THE ESSENTIAL ROCK DISCOGRAPHY

MARTIN C. STRONG

Edinburgh · New York · Melbourne

First published in Great Britain in 2006
by Canongate Books Ltd,
14 High Street, Edinburgh EH1 1TE

British Library Cataloguing-in-Publication Data
A catalogue record for this book is available upon request from the British Library

Hardback
1 84195 827 1 (10 Digit ISBN)
978 184195 827 9 (13 Digit ISBN)

Export Paperback
1 84195 860 3 (10 Digit ISBN)
978 184195 860 6 (13 Digit ISBN)

Typeset by TexturAL, Dundee

Printed and bound in Finland by WS Bookwell

www.canongate.co.uk

This book is dedicated to ...

my mother JEAN FOTHERINGHAM
(born: 6th of January 1929,
died of cancer: 31st of August 1985)

Still missing you
and thanks for still
guiding me through all
the hard times.

my dad GERRY/GEOFF STRONG
(born: 28th of July 1930,
died of a heart attack: 20th October 1998)

Will miss you always.
You were also a great friend, inspiration
and someone who could make me laugh.

Hope you're both getting on up there.
If only ...

* * * * *

Acknowledgements

I'd like to thank Brendon and everyone else who's contributed in their own way. Like last time (7th edition), I'll keep it brief and thank my fiancée Dawn, young daughter Samantha (2), other daughters Suzanne (23) and Shirley (25). Allan and Elaine Brewster get a special mention for mixing up the musical potions, while Vic, Andy and co. were all part of the famous Smith's Lounge Monday club which now has an area in the pavement/road outside for us smokers (thanks Jack McConnell!).

* * * * *

Introduction

This tome (my 15th) comes quite literally to you by accident. The accident (or incident) in question, happened last year (2005) on the 11th of September, three days after my 45th birthday – as a present to myself (I'd also received a new kit and a ball!). I wanted – ironically as it turned out – one last game of football, courtesy of a comeback six-a-side kickabout with pub pals at our local sand-ridden astroturf playing field. What could go wrong? Quite a lot actually.

Around ten minutes into the match, my big frame collapsed when I heard, then felt a snap in my left heel – but no one had tackled me! I couldn't play on (even in goals!) and I trundled off the park to watch the rest of the game from the sidelines; manager and pub owner, Alex Smith, gave me ice in a bucket, telling me it was my Achilles tendon that had ruptured. Sure enough, the hospital doctors diagnosed this to be the case and they put my leg in plaster, gave me crutches and told me to keep my pins horizontal for the next 12 weeks. The problem was I stayed in the top floor (and 39 steps up) of a tenement building.

My regular 60-70 hours I put into my discographies/research/etc., would be drastically cut to er… a big fat zero, although – don't tell the doctors – I steadily worked out a way to keep my leg up while at my computer and extend the hours per day/week gradually. Before the incident, I was working on a secret project that had taken me three years in between my Great Rock Discography work. What has this to do with this book you may well ask? Read on…

On the 8th week, thinking I was going for a second replacement stooky, the nurses un-castigated me and told me I could go home; a third and final cast would not be necessary, and they would give me a tubigrip. Three days after this (the 4th of November, to be exact), I had excruciating pain inside my left rib cage and – after a lot of convincing from my girlfriend, Dawn – I phoned the NHS hotline. They immediately sent round an ambulance and I was duly carted down the 39 steps and off to Stirling Hospital 11 miles away (we have had an adequate hospital in Falkirk for many years, but sections of it were being closed down by TONY BLAIR and the NEW LABOUR/Tories). Anyway, after several hours between waiting and X-rays, it was deemed I had blood clots (Deep Vein Thrombosis) in the lungs and would have to stay in the ward for further observations (in case they spread to my heart or brain), while the taking of the blood-thinning Warfarin (rat poison!) would be compulsory.

After four days, I was fed up and insisted I was sent home, although I had to report daily to Falkirk Royal for my jags – even if I still couldn't walk comfortably for more than a few steps at a time. The 39 steps and the pedestrianised walkway to the taxi rank for the short 1/2 mile journey only had to be tackled once, as I called up my GP to arrange for home visits. I have paid thousands in taxes over the last decade or so, after all. Begrudgingly, he sent a nurse every day for a week, although he did say over the phone, "make an effort, Mr Strong". These words have rung in my ears since he spoke them. "Needles" to say, I now have a new doctor, just in case these little life or death experiences crop up again.

Four months later, the M.C. was off the rat poison and finally finished with a synopsis for that secret project I nearly told you about. Around March, Canongate Books (Jamie Byng and David Graham) convinced me to come out of GRD retirement as they had an idea to make it a little easier and less time-consuming. This proved to be wrong as I had to step up to 70 hours a week again to complete the updates, etc; the deadline was the 30th of June. The rest of each week was spent seeing my new fiancée, Dawn, and my playful toddler, Samantha, while getting to sleep was another major priority. Yes, sleep!

To a vast majority of non-celebrity writers, sleep is probably one of the most important ingredients – bar socialising and er… working – to make a successful author, although we writers wish we needed less snooze time so that we could actually work more each day. It would've helped no end if the noise pollution outside the confines of my old top floor flat could've been spectacularly reduced.

After a rough night listening to drunks singing and shouting sectarian songs from the early hours, it was revving buses that brought me to life from 5.30 a.m. Then the road-sweeper took over from the shitting seagulls and pigeons at 7.30 until the shops opened their shutters at 8.00 (the occasional digging-up of the road to fix burst water mains was frequent), while the rest of the morning/afternoon was spent listening to care-in-the-community lunatics blasting their beatboxes in bus-shelters and car drivers subjecting us to Pinky & Perky rave tunes from rolled down side-windows. While several fire engines, ambulances and police sirens made my area rival something from the streets of New York, a bagpipe-player outside the odd wedding would convince me I was definitely (or defiantly) in Scotland. My Lithuanian neighbours banging doors every five or ten minutes didn't help either and, just what were they selling? From early evening it was the turn of the drunks standing outside the non-smoking pub across the road (thanks again, Jack), shouting, swearing and fighting in front of CCTV cameras; shop alarms pierced both ears into submission at all hours. Where were the police? When the pubs (and local discotheques) shut, the taxi rank became the revellers' meeting square from around 3 a.m. and the vicious 24-hour cycle would be complete.

And on the seventh day, there shall be peace on Earth. Not this side of Falkirk, because Sunday kicked off with Quasimodo-style church and chapel bells competing unceremoniously through all my windows.

I've sold my noisy flat now and have moved into a house on the other side of Falkirk (daft, eh!). Glory be, glory be, and peace to all men/writers… but I see they've just built a 5-storey block across the road . . . arghh!

So here it is then, after all my gripes and woes, THE ESSENTIAL ROCK DISCOGRAPHY, which is, to all intents and purposes, the 8th edition of The Great Rock Discography, condensed and updated, and with the addition of photos. Canongate convinced me to write yet another GRD, although, to save me a little time they suggested this tighter version. The only problem I had with it was the usual one – how and who do I relegate from the book? And by the time we signed contracts (in March '06) could I still cut down the hours each week at the computer and finish by June 30th? I just had to get on with it and solve each problem as it arrived.

The way I picked the entries (omitting all pop and lesser known rock-orientated acts) was as follows: I selected approximately 100 greatest "ROCK" outfits/icons from the 50s/60s, 100 from the 70s, 100 from the 80s, 100 from the 90s and 100 from the 00s, keeping it *current* also by picking 60 newcomers; the rest was made up from 20 INDIE wild cards (one from each major letter) and several POP wild cards. All in all then, around 600 entries including around half that in sub-entries. Taking up a lot of space is the inclusion of even more band pictures than previously – 100 full-page photos to be exact.

For me drastic changes had to be made about the end-of-year cut-off deadline for releases (i.e.

31st December) and when main Canongate man Jamie Byng wanted ARCTIC MONKEYS (a 2006 band really!) in the book, I had my chance not only to include them as newcomers, but also anything else that was issued between 1st January and 30th June 2006. It was a bit of a struggle keeping up to date and re-checking charts, etc, etc, but I think 99% of all these releases are correct. And anyway, the reader gets another 6 months of releases for his/her money.

I've also included DVD-singles (dvd-s) and several DVD-albums (dvd), although the latters' inclusion merits only with a CD-album – DVDs are basically videos in another format and for logistical matters I've never bothered with them. Another new format of recent times came courtesy of the DOWNLOAD-single (dl-s), recordings you can buy through the internet and play on your i-pod thingy; the duo GNARLS BARKLEY making history by hitting the top of the charts on these sales alone.

The biographies, in my opinion, used to lack a little sparkle – due to letting other people contribute to the updates and newcomers in recent years. While I've also contributed greatly to the editing, etc, I thought it was time to return to the basics – myself and co-biographer Brendon Griffin writing together as a partnership (the first time in six years), me with the musical know-all and cheeky wee digs, Brendon with the education and the big words. It was a pleasure to work like this and I know you'll enjoy the book even more.

Martin Strong

Falkirk, August 2006

How To Read The Book

If you're struggling in any way how to comprehend some of the more complex parts of each discography, here are some examples to make it easier. Read below for around 10 minutes, taking a step at a time. The final lines/examples you see will give you a good guide before you proceed with the actual chronological discographies. However, I think that once you've read your own favourites you'll have a good idea.

GROUP / ARTIST

Formed/Born: Where/When . . . biography including style/analysis, songwriters, cover versions, trivia, etc.

Album rating: a rating between 1 and10 – an amalgamation between music press reviews, your letters and my own personal opinion.

SINGER (born; b. day/month/year, town/city, country) – vocals, whatever (ex-GROUP; if any) / **MUSICIAN** (b. BIRTH NAME, 8 Sep'60, Musselburgh, Scotland) – instruments / **OTHER MUSICIANS** – other instruments, vocals, etc.

UK Label US Label

UKdate. (single, ep or album) *(UK cat.no.)* *<US cat.no.>* **THE RELEASE TITLE** US date

Note:– UK label – might be another country's label if not released in UK.

also:- Labels only appear when the group signs to a new one.

Note:– UK date – might be foreign, <even American at times>, if not initially issued in Britain.

Note:– (UK catalogue number in curved brackets) <US cat.no. in angle brackets>

Note:– chart positions, UK and US, are in the boxes below record-labels.

also:- the boxes in the above example have been left blank, meaning they did not hit either UK or US charts.

Note:– US date between the boxes indicates a variation from its UK counterpart.

also:- Any other info between the boxes (e.g. German) indicates it was not issued in the US.

UKdate. (7") *(UK cat.no.)* **A-SIDE. / B-SIDE** –

US date. (7") *<US cat.no.>* **A-SIDE. / DIFFERENT B-SIDE** –

Note:– The two examples above show that the UK + US release did not have an identical A-side & B-side, thus the chart boxes are marked with a – to indicate it was not released in the UK or not released in the US.

UKdate. (7"/c-s) *(CATNO 1/+C)* **A-SIDE. / B-SIDE** –

Note:– above had two formats with the same tracks (i.e. 7"/c-s). However, catalogue numbers will always vary among different formats – often only slightly (e.g. CATNO 1/+C). Each cat.no. would read thus:- (7")=*(CATNO 1)* and (c-s)=*(CATNO 1C)*. To save space the (/) slash comes into effect. The (/) means "or" and in this case it is prefixed with a + sign for the equivalent cassette (c-s).

UKdate. (7"/c-s) *(example same as above)* **SEE ABOVE** –
(12"+=/cd-s+=) *(CATNO 1-12/1-CD)* – Extra tracks.

Note:– If there are more formats with extra or different tracks, a new line would be used. Obviously there would also be alternative catalogue numbers utilising the "(/)" as before. Extra tracks would therefore mean the addition of the sign "(+=)" to each format.

UKdate. (lp/c/cd) *(CATNO 200/+MC/CD)* *<US cat. no. 4509>*
ALBUM TITLE
– Track listing / Track 1 / Track 2 / And so on. *(re-issued = re-iss. A later date, and other 'Label' mentioned, if different from original; new cat.no.) (could be re-iss. many times and if "(+=)" sign occurs there will be extra tracks from the original) <could also apply to the US release if in angle brackets>*

Note:– Album above released in 3 formats, thus 3 catalogue numbers are neccessary. The "long-player" lp *(CATNO 200)* is obvious. The "cassette" c = +MC *(CATNO 200MC)* or "compact disc" CD *(CATNO 200CD)*. The US *<cat.no.>* will normally be just one set of numbers (or see further below for other details).

UKdate. (cd/c/lp) *(CD/TC+/CATNO+200)* *<US cat. no. 4509>*
ALBUM TITLE US date

Note:– This time a prefix is used instead of a suffix, hence the difference before the standard lp catalogue number. For instance, the cd would read as *(CDCATNO 200)*.

Jun 97. (cd/c/lp) *<(5557 49860-2/-4/-1)>* **ALBUM TITLE** 1 May97 1

Note:– Some catalogue numbers don't include any letters, but instead consist of a number sequence followed by one digit which universally corresponds with the format (i.e. 2 = cd / 4 = c / 1 = lp).

also:- If the US numbers are identical, there is no need to list them separately, i.e. *<(the numbers)>*

Note:– I've also marked down an actual date of release and its variant in the US (you'll find this fictitious album also hit No.1 in both charts "and ah've no even heard it yet, man!")

—— **NEW MUSICIAN/SINGER** (b.whenever, etc.) – instruments (ex-GROUP(s)) replaced (repl.) DEPARTING MUSICIAN/SINGER, who joined whatever.

The above denotes a line-up change.

GROUP or ARTIST with major change of name

UK Label US Label

Jun 97. (cd/c/lp; GROUP or ARTIST with minor change of name) *<(5557 49860)>* **ALBUM TITLE** 1 May97 1

– compilations, etc. –

UKdate. (cd) *compilation Label only; (cat.no.)* **ALBUM TITLE** **100** –
– Track listing would be selective, only included if the release was deemed essential.

□ PERSONAL NAME (see under ⇒ GROUP-NAME)
The above is a cross-reference.

Formats & Abbreviations

VINYL (black coloured unless stated)

(lp) = The (LONG PLAYER) record ... circular 12" plays at $33^{1/3}$ r.p.m., and has photo or artwork sleeve. Approximate playing time ... 30–50 minutes with average 10 tracks. Introduced in the mid-'50s on mono until stereo took over in the mid-'60s. Quadrophonic had a spell in the '70s, but only on mainly best-selling lp's, that had been previously released. Because of higher costs to the manufacturer and buyer, the quad sunk around 1978. Also note that around the mid-'50s, some albums were released on 10 inch. Note:– average cost to the customer as of now = £9.00 (new). Collectors can pay anything from £1 to over £500, depending on the quality of the recording. Very scratched records can be worthless, but unplayed mint deletions are worth a small fortune to the right person. Auctions and record fairs can be the place to find that long lost recording that's eluded you. This applies to all other vinyl below.

(d-1p) = The (DOUBLE-LONG PLAYER) record ... as before. Playing time 50–90 minutes on 4 sides, with average 17 tracks. Introduced to rock/pop world in the late '60s, to complement compilations, concept & concert (aka live) albums.[1]
Compilations:– are a selection of greatest hits or rare tracks, demos, etc.
Concepts:– are near-uninterrupted pieces of music, based around a theme.
Note that normal lp's could also be compilations, live or concept. Some record companies through the wishes of their artists, released double lp's at the price of one lp. If not, price new would be around £15.

(t-1p) = The (TRIPLE-LONG PLAYER) record ... as before. Playing time over 100 minutes with normally over 20 tracks. Because of the cost to the consumer, most artists steered clear of this format. Depending on the artwork on the sleeve, these cost over £17.50. (See its replacement, the CD.)

(4-1p-box) = The (BOXED-LONG PLAYER) record (could be between 4 and 10 in each boxed-set). As the triple album would deal with live, concept or compilation side, the boxed-set would be mostly re-issues of all the artist's album material, with probably a bonus lp thrown in, to make it collectable. Could be very pricey, due to lavish outlay in packaging. They cost over £25 new.

(m-lp) = The (MINI-LONG PLAYER) record ... playing time between 20 and 30 minutes and containing on average 7 tracks. Introduced for early '80s independent market, and cost around £5.
= Note:– This could be confused at times with the extended-play 12" single.

(pic-1p) = The (PICTURE DISC-LONG PLAYER) record... as before but with album artwork/ design on the vinyl grooves. Mainly for the collector because of the slightly inferior sound quality. If unplayed, these can fetch between £10 and £250.

(coloured lp) = The (COLOURED-LONG PLAYER) record; can be in a variety of colours including ... white / blue / red / clear / purple / green / pink / gold / silver.

(red-1p) = The (RED VINYL-LONG PLAYER) record would be an example of this.

(7") = The (7-INCH SINGLE). Arrived in the late '50s, and plays at 45 r.p.m. Before this its equivalent was the 10" on 78 r.p.m. Playing time now averages 4 minutes per side, but during the late '50s up to mid-60s, each side averaged $2^{1/2}$ minutes. Punk rock/new wave in 1977/78 resurrected this idea. In the '80s, some disco releases increased playing time. Another idea that was resurrected in 1977 was the picture sleeve. This had been introduced in the '60s, but mostly only in the States.

1: **Note**:– Interview long players, mainly released on 'Babatak' label, have not been included due to the fact this book only gives artists' music discography.

Note:– cost in mid-98 was just under £2.50; second-hand rarities can cost between 25p and £200, depending again on their condition. These might also contain limited freebies/gifts (i.e. posters, patches, stickers, badges, etc). Due to the confusion this would cause, I have omitted this information, and kept to the vinyl aspect in this book. Another omission has been DJ promos, demos, acetates, magazine freebies, various artists' compilations, etc. Only official shop releases get a mention.

(7" m) = The (7-INCH MAXI-SINGLE). Named so because of the extra track, mostly on the B-side. Introduced widely during the early 70s; one being ROCKET MAN by ELTON JOHN.

(7" ep) = The (7-INCH EXTENDED PLAY SINGLE). Plays mostly at 33 1/3 r.p.m., with average playing time 10–15 minutes and 4 tracks. Introduced in the late 50s as compilations for people to sample their albums. These had a *title* and were also re-introduced from 1977 onwards, but this time for punk groups' new songs.

(d7") = The (DOUBLE 7-INCH SINGLE). Basically just two singles combined ... 4 tracks. Introduced in the late 70s for the "new wave/romantics", and would cost slightly more than normal equivalent.

(7" pic-d) = The (7-INCH PICTURE-DISC SINGLE). This was vinyl that had a picture on the grooves, which could be viewed through a see-through plastic cover.

(7" sha-pic-d) = The (7-INCH SHAPED-PICTURE-DISC SINGLE). Vinyl as above but with shape (i.e. gun, mask, group) around the edge of the groove. Awkward because it would not fit into the collector's singles box. Initially limited, and this can still be obtained at record fairs for over £3. Note:– However, in the book the type of shape has not been mentioned, to save space.

(7" coloured) = The (7-INCH COLOURED SINGLE). Vinyl that is not black (i.e. any other colour; red, yellow, etc). Note:– (7" multi) would be a combination of two or more colours (i.e. pink/purple).

(7" flexi) = The (7-INCH FLEXIBLE SINGLE). One-sided freebies, mostly given away by magazines, at concerts or as mentioned here; free with single or lp. Worth keeping in mint condition and well protected.

(12") = The (12-INCH SINGLE). Plays at 45 r.p.m., and can have extended or extra tracks to its 7" counterpart (+=) or (++=). B-side's playing speed could be at 33 r.p.m. Playing time could be between 8 and 15 minutes. Introduced in 1977 with the advent of new wave and punk. They were again a must for collectors, for the new wave of British heavy metal scene.

(12" ep) = The (12-INCH EXTENDED PLAY SINGLE). Virtually same as above but *titled* like the 7" ep. Playing time over 12 minutes, and could have between 3 and 5 tracks.

(d12") = The (DOUBLE 12-INCH SINGLE). See double 7". Can become very collectable and would cost new as normal 12", £4.50.

(12" pic-d) = The (12-INCH PICTURE-DISC SINGLE). As with 7" equivalent ... see above.

(12" sha-pic-d) = The (12-INCH SHAPED-PICTURE-DISC SINGLE). See above 7" equivalent.

(12" colrd) = The (12-INCH COLOURED SINGLE). Not black vinyl ... see above 7" equivalent.

(10") = The (10-INCH SINGLE). Plays at 45 r.p.m. and, like the 12", can have extra tracks (+=). Very collectable, it surfaced in its newer form around the early '80s, and can be obtained in shops at £4.50. Note:– also (10" ep) / (d10") / (10" coloured) / (10" pic-d) / (10" sha-pic-d).

CASSETTES

(c) = The (CASSETTE) album ... size in case 4 1/2 inches high. Playing-time same as lp album, although after the mid-'80s cd revolution, some were released with extra tracks. Introduced in the late '60s, to compete with the much bulkier lp. Until the '80s, most cassettes were lacking in group info, lyric sheets, and freebies. Note:– cost to the consumer as of now = £8 new. But for a few exceptions, most do not increase in price, and can be bought second-hand or budget-priced for around £5.

(d-c) = The (DOUBLE-CASSETTE) album ... as above, and would hold same tracks as d-lp or even t-lp. Price between £12 and £16.

(c-s) = The (CASSETTE-SINGLE). Now released mostly with same two tracks as 7" equivalent. The other side played the same 2 or 3 tracks. Introduced unsuccessfully in the US around the late '60s. Re-introduced there and in Britain in the mid-'80s. In the States, it and its cd counterpart have replaced the charting 7" single for the '90s. Cost new is around £1.50–£2.50, and might well become quite collectable.

(c-ep) = The (CASSETTE-EXTENDED PLAY SINGLE). Same as above but *titled* as 12".

COMPACT DISCS (and others)

(cd) = The (COMPACT DISC) album. All 5" circular and mostly silver on its playing side. Perspex casing also includes lyrics & info, etc. Introduced late in 1982, and widely the following year (even earlier for classical music). Initially for top recording artists, but now in 2004 nearly every release is in cd format. Playing time normally over 50 minutes with some containing extra tracks or mixes. Possible playing time is just over 75 minutes. Marketed as unscratchable, although if they go uncleaned, they will stick just as vinyl. Average price now is £15, and will become collectable if, like most gloomy predictions, they do not deteriorate with time.

(d-cd) = The (DOUBLE-COMPACT DISC) album ... same as above although very pricey, between £20 and £25.

(cd-s) = The (COMPACT DISC-SINGLE). Mainly all 5" (but some 3" cd-s could only be played with a compatible gadget inside the normal cd player). Playing time over 15 minutes to average 25 minutes, containing 4 or 5 tracks. Introduced in 1986 to compete with the 12" ep or cassette. 99% contained extra tracks to normal formats. Cost new: over £4.50.

(pic-cd-s) = The (PICTURE-COMPACT DISC-SINGLE). Has picture on disc, which gives it its collectability. Also on (pic-cd-ep).

(vid-pic-s) = The (VIDEO-COMPACT DISC-SINGLE). A video cd, which can be played through stereo onto normal compatible TV screen. Very costly procedure, but still might be the format of the future. Promo videos can be seen on pub jukeboxes, which has made redundant the returning Wurlitzer style.

(dvd-s) = The (DIGITAL-VIDEO-DISK-SINGLE) can be played on DVD-player, similar to CD-single with visuals, documentary, etc. Cost around £4.99.

(dl-s) = (DOWNLOAD-SINGLE) – Internet single, costing around £1.

(dat) = The (DIGITAL AUDIO TAPE) album. Introduced in the mid-'80s and, except for Japan and the rich yuppie, are not widely issued. It is a smaller version of the cassette, with the quality of the cd.

Another format (which I have not included) is the CARTRIDGE, which was available at the same time as the cassette. When the cassette finally won the battle in the early '80s, the cartridge became redundant. All car-owners of the world were happy when thieves made them replace the stolen cartridge player with the resurrected cassette. You can still buy these second-hand, but remember you'll have to obtain a second-hand 20-year-old player, with parts possibly not available.

Other abbreviations: repl. = replaced / comp. = compilation / re-iss. = re-issued / re-dist. = re-distributed

A

☐ ABBC (see under ⇒ CALEXICO)

AC/DC

Formed: Sydney, Australia ... 1973, by ex-pat Scots brothers MALCOLM and ANGUS YOUNG. After an initial single, 'CAN I SIT NEXT TO YOU', the siblings headed for Melbourne where they recruited another Caledonian exile, wildman BON SCOTT. Stabilizing the line-up with MARK EVANS and PHIL RUDD, the band signed up with 'Albert' records, a company run by the eldest YOUNG brother, GEORGE, and HARRY VANDA (both ex-EASYBEATS). AC/DC's first two releases, 'HIGH VOLTAGE' (1975) and 'TNT' (1976) were Australia-only affairs, competent boogie-rock that established their name on the domestic scene and generated enough interest for 'Atlantic' UK to come sniffing with chequebook in hand. With major label muscle behind them, the band relocated to London just as punk was rearing its snotty, vomit-encrusted head. With their particular brand of no-frills rock and ANGUS' school uniform stage gear, the band were initially loosely affiliated to the scene. But with ANGUS' bowel-quaking riffs and SCOTT's high-pitched bellow, their eventual status as one of the archetypal heavy metal acts was almost inevitable from the off. 'Atlantic' introduced the band to Britain with a compilation drawn from the group's first two Australian releases (confusingly also titled 'HIGH VOLTAGE') and AC/DC's first album proper was 1976's 'DIRTY DEEDS DONE DIRT CHEAP'. While its follow-up, 'LET THERE BE ROCK' gave the band their first taste of chart action, AC/DC were first and foremost a live band. The bare-legged cheek of ANGUS was eminently entertaining, his body contorting and jerking like a clockwork toy on speed (NEIL YOUNG's more frenetic noodlings bear a striking similarity, long lost brothers perhaps?!). After a corking live album, 'IF YOU WANT BLOOD, YOU'VE GOT IT' (featuring that classic paeon to the larger woman, 'WHOLE LOTTA ROSIE', no anorexic waifs for this lot!), the band hit the big time with 'HIGHWAY TO HELL' (1979). Despite a more commercial sheen courtesy of producer Mutt Lange, the likes of 'TOUCH TOO MUCH' and the title track were unforgettable AC/DC moments, utilising the band's trademark steamrolling rhythm section and their inimitable way with a testosterone-saturated chorus. As ever, the group's lyrics were, for the most part, positively neolithic although their reliably unreconstructed, femininst-baiting songs were never without humour, something of a novelty in the metal scene of that era. Being Scottish/Australian, and a rock star to boot, BON SCOTT wasn't exactly a lager shandy man, the 'Uisge Beath' ('Water of life', or whisky to sassenach readers) rather taking away his life after he drank himself into an early grave the following February (1980). Yet incredibly, by July, the band were back with a No. 1 album, 'BACK IN BLACK', a record that saw the band finally break big in America. Ex-GEORDIE singer, BRIAN JOHNSON, had been recruited on vocal duties and his gravelly yelp carried on where SCOTT left off. The likes of 'HELL'S BELLS' and the irrepressible 'YOU SHOOK ME ALL NIGHT LONG' were staples of rock discos (remember them?) up and down the land and the band became a top drawer draw in the age of stadium rock, headlining the legendary Castle Donington Festival in its heyday. Yet from here on in, AC/DC lost their spark somewhat. 'FLICK OF THE SWITCH' and 'FLY ON THE WALL' were metal by numbers although 'WHO MADE WHO' (1986) was an interesting hotch-potch of new and old. 'BLOW UP YOUR VIDEO' (1988) and 'THE RAZOR'S EDGE' (1990) saw a resurgence of sorts, the respective sets making Top 5. The band continued to tour for the metal faithful, 1992's 'LIVE' documenting the visceral thrill of the AC/DC concert experience. But while their formula was wearing a bit thin, nobody seemed to have informed the band, 1995's hilariously titled 'BALLBREAKER' crudely retreading over-familiar ground. Still, in the (supposedly) sophisticated PC world of the 90's, you had to hand it to a band who could still get away with titles like 'COVER YOU IN OIL', 'HARD AS A ROCK' and 'LOVE BOMB'. Signed to 'Liberty' at the turn of the millennium, AC/DC delivered a much improved and even tastier set of numbers via 'STIFF UPPER LIP' (2000). Vive le rock!

• **Songwriters:** Most by YOUNG brothers, some with SCOTT or JOHNSON. Covered; BABY PLEASE DON'T GO / BONNY (trad).

Album rating: HIGH VOLTAGE (UK *8) / DIRTY DEEDS DONE DIRT CHEAP (*6) / LET THERE BE ROCK (*8) / POWERAGE (*6) / IF YOU WANT BLOOD – YOU'VE GOT IT (*8) / HIGHWAY TO HELL (*8) / BACK IN BLACK (*8) / FOR THOSE ABOUT TO ROCK (WE SALUTE YOU) (*4) / FLICK OF THE SWITCH (*5) / FLY ON THE WALL (*5) / WHO MADE WHO part compilation soundtrack to 'Maximum Overdrive' (*7) / BLOW UP YOUR VIDEO (*7) / THE RAZOR'S EDGE (*5) / LIVE (*7) / BALLBREAKER (*6) / STIFF UPPER LIP (*7)

ANGUS YOUNG (b.31 Mar'59, Glasgow, Scotland) – guitar / **MALCOLM YOUNG** (b. 6 Jan'53, Glasgow) – guitar / **DAVE EVANS** – vocals / **ROB BAILEY** – bass / **PETER CLACK** – drums

not iss. Albert

Jul 74. (7") **CAN I SIT NEXT TO YOU. / ROCKIN' IN THE PARLOUR** [–] Aust. [–]

—— When all but the brothers departed, they recruited (i.e.DAVE joined RABBIT) **BON SCOTT** (b.RONALD SCOTT, 9 Jul'46, Kirriemuir, Scotland) – vocals (ex-VALENTINES, ex-FRATERNITY, ex-SPECTORS, ex-MOUNT LOFTY RANGERS) / **MARK EVANS** – (b. 2 Mar'56, Melbourne) – bass (ex-BUSTER BROWN) / **PHIL RUDD** (b.19 May'54, Melbourne) – drums

Jan 75. (lp) *<APLP 009>* **HIGH VOLTAGE** [–] Austra [–]
– Baby please don't go / She's got balls / Little lover / Stick around / Soul stripper / You ain't got a hold of me / Love song / Show business.

1975. (7") **DOG EAT DOG. / CARRY ME HOME** [–] Austra [–]

Dec 75. (lp) *<APLP 016>* **T.N.T.** [–] Austra [–]
– It's a long way to the top (if you wanna rock'n'roll) / The Rock'n'roll singer / The jack / Live wire / T.N.T. / Rocker / Can I sit next to you girl / High voltage / School days.

Atlantic Atco

Apr 76. (7") *(K 10745)* **IT'S A LONG WAY TO THE TOP (IF YOU WANNA ROCK'N'ROLL). / CAN I SIT NEXT TO YOU GIRL** [ ] [–]
(re-iss. Jun80 on 'Heavy Metal-Atlantic'; HM 3) (hit UK 55)

May 76. (lp/c) *(K/K4 50257)* **HIGH VOLTAGE** (compilation from two above) [ ] [–]
– It's a long way to the top (if you wanna rock'n'roll) / The rock'n'roll singer / The jack / Live wire / T.N.T. / Can I sit next to you girl / Little

AC/DC

lover / She's got balls / High voltage. *<US-iss.Apr81; 142> (cd-iss. Oct87; K2 50257) (re-iss. Jul94 cd/c; 7567 92413-2/-4) (cd re-iss. May98 on 'E.M.I.'; 494671-2)*

Aug 76. (7") *(K 10805)* **JAILBREAK. / FLING THING** [ ] [–]
(re-iss. Mar80)

Oct 76. (7") *(K 10860)* **HIGH VOLTAGE. / LIVE WIRE** [ ] [–]
(re-iss. Jun80 on 'Heavy Metal-Atlantic'; HM 1) (hit UK 48)

Dec 76. (7") *<7068>* **HIGH VOLTAGE. / IT'S A LONG WAY TO THE TOP (IF YOU WANNA ROCK'N'ROLL)** [–] [ ]

Dec 76. (lp/c) *(K/K4 50323)* **DIRTY DEEDS DONE DIRT CHEAP** [ ] [–]
– Dirty deeds done dirt cheap / Love at first feel / Big balls / Rocker / Problem child / There's gonna be some rockin' / Ain't no fun (waiting round to be a millionaire) / Ride on / Squealer. *<US-iss.Apr81; 16033> – <hit No.3> (cd-iss. Aug87; K2 50323) (re-iss. Jul94 cd/c; 7567 92448-2/-4) (cd re-iss. May98 on 'E.M.I.'; 494670-2)*

Jan 77. (7"m) *(K 10899)* **DIRTY DEEDS DONE DIRT CHEAP. / BIG BALLS / THE JACK** [ ] [–]
(re-iss. Jun80 on 'Heavy Metal-Atlantic'; HM 2) (hit UK 47)

—— **CLIFF WILLIAMS** (b.14 Dec'49, Romford, England) – bass (ex-HOME, ex-BANDIT) repl. MARK

Sep 77. (7") *(K 11018) <7086>* **LET THERE BE ROCK. / PROBLEM CHILD** [ ] [ ]
(re-iss. Mar80)

Oct 77. (lp/c) *(K/K4 50366) <151>* **LET THERE BE ROCK** [17] [ ]
– Go down / Dog eat dog / Let there be rock / Bad boy boogie / Overdose / Crapsody in blue / Hell ain't a bad place to be / Whole lotta Rosie. *(cd-iss. Jun89; K2 50366) (re-iss. Oct94 cd/c; 7567 92445-2/-4) (cd re-iss. Sep98 on 'E.M.I.'; 497316-2)*

Atlantic Atlantic

May 78. (lp/c) *(K/K4 50483) <19180>* **POWERAGE** [26] [ ]
– Gimme a bullet / Down payment blues / Gone shootin' / Riff raff / Sin city / Up to my neck in you / What's next to the moon / Cold hearted man / Kicked in the teeth. *(cd-iss. Jun89; K 781 548-2) (re-iss. Oct94 cd/c; 7567 92446-2/-4) (cd re-iss. May98 on 'E.M.I.'; 494672-2)*

May 78. (7"/12") *(K 11142/+T)* **ROCK'N'ROLL DAMNATION. / SIN CITY** [24] [–]
(re-iss. Mar80; same)

Jun 78. (7") *<3499>* **ROCK'N'ROLL DAMNATION. / KICKED IN THE TEETH** [–] [ ]

Oct 78. (lp/c) *(K/K4 50532) <19212>* **IF YOU WANT BLOOD, YOU'VE GOT IT (live)** [13] [ ]
– Riff raff / Hell ain't a bad place to be / Bad boy boogie / The jack / Problem child / Whole lotta Rosie / Rock'n'roll damnation / High voltage / Let there be rock / Rocker. *(re-iss. Mar80; same) (cd-iss. Jun89; K 781 553-2) (re-iss. Oct94; 7567 92447-2/-4) (cd re-iss. May98 on 'E.M.I.'; 494669-2)*

Oct 78. (7"/12") *(K 11207/+T) <3553>* **WHOLE LOTTA ROSIE (live). / HELL AIN'T A BAD PLACE TO BE (live)** [ ] [ ]
(re-iss. Mar80; same) (re-iss. Jun80 on 'Heavy Metal-Atlantic'; HM 4) (hit UK 36)

Aug 79. (lp/c) *(K/K4 50628) <19244>* **HIGHWAY TO HELL** [8] [17]
– Highway to Hell / Girls got rhythm / Walk all over you / Touch too much / Beating around the bush / Shot down in flames / Get it hot / If you want blood (you've got it) / Love hungry man / Night prowler. *(cd-iss. Jul87; 250 628-2) (cd re-iss. 1989; K2 50628) (cd re-iss. Jan98 on 'E.M.I.'; 477088-2)*

Aug 79. (7") *(K 11321)* **HIGHWAY TO HELL. / IF YOU WANT BLOOD (YOU'VE GOT IT)** [56] [–]
(re-iss. Mar80; same)

Aug 79. (7") *<3617>* **HIGHWAY TO HELL. / NIGHT PROWLER** [–] [47]

Oct 79. (7") *(K 11406)* **GIRLS GOT RHYTHM. / GET IT HOT** [ ] [–]
(7"ep) *(K 11406E)* – ('A'side) / If you want blood (you've got it) / Hell ain't a bad place to be (live) / Rock'n'roll damnation.

Jan 80. (7"m) *(K 11435)* **TOUCH TOO MUCH (live). / LIVE WIRE (live) / SHOT DOWN IN FLAMES (live)** [29] [–]

Feb 80. (7") *<3644>* **TOUCH TOO MUCH (live). / WALK ALL OVER YOU (live)** [–] [ ]

—— **BRIAN JOHNSON** (b.5 Oct'47, Newcastle, England) – vocals (ex-GEORDIE) repl. BON SCOTT who died 20 Feb'80 after drunken binge.

Jul 80. (lp/c) *(K/K4 50735) <16018>* **BACK IN BLACK** [1] [4]
– Hells bells / Shoot to thrill / What do you do for money honey / Give the dog a bone / Let me put my love into you / Back in black / You shook me all night long / Have a drink on me / Shake a leg / Rock and roll ain't noise pollution. *(cd-iss. Feb87; K2 50735) (re-iss. Aug94 cd/c; 7567 92418-2/-4) (cd re-iss. Jun98 on 'E.M.I.'; 495153-2)*

Sep 80. (7") *(K 11600) <3761>* **YOU SHOOK ME ALL NIGHT LONG. / HAVE A DRINK ON ME** [38] [35]

Nov 80. (7"/12") *(K 11630/+T)* **ROCK'N'ROLL AIN'T NOISE POLLUTION. / HELL'S BELLS** [15] [ ]

Feb 81. (7") *<3787>* **BACK IN BLACK. / WHAT DO YOU DO FOR MONEY HONEY** [–] [37]

Nov 81. (lp/c) *(K/K4 50851) <11111>* **FOR THOSE ABOUT TO ROCK (WE SALUTE YOU)** [3] [1]
– For those about to rock (we salute you) / Put the finger on you / Let's get it up / Inject the venom / Snowballed / Evil walk / C.O.D. / Breaking the laws / Night of the long knives / Spellbound. *(cd-iss. Jul87; K2 50851) (re-iss. Jul94 cd/c; 7567 92412-2/-4) (cd re-iss. Jan98 on 'E.M.I.'; 477090-2)*

Jan 82. (7") *(K 11706)* **LET'S GET IT UP. / BACK IN BLACK (live)** [13] [–]
(12"+=) *(K 11706T)* – T.N.T. (live).

Jan 82 (7")(12") *<3894><3898>* **LET'S GET IT UP. / SNOWBALLED** [–] [44]

Jun 82 (7") *<4029>* **FOR THOSE ABOUT TO ROCK (WE SALUTE YOU). / T.N.T.** [–] [ ]

Jun 82. (7"/ext.12") *(K 11721/+T)* **FOR THOSE ABOUT TO ROCK (WE SALUTE YOU). / LET THERE BE ROCK (live)** [15] [ ]

Aug 83. (lp/c) *(780 100-1/-4) <80100>* **FLICK OF THE SWITCH** [4] [15]
– Rising power / This house is on fire / Flick of the switch / Nervous shakedown / Landslide / Guns for fire / Deep in the hole / Bedlam in Belgium / Badlands / Brain shake. *(re-iss. Jul87 lp/c/cd; K781 455-1/-4/-2) (re-iss. Oct94 cd/c; 7567 92448-2/-4) (cd re-iss. Jan98 on 'E.M.I.'; 477091-2)*

Sep 83. (7"/7"sha-pic-d) *(A 9774/+P) <89774>* **GUNS FOR HIRE. / LANDSLIDE** [37] [84]

Mar 84. (7") *<89722>* **FLICK OF THE SWITCH. / BADLANDS** [–] [ ]

—— **SIMON WRIGHT** (b.19 Jun'63) – drums (ex-A II Z, ex-TYTAN) repl. RUDD

Jul 84. (7"/7"sha-pic-d) *(A 9651/+P)* **NERVOUS SHAKEDOWN. / ROCK'N'ROLL AIN'T NOISE POLLUTION (live)** [35] [ ]
(12"+=/c-s+=) *(A 9651 T/C)* – Sin city (live) / This house is on fire (live).

Jun 85. (7"/7"w-poster/7"sha-pic-d/12") *(A 9532/+W/P/T) <89532>* **DANGER. / BACK IN BUSINESS** [48] [ ]

Jul 85. (lp/c/cd) *(781 263-1/-4/-2) <81263>* **FLY ON THE WALL** [7] [32]
– Fly on the wall / Shake your foundations / First blood / Danger / Sink the pink / Playing with the girls / Stand up / Hell or high water / Back in business / Send for the man. *(cd re-iss. Jan98 on 'E.M.I.'; 477092-2)*

Nov 85. (7") **SHAKE YOUR FOUNDATIONS. / SEND FOR THE MAN** [–] [ ]

Jan 86. (7"/7"w-poster/7"sha-pic-d) *(A 9474/+C/P)* **SHAKE YOUR FOUNDATIONS. / STAND UP** [24] [ ]
(12"+=) *(A 9474T)* – Jailbreak.

May 86. (7"/7"sha-pic-d) *(A 9425/+P) <89425>* **WHO MADE WHO. / GUNS FOR HIRE (live)** [16] [ ]
(12"+=/12"w-poster) *(A 9425T/+W)* – ('A'-Collectors mix).

May 86. (lp/c) *(WX 57/+C) <81650>* **WHO MADE WHO** ('Maximum Overdrive' soundtrack / part compilation) [11] [33]
– Who made who / You shook me all night long / D.T. / Sink the pink / Ride on / Hells bells / Shake your foundations / Chase the ace / For those about to rock (we salute you). *(cd-iss. 1988; 781 650-2) (cd re-iss. Sep98 on 'E.M.I.'; 746299-2) (cd re-iss. Apr03 on 'Columbia'; 510769-2)*

Aug 86. (7"/7"sha-pic-d) *(A 9377/+P) <89377>* **YOU SHOOK ME ALL NIGHT LONG (live). / SHE'S GOT BALLS (live)** [46] [ ]
(12"/12"sha-pic-d) *(A 9377 T/TP)* – ('B'extended) / ('A'live).

Jan 88. (7") *(A 9136) <89136>* **HEATSEEKER. / GO ZONE** [12] [ ]
(12"+=/12"g-f+=/12"pic-d+=/3"cd-s+=) *(A 9136 T/TW/TP/CD)* – Snake high.

Feb 88. (lp/c)(cd) *(WX 144/+C)(781 828-2) <81828>* **BLOW UP YOUR VIDEO** [2] [12]
– Heatseeker / That's the way I wanna rock'n'roll / Meanstreak / Go zone / Kissin' dynamite / Nick of time / Some sin for nuthin' / Ruff stuff / Two's up / Some sin for nuthin' / This means war. *(cd re-iss. Sep98 on 'E.M.I.'; 748977-2)*

Mar 88. (7") *(A 9098) <89098>* **THAT'S THE WAY I WANNA ROCK'N'ROLL. / KISSIN' DYNAMITE** [22] [ ]
(12"+=/12"g-f+=/12"pic-d+=) *(A 9098T/+W/P)* – Borrowed time.
(3"cd-s+=) *(A 9098CD)* – Shoot to thrill (live) / Whole lotta Rosie (live).

— (Apr88) cousin **STEVE YOUNG** – guitar briefly replaced MALCOLM on tour

— (1989) (ANGUS, MALCOLM, BRIAN & CLIFF) bring in **CHRIS SLADE** (b.30 Oct'46) – drums (ex-GARY MOORE, ex-MANFRED MANN EARTHBAND, ex-FIRM) repl. WRIGHT who had joined DIO.

Atco Atco

Sep 90. (7"/c-s/10"pic-d) *(B 8907/+C/P)* **THUNDERSTRUCK. / FIRE YOUR GUNS** [13] [ ]
(12"+=/cd-s+=) *(B 8907 T/CD)* – DT / Chase the ace.

Oct 90. (cd)(lp/pic-lp/c) *(<91413>)(WX 364/+P/+C)* **THE RAZOR'S EDGE** [4] [2]
– Thunderstruck / Fire your guns / Moneytalks / The razor's edge / Mistress for Christmas / Rock your heart out / Are you ready / Got you by the balls / Shot of love / Let's make it / Goodbye & good riddance to bad luck / If you dare. *(cd re-iss. Jun98 on 'E.M.I.'; 495144-2)*

Nov 90. (7"/c-s) *(B 8886/+C)* **MONEYTALKS. / MISTRESS FOR CHRISTMAS** [36] [–]
(12"+=/12"sha-pic-d+=/cd-s+=) *(B 8886 T/P/CD)* – Borrowed time.

Nov 90. (c-s) *<98881>* **MONEYTALKS. / BORROWED TIME** [–] [23]

Apr 91. (7"/7"w-patch/7"s/c-s) *(88830/+X/W/C)* **ARE YOU READY. / GOT YOU BY THE BALLS** [34] [ ]
(12"+=/12"g-f+=/cd-s+=) *(88830 T/TW/CD)* – The razor's edge.

Oct 92. (7") *(B 8479)* **HIGHWAY TO HELL (live) / HELL'S BELLS (live)** [14] [ ]
(12"pic-d) *(B 8479TP)* – ('A'side) / High voltage (live).
(cd-s) *(B 8479CD)* – ('A'side) / High voltage (live) / Hell ain't a bad place to be (live).
(cd-s) *(B 8479CDX)* – ('A'side) / High voltage (live) / The jack (live).

Oct 92. (cd/c/d-lp) *(<7567 92212-2/-4/-1>)* **LIVE (live)** [5] [15]
– Thunderstruck / Shoot to thrill / Back in black / Sin city / Who made who / Fire your guns / Jailbreak / The jack / The razor's edge / Dirty deeds done dirt cheap / Hells bells / Heatseeker / That's the way I wanna rock'n'roll / High voltage / You shook me all night long / Whole lotta Rosie / Let there be rock / Medley:- Bonny – Highway to Hell / T.N.T. / For those about to rock (we salute you). *<in the US, a SPECIAL COLLECTOR'S EDITION hit No.26; 92215-2> (cd/d-cd re-iss. Jun98 on 'E.M.I.'; 49514 5/6-2)*

Feb 93. (12"/cd-s) *(B 6073 T/CD)* **DIRTY DEEDS DONE DIRT CHEAP (live). / SHOOT TO THRILL (live) / DIRTY DEEDS DONE DIRT CHEAP** [68] [ ]

Jun 93. (7"/c-s) *(88396/+C) <98406>* **BIG GUN. / BACK IN BLACK (live)** [23] [65]
(12"+=) *(88396T)* – For those about to rock (live).
(cd-s) *(88396CD)* – ('A'side) / For those about to rock (live).

Sep 95. (7"yellow/cd-s/s-cd-s) *(A 4368 X/CD/CDX)* **HARD AS A ROCK. / CAUGHT WITH YOUR PANTS DOWN** [33] [ ]

Sep 95. (cd/c/lp) *(<7559 61780-2/-4/-2>)* **BALLBREAKER** [6] [4]
– Whisky on the rocks / The honey roll / The furor / Love bomb / Hard as a rock / Hail Caesar / Cover you in oil / Caught with your pants down / Burnin' alive / Boogie man / Ballbreaker. *(cd re-iss. Jun98 on 'E.M.I.'; 495149-2)*

Apr 96. (c-s) *(A 6051C)* **HAIL CAESAR / WHISKEY ON THE ROCKS** [56] [ ]
(cd-s+=) *(A 6051CD)* – Whole lotta Rosie (live).

Jul 96. (cd-s) *(7559-64286-2)* **COVER YOU IN OIL / LOVE BOMB / BALLBREAKER** [ ] [ ]

Liberty Liberty

Feb 00. (cd/c) *(525667-2/-4) <62494>* **STIFF UPPER LIP** [12] [7]
– Stiff upper lip / Meltdown / House of jazz / Hold me back / Safe in New York City / Can't stand still / Can't stop rock'n'roll / Satellite blues / Damned / Come and get it / All screwed up / Give it up.

Apr 00. (cd-s) *(CDSTIFF 100)* **STIFF UPPER LIP / HARD AS A ROCK (live) / BALLBREAKER (live)** [65] [–]

– compilations, others, etc. –

Aug 84. (m-lp) *Atco; <80178>* **JAILBREAK '74** (early demos..) [–] [76]
(UK re-iss. cd Oct94; 7567 92449-2)

Sep 84. (7") *Atlantic; <89616>* **JAILBREAK. / SHOW BUSINESS** [–] [ ]

1991. (3xcd-box) *Atco;* **BOX SET** [ ] [–]
– HIGHWAY TO HELL / BACK IN BLACK / FOR THOSE ABOUT TO ROCK

Nov 97. (d-cd; BON SCOTT & THE FRATERNITY) *Raven; (RVCD 56)* **COMPLETE SESSIONS 1971-1972** [ ] [ ]

Dec 97. (5xcd-box) *(493273-2)* **BONFIRE** [ ] [90]

Jan 98. (cd-s; BON SCOTT) *Head Office; (HOR 002)* **ROUND AND ROUND AND ROUND. /** [ ] [–]

Sep 98. (cd; by BON SCOTT & THE FRATERNITY) *Connoisseur; VSOPCD 261)* **LIVESTOCK – BON SCOTT WITH FRATERNITY** [ ] [–]

ADAM & THE ANTS

Formed: London, England . . . April '77 by STUART GODDARD (aka ADAM ANT) along with LESTER SQUARE, ANDY WARREN and PAUL FLANAGAN. Initially a fairly rote punk act with attitude, what got the band noticed was their lurid stage show and penchant for S&M trappings. Derek Jarman was sufficiently enamoured to offer ADAM a part in his controversial punk flick, 'Jubilee' (released Feb '78), a revised ANTS line-up (featuring new members DAVE BARBE and MARK GAUMONT) recording two songs for the soundtrack, 'Plastic Surgery' and 'Deutcher Girls'. Later that year, the group released a one-off debut single for 'Decca', 'YOUNG PARISIANS', before releasing their rated debut album, 'DIRK WEARS WHITE SOX' in late '79. A morose slab of post-punk doom-mongering, the record stood in stark contrast to their later albums by a remodelled ADAM & THE ANTS. The shake-up came courtesy of none other than ex-SEX PISTOLS svengali, MALCOLM McLAREN, who, after dreaming up the flamboyant new image (a surprisingly effective if retrospectively ridiculous Native Indian cum swashbuckling pirates concept), whisked ADAM's band off to become BOW WOW WOW. Virtually written off by his critics, ADAM came swaggering back with a new line-up (MARCO PIRRONI, CHRIS HUGHES aka MERRICK, KEVIN MOONEY and TERRY LEE MIALL), a new sound and a new album (his first for 'C.B.S.'), 'KINGS OF THE WILD FRONTIER' (1980). Taking their cue from the Burundi drummers of Africa, the band had stumbled on a unique musical mutant which combined retro rock'n'roll with pseudo-tribal, dayglo pouting pop; teenyboppers loved it and a string of anthemic singles, 'DOG EAT DOG', 'ANT MUSIC' and the thundering title track all made the UK Top 5. The album itself rode to the top of the charts (even scaping into the US Top 50) and for a brief but warpainted period, Britain was gripped with "Antmania". The sight of the ever photogenic ADAM striding boldly through his video adventures like some dandy Indiana Jones was the stuff of girly fantasy and if you didn't have a white stripe across your nose, well, you could forget about getting lucky at the school disco. ANT was clever enough to slightly tweak his image on the follow-up set, 'PRINCE CHARMING' (1981), this time going for a dashing highwayman cum 18th century courtier get-up. It was even more effective, the group scoring two No.1 singles in quick succession with 'STAND AND DELIVER' and the title track, while 'ANT RAP' made the Top 3. To be fair to the man, he had the good sense to disband ADAM & THE ANTS at the height of their fame, although by carrying on as ADAM ANT in a vaguely similar vein, he was bound to suffer a backlash sooner or later. Retaining sidekick, PIRRONI, ANT's solo career nevertheless got off to an auspicious start with No.1 single, 'GOODY TWO SHOES', while the accompanying album, 'FRIEND OR FOE' (1982) made the Top 5 (and bizarrely the US Top 20). The following three years brought only one major hit in 'PUSS 'N' BOOTS' and after the 'VIVE LE ROCK' (1985) set, ANT took four years off to develop his acting career while PIRRONI joined SPEAR OF DESTINY. By the turn of the decade, the pair were back with an underwhelming new single, 'ROOM AT THE TOP', and album, 'MANNERS & PHYSIQUE', both enjoying a brief stint in the charts but largely ignored as the nation's pop kids raved to acid house. Of late, the ageing ADAM/STUART has run into a bit of trouble due to him brandishing a WWII gun in a pub when he was refused entry. Early in 2002, he was arrested by police and taken to a mental unit of the Royal Free Hospital in Hampstead, North London.

• **Trivia:** He acted in stage production of 'Entertaining Mr. Sloane'. After retiring to the States in 1986 he took parts in 'Slam Dance' film, and 'Equalizer' TV serial.

Album rating: DIRK WEARS WHITE SOX (*7) / KINGS OF THE WILD FRONTIER (*7) / PRINCE CHARMING (*5) / FRIEND OR FOE (*5) / STRIP (*4) / VIVE LE ROCK (*4) / MANNERS AND PHYSIQUE (*4) / WONDERFUL (*5) / HITS (1980-1985) compilation (*7)

ADAM ANT (b. STUART GODDARD, 3 Nov'54) – vocals, guitar / **MATTHEW ASHMAN** (b.'62) – guitar, vocals (ex-KAMERAS) / **ANDY WARREN** (b.'61) – bass, vocals / **DAVE BARBE** (b.'61) – drums (ex-DESOLATION ANGELS)

Decca | not iss.

Oct 78. (7") *(F 13803)* **YOUNG PARISIANS. / LADY** [ ] [–]
(re-act.Dec80; hit No.9)

Do-It | not iss.

Jun 79. (7") *(DUN 8)* **ZEROX. / WHIP IN MY VALISE** [ ] [–]

—— (some copies had B-side playing 'PHYSICAL (YOU'RE SO)') *(re-act.Jan81; hit No.45)*

Nov 79. (lp/c) *(RIDE 3/+M)* **DIRK WEARS WHITE SOX** [ ] [–]
– Cartrouble (part 1 & 2) / Digital tenderness / Nine plan failed / Day I met God * / Tabletalk / Cleopatra / Catholic day / Never trust a man (with egg on his face) / Animals and men / Family of noise / The idea. *(re-act.Jan81; hit No.16) (remixed & re-iss. Apr83 on 'C.B.S.' lp/c; CBS/40 25361) (track * replaced by)* – Zerox / Kick! / Whip in my valise. *(cd-iss. Jul95 on 'Columbia'; 480521-2) (cd re-mast.Jul04 on 'Columbia'+=; 517081-2)* – (extra demos, etc.).

—— **LEIGH GORMAN** – bass (on B-side) repl. WARREN who joined MONOCHROME SET

Feb 80. (7") *(DUN 10)* **CARTROUBLE. / KICK!** [ ] [–]
(re-act.Jan81; hit No.33)

—— (Jan'80) until (Mar'80 when ADAM brought in entire new group) **MARCO PIRRONI** (b.27 Apr'59) – guitar, vocals (ex-MODELS) repl. ASHMAN / **MERRICK** (b.CHRIS HUGHES, 3 Mar'54) – drums repl. BARBE / **KEVIN MOONEY** – bass, vocals repl. GORMAN (who with above 2 formed BOW WOW WOW) / added **TERRY LEE MIALL** (b. 8 Nov'58) – 2nd drummer (ex-MODELS)

C.B.S. | Columbia

Jul 80. (7") *(CBS 8877)* **KINGS OF THE WILD FRONTIER. / PRESS DARLINGS** [48] [–]
(re-act.Feb81; hit No.2)

Sep 80. (7") *(CBS 9039)* **DOG EAT DOG. / PHYSICAL (YOU'RE SO)** [4] [–]

Nov 80. (lp/c) *(CBS/40 84549)* *<37033>* **KINGS OF THE WILD FRONTIER** [1] Feb81 [44]
– Dog eat dog / Ant music / Feed me to the lions / Los Rancheros / Ants invasion / Killer in the home / Kings of the wild frontier / The magnificent five / Don't be square (be there) / Jolly Roger / Making history / The human beings. *(cd-iss. Oct93 & Dec98 on 'Sony Europe'; 477902-2) (cd re-mast.Jul04 on 'Columbia'; 517082-2)* – (extra demos, etc.).

Nov 80. (7") *(CBS 9352)* **ANT MUSIC. / FALL IN** [2] [–]

Jan 81. (7")(12") *<02042><01061>* **ANT MUSIC. / DON'T BE SQUARE (BE THERE)** [–] [ ]

—— **GARY TIBBS** (b.25 Jan'58)- bass (ex-ROXY MUSIC, ex-VIBRATORS) repl. MOONEY

May 81. (7")<US-12"> *(A-1065)* *<02193>* **STAND AND DELIVER. / BEAT MY GUEST** [1] [ ]

Sep 81. (7") *(A-1408)* **PRINCE CHARMING. / CHRISTIAN D'OR** [1] [–]

Nov 81. (lp/c) *(CBS/40 85268)* *<37615>* **PRINCE CHARMING** [2] [94]
– Prince Charming / The Scorpios / Picasso visita el Planeta de los Simios / 5 guns west / That voodoo / Stand and deliver / Mile high club / Ant rap / Mowhok / S.E.X. *(re-iss. cd Mar96 & Dec03 on 'Columbia'; 474606-2) (cd re-mast.Jul04 on 'Columbia'+=; 517083-2)* – (demo versions, etc.).

Dec 81. (7"/7"pic-d) *(A/+11 1738)* **ANT RAP. / FRIENDS** [3] [–]

—— they broke up early '82

ADAM ANT

continued solo augmented by **PIRRONI** and sessioners

C.B.S. | Epic

May 82. (7"/7"pic-d) *(A/+11 2367)* **GOODY TWO SHOES. / RED SCAB** [1] [–]

Sep 82. (7"/7"pic-d) *(A/+11 2736)* **FRIEND OR FOE. / JUANITO THE BANDITO** [9] [–]

Oct 82. (lp/c) *(CBS/40 25040)* *<38370>* **FRIEND OR FOE** [5] [16]
– Friend or foe / Something girls / Place in the country / Desperate but not serious / Here comes the grump / Hello I love you / Goody two shoes / Crackpot history and the right to lie / Made of money / Cajun twisters / Try this for sighs / A man called Marco. *(cd-iss. Jul96 & Jul03 on 'Columbia'; 484436-2)*

Oct 82. (7") *<03367>* **GOODY TWO SHOES. / CRACKPOT HISTORY** [–] [12]

Nov 82. (7"/7"pic-d) *(A/+11 2892)* **DESPERATE BUT NOT SERIOUS. / WHY DO GIRLS LOVE HORSES?** [33] [–]

Feb 83. (7") *<03688>* **DESPERATE BUT NOT SERIOUS. / PLACE IN THE COUNTRY** [–] [66]

Oct 83. (7"/7"pic-d/ext.12") *(A/WA/TA 3614)* *<04461>* **PUSS 'N' BOOTS. / KISS THE DRUMMER** [5] May84 [ ]

Nov 83. (lp/c) *(CBS/40 25705)* *<39108>* **STRIP** [20] [65]
– Baby let me scream at you / Libertine / Spanish games / Vanity / Puss'n'boots / Playboy / Strip / Montreal / Navel to neck / Amazon. *(cd-iss. Jul84; CD 25705)*

Dec 83. (7"/7"pic-d/ext.12") *(A/WA/TA 3589)* *<04337>* **STRIP. / YOURS, YOURS, YOURS** [41] [42]

Sep 84. (7"/'A'-Orbit mix-12") *(A/TA 4719)* **APOLLO 9. / B SIDE BABY** [13] [ ]
(12") *(QTA 4719)* – ('A'-Splashdown remix & acappella instrumental).

Jul 85. (7") *(A 6367)* *<05574>* **VIVE LE ROCK. / GRETA X** [50] [ ]
(12"+=) *(TA 6367)* – ('A'instrumental dub mix).

Sep 85. (lp/c) *(CBS/40 26583)* *<40159>* **VIVE LE ROCK** [42] [ ]
– Vive le rock / Miss Thing / Razor keen / Rip down / Scorpio rising / Apollo 9 / Hell's eight acres / Mohair lockeroom pin-up boys / No zap / P.O.E. *(c+=)* – Human bondage den. *(cd-iss. 1988+=; CD 26583)* – Apollo 9 (acappella). *(re-iss. cd Mar95 on 'Rewind'; 478504-2)*

—— ADAM retired for 4 years. MARCO joined SPEAR OF DESTINY

ADAM ANT

brought back MARCO to resurrect career.

M.C.A. | M.C.A.

Feb 90. (7"/7"s/c-s) *(MCA/+R/C 1387)* *<53679>* **ROOM AT THE TOP. / BRUCE LEE** [13] [17]
(cd-s+=/12"+=) *(D+/MCAT 1387)* – ('A'house vocals).
(cd-s+=) *(DMCAX 1387)* – ('A'mixes).

Mar 90. (cd/lp)(c) *(D+/MCG 6068)(MCGC 6068)* *<6315>* **MANNERS & PHYSICIQUE** [19] [57]
– Room at the top / If you keep on / Can't set rules about love / Bright lights black leather / Young dumb and full of it / Rough stuff / Manners & physicique / U.S.S.A. / Piccadilly / Anger Inc.

Apr 90. (7"/c-s) *(MCA/+C 1404)* **CAN'T SET RULES ABOUT LOVE. / HOW TO STEAL THE WORLD** [47] [ ]
(cd-s+=/12"+=) *(D+/MCAT 1404)* – Brand new torso.
(cd-s++=) *(DMCAP 1404)* – ('A'-lp version).

Jun 90. (7") *<79042>* **BRIGHT LIGHTS BLACK LEATHER. / ROUGH STUFF** [–] [ ]

—— w/ **PIRRONI** / **BOZ BOORER** – guitars / **BRUCE WITKIN** – bass / **DAVE RUFFY** – drums

E.M.I. | Capitol

Jan 95. (c-s/7") *(TC+/EM 366)* *<58239>* **WONDERFUL. / GOES AROUND** [32] Mar95 [39]
(cd-s+=) *(CDEMS 366)* – Norman / Woman love run through me.
(cd-s) *(CDEM 366)* – ('A'side) / If / Phoenix.

Mar 95. (c-s/7"; withdrawn) **BEAUTIFUL DREAM. / LET'S HAVE A FIGHT** [ ] [ ]
(cd-s+=; w-drawn) – Billy boy / Wonderful (acoustic).
(cd-s; w-drawn) – ('A'side) / Shake your hips / Ant music (acoustic) / ('A'-Lucas master mix).

Apr 95. (cd/c) *(CD/TC EMC 3687)* *<30335>* **WONDERFUL** [24] [39]
– Won't take that talk / Beautiful dream / Wonderful / 1969 again / Yin & Yang / Image of yourself / Alien / Gotta be a sin / Vampires / Angel / Very long ride. *(cd re-iss. Sep97; same)*

May 95. (c-s) *(TCEM 379)* **GOTTA BE A SIN / DOG EAT DOG (live)** [48] [ ]
(cd-s) *(CDEM 379)* – ('A'side) / Cleopatra (live) / Beat my guest (live) / Red scab (live).

(cd-s) *(CDEMS 379)* – ('A'side) / Desperate but not serious (live) / Car trouble (live) / Physical (you're so) (live).

– compilations, others, etc. –

on 'Columbia' unless mentioned otherwise

Feb 82. (7") *E.G.; (EGO 5)* **DEUTCHER GIRLS. / PLASTIC SURGERY** [13] [–]

Mar 82. (7"ep/7"pic-ep) *Do-It; (DUN/+X 20)* **THE B-SIDES** [46] [–]
– Friends / Kick! / Physical (you're so).
(12"ep+=) **ANTMUSIC** *(DUNIT 20)* – Cartrouble (pts. 1 & 2).

1982. (7"; as MANEATERS) *E.G.; (EGO 8)* **NINE TO FIVE. / (SUZI PINNS: Jerusalem)** [ ] [–]
(above another from the film 'Jubilee' & featuring TOYAH)

Sep 86. (lp/c) *C.B.S.; (CBS/40 450074-1/-4)* **HITS** [ ] [ ]
– Kings of the wild frontier / Dog eat dog / Ant music / Stand and deliver / Prince Charming / Ant rap / Goody two shoes / Friend or foe / Desperate but not serious / Puss 'n' boots / Strip / Apollo 9 / Vive le rock. *(re-iss. Jul90 & Jul98 on 'Columbia' cd/c; R 450074-2/-4)*

Jan 88. (7") *Old Gold; (OG 9739)* **ANT MUSIC. / STAND AND DELIVER** [ ] [–]

Oct 89. (12"white/12"pic-d) *Damaged Goods; (FNARR/+P 7)* **YOUNG PARISIANS / LADY. / (interview)** [ ] [–]

Nov 90. (7") *Old Gold; (OG 9953)* **PRINCE CHARMING. / GOODY TWO SHOES** [ ] [–]

Feb 91. (cd/c/lp) *Strange Fruit; (SFR CD/MC/LP 115)* **THE PEEL SESSIONS** (early 1979 material) [ ] [–]

Jun 91. (cd/c) *(468762-2/-4)* **ANTICS IN THE FORBIDDEN ZONE** [ ] [–]

Aug 93. (cd/c) *Arcade; (ARC 31000 5-2/6-4)* **ANTMUSIC – THE VERY BEST OF ADAM ANT** [6] [–]
(re-iss. Mar94 d-cd+ 'LIVE'; ARC 310000-2); hit No.30)

Oct 94. (cd) *(477513-2)* **THE BEST (ADAM ANT)** [ ] [ ]

May 95. (cd) *(480362-2)* **B SIDES BABIES** [ ] [ ]

Mar 99. (cd) *(494229-2)* **THE VERY BEST OF ADAM & THE ANTS** [56] [ ]
(re-iss. May04; same)

Dec 00. (3xcd-box) *(500782-2)* **ANTBOX: THE DEFINITIVE STORY OF ADAM & THE ANTS** [ ] [ ]

Jul 01. (cd) *Strange Fruit; (SFRSCD 099)* **THE COMPLETE RADIO ONE RECORDINGS** [ ] [ ]

Bryan ADAMS

Born: 5 Nov'59, Vancouver, Canada. In 1977 he set up a writing partnership with JIM VALLANCE, drummer with techno-rock band, PRISM. Numerous groups, including LOVERBOY, KISS, BACHMAN-TURNER OVERDRIVE, etc. used their songs before ADAMS signed a contract with 'A&M' early in 1979. While VALLANCE recorded with ADAMS on the low-key debut single and eponymous album, he soon bowed out (the writing partnership continued) and ADAMS assembled a new band for the follow-up, 'YOU WANT IT YOU GOT IT' (1982). However, it wasn't until Spring 1983, with the release of 'STRAIGHT FROM THE HEART', that ADAMS made a significant impact on the US charts. His gravel-voiced, sub-SPRINGSTEEN rock was soon to enter into an ongoing love affair with coffee tables the world over, the follow-up album, 'CUTS LIKE A KNIFE' making the Top 10 album chart in America. ADAMS really hit his stride with 'RECKLESS' (1984), a sturdy, professional set of soft-rockers and ballads. While 'SUMMER OF '69' was an entertaining piece of anthemic pop/rock and the album possessed just enough rough-edged charm to offset the cheese factor, the likes of 'THE KIDS WANNA ROCK' was downright cringeworthy. ADAMS also beat ELTON to a Princess Di tribute with the B-side of the 'HEAVEN' single, entitled, funnily enough, 'DIANA'. The album made the man a household name while the follow-up effort, 'INTO THE FIRE' (1987) marked the end of his songwriting partnerhip with VALLANCE and saw ADAMS lyrics take on a more political bent (the following year saw ADAMS playing the Nelson Mandela benefit concert at Wembley Stadium). Still, any hopes of a radical new direction were dashed several years later upon the release of the unashamed slush-pop ballad, '(EVERYTHING I DO) I DO IT FOR YOU'. The record (featured on the soundtrack to the Kevin Costner film, 'Robin Hood, Prince Of Thieves') went to No. 1 on both sides of the Atlantic for what seemed like an eternity. After 16 weeks of radio overkill, one might have suspected that the populace had satiated their Adams appetite, so to speak, but no, the follow-up, 'CAN'T STOP THIS THING WE STARTED' (more uptempo but equally bland) almost breached the UK Top 10. The album, 'WAKING UP THE NEIGHBOURS' (1992) went to the top of the album charts, although it's safe to say that by now, ADAMS was probably appealing to a slightly different market and had lost any credibility (if, that is, he actually had any in the first place!) with a younger, more discerning audience. More nauseatingly saccharine ballads followed ('ALL FOR LOVE', 'HAVE YOU EVER REALLY LOVED A WOMAN' etc., you get the picture) into the singles charts while his most recent attempts at rock (in the loosest sense of the term, naturally) make HANSON sound dangerous. The icing on ADAMS' sickly-sweet cake came with 'SPIRIT: STALLION OF THE CIMARRON' (2002), a soundtrack for a Disney-style cartoon about a runaway horse. With a single, 'HERE I AM', making the UK Top 5, and the album itself making both the UK Top 10 and the US Top 40, it seems fair to say that come the summer of 2009, ADAMS will still have them rocking in the (cinema) aisles. In the meantime, 'ROOM SERVICE' (2004), was hardly penthouse suite-standard, more like a time-warped Butlins chalet; while America had virtually distanced itself from ADAMS' oil-slick "rock", the Brits were still taking plenty of bookings, elevating the long-player to the Top 5.

• **Covered:** WALKING AFTER MIDNIGHT (D. Hecht / A. Block) / I FOUGHT THE LAW (Sonny Curtis) / LITTLE RED ROOSTER (Willie Dixon).

Album rating: BRYAN ADAMS (*3) / YOU WANT IT YOU GOT IT (*5) / CUTS LIKE A KNIFE (*7) / RECKLESS (*7) / INTO THE FIRE (*5) / WAKING UP THE NEIGHBOURS (*5) / SO FAR SO GOOD compilation (*6) / LIVE! LIVE! LIVE! (*4) / 18 TIL I DIE (*4) / UNPLUGGED (*4) / ON A DAY LIKE TODAY (*4) / THE BEST OF ME compilation (*8) / SPIRIT: STALLION OF THE CIMARRON soundtrack w/ Hans Zimmer (*4) / ROOM SERVICE (*3) / ANTHOLOGY double compilation (*7)

BRYAN ADAMS – vocals, guitar / with **JIM VALLANCE** – drums, keyboards, guitar, bass

A&M A&M

Jul 79. (7"/ext.12") *(AMS/+P 7460) <2163>* **LET ME TAKE YOU DANCIN'. / DON'T TURN ME AWAY** [ ] [ ]

Apr 80. (7") *(AMS 7520) <2220>* **HIDIN' FROM LOVE. / WAIT AND SEE** [ ] [ ]

Mar 81. (lp) *(AMLH 64800) <4800>* **BRYAN ADAMS** [ ] Nov80 [ ]
– Hidin' from love / Win some, lose some / Wait and see / Give me your love / Wastin' time / Don't ya say it / Remember / State of mind / Try to see it my way. *(cd-iss. Jan87; CDA 3100) (re-iss. cd 1988; CDMID 100)*

Apr 81. (7") *<2249>* **GIVE ME YOUR LOVE. / WAIT AND SEE** [–] [ ]

—— now with **TOMMY HANDEL** – keyboards / **BRIAN STANLEY** – bass + **MICKEY CURRY** – drums repl. VALLANCE (he continued to co-write + play piano + percussion for ADAMS until '88).

Mar 82. (7") *(AMS 8183) <2359>* **LONELY NIGHTS. / DON'T LOOK NOW** [ ] [84]

Apr 82. (lp) *(AMLH 64864) <4864>* **YOU WANT IT, YOU GOT IT** [78] Jan82 [ ]
– Lonely nights / One good reason / Don't look now / Jealousy / Coming home / Fits ya good / Tonight / You want it, you got it / Last chance / No one makes it right. *(cd-iss. Aug85; CDA 3154) (re-iss. cd 1988; CDMID 100)*

Jul 82. (7") *<2409>* **COMING HOME. / FITS YA GOOD** [–] [ ]

—— **DAVE TAYLOR** – bass repl. STANLEY

—— added **KEITH SCOTT** – guitar, vocals

Mar 83. (lp) *(SMLH 64919) <4919>* **CUTS LIKE A KNIFE** [ ] Feb83 [8]
– The only one / Take me back / This time / Straight from the heart / Cuts like a knife / I'm ready / What's it gonna be / Don't leave me lonely / The

best has yet to come. *(re-iss. Mar86; same)*; hit UK 21) *(cd-iss. Mar86; CDA 4919)* (cd re-iss. 1988; *CDMID 102*)

Mar 83. (7") *<2536>* **STRAIGHT FROM THE HEART. / ONE GOOD REASON** – 10

Apr 83. (7"/12") *(AM/+X 103)* **STRAIGHT FROM THE HEART. / LONELY NIGHTS** [ ] –

Jun 83. (7") *(2553>* **CUTS LIKE A KNIFE. / LONELY NIGHTS** – 15

Jul 83. (7") *(AM 129)* **CUTS LIKE A KNIFE. / FITS YA GOOD** [ ] –
(12"+=) *(AMP 129)* – Hidin' from love.

Aug 83. (7") *<2574>* **THIS TIME. / FITS YA GOOD** – 24

Nov 83. (7") *<26??>* **THE BEST HAS YET TO COME. / I'M READY** – [ ]

Dec 84. (7") *(AM 224) <2686>* **RUN TO YOU. / I'M READY** 11 Oct84 6
(12"+=) *(AMD 224)* – Cuts like a knife.
(d7"++=) *(AMY 224)* – Lonely nights.

Feb 85. (lp/c/cd) *<(AMA/AMC/CDA 5013)>* **RECKLESS** 7 Nov84 1
– One night love affair / She's only happy when she's dancin' / Run to you / Heaven / Somebody / Summer of '69 / It's only love / Kids wanna rock / Long gone / Ain't gonna cry. *(re-iss. Jul92 & Sep97; 395013-2)*

Feb 85. (7"/7"pic-d/12") *(AM/+P/Y 236) <2701>* **SOMEBODY. / LONG GONE** 35 Jan85 11

Mar 85. (7") *<2722>* **DIANA. / ('A'live)** – [ ]

Apr 85. (7") *<2729>* **HEAVEN. / ('A'live)** – 1
(above/below taken from the 1983! movie, 'A Night In Heaven')

May 85. (7") *(AM 256)* **HEAVEN. / DIANA** 38 –
(12"+=) *(AMY 256)* – Fits ya good / ('A'version).
(d7"+=) *(AMD 256)* – Straight from the heart / You want it, you got it.

Jun 85. (7") *<2739>* **SUMMER OF '69. / THE BEST HAS YET TO COME** – 5

Jul 85. (7") *(AM 267)* **SUMMER OF '69. / KIDS WANNA ROCK (live)** 42 –
(12"+=) *(AMY 267)* – The Bryan Adamix.

Sep 85. (7") *<2770>* **ONE NIGHT LOVE AFFAIR. / LONELY NIGHTS** – 13

Oct 85. (7"/12"; by BRYAN ADAMS & TINA TURNER) *(AM/+Y 285)* **IT'S ONLY LOVE. / THE BEST WAS YET TO COME** 29 –
(d7"+=) *(AMD 285)* – Somebody. / Long gone.

Nov 85. (7"; by BRYAN ADAMS & TINA TURNER) *<2791>* **IT'S ONLY LOVE. / THE ONLY ONE** – 15

Dec 85. (7"/12") *(AM/+Y 297)* **CHRISTMAS TIME. / REGGAE CHRISTMAS** 55 –

Feb 86. (7") *(AM 295)* **THIS TIME. / I'M READY** 41 –
(12"+=) *(AMY 295)* – Lonely nights.

Jul 86. (7") *(AM 322)* **STRAIGHT FROM THE HEART. / FITS YA GOOD** 51 –
(12"+=) *(AMY 322)* – ('A'live).

Mar 87. (7") *(ADAM 2) <2921>* **HEAT OF THE NIGHT. / ANOTHER DAY** 50 6
(12"+=) *(ADAM 2-12)* – ('A'extended remix).

Apr 87. (lp/c/cd) *<(AMA/AMC/CDA 3907)>* **INTO THE FIRE** 10 7
– Heat of the night / Into the fire / Victim of love / Another day / Native son / Only the strong survive / Remembrance day / Rebel rebel / Hearts on fire / Home again. *(re-iss. Mar93 cd/c; CD/C MID 185)*

May 87. (7") *<2948>* **HEARTS ON FIRE. / THE BEST HAS YET TO COME** – 26

May 87. (7"/c-s) *(ADAM/+C 3)* **HEARTS ON FIRE. / RUN TO YOU** 57 –
(12"+=) *(ADAM 3-12)* – Native sun.

Aug 87. (7") *<2964>* **VICTIM OF LOVE. / INTO THE FIRE** – 32

Oct 87. (7"/7"box/c-s) *(AM/+F/C 407)* **VICTIM OF LOVE. / HEAT OF THE NIGHT (live)** 68 –
(12"+=) *(AMY 407)* – ('A'live).

—— BRYAN now used session people?

Jun 91. (7"/c-s) *(AM/+MC 789) <1567>* **(EVERYTHING I DO) I DO IT FOR YOU. / SHE'S ONLY HAPPY WHEN SHE'S DANCING (live)** 1 1
(12"+=/cd-s+=) *(AM Y/CD 789)* – ('A'extended) / Cuts like a knife.

Aug 91. (7"/c-s) *(AM/+MC 812) <1576>* **CAN'T STOP THIS THING WE STARTED. / IT'S ONLY LOVE (live)** 12 2
(etched-12"+=/cd-s+=) *(AM Y/CD 812)* – Hearts on fire.

Sep 91. (cd/c/lp) *(397164-2/-4/-1) <5367>* **WAKING UP THE NEIGHBOURS** 1 6
– Is your mama gonna miss ya? / Hey honey – I'm rockin' you in! / Can't stop this thing we started / Thought I'd died and gone to Heaven / Not guilty / House arrest / Vanishing / Do I have to say the words? / There will never be another tonight / All I want is you / Depend on me / (Everything I do) I do it for you / If you wanna leave me (can I come too?) / Touch the hand / Don't drop that bomb on me.

Nov 91. (7"/c-s) *(AM/+C 838) <1588>* **THERE WILL NEVER BE ANOTHER TONIGHT. / INTO THE FIRE (live)** 32 31
(etched-12"+=/pic-cd-s+=) *(AM Y/CD 838)* – One night love affair (live).

Feb 92. (7"/c-s) *(AM/+C 848) <1592>* **I THOUGHT I'D DIED AND GONE TO HEAVEN. / SOMEBODY (live)** 8 13
(12"+=) *(AMY 848)* – (Everything I do) I do it for you.
(cd-s+=) *(AMCD 848)* – Heart of the night (live).

Jul 92. (7"/c-s) *(AM/+C 879)* **ALL I WANT IS YOU. / RUN TO YOU** 22 –
(12"+=/cd-s+=) *(AM Y/CD 879)* – Long gone.

Sep 92. (7"/c-s) *(AM/+C 0068) <1611>* **DO I HAVE TO SAY THE WORDS?. / SUMMER OF '69** 30 Jul92 11
(12"+=/cd-s+=) *(AM T/CD 0068)* – Kids wanna rock / Can't stop this thing we started.

Oct 93. (7"/c-s) *(580423-7/-4) <0422>* **PLEASE FORGIVE ME. / C'MON EVERYBODY** 2 7
(cd-s+=) *(580423-2)* – Can't stop this thing we started / There will never be another tonight.

Nov 93. (cd/c/lp) *(540157-2/-4/-1) <0157>* **SO FAR SO GOOD** (compilation) 2 7
– Summer of '69 / Straight from the heart / It's only love / Can't stop this thing we started / Do I have to say the words? / This time / Run to you / Heaven / Cuts like a knife / (Everything I do) I do it for you / Somebody / Kids wanna rock / Heat of the night / Please forgive me.

Jan 94. (7"/c-s; BRYAN ADAMS, ROD STEWART & STING) *(580477-7/-4) <0476>* **ALL FOR LOVE. / ('A'instrumental)** 2 Nov93 1
(cd-s) *(580477-2)* – ('A'side) / Straight from the heart (live) (BRYAN ADAMS) / If only (ROD STEWART) / Love is stronger than justice (live) (STING).
(above hit from the film 'The Three Musketeers')

Jul 94. (cd/c) *(397094-2/-4)* **LIVE! LIVE! LIVE!** (rec.live Belgium 1988) 17 –
– She's only happy when she's dancin' / It's only love / Cuts like a knife / Kids wanna rock / Hearts on fire / Take me back / The best was yet to come / Heaven / Heat of the night / Run to you / One night love affair / Long gone / Summer of '69 / Somebody / Walking after midnight / I fought the law / Into the fire.

Apr 95. (7"/c-s/cd-s) *(581028-7/-4/-2) <1028>* **HAVE YOU EVER REALLY LOVED A WOMAN? / LOW LIFE** 4 1

May 96. (c-s/cd-s) *(581579-4/-2) <1578>* **THE ONLY THING THAT LOOKS GOOD ON ME IS YOU / HEY ELVIS / I WANT IT ALL** 6 52
(cd-s) *(581639-2)* – ('A'side) / Summer of '69 / Cuts like a knife / Thought I'd died and gone to Heaven.

Jun 96. (cd/c) *(540675-2/-4) <0551>* **18 TIL I DIE** 1 31
– The only thing that looks good on me is you / Do to you / Let's make a night to remember / 18 til I die / Star / (I wanna be) Your underwear / We're gonna win / I think about you / I'll always be right there / It ain't a party . . . if you can't come 'round / Black pearl / You're still beautiful to me / Have you ever really loved a woman?

Aug 96. (c-ep) *(581865-4)* **LET'S MAKE A NIGHT TO REMEMBER / ROCK STEADY / HEY LITTLE GIRL / IF YA WANNA BE BAD YA GOTTA BE GOOD** 10 –
(cd-ep) *(581865-2)* – (first 3 tracks) / ('A'version).
(cd-ep) *(581867-2)* – ('A'side) / ('A'version) / If ya wanna be bad ya gotta be good / Little red rooster.

Aug 96. (c-s,cd-s) *<1862>* **LET'S MAKE A NIGHT TO REMEMBER / STAR** – 24

Nov 96. (cd-ep) *(582027-2)* **STAR / THE ONLY THING THAT LOOKS GOOD ON ME IS YOU / IT'S ONLY LOVE (with MELISSA ETHERIDGE) / RUN TO YOU** 13 –
(c-ep/cd-ep) *(582025-4/-2)* – ('A'side) / Let's make it a night to remember / All for love / (Everything I do) I do it for you.

Jan 97. (c-s; by BARBRA STREISAND & BRYAN ADAMS) *(582083-4) <78480>* **I FINALLY FOUND SOMEONE / 18 TIL I DIE** 10 Nov96 8
(cd-s) *(582083-2)* – ('A'side) / Star / I think about you / Do to you.
(above from 'The Mirror Has Two Faces' movie on 'Columbia' US)

Apr 97. (c-s/cd-s) *(582183-4/-2)* **18 TIL I DIE / DO TO YOU** 22 [ ]
(cd-s+=) *(582183-5)* – Can't stop this thing we started / Touch the hand.

Dec 97. (cd/c) *<(540831-2/-4)>* **UNPLUGGED (live)** 19 88
– Summer of '69 / Back to you / Cuts like a knife / I'm ready / Fits ya good / When you love someone / 18 til I die / I think about you / If ya wanna be bad ya gotta be good / Let's make a night to remember / The only thing that looks good on me is you / A little love / Heaven / I'll always be right there.

Dec 97. (c-s/cd-s) *(582475-4/-2)* **BACK TO YOU / HEY ELVIS / CAN'T STOP THIS THING WE STARTED – IT AIN'T A PARTY . . . IF YOU CAN'T COME 'ROUND (medley)** [18] [ ]

Mar 98. (c-s/cd-s) *(582535-4/-2)* **I'M READY / (IN WANNA BE YOUR) UNDERWEAR / BACK TO YOU (original) / I'LL ALWAYS BE RIGHT THERE** [20] [–]

Mercury Mercury

Sep 98. (c-s) *(MERMC 516)* **ON A DAY LIKE TODAY / SHE BELIEVES IN ME** [13] [–]
(cd-s+=) *(MERCD 516)* – ('A'-Pants down mix).
(cd-s) *(MERDD 516)* – ('A'side) / The only thing that looks good on me (is you) / Bin there, done that.

Oct 98. (cd/c) *<(541016-2/-4)>* **ON A DAY LIKE TODAY** [11] [ ]
– How do ya feel tonight / C'mon c'mon c'mon / Getaway / On a day like today / Fearless / I'm a liar / Cloud number nine / When you're gone (with MELANIE C) / Inside out / If I had you / Before the night is over / I don't wanna live forever / Where angels fear to tread / Lie to me.

Nov 98. (c-s; by BRYAN ADAMS & MEL C) *(582818-4)* **WHEN YOU'RE GONE / HEY BABY** [3] [–]
(cd-s+=) *(582819-2)* – When you're gone (without Melanie C).
(cd-s) *(582821-2)* – ('A'side) / I love ya too much / What does it do to your heart.

Apr 99. (c-s) *(582646-4)* **CLOUD NUMBER NINE / Bryan Adams & Mel C: WHEN YOU'RE GONE (acoustic)** [6] [–]
(cd-s+=) *(582849-2)* – Let's talk about love.
(cd-s) *(582847-2)* – ('A'mixes; Chicane / Bascombe / medley).

Nov 99. (cd/c) *(490522-2/-4)* **THE BEST OF ME** (compilation) [12] [–]
– The best of me / Can't stop this thing we started / I'm ready / Summer of '69 / Let's make a night to remember / All for love / Have you ever really loved a woman? / Run to you / Cloud number nine / (Everything I do) I do it for you / Back to you / When you're gone / Please forgive me / The only thing that looks good on me is you / Inside out. *(special cd+=; 490559-2)* – South Africa live:- Summer of '69 / Back to you / Can't stop this thing we started / Have you ever really loved a woman / Rock steady. *<US cd-iss. Sep01; 540157>*

Nov 99. (c-s) *(497023-4)* **THE BEST OF ME / CLOUD NUMBER NINE** [47] [–]
(cd-s+=) *(497196-2)* – Fearless.
(cd-s) *(497195-2)* – ('A'side) / Inside out / How do ya feel tonight.

— In Mar'00, ADAMS was credited with CHICANE on their UK No.1 single, 'Don't Give Up'

Universal Universal

Jul 02. (c-s) *(497743-4)* **HERE I AM – END TITLE / I'M READY (live at Slane Castle)** [5] [–]
(cd-s+=) *(497743-2)* – ('A'-soundtrack version) / Cloud number 9 (live at Slane Castle).
(cd-s) *(497744-2)* – ('A'side) / ('A'-instrumental) / You can't take me (alt. version) / ('A'-video).

Jul 02. (cd) *(493362-2) <493304-2>* **SPIRIT: STALLION OF THE CIMARRON** (soundtrack with Hans Zimmer) [8] May02 [40]
– Here I am – end title / I will always return / You can't take me / Get off my back / Brothers under the sun / Don't let go (SARAH McLACHLAN) / This is where I belong / Here I am / Sound the bugle (instrumental) / Run free (instrumental) / Homeland – main title (instrumental) / Rain (instrumental) / The long road back (instrumental) / Nothing I've ever known / I will always return – finale.

Polydor Badman

Sep 04. (cd-s) *(9869053)* **OPEN ROAD / BLESSING IN DISGUISE / FRIDAY NIGHT IN LONDON** [21] [–]

Sep 04. (cd) *(9868245) <9868057>* **ROOM SERVICE** [4] Oct04 [ ]
– East side story / This side of Paradise / Not Romeo not Juliet / Flying / She's a little too good for me / Open road / Room service / I was only dreamin' / Right back where I started from / Nowhere fast / Why do you have to be so hard to love. *(UK+=)* – Blessing in disguise.

Nov 04. (cd-s) *(9869276)* **FLYING / YOU WALKED IN** [39] [–]

Mar 05. (cd-s) *(9871026)* **ROOM SERVICE / OPEN ROAD (stripped)** [ ] [–]
(cd-s+=) *(9871027)* – ('A'-acoustic) / ('A'-video).

Nov 05. (d-cd) *(9835827) <5613>* **ANTHOLOGY** (compilation) [29] Oct05 [65]
– Remember / Lonely nights / Straight from the heart / Cuts like a knife / This time / Run to you / Somebody / Heaven / Summer of '69 / One night love affair / It's only love (w/ TINA TURNER) / Heat of the night / Hearts on fire / (Everything I do) I do it for you / Can't stop this thing we started / There will never be another tonight / Thought I'd died and gone to Heaven / The best of me *[US-only]* // All I want is you *[UK-only]* // Please forgive me / All for love (w/ ROD STEWART & STING) / Have you ever really loved a woman? / Rock steady (live w/ BONNIE RAITT) / The only thing that looks good on me is you / Let's make a night to remember / Star / Back to you (live) / I'm ready (live) / On a day like today / When you're gone (w/ MEL C) *[UK-only]* / Cloud number nine (Chicane mix) / Best of me *[UK-only]* / Don't give up (w/ CHICANE) [UK-only] / Here I am / This side of Paradise *[UK-only]* / Why do you have to be so hard to love *[UK-only]* / Open road / 18 til I die (live) / When you're gone (w/ MEL C) *[US-only]* / So far so good / I'm not the man you think I am *[UK-only]*.

– others, etc. –

Jun 89. (c) *A&M; (AMC 24101)* **CUTS LIKE A KNIFE / RECKLESS** [ ] [–]

— on the 2nd lp below he had replaced NICK GILDER

Jan 92. (cd/lp; SWEENEY TODD featuring BRYAN ADAMS) *Receiver; (RR CD/LP 154)* **IF WISHES WERE HORSES** [ ] [–]
– Tantalize / If wishes were horses / Until I find you / Pushin' and shovin' / No.5243605 Smith / Song for a star / Shut up / All of a sudden / Wastin' time / Say hello wave goodbye.

Ryan ADAMS

Born: DAVID RYAN ADAMS, 5 Nov'74, Jacksonville, North Carolina, USA. Before turning into a music industry brat and hanging around the likes of Elton John and Jon Bon Jovi, RYAN ADAMS used to be a highy respected and low-key member of America's thriving mid-west alt Country scene and the co-founder of the excellent WHISKEYTOWN. After his split with the aforementioned, however, ADAMS cleaned up his act, stopped partying and became friendly with the rich and famous. Luckily for us, he still managed to write songs that could smash most of today's modern singer/songwriter types into tiny pieces. 'HEARTBREAKER' (2000) was a fine example of this: recorded in seventeen days and featuring the likes of EMMYLOU HARRIS, GILLIAN WELCH and her husband DAVID RAWLINGS, the album was full of sweetness, bitterness and of course, downright heartbreak. 'TO BE YOUNG (IS TO BE SAD, IS TO BE HIGH)' was a good ol' country rock'n'roll track, while 'AMY' wouldn't have sounded out of place on the BEATLES 'White Album'. But most impressive of all was the sheer poignancy shot through most of ADAMS' songs, whether it be the soloistic flare of 'IN MY TIME OF NEED' or HARRIS' timely western vocals on the haunting 'OH MY SWEET CAROLINA' (perhaps one of the greatest songs of ADAMS' career, if not one of the greatest ballads ever written). The set also displayed an impressive array of songs and not one would fail to move the listener. After the critical acclaim of 'HEARTBREAKER', ADAMS began work on a more commercial affair, 'GOLD' (2001), a follow-up which saw him moving slowly towards the mainstream and abandoning his lo-fi country roots. To call him a sell-out would be unfair, but ADAMS certainly must have been tempted by the overground to issue such a MOR-tinged, conformist album. Some tracks still hit through (especially in America where it hit the Top 20). For instance 'RESCUE BLUES' and the sweet ballad 'WHEN THE STARS GO BLUE' lived up to the standards of his previous set, but single 'NEW YORK, NEW YORK' (accompanied by a terrible 'nostalgic' music video) was strictly for the Starbucks generation and could've easily featured on BON JOVI's latest. To try to win back some of his indie cred, somewhat lost after 'GOLD', ADAMS set to releasing the quietly admirable demos and rarities compendium 'DEMOLITION' in 2002. Comprised of hastily written and recorded tracks, the album boasted a number of stripped down songs, which, with better production, could've proved to be a hit with his newfound mainstream audience. Whereas 'GOLD' saw him isolate his mawkish fanbase,

'DEMOLITION' did the opposite – not sitting well with the people who made 'NEW YORK . . .' a hit. Nevertheless, a fine addition to his back catalogue and proof that the prolific troubadour was capable of some pretty good stuff, it was back to the usual come the release of the shaky 'ROCK N ROLL' (2003). The "official" follow-up to 'GOLD', ADAMS wanted to issue his "death-threat to himself" album, 'LOVE IS HELL', as the set which would follow hot on its heels. Not if label 'Lost Highway' had anything to do with it; they rejected the album and sent ADAMS back to the studio, with the result being the aforementioned 'ROCK N ROLL'. Slightly hurried and, in some parts, sounding rather drab, the much rawer, depressing 'LOVE IS HELL' was finally available when it was released in two parts at the end of 2003. Sounding somewhat like an ode to those rainy day SMITHS albums ADAMS was so much in love with (and with a production by SMITHS collaborator John Porter), the two mini-LP's delved deeper into his dark psyche and with some impressive submissions aside, you couldn't help wonder if 'Lost Highway' had a point when they noted that the album was "too bleak". ADAMS' long-awaited break into the UK Top 30 singles chart came in summer 2004 via a cover rather than an original, and a strange choice at that: Oasis' 'WONDERWALL'. Making up for a quiet 2004, the former WHISKEYTOWN man went back to his roots on two (very) long-players, 'COLD ROSES' and 'JACKSONVILLE CITY NIGHTS'. Released within months of each other in 2005, they featured ADAMS' new outfit the CARDINALS, backing up ADAMS' JACKSON BROWNE-meets-ROY ORBISON holler with the kind of stone-country he'd steered clear of in recent years. His public responded in kind, sending both records into the middle reaches of the charts. ADAMS overreached himself however, with a third successive album, albeit a solo 1-disc set: '29' (2006). Anybody with even a passing familiarity with the GRATEFUL DEAD will recognise the tongue-trippin' chug of 'Truckin' in the opening title track, even if elsewhere the magpie troubadour exhumed the spectres of both JEFF BUCKLEY and his dad.

• **Covers:** LOVESICK BLUES (Hank Williams).

Album rating: HEARTBREAKER (*9) / GOLD (*6) / DEMOLITION (*5) / ROCK N ROLL (*5) / LOVE IS HELL PT.1 mini (*6) / LOVE IS HELL PT.2 mini (*4) / COLD ROSES (*7) / JACKSONVILLE CITY NIGHTS (*7) / 29 (*4)

RYAN ADAMS – vocals, acoustic guitar, banjo

Cooking Vinyl | Cooking Vinyl

Oct 00. (cd) *<(COOKCD 205)>* **HEARTBREAKER** [ ] [ ]
– (Argument with David Rawlings concerning Morrissey) / To be young (is to be sad, is to be high) / My winding wheel / AMY / Oh my sweet Carolina / Bartering lines / Call me on your way back home / Damn, Sam (I love a woman that rains) / Come pick me up / To be the one / Why do they leave / Shakedown on 9th Street / Don't ask for the water / In my time of need / Sweet lil gal (23rd/1st). *(lp-iss.Jun02; COOK 205)*

Lost Highway | Lost Highway

Sep 01. (cd) *<(170235-2)>* **GOLD** [20] [59]
– New York, New York / Firecracker / Answering bell / Le cienega just smiled / The rescue blues / Somehow, someday / When the stars go blue / Nobody girl / Sylvia Plath / Enemy fire / Gonna make you love me / Wild flowers / Harder now that it's over / Touch, feel & lose / The Toledo's street walkin' blues / Goodnight Hollywood Blvd. *(d-cd+=; 170252-2)* – Rosalie come and go / Fool we are as men / Sweet black magic / Cannonball days / The bar is a beautiful place. *(cd/d-lp-iss.Apr02; 170 262-2/235-1)*

Nov 01. (cd-s) *(172223-2)* **NEW YORK NEW YORK / MARA LISA / FROM ME TO YOU / ('A'-video)** [53] [–]

Apr 02. (cd-s) *(172239-2)* **ANSWERING BELL / SWEET BLACK MAGIC / THE BAR IS A BEAUTIFUL PLACE / ('A'-video)** [39] [–]
(cd-s) *(172240-2)* – ('A'-live) / New York New York (live) / To be young (is to be sad is to be high) (live) / New York New York (video).

Sep 02. (7") *(172259-7)* **NUCLEAR. / SONG FOR KEITH** [37] [–]
(cd-s) *(172259-2)* – ('A') / Blue.

Sep 02. (cd/lp) *<(170333-2/-1)>* **DEMOLITION** [22] [28]
– Nuclear / Hallelujah / You will always be the same / Desire / Cry on demand / Starting to hurt / She wants to play hearts / Tennessee sucks / Dear Chicago / Gimme a sign / Tomorrow / Chin up, cheer up / Jesus (don't touch my baby).

Nov 03. (cd)(lp) *(9861324)(9861004) <13760-2/-1>* **ROCK N ROLL** [41] [33]
– This is it / Shallow / 1974 / Wish you were here / So alive / Luminol / Burning photographs / She's lost total control / Note to self: don't die / Rock n roll / Anybody wanna take me home / Do Miss America / Boys / The drugs not working. *(UK cd+=)* – Hypnotised.

Nov 03. (m-cd) *(9812782) <15480-2>* **LOVE IS HELL PT.1** [62] [78]
– Political scientist / Afraid not scared / This house is not for sale / Love is hell / Wonderwall / The shadowlands / World War 24 / Avalanche.

Dec 03. (m-cd) *(9813667) <15490-2>* **LOVE IS HELL PT.2** [ ] [ ]
– My blue Manhattan / Please do not let me go / City rain, city streets / I see monsters / English girls approximately / Thank you Louise / Hotel Chelsea nights.

Jan 04. (7") *(9861613)* **SO ALIVE. / LUXURY** [21] [–]
(cd-s) *(9861610)* – ('A') / Ah, life / Don't even know her name / ('A'-video).
(cd-s) *(9861611)* – ('A') / I'm coming over.

Mar 04. (cd-ep) *(986214)* **THIS IS IT** [ ] [–]
– This is it / Red lights / Closer when she goes / Twice as bad as love.

May 04. (d-10"lp) *(9861361) <17020-2>* **LOVE IS HELL PT.1 & PT.2** [68] Dec03 [ ]
– (above tracks +) / Fuck the universe / Twice as bad as love.

Jun 04. (7") *(9863099)* **WONDERWALL. / ONE BY ONE** [27] [–]
(cd-s) *(9863097)* – ('A') / This is it (acoustic).
(cd-s) *(9863098)* – ('A') / I want to go home / Suspicion.

RYAN ADAMS & THE CARDINALS

— now with **J.P. BOWERSOCK** – guitars / **JON GRABOFF** – pedal steel / **CATHERINE POPPER** – bass, keyboards, vocals / **BRAD PEMBERTON** – drums

May 05. (d-cd) *(9881827) <B0004343-02>* **COLD ROSES** [20] [26]
– Magnolia mountain / Sweet illusions / Meadowlake street / When will you come back home / Beautiful Sorta / Now that you're gone / Cherry lane / Mockingbird / How do you keep love alive // Easy plateau / Let it ride / Rosebud / Cold roses / If I am a stranger / Dance all night / Blossom / Life is beautiful / Friends. *(UK+=)* – Tonight.

Sep 05. (cd/d-lp) *(9884907) <B0004707-02/-01>* **JACKSONVILLE CITY NIGHTS** [59] [33]
– A kiss before I go / The end / Hard way to fall / Dear John / The hardest part / Games / Silver bullets / Peaceful valley / September / My heart is broken / Trains / PA / Withering heights / Don't fail me now. *(UK cd+=)* – Jeane / Always on my mind. *<US cd++=>* – A kiss before I go (demo) / I still miss someone.

RYAN ADAMS

Jan 06. (cd/lp) *(9887848) <B0005872-02/-01>* **29** [ ] [ ]
– 29 / Strawberry wine / Night birds / Blue sky blues / Carolina rain / Starlite diner / The sadness / Elizabeth, you were born to play that part / Voices.

□ AERIAL-M (see under ⇒ SLINT)

AEROSMITH

Formed: Sunapee, New Hampshire, USA . . . summer 1970, by JOE PERRY and STEVEN TYLER, who, with others (BRAD WHITFORD, TOM HAMILTON and JOEY KRAMER) moved to Boston, Massachusetts. By 1972, through a Max's Kansas City gig, they were signed to 'Columbia' by Clive Davis for a six figure sum. The band released their eponymous debut album the following year and the ROLLING STONES comparisons were inevitable from the off. While The 'Stones had taken American music, translated it and shipped it back across the water, AEROSMITH took the 'Stones interpretation of the Blues and customized it for a younger generation. Comparisons with LED ZEPPELIN were somewhat off the mark, the PERRY/TYLER partnership closely mimicking that of JAGGER and RICHARDS and while the latter two proclaimed themselves the 'Glimmer Twins', so it came to pass that Perry and Tyler were duly christened the 'Toxic Twins' in recognition of their legendary mid-70's decadence. 'MAMA KIN' and the Rufus Thomas cover, 'WALKIN' THE DOG' were fine examples of AEROSMITH's early revved-up R&B strut while the ballad, 'DREAM ON', scraped the lower regions of the US singles chart. The follow-up album, 'GET YOUR WINGS' (1974), consolidated the band's rock'n'raunch but it wasn't until the release of 'TOYS IN THE ATTIC' the following year that the band staked their claim as one of America's biggest and sexiest rock acts. Featuring the swaggering 'SWEET EMOTION' and the supple funk-rock of 'WALK THIS WAY', the record made AEROSMITH a household name, Stateside at least, going on to sell millions. Quintessentially American, the band cut little ice in Britain where punk was the order of the day. While Britain was pogoing to the strains of 'Anarchy in the UK', American heavy metal kids were skinning up to Aerosmith's 'ROCKS' (1976), a seminal record that saw the band at the peak of their powers. Dirty, sinewy riffs gyrated provocatively against diamond melodies, TYLER's pout almost audible as he casually reeled off his lurid tales of life on the road. While the band continued to pack out stadiums across America, their fabled penchant for nose candy was beginning to take its toll on their creative output. 'DRAW THE LINE' (1978) and 'NIGHT IN THE RUTS' (1980) fell woefully short of the band's capabilities, tension between TYLER and PERRY eventually leading to the latter leaving and forming The JOE PERRY PROJECT. Despite a near-fatal road accident, TYLER soldiered on with a revamped line-up for the equally uninspired 'ROCK IN A HARD PLACE' (1982). The all-important chemistry was gone while the chemicals seemingly continued to take their toll. Just as it looked like the end for the band, PERRY and TYLER settled their differences and the original AEROSMITH line-up signed to 'Geffen', getting it together for the 'DONE WITH MIRRORS' (1985) album, their best effort since the 70's heyday. AEROSMITH always had the funk and it seemed fitting that their miraculous commercial and creative rebirth was kickstarted by black hip hop crew RUN DMC. Their reworking of 'WALK THIS WAY' was released at the height of the rock/rap crossover in 1986 when 'Def Jam' was a force to be reckoned with and VW badges were in short supply, duly exposing AEROSMITH to a generation of kids who had never even heard of the band. Bang on cue, the band released 'PERMANENT VACATION' (1987), a masterful return to form which spawned a classic slice of AEROSMITH sleaze in 'DUDE (LOOKS LIKE A LADY)'. Moreover, the band had almost singlehandedly inspired a whole scene; almost every band in the late 80's glam-metal movement modelled themselves on prime 70's AEROSMITH (i.e. GUNS N' ROSES, FASTER PUSSYCAT, JUNKYARD, L.A. GUNS etc.). While the majority of these bands quickly faded into obscurity, AEROSMITH left the young pretenders for dust, releasing the adventurous and critically acclaimed 'PUMP' (1989). The single 'LOVE IN AN ELEVATOR', TYLER's tongue planted, as ever, firmly in cheek (probably not his own though), gave the band their first Top 20 hit in the UK. With the album reaching No.3, it finally seemed Britain had cottoned on, albeit fifteen years later. If 1993's 'GET A GRIP' sounded somewhat formulaic, it was another massive hit nevertheless. After just more than three years away, they returned to 'Columbia', releasing the wittily titled Top 50 hit, 'FALLING IN LOVE (IS HARD ON THE KNEES)', previewing yet another massive selling opus, 'NINE LIVES' (1997). Having scored a modest hit with 'PINK' (an even bigger UK hit in '99), AEROSMITH unplugged their amps to power-ballad to the top of the Hot 100 with 'I DON'T WANT TO MISS A THING'. Almost as sentimental as the film it was lifted from ('Armageddon'), TYLER and his cohorts crooned through every filled up wrinkle whilst leaving a few mascara stains on their female fans. Come the new millennium, the veteran campaigners were back to the hard stuff (music, that is) with 'JUST PUSH PLAY' (2001), the Boneyard Boys (aka producers Mark Hudson and Marti Frederiksen) helping tease out a set which many believed AEROSMITH's best since 'PUMP' more than a decade earlier. Three years on, the Toxic Twins were 'HONKIN' ON BOBO'; no, not some dodgy new drug craze, but a full scale covers set in the grand tradition of 'TRAIN KEPT A-ROLLIN'', etc. Rollin' all the way back to the British blues boom, they indulged themselves with the kind of track listing which their London-centric idols based their career on: Bo Diddley's 'ROAD RUNNER', Big Joe Williams' 'BABY, PLEASE DON'T GO' and Willie Dixon's 'I'M READY'. Critics were divided on both its merits and motives, reflected by fans in a paltry Top 30 UK placing. On the evidence of subsequent live set, 'ROCKIN' THE JOINT' (2005 – recorded 11 January 2002!), TYLER and PERRY still had had their heads stuck in PETER GREEN territory for quite a few years, grinding out 'RATTLESNAKE SHAKE' alongside a set list drawing heavily on their 70s golden era.

• **Songwriters:** PERRY / TYLER (aka TOXIC TWINS) except; COME TOGETHER (Beatles) / REMEMBER WALKIN' IN THE SAND (Shangri-la's) / TRAIN KEPT A-ROLLIN' (Johnny Burnette Trio) / MILK COW BLUES (Kokomo Arnold) / CRY ME A RIVER (Julie London) / MY ADIDAS (Run-DMC) / LOVE ME TWO TIMES (Doors). JOE PERRY PROJECT:- GET IT ON (BANG A GONG) (T. Rex) / BIG TEN-INCH RECORD (F.Weismantel; blues artist?) / ALL YOUR LOVE (Otis Rush) / HELTER SKELTER (Beatles) / CHIP AWAY THE STONE (Richie Supa).

Album rating: AEROSMITH (*8) / GET YOUR WINGS (*7) / TOYS IN THE ATTIC (*9) / ROCKS (*8) / DRAW THE LINE (*7) / LIVE BOOTLEG (*7) / AEROSMITH'S GREATEST HITS compilation (*9) / NIGHT IN THE RUTS (*6) / ROCK IN A HARD PLACE (*6) / DONE WITH MIRRORS (*6) / CLASSICS LIVE collection (*4) / CLASSICS LIVE 2 collection (*5) / PERMANENT VACATION (*8) / GEMS collection (*6) / PUMP (*8) / PANDORA'S BOX compilation boxed-set (*9) / GET A GRIP (*6) / BIG ONES compilation (*8) / NINE LIVES (*6) / JUST PUSH PLAY (*5) / YOUNG LUST – THE AEROSMITH ANTHOLOGY compilation (*8) / O, YEAH! ULTIMATE AEROSMITH ANTHOLOGY compilation (*8) / HONKIN' ON BOBO (*7) / ROCKIN' THE JOINT (*4)

STEVEN TYLER (b. STEVEN TALLARICO, 26 Mar'48, New York City) – vocals / **JOE PERRY** (b.10 Sep'50, Lawrence, Mass.) – guitar (ex-JAM BAND) / **BRAD WHITFORD** (b.23 Feb'52, Winchester, Mass.) – guitar repl. RAY TABANO / **TOM HAMILTON** (b.31 Dec'51, Colorado Springs) – bass (ex-JAM BAND) / **JOEY KRAMER** (b.21 Jun'50, New York City) – drums

C.B.S. Columbia

Jun 73. (lp) *<32005>* **AEROSMITH** – [ ]
– Make it / Somebody / Dream on / One way street / Mama kin / Write me a letter / Movin' out / Walkin' the dog. *(UK-iss.Sep74; CBS 65486) <US re-dist.Mar76 hit No.21> <US re-iss. Sep87/ cd-May88; PC/CK 32005>(cd-iss. Mar92 & Dec93 on 'Columbia'; 469011-2) (cd re-iss. Nov94; CK 64401) (cd re-iss. May97 on 'Columbia'; 474962-2)*

Nov 73. (7") *(CBS 1898) <45894>* **DREAM ON. / SOMEBODY** [ ] Oct73 59
<US ext.re-iss. Jan76; 10278> ; hit No.6 *(re-iss. Apr76; CBS 4000)*

Feb 74. (7") *<46029>* **SAME OLD SONG AND DANCE. / PANDORA'S BOX** – [ ]

Apr 74. (7") *<10034>* **SPACED. / TRAIN KEPT A-ROLLIN'** – [ ]

Jun 74. (7") *<10105>* **S.O.S. (TOO BAD). / LORD OF THE THIGHS** – [ ]

Nov 74. (lp/c) *(CBS/40 80015) <32847>* **GET YOUR WINGS** [ ] Mar74 74
– Same old song and dance / Lord of the thighs / Spaced / Woman of the world / S.O.S. (too bad) / Train kept a-rollin' / Seasons of wither / Pandora's box. *<US re-iss. Sep87/ cd-May88; PC/CK 32847> (UK-cd Mar92 & Dec93 & May97 on 'Columbia'; 474963-2)*

May 75. (7") *<10155>* **SWEET EMOTION. / UNCLE SALTY** – 36

Jul 75. (lp/c) *(CBS/40 80773) <33479>* **TOYS IN THE ATTIC** [ ] Apr75 11
– Toys in the attic / Uncle Salty / Adam's apple / Walk this way / Big ten inch record / Sweet emotion / No more no more / Round and round / You see me crying. *(re-iss. Feb88 on 'Castle' lp/c/cd; CLA LPX/MCX/CDX 135) <US re-iss. Sep87/ cd-iss. May88; PC/CK 33479) (UK re-iss. Apr91 & Nov93 & Jul95 & May97 on 'Columbia'; 480414-2) (re-iss. Oct97 on 'Simply Vinyl'; SVLP 0001)*

Sep 75. (7") *<10206>* **WALK THIS WAY. / ROUND AND ROUND** – [ ]

Nov 75. (7") *<10253>* **TOYS IN THE ATTIC. / YOU SEE ME CRYING** – [ ]

Jun 76. (lp/c) *(CBS/40 81379) <34165>* **ROCKS** [ ] May76 3

AEROSMITH

– Back in the saddle / Last child / Rats in the cellar / Combination / Sick as a dog / Nobody's fault / Get the lead out / Lick and a promise / Home tonight. *<US re-iss. Sep87/ May88; PC/CK 34165> (cd-iss. Jul89; CD 32517) (re-iss. cd Dec93 & May97 on 'Columbia'; 474965-2) (lp re-iss. Feb99 on 'Simply Vinyl'; SVLP 65)*

Aug 76. (7") *(CBS 4452) <10359>* **LAST CHILD. / COMBINATION** [ ] Jun76 [21]

Sep 76. (7") *<10407>* **HOME TONIGHT. / PANDORA'S BOX** [–] [71]

Feb 77. (7") *(CBS 4878) <10449>* **WALK THIS WAY. / UNCLE SALTY** [ ] Nov76 [10]

Apr 77. (7") *<10516>* **BACK IN THE SADDLE. / NOBODY'S FAULT** [–] [38]

Oct 77. (7") *<10637>* **DRAW THE LINE. / BRIGHT LIGHT FRIGHT** [–] [42]

Jan 78. (lp/c) *(CBS/40 82147) <34856>* **DRAW THE LINE** [ ] Dec77 [11]
– Draw the line / I wanna know why / Critical mass / Get it up / Bright light fright / Kings and queens / The hand that feeds / Sight for sore eyes / Milk cow blues. *<US re-iss. Sep87; PC 34856> (re-iss. cd Dec93 & May97 on 'Columbia'; 474966-2)*

Mar 78. (7") *<10699>* **KINGS AND QUEENS. / CRITICAL MASS** [–] [70]

Jun 78. (7") *<10727>* **GET IT UP. / MILK COW BLUES** [–] [ ]

Aug 78. (7") *<10802>* **COME TOGETHER. / KINGS AND QUEENS** [ ] [23]

Jan 79. (d-lp) *(CBS 88325) <35564>* **LIVE! BOOTLEG (live)** [ ] Nov78 [13]
– Back in the saddle / Sweet emotion / Lord of the thighs / Toys in the attic / Last child / Come together / Walk this way / Sick as a dog / Dream on / Chip away the stone / Sight for sore eyes / Mama kin / S.O.S. / I ain't got you / Mother popcorn / Train kept a rollin'. *<US re-iss. Dec87; PC 35564> (re-iss. cd Aug93/Dec93/May97 on 'Columbia'; 469004-2/474967-2)*

Jan 79. (7") *<10880>* **CHIP AWAY THE STONE (live). / CHIP AWAY THE STONE (studio)** [–] [77]

Jan 80. (lp/c) *(CBS/40 83680) <36050>* **NIGHT IN THE RUTS** [ ] Nov79 [14]
– No surprize / Chiquita / Remember (walkin' in the sand) / Cheesecake / Three mile smile / Reefer head woman / Bone to bone (Coney Island white fish boy) / Think about it / Mia. *<US re-iss. Sep87; PC 36050> (cd-iss. Mar92 & Dec93 & May97 & Feb01 on 'Columbia'; 474968-2)*

Feb 80. (7") *(CBS 8220) <11181>* **REMEMBER (WALKIN' IN THE SAND). / BONE TO BONE (CONEY ISLAND WHITE FISH BOY)** [ ] Jan80 [67]

— (Dec79) **JIMMY CREPSO** – guitar (ex-FLAME) repl. JOE PERRY who went solo

— (Feb80) **RICK DUFAY** – guitar repl. WHITFORD who teamed up with ST. HOLMES

Oct 82. (lp/c) *(CBS/40 85931) <38061>* **ROCK IN A HARD PLACE** [ ] Sep82 [32]
– Jailbait / Lightning strikes / Bitch's brew / Bolivian ragamuffin / Cry me a river / Prelude to Joanie / Joanie's butterfly / Rock in a hard place (Cheshire cat) / Jig it up / Push comes to shove. *<US re-iss. Sep87; PC 38061> (cd-iss. Aug93/Dec93/May97 on 'Columbia'; 469006-2/474970-2)*

— (Mar84) original 1970's line-up reform (see above)

Geffen Geffen

Nov 85. (7") *<28814>* **SHEILA. / GYPSY BOOTS** [–] [ ]

Dec 85. (lp/c) *(GEF/40 26695) <24091>* **DONE WITH MIRRORS** [ ] Nov85 [36]
– Let the music do the talking / My fist your face / Shame on you / The reason a dog / Shela / Gypsy boots / She's on fire / The hop / Darkness. *<US cd-iss. Oct87; 20491-2> (UK re-iss. Jun89 on 'W.E.A.'; 924 091-1/-4/-2) (re-iss. Apr92 & Jun94 & Feb98 cd/c; GFLD/GFLC 19052)*

— In Aug'86, AEROSMITH were credited on RUN DMC's hit version of 'WALK THIS WAY'.

Aug 87. (lp/c)(cd) *(WX 126/+C)(924 162-2) <24162>* **PERMANENT VACATION** [37] [11]
– Heart's done time / Magic touch / Rag doll / Simoriah / Dude (looks like a lady) / St. John / Hangman jury / Girl keep coming apart / Angel / Permanent vacation / I'm down / The movie. *(re-iss. Jun94 cd/c; ; GFLD/GFLC 19254) (lp re-iss. Jul98 on 'Simply Vinyl'; SVLP 35)*

Oct 87. (7") *(GEF 29) <28240>* **DUDE (LOOKS LIKE A LADY). / SIMORIAH** [45] Sep87 [14]
(12"+=/12"pic-d+=) *(GEF 29T/+P)* – Once is enough.

Apr 88. (7"/12"/12"pic-d) *(GEF 34/+T/TP) <28249>* **ANGEL. / GIRL KEEPS COMING APART** [69] Jan88 [3]
(3"cd-s+=) *(GEF 34CD)* – Angel (A.O.R. remix) / Dude (looks like a lady).

Jun 88. (12") *<27915>* **RAG DOLL. / ST.JOHN** [–] [17]

Aug 89. (7"/7"s/c-s) *(GEF 63/+X/C) <22845>* **LOVE IN AN ELEVATOR. / YOUNG LUST** [13] [5]
(10"pic-d+=/12"+=/3"cd-s+=) *(GEF 63 TP/T/CD)* – Ain't enough.

Sep 89. (lp/c)(cd) *(WX 304/+C)(924 254-2) <24254>* **PUMP** [3] [5]
– Young lust / F.I.N.E. / Love in an elevator / Monkey on my back / Janie's got a gun / The other side / My girl / Don't get mad, get even / Voodoo medicine man / What it takes. *(re-iss. Jun94 cd/c; GFLD/GFLC 19255) (lp re-iss. Nov98 on 'Simply Vinyl'; SVLP 45)*

Nov 89. (7"/7"sha-pic-d/c-s) *(GEF 68/+P/C) <22727>* **JANIE'S GOT A GUN. / VOODOO MEDICINE MAN** [ ] [4]
(12"+=/3"cd-s+=) *(GEF 68 T/CD)* – Rag doll (live).

Feb 90. (7"/7"sha-pic-d) *(GEF 72/+P)* **DUDE (LOOKS LIKE A LADY) (remix). / MONKEY ON MY BACK** [20] [–]
(12"/cd-s) *(GEF 72 T/CD)* – ('A'extended) / Love in an elevator (live) / Walk this way (live).

Mar 90. (7"/c-s) *<19944>* **WHAT IT TAKES. / MONKEY ON MY BACK** [–] [9]

Apr 90. (7") *(GEF 76)* **RAG DOLL. / SIMORIAH** [42] [–]
(12"/12"s) *(GEF 76 T/TW)* – ('A'side) / Mama kin (live) / Let it rain (live).
(cd-s) *(GEF 76CD)* – ('A'side) / Mama kin (live) / Dream on (live).

Aug 90. (7"/c-s) *(GEF 79/+C) <19927>* **THE OTHER SIDE. / MY GIRL** [46] Jun90 [22]
(12"+=) *(GEFT 79)* – Theme from 'Wayne's World' / ('A'-honky tonk).
(12") *(GEFTW 79)* – ('A'side) / Love in an elevator / Dude (looks like a lady) / Walk this way.

Apr 93. (12"pic-d/cd-s) *(GFST/+D 35) <19149>* **LIVIN' ON THE EDGE. / DON'T STOP / FLESH** [19] [18]
(cd-s) *(GFSTX 35)* – ('A'side) / ('A'acoustic) / Can't stop messin'.

Apr 93. (cd/c/lp) *(GED/GEC/GEF 24444) <24455>* **GET A GRIP** [2] [1]
– Intro / Eat the rich / Get a grip / Fever / Livin' on the edge / Flesh / Walk on down / Shut up and dance / Cryin' / Gotta love it / Crazy / Line up / Can't stop messin' / Amazing / Boogie man.

Jun 93. (10"colrd) *(GFST 46)* **EAT THE RICH. / FEVER / HEAD FIRST** [34] [–]
(cd-s+=) *(GFSTD 46)* – Livin' on the edge (demo).

Oct 93. (c-s) *(GFSC 56) <19256>* **CRYIN' / WALK ON DOWN** [17] Jul93 [12]
(12"white+=) *(GFST 56)* – I'm down.
(cd-s++=) *(GFSTD 56)* – My fist your face.
(cd-s+=) *(GFSXD 56)* – Love in an elevator / Janie's got a gun.

Nov 93. (c-s,cd-s) *<19264>* **AMAZING / FEVER** [–] [24]

Dec 93. (c-s) *(GFSC 63) <19264>* **AMAZING / GOTTA LOVE IT** [57] [–]
(12"colrd+=) *(GFST 63)* – ('A'acoustic).
(cd-s+=) *(GFSTD 63)* – ('A'orchestral).

May 94. (c-s,cd-s) *<19267>* **CRAZY / GOTTA LOVE IT** [–] [17]

Jun 94. (c-s) *(GFSC 75)* **SHUT UP AND DANCE. / DEUCES ARE WILD** [24] [–]
(7"+=) *(GFS 75)* – Crazy (orchestral).
(cd-s++=) *(GFSTD 75)* – Line up.

Oct 94. (c-s) *(GFSC 80)* **CRAZY / BLIND MAN** [23] [–]
(cd-s+=) *(GFSTD 80)* – Shut up and dance (live) / Blind man (mix).

Nov 94. (cd/c/d-lp) *(GED/GEC/GEF 24546) <24716>* **BIG ONES** (compilation) [7] [6]
– Walk on water / Love in an elevator / Rag doll / What it takes / Dude (looks like a lady) / Janie's got a gun / Cryin' / Amazing / Blind man / Deuces are wild / The other side / Crazy / Eat the rich / Angel / Livin' on the edge / Dude (looks like a lady) (live).

Dec 94. (c-s,cd-s) *<19377>* **BLIND MAN / HEAD FIRST** [–] [49]

Columbia Columbia

Mar 97. (7"/c-s) *(664075-7/-4)* **FALLING IN LOVE (IS HARD ON THE KNEES). / FALL TOGETHER** [22] Feb97 [35]
(cd-s+=) *(664075-2)* – Sweet emotion / Seasons of wither.

Mar 97. (cd/c) *(485020-2/-4) <67547>* **NINE LIVES** [4] [1]
– Nine lives / Falling in love (is hard on the knees) / Hole in my soul / Taste of India / Full circle / Something's gotta give / Ain't that a bitch / Farm / Crash / Kiss your past good-bye / Pink / Falling off / Attitude adjustment / Fallen angels.

Jun 97. (7"pic-d) *(664501-7)* **HOLE IN MY SOUL. / NINE LIVES (live)** [29] Aug97 [51]
(cd-s+=) *(664501-2)* – Falling in love (is hard on the knees) (Butcher mix) / Falling in love (is hard on the knees) (Moby flawed mix).
(cd-s) *(664501-5)* – ('A'side) / Falling in love (is hard on the knees) (Moby f**kee mix) / Falling in love (is hard on the knees) (live) / Walk this way (live).

Dec 97. (7"pink) *(664872-7) <78830>* **PINK. / PINK (Chulo mix)** [38] Feb98 [27]
(cd-s) *(664872-2)* – ('A'side) / ('A'-South Beach mix) / ('A'live).

Sep 98. (7"/cd-s) *(666408-7/-2)* *<78952>* **I DON'T WANT TO MISS A THING. / TASTE OF INDIA (rock remix)** [4] Aug98 [1]
(cd-s+=) *(666408-5)* – Pink (live) / Crash.

Jun 99. (c-s) *(667534-4)* **PINK / I DON'T WANT TO MISS A THING (live)** [13] [–]
(cd-s+=) *(667534-2)* – Hole in my soul.
(cd-s) *(667534-5)* – ('A'side) / ('A'mix) / ('A'mix).

Mar 01. (7") *(670931-7)* *<79555>* **JADED. / ANGEL'S EYE** [13] [7]
(cd-s+=) *(670931-2)* – ('A'-stripped down acoustic mix) / ('A'-guitars mix) / Under my skin.
(cd-s+=) *(670931-5)* – ('A'-acoustic mix) / Under my skin (reprise).

Mar 01. (cd/c/lp) *(501535-2/-4/-1)* *<62088>* **JUST PUSH PLAY** [7] [2]
– Beyond beautiful / Just push play / Jaded / Fly away from here / Tip hoppin' / Sunshine / Under my skin / Luv lies / Outta your head / Drop dead gorgeous / The light inside / Avant garden / The face.

Mar 04. (cd/c) *(CK/CT 92079)* *<87025>* **HONKIN' ON BOBO** [28] [5]
– Road runner / Shame, shame, shame / Eyesight to the blind / Baby, please don't go / Never loved a girl / Back back train / You gotta move / The grind / I'm ready / Temperature / Stop messin' around / Jesus is on the main line.

– compilations, others, etc. –

on 'CBS' UK / 'Columbia' US + UK (90's) unless otherwise mentioned

Jan 81. (lp/c) *(CBS/40 84704)* *<36865>* **AEROSMITH'S GREATEST HITS** [ ] Nov80 [53]
– Dream on / Same old song and dance / Sweet emotion / Walk this way / Remember (walking in the sand) / Back in the saddle / Draw the line / Kings and queens / Come together / Last child. *<US re-iss. Sep87/ cd-Feb88; CK/CS 36865> (re-iss. Nov89 pic-lp/cd; 460703-8/-2) (re-iss. cd Dec93 & Jan01 on 'Columbia'; 474969-2)*

Sep 86. (lp/c) *(CBS/40 26901)* *<40329>* **CLASSICS LIVE!** (live 1977-1983) [ ] Apr86 [84]
– Train kept a-rollin' / Kings and queens / Sweet emotion / Dream on / Mama kin / Three mile smile / Reefer head woman / Lord of the thighs / Major Barbra. *<US re-iss. Nov87 lp/c/cd; FC/FCT/CK 40329> (re-iss. cd Dec93 on 'Columbia'; 474971-2)*

Aug 87. (lp/c) *<FC/+T 40855>* **CLASSICS LIVE II (live)** [–] [ ]
– Back in the saddle / Walk this way / Movin' out / Draw the line / Same old song and dance / Last child / Let the music do the talking / Toys in the attic. *(UK cd-iss. Nov89; 460037-2) (cd re-iss. Dec92 on 'Columbia'; 474972-2)*

Jun 88. (d-lp/c/cd) *Raw Power; (RAW LP/TC/CD 037)* **ANTHOLOGY** [ ] [–]

1988. (7") *<08536>* **CHIP AWAY THE STONE. / S.O.S. (TOO BAD)** [–] [ ]

Aug 88. (3"cd-s) *<38K 0795-2>* **WALK THIS WAY / DREAM ON** [–] [ ]

Nov 89. (lp/c/cd) *(463224-1/-4/-2)* *<44487>* **GEMS** [ ] Dec88 [ ]
– Rats in the cellar / Lick and a promise / Chip away the stone / No surprize / Mama kin / Adam's apple / Nobody's fault / Round and round / Critical mass / Lord of the thighs / Jailbait / Train kept a rollin'. *(re-iss. Apr91 & Dec93 on 'Columbia'; 474973-2) (cd re-iss. May98; 491236-2)*

Dec 91. (t-cd/t-c) *(469293-2/-4)* *<46209>* **PANDORA'S BOX** [ ] [45]
– When I needed you / Make it / Movin' out / One way street / On the road again / Mama kin / Same old song and dance / Train kept a-rollin' / Seasons of wither / Write me a letter / Dream on / Pandora's Box / Rattlesnake shake / Walkin' the dog / Lord of the thighs // Toys in the attic / Round and round / Krawhitham / You see me crying / Sweet emotion / No More no more / Walk this way / I wanna know why / Big ten inch record / Rats in the cellar / Last child / All your love / Soul saver / Nobody's fault / Lick and a promise / Adam's apple / Draw the line / Critical mass // Kings and queens / Milk cow blues / I live in Connecticut / Three mile smile / Let it slide / Cheese cake / Bone to bone (Coney Island white fish boy) / No surprize / Come together / Downtown Charlie / Sharpshooter / Shit house shuffle / South station blues / Riff & roll / Jailbait / Major Barbara / Chip away the stone / Helter skelter / Back in the saddle / Circle jerk. *(3xcd-iss. Nov98; 487480-2)*

Jun 93. (cd) *(474038-2)* **TOYS IN THE ATTIC / CLASSICS LIVE** [ ] [–]

Jul 93. (cd) *(463224-2)* **ROCKS / GEMS** [ ] [ ]

Jun 94. (cd/c) *(476956-2/-4)* **PANDORA'S TOYS (BEST)** (compilation of 'PANDORA'S BOX') [ ] [ ]
– Sweet emotion / Draw the line / Walk this way / Dream on / Train kept a rollin' / Mama kin / Nobody's fault / Seasons of wither / Big ten-inch record / All your love / Helter skelter / Chip away the stone.

Aug 94. (c-s) *(660449-4)* *<74101>* **SWEET EMOTION / SUBWAY** [74] Dec91 [ ]
(cd-s+=) *(660449-2)* – Circle jerk.

Dec 94. (12xcd-box) *(477803-2)* **BOX OF FIRE** [ ] [ ]
– (AEROSMITH / GET YOUR WINGS / TOYS IN THE ATTICS / ROCKS / DRAW THE LINE / LIVE BOOTLEG / NIGHT IN THE RUTS / GREATEST HITS / ROCK IN A HARD PLACE / CLASSICS LIVE / CLASSICS LIVE II / GEMS / bonus cd)

May 97. (13xcd-box) *(477803-2)* **BOX OF FIRE** [ ] [ ]

Nov 97. (3xcd-box) *(485312-2)* **TOYS IN THE ATTIC / DRAW THE LINE / ROCKS** [ ] [ ]

Aug 98. (cd) *(487351-2)* **CLASSICS LIVE VOL.1 & 2** [ ] [ ]

Oct 98. (d-cd/d-c) *Geffen; <(GED/GEC 25221)>* **A LITTLE SOUTH OF SANITY (live)** [36] [12]
– Eat the rich / Love in an elevator / Falling in love (is hard on the knees) / Same old song and dance / Hole in my soul / Monkey on my back / Livin' on the edge / Cryin' / Rag doll / Angel / Janie's got a gun / Amazing // Back in the saddle / Last child / The other side / Walk on down / Dream on / Crazy / Mama kin / Walk this way / Dude (looks like a lady) / What it takes / Sweet emotion.

Sep 00. (cd) *(499855-2)* **AEROSMITH / TOYS IN THE ATTIC** [ ] [–]

Oct 00. (d-cd) *Universal; <(E 490433-2)>* **PERMANENT VACATION / DONE WITH MIRRORS** [ ] [ ]

Oct 00. (t-cd) *Universal; <(E 424935-2)>* **PERMANENT VACATION / DONE WITH MIRRORS / PUMP** [ ] [ ]

Nov 00. (t-cd) *Universal; <(E 485312-2)>* **TOYS IN THE ATTIC / DRAW THE LINE / ROCKS** [ ] [ ]

Jan 01. (cd) *Universal; <(E 497441-2)>* **THE UNIVERSAL MASTERS COLLECTION** [ ] [ ]

Nov 01. (d-cd) *Geffen; <(493119-2)>* **YOUNG LUST – THE AEROSMITH ANTHOLOGY** [32] [ ]
– Let the music do the talking / My fist your face / Shame on you / Heart's done time / Rag doll / Dude (looks like a lady) / Angel / Hangman jury / Permanent vacation / Young lust / The other side / What it takes / Monkey on my back / Love in an elevator / Janie's got a gun / Ain't enough / Walk this way (with RUN-D.M.C.) / Eat the rich / Love me two times / Head first / Livin' on the edge (acoustic) / Don't stop / Can't stop messin' / Amazing (orchestral) / Cryin' / Crazy / Shut up and dance / Deuces are wild / WAlk on water / Blind man / Falling in love (is hard on the knees) (live) / Dream on (live) / Hole in my soul (live) / Sweet emotion (live).

Jul 02. (d-cd) *Columbia; (508467-2) / Sony; <86700>* **O, YEAH! – ULTIMATE AEROSMITH HITS** [6] [4]
– Mama kin / Dream on / Same old song and dance / Seasons of wither / Walk this way / Big ten inch record / Sweet emotion / Last child / Back in the saddle / Draw the line / Dude (looks like a lady) / Angel / Rag doll / Janie's got a gun / Love in an elevator / What it takes / The other side / Livin' on the edge / Cryin' / Amazing / Deuces are wild / Crazy / Falling in love (is hard on the knees) / Pink (the South Beach mix) / I don't want to miss a thing / Jaded / Just push play (radio remix) / Walk this way (with RUN-D.M.C.) / Girls of summer / Lay it down.

Oct 05. (cd) *Columbia; (82876 72421-2) / Sony; <97800>* **ROCKIN' THE JOINT** (live at The Hard Rock Hotel Las Vegas 2002) [ ] [ ]
– (Good evening Las Vegas) / Beyond beautiful / Same old song and dance / No more no more / Seasons of wither / Light inside / Draw the line / I don't want to miss a thing / Big ten inch record / Rattlesnake shake / Walk this way / Train kept a rollin'.

AFI

Formed: Ukiah, California, USA . . . 1991 by high school friends DAVEY HAVOK, MARKUS STOPHOLESE, VIC CHALKER and ADAM CARSON. One split 7" EP (with LOOSE CHANGE) and a debut EP, 'BEHIND THE TIMES', later, college commitments led to an inevitable break up. A chance reunion show subsequently went down so well that the AFI crew (now featuring GEOFF KRESGE in place of VIC) got back together permanently, relocating to Berkeley where the likes of RANCID and GREEN DAY had cut their teeth at fabled punk venue, Gillman Street; a debut set, 'ANSWER THAT AND STAY FASHIONABLE' was delivered for 'Wingnut' in '95. After spotting the band at a show in Hollywood, DEXTER HOLLAND (of the OFFSPRING fame) snapped them up for his 'Nitro' label and proceeded to release their follow-up album, 'VERY PROUD OF YA' (1996). Another set of bullseye-aim hardcore followed in 1997: 'SHUT YOUR MOUTH & OPEN

YOUR EYES'. While the band's acronym has been subject to many and varied interpretations over the years, the official line is that it stands for A FIRE INSIDE, the title of a 1998 EP and also the name of AFI's website. Judging by the musical contents of 'BLACK SAILS IN THE SUNSET' (1999), that fire was at least partly fuelled by Old Nick himself. Well, not really, but influences from the darker side of punk – the MISFITS, JOY DIVISION etc – were definitely infiltrating the band's previously straight up sound. Hardcore fans' suspicions were also raised by the fact that HAVOK (now backed by a slightly altered line-up of CARSON, last set recruit HUNTER BURGAN and JADE PUGET) had taken to wearing make-up and black PVC. The transformation was even more pronounced on 'THE ART OF DROWNING' (2000), HAVOK's angst-ridden lyrics mirroring the tortured music. A subsequent deal with 'Dreamworks' meant even more scope for studio experimentation which the band utilised to the full on 'SING THE SORROW' (2003). With Butch Vig and Jerry Finn tweaking the sound into even more of a contemporary mould and the band accommodating luxuries like cello and piano, the record was another sizeable step in AFI's evolution and a canny move into the US Top 5. HAVOK had also been exorcising his more gothic tendencies in SON OF SAM, a side project (featuring hardcore veterans like TODD YOUTH, STEVE ZING and even GLENN DANZIG himself) which released 'SONGS FROM EARTH' a few years previously. AFI returned to the fray in June 2006 with umpteenth album, 'DECEMBERUNDERGROUND', proving that perseverance – and a good bit of growling – pays off in the end: the record topped the American charts, condensing its sub-New Romance and emo-metal into rising-star single, 'MISS MURDER'.

• **Covered:** MAN IN A SUITCASE (Police) / OPEN YOUR EYES (Circus Tents) / VALUES HERE (Dag Nasty) / WHATEVER I DO (Negative Approach) / THE HANGING GARDEN (Cure) / HALLOWEEN + LAST CARESS + DEMONOMANIA (Misfits) / MY MACHINE (Guns N' Roses) / TODAY'S LESSON (Filth).

Album rating: ANSWER THAT AND STAY FASHIONABLE (*6) / VERY PROUD OF YA (*5) / SHUT YOUR MOUTH AND OPEN YOUR EYES (*6) / BLACK SAILS IN THE SUNSET (*7) / THE ART OF DROWNING (*6) / SING THE SORROW (*7) / AFI collection (*5) / DECEMBERUNDERGROUND (*7)

DAVEY HAVOC (b.20 Nov'75, Rochester, NY) – vocals / **MARKUS STOPHOLESE** – guitar / **GEOFF KRESGE** – bass; repl. VIC CHALKER / **ADAM CARSON** (b. 5 Feb'75) – drums

not iss. / Key Lime Pie

Mar 93. (7"ep; split w/ LOOSE CHANGE) **DORK** [–] [ ]
– Red hat / Self pity / Ny-quil / (others by LOOSE CHANGE).

Jun 93. (7"ep) **BEHIND THE TIMES EP** [–] [ ]
– Who said you could touch me? / Rolling balls / High school football hero / Rizzo in the box / Cereal wars / Born in the USA.

Mar 94. (7"ep) **EDDIE PICNIC'S ALL WET EP** (live) [–] [ ]
– Ny-quil / Rizzo in the box / Who said you could touch me? / I wanna mohawk (but mom won't let me get one) / Love is a many splendored thing.

not iss. / Wedge

Mar 95. (7"ep) **FLY IN THE OINTMENT** [–] [ ]
– Theory of a revolution / Crop tub / Cruise control / Open your eyes.

not iss. / Wingnut

Nov 95. (7"split) **HECKLE split** [–] [ ]
– Aspirin free / Advances in modern technology.

Aug 95. (cd/lp) <1370> **ANSWER THAT AND STAY FASHIONABLE** [–] [ ]
– Two of a kind / Half-empty bottle / Yurf rendenmein / I wanna get a Mohawk (but my mom won't let me) / Brownie bottom sundae / The chequered demon / Cereal wars / The mother in me / Rizzo in the box / Kung-fu devil / Your name here / Ny-quil / Don't make me ill / Open your eyes / Highschool football hero. *(lp+=)* – Self-pity / Key lime pie. *<(re-iss. Apr97 on 'Nitro' cd/c/lp; 15811-2/-4/-1)>*

Nitro / Nitro

Oct 96. (cd/c/lp) *<(15805-2/-4/-1)>* **VERY PROUD OF YA** [ ] Jun96 [ ]
– He who laughs last . . . / File 13 / Wake-up call / Cult status / Perfect fit / Advances in modern technolgy / Theory of revolution / This secret Ninja / Soap box derby / Fishbowl / Charles Atlas / Crop tub / Consult my lover / Take the test / Two of a kind / Shatty Fatmas / Yurf Rendenmein / Cruise control / Modern epic. *(cd intro rewind+=)* – No Dave party. *(lp+=)* – Who said you could touch me? / Rolling balls / Love is a many splendored thing.

Jun 97. (7"split) **BOMBING THE BAY. / (other by SWINGIN' UTTERS)** [–] [ ]
(above issued on 'Sessions')

— **HUNTER BURGAN** (b.14 May'76) – bass (ex-the FORCE) repl. GEOFF who formed TIGER ARMY among others

Nov 97. (cd/c/lp) *<(15815-2/-4/-1)>* **SHUT YOUR MOUTH AND OPEN YOUR EYES** [ ] [ ]
– Keeping out of direct sunlight / Three reasons / A single second / ph Low / Let it be broke / Third season / Lower your head and take it in the body / Coin return / The new patron saints and angels / Three seconds notice / Salt for your wounds / Today's lesson / The Devil loves you / Triple zero.

May 99. (7"ep/cd-ep) *<(ADELINE 002/+CD)>* **A FIRE INSIDE EP** [ ] Sep98 [ ]
– 3 1/2 / Over exposure / The hanging garden / Demonomania.
(above issued on 'Adeline')

— **JADE PUGET** (b.28 Nov'72) – guitar (ex-LOOSE CHANGE) repl. MARKUS

Jun 99. (cd-ep) **BLACK SAILS** [–] [ ]
– Porphyria cutanea tarda / Who knew?

Jun 99. (cd/lp) *<(15824-2/-1)>* **BLACK SAILS IN THE SUNSET** [ ] [ ]
– Strength through wounding / Porphyria cutanea tarda / Esanguination / Malleus maleficarum / Narrative of soul against soul / Clove smoke catharsis / The prayer position / No poetic device / Weathered tome / The last kiss / At a glance / God called in sick today.

Dec 99. (cd-ep) *<(15829-2)>* **ALL HALLOWS EP** [ ] [ ]
– Porphryia / Malleus maleficarum / Prayer position / Who knew.

Sep 00. (cd/lp) *<(15835-2/-1)>* **THE ART OF DROWNING** [ ] [ ]
– Initiation / The lost souls / The nephilim / Ever and a day / Sacrifice theory / Of greetings and goodbyes / Smile / A story at three / The days of the phoenix / Catch a hot one / Wester / 6 to 8 / The despair factor / Morningstar / Battled *[cd-only]* / Dream of waking *[lp-only]*.

Apr 01. (cd-ep) *<(15843-2)>* **THE DAYS OF THE PHOENIX E.P.** [ ] [ ]
– The days of the phoenix / A winter's tale / Wester.

— in 2001, HAVOK featured in punk supergroup SON OF SAM

Polydor / Universal

Mar 03. (cd) *(450448-2) <450380>* **SING THE SORROW** [52] [5]
– Miseria cantare – The beginning / The leaving song pt.II / Bleed black / Silver and cold / Dancing through Sunday / Girl's not grey / Death of seasons / The great disappointment / Paper airplanes (makeshift wings) / This celluloid dream / The leaving song / . . .But home is nowhere. *(lp-iss.Mar03 on 'Adeline'; 026)*

Jun 03. (7"grey) *(4504602)* **GIRL'S NOT GREY. / THE HANGING GARDEN** [22] [–]
(cd-s+=) *(4504600)* – Synesthesia (demo) / ('A'-video).
(cd-s) *(4504601)* – ('A') / Reivers music / Now the world (alt. take) / ('A'-prelude / video).

Sep 03. (7") *(4504626)* **THE LEAVING SONG PT.II. / THE GREAT DISAPPOINTMENT (demo)** [43] [–]
(cd-s+=) *(4504627)* – Paper Airplanes (makeshift wings) (demo) / ('A'-video).
(cd-s) *(4504625)* – ('A') / . . .But home is nowhere (demo) / ('A'-demo).

May 06. (cd) *(9858643) <685402>* **DECEMBERUNDERGROUND** [16] Jun06 [1]
– Prelude 12-21 / Kill caustic / Miss murder / Summer shudder / The interview / Love like winter / Affliction / The missing frame / Kiss and control / The killing lights / 37mm / Endlessly, she said.

Jun 06. (7"pic-d) *(9859440) <radio>* **MISS MURDER. / DON'T CHANGE** [ ] Apr06 [24]
(cd-s+=) *(9859439)* – Silver and cold (live acoustic).

– compilations, etc. –

Nov 04. (cd) *Nitro; <(15859-2)>* **AFI** [ ] [88]
– The lost souls / The days of the Phoenix / A winter's tale / Totalimmortal / Fall children / The prayer position / God called in sick today / Lower it / A single second / Third season / He who laughs last / I wanna get a Mohawk (but my mom won't let me get one) / Perfect fit / Rolling balls / Who said you could touch me?

AIR

Formed: Paris, France . . . 1995 by NICOLAS GODIN and JEAN-BENOIT DUNCKEL, who had cut their proverbial teeth waking the neighbours up in punk outfit, ORANGE. Preceded by a string of highly desirable 12" singles and a mini-set 'PREMIERS SYMPTOMES', the gallic duo's sublime 'MOON SAFARI' album ranks as one of 1998's most hypnotic, emotive and consistently listenable long players; the Moog was back. With the added kudos of being an essential purchase for any self respecting fashion victim, the record's unearthly ELO / BURT BACHARACH / CARPENTERS hybrid (be assured that this works considerably more effectively on disc than it does on paper!) had music journalists of all persuasions (with the possible exception of the metal press) reaching for the thesaurus. Those that portrayed AIR as mere faux-space age lounge revivalists were surely missing the point, however; they might've doffed their cap to classic French pop but Messrs GODIN and DUNCKEL were in the business of making music to last, serious business. Seriously sexy in fact, sexy in the way that SAINT ETIENNE used to be, all throbbing bass and breathless melodies. While the likes of 'SEXY BOY' might actually have you questioning your closely guarded conviction that the 80's were shite, the liberal sprinkling of moog synth throughout places the record in a kind of vacuum-packed 70's no-man's land. A damn good place to be, especially if you happen to have a king-sized spliff, a decent pair of "cans" and your favourite armchair to hand. No surprise then, that the album made the UK Top 20, as did the attendant 'KELLY WATCH THE STARS' single. If there was a World Cup for music, AIR would definitely be in there with a shout, the French redrawing of contemporary musical battle lines continuing unabated. At the height of AIR's popularity, 'Virgin' squeezed out their 1997 mini-set for eager fans who surprisingly sent it into the UK Top 20. Meanwhile, the duo were busy constructing the soundtrack to Sofia Coppola's debut movie, 'THE VIRGIN SUICIDES' (2000). This brought AIR into the new millennium although its edited electronica held few surprises (bar hit single, 'PLAYGROUND LOVE') functioning primarily as a cinematic companion. The Gallic duo emerged again the following year with '10,000 Hz LEGEND' (2001), a worthy if more deliberately inscrutable follow-up to 'MOON SAFARI'. The prog-rock cover art was a bit of a giveaway, AIR opting to hue their electronic tapestries from much darker, unsettling source material than the moog-pop references of their debut. It was nevertheless immaculately crafted, flawlessly executed and often eerily beautiful, the likes of BECK and JASON FALKNER enhancing its post-modern appeal. What the album didn't need – in fact what most albums don't need – was a collection of tired remixes, even if the reworkings came from such in demand studio names as the NEPTUNES. 'EVERYBODY HERTZ' (2002) also gets nil points for its title, as insipid as the grooves contained within it. 'CITY READING (TRE STORIE WESTERN)' (2003) was a soundtrack follow-up of sorts, the musical accompaniment to a triptych of spoken-word stories by Italian novelist, Alessandro Baricco. Much more high profile was 'TALKIE WALKIE' (2004), trumpeted as the real follow-up to 'MOON SAFARI', with Nigel "Radiohead" Godrich (who else?) on production and SERGE GAINSBOURG associate/composer Michel Colombier on strings. Just missing out on a UK No.1 spot, the album opened with a couple of bonafide AIR classics: 'VENUS' and 'CHERRY BLOSSOM GIRLS', the kind of goose-down pop that the Americans still haven't quite cottoned on to. The presence of Godrich and Colombier had the effect of channeling the duo's weirder impulses into offbeat curios like the electro-rockin 'SURFING ON A ROCKET', the eerie screen-pulse of 'ANOTHER DAY', the space-whistling of 'ALPHA BETA GAGA' (a UK Top 50 single used for a TV ad) and 'ALONE IN TOKYO', originally written for the feature film, 'Lost In Translation'.

• **Note:** To avoid confusion with another outfit named AIR, "French Band" was incidentally the prefix printed in small writing next to their moniker.

Album rating: PREMIERS SYMPTOMES (*7) / MOON SAFARI (*9) / THE VIRGIN SUICIDES soundtrack (*7) / 10,000hz LEGEND (*7) / EVERYBODY HERTZ remixes (*4) / CITY READING (TRE STORIE WESTERN) book soundtrack w/ Alessandro Baricco (*5) / TALKIE WALKIE (*8)

NICOLAS GODIN (b.1970) – bass, guitar, organ, Minimoog, Vocoder, Korg, percussion, harmonica / **JEAN-BENOIT DUNCKEL** (b.1970) – organ, piano, Rhodes, Korg MS23, Moog, Solins string ensemble, clavinet / with guest vocals **BETH HIRSCH** (on '98 lp)

Source — not iss.

1995. (m-lp) *(894426)* **LE SOLIEL EST PRES DE MOI** — – French –
(UK-iss.Jul97 on 'Source/Virgin'; same)

Nov 95. (12"ep) **MODULAR (mixes)** — – French –
(UK-iss.Aug96 on 'Mo Wax' 12"/cd-s; MW 047/+CD)

Jul 96. (12"ep) *(936576)* **CASANOVA '70 / LES PROFESSIONNELS** — –
(re-iss. Jan98; same)

Jul 97. (m-lp/m-cd) **PREMIERS SYMPTOMES** — – French –
– Modular mix / Casanova 70 / Les professionels / J'ai dormi sous l'eau / Le soleil est pres de moi / California / Gordni mix (Brakes on mix). *(UK-iss.Jan98 on 'Source'; 7243-89428766/+CD) (re-iss. Sep99 on 'Virgin' cd/c/lp; CD/TC+/V 2895)* – Hit UK No.12

Source – Virgin — Caroline

Jan 98. (cd/c/lp) *(CD/TC+/V 2848) <CAR 6644-2>* **MOON SAFARI** — 6
– La femme d'argent / Sexy boy / All I need / Kelly watch the stars / Talisman / Remember / You make it easy / Ce matin la / New star in the sky / Le voyage de Penelope.

Feb 98. (12"/c-s) *(VST/VSC 1672)* **SEXY BOY (mixes; Cassius / Etienne De Crecy & the Flower Pistols)** — 13
(cd-s) *(VSCDT 1672)* – ('A'side) / Jeanne / New star in the sky.

May 98. (c-s) *(VSC 1690)* **KELLY WATCH THE STARS / ('A'mix)** — 18
(12"+=/cd-s+=) *(VS T/CDT 1690)* – Sexy boy (sex kino mix) / Remember (D Whitaker version).
(UK re-iss. Jun98 on 'Source' 7"; 8950727)

Nov 98. (c-s/12"/cd-s) *(VSC/VST/VSCDT 1702)* **ALL I NEED / KELLY WATCH THE STARS (Moog Cookbook mix) / KELLY WATCH THE STARS (American Girls remix by Phoenix)** — 29

Mar 99. (cd-s) *<CAR 6645-2>* **SEXY BOY (Beck remix)** — –

Virgin — Astralwerks

Feb 00. (c-s) *(VSC 1764)* **PLAYGROUND LOVE / BATHROOM GIRL** — 25
(cd-s+=) *(VSCDT 1764)* – ('A'mix).
(12") *(VST 1764)* – ('A'side) / Nosferatu / Highschool prom.
(above 'A' side sung by GORDON TRACKS)

Feb 00. (cd/c/lp) *(CD/TC+/V 2910) <48848>* **THE VIRGIN SUICIDES** (soundtrack) — 14 Mar00
– Playground love / Clouds up / Bathroom girl / Cemetary party / Dark messages / The word 'hurricane' / Dirty trip / Highschool lover / Afternoon sister / Ghost song / Empty house / Dead bodies / Suicide underground.

May 01. (7") *(VS 1803)* **RADIO #1. / FLOWERHEAD** — 31 –
(cd-s+=) *(VSCDT 1803)* – ('A'-JP Cristal remix).
(12") *(VST 1803)* – ('A'side) / ('A'-JP Cristal remix) / ('A'-Senor Coconut's rumbamambochachacha remix).

May 01. (cd/lp) *(CD+/V 2945) <10332>* **10,000Hz LEGEND** — 7 Jun01 88
– Electronic performers / How does it make you feel / Radio #1 / Vagabond / Radian / Lucky and unhappy / Sex born poison / People in the city / Wonder milky bitch / Don't be light / Caramel prisoner.

Feb 02. (cd/d-lp) *(CDV/VD 2956) <11833>* **EVERYBODY HERTZ** (remixes) — 67
– Don't be light (edit) / Don't be light (Mr Ozio remix) / How does it make you feel? (Sherwood remix) / Don't be light (Neptunes remix) / People in the city (Modjo remix) / Don't be light (Hacker remix) / How does it make you feel? (edit) / Don't be light (Malibu remix) / People in the city (Jack Lahana remix) / The way you look tonight / People in the city.

May 03. (cd; w/ Alessandro Baricco) Source; *(CDSOUR 081) <5 81871-2>* **CITY READING (TRE STORIE WESTERN)** (book soundtrack)
– Bird / La Puttana Di Closingtown: Prologo / Se vuoi capire la loro storia /

Pat Cobhan ride / Fanny scivola con le labbra / Pat Cobhan alza gli occhi / Young / 'Affanculo / Quell'uomo bara, dice / Finale / Caccia All'uomo:- Prologo / Il primo giorno / Il secondo giorno / Il terzo giorno / L'urlo / Mondo sparito / Il quarto giorno / Macchie di sangue / Musica.

Jan 04. (cd/lp) *(CD+/V 2980)* *<96632>* **TALKIE WALKIE** [2] Feb04 [ ]
– Venus / Cherry blossom girl / Run / Universal traveller / Mike Mills / Surfing on a rocket / Another day / Alpha beta gaga / Biological / Alone in Kyoto. *(d-cd+=; CDVX 2980)* – live:- Electronic performers / J'ai dormi sous l'eau / Don't be light / People in the city / La femme d'argent.

Feb 04. (12"/cd-s) *<47768/9>* **CHERRY BLOSSOM GIRL (mixes) / FANNY** [–] [ ]

May 04. (12"/cd-s) *(VST 1871)* *<48692>* **SURFING ON A ROCKET (remixes; LP / Juan MacLean / Joakim / Zongamin / Nomo Heroes)** [ ] [ ]

Aug 04. (12"/cd-s) *(VS T/CDX 1880)* **ALPHA BETA GAGA (mixes; 91 BPM edit / Jackson remix / Mark Ronson remix feat. Rhymefest / Mark Ronson dub)** [44] [–]

Oct 04. (cd-ep) *<66699>* **SURFING ON A ROCKET** (remixes by Various Artists) [–] [ ]
– Surfing on a rocket / Alpha Beta gaga / Easy going woman / Surfing on a rocket / Alpha Beta gaga / Surfing on a rocket / Alpha Beta gaga (inmstrumental).

– compilations, etc. –

on 'Virgin' unless mentioned otherwise

Oct 01. (d-cd) *(810875-2)* **MOON SAFARI / PREMIER SYMPTOMES** [ ] [–]

Nov 01. (d-cd) *(810850-2)* **10,000hz LEGEND / THE VIRGIN SUICIDES** [ ] [–]

Sep 04. (t-cd) *(VBK 25)* **PREMIERS SYMPTOMES / MOON SAFARI / 10,000hz LEGEND** [ ] [–]

Sep 04. (d-cd) *(VBK 33)* **MOON SAFARI / THE VIRGIN SUICIDES** [ ] [–]

Nov 04. (d-cd) *(VBK 1)* **TALKIE WALKIE / THE VIRGIN SUICIDES** [ ] [–]

□ Damon ALBARN & . . . (see under ⇒ BLUR)

□ ALICE COOPER (see under ⇒ COOPER, Alice)

ALICE IN CHAINS

Formed: Seattle, Washington, USA ... 1987 as glamsters DIAMOND LIE, then FUCK by main songwriters, LAYNE STALEY and JERRY CANTRELL, who soon opted for the more palatable moniker of ALICE N' CHAINS. They altered this name slightly after enlisting SEAN KINNEY and MIKE STARR, subsequently signing to 'Columbia' in 1989 and debuting the following year with promo EP, 'WE DIE YOUNG. Their debut album, 'FACELIFT' was released to widespread favourable reviews, although it took some time to scale the Billboard Top 100. Later in '91, they finally cracked the Top 50, their cause furthered by the success of new groundbreaking grunge acts like NIRVANA and SOUNDGARDEN giving metal/hard rock a breath of fresh air. A Grammy nomination under their belt (for the track 'MAN IN THE BOX'), the group enjoyed a flurry of activity in '92 with both the release of the easier going 'SAP' EP and a Top 10 follow-up album, 'DIRT', the latter also breaking the band in Britain. In 1993, they lifted no less than four major hits ('WOULD?', 'THEM BONES', 'ANGRY CHAIR' and 'DOWN IN A HOLE') from this critically acclaimed opus. With acoustic sets all the rage, ALICE IN CHAINS then delivered a stripped-down EP, 'JAR OF FLIES', the set being the first mini-cd to top the US charts. When STALEY subsequently formed grunge 'supergroup', The GACY BUNCH (later changing the name to MAD SEASON) alongside PEARL JAM's MIKE McCREADY and BARRETT MARTIN of The SCREAMING TREES, speculation was rife about an ALICE IN CHAINS split. After a one-off album, 'ABOVE' (1995), however, STALEY, CANTRELL & Co. stormed back with the eponymous 'ALICE IN CHAINS' (1995), the record giving the group their second US No.1. The obligatory 'MTV UNPLUGGED' set followed in 1996, ALICE IN CHAINS being only one of a handful of similar acts to be bestowed with such an 'honour'. With AIC out of action for a few years, JERRY CANTRELL decided it was time for a solo piece. 'BOGGY DEPOT' (1998) – which included a track from the earlier made Jim Carrey film, 'The Cable Guy' – hit the US Top 30 for a week and failed miserably to gain much interest in Britain bar Kerrang(!), of course. With ALICE IN CHAINS on hold while STALEY deteriorated into a life of reclusive drug taking, CANTRELL set about recording his sophomore set. Naming it 'DEGRADATION TRIP' (2002), it would be released by 'Roadrunner' a few months after the untimely – but nevertheless expected – drugs death of STALEY c. 5 April 2002 (the anniversary of KURT COBAIN). The aforementioned set fared a little better than his previous effort and, with the help from some top notch backing on session (ROBERT TRUJILLO, CHRIS DeGARMO and MIKE BORDIN), the album peaked into the US Top 40.

• **Songwriters:** CANTRELL solo covered, 'I'VE SEEN ALL THIS WORLD I CARE TO SEE' (Willie Nelson; on a tribute album).

Album rating: FACELIFT (*6) / SAP (*5) / DIRT (*8) / JAR OF FLIES (*7) / ALICE IN CHAINS (*5) / MTV UNPLUGGED (*4) / NOTHING SAFE compilation (*6) / Mad Season: ABOVE (*5) / Jerry Cantrell: BOGGY DEPOT (*5) / DEGRADATION TRIP (*6)

LAYNE STALEY (b.22 Aug'67, Bellevue, WA.) – vocals / **JERRY CANTRELL** (b.18 Mar'66, Tacoma, WA.) – guitar, vocals / **MICHAEL STARR** (b. 4 Apr'66, Honolulu, Hawaii) – bass (ex-SADO) / **SEAN KINNEY** (b.27 May'66, Seattle) – drums, percussion, megaphone

Columbia Columbia

Jul 90. (c-ep/12"ep) *<CAS/CAT 2095>* **WE DIE YOUNG EP** [–] [ ]
– We die young / It ain't like that / Killing yourself.

Sep 91. (cd/c/lp) *(467201-2/-4/-1)* *<46075>* **FACELIFT** [ ] Mar91 [42]
– We die young / Man in the box / Sea of sorrow / Bleed the freak / I can't remember / Love, hate, love / It ain't like that / Sunshine / Put you down / Confusion / I know somethin' ('bout you) / Real thing.

Oct 91. (cd-ep) *<73851>* **MAN IN THE BOX / SEA OF SORROW / BLEED THE FREAK / SUNSHINE** [–] [ ]

Feb 92. (c-ep)(cd-ep) *<74182><74305>* **SAP** [–] [ ]
– Brother / Got me wrong / Right turn / Am I inside / Love song.

—— **MIKE INEZ** (b.14 May'66, San Fernando, California) – bass; repl. MIKE STARR. He formed MY SISTER'S MACHINE, who released album in May'92 'DIVA' on 'Caroline'.

Oct 92. (cd/c/lp) *(472330-2/-4/-1)* *<52475>* **DIRT** [42] [6]
– Them bones / Dam that river / Rain when I die / Down in a hole / Sickman / Rooster / Junkhead / Dirt / God smack / Hate to feel / Angry chair / Would?

Jan 93. (7") *(658888-7)* **WOULD?. / MAN IN THE BOX** [19] [ ]
(12"green+=/pic-cd-s+=) *(658888-6/-2)* – Brother / Right Turn.

Mar 93. (7") *(659090-7)* **THEM BONES. / WE DIE YOUNG** [26] [ ]
(cd-s+=) *(659090-2)* – Got me wrong / Am I inside.

May 93. (7") *(659365-7)* **ANGRY CHAIR. / I KNOW SOMETHIN' ('BOUT YOU)** [33] [ ]
(12"+=) *(659365-6)* – Bleed the freak / It ain't like that.
(cd-s+=) *(659365-2)* – It ain't like that / Hate to feel.

Oct 93. (7"pic-d) *(659751-7)* **DOWN IN A HOLE. / ROOSTER** [36] [ ]
(12"+=) *(659751-6)* – A little bitter / Love, hate, love.
(cd-s+=) *(659751-2)* – What the hell I have I / ('A'radio edit).

Dec 93. (cd-s; w-drawn) *(660047-2)* **ROTTEN APPLE /** [–] [–]

Jan 94. (cd/c/lp) *(475713-2/-4/-1)* *<57628>* **JAR OF FLIES / SAP** [4] [1]
– Rotten apple / Nutshell / I stay away / No excuses / Whale & wasp / Don't follow / Swing on this. (US-version w /out 'SAP')

Oct 95. (7"/c-s) *(662623-7/-4)* **GRIND. / NUTSHELL** [23] [ ]
(cd-s+=) *(662823-2)* – So close / Love, hate, love.

Nov 95. (cd/c/d-lp) *(481114-2/-4/-1)* *<67248>* **ALICE IN CHAINS** [37] [1]
– Grind / Brush away / Sludge factory / Heaven beside you / Head creeps / Again / Shame in you / God am / So close / Nothin' song / Frogs / Over now.

Jan 96. (7"white) *(662893-7)* **HEAVEN BESIDE YOU. / WOULD? (live)** 35 □
(cd-s+=) *(662893-2)* – Rooster (live) / Junkhead (live).
(cd-s) *(662893-5)* – ('A'side) / Angry chair (live) / Man in a box (live) / Love, hate, love (live).

—— added for below only; **SCOTT OLSEN** – guitar

Jul 96. (cd/c/d-lp) *(484300-2/-4/-1) <67703>* **MTV UNPLUGGED (live)** 20 3
– Nutshell / Brother / No excuses / Sludge factory / Down in a hole / Angry chair / Rooster / Got me wrong / Heaven beside you / Would? / Frogs / Over now / Killer is me.

Jul 99. (cd/c) *(494005-2/-4) <63649>* **NOTHING SAFE** (compilation) □ 20
– Get born again / We die young / Man in the box / Them bones / Iron gland / Angry chair / Down in a hole / Rooster / Got me wrong / No excuses / I stay away / What the hell have I / Grind / Again / Would?

– compilations, etc. –

Oct 99. (4xcd-box) *Columbia; (CKX 69580)* **MUSIC BANK** □ □
Dec 00. (cd) *Columbia; <85274>* **LIVE (live)** – □

MAD SEASON

—— were originally called GACY BUNCH with **LAYNE STALEY** – vocals / **MIKE McCREADY** – guitar (of PEARL JAM) / **BARRETT MARTIN** – drums (of SCREAMING TREES)

Mar 95. (cd/c/lp) *(478507-2/-4/-1) <67057>* **ABOVE** 41 24
– Wake up / X-ray mind / I'm above / River of deceit / Lifeless dead / Artificial red / Long gone day / I don't know anything / November hotel / All alone.

—— MARK LANEGAN (of SCREAMING TREES) repl. LAYNE for 2nd set

JERRY CANTRELL

with **SEAN KINNEY** + **MIKE INEZ** / plus bassists **REX BROWN** (PANTERA), **NORWOOD FISHER** (FISHBONE) + **LES CLAYPOOL** (PRIMUS) / guest **ANGELO MOORE** (FISHBONE) – sax

Columbia Columbia

Apr 98. (cd/c/lp) *(488705-2/-4/-1) <68147>* **BOGGY DEPOT** □ 28
– Dickeye / Cut you in / My song / Settling down / Breaks my back / Jesus hands / Devil by his side / Keep the light on / Satisfy / Hurt a long time / Between / Cold piece.

May 98. (cd-ep) *<4704>* **CUT YOU IN** – □
– My song / Leave me alone (remix) / Cut you in.

Roadrunner Roadrunner

Jun 02. (cd) *<(RR 8451-2)>* **DEGRADATION TRIP** □ 33
– Psychotic break / Bargain basement Howard Hughes / Anger rising / Angel eyes / Solitude / Mother's spinning in her grave / Hellbound / Give it a name / Castaway / She was my girl / Chemical tribe / Spiderbite / Locked on / Gone.

ALKALINE TRIO

Formed: Chicago, Illinois, USA . . . 1996 by MATT SKIBA, GLENN PORTER and ROB DORAN. Inspired by 70's punk/pop and drinking, the 'TRIO were all the rage in the late 90's. From 1998's 'GODDAMMIT' to the recent 'FROM HERE TO INFIRMARY' (2001), these square-chinned lads from the Windy City finally came of age by supporting BLINK-182 around the US. However, by the dawn of 2000, they had lost PORTER who was superseded by MIKE FELUMLEE; DAN ANDRIANO had taken DORAN's place a few years earlier (see discography). The group issued 2003's 'GOOD MOURNING', with an album cover that featured all three members dressed in black and looking suspiciously like shifty bouncers at a dodgy goth club. The music within was a blaring blend of squeal-metal and inflammable catchiness, infusing punk-pop melodies with atmospheric emo-rock. The only time ALKALINE TRIO let down their guard was with the set's closing number 'BLUE IN THE FACE', an acoustic-tinged dirge paying homage to broken relationships. In turn, the band managed to mix and match sour glumness with gigantic pop-rock melodies for the masses; it also hit Top 40. From its 80s-style sleeve to its DEPECHE MODE-lite naval-gazing, 'CRIMSON' (2005), was full of the usual rock star-pampered negativity, ruminated over in songs fleshed out by ROGER MANNING's piano (he of JELLYFISH for the uninitiated). The Jerry Finn-produced album hit the Top 40 on both sides of the Atlantic and produced similarly charting singles, 'TIME TO WASTE', 'MERCY ME' and 'BURN'.

• **Covers:** WAIT FOR THE BLACKOUT (Damned) / OVER AT THE FRANKENSTEIN PLACE (Rocky Horror Picture Show).

Album rating: GODAMMIT (*8) / MAYBE I'LL CATCH FIRE (*6) / ALKALINE TRIO collection (*7) / FROM HERE TO INFIRMARY (*8) / GOOD MOURNING (*7) / CRIMSON (*7)

MATT SKIBA (b.24 Feb'76) – vocals, guitar (ex-JERKWATER drummer) / **GLENN PORTER** – drums, vocals (ex-88 FINGER LOUIE) / **ROB DORAN** – bass, vocals

Asian Man Asian Man

Jun 98. (m-cd) *<(AM 028CD)>* **FOR YOUR LUNGS ONLY** □ May98 □
– Snake oil tanker / Southern rock / Cooking wire / For your lungs only.

—— **DAN ANDRIANO** – bass (of SLAPSTICK) repl. DORAN

Oct 98. (lp/cd) *<(AM 034/+CD)>* **GODDAMMIT** □ □
– Cringe / Cop / San Francisco / Nose over tail / As you were / Enjoy your day / Clavicle / My little needle / Southern rock / Message from Kathleen / Trouble breathing / Sorry about that. *(cd re-iss. Apr03 on 'Kung Fu'+=; 78814-2)* – Bleeder / Cooking wine / My friend Peter / 97.

Feb 00. (lp/cd) *<(AM 055/+CD)>* **MAYBE I'LL CATCH FIRE** □ □
– Keep 'em coming Madam me / You've got so far to go / Fuck you Aurora / Sleepyhead / Maybe I'll catch fire / Tuck me in / She took him to the lake / 5-3-10-4 / Radio. *(cd re-iss. Apr03 on 'Kung Fu'+=; 78813-2)*

Apr 00. (lp/cd) *<(AM 058/+CD)>* **ALKALINE TRIO** (collection) □ □
– Goodbye forever / This is getting over you / Bleeder / I lied my face off / My friend Peter / Snake oil tanker / Southern rock / Cooking wine / For your lungs only / Exploding boy / Sun dials / Nose over tail / '97.

—— **MIKE FELUMLEE** – drums (ex-SMOKING POPES) repl. PORTER

Lookout! Lookout!

Apr 01. (7") *<(L 264)>* **HELL YES. / MY STANDARD BREAK FROM LIFE** □ Mar01 □

Vagrant Vagrant

Apr 01. (lp/cd) *<(VR 353/+CD)>* **FROM HERE TO INFIRMARY** □ □
– Private eye / Mr chainsaw / Take lots with alcohol / Stupid kid / Another innocent girl / Steamer trunk / You're dead / Armageddon / I'm dying tomorrow / Bloodied up / Trucks and trains / Crawl. *(cd re-iss. Aug01 on 'B-Unique'+=; BUN 008)* – Standard break / Hell yes. *(cd re-iss. May03 on 'Universal'; 910353-2)*

B-Unique not iss.

Aug 01. (cd-s) *(BUN 007)* **STUPID KID / TRUCKS AND TRAINS / ARMAGEDDON** □ –

Jan 02. (7") *(BUN 013-7)* **PRIVATE EYE. / PRIVATE EYE (original)** 51 –
(cd-s+=) *(BUN 013CDS)* – ('A'-video).
(cd-s) *(BUN 013CDX)* – ('A'-side) / Mr. Chainsaw (live) / Cringe (live).

Mar 02. (7"pic-d/cd-s) *(BUN 016-7/CDS)* **STUPID KID. / METRO** 53 –
(cd-s) *(BUN 016CDX)* – ('A'-side) / She took him to the lake (live) / We've got so far to go (live) / Private eye (video).

Universal Vagrant

May 03. (cd/lp) *(980123-8/-9) <VR 381>* **GOOD MOURNING** 32 20
– This could be love / We've had enough / One hundred stories / Continental / All on black / Emma / Fatally yours / Every thug needs a lady / Blue Carolina / Dooner party (all night) / If we never go inside / Blue in the face. *(cd+=)* – Dead end road / Old school reasons.

Jul 03. (7"pic-d) *(9809024)* **WE'VE HAD ENOUGH. / BLUE IN THE FACE (demo)** 50 –
(cd-s+=) *(9809023)* – One hundred stories (demo) / ('A'-video).

Oct 03. (7"pic-d) *(9811507)* **ALL ON BLACK. / THIS COULD BE LOVE (acoustic SBN session)** 60 –
(cd-s+=) *(9811506)* – ('A'-SBN session).

Vagrant Vagrant

May 05. (cd/lp) *(VRUK 012 CD/LP)* <VR 409/509> **CRIMSON** [34] [25]
– Time to waste / The poison / Burn / Mercy me / Dethbed / Settle for satin / Sadie / Fall victim / I was a prayer / Prevent this tragedy / Back to Hell / Your neck / Smoke. *(d-cd iss.Nov05 +=; VRUK 012CDX)* – (demo tracks of above, videos, etc.)

Jun 05. (7"red) *(VRUK 013S)* **TIME TO WASTE. / DON'T SAY YOU WON'T** [32] [–]
(cd-s+=) *(VRUK 013CDS)* – We can never break up.
(dvd-s++=) *(VRUK 013DVD)* – ('A'-video) / (outtakes).

Nov 05. (7") *(VRUK 024S)* **MERCY ME. / THIS COULD BE LOVE (acoustic)** [30] [–]
(7") *(VRUK 024SX)* – ('A') / Crawl (acoustic).
(cd-s) *(VRUK 024CDS)* – ('A') / Private eye (acoustic) / Buried / ('A'-video).

Feb 06. (7") *(VRUK 029S)* **BURN. / BURN (65DaysOfStatic remix)** [34] [–]
(7") *(VRUK 029SX)* – ('A') / ('A'-Zane Lowe BBC session).
(cd-s) *(VRUK 029CDS)* – ('A') / ('A'-Test Icicles mix) / ('A'-demo) / ('A'-video).

— **DEREK GRANT** – drums (ex-SUICIDE MACHINES) repl. MIKE

– compilations, specials, etc. –

Jan 02. (cd) *Jade Tree;* <1067> **ALKALINE TRIO / HOT WATER MUSIC** [–] [ ]
– Queen of pain / While you're waiting / Rooftops / (HOT WATER MUSIC tracks). *<pic-lp-iss.2005 on 'No Idea'; NIR 160>*

Apr 04. (cd/lp) *Better Youth Org.;* <BYO 96> **ALKALINE TRIO / ONE MAN ARMY** [–] [ ]
– Fine without you / Hating every minute / Dead and broken / Sadie / If you had a bad time . . . / Wait for the blackout / (6 by ONE MAN ARMY).

the ALL-AMERICAN REJECTS

Formed: Stillwater, Oklahoma, USA . . . 2000 as the REJEKTS by TYSON RITTER and NICK WHEELER, who together with drummer TIM CAMPBELL, self-financed mini-CD, 'SAME GIRL, NEW SONGS', in 2001. With the addition of MIKE KENNERTY and new drummer CHRIS GAYLOR, the ALL-AMERICAN REJECTS hooked up with producer Tim O'Heir for the recording of an eponymous debut album. Released on indie label 'Doghouse' in October 2002 (later picked up and re-released into the US Top 30 by 'Dreamworks'), the album was bursting at the seams with adolescent attitude, well-schooled rock classicism and hormone-saturated harmonies exemplified by hit single, 'SWING, SWING'. Having been out of the limelight for a year, the boys returned in 2005 with sophomore set, 'MOVE ALONG', a Top 10-baiting album that courted its opener 'DIRTY LITTLE SECRET', as a Top 10 single (Top 20 in the UK a year later).

Album rating: THE ALL-AMERICAN REJECTS (*7) / MOVE ALONG (*5)

TYSON RITTER (b.24 Apr'84) – vocals, bass / **NICK WHEELER** (b.20 Mar'82) – guitar, keyboards, vocals / **TIM CAMPBELL** – drums

not iss. own label

2001. (m-cd) *<none>* **SAME GIRL, NEW SONGS** [–] [ ]
– One more sad song / Drive away / Too far gone / Don't leave me / Her name rhymes with Mindy / Fembot / Pillsbury doughgirl / She mannequin / Girl of my dreams.

— added **MIKE KENNERTY** (b.20 Jul'80, Houston, Texas) – guitar

— **CHRIS GAYLOR** – drums; repl. CAMPBELL

Doghouse Doghouse

Nov 02. (cd) *<(DOG 092CD)>* **THE ALL-AMERICAN REJECTS** [ ] Oct02 [ ]
– My paper heart / Your star / Swing, swing / Time stands still / One more sad song / Why worry / Don't leave me / Too far gone / Drive away / Happy endings / The last song.

Dreamworks Dreamworks

Jul 03. (re-cd+=) *<(450460-6)>* **THE ALL-AMERICAN REJECTS** [50] Jun03 [25]
– (+=) The cigarette song (acoustic).

Jul 03. (7"orange) *(450461-7)* **SWING, SWING. / TOO FAR GONE (bedroom demo session version)** [13] Aug03 [60]
(cd-s+=) *<(450461-6)>* – The cigarette song (acoustic) / ('A'-video).

Nov 03. (7") *(4504642)* **THE LAST SONG. / TIME STANDS STILL (bedroom demo)** [69] [–]
(cd-s+=) *(4504641)* – Why worry (bedroom demo) / ('A'-video).

Polydor Interscope

Jun 05. (dl-s) *<radio>* **DIRTY LITTLE SECRET** [–] [9]

Jul 05. (cd) *(9883123)* <4791> **MOVE ALONG** [ ] [6]
– Dirty little secret / Stab my back / Move along / It ends tonight / Change your mind / Night drive / 11:11 p.m. / Dance inside / Top of the world / Straitjacket feeling / I'm waiting / Can't take it. *(UK+=)* – Night drive (acoustic) / Eyelash wishes.

Sep 05. (7"pic-d) *(9884359)* **DIRTY LITTLE SECRET. / BITE BACK** [ ] [–]
(cd-s+=) *(9884832)* – Swing, swing (acoustic) / ('A'-video).

Feb 06. (7") *(9851974)* **MOVE ALONG. / KISS YOURSELF GOODBYE** [42] [15]
(cd-s+=) *(9853100)* – Eyelash wishes / ('A'-video).

Jun 06. (7"pic-d) *(9858297)* **DIRTY LITTLE SECRET. / SWING, SWING (live)** [18] [–]
(cd-s+=) *(9858254)* – Move along (live) / ('A'-video).

Jun 06. (re-cd) *(as prev.)* **MOVE ALONG** [45] [–]

the ALLMAN BROTHERS BAND

Formed: Jacksonville, Florida, USA . . . 1967 by brothers DUANE and GREGG. They became the HOURGLASS, after previously gigging under the ALLMAN JOYS banner with others:- BOB KELLER (bass), BILLY CANELL or MANARD PORTWOOD (drums). HOURGLASS released two albums and nearly a third for 'Liberty' before disbanding in 1968. They then returned to their homeland to augment BUTCH TRUCKS in his outfit, 31st OF FEBRUARY, with DUANE also relying on session work for 'Atlantic'. In 1969, all three formed the ALLMAN BROTHERS BAND and moved to Macon, Georgia. The brothers had already signed to the 'Atlantic' distributed label 'Capricorn', run by one-time OTIS REDDING manager, Phil Walden. With a final line-up of GREGG, DUANE, BUTCH TRUCKS, BERRY OAKLEY (bass) and a second percussionist, JAIMO JOHANSON, the band cut their self-titled debut in 1969, following it up a year later with 'IDLEWILD SOUTH'. All the elements that would make the ALLMAN's a legend were in place; the smooth fluidity of the guitar runs, bible belt country and gospel in abundance, jazz-influenced explorations and dyed in the wool Southern-soaked vocals. During this time, DUANE continued his session work for the likes of LAURA NYRO and DELANEY & BONNIE, as well as lending an unmistakable hand to ERIC CLAPTON on DEREK AND THE DOMINOES' 'LAYLA' project (yes, that most famous of English rock refrains was created by the blonde maned all-American boy). Like their spiritual brothers The GRATEFUL DEAD, it was in a live setting that The ALLMAN BROTHERS BAND could really cook up a soulful gumbo stew and 'THE ALLMAN BROTHERS BAND AT FILLMORE EAST' (1971) was possibly the band's defining moment as well as one of rock's great live albums. A sprawling double set, the free flowing jams often tripped out on their own momentum and despite being spaced out over a whole side of vinyl, 'WHIPPING POST' (from the debut) lost none of its hypnotic power. Less than three months later, the band were dealt a potentially fatal blow when DUANE was killed in a motorbike accident. Bloodied but unbowed, the band released the 'EAT A PEACH' (1972) album, a mixture of live tracks left over from the

Fillmore recordings and new studio material. Another double set, three tracks had been recorded prior to the accident, including DUANE's fragile 'LITTLE MARTHA'. The indulgence of the side-long DONOVAN adaptation, 'MOUNTAIN JAM', was balanced by the pastoral beauty of tracks like BETTS' 'BLUE SKY'. After BERRY OAKLEY was killed later that year in a crash spookily reminiscent of DUANE's, BETTS' influence was even more pronounced as the band struggled bravely on with the triumphant 'BROTHERS AND SISTERS' (1973) album. Replacing OAKLEY with LAMAR WILLIAMS and drafting in pianist CHUCK LEAVELL, the rootsier sounding album gave the ALLMAN BROTHERS BAND their first and only No.1. BETTS' glorious country-flavoured 'RAMBLIN' MAN' provided their biggest hit single to date and 'JESSICA' fuelled countless boy racer fantasies after it was used as the theme for Britain's 'Top Gear' TV show. The band then returned to their natural habitat, the tourbus, playing a landmark gig to a crowd of over half a million people in Watkins Glen, New York, alongside The GRATEFUL DEAD and The BAND. Patchy solo projects followed in the shape of GREG's 'LAID BACK' (1973) and BETTS' 'HIGHWAY CALL' (1974), while the next band effort 'WIN, LOSE OR DRAW' (1975) signalled that The ALLMANS' infamous fast living was beginning to sap their creativity. GREG began a brief, torrid marriage with CHER in 1975, releasing the 'TWO THE HARD WAY' album in 1977 under the moniker of ALLMAN AND WOMAN (no, seriously!). The turning point, however, came when GREG testified against his road manager/pusher, SCOOTER HERRING, who was up on a serious drugs rap. After HERRING was sentenced to 75 years(!) in prison, the rest of the band turned their backs on GREG, the all-brothers together bravado gone, at least until the reunion. Splitting and reforming numerous times throughout the 80's, their studio output trawled a creative nadir on their 'Arista' albums. Nevertheless, they can still put bums on seats in the American heartlands and their Southern fried innovation was given official recognition in 1995 when they were inducted into the Rock 'n' Roll Hall Of Fame. In fact they were still cutting it live come the dawn of the new millennium, as 'PEAKIN' AT THE BEACON' (2000) testified. Recorded at one of their annual gigs at New York's Beacon Theater, the record was notable for the last stand of BETTS who was subsequently replaced. While there were rumours that the guitarist was allegedly dropped due to a poor performance on stage, that didn't stop the band trawling through all twenty seven and a half minutes of the man's 'HIGH FALLS'. In the event, BETTS' absence didn't prevent the ALLMANS from turning in one of their best studio outings in the last two decades with 'HITTIN' THE NOTE' (2003). A US Top 40 entry no less, the record was as gritty, soulful, and ambitious as many of their 70's classics, particularly on the more acoustic, country flavoured tracks like 'OLD BEFORE MY TIME'. Even the cover of the Rolling Stones' 'HEART OF STONE' was startling in its delivery. 2004's 'ONE WAY OUT' was yet another live double, the second to originate from dates at New York's Beacon Theater.

• **Songwriters:** The ALLMANS and BETTS. In the 90's most were written by BETTS, HAYNES and NEEL. Covered; STATESBORO BLUES (Blind Willie McTell) / ONE WAY OUT (Elmore James) / I'M YOUR HOOCHIE COOCHIE MAN (Muddy Waters) / SLIP AWAY (Clarence Carter). • **Trivia:** DUANE sessioned for WILSON PICKETT, BOZ SCAGGS, ARETHA FRANKLIN, KING CURTIS, etc, etc . . .

Album rating: THE ALLMAN BROTHERS BAND (*8) / IDLEWILD SOUTH (*7) / AT FILLMORE EAST (*9) / EAT A PEACH (*9) / BROTHERS AND SISTERS (*8) / WIN, LOSE OR DRAW (*4) / WIPE THE WINDOWS, CHECK THE OIL, DOLLAR GAS (*5) / ENLIGHTENED ROGUES (*5) / REACH FOR THE SKY (*4) / BROTHERS OF THE ROAD (*4) / DREAMS boxed-set (*7) / SEVEN TURNS (*6) / A DECADE OF HITS 1969-1979 (*8) / AN EVENING WITH THE ALLMAN BROTHERS (*6) / WHERE IT ALL BEGINS (*5) / PEAKIN' AT THE BEACON (*5) / HITTIN' THE NOTE (*7) / ONE WAY OUT (*6) / Gregg Allman: LAID BACK (*5) / GREGG ALLMAN TOUR (*3) / PLAYIN' UP A STORM (*4) / TWO THE HARD WAY as Allman & Woman (*3) / I'M NO ANGEL (*5) / JUST BEFORE THE BULLETS FLY (*4) / SEARCHING FOR SIMPLICITY (*5)

the HOURGLASS

GREGG ALLMAN (b. 8 Dec'48, Nashville, Tenn.) – vocals, keyboards, guitar / **DUANE ALLMAN** (b.20 Nov'46, Nashville) – guitars / **PAUL HORNSBY** – keyboards, guitar, vocals / **MABRON McKINNEY** – bass / **JOHN SANDLIN** – drums

Liberty Liberty

Feb 68. (7") *<56002>* **HEARTBEAT. / NOTHING BUT TEARS** [–] [ ]

Aug 68. (lp; mono/stereo) *(LBL/LBS 83219E)* *<7536>* **THE HOUR GLASS** [ ] Feb68 [ ]
– Out of the night / Nothing but tears / Love makes the world 'round / Cast off all my fears / I've been trying / No easy way down / Heartbeat / So much love / Got to get away / Silently / Bells.

—— **JESSE WILLARD CARR** – bass, vocals repl. MABRON McKINNEY

Jul 68. (7") *<56029>* **POWER OF LOVE. / I STILL WANT YOUR LOVE** [–] [ ]

Aug 68. (lp) *<7555>* **POWER OF LOVE** [–] [ ]
– Power of love / Changing of the guard / To things before / I'm not afraid / I can stand alone / Down in Texas / I still want your love / Home for the summer / I'm hangin' up my heart for you / Going nowhere / Norwegian wood / Now is the time. *(re-iss. the 1968 lp's; Mar74 on 'United Artists'; USD 303/4)<013G2>*

Sep 68. (7") *<56053>* **CHANGING OF THE GUARD. / D-I-V-O-R-C-E** [–] [ ]

Nov 68. (7") *<56065>* **GOING NOWHERE. / SHE'S MY WOMAN** [–] [ ]

Dec 68. (7") *<56072>* **NOW IS THE TIME. / SHE'S MY WOMAN** [–] [ ]

Feb 69. (7") *<56091>* **I'VE BEEN TRYING. / SILENTLY** [–] [ ]

—— 3rd album was withdrawn

the 31st FEBRUARY

DUANE and **GREGG** with **BUTCH TRUCKS** – drums / **SCOTT BOYER** – guitar, vocals / **DAVID BROWN** – bass

not iss.

Mar 69. (7") **IN THE MORNING WHEN I'M REAL. / PORCELAIN MIRRORS** [–] [ ]

—— An album DUANE AND GREGG was released 1973 on 'Polydor UK'/'Bold' US cont. these demos.

the ALLMAN BROTHERS BAND

(**GREGG** and **DUANE**) plus **DICKEY BETTS** (b.RICHARD, 12 Dec'43, West Palm Beach, Florida) – guitar, vocals / **BERRY OAKLEY** (b. 4 Apr'48, Chicago, Illinois) – bass / **BUTCH TRUCKS** (b.Jacksonville, Florida) – drums, timpani / **JAIMOE JOHANSON** (b.JOHN LEE JOHNSON, 8 Jul'44, Ocean Springs, Miss.) – percussion

Atco Atco

Nov 69. (lp) *(228 033)* *<308>* **THE ALLMAN BROTHERS BAND** [ ] [ ]
– Don't want you no more / It's not my cross to bear / Black hearted woman / Trouble no more / Every hungry woman / Dreams / Whipping post. *(cd-iss. 1994 on 'Polydor'; 823 653-2) (cd re-iss. Jun98; 531257-2)*

Mar 70. (7") *(226 013)* *<8803>* **BLACK HEARTED WOMAN. / EVERY HUNGRY WOMAN** [ ] [ ]

Nov 70. (lp) *(2400 032)* *<342>* **IDLEWIND SOUTH** [ ] [38]
– Revival (love is everywhere) / Don't keep me wonderin' / Midnight rider / In memory of Elizabeth Reed / I'm your hoochie coochie man / Please call home / Leave my blues at home. *(cd-iss. Mar89 on 'Polydor'; 833 334-2) (cd re-iss. Jun98; 531258-2)*

Nov 70. (7") *(2091 040)* *<8011>* **REVIVAL (LOVE IS EVERYWHERE). / LEAVE MY BLUES AT HOME** [ ] [92]

Mar 71. (7") *(2091 070)* *<8014>* **MIDNIGHT RIDER. / WHIPPING POST** [ ] [ ]

Capricorn Capricorn

Jul 71. (d-lp) *(2659 005)* *<802>* **AT FILLMORE EAST (live)** [ ] [13]
– Statesboro blues / Done somebody wrong / Stormy Monday / You don't love me / Hot 'Lanta / In memory of Elizabeth Reed / Whipping post. *(re-iss. Nov74;) (d-cd-iss. 1986 on 'Polydor'; 823 273-2) (d-cd re-iss. Jun98; 531260-2)*

—— On 29 Oct'71, DUANE was killed in a motorcycle accident in Macon. He had already contributed to 3 tracks on below album.

Feb 72. (d-lp) *(67501)* *<0102>* **EAT A PEACH** — 4
– Ain't wastin' time no more / Les brers in A minor / Melissa / Mountain jam / One way out / Trouble no more / Stand back / Blue sky / Little Martha / Mountain jam (reprise). *(re-iss. Nov74;) (cd-iss. 1986 on 'Polydor'; 823 654-2) (cd re-iss. Jun98; 531261-2)*

Apr 72. (7") *<0003>* **AIN'T WASTIN' TIME NO MORE. / MELISSA** – 77

Jul 72. (7") *<0007>* **MELISSA. / BLUE SKY** – 86

Nov 72. (7") *<0014>* **ONE WAY OUT. / STAND BACK** – 86

— (Jan'73) **LAMAR WILLIAMS** (b.1947) – bass; repl. BERRY OAKLEY who also died in a motorcyle accident, again in Macon, 11 Nov'72.

Sep 73. (lp/c) *(2429/3129 102)* *<0111>* **BROTHERS AND SISTERS** 42 Aug73 1
– Wasted words / Ramblin' man / Come and go blues / Jelly jelly / Southbound / Jessica / Pony boy. *(re-iss. Jun81; 2482 504) (cd-iss. 1986 on 'Polydor'; 825 092-2) (cd re-iss. Jun87 on 'Polydor'; 823 721-2) (cd re-iss. Jun98; 531262-2)*

Oct 73. (7") *(2089 005)* *<0027>* **RAMBLIN' MAN. / PONY BOY** Aug73 2

Jan 74. (7") *<0036>* **JESSICA. / WASTED WORDS** – 65

Oct 74. (7") *(2089 006)* **JESSICA. / COME AND GO BLUES** –

Sep 75. (lp) *(2476 116)* *<0156>* **WIN, LOSE OR DRAW** 5
– Can't lose what you never had / Just another love song / Nevertheless / Win, lose or draw / Louisiana Lou And Three Card Monty John / High falls / Sweet mama. *(cd-iss. Aug87; 827586-2) (cd re-iss. Jun98; 531263-2)*

Sep 75. (7") *<0246>* **NEVERTHELESS. / LOUISIANA LOU AND THREE CARD MONTY JOHN** – 67 78

— Jul 76 when GREGG was ostracised by others for giving evidence against convicted drug trafficker and road manager Scooter Herring. GREGG formed his own band. BETTS formed GREAT SOUTHERN and others formed SEA LEVEL who hit US No. 31 Mar 78 with lp 'CATS ON THE COAST'. When rifts were settled **The ALLMAN BROTHERS BAND** re-united early '79. GREGG, DICKEY, BUTCH, JAIMO plus newcomers **DAN TOLER** – guitar / **DAVID GOLDFLIES** – bass (both ex-GREAT SOUTHERN)

Polydor Capricorn

Mar 79. (lp) *(2429 185)* *<0218>* **ENLIGHTENED ROGUES** 9
– Crazy love / Can't take it with you / Pegasus / Need your love so bad / Blind love / Try it one more time / Just ain't easy / Sail away. *(cd-iss. 1987 on 'Polydor'; 831 589-2) (cd re-iss. Jun98; 531265-2)*

Apr 79. (7") *(2089 068)* *<0320>* **CRAZY LOVE. / IT JUST AIN'T EASY** Mar79 29

Jun 79. (7") *<0326>* **CAN'T TAKE IT WITH YOU. / SAIL AWAY** –

Arista Arista

Sep 80. (lp) *(SPART 1146)* *<9535>* **REACH FOR THE SKY** Aug80 27
– Hell & high water / Mystery woman / From the madness of the west / I got a right to be wrong / Angeline / Famous last words / Keep on keepin' on / So long. *(cd-iss. Aug97 on 'Razor & Tie'; RE 2131)*

Sep 80. (7") *<0555>* **ANGELINE. / SO LONG** – 58

Jan 81. (7") *<0584>* **MYSTERY WOMAN. / HELL OR HIGH WATER** –

Sep 81. (lp) *<9564>* **BROTHERS OF THE ROAD** Aug81 44
– Brothers of the road / Leavin' / Straight from the road / The heat is on / Maybe we can go back to yesterday / The judgement / Two rights / Never knew how much (I needed you) / Things you used to do / I beg of you. *(cd-iss. Aug97 on 'Razor & Tie'; RE 2132)*

Sep 81. (7") *(ARIST 432)* *<0618>* **STRAIGHT FROM THE HEART. / LEAVING** Aug81 39

Nov 81. (7") *<0643>* **TWO RIGHTS. / NEVER KNEW HOW MUCH** –

— **CHUCK LEAVELL** rejoined but they soon disbanded once again. Past member **LAMAR** died of cancer on 25 Jan'83.

GREGG ALLMAN BAND

went solo again in 1987 with **DAN TOLER** – guitar / **DAVID 'FRANKIE' TOLER** – drums / **TIM HEDING** – keyboards / **BRUCE WAIBEL** – bass, vocals / **CHAZ TRIPPY** – percussion

Epic Epic

May 87. (lp/c/cd) *<(450392-1/-4/-2)>* **I'M NO ANGEL** Feb87 30
– I'm no angel / Anything goes / Evidence of love / Yours for the asking / Things that might have been / Can't keep running / Faces without names / Lead me on / Don't want you no more / It's not my cross to bear.

Jul 87. (7") *(6507 517)* *<06998>* **I'M NO ANGEL. / LEAD ME ON** Mar87 49

Jul 87. (7") *<07215>* **CAN'T KEEP RUNNING. / ANYTHING GOES** –

Sep 87. (7") *<07430>* **EVIDENCE OF LOVE. / ANYTHING GOES** –

Apr 89. (lp/c/cd) *(462 477-1/-4/-2)* *<44033>* **JUST BEFORE THE BULLETS FLY** Aug88
– Demons / Before the bullets fly / Slip away / Thorn and a wild rose / Ocean awash the gunwale / Can't get over you / Island / Fear of falling / Night games / Every hungry woman.

Apr 89. (7") *<08041>* **SLIP AWAY. / EVERY HUNGRY WOMAN** –

Jan 98. (cd/c) *(481691-2/-4)* *<67143>* **SEARCHING FOR SIMPLICITY** Nov97
– Whipping post / House of blues / Come back and help me / Silence ain't golden no more / Rendezvous with the blues / Wolf's a-howlin' / Love the poison / Don't deny me / Dark end of the street / Neighbor neighbor / I've got news for you / Memphis in the meantime / Startin' over.

– other GREGG ALLMAN releases, etc. –

— with **SCOTT BOYER** – guitar, vocals / **TOMMY TALTON** – slide guitar / **CHUCK LEAVELL** – keyboards / **DAVID BROWN** – bass / **BILL STEWART** – drums / etc.

Capricorn Capricorn

Nov 73. (lp) *(47508)* *<0116>* **LAID BACK** 13
– Will the circle be unbroken / Don't mess up a good thing / Multi-colored lady / Please call home / Queen of hearts / Midnight rider / Don't mess up a good thing / All my friends / These days. *(cd-iss. Aug87 on 'Polydor'; 831 941-2)*

Jan 74. (7") *(2089 002)* *<0035>* **MIDNIGHT RIDER. / MULTI-COLORED LADY** Dec73 19

— (above releases were issued approx.half a year later in UK).

Mar 74. (7") *<0042>* **PLEASE CALL HOME. / DON'T MESS UP A GOOD THING** –

Oct 74. (7") *<0053>* **DON'T MESS WITH A GOOD THING. / MIDNIGHT RIDER** –

Nov 74. (d-lp) *(2659 038)* *<0141>* **GREGG ALLMAN TOUR (live)** 50
– Don't mess up a good thing / Queen of hearts / Feel so bad / Stand back / Time will take us / Where can you go / Double cross / Dreams / Are you lonely for me / Turn on your love light / Oncoming traffic / Will the circle be unbroken?. *(cd-iss. Oct87 on 'Polydor'; 831 940-2)*

— retained **BILL STEWART** and brought in **STEVE BECKMEIER + JOHN HUG** – guitar / **RICKY HIRSCH** – slide guitar / **NEIL LARSEN** – piano / **WILLIE WEEKS** – bass

Jun 77. (lp) *(2476 131)* *<0181>* **PLAYIN' UP A STORM** 42
– Come and go blues / Let this be a lesson to ya / The brightest smile in town / Bring it on back / Cryin' shame / Sweet feelin' / It ain't no use / Matthew's arrival / One more try.

Aug 77. (7") *<0279>* **CRYIN' SHAME. / ONE MORE TRY** –

ALLMAN AND WOMAN

the (Woman being GREGG's wife and singer CHER) (same line-up)

Warners Warners

Nov 77. (lp) *(K 56436)* *<3120>* **TWO THE HARD WAY**
– Move me / I found you love / Can you fool / You've really got a hold on me / We're gonna make it / Do what you gotta do / In for the night / Shadow dream song / Island / I love makin' love to you / Love me.

Dec 77. (7") *(K 17057)* *<8504>* **LOVE ME. / MOVE ME**

— they subsequently split and were divorced on 16th of January '79

the ALLMAN BROTHERS BAND

— re-formed 1989, **GREGG, DICKEY, JAIMO, BUTCH** and newcomers **ALLEN WOODY** – bass / **WARREN HAYES** – guitar / **JOHNNY NEEL** – keyboards

Epic Epic

Jul 90. (7") *<73504>* **GOOD CLEAN FUN. / SEVEN TURNS** –

Jul 90. (cd/c/lp) *(466850-2/-4/-1)* *<46144>* **SEVEN TURNS** 53
– Good clean fun / Let me ride / Low down dirty mean / Shine it on / Loaded dice / Seven turns / Gambler's roll / True gravity / It ain't over yet.

Sep 90. (7") *<73583>* **SEVEN TURNS. / LET ME RIDE** –

Jul 91. (cd/c/lp) *(468525-2/-4/-1)* *<47877>* **SHADES OF TWO WORLDS** 85

– End of the line / Bad rain / Nobody knows / Desert blues / Get on with your life / Midnight man / Kind of bird / Come on in my kitchen.

Jun 92. (cd/c) <48998-2/-4> **AN EVENING WITH THE ALLMAN BROTHERS BAND** [–] [ ]
– Southbound / Nobody knows / Revival (love is everywhere) / Midnight blues / Get on with your life / Dreams / End of the line / Blue sky.

— **MARC QUINONES** – congas, percussion; repl. NEEL

Jul 94. (cd/c) *(476884-2/-4)* <64232> **WHERE IT ALL BEGINS** [ ] May94 [ ]
– All night train / Sailin' 'cross the Devil's sea / Back where it all begins / Soulshine / No one to run with / Change my way of living / Mean woman blues / Everybody's got a mountain to climb / What's done is done / Temptation is a gun.

May 95. (cd,c) <66795> **2ND SET – AN EVENING WITH THE ALLMAN BROTHERS BAND** [–] [88]
– Sailin' 'cross the Devil's sea / You don't love me / Soul shine / Back where it all begins / In memory of Elizabeth Reed / Same thing / No one to run with / Jessica. *(UK-iss.Apr99; 480606-2)*

— added **DEREK TRUCKS** – guitar

Nov 00. (cd) <85205> **PEAKIN' AT THE BEACON (live)** [–] [ ]
– Don't want you no more / It's not my cross to bear / Ain't wastin' time no more / Every hungry woman / Please call home / Stand back / Black hearted woman / Leave my blues alone / Seven turns / High falls.

— **GREGG** plus **WARREN HAYNES** – guitars, vocals / **DEREK TRUCKS** – guitars / **OTEIL BURBRIDGE** – bass / **JAIMOE** – drums / **MARC QUINONES** – percussion

Sanctuary Sanctuary

Apr 03. (cd) *(SANCD 170)* <84599> **HITTIN' THE NOTE** [ ] Mar03 [37]
– Firing line / High cost of low living / Desdemona / Woman across the river / Old before my time / Who to believe / Maydell / Rockin' horse / Heart of stone / Instrumental illness / Old friend.

Mar 04. (d-cd) <84682> **ONE WAY OUT (live)** [–] [ ]
– Statesboro blues / Don't keep me wonderin' / Midnight rider / Rockin' horse / Desdemona / Trouble no more / Wasted words / Good morning little schoolgirl / Instrumental illness / Ain't wastin' time no more / Come and go blues / Woman across the river / Old before my time / Every hungry woman / High cost of low living / Worried down with the blues / Dreams / Whipping post.

– DUANE & GREGG ALLMAN compilations, etc. –

1972. (7") *Bold;* **MORNING DEW. / (pt. 2)** [–] [ ]

1973. (lp) *Polydor; (2310 235) / Bold; <33-301>* **DUANE & GREGG ALLMAN** (rec.'68) [ ] [ ]
– Morning dew / God rest his soul / Nobody knows when you're down and out / Come down and get me / Melissa / I'll change for you / Back down home with you / Well I know too well / In the morning when I'm real.

– ALLMAN BROTHERS compilations, etc. –

Oct 73. (lp; as ALLMAN JOYS) *Mercury; (6398 005) / Dial; <6005>* **EARLY ALLMANS** [ ] [ ]

Nov 74. (d-lp) *Capricorn; (60046) / Atco; <805>* **BEGINNINGS** [ ] Mar73 [25]
– (first 2 ALLMAN BROTHERS BAND lp's) *(cd-iss. Oct87 on 'Polydor'; 827 588-2) (cd re-iss. Jun98; 531259-2)*

1974. (7") *Capricorn; <0050>* **AIN'T WASTIN' TIME NO MORE. / BLUE SKY** [–] [ ]

1974. (7") *Capricorn; <0051>* **MELISSA. / RAMBLIN' MAN** [–] [ ]

Feb 76. (d-lp) *Capricorn; (2637 101) <0164>* **THE ROAD GOES ON FOREVER** [54] Dec75 [43]
– Black hearted woman / Dreams / Whipping post / Midnight rider / Statesboro blues / Stormy Monday / Hoochie coochie man / Stand back / One way out / Blue sky / Hot 'Lanta / Ain't wastin' time no more / Melissa / Wasted words / Jessica / Ramblin' man / Little Martha.

Dec 76. (d-lp) *Capricorn; (2637 103) <0177>* **WIPE THE WINDOWS, CHECK THE OIL, DOLLAR GAS** (demos, rarities recorded live) [ ] [75]
– (introduction) / Wasted words / Southbound / Ramblin' man / In memory of Elizabeth Reed / Ain't wastin' time no more / Come and go blues / Can't lose what you never had / Don't want you no more / It's not my cross to bear / Jessica. *(cd-iss. Jun98; 531264-2)*

Aug 80. (lp) *Capricorn; <6339>* **THE BEST OF THE ALLMAN BROTHERS BAND** [ ] Nov81 [ ]

Jun 81. (d-lp) *Capricorn; (2637 105)* **THE STORY OF THE ALLMAN BROTHERS BAND** [ ] [ ]

Sep 83. (12"ep) *Polydor; (POSP 607)* **JESSICA / SOUTHBOUND. / WHIPPIN' POST / RAMBLIN' MAN** [ ] [–]

Jul 84. (7") *Old Gold; (OG 9437)* **JESSICA. / RAMBLIN' MAN** [ ] [–]

Sep 85. (lp; as HOURGLASS) *C5; (C5-524)* **THE SOUL OF TIME** [ ] [–]

Feb 88. (7") *Old Gold; (OG 4046)* **JESSICA. / (b-side by; Derek & The Dominoes')** [ ] [–]

Jul 88. (lp/c) *Knight; (KNLP/KNMC 10004)* **NIGHTRIDING** [ ] [–]
(cd-iss. Sep89; KNCD 10004)

Apr 89. (6xlp/4xc/4xcd) *Polydor; <(839417-1/-4/-2)>* **DREAMS** [ ] Jul89 [ ]

Jul 90. (d-cd) *Polydor; (843260-2)* **LIVE AT LUDLOW GARAGE 1970 (live)** [ ] [–]

May 92. (cd/c) *Polydor; (511156-2/-4)* **A DECADE OF HITS 1969-1979** [ ] Nov91 [ ]
– Statesboro blues / Ramblin' man / Midnight rider / Southbound / Melissa / Jessica / Ain't wastin' time no more / Little Martha / Crazy love / Revival / Wasted words / Blue sky / One way out / In memory of Elizabeth Reed / Dreams / Whipping post.

May 92. (cd/c) *Castle; (CCS CD/MC 327)* **THE COLLECTION** [ ] [–]

Sep 94. (cd) *R.C.A.; (0782 218724-2)* **HELL & HIGH WATER (The Best Of The Arista Years)** [ ] [–]

Mar 93. (d-cd) *Polydor; (517 294-2)* **THE FILLMORE CONCERTS (live)** [ ] [ ]

Mar 98. (cd) *Camden; (74321 5696124)* **MADNESS OF THE WEST** [ ] [–]

Jun 98. (cd/c) *Epic; (489087-2/-4)* **MYCOLOGY** [ ] [ ]

Sep 98. (cd) *Spectrum; (551824-2)* **THE BEST OF THE ALLMAN BROTHERS BAND LIVE (live)** [ ] [–]

Jan 00. (cd) *Universal; (E 543405-2)* **UNIVERSAL MASTERS COLLECTION** [ ] [–]

Mar 03. (cd) *Universal; (AA314 547899-2)* **20th CENTURY MASTERS** [ ] [ ]

DUANE ALLMAN

exploitation compilations featuring all his guitar/sessions

Oct 74. (d-lp) *Capricorn; <2CP 0108>* **AN ANTHOLOGY** [ ] Dec72 [28]
– B.B. King medley / Hey Jude / The road of love / Goin' down slow / The weight / Games people play / Shake for me / Loan me a dime / Rollin' stone / Livin' on the open road / Down along the cove / lease be with me / Mean old world / Layla / Statesboro blues / Don't keep me wondering / Stand back / Dreams / Little Martha. *(d-cd.iss.Oct87 on 'Polydor'; 831 444-2)*

Jan 75. (d-lp) *Capricorn; <CPN2-0139>* **AN ANTHOLOGY VOL.2** [ ] Jul74 [49]
– Happily married man / It ain't fair / The weight / You reap what you sow / Matchbox / Born to be wild / No money down / Been gone too long / Stuff you gotta watch / Push push / Walk on gilded splinters / Waiting for a train / Don't tell me your troubles / Goin' upstairs / Come on in my kitchen / Dimples / Goin' up the country / Done somebody wrong / Leave my blues at home / Midnight rider. *(d-cd.iss.Oct87 on 'Polydor'; 831 445-2)*

Sep 79. (lp) *Capricorn; (242 919-8)* **THE BEST OF DUANE ALLMAN** [ ] [–]

Marc ALMOND

Born: PETER MARC ALMOND, 9 Jul'59, Southport, England. Having met DAVE BALL at Leeds Polytechnic, the pair formed SOFT CELL and with the help of visual technician, STEVEN GRIFFITHS, they embarked on studio and live work in 1980 with the 'MUTANT MOMENTS' EP. After appearing on the infamous 'Some Bizzare Album', with cut, 'The Girl With The Patent Leather Face', they secured a bonafide deal with the 'Some Bizzare' label. The following year, after a debut single, 'MEMORABILIA' failed to make an impression, a darkly compelling, electro-fuelled cover of 'TAINTED LOVE' (once the dancefloor domain of disco diva, GLORIA JONES) slipped in to the UK chart, peaking at No.1 for two weeks. To end the year, SOFT CELL cracked the Top 5 with both 'BEDSITTER' and their debut album, 'NON-STOP EROTIC CABARET', an early 80's classic which trawled the depths of ALMOND's black-leather, neon-lit fantasies to a sleazy musical backdrop of low-rent alternative disco. Apart from the aforementioned singles, tracks such as 'YOUTH', 'SEX DWARF', 'SEEDY FILMS', 'CHIPS ON MY SHOULDER' and the forthcoming hit, 'SAY HELLO, WAVE GOODBYE', even found a rampant audience in the gay disco community of New York. The extroverted ALMOND was a figurehead for young homosexuals, although the media were scathing in their criticism of what they saw as the singer's effeminate posturing. Nevertheless, SOFT CELL continued to chalk up the hits, 'TORCH' (an exquisite duet featuring CINDY ECSTACY) narrowly missing No.1, while a revamped dance model of the debut, 'NON-STOP ECSTATIC DANCING', marked time as BALL and ALMOND worked on a follow-up. Early in '83, their second set proper, 'THE ART OF FALLING APART', hit the shops and subsequently the Top 5, the record coming with a free 12" single that saw ALMOND bravely attempting a HENDRIX medley. As the pair increasingly concentrated on separate projects, MARC & THE MAMBAS and DAVE BALL solo, a split seemed imminent; by the release of 'THIS LAST NIGHT . . . IN SODOM' in January '84, SOFT CELL was no more. After many threats of impending retirement, ALMOND was back in his beloved spotlight with the 'VERMIN IN ERMINE' (1984) album, cut with new backing band, The WILLING SINNERS. Developing further as an interpretive balladeer/torch singer with each successive release, ALMOND's mid-late 80's output found him marginalised to cult appeal despite an impressive array of cover material from such luminaries as JACQUES BREL, SCOTT WALKER and JOHNNIE RAY. This approach finally resulted in a massive comeback hit duet with GENE PITNEY, the melodramatic 'SOMETHING'S GOTTEN HOLD OF MY HEART', originally a Top 5 hit in 1967 for the singing/songwriting heart-throb. In the early 90's, SOFT CELL enjoyed a bit of a renaissance, remixed versions of 'SAY HELLO WAVE GOODBYE' and 'TAINTED LOVE' making the charts, while ALMOND scored a surprise Top 20 hit with a dancefloor reworking of Jacques Brel's 'JACKY'. Taken from the album, 'TENEMENT SYMPHONY' (1991), this return to form also numbered future hits, 'MY HAND OVER MY HEART' and 'THE DAYS OF PEARLY SPENCER', the latter another blast from the 60's past and originally a hit for DAVID McWILLIAMS. ALMOND continued to work on various idiosyncratic projects, including a set of old French songs and poems, 'ABSINTHE' (1993). Having delivered what was to be a one-off album ('FANTASTIC STAR') for 'Mercury' in early '96, the long-suffering tainted soul that was MARC ALMOND made his re-appearance with the single 'BLACK KISS' in late '98. Having set up his own record label, 'Blue Star', the wee man unleashed his most advanced work since the early days in the shape of 'OPEN ALL NIGHT' (1999). With rave reviews (for once!), ALMOND set about publishing two works, the first a lyrics/poems collection entitled 'A Beautiful Twisted Night', the second an autobiography 'Tainted Life'. 'STRANGER THINGS' (2001) happened to ALMOND in the new millennium as he joined forces with Icelandic leftfield beats merchant JOHAN JOHANNSON. Well, not that strange, merely a trip into more widescreen territory courtesy of JOHANNSON's luxuriant string arrangements, the record even featuring the obligatory guest spot from SHIRLEY BASSEY to add that crucial 007 touch. Spurred on by a UK Top 40 "BEST OF . . ." compilation and with nearly every other post-New Wave outfit re-forming to rake in the spoils of money (or credibility!), it was no surprise that messrs ALMOND and BALL would resurrect SOFT CELL; it had been a full 18 years since their . . . er 'LAST NIGHT IN SODOM' came out. 'CRUELTY WITHOUT BEAUTY' (2002), stepped back to these heady days of yore. Opening with 'DARKER TIMES' and the minor hit single, 'MONOCULTURE', the set showed what might've been had ALMOND not ventured to croon land. Ever the wild card, the man resumed his solo career via a post-Glasnost trek into frost-bitten Russian folk, 'HEART ON SNOW' (2003), backed by native musicians and even singing some original language tracks. From his horizons having widened, they narrowed severely when on the 17th of October the following year, ALMOND was nearly killed travelling as a pillion passenger on a motorcycle in central London. Against the odds, the singer was out of hospital inside a month, although his old sparring partner, GENE PITNEY, wasn't so lucky, suffering a fatal brush with mortality on 5th April, 2006.

• **Covered:** WHERE DID OUR LOVE GO (Supremes). MARC & THE MAMBAS covered IF YOU GO AWAY + THE BULLS (Jacques Brel) / CAROLINE SAYS (Lou Reed) / TERRAPIN (Syd Barrett) / CATCH A FALLEN STAR (Perry Como). MARC ALMOND solo:- A WOMAN'S STORY (Cher) / A SALTY DOG (Procol Harum) / THE LITTLE WHITE CLOUD THAT CRIED (Johnnie Ray) / THE PLAGUE (Scott Walker). • **Trivia:** In 1983, DAVE BALL scored the music for Tennessee Williams' play 'Suddenly Last Summer'. In mid 1987, ALMOND guested and wrote on SALLY TIMMS' single 'This House Is A House Of Tears'.

Album rating: Soft Cell: NON-STOP EROTIC CABARET (*8) / NON-STOP ECSTATIC DANCING remix collection (*4) / THE ART OF FALLING APART (*6) / THIS LAST NIGHT . . . IN SODOM (*5) / MEMORABILIA – THE SINGLES compilation (*8) / CRUELTY WITHOUT BEAUTY (*6) / Marc And The Mambas: UNTITLED (*8) / TORMENT AND TOREROS (*5) / Marc Almond: VERMIN IN ERMINE (*5) / STORIES OF JOHNNY (*5) / MOTHER FIST AND HER FIVE DAUGHTERS (*4) / THE STARS WE ARE (*5) / JACQUES (*5) / ENCHANTMENT (*5) / TENEMENT SYMPHONY (*4) / TWELVE YEARS OF TEARS (*5) / ABSINTHE (*5) / FANTASTIC STAR (*5) / THE SINGLES (1984-1987) compilation (*7) / THE BEST OF MARC ALMOND compilation (*6) / OPEN ALL NIGHT (*7) / STRANGER THINGS (*6) / HEART ON SNOW (*6)

SOFT CELL

MARC ALMOND – vocals / **DAVE BALL** – keyboards, synthesizer, drum programming

Big Frock — not iss.

1980. (7"ep) *(ABF 1)* **MUTANT MOMENTS** [ ] [–]
– Potential / L.O.V.E. feelings / Metro MRX / Frustration.

Some Bizzare — Sire

Mar 81. (7") *(HARD 1)* **MEMORABILIA. / A MAN CAN GET LOST** [ ] [–]
(12") *(HARD 12)* – ('A'extended) / Persuasion (extended).

Jul 81. (7") *(BZS 2)* *<49855>* **TAINTED LOVE. / WHERE DID OUR LOVE GO** [1] Dec81 [8]
(12"+=) *(BZS 2-12)* – Tainted dub / Memorabilia.
(re-iss. Jul82; hit 50, re-iss. Jan85; hit 43)

Nov 81. (7"/ext-12") *(BZS 6/+12)* **BEDSITTER. / FACILITY GIRLS** [4] [ ]

—— guests **CINDY ECSTACY** – dual vox / **DAVE TOFANI** – sax / **JOHN GATHELL** – trumpet

Dec 81. (lp/c) *(BZ LP/MC 2)* *<3647>* **NON-STOP EROTIC CABARET** [5] Jan82 [22]
– Frustration / Tainted love / Seedy films / Youth / Sex dwarf / Entertain me / Chips on my shoulder / Bedsitter / Secret life / Say hello, wave goodbye. *(re-iss. May90 on 'Vertigo' cd/c/lp; 800 061-2/-4/-1)*

Jan 82. (7"/ext-12") *(BZS 7/+12)* **SAY HELLO, WAVE GOODBYE. / FUN CITY** [3] [ ]

May 82. (7"/ext-12") *(BZS 9/+12)* **TORCH. / INSECURE ME** [2] [ ]

—— duo carried on without CINDY, who later formed SIX SEE RED

Jun 82. (m-lp/m-c) *(BZ X/M 1012)* *<23694>* **NON-STOP ECSTATIC DANCING** (remixes) [6] Jul82 [57]
– Memorabilia / Where did our love go / What! / A man could get lost / Chips on my shoulder * / Sex dwarf. *<US version repl.* with =)* – Insecure . . . me? *(re-iss. Mar92 on 'Mercury' cd/c; 510 295-2/-4)* – (extra tracks).

Aug 82. (7"/ext-12") *(BZS 11/+12)* **WHAT! / . . . SO (remix)** [3] [ ]

Nov 82. (7"/ext-12") *(BZS 16/+12)* **WHERE THE HEART IS. / IT'S A MUG GAME** [21] [ ]

Feb 83. (lp/c) *(BIZL/+C 3)* *<23769>* **THE ART OF FALLING APART** [5] [84]
– Forever the same / Where the heart is / Numbers / Heat / Kitchen sink drama / Baby doll / Loving you, hating me / The art of falling apart. *(12"ep with above +=)* – MARTIN. / HENDRIX MEDLEY: HEY JOE – PURPLE HAZE – VOODOO CHILE *(re-iss. Nov87; SOD 2) (re-iss. Mar92 on 'Mercury' cd/c; 510 296-2/-4)* – (extra tracks).

Feb 83. (7"/ext-12") *(BZS 16/+12)* **NUMBERS. / BARRIERS** [25] [–]

Apr 83. (7") **HEAT. / IT'S A MUGS GAME** [–] [ ]

Sep 83. (7") *(BZS 20)* **SOUL INSIDE. / YOU ONLY LIVE TWICE** [16] [–]
(12"+=) *(BZS 20-12)* – Loving you, hating me / 007 theme.
(d7"+=) *(BZS 20-20)* – Loving you, hating me / Her imagination.

Feb 84. (7") *(BZS 22)* **DOWN IN THE SUBWAY. / DISEASE AND DESIRE** [24] [–]
(ext-12"+=/12"remix+=) *(BZS/+R 22-12)* – Born to lose.

Mar 84. (lp/c) *(BIZL/+C 6)* **THIS LAST NIGHT . . . IN SODOM** [12] [–]
– Mr. Self destruct / Slave to this / Little rough rhinestone / Meet murder my angel / The best way to kill / L'Esqualita / Down in the subway / Surrender (to a stranger) / Soul inside / Where was your heart (when you needed it most). *(cd-iss. Aug84; 818 436-2)*

—— split just prior to the above album

– compilations, others, etc. –

1982. (6x12"box) *Some Bizzare; (CELBX 1)* **THE 12" SINGLES** [ ] [–]

Dec 86. (lp/c)(cd) *Some Bizzare; (BZ LP/MC 3)(830 708-2)* **SOFT CELL – THE SINGLES** [58] [–]

Mar 91. (7"/c-s) *Mercury; (SOF T/MC 1)* **SAY HELLO, WAVE GOODBYE '91. / MEMORABILIA (Grid remix)** [38] [–]
(12"+=)(cd-s+=) *(SOFT 1-12)(SOFCD 1)* – ('A'-Mendelsohn extended remix).
(cd-s) *(SOFCP 1)* – ('A'side) / Numbers / Torch (12"version).

May 91. (7"/c-s)(12") *Mercury; (SOF T/MC 2)(SOFT 2-12)* **TAINTED LOVE ('91 remix). / ('A'-Original)** [5] [–]
(cd-s+=) *(SOFCP 2)* – Where did our love go?
(cd-s) *(SOFCD 2)* – Tainted love – Where the heart is / Loving you – hating me / Where the heart is.

May 91. (cd/c/lp) *Mercury; (848 512-2/-4/-1)* **MEMORABILIA – THE SINGLES** [8] [ ]
– Memorabilia '91 / Tainted love / Bedsitter / Torch / What was the matter with Rachmaninov? / Say hello wave goodbye '91 / Where the heart is / I feel love / Tears run rings / A lover spurned / Something's gotten hold of my heart. *(cd+=)* – (Soul inside / Say hello wave goodbye (12"mix) / Waifs and strays (Grid twilight mix).

Mar 94. (cd/c) *Spectrum; (550 189-2/-4)* **DOWN IN THE SUBWAY** [ ] [–]

Mar 96. (cd) *Some Bizarre; (552 086-2)* **SAY HELLO TO SOFT CELL** [ ] [–]

Feb 99. (12"; as SOFT CELL vs CLUB 69) *Twisted; (TWD 55530)* **TAINTED LOVE** [ ] [–]

Apr 02. (cd) *Mercury; (586834-2) <586912>* **THE VERY BEST OF SOFT CELL** [37] [ ]
– Memorabilia / Tainted love / Where did our love go? / Bedsitter / Say hello, wave goodbye / Sex dwarf / Torch / Insecure me / What? / Where the heart is / It's a mugs game / Numbers / Loving you hating me / Soul inside / Down in the subway / Somebody, somewhere, sometime / Divided soul / Tainted love (2XS remix) / Say hello, wave goodbye (almighty radio mix).

MARC AND THE MAMBAS

with **ANNIE HOGAN** – piano / **TIM TAYLOR** – bass / **DAVE BALL** – multi instruments

Mar 82. (12"; mail order) *(BZS 5-12)* **FUN CITY. / SLEAZE (TAKE IT, SHAKE IT) / TAKING IT SHAKING IT** [–] [–]

—— guests on next 2 albums were **GENESIS P. ORRIDGE + MATT JOHNSON**

Oct 82. (lp/c) *(BZA/BZC 13)* **UNTITLED** [42] [–]
– Untitled / Empty eyes / Angels / Big Louise / Caroline says / Margaret / If you go away. *(free-12"ep with above +=)* – Terrapin / Twilights and lowlifes (street walking soundtrack) / Twilights and lowlifes. *(re-iss. Mar92 on 'Mercury' cd/c; 510 298-2/-4)*

Nov 82. (7";w-drawn) *(BZS 15)* **BIG LOUISE. / EMPTY EYES** [–] [–]
(12";w-drawn+=) *(BZS 15-12)* – The dirt behind the neon.

Jun 83. (7") *(BZS 19)* **BLACK HEART. / YOUR AURA** [49] [–]
(12"+=) *(BZS 19-12)* – Mamba.

Aug 83. (d-lp/c) *(BIZL/+C 4)* **TORMENT AND TOREROS** [28] [–]
– The animal in you / Narcissus / Gloomy Sunday / Vision / Your love is a lesson / The untouchable one / My little book of sorrows / In my room / First time / The bulls / Boss cat / Intro / Catch a fallen star / Beat out dat rhythm on a drum / A million manias / Torment / Black heart. *(re-iss. Mar92 on 'Mercury' cd/c; 812 872-2/-4) (cd re-iss. Oct97; SBZCD 028CD)*

Nov 83. (12"ep) *(BZS 21-12)* **TORMENT / FIRST TIME. / YOU'LL NEVER SEE ME ON A SUNDAY / MAGAMILLIONMANIA-MULTIMANIAMIX** [ ] [–]

MARC ALMOND

—— went solo augmented by **The WILLING SINNERS: ANNIE HOGAN** – piano / **BILLY McGEE** – bass / **RICHARD RILEY** – guitar / **STEPHEN HUMPHRIES** – drums / **MARTIN McCARRICK** – cello

May 84. (7") *(BZS 23)* **THE BOY WHO CAME BACK. / JOEY DEMENTO** [52] [ ]
(10"/12") *(BZS 23 10/12)* – ('A'-Loud cut) / ('B'extended).

Sep 84. (7") *(BZS 24)* **YOU HAVE. / SPLIT UP** [57] [ ]
(ext-10"+=) *(BZS 24-10)* – Black mountain blues.
(ext-12"+=) *(BZS 24-12)* – Joey Demento.

Oct 84. (lp/c)(cd) *(BIZL/+C 8)(<822 832-2>)* **VERMINE IN ERMINE** [36] [ ]
– Shining sinners / Hell was a city / You have / Crime sublime / Gutter hearts / Ugly head / The boy who came back / Solo adultos / Tenderness is a weakness. *(c+=/cd+=)* – Pink shack blues / Split lip / Joey Demento.

Nov 84. (7") *(BZS 25)* **TENDERNESS IS A WEAKNESS. / LOVE FOR SALE** [ ] [–]
(10"+=) *(BZS 25-10)* – Pink shack blues (live) / The heel (live).

—— In April '85, he teamed up with BRONSKI BEAT on Top 3 version of 'I FEEL LOVE'. Two months later, he featured anonymously on 12" 'SKIN' as The BURMOE BROTHERS

Aug 85. (7") *(BONK 1)* **STORIES OF JOHNNY. / STORIES OF JOHNNY (with The Westminster City School Choir)** [23] [–]
(12"+=) *(BONK 1-12)* – Take my heart.
(d7"++=/10"++=) *(BONK 1/+10)* – Blond boy.

Sep 85. (lp/c/cd) *(FAITH/TFTH/CDFTH 1)* **STORIES OF JOHNNY** [22] [–]
– Traumas, traumas, traumas / Stories of Johnny / The house is haunted (by the echoes of your last goodbye) / Love letter / The flesh is willing / Always / Contempt / I who never / My candle burns / Love and little white lies. *(c+=/cd+=)* – Take my heart / Blond boy / Stories of Johnny (with The Westminster City School Choir). *<US cd-iss. 1997 on 'Thirsty Ear'; 57039>*

Oct 85. (7") *(BONKP 2)* **LOVE LETTER. / LOVE LETTER (with The Westmonster City School Choir)** [68] [–]
(10"/12") *(BONK 2 10/12)* – ('A'-Special mix) / ('B'side).

Jan 86. (d7") *(GLOW D1)* **THE HOUSE IS HAUNTED (BY THE ECHO OF YOUR LAST GOODBYE). / BROKEN BARRICADES // CARA A CARA (FACE TO FACE). / MEDLEY: (UNCHAIN MY HEART – BLACK HEART – TAKE MY HEART)** [55] [–]
('A'-Ectoplasm mix-12"+=) *(GLOW 1-12)* – Burning boats.

May 86. (7") *(GLOW 2)* **A WOMAN'S STORY. / FOR ONE MOMENT** [41] [ ]
(c-ep+=)(10"pic-d-ep+=)(12"ep+=) **SOME SONGS TO TAKE TO THE TOMB EP** *(TGLOW 2-12)(GLOWY 2-10)(GLOW 2-12)* – The heel / A salty dog / The plague / The little white cloud that cried / Just good friends.

Oct 86. (7") *(GLOW 3)* **RUBY RED. / I'M SICK OF YOU TASTING OF SOMEONE ELSE** [47] [–]
('A'-Arnacoma mix-12"+=) *(GLOW 3-12)* – Broken hearted and beautiful / Jackal jackal (Mustapha Tomb Stone Teeth).
('A'ext.dance mix-12") *(GLOW 3-13)* – ('A'instrumental).

Jan 87. (7") *(GLOW 4)* **MELANCHOLY ROSE. / GYP THE BLOOD** [71] [–]
(12"+=) *(GLOW 4-12)* – A world full of people / Black lullaby.
(d7+=) *(GLOWD 4)* – Surabaya Johnny / Pirate Jenny.

Mar 87. (lp/c/cd) *(FAITH/TFTH/CDFTH 2)* **MOTHER FIST AND HER FIVE DAUGHTERS** [40] [–]
– Mother Fist / There is a bed / Saint Judy / The room below / Angel in her kiss / The hustler / Melancholy rose / Mr. Sad / The sea says / Champ / Ruby red / The river. *<US cd-iss. 1997 on 'Thirsty Ear'; 57038>*

Mar 87. (7") *(GLOW 5)* **MOTHER FIST. / TWO SAILORS ON THE BEACH** [ ] [–]
(12"+=) *(GLOW 5-12)* – The hustler.

Nov 87. (lp/c/cd) *(FAITH/TFTH/CDFTH 3)* **THE SINGLES 1984-1987** (compilation) [ ] [–]
– The boy who came back / You have / Tenderness is a weakness / Stories of Johnny / Love letters / The house is haunted / A woman's story / Ruby red / Melancholy rose / Mother Fist.

—— He was now backed by LA MAGIA. (aka HOGAN, HUMPHRIES + McGEE)

Parlophone Capitol

Aug 88. (7"/7"box) *(R/RX 6186) <44240>* **TEARS RUN RINGS. / EVERYTHING I WANTED LOVE TO BE** [26] Jan89 [67]
(12"+=/cd-s+=) *(12R/CDR 6186)* – ('A'extended).
('A'-Justin Strauss mix-12"+=) *(12RX 6186)* – ('A'-La Magia dance mix).

Sep 88. (cd/c/lp) *(CD/TC+/PCS 7324) <91042>* **THE STARS WE ARE** [41] Jan89 [ ]
– The stars we are / These my dreams are true / Bitter sweet / Only the moment / Your kisses burn / Tears run rings / Something's gotten hold of my heart / The sensualist / She took my soul in Instanbul. *(c+=/cd+=)* – The frost comes tomorrow / Kept boy. *(cd re-iss. Apr02 on 'E.M.I.'+=; 539176-2)* – Something's gotten hold of my heart (w/ GENE PITNEY).

Oct 88. (7"/7"g-f/7"clear) *(R/RG/RC 6194)* **BITTER SWEET. / KING OF THE FOOLS** [40] [–]
(12"+=/12"g-f+=/12"etched+=/'A'-Big Beat mix-12"+=/cd-s+=) *(12R/12RG/12RS/12RX/CDR 6194)* – Tears run rings (Justin Strauss remix).

Jan 89. (7"/7"box; by MARC ALMOND & GENE PITNEY) *(R/RX 6201)* **SOMETHING'S GOTTEN HOLD OF MY HEART. / ('A'-solo version)** [1] [ ]
(12"+=/12"etched+=/cd-s+=) *(12R/12RS/CDR 6201)* – The frost comes tomorrow.

Mar 89. (7",7"clear) *(R 6210)* **ONLY THE MOMENT. / REAL EVIL** [47] [–]
(cd-s+=) *(CDR 6210)* – She took my soul in Instanbul (The Blue Mosque mix).
(12"/12"etched) *(12R/+S 6210)* – ('A'-All The Time In The World mix) / She took my soul in Istanbul (The Blue Mosque mix).

Feb 90. (7"/ext-7"square-pic-d/ext-c-s) *(R/RPD/TCR 6229)* **A LOVER SPURNED. / EXOTICA ROSE** [29] [–]
(12"+=/cd-s+=) *(12R/CDR 6229)* – ('A'version).

May 90. (c-s/7") *(TC+/R 6252)* **THE DESPERATE HOURS. / THE GAMBLER** [45] [–]
(12"+=/12"clear-pic-d+=/cd-s+=) *(12R/12RPD/CDR 6252)* – ('A'extended Flamenco mix).

Jun 90. (cd/c/lp) *(CD/TC+/PCS 7344) <94404>* **ENCHANTED** [52] [ ]
– Madame de la luna / Waifs and strays / The desperate hours / Toreador in the rain / Widow weeds / A lover spurned / Death's diary / Sea still sings / Carnival of life / Orpheus in red velvet. *(cd re-iss. Apr02 on 'E.M.I.'; 539177-2)*

Oct 90. (c-s/7") *(TC+/R 6263)* **WAIFS AND STRAYS. / OLD JACK'S CHARM** [ ] [–]
(12") *(12R 6263)* – (2 'A'-Grid mixes).
(cd-s+=) *(CDR 6263)* – City of nights.

—— Wrote w/**DAVE BALL** + **NORRIS** (The GRID)

W.E.A. Sire

Sep 91. (7"/c-s) *(YZ 610/+C)* **JACKY. / DEEP NIGHT** [17] [–]
(12"+=) *(YZ 610T)* – ('A'-Alpine dub).
(cd-s+=) *(YZ 610CD)* – A love outgrown.

Oct 91. (cd/c/lp) *(9031 75518-2/-4/-1) <26764>* **TENEMENT SYMPHONY** [39] [ ]
– Meet me in my dream / Beautiful brutal thing / I've never seen your face / Vaudeville and burlesque / Champagne / Tenement symphony (i) Prelude, (ii) Jacky, (iii) What is love?, (iv) Trois Chansons de Bilitis – extract, (v) The days of Pearly Spencer, (vi) My hand over my heart. *(re-iss. cd Feb95; same)*

Dec 91. (7"/c-s) *(YZ 633/+C)* **MY HAND OVER MY HEART. / DEADLY SERENADE** [33] [–]
(12"pic-d) *(YZ 633TP)* – ('A'-Grit & Glitter mix) / Money for love (2 versions).
(cd-s) *(YZ 633CD)* – (above 3 tracks) / Night and no morning.

Apr 92. (7"/c-s) *(YZ 638/+C)* **THE DAYS OF PEARLY SPENCER. / BRUISES** [4] [–]
(cd-s+=) *(YZ 638CD)* – Dancing in a golden cage / Extract from 'Trois Chanson De Bilitis'.

—— with **DAVE CLAYTON** – keyboards, musical director / **MARTIN WATKINS** – piano / **ANDY HAMILTON** – saxophone / **MICHELE DREES** – drums, perc. / **CRIS BONACCI** – guitars / **SHIRLEY LEWIS, ANNA ROSS & AILEEN McLAUGHLIN** – b.vox / **TENEMENT SYMPHONY ORCH.**

Mar 93. (7"/c-s) *(YZ 720/+C)* **WHAT MAKES A MAN A MAN (live). / TORCH (live)** [60] [–]
(cd-s+=) *(YZ 720CD)* – The stars we are (live).
(cd-s) *(YZ 720CDX)* – ('A'side) / Tainted love (live) / Vision (live) / Only the moment (live).

Apr 93. (cd/c/lp) *(4509 92033-2/-4/-1) <45247>* **12 YEARS OF TEARS – LIVE AT THE ROYAL ALBERT HALL (live)** [ ] May93 [ ]
– Tears run rings / Champagne / Bedsitter / Mr. Sad / There is a bed / Youth / If you go away / Jacky / Desperate hours / Waifs and strays / Something's gotten hold of my heart / What makes a man a man / Tainted love / Say hello wave goodbye.

Some Bizzare not iss.

Sep 93. (cd/c/lp) *(SBZ CD/MC/LP 10)* **ABSINTHE: THE FRENCH ALBUM** [ ] [–]
– Undress me / Abel and Cain / Lost Paradise / Secret child / Rue Des Blancs Manteaux / The slave / Remorse of the dead / Incestuous love / A man / My little lovers / In your bed / Yesterday when I was young. *<US cd-iss. 1996 on 'Thirsty Ear'; 57026>*

Mercury Mercury

Apr 95. (c-s) *(MERMC 431)* **ADORED AND EXPLORED / ('A'-original)** [25] [–]
(cd-s) *(MERCD 431)* – ('A'side) / The user / Loveless world / ('A'-Andy Meecham's Slow Fat dub).
(cd-s) *(MERDD 431)* – ('A'side) / ('A'-Beatmasters 12 take 1) / ('A'-Andy Meecham club mix) / ('A'-X-Press 2 extre,me excess mix).

Jul 95. (c-s) *(MERMC 437)* **THE IDOL / ('A'-Tin Tin Out mix)** [44] [–]
(cd-s+=) *(MERDD 437)* – ('A'-Idolized mix) / ('A'-Teenage dream mix).
(cd-s) *(MERCD 437)* – ('A'-part 1) / Law of the night / Adored and explored (live) / Bedsitter (live).

Nov 95. (c-s) *(MERMC 450)* **CHILD STAR / EDGE OF HEARTBREAK** [41] [–]
(cd-ep+=) **CHILD STAR EP** *(MERCD 450)* – Christmas in Vegas / My guardian angel.
(cd-ep) **CHILD STAR EP** *(MERDD 450)* – ('A'side) / We need jealousy (live) / The idol (live) / Out there (live).

Feb 96. (c-s) *(MERMC 444)* **OUT THERE / BRILLIANT CREATURES** [ ] [–]
(cd-s+=) *(MERCD 444)* – Lie (Beatmasters mix) / Lie.
(12") *(MERX 444)* – ('A'mixes:- Tony De Vite parts 1 & 2 / Non Eric / House Of Usher / Valerie Singleton).

Feb 96. (cd/c) *(528 659-2/-4)* **FANTASTIC STAR** [54] [–]
– Caged / Out there / We need jealousy / Idol (parts 1 & 2) / All gods fall / Baby night eyes / Adored and explored / Child star / Looking for love (in all the wrong places) / Addicted / Edge of heartbreak / Love to die for / Betrayed / On the prowl / Come in sweet assassin / Brilliant creatures / Shining brightly. *(cd re-iss. Sep97; same)*

—— In Dec'96, MARC was credited on PJ PROBY minor hit single 'YESTERDAY HAS GONE' on 'EMI Premier' (PRESTC/CDPRES/CDPRESX 13).

Echo Instinct

Nov 98. (7"pic-d) *(ECS 58)* **BLACK KISS. / ('A'-DJ mix)** [ ] [–]
(cd-s) *(ECSCD 58)* – ('A'side) / Satan's child / ('A'live).

Blue Star Incense

Mar 99. (cd-s) *(BSRS 001)* **TRAGEDY (TAKE A LOOK AND SEE) / BEAUTIFUL LOSERS / BLACK KISS (hard vocal mix)** [ ] [–]

Apr 99. (cd) *(BSRCD 01) <INS 435-2>* **OPEN ALL NIGHT** [ ] Aug99 [ ]
– Night & dark / Bedroom shine / Tragedy (take a look and see) / Black kiss / Almost diamonds / Scarlet bedroom / My love / Heart in velvet / Open all night / Threat of love / Bad people kiss / Sleepwalker / Midnight soul. *<US+=>* – Satan's child / Lonely go-go dancer / Beautiful losers.

Nov 99. (cd-s) *(BRSCD 002)* **MY LOVE / THREAT OF LOVE / ONE BIG SOUL** [ ] [–]

—— next with **JOHANN JOHANNSON** – keyboards, etc / **JOHNNY GREEN** – strings, keyboards, etc / **PETUR HALLGRIMSSON** – guitar

XIII Bis XIII Bis

Jun 00. (cd) *(<533800-2>)* **STRANGER THINGS** [ ] Jul00 [ ]
– Glorious / Born to cry / Come out / Under your wing / Lights / Tantalise me / Moonbathe skin / Dancer / When it's your time / End in tears / Love in a time of science / Glorious (reprise).

XIII Bis Psychobaby

Nov 03. (cd) *(640326-2) <5029-2>* **HEART ON SNOW** [ ] [ ]
– So long the path (so wide the field) / Strange feeling / Gosudaryunia / Always and everywhere (I will follow you) / Oh my soul / Two guitars / Heart on snow / Nuit de Noel / Romance / The storks / Luna (the Moon) / White flowers of Acacia / The glance of your dark eyes / If your affectionate smile has gone / Sleeping beauty / Just one chance / Gone but not forgotten / So wide the field (reprise).

– compilations, etc. –

Dec 89. (lp/c/cd) *Some Bizzare; (BREL/+C/CD 001)* **JACQUES** (most rec.1986) [ ] [–]
– The Devil (okay) / If you need / The lockman / We must look / Alone / I'm coming / Litany for a return / If you go away / The town fell asleep / The bulls / (Never to be) Next / My death. *<US cd-iss. 1996 on 'Thirsty Ear'; 57025>*

Sep 92. (cd/c) *Virgin; (CD/TC VM 9010)* **A VIRGIN'S TALE VOL.1 (1985-1988)** ☐ [-]

Sep 92. (cd/c) *Virgin; (CD/TC VM 9011)* **A VIRGIN'S TALE VOL.2 (1988-1991)** ☐ ☐
(re-iss. both above Nov92 as d-cd; DCDVM 901 0/1) (both re-iss. Nov97; SBZ 032/033 CD)

Aug 95. (d-cd) *E.M.I.; (CDMATBOX 1)* **TREASURE BOX** ☐ [-]
(re-iss. Apr02 on 'E.M.I.'; 538915-2)

Sep 97. (cd; MARC ALMOND & FOETUS) *Some Bizzare; (SBZ 022CD)* **VIOLENT SILENCE** ☐ ☐

Nov 97. (cd; MARC ALMOND & FOETUS) *Some Bizzare; (SBZ 034CD)* **FLESH VOLCANO / SLUT** ☐ [-]

Nov 98. (cd-enhanced) *Some Bizzare; (SBZ 037)* **LIVE IN CONCERT AT THE ASTORIA (with LA MAGIA)** ☐ [-]

Jun 03. (cd) *Cherry Red; (CDMRED 233)* **THE WILLING SINNER: LIVE AT THE PASSIONCHURCH – BERLIN (live)** ☐ ☐

Aug 03. (cd) *Strange Fruit; (SFRSCD 121)* **THE RADIO 1 SESSIONS VOL.1 1983-1984** ☐ [-]

SOFT CELL

— re-formed with **ALMOND + BALL**

Cooking Vinyl SpinArt

Sep 02. (12")(cd-s) *(FRY 132T)(FRYCD 132)* **MONOCULTURE / MONOCULTURE (extended). / ALL OUT OF LOVE / DANCING ALONE** [52] [-]
(cd-s) *(FRYCD 132X)* – ('A'-mixes; radio / Playgroup / Antoine 909 & Oggie-B).

Sep 02. (cd) *(COOKCD 245)* <*SPIN 116*> **CRUELTY WITHOUT BEAUTY** ☐ Oct02 ☐
– Darker times / Monoculture / Le grand guignol / The night / Last chance / Together alone / Desperate / Whatever it takes / All out of love / Sensation nation / Caligula syndrome / On an up.

Jan 03. (cd-s) *(FRYCD 135)* **THE NIGHT / PERVERSITY / THE NIGHT (almighty mix)** [39] [-]
(cd-s+=) *(FRYCD 135X)* – ('A'-Wayne G Heaven anthem dub) / Say hello wave goodbye (live).

☐ ALT (see under ⇒ CROWDED HOUSE)

☐ ALTER BRIDGE (see under ⇒ CREED)

☐ AMATEUR NIGHT IN THE BIG TOP (see under ⇒ HAPPY MONDAYS)

☐ AMBROSE SLADE (see under ⇒ SLADE)

Tori AMOS

Born: MYRA ELLEN AMOS, 22 Aug'63, Newton, North Carolina, USA. Daughter of a preacher father and part-Cherokee Indian mother, she incredibly scored a scholarship to 'Peabody Conservatory' in Baltimore at five years old (youngest ever admitee!), studying classical piano. Parting company with this illustrious establishment at the age of eleven, AMOS embarked upon her rebellious phase, playing bars and subsequently relocating to L.A. where she was discovered by early 80's sophisto-disco star, NARADA MICHAEL WALDEN. Despite recording some professional demos and releasing a one-off independently released 45, 'BALTIMORE' (1981), it would be a few years down the line before AMOS's career really began. Reinventing herself as TORI, AMOS formed a gaudy glitz-metal band, Y KANT TORI READ, eventually signing to 'Atlantic' and releasing a dodgy eponymous album in 1988. Almost universally lambasted by the critics, TORI underwent a considerably more horrific ordeal when she was raped at gunpoint by a would-be fan after offering him a lift home (this experience was later detailed in the song, 'ME AND A GUN'). Making the transition from leather-clad frontwoman to soul searching singer-songwriter, TORI AMOS "moved along the corridor" to the 'East West' stable and released her solo debut, 'LITTLE EARTHQUAKES' (1991). Breaking initially in Britain, the album's deep subject matter and orchestrated, piano-led atmospherics were the backdrop for AMOS's eye-of-the-hurricane emotional turmoil; from heavy-lidded lullaby to howling, KATE BUSH-esque melodrama, the singer exorcised her demons in compelling fashion. Tracks such as 'SILENT ALL THESE YEARS', 'CHINA', 'WINTER' and 'CRUCIFY' (all UK hit singles in their own right) saw the album eventually scale the American charts; it has since become regarded as one of the all-time classic rock/pop records. AMOS's career trajectory was given a turbo boost in the first days of '94 with the strangely-titled 'CORNFLAKE GIRL', a Top 5 UK hit which helped propel her accompanying album, 'UNDER THE PINK' to the top of the British charts (Top 20 in America). A more probing exploration of the female psyche, the album attempted to reconcile AMOS's religious upbringing and developing identity with songs such as 'PAST THE MISSION', 'GOD' and 'PRETTY GOOD YEAR' (her second Top 10 hit in Britain). In early '96, AMOS released her most commercially successful album to date, 'BOYS FOR PELE' narrowly missing the top slot in both Britain and America despite its overtly experimental nature. Once again it was littered with classy hit singles (albeit with oblique lyrics), 'CAUGHT A LITE SNEEZE', 'TALULA' and double A side 'HEY JUPITER' / 'PROFESSIONAL WIDOW'. The latter track (allegedly written about the death of KURT COBAIN and its controversial aftermath) was subsequently deconstructed in stunning style from its more subdued album counterpart, dance guru ARMAND VAN HELDEN possibly inspired by BT's (BRIAN TRANSEAU) impressive use/sample of TORI's voice on his Top 30 hit, 'Blue Skies'. The remix scaled the British charts in early '97, exposing AMOS's uniquely challenging work to a whole new E-poppin' audience. On the 22nd of February, 1998, she married Mark Hawley, the engineer on her last two albums, her new husband also worked on a mooted fourth set, tentatively titled 'FROM THE CHOIRGIRL HOTEL'. When released that Spring, the record shifted enough units to hit the Top 10 on both sides of the Atlantic, subsequently bringing further well-deserved acclaim to this eclectic but troubled lady; Jools Holland and his TV programme 'Later With . . .' intensified her complex image with a ubiquitous piano-playing performance that would put even RICK WAKEMAN to shame. Just over a year later, she followed this with a double-set helping 'TO VENUS AND BACK', which fused live gems with new studio work. It might have been the new millennium but come 2001, AMOS was not exactly doing anything new. Well, not unless you regard covers set (as in entire covers set) 'STRANGE LITTLE GIRLS' (2001) as breaking new ground. Constructed around a paper thin theme of recapturing the female perspective of songs originally sung about women by men, the record straddled the musical map from NEIL YOUNG to SLAYER, reaching the UK Top 20 and, surprisingly, the US Top 5. While it's unlikely that any TORI AMOS album will ever be described as easily digestible, 'SCARLET'S WALK' (2002) was a tentative return to the cryptic, guardedly accessible alternative pop she excelled at in the early 90's. 'TALES OF A LIBRARIAN: A TORI AMOS COLLECTION' (2003), meanwhile, apart from having a great title, was a more imaginative hits package than most, creatively revising her work rather than just throwing it together. In the same year that KATE BUSH left critics drooling with cyclical reverie, a newly forty-something AMOS also looked to nature – specifically the psychoanalytical minefield of a garden – as metaphor for emotional transition on 'THE BEEKEEPER' (2005), another US Top 5/UK Top 30 success. A record full of the myth and windswept Celticisms of her adopted home, Cornwall (and in 'JAMAICA INN', even referencing a Daphne Du Maurier novel), it also – on the likes of 'WITNESS' and the slinky 'HOOCHIE WOMAN' – unshackled AMOS' funk-hear it to believe it!

• **Covers:** SMELLS LIKE TEEN SPIRIT (Nirvana) / RING MY BELL (Anita Ward) / ANGIE (Rolling Stones) / THANK YOU (Led Zeppelin) / LITTLE DRUMMER BOY (UK-hit 1959) / HOME ON THE RANGE + HAVE YOURSELF A MERRY LITTLE CHRISTMAS (trad.) / IF SIX WAS NINE (Jimi Hendrix Experience) / STRANGE FRUIT (Billie Holliday) / FAMOUS BLUE RAINCOAT (Leonard Cohen) / NEW AGE (Velvet Underground) / '97 BONNIE & CLYDE (Eminem) / STRANGE LITTLE GIRL (Stranglers) / ENJOY THE SILENCE (Depeche Mode) / I'M NOT IN LOVE (10cc) / RATTLESNAKES (Lloyd Cole & The Commotions) / TIME (Tom Waits) / HEART OF GOLD (Neil Young) / I DON'T LIKE MONDAYS (Boomtown Rats) / HAPPINESS IS A WARM GUN (Beatles) / RAINING BLOOD (Slayer) / REAL MEN (Joe Jackson). • **Trivia:** TORI sang backing for AL STEWART on 'Last Days of the Century' album, plus STAN RIDGWAY's 'Mosquitos'.

Album rating: LITTLE EARTHQUAKES (*9) / UNDER THE PINK (*7) / BOYS FOR PELE (*7) / FROM THE CHOIRGIRL MOTEL (*7) / TO VENUS AND BACK (*5) / STRANGE LITTLE GIRLS (*4) / SCARLET'S WALK (*6) / TALES OF A LIBRARIAN compilation (*8) / THE BEEKEEPER (*6)

ELLEN AMOS

not iss. — MEA

Dec 80. (7") *<MEA 5290>* **BALTIMORE. / WALKING WITH YOU** [–] [ ]

Y KANT TORI READ

TORI AMOS – vocals, piano with group: **STEVE FARRIS** – guitar (ex-MR. MISTER) / **MATT SORUM** – drums

not iss. — Atlantic

Jun 88. (7") *<7-89086>* **THE BIG PICTURE. / YOU GO TO MY HEAD** [–] [ ]

Jul 88. (cd,c,lp) *<81845>* **Y KANT TORI READ** [–] [ ]
– The big picture / God on your island / Fayth / Fire on the side / Pirates / Floating city / Heart attack at 23 / On the boundary / You go to my head / Etienne trilogy

Aug 88. (7") *<7-89021>* **COOL ON YOUR ISLAND. / HEART ATTACK AT 23** [–] [ ]

TORI AMOS

— with **STEVE CATON** – guitar / **WILL McGREGOR** – bass / **ERIC ROSSE** – keyboards, co-producer / **JEFF SCOTT** – bass, guitar / **PAULINHO DaCOSTA** – percussion

East West — Atlantic

Nov 91. (7") *(YZ 618/+C)* **SILENT ALL THESE YEARS. / ME AND A GUN** [51] [–]
(12"ep+=)(cd-ep+=) *(YZ 618 T/CD)* – Upside down / Thoughts.

Jan 92. (cd/c/lp) *<(7567 82358-2/-4/-1)>* **LITTLE EARTHQUAKES** [14] Dec91 [54]
– Crucify / Girl / Silent all these years / Precious things / Winter / Happy phantom / China / Leather / Mother / Tear in your hand / Me and a gun / Little earthquakes. *(lp re-iss. Jun99; same)*

Jan 92. (7"/c-s) *(A 7531/+C)* **CHINA. / SUGAR** [51] [–]
(12"+=/cd-s+=) *(A 7531 T/CD)* – Flying Dutchman / Humpty Dumpty.

Mar 92. (7"/c-s) *(A 7504/+C)* **WINTER. / THE POOL** [25] [–]
(cd-s+=) *(A 7504CD)* – Take to the sky / Sweet dreams.
(cd-s) *(A 7504CDX)* – ('A'side) / Angie / Smells like teen spirit / Thank you.

May 92. (cd-ep) *<82399-2>* **CRUCIFY (remix) / WINTER / ANGIE / SMELL LIKE TEEN SPIRIT / THANK YOU** [–] [ ]

Jun 92. (7"/c-s) *(A 7479/+C)* **CRUCIFY (remix). / HERE, IN MY HEAD** [15] [–]
(cd-s+=) *(A 7479CD)* – Mary / Crucify (version).
(cd-s) *(A 7479CDX)* – CRUCIFY LIVE EP – Crucify / Little earthquakes / Precious things / Mother.

Aug 92. (7"/c-s) *(A 7433/+C)* **SILENT ALL THESE YEARS. / SMELLS LIKE TEEN SPIRIT** [26] [–]
(cd-s) *(A 7433CD)* – ('A'side) / Upside down / Me and a gun / Thoughts.
(cd-s) *(A 7433CDX)* – ('A'side) / Ode to the banana king (part 1) / Song for Eric / Happy phantom (live).

Nov 92. (cd-ep) *<85799-2)* **WINTER / THE POOL / TAKE TO THE SKY / SWEET DREAMS / UPSIDE DOWN** [–] [ ]

— now w/ **GEORGE PORTER JR.** – bass / **CARLO NUCCIO** – drums / **ERIC ROSSE** – programming / **STEVE CATON** – drums / **PAULINHO DaCOSTA** – percussion

Jan 94. (7"/c-s) *(A 7281/+C)* **CORNFLAKE GIRL. / SISTER JANET** [4] [–]
(cd-s+=) *(A 7281CD)* – Piano suite: All the girls hate her – Over it.
(cd-s) *(A 7282CDX)* – ('A'side) / A case of you / If 6 was 9 / Strange fruit.

Feb 94. (c-s) *<87250>* **GOD / SISTER JANET** [–] [72]
(cd-s) *<PRCD 5408>* – ('A'side) / Home on the range (Cherokee edition) / Hand suite: All the girls hate her – Over it.

Feb 94. (cd/c/lp) *<(7567 82567-2/-4/-1)>* **UNDER THE PINK** [1] [12]
– Pretty good year / God / Bells for her / Past the mission / Baker baker / The wrong band / The waitress / Cornflake girl / Icicle / Cloud on my tongue / Space dog / Yes, Anastasia.

Mar 94. (7"/c-s) *(A 7263/+C)* **PRETTY GOOD YEAR. / HONEY** [7] [–]
(cd-s+=) *(A 7263CD)* – The black swan.
(cd-s) *(A 7263CDX)* – ('A'side) / Daisy dead petals / Home on the range (Cherokee version).

Apr 94. (cd-ep) *<85655-2>* **CORNFLAKE GIRL / SISTER JANET / DAISY DEAD PETALS / HONEY** [–] [ ]

— TRENT REZNOR of NINE INCH NAILS guested vox on 'Past The Mission'.

May 94. (7"/c-s) *(A 7257/+C)* **PAST THE MISSION. / ('A'live)** [31] [–]
(cd-s) *(A 7257CD)* – Winter (live) / The waitress (live) / Here in my head (live).
(cd-s) *(A 7257CDX)* – ('A'live) / Upside down (live) / Icicle (live) / Flying Dutchman (live).

Oct 94. (7"pic-d/c-s) *(A 7251/+C)* **GOD. / ('A'-Acapella vocal & rain mix)** [44] [–]
(12"+=/cd-s+=) *(A 7251 T/CD)* – ('A'remixes from;- The Joy / Carl Craig / CJ Bolland).

Atlantic — Atlantic

Jan 96. (c-s) *(A 5524C)* **CAUGHT A LITE SNEEZE / GRAVEYARD / TOODLES MR JIM** [20] [–]
(cd-s) *(A 5524CD1)* – ('A'side) / London girls / That's what I like Mick (sandwich song) / Samurai.
(cd-s) *(A 5524CD2)* – ('A'side) / Toodles Mr. Jim / Hungarian wedding song / This old man.

Jan 96. (cd-ep) *<85519>* **CAUGHT A LITE SNEEZE. / SILLY SONGS (medley:- THIS OLD MAN – THAT'S WHAT I LIKE MICK – GRAVEYARD – TOODLES MR. JIM)** [–] [60]

Jan 96. (cd/c) *<(7567 82862-2/-4)>* **BOYS FOR PELE** [2] [2]
– Beauty queen – Horses / Blood roses / Father Lucifer / Professional widow / Mr Zebra / Marianne / Caught a lite sneeze / Muhammed my friend / Hey Jupiter / Way down / Little Amsterdam / Talula / Not the Red Baron / Agent Orange / Doughnut song / In the spring of his voodoo / Putting the damage on / Twinkle.

Mar 96. (c-s) *(A 8512C)* **TALULA / SISTER NAMED DESIRE** [22] [–]
(cd-s+=) *(A 8512CD2)* – Frog on my toe / Alamo.
(cd-s) *(A 8512CD1)* – ('A'-Tornado mix) / ('A'-Synethasia mix) / Til the chicken / Amazing Grace.

May 96. (cd-ep) *<85504>* **TALULA (Tornado version) / SAMURAI / FROG ON MY TOE / LONDON GIRLS / TATULA (BT's synethasia mix)** [–] [ ]

Jul 96. (c-s/12") *(A 5494 C/T)* **HEY JUPITER. / TALULA** [20] Aug96 [94]
(cd-s) *(A 5494CD) <82955-2>* – ('A'-Dakota version) / Professional widow / Sugar (live) / Honey (live). *<US ep+=, hit album chart>* – Somewhere over the rainbow.

Sep 96. (cd-s) *<2-85475>* **IN THE SPRINGTIME OF HIS VOODOO (mixes)** [–] [ ]

— Nov'96, she featured on BT single 'BLUE SKIES', which hit UK 26.

Dec 96. (c-s/12"/cd-s) *(A 5450 C/T/CD) <2-85499>* **PROFESSIONAL WIDOW (IT'S GOT TO BE BIG). / (remixes by Armand Van Helden & Mr. Roy)** [1] Jul96 [ ]

Mar 97. (cd-s) *<2-83001>* **SILENT ALL THESE YEARS (live) / ('A'-album version)** [–] [65]

— now with **MATT CHAMBERLAIN** – drums / **JUSTIN MELDAL-JOHNSEN** + **GEORGE PORTER JR.** – bass / **STEVE CATON** – guitars / **ANDY GRAY** – programming / etc

Apr 98. (c-s) *(AT 0031C) <84104>* **SPARK / PURPLE PEOPLE** [16] Jun98 [49]
(cd-s+=) *(AT 0031CD1)* – Have yourself a merry little Christmas / Bachelorette.
(cd-s) *(AT 0031CD2)* – ('A'side) / Do it again / Cooling.

May 98. (cd/c/lp) *<(7567 83095-2/-4/-1)>* **FROM THE CHOIRGIRL HOTEL** [6] [5]
– Spark / Cruel / Black-dove (January) / Raspberry swirl / Jackie's strength / iieee / Liquid diamonds / She's your cocaine / Northern lad / Hotel / Playboy mommy / Pandora's aquarium.

Aug 98. (cd-s) *<2-84163>* **JACKIE'S STRENGTH / NEVER SEEN BLUE / BEULAH LAND** [–] [54]

Aug 98. (cd-ep) *(AT 0041CD)* **JACKIE'S STRENGTH (Wedding Cake mixes) / FATHER LUCIFER (Silkscreen mixes)** [ ] [–]

Aug 98. (c-s; w-drawn) *(AT 0045C)* **RASPBERRY SWIRL (Lip Gloss version) / ('A'extended)** [ ] [–]
(12"+=/cd-s+=; w-drawn) *(AT 0045 T/CD)* – ('A'-Scarlet Spectrum Feels mix).

Apr 99. (cd-ep) *<2-84412>* **CRUEL (Shady Feline mix) / RASPBERRY SWIRL (Lip Gloss version) / AMBIENT RASPBERRY SWIRL (Scarlet Spectrum Feels) / MAINLINE CHERRY – AMBIENT SPARK** [–] [ ]

Aug 99. (cd-s) *<2-84533>* **BLISS / HEY JUPITER (live) / UPSIDE DOWN (live)** [–] [91]

Sep 99. (d-cd/d-c) *(7567 83242-2) <83230>* **TO VENUS AND BACK** [22] [12]
– Bliss / Juarez / Concertina / Glory of the 80's / Lust / Suede / Riot proof / Datura / Spring haze / 1000 oceans / Precious things / Cornflake girl / Bells for her / Girl / Cooling / Mr. Zebra / Cloud on my tongue / Sugar / Little earthquakes / Space dog / Waitress / Purple people.

Nov 99. (c-s) *(AT 0077 C/CD2)* **GLORY OF THE 80's / BAKER BAKER (live) / WINTER (live)** [46] [–]
(cd-s) *(AT 0077CD)* – ('A'side) / Blue raincoat (live) / Twinkle (live).

Nov 99. (cd-s) *<2-84534>* **1000 OCEANS / BAKER BAKER (live)** [–] [ ]

Sep 01. (cd/c) *<(7567 83486-2/-4)>* **STRANGE LITTLE GIRLS** [16] [4]
– New age / '97 Bonnie and Clyde / Strange little girl / Enjoy the silence / Rattlesnakes / I'm not in love / Time / Heart of gold / I don't like Mondays / Happiness is a warm gun / Raining blood / Real men. *(cd re-iss. Aug02; same)*

Epic Epic

Oct 02. (cd-s) *(673043-2)* **A SORTA FAIRYTALE (route 101 mix) / OPERATION PETER PAN / A SORTA FAIRYTALE / A SCARLET STORY (video)** [41] [–]

Oct 02. (cd) *(508782-2) <86939>* **SCARLET'S WALK** [26] [7]
– Amber waves / A sorta fairytale / Wednesday / Strange / Carbon / Crazy / Wampum prayer / Don't make me come to Vegas / Sweet sangria / Your cloud / Pancake / I can't see New York / Mrs. Jesus / Taxi ride / Another girl's paradise / Scarlet's walk / Virginia / Gold dust. *(cd w/ free dvd; 508782-9)* – (video footage).

Feb 05. (cd) *(519425-2) <92800>* **THE BEEKEEPER** [24] [5]
– Parasol / Sweet the sting / The power of orange knickers / Jamaica Inn / Barons of suburbia / Sleeps with butterflies / General joy / Mother revolution / Ribbons undone / Cars and guitars / Witness / Original sinsuality / Ireland / The beekeeper / Martha's foolish ginger / Hoochie woman / Goodbye Pisces / Marys of the sea / Toast. *(cd w/bonus dvd+=; 519425-9)* – Garlands (documentary).

– compilations, etc. –

Nov 03. (cd) *Atlantic; <(7567 83658-2)>* **TALES OF A LIBRARIAN: A TORI AMOS COLLECTION** (re-workings) [74] [40]
– Precious things / Angels / Silent all these years / Cornflake girl / Mary / God / Winter / Spark / Way down / Professional widow / Mr. Zebra / Crucify / Me and a gun / Bliss / Playboy mommy / Baker, baker / Tear in your hand / Sweet dreams / Jackie's strength / Snow cherries from France. *(dvd+=; 7567 83658-2)* – Pretty good year / Honey / Northern lad / Putting the damage on / Mr. Zebra.

□ the AMPS (see under ⇒ the BREEDERS)

□ Ian ANDERSON (see under ⇒ JETHRO TULL)

□ Jon ANDERSON (see under ⇒ YES)

□ ANGELS & AIRWAVES (see under ⇒ BLINK-182)

the ANIMALS

Formed: Newcastle, England … 1960, as The ALAN PRICE COMBO. BURDON's arrival in 1962 led to tension in the ranks, no doubt a major contributing factor to the band's increasingly manic stage show. After supporting the likes of legendary bluesmen SONNY BOY WILLIAMSON and JOHN LEE HOOKER, they moved to London early in '64 and were promptly signed to EMI's 'Columbia' label by then virtually unknown producer MICKIE MOST. Re-christened The ANIMALS by the fans, the band adopted the name with glee and hit paydirt in summer '64 with the blues standard, 'HOUSE OF THE RISING SUN'. A massive hit on both sides of the Atlantic, with BURDON's ominous vocal phrasing and PRICE's wailing organ, the record remains the band's defining moment. Rarely, if ever, has the United Kingdom produced a white guy who could sing the blues like ERIC BURDON. The whisky-soaked menace of his voice sounded at times like Old Nick incarnate and was a key component in The ANIMALS feisty challenge to The ROLLING STONES' throne at the height of the 60's R&B Boom. Much like The BYRDS, The ANIMALS had an uncanny knack of covering material which, on paper, seemed less than obvious, but worked a treat on vinyl. 'DON'T LET ME BE MISUNDERSTOOD' and 'WE GOTTA GET OUT OF THIS PLACE' both went Top 5 in the UK, ensuring respectable sales of their second album, 'ANIMAL TRACKS'. PRICE left in 1965, beginning a dispute (incredibly still ongoing after more than 30 years) with BURDON over the publishing rights to 'HOUSE OF THE RISING SUN'. With DAVE ROWBERRY as PRICE's replacement, the band cut a few more albums including the semi-classic 'ANIMALIZATION', which contained such powerful tracks as 'INSIDE – LOOKING OUT' and 'GIN HOUSE BLUES'. The original ANIMALS fell apart towards the end of '66, CHAS CHANDLER going on to manage JIMI HENDRIX. BURDON moved to San Francisco, where he immersed himself in the nascent psychedelic scene, consuming liberal quantities of LSD. Under the new and improved moniker ERIC BURDON & THE ANIMALS, he released in 1967 his paeon to the emerging hippy culture, 'WINDS OF CHANGE'. Other highlights of this period include BURDON's tribute to the narcotic delights of the Swiss pharmaceutical industry, 'A GIRL NAMED SANDOZ' and 'MONTEREY', his reverential recollection of the legendary pop festival. BURDON kept his third eye in check enough to release a handful of introspective albums before this particular version of the ANIMALS split at the end of '68. He tasted major success for the last time with soul/funk band WAR, their debut single 'SPILL THE WINE', climbing into the Top 3 in the States mid 1970. The collaboration was short-lived, however, and BURDON went solo with weak support from the public. The original ANIMALS line-up (minus PRICE, of course) re-formed in 1977 and again in '83, although the new material was met with a lukewarm response in the UK. CHAS CHANDLER, who also went onto work with SLADE and others, died of a heart attack on the 17th July '96. While BURDON had busied himself with numerous solo albums over the 70s and 80s (including the 1982 soundtrack, 'COMEBACK', from a neo-autobiographical effort which he also starred in), he continued to earn favourable reviews into the 90s on the likes of 'LOST WITHIN THE HALLS OF FAME' (1995). Following on from his published autobiography, Don't Let Me Be Misunderstood: A Memoir, the former ANIMALS frontman set some of his personal reminiscences and experience to song in quasi-concept set, 'MY SECRET LIFE' (2004), a tribute to the soul, blues and jazz that first inspired him.

• **Songwriters:** BURDON lyrics / PRICE arrangements songs, with covers BOOM BOOM + DIMPLES + I'M MAD AGAIN (John Lee Hooker) / I'M IN LOVE AGAIN (Fats Domino) / TALKIN' ABOUT YOU (Ray Charles) /

GONNA SEND YOU BACK TO GEORGIA (Timmy Shaw) / DON'T LET ME BE MISUNDERSTOOD (hit; Nina Simone) / PRETTY THING (Bo Diddley) / BABY LET ME TAKE YOU HOME (Russell-Farrell) / BRING IT ON HOME TO ME (Sam Cooke) / WE'VE GOTTA GET OUT OF THIS PLACE (Mann-Weil) / DON'T BRING ME DOWN (Goffin-King) / RIVER DEEP MOUNTAIN HIGH (Phil Spector) / PAINT IT BLACK (Rolling Stones) / etc.

Best CD compilation: THE COMPLETE ANIMALS (*9) / Eric Burdon (last four): COMEBACK soundtrack (*5) / I USED TO BE AN ANIMAL (*6) / LOST WITHIN THE HALLS OF FAME (*6) / MY SECRET LIFE (*6)

ERIC BURDON (b.11 May'41, Walker, nr.Newcastle, England) – vocals / **ALAN PRICE** (b.19 Apr'41, Fairfield, Durham, England) – keyboards, vocals / **HILTON VALENTINE** (b.21 May'43, North Shields, England) – guitar / **CHAS CHANDLER** (b.18 Dec'38, Heaton, nr.Newcastle, England) – bass / **JOHN STEEL** (b. 4 Feb'41, Gateshead, England) – drums

Columbia M.G.M.

Apr 64. (7") *(DB 7247)* <K 13242> **BABY LET ME TAKE YOU HOME. / GONNA SEND YOU BACK TO WALKER** (US 'A'side) [21] Sep64 [57]

Jun 64. (7") *(DB 7301)* <K 13264> **THE HOUSE OF THE RISING SUN. / TALKIN' 'BOUT YOU** [1] Jul64 [1]

Sep 64. (7") *(DB 7354)* <K 13274> **I'M CRYING. / TAKE IT EASY** [8] Oct64 [19]

Oct 64. (lp; mono/stereo) *(33SX 1669)* <E/SE 4264> **THE ANIMALS** [6] Sep64 [7]
– Story of Bo Diddley / Bury my body / Dimples / I've been around / I'm in love again / The girl can't help it / I'm mad again / She said yeah / The right time / Memphis / Boom boom / Around and around. *(US diff. tracks +=> – The house of the rising sun. (re-iss. Oct69 on 'Regal Starline'; SRS 5006) (cd-iss. Oct97 on 'E.M.I.'; DORIG 125)*

Nov 64. (7") <K 13298> **BOOM BOOM. / BLUE FEELING** [–] [43]

Jan 65. (7") *(DB 7445)* <K 13311> **DON'T LET ME BE MISUNDERSTOOD. / CLUB A-GO-GO** [3] Feb65 [15]

Mar 65. (lp; mono/stereo) <E/SE 4281> **THE ANIMALS ON TOUR (live)** [–] [99]
– Boom boom / How you've changed / I believe to my soul / Mess around bright lights / Big city / Worried life blues / Let the good times roll / Crying dimples / She said yeah.

Apr 65. (7") *(DB 7539)* <K 13339> **BRING IT ON HOME TO ME. / FOR MISS CAULKER** [7] May 65 [32]

May 65. (lp; mono/stereo) *(33SX 1708)* <E/SE 4305> **ANIMAL TRACKS** [6] Sep65 [57]
– Mess around / How you've changed / Hallelujah, I love her so / I believe to my soul / Worried life blues / Roberta / I ain't got you / Bright lights, big city / Let the good times roll / For Miss Caulker / Roadrunner. *(re-iss. Sep84 on 'Fame' lp/c; FA/TCFA 413110) (cd-iss. Jan99 on 'E.M.I.'; 498936-2)*

Jul 65. (7") *(DB 7639)* <K 13382> **WE'VE GOTTA GET OUT OF THIS PLACE. / I CAN'T BELIEVE IT** [2] Aug65 [13]

Oct 65. (7") *(DB 7741)* <K 13414> **IT'S MY LIFE. / I'M GONNA CHANGE THE WORLD** [7] Nov65 [23]

— **DAVE ROWBERRY** (b.27 Dec'43, Newcastle, England) – keyboards (ex-MIKE COTTON SOUND) repl. PRICE who went solo

Decca M.G.M.

Feb 66. (7") *(F 2332)* **INSIDE – LOOKING OUT. / OUTCAST** [12] [–]

Mar 66. (7") <K 13468> **INSIDE – LOOKING OUT. / YOU'RE ON MY MIND** [–] [34]

— **BARRY JENKINS** (b.22 Dec'44, Leicester, England) – drums (ex-NASHVILLE TEENS) repl. STEEL

May 66. (7") *(F 12407)* <K 13514> **DON'T BRING ME DOWN. / CHEATING** [6] [12]

May 66. (lp) *(LK 4797)* **ANIMALISMS** [4] [–]
– One monkey don't stop no show / Maudie / Outcast / Sweet little sixteen / You're on my mind / Clapping / Gin house blues / Squeeze her – Tease her / What am I living for / I put a spell on you / That's all I am to you / She'll return it. *(cd-iss. Sep99 on 'Repetoire'; RR 4772)*

Aug 66. (lp; mono/stereo) *<E/SE 4384>* **ANIMALIZATION** [–] [20]
– Don't bring me down / One monkey don't stop no show / You're on my mind / She'll return it / Cheating / Inside – looking out / See see rider / Gin house blues / Maudie / What am I living for / Sweet little sixteen / I put a spell on you.

Sep 66. (7") <K 13582> **SEE SEE RIDER. / SHE'LL RETURN IT** [–] [10]

Nov 66. (lp; mono/stereo) <E/SE 4414> **ANIMALISM** [–] [33]
– All night long / Shake / Other side of this life / Rock me baby / Lucille / Smokestack lightning / Hey Gyp / Hit the road Jack / Outcast / Louisiana blues / That's all I am to you / Going down slow. *(cd-iss. Apr03 on 'Repertoire'; REP 4772)*

ERIC BURDON & THE ANIMALS

— ERIC with session musicians incl. BENNY GOULSON

Oct 66. (7") *(F 12502)* **HELP ME GIRL. / SEE SEE RIDER** [14] [–]

Dec 66. (7") <K 13636> **HELP ME GIRL. / THAT AIN'T WHERE IT'S AT** [–] [29]

Mar 67. (lp; mono/stereo) <E/SE 4433> **ERIC IS HERE** [–] [ ]
– Help me girl / In the night / Mama told me not to come / I think it's gonna rain today / This side of goodbye / That ain't where it's at / Wait till next year / Losin' control / It's not easy / Biggest bundle of them all / It's been a long time coming / True love.

— ERIC who had earlier moved to California brought back **BARRY JENKINS** in Jan '67

— recruited **VIC BRIGGS** (b.14 Feb'45, London) – guitar (ex-STEAMPACKET) to finally repl ROWBERRY / **JOHN WIEDER** (b.21 Apr'47, London) – guitar, violin repl. VALENTINE who went solo / **DANNY McCULLOCH** (b.18 Jul'45, London) – bass repl. CHANDLER who became producer

M.G.M. M.G.M.

May 67. (7") *(MGM 1340)* <K 13721> **WHEN I WAS YOUNG. / A GIRL NAMED SANDOZ** [45] Apr67 [15]

Aug 67. (7") *(MGM 1344)* **GOOD TIMES. / AIN'T THAT SO** [20] [–]

Aug 67. (7") <K 13769> **SAN FRANCISCAN NIGHTS. / GOOD TIMES** [–] [9]

Oct 67. (lp; mono/stereo) *(C/CS 8052)* <E/SE 4454> **WINDS OF CHANGE** [ ] Sep67 [42]
– San Franciscan nights / Good times / Winds of change / Poem by the sea / Paint it black / Black plague / Yes I am experienced / Man-woman / Hotel hell / Anything / It's all meat. *(re-iss. Apr71; 2354 001) (cd-iss. Oct85 on 'Polydor'; 825 717-2)*

Oct 67. (7") *(MGM 1359)* **SAN FRANCISCAN NIGHTS. / GRATEFULLY DEAD** [7] [–]

Nov 67. (7") <K 13868> **MONTEREY. / AIN'T IT SO** [–] [15]

Feb 68. (7") *(MGM 1373)* <K 13939> **SKY PILOT (pt.1). / SKY PILOT (pt.2)** [40] Jun68 [14]

Mar 68. (7") <K 13917> **ANYTHING. / IT'S ALL MEAT** [–] [80]

May 68. (7") *(MGM 1412)* **MONTEREY. / ANYTHING** [ ] [–]

May 68. (lp; mono/stereo) *(C/CS 8075)* <E/SE 4537> **THE TWAIN SHALL MEET** [ ] Mar68 [79]
– Just the thought / Closer to the truth / No self pity / Orange and red beans / Sky pilot / We love you Lil / All is one.

— **ZOOT MONEY** – keyboards (ex-BIG ROLL BAND, ex-DANTALIAN'S CHARIOT) / **ANDY SOMERS** (aka SUMMERS) – guitar, bass (ex-BIG ROLL BAND, ex-DANTALIAN'S CHARIOT) repl. BRIGGS and McCULLOCH

Aug 68. (lp; mono/stereo) <E/SE 4553> **EVERY ONE OF US** [–] [ ]
– Uppers and downers / Serenade to a sweet lady / The immigrant lad / Year of the guru / St.James infirmary / New York 1963 – America 1968 / White houses.

Nov 68. (7") <K 14013> **WHITE HOUSES. / RIVER DEEP MOUNTAIN HIGH** [–] [67]

Jan 69. (7") *(MGM 1461)* **RING OF FIRE. / I'M AN ANIMAL** [25] [–]

Dec 68. (lp; mono/stereo) <d-lp> *(C/CS 8105)* <SE 4591-2> **LOVE IS** [ ] [ ]
– River deep, mountain high / I'm the animal / I'm dying, or am I / Gemini / The madman / Ring of fire / Coloured rain / To love somebody / As tears go passing by. *(UK re-iss. Apr71; 2354 006-007) (re-iss. 1973; 2619 002) (cd re-iss/Sep94 on 'One Way'; OW 30338)*

May 69. (7") *(MGM 1481)* **RIVER DEEP, MOUNTAIN HIGH. / HELP ME GIRL** [ ] [–]

— split Feb'69. WIEDER joined FAMILY, ZOOT went solo, JENKINS joined HEAVY JELLY, SOMERS became SUMMERS and joined KEVIN AYERS then KEVIN COYNE; he later helped form the POLICE

ERIC BURDON & WAR

ERIC BURDON – vocals, and WAR: – **LONNIE (LEROY) JORDAN** – keyboards, vocals / **HOWARD SCOTT** – guitar, vocals / **CHARLES MILLER** – saxophone, clarinet / **HAROLD BROWN** – drums, percussion / **B.B. DICKERSON** – bass / **THOMAS 'PAPA DEE' ALLEN** – keyboards / **LEE OSKAR** – harmonica

Polydor M.G.M.

Sep 70. (lp) *(2310 041)* <SE 4663> **ERIC BURDON DECLARES WAR** [50] May70 [18]

– Dedication / Roll on Kirk / Tobacco road / I have a dream / Spill the wine / Blues for Memphis Slim / Birth / Mother Earth / Mr.Charlie / Danish pastry / You're no stranger. *(re-iss. Oct79 on 'MCA'; MCF 3026) <cd-iss. Oct95 on 'Avenue'; 74321 30526-2)*

Jul 70. (7") *(2001 072) <K 14118>* **SPILL THE WINE. / MAGIC MOUNTAIN** [ ] [3]

Liberty M.G.M.

Dec 70. (7") *(LBF 15434) <K 14196>* **THEY CAN'T TAKE AWAY OUR MUSIC. / HOME COOKIN'** [ ] [50]

Feb 71. (d-lp) *(LDS 84003-4) <SE 4710-2>* **BLACK MAN'S BURDON** [ ] Dec70 [82]
– Black on black in black / Paint it black / Laurel and Hardy / P.C. 3 / Black bird / Paint it black / Spirit / Beautiful new born child / Nights in white satin / Bird and the squirrel / Nuts seed and life / Out of nowhere / Sun – Moon / Pretty colours / Gun / Jimbo / Bare back ride / Home cookin' / They can't take away our music. *(re-iss. Oct79 on 'MCA'; MCSP 306) <US-cd 1993 on 'Avenue'; R2 71193>*

U.A. M.G.M.

Jun 71. (7") *(UP 35217)* **PAINT IT BLACK. / SPIRIT** [ ] [–]

ERIC BURDON & JIMMY WITHERSPOON

JIMMY WITHERSPOON – blues guitarist + WAR backing.

U.A. M.G.M.

Aug 71. (7") *(UP 35287) <K 14296>* **SOLEDAD. / HEADIN' FOR HOME** [ ] [ ]

Dec 71. (lp) *(UAG 29251) <SE 4791>* **GUILTY!** [ ] [ ]
– I've been drinking / Once upon a time / Steam roller / The laws must change / Have mercy judge / Goin' down slow / Soledad / Home dream / Wicked wicked man / Headin' for home / The time has come. *<US re-iss. 1976 as 'BLACK AND WHITE BLUES' on 'LA'; GG 58001> (re-iss. Oct79 as 'BLACK AND WHITE BLUES' on 'M.C.A.'; MCF 3024)*

the ERIC BURDON BAND

performed at Reading festival (Aug73), backed by **AARON BUTLER** – guitar / **RANDY RICE** – bass / **ALVIN TAYLOR** – drums. This line-up also featured on his next long awaited album

Capitol Capitol

Dec 74. (7") *<3997>* **THE REAL ME. / LETTER FROM THE COUNTY FARM** [–] [ ]

Feb 75. (lp) *(<E-ST 11359>)* **SUN SECRETS** [ ] Dec74 [51]
– It's my life / Ring of fire / Medley: When I was young – Warchild – The real me / Don't let me be misunderstood – Nina's school / Letter from the county farm / Sun secrets.

Feb 75. (7") *<4007>* **RING OF FIRE. / THE REAL ME** [–] [ ]

—— added **JOHN STERLING** – guitar / **TERRY RYAN** – keyboards / **MOSES WHEELOCK** – percussion / **GEORGE SURANOVICH** – drums / and **KIM KESTERSON** – bass (repl. AARON BUTLER)

Aug 75. (lp/<lp>) *(E-ST/<SMAS 11426>)* **STOP** [ ] [ ]
– City boy / Gotta get it on / The man / I'm lookin' up / Rainbow / All I do / Funky fever / By mine / The way it should be / Stop.

the ORIGINAL ANIMALS

reformed to record below **BURDON, PRICE, VALENTINE, CHANDLER + STEEL**

Barn U.A.

Aug 77. (7") *(2014 109)* **PLEASE SEND ME SOMEONE TO LOVE. / RIVERSIDE COUNTY** [ ] [–]

Aug 77. (lp/c) *(2314 104) <790>* **BEFORE WE WERE SO RUDELY INTERRUPTED** [ ] [70]
– Brother Bill (the last clean shirt) / Many rivers to cross / Lonely avenue / Please send me someone to love / Riverside county / It's all over now, baby blue / Fire on the sun / As the crow flies / Just a little bit / The fool. *(cd-iss. Feb00 on 'Repertoire'; REP 4845)*

Oct 77. (7") *(2014 115)* **MANY RIVERS TO CROSS. / BROTHER BILL (THE LAST CLEAN SHIRT)** [ ] [–]

Nov 77. (7") *<1070>* **FIRE ON THE SUN. / RIVERSIDE COUNTY** [–] [ ]

—— PRICE returned to solo work.

ERIC BURDON

—— solo with many session people.

Polydor not iss.

Mar 78. (lp) *(2302 078)* **SURVIVOR** [ ] [–]
– Rocky / Woman of the rings / The kid / Tomb of the unknown singer / Famous flames / Hollywood woman / Hook of Holland / I was born to live the blues / Highway dealer / P.O. box 500.

1980. (lp) *(2344 147)* **DARKNESS – DARKNESS** [ ] [–]
– Darkness darkness / On the horizon / Rat race / Gospel singer / Ride on / Baby what's wrong / Cry to me / So much love / Ecstasy / Too late.

Ariola not iss.

1981. (lp; as ERIC BURDON'S FIRE DEPT.) *(S 202 800-320)* **THE LAST DRIVE** [–] German [–]
– The last drive / Power company / Bird on the beach / The rubbing out of long hair / Atom-most-fear / Dry / Female terrorist / The last poet.

the ANIMALS

reformed again in 1983

I.R.S. I.R.S.

Sep 83. (7") *(PFP 1019) <9920>* **THE NIGHT. / NO JOHN NO** [ ] [48]
(12"+=) *(PFXS 1019)* – Melt down.

Sep 83. (lp) *(<SP 70037>)* **ARK** [ ] [66]
– Loose change / Love is for all time / My favourite enemy / Prisoner of the light / Being there / Hard times / The night / Trying to get to you / Just can't get enough / Melt down / Gotta get back to you / Crystal nights. *(cd-iss. Nov96 on 'Castle'; CLACD 412) (cd re-iss. Jan00 on 'Essential'; ESMCD 801)*

Nov 83. (7"/12") *(PFP/+X 1030) <9923>* **LOVE IS FOR ALL TIME. / JUST CAN'T GET ENOUGH** [ ] [ ]

Sep 84. (lp) *(<IRSA 70043>)* **RIP IT TO SHREDS – THE GREATEST HITS LIVE (live 1983)** [ ] [ ]
– It's too late / House of the rising Sun / It's my life / Don't bring me down / Don't let me be misunderstood / I'm cryin' / Bring it on home to me / O lucky man / Boom boom / We've gotta get out of this place.

—— (split though they did reunion gigs)

– (selective) compilations, etc. –

on 'Columbia' UK / 'MGM' US, unless stated otherwise

Feb 66. (lp; mono/stereo) *<E/SE 4324>* **THE BEST OF THE ANIMALS** [–] [6]
– It's my life / Gonna send you back to Walker / Bring it on home to me / I'm mad again / The house of the rising sun / We've gotta get out of this place / Boom boom / I'm in love again / I'm crying / Don't let me be misunderstood. *(UK iss.Mar89 on 'Crusader')*

Apr 66. (lp) *(SX 6035)* **MOST OF THE ANIMALS** [4] [–]
– The house of the rising sun / We've gotta get out of this place / Roadrunner / Let the good times roll / Hallelujah I love her so / It's going to change the world / Bring it on home to me / Worried life blues / Baby let me take you home / For Miss Caulker / I believe to my soul / How you've changed. *(re-iss. Sep71 on 'Music For Pleasure'; MFP 5218,* hit no.18) *(cd-iss. Feb92; CDMFP 5218) (cd re-iss. Mar02 on 'EMI Gold'+=; 538296-2)* – Don't let me be misunderstood / It's my life / Club a-go-go / I'm crying.

Jun 67. (lp; mono/stereo) *<E/SE 4454>* **THE BEST OF ERIC BURDON & THE ANIMALS VOL.2** [–] [71]

Sep 72. (7"m) *R.A.K.; (RR 1)* **THE HOUSE OF THE RISING SUN. / DON'T LET ME BE MISUNDERSTOOD / I'M CRYING** [25] [–]
(re-iss. Sep82 7",7"pic-d; RR/+P 1, hit UK No.11)

Apr 76. (lp) *D.J.M.; (DJSL 069)* **IN CONCERT FROM NEWCASTLE** (live '63) [ ] [–]
(re-iss. Dec 76 as 'LIVE IN NEWCASTLE'; DJB 26069) (re-iss. Jan 77 as 'NEWCASTLE '63 on 'Charly'; CR 30016) (re-iss. Feb81; CR 30197) (re-iss. Nov88 as 'LIVE AT THE CLUB A GO GO, NEWCASTLE' on 'Decal'; LIK 88) (cd-iss. Feb93 on 'Charly'; CDCD 1037) (cd re-iss. Jun97 on 'Spalax'; 14550) (re-iss. Oct97 on 'Hallmark' cd/c; 30814-2/-4)

Dec 88. (lp/c/cd) *See For Miles; (SEE/+K/CD 244)* **THE EP COLLECTION** [ ] [–]
(cd re-iss. Mar99; same)

Jul 90. (d-cd/d-c/d-lp) *E.M.I.; (CD/TC+/EM 1367)* **THE COMPLETE ANIMALS** [ ] [–]

Dec 90. (cd/c/lp) *Decal; (CD/C+/LIK 72)* **TRACKIN' THE HITS** [ ] [–]

Mar 91. (cd/d-lp) *Sequel; (NEXCD/NEDLP 153)* **INSIDE LOOKING OUT (THE 1965-1966 SESSIONS)**(cd+= extra tracks) [ ] [–]

1993. (cd; ERIC BURDON) *Avenue; <R2 71219>* **SUN SECRETS / STOP** [–] [ ]

Jun 02. (cd) *A.Z.; (AZCD 04)* **INTERESTING LIFE: NEW RECORDINGS OF THEIR GREATEST HITS**
Mar 03. (cd) *Magic; (3930295)* **THE COMPLETE FRENCH CD EP COLLECTION**
Aug 03. (cd) *Castle; (CMRCD 766)* **DON'T BRING ME DOWN: THE DECCA YEARS**
Jun 04. (cd) *Raven; (<RVCD 194>)* **GRATEFULLY DEAD 1964-1968**
Jul 04. (cd) *EMI Gold; (473272-2)* **THE ANIMALS / ANIMAL TRACKS**
Jul 04. (cd) *Abkco; <719325>* **RETROSPECTIVE**

the ERIC BURDON BAND

with **JOHN STERLING + SNUFFY WALDEN** – guitar / **STEVE GOLDSTEIN + LUIS CABAZA + RONNIE BARRON** – keyboards / **BILL McCUBBIN + TERRY WILSON** – bass / **TONY BRUANAGLE** – drums

Blackline not iss.

1983. (lp) *(BL 712)* **COMEBACK** (soundtrack) German
– No more Elmore / The road / Crawling King Snake / Take it easy / Dey won't / Wall of silence / Streetwalker / It hurts me too / Lights out / Bird on the beach. *(UK-iss.Jun84 as 'THE ROAD' on 'Thunderbolt'; THBL 1017) (cd-iss. Sep94 on 'Line'; LICD 900058) <(d-cd iss.Apr01 on 'Burning Airlines'+=; PILOT 081)>* – (extra tracks).

Bullfrog Carrere

Mar 84. (lp) *(BDL 4006) <267.003>* **POWER COMPANY** Dec83
– Power company / Devil's daughter / You can't kill my spirit / Do you feel it (today) / Wicked man / Heart attack / Who gives a f*** / Sweet blood call / House of the rising Sun / Comeback. *<US-iss.1988 as 'WICKED MAN on 'GNP Crescendo' lp/c/cd; GNP S/C/D 2194)*

Striped Horse not iss.

Aug 88. (12") *(SH12 615)* **RUN FOR YOUR LIFE (extended). / RUN FOR YOUR LIFE / RUN FOR YOUR LIFE (instrumental)**
(cd-s+=) *(SHCD 615)* – Run for your life (Animal remix).
Aug 88. (cd) *<SHD 5006>* **I USED TO BE AN ANIMAL**
– I used to be an animal / The dream / American dreams / Going back to Memphis / Leo's place / Run for your life / Don't give a damn / Living in fear / I will be with you again. *(re-iss. Jul94 on 'Success' cd/c; 2326) (cd re-iss. Oct03 on 'Falcon'; UN 3215)*

Rhino Rhino

1990. (c-s) *(4JM 74425)* **SIXTEEN TONS / ('A'instrumental)**

ERIC BURDON

Jet not iss.

Apr 95. (cd) *(JETCD 1011)* **LOST WITHIN THE WALLS OF FAME**
– I used to be an animal / When we were a gang / American dreams / Rock & roll shoes / Memories of Anna / New Orleans rap / I will be with you again / Brand new day / Nightrider / Going back to Memphis / Leo's place / Woman's touch / Is there another world / Don't shoot me. *(re-iss. Jul00 on 'Mooncrest'; CRESTCD 050)*

S.P.V. not iss.

Apr 04. (cd) *(SPV 085-7003-2)* **MY SECRET LIFE**
– Once upon a time / Motorcycle girl / Over the border / The secret / Factory girl / Highway 62 / Jazzman / Black and white world / Heaven / Devil slide / Broken records / Can't kill the boogieman / My secret life.

□ ANOTHER PRETTY FACE
(see under ⇒ the WATERBOYS)

□ Adam ANT (see under ⇒ ADAM & THE ANTS)

ANTHRAX

Formed: Queens, New York, USA . . . mid '81, by NEIL TURBIN and DAN LILKER. SCOTT 'NOT' IAN, CHARLIE BENANTE and the diminutive DAN SPITZ completed the line-up, the band consequently spotted and signed to the 'Megaforce' label (licensed to 'Music For Nations' in Europe) by the legendary JOHNNY Z. The 1984 debut, 'FISTFUL OF METAL' (if you think the title's cheesy, wait till you see the cover!) hardly set the rock world alight, although 'METAL THRASHING MAD' was good for a laugh and the ALICE COOPER cover, 'I'M EIGHTEEN' was passable. By the release of the mini album, 'ARMED AND DANGEROUS', the following year, the more traditional metal tonsils of JOEY BELLADONNA were employed, a canny move that lent the band a modicum of style and sophistication. This was evident on ANTHRAX's first outing for 'Island', 'SPREADING THE DISEASE', a classy thrash metal affair that frequently rose above the narrow confines of the genre. By turns humorous, impassioned, and bloody loud, the likes of 'MADHOUSE' (a must-see video), 'AFTERSHOCK', 'ARMED AND DANGEROUS' and 'MEDUSA' made this one of the key metal releases of the 80's. 'AMONG THE LIVING' (1987) was almost as good and for many aging metallers, 'I AM THE LAW' is the definitive ANTHRAX track, a tribute to the meanest cop in Mega City One, Judge Dredd. 'INDIANS', meanwhile, was a more serious affair, dealing with the plight of their Native American brethren. Yet accomplished as the music was, it was almost overshadowed by the band's image. A case of bullet belts (!) out, skateboards and surf shorts in; for a brief, heady time in the late 80's, ANTHRAX almost made metal (whisper it now) trendy. Proving there was always a hip-hop element to their hardcore, the band released 'I'M THE MAN', a rap/metal pastiche that quite probably pissed off SAXON fans everywhere. At this point, the band were up there with METALLICA as the great white hopes of thrash and fans waited with baited breath for their next album, 'STATE OF EUPHORIA' (1988). Inevitably, perhaps, the record was a letdown; on first listen it sounded dense, promising, on repeated listening it became obvious the songs just weren't there. Equally inevitably, the band's dayglo image prompted a backlash. They retaliated with a considerably darker, more introspective opus, 'PERSISTENCE OF TIME' (1990). While the JOE JACKSON cover, 'GOT THE TIME', was engaging, the songwriting still wasn't up to scratch. A 1991 collaboration with CHUCK D on a storming cover of PUBLIC ENEMY's 'BRING THE NOISE' was the band's most effective effort for years and showed what they were obviously still capable of. The single was included on 'ATTACK OF THE KILLER B's', a compilation of B-sides and rare tracks, while ANTHRAX went on to tour with PUBLIC ENEMY on a genre busting double bill. Signing a new contract with 'Elektra', the band promptly ditched BELLADONNA in favour of ex-ARMOURED SAINT man, JOHN BUSH. These were tough times for ANTHRAX, as every metal band on the planet purchased a distortion pedal, grew a goatee, and insisted they weren't actually metal after all, no, they were GRUNGE!! (of course). All credit to ANTHRAX then, for sticking to their metal guns and releasing 'THE SOUND OF WHITE NOISE' (1993), a barrage of furious riffing that almost topped the work of their mid-80's golden period. 'STOMP 442' (1995) was equally ferocious, and while ANTHRAX mightn't sell as many records as they used to, they remain one of metal's best loved bands. The ever productive IAN had also turned his hand to side project STORMTROOPERS OF DEATH aka S.O.D. back in the mid-80's. A collaboration with BENANTE, LILKER and ANTHRAX roadie BILLY MILANO, the project came to life with the release of 1985's legendary 'SPEAK ENGLISH OR DIE'. Regarded as one of the pivotal records in the cross-fertilisation of punk/hardcore and thrash metal, the album was a riot of 2-minute-wonder noise, fury and irreverent humour which brought charges (not altogether unjustified) of sexism and racism. Incredibly, sales of this cult record eventually topped one million and prompted 'Megaforce' to release a millennial remastered edition complete with new studio tracks and live material. While it was originally intended as a one-off affair – MILANO going off to form M.O.D. – the group reformed in 1992 for the ironically titled 'LIVE AT BUDOKAN' (actually recorded live in New York). From the hilarious IRON MAIDEN pastiche of the cover art to MILANO's crowd baiting, the record was a treat for fans of the original album from which much of the material was used (alongside a few choice covers). Finally, the cult of S.O.D. demanded a follow-up studio album and in 1999, possibly the most belated sophomore effort in recorded history hit the shelves. 'BIGGER THAN THE DEVIL' carried on where their debut had left off all those years ago, showing the young pretenders how to really mosh and how to get a proper sense of humour. No target was too soft for MILANO's caustic gaze with both mealy-mouthed liberals and bigots coming under attack; they mightn't be bigger than the Devil but SOD probably have all the best jokes. Given the musical climate into which ANTHRAX returned in 2003, 'WE'VE COME FOR YOU ALL' was almost revolutionary in its no-frills thrash metal. While new guitarist and co-producer ROB CAGGIANO lent a competitive edge to proceedings, there were precious few, if any, concessions to contemporary trends. But then ANTHRAX were always one step removed from their peers. With spandex-rock the unlikeliest of candidates for a fashion resurrection, it wouldn't be so surprising to see an 80's back-to-the-roots thrash revival in the not too distant future. What certainly was surprising was the appearance of ROGER DALTREY (on 'TAKING THE MUSIC BACK'), not quite as revolutionary a collaboration as the CHUCK D one, but effective nonetheless. The band's undying popularity fired concert set 'MUSIC OF MASS DESTRUCTION: LIVE FROM CHICAGO' (2004), frontman BUSH even re-branding a whole album's worth of back catalogue classics, 'THE GREATER OF TWO EVILS' (2004), featuring a fan-tasy track listing selected via internet message board. Yet more revisionism was on the cards with 'ALIVE 2' (2005), a cd/dvd package celebrating the return of JOEY BELLADONNA in place of BUSH.

• **Songwriters:** SCOTT IAN except; I'M EIGHTEEN (Alice Cooper) / SABBATH BLOODY SABBATH (Black Sabbath) / GOD SAVE THE QUEEN and FRIGGIN' IN THE RIGGIN' (Sex Pistols) / GOT THE TIME (Joe Jackson) / BRING THE NOISE (Public Enemy) / PROTEST AND SURVIVE (Discharge), LOOKING DOWN THE BARREL OF A GUN (Beastie Boys) / SHE (Kiss) / THE BENDS (Radiohead). • **Trivia:** DAN SPITZ's older brother DAVID played bass in the mid'80's with BLACK SABBATH. ANTHRAX an acting/ singing appearance on a 1992 showing of US TV sit-com 'Married With Children'. • **Note:** Not to be confused with UK "oi" band of the same name.

Album rating: FISTFUL OF METAL (*4) / SPREADING THE DISEASE (*8) / AMONG THE LIVING (*8) / STATE OF EUPHORIA (*5) / PERSISTENCE OF TIME (*7) / SOUND OF WHITE NOISE (*6) / STOMP 442 (*5) / WE'VE COME FOR YOU ALL (*6) / MUSIC OF MASS DESTRUCTION: LIVE FROM CHICAGO (*6) / THE GREATER OF TWO EVILS re-recordings (*6) / ALIVE 2 (*7) / ANTHROLOGY (NO HIT WONDERS 1985-1991) compilation (*7)

NEIL TURBIN – vocals / **DAN SPITZ** (b.28 Jan'63) – lead guitar / **SCOTT 'Not' IAN** (b.31 Dec'63) – rhythm guitar / **DAN LILKER** (b.18 Oct'64) – bass / **CHARLIE BENANTE** (b.27 Nov'62, The Bronx) – drums

Music For Nations | Megaforce

Nov 83. (7") **SOLDIERS OF DEATH. / HOWLING FURIES** [–] [ ]

Jan 84. (lp) *(MFN 14) <MRS 469>* **FISTFUL OF METAL** [ ] [ ]
– Deathrider / Metal thrashing mad / I'm eighteen / Panic / Subjagator / Death from above / Across the river / Anthrax. *(re-iss. Apr87 lp/pic-lp; MFN 14DM/P) (c+=/cd+=; CD/T MFN 14)* – Soldiers of metal / Howling furies. *<US-cd-iss. 1987 on 'Caroline'; CAROLCD 1383> (re-iss. cd Sep95 on 'Bulletproof'; CDMVEST 56)*
(Mid'84) **MATT FALLON** – vocals repl. TURBIN

— **FRANK BELLO** (b. 7 Sep'65) – bass (ex-roadie) repl. LILKER

— (Aug'84) **MATT** was replaced by **JOEY BELLADONNA** (b.30 Oct'60, Oswego, NY) – vocals (ex-BIBLE BLACK)

Feb 85. (m-lp/pic-m-lp) *<MRS 05/+P>* **ARMED AND DANGEROUS** [–] [ ]
– Armed and dangerous / Raise Hell / God save the Queen / Metal thrashing mad / Panic. *(UK-iss.Aug87 on 'Music For Nations' lp/c; MFN/CMFN 123) (cd-iss. Nov91; CDMFN 123) (cd re-iss. Sep95 on 'Bulletproof'; CDMVEST 55)*

Music For Nations | Megaforce-Island

Feb 86. (lp/c) *(MFN/TMFN 62) <90460>* **SPREADING THE DISEASE** [ ] Dec85 [ ]
– A.I.R. / Lone justice / Madhouse / S.S.C – Stand or fall / The enemy / Aftershock / Armed and dangerous / Medusa / Gung ho. *(cd-iss. May86 on 'Island'; CID 9806) (pic-lp Sep87; MFNP 62) (re-iss. Aug91 on 'Island' cd)(c; IMCD 136)(ICM 9806)*

Island | Island

May 86. (12"/12"s/12"pic-d) *(12IS/+B/P 285)* **MADHOUSE. / A.I.R. / GOD SAVE THE QUEEN** [ ] [ ]

Feb 87. (7"pic-d)(12") *(LAWP 1)(12IS 316)* **I AM THE LAW. / BUD E. LUVBOMB AND SATAN'S LOUNGE BAND** [32] [ ]
('A'live-7"red+=) *(ISX 316)* – Madhouse (live).

Apr 87. (lp/pic-lp/c/cd) *(ILPS/PILPS/ICT/CID 9865) <90584>* **AMONG THE LIVING** [18] [62]
– Among the living / Caught in the mosh / I am the law / Efilnikufesin (N.F.L.) / A skeleton in the closet / One world / A.D.I.- horror of it all / Imitation of life. *(cd re-iss. Mar94; IMCD 186)*

Jun 87. (7"orange/7"pic-d) *(IS/+P 325)* **INDIANS. / SABBATH BLOODY SABBATH** [44] [ ]
(12"+=/12"pic-d+=) *(12IS/+P 325)* – Taint.

Nov 87. (7"/7"sha-pic-d) *(IS/+P 338)* **I'M THE MAN. / CAUGHT IN THE MOSH** [20] [–]
(12"+=) *(12IS 338)* – I am the law (live).

Dec 87. (m-lp,c,cd) *<90685>* **I'M THE MAN** [–] [53]
– I'm the man (censored version) / I'm the man (Def uncensored version) / Sabbath bloody sabbath / I'm the man (live & extremely Def II uncensored version) / Caught in a mosh (live) / I am the law (live).

Sep 88. (7"yellow) *(IS 379)* **MAKE ME LAUGH. / ANTI SOCIAL (live)** [26] [ ]
(12"+=/cd-s+=) *(12IS/CIDP 379)* – Friggin' in the riggin'.

Sep 88. (lp/c/cd) *(ILPS/ICT/CID 9916) <91004>* **STATE OF EUPHORIA** [12] [30]
– Be all, end all / Out of sight, out of mind / Make me laugh / Anti-social / Who cares wins / Now it's dark / Schism / Misery loves company / 13 / (finale). *(re-iss. cd Apr94; IMCD 187)*

Mar 89. (7"/7"amber/7"blue/7"red) *(IS/+A/B/R 409)* **ANTI-SOCIAL. / PARASITE** [44] [ ]
(12"+=/12"amber+=/12"blue+=/12"red+=)(3"cd-s+=) *(12IS/+A/B/R 409)(CIDX 409)* – Le sects.

Island | Megaforce

Aug 90. (7") *(IS 470)* **IN MY WORLD. / KEEP IT IN THE FAMILY** [29] [ ]
(10"+=/12"+=/cd-s+=) *(10IS/12IS/CID 470)* – ('A'&'B'extended).

Aug 90. (cd/c/lp) *(CID/ICT/ILPS 9967) <846480>* **PERSISTENCE OF TIME** [13] [24]
– Time / Blood / Keep it in the family / In my world / Gridlock / Intro to reality / Belly of the beast / Got the time / H8 red / One man stands / Discharge. *(pic-lp.Jan91; ILPSP 9967) (re-iss. Apr94 cd)(c; IMCD 178)(ICM 9967)*

Nov 90. (c-s/10"/7") *(C/10+/CIS 476)* **GOT THE TIME. / WHO PUT THIS TOGETHER** [16] [ ]
(12"+=/cd-s+=) *(12IS/CID 476)* – I'm the man (live).

Jun 91. (c-s/7"; ANTHRAX featuring CHUCK D) *(C+/IS 490)* **BRING THE NOISE. / I AM THE LAW '91** [14] [ ]
(10"+=/12"+=/cd-s+=)(10"pic-d+=/12"pic-d+=) *(10IS/12IS/CID 490)(10/12 ISP 490)* – Keep it in the family (live).

— CHUCK D. (of-PUBLIC ENEMY)

Jun 91. (cd/c/lp) *(CID/ICT/ILPS 9980) <848804>* **ATTACK OF THE KILLER B's** (rare studio) [13] [27]
– Milk (ode to Billy) / Bring the noise / Keep it in the family (live) / Startin' up a posse / Protest and survive / Chromatic death / I'm the man '91 / Parasite / Pipeline / Sects / Belly of the beast (live) / N.F.B. (dallabnikufesin). *(re-iss. Apr94 cd)(c; IMCD 179)(ICM 9980)*

— (May'92) **JOHN BUSH** (b.24 Aug'63, L.A.) – vocals (ex-ARMOURED SAINT) repl. MARK OSEGUEDA who had replaced BELLADONNA

Elektra | Elektra

Apr 93. (7"/c-s) *(EKR 166/+C)* **ONLY. / ONLY (mix)** [36] [ ]
(cd-s+=) *(EKR 166CD1)* – Cowboy song / Sodium pentaghol.
(cd-s) *(EKR 166CD2)* – ('A'side) / Auf wiedersehen / Noisegate.

May 93. (cd/c/lp) *<(7559 61430-2/-4/-1)>* **SOUND OF WHITE NOISE** [14] [7]
– Potter's field / Only / Room for one more / Packaged rebellion / Hy pro glo / Invisible / 1000 points of hate / C11 H17 N2 O2 SNA / Burst / This is not an exit. *(cd+=)* – Black lodge. *(cd re-iss. Jap version Apr98 on 'Victor'; VICP 80320)*

Sep 93. (7"/c-s) *(EKR 171/+W)* **BLACK LODGE. / ('A'-Black strings mix)** [53] [ ]
(10"+=/12"pic-d+=/cd-s+=) *(EKR 171 TE/TP/CD)* – Pottersfield / Love her all I can.

Nov 93. (7"/c-s) *(EKR 178/+C)* **HY PRO GLO. / LONDON** [ ] [ ]
(12"+=/cd-s+=) *(EKR 178 T/CD)* – Room for one more (live).

Oct 95. (cd/c) *<(7559 61856-2/-4)>* **STOMP 442** [ ] [47]
– Random acts of senseless violence / Fueled / King size / Riding shotgun / Perpetual motion / In a zone / Nothing / American Pompeii / Drop the ball / Tester / Bare.

Jan 96. (c-s) *(EKR 216C)* **NOTHING / FUELLED (remix)** [ ] [ ]
(cd-s+=) *(EKR 216CD1)* – Remember tomorrow / Grunt and click.
(cd-s) *(EKR 216CD2)* – ('A'side) / Dethroned emperor / No time this time.

Ignition – Tommy Boy | Ignition – Tommy Boy

Jul 98. (cd/c) *<(IGN7 4034-3/-4)>* **VOLUME 8 – THE THREAT IS REAL!** [73] [ ]
– Crush / Catharsis / Inside out / Piss n vinegar / 604 / Toast to the extras / Born again idiot / Killing box / Harms way / Hog tied / Big fat / Cupajoe / Alpha male / Stealing from a thief.

Oct 98. (7") *(IGN 740516)* **INSIDE OUT. / GIVING THE HORNS** [ ] [–]
(cd-s+=) *(IGN 740513)* – The bends.

—— line-up:- **JOHN BUSH** + **SCOTT IAN** + **CHARLIE BENANTE** + **FRANK BELLO** recruited **ROB CAGGIANO** – lead guitar

Nuclear Blast | Sanctuary

Feb 03. (cd) *(NB 699DP)* *<84609>* **WE'VE COME FOR YOU ALL** [ ] May03 [ ]
– Contact / What doesn't lie / Superhero / Refuse to be denied / Safe home / Any place but here / Nobody knows anything / Strap it on / Black dahlia / Cadillac rock box / Taking the music back / Crash / Think about an end / W.C.F.Y.A. *(lp-iss.Apr03; 121095) (d-cd-iss. Jun03 +=; NB 6995)*

Sep 04. (cd) *(NB 1297CDD)* *<84688>* **MUSIC OF MASS DESTRUCTION: LIVE FROM CHICAGO** (live) [ ] Apr04 [ ]
– What doesn't die / Got the time / Caught in a mosh / Safe home / Room for one more / Antisocial / Nobody knows anything / Fueled / Inside out / Refuse to be denied / I am the law / Only. // (DVD tracks).

Nov 04. (cd) *(NB 1274CD)* *<84709>* **THE GREATER OF TWO EVILS** (re-recordings) [ ] [ ]
– Deathrider / Metal thrashing mad / Caught in a mosh / A.I.R. / Among the living / Keep it in the family / Indians / Madhouse / Panic / I am the law / Belly of the beast / NFL / Be all, end all / Gung-ho.

—— **JOEY BELLADONNA** – vocals; returned to repl. BUSH

Nov 05. (cd+dvd) *(NB 1583DCD)* *<84764>* **ALIVE 2** (live) [ ] Sep05 [ ]
– Among the living / Caught in a mosh / A.I.R. / Antisocial / NFL / Deathrider / Medusa / In my world / Indians / Time / Be all, end all / I am the law // (DVD equivalents & outtakes/documentary).

– compilations, others, etc. –

Nov 92. (d-cd) *Island; (ITSCD 6)* **AMONG THE LIVING / PERSISTENCE OF TIME** [ ] [–]

Apr 94. (cd/c/lp) *Island; (CID/ICT/ILPS 8027)* *<518920>* **ANTHRAX LIVE – THE ISLAND YEARS (live)** [ ] [ ]

Mar 98. (cd) *Connoisseur; (VSOPCD 252)* **MOSHERS 1986-1991** [ ] [–]

Feb 99. (d-cd) *S.P.V.; (SPV 0761818-2)* **FISTFUL OF METAL / ARMED AND DANGEROUS** [ ] [–]

Nov 99. (cd) *Beyond; <(63985 78067-2)>* **RETURN OF THE KILLER A's** [ ] [ ]
(re-iss. Jan00 on 'Spitfire'; SPITCD 057)

Oct 01. (cd) *Universal; <(E 586324-2)>* **CLASSIC ANTHRAX: THE UNIVERSAL MASTERS COLLECTION** [ ] Feb02 [ ]

Aug 02. (cd) *Universal; <(5 44991-2)>* **THE COLLECTION** [ ] Jun02 [ ]

Mar 03. (cd) *Universal; <(AA314 586004-2)>* **MADHOUSE – THE VERY BEST OF ANTHRAX** [ ] Jun01 [ ]

Sep 05. (d-cd) *Universal; (9883263)* *<4996>* **ANTHROLOGY (NO HIT WONDERS 1985-1991)** [ ] [ ]
– A.I.R. / Lone justice / Madhouse / The enemy / Armed and dangerous / Medusa / Gung-ho / Among the living / Caught in a mosh / I am the law / Efilnikufesin (NFL) / A skeleton in the closet / Indians / Sabbath bloody sabbath / I'm the man (version) / Be all, end all / Make me laugh / Antisocial / Who cares wins / Now it's dark / Finale / Time / Keep it in the family / In my world / Intro to reality / Belly of the beast / Got the time / Discharge / Bring the noise / Antisocial (French version).

ANTONY AND THE JOHNSONS

Born: ANTONY HEGARTY, 1971, Chichester, West Sussex, England. Relocating to California as a teenager, ANTONY discovered a role model in BOY GEORGE, at the time enjoying taboo-busting, tabloid-scoffing stardom with CULTURE CLUB. By his late teens, he'd based himself in the more sympathetic environs of New York, where he performed, shaven headed, with cabaret collective Blacklips. Although recorded in 1998, ANTONY's eponymous debut album didn't see a release until 2000, when onetime Psychic TV member, Current 93 mainman and NICK CAVE collaborator DAVID TIBET issued it on his own 'Durtro' label. With such impeccably underground credentials, it's surprising that ANTONY AND THE JOHNSONS breached the mainstream at all, yet a series of connections and coincidences rapidly fell into place: LOU REED copped an earful of follow-up EP, 'I FELL IN LOVE WITH A DEAD BOY' (featuring covers of Tibet's 'Soft Buck Stars' and David Lynch/Angelo Badalamenti's 'Mysteries Of Love'), and promptly called on ANTONY's talents for his Edgar Allen Poe adaptation, 'The Raven' (2003). REED returned the favour by guesting on subsequent EP, 'THE LAKE', released on the more widely distributed 'Secretly Canadian' label following a couple of split singles with Current 93. Having already re-released the debut album, the label issued belated sophomore set, 'I AM A BIRD NOW', in 2005 to ecstatic reviews and a Mercury Music Prize. In trying to get to grips with ANTONY's androgynous soliloquies, critics consistently namechecked NINA SIMONE. The similarity was obvious but hardly definitive: a SIMONE without enmity, born-again and beset by visions, a voice polarising in its vibrato-rich queerness, liberating in its gospel-like intimacy. Nor were the august chamber arrangements the stuff of a typical Mercury Music winner, but that didn't stop sublime opener, 'HOPE THERE'S SOMEONE', from scraping the Top 40. ANTONY even got to duet with his old hero, BOY GEORGE, who joined the likes of RUFUS WAINWRIGHT, DEVENDRA BANHART and LOU REED on a privileged guestlist.

Album rating: ANTONY AND THE JOHNSONS (*7) / I AM A BIRD NOW (*8)

ANTONY – vocals, piano / with **FRANCOIS GEHEN** – bass / **TODD COHEN** – drums / **BABY DEE** – harp / **WILLIAM BASINSKI** – clarinet / **CADY FINLAYSON** + **LIZ MARANVILLE** – violins / **MARIANA DAVENPORT** – flute / **BARB MORRISON** – clarinet, saxophone / **VICKY LEAVITT** – cello / **CHARLES NEILSON** – guitar effects

not iss. | Durtro

2000. (cd) *<DURTRO 050CD>* **ANTONY AND THE JOHNSONS** [–] [ ]
– Twilight / Cripple and the starfish / Hitler in my heart / The atrocities / River of sorrow / Rapture / Deeper than love / Divine / Blue angel.

—— retained **TODD** + recruited **REUBEN BUTCHART** – piano / **STEVE BROWN** – bass / **JOAN WASSER** – viola / **MAXIM MOSTON** + **JULIANN KLOPOTIC-JOHNSON** – violins / **JULIA KENT** – cello

not iss. | Rebis

2001. (cd-ep) *<Rebis 01CD>* **I FELL IN LOVE WITH A DEAD BOY** [–] [ ]
– I fell in love with a dead boy / Mysteries of love / Soft black stars.

Secretly Canadian | Secretly Canadian

Jul 04. (re-cd) *<(SC 104CD)>* **ANTONY AND THE JOHNSONS** [ ] [ ]
(re-iss. Aug05; same)

—— now with **JULIA KENT** + **KEVIN BARKER**

Nov 04. (12"ep/cd-ep) *<(SC 113/+CD)>* **THE LAKE ep** [ ] [ ]
– The lake / Fistful of love (w/ LOU REED) / The horror has gone. *(re-iss. Aug05; same)*

Rough Trade | Secretly Canadian

Jan 05. (cd/lp) *(RTRAD CD/LP 223)* *<SC 105>* **I AM A BIRD NOW** [16] Feb05 [ ]
– Hope there's someone / My lady story / For today I am a boy / Man is the baby / You are my sister / What can I do? / Fistful of love / Spiralling / Free at last / Bird Gerhl.

May 05. (cd-s) *(RTRADSCD 229)* *<SC 114>* **HOPE THERE'S SOMEONE / FRANKENSTEIN / JUST ONE STAR / ('A'-video)** [44] Dec04 [ ]

Oct 05. (cd-s) *<SC 130>* **YOU ARE MY SISTER / POOREST EAR / FOREST OF LOVE / PADDY'S GONE** [–] [ ]

Nov 05. (7"/cd-s; feat. BOY GEORGE) *(RTRADS/+CD 276)* **YOU ARE MY SISTER. / POOREST EAR** [39] [–]
(cd-s) *(RTRADSCDX 276)* – ('A') / Forest of love / Paddy's gone / ('A'-video).

Fiona APPLE

Born: FIONA APPLE MAGGART, 13 Sep'77, New York City, New York, USA; her unmarried parents were separated when she was four. Raised most of her childhood by her jazz-loving mother and her BEATLES-obsessed step-father, FIONA found her solace in the poetry of Maya Angelou. However, more trauma was just around the corner when at the age of only twelve, she was raped outside her mother's apartment. Taking up singing as a way of channeling her emotions, FIONA was discovered by music publicist, Kathy Schenker (her babysitter at the time!), who sent her bedroom-cut demo on to 'Clean Slate' records boss, Andy Slater ('Sony'/'Work' would subsequently give it backing). In July '96 and after over eighteen months in the making, FIONA's debut album 'TIDAL' made the shops. Described as ALANIS MORISSETTE or LAURA NYRO with angst to spare, the impressive album subsequently caught the attention of the American buying public and finally crawled all the way up to No.15 in the charts. One of it's highlights, 'CRIMINAL', took the Best Female Rock Performance Award at the 1998 Grammies, while another 'SLEEP TO DREAM' was released as a UK single. At the turn of the century, FIONA was already setting new boundaries by releasing her follow-up set, 'WHEN THE PAWN HITS . . .', the longest album title ever! (the full title taken from a poem). Released late into 1999 (early 2000 in Britain), the album hit No.13 in the Billboard charts, producer Jon Brion getting results from the youngest and most promising lady in recent years to grace the jazz-pop music world. In the ensuing saga of recording 'EXTRAORDINARY MACHINE', unreleased – whether at the behest of 'Sony' or APPLE herself – tracks found their way on to the internet, although the version which finally reached the shops in October 2005, had been completed by Mike Elizondo, finishing the production work that Jon Brion had originally started. Given APPLE's increasingly oblique, elongated style, a hit single was always unlikely although the album itself reached the US Top 10 (a personal record).

Album rating: TIDAL (*7) / WHEN THE PAWN . . . (*8) / EXTRAORDINARY MACHINE (*8)

FIONA APPLE – vocals, piano / with session people

Columbia | Clean Slate – Epic

Sep 96. (cd/c) *(483750-2/-4)* *<67439>* **TIDAL** [ ] Jul96 [15]
– Sleep to dream / Sullen girl / Shadowboxer / Criminal / Slow like honey / The first taste / Never is a promise / The child is gone / Pale September / Carrion. *(cd re-iss. Apr00; same)*

Apr 97. (c-s) *(664428-4)* **SLEEP TO DREAM / PALE SEPTEMBER** [ ] [–]
(10"+=/cd-s+=) *(664428-0/-2)* – Never is a promise / Sullen girl.

Jun 98. (c-s/cd-s) *(6834)* *<78595>* **CRIMINAL / SLEEP TO DREAM (live)** [ ] Sep97 [21]

Jul 98. (c-s/cd-s) *<110509>* **SHADOWBOXER / (version) / NEVER IS A PROMISE / CARRION (live)** [–] [ ]

Feb 00. (cd-s) *(668996-2)* *<4630>* **FAST AS YOU CAN / SLEEP TO DREAM / I KNOW** [ ] Nov99 [33]
(cd-s) *(668996-5)* – ('A') / Never is a promise (live) / Across the universe (live).

Feb 00. (cd/c) *(496428-2/-4)* *<69195>* **WHEN THE PAWN HITS THE CONFLICTS HE THINKS LIKE A KING WHAT HE KNOWS THROWS THE BLOWS WHEN HE GOES TO THE FIGHT AND HE'LL WIN THE WHOLE THING 'FORE HE ENTERS THE RING THERE'S NOBODY TO BATTER WHEN YOUR MIND IS YOUR MIGHT SO WHEN YOU GO SOLO, YOU HOLD YOUR OWN HAND AND REMEMBER THAT DEPTH IS THE GREATEST OF HEIGHTS AND IF YOU KNOW WHERE YOU STAND, THEN YOU KNOW WHERE TO LAND AND IF YOU FALL IT WON'T MATTER, CUZ YOU'LL KNOW THAT YOU'RE RIGHT** [46] Nov99 [13]
– On the bound / To your love / Limp / Love ridden / Paper bag / A mistake / Fast as you can / The way things are / Get gone / I know.

Jul 00. (cd-s) *(669633-2)* **PAPER BAG / FAST AS YOU CAN (video) / LIMP (video) / PAPER BAG (video)** [ ] [–]

Epic | Epic

Oct 05. (cd/d-lp) *<(82876 73636-2)>* *<86683-2/S1>* **EXTRAORDINARY MACHINE** [ ] [7]
– Extraordinary machine / Get him back / O' sailor / Better version of me / Tymps (the sick in the head song) / Parting gift / Window / Oh well / Please please please / Red red red / Not about love / Waltz (better than fine). *(d-cd w/dvd+=)* – Not about love (video) / Extraordinary machine (live) / River, stay away from my door (live) / Fast as you can (live) / You belong to me (live) / Parting gift (live).

ARAB STRAP

Formed: Falkirk, Scotland . . . 1995 by AIDAN MOFFAT and MALCOLM MIDDLETON. The former had already given up his day job at the local Sleeves record shop to team up with songwriter, JASON "JT" TAYLOR, in his outfit, BAY. This low-key band with drummer! AIDAN (augmented on their second release by RONNIE YOUNG, WILL HEGGIE – ex-COCTEAU TWINS – and ROSS BALLANY), released a couple of RED HOUSE PAINTERS-esque CD's, namely 'HAPPY BEING DIFFERENT' (1994) and 'ALISON RAE' (1995), the latter including a Lo-Fi cover of Roxy Music's 'IN EVERY DREAM HOME A HEARTACHE' and also coming free with an acoustic CD featuring a version of Nick Drake's 'WHICH WILL'. AIDAN, meanwhile, was plotting his own breakaway group, ARAB STRAP (named after a device used for horse-breeding and better known for something bought from a sex shop), re-establishing a friendship with MALCOLM while writing songs together in the latter's bedroom. A debut ARAB STRAP single, 'THE FIRST BIG WEEKEND', was warmly received by the music press in September '96, critics describing it as "trainspotting for the music world". AIDAN's drug/drink-fuelled life was portrayed in painful detail in a couple of the narrative songs from debut album, 'THE WEEK NEVER STARTS ROUND HERE' (incidentally the rhythm section was completed by GARY MILLER and DAVID GOW). His bittersweet, off-the-cuff, Scots-accented sagas of broken romance were squeezed between Lo-Fi mumblings of occasional pure genius – several of these provided by their equally wasted pal, JOHN MAUCHLINE. MALCOLM's guitar-plucking, meanwhile, came from the laid back school of cool, often played while literally lying on his back. The album was heralded by many (including John Peel) as the next big thing in exotic sound. It included seminal classics, 'THE CLEARING', 'COMING DOWN', 'I WORK IN A SALOON', 'WASTING' and 'DEEPER'. Their live set (including an early afternoon spot at Scotland's 'T In The Park' that added a host of singalong friends), was a mixture of apathy-in-concrete attitude with most people shouting for their favourite, 'THE FIRST BIG

WEEKEND'; the track was subsequently used as the backing (with a new coherent talker!) on the Guinness ad (yes, that one that says about 38 per cent of all strippers were educated in a convent!). A year on, with word of mouth cult status ensured, ARAB STRAP finally achieved minor chart glory when 'THE GIRLS OF SUMMER' EP dented the Top 75. Following on from a double header tour with drinking buddies, MOGWAI, the now bearded AIDAN and Co delivered a surprise Top 50 hit, 'HERE WE GO' (a double A-side with 'TRIPPY'), one of the many low-rent, X-rated classics on their Top 40 Spring 1998 follow-up, 'PHILOPHOBIA'. Having signed up with 'Go Beat' early in '99, ARAB STRAP proceeded to deliver a disappointing stop-gap limited-edition live set, 'MAD FOR SADNESS'. Four months later, the 'CHERUBS' EP made amends and was one of the highlights of their rush-released third studio album, the over commercialised 'ELEPHANT SHOE'. However, after a two year vacation from the music scene, The 'STRAP returned in 2001 with their deeply poetic fourth outing 'THE RED THREAD'. Theme'd, as ever, around sex and love and drinking in the central belt of Scotland, the duo refused to change their style of song structure. But with single 'LOVE DETECTIVE' harking back to ARAB STRAP's earlier moments (thumping house beats, accompanied by MIDDLETON's sparse guitar playing) and closing track 'TURBULENCE' delivering a fine closure – if not conclusion – it's a wonder why this pair of talented musicians even strayed from their nest in the first place. Of late, AIDAN and a plethora of other, mainly Scottish musicians/singers, have got together for one set, 'Y'ALL GET SCARED NOW, YA HEAR' (2001) under the REINDEER SECTION banner. September 2002 was certainly an eventful month for MOFFAT and MIDDLETON with the release of both solo projects: the former with the LUCKY PIERRE minimalist instrumental set, 'HYPNOGOGIA', the latter with his solo effort, '5.14 FLUOXYTINE SEAGULL ALCOHOL JOHN NICOTINE' – the jury was certainly out on MOFFAT's noodlings. The Falkirk duo returned in 2003 with possibly their most courageous and adventurous work to date, the brilliant 'MONDAY AT THE HUG AND PINT'. A gloomy affair in places, but uplifting in others, MOFFAT and MIDDLETON added local jazzman BILL WELLS to the mix along with pipers, wind instruments and celloists to create an altogether alt-Celtic album (check out the beautiful chanter solo of 'LOCH LEVEN INTRO'). Highlights included the stinging revenge song 'FUCKING LITTLE BASTARDS' in which MOFFAT rebuked his "fake friends", the eerie slide-guitar driven 'PEEP-PEEP', which was just classic STRAP, and the fact that AIDAN attempted to sing in tune and pulled it off added to its appeal. After a quiet 2004, the following year saw the release of two 'STRAP-related projects: MALCOLM MIDDLETON's sophomore solo album, 'INTO THE WOODS' and – though it seems hard to believe – ARAB STRAP's 7th long-player, 'THE LAST ROMANCE'. Which didn't mean that AIDAN was the last romantic, although the brassy 'THERE IS NO ENDING' almost approached BELLE & SEBASTIAN levels of carefree abandon. Diehard miserabilists take heart though; most of the rest of the album found the MOFFAT man slouching between Trainspotting monologue and closing-time poetry.

• **Covers:** IS YOUR LOVE IN VAIN? (Bob Dylan) / YOU ONLY TELL ME YOU LOVE ME WHEN YOU'RE DRUNK (Pet Shop Boys) / NEW YEAR (Sugababes) / WHY CAN'T THIS BE LOVE (Van Halen) / YOU SHOOK ME ALL NIGHT LONG (Ac/Dc).

Album rating: THE WEEK NEVER STARTS ROUND HERE (*8) / PHILOPHOBIA (*8) / MAD FOR SADNESS (*6) / ELEPHANT SHOE (*7) / THE RED THREAD (*8) / MONDAY AT THE HUG AND PINT (*7) / THE LAST ROMANCE (*7) / Lucky Pierre: HYPNOGOGIA (*4) / Malcolm Middleton: 5.14 FLUOXYTINE SEAGULL ALCOHOL JOHN NICOTINE (*6) / INTO THE WOODS (*7)

AIDAN MOFFAT – vocals, keyboards (ex-BAY) / **MALCOLM MIDDLETON** – guitar / **GARY MILLER** – bass / **DAVID GOW** – drums

Chemikal Underground | Chemikal Undergrou

Sep 96. (7") *(Chem 007)* **THE FIRST BIG WEEKEND. / GILDED** | | -

— interruptions/tape narrative by **JOHN MAUCHLINE**

Nov 96. (lp/cd) *(<Chem 010/+cd>)* **THE WEEK NEVER STARTS ROUND HERE** | | 1997
– Coming down / The clearing / Driving / Gourmet / I work in a saloon / Wasting / General plea to a girlfriend / The first big weekend / Kate Moss / Little girls / Phone me tonight / Blood / Deeper.

Mar 97. (12"/cd-s) *(Chem 013/+cd)* **THE CLEARING (guest starring Isobel Campbell & Chris Geddes). / (remixed by Hungry Lions) (remixed by Iain Hanlon & Jonathan Hilditch)** | | -

Sep 97. (12"ep/cd-ep) *(Chem 017/+cd)* **THE GIRLS OF SUMMER E.P.** | 74 | -
– Hey! fever / Girls of summer / The beautiful barmaids of Dundee / One day, after school.

Nov 97. (7"m) *(LISS 22)* **THE SMELL OF OUTDOOR COOKING. / THEME TUNE / BLACKSTAR** | | -
(above issued on 'Lissy's', below on 'Too Many Cooks')

1998. (7") *(BROTH 001)* **LIVE: PACKS OF THREE. / BLOOD** | | -

Chemikal Underground | Matador

Mar 98. (10"/cd-s) *(Chem 20 t/cd)* **HERE WE GO. / TRIPPY** | 48 | -

Apr 98. (cd) *(Chem 21cd)* <OLE 315> **PHILOPHOBIA** | 37 | May98
– Packs of three / Soaps / Here we go / New birds / One day, after school / Islands / The night before the funeral / Not quite a yes / Piglet / Afterwards / My favourite muse / I would've liked me a lot last night / The first time you're unfaithful.

Sep 98. (7") *(Chem 27)* **(AFTERNOON) SOAPS. / PHONE ME TOMORROW** | 74 | -
(12"+=/cd-s+=) *(Chem 27 t/cd)* – ('A') / Toy fights / Forest hills.

Go Beat | not iss.

May 99. (cd/lp) *(547387-2/-1)* **MAD FOR SADNESS (live)** | | -
– Intro – My favourite muse / Packs of three / New birds / Toy fights / Here we go / Phone me tomorrow / Girls of summer / Piglet / Blood / Afterwards. *<US cd-iss. Jul00 on 'Jetset'; 029>*

Aug 99. (12"ep/cd-ep) *(GOB X/CD 21 – 561263-1/-2)* **CHERUBS E.P.** | | -
– Cherubs / Motown answers / An eventful day / Pulled.

— next with guests, CORA BISSETT, BARRY BURNS + ALAN WYLIE

Sep 99. (cd/lp) *(547805-2/-1)* **ELEPHANT SHOE** | | -
– Cherubs / One four seven one / Pyjamas / Autumnal / Lay the day free / Direction of strong man / Tanned / Aries the ram / The drinking eye / Pro-(your) life / Hello daylight. *<US cd-iss. Jun00 on 'Jetset'; 028>*

Chemikal Underground | Matador

Nov 00. (12"/cd-s) *(Chem 048/+cd)* **FUKD ID VOL.2 EP** | | -
– Rocket, take your turn / Blackness.

Jan 01. (12"/cd-s) *(Chem 049/+cd)* **LOVE DETECTIVE. / BULLSEYE / WE KNOW WHERE YOU LIVE** | 66 | -

Feb 01. (lp/cd) *(Chem 050/+cd)* <OLE 503> **THE RED THREAD** | |
– Amor veneris / Last orders / Scenery / The Devil-tips / The long sea / Love detective / Infrared / Screaming in the trees / Haunt me / Turbulence.

May 01. (12"/cd-s) *(Chem 051/+cd)* **TURBULENCE (mixes by BIS, ARAB STRAP & JASON FAMOUS)** | | -

— now without GOW + MILLER

Apr 03. (lp/cd) *(Chem 065/+cd)* <OLE 577> **MONDAY AT THE HUG AND PINT** | |
– The shy retirer / Meanwhile, at the bar, a drunkard muses / Fucking little bastards / Peep-peep / Flirt / Who named the days? / Loch Leven intro / Loch Leven / Glue / Act of war / Serenade / The week never starts round here / Pica Luna.

Sep 03. (12"ep/cd-ep) *(Chem 067/+cd)* **THE SHY RETIRER** | | -
– The shy retirer (radio mix) / Why can't this be love / The good part / The new Saturday / You shook me all night long / The shy retirer (Dirty Hospital remix).

Chemikal Underground | Transdreame

Oct 05. (7") *(Chem 081)* **DREAM SEQUENCE. / DEAD AIR** | | -

Oct 05. (cd) *(Chem 082cd)* <2031> **THE LAST ROMANCE** | | Feb06
– Stink / (If there's) No hope for us / Chat in Amsterdam, Winter 2003 / Don't ask me to dance / Confessions of a big brother / Come round and

love me / Speed-date / Dream sequence / Fine tuning / There is no ending. <*US*+=> – El Paso song / Go back to the sea.

Feb 06. (7") *(Chem 086)* **SPEED-DATE. / (PREFACE) SET THE SCENE / GIRL I LOVED BEFORE I FUCKED** [ ] [–]

LUCKY PIERRE

— aka (French DJ) AIDAN MOFFAT with the FORCE

Lucky not iss.

Feb 99. (7"promo) *(LUCKY 1)* **PIERRE'S FINAL THOUGHT: TWO SONGS BY LUCLY PIERRE** [–] [–]
– Chloe / Sometimes I feel like a motherless child.

Jul 99. (12"promo) *(LUCKY 2)* **BLANK FOR YOUR OWN MESSAGE. / (+ 2)** [–] [–]

Melodic not iss.

May 02. (7") *(MELO 011)* **ANGELS ON YOUR BODY. / BOGEY ON MY SIX** [ ] [–]

Sep 02. (lp/cd) *(MELO 013/+CD)* **HYPNOGOGIA** [ ] [–]
– Angels of your body / Nurse flamingo / Shatterproof / Ghost two / The heart of all that is / The bit in the woods / Sometimes I feel like a motherless child / White Heaven in Hell / Ghost one / Bedwomb.

BEN TRAMER

aka **AIDAN MOFFAT** with **JASON FAMOUS** (of JOHNNY 7)

Chemikal Underground not iss.

Oct 02. (12"/cd-s) *(Chem 059 t/cd)* **HALLOWEEN THEME. / THE SHAPE LURKS / LAURIE'S THEME (HALLOWEEN 1978)** [ ] [–]

MALCOLM MIDDLETON

with **JEANNY REAVE** – vocals (of EVA) + **BARRY BURNS**

Chemikal Underground Chemikal Underground

Sep 02. (cd) *(<Chem 062cd>)* **5.14 FLUOXYTINE SEAGULL ALCOHOL JOHN NICOTINE** [ ] Oct03 [ ]
– Crappo the clown / Wake up / The loneliest night of my life come calling / Best in me / Cold winter / Bring down (preprise) / Rotten heart / Speed on the M9 / 1, 2, 3, 4 / Birdwatcher / The king of bring / Devil and the angel.

May 05. (7") *(Chem 080)* **LONELINESS SHINES. / NO MODEST BEAR** [ ] [–]

May 05. (cd) *(<Chem 076cd>)* **INTO THE WOODS** [ ] Aug05 [ ]
– Break my heart / Devastation / Loneliness shines / No modest bear / Monday night nothing / Bear with me / A happy medium / Autumn / Burst Noel / Choir / Solemn thirsty / A new heart.

Sep 05. (7") *(Chem 085)* **BREAK MY HEART. / A NEW HEART / A MOANING SHITE** [ ] [–]

Ryanair not iss.

Dec 05. (7") *(SLOW 02)* **RYANAIR SONG. / CIGARETTE** [ ] [–]

the ARCADE FIRE

Formed: Montreal, Quebec, Canada . . . June 2003 by songwriting team, WIN BUTLER and his Haitian-descended wife-to-be REGINE CHASSAGNE. Recruiting fellow multi-instrumentalists RICHARD REED PARRY, TIMOTHY KINGSBURY, HOWARD BILERMAN, WILLIAM BUTLER and occasional friends to their ARCADE army, the band condensed their avant-garde, new wave and native French-Canadian influences into an eponymous, self-financed debut EP. Doubtless on the strength of hearing the record, Chapel Hill-based US indie 'Merge' signed them for North America, generating an almost universal critic concensus with the delivery of debut album, 'FUNERAL' (2004). British fans had to make do with imports until a re-ignited 'Rough Trade' fanned the flames with a general release early in 2005. Like a New Wave chamber-music reincarnation of the HANDSOME FAMILY, the BUTLER-CHASSAGNE aesthetic jerked to the dysfunctional groove of early TALKING HEADS and reeked of quasi-Gallic intrigue/WATERBOYS-esque Celtic mysticism, flaying the competition with a series of baroquely-linked (via a bizarre 'NEIGHBORHOOD' theme) hit singles/tracks: '#1 (TUNNELS)', '#2 (LAIKA), '#3 (POWER OUT' and '#4 (KETTLES)'. Epic in scale and anthemic of chorus, successive hit singles, 'REBELLION (LIES)' and 'WAKE UP', rekindled 'FUNERAL's chart pyre.

• **Covers:** MY BUDDY (Alvino Rey) / BRAZIL (Ary Baroso & Ed Russell) / THIS MUST BE THE PLACE (NAIVE MELODY) (Talking Heads).

Album rating: FUNERAL (*9)

WIN BUTLER – vocals, guitars, piano, synth, bass / **REGINE CHASSAGNE** – vocals, drums, synth, piano, accordion, xylophone, recorders, percussion / **RICHARD REED PARRY** – rickenbacker, synth, organ, piano, accordion, xylophone, percussion, upright bass / **TIMOTHY KINGSBURY** – bass, guitars / **HOWARD BILERMAN** – drums, guitar / **WILLIAM BUTLER** – bass, xylophone, percussion, synth / plus **SARAH NEUFELD** – violin / **OWEN PALLETT** – violin / **MICHAEL OLSEN** – cello

not iss. own label

Nov 03. (cd-ep) <*29569*> **ARCADE FIRE** [–] [ ]
– Old flame / I'm sleeping in a submarine / No cars go / The woodlands national anthem / My heart is an apple / Headlights look like diamonds / Vampire – Forest fire.

Rough Trade Merge

Jun 04. (ltd;cd-s) <*MRG 253*> **NEIGHBORHOOD #1 (TUNNELS) / MY BUDDY** [–] [ ]

Feb 05. (cd/lp) *(RTRAD CD/LP 219)* <*MRG 255*> **FUNERAL** [ ] Sep04 [ ]
– Neighborhood #1 (Tunnels) / Neighborhood #2 (Laika) / Une Annee sans lumiere / Neighborhood #3 (Power out) / Neighborhood #4 (Kettles) / Crown of love / Wake up / Haiti / Rebellion (Lies) / In the backstreet.

Mar 05. (7"/cd-s) *(RTRAD S/CD 225)* **NEIGHBORHOOD #2 (LAIKA). / MY BUDDY** [30] [–]

May 05. (7"/cd-s) *(RTRAD S/CD 232)* **NEIGHBORHOOD #3 (POWER OUT). / POWER OUT (August session)** [26] Oct05 [ ]
(7") *(RTRADSX 232)* – ('A') / This Must Be The Place (Naive Melody).

Aug 05. (7"clear) *(RTRADS 254)* <*MRG 275*> **COLD WIND. / BRAZIL** [52] [ ]

Aug 05. (cd-ep;re-) <*MRG 248*> **ARCADE FIRE** [–] [ ]

Sep 05. (7"white) *(RTRADS 252)* **REBELLION (LIES). / REBELLION (LIES) (live)** [19] [–]
(dvd-s+=) *(RTRADSDVD 252)* – ('A'-live from the Much..).
(cd-s) *(RTRADSCD 252)* – ('A') / Brazil.

Nov 05. (7"etched) *(RTRADS 286)* **WAKE UP** [29] [–]

Jan 06. (cd; re-) *(as prev)* **FUNERAL** [33] [–]

□ ARCADIA (see under ⇒ DURAN DURAN)

ARCTIC MONKEYS

Formed: Sheffield, England . . . 2003 by ALEX TURNER, JAMIE COOK, ANDY NICHOLSON and MATT HELDERS. So popular now that their 2005 debut single, 'FIVE MINUTES WITH..' changes hands for over £300, ARCTIC MONKEYS success story is one of the more unlikely of recent years, built on the digital DIY ethos of internet self-promotion. Caged by 'Domino' (home of FRANZ FERDINAND) for over a year, the Sheffield simians finally released their debut single proper, 'I BET YOU LOOK GOOD ON THE DANCEFLOOR' in the autumn of '05. Charming record buyers with its lippy, cram-it-all-in phrasing and tales-of-everyday-insight lyrics, the track entered the charts at No.1, confounding commercial and critical expectation. Early 2006 saw the 'MONKEYS climb to the top of the charts again via follow-up single, 'WHEN THE SUN GOES DOWN', another shrewdly observed urban vignette tracing the missing link between modish punk, Brit-Pop and the LIBERTINES. The old guitar-music-is-dead proclamations were definitively shot out of the water with the release of 'WHATEVER PEOPLE SAY I AM, THAT'S WHAT I'M NOT' (2006) the fastest selling debut album in rock/pop history. The 'MONKEYS were even in the US Top 30 while the Brits & NME hailed them as "Best New Act/Band" at their annual awards.

Alex Turner of ARCTIC MONKEYS

Album rating: WHATEVER PEOPLE SAY I AM, THAT'S WHAT I'M NOT (*9)

ALEX TURNER (b. 1986) – vocals, lead guitar / **JAMIE "Cookie" COOK** – rhythm guitar / **ANDY NICHOLSON** – bass / **MATT "The Cat" HELDERS** (b. 1986) – drums

Bang Bang | not iss.

May 05. (ltd;7"/cd-s) *(BANGB 7/CD 1)* **FIVE MINUTES WITH ARCTIC MONKEYS** [ ] [–]
– Fake Tales Of San Francisco / From The Ritz To The Rubble.

Domino | Domino

Oct 05. (7") *(RUG 212)* **I BET YOU LOOK GOOD ON THE DANCEFLOOR. / BIGGER BOYS AND STOLEN SWEETHEARTS** [1] Mar06 [ ]
(cd-s+=)<10"+=> *(RUG 212CD)* <DNO 070> – Chun Li's Spinning Bird Kick.

Jan 06. (7") *(RUG 216)* **WHEN THE SUN GOES DOWN. / SETTLE FOR A DRAW** [1] [ ]
(cd-s) *(RUG 216-1)* – ('A') / Settle for a draw / Seven.
(12") <DNO 080> – (all above).

Feb 06. (cd/lp) *(WIG CD/LP 162)* <DNO 086> **WHATEVER PEOPLE SAY I AM, THAT'S WHAT I'M NOT** [1] [24]
– The view from the afternoon / I bet you look good on the dancefloor / Fake tales of San Francisco / Dancing shoes / You probably couldn't see for the lights but you were looking straight at me / Still take you home / Riot van / Red light indicates doors are secured / Mardy bum / Perhaps vampires is a bit strong but.. / When the sun goes down / From the Ritz to the rubble / A certain romance.

Apr 06. (10"ep/cd-ep) *(RUG 226/+CD)* **WHO THE FUCK ARE ARCTIC MONKEYS EP** [36] dl-s [–]
– The view from the afternoon / Cigarette smoker Fiona / Despair in the departure lounge / No buses / Who the fuck are Arctic Monkeys?

— **NICK O'MALLEY** – bass (ex-DODGEMS) repl. NICHOLSON

ASH

Formed: Downpatrick, County Down, N. Ireland ... 1989 by TIM WHEELER (then 12 years of age) and MARK HAMILTON, although it would take a few years before they completed the trio with RICK McMURRAY. ASH's precocious talents were quickly spotted by American record moguls eager for more punk-centric guitar music which would also cross over to the pop market. Though they eventually opted to sign with 'Reprise', the trio had already released their debut set, 'TRAILER' on 'Infectious'. Their starry-eyed, bushy-tailed but ultimately derivative blend of indie punk finally became a part of the pop vocabulary when the catchy 'GIRL FROM MARS' sky-rocketed into the UK Top 20 in summer '95. This was pursued by another Top 20 hit later that year in 'ANGEL INTERCEPTOR'. With the hype machine going into overload, the group hit the UK Top 5 in spring of the following year with 'GOLDFINGER', the single trailing a No.1 album, '1977' (1996). Apparently a reference to the year 'Star Wars' was released rather than any reference to safety-pins and saliva, the record included all their hit singles to date and confirmed their increasingly melodic approach. Keeping their profile high with festival appearances, the band later added another guitarist, CHARLOTTE HATHERLEY in summer '97. She made her debut on ASH's theme for the much lauded Ewan McGregor/Cameron Diaz film, 'A LIFE LESS ORDINARY', another Top 10 in late '97. While the indie scene continues to cry out for something innovative, it remains difficult to envisage any figureheads less ordinary than ASH (songs!). Surprisingly 'Kerrang!-friendly, the quartet lost a little of their indie cred with the release of their third album proper, 'NU-CLEAR SOUNDS' (1998), a record that quickly vacated the Top 10 with the accompanying single, 'JESUS SAYS', only managing to make a Top 20 placing. With sex (group, that is), drugs (abuse) and rock'n'roll (Tim Wheeler in the buff!) all the ingredients were in the latest promo instalment for ASH's single 'NUMBSKULL'. Unfortunately the viewing public, and for that matter the buying public, didn't get much of a look-in, as the EP (like many others at the turn of the century) was ineligible for the charts via a new ruling by those pesky compilers. Older and wiser, the ASH posse returned in 2001 with their first material of the new millennium, 'FREE ALL ANGELS'. Previewed by the hits, 'SHINING LIGHT' and 'BURN BABY BURN' (also to feature on forthcoming compilation, 'INTERGALACTIC SONIC SEVENS'), the record recaptured some of their mid-period spunk and used it to temper the aural hangover of its predecessor. While there was plenty of Americanised muscle, 'MELTDOWN's flaming heavy-metal sleeve wasn't the whole story. Released in 2004, the record went Top 5, covering all the usual bases from post-grunge to power ballad on hits, 'ORPHEUS', 'STARCROSSED' and 'RENEGADE CAVALCADE'. The album was also the last to feature solo bound CHARLOTTE HATHERLEY, who'd released her own LP, 'Grey Will Fade' (2004).

• **Songwriters:** WHEELER or w/ HAMILTON except covers; PUNKBOY (Helen Love) / GET READY (Temptations) / DOES YOUR MOTHER KNOW (Abba) / LOSE CONTROL (Backwater) / BLEW (Nirvana) / WHO YOU DRIVIN' NOW? (Mudhoney) / EVERYBODY'S HAPPY NOWADAYS (Buzzcocks). • **Trivia:** The cover sleeve of their single, 'KUNG FU', had a photo of French former Man U star footballer, Eric Cantona, giving his famous throat and neck tackle on an abusive Crystal Palace supporter in 1995.

Album rating: TRAILER mini (*7) / 1977 (*9) / LIVE AT THE WIRELESS live official bootleg (*5) / NU-CLEAR SOUNDS (*7) / FREE ALL ANGELS (*6) / INTERGALACTIC SONIC SEVENS compilation (*8) / MELTDOWN (*7)

TIM WHEELER (b. 4 Jan'77) – vocals, guitar / **MARK HAMILTON** – bass / **RICK McMURRAY** – drums

La La Land | not iss.

Feb 94. (7") *(LA LA 001)* **JACK NAMES THE PLANETS. / DON'T KNOW** [ ] [–]

Infectious | Reprise

Aug 94. (7"ep) *(INFECT 13S)* **PETROL. / THE LITTLE POND / A MESSAGE FROM OSCAR WILDE AND PATRICK THE BREWER** [ ] [–]
(cd-s+=) *(INFEVT 13CD)* – Things. *(re-iss. Nov96; same)*

Oct 94. (cd/c/lp) *(INFECT 14 CD/MC/LP)* <45985> **TRAILER** [ ] Oct95 [ ]
– Season / Message from Oscar Wilde and Patrick the brewer / Jack names the planets / Intense thing / Uncle Pat / Message from Mr. Waterman / Get out / Petrol / Obscure thing. *(lp w/ free 7"yellow) (INFECT 14S)* SILVER SURFER. / JAZZ '59 *<diff.tracks US> (re-iss. Jan01 cd/c/lp; INFECT 14 CD/MC/LPX)*

Oct 94. (7") *(INFECT 16S)* **UNCLE PAT. / DIFFERENT TODAY** [ ] [–]
(cd-s+=) *(INFECT 16CD)* – Hulk Hogan bubble bath. *(re-iss. Nov96; same)*

Mar 95. (7") *(INFECT 21J)* <17706> **KUNG FU. / DAY OF THE TRIFFIDS** [57] Nov95 [ ]
(cd-s+=) *(INFECT 21CD)* – Luther Ingo's star cruiser. *(re-iss. Nov96 & Jan01; same)*

Jul 95. (7"/c-s) *(INFECT 24S/24MC)* **GIRL FROM MARS. / CANTINA BAND** [11] [–]
(cd-s+=) *(INFECT 24CD)* – Astral conversations with Toulouse Lautrec. *(re-iss. Nov96 & Jan01; same)*

Sep 95. (7"colrd-various) <G26> **PETROL. / PUNKBOY** [–] [ ]

Oct 95. (7"/c-s/cd-s) *(INFECT 27S/27MC/27CD)* **ANGEL INTERCEPTOR. / 5 A.M. ETERNAL / GIVE ME SOME TRUTH** [14] [–]
(re-iss. cd-s Nov96 & Jan01; same)

Dec 95. (7"red) *(FP 004)* **GET READY. / ZERO ZERO ZERO** [ ] [–]
(above 45 issued on 'Fantastic Plastic')

Apr 96. (7"/c-s) *(INFECT 39 S/MC)* **GOLDFINGER. / I NEED SOMEBODY / SNEAKER** [5] [–]
(cd-s+=) *(INFECT 39CD)* – Get ready. *(re-iss. Nov96 & Jan01; same)*

May 96. (cd/c/lp) *(INFECT 40 CD/MC/LP)* <46191> **1977** [1] [ ]
– Lose control / Goldfinger / Girl from Mars / I'd give you anything / Gone the dream / Kung Fu / Oh yeah / Let it flow / Innocent smile / Angel interceptor / Lost in you / Darkside lightside. *(cd+=hidden track)* – Sick of vomiting. *(lp re-iss. Jan01; same)*

Jun 96. (7"yellow/c-s) *(INFECT 41 S/MC)* **OH YEAH / T. REX / EVERYWHERE IS ALL AROUND / OH YEAH (quartet version)** [6] [–]
(cd-s) *(INFECT 41CD)* – (first 3 tracks) / Does your mother know. *(re-iss. Nov96 & Jan01; same)*

— added **CHARLOTTE HATHERLEY** (b.20 Jun'79, England) – guitar (ex-NIGHTNURSE)

Infectious Dreamworks

Oct 97. (7"blue/c-s) *(INFECT 50 S/MC)* **A LIFE LESS ORDINARY. / WHERE IS LOVE GOING / WHAT DEANER WAS TALKING ABOUT** [10] [–]
(cd-s+=) *(INFECT 50CD)* – Halloween. *(re-iss. Jan01; same)*

Sep 98. (7") *(INFECT 059S)* **JESUS SAYS. / TAKEN OUT** [15] [–]
(c-s+=/cd-s+=) *(INFECT 059 MCS/CDS)* – Heroin, vodka, white noise.
(cd-s) *(INFECT 059CDSX)* – ('A'side) / Radiation / Dancing on the Moon. *(re-iss. Jan01; same)*

Oct 98. (cd/c/lp) *(INFECT 060 CD/MC/LP)* <50121> **NU-CLEAR SOUNDS** [7] Sep99 [ ]
– Projects / Low ebb / Jesus says / Wild surf / Death trip 21 / Folk song / Numbskull / Burn out / Aphrodite / Fortune teller / I'm gonna fall. *(re-iss. Jan01; same)*

Nov 98. (7") *(INFECT 061S)* **WILD SURF. / STORMY WATERS** [31] [–]
(c-s+=/cd-s+=) *(INFECT 061 MCS/CDS)* – When I'm tired.
(cd-s) *(INFECT 061CDSX)* – ('A'side) / Lose control / Gonna do it soon. *(re-iss. Jan01; same)*

— added on tour **DJ DICK KURTAINE** – turntables

Apr 99. (d7"red-ep) *(INFECT 62)* **NUMBSKULL EP** [ ] [–]
– Numbskull / Blew / Who you drivin' now? / Jesus says (live).
(cd-ep+=) *(INFECT 62EP)* – Girl from Mars (live) / Fortune teller (live). *(re-iss. Jan01; same)*

Jan 01. (7"/c-s) *(INFECT 98 S/MCS)* **SHINING LIGHT. / WARMER THAN FIRE** [8] [–]
(cd-s+=) *(INFECT 98CDS)* – Gabriel.
(cd-s) *(INFECT 98CDSX)* – ('A'side) / Feel no pain / Jesus says (headrock valley beats lightyear 12"mix) / ('A'-CD-ROM video).

Apr 01. (7") *(INFECT 99S)* **BURN BABY BURN. / THINKING ABOUT YOU** [13] [–]
(cd-s+=) *(INFECT 99CDSX)* – Submission (Arthur Baker remix).
(cd-s) *(INFECT 99CDS)* – ('A'side) / 13th floor (session) / Only in dreams (session).

Apr 01. (cd/c/lp) *(INFECT 100 CD/MC/LP)* **FREE ALL ANGELS** [1] [–]
– Walking barefoot / Shining light / Burn baby burn / Candy / Submission / Someday / Pacific palisades / Shark / Sometimes / Nicole / There's a star / World domination.

Jul 01. (d7") *(INFEC 101S)* **SOMETIMES. / SKULLFULL OF SULPHUR / SO THE STORY GOES. / TEENAGE KICKS** [21] [–]
(cd-s) *(INFEC 101CDS)* – (first 3 tracks) / ('A'-video).
(cd-s) *(INFEC 101CDSX)* – (first & fourth tracks) / Melon farmer (live) / (video mixer update).

Oct 01. (d7") *(INFEC 106S)* **CANDY. / WATERFALL // NOCTURNE. / STAY IN LOVE FOREVER** [20] [–]
(cd-s) *(INFEC 106CDS)* – (first 3 tracks) / ('A'-video).
(cd-s) *(INFEC 106CDSX)* – (first & fourth tracks) / Sweetness of death by the obsidian knife.

Jan 02. (cd-s) *(INFEC 112CDS)* **THERE'S A STAR / NO PLACE TO HIDE / COASTING / THERE'S A STAR (video)** [13] [–]
(cd-s) *(INFEC 112CDSX)* – ('A'side) / Here comes the music / Grey will fade / (video excerpts).

Aug 02. (cd-s) *(INFEC 119CDS)* **ENVY / TONIGHT YOU BELONG TO ME / I SHALL NOT DIE** [21] [–]
(cd-s) *(INFEC 119CDSX)* – ('A'side) / Bad karma blues / I don't mind.
(d7"+=) *(INFEC 119S)* – I shall not die.

Sep 02. (cd/d-lp) *(INFEC 120 CD/LP)* **INTERGALACTIC SONIC SEVENS** (compilation) [3] [–]
– Burn baby burn / Envy / Girl from Mars / Shining light / A life less ordinary / Goldfinger / Jesus says / Oh yeah / Jack names the planets / Sometimes / Kung Fu / Candy / Angel interceptor / Uncle Pat / Wildsurf / Walking barefoot / Petrol / There's a star / Numbskull. *(2xcd+=/4xlp+=; INFEC 120CDB)* – No place to hide / Warmer than fire / Where is our love going / Taken out / 13th floor / Stormy waters / Message from Oscar Wilde / Who you drivin' now / Stay in love forever / Sweetness of death by the obsidian knife / Melon farmer / Nocturne / Gabriel / Coasting / Lose control / I need somebody / Sneaker / Cantina band / Astral conversations with Toulouse Lautrec / Day of the triffids / Hallowe'en / Thinking about you.

May 04. (7") *(ASH 01)* **ORPHEUS. / EVERYBODY'S HAPPY NOWADAYS** [13] [–]
(cd-s+=) *(ASH 01CD)* – Tinsel town.
(dvd-s) *(ASH 01DVD)* – ('A') / Tinsel town / ('A'-video) / Clones (video) / (making of Orpheus – behind the scenes video).

May 04. (cd) *(5046 73197-2)* <3197> **MELTDOWN** [5] Jun04 [ ]
– Meltdown / Orpheus / Evil eye / Clones / Starcrossed / Out of the blue / Renegade cavalcade / Detonator / On a wave / Won't be saved / Vampire love. *(d-cd+=; 5046 73246)* – (live versions).

Jul 04. (7") *(ASH 02)* **STARCROSSED. / COOL IT DOWN** [22] [–]
(dvd-s+=) *(ASH 02DVD)* – ('A'-video) / Girl from Mars (video) / Star Wars Republic Commander (video trailer).
(cd-s) *(ASH 02CD)* – ('A') / Solace.

Oct 04. (7") *(ASH 03)* **RENEGADE CAVALCADE. / SHOCKWAVE** [33] [–]
(cd-s) *(ASH 03CD)* – ('A') / We don't care.
(dvd-s) *(ASH 03DVD)* – ('A') / ('A'-video) / Jesus says (video) / ('A'-unseen video clip).

— CHARLOTTE HATHERLEY released her debut solo single, 'SUMMER' (UK No.31), from her set, 'GREY WILL FADE', in Aug'04 (UK hit 51)

— she would leave ASH early 2006

– compilations, etc. –

Feb 97. (cd) *Death Star; (DEATH 3)* **LIVE AT THE WIRELESS** (live) [ ] [–]
– Darkside lightside / Girl from Mars / Oh yeah / T.Rex / I'd give you anything / Kung Fu / What Deaner was talking about / Goldfinger / Petrol / A clear invitation to party. *(lp-iss.Jan01; DEATH 3LP)*

Dec 02. (cd-s) *Double Dragon; (DD 2007)* **JACK NAMES THE PLANETS** [ ] [–]

☐ Richard ASHCROFT (see under ⇒ the VERVE)

☐ ASPHALT RIBBONS (see under ⇒ TINDERSTICKS)

ASSOCIATES

Formed: Dundee, Scotland ... 1979 by BILLY MACKENZIE and ALAN RANKINE, who had worked as a duo in 1976 (the ABSORBIC ONES). After a debut single on their own 'Double-Hip' label, they signed to Chris Parry's 'Fiction', a subsidiary of 'Polydor' records. Their glorious debut set, 'THE AFFECTIONATE PUNCH', was followed by a series of highly rated 45's for the independent 'Situation 2' label. In 1982, they enjoyed their first taste of success when stylish 'PARTY FEARS TWO' and 'CLUB COUNTRY' both hit the UK Top 20. Energetic alternative dance rock, featuring high, passionate vocals of MACKENZIE, the ASSOCIATES inimitable, unclassifiable sound enjoyed only a very brief liaison with the pop charts. Now signed to 'Warners', the group's more accessible 'SULK' (1982) album made the UK Top 10, its lavish arrangements, white funk and stirring vocal histrionics going down well amid the craze for all things "New Romantic". Despite this belated recognition, the pair subsequently went their separate ways, losing their commercial momentum in the process. When they finally got back together in 1984 (with a line-up of STEVE GOULDING, IAN McINTOSH, ROBERT SUAVE and L. HOWARD JONES), MACKENZIE and RANKINE recorded only one further single together, 'THOSE FIRST IMPRESSIONS', before the latter finally bowed out. The remaining members recorded the 'PERHAPS' (1985) album, a relative flop which saw a further set, 'THE GLAMOUR CHASE' shelved and MACKENZIE returned in 1990 with an album on the 'Circa' label, 'WILD AND LONELY', to little reaction. The ASSOCIATES name had seemingly been laid to rest when, a couple of years later, the singer released a solo set, 'OUTERNATIONAL'. The next five years were quiet as MACKENZIE attended to his beloved greyhounds in his native Dundee. The music world was shocked, when, on the 22nd January '97, it was announced that he had taken his own life (overdose of presciption drugs), reportedly depressed after the death of his mother a little earlier. Ironically, MACKENZIE had signed to the hip 'Nude' label (home of SUEDE), and had been working on new material at the time of his death. This material was posthumously released as 'BEYOND THE SUN', pundits and public alike mourning the death at 39 of one of music's forgotten geniuses.

• **Songwriters:** Lyrics / music by duo (until RANKINE's departure), except BOYS KEEP SWINGING (David Bowie) / LOVE HANGOVER (Diana Ross) / GLOOMY SUNDAY (Lewis-Seress) / GOD BLESS THE CHILD (Billie Holiday) / HEART OF GLASS (Blondie) / KITES (Simon Dupree & The Big Sound) / GROOVIN' WITH MR. BLOE (Mr. Bloe) / GREEN TAMBOURINE (Lemon Pipers) / I'M GONNA RUN AWAY FROM YOU (Tammi Lynn).
• **Trivia:** MACKENZIE featured on B.E.F.'s (HEAVEN 17) single 'IT'S OVER' circa '82.

Album rating: THE AFFECTIONATE PUNCH (*6) / FOURTH DRAWER DOWN singles compilation (*9) / SULK (*7) / PERHAPS (*5) / WILD AND LONELY (*4) / POPERA: THE SINGLES COLLECTION compilation (*8) / DOUBLE HIPNESS collection (*4) / SINGLES double compilation (*8) / Billy MacKenzie: OUTERNATIONAL (*5) / BEYOND THE SUN (*8)

BILLY MACKENZIE (b. WILLIAM MacARTHUR MacKENZIE, 27 Mar'57) – vocals / **ALAN RANKINE** – keyboards, guitar, etc

Double Hip | not iss.

Oct 79. (7") *(DHR 1)* **BOYS KEEP SWINGING. / MONA PROPERTY GIRL** [ ] [–]
(re-iss. Dec79 on 'M.C.A.'; MCA 537)

— added **NIGEL GLOCKER** – drums / guest **ROBERT SMITH** – guitar (of-CURE) who replaced unknown guitarist

Fiction | not iss.

Aug 80. (7") *(FICS 11)* **THE AFFECTIONATE PUNCH. / YOU WERE YOUNG** [ ] [–]
Aug 80. (lp/c) *(FIX/+C 5)* **THE AFFECTIONATE PUNCH** [ ] [–]
– The affectionate punch / Amused as always / Logan time / Paper house / Trans-port to Central / A matter of gender / Even dogs in the wild / Would I . . . bounce back / Deeply concerned / A. *(remixed & re-iss. Nov82; FIXD 5) (re-iss. Aug83 on 'Polydor' lp/c; SPE LP/MC 33) (cd-iss. Oct04 on 'POlydor'; 9821060)*

— **JOHN MURPHY** (b. Australia) – drums repl. GLOCKER (to TOYAH)

Situation 2 | not iss.

Apr 81. (7"/12") *(SIT 1/+12)* **TELL ME EASTER'S ON FRIDAY. / STRAW TOWELS** [ ] [–]
(re-iss. but w-drawn Nov82 on 'Beggars Banquet'; BEG 86)
Jun 81. (7") *(SIT 4)* **Q: QUARTERS. / KISSED** [ ] [–]
(12"+=) *(SIT 4T)* – Q: Quarters (original).
Aug 81. (7"/12") *(SIT 7/+T)* **KITCHEN PERSON. / AN EVEN WHITER CAR** [ ] [–]
Oct 81. (7"/12") *(SIT 10/+T)* **MESSAGE OBLIQUE SPEECH. / BLUE SOAP** [ ] [–]
Nov 81. (7"/12") *(SIT 11/+T)* **WHITE CAR IN GERMANY. / THE ASSOCIATE** [ ] [–]
Jan 82. (lp/c) *(SITU 2/+C)* **FOURTH DRAWER DOWN** [ ] [–]
– White car in Germany / A girl named Property / Kitchen person / Q; quarters / Tell me Easter's on Friday / The associate / Message oblique speech / An even whiter car. *(re-iss. Nov82 on 'Beggars Banquet' lp/c; BEGA/BEGC 43) (cd-iss. Apr02 on 'V2'+=; VVR 101202-2)* – Fearless (it takes a full moon) / Point St. / Straw towels / Kissed / Blue soap.

R.S.O. | not iss.

1981. (7"/12"; as 39, LYON STREET) *(RSO/+X 78)* **KITES. / A GIRL NAMED POVERTY** [ ] [–]

— added **MICHAEL DEMPSEY** – bass (of CURE) / **MARTHA LADLY** – backing vocals (ex-MARTHA & THE MUFFINS)

Associates | WEA

Mar 82. (7"/12") *(ASC 1/+T)* **PARTY FEARS TWO. / IT'S BETTER THIS WAY** [9] [ ]
May 82. (7") *(ASC 2)* **CLUB COUNTRY. / IT'S YOU AGAIN** [13] [ ]
(12"+=) *(ASC 2T)* – Ulcragyceptemol.
Jun 82. (lp/c) *(ASCL/ASCC 1)* **SULK** [10] [–]
– It's better this way / Party fears two / Club country / Love hangover / 18 carat love affair / Arrogance gave him up / No / Skipping / Nothing in something particular / Arrogance gave him up / White car in Germany / Gloomy Sunday / The associate. *(re-iss. Oct82 on 'WEA' lp/c; 240 005-1/-4) (cd-iss. Jul88 on 'WEA'; K 240005-2) (cd re-iss. Apr02 on 'V2'; VVR 101201-2)*
Jul 82. (7") *(ASC 3)* **18 CARAT LOVE AFFAIR. / LOVE HANGOVER** [21] [ ]
(12"+=) *(ASC 3T)* – Voluntary wishes, swapit production.

— split & re-formed 1984 by **MACKENZIE + RANKINE** recruiting **STEVE GOULDING** – drums / **IAN McINTOSH** – rhythm guitar / **ROBERT SUAVE** – bass / **L. HOWARD JONES** – keyboards

WEA | WEA

May 84. (7"/ext.12") *(YZ 6/+T)* **THOSE FIRST IMPRESSIONS. / THIRTEEN FEELINGS** [43] [ ]

— **STEPHEN REID** – guitar; repl. RANKINE who joined PAUL HAIG. He also had a solo career between 1986-87, releasing two albums, 'THE WORLD BEGINS TO LOOK HER AGE' for 'Crepescule' and 'SHE LOVES ME NOT' for 'Virgin'

Aug 84. (7"/ext.12") *(YZ 16/+T)* **WAITING FOR THE LOVE BOAT. / SCHAMP OUT** [53] [ ]
Jan 85. (7"/7"pic-d) *(YZ 28/+P)* **BREAKFAST. / BREAKFAST ALONE** [49] [ ]
(12"+=) *(YZ 28T)* – Kites.
Feb 85. (lp/c) *(WX 9/+C)* **PERHAPS** [23] [ ]
– Those first impressions / Waiting for the love boat / Perhaps / Schampout / Helicopter helicopter / Breakfast / Thirteen feelings / The stranger in your voice / The best of you / Don't give me that I told you so look.
Oct 85. (7") *(YZ 47)* **TAKE ME TO THE GIRL. / PERHAPS** [ ] [–]
(ext.12"+=) *(YZ 47T)* – The girl that took me / ('A'instrumental).
(10"+=) *(YZ 47TE)* – God bless the child (live) / Even dogs in the wild (live) / The boy that Santa Claus forgot (live).

— The above 'A'side was later (in Mar88) covered by group/artist JIH.

— (early 1986) HUGHES and SUAVE joined PETE MURPHY

— **MACKENZIE** now used session people under The ASSOCIATES

Sep 88. (7") *(YZ 310)* **HEART OF GLASS. / HER ONLY WISH** [56] [ ]
(3"cd-s+=) *(YZ 310CD)* – Breakfast / Those first impressions.
('A'-Auchterhouse mix-12"+=) *(YZ 310T)* – ('A'-Auchterhouse instrumental).
(12"+=) *(YZ 310TX)* – ('A'-Temperamental mix) / Heavens blue.
Nov 88. (w-drawn lp/c)(cd) *(WX 222/+C)(244619-2)* **THE GLAMOUR CHASE** [–] [–]
Jan 89. (w-drawn 7") *(YZ 329)* **COUNTRY BOY. / JUST CAN'T SAY GOODBYE** [–] [–]
(w-drawn 12"+=) *(YZ 329T)* – Heart of glass (dub mix).
(w-drawn 3"cd-s++=) *(YZ 329CD)* – Take me to the girl.

Circa | Charisma

Mar 90. (c/cd/lp) *(CIRC/+D/A 11)* **WILD AND LONELY** [71] [ ]
– Fire to ice / Fever / People we meet / Just can't say goodbye / Calling all around the world / The glamour chase / Where there's love / Something's got to give / Strasbourg Square / Ever since that day / Wild and lonely / Fever in the shadows.
Apr 90. (7"/c-s) *(YR/+C 46)* **FEVER. / FEVER IN THE SHADOWS** [ ] [–]
(12"+=/s12"+=/3"cd-s+=/cd-s+=) *(YR T/TB/CD/CDT 46)* – Groovin' with Mr.Bloe.
Aug 90. (7"/c-s) *(YR/+C 49)* **FIRE TO ICE. / GREEN TAMBOURINE** [ ] [–]
(ext.12"+=) *(YRT 49)* – The glamour chase.
(10"++=/ext.cd-s++=) *(YR TX/CD 49)* – Groovin' with Mr.Bloe.
Sep 90. (12"ep) *<096448>* **FIRE TO ICE (mixes) / GREEN TAMBOURINE** [–] [ ]
Jan 91. (7"/c-s) *(YR/+C 56)* **JUST CAN'T SAY GOODBYE. / ONE TWO THREE** [ ] [–]
(12") *(YRT 56)* – ('A'-Time Unlimited mix) / ('A'-Time Unlimited instrumental) / ('A'-US mix).
(12") *(YRTX 56)* – ('A'-Time Unlimited mix) / ('A'-Time Unlimited instrumental) / ('A'-Karma mix).
(cd-s) *(YRCD 56)* – ('A'side) / ('A'-Time Unlimited piano mix) / ('A'-US version) / I'm gonna run away from you.

BILLY MACKENZIE

Jun 92. (7") *(YR 86)* **BABY. / SACRIFICE AND BE SACRIFICED (CH 8032 mix)** [ ] [–]
(cd-s+=) *(YRCD 86)* – Grooveature (D 1000 mix) / Colours will come (US 60659 mix).
(12") *(YRT 86)* – ('A'side) / Colours will come (Larry Heard remix) / Opal krush / Colours will come (Raw Stylus remix).
Aug 92. (7") *(YR 91)* **COLOURS WILL COME. / OPAL KRUSH** [ ] [–]
(12"+=/cd-s+=) *(YRT/YRCD 91)* – Look what you've done / Feels like the richtergroove.
Sep 92. (c/cd) *(CIRC/+D 22)* **OUTERNATIONAL** [ ] [–]

– Outernational / Feels like the richtergroove / Opal krusch / Colours wil come / Pastime paradise / Groovecture / Sacrifice and be sacrificed / Baby / What made me turn on the lights / Windows cell.

— In Jul'96, BILLY was featured on a single by LOOM, 'ANACOSTIA BAY'.

— Tragically on the 22nd January 1997, BILLY committed suicide in his father's garden shed; he had recently signed to 'Nude' records.

		Nude	not iss.
Oct 97.	(cd) *(NUDE 8CD)* **BEYOND THE SUN**	64	–

– Give me time / Winter academy / Blue it is / 14 mirrors / At the edge of the world / Beyond the sun / And this she knows / Sour jewel / 3 gypsies in a restaurant / Nocturne VII.

— early in 2000, a posthumous CD-album, 'MEMORY PALACE' (credited with PAUL HAIG) was released on 'Rhythm Of Life' *(ROL 003)*

		Rhythm Of Life	not iss.
Mar 01.	(cd; as BILLY MACKENZIE & STEVE AUNGLET) *(ROL 005)* **EUROCENTRIC**		–

– Falling out with the future / Homophobic / 14th Century nightlife / Liberty lounge / When the world was young / Sing that song again / Soul that sighs / Wild is the wind / Mother Earth / Return to love.

– (ASSOCIATES) compilations, others, etc. –

Sep 81.	(7"/12") *Fiction; (FICS/+X 13)* **A. / WOULD I . . . BOUNCE BACK**		–
Nov 82.	(7"/12") *Fiction; (FIXS/+X 16)* **A MATTER OF GENDER. / EVEN DOGS IN THE WILD**		–
Oct 89.	(12"ep/cd-ep) *Strange Fruit; (SFPS/+CD 075)* **THE PEEL SESSIONS** ('82)		–

– It's better this way / Nude spoons / Me myself and the tragic story / Natural gender / Ulcragyceptemol.

Jan 91.	(cd)(lp/c) *East West; (9031 72414-2)(WX 363/+C)* **POPERA**		–

– Party fears two / Club country / 18 Carat love affair / Love hangover / Those first impressions / Waiting for the loveboat / Breakfast / Take me to the girl / Heart of glass / Country boy / The rhythm divine / Waiting for the loveboat (slight return) / Tell me Easter's on Friday / Q; quarters / Kitchen person / Message oblique speech / White car in Germany.

Jan 91.	(7"/c-s) *East West; (YZ 534/+C)* **POPERETTA EP: WAITING FOR THE LOVEBOAT (Slight Return). / CLUB COUNTRY CLUB**		–

(12"+=/cd-s+=) *(YZ 534 T/CD)* – Waiting for the loveboat (extended voyage) / Club country club (Time Unlimited).

Sep 94.	(cd) *Nighttracks; (CDNT 006)* **THE RADIO ONE SESSION**		–
Apr 02.	(d-cd) *V2; (VVR 101203-2)* **DOUBLE HIPNESS** (outtakes, extras & 1993 reunion)		–
May 02.	(d-cd) *Warners; (8573 88496-2)* **THE GLAMOUR CHASE / PERHAPS**		–
Feb 03.	(cd) *Strange Fruit; (SFRSCD 115)* **THE RADIO ONE SESSIONS 1981-1983**		
Jun 03.	(cd) *Strange Fruit; (SFRSCD 118)* **THE BBC RADIO 1 SESSIONS VOL.2 1984-1985**		
May 04.	(d-cd) *V2; (VVR 102771-2)* **SULK / FOURTH DRAWER DOWN**		
Jul 04.	(d-cd) *W.S.M.; (<5046 74010-2>)* **SINGLES**		

☐ Ian ASTBURY (see under ⇒ CULT)

AT THE DRIVE-IN

Formed: El Paso, Texas, USA . . . 1994 by frontman CEDRIC BIXLER and twin guitarists OMAR RODRIGUEZ and JIM WARD. Recorded between bouts of hard-bitten touring, the band's first two 7" singles, 'HELL PASO' and 'ALFARO VIVE, CARAJO' served notice of a hardcore storm brewing in the Texas badlands. Night after night spent playing to dismal crowds was rewarded when 'Flipside' caught them at an empty L.A. bar and signed them up for a debut album, 'ACROBATIC TENEMENT'. Released in early '97, the record's blistering emotional outpourings and precocious mastery of punk dynamics won over critics across the board while another stint of touring – with new recruits TONY and PALL – cultivated a grassroots fanbase. A subsequent mini-set, 'EL GRAN ORGO' was issued on the 'Offtime' imprint later that year, after which followed a period of insecurity as the band searched in vain for a label willing to take on their sophomore album. 'IN CASINO OUT' (1998) was finally sponsored by the independent 'Fearless' operation, a label more often associated with pop/punk fare. Nevertheless, the album – recorded almost entirely live with only a few overdubs – represented the closest ATD-I had yet come to capturing the passionate drive of their live work. Yet more touring ensued as the band played with the likes of FUGAZI and ARCHERS OF LOAF before undertaking their first European jaunt in Spring '99. Later that summer the 'VAYA' EP showed that their relentless road schedule was paying handsome dividends in terms of musical sharpness and songwriting depth, 'Virgin' records signing up the Texas troopers for their third and most highly acclaimed album to date, 'RELATIONSHIP OF COMMAND' (2000). Released on the BEASTIE BOYS' 'Grand Royal' (with whom 'DEN' had merged), produced by Ross 'SLIPKNOT' Robinson and mixed by Andy Wallace, the record had critics reaching for the superlatives in an attempt to describe their unflinchingly honest and unrelentingly intense sound. After disclaiming "indefinite hiatus", ATD had literally split into two camps, the MARS VOLTA, which featured members BIXLER and RODRIGUEZ, and SPARTA, set up by WARD, HINOJOS and HAJJAR. The former, who issued the brilliant 'TREMULANT' EP in 2002, had strayed away from their restrictive "emo" tag and began performing rambunctious live shows which often leaned towards the experimental. IKEY OWENS of the Long Beach Dub All-Stars lended a hand, as did MICHAEL WARD (both flirted with prog-dub outfit DE FACTO). While the MARS VOLTA recreated the same volatile intensity as SCRATCH ACID and MELT BANANA, SPARTA would ultimately stick with the hard-edged punk formula of early BLACK FLAG and FUGAZI (circa 'Repeater'). After issuing the heavily criticised 'AUSTERE' EP on Spielberg/Geffen's 'Dreamworks' imprint, the group issued the overtly angst and typically difficult 'WIRETAP SCARS' (2002), a mixed bag of guitar-fuelled disdain and post-punk noise that had a distinct aftertaste of regret, worry and self-doubt. After ATD-I went their separate ways, much was hanging on what its abandoned members would do next. RODRIGUEZ and CEDRIC BIXLER were obviously going to stick together, as they had been best friends since childhood and shared the same enthusiastic and diverse musical tastes. It came as no surprise then when they announced their new project, the MARS VOLTA and issued an EP 'TREMULANT' in 2002, a record which whet the appetites of music critics and fans alike. Also recruiting JEREMY MICHAEL WARD and IKEY OWENS, they headed into the studio to record the schizophrenic and fractured debut album 'DE-LOUSED IN THE COMATORIUM' (2003), which took ATD-I's hardcore punk edge, put it in a blender and mixed it all up until it was practically unrecognisable. Mixing free-jazz, funk, metal and prog, the album truly did amaze and the MARS VOLTA were critically hailed by many as the new KING CRIMSON. After touring with the RED HOT CHILI PEPPERS, WARD sadly died of a drug overdose at the age of 27. SPARTA returned with their sophomore set, 'PORCELAIN', in summer 2004, an album of market-ready post-grunge which, while not scaling the heights of the emo hordes, managed a respectable Top 60 place. Meanwhile, back at the MARS VOLTA station, OMAR A. RODRIGUEZ-LOPEZ ventured into a deep space solo mission, 'A MANUAL DEXTERITY: SOUNDTRACK VOLUME ONE' (2004). Music for an unfinished movie, the mostly instrumental album saw OMAR orbiting around radioactive clusters of jazz noise, warped salsa and black hole ambience. Like a Krautrock OS MUTANTES beaming up LED

ZEPPELIN in a parallel dimension, MARS VOLTA's 'FRANCES THE MUTE' (2005) ranked as some of the most wigged-out music to ever grace the US Top 5 (UK Top 30), and certainly the most wigged-out music with Latin spirit. As 'SCAB DATES' (2005) suggested though, the songs rarely remained the same, at least in a live environment where the likes of '..COMATORIUM' highlight 'CICATRIZ' shapeshifted into a five part psychedelic suite.

• **Covered:** TAKE UP THY STETHOSCOPE AND WALK (Pink Floyd) / THIS NIGHT HAS OPENED MY EYES (Smiths).

Album rating: ACROBATIC TENEMENT (*7) / IN/CASINO/OUT (*7) / RELATIONSHIP OF COMMAND (*7) / THIS STATION IS NON-OPERATIONAL anthology (*8) / Sparta: WIRETAP SCARS (*7) / PORCELAIN (*7) / the Mars Volta: DE-LOUSED IN THE COMATORIUM (*7) / FRANCES THE MUTE (*8) / SCAB DATES (*6) / Omar A. Rodriguez-Lopez: A MANUAL DEXTERITY: SOUNDTRACK VOLUME ONE (*6)

CEDRIC BIXLER-ZAVALA (b. 4 Nov'74, Redwood City, Calif.) – vocals / **OMAR RODRIGUEZ-LOPEZ** (b. 1 Sep'75, Bayamon, Puerto Rico) – guitar / **JIM WARD** (b.21 Sep'76) – guitar, vocals

not iss. | Western Breed – Offtime

Dec 94. (7"m) **HELL PASO. / RED PLANET / EMPTINESS IS A MULE** [–] [ ]

Jun 95. (7"ep) **ALFARO VIVE, CARAJO!. / BRADLEY SMITH / INSTIGATE THE ROLE** [–] [ ]
<re-iss. 1990's on 'Headquarter'>

not iss. | Flipside

Feb 97. (cd) *<FLIP 94CD>* **ACROBATIC TENEMENT** [–] [ ]
– Star flight / Schaffino / Ebroglio / Initiation / Communication drive-in / Skips on the record / Paid vacation time / Ticklish / Blue tag / Coating of arms / Porfirio Diaz. *(UK-iss.Jan00; same as US) (UK re-iss. Aug04 on 'Restart'; RES 94CD) (UK re-iss. Dec04 on 'V2'; VVR 103030-2)*

—— added **PALL HINOJOS** (b.17 Jul'75, Los Angeles, Calif.) – bass / **TONY HAJJAR** (b.17 Aug'74) – drums

not iss. | One Foot – Offtime

Sep 97. (cd-ep) *<62>* **EL GRAN ORGO** [–] [ ]
– Give it a name / Honest to a fault / Winter month novelty / Fahrenheit / Picket fence cartel / Speechless.

Fearless | Fearless

Jul 98. (cd) *<F 034CD>* **IN/CASINO/OUT** [–] [ ]
– Alpha Centauri / Chanbara / Hulahoop wounds / Napoleon Solo / Pickpocket / For now . . . we toast / A devil among tailors / Shaking hand incision / Lopsided / Hourglass / Transatlantic foe. *(UK-iss.Aug00; same as US) (UK re-iss. Dec04 on 'V2'; VVR 103027-2)*

Nov 98. (7") **DOORMAN'S PLACEBO. / (other track by AASSEE LAKE)** [–] [ ]

—— <above iss. on 'Nerd' records>

Oct 99. (12"ep) *(F 040-1)* **VAYA** [–] [ ]
– Rascuache / Proxima centauri / Ursa minor / Heliotrope / Metrognome arthritis / 300 MHz / 198d. *(UK-iss.Oct99; same as US) (cd-ep iss.Aug00; FO 40CD) (cd-ep re-iss. Dec04 on 'V2'; VVR 103028-2)*

Thick | Thick

Mar 00. (7"pic-d) *<(THK 066)>* **CATACOMBS. / (other by Burning Airlines)** [ ] [ ]
(UK re-iss. Oct00; same)

Big Wheel | Big Wheel

May 00. (12"ep/cd-ep) *<(BWR 0223/+CD)>* **BIG WHEEL RECREATION** [ ] [ ]
– Extracurricular / Autorelocator / (two others by Sunshine).

Grand Royal | Grand Royal

Aug 00. (7") *<(GR 91)>* **ONE ARMED SCISSOR. / PATTERN AGAINST USER** [64] [ ]
(cd-s+=) *<(GR 91CD)>* – Incetardis.

Virgin | Virgin

Sep 00. (cd/lp) *(CDVUS/VUSLP 184) <49999>* **RELATIONSHIP OF COMMAND** [33] [ ]
– Arcarsenal / Pattern against user / One armed scissor / Sleepwalk capsules / Invalid litter dept. / Mannequin republic / Enfilade / Rolodex propaganda / Quarantined / Cosmonaut / Non-zero possibility / Catacombs. *(UK re-iss. Dec04 on 'V2'; VVR 103029-2)*

Oct 00. (7"colrd) **BUDDYHEAD. / (other by Murder City Devils)** [–] [ ]

Dec 00. (7") *(VUS 189)* **ROLODEX PROPAGANDA. / EXTRACURRICULAR** [54] [–]
(cd-s+=) *(VUSCD 189)* – One armed scissor (Lamacq version).

Mar 01. (7") *(VUS 193)* **INVALID LITTER DEPT. / INITIATION (Lamacq version)** [50] [–]
(cd-s+=) *(VUSCD 193)* – Quarantined (Lamacq version).
(cd-s) *(VUSDX 193)* – ('A'side) / Take up thy stethoscope and walk (Lamacq version) / Metrognome arthritis.

—— split later in 2001

– compilations, etc. –

May 05. (cd) *V2; (VVR 103246-2) / Fearless; <30074>* **THIS STATION IS NON-OPERATIONAL** [ ] [ ]
– Fahrenheit / Picket fence cartel / Chanbara / Lopsided / Napoleon Solo / Pickpocket / Metronome arthritis / 1986 / One armed scissor / Enfilade / Non-zero possibility / Incetardis / Doorman's placebo / Autorelocator / Rascuache / This night has opened my eyes / Take up thy stethoscope and walk. *(special cd w/dvd+=; VVR 103246-8)* – (videos).

the MARS VOLTA

CEDRIC BIXLER-ZAVALA + OMAR RODRIGUEZ-LOPEZ with **JEREMY MICHAEL WARD + IKEY OWENS**

Gold Standard | Gold Standard

Mar 02. (12"ep/cd-ep) *<(GSL 54/+CD)>* **TREMULANT EP** [ ] [ ]
– Cut that city / Concertina / Eunuch provocateur.

Universal | Universal

Jun 03. (cd) *(9860460) <59302>* **DE-LOUSED IN THE COMATORIUM** [43] [39]
– Son et lumiere / Inertiatic ESP / Roulette dares (the haunt of) / Tira me a las Aranas / Drunkship of lanterns / Eriatarka / Cicatriz ESP / This apparatus must be unearthed / Televators / Take the veil Cerpin taxt. *(d-lp iss.Jul03 on 'Gold Standard' +=; GSL 75LP)* – Ambuletz.

M.C.A. | Universal

Sep 03. (10") *(MCST 40352)* **INERTIATIC ESP. / DRUNKSHIP OF LANTERNS (FM session)** [42] [–]
(cd-s) *(MCSTD 40352)* – ('A'side) / Roulette dares (the haunt of) (XFM session) / ('A'-video).

Mar 04. (10"yellow) *(MCST 40352)* **TELEVATORS. / ERIATARKA (live from the Electric Ballroom)** [41] [–]
(cd-s+=) *(MCSTD 40352)* – ('A'-video).

Apr 04. (cd-ep) *<620921>* **TELEVATORS EP** [–] [ ]
– Televators / Roulette dares (the haunt of) / Drunkship of lanterns / Cicatriz ESP (live) / Televators (live).

—— added **JUAN ALDERETE** – bass / **MARCEL RODRIGUEZ** – percussion

Nov 04. (12"green) *<GSL 95>* **FRANCES THE WIDOW. / THE WIDOW (live acoustic version)** [–] [95]
(above on 'Gold Standard')

Feb 05. (cd) *(2103977) <00041290-2>* **FRANCES THE MUTE** [23] Mar05 [4]
– Cygnus . . . Vismund Cygnus: a) Sarcophagi, b) Umbilical syllables, c) Facilis descenus averni, d) Con safo / The widow / L'via l'viaquez / Miranda that ghost just isn't holy anymore: a) Vade mercum, b) Pour another icepick, c) Pisacis (phra-men-ma), d) Con safo / Cassandra Geminni: a) Tarantism, b) Plant a nail in the naval stream, c) Faminepulse, d) Multiple spouse wounds, e) Sarcophagi. *<US t-lp on 'Gold Standard'; GSL 96>*

Mar 05. (12"pic-d/cd-s) *(MCST/+D 40408)* **THE WIDOW. / FRANCES THE MUTE** [20] [–]
(dvd-s) *(MCSVD 40808)* – ('A'-video) / Roulette dares (the haunt of) (video) / Televators (video).

Jul 05. (10"pic-d) *(MCST 40420)* **L'VIA L'VIAQUEZ. / THE BIBLE AND THE BREATHALYZER** [53] [–]
(cd-s) (MCSTD 40420) – ('A'-video).

Nov 05. (cd) *(9886788) <56440-2>* **SCAB DATES** (live) [ ] [76]
– Abrasions mount the timpani / Take the veil carpin taxt / Gust of mutts / And ghosted pouts / Caviglia / Concertina / Haruspex / Cicatrix / Cicatrix (part 1) / Cicatrix (part 2) / Cicatrix (part 3) / Cicatrix (part 4). *(<d-lp iss.Jan06 on 'Gold Standard'; GSL 118>)*

OMAR A. RODRIGUEZ-LOPEZ

Gold Standard | Gold Standard

Aug 04. (cd) *<(GLS 90CD)>* **A MANUAL DEXTERITY: SOUNDTRACK VOLUME ONE** [ ] [ ]
– Around knuckle white tile / Dyna sark arches / Here the tame go by /

Deus ex machina / Dramatic theme / A dressing failure / Sensory decay part 2 / Of blood blue blisters / Dream sequence / The palpitations from a limit.

SPARTA

JIM WARD – vocals, guitar / **PAUL HINOJOS** – guitar / **TONY HAJJAR** – drums / **MATT MILLER** – bass (ex-BELKNAP)

Dreamworks Dreamworks

Apr 02. (cd-s) *(450844-2)* **AUSTERE EP** [ ] [–]
– Mye / Cataract / Vacant skies / Echodyne harmonic (de-mix).

Aug 02. (cd) *(450393-2) <450366>* **WIRETAP SCARS** [ ] [ ]
– Cut your ribbon / Air / Mye / Collapse / Sans cosm / Light burns clear / Cataract / Red alibi / Rx coup / Glasshouse tarot / Echodyne harmonic / Assemble the empire.

Geffen Geffen

Jul 04. (cd) *(9862906) <00028180-2>* **PORCELAIN** [ ] [60]
– Guns of Memorial Park / Hiss the villain / While Oceana sleeps / La cerca / Breaking the broken / Lines in sand / End Moraine / Death in the family / Syncope / Tensioning / Travel by bloodline / P.O.M.E. / FRom now to never / Splinters.

— PAUL HINOJOS became a member of the MARS VOLTA

ATHLETE

Formed: Deptford, South London, England ... early 2000 by longtime friends JOEL POTT, CAREY WILLETS, TIM WANSTALL and STEVE ROBERTS. Alternative-type mavericks with a sound which can readily be deemed undefinable in the same way that the likes of the BETA BAND and SUPER FURRY ANIMALS defy lazy categorization, ATHLETE limbered up in style with their debut EP, 'WESTSIDE'. Released on 'Regal', the track earned a Single Of The Week award from Radio One's Jo Whiley, with follow-up 'YOU GOT STYLE' entering the UK Top 40 a few months later and engendering a major label deal with 'Parlophone' – 'BEAUTIFUL' and 'EL SALVADOR' continuing the minor hit formula. Debut UK Top 20 album 'VEHICLES & ANIMALS' (2003) was unsurprisingly the kind of loose-limbed, horizontally chilled noodling that could only have been made in Britain, with gloriously insinuating hooks and midsummer harmonies easily taking up the slack. In fact if there was a songwriting Olympics, ATHLETE might well run away with a few medals: in 2006, the Top 5 single 'WIRES' scooped an Ivor Novello award for Best Contemporary Song, a track which hailed from acclaimed sophomore album, 'TOURIST' (2005). Like COLDPLAY with exercise-induced endomorphines, ATHLETE's slo-mo chart run continued with 'HALF LIGHT' and minor hits, 'TOURIST' and 'TWENTY FOUR HOURS'.

Album rating: VEHICLES & ANIMALS (*6) / TOURIST (*7)

JOEL POTT – vocals, guitar / **CAREY WILLETS** – bass, vocals / **TIM WANSTALL** – keyboards, vocals / **STEVE ROBERTS** – drums, vocals

Regal not iss.

Mar 02. (10"/cd-s) *(REG 72/+CD)* **WESTSIDE. / DUNGENESS / ONE OF THOSE DAYS** [ ] [–]

Parlophone Astralwerks

Jun 02. (etched-10"/cd-s) *(10/CD ATH 001)* **YOU GOT THE STYLE. / A FEW DIFFERENCES / YOU GOT THE STYLE (remix)** [37] [–]

Nov 02. (7") *(ATH 002)* **BEAUTIFUL. / ON AND ON** [41] [–]
(cd-s+=) *(CDATH 002)* – Another kind of beautiful / ('A'-video).

Mar 03. (7") *(ATH 003)* **EL SALVADOR. / MOVING OUT** [31] [–]
(cd-s+=) *(CDATH 003)* – Loose change.
(cd-s) *(CDATHS 003)* – ('A'side) / Dungeness (live) / You got the style (live) / ('A'-video).

Apr 03. (cd/lp) *(582291-2/-1) <82291>* **VEHICLES & ANIMALS** [19] May04 [ ]
– El Salvador / Westside / One million / Shake those windows / Beautiful / New project / You got the style / Vehicles and animals / Out of nowhere / Dungeness / You know / Le casio. *<US cd+=>* – A few differences / You got the style (CD-rom).

Jun 03. (12") *(12ATH 005)* **WESTSIDE. / COUNT ME IN / WESTSIDE (Elbow mix)** [42] [–]
(cd-s+=) *(CDATHS 005)* – ('A'-video).
(cd-s) *(CDATH 005)* – ('A'live) / Vehicles and animals (live) / One million (live).

Sep 03. (7") *(ATH 006)* **YOU GOT THE STYLE. / HOT SUN PAVEMENT** [42] [–]
(cd-s) *(CDATH 006)* – ('A'side) / Beautiful (live).

Jan 05. (7") *(ATH 007)* **WIRES. / TRANSFORMER MAN** [4] [–]
(cd-s) *(CDATH 007)* – ('A') / Never running out.
(cd-s+=) *(CDATHS 007)* – Get it back / ('A'-video).

Jan 05. (cd) *(560740-2) <73951>* **TOURIST** [1] Mar05 [ ]
– Chances / Half light / Tourist / Trading air / Wires / If I found out / Yesterday threw everything at me / Street map / Modern mafia / Twenty four hours / I love. *(cd w/dvd; 5637040)* – (video versions). *(d-lp iss.Nov05; 560740-1)*

Apr 05. (7") *(ATH 008)* **HALF LIGHT. / HALF LIGHT (Eddy TM losers remix)** [16] [–]
(cd-s) *(CDATH 008)* – ('A') / I've got a question.
(cd-s) *(CDATHS 008)* – ('A') / Forest fire / Wires (live Jo Whiley session).

Aug 05. (7"pic-d) *(ATH 009)* **TOURIST. / HALF LIGHT (BBC6 Music Session)** [43] [–]
(cd-s) *(CDATH 009)* – ('A') / ('A'-Roots Manuva remix).

Nov 05. (7") *(ATH 010)* **TWENTY FOUR HOURS. / BEFORE TOMORROW** [42] [–]
(cd-s) *(CDATH 010)* – ('A') / Stand in the sun / Lay your head.

□ AUDIOSLAVE
(see under ⇒ RAGE AGAINST THE MACHINE)

the AUTOMATIC

Formed: Cowbridge, nr. Cardiff, Wales ... 2002 by ROB HAWKINS, ALEX PENNIE, JAMES FROST and IWAN GRIFFITHS. The latest of a new breed of Welsh gonzoid-poppers, the AUTOMATIC's push-button blend of razorwire indie and hyperkinetic melody together with their 80s fashion sense, saw them find a happy home at 'B-Unique' (alongside KAISER CHIEFS and the ORDINARY BOYS). In the twilight of 2005, the lads issued their debut single, 'RECOVER', also its limited edition status witnessed it falling foul of ever-stricter chart bureaucracy. No such obstacles befell them the following year as 'RAOUL' hit the Top 40 and the NME adopted them as Welsh rarebits, sponsoring a tour with BOY KILL BOY, !FORWARD, RUSSIA! and the LONG BLONDES. One of the most hyped bands since er.. the last one, the AUTOMATIC justified at least some of it by hitting the UK Top 5 with raving festival anthem, 'MONSTER', and the Top 3 with their debut album, 'NOT ACCEPTED ANYWHERE' (2006).

Album rating: NOT ACCEPTED ANYWHERE (*8)

ROB HAWKINS – vocals, bass / **JAMES FROST** – guitar / **ALEX PENNIE** – keyboards / **IWAN GRIFFITHS** – drums

B-Unique Universal

Nov 05. (7") *(BUN 101-7)* **RECOVER. / SONG 6** [ ] [–]
(cd-s+=) *(BUN 101CD)* – ('A') / Jack Daniels.

Mar 06. (7") *(BUN 104-6)* **RAOUL. / TROPHY WIVES** [32] [–]
(cd-s) *(BUN 104CD)* – ('A') / On the campaign trail.

Jun 06. (7") *(BUN 106-7)* **MONSTER. / MONSTER (Trey Prefontaine mix)** [4] [–]
(cd-s) *(BUN 106CD)* – ('A') / Night drive.
(cd-s) *(BUN 106CDX)* – ('A') / High tide on Caroline Street / ('A'-Culprit One remix) / ('A'-video).

Jun 06. (cd) *(BUN 107)* **NOT ACCEPTED ANYWHERE** [3] [–]
– That's what she said / Raoul / You shout, you shout, you shout / Recover / Monster / Lost at home / Keep your eyes peeled / Seriously guys . . . I hate you / On the campaign trail / Team drama / By my ride / Rats.

AZTEC CAMERA

Formed: East Kilbride, Scotland ... early 1980 by 15 year-old, RODDY FRAME, who released two independent 45's on ALAN HORNE's now semi-famous 'Postcard' label, before moving on to 'Rough Trade' in 1982. The following year, RODDY and Co. hit the top of the indie charts (reached Top 30 nationally) with debut album, 'HIGH LAND, HARD RAIN', a largely acoustic-based affair combining folkish flights of fancy, Latin/jazz rhythms and an incisive lyrical flair with stunning results. The record's breezy lead track, 'OBLIVIOUS', was re-issued by new label 'Warners' later that year on the back of the album's success, one of the few AZTEC CAMERA singles to break the Top 20. FRAME brought in a new cast of musicians for 1984's MARK KNOPFLER-produced 'KNIFE' set, including seasoned Scots players CRAIG GANNON and MALCOLM ROSS. A more commercial offering, the record almost made the UK hit in 'ALL I NEED IS EVERYTHING'. After a world tour, FRAME laid low for more than two years, penning material for 'LOVE' (1987), the most successful album of his career. Initially something of a non-starter, this over-produced yet affecting album eventually made the Top 10 almost a year after its release following the massive Top 5 success of the plaintive 'SOMEWHERE IN MY HEART' single. Despite courting the pop mainstream, FRAME's subsequent effort, 'STRAY' (1990) veered off into more eclectic territory, the Top 20 hit, 'GOOD MORNING BRITAIN', featuring MICK JONES of BIG AUDIO DYNAMITE / CLASH fame. The 90's witnessed FRAME developing his earlier style, especially on the 1995 set, 'FRESTONIA'. Come 1998, the Scots veteran had signed to 'Independiente', releasing a minor hit, 'REASON FOR LIVING' which accompanied the relatively low-key pop-rock album, 'THE NORTH STAR'. FRAME was back in 2002 with 'SURF', his most unassuming and low-key recording to date. Stripped back to the bare bones of vocals and acoustic guitar, the record proved that the Scotsman's astute, shrewdly observed and lovingly crafted material needed little or no sonic froth to get its point across. More likely to be playing Ronnie Scott's or the Cambridge Folk Festival than rock venues these days, the forty-something FRAME mellowed out with his third solo set, 'WESTERN SKIES' (2006), its title track originating in a one-off link-up with Radio One DJ, ROB DA BANK.

• **Covered:** JUMP (Van Halen) / DO I LOVE YOU (Cole Porter) / I THREW IT ALL AWAY (Bob Dylan) / BAD EDUCATION (Blue Orchids) / IF PARADISE WAS HALF AS NICE (Amen Corner). • **Trivia:** In autumn '83, while in the States supporting ELVIS COSTELLO, he lied about his age (19) to get into the country.

Album rating: HIGH LAND, HARD RAIN (*8) / KNIFE (*6) / LOVE (*5) / STRAY (*6) / DREAMLAND (*6) / FRESTONIA (*5) / THE BEST OF AZTEC CAMERA compilation (*8) / Roddy Frame: THE NORTH STAR (*5) / SURF (*7) / WESTERN SKIES (*7)

RODDY FRAME (b.29 Jan'64) – vocals, acoustic guitar / **DAVE MULHOLLAND** – drums / **CAMPBELL OWENS** – bass; who repl. ALAN WELSH late in 1980

Postcard — not iss.

Mar 81. (7") *(81-3)* **JUST LIKE GOLD. / WE COULD SEND LETTERS** — –

Jul 81. (7") *(81-8)* **MATTRESS OF WIRE. / LOOK OUTSIDE THE TUNNEL** — –

Sep 81. (lp; w-drawn) *(81-13)* **GREEN JACKET GREY** – –

— (mid-'82) added temp. member **BERNIE CLARK** – keyboards / **DAVE RUFFY** – drums (ex-RUTS) repl. MULHOLLAND

Rough Trade — Sire

Aug 82. (7"/7"pic-d) *(RT 112/+P)* **PILLAR TO POST. / QUEEN'S TATTOO** — –

Jan 83. (7") *(RT 122)* **OBLIVIOUS. / ORCHARD GIRL** 47 –
(12"+=) *(RT 122T)* – Haywire.

Apr 83. (lp) *(ROUGH 47)* *<23899>* **HIGH LAND, HARD RAIN** 22 Aug83
– Oblivious / The boy wonders / Walk out to winter / The bugle sounds again / We could send letters / Pillar to post / Release / Lost outside the tunnel / Back on board / Down the dip. *(cd-iss. Feb87 +=; ROUGHCD 47)* – Haywire / Queen's tattoo / Orchard girl. *(re-iss. Sep93 on 'WEA' cd/c; 4509 92849-2/-4)*

May 83. (7"/12") *(RT/+T 132)* **WALK OUT TO WINTER. / SET THE KILLING FREE** 64

WEA — Sire

Oct 83. (d7") *(AZTEC 1)* **OBLIVIOUS. / ORCHARD GIRL // WE COULD SEND LETTERS (live). / BACK ON BOARD (live)** 18

— **RODDY FRAME** retained **RUFFY** and brought into line-up:- **CRAIG GANNON** – bass (ex-BLUEBELLS) repl. OWENS / added **MALCOLM ROSS** – guitar (ex-ORANGE JUICE, ex-JOSEF K) / guest / **GUY FLETCHER** – keyboards

Aug 84. (7") *(AC 1)* **ALL I NEED IS EVERYTHING. / JUMP** 34
(12") *(AC 1T)* – ('A'-Latin mix) / Jump (Loaded version).

Sep 84. (lp/c)(cd) *(WX 8/+C)(240 483-2)* *<25183>* **KNIFE** 14
– Still on fire / Just like the U.S.A. / Head is happy (heart's insane) / The back door to Heaven / All I need is everything / Backwards and forwards / Birth of the true / Knife. *(cd-iss. Sep93; same)* *(cd re-iss. Jun02 on 'Wounded Bird'+=; WOU 5183)* – AZTEC CAMERA mini-lp tracks.

Nov 84. (7"/7"sha-pic-d) *(AC 2/+P)* **STILL ON FIRE. / WALK OUT TO WINTER**
(12"+=) *(AC 2T)* – Mattress of wire (live) / The boy wonders (live) / The bugle sounds again (live).

Apr 85. (10"m-lp) *<25285>* **AZTEC CAMERA (live)** –
– Birth of the true / Mattress of wire / Jump / The bugle sounds again / Backwards and forwards.

— **FRAME + RUFFY** alongside other session musicians **MARCUS MILLER** – bass / **DAVID FRANK** – keyboards (ex-SYSTEM) / **STEVE JORDAN** – guitar

Sep 87. (7"/ext-12") *(YZ 154/+T)* **DEEP AND WIDE AND TALL. / BAD EDUCATION**

Oct 87. (lp/c)(cd) *(WX 128/+C)(242 202-2)* *<25646>* **LOVE** 10
– Deep and wide and tall / How men are / Everybody is a number one / More than a law / Somewhere in my heart / Working in a goldmine / One and one / Paradise / Killermont Street. *(cd-iss. Sep93; same)*

Jan 88. (7") *(YZ 168)* **HOW MEN ARE. / THE RED FLAG** 25
(12"+=) *(YZ 168T)* – Killermont Street (live) / Pillar to post (live).
(cd-s+=) *(248 028-2)* – Oblivious / All I need is everything.

Apr 88. (7") *(YZ 181)* **SOMEWHERE IN MY HEART. / EVERYBODY IS A NUMBER ONE '86** 3
(12"+=) *(YZ 181T)* – Down the dip / Jump.
(cd-s+=) *(YZ 181CD)* – Walk out to winter / Still on fire.

Jul 88. (7") *(YZ 199)* **WORKING IN A GOLDMINE. / I THREW IT ALL AWAY** 31
(12"+=/12"s+=) *(YZ 199 T/W)* – ('A'version).
(cd-s++=) *(YZ 199CD)* – How men are.

Sep 88. (7") *(YZ 154)* **DEEP AND WIDE AND TALL. / BAD EDUCATION** 55
(12"+=/cd-s+=) *(YZ 154 T/CD)* – More than a law.

— (live band '88: augmenting **FRAME + RUFFY**) **EDDIE KULAK** – keyboards / **GARY SANFORD** – guitar / **PAUL POWELL** – bass

— (by 1990, **FRAME** had lost RUFFY but retained **POWELL** / and new **GARY SANCTUARY** – keyboards / **FRANK TONTOH** – drums / guests **PAUL CARRACK, EDWYN COLLINS, MICKEY GALLAGHER & STEVE SIDELYNK.**

Jun 90. (cd)(lp/c) *(<9031 71694-2>)(WX 350/+C)* **STRAY** 22
– Stray / The crying scene / Get outta London / Over my head / How it is / Good morning Britain (featuring MICK JONES) / The gentle kind / Notting Hill blues / Song for a friend. *(re-iss. cd+c Sep93)*

Jun 90. (7") *(YZ 492)* **THE CRYING SCENE. / TRUE COLOURS** 70
(12"+=/cd-s+=) *(YZ 492 T/CD)* – Salvation.
(10"+=) *(YZ 492X)* – I threw it all away (live).

Sep 90. (7"/c-s; AZTEC CAMERA and MICK JONES) *(YZ 521/+C)* **GOOD MORNING BRITAIN. / ('A'live version)** 19
(12"+=) *(YZ 521T)* – ('A'remix)
(cd-s+=) *(YZ 521CD)* – Consolation prize. (with EDWYN COLLINS)

Jul 92. (7"/c-s) *(YZ 688/+C)* **SPANISH HORSES. / JUST LIKE THE U.S.A. (live)** 52
(cd-s) *(YZ 688CD1)* – ('A'side) / Killermont street (live) / The birth of the true (live) / Song for a friend (live).

(cd-s) *(YZ 688CD2)* – ('A'live version) / Stray (live) / The bugle sounds again (live) / Dolphins (live).

Apr 93. (7"/c-s) *(YZ 740/+C)* **DREAM SWEET DREAMS. / GOOD MORNING BRITAIN (live)** 67 –
(cd-s+=) *(YZ 740CD1)* – Sister Anne (live) / How men are (live).
(cd-s) *(YZ 740CD2)* – ('A'side) / Mattress of wire (live) / Let your love decide (live) / Orchid girl (live).

May 93. (cd/c/lp) *(<4509 92492/-2/-4/-1>)* **DREAMLAND** 21 –
– Birds / Safe in sorrow / Black Lucia / Let your love decide / Spanish horses / Dream sweet dreams / Piano's and clocks / Sister Ann / Vertigo / Valium Summer / Belle of the ball.

Jun 93. (7"/c-s) *(YZ 754/+C)* **BIRDS. / DEEP AND WIDE AND TALL**
(cd-s) *(YZ 754CD1)* – ('A'side) / Working in a goldmine / Knife.
(cd-s) *(YZ 754CD2)* – ('A'side) / Somewhere in my heart / Oblivious / Good morning Britain.

WEA Reprise

Oct 95. (c-s) *(WEA 007C)* **SUN / SUNSET**
(cd-s+=) *(WEA 007CD)* – The crying scene (live).
(cd-s) *(WEA 007CDX)* – ('A'side) / We could send letters (live) / Black Lucia (live) / The rainy season (live).

Nov 95. (cd/c) *(<0630 11929-2/-4>)* **FRESTONIA**
– The rainy season / Sun / Crazy / On the avenue / Imperfectly / Debutante / Beautiful girl / Phenomenal world / Method of love / Sunset.

– compilations, etc. –

Sep 90. (7") *Old Gold; (OG 9945)* **SOMEWHERE IN MY HEART. / OBLIVIOUS** –

— In Nov'90, 'DO I LOVE YOU?' appeared as the extra track on the 12" & cd-s of a Cole Porter tribute by The POGUES and KIRSTY MacCOLL

Oct 94. (cd) *Windsong; (WHISCD 006)* **LIVE ON THE TEST (live)** –

Jul 99. (cd/c) *WEA; (3984 28984-2/-4)* **THE BEST OF AZTEC CAMERA** 36 –
– Oblivious / Good morning Britain / Somewhere in my heart / Working in a goldmine / How men are / Birth of the true / Walk out to winter / Jump / All I need is everything / Deep & wide & tall / The crying scene / Killermont street / Spanish horses / Reason for living.

RODDY FRAME

Independiente Sony

Sep 98. (c-s) *(ISOM 18CS)* **REASON FOR LIVING / WINTER HAVEN HIGH** 45 Nov98
(cd-s) *(ISOM 18MS)* *<66231A>* – Rainy greys and blues.
(cd-s) *(ISOM 18SMS)* *<66231B>* – ('A'side) / Biba nova / The sea is wide.

Sep 98. (cd) *(ISOM 7CD)* *<120123>* **THE NORTH STAR** 55 Nov98
– Back to the one / The north star / Here comes the ocean / River of brightness / Strings / Bigger brighter better / Autumn flower / Reason for living / Sister shadow / Hymn to grace.

Redemption Cooking Vinyl

Aug 02. (cd) *(RRUK 2)* *<COOKCD 117>* **SURF** Oct02
– Over you / Surf / Small world / I can't start now / Abloom / Tough / Big Ben / High class music / Turning the world around / Mixed up love / For what it was.

May 06. (cd) *(RRUK 6)* **WESTERN SKIES** –
– Western skies / The coast / Marble arch / She wolf / Tell the truth / Rock god / Day of reckoning / Shore song / Dry land / Worlds in worlds / Portastudio. *(lp-iss.Jun06 on 'Tuition'; TIN 00901)*

☐ BABYSHAMBLES (see under ⇒ LIBERTINES)

BAD COMPANY

Formed: In late Summer 1973, by the English seasoned-pro foursome of PAUL RODGERS and SIMON KIRKE (both ex-FREE), plus MICK RALPHS and BOZ BURRELL. They got together to form this power-rock supergroup, taking their name from a 1972 Western film starring Jeff Bridges. LED ZEPPELIN manager, PETER GRANT, signed the band to his new 'Swan Song' label in 1974 and they hit the big time almost immediately. No.1 in America, No.3 in the UK, their eponymous debut album set the blueprint; driving music par excellence with RODGERS' heavy, soulful vocals set against a rock solid musical backdrop. These were songs that were built to last, and indeed they have, it's just a pity the cock-rock lyrics haven't aged quite so well. Then again, with such timeless melodic fare as 'CAN'T GET ENOUGH OF YOUR LOVE' and 'BAD COMPANY', maybe the lyrics are beside the point (it was the 70's after all). 'STRAIGHT SHOOTER' (1975) was a bit tougher, yet ultimately more of the same. No bad thing, with the classic 'FEEL LIKE MAKIN' LOVE' on a par with FREE's best efforts. Within such a limited framework, however, there was never much room for experimentation and it was probably inevitable that BAD COMPANY would begin to tread water as they waded through the murky tail end of the 70's. Nevertheless, they continued to sell bucketloads of records and put bums on seats right up until their 1983 parting shot, 'ROUGH DIAMONDS'. While RODGERS went on to solo work, BAD CO. reformed three years later with ex-TED NUGENT frontman, BRIAN HOWE, taking RODGERS' place. Their subsequent releases were lukewarm AOR fodder without the saving grace of the latter's voice, although they sold moderately. Come the 90's, RALPHS was the only remaining member from the original line-up, 'COMPANY OF STRANGERS' in '95 being their last new UK-issued effort to date.

• **Songwriters:** RALPHS penned most. In the 90's RALPHS and HOWE individually co-wrote with THOMAS. • **Note:** watch out! a dance act going by the name of BAD COMPANY exists.

Album rating: BAD CO. (*7) / STRAIGHT SHOOTER (*8) / RUN WITH THE PACK (*4) / BURNIN' SKY (*4) / DESOLATION ANGELS (*5) / ROUGH DIAMONDS (*4) / 10 FROM 6 compilation (*7) / FAME AND FORTUNE (*3) / DANGEROUS ACE (*3) / HOLY WATER (*4) / HERE COMES TROUBLE (*3) / THE BEST OF BAD COMPANY LIVE . . . WHAT YOU HEAR IS WHAT YOU GET collection (*5) / COMPANY OF STRANGERS (*4) / STORIES TOLD AND UNTOLD (*4) / THE ORIGINAL BAD CO. ANTHOLOGY compilation (*8) / IN CONCERT – MERCHANTS OF COOL (*5)

PAUL RODGERS (b.12 Dec'49) – vocals, piano (ex-FREE) / **MICK RALPHS** (b.31 Mar'48) – guitar, piano (ex-MOTT THE HOOPLE) / **BOZ BURRELL** (b. RAYMOND BURRELL, 1946) – bass, vocals (ex-KING CRIMSON, ex-SNAFU) / **SIMON KIRKE** (b.28 Jul'49) – drums (ex-FREE)

Island — Swan Song

May 74. (7") *(WIP 6191)* <70015> **CAN'T GET ENOUGH. / LITTLE MISS FORTUNE** [15] [5]

Jun 74. (lp/c) *(ILPS/ICT 9279)* <8410> **BAD CO.** [3] [1]
– Can't get enough / Rock steady / Ready for love / Don't let me down / Bad company / The way I choose / Movin' on / Seagull. *(cd-iss. Oct94 on 'Atlantic'; 7567 92441-2)*

Jan 75. (7") <70101> **MOVIN' ON. / EASY ON MY SOUL** [–] [19]

Mar 75. (7") *(WIP 6223)* <70103> **GOOD LOVIN' GONE BAD. / WHISKEY BOTTLE** [31] [36]

Apr 75. (lp/c) *(ILPS/ICT 9304)* <8413> **STRAIGHT SHOOTER** [3] [3]
– Good lovin' gone bad / Feel like makin' love / Weep no more / Shooting star / Deal with the preacher / Wild fire woman / Anna / Call on me. *(cd-iss. Oct88 on 'Swan Song'; SS 8502-2) (cd re-iss. Jul94 on 'Atlantic'; 7567 82637-2)*

Aug 75. (7") *(WIP 6242)* <70106> **FEEL LIKE MAKIN' LOVE. / WILD FIRE WOMEN** [20] Jul75 [10]

Feb 76. (lp/c) *(ILPS/ICT 9346)* <8415> **RUN WITH THE PACK** [4] [5]
– Live for the music / Simple man / Honey child / Love me somebody / Run with the pack / Silver, blue & gold / Young blood / Do right by your woman / Sweet lil' sister / Fade away. *(cd-iss. Oct88 on 'Swan Song'; SS 8503-2) (cd re-iss. Jul94 on 'Atlantic'; 7567 92435-2)*

Mar 76. (7") *(WIP 6263)* **RUN WITH THE PACK. / DO RIGHT BY YOUR WOMAN** [ ] [–]

Mar 76. (7") <70108> **YOUNG BLOOD. / DO RIGHT BY YOUR WOMAN** [–] [20]

Jul 76. (7") <70109> **HONEY CHILD. / FADE AWAY** [–] [59]

Feb 77. (7") *(WIP 6381)* **EVERYTHING I NEED. / TOO BAD** [ ] [ ]

Mar 77. (lp/c) *(ILPS/ICT 9441)* <8500> **BURNIN' SKY** [17] [15]
– Burnin' sky / Morning Sun / Leaving you / Like water / Everything I need / Heartbeat / Peace of mind / Passing time / Too bad / Man needs a woman / Master of ceremony. *(cd-iss. Oct94 on 'Atlantic'; 7567 92450-2)*

May 77. (7") <70112> **BURNIN' SKY. / EVERYTHING I NEED** [–] [78]

Swan Song — Swan Song

Mar 79. (7") *(K 19416)* <70119> **ROCK'N'ROLL FANTASY. / CRAZY CIRCLES** [ ] [13]

Mar 79. (lp/c) *(SS K/4 59408)* <8506> **DESOLATION ANGELS** [10] [3]
– Rock'n'roll fantasy / Crazy circles / Gone, gone, gone / Evil wind / Early in the morning / Lonely for your love / Oh, Atlanta / Take the time / Rhythm machine / She brings me love. *(cd-iss. Sep94 on 'Atlantic'; 7567 92451-2)*

Jul 79. (7") <71000> **GONE, GONE, GONE. / TAKE THE TIME** [–] [56]

Aug 82. (lp/c) *(SS K/4 59419)* <90001> **ROUGH DIAMONDS** [15] [26]
– Electricland / Untie the knot / Nuthin' on T.V. / Painted face / Kickdown / Ballad of the band / Cross country boy / Old Mexico / Downhill ryder / Racetrack. *(cd-iss. Oct94 on 'Atlantic'; 7567 92452-2)*

Sep 82. (7") <99966> **ELECTRICLAND. / UNTIE THE KNOT** [–] [74]

—— (mid'83) Disbanded. RODGERS went solo before joining The FIRM. KIRKE played with WILDFIRE. BURRELL sessioned for ROGER CHAPMAN.

—— **BAD COMPANY** reformed 1986. **RALPHS, KIRKE, BURRELL** and the incoming **BRIAN HOWE** – vocals (ex-TED NUGENT)

Atlantic — Atlantic

Jan 86. (lp/c)(cd) *(WX 31/+C)(781625-2)* <81625> **10 FROM 6** (compilation) [ ] [ ]
– Can't get enough / Feel like makin' love / Run with the pack / Shooting star / Movin' on / Bad company / Rock'n'roll fantasy / Electricland / Ready for love / Live for the music.

Oct 86. (lp/c)(cd) *(WX 69/+C)(781684-2)* <81684> **FAME AND FORTUNE** [ ] [ ]
– Burning up / This love / Fame and fortune / That girl / Tell it like it is / Long walk / Hold on my heart / Valerie / When we made love / If I'm sleeping.

Nov 86. (7") *(A 9355)* <89355> **THIS LOVE. / TELL IT LIKE IT IS** [ ] Oct86 [85]
(12"+=) *(TA 9355)* – Burning up / Fame & fortune.

Feb 87. (7") *(A 9296)* **FAME AND FORTUNE. / WHEN WE MADE LOVE** [ ] [–]
Feb 87. (7") *<89299>* **THAT GIRL. / IF I'M SLEEPING** [–] [ ]
Aug 88. (7") *<89035>* **NO SMOKE WITHOUT FIRE. / LOVE ATTACK** [–] [ ]
Aug 88. (lp/c/cd) *(K 781884-1/-4/-2) <81884>* **DANGEROUS AGE** [ ] [58]
– One night / Shake it up / No smoke without fire / Bad man / Dangerous age / Dirty boy / Rock of America / Something about you / The way it goes / Love attack. *(cd+=)* – Excited.
Apr 89. (7") *<88939>* **SHAKE IT UP. / DANGEROUS AGE** [–] [82]
Mar 90. (7"/c-s) *(A 7954/+MC)* **CAN'T GET ENOUGH. / BAD COMPANY** [ ] [–]
(12"+=/cd-s+=) *(A 7954 T/CD)* – No smoke without fire / Shake it up.

— **GEOFF WHITEHORN** – guitar (ex-BACK STREET CRAWLER) repl. RALPHS / **PAUL CULLEN** – bass repl. BURRELL / added **DAVE COLWELL** – keyboards (ex-ASAP)

Atco Atco
Jul 90. (cd/c/lp) *(<7567 91371-2/-4/-1>)* **HOLY WATER** [ ] Jun90 [35]
– Holy water / Walk through fire / Stranger stranger / If you needed somebody / Fearless / Lay your love on me / Boys cry tough / With you in a heartbeat / I don't care / Never too late / Dead of the night / I can't live without you / 100 miles.
Jul 90. (7") *<98944>* **HOLY WATER. / I CAN'T LIVE WITHOUT YOU** [–] [89]
(12"+=/cd-s+=) – Love attack.
Apr 91. (7") *<98914>* **IF YOU NEEDED SOMEBODY. / DEAD OF THE NIGHT** [ ] Nov90 [16]
(12"+=/cd-s+=) – Love attack.
Jul 91. (c-s,cd-s) *<98748>* **WALK THROUGH FIRE / LAY YOUR LOVE ON ME** [–] [28]

— (May'91) **STEVE WALSH** – vocals (ex-KANSAS) repl. HOWE / **MICK RALPHS** also returned

Sep 92. (c-s,cd-s) *<98509>* **HOW ABOUT THAT / BROKENHEARTED** [–] [38]
Sep 92. (7"/c-s) **HOW ABOUT THAT. / HERE COMES TROUBLE** [ ] [–]
(12") – No smoke without a fire (remix) / Stranger stranger.
(cd-s+=) – No smoke without a fire (remix) / If you needed somebody.
Sep 92. (cd/c/lp) *(<7567 91759-2/-4/-1>)* **HERE COMES TROUBLE** [ ] [40]
– How about that / Stranger than fiction / Here comes trouble / This could be the one / Both feet in the water / Take this town / What about you / Little angel / Hold on to my heart / Brokenhearted / My only one.
Nov 92. (c-s,cd-s) *<98463>* **THIS COULD BE THE ONE / BOTH FEET IN THE WATER** [–] [87]

— **RICK WILLS** – bass (ex-ROXY MUSIC, ex-FOREIGNER, ex-PETER FRAMPTON) repl. WALSH

Dec 93. (cd/c) *(<7567 92307-2/-4>)* **WHAT YOU HEAR IS WHAT YOU GET (The Best Of Bad Company – live)** [ ] [ ]
– How about that / Holy water / Rock'n'roll fantasy / If you needed somebody / Here comes trouble / Ready for love / Shooting star / No smoke without a fire / Feel like makin' love / Take this town / Movin' on / Good lovin' gone bad / Fist full of blisters / Can't get enough / Bad company.

— **RALPHS, KIRKE, COLWELL + WILLS** recruited **ROBERT HART** – vox

Jul 95. (cd/c) *(<7559-61808-2/-4>)* **COMPANY OF STRANGERS** [ ] [ ]
– Company of strangers / Clearwater highway / Judas my brother / Little Martha / Gimme gimme / Where I belong / Down down down / Abandoned and alone / Down and dirty / Pretty woman / You're the only reason / Dance with the Devil / Loving you out loud.
Nov 96. (cd) *(7559 61976-2)* **STORIES TOLD & UNTOLD** (new & old) [–] German [–]
– One on one / Oh Atlanta / You're never alone / I still believe in you / Ready for love / Waiting on love / Can't get enough / Is that all there is to love / Love so strong / Silver, blue and gold / Downpour in Cairo / Shooting star / Simple man / Weep no more. *(UK-iss.Jan98; same)*
Mar 99. (d-cd) *<(7559 62391-2)>* **THE ORIGINAL BAD CO. ANTHOLOGY** (compilation) [ ] [ ]
– Can't get enough / Rock steady / Bad company / Seagull / Superstar woman / Little Miss Fortune / Good lovin' gone bad / Shooting star / Deal with the preacher / Wildfire woman / Easy on my soul / Whiskey bottles / Honey child / Run with the pack / Silver, blue and gold / Do right by your woman / Burnin' sky / Heartbeat / Too bad / Smoking / Rock'n'roll fantasy / Evil wind / Oh Atlanta / Rhythm machine / Untie the knot / Downhill rider / Track down a runaway / Ain't it good / Hammer of love / Hey hey.

— **RODGERS + KIRKE** now with **DAVE COLWELL** – guitar / **JAZ LOCHRIE** – bass

Sanctuary Sanctuary
May 02. (cd) *(SANCD 115) <84549>* **IN CONCERT: MERCHANTS OF COOL (live)** [ ] [ ]
– Burnin' sky / Can't get enough / Feel like makin' love / Rock steady / Movin' on / Deal with the preacher / Ready for love / Rock'n'roll fantasy – Ticket to ride / All right now / Bad company / Silver, blue and gold / Shooting star / Joe Fabulous / Saving grace.

BADFINGER

Formed: Swansea, South Wales . . . 1964 as The IVEYS by PETER HAM, RON GRIFFITHS, DAVID JENKINS and drummer TERRY GLEASON; the following year MIKE GIBBINS replaced the latter. The IVEYS were a melodic pop group in the vein of The HOLLIES. By the time they'd signed to The BEATLES' fledgling 'Apple' London-based label in 1968, Liverpudlian TOMMY EVANS had joined the group, replacing DAVID JENKINS. After one minor hit 'MAYBE TOMORROW', they ditched the IVEYS moniker in favour of the more late 60's sounding BADFINGER. They scored their first major hit in the first month of the new decade with the PAUL McCARTNEY-penned 'COME AND GET IT'. JOEY MOLLAND then replaced other original RON GRIFFITHS during its chart run, while EVANS switched to bass. The BEATLES comparisons were unavoidable and their next 45, 'NO MATTER WHAT', was as close an approximation of The Fab Four's mid-60's amphetamine kick as you're likely to hear. The BEATLES' connection continued with contributions to the soundtrack for the movie, 'MAGIC CHRISTIAN MUSIC' and guest appearances on GEORGE HARRISON's 'All Things Must Pass' and JOHN LENNON's 'Imagine'. HARRISON returned the favour by producing 'DAY AFTER DAY', an American Top 5 hit from the 'STRAIGHT UP' album late in '71. The songwriting skills of the HAM-EVANS team were finally recognised in 1972, when NILSSON transformed their 'WITHOUT YOU' into his own tortured No.1 classic. Ironically, the band failed to capitalise on this and their subsequent material was fairly lacklustre. A reputed deal with 'Warner Bros.' for a $3 million advance was struck prior to their last album for 'Apple', 1973's 'ASS'. However, their 'WISH YOU WERE HERE' album in '74 was shifting plenty of units in the States when money in their account went mysteriously missing, the record removed from retail sale soon after. Frustrated by his band's lack of success and MOLLAND's departure, and troubled by personal worries, PETE HAM hanged himself on the 23rd April '75 in his London home. Reeling from this tragedy, the band split, only to be re-formed by EVANS and part-time pipefitter, MOLLAND, in 1978. They even secured a deal with 'Elektra' but again failed to achieve any real success. Incredibly, history repeated itself when, on the 19th of November '83, TOMMY EVANS also hanged himself amid fits of depression and financial troubles. Business problems were sorted out around a year and a half later, too late, of course, to bring back these lost songwriters of the 70's. Fans had to wait a decade and a half for the belated release of long lost album, 'HEAD FIRST' (2000), the record which the band had dutifully recorded – and then had rejected – by Warners after 'WISH YOU WERE HERE' was taken out of circulation back in the mid-70's. While it's difficult to listen to without the weight of attendant events hanging over it, this double disc set (compete with outtakes and demos) proved that BADFINGER were far from a spent force when they recorded it. On the contrary, its musclebound pop was among the best of the day, begging the unavoidable what if.. question. Another greatest hits package was released around the same time, only underlining the band's underrated talent.

Album rating: MAGIC CHRISTIAN MUSIC (*5) / NO DICE (*7) / STRAIGHT UP (*7) / ASS (*5) / BADFINGER (*3) / WISH YOU WERE HERE (*5) / AIRWAVES (*4) / SAY NO MORE (*3) / COME AND GET IT – THE BEST OF . . . compilation (*7) / THE VERY BEST OF . . . compilation (*8) / HEAD FIRST (*7) / Pete Ham: 7 PARK AVENUE (*7)

the IVEYS

PETE HAM (b.27 Apr'47, Swansea, Wales) – guitar, vocals / **TOM EVANS** (b. 5 Jun'47, Liverpool, England) – guitar; repl. DAVID JENKINS / **RON GRIFFITHS** – bass, vocals / **MIKE GIBBINS** (b.12 Mar'49, Swansea) – drums; repl. TERRY GLEASON

Apple Apple

Nov 68. (7") *(APPLE 5)* <1803> **MAYBE TOMORROW. / AND HER DADDY'S A MILLIONAIRE** [ ] Jan69 [67]

Jul 69. (lp) *(SAPCOR 8)* **MAYBE TOMORROW** [–] Europe [–]
(UK-iss.Jun92; same) (with free 12"; SAPCOR 82)

Jul 69. (7") *(APPLE 14)* **DEAR ANGIE. / NO ESCAPING YOUR LOVE** [–] Europe [–]

— Also appeared on Various Artists 'Apple' records comp. EP for Walls ice cream, singing 'STORM IN A TEACUP'.

BADFINGER

supplied 3 tracks (*) for 'The Magic Christian' film soundtrack released Apr'70 on 'Pye Int.'

Dec 69. (7") *(APPLE 20)* <1815> **COME AND GET IT. / ROCK OF ALL AGES** [4] Jan70 [7]

— **JOEY MOLLAND** (b.21 Jun'47, Liverpool) – lead guitar (ex-MERSEYS, etc) repl. GRIFFITHS. (EVANS switched to bass guitar)

Jan 70. (lp) *(SAPCOR 12)* <3364> **MAGIC CHRISTIAN MUSIC** [ ] Mar70 [55]
– Come and get it / Crimson ship / Dear Angie / Fisherman / Midnight sun / Beautiful and blue / Rock of all ages / Carry on till tomorrow / Fisherman / I'm in love / Walk out in the rain / Knocking down our home / Give it a try / Maybe tomorrow. *(re-iss. Oct91 cd+=/c/d-lp; same)* – Storm in a teacup / Arthur.

Oct 70. (7") <1822> **NO MATTER WHAT. / CARRY ON UNTIL TOMORROW** [–] [8]

Dec 70. (7") *(APPLE 31)* **NO MATTER WHAT. / BETTER DAYS** [5] [–]

Dec 70. (lp) *(SAPCOR 16)* <3367> **NO DICE** [ ] Nov70 [28]
– I can't take it / I don't mind / Love me do / Midnight caller / No matter what / Without you / Blodwyn / Better days / It had to be / Watford John / Believe me / We're for the dark. *(cd-iss. Jun92+=;)* – Get down / Friends are hard to find / Mean mean Jemima / Loving you / I'll be the one.

Nov 71. (7") <1841> **DAY AFTER DAY. / MONEY** [–] [4]

Dec 71. (lp) *(SAPCOR 19)* <3387> **STRAIGHT UP** [ ] [31]
– Money / Flying / Suitcase / Sweet Tuesday morning / Perfection / I'd die babe / Take it all / Baby blue / Name of the game / Day after day / Sometimes / It's over. *(cd-iss. Mar93 cd/c/lp; same)* – (original sessions of songs).

Jan 72. (7") *(APPLE 40)* **DAY AFTER DAY. / SWEET TUESDAY MORNING** [10] [–]

Apr 72. (7"; w-drawn UK) *(APPLE 42)* <1844> **BABY BLUE. / FLYING** [ ] Mar72 [14]

Mar 74. (7") *(APPLE 49)* **APPLE OF MY EYE. / BLIND OWL** [ ] [ ]

Mar 74. (lp) *(SAPCOR 27)* <3411> **ASS** [ ] Dec73 [ ]
– Apple of my eye / Get away icicles / The winner / Blind owl / Constitution / When I say / Cowboy / Timeless / I can love you. *(cd-iss. Feb97; CDSAPCOR 27)*

Warners Warners

Jun 74. (lp) *(K 56023)* <2762> **BADFINGER** [ ] Mar74 [ ]
– I miss you / Shine on / Love is easy / Song for a lost friend / Why don't we talk / Island / Matted spam / Where do we go from here? / My heart goes out / Lonely you / Give it up / Andy Norris. *(<cd-iss. Mar00; 7599 26539-2>)*

Jul 74. (7") **I MISS YOU. / SHINE ON** [–] [ ]

Oct 74. (7") *(K 16323)* **LOVE IS EASY. / MY HEART GOES OUT** [ ] [ ]

Oct 74. (lp) *(K 56076)* <2827> **WISH YOU WERE HERE** [ ] [ ]
– Just a chance / You're so fine / Got to get out of here / Know one knows / Dennis / In the meantime / Love time / Some other time / King of the load (T) / Meanwhile, back at the ranch – Should I smoke. *(<cd-iss. Mar00; 7599 26540-2>)*

— added **BOB JACKSON** – keyboards (MOLLAND also left to join NATURAL GAS) They split just after PETE HAM commited suicide on 23rd April. EVANS joined DODGERS. Re-formed '76 by **MOLLAND + EVANS** who recruited new members / **KENNY HARCK** – drums / **JOE TANZIN** – guitar / session man **ANDY NEWMARK** – drums repl. HARCK on half of album

Elektra Elektra

Apr 79. (7") *(K 12345)* **LOST INSIDE YOUR LOVE. / COME DOWN HARD** [ ] [ ]

Apr 79. (lp) *(K 52129)* <6E 175> **AIRWAVES** [ ] [ ]
– Airwaves / Look out California / Lost inside your love / Love is gonna come at last / Sympathy / The winner / The dreamer / Come down hard / Sail away. *(cd-iss. Mar99 on 'Permanent Press'; 70267 52712-2)*

Jun 79. (7") *(K 12369)* <46025> **LOVE IS GONNA COME AT LAST. / SAIL AWAY** [ ] Mar79 [69]

— **MOLLAND + EVANS** brought in **TONY KAYE** – keyboards (ex-YES, ex-BADGER) / **GLENN SHERBA** – guitar / **RICHARD BRYANS** – drums

not iss. Radio-Atlantic

Feb 81. (7") <3793> **HOLD ON./ PASSIN' TIME** [–] [56]

Mar 81. (lp) <16030> **SAY NO MORE** [–] [ ]
– Hold on / I got you / Come on / Because I love you / Rock'n'roll contract / Passin' time / Three time loser / Too hung up on you / Crocadillo / No more.

May 81. (7") <3815> **I GOT YOU. / ROCK'N'ROLL CONTRACT** [–] [ ]

Jul 81. (7") <3833> **BECAUSE I LOVE YOU. / TOO HUNG UP ON YOU** [–] [ ]

— They split again in '83. JOEY MOLLAND released solo album AFTER THE PEARL. He later (1992) released cd 'THE PILGRIM' for 'Rykodisc'. TOM EVANS also tragically killed himself 23 Nov'83. MOLLAND and MIKE GIBBINS still tour as BADFINGER in US 60's tour.

— they reformed with **MOLLAND, GIBBINS** plus **RANDY ANDERSON** – guitar / **A.J. NICHOLAS** – bass

not iss. Independent

1988. (lp) **TIMELESS** [–] [ ]

– compilations, others, etc. –

Apr 89. (lp/cd) *Edsel; (ED/+CD 302)* **SHINE ON** [ ] [–]

Nov 90. (cd/c/lp) *Essential; (ESS CD/MC/LP 135)* **DAY AFTER DAY (live)** [ ] [–]
– Sometimes / I don't mind / Blind owl / Give it up / Constitution / Baby blue / Name of the game / Day after day / Timeless / I can't take it.

Jul 92. (cd) *Raven;* **APPLE DAZE** (TOM EVANS interview) [ ] [–]

Sep 93. (cd/c) *Gipsy;* **THE FINAL TRACKS** [ ] [–]

Apr 95. (cd/lp) *Apple; (CD+/SAPCOR 28)* **COME AND GET IT – THE BEST OF BADFINGER** [ ] [–]
– Come and get it / Maybe tomorrow / Rock of all ages / Dear Angie / Carry on till tomorrow / No matter what / Believe me / Midnight caller / Better days / Without you / Take it all / Money / Flying / The name of the game / Suitcase / Day after day / Baby blue / When I say / Icicles / I can love you / Apple of my eye.

Jun 97. (cd) *Strange Fruit; (SFRSCD 031)* **BBC LIVE IN CONCERT (live)** [ ] [–]
(d-lp re-iss. Dec99 on 'Turning Point'; TPM 99201)

Oct 00. (cd) *Apple/Capitol; (<5 26974-2>)* **THE VERY BEST OF BADFINGER** [ ] Sep00 [ ]
– No matter what / Day after day / Baby blue / Name of the game / Maybe tomorrow / Come and get it / Rock of all ages / Carry on till tomorrow / Midnight caller / We're for the dark / I'll be the one / Without you / I'd die babe / It's over / When I say / Dennis / Lonely you / Love time / Meanwhile, back at the ranch – Should I smoke.

Nov 00. (d-cd) *Artisan – Snapper; (<SMADD 829>)* **HEAD FIRST** (shelved LP) [ ] [ ]
– Lay me down / Hey, Mr. Manager / Keep believing / Passed first / Rock'n'roll contract / Saville Row / Moonshine / Back again / Turn around / Rockin' machine / Time is mine / Smokin' gun / Old fashioned notions / Nothing to show / You ask yourself why / Keep your country tidy / To say goodbye / Queen of darkness / I can't believe in / Thanks to you all / Lay me down. *(re-iss. Sep02; SMDCD 395)*

PETE HAM

— posthumous solo release

Rykodisc Rykodisc

Apr 97. (cd) *<(RCD 10349)>* **7 PARK AVENUE** [ ] [ ]
– Catherine cares / Coppertone blues / It really doesn't matter / Live love all of your days / Would you deny / Dear father / Matted spam / No matter what / Leaving on a midnight train / Weep baby / Hand in hand / Sille veb / I know that you should / Island / Just look inside the cover / Just how lucky we are / No more / Ringside.

BADLY DRAWN BOY

Formed: Bolton, England . . . early 1997, as a one-man vehicle for the highly charged but eccentric DAMON GOUGH. The Bolton-born – or at least in a village outside it – first initiated his weird brand of gnome-ish psychedelia when he self-financed (with graphic designer ANDY VOTEL) an EP on his own 'Twisted Nerve' label. 'EP1' (released in September '97) was quickly pursued by the following year's 'EP2', a contract with 'XL Recordings' (home of the the PRODIGY) just around the corner. In the Autumn of '98, his third set, the imaginatively titled 'EP3' hit the shops, this BECK-esque trio of tracks finally making the more discerning music punter sit up and listen. Prior to this, GOUGH had contributed the track, 'Nursery Rhyme', to the acclaimed UNKLE album, 'Psyence Fiction'. Minor hits 'ONCE AROUND THE BLOCK' and 'ANOTHER PEARL' preceded a long-awaited debut set, 'THE HOUR OF THE BEWILDERBEAST' (2000), the UK Top 20 entry a mixture of NICK DRAKE's quiet, cello-driven folk and SPRINGSTEEN's poor-man's blues. Three Top 30 singles followed the Mercury Prize-winning album; 'DISILLUSION', 'ONCE AROUND THE BLOCK' and 'PISSING IN THE WIND', with the latter video starring Joan Collins. GOUGH subsequently put his artistry on the line by cutting a full-on soundtrack as his next release, an increasingly rare career move these days. 'ABOUT A BOY' (2002) was music for the adaptation of Nick Hornby's novel of the same name, a romantic/coming-of-age saga with which GOUGH's flittering acoustica dovetailed perfectly, especially on the hit singles, 'SOMETHING TO TALK ABOUT' and the gorgeous 'SILENT SIGH'. Some of the soundtrack's spare grace would've been useful on third serving, 'HAVE YOU FED THE FISH?' (2002), an L.A. recorded opus criticised for its sonic flab. Nevertheless it did feature three UK hits, 'YOU WERE RIGHT', 'BORN AGAIN' and 'ALL POSSIBILITIES'. 2004's 'ONE PLUS ONE IS ONE' was BDB's third consecutive Top 10 album, an Andy Votel-produced return to form skipping between eclectic updates of late 60s/early 70s 'Island' (i.e. JETHRO TULL, NICK DRAKE again!, the INCREDIBLE STRING BAND, etc.) and Bewilderbeast-ian ballads such as the children's choir-enhanced single, 'YEAR OF THE RAT'.

Album rating: THE HOUR OF THE BEWILDERBEAST (*8) / ABOUT A BOY soundtrack (*7) / HAVE YOU FED THE FISH? (*5) / ONE PLUS ONE IS ONE (*6)

DAMON GOUGH (b. 2 Oct'70, Dunstable, England) – vocals, instruments & things / with various session people

Twisted Nerve not iss.

Sep 97. (7"ep) *(TN 001)* **EP1** [ ] [–]
– Riding with Gabriel Greenburg / Shake the rollercoaster / No point in living / Sugarstealer / No point in living (reprise).

Apr 98. (7"ep) *(TN 002)* **EP2** [ ] [–]
– I love you all / The treeclimber / I love you all (I loop you all Andy Votel mix) / Thinking of you.

Twisted Nerve – X.L. Toy

Oct 98. (7") *(TNXL 001R)* **ROAD MOVIE. / MY FRIEND CUBILAS** [ ] [–]
(10"ep) *(TNXL 001T)* – ('A'side) / Spooky driver / I need a sign / Meet me on the horizon.
(cd-ep) *(TNXL 001CD)* – ('B'side) / Interlude / Kerplunk by candlelight / Meet me on the horizon.

Mar 99. (10"ep) *(TNXL 002T)* **IT CAME FROM THE GROUND / WALKMAN (demo 1) / OUTSIDE A LIGHT (1 & 2) / WALKMAN (demo 2)** [ ] [–]
(cd-ep+=) *(TNXL 002CD)* – ('A'-Andy Votel remix).
(7") *(TNXL 002R)* – (above remix) / Whirlpool.

Aug 99. (7") *(TNXL 003)* **ONCE AROUND THE BLOCK. / SOUL ATTITUDE** [46] [–]
(cd-s+=) *(TNXL 003CD)* – ('A'-Radio Luxembourg mix).
(7") *(TNXL 003R)* – ('A'-Andy Votel mix) / Another pearl.

Dec 99. (cd) *<1>* **HOW DID I GET HERE?** [–] [ ]
– My friend Cubilas / I need a sign / Interlude / Meet on the horizon / Road movie / Kerplunk by candlelight / It came from the ground / Outside is a light (one) / Soul attitude / Whirlpool / It came from the ground (Andy Votel mix).

Twisted Nerve – XL XL – B.M.G.

Jun 00. (10"/cd-s) *(TNXL 004 T/CD)* **ANOTHER PEARL. / DISTANT TOWN / CHAOS THEORY** [41] [–]
(cd-s) *(TNXL 004CD2)* – ('A'mixes).

Jun 00. (cd/c/lp) *(TNXL CD/MC/LP 133)* *<87211>* **THE HOUR OF THE BEWILDERBEAST** [13] [ ]
– The shining / Everybody's stalking / Bewilder / Fall in a river / Camping next to water / Stone on the water / Another pearl / Body rap / Once around the block / This song / Bewilderbeast / Magic in the air / Cause a rockslide / Pissing in the wind / Blistered heart / Disillusion / Say it again / Epitaph.

Sep 00. (10") *(TNXL 005T)* **DISILLUSION. / WERECKING THE STAGE / DISILLUSION (Mr Scruff mix)** [26] [–]
(cd-s) *(TNXL 005CD)* – (first 2) / Bottle of tears.
(cd-s) *(TNXL 005CD2)* – ('A'side) / ('A'-Blue States mix) / ('A'-Black lodge mix).

Nov 00. (ltd-10") *(TNXL 008T)* **THE SHINING** [–] wdrawn [–]

Nov 00. (7") *(TNXL 009)* **ONCE AROUND THE BLOCK. / TUMBLEWEED / THE SHINING (Avalanches good for the weekend mix)** [27] [–]
(cd-s+=) *(TNXL 009CD)* – (first & third tracks) / The shining (Capitol K mix).
(cd-s) *(TNXL 009CD2)* – ('A'side) / ('A'-Andy Votel mix) / ('A'-Nick Faber mix).

May 01. (10"/cd-s) *(TNXL 010 T/CD)* **PISSING IN THE WIND. / SPITTING IN THE WIND / THE SHINING (minotaur shock mix)** [22] [–]
(cd-s) *(TNXL 010CD2)* – ('A'side) / Magic in the air (WDET Detroit mix) / Everybody's stalking (WDET Detroit mix).

Twisted Nerve B.M.G.

Mar 02. (7") *(TNXL 012)* **SILENT SIGH. / DONNA AND BLITZEN (KCRW acoustic session) / PIANO MEDLEY (KCRW acoustic session)** [16] [–]
(cd-s) *(TNXL 012CD)* – ('A'side) / ('A'-acoustic) / Better way / ('A'-version).
(cd-s) *(TNXL 012CD2)* – ('A'side) / ('A'-Broadway project mix) / ('A'-Zongamin remix).

Apr 02. (cd/lp) *(TNXL CD/LP 152)* *<1019>* **ABOUT A BOY** (soundtrack) [6] [ ]
– Exit stage right / A peak you reach / Something to talk about / Dead duck / Above you, below me / I love N.Y.E. / Silent sigh / Wet, wet, wet / River, sea, ocean / S.P.A.T. / Rachel's flat / Walking out of stride / File me away / A minor incident / Delta (little boy blues) / Donna and Blitzen.

Jun 02. (7") *(TNXL 014)* **SOMETHING TO TALK ABOUT. / WALK IN THE PARK WITH ANGIE / HAMSTER COUNTDOWN** [28] [–]
(cd-s) *(TNXL 014CD)* – ('A'-side) / ('A'-Four Tet convention mix) / ('A'-Misty Dixon mix).
(cd-s) *(TNXL 014CD2)* – ('A'side) / Above you below me (electric bedroom version) / My name's not down.

Oct 02. (7") *(TNXL 015)* **YOU WERE RIGHT. / LAST FRUIT** [9] [–]
(cd-s+=) *(TNXL 015CD)* – ('A'-live at Glastonbury).

Nov 02. (cd/lp) *(TNXL CD/LP 156)* *<1066>* **HAVE YOU FED THE FISH?** [10] [ ]
– Coming in to land / Have you fed the fish? / Born again / 40 days, 40 nights / All possibilities / I was wrong / You were right / Centrepeace / How? / The further I slide / Imaginary lines / Using our feet / Tickets to what you need / What is it now? / Bedside story.

Jan 03. (7") *(TNXL 016)* **BORN AGAIN. / THERE'S A STORM** [16] [–]
(cd-s+=) *(TNXL 016CD)* – Golden days.

Apr 03. (7") *(TNXL 017)* **ALL POSSIBILITIES. / WALK AWAY RENEE** [24] [–]
(cd-s) *(TNXL 017CD)* – ('A'side) / Where were you (live) / Let the sunshine (live).

Twisted Nerve – XL | Astralwerks

Jun 04. (cd/lp) *(TNXL CD/LP 179)* <73986> **ONE PLUS ONE IS ONE** [9] Jul04 [ ]
– One plus one is one / Easy love / Summertime in wintertime / This is that new song / Another devil dies / The blossoms / Year of the rat / Four leaf clover / Fewer words / Logic of a friend / Stockport / Life turned upside down / Take the glory / Holy grail. *<US cd+=>* – Don't ask me I'm just the president / Plan-B.

Jul 04. (7") *(TNXL 018)* **YEAR OF THE RAT. / ONE PLUS ONE IS ONE (live in Nashville)** [38] [–]
(cd-s) *(TNXL 018CD)* – ('A') / Don't ask me I'm just the president / Plan-B.
(dvd-s) *(TNXL 018DVD)* – ('A'-video) / Fewer words (live video).

Joan BAEZ

Born: 9 Jan'41, Staten Island, New York, USA. After a successful 1959 Newport festival appearance, she signed to the 'Vanguard' label in the States. An innovator of protest folk music that leant on early PETE SEEGER, BAEZ was an inspiration to the likes of DYLAN etc. Her defiant protest anthems made her the darling of the intellectual beatnik scene developing in America at the time. Although her early material concentrated on traditional folk fare delivered in a crystal pure vocal style, BAEZ became a figurehead for the protest movement in the mid-60's with her anthemic 'WE SHALL OVERCOME'. On 'JOAN BAEZ 5' (1965), she showcased her move towards interpreting more contemporary artists, covering Phil Och's 'THERE BUT FOR FORTUNE' and Bob Dylan's 'IT AIN'T ME BABE'. As well as becoming a celebrated interpreter of the latter's work, BAEZ and DYLAN became lovers, the King and Queen of folk, as the couple were dubbed (their relationship was well documented in the film, 'Don't Look Back'). The aforementioned album went Top 5 in the UK as did her sixth set 'FAREWELL ANGELINA' (1965), a record featuring a further two DYLAN covers in 'IT'S ALL OVER NOW, BABY BLUE' and 'A HARD RAIN'S A-GONNA FALL'. The same year, BAEZ founded the Institute For The Study Of Nonviolence in California, her increasingly political activism directed mainly against US involvement in the Vietnam war. In 1968, the singer married fellow protest leader DAVID HARRIS, although he was subsequently jailed for resisting the draft. '68 also saw BAEZ's most ambitious album to date, 'BAPTISM – A JOURNEY THROUGH OUR TIME' (1968), wherein she turned her head to spoken word poems etc. The early 70's found the folk veteran covering material by more mainstream artists such as The BEATLES and The BAND, her reading of the latter's 'THE NIGHT THEY DROVE OLD DIXIE DOWN', making the US Top 3. Her commitment to humanitarian protest remained steadfast and indeed, throughout the first half of the 70's, the singer's political activities (she was a high profile opponent of the military coup in Chile) overshadowed her recorded output. With 'DIAMONDS AND RUST' (1975), however, BAEZ emerged as an important figure in the American singer/songwriter movement, the album making the US Top 20 and becoming one of her best loved works. The mid-70's also saw a belated reunion with DYLAN, the pair hooking up in the Rolling Thunder Revue. Autobiographical efforts such as 'GULF WINDS' (1976) and 'BLOWIN' AWAY' (1977) marked the end of BAEZ's career for almost a decade as she found herself without a record label. She nevertheless continued to perform throughout the 80's, playing benefit concerts for Amnesty International and, of course, appearing at Live Aid in 1985. Perhaps inspired by the new wave of young female troubadours (SUZANNE VEGA, TRACY CHAPMAN etc.), BAEZ returned to the recording front in the late 80's/early 90's, the 'PLAY ME BACKWARDS' (1993) set seeing her court an adult MOR audience, while a live set, 'RING THEM BELLS' (1995) featured duets with JANIS IAN, MARY CHAPIN-CARPENTER and MARY BLACK amongst others. Of late, BAEZ has completed a further studio set, 'GONE FROM DANGER' (1997), which didn't see light of day in the UK until a few years later. 'DARK CHORDS ON A BIG GUITAR' (2003) meanwhile, built on the achievements of its predecessor, bravely taking on material by such free musical spirits as STEVE EARLE, JOSH RITTER, RYAN ADAMS, NATALIE MERCHANT and GILLIAN WELCH. Bringing the whole weight and depth of her considerable talent and experience to bear on the likes of Earle's 'CHRISTMAS IN WASHINGTON' and Merchant's 'MOTHERLAND', BAEZ succeeded in infusing them with the kind of crackling emotional charge their original authors had perhaps only partly realised. 2005's 'BOWERY SONGS' featured many of the same songs in a live performance context at New York's Bowery Ballroom.

• **Songwriters:** She writes her own work interspersed with covers:- (Her debut album contained some Scottish traditional ballads). She recorded a whole lp 'ANY DAY NOW' of DYLAN material) and 'PACK UP YOUR SORROWS' (Richard Farina, her brother-in-law, who was killed in a motorcycle accident, summer '66) / IN THE QUIET MORNING (Mimi Farina, her sister) / LET IT BE (Beatles) / AMSTERDAM (Janis Ian) / STONES IN THE ROAD (Mary-Chapin Carpenter) / STRANGE RIVERS (John Stewart) / STEAL ACROSS THE BORDER (Ron Davies) / THROUGH YOUR HANDS (John Hiatt) / lots more . . .

Album rating: JOAN BAEZ (*8) / JOAN BAEZ 2 (*5) / JOAN BAEZ IN CONCERT (*7) / JOAN BAEZ IN CONCERT PART 2 (*5) / JOAN BAEZ 5 (*6) / FAREWELL ANGELINA (*6) / PORTRAIT (*5) / NOEL (*4) / JOAN (*5) / BAPTISM (*5) / ANY DAY NOW (*5) / DAVID'S ALBUM (*4) / ONE DAY AT A TIME (*5) / BLESSED ARE (*5) / CARRY IT ON soundtrack (*5) / COME FROM THE SHADOWS (*5) / WHERE ARE YOU NOW, MY SON? (*4) / GRACIAS A LA VIDA (*4) / DIAMONDS AND RUST (*7) / FROM EVERY STAGE (*4) / GULF WINDS (*4) / BLOWING AWAY (*5) / HONEST LULLABY (*4) / LIVE EUROPE 83 (*5) / RECENTLY (*6) / DIAMONDS AND RUST IN THE BULLRING (*3) / SPEAKING OF DREAMS (*5) / PLAY ME BACKWARDS (*5) / RING THEM BELLS (*4) / GONE FROM DANGER (*5) / GREATEST HITS compilation (*7) / DARK CHORDS ON A BIG GUITAR (*6) / BOWERY SONGS (*6)

JOAN BAEZ – vocals, acoustic guitar

Fontana | Vanguard

Nov 60. (lp) *(STFL 6002)* <VSD 2077> **JOAN BAEZ** [ ] [ ]
– Silver dagger / East Virginia / Ten thousand miles / House of the rising sun / All my trials / Wildwood flower / Donna Donna / John Riley / Rake and rambling boy / Little Moses / Mary Hamilton / Henry Martin / El preso numero nuevo (the ninth prisoner). *<re-dist.US Apr62 hit No.15> (re-iss. UK Jun65 hit No.9) (re-iss. 1973 on 'Vanguard'; VSD 79073) (cd-iss. Oct88 on 'Start'; VFCD 7101) (cd-iss. Jan94 & Oct95 on 'Vanguard; VMD 2077) <(cd re-mast.Nov01 +=; VMD 79594)>* – Girl of constant sorrow / I know you rider / John Riley.

Oct 61. (lp) *(STFL 6025)* <VSD 2097> **JOAN BAEZ 2** [ ] [13]
– Wagoner's lad / The trees they do grow high / The lily of the west / Silkie / Engine 143 / Once I knew a pretty girl / Lonesome road / Banks of the Ohio / Pal of mine / Barbara Allen / The cherry tree carol / Old blue / Railroad boy / Plaisir d'amour. *(re-iss. 1973 on 'Vanguard'; VSD 79094) (cd-iss. Oct88 on 'Start'; VFCD 7102) (cd-iss. Jan94 & Oct95 on 'Vanguard'; VMD 2097) <(cd re-mast.Nov01 +=; VCD 79595)>* – I once loved a boy / Poor boy / The longest train I ever saw.

Oct 61. (7") <35012> **BANKS OF THE OHIO. / OLD BLUE** [–] [ ]

Feb 62. (7") <35013> **LONESOME ROAD. / PAL OF MINE** [–] [ ]

Oct 62. (lp) *(STFL 6035)* <VSD 2122> **JOAN BAEZ IN CONCERT (live)** [ ] [10]
– Babe, I'm gonna leave you / Geordie / Copper kettle / Kumbaya / What have they done to the rain / Black is the colour of my true love's hair / Danger waters / Gospel ship / The house carpenter / Pretty Boy Floyd / Lady Mary / Ate Amanha / Matty Groves. *(re-iss. 1973 on 'Vanguard'; VSD 79112) (cd-iss. Jan96 on 'Vanguard'; VMD 2122) <(cd re-mast.May02 +=; VMD 79598)>* – Streets of Laredo / My good old man / My Lord what a morning.

Nov 62. (7") <35018> **WHAT HAVE THEY DONE TO THE RAIN. / DANGER WATERS** [–] [ ]

Oct 63. (7") <35023> **WE SHALL OVERCOME (live). / WHAT HAVE THEY DONE TO THE RAIN (live)** [–] [90]

May 64. (lp) *(STFL 6033)* <VSD 2123> **JOAN BAEZ IN CONCERT, PART 2 (live)** [8] Dec63 [7]
– Once I had a sweetheart / Jackaroe / Don't think twice, it's all right / We shall overcome / Portland town / Queen of hearts / Manha de carnaval –

Te ador / Long black veil / Fennario / 'Nu bello cardillo / With God on our side / Three fishers / Hush little baby / Battle hymn of the republic. *(re-iss. 1973 on 'Vanguard'; VSD 79113) (cd-iss. Jan96 on 'Vanguard'; VMD 2123) <(cd re-mast.May02 +=; VMD 79240)>* – Rambler gambler / Railroad Bill / Death of Emmett Till / Tomorrow is a long time / When first unto this country a stranger I came.

Jun 64. (7") *<35026>* **WITH GOD ON OUR SIDE. / RAILROAD BILL – DADDY YOU BEEN ON MY MIND (MEDLEY)** [–] [ ]

Nov 64. (7") *(TF 561)* **IT AIN'T ME BABE. / GO 'WAY FROM MY WINDOW** [ ] [–]

Apr 65. (lp) *(STFL 6043) <VSD 79160>* **JOAN BAEZ 5** [3] Nov64 [12]
– There but for fortune / Stewball / It ain't me babe / The death of Queen Jane / Villa lobos: Bachianas Brasileias No.5 – aria / Go 'way from my window / I still miss someone / When you hear them cuckoos hollerin' / Birmingham Sunday / So we'll go no more a-rovin' / O'cangaceiro / The unquiet grave. *(re-iss. 1973 on 'Vanguard'; VSD 79160) (cd-iss. Apr97 on 'Vanguard'; VMD 79160) <(cd re-mast.Sep02 on 'Vanguard'+=; VMD 79700)>* – Tramp on the street / Long black veil.

Mar 65. (7") *(TF 564)* **WE SHALL OVERCOME. / DON'T THINK TWICE** [26] [–]

Jun 65. (7") *<35031>* **THERE BUT FOR FORTUNE. / DADDY YOU BEEN ON MY MIND** [–] [50]

Jul 65. (7") *(TF 587)* **THERE BUT FOR FORTUNE. / PLAISIR D'AMOUR** [8] [–]

Aug 65. (7") *(TF 604)* **IT'S ALL OVER NOW, BABY BLUE. / DADDY YOU'VE BEEN ON MY MIND** [22] [–]

Nov 65. (lp) *(STFL 6058) <VSD 79200>* **FAREWELL ANGELINA** [5] Oct65 [10]
– Farewell Angelina / Daddy, you been on my mind / It's all over now, baby blue / The ranger's command / Colours / A satisfied mind / The river in the pines / Pauvre Ruteboeuf / Sagt mir wo die blumen sind / A hard rain's a-gonna fall. *(re-iss. 1973 on 'Vanguard'; VSD 23006) (re-iss. Oct88 on 'Start' lp/c/cd; VFLP5/VFTC6/VFCD7 105) (cd-iss. Jan94 & Oct95 on 'Vanguard'; VMD 79200) <(cd re-mast.Sep02 +=; VMD 79701)>* – One too many mornings / Rock, salt and nails / Water is wide.

Dec 65. (7") *(TF 639)* **FAREWELL ANGELINA. / QUEEN OF HEARTS** [35] [–]

Jun 66. (7") *(TF 727) <35040>* **PACK UP YOUR SORROWS. / SWALLOW SONG** [50] [ ]

Aug 66. (lp) *(STFL 6082) <VSD 79240>* **JOAN** [ ] [38]
– Be not too hard / Eleanor Rigby / Turquoise / La colombe – the dove / Dangling conversation / The lady came from Baltimore / North / Children of darkness / The greenwood side / If you were a carpenter / Annabel Lee / Saigon bride. *(re-iss. 1973 on 'Vanguard'; VSD 23011) (cd-iss. Apr97 on 'Vanguard'; VMD 79240)*

Nov 66. (7") *<35046>* **CANTIQUE DE NOEL. / LITTLE DRUMMER BOY** [–] [ ]

Nov 66. (lp) *(STFL 6082) <VSD 79240>* **NOEL** (festive album) [ ] [ ]
– O come, o come Emmanuel / Coventry carol / Good King Wencelas / Little drummer boy / Wonder as I wander, bring a torch Jeanette Isabella / Down in yon forest / Carol of the birds / Angels we have heard on high / Ave Maria / Medley:- Deck the halls – Mary's wandering – Away in a manger – Adieste fidelis / Cantique de noel (O holy night) / What child is this / Silent night. *(re-iss. 1973 on 'Vanguard'; VSD 23018) (re-iss. Oct88 on 'Start' lp/c/cd; VFLP5/VFTC6/VFCD7 107) (cd re-iss. Oct96 on 'Vanguard'; VMD 79230) <(cd re-mast.Nov01 +=; VMD 79596)>* – The first noel / We three kings / Virgin Mary / Good christian men / Burgundian carol / Away in a manger (French version).

Jun 67. (7") *(TF 865) <35055>* **BE NOT TOO HARD. / NORTH** [ ] [ ]

Vanguard Vanguard

Aug 68. (lp) *(SVRL 19000) <VSD 79275>* **BAPTISM – A JOURNEY THROUGH OUR TIME** [ ] [84]
– Old Welsh song / I saw the vision of armies / Minister of war / Casida of the lament / Of the dark past / London / In Guernica / Who murdered the minutes / Oh, little child / No man is an island / From portrait of the artist as a young man / All the pretty little horses / Childhood III / The magic wood / Poems from the Japanese / Colours / All in green went my love riding / Gacela of the dark death / The parable of the old man and the young / Evil / Epitaph for a poet / Old Welsh song (reprise). *(re-iss. Aug89 on 'Start' lp/c/cd; VFLP5/VFTC6/VFCD7 103) <(cd re-iss. Jun98 on 'Vanguard';* **VMD 79275)>**

— added many session people **NORMAN PUTTNAM** – bass / **KEN BUTTREY** – drums / **DAVID BRIGGS** – keyboards / **GRADY MARTIN** – dobro / **PETE WADE** – guitar / etc.

Jan 69. (d-lp) *(55-66) <VSD 79306-7>* **ANY DAY NOW** [ ] [30]
– Love minus zero – No limit / North country blues / You ain't goin' nowhere / Drifter's escape / I pity the poor immigrant / Tears of rage / Sad eyed lady of the Lowlands / Love is just a four-letter word / I dreamed I saw St. Augustine / The walls of Redwing / Dear landlord / One too many mornings / I shall be released / Boots of Spanish leather / Walkin' down the line / Restless farewell. *(re-iss. Sep89 on 'Start' d-lp/d-c/cd; VSD/CVSD/VCD 79306-7)*

Apr 69. (7") *(VA 2) <35088>* **LOVE IS JUST A FOUR-LETTER WORD. / LOVE MINUS ZERO – NO LIMIT** [ ] [86]

Jun 69. (7") *<35092>* **IF I KNEW. / ROCK, SALT AND NAILS** [–] [ ]

Jun 69. (lp) *(SVRL 19050) <VSD 79308>* **DAVID'S ALBUM** [ ] [36]
– If I knew / Rock / Salt and nails / Glad bluebird of happiness / Green, green grass of home / Will the circle be unbroken / Tramp on the street / I'm a poor wayfaring stranger / Just a closer walk with thee / Hickory wind / My home's across the blue ridge mountains. *<(cd-iss. Jan94 & Oct98; VMD 79308)>*

Aug 69. (7") *<35098>* **HICKORY WIND. / FOUR DAYS GONE** [–] [ ]

Mar 70. (7") *<35103>* **NO EXPECTATIONS. / ONE DAY AT A TIME** [–] [ ]

Apr 70. (lp) *(VSD 23010) <VSD 79310>* **ONE DAY AT A TIME** [ ] Mar70 [80]
– Seven bridges road / David's song / Sweet Sir Galahad / Long black veil / Ghetto / Carry it on / Jolie blonde / Joe Hill / No expectations / Take me back to the sweet sunny south / One day at a time. *(cd-iss. Oct96; VMD 79310)*

Jun 70. (7") *<35106>* **SWEET SIR GALAHAD. / GHETTO** [–] [ ]

Jan 71. (7") *<35114>* **CARRY IT ON. / ROCK SALT & NAILS** [–] [ ]

Sep 71. (7") *<(VRS 35138)>* **THE NIGHT THEY DROVE OLD DIXIE DOWN. / WHEN TIME IS STOLEN** [6] Aug71 [3]

Sep 71. (d-lp) *<(VSD 6570-1)>* **BLESSED ARE** [ ] [11]
– Blessed are . . . / The night they drove old Dixie down / The salt of the Earth / Three horses / Brand new Tennessee waltz / Lost lonely and wretched / Lincoln freed me today / Outside the Nashville limits / San Francisco Mabel Joy / When time is stolen / Heaven help us all / Angeline / Help me make it through the night / Let it be / Put your hand in the hand / Gabriel and me / Milanese waltz / Marie Flore / The hitch-hiker's song / The 23rd of August / Fifteen months. *(d-cd-iss. Jan97; VCD2 6570)*

Nov 71. (7") *<35145>* **LET IT BE. / POOR WAYFARING STRANGER** [–] [49]

Nov 71. (7") *(VAN 1002)* **LET IT BE. / GABRIEL AND ME** [ ] [–]

Jan 72. (7") *<35148>* **WILL THE CIRCLE BE UNBROKEN. / JUST A CLOSER WALK WITH THEE** [–] [ ]

Apr 72. (7") *<35158>* **BLESSED ARE. / THE BRAND NEW TENNESSEE WALTZ** [–] [ ]

Jul 72. (lp) *<(VSD 79313)>* **CARRY IT ON** (soundtrack compilation w/ spoken word *) [ ] Dec71 [ ]
– Oh, happy day / Carry it on / In forty days (* w/ DAVID HARRIS) / Hickory wind / The last thing on my mind / Life is sacred (* by DAVID HARRIS) / Joe Hill / I shall be released / Do right woman, do right man / Love is just another four-letter word / Suzanne / Idols and heroes (* by DAVID HARRIS) / We shall overcome (by DAVID HARRIS). *<(cd-iss. Sep99; VCD 79313)>*

— she also issued 2 film s-tracks 'Sacco & Vanzetti' & 'Silent Running'

A&M A&M

Apr 72. (7") *<1334>* **PRISON TRILOGY (BILLY ROSE). / SONG OF BANGLADESH** [–] [ ]

May 72. (lp/c) *(AMLH/CAM 64339) <4339>* **COME FROM THE SHADOWS** [ ] [48]
– Prison trilogy (Billy Rose) / Rainbow road / Love song to a stranger / Myths / In the quiet morning / Weary mothers / To Bobby / Song of Bangladesh / A stranger in my place / Tumbleweed / The partisan / Imagine.

Jul 72. (7") *(AMS 7011)* **IN THE QUIET MORNING. / SONG OF BANGLADESH** [ ] [–]

Jul 72. (7") *<1362>* **IN THE QUIET MORNING. / TO BOBBY** [–] [69]

Sep 72. (7") *<1393>* **LOVE SONG TO A STRANGER. / TUMBLEWEED** [–] [ ]

Mar 73. (7") *<1454>* **BEST OF FRIENDS. / MARY CALL** [–] [ ]

Apr 73. (lp/c) *(AMLH/CAM 64390) <4390>* **WHERE ARE YOU NOW, MY SON?** [ ] [ ]
– Only Heaven knows / Less than the song / A young gypsy / Mary call / Rider pass by / Best of friends / Windrose / Where are you now, my son? / *(one side was devoted to Vietnam bombing noises).*

— now with complete new set of session people.

Jun 73. (7") *<1472>* **LESS THAN A SONG. / WINDROSE** [–] [ ]

Jun 73. (7") *(AMS 7072)* **LESS THAN A SONG. / MARY CALL** [ ] [–]

May 74. (lp/c) *(AMLH 63614)* **GRACIAS A LA VIDA (HERE'S TO LIFE)** [ ] [–]

– Gracias a la vida / Ilego contres heridas (Come with three wounds) / La Ilorona (The weeping woman) / El preso numero (Prisoner number nine) / Guantanamera / Te recuerdo Amanda (I remember Amanda) / Dida / Cucurrucucu Paloma / Paso Rio (I pass a river) / El rossinyol (The nightingale) / De colores (In colours) / Las madras cansades (All the weary mothers of the Earth) / No nos moveran (We shall not be moved) / Esquinazo del guerrillo (The guerilla's serenade). *<(cd-iss. Mar03 on 'Universal'; E 393614-2)>*

Jun 74. (7") *<1516>* **GUANTANAMERA. / FOREVER YOUNG** [–] [ ]

May 75. (lp/c) *(AMLH 64527) <4527>* **DIAMONDS & RUST** [ ] [11]
– Diamonds and rust / Fountain of sorrow / Never dreamed you'd leave me in summer / Children and all that jazz / Simple twist of fate / Blue sky / Hello in there / Jesse / Winds of the old days / Dida / I dream of Jeannie / Danny boy. *(cd-iss. Feb03 on 'Spectrum'; 393233-2)*

Jun 75. (7") *<1703>* **BLUE SKY. / DIDA** [–] [57]

Jul 75. (7") **NEVER DREAMED YOU'D LEAVE ME IN SUMMER. / LAST SUMMER** [ ] [–]

Oct 75. (7") *(AMS 7200) <1737>* **DIAMONDS AND RUST. / WINDS OF THE OLD DAYS** [ ] Sep75 [35]

Jan 76. (7") **CHILDREN AND ALL THAT JAZZ. / NEVER DREAMED YOU'D LEAVE ME IN SUMMER** [–] [ ]

Mar 76. (d-lp) *(AMLH 64704) <3704>* **FROM EVERY STAGE (live)** [ ] Jan76 [34]
– (Ain't gonna let nobody) Turn me around / Blessed are . . . / Suzanne / Love song to a stranger / I shall be released / Blowin' in the wind / Stewball / Natalia / The ballad of Sacco & Vanzetti / Joe Hill / Love is just a four-letter word / Forever young / Diamonds and rust / Boulder to Birmingham / Swing low sweet chariot / Oh, happy day / Please come to Boston / Lily, Rosemary and the jack of hearts / The night they drove old Dixie down / Amazing Grace. *<(d-cd-iss. Jul94 on 'Universal'; E 396506-2)>*

Apr 76. (7") *(AMS 7226) <1802>* **PLEASE COME TO BOSTON. / LOVE SONG TO A STRANGER** [ ] [ ]

Nov 76. (lp/c) *(AMLH/CAM 64603) <4603>* **GULF WINDS** [ ] [62]
– Sweeter for me / Seabirds / Caruso / Still waters at night / Kingdom of childhood / O brother! / Time is passing us by / Stephanie's room / Gulf winds.

Nov 76. (7") *<1884>* **CARUSO. / TIME IS PASSING US BY** [–] [ ]

Feb 77. (7") *<1906>* **O BROTHER!. / STILL WATERS AT NIGHT** [–] [ ]

Portrait Portrait

Jul 77. (lp/c) *(PRT/40 82011) <34697>* **BLOWIN' AWAY** [ ] Jun77 [54]
– Sailing / Many a mile to freedom / Miracles / Yellow coat / Time rag / A heartfelt line or two / I'm blowin' away / Luba the baroness / Alter boy and the thief / Cry me a river.

Jul 77. (7") *<70006>* **I'M BLOWIN' AWAY. / ALTAR BOY AND THE THIEF** [–] [ ]

Jul 77. (7") *(PRT 5442)* **I'M BLOWIN' AWAY. / LUBA THE BARONESS** [ ] [–]

Nov 77. (7") *(PRT 5759) <70009>* **TIME RAG. / MIRACLES** [ ] [ ]

Jul 79. (lp/c) *(PRT/40 83474) <35766>* **HONEST LULLABY** [ ] [ ]
– Let your love flow / No woman, no cry / Light a light / The song at the end of the movie / Before the deluge / Honest lullaby / Michael / For Sasha / For all we know / Free at last. *(cd-iss. Feb97 on 'Columbia'; 473695-2)*

Feb 81. (lp/c) *(PRT/40 84790)* **EUROPEAN TOUR (live)** [ ] [–]
– The boxer / Don't cry for me Argentina / Gracias a la vida / The rose / For Sasha / Diamonds and rust / Soyuz druzyei / Cambodia / Kinder (sind so kleine hande) / Here's to you / Blowin' in the wind.

— retired for several years, although she toured Europe again in '83

Goldcastle Ccapitol

May 88. (cd/c/lp) *(CD/TC+/VGC 1) <71304>* **RECENTLY** [ ] [ ]
– Brothers in arms / Recently / Asimbonanga / The Moon is a harsh mistress / James and the gang / Let us break bread together (freedom) / MLK / Do right woman, do right man / Biko. *(re-iss. Aug91 on 'Virgin' lp/c; OVED/+C 354) (cd re-iss. Dec03; same)*

Apr 89. (cd/c/lp) *(CD/TC+/VGC 9) <71321>* **DIAMONDS AND RUST IN THE BULLRING (live)** [ ] [ ]
– Diamonds and rust / (Ain't gotta let nobody) Turn me around / No woman, no cry / Famous blue raincoat / Swing low sweet chariot / Let it be / El preso numero nueve / Ilego contres Heridas / Txoria Txoria / Ellas danzan solas (cueca sola) / Gracias a la vida / No nos moveran. *(re-iss. Aug91 on 'Virgin' lp/c; OVED/+C 370)*

Nov 89. (cd/c/lp) *(CD/TC+/VGC 12) <71324>* **SPEAKING OF DREAMS** [ ] [ ]
– China / Warriors of the sun / Carrickfergus / Hand to mouth / Speaking of dreams / El Salvador / Rambler gambler – Whispering bells / Fairfax country / A mi manera. *(re-iss. Aug91 on 'Virgin' lp/c; OVED/+C 371) (cd re-iss. Dec03; same)*

— now co-wrote with producers **WALLY WILSON** – (also) synthesizers / **KENNY GREENBERG** (also) guitars Other co-writers **KAREN O'CONNOR** or **PAT BUNCH.** Musicians:- **CHAD CROMWELL** – drums / **JERRY DOUGLAS** – various / **MARCOS SUZANO** – percussion / **EDGAR MEYER** – upright bass

Virgin Virgin

Jan 93. (cd/c) *(CD/TC 2705) <86458>* **PLAY ME BACKWARDS** [ ] Nov92 [ ]
– Play me backwards / Amsterdam / Isaac & Abraham / Stones in the road / Steal across the border / I'm with you / I'm with you (reprise) / Strange rivers / Through your hands / The dream song / Edge of glory. *(cd re-iss. Oct96 & Dec03 on 'Virgin-VIP'; CDVIP 164) (cd re-iss. Nov96 on 'Disky'; VI 87484-2)*

— next feat. duets w/ JANIS IAN, MARY CHAPIN-CARPENTER, MARY BLACK . . .

Grapevine Capitol

Sep 95. (cd/c) *(GRA CD/MC 208) <34989>* **RING THEM BELLS (live)** [ ] [ ]
– Lily of the west / Sweet Sir Galahad / The band played Waltzing Matilda / Willie Moore / Swallow song / Don't make promises / Jesse / Ring the bells / Welcome me / Suzanne / You're ageing well / Pajarillo Barranqueno / Don't think twice it's all right / Diamonds and rust / The night they drove old Dixie down. *(re-iss. May99; same)*

May 99. (cd) *(GRACD 223) <59357>* **GONE FROM DANGER** [ ] Sep97 [ ]
– No mermaid / Reunion hill / Crack in the mirror / February / Fishing / If I wrote you / Lily / Who do you think I am / Mercy bound / Money for floods.

Sep 99. (cd-s) *(CDGPS 269)* **NO MERMAID / FUSHING / DIAMONDS AND RUST (with Mary-Chapin Carpenter)** [ ] [–]

Sanctuary Koch

Sep 03. (cd) *(SANCD 218) <862-2>* **DARK CHORDS ON A BIG GUITAR** [ ] [ ]
– Sleeper / In my time of need / Rosemary Moore / Caleb Meyer / Motherland / Wings / Rexroth's daughter / Elvis Presley blues / King's highway / Christmas in Washington.

Proper Koch

Feb 06. (cd) *(PRPCD 029) <5714>* **BOWERY SONGS** (live) [ ] Sep05 [ ]
– Finlandia / Rexroth's daughter / Deportee (plane wreck at Los Gatos) / Joe Hill / Christmas in Washington / Farewell, Angelina / Motherland / Carrickfergus / Jackaroe / Seven curses / Dink's song / Silver dagger / It's all over now, baby blue / Jerusalem.

– (selective) compilations, etc. –

on 'Vanguard' unless mentioned otherwise

Nov 63. (lp) *Squire; <33001>* **THE BEST OF JOAN BAEZ** (early '59 live Newport) [–] [45]

Jun 69. (lp) *(SVXL 100)* **JOAN BAEZ ON VANGUARD** [15] [–]

Dec 70. (d-lp) *<(VSD 6560-1)>* **THE FIRST 10 YEARS** [41] Nov70 [73]
<(cd-iss. Nov00; VCD 6560)>

Nov 72. (d-lp) *<(VSD 41-42)>* **THE JOAN BAEZ BALLAD BOOK** [ ] [ ]
(re-iss. Aug89 on 'Start' lp/c/cd; VFLP5/VFTC6/VFCD7 108)

Dec 93. (3xcd-box) *Virgin; (TPAK 30)* **THE COMPACT COLLECTION** [ ] [–]
– (RECENTLY / DIAMONDS AND RUST / SPEAKING OF DREAMS)

Apr 94. (3xcd-box) *(VCD 3125)* **RARE, LIVE AND CLASSIC 1958-1989** [ ] [–]

Apr 96. (d-cd) *A&M; (540 500-2)* **DIAMONDS (A JOAN BAEZ ANTHOLOGY)** [ ] [–]

Sep 98. (cd) *<(VCD 79512)>* **BAEZ SINGS DYLAN** [ ] [ ]

Jan 01. (cd) *Universal; (E 497440-2)* **UNIVERSAL MASTERS COLLECTION** [ ] [ ]

Jan 03. (cd) *Ariola; (610586)* **LIVE – EUROPE 1983** [ ] [–]

Mar 03. (cd) *Universal; (AA694 90418-2)* **20TH CENTURY MASTERS** [ ] [ ]

Sep 03. (4xcd-box) *A&M; (9860479)* **THE COMPLETE A&M RECORDINGS** [ ] [ ]

the BAND

Formed: 1967, by expatriate Canadians ROBBIE ROBERTSON, RICK DANKO, RICHARD MANUEL, LEVON HELM and GARTH HUDSON. Having previously backed up rockabilly singer RONNIE HAWKINS, the group recorded under the name The CANADIAN SQUIRES and later LEVON AND THE HAWKS. As the HAWKS, the group also backed BOB DYLAN on his 1965-66 world tour, HELM having fallen out with DYLAN at an earlier gig, the infamous Forest Hills concert where the folk messiah has "gone electric" much to the chagrin of his more purist fans. Following DYLAN's 1966 motorcycle accident and subsequent seclusion at Woodstock, the group also relocated to the area, HELM rejoining them. They then began work on a series of laid back, informal sessions with DYLAN which would later see the light of day as 'THE BASEMENT TAPES', released by DYLAN's label, 'Columbia', in 1975. A seminal set of experimental proto-country rock, the legendary recording sessions from which the album resulted saw The BAND developing their distinctive instrumental, vocal and songwriting dexterity which would mark out 'MUSIC FROM BIG PINK' (1968) as one of the pivotal debut releases of the decade. Named after the group's communal Woodstock home, it stood alongside 'Sweetheart Of The Rodeo' and 'John Wesley Harding' as a quietly confident display of back to basics musical integrity and an antidote to the psychedelic excesses of the previous year. The record highlighted the vocal diversity of HELM, DANKO and MANUEL both individually and collectively whether covering DYLAN material ('TEARS OF RAGE', 'I SHALL BE RELEASED') or tackling the compelling ROBERTSON / MANUEL penned originals. From the former's prudent guitar playing to the eclecticism of HUDSON's organ runs, the musicianship was flawless and while songs like 'THE WEIGHT' were deceptively simple, they possessed an air of strange grace. If this album introduced The BAND as major contenders, then their eponymous follow-up assured them of a place in rock history. A veritable distillation of classic American musical tradition, 'THE BAND' (1969) put rock into a bit of much needed perspective, its rich beauty a reminder of why people set words to song in the first place. Vivid narratives like 'THE NIGHT THEY DROVE OLD DIXIE DOWN' and 'KING HARVEST (HAS SURELY COME)' resonated as deeply as any Steinbeck novel yet no one could accuse ROBERTSON of misty eyed nostalgia; the characters and their attendant burdens that inhabit these songs were genuine, holding up a mirror to the struggles of modern society. By 'STAGE FRIGHT' (1970), ROBERTSON's songwriting prowess was becoming a little blunted. Much of the material centered around his on-the-road experiences and while the likes of 'THE SHAPE I'M IN' and the title track were enjoyable enough, there was nothing to match the depths of its predecessor. 'CAHOOTS' (1971) was even more bereft of fresh ideas, a VAN MORRISON collaboration, '4% PANTOMINE', one of the record's few saving graces. 'ROCK OF AGES' (1972) was a competent, if pointless, double live effort, embellished with horns courtesy of the ubiquitous ALLEN TOUSSAINT while 'MOONDOG MATINEE' (1973) was an even more inessential collection of rock'n'roll covers. 'NORTHERN LIGHTS – SOUTHERN CROSS' (1975) saw the verve (small V!) returning to ROBERTSON's songwriting while HUDSON's keyboard work came into its own. By the following year, however, they'd decided enough was enough, playing their farewell concert at San Francisco's Winterland ballroom on Thanksgiving Day. The event was recorded for posterity as 'THE LAST WALTZ', a triple album set that also served as a soundtrack for the rockumentary of the same name. With an all-star cast including the likes of NEIL YOUNG and JONI MITCHELL, the record was a spirited, poignant farewell to a group that had helped define an era. After a final album to fulfil contractual obligations, the rank 'ISLANDS' (1977), the various members went off to do their own thing and that should've been the end of it. Inevitably it wasn't, and while an initial comeback album attempt was dealt a severe blow when RICHARD MANUEL took his own life in 1986, The BAND did reform the following decade (minus ROBERTSON who knocked back an invitation to join). Without two of their mainstays, the group were always going to find it difficult and indeed, both their albums, 'JERICHO' (1994) and 'HIGH ON THE HOG' (1996) consisted largely of well below par cover material. 1998's 'JUBILATION' was a more worthwhile proposition, a solid, earthy set of largely self-penned songs which included a cover of Allen Toussaint's 'YOU SEE ME' and featured guest appearances from both ERIC CLAPTON and JOHN HIATT. Sadly, just over a year later, RICK DANKO was found dead in his New York home on the 10th of December, 1999.

• **Covered:** WHEN I PAINT MY MASTERPIECE + FOREVER YOUNG + I MUST LOVE YOU TOO MUCH (Bob Dylan) / DON'T DO IT (Holland-Dozier-Holland) / LONG BLACK VEIL (Wilkin-Dill) / MYSTERY TRAIN (Elvis Presley) / THE GREAT PRETENDER (Platters) / SHE KNOWS (Procol Harum) / CRAZY MAMA (JJ Cale) / FREE YOUR MIND (D.Foster / T.McElroy) / WHERE SHOULD I ALWAYS BE (Bill Chaplin) / BACK TO MEMPHIS / STAND UP (B.Channel / R.Rector) / etc.

Album rating: MUSIC FROM BIG PINK (*8) / THE BAND (*10) / STAGE FRIGHT (*7) / CAHOOTS (*5) / ROCK OF AGES (*7) / MOONDOG MATINEE (*5) / NORTHERN LIGHTS – SOUTHERN CROSS (*6) / ISLANDS (*4) / THE LAST WALTZ with various artists (*8) / THE BEST OF THE BAND – ANTHOLOGY compilation (*7) / TO KINGDOM COME – THE DEFINITIVE COLLECTION compilation (*7) / JERICHO (*5) / LIVE AT WATKINS' GLEN live '73 (*6) / HIGH ON THE HOG (*2) / ACROSS THE GREAT DIVIDE boxed-set (*6) / JUBILATION (*5)

ROBBIE ROBERTSON (b. 4 Jul'44, Toronto, Canada) – guitar, vocals / **RICHARD MANUEL** (b. 3 Apr'45, Stratford, Canada) – piano, vocals, drums, sax / **RICK DANKO** (b. 9 Dec'43, Simcoe, Canada) – vocals, bass, violin, trombone / **GARTH HUDSON** (b. 2 Aug'37, London, Canada) – organ, saxophone, accordion / **LEVON HELM** (b.26 May'42, Marvel, Arizona) – drums, vocals, mandolin, guitar

not iss. | Apex

1964. (7"; as CANADIAN SQUIRES) **UH-UH-UH. / LEAVE ME ALONE** [–] [ ]
<re-iss. 1965 on 'Ware'; >

Atlantic | Atco

Nov 65. (7"; as LEVON AND THE HAWKS) *(4054) <6383>* **THE STONES I THROW. / HE DON'T LOVE YOU AND HE'LL BREAK YOUR HEART** [ ] Mar65 [ ]

1968. (7"; as LEVON AND THE HAWKS) *<6625>* **GO GO LISA JANE. / HE DON'T LOVE YOU AND HE'LL BREAK YOUR HEART** [–] [ ]

Capitol | Capitol

Aug 68. (lp; stereo/mono) *(S+/ST <2955>)* **MUSIC FROM BIG PINK** [ ] [30]
– Tears of rage / To kingdom come / In a station / Caledonian mission / The weight / We can talk / Long black veil / Chest fever / Lonesome Suzie / This wheel's on fire / I shall be released. *(re-iss. Jun81 on 'Greenlight' lp/c; GO/TC-GO 2001) (cd-iss. May87; CDP 746 069-2) (lp re-iss. Apr99 on 'E.M.I.'; 499465-2) <cd re-mast.Sep00 on 'E.M.I.'+=; 5 25390-2>* – Yazoo street scandal / Tears of rage (alt.) / Katie's been gone / If I lose / Long distance operator / Lonesome Suzie (alt.) / Orange juice blues (blues for breakfast) / Key to the highway / Ferdinand the imposter. *(lp-iss.Jun01 on 'Simply Vinyl'; SVLP 338)*

Sep 68. (7") *(CL 15559) <2269>* **THE WEIGHT. / I SHALL BE RELEASED** [21] Aug68 [63]

Jan 70. (lp) *<(EST 132)>* **THE BAND** [25] Sep69 [9]
– Across the great divide / Rag mama rag / The night they drove old Dixie down / When you awake / Up on Cripple Creek / Whispering pines / Jemima surrender / Rockin' chair / Look out Cleveland / Jawbone / The unfaithful servant / King Harvest (has surely come). *(re-iss. Aug86 lp/c; EMS/TCEMS 1192) (cd-iss. Aug88 on 'E.M.I.'; CZ 70) (cd re-iss. Aug97 on 'E.M.I.' hit UK No.41; CDP 746493-2) <cd re-mast.Sep00 +=; 5 25389-2>* – Get up Jake / Rag mama rag (alt.) / The night they drove old Dixie down (alt.) / Up on Cripple Creek (alt.) / Whispering pines (alt.) / Jemima surrender (alt.) / King Harvest (has surely come) (alt.). *(lp re-iss. Jun01 on 'Simply Vinyl'; SVLP 326)*

Oct 69. (7") *(CL 15613)* *<2635>* **UP ON CRIPPLE CREEK. / THE NIGHT THEY DROVE OLD DIXIE DOWN** [ ] [25]

Feb 70. (7") *(CL 15629)* *<2705>* **RAG MAMA RAG. / THE UNFAITHFUL SERVANT** [16] [57]

Oct 70. (lp) *<(EASW 425)>* **STAGE FRIGHT** [15] Sep70 [5]
– Strawberry wine / Sleeping / Time to kill / Just another whistle stop / All la glory / The shape I'm in / The W.S. Walcott medicine show / Daniel and the sacred harp / Stage fright / The rumor. *(re-iss. Jun81 on 'Greenlight' lp/c; GO/TC-GO 2003) (cd-iss. Mar91; CZ 405) <(cd re-mast.Sep00 +=; 5 25395-2)>* – Daniel and the sacred harp (alt.) / Time to kill (alt.) / The W.S. Walcott medicine show (alt.) / Radio commercial.

Oct 70. (7") *<2870>* **TIME TO KILL. / THE SHAPE I'M IN** [–] [77]

Oct 70. (7") *(CL 15659)* **TIME TO KILL. / SLEEPING** [ ] [–]

Mar 71. (7") *(CL 15675)* **THE SHAPE I'M IN. / THE RUMOR** [ ] [–]

Oct 71. (lp) *<(EAST 651)>* **CAHOOTS** [41] [21]
– Life is a carnival / When I paint my masterpiece / Last of the blacksmiths / Where do we go from here? / 4% pantomime / Shoot out in Chinatown / The Moon struck one / Thinkin' out loud / Smoke signal / Volcano / The river hymn. *(re-iss. Jun81 on 'Greenlight' lp/c; GO/TC-GO 2015) (cd-iss. May89; CZ 138) <(cd re-mast.Sep00 +=; 5 25391-2)>* – Endless highway / When I paint my masterpiece (alt.) / Bessie Smith / Don't do it / Radio commercial.

Oct 71. (7") *(CL 15700)* *<3199>* **LIFE IS A CARNIVAL. / THE MOON STRUCK ONE** [ ] [72]

Dec 71. (7") *<3249>* **WHEN I PAINT MY MASTERPIECE. / WHERE DO WE GO FROM HERE?** [–] [ ]

Aug 72. (d-lp) *<(SABB 11045)>* **ROCK OF AGES (live)** [ ] [6]
– (introduction) / Don't do it / King harvest (has surely come) / Caledonia mission / Get up Jake / The W.S. Walcott medicine show / Stage fright / The night they drove all Dixie down / Across the great divide / This wheel's on fire / Rag mama rag / The weight / The shape I'm in / The unfaithful servant / Life is a carnival / The genetic method * / Chest fever / (I don't want to) Hang up my rock and roll shoes. *(re-iss. Jul83 on 'E.M.I.';) (re-iss. Apr87 – =*; CDP 746 617-2) <d-cd-iss. 1990 += *> <(d-cd re-iss. May01 +=; 530181-2)>* – Loving you is sweeter than ever / I shall be released / Up on Cripple Creek / The rumor / Rockin' chair / Time to kill / Down in the flood (with BOB DYLAN) / When I paint my masterpiece (with BOB DYLAN) / Don't ya tell Henry (with BOB DYLAN) / Like a rolling stone (with BOB DYLAN).

Nov 72. (7") *(CL 15737)* *<3433>* **DON'T DO IT (live). / RAG MAMA RAG (live)** [ ] Sep72 [34]

Feb 73. (7") *<3500>* **CALEDONIA MISSION. / (I DON'T WANT TO) HANG UP MY ROCK AND ROLL SHOES** [–] [ ]

Nov 73. (7") *(CL 15767)* *<3758>* **AIN'T GOT NO HOME. / GET UP JAKE** [ ] [73]

Dec 73. (lp) *<(ESW 11214)>* **MOONDOG MATINEE** [ ] Nov73 [28]
– Ain't got no home / Holy cow / Share your love / Mystery train / The Third Man theme / The promised land / The great pretender / I'm ready / Saved / A change is gonna come. *(cd-iss. Jun98; 793592-2) <(cd re-iss. May01 on 'E.M.I.'+=; 5 25393-2)>* – Didn't it rain / Crying heart blues / Shakin' / What am I living for / Going back to Memphis / Endless highway.

— late '73, they renewed association with BOB DYLAN, helping out on album 'PLANET WAVES' and more so 'BEFORE THE FLOOD' a live album credited to BOB DYLAN / THE BAND. In '75 The BAND returned with brand new material.

Feb 74. (7") *<3828>* **THE THIRD MAN THEME. / THE W.S. WALCOTT MEDICINE SHOW** [–] [ ]

Dec 75. (lp) *<(ST 11440)>* **NORTHERN LIGHTS – SOUTHERN CROSS** [ ] [26]
– Forbidden fruit / Hobo jungle / Ophelia / Acadian driftwood / Ring your bell / It makes no difference / Jupiter hollow / Rags and bones. *(cd-iss. Mar91; CZ 404) <(cd re-iss. May01 +=; 5 25394-2)>* – Twilight (early take) / Christmas must be tonight (alt.).

Feb 76. (7") *<4230>* **OPHELIA. / HOBO JUNGLE** [–] [62]

Mar 76. (7") *(CL 15861)* **RING YOUR BELL. / FORBIDDEN FRUIT** [ ] [–]

Nov 76. (7") *<4316>* **TWILIGHT. / ACADIAN DRIFTWOOD** [–] [ ]

Apr 77. (lp) *<(EST 11602)>* **ISLANDS** [ ] Mar77 [64]
– Right as rain / Street walker / Let the night fall / Ain't that a lot of love / Christmas must be tonight / Islands / The saga of Pepote Rouge / Georgia on my mind / Knockin' lost John / Livin' in a dream. *(cd-iss. Mar91; CZ 406) (cd re-iss. May01 on 'E.M.I'+=; 525392-2)* – Twilight / Georgia on my mind (alt.).

Apr 77. (7") *<4361>* **GEORGIA ON MY MIND. / THE NIGHT THEY DROVE OLD DIXIE DOWN** [–] [ ]

Apr 77. (7") *(CL 15921)* **RIGHT AS RAIN. / KNOCKIN' LOST JOHN** [ ] [–]

— Joined by guests BOB DYLAN, NEIL YOUNG, RONNIE HAWKINS, JONI MITCHELL, ERIC CLAPTON, VAN MORRISON, NEIL DIAMOND, MUDDY WATERS, PAUL BUTTERFIELD, BOBBY CHARLES and DR. JOHN etc. Jams were from STEPHEN STILLS, RINGO STARR and RONNIE WOOD

Warners Warners

Apr 78. (t-lp) *(K 66076)* *<3WS 3146>* **THE LAST WALTZ** (live 25th Nov'76 – film soundtrack) [39] [16]
– Theme from the last waltz / Up on cripple creek / Who do you love? / Helpless / Stage fright / Coyote / Dry your eyes / Such a night / It makes no difference / Mystery train / The shape I'm in / The night they drove old Dixie down / Mannish boy / Further on up the road / The shape I'm in / Down south in New Orleans / Ophelia / Tura lura lural (that's an Irish lullaby) / Caravan / Life is a carnival / Baby let me follow you down / I don't believe you (she acts like we never have met) / Forever young / Baby let me follow you down (reprise) / I shall be released / The Last Waltz suite: The well – Evangeline – Out of the blue – The weight – The last waltz refrain – Theme from the last waltz. *(d-cd-iss. Jul88; K 266076) <(d-cd re-iss. Oct03 on 'Rhino'; 8122 73925-2)> <(4xcd-box iss.Apr02 on 'Rhino'+=; 8122 782782-3)>* – (extra tracks).

Jun 78. (7") *(K 17187)* **THEME FROM THE LAST WALTZ (live). / OUT OF THE BLUE (live)** [ ] [–]

Nov 78. (7") *<8592>* **OUT OF THE BLUE (live). / THE WELL (live)** [–] [ ]

— After their official split in 1978, HUDSON and MANUEL went into sessions. MANUEL hung himself 6 Mar'86, after a fit of depression. RICK DANKO and LEVON HELM went solo. In 1980, ROBBIE wrote score for film CARNY, before finally getting around to recording solo album in 1987.

— re-formed (now studio / earlier live) with **DANKO, HELM, HUDSON + JIM WEIDER** – bass / **RICHARD BELL** – piano / **RANDY CIARLANTE** – drums

Essential Pyramid

Feb 94. (cd/c) *(ESS CD/MC 199)* *<71564>* **JERICHO** [ ] Nov93 [ ]
– Remedy / Blind Willie McTell / The caves of Jericho / Atlantic City / Too soon gone / Country boy / Move to Japan / Amazon (river of dreams) / Stuff you gotta watch / Same thing / Shine a light / Blues stay away from me.

Transatla. Rhino

Apr 96. (cd/c) *(TRA CD/MC 228)* *<R2/R4 72404>* **HIGH ON THE HOG** [ ] [ ]
– Stand up / Back to Memphis / Where I should always be / Free your mind / Forever young / The high price of love / Crazy mama / I must love you too much / She knows / Ramble jungle.

not iss. Platinum

Sep 98. (cd) *<161420>* **JUBILATION** [–] [ ]
– Book faded brown / Don't wait / Last train to Memphis / High cotton / Kentucky downpour / Bound by love / White cadillac (ode to Ronnie Hawkins) / If I should fail / Spirits of the dance / You see me / French girls (instrumental). *(UK-iss.Jun00 on 'River North'; 514 161420-2) (UK re-iss. Oct03 on 'Solo'; 221416)*

– compilations, etc. –

on 'Capitol' unless stated otherwise

Sep 76. (d-lp) *(ST 3927)* *<ST 11553>* **THE BEST OF THE BAND** [ ] Jul76 [51]
– Up on Cripple Creek / The shape I'm in / The weight / It makes no difference / Life is a carnival / Twilight / Tears of rage / Stage fright / Ophelia / ,The night they drove old Dixie down. *(re-iss. Jun82 on 'Fame' lp/c; FA/TC-FA 3016) (cd-iss. May87; CDP 746 070-2)*

Oct 76. (7") *(CL 115887)* **TWILIGHT. / THE WEIGHT** [ ] [–]

Jan 79. (d-lp) *(ESTSP 19)* *<SKBO 11856>* **ANTHOLOGY** [ ] [ ]
(cd-iss. May89; CZ 63)

Jul 84. (7") *EMI Gold; (G45 28)* **RAG MAMA RAG. / THE WEIGHT** [ ] [–]

Oct 89. (t-lp/d-c)(d-cd) *(EN/TCEN 5010)(CDS 792 169-2)* **TO KINGDOM COME – THE DEFINITIVE COLLECTION** [ ] [ ]

May 92. (cd) *Castle; (CCS CD/MC 333)* **THE COLLECTION** [ ] [–]
– Back to Memphis / Tears of rage / To kingdom come / Long black veil / Chest fever / The weight / I shall be released / Up on Cripple Creek / Loving you is sweeter than ever / Rag mama rag / The night they drove old Dixie down / Unfaithful servant / King Harvest (has surely come) / The shape I'm in / The W.S.Walcott medicine show / Daniel and the sacred

harp / Stage fright / Don't do it (baby don't do it) / Life is a carnival / When I paint my masterpiece / 4% pantomine / The river hymn / Mystery train / Endless highway / Get up Jake / It makes no difference / Ophelia / Arcadian driftwood / Christmas must be tonight / The saga of Peopote rouge / Knockin' lost John.

Nov 94. (3xcd-box) *(CDBAND 1)* **ACROSS THE GREAT DIVIDE** ☐ ☐

Apr 95. (cd) *(CDP 831742-2)* **LIVE AT WATKINS GLEN (live)** ☐ ☐-
– Back to Memphis / Endless highway / I shall be released / Loving you is sweeter than ever / Too wet to work / Don't ya tell Henry / The rumour / Time to kill / Jam / Up on Cripple Creek.

Nov 96. (cd) *Disky; (DC 86716-2)* **THE WEIGHT** ☐ ☐-

Aug 98. (cd) *E.M.I.; (495051-2)* **THE SHAPE I'M IN (THE VERY BEST OF THE BAND)** ☐ ☐-
– The shape I'm in / Across the great divide / The night they drove old Dixie down / Stage fright / Rag mama rag / Ophelia / Up on Cripple Creek / Twilight / King Harvest (has surely come) / Life is a carnival / I shall be released / Tears of rage / Acadian driftwood / The weight / It makes no difference / Chest fever / Share your love with me / Don't do it (baby don't do it).

Feb 01. (cd) *Capitol; <(5 24941-2)>* **GREATEST HITS** ☐ Sep00 ☐
– The weight / Tears of rage / Chest fever / I shall be released / Up on Cripple Creek / The night they drove old Dixie down / Rag mama rag / King harvest (has surely come) / The shape I'm in / Stage fright / Time to kill / Life is a carnival / When I paint my masterpiece / Ain't got no home / It makes no difference / Ophelia / Acadian driftwood / The saga of Pepote Rouge.

Mar 02. (cd) *EMI Gold; (CDGOLD 1075)* **THE COLLECTION** (different) ☐ ☐-

Oct 02. (cd) *Disky; (SI 905050)* **THE MOON STRUCK ONE** ☐ Dec02 ☐

Mar 03. (cd) *E.M.I.; (583268-2)* **THE ESSENTIAL BAND** ☐ ☐-

☐ Thomas BANGALTER (see under ⇒ DAFT PUNK)

Syd BARRETT

Born: ROGER KEITH BARRETT, 6 Jan'46, Cambridge, England. Earned the nickname SID (which he later changed to SYD), after regulars at the local Riverside Jazz Club found out his surname and christened him after an old drummer from the area, SID BARRET. SYD was talented enough to secure a place at the prestigious Camberwell Art School in 1963 and once in London, he teamed up with his old friend ROGER WATERS, who had asked him to join his band The SCREAMING ABDABS. At SYD's suggestion, the band renamed themselves PINK FLOYD after two Georgia bluesmen featured on an old record he owned. Turned onto LSD by a friend, he became fascinated by the mysteries of the Universe, even carrying around a Times Astronomical Atlas. This obsession would later inspire such FLOYD classics as 'ASTRONOMY DOMINE' and 'INTERSTELLAR OVERDRIVE'. The latter's main riff was famously derived from a chord pattern SYD worked out after hearing manager PETER JENNER attempting to hum LOVE's version of BURT BACHARACH's 'My Little Red Book'. The 1967 album 'THE PIPER AT THE GATES OF DAWN' on which these two tracks appeared, made the group and especially BARRETT, major league pop stars. This was something that did SYD's increasingly erratic mental health no good whatsoever. By the time of the album's release, he had moved into the infamous Cromwell Road flat in London, living on a daily diet of hallucinogenics and was beginning to develop a piercing stare, which would scare even the most hardened person in his company. At EMI's request, BARRETT recorded two further tracks, 'SCREAM THY LAST SCREAM' and 'VEGETABLE MAN', which were unsurprisingly rejected, EMI staff producer NORMAN SMITH dubbing them "lunatic ravings". His penultimate offering for FLOYD, 'APPLES AND ORANGES', flopped, and SYD's mental condition deteriorated further. After missing some shows and performances, WATERS eventually made it clear he was surplus to requirement. His last effort with PINK FLOYD, 'JUGBAND BLUES', appeared after his departure, on the second FLOYD album 'A SAUCERFUL OF SECRETS' (mid-68). It was his last poignant statement for FLOYD, a self-diagnosis of his encroaching schizophrenia. EMI (actually 'Harvest') still had enough confidence in SYD to offer him a solo deal, as he set about recording his debut, 'THE MADCAP LAUGHS'. Released early in 1970 after a laborious year in the studio, it featured drummer NICK MASON and other FLOYD-ians, thus its brief entry into the UK Top 40. Despite SYD being high on the tranquiliser Mandrax, the album had its moments, with the likes of 'OCTOPUS', 'DARK GLOBE', 'TERRAPIN', 'NO GOOD TRYIN' and 'LONG GONE', making up for the other lost-in-the-ether tracks. The hastily recorded 'BARRETT', released later the same year, used a band featuring DAVE GILMOUR (the friend who replaced him in PINK FLOYD), RICK WRIGHT and JERRY SHIRLEY, giving him some cohesion, and although it was more assured in depth, it lacked the fragility of its predecessor. The album was poorly received and SYD retreated to the cellar of his mother's home in Cambridge. He resurfaced in 1972 as part of the doomed STARS project (with TWINK & JACK MONK), before finally giving up music altogether. He never fully recovered from his debilitating mental illness and tragically, he's become almost blind due to diabetes related problems. Whether the drugs actually caused his decline or merely assisted it is something that will no doubt continue to be debated long into the future, although you can be sure SYD won't care to listen. A flawed genius whose legend and influence grows stronger with each passing year, SYD BARRETT was the whimsical child-like star, burning brightly in a kaleidoscope of technicolour sound, before dropping out into a haze of drug-induced psychosis. He has since been tributed and stylised by many, including TELEVISION PERSONALITIES, ROBYN HITCHCOCK and the LEGENDARY PINK DOTS. Sadly, having lived alone at his late mother's home in Cambridge, SYD died of a diabetes related illness in early July 2006. Shine on Syd . . .

• **Trivia:** In 1975, PINK FLOYD paid homage to SYD on the classic track, 'Shine On You Crazy Diamond' from the album 'Wish You Were Here'; SYD attended these sessions but didn't contribute.

Album rating: THE MADCAP LAUGHS (*8) / BARRETT (*6) / collections: OPEL (*6) / OCTOPUS – THE BEST OF SYD BARRETT (*7) / WOULDN'T YOU MISS ME – THE BEST OF SYD BARRETT (*8) / THE RADIO ONE SESSIONS mini (*6)

SYD BARRETT – vocals, guitar; augmented by **DAVID GILMOUR** + **ROGER WATERS** with **MIKE RATLEDGE** – keyboards / **HUGH HOPPER** – bass / **ROBERT WYATT** – drums (all of SOFT MACHINE) plus **JOHN 'WILLIE' WATSON** + **JERRY SHIRLEY** – rhythm (latter of HUMBLE PIE)

Harvest Harvest

Oct 69. (7") *(HAR 5009)* **OCTOPUS. / GOLDEN HAIR** ☐ ☐

Jan 70. (lp) *(SHVL 765) <SABB 11314>* **THE MADCAP LAUGHS** 40 ☐
– Terrapin / No good trying / Love you / No man's land / Dark globe / Here I go / Octopus / Golden Hair / Long gone / She took a long cold look / Feel / If it's in you / Late night. *(cd-iss. Oct87; CDP 746 607-2) (re-iss. cd Jun94; CDGO 2053) (re-iss. Feb97 on 'E.M.I.'; LPCENT 1) (lp re-iss. Jan01 on 'Simply Vinyl'; SVLP 289)*

— SYD retained GILMOUR, SHIRLEY + WILSON adding **RICK WRIGHT** – keyboards (of PINK FLOYD) and guest on one **VIC SAYWELL** – tuba

Nov 70. (lp) *(SHSP 4007)* **BARRETT** ☐ ☐-
– Baby lemonade / Love song / Dominoes / It is obvious / Rats / Maisie / Gigolo aunt / Waving my arms in the air / Wined and dined / Wolfpack / Effervescing elephant / I never lied to you. *(cd-iss. May87; CDP 746 606-2) (re-iss. cd Jun94; CDGO 2054) (lp re-iss. Jan01 on 'Simply Vinyl'; SVLP 281)*

— his solo career ended and he formed short-lived STARS early in '72, with **TWINK** – drums (ex-PINK FAIRIES) + **JACK MONK** – bass (they made no recordings)

— in 1982 he was living with his mother having hung up his guitar

— in early July 2006, SYD died of a diabetes related illness

– compilations, others, etc. –

Sep 74. (d-lp) *Harvest; (SHDW 404)* **SYD BARRETT** □ –
– (THE MADCAP LAUGHS / BARRETT). *(d-cd-iss. Mar03; 582346-2)*

Jan 88. (12"ep) *Strange Fruit; (SFPS/+CD 043) / Dutch East India; <8307>* **THE PEEL SESSIONS** (24.2.70) □ □
– Terrapin / Gigolo aunt / Baby lemonade / Two of a kind / Effervescing elephant. *(cd re-iss. Sep95; same)*

Oct 88. (cd)(c/lp) *Harvest; (CDP 791 206-2)(TC+/SHSP 4126) / Capitol; <91206>* **OPEL** (recorded 68-70) □ Apr89 □
– Opel / Clowns and daggers (Octopus) / Rats / Golden hair (vocal) / Dollyrocker / Word song / Wined and dined / Swan Lee (Silas Lang) / Birdie hop / Let's split / Lanky (part 1) / Wouldn't you miss me / Golden hair (instrumental). *(re-iss. cd Jun94; CDGO 2055) (lp re-iss. Dec99 on 'Simply Vinyl'; SVLP 153)*

Apr 93. (3xcd-box) *E.M.I.; (SYDBOX 1)* **CRAZY DIAMOND – THE COMPLETE SYD BARRETT** □ □
– (all 3 albums above)

Apr 94. (cd) *Cleopatra; (<CLEO 5771-2>)* **OCTOPUS – THE BEST OF SYD BARRETT** □ May92 □
– Octopus / Swan Lee (Silas Lang) / Baby lemonade / Late night / Wined and dined / Golden hair / Gigolo aunt / Wolfpack / It is obvious / Lanky (pt.1) / No good trying / Clowns and jugglers (Octopus) / Waving my arms in the air / Opel. *(re-iss. Jul01; CLP 2200CD)*

Apr 01. (cd) *Harvest; (532320-2)* **WOULDN'T YOU MISS ME – THE BEST OF SYD BARRETT** □ □
– Octopus / Late night / Terrapin / Swan Lee / Wolfpack / Golden hair / Here I go / Long gone / No good trying / Opel / Baby lemonade / Gigolo aunt / Dominoes / Wouldn't you miss me / Wined and dined / Efferverscing elephant / Waving my arms in the air / I never lied to you / Love song / Two of a kind / Bob Dylan blues / Golden hair (instrumental).

Mar 04. (m-cd) *Strange Fruit; (<SFRSCD 127>)* **THE RADIO ONE SESSIONS** (live) □ May04 □

BASEMENT JAXX

Formed: Brixton, South London, England . . . 1993 by producer & DJ duo SIMON RATCLIFFE and FELIX BUXTON. The pair met at a Thames party organised by the latter on a riverboat. After conversation, sparks flew between the two DJs and they promptly set up 'Atlantic Jaxx' records in the summer of 1994. The pair were astounded when their idol and key influence TONY HUMPHRIES played 'DA UNDERGROUND' (a song from their first EP with the same title) to near annihilation on his 'Mix-show' in 1995. Later the same year the group also released 'SAMBA MAGIC' on single and conscripted vocalist CORRINA JOSEPHS into the outfit. 1996 was spent doing remixes for the PET SHOP BOYS, 'LIL' MO YIN' and various other artists. The collective also released an eponymous EP, which saw the track 'FLY LIFE' reach the British Top 20 and go on to become a massive house anthem. Relentlessly being pursued by major labels, RATCLIFFE and BUXTON settled for imprint 'X.L.' (home of The PRODIGY), where the band went on to issue their first major album 'REMEDY' (1999). The obvious highlight was the rare 12" single, 'SAME OLD SHOW', a sampletastic "rude girl!" beatbox of a song that incorporated the Selecter's 1980 hit 'On My Radio'; a ska influence (as well as a Latin one) was also evident on the PIGBAG-humping 'BINGO BANGO'. Two singles, 'RED ALERT' and the bass-breaking 'RENDEZ-VU', both became massive Ibiza and London house tracks, mixing styles as far apart as Chicago (drum'n'bass) to eclectic Latin disco-funk, the scope was undeniably wide. The pair of Brixton beatbreakers returned in the summer of 2001 with an album to equal that of 'REMEDY', named after their now de-funked private nightclub 'ROOTY'. Not only was 'ROOTY' better in terms of music, production and eclecticness (check out the funky PRINCE grooves on 'SEXY FELINE MACHINE'), but the album also boasted fantastic singles 'ROMEO' and the macabre GARY NUMAN-sampled 'WHERE'S YOUR HEAD AT?', which featured an equally wacked-out video starring some very scary monkeys. Other highlights included the KELE LA ROC fronted 'CRAZY GIRL', the Ibiza club floor-piece 'JUS 1 KISS' and the very laid bare 'BROKEN DREAMS', with its chilled, lounge-feel sweetness. It was inevitable that, due to the success of 'RED ALERT', the 'JAXX would spawn a whole host of hit singles, with both of the aforementioned reaching the Top 10 and the album crashing into the Top 5. 'KISH KASH' (2003) completed a home run of incredible records and even if it wasn't as groundbreaking as its predecessors, the very fact that they'd breathed life into that most difficult of music mediums – the dance long player – was surely an achievement in itself. The PRINCE influence was more notable than ever, while a raft of unlikely guest stars – from ME'SHELL NDEGEOCELLO to DIZZEE RASCAL to SIOUXSIE SIOUX – kept things interesting. Long since a Household name, BASEMENT JAXX proved their staying power with a UK No.1 anthology, 'THE SINGLES' (2005). Alongside the familiar hits were a couple of new ones, the fly girly-beat of 'OH MY GOSH' and the very DONNA SUMMER-esque 'U DON'T KNOW ME'.

Album rating: ATLANTIC JAXX – A COMPILATION (*6) / REMEDY (*9) / ROOTY (*8) / KISH KASH (*7) / THE SINGLES compilation (*8)

SIMON RATCLIFFE + FELIX BUXTON – electronics, samples

Atlantic Jaxx unknown

Mar 96. (12"; by CORRINA JOSEPH) *(JAXX 005)* **I WANNA GET DOWN (WHEN U GET DOWN). /** □ –

Jun 96. (12"ep) *(JAXX 001)* **BASEMENT JAXX E.P. 1** □ □

Jul 96. (12"ep) *(JAXX 002)* **BASEMENT JAXX E.P. 2** □ □
– Be free / Deep jackin' / I'm thru with you / Dusk till dawn.

Jul 96. (12"ep) *(JAXX 003)* **SUMMER DAZE E.P.** □ □
– Paradise / Phase 2 hi / Aprino jam / Samba magic.

Jul 96. (12"ep; by RATCLIFFE) *(JAXX 004)* **RATCLIFFE E.P.** □ □

Jul 96. (12"ep) *(JAXX 006)* **BASEMENT JAXX E.P. 3** □ □
– Daluma / Jus becuz / Fly life / Slide slide.

Nov 96. (12"; by HEARTISTS) *(JAXX 009)* **BELO HORIZONTI. /** □ –
(re-iss. Jul97 c-s/12"/cd-s; VCR C/T/D 23)

Feb 97. (12"ep) *(JAXX 008)* **SLEAZYCHEEKS E.P.** □ □
– Ennao / Moradi / Get down, get horny / Jump / Stanley.

Mar 97. (12"ep) *(JAXX 010)* **URBAN HAZE E.P.** □ □
– City people / Urban haze / Set yo' body free / Raw shit.

Multiply not iss.

May 97. (c-s/12"/cd-s) *(CA/12/CD MULTY 21)* **FLY LIFE (mixes)** 19 –
(12") *(12MULTY 21X)* – ('A'mixes).

Banana Krew not iss.

Aug 98. (12") *(001)* **SAME OLD SHOW. / AUTOMATIC** □ –

Nov 98. (12") *(JAXL 001)* **RED ALERT. / YO-YO** □ –

X.L. Astralwerks

Apr 99. (12")(cd-s) *(XLT 100)(XLS 100CD2) <6273>* **RED ALERT (mixes; Jaxx club / Eric Morillo & Harry Choo Choo Romero dub / Steve Gurley)** 5 Jul99 □
(cd-s) *(XLS 100CD) <6274>* – ('A'side) / Razocaine / ('A'-Jaxx nite dub).

May 99. (cd/c/d-lp) *(XL CD/MC/LP 129) <6270>* **REMEDY** 4 Aug99 □
– Rendez-vu / Yo-yo / Jump n' shout / U can't stop me / Jaxxalude / Red alert / Jazzalude / Always be there / Sneakalude / Same old show / Bingo bango / Gemilude / Stop 4 love / Don't give up / Being with U.

Jul 99. (c-s) *(XLC 110) <6281>* **RENDEZ-VU / MUSIC KEEPS ON PLAYIN' (Miracles mix of Red Alert)** 4 Oct99 □
(12") *(XLT 110)* – All U crazies.
(cd-s) *(XLS 110CD)* – (some of above).

Oct 99. (c-s)(cd-s) *(XLC 116)(XLS 116CD)* **JUMP N' SHOUT / LA PHOTO / I BEG YOU** 12 □
(12") *(XLT 116)* – ('A'side) / I Beg U / Boo slings dub.

Apr 00. (c-s) *(XLC 120)* **BINGO BANGO / (mix)** 13 □
(12"+=)(cd-s+=) *(XLT 120)(XLS 120CD)* – Jump 'n' shout.

Jun 01. (c-s/12") *(XLC/XLT 132)* **ROMEO. / BONGOLOID / CAMBERWELL SKIES** 6 □
(cd-s+=) *(XLS 132CD)* – ('A'mixes).

Jun 01. (cd/c/d-lp) *(XL CD/MC/LP 143) <10423>* **ROOTY** 5 □
– Romeo / Breakaway / SFM / Kissalude / Jus 1 kiss / Broken dreams / I want U / Get me off / Where's your head at / Freakalude / Crazy girl / Do your thing / All I know.

Sep 01. (cd-s) *(XLS 136CD)* **JUS 1 KISS / TWILITE / JUS 1 KISS (Jaxx nite club) / JUS 1 KISS (video)** 23 –
(12")(cd-s) *(XLT 136)(XLS 136CD2)* – ('A'-extended) / ('A'-Sunship mix) / ('A'-Boris Dlugosch mix).
Nov 01. (cd-s) *(XLS 140CD)* **WHERE'S YOUR HEAD AT / (acoustic version)** 9 –
(12") *(XLT 140)* – ('A'extended) / ('A'-Stanton Warriors remix) / ('A'-Sounds Of Da Future mix).
Jun 02. (cd-s) *(XLS 146CD)* **GET ME OFF / DO YOUR THING (Jaxx Club remix) / BROKEN DREAMS (Los Amigos Invisibles mix)** 22 –
(12")(cd-s) *(XLT 146)(XLS 146CD2)* – ('A'-2002 club mix) / ('A'-Peaches remix) / ('A'-Superchumbo 'Supergetoff' remix).
Oct 03. (cd/lp) *(XLCD/XLLP 174)* <93878> **KISH KASH** 17
– Good luck (with LISA KEKAULA) / Right here's the spot (with ME'SHELL NDEGEOCELLO) / Benjilude / Lucky star (with DIZZEE RASCAL) / Petrilude / Supersonic (with TOTLYN JACKSON) / Plug it in (with JC CHASEZ) / Cosmolude / If I ever recover / Cish cash (with SIOUXSIE SIOUX) / Tonight (with PHOEBE) / Hot 'n cold / Living room / Feels like home (with ME'SHELL NDEGEOCELLO).
Nov 03. (cd-s; by BASEMENT JAXX feat. DIZZEE RASCAL) *(XLS 172CD)* **LUCKY STAR / ('A'-Jaxx club remix) / ('A'-Dillinja remix)** 23 –
(12") *(XLT 172)* – ('A'-extended / Jaxxhouz dub / Jaxx club).
(12") *(XLR 172)* – ('A'-remixes; Dillinja / Dillinja dub).
Jan 04. (cd-s: by BASEMENT JAXX feat. LISA KEKAULA) *(XLS 178CD)* <618670> **GOOD LUCK / MERE PASS** 12
Mar 04. (cd-s; by BASEMENT JAXX feat. JC CHASEZ) *(XLS 180CD)* **PLUG IT IN / RENDEZ-VU (Rogers secret mix) / PLUG IT IN (mixes; Tab / Armand Van Helden / enhanced house)** 22 –
Jun 04. (cd-s; by BASEMENT JAXX feat. LISA KEKAULA) *(XLS 190CD)* **GOOD LUCK / MERE PASS / GOOD LUCK (Tim Deluxe & Roni Size mixes)** 14 –
Mar 05. (cd-s) *(XLS 209CD1)* **OH MY GOSH / OH MY GOSH (Old Skool dub)** 8 –
(12") *(XLT 209)* – ('A'-Jaxx club edit) / ('A'-KneeDeep club edit) / ('A'-Bugs in the attic mix).
(cd-s+=) *(XLS 209CD2)* – Oh my dub.
Apr 05. (d-cd) (*<XLCD 187>*) **THE SINGLES** (compilation) 1
– Red alert / Good luck / Romeo / Oh my gosh / Bingo bango / Where's your head at / Rendez-vu / Jump n' shout / Lucky star / Plug it in / U don't know me / Do your thing / Jus 1 kiss / Flylife / Samba magic // Magnificent Romeo / I beg U / Mere pass / Miracles keep on playin' (Red Alert remix) / Bongoloid / Good luck (live) / Rendez-vu / Broken dreams / Ha choo / Onyx / I live in Camberwell / Camberskank / Jus 1 kiss – the Isley bootleg / Romeoo – acoustic.
Jun 05. (cd-s; by BASEMENT JAXX feat. LISA KEKAULA) *(XLS 215CD1)* **U DON'T KNOW ME (Jaxxhouz Klubmix) / (original)** 26 –
(12") *(XLT 215)* – ('A') / ('A'-Solid Groove remix).
(cd-s+=) *(XLS 215CD2)* – Close 2 U.
Sep 05. (cd-s) *(XLS 220CD)* **DO YOUR THING / (Seiji mix)** 32 –
(12") *(XLT 220)* – ('A'-Jaxx club mix) / ('A'-Acid dub mix) / ('A'-Gadjo mix).
(12") *(XLR 220)* – ('A'-Seiji mix) / ('A'-Rubble Riviera juicy summer mix + dub).

– compilations, others, etc. –

on 'Atlantic Jaxx' unless otherwise stated
Oct 97. (cd/d-lp) *(JAXX CD/LP 001)* **ATLANTIC JAXX – A COMPILATION** –
– Intro / Be free / Samba magic / CORRINA JOSEPH: Live your life / Fly life / Ennao / HEARTISTS: Belo horizonti / CORRINA JOSEPH: Lonely / Set yo' body free / CORRINA JOSEPH: Daluma / RATCLIFFE: Grapesoda / RONNIE RICHARDS: Missing you / Undaground.
Aug 99. (12") *(JAXX 013)* **BETTA DAZE** –
Aug 02. (d12") *(JAXL 009)* **DO YOUR THING (mixes)** –
Oct 05. (12") *(JAXX 029)* **FLYLIFE XTRA. / (Switch mix) / (Dub 3 by Mr. Dan & Raf Daddy)** –

the BEACH BOYS

Formed: Hawthorne, Los Angeles, California, USA . . . 1961 by WILSON brothers BRIAN, DENNIS and CARL, who were soon joined by their cousin MIKE LOVE and neighbour AL JARDINE. They went through a series of cringe-inducing names before being individually christened The BEACH BOYS by a local DIY studio, who had released their first single 'SURFIN' on their small 'Candix' label. As sales of the record mushroomed, the band decided to keep the name. Murray Wilson, the brothers' tyrannical father, seized the opportunity to become their manager, producer and song publisher; not exactly a healthy combination and one which the band would come to regret when financial troubles dogged them throughout the next decade and beyond. For the moment however, on the surface at least, everything was hunky dory, the band riding the commercial crest of their surfing wave as they signed to 'Capitol' in 1962 and became the very essence of the sun-tanned, Californian dream. The hits came thick and fast with the prodigiously talented BRIAN writing most of the material. Songs like 'SURFIN SAFARI' and 'SURFIN U.S.A.' were effervescent feelgood anthems, their jaw dropping vocal harmonies framing images of surf, sea and beautiful girls. Early glimpses of BRIAN's penchant for introspection are evident on tracks like the poignant 'IN MY ROOM', co-written with GARY USHER, the first of many songwriters BRIAN would collaborate with during the course of his career. The execrable sentiments of songs like 'BE TRUE TO YOUR SCHOOL', were a result of a period of collaboration with lyricist ROGER CHRISTIAN, although this partnership also created livelier gems like 'LITTLE DEUCE COUPE' and 'I GET AROUND'. The latter song was probably the highlight of 'ALL SUMMER LONG', the 1964 album which saw the band make the leap from being primarily a singles act to creating consistent long players. By Christmas of that year, however, the strain of their horrendous recording/touring treadmill was too much for BRIAN and he suffered a series of nervous breakdowns. Producing and arranging 6 albums in just over 2 years as well as writing over 60 songs in the same period would've been too much for the hardiest of souls, let alone the painfully shy and sensitive BRIAN. This episode signalled the end of BRIAN's live commitment to the band, allowing him to concentrate solely on composing and recording. 'BEACH BOYS – TODAY' and 'SUMMER DAYS (AND SUMMER NIGHTS)' represented a career high with breathtaking material highlighting his preoccupation with achieving the perfect sound. BRIAN WILSON had become obsessed with outdoing The BEATLES who he saw as a threat, a paranoia that grew stronger after his first forays into the world of LSD. He first took the drug in the summer of '65 and it changed his approach to music, to his whole life in fact, with BRIAN later stating that his mind was opened and it scared the shit out of him. BRIAN then enlisted the unlikely help of erstwhile ad sloganeer Tony Asher to express the lyrical mood of these new pieces, and the result was 'PET SOUNDS'. Released in May '66, it still holds the coveted "best album of all-time" position among many critics, with fragile highlights being 'GOD ONLY KNOWS', 'WOULDN'T IT BE NICE' and 'CAROLINE NO', which perfectly evoked BRIAN's turbulent emotional state. Reportedly devastated at the album's lack of success in his home country (yes, it did hit Top 10) and feeling outdone by The BEATLES' 'Revolver' and DYLAN's 'Blonde On Blonde', he upped his drug use and vowed to go one better, dreaming of the ultimate studio masterpiece. Initially pencilled in for inclusion on 'PET SOUNDS' in its earliest incarnation, 'GOOD VIBRATIONS' was released in October that year and soon became their biggest ever selling single. With its pioneering use of the theramin and complex vocal arrangements, its success vindicated BRIAN's vision

The BEACH BOYS

of grand sonic tapestries over the formulaic pop that other members (most notably MIKE LOVE and his father) wanted to churn out. Around this time, BRIAN began working on his masterpiece (with self-styled L.A. boho scenester/songwriter VAN DYKE PARKS), which had a working title of 'DUMB ANGEL', later changing to 'SMILE'. The sessions that resulted are the stuff of legend, with BRIAN's mental condition deteriorating rapidly under the weight of his own expectation. Among BRIAN's more whimsical foibles were having a box filled with sand so he could play piano barefoot "like on the beach, man" (Surf's Up, indeed). More worrying was the pathological superstition which saw him attempt to destroy tapes of the abandoned 'SMILE' album, although these did surface later on albums 'SMILEY SMILE', 'HEROES AND VILLAINS' and 'SURF'S UP'. From this point on, BRIAN retreated even further from the world at large and spent much of the following decade in bed. A string of average, occasionally good albums followed with DENNIS emerging as a fairly talented songwriter. Recorded after the band's acrimonious split with 'Capitol', 1971's 'SURF'S UP' was the highlight of this period with its 'SMILE'-era title track and spirited contributions from other band members. DENNIS WILSON's association with the infamous Charles Manson, albeit before he went on his killing spree in 1969, probably brought more attention than any music the band released at this time. With the exception of one outstanding BRIAN-penned song 'SAIL ON SAILOR' from the disappointing 'HOLLAND' set, much of the 70's material was creatively bland to say the least. On the 4th June 1973, their father died and eventually MIKE LOVE's brothers STAN and STEVE were removed from management after STEVE was found guilty of embezzling around $1 million. 1977's 'BEACH BOYS LOVE YOU' album saw BRIAN return to take the reins again for the first time in 10 years, and included some fine material. From here on in, The BEACH BOYS became nothing more than a nostalgic novelty act, living on past glories while producing stagnant albums for the over 40's. On the 28th December '83, tragedy struck when DENNIS drowned during a diving trip in Marina Del Ray. The band struggled on minus BRIAN who'd been sacked a year earlier. The band scored a surprise US No.1 hit in 1988 with the soppy 'KOKOMO', which was co-written with former MAMAS & THE PAPAS singer JOHN PHILLIPS. Meanwhile, BRIAN released a competent, not to mention long-awaited solo album under the guidance of his controversial therapist EUGENE LANDY. He even recorded a second album, which was strangely turned down by his new label 'Sire', despite garnering rave reviews from critics who'd heard the pre-release tapes. 1995 saw the release of BRIAN's 'I JUST WASN'T MADE FOR THESE TIMES', an album project combining re-working of older and rare material. A year later The BEACH BOYS scraped the barrel of banality when they did a nauseating run through of their 60's hit 'FUN, FUN, FUN' with STATUS QUO. This was surely the end of the sandy road for the once inspirational outfit; tragedy struck with the lung cancer death (on the 6th of February) of CARL. Remaining brother BRIAN carried on, his 'IMAGINATION' (1998) set receiving rave reviews from the "old fogey" brigade while reaching the Top 100 (Top 30 in Britain); he subsequently teamed up with BRIAN SETZER (ex-STRAY CATS) to record 'LITTLE DEUCE COUPE' for a V/A "save our beaches" benefit album, 'Music For Our Mother Ocean'. BRIAN's musical rehabilitation went from strength to strength in the new millennium: a live solo album from the troubled genius would've been unimaginable only a decade earlier yet 'LIVE AT THE ROXY THEATRE' (2000) was just that, an internet-only release delving into at least some of the kind of difficult, introspective material which the BEACH BOYS steered clear of on stage. When the man went the whole hog and performed 'PET SOUNDS LIVE' (2002) over a four-night run at London's Royal Festival Hall, it was, understandably, the cue for grown men to weep in the aisles. Though the album was hardly a substitute for the living history of actually being there, critics were generally kind to it, and to WILSON's weathered vocals/erratic stage presence. 'GETTIN' IN OVER MY HEAD' (2004) took the same troupe of sympathetic and dedicated musicians into the studio alongside guests like PAUL McCARTNEY, ELTON JOHN and – with the help of studio technology – his late brother CARL. An obsession with studio possibilities had originally helped put the lid on 'SMILE' (2004), the would-be masterpiece he abandoned in 1967. Re-recorded and finally released in full, as a gloriously seamless whole, the album was final proof that WILSON was more than capable of making up for vanished years and genius overreached. The chart positions – UK Top 10, US Top 20 – were the best he'd scored in decades, reflecting the magnitude of the project. 'WHAT I REALLY WANT FOR CHRISTMAS' (2005) wasn't the most likely of follow-ups, even if the scope of the arrangements was as dazzling as ever, with contributions from the likes of Bernie Taupin and JIMMY WEBB.

• **Covered:** THE TIMES THEY ARE A-CHANGIN' (Bob Dylan) / PAPA OOM MOW MOW (Rivingtons) / I CAN HEAR MUSIC (Ronettes) / BARBARA ANN (Regents) / LOUIE LOUIE (Kingsmen) / WHY DO FOOLS FALL IN LOVE? (Frankie Lymon & the Teenagers) / MONSTER MASH (Bobby Pickett) / JOHNNY B. GOODE (Chuck Berry) / DO YOU WANNA DANCE (Bobby Freeman) / YOU'VE GOT TO HIDE YOUR LOVE AWAY + I SHOULD HAVE KNOWN BETTER (Beatles) / ALLEY OOP (Hollywood Argyles) / BLUEBIRDS OVER THE MOUNTAIN (Ersel Hickey) / THEN I KISSED HER (Crystals) / COME GO WITH ME (Del-Vikings) / CALIFORNIA DREAMIN' (Mamas & The Papas) / THE WANDERER (Dion) / ROCK AND ROLL MUSIC (Chuck Berry) / BLUEBERRY HILL (Fats Domino) / MONA (Bo Diddley) / PEGGY SUE (Buddy Holly) / THE AIR THAT I BREATHE (Hollies) / HOT FUN IN THE SUMMERTIME (Sly & The Family Stone) / WALKING IN THE SAND (Shangri-la's) / UNDER THE BOARDWALK (Drifters) / etc.

Album rating: SURFIN' SAFARI (*4) / SURFIN' U.S.A. (*7) / SURFER GIRL (*5) / LITTLE DEUCE COUPE (*4) / SHUT DOWN VOL.2 (*6) / ALL SUMMER LONG (*7) / THE BEACH BOYS CONCERT (*4) / THE BEACH BOYS – TODAY! (*7) / SUMMER DAYS (AND SUMMER NIGHTS!!) (*7) / THE BEACH BOYS PARTY (*4) / PET SOUNDS (*10) / SMILEY SMILE (*7) / WILD HONEY (*6) / FRIENDS (*5) / 20/20 (*6) / SUNFLOWER (*7) / SURF'S UP (*7) / CARL AND THE PASSIONS: SO TOUGH (*4) / HOLLAND (*6) / THE BEACH BOYS IN CONCERT (*5) / ENDLESS SUMMER compilation (*8) / 15 BIG ONES (*5) / THE BEACH BOYS LOVE YOU (*5) / M.I.U. ALBUM (*5) / L.A. (LIGHT ALBUM) (*5) / KEEPIN' THE SUMMER ALIVE (*2) / THE BEACH BOYS (*4) / STILL CRUISIN' collection (*3) / SUMMER IN PARADISE (*2) / THE VERY BEST OF THE BEACH BOYS compilation (*9) / CLASSICS: SELECTED BY BRIAN WILSON compilation (*7) / Brian Wilson: BRIAN WILSON (*6) / I JUST WASN'T MADE FOR THOSE TIMES (*6) / IMAGINATION (*7) / LIVE AT THE ROXY THEATRE (*6) / PET SOUNDS LIVE (*4) / GETTIN' IN OVER MY HEAD (*5) / SMiLE (*8) / WHAT I REALLY WANT FOR CHRISTMAS (*4)

BRIAN WILSON (b.20 Jun'42, Inglewood, California) – vocals, percussion / **CARL WILSON** (b.21 Dec'46) – guitar, vocals / **DENNIS WILSON** (b. 4 Dec'44) – vocals, drums / **MIKE LOVE** (b.15 Mar'44, Baldwin Hills, California) – vocals / **AL JARDINE** (b. 3 Sep'42, Lima, Ohio) – vocals, guitar

		not iss.	Candix
Dec 61.	(7") *<301>* **SURFIN'. / LUAU**	–	
Feb 62.	(7") *<331>* **SURFIN'. / LUAU**	–	75

—— **DAVID MARKS** – vocals repl. JARDINE who became a dentist

		Capitol	Capitol
Aug 62.	(7") *(CL 15273) <4777>* **SURFIN' SAFARI. / 409**		14 / 76
Nov 62.	(lp) *<T 1808>* **SURFIN' SAFARI** – Surfin' safari / County fair / Ten little indians / Chug-a-lug / Little girl (you're my Miss America) / 409 / Surfin' * / Heads you win – tails I lose / Summertime blues / Cuckoo clock * / Moon dawg / The shift. *(UK-iss.Apr63; SY 4572) (re-iss. Jun81 on Greenlight'; GO 2014)* – omitted *	–	32
Jan 63.	(7") *(CL 15285) <4880>* **TEN LITTLE INDIANS. / COUNTY FAIR** *(re-iss. Jun79; CL 16041)*		Nov62 49
Mar 63.	(7") *(CL 15305) <4932>* **SURFIN' U.S.A.. / SHUT DOWN** *(re-iss. Jun79; CL 16042)*	34	3 / 23

Apr 63. (lp; stereo/mono) <S+/T 1890> **SURFIN' U.S.A.** [–] [2]
– Surfin' U.S.A. / Farmer's daughter / Misirlou / Stoked / Lonely sea / Shut down / Noble surfer / Honky tonk / Lana / Surf jam / Let's go trippin' / Finders keepers. *(UK-iss.Aug65; same); hit No.17)*

— **AL JARDINE** – vocals returned to repl. MARKS

Jul 63. (7") *<5009>* **SURFER GIRL. / LITTLE DEUCE COUPE** [–] [7] [15]

Sep 63. (lp; stereo/mono) <S+/T 1981> **SURFER GIRL** [–] [7]
– Surfer girl / Catch a wave / Surfer Moon / South bay surfer / Rocking surfer / Little deuce Coupe / In my room / Hawaii / Surfer's rule / Our car club / Your summer dream / Boogie woogie. *(UK-iss.Mar67; same); hit No.13) (re-iss. Aug86 lp/c; EMS/TC-EMS 1175)*

Oct 63. (lp; stereo/mono) <*(S+/T 1998)*> **LITTLE DEUCE COUPE** [ ] [4]
– Little deuce Coupe / Ballad of ole' Betsy / Be true to your school / Car crazy cutie * / Cherry, cherry Coupe / 409 / Shut down / Spirit of America / Our car club * / No-go showboat / A young man is gone / Custom machine. *(re-iss. Jun81 on 'Greenlight'; GO 2025)* – omitted * *(re-iss. Aug86 lp/c; EMS/TC-EMS 1174)*

Nov 63. (7") *<5069>* **BE TRUE TO YOUR SCHOOL. / IN MY ROOM** [–] [6] [23]

Dec 63. (7") *<5096>* **LITTLE SAINT NICK. / THE LORD'S PRAYER** [–] xmas [ ]

Jan 64. (7"; as SURVIVORS) *<5102>* **PAMELA JEAN. / AFTER THE GAME** [–] [ ]

Mar 64. (7") *(CL 15339) <5118>* **FUN, FUN, FUN. / WHY DO FOOLS FALL IN LOVE** [ ] Feb64 [5]
(re-iss. Jun79; CL 16043)

Jul 64. (lp; stereo/mono) <*(S+/T 2027)*> **SHUT DOWN, VOLUME 2** [ ] Apr64 [13]
– Fun, fun, fun / Don't worry baby / In the parkin' lot / "Cassius" Love vs "Sonny" Wilson / The warmth of the sun / This car of mine / Why do fools fall in love / Pom-pom play girl / Keep an eye on summer / Shut down (pt.II) / Louie louie / Denny's drum. *(re-iss. May89 on 'C5'; C5-535)*

— Note:- 'SHUT DOWN' was a various artists surf US-lp issued Jul63 reaching No.7. It contained two BEACH BOYS tracks; 409 / Shut down.

Jun 64. (7") *(CL 15350) <5174>* **I GET AROUND. / DON'T WORRY BABY** [7] May64 [1]
(re-iss. Jun79; CL 16044)

Jul 64. (lp; stereo/mono) *<S+/T 2110>* **ALL SUMMER LONG** [–] [4]
– I get around / All summer long / Hushabye / Little Honda / We'll run away / Carl's big chance / Wendy / Do you remember? / Girls on the beach / Drive-in / Our favourite recording session / Don't back down. *(UK-iss.Jun65; same) (re-iss. Jul73 on 'Music For Pleasure'; MfP 50065) (re-iss. Aug86 lp/c; EMS/TC-EMS 1176)*

Oct 64. (7") *(CL 15361) <5245>* **WHEN I GROW UP (TO BE A MAN). / SHE KNOWS ME TOO WELL** [27] Aug64 [9]
(re-iss. Jun79; CL 16045)

Oct 64. (7"ep) *<R-5267>* **LITTLE HONDA / DON'T BACK DOWN. / WENDY / HUSHABYE** [–] [65] [44]

Dec 64. (7") *<5312>* **THE MAN WITH ALL THE TOYS. / BLUE CHRISTMAS** [–] xmas [ ]

Jan 65. (7") *(CL 15370) <5306>* **DANCE, DANCE, DANCE. / THE WARMTH OF THE SUN** [24] Oct64 [8]
(re-iss. Jun79; CL 16046)

Feb 65. (lp; stereo/mono) <*(S+/T 2198)*> **BEACH BOYS CONCERT (live)** [ ] Nov64 [1]
– Fun, fun, fun / The little old lady from Pasadena / Little deuce Coupe / Long tall Texan / In my room / Monster mash / Let's go trippin' / Papa-oom-mow-mow / The wanderer / Hawaii / Graduation day / I get around / Johnny B. Goode. *(re-iss. Jun81 on 'Greenlight' lp/c; GO/TCGO 2005)*

— **GLEN CAMPBELL** – vocals (on tour) repl. BRIAN who suffered breakdown. However BRIAN did stay as writer/producer (6th member)

Feb 65. (7") *<5372>* **DO YOU WANNA DANCE?. / PLEASE LET ME WONDER** [–] [12] [52]

Mar 65. (7") *(CL 15384)* **ALL SUMMER LONG. / DO YOU WANNA DANCE?** [ ] [–]
(re-iss. Jun79; CL 16047)

Mar 65. (lp; stereo/mono) <*(S+/T 2269)*> **THE BEACH BOYS TODAY!** [–] [4]
– Do you wanna dance? / Good to my baby / Don't hurt my little sister / When I grow up (to be a man) / Help me, Rhonda / Dance, dance, dance / Please let me wonder / I'm so young / Kiss me baby / She knows me too well / In the back of my mind / She knew me too well. *(UK-iss.Apr66; same); hit No.6) (re-iss. Jan72 as 'DO YOU WANNA DANCE' on 'Music For Pleasure'; MFP 5235)*

— **BRUCE JOHNSTON** – vocals (ex-his combo) repl. GLEN CAMPBELL who went solo

May 65. (7") *(CL 15392) <5395>* **HELP ME, RHONDA. / KISS ME BABY** [27] Apr65 [1]
(re-iss. Jun79; CL 16048)

Jul 65. (lp; stereo/mono) <*(S+/T 2354)*> **SUMMER DAYS (AND SUMMER NIGHTS!!)** [–] [2]
– The girl from New York City / Amusements parks U.S.A. / Then I kissed her / Salt Lake City / Girl don't tell me / Help me Rhonda / Let him run wild / You're so good to me / Summer means new love / I'm bugged at my ol' man / And your dream comes true. *(UK-iss.Jul66; same); hit No.4) (re-iss. Jun78; CAPS 1023) (re-iss. Aug86 lp/c; EMS/TC-EMS 1178)*

Aug 65 (7") *(CL 15409) <5464>* **CALIFORNIA GIRLS. / LET HIM RUN WILD** [26] Jul65 [3]
(re-iss. Jun79; CL 16049)

Dec 65. (7") *(CL 15425) <5540>* **THE LITTLE GIRL I ONCE KNEW. / THERE'S NO OTHER (LIKE MY BABY)** [ ] Nov65 [20]
(re-iss. Jun79; CL 16050)

Feb 66. (7") *(CL 15432) <5561>* **BARBARA ANN. / GIRL DON'T TELL ME** [3] Dec65 [2]
(re-iss. Jun79; CL 16051)

Feb 66. (lp; stereo/mono) <*(S+/T 2398)*> **BEACH BOYS' PARTY!** [3] Nov65 [6]
– Hully gully / I should have known better / Tell me why / Papa-oom-mow-mow / Mountain of love / You've got to hide your love away / Devoted to you / Alley oop / There's no other (like my baby) / I get around – Little deuce Coupe / The times they are a-changin' / Barbara Ann. *(re-iss. Aug86 lp/c; EMS/TC-EMS 1177)*

Apr 66. (7"; by BRIAN WILSON *(CL 15438) <5610>* **CAROLINE, NO. / SUMMER MEANS NEW LOVE** [ ] Mar66 [32]

Apr 66. (7") *(CL 15441) <5602>* **SLOOP JOHN B. / YOU'RE SO GOOD TO ME** [2] Mar66 [3]
(re-iss. Jun79; CL 16052)

May 66. (lp; stereo/mono) <*(S+/T 2458)*> **PET SOUNDS** [2] [10]
– Wouldn't it be nice / You still believe in me / That's not me / Don't talk (put your head on my shoulder) / I'm waiting for the day / Let's go away for awhile / Sloop John B. / God only knows / I know there's no answer / Here today / I just wasn't made for these times / Pet sounds / Caroline, no. *(re-iss. Jun81 on 'Greenlight'; GO 2002) (re-iss. May82 on 'Fame'; FA 3018) (re-iss. Aug86 lp/c; EMS/TC-EMS 1179)* <*(cd-iss. Jun90; 7-48421)*> – Hang on to your ego / Trombone Dixie. *(re-iss. Nov93 on 'Fame' cd/c; CD/TC FA 3298)* – hit No.70 Sep95 & No.59 Aug02 – *(lp re-iss. Dec99 on 'Simply Vinyl'; SVLP 149) (cd re-iss. Sep00 mono; 527319-2)*

Jul 66. (7") *(CL 15459) <5706>* **GOD ONLY KNOWS. / WOULDN'T IT BE NICE** [2] [39] [8]
(re-iss. Jun79; CL 16053)

Oct 66. (7") *<5676>* **GOOD VIBRATIONS. / LET'S GO AWAY FOR AWHILE** [–] [1]

Oct 66. (7") *(CL 15475)* **GOOD VIBRATIONS. / WENDY** [1] [–]
(re-iss. Jun79; CL 16054)

Apr 67. (7") *(CL 15502)* **THEN I KISSED HER. / MOUNTAIN OF LOVE** [4] [–]
(re-iss. Jun79; CL 16055)

Capitol Brother

Aug 67. (7") *(CL 15510) <1001>* **HEROES AND VILLAINS. / YOU'RE WELCOME** [8] Jul67 [12]
(re-iss. Jun79; CL 16056)

Sep 67. (7"; BRIAN WILSON & MIKE LOVE) *(CL 15513) <1002>* **GETTIN' HUNGRY. / DEVOTED TO YOU** [ ] [ ]

Nov 67. (lp; stereo/mono) <*(S+/T 9001)*> **SMILEY SMILE** [9] Sep67 [41]
– Heroes and villains / Vegetables / Fall breaks and back to winter / She's goin' bald / Little pad / Good vibrations / With me tonight / Wind chimes / Gettin' hungry / Wonderful / Whistle in. *(cd-iss. Nov98 on 'Magic'; 497576-2)*

Capitol Capitol

Nov 67. (7") *(CL 15521) <2028>* **WILD HONEY. / WIND CHIMES** [29] [31]
(re-iss. Jun79; CL 16057)

Dec 67. (7") *<2068>* **DARLIN'. / HERE TODAY** [–] [19]

Jan 68. (7") *(CL 15527)* **DARLIN'. / COUNTRY AIR** [11] [–]
(re-iss. Jun79; CL 16058)

Mar 68. (lp; stereo/mono) <*(S+/T 2859)*> **WILD HONEY** [7] Dec67 [24]
– Wild honey / Aren't you glad / I was made to love her / Country air /

A thing or two / Darlin' / I'd love just once to see you / Here comes the night / Let the wind blow / How she boogalooed it / Mama says.

May 68. (7") *(CL 15545)* *<2160>* **FRIENDS. / LITTLE BIRD** 25 47
(re-iss. Jun79; CL 16059)

Jul 68. (7") *(CL 15554)* *<2239>* **DO IT AGAIN. / WAKE THE WORLD** 1 20
(re-iss. Jun79; CL 16060)

Sep 68. (lp; stereo/mono) *<(S+/T 2895)>* **FRIENDS** 13 Jun68 –
– Meant for you / Friends / Wake the world / Be here in the mornin' / When a man needs a woman / Passing by / Anna Lee, the healer / Little bird / Be still / Busy doing nothin' / Diamond head / Transcendental meditation.

Dec 68. (7") *(CL 15572)* *<2360>* **BLUEBIRDS OVER THE MOUNTAIN. / NEVER LEARN NOT TO LOVE** 33 61
(re-iss. Jun79; CL 16061)

Feb 69. (7") *(CL 15584)* *<2432>* **I CAN HEAR MUSIC. / ALL I WANT TO DO** 10 24
(re-iss. Jun79; CL 16062)

Feb 69. (lp) *<(EST 133)>* **20/20** 3 68
– Do it again / I can hear music / Bluebirds over the mountain / Be with me / All I want to do / The nearest faraway place / Cottonfields / I went to sleep / Time to get alone / Never learn not to love / Our prayer / Cabinessence.

Jun 69. (7") *(CL 15598)* *<2530>* **BREAK AWAY. / CELEBRATE THE NEWS** 6 63
(re-iss. Jun79; CL 16063)

Stateside Reprise

Feb 70. (7") *<0894>* **ADD SOME MUSIC TO YOUR DAY. / SUSIE CINCINNATTI** – 64

Sep 70. (7") *<0929>* **SLIP ON THROUGH. / THIS WHOLE WORLD** – –

Nov 70. (7") *(SS 2181)* *<0957>* **TEARS IN THE MORNING. / IT'S ABOUT TIME**

Nov 70. (lp) *(SSL 8251)* *<6382>* **SUNFLOWER** 29 Sep70
– Slip on through / This whole world / Add some music to your day / Got to know the woman / Deirdre / It's about time / Tears in the morning / All I wanna do / Forever / Our sweet love / At my window / Cool, cool water. *(re-iss. Nov80 on 'Caribou'; 31773>* – Cottonfields. *(re-iss. Jul91 on 'Epic' cd/c; 467836-2/-4)*

Dec 70. (7"; by DENNIS WILSON & RUMBO) *(SS 2184)* **SOUND OF FREE. / LADY** –

Feb 71. (7") *<0998>* **COOL, COOL WATER. / FOREVER** –

Jun 71. (7") *(SS 2190)* *<1015>* **LONG PROMISED ROAD. / DEIRDRE**

Oct 71. (7") *<1047>* **LONG PROMISED ROAD. / TILL I DIE** – 89

Nov 71. (7") *(SS 2194)* **DON'T GO NEAR THE WATER. / STUDENT DEMONSTRATION TIME**

Nov 71. (lp) *(SSL 10313)* *<6453>* **SURF'S UP** 15 Aug71 29
– Don't go near the water / Long promised road / Take a load off your feet / Disney girls (1957) / Student demonstration time / Feel flows / Lookin' at tomorrow / A day in the life of a tree / 'Til I die / Surf's up. *<re-iss. Nov80 on 'Caribou'; 31774>* *(re-iss. Jul91 on 'Epic' cd/c; 467835-2/-4)*

Nov 71. (7") *<1058>* **SURF'S UP. / DON'T GO NEAR THE WATER** –

— **BLONDIE CHAPLIN** – guitar repl. JOHNSTON who later went solo added **RICKY FATAAR** – drums (DENNIS now just vocals)

Reprise Reprise

May 72. (7") *(K 14173)* *<1091>* **YOU NEED A MESS OF HELP TO STAND ALONE. / CUDDLE UP**

Jun 72. (d-lp) *(K 44184)* *<2083>* **CARL AND THE PASSIONS – SO TOUGH** 25 May72 50
– You need a mess of help to stand alone / Here she comes / He come down / Marcella / Hold on dear brother / Make it good / All this is that / Cuddle up. *(w/ 'PET SOUNDS') (re-iss. Jul91 on 'Epic' cd/c; 468349-2/-4)*

Aug 72. (7") *<1101>* **MARCELLA. / HOLD ON DEAD BROTHER** –

Jan 73. (lp) *(K 54008)* *<2118>* **HOLLAND** 20 36
– Sail on sailor / Steamboat / California saga (on my way to sunny Californ-i-a (medley):- Big surf – Beaks of eagles – California / The trader / Leaving this town / Only with you / Funky pretty. *(7"ep free-w/a) <2118>* **MOUNT VERNON AND FAIRWAY (A FAIRY TALE)** – Better get back in bed / Magic transistor radio / Mount Vernon and Fairway / I'm the pied piper / Radio King Dom. *(re-iss. Jul91 on 'Epic' cd/c; 467837-2/-4)*

Feb 73. (7") *<1138>* **SAIL ON SAILOR. / ONLY WITH YOU** – 79

Feb 73. (7") *(K 14232)* **CALIFORNIA SAGA: CALIFORNIA. / SAIL ON SAILOR** 37 –

May 73. (7") *<1156>* **CALIFORNIA SAGA (ON MY WAY TO SUNNY CALIFORN-I-A). / FUNKY PRETTY** – 84

Nov 73. (d-lp) *(K 84001)* *<6484>* **THE BEACH BOYS IN CONCERT (live)** 25
– Sail on sailor / Sloop John B. / The trader / You still believe me / California girls / Darlin' / Marcella / Caroline, no / Leaving this town / Heroes and villains / We got love / Don't worry baby / Surfin' U.S.A. / Good vibrations / Fun, fun, fun / Funky pretty / Let the wind blow / Help me Rhonda / Surfer girl / Wouldn't it be nice. *(re-iss. Jun91 on 'Epic' cd/c; 468345-2/-4)*

Jul 74. (7") *<1310>* **I CAN HEAR MUSIC (live). / LET THE WIND BLOW (live)** –

Aug 74. (7"ep) *(K 14346)* **CALIFORNIA SAGA: CALIFORNIA / SAIL ON SAILOR. / MARCELLA / I'M THE PIED PIPER** –

— **JAMES GUERICO** – bass (on tour) repl. BLONDIE and RICKY /
— **DENNIS** returned to his drums

Jun 75. (7") *(K 14394)* *<1325>* **SAIL ON SAILOR. / ONLY WITH YOU** 49

Dec 75. (7"w-drawn) *(K 14411)* *<1321>* **CHILD OF WINTER. / SUSIE CINCINNATI** – Dec74

— **BRIAN** returned to live work

— After this point, The BEACH BOYS abandoned even the slightest attempt to push their own musical boundaries. Instead relying upon tired retreads of their earlier sound.

Jul 76. (7") *(K 14440)* *<1354>* **ROCK AND ROLL MUSIC. / THE T.M. SONG** 36 May76 5

Jul 76. (lp/c) *(K/K4 54079)* *<MSK 2251>* **15 BIG ONES** 31 8
– Rock and roll music / It's O.K. / Had to phone ya / Chapel of love / Everyone's in love with you / Talk to me / That same song / The T.M. song / Palisades park / Susie Cincinatti / A casual look / Blueberry Hill / Back home / In the still of the night / Just once in my life. *(re-iss. Jul91 on 'Epic' cd/c; 468346-2/-4)*

Aug 76. (7") *(K 14448)* *<1368>* **IT'S O.K. / HAD TO PHONE YA** 29

Nov 76. (7") *<1375>* **SUSIE CINCINNATI. / EVERYONE'S IN LOVE WITH YOU** –

Apr 77. (7") *<1389>* **HONKIN' DOWN THE HIGHWAY. / SOLAR SYSTEM** –

Apr 77. (lp/c) *(K/K4 54079)* *<MSK 2258>* **THE BEACH BOYS LOVE YOU** 26 53
– Roller skating child / I'll bet he's nice / Airplane / Love is a woman / Johnny Carson / Let us go on this way / I wanna pick you up / Let's put our hearts together / Solar system / The night was so young / Ding dang / Mona / Honkin' down the highway / Good time. *(re-iss. Jun91 on 'Epic' cd/c; 468347-2/-4)*

Aug 77. (7"ep) *(K 14481)* **MONA / ROCK AND ROLL MUSIC. / SAIL ON SAILOR / MARCELLA** –

Sep 78. (lp/c) *(K/K4 54102)* *<MSK 2268>* **M.I.U. ALBUM**
– She's got rhythm / Come go with me / Hey little tomboy / Kona coast / Peggy Sue / Wontcha come out tonight / Sweet Sunday kinda love / Belles of Paris / Pitter patter / My Diane / Match point of your love / Winds of change. *(re-iss. Jul91 on 'Epic' cd/c; 468348-2/-4)*

Oct 78. (7") *(K 14489)* *<1394>* **PEGGY SUE. / HEY LITTLE TOMBOY** Aug78 59

Dec 78. (7") *(K 14494)* **KONA COAST. / SWEET SUNDAY KINDA LOVE** –

— **BRUCE JOHNSTON** – vocals, returned to add to DENNIS, CARL, AL, MIKE + BRIAN

Caribou Caribou

Mar 79. (7") *(CRB 7204)* *<9026>* **HERE COMES THE NIGHT. / BABY BLUE** 37 44
(12"blue+=) *(CRB 12-7204)* – ('A'-disco version).

Apr 79. (lp/c/pic-lp) *(CRB/40/11 86081)* *<35752>* **L.A. (LIGHT ALBUM)** 32 100
– Angel come home / Baby blue / Love surrounds me / Good timin' / Goin' south / Shortenin' bread / Lady Lynda / Sumahama / Full sail / Sumahama / Here comes the night. *(re-iss. Aug86; 4032806) (cd-iss. Jul89 on 'Pickwick'; 902127-2)*

May 79. (7") *<9029>* **GOOD TIMIN'. / LOVE SURROUNDS ME** – 40

Jun 79. (7") *(CRB 7427)* *<9030>* **LADY LYNDA. / FULL SAIL** 6

Aug 79. (7") *(CRB 7846)* **SUMAHAMA. / ANGEL COME HOME** 6

Sep 79. (7") *<9031>* **SUMAHAMA. / IT'S A BEAUTIFUL DAY** –

Nov 79. (7") *(CRB 8055)* **GOOD TIMIN'. / GOIN' SOUTH** [ ] [–]
Mar 80. (7") *<9032>* **GOIN' ON. / ENDLESS HARMONY** [–] [83]
Mar 80. (7") *(CRB 8367)* **OH DARLING. / ENDLESS HARMONY** [ ] [–]
Mar 80. (lp) *(CRB 86109) <36283>* **KEEPIN' THE SUMMER ALIVE** [54] [75]
– Endless harmony / When girls get together / School day (ring! ring! goes the bell) / Sunshine / Santa Ana winds / Goin' on / Some of your love / Oh darlin' / Livin' with a heartache / Keepin' the summer alive. *(re-iss. Jun91 on 'Epic' cd/c; 468350-2/-4)*
Jun 80. (7") *(CRB 8663)* **KEEPIN' THE SUMMER ALIVE. / WHEN GIRLS GET TOGETHER** [ ] [–]
Jul 80. (7") *<9033>* **LIVING WITH A HEARTACHE. / SANTA ANA WINDS** [–] [ ]
Jul 80. (7") *(CRB 8633)* **SANTA ANA WINDS. / SUNSHINE** [ ] [–]

— **ADRIAN BAKER** – vocals (ex-solo) repl. CARL and BRUCE

— **CARL WILSON** returned after short solo career

Feb 82. (7") *(CRBA 2015) <02633>* **COME GO WITH ME. / DON'T GO NEAR THE WATER** [ ] Nov81 [18]

— Tragically on 28th Dec83, DENNIS drowned (see above). The other original 4 (BRIAN, CARL, AL and MIKE) carried on. Mar'85, ere credited on JULIO IGLESIAS single 'THE AIR THAT I BREATHE' *(CBS A 5009)*

May 85. (7") *(A 6324) <04913>* **GETCHA BACK. / MALE EGO** [ ] [26]
(12"+=) *(TA 6324)* – Here comes the night / Lady Lynda.
Jun 85. (lp/c/cd) *(CRB/40/CD 26378) <39946>* **THE BEACH BOYS** [60] [52]
– Getcha back / It's gettin' late / Crack at your love / Maybe I don't know / She believes in love again / California calling / Passing friend / I'm so lonely / Where I belong / I do love you / It's just a matter of time. *(cd+=)* – Male ego. *(re-iss. Ovt90 on 'C.B.S.' cd/c/lp; 467363-2/-4/-1)*
Jul 85. (7") *<05433>* **IT'S GETTIN' LATE. / IT'S O.K.** [–] [82]
Aug 85. (7") *(A 6471)* **PASSING FRIEND. / IT'S O.K.** [ ] [–]
Nov 85. (7") *<05624>* **SHE BELIEVES IN LOVE AGAIN. / IT'S JUST A MATTER OF TIME** [–] [ ]

Capitol Capitol

Jun 86. (7") *<5595>* **ROCK'N'ROLL TO THE RESCUE. / GOOD VIBRATIONS (live)** [–] [68]
Sep 86. (7") *(CL 425) <5630>* **CALIFORNIA DREAMIN'. / LADY LIBERTY** [ ] [57]
(12"+=) *(12CL 425)* – (Ballads medley).

— BRIAN now departed to go solo, the rest did one-off (Jul'87) with The FAT BOYS on their UK No.2 hit single 'WIPE OUT' *(Urban; URB 5)* Also hit No.12 in the US on 'Tin Pan'; *<885960>*

Nov 88. (7"/12") *(EKR 85/+T) <69385>* **KOKOMO. / TUTTI FRUTTI (by 'Little Richard')** [25] Aug88 [1]
above single was from the film 'Cocktail' on 'Elektra' label / below from 'Lethal Weapon 2'
Aug 89. (7") *(CL 549) <44445>* **STILL CRUISIN'. / KOKOMO** [ ] [93]
(cd-s+=) *(CDCL 549)* – Rock'n'roll to the rescue (mix) / Lady Liberty.
(12"+=) *(12CL 549)* – Beach Boys Medley.
Jul 90. (c-s/cd-s) *<44475>* **SOMEWHERE NEAR JAPAN / KOKOMO** [–] [ ]

— **MIKE LOVE, CARL WILSON, AL JARDINE, BRUCE JOHNSTON** (now keyboards), **MELCHER** (keyboards + co-writer w/LOVE), **ADRIAN BAKER** (backing vocals), **KEITH WECHSLER** (keyboards / some drums), **CRAIG FALL** – guitar, keyboards / **ROD CLARK** – bass / **SAMMY MERENDINO** – drums / **VAN DYKE PARKS** – accordion, keyboards / **DANNY KORTCHMAR** – guitars / **JOEL PESKIN** – saxophone / **JOHN WESTON** – pedal steel

E.M.I. Brother

Jun 93. (cd/c) *(CD/TC EMD 1046) <727>* **SUMMER IN PARADISE** [ ] Aug92 [ ]
– Hot fun in the summertime / Surfin' / Slow summer dancin' (one summer night) / Strange things happen / Remember walking in the sand / Lahaina aloha / Under the boardwalk / Summer in Paradise forever. *(re-iss. cd May95 on 'Fame'; CDFA 3321)*

— guested on STATUS QUO's hit version of their 'FUN FUN FUN'.

not iss. Sub Pop

Jun 96. (7"m) *<SP 363>* **I JUST WASN'T MADE FOR THESE TIMES. / WOULDN'T IT BE NICE / HERE TODAY** [–] [ ]

— **MIKE LOVE** brought in various vocalists

not iss. River North

Aug 96. (cd) *<51416 1205-2>* **STARS AND STRIPES VOL.1** [–] [ ]
– Don't worry baby / Little deuce coupe / 409 / Long tall Texan / I get around / Be true to your school / Fun, fun, fun / Help me, Rhonda / The warmth of the sun / Sloop John B. / I can hear music / Caroline no. *(UK-iss.Jun00; same as US)*

– (selective) compilations, etc. –

on 'Capitol' unless stated otherwise

Oct 66. (lp; stereo/mono) *(S+/T 20856) <2545>* **THE BEST OF THE BEACH BOYS** [2] [8]
Oct 67. (lp; stereo/mono) *(S+/T 20956) <2706>* **THE BEST OF THE BEACH BOYS VOL.2** [3] Aug67 [50]
Nov 68. (lp; stereo/mono) *(S+/T 21142) <2905>* **THE BEST OF THE BEACH BOYS VOL.3** [8] Sep68 [ ]
May 70. (7") *(CL 15640) <2765>* **COTTONFIELDS. / THE NEAREST FARAWAY PLACE** [5] [ ]
Sep 70. (lp) *(T 21628)* **GREATEST HITS** [5] [–]
Aug 72. (lp) *(ST 21715) <11584>* **LIVE IN LONDON (live 1969)** [ ] Dec76 [75]
(re-iss. Sep77 on 'Music For Pleasure'; 50345)
Jul 74. (d-lp) *<2166>* **WILD HONEY / 20-20** [–] [50]
Aug 74. (7") *<3924>* **SURFIN' U.S.A. / THE WARMTH OF THE SUN** [–] [36]
Nov 74. (d-lp) *<(EA-ST 11307)>* **ENDLESS SUMMER** [ ] Jul74 [1]
(re-iss. Sep81 on 'Music For Pleasure'; MfP 50528) (cd-iss. Feb87 on 'E.M.I.'; CDP 746 467-2) (cd re-iss. May99; CDMFP 50528)
Apr 75. (d-lp) *(VMP 1007) <SVBB 11384>* **SPIRIT OF AMERICA** [ ] [8]
(cd-iss. Jun87; CDP7 746 618-2)
Oct 75. (lp) *Music For Pleasure; (MFP 50234) / Brother; <2223>*
GOOD VIBRATIONS – THE BEST OF BEACH BOYS [ ] Jul75 [25]
Jun 76. (7") *(CL 15875)* **GOOD VIBRATIONS. / WOULDN'T IT BE NICE** [18] [–]
Jul 76. (lp/c) *E.M.I.; (EMTV/TC-EMTV 1)* **20 GOLDEN GREATS** [1] [ ]
(cd-iss. Nov87; CDEMTV 1) (re-iss. 1979 blue-lp; same) (re-iss. cd+c Sep94)
Aug 81. (7") *(CL 213) <5030>* **BEACH BOYS MEDLEY. / GOD ONLY KNOWS** [47] [12]
Jul 83. (d-lp) *(BBTV 1867193)* **THE VERY BEST OF THE BEACH BOYS** [1] [ ]
– Surfin' safari / Surfin' U.S.A. / Shut down / Little deuce Coupe / In my room / Fun, fun, fun / I get around / Don't worry baby / When I grow up (to be a man) / Wendy / Little Honda / Dance dance dance / All summer long / Do you wanna dance / Help me Rhonda / California girls / Little girl I once knew / Barbara Ann / You're so good to me / Then I kissed her / Sloop John B. / God only knows / Wouldn't it be nice / Here today / Good vibrations / Heroes and villains / Wild honey / Darlin' / Country air / Here comes the night / Friends / Do it again / Bluebirds over the mountain / I can hear music / Break away / Cottonfields.
Dec 84. (d-lp/d-c) *C.B.S.; (22178) / Caribou; <37445>* **TEN YEARS OF HARMONY (1970-1980)** [ ] Dec81 [ ]
Aug 86. (cd/c/d-lp) *(CD/TC+/EN 5005) <12396>* **MADE IN THE U.S.A.** [ ] Jul86 [96]
Jun 90. (7") *(CL 579)* **WOULDN'T IT BE NICE. / I GET AROUND** [58] [ ]
(12"+=/cd-s+=) *(12/CD CL 579)* – Medley of hits.
Jun 90. (cd)(c/d-lp) *(CDP7 94620-2)(TC+/EMTVD 51)* **SUMMER DREAMS** [2] [–]
Jun 90. (cd) *(CDP7 93691-2)* **SURFIN' SAFARI / SURFIN' U.S.A.** [ ] [ ]
(contains extra tracks) (c-iss.Jul91; C 493691)
Jun 90. (cd) *(CDP7 93692-2)* **SURFER GIRL / SHUT DOWN, VOLUME 2** [ ] [ ]
(contains extra tracks) (c-iss.Jul91; C 493692)
Jul 90. (cd) *(CDP7 93693-2)* **LITTLE DEUCE COUPE / ALL SUMMER LONG** [ ] [ ]
(contains extra tracks) (c-iss.Aug91; C 493693)
Aug 90. (cd) *(CDP7 93694-2)* **TODAY / SUMMER DAYS (AND SUMMER NIGHTS!!)** [ ] [ ]
(contains extra tracks) (c-iss.Aug91; C 493694)
Aug 90. (cd) *(CDP7 93695-2)* **BEACH BOYS' CONCERT / LIVE IN LONDON** [ ] [ ]
(contains extra tracks) (c-iss.Aug91; C 493695)
Aug 90. (cd) *(CDP7 93696-2)* **WILD HONEY / SMILEY SMILE** [ ] [ ]
(contains extra tracks) (c-iss.Aug91; C 493696)
Aug 90. (cd) *(CDP7 93697-2)* **FRIENDS / 20-20** [ ] [ ]
(contains extra tracks) (c-iss.Aug91; C 493697)
Aug 90. (cd) *(CDP7 93698-2)* **BEACH BOYS' PARTY / STACK O-TRACKS** [ ] [ ]
(contains extra tracks) (c-iss.Aug91; C 493698)

Jun 91. (7"/c-s) *E.M.I.; (EM/+C 1)* **DO IT AGAIN. / GOOD VIBRATIONS** [61] [ ]
(cd-s+=) *(EMCT 1)* – Wouldn't it be nice.

Jul 93. (5xcd-box) *(CDS 789936-2)* **GOOD VIBRATIONS – 30 YEARS OF THE BEACH BOYS** [ ] [ ]

Jun 95. (d-cd/d-c) *E.M.I.; (CD/TC ESTVD 3)* **THE BEST OF THE BEACH BOYS** [26] [ ]

Apr 96. (cd) *<29418>* **20 GOOD VIBRATIONS – THE GREATEST HITS** [–] [ ]

Oct 97. (4xcd-box) *(CDS 837662-2)* **THE PET SOUNDS SESSIONS** [ ] [–]

Jun 98. (cd/c) *E.M.I.; (495696-2/-4)* **GREATEST HITS** [28] [ ]

Sep 98. (cd) *E.M.I.; (496391-2)* **ENDLESS HARMONY SOUNDTRACK** [56] [ ]

Nov 98. (cd) *E.M.I.; <(4 95734-2>)* **ULTIMATE CHRISTMAS** [ ] Nov00 [20]

Mar 00. (cd) *<21860>* **THE GREATEST HITS – VOLUME 1: 20 GOOD VIBRATIONS** [–] [95]

Mar 00. (cd) *<20238>* **THE GREATEST HITS – VOLUME 2: 20 MORE GOOD VIBRATIONS** [–] [ ]

Jun 00. (cd) *(525000-2) <19707>* **THE BEST OF THE BEACH BOYS 1970-1986: THE BROTHER YEARS** [ ] Mar00 [26]

Jul 00. (cd) *Burning Airlines; (PILOT 062)* **STUDIO SESSIONS 1961-1962** [ ] [ ]

Aug 00. (cd) *<(525692-2)>* **SUNFLOWER / SURF'S UP** [ ] [ ]

Aug 00. (cd) *<(525694-2)>* **CARL AND THE PASSIONS – SO TOUGH / HOLLAND** [ ] [ ]

Sep 00. (cd) *<(527945-2)>* **15 BIG ONES / THE BEACH BOYS LOVE YOU** [ ] [ ]

Sep 00. (cd) *<(527948-2)>* **KEEPING THE SUMMER ALIVE / THE BEACH BOYS** [ ] [ ]

Sep 00. (cd) *<(527950-2)>* **M.I.U. / L.A. (LIGHT ALBUM)** [ ] [ ]

Apr 01. (cd) *<(531861-2)>* **BEACH BOYS CONCERT / LIVE IN LONDON 1969** [ ] [ ]

May 01. (d-cd) *<(531583-2)>* **HAWTHORNE, CA. – BIRTHPLACE OF A MUSICAL LEGACY (live)** [ ] [ ]

Jul 01. (cd/c) *(532615-2/-4)* **THE VERY BEST OF THE BEACH BOYS** [31] [ ]
– Good vibrations / California girls / I get around / Wouldn't it be nice / Surfin' safari / Fun, fun, fun / Surfin' USA / Help me, Rhonda / Don't worry baby / When I grow up (to be a man) / Little deuce coupe / Dance, dance, dance / Little Honda / Do you wanna dance / Surfer girl / Then I kissed her / God only knows / Caroline, no / Sloop John B. / Barbara Ann / Heroes and villains / Do it again / Darlin' / Wild honey / Break away / Rock & roll music / I can hear music / Cottonfields / Lady Lynda / Kokomo.

Jul 02. (cd) *<(540087-2)>* **CLASSICS: SELECTED BY BRIAN WILSON** [ ] [ ]
– Surfer girl / The warmth of the sun / I get around / Don't worry baby / In my room / California girls / God only knows / Caroline, no / Good vibrations / Wonderful / Heroes and villains / Surf's up / Busy doin' nothin' / We're together again / Time to get alone / This whole world / Marcella / Sail on sailor / 'Til I die / California feelin'.

Aug 02. (cd) *Eagle; (EAGCD 155)* **LIVE AT KNEBWORTH 1980** [ ] [–]

Dec 02. (cd) *<66035>* **I CAN HEAR MUSIC** [–] [ ]

Jun 03. (cd) *<82710-2>* **SOUNDS OF SUMMER: THE VERY BEST OF THE BEACH BOYS** [–] [16]
– California girls / I get around / Surfin' safari / Surfin' U.S.A. / Fun, fun, fun / Surfer girl / Don't worry baby / Little Deuce Coupe / Shut down / Help me, Rhonda / Be true to your school / When I grow up (to be a man) / In my room / God only knows / Sloop John B / Wouldn't it be nice / Getcha back / Come go with me / Rock & roll music / Dance, dance, dance / Barbara Ann / Do you wanna dance / Heroes and villains / Good timin' / Kokomo / Do it again / Wild honey / Darlin' / I can hear music / Good vibrations.

May 05. (cd) *(571345-2)* **THE PLATINUM COLLECTION** [30] [–]

BRIAN WILSON

Sire Sire

May 87. (7") *<28350>* **LET'S GO TO HEAVEN IN MY CAR. / TOO MUCH SUGAR** [–] [ ]

Jul 88. (lp/c)(cd) *(WX 157/+C)<(925669-2)>* **BRIAN WILSON** [ ] [54]
– Love and mercy / Walkin' the line / Melt away / Baby let your hair grow long / Little children / One of the boys / There's so many / Night time / Let it shine / Meet me in my dreams tonight / Rio Grande. *(re-iss. cd Dec95; 7599 25669-2) <(cd re-iss. Sep00 on 'Rhino'+=; 8122 79960-2)>* – Brian on 'Love And Mercy' / He couldn't get his poor old body to move / Being with the one you love / Let's go to Heaven in my car / Too much sugar / There's so many (demo) / Walkin' the line (demo) / Melt away / Night time (instrumental) / Little children (demo) / Night blooming Jasmine (demo) / Rio Grande / Brian on 'Rio Grande' / Brian on 'The Source'.

Aug 88. (7") *(W 7814) <27814>* **LOVE AND MERCY. / HE COULDN'T GET HIS POOR OLD BODY TO MOVE** [ ] [ ]
(12"+=/3"cd-s+=) *(W 7814 T/CD)* – One for the boys.

Nov 88. (7") *(W 7787)* **NIGHT TIME. / ONE FOR THE BOYS** [ ] [–]
(12"+=/3"cd-s+=) *(W 7787 T/CD)* – Being with the one you love.

Feb 89. (7") *<27694>* **MELT AWAY. / BEING WITH THE ONE YOU LOVE** [–] [ ]

—— with musicians **JIM KELTNER** – drums / **JAMES HUTCHINSON** – bass / **BENMONT TENCH** – keyboards / **MARK GOLDENBERG** + **WADDY WACHTEL** – guitar / **DAVID McMURRAY** – sax, flute

M.C.A. M.C.A.

Sep 95. (cd) *<(MCD 11270)>* **I JUST WASN'T MADE FOR THOSE TIMES** [59] [ ]
– Meant for you / This whole world / Caroline, no / Let the wind blow / Love and mercy / Do it again / The warmth of the sun / Wonderful / Still I dream of it / Melt away / 'Til I die. *(re-iss. May02; same)*

—— a few months later, BRIAN teamed up with VAN DYKE PARKS (the main writer) on an album, 'ORANGE CRATE ART' for 'Warners'

R.C.A. Paladin-Giant

May 98. (c-s/cd-s) *<17216>* **YOUR IMAGINATION / YOUR IMAGINATION (a cappella) / HAPPY DAYS** [–] [ ]

Jun 98. (cd) *(74321 57303-2) <24703>* **IMAGINATION** [30] [88]
– Your imagination / She says that she needs me / South American / Where has love been? / Keep an eye on summer / Dream angel / Cry / Lay down burden / Let him run wild / Sunshine / Happy days.

Oglio BriMel

Jun 01. (d-cd) *(OGL 8201-2) <1001>* **LIVE AT THE ROXY THEATRE (live)** [ ] i-net [–]
– Little girl (intro) / Little girl I once knew / This whole world / Don't worry baby / Kiss me baby / Do it again / California girls / I get around / Back home / In my room / Surfer girl / First time / This isn't love / Add some music to your day / Please let me wonder / Band intro / Brian Wilson / 'Til I die / Darlin' / Let's go away for awhile / Pet sounds / God only knows / Lay down Burden / Be my baby / Good vibrations / Caroline, no / All summer long / Love and mercy. *(re-iss. Jan02 on 'Sanctuary'; SANDD 107) (re-iss. Jan02 on 'Victor'; VICP 61788/9)*

Sanctuary Sanctuary

May 02. (cd) *(SANCD 118) <84556>* **PET SOUNDS LIVE** (live) [ ] Jun02 [ ]
– Show intro / Wouldn't it be nice / You still believe in me / That's not me / Don't talk (put your head on my shoulder) / I'm waiting for the day / Let's go away for awhile / Sloop John B. / God only knows / I know there's an answer / Here today / I just wasn't made for these times / Pet sounds / Caroline no.

Brimel-Rhino Brimel-Rhino

Jun 04. (cd) *<(8122 76471-2)>* **GETTIN' IN OVER MY HEAD** [53] [100]
– How could we still be dancin' / Soul searchin' / You've touched me / Gettin' in over my head / City blues / Desert drive / A friend like you / Make a wish / Rainbow eyes / Saturday morning in the city / Fairy tale / Don't let her know she's an angel / The waltz.

Must Destroy not iss.

Sep 04. (7"green/blue/yellow) *(MDA 001/+X/XX)* **WONDERFUL. / WIND CHIMES** [29] [–]

Nonesuch Nonesuch

Sep 04. (cd) *<(7559 79846-2)>* **SMiLE** [7] [13]
– Our prayer – Gee / Heroes and villains / Roll Plymouth rock / Barnyard / Old master painter – You are my sunshine / Cabin essence / Wonderful / Song for children / Child is father of the man / Surf's up / I'm in great shape – I wanna be around – Workshop / Vega-tables / On a holiday / Wind chimes / Mrs. O'Leary's cow / In Blue Hawaii / Good vibrations. *(d-lp iss.Nov04 +=; 7559 79846-1)* – (instrumentals):- Heroes and villains / Cabin essence / On a holiday / Wind chimes.

Dec 04. (7"/cd-s) *(NS 001/+CD)* **GOOD VIBRATIONS. / IN BLUE HAWAII** [30] [–]

Arista Arista

Oct 05. (cd) *(82876 71809-2) <70300>* **WHAT I REALLY WANT FOR CHRISTMAS** (festive songs) [ ] [ ]

Oct 05. (cd-s) *(82876 76480-2)* **WHAT I REALLY WANT FOR CHRISTMAS / WE WISH YOU A MERRY CHRISTMAS / BRIAN'S CHRISTMAS MESSAGE** [ ] [–]

BEASTIE BOYS

Formed: Greenwich Village, New York, USA ... 1981 by ADAM YAUCH and MIKE DIAMOND. They recruited ADAM HOROWITZ to replace two others (KATE SCHELLENBACH and JOHN BERRY), and after two US indie releases they signed to 'Def Jam', the label run by the BEASTIE's friend and sometime DJ, RICK RUBIN. RUBIN paired with the BEASTIE BOYS was a match made in Heaven (or Hell, if you were unfortunate enough to own a Volkswagen) and the debut album 'LICENSED TO ILL' (1986) was the first real attempt to create a white, rock-centric take on of Afro-American Hip Hop. At turns hilarious and exhilarating, RUBIN and the BEASTIE's shared taste in classic metal was evident with samples from the likes of AC/DC and LED ZEPPELIN along with the theme tune from American TV show 'Mr. Ed'. With snotty rapping and riff-heavy rhymes, tracks like 'FIGHT FOR YOUR RIGHT (TO PARTY) and 'NO SLEEP TILL BROOKLYN' stormed the charts on both sides of the Atlantic, 'LICENSED TO ILL' becoming the fastest selling debut in Columbia's history. The record turned the band into a phenomenon and in 1987 they undertook a riotous headlining tour. Courting controversy wherever they played, the band were savaged by the press, a dispute with 'Def Jam' not helping matters any. Despite all the upheaval, by the release of 'PAUL'S BOUTIQUE' in 1989, the group's profile was negligible and the album was more or less passed over. A tragedy, as it remains one of hip hop's lost gems, a widescreen sampladelic collage produced by the ultra-hip DUST BROTHERS (US). Bypassing the obvious guitar riffs for samples of the BEATLES, CURTIS MAYFIELD and PINK FLOYD along with a kaleidoscopic array of cultural debris and hip references, the album was a funky tour de force. After another extended sabbatical during which the group relocated to California, the BEASTIE BOYS returned in 1992 with 'CHECK YOUR HEAD'. Hipness and attitude were still there in abundance but by now, the group were using live instrumentation. Despite veering from all out thrash to supple funk, the record was a success and only the BEASTIE BOYS could get away with a TED NUGENT collaboration ('THE BIZ VS THE NUGE'). 'ILL COMMUNICATION' (1994) developed this strategy to stunning effect. From the irresistible funk of 'SURE SHOT' and 'ROOT DOWN' to the laid back swing of 'GET IT TOGETHER' and 'FLUTE LOOP', this was the group's most mature and accomplished work to date. The hardcore was still there, 'TOUGH GUY' and 'HEART ATTACK MAN' but it was offset by the sombre strings of 'EUGENE'S LAMENT' and the mellow 'RICKY'S THEME'. A double A-side 'GET IT TOGETHER' and the screechingly brilliant 'SABOTAGE' (complete with entertaining cop-pastiche video) quite rightly returning them into the UK Top 20. From the artwork to the meditative feel of the music (well o.k., maybe not the punk numbers) it was no surprise that YAUCH had become a buddhist and the band subsequently played a high profile benefit for the oppressed nation of Tibet. Ever industrious, the group also started their own label and fanzine 'Grand Royal', signing the likes of LUSCIOUS JACKSON and the now "Big In Japan" BIS. Between development on their magnum-opus comeback (see below), The BEASTIE BOYS dabbled in more electronic/hardcore/instrumental tomfoolery via three mini-albums/EP's, 'ROOT DOWN' (1995), 'AGLIO E OLIO' (1995) and 'THE IN SOUND FROM WAY OUT!' (1996). 1998's 'INTERGALACTIC' single (along with bizarre Power-Rangers-esque video) led the way for the release of the eagerly-awaited 5th set proper, 'HELLO NASTY', an uncompromising, no-holds barred 23-track blinder. With reviews getting near perfect results it was inevitable that The BEASTIE's would have their first transatlantic chart-topper. The band had not lost their tongue-in-cheek attitude despite their recent shifts to a more harmonic religion. Such examples of this would be UK hit singles, 'BODY MOVIN' and 'REMOTE CONTROL', which would also turn up on double-CD anthology 'THE SOUNDS OF SCIENCE' (1999). Meanwhile, inbetween meditating and freestyling, ADAM HOROVITZ collaborated (from the East-Side of America) with the BEASTIE's live drummer AMERY SMITH on the West Coast to create an album of sheer lunacy under the mysterious guise of BS2000. An eponymous album was issued in 1997 on limited vinyl release through Grand Royal's website and immediately became an underground classic amongst the DJ's and The B-Boyz of Brooklyn. Mixing thrashing electronica with phat beats, cheesy hooks and throbbing bass, the set sat on the line between genius masterstroke and faltering mess. Imagine if Aldous Huxley and Albert Einstein had both taken mescaline and turned their mathematical theories into music. The side project returned three years later with the more musically accessible 'SIMPLY MORTIFIED' (2000). Much the same fare, but with distorted vocals, fantastic scratching and less songs, at least the passion was all there even if HOROVITZ's and SMITH's brains were somewhere else. Many would've liked to dismiss BS2000 as a sad joke or just another example of the BEASTIE's ever-increasing oddness – and perhaps it was, but that still didn't diminish the fact that it was as zany, as lo-fi and as nuts as anything to grace the underground indie scene that year. When the original caucasian B-Boys finally got around to releasing a follow-up some six years later, EMINEM had long since had the monopoly on petulant sneer, and the American cultural landscape had changed almost beyond recognition. Rather than kowtowing to contemporary production – not that they'd ever done that anyway – 'TO THE 5 BOROUGHS' (2004) found the BEASTIEs reliving the thrill of misspent youth through the prism of middle age. As the follow-up to 'LICENSED TO ILL' that never was, '..BOROUGHS' revelled in some of the oldest skool ryhmes and beats (check out 'TRIPLE TROUBLE') to ever top the American charts. In terms of sheer, in your face directness, honky funk and sibling joie de vivre, it also sparked a fading memory of how great hip hop could really be, even with the – admissible in the circumstances – politicised overtones. For 'SOLID GOLD HITS' (2005) – an abbreviated version of the previous anthology – the ageing science-smiths went one better with a classic beatbox'n'trackies cover shot, just steering shy of the US Top 40.

• **Songwriters:** Although they released few cover versions, they sampled many songs (see above). In 1992, they covered JIMMY JAMES (Jimi Hendrix) + TIME FOR LIVIN' (Stewart Frontline), also collaborating with NISHITA. • **Trivia:** ADAM HOROWITZ is the son of playwrite ISRAEL. HOROWITZ played a cameo role in TV serial 'The Equalizer' (circa '88).

Album rating: LICENSED TO 'ILL (*8) / PAUL'S BOUTIQUE (*7) / CHECK YOUR HEAD (*7) / ILL: COMMUNICATION (*9) / HELLO NASTY (*9) / THE SOUNDS OF SCIENCE compilation (*8) / TO THE 5 BOROUGHS (*7) / SOLID GOLD HITS compilation (*7)

'MCA' ADAM YAUCH (b. 5 Aug'65, Brooklyn, New York) – vocals / **'MIKE D' MIKE DIAMOND** (b.20 Nov'66, New York) – vocals / **KATE SCHELLENBACH** (b. 5 Jan'66, New York City) – drums / **JOHN BERRY** – guitar

Ratcage Ratcage

Nov 82. (7"ep) <*(MOTR 21)*> **POLLY WOG STEW EP** □ □
– B.E.A.S.T.I.E. boys / Transit cop / Jimi / Holy snappers / Riot fight / Ode to . . . / Michelle's farm / Egg raid on mojo. *(UK-iss.Apr88 12"/c-s; same) (re-iss. 12"ep/c-ep/cd-ep Feb93; same)*

—— **AD ROCK – ADAM HOROWITZ** (b.31 Oct'67, New York City) – vocals, guitar (ex-The YOUNG & THE USELESS) repl.BERRY + SCHELLENBACH (she later joined LUSCIOUS JACKSON)

Aug 83. (7") <*MOTR 26*> **COOKY PUSS. / BEASTIE REVOLUTION** - □
(UK-iss.Jan85 + Jul87; MOTR 26 C/CD) (cd-ep-iss.Dec87; same) (re-issues

The BEASTIE BOYS

+=) – Bonus batter / Cooky puss (censored version). *(re-iss. 12"ep/c-ep/cd-ep Feb93; same)*

— added guest RICK RUBIN – scratcher, DJ

Def Jam Def Jam

Dec 85. (12"ep; w-drawn) *<002>* **ROCK HARD / BEASTIE GROOVE. / THE PARTY'S GETTING ROUGH / BEASTIE GROOVE (instrumental)** [–] [–]

Jan 86. (7"/12") *(A/TA 6686)* *<05683>* **SHE'S ON IT. / SLOW AND LOW** [ ] [ ]

May 86. (7"/12") *(A/TA 7055)* *<05864>* **HOLD IT NOW, HIT IT. / ACAPULCO (Hold it now, hit it acapella)** [ ] [ ]

Sep 86. (7") *(650 114-7)* **SHE'S ON IT. / SLOW AND LOW** [ ] [–]
(12"+=) *(650 114-6)* – Hold it now, hit it.

Nov 86. (7") *(650 169-7)* *<06341>* **IT'S THE NEW STYLE. / PAUL REVERE** [ ] [–]
(12"+=) *(650 169-6)* – ('A'&'B'instrumentals).
(d12"++=) *(650 169-8)* – Hold it now, hit it / Hold it now, hit it (Acapulco version) / Hold it now, hit it (instrumental).

Nov 86. (lp/c/cd) *(450 062-1/-4/-2)* *<40238>* **LICENSED TO 'ILL** [7] [1]
– Rhymin and stealin' / The new style / She's crafty / Posse in effect / Slow ride / Girls / (You gotta) Fight for your right (to party) / No sleep till Brooklyn / Paul Revere / Hold it now, hit it / Brass monkey / Slow and low / Time to get ill. *(re-iss. Nov89 on 'Capitol'; 460 949-1) (re-iss. Jun94 cd/c; 460 949-2/-4) (cd re-iss. Jul95 & Nov99; 527351-2)*

Dec 86. (7") *<06595>* **(YOU GOTTA) FIGHT FOR YOUR RIGHT (TO PARTY). / PAUL REVERE** [–] [7]

Feb 87. (7") *(650 418-7)* **(YOU GOTTA) FIGHT FOR YOUR RIGHT (TO PARTY). / TIME TO GET ILL** [11] [–]
(12"+=) *(650 418-6)* – No sleep till Brooklyn.

Apr 87. (7") *<06675>* **NO SLEEP TILL BROOKLYN. / SHE'S CRAFTY** [–] [ ]

May 87. (7"/7"sha-pic-d) *(BEAST/+P 1)* **NO SLEEP TILL BROOKLYN. / POSSE IN EFFECT** [14] [–]
(12"+=) *(BEASTT 1)* – Hold it now, hit it / Brass monkey.

Jul 87. (7"/7"s/7"s) *(BEAST/+B/D 2)* **SHE'S ON IT. / SLOW AND LOW** [10] [–]
(12"+=) *(BEASTT 2)* – Hold it now, hit it.

Sep 87. (7"/7"s/7"s/7"s/10"sha-pic-d) *(BEAST/+P/S/Q/W 3)* **GIRLS. / SHE'S CRAFTY** [34] [–]
(12"+=/12"s+=) *(BEASTT/+Q 3)* – Rock hard.

Mar 88. (7") *<07020>* **BRASS MONKEY. / POSSE IN EFFECT** [–] [48]

— no more RICK RUBIN as DJ

Capitol Capitol

Jul 89. (7") *(CL 540)* *<44454>* **HEY LADIES. / SHAKE YOUR RUMP** [ ] [36]
(12"ep+=/cd-ep+=) *(12/CD CL 540)* **LOVE AMERICAN STYLE** – 33% God / Dis yourself in '89 (just do it). *(re-iss. Jul98 on 'Grand Royal'; GR 064)*

Jul 89. (cd/c/lp) *(DE/TC+/EST 2102)* *<91743>* **PAUL'S BOUTIQUE** [44] [14]
– To all the girls / Shake your rump / Johnny Ryall / Egg man / High plains drifter / The sound of science / 3-minute rule / Hey ladies / 5-piece chicken dinner / Looking down the barrel of a gun / Car thief / What comes around / Shadrach / Ask for Janice / B-boy bouillabaisse:- (a) 59 Chrystie Street, (b) Get on the mic, (c) Stop that train, (d) A year and a day, (e) Hello Brooklyn, (f) Dropping names, (g) Lay it on me, (h) Mike on the mic, (i) A.W.O.L.

Aug 89. (12"ep) *<Y 15523>* **AN EXCITING EVENING AT HOME WITH SHADRACH, MESHACH AND ABEDNEGO EP** [–] [ ]
– Shadrach / Caught in the middle of a 3-way mix / And what you give is what you get / Car thief / Some dumb cop gave me two tickets already / Your sister's def.

— trio now also on instruments; MCA – bass / **AD ROCK** – keyboards / **MIKE D** – drums

Apr 92. (c-s/7") *(TC+/CL 653)* **PASS THE MIC. / PROFESSOR BOOTY** [47] [ ]
(etched-12"+=/c-s+=) *(12CL/TCCLX 653)* – Time for livin' / Drunken Praying Mantis style.
(cd-s) *(CDCL 653)* – ('A'side) / Netty's girl / Something's got to give / ('A'-pt.2 – The skills to pay the bills).

May 92. (cd/c/d-lp) *(CD/TC+/EST 2171)* *<98938>* **CHECK YOUR HEAD** [ ] [10]
– Jimmy James / Funky boss / Pass the mic / Gratitude / Lighten up / Finger lickin' good / So what 'cha want / The biz .vs. the Nuge (with TED NUGENT) / Time for livin' / Something's got to give / The blue nun / Stand together / Pow / The maestro / Groove Holmes / Live at P.J.'s / Mark on the bus / Professor Booty / In 3's / Namaste. *(re-iss. Sep94; CDP 798938-2/-4) (d-lp re-iss. Nov98; GR 066)*

May 92. (12"ep/c-ep/cd-ep) *<Y/4Y/C2 15836>* **JIMMY JAMES / THE MAESTRO / JIMMY JAMES (album version) / BOOMIN' GRANNY / JIMMY JAMES (original) / DRINKIN' WINE** [–] [ ]

Jun 92. (12"ep/12"white-ep/c-ep) *(12CL 665)* **FROZEN METAL HEAD EP** [55] [–]
– Jimmy James / So what'cha want (All the way live freestyle version) / Jimmy James (original) / Drinkin' wine.
(cd-ep) *(CDCL 665)* – The blue nun *[repl. original]*

Jun 92. (cd-ep) *<15847>* **SO WHAT'CHA WANT (3 versions; including pt.2 – The Skills to pay the bills) / GROOVE HOLMES (2 versions)** [–] [93]

Dec 92. (12"ep/cd-ep) *<Y/C2 07777>* **GRATITUDE EP** [–] [ ]
– Gratitude / Stand together (live) / Finger lickin' good (remix) / Gratitude (live) / Honkey rink.

Capitol Grand Royal

May 94. (cd/c/d-lp) *(CD/TC+/EST 2229)* *<28599>* **ILL: COMMUNICATION** [10] [1]
– Sure shot / Tough guy / Freak freak / Bobo on the corner / Root down / Sabotage / Get it together / Sabrosa / The update / Futterman's rule / Alright hear this / Eugene's lament / Flute loop / Do it / Rick's theme / Heart attack man / The scoop / Shambala / Bodhisattva vow / Transitions. *(lp re-iss. Apr97 on 'Grand Royal'; GR 006LP)*

Jul 94. (c-s/7"green) *(TC+/CL 716)* **GET IT TOGETHER. / SABOTAGE / DOPE LITTLE SONG** [19] [ ]
(10") *(10CL 716)* – (first 2 tracks) / ('A'-Buck Wild remix) / ('A'instrumental).
(cd-s) *(CDCL 716)* – (first 2 tracks) / ('A'-A.B.A. remix) / Resolution time.

Nov 94. (7"maroon) *(CL 726)* **SURE SHOT. / MULLET HEAD / SURE SHOT (Mario mix)** [27] [ ]
(10"+=) *(10CL 726)* – The vibes.
(cd-s+=) *(CDCLS 726)* – Son of neck bone.
(cd-s) *(CDCL 726)* – ('A'mixes:- Pruins – European B-Boy / Nardone / Large Professor / instrumental).

Jun 95. (m-cd/m-c/m-lp) *(CD/TC+/EST 2262)* *<33603>* **ROOT DOWN EP** (some live) [23] [50]
– Root down (free zone mix) / Root down / Root down (PP balloon mix) / Time to get ill / Heart attack man / The maestro / Sabrosa / Flute loop / Time for livin' / Something's got to give / So what'cha want. *(m-lp-iss.Apr97 on 'Grand Royal'; GR 018)*

Dec 95. (12"ep/cd-ep) *<GR 026/+CD>* **AGLIO E OLIO** (11 minutes of hardcore) [–] [ ]
– Brand new / Deal with me / Believe me / Nervous assistant / Square wave in unison / You catch a bad one / I can't think straight / I want some. *(UK-iss.Mar98; same)*

— added guest co-writers **(MONEY) MARK RAMOS NISHITA** – claviers / **ERIC BOBO** – percussion / **EUGENE GORE** – violin

Mar 96. (cd/c) *(CD/TC EST 2281)* *<7243 8 33590-2/-4>* **THE IN SOUND FROM WAY OUT!** (instrumental) [45] [45]
– Groove Holmes / Sabrosa / Namaste / Pow / Son of neckbone / In 3's / Eugene's lament / Bobo on the corner / Shambala / Lighten up / Ricky's theme / Transitions / Drinkin' wine. *(lp re-iss. Jan99 on 'Grand Royal'; GRA 80013)*

Jun 98. (c-s) *(TCCL 803)* *<58705>* **INTERGALACTIC / HAIL SAGAN (Special K)** [5] Jul98 [28]
(cd-s+=) *(CDCL 803)* – ('A'-Prisoners Of Technology TMSI remix).
(10") *(10CL 803)* – ('A'side) / ('A'-Prisoners Of . . . remix).

Jul 98. (cd/c/d-lp) *(495723-2/-4/-1)* *<37716>* **HELLO NASTY** [1] [1]
– Super disco breakin' / The move / Remote control / Song for the man / Just a test / Body movin' / Intergalactic / Sneakin' out of hospital / Putting shame in your game / Flowin' prose / And me / Three MC's and one DJ / Can't, won't, don't stop / Song for Junior / I don't know / The negotiation Limerick file / Electrify / Picture this / Unite / Dedication / Dr. Lee PhD / Instant death.

Oct 98. (cd-s) *(CDCLS 809)* **BODY MOVIN' / (Mickey Finn mix) / DR. LEE phD (dub mix)** [15] [ ]
(cd-s) *(CDCL 809)* – ('A'side) / (Fatboy Slim remix) / (Peanut butter and jelly mix).
(12") *(12CL 809)* – ('A'side) / (Kut Masta Kurt remix) / (Erick Sermon remix) / (instrumental).
(re-iss. /re-mixed May99; GR 069/063)

May 99. (12"/cd-s) *(12CL/CDCLS 812)* **REMOTE CONTROL / THREE MC'S AND ONE DJ / THE NEGOTIATION LIMERICK FILE (Ganja Kru – or – the 41 Small Star remix)** 21 ☐
(cd-s) *(CDCL 812)* – ('A'side) / Three MC's and one DJ (live video version) / Putting shame in your game (mix) / Three MC's and one DJ (enhanced video).

Aug 99. (12"ep) *<(GR 071)>* **SCIENTIST OF SOUND** ☐ ☐
– Negotiation Limerick file (mixes) / Intergalactic / Three MC's and one DJ / Body movin' (mixes) / Putting shame in your game.

Nov 99. (d-cd/d-c) *(522940-2/-4) <22940>* **THE SOUNDS OF SCIENCE** (compilation) 36 19
– Beastie Boys / Slow and low / Shake your rump / Gratitude / Skills to pay the bills / Root down / Believe me / Sure shot / Body movin' / Boomin' granny / (You gotta) Fight for your right (to party) / Country Mike's theme / Pass the mic / Something's got to give / Bodhisattva vow / Sabrosa / Song for the man / Soba violence / Alive / Jimmy James / Three MC's and one DJ / Biz vs. the Nuge / Sabotage / Shadrach / Brass monkey / Time for livin' / Dub the mic / Benny and the jets / Negotion limerick file / I want some / She's on it / Son of neckbone / Get it together / Twenty questions / Remote control / Railroad blues / Live wire / So what'cha want / Netty's girl / Egg raid on mojo / Hey ladies / Intergalactic.

Dec 99. (10") *(10CL 818)* **ALIVE / START! / ALIVE (B.R.A. remix)** 28 –
(cd-s+=) *(CDCLS 818)* – Start! (video).
(cd-s) *(CDCL 818)* – ('A'side) / You and me together / Big shot (live) / ('A'-video).

May 04. (cd-s) *(CDCLS 857)* **CH-CHECK IT OUT / (Just Blaze remix)** 8 –
(12"+=) *(12CL 857)* – ('A'-instrumental) / ('A'-A Cappella).
(cd-s) *(CDCLS 857)* – ('A') / (instrumental) / And then I / ('A'-video).

Jun 04. (cd)(d-lp) *(4733310)(4733971) <84571>* **TO THE 5 BOROUGHS** 2 1
– Ch-check it out / Right right now now / 3 the hard way / Time to build / Rhyme the rhyme well / Triple trouble / Hey fuck you / Oh word? / That's it that's all / All lifestyles / Shazam! / An open letter to NYC / Crawlspace / The brouhaha / We got the. *(ltd-cd+=; 4733390)* – Rhyme the rhyme well (video).

Sep 04. (cd-s) *(CDCL 859)* **TRIPLE TROUBLE / (J. Wizzle remix)** 37 ☐
(12"+=) *(12CL 859)* – ('A'-instrumental) / ('A'-A Cappella).
(cd-s+=) *(CDCLS 859) <867246>* – ('A'-Graham Coxon remix) / ('A'-video).

Nov 04. (cd-s) *(CDCL 867)* **AN OPEN LETTER TO NYC / MTL REPPIN' FOR THE 514** 38 –
(cd-s) *(CDCLS 867)* – ('A') / Rizzle rizzle nizzle nizzle / Sabotage (live) / ('A'-video).

Parlophone Capitol

Nov 05. (cd)(lp) *(344049-2)(344667-1) <44167>* **SOLID GOLD HITS** (compilation) ☐ 42
– So what'cha want / Brass monkey / Ch-check it out / No sleep till Brooklyn / Hey ladies / Pass the mic / An open letter to NYC / Root down / Shake your rump / Intergalactic / Sure shot / Body movin' (Fatboy Slim remix) / Triple trouble / Sabotage / Fight for your right. *(ltd-d-cd+=; 344550-2)* – (videos/dvd's).

– compilations, others, etc. –

Feb 94. (cd/c) *Honey World; (CD/TC EST 2225) / Grand Royal; <89843>* **SOME OLD BULLSHIT** ☐ 46
– (compilation of 1st 2 EP's) *(re-iss. Jan99; same)*

Oct 05. (12") *Def Jam; (9829784)* **YOU GOTTA FIGHT FOR YOUR RIGHT TO PARTY. / TIME TO GET ILL / NO SLEEP TILL BROOKLYN** ☐ –

the BEATLES

Formed: Liverpool, England . . . by JOHN LENNON and PAUL McCARTNEY as schoolboy band The QUARRYMEN in 1957. GEORGE HARRISON joined up the following year, although they split late '59. They reformed in the Spring of 1960 as The SILVER BEATLES, adding PETE BEST and STU SUTCLIFFE. Dropping the SILVER part of their name, they employed manager Alan Williams, who secured them local gigs. Later that year, they toured Hamburg, West Germany, although they had to return when HARRISON was deported for being under eighteen. On the 21st of March '61, they debuted at Liverpool's 'Cavern Club', preceding another 3-month stint in Hamburg. While there, they recorded for 'Polydor' records, backing cabaret-type pop singer TONY SHERIDAN. (These recordings were later released, when the band were at the peak of their popularity). Around mid-'61, STU stayed in Hamburg to get married and study art. There, he was to tragically die of a brain haemorrhage on the 10th April of 1962. With PAUL now on bass and BRIAN EPSTEIN as their new manager, they laid down a demo for 'Decca', which was subsequently discarded by DICK ROWE. Instead he signed BRIAN POOLE & THE TREMELOES (!), although he soon found consolation when he contracted rivals-to-be The ROLLING STONES. Summer '62 brought sunshine when George Martin introduced them to EMI's 'Parlophone' label. During rehearsals BEST was fired and replaced by the more experienced drummer RINGO STARR. By the end of 1962 their debut single 'LOVE ME DO' was in the UK Top 20. The follow-up 'PLEASE PLEASE ME' (1963) reached No.2 and The BEATLES had arrived, their breezy, fresh-faced pop striking a chord in a music scene that was crying out for a band with the effortless charisma of the cheeky Scousers. More, their mop-topped, sharp-suited image (courtesy of BRIAN EPSTEIN) remains one of the most enduring impressions in the history of pop culture. And thus did that dog-eared cliche of a phenomenon, 'BEATLEMANIA' tighten its grip as the band toured above ROY ORBISON later that year to unprecedented scenes of teenage delirium. They also found time to knock out a debut album, 'PLEASE PLEASE ME' (1963), produced by their mentor George Martin and featuring a heady cocktail of live wig-outs ('I SAW HER STANDING THERE', 'TWIST AND SHOUT'etc.) and LENNON/McCARTNEY originals. This precocious songwriting partnership was entering its golden period as the band notched up an incredible string of No.1 singles in quick succession, 'FROM ME TO YOU' (1963), 'SHE LOVES YOU' (1963), 'I WANT TO HOLD YOUR HAND' (1963) and 'CAN'T BUY ME LOVE' (1964). The BEATLES finished 1963 in fine style; a No.1 follow-up album, 'WITH THE BEATLES', the biggest selling single in British history, 'SHE LOVES YOU' and a performance before the Queen Mother at the Royal Command Variety Performance. With British domination well under way, the band flew to America in February 1964, droves of hysterical fans greeting them upon their landing at New York's Kennedy Airport. They made a legendary appearance on the 'Ed Sullivan Show' and by April The BEATLES held the top five positions in the American Billboard singles charts (i.e. No.1:- CAN'T BUY ME LOVE, 2:- TWIST AND SHOUT, 3:- SHE LOVES YOU, 4:- I WANT TO HOLD YOUR HAND, 5:- PLEASE PLEASE ME). Flying high, that summer saw the release of The BEATLES' first movie and accompanying soundtrack, 'A HARD DAY'S NIGHT'. The band proved themselves as compelling on screen as on stage, and the film's revolutionary shooting technique created the blueprint for decades of rockumentaries to come. The same year also saw the release of the band's third album, 'BEATLES FOR SALE', a record which included some of the last genuine LENNON/McCARTNEY collaborations. Each were developing their own particular style and although all their songs continued to be credited as joint efforts, by the following year the pair seldom wrote together. 'HELP' (1965), a filmic follow-up to 'A HARD DAY'S NIGHT', featured some of LENNON and McCARTNEY's most focused songwriting to date (notably the title track and 'YESTERDAY') and was filmed at various locations around the globe. The BEATLES performed before a record number of fans at New York's Shea Stadium in August, the same month as 'HELP' was opened in the U.S. By this point The BEATLES were undoubtedly the biggest pop/rock band in the world, unique in their abilty to produce music that seemingly

The BEATLES

crossed all boundaries of age, race, class and gender. Even so, it was a shock to the rock world when the Queen announced in the summer of '65 that the band were each to receive an M.B.E.. It was almost unthinkable that bad boy rivals The ROLLING STONES would be given such a (dubious) honour, and while the two bands were poles apart musically, LSD and the burgeoning psychedelic culture brought them together briefly. 'RUBBER SOUL' (1965), written and recorded in just over a month, was the sound of The BEATLES in flux, shedding their clean cut image and interpreting the influence of BOB DYLAN's pioneering folk-rock experiments. Despite the transformation taking place, the sound was more fluid and assured, the songwriting more mature. LENNON's 'IN MY LIFE' was beautifully bittersweet while McCARTNEY almost equalled 'YESTERDAY' with 'MICHELLE' and the lilting 'NORWEGIAN WOOD' saw HARRISON's first forays into sitar work. The album was sandwiched between pioneering double A-sided singles 'DAY TRIPPER' / 'WE CAN WORK IT OUT' (1965) and 'PAPERBACK WRITER' / 'RAIN' (1966). 'RAIN' was the first overtly psychedelic BEATLES record, innovative in its use of rhythm and featuring an undulating LENNON vocal (a style much mimicked by many of todays crop of young bands). Its potential was fully realised on 'REVOLVER' (1966), oft cited as The BEATLES' pinnacle achievement and as one of the best albums ever made. McCARTNEY excelled himself with the string-cloaked melancholy of 'ELEANOR RIGBY', while HARRISON's biting 'TAXMAN' kicked off the album in strident style. But it was the psychedelic numbers which made most impact. 'SHE SAID SHE SAID' was a swirling piece of trip-pop, while 'TOMORROW NEVER KNOWS' remains one of the most bizarre and enigmatic songs in The BEATLES' canon. With a working title of 'THE VOID', the song was based on one of LENNON's first profound acid trips and was partly inspired by the ancient religious text beloved of hippies at the time, 'The Tibetan Book Of The Dead'. With a hypnotic drum sound that many have since tried and failed to recreate, backwards guitar that sounded like a flock of screeching pterodactyls and LENNON's mantra-like vocals, the record set a precedent in psychedelic rock. At this stage The BEATLES were already preoccupied with the possibilities of the recording studio and significantly, the band played their last gig in San Francisco's Candlestick Park the same month 'REVOLVER' was released. Ensconced in Abbey Road Studios, the band came up with the double A-side, 'PENNY LANE' / 'STRAWBERRY FIELDS FOREVER'. Released in February '67, the single's effects-laden innovation was a taster for The BEATLES' much heralded psychedelic concept album 'SGT. PEPPER'S LONELY HEARTS CLUB BAND'. Its release coinciding perfectly with the fabled 1967 'Summer Of Love', the record was a landmark in new studio technique. Utilising the (then) pioneering four-track recording process, the band painstakingly pieced together ornate pieces of sonic intricacy that set new standards. It contained many classics such as 'LUCY IN THE SKY WITH DIAMONDS' (wrongly thought by many to be about L.S.D.), 'SHE'S LEAVING HOME' and the never-ending 'A DAY IN THE LIFE', complete with prolonged intentionally stuck-in-the-groove outro. Fans and critics alike made it "their greatest album of all time", although many others thought it too overblown as well as over-produced. A month later, the anthemic 'ALL YOU NEED IS LOVE' gave them another No.1, helped no doubt by its simultaneous worldwide TV broadcast. The death of BRIAN EPSTEIN cast a shadow over the celebrations but the band moved on, filming/recording 'MAGICAL MYTERY TOUR' (1967). A trippy film and soundtrack inspired by KEN KESEY and his bunch of technicolour minstrels, it contained the infamous LENNON-penned surrealism of 'I AM THE WALRUS'. Screened on British TV on Boxing Day 1967, the film was almost universally panned. Unbowed, The BEATLES decamped to India for spiritual retreat with the Maharishi Mahesh Yogi, during which time they accumulated much of the material that would form the 'WHITE ALBUM'. Upon their return to English shores, they set about forming the 'Apple Corporation', which would handle all the business dealings of the band as well as functioning as a label for The BEATLES and likeminded talent. The first release was 'HEY JUDE' / 'REVOLUTION' (1968), the former a rousing torch song, the latter a stinging attack by LENNON on would-be radicals. Eventually released in November '68, 'THE BEATLES (White Album)' was a sprawling double set recorded in an environment of tension and breakdown of inter-band communications. Yet it contained some of The BEATLES finest songs, 'HARRISON's solemn 'WHILE MY GUITAR GENTLY WEEPS', LENNON's gorgeous 'DEAR PRUDENCE' and 'JULIA', a moving tribute to his mother. The album also included the cryptic genius of LENNON's 'HAPPINESS IS A WARM GUN' while 'REVOLUTION No.9' was The BEATLES at their most defiantly experimental. Nevertheless, the recording had strained relationships within the band to breaking point and the subsequent back to basics sessions in 1969 (eventually emerging as the 'LET IT BE' album) broke down in disarray. Incredibly, the band got it together one last time for 'ABBEY ROAD' (1969), a breathtaking sweep through the diverse styles of each of the songwriters. GEORGE HARRISON contributed two of his best tracks, 'SOMETHING' and the pastoral beauty of 'HERE COMES THE SUN'. McCARTNEY penned most of the medley which formed a sizeable chunk of the album and which included one of his most heartbreakingly lovely songs, 'GOLDEN SLUMBERS'. 'LET IT BE', eventually released in 1970 was hardly a fitting epitaph for The BEATLES, PHIL SPECTOR's production coming in for some flak. It did, however, contain such definitive BEATLES moments as the deeply reflective title track, the sleepy 'ACROSS THE UNIVERSE' and the beguiling 'THE LONG AND WINDING ROAD'. The BEATLES had officially split a couple of months before the album's release in April 1970, estranged amid personal rows and more serious business disagreements. LENNON, McCARTNEY and HARRISON all went on to respectable solo careers, although none of the subsequent recordings had quite the same impact as The BEATLES' material. Come the 90's, there was still a voracious market for anything BEATLES-related and fans were treated to successive live and outtakes sets, most of which topped the charts in both America and Britain. 1994's 'LIVE AT THE BBC was the first of these monster doubles, showcasing the band's early, rock'n'roll-influenced years with a slew of previously unissued material including many incendiary covers of both well known and more obscure songs. The three mid-90's volumes of 'ANTHOLOGY' meanwhile, trawled the archives for alternate takes, rough demos, live cuts and other odds 'n'sods, releasing them chronologically with each covering a distinct phase of the band's 60's career. Pick of the bunch was probably the third and final one, if for no other reason than the sheer experimentalism of their latter years and the inevitable, fascinating cast-offs which that produced (including acoustic demos from 'THE WHITE ALBUM' sessions and the semi-legendary stringless version of 'THE LONG AND WINDING ROAD'). The rather unnecessary '1' (2000) collected the complete sweep of the band's No.1 singles in both America and the States while 'LET IT BE . . .NAKED' (2003) offered an alternate take on the controversial original. While the record purported to be the finished article as originally envisioned, it certainly wasn't a warts'n'all release of the abandoned 'GET BACK' sessions and, in dispensing with the banter and asides of 'LET IT BE', sacrificed some of the original's spontaneity. In its favour was the inclusion of the aforementioned stringless ' . . .WINDING ROAD' and pre-SPECTOR versions of both 'ACROSS THE UNIVERSE' and 'I ME MINE' as well as a much better overall sound quality. Whether these and other minor differences warranted its release is another matter. Sadly, another chapter in the BEATLES saga drew to a close when

GEORGE HARRISON finally succumbed to cancer on the 29th of November, 2001, a star-studded concert at London's Royal Albert Hall paying tribute to perhaps the greatest and most underrated Beatle of them all. The band remain one of the greatest cultural icons of the 20th Century with a back catalogue that even OASIS will never be able to match.

• **Covered:** TWIST AND SHOUT (Isley Brothers) / A TASTE OF HONEY (Bobby Scott) / MONEY (Barrett Strong) / ROLL OVER BEETHOVEN + ROCK AND ROLL MUSIC (Chuck Berry) / YOU REALLY GOT A HOLD ON ME (Miracles) / PLEASE MR. POSTMAN (Marvelettes) / KANSAS CITY (Wilbert Harrison) / WORDS OF LOVE (Diamonds) / CHAINS (Cookies) / BABY IT'S YOU (Shirelles) / etc.

Album rating: PLEASE PLEASE ME (*8) / WITH THE BEATLES (*8) / A HARD DAY'S NIGHT soundtrack (*8) / BEATLES FOR SALE (*7) / HELP! soundtrack (*8) / RUBBER SOUL (*9) / REVOLVER (*10) / SGT. PEPPER'S LONELY HEARTS CLUB BAND (*10) / MAGICAL MYSTERY TOUR soundtrack (*8) / THE BEATLES 'White Album' (*10) / YELLOW SUBMARINE soundtrack (*6) / ABBEY ROAD (*9) / LET IT BE soundtrack (*7) / THE BEATLES 1967-70 compilation (*10) / THE BEATLES 1962-66 compilation (*10) / LIVE AT THE BBC collection (*8) / 1 compilation (*10) / LET IT BE . . . NAKED (*6)

JOHN LENNON (b. JOHN WINSTON LENNON, 9 Oct'40) – vocals, rhythm guitar / **PAUL McCARTNEY** (b. JAMES PAUL McCARTNEY, 18 Jun'42) – vocals, guitar / **GEORGE HARRISON** (b.25 Feb'43) – vocals, lead guitar/ **STU SUTCLIFFE** (b. STUART, 23 Jun'40, Edinburgh, Scotland) – bass/ **PETE BEST** (b.1941) – drums

Polydor — Decca

Jan 62. (7"; as TONY SHERIDAN & THE BEATLES) *(NH 66-833)* <31382> **MY BONNIE. / THE SAINTS** [ ] Apr62 [ ]
(re-iss. May63 hit UK No.48; same) (re-iss. Feb64; same) <US re-iss. Jan64 on 'M.G.M.'; K 13213>; hit No. 26) (above A-side was released Aug61 in Germany as TONY SHERIDAN & The BEAT BROTHERS)

— Were a quartet at the time, STU stayed in Germany, died 10 Apr'62 of brain haemorrhage. McCARTNEY now on bass and vocals.

— (Aug62) **RINGO STARR** (b.RICHARD STARKEY, 7 Jul'40) – drums (ex-RORY STORM & THE HURRICANES)repl. BEST

Parlophone — not iss.

Oct 62. (7") *(R 4949)* **LOVE ME DO. / P.S. I LOVE YOU** [17] [–]
(re-iss. Feb63; same) <US-iss.Apr64 on 'Tollie'; 9008>; hit Nos. 1+10> <US re-iss. Aug64 on 'Oldies'; 45 OL 151> <US re-iss. Oct65 on 'Capitol Starline'; 6062> (re-iss. Oct82; same); hit No.4) (re-iss. cd-s.1989) (re-iss. Oct92; same); hit No.53)

Parlophone — Vee Jay

Jan 63. (7") *(R 4983)* <VJ 498> **PLEASE PLEASE ME. / ASK ME WHY** [2] [ ]
(re-iss. Feb63; same) (re-iss. Jan83; same); hit 29) (re-iss. cd-s.1989)

Mar 63. (lp; mono)(lp; stereo) *(PMC 1202)(PCS 3042)* **PLEASE PLEASE ME** [1] [–]
– I saw her standing there / Misery / Anna (go to him) / Chains / Boys / Ask me why / Please please me / Love me do / P.S. I love you / Baby, it's you / Do you want to know a secret / A taste of honey / There's a place / Twist and shout. *(c-iss.1970's) (cd-iss. Feb87; CDP 746435-2); hit 32) (re-iss. Nov88 lp/c; PMC/TC-PMC 1202)*

Apr 63. (7") *(R 5015)* <VJ 522> **FROM ME TO YOU. / THANK YOU GIRL** [1] [ ]
(re-iss. Apr83; same); hit No.40) (re-iss. cd-s.1989)

Jul 63. (lp) <1062> **INTRODUCING . . . THE BEATLES** [–] Feb64 [2]
-(tracks nearly same as UK debut)

Aug 63. (7") *(R 5055)* <Swan; S-4152> **SHE LOVES YOU. / I'LL GET YOU** [1] Sep63 [1]
(re-iss. Aug83; same); hit No.45) (re-iss. cd-s.1989)

Nov 63. (lp; mono)(lp; stereo) *(PMC 1206)(PCS 3042)* **WITH THE BEATLES** [1] [–]
– It won't be long / All I've got to do / All my loving / Don't bother me / Little child / Till there was you / Please Mr. Postman / Roll over Beethoven / Hold me tight / You really got a hold on me / I wanna be your man / Roll over Beethoven / Devil in her heart / Not a second time / Money. *(c-iss.1970's) (cd-iss. Feb87; CDP 746436-2); hit No.40) (re-iss. Nov88 lp/c; PMC/TC-PMC 1206)*

Nov 63. (7") *(R 5084)* **I WANT TO HOLD YOUR HAND. / THIS BOY** [1] [–]
(re-iss. Nov83; same); hit No.62) (re-iss. cd-s.1989)

Jan 64. (7") <VJ 581> **PLEASE PLEASE ME. / FROM ME TO YOU** [–] [3]
<US re-iss. Aug64 on 'Oldies'; 45 OL 150> <US re-iss. Oct65 on 'Capitol Starline'; 6063>

Parlophone — Capitol

Jan 64. (7") <5112> **I WANT TO HOLD YOUR HAND. / I SAW HER STANDING THERE** [–] [1] [14]

Jan 64. (lp) <2047> **MEET THE BEATLES!** [–] [1]
– I want to hold your hand / I saw her standing there / This boy / It won't be long / All I've got to do / All my loving / Don't bother me / Little child / Till there was you / Hold me tight / I wanna be your man / Not a second time.

Mar 64. (7") *(R 5114)* <5150> **CAN'T BUY ME LOVE. / YOU CAN'T DO THAT** [1] [1]
(re-iss. Mar84; same); hit No.53) (re-iss. cd-s.1989)

Apr 64. (lp) <2080> **THE BEATLES' SECOND ALBUM** [–] [1]
– Roll over Beethoven / Thank you girl / You really got a hold on me / Devil in her heart / Money / You can't do that / Long tall Sally / I call your name / Please Mr. Postman / I'll get you / She loves you.

Jul 64. (7") *(R 5160)* **A HARD DAY'S NIGHT. / THINGS WE SAID TODAY** [1] [–]
(re-iss. Jul84; same); hit No.52) (re-iss. cd-s.1989)

Jul 64. (7") <5222> **A HARD DAY'S NIGHT. / I SHOULD HAVE KNOWN BETTER** [–] [1] [53]

Jul 64. (lp; mono)(lp; stereo) *(PMC 1230)(PCS 3058)* <6366> **A HARD DAY'S NIGHT** (soundtrack) [1] [1]
– A hard day's night / I should have known better / If I fell / I'm happy just to dance with you / And I love her / Tell me why / Can't buy me love / Anytime at all / I'll cry instead / Things we said today / When I get home / You can't do that / I'll be back. *(re-iss. Jan71; same); hit 39) (cd-iss. Feb87; CDP 746437-2); hit No.30) (re-iss. Nov88 lp/c; PMC/TC-PMC 1230)*

Aug 64. (7") <5234> **I'LL CRY INSTEAD. / I'M HAPPY JUST TO DANCE WITH YOU** [–] [25] [95]

Aug 64. (7") <5235> **AND I LOVE HER. / IF I FELL** [–] [12] [53]

Sep 64. (7") <5255> **MATCHBOX. / SLOW DOWN** [–] [17] [25]

Nov 64. (7") *(R 5200)* <5327> **I FEEL FINE. / SHE'S A WOMAN** [1] [1] [4]
(re-iss. Nov84; same) ; hit No.65) (re-iss. cd-s.1989)

Dec 64. (lp; mono)(lp; stereo) *(PMC1240)(PCS 3062)* **BEATLES FOR SALE** [1] [–]
– No reply / I'm a loser / Baby's in black / Rock and roll music / I'll follow the sun / Mr. Moonlight / Medley: Kansas City – Hey hey hey hey / Eight days a week / Words of love / Honey don't / Every little thing / I don't want to spoil the party / What you're doing / Everybody's trying to be my baby. *(c-iss.1970's) (cd-iss. Feb87; CDP 746438-2); hit No.45) (re-iss. Nov88 lp/c; PMC/TC-PMC 1240)*

Jan 65. (lp) <2228> **BEATLES '65** [–] [1]
– (track listing near as above)

Feb 65. (7") (5371> **EIGHT DAYS A WEEK. / I DON'T WANT TO SPOIL THE PARTY** [–] [1] [39]

Apr 65. (7") *(R 5265)* <5407> **TICKET TO RIDE. / YES IT IS** [1] [1]
(re-iss. Apr85; same); hit No.70) (re-iss. cd-s.1989)

Jul 65. (lp) <2358> **BEATLES VI** [–] [1]
– Kansas City / Eight days a week / You like me too much / Bad boy / I don't want to spoil the party / Words of love / What you're doing / Yes it is / Dizzy Miss Lizzy / Tell me what you see / Every little thing.

Jul 65. (7") *(R 5305)* <5476> **HELP!. / I'M DOWN** [1] [1]
(re-iss. Apr76; same); hit No.37) *(re-iss. Jul85; same) (re-iss. cd-s.1989)*

Jul 65. (lp; mono)(lp; stereo) *(PMC 1255)(PCS PCS 3071)* <2386> **HELP!** (soundtrack) [1] Aug65 [1]
– Help! / The night before / You've got to hide your love away / I need you / Another girl / You're going to lose that girl / Ticket to ride / Act naturally / It's only love / You like me too much / Tell me what you see / I've just seen a face / Yesterday / Dizzy Miss Lizzy. *(re-iss. Jul71 lp/c; same); hit No.33) (cd-iss. Apr87; CDP 746439-2); hit No.61) (re-iss. Nov88 lp/c; PMC/TC-PMC 1255)*

Sep 65. (7") <5498> **YESTERDAY. / ACT NATURALLY** [–] [1]

Dec 65. (7") *(R 5389)* <5555> **DAY TRIPPER. / WE CAN WORK IT OUT** [1] [5] [1]
(re-iss. Dec85; same) (re-iss. cd-s.1989)

Dec 65. (lp; mono)(lp; stereo) *(PMC 1267)(PCS 3075)* <2442> **RUBBER SOUL** [1] [1]

– Drive my car / Norwegian wood (this bird has flown) / You won't see me / Nowhere man / Think for yourself / The word / Michelle / What goes on? / Girl / I'm looking through you / In my life / Wait / If I needed someone / Run for your life. *(c-iss.1970's) (cd-iss. Apr87; CDP 746440-2); hit UK No.60) (re-iss. Nov88 lp/c; PMC/TC-PMC 1267)*

Feb 66. (7") *<5587>* **NOWHERE MAN. / WHAT GOES ON** – 3 81

Jun 66. (7") *(R 5452) <5651>* **PAPERBACK WRITER. / RAIN** 1 1 23
(re-iss. Mar76; same); hit No.23) (re-iss. Jun86; same) (re-iss. cd-s.1989)

Aug 66. (7") *(R 5493) <5715>* **YELLOW SUBMARINE. / ELEANOR RIGBY** 1 2 11
(re-iss. Aug86; same); hit No.63) (re-iss. cd-s.1989)

Aug 66. (lp; mono/stereo) *(PMC/PCS 7009) <2576>* **REVOLVER** 1 1
– Taxman / Love you to / I want to tell you / Eleanor Rigby / Here, there and everywhere / Good day sunshine / For no one / Got to get you into my life / I'm only sleeping / She said she said / And your bird can sing / Doctor Robert / Tomorrow never knows / Yellow submarine. *(c-iss.1970's) (cd-iss. Apr87; CDP 746441-2); hit UK No.55) (re-iss. Nov88 lp/c; PMC/TC-PMC 7009)*

Feb 67. (7") *(R 5570) <5810>* **PENNY LANE. / STRAWBERRY FIELDS FOREVER** 2 1 8
(re-iss. Mar76; same); hit No.32) (re-iss. Feb87; same); hit No.65) (re-iss. cd-s.1989)

Jun 67. (lp; mono/stereo) *(PMC/PCS 7027) <2653>* **SGT. PEPPER'S LONELY HEARTS CLUB BAND** 1 1
– Sgt.Pepper's lonely hearts club band / With a little help from my friends / Lucy in the sky with diamonds / Getting better / Fixing a hole / She's leaving home / Being for the benefit of Mr.Kite / Within you without you / When I'm sixty-four / Lovely Rita / Good morning, good morning / Sgt. Pepper's lonely hearts club band (reprise) / A day in the life. *(c-iss.1970's) (cd-iss. Jun87; CDP 746442-2); hit UK No.3) (re-iss. Nov88 lp/c; PMC/TC-PMC 7027) (re-iss. Jun92; same); hit UK No.6)*

Jul 67. (7") *(R 5620) <5964>* **ALL YOU NEED IS LOVE. / BABY YOU'RE A RICH MAN** 1 1 34
(re-iss. Jul87; same); hit No.47) (re-iss. cd-s.1989)

Nov 67. (7") *(R 5655) <2056>* **HELLO GOODBYE. / I AM THE WALRUS** 1 1 56
(re-iss. Nov87; same); hit No.63) (re-iss. cd-s.1989)

Dec 67. (d7"ep; stereo/mono) *(S+/MMT 1)* **MAGICAL MYSTERY TOUR** 2 –
– Magical mystery tour / Your mother should know / Flying / Fool on the hill / Blue Jay way / I am the walrus.

Dec 67. (lp) *(imported) <2835>* **MAGICAL MYSTERY TOUR** (soundtrack) 31 1
– (above UK-ep, plus 1967 singles) *(UK-iss.Oct76, cd-iss. Sep87; CDP 748 062-2); hit UK 52)*

Mar 68. (7") *(R 5675) <2138>* **LADY MADONNA. / THE INNER LIGHT** 1 4 96
(re-iss. Mar88; same); hit No.67) (re-iss. cd-s.1989)

Apple Apple

Aug 68. (7") *(R 5722) <2276>* **HEY JUDE. / REVOLUTION** 1 1 12
(re-iss. Mar76; same); hit No.12) (re-iss. Aug88; same); hit No.52) (re-iss. cd-s.1989)

Nov 68. (d-lp; mono/stereo) *(PMC/PCS 7067-8) <101>* **THE BEATLES (White Album)** 1 1
– Back in the U.S.S.R / Dear Prudence / Glass onion / Ob-la-di-ob-la-da / Wild honey pie / The continuing story of Bungalow Bill / While my guitar gently weeps / Happiness is a warm gun / Martha my dear / I'm so tired / Blackbird / Piggies / Rocky raccoon / Don't pass me by / Why don't we do it in the road / I will / Julia / Birthday / Yer blues / Mother nature's son / Everybody's got something to hide except me and my monkey / Sexy Sadie / Helter skelter / Long long long / Revolution 1 / Honey pie / Savoy truffle / Cry baby cry / Revolution 9 / Good night. *(re-iss. Sep78 white-lp; same) (cd-iss. Aug87; CDP CDS 746443-2); hit UK No.18) (re-iss. Nov88 lp/c; PCS/TCPCS 7067) (d-cd re-iss. Nov98; 496895-2)*

Jan 69. (lp; mono/stereo) *(PMC/PCS 7070) <153>* **YELLOW SUBMARINE (Soundtrack)** 4 2
– Yellow submarine / Only a northern song / All together now / Hey bulldog / It's all too much / All you need is love / Pepperland / Sea of time / Sea of holes / Sea of monsters / March of the Meanies / Pepperland laid waste / Yellow submarine in Pepperland. (with GEORGE MARTI[N] ORCHESTRA) *(re-iss. Aug87; CDP 746445-2); hit UK 60) (re-iss. Nov8[8] lp/c; PCS/TC-PCS 7070)*

Apr 69. (7"; by BEATLES with BILLY PRESTON) *(R 5777) <2490>* **GET BACK. / DON'T LET ME DOWN** 1 1 35
(re-iss. Mar76; same); hit No.28) (re-iss. Apr89; same); hit 74) (re-iss cd-s.1989)

May 69. (7") *(R 5786) <2531>* **THE BALLAD OF JOHN AND YOKO. / OLD BROWN SHOE** 1 8
(UK re-iss. May89) (re-iss. cd-s.1989)

Sep 69. (lp/c) *(PCS/TC-PCS 7088) <383>* **ABBEY ROAD** 1 1
– Come together / Maxwell's silver hammer / Something / Oh darling Octopus's garden / I want you (she's so heavy) / Here comes the sun Because / You never give me your money / Sun king / Mean Mr. Mustard Polythene Pam / She came in through the bathroom window / Golde[n] slumbers / Carry that weight / The end / Her majesty. *(UK re-iss. Oct87 CDP 746 446-2); hit No.30) (re-iss. Nov88 lp/c; PCS/TC-PCS 7088)*

Oct 69. (7") *(R 5814) <2654>* **SOMETHING. / COME TOGETHER** 4 3 1
(UK re-iss. Oct89) (re-iss. cd-s.1989)

Mar 70. (7") *(R 5833) <2764>* **LET IT BE. / YOU KNOW MY NAME (LOOK UP THE NUMBER)** 2 1
(UK re-iss. Mar90) (re-iss. cd-s.1989)

May 70. (lp/c) *(PCS/TC-PCS 7096) <34001>* **LET IT BE** (soundtrack) 1 1
– Two of us / Dig a pony / Across the universe / I me mine / Dig it / Le[t] it be / Maggie Mae / I've got a feeling / The one after 909 / The long an[d] winding road / For you blue / Get back. *(cd-iss. Oct87; CDP 746 447-2); hi[t] No.50) (re-iss. Nov88 lp/c; PCS/TC-PCS 7096)*

May 70. (7") *<2832>* **THE LONG AND WINDING ROAD. / FOR YOU BLUE** – 1

—— officially disbanded April 1970 – all 4 had released, or were due to release own albums. See **Paul McCARTNEY ⇒ , John LENNON ⇒ , Georg[e] HARRISON ⇒ , Ringo STARR ⇒ .**

– (selective) compilations, etc. –

on 'Parlophone' UK / 'Capitol' US unless otherwise mentioned

Jul 63. (7"ep) *(GEP 8880)* **TWIST AND SHOUT** 2 –
– Twist and shout / A taste of honey / Do you want to know a secret / There's a place.

Sep 63. (7"ep) *(GEP 8882)* **THE BEATLES HITS** 14 –
– From me to you / Thank you girl / Please please me / Love me do.

Nov 63. (7"ep) *(GEP 8883)* **THE BEATLES (No.1)** 19 –
– I saw her standing there / Misery / Chains / Anna (go to him).

Jan 64. (7"; by TONY SHERIDAN & THE BEATLES) *Polydor; (NH 52-906)* **SWEET GEORGIA BROWN. / NOBODY'S CHILD** –

Feb 64. (7"ep) *(GEP GEP 8891)* **ALL MY LOVING** 12 –
– All my loving / Ask me why / Money / P.S. I love you.

Mar 64. (7"; by TONY SHERIDAN & THE BEATLES) *M.G.M.; <K 13227>* **WHY. / CRY FOR A SHADOW** – 88

Mar 64. (7") *Tollie; <9001>* **TWIST AND SHOUT. / THERE'S A PLACE** – 2 74

Apr 64. (7") *Vee Jay; <VJ 587>* **DO YOU WANT TO KNOW A SECRET. / THANK YOU GIRL** – 2 35

May 64. (7") *Swan; <S-4182>* **SIE LIEBT DICH. / I'LL GET YOU** – 97

May 64. (7"; by TONY SHERIDAN & THE BEATLES) *Polydor; (NH 52-317)* **AIN'T SHE SWEET. / IF YOU LOVE ME BABY** 29 –

Jun 64. (lp; by TONY SHERIDAN & THE BEATLES) *Polydor Special; (236 201)* **THE BEATLES' FIRST** –
(re-iss. Jun71 as THE EARLY YEARS on 'Contour') (re-iss. as 'THE FIRST ALBUM' cd+c May93 on 'Spectrum', credited to TONY SHERIDAN & THE BEATLES)

Jun 64. (7"; by TONY SHERIDAN & THE BEATLES) *Atco; <6302>* **SWEET GEORGIA BROWN. / TAKE OUT SOME INSURANCE ON ME BABY** –

Jun 64. (7"ep) *(GEP 8913)* **LONG TALL SALLY** 14 –
– Long tall Sally / I call your name / Slow down / Matchbox.

Jun 64. (7"ep) *<EAP 2121>* **FOUR BY THE BEATLES** – 92
– All my loving / This boy / Roll over Beethoven / Please Mr.Postman.

Jul 64. (7"; by TONY SHERIDAN & THE BEATLES) *Atco;* *<6308>* **AIN'T SHE SWEET. / NOBODY'S CHILD** [–] [19]

Aug 64. (lp) *<2108>* **SOMETHING NEW** [–] [2]

Nov 64. (7"ep) *(GEP 8920)* **EXTRACTS FROM THE FILM 'A HARD DAY'S NIGHT'** [34] [–]
– I should have known better / If I fell / Tell me why / And I love her.

Dec 64. (7"ep) *(GEP 8924)* **EXTRACTS FROM THE ALBUM 'A HARD DAY'S NIGHT' 2** [ ] [–]
– Anytime at all / I'll cry instead / Things we said today / When I get home.

Dec 64. (lp) *<2222>* **THE BEATLES' STORY (narrative)** [–] [7]

Jul 66. (lp) *(2553>* **YESTERDAY . . . AND TODAY** [–] [1]

Dec 66. (lp) *(PMC/PCS 7016)* **A COLLECTION OF BEATLES OLDIES** [7] [–]
– She loves you / From me to you / We can work it out / Help! / Michelle / Yesterday / I feel fine / Yellow submarine / Can't buy me love / Bad boy / Day tripper / A hard day's night / Ticket to ride / Paperback writer / Eleanor Rigby / I want to hold your hand. *(re-iss. Oct83 on 'Fame' lp/c; FA/TC-FA 3081)*

Mar 70. (lp) *Apple; <385>* **HEY JUDE** [–] [2]
(UK-iss.May79 on 'Parlophone' lp/c; PCS/TC-PCS 7184)

Apr 73. (d-lp/d-c) *Apple; (PCSP/TC2-PCSP 717) <3403>* **THE BEATLES 1962-1966** [3] [3]
– Love me do / Please please me / She loves you / From me to you / She loves you / I want to hold your hand / All my loving / Can't buy me love / A hard day's night / And I love her / Eight days a week / I feel fine / Ticket to ride / Yesterday / Help! / You've got to hide your love away / We can work it out / Day tripper / Drive my car / Norwegian wood (this bird has flown) / Nowhere man / Michelle / In my life / Girl / Paperback writer / Eleanor Rigby / Yellow submarine. *(re-iss. Sep78 & Feb94 red-lp) (d-cd-iss. Jul91; CDPCSP 717) (re-iss. d-cd Sep93 on 'Apple-Parlophone'; same)* – hit UK No.3

Apr 73. (d-lp/d-c) *Apple; (PCSP/TC2-PCSP 718) <3404>* **THE BEATLES 1967-1970** [2] [1]
– Strawberry fields forever / Penny lane / Sgt. Pepper's lonely hearts club band / With a little help from my friends / Lucy in the sky with diamonds / A day in the life / All you need is love / I am the Walrus / Hello, goodbye / The fool on the hill / Magical mystery tour / Lady Madonna / Hey Jude / Revolution / Back in the U.S.S.R / While my guitar gently weeps / Ob-la-di, ob-la-da / Get back / Don't let me down / The ballad of John and Yoko / Old brown shoe / Here comes the sun / Come together / Something / Octopus's Garden / Let it be / Across the universe / The long and winding road. *(re-iss. Sep78 & Feb94 blue-lp) (d-cd-iss. Jul91; CDPCSP 718) (re-iss. d-cd Sep93 on 'Apple-Parlophone'; same)* – hit UK No.4

Mar 76. (7") *(R 6013)* **YESTERDAY. / I SHOULD HAVE KNOWN BETTER** [8] [–]

Jun 76. (lp/c) *(PCSP/TC-PCSP 719) <11537>* **ROCK'N'ROLL MUSIC** [11] [2]
(re-iss. Nov80 as . . . VOL.1 / . . . VOL.2 both on 'MfP')

Jun 76. (7") *<4274>* **GOT TO GET YOU INTO MY LIFE. / HELTER SKELTER** [–] [7]

Jul 76. (7") *(R 6016)* **BACK IN THE U.S.S.R. / TWIST AND SHOUT** [19] [–]

Aug 76. (d-lp) *Polydor; (2683 068)* **THE BEATLES TAPES (interviews)** [45] [–]

Nov 76. (7") *<4347>* **OB-LA-DI, OB-LA-DA. / JULIA** [–] [49]

May 77. (lp/c) *(EMTV/TC-EMTV 4) <11638>* **THE BEATLES AT THE HOLLYWOOD BOWL (live)** [1] [2]
(UK re-iss. Sep84 on 'MfP')

Dec 77. (d-lp/d-c) *(PCSP/TC-PCSP 721) <11711>* **LOVE SONGS** [7] [24]

Sep 78. (7") *(R 6022) <4612>* **SGT. PEPPER'S LONELY HEARTS CLUB BAND – WITH A LITTLE HELP FROM MY FRIENDS. / A DAY IN THE LIFE** [63] [71]

Nov 78. (14xlp-box) *(BBX 1)* **THE BEATLES COLLECTION** [ ] [ ]
– (all original albums boxed)

Oct 79. (lp/c) *(PCM/TC-PCM 1001) <12060>* **RARITIES** [71] Apr80 [21]

Nov 80. (lp/c) *(PCS/TC-PCS 7214)* **BEATLES BALLADS** [17] [ ]

Apr 82. (lp/c) *<12199>* **REEL MUSIC** [–] [19]

May 82. (7") *(R 6055) <5107>* **BEATLES MOVIE MEDLEY. / I'M HAPPY JUST TO DANCE WITH YOU** [10] Mar82 [12]
– ('A'medley); Magical Mystery Tour – All You Need Is Love – You've Got To Hide Your Love Away – I Should Have Known Better – A Hard Day's Night – Ticket To Ride – Get Back.

Oct 82. (d-lp/d-c) *(PCTC/TC-PCTC 260) <12245>* **20 GREATEST HITS** [10] [50]

Feb 88. (cd/c/d-lp) *E.M.I.; (CD/TC+/BPM 1)* **PAST MASTERS VOL.1** [49] [ ]

Feb 88. (cd/c/d-lp) *E.M.I.; (CD/TC+/BPM 2)* **PAST MASTERS VOL.2** [46] [ ]

Apr 92. (cd-epx14-box) *(CDBEP 14)* **THE BEATLES EP COLLECTION** [ ] [–]

Dec 94. (d-cd/d-c/d-lp) *Apple; (CD/TC+/PCSP 726)* **LIVE AT THE BBC (live)** [1] [3]
– Beatle greetings / From us to you / Riding on a bus / I got a woman / Too much monkey business / Keep your hands off my baby / I'll be on my way / Young blood / A shot of rhythm and blues / Sure to fall (in love with you) / Some other guy / Thank you girl / Sha la la la la! / Baby it's you / That's all right (mama) / Carol / Soldier of love / A little rhyme / Clarabella / I'm gonna sit right down and cry (over you) / Crying, waiting, hoping / Dear Wack! / You really got a hold on me / To know her is to love her / A taste of honey / Long tall Sally / I saw her standing there / The honeymoon song / Johnny B Goode / Memphis, Tennessee / Lucille / Can't buy me love / From Fluff to you / Till there was you // Crinsk Dee night / A hard day's night / Have a banana! / I wanna be your man / Just a rumour / Roll over Beethoven / All my loving / Things we said today / She's a woman / Sweet little sixteen / 1882! / Lonesome tears in my eyes / Nothin' shakin' / The hippy hippy shake / Glad all over / I just don't understand / So how come (no one loves me) / I feel fine / I'm a loser / Everybody's trying to be my baby / Rock and roll music / Ticket to ride / Dizzy Miss Lizzy / Medley: Kansas City – Hey! hey! hey! hey! / Set fire to that lot! / Matchbox / I forgot to remember to forget / Love these Goon shows! / I got to find my baby / Ooh! my soul / Ooh! my arms / Don't ever change / Slow down / Honey don't / Love me do.

Mar 95. (c-s/7") *Apple; (TC+/R 6406) <58348>* **BABY IT'S YOU / I'LL FOLLOW THE SUN** [7] [67]
(cd-s+=) *(CDR 6406)* – Devil in her heart / Boys.

Nov 95. (d-cd/d-c/t-lp) *Apple; (CD/TC+/PCSP 727) <34445>* **ANTHOLOGY 1** [2] [1]
– Free as a bird / Speech (by JOHN LENNON) / That'll be the day / In spite of all the danger / Sometimes I'd borrow (speech by PAUL McCARTNEY) / Hallelujah I love her so / You'll be mine / Cayenne / First of all (speech by PAUL) / My Bonnie (w/ TONY SHERIDAN) / Ain't she sweet / Cry for a shadow / Brian was a beautful guy (speech by JOHN) / Secured them an audition (speech by BRIAN EPSTEIN) / Searchin' / Three cool cats / The Sheik of Araby / Like dreamers do / Hello little girl / Well, the recording test (speech by BRIAN) / Besame mucho / Love me do / How do you do it? / Please please me / One after 909 (sequence) / One after 909 (complete) / Lend me your comb / I'll get you / We were performers (speech by JOHN) / I saw her standing there / From me to you / Money (that's what I want) / You really got a hold on me / Roll over Beethoven / She loves you / Till there was you (music man) / Twist and shout / This boy / I want to hold your hand / Boys, what I was thinking (speech by The BEATLES and MORECAMBE & WISE) / Moonlightbay (w/ MORECAMBE & WISE) / Can't buy me love / All my loving / You can't do that / And I love her / A hard day's night / I wanna be your man / Long tall Sally / Boys / Shout / I'll be back (take 2) / I'll be back (take 3) / You know what to do / No reply (demo) / Mr.Moonlight / Leave my kitten alone / No reply / Eight days a week (sequence) / Eight days a week (complete) / Kansas City – hey, hey, hey.
(below single was recently re-recorded from JOHN LENNON's 1977 cut)

Dec 95. (c-s/7") *Apple; (TC+/R 6422) <58497>* **FREE AS A BIRD. / CHRISTMAS TIME (IS HERE AGAIN)** [2] [6]
(cd-s+=) *(CDR 6422)* – I saw her standing there (take 9) / This boy (take 13).

Mar 96. (c-s/7") *Apple; (TC+/R 6425) <58544>* **REAL LOVE / BABY'S IN BLACK** [4] [11]
(cd-s+=) *(CDR 6425)* – Yellow submarine / Here, there and everywhere.

Mar 96. (d-cd/d-c/t-lp) *(CD/TC+/PCSP 728) <34448>* **ANTHOLOGY 2** [1] [1]
– Real love / Yes it is (version) / I'm down / You've got to hide your love away / If you've got trouble / That means a lot / Yesterday (take) / It's only love (take) / I feel fine / Ticket to ride / Yesterday (take) / Help! (version) / Everybody's trying to be my baby / Norwegian wood (this bird has flown) / I'm looking through you / 12-bar original / Tomorrow never knows / Got to get you into my life / And your bird can sing (version) / Taxman / Eleanor Rigby (strings only) / I'm only sleeping (rehearsal) / I'm only sleeping (take 1) / Rock & roll music / She's a woman / Strawberry fields forever (demo sequence) / Strawberry fields forever (take 1) / Strawberry fields forever (take 7 and edit piece) / Penny Lane (take) / A day in the life (version) / Good morning, good morning (version) / Only a Northern song / Being for the benefit of Mr. Kite (takes 1 & 2) / Being for the benefit of Mr. Kite (take 7) / Lucy in the sky with diamonds (take) / Within you, without you (instrumental) / Sgt. Pepper's lonely hearts club band (take) / You know my name (look up my number) / I am the walrus (version) / Fool on the hill (demo) / Your mother should know / Fool on the hill (take

4) / Hello, goodbye (version) / Lady Madonna (take) / Across the universe (alt. take).

Oct 96. (d-cd/d-c/t-lp) *(CD/TC+/PCSP 729) <46332>* **ANTHOLOGY 3** [4] [1]
– A beginning / Happiness is a warm gun / Helter skelter / Mean Mr. Mustard (take) / Polythene Pam / Glass onion (version) / Junk (take) / Piggies / Honey pie / Don't pass me by / Ob-la-di, ob-la-da / Good night (version) / Cry baby cry (version) / Blackbird / Sexy Sadie / While my guitar gently weeps / Hey Jude / Not guilty / Mother nature's son (take) / Glass onion (version) / Rocky racoon (take) / What's the new Mary Jane? / Step inside love / I'm so tired / I will / Why don't we do it in the road? (version) / Julia (take) / I've got a feeling (version) / She came in through the bathroom window / Dig a pony (version) / Two of us (take) / For you blue / Teddy boy / Medley: Rip it up – Shake, rattle and roll – Blue suede shoes / The long and winding road / Oh! darling (take) / All things must pass / Mailman, bring me no more blues / Get back / Old brown shoe / Octopus's garden / Maxwell's silver hammer (take) / Something / Come together (version) / Come and get it / Ain't she sweet / Because (version) / Let it be / I me mine / The end.

Sep 99. (cd/c/lp) *(<5 21481-2/-4/-1>)* **YELLOW SUBMARINE SONGTRACK** [8] [15]
– Yellow submarine / Hey bulldog / Eleanor Rigby / Love you to / All together now / Lucy in the sky with diamonds / Think for yourself / Sgt. Pepper's lonely hearts club band / With a little help from my friends / Baby you're a rich man / Only a northern song / All you need is love / When I'm sixty-four / Nowhere man / It's all too much.

Nov 00. (cd/c)(d-lp) *(529970-2/-4)(529325-1) <29325>* **1** [1] [1]
– Love me do / From me to you / She loves you / I want to hold your hand / Can't buy me love / A hard day's night / I feel fine / Eight days a week / Ticket to ride / Help! / Yesterday / Day tripper / We can work it out / Paperback writer / Yellow submarine / Eleanor Rigby / Penny Lane / All you need is love / Hello, goodbye / Lady Madonna / Hey Jude / Get back / The ballad of John and Yoko / Something / Come together / Let it be / The long and winding road.

Nov 01. (d-cd) *Bear Family; (<BCD 16447)* **BEATLES BOP – HAMBURG DAYS** [ ] [ ]

Nov 03. (cd)(lp) *(595713-2)(595438-0)* **LET IT BE . . . NAKED** [7] [–]
– Get back / Dig a pony / For you blue / The long and winding road / Two of us / I've got a feelin / One after 909 / Don't let me down / I me mine / Across the universe / Let it be. *(cd w/ dvd+=)* – (fly on the wall outtakes). *(lp w/ free 7"+=)* – (interview).

□ BEATS INTERNATIONAL
(see under ⇒ COOK, Norman)

BECK

Born: BECK HANSEN, 8 Jul'70, Los Angeles, California, USA. After absorbing the strains of primitive country blues artists like LEADBELLY and MISSISSIPPI JOHN HURT, along with the aural terrorism of hardcore noise, the 17-year old BECK relocated to New York in 1989 to try his hand on the post-punk East Village folk scene. Broke, he retired to L.A., setting himself up in the (now) trendy Silverlake district, playing low key gigs in local coffeehouses. Spotted by 'Bongload' owner TOM ROTHROCK, he was offered some studio time and the resulting sessions produced the 'LOSER' (1993) single. Caned by L.A.'s alternative radio stations, its popularity led to BECK signing with 'Geffen'. 'LOSER' (1994) in its re-issued, major label form went top 20 in both Britain and America, its slow burning hip hop blues turning the rosy cheeked BECK into an overnight slacker anti-hero. The 'MELLOW GOLD' (1994) album went some way towards crystallising BECK's skewed vision of a modern folk music that encapsulated roots blues, hip hop, country, noise-core and psychedelia. While the record went on to sell half a million copies, BECK's unique contract allowed him the option of recording for other labels. 'STEREOPATHIC SOUL MANURE' (1994) was a U.S. only release of rough early material on the small 'Flipside' label, while 'ONE FOOT IN THE GRAVE' (1995) was a mainly acoustic set released on CALVIN JOHNSON's 'K' records, its stark harmonica-driven title track remaining a highlight of the BECK live experience. Any dubious whispers of "one-hit wonder" were cast aside with the release of 1996's 'ODELAY', a record that topped many end of year polls and turned BECK into the music world's coolest hep cat. Garnering gushing praise from the dance, rock and hip hop communities alike, the album's effortless fusion of disparate styles was breathtaking. The cut'n'paste surrealism of the lyrics flourished imagery of a lucidness to match BOB DYLAN's 60's work and indeed, the gorgeously bittersweet 'JACKASS' used Dylan's 'IT'S ALL OVER NOW BABY BLUE' as a shimmering harmonic backdrop. The album segued smoothly from distortion and dissonance into downhome steel guitar hoedown, all the while retaining an irresistibly funky backbeat. For now, this pop auteur/wunderkid can do no wrong, his live experience is a dayglo potted history of American music and any readers who were lucky enough to catch his glorious set at the Chelmsford V97 festival, will know that BECK doesn't take too kindly to bottle throwing eunuchs! Towards the end of 1998, BECK found himself in the midst of another legal wrangle with label 'Geffen' when a dispute over who was to release his new 14-day recorded 'MUTATIONS' resulted in the label taking full control. The latter was subsequently released to critical acclaim due to Nigel Godrich's production of BECK's live direction. With less label fuss but with more media frenzy, the Lo-Fi loner issued his 4th 'Geffen' set, 'MIDNITE VULTURES' (1999), which proved to be a dark contrast between that and the aforementioned 'MUTATIONS'. After the strange kitsch-adelic sound of 'MIDNITE VULTURES', BECK reverted back to folksy troubadour mode once again complemented by producer Nigel Godrich. A wistful seventh album from the ever eclectic, robot-dancing HANSEN, 'SEA CHANGE' (2002) saw him revisiting the days of 'ONE FOOT IN THE GRAVE' and the Godrich produced no-fi album 'MUTATIONS'. With its gentle melodies and sombre, quasi-romantic overtones, BECK, as always, spiced up the mix by adding harpsicord, trombone, violins and pedal steel to give the set a swift breezy sound – like a psychedelic GRAM PARSONS. Well, he always has been really. Now – as we're constantly reminded – a husband and father, with his demons at least partly exorcised, and with enough time lapsed since his mid-90's entree, a seriously thirty something BECK revisited the classic, Dust Brothers-produced soundclash of yore with 'GUERO' (2005). Had it arrived a year later, 'E-PRO', would've made a great de-facto World Cup theme tune for a hybrid, fictionalised country. As it was, it scraped into the UK Top 40 and lingered in the lower reaches of the US charts, even if the album itself clocked up the best chart showing of BECK's career (No.2). Among the typically quixotic compendium of constituent parts – everything from Peter Frampton-esque fret-gasm to parlour funk – it was HANSEN's vocals which dug deepest, finally mellow enough to sink some real depth into his magpie laments. A remix album, coyly titled 'GUEROLITO' (as in "little Guero"), appeared later the same year, featuring reworkings from the likes of AIR amongst others.

• **Songwriters:** BECK writes most of his material, some with KARL STEPHENSON. 'LOSER' used a sample of DR.JOHN's 'I Walk On Guilded Splinters'. Covered: I'M SO GREEN (Can) / HALO OF GOLD (Moby Grape).
• **Trivia:** The 'Geffen Rarities Vol.1' album of various artists, featured the BECK track, 'Bogusflow'.

Album rating: A WESTERN HARVEST FIELD BY MOONLIGHT (*4) / GOLDEN FEELINGS mini (*3) / MELLOW GOLD (*7) / STEREOPATHETIC SOULMANURE (*4) / ONE FOOT IN THE GRAVE (*6) / ODELAY (*9) / MUTATIONS (*7) / MIDNITE VULTURES (*8) / SEA CHANGE (*7) / GUERO (*7) / GUEROLITO (*4)

BECK (HANSEN) – vocals, acoustic guitar with guests **RACHEL HADEN** – drums, vocals / **ANNA WARONKER** – bass, vocals / **PETRA HADEN** – violin, vocals / **MIKE BOITO** – organ / **DAVID HARTE** – drums / **ROB ZABRECKY** – bass not iss. Flipside

1992. (ltd-7"blue-ep) *<FLIP 46>* **TO SEE THAT WOMAN OF MINE / MTV MAKES ME WANNA SMOKE CRACK. / (other side 2 tracks by BEAN)** [–] [ ]

not iss. Sonic Enemy

Jan 93. (c) *<none>* **GOLDEN FEELINGS** [–] [ ]
– The fucked up blues / Special people / Magic stationwagon / No money no honey / Trouble all my days / Bad energy / Schmoozer / Heartland feeling / Super golden black sunchild / Soul sucked dry / Feelings / Gettin home / Will I be ignored by the Lord / Bogus soul / Totally confused / Muthafukka / People gettin busy.

not iss. Bongload

1993. (ltd-12") *<BL 5>* **LOSER. / STEAL MY BODY HOME** [–] [ ]

1994. (ltd-7") *<BL 11>* **STEVE THREW UP. / MUTHERFUCKER / (CUPCAKE)** [–] [ ]
(both above UK-iss.Jan95; same) (cd-s iss.Dec97 & Oct00; BL 11CDS)

not iss. Fingerpaint

1994. (10"m-lp) *<FP 02>* **A WESTERN HARVEST FIELD BY MOONLIGHT** [–] [ ]
– Totally confused / Mayonaisse salad / Gettin' home / Blackfire choked our death / Feel like a piece of shit (mind control) / She is all (gimme something to eat) / Pinefresh / Lampshade / Feel like a piece of shit (crossover potential) / Mango (Vader rocks!) / Feel like a piece of shit (cheetoes time) / Styrofoam chicken (quality time). *<re-iss. Sep95; same> (UK cd-iss. Oct97 & May98; same)*

Geffen D.G.C.

Mar 94. (7"/c-s) *<DGC S7-19/CS-12 270>* **LOSER. / ALCOHOL** [–] [10]
(cd-s+=) *<DGCDM-21930>* – Corvette bumper / Soul suckin' jerk (reject) / Fume.

Mar 94. (7"/c-s) *(GFS/+C 67)* **LOSER. / ALCOHOL / FUME** [15] [–]
(cd-s) *(GFSTD 67)* – ('A'side) / Totally confused / Corvette bumper / MTV makes me want to smoke crack.

Mar 94. (cd/c/lp) *(GED/GEC/GEF 24634) <DGCD/DGC 24634>* **MELLOW GOLD** [41] [13]
– Loser / Pay no mind (snoozer) / Fuckin with my head (mountain dew rock) / Whiskeyclone, Hotel City 1997 / Soul suckin jerk / Truckdrivin neighbors downstairs (yellow sweat) / Sweet sunshine / Beercan / Steal my body home / Nitemare hippy girl / Motherfuker / Blackhole. *<lp-iss. on 'Bongload'(hidden track cd+=)* – Analog odyssey. *(lp re-iss. Apr97 & Sep99 & Jan01 on 'Bongload'; BL 12> (lp re-iss. Nov98 on 'Simply Vinyl'; SVLP 44)*

May 94. (cd-ep) *<DM-22000>* **BEERCAN / GOT NO MIND / ASSKIZZ POWERGRUDGE (PAYBACK '94) / TOTALLY CONFUSED / SPANKING ROOM / BONUS NOISE** [–] [ ]

May 94. (7"/c-s; w-drawn) *(GFS/+C 73)* **PAY NO MIND (SNOOZER). / SPECIAL PEOPLE** [–] [ ]
(12"+=/cd-s+=)<US cd-ep> *(GFST/+D 73)<GED 21911>* – Trouble all my days / Supergolden (sunchild).

— BECK featured on Various Artists 'Mammoth' EP 'JABBERJAW: GOOD TO THE LAST DROP'. In the same year, with CHRIS BALLEW of The PRESIDENTS . . . and under the moniker of CASPAR AND MOLLUSK, they issued the single, 'TWIG'. He was also featured on below alongside CALVIN JOHNSON – vocals (ex-BEAT HAPPENING), SCOTT PLOUFF – drums / JAMES BERTRAM – bass / +2

not iss. K

Aug 94. (cd/c) *<(KLP 28 CD/C)>* **ONE FOOT IN THE GRAVE** [–] [ ]
– He's a mighty good leader / Sleeping bag / I get lonesome / Burnt orange peel / Cyanide breath mint / See water / Ziplock bag / Hollow log / Forcefield / Fourteen rivers fourteen floods / Asshole / I've seen the land beyond / Outcome / Girl dreams / Painted eyelids / Atmospheric conditions. *(UK-iss.Nov95; lp-iss.Jun97; KLP 28) (re-iss. Oct98; same)*

Nov 94. (7",7"brown) *<iPU 45>* **IT'S ALL IN YOUR MIND. / FEATHER IN YOUR CAP / WHISKEY CAN CAN** [–] [ ]
(UK-iss.Jan02; same as US)

D.G.C. D.G.C.

Jun 96. (c-s) *(GFSC 22156)* **WHERE IT'S AT / WHERE IT'S AT (Mario C & Mickey P remix)** [35] [61]
(cd-s+=)<US cd-ep> *(GFSTD 22156)<DGC CD-22214>* – Bonus beats.
(12"++=)<US 12"ep> *(GFST 22156)<DGC 12-22214>* – ('A'-U.N.K.L.E. remix).

Jun 96. (cd/c; as BECK!) *(GED/GEC 24908) <DGCD/DGC 24823>* **ODELAY** [18] [16]
– Devils haircut / Hotwax / Lord only knows / The new pollution / Derelict / Novacane / Jack-ass / Where it's at / Minus / Sissyneck / Readymade / High 5 (rock the catskills) / Ramshackle / Diskobox. *<lp-iss.Apr97 & Sep99 on 'Bongload'; BL 030LP> (lp-iss.Nov98 on 'Simply Vinyl'; SVLP 51)*

Nov 96. (7") *(GFSC 22183)* **DEVILS HAIRCUT. / LLOYD PRICE EXPRESS** [22] [94]
(cd-s)<US cd-ep> *(GFSTD 22183)<GED 22175>* – ('A'side) / Dark and lovely (Dust Brothers remix) / American wasteland (Mickey P remix).
<US 12"ep++=> *<DGC 12-22222>* – Lloyd Price express / Clock.
(cd-s) *(GFSXD 22183)* – ('A'side) / ('A'-Noel Gallagher remix) / Groovy Sunday (Mike Simpson remix) / Trouble all my days.

Mar 97. (7") *(GFS 22205)* **THE NEW POLLUTION. / ELECTRIC MUSIC AND SUMMER PEOPLE** [14] [78]
(c-s) *(GFSC 22205)* – ('A'side) / Richard's hairpiece (Aphex Twin remix).
(cd-s)<US cd-ep> *(GFSTD 22205) <GED 22204>* – (all 3 tracks).
(cd-s)<US 12"ep> *(GFSTXD 22205) <DGC12 22300>* – ('A'side) / ('A'-Mario C & Mickey P remix) / Lemonade.
(rel.Europe 12" May97 on 'Play It Again Sam'; 22300)

May 97. (7") *(GFS 22253)* **SISSYNECK. / FEATHER IN YOUR CAP** [30] [ ]
(c-s) *(GFSC 22253)* – ('A'side) / The new pollution (remix by Mickey P).
(cd-s) *(GFSTD 22253)* – (all 3 tracks).

Aug 97. (d7"/cd-ep) *(GFS/+TD 22276) <22303>* **JACK-ASS (Butch Vig mix). / STRANGE INVITATION (orchestral version) / DEVIL GOT MY WOMAN // JACK-ASS (Lowrider mix). / BURRO / BROTHER** [ ] [–]

Aug 97. (12"ep) *<DGC12 22303>* **JACK-ASS / BURRO. / STRANGE INVITATION / BROTHER** [–] [97]

Oct 97. (7"/c-s) *(GFS/+C 22293)* **DEADWEIGHT / ERASE THE SUN** [23] [ ]
(cd-s+=) *(GFSTD 22293)* – SA-5.

— BECK with **SMOKEY HORMEL** – guitar / **ROGER MANNING** – keyboards, percussion / **JUSTIN MELDAL JOHNSON** – bass / **JOEY WARONKER** – drums

Nov 98. (cd/c) *(GED/GEC 25184) <25309>* **MUTATIONS** [24] [13]
– Cold brains / Nobody's fault but my own / Lazy flies / Cancelled check / We live again / Tropicalia / Dead melodies / Bottle of blues / O Maria / Sing it again / Static / Diamond bollocks / Runners dial zero. *(lp/7"box-iss. on 'Bongload'; BL 39)*

Dec 98. (7"/c-s) *(GFS/+C 22365)* **TROPICALIA. / HALO OF GOLD** [39] [ ]
(cd-s+=) *(GFSTD 22365)* – Black balloon.

Oct 99. (7"pic-d/c-s) *(497181-7/-4)* **SEXX LAWS. / SALT IN THE WOUND** [27] [ ]
(cd-s+=) *(497181-2)* – ('A'-Wizeguyz mix).
(cd-s) *(497182-2)* – ('A'side) / This is my crew / ('A'-Malibu mix).

Nov 99. (cd/c) *<(490485-2/-4)>* **MIDNITE VULTURES** [19] [34]
– Sexx laws / Nicotine & gravy / Mixed bizness / Get real paid / Hollywood freaks / Peaches & cream / Broken train / Milk & honey / Beautiful way / Pressure zone / Debra. *(lp-iss.Mar00 on 'Bongload'; BL 46)*

Mar 00. (7") *(497312-7)* **MIXED BIZNESS. / DIRTY DIRTY** [34] [–]
(cd-s+=) *(497300-2)* – ('A'video).
(cd-s) *(497301-2)* – ('A'side) / Sexx laws (video).

Apr 00. (cd-s) *<069497272-2>* **MIXED BIZNESS / (mixes; Nu Wave Dreamix by Les Rhythmes / Cornelious / DJ Me DJ You) / DIRTY DIRTY / SAXX LAWS (Night Flight To Ojai)** [–] [ ]

Sep 02. (cd) *<(493393-2)>* **SEA CHANGE** [20] [8]
– The golden age / Paper tiger / Guess I'm doing fine / Lonesome tears / Lost cause / End of the day / It's all in your mind / Round the bend / Already dead / Sunday sun / Little one / Side of the road.

Mar 05. (7"pic-d) *(9880053)* **E-PRO. / BAD CARTRIDGE** [38] [65]
(cd-s) *<(9880052)>* – ('A') / Venom confection (E-Pro remix by Green, Music and Gold) / Ghost range (E-Pro remix by Homelife) / ('A'-video).

Mar 05. (cd)(d-lp) *(9880288)(9864087) <348102>* **GUERO** [15] [2]
– E-Pro / Que onda Guero / Girl / Missing / Black tambourine / Earthquake weather / Hell yes / Broken drum / Scarecrow / Go it alone / Farewell ride / Rental car / Emergency exit. *(ltd-cd w/dvd++; 9880290)* – (audio/DVD tracks).

Jul 05. (7"pic-d) *(9882471)* **GIRL. / GIRL (Octet remix)** [??] [100]
(cd-s+=) *<(9882469)>* – ('A'-Paza remix – The X-Dump) / ('A'-video).

Dec 05. (7") *(9889111)* **HELL YES** [ ] [–]
– Gettochip Malfunction (remixed by 8Bit) / Gucci Bag In Flames (remixed by Green, Music and Gold).

Jan 06. (cd)(d-lp) *(9888858)<(565001)>* **GUEROLITO** (remixes) [ ] Dec05 [ ]
– Ghost range (E-Pro) / Que onda Guero / Girl / Heaven hammer (Missing) / Shake shake tambourine (Black tambourine) / Terremoto tempo (Earthquake weather) / Gettochip malfunction (Hell yes) / Broken drum / Scarecrow / Wish coin / Farewell ride / Rental car / Emergency exit / Clap hands.

– compilations, etc. –

Apr 94. (cd) *Flipside;* <*FLIP 60*> **STEREOPATHETIC SOULMANURE** (home recordings '88-'93) [–] [ ]
– Pink noise (rock me Amadeus) / Rowboat / Thunder peel / Waitin' for a train / The spirit moves me / Crystal clear (beer) / No money no honey / 8.6.82 / Total soul future (eat it) / One foot in the grave / Aphid manure heist / Today has been a fucked up day / Rollins power sauce / Puttin it down / 11.6.45 / Cut 1/2 blues / Jagermeister pie / Ozzy / Dead wildcat / Satan gave me a taco / 8.4.82 / Tasergun / Modesto. *(UK-iss.Dec95 & Nov97 & Sep00 d-lp/cd; FLIP 660/+CD)*

Jeff BECK

Born: 24 Jun'44, Surrey, England. His solo career began in earnest at the start of '67, BECK having successfully filled the shoes of ERIC CLAPTON in The YARDBIRDS over the preceding two years. Under the wing of pop maestro MICKIE MOST, he scored an immediate UK hit with the anthemic 'HI HO SILVER LINING'. Two further commercial pop-rock numbers, 'TALLYMAN' and 'LOVE IS BLUE' signalled the end of BECK's brief chart liaison, also terminating his period with MOST. With blues-rock back in vogue, the axeman steered a course back into heavier territory, forming The JEFF BECK GROUP alongside old cohorts, ROD STEWART (vocals), RON WOOD (guitar), NICKY HOPKINS (piano) and MICKY WALLER (drums). The resulting two albums, 'TRUTH' (1968) and 'BECK-OLA' (1969), established BECK and co. as a major UK export across the Atlantic, both sets making the US Top 20. With ROD STEWART striking out his own, BECK turned to the unlikely source of hippy-dippy popster DONOVAN, who combined with the group on the summer '69 single, 'GOO GOO BARABAJAGAL'. In the early 70's, The JEFF BECK GROUP was re-modelled around newcomers COZY POWELL (drums) and BOBBY TENCH (vocals), the resulting two albums both making US Top 50 placings. With the country's top guitarist, ERIC CLAPTON, now partially sidelined, BECK took the opportunity to form his own supergroup, BECK, BOGART & APPICE. However, after only one album with the former VANILLA FUDGE heavyweights, BECK resumed a solo career. In the mid 70's he returned to form with the highly successful 'BLOW BY BLOW' opus, regarded by many as his finest hour. Along with many in the rock fraternity, BECK subsequently veered towards jazz-fusion, collaborating with JAN HAMMER on two albums, 'WIRED' (1976) and 'LIVE' (1977). After going to ground for a few years, BECK was 'THERE AND BACK' in the early 80's, although he spent the same amount of time recording his follow-up set, 'FLASH' (1985). This featured a belated reunion with old mucker, ROD STEWART, on the collaborative hit 45, 'PEOPLE GET READY'. After working with MICK JAGGER on his 1987 album, 'Primitive Cool', BECK returned in '89 with his 'GUITAR SHOP' project/album. In the early 90's, he collaborated (yet again!), this time with blues legend, BUDDY GUY, on a superb interpretation of the standard soul/blues classic, 'MUSTANG SALLY'. JEFF showcased yet another dimension to his talent when he recorded a 1993 GENE VINCENT tribute album, 'CRAZY LEGS', with his BIG TOWN PLAYBOYS. A six-year long wait resulted in 1999's 'WHO ELSE!', minor chart positions on both sides of the Atlantic reminding us that in some quarters the man has not been forgotten. Come the new millennium, BECK once again illustrated his instinctive ability to absorb outside influences and adapt his talents to the prevailing musical climate. Thus the digitised beats and bleeps of 'YOU HAD IT COMING' (2001) where the veteran guitarist places his six-string talents in a surprisingly effective contemporary setting. A departure from his familiar sound but an admirable attempt to get to grips with new technology. BECK upped the ante even further with 2003's 'JEFF', finishing what he started with producer Andy Wright. Immersing himself in cutting edge electronica, the guitarist pushed at the conceptual limits of conventional meets contemporary and in so doing, left most of his noodling peers for dust. Roping in the likes of APOLLO 440 and SPLATTERCELL (aka DAVID TORN), BECK grooved on the resulting electric sparks, tearing at the seams of his instrument and its potential. While the likes of 'J.B.'s BLUES' or at a push, the Delta meets drum and bass rollercoaster of 'HOT ROD HONEYMOON' was about as close as he came to his bluesy roots, few real fans could argue with the record's dizzying, feral dynamism.

• **Songwriters:** BECK with covers being; HI HO SILVER LINING (Scott English & Larry Weiss) / TALLYMAN (Graham Gouldman) / ALL SHOOK UP + JAILHOUSE ROCK (Leiber – Stoller) / I'VE BEEN DRINKIN' (D.Tauber & J.Mercer) / I AIN'T SUPERSTITIOUS (Willie Dixon) / MORNING DEW (Tim Rose) / SUPERSTITIOUS + CAUSE WE'VE ENDED AS LOVERS (Stevie Wonder) / GREENSLEEVES (trad.) / OL' MAN RIVER ('Showboat' musical) / GOODBYE PORK PIE HAT (Charlie Mingus) / SHE'S A WOMAN (Beatles) / STAR CYCLE (Jan Hammer) / WILD THING (Troggs) / etc. • **Trivia:** His song 'STAR CYCLE' (written by band members Hymas & Philips), became theme tune for 'The Tube' in 1983.

Album rating: TRUTH (*6) / BECK-OLA (*6) / ROUGH AND READY (*7) / BLOW BY BLOW (*6) / WIRED (*5) / JEFF BECK WITH THE JAN HAMMER GROUP LIVE (*4) / THERE AND BACK (*5) / FLASH (*4) / JEFF BECK'S GUITAR SHOP (*6) / THE BEST OF BECKOLOGY compilation (*7) / FRANKIE'S HOUSE soundtrack w/ Jed Leiber (*3) / CRAZY LEGS (*4) / UP (*4) / WHO ELSE! (*5) / YOU HAD IT COMING (*5) / JEFF (*6)

JEFF BECK (solo) – vocals, lead guitar (ex-YARDBIRDS) with **JET HARRIS** – bass (ex-SHADOWS) / **VIV PRINCE** – drums (ex-PRETTY THINGS)

Columbia Epic

Mar 67. (7") *(DB 8151)* <*10157*> **HI-HO SILVER LINING. / BECK'S BOLERO** [14] [ ]

— **RAY COOK** – drums repl. PRINCE

Jul 67. (7") *(DB 8227)* **TALLYMAN. / ROCK MY PLIMSOUL** [30] [–]

Feb 68. (7") *(DB 8359)* **LOVE IS BLUE. / I'VE BEEN DRINKING** [23] [–]

JEFF BECK GROUP

— with **ROD STEWART** – vocals (also a solo artist, who sang on BECK's last 'B'side) / **RON WOOD** – bass (ex BIRDS) / **MICKY WALLER** (b. 6 Sep'44) – drums / **NICKY HOPKINS** – keyboards

Jul 68. (lp; stereo/mono) *(S+/CX 6293)* <*26413*> **TRUTH** [ ] [15]
– Shapes of things / Let me love you / Morning dew / You shook me / Ol' man river / Greensleeves / Rock my plimsoul / Beck's bolero / Blues de luxe / I ain't superstitious. *(re-iss. 1985 lp/c; ATAK/TC-ATAK 42) (re-iss. Jun86 on 'Fame' lp/c; FA/TC-FA 3155)*

— **TONY NEWMAN** – drums repl. WALLER

— (mid'69) The JEFF BECK GROUP teamed up with ⇒ DONOVAN, on their joint hit GOO GOO BARABAJAGAL (LOVE IS HOT). (see ⇒ DONOVAN)

Jul 69. (lp) *(SCX 6351)* <*26478*> **BECK-OLA** [39] [15]
– All shook up / Spanish boots / Girl from Mill Valley / Jailhouse rock / Plynth (water down the drain) / The hangman's knee / Rice pudding. *(re-iss. Jul85 on 'Capitol' lp/c; ED 260600-1/-4)*

Sep 69. (7"; w-drawn) *(DB 8590)* **PLYNTH (WATER DOWN THE DRAIN). / HANGMAN'S KNEE** [–] [–]

— split (Sep'69) when ROD STEWART and RON WOOD joined The FACES.

JEFF BECK GROUP reformed (Apr'71) with **JEFF BECK** – guitar (only) plus **BOBBY TENCH** – vocals / **MAX MIDDLETON** – keyboards / **CLIVE CHAPMAN** – bass / **COZY POWELL** – drums (ex-BIG BERTHA, ex-ACE KEFFORD STAND, ex-SORCERORS)

Epic Epic

Oct 71. (lp/c) *(EPC/40 64619)* <*30973*> **ROUGH AND READY** [ ] [46]
– Got the feeling / Situation / Short business / Max's tune / I've been used / New ways – Train train / Jody. *(re-iss. Aug84 lp/c; EPC/40 32037) (quad-lp 1974; Q 64619) (cd-iss. 1990; 471047-2)*

Jan 72. (7") *(EPC 7720)* <*10814*> **GOT THE FEELING. / SITUATION** [ ] [ ]

Jul 72. (lp/c) *(EPC/40 64899)* <*31331*> **JEFF BECK GROUP** [ ] May72 [19]
– Ice cream cakes / Glad all over / Tonight I'll be staying here with you / Sugar cane / I can't give back the love I feel for you / Going down / I got

to have a song / Highways / Definitely maybe. *(quad-lp 1974 on 'C.B.S.'; Q 31331) (cd-iss. 1990; 471047-2)*

Aug 72. (7") <10938> **DEFINITELY MAYBE. / HI HO SILVER LINING** [–] [ ]

— Broke-up when COZY POWELL went solo & joined BEDLAM. Later to RAINBOW, etc. TENCH joined STREETWALKERS then VAN MORRISON. **JEFF** formed supergroup

BECK, BOGERT, APPICE

— with **TIM BOGERT** – bass, vocals / **CARMINE APPICE** – drums (both ex-VANILLA FUDGE, etc.) plus **DUANE HITCHINS** – keyboards / **JIMMY GREENSPOON** – piano / **DANNY HUTTON** – vox

Mar 73. (7") *(EPC 1251)* **BLACK CAT MOAN. / LIVIN' ALONE** [ ] [–]

Apr 73. (7") <11027> **LADY. / OH TO LOVE YOU** [–] [ ]

Jul 73. (7") <10998> **I'M SO PROUD. / OH TO LOVE YOU** [–] [ ]

Apr 73. (lp/c) *(EPC/40 65455)* <32140> **BECK, BOGERT, APPICE** [28] [12]
– Black cat moan / Lady / Oh to love you / Superstition / Sweet sweet surrender / Why should I care / Love myself with you / Livin' alone / I'm so proud. *(re-iss. Sep84 lp/c; EPC/40 32491) (re-iss. Nov89 on 'Essential' lp/c/cd; ESS LP/MC/CD 011) (quad-lp 1975 on 'C.B.S.'; Q 65455)*

— This trio, also released widely available (JAP-import Nov74 d-lp) LIVE IN JAPAN

JEFF BECK

— group reformed as instrumental line-up, **BECK + MIDDLETON / PHILIP CHEN** – bass / **RICHARD BAILEY** – drums

Mar 75. (lp/c) *(EPC/40 69117)* <33409> **BLOW BY BLOW** [ ] [4]
– It doesn't really matter / You know what I mean / She's a woman / Constipated duck / Air blower / Scatterbrain / Cause we've ended as lovers / Thelonius / Freeway jam / Diamond dust. *(re-iss. Sep83 lp/c; EPC/40 32367) (re-iss. May94 & Nov95 & Sep99 cd/c; 469012-2/-4)*

May 75. (7") *(EPC 3334)* **SHE'S A WOMAN. / IT DOESN'T REALLY MATTER** [ ] [–]

Jun 75. (7") <50112> **CONSTIPATED DUCK. / YOU KNOW WHAT I MEAN** [–] [ ]

— **JAN HAMMER** (b.1950, Prague, Czechoslavakia) – drums, synthesizer / **MICHAEL NARADA WALDEN** – keyboards, drums (both ex-MAHAVISHNU ORCHESTRA) / **WILBUR BASCOMBE** – bass (all 3 replaced CHEN)

Jul 76. (lp/c) *(EPC/40 86012)* <33849> **WIRED** [38] Jun76 [16]
– Led boots / Come dancing / Goodbye pork pie hat / Head for backstage pass / Blue wind / Sophie / Play with me / Love is green. *(re-iss. Mar82 lp/c; EPC/40 32067) (cd-iss. 1988; CD 86012)*

Aug 76. (7") <50276> **COME DANCING. / HEAD FOR BACKSTAGE PASS** [–] [ ]

— (**BECK, HAMMER**) plus **TONY SMITH** – drums / **FERNANDO SAUNDERS** – bass / **STEVE KINDLER** – violin, synth.

Mar 77. (lp/c) *(EPC/40 86025)* <34433> **LIVE . . . WITH THE JAN HAMMER GROUP (live)** [ ] [23]
– Freeway jam / Earth (still our only home) / She's a woman / Full Moon boogie / Darkness – Earth in search of a sun / Scatterbrain / Blue wind. *(re-iss. Jun85 lp/c; EPC/40 32297)*

— with **TONY HYMAS** – keyboards / **MO FOSTER** – bass / **SIMON PHILLIPS** – drums

Jul 80. (lp/c) *(EPC/40 83288)* <35684> **THERE AND BACK** [38] [21]
– Star cycle / Too much to lose / You never know / The pump / El Becko / The golden road / Space boogie / The final peace. *(re-iss. Aug84 lp/c; EPC/40 32197) (cd-iss. Jan89; CD 83288)*

Jul 80. (7") *(EPC 8806)* **THE FINAL PEACE. / SPACE BOOGIE** [ ] [–]

Aug 80. (7") <50914> **THE FINAL PEACE. / TOO MUCH TO LOSE** [–] [ ]

Feb 81. (12"ep) *(EPCA 1009)* **THE FINAL PEACE / SCATTERBRAIN. / TOO MUCH TO LOSE / LED BOOTS** [ ] [–]

— retired from the studio for half a decade, before returning 1985 with **HAMMER, APPICE, HYMAS** and **JIMMY HALL** – vocals

Jun 85. (7") *(EPCA 6387)* <05416> **PEOPLE GET READY. / BACK ON THE STREET** [ ] [48]
(12"+=) *(TA 6387)* – You know, we know.
(above single featured ROD STEWART on vox)

Jul 85. (lp/c) *(EPC/40 26112)* <39483> **FLASH** [83] [39]
– Ambitious / Gets us all in the end / Escape / People get ready / Stop, look and listen / Get workin' / Ecstasy / Night after night / You know, we know. *(re-iss. Jan89; CD 26112) (re-iss. Mar94 on 'Pickwick' cd/c; 982838-2/-4)*

Sep 85. (7") <05595> **GETS US ALL IN THE END. / YOU KNOW, WE KNOW** [–] [ ]

Sep 85. (7") *(EPCA 6587)* **STOP, LOOK AND LISTEN. / YOU KNOW, WE KNOW** [ ] [–]
(12"+=) *(TA 6587)* – ('A'remix).

Mar 86. (7"/12") *(EPCA/TA 6981)* **AMBITIOUS. / ESCAPE** [ ] [ ]

Jul 86. (7") *(EPCA 7271)* **WILD THING. / GETS US ALL IN THE END** [ ] [ ]
(12"+=) *(TA 7271)* – Nighthawks.

— In 1987, BECK went to session with MICK JAGGER on his 2nd album.

Oct 89. (lp/c/cd; JEFF BECK with TERRY BOZZIO & TONY HYMAS) *(463472-1/-4/-2)* <44313> **JEFF BECK'S GUITAR SHOP** [ ] [49]
– Guitar shop / Savoy / Behind the veil / Big block / Where were you / Stand on it / Day in the house / Two rivers / Sling shot.

Oct 89. (7") *(BECK 1)* **DAY IN THE HOUSE. / PEOPLE GET READY** [ ] [ ]
(cd-s+=) *(BECK 1CD)* – Cause we've ended as lovers / Blue wind.
(12") *(BECK 1T)* – ('A'side) / Guitar shop (guitar mix) / Cause we've ended as lovers.

— In Sep'91 JEFF collaborated with BUDDY GUY on a single 'MUSTANG SALLY' on 'Silvertone'.

Nov 92. (cd/c/lp) *(472494-2/-4)* <EK/ET 53194> **FRANKIE'S HOUSE** (soundtrack w/ Jed Leiber) [ ] Jan93 [ ]
– The jungle / Requiem for the Bao-Chi / Hi-heel sneakers / Thailand / Love and death / Cathouse / In the dark / Sniper patrol / Peace island / White mice / Tunnel rat / Vihn's funeral / Apocalypse / Innocent victim / Jungle reprise.

— now with **MIKE SANCHEZ** – vocals, piano / **IAN JENNINGS** – bass, vocals / **ADRIAN UTLEY** – rhythm guitar / **CLIVE DENVER** – drums, vocals / **LEO GREEN** – tenor sax / **NICK HUNT** – baritone sax

Jun 93. (cd/c/lp; as JEFF BECK & THE BIG TOWN PLAYBOYS) *(473597-2/-4/-1)* <53562> **CRAZY LEGS** [ ] [ ]
– Race with the devil / Cruisin' / Crazy legs / Double talkin' baby / Woman love / Lotta lovin' / Catman / Pink thunderbird / Baby blue / You better believe / Who slapped John? / Say mama / Red blue jeans and a pony tail / Five feet of lovin' / B-i-bickey-bi-bo-bo-go / Blues stay away from me / Pretty, pretty baby / Hold me, hug me, rock me.
(above was a tribute to GENE VINCENT & HIS BLUE CAPS)

— 1999 with **TONY HYMAS** – keyboards, co-producer / **JENNIFER BATTEN** – guitars / **RANDY HOPE-TAYLOR – bass / STEVE ALEXANDER** – drums

Columbia Epic

Mar 99. (cd/c) *(493041-2/-4)* <67987> **WHO ELSE!** [74] [99]
– What mama said / Psycho Sam / Brush with the blues / Blast from the east / Space for the papa / Angel (footsteps) / THX138 / Hip-notica / Even odds / Declan / Another place. *(cd re-iss. Jan01; same)*

Epic Epic

Feb 01. (cd) *(501018-2)* <61625> **YOU HAD IT COMING** [ ] [ ]
– Earthquake / Roy's toy / Dirty mind / Rollin' and tumblin' / Badia / Loose cannon / Rosebud / Left hook / Blackbird / Suspension.

— 2003 with **HYMAS** plus **DEAN GARCIA + STEVE BARNEY** – rhythm

Aug 03. (cd) *(510820-2)* <86941> **JEFF** [ ] [ ]
– So what / Plan B / Pork-u-pine / Seasons / Trouble man / Grease monkey / Hot rod honeymoon / Line dancing with monkeys / JB's blues / Pay me no mind / My thing / Bulgaria / Why Lord oh why?

– compilations, etc. (selective) –

1969. (lp) *Music For Pleasure; (MFP 5219)* **THE MOST OF JEFF BECK** [ ] [–]

Oct 72. (7"m) *RAK; (RR 3)* **HI HO SILVER LINING. / BECK'S BOLERO / ROCK MY PLIMSOUL** [14] [–]
(re-iss. Oct82 7"pic-d/12"; RRP/12RR 3); hit No.62.

Apr 73. (7"m; JEFF BECK AND ROD STEWART) *RAK; (RR 4)* **I'VE BEEN DRINKING. / MORNING DEW / GREENSLEEVES** [ ] [–]

May 89. (d-lp/d-c/d-cd) *That's Original; (TFO LP/MC/CD 19)* **JEFF BECK GROUP / ROUGH & READY** [ ] [–]

Feb 91. (cd)(c) *E.M.I.; (CZ 374)(TCEMS 1379)* **TRUTH / BECK-OLA** [ ] [–]

Feb 92. (7"/c-s; by JEFF BECK & ROD STEWART) *Epic; (657756-7/-4)* **PEOPLE GET READY. / TRAIN KEPT A ROLLIN'** [49] [–]
(cd-s) *(657756-2)* – ('A') / Cause we've ended as lovers / Where were you.

(cd-s) *(657756-5)* – ('A') / Train train / New ways.
Feb 92. (3xcd/3xc;box) *Epic; (469262-2/-4)* <48661> **BECKOLOGY** ☐ ☐
(re-iss. May94 & Apr98; same)
Mar 92. (cd/c/lp) *Epic; (471348-2/-4/-1)* <64689> **THE BEST OF BECKOLOGY** ☐ Aug95 ☐
– Heart full of soul (YARDBIRDS) / Shapes of things (YARDBIRDS) / Over under sideways down (YARDBIRDS) / Hi ho silver lining / Tallyman / Jailhouse rock / I've been drinking / I ain't superstitious / Superstition (BECK, BOGART & APPICE) / Cause we've ended as lovers / The pump / Star cycle (theme from 'The Tube') / People get ready (with ROD STEWART) / Wild thing / Where were you (w/ TERRY BOZZIO & TONY HYMAS) / Trouble in mind (TRIDENTS).
Mar 93. (3xcd-box) *Epic; (468802-2)* <64808> **FLASH / BLOW BY BLOW / THERE & BACK** ☐ Oct95 ☐
Apr 98. (cd) *Hallmark; (30858-2)* **GUITAR LEGENDS** ☐ -
(<re-iss. Feb01 on 'EMI Plus'; 576228-2>)

☐ Walter BECKER (see under ⇒ STEELY DAN)

the BEE GEES

Formed: By the GIBB brothers in Brisbane, Australia (where they had emigrated from Manchester, England) in 1958. The boys' inaugural performance had taken place three years previous at their dad's Manchester 'Blue Cats' residency where they played skiffle covers (yes, LONNIE DONEGAN had a lot to answer for!). The brothers continued to cut their teeth (quite, er, literally!?) in the parochial talent contests/amateur shows in their new hometown of Brisbane, going under name of the BROTHERS GIBB before abbreviating it to The BEE GEES. Interest in the talented schoolboy group was not long in coming and in 1959, DJ Bill Gates (no, not THE Bill Gates!) offered to manage the trio, promising them more lucrative gigs and air space. Becoming ever more adept at songwriting, the lads were subsequently signed to local label 'Leedon' where they released numerous 45's to moderate success. Realising that they were potentially big fish in the small Aussie music biz pond, they packed their bags and headed back to England in 1966. Ironically, as they made their plans to travel to the mother country, the title track from their album, 'SPICKS AND SPECKS', reached No.1 down under. However, their collective minds were made up and they settled in London, virtually unknown but totally confident of their ability to storm the world leading UK charts. Recruiting a drummer (COLIN PETERSON), bass player (VINCE MELOUNEY) and manager (the notorious ROBERT STIGWOOD), they secured a deal with 'Polydor' and released their debut British single, 'NEW YORK MINING DISASTER 1941' (suffixed in the USA with the chorus, "Have You Seen My Wife, Mr. Jones"). Their distinctive combination of good looks, vocal harmony and astute lyrics slotted in seamlessly with other contemporary Brit beat groups and the single soon went Top 20. Hot on its heels came further classic singles, 'TO LOVE SOMEBODY', 'MASSACHUSETTS' (a UK No.1), 'WORDS' and 'I'VE GOT TO GET A MESSAGE TO YOU'. On the album front, the lads also scored a number of successes culminating in Spring '69 with an obligatory pseudo-psychedelic (double!) album, 'ODESSA'. Around the same time, MAURICE tied the knot with diminutive Glasgow popster LULU while the latter album's release marked the departure of solo bound ROBIN. He made it in his own right later that year with the massive selling single, 'SAVED BY THE BELL' as the remaining MAURICE and BARRY retaliated chart-wise with 'DON'T FORGET TO REMEMBER ME'. As the decade drew to a close, it seemed that the once mighty BEE GEES were falling apart; not for the first time the brothers had surfed the big pop wave only to wipeout! Even after ROBIN's return in 1970, their moment seemed to have passed in the UK at least. However, their Stateside momentum continued, hits such as 'LONELY DAYS' and the No.1 'HOW CAN YOU MEND A BROKEN HEART' keeping their name in the spotlight. The first years of the new decade found them quite possibly at their lowest creative ebb as the albums 'TRAFALGAR' (1972) and 'TO WHOM IT MAY CONCERN'(1973) sank without trace. Subsequently signing to Stigwood's new 'R.S.O.' label (also home of ERIC CLAPTON), The BEE GEES released 'LIFE IN A TIN CAN' (1973) to little response. Something different was needed to re-ignite the ol' Antipodean magic and the 1974 arrival of producer Arif Mardin for their 'MR. NATURAL' album marked a watershed in the brothers' career. Adopting a new dance-based sound, the icing on their funky rhythm-rich cake came in the form of the (then rare) falsetto harmonies, destined to become their trademark. Again guided by Mardin, they were on to a winner with 1975's 'MAIN COURSE'. Comeback single, 'JIVE TALKIN' deftly captured the essence of mid-70's funk and became a huge Stateside chart topper (Top 5 in Britain). 'NIGHTS ON BROADWAY' and er, 'FANNY (BE TENDER WITH MY LOVE)' repeated the formula as did the 'CHILDREN OF THE WORLD' album and its famous No.1 single, 'YOU SHOULD BE DANCING'. Yet again on the crest of a popular wave, their songs were much in demand by the disco/soul artists of the day including TAVARES and YVONNE ELLIMAN. They also ensured the success of a 1977 mid-budget movie entitled 'Saturday Night Fever' (which attempted to cash-in on the disco phenomenon) and an unknown young actor called John Travolta by penning a ditty or two for inclusion in its screenplay. One of the biggest grossing soundtracks of all-time, 'SATURDAY NIGHT FEVER', included THE "medallion man" anthem, 'STAYIN' ALIVE'. Never one to miss an opportunity, Stigwood lifted another two huge No.1 singles from the soundtrack, 'HOW DEEP IS YOUR LOVE' and 'NIGHT FEVER'. A rather bad career move in the form of the Stigwood-conceived musical version of the BEATLES' 'Sgt. Pepper' occupied them for much of the following year. In 1979, the album 'SPIRITS HAVING FLOWN' spawned three further US No.1's, 'TOO MUCH HEAVEN', 'TRAGEDY' and 'LOVE YOU INSIDE OUT', The BEE GEES continuing to flash their hairy chests as if Punk had never happened. Yet 1981's effort, 'LIVING EYES' surprisingly sank like a lead balloon, failing to break into either US or UK Top 40's. There were contributions to follow-up film 'STAYING ALIVE' but the disco medium was truly dead and the Brothers GIBB strategically withdrew to count their millions, do a bit of outside songwriting (for the likes of BARBRA STREISAND, DIONNE WARWICK, etc.) and ponder the next big thing. It was 1987 when they re-emerged on 'Warners' with 'ESP' and its hit single, 'YOU WIN AGAIN' although the storm clouds were gathering once again. Young brother, ANDY GIBB (who had a few hits in the latter half of '77) was found dead from a cocaine overdose. During the next four years, they released three fairly successful albums, 'ONE' (1989), 'HIGH CIVILIZATION' (1991) and 'SIZE ISN'T EVERYTHING' (1993). In 1997 the brothers became immortalised after their induction into the Rock'n'Roll Hall of Fame, releasing 'STILL WATERS' at the same time. In conclusion, there have been few more resilient bands through the last four decades. Just when they're considered dead and buried they reappear in a new and more commercial guise, always in command of melody, harmony and rhythm, with fingers and ears shrewdly on the pulse of musical fashion. 2001's transatlantic Top 20 success, 'THIS IS WHERE I CAME IN', saw them enter their fifth decade of recording with nary a hint of the jaded, faded listlessness that often permeates the umpteenth releases of certified rock dinosaurs. Nods to both the psych-pop era and their airbrushed heyday resist revelling in nostalgia, the brothers even making a passable stab at post-modern electronica. However, the BEE GEES were now two when MAURICE died (12th January, 2003) after receiving treatment for an intestinal blockage.

Album rating: BEE GEES' FIRST (*6) / HORIZONTAL (*6) / IDEA (*4) / ODESSA (*7) / THE BEST OF THE BEE GEES VOL.1 compilation (*8) / CUCUMBER CASTLE soundtrack (*3) / TWO YEARS ON (*5) / TRAFALGAR (*4) / TO WHOM IT MAY CONCERN (*4) / LIFE IN A TIN CAN (*4) / THE BEST OF THE BEE GEES VOL.2 compilation (*7) / MR. NATURAL (*3) / MAIN COURSE (*7) / CHILDREN OF THE WORLD (*5) / BEE GEES GOLD VOL.1 compilation (*7) / HERE AT LAST . . . BEE GEES LIVE (*5) / SATURDAY NIGHT FEVER with Various Artists soundtrack (*8) / SPIRITS HAVING FLOWN (*6) / GREATEST compilation (*7) / LIVING EYES (*4) / STAYING ALIVE soundtrack (*4) / E.S.P. (*4) / ONE (*5) / HIGH CIVILIZATION (*3) / SIZE ISN'T EVERYTHING (*4) / STILL WATERS (*5) / THIS IS WHERE I CAME IN (*5) / THE RECORD – THEIR GREATEST HITS compilation (*7)

BARRY GIBB (b. 1 Sep'47, Manchester, England) – vocals, guitar / **MAURICE GIBB** (b.22 Dec'49, Isle Of Man) – vocals, bass / **ROBIN GIBB** (b.22 Dec'49, Isle Of Man) – vocals

Leedon not iss.

Mar 63. (7") *(LK 346)* **THE BATTLE OF THE BLUE AND GREY. / THE THREE KISSES OF LOVE** – Austra –

Jun 63. (7") *(LK 412)* **TIMBER! / TAKE HOLD OF THAT STAR** – Austra –

Feb 64. (7") *(LK 534)* **DON'T SAY GOODBYE. / PEACE OF MIND** – Austra –

— in Jun'64, they backed JOHNNY DEVLIN on 'Festival' label single, 'BLUE SUEDE SHOES'. / 'WHOLE LOTTA SHAKIN' GOIN' ON'

Aug 64. (7") *(LK 696)* **CLAUSTROPHOBIA. / COULD IT BE** – Aussie –

Oct 64. (7") *(LK 745)* **TURN AROUND LOOK AT ME. / THEME FROM THE TRAVELS OF JAMIE McPHEETERS** – Aussie –

Dec 64. (7"; with TREVOR GORDON) *(LK 829* **HOUSE WITHOUT WINDOWS. / I'LL BE HAPPY** – Austra –

Apr 65. (7") *(LK 920)* **EVERY DAY I HAVE TO CRY. / YOU WOULDN'T KNOW IT** – Austra –

May 65. (7"; with TREVOR GORDON) *(LK 924)* **LITTLE MISS RHYTHM AND BLUES. / HERE I AM** – Austra –

Aug 65. (7") *(LK 1070)* **WINE AND WOMEN. / FOLLOW THE WIND** – Austra –

Nov 65. (7") *(LK 1150)* **I WAS A LOVER, A LEADER OF MEN. / AND THE CHILDREN LAUGHING** – Austra –

Nov 65. (lp) *(LL 31801)* **BARRY GIBB AND THE BEE GEES SING AND PLAY 14 BARRY GIBB SONGS** – Austra –
(re-iss. 1968 as 'BARRY GIBB AND THE BEE GEES' on 'Calendar', R 66241)

Mar 66. (7") *(LK 1282)* **CHERRY RED. / I WANT HOME** – Austra –

Spin not iss.

Jun 66. (7") *(EK 1384)* **MONDAY'S RAIN. / ALL OF MY LIFE** – Austra –

Sep 66. (7") *(EK 1474)* **SPICKS AND SPECKS. / I AM THE WORLD** – Austra –

Nov 66. (lp) *(EL 32031)* **SPICKS AND SPECKS** – Austra –
(UK-iss.Sep93 on 'Remember' cd/c; RMB 7/4 5068)

Jan 67. (7") *(EK 1634)* **BORN A MAN. / BIG CHANCE** – –
(also iss.AUST. ep's THE BEE GEES (1964) / **WINE AND WOMEN** (1966) / **SPICKS AND SPECKS** (1967).

— added **VINCE MELOUNEY** (b. Australia) – guitar / **COLIN PETERSON** (b. Australia) – drums

Polydor Atco

Feb 67. (7") *(56727)* **SPICKS AND SPECKS. / I AM THE WORLD** –

Apr 67. (7") *(56161) <6487>* **NEW YORK MINING DISASTER 1941. / I CAN'T SEE NOBODY** 12 May67 14
(above 'A'side was prefixed with 'HAVE YOU SEEN MY WIFE, MR. JONES')

Jun 67. (7") *(56178) <6503>* **TO LOVE SOMEBODY. / CLOSE ANOTHER DOOR** 41 Jul67 17

Jul 67. (lp; mono/stereo) *(582/583 012) <223>* **BEE GEES' FIRST** 8 Aug67 7
– Close another door / Craise Finton Kirk Royal Academy of Arts / Cucumber castle / Every Christian lion-hearted man will show you / Holiday / I can't see nobody / I close my eyes / In my own time / New York mining disaster 1941 / One minute woman / Please read me / Red chair / Fade away / To love somebody / Turn of the century. *(re-iss. Nov83 lp/c; SPE LP/MC 56) (cd-iss. 1985; 825220-2)*

Sep 67. (7") *(56192)* **MASSACHUSETTS. / BARKER OF THE F.O.** 1 –

Sep 67. (7") *<6521>* **HOLIDAY. / EVERY CHRISTIAN LION HEARTED MAN WILL SHOW YOU** – 16

Nov 67. (7") *<6532>* **(THE LIGHTS WENT OUT IN) MASSACHUSETTS. / SIR GEOFFREY SAVED THE WORLD** – 11

Nov 67. (7") *(56220)* **WORLD. / SIR GEOFFREY SAVED THE WORLD** 9 –

Jan 68. (7") *(56229) <6548>* **WORDS. / SINKING SHIPS** 8 15

Feb 68. (lp; mono/stereo) *(582/583 020) <233>* **HORIZONTAL** 16 12
– World / And the sun will shine / Lemons never forget / Really and sincerely / Birdie told me / With the sun in my eyes / Massachusetts / Harry Braff / Day time girl / The earnest of being George / Change is made / Horizontal. *(cd-iss. Feb90; 833659-2)*

Mar 68. (7") *(56242) <6570>* **JUMBO. / THE SINGER SANG HIS SONG** 25 57

Aug 68. (7") *(56273) <6603>* **I'VE GOTTA GET A MESSAGE TO YOU. / KITTY CAN** 1 8

Sep 68. (lp; mono/stereo) *(582/583 036) <253>* **IDEA** 4 Aug68 17
– Let there be love / In the summer of his years / Down to earth / I've gotta get a message to you / When the swallows fly / I started a joke / Swan song / Kitty can / Indian gin and whisky dry / Such a shame / I dea / I have decided to join the airforce / Kilburn Towers. *(cd-iss. Nov89; 833660-2)*

Dec 68. (7") *<6639>* **I STARTED A JOKE. / KILBURN TOWERS** – 6

Feb 69. (7") *(56304) <6657>* **FIRST OF MAY. / LAMPLIGHT** 6 Mar69 37

Mar 69. (d-lp) *(582 049-050) <702>* **ODESSA** 10 Feb69 20
– Odessa (city on the Black Sea) / You'll never see my face again / Black diamond / Marley Purt drive / Edison / Melody fair / Give your best / Seven sea symphony with all nations (international anthem) * / Laugh in your face / Never say never again / First of May / The British opera. *(cd-iss. May85 – * track; 825451-2)*

— **BARRY + MAURICE** continue as a duo when ROBIN GIBB went solo (VINCE + COLIN also departed)

May 69. (7") *(56331) <6682>* **TOMORROW TOMORROW. / SUN IN THE MORNING** 23 54

Aug 69. (7") *(56343) <6702>* **DON'T FORGET TO REMEMBER. / THE LORD** 2 Sep69 73

Mar 70. (7") *<6741>* **IF ONLY I HAD MY MIND ON SOMETHING ELSE. / SWEETHEART** – 91

Mar 70. (7") *(56377)* **I.O.I.O. / SWEETHEART** 49 –

Apr 70. (lp) *(2383 010) <327>* **CUCUMBER CASTLE** (TV soundtrack) 57 94
– If only I had my mind on something else / I.O.I.O. / Then you left me / The Lord / I was the child / I lay down and die / Sweetheart / Bury me down by the river / My thing / The chance of love / Turning tide / Don't forget to remember. *(cd-iss. Nov89; 833783-2)*

Jun 70. (7") *<6752>* **I.O.I.O. / THEN YOU LEFT ME** – 94

— **ROBIN** returned to make up the trio once again

Nov 70. (7") *(2001 104) 6795>* **LONELY DAYS. / MAN FOR ALL SEASONS** 33 3

Dec 70. (lp) *(2310 069) <353>* **TWO YEARS ON** Jan71 32
– Two years on / Portrait of Louise / Man for all seasons / Sincere relation / Back home / The first mistake I made / Lonely days / Alone again / Tell me why / Lay it on me / Every second, every minute / I'm weeping. *(cd-iss. Mar90; 833785-2)*

Jun 71. (lp) *(2383 043) <SD33 363>* **MELODY** (soundtrack with RICHARD HEWSON ORCHESTRA, etc.)
– In the morning / In the morning (reprise) / Melody fair / Melody fair (reprise) / Spicks and specks / Romance theme in F / Give your best / To love somebody / Working on it night and day / First of May / First of May (reprise) / Seaside banjo / Teachers chase / Teach your children (CROSBY, STILLS, NASH & YOUNG). *<cd-iss. 2002 in Japan'; POCP 2007>*

Jun 71. (7") *(2058 115) <6824>* **HOW CAN YOU MEND A BROKEN HEART. / COUNTRY WOMAN** 1

— added **GEOFF BRIDGEFORD** – drums / **ALAN KENDALL** – lead guitar

Oct 71. (7") *<6847>* **DON'T WANNA LIVE INSIDE MYSELF. / WALKING BACK TO WATERLOO** – 53

Nov 71. (lp) *(2383 052) <7003>* **TRAFALGAR** Sep71 34
– How can you mend a broken heart / Israel / The greatest man in the world / It's just the day / Remembering / Somebody stop the music / Trafalgar / Don't wanna live inside myself / When do I / Dearest / Lion in winter / Walking back to Waterloo. *(cd-iss. Mar90; 833786-2)*

Jan 72. (7") *(2058 185) <6871>* **MY WORLD. / ON TIME** 16 16

Jul 72. (7") *(2058 255) <6896>* **RUN TO ME. / ROAD TO ALASKA** 9 16

Oct 72. (lp) *(2383 139) <7012>* **TO WHOM IT MAY CONCERN** 35
– Run to me / We lost the road / Never been alone / Paper mache, cabbages & kings / I can bring love / I held a party / Please don't turn out the lights /

Sea of smiling faces / Bad bad dreams / You know it's for you / Alive / Road to Alaska / Sweet song of summer. *(cd-iss. Apr93; 833787-2)*

Nov 72. (7") *(2058 304)* <6909> **ALIVE. / PAPER MACHE, CABBAGES AND KINGS** [ ] [34]

R.S.O. R.S.O.

Mar 73. (7") *(2090 105)* <401> **SAW A NEW MORNING. / MY LIFE HAS BEEN A SONG** [ ] [94]

—— now with **RIC GRECH** – bass / **SNEAKY PETE** – pedal steel / **JIM KELTNER** – drums / **JEROME RICHARDSON** – flute / **TOMMY MORGAN** – harmonica

Mar 73. (lp) *(2394 102; w-drawn)* <870> **LIFE IN A TIN CAN** [–] Jan73 [69]
– Saw a new morning / I don't wanna be the one / South Dakota morning / Living in Chicago / While I play / My life has been a song / Come home Johnny Bridie / Method to my madness. *(cd-iss. Apr93; 833788-2)*

Jun 73. (7") *(2090 111)* <404> **WOULDN'T I BE SOMEONE. / ELISA** [ ] [ ]

Mar 74. (7") *(2090 128)* <408> **MR. NATURAL. / IT DOESN'T MATTER MUCH TO ME** [ ] [93]

Jun 74. (7") <410> **THROW A PENNY. / I CAN'T LET YOU GO** [–] [ ]

Jul 74. (lp) *(2394 132)* <4800> **MR. NATURAL** [ ] Jun74 [ ]
– Charade / Throw a penny / Down the road / Voices / Give a hand take a hand / Dogs / Mr. Natural / Lost in your love / I can't let you go / Heavy breathing / Had a lot of love last night. *(cd-iss. Apr93; 833789-2)*

Aug 74. (7") *(2090 136)* <501> **CHARADE. / HEAVY BREATHING** [ ] [ ]

—— back-up now from **ALAN KENDALL** – guitar / **BLUE WEAVER** – keyboards / **DENNIS BYRON** – drums

May 75. (7") *(2090 160)* <510> **JIVE TALKIN'. / WIND OF CHANGE** [5] [1]

Jun 75. (lp)(c) *(2394 150)(3216 050)* <4807> **MAIN COURSE** [ ] [14]
– Nights on Broadway / Jive talkin' / Winds of change / Songbird / Fanny (be tender with my love) / All this making love / Country lanes / Come on over / Edge of the universe / Baby as you turn away. *(re-iss. Aug84 lp/c; SPE LP/MC 111) (cd-iss. May88; 833790-2)*

Sep 75. (7") *(2090 171)* <515> **NIGHTS ON BROADWAY. / EDGE OF THE UNIVERSE** [ ] [7]

Jan 76. (7") *(2090 179)* <519> **FANNY (BE TENDER WITH MY LOVE). / COUNTRY LANES** [ ] Dec75 [12]

Jul 76. (7") *(2090 195)* <853> **YOU SHOULD BE DANCING. / SUBWAY** [5] [1]

Sep 76. (7") *(2090 207)* <859> **LOVE SO RIGHT. / YOU STEPPED INTO MY LIFE** [41] [3]

Oct 76. (lp) *(2394 169)* <3003> **CHILDREN OF THE WORLD** [ ] Sep76 [8]
– You should be dancing / You stepped into my life / Love so right / Lovers / Can't keep a good man down / Boogie child / Love me / Subway / The way it was / Children of the world. *(cd-iss. Nov89; 623658-2)*

Jan 77. (7") <867> **BOOGIE CHILD. / LOVERS** [–] [12]

Feb 77. (7") *(2090 224)* **CHILDREN OF THE WORLD. / BOOGIE CHILD** [ ] [–]

Jun 77. (d-lp)(d-c) *(2658 120)(3517 013)* <3901> **HERE AT LAST . . . BEE GEES . . . LIVE (live)** [ ] May77 [8]
– I've gotta get a message to you / Love so right / Edge of the universe / Come on over / Can't keep a good man down / New York mining disaster 1941 / Run to me / World / Holiday / I can't see nobody / I started a joke / Massachusetts / How can you mend a broken heart / To love somebody / You should be dancing / Boogie child / Down the road / Words / Winds of change / Nights on Broadway / Jive talkin' / Lonely days. *(re-iss. Oct84; 3517013)*

Jul 77. (7") <880> **EDGE OF THE UNIVERSE (live). / WORDS (live)** [–] [26]

Oct 77. (7") *(2090 259)* <882> **HOW DEEP IS YOUR LOVE. / CAN'T KEEP A GOOD MAN DOWN** [3] Sep77 [1]

Jan 78. (7") *(2090 267)* <885> **STAYIN' ALIVE. / Yvonne Elliman: IF I CAN'T HAVE YOU** [4] Dec77 [1]

Mar 78. (d-lp)(d-c) *(2658 123)(3517 014)* <4001> **SATURDAY NIGHT FEVER (soundtrack w/ Various Artists)** [1] Nov77 [1]
– Stayin' alive / How deep is your love / Night fever / More than a woman / If I can't have you (YVONNE ELLIMAN) / A fifth of Beethoven (WALTER MURPHY) / More than a woman (TAVARES) / Manhattan skyline (DAVID SHIRE) / Calypso breakdown (RALPH MacDONALD) / If I can't have you (YVONNE ELLIMAN) / Night on disco mountain (DAVID SHIRE) / Open sesame (KOOL & THE GANG) / Jive talkin' / You should be dancing / Boogie shoes (K.C. & THE SUNSHINE BAND) / Salsation (DAVID SHIRE) / K-Jee (M.F.S.B.) / Disco inferno (TRAMMPS). *(d-cd-iss. Nov83; 800068-2) (d-lp re-iss. Jan84; SPDLP 5) (d-cd re-iss. Oct95; 825389-2)*

Apr 78. (7") *(2090 272)* <889> **NIGHT FEVER. / DOWN THE ROAD (live)** [1] Jan78 [1]

Nov 78. (7") *(RSO 25)* <913> **TOO MUCH HEAVEN. / REST YOUR LOVE IN ME** [3] [1]

Feb 79. (7") *(RSO 27)* <918> **TRAGEDY. / UNTIL** [1] [1]

Feb 79. (lp/c) *(RSBG/TRSBG 1)* <3041> **SPIRITS HAVING FLOWN** [1] [1]
– Tragedy / Too much Heaven / Love you inside out / Reaching out / Search find stop (think again) / Spirits (having flown) / Living together / I'm satisfied / Until. *(re-iss. Sep83 lp/c; SPE LP/MC 48) (also iss.on US pic-lp) (cd-iss. Nov89; 827335-2)*

Apr 79. (7") *(RSO 31)* <925> **LOVE YOU INSIDE OUT. / I'M SATISFIED** [13] [1]

Nov 79. (d-lp/d-c) *(RSDX/+C 001)* <4200> **BEE GEES GREATEST** (compilation) [6] [1]
– Children of the world / Don't throw it all away / Fanny (be tender with my love) / How deep is your love / If I can't have you / Jive talkin' / Love me / Love so right / Love you inside out / More than a woman / Night fever / Nights on Broadway / Rest of your love on me / Spirits (having flown) / Stayin' alive / Too much Heaven / Tragedy / Wind of change / You should be dancing / You stepped into my life. *(cd-iss. 1983; 800071-2)*

Dec 79. (7") *(RSO 52)* **SPIRITS (HAVING FLOWN). / WINDS OF CHANGE** [16] [–]

—— the trio were now augmented by many session people

Sep 81. (7") *(RSO 81)* <1066> **HE'S A LIAR. / (instrumental)** [ ] [30]

Nov 81. (lp/c) *(RSBG/TRSBG 2)* <3098> **LIVING EYES** [73] [41]
– Living eyes / He's a liar / Paradise / Don't fall in love with me / Soldiers / I still love you / Wild flower / Nothing could be good / Cryin' every day / Be who you are. *(re-iss. Aug83 lp/c; SPE LP/MC 22) (cd-iss. Aug84; 813642-2)*

Nov 81. (7") *(RSO 85)* <1067> **LIVING EYES. / I STILL LOVE YOU** [ ] [45]

Jul 83. (7") *(RSO 94)* <813 713-7> **THE WOMAN IN YOU. / STAYIN' ALIVE** [ ] May83 [24]
(12") *(RSOX 94)* – ('A'side) / Saturday night segue.

Jul 83. (lp/c)(cd) *(RSBG/TRSBG 3)(<813 269>)* **STAYING ALIVE** (soundtrack with Various Artists) [14] [6]
– The woman in you / I love you too much / Breakout / Someone belonging to someone / Life goes on / Stayin' alive / (other artists).

Sep 83. (7") *(RSO 96)* <815 235-7> **SOMEONE BELONGING TO SOMEONE. / I LOVE YOU TOO MUCH** [49] Aug83 [49]
(12") *(RSOX 96)* – ('A'side) / Saturday night fever medley.

Warners Warners

Sep 87. (7"/c-s/12"/12"pic-d) *(W 8351/+C/T/TP)* <28351> **YOU WIN AGAIN. / BACKTAFUNK** [1] [75]

Sep 87. (lp/c)(cd) *(WX 83/+C)(925541-2)* <25541> **E.S.P.** [5] Oct87 [96]
– E.S.P. / You win again / Live or die / Giving up the ghost / The longest night / This is your life / Angela / Overnight / Crazy for your love / Backtafunk. *(re-iss. cd Feb95; same)*

Dec 87. (7") *(W 8139)* <28139> **E.S.P. / OVERNIGHT** [51] [ ]
(ext-12"+=) *(W 8139T)* – ('A'-Extra house vocals mix).

Feb 88. (7") *(W 7966)* **CRAZY FOR YOUR LOVE. / YOU WIN AGAIN** [ ] [–]
(12"+=) *(W 7966T)* – Giving up the ghost.

Mar 89. (7"/c-s) *(W 7523/+C)* **ORDINARY LIVES. / WING AND A PRAYER** [54] [–]
(12"+=/cd-s+=) *(W 7523 T/CD)* – ('A'extended).

Apr 89. (lp/c)(cd) *(WX 252/+C)(925887-2)* <25887> **ONE** [29] Aug89 [68]
– Ordinary lives / Bodyguard / Tears / Flesh and blood / House of shame / One / It's my neighbourhood / Tokyo nights / Wish you were here / Will you ever let him. *(re-iss. cd Feb95; same)*

Jun 89. (7"/c-s) *(W 2916/+C)* **ONE. / FLESH AND BLOOD** [71] [–]
(12"+=/cd-s+=) *(W 2916 T/CD)* – ('A'dance mix).

Jul 89. (7") <22899> **ONE. / WING AND A PRAYER** [–] [7]

Nov 89. (7") <22733> **YOU WIN AGAIN. / WILL YOU EVER LET ME** [–] [ ]

Feb 91. (7"/c-s) *(W 0014/+C)* **SECRET LOVE. / TRUE CONFESSIONS** [5] [ ]
(12"+=/cd-s+=) *(W 0014 T/CD)* – Human sacrifice.

Mar 91. (cd)(lp/c) *(<7599 26530-2>)(WX 417/+C)* **HIGH CIVILIZATION** [24] [ ]
– High civilization / Secret love / When he's gone / Happy ever after / Party with no name / Ghost train / Dimensions / The only one / Human sacrifice / Evolution. *(re-iss. cd Feb95; same)*

May 91. (7"/c-s) **WHEN HE'S GONE. / MASSACHUSETTS (live)** [ ] [–]
(12"+=/cd-s+=) – You win again (live).

— now with **ALAN KENDALL + TIM CANSFIELD** – guitars / **GEORGE PERRY** – bass / **TIM MOORE** – keyboards / **TREVOR MURRELL** – drums / **LUIS JARDIM** – percussion / **ED CALLE** – sax / **GUSTAVO LEZCANO** – harmonica

Polydor Polydor

Aug 93. (7") *(PO 284)* <859164> **PAYING THE PRICE OF LOVE. / MY DESTINY** 23 Oct93 74
(cd-s+=) *(PZCD 284)* – (2-'A'mixes)

Sep 93. (cd/c) *(519945-2/-4)* <521055> **SIZE ISN'T EVERYTHING** 28 Oct93
– Paying the price of love / Kiss of life / How to fall in love, pt.1 / Omega man / Haunted house / Heart like mine / Anything for you / Blue island / Above and beyond / For whom the bell tolls / Fallen angel / Decadence.

Nov 93. (cd-s) *(PZCD 299)* **FOR WHOM THE BELL TOLLS. / DECADENCE (YOU SHOULD BE DANCING)** 4
(12"/c-s) – ('A'side) / Staying alive / Too much Heaven / Massachusetts.

Apr 94. (7"/c-s) *(PO/+CS 311)* **HOW TO FALL IN LOVE PART 1. / 855 7019** 30
(cd-s+=) *(PZCD 311)* – Fallen angel.
(cd-s) *(PZDD 311)* – ('A'side) / I've gotta get a message to you / Tragedy / New York mining disaster 1941.

Feb 97. (c-s/cd-s) *(573527-4/-2)* **ALONE / CLOSER THAN CLOSE / RINGS AROUND THE MOON** 5 May97 28
(cd-s) *(573529-2)* – ('A'side) / How deep is your love / Words / I've gotta get a message to you.

Mar 97. (cd/c) *(<537302/-2/-4>)* **STILL WATERS** 2 May97 11
– Alone / I surrender / I could not love you more / Still waters (run deep) / My lover's prayer / With my eyes closed / Irresistible force / Closer than close / I will / Obsessions / Miracles happen / Smoke and mirrors.

Jun 97. (c-s) *(571220-4)* **I COULD NOT LOVE YOU MORE / (Brits medley)** 14
(cd-s) *(571299-2)* – ('A'side) / Stayin' alive / Jive talkin'.
(cd-s) *(571223-2)* – ('A'side) / To love somebody / Love never dies.

Oct 97. (c-s/cd-s) *(571628-4/-2)* <569218> **STILL WATERS (RUN DEEP) / OBSESSIONS** 18 57
(cd-s) *(571885-2)* – ('A'side) / Night fever / More than a woman / You should be dancing.

Sep 98. (cd/c) *(<559220-2/-4>)* **LIVE ONE NIGHT ONLY (live)** 4 Nov98 72
– Intro – You should be dancing – Alone / Massachusetts / To love somebody / Words / Closer than close / Islands in the stream / Our love (don't throw it all away) / Night fever – More than a woman / Lonely days / New York mining disaster 1941 / I can't see nobody / And the sun will shine / Nights on Broadway / How can you mend a broken heart / Heartbreaker / Guilty / Immortality (BEE GEES & CELINE DION) / Tragedy / I started a joke / Grease / Jive talking / How deep is your love / Stayin' alive / You should be dancing. *(re-iss. Nov99; same)*

Mar 01. (c-s) *(587977-4)* **THIS IS WHERE I CAME IN / JUST IN CASE** 18
(cd-s+=) *(587977-2)* – I will be there / ('A'-video).

Apr 01. (cd/c) *(<549458-2/-4>)* **THIS IS WHERE I CAME IN** 6 May01 16
– This is where I came in / She keeps on coming / Sacred trust / Wedding day / Man in the middle / Deja vu / Technicolour dreams / Walking on air / Loose talk costs lives / Embrace / The extra mile / Voice in the wilderness.

— sadly, on the 12th of January 2003, MAURICE died of a cardiac arrest while having an intestinal operation

– compilations, etc. –

Note; all below on 'Polydor' UK / 'Atco' US until stated otherwise

Nov 68. (lp) *(236 221)* <264> **RARE, PRECIOUS & BEAUTIFUL** 99

Oct 69. (lp) *(583063)* <292> **BEST OF THE BEE GEES** 7 Jul69 9
– Holiday / I've got to get a message to you / I can't see nobody / Words / I started a joke / Spicks and specks / First of May / World / Massachusetts / To love somebody / Every Christian lion hearted man will show you / New York mining disaster 1941. *(cd-iss. Mar87 on 'R.S.O.'; 831594-2)*

Mar 70. (lp) *(236 513)* <321> **RARE, PRECIOUS & BEAUTIFUL VOL.2** 100

Apr 70. (lp) *(236 556)* **RARE, PRECIOUS & BEAUTIFUL VOL.3** –

Jun 71. (lp) *(2447 012)* **MARLEY PURT DRIVE** –
– Odessa (city on the black sea) / You'll never see my face again / Black diamond / Marley Purt drive / Edison / Melody fair / Suddenly / Whisper whisper.

Jun 73. (lp) *(234 106)* / *R.S.O.;* <875> **THE BEST OF THE BEE GEES, VOL.2** Jul73 98
(re-iss. Nov85; SPELP 90) (cd-iss. 1988 on 'R.S.O.'; 831960-2)

Nov 76. (lp) *R.S.O.;* <3006> **BEE GEES GOLD, VOLUME ONE** – 50

Nov 90. (cd/c/lp) *(847339-2/-4/-1)* **THE VERY BEST OF THE BEE GEES** 8
– You win again / How deep is your love / Night fever / Tragedy / Massachusetts / I've gotta get a message to you / You should be dancing / New York mining disaster 1941 / World / First of May / Don't forget to remember / Saved by the bell (ROBIN GIBB) / Run to me / Jive talkin' / More than a woman / Stayin' alive / Too much Heaven / Ordinary lives. *(cd+=/c+=)* – To love somebody / Nights on Broadway. *(re-iss. Mar97; same)* – hit UK No.6

Dec 90. (4xcd-box/4xc-box) *(843911-2/-4)* **TALES FROM THE BROTHERS GIBB: A HISTORY IN SONG 1967-1990**
(re-iss. Nov99; same)

Nov 01. (d-cd/d-c) *(589449-2/-4)* <589400> **THE RECORD – THEIR GREATEST HITS** 5 49
– Stayin' alive / How deep is your love / Night fever / More than a woman / Emotion / Too much heaven / Tragedy / Love you inside out / Guilty / Heartbreaker / Islands in the sun / You win again / One / Secret love / For who the bells toll / Alone / Immortality / This is where I came in / Spicks & specks.

Nov 04. (cd) *(<9868840>)* **NUMBER ONES** 7 Jan05 23

Nov 05. (cd) *(9874225)* <5561> **LOVE SONGS** 51

the BEES

Formed: Isle Of Wight, England . . . early 2000 by PAUL BUTLER and AARON FLETCHER, who subsequently brought in KRIS BIRKIN, MICHAEL CLEVETT, WARREN HAMPSHIRE and TIM PARKIN. Like the BETA BAND fronting a scratchy old rocksteady 45, the band's first single, 'NO TROPHY', sounded like it'd been recorded in a shed; in fact, the whole of their debut LP, 'SUNSHINE HIT ME' (2002), was recorded in a shed (in BUTLER's folks' garden!) and sounded all the better for it. Obvious vinyl connoisseurs with a recurring fondness for early 70s PINK FLOYD, the BEES (or A BAND OF BEES, as they were forced to style themselves in the US of A) clearly got a buzz from all things analogue, even translating some of the lyrics on a great cover of the Jorge Ben/Os Mutantes classic 'A MINHA MENINA'. The people behind the Mercury Music Awards were also impressed, nominating it for the 2003 prize. 'Virgin' records were suitably keen to dip their fingers in their psychedelic honey-pot, coaxing out a much more raucous 60's-orientated sound on 'FREE THE BEES' (2004). The vintage organ-grind of SYD BARRETT-ish lead single, 'WASH IN THE RAIN', paved a chart path for the album, while subsequent singles 'HORSEMEN' and the do-the-funky 'CHICKEN PAYBACK' extended its shelflife. If you think you've never been stung by the BEES, think again: the latter Top 30 single was used to harmonal effect in a 'Sure' TV ad.

Album rating: SUNSHINE HIT ME (*8) / FREE THE BEES (*8)

PAUL BUTLER – vocals / **AARON FLETCHER** – guitar / **KRIS BIRKIN** – bass / **MICHAEL CLEVETT** – drums / **WARREN HAMPSHIRE** – hammond organ / **TIM PARKIN** – trumpet

We Love You Astralwerks

Jan 01. (7") *(AMOUR 8S)* **NO TROPHY. / (dub version)** –

Jun 01. (7") *(AMOUR 10S)* **PUNCHBAG. / A MINHA MENINA** –
(cd-s+=) *(AMOUR 10D)* – Town version.

Feb 02. (d7"ep/cd-ep) *(AMOUR 12 S/D)* **YOU GOT TO LEAVE EP** –
– You got to leave / Elain / Whistle stop / Jackel head.

Mar 02. (cd/lp) *(AMOUR 6 CD/LP)* <42236> **SUNSHINE HIT ME** 2003
– Punchbag / Angryman / No trophy / Binnel Bay / Sunshine / A minha menina / This town / Sweet like a champion / Lying in the snow / Zia / Sky holds the sun. *(cd re-iss. Sep03 +=; same)* – You've got to leave.

Jun 02. (7") *(AMOUR 14S)* **A MINHA MENINA. / OUT FOR THE COUNT** –
(cd-s+=) *(AMOUR 14D)* – Punchdub.

Virgin E.M.I.

Apr 04. (7"/cd-s) *(VS/+CDT 1868)* **WASH IN THE RAIN. / NOTHIN' (live)** 31 –

Jun 04. (7"/cd-s) *(VS/+CDT 1869)* **HORSEMEN. / THE START** 41 –
(cd-s) *(VSCDX 1869)* – ('A') / It isn't exact / March of the Bees / ('A'-video).

Jun 04. (cd/d-lp) *(CD+/V 2983) <578326>* **FREE THE BEES** 26 Aug04
– These are the ghosts / Wash in the rain / No atmosphere / Horsemen / Chicken payback / The Russian / I love you / The start / Hourglass / Go karts / One glass of water / This is the land.

— in Aug'04, the BEES featured on the ASPECTS single, 'Off The Lip'

Apr 05. (7") *(VS 1884)* **CHICKEN PAYBACK. / THESE ARE THE GHOSTS (undead version)** 28 –
(cd-s+=) *(VSCDX 1884)* – ('A'-Madlib's soul distortion vocal).
(cd-s) *(VSCDT 1884)* – ('A') / Wash in the rain.

BELLE AND SEBASTIAN

Formed: Glasgow, Scotland . . . early '96 by ex-choirboy/boxer!, STUART MURDOCH (the main songwriter) and ISOBEL CAMPBELL, who met and recruited additional members STUART DAVID, RICHARD COLBURN, STEVIE JACKSON and CHRIS GEDDES in a local cafe. They borrowed the group name from a popular 70's children's TV series (from France) about a young boy and his Pyrenees mountain dog. Two months into their career, the expanded outfit released a very limited (1000 copies) college financed album, 'TIGERMILK', which gained sufficient airplay on national radio to ensure encroaching cult status. By the end of the year (and now with 7th member, SARAH MARTIN) they had unleashed their second set, 'IF YOU'RE FEELING SINISTER', which went on to sell in excess of 15,000 copies and gained much respect from end of the year critic polls. Since then, BELLE AND SEBASTIAN have hit the singles chart three times with a series of highly desirable EP's, 'DOGS ON WHEELS', 'LAZY LINE PAINTER JANE' (with former THRUM larynx-basher MONICA QUEEN on excellent form) and culminating with their critically acclaimed Top 40 entry, '3.. 6.. 9 SECONDS OF LIGHT'. The fact that they've scaled such giddy heights of indie stardom with only a minimum of promotion and a handful of gigs speaks volumes for the quality of their vintage twee C-86-esque sound. By late summer '98, expectations for a new album had reached fever pitch, critics unanimously hailing 'THE BOY WITH THE ARAB STRAP' as one of the year's finest (sadly, too late for esteemed Mercury Prize) and helped ease it into the Top 20. Their by now trademark combination of fey vocals, killer hooklines and avant-pop experimentalism resulted in some of B&S's most infectious tracks to date. With the spirit of NICK DRAKE ghosting in and out of focus (especially on 'SLEEP THE CLOCK AROUND' and 'A SUMMER WASTING'), this troupe of Glaswegian revivalists succeeded in putting the 60's and 70's through an 80's filter, incredibly coming up with something quintessentially 90's! The uninitiated should head straight for the holy trinity of tracks opening side two wherein BELLE & SEBASTIAN do an "ARAB STRAP" so to speak, the "Bairn"-like narrative of 'A SPACE BOY DREAM' complementing the BOLAN-esque stomp of the title track and sandwiching the brassy, BOO RADLEYS (but don't let that put you off!) style 'DIRTY DREAM NUMBER TWO'. Fans eager to get a glimpse of these elusive Scots shysters in the flesh should keep their eyes peeled, actual gigs are woefully few and far between. Extra-curricular activities, meanwhile, included a US 'Sub Pop' 7" from STUART DAVID's spoken word/electro outfit, LOOPER (with also his wife, Wee KARN and his brother, RONNIE BLACK). They would continue as a unit early in 1999, releasing a debut album for 'Jeepster', while ISOBEL's side project, the GENTLE WAVES, also released a long-player on the same label. In July that year and due to demand from everybody bar possibly PETE WATERMAN and his STEPS (who were somewhat peeved about losing the recent Brit Newcomers award due to internet voting), BELLE & SEBASTIAN re-distributed their semi-quasi debut 'TIGERMILK'; this time it hit the UK Top 20. After a two-year recording gap, B&S confidently returned with their fourth studio outing, the sublime, if not translucent 'FOLD YOUR HANDS CHILD, YOU WALK LIKE A PEASANT'. From its flaky opener, 'I FOUGHT IN THE WAR', listeners could detect that this album would be pale in comparison to the aforementioned 'BOY WITH THE . . .'. It seemed that, since the band had apparently broken into the mainstream of America, that their sound was becoming more MOR, more tweaked, more . . . STUART MURDOCH. With that in mind, however, MURDOCH did allow other band members to take the artistic reins: JACKSON and CAMPBELL sang on more songs than usual, slightly thwarting the ever-impending NICK DRAKE references. It could be just that B&S, like many other artists, followed a pivotal record with one that was weaker. Or maybe the group had simply lost their edge. On the eve of the release for this album they started doing press interviews – something that was frowned upon during their earlier years. The band also covered uncharted territory by issuing the album 'STORYTELLING' (2002), the "unofficial" soundtrack to the Todd Solondz film of the same name. A bleak look into American suburbia, the movie was a follow-up to the highly controversial (and highly uncomfortable) work 'Happiness'. It eventually got edited so much by the producers that Solondz vowed never to make another movie again. Unfortunately, so was the B&S score, which didn't make the final cuts. And it's a shame really, because the group almost redeemed themselves by attempting to create proper film music. 'FREAK', 'FUCK THIS SHIT' and the humourously entitled 'BLACK AND WHITE UNITE' (believe it, you have to see the film to get the joke) all made for good soundtrack material. The only let down being the inclusion of 'sound-bites' from the film which were inter-spliced with the music. Unnecessary, and ultimately tiring, dialogue such as "Nigger, fuck me . . ." was hardly worthy of 'Pulp Fiction' proportions. Still, an interesting enough album to accompany an interesting enough film. ISOBEL, meanwhile, collaborated with celebrated Falkirk-born avant-jazz man, BILL WELLS, on the album 'GHOST OF YESTERDAY' (a take on the legendary BILLIE HOLIDAY). Now signed to 'Rough Trade' records, B&S enlisted pop producer Trevor Horn to ride the faders, and while many thought it was the band committing indie suicide or selling out (more than they had already done), it was a blessing for MURDOCH and Co's camp. 'DEAR CATASTROPHE WAITRESS' (2003) re-instated BELLE & SEBASTIAN's indie cred, as well as harnessing new fans to the fore, much in the same way 'THE BOY WITH THE ARAB STRAP' had done five years previously. The songs were mostly uptempo numbers helmed by MURDOCH's keen ear for a good tune, with the band following tightly behind him incognito. Trevor Horn's production, while far from the nonsense pop of TATU and ABC, gave the B&S crowd the unthinkable – a straight up, clean and commercially viable record. Strange, but rather beautiful. Ten years into a glorious pop career (summed up by 2005's EP anthology, 'PUSH BARMAN TO OPEN OLD WOUNDS'), the mercurial MURDOCH still had the best lyrics in the business and the tunes to back them up: 'THE LIFE PURSUIT' (2006) served notice that B&S weren't going to relinquish their official title as the best Scottish band ever (as voted by the great Scottish public and awarded by The List) any time soon, nor their claim on the Top 10 (the album even edged into the US Top 75). Produced by Tony Hoffer (AIR, BECK etc.), the record continued to cultivate the bolder airs of its predecessor, flirting with BOLAN-esque stomp, 70's-vintage L.A. soul and early 80's electro-funk (yes, MURDOCH as fey funkateer, hear it to believe it..) while never forsaking the parochial charm. The band's chameleonic frontman proved he could still break hearts with a flourish of that falsetto ('FUNNY LITTLE FROG') and slay a crowd with his words ("she didn't enrol but she wiped the floor with all the arseholes"), while referencing the past with the kind of intelligence and perception that's way beyond most – if not all – of the competition. Best British indie band ever?

• **Covered:** WHISKEY IN THE JAR (trad) / BABY JANE (Rod Stewart).

Album rating: TIGERMILK (*8) / IF YOU'RE FEELING SINISTER (*8) / THE BOY WITH THE ARAB STRAP (*9) / FOLD YOUR HANDS CHILD, YOU WALK LIKE A PEASANT (*7) / STORYTELLING soundtrack (*6) / DEAR CATASTROPHE WAITRESS (*7) / PUSH BARMAN TO OPEN OLD WOUNDS compilation (*8) / THE LIFE PURSUIT (*9)

STUART MURDOCH (b.25 Aug'68) – vocals, acoustic guitar / **ISOBEL CAMPBELL** (b.27 Apr'76) – cello, vocals / **STEVIE JACKSON** – guitars, vocals (ex-MOONDIALS) / **STUART DAVID** – bass / **RICHARD COLBURN** – drums / **CHRIS GEDDES** – piano

Electric Honey not iss.

May 96. (lp) *(EHRLP 5)* **TIGERMILK** [ ] [–]
– The state I am in / Expectations / She's losing it / You're just a baby / Electronic renaissance / I could be dreaming / We rule the school / My wandering days are over / I don't love anyone / Mary Jo. *(re-iss. Jul99 on 'Jeepster' cd/c/lp; JPR CD/MC/LP 007)* – hit No.13

— added **SARAH MARTIN** – violin, saxophone / and also extra member **MICK COOKE** – trumpet

Jeepster Enclave-Capitol

Nov 96. (cd/c/lp) *(JPR CD/MC/LP 001) <56713>* **IF YOU'RE FEELING SINISTER** [ ] Feb97 [ ]
– Stars of track and field / Seeing other people / Me and the Major / Like Dylan in the movies / The fox in the snow / Get me away from here, I'm dying / If you're feeling sinister / Mayfly / The boy done wrong again / Judy and the dream of horses.

May 97. (7") *(JPR7 001)* **DOG ON WHEELS. / THE STATE I AM IN (demo)** [59] [–]
(12"+=/cd-s+=) *(JPR 12/CDS 001)* – String bean Jean / Belle & Sebastian.

— guest on below, **MONICA QUEEN** – vocals (of THRUM)

Aug 97. (7") *(JPR7 002)* **LAZY LINE PAINTER JANE. / YOU MADE ME FORGET MY DREAMS** [41] [–]
(12"+=/cd-s+=) *(JPR 12/CDS 002)* – Photo Jenny / A century of Elvis.

Oct 97. (7"ep) *(JPR7 003)* **3.. 6.. 9 SECONDS OF LIGHT EP** [32] [–]
– A century of fakers / Le pastie de la bourgeoisie.
(12"ep+=/cd-ep+=) *(JPR 12/CDS 003)* – Beautiful / Put the book back on the shelf / *(hidden track-)* Songs for children.

— added guest **NEIL ROBERTSON** – bass

Jeepster Matador

Sep 98. (cd/c) *(JPR CD/MC 003) <OLE 311>* **THE BOY WITH THE ARAB STRAP** [12] [ ]
– It could have been a brilliant career / Sleep the clock around / Is it wicked not to care? / Ease your feet in the sea / A summer wasting / Seymour Stein / A space boy dream / Dirty dream number two / The boy with the arab strap / Chickfactor / Simple things / The rollercoaster ride.

Dec 98. (12"ep/cd-ep) *(JPR 12/CDS 009)* **THIS IS JUST A MODERN ROCK SONG / I KNOW WHERE THE SUMMER GOES. / THE GATE / SLOW GRAFFITI** [–] -chart [–]
below featured the MAISONETTES

May 00. (7") *(JPR7 018)* **LEGAL MAN. / WINTER WOOSKIE** [15] [–]
(cd-s+=) *(JPRCDS 018) <OLE 448>* – Judy is a dick slap.
(12") *(JPR12 018)* – ('A'side) / Judy is a dick slap (extended).

Jun 00. (cd/md/lp) *(JPR CD/MD/LP 010) <OLE 429>* **FOLD YOUR HANDS CHILD, YOU WALK LIKE A PEASANT** [10] [80]
– I fought in a war / The model / Beyond the sunrise / Waiting for the moon to rise / Don't leave the light on baby / The wrong girl / The chalet lines / Nice day for a sulk / Woman's realm / Family tree / There's too much love.

— **BOBBY KILDEA** – bass, guitar; repl. STUART DAVID

Jun 01. (7") *(JPR7 022)* **JONATHAN DAVID. / THE LONELINESS OF A MIDDLE DISTANCE RUNNER** [31] [–]
(12"+=/cd-s+=) *(JPR 12/CD 022)* – Take your carriage clock and shove it.

Nov 01. (7") *(JPR7 023)* **I'M WAKING UP TO US. / I LOVE MY CAR** [39] [–]
(12"+=/cd-s+=) *(JPRCDS 023)* – Marx and Engels.

Jun 02. (cd/lp) *(JPR CD/LP 014) <OLE 512>* **STORYTELLING** (soundtrack) [26] [ ]
– Fiction / Freak / Dialogue: Conan, early Letterman / Fuck this shit / Night walk / Dialogue: Jersey's where it's at / Black and white unite / Consuelo / Dialogue: Toby / Storytelling / Dialogue: Class rank / I don't want to play football / Consuelo leaving / Wandering alone / Dialogue: Mandingo cliche / Scooby driver / Fiction (reprise) / Big John Shaft.

— now without ISOBEL CAMPBELL who went solo

Rough Trade Sanctuary

Oct 03. (cd/d-lp) *(RTRADE CD/LP 080) <83216>* **DEAR CATASTROPHE WAITRESS** [21] [84]
– Step into my office, baby / Dear catastrophe waitress / If she wants me / Piazza, New York catcher / Asleep on a sunbeam / I'm a cuckoo / You don't send me / Wrapped up in books / Lord Anthony / If you find yourself caught in love / Roy Walker / Stay loose.

Nov 03. (7") *(RTRADS 128)* **STEP INTO MY OFFICE, BABY. / LOVE ON THE MARCH** [32] [–]
(cd-s+=) *(RTRADSCD 128)* – Desperation made a fool of me / Untitled.

Feb 04. (7") *(RTRADS 157)* **I'M A CUCKOO. / (I BELIEVE IN) TRAVELLIN' LIGHT** [14] [–]
(cd-s+=) *(RTRADSCD 157)* – Stop, look and listen / ('A'-Avalanches mix) / ('A'-video).
(dvd-s) *(RTRADSDVD 157)* – (above tracks).

Jun 04. (12"ep) *(RTRADS 180)* **BOOKS EP** [20] [–]
– Your cover's blown / Wrapped up in books / Your secrets / Cover (version).
(cd-ep+=) *(RTRADSCD 180)* – Wrapped up in books (video).

Rough Trade Matador

Jan 06. (7") *(RTRADS 283)* **FUNNY LITTLE FROG. / THE 8TH STATION OF THE CRODD KEBAB HOUSE** [13] [–]
(cd-s) *(RTRADSCD 283)* – ('A') / Meat and potatoes / I took a long hard look.
(dvd-s) *(RTRADSDVD 283)* – ('A'-video) / Lazy line painter Jane (live).

Feb 06. (cd/d-lp) *(RTRAD CD/LP 280) <OLE 687>* **THE LIFE PURSUIT** [8] [65]
– Act of the Apostle / Another sunny day / White collar boy / The blues are still blue / Dress up in you / Sukie in the graveyard / We are the sleepyheads / Song for sunshine / Funny little frog / To be myself completely / Act of the Apostle II / For the price of a cup of tea / Mornington Crescent. *(ltd-cd w/dvd+=; RTRADCDX 280)* – (bonus videos).

Apr 06. (7"blue) *(RTRADS 313)* **THE BLUES ARE STILL BLUE. / WHISKEY IN THE JAR** [25] [–]
(cd-s+=) *(RTRADSCD 313)* – ('A'-version) / The life pursuit / Mr. Richard.

Jun 06. (7") *(RTRADS 355)* **WHITE COLLAR BOY. / BABY JANE (live at Sirius)** [45] [–]
(cd-s) *(RTRADSCD 355)* – ('A') / Long black scarf / Heaven in the afternoon.
(dvd-s) *(RTRADSDVD 355)* – ('A') / Sukie in the graveyard (live at BBC Scotland).

– compilations, etc. –

Mar 00. (cd) *Jeepster; (JPRBOX 001) / Matador; <OLE 313>* **LAZY LINE PAINTER JANE** (the first 3 EP's) [ ] Oct00 [ ]

May 05. (d-cd) *Jeepster; (JPRCD 015) / Matador; <OLE 658>* **PUSH BARMAN TO OPEN OLD WOUNDS** [40] [ ]
– (the EP tracks 1997-2001)

☐ BEN TRAMER (see under ⇒ ARAB STRAP)

Chuck BERRY

Born: CHARLES EDWARD ANDERSON BERRY, 18 Oct'26, St. Louis, Missouri, USA. Having learned the guitar while at school, BERRY had his first run-in with the law in his late teens, when he was sent to reform school for a 3-year stretch after being convicted of armed attempted robbery. Upon his release, he worked blue collar jobs by day, perfecting his playing and songwriting by night; BERRY's first professional combo (with pianist JOHNNIE JOHNSON and drummer EBBY HARDY) became a regular local attraction during the early to mid-50's with their upbeat blend of R&B/C&W. During a trip to Chicago ("home of the blues"), BERRY enjoyed an opportunistic encounter with the legendary MUDDY WATERS, who in turn, put him in touch with 'Chess' records. By the summer of '55, his first recording, 'MAYBELLENE' (an adaptation of an old country standard), was riding high in the US singles chart; this rock'n'roll template would be successfully utilised by BERRY right through to the end of the decade on such definitive R&B gems as 'TOO MUCH MONKEY BUSINESS', 'ROLL OVER BEETHOVEN', 'ROCK AND ROLL MUSIC', 'SWEET LITTLE SIXTEEN' and 'JOHNNY B. GOODE'. As well as inventing his inimitable stage party piece, the "duck-walk", BERRY injected a quintessentially Afro-American element of humour, wit and innuendo into the concept of pop music as teen rebellion, reclaiming the rock'n'roll crown from white pretenders such as BILL HALEY and ELVIS PRESLEY. However, the position of a famous black, anti-establishment star was a precarious one and BERRY fell foul of the authorities after employing a 14-year old Apache Indian as a hat-check girl in his nightclub. Unbeknown to BERRY, the girl had allegedly worked as a prostitute, and he was subsequently found guilty of contravening the 'Mann act' by bringing an under-age child across the Texas-Missouri border. In October '61, he was sentenced to jail for five years, although due to the judge's racist remarks, he was given a retrial. He was later successfully tried and sentenced to three years, although with good behaviour, he was out early in '64. While in jail, BERRY's work was being successfully reappraised with many British-invasion artists, including The BEATLES and The ROLLING STONES, covering his early material as a sizeable part of their repertoire. Inspired, "Crazy Legs" (as he was nicknamed) returned to the studio to record a new song, 'NADINE', the single becoming a Top 30 hit on both sides of the Atlantic. BERRY also set foot in Britain for the first time, wowing audiences with a further brace of recent hits including 'NO PARTICULAR PLACE TO GO' and 'YOU NEVER CAN TELL'. In June 1966, with flower-power just over the horizon, he signed to 'Mercury', although this ill-advised partnership proved commercially fruitless. In 1972, following a return to the 'Chess' label three years previous, he scored a UK No.1 novelty hit with the embarrassing 'MY DING-A-LING'. Its double entendre lyrical content sufficiently enraged morality pest, Mary Whitehouse, for her to press for a media ban. In June 1979, BERRY was again imprisoned (100 days this time) for tax evasion, although during this period he signed a deal with 'Atlantic'. Throughout the 80's, he continued to work sporadically, a docu-film 'HAIL! HAIL! ROCK'N'ROLL' being released early in '88, featuring footage from his 60th birthday concert (KEITH RICHARDS – his biggest fan – along with other star names formed his backing band at the time). BERRY subsequently retired from recording, choosing to live in his own amusement park in Wentzville, Missouri. He did, however, play live again in a November '89 revival concert alongside BO DIDDLEY, The COASTERS etc. The following month, more controversy surrounded him when it was claimed he had been videoing a ladies rest-room for immoral purposes! In June 1990, his house was raided by the drugs squad, who seized marijuana, guns and homemade pornography. He was later charged with possession of drugs and child abuse, although he was cleared of the latter and handed a fine and a 6-month suspended prison sentence for the drugs misdemeanour. Hail! hail!, rock'n'roll! right enough!

Best CD compilation: THE BEST OF CHUCK BERRY (*9)

CHUCK BERRY – vocals, guitar with **JOHNNIE JOHNSON** – piano / **JASPER THOMAS** – drums / **WILLIE DIXON** – bass / etc.

		London		Chess
Jul 55.	(7") <1604> **MAYBELLENE. / WEE WEE HOURS**	–		5
Oct 55.	(7") <1610> **THIRTY DAYS. / TOGETHER WE WILL ALWAYS BE**	–		
May 56.	(7",78) *(HLU 8275)* <1615> **NO MONEY DOWN. / THE DOWNBOUND TRAIN**		Feb56	
May 56.	(7") <1626> **ROLL OVER BEETHOVEN. / DRIFTING HEART** *(UK-iss.May57 – 7",78; HLU 8428)*	–		29
Aug 56.	(7") <1635> **TOO MUCH MONKEY BUSINESS. / BROWN EYED HANDSOME MAN**	–		
Feb 57.	(7",78) *(HLN 8375)* <1645> **YOU CAN'T CATCH ME. / HAVANA MOON**		Nov56	29
Jun 57.	(7",78) *(DB 3951)* <1653> **SCHOOL DAY (RING! RING! GOES THE BELL). / DEEP FEELING** *(above was issued in UK on 'Columbia')*	24	Mar57	3

—— He retained **DIXON** and enlisted on most of 50's **FRED BELOW** – drums / **LAFAYETTE LEAKE** – piano

Date	Release	UK		US
Jun 57.	(7") <1664> **OH BABY DOLL / LA JAUNDA**	–		57
Dec 57.	(7",78) *(HLM 8531)* <1671> **ROCK AND ROLL MUSIC. / BLUE FEELING**		Sep57	8
1958.	(lp) <1426> **AFTER SCHOOL SESSIONS** – School day / Deep feeling / Too much monkey business / Wee wee hours / Roly poly / No money down / Brown-eyed handsome man / Berry pickin' / Together we will always be / Havana Moon / Downbound train / Drifting heart.	–		
Mar 58.	(7",78) *(HLM 8585)* <1683> **SWEET LITTLE SIXTEEN. / REELIN' AND ROCKIN'**	16	Jan58	2
May 58.	(7",78) *(HLM 8629)* <1691> **JOHNNY B. GOODE. / AROUND AND AROUND**		Apr58	8
Aug 58.	(7",78) *(HL 8677)* <1697> **BEAUTIFUL DELILAH. / VACATION TIME**		Jun58	81
Oct 58.	(7",78) *(HL 8712)* <1700> **CAROL. / HEY PEDRO**		Aug58	18
Nov 58.	(lp; stereo/mono) *(HA/+M 2132)* <1432> **ONE DOZEN BERRYS** – Sweet little sixteen / Blue feeling / La juanda / Rockin' at the Philharmonic / Oh baby doll / Reelin' & rockin' / In-go / Rock and roll music / How you've changed / Low feeling / It don't take but a few minutes.			
Dec 58.	(7",78) *(HLM 8767)* <1709> **SWEET LITTLE ROCK AND ROLLER. / JOE JOE GUN**		Oct58	47 / 83
Dec 58.	(7") <1714> **RUN RUDOLPH RUN. / MERRY CHRISTMAS BABY**	–		69 / 71
Jan 59.	(7") <1716> **ANTHONY BOY. / THAT'S MY DESIRE**	–		60
Apr 59.	(7",78) *(HLM 8853)* <1722> **ALMOST GROWN. / LITTLE QUEENIE**		Mar59	32 / 80
Jul 59.	(7",78) *(HLM 8921)* <1729> **BACK IN THE U.S.A. / MEMPHIS, TENNESSEE**		Jun59	37
1959.	(lp) <1435> **CHUCK BERRY IS ON TOP** – Almost grown / Carol / Maybellene / Sweet little rock and roller / Anthony boy / Johnny B. Goode / Little Queenie / Jo Jo Gunne / Roll over Beethoven / Around and around / Hey Pedro / Blues for Hawaiians. *(UK-iss.Oct87;) (re-iss. Oct94 cd/c;)*	–		
Oct 59.	(7") <1737> **CHILDHOOD SWEETHEART. / BROKEN ARROW**	–		
Mar 60.	(7") *(HLM 9069)* <1747> **LET IT ROCK. / TOO POOPED TO POP**		Jan60	64 / 42
Apr 60.	(7") <1754> **BYE BYE JOHNNY. / WORRIED LIFE BLUES**	–		
Jun 60.	(7") *(HLM 9159)* **BYE BYE JOHNNY. / MAD LAD**			–
Jun 60.	(7") <1763> **MAD LAD. / I GOT TO FIND MY BABY**	–		
1960.	(lp) <1448> **ROCKIN' AT THE HOPS** – Bye bye Johnny / Worried life blues / Down the road apiece / Confessin' the blues / Too pooped to pop ("Casey") / Mad lad / I got to find my baby / Betty Jean / Childhood sweetheart / Broken arrow / Driftin' blues / Let it rock. *(re-iss. +c.Aug87)*	–		
Sep 60.	(7") <1767> **JAGUAR AND THUNDERBIRD. / OUR LITTLE RENDEZVOUS**	–		

		Pye Int.		Chess
Sep 61.	(7") *(7N 25100)* <1779> **I'M TALKIN' 'BOUT YOU. / LITTLE STAR**		Feb61	

—— BERRY was convicted of an earlier crime of transporting a minor (14 year-old) across the border. He served two years in prison.

– early recordings, compilations, etc, while in prison –

Jun 62.	(lp) *(NPL 28019)* <1456> **NEW JUKE BOX HITS** – I'm talking about you / Diploma for two / Thirteen question method / Away from you / Don't you lie to me / The way it was before / Little star / Route 66 / Sweet sixteen / Run around / Stop and listen / Rip it up.		Nov61	

May 63. (lp) *(NPL 28024)* <1465> **CHUCK BERRY** (compilation) <US-title 'CHUCK BERRY TWIST' different tracks> [12] 1962 [ ]
– Come back / Maybellene / Down the road apiece / Mad lad / School day (ring ring goes the bell) / Sweet little sixteen / Confessin' the blues / Back in the U.S.A. / Johnny B. Goode / Oh, baby doll / Come on / I got to find my baby / Betty Jean / Round and round / Almost grown. *(re-iss. US Dec63 as 'MORE CHUCK BERRY')(re-iss. 1984 on 'Audio Fidelity') (re-iss. Dec85 on 'Astan')*

Jul 63. (7") *(7N 25209)* <1799> **GO GO GO. / COME ON** [38] Jun61 [ ]

Aug 63. (7") <1853> **I'M TALKIN' 'BOUT YOU. / DIPLOMA FOR TWO** [–] [ ]

Oct 63. (lp) *(NPL 28027)* <1480> **CHUCK BERRY ON STAGE (fake live)** [6] Aug63 [29]
– Go go go / Memphis, Tennessee / Maybellene / Surfin' steel (blues for Hawaiians) / Rockin' on the railroad (let it rock) / Brown eyed handsome man (new version) / I still got the blues / Surfin' USA (sweet little sixteen) / Jaguar and thunderbird / I just want to make love to you / All aboard / Trick or treat / Man and the donkey / How high the moon.

Oct 63. (7") <1866> **MEMPHIS, TENNESSEE. / SWEET LITTLE SIXTEEN** [–] [ ]

Oct 63. (7") *(7N 25218)* **MEMPHIS, TENNESSEE. / LET IT ROCK** [6] [–]

Dec 63. (7") *(7N 25228)* **RUN RUDOLPH RUN. / JOHNNY B. GOODE** [36] [–]

—— Released from prison early '64. New recordings . . .

Feb 64. (7") *(7N 25236)* <1883> **NADINE (IS IT YOU?). / O RANGUTANG** [27] [23]

Apr 64. (7") *(7N 25242)* **NO PARTICULAR PLACE TO GO. / LIVERPOOL DRIVE** [3] [–]

May 64. (7") <1898> **NO PARTICULAR PLACE TO GO. / YOU TWO** [–] [10]

May 64. (lp) *(NPL 28031)* **THE LATEST AND THE GREATEST** [8] [–]
– Nadine / Fraulein / Guitar boogie / Things I used to do / Don't you lie to me / Driftin' blues / Liverpool drive / No particular place to go / Lonely all the time (crazy arms) / Jaguar and Thunderbird / O rangutang / You two / Deep feeling / Bye bye Johnny.

Aug 64. (7") *(7N 25257)* <1906> **YOU NEVER CAN TELL. / BRENDA LEE** [23] Jul64 [14]

Sep 64. (lp) *(NPL 28039)* **YOU NEVER CAN TELL** [18] [–]
– You never can tell / Diploma for two / The little girl from Central / The way it was before / Around and around / Big Ben / Promised land / Back in the USA / Run around / Brenda Lee / Reeling and rockin' / Come on. *(re-iss. Dec67 on 'Marble Arch';)*

Oct 64. (7") *(7N 25271)* <1912> **LITTLE MARIE. / GO BOBBY SOXER** [ ] Sep64 [54]

—— Late in '64, he paired up with BO DIDDLEY to record single CHUCK'S BEAT. / BO'S BEAT; <1089> and album TWO GREAT GUITARS. They had already appeared together on 1963 EP's 'CHUCK AND BO' Volumes 1,2 & 3.

Dec 64. (lp) <1488> **ST. LOUIS TO LIVERPOOL (live)** [–] [ ]
– Little Marie / Our little rendezvous / No particular place to go / You two / Promised land / You never can tell / Go Bobby soxer / Things I used to do / Night beat / Liverpool drive / Merry Christmas baby / Brenda Lee. *(re-iss. Aug86)*

Jan 65. (7") *(7N 25285)* <1916> **THE PROMISED LAND. / THINGS I USED TO DO** [26] [ ]

Chess Chess

Mar 65. (7") *(CRS 8006)* **LONELY SCHOOL DAYS. / I GOT A BOOKING** [ ] [–]

Mar 65. (lp) *(CRL 4005)* <1495> **CHUCK BERRY IN LONDON (live)** [ ] [ ]
– My little love light / She once was mine / After it's over / I got a booking / Night beat / His daughter Caroline / You came a long way from St. Louis / St. Louis blues / Jamaica farewell / Dead dad / Butterscotch / The song of my love / Why should we end this way / I want to be your driver.

May 65. (7") *(CRS 8012)* <1926> **DEAR DAD. / MY LITTLE LOVELIGHT** [ ] Mar65 [95]

Oct 65. (7") <1943> **IT WASN'T ME. / WELCOME BACK PRETTY BABY** [–] [ ]

Oct 65. (7") *(CRS 8022)* **IT WASN'T ME. / IT'S MY OWN BUSINESS** [ ] [–]

Nov 65. (lp) *(CRL 4506)* <1498> **FRESH BERRYS** [ ] [ ]
– It wasn't me / Run Joe / Everyday we rock and roll / One for my baby / Sad day long night * / It's my own business / Right off Rampart Street / Vaya con dios / Merrily we rock and roll / My Mustang Ford / Ain't that just like a woman / Wee hours blues. *<US version omitted * for 'Welcome back pretty baby'>*

Jul 66. (7") *(CRS 8037)* <1963> **RAMONA SAY YES. / LONELY SCHOOL DAYS** [ ] Jun66 [ ]

Mercury Mercury

Dec 66. (7") *(MF 958)* <72643> **CLUB NITTY GRITTY. / LAUGH AND CRY** [ ] Nov66 [ ]

Jul 67. (7") *(MF 994)* <72680> **BACK TO MEMPHIS. / I DO REALLY LOVE YOU** [ ] Jun67 [ ]

Nov 67. (7") <72748> **FEELIN' IT. / IT HURTS ME TOO** [–] [ ]

Dec 67. (lp) *(SMCL 20110)* **IN MEMPHIS** [ ] [–]
– Back to Memphis / I do really love you / My heart will always belong to you / Ramblin' Rose / Sweet little rock and roller / Oh baby doll / Check me out / It hurts me too / Bring another drink / So long / Goodnight, well it's time to go.

Apr 68. (lp) *(MCL 20112)* <SR 61138> **LIVE AT THE FILLMORE AUDITORIUM (live)** [ ] [ ]
– Medley: Rockin' at the Fillmore – Everyday I have the blues / C.C. rider / Driftin' blues / Feelin' it / Flying home / Hoochie coochie man / It hurts me too / Fillmore blues / Wee baby James / Johnny B. Goode.

Oct 68. (7") *(MF 1057)* <7840> **ST. LOUIS TO FRISCO. / MA DEAR** [ ] Aug68 [ ]

Nov 68. (lp) <6463 015> **FROM ST. LOUIS TO FRISCO** [ ] [–]
– St. Louis to Frisco / Ma dear / The love I lost / I love her, I love her / Little fox / Rock cradle rock / Soul rockin' / I can't believe / Misery / My tambourine / Oh captain / Mum's the word.

Aug 69. (7") <72963> **GOOD LOOKING WOMAN. / IT'S TOO DARK IN THERE** [–] [ ]

Nov 69. (lp) <SMCL 20162> **CONCERTO IN B. GOODE** [ ] [–]
– Good looking woman / My woman / It's too dark in there / Put her down / Concerto in 'B Goode'.

Chess Chess

Aug 70. (7") <2090> **TULANE. / HAVE MERCY JUDGE** [–] [ ]

Jan 71. (lp) *(6310 13)* <1550> **BACK HOME** [ ] 1970 [ ]
– Tulane / Have mercy judge / Instrumental / Christmas / Gun / I'm a rocker / Flyin' home / Fish and chips / Some people.

1971. (lp) *(6310 115)* **SAN FRANCISCO DUES** [ ] [–]
– Oh Louisiana / Let's do our thing together / Your lick / Festival / Bound to lose / Bordeaux in my pirough / San Francisco dues / Viva rock and roll / My dream / Lonely school days (version 2).

Jun 72. (lp) *(6310 122)* **THE LONDON SESSIONS** [8] [–]
– Let's boogie / Mean old world / I will not let you go / London Berry blues / I love you / Reeling and rockin'(live) / My ding-a-ling (live) / Johnny B. Goode (live).

Aug 72. (7") *(6145 012)* **DOWN THE ROAD APIECE. / JOHNNY B. GOODE** [ ] [–]

Aug 72. (7") <2131> **MY DING-A-LING. / JOHNNY B. GOODE** [–] [1]

Oct 72. (7") *(6145 019)* **MY DING-A-LING. / LET'S BOOGIE** [1] [–]

Dec 72. (7") <2136> **REELIN' AND ROCKIN' (live). / LET'S BOOGIE** [–] [27]

Jan 73. (7") *(6145 020)* **REELIN' AND ROCKIN' (live). / I WILL NOT LET YOU GO** [18] [–]

Sep 73. (7") <2140> **BIO. / ROLL 'EM PETE** [–] [ ]

Oct 73. (lp) *(6499 650)* **BIO** [ ] [–]
– Bio / Hello little girl, goodbye / Woodpecker / Rain eyes / Aimlessly driftin' / Got it and gone / Talkin' about my buddy. *(re-iss. May88)*

Nov 73. (7") *(6145 027)* **SOUTH OF THE BORDER. / BIO** [ ] [–]

—— duets with daughter INGRID GIBSON on some tracks in 1975

Feb 75. (7") <2169> **SHAKE, RATTLE AND ROLL. / BABY WHAT YOU WANT ME TO DO** [–] [ ]

Mar 75. (7") *(6145 038)* **SHAKE, RATTLE AND ROLL. / I'M JUST A NAME** [ ] [–]

Apr 75. (lp) *(9109 101)* **CHUCK BERRY '75** [ ] [ ]
– Swanee river / I'm just a name / I just want to make love to you / Too late / South of the border / Hi-heel sneakers / You are my sunshine / My babe / Baby what you want me to do / A deuce / Shake, rattle and roll / Sue answer / Don't you to me.

—— on the 10th July '79, he was sentenced to four months in jail

Atlantic Atlantic

Aug 79. (7") *(K 11354)* <7203> **OH WHAT A THRILL. / CALIFORNIA** [ ] [ ]

Oct 79. (lp) *(50648)* <SD 38118> **ROCKIT** [ ] Aug79 [ ]
– Move it / Oh what a thrill / I need you baby / If I were / House lights / I never thought / Havana moon / Pass away. *(re-iss. +cd.Nov88 on 'Magnum Force')*

—— virtually retired from the studio

– (selective) compilations, etc. –

on 'Chess' unless mentioned otherwise

May 64. (lp) *<1485>* **GREATEST HITS** [–] [34]

May 72. (d-lp) *(6641 177) <LPS 1514D>* **GOLDEN DECADE VOL.1** [ ] [72]

1973. (d-lp) *<2CH 60023>* **GOLDEN DECADE VOLUME 2** [–] [ ]

Jan 77. (lp) *(9288 690)* **MOTORVATIN'** (Greatest live) [7] [–]
(re-iss. Dec87 on 'Starblend'; SMT 009)

Feb 88. (lp/c/cd) *M.C.A.; (MCF/MCFC/DMCF 3411) <80465>* **HAIL! HAIL! ROCK'N'ROLL** (soundtrack) [ ] [ ]
– Maybellene / Around and around / Sweet little sixteen / Brown eyed handsome man (with ROBERT CRAY) / Memphis Tennessee / Too much monkey business / Back in the U.S.A. (with LINDA RONSTADT) / Wee wee hours (with ERIC CLAPTON) / Johnny B. Goode (with JULIAN LENNON) / Little Queenie / Rock and roll music (with ETTA JAMES) / Roll over Beethoven / I'm through with love.

Sep 89. (3xlp-box/3xc-box/3xcd-box) *M.C.A,; (CH6/CHC4/CD 8001)* **CHESS BOX** [ ] [ ]

Nov 89. (3xcd-box/3xc-box/3xlp-box) *Charly; (CD/TC+/BOX 256)* **CHUCK BERRY BOX SET** [ ] [ ]

Nov 96. (cd/c) *M.C.A.; <(MCD/MCC 11560)>* **THE BEST OF CHUCK BERRY** [ ] [ ]
– Roll over Beethoven / Sweet little sixteen / Johnny B Goode / You never can tell / You can't catch me / Downbound train / Too much monkey business / Havana moon / School days / Oh baby doll / Beautiful Delilah / Sweet little rock'n'roller / Anthony boy / Little Queenie / Almost grown / Let it rock / Back in the USA / Reelin' and rockin' / Around and around / Brown eyed handsome man / Maybelline / No particular place to go / Rock'n'roll / Run Rudolph run / Jo Jo Gunne / Carol / Confessin' the blues / Jaguar and Thunderbird / Down the road apiece / Thirty days / Merry Christmas baby / My ding-a-ling / I'm talking about you / Too pooped to pop / Bye bye Johnny / Promised land / Tulane / Come on / Nadine (is it you) / Memphis, Tennessee.

Dec 98. (cd) *Beat Goes On; (BGOCD 428)* **YOU NEVER CAN TELL / THE LATEST AND GREATEST** [ ] [–]

Aug 99. (cd) *Beat Goes On; (BGOCD 458)* **ONE DOZEN BERRYS / JUKE BOX HITS** [ ] [–]

Jun 00. (d-cd) *<112304-2>* **THE ANTHOLOGY** [ ] [ ]
<(re-iss. Jun05 as 'GOLD' on 'Universal'; 9880558)>

Aug 03. (cd) *<(A000 53002-2)>* **BLUES** [ ] [ ]

Apr 06. (cd) *Geffen; <44170-2>* **THE DEFINITIVE COLLECTION** [–] [ ]

the BETA BAND

Formed: London, England ... 1994 by ex-patriate Scotsman, STEVE MASON, the St. Andrews-born singer meeting up with Edinburgh University students, decksman JOHN MacLEAN, drummer ROBIN JONES and GORDON ANDERSON on a train down to the capital. There they worked at various day jobs while sharing a flat in Shepherd's Bush, although ill-health forced ANDERSON to return home in August '96. Portsmouth-born RICHARD GREENTREE, formerly bassist of SINISTER FOOTWEAR would become part of the zany quartet in early '97 after being introduced through mutual friends, PUSHERMAN. Discovered and subsequently produced by THE VERVE's NICK McCABE (who saw some potential in their psychedelic transcendental dub malarky), they were signed to 'Regal' records. A pot-pourri of sound right enough (STONE ROSES or The MOONFLOWERS – remember them? – on a mantric mission!), the lads issued three EP's in the space of a year, 'CHAMPION VERSIONS', 'THE PATTY PATTY SOUND' and the excellent 'LOS AMIGOS DEL BETA BANDIDOS'. By popular demand (the vinyl was changing hands for upwards of £40 a time!) these were soon collected together on one shiny cd/album, simply titled 'THE THREE E.P.'S'. Lauded by the more discerning factions of the music press, the bumbling art-rockers (by-passing the fashion stakes completely; safari suits, judo gear and horror of horrors, STEVE's "smart-arse" shell-suit being the disorder of the day) found themselves in the Top 40 by Autumn '98 with a long player that hung together surprisingly well. The sound of "baggy" ten years on, filtered through a kingsized bong, BETA standards such as 'DRY THE RAIN' ("It Will Be Alright"), 'INNER MEET ME', 'SHE'S THE ONE', 'DR. BAKER' and 'NEEDLES IN MY EYES' have since become underground classics. To end the year, MASON moonlighted as KING BISCUIT TIME, releasing (to coincide with the latest edition of the band's zany in-house comic) a bizarre EP of spaced-out drum'n'bass, '"SINGS" NELLY FOGGIT'S BLUES IN "ME AND THE PHARAOHS"'. With expectation and hype rife about the recording schedules and rumoured double-disc set of their debut set proper, the band were finally ready to promote 'THE BETA BAND' long-player in June '99. However, delays due to an objection from JIM STEINMAN (for the sample/use of his BONNIE TYLER – 'Total Eclipse Of The Heart' collaboration) and the band's post-release qualms that it was "fucking awful" contributed to complete bewilderment within the press and its readers. At the end of June, the album shot into the Top 20 despite poor reviews stating over-production was its downfall (or was it just plain arsing about?). Opening with the self-explanatory 'THE BETA BAND RAP' (which might've been handled better by the BONZO's in the 60's . . .) and finishing with the baffling 'THE COW'S WRONG', the album shocked fans who thought the quartet were perhaps a tad over-indulgent. On reflection though, The BETA BAND's original stage interpretations of the tracks could not be faulted. It's just a pity that critical cohorts like the MANICS were beginning to be proved right. As unfazed as ever, The BETA BAND shambled back into the fray with 'HOT SHOTS II' (2001; and a Top 20 hit!), the irony of the self-mocking title belying a half decent, occasionally brilliant set which certainly came closer to realising the promise of their early EP's. There was more focus, less sonic soup for the sake of it and more determined attempts at discernible songs. Which isn't to say they no longer walked that tightrope between endearingly wayward invention and rampant self-indulgence, the guiding hand of R&B producer C-Swing lending a contemporary edge to their urban meta-folk. Another self-mocking title, another BETA BAND album: 'HEROES TO ZEROS' (2004) met with the same mixture of bafflement and wonderment that's greeted everything they've put their name to, even if MASON and co resisted at least some of their flightier impulses: lead single 'ASSESSMENT' (a minor Top 40 hit) ranks as one of most straightforward alterna-pop epistles in their catalogue. There was still enough record collection saturation, glo-worm revelation and lost-in-headspace charm to satisfy longtime fans and earn a Top 20 placing; maybe not enough to satisfy them indefinitely but with the announcement of their retiral it ultimately ended up as their epitaph. Half anthology/half live, 'THE BEST OF THE BETA BAND' (2005), summed up why Scotland has consistently shown itself to be a breeding ground for some of Britain's most imaginative, intelligent and attitude-free pop music. The talented Mr MASON has since mainlined the BETA mindset with KING BISCUIT TIME, releasing the 'BLACK GOLD' album in 2006.

• **Covered:** ONE (Nilsson). • **Trivia:** They guested on SPIRITUALIZED's 'Abbey Road' EP early '98.

Album rating: THE THREE E.P.'S (*9) / THE BETA BAND (*7) / HOT SHOTS II (*7) / HEROES TO ZEROS (*7) / THE BEST OF THE BETA BAND compilation (*8) / King Biscuit Time: BLACK GOLD (*7)

STEVE MASON – vocals, guitar, percussion, drums, etc / **JOHN MacLEAN** – turntable, sampling / **RICHARD GREENTREE** – bass (ex-SINISTER FOOTWEAR) / **ROBIN JONES** – drums, percussion / GORDON ANDERSON departed before any recordings (now LONE PIGEON)

Regal / Astralwerk

Jul 97. (12"ep) *(REG 16)* **CHAMPION VERSIONS** [ ] [–]
– Dry the rain / I know / B + A / Dogs got a bone.

Mar 98. (2x12"ep/cd-ep) *(REG 18/+CD)* **THE PATTY PATTY SOUND** [ ] [–]

– Inner meet me / The house song / The monolith / She's the one.

Jul 98. (cd-ep) *(REG 20CD)* **LOS AMIGOS DEL BETA BANDIDOS** ☐ –
– Push it out / It's over / Dr. Baker / Needles in my eyes.

Sep 98. (cd) *(7243 4 97385 2 2)* <6252> **THE THREE E.P.'S** (compilation) 35 ☐

Jun 99. (cd/d-lp) *(REG 30 CD/LP)* <6268> **THE BETA BAND** 18 ☐
– The Beta Band rap / It's not too beautiful / Simple boy / Round the bend / Dance o'er the border / Brokenupadingdong / Number 15 / Smiling / The hard one / The cow's wrong.

Jan 00. (12"/cd-s) *(REG 40/+CD)* **TO YOU ALONE. / SEQUINSIZER** ☐ –

Jul 01. (12"/cd-s) *(REG 60/+CD)* **BROKE. / WON / DANCE O'ER THE BORDER** 30 –

Jul 01. (d-lp/cd) *(REG 59/+CD)* <10446> **HOT SHOTS II** 13 ☐
– Squares / Al Sharp / Humanbeing / Gone / Dragon / Broke / Quiet / Alleged / Life / Eclipse. *(bonus cd+=; REG 59CDL)* – Won.

Oct 01. (12"/cd-s) *(REG 65/+CD)* **HUMAN BEING. / UNKNOWN / THE HARD ONE** 57 –

Jan 02. (12"/cd-s) *(REG 69/+CD)* **SQUARES. / SQUARES (Bloah mix) / QUIET (acoustic – from 99X Atlanta session)** 42 –

Apr 04. (cd-s) *(REG 102CD)* **ASSESSMENT / SHREK** 31 –
(12"+=) *(REG 102)* – ('A'-C Swing's bootleg mix).
(cd-s++=) *(REG 102CDS)* – ('A'-video).

Apr 04. (lp/cd) *(REG 101/+CD)* <78005> **HEROES TO ZEROS** 18 May04 ☐
– Assessment / Space / Lion thief / Easy / Wonderful / Troubles / Out-side / Space beatle / Rhododendron / Liquid bird / Simple / Pure for.

Jul 04. (7"/cd-s) *(REG 110/+CD)* **OUT-SIDE. / OUT-SIDE (Roman Nose edit)** 54 –
(cd-s+=) *(REG 110CDS)* – ('A'-Depth Charge remix) / ('A'-video).

— disbanded later in 2004

– compilations, etc. –

Oct 05. (d-cd) *Regal; (REG 126CDX) / Astralwerks; <36621>* **THE BEST OF THE BETA BAND** ☐ ☐
– Dry the rain / Inner meet me / She's the one / Dr. Baker / It's not too beautiful / Smiling / To you alone / Squares / Human being / Gone / Broke / Assessment / Easy / Wonderful / Troubles / Simple // live:- It's not too beautiful / Squares / Inner meet me / Simple / She's the one / Easy / Dr. Baker / Dry the rain / Quiet / Broke / Assessment / Dog's got a bone / House song.

KING BISCUIT TIME

aka **STEVE MASON** – vocals, etc

Regal Astralwerks

Dec 98. (12"ep/cd-ep) *(REG 025/+CD)* **"SINGS" NELLY FOGGIT'S BLUES IN "ME AND THE PHARAOHS"** ☐ –
– Fatheriver / Niggling discrepancy / Little white / Eye o' the dug.

Jun 00. (12"ep/cd-ep) *(REG 049/+CD)* <49657> **NO STYLE EP** ☐ Jul00 ☐
– I walk the earth / Untitled / I love you / Time to get up. *<US cd-ep+=>* – . . . NELLY FOGGIT'S BLUES . . . tracks

Poptones not iss.

Sep 05. (7"; feat. TOPCAT) *(MC 5103S)* **C I AM 15. / C I AM 15 (swing remix)** 67 –
(7") *(MC 5103VS)* – ('A') / ('A'-infidel mix by Junior Mason Mumbazza)
(cd-s) *(MC 5103SCD)* – ('A') / People happy.

Apr 06. (7") *(MC 5106S)* **KWANGCHOW. / TEARS DRY** ☐ –
(cd-s+=) *(MC 5106SCD)* – ('A'-Doctors of love remix) / ('A'-Suicide D.O.G.Z. – Faudels Hash Den remix).

May 06. (cd/lp) *(MC 5104 CD/LP)* **BLACK GOLD** ☐ –
– C I am 15 / Izzum / Impossible ride / Kwangchow / Lefteye / All over you / The way you walk / Paperhead / Rising son / Metal biscuit.

the B-52's

Formed: Athens, Georgia, USA . . . late '76, by KATE PIERSON, FRED SCHNEIDER, KEITH STRICKLAND, RICKY WILSON and his sister CINDY. After one self-financed 45 sold out its limited 2,000 copies, they drew the attention of Island's Chris Blackwell, who signed them after they played residency at Max's Kansas City late in 1978. They subsequently re-issued their 'ROCK LOBSTER' debut, the single making UK Top 40 lists the following year. Combining a kitsch image and sound which took in everything from rock'n'roll and 60's beat to new wave REZILLOS-style dual harmonies, The B-52's brightened up the increasingly dour late 70's/early 80's punk/pop scene. The marine madness of the classic 'ROCK LOBSTER' eventually made its way into the US charts in early 1980, by which time the eponymous '79 debut album had made UK Top 30. Even JOHN LENNON was a fan, the former BEATLES man surprisingly admitting that The B-52's were one of the groups who inspired him to start writing again. A strong follow-up set, 'WILD PLANET' (1980), made the Top 20 in both Britain and America, although critics weren't quite so enamoured with the more mannered 'MESOPOTAMIA' set (1982), produced by DAVID BYRNE of TALKING HEADS. The mid-80's were a bleak time for the band as RICKY finally died from AIDS on the 12th October, 1985, and the group struggled to capture the inspired creativity of their earlier period (fans were content in making 'ROCK LOBSTER' an even bigger UK hit than before). Signing a new deal with 'Reprise', The B-52's reunited with their roots on the 'BOUNCING OFF SATELLITES', an album which should have spawned a hit single, 'WIG'. DON WAS / NILE RODGERS-produced 'COSMIC THING' (1989), a remarkable comeback that showcased their alternative dancefloor smash, 'LOVE SHACK', the album becoming their most successful release to date, making the US Top 5. Trimmed to a trio of PIERSON, SCHNEIDER and STRICKLAND following the departure of CINDY in 1992, the group recorded another album in the classic B-52's style, 'GOOD STUFF', before setting to work on the soundtrack for the revamped 'Flintstones' movie. Something of a canny pairing, SCHNEIDER's nasal-voiced nonsense was a perfect backdrop for Fred and family's stone age adventures.

• **Songwriters:** All mainly STRICKLAND or group compositions. PLANET CLAIRE (w/ Henry Mancini) • **Trivia:** In 1981, during lay-off, STRICKLAND, PIERSON and CINDY WILSON did one-off Japan venture as "MELON" with group The PLASTICS and ADRIAN BELEW. Late 1990, PIERSON contributed on singles by IGGY POP (Candy) and R.E.M. (Shiny Happy People).

Album rating: THE B-52's (*8) / WILD PLANET (*6) / PARTY MIX! remixes (*3) / MESOPOTAMIA mini (*4) / WHAMMY! (*5) / BOUNCING OFF THE SATELLITES (*4) / COSMIC THING (*7) / DANCE THIS MESS AROUND – THE BEST OF THE B-52's compilation (*9) / GOOD STUFF (*5) / TIME CAPSULE: SONGS FOR A FUTURE GENERATION compilation (*7) / NUDE ON THE MOON: THE B-52'S ANTHOLOGY double compilation (*7) / Fred Schneider: FRED SCHNEIDER AND THE SNAKE SOCIETY (*5) / JUST . . . FRED (*5)

KATE PIERSON (b.27 Apr'48, Weehawken, N.J.) – vocals, organ, bass / **CINDY WILSON** (b.28 Feb'57) – vocals, percussion, guitar / **RICKY WILSON** (b.19 Mar'53) – guitar / **FRED SCHNEIDER** (III) (b. 1 Jul'56, Newark, N.J.) – vocals, keyboards / **KEITH 'Julian' STRICKLAND** (b.26 Oct'53) – drums

not iss. Boo-Fant

Nov 78. (7") <DB-52> **ROCK LOBSTER. / 52 GIRLS** – ☐

Island Warners

Jul 79. (7") *(WIP 6506)* **ROCK LOBSTER. / RUNNING AROUND** 37 –

Jul 79. (lp/c) *(WIP/ICT 9580)* <3355> **THE B-52's** 22 59
– Planet Claire / 52 girls / Dance this mess around / Rock lobster / Lava / There's a Moon in the sky (called the Moon) / Hero worship / 6060-842 / Downtown. *(lp w/ free 7") (PSR 438)* – ROCK LOBSTER. / 52 GIRLS *(re-iss. May86; same) (cd-iss. Jan87; CID 9580) (re-iss. Jan94 + May94;)*

Sep 79. (7") *(WIP 6527)* **6060-842. / HERO WORSHIP** ☐ ☐

Nov 79. (7"pic-d/7") *(P+/WIP 6551)* <WBS 49212> **PLANET CLAIRE. / THERE'S A MOON IN THE SKY (CALLED THE MOON)** ☐ May80 ☐

Jan 80. (7") <WBS 49173> **ROCK LOBSTER. / 6060-842** – 56

Jul 80. (7") *(WIP 6579)* **GIVE ME BACK MY MAN. / STROBE LIGHT** 61 –

Sep 80. (lp/c) *(ILPS/ICT 9622)* <BSK 3471> **WILD PLANET** 18 18
– Party out of bounds / Dirty back road / Runnin' around / Give me back

my man / Private Idaho / Devil in my car / Quiche Lorraine / Strobe light / 53 miles west of Venus. *(cd-iss. May90; 842436-2)*

Oct 80. (7") *<WBS 49537>* **PRIVATE IDAHO. / PARTY OUT OF BOUNDS** [–] [74]

Nov 80. (7") *(WIP 6685)* **DIRTY BACK ROAD. / STROBE LIGHT** [ ] [–]

Jan 81. (7") *<WBS 49717>* **QUICHE LORRAINE. / LAVA** [–] [ ]

Jul 81. (m-lp/c) *(IPM/ICT 1001) <MINI 3596>* **THE PARTY MIX ALBUM** (remixes) [36] [55]
– Party out of bounds / Private Idaho / Give me back my man / Lava / Dance this mess around / 52 girls. *(cd-iss. May90; 846044-2)*

Aug 81. (7") *(WIP 6727)* **GIVE ME BACK MY MAN (Party mix). / PARTY OUT OF BOUNDS (version)** [ ] [–]

Feb 82. (m-lp/c) *(ISSP/ICT 4006) <3641>* **MESOPOTAMIA** [18] [35]
– Loveland / Deep sleep / Mesopotamia / Cake / Throw that beat in the garbage can / Nip it in the bud. *(cd-iss. May90; 846239-2) (cd re-iss. Aug01; IMCD 107)*

Mar 82. (7") *<50064>* **DEEP SLEEP. / NIP IT IN THE BUD** [–] [ ]

Jun 82. (7") *<29971>* **MESOPOTAMIA. / THROW THAT BEAT IN THE GARBAGE CAN** [–] [ ]

Apr 83. (7") *(IS 107)* **SONG FOR A FUTURE GENERATION. / ('A'instrumental)** [63] [–]
(12"+=) *(12IS 107)* – Planet Claire.
(d7"++=) *(ISD 107)* – There's a moon in the sky (called the moon).

May 83. (lp/c) *(ILPS 9759) <23819>* **WHAMMY!** [33] [29]
– Legal tender / Whammy kiss / Song for a future generation / Butterbean / Trism / Queen of Las Vegas / Don't worry / Big bird / Work that skirt. *(cd-iss. May90; 842445-2) (cd re-iss. Aug01; IMCD 109)*

Jul 83. (7") *<29579>* **LEGAL TENDER. / MOON 83** [–] [81]

Oct 83. (7") *<29561>* **SONG FOR A FUTURE GENERATION. / TREASON** [–] [ ]

—— **RICKY** suffering from full blown AIDS, died 12 Oct'85.

May 86. (7"/7"sha-pic-d; rock/planet/lobster) *(BFT+/G/P/L 1)* **ROCK LOBSTER (new version). / PLANET CLAIRE** [12] [–]
(d7"+=) *(BFTD 1)* – Song for a future generation / 52 girls.
(12"+=) *(12BFT 1)* – Song for a future generation / Give me back my man.

—— They carry on, augmented by session man **RALPH CARNEY** – guitar

Jun 87. (7"/7"pic-d) *(BFT/+P 2)* **WIG. / SUMMER OF LOVE** [ ] [ ]
(c-s+=/12+=) *(BFTD/12BFT 2)* – Song for a future generation.

Jul 87. (lp/c/cd) *(ILPS/ICT/CID 9871) <25504>* **BOUNCING OFF THE SATELLITES** [74] Sep86 [85]
– Summer of love / Girl from Ipanema goes to Greenland / Housework / Detour thru your mind / Wig / Theme for a nude beach / Ain't it a shame / Juicy jungle / Communicate / She brakes for rainbows. *(cd-iss. May90; 842480-2)*

Sep 87. (7") **SUMMER OF LOVE. / HOUSEWORK** [–] [ ]

—— added on tour **PAT IRWIN** – keyboards / **ZACH ALFORD** – drums / **PHILIPPE SASSE** – (studio keyboards) / **SARA LEE** – bass (ex-GANG OF FOUR) (also studio)

Reprise Reprise

Jul 89. (lp/c)(cd) *(WX 283/+C)(925854-2) <25854>* **COSMIC THING** [8] [4]
– Cosmic thing / Dry country / Deadbeat club / Love shack / Junebug / Roam / Bushfire / Channel Z / Topaz / Follow your blues.

Aug 89. (7") *<22817>* **LOVE SHACK. / CHANNEL Z** [–] [3]

Sep 89. (7") *(W 2831)* **CHANNEL Z (remix). / JUNEBUG** [61] [–]
(12")(cd-s) *(W 2831 T/CD)* – ('A'-Rock mix) / ('A'side) / ('A'dub mix). *(re-iss. Aug90;)*

Dec 89. (7") *<22667>* **ROAM. / BUSHFIRE** [–] [3]

Feb 90. (7"/7"g-f/7"pic-d/c-s/cd-s) *(W 9917/+X/P/C/CD)* **LOVE SHACK. / PLANET CLAIRE (live) / ROCK LOBSTER (live)** [2] [–]
(12") *(W 9917T)* – ('A'-Dany Rampling remix) / ('A'-Ben Grosse mix) / ('A'side).

Apr 90. (7") *<19938>* **DEADBEAT CLUB. / PLANET CLAIRE** [–] [30]

May 90. (7"/c-s/cd-s) *(W 9827/+C/CD)* **ROAM. / WHAMMY KISS (live) / DANCE THIS MESS AROUND (live)** [17] [–]
(12"/12"w-poster) *(W 9827T/+W)* – ('A'-Radio mix) / ('A'remix) / ('A'extended remix).

Sep 90. (7"/c-s) **DEADBEAT CLUB. / LOVE SHACK** [ ] [–]
(12"+=/cd-s+=) – B-52's megamix.

—— now trimmed to basic trio of **PIERSON, SCHNEIDER** – vox / + **STRICKLAND** – guitar with guest musicians **IRWIN / ALFORD / LEE /** plus **JEFF PORCARO + STERLING CAMPBELL** – drums / **DAVID McMURRAY** – sax / **JAMIE MULHOBERAC + RICHARD HILTON** – keyboards / **LENNY CASTRO** – percussion / **TRACY WORMWORTH** – bass

Jun 92. (7"/c-s) *(W 0109/+C) <18895>* **GOOD STUFF. / BAD INFLUENCE** [21] [28]
(12"+=/cd-s+=) *(W 0109 T/CD)* – Return to Dreamland.
(12") *(W 0109TX)* – (4-'A'mixes).

Jul 92. (cd/c/lp) *<(7599 26943-2/-4/-1)>* **GOOD STUFF** [8] [16]
– Tell it like it t-i-is / Hot pants explosion / Good stuff / Revolution Earth Dreamland / Is that you Mo-Dean? / The world's green laughter / Vision of a kiss / Breezin' / Bad influence. *(re-iss. Feb95 cd/c; same)*

Sep 92. (7"/c-s) *(W 0130/+C)* **TELL IT LIKE IT T-I-IS. / THE WORLD'S GREEN LAUGHTER** [61] [ ]
(12"/cd-s) *(W 0130 T/CD)* – ('A'-4 other mixes).

Nov 92. (7"/c-s) *(W 0141/+C)* **IS THAT YOU MO-DEAN? / ('A'-Moby mix)** [ ] [ ]
(12"+=/cd-s+=) *(W 0141 T/CD) <40642-2>* – ('A'-2 other mixes) / Tell it like it t-i-is.

Feb 93. (7"/c-s) *(W 0156/+C)* **HOT PANTS EXPLOSION. / LOVE SHACK** [ ] [–]
(cd-s+=) *(W 0156CD)* – Channel Z / Roam.

—— **SCHNEIDER, PIERSON + STRICKLAND**

M.C.A. M.C.A.

Jun 94. (7"/c-s; BC-52's) *(MCS/+CS 1986) <54839>* **(MEET) THE FLINTSTONES. / ('A'-Barney's mix)** [3] May94 [33]
(cd-s+=) *(MCSTD 1986)* – (2-'A'mixes).
(above from that year's movie, 'The Flintstones')

—— disbanded in 1994

– compilations, others, etc. –

Jun 90. (cd/c/lp) *Island; (ILPS/ICT/CID 9959)* **DANCE THIS MESS AROUND THE BEST OF THE B-52's** [36] [–]
– Party out of bounds / Devil in my car / Dirty back road / 6060-842 / Wig / Dance this mess around / Private Idaho / Rock lobster / Strobe light / Give me back my man / Song for a future generation / Planet Claire / 52 girls *(cd+=)* – (2 extra mixes).

Feb 91. (cd) *Reprise; <26401>* **PARTY MIX! / MESOPOTAMIA** [–] [ ]

Nov 92. (d-cd) *Island; (ITSCD 1)* **THE B-52'S / WILD PLANET** [ ] [–]

Sep 95. (cd) *Spectrum; (551210-2)* **PLANET CLAIRE** [ ] [–]

Jul 98. (cd/c) *Reprise; (9362 46995-2/-4) <46920>* **TIME CAPSULE – SONGS FOR A FUTURE GENERATION** [ ] Jun98 [93]
– Planet Claire / 52 girls *[US-only]* / Rock lobster / Party out of bounds *[US-only]* / Strobelight *[US-only]* / Private Idaho / Quiche Lorraine (live) / Mesopotamia / Songs for a future generation *[US-only]* / Summer of love (original unreleased mix) / Channel Z / Deadbeat club / Love shack / Roam / Good stuff / Is that you Mo-Dean? / (Meet) The Flintstones *[UK-only]* / Debbie / Hallucinating Pluto.

Jan 99. (c-s) *Reprise; (W 0461C)* **LOVE SHACK '99 (mix) / (DJ Tonka remix)** [66] [–]
(cd-s+=) *(W 0461CD)* – ('A'-album mix).

Jan 02. (d-cd) *Rhino; <78357>* **NUDE ON THE MOON: THE B-52'S ANTHOLOGY** [–] [ ]

Aug 03. (3xcd-box) *Spectrum; (9808959)* **MESOPOTAMIA / PLANET CLAIRE / WHAMMY** [ ] [–]

□ BIG BROTHER & THE HOLDING CO.
(see under ⇒ JOPLIN, Janis)

BIG COUNTRY

Formed: Dunfermline, Scotland ... Autumn 1981 by STUART ADAMSON and BRUCE WATSON, following the former's departure from The SKIDS. They recruited brothers PETER (keyboards) and ALAN WISHART (bass) plus CLIVE PARKER (drums, ex-SPIZZ ...) although by early 1982, the latter three had been replaced by the lynchpin rhythm section of MARK BRZEZICKI and TONY BUTLER. After they turned down a contract with 'Ensign', the band signed to 'Mercury-Phonogram' in Spring '82, soon moving to London where they began work on a debut set, 'THE CROSSING' (1983). Previewed by the classic singles, 'FIELDS OF FIRE' & 'IN A BIG COUNTRY', the album traversed the charts in both Britain and America, introducing the famous (and, in certain quarters, much maligned) 'bagpipe' twin-guitar sound. Very much in the Celtic, stir-the-blood tradition, 'THE CROSSING' was a call to arms in a posturing, terminally pretentious early 80's music scene, its expansive, soaring sound transporting even the most smog-bound city dweller to the Scottish highlands. ADAMSON somehow managed to sing from the heart without sounding earnest, the chiming lament, 'CHANCE', displaying the raw emotive power this band once harnassed. Despite their straightforward approach, BIG COUNTRY were initially lauded by the press, even making something of a fashion statement with their trademark check shirts. With follow-up set, 'STEELTOWN' (1984), ADAMSON's voice of conscience examined Scottish industrial and economic decay; despite the subject matter, tracks such as the rousing 'FLAME OF THE WEST' burned with hope and optimism. Though the record entered the British chart at No.1, its less immediate appeal failed to translate into further Stateside success. This is where BIG COUNTRY began to lose their vision; although subsequent releases like 'THE SEER' (1986) and 'PEACE IN OUR TIME' (1988) continued to chart high and feature some inspired moments, creatively the band were merely treading water. The fact that the track 'ONE GREAT THING' was used on a Tennent's lager advert only seemed to underline its more pedestrian qualities. Despite periods where the band came perilously close to splitting, BIG COUNTRY survived into the 90's, their albums never breaking the mould but eagerly received by the band's fiercely partisan fans. ADAMSON had always addressed social/political issues in a challenging and often sympathetic fashion, the band releasing a 1995 EP, 'NON!', in protest at France's nuclear testing programme. Signed to 'Transatlantic', however, the poor commercial showing of the band's last two albums, 'WHY THE LONG FACE?' (1995) and 'ECLECTIC' (1996), suggested that their appeal was waning. Late in 1999, and thought to be because of his alcohol problems, STUART moved to Nashville, Tennessee. There, he formed The RAPHAELS, a roots country-orientated outfit who released one set, 'SUPERNATURAL' (2001). Sadly, this was to be ADAMSON's last outing. For nearly two months the man went AWOL and was subsequently found dead in a Hawaiian hotel room on the 16th of December, 2001. Scotland, and indeed the world of music, would mourn the death of such an enigmatic figure.

• **Songwriters:** Mostly ADAMSON / WATSON, except TRACKS OF MY TEARS (Smokey Robinson & The Miracles) / HONKY TONK WOMAN + RUBY TUESDAY (Rolling Stones) / AULD LANG SYNE (trad.) / ROCKIN' IN THE FREE WORLD (Neil Young) / FLY LIKE AN EAGLE (Steve Miller) / BLACK SKINNED BLUE EYED BOYS (Equals / Eddy Grant) / OH WELL (Fleetwood Mac) / (DON'T FEAR) THE REAPER (Blue Oyster Cult) / WOODSTOCK + BIG YELLOW TAXI (Joni Mitchell) / CRACKED ACTOR (David Bowie) / PARANOID (Black Sabbath) / SUMMERTIME (Gershwin – Du Bose Heyward) / ELEANOR RIGBY (Beatles) / SLING IT (Steve Harley) / I'M ON FIRE (Bruce Springsteen) / VICIOUS (Lou Reed) / I'M EIGHTEEN (Alice Cooper) / ON THE ROAD AGAIN (Canned Heat).

Album rating: THE CROSSING (*8) / STEELTOWN (*7) / THE SEER (*6) / PEACE IN OUR TIME (*4) / NO PLACE LIKE HOME (*5) / THE BUFFALO SKINNERS (*4) / WHY THE LONG FACE? (*4) / THROUGH A BIG COUNTRY – GREATEST HITS compilation (*8) / ECLECTIC (*4) / DRIVING TO DAMASCUS (*4) / COME UP SCREAMING (*6)

STUART ADAMSON (b.11 Apr'58, Manchester, England) – vocals, lead guitar, synthesizer (ex-SKIDS) / **BRUCE WATSON** (b.11 Mar'61, Timmins, Ontario, Canada) – guitar (ex-DELINX) / **TONY BUTLER** (b. 3 Feb'57, London, England) – bass (ex-ON THE AIR) / **MARK BRZEZICKI** (b.21 Jun'57, Slough, England) – drums (ex-ON THE AIR); the latter two repl. Scots-born brothers PETER and ALAN WISHART

Mercury Mercury

Sep 82. (7") *(COUNT 1)* **HARVEST HOME. / BALCONY**
(12"+=)(12"clear+=) *(COUNT 12)(COUNX 1)* – Flag of nations (swimming).

Feb 83. (7") *(COUNT 2) <811450>* **FIELDS OF FIRE. / ANGLE PARK** 10 Jan84 52
(12"+=/12"clear+=) *(COUN T/X 2-12)* – ('A'-alternative mix).
(7"sha-pic-d+=) *(COUP 2)* – Harvest home.

May 83. (7") *(COUNT 3) <814467>* **IN A BIG COUNTRY. / ALL OF US** 17 Sep83 17
(12"+=) *(COUNT 3-12)* – ('A'-pure mix).
(12"++=) *(COUNT 313)* – Heart and soul.

Jun 83. (lp/c) *(MERH/+C 27) <812870>* **THE CROSSING** 3 Jul83 18
– In a big country / Inwards / Chance / 1,000 stars / The storm / Harvest home / Lost patrol / Close action / Fields of fire / Porrohman. *(c+=)* – (4 remixes). *(re-dist.Mar84 lp/c; MERS/+C 27) (cd-iss. 1986; 812 870-2)*

Aug 83. (7") *(COUNT 4)* **CHANCE. / TRACKS OF MY TEARS (live)** 9
(ext.12"+=)(ext.12"pic-d+=) *(COUNT 4-12)(COUP 4)* – The crossing.

Jan 84. (7") *(COUNT 5) <818834>* **WONDERLAND. / GIANT** 8 86
(12"+=) *(COUNT 5-12)* – ('A'extended).
(12"clear+=) *(COUNX 5)* – Lost patrol (live).
(d7"+=) *(COUNT 5-5)* – Lost patrol (live – parts one & two).

Apr 84 (m-lp) *<818835>* **WONDERLAND** – 65
– Wonderland / Angle park / The crossing / All fall together.

Sep 84. (7"/7"w-poster) *(MER/+P 175)* **EAST OF EDEN. / PRAIRIE ROSE.** 17
(12"+=/12"w-poster+=) *(MERX/+P 175)* – ('A'extended).

Oct 84. (lp/c) *(MERH/+C 49) <822831>* **STEELTOWN** 1 70
– Flame of the west / East of Eden / Steeltown / Where the rose is sown / Come back to me / Tall ships go / Girl with grey eyes / Rain dance / The great divide / Just a shadow. *(cd-iss. 1986; 822 831-2) (re-iss. May93 on 'Spectrum' cd/c;)*

Nov 84. (7") *(MER 185)* **WHERE THE ROSE IS SOWN. / BELIEF IN THE SMALL MAN** 29
(12"+=) *(MERX 185)* – ('A'extended remix) / Bass dance.
(d7"+=) *(MERD 185)* – Wonderland (live) / In a big country (live) / Auld Lang Syne (live).

Jan 85. (7") *(BCO 8)* **JUST A SHADOW. / WINTER SKY** 26
(12"+=) *(BCO 8-12)* – ('A'extended remix).

Apr 86. (7"/7"sha-pic-d) *(BIGC/+P 1)* **LOOK AWAY. / RESTLESS NATIVES** 7
(d7"+=) *(BIGCD 1)* – Margo's theme / Highland scenery.
(ext.12"+=) *(BIGCX 1-1)* – ('A'-Outlaw mix).
(12") *(BIG CX 1)* – ('A'extended) / Restless natives (soundtrack part one).

Jun 86. (7") *(BIGC 2)* **THE TEACHER. / HOME CAME THE ANGELS** 28
(12") *(BIGCX 2)* – ('A'-Mystery mix) / Restless natives (soundtrack part two).

Jul 86. (lp/c/cd) *(MERH/+C 87)(826 844-2) <826 844>* **THE SEER** 2 59
– Look away / The seer / The teacher / I walk the hill / Eiledon / One great thing / Hold the heart / Remembrance day / The red fox / The sailor. *(re-iss. cd Aug94 on 'Vertigo';)*

Sep 86. (7"/s7")('A'-Boston mix-12") *(BIGC/+G 3)(BIGCX 3-3)* **ONE GREAT THING. / SONG OF THE SOUTH** 19
(d7"+=) *(BIGCD 3)* – Porrohman (live) / Chance (live).
(d7"+=) *(BIGCE 3)* – Wonderland (live) / Inwards (live).
('A'-Big Baad Country mix.c-s+=) *(BIGCM 3)* – In a big country (pure mix) / Fields of fire (live).
('A'-Big Baad Country mix.12"+=) *(BIGCR 3)* – Look away (outlaw mix).

Nov 86. (7"/remix-12") *(BIGC/+X 4)* **HOLD THE HEART. / HONKY TONK WOMAN (live)** 55
(d12"+=) *(BIGCX 4-4)* – (interview parts one & two).

—— added on tour **JOSS PHILIP-GORSE** – keyboards

Mercury Reprise

Aug 88. (7") *(BIGC 5)* **KING OF EMOTION. / THE TRAVELLERS** 16
(12"+=) *(BIGC 5-12)* – Starred and Crossed.
(cd-s++=) *(BIGCD 5)* – Not waving but drowning.
(c-s+=) *(BIGMC 5)* – Starred and crossed / On the shore.

Sep 88. (7") **KING OF EMOTION. / IN A BIG COUNTRY** –

Sep 88. (lp/c)(cd) *(MERH/+C 130)(836 325-2) <25787>* **PEACE IN OUR TIME** 9
– King of emotion / Broken heart (thirteen valleys) / Thousand yard stare / From here to eternity / Everything I need / Peace in our time / Time for leaving / River of hope / In this place / I could be happy here. *(cd+=)* – The travellers.

Oct 88. (7") *(BIGC 6)* **BROKEN HEART (THIRTEEN VALLEYS). / SOAPY SOUTAR STRIKES BACK** 47
(12"+=/12"red+=) *(BIGC/R 6-12)* – When a drum beats / On the shore.

(cd-s+=) *(BIGCD 6)* – Wonderland (12"mix).
(cd-s+=) *(BIGCDR 6)* – Made in Heaven / When a drum beats.

Jan 89. (7"/s7") *(BIGC/+P 7)* **PEACE IN OUR TIME. / PROMISED LAND** 39
(12"+=) *(BIGC 7-12)* – Over the border / The longest day.
(12"+=) *(BIGCR 7-12)* – In a big country (live) / Chance (live).
(cd-s+=) *(BIGCD 7)* – Chance / The longest day.

—— (Feb'90) **PAT AHERN – drums (ex-DAVE HOWARD SINGERS) repl. BRZEZICKI who joined PRETENDERS**

Apr 90. (7"/c-s) *(BIG C/MC 8)* **SAVE ME. / PASS ME BY** 41
(12"+=) *(BIGC 8-12)* – Dead on arrival.
(cd-s+=) *(BIGCD 8)* – World on fire.
(cd-s+=) *(BIGCD 8-12)* – Wonderland (live) / Thousand yard stare (live).

May 90. (cd/c/lp) *(846 022-2/-4/-1)* **THROUGH A BIG COUNTRY – GREATEST HITS** (compilation) 2 –
– Save me / In a big country / Fields of fire / Chance / Wonderland / Where the rose is sown / Just a shadow / Look away / King of emotion / East of Eden / One great thing / The teacher / Broken heart (thirteen valleys) / Peace in our time. *(c+=/cd+=)* – Eiledon / The seer / Harvest home. *(re-iss. Feb93 cd/c;)*

Jul 90. (7"/c-s) *(BIG C/MC 9)* **HEART OF THE WORLD. / BLACK SKINNED BLUE EYED BOYS** 50
(12"+=) *(BIGC 9-12)* – Broken heart (thirteen valleys) (acoustic) / Peace in our time (acoustic).
(cd-s+=) *(BIGCD 9)* – Restless Natives.

Vertigo not iss.

Aug 91. (7") *(BIC 1)* **REPUBLICAN PARTY REPTILE. / COMES A TIME / YOU, ME AND THE TRUTH** 37 –
(10"ep+=/12"ep+=) *(BIC T/X 1)* – Comes a time.
(cd-ep) *(BIGCD 1)* – ('A'side) / Freedom song / Kiss the girl goodbye / I'm only waiting.

Sep 91. (cd/c/lp) *(510230-2/-4/-1)* **NO PLACE LIKE HOME** 28 –
– We're not in Kansas / Republican party reptile / Dynamic lady / Keep on dreaming / Beautiful people / The hostage speaks / Beat the Devil / Heap of faith / Ships / Into the fire. *(cd+=)* – You, me and the truth / Comes a time. *(re-iss. Aug94; same)*

Oct 91. (7"/c-s) *(BIC/+C 2)* **BEAUTIFUL PEOPLE. / RETURN OF THE TWO HEADED KING** 72 –
(12"pic-d+=) *(BICX 2)* – Fly like an eagle.
(cd-s+=) *(BICCD 2)* – Rockin' in the free world (live).

—— **ADAMSON, BUTLER + WATSON** were joined by session men **SIMON PHILLIPS** – drums / **COLIN BERWICK** – keyboards

Compulsion Fox-RCA

Mar 93. (c-s/7") *(TC+/PULSS 4)* **ALONE. / NEVER TAKE YOUR PLACE** 24
(12"pic-d+=) *(12PULSS 4)* – Winter sky / Look away.
(cd-s) *(CDPULSS 4)* – ('A'side) / Chance / Rockin' in the free world / Eastworld.

Mar 93. (cd/c/lp) *(CD/TC+/NOIS 2)* <66294> **THE BUFFALO SKINNERS** 25 Sep93
– Alone / Seven waves / What are you working for / The one I love / Long way home / The selling of America / We're not in Kansas / Ships / All go together / Winding wind / Pink marshmallow moon / Chester's farm. *(re-iss. Sep94; same) (cd re-iss. May02 on 'EMI Gold'; 321988-2)*

Apr 93. (c-s/7") *(TC+/PULSS 6)* **SHIPS (WHERE WERE YOU). / OH WELL** 29
(12"+=/cd-s+=) *(12/CD PULSS 6)* – (Don't fear) The reaper / Woodstock.
(cd-s+=) *(CDXPULSS 6)* – The buffalo skinners / Cracked actor / Paranoid.

Jun 94. (cd/c/lp) *(CD/TC+/NOIS 5)* **WITHOUT THE AID OF A SAFETY NET (live)** 35 –
– Harvest home / Peace in our time / Just a shadow / Broken heart (thirteen valleys) / The storm / Chance / Look away / Steeltown / Ships / Wonderland / What are you working for / Long way home / In a big country / Lost patrol. *(cd re-iss. Mar03 on 'Disky'; 76207-2)*

Transatla. Pure

May 95. (c-ep/cd-ep) *(TRAM/TRAX 1009)* **I'M NOT ASHAMED / ONE IN A MILLION (1st visit) / MONDAY TUESDAY GIRL / ('A'edit)** 69 –
(cd-ep) *(TRAX 1010)* – ('A'side) / Crazytimes / In a big country / Blue on a green planet.

Jun 95. (cd/c) *(TRA CD/MC/LP 109)* <2200> **WHY THE LONG FACE?** 48
– You dreamer / Message of love / I'm not ashamed / ail into nothing / Thunder & lightning / Send you / One in a million / God's great mistake / Wild land in my heart / Thank you to the Moon / Far from me to you / Charlotte / Post nuclear talking blues / Blue on a green planet.

Aug 95. (12"ep/cd-ep) *(TRAT/TRAD 1012)* **YOU DREAMER EP** –
– You dreamer / Ice cream smile / Magic in your ice / Bianca.
(cd-ep) *(TRAX 1012)* – ('A'side) / I'm eighteen / Vicious / On the road again.

Nov 95. (cd-ep) *(TRAD 1013)* **NON!** –
– Post nuclear talking blues / Blue on a green planet / God's great mistake / All go together.
above was an action awareness record for Greenpeace.
below featured guests **BOBBY VALENTINO** – violin / **AARON EMERSON** – keyboards / **HOSSAM RAMZY + MOHAMMED TOUFIQ** – percussion / **CAROL LAULA + STEVE HARLEY + KYM MAZELLE** – vocals

Aug 96. (cd/c) *(TRA CD/MC 234)* **ECLECTIC** 41 –
– River of hope / King of emotion / Big yellow taxi / The buffalo skinners / Summertime / The night they drove old Dixie down / Eleanor Rigby / Winter sky / Sling it / I'm on fire / Where the rose is sown / Come back to me / Ruby Tuesday.

Track Record not iss.

Aug 99. (10"; BIG COUNTRY featuring EDDI READER) *(TRACK 0004C)* **FRAGILE THING. / I GET HURT / LOSERVILLE** 69 –
(cd-s) *(TRACK 0004A)* – (first & third tracks) / Dust on the road.
(cd-s) *(TRACK 0004B)* – (first two tracks) / John Wayne's dream.

Sep 99. (cd/c) *(TRK 1000 CD/CAS)* **DRIVING TO DAMASCUS** –
– Driving to Damascus / Dive in to me / See you / Perfect world / Somebody else / Fragile thing / The president slipped and fell / Devil in the eye / Trouble the waters / Bella / Your spirit to me / Grace. *(special cd+=; TRK 1000CDSP)* – Shattered cross / Too many ghosts.

Nov 99. (c-s) *(TRACK 0005C)* **SEE YOU / PERFECT WORLD** –
(cd-s+=) *(TRACK 0005A)* – This blood's for you.
(cd-s+=) *(TRACK 0005B)* – Camp Smedley's theme.

—— STUART ADAMSON retired for a while – late in '99

Oct 00. (d-cd) *(TRK 1003CD)* **COME UP SCREAMING (live)** –
– Harvest home / King of emotion / Driving to Damascus / John Wayne's dream / The storm / Where the rose is sown / Come back to me / Somebody else / Look away / You dreamer / Your spirit to me / The president slipped and fell / Drive in to me / Lost patrol / 13 valleys inwards / Wonderland / We're not in Kansas / Porroh man / Chance / In a big country / Fields of fire.

– compilations, etc. –

Aug 94. (cd) *Nighttracks; (CDNT 007)* **RADIO 1 SESSIONS** –
Aug 94. (cd) *Legends In Music; (LECD 043)* **BIG COUNTRY** –
Aug 95. (cd) *Spectrum; (550 879-2)* **IN A BIG COUNTRY** –
Oct 95. (cd) *Windsong; (WINCD 075)* **BBC LIVE IN CONCERT (live)** –
Mar 97. (cd) *Disky; (DC 87863-2)* **THE GREATEST HITS LIVE** –
May 00. (cd) *Snapper; (SMMCD 557)* **BRIGHTON ROCK** –
Mar 01. (cd) *Big Country Tracks; (<BCRTRK 001>)* **UNDERCOVER** (cover versions) May01
Apr 01. (cd) *Big Country Tracks; (<BCRTRK 002>)* **RARITIES** May01
Jun 01. (cd) *Big Country Tracks; (BCRTRK 003) / Cleopatra; <71146>* **ONE IN A MILLION** Jul01
Aug 01. (cd) *Big Country Tracks; (<BCRTRK 005>)* **GREATEST 12" HITS VOL.1** Sep01
Oct 01. (cd) *Universal; (E 586314-2)* **UNIVERSAL MASTERS COLLECTION** –
May 02. (d-cd) *Universal TV; (586989-2)* **GREATEST HITS** (BIG COUNTRY & The SKIDS) 71 –
Jul 02. (6xcd-s-box) *Track; (<TRKSP 001>)* **SINGLES COLLECTION**
Oct 02. (7xcd-s-box) *Track; (<TRKSP 002>)* **SINGLES COLLECTION VOL.2**
Jan 03. (cd) *Track; (<BCRTRK 006>)* **RARITIES VOL.3**
Mar 03. (cd) *Track; (TRK 1026CD)* **PEACE IN OUR TIME / NO PLACE LIKE HOME** –
Mar 03. (7xcd-s-box) *Track; (<TRKSP 003>)* **SINGLES COLLECTION VOL.3**
Jun 03. (7xcd-s-box) *Track; (<TRKSP 004>)* **SINGLES COLLECTION VOL.4**
Oct 03. (cd) *Spectrum; (063612-2)* **THE COLLECTION** –

the RAPHAELS

ADAMSON plus **MARCUS HUMMON** – acoustic guitar / + others

Track Track

May 01. (cd) *(<TRK 0005CD>)* **SUPERNATURAL** Aug01
– Supernatural / Simple man / Private battlefield / Old country, country / Learning to row / Shattered cross / Toujour aimez / My only crime / Stand up / Too many ghosts / Blue rose / Mexican trout / Life is a church.

— ADAMSON was to die late 2001

BIG STAR

Formed: when ALEX CHILTON headed back to Memphis, where he hooked up with his old schoolfriend CHRIS BELL to form the hugely influential but desperately unlucky BIG STAR. The first two albums sounded like a rougher take on the pop sensibilities of The BEATLES and The BEACH BOYS, with the 1972 debut 'NO.1 RECORD', especially, having great commercial potential. Guitarist BELL acted as a foil for CHILTON's inspired outpourings and the album contained such acoustic gems as 'BALLAD OF EL GOODOO'. Despite garnering rave reviews, the album failed to sell, due almost wholly to the distribution problems of their label 'Ardent' (a 'Stax' offshoot). BELL left at the end of '72, after a fallout with CHILTON over live work, the upshot being that BIG STAR became CHILTON's "power-pop" baby. Generally thought to be his artistic peak, early '74's 'RADIO CITY' had a gloriously raw spontaneity, with 'SEPTEMBER GURLS' proving the pained highlight. Distribution problems continued to dog Ardent and as the record stiffed, BIG STAR gradually broke up. Although released under the BIG STAR moniker, 'BIG STAR'S THE THIRD ALBUM', later re-released as 'SISTER LOVERS', was more or less the work of CHILTON. A difficult album, although none the less rewarding, it showcased a vulnerable man exorcising his demons in haunting and deeply introspective songs. CHRIS BELL's similarly downbeat 'I AM THE COSMOS', was recorded just before his death in a car accident in 1978, and was posthumously released by 'Rykodisc' in the early 90's. In 1979, CHILTON re-surfaced after a quiet period in New York, where his makeshift band toured with the likes of TELEVISION and The CRAMPS, whom he went on to produce. That same year saw him record the folk-punk 'BANGKOK' single and 'FLIES ON SHERBET', a cult classic which featured a hotch-potch of inspired covers and CHILTON originals. In the 80's, he worked with TAV FALCO under the name The PANTHER BURNS before releasing a solo album 'HIGH PRIEST' in 1987, a fairly enjoyable romp through a patchwork of ragged styles. The praise lavished upon BIG STAR by the likes of PRIMAL SCREAM and TEENAGE FANCLUB, brought about a renaissance of sorts, and CHILTON re-formed the band in 1993. He also released a further solo album in 1995, 'A MAN CALLED DESTRUCTION'.

Album rating: Big Star: #1 RECORD (*7) / RADIO CITY (*7) / SISTER LOVERS – THIRD ALBUM (*8) / Alex Chilton: LIKE FLIES ON SHERBET (*3) / BLACK LIST (*4) / 19 YEARS: A COLLECTION compilation (*7) / COLUMBIA: LIVE AT MISSOURI UNIVERSITY (*4; Big Star) / CLICHES (*5) / A MAN CALLED DESTRUCTION (*3)

CHRIS BELL (b.12 Jan'51, Memphis) – vocals, guitar / plus **ALEX CHILTON / ANDY HUMMEL** (b.26 Jan'51) – bass / **JODY STEPHENS** (b. 4 Oct'52) – drums

not iss. Ardent

Apr 72. (lp) *<ADS 1501>* **#1 RECORD** –
– Feel / The ballad of El Goodo / In the street / Don't lie to me / Thirteen / The India song / When my baby's beside me / My life is right / Give me another chance / Try again / Watch the sunrise / St 100-6. *(re-iss. Nov86 & Jan90 on 'Big Beat' lp/c; WIK/+C 53)*

Apr 72. (7") *<2902>* **IN THE STREET. / WHEN MY BABY'S BESIDE ME** –

Jul 72. (7") *<2904>* **DON'T LIE TO ME. / WATCH THE SUNRISE** –

— now trio when BELL left to go solo, He's killed in car crash 27th Dec'78.

Feb 74. (lp) *<ADS 2803>* **RADIO CITY** –
– O, my soul / Life is white / Way out west / What's going on / You got what you deserve / Mod Lang / Back of a car / Daisy glaze / She's a mover / September gurls / Morpha too – I'm in love with a girl. *(re-iss. Nov86 & Mar95 on 'Big Beat' lp/c; WIK/+C 54)*

Feb 74. (7") *<2909>* **O, MY SOUL. / MORPHATOO – I'M IN LOVE WITH A GIRL** –

May 74. (7") *<2912>* **SEPTEMBER GURLS. / MOD LANG** –
(UK-iss.Sep78 on 'Stax'; *STAX 504)*

1974. (7"; as BOX TOPS) *<0199>* **WILLOBEE AND DALE. / I'M GONNA BE ALRIGHT** –

— ALEX CHILTON now sole BIG STAR with session people, incl. STEPHENS + STEVE CROPPER. In 1975, after recording below album, they disbanded. It was finally released.

Aura P.V.C.

Jul 78. (lp) *(AUL 703) <7903>* **BIG STAR'S THE THIRD ALBUM**
– Stroke it Noel / For you / Kizza me / You can't have me / Nightime / Blue moon / Take care / Jesus Christ / Femme fatale / O Dana / Big black car / Holocaust / Kangaroo / Thank you friends. *(re-iss. 1987 on 'Dojo' lp/cd; DOJO LP/CD 55) <US re-iss. Nov87 lp/c/cd; PVC/+C/CD 8917> (UK cd-iss. Mar92 & Apr97 on 'Rykodisc'; RCD 10220) (cd re-iss. Oct94 on 'Line'; LICD 900492)*

Jul 78. (7") *(AUS 103)* **KIZZA ME. / DREAM LOVER** –

Dec 78. (7") *(AUS 107)* **JESUS CHRIST. / BIG BLACK CAR** –

– (BIG STAR) compilations etc. –

Jul 78. (d-lp) *Stax; (SXSP 302)* **#1 RECORD / RADIO CITY**
(cd-iss. Jun87 & Jan90 on 'Big Beat'; CDWIK 910) – (omits; In the street / St 100-6.

1988. (lp) *Line; (LILP 400509)* **BIG STAR'S BIGGEST** – German –
– The ballad of El Goodo / In the street / Don't lie to me / When my baby's beside me / Try again / Watch the sunrise / Life is white / What's goin' ahn / Back of a car / She's a mover / Way out west / September gurls / Jesus Christ / O'Dana / Holocaust / Kangaroo / Big black car / Thank you friends. *(UK cd-iss. Oct94; LICD 900509)*

Mar 92. (cd) *Rykodisc; (RCD 10221)* **LIVE** –
(re-iss. Apr97; same)

Dec 99. (cd) *Big Beat; (CDWIKK 197)* **THE BEST OF BIG STAR** –

BIG STAR

re-formed with **CHILTON / JONATHAN BAUER** – guitar, vocals / **KEN STRINGFELLOW** – guitar, bass (ex-POSIES)

Zoo Zoo

Sep 93. (cd/c) *<(11060-2/-4)>* **LIVE AT MISSOURI UNIVERSITY (4.25.93)** (live)
– In the street / Don't lie to me / When my baby's beside me / I am the cosmos / The ballad of El Goodo / Back of a car / Way out west / Daisy glaze / Baby strange / For you / Fool / September gurls / Thank you friends / Slut / Jeepster.

— CHILTON teamed up with VEGA (from SUICIDE) and BEN VAUGHN on album 'CUBIST BLUES' for 'Last Call'; *(7422466)*

☐ the BIRTHDAY PARTY (see under ⇒ CAVE, Nick)

BJORK

Born: BJORK GUDMUNDSDOTTIR, 21 Oct'65, Reykjavik, Iceland. Growing up in a creative communal family and something of a child prodigy, the strikingly unique BJORK enjoyed her first taste of the music business at the age of 11 when she impressed her teachers with her rendition of TINA CHARLES' No.1 'I LOVE TO LOVE', who in turn convinced a local radio station to play it. This led to her recording a self-titled album with many of Iceland's top musicians. It also included other covers; YOUR KISS IS SWEET (hit; Syreeta) / ALFUR UT UR HOL (FOOL ON THE HILL; Beatles) / CHRISTOPHER ROBIN (Melanie) / ALTA MIRA (Edgar Winter). BJORK graduated to her first band EXODUS, and in 1981 aged 14, she instigated another; TAPPI TIKARRASS, which meant 'Cork The Bitch's Arse'. In the next two

BIG STAR

years, the X-RAY SPEX-type outfit completed two albums 'BITID FAST I VITID' and 'MIRANDA'. She subsequently worked with KILLING JOKE theorists, JAZ COLEMAN and YOUTH, who had both fled to the frozen north in fear of a supposed impending apocalypse. In the interim, she guested for free-form jazz-rock duo STIFGRIM, who comprised of comedian/vocalist KRISTINN JON GUDMUNDSSON and guitarist STEINN SKAPTASON. They went down in the record books as one of over a hundred bands who took part in the longest ever continuous live performances (seven weeks!). She then spent two summer seasons playing synthesizer in a covers band named, CACTUS. In 1984, she teamed up with friends EINAR ORN BENEDIKTSSON (he of the legendary, erm, rapping "talent") and SIGTRYGGUR 'SIGGI' BALDERSSON to form KUKL ('Sorcery'), this FALL/BANSHEES influenced lot finding their way into Britain's earlobes (via the 'Crass' label) with two albums 'THE EYE' and 'HOLIDAYS IN EUROPE'. During this mid 80's period, she was also part of ROKHA ROKHA DRUM (as a drummer! and voice). They included lead vocalist JOHNNY TRIUMPH (b. SJON), who collaborated with BJORK's most famous and productive outfit The SUGARCUBES. Hooking up with BRAGI OLAFSSON, THOR ELDON (the father of BJORK's son, Sindri) and EINAR MELLAX, BJORK and Co. formed Iceland's first (and so far only) internationally renowned band. Signed to Derek Birkett's 'One Little Indian', the group had the critics frothing with their debut single, the sublime 'BIRTHDAY'. Like pop music from another planet, the song's reverberating bassline, celestial brass and ethereal production conspired to make this the aural equivalent of a particularly sensual massage. The track also introduced BJORK's inimitable vocals, a perversely melodic combination of wide-eyed child and Icelandic banshee. A further two slices of avant-garde strangeness, 'COLD SWEAT' and 'DEUS' followed into the UK Top 75 before a debut album, 'LIFE'S TOO GOOD', crashed into the Top 20 in Spring '88. An intoxicating blend of jazzy instrumentation, indie stylings and wilful weirdness, the album's success allowed the band to set up their own multi-media enterprise, 'Bad Taste Ltd.' back in Iceland. Though a follow-up, 'HERE TODAY, TOMORROW, NEXT WEEK' (1989) again made the UK Top 20, the critical reception was poor, particular vitriol reserved for EINER's (ORN) jarring vocal exhortations. After extensive touring the band headed back to Iceland to work on various outside jazz-styled projects, BJORK keeping her name in the music press via collaborative work with 808 STATE on their 'Ex:El' album. Then, in late '91, The SUGARCUBES bounced back with the celebratory avant-funk of 'HIT', the band putting in an unforgettable performance on Channel 4's 'The Word'. The accompanying album, 'STICK AROUND FOR JOY' (1992) saw the group back in critical favour, a brassy pot-pourri of spiked melody and faultless instrumental dexterity. To consolidate the new dancefloor-friendly direction, a set of remixes, 'IT'S-IT', was released in late '92, coinciding with the voluntary demise of The SUGARCUBES. It had been a short strange trip, but not as strange as BJORK's forthcoming rise to international pop superstardom. While she undoubtedly had a distinctive, beguiling charm, few would've predicted the massive critical and commercial achievements of her solo debut, entitled, er . . . 'DEBUT' actually. Released in summer '93, co-written with ex-SOUL II SOUL/MASSIVE ATTACK guru, NELLEE HOOPER and featuring such underrated talents as TALVIN SINGH and JHELISA ANDERSON, proceedings were dominated by pulsing, house-orientated material, although there was a fair smattering of off-the-wall BJORK oddities. Lauded by the indie and dance press alike, the album's kudos was further boosted by the success of the 'PLAY DEAD' single, a collaboration with soundtrack man, DAVID ARNOLD recorded for the movie, 'Young Americans'. A UK Top 3 success and a Mercury Music Prize nominee, 'DEBUT' turned BJORK into a household name, remixers clamouring to get to grips with her work. A true celebrity hobnobber, BJORK co-wrote the title track to MADONNA's 'Bedtime Stories' set, while 1995's follow-up album, 'POST', saw her working with everyone from TRICKY and SKUNK ANANSIE to The BRODSKY QUARTET and EVELYN GLENNIE! The latter two featured on the experimental/schizophrenic (delete according to taste) Top 5 hit, 'IT'S OH SO QUIET', an, ahem, 'adaptation' of Betty Hutton's 40's big band number which saw BJORK veer wildly from hushed reverence to shouting the rafters down in fine style. The song was characteristic of the album's more fragmented nature, a challenging listen but proof positive that the elfen firebrand wasn't content to rest on her laurels. The following year saw BJORK take up residence in the gossip columns rather than the charts, what with her highly publicised relationship with GOLDIE and her unfortunate fracas with a reporter at Bangkok airport (19th February '96). In September, an obsessed fan from Florida blew his brains out after sending a letter bomb to BJORK. Luckily neighbours contacted police after smelling his decomposed body and the bomb was averted, although unsurprisingly it caused her much distress. The stresses and strains of stardom formed the lyrical backbone for her acclaimed 1997 set, 'HOMOGENIC', a return to more electronic waters that was nevertheless more downbeat than dancefloor. One of the music world's more unpredictable stars, her maverick genius is sorely needed in a chart choked with indie loser clones. With a plethora of mixes behind her, BJORK looked set to be a film star, her part in the film, 'Dancer In The Dark' (alongside Catherine Deneuve) won her praise at Cannes 2000; she also wrote the score. With help from conductor/arranger Vincent Mendoza, she composed the musical fantasies of her doomed character, Selma (as full-set 'SELMASONGS'). Deliciously different from her studio albums, the soundtrack presented a forum for BJORK's more esoteric ideas, poignantly capturing the light, shade and emotional extremes of Selma's life. In contrast, the celestial calm of 'VESPERTINE' (2001) was located squarely inside the meditative confines of the author's immediate environment. A reclusive rhapsody to private contentment, the record's spectral choir, angelic harp and head-nodding beats (courtesy of MATMOS) weaved a suitably spiritual spell to accommodate BJORK's uncharacteristically restrained and subdued vocals. Listen for instance to its heart-rending and emotive hit singles, 'THE HIDDEN PLACE' and 'PAGAN POETRY', to find out exactly how much this little lady had progressed. A multi-cultural cast of collaborators were rounded up for her latest pet project, 'MEDULLA' (2004), her most challenging piece since 'SELMASONGS'. Such distinctive characters as ROBERT WYATT, MIKE PATTON, RAHZEL and one-time LFO electroid boffin, MARK BELL, helped shape the kind of stark, ethnically-inclined canvas normally the preserve of specialist media rather than the Top 20. One of the most accessible highlights from an album constructed almost wholly from diverse human voices was 'OCEANIA', written specifically for the opening ceremony at the 2004 Athens Olympics. Keeping on her world music trip, BJORK returned to the even more freeform sphere of avant-garde cinema and soundtracks, via her collaboration with filmmaking beau, Matthew Barney. Like MADONNA's keep-it-in-the-family venture, 'Swept Away', 'DRAWING RESTRAINT 9' (2005) was a maritime meditation; unlike Madge's movie, it featured whaling culture, Japanese myth and symbolism, and even a soundtrack cameo for indie actor, WILL OLDHAM, alongside the obligatory BJORK-ian strangeness.

• **Songwriters:** SUGARCUBES – all written by BJORK and EINAR, except TOP OF THE WORLD (Carpenters) / MOTORCYCLE MAMA (Sailcat).
• **Trivia:** BJORK was married to THOR, although after they had a child, he soon married new SUGARCUBE, MAGGI. SIGGI and BRAGI were former brother-in-laws who were married to twin sisters. In 1989, they divorced

and moved to Denmark to get married to each other!. The first openly gay marriage in rock/pop history.

Album rating: Tappi Tikarrass: MIRANDA (*4) / Kukl: THE EYE mini (*4) / HOLIDAYS IN EUROPE mini (*4) / Sugarcubes: LIFE'S BEEN GOOD (*9) / STICK AROUND FOR JOY (*8) / HERE TODAY, TOMORROW, NEXT WEEK (*8) / IT'S-IT remixes (*6) / THE GREAT CROSSOVER POTENTIAL compilation (*7) / Bjork: DEBUT (*9) / POST (*8) / TELEGRAM remixes (*7) / HOMOGENIC (*7) / SELMASONGS soundtrack (*7) / VESPERTINE (*7) / GREATEST HITS compilation (*9) / FAMILY TREE boxed collection (*6) / MEDULLA (*7) / DRAWING RESTRAINT 9 soundtrack (*6)

BJORK GUDMUNDSDOTTIR

Falkinn — not iss.

Dec 77. (lp/c) *(FA 006/+C)* **BJORK** [–] Icelan [–]
– Arabadrengurinn / Bukolla / Alta mira / Johannes Kjarvalv / Fusi Hreindyr / Himnafor / Oliver / Alfur ut ur hol / Musastiginn / Baenin.

TAPPI TiKARRASS

BJORK – vocals, keyboards, etc / **JAKOB MAGNUSSON** – bass (ex-EXODUS) / etc.

Spor — not iss.

Sep 81. (m-lp) *(SPOR 4)* **BITID FAST I VITID** [–] Icelan [–]

Gramm — not iss.

Aug 83. (lp) *(GRAMM 16)* **MIRANDA** [–] Icelan [–]

KUKL

BJORK – vocals, keyboards / **EINAR ORN BENEDIKTSSON** (b.29 Oct'62, Copenhagen, Denmark) – trumpet, vocals / **SIGTRYGGUR 'Siggi' BALDURSSON** (b. 2 Oct'62, Stavanger, Norway) – drums, percussion / **EINAR MELLAX** – keyboards

Gramm — not iss.

Sep 83. (7") *(GRAMM 17)* **SONGULL. / POKN FYRIR BYRJENDUR** [–] Icelan [–]

Crass — not iss.

Nov 84. (m-lp) *(1984-1)* **THE EYE** [ ] [–]
– Dismembered / Assassin / Anna. *(cd-iss. Mar97; 1984 2CD)*

Mar 86. (m-lp) *(Cat.No.4)* **HOLIDAYS IN EUROPE (THE NAUGHTY NOUGHT)** [ ] [–]
– (8 untitled tracks).

the SUGARCUBES

BJORK, EINAR, EINAR + SIGGI recruited **THOR ELDON JONSON** (b. 2 Jun'62, Reykjavik) – guitar / **BRAGI OLAFSSON** (b.11 Aug'62, Reykjavik) – bass

One Little Indian — Elektra

Sep 87. (7") *(7TP 7)* **BIRTHDAY. / BIRTHDAY (Icelandic)** [65] [–]
(12"+=) *(12TP 7)* – Cat (Icelandic).
(cd-s;Dec87;++=) *(7TP 7CD)* – Motorcrash.

Feb 88. (7") *(7TP 9)* **COLD SWEAT. / DRAGON (Icelandic)** [56] [–]
(12"+=) *(12TP 9)* – Traitor (Icelandic).
(12"++=) *(L12TP 9)* – Birthday (demo).
(cd-s+=) *(7TP 9CD)* – Traitor (Icelandic) / Revolution.

Apr 88. (7") *(7TP 10)* **DEUS. / LUFTGITAR (Icelandic) (with JOHNNY TRIUMPH)** [51] [–]
(10"+=/12"+=) *(10TP/12TP 10)* – Organic prankster.
(cd-s+=) *(7TP 10CD)* – Night of steel (Icelandic).

Apr 88. (lp/c/cd/dat) *(TPLP/TPC/TPCD/DTPLP 5)* **LIFE'S TOO GOOD** [14] Jun 88 [54]
– Mama / Delicious demon / Birthday / Traitor / Blue eyed pop / Petrol / F***ing in rhythm and sorrow / Cold sweat / Deus / Sick for toys. *(cd+=)* – I want.

May 88. (12"ep)(cd-ep) **COLD SWEAT / COLD SWEAT (meat mix). / BIRTHDAY (Icelandic) / DELICIOUS DEMON / COLD SWEAT (instrumental)** [–] [ ]

— **MARGRET 'Magga' ORNOLFSDOTTIR** (b.21 Nov'67, Reykjavik) – keyboards repl. MELLAX

Sep 88. (7") *(7TP 11)* **BIRTHDAY. / CHRISTMAS (with Jesus & Mary Chain)** [65] [–]
(12")(cd-s) *(12TP 11)(7TP 11CD)* – ('A'side) / Fucking in rhythm and sorrow (live) / Cowboy (live) / Cold sweat (live).
(12")(cd-s) *(12TP 11L)(7TP 11CDL)* – BIRTHDAY CHRISTMAS MIX: – Christmas eve – Christmas day / Christmas present / Petrol (live).
(US-green-ep title 'DELICIOUS DEMONS')

Dec 88. (c-s) **MOTORCRASH (live) / POLO** [–] [ ]
(12"+=)(3"cd-s+=) – Blue eyed pop.

Aug 89. (7"/c-s) *(26 TP7/+C)* **REGINA. / HOT MEAT** [55] [ ]
(7"ep+=) *(26 TP7L)* – Hey / Propeller vs jet.
(12"+=) *(26 TP12)* – Regina (Icelandic).
(cd-s+=) *(26 TP7CD)* – Hey / Regina (Icelandic).
(12") *(26 TP12L)* – ('A'-Propeller mix) / ('A'-Jet mix).

Oct 89. (lp/silver-lp/c)(cd) *(TPLP 15/+SP/C)(TPCD 15)* **HERE TODAY, TOMORROW, NEXT WEEK** [15] [70]
– Tidal wave / Regina / Speed is the key / Dream T.V. / Nail / Pump / Eat the menu / Bee / Dear plastic / Shoot him / Water / Day called Zero / Planet. *(cd+=)* – Hey / Dark disco! / Hot meat.

Feb 90. (7") *(32 TP7)* **PLANET. / PLANET (somersault version)** [ ] [ ]
(12"+=/cd-s+=) *(32 TP 12/7CD)* – Planet (Icelandic) / Cindy.

Dec 91. (7") *(62 TP7)* **HIT. / HIT (instrumental)** [17] [ ]
(12"+=) *(62 TP12)* – Theft.
(cd-s++=) *(62 TP7CD)* – Chihuahua (instrumental).
(12"+=) *(62 TP12L)* – Leash called love.

Feb 92. (lp/c/cd) *(TPLP 30/+C/CD)* **STICK AROUND FOR JOY** [16] [95]
– Gold / Hit / Leash called love / Lucky night / Happy nurse / I'm hungry / Walkabout / Hetero scum / Vitamin / Chihuahua.

Mar 92. (7"/c-s) *(72 TP7/+C)* **WALKABOUT (remix). / STONE DRILL (IN THE ROCK)** [ ] [ ]
(12"+=) *(72 TP12)* – Top of the world (live).
(cd-s++=) *(72 TP7CD)* – Bravo pop.

Aug 92. (12"ep) *(102 TP12)* **VITAMIN REMIXES** [ ] [–]
– ('A'-Babylon's Burnin mix) / ('A'-Earth dub) / ('A'-Laser dub in Hell mix) / ('A'-Decline of Rome part II & III) / ('A'-Meditation mix).
(cd-ep+=) *(102 TP7CD)* – ('A'-E mix).

Sep 92. (c-ep/12"ep/cd-ep) *(104 TP 7C/12/7CD)* **BIRTHDAY REMIX EP** [64] [ ]
– ('A'-Justin Robertson remix) / ('A'-Tommy D. dub mix) / ('A'-Jim & William Reid Christmas Eve mix) / ('A'original) / ('A'-Tommy D. 12" or dub mix) / ('A'-Justin Robertson dub) / ('A'-Jim & William Reid Christmas Day mix) / ('A'demo).
(cd-ep) *(104 TP7CDL)* – Birthday (Justin Robertson edit) / Birthday (Tommy D. edit) / Hit (Tony Humphries mix) / Mama (Mark Saunders mix).

Oct 92. (lp/c/cd/d-cd) *(TPLP 40/+C/CD/CDL)* <61426> **IT'S-IT (remixes)** [47] [ ]
– Birthday (Justin Robertson 12" mix) / Leash called love / Blue eyed pop / Motorcrash (Justin Robertson mix) / Planet / Gold (Todd Terry mix) / Water / Regina (Sugarcubes mix) / Mama (Mark Saunders mix) / Pump (Marius De Vries mix) / Hit (Tony Humphries sweet and low mix) / Birthday (Tommy D mix) / Coldsweat (DB/BP mix). *(cd w/ bonus cd)*

— officially disbanded late 1992

– compilations, others, etc. –

all on 'One Little Indian' ('Elektra' US)

Apr 90. (11x12"box) *(TP BOX 1)* **12.11** (box set) [ ] [–]
Apr 90. (8x7"box) *(TP BOX 2)* **7.8** (box set) [ ] [–]
Apr 90. (6xcd-s-box) *(TP BOX 3)* **CD.6** [ ] [–]
Jul 98. (cd/c/lp) *(TPLP 333 CD/MC/LP)* <62102> **THE GREAT CROSSOVER POTENTIAL** [ ] [ ]
– Birthday / Cold sweat / Mama / Motor crash / Deus / Regina / Pump / Planet / Water / Hit / Vitamin / Walkabout / Gold / Chihuahua.

BJORK GUDMUNDSDOTTIR & TRIO GUDMUNDAR INGOLFSSONAR

Smekkleysa — not iss.

Oct 90. (lp/c/cd) *(SM 27/+C/CD)* **GLING-GLO** [–] Icelan [–]
– Gling-glo / Luktar-gvendur / Kata rokkar / Pabbi minn / Brestir og brak / Astartofrar / Bella simamaer / Litli tonlistarmadurinn / Pad sest ekki saetari mey / Bilavisur / Tondelevo / Eg veit ei hvad skal segja / I dansi med per / Bornin vid tjornina / Ruby baby / I can't help loving that man.

BJORK

— solo, with **MARIUS DE VRIES, PAUL WALLER, MARTIN VIRGO + GARRY HUGHES** – keyboards / **NELLEE HOOPER** (co-writer of some), **LUIS JARDIM** (also bass) + **BRUCE SMITH** – drums, percussion / **JON MALLISON** – guitar / **TALVIN SINGH** – tabla / **CORKI HALE** – harp / **JHELISA ANDERSON** – backing vocals / **OLIVER LAKE, GARY BARNACLE, MIKE MOWER** – brass

One Little Indian | Elektra

Jun 93. (c-s) *(112 TP7C)* **HUMAN BEHAVIOUR / ATLANTIC** [36] [ ]
(12") *(112 TP12)* – ('A'-Underworld mix) / ('A'-Close to human mix) / ('A'-Dom T. mix).
(cd-s) *(112 TP7CD)* – ('A'side) / (above extras) / ('A'-Bassheads edit).

Jul 93. (cd/c/lp) *(TPLP 31 CD/C/L) <61468>* **DEBUT** [3] [61]
– Human behaviour / Crying / Venus as a boy / There's more to life than this recorded live at the Milk Bar toilets / Like someone in love / Big time sensuality / One day / Aeroplane / Come to me / Violently happy / The anchor song. *(re-iss. Nov93 cd/c; TPLP 31 CDX/CX)(+=)* – Play dead.

Aug 93. (7"/c-s) *(122 TP7/+C)* **VENUS AS A BOY. / ('A'-Dream mix)** [29] [ ]
(cd-s) *(122 TP7CD)* – ('A'side) / ('A'-Mykaell Riley mix) / There's more to life than this (non toilet mix) / Violently happy.
(cd-s) *(122 TP7CDL)* – ('A'side) / Stigdu mig / Anchor song (Black Dog mix) / I remember you.
(below single credited with DAVID ARNOLD and from the movie 'Young Americans', released on 'Island' records)

Oct 93. (7"/c-s) *(IS/CIS 573)* **PLAY DEAD. / ('A'-Tim Simenon remix)** [12] [ ]
(12"+=/cd-s+=) *(12IS/CID 573)* – ('A'-Tim Simenon mixes; Orchestral / 12" / Instrumental) / ('A'-Original film mix).

Nov 93. (c-s) *(132 TP7C)* **BIG TIME SENSUALITY / SiDASTA EG** [17] [–]
(cd-s+=) *(132 TP7CD)* – Gloria / Come to me (Black Dog Productions).
(12"/cd-s) *(132 TP 12/7CDL)* – ('A'-Dave Morales def radio mix) / ('A'-Fluke mixes) / ('A'-Justin Robertson – Lionrock Wigout & Prankster's Joyride mix) / ('A'-Dom T. mix).

Jan 94. (c-s) *<64561>* **BIG TIME SENSUALITY / THERE'S MORE TO LIFE THAN THIS** [–] [88]

— In Mar'94, BJORK was accused by SIMON FISHER (LOVEJOY) of not crediting him on 4 of her songs on her 'DEBUT' album.

Mar 94. (c-s) *(142 TP7C)* **VIOLENTLY HAPPY. / ('A'-Fluke mix)** [13] [ ]
(cd-s) *(142 TP7CD)* – ('A'side) / Anchor song (acoustic) / Come to me (acoustic) / Human behavior (acoustic).
(d-cd-s) *(142 TP7CDL)* – ('B'side) / ('A'-5 other mixes).

Sep 94. (cd/c) *(MUM CD/SC 59)* **BEST MIXES FROM THE ALBUM DEBUT (For All The People Who Don't Buy White Labels)** [ ] [–]
(above rel. on 'Mother')

Apr 95. (c-s) *(162 TP7C)* **ARMY OF ME / ('A'-ABA All-Stars mix)** [10] [ ]
(cd-s+=) *(162 TP7CD)* – You've been flirting again / Sweet intuition.
(cd-s+=) *(162 TP7CDL)* – ('A'-Massey mix) / ('A'-featuring SKUNK ANANSIE) / ('A'-ABA All-Stars instrumental).
(cd-s) *(162 TP7)* – ('A'side) / Cover me.

Jun 95. (cd/c/lp) *(TPLP 51 CD/C/L) <612740>* **POST** [2] [32]
– Army of me / Hyper-ballad / The modern things / It's oh so quiet / Enjoy / You've been flirting again / Isobel / Possibly maybe / I miss you / Cover me / Headphones. *(cd re-iss. Oct99; TPLP 51CD)*

Aug 95. (c-s/cd-s) *(172 TP7 C/CD)* **ISOBEL / CHARLENE (Black Dog mix) / I GO HUMBLE / VENUS AS A BOY (harpsicord version)** [23] [ ]
(cd-s) *(172 TP7CDL)* – ('A'side) / ('A'-Goldie mix) / ('A'-Eumir Deodato mix) / ('A'-Siggi mix).

Nov 95. (c-s) *(182 TP7C)* **IT'S OH SO QUIET / YOU'VE BEEN FLIRTING AGAIN (flat is a promise mix)** [4] [ ]
(cd-s+=) *(182 TP7CD)* – Hyper-ballad (Over the edge mix) / Sweet sweet intuition.
(cd-s) *(182 TP7CDL)* – ('A'side) / Hyper-ballad (Girl's blouse mix) / Hyper-ballad (with The Brodsky Quartet) / My spine (featuring Evelyn Glennie).

Feb 96. (c-s) *(192 TP7C)* **HYPER-BALLAD / HYPER-BALLAD (Robin Hood riding through the glen mix)** [8] [ ]
(cd-s+=) *(192 TP7CD)* – ('A'-The stomp remix) / ('A'-Fluke mix) / ('A'-Subtle abuse mix) / ('A'-Tee's freeze mix).
(cd-s) *(192 TP7CDL)* – ('A'side) / Isobel (the Carcass remix) / Cover me (Plaid mix) / ('A'-Towa Tei remix).

Oct 96. (cd-s) *(193 TP7CD)* **POSSIBLY MAYBE (mixes; Lucy / Calcutta Cyber Cafe / Dalas Austin)** [13] [ ]
(cd-s) *(193 TP7CDT)* – ('A'-Calcutta Cyber Cafe dub) / Cover me (Dillinja mix) / One day (Trevor Morais mix) / I miss you (Photek mix).
(cd-s) *(193 TP7CDL)* – ('A'live mix) / Big time sensuality (Plaid remix) / Visur vatnsenda-rosu / Hyper-ballad (live).

Nov 96. (cd/c/lp) *(TPLP 51 CDT/CT/T) <61897>* **TELEGRAM** (remixes) [ ] Jan97 [66]
(cd re-iss. Aug99; TPLP 51CDT)

Feb 97. (c-s) *(194 TP7C)* **I MISS YOU / I MISS YOU (Photek mix)** [36] [ ]
(cd-s) *(194 TP7CD)* – ('A'side) / ('A'-Dobie part 2) / ('A'Darren Emerson mix) / Karvel (Graham Massey mix).
(cd-s) *(194 TP7CDL)* – ('A'-Dobie part 1) / Hyperballad (LFO) Violently happy (live) / Headphones (Miko Vainio remix).

Sep 97. (cd-s) *(202 TP7CD)* **JOGA (mixes; album / Alec Empire / Alec Empire Digital Hardcore 1 & 2)** [ ] [ ]
(cd-s) *(202 TP7CDL)* – ('A'album mix) / Sod off / Immature (Bjork's version) / So broken.
(cd-s) *(202 TP7CDX)* – (mixes; Howie B. main / String & Vocal / Buzzwater) / All is full of love (original).

Sep 97. (lp/c/cd) *(TPLP 71/+C/CD) <62061>* **HOMOGENIC** [4] [28]
– Hunter / Joga / Unravel / Bachelorette / All neon like / 5 years / Immature / Alarm call / Pluto / All is full of love.

Dec 97. (c-s) *(212 TP7C)* **BACHELORETTE / ('A'-Howie "Spread" mix)** [21] [ ]
(cd-s+=) *(212 TP7CD)* – My snare / Scary.
(12") *(212 TP12P1)* – ('A'-Alec Empire remix) / ('B'side).
(12") *(212 TP12P2)* – ('A'-Mark Bell "Optimism" remix) / ('A'-Mark Bell "Zip" remix).
(cd-s) *(212 TP7CDL)* – (mixes; above + RZA / Grooverider / etc).

— In Aug'98. BJORK collaborated with FUNKSTORUNG on a single, 'ALL IS FULL OF LOVE', released on 'Fat Cat' cd-s; *CDFAT 022)*

Oct 98. (cd-s) *(222 TP7CD)* **HUNTER / ALL IS FULL OF LOVE (In Love With Funkstorung remix) / ('A'-U-Ziq remix)** [44] [ ]
(cd-s) *(222 TP7CDL)* – ('A'side) / ('A'-State Of Bengal mix) / ('A'-Skothus mix).
(cd-s) *(222 TP7CDX)* – ('A'-Moodswing mix) / So broken (DK Krust remix) / ('A'live).

Nov 98. (cd-s) *(232TP7CD)* **ALARM CALL (mixes; radio / Rhythmic Phonetics / Bjeck)** [33] [ ]
(cd-s) *(232 TP7CDL)* – (mixes; Potage du jour / French edit / French dub).
(cd-s) *(232 TP7CDX)* – (mixes; Phunk you / Gangsta / Locked).
(12") *(232 TP12P1)* – (mixes; Bjeck [Beck] / Rhythmic Phonetics [Matmos] / Speech therapy [Matmos]).
(12") *(232 TP12P2)* – (mixes; Enough is enough [Mark Bell] / Rise & shine [Mark Bell]) / All is full of love (Mark Bell mix).
(12") *(232 TP12P3)* – (mix; Reprosession [DJ Krust] / So broken (DJ Krush mix).
(12") *(232 TP12P4)* – (mixes; Alan Braxe & Ben Diamond [Stardust] / Teesmade dub [Swag] / Alan Braxe & Ben Diamond).
(12") *(232 TP12P5)* – (mixes; Andy Bradford & Mark Bell / album / Snooze button [Dom T] / (Moodswing [Mark Bell]).

Jun 99. (cd-s) *(242 TP7CD)* **ALL IS FULL OF LOVE (mixes; original / Funkstorung exclusive / strings)** [24] [ ]
(cd-s) *(242 TP7CDL)* – ('A'mixes; Howie B / Plaid / Guy Sigsworth).
(12") *(242 TP12)* – ('A'mixes; Mark Stent / Funkstorung exclusive / Mark Stent radio strings).
(12") *(242 TP12L)* – ('A'mixes; U-Ziq 7 minute / U-Ziq 1 minute / Funkstorung exclusive).

Sep 00. (lp/cd) *(TPLP 151/+CD) <62533>* **SELMASONGS: Music From The Motion Picture Dancer In The Dark** [34] [41]
– Overture / Cvalda / I've seen it all (with THOM YORKE) / Scatterheart / In the musicals / 107 steps / New world.

Aug 01. (cd-s) *(332 TP7CD)* **HIDDEN PLACE / GENEROUS PALMSTROKE / VERANDI** [21] [–]
(cd-s) *(332 TP7CDL)* – ('A'-acapella) / Mother heroic / Foot soldiers.

Aug 01. (d-lp/c/cd) *(TPLP 101/+C/CD) <62653>* **VESPERTINE** [8] [19]
– Hidden place / Cocoon / It's not up to you / Undo / Pagan poetry / Frosti / Aurora / An echo, a stain / Sun in my mouth / Heirloom / Harm of will / Unison.

Nov 01. (cd-s) *(352 TP7CD)* **PAGAN POETRY / DOMESTICA / BATABID (DVD)** [38] [–]
(cd-s) *(352 TP7CDL)* – ('A'side) / ('A'-Matthew Herbert mix) / Aurora (opiate mix).

Mar 02. (cd-s) *(332 TP7CD1)* **COCOON / PAGAN POETRY (new music box version) / SUN IN MY MOUTH (recomposed by ensemble)** 35 –
(cd-s) *(332 TP7CD2)* – ('A'-radio) / Aurora (new music box version) / Amphibian (DVD) / ('A'-video).

Nov 02. (d-lp/cd) *(TPLP 359/+CD) <62787>* **GREATEST HITS** (compilation) 53
– All is full of love / Hyperballad / Human behaviour / Joga / Bachelorette / Army of me / Pagan poetry / Big time sensuality (the Fluke minimix) / Venus as a boy / Hunter / Hidden place / Isobel / Possibly maybe / Play dead / It's in our hands.

Nov 02. (6xcd-box) *(TPLP 365CD) <62815>* **FAMILY TREE** (collection)
– Sidasta eg / Giora / Fuglar / Ammaeli / Mamma / Immature / Cover me / Generous palmstroke / Joga / Mother heroic / The modern things / Karvel / I go humble / Nature is ancient / Unravel / Cover me / Possibly maybe / The anchor song / Hunter / All neon like / I've seen it all / Bachelorette / Play dead / Venus as a boy / Hyperballad / You've been flirting again / Isobel / Joga / Unravel / Bachelorette / All is full of love / Scatterheart / I've seen it all (with THOM YORKE) / Pagan poetry / It's not up to you.

Nov 02. (cd-s) *(366 TP7CD1)* **IT'S IN OUR HANDS / COCOON (rectangled by ensemble) / HUMAN BEHAVIOUR (live)** 37 –
(cd-s) *(366 TP7CD2)* – ('A'side) / Matmos (mix) / Arcade (mix).

Aug 04. (d-lp/cd) *(TPLP 358/+CD) <62984>* **MEDULLA** 9 14
– Pleasure is all mine / Show me forgiveness / Where is the line / Vokuro / Oll Birtan / Who is it / Submarine / Desired constellation / Oceania / Sonnets – Unrealities XI / Ancestors / Mouth's cradle / Midvikudags / Triumph of a heart.

Oct 04. (cd-s) *(446 TP7CD1)* **WHO IS IT (CARRY MY JOY ON THE LEFT, CARRY MY PAIN ON THE RIGHT) / OCEANIA (featuring KELIS)** 26 –
(cd-s) *(446 TP7CD2)* – ('A'-C2N Dattasette mix) / ('A'-Fruit Machine mix) / ('A'-Bell Choir mix).
(dvd-s) *(446 TP7DVD)* – ('A'-video) / ('A'-Choir mix) / Mouth's cradle (Cortejo Affro Ile Aiye mix).

Mar 05. (cd-s) *(447 TP7CD1)* **TRIUMPH OF A HEART / DESIRED CONSTELLATION (Ben Frost's School Of Emotional Engineering mix)** 31 –
(cd-s) *(447 TP7CD2)* – ('A'-Audition mix) / Vokuro (V V mix) / Mouth's cradle mouth (recomposed by Ensemble).
(dvd-s) *(447 TP7DVD)* – ('A'-video) / Oceania (piano & vocal) / Desired constellation (choir mix).

One Little Indian One Little Indian

Jul 05. (cd) *(<TPLP 459CD>)* **DRAWING RESTRAINT 9** (soundtrack) Aug05
– Gratitude / Pearl / Ambergris march / Bath / Hunter vessel / Shimenawa / Vessel Shimenawa / Storm / Holographic entrypoint / Cetacea / Antarctic return.

– others, etc. –

Aug 96. (12"ltd) *(193 TP12TD)* **POSSIBLY MAYBE (Talvin Singh mix). / I MISS YOU (Dobie mix)** –

Sep 96. (12"ltd) *(193 TP12DM)* **POSSIBLY MAYBE (LFO mix). / ENJOY (Dom T mix)** –

Oct 96. (12"ltd) *(193 TP12PT)* **BIG TIME SENSUALITY (Plaid mix). / ONE DAY (Trevor Morais mix)** –

Jun 97. (12"ltd) *(193 TP12PT)* **BIG TIME SENSUALITY. / ONE DAY** –

Jun 97. (12"ltd) *(193 TP12PD)* **I MISS YOU (Photek mix). / COVER ME (Dillinja mix)** –

Jun 97. (12"ltd) *(193 TP12GH)* **ISOBEL'S LONELY HEART (Goldie remix). / HYPERBALLAD (Robin Hood Riding Through The Glen mix)** –

Jun 97. (12"ltd) *(193 TP12MO)* **POSSIBLY MAYBE (Lucy mix – Mark Bell). / ENJOY (Further Over The Edge mix – Outkast)** –

Jun 97. (12"ltd) *(193 TP12TT)* **HYPERBALLAD (Towa Tei remix). / ENJOY (The Beats mix – Dom T)** –

Aug 98. (12"/cd-s; BJORK & FUNKSTORUNG) *Fat Cat; (12/CD FAT 022)* **ALL IS FULL OF LOVE (mixes)** –

Mar 00. (4xcd-box) *(252TP 7BOX)* **A COLLECTION OF SINGLES** –

□ Frank BLACK (see under ⇒ PIXIES)

the BLACK CROWES

Formed: Atlanta, Georgia, USA ... 1984 under the name MR CROWE'S GARDEN by the ROBINSON brothers, CHRIS and RICH (sons of STAN ROBINSON, who had a minor US hit in 1959 with 'Boom A Dip Dip'). By 1988, they'd adopted the BLACK CROWES moniker and assembled the line-up that would remain more or less stable throughout their career. Picked up by the ever eclectic RICK RUBIN, for his fledgling 'Def American' label, the band released their debut album in 1990 to almost universal acclaim. Taking its title from an old ELMORE JAMES song, the record was steeped in classic American musical tradition; a seamless mesh of hard-rock, blues, soul, country and R&B that drew inevitable comparisons with The FACES and The ROLLING STONES. Yet the BLACK CROWES were unmistakably American, Southern American in the tradition of The ALLMAN BROTHERS and LYNYRD SKYNYRD. The songwriting was simple but effective, while CHRIS ROBINSON's voice was a revelation, if a little wearing after prolonged exposure. This was feelgood music, genuine rough'n'ready soul music as opposed to the slick, neutered wallpaper that passes for much modern black soul. 'TWICE AS HARD', 'JEALOUS AGAIN', 'COULD'VE BEEN SO BLIND' and a rough hewn cover of OTIS REDDING's 'HARD TO HANDLE' sounded effortless, while ROBINSON put in a spine-tingling vocal performance on the emotive ballad, 'SHE TALKS TO ANGELS'. Live, the BLACK CROWES were naturally in their element and following the album's release, the band embarked on a punishing touring schedule, playing with everyone from DOGS D'AMOUR to ZZ TOP (in a well documented incident, the band were dropped from the ZZ TOP tour following CHRIS ROBINSON's criticisms of corporate sponsorship). With the permanent addition of keyboardist EDDIE HAWRYSCH to flesh out the sound, and replacing guitarist JEFF CEASE with MARC FORD (ex-BURNING TREE), the band cut 'THE SOUTHERN HARMONY AND MUSICAL COMPANION'. Produced by CHUCK LEAVELL (ex-ALLMANS) and released May 1992 (incredibly, recorded in just over a week), the album built on the solid blueprint of the debut. The band had amassed a sizeable following through their ceaseless live work and the album deservedly hit the top spot in America, No.2 in the UK. With the songwriting more assured and the arrangements more ambitious, The 'CROWES succeeded in carving out a musical identity distinct from their weighty musical influences. The addition of female backing singers added a richness to the sound and the record segued smoothly from the raucous R&B of opener 'STING ME' to the stoned melancholy of 'THORN IN MY PRIDE' and on to the darker, 'Midnight Rambler'-esque 'BLACK MOON CREEPING'. Just to make sure people knew where he was coming from (man), ROBINSON closed the set with a mellow, acoustic reading of Bob Marley's 'TIME WILL TELL'. Soon after the album's release, the band hit the road once more, a headlining spot at the 1994 Glastonbury Festival illustrating just how high the 'CROWES had flown. Released later that year amid a storm of controversy over the cover shot (Uncle Sam[antha] in a compromising position, you could say), 'AMORICA' was something of a disappointment. Perhaps the relentless touring was beginning to take its toll, as the record sounded claustrophobic and turgid, the pace rarely rising above a monotonous plod. The songs were also lacking in cohesion and focus, although moments of genius were still evident on the likes of 'A CONSPIRACY' and the single, 'WISER TIME'. The band continued to cut it live, getting further out both musically and image wise. While The 'CROWES had always been defiantly 70's in their choice of apparel, CHRIS ROBINSON, in particular, had graduated from a vaguely glam look to a latter day CHARLES MANSON-alike. This was the revenge of the 70's; oriental rugs, ragged denim flares, bare feet, hell, even a GRATEFUL DEAD t-shirt! Rambling organ solos were also de rigeur of course, but fans lucky enough to catch the band at their low-key London gigs at the tail end of '96/early '97, were treated to a stripped down, largely acoustic set. While completely clueless, mullet headed, rock bores voiced their disapproval, the Christ-like ROBINSON mesmerised the more discerning 'CROWES fans with sterling covers of BOB DYLAN, BYRDS and LITTLE FEAT material. The 1996 album, 'THREE SNAKES AND ONE CHARM' was also a return to form, encompassing a greater diversity of styles and adding a bit of SLY STONE-style funkiness to their ragged retro patchwork. Where the band go from here is anybody's guess although a drum'n'bass remix is unlikely. With bassist JOHNNY COLT and guitarist FORD both leaving within a few months of each other, things didn't look too good. However, all was well again by early '99 with the release of their fifth set, 'BY YOUR SIDE', a typical FACES-meets-'STONES effort that highlighted their best track for some time, 'KICKIN' MY HEART AROUND' (a minor hit from late the previous year). After a much-praised one nighter with 'ZEPPELIN's axe king JIMMY PAGE (an album, 'LIVE AT THE GREEK' was issued in 2000), the BLACK CROWES returned the following year with 'LIONS' on the 'V2' (Virgin/Branson) imprint. While the album notched up a respectable US Top 20 chart placing, the CROWES ultimately decided that they'd reached the end of the line with 2002's 'LIVE' documenting the ensuing farewell tour. Tight, raucous, and as close to the spirit of unpretentious rock'n'roll as you're likely to hear these days, the album was as fitting an epitaph as any given the 'CROWES' career-long commitment to the stage. If there was any criticism at all, it was the almost complete absence of covers, the reverence of which always made this band's readings of other people's songs worthwhile. Songwriters CHRIS and RICH took their respective chops in different directions, the former living out his more pastoral-minded early-mid 70s fantasies on solo debut, 'NEW EARTH MUD' (2002), spicing it up with a dash of old school funk. 'THIS MAGNIFICENT DISTANCE' (2004) was tougher and more complex both musically and lyrically, going off at tangents the BLACK CROWES had only occasionally hinted at. Meanwhile, brother RICH occupied himself with the soundtrack for a straight-to-DVD feature, 'Highway' (2001), before briefly touring with HOOKAH BROWN. Finally tiring of a band format, the guitarist took the plunge and recorded a full-on solo debut, 'PAPER' (2004), revealing a STEVE MILLER-esque vocal and a bluesier spin on 70s retro than CHRIS. Likely hanging on the old adage that two heads are better than one, the siblings finally reformed the BLACK CROWES in 2005.

• **Covers:** HARD TO HANDLE (Otis Redding) / RAINY DAY WOMAN NOS.12 & 35 + WHEN THE NIGHT COMES FALLING FROM THE SKY (Bob Dylan) / TIME WILL TELL (Bob Marley) / DREAMS (Allman Brothers). • **Trivia:** CHRIS and RICH's father STAN ROBINSON had a minor US hit in '59 with 'BOOM-A-DIP-DIP'.

Album rating: SHAKE YOUR MONEY MAKER (*9) / THE SOUTHERN HARMONY AND MUSICAL COMPANION (*9) / AMORICA (*7) / THREE SNAKES AND ONE CHARM (*7) / SHO' NUFF: THE COMPLETE BLACK CROWES boxed set (*7) / BY YOUR SIDE (*7) / GREATEST HITS 1990-1999 – A TRIBUTE TO A WORK IN PROGRESS compilation (*8) / LIONS (*5) / LIVE (*5) / Chris Robinson: NEW EARTH MUD (*5) / THIS MAGNIFICENT DISTANCE (*6) / Rich Robinson: PAPER (*4)

CHRIS ROBINSON (b.20 Dec'66) – vocals / **'Young' RICH ROBINSON** (b. RICHARD, 24 May'69) – guitar / **JEFF CEASE** (b.24 Jun'67, Nashville, USA) – guitar / **JOHNNY COLT** (b. 1 May'68, Cherry Point, New Connecticut) – bass (repl. 2 earlier) / **STEVE GORMAN** (b.17 Aug'65, Hopkinsville, Kentucky) – drums (repl. 5 earlier)

Def American / Def American

Mar 90. (cd/c/lp) *(842515-2/-4/-1)* *<24278>* **SHAKE YOUR MONEY MAKER** — [ ] Oct89 [4]
– Twice as hard / Jealous again / Sister luck / Could I've been so blind / Hard to handle / Seeing things / Thick'n'thin / She talks to angels / Struttin' blues / Stare it cold. *(finally hit UK No.36 Aug91 – re-dist.Sep92) (re-iss. Dec94 on 'American-BMG' cd/c; 74321 24839-2/-4) (cd re-iss. Feb99 on 'Columbia'; 491790-2) (cd re-iss. Aug00; 499653-2)*

May 90. (7") *(DEFA 4)* *<19697>* **JEALOUS AGAIN. / THICK'N'THIN** — [ ] Apr90 [75]
(12"+=/12"pic-d+=)(cd-s+=) (DEFA/+P 4-12)(DEFAC 4) – Waitin' guilty.

Aug 90. (7"/c-s) *(DEFA/+M 6)* *<19668>* **HARD TO HANDLE. / JEALOUS AGAIN (acoustic)** — [45] Oct90 [45]
(12"+=/12"sha-pic-d+=) *(DEFA/+P 6-12)* – Twice as hard / Stare it cold (both live).
(cd-s+=) *(DEFAC 6)* – Twice as hard (remix).

Jan 91. (7"/c-s) *(DEFA/+M 7)* **TWICE AS HARD. / JEALOUS AGAIN (live)** — [47] [–]
(12"+=)(cd-s+=) *(DEFA 7-12)(DEFAC 7)* – Jealous guy (live).
(12"pic-d+=) *(DEFAP 7-12)* – Could I've been so blind (live).

Mar 91. (c-s/7") *<19403>* **SHE TALKS TO ANGELS. / ('A'live video version)** — [–] [30]

Jun 91. (7") *(DEFA 8)* **JEALOUS AGAIN. / SHE TALKS TO ANGELS** — [70] [–]
(12"+=) *(DEFA 8-12)* – She talks to angels (live).
(cd-s++=) *(DEFAC 8)* – Could I've been so blind (live).
(12"pic-d) *(DEFAP 8-12)* – ('A'acoustic) / ('B'acoustic) / Waitin' guilty / Struttin' blues.

Jun 91. (7") *<19245>* **HARD TO HANDLE. / WAITIN' GUILTY** — [–] [26]

Aug 91. (7") *(DEFA 10)* **HARD TO HANDLE. / SISTER LUCK (live)** — [39] [–]
(cd-s+=) *(DEFCD 10)* – Sister Luck (live).
(7"sha-pic-d) *(DEFAP 10)* – Hard to handle / Stare it cold (live).
(12"+=) *(DEFA 10-12)* – Dreams (live).

Oct 91. (7") *(DEFA 13)* **SEEING THINGS. / COULD I'VE BEEN SO BLIND (live)** — [72] [–]
(12"+=) *(DEFAG 13-12)* – She talks to angels (live) / Sister luck (live).
(cd-s) *(DEFAC 13)* – ('A'side) / Hard to handle / Jealous again / Twice as hard.

—— **MARK FORD** (b.13 Apr'66, Los Angeles, Calif.) – guitar (ex-BURNING TREE) repl. CEASE / added **EDDIE HAWRYSCH** – keyboards

Apr 92. (etched-7") *(DEFA 16)* *<18877>* **REMEDY / DARLING OF THE UNDERGROUND PRESS** — [24] Jun92 [48]
(12"+=)(cd-s+=) *(DEFA 16-12)(DEFCD 16)* – Time will tell.

May 92. (cd/c/lp) *(512263-2/-4/-1)* *<26916>* **THE SOUTHERN HARMONY AND MUSICAL COMPANION** — [2] [1]
– Sting me / Remedy / Thorn in my pride / Bad luck blue eyes goodbye / Sometime salvation / Hotel illness / Black moon creeping / No speak, no slave / My morning song / Time will tell. *(re-iss. Dec94 on 'American-BMG' cd/c; 74321 24840-2/-4) (cd re-iss. Feb99 on 'Columbia'; 491791-2) (cd re-iss. Aug01 on 'American'; 499654-2)*

Aug 92. (c-s,cd-s) *<18803>* **THORN IN MY PRIDE. / STING ME** — [–] [80]

Sep 92. (7") *(DEFA 21)* **STING ME. / RAINY DAY WOMEN NOS.12 & 35** — [42] [–]
(cd-s) *(DEFCD 21)* – ('A'side) / She talks to angels / Thorn in my pride / Darling of the underground press.

Nov 92. (7") *(DEFA 23)* **HOTEL ILLNESS. / NO SPEAK, NO SLAVE** — [47] [–]
(12"clear) *(DEFX 23)* – ('A'side) / Words you throw away / Rainy day women Nos.12 & 35.
(cd-s) *(DEFCD 23)* – ('A'side) / Rainy day / (Chris interview).
(cd-s) *(DEFCB 23)* – ('A'side) / Words you throw away / (Rich interview).

Jun 93. (7"/cd-s) *(862202-7/-2)* **REMEDY. / HARD TO HANDLE** — [ ] [–]
(12"+=/cd-s+=) *(862203-1/-2)* – Hotel illness / Jealous again.

—— added **EDDIE HARSCH** (b.27 May'57, Toronto, Ontario) – keyboards

American-BMG / American-BMG

Nov 94. (cd/c/lp) *(74321 23682-2/-4/-1)* *<43000>* **AMORICA** — [8] [11]
– Gone / A conspiracy / High head blues / Cursed diamond / Non-fiction / She gave good sunflower / P.25 London / Ballad in urgency / Wiser time / Downtown money waster / Descending. *(cd+=/c+=)* – Tied up and swallowed. *(cd re-iss. Feb99 on 'Columbia'; 491792-2)*

Jan 95. (7"blue) *(74321 25849-7)* **HIGH HEAD BLUES. / A CONSPIRACY / REMEDY (live)** — [25] [–]
(ext'B'live; 12"+=) *(74321 25849-6)* – Thick'n'thin (live).
(cd-s++=) *(74321 25849-2)* – ('A'extended).
('B'live-cd-s+=) *(74321 25849-5)* – P25 London (live).

Jul 95. (7") *(74321 27267-7)* **WISER TIME. / CHEVROLET** [34] [–]
('A'-Rock mix; cd-s+=) (74321 27267-2) – She talks to angels (acoustic). (cd-s) *(74321 29827-2)* – ('A'acoustic) / Jealous again (acoustic) / Non fiction (acoustic) / Thorn in my pride (acoustic).

Jul 96. (10"pic-d/cd-s) *(74321 39857-1/-2)* **ONE MIRROR TOO MANY. / PIMPERS PARADISE / SOMEBODY'S ON YOUR CASE** [51] [–]

Jul 96. (cd/c) *(74321 38484-2/-4) <43082>* **THREE SNAKES AND ONE CHARM** [17] [15]
– Under a mountain / Good Friday / Nebakanezer / One mirror too many / Blackberry / Girl from a pawnshop / (Only) Halfway to everywhere / Bring on, bring on / How much for your wings? / Let me share the ride / Better when you're not alone / Evil eye. *(cd re-iss. Feb99 on 'Columbia'; 491793-2)*

— COLT + FORD left; repl. by **SVEN PIPPEN** – bass (ex-MARY MY HOPE)

— added touring guitarist **AUDLEY FREED** (ex-CRY OF LOVE)

Columbia Columbia

Oct 98. (c-s) *(666666-4)* **KICKIN' MY HEART AROUND / IT MUST BE OVER** [55] [–]
(cd-s+=) *(666666-2)* – You don't have to go.
(cd-s+=) *(666666-5)* – Diamond ring (version).

Jan 99. (cd/c) *(491669-2/-4) <69361>* **BY YOUR SIDE** [34] [26]
– Go faster / Kickin' my heart around / By your side / Horsehead / Only a fool / Heavy / Welcome to the goodtimes / Go tell the congregation / Diamond ring / Then she said my name / Virtue and vice. *(cd re-iss. Aug01; same)*

Jul 99. (7"/cd-s) *<41902>* **ONLY A FOOL. / WHEN THE NIGHT COMES FALLING FROM THE SKY** [–] [ ]

Jun 00. (cd/c) *<63666>* **GREATEST HITS 1990-1999 – A TRIBUTE TO A WORK IN PROGRESS** (compilation) [–] [ ]
– Jealous again / Twice as hard / Hard to handle / She talks to angels / Remedy / Sting me / Thorn in my pride / Bad luck blue eyes goodbye / A conspiracy / Wiser time / Good Friday / Blackberry / Kickin' my heart around / Go faster / Only a fool / By your side. *(UK-iss.Mar02 on 'Universal'; 314 586789-2)*

— In Jul'00, The BLACK CROWES were credited with JIMMY PAGE on a special 2CD-set, 'LIVE AT THE GREEK' (recorded late '99)

V2 V2

May 01. (cd) *(VVR 1015678) <27091>* **LIONS** [37] [20]
– Midnight from the inside out / Lickin' / Come on / No use lying / Losing my mind / Ozone mama / Greasy grass river / Soul singing / Miracle to me / Young man, old man / Cosmic friend / Cypress tree / Lay it all on me.

Jul 01. (cd-s) *(VVR 501657-3)* **SOUL SINGING / LOVE IS NOW / ALWAYS THE LAST TIME** [ ] [–]
(cd-s) *(VVR 501657-8)* – ('A'side) / Sleepyheads / ('A'live).

— the band split after a farewell tour in 2001

Aug 02. (d-cd) *(VVR 102077-2) <27134>* **LIVE (live)** [ ] [ ]
– Midnight from the inside out / Sting me / Thick n thin / Greasy grass river / Sometimes salvation / Cursed diamond / Miracle to me / Wiser time / Girl from a pawnshop / Cosmic friend / Black moon creeping / High head blues / Title song / She talks to angels / Twice as hard / Lickin' / Soul singing / Hard to handle / Remedy.

— GORMAN departed + group when on hiatus

– compilations, etc. –

Aug 98. (5xcd-box) *Columbia; (C5K 65741)* **SHO 'NUFF: THE COMPLETE BLACK CROWES** [ ] [ ]
(re-iss. Jun02; 586946-2)

Aug 00. (d-cd) *Columbia; (499857-2)* **AMORICA / THREE SNAKES AND ONE CHARM** [ ] [ ]

CHRIS ROBINSON

with **PAUL STACEY** – guitar, multi, producer / etc.

Redline Redline

May 03. (cd) *(308206-2) <70009-2>* **NEW EARTH MUD** [ ] Oct02 [ ]
– Safe in the arms of love / Silver car / Kids that ain't got none / Could you really love me? / Untangle my mind / Fables / Sunday sound / Barefoot by the cherry tree / Katie dear / Ride / Better than the sun / She's on her way. *(ltd-cd+=; 308220-2)* – Silver car (live) / Sunday sound (live) / Untangle my mind (live). *(w/ dvd++=)* – Mother of stone (live) / Mint tea (live) / Beginners (live) / Sinners (live).

— added **GEORGE REIFF** – bass

Vector Vector

Feb 05. (cd) *<(2 48821>)* **THIS MAGNIFICENT DISTANCE** [ ] Jun04 [ ]
– 40 days / Girl on the mountain / Mother of stone / Train robbers / Like a tumbleweed in Eden / When the cold wind blows at the dark edge of night / ...If you see California / The never empty table / Eagles on the highway / Surgical glove / Sea of love / Piece of land.

RICH ROBINSON

with **JOE MAGISTRO** – drums / + guests

Compadre Keyhole

Sep 04. (cd) *<(591587-2)>* **PAPER** [ ] Aug04 [ ]
– Yesterday I saw you / Enemy / Leave it alone / Know me / Forgiven song / Veil / When you will / Places / Begin / Falling away / Baby / Oh no / Answers / It's over.

□ BLACK GRAPE (see under ⇒ HAPPY MONDAYS)

□ BLACKMORE'S RAINBOW (see under ⇒ RAINBOW)

BLACK REBEL MOTORCYCLE CLUB

Formed: San Francisco, California, USA . . . late '98 by high school musicians ROBERT LEVON BEEN and PETER HAYES (the latter a former member of BRIAN JONESTOWN MASSACRE), eventually recruiting drummer NICK JAGO from the garage club scene around the city's Bay Area. If the film 'The Wild One' – from which BLACK REBEL MOTORCYCLE CLUB had grabbed their name – had been soundtracked by this particular group, all proverbial hell would have ensued. After extensively touring between San Francisco and L.A., the trio of leather-clad, brooding dirty rock'n'rollers decided to issue a self-produced demo of thirteen tracks, which finally wormed its way onto the A&R desk of 'Virgin' records. The group were signed in late 2000, and headed off on a tour with the DANDY WARHOLS across America, pulling in much praise and fanbase from the college circuit. They arrived on the shores of Britain just in time to feel the hype of the new garage revival (the STROKES et al), and were thoroughly lauded by the NME and rock stars such as NOEL GALLAGHER and JIM REID. This was even before the debut album, 'B.R.M.C.' (2001) was released, so one can imagine the commotion when it turned out to be one of the finest rock'n'roll albums of the last decade. Fuzzy guitar, jiving choruses, big hairy sweaty percussion – it had it all. The LP entered the Top 20 and they sold out an entire tour before going on the road with OASIS. The defiantly titled 'TAKE THEM ON, ON YOUR OWN' (2003), took them into the UK Top 3 (US Top 50), defragging the vocals and letting rip on high-octane protest songs such as 'STOP' (a UK Top 20 hit). Such ill communication didn't stop them getting dropped by 'Virgin', and when they next showed up on 'R.C.A.', BRMC were more folk-club than motorbike club. In the spirit of fellow rock'n'roll believers PRIMAL SCREAM, BRMC let their roots flag fly on 'HOWL' (2005), an album which could have been recorded by different artists in a different decade: the title referenced Allen Ginsburg, HAYES sang like a Beat-fevered bard and the band made like, well.. the BAND, at least in spirit. Chart wise, the born-again makeover didn't do much harm either, with the vintage blues, 'AIN'T NO EASY WAY', almost making the Top 20, and the album itself within howling distance of the UK Top 10.

Album rating: B.R.M.C. (*8) / TAKE THEM ON, ON YOUR OWN (*7) / HOWL (*6)

PETER HAYES – vocals, guitar, bass, harmonica, keyboards (ex-BRIAN JONESTOWN MASSACRE) / **ROBERT LEVON BEEN** – vocals, bass, guitar, keyboards (ex-BEGGARS) / **NICK JAGO** – drums, percussion not iss. own label

Feb 01. (d7") *<none>* **RED EYES AND TEARS / SCREAMING GUN. / AS SURE AS THE SUN / WHITE PALMS** – promo –

Mar 01. (d7") *<none>* **RIFLES. / AWAKE // SPREAD YOUR LOVE. / AT MY DOOR** – promo –

May 01. (d7") *<none>* **LOVE BURNS. / DOWN HERE // TOO REAL. / SALVATION** – promo –

Virgin Virgin

Oct 01. (d7") *(VUS 224)* **WHATEVER HAPPENED TO MY ROCK'N'ROLL (PUNK SONG). / RED EYES AND TEARS // FAIL-SAFE. / DOWN HERE** Nov01
(cd-s+=) *(VUSCD 224)* – ('A'-video).

Nov 01. (cd-ep) *<none>* **SCREAMING GUN EP** – promo –
– Fail-safe / Down here / At my door / Screaming gun / TV loop (down deep).

Jan 02. (cd/d-lp) *(CDVUS/VUSLP 207)* *<10045>* **BLACK REBEL MOTORCYCLE CLUB** 25 Apr01
– Love burns / Red eyes and tears / Whatever happened to my rock'n'roll (punk song) / Awake / White palms / As sure as the sun / Rifles / Too real / Spread your love / Head up high / Salvation.

Jan 02. (7") *(VUS 234)* **LOVE BURNS. / AT MY DOOR** 37 –
(cd-s) *(VUSCD 234)* – ('A') / Screaming gun / Rifles.

May 02. (7") *(VUS 245)* **SPREAD YOUR LOVE. / TONIGHT'S WITH YOU** 27 –
(cd-s+=) *(VUSDX 245)* – Simple words.
(cd-s) *(VUSCD 245)* – ('A'side) / The weight is more / Loaded gun.

Sep 02. (7") *(VUS 257)* **WHATEVER HAPPENED TO MY ROCK'N'ROLL (PUNK SONG). / RIFLES (live)** 46 –
(cd-s) *(VUSCD 257)* – ('A'side) / Shuffle your feet (XFM session) / ('A'-video).

Aug 03. (7") *(VUS 273)* **STOP. / HIGH – LOW** 19 –
(cd-s+=) *(VUSCD 273)* – Take them on on your own.

Aug 03. (cd/d-lp) *(CDVUS/VUSLP 245)* *<80095/91618>* **TAKE THEM ON, ON YOUR OWN** 3 Sep03 47
– Stop / Six barrel shotgun / We're all in love / In like the rose / Ha ha high babe / Generation / Shade of blue / U.S. government / And I'm aching / Suddenly / Rise or fall / Heart + soul.

Nov 03. (7") *(VUS 279)* **WE'RE ALL IN LOVE. / WAITING HERE** 45 –
(cd-s+=) *(VUSCDX 279)* – Abstract dragon / ('A'-video).

Echo Red Ink

Aug 05. (7") *(ECS 175)* **AIN'T NO EASY WAY. / STILL SUSPICION HOLDS YOU TIGHT** 21 –
(cd-s) *(ECSCX 175)* – Grind my bones.

Aug 05. (cd) *(ECHCD 67)* *<71601>* **HOWL** 14 90
– Shuffle your feet / Howl / Devil's waitin' / Ain't no easy way / Still suspicion holds you tight / Fault line / Promise / Weight of the world / Restless sinner / Gospel song / Complicated situation / Sympathetic noose / The line.

Feb 06. (cd-ep) *<81250>* **HOWL SESSIONS** – promo –
– Grind my bones / Mercy / Wishing well / Steal a ride / Feel it now / Pretend.

☐ BLACK ROSE (see under ⇒ CHER)

BLACK SABBATH

Formed: Aston, Birmingham, England . . . early 1969 by TONY IOMMI, OZZY OSBOURNE, TERRY 'GEEZER' BUTLER and BILL WARD, out of the jazz fusion combo, EARTH (IOMMI had also filled in as JETHRO TULL guitarist for a few weeks). Taking the name, BLACK SABBATH from a horror film adapted from a Dennis Wheatley novel of the same name, they signed to 'Fontana' in late '69. After a flop single, 'EVIL WOMAN (DON'T PLAY YOUR GAMES WITH ME)', they were shunted to the more progressive 'Vertigo' label in early 1970. The inimitable SABBATH sound was stunningly defined on the opening title cut from the self-titled debut album, the record storming into the UK Top 10. Occult influenced, BLACK SABBATH fused IOMMI's deceptively basic, doom-laden guitar riffs with OZZY's (much-mimicked since) banshee shriek. Lyrically morbid, with futuristic/medieval themes, tracks like 'THE WIZARD' highlighting their tongue-in-cheek protest against God! The band then branded their name on the nation's musical consciousness with a Top 5 hit single!!! 'PARANOID', a skullcrushing but strangely melodic track which remains one of the most (in)famous metal songs of all time. Not surprisingly, the album of the same name (also in 1970!) bludgeoned its way straight to No.1, a metal classic rammed full of blinding tracks, not least the stop-start dynamics of 'WAR PIGS', the spiralling melancholy of 'IRON MAN' and the doom-driven 'FAIRIES WEAR BOOTS' ("and you gotta believe me!"). Their third set, 'MASTER OF REALITY' (1971), was another dark jewel in the SABBATH legend, softer tracks like 'EMBRYO' and 'ORCHID' sledgehammered into oblivion by mogadon monsters, 'CHILDREN OF THE GRAVE' and 'SWEET LEAF'. The last two years had witnessed SABBATH taking America by the throat, 'VOL. 4' in '72 loosening the grip somewhat, although it did boast a classic rock ballad, 'CHANGES'. Returning to more pseudo-satanic territory, 'SABBATH BLOODY SABBATH' was another milestone, its demonic credibility nevertheless diminished somewhat by the fact that the instrumental, 'FLUFF', was subsequently adopted by namesake Radio One DJ ALAN FREEMAN on his Saturday afternoon prog-rock show! Returning from a year-long sabbatical, the release of the largely disappointing sixth album, 'SABOTAGE', was indicative of the cracks appearing in the IOMMI/OSBOURNE relationship. However, the album did contain two brilliant opening salvos, 'HOLE IN THE SKY' and 'SYMPTOM OF THE UNIVERSE'. The beginning of the end came with the ill-advised experimentation of 'TECHNICAL ECSTASY' (1976), an album which led to OZZY's brief departure (his supernatural consumption of the demon drink was also a factor). However, a newly rehabilited OSBOURNE was back at the helm for 1978's 'NEVER SAY DIE', sales of which were boosted by a near UK Top 20 title track. In 1979, OZZY took off on a solo career, leaving behind IOMMI, BUTLER and WARD to pick up the pieces in LA (where the band had relocated). With a new manager, Don Arden, in tow, they finally recruited American, RONNIE JAMES DIO (from RAINBOW), after auditioning many would-be OZZY clones. This proved to be SABBATH's blackest period, pitch in fact, with the release of two mediocre albums in the early 80's, 'HEAVEN AND HELL' and 'MOB RULES'. Things went from bad to ridiculous in 1983, when DIO was substituted by another hard-rock frontman celebrity, IAN GILLAN, taken straight from the proverbial heart of DEEP PURPLE. The resulting, ironically-titled album, 'BORN AGAIN', was an exercise in heavy-metal cliche, although it still managed to hit the UK Top 5. The original SABBATH reunited on the 13th of July '85 for a rather disappointing one-off performance at the 'Live Aid' concert in Philadelphia. In 1986, IOMMI was in full control once more, even giving his name co-billing on the appalling, 'SEVENTH STAR' set. Astonishingly, SABBATH were given another chance by Miles Copeland's 'I.R.S.' records, IOMMI having found a new vocalist, TONY MARTIN, also securing the services of veteran drummer, COZY POWELL (ex-everyband) to boost the sales of their comeback album, 'HEADLESS CROSS' (1989). The 1990's saw IOMMI and group trying to relive past glories, the 1995 album 'FORBIDDEN' even including a vocal piece from US rapper, ICE-T. At the turn of 1997/8, IOMMI and OZZY had finally settled their differences, coming together in a much heralded SABBATH reunion, which will apparently result in a comeback album, 20 years too late for some! IOMMI finally released his first – eponymous – solo album in 2000, an all-star project that had the cream of the rock/metal world queuing up to work with the legendary riffmeister. Alongside OZZY himself, guest vocalists included HENRY ROLLINS, SKIN (of SKUNK ANANSIE), DAVE GROHL (NIRVANA/FOO FIGHTERS), PHIL ANSELMO (PANTERA), BILLY CORGAN – again! – (SMASHING PUMPKINS), IAN ASTBURY (CULT), PETER STEELE (TYPE O

NEGATIVE), SERJ TANKIAN (SYSTEM OF A DOWN) and even BILLY IDOL while the likes of MATT CAMERON (PEARL JAM), BEN SHEPHERD (SOUNDGARDEN) and even BRIAN MAY (!!?!?) lent their musical talents. If not exactly a classic in the BLACK SABBATH mould, the record was certainly diverse enough to offer most fans some value for money. Almost two decades on from their initial collaboration on 'SABBATH's 'SEVENTH STAR', IOMMI and former DEEP PURPLE man GLENN HUGHES released a full-scale joint solo offering, 'FUSED' (2005), a power-trio affair anchored by session drummer KENNY ARONOFF.

• **Footnote:** Not a band for the easily-led and weak-minded, as the blame for teenage suicide attempts was always laid at their darkened door. Nevertheless, their influence on the worldwide metal scene is inestimable; as well as playing grunge before it was even invented, the likes of METALLICA et al, owe SABBATH a massive debt. • **Songwriters:** Mainly group compositions. Covered EVIL WOMAN (DON'T PLAY YOUR GAMES WITH ME) (Crow) / WARNING (Aynsley Dunbar).

Album rating: BLACK SABBATH (*8) / PARANOID (*9) / MASTER OF REALITY (*9) / VOLUME 4 (*8) / SABBATH BLOODY SABBATH (*8) / SABOTAGE (*7) / WE SOLD OUR SOULS FOR ROCK'N'ROLL compilation (*8) / TECHNICAL ECSTASY (*5) / NEVER SAY DIE (*5) / HEAVEN AND HELL (*7) / LIVE AT LAST (*4) / MOB RULES (*6) / LIVE EVIL (*7) / BORN AGAIN (*5) / SEVENTH STAR (*4) / THE ETERNAL IDOL (*4) / HEADLESS CROSS (*6) / BLACKEST SABBATH compliation (*7) / TYR (*5) / DEHUMANIZER (*5) / CROSS PURPOSES (*5) / FORBIDDEN (*4) / REUNION (*6) / THE BEST OF BLACK SABBATH compilation (*8) / Tony Iommi: IOMMI (*6) / FUSED w/ Glenn Hughes (*6)

OZZY OSBOURNE (b. JOHN, 3 Dec'48) – vocals / **TONY IOMMI** (b.19 Feb'48) – guitars / **TERRY 'GEEZER' BUTLER** (b.17 Jul'49) – bass / **BILL WARD** (b. 5 May'48) – drums

Fontana not iss.

Jan 70. (7") *(TF 1067)* **EVIL WOMAN, DON'T PLAY YOUR GAMES WITH ME. / WICKED WORLD** [ ] [–]

Vertigo Warners

Feb 70. (lp) *(VO 6)* <1871> **BLACK SABBATH** [8] Jul70 [23]
– Black Sabbath / The wizard / Behind the wall of sleep / N.I.B. / Evil woman, don't play your games with me / Sleeping village / Warning. *(re-iss. Jan74 on 'W.W.A.'; WWA 006) (re-iss. Jun80 + Nov85 on 'NEMS'; NEL 6002) (cd-iss. Dec86+=; NELCD 6002)* – Wicked world. *(cd/c re-iss. Oct96/Oct97 on 'Essential'; ESM CD/MC 301) (lp re-iss. Jan97 on 'Original Recordings'; ORRLP 004) (cd re-iss. Sep00 on 'Essential'; CMTCD 003)*

Mar 70. (7") *(V2)* **EVIL WOMAN (DON'T PLAY YOUR GAMES WITH ME). / WICKED WORLD** [ ] [–]

Aug 70. (7") *(6059 010)* *<7437>* **PARANOID. / THE WIZARD** [4] Nov70 [61]

Sep 70. (lp) *(6360 011)* *<1887>* **PARANOID** [1] Feb71 [12]
– War pigs / Paranoid / Planet Caravan / Iron man / Electric funeral / Hand of doom / Rat salad / Fairies wear boots. *(re-iss. Jan74 on 'W.W.A.'; WWA 007) (re-iss. Jun80 on 'NEMS'; NEL 6003); hit UK 54. (re-iss. Nov85 on 'NEMS' lp/pic-lp/c/cd; NEL/NEP/NELMC/NELCD 6003) (re-iss. Jun89 on 'Vertigo' lp/c/cd+=; 832701-1/-4/-2)* – Tomorrow's world (live). *(cd/c re-iss. Feb96/Oct97 on 'Essential'; ESM CD/MC 302) (cd re-iss. Sep00 on 'Essential'; CMTCD 004)* – hit No.63 Jul02

Aug 71. (lp) *(6360 050)* *<2562>* **MASTER OF REALITY** [5] [8]
– Sweet leaf / After forever / Embryo / Children of the grave / Orchid / Lord of this world / Solitude / Into the void. *(re-iss. Jan74 on 'W.W.A.'; WWA 008) (re-iss. Nov80 on 'NEMS'; NEL 6004) (re-iss. Nov85 on 'NEMS' lp/c/cd; NEL/+MC/CD 6004) (re-iss. cd Jun89 on 'Vertigo' lp/c/cd+=; 832707-1/-4/-2)* – Killing yourself to live (live). *(cd/c re-iss. Feb96/Oct97 on 'Essential'; ESM CD/MC 303) (cd re-iss. Sep00 on 'Essential'; CMTCD 005)*

Jan 72. (7") *<7530>* **IRON MAN. / ELECTRIC FUNERAL** [–] [52]
<re-iss. 1974; 7802>

Sep 72. (7") *(6059 061)* *<7625>* **TOMORROW'S DREAM. / LAGUNA SUNRISE** [ ] [ ]

Sep 72. (lp) *(6360 071)* *<2602>* **BLACK SABBATH VOL.4** [8] Oct72 [13]
– Wheels of confusion / Tomorrow's dream / Changes / FX / Supernaut / Snowblind / Cornucopia / Laguna sunrise / St. Vitus' dance / Under the sun. *(re-iss. Jan74 on 'W.W.A.'; WWA 009) (re-iss. Jun80 on 'NEMS'; NEL 6005) (c/cd-iss. 1988+=; NEL MC/CD 6005)* – Children of the grave (live). *(cd/c re-iss. Feb96/Oct97 on 'Essential'; ESM CD/MC 304) (cd re-iss. Sep00 on 'Essential'; MCTCD 006)*

W.W.A. Warners

Oct 73. (7") *(WWS 002)* *<7764>* **SABBATH BLOODY SABBATH. / CHANGES** [ ] [ ]

Dec 73. (lp) *(WWA 005)* *<2695>* **SABBATH BLOODY SABBATH** [4] Jan74 [11]
– Sabbath bloody sabbath / A national acrobat / Fluff / Sabbra cadabra / Killing yourself to live / Who are you? / Looking for today / Spiral architect. *(w-drawn copies were on 'Vertigo'; 6360 115) (re-iss. Jun80 on 'NEMS'; NEL 6017) (re-iss. Nov85 c/cd; NEL MC/CD 6017) (re-iss. Jun89 on 'Vertigo' lp/c/cd+=; 832700-1/-4/-2)* – Cornucopia (live). *(cd/c re-iss. Feb96/Oct97 on 'Essential'; ESM CD/MC 305)*

N.E.M.S. Warners

Sep 75. (lp) *(9119 001)* *<2822>* **SABOTAGE** [7] [28]
– Hole in the sky / Don't start (too late) / Symptom of the universe / Megalomania / Thrill of it all / Supertzar / Am I going insane (radio) / The writ. *(re-iss. Nov80 on 'NEMS'; NEL 6018) (re-iss. Nov85 c/cd; NEL MC/CD 6018) (re-iss. Jun89 on 'Vertigo' lp/c/cd+=; 832706-1/-4/-2)* – Sweat leaf (live). *(cd/c re-iss. Feb96/Oct97 on 'Essential'; ESM CD/MC 306)*

Feb 76. (d-lp) *(6641 335)* *<2923>* **WE SOLD OUR SOULS FOR ROCK'N'ROLL** (compilation) [35] [48]
– Black sabbath / The wizard / Warning / Paranoid / Wicked world / Tomorrow's dream / Fairies wear boots / Changes / Sweet leaf / Children of the grave / Sabbath bloody sabbath / Am I going insane (radio) / Laguna sunrise / Snowblind / N.I.B. *(re-iss. Nov80; NELD 101) (re-iss. Apr86 on 'Raw Power' d-lp/c/cd; RAW LP/TC/CD 017) (re-iss. Dec90 on 'Castle' cd/c/d-lp; CCS CD/MC/LP 249) (cd re-iss. Jan98 on 'Essential'; ESDCD 605) <(d-cd iss.Oct04 on 'Sanctuary'; SMDDD 078)>*

Feb 76. (7") *(6165 300)* **AM I GOING INSANE (RADIO). / HOLE IN THE SKY** [ ] [ ]

Vertigo Warners

Oct 76. (lp) *(9102 750)* *<2969>* **TECHNICAL ECSTASY** [13] [51]
– Back street kids / You won't change me / It's alright / Gypsy / All moving parts (stand still) / Rock'n'roll doctor / She's gone / Dirty women. *(re-iss. Aug83 lp/c; PRICE/PRIMC 40) (cd-iss. Jun89; 838224-2) (cd/c re-iss. Jan96/Oct97 on 'Essential'; ESM CD/MC 328)*

Nov 76. (7") *<8315>* **IT'S ALRIGHT. / ROCK'N'ROLL DOCTOR** [–] [ ]

—— Late '77 OZZY leaves and is briefly repl. by **DAVE WALKER** (ex-SAVOY BROWN) Early 1978 **OZZY** returned.

May 78. (7") *(SAB 001)* **NEVER SAY DIE. / SHE'S GONE** [21] [–]

Sep 78. (7",7"purple) *(SAB 002)* **HARD ROAD. / SYMPTOM OF THE UNIVERSE** [33] [–]

Oct 78. (lp) *(9102 751)* *<3186>* **NEVER SAY DIE!** [12] [69]
– Never say die / Johnny Blade / Juniors eyes / Hard road / Shock wave / Air dance / Over to you / Breakout / Swinging the chain. *(re-iss. May83 lp/c; PRICE/PRIMC 9) (re-iss. Sep93 on 'Spectrum' cd/c;) (cd/c re-iss. Jan96/Oct97 on 'Essential'; ESM CD/MC 329)*

—— **RONNIE JAMES DIO** (b.1950, Cortland, N.J.) – vocals (ex-(RITCHIE BLACKMORE'S) RAINBOW, ex-ELF etc.) repl.OZZY who went solo.

Apr 80. (lp)(c) *(9102 752)(7231 402)* *<3372>* **HEAVEN AND HELL** [9] Jun80 [28]
– Neon knights / Children of the sea / Lady evil / Heaven and Hell / Wishing well / Die young / Walk away / Lonely is the word. *(re-iss. May83 lp/c; PRICE/PRIMC 10) (cd-iss. 1987; 830171-2) (re-iss. May93 on 'Spectrum' cd/c;) (cd/c re-iss. Jan96/Oct97 on 'Essential'; ESM CD/MC 330) (cd/c re-iss. Apr96 on 'Raw Power'; RAW CD/MC 104)*

Jun 80. (7") *(SAB 3)* **NEON KNIGHTS. / CHILDREN OF THE SEA** [22] [–]

Jul 80. (7") *<49549>* **LADY EVIL. / CHILDREN OF THE SEA** [–] [ ]

Nov 80. (7"/ext.12") *(SAB 4/+12)* **DIE YOUNG. / HEAVEN AND HELL (live)** [41] [–]

—— **VINNIE APPICE** (b.Staten Island, N.Y.) – drums, percussion repl. WARD

Oct 81. (7"/12") *(SAB 5/+12)* **MOB RULES. / DIE YOUNG** [46] [–]

Nov 81. (lp/c) *(6302/7144 119)* *<3605>* **MOB RULES** [12] [29]
– Turn up the night / Voodoo / The sign of the southern cross / E5150 / The mob rules / Country girl / Slippin' away / Falling off the edge of the world / Over and over. *(re-iss. Jan85 lp/c; PRICE/PRIMC 77) (cd/c re-iss. Jan96/Oct97 on 'Essential'; ESM CD/MC 332)*

Feb 82. (7")(12"/12"pic-d) *(SAB 6)(SABP 6/+12)* **TURN UP THE NIGHT. / LONELY IS THE WORD** [37] [–]

Jan 83. (d-lp/d-c) *(SAB/+M 10)* *<23742>* **LIVE EVIL (live)** [13] [37]
– E5150 / Neon knights / N.I.B. / Children of the sea / Voodoo / Black sabbath / War pigs / Iron man / Mob rules / Heaven and Hell / The sign of the southern cross / Heaven and Hell (continued) / Paranoid / Children of the grave / Fluff. *(re-iss. Apr86 lp/c; PRID/+C 11) (cd/c re-iss. Apr96/Oct97 on 'Essential'; ESM CD/MC 333)*

—— **IAN GILLAN** (b.19 Aug'45, Hounslow, England) – vocals (ex-DEEP PURPLE, ex-GILLAN) repl. RONNIE who formed DIO. **BILL WARD** –

drums returned replacing VINNIE who also joined DIO. **BEV BEVAN** – drums (ex-ELECTRIC LIGHT ORCHESTRA) repl. BILL, only originals in band were IOMMI and BUTLER

Sep 83. (lp/c) *(VERL/+C 8)* *<23978>* **BORN AGAIN** [4] [39]
– Trashed / Stonehenge / Disturbing the priest / The dark / Zero the hero / Digital bitch / Born again / Hot line / Keep it warm. *(cd/c re-iss. Apr96/Oct97 on 'Essential'; ESM CD/MC 334)*

Oct 83. (7") *<29434>* **STONEHENGE. / THRASHED** [-] [ ]

— **DAVE DONATO** – vocals repl. GILLAN who rejoined DEEP PURPLE

— **TONY IOMMI** recruited **GLENN HUGHES** – vocals (ex-DEEP PURPLE, etc.) repl. DONATO / **DAVE SPITZ** (b. New York City) – bass repl. BUTLER / **ERIC SINGER** (b.Cleveland, Ohio) – drums repl. BEVAN / added **GEOFF NICHOLLS** (b.Birmingham) – keyboards (ex-QUARTZ) had toured '79.

Feb 86. (lp/c)(cd; as BLACK SABBATH featuring TONY IOMMI) *(VERH/+C 29)(826704-2)* *<25337>* **SEVENTH STAR** [27] [78]
– In for the kill / No stranger to love / Turn to stone / Sphinx (the guardian) / Seventh star / Danger zone / Heart like a wheel / Angry heart / In memory. *(cd/c re-iss. Apr96/Oct97 on 'Essential'; ESM CD/MC 335)*

— **TONY IOMMI** again added **BOB DAISLEY** – bass / **BEV BEVAN** – percussion / **TONY MARTIN** – vocals repl. HUGHES

Nov 87. (lp/c)(cd) *(VERH/+C 51)(832708-2)* *<25548>* **THE ETERNAL IDOL** [66] [ ]
– The shining / Ancient warrior / Hard life to love / Glory ride / Born to lose / Scarlet Pimpernel / Lost forever / The eternal idol. *(cd+=)* – Nightmare. *(cd/c re-iss. Apr96/Oct97 on 'Essential'; ESM CD/MC 336)*

— **IOMMI + MARTIN** recruited **COZY POWELL** – drums (ex-RAINBOW, ex-ELP) **LAURENCE COTTLE** – bass (on session)

I.R.S. I.R.S.

Apr 89. (7"/7"s) *(EIRS/+CB 107)* **HEADLESS CROSS. / CLOAK AND DAGGER** [62] [ ]
(12"+=/12"w-poster+=) *(EIRST/+PB 107)* – ('A'extended).

Apr 89. (lp/pic-lp/c/cd) *(EIRSA/+PD/C/CD 1002)* *<82002>* **HEADLESS CROSS** [31] [ ]
– The gates of Hell / Headless cross / Devil & daughter / When death calls / Kill in the spirit world / Call of the wild / Black moon / Nightwing. *(pic-lp+=)* – Cloak and dagger. *(re-iss. cd Apr94;) (cd re-iss. Aug99 on 'E.M.I.'; 521299-2)*

Jun 89. (one-sided; 7"/7"s/7"pic-d) *(EIRS/+B/PD 115)* **DEVIL AND DAUGHTER** [ ] [ ]
(12"+=) *(EIRST 115)* – (15 minute interview).

— **NEIL MURRAY** – bass (ex-VOW WOW, etc.) joined mid'89 repl.COTTLE

Aug 90. (lp/pic-lp/c/cd) *(EIRSA/+PD/C/CD 1038)* *<X2-13049>* **TYR** [24] [ ]
– Anno Mundi / The law maker / Jerusalem / The sabbath stones / The battle of Tyr / Odin's court / Valhalla / Feels good to me / Heaven in black. *(pic-lp+=)* – Paranoid (live) / Heaven and Hell (live). *(re-iss. cd Apr94) (cd re-iss. Aug99 on 'E.M.I.'; 521298-2)*

Sep 90. (7"/c-s) *(EIRS/C 148)* **FEELS GOOD TO ME. / PARANOID (live)** [ ] [ ]
(12"+=/cd-s+=) *(EIRS T/CD 148)* – Heaven and Hell (live).

— the 1981-83 line-up re-formed Oct91, **IOMMI, GEEZER, VINNIE** and **R.JAMES DIO**

I.R.S. Reprise

Jun 92. (lp/c/cd) *(EIRS A/C/CD 1064)* *<26965>* **DEHUMANIZER** [28] [44]
– Computer god / After all (the dead) / TV crimes / Letters from Earth / Masters of insanity / Time machine / Sins of the father / Too late / I / Buried alive. *(re-iss. cd Apr94 & Feb99; same)*

Jun 92. (7"pic-d) *(EIRSP 178)* **TV CRIMES. / LETTERS FROM EARTH** [33] [-]
(12"pic-d+=) *(12EIRSPD 178)* – Mob rules (live).
(cd-s+=) *(CDEIRS 178)* – Paranoid (live).
(cd-s+=) *(CDEIRSS 178)* – Heaven and Hell (live).

— **TONY MARTIN** returned on vocals to repl. DIO

— **BOBBY RONDINELLI** – drums (ex-RAINBOW) repl. APPICE

Feb 94. (cd/c/lp) *(EIRS CD/TC/LP 1067)* *<13222>* **CROSS PURPOSES** [41] [ ]
– I witness / Cross of thorns / Psychophobia / Virtual death / Immaculate deception / Dying for love / Back to Eden / The hand that rocks the cradle / Cardinal sin / Evil eye.

— The 1990 line-up was once again in force although COZY departed once again after below to be repl. by the returning RONDINELLI

I.R.S. Capitol

Jun 95. (cd/c) *(EIRS CD/TC 1072)* *<30620>* **FORBIDDEN** [71] [ ]
– The illusion of power / Get a grip / Can't get close enough / Shaking off the chains / I won't cry for you / Guilty as hell / Sick and tired / Rusty angels / Forbidden / Kiss of death.

— the original BLACK SABBATH reformed for live gigs

Epic Epic

Oct 98. (d-cd/d-c) *(491954-2/-4)* *<69115>* **REUNION** (live late '97) [41] [11]
– War pigs / Beyond the wall of sleep / N.I.B. / Fairies wear boots / Electric funeral / Sweet leaf / Spiral architect / Into the void / Snowblind / Sabbath bloody sabbath / Orchid – Lord of this world / Dirty women / Black sabbath / Iron man / Children of the grave / Paranoid / Psycho man (studio) / Selling my soul (studio). *(also d-cd; 491954-9)*

N.M.C. not iss.

Dec 99. (cd-ep) *(PILOT 49)* **BLACK MASS** [ ] [-]
– Paranoid / Black sabbath / Iron man / Blue suede shoes.

– compilations etc. –

on 'NEMS' / 'Warners' unless otherwise stated

Dec 77. (lp) *(NEL 6009)* **BLACK SABBATH'S GREATEST HITS** [ ] [ ]
(re-iss. Nov90 on 'Castle' lp/c/cd+=; CLA LP/MC/CD 200)

Aug 78. (7") *(NES 121)* **PARANOID. / SNOWBLIND** [ ] [-]

Jun 80. (lp) *(BS 001)* **LIVE AT LAST** (live) [5] [ ]
– Tomorrow's dream / Sweet leaf / Killing yourself to live / Cornucopia / Snowblind / Children of the grave / War pigs / Wicked world / Paranoid. *(cd-iss. Aug96 on 'Essential'; ESMCD 331) (<d-cd re-iss. Sep02 as 'PAST LIVES' on 'Sanctuary'+=; SANDP 138 / 84561>)* – Hand of doom / Hole in the sky / Symptom of the universe / Megalomania / Iron man / Black sabbath / N.I.B. / Behind the wall of sleep / Fairies wear boots.

Aug 80. (7") *(BSS 101)* **PARANOID. / SABBATH BLOODY SABBATH** [14] [-]

Aug 82. (7"pic-d) *(NEP 1)* **PARANOID. / IRON MAN** [ ] [ ]
(12"+=) *(12NEX 01)* – Fairies wear boots / War pigs.

Aug 85. (d-lp/c) *Castle; (CCS LP/MC 109)* **THE COLLECTION** [ ] [-]
(cd-iss. 1986; CCSCD 109)

Dec 85. (7xlp-box) *Castle; (BSBOX 01)* **BOXED SET** [ ] [-]
– (all albums with OZZY)

Jun 86. (12"ep) *That's Original; (TOF 101)* **CLASSIC CUTS FROM THE VAULTS** [ ] [-]
– Paranoid / War pigs / Iron man / Black sabbath.

Jun 88. (d-lp/d-c/d-cd) *That's Original; (TFO LP/MC/CD 10)* **SABBATH BLOODY SABBATH / BLACK SABBATH** [ ] [-]

Nov 88. (3"cd-ep) *Castle; (CD 3-5)* **BLACK SABBATH LIMITED EDITION** [ ] [-]
– Paranoid / Iron man / War pigs.

Dec 88. (6xcd-box) *Castle; (BSBCD 001)* **THE BLACK SABBATH CD COLLECTION** [ ] [-]

Mar 89. (cd-ep) *Old Gold; (OG 6129)* **PARANOID / ELECTRIC FUNERAL / SABBATH BLOODY SABBATH** [ ] [-]

Nov 89. (d-lp/c/cd) *Vertigo; (838 818-1/-4/-2)* **BLACKEST SABBATH** [ ] [ ]

Dec 89. (d-lp/d-c/cd) *Masterpiece; (TRK LP/MC/CD 103)* **BACKTRACKIN' (20th ANNIVERSARY EDITION)** [ ] [-]

Mar 90. (7") *Old Gold; (OG 9467)* **PARANOID. / IRON MAN** [ ] [-]

Oct 90. (cd/c/lp) *Castle; (CCS CD/MC/LP 199)* **THE BLACK SABBATH COLLECTION VOL.II** [ ] [-]

May 91. (3xcd/5xlp-box) *Essential; (ESB CD/LP 142)* **THE OZZY OSBOURNE YEARS** [ ] [-]
– (features first 6 albums)

Sep 94. (cd/c) *Spectrum; (550720-2/-4)* **IRON MAN** [ ] [-]

1995. (cd-box with video) *P.M.I.; (7243-8-30069-2)* **CROSS PURPOSES LIVE (live 1994)** [ ] [-]

Sep 95. (cd/c) *Raw Power; (RAW CD/MC 104)* **BETWEEN HEAVEN AND HELL (THE BEST OF BLACK SABBATH)** [ ] [-]

Nov 95. (3xcd-box) *E.M.I.; (CDOMB 014)* **THE ORIGINALS** [ ] [-]
– (HEADLESS CROSS / TYR / DEHUMANISER)

Apr 96. (cd/c) *Essential; (EIRS CD/TC 1076)* **THE SABBATH STONES** [ ] [-]

Nov 96. (4xcd-box) *Essential; (ESFCD 419)* **UNDER THE WHEELS OF CONFUSION** [ ] [-]

Oct 98. (3xcd-box) *Essential; (ESMBX 300)* **BLACK SABBATH / PARANOID / MASTER OF REALITY** [ ] [-]

Oct 98. (3xcd-box) *Essential; (ESMBX 301)* **TECHNICAL ECSTASY / NEVER SAY DIE / HEAVEN AND HELL** [ ] [–]

Jun 00. (d-cd/q-lp) *Raw Power; (RAW DD/LP 145)* **THE BEST OF BLACK SABBATH** [24] [–]

Sep 00. (6xcd-s-box) *Essential; (CMKBX 002)* **THE SINGLES BOX SET** [ ] [–]

Oct 02. (d-cd) *Rhino; <(8122 73772-2)>* **SYMPTOM OF THE UNIVERSE: THE ORIGINAL BLACK SABBATH 1970-1978** [ ] [ ]

Apr 04. (4xcd-box) *Rhino; (<8122 73923-2)>* **BLACK BOX: THE COMPLETE ORIGINAL BLACK SABBATH 1970-1978** [ ] [ ]

Nov 04. (6x7"-box) *Earmark; (41031)* **THE SINGLES** [ ] [–]

Jan 06. (d-cd) *Sanctuary; (SANDD 325) <367>* **THE BEST OF BLACK SABBATH** [ ] Apr05 [ ]

Mar 06. (cd) *R.R.W.; <73365-2>* **GREATEST HITS 1970-1978** [–] [96]

TONY IOMMI

with **BILL WARD** plus guests vocalists (see below) + **MATT CAMERON** + **JOHN TEMPESTA** + **KENNY ARONOFF** – drums / **BEN SHEPHERD** + **LAURENCE COTTLE** – bass / **BRIAN MAY** – guitar

Priority Priority

Oct 00. (cd) *(CDPTY 207) <27857>* **IOMMI** [ ] [ ]
– Laughing man (in the devil mask) (w/ HENRY ROLLINS) / Meat (w/ SKIN) / Goodbye lament (w/ DAVE GROHL) / Time is mine (w/ PHIL ANSELMO) / Patterns (w/ SERJ TANKIAN) / Black oblivion (w/ BILLY CORGAN) / Flame on (w/ IAN ASTBURY) / Just say no to love (w/ PETER STEELE) / Who's fooling who (w/ OZZY OSBOURNE) / Into the night (w/ BILLY IDOL).

—— next with **GLENN HUGHES** – vocals, bass, etc.

Sanctuary Sanctuary

Jul 05. (cd; TONY IOMMI / GLENN HUGHES) *(SANCD 372) <84759>* **FUSED** [ ] [ ]
– Dopamine / Wasted again / Saviour of the real / Resolution song / Grace / Deep inside a shell / What you're living for / Face your fear / The spell / I go insane.

– others, etc. –

Oct 04. (cd; IOMMI with GLENN HUGHES) *Mayan; (MYNCD 020) / Sanctuary; <84724>* **THE 1996 DEP SESSIONS** [ ] Oct04 [ ]
– Gone / From another world / Don't you tell me / Don't drag the river / Fine / Time is the healer / I'm not the same man / It falls through me.

☐ BLIND FAITH (see under ⇒ CLAPTON, Eric)

BLINK-182

Formed: Poway, nr. San Diego, California, USA ... 1992 by vocalist/guitarist TOM DeLONGE, bassist MARK HOPPUS and drummer SCOTT RAYNOR. This post new cartoon punk outfit began when DELONGE and BARKER met in college. Soon, they were distributing their collection of demos (all which would later appear on 'BUDDHA' debut set) to A&R upstarts. Unfortunately their quest did not succeed, forcing our mangled, spiky-haired heroes to issue their second, self-financed set 'CHESHIRE CAT' (1995), whilst still under the name of BLINK. However, with pressures from an Irish group of the same name, the band re-emerged as BLINK-182 – the 182 in question, being the number of times Al Pacino said "fuck" in the movie, 'Scarface' – and issued the more successful 'DUDE RANCH' (1997). The album boasted college anthem 'DICK LIPS' which sent the boys quite literally on the road to semi-stardom via a little help from supportive peers GREEN DAY and NOFX. Major labels began to show interest, BLINK-182 (with new drummer TRAVIS BARKER) finally signing on the dotted line with 'M.C.A.' at the beginning of 1999. 'ENEMA OF THE STATE' (which featured porn actress Janine scantily clad in a nurse's uniform) surfaced in that summer and went on to achieve double platinum sales throughout America and Europe. Memorable single, 'WHAT'S MY AGE AGAIN?' (a catchy two minute punk/pop rant), saw the trio run naked through L.A. (in the video at least!) and earned them a cameo performance in "ironic" teen sex movie, 'American Pie'. No underlying message, it seemed that BLINK-182 were just out to drink, party and get nekid! Indeed, their next offering hinted as much. Forgetting the decidedly dismal 'THE MARK, TOM & TRAVIS SHOW' a year earlier, 'TAKE OFF YOUR PANTS AND JACKET' (2001), smashed in at No.1 in the US album charts and also broke into the UK Top 5, thanks to the hit single, 'THE ROCK SHOW'. In 2002, and with spare studio time in hand, TOM and TRAVIS (and producer JERRY FINN) formed side-project, BOXCAR RACER. Recruiting new kids on the block, guitarist DAVID KENNEDY and bassist ANTHONY CELESTINO, BLINK-182 surprised fans and critics alike with a more mature and darker sound on their eponymous album, issued in 2003. The riffs and teen-punk harmonies were still intact, but the band had created a richer atmosphere than on previous records. Think GREEN DAY's seminal 'Kerplunk', all twisted guitar hooks and downbeat lyrics of genuine angst and loss of self-control; example 'I MISS YOU'. Hell, even the Cure's ROBERT SMITH popped up to lend his vocals on the LP, and while it ain't no classic, it's still a departure from porn star covers and silly songs about masturbating and snot. With more than a decade's worth of recordings behind them (and 20 million album sales), it was inevitable that a 'GREATEST HITS' set would surface sooner or later; it arrived in the Top 10 just in time for the Xmas 2005 rush, almost a year after their split. The album also featured a posthumous UK Top 30 single, 'NOT NOW' (from the outtakes of their previous LP) and a cover of the Only Ones' 'ANOTHER GIRL ANOTHER PLANET'. For his next move, DeLONGE (and his new ANGELS & AIRWAVES associates, DAVID KENNEDY, ATOM WILLARD and RYAN SINN) made a by-the-book bid for "serious artist" status with an 80s-centric attempt at stadium cerebro-rock, 'WE DON'T NEED TO WHISPER' (2006), a guaranteed transatlantic Top 10.

Album rating: BUDDHA (*5) / CHESHIRE CAT (*6) / DUDE RANCH (*7) / ENEMA OF THE STATE (*6) / THE MARK, TOM & TRAVIS SHOW (*4) / TAKE OFF YOUR PANTS AND JACKET (*6) / BLINK-182 (*7) / GREATEST HITS compilation (*7) / Boxcar Racer: BOXCAR RACER (*6) / Angels & Airwaves: WE DON'T NEED TO WHISPER (*6)

TOM DeLONGE (b.13 Dec'75) – vocals, guitar / **MARK HOPPUS** (b.15 Mar'72) – bass / **SCOTT RAYNOR** – drums

not iss. unknown

1993. (7"ep; as BLINK) **FLY SWATTER EP** [–] [ ]

not iss. Kung Fu

1994. (cd/lp) *<78765-2/-1>* **BUDDHA** [–] [ ]
– Carousel / T.V. / Strings / Fentoozler / Time / Romeo & Rebecca / 21 days / Sometimes / Degenerate / Point of view / My pet Sally / Reebok commercial / Toast and bananas / The girls next door / Don't. *(re-iss. Jan99 & Jul99; same)*

not iss. Rapido

Jun 96. (cd-ep) *<RAP 14>* **WASTING TIME – 1996 AUSTRALIAN TOUR EP** [–] [ ]
– Wasting time / Wrecked him / Lemmings / Enthused. *(UK-iss.Apr98; RAP 30)*

Grilled Cheese Grilled Cheese

Nov 96. (cd) *<(GRL 001)>* **CHESHIRE CAT** [ ] May95 [ ]
– Carousel / M + M's / Fentoozler / Touchdown boy / Strings / Peggy Sue / Sometimes / Does my breath smell? / Cacophony / T.V. / Toast and bananas / Wasting time / Romeo and Rebecca / Ben wah balls / Just about done / Depends. *(re-iss. Nov00 on 'M.C.A.'; 488136-2)*

Nov 96. (cd-s) *<(GRL 701)>* **THEY CAME TO CONQUER . . . URANUS** [ ] Dec95 [ ]
– Waggy / Wrecked him / Zulu.

May 97. (cd-ep) *<(CSGRL 004)>* **DICK LIPS EP** [ ] [ ]
– Dick lips / Apple shampoo / Wrecked him / Zulu.

Jul 97. (cd/lp) *<(CRGD/LPGRL 4)>* **DUDE RANCH** [ ] [67]
– Pathetic / Voyeur / Dammit / Boring / Dick lips / Waggy / Enthused / Untitled / Apple shampoo / Emo / Josie / A new hope / Degenerate / Lemmings / I'm sorry. *<(cd re-iss. Nov97 on 'M.C.A.'; MCD 11624)>*

Dec 97.	(7") **DAMMIT. / DAMMIT (Growing Up edit)**	–	

— **TRAVIS BARKER** (b.14 Nov'75) – drums (ex-AQUABATS, ex-PSYCHO BUTTERFLY) repl. SCOTT

Nov 98. (cd-ep) *<55513>* **JOSIE / WASTING TIME / CAROUSEL / I WON'T BE HOME FOR CHRISTMAS** [–] [ ]

Dec 98. (7") **I WON'T BE HOME FOR CHRISTMAS** [–] [–]

M.C.A. M.C.A.

Sep 99. (c-s) *(MCSC 40219) <radio cut>* **WHAT'S MY AGE AGAIN? / PATHETIC (live)** [38] Jul99 [59]
(cd-s+=) *<(MCSTD 40219)>* – Untitled (live).
(cd-s) *<(MCSXD 40219)>* – ('A'side) / Josie (live) / Aliens exist (live).

Oct 99. (cd) *(MCD 11950) <111950>* **ENEMA OF THE STATE** [15] Jun99 [9]
– Don't leave me / Adam's song / The party song / Wendy clear / Going away to college / Dysentery Gary / Aliens exist / All the small things / Mutt / Anthem / What's my age again? / Dumpweed.

Mar 00. (c-s) *(MCSC 40223) <155606>* **ALL THE SMALL THINGS DAMMIT (live)** [2] Nov99 [6]
(cd-s+=) *(MCSXD 40223)* – ('A'live) / ('A'-CD-Rom video).
(cd-s) *(MCSTD 40223)* – ('A'side) / Dumpweed (live) / What's my age again? (live).

Jun 00. (c-s) *(MCSC 40219)* **WHAT'S MY AGE AGAIN? / PATHETIC (live)** [17] [–]
(cd-s+=) *(MCSZD 40219)* – Untitled (live) / ('A'-CD-Rom).
(cd-s) *(MCSYD 40219)* – ('A'side) / Josie (live) / (interview on CD-Rom).

Nov 00. (cd) *<(112379-2)>* **THE MARK, TOM AND TRAVIS SHOW – THE ENEMA STRIKES BACK! (live)** [69] [8]
– Dumpweed / Don't leave me / Alines exist / Family reunion / Going away to college / What's my age again? / Dick lips / Blow job / Untitled / Voyeur / Pathetic / Adam's song / Peggy Sue / Wendy clear / Carousel / All the small things / Mutt / The country song / Dammit / Man overboard / (plus a whole bunch of funny shit in between).

Jun 01. (cd) *<(112627-2)>* **TAKE OFF YOUR PANTS AND JACKET** [4] [1]
– Anthem (part 2) / Online songs / First date / Happy holidays you bastard / Story of a lonely guy / The rock show / Stay together for the kids / Roller coaster / Reckless abandon / Everytime I look for you / Give me one good reason / Shut up / Please take me home / What went wrong / Time to break up / Fuck a dog / Man overboard (video).

Jul 01. (cd-s) *(MCSTD 40259) <radio cut>* **THE ROCK SHOW / TIME TO BREAK UP / MAN OVERBOARD** [14] [71]

Sep 01. (7") *(MCS 40264)* **FIRST DATE. / DON'T TELL ME IT'S OVER** [31] [ ]
(cd-s+=) *(MCSTD 40264)* – Mother's day.

Nov 03. (cd) *(9861408) <133612>* **BLINK-182** [22] [3]
– Feeling this / Obvious / I miss you / Violence / Stockholm syndrome / Down / The fallen interlude / Go / Asthenia / Always / Easy target / All of this / Here's your letter / I'm lost without you. *(UK+=)* – Not now / Anthem (part 2 – live in Chicago) / Feeling this (video) / Obvious (video) / Down / The fallen interlude (video) / Violence (video).

Nov 03. (7"/cd-s) *(MCS/+TD 40347) <981409>* **FEELING THIS. / ROCK SHOW (live)** [15] Dec03 [ ]

— early 2005, BLINK-182 were no more . . . for now (BARKER formed PLUS 44)

Nov 05. (cd) *(9886987) <55800-2>* **GREATEST HITS** (compilation) [6] [6]
– Carousel / M + M's / Dammit / Josie / What's my age again? / All the small things / Adam's song / Man overboard / The rock show / First date / Stay together for the kids / Feeling this / I miss you / Down / Always / Not now / Another girl another planet. *(UK+=)* – I won't be home for Christmas / Go (BBC Radio 1 session). *(ltd-cd w/dvd+=; 9887099)* – (bonus live tracks + behind the scenes videos).

Nov 05. (7"/cd-s) *(MCS/+TD 40440)* **NOT NOW. / DAMMIT (dirty edit)** [30] [–]
(7") *(MCSX 40440)* – ('A') / All the small things.

BOXCAR RACER

TOM DeLONGE + **TRAVIS BARKER** plus **DAVID KENNEDY** – guitar / **ANTHONY CELESTINO** – bass

M.C.A. M.C.A.

May 02. (cd) *(112947-2) <112894-2>* **BOXCAR RACER** [27] [12]
– I feel so / All systems go / Watch the world / Tiny voices / Cat like thief / And I / Letters to God / My first punk song / Sorrow / There is / The end with you / Elevator / Instrumental.

Jun 02. (7") *(MCS 40290)* **I FEEL SO. / CAT LIKE THIEF** [41] [–]
(cd-s+=) *(MCSTD 40290)* – ('A'-guitar intro) / ('A'-video).

ANGELS & AIRWAVES

TOM DeLONGE – vocals, guitar / **DAVID KENNEDY** – guitar / **RYAN SINN** – bass (ex-DISTILLERS) / **ATOM WILLARD** – drums (ex-ROCKET FROM THE CRYPT, ex-MOTH)

M.C.A. Geffen

May 06. (7"pic-d; 1-sided) *(MCS 40461)* **THE ADVENTURE** [20] [65]
(cd-s+=) *(MCSTD 40461)* – ('A'-version).

May 06. (cd) *(9878574) <B0006696-2>* **WE DON'T NEED TO WHISPER** [6] [4]
– Valkyrie missile / Distraction / Do it for me now / The adventure / A little's enough / The war / The gift / It hurts / Good day / Start the machine.

BLOC PARTY

Formed: South London, England . . . 2002 originally as SUPERHEROES OF MBX, ANGEL RANGE, DIET and UNION before opting for BLOC PARTY in 2003. KELE OKEREKE and RUSSELL LISSACK expanded the band to a quartet shortly after with the addition of GORDON MOAKES and MATT TONG. A 'Domino' records 10th anniversary shindig later in the year presented a prime opportunity for BLOC PARTY to make the right connections: with both ALEX KAPRANOS and Radio One presenter Steve Lamacq on the case, the interracial art-rockers had set the stage for the release of independently-released debut 45, 'SHE'S HEARING VOICES'. Uniquely among the neo-wave of GANG OF FOUR, JOY DIVISION devotees, BLOC PARTY boasted a black singer; on the pulverising debut at least, OKEREKE effortlessly morphed between the wounded wail of ROBERT SMITH and IAN CURTIS-haunted gothic soul. Another one-off indie 45, 'BANQUET' (on 'Moshi Moshi'), nearly cracked the Top 50, preceding a full-time move to WEBB BROTHERS imprint, 'Wichita'. With Top 40 success imminent, the band inevitably cracked the charts via 'LITTLE THOUGHTS' and the overtly political 'HELICOPTER', both revolving on the kind of trendy coloured vinyl originally popularised by their New Wave/Punk forebears a quarter of a century earlier. 2005 kicked off with the chiming crescendos of 'SO HERE WE ARE', sparking fears of a shoegazing revival but making the Top 5 all the same. Their unlikely rebirth as pop stars pretty much guaranteed a Top 3 place for debut album, 'SILENT ALARM', and a wider audience for further hits, 'BANQUET' (again!) and 'THE PIONEERS'. Having become the latest indie band to collaborate with the CHEMICAL BROTHERS (on their 'Push The Button' LP), BLOC PARTY were honoured with a full-blow remix set, featuring peer pressure makeovers from the likes of MOGWAI, FOUR TET and DEATH FROM ABOVE 1979. New material arrived courtesy of the 'TWO MORE YEARS' single, a Top 10 hit subsequently tacked on (together with the aforementioned 'LITTLE THOUGHTS') to a re-issue of the original 'SILENT ALARM', voted Album Of The Year in the NME's annual round-up.

Album rating: SILENT ALARM (*9)

KELE OKEREKE (b.13 Oct'81, Bethnal Green, London) – vocals, guitar / **RUSSELL LISSACK** (b.11 Mar'61, Chingford, nr. London) – guitar / **GORDON MOAKES** (b.22 Jun'76, Milton Keynes, England) – bass, vocals / **MATT TONG** (b.29 Apr'79, Bournemouth, England) – drums

Trash Aesthetics not iss.

Feb 04. (7"clear) *(EP-TA 701)* **SHE'S HEARING VOICES. / THE MARSHALS ARE DEAD / THE ANSWER** [ ] [–]

Moshi Moshi not iss.

May 04. (7"/cd-s) *(MOSHI 10/+CD)* **BANQUET. / STAYING FAT** [51] [–]

Wichita Dim Mak

Jul 04. (7"blue) *(WEBB 067S)* **LITTLE THOUGHTS. / STORM AND STRESS** [38] [–]
(cd-s) *(WEBB 067SCD)* – ('A') / Tulips / Banquet (phones disco edit).

Sep 04. (cd-ep) *<DM 069>* **BLOC PARTY** (compilation) [–] [ ]

Oct 04. (7"green) *(WEBB 070S)* **HELICOPTER. / SKELETON** [26] [–]
(cd-s) *(WEBB 070SCD)* – ('A') / Always new depths / Tulips (Minotaur Shock mix).

Jan 05. (12"/cd-s) *<DM 076>* **TULIPS. / TULIPS (Minotaur Shock mix)** [–] [ ]

Jan 05. (7"green) *(WEBB 076S)* **SO HERE WE ARE. / THE MARSHALS ARE DEAD** [5] [–]
(dvd-s+=) *(WEBB 076DVD)* – ('A'-video) / Tulips (video).
(cd-s) *(WEBB 076SCD)* – ('A') / Positive tension / Helicopter (Sheriff Whitey mix).

Feb 05. (cd/lp/pic-lp) *(WEBB 075 CD/LP/PD) <DM 080>* **SILENT ALARM** [3] Mar05 [ ]
– Like eating glass / Helicopter / Positive tension / Banquet / Blue light / She's hearing voices / This modern love / The pioneers / Price of gasoline / Little thoughts *[US-only + UK cd re-iss]* / So here we are / Luno / Plans / Compliments. *<US 3xlp +=>* – Positive tension (Blackbox remix) / Positive tension (Johnny Whitney remix) / Price of gasoline (Automato remix) / Price of gasoline (Jus Ske remix). *<US re-iss. Apr05 on 'Vice-Atlantic'; 93815> (re-iss. Oct05 +=; WEBB 075CDB)* – Two more years.

Apr 05. (7"gold) *(WEBB 078S)* **BANQUET. / TULIPS (Peel session)** [13] [–]
(cd-s) *(WEBB 078SCD)* – ('A') / Compliments (Peel session) / ('A'-another version by the Glimmers).
(dvd-s) *(WEBB 078DVD)* – ('A') / So here we are (Peel session) / ('A'-video) / Little thoughts (video).

Jul 05. (7"pic-d) *(WEBB 088S)* **THE PIONEERS. / THE PIONEERS (Bloc Party vs. Mystery Jets)** [18] [–]
(cd-s) *(WEBB 088SCD)* – ('A') / Plans (acoustic) / Storm and stress (acoustic).
(dvd-s) *(WEBB 088DVD)* – ('A'-video) / Banquet (video).

Aug 05. (cd/d-lp) *(WEBB 090 CD/LP) <DM 093>* **SILENT ALARM REMIXED** [54] Sep05 [ ]
– (remixes by/w/ Various Artists). *<US+=>* – Storm and stress / Always new depths / Skeleton / Plans (acoustic) / Storm and stress (acoustic).

Oct 05. (7"green) *(WEBB 095S)* **TWO MORE YEARS. / HERO** [7] [–]
(dvd-s+=) *(WEBB 095DVD)* – ('A'-video) / Banquet (the Streets mix video).
(cd-s) *(WEBB 095SCD)* – ('A') / Banquet (the Streets mix).

Feb 06. (12") *<DM 095>* **HELICOPTER (Diplo remix). / HELICOPTER (Weird Science remix)** [–] [ ]
(cd-s+=) *<DM 095>* – ('A'-Whitey mix) / ('A'-original).

BLONDIE

Formed: New York City, New York, USA . . . August 1974 by former Playboy bunny girl, DEBBIE HARRY and boyfriend CHRIS STEIN. Other original members excluding female backing singers were sticksman, BILLY O'CONNOR (soon replaced by CLEM BURKE), bassist FRED SMITH (later of TELEVISION) and guitarist IVAN KRAL (later of PATTI SMITH GROUP). After line-up changes which saw the latter two replaced by GARY VALENTINE and JIMMY DESTRI respectively, the group soon found themselves supporting the likes of punk legend, IGGY POP. Subsequently hooking up with veteran producer, Richard Gottehrer, the group released their debut single, 'X-OFFENDER', on his 'Private Stock' label in late '76. This was followed up with a second track, 'IN THE FLESH', while the eponymous debut hit the shelves later that Spring. Trawling tacky 60's girly pop and sprucing it up with a healthy dose of punk muscle and attitude, BLONDIE laid the foundations for their swoonsomely infectious late 70's/early 80's hits. With HARRY as the peroxide Marilyn Monroe of new wave, BLONDIE almost immediately caught the eye of the UK scene, where a follow-up album, 'PLASTIC LETTERS', made the Top 10 in Spring '78. By this point BLONDIE had signed to 'Chrysalis' (who had reputedly bought the contract out for $500,000 in August of the previous year) and had replaced VALENTINE with FRANK INFANTE. A cover of Randy & The Rainbows 60's nugget 'DENISE' (aka 'DENIS') almost topped the British charts, while another single pulled from the album, '(I'M ALWAYS TOUCHED BY YOUR) PRESENCE DEAR', made the Top 10. With the subsequent recruitment of bassist NIGEL HARRISON, INFANTE switched to rhythm guitar, the music taking on a whole new dimension with the seminal 'PARALLEL LINES' (1978). Produced by legendary pop picker, MIKE CHAPMAN, the album spawned a UK Top 5 in 'HANGING ON THE TELEPHONE', plus two No.1's with 'SUNDAY GIRL' and 'HEART OF GLASS'. The latter track's throbbing disco feel was further developed on fourth album, 'EAT TO THE BEAT', a set which featured yet another UK chart topper in the moody dancefloor classic, 'ATOMIC' (later famous for providing the aural backdrop to the disco scene in 'Trainspotting'). BLONDIE even teamed up with electro disco guru, GEORGIO MORODER, for 'CALL ME' (recorded for the soundtrack to 'American Gigolo'), the band's second transatlantic No.1. They repeated this feat with 'THE TIDE IS HIGH', a wonderfully dreamy cover of a track originally cut by reggae outfit, The PARAGONS while also having a bash at hip hop with 'RAPTURE', their fourth US No.1. Both tracks were included on 1980's 'AUTOAMERICAN', an album which suggested BLONDIE were beginning to lose their musical curls. Although 'THE HUNTER' (1982) spawned a further British No.1 in 'ISLAND OF LOST SOULS', the album met with a less than rapturous reception, likewise their final tour. The band finally split in summer '82, STEIN forming his own 'Chrysalis'-backed label, 'Animal', before falling ill the following year. This put HARRY's solo career (begun rather noneventfully with 1981's BERNARD EDWARDS / NILE RODGERS collaborative set, 'KOO KOO') temporarily on the back burner, the singer re-emerging in late '86 with the UK Top 10, 'FRENCH KISSIN' IN THE U.S.A.'. The accompanying album, 'ROCKBIRD' made the Top 40 although 1989's 'DEF, DUMB AND BLONDE' was more successful, its shiny poppy single 'I WANT THAT MAN' making the UK Top 20. If nothing else, she proved herself an adaptable stylist although much more interesting was a tongue in cheek duet with IGGY POP in 1990, 'WELL, DID YOU EVAH!'. Throughout her career, HARRY had also made the occasional venture into celluloid (see below). At the tender age of 53, but still looking every inch (or two) the ideal peroxide sex symbol, DEBBIE and her slightly younger crew of CHRIS, JIMMY and CLEM, re-formed BLONDIE for round the world tours. By early 1999, the band were topping the UK charts with the catchy 'MARIA', a song lifted from their aptly-titled Top 5 (US Top 40) parent album, 'NO EXIT'. A year later, BLONDIE opted for a quick follow-up, the 'greatest hits live' package 'LIVID' (2000) – I know I was. The aptly titled 'CURSE OF BLONDIE' (2003), meanwhile, was an altogether unnecessary addition to the band's revered catalogue, an ill-advised attempt to milk the reunion for more than it could conceivably have provided. Largely directionless and tired, HARRY (on the cusp of 60!) would have done well to resurrect her solo career instead. Proving that you could still see DEBBIE in the flesh, 'LIVE BY REQUEST' (2004) documented most of the original BLONDIE line-up playing to their strengths.

• **Songwriters:** Most written by STEIN-HARRY except; HANGING ON THE TELEPHONE (Jack Lee; Nerves) / RING OF FIRE (Johnny Cash) / HEROES (David Bowie). • **Trivia:** DEBBIE HARRY starred in a Broadway play 'TEANECK TANZI: THE VENUS FLYTRAP' (1983), which bombed after one night. She also appeared on 'The Muppet Show' circa 1980.

Album rating: BLONDIE (*6) / PLASTIC LETTERS (*7) / PARALLEL LINES (*8) / EAT TO THE BEAT (*6) / AUTOAMERICAN (*5) / THE BEST OF BLONDIE compilation (*9) / THE HUNTER (*4) / THE COMPLETE PICTURE – THE VERY BEST OF DEBORAH HARRY & BLONDIE compilation (*9) / BLONDE AND BEYOND compilation (*5) / NO EXIT (*6) / LIVID (*3) / THE

BLONDIE

CURSE OF BLONDIE (*4) / LIVE BY REQUEST (*6) / Debbie Harry: KOOKOO (*5) / ROCKBIRD (*6) / ONE MORE INTO THE BLEACH compilation w/ Blondie (*6) / DEF, DUMB & BLONDE (*5) / DEBRAVATION (*4)

DEBBIE HARRY (b. 1 Jul'45, Miami, Florida) – vocals (ex-WIND IN THE WILLOWS) / **CHRIS STEIN** (b. 5 Jan'50, Brooklyn, New York) – guitar / **JIMMY DESTRI** (b.13 Apr'54) – keyboards (ex-KNICKERS) / **GARY VALENTINE** – bass / **CLEM BURKE** (b.CLEMENT, 24 Nov'55) – drums (ex-SWEET REVENGE)

Private Stock — Private Stock

Dec 76. (7") *<PVT 90>* **X OFFENDER. / IN THE SUN** [–] [ ]

Dec 76. (lp) *<PS 2023>* **BLONDIE** [–] [ ]
– X offender / Little girl lies / In the flesh / Look good in blue / In the sun / A shark in jet's clothing / Man overboard / Rip her to shreds / Rifle range / Kung Fu girls / The attack of the giant ants. *<re-iss. Feb77; PVLP 1017> (UK-iss.Dec77 on 'Chrysalis'; CHR 1165)* – (hit UK No.75 in Mar79) *(re-iss. Oct82 on 'Hallmark' lp/c; SHM/HSC 3119) (re-iss. Apr85 on 'M.F.P.' lp/c; MFP 41-5696-1/-4) (cd-iss. Sep94 on 'Chrysalis'; CDCHR 6081)*

Feb 77. (7") *<PVT 105>* **IN THE FLESH. / MAN OVERBOARD** [–] [ ]

May 77. (7") *(PVT 105)* **IN THE FLESH. / X OFFENDER** [ ] [–]

Chrysalis — Chrysalis

Nov 77. (7"m/12"m) *<CHS 2180/+12>* **RIP HER TO SHREDS. / IN THE FLESH / X OFFENDER** [ ] [–]
(re-iss. 12"m Dec81; same)

— (Oct'77) **FRANK INFANTE** – bass (ex-WORLD WAR III) repl. VALENTINE

Feb 78. (7"m/12"m) *<(CHS 2180/+12)>* **DENIS. / CONTACT IN RED SQUARE / KUNG FU GIRLS** [2] [ ]
(re-iss. 12"white Dec81; same)

Feb 78. (lp/c) *<(CHR/ZCHR 1166)>* **PLASTIC LETTERS** [10] Feb78 [72]
– Fan mail / Denis / Bermuda Triangle blues (Flight 45) / Youth nabbed as sniper / Contact in Red Square / (I'm always touched by your) Presence, dear / I'm on E / I didn't have the nerve to say no / Love at the pier / No imagination / Kidnapper / Detroit 442 / Cautious lip. *(cd-iss. Sep94; CDCHR 6085)*

Apr 78. (7"m/12"m) *<(CHS/+12 2217)>* **(I'M ALWAYS TOUCHED BY YOUR) PRESENCE, DEAR. / POET'S PROBLEM / DETROIT 442** [10] [ ]
(re-iss. Dec81; same)

— (Nov77 on recording of 2nd lp) added **NIGEL HARRISON** – bass (b.24 Apr'51, Stockport, England) now sextet with **INFANTE** – now on rhythm guitar

Aug 78. (7"yellow) *<(CHS 2204)>* **PICTURE THIS. / FADE AWAY (AND RADIATE)** [12] [ ]

Sep 78. (7") *<2251>* **I'M GONNA LOVE YOU TOO. / JUST GO AWAY** [–] [ ]

Sep 78. (lp/c) *<(CHR/ZCHR 1192)>* **PARALLEL LINES** [1] [6]
– Fade away (and radiate) / Hanging on the telephone / One way or another / Picture this / Pretty baby / I know but I don't know / 11:59 / Will anything happen / Sunday girl / Heart of glass / I'm gonna love you too / Just go away. *(re-iss. Nov83 on 'Fame' lp/c; FA/TCFA 3089-1/-4) (re-iss. Jul88 lp/c/cd; CDL/ZCDL/CCD 1192) (re-iss. Dec92 on 'Fame' cd/c; CD/TC FA 3282) (re-iss. Jul94 cd/c; CCD/ZCDL 1192)*

Nov 78. (7") *(CHS 2266)* **HANGING ON THE TELEPHONE. / WILL ANYTHING HAPPEN** [5] [–]

Nov 78. (7") *<CHS 2266>* **HANGING ON THE TELEPHONE / FADE AWAY AND RADIATE** [–] [ ]

Jan 79. (7") *(CHS 2275)* **HEART OF GLASS. / RIFLE RANGE** [1] [–]
(12"+=) – ('A'instrumental). *(re-iss. 12" Dec81; same)*

Feb 79. (7") *<CHS 2275>* **HEART OF GLASS. / 11:59** [–] [1]

May 79. (7") *(CHS 2320)* **SUNDAY GIRL. / I KNOW BUT I DON'T KNOW** [1] [–]
(12"+=) *(CHS/+12 2320)* – ('A' French version).
(re-iss. 12"clear Dec81; same)

May 79. (7") *<CHS 2336>* **ONE WAY OR ANOTHER. / JUST GO AWAY** [–] [24]

Sep 79. (7") *(CHS 2350)* **DREAMING. / SOUND ASLEEP** [2] [–]

Sep 79. (7") *<CHS 2379>* **DREAMING. / LIVING IN THE REAL WORLD** [–] [27]

Oct 79. (lp/c) *<(CHR/ZCHR 1225)>* **EAT TO THE BEAT** [1] [17]
– Dreaming / The hardest part / Union city blue / Shayla / Eat to the beat / Accidents never happen / Die young stay pretty Slow motion / / Atomic / Sound-a-sleep / Victor / Living in the real world. *(cd-iss. Jun87; CPCD 1225) (cd-iss. Nov92; CDCHR 1225)*

Nov 79. (7") *(CHS 2400)* **UNION CITY BLUE. / LIVING IN THE REAL WORLD** [13] [ ]

Jan 80. (7") *<CHS 2408>* **THE HARDEST PART. / SOUND-A-SLEEP** [–] [84]

Feb 80. (7") *<(CHS 2410)>* **ATOMIC. / DIE YOUNG STAY PRETTY** [1] May80 [39]
(12"+=) *(CHS12 2410)* – Heroes. *(re-iss. 12" Dec81; same)*

Apr 80. (7") *<(CHS 2414)>* **CALL ME. / (instrumental by GIORGIO MORODER)** [1] Feb80 [1]
(12"+=) *(CHS12 2414)* – ('A'-Spanish version).

Oct 80. (7") *<(CHS 2465)>* **THE TIDE IS HIGH. / SUZIE AND JEFFREY** [1] Nov80 [1]

Nov 80. (lp/c) *<(CDL/ZCDL 1290)>* **AUTOAMERICAN** [3] [7]
– Europa / Live it up / Here's looking at you / The tide is high / Angels on the balcony / Go through it / Do the dark / Rapture / Faces / Do the dark / T-Birds / Walk like me / Follow me. *(cd-iss. Sep94; CDCHR 6084)*

Jan 81. (7") *<(CHS 2485)>* **RAPTURE. / WALK LIKE ME** [5] [1]
(12") *(CHS12 2485)* – ('A'side) / Live it up.

Oct 81. (lp/c) *(CDLTV/ZCLTV 1) <1371>* **THE BEST OF BLONDIE** (compilation) [4] [30]
– Denis / The tide is high / In the flesh / Sunday girl / (I'm always touched by your) Presence dear / Dreaming / Hanging on the telephone / Rapture / Picture this / Union city blue / Call me / Atomic / Rip her to shreds / Heart of glass. *(cd-iss. Jan88; CCD 1371)*

Apr 82. (7"/7"pic-d) *<(CHS/+P 2608)>* **ISLAND OF LOST SOULS. / DRAGONFLY** [1] May82 [37]

May 82. (lp/c/pic-lp) *<(CDL/ZCDL/PCDL 1384)>* **THE HUNTER** [9] [33]
– Orchid club / Island of lost souls / Dragonfly / For your eyes only / The beast / War child / Little Caesar / Danceaway / (Can I) Find the right words (to say) / English boys / The hunter gets captured by the game. *(cd-iss. Sep94; CDCHR 6083)*

Jul 82. (7"/7"pic-d/12") *<(CHS/+P/12 2624)>* **WAR CHILD. / LITTLE CAESAR** [39] [ ]

— (Aug'82) STEIN formed own 'Animal' label through 'Chrysalis'. CLEM BURKE joins EURYTHMICS and later RAMONES. He also teams up with HARRISON to form CHEQUERED PAST. A solo album, 'HEART ON THE WALL', was released by JIMMY DESTRI in 1982 and featured most of BLONDIE.

DEBBIE HARRY

solo, with **NILE RODGERS** and **BERNARD EDWARDS** on production, etc.

Chrysalis — Chrysalis

Jul 81. (7"/12") *<(CHS/+12 2526)>* **BACKFIRED. / MILITARY RAP** [32] [43]

Aug 81. (lp/c) *<(CHR/ZCCHR 1347)>* **KOO KOO** [6] [23]
– Jump jump / The jam was moving / Chrome / Under arrest / Inner city spillover / Surrender / Backfired / Now I know you / Military rap / Oasis. *(cd-iss. Sep94; CDCHR 6082)*

Sep 81. (7") *<(CHS 2554)>* **THE JAM WAS MOVING. / CHROME** [ ] [82]
(12"+=) *(CHS12 2554)* – Inner city spillover.

— now worked with various session musicians.

Chrysalis — Geffen

Jan 84. (7") **RUSH RUSH. / (other by Beth Anderson)** [–] [ ]

Jan 84. (7"/12") *(CHS/12CHS 2752)* **RUSH RUSH. / (other by Giorgio Moroder)** [ ] [–]

Nov 86. (7") *(CHS 3066)* **FRENCH KISSIN' IN THE U.S.A. / ROCKBIRD** [8] [–]
('A'dance; 12"+=/12"pic-d+=) *(CHS12 3066/+B)* – ('A'dub version).

Nov 86. (7") *<28546>* **FRENCH KISSIN' IN THE U.S.A. / BUCKLE UP** [–] [57]

Nov 86. (lp/c/cd) *(CHR/ZCHR/CCD 1540) <24123>* **ROCKBIRD** [31] [97]
– I want you / French kissin' in the U.S.A. / Buckle up / In love with love / You got me in trouble / Free to fall / Rockbird / Secret life / Beyond the limit. *(cd re-iss. Sep94; CCD 1540)*

Feb 87. (7") *<(CHS 3093)>* **FREE TO FALL. / FEEL THE SPIN** [46] [ ]
(12"+=/12"pic-d+=) *(CHS12 3093/+B)* – Secret life.
(d7"+=) *(CHSD 3093)* – French kissin' in the U.S.A. / Rockbird.

Apr 87. (7") *(CHS 3128)* **IN LOVE WITH LOVE. / FEEL THE SPIN** [45] [–]
(12"+=/12"pic-d+=) *(CHS/+P 12-3128)* – French kissin' in the U.S.A. (French version).

Jun 87. (7") *<28476>* **IN LOVE WITH LOVE. / SECRET LIFE** [–] [70]

DEBORAH HARRY

— with **CHRIS STEIN** – guitar / **LEIGH FOXX** – bass / **TERRY BOZZIO** – drums / **TOMMY PRICE** – drums / **PHIL ASHLEY** – synthesizers / **STEVE GOLDSTEIN** – keyboards, etc.

Chrysalis Sire

Sep 89. (7"/c-s) *(CHS/+MC 3369)* **I WANT THAT MAN. / BIKE BOY** 13
(12"pic-d+=/cd-s+=) *(CHS 12P/CD 3369)* – ('A'remix) / ('A'instrumental).

Oct 89. (lp/c/cd) *(CHR/ZCHR/CCD 1650) <25938>* **DEF, DUMB AND BLONDE** 12
– I want that man / Lovelight / KIss it better / Bike boy * / Get your way / Maybe for sure / I'll never fall in love / Calmarie / Sweet and low / He is so / Bugeye / Comic books / Brite side / End of the run *. *(cd+=*) (cd re-iss. Sep94; CCD 1650)*

Nov 89. (7"/7"s) *(CHS/+PB 3452)* **BRITE SIDE. / BUGEYE** 59
(12"+=/cd-s+=) *(CHS 12/CD 3452)* – In love with love.
('A'remix-cd-s++=) *(CHSCCD 3452)* – French kissin' in the U.S.A.

— Her touring group at time included **STEIN** and **FOXX** plus **SUZY DAVIS** – keyboards / **CARLA OLLA** – rhythm guitar / **JIMMY CLARK** – drums

Mar 90. (7"/7"s) *(CHS/+PB 3491)* **SWEET AND LOW. / LOVELIGHT** 57
(12"/12"pic-d/cd-s) *(CHS 12/P12/CD 3491)* – (3-'A'mixes).

May 90. (7") *(CHS 3537)* **MAYBE FOR SURE. / GET YOUR WAY**
(12"+=/cd-s+=) *(12/CD CHS 3537)* – ('A'extended).
below featured on a Cole Porter tribute album, 'Red Hot & Blue'.

Dec 90. (7"/12"; by DEBORAH HARRY & IGGY POP) *(CHS/+12 3646)* **WELL DID YOU EVAH! / (b-side by The Thompson Twins)** 42
(cd-s+=) *(CHSCD 3646)* – (track by 'Aztec Camera').

Jun 93. (c-s/7") *(TC+/CHS 4900)* **I CAN SEE CLEARLY. / STANDING IN MY WAY** 23
(12"+=/cd-s+=) *(12/CD CHS 4900)* – Atomic / Heart of glass.
(cd-s+=) *(CDCHSS 4900)* – Call me / In love with love.

Jul 93. (cd/c/lp) *(CD/TC+/CHR 6033)* **DEBRAVATION** 24
– I can see clearly / Stability / Strike me pink / Rain / Communion / Lip service / Mood ring / Dancing down the moon / Standing in my way / The fugitive / Dog star girl.

Sep 93. (c-s) *(TCCHS 5000)* **STRIKE ME PINK / 8 AND A HALF RHUMBA** 46
(cd-s) *(CDCHS 5000)* – Dreaming.
(12"pic-d/cd-s) *(12CHSPD/CDCHSS 5000)* – ('A'side) / Sweet and low / On a breath.

BLONDIE

— re-formed in 1998 with **DEBBIE, CHRIS, CLEM + JIMMY**

Beyond-RCA Logic

Feb 99. (c-s) *(74321 64563-4) <78040>* **MARIA / MARIA (Soul Soultion mix)** 1 Mar99 82
(cd-s+=) *(74321 64563-2)* – Maria (Talvin Singh remix).
(cd-s) *(74321 63737-2)* – ('A'side) / In the flesh (live) / Screaming skin (live).

Feb 99. (cd/c) *(74321 64114-2/-4) <78003>* **NO EXIT** 3 18
– Screaming skin / Forgive & forget / Maria / No exit / Double take / Nothing is real but the girl / Boom boom in the zoom zoom room / Night wind sent / Under the gun / Out in the streets / Happy dog (for Caggy) / The dream's lost on me / Divine / Dig up the Congo. *(cd re-iss. Aug02 on 'Epic'+=; 501408-2)* – Hot shot / Rapture (live) / Heart of glass (live).

Jun 99. (c-s) *(74321 66948-4)* **NOTHING IS REAL BUT THE GIRL (Boilerhouse mix) / RIP HER TO SHREDS (live)** 26 –
(cd-s) *(74321 66380-2)* – ('A'side) / ('A'-Danny Tenaglia mix) / ('A'-Danny Tenaglia instradub).
(cd-s) *(74321 66947-2)* – ('A'-US radio mix) / Hanging on the telephone (live) / Shayla (live).

Nov 99. (cd-ep) *(74321 71653-2)* **NO EXIT / MARIA (J&B mix) / MARIA (Talvin Singh rhythmic mix) / NOTHING IS REAL BUT THE GIRL (Danny Tenaglia mix & his trance version)** –

Feb 00. (cd/c) *(501409-2)* **LIVID – THE GREATEST HITS LIVE (live)**
– Dreaming / Hanging on the telephone / Screaming skin / Atomic / Forgive and forget / The tide is high / Shayla / Sunday girl / Maria / Call me / Under the gun / Rapture / Rip her to shreds / X-offender / No exit / Heart of glass / One way or another.

— now without DESTRI

Epic Sanctuary

Oct 03. (cd-s) *(674399-2)* **GOOD BOYS / MARIA (live) / RAPTURE (live) / GOOD BOYS (live)** 12 –
(cd-s) *(674399-5)* – ('A'side) / ('A'-Giorgio Moroder extended).
(12") *(674399-6)* – ('A'-Giorgio Moroder extended) / ('A'-Scissor Sisters' gyad byas myax mix) / ('A'-return to New York mix).

Oct 03. (cd) *(5119219) <84666>* **THE CURSE OF BLONDIE** 36 Apr04
– Shake down / Good boys / Undone / Golden rod / Rules for living / Background melody (the only one) / Magic (Asaadoya Yunta) / End to end / Hello Joe / The tingler / Last one on the planet / Diamond bridge / Desire brings me back / Songs of love.

Cooking Vinyl Sanctuary

Oct 05. (cd) *(COOKCD 332) <84712>* **LIVE BY REQUEST** (live 2004) Sep04
– Dreaming / Hanging on the telephone / Accidents never happen / Tide is high / Good boys / Rip her to shreds / One way or another / Rapture / X offender / Call me / Union City blues / Heart of glass / The dream's lost on me / (I'm always touched by your) Presence dear.

– compilations, etc. (selective) –

on 'Chrysalis' unless mentioned otherwise

Nov 88. (7") *(CHS 3328)* **DENIS (remix). / RAPTURE (Teddy Riley remix)** 50 –
(12"+=/12"pic-d+=/cd-s+=) *(CHS/+12/12P/CD 3328)* – Heart of glass (remix) / Atomic (remix).

Dec 88. (lp/c/cd) *(CJB/ZCJB/CDJB 2)* **ONCE MORE INTO THE BLEACH (GREATEST HITS)** 50 –
– Denis / Heart of glass / Call me / Rapture / Rapture (bonus beats) / The tide is high / The jam was moving (DEBBIE HARRY) / In love with love (DEBBIE HARRY) / Rush rush (DEBBIE HARRY) / French kissin' in the U.S.A. (DEBBIE HARRY) / Feel the spin (DEBBIE HARRY) / Backfired (DEBBIE HARRY) / Sunday girl (French version).

Feb 89. (7") *(CHS 3342)* **CALL ME. / CALL ME (version)** 61 –
(12"+=/cd-s+=) *(CHS 12/CD 3342)* – Backfired (DEBBIE HARRY).

Mar 91. (cd/c/d-lp) *(CCD/ZCHR/CHR 1817)* **THE COMPLETE PICTURE – THE VERY BEST OF DEBORAH HARRY & BLONDIE** 3
– Heart of glass / I want that man / Call me / Sunday girl / French kissin' in the USA / Denis / Rapture / Brite side / (I'm always touched by your) Presence dear / Well, did you evah! / The tide is high / In love with love / Hanging on the telephone / Island of lost souls / Picture this / Dreaming / Sweet and low / Union city blue / Atomic / Rip her to shreds.

Jan 94. (cd/c) *(CD/TC CHR 6063)* **BLONDIE AND BEYOND – RARITIES AND ODDITIES** –

Aug 94. (c-s/12"/cd-s) *(12/ZC/CD CHS 5013)* **ATOMIC (re-mix). / ('A'mixes by Diddy & Alan Thompson)** 19 –
(cd-s) *(CDCHSS 5013)* – ('A') / Sunday girl (re-mix) / Union City blues (re-mix).

Nov 94. (d-cd) *(CDCHR 6089)* **THE PLATINUM COLLECTION** –

Jun 95. (12") *(12CHS 5023) HEART OF GLASS (re-mix). / CALL ME (re-mix)* 15
(c-s) *(CDCHS 5023)* – ('A') / Rapture (re-mix) / Atomic (re-mix).
(cd-s+=) *(CDCHSS 5023)* – ('A'-mixes).

Jul 95. (cd/c/d-lp) *(CD/TC+/CHR 6105)* **BEAUTIFUL – THE REMIX ALBUM** 25 –

Oct 95. (12"blue/cd-s) *(12/CD CHS 5027)* **UNION CITY BLUE (re-mix) / I FEEL LOVE (live)** 31 –
(cd-s) *(CDCHSS 5027)* – (other mixes by:- Diddy / The Burger Queens / OPM / Vinny Vero & Jammin' Hot).

Jul 98. (cd/c) *E.M.I.; (494996-2/-4)* **ATOMIC – THE VERY BEST OF . . .** 12
(d-cd-iss. Feb99 +=; 499288-2) – ATOMIX

Jul 98. (c-s) *E.M.I.; (TCATOM 150)* **ATOMIC (1998 remix)** –
(12"+=/cd-s+=) *(12/CD ATOM 150)* – ('A'-mixes).

Mar 99. (cd) *EMI Gold; (499421-2)* **THE ESSENTIAL COLLECTION** –

Jun 99. (cd) *E.M.I.; (521233-2)* **LIVE** (live Philadelphia 1978 / Dallas 1980) –

Oct 02. (cd) *E.M.I.; (543105-2)* **GREATEST HITS** 38
– Dreaming / Call me / One way or another / Heart of glass / The tide is high / X-offender / Hanging on the telephone / Rip her to shreds / Rapture / Atomic / Picture this / In the flesh / Denis / I'm always touched by your presence dear / Union city blue / The hardest part / Island of lost souls / Sunday girl / Maria.

Sep 03. (d-cd) *(592228-2)* **BLONDIE / PLASTIC LETTERS** –

the BLUE NILE

Formed: Glasgow, Scotland ... 1981 by songwriter PAUL BUCHANAN, PAUL JOSEPH MOORE and ROBERT BELL; took the name from a classic 1962 Alan Moorehead novel. After a debut 45 on 'R.S.O.' (just prior to the label going belly up!), they were offered an unusual record contract by East Lothian label, 'Linn', the hi-fi manufacturer using their tape as a demo and subsequently being sufficiently impressed to sign the band up for their recently formed music business venture. After an initial single, 'STAY', in spring '84, the label issued the languorous debut album, 'A WALK ACROSS THE ROOFTOPS'. Garnering gushing reviews, this classic set of understated pop elegance created enough of a buzz for 'Virgin' to take over distribution. Its relatively lowly final chart position of No.80 belied the record's influence and impact, although it would be another five years before a follow-up as the trio locked themselves in the studio and diligently attempted to create another masterpiece. After a few false starts, they finally emerged in 1989 with 'HATS', a record which arguably topped their debut in the late night sophistication stakes, its moody atmospherics delicately caressed by PAUL BUCHANAN's silky croon (a singer who undoubtedly has the potential of being the next SINATRA). A UK Top 20 hit, the record's success saw the BLUE NILE leave their studio cocoon in the early 90's for a tour of America where they ended up working with such luminaries as ROBBIE ROBERTSON and RICKIE LEE JONES amongst others. Now signed to 'Warners', it looked as if the BLUE NILE were finally destined to leave cultdom behind with a third set, 'PEACE AT LAST' (1996). Another classy effort, again the trio enjoyed critical plaudits and modest chart success while simultaneously failing to corner the wider pop market. With exponentially wider gaps between album releases, you might expect the BLUE NILE's fanbase to have floated away down the proverbial Swanee, yet the 8 year-coming 'HIGH' (2004) – on 'Sanctuary' records – was another instant UK Top 10, and in most quarters another unqualified critical success. Of late, 2006, PAUL BUCHANAN has made a series of rare solo appearances; whether this signals that the BLUE NILE has finally run dry, we probably won't know for another decade.

Album rating: A WALK ACROSS THE ROOFTOPS (*9) / HATS (*8) / PEACE AT LAST (*6) / HIGH (*7)

PAUL BUCHANAN – vocals, guitar, synthesizer / **PAUL JOSEPH MOORE** – keyboards, synthesizer, etc. / **ROBERT BELL** – bass, synthesizer, etc.

R.S.O. / not iss.

Oct 81. (7") *(RSO 84)* **I LOVE THIS LIFE. / SECOND ACT** [ ] [–]

— added guests **CALUM MALCOLM** – keyboards, vocals (ex-BADGER, ex-HEADBOYS) / **NIGEL THOMAS** – drums

Linn-Virgin / A&M

Apr 84. (7"/12") *(LKS 1/+12)* **STAY. / SADDLE THE HORSES** [ ] 1985 [ ]
(re-iss. Jan89 remixed 7"/12"/d7"+=; same/same/LKSD 1) – Tinseltown in the rain / Heatwave (instrumental).

Apr 84. (lp/c) *(LKH/+C 1)* **A WALK ACROSS THE ROOFTOPS** [80] 1985 [ ]
– A walk across the rooftops / Tinseltown in the rain / From rags to riches / Stay / Easter parade / Heatwave / Automobile noise. *(cd-iss. Jan89; LKHCD 1)*

Jul 84. (7") *(LKS 2)* **TINSELTOWN IN THE RAIN. / HEATWAVE (instrumental)** [ ] [–]
('A'ext-12") *(LKS 2-12)* – Regret.

— now a basic trio plus session musicians.

Sep 89. (7") *(LKS 3)* **THE DOWNTOWN LIGHTS. / THE WIRES ARE DOWN** [67] [ ]
(12"+=/3"cd-s+=) *(LKS 3-12/CD3)* – Halfway to Paradise (TV theme).

Oct 89. (lp/c/cd) *(LKH/+C/CD 2)* *<5284>* **HATS** [12] [ ]
– Over the hillside / The downtown lights / Let's go out tonight / Headlights on the parade / From a late night train / Seven a.m. / Saturday night. *(re-iss. Apr92 on 'Virgin' cd/c; OVED CD/C 391)*

Sep 90. (7"/c-s) *(LKS/+C 4)* **HEADLIGHTS ON THE PARADE (Bob Clearmount mix). / ('A'-lp version)** [72] [ ]
(12"+=/cd-s+=) *(LKS 4-12/CD4)* – Easter parade (with RICKIE LEE JONES).

Jan 91. (7"/c-s) *(LKS/+C 5)* **SATURDAY NIGHT. / ('A'version)** [50] [ ]
(12"+=/cd-s+=) *(LKS 5-12/CD5)* – Seven a.m. (live in the U.S.) / or / Our lives.

Warners / Warners

Jun 96. (cd/c/lp) *(<9362 45848-2/-4/-1>)* **PEACE AT LAST** [13] [ ]
– Happiness / Tomorrow morning / Sentimental man / Love came down / Body and soul / Holy love / Family life / War is love / God bless you kid / Soon.

Sep 96. (c-ep/cd-ep) *(W 0373 C/CD2)* **HAPPINESS / NEW YORK MAN / WISH ME WELL** [ ] [–]
(cd-ep) *(W 0373CD1)* – ('A') / War is love / O Lolita.

Sanctuary / Sanctuary

Aug 04. (cd-s) *(SANXCD 305)* **I WOULD NEVER / I LOVE THIS LIFE / THE SECOND ACT** [52] [–]

Aug 04. (cd) *(SANCD 285)* *<86368>* **HIGH** [10] [ ]
– The days of our lives / I would never / Broken loves / Because of Toledo / She saw the world / High / Soul boy / Everybody else / Stay close.

□ the BLUE RIDGE RANGERS (see under ⇒ CREEDENCE CLEARWATER REVIVAL)

□ the BLUE VELVETS (see under ⇒ CREEDENCE CLEARWATER REVIVAL)

□ BLUESBREAKERS (see under ⇒ MAYALL, John)

□ BLUESOLOGY (see under ⇒ JOHN, Elton)

James BLUNT

Born: JAMES HILLIER BLOUNT, 22 Feb'74, Tidworth, Wiltshire, England. Hardly your average rock'n'roller, JAMES B took the military route to pop stardom: rather than burning his draft card, he graduated from Sandhurst and became a British Army captain. Serving time in post-conflict Kosovo amongst other places, he'd later make quips about his career having been more dangerous than a leading rapper. Subsequently posting himself to Texas, the civvy street ex-soldier commandeered the attention of songwriter/producer LINDA PERRY (ex-4 NON BLONDES) at the 2003 South By Southwest Festival. BLUNT quickly signed a deal with her 'Custard' imprint (through 'Atlantic'), co-writing a debut single, 'HIGH', with DEACON BLUE's RICKY ROSS. Hot on its heels came parent album, 'BACK TO BEDLAM' (2004), a record which initially went unnoticed as did follow-up single, 'WISEMEN'. However, the blue-eyed boy wonder (he was actually thirty!) finally harnessed the nation's heart-strings in summer 2005 with international chart-topper, 'YOU'RE BEAUTIFUL'. A falsetto fable on lost love, the song was accompanied by an equally morbid video. Its success was the cue for '..BEDLAM' to finally take off, scaling the charts as BLUNT became a household/housewives' choice (the husbands' choice – at least in East London – was the newly coined Cockney rhyming slang "a right James"). While old guard stars have sung his praises, youth culture mouthpiece the NME has chosen to virtually ignore him and his volley of hit singles (including re-issues of his earlier songs and 'GOODBYE MY LOVER').

• **Covers:** FALL AT YOUR FEET (Crowded House) / IN A LITTLE WHILE (U2).

Album rating: BACK TO BEDLAM (*6)

JAMES BLUNT – vocals, piano, guitar, etc. / with various

		Atlantic	Atlantic
Oct 04.	(cd-s) *(AT 0184CD)* **HIGH / SUGAR-COATED**		–
Nov 04.	(cd) *(<7567 83752-2>)* **BACK TO BEDLAM** – High / You're beautiful / Wisemen / Goodbye my lover / Tears and rain / Out of my mind / So long Jimmy / Billy / Cry / No bravery. *(re-iss. Mar05; same)*	Jan05	
Mar 05.	(7"/cd-s) *(AT 0198/+CD)* **WISEMEN. / NO BRAVERY (live)** (dvd-s+=) *(AT 0198DVD)* – ('A'-video).		–
May 05.	(7") *(AT 0207)* *<radio>* **YOU'RE BEAUTIFUL. / SO LONG JIMMY** (cd-s) *(AT 0207CD)* – ('A') / Fall at your feet (acoustic). (cd-s) *(AT 0207CDX)* – ('A') / High (acoustic) / (making of the..) / ('A'-video).	1	1
Jun 05.	(re-cd) *(<7567 93451-2>)* **BACK TO BEDLAM**	1	2
Oct 05.	(7") *(AT 0222)* **HIGH. / BUTTERFLY** (cd-s) *(AT 0222CD)* – ('A') / In a little while ((Whiley session). (cd-s) *(AT 0222CDX)* – ('A') / You're beautiful (radio session) / (making of the..) / ('A'-video).	16	–
Dec 05.	(7") *(AT 0230)* **GOODBYE MY LOVER. / WHERE IS MY MIND? (live in Manchester)** (cd-s+=) *(AT 0230CDX)* – (making of the..) / ('A'-video). (cd-s) *(AT 0230CD)* *<94060>* – ('A') / Close your eyes.	9	66
Feb 06.	(cd w/dvd) *(7567 93512-2)* **CHASING TIME – THE BEDLAM SESSIONS** (live in Ireland) – Wisemen / High / Cry / Goodbye my lover / So long Jimmy / Sugar-coated / You're beautiful / Billy / Fall at your feet / Tears and rain / No bravery / Where is my mind // (DVD tracks).	– non-ch	–
Mar 06.	(etched-7") *(AT 0236)* **WISEMEN** (cd-s+=) *(AT 0236CD)* – Out of my mind (live @ Bowery Ballroom).	23	–

BLUR

Formed: Colchester, Essex, England … 1989 by DAMON ALBARN, GRAHAM COXON, ALEX JAMES and DAVE ROWNTREE. Initially they went under the moniker of SEYMOUR before opting for The GREAT WHITE HOPES. Finally settling with BLUR, they soon were on the books of David Balfe's 'Food' label, a subsidiary of Parlophone. There, they secured their first UK Top 50 entry with 'SHE'S SO HIGH', an early PINK FLOYD-influenced tune, that rode the coat-tails of the baggy brigade. With the ghost of SYD BARRETT even more pronounced, they created one of the more psychedelic singles of the era in 'THERE'S NO OTHER WAY', the record hitting Top 10 in '91. Another single, 'BANG', preceded their debut album, 'LEISURE', a record that received mixed reviews at the time. Still mainly a singles orientated outfit, they progressed dramatically with the much-improved, 'MODERN LIFE IS RUBBISH' (1993) album, which featured some classy tracks including the hits, 'FOR TOMORROW', 'CHEMICAL WORLD' and 'SUNDAY SUNDAY'. Although they had come on leaps and bounds creatively, this wasn't translated into sales. With the release of 'GIRLS AND BOYS', however, they embarked upon a commercial renaissance that saw the record become their biggest hit to date. It was the opening track on the critically approved 'PARKLIFE' album, which also spawned further hits, 'TO THE END' and the title track (co-sung with actor PHIL DANIELS). By this point they had evolved into a mod-ish indie-pop combo, ALBARN supplying the cockney barra-boy delivery over a musical backdrop that drew from the rich English pop heritage, once the domain of such luminaries as The SMALL FACES and The KINKS. The following year, 1995, saw them win the battle to the coveted No.1 spot with 'COUNTRY HOUSE', beating rivals OASIS who were sharpening their tongues for an onslaught of media slagging. However, BLUR lost ground in the credibility stakes, when their 'GREAT ESCAPE' album failed to impress the critics. OASIS, on the other hand, were scaling new heights with their 2nd album. 1997 marked a slight return to favour, both the single, 'BEETLEBUM', and their eponymous 5th album hitting pole position. With BLUR taking a slight sabbatical from the recording studio, GRAHAM COXON took the opportunity to release a respectable solo effort, 'THE SKY IS TOO HIGH', the BLUR factor and a few good reviews nearly carrying it into the Top 30. Having involved themselves with various remixers (including WILLIAM ORBIT, MOBY, THURSTON MOORE, ADRIAN SHERWOOD and JOHN McENTIRE on the once Japanese-only 'BUSTIN' & DRONIN') over the course of the last year or so, BLUR were seeing clearly once again. In March '99, the gospel-led 'TENDER' went straight to No.2 while the accompanying album, '13' (DAMON had recently split with ELASTICA's JUSTINE FRISCHMANN) topped the chart. Further singles, 'COFFEE & TV' (with COXON taking the lead) and 'NO DISTANCE LEFT TO RUN', only managed to reach the Top 20, it would seem BLUR (like possibly OASIS to come?) were beginning to falter slightly. A good time to release a greatest hits set then, 'BEST OF BLUR' (2000) – only a UK Top 3 – coming exactly a decade after the release of their debut single. The album charted Colchester's own pop idols through the various incarnations of their career with the conspicuous underrepresentation of 'MODERN LIFE …', their transitional but commercially flat 1993 effort. GRAHAM COXON also released his second solo effort, 'GOLDEN D', the same year, a spiky, DIY follow-up to his debut which found him revisiting Mission Of Burma's 'FAME AND FORTUNE' and 'THAT'S WHEN I REACH FOR MY REVOLVER'. The most pertinent millennial development in the BLUR camp, however, arguably came with the inception of GORILLAZ, the pop world's very first "virtual" dub/hip hop outfit. The brainchild of ALBARN and cartoonist JAMIE HEWLETT (creator of cult comic heroine 'Tank Girl', herself the inspiration for Lara Croft and a forerunner of the "girlpower" shenanigans), this cutting edge project also benefitted from the talents of CIBO MATTO's MIHO MATORI, hip hop beats merchant DAN 'THE AUTOMATOR' NAKAMURA, reggae bassist DAN JUNIOR and white funk veterans TINA WEYMOUTH and CHRIS FRANTZ (ex-TALKING HEADS, TOM TOM CLUB). As for the band "members", they were cute but dim lead singer 2-D (NOT based on DAMON as everyone thought), sinister, scowling guitarist MURDOC, b-boy RUSSEL and the mysterious, oriental NOODLE. GORILLAZ' debut EP, 'TOMORROW COMES TODAY' arrived in late 2000 while the seminal 'CLINT EASTWOOD' single was released the following year. A lurching slice of feelgood dub-hop which made the UK Top 5 and even the Italian Top 10, the track was a definite contender for single of the year. More importantly for a virtual band, the brilliantly inventive video brought the characters to life in a way that the eponymous 'GORILLAZ' (2001) album did not. Still, there were plenty of sterling pop thrills to be had amidst the occasionally unfocused dubscapes while ironically, perhaps, ALBARN's cockney leer sounded better in this environment than in the confines of BLUR. While the live shows may not quite have lived up to the hype, hits to the band's web site (www.gorillaz.com) dominate the EMI server's traffic. When BLUR did eventually get it together for the long awaited 'THINK TANK' (2003), the results were less than spectacular. Despite the presence of such savvy producers as FATBOY SLIM and WILLIAM ORBIT, the chilly, directionless experimentation of much of the album wasn't so much of a surprise given the acrimonious departure of COXON. ALBARN's recent dalliances with world music flitered through to a certain extent, with strings employed by a cast of North African musicians. Yet even this exotica wasn't enough to redeem the record, its emotionally barren soundscapes skewering the band's trademark pop aesthetic. Among the few high points was the UK Top 5 single, 'OUT OF TIME'. Amid the apocalyptic, geopolitical jungle of the mid-noughties, GORILLAZ (ALBARN, HEWLETT and holographic

BLUR

mates) approximated the aural equivalent of life lived in a technological cage with comeback album, 'DEMON DAYS' (2005). Even daisy-agers DE LA SOUL were feeling the paranoia, back on the cutting edge with collaborative lead hit, 'FEEL GOOD INC.'. Also referencing prime 80s electro was 'DARE', SHAUN RYDER's degenerate slur (and head!) gracing a UK No.1 for the first time in his chequered career. The Clint Eastwood cred continued with third hit, 'DIRTY HARRY', aka Another Brick In The Wall, part 2005, as consumed by the post-E generation. ALBARN's ear for the next big thing was further underlined with his choice of producer, DANGER MOUSE, currently laying waste to the charts under the guise of GNARLS BARKLEY. It's a pity then that ALBARN and Co have recently decided to consign his animated primates to digital memory.

• **Covered:** MAGGIE MAY (Rod Stewart) / LAZY SUNDAY (Small Faces).
• **Trivia:** DAMON's father, KEITH ALBARN, used to be the manager of 60's rock outfit, the SOFT MACHINE.

Album rating: LEISURE (*6) / MODERN LIFE IS RUBBISH (*8) / PARKLIFE (*9) / THE GREAT ESCAPE (*7) / BLUR (*8) / 13 (*6) / THE BEST OF BLUR compilation (*9) / THINK TANK (*5) / Gorillaz: GORILLAZ (*9) / G SIDES collection (*7) / LAIKA COME HOME w/ Space Monkeyz (*5) / DEMON DAYS (*9) / Damon Albarn: RAVENOUS soundtrack w/ Michael Nyman (*6) / ORDINARY DECENT CRIMINAL soundtrack w/ Various Artists (*5) / 101 REYKJAVIK soundtrack w/ Einer Orn Benediktsson (*6)

DAMON ALBARN (b.23 Mar'68, Whitechapel, London) – vocals / **GRAHAM COXON** (b.12 Mar'69, Hanover, West Germany) – guitars, vocals / **ALEX JAMES** (b.21 Nov'68, Dorset, England) – bass, vocals / **DAVE ROWNTREE** (b. 8 Apr'63) – drums

Food-EMI S.B.K.

Oct 90. (c-s/7") *(TC+/FOOD 26)* **SHE'S SO HIGH. / I KNOW** 48 –
(12") *(12FOOD 26)* – ('A'-Definitive) / Sing / I know (extended).
(cd-s) *(CDFOOD 26)* – ('A'side) / I know (extended) / Down.

Apr 91. (c-s/7") *(TC+/FOOD 29)* **THERE'S NO OTHER WAY. / INERTIA** 8 –
(ext.12"+=/cd-s+=) *(12/CD FOOD 29)* – Mr.Briggs / I'm all over.
(12") *(12FOODX 20)* – ('A'remix). / Won't do it / Day upon day (live).

Jul 91. (c-s/7") *(TC+/FOOD 31)* **BANG. / LUMINOUS** 24
(ext.12"+=) *(12FOOD 31)* – Explain / Uncle Love.
(cd-s+=) *(CDFOOD 31)* – Explain / Beserk.

Aug 91. (cd/c/lp) *(FOOD CD/TC/LP 6)* *<97880>* **LEISURE** 7
– She's so high / Bang / Slow down / Repetition / Bad day / Sing / There's no other way / Fool / Come together / High cool / Birthday / Wear me down.

Dec 91, (c-s,cd-s) *<07374>* **THERE'S NO OTHER WAY / EXPLAIN** – 82

Mar 92. (c-s/7") *(TC+/FOOD 37)* **POPSCENE. / MACE** 32
(12"+=) *(12FOOD 37)* – I'm fine / Garden central.
(cd-s+=) *(CDFOOD 37)* – Badgeman Brown.

Apr 93. (c-s) *(TCFOOD 40)* **FOR TOMORROW. / INTO ANOTHER / HANGING OVER** 28
(12"+=) *(12FOOD 40)* – Peach.
(cd-s) *(CDFOOD 40)* – ('A'extended) / Peach / Bone bag.
(cd-s) *(CDSFOOD 40)* – ('A'side) / When the cows come home / Beachcoma / For tomorrow (acoustic).

May 93. (cd/c/lp) *(FOOD CD/TC/LP 9)* *<89442>* **MODERN LIFE IS RUBBISH** 15
– For tomorrow / Advert / Colin Zeal / Pressure on Julian / Star shaped / Blue jeans / Chemical world / Sunday Sunday / Oily water / Miss America / Villa Rosie / Coping / Turn it up / Resigned.

Jun 93. (7"red) *(FOODS 45)* **CHEMICAL WORLD. / MAGGIE MAY** 28
(12"/cd-s) *(12/CD FOOD 45)* – ('A'side) / Es Schmecht / Young and lovely / My ark.
(cd-s) *(CDFOODS 45)* – ('A'side) / Never clever (live) / Pressure on Julian (live) / Come together (live).

Oct 93. (7"yellow) *(FOODS 46)* **SUNDAY SUNDAY. / TELL ME, TELL ME** 26
(12") *(12FOODS 46)* – ('A'side) / Long legged / Mixed up.
(cd-s) *(CDFOODS 46)* – ('A'side) / Dizzy / Fried / Shimmer.
(cd-s) *(CDFOODX 46)* – ('A'side) / Daisy bell / Let's all go The Strand.

Mar 94. (7"/c-s) *(FOODS/TCFOOD 47)* **GIRLS AND BOYS. / MAGPIE / PEOPLE IN EUROPE** 5 –
(cd-s) *(CDFOOD 47)* – ('A'side) / People in Europe / Peter Panic.
(cd-s) *(CDFOODS 47)* – ('A'side) / Magpie / Anniversary waltz.

Apr 94. (cd/c/lp) *(FOOD CD/TC/LP 10)* *<29194>* **PARKLIFE** 1 Jun94
– Girls and boys / Tracy Jacks / End of a century / Park life / Bank holiday / Bad head / The debt collector / Far out / To the end / London loves / Trouble in the message centre / Clover over Dover / Magic America / Jubilee / This is a low / Lot 105.

May 94. (c-s) *(TCFOOD 50)* **TO THE END / GIRLS AND BOYS (Pet Shop Boys remix) / THREADNEEDLE STREET** 16
(12"/cd-s) *(12/CD FOOD 50)* – (1st 2 tracks; 2 versions of 2nd).
(cd-s) *(CDFOODS 50)* – ('A'side) / Threadneedle Street / Got yer.
(above featured LETITIA of STEREOLAB. Next with actor PHIL DANIELS.

Jun 94. (c-s,cd-s) *<58155>* **GIRLS AND BOYS / GIRLS AND BOYS (Pet Shop Boys radio mix) / MAGGIE MAY** – 59

Aug 94. (c-s/cd-s) *(TC/CDS FOOD 53)* **PARKLIFE. / SUPA SHOPPA / THEME FROM AN IMAGINARY FILM** 10
(12") *(12FOOD 53)* – (1st 2 tracks) / To the end (French version).
(cd-s) *(CDFOOD 53)* – (1st track) / Beard / To the end (French version).

Nov 94. (c-s/7") *(TCFOOD/FOODS 56)* **END OF A CENTURY. / RED NECKS** 19
(cd-s+=) *(CDFOOD 56)* – Alex's song.

Food Virgin

Aug 95. (c-s/7") *(TC+/FOOD 63)* **COUNTRY HOUSE. / ONE BORN EVERY MINUTE** 1 –
(cd-s+=) *(CDFOOD 63)* – To the end (with FRANCOISE HARDY).
(cd-ep) *(CDFOODS 63)* ('A'live) / Girls and boys (live) / Parklife (live) / For tomorrow (live).

Sep 95. (cd/c/lp) *(FOOD CD/MC/LP 14)* *<40855>* **THE GREAT ESCAPE** 1
– Stereotypes / Country house / Best days / Charmless man / Fade away / Top man / The universal / Mr. Robinson's quango / He thought of cars / It could be you / Ernold Same / Globe alone / Dan Abnormal / Entertain me / Yuko and Hiro.

Nov 95. (c-s) *(TCFOOD 69)* **THE UNIVERSAL / ENTERTAIN ME (the live it! remix)** 5 –
(cd-s+=) *(CDFOODS 69)* – Ultranol / No monsters in me.
(cd-ep) *(CDFOOD 69)* – ('A'live) / Mr. Robinson's quango (live) / It could be you (live) / Stereotypes (live).

Feb 96. (c-s/7") *(TC+/FOOD 73)* **STEREOTYPES. / THE MAN WHO LEFT HIMSELF / TAME** 7 –
(cd-s+=) *(CDFOOD 73)* – Ludwig.

Apr 96. (c-s/7") *(TC+/FOOD 77)* **CHARMLESS MAN. / THE HORRORS** 5 –
(cd-s+=) *(CDFOOD 77)* – A song / St. Louis.

—— BLUR were joint winners (with rivals OASIS; NOEL) of the Ivor Novello Award for songwriter of the year.

May 96. (d-cd; ltd on 'EMI Japan') *(TOCP 8400)* **LIVE AT THE BUDOKAN (live)** – –

—— ALEX JAMES helped to form one-off indie supergroup ME ME ME alongside JUSTIN WELCH (Elastica –), STEPHEN DUFFY and CHARLIE BLOOR. Had a UK Top 20 hit in Aug'96 with 'HANGING AROUND'.

Food Virgin

Jan 97. (7"red) *(FOOD 89)* **BEETLEBUM. / WOODPIGEON SONG** 1 –
(cd-s+=) *(CDFOODS 89)* – ('A'-Mario Caldato Jr mix) / Dancehall.
(cd-s) *(CDFOOD 89)* – ('A'side) / All your life / A spell for money.

Feb 97. (cd/c/lp) *(FOOD CD/TC/LP 19)* *<42876>* **BLUR** 1 61
– Beetlebum / Song 2 / Country sad ballad man / M.O.R. / On your own / Theme from retro / You're so great / Death of a party / Chinese bombs / I'm just a killer for your love / Look inside America / Strange news from another star / Movin' on / Essex dogs.

Apr 97. (7"purple) *(FOOD 93)* **SONG 2 / GET OUT OF THE CITIES** 2 –
(cd-s+=) *(CDFOODS 93)* – Polished stone.
(cd-s) *(CDFOOD 93)* – ('A'side) / Bustin' & dronin' / Country sad ballad man (live acoustic).

Jun 97. (7"white) *(FOOD 98)* **ON YOUR OWN. / POP SCENE (live) / SONG 2 (live)** 5 –
(cd-s+=) *(CDFOOD 98)* – On your own (live).
(cd-s) *(CDFOODS 98)* – ('A'side) / Chinese bombs (live) / Moving on (live) / M.O.R. (live).

Sep 97. (c-s/7"orange) *(TC+/FOOD 107)* **M.O.R. (Alan Moulder road version). / SWALLOWS IN THE HEATWAVE** [15] [–]
(cd-s+=) *(CDFOOD 107)* – Movin' on (William Orbit mix) / Beetlebum (Moby's minimal house mix).

Mar 98. (d-cd) *(TOCP 504445)* **BUSTIN' AND DRONIN'** [ ] [–]

Mar 99. (c-s/7"blue) *(TC+/FOOD 117)* **TENDER. / ALL WE WANT** [2] [–]
(cd-s+=) *(CDFOOD 117)* – Mellow jam (short version).
(cd-s) *(CDFOODS 117)* – ('A'side) / French song (full version) / Song 2 (video).

Mar 99. (cd/c/d-lp) *(FOOD CD/MC/LP 29)* *<99129>* **13** [1] [80]
– Tender / Bugman / Coffee & TV / Swamp song / 1992 / B.L.U.R.E.M.I. / Battle / Mellow song / Trailerpark / Caramel / No distance left to run / Trimm trabb / Optigan 1.

Jun 99. (c-s) *(TCFOOD 122)* **COFFEE & TV / X-OFFENDER (Damon – Controls freaks bugman remix)** [11] [–]
(cd-s+=) *(CDFOOD 122)* – Coyote (Dave's bugman remix).
(12"++=) *(12FOOD 122)* – Trade stylee (Alex's bugman remix) / Metal hip slop (Graham's bugman remix).
(cd-s) *(CDFOODS 122)* – ('A'side) / (above 2).

Nov 99. (c-s) *(TCFOOD 123)* **NO DISTANCE LEFT TO RUN / BEAGLE 2 / SO YOU** [14] [–]
(cd-s) *(CDFOODS 123)* – ('A'side) / Battle (U.N.K.L.E. remix).
(cd-s) *(CDFOOD 123)* – ('A'side) / Tender (Cornelius mix).

Oct 00. (12") *(12FOOD 135)* **MUSIC IS MY RADAR. / BLACK BOOK** [10] [ ]
(cd-s+=) *(CDFOOD 135)* – Headist / Into another (live).
(c-s+=) *(TCFOOD 135)* – She's so high.
(cd-s) *(CDFOODS 135)* – ('A'side) / She's so high / Seven days (live).

Oct 00. (cd/c/d-lp) *(FOOD CD/TC/LPD 33)* *<50457>* **BLUR: THE BEST OF** (compilation) [3] Nov00 [ ]
– Beetlebum / Song 2 / There's no other way / The universal / Coffee & TV / Parklife / End of a century / No distance left to run / Tender / Girls and boys / Charmless man / She's so high / Country house / To the end / On your own / This is a low / For tomorrow (visit to Primrose Hill extended) / Music is my radar. *(d-cd+=; FOODCDS 33)* – LIVE: She's so high / Girls and boys / To the end / End of a century / Charmless man / Beetlebum / MOR / Tender / No distance left to run.

—— now without COXON who continued with his own solo career

Apr 03. (7") *(R 6606)* **OUT OF TIME. / MONEY MAKES ME CRAZY (Marrakesh mix)** [5] [–]
(cd-s+=) *(CDRS 6606)* – Tune 2 / ('A'-video in Morocco).

May 03. (cd/d-lp) *(582997-2/-1)* *<84244>* **THINK TANK** [1] [ ]
– Ambulance / Out of time / Crazy beat / Good song / On the way to the club / Brothers and sisters / Caravan / We've got a file on you / Moroccan peoples revolutionary bowls club / Sweet song / Jets / Gene by gene / Battery in your leg. *(ltd-cd+=; 582997-0)* – Ambulance (live at MTV) / Crazy beat (live at MTV) / Caravan (live at MTV).

Jul 03. (7"red) *(R 6610)* **CRAZY BEAT. / THE OUTSIDER** [18] [–]
(cd-s+=) *(CDRS 6610)* – Don't be / ('A'-alt. video).

Oct 03. (7"red) *(R 6619)* **GOOD SONG. / MORRICONE** [22] [–]
(cd-s) *(CDRS 6619)* – ('A'side) / Me – White noise (alternate version).

– compilations, etc. –

all on 'Food' except where indicated

Sep 99. (cd-ep-box) *(BLURBOX 10)* **10th ANNIVERSARY BOX SET** [ ] [–]
– (all 22 hit singles)

Sep 03. (d-cd) *(592001-2)* **BLUR / 13** [ ] [–]

Sep 03. (d-cd) *(592002-2)* **PARKLIFE / MODERN LIFE IS RUBBISH** [ ] [–]

GORILLAZ

DAMON ALBARN – vocals (of DELTRON 3030) / **DAN "THE AUTOMATOR" NAKAMURA** – producer / **MIHO HATORI** – vocals (of CIBO MATTO) / **JAMIE HEWLETT** – visuals / plus **KID KOALA + DEL THA FUNKEE HOMOSAPIEN** – vocals / **2-D** – keyboards / **MURDOC** – bass / **RUSSEL** – drums / **NOODLE** – guitar / + **TINA WEYMOUTH** – vocals (ex-TALKING HEADS)

Parlophone Virgin

Nov 00. (12") *(12R 6545)* **TOMORROW COMES TODAY. / ROCK THE HOUSE / LATIN SIMONE** [ ] [–]
(cd-s+=) *(CDR 6545)* – ('A'-video).

Mar 01. (c-s) *(TCR 6552)* *<radio cut>* **CLINT EASTWOOD / CLINT EASTWOOD (Ed Case refix) / DRACULA** [4] Aug01 [57]
(cd-s+=) *(CDR 6552)* – ('A'CD-Rom).
(12") *(12R 6552)* – ('A'side) / ('A'-Ed Case refix full) / ('A'-Phil Life cypher version).

Mar 01. (cd/d-lp) *(531138-2/-1)* *<33748>* **GORILLAZ** [3] Jun00 [14]
– Re-hash / 5-4 / Tomorrow comes today / New genius (brother) / Clint Eastwood / Man research (clapper) / Punk / Sound check (gravity) / Double bass / Rock the house / 19-2000 / Latin Simone / Starshine / Slow country / M1 A1 / Clint Eastwood (Ed Case refix full version) / 19-2000 (soul child mix). *(cd+=)* – Dracula / Left hand Suzuki method. *(re-iss. Sep04 as d-cd+=; EBX 13)* – LAIKA COME HOME

Jun 01. (c-s) *(TCR 6559)* **19-2000 / HIP ALBATROSS** [6] [–]
(cd-s) *(CDR 6559)* – ('A'side) / ('A'-Soulchild remix) / Left hand Suzuki method.
(12"++=) *(12R 6559)* – ('A'-Wiseguys house of wisdom remix).

Oct 01. (c-s) *(TCR 6565)* **ROCK THE HOUSE / GHOST TRAIN** [18] [–]
(cd-s+=) *(CDR 6565)* – 19-2000 (video).
(cd-s) *(CDRS 6565)* – ('A'side) / Sounder / Faust / (making of the 'Rock The House' video).

Feb 02. (12") *(12R 6573)* **TOMORROW COMES TODAY. / TOMORROW (dub) / FILM MUSIC (mode remix)** [33] [–]
(cd-s) *(CDR 6573)* – ('A'side) / Film music / Tomorrow dub (Space Monkeyz mix) / ('A'-video).

Mar 02. (cd) *(536942-0)* *<11967>* **G SIDES** (compilation) [65] [84]
– 19/2000 (Soulchild remix) / Dracula / Rock the house / The sounder / Faust / Clint Eastwood (Phi life cypher version) / Ghost train / Hip albatross / Left hand Suzuki method / 12D3 / Clint Eastwood (video) / Rock the house (video).

below 2 as SPACE MONKEYZ VERSUS GORILLAZ; aka ALBARN + NAKAMURA feat. TERRY HALL, EARL 16, etc.

Parlophone Astralwerks

Jul 02. (cd-s) *(CDR 6584)* **LIL' DUB CHEFIN' (album + radio version) / SPACE MONKEYZ THEME / ('A'-video)** [73] [–]

Jul 02. (cd/d-lp) *(540362-2)(539982-1)* *<40522>* **LAIKA COME HOME** (dub mixes) [ ] [ ]
– Jungle fresh (19/2000) / Strictly rubbadub (Slow country) / Banana baby (Tomorrow comes today) / Monkey racket (Man research) / De-punked (Punk) / P45 (5/4) / Dub D9 (Starshine) / Crooked dub (Soundcheck) (Gravity) / Mutant genius (New genius) / Come again (Re-hash) / A fistful of peanuts (Clint Eastwood) / Lil' dub chefin' (M1 A1). *(d-lp+=)* – Strictly rubbadub version / A fistful of peanuts version.

—— next feat. **DE LA SOUL**

Parlophone Virgin

May 05. (cd-s) *(CDR 6663)* *<86988-2>* **FEEL GOOD INC. / SPITTING OUT THE DEMONS** [2] [14]
(dvd-s+=) *(DVDR 6663)* – Bill Murray.

May 05. (cd)(d-lp) *(311691-2)(<8 73838-1>)* **DEMON DAYS** [1] [6]
– Intro / Last living souls / Kids with guns / O grren world / Dirty Harry / Feel good inc. / El manana / Every planet we reach is dead / November has come / All alone / White light / Dare / Fire coming out of the monkey's head / Don't get lost in Heaven / Demon days. *<US+=>* *(ltd-cd w/dvd+=; 474407-0)* – The swagga / Feel good inc. / Feel good inc. (animatics) / Feel good inc. (audio commentary) / Gorillaz talent quest – G bite animation / Gorillaz on set – G bite animation.

below feat. **SHAUN RYDER** – vocals (ex-HAPPY MONDAYS)

Aug 05. (cd-s) *(CDR 6668)* **DARE / CLINT EASTWOOD (live)** [1] [ ]
(cd-s) *(DVDR 6668)* – ('A') / Highway (under construction) / ('A'-Soulwax remix).

Nov 05. (cd-s) *(CDR 6676)* **DIRTY HARRY / ALL ALONE (live)** [6] [–]
(cd-s) *(CDRS 6676)* – ('A') / Hongkongaton / ('A'-Chopper remix).
(dvd-s) *(DVDR 6676)* – ('A') / Murdoc is God / ('A'-animatic with Dirty Harry instrumental).

Apr 06. (7"red) *(R 6685)* **KIDS WITH GUNS. / EL MANANA** [??] [–]
(cd-s+=) *(CDR 6685)* – Stop the damns.
(dvd-s) *(DVDR 6685)* – ('AA'-videos) / Don't get lost in Heaven (original demo) / El manana (animatic).

DAMON ALBARN & . . .

E.M.I. Virgin

Sep 99. (cd; by DAMON ALBARN & MICHAEL NYMAN) *(522370-2)* *<47126-2>* **RAVENOUS** (soundtrack) [ ] Mar99 [ ]
– Hail Columbia / Boyd's journey / Welcome to Fort Spencer (FOSTER'S SOCIAL ORCHESTRA) / Noises off (FOSTER'S SOCIAL

ORCHESTRA) / Stranger at the window / Colquhoun's story / Weendigo myth (QUILTMAN) / Trek to the cave / He was licking me / The cave (MICHAEL NYMAN ORCHESTRA) / Run (MICHAEL NYMAN ORCHESTRA) / Let's go kill that bastard / The pit / Ives returns / Cannibal fantasy / Game of two shoulders / Checkmate / Martha and the horses / Ives torments Boyd and kills Knox / Manifest destiny / Saveoursoulissa / End titles.

Atlantic Atlantic

Mar 00. (cd) *(<7567 83316-2>)* **ORDINARY DECENT CRIMINAL** (soundtrack w/ Various Artists) ☐ May00 ☐
– One day at a time (w/ ROBERT '3D' DEF NAJA) / Kevin on a motorbike / Chase after gallery / Bank job / Dying isn't easy / (+ other artists).

E.M.I. E.M.I.

May 01. (cd; by DAMON ALBARN & EINAR ORN BENEDIKTSSON) *(<532989-2>)* **101 REYKJAVIK** (soundtrack) ☐ Sep01 ☐
– 101 Reykjavik theme / 101 Reykjavik theme (Emiliana Torrini remix) / Bath (ATLANTA) / Frost (JOURNEY CLUB) / Bar beaten / Bar beaten (101 Terror City remix) / Flamenco Lola / Shooting gallery / Suitcase / Suitcase (101 hangovers) (Hilmar Orn Hilmarsson remix) / Bar hip hop / Teapot / Teapot (Egil S. remix) / Fireworks organ / New year (part 1) / New year (part 1 – Bang Gang remix) / New year (part 2) / Glacier memory / Morning beer / University / Dream scene / Stereo blasting / Out of church / Man's world / Bar fight / Bar fight (Minus remix) / Big party / Glacier / Dub Lola / Dub Lola (Gus Gus remix).

BOARDS OF CANADA

Formed: Pentland Hills, nr. Edinburgh . . . 1995 by MICHAEL SANDISON and MARCUS EOIN. The group earned their acclaim after recording a ridiculous amount of tracks which became available on the now legendary 'TWOISM' mini-LP – limited to 100 copies and ever so collectable. Next up was for experimental electronica label 'Skam' who signed the pair in 1996. Hailed as 'Skam's greatest release to date, the 'HI SCORES' EP set the ball rolling for the team in 1996 (now worth over £500). Audiences couldn't get enough of its catchy but simple, A-B-C (or L.F.O.) synth formats and melodies. References were, of course, made to the APHEX TWIN and JEGA, however 'HI SCORES' had a better twisted back-beat to it than, say, RICHARD D. JAMES' cult 'ANALOGUE BUBBLEBATH VOL.1'. It fooled listeners into thinking the band were American by its sheer 1992 hip-hop nostalgia and chilled out beach party vibes. This impressive debut was quickly followed up in late 1996 by a series of tracks for 'UMV' and 'Slam/Musik Aus Strom' side project label 'Mask', with 1998 witnessing the unfettering of the excellent "difficult" third release, 'MUSIC HAS THE RIGHT TO CHILDREN'. Cool as well as deeply serene, the album (distributed by 'Warp' and 'Matador') intensified that early 90's Miami trip-hop identity and added in a little scratching and sampling for good measure. A prime example of this was the single out-take, and the most famous track you'll hear from the album, 'ROYGBIV', which sounded like the Terminator doing slow motion break dancing in a crowded Beverly Hills house party. 1999 saw the latest from BOC, a PEEL SESSIONS EP, another triumph from the Peel acres and an entry into the 'Matador' 10th anniversary collection, 'Everything Is Nice'. The duo finally returned with a two track EP, 'A BEAUTIFUL PLACE IN THE COUNTRY', towards the end of 2000. The single was an unexpected trip into the psychedelic shenanigans that were about to be, once again, explored by the BOARDS OF CANADA. In February 2002, their long-awaited sophomore album, 'GEOGADDI', was released to huge critical acclaim, which resulted in their first interview with the NME. For this they described the open Scottish wilderness as an inspiration for their hallucinogenic, spaced-out synth doodlings. They also declared that the meaning of their moniker was indeed (as older readers may recall!) lifted from an educational company whose films on science and nature had been shown while the pair had attended school. This reflected a lot of the new album; one track in question 'DANDELION' had a backwards moog drone accompanied by a man (actor Leslie Nielsen from 'Naked Gun' fame!) narrating a TV documentary about a diving team; this segued into the six and a half minute epic 'SUNSHINE RECORDER'. Track 16, 'THE DEVIL IN THE DETAILS', had a simple keyboard riff on a loop which played the insane shrills of a child and the voice of a distorted, disjointed telephone operator. 'GEODADDI' (a near Top 20 entry) was much darker and yet much more layered in terms of themes, music and ambience. For two guys living in the countryside this was quite a feat, a real slice of math-electronica that was both gentle and eerily sublime. Three years in the lab, 'THE CAMPFIRE HEADPHASE' (2005) introduced straight up guitars into the mix, although the overall effect was erring towards BoC-by-numbers, loitering on the outskirts of the UK Top 40. The following May, they finally issued a belated single, or rather an EP 'TRANS CANADA HIGHWAY', featuring 'CAMPFIRE..' twiddle-along, 'DAYVAN COWBOY'.

Album rating: TWOISM mini (*7) / HI SCORES mini (*7) / MUSIC HAS THE RIGHT TO CHILDREN (*9) / PEEL SESSIONS (*7) / GEOGADDI (*9) / THE CAMPFIRE HEADPHASE (*6)

MICHAEL SANDISON (b.10 Jun'69) – electronics / **MARCUS EOIN** (b.21 Sep'70) – electronics

Music 70 not iss.

Aug 95. (ltd; m-lp) *(BOARD 1)* **TWOISM** ☐ –
– Sixtyniner / Directline / Iced cooly / Basefree / Twoism / Seeya later / Melissa juice / Smokes quantity. *(re-iss. Nov02 on 'Warp' m-lp/m-cd+=; WARP LP/CD 70)* – 1986 summer fire.

Skam not iss.

Dec 96. (m-lp) *(SKA 8)* **HIGH SCORES** ☐ –
– Hi scores / Turquoise hexagon sun / Nlogax / June 9th / Seeya later / Everything you do is a balloon. *(m-cd-iss. Nov02; SKA 8CD)*

Jan 98. (7") *(KMAS 1)* **AQUARIUS. / CHINOOK** ☐ –

Warp – Skam Matador

Mar 98. (10") *(WAP10 55)* **ROYGBIV. / TELEPHASIC WORKSHOP** ☐ –

Apr 98. (cd/d-lp) *(WARP CD/LP 55 – SKALD 1)* *<OLE 299-2/-1>* **MUSIC HAS THE RIGHT TO CHILDREN** ☐ ☐
– Wildlife analysis / An eagle in your mind / The color of the fire / Telephasic workshop / Triangles & rhombuses / Sixtyten / Turquoise hexagon sun / Kaini industries / Bocuma / Roygbiv / Rue the whirl / Aquarius / Olson / Pete standing alone / Smokes quantity / Open the light / One very important thought. *(d-lp+=)* – Happy cycling.

Warp Warp

Jan 99. (cd-ep) *(<WAP 114CD>)* **PEEL SESSIONS** ☐ Mar99 ☐
– Aquarius (version 3) / Happy cycling / Olson (version 3).

Nov 00. (12"/cd-s) *(<WAP 144/+CD>)* **IN A BEAUTIFUL PLACE OUT IN THE COUNTRY EP** ☐ ☐
– Kid for today / Amo bishop Roden / In a beautiful place out in the country / Zoetrope.

Feb 02. (cd/t-lp) *(<WARP CD/LP 101>)* **GEOGADDI** 21 ☐
– Ready let's go / Music is math / Beware the friendly stranger / Gyroscope / Dandelion / Sunshine recorder / In the annexe / Julie and Candy / The smallest weird number / 1969 / Energy warning / The beach at Redpoint / Opening the mouth / Alpha and Omega / I saw drones / The devil in the details / A is to B as B is to C / Over the horizon radar / Dawn chorus / Diving station / You could feel the sky / Corsair / Magic window.

Oct 05. (cd/lp) *(<WARP CD/LP 123>)* **THE CAMPFIRE HEADPHASE** 41 ☐
– Into the rainbow vein / Chromakey dreamcoat / Satellite anthem Icarus / Peacock tail / Dayvan cowboy / A moment of clarity / '84 Pontiac dream / Sherbet head / Oscar see through red eye / Ataronchronon / Hey Saturday sun / Constants are changing / Slow this bird down / Tears from the compound eye / Farewell fire.

May 06. (12"ep/cd-ep) *(<WAP 200/+CD>)* **TRANS CANADA HIGHWAY** ☐ ☐
– Dayvan cowboy / Left side drive / Heard from telegraph lines / Skyliner / Under the Coke sign / Dayvan cowboy (odd Nosdam remix).

☐ BODY COUNT (see under ⇒ ICE-T)

Marc BOLAN

Born: MARC FELD, 30 Sep'47, London, England. He began his performing career under the improbable moniker of TOBY TYLER, before ditching it and signing to 'Decca'. After 3 flop singles, he enjoyed a brief stint with JOHN'S CHILDREN ('Desdemona') before teaming up in 1968 with bongo player STEVE PEREGRINE TOOK to form TYRANNOSAURUS REX. Far from the hoary, chest-beating proto-metal that name might imply, the band's sound was a folky melange of acoustic guitar, manic bongos and pop melodies. Unfortunately the band were victims of their era and prone to lyrical flights of fancy that often broke down into hippy cliche, just check out the title of their debut mid-68 album 'MY PEOPLE WERE FAIR AND HAD SKY IN THEIR HAIR . . . BUT NOW THEY'RE CONTENT TO WEAR STARS ON THEIR BROWS'. A bit of a hippy himself at the time, Radio One DJ JOHN PEEL championed their first single 'DEBORA', as well as material from their next 3 albums. They became a big draw on the underground circuit, helping the albums gain minor placings in the UK charts. MARC's ex-model features and effeminate charisma did no harm in making him an object of hippy chick lust, and it was about time the band had a sexier name to match. Just before the group became T.REX, TOOK was replaced by MICKEY FINN, as they gradually adopted an all-electric sound. The spanking new single 'RIDE A WHITE SWAN', nearly nailed the No.1 spot in October 1970 and made BOLAN a fully fledged pop idol. A jaunty little number with a stabbing guitar-line, it heralded the band's strident new sound, although it retained the quasi-mystical lyrical schtick. STEVE CURRY and BILL LEGEND were drafted in and the band notched up 8 consecutive Top 3 hits, including 4 UK chart-toppers. The celebratory 'HOT LOVE' and the timeless 'GET IT ON' both hit the top spot as did the 'ELECTRIC WARRIOR' album, displaying a welcome move to raunchier (but often equally silly) lyrics. BOLAN then set up his own label through EMI after 'JEEPSTER' was re-issued without his consent. He almost single handedly invented the "glam-rock" phenomenon, achieving the rare feat of being a rock idol and pop star at the same time. 'TELEGRAM SAM', 'METAL GURU' and the evergreen '20th CENTURY BOY' are still guaranteed to get you dusting down your 6" platforms a quarter of a century on. After the single 'THE GROOVER' was released in 1973 and after splitting with his wife JUNE CHILD, BOLAN brought in his new girlfriend GLORIA JONES to record 'TRUCK ON (TYKE)'. This was the first single by T.REX not to make the Top 10. His creativity was ebbing and he moved to America to record some lacklustre formulaic material in a variety of styles. Like early fan JOHN PEEL, BOLAN embraced the subsequent punk takeover and had a new deal with 'R.C.A.' before he met his untimely end on 16th September 1977. In yet another bizarre rock'n'roll death, his girlfriend crashed their car into a tree near Barnes Common, which soon became a shrine. Since his death, obsessive fans and curious observers alike have lapped up a stream of documentaries, greatest hits packages, tributes and re-issues (mostly on fan club label 'Marc On Wax'), which show no sign of abating.

• **Covers:** SUMMERTIME BLUES (Eddie Cochran) / DO YOU WANNA DANCE (Bobby Freeman) / DOCK OF THE BAY (Otis Redding) / TO KNOW HIM IS TO LOVE HIM (Teddy Bears) / RIP IT UP (Little Richard) / ENDLESS SLEEP (Joey Reynolds) / A TEENAGER IN LOVE (Dion).

Album rating: Tyrannosaurus Rex: MY PEOPLE WERE FAIR AND HAD SKY IN THE HAIR, BUT NOW THEY'RE CONTENT TO WEAR STARS ON THEIR BROWS (*6) / PROPHETS, SEERS AND SAGES, THE ANGEL OF THE AGES (*6) / UNICORN (*7) / A BEARD OF STARS (*6) / T.Rex: T.REX (*5) / ELECTRIC WARRIOR (*8) / THE SLIDER (*7) / TANX (*6) / ZINC ALLOY & THE HIDDEN RIDERS OF TOMORROW (*4) / BOLAN'S ZIP GUN (*4) / FUTURISTIC DRAGON (*5) / DANDY IN THE UNDERWORLD (*5) / THE ULTIMATE COLLECTION compilation (*9) / THE ESSENTIAL . . . compilation (*9)

MARC BOLAN

— solo using session men

Decca | not iss.

Nov 65. (7") *(F 12288)* **THE WIZARD. / BEYOND THE RISING SUN** | – |

Jun 66. (7") *(F 12413)* **THE THIRD DEGREE. / SAN FRANCISCO POET** | – |

Parlophone | not iss.

Dec 66. (7") *(R 5539)* **HIPPY GUMBO. / MISFIT** | – |

— BOLAN then joined JOHN'S CHILDREN before forming own band

TYRANNOSAURUS REX

MARC – vocals, guitars / **STEVE PEREGRINE TOOK** (b.28 Jul'49, London) – bongos, vocals

Regal Zonophone | A&M

Apr 68. (7") *(RZ 3008)* **DEBORA. / CHILD STAR** | 34 |

Jun 68. (lp; stereo/mono) *(S+/LRZ 1003)* **MY PEOPLE WERE FAIR AND HAD SKY IN THEIR HAIR . . . BUT NOW THEY'RE CONTENT TO WEAR STARS ON THEIR BROWS** | 15 |
– Red hot mama / Scenesof / Child star / Strange orchestras / Chateau in Virginia Waters / Dwarfish trumpet blues / Mustang Ford / Afghan woman / Knight / Graceful fat shake / Weilder of words / Frowning Atahuallpa. *(re-iss. May85 on 'Sierra' lp/c; FEDB/CFEDB 5013) (cd-iss. Oct98 on 'Polydor'; 541009-2)*

Regal Zonophone | Blue Thumb

Aug 68. (7") *(RZ 3011)* **ONE INCH ROCK. / SALAMANDA PALAGANDA** | 28 |

Oct 68. (lp; stereo/mono) *(S+/LRZ 1005)* **PROPHETS, SEERS AND SAGES, THE ANGELS OF THE AGES**
– Deboraarobed / Stacey grove / Wind quartets / Conesuala / Trelawny lawn / Aznagell the mage / The friends / Salamanda Palaganda / Our wonderful brownskin man / Oh Harley (the Saltimbanques) / Eastern spell / The travelling tragition / Juniper suction / Scenes of dynasty. *(re-iss. May85 on 'Sierra' lp/c; FEDB/CFEDB 5022) (cd-iss. Oct94 on 'Disky'; CUCD 10) (cd re-iss. Oct98 on 'Polydor'; 541010-2)*

Jan 69. (7") *(RZ 3016)* **PEWTER SUITOR. / WARLORD OF THE ROYAL CROCODILES**

May 69. (lp; stereo/mono) *(S+/LRZ 1007)* **UNICORN** | 12 |
– Chariots of silk / 'Pon a hill / The seal of seasons / The throat of winter / Cat black (the wizard's hat) / Stones of Avalon / She was born to be my unicorn / Like a white star, tangled and far, Tulip that's what you are / Warlord of the royal crocodiles / Evenings of Damask / The sea beasts / Iscariot / Nijinsky hind / The pilgrim's tale / The misty coast of Albany / Romany soup. *(re-iss. May85 on 'Sierra' lp/c; FEDB/CFEDB 5024) (cd-iss. Oct94 on 'Disky'; CUCD 11) (cd re-iss. Oct98 on 'Polydor'; 541012-2)*

Jul 69. (7") *(RZ 3022)* **KING OF THE RUMBLING SPIRES. / DO YOU REMEMBER?** | 44 |

— **MICKEY FINN** (b. 3 Jan'47) – bongos, vocals repl. TOOK who joined PINK FAIRIES (He died Nov80)

Jan 70. (7") *(RZ 3025)* **BY THE LIGHT OF THE MAGICAL MOON. / FIND A LITTLE WOOD**

Mar 70. (lp) *(SLRZ 1013)* **A BEARD OF STARS** | 21 |
– Prelude / A day laye / The woodland bop / First heart mighty dawn dart / Pavillions of sun / Organ blues / By the light of the magical Moon / Wind cheetah / A beard of stars / Great horse / Dragon's ear / Lofty skies / Dove / Elemental child. *<US-import had free 7"; BLUE THING> (re-iss. May85 on 'Sierra' lp/c; FEDB/CFEDB 5035) (cd-iss. Oct98 on 'Polydor'; 541003-2)*

T. REX

Fly | Blue Thumb

Oct 70. (7"m) *(BUG 1) <121>* **RIDE A WHITE SWAN. / IS IT LOVE / SUMMERTIME BLUES** | 2 | Jan71 | 76 |

— added **STEVE CURRY** (b.21 May'47, Grimsby, England) – bass / **BILL LEGEND** (b. 8 May'44, Essex, England) – drums

Fly | Reprise

Dec 70. (lp/c) *(HIFLY/ZCFLY 2) <6440>* **T.REX** | 13 | Apr71 |
– The children of Rarn / Jewel / The visit / Childe / The time of love is

now / Diamond meadows / Root of star / Beltane walk / Is it love / One inch rock / Summer deep / Seagull woman / Sun eye / The wizard / The children of Rarn (reprise). *(re-iss. Mar78 + Oct81; same) (re-iss. May85 on 'Sierra' lp/c; FEDB/CFEDB 5010) (cd-iss. May92 on 'Castle';) (cd re-iss. Oct98 on 'Polydor'; 541011-2)*

Feb 71. (7"m) *(BUG 6)* **HOT LOVE. / WOODLAND ROCK / KING OF THE MOUNTAIN COMETH** [1] [–]

Apr 71. (7"m) *<1006>* **HOT LOVE. / ONE INCH ROCK / SEAGULL WOMAN** [–] [72]

Jul 71. (7"m) *(BUG 10)* **GET IT ON (BANG A GONG). / THERE WAS A TIME / RAW RAMP** [1] [–]

Sep 71. (lp/c) *(HIFLY/ZCFLY 6) <6466>* **ELECTRIC WARRIOR** [1] Oct71 [32]
– Mambo sun / Cosmic dancer / Jeepster / Monolith / Lean woman blues / Get it on (bang a gong) / Planet queen / Girl / The motivator / Life's a gas / Rip off. *(re-iss. Mar78 + Oct81; same) (cd-iss. May87 on 'Sierra; CDTR 2) (re-iss. Apr90 on 'Castle' c/cd+=; CLA MC/CD 180)* – Hot love / Deborah. *(cd re-iss. Oct98 on 'Polydor'; 541007-2) (lp re-iss. Sep99 on 'Simply Vinyl'; SVLP 117) (deluxe cd-iss. Sep01 on 'Polydor'+=; 493113-2)* – (work in progress tracks)

Nov 71. (7") *(BUG 16)* **JEEPSTER. / LIFE'S A GAS** [2] [–]

Dec 71. (7") *<1032>* **BANG A GONG (GET IT ON). / RAW RAMP** [–] [10]

E.M.I. Reprise

Jan 72. (7"m) *(T REX 1) <1078>* **TELEGRAM SAM. / CADILLAC / BABY STRANGE** [1] Apr72 [67]
(re-iss. Mar82; same); hit No.69)

Feb 72. (7") *<1056>* **JEEPSTER. / RIP OFF** [–] [ ]

May 72. (lp/c) *(HIFLY/ZCFLY 8)* **BOLAN BOOGIE** (compilation) [1] [–]
– Get it on (bang a gong) / The king of the mountain cometh / She was born to be my unicorn / Dove / Woodland bop / Ride a white swan / Raw ramp / Jeepster / First heart mighty dawn dart / By the light of the magical Moon / Summertime blues / Hot love. *(re-iss. Mar78 & Oct81; same) (re-iss. Apr89 on 'Castle' lp/c/cd; CLA LP/MC/CD 145) (cd re-iss. Oct98 on 'Polydor'; 541006-2)*

May 72. (7"m) *(MARC 1) <1095>* **METAL GURU. / LADY / THUNDERWING** [1] [ ]

Jul 72. (lp/c) *(BLN/ 5001) <2095>* **THE SLIDER** [4] Aug72 [17]
– Metal guru / Mystic lady / Rock on / The slider / Baby boomerang / Spaceball ricochet / Buick MacKane / Telegram Sam / Rabbit fighter / Baby strange / Ballrooms of Mars / Chariot choogle / Main man. *(re-iss. Nov89 on 'Marc On Wax' lp/c/cd; MARC L/K/D 503) (cd re-iss. Jul94 on 'Edsel'; EDCD 390) (deluxe d-cd-iss. Jun02 on 'Edsel'+=;* **MEDCD 715)** – (alt. takes).

Jul 72. (7") *<1122>* **THE SLIDER. / ROCK ON** [–] [ ]

Sep 72. (7"m) *(MARC 2)* **CHILDREN OF THE REVOLUTION. / JITTERBUG LOVE / SUNKEN RAGS** [2] [ ]

Dec 72. (7") *(MARC 3)* **SOLID GOLD EASY ACTION. / BORN TO BOOGIE** [2] [ ]

Mar 73. (7") *(MARC 4)* **20th CENTURY BOY. / FREE ANGEL** [3] [ ]

Mar 73. (lp/c) *(BLN/ 5002) <2132>* **TANX** [4] [ ]
– Tenement lady / Rapids / Mister mister / Broken hearted blues / Shock rock / Country honey / Electric Slim and the factory man / Mad Donna / Born to boogie / Life is strange / The street and the babe shadow / Highway knees / Left hand Luke and the beggar boys. *(re-iss. Oct87 on 'Marc On Wax' lp/pic-lp/c/cd; RAP/+D/C/CD 504) (re-iss. Nov89 lp/c/cd; MARC L/K/D 504) (cd re-iss. Jul94 on 'Edsel'; EDCD 391) (cdluxe d-cd-iss. Aug02 +=; MEDCD 716)* – (alt. takes).

Jun 73. (7") *(MARC 5)* **THE GROOVER. / MIDNIGHT** [4] [–]

Jun 73. (7") **THE GROOVER. / BORN TO BOOGIE** [–] [ ]

—— added **JACK GREEN** – guitar (plus 3 female backing singers incl. **GLORIA JONES**)

Nov 73. (7") *(MARC 6)* **TRUCK ON (TYKE). / SITTING HERE** [12] [–]

—— (T.REX = FINN, CURRIE, GREEN, JONES – keyboards, vocals) / **DAVY LUTTON** – drums (ex-HEAVY JELLY), repl. LEGEND (2 more female singers)

Feb 74. (7"; as MARC BOLAN & T.REX) *(MARC 7)* **TEENAGE DREAM. / SATISFACTION PONY** [13] [ ]

Mar 74. (lp/c; as MARC BOLAN & T.REX) *(BNLA 7751)* **ZINC ALLOY AND THE EASY RIDERS OF TOMORROW** [12] [ ]
– Venus loon / Sound pit / Explosive mouth / Galaxy / Orange / Nameless wildness / Teenage dream / Liquid gang / Carsmile Smith & the old one / You've got to jive to stay alive – Spanish midnight / Interstellar soul / Painless persuasion and the meathawk / Immaculate / The avengers (superbad) / The leopards (featuring Gardinia and The Mighty Slug). *(re-iss. Oct87 on 'Marc On Wax' lp/pic-lp/c/cd; RAP/+D/C/CD 505) (re-iss. Nov89 lp/c/cd; MARC L/K/D 505) (cd re-iss. Jul94 on 'Edsel'; EDCD 392) (deluxe d-cd-iss. Jul02 +=; MEDCD 717)* – (alt. takes).

Jul 74. (7") *(MARC 8)* **LIGHT OF LOVE. / EXPLOSIVE MOUTH** [22] [–]

—— added **DINO DINES** – keyboards

Nov 74. (7") *(MARC 9)* **ZIP GUN BOOGIE. / SPACE BOSS** [41] [–]

Feb 75. (lp/c) *(BNLA/ 7752)* **BOLAN'S ZIP GUN** [ ] [ ]
– Light of love / Solid baby / Precious star / Zip gun boogie / Token of my love / Think zine / 'Till dawn / Girl in the thunderbolt suit / I really love you baby / Golden belt. *(re-iss. Jul87 on 'Marc On Wax' lp/pic-lp/c/cd; RAP/+D/C/CD 506) (re-iss. Nov89 lp/c/cd; MARC L/K/D 506) (cd re-iss. Jul94 on 'Edsel'; EDCD 393) (deluxe d-cd-iss. Aug02 +=; MEDCD 718)* – (alt. takes).

—— members FINN and GREEN departed. The latter to PRETTY THINGS. Now 5-piece comprising **BOLAN, JONES, CURRIE, LUTTON + DINES**

Jul 75. (7") *(MARC 10)* **NEW YORK CITY. / CHROME SITAR** [15] [–]

—— next with **BILLY PRESTON** – keyboards

Oct 75. (7"m; as T.REX DISCO PARTY) *(MARC 11)* **DREAMY LADY. / DO YOU WANNA DANCE / DOCK OF THE BAY** [30] [–]

Feb 76. (lp/c) *(BLNA/ 5004)* **FUTURISTIC DRAGON** [50] [ ]
– Futuristic dragon / Jupiter lion / All alone / Chrome sitar / New York City / My little baby / Calling all destroyers / Theme for a dragon / Sensation boulevard / Ride my wheels / Dreamy lady / Dawn storm / Casual agent. *(re-iss. Oct87 on 'Marc On Wax' lp/pic-lp/c/cd; RAP/+D/C/CD 507) (re-iss. Nov89 lp/c/cd; MARC L/K/D 507) (cd re-iss. Jul94 on 'Edsel'; EDCD 394) (deluxe d-cd-iss. Jun02 +=; MEDCD 719)* – (alt. takes).

Feb 76. (7") *(MARC 13)* **LONDON BOYS. / SOLID BABY** [40] [–]

Jun 76. (7") *(MARC 14)* **I LOVE TO BOOGIE. / BABY BOOMERANG** [13] [–]

Sep 76. (7") *(MARC 15)* **LASER LOVE. / LIFE'S AN ELEVATOR** [41] [–]

Jan 77. (7"; by MARC BOLAN & GLORIA JONES) *(EMI 2572)* **TO KNOW HIM IS TO LOVE HIM. / CITY PORT** [ ] [–]

—— now comprised BOLAN and DINES who brought in **MILLER ANDERSON** – guitar (ex-SAVOY BROWN) repl. GLORIA JONES who went solo / **HERBIE FLOWERS** – bass repl. CURRIE who went into sessions **TONY BRENNAN** – drums repl. LUTTON who joined WRECKLESS ERIC

Mar 77. (7") *(MARC 16)* **THE SOUL OF MY SUIT. / ALL ALONE** [42] [–]

Mar 77. (lp/c) *(BLNA 5005)* **DANDY IN THE UNDERWORLD** [26] [ ]
– Dandy in the underworld / Crimson moon / Universe / I'm a fool for you / I love to boogie / Visions of Domino / Jason B. Sad / Groove a little / Hang-ups / The soul of my suit / Pain and love / Teen riot structure. *(re-iss. Oct87 on 'Marc On Wax'; lp/pic-lp/c/cd; RAP/+D/C/CD 508) (re-iss. Nov89 lp/c/cd; MARC L/K/D 508) (cd re-iss. Jul94 on 'Edsel'; EDCD 395) (deluxe d-cd-iss. Jul02 +=; MEDCD 720)* – (alt. takes).

May 77. (7") *(MARC 17)* **DANDY IN THE UNDERWORLD. / GROOVE A LITTLE** [ ] [–]

Aug 77. (7") *(MARC 18)* **CELEBRATE SUMMER. / RIDE MY WHEELS** [ ] [–]

—— On 16th Sep'77 MARC BOLAN died when his car driven by GLORIA hit a tree. ANDERSON joined SOUTHSIDE JOHNNY and FLOWERS formed SKY.

Apr 78. (7") *(MARC 19)* **CRIMSON MOON. / JASON B. SAD** [ ] [–]

– (selective) compilations, etc. –

on 'Fly' UK / 'Reprise' US unless mentioned otherwise.

Aug 71. (lp/c) *(TON/CTON 2)* **THE BEST OF T. REX** [21] [ ]

Mar 72. (d-lp/d-c) *(TOOFA/ZCTOF 3-4) / A&M; <3514>* **PROPHETS, SEERS AND SAGES, THE ANGELS OF THE AGES / MY PEOPLE WERE FAIR . . .** <US-title 'TYRANNOSAURUS REX – A BEGINNING'> [1] [ ]
(re-iss. Oct81; same)

Mar 72. (7"ep) *Magni Fly; (ECHO 102)* **DEBORA / ONE INCH ROCK. / WOODLAND BOP / SEAL OF SEASONS** [7] [ ]

Dec 72. (d-lp/d-c) *Cube; (TOOFA/ZCTOF 9-10)* **A BEARD OF STARS / UNICORN** [44] [ ]
(re-iss. Mar78 + Oct81; same) (re-iss. Sep88 on 'That's Original' d-lp/c/cd;) (re-iss. cd Oct94 on 'Disky';)

Sep 73. (7"; as BIG CARROT) *E.M.I.; (EMI 2047)* **BLACKJACK. / SQUINT EYE MANGLE** [ ] [–]

Nov 73. (lp/c) *E.M.I.; (BLN/ 5003)* **GREAT HITS** [32] [ ]

Jun 74. (lp; by MARC BOLAN) *Track; (2410 201)* **THE BEGINNING OF DOVES** [ ] [–]

(re-iss. Aug89 on 'Media Motion' lp/c/cd; MEDIA/+C/CD 2) (cd-iss. Oct91 on 'Receiver';)

Jun 74. (7"m; by MARC BOLAN) *Track; (2094 013)* **JASPER C. DEBUSSY. / HIPPY GUMBO / THE PERFUMED GARDEN OF GULLIVER SMITH** [ ] [–]

Jun 79. (lp/c) *E.M.I.; (NUT 5)* **SOLID GOLD T.REX** [51] [ ]
(re-iss. May82 on 'Fame' lp/c; FA/TC-FA 3005) (cd-iss. Feb99 on 'Repertoire'; RR 4800)

Mar 81. (12"pic-ep/12"clear-ep) *Rarn; (MBFS 001 C/P)* **THE RETURN OF THE ELECTRIC WARRIOR** [50] [–]
– Sing me a song / Endless sleep (extended) / The lilac hand of Menthol Dan. *(re-iss. 7"pic-d.Jul82;)*

Aug 81. (pic-lp; 2 diff) *Marc; (ABOLAN 1P)* **T.REX IN CONCERT (live)** [35] [–]

Sep 81. (7"/7"pic-d; by MARC BOLAN) *Cherry Red: (CHERRY/+P 29)* **YOU SCARE ME TO DEATH. / THE PERFUMED GARDEN OF GULLIVER SMITH** [51] [–]

Oct 81. (pic-lp/lp; by MARC BOLAN) *Cherry Red; (P+/ERED 20)* **YOU SCARE ME TO DEATH** [88] [–]
(re-iss. Nov94 on 'Emporio' cd/c; EMPR CD/MC 545)

Sep 83. (lp/c; by MARC BOLAN) *Marc On Wax; (MARC L/K 501)* **DANCE IN THE MIDNIGHT** [83] [–]
(re-iss. Apr85; same)

Apr 85. (d-lp/d-c; as MARC BOLAN & T.REX) *K-Tel; (NE/CE 1297)* **THE BEST OF THE 20th CENTURY BOY** [5] [–]
(cd-iss. Oct87; NCD 3325)

May 85. (7"ep) *Marc On Wax; (TANX 1)* **MEGAREX 1 (medley). / CHARIOT CHOOGLE / LIFE'S AN ELEVATOR** [72] [–]
(12"+=) *(12TANX 1)* – Solid baby.

May 87. (7"; as MARC BOLAN & T. REX) *Marc On Wax; (MARC 10)* **GET IT ON. / JEEPSTER** [54] [–]
(12"+=/c-s+=/cd-s+=) *(MARC B/C/CD 10)* – Cadillac.

Aug 87. (12"ep) *Strange Fruit; (SFPS 031)* **THE PEEL SESSIONS** (27.10.70) [ ] [–]
– Jewel / Ride a white swan / Elemental child / Sun eye. *(cd-ep-iss.Dec94; SFPSCD 031)*

Jun 91. (cd/c) *Music Club; (MC CD/TC 030)* **THE VERY BEST OF MARC BOLAN & T.REX** [ ] [–]
(gold-cd-iss. Mar96; MCCDSE 030)

Aug 91. (7"/c-s; as MARC BOLAN & T.REX) *Marc On Wax; (MARC/+C 501)* **20th CENTURY BOY. / MIDNIGHT / THE GROOVER** [13] [–]
(12"+=/cd-s+=) *(MARC T/CD 501)* – Telegram Sam.

Sep 91. (cd/c/lp; MARC BOLAN & T.REX) *Telstar; (TCD/STAC/STAR 2539)* **THE ULTIMATE COLLECTION** [4] [–]
– 20th century boy / Metal guru / I love to boogie / Debora / New York City / Telegram Sam / Hot love / Dreamy lady / One inch rock / The soul of my suit / London boys / Ride a white swan / Get it on / Light of love / Children of the revolution / Jeepster / Laser love / Zip gun boogie / The groover / King of the rumbling spires / Plateau skull / Truck on (Tyke) / Solid gold easy action / Teenage dream. *(cd has 4 extra above)*

Sep 95. (cd/c; as MARC BOLAN & T. REX) *Polygram TV; (525 961-2/-4)* **THE ESSENTIAL COLLECTION** [24] [–]
(re-iss. Oct00 on 'Universal TV'; same) – (hit UK No.34)

Apr 99. (4xcd-box) *Burning Airlines; (XPILOT 017)* **THE WARRIOR BOX SET** [ ] [–]
– (ELECTRIC WARRIOR SESSIONS / ELECTRIC BOOGIE / SPACEBALL / T.REX)

Sep 99. (d-cd) *Cleopatra; (CLP 577)* **T. REX CLASSICS** [ ] [–]

Sep 02. (cd) *Universal TV; (493432-2)* **THE ESSENTIAL COLLECTION (25th ANNIVERSARY EDITION)** [18] [–]
– 20th Century boy / Get it on / Telegram Sam / Ride a white swan / Jeepster / Hot love / Children of the revolution / Metal guru / I love to boogie / Debora (original full length version) / The groover / Truck on (tyke) / Teenage dream / New York City / King of the rumbling spires / By the light of the magical moon / Summertime blues / Cosmic dancer / Light of love / Dreamy lady / London boys / Laser love / One inch rock / Solid gold easy action. *(cd w/ dvd+=)* – (videos).

Nov 03. (d-cd) *Chrome Dreams; (<CDCD 5004>)* **FOR THE LION AND THE UNICORN IN THE OAK FORESTS OF FAUN** [ ] [ ]

Jan 04. (cd) *Universal; (<E 493718-2>)* **THE UNIVERSAL MASTERS COLLECTION** [ ] [ ]

Sep 04. (cd) *Thunderwing; (TPLCD 4)* **BUMP 'N' GRIND** [ ] [–]

Mar 05. (cd) *Classic Rock Legends; (CRP 1769)* **INSIDE T. REX** [ ] [ ]

BON JOVI

Formed: Sayreville, New Jersey, USA . . . spring '83, by JON BON JOVI and DAVID BRYAN, who duly recruited RICHIE SAMBORA, ALEC SUCH and TICO TORRES. Gaining a toehold on the music business ladder by helping out at his cousin's recording studio, JON found time to cut a rough demo of 'RUNAWAY', which subsequently gained radio play after being featured on a local various artists compilation. A line-up that would remain stable throughout BON JOVI's career was soon established and by the summer of 1983, the band had signed to a worldwide deal with 'Polygram'. The first two albums, 'BON JOVI' (1984) and '7800 DEGREES FAHRENHEIT' (1985) were generally derided by critics for their formulaic, glossy pop-metal content, yet the latter sold respectably, 'Polygram's marketing muscle and JON's pretty boy looks certainly not doing the band any harm. At this point, BON JOVI were just another name in an endless sea of wet-permed 'hair' bands on the hard-rock circuit and no one was quite expecting the splash that 'SLIPPERY WHEN WET' would make upon its release in 1986. Preceded by the squalling riff and anthemic chorus of 'YOU GIVE LOVE A BAD NAME', the album was heavy metal (in the broadest possible sense) for people who didn't like heavy metal (housewives, junior schoolgirls, construction workers, etc.). The next single taken from it was 'LIVIN' ON A PRAYER', a hard bitten tale of love on the breadline (rather ironic considering the moolah rolling into BON JOVI's coffers) that featured what must rank as one of the most bombastic choruses in the history of rock. Elsewhere on the record, the production loomed equally large and the songs were relentlessly hook-laden, with just enough edge to convince "real" rock fans that the band hadn't sold out. 'WANTED DEAD OR ALIVE' marked the beginning of JON's cowboy fantasies while 'I'D DIE FOR YOU' and 'NEVER SAY GOODBYE' were the obligatory 'sensitive' numbers. The album's success was partly down to the band hiring soft rock songsmith extrordinaire, DESMOND CHILD, whose unerringly catchy way with a tune saw the album going on to sell millions. BON JOVI were at the top of their career already, headlining the Monsters Of Rock shows in Britain and Europe. No doubt feeling more confident about his songwriting abilities, JON BON JOVI followed a more SPRINGSTEEN-esque direction on 'NEW JERSEY' (1988); more rock, less metal, while still retaining the spotless production and impeccable hooks. 'LIVING IN SIN', 'BLOOD ON BLOOD' (title taken from SPRINGSTEEN's 'HIGHWAY PATROLMAN', perchance?) and 'WILD IS THE WIND' were all reassuringly strident, the album again selling in mindboggling quantities. In many ways, JON BON JOVI is BON JOVI, so when JON-boy released his 'BLAZE OF GLORY' solo effort (a result of his acting role in 'YOUNG GUNS II'), it was a case of more of the same. When the band re-emerged in 1992 with 'KEEP THE FAITH', there was no question of the album failing to scale the heights of its predecessors. The songs were intact although the likes of 'I'LL SLEEP WHEN I'M DEAD' were verging on self-parody. Needless to say, a compilation, 'CROSSROADS', sold phenomenally with the subsequent studio album, 'THESE DAYS' also hitting No.1 in Britain. While the band continue to win the hearts of coffee table browsers the world over, most metal fans probably lost interest years ago. Something of a celeb these days with his short(er) hair, pseudo-trendy image and acting career, JON recently completed his own short film and accompanying soundtrack (he'd previously made his acting debut proper, in the 1996 film, 'Moonlight And Valentino'). In fact the man could do no wrong, going on to have further major chart success with his 'DESTINATION ANYWHERE' (1997) solo set and its UK Top 5 single, 'MIDNIGHT IN CHELSEA'. He even turned up on

Chris Evans' TFI Friday with a rough'n'ready cover of Simon & Garfunkel's 'MRS. ROBINSON'. BON JOVI the band, meanwhile, returned in spring '99 with a one-off single, 'REAL LIFE', followed a year later by the 'CRUSH' album. The only surprises on offer – apart from the fact that JON BON seems immune to the ageing process – were that if anything, the band's sound was even more mainstream than before while previously undetectable influences of British 60's/70's pop/glam were apparent. As if to prove they could still rock it like a proverbial mother, the veterans released the 'ONE WILD NIGHT' live set in 2001. Unfortunately, they rocked out just a little too much on the self-conscious 'BOUNCE' (2002), its title something of a misnomer for so turgid an album. Unadvised forays into social commentary and an inexplicable absence of their trademark melodic gusto left something of an anaemic aftertaste. Almost as uninspired, or perhaps even more so, was 2003's 'THIS LEFT FEELS RIGHT', a rather pointless set of reworkings running the breadth of their career but failing to point the way to the future. Tastefully executed and designed to fit within the boundaries of their ageing audience's comfort zone, the songs nevertheless sounded glaringly out of context. 'HAVE A NICE DAY' (2005) suggested BON JOVI's mainman was unhappier than ever with the world. Always an unlikely protest singer, his digs at American politics were necessarily framed in the kind of moulderingly familiar arrangements that made the message harder to hit home. The US election-bashing title track lingered uncertainly outside the Billboard Top 40, although they did break the British Top 20 with the anthemically pointless 'WELCOME TO WHEREVER YOU ARE'. JBJ referenced his hero's hero (DYLAN via SPRINGSTEEN) with 'BELLS OF FREEDOM', while his engaging duet with SUGARLAND's JENNIFER NETTLES, 'WHO SAYS YOU CAN'T GO HOME', made the US Top 30.

• **Covered:** IT'S ONLY ROCK'N'ROLL (Rolling Stones) / WITH A LITTLE HELP FROM MY FRIENDS + HELTER SKELTER (Beatles) / I DON'T LIKE MONDAYS (Boomtown Rats) / ROCKIN' IN THE FREE WORLD (Neil Young) / HOUSE OF THE RISING SUN (trad). • **Miscellaneous:** April 1988 saw their manager DOC McGEE convicted for drug offences. He was sentenced to five years suspended, although he ended up doing community work. JON married his childhood sweetheart Dorothea Hurley on the 29th April '89. SAMBORA is married to actress Heather Locklear, while TORRES tied the knot with supermodel Eva Herzigova on the 7th of September '96.

Album rating: BON JOVI (*6) / 7800° FAHRENHEIT (*5) / SLIPPERY WHEN WET (*9) / NEW JERSEY (*7) / BLAZE OF GLORY solo (*5) / STRANGER IN THIS TOWN; Sambora solo (*6) / KEEP THE FAITH (*8) / CROSS ROAD – THE BEST OF BON JOVI compilation (*8) / (THESE DAYS) (*6) / DESTINATION ANYWHERE solo (*6) / CRUSH (*5) / ONE WILD NIGHT (*5) / BOUNCE (*4) / THIS LEFT FEELS RIGHT (*4) / HAVE A NICE DAY (*4)

JON BON JOVI (b. JOHN BONGIOVI, 2 Mar'62) – vocals, guitar / **RICHIE SAMBORA** (b.11 Jul'59, Woodbridge, N.J.) – lead guitar / **DAVID BRYAN** (b. DAVID BRYAN RASHBAUM, 7 Feb'62, New York City) – keyboards / **ALEC JOHN SUCH** (b.14 Nov'56, Yonkers, N.Y.) – bass (ex-PHANTON'S OPERA) / **TICO 'Tar Monster' TORRES** (b. HECTOR TORRES, 7 Oct'53, New York City) – drums (ex-FRANKIE & THE KNOCKOUTS)

Vertigo / Mercury

Feb 84. (7") *<818309>* **RUNAWAY. / LOVE LIES** [–] [39]

Apr 84. (lp/c) *(VERL/+C 14) <814982>* **BON JOVI** [71] Feb84 [43]
– Runaway / Roulette / She don't know me / Shot through the heart / Love lies / Breakout / Burning for love / Come back / Get ready. *(cd-iss. Jul86; 814 982-2) (cd-enhanced.Oct98 & Sep00 on 'Jambco'; 538023-2)*

May 84. (7"/12") *(VER/+X 11)* **SHE DON'T KNOW ME. / BREAKOUT** [ ] [–]

May 84. (7") *<818958>* **SHE DON'T KNOW ME. / BURNING FOR LOVE** [–] [48]

Oct 84. (7") *(VER 14)* **RUNAWAY. / BREAKOUT (live)** [ ] [–]
(12"+=) *(VERX 14)* – Runaway (live).

Apr 85. (7") *<880736>* **ONLY LONELY. / ALWAYS RUN TO YOU** [–] [54]

May 85. (lp/c) *(VERL/+H 24) <824509>* **7800° FAHRENHEIT** [28] [37]
– In and out of love / The price of love / Only lonely / King of the mountain / Silent night / Tokyo road / The hardest part is the night / Always run to you / To the fire / Secret dreams. *(cd-iss. Jul86; 824 509-2) (cd-enhanced.Oct98 & Sep00 on 'Jambco'; 538026-2)*

May 85. (7"/7"pic-d) *(VER/+P 19)* **IN AND OUT OF LOVE. / ROULETTE (live)** [ ] [–]
(12"+=) *(VERX 19)* – Shot through the heart (live).

Jul 85. (7") *<880951>* **IN AND OUT OF LOVE. / BREAKOUT (Japanese live version)** [–] [69]

Jul 85. (7") *(VER 22)* **THE HARDEST PART IS THE NIGHT. / ALWAYS RUN TO YOU** [68] [–]
(12"+=) *(VERX 22)* – Tokyo Road (live).
(d7"++=) *(VERDP 22)* – Shot through the heart (live).
(12"red) *(VERXR 22)* – ('A'side) / Tokyo Road (live) / In and out of love (live).

Aug 86. (7"/10"sha-pic-d) *(VER/+P 26)* **YOU GIVE LOVE A BAD NAME. / LET IT ROCK** [14] [–]
(12"+=) *(VERX 26)* – Borderline.
(12"blue+=) *(VERXR 26)* – The hardest part is the night (live) / Burning for love (live).

Aug 86. (7") *<884953>* **YOU GIVE LOVE A BAD NAME. / RAISE YOUR HANDS** [–] [1]

Sep 86. (lp/c)(cd) *(VERH/+C 38)(<830 264-2>)* **SLIPPERY WHEN WET** [6] [1]
– Let it rock / You give love a bad name / Livin' on a prayer / Social disease / Wanted dead or alive / Raise your hands / Without love / I'd die for you / Never say goodbye / Wild in the streets. *(pic-lp Aug88; VERHP 38) (re-iss. Dec90; same); hit 46) (re-charted.Jun91 No.42, Sep92 re-issue) (cd-enhanced.Oct98 & Sep00 on 'Jambco'; 538025-2) (lp re-iss. Jun99 & Mar00 on 'Simply Vinyl'; SVLP 93)*

Oct 86. (7"/7"pic-d/7"w-patch) *(VER/+P/PA 28) <888184>* **LIVIN' ON A PRAYER. / WILD IN THE STREETS** [4] Dec86 [1]
(12"+=/12"green+=) *(VERX/+P 28)* – Edge of a broken heart.
(d12"+=) *(VERXG 28)* – Only lonely (live) / Runaway (live).

Mar 87. (7"/7"s) *(JOV/+S 1)* **WANTED DEAD OR ALIVE. / SHOT THROUGH THE HEART** [13] [–]
(12"+=) *(JOV 1-12)* – Social disease.
(12"silver++=) – *(JOVR 1-12)* – Get ready (live).

Mar 87. (7") *<888467>* **WANTED DEAD OR ALIVE. / I#D DIE FOR YOU** [–] [7]

Aug 87. (7") *(JOV 2)* **NEVER SAY GOODBYE. / RAISE YOUR HANDS** [21] [–]
(c-s+=) *(JOVC 2)* – ('A'acoustic).
(12"+=/12"yellow+=) *(JOV/+R 2-12)* – Wanted dead or alive (acoustic).

Sep 88. (7") *(JOV 3)* **BAD MEDICINE. / 99 IN THE SHADE** [17] [1]
(12"+=/cd-s+=) *(JOV 3-12/CD3)* – Lay your hands on me.
(12") *(JOVR 3-12)* – ('A'side) / You give love a bad name / Livin' on a prayer (live).

Sep 88. (lp/c)(cd) *(VERH/+C 62)(<836 345-2>)* **NEW JERSEY** [1] [1]
– Lay your hands on me / Bad medicine / Born to be my baby / Living in sin / Blood on blood / Stick to your guns / Homebound train / I'll be there for you / 99 in the shade / Love for sale / Wild is the wind / Ride cowboy ride. *(re-iss. Mar93 cd/c; same) (cd-enhanced.Oct98 & SEp00 on 'Jambco'; 538024-2)*

Nov 88. (7"/7"s) *(JOV/+S 4) <872156>* **BORN TO MY BABY. / LOVE FOR SALE** [22] [3]
(12"+=/12"g-f+=/12"pic-d+=) *(JOV/+R/P 4-12)* – Wanted dead or alive.
(cd-s+=) *(JOVCD 4)* – Runaway / Livin' on a prayer.

Apr 89. (7"/7"w-poster) *(JOV/+PB 5) <872564>* **I'LL BE THERE FOR YOU. / HOMEBOUND TRAIN** [18] Feb89 [1]
(12"+=) *(JOV 5-12)* – Wild in the streets (live).
(cd-s+=) *(JOVCD 5)* – Borderline / Edge of a broken heart.

May 89. (7") *<874452>* **LAY YOUR HANDS ON ME. / RUNAWAY (live)** [–] [7]

Aug 89. (7"/c-s)(7"red/7"white/7"blue) *(JOV/+MC 6)(JOVS 6 61/62/63)* **LAY YOUR HANDS ON ME. / BAD MEDICINE** [18] [–]
(10"pic-d+=) *(JOV 6-10)* – Blood on blood.
(12") *(JOVG 6-12)* – ('A'side) / Blood on blood (live) / Born to be my baby (acoustic).
(cd-s) *(JOVCD 6)* – ('A'side) / You give love a bad name / Let it rock.

Nov 89. (7"/c-s) *(JOV/+MC 7) <876070>* **LIVING IN SIN. / LOVE IS WAR** [35] Oct89 [9]
(12"+=/box-cd-s+=) *(JOV 7-12/CD7)* – Ride cowboy ride / Stick to your guns.
(12"white+=) *(JOVR 7-12)* **The boys are back in town.**

JON BON JOVI

Jul 90. (7") *(JBJ 1) <875896>* **BLAZE OF GLORY. / YOU REALLY GOT ME NOW (with LITTLE RICHARD)** 13 1
(12"+=/cd-s+=) *(JBJ T/CD 1)* – Blood money.
Aug 90. (cd/c/lp) *<(846473-2/-4/-1)>* **BLAZE OF GLORY – YOUNG GUNS II** (soundtrack) 2 3
– Billy get your guns / Miracle / Blaze of glory / Blood money / Santa Fe / Justice in the barrel / Never say die / You really got me now / Bang a drum / Dyin' ain't much of a livin' / Guano city. *(re-iss. Apr95 cd/c; same)*
Oct 90. (c-s) *<878392>* **MIRACLE / BLOOD MONEY** – 12
Nov 90. (7"/c-s) *(JBJ/+C 2)* **MIRACLE. / BANG A DRUM** 29 –
(12"+=/cd-s+=) *(JBJ T/CD 2)* – Dyin' ain't much of a livin' / (interview).

BON JOVI

Jambco Jambco

Oct 92. (7"/c-s) *(JOV/+MC 8) <864432>* **KEEP THE FAITH. / I WISH EVERYDAY COULD BE CHRISTMAS** 5 29
(cd-s+=) *(JOVCB 8)* – Living in sin.
(cd-s+=) *(JOVCA 8)* – Little bit of soul.
Nov 92. (cd/c/lp) *(514197-2/-4/-1) <514045>* **KEEP THE FAITH** 1 5
– I believe / Keep the faith / I'll sleep when I'm dead / In these arms / Bed of roses / If I was your mother / Dry country / Woman in love / Fear / I want you / Blame it on the love of rock'n'roll / Little bit of soul. *(d-cd-iss. Aug93; 518 019-2)* – (live versions). *(cd-enhanced.Oct98 & Sep00; 538034-2)*
Jan 93. (c-s) *<864852>* **BED OF ROSES / LAY YOUR HANDS ON ME (live)** – 10
Jan 93. (7"/c-s) *(JOV/+MC 9)* **BED OF ROSES. / STARTING ALL OVER AGAIN** 13 –
(12"+=) *(JOVT 9)* – Lay your hands on me (live).
(cd-s) *(JOVCD 9)* – ('A'side) / Lay your hands on me (live) / I'll be there for you (live) / Tokyo road (live).
May 93. (cd-s) *<862088>* **IN THESE ARMS / SAVE A PRAYER / IN THESE ARMS (live)** – 27
May 93. (7") *(JOV 10)* **IN THESE ARMS. / BED OF ROSES (acoustic)** 9 –
(cd-s) *(JOVCD 10)* – ('A'side) / Keep the faith (live) / In these arms (live).
(c-s) *(JOVMC 10)* – ('A'side) / Blaze of glory (acoustic).
Jul 93. (7"/c-s) *(JOV/+MC 11) <862428>* **I'LL SLEEP WHEN I'M DEAD. / NEVER SAY GOODBYE (live acoustic)** 17 97
(cd-s) *(JOVCD 11)* – ('A'side) / Blaze of glory / Wild in the streets (both live).
(cd-ep) **HITS LIVE EP** *(JOVD 11)* – ('A'side) / Blaze of glory / You give love a bad name / Bad medicine.
Sep 93. (7"/c-s) *(JOV/+MC 12)* **I BELIEVE (Clearmountain mix). / ('A'live)** 11 –
(cd-s) *(JOVCD 12)* – ('A'side) / Runaway (live) / Livin' on the prayer (live) / Wanted dead or alive ('HITS LIVE PART 2 EP').
(cd-s) *(JOVCB 12)* – ('A'side) / You give love a bad name (live) / Born to be my baby (live) / I'll sleep when I'm dead (live).
Mar 94. (7"/c-s) *(JOV/+MC 13)* **DRY COUNTY. / STRANGER IN THIS TOWN (live)** 9 –
(gold-cd-s+=) *(JOVBX 13)* – Blood money (live).
(cd-s) *(JOVCD 13)* – ('A'side) / It's only rock'n'roll (live) / Waltzing Matilda (live).
Sep 94. (c-s) *(JOVMC 14)* **ALWAYS. / THE BOYS ARE BACK IN TOWN** 2 –
(12"colrd) *(JOVT 14)* – ('A'side) / Prayer '94.
(cd-s) *(JOVCD)* – ('A'side) / ('A'mix) / Edge of a broken heart.
Sep 94. (cd-s) *<856227>* **ALWAYS / NEVER SAY GOODBYE / EDGE OF A BROKEN HEART** – 4
Oct 94. (cd/c/lp) *(522 936-2/-4/-1) <526013>* **CROSS ROAD – THE BEST OF BON JOVI** (compilation) 1 8
– Livin' on a prayer / Keep the faith / Someday I'll be Saturday night / Always / Wanted dead or alive / Lay your hands on me / You give love a bad name / Bed of roses / Blaze of glory / In these arms / Bad medicine / I'll be there for you / In and out of love / Runaway / Never say goodbye. *(cd-enhanced.Oct98; same)*
Dec 94. (7"pic-d/c-s) *(JOV P/MC 16)* **PLEASE COME HOME FOR CHRISTMAS / BACK DOOR SANTA** 7 –
(cd-s+=) *(JOVCD 16)* – I wish every day could be like Christmas.
Feb 95. (7"pic-d/c-s) *(JOV P/MC 15)* **SOMEDAY I'LL BE SATURDAY NIGHT. / GOOD GUYS DON'T ALWAYS WEAR WHITE (live)** 7 –
(cd-s+=) *(JOVCD 15)* – With a little help from my friends (live).
(cd-s+=) *(JOVDD 15)* – Always (live).
May 95. (c-s) *(JOVMC 17)* **THIS AIN'T A LOVE SONG. / LONELY AT THE TOP** 6 –
(cd-s+=) *(JOVCX 17)* – The end.
(cd-s) *(JOVCD 17)* – ('A'side) / When she comes / Wedding day / Prostitute.
May 95. (c-s) *<856227>* **THIS AIN'T A LOVE SONG / ALWAYS (live) / PROSTITUTE** – 14
Jun 95. (cd/c/d-lp) *(528 248-2/-4/-1) <528181>* **(THESE DAYS)** 1 9
– Hey God / Something for the pain / This ain't a love song / These days / Lie to me / Damned / My guitar lies bleeding in my arms / (It's hard) Letting you go / Hearts breaking even / Something to believe in / If that's what it takes / Diamond ring / All I want is everything / Bitter wine. *(re-iss. w/ free cd+=)* – (8 tracks). *(iss.w/ tour pack Jun96; 532 644-2) (cd-enhanced.Oct98; 538036-2)*
Sep 95. (c-s) *(JOVMC 18)* **SOMETHING FOR THE PAIN / THIS AIN'T A LOVE SONG** 8 –
(cd-s+=) *(JOVCX 18)* – I don't like Mondays.
(cd-s) *(JOVCD 18)* – ('A'side) / Living on a prayer / You give love a bad name / Wild in the streets.
Nov 95. (c-s) *(JOVMC 19) <852296>* **LIE TO ME / SOMETHING FOR THE PAIN (live)** 10 88 76
(cd-s+=) *(JOVCX 19)* – Always (live) / Keep the faith (live).
(cd-s) *(JOVCD 19)* – ('A'side) / Something for the pain / Hey God (live) / I'll sleep when I'm dead (live).
Feb 96. (c-s) *(JOVMC 20)* **THESE DAYS / 634-5789** 7 –
(cd-s+=) *(JOVCX 20)* – Rockin' in the free world (live) / (It's hard) Letting you go (live).
(cd-s) *(JOVCD 20)* – ('A'side) / Someday I'll be Saturday night / These days (live) / Helter skelter (live).
Jun 96. (c-s) *(JOVMC 21)* **HEY GOD / LIE TO ME (remix)** 13 –
(cd-s+=) *(JOVCX 21)* – House of the rising sun / Livin' on a prayer.
(cd-s) *(JOVCD 21)* – ('A'side) / The end / When she comes / ('A'live).

JON BON JOVI

— with **DAVID BRYAN** – keyboards / **KENNY ARONOFF** – drums / **ERIC BAZILIAN + DAVE STEWART**

Mercury Mercury

Jun 97. (c-s) *(MERMC 488)* **MIDNIGHT IN CHELSEA / MIDNIGHT IN CHELSEA (album version)** 4 –
(cd-s+=) *(MERCD 488)* – Sad song tonight / August 7th (acoustic).
(cd-s+=) *(MERCX 488)* – Drive / Every word was a piece of my heart.
Jun 97. (cd/c) *(536 011-2/-4) <534903>* **DESTINATION ANYWHERE** 2 31
– Queen of New Orleans / Janie, don't take your love to town / Midnight in Chelsea / Ugly / Staring at your window with a suitcase in my hand / Every word was a piece of my heart / It's just me / Destination anywhere / Learning how to fall / Naked / Little city / August 4, 4:15 / Cold hard heart. *(cd re-iss. Dec97 with bonus cd of live tracks; 536 758-2)* – Queen of New Orleans / Midnight in Chelsea / Destination anywhere / Ugly / It's just me / August 7, 4:15 / Jailbreak / Not fade away / Janie, don't take your love to town.
Aug 97. (c-s) *(MERMC 493)* **QUEEN OF NEW ORLEANS / MIDNIGHT IN CHELSEA (live)** 10 –
(cd-s+=) *(MERCD 493)* – ('A'album version) / Destination anywhere (live).
(cd-s) *(MERCX 493)* – ('A'side) / ('A'album version) / Every piece of my heart (acoustic) / Jailbreak (live).
Nov 97. (c-s) *(574986-4)* **JANIE, DON'T TAKE YOUR LOVE TO TOWN / TALK TO JESUS (demo)** 13 –
(cd-s+=) *(574987-2)* – Billy get your guns (live).
(cd-s) *(574989-2)* – ('A'album version) / Destination anywhere (MTV acoustic) / It's just me (MTV acoustic) / ('A'-MTV acoustic).

– (JOHN BONGIOVI) compilations, etc. –

Jul 97. (cd/c) *Masquerade; (MASQ CD/MC 1011)* **THE POWER STATION YEARS** (rec.1980-1983; remixed 1997)
(re-iss. Feb99; same)
Aug 97. (cd-ep) *Masquerade; (MASSCD 1001)* **MORE THAN WE BARGAINED FOR**
Nov 99. (cd) *Laserlight; (21490)* **JOHN BONGIOVI** –

BON JOVI

— same line-up

Warners Reprise

Mar 99. (c-s) *(W 479C)* **REAL LIFE / KEEP THE FAITH (live)** [21] [–]
(cd-s+=) *(W 479CD)* – Real life (instrumental).

Jambco Jambco

May 00. (c-s) *(562753-4)* **IT'S MY LIFE / HUSH** [3] [33]
(cd-s+=) *(562752-2)* – You can't lose at love.
(cd-s) *(562768-2)* – ('A'side) / Temptation / I don't want to live forever / ('A'-CD-Rom).

May 00. (cd/c) *(54256-22/-14)* *<542474>* **CRUSH** [1] [9]
– It's my life / Say it isn't so / Thank you for loving me / Two storey town / Next 100 years / Just older / Mystery train / Save the world / Captain Crash and the beauty queen from Mars / She's a mystery / I got the girl / One wild night.

Aug 00. (c-s) *(568898-4)* **SAY IT ISN'T SO / AIN'T NO CURE FOR LOVE (demo)** [10] [–]
(cd-s+=) *(568897-2)* – Stay (demo).
(cd-s) *(568898-2)* – ('A'side) / Ordinary people (demo) / Welcome to the good times (demo).

Nov 00. (c-s) *(572730-4)* *<radio play>* **THANK YOU FOR LOVING ME / CAPTAIN CRASH AND THE BEAUTY QUEEN FROM MARS (live)** [12] [57]
(cd-s+=) *(572730-2)* – Runaway (acoustic live).
(cd-s) *(572731-2)* – ('A'side) / Just older (live) / Born to be my baby (live).

May 01. (c-s) *(572949-4)* **ONE WILD NIGHT (2001 version) / LAY YOUR HANDS ON ME (live)** [10] [–]
(cd-s+=) *(572949-2)* – I believe (live).
(cd-s) *(572950-2)* – ('A'side) / Hey God (live) / Tokyo road (live).

May 01. (cd) *<(548865-2)>* **ONE WILD NIGHT** (live 1985-2001) [2] [20]
– It's my life / Livin' on a prayer / You give love a bad name / Keep the faith / Saturday night / Rockin' in the free world / Something to believe in / Wanted dead or alive / Runaway / In and out of love / I don't like Mondays / Just older / Something for the pain / Bad medicine / One wild night.

Mercury Island

Sep 02. (cd-s) *(063937-2)* **EVERYDAY / LUCKY (demo) / NO REGRETS (demo) / EVERYDAY (video)** [5] [–]
(cd-s) *(063936-2)* – ('A'side) / Standing (demo) / Another reason to believe (demo) / (the making of Everyday – CD-ROM).

Oct 02. (cd/c) *(63395-2/-4)* *<063055>* **BOUNCE** [2] [2]
– Undivided / Everyday / The distance / Joey / Misunderstood / All about lovin' you / Hook me up / Right side of wrong / Love me back to life / You had me from hello / Bounce / Open all night.

Dec 02. (c-s) *(63808-4)* **MISUNDERSTOOD / EVERYDAY (acoustic)** [21] [–]
(cd-s+=) *(63815-2)* – Undivided (demo) / ('A'video).
(cd-s) *(63816-2)* – ('A'side) / Celluloid heroes (live) / Joey (demo).

May 03. (cd-s) *(980024-2)* **ALL ABOUT LOVIN' YOU / ALL ABOUT LOVIN' YOU (acoustic) / POSTCARD FROM THE WASTELAND (demo) / ALL ABOUT LOVIN' YOU (video)** [9] [ ]

Nov 03. (cd) *(986139-2)* *<15400-2>* **THIS LEFT FEELS RIGHT** (live acoustic) [4] [14]
– Wanted dead or alive / Livin' on a prayer (with OLIVIA D'ABO) / Bad medicine / It's my life / Lay your hands on me / You give love a bad name / Bed of roses / Everyday / Born to be my baby / Keep the faith / I'll be there for you / Always. *(ltd-cd+=; 986138-9)* – Distance (live) / Joey (live).

Sep 05. (cd-s) *(9885841)* *<radio>* **HAVE A NICE DAY / THE RADIO SAVED MY LIFE TONIGHT (live)** [6] [53]
(cd-s) *(9884894)* – ('A') / I get a rush (live) / Miss Fourth of July (live) / ('A'-CD-Rom video).

Sep 05. (cd) *(2103556)* *<5371>* **HAVE A NICE DAY** [2] [2]
– Have a nice day / I want to be loved / Welcome to wherever you are / Who says you can't go home / Last man standing / Bells of freedom / Wildflower / Last cigarette / I am / Complicated / Novocaine / Story of my life / Who says you can't go home *[US-only]* / Dirty little secret *[UK-only]* / Unbreakable *[UK-only]*. *(ltd-cd w/ dvd+=; 9884960)* – Live in Atlantic City '04:- Everyday / Miss Fourth of July / I get a rush / These arms are open all night / The radio saved my life tonight.

Jan 06. (-)

Jan 06. (cd-s) *(9879525)* **WELCOME TO WHEREVER YOU ARE (Jeremy Wheatley mix) / LAST MAN STANDING (live)** [19] [–]
(cd-s) *(9879526)* – ('A') / Someday I'll be Saturday night (live) / Wanted dead or alive (live) / Wanted dead or alive (video).
(dvd-s) *(9879529)* – ('A'-video) / Have a nice day (live) / Who says you can't go home (live).

Jun 06. (7"pic-d)(cd-s) *(9859749)(9858238)* *<radio>* **WHO SAYS YOU CAN'T GO HOME. / COMPLICATED (live in Boston, MA 12/10/05)** [5] Jan06 [23]
(cd-s) *(9858248)* – ('A') / Last man standing (live in Boston, MA 12/10/05) / Raise your hands (live in Boston..) / ('A'-video).

RICHIE SAMBORA

(solo with **BRYAN** + **TORRES** + **TONY LEVIN** – bass)

Mercury Mercury

Aug 91. (7") *(MER 350)* *<868790>* **BALLAD OF YOUTH. / REST IN PEACE** [59] [63]
(12"+=/cd-s+=) *(MER X/CD 350)* – The wind cries Mary.

Sep 91. (cd/c/lp) *(<848895-2/-4/-1>)* **STRANGER IN THIS TOWN** [20] [36]
– Rest in peace / Church of desire / Stranger in this town / Ballad of youth / One light burning / Mr. Bluesman / Rosie / River of love / Father time / The answer. *(re-iss. Apr95 cd/c; same)*

Feb 98. (cd-s) *(568503-2)* **HARD TIMES COME EASY / MIDNIGHT RIDER – WANTED DEAD OR ALIVE (live) / WE ALL SLEEP ALONE (live) / BAD MEDICINE (live)** [37] [ ]
(cd-s) *(568503-5)* – ('A'side) / Little help from my friends (live) / Stranger in this town (live) / I'll be there for you (live).

Mar 98. (cd/c) *<(536972-2/-4)>* **UNDISCOVERED SOUL** [24] [ ]
– Made in America / Hard times come easy / Fallen from Graceland / If God was a woman / All that really matters / You're not alone / In it for love / Chained / Harlem rain / Who am I / Downside of love / Undiscovered soul.

Jul 98. (cd-s) *(566063-2)* **IN IT FOR LOVE / MADE IN AMERICA (German acoustic) / IN IT FOR LOVE (German acoustic)** [58] [ ]
(cd-s) *(568825-2)* – ('A'side) / Livin' on a prayer (live at Ronnie Scott's) / I'll be there for you (live '91).

☐ BONNIE 'PRINCE' BILLY (see under ⇒ OLDHAM, Will)

the BOOMTOWN RATS

Formed: Dun Laoghaire (near Dublin), Ireland . . . 1975 by former NME journalist BOB GELDOF, JOHNNIE FINGERS, GERRY COTT, PETE BRIQUETTE, GERRY ROBERTS and SIMON CROWE. Moving to London in late 1976, they signed to the newly formed 'Ensign' records. Though their music was rooted in R&B and they were more of a New Wave outfit than anything, The BOOMTOWN RATS were loosely affiliated with the burgeoning punk scene, at least initially. In the long, hot summer of '77, their debut single, 'LOOKIN' AFTER No.1' made the UK Top 20. This was closely followed by a similarly successful eponymous debut album and a second Top 20 hit, 'MARY OF THE 4th FORM'. With a lean sound lying somewhere between EDDIE & THE HOT RODS and The ROLLING STONES, The BOOMTOWN RATS were also a compelling live proposition, GELDOF's moody charisma helping to give the band a distinct identity. Major success came with 'A TONIC FOR THE TROOPS' (1978), this album spawning a number of hits including their first No.1 in the insistent 'RAT TRAP'. They scored a second number one and a massive worldwide hit with 'I DON'T LIKE MONDAYS', a stunningly effective, piano-driven belter inspired (if that's the appropriate word) by schoolgirl Brenda Spencer, who snipered/shot dead several of her school colleagues. The accompanying album, 'THE ART OF SURFACING' (1979) showed the 'RATS at the peak of their power, although subsequent albums increasingly followed a more mundane pop/rock direction and the band slowly faded from view, finally splitting in 1984. GELDOF's profile remained high, however, the Irishman helping to mastermind the mammoth undertaking that was LIVE AID. He and ULTRAVOX's MIDGE URE, assembled together all the major stars of the time to sing 'DO THEY KNOW IT'S CHRISTMAS', the resulting 45 making millions of pounds/dollars/etc for famine relief in Ethiopia. Not content with this, BOB and MIDGE reunited most of them again for the LIVE AID concert at Wembley Stadium on the 13th of July '85 (this was simultaneously broadcast over the Atlantic at JFK Stadium, Philadelphia). At the time, it amassed well over £10m, the money also being spread around other needy charities as well as Ethiopia (the total at the end of 1991 was over £100m). In June 1986, BOB was now Sir BOB GELDOF, after being knighted by the Queen and two months later he married long-time fiance, PAULA YATES (TV presenter/writer/etc). She gave birth to FIFI TRIXIBELLE and in 1989, their second daughter, PEACHES, was born. During the latter half of a very busy decade for GELDOF, he managed to maintain a solo career, a hit single, 'THIS IS THE WORLD CALLING', was appropriate enough to become a Top 30 hit in 1986, while 1990's 'THE GREAT SONG OF INDIFFERENCE' went one step better. His backing band at the time, The VEGETARIANS OF LOVE, provided the title of the single's folky/cajun parent album, which also sold reasonably well. His last solo album, 'THE HAPPY CLUB' (1992), was something of a disappointment and Sir BOB virtually retired from the studio side of things to run his own Planet 24 company and The Big Breakfast on Channel 4. Paula was also part of the latter, although by 1995, she had opted to bed MICHAEL HUTCHENCE of INXS, citing BOB as the cause. BOB and Paula were subsequently divorced as the new couple became the media focal point (tragically, this was cut short when MICHAEL took his own life on the 22nd November, 1997 – see INXS). GELDOF was dealt yet another brutal blow when his tormented ex died from an overdose on the 17th September, 2000; BOB finally won custody of his children, and even their half-sister, daughter of Paula and Michael. Come the new millennium, busy BOB finally returned to the thing which fired his adult life in the first place: angry, questioning rock'n'roll music. There aren't many guys his age making records like 'SEX, AGE & DEATH' (2002), still railing against complacency and inertia with all the spasmodic energy of youth. Fittingly, GELDOF embraced contemporary studio trends rather than relying completely on conventional instruments, bringing a modern edge to the menace his muse has always possessed.

• **Songwriters:** Most written by GELDOF except; BAREFOOTIN' (Robert Parker). GELDOF solo covered SUNNY AFTERNOON (Kinks). • **Trivia:** GELDOF starred in the feature films, 'The Wall' (1982) and 'Number One' (1984).

Album rating: THE BOOMTOWN RATS (*6) / A TONIC FOR THE TROOPS (*5) / THE FINE ART OF SURFACING (*5) / MONDO BONGO (*4) / V DEEP (*4) / IN THE LONG GRASS (*5) / Bob Geldof: DEEP IN THE HEART OF NOWHERE (*5) / THE VEGETARIANS OF LOVE (*5) / THE HAPPY CLUB (*4) / LOUDMOUTH – THE BEST OF THE BOOMTOWN RATS AND BOB GELDOF compilation (*8) / SEX, AGE & DEATH (*6)

BOB GELDOF (b. 5 Oct'54, Dublin, Ireland) – vocals / **JOHNNIE FINGERS** (b. JOHNNY MOYLETT) – keyboards, vocals / **GERRY COTT** – guitar / **PETE BRIQUETTE** (b. PATRICK CUSACK) – bass / **GERRY ROBERTS** – guitar, vocals / **SIMON CROWE** – drums, vocals

Ensign Mercury

Aug 77. (12"m) *(ENY 4)* **LOOKIN' AFTER No.1. / BORN TO BURN (live) / BAREFOOTIN' (live)** [11] [–]

Sep 77. (lp/c) *(ENVY/ENCAS 1) <SRM 1188>* **THE BOOMTOWN RATS** [18] [ ]
– Lookin' after No.1 / Neon heart / Joey's on the street again / Never bite the hand that feeds / Mary of the 4th form / (She gonna) Do you in / Close as you'll ever be / I can make it if you can / Kicks. *(re-iss. Dec83 on 'Mercury' lp/c; PRICE/PRIMC 57)*

Nov 77. (7") *(ENY 9)* **MARY OF THE 4th FORM. / DO THE RAT** [15] [–]

Ensign Columbia

Mar 78. (7") *(ENY 13)* **SHE'S SO MODERN. / LYING AGAIN** [12] [ ]

Jun 78. (7") *(ENY 14)* **LIKE CLOCKWORK. / HOW DO YOU DO?** [6] [ ]

Jul 78. (lp/c) *(ENVY/ENCAS 3) <35750>* **A TONIC FOR THE TROOPS** [8] [ ]
– Like clockwork / Blind date / (I never loved) Eva Braun / Living i an island / Don't believe what you read / She's so modern / Me an Howard Hughes / Can't stop * / (Watch out for) The normal people Rat trap. *<US version repl.* with – Joey> (re-iss. Dec83 on 'Mercury' lp/ PRICE/PRIMC 58)*

Oct 78. (7") *(ENY 16)* **RAT TRAP. / SO STRANGE** [1] [–]

Nov 78. (7") **RAT TRAP. / DO THE RAT** [–] [ ]

Jul 79. (7") *(ENY 30) <11117>* **I DON'T LIKE MONDAYS. / IT'S ALL THE RAGE** [1] Jan80 [73]

Oct 79. (lp/c) *(ENROX/ENCAS 11) <36248>* **THE FINE ART OF SURFACING** [7] [ ]
– Someone's looking at you / Diamond smiles / Wind chill factor (minu zero) / Having my picture taken / Sleep (Fingers' lullaby) / I don't lik Mondays / Nothing happened today / Keep it up / Nice 'n' neat / Whe the night comes. *(re-iss. Nov84 on 'Mercury' lp/c; PRICE/PRIMC 73)*

Nov 79. (7") *(ENY 33)* **DIAMOND SMILES. / LATE LAST NIGHT** [13] [–]

Jan 80. (7",12") *(ENY 34)* **SOMEONE'S LOOKING AT YOU. / WHEN THE NIGHT COMES** [4] [–]

May 80. (7") *<11248>* **SOMEONE'S LOOKING AT YOU. / I DON'T LIKE MONDAYS (live)** [–] [ ]

Mercury Colum

Nov 80. (7") *(BONGO 1)* **BANANA REPUBLIC. / MAN AT THE TOP** [3] [–]

Dec 80. (lp/c) *(6359/7150 042) <37062>* **MONDO BONGO** [6] [ ]
– Please don't go / The elephant's graveyard (guilty) / Banana republic Fall down / Hurt hurts / Whitehall 1212 * / Mood mambo / Straight up This is my room / Another piece of red / Under their thumb . . . is unde my thumb / Go man go. *<US version repl. * with – Don't talk to me>*

Jan 81. (7") *(BONGO 2)* **THE ELEPHANT'S GRAVEYARD (GUILTY). / REAL DIFFERENT** [26] [–]

—— (Mar'81) trimmed to a quintet when GERRY COTT left to go solo

Nov 81. (7") *<60512>* **UP ALL NIGHT. / ANOTHER PIECE OF RED** [–] [ ]

Nov 81. (7") *(MER 87)* **NEVER IN A MILLION YEARS. / DON'T TALK TO ME** [62] [–]

Mar 82. (7"/12") *(MER/+X 91)* **HOUSE ON FIRE. / EUROPE LOOKED UGLY** [24] [–]

Mar 82. (lp/c) *(6359/7150 082)* **V DEEP** [64] [ ]
– Never in a million years / The bitter end / Talking in code / He watche it all / Storm breaks / Charmed lives / House on fire / Up all night / Ski on skin / Little death.

Jun 82. (7") *(MER 106)* **CHARMED LIVES. / NO HIDING PLACE** [ ] [–]
(d7"+=) *(MER 106-2)* – Nothing happened today (live) / Storm break (instrumental).
(12") *(MERX 106)* – ('A'side) / A storm breaks.

Aug 82. (7") *<03386>* **CHARMED LIVES. / NEVER IN A MILLION YEARS** [–] [ ]

Jan 84. (7") *(MER 154)* **TONIGHT. / PRECIOUS TIME** [73] [–]
(12"+=) *(MERX 154)* – Walking downtown.

May 84. (7") *(MER 163)* **DRAG ME DOWN. / AN ICICLE IN THE SUN** [50] [–]
(12"+=) *(MERX 163)* – Rat trap / She's so modern.

Nov 84. (7"pic-d) *(MER 179)* **DAVE. / HARD TIMES** [ ] [–]
(d7"+=) *(MER 179-2)* – I don't like Mondays / It's all the rage.
(12"+=) *(MERX 179)* – Banana republic (live) / Close as you'll ever b (live).

Dec 84. (lp/c) *(MERL/+C 38) <39335>* **IN THE LONG GRASS** [ ] [ ]
– A hold of me / Drag me down / Dave / Over again / Another sad story Tonight / Hard times / Lucky / Icicle in the Sun / Up or down.

Feb 85. (7") *(MER 184)* **A HOLD OF ME. / NEVER IN A MILLION YEARS** [ ] [–]
(12"+=) *(MERX 184)* – Say hi to Mick.

Mar 85. (7") *<04892>* **ICICLE IN THE SUN. / RAIN** [–] [ ]

Jun 85. (7") *<05590>* **DRAG ME DOWN. / HARD TIMES** [–] [ ]

—— had already split late '84. FINGERS and CROWE formed GUNG HO. BOB GELDOF pieced together BAND/LIVE AID before going solo.

– compilations, others, etc. –

Dec 83. (6x7"box) *Mercury; (none)* **RAT PACK** (6 best of singles pack) [ ] [–]

Jan 88. (7") *Old Gold; (OG 9790)* **I DON'T LIKE MONDAYS. / RAT TRAP** [ ] [–]

BOB GELDOF

solo, with guests **DAVE STEWART, ERIC CLAPTON**, etc.

Mercury Atlantic

Oct 86. (7"/12") *(BOB/+X 101)* <89341> **THIS IS THE WORLD CALLING. / TALK ME UP** [25] [82]

Nov 86. (lp/c)(cd) *(BOB LP/MC 1)(830 607-2)* <812687> **DEEP IN THE HEART OF NOWHERE** [79] [ ]
– Love you like a rocket / In the pouring rain / This heartless night / Words from Heaven / Deep in the heart of nowhere / Night turns to day / I cry too / The beat of the night / When I was young / This is the world calling / August was a heavy month. *(cd+=)* – Pulled apart by horses / Good boys in the wrong / Truly true blue.

Jan 87. (7") *(BOB 102)* **LOVE YOU LIKE A ROCKET. / THIS IS THE WORLD CALLING** [61] [-]
(12"+=) *(BOBX 102)* – ('A'extended).
(cd-s+=) *(BOBCD 102)* – Pulled apart by horses / Truly true blue.

Mar 87. (7") *<89309>* **LOVE YOU LIKE A ROCKET. / PULLED APART BY HORSES** [-] [ ]

Jun 87. (7") *<89261>* **THE HEARTLESS NIGHT. / PULLED APART BY HORSES** [-] [ ]

Jun 87. (7") *(BOB 103)* **I CRY TOO. / LET'S GO** [ ] [ ]
(12"+=) *(BOBX 103)* – Night turns to day / Deep in the heart of nowhere.

— He was now augmented by his **VEGETARIANS OF LOVE** backing band **GEOFF RICHARDSON** – viola, clarinet, etc. / **BOB LOVEDAY** – violin, bass, penny whistle / **PETE BRIQUETTE** – bass, keyboards / **PHIL PALMER** – guitars / **STEVE FLETCHER** – keyboard ALUN DUNN – accordion, organ / **RUPERT HINE** – keyboards, percussion, producer,

Jun 90. (7") *(BOB 104)* **THE GREAT SONG OF INDIFFERENCE. / HOTEL 75** [15] [ ]
(12"+=/cd-s+=) *(BOB X/CD 104)* – In the pouring rain.

Jul 90. (cd/c/lp) *(846 250-2/-4/-1)* *<82041-2/-4/-1>* **THE VEGETARIANS OF LOVE** [21] [ ]
– A gospel song / Love or something / Thinking Voyager 2 type things / The great song of indifference / Crucified me / Big romance stuff / The chains of pain / A rose at night / Let it go / No small wonder / Walking back to happiness / The end of the world. *(cd re-iss. Jun03; same)*

Aug 90. (7") *(BOB 105)* **LOVE OR SOMETHING. / OUT OF ORDER** [ ] [-]
(12"+=/cd-s+=) *(BOB X/CD 105)* – The great song of indifference (mix) / Friends for life / One of these girls.

Nov 90. (7") *(BOB 106)* **A GOSPEL SONG. / VEGETARIANS OF LOVE** [ ] [-]
(12"+=/cd-s+=) *(BOB X/CD 106)* – The warmest fire.

— now with The HAPPY CLUBSTERS (same as last)

Vertigo Polygram

Jun 92. (7") *(BOB 107)* **ROOM 19 (SHA LA LA LA LEE). / HUGE BIRDLESS SILENCE** [ ] [-]
(cd-s+=) *(BOBCD 107)* – The great song of indifference / Sweat for you (BRIQUETTE & SHARKEY CO.).

Sep 92. (7") *(BOB 108)* **MY HIPPY ANGEL. / MAYBE HEAVEN** [ ] [-]
(cd-s+=) *(BOBCD 108)* – Love or something / ('A'extended).

Oct 92. (cd/c/lp) *(512 896-2/-4/-1)* *<519132>* **THE HAPPY CLUB** [ ] [ ]
– Room 19 (sha la la la lee) / Attitude chicken / The soft soil / A hole to fill / The song of the emergent nationalist / My hippy angel / The happy club / Like down on me / Too late God / Roads of Germany (after BD) / A sex thing / The house at the top of the world.

Apr 94. (7"/c-s) *(MER/+MC 85)* **CRAZY. / THE HAPPY CLUB** [65] [-]
(cd-s) *(MERCX 85)* – ('A'side) / Room 19 (sha la la la lee) (live) / The beat of the night (live) / Rat trap (live).

Note; below single by BOOMTOWN RATS (also compilation tracks *)

Jun 94. (7"colrd/c-s) *(VER/+MC 87)* **I DON'T LIKE MONDAYS. / BORN TO BURN / DO THE RAT** [38] [ ]
(cd-s) *(MERCD 87)* – ('A'side) / Looking after No.1 / Mary of the 4th form / She's so modern.
(cd-s) *(MERCX 87)* – ('A'side) / Rat trap / Someone's looking at you / Banana republic.

Jul 94. (cd/c) *(522 283-2/-4)* **LOUDMOUTH – THE BEST OF THE BOOMTOWN RATS & BOB GELDOF** (compilation) [10] [ ]
– I don't like Mondays * / This is the world calling / Rat trap * / The great song of indifference / Love or something / Banana republic * / Crazy / The elephant's graveyard (guilty) * / Someone's looking at you * / She's so modern * / House on fire * / The beat of the night / Diamond smiles * / Like clockwork * / Room 19 (sha la la la lee) / Mary of the 4th form * / Looking after No.1 *. *(* tracks by The BOOMTOWN RATS)*

Eagle Koch

Oct 01. (cd) *(EAGCD 187)* *<8415>* **SEX, AGE AND DEATH** [ ] Jun02 [ ]
– One for me / $6,000,000 loser / Pale white girls / The new routine / Mudslide / Mind in pocket / My birthday suit / Scream in vain / Inside your head / 10:15. *<US+=>* – Cool, blue and easy / The original Miss Jesus.

Jan 03. (cd-s) *(EAGXS 220)* **PALE WHITE GIRLS** [ ] [-]

☐ Tim BOOTH / BOOTH AND THE BAD ANGEL

(see under ⇒ JAMES)

David BOWIE

Born: DAVID ROBERT JONES, 8 Jan'47, Brixton, London. In 1964 he formed The KING BEES with schoolmate GEORGE UNDERWOOD but after one single they split when BOWIE joined The MANNISH BOYS. They also lasted half a year, DAVID going solo with backing from The LOWER THIRD. In early 1966, he became DAVID BOWIE and signed to 'Pye' although commercial success continued to elude him. After three years of trying, he finally charted with 'SPACE ODDITY', a classic that introduced his "MAJOR TOM" character. That year (1969) his father died, but he was compensated by the introduction to ANGIE, his future wife. Although he was regarded as one of the top newcomers to the rock/pop scene, it took him until 1972 to finally establish himself as *the* rock star. He formed his now famous backing band, The SPIDERS, and announced his bisexuality to the music press. The single, 'STARMAN', and parent album, 'ZIGGY STARDUST' (an archetype alter-ego), were to hit the UK top 10. By this stage he'd come a long way from being a 60's ANTHONY NEWLEY copyist, innovating a risqué, glam rock style and pioneering the 'feathercut', make-up for men and stage-mime (the latter being learnt from LINDSEY KEMP). Signed to 'R.C.A.', the company duly re-issued his past three albums which all broke into the UK charts and 'ALADDIN SANE' (1973) was the first of his many No.1 albums. 'DIAMOND DOGS' (1974) represented the finale of his futuristic concept work and bore the hit single, 'REBEL, REBEL', while the follow-up concert album, 'DAVID LIVE' (1974), documented the mammoth tour that followed. With 'YOUNG AMERICANS' in 1975, his music took a dramatic and not entirely well-received turn towards Philadelphia soul/disco. Nevertheless, the album hit No.2 in the UK and a collaborative single with JOHN LENNON, 'FAME', gave him a US No.1. BOWIE then made yet another about face; dallying briefly with themes of fascism and dictatorship, he recorded the stark 'STATION TO STATION' (1976) album, before relocating to Berlin with BRIAN ENO and continuing his move towards experimental/avant-garde rock. The resulting albums, 'LOW' and 'HEROES', both released in 1977, were fairly successful in the UK despite containing some of BOWIE's most uncommercial work to date. After a final album with ENO, BOWIE returned to more conventional rock, gaining another No.1 hit with his resurrection of Major Tom on 'ASHES TO ASHES' (1980). After a two and a half year hiatus, he returned with the NILE RODGERS-produced 'LET'S DANCE' album. A typically polished, 80's-sounding record, it featured the single 'CHINA GIRL', complete with controversial video (in 1977, BOWIE had originally collaborated on the track with IGGY POP for the wild man's 'The Idiot' album). The rest of BOWIE's 80's output was hardly essential and at the turn of the decade he set up the embarrassing TIN MACHINE project, a misguided attempt at a return to spontaneous rock'n'roll. Ignoring the critical barbs, he carried on with this set-up until 1991 but couldn't substantiate any major hits. The release of 'OUTSIDE' (1995), (a collaboration with

DAVID BOWIE

his old mucker ENO) saw BOWIE back in critical favour, while 'EART HL ING' (1997) was an admirable attempt to incorporate cutting edge dance styles into his music, collaborating with drum 'n' bass don, A GUY CALLED GERALD. More recently and trying desperately to get his new material noticed by an ailing public (he was still excellent live), BOWIE delivered his final set towards the end of the 90's, 'HOURS . . .' – it had in fact been "years . . ." since his last great album. While 2002's 'HEATHEN' wasn't quite great, it was definitely getting there, a sure-footed beginning to a new decade which saw BOWIE revisiting his past in the shape of producer Tony Visconti. Although a fairly bold step for an artist of such tireless experimentation, the record was by no means a retreat into rose-tinted nostalgia. Visconti seemed to coax out the generous side to BOWIE's muse while utilising studio technology to achieve an authentic updating of the feel – if not quite the sound – of their 70's recordings. Also placing the record in a contemporary context were fairly radical reworkings of both Neil Young's 'I'VE BEEN WAITING FOR YOU' and early Pixies classic, 'CACTUS'. The partnership proved so successful in fact, that BOWIE and Visconti kept it going for 2003's 'REALITY', another very self-assured, if slightly more angular set which again featured some choice covers (Jonathan Richman's 'PABLO PICASSO' and George Harrison's 'TRY SOME, BUY SOME') and which suggested the veteran starman's retirement is more far off than ever.

• **Songwriters:** He wrote all his own material even managing some for others (e.g. ALL THE YOUNG DUDES for (Mott The Hoople) / OH YOU PRETTY THINGS (Peter Noone) / THE MAN WHO SOLD THE WORLD / (Lulu) / PINK ROSE (Adrian Belew) / etc. He produced 'RCA' acts LOU REED (Transformer) / MICK RONSON (Slaughter on Tenth Avenue) / etc. BOWIE's cover album PIN-UPS featured SORROW (Merseys) / ROSALYN (Pretty Things) / HERE COMES THE NIGHT (Them) / SHAPES OF THINGS (Yardbirds) / FRIDAY ON MY MIND (Easybeats) / ANYWAY ANYHOW ANYWHERE + I CAN'T EXPLAIN (Who) / SEE EMILY PLAY (Pink Floyd) / WHERE HAVE ALL THE GOOD TIMES GONE (Kinks) / DON'T BRING ME DOWN + I WISH YOU WOULD (Pretty Things) / EVERYTHING'S ALRIGHT (Mojos) /. Other covers:- LET'S SPEND THE NIGHT TOGETHER (Rolling Stones) / KNOCK ON WOOD (Eddie Floyd) / ALABAMA SONG (Brecht-Weill) / DANCING IN THE STREET (Martha & The Vandellas). I FEEL FREE (Cream) / NITE FLIGHT (Scott Walker) / I KNOW IT'S GONNA HAPPEN SOMEDAY (Morrissey) / DON'T LET ME DOWN & DOWN (Tacha-Valmont) / THE SEEKER (Who). – TIN MACHINE :- He co-wrote with GABRELS except MAGGIE'S FARM (Bob Dylan) / WORKING CLASS HERO (John Lennon, who also co-wrote FAME for BOWIE in 1975) / IF THERE IS SOMETHING (Roxy Music).

• **Trivia:** BOWIE'S acting career started in 1976 with the film 'THE MAN WHO FELL TO EARTH' and 'JUST A GIGOLO' (1978). After starring in stage production of ELEPHANT MAN in 1980, he returned to films THE HUNGER (1982) / MERRY XMAS MR. LAWRENCE (1983) / LABYRINTH (1986) / ABSOLUTE BEGINNERS (1986) / THE LAST TEMPTATION OF CHRIST (1989). In 1985, he was one of the major stars of LIVE AID concert, and co-sang on 'DANCIN' IN THE STREET' with MICK JAGGER.

Album rating: DAVID BOWIE (*4) / MAN OF WORDS, MAN OF MUSIC aka SPACE ODDITY (*6) / THE MAN WHO SOLD THE WORLD (*9) / HUNKY DORY (*9) / THE RISE AND FALL OF ZIGGY STARDUST . . . (*10) / ALADDIN SANE (*10) / BOWIE PIN-UPS (*5) / DIAMOND DOGS (*6) / DAVID LIVE (*5) / YOUNG AMERICANS (*6) / STATION TO STATION (*8) / LOW (*10) / HEROES (*9) / STAGE (*5) / LODGER (*4) / SCARY MONSTERS (AND SUPER CREEPS) (*8) / CHANGESONEBOWIE compilation (*10) / CHRISTIANE F. live soundtrack (*6) / LET'S DANCE (*6) / ZIGGY STARDUST – THE MOTION PICTURE live soundtrack (*4) / TONIGHT (*4) / LABYRINTH shared soundtrack (*5) / NEVER LET ME DOWN (*4) / CHANGESBOWIE compilation (*9) / Tin Machine: TIN MACHINE (*5) / TIN MACHINE II (*3) / OY, VEY BABY (*3) / David Bowie: BLACK TIE, WHITE NOISE (*5) / THE BUDDHA OF SUBURBIA soundtrack for TV (*5) / OUTSIDE (*6) / EART HL ING (*6) / HOURS . . . (*6) / HEATHEN (*7) / BEST OF BOWIE compilation (*8) / REALITY (*7)

DAVID BOWIE – vocals, acoustic guitar / with session people

Vocalion — not iss.

Jun 64. (7"; as DAVIE JONES with The KING BEES) *(Pop V 9221)* **LIZA JANE. / LOUIE LOUIE GO HOME** — -
(re-iss. Sep78 on 'Decca'; F 13807)

Parlophone — not iss.

Mar 65. (7"; as The MANNISH BOYS) *(R 5250)* **I PITY THE FOOL. / TAKE MY TIP** — -

Aug 65. (7"; as DAVY JONES) *(R 5315)* **YOU'VE GOT A HABIT OF LEAVING. / BABY LOVES THAT WAY** — -

Pye — Warners

Jan 66. (7"; as DAVID BOWIE with The LOWER THIRD) *(7N 17020)* *<5814>* **CAN'T HELP THINKING ABOUT ME. / AND I SAID TO MYSELF**

Apr 66. (7") *(7N 17079)* **DO ANYTHING YOU SAY. / GOOD MORNING GIRL** — -

Aug 66. (7") *(7N 17157)* **I DIG EVERYTHING. / I'M NOT LOSING SLEEP** — -

Deram — Deram

Dec 66. (7") *(DM 107)* **RUBBER BAND. / THE LONDON BOYS** — -

Feb 67. (7") *<85009>* **RUBBER BAND. / THERE IS A HAPY LAND** - —

Apr 67. (7") *(DM 123)* **THE LAUGHING GNOME. / THE GOSPEL ACCORDING TO TONY DAY** — -
(re-iss. Sep73; same); hit UK No.6 (re-iss. Jun82)

Jun 67. (lp; mono/stereo) *(DML/SML 1007)* **DAVID BOWIE** — -
– Uncle Arthur / Sell me a coat / Rubber band / Love you till Tuesday There is a happy land / We are hungry men / When I live my dream / Little bombadier / Silly boy blue / Come and buy me toys / Join the gang / She's got medals / Maids of Bond Street / Please Mr. Gravedigger. *(re-iss. Nov69 on 'Philips'; SBL 7912) (re-iss. Aug84 lp/c; DOA 1) (cd-iss. Oct88; 800 087-2)*

Jul 67. (7") *(DM 135)* *<85016>* **LOVE YOU TILL TUESDAY. / DID YOU EVER HAVE A DREAM**

— (Jul68-Feb69) **BOWIE** formed FEATHERS with girlfriend **HERMOINE FARTHINGALE + JOHN HUTCHINSON** – bass. BOWIE went solo, recording solo album with session players **RICK WAKEMAN** – keyboards

Philips — Mercury

Jul 69. (7") *(BF 1801)* *<72949>* **SPACE ODDITY. / THE WILD EYED BOY FROM FREECLOUD** 5 —

Nov 69. (lp) *(SBL 7912)* **DAVID BOWIE – MAN OF WORDS MAN OF MUSIC** — -
– Space oddity / Unwashed and somewhat slightly dazed / Letter to Hermione / Cygnet committee / Janine / An occasional dream / The wild eyed boy from Freecloud / God knows I'm good / Memory of a free festival. *(re-iss. Nov72 as 'SPACE ODDITY' on 'RCA' lp/c; LSP/PK 4813) (hit No.17 UK + No.16 US; <ST 61246>) (re-iss. Oct84 on 'RCA' lp/c/cd; PL/PK/PD 84813) (re-iss. Apr90 on 'EMI' cd/c/lp; CD/TC+/EMC 3571) (+=)* – Conversation piece / Don't sit down. *(hit UK No.64) (cd re-iss. Sep97 on 'Premier-EMI'; CDP 791835-2)*

— **BOWIE** formed backing band **HYPE** with **TONY VISCONTI** – bass / **MICK RONSON** – guitar / **JOHN CAMBRIDGE** – drums

Mercury — Mercury

Mar 70. (7") *(MF 1135)* **THE PRETTIEST STAR. / CONVERSATION PIECE** — -

— **MICK 'Woody' WOODMANSEY** – drums repl. CAMBRIDGE

Jun 70. (7") *(6052 026)* *<73075>* **MEMORY OF A FREE FESTIVAL (part 1). / (part 2)**

Jan 71. (7") *(6052 049)* **HOLY HOLY. / BLACK COUNTRY ROCK** — -

Apr 71. (lp) *(6338 041)* *<61325>* **THE MAN WHO SOLD THE WORLD**
– The width of a circle / All the madmen / Black country rock / After all / Running gun blues / Saviour machine / She took me cold / The man who sold the world / The supermen. *(re-iss. Nov72 on 'RCA' lp/c; LSP/PK 4816) (hit No.26 UK) (re-iss. Apr83 on 'RCA' lp/c; INTS/INTK 5237) (hit UK 64) (re-iss. Oct84 on 'RCA Int.' lp/c/cd; NL/NK/PD 84654) (re-iss. Apr90 on 'EMI' cd/c/lp; CD/TC+/EMC 3573) (+=)* – Lightning frightening / Moonage daydream / Holy holy / Hang on to yourself. *(hit UK No.66) (cd re-iss. Sep97 on 'Premier-EMI'; CDP 791837-2)*

Jun 71. (7") *<73175>* **ALL THE MADMEN. /** - —

— Became **SPIDERS FROM MARS (BOWIE, RONSON, WOODMANSEY), TREVOR BOULDER** – bass repl. VISCONTI

R.C.A. — R.C.A.

Dec 71. (lp/c) *(SF/PK 8244)* *<AFL-1 4623>* **HUNKY DORY** — 93
– Changes / Oh! you pretty things / Eight line poem / Life on Mars? /

Kooks / Quicksand / Fill your heart – Andy Warhol / Song for Bob Dylan / Queen bitch / The Bewlay Brothers. *(re-dist.Sep72 reached No.3 UK) (re-iss. Jan81 lp/c; INTS/INTK 5064) (hit No.32 UK) (pic-lp Apr84; BOPIC 2) (re-iss. Oct84 on 'RCA Int.' lp/c/cd; NL/NK/PD 83844) (re-iss. Apr90 on 'EMI' cd/c/lp; CD/TC+/EMC 3572) (+=)* – Bombers / The supermen (alt.) / Quicksand (demo) / The Bewlay Brothers (alt.). *(hit UK No.39) (cd re-iss. Sep97 on 'Premier-EMI'; LPCENT 21) (lp re-iss. Nov97 on 'E.M.I.'; CDP 791843-2)*

Jan 72. (7") *(RCA 2160) <74-0605>* **CHANGES. / ANDY WARHOL** [ ] Apr72 [66]
(re-iss. Dec74; same); reached No.41 UK

Apr 72. (7") *(RCA 2199) <74-0719>* **STARMAN. / SUFFRAGETTE CITY** [10] Jun72 [65]

Jun 72. (lp/c) *(SF/PK 8267) <AFL-1 4702>* **THE RISE AND FALL OF ZIGGY STARDUST AND THE SPIDERS FROM MARS** [5] [75]
– Five years / Soul love / Moonage daydream / Starman / It ain't easy / Lady Stardust / Star / Hang on to yourself / Ziggy Stardust / Suffragette city / Rock'n'roll suicide. *(re-iss. Jan81 lp/c; INTS/INTK 5063) (hit No.33 UK) (pic-lp Apr84; BOPIC 3) (re-iss. Oct84 on 'RCA Int.' lp/c/cd; NL/NK/PD 83843) (re-iss. Apr90 on 'EMI' cd+=/c+=/lp; CD/TC+/EMC 3577) <re-iss. Jun90 on 'Rykodisc'+=; 10134>; hit No.93.* – John, I'm only dancing (demo) / Velvet goldmine / Sweet head / Ziggy Stardust (demo) / Lady Stardust (demo). *(hit UK No.25) (re-iss. Feb97 on 'E.M.I.'; LPCENT 4)*

Sep 72. (7") *(RCA 2263)* **JOHN, I'M ONLY DANCING. / HANG ON TO YOURSELF** [12] [–]

Nov 72. (7") *(RCA 2302)* **THE JEAN GENIE. / ZIGGY STARDUST** [2] [–]

Nov 72. (7") *<74-0838>* **THE JEAN GENIE. / HANG ON TO YOURSELF** [–] [71]

Jan 73. (7") *<74-0876>* **SPACE ODDITY. / THE MAN WHO SOLD THE WORLD** [–] [15]

Apr 73. (7") *(RCA 2352)* **DRIVE-IN-SATURDAY. / ROUND AND ROUND** [3] [–]

— with guests **MIKE GARSON** – piano / **KEN FORDHAM** and **BUX** – saxophone, flute

Apr 73. (lp/c) *(RS/PK 1001) <AFL-1 4852>* **ALADDIN SANE** [1] May73 [17]
– Watch that man / Aladdin Sane (1913-1938-197?) / Drive-in Saturday / Panic in Detroit / Cracked actor / Time / The prettiest star / Let's spend the night together / The Jean genie / Lady grinning soul. *(re-iss. Feb81 on 'RCA Int.' lp/c; INTS/INTK 5067) (hit No.49 UK Feb82) (re-iss. Mar84 on 'RCA Int.' lp/c; NL/NK 83890) (pic-lp Apr84; BOPIC 1) (cd-iss. Jun85; PD 83890) (re-iss. Jul90 on 'EMI' cd/c/lp; CD/TC+/EMC 3579)(+=)* – (other rare tracks). *(hit UK No.43) (cd re-iss. Sep97 on 'Premier-EMI'; CDP 794768-2)*

Jun 73. (7") *<APBO 0001>* **TIME. / THE PRETTIEST STAR** [–] [ ]

Jun 73. (7") *(RCA 2316)* **LIFE ON MARS. / THE MAN WHO SOLD THE WORLD** [3] [–]

Aug 73. (7") *<APBO 0028>* **LET'S SPEND THE NIGHT TOGETHER. / LADY GRINNING SOUL** [–] [ ]

— **AYNSLEY DUNBAR** – drums repl. WOODY

Oct 73. (7") *(RCA 2424) <APBO 0160>* **SORROW. / AMSTERDAM** [3] Nov73 [ ]

Oct 73. (lp/c) *(RS/PK 1003) <AFL-1 0291>* **PIN-UPS** [1] [23]
– Rosalyn / Here comes the night / I wish you would / See Emily play / Everything's alright / I can't explain / Friday on my mind / Sorrow / Don't bring me down / Shapes of things / Anyway anyhow anywhere / Where have all the good times gone!. *(re-iss. Sep81 lp/c; RCA LP/K 3004) (re-iss. Apr83 on 'RCA Int.' lp/c; INTS/INTK 5236) (hit UK 57) (pic-lp Apr84; BOPIC 4) (re-iss. Jul90 on 'EMI' cd/c/lp; CD/TC+/EMC 3580) (hit No.52)*

— **DUNBAR** and **TONY NEWMAN** – drums / **HERBIE FLOWERS** – bass / **MIKE GARSON** – keyboards

Feb 74. (7") *(LPBO 5009)* **REBEL REBEL. / QUEEN BITCH** [5] [–]

Apr 74. (7") *(LPBO 5021)* **ROCK'N'ROLL SUICIDE. / QUICKSAND** [22] [–]

May 74. (7") *<APBO 0287>* **REBEL REBEL. / LADY GRINNING SOUL** [–] [64]

May 74. (lp/c; as BOWIE) *(<APL/APK 1-0576>)* **DIAMOND DOGS** [1] [ ]
– Future legend / Diamond dogs / Sweet thing / Candidate / Sweet thing (reprise) / Rebel rebel / Rock'n'roll with me / We are the dead / 1984 / Big brother (including 'Chant of the ever circling skeletal family'). *(re-iss. Feb81 on 'RCA Int.' lp/c; INTS/INTK 5068) (hit UK 60 in May83) (re-iss. Mar84 on 'RCA Int.' lp/c/cd; NL/NK/PD 83889) (pic-lp Apr84; BOPIC 5) (re-iss. Jun90 on 'E.M.I.' cd/c/lp; CD/TC+/EMC 3584) (+=)* – Dodo / Candidate. *(hit UK No.67)*

Jun 74. (7") *(<APBO 0293>)* **DIAMOND DOGS. / HOLY HOLY** [21] [ ]

— added **EARL SLICK** – guitar / **DAVID SANBORN** – saxophone

Sep 74. (7") *(RCA 2466)* **KNOCK ON WOOD (live). / PANIC IN DETROIT (live)** [10] [–]

Oct 74. (7") *<10026>* **1984 (live). / QUEEN BITCH** [–] [ ]

Nov 74. (d-lp/c) *(<APL/APK 2-0771>)* **DAVID LIVE (live at the Tower theatre Philadelphia '74)** [2] [8]
– 1984 / Rebel rebel / Moonage daydream / Sweet thing / Changes / Suffragette city / Aladdin Sane (1913-1938-197?) / All the young dudes / Cracked actor / Rock'n'roll with me / Watch that man / Knock on wood / Diamond dogs/ Big brother / The width of a circle / The Jean genie / Rock'n'roll suicide. *(re-iss. May84 lp/c; PL/PK 80771) (re-iss. Jun90 on 'EMI' cd/c/d-lp+=; CD/TC+/DBLD 1)* – (band intro) / Here today, gone tomorrow / Time. *(re-iss. d-cd Jun95 on 'EMI'; same)*

Dec 74. (7") *<10105>* **ROCK'N'ROLL WITH ME (live). / PANIC IN DETROIT (live)** [–] [ ]

— **ANDY NEWMARK** – drums / **WILLIE WEEKS** – bass / **CARLOS ALOMAR** – guitar / **EARL SLICK** – guitar / guests **LUTHER VANDROSS** + **JOHN LENNON** – backing vocals

Feb 75. (7") *(RCA 2523)* **YOUNG AMERICANS. / SUFFRAGETTE CITY** [18] [–]

Mar 75. (7") *<10152>* **YOUNG AMERICANS. / KNOCK ON WOOD (live)** [–] [28]

Mar 75. (lp/c) *(APL/APK 1-1006) <0998>* **YOUNG AMERICANS** [2] [9]
– Young Americans / Win / Fascination / Right / Somebody up there like me / Across the universe / Can you hear me / Fame. *(re-iss. Sep81 lp/c; RCA LP/K 3009) (re-iss. Oct84 lp/c/cd; PL/PK/PD 80998) (re-iss. Apr91 on 'E.M.I.' cd+=/c+=/lp; CD/TC+/EMD 1021)* – Who can I be now? / John, I'm only dancing (again) (1975) / It's gonna be me. *(hit UK No.54)*

Jul 75. (7") *(RCA 2579) <10320>* **FAME. / RIGHT** [17] Jun75 [1]

Sep 75. (7"m) *(RCA 2593)* **SPACE ODDITY. / CHANGES / VELVET GOLDMINE** [1] [–]

— retained **SLICK** + **ALOMAR**

— **GEORGE MURRAY** – bass + **DENNIS DAVIS** – drums repl. WEEKS + NEWMARK

Nov 75. (7") *(RCA 2640) <10441>* **GOLDEN YEARS. / CAN YOU HEAR ME** [8] [10]

Jan 76. (lp/c) *(<APL/APK 1-1327>)* **STATION TO STATION** [5] [3]
– Station to station / Golden years / Word on a wing / TVC 15 / Stay / Wild is the wind. *(re-iss. Sep81 lp/c; RCA LP/K 3013) (re-iss. Oct84 lp/c/cd; PL/PK/PD 81327) (re-iss. Apr91 on 'E.M.I.' cd/c/lp; CD/TC+/EMD 1020) (+=)* – Word on the wing (live) / Stay (live). *(hit UK No.57)*

May 76. (7") *(RCA 2682) <10664>* **TVC 15. / WE ARE THE DEAD** [33] [64]

Jun 76. (lp/c) *(RS/PK 1055) <1732>* **CHANGESONEBOWIE** (compilation) [2] [10]
– Space oddity / John, I'm only dancing / Changes / Ziggy Stardust / Suffragette city / The Jean genie / Diamond dogs / Rebel rebel / Young Americans / Fame / Golden years. *(re-iss. May84 lp/c/cd; PL/PK/PD 81732)*

Jul 76. (7") *(RCA 2726)* **SUFFRAGETTE CITY. / STAY** [ ] [–]

Aug 76. (7") *<10736>* **STAY. / WORD ON A WING** [–] [ ]

— now collaborated with **BRIAN ENO** – synthesizers

— **RICKY GARDINER** – guitar repl. SLICK

Jan 77. (lp/c) *(PL/PK 12030) <2030>* **LOW** [2] [11]
– Speed of life / Breaking glass / What in the world / Sound and vision / Always crashing in the same car / Be my wife / A new career in a new town / Warszawa / Art decade / Weeping wall / Subterraneans. *(re-iss. Dec80 on 'RCA Int.' lp/c; INTS/INTK 5065) ;hit UK 85 in Jun83) (re-iss. Mar84 on 'RCA Int.' lp/c/cd; NL/NK/PD 83856) (re-iss. Aug91 on 'E.M.I.' cd/c/lp; CD/TC+/EMD 1027) (+=)* – (bonus tracks). *(hit UK No.64)*

Feb 77. (7") *(PB 0905) <10905>* **SOUND AND VISION. / A NEW CAREER IN A NEW TOWN** [3] [69]

Jun 77. (7") *(PB 1017) <11017>* **BE MY WIFE. / SPEED OF LIFE** [ ] [ ]

— next guest **ROBERT FRIPP** – guitar who repl. RICKY GARDINER.

Oct 77. (7") *(PB 1121) <11121>* **HEROES. / V2-SCHNEIDER** [24] [ ]

Oct 77. (lp/c) *(PL/PK 12522) <2522>* **HEROES** [3] [35]
– Beauty and the beast / Joe the lion / Heroes / Sons of the silent age / Blackout / V-2 Schneider / Sense of doubt / Moss garden / Neukoln / Black out / The secret life of Arabia. *(re-iss. Dec80 lp/c; INTS/INTK 5066) (hit UK 75 in Jun83) (re-iss. Nov84 lp/c/cd; NL/NK/PD 83857) (re-iss. Apr91 on 'E.M.I.' cd/c/lp; CD/TC+/EMD 1025) (+=)* – Joe the Lion (1991 remix) / Abolumajor.

Jan 78. (7") *(PB 1190) <11190>* **THE BEAUTY AND THE BEAST. / SENSE OF DOUBT** [39] [ ]

— added **ADRIAN BELEW** – guitar / **SIMON HOUSE** – violin (ex-HIGH TIDE, ex-HAWKWIND) / **SEAN MAYES** – piano

Sep 78. (d-lp,yellow-d-lp/d-c) *(PL/PK 02913) <2913>* **STAGE (live)** 5 44
– Hang on to yourself / Ziggy Stardust / Five years / Soul love / Star / Station to station / Fame / TVC 15 / Warszawa / Speed of life / Art decade / Sense of doubt / Breaking glass / Heroes / What in the world / Blackout / Beauty and the beast. *(re-iss. Jul84 d-lp/cd; PL/PD 89002) (re-iss. Feb92 on 'EMI' d-cd/c; CD/TC EMD 1030)* – (bonus tracks).

Oct 78. (7"ep) *(BOW 1)* **BREAKING GLASS (live). / ZIGGY STARDUST (live) / ART DECADE (live)** 54 –

Apr 79. (7") *(BOW 2) <11585>* **BOYS KEEP SWINGING. / FANTASTIC VOYAGE** 7

May 79. (lp/c) *(BOW LP/K 1) <3254>* **LODGER** 4 20
– Fantastic voyage / African night flight / Move on / Yassassin / Red sails / D.J. / Look back in anger / Boys keep swinging / Repetition / Red money. *(re-iss. May82 on 'RCA Int.' lp/c; INTS/INTK 5212) (re-iss. Mar84 on 'RCA Int.' lp/c/cd; NL/NK/PD 84234) (re-iss. Aug91 on 'E.M.I.' cd/c/lp; CD/TC+/EMD 1026)* – (2 tracks).

Jul 79. (7",7"green) *(BOW 3)* **D.J. / REPETITION** 29 –

Aug 79. (7") *<11661)* **D.J. / FANTASTIC VOYAGE** –

Oct 79. (7") *<11724>* **LOOK BACK IN ANGER. / REPITITION** –

Dec 79. (7"/ext.12") *(BOW 4/12-4)* **JOHN, I'M ONLY DANCING (AGAIN) (1975). / JOHN, I'M ONLY DANCING (1972)** 12 –

Jan 80. (7") *<11887>* **JOHN, I'M ONLY DANCING (1972). / JOE THE LION** –

Feb 80. (7") *(BOW 5)* **ALABAMA SONG. / SPACE ODDITY** 23

— guest **ROBERT FRIPP** – guitar repl. BRIAN ENO

Aug 80. (7") *(BOW 6)* **ASHES TO ASHES. / MOVE ON** 1 –

Sep 80. (7") *<12078>* **ASHES TO ASHES. / IT'S NO GAME** –

Sep 80. (lp/c) *(BOW LP/K 2) <3647>* **SCARY MONSTERS** 1 12
– It's no game (No.1) / Up the hill backwards / Scary monsters (and super creeps) / Ashes to ashes / Fashion / Teenage wildlife / Scream like a baby / Kingdom come / Because you're young / It's no game (No.2). *(re-iss. Oct84 lp/c/cd; PL/PK/PD 83647) (re-iss. Jun92 on 'EMI' cd/c; CD/TC EMD 1029) (+=)* – Space oddity / Panic in Detroit / Crystal Japan / Alabama song.

Oct 80. (7"/12") *(BOW/+T 7) <12134>* **FASHION. / SCREAM LIKE A BABY** 5 70

Jan 81. (7"/c-s) *(BOW/+C 8)* **SCARY MONSTERS (AND SUPER CREEPS). / BECAUSE YOU'RE YOUNG** 20 –

Mar 81. (7"/c-s) *(BOW/+C 9)* **UP THE HILL BACKWARDS. / CRYSTAL JAPAN** 32 –

— (next single "UNDER PRESSURE" was a No.1 collaboration w/ "QUEEN")

Nov 81. (7"/12") *(BOW/+T 10)* **WILD IS THE WIND. / GOLDEN YEARS** 24 –

Nov 81. (lp/c) *(BOW LP/K 3) <4202>* **CHANGESTWOBOWIE** (compilation) 24 68
– Aladdin Sane / Oh you pretty things / Starman / 1984 / Ashes to ashes / Sound and vision / Fashion / Wild is the wind / John, I'm only dancing (again) (1975) / D.J. *(re-iss. May84 lp/c/cd; PL/PK/PD 84202)*

Feb 82. (7"ep) *(BOW 11)* **BAAL'S HYMN** 29 –
– Baal's hymn / Remembering Marie / Ballad of the adventurers / The drowned girl / The dirty song.

Apr 82. (7"/ext.12") *(MCA/+T 770) <52024>* **CAT PEOPLE (PUTTING OUT FIRE). / (other by Giorgio Moroder)** 26 67
(above single taken from the film of the same name on 'M.C.A.')

Nov 82. (7"/12"; by DAVID BOWIE & BING CROSBY) *(BOW/+T 12) <13400>* **PEACE ON EARTH – LITTLE DRUMMER BOY. / FANTASTIC VOYAGE** 3
(cd-s iss.Oct02 on 'Oglio'+=; OGL 85001) – (video).

— now with **NILE RODGERS + STEVIE RAY VAUGHAN** – guitar / **BERNARD EDWARDS + CARMINE ROJAS** – bass / **OMAR HAKIM + TONY THOMPSON** – drums / **SAMMY FIGUEROA** – percussion

EMI America EMI America

Mar 83. (7"/12"/c-s) *(EA/12EA/45-TCEA 152) <8158>* **LET'S DANCE. / CAT PEOPLE (PUTTING OUT FIRE)** 1 1

Apr 83. (lp/pic-lp/c) *(AML/AMLP/TCAML 3029) <17093>* **LET'S DANCE** 1 4
– Modern love / China girl / Let's dance / China girl / Without you / Ricochet / Criminal world / Cat people (putting out fire) / Shake it. *(cd-iss. Jan84; CDP 7460022) (re-iss. cd Nov95 on 'Virgin American'; CDVUS 96) (cd re-iss. Jan98 on 'E.M.I.'; 493094-2)*

Jun 83. (7"/7"pic-d/12") *(EA/EAP/12EA 157) <8165>* **CHINA GIRL. / SHAKE IT** 2 10

Sep 83. (7"/12") *(EA/12EA 158) <8177>* **MODERN LOVE. / MODERN LOVE (live)** 2 14

Feb 84. (7") *<8190>* **WITHOUT YOU. / CRIMINAL WORLD** – 73

— retained **HAKIM, ROJAS, FIGUEROA** / brought back **ALOMAR** and recruited **DEREK BRAMBLE** – bass, snyths, etc.

Sep 84. (7"/12") *(EA/12EA 181) <8231>* **BLUE JEAN. / DANCING WITH THE BIG BOYS** 6 8

Sep 84. (lp/c)(cd) *(DB/TCDB 1)(CDP 746047-2) <17138>* **TONIGHT** 1 11
– Loving the alien / Don't look down / God only knows / Tonight / Neighbourhood threat / Blue Jean / Tumble and twirl / I keep forgetting / Dancing with the big boys. *(re-iss. cd Nov95 on 'Virgin American'; CDVUS 97) (cd re-iss. Jan 98 on 'E.M.I.'; 493102-2)*

Nov 84. (7") *(EA 187) <8246>* **TONIGHT. / TUMBLE AND TWIRL** 53 53
(12") *(12EA 187)* – ('A'vocal dance mix) / ('B'extended dance mix) / ('A'dub mix).

— (next single, from the film "Falcon And The Snowman")

Jan 85. (7"/12"; by DAVID BOWIE with The PAT METHENY GROUP) *(EA 190) <8251>* **THIS IS NOT AMERICA. / ('A'instrumental by The PAT METHENY GROUP)** 14 32

May 85. (7"/7"pic-d) *(EA/+P 195) <8271>* **LOVING THE ALIEN. / DON'T LOOK DOWN** 19
(ext.12"+=/ext.12"sha-pic-d+=) *(12EA/+P 195)* – ('A'extended dub mix).

Sep 85. (7"; by DAVID BOWIE & MICK JAGGER) *(EA 204) <8288>* **DANCING IN THE STREET (Clearmountain mix). / ('A'instrumental)** 1 7
(12") *(12EA 204)* – ('A'-Steve Thompson mix) / ('A'dub version) / ('A'edit).
(below single from 'Virgin' records film & album of the same name, cont. 3 BOWIE tracks, album reached No.19 UK)

Mar 86. (7"/7"sha-pic-d)(ext.12") *(VS/+S 838)(VS 838-12) <8308>* **ABSOLUTE BEGINNERS. / ('A'dub version)** 2 53
(re-iss. 3"cd-s Nov88; CDT 20)

— now with **ALOMAR, ROJAS + ERDAL KIZILCAY** – keyboards / **PHILIPPE SAISSE** – keyboards, etc. / **PETER FRAMPTON** – guitar

Jun 86. (7"/7"sha-pic-d) *(EA/+P 216) <8323>* **UNDERGROUND. / ('A'instrumental)** 21

Jun 86. (lp/c) *(AML/TCAML 3104) <17206>* **LABYRINTH** (soundtrack; shared with Trevor Jones *) 38 Jul86 68
– Opening titles including Underground / Magic dance / Chilly down / As the world falls down / Within you / Underground / (others by *) *(cd-iss. Sep86 & Feb90; CDP7 46312-2)*

— (next was from animated film of the same name on 'Virgin')

Nov 86. (7"/7"sha-pic-d) *(VS/+S 906)* **WHEN THE WIND BLOWS. / ('A'-instrumental)** 44 –
(ext.dance-12"+=) *(VS 906-12)* – ('A'-dub).

Mar 87. (7"/7"red) *(EA/+X 230) <8380>* **DAY-IN DAY-OUT. / JULIE** 17 21
(ext.dance-12"+=/remix-12"+=)(ext.dance c-s+=) *(12EA/+X 230)(TCEA 230)* – ('A'extended dub).

Apr 87. (lp/c/cd) *(AMLS/TCAMLS/CDAMLS 3117) <17267>* **NEVER LET ME DOWN** 6 34
– Day-in day-out / Time will crawl / Beat of your drum / Never let me down / Zeroes / Glass spider / Shining star (makin' my love) / New York's in love / '87 and cry / Bang bang / Too dizzy. *(cd+=)* – Time will crawl (extended dance) / Never let me down (version) / Day-in day-out (Groucho mix). *(re-iss. cd Nov95 on 'Virgin American'; CDVUS 98) (cd re-iss. Jan98 on 'E.M.I.'; 493097-2)*

Jun 87. (7"/7"w-poster) *(EA/+P 237) <43020>* **TIME WILL CRAWL. / GIRLS** 33
(12") *(12EA 237)* – ('A'extended dance mix) / ('A'version) / ('B'extended).
(12") *(12EAX 237)* – ('A'dance crew mix) / ('A'dub) / ('B'-Japanese version).

Aug 87. (7"/7"pic-d) *(EA/+P 239) <43031>* **NEVER LET ME DOWN. / '87 AND CRY** 34 27
(c-s+=) *(TCEA 239)* – Time will crawl (extended dance mix) / Day-in day-out (Groucho mix).
(ext.dance-12"+=) *(12EA 239)* – ('A'dub) / ('A'acappella).

TIN MACHINE

was the name of **BOWIE's** next project/band. **DAVID BOWIE** – vocals, saxophone / **REEVES GABRELS** – lead guitar / **TONY SALES** – bass / **HUNT SALES** – drums (both ex-IGGY POP, ex-TODD RUNDGREN RUNT)plus p/t member **KEVIN ARMSTRONG** – guitar

Manhattan Manhattan

May 89. (cd/c/lp) *(CD/MC+/MTLS 1044)* <91990> **TIN MACHINE** [3] [28]
– Heaven's in here / Tin machine / Prisoner of love / Crack city / I can't read / Under the god / Amazing / Working class hero / Bus stop / Pretty thing / Video crimes / Run * / Sacrifice yourself * / Baby can dance. *(cd+= *) (re-iss. cd Nov95 on 'Virgin American'; CDVUS 99)*

Jun 89. (7"/c-s) *(MT/TCMT 68)* **UNDER THE GOD. / SACRIFICE YOURSELF** [51] [ ]
(10"+=/12"+=/cd-s+=) *(10/12/CD MT 68)* – (the interview).

Aug 89. (7"/7"s/7"sha-pic-d/c-s) *(MT/MTG/MTPD/TCMT 73)* **TIN MACHINE. / MAGGIE'S FARM (live)** [48] [ ]
(12"+=) *(12MT 73)* – I can't read (live).
(cd-s++=) *(CDMT 73)* – Bus stop (live country version).

Oct 89. (7"/7"s/7"sha-pic-d/c-s) *(MT/MTS/MTPD/TCMT 76)* **PRISONER OF LOVE. / BABY CAN DANCE (live)** [ ] [ ]
(12"+=) *(12MT 76)* – Crack city (live).
(cd-s++=) *(CDMT 76)* – ('A'version).

London Victory

Aug 91. (7"/12") *(LON/+X 305)* **YOU BELONG IN ROCK'N'ROLL. / AMLAPURA** [33] [ ]
(pic-cd+=) *(LONCD 305)* – Stateside / Hammerhead.

Sep 91. (cd/c/lp) *(828 272-2/-4/-1)* <511216> **TIN MACHINE II** [23] [ ]
– Baby universal / One shot / You belong in rock'n'roll / If there is something / Amlapura / Betty wrong / You can't talk / Stateside / Shopping for girls / Big hurt / I'm sorry / Goodbye Mr. Ed / Hammerhead.

Oct 91. (7"/c-s) *(LON/+CS 310)* **BABY UNIVERSAL. / YOU BELONG IN ROCK'N'ROLL** [48] [ ]
(12") *(LONT 310)* – ('A'side) / A big hurt (live) / ('A'live).
(cd-s) *(LONCD 310)* – ('A'side) / Stateside (live) / If there is something (live) / Heaven's in here (live).

— In Feb'92, BOWIE's song 'SOUND AND VISION (remix)' was re-done with himself and 808 STATE on label 'Tommy Boy'.

Jul 92. (cd/c/lp) *(828 328-2/-4/-1)* <480004> **TIN MACHINE LIVE – OY VEY, BABY (live)** [ ] [ ]
– If there is something / Amazing / I can't read / Stateside / Under the god / Goodbye Mr. Ed / Heaven's in here / You belong in rock'n'roll.

DAVID BOWIE

(solo again) and starred in the film 'THE LINGUINI INCIDENT'.

Warners Warners

Aug 92. (7"/c-s) *(W 0127/+C)* **REAL COOL WORLD. / ('A'instrumental)** [53] [ ]
(12") *(W 0127T)* – ('A'club) / ('A'dub thing 1 & 2) / ('A'dub overture).
(cd-s+=) *(W 0127CD)* – (2 more 'A'mixes).

— with **NILE RODGERS** – guitar, co-producer / **DAVE RICHARDS + RICHARD HILTON + PHILIPPE SAISSE + RICHARD TEE** – keyboards / **BARRY CAMPBELL + JOHN REGAN** – bass / **PUGI BELL + STERLING CAMPBELL** – drums / **GERADO VELEZ** – percussion. Plus guests **MICK RONSON** – guitar / **LESTER BOWIE** – trumpet / **REEVES GABRELS** – guitar / **MIKE GARSON** – piano / **AL B.SURE!** – vocals / **WILD T.SPRINGER** – guitar

Savage-BMG Savage-BMG

Mar 93. (c-s) *(74321 139424)* **JUMP THEY SAY. / PALLAS ATHENA (Don't Stop Praying mix)** [9] [ ]
(cd-s+=) *(74321 139422)* – ('A'-Hard Hands mix) / ('A'-JAE-E remix).
(cd-s) *(74321 139432)* – ('A'-Brothers In Rhythm mix) / ('A'-Brothers In Rhythm instrumental) / ('A'-Leftfield vocal) / ('A'ext).
(12") *(74321 139424-1)* – ('A'-Hard Hands mix) / ('A'version) / ('A'-Leftfield 12" vocal) / ('A'-extended).

Apr 93. (cd/c/lp) *(<74321 13697-2/-4/-1>)* **BLACK TIE WHITE NOISE** [1] [39]
– The wedding / You've been around / I feel free / Black tie white noise / Jump they say / Nite flight / Pallas Athena / Miracle tonight / Don't let me down & down / Looking for Lester / I know it's gonna happen someday / The wedding song / Jump they say (alternate mix) / Lucy can't dance.

Jun 93. (7"/c-s) *(74321 14868-7/-4)* **BLACK TIE WHITE NOISE. / YOU'VE BEEN AROUND (Jack Dangers remix)** [36] [ ]
(cd-s+=) *(74321 14868-2)* – ('A'extended remix) / ('A'-Urban).
(12") *(74321 14868-1)* – ('A'extended) / ('A'trance mix) / ('A'version) / ('A'club mix with AL B.SURE!) / ('A'extended urban mix).

Oct 93. (7"/c-s) *(74321 16226-7/-4)* **MIRACLE TONIGHT. / LOOKING FOR LESTER** [40] [ ]
(cd-s+=) *(74321 16226-2)* – ('A'-Philly mix) / ('A'-Masereti mix).
(12") *(74321 16226-1)* – ('A'-Blunted mix) / ('A'-Make believe mix) / ('A'-Philly mix) / ('A'dance dub).

Nov 93. (7"/c-s) *(74321 17705-7/-4)* **BUDDHA OF SUBURBIA. / DEAD AGAINST IT** [35] [–]
(cd-s+=) *(74321 17705-2)* – South horizon / ('A'-Lenny Kravitz rock mix).

Nov 93. (cd/c) *(74321 17004-2/-4)* <40988> **THE BUDDHA OF SUBURBIA** (TV soundtrack) [ ] Oct95 [ ]
– Buddha of suburbia / Sex and the church / South horizon / The mysteries / Bleed like a craze, dad / Strangers when we meet / Dead against it / Untitled No.1 / Ian Fish, U.K. heir / Buddha of suburbia (featuring LENNY KRAVITZ).

— now with **ENO** – synthesizers, co-writer (on most) / **REEVES GABRELS / ERDAL KIZILCAY / MIKE GARSON / STERLING CAMPBELL / CARLOS ALOMAR / JOEY BARON / YOSSI FINE**

R.C.A. Virgin

Sep 95. (c-s/cd-s) *(74321 30703-4/-2)* **THE HEARTS FILTHY LESSON / I AM WITH NAME** [35] [–]
(cd-s+=) *(74321 30703-2)* – ('A'-Bowie mix) / ('A'-Trent Reznor alt.remix) / ('A'-Tony Maserati remix).
(12"pic-d) *(74321 30703-1)* – (5-'A'mixes; Bowie / alt. / Rubber / Simple text / Filthy).

Sep 95. (cd/c/d-lp) *(<74321 30702-2/-4/-1>)* **OUTSIDE** [8] [21]
– THE NATHAN ADLER DIARIES: A Hyper Cycle:- Leon takes us outside / Outside / The hearts filthy lesson / A small plot of land / segue – Baby Grace (a horrid cassette) / Hallo spaceboy / The motel / I have not been to Oxford Town / No control / segue – Algeria touchshriek / The voyeur of utter destruction (as beauty) / segue – Ramona A. Stone – I am with name / Wishful beginnings / We prick you / segue – Nathan Adler / Strangers when we meet.

Sep 95. (c-s) <38518> **THE HEARTS FILTHY LESSON / NOTHING TO BE DESIRED** [–] [92]

Nov 95. (7"/c-s) *(74321 32940-7/-4)* **STRANGERS WHEN WE MEET. / THE MAN WHO SOLD THE WORLD (live)** [39] [ ]
(cd-s+=) *(74321 32940-2)* – ('A'side again) / Get real.
(12") *(74321 32940-1)* – ('A'side) / The seeker / Hang ten high.

Feb 96. (7"pink/c-s) *(74321 35384-7/-4)* **HALLO SPACEBOY. / THE HEARTS FILTHY LESSON** [12] [ ]
(cd-s+=) *(74321 35384/-2)* – Moonage daydream (live) / Under pressure (live).

below a collaboration with A GUY CALLED GERALD. His main band:- REEVES GABRELS, MIKE GARSON + ZACHARY ALFORD + GAIL ANN DORSEY – vocals

Nov 96. (12"/cd-s) *(74321 39741-1/-2)* **TELLING LIES (mixes; Paradox / Feelgood / Adam F)** [ ] [–]

Jan 97. (12"/cd-s) *(74321 45207-1/-2)* **LITTLE WONDER. / TELLING LIES (Adam F mix)** [14] [ ]
(cd-s) *(74321 45208-2)* – ('A'mixes by Junior Vasquez & Danny Saber) / Jump they say (Leftfield mix).

Feb 97. (cd/c) *(<74321 44944-2/-4>)* **EART HL ING** [6] [39]
– Little wonder / Looking for satellites / Battle for Britain (the letter) / Seven years in Tibet / Dead man walking / Telling lies / Last thing you should do / I'm afraid of Americans / Law (earthlings on fire).

Apr 97. (12"/cd-s) *(74321 47584-1/-2)* **DEAD MAN WALKING. / TELLING LIES** [32] [ ]
(cd-s) *(74321 47585-2)* – ('A'mixes) / I'm deranged / Heart's filthy lesson.

Aug 97. (12"clear/cd-s) *(74321 51254-7/-2)* **SEVEN YEARS IN TIBET (mixes; Mandarin). / PALLAS ATHENA** [61] [ ]

Nov 97. (c-s,cd-s) <38618> **I'M AFRAID OF AMERICANS (versions V1, V2, V3 – with ICE CUBE, V4, V5, V6)** [–] [56]

Velvel not iss.

Feb 98. (cd-ep) *(ZYX 87578)* **I CAN'T READ (short & long version) / THIS IS NOT AMERICA** [73] [–]

Virgin Virgin

Sep 99. (c-s/cd-s) *(VSC/+DT 1753)* **THURSDAY'S CHILD / WE ALL GO THROUGH / NO ONE CALLS** [16] [–]
(cd-s) *(VSCDTX 1753)* – ('A'-Rock mix) / We shall all go to town / 1917 / ('A'-CD-Rom video).

Oct 99. (cd/c) *(CDV/TCV 2900)* <48157> **HOURS . . .** [5] [47]
– Thursday's child / Something in the air / Survive / If I'm dreaming my life / Seven / What's really happening? / The pretty things are going to hell / New angels of promise / Brilliant adventure / The dreamers.

— in Dec'99, BOWIE and QUEEN were back in the charts (UK No.14) with the remix of 'Under Pressure'

Jan 00. (cd-s) *(VSCDT 1767)* **SURVIVE / SURVIVE (Marius De Vries mix) / THE PRETTY THINGS ARE GOING TO HELL (from 'The Matrix')** | 28 | [ ]
(cd-s) *(VSCDX 1767)* – ('A'side) / Thursday's child (live) / Seven (live).

Jul 00. (cd-s) *(VSCDT 1776)* **SEVEN (mixes; Marius DeVries / Beck / demo)** | 32 | [ ]
(cd-s) *(VSCDX 1776)* – ('A'mix) / I'm afraid of Americans (Nine Inch Nails mix).
(cd-s) *(VSCDXX 1776)* – ('A'mix) / ('A'live) / Something in the air (live) / Pretty things are going to hell (live).

— in May'02, SCUMFROG feat. BOWIE on hit version of 'LOVING THE ALIEN'

I.S.O. – Columbia | I.S.O. – Columbia

Jun 02. (cd/lp) *(508222-2/-1)* *<86630>* **HEATHEN** | 5 | 14
– Sunday / Cactus / Slip away / Slow burn / Afraid / I've been waiting for you / I would be your slave / I took a trip on a Gemini spaceship / 5.15 the angels have gone / Everyone says 'Hi' / A better future / Heathen (the rays). *(d-cd+=; 508222-9)* – Sunday (Moby remix) / Better future (air remix) / Conversation piece / Panic in Detroit (1979 recording).

Sep 02. (cd-s) *(673134-2)* **EVERYONE SAYS 'HI' / SAFE / WOOD JACKSON** | 20 | –
(cd-s) *(673134-5)* – ('A'side) / Baby loves that way / You've got a habit of leaving.
(cd-s) *(673134-3)* – ('A'side) / When the boys come marching home / The shadow man.

— in Jul'03, DAVID GUETTA vs BOWIE hit the UK Top 75 with 'JUST FOR ONE DAY (HEROES)'

Sep 03. (cd) *(512555-2)* *<90576>* **REALITY** | 3 | 29
– New killer star / Pablo Picasso / Never get old / The loneliest guy / Looking for water / She'll drive the big car / Days / Fall dogs bombs the moon / Try some, buy some / Reality / Bring me the disco king.

Sep 03. (dvd-s) *(674279-9)* **NEW KILLER STAR (video) / REALITY / LOVE MISSILE F1-11** | [ ] | –

– compilations, etc. –

note; All below on 'RCA' unless otherwise mentioned

Mar 70. (lp; mono/stereo)(c) *Decca; (PA/SPA 58)(KCSP 58)* **THE WORLD OF DAVID BOWIE** | [ ] | –

May 75. (d-lp) *Decca; (DPA 3017-8) / London; <628-9>* **IMAGES 66-67** | [ ] | [ ]

Dec 80. (lp/c) *K-Tel; (NE/+C 1111)* **THE BEST OF DAVID BOWIE** | 3 | –

Apr 81. (lp/c) *Decca; (TAB/KTAB 17)* **ANOTHER FACE** | [ ] | –

May 81. (lp/c) *(RCA LP/K 3074)* *<AFI/AFK1 4239>* **CHRISTIANE F. – WIR KINDER VOM BAHNHOF ZOO** (live soundtrack) | [ ] | Mar82 [ ]
– V-2 Schneider / TVC 15 / Heroes (Helden) / Boys keep swinging / Sense of doubt / Station to station / Look back in anger / Stay / Warszawa. *(<cd-iss. Aug01 on 'E.M.I.'; 5 33093-2>)*

Dec 82. (10x7"pic-d-singles) *(BOW 100)* **FASHIONS** | [ ] | –
– SPACE ODDITY / LIFE ON MARS / THE JEAN GENIE / REBEL REBEL / SOUND & VISION / DRIVE-IN SATURDAY / SORROW / GOLDEN YEARS / BOYS KEEP SWINGING / ASHES TO ASHES

Jan 83. (lp/c) *(PL/PK 45406)* **RARE** | 34 | –

Aug 83. (lp/c) *(BOW LP/K 004)* *<4792>* **GOLDEN YEARS (live recent)** | 33 | 99

Aug 83. (lp) *Decca Rock Echoes; (TAB 71)* **A SECOND FACE** | [ ] | –

Oct 83. (d-lp/d-c) *(PL/PK 84862)* *<AFI/AFK1 4862>* **ZIGGY STARDUST – THE MOTION PICTURE** (live soundtrack from 1973) | 17 | 89
– Hang on to yourself / Ziggy Stardust / Watch that man / Wild eyed boy from Freecloud / All the young dudes – Oh! you pretty things / Moonage daydream / Space oddity / My death / Cracked actor / Time / Width of a circle / Changes / Let's spend the night together / Suffragette city / White light – white heat / Rock and roll suicide. *(cd-iss. Sep92 on 'EMI'; CDP 780411-2)*

Oct 83. (7") *(RCA 372)* *<13660>* **WHITE LIGHT – WHITE HEAT (live). / CRACKED ACTOR (live)** | 46 | [ ]

Apr 84. (lp/c/cd) *(PL/PK/PD 84919)* *<4919>* **FAME AND FASHION (ALL TIME GREATEST HITS)** | 40 | [ ]

May 84. (lp/c) *Deram; (BOWIE/BOWMC 1)* **LOVE YOU TILL TUESDAY** | 53 | –

Sep 89. (cd) *Rykodisc; <0120>* **SOUND + VISION** | – | 97

Mar 90. (c-s/7") *EMI-USA; (TC+/FAME 90)* **FAME 90 (Gass mix). / ('A'-Queen Latifah's version)** | 28 | [ ]
(cd-s+=) *(CDFAME 90)* – ('A'house mix) / ('A'hip hop mix).
(12") *(12FAME 90)* – ('A'side) / ('A'house) / ('A'hip hop).
(7"pic-d) *(FAMEPD 90)* – ('A'side) / ('A'-bonus beats mix).

Apr 90. (cd/c/d-lp) *E.M.I.; (CD/TC+/DBTV 1) / Rykodisc; <20171>* **CHANGESBOWIE** | 1 | 39
– Space oddity / John, I'm only dancing / Changes / Ziggy stardust / Suffragette city / The Jean genie / Diamond dogs / Rebel rebel / Young Americans / Fame ('90 remix) / Golden years / Heroes / Ashes to ashes / Fashion / Let's dance / China girl / Modern love / Blue Jean.

Nov 93. (d-cd/d-c/t-lp) *E.M.I.; (7243 828099-2/-4/-1)* **THE SINGLES COLLECTION** | 9 | [ ]
(re-iss. Nov95 d-cd/d-c/t-lp; CD/TC+/EM 1512)

May 94. (cd/c/d-lp) *Trident; (GY/+MC/LP 002)* **SANTA MONICA '72 (live)** | 74 | –

Oct 97. (cd/c) *E.M.I.; (821849-2/-4)* **THE BEST OF DAVID BOWIE 1969-1974** | 13 | [ ]

Apr 98. (cd/c) *E.M.I.; (494300-2/-4)* **THE BEST OF DAVID BOWIE 1974-1979** | 39 | [ ]

Sep 00. (3xcd-box) *E.M.I.; (528958-2) / Virgin; <28958>* **BOWIE AT THE BEEB – THE BEST OF THE BBC RECORDINGS 1968-1972** | 7 | [ ]

Nov 02. (d-cd) *E.M.I.; (539821-2)* **BEST OF BOWIE** | 11 | [ ]

□ BOXCAR RACER (see under ⇒ BLINK-182)

BOY KILL BOY

Formed: Leytonstone, East London, England . . . 2004 by CHRIS PECK, PETE CARR, KEV CHASE and SHAZ MAHMOOD. Despite the homicidal name, BOY KILL BOY were actually a bouncy indie-pop quartet from the heart of chirpy Cockney land. Like many a current alt-pop superstar, they started out on 'Fierce Panda', releasing a one-off single, 'SUZIE', in May 2005. Graduating to 'Vertigo' via 'Island' records (for whom they cut 'CIVIL SIN'), BKB were 'BACK AGAIN' and in the Top 30 come February 2006. They subsequently took off for Texas' 'South By Southwest' forum, returning to an NME tour alongside the AUTOMATIC and a hit re-issue of 'SUZIE'. A John Cornfield-produced debut album, 'CIVILIAN' (2006), wasn't long in joining their punk-rooted peers in the Top 20, its addictive hooks promising a few more hit singles in the bag.

• **Covers:** IT'S DIFFERENT FOR GIRLS (Joe Jackson).

Album rating: CIVILIAN (*8)

CHRIS PECK – vocals, guitar / **PETE CARR** – keyboards / **KEV CHASE** – bass, vocals / **SHAZ MAHMOOD** – drums

Fierce Panda | not iss.

May 05. (cd-s) *(NING 170CD)* **SUZIE / LAST OF THE GREAT** | [ ] | –

Island | not iss.

Sep 05. (7"/cd-s) *(IS/CID 907)* **CIVIL SIN. / KILLER / ON AND ON** | [ ] | –

Vertigo | Island

Feb 06. (cd-s) *(9876834)* **BACK AGAIN / CHEAPER** | 26 | –
(7"+=) *(9876835)* – Number one.

May 06. (7") *(9856257)* **SUZIE. / LAST OF THE GREAT** | 17 | –
(cd-s) *(9856255)* – ('A') / It's different for girls.
(cd-s) *(9856256)* – ('A') / Orphan / 6 minutes (live at King Tut's Glasgow 23rd October 2005).

May 06. (cd/lp) *(9877 358/180)* *<9873781>* **CIVILIAN** | 16 | Jun06 [ ]
– Back again / On and on / Suzie / Six minutes / On my own / Ivy Parker / Civil sin / Killer / Friday Friday / Showdown / Shoot me down. *(cd+=)* – (hidden track).

□ BOYS NEXT DOOR (see under ⇒ CAVE, Nick)

Billy BRAGG

Born: STEVEN WILLIAM BRAGG, 20 Dec'57, Barking, Essex, England. Inspired by The CLASH, he formed Peterborough-based R&B/punk band, RIFF RAFF, in 1977. After releasing a string of indie 7" singles, (including the wonderfully titled 'I WANNA BE A COSMONAUT'), the band split in 1981, BILLY incredibly going off to join the army. Thankfully, a career in the military wasn't to be though, and he bought himself out after only 90 days. Complete with amplifier and guitar, he busked around Britain, finally furnished with some studio time in 1983 courtesy of 'Charisma' indie subsidiary, 'Utility'. The result was 'LIFE'S A RIOT WITH SPY VS SPY', and with the help and distribution of new label 'Go! Discs', the record finally hit the UK Top 30 in early '84. BRAGG's stark musical backdrop (for the most part, a roughly strummed electric guitar) and even starker vocals, belied a keen sense of melody and passionate, deeply humane lyrics. 'THE MILKMAN OF HUMAN KINDNESS' was a love song of the most compassionate variety which illustrated that BRAGG approached politics from a humanist perspective rather than a soapbox. After seeing firsthand how Thatcher had decimated mining communities, BRAGG's songs became more overtly political. 'BREWING UP WITH BILLY BRAGG' (1984) opened with the fierce 'IT SAYS HERE', but again the most affecting moments were to be found on heartfelt love songs like the wistful 'ST. SWITHIN'S DAY'. It would be another two years before he released a new album, in the interim taking time to make his Top Of The Pops debut and play a lead role in the 'Red Wedge' campaign. A well intentioned but ultimately hopeless initiative to persuade people to vote Labour, BRAGG toured alongside The STYLE COUNCIL, MADNESS, The COMMUNARDS and MORRISSEY. As the Conservatives romped home to another sickening victory, BRAGG licked his wounds and bounced back with a third album, 'TALKING WITH THE TAXMAN ABOUT POETRY' (1986). His most successful and accomplished release to date, the record spawned the classic single, 'LEVI STUBBS' TEARS' as well as the JOHNNY MARR collaboration, 'GREETINGS TO THE NEW BRUNETTE'. And of course, who could argue with the sentiments of 'HELP SAVE THE YOUTH OF AMERICA'?! Not content with saving our Transatlantic cousins, BRAGG also did his bit for kids back in Blighty. Recording a cover of 'SHE'S LEAVING HOME' with CARA TIVEY, BRAGG found himself at No.1 when the song was released as the B-side to WET WET WET's cover of 'WITH A LITTLE HELP FROM MY FRIENDS', the not inconsiderable proceeds going to the Childline charity. BRAGG's next album, 'WORKER'S PLAYTIME' (1988), saw a move away from the sparse accompaniment of old, while lyrically the record focused more on matters of the heart than the ballot box. 'THE INTERNATIONALE' (1990), meanwhile, was BRAGG's most political work to date, with the likes of 'NICARAGUITA' and 'THE RED FLAG'. On 'DON'T TRY THIS AT HOME' (1991), BRAGG enlisted a cast of musicians to flesh out the sound, a tactic that elicited mixed results. His stance with CND and anti-apartheid, anti-poll tax, etc, often saw him on wrong side of the law. For the 90's it looked as though he would become a bit more cosmopolitan but still ungagged. In 1998, BILLY and the alt-country group WILCO decided to do a tribute album dedicated to their dustbowl hero, WOODY GUTHRIE. 'MERMAID AVENUE' (a street in Coney Island where WOODY lived with his family in the late 40's and early 50's) was the title, the lyrics seemingly found in an attic while messers BRAGG and WILCO set them to tunes. From the bawdy, singalong raucousness of opener 'WALT WHITMAN'S NIECE' to the gorgeous, yawning back porch swing of 'CALIFORNIA STARS' and the desolate fragility of 'BIRDS AND SHIPS' (featuring a heart-stopping guest vocal by NATALIE MERCHANT), this ranked among the cream of both artists' back catalogues. While they each interpreted the material in their own way – BRAGG obviously coming closer to the mould of GUTHRIE's worldly, open hearted troubadour – both WILCO and BRAGG brought their own personality to bear on WOODY's words of wisdom. As well as being a great record in its own right – surely a contender for album of the year – this collection served to underline just how unceasingly prolific and inventive a songwriter GUTHRIE really was. The spirit of this work cut to the heart of popular music's foundations, no argument. Inevitably, 'MERMAID AVENUE VOL.2' (2000) couldn't quite match that high standard but was nevertheless an enjoyable companion piece to its predecessor.

• **Covered:** WALK AWAY RENEE (Four Tops) / SHE'S LEAVING HOME + REVOLUTION (Beatles) / JEANE (Smiths) / SEVEN AND SEVEN IS (Love) / THERE IS POWER IN A UNION (trad.new words) / THINK AGAIN (Dick Gaughan) / CHILE YOUR WATERS RUN RED THROUGH SOWETO (B.Johnson Reagan) / TRAIN TRAIN (Z.Delfeur) / DOLPHINS (Fred Neil) / EVERYWHERE (Sid Griffin-Greg Trooper) / JERUSALEM (William Blake) / WHEN WILL I SEE YOU AGAIN (Three Degrees) / NEVER HAD NO ONE EVER (Smiths) / FEAR IS A MAN'S BEST FRIEND (John Cale)/ SHE SMILED SWEETLY (Rolling Stones) / A13, TRUNK ROAD TO THE SEA (Bobby Troup) / DRY BED (Woody Guthrie).

Album rating: LIFE'S A RIOT WITH SPY VS. SPY mini (*7) / BREWING UP WITH BILLY BRAGG (*8) / TALKING WITH THE TAXMAN ABOUT POETRY (*8) / BACK TO BASICS compilation (*7) / WORKERS PLAYTIME (*7) / THE INTERNATIONALE (*5) / DON'T TRY THIS AT HOME (*8) / WILLIAM BLOKE (*7) / BLOKE ON BLOKE (*6) / MERMAID AVENUE with Wilco (*8) / REACHING TO THE CONVERTED (MINDING THE GAPS) collection (*7) / MERMAID AVENUE VOL.II with Wilco (*6) / ENGLAND, HALF ENGLISH (*5) / MUST I PAINT YOU A PICTURE?: THE ESSENTIAL . . . compilation (*8)

RIFF RAFF

BILLY BRAGG – vocals, guitar and other members

Chiswick | not iss.

May 78. (7"ep) *(SW 34)* **I WANNA BE A COSMONAUT** [ ] [–]
– Cosmonaut / Romford girls / What's the latest? / Sweet as pie.

Geezer | not iss.

Oct 80. (7") *(GZ 1)* **EVERY GIRL AN ENGLISH ROSE. / U SHAPED HOUSE** [ ] [–]

Oct 80. (7") *(GZ 2)* **KITTEN. / FANTOCIDE** [ ] [–]

Oct 80. (7") *(GZ 3)* **LITTLE GIRLS KNOW. / SHE DON'T MATTER** [ ] [–]

Oct 80. (7") *(GZ 4)* **NEW HOME TOWN. / RICHARD** [ ] [–]

BILLY BRAGG

Utility | not iss.

Jun 83. (m-lp) *(UTIL 1)* **LIFE'S A RIOT WITH SPY VS. SPY** [30] [–]
– The milkman of human kindness / To have and have not / A new England / The man in the iron mask / The busy girl buys beauty / Lover's town revisited / Richard. *(re-iss. Jan84 on 'Go! Discs' lp/c; UTIL/+C 1) (cd-iss. Sep96 on 'Cooking Vinyl'; COOKCD 106)*

— added for back-up **KENNY CRADDOCK** – organ / **DAVE WOODHEAD** – trumpet

Go! Discs | Elektra

Oct 84. (lp/c) *(A/Z GOLP 4)* **BREWING UP WITH BILLY BRAGG** [16] [–]
– It says here / Love gets dangerous / The myth of trust / From a Vauxhall Velox / The Saturday boy / Island of no return / St. Swithin's Day / Like soldiers do / This guitar says sorry / Strange things happen / A lover sings. *(cd-iss. Sep96 on 'Cooking Vinyl'; COOKCD 107)*

Feb 85. (7") **ST. SWITHIN'S DAY. / A NEW ENGLAND** [–] Euro [–]

Mar 85. (7"ep) *(AGOEP 1)* **BETWEEN THE WARS** [15] [–]
– Between the wars / Which side are you on? / World turned upside down / It says here.

Dec 85. (7"m) *(GOD 8)* **DAYS LIKE THESE. / I DON'T NEED THIS PRESSURE RON / SCHOLARSHIP IS THE ENEMY OF ROMANCE** [43] [–]

— + guests **JOHNNY MARR** – guitar / **KIRSTY MacCOLL** – b.vocals / **KENNY**

JONES – drums, co-producer / **JOHN PORTER** – bass, co-producer / **SIMON MORTEON** – percussion / **BOBBY VALENTINO** – violin

Jun 86. (7"m) *(GOD 12)* **LEVI STUBBS' TEARS. / THINK AGAIN / WALK AWAY RENEE** [29] [–]
(12"+=) *(GODX 12)* – Between the wars (live).

Sep 86. (lp/c) *(A/Z GOLP 6)* **TALKING WITH THE TAXMAN ABOUT POETRY** [8] [ ]
– Greetings to the new brunette / Train train / The marriage / Ideology / Levi Stubbs' tears / Honey, I'm a big boy now / There is power in a union / Help save the youth of America / Wishing the days away / The passion / The warmest room / The home front. *(cd-iss. May87; AGOCD 6) (cd re-iss/Sep96 on 'Cooking Vinyl'; COOKCD 108)*

Nov 86. (7"m) *(GOD 15)* **GREETINGS TO THE NEW BRUNETTE. / DEPORTEES / THE TATLER** [58] [–]
(12"+=) *(GODX 15)* – Jeane / There is power in a union (instrumental).

— Oct'87, BRAGG is credited with OYSTER BAND backing **LEON ROSSELSON** on his single **BALLAD OF A SPYCATCHER** (Upside Down records)

— May'88, he's credited with **CARA TIVEY** on 45 **SHE'S LEAVING HOME** the B-side of **WET WET WET** – With A little Help From My Friends. This UK No.1 single issued on 'Childline' gave all proceeds to children's charity, with backing including his usual friends.

Go! Discs / Elektra

May 88. (12"ep/cd-ep) *(A/ZA GOLP 1) <960-787-2>* **HELP SAVE THE YOUTH OF AMERICA (LIVE AND DUBIOUS)** [ ] [ ]
– Help save the youth of America / Think again / Chile your waters run red through Soweto / Days like these (DC mix) / To have and have not / There is power in a union (with The PATTERSONS).

Aug 88. (7"m) *(GOD 23)* **WAITING FOR THE GREAT LEAP FORWARD. / WISHING THE DAYS AWAY / SIN CITY** [52] [–]

Sep 88. (lp/c/cd) *(AGOLP/ZGOLP/AGOCD 15) <60824>* **WORKER'S PLAYTIME** [17] [ ]
– She's got a brand new spell / Must I paint you a picture / Tender comrade / The price I pay / Little timb-bomb / Rotting on demand / Valentine's day is over / Life with the lions / The only one / The short answer / Waiting for the great leap forward. *(cd re-iss. Sep96 on 'Cooking Vinyl'; COOKCD 109)*

Nov 88. (7") *(GOD 24)* **SHE'S GOT A BRAND NEW SPELL. / MUST I PAINT YOU A PICTURE** [ ] [–]

— In Jul'89, BRAGG was credited on a NORMAN COOK Top 30 single 'Won't Talk About it'.

May 90. (m-lp/m-c/m-cd; on 'Utility') *(UTIL/+C/CD 011) <60960>* **THE INTERNATIONALE** [34] Jun90 [ ]
– The internationale / I dreamed I saw Phil Ochs last night / The marching song of the convent battalions / Jerusalem / Nicaraguita / The red flag / My youngest son came home today.

— still holding on to **MARR, MacCOLL, TIVEY** (keyboards) and WOODHEAD plus **WIGGY** – guitar, bass / **J.F.T. HOOD** – drums / **AMANDA VINCENT** – keyboards / etc.

Jun 91. (7") *(GOD 56)* **SEXUALITY. / BAD PENNY** [27] [–]
(12"+=/cd-s+=) *(GOD X/CD 56)* – (2 'A'mixes).

Aug 91. (7") *(GOD 60)* **YOU WOKE UP MY NEIGHBOURHOOD. / ONTARIO, QUEBEC AND ME** [54] [–]
(12"+=/cd-s+=) *(GOD X/CD 60)* – Bread and circuses / Heart like a wheel.
(above single 'A'featured **MICHAEL STIPE and PETER BUCK (R.E.M.)** with first 12"extra track with **NATALIE MERCHANT** (10,000 MANIACS) – also backing vocals

Sep 91. (cd/c/d-lp)(8x7"box) *(828279-2/-4/-1) <61121>* **DON'T TRY THIS AT HOME** [8] [ ]
– Accident waiting to happen / Moving the goalposts / Everywhere / Cindy of a thousand lives / You woke up my neighbourhood / Trust / God's footballer / The few / Sexuality / Mother of the bride / Tank park salute / Dolphins / North sea bubble / Rumours of war / Wish you were here / Body of water. *(re-iss. Nov93 & Apr98 on 'Cooking Vinyl' lp/c/cd; COOK/+C/CD 062) (cd re-iss. Sep96; COOKCD 110)*

Feb 92. (7"ep) *(GOD 67)* **ACCIDENT WAITING TO HAPPEN (Red Star version) / SULK. / THE WARMEST ROOM (live) / REVOLUTION** [33] [–]
(12"+=/cd-s+=) *(GOD X/CD 67)* – ('A'live version) / Levi Stubbs' tears / Valentine's day is over / North Sea bubble.

Cooking Vinyl / Elektra

Aug 96. (7"/c-s) *(FRY/+C 051)* **UPFIELD / THATCHERITES** [46] [–]
(cd-s+=) *(FRYCD 051)* – Rule nor reason.

Sep 96. (lp/c/cd) *(COOK/+C/CD 100) <61935>* **WILLIAM BLOKE** [16] [ ]
– From red to blue / Upfield / Everybody loves you babe / Sugardaddy / A Pict song / Brickbat / The space race is over / Northern industrial town / The fourteenth of February / King James version / Goalhanger.

May 97. (7") *(FRY 064)* **THE BOY DONE GOOD. / SUGARDADDY** [55] [ ]
(cd-s+=) *(FRYCD 064)* – Just one victory / Qualifications.
(cd-s+=) *(FRYCDX 064)* – Never had no one ever / Run out of reasons.

Jun 97. (cd) *(COOKCD 127)* **BLOKE ON BLOKE** [72] [–]
– The boy done good / Just one victory / Qualifications / Sugar daddy / Never had no one ever / Run out of seasons / Rule nor reason / Thatcherites.

BILLY BRAGG & WILCO

— **WILCO** were **JEFF TWEEDY** and Co

Elektra / Elektra

Jun 98. (cd/c) *(<7559 62204-2/-4>)* **MERMAID AVENUE** [34] [90]
– Walt Whitman's niece / California stars / Way over yonder in the minor key / Birds and ships / Hoodoo voodoo / She came along to me / At my window sad and lonely / Ingrid Bergman / Christ for President / I guess I planted / One by one / Eisler on the go / Hesitating beauty / Another man's done gone / The unwelcome guest.

Nov 98. (7"/c-s) *(E 3798/+C)* **WAY OVER YONDER IN THE MINOR KEY. / MY THIRTY THOUSAND** [ ] [–]
(cd-s+=) *(E 3798CD)* – Bug-eyed Jim.

May 00. (cd/c) *<(7559 62522-2/-4)>* **MERMAID AVENUE VOL.II** [61] [88]
– Airline to Heaven / My flying saucer / Feed of man / Hot rod hotel / I was born / Secret of the sea / Stetson Kennedy / Remember the mountain bed / Blood of the lamb / Against th' law / All you fascists / Joe Dimaggio done it again / Meanest man / Black wind blowing / Someday some morning sometime.

BILLY BRAGG AND THE BLOKES

with **IAN McLAGAN** – keyboards, accordion / **MARTYN BARKER** – drums, percussion / **SIMON EDWARDS** – bass / **BEN MANDELSON** – bouzouki, mandolin, guitars / **DAVE WOODHEAD** – trumpet / **LU** – guitars

Cooking Vinyl / Elektra

Feb 02. (cd-s) *(FRYCD 120)* **ST. MONDAY / ENGLAND, HALF ENGLISH** [ ] [–]

Mar 02. (lp/cd) *(COOK/+CD 222) <62743>* **ENGLAND, HALF ENGLISH** [51] [ ]
– St. Monday / Jane Allen / Distant shore / England, half English / Npwa / Some days I see the point / Baby Faroukh / Take down the Union Jack / Another kind of Judy / He'll go down / Dreadbelly / Tears of my tracks.

May 02. (cd-s) *(FRYCD 131)* **TAKE DOWN THE UNION JACK / MYSTERY SHOES / ENGLAND, HALF ENGLISH (7" remix)** [22] [–]
(cd-s) *(FRYCD 131X)* – ('A'-band version) / Yarra song / England, half English (12" remix).
(cd-s) *(FRYCD 131XX)* – ('A'side) / You pulled the carpet out / England, half English (ambient remix) / ('A'video).

– compilations, etc. –

May 87. (12"ep) *Strange Fruit; (SFPS 027)* **THE PEEL SESSIONS** [ ] [–]
– A new England / Strange things happen / This guitar says sorry / Love gets dangerous / A13 trunk road to the sea / Fear . . . *(cd-iss. 1988; SFPSCD 027)*

Jun 87. (d-lp/d-c/cd) *Go! Discs; (AGOLP/ZGOLP/AGOCD 8)* **BACK TO BASICS** (best 83-85 material) [37] [–]
(re-iss. Apr98 on 'Cooking Vinyl' d-lp/c/cd; COOK/+C/CD 060)

Feb 92. (cd/c/lp) *Strange Fruit; (SFR CD/MC/LP 117)* **THE PEEL SESSIONS ALBUM** [ ] [–]
(cd with extra tracks)

Nov 93. (d-lp/c/cd) *Cooking Vinyl; (COOK/+C/CD 061)* **VICTIM OF GEOGRAPHY** [ ] [–]
– Greetings to the new brunette / Train train / Marriage / Idealogy / Levi Stubbs' tears / Honey I'm a big boy now / There is a power in a union / Help save the youth of America / Wishing the days away / Passion / The warmest room / Home front / She's got a new spell / Must I paint you a picture / Tender comrade / The price I pay / Little time bomb / Rotting on demand / Valentine's day is over / Life with the lions / The only one / Short answer / Waiting for the great leap forward. *(re-iss. Apr98 cd/c; same)*

Aug 99. (cd/c/lp) *Cooking Vinyl; (COOK CD/MC/LP 186) / Rhino; <75962>* **REACHING TO THE CONVERTED (MINDING THE GAPS)** 41
– Shirley / Sulk / Accident waiting to happen / Boy done good / Heart like a wheel / Bad penny / Ontario Quebec and me / Walk away Renee / Rule nor reason / Days like these / Think again / Scholarship is the enemy of romance / Wishing the days away (ballad version) / Tatler / Jeane / She's leaving home.

Oct 03. (d-cd) *Cooking Vinyl; (COOKCD 266) / Rhino; <73993>* **MUST I PAINT YOU A PICTURE?: THE ESSENTIAL BILLY BRAGG** 49
– A new England / The man in the iron mask / The milkman of human kindness / To have and to have not / A lover sings / St. Swithin's Day / The Saturday boy / Between the wars / The world turned upside down / Levi Stubbs' tears / Walk away Renee / Greetings to the new brunette / There is power in a union / Help save the youth of America / The warmest room / Must I paint you a picture? / She's got a new spell / The price I pay / Valentine's Day is over / Waiting for the great leap forward / Sexuality / Cindy of a thousand lives / Moving the goalposts / Tank park salute / You woke up my neighbourhood / Accident waiting to happen (red stars version) / Sulk / Upfield / The fourteenth of February / Brickbat / The pace race is over / The boy done good / Ingrid Bergman (with WILCO) / WAy over yonder in the minor key (with WILCO) / My flying saucer (with WILCO) / All you fascists bound to lose (Blokes version) / NPWA / St. Monday / Some days I see the point / Take down the Union Jack (band version). *(ltd t-cd+=; COOKCD 266X)* – A13, trunk road to the sea / Fear is a man's best friend / Cold and bitter tears (live with TED HAWKINS) / Seven and seven is / When will I see you again / Rule nor reason (live) / Debris (live) / My bed (demo) / She smiled sweetly / Take down the Union Jack.

□ BRAIN DONOR (see under ⇒ COPE, Julian)

the BRAVERY

Formed: New York City, New York, USA … early 2003 by SAM ENDICOTT (the songwriter), JOHN CONWAY, MICHAEL ZAKARIN, ANTHONY BURULCICH and MIKE HINDERT. Wishing dearly for a Tardis-style trip back to the early 80s (ENDICOTT even gelling his comb-over in A FLOCK OF SEAGULLS-esque anticipation), in-CURE-able throwbacks the BRAVERY signed to 'Fiction' for debut EP/single, 'UNCONDITIONAL', released late in 2004. Following the footsteps of fellow New Yorkers the STROKES, INTERPOL, et al, the synth-warriors broke the UK Top 10 with second single, 'AN HONEST MISTAKE'. Their devotion to DEPECHE MODE, DURAN DURAN, early U2 and GARY NUMAN was probably more deliberate, as heard on their eponymous Top 5 (US Top 20) debut album early 2005. Their carefully manicured New Romantic image took a good smearing that summer with the revelations that both ENDICOTT and analogue keyboardist CONWAY had previously plied their trade (alongside CSI: Miami star, Jonathan Togo) in cod-reggae outfit, SKABBA THE HUTT.

Album rating: THE BRAVERY (*7)

SAM ENDICOTT (b. 1978, Washington, DC) – vocals, guitar (ex-SKABBA THE HUTT) / **MICHAEL ZAKARIN** – guitar / **JOHN CONWAY** – keyboards (ex-SKABBA THE HUTT) / **MIKE HINDERT** – bass / **ANTHONY BURULCICH** – drums

Fiction Island

Nov 04. (12"/cd-s) *(986886 2/1)* **UNCONDITIONAL. / NO BRAKES / OUT OF LINE** –

Feb 05. (7") *(9880264)* **AN HONEST MISTAKE. / HOT PURSUIT (duet)** 7 97
(cd-s) *(9880300)* – ('A') / Hey sunshiney day.
(dvd-s) *(9880301)* – ('A'-video) / Unconditional (video) / Unconditional (making of the video).
(10") *(9880023)* – ('A'-Superdiscount mix).

Mar 05. (cd/lp) *(988026 1/3) <41630-2/-1>* **THE BRAVERY** 5 18
– An honest mistake / No brakes / Fearless / Tyrant / Give in / Swollen summer / Public service announcement / Out of line / Unconditional / The ring song / Rites of spring. *(hidden+=)* – Hot pursuit.

May 05. (7") *(9882340)* **FEARLESS. / IT'S ALL I CAN DO** 43 –
(cd-s) *(9882338)* – ('A') / An cat dubh.
(dvd-s) *(9882504)* – ('A'-video) / No brakes (live video).

Jul 05. (ltd-7") *(LOGO 009)* **AN HONEST MISTAKE (live). / UNCONDITIONAL (live)** –
(above issued on 'Loog')

Aug 05. (7") *(9884838)* **UNCONDITIONAL. / AN HONEST MISTAKE (acoustic)** 49 –
(cd-s) *(9885196)* – ('A') / ('A'-Benny Benassi mix).
(dvd-s) *(988519-7)* – ('A') / Oh glory / An honest mistake (superdiscount mix) / ('A'-video).

the BREEDERS

Formed: Boston, Massachusetts, USA … 1989 by TANYA DONELLY (of THROWING MUSES) and KIM DEAL (of PIXIES) as a side project to their respective musical careers, an opportunity to exercise their frustrated songwriting talent. Recruiting JOSEPHINE WIGGS (of PERFECT DISASTER) on bass and SHANNON DOUGHTY (of the late, great SLINT) on drums, the BREEDERS cut their debut outing, 'POD', in a matter of weeks. Released in May 1990, the album rapidly achieved cult status, even enjoying a hearty endorsement from one KURT COBAIN. Inevitably, the record was compared with the PIXIES by critics although in reality there was little in common between the two bands. Where PIXIES were enigmatic and frenetic, the BREEDERS were deliberate, dark and intense. While the pace picked up with 'HELLBOUND', tracks like the opener, 'GLORIOUS' and 'IRIS' were more representative of the record as a whole and if their cover of LENNON's 'HAPPINESS IS A WARM GUN' didn't add much to the original, it sounded so BREEDERS-like within the context of the album that they could've conceivably penned it themselves. The group recorded a further EP, 'SAFARI' (1992), with the original line-up before DONELLY went off to work full-time with her own outfit, BELLY. Following The PIXIES' demise later that year, DEAL devoted all her energies to a BREEDERS follow-up album. Enlisting her sister KELLEY in place of the departed DONELLY, the band released the 'CANNONBALL' single in Autumn '93. With its undulating guitar riff and pneumatic rhythm section, the track became an alternative classic, tearing up indie dancefloors across the country. The subsequent album, 'LAST SPLASH', powered into the UK Top 5 upon its release the following month. While much of the set sounded less focused than the debut, it nevertheless contained another stellar guitar pop moment in 'DIVINE HAMMER', also released as a single. Although the album's sales topped the million mark, things went quiet on the BREEDERS front, save for a lone 10" EP in 1994. The following year, (KIM) DEAL did surface in the guise of The AMPS, releasing an album, 'PACER', on '4 a.d.'. A near decade long wait for a follow-up album was primed to erase expectations completely rather than build them up. For fans who hadn't grown out of barbed femme-punk in the meantime, 'TITLE TK' (2002) provided rich if not exactly cutting edge pickings. There was no 'CANNONBALL' this time around although there were moments of sparky, irreverent genius and hallucinatory hints of the sinister sensuality of old. If KIM DEAL sounded longer in both the tooth and throat, her lyrics were as impenetrably enthralling as ever, while sister KELLEY's slightly smoother vocals served as a intriguing foil.

• **Songwriters:** KIM DEAL wrote bulk from 1992 onwards. • **Covered:** HAPPINESS IS A WARM GUN (Beatles / George Harrison) / LORD OF THE THIGHS (Aerosmith) / SO SAD ABOUT US (Who). The AMPS covered JUST LIKE A BRIAR (Tasties).

Album rating: POD (*7) / LAST SPLASH (*9) / TITLE TK (*7) / Amps: PACER (*6)

TANYA DONELLY (b.14 Jul'66, Newport, Rhode Island) – rhythm guitar, vocals (of THROWING MUSES) / **KIM DEAL** (b.10 Jun'61, Dayton, Ohio, USA) – guitar, vocals (of The PIXIES) / **JOSEPHINE WIGGS** (b.26 Feb'65, Letchworth, England) – bass, cello, vocals (of PERFECT DISASTER) / **SHANNON DOUGHTY** (aka MIKE HUNT) (b. BRITT WALFORD, Louisville, Kentucky) – drums (of SLINT) repl. NARCIZO and another from HUMAN SEXUAL RESPONSE

		4 a.d.	Elektra
May 90.	(cd)(lp/c) *(CAD 0006CD)(CAD/+C 0006) <61331>* **POD**	22	
	– Glorious / Doe / Happiness is a warm gun / Oh! / Hellbound / When I was a painter / Fortunately gone / Iris / Opened / Only in 3's / Limehouse / Metal man.		

— **DONELLY, KIM DEAL, JO WIGGS + JON MATLOCK** (of SPIRITUALIZED)

Apr 92.	(12"ep/cd-ep) *(BAD 2003/+CD)* **SAFARI**	69	
	– Safari / So sad about us / Do you love me now? / Don't call home.		

— now **KIM** her sister **KELLEY DEAL** (b.10 Jun'61, Dayton) – guitar, vocals / **JO WIGGS** – bass, vox / **JIM MacPHERSON** (b.23 Jun'66, Dayton) – drums, vocals (ex-RAGING MANTRAS) / (DONELLY formed BELLY)

Aug 93.	(12"ep/cd-ep) *(BAD 3011/+CD) <64566>* **CANNONBALL. / CRO-ALOHA / LORD OF THE THIGHS / 900**	40	Nov93 44
Sep 93.	(cd)(lp/c) *(CAD 3014CD)(CAD/+C 3014) <61508>* **LAST SPLASH**	5	33
	– New Year / Cannonball / Invisible man / No aloha / Roi / Do you love me now? / Flipside / I just wanna get along / Mad Lucas / Divine hammer / S.O.S./ Hag / Saints / Drivin' on 9 / Roi (reprise).		
Oct 93.	(7"clear/c-s) *(AD/+C 3017) <66260>* **DIVINE HAMMER. / HOVERIN'**	59	
	(10"ep+=)(cd-ep+=) *(BADD 3017)(BAD 3017CD)* – I can't help it (if I'm still in love with you) / Do you love me now Jr (J. Mascis remix).		
Jul 94.	(10"ep) *(BADD 4012)* **HEAD TO TOE. / SHOCKER IN GLOOMTOWN / FREED PIG**	68	–
	(cd-ep+=) *(BAD 4014CD)* – Saints.		

the AMPS

KIM DEAL / JIM MacPHERSON / NATHAN FARLEY + LUIS LERMA

		4 a.d.	4 a.d.
Oct 95.	(12"ep/cd-ep) *(BAD 5015/+CD)* **TIPP CITY / JUST LIKE A BRIAR. / EMPTY GLASSES (Kim's basement 4 track version)**	61	–
Oct 95.	(cd)(lp/c) *(CAD 5016CD)(CAD/+C 5016) <61623>* **PACER**	60	
	– Pacer / Tipp city / I am decided / Mom's drunk / Bragging party / Hoverin' / First revival / Full on idle / Breaking the split screen barrier / Empty glasses / She's a girl / Dedicated. *(cd re-iss. Jul98; GAD 5016CD)*		

the BREEDERS

— new 1997 line-up, included **KIM DEAL + JIM MacPHERSON** plus **MICHAEL O'DEAN** – guitar / **NATE FARLEY** – guitar / **LOUIS NERMA** – bass / **CARRIE BRADLEY** – violin

— **TYLER TRENT** – drums; repl. MacPHERSON who later joined GUIDED BY VOICES

— 2001/2 line-up **KIM + KELLEY** with **RICHARD PRESLEY** – guitar (ex-FEAR) / **MANDO LOPEZ** – bass / **JOSE MEDELES** – drums

		4 a.d.	Elektra
Mar 02.	(10"ep) *(TAD 2203)* **OFF YOU. / LITTLE FURY / THE SHE**		–
	(cd-s iss.May02; TAD 2203CDP)		
May 02.	(lp/cd) *(CAD 2205/+CD) <62766>* **TITLE TK**	51	
	– Little fury / London song / Off you / The she / Too alive / Son of three / Put on a side / Full on idle / Sinister Foxx / Forced to drive / T and T / Huffer.		
Sep 02.	(7") *(AD 2213)* **SON OF THREE. / BUFFY THEME**	72	–
	(cd-s+=) *(BAD 2213CD)* – Safari (live).		

BRIGHT EYES

Formed: Omaha, Nebraska, USA . . . by 15 year-old singer/guitarist CONNOR OBERST and a rotating cast of musicians. Incredibly OBERST already had two albums under his belt as frontman with slacker band COMMANDER VENUS. Formed in 1994 and comprising OBERST, BEN ARMSTRONG, ROBB NANSEL and TOM BAECHLE, COMMANDER VENUS released their debut 'DO YOU FEEL AT HOME?' on their own 'Saddle Creek' label in 1995. The next two years saw the departure of ARMSTRONG and BAECHLE, who were replaced by TIM KASHER and MATT BOWEN, before the release of their second and final album 'THE UNEVENTFUL VACATION'. OBERST had clearly been thinking about a long term career in the music industry and not only had he invested in the 'Saddle Creek' record label he had been holding back a number of songs for future release. These songs, which were recorded between 1995-1997, became the first BRIGHT EYES album. Informatively called 'A COLLECTION OF SONGS: RECORDED 1995-1997', it was released in 1998 and further cemented OBERST's reputation as a prodigious talent worth watching out for. Another equally impressive album 'LETTING OFF HAPPINESS' was released the same year. OBERST's work rate was as astonishing as his songwriting ability. He released the album, which really saw him coming of age, 'FEVERS AND MIRRORS' in 2000, before contributing to a split album, 'OH HOLY FOOL: THE MUSIC OF SON, AMBULANCE & BRIGHT EYES' and then a further solo album, 'LIFTED OR THE STORY IS IN THE SOIL, KEEP YOUR EAR TO THE GROUND' (2002). With his side-project, DESAPARECIDOS, OBERST – alongside LANDON HEDGES, DENVER DALLEY, IAN McELROY and MATT BAUM – released their take-on acoustic-based indie rock in the shape of emo-spiked set, 'RED MUSIC / SPEAK SPANISH' (2002). After a year's hiatus, OBERST resurrected BRIGHT EYES for two split EP's, the first was 'HOME VOL.4' with BRITT DANIEL (of SPOON), the second 'ONE JUG OF WINE, TWO VESSELS' (2004) with JAKE BELLOWS' sad-pop outfit NEVA DINOVA. An unlikely link-up with country waif EMMYLOU HARRIS showed some genre-crossing bravado even if OBERST is no GRAM PARSONS. HARRIS appeared on the first of two simultaneously released sets early the following year, 'I'M WIDE AWAKE, IT'S MORNING' (2005), supplying her unmistakeable harmonies on three numbers. The collaborative fires burned bright and OBERST swept out the electro-industrial ashes on partner set 'DIGITAL ASH IN A DIGITAL URN', featuring sonic support from YEAH YEAH YEAH's guitarist NICK ZINNER. A brave move for what was at the end of the day a cult artist with clout, this incongruous double-header earned BRIGHT EYES (and hip Lo-Fi stable, 'Saddle Creek') a twin US Top 20 placing.

• **Covers:** I WOKE UP WITH THIS SONG IN MY HEAD THIS MORNING (Bruces) / BURN RUBBER (Simon Joyner).

Album rating: Commander Venus: THE UNEVENTFUL VACATION (*5) / Bright Eyes: A COLLECTION OF SONGS (*5) / LETTING OFF THE HAPPINESS (*7) / FEVERS AND MIRRORS (*7) / LIFTED OR THE STORY IS IN THE SOIL, KEEP YOUR EAR TO THE GROUND (*7) / I'M WIDE AWAKE, IT'S MORNING (*8) / DIGITAL ASH IN A DIGITAL URN (*8) / MOTION SICKNESS (*6) / Desaparecidos: READ MUSIC – SPEAK SPANISH (*7)

COMMANDER VENUS

CONOR OBERST (b.15 Feb'80) – vocals, guitar / **ROBB NANSEL** – guitar / **TODD BAECHLE** – bass / **BEN ARMSTRONG** – drums

		not iss.	Saddle Creek
1995.	(cd) **DO YOU FEEL AT HOME?**	–	
	– Peppermints / Showcase showdown / My other car is a spaceship / Judy Blume / Radio announcer / It is fun to grow ornamental peppers / Calling		

Sooyoung / When two vowels go walking; the first one does the talking / Sunny slope / Pennsylvania made you sick / Do you feel at home?

— **CONOR + ROBB** added **MATT BOWEN + TIM KASHER**

not iss. Thick

Jul 97. (cd) *<THK 49>* **THE UNEVENTFUL VACATION** [–] [ ]
– Jean's T.V. / Refused by light / We'll always have Paris / Uneventful vacation (pt.1) / Lock n' chase / Life as expected / The way things had to be / Dress to please / The walk-around problem / My collapsing frame / Raining holiday (part 2) / The role of the hero in antiquity.

BRIGHT EYES

CONOR OBEREST – vocals, guitar, keyboards / with **ANDY LeMASTER** – bass, guitar / **MIKE MOGIS** – multi / **KEVIN BARNES** – keyboards / **TED STEVENS + JEREMY BARNES** – drums, percussion

Saddle Creek Saddle Creek

Jan 98. (cd) *<LBJ 19>* **A COLLECTION OF SONGS WRITTEN AND RECORDED 1995-1997** [–] [ ]
– The invisible gardener / Patient hope in new show / Saturday as usual / Falling out of love at this volume / Exaltation on a cool, kitchen floor / The awful sweetness of escaping sweet / Puella quam amo est pulchra / Driving fast through a big city at night / How many lights do you see? / I watched you taking off / A celebration upon completion / Emily, sing something sweet / All of the truth / One straw (please) / Lila / A few minutes on Friday / Supriya / Solid Jackson / Feb. 15th / The 'feel good' revolution. *<re-iss. Jun00; same>*

Mar 99. (cd) *<(LBJ 23)>* **LETTING OFF THE HAPPINESS** [ ] Nov98 [ ]
– If winter ends / Padraic my prince / Contrast and compare / The city has sex / The difference in the shades / Touch / June on the West Coast / Pull my hair / A poetic retelling of an unfortunate seduction / Tereza and Thomas. *<(re-iss. Apr01 on 'Wichita'; WEBB 011)>*

— **JOE KNAPP** – percussion (of SON, AMBULANCE) repl. TED + JEREMY

Wichita Saddle Creek

Jun 00. (cd-ep) *<LBJ 30>* **EVERY DAY AND EVERY NIGHT** [–] [ ]
– A line allows progress, a circle does not / A perfect sonnet / On my way to work / A new arrangement / Neely O'Hara. *(UK-iss.Nov02; same as US)*

Jul 00. (cd) *(WEBB 001) <LBJ 32>* **FEVERS AND MIRRORS** [ ] Jan00 [ ]
– A spindle, a darkness, a fever, and a necklace / A scale, a mirror, and these indifferent clocks / The calendar hung itself / Something vague / The movement of a hand / Arienette / When the curious girl realizes she is under glass / Haligh, haligh, a lie, Haligh / The center of the world / Sunrise, sunset / An attempt to tip the scales / A song to pass the time.

Sep 00. (7") *(WEBB 005S)* **THE CALENDAR HUNG ITSELF. / (other by HER SPACE HOLIDAY)** [ ] [–]
(cd-s+=) *(WEBB 005SCD)* – (2 by HER SPACE HOLIDAY).

Jan 01. (cd/lp; split w/ SON, AMBULANCE) *<LBJ 34>* **OH HOLY FOOLS** [–] [ ]
– (S,A track) / Going for the gold / (S,A track) / Oh, you are the roots that sleep beneath my feet . . . (. . .and hold the earth in place) / (S,A track) / No lies, just love / (S, A track) / Kathy's with a K's song. *(UK-iss.Nov02; same as US)*

Mar 01. (7") *<SP 528>* **I WILL BE GRATEFUL FOR THIS DAY. / WHEN THE CURIOUS GIRL REALIZES SHE IS UNDER GLASS AGAIN** [–] [ ]
(above issued on 'Sub Pop')

May 01. (7") *(WEBB 012S)* **DRUNK KID CATHOLIC. / FEBRUARY 15th** [ ] [–]
(cd-s+=) *(WEBB 012SCD)* – I have been eating for you.

— **MIKE SWEENEY** – drums; repl. KNAPP

Jul 02. (cd-ep) *(WEBB 031SCD)* **THERE IS NO BEGINNING TO THE STORY EP** [ ] [–]
– From a balance beam / The messenger bird's song / We are free men / Loose leaves.

Aug 02. (cd) *(WEBB 034) <LBJ 46>* **LIFTED OR THE STORY IS IN THE SOIL, KEEP YOUR EAR TO THE GROUND** [ ] [ ]
– Big picture / Method acting / False advertising / You will, you will, you will, you will / Lover I don't have to love / Bowl of oranges / Don't know when but a day is gonna come / Nothing gets crossed out / Make war / Waste of paint / From a balance beam / Laura Laurent / Let's not shit ourselves (to love and to be loved).

Nov 02. (7") *(WEBB 037S)* **LOVER I DON'T HAVE TO LOVE. / AMY IN THE WHITE COAT** [ ] [–]
(cd-s+=) *(WEBB 037SCD)* – Out on the weekend.

Mar 04. (cd-ep; w/ BRITT DANIEL) *<(PPE 020CD)>* **HOME VOL.4** [ ] [ ]
– Spent on rainy days / You get yours / Southern state / Let the distance bring us together.
(above issued on 'Post Parlo')

— <below issued on 'Crank!: A Record Company' US-only>

Apr 04. (m-cd; BRIGHT EYES & NEVA DINOVA) *(SCE 60-2) <40>* **ONE JUG OF WINE, TWO VESSELS** [ ] [ ]
– Tripped / Black comedy / Poison / I'll be your friend / Get back / Spring cleaning.

— **JASON BOESEL** – drums; repl. SWEENEY

Nov 04. (7") *<(SCE 68)>* **LUA. / I WOKE UP WITH THIS SONG IN MY HEAD THIS MORNING** [ ] Oct04 [ ]
(cd-s+=) *<(SCE 68CD)>* – Well whiskey / True blue.

Nov 04. (7") *<(SCE 69)>* **TAKE IT EASY (LOVE NOTHING). / CREMATION** [ ] Oct04 [ ]
(cd-s+=) *<(SCE 69CD)>* – Burn rubber.
below featured **EMMYLOU HARRIS** – vocals

Jan 05. (lp/cd) *<(SCE 72 V/CD)>* **I'M WIDE AWAKE, IT'S MORNING** [23] [10]
– At the bottom of everything / We are nowhere and it's now / OLd soul song (for the new world order) / Lua / Train under water / First day of my life / Another travelin' song / Land locked blues / Poison oak / Road to joy.
below featured **NICK ZINNER** – guitar (of YEAH YEAH YEAHS)

Jan 05. (lp/cd) *<(SCE 73/+CD)>* **DIGITAL ASH IN A DIGITAL URN** [43] [15]
– Time code / Gold mine gutted / Arc of time (Time code) / Down in a rabbit hole / Take it easy (love nothing) / Hit the switch / I believe in symmetry / Devil in the details / Ship in a bottle / Light pollution / Theme to Pinata / Easy – lucky – free.

Apr 05. (7") *(SCE 79V)* **FIRST DAY OF MY LIFE. / WHEN THE PRESIDENT TALKS TO GOD** [37] [–]
(cd-s+=) *(SCE 79CD)* – True blue.

Jul 05. (7") *(SCE 84V)* **GOLD MINE GUTTED. / EASY – LUCKY – FREE** [42] [–]
(cd-s+=) *(SCE 84CD)* – Easy – lucky – free (Danger Mouse remix).
(7") *(SCE 84V2)* – ('A'-Jimmy Tamborella remix) / Easy – lucky – free (Chip remix).

— **NICK WALCOTT** – trumpet; repl. BOESEL

Nov 05. (cd) *(SCE 88CD)* **MOTION SICKNESS** (live recordings) [ ] [–]
– At the bottom of everything / We are nowhere and it's now / Old soul song / Make war (short version) / Make war (long version) / Scale / Landlocked blues / Method acting / Train underwater / When the President talks to God / Road to joy / Mushaboom / True blue / Southern state / Biggest lie.

– compilations, etc. –

Nov 03. (7xlp-box) *Saddle Creek; <(LBJ 33)>* **VINYL BOX SET** [ ] [ ]
– (includes 7 extra tracks).

DESAPARECIDOS

CONOR OBERST – vocals, guitar / with **DENVER DALLEY** – vocals, guitar / **LANDON HEDGES** – bass / **MATT BAUM** – drums / **IAN McELROY** – keyboards

Wichita Saddle Creek

Feb 02. (7") *(WEBB 027S) <LBJ 40>* **WHAT'S NEW FOR FALL. / THE HAPPIEST PLACE ON EARTH** [ ] Dec01 [ ]
(cd-s+=) *(WEBB 027SCD)* – Give me the pen.

Apr 02. (cd) *(WEBB 028) <LBJ 42>* **READ MUSIC – SPEAK SPANISH** [ ] Feb02 [ ]
– What's new for fall / Man and wife, the former (financial planning) / Manana / Greater Omaha / Man and wife, the latter (damaged goods) / Mall of America / The happiest place on earth / Survival of the fittest – It's a jungle out there / $$$$ / Hole in one.

BRITISH SEA POWER

Formed: Brighton, England . . . late 2000 by Kendal lads YAN (aka SCOTT WILKINSON), his brother HAMILTON (NEIL WILKINSON), NOBLE and WOOD; keyboards provided by EAMON on tour only until '05. This eccentric quartet created ripples of interest with their JOY DIVISION-inspired indie-rock gigs and unusual stage aesthetics (large stuffed birds and matching military uniforms!). Releasing first single, 'FEAR OF DROWNING' on their own 'Golden Chariot' label in spring 2001, BSP also continued to run their own monthly club night, Club Sea Power, at Brighton venues The Lift and The Freebutt. After witnessing BRITISH SEA POWER in their natural environment, an impressed Geoff Travis of 'Rough Trade' promptly signed them up. Subsequently releasing two singles, 'REMEMBER ME' and 'THE SPIRIT OF ST. LOUIS', the lads continue to pay rock homage to British marine wildlife. BSP finally issued their long awaited debut album 'THE DECLINE OF . . .' in 2003, a brash, brooding exploration into what could only be described as a psychedelic mish-mash of pop and rock, set to melodic guitar hooks and well-read quasi romantic lyrics. A tough but rewarding listen, the group not only proved that, like their more accessible musical cousins the POSTAL SERVICE, they could successfully bring epic songscapes and tender melodics to the forum of indie rock. This album was crammed with great tracks, from the tense opener 'MEN TOGETHER TODAY', recalling NEW ORDER at their best, to the 13-minute acid-jam rock of 'LATELY' which sounded like YO LA TENGO on bad drugs. Elsewhere, spiky punk rock in the form of 'REMEMBER ME' and the thunderous 'FEAR OF DROWNING', which would make the late IAN CURTIS proud of his legacy. As for lyrics, it's not every day you hear a British indie band quote famous Russian poets and Czech philosophers, well, not unless you're the MANICS, which, fortunately BSP are not. The cheeky title is another quirk added to this strange and sometimes bewildering set, but unlike it suggests, BRITISH SEA POWER were not in decline at all, and that is what made it all the more of a celebrated experience. 2004 saw another quirky ploy with the release of one-off single, 'A LOVELY DAY TOMORROW' (a re-record of an early B-side), released that is, in the Czech Republic; British fans had to acquire it by post. Both an English and a Czech language version were sung by KATERINA WINTEROVA (of the ECSTASY OF ST. THERESA), while B-side 'FAKIR' was a traditional folk song from the land of Budvar and Staropramen. BSP were on the crest of a gentle wave with 'OPEN SEASON' (2005), their most accessible and successful release to date. YAN's whispering, BOWIE-esque whimsy made the UK Top 20, powered by hit singles, 'IT ENDED ON AN OILY STAGE' and 'PLEASE STAND UP'. Their studiedly eccentric Englishness reached a peak (a nadir?) via a song-swapping 7" cut in tandem with legendary yokels the WURZELS: while BSP tackled mid-70s novelty nugget 'I AM A CIDER DRINKER', the ageing combine-pilots got stuck in to 'REMEMBER ME'.

Album rating: THE DECLINE OF BRITISH SEA POWER (*8) / OPEN SEASON (*7)

YAN (b. SCOTT WILKINSON) – vocals, guitar, keyboards / **NOBLE** (b. MARTIN NOBLE, Bury, Gtr. Manchester, England) – guitar / **HAMILTON** (b. NEIL WILKINSON) – bass, vocals / **WOOD** (b. MATTHEW WOOD) – drums

Golden Chariot — not iss.

Aug 01. (7") *(none)* **FEAR OF DROWNING. / A WOODEN HORSE** [ ] [–]

Rough Trade — Sanctuary

Dec 01. (7") *(RTRADES 032)* **REMEMBER ME. / A LOVELY DAY TOMORROW** [ ] [–]
(cd-s+=) *(RTRADESCD 032)* – Birdy.

Apr 02. (7") *(RTRADES 048)* **THE SPIRIT OF ST. LOUIS. / THE LONELY** [ ] [–]
(cd-s+=) *(RTRADESCD 048)* – No Red Indian.

Nov 02. (7") *(RTRADES 069)* **CHILDHOOD MEMORIES. / FAVOURS IN THE BEETROOT FIELDS** [ ] [–]
(cd-s+=) *(RTRADESCD 069)* – Strange communication.

Jun 03. (cd/lp) *(RTRADE CD/LP 090)* *<83214>* **THE DECLINE OF BRITISH SEA POWER** [54] Sep03 [ ]
– Men together today / Apologies to insect life / Favours in the beetroot fields / Something wicked / Remember me / Fear of drowning / The lonely / Carrion / Blackout / Lately / A wooden horse. *<US cd+=>* – Childhood memories / Heavenly waters.

Jun 03. (7") *(RTRADES 092)* **CARRION. / APOLOGIES TO INSECT LIFE** [36] [–]
(cd-s+=) *(RTRADESCD 092)* – Heavenly waters.
(cd-s) *(RTRADESCD 092X)* – ('A'-Ridgeway mix) / ('B'-Russian rock demo) / Albert's eyes.

Oct 03. (7") *(RTRADES 125)* **REMEMBER ME. / THE SCOTTISH WILDLIFE EXPERIENCE** [30] [–]
(cd-s) *(RTRADESCD 125)* – ('A') / Salty water / Good good boys.
(cd-s) *(RTRADESCD 126)* – ('A') / Moley & me / The smallest church in Sussex.

Apr 04. (cd-s) *(RTRADSCD 179)* **A LOVELY DAY TOMORROW / ZITRA BUDE KRASNY DEN / FAKIR** [ ] [–]
(above with the ECSTASY OF SAINT THERA)

Rough Trade — Rough Trade

Mar 05. (7") *(RTRADS 220)* **IT ENDED ON AN OILY STAGE. / DON'T YOU WANT TO BE A BIRD?** [18] [–]
(cd-s) *(RTRADSCD 220)* – ('A') / Green grass of tunnel.
(cd-s) *(RTRADSCDX 220)* – ('A') / When I go out / Crystal horse / ('A'-video).

Apr 05. (cd/lp) *(RTRAD CD/LP 300)* *<3356>* **OPEN SEASON** [13] [ ]
– It ended on an oily stage / Be gone / How will I ever find my way home? / Like a honeycomb / Please stand up / North hanging rock / To get to sleep / Victorian ice / Oh Larsen B / The land beyond / True adventures.

Jun 05. (7") *(RTRADS 242)* **PLEASE STAND UP. / GALE WARNINGS IN VIKING NORTH** [34] [–]
(cd-s) *(RTRADSCD 242)* – ('A') / Over in the corner.
(cd-s) *(RTRADSCDX 242)* – ('A') / Grey goose / Chicken pig – True adventures instrumental demo / ('A'-video).

Nov 05. (7") *(RTRADS 302)* **REMEMBER ME (by the WURZELS). / I AM A CIDER DRINKER** [ ] [–]

Ian BROWN

Born: 20 Feb'63, Ancoats, Manchester, England. Having hit the heights with the iconic STONE ROSES for nearly a decade, IAN was ready to hit out on his own. In early '98, the man launched his solo career (via a new deal with 'Polydor') by releasing the single, 'MY STAR', a taster from his debut album, 'UNFINISHED MONKEY BUSINESS', which also reached the Top 5. However, BROWN subsequently landed himself in deep water when he was charged with threatening behaviour on a flight between Paris and Manchester. Astonishingly sentenced to four months in prison at the end of October, the singer was released a couple of months early that Christmas eve. Back in circulation the following year, BROWN guested for 'Mo Wax' duo U.N.K.L.E. on the track, 'BE THERE'. Album No.2, 'GOLDEN GREATS', was completed and in the Top 20 towards the end of 1999. Previewed by the hit single, 'LOVE LIKE A FOUNTAIN', the set showed IAN (and co-writer DAVE McCRACKEN) venturing away from the staid and into every funkin' Rock genre under the sun. BROWN surfaced almost two years later with the brilliant orchestral driven single 'F.E.A.R.', in which he turned the letters of the word into a poetic acronym which resulted in a Top 20 hit. His third album proper, 'MUSIC OF THE SPHERES' was issued in October 2001 to almost unanimous critical acclaim and reinforced his self-confidence as an artist when it climbed into the Top 3. 'SOLARIZED' (2004) continued his international, interstellar DIY, with diversions into mariachi (his wife is Mexican after all), delivered as ever in his cocky simian slur. BROWN and Mancunian mate, NOEL GALLAGHER, put their eyebrows together for one of the album's highlights, the Top 20 track, 'KEEP WHAT YA GOT'. Both this and 'TIME IS MY EVERYTHING' were elevated to BROWN's personal hall of fame on the self-referentially titled 'THE GREATEST' (2005) – well he was bestowed with the title/award "Godlike Genius" by the NME in 2006.

• **Covered:** BILLIE JEAN + THRILLER (Michael Jackson) / COKANE IN MY BRAIN (Dillinger).

Album rating: UNFINISHED MONKEY BUSINESS (*6) / GOLDEN GREATS (*7) / MUSIC OF THE SPHERES (*7) / REMIXES OF THE SPHERES (*4) / SOLARIZED (*6) / THE GREATEST compilation (*7)

IAN BROWN on mostly all vocals/instruments except co-writers **AZIZ IBRAHIM** – guitars, etc / **SIMON MOORE** – drums / **NIGEL IPPINSON** – keyboards, bass / guests **MANI MOUNFIELD + NOEL GALLAGHER + DENISE JOHNSON** + co-writer/mixer **ROBBIE MADDIX**

Polydor Polydor

Jan 98. (7") *(571 987-7)* **MY STAR. / SEE THE DAWN** 5 –
(cd-s+=) *(571 987-2)* – Fourteen.

Feb 98. (cd/c/lp) *(539 565-2/-4/-1)* **UNFINISHED MONKEY BUSINESS** 4 –
– Intro under the paving stones: The beach / My star / Can't see me / Ice cold cube / Sunshine / Lions / Corpses in their mouths / What happened to ya part 1 / What happened to ya part 2 / Nah nah / Deep pile dreams / Unfinished monkey business.

Mar 98. (7") *(569 654-7)* **CORPSES. / JESUS ON THE MOVE / COME AGAIN (part one)** 14 –
(cd-s) *(569 657-2)* – (first 2 tracks) / Lions (with Denise).

Jun 98. (7") *(567 092-7)* **CAN'T SEE ME (Bacon & Quarmby remix). / CAN'T SEE ME (Bacon & Quarmby vocal dub)** 21 –
(cd-s+=) *(044 045-2)* – Under the paving stones: The beach (Gabriel's 13th dream remix) / ('A'video).
(cd-s) *(044 047-2)* – ('A'side) / ('A'-Harvey's invisible mix) / Come again part 2 / My star (CD-ROM video).
(12"++=) *(044 047-6)* – ('A'-Harvey's instrumental).

Oct 99. (7") *(561 516-7)* **LOVE LIKE A FOUNTAIN. / THE FISHERMAN** 23 –
(cd-s+=) *(561 516-2)* – ('A'-CD-Rom mix).
(cd-s) *(561 517-2)* – ('A'side) / ('A'-Stereo MC's mix) / ('A'-Aim mix).

Nov 99. (cd/c/lp) *(543 141-2/-4/-1)* <543720> **GOLDEN GREATS** 14 Feb00
– Gettin' high / Love like a fountain / Free my way / Set my baby free / So many sisters / Golden gaze / Dolphins were monkeys / Neptune / First world / Babasonicos.

Feb 00. (7") *(561 637-7)* **DOLPHINS WERE MONKEYS. / CORPSES (live radio session)** 5 –
(cd-s) *(561 637-2)* – ('A'side) / Billie Jean / ('A'-Goldfinger mix) / ('A'-CD-Rom).
(cd-s) *(561 638-2)* – ('A'side) / ('A'-Unkle vs. South mix) / Love like a fountain (Andy Votel's remix).

Jun 00. (7") *(561 844-7)* **GOLDEN GAZE. / SUNSHINE (live radio session)** 29 –
(cd-s) *(561 844-2)* – ('A'side) / ('A'-Andy Gray remix) / Love like a fountain (Laj & Quakerman remix) / ('A'-CD-Rom).
(cd-s) *(561 845-2)* – ('A'side) / Thriller / ('A'-Sharktank's dirt it up remix).

Sep 01. (7") *(587 284-7)* **F.E.A.R. / (instrumental)** 13 –
(c-s) *(587 284-4)* – ('A'side) / ('A'-side with DANN).
(cd-s+=) *(587 284-2)* – Hear no see no speak no (extended) / ('A'video).

Oct 01. (cd/c) *(<589 126-2/-4>)* **MUSIC OF THE SPHERES** 3
– F.E.A.R. / Stardust / The gravy train / Bubbles / Hear no see no / Northern lights / Whispers / El mundo pequeno / Forever and a day / Shadow of a saint.

Feb 02. (7") *(570538-7)* **WHISPERS. / EL MUNDO PEQUENO** 33 –
(cd-s) *(570538-2)* – ('A') / ('A'video) / Superstar / My star (remix).

Nov 02. (cd/d-lp) *(<065927-2/-1>)* **REMIXES OF THE SPHERES** (remixes)
– F.E.A.R. (U.N.K.L.E. mix) / Northern lights (Freelance Hellraiser mix) / The gravy train (Nightmares On Wax mix) / Forever and a day (Cedar Blue mix) / Shadow of a saint (Boy Bierton mix) / Superstar / My star (2002 version) / Hear no see no speak no / Cokane in my brain (DJ Mek Nuremberg scratch mix) / The gravy train (instrumental) / El mundo pequeno (live acoustic version) / F.E.A.R. (U.N.K.L.E. instrumental).

Fiction Fiction

Sep 04. (cd)(lp) *(9867772)(9867843)* <9868063> **SOLARIZED** 7 Nov04
– Longsight M13 / Time is my everything / Destiny or circumstance / Upside down / Solarized / The sweet fantastic / Keep what ya got / Home is where the heart is / One way ticket to Paradise / Kiss ya lips (no I.D.).

Sep 04. (7") *(9867774)* **KEEP WHAT YA GOT. / LOVEBUG** 18 –
(cd-s+=) *(9868284)* – Solarized (instrumental) / ('A'-video).

Jan 05. (7") *(9870065)* **TIME IS MY EVERYTHING. / WHERE ANGELS PLAY** 15 –
(cd-s+=) *(9869961)* – ('A'-Stateside Hombres Over Easy mix) / ('A'-CD-Rom video).
(cd-s) *(9869960)* – ('A') / ('A'-U.N.K.L.E. reconstruction).

Sep 05. (7"clear) *(9873253)* **ALL ABLAZE. / DESTINY OR CIRCUMSTANCE (live at Brixton Academy)** 20 –
(cd-s+=) *(9873252)* – The sweet fantastic (live at Brixton Academy) / ('A'-CD-Rom video).

Sep 05. (cd) *(9872874)* **THE GREATEST** (compilation) 5 –
– My star / Corpses in their mouths / Can't see me / Be there / Love like a fountain / Dolphins were monkeys / Golden gaze / F.E.A.R. / Forever and a day / Keep what ya got / Time is my everything / Longsight M13 / Reign / Lovebug / All ablaze.

James BROWN

Born: 3 May'33 in Barnwell, South Carolina. At the age of five, BROWN moved to his Aunt's brothel in Augusta, Georgia, during which time he learned to play piano, drums and guitar. By the time he was nineteen, after a brief spell as a semi-pro boxer and a brief spell in jail, he had settled in Georgia and was a member of BOBBY BYRD's quartet, the GOSPEL STARLIGHTERS. A raw Southern gospel group, they subsequently evolved into a R&B outfit, in the process changing their name to the AVONS, then the FLAMES. The band performed R&B covers, among them an ORIOLES song, 'BABY PLEASE DON'T GO'. After some fine tuning, BROWN brought the "please" to the forefront, crafting the showstopping 'PLEASE, PLEASE, PLEASE'. On hearing the tune, LITTLE RICHARD, at the time Georgia's most celebrated black musician, told Brown to move to Macon, Georgia, where the song was cut at a local radio station under the band name the FAMOUS FLAMES, the prefix added coutesy of Richard's manager, Clint Brantly. Although the song was refused by a number of labels, when Ralph Bass of 'King' Records heard the tune, he immediately signed the group and the track was re-recorded at King's Ohio studio. The session proved to be more troublesome than expected, as the musical director and owner of the label couldn't come to grips with BROWN's unusual and now heavily influential writing style of hitting on the downbeat instead of the upbeat. Nevertheless, the track was eventually released on King's 'Federal' label in March '56, making No.5 on the Billboard R&B chart. It would be another three years before their next hit, the infectious 'TRY ME' reaching No.1 on the R&B chart and crucially creating enough money for BROWN to hire a backing band, the first quintet led by the tenor sax of J.C. DAVIS. It was during the end of the 50's, with the components all in place, that the band set about touring to sharpen their sound and BROWN's routines of knee-drops, flying splits and cochlea-piercing screams. Whilst BROWN continued to supply hits for 'King', he still hadn't hit the big time, subsequently trying to persuade the label to front the money for a live recorded performance. With 'King' not convinced that such a record would sell, BROWN decided to put up his own cash, coming up with one of the most successful live LP's of all time, the '63 killer 'LIVE AT THE APOLLO'. The record not only made it to No.2 on the Billboard album charts, it also had the knock-on effect of mammoth audience attendances, and in turn increased sales figures and the high profile that BROWN craved. This mushroomed to an even greater height when, in '65, he released the definitive funk single, 'PAPA'S GOT A BRAND NEW BAG', featuring a larger band led by the trumpet of LEWIS HAMLIN, in the process modifying his style from the gospel and blues structure to a more straight ahead approach. His singing was also reaching new heights of primordial intensity, fusing with a tight and oh-so-funky backing band. The middle to late 60's proved a purple patch for BROWN, with one classic single following another; 'IT'S A MAN'S WORLD' in '66, 'COLD SWEAT' in '67, 'SAY IT LOUD – I'M BLACK AND PROUD' in '68 and 'GET UP / I FEEL LIKE BEING A SEX MACHINE' in

70, his backing band including the likes of the PARKER brothers (MACEO and MELVIN) and older stalwarts like JIMMY NOLAN and ALPHONSO KELLUM on guitars. The early 70's saw the line-up constantly changing, PEE WEE ELLIS, BOOTSY COLLINS and PHELPS COLLINS the leading lights in the backing band dubbed first The PACEMAKERS, then latterly the now familiar J.B.'s, FRED WESLEY joining soon after to form the backbone of the band alongside MACEO. BROWN's '72 single, 'KING HEROIN' is often cited as the first rap record (although the waters are cloudy on this one), and he even made it to Zaire for the "Rumble In The Jungle", solidifying his status as Soul Brother Number One. He continued to tour the world throughout the '70s, simultaneously influencing popular music styles wherever he went, although the quality of his recordings became ever more infrequent set next to the standards he had already set, a prime example being the '79 offering 'TAKE A LOOK AT THOSE CAKES'. However, his spectacular cameo as the rocking reverend in the '80 cult classic film, 'The Blues Brothers' opened the gates to a whole new generation of fans, and as the Stars & Stripes clad special guest in 'Rocky IV', he stole the show whilst achieving yet another Top 10 hit with the cheesy 'LIVING IN AMERICA'. BROWN has had his problems with the law along the way, the most publicised event occurring in September '88, when he walked into an insurance seminar with a shotgun in an attempt to find out who had used his private toilet, the tale ending in a two-state police chase and two years in jail. Having amassed 98 entries on Billboard's Top 40 R&B singles chart over his career, earning the nickname 'the hardest working man in showbusiness', as well as being sampled by other musicians an estimated 4000 times, his journey from juvenile delinquent to the Godfather Of Soul bears all the hallmarks of greatness.

Album rating (selective): PLEASE, PLEASE, PLEASE (*6) / TRY ME! (*6) / LIVE AT THE APOLLO (*9) / PURE DYNAMITE! LIVE AT THE ROYAL (*6) / LIVE AT THE APOLLO, VOL.II (*7) / REVOLUTION OF THE MIND – LIVE AT THE APOLLO, VOL. III (*8) / THERE IT IS (*7) / THE PAYBACK (*7) / HELL (*7) / FUNKY PRESIDENT (*7) / THE BEST OF JAMES BROWN (THE GODFATHER OF SOUL) compilation (*9) / STAR TIME boxed set (*9) / THE GODFATHER (THE VERY BEST OF JAMES BROWN) compilation (*8) / THE NEXT STEP (*5)

JAMES BROWN & THE FAMOUS FLAMES

JAMES BROWN – vocals, multi / **BOBBY BYRD** – organ / **JOHNNY TERRY** - / **SYLVESTER KEELS** - / **NAFLOYD SCOTT** – guitar / **etc.**

not iss. Federal

Feb 56. (7") *<12258>* **PLEASE, PLEASE, PLEASE. / WHY DO YOU DO ME** [-] [ ]

May 56. (7") *<12264>* **I DON'T KNOW. / I FEEL THAT OLD FEELING COMING ON** [-] [ ]

Aug 56. (7") *<12277>* **NO, NO, NO, NO. / HOLD MY BABY'S HAND** [-] [ ]

Dec 56. (7") *<12289>* **JUST WON'T DO ME RIGHT. / LET'S MAKE IT** [-] [ ]

Jan 57. (7") *<12290>* **CHONNIE-ON-CHON. / I WON'T PLEAD NO MORE** [-] [ ]

Feb 57. (lp) *<610>* **PLEASE, PLEASE, PLEASE** [-] [ ]
– Please, please, please / Chonnie-on-chon / Hold my baby's hand / I feel that same old feeling coming on / Just won't do right / Baby cries over the ocean / I don't know / Tell me what I did wrong / Try me / That dood it / Begging, begging / I walked alone / No, no, no, no / That's when I lost my heart / Let's make it / Love or a game.

Mar 57. (7") *<12292>* **CAN'T BE THE SAME. / GONNA TRY** [-] [ ]

Jul 57. (7") *<12295>* **LOVE OR A GAME. / MESSING WITH THE BLUES** [-] [ ]

Nov 57. (7") *<12300>* **YOU'RE MINE, YOU'RE MINE. / I WALKED ALONE** [-] [ ]

Mar 58. (7") *<12311>* **THAT DOOD IT. / BABY CRIES OVER THE OCEAN** [-] [ ]

May 58. (7") *<12316>* **BEGGING, BEGGING. / THAT'S WHEN I LOST MY HEART** [-] [ ]

Nov 58. (7") *<12337>* **TRY ME. / TELL ME WHAT I DID WRONG** [-] [48]

Apr 59. (7") *<12348>* **I WANT YOU SO BAD. / THERE MUST BE THE REASON** [-] [ ]

Jun 59. (7") *<12352>* **I'VE GOT TO CHANGE. / IT HURTS TO TELL YOU** [-] [ ]

Jul 59. (lp) *<635>* **TRY ME** [-] [ ]
– Try me / There must be a reason / Strange things happen / Messing with the blues / Why do you do me / I've got to cry / Fine old foxy self / I want you so bad / It was you / I've got to change / Can't be the same / It hurts to tell you / I won't plead no more / You're mine, you're mine / Gonna try / Don't let it happen to me.

Oct 59. (7") *<12361>* **GOOD GOOD LOVIN'. / DON'T LET IT HAPPEN TO ME** [-] [ ]

Dec 59. (7") *<12364>* **IT WAS YOU. / GOT TO CRY** [-] [ ]

—— Released MASHED POTATOES on 'Dade' label, as NAT KENDRICK & THE SWANS.

Feb 60. (lp) *<683>* **THINK** [-] [ ]
– Think / Good good lovin' / Wonder when you're coming home / I'll go crazy / This old heart / I know it's true / Bewildered / I'll never never let you go / You've got the power / If you want me / Baby, you're right / So long.

Mar 60. (7") *<12369>* **I'LL GO CRAZY. / I KNOW IT'S TRUE** [-] [ ]

Parlophone Federal

Jun 60. (7") *(R 4667) <12370>* **THINK. / YOU'VE GOT THE POWER** [ ] Apr60 [33] [86]

Nov 60. (7") *(H 273) <12378>* **THIS OLD HEART. / WONDER WHEN YOU'RE GOING HOME** [-] Jul60 [79]
(above issued on 'Fontana' UK)

Parlophone King

Nov 60. (7") *<5423>* **THE BELLS. / AND I DO JUST WHAT I WANT** [-] [68]

Jan 61. (7") *<5438>* **HOLD IT (instrumental). / THE SCRATCH (instrumental)** [-] [ ]

Feb 61. (7") *<5442>* **BEWILDERED. / IF YOU WANT ME** [-] [40]

Apr 61. (7") *<5466>* **I DON'T MIND. / LOVE DON'T LOVE NOBODY** [-] [47]

Jun 61. (7") *<5485>* **SUDS (instrumental). / STICKY (instrumental)** [-] [ ]

Aug 61. (7") *<5519>* **CROSSFIRING (instrumental). / NIGHT FLYING (instrumental)** [-] [ ]

Sep 61. (7") *<5524>* **BABY, YOU'RE RIGHT. / I'LL NEVER NEVER LET YOU GO** [-] [47]

1961. (lp) *<743>* **THE AMAZING JAMES BROWN** [-] [ ]
– I love you, yes I do / Lost someone / You don't have to go / Dancin' little thing / The bells / Tell me what you're gonna do / So long / Just you and me / And I do just what I want / Come over here / I don't mind / Love don't love nobody.

Nov 61. (7") *<5547>* **I LOVE YOU, YES I DO. / JUST YOU AND ME DARLING** [-] [ ]

Jan 62. (7") *<5573>* **LOST SOMEONE. / CROSS FIRING (instrumental)** [-] [48]

Jul 62. (7") *(R 4922) <5614>* **NIGHT TRAIN (instrumental). / WHY DOES EVERYTHING HAPPEN TO ME** [ ] Apr62 [35]
(re-iss. Dec64 on 'Sue'; WI 360)

Aug 62. (7") *(R 4952) <5657>* **SHOUT AND SHIMMY. / COME OVER HERE** [ ] [61]

Sep 62. (7") *<5672>* **MASHED POTATOES U.S.A. / YOU DON'T HAVE TO GO** [-] [82]

Nov 62. (7") *<5698>* **(CAN YOU) FEEL IT. / (part 2)** [-] [ ]

Dec 62. (7") *<5701>* **THREE HEARTS IN A TANGLE. / I'VE GOT MONEY** [-] [93]

London King

Dec 62. (lp) *<826>* **LIVE AT THE APOLLO (live)** [-] [2]
– I'll go crazy / Try me / Think / I don't mind / Lost someone (part 1 & 2) / Please, please, please / You've got the power / I found someone / Why do you do me like you do / I want you so bad / I love you yes I do / Why does everything happen to me / Bewildered / Please don't go / Night train. *(UK-iss.Sep64; HA 8184) (re-iss. Aug75 on 'Polydor') <re-iss. Nov80 as 'LIVE AND LOWDOWN AT THE APOLLO, VOL.1' on 'Solid Smoke'; 8006> (re-iss. Sep73 on 'Polydor' lp/c; SPE LP/MC 46) (cd-iss. Jul90; 843479-2)*

Jan 63. (7") *<5710>* **EVERY BEAT OF MY HEART (instrumental). / LIKE A BABY** [-] [99]

Apr 63. (7") *(HL 9730) <5739>* **PRISONER OF LOVE. / CHOO CHOO (LOCOMOTION)** [ ] [18]

Jun 63. (7") *(HL 9775) <5767>* **THESE FOOLISH THINGS. / (CAN YOU) FEEL IT** [ ] [55]

Sep 63. (lp) *<851>* **PRISONER OF LOVE** – 73
– Prisoner of love / Waiting in vain / Again / Lost someone / Bewildered / So long / Signed, sealed & delivered / Try me / (Can you) Feel it (pt.1) / How long darling / The thing in 'G'. *(re-iss. Nov83 on 'Polydor'; 8134 911)*

Oct 63. (7") *<5803>* **SIGNED, SEALED AND DELIVERED. / WAITING IN VAIN** – 77

Jan 64. (7") *<5829>* **I'VE GOT TO CHANGE. / THE BELLS** –

Feb 64. (7") *<5842>* **OH BABY DON'T YOU WEEP. / (part 2)** – 23

Mar 64. (7") *<5853>* **PLEASE, PLEASE, PLEASE. / IN THE WEE WEE HOURS** – 95

— He signed to 'Smash' records in the US and was also retained by 'King'. In the UK, 'King' was licensed by 'London' until late '65. The releases on 'Smash' US were on 'Philips' UK, and marked *.

May 64. (7") **<1898>* **CALEDONIA. / EVIL** – 95

Jun 64. (7") *<5876>* **AGAIN. / HOW LONG DARLING** –

Jul 64. (lp) *(HA 8177) <883>* **PURE DYNAMITE! LIVE AT THE ROYAL (live)** Feb64 10
– Shout and shimmy / These foolish things / Signed, sealed and delivered / Like a baby / I'll never let you go / Please, please, please / Oh, baby, don't you weep / Good, good lovin'.

Jul 64. (7") *<5899>* **SO LONG. / DANCIN' LITTLE THING** –

Aug 64. (7") **<1908>* **THE THINGS I USED TO DO. / OUT OF THE BLUE** – 99

Sep 64. (7") *(BF 1368)*<1919>* **OUT OF SIGHT. / MAYBE THE LAST TIME** Aug64 24

Jun 64. (7") *<5922>* **TELL ME WHAT YOU'RE GONNA DO. / I DON'T CARE** –

Sep 64. (lp) *(BL 7630)*<67054>* **SHOWTIME (live)** May64 61

Sep 64. (lp) *Ember; (EMB 3357)* **TELL ME WHAT YOU'RE GONNA DO** –
– Just you and me darling / I love, yes I do / I don't mind / Come over here / The bells / Love don't love nobody / Dancin' little thing / Lost someone / And I do just what I want / So long / You don't have to go / Tell me what you're gonna do. *(cd-iss. Mar95 on 'Charly'; CPCD 8053)*

Oct 64. (7") *<5952>* **THINK. / TRY ME** –

Oct 64. (7") *<5956>* **FINE OLD FOXY SELF. / MEDLEY** –

Dec 64. (7") *(HL 9945) <5968>* **HAVE MERCY BABY. / JUST WON'T DO RIGHT** 92

Mar 65. (7") **<1975>* **DEVIL'S HIDEAWAY (instrumental). / WHO'S AFRAID OF VIRGINIA WOOLF (instrumental)** –

Apr 65. (lp) *(BL 7664)*<67057>* **GRITS AND SOUL (instrumental)**
– Grits / Tempted / There / After you're through / Devil's den / Who's afraid of Virginia Woolf / Infatuation / Wee wee / Mister hip / Headache.

Apr 65. (7") *<5995>* **THIS OLD HEART. / IT WAS YOU** –

Jul 65. (lp) *(HA 8231) <909>* **PLEASE, PLEASE, PLEASE**
– Try me / Please, please, please / I feel that old feeling coming on / That's when I lost my heart / Chonnie on chon / Hold my baby's hand / Tell me what I did wrong / Baby cries over the ocean / Begging, begging / No, no, no, no / That dood it / I don't know / I walked alone / Love or a game / Let's make it / Just won't do right. *(re-iss. Nov83; 2489 194)*

— His UK touring band 1965 **BOBBY BYRD, BOBBY BENNETT, JAMES CRAWFORD + LLOYD STALLWORTH**

Aug 65. (7") *(HL 9990) <5999>* **PAPA'S GOT A BRAND NEW BAG. / (part 2)** 25 Jul65 8

Sep 65. (lp) *<938>* **PAPA'S GOT A BRAND NEW BAG** – 26
– Papa's got a brand new bag / Mashed potatoes U.S.A. / This old heart / Cross firing / Doin' the limbo / Baby, you're right / Love don't love nobody / Have mercy baby / And I do just what I want / I stay in the chapel every night / You don't have to go. *(UK-iss.Mar66; HA 8262) (re-iss. May67 on 'Pye International'; NPL 28099) (re-iss. Nov83 on 'Polydor'; 2489 195)*

Oct 65. (lp) *(HA 8240)* **JAMES BROWN AND HIS FAMOUS FLAMES TOUR THE U.S.A. (live)** –

Dec 65. (7") *(BF 1458)*<2008>* **TRY ME (instrumental) / PAPA'S GOT A BRAND NEW BAG (instrumental)** 63

Dec 65. (lp) *(BL 7697)*<67072>* **JAMES BROWN PLAYS JAMES BROWN TODAY AND YESTERDAY** Nov65 42
– Papa's got a brand new bag / Oh baby don't you weep / Every beat of my heart / Out of sight / Sidewinder / Maybe the last time / Hold it / Song for my father.

Pye Int. King

Feb 66. (7") *(7N 25350) <6015>* **I GOT YOU (I FEEL GOOD). / I CAN'T HELP IT** 29 Nov65 3

Mar 66. (7") *<6020>* **LOST SOMEONE. / I'LL GO CRAZY** – Jan66 94 73

Apr 66. (lp) *(NPL 29072) <946>* **I GOT YOU (I FEEL GOOD)** Jan66 36
– I got you (I feel good) / Good good lovin' / Lost someone / I can't help it / You've got the power / Night train / I've got money / Dancin' little thing / Three hearts in a tangle / Suds / Love don't love nobody.

Apr 66. (7") *(7N 25367) <6025>* **AIN'T THAT A GROOVE. / (part 2)** Feb66 42

Apr 66. (7") *<6029>* **PRISONER OF LOVE. / I'VE GOT TO CHANGE** –

May 66. (7") *<6032>* **COME OVER HERE. / TELL ME WHAT YOU'RE GONNA DO** –

Apr 66. (7") *(BF 1481)*<2028>* **NEW BREED (instrumental) / (part 2)**

May 66. (lp) *(BL 7718)*<67090>* **JAMES BROWN PLAYS NEW BREED** Apr66
– New breed / Slow walk / Fat bag / Vanshelia / Jabo / Lost in the mood of changes / All about my girl / Hooks / Something else.

Jun 66. (7") *(7N 25371) <6035>* **IT'S A MAN'S MAN'S MAN'S WORLD. / IS IT YES OR IS IT NO?** 13 Apr66 8

Jun 66. (7") *<6037>* **JUST WON'T DO RIGHT. / I'VE GOT MONEY** –

Jun 66. (7") **<2042>* **JAMES BROWN'S BOO-GA-LOO (instrumental) / LOST IN A MOOD OF CHANGES (instrumental)** –

Jul 66. (lp) *(NPL 28079) <985>* **IT'S A MAN'S, MAN'S, MAN'S WORLD** 90
– It's a man's, man's, man's world / Is it yes or is it no? / Ain't that a groove (pt.1 & 2) / The scratch / Bewildered / The bells in the wee wee hours / Come over here / I don't mind / Just you and me / I love you, yes I do. *(re-iss. Nov83 on 'Polydor'; 2489 197)*

Jul 66. (7") *<6040>* **IT WAS YOU. / I DON'T CARE** –

Aug 66. (7") *<6044>* **THIS OLD HEART. / HOW LONG DARLING** –

Sep 66. (7") *(7N 25379) <6048>* **MONEY WON'T CHANGE YOU. / (pt.2)** Jul66 53

Nov 66. (7") *<6056>* **DON'T BE A DROP-OUT. / TELL ME THAT YOU LOVE ME** – 50

Dec 66. (7") *<6064>* **THE CHRISTMAS SONG. / (pt.2)** –

Dec 66. (7") *<6065>* **SWEET LITTLE BABY BOY. / (pt.2)** –

Dec 66. (lp) *(NPL 28097)* **THE JAMES BROWN CHRISTMAS ALBUM** (festive songs) –

Dec 66. (7") *(7N 25411) <6071>* **BRING IT UP. / NOBODY KNOWS** 29

Dec 66. (7") *<6072>* **LET'S MAKE CHRISTMAS MEAN SOMETHING THIS YEAR. / (pt.2)** –

Feb 67. (lp) *(NPL 28093)* **MIGHTY INSTRUMENTALS** –
– Papa's got a brand new bag (part 1) / Feel it / Hold it / Sticky / Scratch / James Brown's house party / Night train / Every beat of my heart / Cross firing / Suds / Doin' the limbo / Choo choo.

Mar 67. (7") **<2064>* **LET'S GO GET STONED (instrumental) / OUR DAY WILL COME (instrumental)** –

Mar 67. (lp; stereo/mono) *(S+BL 7761)*<67084>* **HANDFUL OF SOUL** Nov66
– Our day will come / Get loose / Oh Henry / Let's go get stoned / Hot mix / Hold on, I'm coming / King / When a man loves a woman / Message to Michael / 6345-789.

Apr 67. (7") *(7N 25418) <6086>* **KANSAS CITY. / STONE FOX (instrumental)** 55

May 67. (lp) *(NPL 28103) <1016>* **SINGS RAW SOUL** Apr67 88
– Bring it up / Don't be a drop out / Till then / Tell me that you love me / Yours and mine / Money won't change you (part 1 & 2) / Only you / Let yourself go / The nearness of you / Nobody knows / Stone fox.

— In May '67, he issued 7" 'THINK' a collaboration with VICKI ANDERSON hit No.100 in the US.

Nov 67. (lp) *(NPL 28104) <1018>* **LIVE AT THE GARDEN (live)** Jun67 41
– Out of sight / Bring it up / Try me / Let yourself go / Hip bag '67 / Prisoner of love / It may be the last time / I got you / Ain't that a groove (parts 1 & 2) / Please, please, please / Bring it up.

Jul 67. (7") *(7N 25423) <6100>* **LET YOURSELF GO. / GOOD ROCKIN' TONIGHT** 46

Jul 67. (lp) *(NPL 28100)* **MR. EXCITEMENT** (recordings from 1962) –
(re-iss. Nov83 on 'Polydor')

Jul 67. (7") **<2093>* **JIMMY MACK (instrumental) / WHAT DO YOU LIKE (instrumental)** –

— In mid'67, he released 'I LOVE YOU PORGY'. / 'YOURS AND MINE' on 'Bethlehem' <3089>.

— **ALFRED 'Pee-Wee' ELLIS** – brass; repl. JONES new **JIMMY NOLEN** – guitar / **CLYDE STUBBLEFIELD** – drums / **MACEO PARKER** – tenor sax / **ST. CLAIR PINCKNEY** – tenor sax / etc.

Sep 67. (7") *(7N 25430)* <6110> **COLD SWEAT. / (pt.2)** [ ] Jul67 [7]

Oct 67. (lp) *(658 043)* <1020> **COLD SWEAT** [ ] Sep67 [35]
– Cold sweat (pt.1 & 2) / Nature boy / Come rain or come shine / I love you Porgy / Back stabbin' / Fever / Mona Lisa / I want to be around / Good rockin' tonight / Stagger Lee / Kansas City. *(re-iss. Nov83 on 'Polydor')*

Oct 67. (7") <6112> **AMERICA IS MY HOME. / (part 2)** [–] [ ]
<hit US No.52 in May68>

Nov 67. (lp) *(582 703)* **THE JAMES BROWN SHOW (live)** [ ] [–]
– I'll go crazy / Try me / Think / I don't mind / Lost someone / Please, please, please / You've got the power / I found someone / Why do you do me / I want you so bad / I love you yes I do / Why does everything happen to me / Bewildered / Please don't go / Night train.

Nov 67. (7") *(7N 25441)* <6122> **GET IT TOGETHER. / (pt.2)** [ ] Oct67 [40]

Nov 67. (7") <6133> **FUNKY SOUL No.1 (instrumental) / THE SOUL OF J.B. (instrumental)** [–] [ ]

Nov 67. (7") <6141> **I GUESS I'LL HAVE TO CRY, CRY, CRY. / JUST PLAIN FUNK (instrumental)** [–] [ ]
<hit No.US 55 in Jul68>

Polydor King

Dec 67. (7") *(56740)* <6144> **I CAN'T STAND MYSELF (WHEN YOU TOUCH ME). / THERE WAS A TIME** [ ] [28] [36]

Mar 68. (lp) *(184 136)* <1030> **I CAN'T STAND MYSELF (WHEN YOU TOUCH ME)** [ ] [17]
– I can't stand myself (when you touch me) (part 1) / There was a time / Get it together (part 1) / Baby, baby, baby, baby / Time after time / The soul of J.B. (instrumental) / I can't stand myself (when you touch me) (part 2) / Get it together (part 2) / Why did you take your love away from me / Need your love so bad / You've got to change your mind / Fat Eddie *[US]* / Funky soul #1 *[UK]*.

Mar 68. (7"; with BOBBY BYRD) <6151> **YOU'VE GOT TO CHANGE YOUR MIND. / I'LL LOSE MY MIND** [–] [ ]

Mar 68. (7"; with VICKI ANDERSON) <6152> **YOU'VE GOT THE POWER. / WHAT THE WORLD NEEDS NOW IS LOVE** [–] [ ]

May 68. (7") *(56743)* <6155> **I GOT THE FEELIN'. / IF I RULED THE WORLD** [ ] Mar68 [6]

Apr 68. (lp) *(623 032)* **MR. DYNAMITE** [ ] [–]
– Money won't change you (part 1 & 2) / I don't mind / Doin' the limbo / I stay in the chapel every night / Scratch / Night train / I can't help it / Is it yes or is it no / Come over here / In the wee wee hours / Choo choo.

Apr 68. (7") <6159> **MAYBE GOOD, MAYBE BAD (instrumental). / (pt.2)** [–] [ ]

May 68. (7") <6164> **SHHHHHHHH (FOR A LITTLE WHILE) (instrumental). / HERE I GO (instrumental)** [–] [ ]

May 68. (lp) <1031> **I GOT THE FEELIN'** [–] [ ]
– I got the feelin' / Maybe I'll understand – part 1 / You've got the power / Maybe good, maybe bad – part 1 / Shhhhhhh (for a little while) / Just plain funk / If I ruled the world / Maybe I'll understand – part 2 / Stone fox / It won't be me / Maybe good, maybe bad – part 2 / Here I go.

Jun 68. (7") *(56744)* <6166> **LICKING STICK, LICKING STICK. / (pt.2)** [ ] May68 [14]

JAMES BROWN

— solo, but still with The FAMOUS FLAMES

Sep 68. (7") *(56752)* <6187> **SAY IT LOUD – I'M BLACK AND I'M PROUD. / (pt.2)** [ ] [10]

Sep 68. (d-lp) <1022> **LIVE AT THE APOLLO VOLUME 2 (live)** [–] [32]
– Introduction / Think / I want to be around / Thanks / That's life / Kansas City / Let yourself go / There was a time / I feel all right / Cold sweat / It may be the last time / I feel good / Prisoner of love / Out of sight / Try me / Bring it up / It's a man's man's world / Lost someone / Please, please, please. *(UK-iss.Jun69; 583 729/30) (re-iss. Jun70; 2612 005) (cd-iss. Dec88 on 'Polydor') (cd-iss. Jan 93)*

Nov 68. (7") <6198> **GOODBYE MY LOVE. / SHADES OF BROWN (instrumental)** [–] [31]

Nov 68. (7") *(BM 56540)* **THAT'S LIFE. / PLEASE, PLEASE, PLEASE** [ ] [–]

Dec 68. (7") <6203> **SANTA CLAUS GOES STRAIGHT TO THE GHETTO. / YOU KNOW IT (instrumental)** [–] [ ]

Dec 68. (7") <6204> **TIT FOR TAT (AIN'T NO TAKING BACK). / BELIEVERS SHALL ENJOY** [–] [86]

Dec 68. (7") <6205> **LET'S UNITE THE WHOLE WORLD AT CHRISTMAS. / IN THE MIDDLE (pt.1)** [–] [ ]

Jan 69. (7") <6213> **GIVE IT UP OR TURNIT A LOOSE. / I'LL LOSE MY MIND** [–] [15]

Jan 69. (lp) *(580 701)* **TURN IT LOOSE** [ ] [–]
– Give it up or turnit a loose / I'll lose my mind / I don't want nobody to give me tonight (open up the door, I'll get it myself) (parts 1 & 2).

Mar 69. (7") <6216> **ATTACK WITH THE NEWS. / SHADES OF BROWN (pt.2)** [–] [ ]

Mar 69. (7"; with MARVA WHITNEY) <6218> **YOU'VE GOT TO HAVE A JOB. / I'M TIRED, I'M TIRED, I'M TIRED** [–] [ ]

Mar 69. (7") <6222> **SOUL PROUD. / (pt.2)** [–] [ ]

Mar 69. (7") <6223> **YOU'VE GOT TO HAVE A MOTHER FOR ME. / (part 2)** [–] [ ]

Apr 69. (7") <6224> **I DON'T WANT NOBODY TO GIVE ME NOTHIN' (OPEN UP THE DOOR, I'LL GET IT MYSELF). / (pt.2)** [–] [20]

Apr 69. (lp) <1047> **SAY IT LOUD – I'M BLACK AND I'M PROUD** [–] [53]
– Say it loud I'm black and proud (parts 1 & 2) / I guess I'll have to cry, cry, cry / Goodbye my love (parts 1 & 2) / Shades of brown / Licking stick / I love you / Then you can tell me goodbye / Let them talk / Maybe I'll understand / I'll lose my mind. *(UK-iss.Sep69; 583 741)*

May 69. (7") <6235> **THE LITTLE GROOVE MAKER ME. / I'M SHOOK** [–] [ ]

May 69. (lp) <1051> **GETTIN' DOWN TO IT** [–] [99]
– Sunny / That's life / Strangers in the night / Willow weep for me / Cold sweat / There was a time / Chicago / For sentimental reasons / Time after time / All the way / It had to be you / Uncle. *(UK-iss.Jan70; 583 742)*

Jun 69. (7") <6240> **THE POPCORN (instrumental) / THE CHICKEN (instrumental)** [–] [30]

Jul 69. (7") *(56776)* <6245> **MOTHER POPCORN (YOU GOT TO HAVE A MOTHER FOR ME). / (pt.2)** [ ] Jun69 [11]

Aug 69. (7") <6250> **LOWDOWN POPCORN (instrumental) / TOP OF THE STACK (instrumental)** [–] [41]

Aug 69. (lp) <1055> **JAMES BROWN PLAYS AND DIRECTS THE POPCORN** [–] [40]
– The popcorn / Why am I treated so bad / In the middle / Soul pride / A new shift / Sudsy / The chicken / The chase. *(UK-iss.Mar70 as 'THE POPCORN'; 184 319)*

Sep 69. (7") <6255> **LET A MAN COME IN AND DO THE POPCORN PART ONE. / SOMETIME** [–] [21]

Sep 69. (7") *(56780)* <6258> **THE WORLD. / (pt.2)** [ ] [37]

Oct 69. (lp) *(583 768)* <1063> **IT'S A MOTHER** [ ] Sep69 [26]
– Mother popcorn (you got to have a mother for me) (parts 1 & 2) / Mashed potato popcorn (parts 1 & 2) / I'm shook / Popcorn with a feeling / Little groove maker me (parts 1 & 2) / Any day now (my wild beautiful bird) / If I ruled the world / You're still out of sight / Top of the stack.

Nov 69. (7") <6273) **I'M NOT DEMANDING. / (part 2)** [–] [ ]

Dec 69. (7") <6275> **PART TWO (LET A MAN COME IN AND DO THE POPCORN). / GETTIN' A LITTLE HIPPER (pt.1)** [–] [40]

Dec 69. (7") <6277> **IT'S CHRISTMAS TIME. / (pt.2)** [–] [ ]

Jan 70. (7") *(56787)* **THERE WAS A TIME. / I CAN'T STAND MYSELF (WHEN YOU TOUCH ME)** [ ] [–]

Jan 70. (7") <6285> **BROTHER RAPP. / (part 2)** [–] [ ]

Feb 70. (7") <6290> **FUNKY DRUMMER (instrumental) / (pt.2)** [–] [51]

Feb 70. (7") <6292> **IT'S A NEW DAY. / (pt.2)** [–] [32]

Feb 70. (lp) <1092> **AIN'T IT FUNKY** [–] [43]
– Ain't it funky now (parts 1 & 2) / Fat wood (parts 1 & 2) / Cold sweat / Give it up or turnit a loose / Nose job / Use your mother / After you done it. *(UK-iss.Aug70; 2343 010)*

Mar 70. (7") *(56793)* <6280> **AIN'T IT FUNKY NOW (instrumental). / (pt.2)** [ ] Nov69 [24]

Mar 70. (7") <6300> **TALKIN'' LOUD AND SAYIN' NOTHIN'. / (part 2)** [–] [ ]

Apr 70. (7") <6310> **BROTHER RAPP (pt.1). / BEWILDERED** [–] [32]

Jul 70. (7") *(2001 018)* **IT'S A NEW DAY. / GEORGIA ON MY MIND** [ ] [–]

Jul 70. (lp) *(2310 029)* <1095> **IT'S A NEW DAY SO LET A MAN COME IN** [ ] [ ]
– It's a new day so let a man come in / Do the popcorn / World / Georgia on my mind / It's a man's man's world / Give it up or turn

it a loose / If I ruled the world / The man in the glass / I'm not demanding.

— (Also released lp SOUL ON TOP with The LOUIE BELLSON ORCHESTRA (Jul70) Released another duet 7" with VICKI ANDERSON – Let It Be Me.

— He breaks up The FAMOUS FLAMES to introduce his new band The JB's. They included **BOOTSY COLLINS, FRED WESLEY, BOBBY BYRD, JIMMY PARKER**, etc.

Sep 70. (7") *(2001 071) <6318>* **GET UP, I FEEL LIKE BEING A SEX MACHINE. / (pt.2)** [32] Jul70 [15]

— (released gospel 45, A MAN HAS TO GO BACK TO THE CROSSROADS on 'Bethlehem')

Sep 70. (7") *<6322>* **I'M NOT DEMANDING. / (part 2)** [–] [ ]

Nov 70. (7") *(2001 097) <6329>* **CALL ME SUPER BAD. / (pt.2)** [ ] Sep70 [13]

Nov 70. (7") *<6339>* **HEY AMERICA (vocal). / (instrumental)** [–] [ ]

Dec 70. (d-lp) *(2625 004) <1115>* **SEX MACHINE (live)** [ ] Sep70 [29]
– Get up I feel like being a sex machine / Brother Rapp (parts 1 & 2) / Bewildered / I got the feelin' / Give it up or turn it a loose / I don't want nobody / To give me nothing / Licking stick / Lowdown / Popcorn / Spinning wheel / If I ruled the world / There was a time / It's a man's man's world / Please, please, please / I can't stand myself / Mother popcorn. *(cd-iss. Sep98; 517984-2)*

Dec 70. (7") *<6340>* **SANTA CLAUS IS DEFINITELY HERE TO STAY. / (instrumental)** [–] [ ]

Jan 71. (7") *<6347>* **GET UP, GET INTO IT, GET INVOLVED. / (pt.2)** [–] [34]

Feb 71. (7") *<6359>* **TALKING LOUD AND SAYING NOTHING. / (pt.2)** [–] [ ]

Feb 71. (7") *<6366>* **SPINNING WHEEL (instrumental) / (part 2)** [–] [90]

Mar 71. (7") *(2001 163) <6368>* **SOUL POWER. / (pt.2)** [ ] Feb71 [29]

May 71. (7") *(2001 190) <6363>* **I CRIED. / GET UP, GET INTO IT, GET INVOLVED** [ ] Feb71 [50]

May 71. (lp) *(2310 089) <1127>* **SUPER BAD** [ ] Jan71 [61]
– Superbad (parts 1 & 2) / Let it be me / Sometime a man has to go back to the crossroads / Giving out my juice / By the time I get to Phoenix.

— Most of his band except WESLEY, joined PARLIAMENT/FUNKADELIC.

Polydor People

Jun 71. (7") *<2500>* **ESCAPE-ISM. / (part 2)** [–] [35]

Jul 71. (7") *(2001 213) <2501>* **HOT PANTS (SHE GOT TO USE WHAT SHE GOT, TO GET WHAT SHE WANTS). / (pt.2)** [ ] [15]

Polydor Polydor

Sep 71. (lp) *(2425 086) <4054>* **HOT PANTS** [ ] Aug71 [22]
– Blues and pants / Can't stand it / Escape-ism (part 1) / Escape-ism (Part 2) / Hot pants (she got to use what she got to get what she wants) / Escape-ism. *(re-iss. Sep98 lp/cd; 517985-1/-2)*

Sep 71. (7") *(2001 223) <14088>* **MAKE IT FUNKY. / (pt.2)** [ ] [22]

Oct 71. (7") *<14098>* **MY PART: MAKE IT FUNKY PART 3. / (other version)** [–] [68]

Nov 71. (7") *(2066 153) <14100>* **I'M A GREEDY MAN. / (part 2)** [ ] [35]

Feb 72. (d-lp) *(2659 011) <3003>* **REVOLUTION OF THE MIND – LIVE AT THE APOLLO, VOLUME III (live)** [ ] Dec71 [39]
– It's a new day so let a man come in and do the popcorn / Bewildered / Sex machine / Escape-ism / Make it funky / Try me / Fast medley: I can't stand myself – Mother popcorn – I got the feelin' / Give it up or turn it a loose / Call me Superbad / Get up, get into it, get involved (parts 1 & 2) / Soul power / Hot pants (she got to use what she got to get what she wants). *(cd-iss. Sep98; 517983-2)*

Feb 72. (7") *(2066 185) <14116>* **KING HEROIN. / THEME FROM KING HEROIN** [ ] [40]

Apr 72. (7") *(2066 210) <14126>* **THERE IT IS. / (part 2)** [ ] [43]

Jun 72. (7") *(2066 216) <14129>* **HONKY TONK. / (part 2)** [ ] [44]

Aug 72. (7") *(2066 231) <14139>* **GET ON THE GOOD FOOT. / (part 2)** [ ] [18]

Nov 72. (lp) *(2391 033) <5028>* **THERE IT IS** [ ] Jun72 [ ]
– There it is (parts 1 & 2) / King heroin / I'm a greedy man (parts 1 & 2) / Who am I / Talkin' loud and sayin' nothing / Public enemy #1 (part 1) / Public enemy #1 (part 2) / I need help (I can't do it alone) / Never can say goodbye. *(re-iss. Sep98 lp/cd; 517986-1/-2)*

Nov 72. (7") *(2066 283) <14157>* **WHAT MY BABY NEEDS NOW IS A LITTLE MORE LOVIN'. / THIS GUY'S IN LOVE WITH YOU (with LYN COLLINS)** [ ] Dec72 [56]

Dec 72. (7") *(2066 285) <14153>* **I GOT A BAG OF MY OWN. / I KNOW IT'S TIME** [ ] Nov72 [44]

Dec 72. (7") *<14161>* **SANTA CLAUS GOES STRAIGHT TO THE GHETTO. / SWEET LITTLE BABY BOY** [–] [ ]

Jan 73. (7") *<14162>* **I GOT ANTS IN MY PANTS (AND I WANT TO DANCE). / (part 2)** [–] [27]

Jan 73. (d-lp) *(2659 018) <3004>* **GET ON THE GOOD FOOT** [ ] Dec72 [68]
– Get on the good foot (parts 1 & 2) / The whole world needs liberation / Your love was good for me / Cold sweat / Recitation by Hank Ballard / I got a bag of my own / Nothing beats a try but a fail / Lost someone / Funky side of town / Please, please, please / Ain't it a groove / My part – Make it funky (parts 3 & 4) / Dirty Harry / I know it's a true. *(cd-iss. Mar99 on 'IMS-Universal'; E 523982-2)*

Mar 73. (7") *<14168>* **DOWN AND OUT IN NEW YORK CITY. / MAMA'S DEAD** [–] [50]

Mar 73. (7") *<14169>* **LIKE IT IS, LIKE IT WAS. / THE BOSS** [–] [ ]

May 73. (lp) *(2490 117) <PD 6014>* **BLACK CAESAR (Soundtrack)** [ ] Feb73 [31]
– Down and out in New York city / Blind man can see it / Sportin' life / Dirty Harri / The boss / Make it good to yourself / Mama Feelgood / Mama's dead / White lightning (I mean moonshine) / Chase / Like it is, like it was. *<(re-iss. Sep98 lp/cd; 517135-1/-2)>*

May 73. (7") *(2066 329) <14177>* **THINK. / SOMETHING** [ ] [77]
(above and below 2 different versions)

Jun 73. (7") *<14185>* **THINK. / SOMETHING** [–] [80]

Jul 73. (7") *<14193>* **WOMAN. / (part 2)** [–] [ ]

Aug 73. (lp) *(2391 084) <PD 6015>* **SLAUGHTER'S BIG RIP-OFF (Soundtrack)** [ ] Jul73 [92]
– Slaughter theme / Tryin' to get over / Transmograpfication / Happy for the poor / Brother rap / Big strong / Really, really, really / Sexy, sexy, sexy / To my brother / How long can I keep it up / People get up and drive your funky soul / King Slaughter / Straight ahead. *<(cd-iss. Aug96 & Sep98; 314 517136-2)>*

Aug 73. (7") *<14194>* **SEXY, SEXY, SEXY. / SLAUGHTER THEME** [–] [50]

Sep 73. (7"; JAMES BROWN with LYN COLLINS) *<14199>* **LET IT BE ME. / IT'S ALL RIGHT** [–] [ ]

Oct 73. (7") *<14206>* **I'VE GOT A GOOD THING. / (part 2)** [–] [ ]

Nov 73. (7") *<14210>* **STONED(D) TO THE BONE. / (part 2)** [–] [58]

Jan 74. (7") *(2066 411)* **STONE(D) TO THE BONE. / SEXY, SEXY, SEXY** [ ] [–]

Mar 74. (7") *<14223>* **THE PAYBACK. / (part 2)** [–] [26]

Apr 74. (d-lp) *(2659 030) <3007>* **THE PAYBACK** [ ] Jan74 [34]
– The payback / Doing the best I can / Take some – leave some / Shoot your shot / Forever suffering / Time is running out fast / Stoned to the bone / Mind power. *(cd-iss. Sep98; 517137-2)*

Jun 74. (7") *(2066 485)* **MY THANG. / THE PAYBACK** [ ] [–]

Jul 74. (7") *<14244>* **MY THANG. / PUBLIC ENEMY #1** [–] [29]

Sep 74. (7") *<14255>* **PAPA DON'T TAKE NO MESS. / (part 2)** [–] [31]

Sep 74. (d-lp) *(2659 036) <9001>* **IT'S HELL** <US-title 'HELL'> [ ] Jul74 [35]
– Coldblooded / Hell / My thang / Savin' it and doin' it / Please, please, please / When the saints go marching in / These foolish things / Storming Monday / A man has to go back to the cross road before he finds himself / Sometime / I can't stand it / Lost someone / Don't tell a lie about me and I won't tell the truth about you / Papa don't take no mess. *(re-iss. Jul88)*

Jan 75. (7") *(2066 520) <14258>* **FUNKY PRESIDENT (PEOPLE IT'S BAD). / COLD BLOODED** [ ] Nov74 [44]

Feb 75. (7") *<14268>* **REALITY. / TWIST** [–] [80]

Mar 75. (lp) *(2391 164) <6039>* **REALITY** [ ] Jan75 [56]
– Reality / Funky President (people it's bad) / Further on up the road / Check your body / Don't fence me in / All for one / I'm broken hearted / The twist / Who can I turn to.

Apr 75. (7") *<14270>* **SEX MACHINE (remix). / (part 2)** [–] [ ]

May 75. (lp) *(2391 175) <6042>* **SEX MACHINE TODAY** [ ] [ ]
– Sex machine (pt.1 & 2) / I feel good / Problems / Dead on it / Get up off of me / Deep in it.

Jun 75. (7") *<14279>* **DEAD ON IT. / (part 2)** [–] [ ]

Jul 75. (7") *<14281>* **HUSTLE!!! (DEAD ON IT). / (part 2)** [–] [ ]

Nov 75. (7") *<14295>* **SUPERBAD, SUPERSLICK. / (part 2)** [–] [ ]

Dec 75. (lp) *(2391 197) <6054>* **EVERYBODY'S DOIN' THE HUSTLE AND DEAD ON THE DOUBLE BUMP** [ ] Oct75 [ ]
– Hustle!!! (dead on it) / Papa's got a brand new bag / Your love / Turn on the heat and build some fire / Superbad, superslick / Calm & cool / Kansas City.

Jan 76. (7") *(2066 642) <14301>* **HOT (I NEED TO BE LOVED, LOVED, LOVED). / SUPERBAD, SUPERSLICK (part 1)** [ ] [ ]

Feb 76. (7") *<14303>* **DOOLEY'S JUNKYARD DOGS. / (part 2)** [–] [ ]

Feb 76. (7") *<14304>* **(I LOVE YOU) FOR SENTIMENTAL REASONS. / GOODNIGHT MY LOVE** [–] [ ]

Mar 76. (lp) *(2391 214)* **HOT** [ ] [–]
– Hot (I need to be loved, loved, loved) / so long / For sentimental reasons / Try me / The future shock of the world / woman / Most of all / Goodnight my love / Please, please, please. *(re-iss. Jul88; PD 6059)*

Jul 76. (7") *(2066 687) <14326>* **GET UP OFFA THAT THING. / RELEASE THE PRESSURE** [22] [45]

Sep 76. (lp) *(2391 228) <6071>* **GET UP OFFA THAT THING** [ ] Aug76 [ ]
– Get up offa that thing / Release the pressure / You took my heart / I refuse to lose / Can't take it with you / Home again / This feeling.

Nov 76. (7") *<14354>* **I REFUSE TO LOSE. / HOME AGAIN** [–] [ ]

Jan 77. (7") *(2066 763) <14360>* **BODYHEAT. / (part 2)** [36] [88]

Feb 77. (lp) *(2391 258) <6093>* **BODYHEAT** [ ] Jan77 [ ]
– Bodyheat / Woman / Kiss in '77 / I'm satisfied / What the world needs now is love / Wake up and give yourself a chance / Don't feel it. *(re-iss. Oct82 on 'Phoenix'; PHX 1025) (re-iss. Jul88; PD 6093)*

Jun 77. (7") *<14388>* **KISS IN '77. / WOMAN** [–] [ ]

Jul 77. (7") *(2066 834)* **HONKY TONK. / BROTHER RAPP** [ ] [–]

Sep 77. (7") *<14409>* **GIVE ME SOME SKIN. / PEOPLE WAKE UP AND LIVE** [–] [ ]

Sep 77. (lp) *(2391 300) <6111>* **MUTHA'S NATURE** [ ] [ ]
– Give me some skin / People who criticize / Have a happy day / Bessie / If you don't give a doggone about it / Summertime / People wake up and live / Take me higher and groove me.

Nov 77. (7") *<14433>* **TAKE ME HIGHER AND GROOVE ME. / SUMMERTIME (Martha & James)** [–] [ ]

Jan 78. (7") *<14438>* **IF YOU DON'T GIVE A DOGGONE ABOUT IT. / PEOPLE WHO CRITICIZE** [–] [ ]

— His backing group, left for a while, but soon returned. JIMMY NOLAN was to die of a heart attack 18 Dec'83.

May 78. (7") *<14460>* **LOVE ME TENDER. / HAVE A HAPPY DAY** [–] [ ]

May 78. (lp) *(2391 342) <6140>* **JAM / 1980's** [ ] [ ]
– Jam / The spank / Nature / Eyesight / I never never never will forget.

Jun 78. (7") *(2066 915) <14465>* **EYESIGHT. / NEVER, NEVER, NEVER WILL FORGET** [ ] [ ]

Aug 78. (7") *<14487>* **LOVE ME TENDER. / THE SPANK** [–] [ ]

Oct 78. (7") *(2066 984) <14512>* **NATURE. / (part 2)** [ ] [ ]

Dec 78. (7") *<14522>* **FOR GOODNESS SAKES, LOOK AT THOSE CAKES. / (part 2)** [–] [ ]

Jan 79. (7") *(POSP 24)* **FOR GOODNESS SAKES, LOOK AT THOSE CAKES. / GET UP, I FEEL LIKE BEING A SEX MACHINE** [ ] [–]

Jan 79. (lp) *(2391 384) <6181>* **TAKE A LOOK AT THOSE CAKES** [ ] [ ]
– For goodness sakes, take a look at those cakes / A man understands / As long as I love you / Someone to talk about / Spring.

Apr 79. (7") *<14540>* **SOMEONE TO TALK ABOUT. / (part 2)** [–] [ ]

Jul 79. (7") *(POSP 68) <14557>* **IT'S TOO FUNKY IN HERE. / ARE WE REALLY DANCING** [ ] [ ]

Aug 79. (lp) *(2391 412) <6212>* **THE ORIGINAL DISCO MAN** [ ] [ ]
– It's too funky in here / Let the boogie do the rest / Still / The original disco man / Star generation / Women are something else.

Aug 79. (7") *<2005>* **STAR GENERATION. / WOMEN ARE SOMETHING ELSE** [–] [ ]

Sep 79. (7"/12") *(STEP/+X 2)* **STAR GENERATION. / LET THE BOOGIE DO THE REST** [ ] [–]

Nov 79. (7") *<2034>* **THE ORIGINAL DISCO MAN. / LET THE BOOGIE DO THE REST** [–] [ ]

Feb 80. (7") *(POSP 121) <2054>* **REGRETS. / STONE COLD DRAG** [ ] [ ]

Apr 80. (lp) *(2391 446) <6258>* **PEOPLE** [ ] [ ]
– Regrets / Don't stop the funk / That's sweet music / Let the funk flow / Stone cold drag / Are we really dancing / Sometimes that's all there is. *(re-iss. Jul88; PD 16258)*

May 80. (7") *<2078>* **LET THE FUNK FLOW. / SOMETIMES THAT'S ALL THERE IS** [–] [ ]

Aug 80. (7") *<2129>* **IT'S TOO FUNKY FOR ME IN HERE. / GET UP OFFA THAT THING** [–] [ ]

Oct 80. (d-lp) *(2683 085) <6290>* **JAMES BROWN . . . LIVE – HOT ON THE ONE (live)** [ ] Aug80 [ ]
– It's too funky in here / Gonna have a funky good time / Get up offa that thing / Bodyheat / I got the feelin' / Try me / Sex machine / It's a man's man's man's world / Get on the good foot / Papa's got a brand new bag / Please, please, please / Jam. *(cd-iss. Apr91; 847856-2)*

Oct 80. (7") *<2167>* **GIVE THE BASS PLAYER SOME. / (part 2)** [–] [ ]

R.C.A. / T.K.

Dec 80. (7"/12") *(RCA/+T 28) <1039>* **RAPP PAYBACK (WHERE IZ MOSES?). / (pt.2)** [39] [ ]

Dec 80. (lp) *(RCALP 5006) <5334>* **SOUL SYNDROME** [ ] [ ]
– Rapp payback / Mashed potatoes / Smokin' and drinkin' / Stay with me / Honky tonk. *(re-iss. Sep81 lp/c; RCA LP/K 3048)*

Feb 81. (7") *(RCA 44) <1042>* **STAY WITH ME. / SMOKIN' AND DRINKIN'** [ ] [ ]

May 81. (7") *(RCA 65)* **FUNKY MAN. / (part 2)** [ ] [ ]
(12"+=) *(RCAT 65)* – Mashed potatoes.

Polydor / not iss.

Apr 81. (lp) *(POLS 1029)* **THE THIRD COMING** [ ] [ ]
– Popcorn 80's / Give that bass player some / You're my only love / World cycle inc. / Superball / Superbad 80's / I go crazy.

Jun 81. (7") *(POSP 290)* **I GO CRAZY. / WORLD CYCLE INC.** [ ] [–]

Sonet / not iss.

Jun 83. (7"/12") *(SON/+L 2258)* **BRING IT ON . . . BRING IT ON. / NIGHT TIME IS THE RIGHT TIME** [45] [–]

Sep 83. (lp) *(SNTF 906)* **BRING IT ON** [ ] [–]
– Bring it on . . . bring it on / Today / You can't keep a good man down / Nighttime is the right time / Tennessee waltz / For your precious love.

— In Aug'84, he teamed up with **AFRIKA BAMBAATAA** for one-off 7+12" **UNITY** (THE THIRD COMING) on 'Tommy Boy' (US No.49).

Scotti Bros / Scotti Bros

Jan 86. (7") *(A 6701) <05682>* **LIVING IN AMERICA. / Vince Di Cola: FAREWELL** [5] Dec85 [4]
(12"+=) *(TA 6701)* – ('B'extended).

— (above from the film 'Rocky IV', and written by DAN HARTMAN)

Oct 86. (7") *(650059-7) <06275>* **GRAVITY. / GRAVITY (dub)** [65] [93]
(12") *(650059-6)* – ('A'side) / The big G (dig this myth).

Oct 86. (lp/c) *(SCT/40 57108) <40380>* **GRAVITY** [85] [ ]
– How do you stop / Turn me loose, I'm Dr.Feelgood / Living in America / Goliath / Repeat the beat (faith) / Return to me / Gravity. *(cd-iss. Mar87; CD 57108) (re-iss. Jul88; FZ 40380)*

Mar 87. (7") *<06568>* **HOW DO YOU STOP. / HOUSE OF ROCK** [–] [ ]

Apr 87. (7") *(JAMES 1)* **HOW DO YOU STOP. / REPEAT THE BEAT (FAITH)** [ ] [–]
(12"+=) *(JAMEST 1)* – Living in America.
(12"+=) *(JAMESQ 1)* – ('A'-House mix).

Jun 87. (7") *<07090>* **LET'S GET PERSONAL. / REPEAT THE BEAT** [–] [ ]

Urban-Polydor / Scotti Bros

May 88. (7") *<07783>* **I'M REAL. / TRIBUTE** [–] [ ]

May 88. (7") *(JSB 1)* **I'M REAL. / KEEP KEEPING** [31] [–]
(12"+=) *(JSBX 1)* – Tribute.
(cd-s++=) *(JSBCD 1)* – ('A'-Hype mix).

Jun 88. (lp/c)(cd) *(POLD/+C 5230)(834755-2) <44241>* **I'M REAL** [27] [96]
– Tribute / I'm real / Static / Time to get busy / She looks types a good / Keep keeping / Can't git enuf / It's your money / Godfather runnin' the joint.

Aug 88. (7") *(JSB 1) <07975>* **STATIC. / GODFATHER RUNNIN' THE JOINT** [ ] [ ]
(12"+=) *(JSBX 2)* – I'm real (US remix).
(cd-s++=) *(JSBCD 2)* – ('A'-Full Force mix).

Nov 88. (7") *<08088>* **TIME TO GET BUSY. / BUSY J.B.** [–] [ ]

Feb 89. (7") *<68559>* **IT'S YOUR MONEY. / YOU AND ME** [–] [ ]

— He guested on ARETHA FRANKLIN single Nov88, 'GIMME YOUR LOVE'.

— In Apr-May'88, JAMES and his wife ADRIANNE were arrested for possession of substances and guns. She also filed for divorce and pleaded not guilty. Later that year, after resisting arrest in a car chase, etc., he was sentenced to 6 years. He was released on parole on 27th Feb'91, but had to return until late 1993 to serve full sentence. In 1992, he was awarded a special grammy award, for his contribution to music. He appeared there with his wife, to sing finale.

Polydor / Polydor

Jul 91. (cd/c/lp) *(510079-2/-4/-1)* **LOVE OVERDUE** [ ] [ ]
– (So tired of standing still we got to) Move on / Show me – dance, dance, dance / To the funk / Teardrops on your letter / Standing on higher ground / Later for dancing / You are my everything / It's time for love (put a little love).

Jul 91. (7") **(SO TIRED OF STANDING STILL WE GOT TO) MOVE ON / YOU ARE MY EVERYTHING** [ ] [-]
(12"+=) – ('A' extended).

Mar 93. (cd/c) *(514329-2/-4)* **UNIVERSAL JAMES** [ ] [ ]
– Can't get any harder / Just do it / Mine all mine / Watch me / Georgia-Lina / Show me your friends / Everybody's got a thang / How long / Make it funky 2000 / Moments.

Apr 93. (7"/c-s) *(PO/+CS 262)* **CAN'T GET ANY HARDER. / ('A'-O.B.C. mix)** [59] [ ]
(12"+=/cd-s+=) *(PZ/+CD 262)* – ('A'mixes).

Eagle Crash

Nov 98. (cd) *(EAGCD 054)* *<417081>* **I'M BACK** [ ] [ ]
– Can't stand it / Funk on ah roll / Kare / What it takes / Papa's got a brand new bag / Break away / Funk on ah roll / Lucky old sun / I don't hear no music / Every part of my heart / Eden / Peace in the world / Funk on ah roll / James on the loose.

Apr 99. (12"/cd-s) *(EAG 12/XS 073)* **FUNK ON AH ROLL / ('A'mix)** [40] [ ]
(cd-s) *(EAGXA 073)* – ('A'mixes).

C.N.R. Red Ink

Jun 03. (cd) *(2299999-2)* *<13943>* **THE NEXT STEP** [ ] Aug02 [ ]
– Automatic (remix) / Send her back to me (remix) / Motivation / Sunshine / Nothing but a jam / Baby you've got what it takes / It's time / Why did this happen to me / Good and natural / Killing is out, school is in.

– (selective) compilations, etc. –

on Polydor UK / King + Polydor (+'75) US, unless mentioned otherwise

Aug 72. (lp) *(2391 057)* *<5401>* **JAMES BROWN SOUL CLASSICS** [ ] [83]

May 75. (7") *<14270>* **SEX MACHINE (part 1). / (part 2)** [-] [61]

Feb 90. (cd/c/lp) *(841516-2/-4/-1)* **DUETS** [ ] [ ]

Jan 91. (d-cd) *(847258-2)* **MESSIN' WITH THE BLUES** (rare R&B/Blues) [ ] [ ]

May 91. (4xcd-box/4xc-box) *(849 108-2/-4)* **STAR TIME** [ ] [-]

Nov 91. (cd/c/lp) *(845 828-2/-4/-1)* **SEX MACHINE – THE VERY BEST OF JAMES BROWN** [19] [ ]
– (see K-Tel album except replacement of tracks marked * by:-) Night train / Out of sight / I'm a greedy man (pt.1) / Get up offa that thing / I'm real / It's too funky in here / Soul power (live).

Apr 85. (7") *Boiling Point; (FROG 1)* **FROGGY MIX. / (pt.2)** [50] [ ]
(12"+=) *(FROGX 1)* – (extra mixes).

Jun 85. (7") *(POSP 751)* **GET UP, I FEEL LIKE BEING A SEX MACHINE (pt.2). / PAPA'S GOT A BRAND NEW BAG** [47] [ ]
(12"+=) *(POSPX 751)* – Get up offa that thing (release the pressure) / Get on the good foot. *(re-iss. Feb86 hit UK-No.46)*

Apr 86. (7") *(POSP 783)* **SOUL POWER (pt.1). / IT'S A MAN'S, MAN'S, MAN'S WORLD** [ ] [ ]
(12"+=) *(POSPX 783)* – King Heroin / Don't tell it.

May 86. (d-lp) *Urban; (URB LP/DC 11)* **IN THE JUNGLE GROOVE** [ ] [ ]
(cd-iss. May88 on 'Polydor'; 829624-2)

Sep 87. (lp/c/cd) *K-Tel; (NE1/CE2/NCD3 376)* **THE BEST OF JAMES BROWN (THE GODFATHER OF SOUL)** [17] [-]
– Living in America /* Body heat / Hey America / Please, please, please / Hot pants (pt.1) / Think / I got you (I feel good) / Say it loud, I'm black and proud (pt.1) / Get up (I feel like being a) sex machine / Make it funky (pt.1) / Papa's got a brand new bag (pt.1) / Get on the good foot / * Gonna have a funky good time / Cold sweat / * Honky tonk / It's a man's man's man's world / * Gravity.

Jan 88. (7") *Urban; (URB 13)* **SHE'S THE ONE. / FUNKY PRESIDENT (PEOPLE IT'S BAD)** [45] [ ]
(12"+=) *(URBX 13)* – Funky drummer (edit) / Funky drummer (boms beat reprise).

Apr 88. (7") *Urban; (URB 17)* **THE PAYBACK MIX (pt.1). / GIVE IT UP OR TURNIT A LOOSE** [ ] [ ]
(12") *(URBX 17)* – ('A'side) / Keep on doing what you're doing but keep it funky / Stoned to the bone / Cold sweat.

— May'88 'A&M' released 'I GOT YOU (I FEEL GOOD)' hit UK 52, from the film 'Good Morning Vietnam', B-side by Martha Reeves & The Vandellas.

Oct 92. (7"; JAMES BROWN VS DAKEYNE) *F.B.I.; (FBI 9)* **I GOT YOU (I FEEL GOOD) (remix). / PROCESSED B'S** [72] [-]
(cd-s+=) *(FBICD 9)* – B-Funked.

Apr 02. (cd) *Universal TV; (589841-2)* **THE GODFATHER: THE VERY BEST OF JAMES BROWN** [30] [-]
– Papa's got a brand new bag / I got you (I feel good) / It's a man's man's man's world / Please please please / Think / Night train / Cold sweat / Give it up or turn it loose / Funky drummer (parts 1 & 2) / Get up I feel like being a sex machine / Soul power / Get on the good foot / Doing it to death / Get up offa that thing / I'm real / It's too funky in here / Living in America / Super bad / The boss / The payback mix.

Jackson BROWNE

Born: 9 Oct'48, Heidelberg, Germany. BROWNE's parents were actually American (father was in the Army) and the family subsequently moved back to Orange County, California. During the 60's, the budding singer/songwriter worked with the likes of TIM BUCKLEY, NITTY GRITTY DIRT BAND and even NICO, BROWNE later providing material for such luminaries as The BYRDS and LINDA RONSTADT. He duly signed a solo deal with 'Elektra', initially as a house writer, before being picked up by David Geffen's new 'Asylum' label in 1971. With the help of a number of high profile cover versions, 'DOCTOR MY EYES' (Jackson 5) / 'SHADOW DREAM SONG' (Tom Paxton), BROWNE's eponymous debut album hit the US Top 60. Featuring such ubiquitous L.A. session men as LELAND SKLAR and RUSS KUNKEL alongside such esteemed company as DAVID CROSBY, CLARENCE WHITE and SNEAKY PETE KLEINOW, the album established BROWNE at the forefront of the navel-gazing Californian singer/songwriter scene. His fragile melodies and bookish, confessional lyrics saw him adopted as a kind of genre figurehead, BROWNE garnering further kudos after co-penning the classic EAGLES track, 'TAKE IT EASY'. But while The EAGLES took that song's philosophy to its ultimate conclusion, BROWNE continued to analyse himself and his relationships on classic sets, 'FOR EVERYMAN' (1973) and 'LATE FOR THE SKY' (1974). Tragedy struck on 25th March 1976, when his wife, PHYLLIS, committed suicide, something that undoubtedly contributed to the bleak feel of 'THE PRETENDER' (1976), BROWNE's first album to make the US Top 10. The singer forged on nevertheless, releasing a further set, 'RUNNING ON EMPTY' (1978), which featured previously unreleased material and songs recorded on the road, notably a smash hit version of Maurice Williams & the Zodiacs' 'STAY'. His popularity had been steadily increasing as the decade wore on and BROWNE finally topped the American charts in summer 1980 with the 'HOLD OUT' album. The new decade saw BROWNE becoming increasingly politically active and outspoken on such controversial issues as nuclear power and US foreign policy. Inevitably, this was reflected in BROWNE's writing, the 'LAWYERS IN LOVE' set marking a move away from the personal towards the socially conscious. Subsequent politicised sets, 'LIVES IN THE BALANCE' (1986) and 'WORLD IN MOTION' (1989) were relative commercial failures, some sections of BROWNE's fanbase perhaps not impressed with his liberal convictions. With a star cast including DAVID CROSBY, JENNIFER WARNES, DON HENLEY and longtime collaborator, DAVID LINDLEY, BROWNE returned to more personal fare on 1993's 'I'M ALIVE'. While he might not enjoy the critical and commercial plaudits of his 70's heyday, the singer retains a loyal following, even in Britain, where he made a rare appearance, headlining the 1997 Cambridge Folk Festival. With his first album of the new millennium, 'THE NAKED RIDE HOME' (2002), the ageing songwriter was still picking apart the increasingly perilous state of his homeland, a subject which seems to propel his muse more effectively than most. Musically, there were no great surprises, in itself perhaps a relief given the ill-advised experimentation of some of his contemporaries. With no new material in the offing, BROWNE kept his name on the chart listings via a 'VERY BEST OF..' (2004) set and a live round-up 'SOLO ACOUSTIC VOL.1' (2005).

Album rating: JACKSON BROWNE (*8) / FOR EVERYMAN (*7) / LATE FOR THE SKY (*8) / THE PRETENDER (*6) / RUNNING ON EMPTY (*6) / HOLD OUT (*4) / LAWYERS IN LOVE (*5) / LIVES IN THE BALANCE (*6) / WORLD IN MOTION (*4) / I'M ALIVE (*6) / LOOKING EAST (*5) / THE NEXT VOICE YOU HEAR – THE BEST OF JACKSON BROWNE compilation (*7) / THE NAKED RIDE HOME (*5) / THE VERY BEST OF JACKSON BROWNE compilation (*8) / SOLO ACOUSTIC VOL.1 (*6)

JACKSON BROWNE – vocals, guitar, piano / with **CRAIG DOERGE** – keyboards / **LELAND SKLAR** – bass / **RUSS KUNKEL** – drums / **CLARENCE WHITE** – guitar / **DAVID CROSBY** – b.vocals

Asylum Asylum

Mar 72. (7") *(K 13043)* <11004> **DOCTOR MY EYES. / I'M LOOKING INTO YOU** [ ] Feb72 8

Apr 72. (lp) *(SYL 9002)* <5051> **JACKSON BROWNE** [ ] Mar72 53
– Jamaica say you will / A child in these hills / Song for Adam / Doctor my eyes / From Silver Lake / Something fine / Under the falling sky / Looking into you / Rock me on the water / My opening farewell. *(re-iss. Jun76 lp/c; K/K4 53022) (cd-iss. Jan87; K2 53022)*

Aug 72. (7") *(AYM 506)* <11006> **ROCK ME ON THE WATER. / SOMETHING FINE** [ ] Jul72 48

— added **DAVID LINDLEY** – guitar, violin, etc. (ex-KALEIDOSCOPE)

Nov 73. (7") *(AYM 522)* <11023> **REDNECK FRIEND. / THE TIMES YOU'VE COME** [ ] Sep73 85

Dec 73. (lp/c) *(K/K4 43003)* <5067> **FOR EVERYMAN** [ ] Nov73 43
– Take it easy / Our lady of the well / Colors of the sun / I thought I was a child / These days / Redneck friend / The times you've come / Ready or not / Sing my songs to me / For everyman. *(cd-iss. Jan87; K2 43003)*

Apr 74. (7") *(AYM 526)* <11030> **TAKE IT EASY. / READY OR NOT** [ ] [ ]

— retained **LINDLEY** and brought in **JAI WINDING** – keyboards / **DOUG HAYWOOD** – bass, vocals / **LARRY ZACK** – drums

Oct 74. (7") <45227> **WALKING SLOW. / BEFORE THE DELUGE** – [ ]

Nov 74. (7") *(AYM 535)* **WALKING SLOW. / THE LATE SHOW** [ ] –

Dec 74. (lp/c) *(SYL 9018)* <EQ 1017> **LATE FOR THE SKY** [ ] Oct74 14
– Late for the sky / Fountain of sorrow / Farther on / The late show / The road and the sky / For a dancer / Walking slow / Before the deluge. *(re-iss. Jun76 lp/c; K/K4 43007) (cd-iss. Jan87; K2 43007)*

Mar 75. (7") *(K 13022)* <45242> **FOUNTAIN OF SORROW. / THE LATE SHOW** [ ] [ ]

— now with **KUNKEL, SKLAR, DOERGE and LINDLEY** plus **JEFF PORCARO** – drums / **JIM GORDON** – drums / **BOB GLAUB and CHUCK RAINEY** – bass / **ROY BITTAN and BILL PAYNE** – organ / **LUIS F.DAMIAN** – guitar / etc.

Nov 76. (lp/c) *(K/K4 53048)* <7E 1079> **THE PRETENDER** 26 5
– The fuse / Your bright baby blues / Linda Paloma / Here come those tears again / Daddy's tune / The only child / Daddy's tune / Sleep's dark and silent gate / The pretender. *(cd-iss. Jan87)*

Feb 77. (7") *(K 13073)* <45379> **HERE COME THOSE TEARS AGAIN. / LINDA PALOMA** [ ] 23

Jul 77. (7") *(K 13086)* <45399> **THE PRETENDER. / DADDY'S TUNE** [ ] May77 58

Jan 78 (7") *(K 13105)* **YOU LOVE THE THUNDER. / COCAINE** [ ] –

Jan 78. (lp/c) *(K/K4 53070)* <6E 113> **RUNNING ON EMPTY** 28 3
– Running on empty / The road / Rosie / You love the thunder / Cocaine / Shaky town / Love needs a heart / Nothing but time / The load-out / Stay. *(cd-iss. Jan87; K2 53070)*

Mar 78. (7") *(K 13118)* <45460> **RUNNING ON EMPTY. / NOTHING BUT TIME** [ ] Feb78 11

Jun 78. (7") *(K 13128)* **STAY. / ROSIE** 12 –

Sep 78. (7") <45485> **STAY. / THE LOAD-OUT** – 20

Nov 78. (7") <45543> **THE ROAD. / YOU LOVE THE THUNDER** – [ ]

Jul 80. (7") *(K 12466)* <47003> **BOULEVARD. / CALL IT A LOAN** [ ] 19

Jul 80. (lp/c) *(K/K4 52226)* <5E 511> **HOLD OUT** 44 1
– Disco apocalypse / Hold out / That girl could sing / Boulevard / Of missing persons / Call it a loan / Hold on hold out. *(cd-iss. Jan87; K2 52226)*

Oct 80. (7") *(K 12479)* **DISCO APOCALYPSE. / BOULEVARD** [ ] –

Oct 80. (7") <47036> **THAT GIRL COULD SING. / OF MISSING PERSONS** – 22

— next single was from 'Fast Times at Ridgemont High' soundtrack – B-side featured GRAHAM NASH + DAVID LINDLEY

Aug 82. (7") *(K 13185)* <69982> **SOMEBODY'S BABY. / THE CROW ON THE CRADLE** [ ] Jul82 7

— **BROWNE** retained **KUNKEL, DOERGE, HAYWOOD, GLAUB / + RICK VITO** – guitar repl. LINDLEY

Elektra Asylum

Jul 83. (7") *(E 9826)* <69826> **LAWYERS IN LOVE. / SAY IT ISN'T TRUE** [ ] 13
(with free 7") – TENDER IS THE NIGHT. / ON THE DAY

Aug 83. (lp/c) *<(960 268-1/-4)>* **LAWYERS IN LOVE** 37 8
– Lawyers in love / On the day / Cut it away / Downtown / Tender is the night / Knock on any door / For a rocker. *(cd-iss. Jul87; 960 268-2)*

Oct 83. (7") *(E 9791)* <69791> **TENDER IS THE NIGHT. / ON THE DAY** [ ] Sep83 25

Jan 84. (7") <69764> **FOR A ROCKER. / DOWNTOWN** – 45

— Late '85 / early in '86, JACKSON was credited on US Top 20 single 'You're A Friend Of Mine', with CLARENCE CLEMONS (ex-BRUCE SPRINGSTEEN). His girlfriend DARRYL HANNAH guested, backing vocals.

Feb 86. (lp/c)(cd) *(EKT 31/+C)*<(960 457-2)> **LIVES IN THE BALANCE** 36 23
– For America / Soldier of plenty / In the shape of a heart / Candy / Lawless avenues / Lives in the balance / Till I go down / Black and white.

Feb 86. (7"/7"sha-pic-d) *(EKR 35/+P)* <69566> **FOR AMERICA. / TILL I GO DOWN** [ ] 30

Oct 86. (7"/7"sha-pic-d) *(EKR 42/+P)* <69543> **IN THE SHAPE OF A HEART. / VOICE OF AMERICA** 66 Jun86 70
(d7"+=) *(EKR 42)* – Running on empty / The pretender.

Jan 87. (7"/12") *(W 8698/+T)* **EGO MANIAC. / LOVE'S GONNA GET YOU** [ ] –
(above single on 'Warners')

Jun 89. (lp/c)(cd) *(EKT 50/+C)*<(960 832-2)> **WORLD IN MOTION** 39 45
– World in motion / Enough of the night / Chasing you into the light / How long / Anything can happen / When the stone begins to turn / The word justice / My personal revenge / I am a patriot / Lights and virtues. *(cd re-iss. Feb95; same)*

Jun 89. (7") <69292> **WORLD IN MOTION. / PERSONAL REVENGE** – [ ]

Oct 89. (7") <69284> **ANYTHING CAN HAPPEN. / LIGHTS AND VIRTUES** – [ ]

Jan 90. (7") <69262> **CHASING YOU INTO THE NIGHT. / HOW LONG** – [ ]

— now with **DAVID LINDLEY, MARK GOLDENBERG, SCOTT THURSTON, MIKE CAMPBELL, WALLY WACHTEL** – guitars / **KEVIN McCORMICK** – bass / **BENMONT TENCH** – organ / **MAURICIO LEWAK** – drums / **LUIS CONTE + LENNY CASTRO** – percussion / plus guests **DAVID CROSBY / DON HENLEY / JENNIFER WARNES / SWEET PEA ATKINSON + SIR HARRY BOWENS**

Oct 93. (cd/c) *<(7559 61524-2/-4)>* **I'M ALIVE** 35 40
– I'm alive / My problem is you / Everywhere I go / I'll do anything / Miles away / Too many angels / Take this rain / Two of me, two of you / Sky blue and black / All good things.

Nov 93. (7"/c-s) *(EKR 176/+C)* **I'M ALIVE / TOO MANY ANGELS** [ ] [ ]
(cd-s) *(EKR 176CD)* – ('A'side) / Late for the sky / Running on empty / The pretender.

Jun 94. (7"/c-s) *(EKR 184/+C)* **EVERYWHERE I GO. / I'M ALIVE (live)** 67 [ ]
(cd-s+=) *(EKR 184CD2)* – The pretender (live) / Running on empty (live).
(cd-s) *(EKR 184CD1)* – ('A'side) / Take it easy / Doctor my eyes / In the shape of a heart.

Nov 94. (7"/c-s) *(EKR 193/+C)* **SKY BLUE AND BLACK. / TENDER IS THE NIGHT** [ ] [ ]
(12"+=/cd-s+=) *(EKR 193 T/CD)* – Everywhere I go.

— guests on below; BONNIE RAITT / RY COODER / DAVID CROSBY / DAVID LINDLEY / etc.

Feb 96. (cd/c) *<(7559 61867-2/-4)>* **LOOKING EAST** 47 36
– Looking east / The barricades of Heaven / Some bridges / Information wars / I'm the cat / Culver moon / Baby how long / Nino / Alive in the world / It is one.

Jul 96. (c-s/cd-s) *(EKR 221 C/CD)* **I'M THE CAT / BEFORE THE DELUGE** [ ] [ ]

Nov 97. (cd/c) *<(7559 62111-2/-4)>* **THE NEXT VOICE YOU HEAR – THE BEST OF JACKSON BROWNE** (compilation) □ Oct97 47
– Doctor my eyes / These days / Late for the sky / Fountain of sorrow / The pretender / Running on empty / Call it a loan / Somebody's baby / Tender is the night / Lives in the balance / In the shape of a heart / Sky blue and black / Barricades of Heaven / The rebel Jesus / The next voice you hear. *(cd re-iss. Sep05; same)*

Oct 02. (cd) *<(7559 62793-2)>* **THE NAKED RIDE HOME** 53 Sep02 36
– The naked ride home / The night inside me / Casino nation / For taking the trouble / Never stop / Walking town / About my imagination / Sergio Leone / Don't you want me to be there / My stunning mystery companion.

Angel Inside

Oct 05. (cd) *(CDANGE 01)* *<15251>* **SOLO ACOUSTIC VOL.1** (live) □ 55
– The barricades of Heaven / (intro) – These days / (intro) – The birds of St. Marks / (intro) – Fountain of sorrow / Your bright baby blues / For a dancer / Too many angels / (intro) – For everyman / (intro) – Lives in the balance / (intro) – Looking east / (intro) – The pretender / (intro) – Take it easy.

– compilations, etc. –

on 'Asylum' unless mentioned otherwise

Sep 76. (7") *(K 13043)* **DOCTOR MY EYES. / TAKE IT EASY** □ –

Oct 82. (d-c) *(K4 62041)* **THE PRETENDER / LATE FOR THE SKY** □ –

Nov 83. (d-c) *(960 277-4)* **JACKSON BROWNE / RUNNING ON EMPTY** □ –

Oct 04. (d-cd) *Rhino; <(8122 78091-2)>* **THE VERY BEST OF JACKSON BROWNE** 53 46
– Doctor my eyes / Jamaica, say you will / Rock me on the water / Take it easy / These days / Redneck friend / For everyman / For a dancer / Fountain of sorrow / Late for the sky / Before the deluge / Your bright baby blues / The pretender / Here come those tears again / The load-out (live) / Stay (live) / Running on empty (live) / You love the thunder (live) // Boulevard / Somebody's baby (from 'Fast Times At Ridgemont High') / Tender is the night / Lawyers in love / In the shape of a heart / Lawless avenues / Lives in the balance / I am a patriot / Sky blue and black / I'm alive / The barricades of Heaven / Looking east / The naked ride home / The night inside me.

Jeff BUCKLEY

Born: 17 Nov'66, Orange County, California, USA. The offspring of the late, great TIM BUCKLEY, JEFF's chosen career as a musician, singer and songwriter was always destined to bear the heavy burden of his father's unique legacy (note: in this instance JEFF appears out of alphabetical sequence). To his credit, BUCKLEY Jnr. persevered at carving out a distinctive niche in the musical landscape of the early 90's, plugging away on the once legendary Greenwich Village scene of New York. Torch rather than tortured, JEFF utilised his inherited multi-octave vocal chords in ever more impressive and innovative fashion, both in tackling an eclectic variety of cover material (see below) and lavishly dramatic originals. Given his first British break in 1994, via 'LIVE AT THE SIN-E' EP (1992 in America) on the 'Big Cat' label, BUCKLEY was a surprise success at the grunge overload of Reading 1994. Coinciding with his appearance was the release of his major label ('Columbia') debut, 'GRACE', an emotionally raw and occasionally claustrophobic listen that gained almost unanimous praise from UK critics and enjoyed a brief residence in the Top 50. Tracks such as 'SO REAL', 'LAST GOODBYE' and 'DREAM LOVER', suggested a mercurial talent in the ascendant, although the lad had possibly listened to too much LED ZEPPELIN as a youth. Eventually resuming his recording career early in 1997 with TOM VERLAINE (ex-TELEVISION) at the controls, JEFF looked like making a severe dent in the rock mainstream with a follow-up to 'GRACE', although subsequent sessions proved problematic. Fate was to deal a cruel hand when, on the 29th of May '98, JEFF, like his father before him, was cut down in his prime; hardly a typical rock'n'roll death, the young singer was swept away by a powerful current while swimming in Memphis harbor. Exactly a year later, the half-finished project BUCKLEY had been working on at the time of his death was posthumously released as 'SKETCHES FOR MY SWEETHEART THE DRUNK'. A double CD partly curated by his mother, the UK Top 10 set gave an indication as to where JEFF was headed as well as serving as a convincing last word on the career of a man many considered a genius. Well, it wasn't quite the last word, that honour falling to 'MYSTERY WHITE BOY: LIVE '95-'96 (2000), a collection of live performances culled from the DAT recordings of his 'Grace' tour. Like the posthumous live recordings of his father, this record will no doubt be cherished by hardcore fans although its interest to the wider music buying public (outside the UK where it hit the Top 10) might well be more limited.

• **Covers:** JE N'EN CONNAIS PAS LA FIN (Edith Piaf) / THE WAY YOUNG LOVERS DO (Van Morrison) / LILAC WINE (Elkie Brooks) / HALLELUJAH (Leonard Cohen) / KANGA ROO (Big Star) / KICK OUT THE JAMS (MC5) / YARD OF BLONDE GIRLS (Audrey Clark) / BACK IN N.Y.C. (Genesis) / SATISFIED MIND (J.Hayes & J.Rhodes).

Album rating: LIVE AT SIN-E mini (*6) / GRACE (*8) / SKETCHES FOR MY SWEETHEART THE DRUNK (*8) / MYSTERY WHITE BOY (*6) / LIVE A L'OLYMPIA (*5)

JEFF BUCKLEY – vocals, guitars, harmonium, organ, dulcimer / with **MICK GRONDAHL** – bass / **MATT JOHNSON** – drums, percussion / plus MICHAEL TIGHE – guitar / **GARLY LUCAS** – magicalguitarness

Big Cat Columbia

Apr 94. (m-lp/m-cd) *(ABB 61/+CD)* *<77296>* **LIVE AT SIN-E (live)** □ □
– Mojo pin / Eternal life / Je n'en connais pas la fin / The way young lovers do.

Columbia Columbia

Aug 94. (cd/c/lp) *(475928-2/-4/-1)* *<57528>* **GRACE** 42 □
– Mojo pin / Grace / Last goodbye / Lilac wine / So real / Hallelujah / Lover, you should've come over / Corpus christi Carol / Eternal life / Dream brother. *(lp re-iss. Jun99 on 'Simply Vinyl'; SVLP 77) (cd re-expanded Dec04 +=; 475928-5)* – Forget her.

May 95. (cd-s) *<475928>* **LAST GOODBYE / LAST GOODBYE (edit) / KANGA-ROO** – □

May 95. (10"ep/cd-ep) *(662042-0/-2)* **LAST GOODBYE. / LOVER, YOU SHOULD'VE COME OVER (live) / TONGUE (live)** 54 –
(cd-ep) *(662042-5)* – ('A') / Dream brother (live) / So real (live).

1996. (m-cd) *<662155>* **LIVE FROM THE BATACLAN (live)** – □
– Dream brother / The way young lovers do / Je n'en connais pas la fin / Hallelujah.

—— sadly, JEFF was to die in a drowning accident on the 29th of May '97

– posthumous releases, etc. –

May 98. (d-cd/d-c/d-lp) *(488661-2/-4/-1)* *<67228>* **SKETCHES FOR MY SWEETHEART THE DRUNK** 7 64
– The sky is a landfill / Everybody here wants you / Opened once / Nightmares by the sea / Yard of blonde girls / Witches' rave / Morning theft / Vancouver / You & I // Nightmares by the sea / New Year's prayer / Haven't you heard / I know we could be so happy baby (if we wanted to be) / Murder suicide meteor slave / Back in N.Y.C. / Gunshot glitter *[cd-only]*/ Demon John / Your flesh is so nice / Jewel box / Satisfied mind.

May 98. (cd-ep) *(665791-2)* **EVERYBODY HERE WANTS YOU / THOUSAND FOLD / ETERNAL LIFE (road version) / HALLELUJAH (live)** 43 –
(cd-ep) *(665791-5)* – ('A') / Lover, you should've come over (live and acoustic) / Tongue (live).

May 00. (cd/c/lp) *(497972-2/-4/-1)* *<69592>* **MYSTERY WHITE BOY – LIVE '95-'96** 8 □
– Dream brother / I woke up in a strange place / Mojo pin / Lilac wine / What will you say / Last goodbye / Eternal life / Grace / Moodswing whiskey / The man that got away / Kanga-roo / Hallelujah – I know it's over. *(d-cd+=; 497972-9)* – That's all I ask / Lover, you should've come over / So real. *(cd re-iss. Apr02; same)*

Oct 01. (cd) *<(503204-9)>* **LIVE A L'OLYMPIA** (live) □ Jul01 □
– Lover, you should have come over / Dream brother / Eternal life / Kick

JEFF BUCKLEY

out the jams / Lilac wine / Grace / That's all I ask / Kashmir / Je n'en connais pas la fin / Hallelujah / What will you say (with ALIM QASIMOV).

Nov 02. (5xcd-s-box) *(501178-2)* <87077> **THE GRACE EP'S**

Sep 03. (d-cd) *(512257-2)* <89202> **THE COMPLETE LIVE AT SIN-E** (adds extra tracks + monologue)

Aug 04. (d-cd) *(517460-2)* **GRACE** (10th ANNIVERSARY LEGACY EDITION) **44** –
– Grace (tracks) / (extra tracks) / DVD tracks).

Sep 05. (d-cd) *(520265-2)* **GRACE / MYSTERY WHITE BOY**

– others, etc. –

Oct 02. (cd; with GARY LUCAS) *Circus; (FYL 014)* **SONGS TO NO ONE 1991-1992** –

Tim BUCKLEY

Born: 14 Feb'47, Washington DC, USA. Signed to 'Elektra' in 1966 by FRANK ZAPPA manager HERB COHEN, who'd discovered him playing folk clubs around L.A. He recorded an eponymous debut with ZAPPA's musicians backing him up, before moving to New York where he was influenced by Greenwich Village troubadour FRED NEIL (whose 'DOLPHINS', he would later cover on 1973 album 'SEFRONIA'). 1967's 'GOODBYE AND HELLO', wore its influences on its sleeve but won critical plaudits for its cascading vocal versatility and meandering grace. Released a couple of years later, 'HAPPY / SAD's introspective intimations abandoned conventional song structures for abstract folk-jazz workouts. Despite their more experimental nature, the songs retained a tangible warmth of feeling, especially the lovely 'BUZZIN' FLY'. A frenetic period of creativity followed in 1970, with BUCKLEY releasing three albums in the space of a year. 'BLUE AFTERNOON' carried on in much the same vein while he took a further sidestep into improvisation with 'LORCA', culminating in the uncompromising 'STARSAILOR'. In true BUCKLEY fashion, he veered wildly into new territory with the sexually explicit 1972 album 'GREETINGS FROM L.A.', which exhibited an interest in black music. The doomed singer recorded two final rather patchy and self-indulgent albums before he died of an accidental drug overdose on 29th June '75. His poetic awareness and uncompromising efforts to push musical boundaries had taken him down a solitary path that bypassed commercial success and eventually led to disillusionment and death, although he left behind a musical legacy of shimmering beauty. In 1990, 'DREAM LETTER', an album of live material from 1968, was unearthed to critical acclaim and along with various other re-issues, has only served to feed the myth of one of rock's greatest enigmas.

• **Covered:** SALLY GO ROUND THE ROSES (Jaynettes). • **Trivia:** His songs were later recorded by THIS MORTAL COIL (Song To The Siren + I Must Have Been Blind) and BLOOD, SWEAT & TEARS (Morning Glory).

Album rating: TIM BUCKLEY (*7) / GOODBYE & HELLO (*7) / HAPPY SAD (*7) / BLUE AFTERNOON (*7) / LORCA (*5) / STARSAILOR (*7) / GREETINGS FROM L.A. (*7) / SEFRONIA (*4) / LOOK AT THE FOOL (*4) / posthumous: BEST OF TIM BUCKLEY – 1983 US-import lp (*8) / DREAM LETTER – LIVE IN LONDON (*8) / LIVE AT THE TROUBADOUR 1969 (*5) / HONEYMAN (*5) / COPENHAGEN TAPES (*7) / MORNING GLORY – ANTHOLOGY double compilation (*9)

TIM BUCKLEY – vocals, guitar with **LEE UNDERWOOD** – guitar, keyboards / **BILLY MUNDI** – drums / **JIM FIELDER** – bass / **VAN DYKE PARKS** – piano / **JACK NITZSCHE** – string arrangements

Elektra Elektra

Nov 66. (7") <45606> **GRIEF IN MY SOUL. / WINGS** –

Dec 66. (lp; mono/stereo) *(EKL/EKS 4004)* <74004> **TIM BUCKLEY** Oct66
– I can't see you / Wings / Song of the magician / Strange street affair under blue / Valentine melody / Aren't you the girl / Song slowly sung / It happens every time / Song for Jainie / Grief in my soul / She is / Understand your man. *<re-iss. Jul71 & Mar75; same> <cd-iss. 1990's; 61338>*

Jan 67. (7") *(EKSN 45008)* <45612> **AREN'T YOU THE GIRL. / STRANGE STREET AFFAIR UNDER BLUE**

— BUCKLEY retained only UNDERWOOD, recruiting **CARTER C. COLLINS** – congas

Aug 67. (7") <45618> **LADY GIVE ME YOUR HEART. / ONCE UPON A TIME** –

Oct 67. (7") <45623> **MORNING GLORY. / ONCE I WAS** –

Nov 67. (7") *(EKSN 45018)* **MORNING GLORY. / KNIGHT-ERRANT** –

Dec 67. (lp; mono/stereo) *(EKL/EKS 318)* <7318> **GOODBYE AND HELLO** Oct67
– No man can find the war / Carnival song / Pleasant street / Hallucinations / I never asked to be your mountain / Once I was / Phantasmagoria in two / Knight-Errant / Goodbye and hello / Morning glory. *(re-iss. Jul71; K 42070) (re-iss. Mar93 & Sep95 & Mar00 on 'Warners' cd/c; 7559 60896-2/-4)*

Jan 68. (7") *(EKSN 45023)* **ONCE I WAS. / PHANTASMAGORIA IN TWO** –

Mar 68. (7") *(EKSN 45031)* **WINGS. / I CAN'T SEE YOU**

— added **JOHN MILLER** – acoustic & electric bass / **DAVID FREEDMAN** – vibes, percussion

Oct 68. (7") *(EKSN 45041)* **PLEASANT STREET. / CARNIVAL SONG**

Jul 69. (lp) *<(EKS 74045)>* **HAPPY – SAD** **81**
– Strange feeling / Buzzin' fly / Love from room 109 at the Islander (on Pacific Coast Highway) / Dream letter / Gypsy woman / Sing a song for you. *(re-iss. Jul71; K 42072) (cd-iss. Feb93; 7559 74045-2)*

— added **JIMMY MADISON** – drums

Straight Straight

Feb 70. (7") *(S 4799)* **HAPPY TIME. / SO LONELY**

Feb 70. (lp) *<(STS 1060)>* **BLUE AFTERNOON**
– Happy time / Chase the blues away / I must have been blind / The river / So lonely / Cafe / Blue melody / Train. *<US re-iss. Jul71 on 'Warners'; WS 1842> <cd-iss. 1990's; 70356>*

— BUCKLEY retained only UNDERWOOD and COLLINS, recruiting **JOHN BLAKIN** – bass

Elektra Elektra

Oct 70. (lp) *(2410 005)* *<EKS 74074>* **LORCA**
– Lorca / Anonymous proposition / I had a talk with a woman / Driftin' / Nobody walkin'. *<US re-iss. Jul71; K 42053> (re-iss. Mar75; same) <cd-iss. 1990's; 61339>*

— BUCKLEY retained only UNDERWOOD and BALKIN, recruiting co-write **LARRY BECKETT / MAURI BAKET** – timpani / **BUZZ GARDNER** + **BUNK GARDNER** on wind and horns

Straight Straight

Jan 71. (lp) *<(STS 1064)>* **STARSAILOR**
– Come here woman / I woke up / Monterey / Moulin Rouge / Song to the siren / Jungle fire / Starsailor / The healing festival / Down by the borderline. *<US re-iss. Jul71 on 'Warners'; WS 1881> <cd-iss. 1991 on 'Rhino'; 70360>*

— from now on BUCKLEY used loads of session people plus past friends.

Warners Warner

Oct 72. (7") <7623> **MOVE WITH ME. / NIGHTHAWKIN'** –

Oct 72. (lp) *(K 46176)* <BS 2631> **GREETINGS FROM L.A.**
– Move with me / Get on top / Sweet surrender / Nighthawkin' / Devil eyes / Hong Kong bar / Make it right. *<cd-iss. Jul89 on 'Disc Int.'; EN 73506> <(cd-iss. Feb96; 7599 27261-2)>*

Discreet-Warners Discreet-Warner

May 74. (lp) *(K 49201)* <MS 2157> **SEFRONIA**
– Dolphins / Honeyman / Because of you / Peanut man / Martha / Quicksand / I know I'd recognise your face / Stone in love / Sefronia – After Asklepiades, after Kafka / Sefronia – The King's chain / Sally go 'round the roses. *(re-iss. Oct89 on 'Edsel' lp/cd; ED/+CD 277) (cd re-iss. Feb97 on 'Manifesto'; PT 340701) (cd re-iss. Apr01 on 'Manifesto'; MFO 40701CD)*

May 74. (7") <1187> **STONE IN LOVE. / QUICKSAND** –

Jul 74. (7") <1189> **HONEYMAN. / DOLPHINS** –

Nov 74. (lp) *(K 59204)* <DS 2201> **LOOK AT THE FOOL**
– Look at the fool / Bring it on up / Helpless / Freeway blues / Tijuana moon / Ain't it peculiar / Who could deny you? / Mexicali voodoo / Down in the street / Wanda Lu. *(re-iss. Oct89 on 'Edsel' lp/cd; ED/+CD 294) (cd re-iss. Feb97 on 'Manifesto'; PT 340702) (cd re-iss. Apr01 on 'Manifesto'; MFO 40702CD)*

Nov 74. (7") <1311> **WANDA LU. / WHO COULD DENY YOU** –

— TIM died on the 29th of June '75 (see biog.)

TIM BUCKLEY

– compilations, etc. –

Sep 76. (7") *Elektra; (K 12223)* **MORNING GLORY. / ONCE I WAS** ☐ ☐

Jun 90. (d-lp/d-cd) *Demon; (DFIEND/+CD 200) / Enigma; <73507>* **DREAM LETTER – LIVE IN LONDON 1968 (live)** ☐ May90 ☐
– Introduction / Buzzin' fly / Phantasmagoria in two / Morning glory / Dolphins / I've been out walking / The earth is broken / Who do you love / Pleasant Street – You keep me hanging on / Love from room 109 – Strange feelin' / Carnival song – Hi lily, hi lo / Hallucinations / Troubadour / Dream letter – Happy time / Wayfaring stranger – You got me runnin' / Once I was. *(d-cd re-iss. Feb97 on 'Manifesto'; PT 340703) (d-cd re-iss. Apr01 on 'Manifesto'; MFO 40703CD)*

Aug 91. (cd-ep) *Strange Fruit; (SFPSCD 082)* **THE PEEL SESSIONS** ☐ –
– Morning glory / Coming home to you / Sing a song for you / Hallucinations / Troubadour / Once I was.

Mar 94. (cd) *Demon; (EDCD 400) / Rhino; <71663>* **LIVE AT TROUBADOUR 1969 (live)** ☐ ☐
– Strange feelin' / Venice mating call / I don't need it to rain / I had a talk with my woman / Gypsy woman / Blue melody / Chase the blues away / Driftin' / Nobody walkin'. *<(US+re-iss. May97 on 'Manifesto'; PT 340705)> <(re-iss. Apr01 on 'Manifesto'; MFO 40705CD)>*

Aug 94. (cd) *Band Of Joy; (BOJCD 009)* **MORNING GLORY** ☐ –

Sep 95. (cd) *Edsel; (EDCD 450)* **HONEYMAN** (live 27th Nov'73) ☐ –
– Dolphins / Buzzin' fly / Get on top / Devil eyes / Pleasant Street / Sally, go 'round the roses / Stone in love / Honey man / Sweet surrender. *(re-iss. Apr01 on 'Manifesto'; MFO 40704CD)*

Jul 99. (cd) *Strange Fruit; (SFRSCD 084)* **ONCE I WAS** (the BBC sessions) ☐ –
– Dolphins / Honey man / Morning glory / Coming home to you (happy time) / Sing a song for you / Hallucinations – Troubadour / Once I was / I don't need it to rain. *(re-iss. Apr00 on 'Varese Sarabande'; 0302 061056-2) (lp-iss.Apr00 on 'Get Back'; TPM 205)*

Jul 00. (cd) *Pinnacle; (PLRCD 018)* **THE COPENHAGEN TAPES (live 1968)** ☐ –
– I don't need it to rain / Buzzin' fly / Strange feelin' / Gypsy woman.

Apr 01. (d-cd) *Rhino; <(8122 76722-2)>* **MORNING GLORY – THE ANTHOLOGY** ☐ Mar01 ☐
– Wings / She is / Song slowly song / It happens every time / Aren't you the girl / Pleasant street / Hallucinations / No man can find the war / Once I was / Morning glory / Goodbye and hello / Buzzin' fly / Strange feelin' / Sing a song for you / Phantasmagoria in two (live) / I've been out walking (live) / Troubadour (live) / Happy time / Chase the blues away / I must have been blind / The river / So lonely / Blue melody / I had a talk with my woman (live) / Moulin Rouge / Song to the siren / Monterey / Sweet surrender / Hong Kong bar / Make it right / Sally go 'round the roses / Who could deny you / Song to the siren (from the 'Monkees' TV show).

May 01. (cd) *Maestro; <(MFO 40706CD)>* **THE DREAM BELONGS TO ME: RARE AND UNRELEASED RECORDINGS 1968-1973** ☐ ☐

Oct 01. (cd) *Elektra; <(8122 73569-2)>* **TIM BUCKLEY / GOODBYE AND HELLO** ☐ ☐

☐ BUENA VISTA SOCIAL CLUB
(see under ⇒ COODER, Ry)

BUFFALO SPRINGFIELD

Formed: Los Angeles, California, USA ... March '66. In a well-documented incident, STEPHEN STILLS and guitarist RICHIE FUREY were caught in a traffic jam on Sunset Strip, when by pure chance, STILLS recognised the driver of a black hearse, NEIL YOUNG. Along with bass player and fellow Canadian BRUCE PALMER, YOUNG had travelled down to Hollywood to try his luck in the fabled City of Angels. This fated get-together also led to another member being recruited, drummer DEWEY MARTIN. STILLS and YOUNG clashed right from the off, but it was essentially this tension that fuelled the band's creative spark in a JAGGERS/RICHARDS kind of fashion. Taking their name from a type of steamroller, and with the help of the SONNY & CHER management team of CHARLIE GREENE and BRIAN STONE, the band were signed to Atlantic offshoot 'Atco' in a matter of months. With the combined talent of STILLS and YOUNG's soaring harmonies and driving rhythm, the band often came on like a country-fied BEATLES, although their albums are notable for their striking stylistic diversity. The ambitiously eccentric, YOUNG-penned debut single, 'NOWADAYS CLANCY CAN'T EVEN SING', did nothing, while 'BURNED', the 2-minute pop thrill of a follow-up, fared equally badly. But then STILLS struck gold with the famous protest anthem 'FOR WHAT IT'S WORTH', released in the same month as the band's fine eponymous debut album. The song concerned itself with the previous summer's riots whereby a coterie of businessmen had threatened Sunset Strip's nightlife by proposing the building of a business district. Of course the students were none too happy, especially when 300 protesters were arrested. The song was duly adopted by rebels everywhere as a general mascot for fighting the good fight, and its vaguely psychedelic, menacing tone perfectly evoked the feelings of persecution felt by the emerging flower children. Throughout 1967, the band was rocked by internal squabbling with various members coming and going. An album, 'STAMPEDE', was recorded but never quite completed. It later surfaced as a bootleg and one track from it, 'DOWN TO THE WIRE', featuring an impassioned YOUNG vocal, was included on his, 'DECADE' (1976) compilation. YOUNG also missed the bands slot at the Monterey Pop Festival, DAVID CROSBY taking his place. Despite all this, the band completed a follow-up, 'BUFFALO SPRINGFIELD AGAIN', which was issued in late '67. Opinions on the album are mixed with some critics deeming it a classic of its time, others criticising its watered down production. The best moments are YOUNG's JACK NITZSCHE-arranged numbers, 'BROKEN ARROW' and 'EXPECTING TO FLY', the latter possessed a haunting, lysergic quality. STILL's compositions, 'BLUEBIRD' and 'ROCK AND ROLL WOMAN', lack the sophistication of YOUNG's surreal epics but are enjoyable none the less. The tension between YOUNG and STILLS eventually finished the band (DAVID CROSBY once commenting that they used their guitars as weapons, on stage and off!) with a final album, 'LAST TIME AROUND', released after the split. YOUNG contributed the fragile 'I AM A CHILD' and one other song before leaving the band early on during the sessions. YOUNG went on to an erratic, often mercurial career, while STILLS went off to help form CROSBY, STILLS and NASH (re-united with YOUNG in 1970). FURAY meanwhile, went off to join country rockers POCO. Along with The BYRDS and LOVE, BUFFALO SPRINGFIELD were one of the most influential, if somewhat short-lived bands to come out of L.A.

Album rating: BUFFALO SPRINGFIELD (*7) / BUFFALO SPRINGFIELD AGAIN (*9) / LAST TIME AROUND (*6) / THE BEST OF BUFFALO SPRINGFIELD ... RETROSPECTIVE compilation (*8) / EXPECTING TO FLY compilation (*7)

STEPHEN STILLS (b. 3 Jan'45, Dallas, Texas) – lead guitar, vocals / **NEIL YOUNG** (b.12 Nov'45, Toronto, Canada) – lead guitar, vocals / **RICHIE FURAY** (b. 9 May'44, Dayton, Ohio) – vocals, guitar / **BRUCE PALMER** (b. 1944, Liverpool, Canada) – bass; repl. KEN KOBLUN / **DEWEY MARTIN** (b.30 Sep'42, Chesterfield, Canada) – drums (ex-DILLARDS)

Atlantic Atco

Oct 66. (7") *<6428>* **NOWADAYS CLANCY CAN'T EVEN SING. / GO AND SAY GOODBYE** – ☐

Dec 66. (7"w-drawn) *<6452>* **BURNED. / EVERYBODY'S WRONG** – ☐

Jan 67. (lp; stereo/mono) *(588/587 070) <SD+/33-200>* **BUFFALO SPRINGFIELD** ☐ Dec66 ☐
– Don't scold me (*) / Go and say goodbye / Sit down I think I love you / Nowadays Clancy can't even sing / Everybody's wrong / Hot dusty roads / Flying on the ground / Burned / Do I have to come right out and say it?

Leave / Pay the price / Out of my mind. <*re-iss. Feb67 stereo/mono; SD+/33-200-A*> – For what it's worth (repl.track (*) ; hit US No.80> *(re-iss. 1971; K 30028) (cd-iss. Feb93; 7567 90389-2)*

Jan 67. (7") *(584 077)* <*6459*> **FOR WHAT IT'S WORTH. / DO I HAVE TO COME RIGHT OUT AND SAY IT?** [ ] [7]

— on stage **KEN KOBLUN** and **JIM FIELDER**, latter of The MOTHERS, repl. PALMER, although PALMER did return occasionally. / **DOUG HASTINGS** – guitar repl. YOUNG (also DAVID CROSBY guested at Monteray)

— **BOB WEST** – bass & CHARLIE CHIN – banjo deputise for above reshuffles

Jul 67. (7") <*6499*> **BLUEBIRD. / MR. SOUL** [–] [58]

— **STILLS, FURAY, MARTIN** and the returning **YOUNG** recruit **JIM MESSINA** (b. 5 Dec'47, Maywood, Calif.) – bass repl. FIELDER who joined BLOOD SWEAT & TEARS

Oct 67. (7") *(584 145)* <*6519*> **ROCK'N'ROLL WOMAN. / A CHILD'S CLAIM TO FAME** [ ] Sep67 [44]

Jan 68. (lp; stereo/mono) *(588/587 091)* <*SD+/33-226*> **BUFFALO SPRINGFIELD AGAIN** [ ] Nov67 [44]
– Mr. Soul / A child's claim to fame / Everydays / Expecting to fly / Bluebird / Hung upside down / Sad memory / Good time boy / Rock'n'roll woman / Broken arrow. *(re-iss. 1971; K 40014) (cd-iss. Jul88; 790-391-2)*

Feb 68. (7") *(584 165)* <*6545*> **EXPECTING TO FLY. / EVERYDAYS** [ ] Jan68 [98]

Jun 68. (7") *(584 189)* <*6572*> **UNO MUNDO. / MERRY-GO-ROUND** [ ] [ ]

Aug 68. (7") <*6602*> **KIND WOMAN. / SPECIAL CARE** [–] [ ]

— with original line-up they recorded another album, but they had split by May'68. MESSINA who had always been their sound recordist posthumously assembled line-up

Oct 68. (7") <*6615*> **ON THE WAY HOME. / FOUR DAYS GONE** [–] [82]

Dec 68. (lp) *(228 024)* <*SD33-256*> **LAST TIME AROUND** [ ] Aug68 [42]
– On the way home / It's so hard to wait / Pretty girl why / Four days gone / Carefree country day / Special care / The hour of not quite rain / Questions / I am a child / Merry-go-round / Uno mundo / Kind woman. *(re-iss. 1971; K 40077) (cd-iss. Mar94 on 'Atco'; 7567 90393-2)*

— After their split, NEIL YOUNG went solo and joined STEPHEN STILLS in CROSBY, STILLS NASH & YOUNG. FURAY formed POCO adding later MESSINA. DEWEY MARTIN tried in vain to use BUFFALO SPRINGFIELD name.

– compilations, etc. –

on 'Atlantic' UK / 'Atco' US; unless otherwise mentioned

Mar 69. (lp) *(228 012)* <*SD33-283*> **RETROSPECTIVE – THE BEST OF BUFFALO SPRINGFIELD** [ ] Feb69 [42]
– For what it's worth / Mr. Soul / Sit down I think I love you / Kind woman / Bluebird / On the way home / Nowadays Clancy can't even sing / Broken arrow / Rock'n'roll woman / I am a child / Go and say goodbye / Expecting to fly. *(re-iss. 1971; K 40071) (cd-iss. Jul88; 790 417-2)*

Oct 69. (7") *Atco; (226 006)* **PRETTY GIRL WHY / QUESTIONS** [ ] [–]

Oct 70. (lp) *(K 2462 012)* **EXPECTING TO FLY** [ ] [–]

Oct 72. (7"ep) *(K 10237)* **BLUEBIRD / MR. SOUL. / ROCK'N'ROLL WOMAN / EXPECTING TO FLY** [ ] [–]

Dec 73. (d-lp) *(K 70001)* <*SD2 806*> **BUFFALO SPRINGFIELD** [ ] [ ]

Jul 01. (4xcd-box) *Rhino; <(8122 74324-2)>* **BOX SET** [ ] [ ]

— some BUFFALO SPRINGFIELD live tracks appeared on NEIL YOUNG's compilation lp 'JOURNEY THROUGH THE PAST', and two on his 'DECADE' triple in '77.

BULLET FOR MY VALENTINE

Formed: Bridgend, Wales ... 2003 originally as JEFF KILLED JOHN by MATTHEW TUCK, MICHAEL PADGET, MICHAEL 'Moose' THOMAS and NIK CRADLE (the latter soon replaced by JASON JAMES). With the Welsh valleys now ringing to the sound of death growls (step up LOSTPROPHETS and FUNERAL FOR A FRIEND) rather than male voice choirs, the romantically monikered BULLET FOR MY VALENTINE became the latest British band to co-opt the quintessentially American, metalcore ear-bashing plied by the likes of TAKING BACK SUNDAY and THRICE. In November 2004, the BULLET boyos opened their sonic account via an eponymous EP, the lead track of which, 'HAND OF BLOOD', served as the title of the US version (released the following August). Over the course of the following year, they grazed the UK Top 40 courtesy of singles, '4 WORDS (TO CHOKE UPON)', 'SUFFOCATING UNDER WORDS OF SORROW (WHAT CAN I DO)' and 'ALL THESE THINGS I HATE (REVOLVE AROUND YOU)'. 'THE POISON' (2005), meanwhile, just missed out on a UK Top 20 place, persuading Kerrang! to name them Best British Newcomer at their annual awards.

Album rating: THE POISON (*7)

MATTHEW TUCK – vocals, guitar / **MICHAEL PADGET** – guitar, vocals / **JASON JAMES** – bass, vocals; repl. NIK CRADLE / **MICHAEL 'Moose' THOMAS** – drums

Visible Noise Trustkill

Nov 04. (cd-ep) *(TORMENT 45CD)* **BULLET FOR MY VALENTINE** [ ] [–]
– Hand of blood / Cries in vain / Curses / No control / Just another star / Hand of blood (video). <*US-iss.Aug05 as 'HAND OF BLOOD' on 'Trustkill'+=; <TKL 67-2>* – 4 words (to choke upon).

Mar 05. (etched-7") *(TORMENT 52)* **4 WORDS (TO CHOKE UPON)** [40] [–]
(cd-s+=) *(TORMENT 51CD)* – Curses (unedited).

Sep 05. (etched-7") *(TORMENT 60)* **SUFFOCATING UNDER THE WORDS OF SORROW (WHAT CAN I DO)** [37] [–]
(7"+=) *(TORMENT 59)* – Room 409 (live).
(cd-s+=) *(TORMENT 58CD)* – Spit you out (live).

Oct 05. (cd/lp) *(TORMENT 50 CD/LP)* <*TKL 74-2*> **THE POISON** [21] Feb06 [ ]
– Intro / Her voice resides / 4 words (to choke upon) / Tears don't fall / Suffocating under words of sorrow (what can I do) / Hit the floor / All these things I hate (revolve around me) / Room 409 / The poison / 10 years today / Cries in vain / Spit you out / The end.

Feb 06. (etched-7") *(TORMENT 65)* **ALL THESE THINGS I HATE (REVOLVE AROUND ME)** [29] [–]
(cd-s+=) *(TORMENT 64CD)* – My fist, your mouth, her scars.
(cd-s+=) *(TORMENT 63CD)* – Seven days.

□ Eric BURDON (see under ⇒ ANIMALS)

□ Tim BURGESS (see under ⇒ CHARLATANS)

BUSH

Formed: Kilburn, London, England ... 1992 as FUTURE PRIMITIVE by the seasoned Brit team of singer and lyricist GAVIN ROSSDALE (of mixed Russian Jewish/Scottish parentage), guitarist NIGEL PULSFORD, bassist DAVE PARSONS (from TRANSVISION VAMP!) and drummer ROBIN GOODRIDGE. Virtually ignored outright in the capital, BUSH's luck changed after American label 'Trauma' got hold of a demo, their signature obviously worth its weight in gold to US A&R men looking for the British answer to the recently defunct grungesters, NIRVANA. They relocated to the States early '95, a highlight at this point playing New York's CBGB's. The following year, they issued their debut, 'SIXTEEN STONE', an album that garnered critical acclaim from more rockcentric quarters and massive US sales from all quarters. Finally hitting the Top 5, the set contained a handful of impressive NIRVANA-esque numbers, among them 'EVERYTHING ZEN', 'COMEDOWN' and 'TESTOSTERONE', tracks that were to break the band in the UK a year later. By the end of 1996, BUSH were burning a proverbial trail with their chart-topping follow-up, 'RAZORBLADE SUITCASE', an album that made the UK Top 5 early the next year. A string of British hit singles completed their rise to transatlantic fame, the Top 10 'SWALLOWED' being one of their more memorable efforts. Stepping a little into the world of electronica, BUSH delivered a remixed set, 'DECONSTRUCTED' (1997), although this recording (complete with help from TRICKY and GOLDIE) was only for the initiated. Towards the end of the millennium, BUSH were back to offer up their third album proper, 'THE SCIENCE OF THINGS' (1999), a Top 30 breaker in Britain and even bigger in the States. Two years on, ROSSDALE and Co were back to basics with album No.4, 'GOLDEN STATE' (2001), a rather disappointing set that failed to win any new fans. With BUSH subsequently put out to pasture, media attention focused on ROSSDALE's marriage – on September 14th 2002 – to (NO DOUBT's) GWEN STEFANI; the celebrity couple recently (May 2006) announced the birth of a son. Musically, he'd been keeping busy via new alt-rock outfit, INSTITUTE (together with CHRIS TRAYNOR, CACHE TOLMAN and CHARLIE WALKER); while lead single 'BULLET-PROOF SKIN' was featured in the movie, 'Stealth', the album 'DISTORT YOURSELF' (2005) fell victim to changing music fashions, languishing just inside the US Top 100. ROSSDALE's acting career looked more promising, with a role as Balthazar in the Keanu Reeves thriller, 'Constantine'.

• **Covers:** REVOLUTION BLUES (Neil Young).

Album rating: SIXTEEN STONE (*7) / RAZORBLADE SUITCASE (*6) / DECONSTRUCTED (*5) / THE SCIENCE OF THINGS (*6) / GOLDEN STATE (*5) / Institute: DISTORT YOURSELF (*5)

GAVIN ROSSDALE (b.30 Oct'65, London) – vocals, guitar (ex-MIDNIGHT) / **NIGEL PULSFORD** (b.11 Apr'65, Newport, Wales) – guitar (ex-KING BLANK) / **DAVE PARSONS** (b. 2 Jul'66, Uxbridge, England) – bass (ex-TRANSVISION VAMP) / **ROBIN GOODRIDGE** (b.10 Sep'66, Crawley, England) – drums (ex-BEAUTIFUL PEOPLE)

Atlantic Trauma

Apr 95. (c-s) *(A 8196C)* **EVERYTHING ZEN / BUD** [ ] [-]
(12"+=/cd-s+=) *(A 8196 T/CD)* – Monkey.

May 95. (cd/c/lp) *(<6544-92531-2/-4/-1>)* **SIXTEEN STONE** [ ] [4]
– Everything zen / Swim / Bomb / Little things / Comedown / Body / Machinehead / Testosterone / Monkey / Glycerine / Alien / X-girlfriend. *(re-iss. Jun96 on 'Interscope' cd/c; IND/INC 92531)* – w/ bonus cd; hit UK 42) *(cd re-iss. Nov01 on 'S.P.V.'; 0767287-2)*

Jul 95. (5"ltd/c-s) *(A 8160/+C)* **LITTLE THINGS. / X-GIRLFRIEND** [ ] [-]
(cd-s+=) *(A 8160CD)* – Swim.

Aug 95. (c-s) <98134> **COMEDOWN / TESTOSTERONE** [-] [30]

Dec 95. (c-s) *(A 8152C)* **COMEDOWN / REVOLUTION BLUES** [ ] [-]
(cd-s+=) *(A 8152CD)* – Testosterone.

Jan 96. (c-s) <98088> **GLYCERINE / SOLOMON'S BONES** [-] [28]

Interscope Trauma

Apr 96. (c-s) <98079> **MACHINEHEAD / ALIEN (live)** [-] [43]

May 96. (10"ep) *(INV 95505)* **MACHINEHEAD. / COMEDOWN / SOLOMON'S BONES** [48] [-]
(cd-s) *(IND 95505)* – (first & third track) / Bud.
(cd-s) *(INDX 95505)* – (first & second track) / X-girlfriend.

Jan 97. (cd/c) *(<IND/INC 90091>)* **RAZORBLADE SUITCASE** [4] Nov96 [1]
– Personal Holloway / Greedy fly / Swallowed / Insect kin / Cold contagious / Tendency to start fires / Mouth / Straight no chaser / History / Synapse / Communicator / Bonedriven / Distant voices. *(d-lp-iss.Sep99 on 'Simply Vinyl'; SVLP 120) (cd re-iss. Nov01 on 'S.P.V.'; 0767286-2)*

Feb 97. (c-ep/cd-ep) *(INC/IND 95528)* **SWALLOWED / BROKEN TV. / GLYCERINE / IN A LONELY PLACE** [7] [-]
(cd-ep) *(INDX 95528)* – ('A'side) / ('A'-Toasted both sides) / Insect kin (live) / Cold contagious (16oz demo).

May 97. (c-s) *(INC 95536)* **GREEDY FLY / GREEDY FLY (album version)** [22] [-]
(cd-s+=) *(IND 95536)* – ('A'-16 oz demo).
(cd-s) *(INDX 95536)* – ('A'side) / Old / Insect kin (live) / Personal Holloway (live).

Nov 97. (c-s) *(INC 95553)* **BONEDRIVEN / SYNAPSE (Philip Steir remix)** [49] [-]
(cd-s+=) *(IND 95553)* – Personal Holloway (Soundclash Republic remix) / Straight no chaser.
(cd-s) *(INDX 95553)* – ('A'version) / ('A'-Beat Me Clever mix) / Everything zen (Derek DeLarge mix) / ('A'-Video cd-rom).

Nov 97. (cd) *(<IND 90161>)* **DECONSTRUCTED** [ ] [36]
– Everything zen (The lhasa fever mix) / Mouth (the stingray mix) / Swallowed (toasted both sides please – Goldie remix) / Synapse (my ghost in the bush of life remix) / History (Dub Pistols mix) / Personal Holloway (Fablo Paras Soundclash Republic mix) / Bonedriven (Mekon beat me clever mix) / Insect kin (Jack Dangers drum and bees mix) / Comedown (Lunatic calm mix) / Everything zen (Derek DeLarge mix) / In a lonely place (Tricky mix). *(re-iss. Nov01 on 'S.P.V.'; 0767284-2)*

Oct 99. (cd/c/lp) *<(490483-2/-4/-1)>* **THE SCIENCE OF THINGS** [28] [11]
– Warm machine / Jesus online / The chemicals between us / English fire / Spacetravel / 40 miles from the sun / Prizefighter / The disease of the dancing cats / Altered states / Dead meat / Letting the cables sleep / Mindchanger. *(cd re-iss. Nov01 on 'S.P.V.'; 0767285-2)*

Nov 99. (7"clear) *(497222-7)* *<album cut>* **THE CHEMICALS BETWEEN US. / HOMEBODY** [46] Sep99 [67]
(cd-s+=) *(497223-2)* – Letting the cables sleep (original demo).
(cd-s) *(497222-2)* – ('A'side) / ('A'-Supercollider remix) / ('A'-video).

Mar 00. (cd-s) *(497275-2)* **WARM MACHINE / SWALLOWED (live) / IN A LONELY PLACE (Tricky mix)** [45] [ ]
(cd-s) *(497276-2)* – ('A'side) / Greedy fly (live) / The chemicals between us (original demo).

May 00. (7") *(497336-7)* **LETTING THE CABLES SLEEP. / MOUTH (Stingray remix)** [51] [ ]
(cd-s+=) *(497336-2)* – ('A'-Apocalyptic version).
(cd-s) *(497335-2)* – ('A'side) / ('A'-Nightmares On Wax remix) / ('A'-original demo).

Atlantic Atlantic

Oct 01. (cd/c) *<(7567 83488-2/-4)>* **GOLDEN STATE** [53] [22]
– Solutions / Headful of ghosts / The people that we love / Superman / Fugitive / Hurricane / Inflatable / Reasons / Land of the living / My engine is with you / Out of this world / Float.

Nov 01. (c-s) *(AT 0116C)* **THE PEOPLE THAT WE LOVE / AMERICAN EYE** [ ] [-]
(cd-s+=) *(AT 0116CD)* – ('A'-Golden dub mix).

Feb 02. (7") *(AT 0129)* **INFLATABLE. / HEADFUL OF GHOSTS (live)** [ ] [-]

INSTITUTE

GAVIN ROSSDALE – vocals / **CHRIS TRAYNOR** – guitar (ex-ORANGE 9mm, ex-HELMET) / **CACHE TOLMAN** – bass (ex-CIV, ex-RIVAL SCHOOLS) / **CHARLIE WALKER** – drums (ex-SPLIT LIP, CHAMBERLAIN)

Mercury Interscope

Sep 05. (cd) *(9884903)* <4968> **DISTORT YOURSELF** [ ] [81]
– Bullet-proof skin / When animals attack / Come on over / Information age / Wasteland / Boom box / Seventh wave / The heat of your love / Ambulances / Secrets and lies / Mountains / Save the robots.

Sep 05. (7"clear) *(9885135)* **BULLET-PROOF SKIN. / ART OF WALKING** [ ] [-]

Kate BUSH

Born: CATHERINE BUSH, 30 Jul'58. Bexleyheath, Kent, England. In 1974, this child prodigy formed her own K.T.BUSH band with brother PADDY and future boyfriend DEL PALMER, having already stockpiled a sizeable number of songs. By summer '76, with help from DAVE GILMOUR (Pink Floyd), she had secured a development contract with EMI, subsequently setting to work on the songs which would make up her debut set. Things couldn't have got off to a better start in early '78 when the classic 'WUTHERING HEIGHTS' warbled its way to the top of the charts. The single announced the arrival of a distictively original talent, a swooping, soaring epic of a track which fully exhibited BUSH's stunning four-octave vocal range. The debut album, 'THE KICK INSIDE', followed into the Top 3 shortly after, the singer's ambitious, idiosyncratic brand of art-rock set to probing, intelligent and often fantastical lyrics. A second track, 'THE MAN WITH THE CHILD IN HIS EYES', also made the Top 10, while a hastily recorded follow-up album, 'LIONHEART' was released later that year. BUSH subsequently undertook her first and only tour, the experience proving so trying that she'd later keep her promotional work to a minimum. This freed her up to concentrate on lavish videos, characterised by her inspired eccentricity and imaginative choreography. Fuelled by the Top 5 success of the sassy 'BABOOSHKA', a third set, 'NEVER FOR EVER' (1980) became her first No.1 album, the record spawning further hits in 'ARMY DREAMERS' and the bizarre 'BREATHING'. The latter track's overtly experimental nature was carried over into her next album, 'THE DREAMING' (1982). Her first self-produced effort, the record's intricate inaccessiblity and conceptual weirdness tested even her most devoted fans. Although it made the UK Top 3, the record sold relatively poorly and BUSH retreated to her newly built, hi-tech home studio to create as near as she could get to a perfect album. She eventually emerged in summer '85 with the hypnotic grace of 'RUNNING UP THAT HILL', its foghorn-like synth refrain and mature, sensual vocals taking BUSH back into the Top 5 in the first time in five years and even giving her a rare US hit. The accompanying album, 'HOUNDS OF LOVE' (1985), was raved over by a wide cross section of critics, BUSH at her creative peak on a record which saw the singer rein in her more wayward tendencies and achieve a perfect balance of melody, drama and mystery. The album spawned a further two Top 20 hits in 'CLOUDBUSTING' and the title track while late in '86, she teamed up with hero PETER GABRIEL on the Top 10 hit, 'DON'T GIVE UP'. After this critical and commercial rebirth, BUSH returned in 1989 with 'THE SENSUAL WORLD', a markedly more reflective affair, its title track inspired by the Molly Bloom character in James Joyce's classic novel, 'Ulysses'. The record narrowly missed the No.1 spot and consolidated BUSH's position as the elder stateswoman of fiercely original femme-pop. Though her most recent album, 'THE RED SHOES' received a mixed critical reception, the singer remains a towering influence on today's more erm, wayward songstresses, step forward TORI AMOS. In 2005, a young retro-punk outfit, the FUTUREHEADS, took the UK charts by storm with their re-vamped version of 'HOUNDS OF LOVE'. The timing was impeccable. KATE's recent work rate may make DONALD FAGEN look like NEIL YOUNG, but her open ended schedules certainly create anticipation: when 'AERIAL' finally arrived in late 2005, the press – not least Mojo who awarded it "instant classic" status – hailed the album as a pop landmark, a flawed double-set in the great British tradition of flawed double sets. Split roughly into meditations on inner and outer worlds, it even came with prog-ish (small "p") theme titles for each disc: 'A SEA OF HONEY' and 'A SKY OF HONEY' respectively. Lead track/single 'KING OF THE MOUNTAIN' was classic BUSH but still one of the most unlikely Top 5 hits (the album itself went Top 3), a synth-percolating, back-loaded ELVIS reverie projecting the rocker's awol spirit into snowy, Citizen Kane-referencing seclusion. Now a mother on the cusp of 50, her take on domesticity was never going to be humdrum: 'BERTIE' serenaded her son medieval style; 'MRS. BARTOLOZZI' reimagined the minutia of clothes washing as sensuous rite. 'A SEA OF HONEY' was even riper with possibility, invoking Wordsworthian communion and pastoral flight against digitised birdsong and acoustic jazz.

• **Covered:** ROCKET MAN + CANDLE IN THE WIND (Elton John) / I'M STILL WAITING (Diana Ross) / WHEN YOU WISH UPON A STAR (Disney soundtrack) / SEXUAL HEALING (Marvin Gaye). • **Trivia:** Her first major tour came in April'79, and although it was mildly successful, she only once appeared live again at 'The Secret Policeman's Third Ball' in 1987. Actor Donald Sutherland appeared in her video for 'CLOUDBUSTING' 45.

Album rating: THE KICK INSIDE (*7) / LIONHEART (*5) / NEVER FOR EVER (*6) / THE DREAMING (*6) / HOUNDS OF LOVE (*7) / THE WHOLE STORY compilation (*9) / THE SENSUAL WORLD (*7) / THE RED SHOES (*5) / AERIAL (*7)

KATE BUSH – vocals, keyboards with **PADDY BUSH** – mandolin, etc. / **DEL PALMER** – bass / **IAN BAIRNSON** – guitar / **DUNCAN MACKAY** – keyboards / **ANDREW POWELL** – keyboards / **STUART ELLIOTT** – drums / **DAVID PATON** – bass / **MORRIS PERT** – percussion / **BRIAN BATH** – guitar / + others (her backing musicians changed from time to time, see 2nd edition)

E.M.I. | EMI America

Jan 78. (7") *(EMI 2719)* <8003> **WUTHERING HEIGHTS. / KITE** 1 |

Feb 78. (lp/c) *(EMC/TC-EMC 3223)* <11761> **THE KICK INSIDE** 3 |
– Moving / The saxophone song / Strange phenomena / Kite / The man with the child in his eyes / Wuthering heights / James and the cold gun / Feel it / Oh to be in love / L'amour looks something like you / Them heavy people / Room for the life / The kick inside. *(pic-lp 1979; EMPC 3223) (cd-iss. Jan84; CDP 746012-2) (re-iss. Oct88 on 'Fame' lp/c/cd; FA/TCFA/CDFA 3207) (re-iss. Sep94 cd/c; CD/TC EMS 1522)*

May 78. (7") *(EMI 2806)* <8006> **THE MAN WITH THE CHILD IN HIS EYES. / MOVING** 6 | Feb79 85

Nov 78. (7") *(EMI 2887)* **HAMMER HORROR. / COFFEE HOMEGROUND** 44 | –

Nov 78. (lp/c) *(EMA/TC-EMA 787)* <1978> **LIONHEART** 6 |
– Symphony in blue / In search of Peter Pan (incl. When you wish upon a star) / Wow / Don't push your foot on the heartbrake / Oh England my lionheart / Fullhouse / In the warm room / Hammer horror / Kashka from Baghdad / Coffee homeground / Hammer horror. *(re-iss. Apr84 on 'Fame' lp/c; FA 41-3094-1/-4) (re-iss. Oct88 on 'Fame' lp/c/cd; FA/TCFA/CDFA 3094) (re-iss. Sep94 cd/c; CD/TC EMS 1523)*

Mar 79. (7") *(EMI 2911)* **WOW. / FULLHOUSE** 14 | –

Sep 79. (d7"ep) *(MIEP 2991)* **KATE BUSH ON STAGE (live)** 10 | –
– Them heavy people / Don't put you foot on the heartbrake / James and the cold gun / L'amour looks something like you.

Apr 80. (7") *(EMI 5058)* **BREATHING. / THE EMPTY BULLRING** 16 | –

Jun 80. (7") *(EMI 5085)* **BABOOSHKA. / RAN TAN WALTZ** 5 | –

Sep 80. (lp/c) *(EMA/TC-EMA 794)* **NEVER FOR EVER** 1 |
– Babooshka / Delius / Blow away / All we ever look for / Egypt / The wedding list / Violin / The infant kiss / Night scented stock / Army dreamers / Breathing. *(re-iss. Sep82 lp/c; ATAK/TCATAK 91) (cd-iss. Mar87; CDP 746360-2) (cd-iss. Oct90; CDP 746360-2)*

Sep 80. (7"m) *(EMI 5106)* **ARMY DREAMERS. / DELIUS / PASSING THROUGH THE AIR** 16 | –

Nov 80. (7") *(EMI 5121)* **DECEMBER WILL BE MAGIC AGAIN. / WARM AND SOOTHING** 29 | –

Jul 81. (7") *(EMI 5201)* **SAT IN YOUR LAP. / LORD OF THE REEDY RIVER** 11 | –

Jul 82. (7") *(EMI 5296)* **THE DREAMING. / DREAMTIME (instrumental)** 48 | –

Sep 82. (lp/c) *(EMC/TC-EMC 3419)* <17084> **THE DREAMING** 3 |
– Sat in your lap / There goes a tenner / Pull out the pin / Suspended in Gaffa / Leave it open / The dreaming / Night of the swallow Houdini / Get out of my house / All the love. *(cd-iss. Jan87; CDP 746361-2) (re-iss. Mar91 lp/c; ATAK/TCATAK 45) (cd-iss. Mar91; CDP 746361-2)*

Nov 82. (7") *(EMI 5350)* **THERE GOES A TENNER. / NE T'ENFUIS PAS** |

Aug 85. (7") *(KB 1)* <8285> **RUNNING UP THAT HILL. / UNDER THE IVY** 3 | 30
(ext.12"+=) *(12KB 1)* – ('A'instrumental).

Sep 85. (lp/c)(cd) *(KAB/TC 1)(CDP 746164-2)* <17171> **HOUNDS OF LOVE** 1 | 30
– Running up that hill / Hounds of love / The big sky / Mother stands for comfort / Cloudbusting / And dream of sheep / Under ice / Waking the witch / Watching you without me / Jig of life / Hello Earth / The morning fog. *(cd+=)* – Cloudbusting (extended). *(re-iss. Oct90 lp/c; ATAK/TCATAK 157) (<cd-iss. Sep90; CDP 746164-2>) (cd re-iss. Jun97 +=; CDCNTAV 3)* (cd re-iss. Jan00 +=; *525239-2)* – Big sky (meteorogical mix) / Running up that hill (12" mix) / Be kind to my mistakes / Under the ivy / Burning bridge / My lagan love. *(lp re-iss. Jan01 on 'Simply Vinyl'; SVLP 290)*

Oct 85. (7") *(KB 2)* **CLOUDBUSTING. / BURNING BRIDGES** 20 | –
('A'-Organon mix-12"+=) *(12KB 2)* – My Lagan Love.

Feb 86. (7") *(KB 3)* **HOUNDS OF LOVE. / HANDSOME CABIN BOY** 18 | –
(12"+=) *(12KB 3)* – The alternative hounds of love / Jig of life.

May 86. (7"/7"pic-d) *(KB/+P 4)* **THE BIG SKY. / NOT THIS TIME** 37 | –
(12"+=) *(12KB 4)* – The morning fog.

— In Oct 86, she did a duet **DON'T GIVE UP** with **PETER GABRIEL** which hit for 'Geffen' UK No.9 / US No.72.

Nov 86. (7") *(KB 5)* **EXPERIMENT IV. / WUTHERING HEIGHTS (vocal)** [23] [–]
(12"+=) *(12KB 5)* – December will be magic again.

Nov 86. (lp/c)(cd) *(KBTV/TCKBTV 1)(CDP 746414-2) <17242>* **THE WHOLE STORY** (compilation) [1] [76]
– Wuthering heights / Cloudbusting / The man with the child in his eyes / Breathing / Wow / Hounds of love / Running up that hill / Army dreamers / Sat in your lap / Experiment IV / The dreaming / Babooshka. *(lp re-iss. Nov00 on 'Simply Vinyl'; SVLP 268)*

E.M.I. Columbia

Sep 89. (7"/c-s) *(EM/TCEM 102)* **THE SENSUAL WORLD. / WALK STRAIGHT DOWN THE MIDDLE** [12] [–]
(ext.12"+=/ext.cd-s+=) *(12/CD EM 102)* – ('A'instrumental).

Oct 89. (lp/c)(cd) *(EMD/TCEMD/CDEMD 1010) <44164>* **THE SENSUAL WORLD** [2] [43]
– The sensual world / Love and anger / The fog / Reaching out / Heads we're dancing / Deeper understanding / Between a man and a woman / Never be mine / Rocket's tail / This woman's work. *(cd+=)* – Walk straight down the middle.

Nov 89. (7"/7"pic-d) *(EM/TCEM 119)* **THIS WOMAN'S WORK. / BE KIND TO MY MISTAKES** [25] [–]
(12"+=/cd-s+=) *(12/CD EM 119)* – ('A'version) / I'm still waiting.

Mar 90. (7"/c-s) *(EM/TCEM 134)* **LOVE AND ANGER. / KEN** [38] [–]
(12"+=/cd-s+=) *(12/CD EM 134)* – The confrontation / Just one last look around the house before we go.

Apr 90. (7") *<73092>* **LOVE AND ANGER. / WALK STRAIGHT DOWN THE MIDDLE** [–] [ ]
(c-s+=) *<73098>* – This woman's work.

Nov 91. (7"/c-s) *(TRIBO/+C 2)* **ROCKET MAN (I THINK IT'S GOING TO BE A LONG LONG TIME). / CANDLE IN THE WIND** [12] [ ]
(12"+=/cd-s+=) *(TRIBOT 2)* – ('B'instrumental).
(above single on 'Mercury')

— with **STUART ELLIOTT** – drums / **JOHN GIBLIN** – bass / **DANNY McINTOSH** – guitar / **GARY BROOKER** – hammond organ / **PADDY BUSH** + **COLIN LLOYD TUCKER** – vocals / **PAUL SPONG** + **STEVE SLOWER** – trumpet / **NEIL SIDWELL** – trombone / **NIGEL HITCHCOCK** – sax / **NIGEL KENNEDY** – violin / + guests **PRINCE** + **ERIC CLAPTON**

Sep 93. (7"/c-s) *(EM/TCEM 280)* **RUBBERBAND GIRL. / BIG STRIPEY LIE** [12] [–]
(12"pic-d+=/cd-s+=) *(12/CD EM 280)* – ('A'extended remix).

Nov 93. (cd/c/lp) *(CD/TC+/EMD 1047) <53737>* **THE RED SHOES** [2] [28]
– Rubberband girl / And so is love / Eat the music / Moments of pleasure / The song of Solomon / Lily / The red shoes / Top of the city / Constellation of the heart / Big stripey lie / Why should I love you? / You're the one.

Nov 93. (7"/c-s) *(EM/TCEM 297)* **MOMENTS OF PLEASURE. / SHOW A LITTLE DEVOTION** [26] [ ]
(12") *(12EM 297)* – ('A') / ('A'instrumental) / Home for Christmas.
(cd-s) *(CDEM 297)* – ('A') / December will be magic again / Experiment IV.

Dec 93. (c-s) *<77280>* **RUBBERBAND GIRL / THIS WOMAN'S WORK** [–] [88]

Apr 94. (7"/c-s) *(EMS/TCEM 316)* **THE RED SHOES. / YOU WANT ALCHEMY** [21] [–]
(cd-s+=) *(CDEM 316)* – Cloudbusting (video) / This woman's work.
(cd-s) *(CDEMX 316)* – ('A'-Shoedance mix) / The big sky / Running up that hill.

— In Jul 94, KATE partnered LARRY ADLER on 'Mercury' single 'THE MAN I LOVE'; *MER/+C/CD 408)*. It hit UK No.27, and was from his tribute album 'The Glory Of Gershwin'.

Nov 94. (7"pic-d/c-s) *(EMS/TCEMS 355)* **AND SO IS LOVE. / RUBBERBAND GIRL (U.S. mix)** [26] [–]
(cd-s+=) *(CDEM 355)* – Eat the music (U.S. mix).

Oct 05. (7"pic-d/cd-s) *(EM/CDEM 674)* **KING OF THE MOUNTAIN. / SEXUAL HEALING** [4] [–]

Nov 05. (d-cd/d-lp) *(343960-2/-1) <97772>* **AERIAL** [3] [48]
– A Sea Of Honey:- King of the mountain / Pi / Bertie / Mrs. Bartolozzi / How to be invisible / Joanni / A coral room // A Sky Of Honey:- Prelude / Prologue / An architect's dream / The painter's link / Sunset / Aerial tal / Somewhere in between / Nocturn / Aerial.

– compilations, others, etc. –

Jun 83. (m-lp) *EMI America; <19004>* **KATE BUSH** [–] [ ]

Oct 83. (7") *Old Gold; (OG 9380)* **WUTHERING HEIGHTS. / THE MAN WITH THE CHILD IN HIS EYES** [ ] [–]

Jan 84. (7"x13) *E.M.I.; (KBS 1)* **THE SINGLES FILE** [ ] [–]
– (all previous singles +) NE T'ENFUIS PAS. / UN BAISER D'ENFANT

Oct 90. (9xcd-box/8xc-box/8xlp-box) *(KBBX/+CD/C 1)* **THIS WOMAN'S WORK – ANTHOLOGY 1978-1990** [ ] [–]

Oct 92. (12"-box+cd) *(KB 2)* **NEVER FOREVER** [ ] [–]
(above issued w / free booklet & T-shirt)

Aug 94. (cd-vid) *E.M.I.; (SAV 4913063)* **LIVE AT HAMMERSMITH ODEON (live)** [ ] [–]
– (a complete history of all her songs, re-issuing albums)

Mar 03. (d-cd) *E.M.I.; (582364-2)* **THE DREAMING / LIONHEART** [ ] [–]

BUSTA RHYMES

Born: TREVOR SMITH, 20 May'72, Brooklyn, New York, USA. Growing up as a teenager in Long Island, NY (or Strong Island as it was known among the hip hop fraternity, subsequently immortalised in song by JVC FORCE), the young BUSTA RHYMES hooked up with MC's CUT MONITOR MILO, DINCO D and CHARLIE BROWN to form LEADERS OF THE NEW SCHOOL. A well established hotbed of talent, Long Island had already spawned the likes of PUBLIC ENEMY, RAKIM and EPMD. LEADERS OF THE NEW SCHOOL were next in line, 'Elektra' picking up BUSTA & Co when the frontman was barely out of school. Touting a distinctive rapping style influenced by his Jamaican background and the freestyle ethos of the genre's pioneers, RHYMES stamped his not inconsiderable personality firmly over the group's debut album, 'FUTURE WITHOUT A PAST' (1991). Although they only recorded one more long player before breaking up, 'T.I.M.E.' (1993), they left behind a couple of interesting collaborations, with funk godfather JAMES BROWN on 'CAN'T GET ANY HARDER' and A TRIBE CALLED QUEST on the freestyling classic, 'SCENARIO'. After working with various artists in the soul/R&B field including the delectable MARY J. BLIGE, BUSTA RHYMES launched his solo career with the wild 'WOO-HAH!! GOT YOU ALL IN CHECK', making the US Top 10 and boosting sales of debut album, 'THE COMING' (1996). The man's finest moment, however, arguably arrived with the gloriously funky 'PUT YOUR HANDS WHERE MY EYES CAN SEE' leaving the cliched world of gangsta rap for dead and proving that less is more with a minimalist, shuffling rhythm, spooked-out rapping and a rivetting dayglo video. The accompanying album, 'WHEN DISASTER STRIKES' (1997) entered the US chart at No.3 and confirmed RHYMES' place among the new Hip Hop elite. The rapper wasted little time in consolidating his success, releasing a third set, 'EXTINCTION LEVEL EVENT – THE FINAL WORLD FRONT', a year later. As a singles artist he was more popular than ever, notching up another two sizeable Top 10 UK hits – 'GIMME SOME MORE' and 'WHAT'S IT GONNA BE?!' in 1999. This was no mean feat for a hardcore rapper, especially given the man's relentless creative output. The new millennium found him as busy as ever, still hanging on the theme of imminent chaos for humankind with 'ANARCHY' (2000). The following year also saw a compilation set ('TURN IT UP') and a fresh batch of tracks, 'GENESIS', an album which featured MARY J BLIGE, KELIS and P DIDDY (or PUFF DADDY to the uninitiated). Of all the guest spots, most memorable was KELIS' android vocal on 'WHAT IT IS', another RHYMES masterclass in sinewy, post-modern funk. A radical reworking of Public Enemy's 'SHUT 'EM DOWN', meanwhile, was as fresh as it was timely. The rap maverick was back in 2002 with 'IT AIN'T SAFE NO MORE', another swaggering trip through New York's ᵒost-9/11 musical landscape with RHYMES as guide, spitting out ₗyrics with the kind of eloquent fury few old hands can muster. ˌike its predecessor, the often ominous synth-cloaked production eemed tailor-made for BUSTA's post-millennial misgivings while he brilliant 'MAKE IT CLAP' ranked as his most compelling hit ingle of the new decade. Managing to stay in the limelight via both ilm work (his latest box-office smash being 'Narc') and a series f rap cameos (for METHOD MAN and the PUSSYCAT DOLLS), BUSTA finally came up with some original rhymes on 2006's US hart-topper 'THE BIG BANG'. Accompanying hit single, 'TOUCH T' (or rather its video promo), found the veteran rapper embroiled n controversy after the fatal shooting of his bodyguard, Israel Izzy" Ramirez; the police were allegedly obliged to subpoena both RHYMES and 'Aftermath' labelmate Tony Yayo.

ˌlbum rating: THE COMING (*6) / WHEN DISASTER STRIKES (*7) / ːXTINCTION LEVEL EVENT – THE FINAL WORLD FRONT (*7) / ANARCHY *6) / TURN IT UP – THE VERY BEST OF . . . compilation (*8) / GENESIS (*6) / T AIN'T SAFE NO MORE (*6) / THE BIG BANG (*7)

ƁUSTA RHYMES – vocals / with various personnel

Elektra Elektra

ɪar 96. (cd/c/lp) *<(7559 61742-2/-4/-1)>* **THE COMING** [ ] [6]
– The coming / Do my thing / Abandon ship / Everything remains raw / Hot fudge – interlude / Flipmode squad meets the Def squad / Keep it movin' / End of the world / Finish line / Still shining / Ill vibe / It's a party / Woo-hah!! got you all in the check.

ɪay 96. (c-s) *(EKR 220C) <64335>* **WOO-HAH!! GOT YOU ALL IN CHECK / EVERYTHING REMAINS RAW** [ ] Feb96 [8]
(12"+=/cd-s+=) *(EKR 220 T/CD)* – ('A'mix).

ul 96. (c-s; BUSTA RHYMES featuring ZHANE) *<64268>* **IT'S A PARTY / ILL VIBE (with Q-TIP)** [–] [52]

ep 96. (c-s; BUSTA RHYMES featuring ZHANE) *(EKR 226C) <64268>* **IT'S A PARTY / EVERYTHING REMAINS RAW** [23] [–]
(12"+=/cd-s+=) *(EKR 226 T/CD)* – ('A'mixes).

— In Mar'97, BUSTA featured on B REAL UK Top 10 single, 'HIT EM HIGH (THE MONSTARS' ANTHEM)'.

ᴀpr 97. (c-s) *(EKR 235C)* **DO MY THING / (DJ Scratch remix)** [39] [ ]
(12"+=/cd-s+=) *(EKR 235 T/CD)* – ('A'-Fila Brazillia mixes + instrumental).

ul 97. (cd) *(7559 63992-2)* **FLIPMODE REMIXES** [ ] [ ]
– Woo-hah!! got you all in check / It's a party / Do my thing / Abandon ship.

ep 97. (cd/c) *<(7559 62064-2/-4)>* **WHEN DISASTER STRIKES** [34] [3]
– (intro) / Whole world lookin' at me / Survival hungry / When disaster strikes / So hardcore / Get high tonight / Turn it up / Put your hands where my eyes can see / It's all good / There's not a problem my squad can't fix / We can take it outside / Rhymes galore / Thing we be doin' for money (parts 1 & 2) / One / Dangerous / Body rock / Get off my block / (outro).

)ct 97. (c-s) *(E 3900C)* **PUT YOUR HANDS WHERE MY EYES CAN SEE / ('A'mix)** [16] [ ]
(12"+=/cd-s+=) *(E 3900 T/CD)* – ('A'mixes).

)ec 97. (c-s) *(E 3877C) <64131>* **DANGEROUS / ('A'mix)** [32] [9]
(12"+=/cd-s+=) *(E 3877 T/CD)* – ('A'mixes).

— In Mar'98, the BUSTA man featured with The NOTORIOUS B.I.G. on PUFF DADDY & THE FAMILY's Top 20 (US) hit, 'Victory'.

ᴀpr 98. (c-s) *(E 3847C) <64104>* **TURN IT UP / FIRE IT UP** [2] [10]
(12"+=/cd-s+=) *(E 3847 T/CD)* – ('A'&'B'mixes).

un 98. (c-s/cd-s; BUSTA RHYMES featuring ERYKAH BADU) *(E 3833 C/CD1)* **ONE / FIRE IT UP / WOO HAH** [23] [ ]
(12"+=/cd-s+=) *(E 3833 T/CD2)* – ('A'side) / Rhymes galore.

)ec 98. (cd/c/lp) *<(7559 62211-2/-4/-1)>* **EXTINCTION LEVEL EVENT – THE FINAL WORLD FRONT** [65] [12]
– There's only one year left!!! (intro) / Everybody rise / Where we're about to take it / Extinction level event (the song of salvation) / Tear da roof off / Against all odds (with FLIPMODE SQUAD) / Just don't give it to me raw (what U asking 4) / Do it to death / Keepin' it tight / Gimme some more / Iz they wildin' wit' us or gettin' rowdy wit' us? (with MYSTIKAL) / A party goin' on over here / Do the bus a bus / Take it off / What's it gonna be?! (with JANET JACKSON) / Hot shit makin' ya bounce / What the fuck you want!! / This means war!! (with OZZY OSBOURNE) / The burial song (outro).

Jan 99. (c-s/12"/cd-s) *(E 3782 C/T/CD)* **GIMME SOME MORE. / DO IT LIKE NEVER BEFORE** [5] [ ]

Apr 99. (c-s/12"/cd-s; BUSTA RHYMES featuring JANET) *(E 3762 C/T/CD1) <64051>* **WHAT'S IT GONNA BE?! / TEAR DA ROOF OFF** [6] Mar99 [3]
(cd-s) *(E 3762CD2)* – ('A'mixes).

Jun 00. (cd/c/lp) *<(7559 62517-2/-4)>* **ANARCHY** [38] [4]
– The current state of anarchy – intro / Salute da gods!! / Enjoy da ride / We put it down for y'all / Bladow!! / Live it up / Fire / All night / Show me what you got / Get out!! / The heist / A trip out of town / How much we grew / Here we go again / We comin' through / C'mon all my niggaz, c'mon all my bitches / Make noise / Ready for war / Why we die / Anarchy / Outro.

Jul 00. (c-s/12"/cd-s) *(E 7075 C/T/CD)* **GET OUT / DO THE BUS A BUS / WHAT'S IT GONNA BE?! (featuring Janet Jackson)** [57] [ ]

Dec 00. (c-s/12"/cd-s) *(E 7136 C/T/CD)* **FIRE (mixes; original / KMG RMX radio / Gorch fonk RMX radio / original instrumental / KMG instrumental / Gorch fonk RMX instrumental)** [60] [ ]

— in Jun'01, BUSTA featured on VIOLATOR's hit single, 'What It Is'

— in Aug'01, the man featured on MOP's massive hit, 'Ante Up'

Sep 01. (cd) *<(8122 73559-2)>* **TURN IT UP – THE VERY BEST OF BUSTA RHYMES** (compilation) [44] [ ]
– Turn it up / Fire it up / Woo has got it all in check / Gimme some more / What's it gonna be (with JANET JACKSON) / Dangerous / It's a party (with ZHANE) / One (with ERYKAH BADU) / Hit 'em high (with B-REAL & COOLIO) / Do my thing / Do the bus a bus / The party is going on over here / Get out / Sobb story (with LEADERS OF THE NEW SCHOOL) / Scenario (with A TRIBE CALLED QUEST) / Dangerous (Soul Society mix) / Turn it up (Soul Society extended mix) / Fire (Gorch funk mix).

J – Arista J – Arista

Dec 01. (cd/d-lp) *<(80813 20009-2)>* **GENESIS** [ ] Nov01 [7]
– (intro) / Everybody rise again / As I come back / Shut 'em down 2002 / Genesis / Betta stay up in your home (with RAH DIGGA) / We got what you want / Truck volume / Pass the courvoisier (with P. DIDDY) / Break ya neck / Bounce / Holla / Wife in-law / Ass on your shoulders / Make it hurt / What ii is (with KELIS) / There's only one (with MARY J. BLIGE) / You ain't fuckin' wit me / Match the name with the voice (with FLIPMODE SQUAD) / Bad dreams. *(re-dist.Mar02)* – hit No.58

Mar 02. (12"/cd-s) *(74321 92233-1/-2) <21061>* **BREAK YA NECK. / AS I COME BACK / BETTA STAY UP IN YOUR HOUSE** [11] Oct01 [26]

May 02. (c-s; by BUSTA RHYMES featuring P. DIDDY & PHARRELL) *(74321 93790-4) <21154>* **PASS THE COURVOISIER PART II / (version)** [16] Feb02 [11]
(12"+=/cd-s+=) *(74321 93790-1/-2)* – Shut 'em down 2002.

Nov 02. (cd) *(74321 98125-2) <020043>* **IT AIN'T SAFE NO MORE** [ ] [43]
– Intro / It ain't safe no more / What do you do when you're branded / Call the ambulance (with PHARRELL WILLIAMS & CHAD HUGO) / We goin' to do it to ya / What up / Turn me up some / Make it clap (with SPLIFF STAR) / Take it off – part 2 (with MEKA) / Taste it / Hey ladies / I know what you want (with MARIAH CAREY & FLIPMODE SQUAD) / Riot / Hop / Together (with RAH DIGGA) / Struttin' like a G.O.D. / The struggle will be lost (with CARL THOMAS) / Till it's gone.

Jan 03. (c-s; by BUSTA RHYMES & SPLIFF STAR) *(82876 50206-4) <21236>* **MAKE IT CLAP / (instrumental)** [16] Oct02 [46]
(12"+=/cd-s+=) *(82876 50206-1/-2)* – What do you do when you're branded.

May 03. (c-s; by BUSTA RHYMES with MARIAH CAREY & FLIPMODE SQUAD) *(82876 52829-4) <21258>* **I KNOW WHAT YOU WANT / CALL THE AMBULANCE (M.O.P. remix)** [3] Mar03 [3]
(12"+=/cd-s+=) *(82876 52829-1/-2)* – ('A'-instrumental).

Nov 03. (12"/cd-s; by BUSTA RHYMES & PHARRELL) *(82876 57251-1/-2) <54245>* **LIGHT YOUR ASS ON FIRE. / BLAZE OF GLORY / (instrumental)** [62] Aug03 [58]
in May'04, BUSTA feat. on METHOD MAN's hit, 'What's Happenin'
in Sep'05, the PUSSYCAT DOLLS feat. BUSTA on No.1, 'Don't Cha'

Universal Universal

May 06. (12") *(9855967) <615011>* **TOUCH IT. / TOUCH IT (remix w/ MARY J. BLIGE, RAH DIGGA & MISSY ELLIOTT) / TOUCH IT (w/ DMX)** [6] Jan06 [16]
(cd-s) *<(9855966)>* – ('A') / ('A'-mix w/ LLOYD BANKS & PAPOUSE).

Jun 06. (cd) *(9878436) <6748-02>* **THE BIG BANG** [19] [1]
– Get you some (w/ Q-TIP & MARSHA AMBROSIUS) / Touch it / How we do it over here / New York shit / Been through the storm / In the ghetto / Cocaina / You can't hold the torch / Goldmine / I love my bitch / Don't get carried away / They're out to get me / Get down / I'll do it all / Legend of the fall offs.

Jun 06. (12")(cd-s) *<708111><1702199>* **I LOVE MY BITCH** [–] [41]

BUZZCOCKS

Formed: Manchester, England ... April 1976 by HOWARD DEVOTO and PETE SHELLEY who met at Bolton Institute Of Higher Education. Having recruited STEVE DIGGLE and JOHN MAHER, they played their first gig on the 20th of July '76 supporting the SEX PISTOLS. Early the following year, they released the first ever DIY punk "indie" 45 on 'New Hormones' in the form of the 'SPIRAL SCRATCH' EP. They then suffered a major bust up when frontman DEVOTO departed (to form MAGAZINE), although the rest carried on having signed to 'United Artists' on the strength of featuring on the now famous 'LIVE AT THE ROXY' Various artists compilation (with tracks 'Breakdown' and 'Love Battery'). By this time, SHELLEY had taken over vocal duties, while DIGGLE switched to guitar, having found a new bassist, GARTH SMITH. Early in 1978, they stormed the charts with the brooding love gem, 'WHAT DO I GET', a two-minute rush of bittersweet pop/punk angst which saw SHELLEY emerging as a strong frontman in his own right. The previous year's masturbating classic, 'ORGASM ADDICT', was too frenetic to allow SHELLEY's effeminate romance'n'roll stylings a look-in, although he blossomed on subsequent releases. A debut album, 'ANOTHER MUSIC IN A DIFFERENT KITCHEN' (1978), made the UK Top 20, while another SHELLEY-penned classic, 'EVER FALLEN IN LOVE (WITH SOMEONE YOU SHOULDN'T'VE?)', almost made the Top 10 later that year. With fervent support from Radio One DJ, John Peel, the band had squarely cornered the more accessible end of the punk market, although the 'LOVE BITES' album marked a move away from the short, sharp melodic shock which had become their trademark as songwriting duties were more democratically distributed. A final clutch of Top 30 hits, 'PROMISES' (their fifth hit in 1978), 'EVERYBODY'S HAPPY NOWADAYS' and 'HARMONY IN MY HEAD', saw the increasing influence of DIGGLE. 1979's 'A DIFFERENT KIND OF TENSION' saw SHELLEY's influence begin to dissipate and the album's mixed reviews signalled the band were running out of creative steam. After 'Liberty' took over their contract in 1980 and a further three 45's flopped, the BUZZCOCKS split, DIGGLE forming FLAG OF CONVENIENCE with MAHER. SHELLEY, meanwhile, went solo, making his debut in 1981 with the 'HOMOSAPIEN' album. Although the album made little commercial headway in Britain, the title track, bizarrely enough, topped the Australian charts. He released another two sets, 'XL-1' (1983) and 'HEAVEN AND THE SEA' (1986) to mild interest; far more newsworthy was the band's reformation in 1990 with a line-up of SHELLEY, DIGGLE, STEVE GARVEY and ex-SMITHS drummer, MIKE JOYCE. A comeback album, 'TRADE TEST TRANSMISSION' (1993) was lapped up by old punks and new converts alike, while a slightly modified line-up undertook a heartily received tour. A live set culled from the dates, 'FRENCH', was released in 1995, while a follow-up album, 'ALL SET' appeared a year later. The band's classic late 70's output remains one of the most influential bodies of work from the punk era, second only to perhaps the SEX PISTOLS. While 1999's 'MODERN' was a slightly turgid affair and never really troubled that legacy, it far outflanked the amateurish flailings of the young – largely American – bands who'd supposedly carry their flame. Much more satisfying was 2003's 'BUZZCOCKS', the eponymous title perhaps serving notice that the reformed band (with a new rhythm section of TONY BARBER and PHIL BARKER) were, at the end o the day, the guardians of that classic buzzsaw sound and the onl ones with the ability to carry it forward. That said, the record wasn' exactly a transformation although it did carry the weight that migh be expected from these veterans, the resumption of the SHELLEY DEVOTO writing partnership on two tracks (having alread worked together on experimental electronica set, 'BUZZKUNST' the previous year) making things even more interesting. Celebratin an on/off thirty year musical relationship, BUZZCOCKS returne in 2006 with 'FLAT-PACK PHILOSOPHY', another dose of AO (Adult Orientated Punk) concerned with the trials of responsibilit rather than rebellion.

• **Covered:** HERE COMES THE NICE (Small Faces). • **Trivia:** In 197 SHELLEY produced fun group, ALBERTO Y LOST TRIOS PARANOIAS.

Album rating: ANOTHER MUSIC IN A DIFFERENT KITCHEN (*9) / LOV BITES (*7) / DIFFERENT KIND OF TENSION (*6) / SINGLES – GOING STEAD compilation (*9) / TRADE TEST TRANSMISSION (*5) / FRENCH (*4) / ALL SE (*5) / MODERN (*5) / BUZZCOCKS (*6) / FLAT-PACK PHILOSOPHY (*6) / Pet Shelley: SKY YEN (*4) / HOMOSAPIEN (*7) / XL-1 (*5) / HEAVEN AND TH SEA (*6) / ShelleyDevoto: BUZZKUNST (*5)

HOWARD DEVOTO (b. HOWARD TROTTER, 1955) – vocals / **PET SHELLEY** (b.PETER McNEISH, 17 Apr'55) – guitar, vocals / **STEV DIGGLE** – bass, vocals / **JOHN MAHER** – drums

New Hormones — not is

Jan 77. (7"ep) *(ORG 1)* **SPIRAL SCRATCH** [ ] [–]
– Breakdown / Times up / Boredom / Friends of mine. *(re-iss. Aug7 credited as "BUZZCOCKS with HOWARD DEVOTO"; same); hit No.3 (re-iss. 1994 on 'Document' 12"ep/cd-ep)*

—— (Mar'77) **GARTH SMITH** – bass; repl. DEVOTO who formed MAGAZIN **SHELLEY** now lead vocals, guitar / **DIGGLE** switched to guitar, vocals

U.A. — not is

Oct 77. (7") *(UP 36316)* **ORGASM ADDICT. / WHATEVER HAPPENED TO . . . ?** [ ] [–]

—— **STEVE GARVEY** – bass repl. GARTH (on tour at first)

Jan 78. (7") *(UP 36348)* **WHAT DO I GET?. / OH SHIT** [37] [–]

U.A. — I.R.S

Mar 78. (lp/c) *(UAG/TCK 30159)* **ANOTHER MUSIC IN A DIFFERENT KITCHEN** [15] [–]
– Fast cars / No reply / You tear me up / Get on our own / Love battery 16 / I don't mind / Fiction romance / Autonomy / I need / Moving awa from the pulsebeat. *(re-iss. Aug85 on 'Liberty' lp/c; ATAK/TC-ATAK 51) (re iss. Jun87 on 'Fan Club' blue-lp; FC 021) (re-iss. May88 on 'Fame' lp/c/c FA/TC-FA/CD-FA 3199) (re-iss. cd Jul88 on 'E.M.I.'; CDP 790299-2) (cd re iss. Jul96; PRDFCD 3) (cd re-iss. Aug01 on 'E.M.I.'+=; 534405-2)* – Orgasn addict / Whatever happened to? / What do I get / Oh shit.

Apr 78. (7") *(UP 36386)* **I DON'T MIND. / AUTONOMY** [55] [–]

Jul 78. (7") *(UP 36433)* **LOVE YOU MORE. / NOISE ANNOYS** [34] [–]

Sep 78. (7") *(UP 36455)* **EVER FALLEN IN LOVE (WITH SOMEONE YOU SHOULDN'T'VE?). / JUST LUST** [12] [–]

Sep 78. (lp/c) *(UAG/TCK 30197)* **LOVE BITES** [13] [–]
– Real world / Ever fallen in love with someone you shouldn't've Operator's manuel / Nostalgia / Just lust / Sixteen again / Walkin distance / Love is lies / Nothing left / E.S.P. / Late for the train. *(re-is Mar87 on 'Fame' lp/c; FA/TC-FA 3174) (re-iss. Jun87 on 'Fan Club' blue lp; FC 022) (cd-iss. Jul88 on 'Fame'; CD-FA 3174) (cd re-iss. Jul96; PRDFC 4) (cd re-iss. Aug01 on 'E.M.I.'+=)* – Love you more / Noise annoys Promises / Lipstick.

Nov 78. (7") *(UP 36471)* **PROMISES. / LIPSTICK** [20] [–]

Mar 79. (7") *(UP 36499)* **EVERYBODY'S HAPPY NOWADAYS. / WHY CAN'T I TOUCH IT?** [29] [–]

Jul 79. (7") *(UP 36541)* **HARMONY IN MY HEAD. / SOMETHING'S GONE WRONG AGAIN** [32] [–]

Sep 79. (7") *(BP 316)* **YOU SAY YOU DON'T LOVE ME. / RAISON D'ETRE** [ ] [–]

Sep 79. (lp/c) *(UAG/TCK 30260) <SP 009>* **A DIFFERENT KIND OF TENSION** [26] [ ]
– Paradise / Sitting round at home / You say you don't love me You know you can't help it / Mad mad Judy / Raison d'etre / I don' know what to do with my life / Money / Hollow inside / A differen kind of tension / I believe / Radio Nine. *(initial copies cont. previou*

BUZZCOCKS

45) (re-iss. Jun87 on 'Fan Club' blue-lp; FC 023) (cd-iss. Jul88 on 'E.M.I.'; CZ 93)

Nov 79. (lp/c) *<010>* **SINGLES – GOING STEADY** (compilation) [–] [ ]
– Orgasm addict / What do I get / I don't mind / Love you more / Ever fallen in love with someone you shouldn't've / Promises / Everybody's happy nowadays / Harmony in my head / Whatever happened to . . . ? / Oh shit! / Autonomy / Noise annoys / Just luck / Lipstick / Why can't I touch it / Something's gone wrong again. *(UK-iss.Nov81 on 'Liberty' lp/c; LBR/TC-LBR 1043) (re-iss. Aug85 lp/c; ATAK/TC-ATAK 52) (cd-iss. Jun87 + Jun88 on 'E.M.I.'; CDP 746449-2) (re-iss. Sep90 cd/c/lp; CD/TC+/FA 3241) (cd re-iss. Aug01 on 'E.M.I.'+=; 534442-2)* – (extra tracks).

Feb 80. (7") *<IR 9010>* **I BELIEVE. / SOMETHING'S GONE WRONG AGAIN** [–] [ ]

Liberty I.R.S.

Aug 80. (7") *(BP 365)* **WHY SHE'S A GIRL FROM THE CHAINSTORE. / ARE EVERYTHING** [61] [–]

Oct 80. (7") *(BP 371)* **STRANGE THING. / AIRWAVES DREAM** [ ] [–]

Nov 80. (7") *(BP 392)* **RUNNING FREE. / WHAT DO YOU KNOW** [ ] [–]

— (split Feb'81) **DIGGLE** went solo and formed FLAG OF CONVENIENCE, with MAHER

PETE SHELLEY

— augmented by **STEVE GARVEY** – bass / **JIM RUSSELL** – drums

Genetic-Island Arista

Aug 81. (7"/12") *(WIP/12WIP 6720)* **HOMOSAPIEN. / KEAT'S SONG** [ ] [–]

Sep 81. (lp/c) *(ILPS/ICT 9676)* **HOMOSAPIEN** [ ] Jun82 [ ]
– Homosapien / Yesterday's here / I generate a feeling / Keat's song / Qu'est-ce que c'est que ca / I don't know what it is / Guess I must have been in love with myself / Pusher man / Just one of those affairs / It's hard enough knowing. *(re-iss. cd Sep94 on 'Grapevine'; GRACD 201) (cd re-iss. May98 on 'Razor & Tie'; RE 2126)*

Nov 81. (d7"/12") *(U/12 WIP 6740)* **I DON'T KNOW WHAT IT IS. / WITNESS THE CHANGE/ / IN LOVE WITH SOMEBODY ELSE. / MAXINE** [ ] [–]

Apr 82. (7"/12") *(WIP/12WIP 6720)* **HOMOSAPIEN. / LOVE IN VAIN** [ ] [–]

— **BARRY ADAMSON** – bass (ex-MAGAZINE, ex-BIRTHDAY PARTY) repl. GARVEY / added **MARTIN RUSHENT** – keyboards, producer

Island Arista

Feb 83. (7"/12") *(XX/+T 1)* **TELEPHONE OPERATOR. / MANY A TIME** [66] [–]

Apr 83. (lp) *(XL 1)* **XL-1** [42] Jul83 [ ]
– Telephone operator / If you ask me (I won't say no) / What was Heaven? / You better than I know / Twilight / (Millions of people) No one like you / Many a time / I just wanna touch / You and I / XL-1 *. (c+= dub tracks) (track* = only playable on ZX Spectrum computer) *(re-iss. cd Sep94 on 'Grapevine'; GRACD 202)*

Immaculate not iss.

Nov 84. (7") *(IMMAC 1)* **NEVER AGAIN. / ONE ONE ONE** [ ] [–]
(12"+=) *(12IMMAC 1)* – Give it to me.

— **SHELLEY** brought in new **JOHN DOYLE** – drums / **MARK SANDERSON** – bass / **NORMAN FISCHER-JONES** – guitar / **GERARD COOKSON** – keyboards / **JIM GARDNER** – synth.

Mercury Mercury

Mar 86. (7"/12") *(MER/+X 215)* **WAITING FOR LOVE. / DESIGNER LAMPS** [ ] [–]

May 86. (7"/12") *(MER/+X 221)* **ON YOUR OWN. / PLEASE FORGIVE ME . . . BUT I CANNOT ENDURE IT ANY LONGER** [ ] [–]

Jun 86. (lp/c)(cd) *(MERH/+C 90)(830004-2)* **HEAVEN AND THE SEA** [ ] [ ]
– Never again / My dreams / Blue eyes / You can't take that away / No Moon . . . / Waiting for love / On your own / They're coming for you / I surrender / Life without reason / Need a minit.

Aug 86. (7"/12") *(MER/+X 225)* **BLUE EYES. / NELSON'S RIDDLE** [ ] [–]

Nov 86. (7"/12") *(MER/+X 234)* **I SURRENDER. / I NEED A MINUTE** [42] [–]

— In 1988, **SHELLEY** formed **ZIP** with COOKSON and SANDERSON.

– his compilations, others, etc. –

Apr 80. (m-lp) *Groovy; (STP 2)* **SKY YEN** (rec.1974) [ ] [–]

Apr 89. (7"/12") *Immaculate; (IMMAC/12IMMAC 11)* **HOMOSAPIEN. PETE SHELLEY VS. POWER, WONDER AND LOVE / ('A'mix)** [ ] [–]
(3"cd-s+=) *(IMMACD 11)* – ('A'-Icon mix) / ('A'-shower mix).

BUZZCOCKS F.O.C.

— **DIGGLE, HAMMER** + **ANDY COUZENS** – guitar / **CHRIS GOODWIN** – drums

Thin Line not iss

Jul 89. (12"/cd-s) *(THIN 003/+CD)* **TOMORROW'S SUNSET. / LIFE WITH THE LIONS / ('A'version)** [ ] [–]

BUZZCOCKS

— re-formed in 1990 **SHELLEY, DIGGLE, GARVEY** and **MIKE JOYCE** – drums (ex-SMITHS) repl. ANDY and CHRIS who formed The HIGH

Planet Pacific not iss

Apr 91. (7"ep/12"ep/c-ep/cd-ep) **ALIVE TONIGHT** [ ] [–]
– Alive tonight / Successful street / Serious crime / Last to know.

— **JOHN MAHER** – drums returned to repl. MIKE who joined PIL.

— **TONY BARBER** – bass / **PHIL BARKER** – drums repl.GARVEY and MAHER

Essential Carolir

May 93. (7") *(ESS 2025)* **INNOCENT. / WHO'LL HELP ME TO FORGET** [ ] [–]
(12"+=/cd-s+=) *(ESS T/X 2025)* – Inside.

Jun 93. (cd/c/lp) *(ESM CD/MC/LP 389) <1747>* **TRADE TEST TRANSMISSION** [ ] [ ]
– Innocent / Smile / Palm of your hand / Last to know / Do it/ Who will help me to forget / Energy / Alive tonight / Inside / Isolation / Never gonna give it up / Crystal night / 369 / Chegga / It's unthinkable / Somewhere. *(reiss.cd Jul96; same)*

Aug 93. (12"/cd-s) *(ESS T/X 2031)* **DO IT. / TRASH AWAY / ALL OVER YOU** [ ] [–]

Apr 94. (12"/cd-s) **LIBERTINE ANGEL. / ROLL IT OVER / EXCERPT FROM PRISON RIOT HOSTAGE** [ ] [–]

Dojo I.R.S.

Nov 95. (cd) *(DOJOCD 237) <36761>* **FRENCH (live in Paris 12th April 1995)** [ ] Jan96 [ ]
– I don't mind / Who'll help me to forget / Get on our own / Unthinkable / Strange thing / Energy / Breakdown / Innocent / Roll it over / Why she's a girl from the chainstore / Last to know? / Running free / Libertine angel / Why can't I touch it / Noise annoys / Isolation / Boredom / Do it / Harmony in my head / I believe.

I.R.S. I.R.S.

Apr 96. (cd) *(EIRSCD 1078) <36962>* **ALL SET** [ ] [ ]
– Totally from the heart / Without you / Give it to me / Your love / Point of no return / Hold me close / Kiss & tell / What am I supposed to do? / Some kind of wonderful / (What you) Mean to me / Playing for time / Pariah / Back with you.

Go Kart Go Kar

Mar 00. (lp/cd) *(<GK 058/+CD>)* **MODERN** [ ] Sep99 [ ]
– Soul on a rock / Rendezvous / Speed of life / Thunder of hearts / Why compromise? / Don't let the car crash / Runaround / Doesn't mean anything / Phone / Under the sun / Turn of the screw / Sneaky / Stranger in your town / Choices.

SHELLEYDEVOTO

Cooking Vinyl Cookin Vinyl

Feb 02. (cd) *(<COOKCD 230>)* **BUZZKUNST** [ ] Mar02 [ ]
– Can you see me shining? / Strain of bacteria / Deeper / 'Til the stars in his eyes are dead / On solids / Self-destruction / You are still there / God's particle / A world to give away / Stupid kunst / System blues / So there I was / Wednesday's emotional setup / Going off.

BUZZCOCKS

SHELLEY + **DIGGLE** with **TONY BARBER** – bass / **PHILIP BARKER** – drums

Cherry Red Merge

Apr 03. (cd/lp) *(CD+/BRED 226)* <*MRG 227*> **BUZZCOCKS**
– Jerk / Keep on / Wake up call / Friends / Driving you insane / Morning after / Sick city sometimes / Stars / Certain move / Lester Sands / Up for the crack / Useless situation.

Damaged Goods not iss.

Apr 03. (7") *(DAMGOOD 214)* **JERK. / DON'T COME HOME / OH SHIT (live)** –

Feb 06. (7") *(DAMGOOD 261)* **WISH I NEVER LOVED YOU. / DON'T MATTER WHAT YOU SAY / LOVE BATTERY (live)** –
(cd-s) *(Cooking Vinyl; FRYCD 261)* – (first 2 tracks) / Orion.

Cooking Vinyl Cooking Vinyl

Mar 06. (cd) *(COOKCD 370)* <*4772*> **FLAT-PACK PHILOSOPHY**
– Flat-pack philosophy / Wish I never loved you / Sell you everything / Reconcilliation / I don't exist / Survivor / God, what have I done / Credit / Big Brother wheels / Dreamin' / Sound of a gun / Look at you now / I've had enough / Between Heaven and Hell. *(lp-iss. on 'Damaged Goods'; DAMGOOD 262LP)*

– compilations, others, etc. –

Apr 87. (lp/c) *Weird Systems; (WS 021/+X1)* **TOTAL POP** –
Jan 88. (12"ep) *Strange Fruit; (SFPS 044)* **THE PEEL SESSIONS (7.9.77)** –
– Fast cars / What do I get / Moving away from the pulsebeat.
Oct 88. (c) *R.O.I.R.; (A 158)* **LEST WE FORGET (live)** –
(cd-iss. Nov94; RE 158CD)
Sep 89. (lp/cd) *Absolutely Free; (FREE LP/CD 002)* **LIVE AT THE ROXY CLUB, 2 APRIL 1977** (live) –
(cd+=) – (1 extra track). *(re-iss. Jul90 & Jul93 on 'Receiver'; RR CD/LC/LP 131)*
Oct 89. (7"ep/12"ep/cd-ep) *E.M.I.; (EM/12EM/CDEM 104)* **THE FAB FOUR** –
– Ever fallen in love with someone you shouldn't've / Promises / Everybody's happy nowadays / Harmony in my head.
Nov 89. (4xlp/2xd-c/2xd-cd) *E.M.I.; (LP/TC/CD PROD 1)* **PRODUCT** –
– (cont. first 3 albums + 1 live and rare) *(re-iss. May95 cd; PRODUCT 1)*
Feb 90. (cd/lp) *Strange Fruit; (SFR CD/LP 104)* **THE PEEL SESSIONS ALBUM** –
Sep 91. (cd/c/d-lp) *E.M.I.; (CD/TC+/EM 1421)* **OPERATOR'S MANUAL (BUZZCOCKS BEST)** –
May 92. (cd) *EMI Gold; (CDGOLD 1029)* **ENTERTAINING FRIENDS LIVE AT THE HAMMERSMITH ODEON – MARCH 1979** (live) –
Oct 92. (cd-s) *Old Gold; (OG 6182)* **EVER FALLEN IN LOVE WITH SOMEONE . . . / WHAT DO I GET / PROMISES** –
Apr 94. (cd) *E.M.I.; (CDPRDT 12)* **ANOTHER MUSIC IN A DIFFERENT KITCHEN / LOVE BITES** –
1995. (7") *One Stop Music; (ONE 7001)* **NOISE ANNOYS. / ISOLATION (live)** –
Jul 95. (cd) *Dojo; (DLP 2)* **TIME'S UP** –
(re-iss. Mar00 on 'The Grey Area'; SCRATCH 2/+CD)
Nov 95. (cd-s) *Old Gold; (12623 6332-2)* **EVER FALLEN IN LOVE WITH SOMEONE YOU SHOULDN'T HAVE FALLEN IN LOVE WITH / PROMISES** –
Jun 97. (cd) *EMI Gold; (CDGOLD 2073)* **CHRONOLOGY** –
Sep 97. (cd) *EMI Gold; (CDGOLD 1093)* **I DON'T MIND** –
Oct 98. (cd) *E.M.I.; (497771-2)* **THE BBC SESSIONS** –
Jun 99. (cd) *Almafame; (<YEAAH 1>)* **PARIS ENCORE DU PAIN**
Sep 99. (d-cd) *E.M.I.; (521767-2)* **MODERN / A DIFFERENT KIND** –
Jul 00. (d-cd) *Burning Airlines; (PILOT 078)* **BEATING HEARTS (LIVE IN MANCHESTER 1978)** –
(d-lp-iss.Feb01 on 'Get Back'; GET 74)
Jul 01. (cd) *Castle Pie; (PIESD 259)* **LIVE IN PARIS** (live) –
Sep 01. (d-lp) *Get Back; (GET 80)* **SMALL SONGS WITH BIG HEARTS** –
Nov 01. (cd) *Dressed To Kill; (MIDRO 805)* **ORGASM ADDICTS** –
Apr 02. (cd) *EMI Gold; (538464-2)* **FINEST (EVER FALLEN IN LOVE)** –
Jun 02. (cd) *N.M.C.; (SJLTD 01)* **NOISE ANNOYS – MANCHESTER APOLLO 1978** (live) –
Jun 02. (cd) *N.M.C.; (SJLTD 02)* **LIVE TENSION – RAINBOW THEATRE, LONDON, 09/11/79)** –
Jul 02. (lp) *Get Back; (GET 92)* **FAST CARS** –
Mar 03. (d-cd) *E.M.I.; (582350-2)* **ANOTHER MUSIC IN ANOTHER KITCHEN / LOVE BITES** –
– (with extra tracks).
May 03. (14xcd-box) *E.M.I.; (551824-2)* **INVENTORY** –

the BYRDS

Formed: Los Angeles, California, USA ... 1964 as The JETSET by JIM McGUINN, GENE CLARK and DAVID CROSBY. All three had come from folky backgrounds, McGUINN having toured with The CHAD MITCHELL TRIO as a teenager and CLARK already having proved an accomplished songwriter with The NEW CHRISTY MINSTRELS. CROSBY, meanwhile was an ambitious singer/songwriter who'd performed with LES BAXTER'S BALLADEERS. The JETSET recorded a one-off flop single for 'Elektra', 'PLEASE LET ME LOVE YOU', under the pseudonym of The BEEFEATERS. Later the same year, they recruited expert bluegrass player CHRIS HILLMAN, previously of The HILLMEN, who'd incorporated his instrumental dexterity on the mandolin into his bass playing. Drummer MICHAEL CLARKE, with his chiselled, BRIAN JONES-esque looks, completed the line-up, initially playing on cardboard boxes when the band were too hard-up to afford a real drum-kit! Profoundly influenced by The BEATLES, they soon changed their name to The BYRDS (the mis-spelling a tribute to their heroes), and set about realising their vision of marrying the fab four's electric energy to the folk music which was their stock in trade. With the help of long-time manager JIM DICKSON and the unlikely recommendation of MILES DAVIS, the band signed to 'Columbia'. At the insistence of DICKSON and producer TERRY MELCHER, the reluctant BYRDS eventually agreed to re-work their earlier demo of 'MR. TAMBOURINE MAN' (this and other demos later surfaced on 'PREFLYTE'). It was a canny decision which did nothing less than change the course of pop/rock history. The resulting song's unforgettable euphoric rush charged DYLAN's lyrics with a youthful romanticism, encapsulating in 3 minutes, what it was to be young and have the world at your feet. It soon hit No.1 on both sides of the Atlantic and it still sounds as fresh today as it did then, a timeless slice of hypnotic, bittersweet pop with McGUINN's delivery forging an affecting DYLAN / LENNON hybrid. Much has since been made of the fact that only one BYRD, McGUINN, actually played on the record, with MELCHER hiring session musicians like LEON RUSSELL, LARRY KNECHTAL and HAL BLAINE. However, any doubts about The BYRDS' ability as a band were dispelled with the self-titled debut album, a folk-rock classic. It was a case of more of the same really, with the band turning in a dazzling string of DYLAN covers, making the songs distinctly their own. 'CHIMES OF FREEDOM' was a ringing, hippy call to arms, fuelled by a starry-eyed optimism and they even managed to transform the Welsh mining disaster ballad 'BELLS OF RHYMNEY', into an effervescent swirl. GENE CLARK was the band's chief songwriter at this stage, contributing the classic BEATLES-esque originals 'FEEL A WHOLE LOT BETTER', 'I KNEW I'D WANT YOU' and 'HERE WITHOUT YOU'. In the summer of '65, they played a residency at Ciro's nightclub on Sunset Strip, often cited as the origin of the L.A. hippy movement (described by the L.A. Times as being frequented by people who looked like they'd been dragged from Sherwood Forest!). They were back at No.1 by the end of 1965, when they managed to transform PETE SEEGER's Book Of Ecclesiastes-adaptation 'TURN! TURN! TURN!' into a classic pop record, a miracle of biblical proportions. Very early the next year, the second album boasted two more DYLAN covers, an uninspiring update

The BYRDS

of 'THE TIMES THEY ARE A-CHANGIN' and 'LAY DOWN YOUR WEARY TUNE', apparently the song that finally persuaded DYLAN that The BYRDS were doing something above and beyond mere imitation. McGUINN contributed two songs, one of which was his tribute to the assassinated JOHN F. KENNEDY, 'HE WAS A FRIEND OF MINE', while CLARK offered three originals, including the classic 'SET YOU FREE THIS TIME'. Recorded the previous January, 'EIGHT MILES HIGH' pioneered psychedelic rock, predating the efforts of The BEATLES, The BEACH BOYS and the San Franciscan bands. The JOHN COLTRANE-inspired track was promptly vetoed by radio stations on its spring '66 release, amid allegations that the song was an explicit account of an LSD trip. After the completion of the third album 'FIFTH DIMENSION', CLARK departed, citing his paranoia-fuelled fear of flying and CROSBY's digs regarding his tambourine playing. The new album heralded a move away from sparkling pop to a more complex, ambitious and intelligent sound. Influenced heavily by Indian sitar player RAVI SHANKAR, and modal jazz, the record didn't fulfil the promise of the preceding single but still contained some memorable moments. McGUINN's 'MR SPACEMAN' hinted at the country sound the band would later embrace. Just prior to releasing the fourth album, 'YOUNGER THAN YESTERDAY', the band issued 'SO YOU WANT TO BE A ROCK'N'ROLL STAR', a sarcastic reaction to manufactured bands by a group that had fallen out of favour with the Hollywood set. The album was an assorted bag of styles, with HILLMAN emerging as a talented songwriter on the likes of 'TIME BETWEEN' and 'THOUGHTS AND WORDS', while CROSBY had his finest moment with the haunting 'EVERYBODY'S BEEN BURNED'. Despite the melange of styles, the album predated 'SGT PEPPER', once again proving that The BYRDS were ahead of their time. By the time of 'THE NOTORIOUS BYRD BROTHERS' in 1968, CROSBY's dictatorial manner had led to his ejection from the band, along with MICHAEL CLARKE. A contender for the The BYRDS best album, the record was again stylistically diverse but included possibly the band's finest moment in the GOFFIN/KING number, 'GOIN' BACK' (later a hit for DUSTY SPRINGFIELD). Its wistful musings on the passage from childhood to maturity were set against a backdrop of heavenly harmonies and celestial pedal steel while 'WASN'T BORN TO FOLLOW' (another GERRY GOFFIN-CAROLE KING cover), was a triumphant clarion call of phased, psychedelic country. With the addition of GRAM PARSONS and HILLMAN's cousin KEVIN KELLEY, the band steered radically away from the studio-enhanced sound of 'NOTORIOUS', straight into the heart of country, once again staying one step ahead of their peers and foreshadowing the country-rock boom of the early 70's. 'SWEETHEART OF THE RODEO', with its purist sound, confounded the hippies and despite playing a show at the Grand Ole Opry, and even, God forbid, cutting their hair! for the occasion, the country crowd remained suspicious of their druggy image, thereby ensuring little commercial success. Released in '68, PARSONS was the driving force behind the album, contributing beautiful songs like 'HICKORY WIND' and 'ONE HUNDRED YEARS FROM NOW', which sat majestically alongside covers of LOUVIN BROTHERS and DYLAN material. The gypsy-like PARSONS soon left, taking HILLMAN with him to form The FLYING BURRITO BROTHERS. McGUINN (who'd now changed his name to ROGER, following his immersion in the Indonesian religion, Subud) recruited country guitar maestro CLARENCE WHITE along with a cast of other musicians. The albums that followed were inconsistent, although they contained a few BYRDS classics and highlighted WHITE's virtuoso guitar playing. 'DR BYRDS & MR HYDE', featured the ironic stab at the country establishment, 'DRUG STORE TRUCK DRIVING MAN', while 'BALLAD OF EASY RIDER's gentle meandering title track was a minor classic. The half live/half studio set, 'UNTITLED', from 1970, included an impassioned performance from WHITE on 'LOVER ON THE BAYOU' and a lovely version of LOWELL GEORGE's 'TRUCK STOP GIRL'. Probably the strongest set of the latter day BYRDS, it also included the single 'CHESTNUT MARE', and the evocative McGUINN and JACQUES LEVY song 'ALL THE THINGS'. Much of McGUINN's songs during this period came from the abandoned 'Gene Tryp' project which he had begun with New York psychologist LEVY to chart the history of American music. The last few albums weren't quite as ambitious in their scope, but 'BYRDMANIAX' and 'FARTHER ALONG' were enjoyable despite having the weight of such an illustrious career on their shoulders. McGUINN did the right thing and called it a day at last in mid-72, later joining up with the original BYRDS for an uninspired album a year later. Two of the BYRDS most talented members died in separate incidents in the early 70's, CLARENCE WHITE killed by a drunken driver, GRAM PARSONS from a heroin overdose. CROSBY survived a descent into free-base cocaine addiction and a liver transplant to record songs in Nashville with McGUINN and HILLMAN in 1990. McGUINN's solo career proved to be fairly prolific, kicking off with an eponymous solo debut in early 1973, revisiting the eclecticism of mid-period BYRDS. 'PEACE ON YOU' followed in '74, while 'ROGER McGUINN & HIS BAND' foreshadowed the guitarist's stint with BOB DYLAN and *his* band (as part of DYLAN's famous Rolling Thunder Revue) through the mid-70s. Forging an unlikely friendship with MICK RONSON, McGUINN teamed up with the ex-BOWIE acolyte (together with assorted Rolling Thunder stragglers) on what was hailed as the man's most accomplished solo work, 'CARDIFF ROSE' (1976). With the musical climate not exactly receptive to roots rock, the veteran jangler went to ground after 1977's 'THUNDERBYRD'. Save for a one-off 1981 collaboration with CHRIS HILLMAN ('MEAN STREETS'), it'd be 14 long years before he re-emerged with a US Top 50 comeback set on 'Arista', 'BACK FROM RIO' (1991), roping in TOM PETTY, DAVID CROSBY and CHRIS HILLMAN. McGUINN was subsequently sighted running through some old numbers on 'Later With Jools (Holland)' in true troubadour style, although he was hardly stuck in the past: since the mid-90s, he'd been one of the first of the old guard to harness the power of the internet, posting traditional folk songs recorded in various home studios. He took the same concept into the physical realm with 'TREASURES FROM THE FOLK DEN' (2001), cutting a swathe through the traditional landscape in the company of PETE SEEGER, ODETTA, JOAN BAEZ, JUDY COLLINS and ELIZA CARTHY, amongst others. McGUINN plugged in once more for 'LIMITED EDITION' (2004), a folk-rock return to BYRDS-ian fare. An endless list of artists and bands (TOM PETTY, R.E.M., the LONG RYDERS, the SMITHS, PRIMAL SCREAM, RIDE, etc), have kept alive the spirit of the BYRDS in their own particular style, while the band's own recordings remain timeless treasures.

Album rating: MR. TAMBOURINE MAN (*8) / TURN! TURN! TURN! (*8) / FIFTH DIMENSION (*6) / YOUNGER THAN YESTERDAY (*8) / THE BYRDS' GREATEST HITS compilation (*10) / THE NOTORIOUS BYRD BROTHERS (*9) / SWEETHEART OF THE RODEO (*8) / DR. BYRDS & MR. HYDE (*5) / BALLAD OF EASY RIDER (*5) / UNTITLED (*6) / BYRDMANIAX (*4) / GREATEST HITS VOL.2 compilation (*8) / FARTHER ALONG (*4) / THE BYRDS (*4) / THE VERY BEST OF THE BYRDS compilation (*8) / Roger McGuinn: ROGER McGUINN (*6) / PEACE ON YOU (*5) / ROGER McGUINN & HIS BAND (*5) / CARDIFF ROSE (*8) / THUNDERBYRD (*5) / McGUINN, CLARK & HILLMAN (*6) / CITY (*4) / MEAN STREETS with Chris Hillman (*3) / BACK FROM RIO (*6) / BORN TO ROCK'N'ROLL compilation (*7) / LIVE FROM MARS (*5) / TREASURES FROM THE FOLK DEN (*5) / LIMITED EDITION (*5)

GENE CLARK (b. HAROLD EUGENE CLARK, 17 Nov'41, Tipton, Missouri, USA) – vocals, tambourine / **JIM McGUINN** (b. JAMES JOSEPH McGUINN, 13 Jul'42, Chicago, Illinois, USA) – guitar, vocals / **DAVID CROSBY** (b. DAVID VAN CORTLAND, 14 Aug'41, L.A.) – guitar, vocals

Pye Inter. Elektra

Nov 64. (7"; as BEEFEATERS) *(7N 25277)* *<45013>* **PLEASE LET ME LOVE YOU. / DON'T BE LONG** [ ] Sep64 [ ]

— added **CHRIS HILLMAN** (b. 4 Dec'42, L.A.) – bass, vocals (ex-HILLMEN) / **MICHAEL CLARKE** (b. 3 Jun'43, New York City) – drums

C.B.S. Columbia

Jun 65. (7") *(201765)* *<43271>* **MR. TAMBOURINE MAN. / I KNEW I'D WANT YOU** [1] May65 [1]

Aug 65. (7") *(201796)* *<43332>* **ALL I REALLY WANT TO DO. / I'LL FEEL A WHOLE LOT BETTER** [4] Jul65 [40]

Aug 65. (lp; stereo/mono) *(S+/BPG 62571)* *<9172>* **MR. TAMBOURINE MAN** [7] Jun65 [6]
– Mr. Tambourine man / I'll feel a whole lot better / Spanish Harlem incident / You won't have to cry / Here without you / The bells of Rhymney / All I really want to do / I knew I'd want you / It's no use / Don't doubt yourself, babe / Chimes of freedom / We'll meet again. *(re-iss. Jul77; CBS/40 31503) <(cd re-mast.May96 on 'Columbia'+=; 483705-2)<64845>* – She has a way * / I'll feel a whole lot better / It's no use / You won't have to cry / All I really want to do / You and me (instrumental) *. *(lp re-iss. Jul98 on 'Simply Vinyl'; SVLP 32) <(lp re-iss. Jun99 on 'Sundazed'+= *; SCLP 5057)>*

Oct 65. (7") *(202008)* *<43424>* **TURN! TURN! TURN!. / SHE DON'T CARE ABOUT TIME** [26] [1]

Feb 66. (7") *(202037)* *<43501>* **SET YOU FREE THIS TIME. / IT WON'T BE WRONG** [ ] [79] [63]

Mar 66. (lp; stereo/mono) *(S+/SPG 62652)* *<9254>* **TURN! TURN! TURN!** [11] Dec65 [17]
– Turn! Turn! Turn! (to everything there is a season) / It won't be wrong / Set you free this time / Lay down your weary tune / He was a friend of mine / The world turns all around her / Satisfied mind / If you're gone / The times they are a-changin' / Wait and see / Oh! Susannah. *(re-iss. Jul77; CBS/40 31526) <(cd re-mast.May96 on 'Columbia'+=; 483706-2)<64846>* – The day walk (never before) / She don't care about time (mono) * / The times they are a-changin' (mono) * / It's all over now, baby blue (version 1) / She don't care about time (version 1) / The world turns all around her (alt.) / Stranger in a strange land (instrumental) *. *(lp re-iss. Nov98 on 'Simply Vinyl'; SVLP 27) <(lp re-iss. Jun99 on 'Sundazed'+= *; SCLP 5058)>*

— trimmed to a quartet when GENE CLARK went solo

Apr 66. (7") *(202067)* *<43578>* **EIGHT MILES HIGH. / WHY?** [24] [14]

Jul 66. (7") *(202259)* *<43702>* **5D (FIFTH DIMENSION). / CAPTAIN SOUL** [ ] [44]

Sep 66. (lp; stereo/mono) *(S+/BPG 62783)* *<9349>* **FIFTH DIMENSION** [27] Aug66 [24]
– 5D (Fifth Dimension) / Wild mountain thyme / Mr. Spaceman / I see you / What's happening?!?! / I come and stand at every door / Eight miles high / Hey Joe / John Riley / Captain Soul / 2-4-2 Foxtrot (the Lear jet song). *(re-iss. Jul83 lp/c; CBS/40 32284) <(cd re-mast.May96 on 'Columbia'+=; 483707-2)<64847>* – Why? / I know my rider (I know you rider) * / Psychodrama city / Eight miles high (alt.) * / Why? * / John Riley (instrumental). *(lp re-iss. Nov98 on 'Simply Vinyl'; SVLP 47) <(lp re-iss. Jun99 on 'Sundazed'+= *; SCLP 5059)>*

Oct 66. (7") *(202295)* *<43766>* **MR. SPACEMAN. / WHAT'S HAPPENING?!?!** [ ] Sep66 [36]

Feb 67. (7") *(202559)* *<43987>* **SO YOU WANT TO BE A ROCK'N'ROLL STAR. / EVERYBODY'S BEEN BURNED** [ ] Jan67 [29]

Apr 67. (lp; stereo/mono) *(S+/BPG 62988)* *<9442>* **YOUNGER THAN YESTERDAY** [37] Mar67 [24]
– So you want to be a rock'n'roll star / Have you seen her face / C.T.A. – 102 / Renaissance fair / Time between / Everybody's been burned / Thoughts and words / Mind gardens / My back pages / The girl with no name / Why? *(re-iss. Mar87 on 'Edsel' cd/c/lp; CD/C+/ED 227) (cd re-mast.May96 on 'Columbia'+=; 483708-2)<64848>* – It happens each day * / Don't make waves * / My back pages / Mind gardens / Lady friend / Old John Robertson. *(lp re-iss. Oct97 on 'Simply Vinyl'; SVLP 7) <(lp re-iss. Jun99 on 'Sundazed'+= *; SUNLP 5060)>*

May 67. (7") *(2648)* *<44054>* **MY BACK PAGES. / RENAISSANCE FAIR** [ ] Mar67 [30]

Jun 67. (7") *<44157>* **HAVE YOU SEEN HER FACE. / DON'T MAKE WAVES** [–] [74]

Sep 67. (7") *<44230>* **LADY FRIEND. / OLD JOHN ROBERTSON** [–] [82]

Sep 67. (7") *(2924)* **LADY FRIEND. / DON'T MAKE WAVES** [ ] [–]

Oct 67. (lp; stereo/mono) *(S+/BPG 63107)* *<9516>* **THE BYRDS' GREATEST HITS** (compilation) [ ] Aug67 [6]
– Mr. Tambourine man / I'll feel a whole lot better / Bells of rhymney / Turn! turn! turn! / All I really want to do / Chimes of freedom / Eight miles high / Mr.Spaceman / 5D (Fifth Dimension) / So you want to be a rock'n'roll star / My back pages. *(re-iss. Jan84; CBS/40 32068) (cd-iss. Jun89; CD 32068) (cd re-mast.Feb91; 467843-2) (cd re-mast.May96 on 'Columbia'; 483705-2)*

— **GENE CLARK** – guitar, vocals returned to repl. DAVID who formed CROSBY, STILLS and NASH (JIM also changed name to ROGER McGUINN)

Dec 67. (7") *(3093)* *<44362>* **GOIN' BACK. / CHANGE IS NOW** [ ] Nov67 [89]
(re-iss. Jun77; 5300)

Now a trio of **McGUINN, HILLMAN and CLARKE** (GENE continued solo career)

Apr 68. (lp; stereo/mono) *(S+/BPG 63169)* *<9575>* **THE NOTORIOUS BYRD BROTHERS** [12] Jan68 [47]
– Artificial energy / Goin' back / Natural harmony / Draft morning / Wasn't born to follow / Get to you / Change is now / Old John Robertson / Tribal gathering / Dolphin's smile / Space odyssey. *(re-iss. Aug88 on 'Edsel' cd/lp; CD+/ED 262) <(cd re-iss. Mar97 on 'Columbia'+=; 486751-2)<65151* – Moog raga (instrumental) / Bound to fall (instrumental) / Triad / Goin' back / Draft morning / Universal mind decoder (instrumental). *(lp re-iss. Oct97 on 'Simply Vinyl'; SVLP 6)*

— **KEVIN KELLEY** (b.1945, California) – drums (ex-RISING SONS) repl. MICHAEL who joined DILLARD & CLARK. Also added **GRAM PARSONS** (b.INGRAM CECIL CONNOR III, 5 Nov'46, Winterhaven, Florida) – guitar, vocals, keyboards (ex-INTERNATIONAL SUBMARINE BAND) / guests on album – **SNEAKY PETE** – pedal steel guitar / **DOUG DILLARD** – banjo

May 68. (7") *(3411)* *<44499>* **YOU AIN'T GOING NOWHERE. / ARTIFICIAL ENERGY** [45] [74]

Sep 68. (lp) *(63353)* *<9670>* **SWEETHEART OF THE RODEO** [ ] Aug68 [77]
– You ain't going nowhere / I am a pilgrim / The Christian life / You're still on my mind / Pretty Boy Floyd / You don't miss your water / Hickory wind / One hundred years from now / Blue Canadian Rockies / Life in prison / Nothing was delivered. *(re-iss. Jun87 on 'Edsel' cd/lp; CD+/ED 234) <(cd re-iss. Mar97 on 'Columbia'+=; 486752-2)<65150>* – You got a reputation / Lazy days / Pretty Polly The Christian life (Gram Parsons vocal) / Life in prison (alt.) / You're still on my mind (alt.) / One hundred years from now (Gram Parsons vocal) / All I have are memories (instrumental). *(lp re-iss. Nov98 on 'Simply Vinyl'; SVLP 57) (cd re-iss. Oct99 on 'Columbia'; MILLEN 6) <(d-cd iss.Sep03 on 'Columbia'+=; 510921-2)<505473>* – (bonus cd of alt. takes).

Oct 68. (7") *(3752)* *<44643>* **PRETTY BOY FLOYD. / I AM A PILGRIM** [ ] [ ]

— **CARLOS BERNAL** – guitar played on US tour replacing GRAM who joined FLYING BURRITO BROTHERS alongside HILLMAN and SNEAKY PETE. Soon McGUINN recruited entirely new members **CLARENCE WHITE** (b. 6 Jun'44, Lewiston, Maine, USA) – guitar, vocals (ex-NASHVILLE WEST) repl. BERNAL / **GENE PARSONS** (b. 9 Apr'44) – drums, vocals (ex-NASHVILLE WEST) repl. KELLEY / **JOHN YORK** – bass, vocals repl. HILLMAN

Mar 69. (7") *(4055)* *<44746>* **BAD NIGHT AT THE WHISKEY. / DRUG STORE TRUCK DRIVIN' MAN** [ ] [ ]

Apr 69. (lp) *(63545)* *<9755>* **DR. BYRDS AND MR. HYDE** [15] Mar69 [ ]
– This wheel's on fire / Old blue / Your gentle way of loving me / Child of the universe / Nashville West / Drug store truck drivin' man / King Apathy III / Candy / Bad night at the Whiskey / My back pages – B.J. blues – Baby what you want me to do. *(cd-iss. Aug91 on 'Beat Goes On'; BGOCD 107) <(cd re-mast.Mar97 & Jul03 on 'Columbia'+=; 486753-2)<65113>* – Stanley's song / Lay lady lay / This wheel's on fire / My back pages – B.J. blues – Baby what you want me to do (alt.) / Nashville west (alt.). *(lp re-iss. Feb99 on 'Simply Vinyl'; SVLP 70)*

Jun 69. (7") *(4284)* *<44868>* **LAY LADY LAY. / OLD BLUE** [ ] [ ]

Sep 69. (7") *(4572)* **WASN'T BORN TO FOLLOW. / CHILD OF THE UNIVERSE** [ ] [–]

Oct 69. (7") *<44990>* **THE BALLAD OF EASY RIDER. / WASN'T BORN TO FOLLOW** [–] [5]

Jan 70. (lp) *(63795)* *<9942>* **BALLAD OF EASY RIDER** [41] Dec69 [36]
– Ballad of Easy Rider / Fido / Oil in my lamp / Tulsa County / Jack Tarr the sailor / Jesus is just alright / It's all over now, baby blue / There must be someone / Gunga Din / Deportee (plane wreck at Los Gatos) / Armstrong, Aldrin and Collins. *<(cd re-mast.Mar97 & Jul03 on 'Columbia'+=; 486751-2)<65114>* – Way beyond the sun / Mae Jean goes to Hollywood / Oil in my lamp (alt.) / Tulsa County (alt.) / Fiddler a dram (moog experiment) / Ballad of easy rider (long version) / Build it up (instrumental).

Feb 70. (7") *(4753)* *<45071>* **JESUS IS JUST ALRIGHT. / IT'S ALL OVER NOW, BABY BLUE** [ ] [97]

— **SKIP BATTIN** (b. 2 Feb'34, Gallipolis, Ohio) – bass; repl. YORK

Nov 70. (d-lp) *(66253)* *<30127>* **UNTITLED (1/2 live)** 11 Oct70 40
– Lover of the bayou / Positively 4th Street / Nashville West / So you want to be a rock'n'roll star / Mr. Tambourine man / Mr. Spaceman / Eight miles high // Chestnut mare / Truck stop girl / All the things / Yesterday's train / Hungry planet / Just a season / Take a whiff (on me) / You all look alike / Welcome back home. *<(d-cd re-mast.Feb00 on 'Columbia'+=; 495077-2)<65847>* – All the things / Yesterday's train / Lover of the bayou / Kathleen's song / White's lightning (part 2) / Willin' / You ain't goin' nowhere (live) / Old Blue (live) / It's alright, ma (I'm only bleeding) (live) / Ballad of easy rider (live) / My back pages (live) / Take a whiff on me (live) / Jesus is just alright (live) / This wheel's on fire (live). *(3xlp-set-iss.JUn02 on 'Simply Vinyl'+=; SVLP 381)*

Dec 70. (7") *(5322)* *<45259>* **CHESTNUT MARE. / JUST A SEASON** 19

May 71. (7") *(7253)* **I TRUST (EVERYTHING'S GONNA WORK OUT FINE). / THIS IS MY DESTINY** –

Aug 71. (lp) *(64389)* *<30640>* **BIRDMANIAX** Jul71 46
– Glory, glory / Pale blue / I trust / Tunnel of love / Citizen Kane / I wanna grow up to be a politician / Absolute happiness / Green apple quick step / My destiny / Kathleen's song / Jamaica say you will. *(cd-iss. Sep90 on 'Line'; CLCD 900930) <(cd re-mast.Feb00 on 'Columbia'+=; 495079-2)<65848>* – Just like a woman / Pale blue (alt.) / Think I'm gonna feel better.

Oct 71. (7") *(7501)* *<45440>* **GLORY, GLORY. / CITIZEN KANE**

Oct 71. (lp) *(64650)* *<31795>* **THE BYRDS' GREATEST HITS VOLUME 2** (compilation) <US title 'THE BEST OF THE BYRDS (GREATEST HITS, VOLUME II'> Dec72
– The ballad of Easy rider / Jesus is just alright / Chestnut mare / You ain't goin' nowhere / I am a pilgrim / Goin' back / I trust / Lay lady lay / Wasn't born to follow / The times they are a-changin' / Drug store truck drivin' man / Get to you.

Jan 72. (lp) *(64676)* *<31050>* **FARTHER ALONG** Dec71
– Tiffany queen / Get down your line / Farther along / B.B. class road / Bugler / America's great national pastime / Antique Sandy / Precious Kate / So fine / Lazy waters / Bristol steam convention blues. *<(cd re-mast.Feb00 on 'Columbia'+=; 495078-2)<65849>* – Lost my drivin' wheel / Born to rock & roll / Bag full of money / Bristol steam convention blues (alt.).

Jan 72. (7") *(7712)* *<45514>* **AMERICA'S GREAT NATIONAL PASTIME. / FARTHER ALONG**

— They split mid '72, SKIP joined NEW RIDERS OF THE PURPLE SAGE. CLARENCE WHITE was killed in a road accident 14 Jul'73. / **JOHN GUERRIN** – drums (session men) took over briefly when reforming

— **McGUINN** then re-formed the original **"BYRDS"** Himself, **CROSBY, CLARK, HILLMAN + CLARKE**

Asylum Asylum

Apr 73. (lp) *(SYLA 8754)* *<5058>* **THE BYRDS** 31 Mar73 20
– Full circle / Sweet Mary / Changing heart / For free / Born to rock'n'roll / Things will be better / Cowgirl in the sand / Long live the King / Borrowing time / Laughing / (See the sky) about to rain. *(cd-iss. Feb93 on 'Warners; 7559 60955-2)*

May 73. (7") *(AYM 516)* **THINGS WILL BE BETTER. / FOR FREE** –

Jun 73. (7") *(AYM 517)* *<11016>* **FULL CIRCLE. / LONG LIVE THE KING** Apr73

Jul 73. (7") *<11019>* **COWGIRL IN THE SAND. / LONG LIVE THE KING** –

— McGUINN, HILLMAN and CLARK all went solo, later teaming up together on album. CROSBY re-formed CROSBY, STILL and NASH. Sadly, MICHAEL CLARKE was to die of liver failure 19th December '93.

– compilations, etc. –

On 'CBS' / 'Columbia' unless mentioned otherwise.

Feb 66. (7"ep) *(EP 6069)* **THE TIMES ARE A-CHANGING** 15 –

Oct 66. (7"ep) *(EP 6077)* **EIGHT MILES HIGH** 18 –

Aug 69. (lp) *Together;* *<ST-T 1001>* **PREFLYTE (demo recordings of '64)** –
<re-iss. 1973 on 'Columbia'; C 32183> (UK-iss.Sep73 on 'Bumble'; GEXP 8001)

Dec 69. (lp) *Together;* *<ST-T 1019>* **EARLY L.A.** –

May 73. (d-lp) *(68242)* **THE HISTORY OF THE BYRDS** 47 –
– Mr. Tambourine man / Turn! turn! turn! / She don't care about time / Wild mountain thyme / Eight miles high / Mr.Spaceman / 5D (Fifth Dimension) / So you want to be a rock'n'roll star / Time between / My back pages / Lady friend / Goin' back / Old John Robertson / Wasn't born to follow / You ain't goin' nowhere / Hickory wind / Nashville West / Drug store truck drivin' man / Gunga Din / Jesus is just alright / The ballad of Easy Rider / Chestnut mare / Yesterday's train / Just a season / Citizen Kane / Jamaica say you will / Tiffany queen / America's great national pastime. *(re-iss. Sep87 d-lp/c; 460115-1/-4)*

Feb 80. (lp/c) *(CBS/40 31795)* **THE BYRDS PLAY DYLAN**
(cd-iss. Apr94 & Feb96 on 'Sony'; 476757-2)

Aug 80. (lp/c) *(CBS/40 31851)* **THE ORIGINAL SINGLES 1965-1967**
(re-iss. Nov81 lp/c; CBS/40 32069)

Feb 82. (lp/c) *(CBS/40 32103)* **THE ORIGINAL SINGLES 1967-1969**

Feb 91. (cd/c) *Raven; (RV CD/CA 10)* **FULL FLYTE 1965-1970** –

Jul 91. (3xcd-box) *Columbia; (468338-2)* **MR. TAMBOURINE MAN / TURN! TURN! TURN! / YOUNGER THAN YESTERDAY** –

Mar 93. (cd/c) *Columbia; (471665-2/-4) <32644>* **20 ESSENTIAL TRACKS FROM THE BOXED SET: 1965-1990**

Jun 97. (d-cd) *Columbia; (487995-2)* **THE VERY BEST OF THE BYRDS** –
– Mr. Tambourine man / All I really want to do / Chimes of freedom / I'll feel a whole lot better / Turn! turn! turn! (there is a season) / The times they are a-changin' / The world turns all around her / It won't be wrong / He was a friend of mine / Eight miles high / 5D (Fifth dimension) / Mr. Spaceman / So you want to be a rock & roll star / My back pages / Renaissance fair / Goin' back / Wasn't born to follow / Dolphin's smile / You ain't goin' nowhere / One hundred years from now / You're still on my mind / Hickory wind / Ballad of easy rider / Jesus is just alright / It's all over now, baby blue / Lay lady lay / Chestnut mare. *(d-lp-iss.Apr02 on 'Simply Vinyl'; SVLP 375)*

Jun 00. (lp) *Sundazed; <(SCLP 5061)>* **SANCTUARY**

Nov 00. (lp) *Sundazed; <(SCLP 5065)>* **SANCTUARY II**

Dec 01. (lp) *Sundazed; <(SCLP 5066)>* **SANCTUARY III**

Oct 02. (3xcd-box) *Columbia; (509502-2)* **YOUNGER THAN YESTERDAY / THE NOTORIOUS BYRD BROTHERS / SWEETHEART OF THE RODEO** –

Nov 02. (cd-ep) *Magic; (3930244)* **SET YOU FREE THIS TIME / THE TIMES THEY ARE A-CHANGIN' / IT WON'T BE WRONG / OH SUSANNA** –

Jul 03. (cd) *(495080-2)* **FILMORE WEST 1969**

Sep 03. (cd) *(512778-2)* **MOJO PRESENTS . . . THE BYRDS**

ROGER McGUINN

C.B.S. Columbia

Jun 73. (7") *<45931>* **DRAGGIN'. / TIME CUBE** –

Jun 73. (lp) *(CBS 65274)* *<31946>* **ROGER McGUINN**
– I'm so restless / My new woman / Lost my drivin' wheel / Draggin' / Time cube / Bag full of money / Hanoi Hannah / Stone / Heave away / M'Linda / The water is wide. *(re-iss. Jul88 on 'Edsel'; ED 281) (cd-iss. Feb91; EDCD 281) <(cd re-iss. Feb04 on 'Sundazed'+=; SC 6201)>* – John John / Jamaica say you will.

Jul 74. (7") *<10019>* **SAME OLD SOUND. / GATE OF HORN** –

Sep 74. (lp) *(CBS 80171)* *<32956>* **PEACE ON YOU** 92
– Peace on you / Without you / Going to the country / One more time / Same old sound / Do what you want to / Together / Better change / Gate of horn / Lady. *<(cd-iss. Feb04 on 'Sundazed'+=; SC 6202)>** - Rock'n'roll time.

Sep 74. (7") *(2649)* *<10044>* **PEACE ON YOU. / WITHOUT YOU**

— his band; **GREG ATTAWAY / STEVE LOVE / DAVID LOVELACE**

Jul 75. (lp; as ROGER McGUINN & BAND) *(CBS 80877)* *<33541>* **ROGER McGUINN AND BAND** Jun75
– Somebody loves you / Knockin' on Heaven's door / Bull Dog / Painted lady / Lover of the bayou / Lisa / Circle song/ So long / Easy does it / Born to rock and roll.

Jul 75. (7"; as ROGER McGUINN & BAND) *<10181>* **SOMEBODY LOVES YOU / EASY DOES IT** –

Oct 75. (7"; as ROGER McGUINN & BAND) *<10201>* **LOVER OF THE BAYOU. / EASY DOES IT** –

Jun 76. (7") *<10385>* **TAKE ME AWAY. / FRIEND** –

Jun 76. (lp) *(CBS 81369)* *<34154>* **CARDIFF ROSE**
– Jolly Roger / Take me away / Rock and roll time / Partners in crime / Friend / Up to me / Round table / Prettly Polly / Dream land.

May 77. (lp) *(CBS 81883)* *<34656>* **THUNDERBYRD**
– All night long / It's gone / Dixie highway / American girl / We can do it all over again / Why, baby why / I'm not lonely anymore / Golden loom / Russian Hill.

May 77. (7") *(5231)* **AMERICAN GIRL. / RUSSIAN HILL** [ ] [–]
May 77. (7") *(10543>* **AMERICAN GIRL. / I'M NOT LONELY ANYMORE** [–] [ ]

McGUINN, CLARK & HILLMAN

(nearly a BYRDS reformation; ROGER, GENE & CHRIS)

Capitol Capitol

Feb 79. (7") *(CL 16065)* **SURRENDER TO ME. / BYE BYE BABY** [ ] [–]
Feb 79. (lp/c) *<(EST/TC-EST 11910)>* **McGUINN, CLARK & HILLMAN** [ ] [39]
– Long long time / Little mama / Don't you write her off / Sad boy / Surrender to me / Backstage pass / Stopping traffic / Feeling higher / Release me girl / Bye bye baby. *(cd-iss. Feb99 on 'E.M.I.'; CDP 796355-2)*
Apr 79. (7") *(CL 16077) <4693>* **DON'T YOU WRITE HER OFF. / SAD BOY** [ ] Mar79 [33]
Jun 79. (7") *<4739>* **SURRENDER TO ME. / LITTLE MAMA** [–] [ ]
Sep 79. (7") *<4763>* **BYE BYE BABY. / BACKSTAGE PASS** [–] [ ]
Jan 80. (lp; by ROGER McGUINN and CHRIS HILLMAN featuring GENE CLARK) *<(EST/TC-EST 12043)>* **CITY** [ ] [ ]
– Who taught the night / One more chance / Won't let you down / Street talk / City / Skate date / Givin' herself away / Let me down easy / Deeper in / Painter fire.
Feb 80. (7") *<4821>* **STREET TALK. / ONE MORE CHANCE** [–] [ ]
Apr 80. (7") *<4855>* **CITY. / DEEPER IN** [–] [ ]

McGUINN / HILLMAN

Mar 81. (lp/c) *<(EST/TC-EST 12108)>* **McGUINN / HILLMAN – MEAN STREETS** [ ] [ ]
– Mean streets / Entertainment / Soul shoes / Between you and me / Angel / Ain't no money / Love me tonight / King for a night / A secret side of you / Turn your radio on. *(cd-iss. Feb91;)*
Mar 81. (7") *(4952>* **TURN YOUR RADIO ON. / MAKING MOVIES** [–] [ ]
May 81. (7") *<4973>* **LOVE ME TONIGHT. / KING FOR A NIGHT** [–] [ ]

not iss. Universal

1983. (7") *<66006>* **YOU AIN'T GOIN' NOWHERE. / DON'T YOU HEAR JERUSALEM MOAN** [–] [ ]

ROGER McGUINN

used session people **STAN LYNCH** – drums / **GEORGE HAWKINS** – bass / **DAVID COLE** – acoustic guitar / **JOHN JORGENSEN** – guitar / **BELMONT TENCH** – keyboards / **MICHAEL THOMPSON** – acoustic guitar

Arista Arista

Feb 91. (cd/c/lp) *(261/411/211 348) <8648>* **BACK FROM RIO** [ ] Jan91 [44]
– Someone to love / Car phone / You bowed down / Suddenly blue / The trees are all gone / king of the hill / Without your love / The time has come / Your love is a gold mine / If we never meet again.
Feb 91. (7") *(113 993)* **KING OF THE HILL. / YOUR LOVE IS A GOLD MINE** [ ] [–]
(cd-s+=) *(663 993)* – The time has come.

Polydor Hollywood

Jan 97. (cd) *<(162090-2)>* **LIVE FROM MARS** (live) [ ] Nov96 [ ]
– Heartbreak hotel / Daddy roll 'em / Gate of Horn / Chestnut mare / Bells of rhymney / Turn! turn! turn! (to everything there is a season) / Beach ball / Wild mountain thyme / You showed me / Mr. Tambourine man (acoustic) / Mr. Tambourine man (electric) / Mr. Spaceman / Eight miles high / So you want to be a rock & roll star / King of the hill / May the road rise / Fireworks / May the road rise.

not iss. mp3

2000. (cd) *<2720>* **McGUINN'S FOLK DEN VOL.1** [–] [ ]
– Mighty day / Pushboat / John the revelator / Bonny ship the Diamond / John Henry / Handsome cabin boy / Wayfaring stranger / Finnegan's wake / James alley blues / Home on the range / Mary had a baby.
2000. (cd) *<12919>* **McGUINN'S FOLK DEN VOL.2** [–] [ ]
– John Riley / Virgin Mary / 900 miles / Old paint / Easter morn / Old Texas / Springfield mountain / Buffalo skinners / Argonaut / Liverpool girls / Evenin' blues.
2000. (cd) *<31893>* **McGUINN'S FOLK DEN VOL.3** [–] [ ]
– I'm Alabama bound / Sail away lady / Get along little doggies / Brisbane ladies / Cane blues / Blood red roses / Oh you New York girls / Gold coast of Greenland / Trouble in mind / I saw 3 ships / Greenland whale.
2000. (cd) *<63938>* **McGUINN'S FOLK DEN VOL.4** [–] [ ]
– Willie Moore / The star spangled banner / Alberta / If I had wings / East Virginia blues / Faithless Floa / South Australia / Boatman / Whiskey in the jar / Cruel war / Auld lang syne.

Appleseed Appleseed

Aug 01. (cd) *<(APRCD 1046)>* **TREASURES FROM THE FOLK DEN** (original mp3 recordings) [ ] [ ]
– Wagoner's load / Dink's song / Bonnie ship the Diamond / Cane blues / Reel / Fair Nottamun town / John the revelator / Alabama bound / Finnegan's wake / In the evenin' / Willie Moore / The Brazos river / Sail away lady / John Riley / Trouble in mind / Whiskey in the jar / The Virgin Mary / Pete's song.

not iss. April Fir

Apr 04. (cd) *<0401>* **LIMITED EDITION** [–] [ ]
– If I needed someone / Parade of lost dreams / Shady grove / James alley blues / On and on / Southbound 95 / Castanet dance / Shenandoah / When the saints go marching in / Saint James infirmary / May the road rise to meet you / Echoes live / Made in China.

– compilations, etc. –

Mar 92. (cd/c) *Columbia; (471269-2/-4) <CK/CT 47494>* **BORN TO ROCK AND ROLL** [ ] [ ]
Dec 92. (cd; McGUINN / CLARK / HILLMAN) *Edsel; (EDCD 358)* **RETURN FLYTE** [ ] [–]
Jun 93. (cd) *Edsel; (EDCD 373)* **RETURN FLIGHT VOL.2** [ ] [ ]
Feb 97. (d-cd; McGUIIN, HILLMAN & CLARK) *Strange Fruit (SFRCD 001)* **3 BYRDS LAND IN LONDON** [ ] [–]
Apr 04. (cd) *Beat Goes On; (BGOCD 620)* **ROGER McGUINN / PEACE ON YOU** [ ] [–]

☐ David BYRNE (see under ⇒ TALKING HEADS)

CABARET VOLTAIRE

Formed: Sheffield, England . . . 1973 by STEPHEN MALLINDER, RICHARD H. KIRK and CHRIS WATSON, naming themselves after the experimental Parisian Dadaist performances of pre-20's France. A farcical 1975 debut gig saw them using a backing tape of a steamhammer while KIRK played clarinet; his jacket was also covered in fairy lights (!), the whole set up not going down with a rioting audience who proceeded to beat him up! Inspired by the likes of CAN and BRIAN ENO, the CABS contributed two songs (one of them, 'BAADER MEINHOF', was nearly chosen as a debut 45!) to a 1978 various artists double EP, 'A FACTORY SAMPLER', before they signed to Geoff Travis's new independent operation, 'Rough Trade'. Later that year, the trio issued their debut release, 'EXTENDED PLAY', a four track EP that included their industrial mangling of The Velvet Underground's 'HERE SHE COMES NOW'. A classic follow-up, 'NAG NAG NAG', fused electronic sound with the yobbish rush of adrenaline-fuelled punk to devastating effect. 1979 also saw the release of their debut long-player, 'MIX-UP', a pivotal experimental affair which, although marking out new territory, was a challenging listen end to end. The early years of the following decade found CABARET VOLTAIRE ploughing their own idiosyncratic furrow over the course of three studio albums (two live events were also issued), namely 'THE VOICE OF AMERICA' (1980), 'RED MECCA' (1981) and '2 X 45' (1982), before WATSON's departure left MALLINDER and KIRK as a duo. In 1983, they were sought out by Virgin off-shoot, 'Some Bizzare', their avant-garde inaccessibility now taking on a more commercial hue with 'THE CRACKDOWN', an album which nearly took them into the UK Top 30. Incorporating elements of Eastern exotica, the record was also more dancefloor friendly than anything they had recorded to date; tracks such as 'JUST FASCINATION', '24-24', 'ANIMATION' and 'WHY KILL TIME (WHEN YOU CAN KILL YOUSELF)', were lent the rhythmic expertise of SOFT CELL's DAVE BALL (later of The GRID). Ironically, the more overtly pop approach of SOFT CELL and their ilk (DEPECHE MODE, HUMAN LEAGUE and OMD) led to the more adventurous CABS being squeezed out of the market. They did, however, maintain a loyal if not massive following who stuck by them through a series of lesser mid-80's albums, 'MICRO-PHONIES' (1984), 'THE COVENANT, THE SWORD AND THE ARM OF THE LORD' (1985) and 'CODE' (1987), the latter set their first for 'Parlophone'. Since 1983, both MALLINDER and KIRK had moonlighted in various side projects, the former releasing a solo album, 'POW-WOW', the latter far more prolific in his output with 'BLACK JESUS VOICE' (1986) the pick of the bunch. The late 80's house scene, meanwhile, saw CABARET VOLTAIRE cited as a prominent influence on many of the genre's prime movers; the result was a creative renaissance of sorts which led to a remix by PETE WATERMAN (!) for the 'KEEP ON' single, while house producer, MARSHALL JEFFERSON, took controls on the comeback set, 'GROOVY, LAID BACK AND NASTY' (1990). Despite this uncharacteristic dalliance with the mainstream, the CABS slipped back into semi-obscurity with their former Belgian label, 'Les Disques Du Crepescule' releasing a handful of low profile sets, 'BODY AND SOUL' (1991), 'PERCUSSION FORCE' (1991), 'INTERNATIONAL LANGUAGE' (1993) and 'THE CONVERSATION' (1994).

Album rating: MIX-UP (*5) / THE VOICE OF AMERICA (*4) / RED MECCA (*7) / 2x45 (*7) / JOHNNY YES NO soundtrack (*3) / THE CRACKDOWN (*8) / MICRO-PHONIES (*6) / DRINKING GASOLINE (*6) / THE COVENANT, THE SWORD & THE ARM (*6) / CODE (*7) / GROOVY, LAIDBACK & NASTY (*6) / THE LIVING LEGENDS compilation (*9) / THE GOLDEN MOMENTS OF CABARET VOLTAIRE compilation (*7) / LISTEN UP WITH CABARET VOLTAIRE compilation (*7) / COLOURS (*5) / PLASTICITY (*5) / Stephen Mallinder: POW WOW (*6) / Richard H. Kirk: BLACK JESUS VOICE (*6)

STEPHEN MALLINDER – vocals, bass, electronics, percussion, trumpet, piano / **RICHARD H. KIRK** – guitar, vocals, synthesizer, bongos, piano / **CHRISTOPHER R. WATSON** – electronics, tapes

(issued cassette 25 copies LIMITED EDITION in 1976 on own label)

Rough Trade | not iss.

Nov 78. (7"ep) *(RT 003)* **EXTENDED PLAY** [ ] [–]
– Talkover / Here she comes now / Do the Mussolini – headkick / The set up.

Jun 79. (7") *(RT 018)* **"NAG NAG NAG." / IS THAT ME (FINDING SOMEONE AT THE DOOR AGAIN)?** [ ] [–]

Oct 79. (lp) *(ROUGH 4)* **MIX-UP** [ ] [–]
– Kurlian photograph / No escape / 4th shot / Heaven and Hell / Eyeless sight (live) / Photophobia / On every other street / Expect nothing / Capsules. *(re-iss. Sep90 on 'Mute' lp/cd; CABS 8/+CD)*

Dec 79. (7") *(RT 035)* **SILENT COMMAND. / The Soundtrack 'CHANCE VERSUS CAUSALITY'** [ ] [–]

— added guest **MARK TATTERSALL** – drums

Jan 80. (lp) *(ROUGH 7)* **LIVE AT THE Y.M.C.A. 27.10.79 (live)** [ ] [–]
– Untitled / On every other street / Nag nag nag / The set up / Havoc / Expect nothing / Here she comes now / No escape / Baader Meinhof. *(re-iss. Jun90 on 'Mute' lp/cd; CABS 4/+CD)*

— now with guests **JOHN CLAYTON** – percussion / **JANE** – tapes

Mar 80. (12"ep) *(RT 038)* **THREE MANTRAS** [ ] [–]
– Eastern mantra / Western mantra. *(re-iss. Jun90 on 'Mute' m-lp/cd; CABS 7/+CD)*

— with guest **HAYDN BOYES-WESTON** – drums (ex-2.3) (also on debut lp)

Jul 80. (lp) *(ROUGH 11)* **THE VOICE OF AMERICA** [ ] [–]
– The voice of America / Damage is done / Partially submerged / Kneel to the boss / Premonition / This is entertainment / If the shadows could march? / Stay out of it / Obsession / News from nowhere / Messages received. *(re-iss. Jun90 on 'Mute' lp/cd; CABS 2/+CD)*

Nov 80. (7") *(RT 060)* **SECONDS TOO LATE. / CONTROL ADDICT** [ ] [–]

Jul 81. (12"ep) *(TWI 018)* **3 CREPUSCULE TRACKS** [–] Belg. [–]
– Sluggin' fer Jesus (Pt.1) / Your agent man / Sluggin' fer Jesus (Pt.2). (above released on 'Crepuscule')

— **NICK ALLDAY** – drums (ex-GRAPH) repl. HAYDN

Aug 81. (lp) *(ROUGH 27)* **RED MECCA** [ ] [–]
– Touch of evil / Sly doubt / Landslide / A thousand ways / Red mask / Split second feling / Black mask / Spread the virus / A touch of evil (reprise). *(re-iss. Jun90 on 'Mute' lp/cd; CABS 3/+CD)*

Sep 81. (lp) *(COPY 002)* **LIVE AT THE LYCEUM (live)** [ ] [–]
– Taxi music / Seconds too late / Your agent man / Split second feeling / Sluggin' fer Jesus (Pt.1) / Kneel to the bass / Obsession / A thousand ways. *(re-iss. Sep90 on 'Mute' lp/cd; CABS 13/+CD)*

Nov 81. (7") *(RT 095)* **JAZZ THE GLASS. / BURNT TO THE GROUND** –

Dec 81. (12") *(RT 096)* **EDDIE'S OUT. / WALLS OF JERICHO** –
(limited copies contained last 7" free) (below on 'Solidarity')

Mar 82. (12"ep; by PRESSURE COMPANY) *(SOLID 1)* **LIVE IN SHEFFIELD 19th JANUARY 1982 (live)** –
– War of nerves / Wait & shuffle / Get out of my face / Vitrions China (paradox).

— **ALAN FISH** – drums, percussion (of HULA) repl. **ALLDAY** / guest **ERIC RANDOM** – guitar (also a solo artist)

Jun 82. (2x12"lp) *(ROUGH 42)* **2 x 45** 98 –
– Breathe deep / Yashar / Protection / War of nerves (T.E.S.) / Wait and shuffle / Get out of my face. *(re-iss. Sep90 on 'Mute' lp/cd; CABS 9/+CD)*

Nov 82. (lp) *(RTD 1)* **HAI! (live)** – German –
– Walls of Kyoto / 3 days monk / Yashar (version) / Over and over / Diskono / Taxi music (version). *(re-iss. Sep90 on 'Mute' lp/cd; CABS 11/+CD)*

— trimmed to a duo (**MALLINDER** + **KIRK**) when WATSON departed. Retained **ALAN FISH** and brought in **DAVE BALL** – keyboards (of SOFT CELL)

Feb 83. (12") *(TWI 020)* **FOOLS GAME (SLUGGIN' FER JESUS Pt.3). / GUT LEVEL** – Belg. –
(above released on 'Crepuscule')

Some Bizzare – Virgin not iss.

Jul 83. (7") *(CVS 1)* **JUST FASCINATION. / EMPTY WALLS** –
(12") *(CVS 1-12)* – ('A'side) / The crackdown.

Aug 83. (lp/c) *(CV/TCV 1)* **THE CRACKDOWN** 31 –
– 24-24 / In the shadows / Talking time / Animation / Over and over / Just fascination / Why kill time (when you can kill yourself) / Haiti / Crackdown. *(free 12"w/ above + on c+cd)* – MOSCOW / BADGE OF EVIL. / DISKONO / DOUBLE VISION *(cd-iss. 1984; CDCV 1) (re-iss. Aug86 lp/c; OVED/+C 156)*

Nov 83. (lp) *(DVR 1)* **JOHNNY YESNO** (1982 video) –
– Taxi music / Hallucination sequence / D.T.'s – Cold turkey / The quarry (in the wilderness) / Title sequence / Taxi music dub. *(re-iss. Sep90 on 'Grey Area-Mute' lp/cd; CABS 10/+CD) <US cd-iss. Sep90 on 'Mute-Elektra'; 61004-2>*
(above released on 'DoubleVision')

Dec 83. (7"/ext.12") *(CVS 2/+12)* **THE DREAM TICKET. / SAFETY ZONE** –

Sep 84. (7"/ext.12") *(CVS 3/+12)* **SENSORIA. / CUT THE DAMN CAMERA** –

Nov 84. (lp/c/cd) *(CV/TCV/CVCD 2)* **MICRO-PHONIES** 69 –
– Do right / The operative / Digital rasta / Spies in the wires / Theme from Earthshaker / James Brown / Slammer / Blue heat / Sensoria. *(cd+=)* – Blue heat (extended) / Sensoria (extended). *(re-iss. Sep91 on 'Virgin'; cd/c; same)*

Jan 85. (7"/12") *(CVS 4/+12)* **JAMES BROWN. / BAD SELF (part 1)** –

Jun 85. (2x12"/c) *(CVM/TCVM 1)* **DRINKING GASOLINE** 71 –
– Kino / Sleepwalking / Big funk / Ghost talk. *(re-iss. Sep91 on 'Virgin'; same)*

Sep 85. (7") *(CVS 5)* **I WANT YOU. / DRINK YOUR POISON** –
(12") *(CVS 5-12)* – ('A'side) / Drink your poison, C.O.M.A.

Oct 85. (lp/c/cd) *(CV/TCV/CDCV 3)* **THE COVENANT, THE SWORD AND THE ARM OF THE LORD** 57 –
– L21st / I want you / Hell's home / Kickback / The arm of the Lord / Warm / Golden halos / Motion rotation / Whip blow / The web. *(cd+=)* – Sleepwalking / Big funk *(re-iss. Sep91 on 'Virgin'; same)*

— guest **DEE BOYLE** – drums (of CHAAK) repl. FISH

DoubleVision not iss.

Jun 86. (12"ep) *(DVR-DVRP 21)* **THE DRAIN TRAIN** –
– Shakedown (the whole thing) / Menace / Electro-motive.
(w/ free-12") – SHAKEDOWN (The Whole Thing). / SHAKEDOWN (dub).

Parlophone Manhattan

Jul 87. (7") *(R 6157)* **DON'T ARGUE. / DON'T ARGUE (WHO'S ARGUING)** 69 –
(12") *(12R 6157)* – ('A'extended) / ('A'-Hate & Destroy mix).
(12") *(12RX 6157)* – ('A'dance mix) / ('A'dub).

Sep 87. (7") *(R 6166)* **HERE TO GO. / HERE TO GO (dub)**
(12") *(12R 6166)* – ('A'extended mix) / ('A'-Space dub mix).
(12") *(12RX 6166)* – ('A'-Linn drum mix) / ('A'-Eleven Eleven mix).

Oct 87. (lp/c/cd) *(PCS/TCPCS/CDPCS 7312)* <46999> **CODE**
– Don't argue / Sex, money, freaks / Thank you America / Here to go / Trouble (won't stop) / White car / No one here / Life slips by / Code *(cd+=)* – Here to go (little dub) / Hey hey.

Oct 89. (7") *(RS 6227)* **HYPNOTISED (Daniel Miller mix). / ('A'-Gerald's vocal mix)** 66 –
(12") *(12RS 6227)* – ('A'-Fon Force mix) / ('A'-Fon Force dub) / ('A'-Danie Miller dub mix) / ('A'-Robert Gordon mix).
(cd-s) *(CDCDR 6227)* – ('A'-Fon Force mix) / ('A'-Gerald's vocal mix).
(12") *(12RX 6227)* – (cd tracks) / ('A'-A Guy Called Gerald's music mix) / ('A'-Western Works mix).

Mar 90. (7") *(R 6250)* **KEEP ON. / KEEP ON (Les dub)** 55 –
(12") *(12R 6250)* – ('A'-Sweet Exorcist mix) / ('A'-Sleazy Dog mix) / ('A'-Mayday mix).
(cd-s) – ('A'-western works mix) / ('A'club mix).

Jun 90. (cd/c/lp) *(CD/TC+/PCS 7338)* <92249> **GROOVY, LAIDBACK AND NASTY**
– Searchin' / Hypnotised / Minute by minute / Runaway / Keep on (I got this feeling) / Magic / Time beats / Easy life. *(free 12"ep w/ above,* **GROOVY, LAIDBACK AND NASTY** (remixes) – Runaway / Magic / Searchin' / Rescue me (city lights) * / Easy life. *(cd+= *)*

Jul 90. (7") *(R 6261)* **EASY LIFE. / ('A'-Robert Gordon mix)** 61
(12") *(12R 6261)* – ('A'side) / Fluid / Positive I.D.
(cd-s) *(CDR 6261)* – ('A'side) / ('A'-Jive Turkey mix) / Fluid.
(12") *(12RX 6261)* – ('A'vocal) / ('A'-Strange mix) / ('A'-Very strange mixes by Robert Gordon and Fon Force).

Crepescule not iss.

Feb 91. (12") *(TWI 948)* **WHAT IS REAL. / ('A'-Virtual reality mix)** –
(cd-s+=) *(TWI 948-2)* – Legacy of a computer.

Mar 91. (lp/cd) *(TWI 944/+2)* **BODY AND SOUL** –
– No resistance / Shout / Happy / Decoy / Bad chemistry / Vibration / What is real / Western land. *(cd+=)* – What is real (dreamtime mix).

Jul 91. (m-lp/cd) *(TWI 951/+2)* **PERCUSSION FORCE** –
– Don't walk away / Keep on pushin' / Don't walk away (Robert Gordon mix) / Dynamic zone / Jazz the computer (part 1) / Keep on pushin (version). *(cd+=)* – T.Phunk / Don't walk away (version) / Jazz the computer part 2.

Plastex Instinc

Oct 91. (m-lp) *(EXL 001)* <93> **COLOURS**
– Colours (original style mix) / Alright / Smooth / Colours (thunder mix) / Wildlife / Colours (club mix) / Ex.

Oct 92. (d-lp/c/cd) *(EXL/+C/CD 003)* <255> **PLASTICITY**
– Low cool / Soul vine (70 billion people) / Resonator /Inside the electronic revolution / From another source / Deep time / Back to Brazilia / Neuron factory / Delmas 19 / Cooled out / Invisible generation / Soulenoid (scream at the right time). *(cd re-iss. Mar96 on 'Crepescule'; TWI 975-2)*

Jun 93. (cd) *(EXLCD 004)* <264> **INTERNATIONAL LANGUAGE** –
– Everything is true / Radical chic / Taxi mutant / Let it come down / Afterglow / The rest / Millenium / Belly of the beast (back in Babylon) / Other world.

Apollo-R&S Instinc

Jul 94. (q-lp/d-cd) *(AMB 4934/+CD)* <273> **THE CONVERSATION**
– Exterminating angel (intro) / Brutal but clean / The message / Let's start / Night rider / Night rider / I think / The heat / Harmonic parallel / Project 80 (parts 1-4) / Exterminating angel (outro).

— disbanded soon after above

– compilations, others, etc. –

1981. (c) *Industrial; (IRC 35)* **74-76** –
(cd-iss. Jun92 on 'Grey Area-Mute'; CABS 15CD)

Feb 88. (lp/cd) *Crepuscule; (TWI 749/+2)* **8 CREPESCULE TRACKS** – Belgium –
(cd re-iss. Mar96; same)

Jul 83. (12") *Factory Benelux; (FBN 25)* **YASHAR (5.00). / YASHAR (7.20)** – Belgium –

Nov 87. (cd) *Rough Trade; (RUFCD 6001)* **THE GOLDEN MOMENTS OF CABARET VOLTAIRE** –
– Do the Mussolini (Head Kick) / Nag nag nag / Photophobia / Expect nothing / Seconds Too late / This is entertainment / Obsession / Sluggin for Jesus / Landslide / Red mask / Get out of my face.
(below releases on 'Mute' unless otherwise mentioned)

May 90. (cd-ep) *(CABS 1CD)* **"NAG NAG NAG." / YASHAR / YASHAR (John Robie remixes)** –

Jun 90. (lp/c/cd) *(CABS 5/+C/CD)* **LISTEN UP WITH CABARET VOLTAIRE** (rare demos) –

Jun 90. (d-lp/c/cd) *(CABS 6/+C/CD)* **THE LIVING LEGENDS . . . CABARET VOLTAIRE** (the singles)
– Do the Mussolini (head kick) / Talk over / Here she comes now / The set up / Nag, nag, nag / Silent command / Jazz the glass / Walls of Jericho / Seconds too late / Eddie's out / Burnt to the ground / Extract from : Chance Verses Casuality / Control addict / Is that me (finding someone at the door again).

Jun 90. (c) *(CABS 2C)* **LIVE AT THE LYCEUM / THE VOICE OF AMERICA** –

Jun 90. (c) *(CABS 7C)* **THE DRAIN TRAIN / THREE MANTRAS** –

Jun 90. (c) *(CABS 8C)* **MIX-UP / LIVE AT THE Y.M.C.A.** –

Jun 90. (c) *(CABS 10C)* **2 x 45 / JOHNNY YESNO** –

Jun 90. (c) *(CABS 11C)* **HAI! / RED MECCA** –

Apr 92. (12"ep/cd-ep) *Virgin; (CVT 5)* **I WANT YOU hardcore hell) / KINO 4. / I WANT YOU (808 heaven mix) / KINO 5** –
– (Altern 8 remixes / Western re-works '92)

May 92. (d-lp/cd)(c) *Virgin; (CV/+CD 4)(TCV 4)* **TECHNOLOGY** (remixes late 70's & early 80's) –

Oct 00. (cd) *Burning Airlines; (<PILOT 039>)* **RADIATION (BBC SESSIONS)**
(lp-iss.Sep01 on 'Get Back'; GET 82)

Apr 01. (cd) *E.M.I.; (532573-2)* **REMIXED** –

Nov 01. (3xcd-box) *Virgin; (CVBOX 1)* **CONFORM TO DEFORM – THE VIRGIN YEARS** –

Dec 01. (cd) *Virgin; (CVCD 5) / Superfecto; <1>* **THE ORIGINAL SOUND OF SHEFFIELD – THE BEST OF THE VIRGIN/EMI YEARS**

Oct 02. (12") *Nova Mute; (12NOMU 103)* **NAG NAG NAG. / NAG NAG NAG (R.H. Kirk 4 remix)** –
(12") *(L12NOMU 103)* – ('A'-Tiga & Zyntherius radio version) / ('A'Akufen's karaoke slam mix).
(cd-s) *(CDNOMU 103)* – (all of the above).

Oct 02. (cd) *The Grey Area; (CABS 16CD) / Mute; <9190>* **THE ORIGINAL SOUND OF SHEFFIELD – THE BEST OF CABARET VOLTAIRE 1978-1982**
– Do the Mussolini (headkick) / Set up / Baader Meinhof / Nag nag nag / Silent command / No escape / This is entertainment /Obsession / Seconds too late / Split second feeling / Spread the virus / Yashar / Wait and shuffle / Loosen the clamp.

Jan 03. (cd) *Cherry Red; (<CDMRED 220>)* **LIVE AT THE HACIENDA 1983-1986 (live)** Feb03

Jun 03. (3xcd-box) *The Grey Area; (CABS 17CD) / Mute; <9211>* **METHODOLOGY '74/'78. ATTIC TAPES!**

John CALE

Born: 9 Mar'42, Garnant, Carmarthen, Wales. He studied classical piano and later viola at London's Guildhall School Of Music. As an 8 year old schoolboy prodigy, he'd already composed music for the BBC. In 1963, he moved to New York on a scholarship, and under JOHN CAGE and LaMONTE YOUNG's tuition, he experimented with avant-garde music. In 1965, he met LOU REED, and formed the legendary VELVET UNDERGROUND, CALE's wailing viola and white noise experimentation meshing with REED's pop sensibilities and dark lyrics to create their distinctive sound. After being fired by the band in 1968, he went solo, releasing a couple of albums for 'Columbia'. His debut in 1970 'VINTAGE VIOLENCE', saw him exhibiting a more traditional side to his enigmatic persona, with gentle folky songs. A collaboration entitled 'CHURCH OF ANTHRAX', with minimalist composer TERRY RILEY, followed in 1971. CALE continued the trend towards his baroque'n'roll roots with 'ACADEMY OF PERIL', before returning once more to the songwriter format of his first album. With LITTLE FEAT members LOWELL GEORGE and RICHIE HAYWARD among his backing band, he cut the classic 'PARIS 1919', which infused his melancholic songwriting with a disturbing unease. This was the template for much of CALE's 70's output with 1974's 'FEAR' also introducing a more aggressive element. 'HELEN OF TROY' (1975), featured a version of 'HEARTBREAK HOTEL' guaranteed to send a shiver up anyone's spine, although the album was generally disappointing overall. In 1976, he cemented his reputation by producing the legendary PATTI SMITH album, 'HORSES', having previously worked on the classic blast of primal noise that was THE STOOGES first album. His career went into a bit of a slump in the latter half of the 70's, and after an infamous incident in which he allegedly beheaded a chicken onstage (!), he had a brief dalliance with the New York punk scene. He regained his footing with 1982's 'MUSIC FOR A NEW SOCIETY', an intelligent, minimalistic affair. The mid-80's saw him sign to British label 'Beggars Banquet', and release the more mainstream 'ARTIFICIAL INTELLIGENCE'. 'WORDS FOR THE DYING', released in 1989, was a return to the classical field which included a collaboration with BRIAN ENO. They also teamed up on the sparse 'WRONG WAY UP' from 1990. 'SONGS FOR DRELLA' (a tribute to mentor ANDY WARHOL), saw CALE hook up once more with his old sparring partner LOU REED, together producing an album that outshone CALE's more recent solo outings. He and REED re-united with the others in VELVET UNDERGROUND for live work which resulted in the comeback album 'LIVE MCMXCIII'. A year later, another collaboration, this time with BOB NEUWIRTH, was largly ignored by the public. Throughout his career, he also sessioned for others, including ENO, and produced the MODERN LOVERS (JONATHAN RICHMAN), SQUEEZE, etc. CALE's first record of the new millennium, 'HOBOSAPIENS' (2003), was also his most adventurous for more than a decade. With ENO returning the guest favours alongside a host of hired hands, the album was alive with spontaneous creativity and freewheeling imagination. Embracing contemporary musical trends and technology, CALE gave free rein to a muse that only seems to have become even more literate, erudite and waggish with age. Released almost simultaneously with his umpteenth soundtrack effort, 'THE PROCESS', 'BLACK ACETATE' (2005) was another cult critical favourite evidencing CALE's refusal to grow old gracefully; while citing the likes of the NEPTUNES and GORILLAZ as influences, he was still forging ahead with his own avant-garde impulses.

Album rating: VINTAGE VIOLENCE (*5) / CHURCH OF ANTHRAX with Terry Riley (*5) / THE ACADEMY IN PERIL (*5) / PARIS 1919 (*8) / FEAR (*7) / SLOW DAZZLE (*6) / HELEN OF TROY (*5) / GUTS compilation (*7) / SABOTAGE – LIVE (*4) / HONI SOIT (*4) / MUSIC FOR A NEW SOCIETY (*6) / CARIBBEAN SUNSET (*4) / COMES ALIVE (*4) / ARTIFICIAL INTELLIGENCE (*5) / WORDS FOR THE DYING (*6) / SONGS FOR DRELLA with Lou Reed (*7) / WRONG WAY UP with Eno (*7) / EVEN COWGIRLS GET THE BLUES live collection (*5) / FRAGMENTS OF A RAINY SEASON (*7) / LAST DAYS ON EARTH with Bob Neuwirth (*5) / SEDUCING DOWN THE DOOR a collection (*7) / PARIS S'EVEILLE soundtrack (*5) / 23 SOLO PIECES FOR LA NAISSANCE DE L'AMOUR soundtrack (*5) / THE ISLAND YEARS compilation (*7) / WALKING ON LOCUSTS (*4) / ANTARTIDA soundtrack (*5) / N'OUBLIE PAS QUE TU VAS MOURIR (*5) / EAT/KISS: MUSIC FOR THE FILMS OF ANDY WARHOL (*5) / SOMEWHERE IN THE CITY soundtrack (*5) / LE VENT DE LA NUIT soundtrack (*5) / LOVE ME soundtrack (*5) / SAINT-CYR soundtrack (*6) / HOBOSAPIENS (*8) / PROCESS soundtrack (*7) / BLACK ACETATE (*7)

JOHN CALE – vocals, viola, keyboards, bass, guitar (with session people)

C.B.S. Columbia

Nov 70. (7") *<45154>* **FAIRWEATHER FRIEND. / CLEO** –

Dec 70. (lp) *(64256) <CS 1037>* **VINTAGE VIOLENCE**
– Hello there / Gideon's bible / Adelaide / Big white cloud / Cleo / Please / Charlemange / Bring it on up / Amsterdam / Ghost story / Fairweather friend. *(re-iss. May87 on 'Edsel' lp/cd; ED/+CD 230) (cd-iss. Sep94 on 'Columbia'; 477356-2) (<cd re-iss. Jul03 on 'Legacy'+=; 499945-2>)* – Fairweather friend (alt.) / Wall.

Jan 71. (7") *<45266>* **GIDEON'S BIBLE. / BIG WHITE CLOUD** –

Apr 71. (lp; JOHN CALE & TERRY RILEY) *(64259) <CS 30131>* **CHURCH OF ANTHRAX**
– Church of anthrax / The hall of mirrors in the palace at Versailles / The soul of Patrick Lee / Ides of March / The protege. *(cd-iss. Oct93 on 'Sony Europe';) (cd re-iss. Mar96 on 'Columbia'; 476640-2)*

Reprise Reprise

Apr 72. (lp) *(K 44212) <MS 2079>* **ACADEMY IN PERIL**
– The philosopher / Brahms / Legs Larry at Television Centre / Academy in peril / Intro: days of steam / 3 orchestral pieces: (a) Faust, (b) The balance, (c) Capt. Morgan's lament / King Harry / John Milton. *(re-iss. Apr86 on 'Edsel'; XED 182) (cd-iss. Apr89; EDCD 182) (cd-iss. Oct93 on 'Warners'; 7599 26930-2)*

May 72. (7") *<1108>* **DAYS OF STEAM. / LEGS LARRY AT TELEVISION CENTER** –

Mar 73. (lp) *(K 44239) <MS 2131>* **PARIS 1919**
– Child's Christmas in Wales / Hanky panky nohow / The endless plain of fortune / Andalucia / Macbeth / Paris 1919 / Graham Greene / Half past France / Antartica starts here. *(cd-iss. Oct93 on 'Warners'; 7599 25926-2)*

— Around this time he contributed to album 'JUNE 1st, 1974' on 'Island' with others ENO, NICO, KEVIN AYERS. *(ILPS 9291)*

— now with **ENO** – synth / **PHIL MANZANERA** – guitar / **ARCHIE LEGGAT** – bass / **FRED SMITH** – drums guest on below 'A'side **JUDY NYLON** – vocals

Island A&M

Jul 74. (7") *(WIP 6202)* **THE MAN WHO COULDN'T AFFORD TO ORGY. / SYLVIA SAID** –

Sep 74. (lp) *(ILPS 9301)* **FEAR** –
– Fear is a man's best friend / Buffalo ballet / Barracuda / Emily / Ship of fools / Gun / The man who couldn't afford to orgy / You know more than I know / Momamma scuba. *(re-iss. Aug91 cd)(c; IMCD 140)(ICM 9301)*

— with **CHRIS SPEDDING** + **PHIL MANZANERA** – guitar / **PAT DONALDSON** – bass / **TIMI DONALD** + **GERRY CONWAY** – drums / **ENO** – synthesizer / **CHRIS THOMAS** – violin, electric piano

Apr 75. (lp) *(ILPS 9317)* **SLOW DAZZLE** –
– Mr. Wilson / Taking it all away / Dirty ass rock'n'roll / Darling I need you / Rollaroll / Heartbreak hotel / Ski patrol / I'm not the loving kind / Guts / The jeweller. *(cd-iss. Jun88; CID 9317) (re-iss. cd Aug94; IMCD 202) (cd re-iss. Jun03; 846069-2)*

— **PHIL COLLINS** – drums; repl. CONWAY, MANZANERA + THOMAS.

Nov 75. (lp) *(ILPS 9350)* **HELEN OF TROY** –
– My Maria / Helen of Troy / China sea / Engine / Save us / Cable Hogue / I keep a close watch / Pablo Picasso / Leaving it up to you * / Baby what you want me to do? / Sudden death. *(some copies repl.* by)* – Coral Moon'. *(cd-iss. Apr94; IMCD 177)*

Feb 77. (lp) *(ILPS 9459)* **GUTS** (compilation) –
– Guts / Mary Lou / Helen of Troy / Pablo Picasso / Leaving it up to you / Fear is a man's best friend / Gun / Dirty ass rock 'n' roll / Heartbreak hotel. *(cd-iss. Aug94; IMCD 203)*

— with **RITCHIE FLIEGLER** – lead guitar / **BRUCE BRODY** – mogg synthesizer / **JIMMY BAIN** – bass / **KEVIN CURRIE** – drums

Illegal not iss.

Sep 77. (7"ep) *(ILL 003)* **ANIMAL JUSTICE** –
– Chicken shit / Memphis / Hedda Gabbler.

— with **MARK AARON** – guitar / **JOE BIDWELL** – keyboards / **GEORGE SCOTT** – bass / **DOUG BROWN** – drums / **DEERFRANCE** – vocals

not iss. Spy

Dec 79. (lp) *<SP 004>* **SABOTAGE (live)** –
– Mercenaries (ready for war) / Baby you know / Evidence / Dr.Mudd / Walkin' the dog / Captain Hook / Only time will tell / Sabotage / Chorale. *(UK cd-iss. Apr01 on 'Doesel Motor'+=; MOTORCD 1002)* – Chickenshift / Memphis / Hedda Gabler / Rosegarden full of sores.

not iss. I.R.S.

1980. (7") *<9008>* **MERCENARIES (READY FOR WAR). / ROSEGARDEN FUNERAL OF SORES** –

— with **STURGIS NIKIDES** – guitar, vocals / **JIM GOODWIN** – keyboards, synth. / **PETER MUNY** – bass / **ROBERT MEDECI** – drums

A&M A&M

Mar 81. (lp) *(AMLH 64849)* **HONI SOIT**
– Dead or alive / Strange times in Casablanca / Fighter pilot / Wilson Joliet / Streets of Laredo / Honi soit (la premiere Lecon de Francaise) / Riverbank / Russian roulette / Magic & lies. *(cd-iss. Jul94; CDMID 1936)*

Apr 81. (7") *(AMS 8130)* **DEAD OR ALIVE. / HONI SOIT**

— now w/ **ALAN LANIER** – keyboards / **D. J. YOUNG** – guitar / **DAVID LICHTENSTEIN** – drums / **JOHN WONDERLING** / **MIKE McCLINTOCK** / **ROBERT ELK**

Ze-Island Passport

Aug 82. (lp/c) *(ILPS/ICT 7019) <PB 6019>* **MUSIC FOR A NEW SOCIETY**
– Taking your life in your hands / Thoughtless kind / Sanities / If you were still around / Close watch / Mama's song / Broken bird / Chinese envoy / Changes made / Damn life / Rise, Sam and Rimsky Korsakov. *(cd-iss Mar94 on 'Yellow Moon'; YMCD 003)*

Apr 83. (7") *(IS 113)* **I KEEP A CLOSE WATCH. / CLOSE WATCH (instrumental)**

— **ANDY HEERMANS** – bass, vocals repl. LANIER

Ze-Island Ze-Islan

Jun 83. (lp/c) *(<ILPS/ICT 7024>)* **CARIBBEAN SUNSET**
– Hungry for love / Experiment number 1 / Model Beirut recital / Caribbean sunset / Praetorian underground / Magazines / Where there's a will / The hunt / Villa Albani.

Aug 84. (7") *(IS 197)* **OOH LA LA. / MAGAZINES** –

Sep 84. (lp/c) *(ILPS/ICT 7026) <8402>* **JOHN CALE COMES ALIVE (live)**
– Ooh la la / Evidence / Dead or alive / Chinese envoy / Leaving it up tc you / Dr. Mudd / Waiting for the man / Heartbreak hotel / Fear / Never give up on you.

— with **DAVID YOUNG** – guitar / **JAMES YOUNG** – keyboards / **GRAHAM DOWDALL** – percussion

Beggars Banquet P.V.C.

Jul 85. (7"/12") *(BEG 145/+T)* **DYING ON THE VINE. / EVERYTIME THE DOGS BARK** –

Nov 85. (lp/c) *(BEG A/C 68) <PVC 8947>* **ARTIFICIAL INTELLIGENCE**
– Everytime the dogs bark / Dying on the vine / The sleeper / Vigilante lover / Chinese takeaway (Hong Kong 1997) (medley) / Song of the valley / Fade away tomorrow / Black rose / Satellite walk. *(re-iss. Jan89 on 'Lowdown-Beggars Banquet' lp/c; BBL/+C 68) (cd-iss. Mar96; BBL 68CD)*

Nov 85. (12"m) *(BEG 153T)* **SATELLITE WALK. / DYING ON THE VINE / CRASH COURSE IN HARMONICS** –

— now w/ **BRIAN ENO** – synthesizers, keyboards / **NEIL CATCHPOLE** – viola violin / choir

Land Warner

Oct 89. (lp/c/cd) *(LAND/+C/CD 009) <26024>* **WORDS FOR THE DYING**
– The Falkland suite:- Introduction-There was a saviour – Interlude 1 / On a wedding anniversary – Interlude II – Lie still, sleep becalmed – Do not go gentle into that good night / Songs without words 1 & 2 / The soul of Carmen Miranda. *(re-iss. cd Oct95 & Aug99 on 'All Saints'; ASCD 009)*

— Apr'90, CALE & Lou REED⇒, collaborated on Andy Warhol tribute album SONGS FOR DRELLA. On 'Warners' records lp/c//cd *WX 345/+C //7599 26140-2*. It was CALE's first excursion into the Top 30.

— Oct'90, he teamed up with ENO on the album 'WRONG WAY UP' on 'Land'

Delabel not iss

Dec 91. (cd) *(DE 035080)* **PARIS S'EVEILLE** (soundtrack) – France –
– Paris S'eveille, suivi d'autres / Sanctus (four etudes for electronic orchestra) / Animals at night / The cowboy laughs at round-up. *(UK-iss.Mar93 on 'Crepuscule'+=; TWI 952-2)* – Primary motive: 1) Factory speech, 2) Strategy session, 3) Closing titles / Antarctica starts here / Booker T. (by VELVET UNDERGROUND). *(re-iss. Nov95 on 'Yellow Moon'+=; YMCD 007)*

Crepuscule not iss.

Nov 93. (cd) *(TWI 954-2)* **23 SOLO PIECES FOR LA NAISSANCE DE L'AMOUR** (soundtrack work) –
– La naissance de l'amour / If you love me no more / And if I love you still / Judith / Converging themes / Opposites attract / I will do it, I will keep it / Keep it to yourself / Walk towards the sea / Unquiet heart / Waking up to love / Mysterious relief / Never been so hapy / Beyond expectations / Conversations in the garden / La naissance de l'amour II / Secret dialogue / Roma / On the dark side / La naissance de l'amour III / Eye to eye / Maria's car crash and hotel rooms / La naissance de l'amour IV. *(re-iss. Nov95 on 'Yellow Moon'; YMCD 007)*

M.C.A. M.C.A

May 94. (cd; JOHN CALE / BOB NEUWIRTH) *(11037)* **LAST DAY ON EARTH**
– Overture:- a) A tourist, b) A contract, c) A prisoner / Cafe Shabu / Pastoral angst / Who's in charge? / Short of time / Angel of death / Paradise Nevada / Old China / Ocean life / Instrumental / Modern world / Streets come alive / Secrets / Maps of the world / Broken hearts / The high and the mighty road.

Crepuscule not iss.

Nov 95. (cd) *(TWI 1008)* **ANTARTIDA** (soundtrack) –
– Flashback 1 #1 / Antartida / Velasco's theme / Maria's appartement / Flashback 1 #2 / On the waterfront / Pasodoble mortal / Maria's dream

Flashback 1 #3 / Antarctica starts here / Flashback 3 / Sunset / Get away / Flashback 1 #4 / Antartida starts here / Frame up / Barn / People who died (by JIM CARROLL) / Flashback 1 #5. *(re-iss. Jan03; same)*

Mar 96. (cd) *(TWI 1028)* **N'OUBLIE PAS QUE TU VAS MOURIR** (soundtrack) [ ] [-]
– The Pianos part I:- Welcome to Europe / Everybody's cold sometimes / A snake in China? / First train to Heaven / Martyrs and madmen / Take a deep breath / The String Quartets:- Never seen anything so beautiful / Angels in the cloud / Madonna's blues / Sunflowers fields / Al dente / Hadrian was here / Kiss me once more my love / Alive at dawn / The Pianos part II:- Skin in the mirror / Who said love's safe? / 100% pure / Do not forget / Last train to Bosnia / Gold and crimson / So far so good. *(re-iss. Jan03; same)*

Hannibal Hannibal

Sep 96. (cd) *(<HNCD 1395>)* **WALKING ON LOCUSTS** [ ] [ ]
– Dancing undercover / Set me free / So what / Crazy Egypt / So much for love / Tell me why / Indistinct notion of cool / Secret corrida / Circus / Gatorville and points east / Some friends / Entre nous.

Jun 97. (cd) *(<HNCD 1407>)* **EAT / KISS – MUSIC FOR THE FILMS OF ANDY WARHOL** [ ] [ ]
– KISS:- Infinite guitar, quartet / Frozen warning, Jimmy, metal-violin solo – Daid Tiye (backing vocal) / B.J., quartet, Moe / Violin solo – Todd, Tiye, quartet / Harpsichord, infinite guitar / Quartet, Moe – Harpsichord, Tiye – percussion / Quartet, cello solo – Dawn, harpsichord / B.J., quartet, electric piano / B.J., quartet, electric piano / Quartet solo / Solo Tiye, strings // EAT:- B.J., 12-string guitar intro – David / Reading from 'Melanethon' (Swedenborg) / Todd solo, 12-string, Moe / Piano, B.J.

not iss. Velvel

Aug 98. (cd) *<VEL 79717>* **SOMEWHERE IN THE CITY** (soundtrack w/ Various Artists) [-] [ ]
– Marta and Frankie / Love scene / Pennywhistle / Drive up to robbery / Marta and Frankie (reprise) / Indistinct notion of cool / (other artists).

— In Nov'98, JOHN CALE, ED WUBBE featured on ICE NINE's 'Nico' live set on 'Erato Detour' *(3984 22122-2)*

Crepuscule not iss.

Apr 99. (cd) *(TWI 1083)* **LE VENT DE LA NUIT** (soundtrack) [-] Europe [-]
– On the road to Portofino / At the boats / Naples / On the road to Turin / Turin at night / The Seine at night / Suicide 1 / Truck parking lot at night / On the road to Germany / Waiting / Thinking and acting / Suicide 2 / Memories Of Paris:- President Y is still stable / B. calls / Darkness on the delta / What Mrs. Ives said to Mr. Ives / My piano thanks you for visiting. *(UK-iss.Jan03; same)*

Mercury FR not iss.US

2000. (cd) *(542 373-2)* **LOVE ME** (soundtrack) [-] French [-]
– A thrill and a half / A thrill and a half II / Love theme / Love theme electric / Love theme acoustic / Love theme acoustic II / Solitary / Sailor theme / Rocking chair / Heartbreak hotel (live).

Archipel 35 – Virgin FR not iss.US

Dec 00. (cd) *(8 49545-2)* **SAINT-CYR** (soundtrack) [-] French [-]
– Opening theme / Ironic trumpet / Stately / Esther (J.B. Moreau) / Opening theme No.2 / Pillar theme / Pillar theme No.2 / 2nd theme / 2nd theme No.2 / War time / War time No.2.

E.M.I. E.M.I.

May 03. (cd-ep) *(CDEM 621)* **5 TRACKS** [ ] [-]
– Verses / Waiting for blonde / Chums of Dumpty / E is missing / Wilderness approaching.

Oct 03. (cd) *<(591711-2)>* **HOBOSAPIENS** [ ] Nov03 [ ]
– Zen / Reading my mind / Things / Look horizon / Magritte / Archimedes / Caravan / Bicycle / Twilight zone / Letter from abroad / Things X / Over her head / Set me free.

Oct 03. (12") *(12EM 628)* **BICYCLE. / LOOK HORIZON** [ ] [-]

Oct 03. (12") *(12EM 629)* **THINGS. / THINGS X** [ ] [-]

Jul 05. (cd) *(<50245 453351-25>)* **PROCESS** (soundtrack) [ ] Aug05 [ ]
– Theme intro / Theatre / Post sex / Museum / Radiology / Candles / Bedroom / Car blue / Packing books / Reading poem / Burning – Painting / La defense – Metro / Suicide theme / Ascention.
(above issued on 'Syntax')

Oct 05. (cd) *(<334378-2>)* **BLACK ACETATE** [ ] Sep05 [ ]
– Outta the bag / Foraride / Brotherman / Satisfied / In a flood / Hush / Gravel drive / Perfect / Sold-motel / Woman / Wasteland / Turn the lights on / Mailman (the lying song).

– compilations, others, etc. –

Jul 91. (c) *Danceteria; (DANC 113)* **EVEN COWGIRLS GET THE BLUES** (live 1978-79 at CBGB's) [ ] [ ]
– Dance of the seven veils / Helen of Troy / Casey at the bat / Even cowgirls get the blues / Don't know why she came / Somebody should have told / Decade / Magic & lies. *(cd-iss. Jun97 +=; DANCD 113)* – Memphis.

Oct 92. (cd) *Hannibal; (HNCD 1372)* **FRAGMENTS OF A RAINY SEASON (live)** [ ] [-]

Oct 92. (cd) *Traditional Line; (TL 001326)* **BROKEN HEARTS LIVE 1984-1992 (live)** [ ] [-]

Jul 94. (d-cd) *Rhino; <R2 71685>* **SEDUCING DOWN THE DOOR: A JOHN CALE COLLECTION** [-] [ ]

Sep 96. (d-cd) *Island; (524235-2)* **THE ISLAND YEARS ANTHOLOGY** [ ] [-]

Feb 99. (cd) *Island; (IMCD 259)* **CLOSE WATCH (AN INTRODUCTION TO JOHN CALE)** [ ] [ ]
– Paris 1919 / Mr. Wilson / Leaving it up to you / Dying on the vine / Guts / Heartbreak hotel / Ship of fools / Cable hogue / Gun / Riverbank / Child's Christmas in Wales / Fear is a man's best friend / If you were still around / Wilson Joilet / I keep a close watch.

1999. (cd) *Les Disques . . .; (TWI 1023)* **THE UNKNOWN** [ ] [-]
– Parts 1-8. *(re-iss. Jan03; same)*

May 00. (cd) *Table Of The Elements; <(TOECD 74)>* **INSIDE THE DREAM SYNDICATE VOL.1: DAY OF NIAGARA** [ ] [ ]

Apr 01. (cd) *Table Of The Elements; (TOECD 75)* **SUN BLINDNESS MUSIC** [ ] [-]

Dec 01. (cd) *Table Of The Elements; <(TOECD 79)>* **INSIDE THE DREAM SYNDICATE VOL.2: DREAM INTERPRETATION** [ ] [ ]

Dec 01. (cd) *Table Of The Elements; <(TOECD 80)>* **INSIDE THE DREAM SYNDICATE VOL.3: STAINLESS STEEL GAMELAN** [ ] [ ]

CALEXICO

Formed: California, USA . . . 1990 by JOEY BURNS and JOHN CONVERTINO. CALEXICO had always been known as the obscure offshoot band to HOWE GELB's masters of alt country, GIANT SAND. True, both BURNS and CONVERTINO have enjoyed success in GELB's weird, tumbling desert band, but CALEXICO had moved from "backing band" with their third album proper, 'HOT RAIL'. It all began when BURNS met session musician CONVERTINO in L.A. At that point, he was touring with GIANT SAND and invited CONVERTINO to accompany the band on their European tour. After the tour had ended, the duo moved to Tucson, Arizona and began playing and collecting weird instruments from a down-town store Chicago Music. A group was formed, FRIENDS OF DEAN MARTINEZ and the strange musical instruments were put to good use: harps, accordions, marimba and vibraphone were all added to the mix of jazzy lounge music, which, in turn, was so bad it was sheer brilliant. But the band were to split after a disagreement with founder BILL ELM. Session work followed, and BURNS and CONVERTINO were beginning to build a strong musical prowess. They finally put the plan into action in 1996, recording and issuing the lo-fi porch soundtrack 'SPOKE' (issued on the German label 'Haus Musik'), which caught the attention of 'Touch & Go' records. 'THE BLACK LIGHT', arguably their best work, was unfettered in 1998 to widespread critical acclaim. It was hard to categorise CALEXICO's music: a strange amalgamation of blues, post-rock, surf music, Portuguese/Mexican Mariachi fused with MORRICONE's sweeping soundtracks. Basically, it sounded like CALEXICO's (a small railway town on the Californian/Mexican border) national anthem, if it were to have one. The same energy could be heard on the follow-up, 'HOT RAIL' (2000). Much the same record (almost like a Part 2), but slightly inferior, the set again treated us to the Desert experience with singles 'BALLAD OF CABLE HOGUE' and 'SERVICE AND REPAIR' to boot. The group were still faithful to GELB, however, appearing on albums 'Chore Of Enchantment' (in 2000) and 'Confluence' (in 2001). Meanwhile, CONVERTINO and BURNS moonlighted with yet another outfit, ABBC, along with Parisians GABRIEL NAIM AMOR and THOMAS

BELHOM. Their collaborative work, 'TETE A TETE, was released towards the end 2000 – think eerie westerns and experimental textured jazz. CALEXICO's fourth album came in the form of 'FEAST OF WIRE' (2003), a dark follow-up to the aforementioned 'HOT RAIL'. Sticking along the same lines (no pun intended), the CONVERTINO and BURNS partnership had seemed to restrain itself, with the songs either cut short or lacking in the epic intensity of some of their earlier work. Tracks such as 'DUB LATINO' and 'QUATTRO (WORDS DRIFT IN)' all had that sparse desert drift to them, but essentially it seemed as if the band had remade the same album three times over, as the template for 1998's 'BLACK LIGHT' was much different from that of the whispered acoustic affair 'SPOKE'. But then again music fans were not complaining – CALEXICO keep doing their thing, whilst we quite happily swing. For all the vaulting reach of their sound, there is an argument that one of America's greatest – and most unsung – modern bands had manoeuvred themselves into an aesthetic cul de sac over the course of their decade long career. The idea of JOEY BURNS and co jangling and ba-ba-ing in 60s harmony, however, was always likely to have hardcore fans running for the pop-art shelter of their Ennio Morricone re-issues. In practice, 'GARDEN RUIN' (2006) – the album where CALEXICO finally hitched up after endless days and nights in the desert – worked as a decent album on its own terms. If lead track 'CRUEL' flaunted CALEXICO's claim as natural inheritors of trad college rock, and the likes of 'BISBEE BLUE' was barely even recognisable as the Tucson troupe ('LUCKY DIME' made the LOVIN' SPOONFUL sound dangerous), there was just enough frontier twang, Latin spirit and confidential menace (check the GAINSBOURG-ian 'NOM DE PLUME') to keep longtime fans interested.

• **Covered:** CHANEL NO.5 (Mark Eitzel) / CLOTHES OF SAND (Nick Drake) / TULSA TELEPHONE BOOK (Tom T. Hall) / DRIVING ON 9 (Minutemen) / SUNDOWN, SUNDOWN (Lee Hazlewood) / CASEY'S LAST RIDE (Kris Kristofferson) / ALONE AGAIN OR (Love).

Album rating: "SPOKE" (*7) / THE BLACK LIGHT (*8) / HOT RAIL (*8) / EVEN MY SURE THINGS FALL THROUGH collection (*4) / FEAST OF WIRE (*7) / GARDEN RUIN (*7) / ABBC: TETE A TETE (*6)

JOEY BURNS – vocals, guitar, bass, cello, accordion, organ (of GIANT SAND) / **JOHN COVERTINO** – drums, vibes, organ, marimba, percussion, accordion (of GIANT SAND) / **TASHA BUNDY** – drums

not iss. / All City

1996. (7") <*ALLCITY 2*> **LAQUER. / DRAPE** [–] [ ]
(UK-iss.Oct97 on 'All City'; same)

not iss. / Wabana

1996. (7") <*ORE 004*> **SPARK. / THE RIDE** [–] [ ]

— guests **BRIDGET KEATING** – violin / **DAVID COFFMAN** – guitar

Quarter Stick / Quarter Stick

Sep 97. (cd) <*(QS 51CD)*> **"SPOKE"** [ ] Aug97 [ ]
– Low expectations / Mind the gap / Mazurra / Sanchez / Haul / Slag / Paper route / Glimpse / Navy cut / Spokes / Scout / Point Vicente / Wash / Ice cream jeep / Windjammer / Mazurka / Removed / Hitch / Stinging nettle. *(re-iss. May00; same)*

— **NICK LUCA** – Spanish guitar; repl. COFFMAN

— + guests **HOWE GELB** + **NEIL HARRY** + **GABRIEL LANDIN**

City Slang / Quarter Stick

Oct 98. (cd/d-lp) *(efa 08707-2/-1)* <*QS 54CD*> **THE BLACK LIGHT** [ ] May98 [ ]
– Gypsy's curse / Fake fur / Ride (part II) / Where water flows / The black light / Sideshow / Chach / Missing / Minas de cobre (for better metal) / Over your shoulder / Vinegaroon / Trigger / Sprawl / Stray / Old man waltz / Bloodflow / Frontera.
Oct 98. (cd-s) *(08713-2)* **STRAY / LAQUER / DRAPE** [ ] [–]
Apr 99. (7"/cd-s) *(08719-7/-2)* **THE RIDE (PART II). / MINAS DE COBRE (mixes; extend-o-mix / Spatial / acoustic)** [ ] [–]

— they also issued a few concert/gig ltd-CD's 'ROAD MAP' (1999) and 'TRAVELALL' (2000); 'AEROCALEXICO' (2001) and 'SCRAPING' (2000) followed

— **JOHN + JOEY** with **NICK LUCA** – guitar / **RUBEN MORENO + MARTIN WENK** – trumpets / **MADELEINE SOSIN** – violin / etc

Apr 00. (7") *(20154-7)* **BALLAD OF CABLE HOGUE. / CRYSTAL FRONTIER** [ ] [–]
(cd-s+=) *(20154-2)* – Hard hat.
May 00. (cd/lp) *(20153-2/-1)* <*2006-2*> **HOT RAIL** [57] [ ]
– El picador / Ballad of Cable Hogue / Ritual road map / Fade / Untitled III / Sonic wind / Muleta / Mid-town / Service and repair / Untitled II / Drenched / 16 track scratch / Tree avisos / Hot rail.
Sep 00. (cd-s) *(20167-2)* **SERVICE AND REPAIR / CROOKED ROAD AND THE BRIAR / BANDERILLA** [ ] [–]
Mar 01. (d7"ep) *(20173-7)* **CRYSTAL FRONTIER / CHANEL #5. / CROOKED ROAD AND THE BRIAR / BANDERILLA** [ ] [–]
(cd-s) *(20173-2)* – (first 2 tracks) / ('A'-widescreen mix) / ('A'-acoustic).
(12") *(20173-6)* – ('A'-widescreen mix) / ('A'-Buscemi remix) / Untitled 3 (virus style mix).
Feb 03. (cd/lp) *(20213-2/-1)* <*QS 78*> **FEAST OF WIRE** [71] [ ]
– Sunken waltz / Quattro (world drifts in) / Stucco / Black heart / Pepita / Not even Stevie Nicks . . . / Close behind / Woven birds / The book and the canal / Attack el robot! attack! / Across the wire / Dub Latina / Guero Canelo / Whipping the horse's eyes / Crumble / No doze. *(ltd d-cd+=; 593147-0)* – Alone again or / Woven birds (Cinematic Orchestra mix) / Convict pool / Woven birds (stratus mix).
Apr 03. (cd-s) *(20215-2)* **QUATTRO (WORLD DRIFTS IN) / PRASKOVIA / PAMPA** [ ] [–]
Jul 03. (12") *(20223-6)* **ALONE AGAIN OR. / WOVEN BIRDS (Cinematic Orchestra mix) / WOVEN BIRDS (Stratus mix)** [ ] [–]
(cd-s+=) *(20223-2)* – Convict pool.

— in 2005, CALEXICO feat. on IRON & WINE's set, 'In The Reins'

Apr 06. (cd/lp) *(SLANG 103857-2/-1)* <*QS 97/+CD*> **GARDEN RUIN** [ ] [ ]
– Cruel / Yours and mine / Bisbee blue / Panic open string / Letter to Bowie knife / Roka / Lucky dime / Smash / Deep down / Nom de plume / All systems red. *(ltd-cd w/dvd+=; SLANG 103857-8)* – (DVD tracks).
Apr 06. (ltd-7") *(SLANG 503930-7)* **BISBEE BLUE. / LUCKY DIME (alt)** [ ] [–]

– compilations, etc. –

May 01. (cd) *QuarterStick;* <*QS 67*> **EVEN MY SURE THINGS FALL THROUGH** [–] [ ]
– Sonic wind (instrumental) / Crystal frontier / Untitled III / Chanel No.5 / Banderilla / Crooked road and the briar / Crystal frontier / Hard hat / Crystal frontier / Ballad of Cable Hogue / The black light.

ABBC

CONVERTINO + BURNS with **GABRIEL NAIM AMOR** – guitar, violin + **THOMAS BELHOM** – percussion, etc.

Wabana / Wabana

Nov 00. (cd/lp) <*(ORE 24/+CD)*> **TETE A TETE** [ ] [ ]
– La valse des 24 heures / Elevator baby / En route to the blanchisserie / Mobile home / Orange trees in the yard / Gilbert / Pluie sans nuages / The wrestler's masque / Je voudrais me rappeller / Le savon se dissout dans la rigole. *(re-iss. Jul01 on 'Cargo' cd/lp; CAR 031 CD/LP)*

Easy Tiger! / not iss.

Apr 01. (7") *(MUSE 009)* **GILBERT. / BUTTERFLY MOUTH** [ ] [–]

□ Randy CALIFORNIA (see under ⇒ SPIRIT)

CAN

Formed: Cologne, Germany . . . 1968 initially as INNER SPACE by HOLGER CZUKAY and IRMIN SCHMIDT. MICHAEL KAROLI and JAKI LIEBEZEIT were soon recruited along with DAVID JOHNSON and black American vocalist MALCOLM MOONEY. Later that year, JOHNSON bailed out prior to their debut album, 'MONSTER MOVIE' (1970). Having studied under KARL-HEINZ STOCKHAUSEN, CZUKAY and SCHMIDT (who were also influenced by JOHN CAGE, TERRY RILEY and

CAN

The VELVET UNDERGROUND) pioneered their own take on avant-garde minimalism, creating a hypnotic, free-form sound, relentless in its intensity. The album included a 20-minute piece, 'YOU DOO RIGHT', extracted from a marathon improv-session and highlighting the very real dementia of MOONEY's ravings. He suffered a nervous breakdown soon after and was subsequently replaced by the Japanese 'vocalist' DAMO SUZUKI prior to recording 'SOUNDTRACKS'. More improvised beauty was evidenced on their next set, the German Top 40 classic, 'TAGO MAGO' (1971), a sprawling double-set that featured two of their more hypnotic tracks, 'HALLELUWAH' and 'MUSHROOM'. On their next two releases, 'EGE BAMYASI' and 'FUTURE DAYS', CAN explored even more ritualistic textures alongside SUZUKI's partly-spoken tri-lingual ramblings. SUZUKI subsequently returned to Japan to become a Jehovah's Witness, after a final gig at the 1973 Edinburgh Festival. Vocal duties were now shared by KAROLI and SCHMIDT on the more percussive 'SOON OVER BABALUMA' album (1974). They signed to Richard Branson's innovative 'Virgin' label the following year, 'LANDED' being a prime example of British-influenced avant-garde rock. In 1976, they surprised many by having a Top 30 hit, 'I WANT MORE', penned by PINK FLOYD's DAVID GILMOUR. With the addition of ROSKO GEE and sessionman REEBOP KWAKU BAAH, they moved in a more African/reggae influenced direction; CZUKAY having already withdrawn from most of the proceedings. Their final efforts were of little significance, the 1979 album interesting only for its re-hash of Offenbach's 'CAN-CAN', which had previously been released as a single. KAROLI, SCHMIDT and CZUKAY all continued in the 80's as solo artists, the latter teaming up once again with LIEBEZEIT (and JAH WOBBLE) on the 1982 album 'FULL CIRCLE'. The original line-up reformed in 1986 for an album, 'RITE TIME', but the record lacked the inspiration and originality that characterised CAN's earlier work. The band remain highly regarded, cited as a major influence by artists as diverse as CARL CRAIG and PRIMAL SCREAM. Even The FALL paid homage to them by crediting a song as 'I AM DAMO SUZUKI'. A plethora of post-CAN work (mainly from CZUKAY) appeared from time to time, although their legacy was always from the experimental 70's. More recently (on the 17th of November, 2001), the death of MICHAEL KAROLI filtered through to the media. He would be sadly missed by his great friend CZUKAY.

Album rating: MONSTER MOVIE (*7) / SOUNDTRACKS compilation (*6) / TAGO MAGO (*7) / EGE BAMYASI (*7) / FUTURE DAYS (*7) / LIMITED EDITION collection (*6) / SOON OVER BABALUMA (*6) / LANDED (*5) / FLOW MOTION (*5) / UNLIMITED EDITION collection (*5) / SAW DELIGHT (*6) / CANNIBALISM compilation (*7) / OUT OF REACH (*3) / CAN (*4) / DELAY 1968 exploitation (*5) / RITE TIME (*5) / CANNIBALISM II compilation (*6) / CANNIBALISM III compilation (*5) / ANTHOLOGY 1968-1993 compilation (*8)

IRMIN SCHMIDT (b.29 May'37, Berlin, Germany) – keyboards / **HOLGER CZUKAY** (b.24 Mar'38, Danzig, Germany) – bass, electronics / **DAVID JOHNSON** – flute / **MICHAEL KAROLI** (b.29 Apr'48, Straubing, Germany) – guitar, violin / **JAKI LIEBEZEIT** (b.26 May'38, nr.Dresden, Germany) – drums / **MALCOLM MOONEY** – vocals

Music Factory — not iss.

Nov 68. (7"; by IRMIN SCHMIDT) **KAMA SUTRA. /** [–] German [–]

— now a quintet when JOHNSON departed (below issued Germany Aug'69)

U.A. — U.A.

May 70. (lp) *(UAS 29094)* **MONSTER MOVIE** [ ] [–]
– Father cannot yell / Mary, Mary so contrary / You doo right / Outside my door. *(cd-iss. Jun89 on 'Spoon-Mute'; SPOONCD 004)*

— **KENJI 'DAMO' SUZUKI** (b.16 Jan'50, Japan) – vocals repl.MOONEY who suffered a nervous breakdown

Sep 70. Liberty; (7") **SOUL DESERT. / SHE BRINGS THE RAIN** [–] German [–]

Sep 71. (lp) *(UAS 29283)* **SOUNDTRACKS** (soundtrack compilation) [ ] [–]
– Deadlock / Tango whiskyman / Deadlock (instrumental) / Don't tur the light on, leave me alone / Soul desert / Mother sky / She brings th rain. *(cd-iss. Jun89 on 'Spoon-Mute'; SPOONCD 005)*

1971. (7") **TURTLES HAVE SHORT LEGS. / HALLELUWAH (edit)** [–] German [–]

1971. (7") **SPOON. / SHIKAKO MARU TEN** [–] German [–]

Feb 72. (d-lp) *(UAD 60009-10)* **TAGO MAGO** [ ] [–]
– Paperhouse / Mushroom / Oh yeah / Halleluwah / Aumgn / Peking O Bring me coffee or tea. *(cd-iss. Jul89 on 'Spoon-Mute'; SPOONCD 006-007)*

Nov 72. (lp) *(UAS 29414)* <063> **EGE BAMYASI** [ ] [ ]
– Pinch / Sing swan song / One more night / Vitamin C / Soup / I'm s green / Spoon. *(cd-iss. Jun89 on 'Spoon-Mute'; SPOONCD 008)*

Feb 73. (7") *(UP 35506)* **SPOON. / I'M SO GREEN** [ ] [–]

Jun 73. (lp) *(UAS 29505)* <213> **FUTURE DAYS** [ ] [ ]
– Future days / Spray / Moonshake / Bel Air. *(cd-iss. Jun89 on 'Spoon Mute'; SPOONCD 009)*

Oct 73. (7") *(UP 35596)* <446> **MOONSHAKE. / FUTURE DAYS (edit)** [ ] [ ]

— trimmed to a quartet when DAMO SUZUKI left to become a Jehovah Witness. Now **SCHMIDT / KAROLI** (shared vocals) **CZUKAY LIEBEZEIT**

Nov 74. (lp) *(UAG 29673)* <343> **SOON OVER BABALUMA** [ ] [ ]
– Dizzy dizzy / Come sta, la luna / Splash / Chain reaction / Quantur physics. *(cd-iss. Jun89 on 'Spoon-Mute'; SPOONCD 010)*

Dec 74. (7") *(UP 35749)* **DIZZY DIZZY. / SPLASH** [ ] [–]

Virgin — Polyd

Sep 75. (lp) *(V 2041)* **LANDED** [ ] [ ]
– Full moon on the highway / Half past one / Hunters and collectors Vernal equinox / Red hot Indians / Unfinished. *(cd-iss. Jun87; CDV 204. (re-iss. Aug88; OVED 194)*

— approx Mar76, tried two vocalists one a Malayan, the other **MICHAE COUSINS** (English). added **DAVID GILMOUR** – guest/composer (³ b.vocals of PINK FLOYD

Jul 76. (7") *(VS 153)* **I WANT MORE. / . . . AND MORE** [26] [ ]

Oct 76. (lp) *(V 2071)* **FLOW MOTION** [ ] [ ]
– I want more / Cascade waltz / Laugh till you cry . . . live till you die . . .And more / Babylonian pearl / Smoke (E.F.S. No.59) / Flow motior *(cd-iss. Jun87; CDV 2071) (re-iss. Aug88; OVED 88)*

Nov 76. (7") *(VS 166)* **SILENT NIGHT. / CASCADE WALTZ** [ ] [–]

— added **ROSKO GEE** – bass + **REEBOP KWAKU BAAH** (b. Konong Ghana) – percussion (both ex-TRAFFIC) (HOLGER now synths., samplers

Mar 77. (lp) *(V 2079)* **SAW DELIGHT** [ ] [ ]
– Don't say no / Sunshine day and night / Call me / Animal waves / Fly b night. *(cd-iss. Jun87; CDV 2079) (re-iss. Aug88; OVED 195)*

Apr 77. (7") *(VS 172)* **DON'T SAY NO. / RETURN** [ ] [–]

— HOLGER went on a few holidays (& solo). The rest of the band belov (**SCHMIDT, KAROLI, LIEBEZEIT, BAAH & GEE**) recorded album.

Lightning — Peters

Jun 78. (7") *(LIG 545)* **CAN-CAN. / CAN BE** [ ] [–]

Jul 78. (lp) *(LIP 4)* <9024> **OUT OF REACH** [ ] [ ]
– Serpentine / Pauper's daughter and I / November / Seven days awake Give me no roses / Like Inobe God / One more day. *(re-iss. Jun86 o 'Thunderbolt'; THBL 025) (cd-iss. Nov88; CDTB 025) (cd re-iss. May99 o 'MagMid'; MM 030)*

Laser — not is

Jul 79. (lp) *(LASL 2)* **CAN** [ ] [–]
– All gates open / Safe / Sunday jam / Sodom / Aspectacle / E.F.S. No.9 "can can" / Ping pong / Can be. *(re-iss. Feb85 as 'INNER SPACE' o 'Thunderbolt'; THBL 020) (cd-iss. Jun87; THBL 020)*

— had already split late '78. JAKI formed PHANTOM BAND and collaborate with HOLGER. IRMIN went solo and formed BRUNO SPOERR MICHAEL in '84 went solo. All their releases were mainly German only **CAN** re-formed 1969 line-up 20 years on.

Mercury — not is

Oct 89. (lp/c/cd) *(838 883-1/-4/-2)* **RITE TIME** [ ] [–]
-On the beautiful side of a romance / The without law man / Below thi level (patient's song) / Movin' right along / Like a new world / Hoola hoolah / Give the drummer some / In the distance lies the future. *(cd-is. Oct94 on 'Spoon-Mute'; SPOONCD 029)*

White Label — not is

Sep 90. (cd)(c)(lp) **FISHERMAN'S FRIEND REMIXES** [ ] [–]

– compilations, others, etc. –

on 'United Artists' unless otherwise mentioned

Aug 74. (lp) *(USP 103)* **LIMITED EDITION** ☐ –
May 76. (d-lp) *Caroline; (CAD 3001)* **UNLIMITED EDITION** ☐ –
Nov 76. (lp) *Sunset; (SLS 50400)* **OPENER** (71-74 material) ☐ –
Oct 78. (d-lp) *(UDM 105-6)* **CANNIBALISM** ☐ –
May 81. (7") *Virgin; (VS 422) / Polydor;* **I WANT MORE. / . . . AND MORE** ☐ ☐
(12"+=) *(VS 422-12)* – Silent night.
1981. (lp) *(SPOON 012)* **DELAY 1968** – German –
– Butterfly / Pnoom / 19th century man / Thief / Man named Joe / Uphill / Little star of Bethlehem. *(cd-iss. Jun89 on 'Spoon-Mute'; SPOONCD 012)*
Oct 81. (lp) *Virgin; (OVED 3)* **INCANDESCENCE** ☐ –
1982. (c) *Pure Freude; (PF 23)* **ONLYOU** – German –
Mar 83. (12"ep) *Cherry Red; (12CHERRY 57)* **MOONSHAKE. / TURTLES HAVE SHORT LEGS / ONE MORE NIGHT** ☐ –
Jan 85. (c) *Tago Mago; (TM 4755)* **PREHISTORIC FUTURE** – France –
Jun 91. (cd) *Spoon-Mute; (SPOONCD 23-24)* **UNLIMITED EDITION** (new collection) ☐ –
Nov 92. (cd) *Spoon-Mute; (SPOONCD 021)* **CANNIBALISM II** ☐ –
– Uphill / Pnoom / Connection / Mother Upduff / Little star / T.V. spot / Doko E. / Turtles have short legs / Shikaku maru ten / Gomorrha / Blue bag / Red hot Indians / Half past one / Flow motion / Smoke / I want more . . .and more / Laugh till you cry / Aspectacle animal waves / Sunshine day and night / E.F.S. No.7 / Melting away.
Oct 94. (cd) *Spoon-Mute; (SPOONCD 3031)* **ANTHOLOGY 1968-1993** ☐ –
Feb 95. (cd) *Spoon-Mute; (SPOONCD 022)* **CANNIBALISM III** ☐ –
– (solo work 1979-1991 from CZUKAY, SCHMIDT, LIEBEZEIT & KAROLI)
Oct 95. (cd) *Strange Fruit; (SFRCD 135)* **LIVE AT THE BBC (Peel sessions)** ☐ –
May 97. (t-lp/d-cd) *Grey Area; (SPOON/+CD 39-40)* **SACRILEGE** ☐ –
Mar 99. (d-cd+video+book) *Spoon-Mute; (SPOON 041)* **CAN BOX** ☐ ☐
Sep 99. (d-cd) *Spoon-Mute; (SPOON 042/043)* **CAN LIVE (live)** ☐ ☐

CANNED HEAT

Formed: 1966, Los Angeles, California, USA by ALAN WILSON and BOB HITE. WILSON, nicknamed 'BLIND OWL' because of his thick-lensed glasses, was already a renowned harmonica player and had accompanied SON HOUSE on his album, 'FATHER OF FOLK BLUES'. He met HITE (known as 'THE BEAR' due to his massive 300 pound frame) in 1965 and they soon discovered a shared passion for blues archives (WILSON had studied music at Boston University and did a thesis on blues music while HITE had a collection of blues 78s that numbered in the thousands). They were joined by FRANK COOK on drums and HENRY 'SUNFLOWER' VESTINE, a former member of The MOTHERS OF INVENTION, on guitar. Taking their name from TOMMY JOHNSON, 'CANNED HEAT BLUES' they completed the line-up with the addition of LARRY 'THE MOLE' TAYLOR who was a session bass player with CHUCK BERRY, JERRY LEE LEWIS and The MONKEES. CANNED HEAT's eponymous debut album was released in 1967 and showed some promise, although it only offered copies of 12-bar standards such as, 'ROLLIN' AND TUMBLIN'', 'DUST MY BROOM' and 'BULLFROG BLUES'. Later the same year they performed with distinction at the Monterey Festival, while things got even better with the arrival of new drummer ALFREDO FITO and the subsequent release of the second album, 'BOOGIE WITH CANNED HEAT' in 1968. This was an impressive selection which included, 'FRIED HOCKEY BOOGIE' (a song destined to become a concert favourite) and the hypnotic 'ON THE ROAD AGAIN' (originally recorded by The MEMPHIS JUG BAND in the early Twenties) which gave them a UK Top 10 and US Top 20 hit single. For the next album, 'LIVIN' THE BLUES', WILSON adapted a HENRY THOMAS song, 'BULLDOZE BLUES', by keeping the tune and rewriting the lyric, the result being 'GOIN' UP THE COUNTRY', which highlighted WILSON's trademark falsetto (seemingly taken from SKIP JAMES) and gave them a UK and US Top 20 hit as well as being one of the highlights of the Woodstock movie. Their newfound chart status allowed them to bully their record company, 'Liberty', into giving ALBERT COLLINS a deal with their subsidiary, 'Imperial'. CANNED HEAT recorded a further four albums between 1969-70 including a self financed collaboration with JOHN LEE HOOKER (which gave HOOKER his first chart album). For 'HALLELUJAH', guitarist HARVEY MANDEL replaced HENRY VESTINE who could no longer work with LARRY TAYLOR. They enjoyed further UK hits with a cover of WILBERT HARRISON's, 'LET'S WORK TOGETHER', which reached number 2, and the cajun-like, 'SUGAR BEE' (originally by CLEVELAND CROCHET) but they were shocked by the suicide of ALAN WILSON, whose body was found in HITE'S backyard on the 3rd of September 1970. His death brought about a major reshuffle with TAYLOR and MANDEL going to JOHN MAYALL's BLUESBREAKERS, VESTINE returning and ANTONIO DE LA BARREDA becoming the new bassist. The new line-up completed one album, 'HISTORICAL FIGURES AND ANCIENT HEADS', before BOB HITE's brother RICHARD, replaced BARREDA for the 1973 release, 'THE NEW AGE'. Throughout the next decade, HITE tried to keep the band going although he was unable to get a permanent record deal. A new impetus came with 'HUMAN CONDITION' but the years of struggle took their toll on HITE, who collapsed and died after a gig on the 5th of April 1981. The band's name lived on with TAYLOR and DE LA PARRA recruiting new guitarists JAMES THORNBURY and JUNIOR WATSON and they still tour today although their line-up is constantly changing. The band were still cranking it out come the end of the 90's: while 'BOOGIE 2000' (1999) suggested there was precious little pre-millennial tension in the CANNED HEAT camp (although the music could've done with some), the record was admittedly better than 1996's dismal 'CANNED HEAT BLUES BAND'. 'FRIENDS IN THE CAN' (2003), meanwhile, found the likes of WALTER TROUT, TAJ MAHAL and even the late JOHN LEE HOOKER guesting (the latter on 'LITTLE WHEEL', resurrected from sessions for the late, great bluesman's 1989 album, 'The Healer'), contributing to an infectiously upbeat vibe missing on many oldsters' sets.

• **Songwriters:** HITE and WILSON, except ROLLIN' AND TUMBLIN' (Muddy Waters) / WOOLY BULLY (Sam The Sham & The Pharoahs) / SUGAR BEE (Cleveland Crotchet) / BULLDOZE BLUES (Henry Thomas).
• **Trivia:** 'Blind Owl' WILSON was so-called due to his bespectacled eyes.

Album rating: CANNED HEAT (*6) / BOOGIE WITH CANNED HEAT (*6) / LIVIN' THE BLUES (*6) / HALLELUJAH (*7) / CANNED HEAT '70 CONCERT (*4) / CANNED HEAT COOKBOOK compilation (*9) / FUTURE BLUES (*5) / HOOKER 'N' HEAT with John Lee Hooker (*5) / HISTORICAL FIGURES AND ANCIENT HEADS (*5) / NEW AGE (*3) / ONE MORE RIVER TO CROSS (*3) / LIVE AT TOPANGA CORRAL (*3) / THE HUMAN CONDITION (*4) / KINGS OF THE BOOGIE (*4) / THE BOOGIE ASSAULT – LIVE IN AUSTRALIA (*3) / RE-HEATED (*3) / INTERNAL COMBUSTION (*4) / UNCANNED – THE BEST OF CANNED HEAT compilation (*8) / BLUES BAND (*2) / BOOGIE 2000 (*3) / LIVE IN OZ (*4) / FRIENDS IN THE CAN (*5)

BOB 'THE BEAR' HITE (b.26 Feb'45, Torrance, California) – vocals, harmonica / **AL 'BLIND OWL' WILSON** (b. 4 Jul'43, Boston, Mass.) – vocals, guitar, harmonica / **HENRY VESTINE** (b.25 Dec'44, Washington, D.C.) – guitar (ex-MOTHERS OF../ ZAPPA) / **LARRY TAYLOR** (b.SAMUEL TAYLOR, 26 Jun'42, Brooklyn, N.Y.) – bass repl. MARK ANDES who had repl. STUART BROTMAN (to KALEIDOSCOPE) / **FRANK COOK** – drums

Liberty Liberty

Aug 67. (lp; mono/stereo) *(LBL/LBS 83059)* <7526> **CANNED HEAT** ☐ 76
– Rollin' and tumblin' / Bullfrog blues / Evil is going on / Goin' down slow / Catfish blues / Dust my broom / Help me / Big road blues / The story of my life / The road song / Rich woman. *(re-iss. Feb73 as 'ROLLIN'*

& TUMBLIN" on 'Sunset'; SLS 50321) (re-iss. Jun89 on 'See for Miles'; SEE 268) (cd-iss. Aug90; SEECD 268)

Jan 68. (7") *(LBF 150)* *<55979>* **ROLLIN' AND TUMBLIN'. / BULLFROG BLUES** [ ] [ ]

— **FITO 'ADOLPHO' DE LA PARRA** (b. 3 Feb'46, Mexico City, Mexico) – drums (ex-BLUESBERRY JAM) repl. COOK

Mar 68. (7") *<56005>* **EVIL WOMAN. / THE WORLD IS A JUDGE** [–] [ ]

May 68. (7") *(LBF 15090)* **ON THE ROAD AGAIN. / THE WORLD IN A JUG** [8] [–]
(re-iss. Sep75 on 'United Artists'; UP 36001)

Jun 68. (lp; mono/stereo) *(LBL/LBS 83103)* *<7541>* **BOOGIE WITH CANNED HEAT** [5] Feb68 [16]
– Evil woman / My crime / On the road again / World in a jug / Turpentine moan / Whiskey headed woman No.2 / Amphetamine Annie / An owl song / Marie Laveau / Fried hockey boogie. *(re-iss. Feb86 on 'See for Miles'; SEE 62) (cd-iss. Feb90; SEECD 62)*

Jul 68. (7") *<56038>* **ON THE ROAD AGAIN. / BOOGIE MUSIC** [–] [16]

Nov 68. (7") *(LBF 15169)* *<56077>* **GOING UP THE COUNTRY. / ONE KIND FAVOUR** [19] [11]

Dec 68. (d-lp) *(LDS 84001)* *<27200>* **LIVING THE BLUES** [ ] [18]
– Pony blues / My mistake / Sandy's blues / Going up the country / Walking by myself / Boogie music / One kind favour / Parthenogenesis:- Nebulosity – Rollin' and tumblin' – Five owls – Bear wires – Snooky flowers – Sunflower power – Ragi Kafi – Icebag – Childhood's / Refried the boogie (part 1 – live) / Refried the boogie (part 2 – live). *(re-iss. Jul87 on 'See for Miles' lp; SEE 97) (cd-iss. Feb90; SEECD 97) (re-iss. May99 on 'Akarma' d-cd/d-lp; AK 051 CD/LP)*

Apr 69. (7") *(LBF 15200)* *<56097>* **TIME WAS. / LOW DOWN** [ ] Mar69 [67]

— **HARVEY MANDEL** (b.11 Mar'45, Detroit, Mich.) – guitar (+ solo artist) repl. VESTINE

Aug 69. (lp) *(LBS 83239)* *<7618>* **HALLELUJAH** [ ] [37]
– Same all over / Change my ways / Canned Heat / Sic 'em pigs / I'm her man / Time was / Do not enter / Big fat / Huautla / Get off my back / Down in the gutter, but free. *(re-iss. Feb89 on 'See for Miles'; SEE 248) (cd-iss. Aug90; SEECD 248)*

Sep 69. (7") *(LBF 15255)* **POOR MAN. / SIC 'EM PIGS** [ ] [ ]

Dec 69. (7") *<56140>* **CHANGE MY WAYS. / GET OFF MY BACK** [–] [ ]

Jan 70. (lp) *(LBS 83303)* *<11000>* **CANNED HEAT COOKBOOK** (compilation) [8] Nov69 [86]
– Bullfrog blues / Rollin' and tumblin' / Going up the country / Time was / Boogie music / On the road again / Same all over / Sic 'em pigs / Fried hockey boogie / I will wait for you. *(re-iss. Nov75 on 'Sunset'; SLS 50377)*

Jan 70. (7") *(LBF 15302)* *<56151>* **LET'S WORK TOGETHER. / I'M HER MAN** [2] Sep70 [26]

Jun 70. (7") *(LBF 15350)* **SUGAR BEE. / SHAKE IT AND BREAK IT** [49] [–]

Jun 70. (lp) *(LBS 83333)* *<5509>* **CANNED HEAT '70 CONCERT (live in Europe)** [15] Jul71 [ ]
– That's all right mama / Bring it on home / Pulling hair blues / Back out on the road – On the road again / London blues / Let's work together / Goodbye for now. *(re-iss. Oct88 as '70: LIVE IN EUROPE' on 'Beat Goes On'; BGOLP 12) (cd-iss. Sep89; BGOCD 12)*

— **ANTONIO DE LA BARREDA** (aka TONY OLAV) – bass repl. LARRY TAYLOR

Sep 70. (7") *(LBF 15395)* **FUTURE BLUES. / SKAT** [ ] [–]

Sep 70. (lp) *(LBS 83364)* *<11002>* **FUTURE BLUES** [27] [59]
– Sugar bee / Shake it and break it / That's all right mama / My time ain't long / Scat / Let's work together / London blues / So sad (the world's in a tangle) / Future blues. *(re-iss. Jul89 on 'Beat Goes On' lp/cd; BGO LP/CD 49)*

— On 3rd Sep70, **AL WILSON** suffering depression died of drug o/d. He appeared on the releases below until stated.

Dec 70. (7") *(LBF 15429)* **CHRISTMAS BLUES. / DO NOT ENTER** [ ] [–]

Jan 71. (7") *(LBF 15439)* **WOOLY BULLY. / MY TIME AIN'T LONG** [ ] [ ]

— **HENRY VESTINE** – guitar returned to repl. MANDEL who returned to JOHN MAYALL (next with veteran US blues legend)

Mar 71. (d-lp; by CANNED HEAT / JOHN LEE HOOKER) *(LPS 103-4)* *<35002>* **HOOKER'N'HEAT** [ ] Feb71 [73]
– Messin' with the Hook / The feelin' is gone / Send me your pillow / Sittin' here thinkin' / Meet me in the bottom / Altmonia blues / Drifter / You talk too much / Burning Hell / Bottle up and go / The world today / I got my eyes on you / Whiskey and wimmen' / Just you and me / Let's make it / Peavine / Boogie chillen No.2. *<re-iss. Oct71 on 'United Artists'; 9955> (re-iss. Sep88 as lp 'THE BEST OF HOOKER'N'HEAT' on 'See for Miles'; SEE 234) (cd-iss. Aug89 as 'HOOKER'N'HEAT (THE BEST OF PLUS)'; SEECD 234)*

— **JOEL SCOTT HILL** – guitar, vocals finally repl. AL WILSON, now alongside **HITE, BARREDA, PARRA and VESTINE**

U.A. U.A.

Mar 71. (7"; CANNED HEAT & JOHN LEE HOOKER) *<50779>* **LET'S MAKE IT. / WHISKEY AND WIMMEN** [–] [ ]

Sep 71. (7") *(UP 35279)* *<50831>* **LONG WAY FROM L.A.. / HILL'S STOMP** [ ] [ ]

— **LITTLE RICHARD** – piano, vocals guested on next album

Mar 72. (lp) *(UAG 29304)* *<5557>* **HISTORICAL FIGURES AND ANCIENT HEADS** [ ] Feb72 [87]
– Sneakin' around / Hill's stomp / Rockin' with the king / I don't care what you tell me / Long way from L.A. / Cherokee dance / That's all right / Utah. *(re-iss. Aug90 on 'Beat Goes On' cd/lp; BGO CD/LP 83)*

Apr 72. (7") *(UP 35348)* *<50892>* **ROCKIN' WITH THE KING. / I DON'T CARE WHAT YOU TELL ME** [ ] Mar72 [88]

Jul 72. (7") *<50927>* **CHEROKEE DANCE. / SNEAKIN' AROUND** [–] [ ]

— **RICHARD HITE** – bass (BOB's brother) (ex-POPPA HOP) repl. BARREDA / added **JAMES SHANE** – guitar / **ED BEYER** – keyboards

Jun 73. (7") *(UP 35562)* **KEEP IT CLEAN. / YOU CAN RUN, BUT YOU SURE CAN'T HIDE** [ ] [–]

Sep 73. (lp) *(UAS 29455)* *<049F>* **NEW AGE** [ ] [ ]
– Keep it clean / Harley Davidson blues / Don't deceive me / You can run, but you sure can't hide / Rock and roll music / Lookin' for my rainbow / Framed / Election blues / So long wrong *(cd-iss. May91 on 'Beat Goes On'; BGOCD 85)*

Sep 73. (7") *<167>* **LOOKIN' FOR MY RAINBOW. / ROCK AND ROLL MUSIC** [–] [ ]

Nov 73. (7") *<243>* **HARLEY DAVIDSON BLUES. /** [–] [ ]

Atlantic Atlantic

Feb 74. (7") *(K 10420)* *<3010>* **ONE MORE RIVER TO CROSS. / HIGHWAY 401** [ ] [ ]

Mar 74. (lp) *(K 50026)* *<SD 7289>* **ONE MORE RIVER TO CROSS** [ ] [ ]
– L.A. town / I need someone / Bagful of boogie / I'm a hog for you baby / You am what I am / Shake rattle & roll / Bright times are comin' / Highway 401 / We remember Fats.

Jan 75. (7") *<3236>* **THE HARDER THEY COME. / ROCK 'N' ROLL SHOW** [–] [ ]

— **RICHARD HITE + FITO DE LA PARRA** took over control of band when BOB & HENRY got stoned. ED BAYER also departed. Recruited **CHRIS MORGAN** – guitar / **GENE TAYLOR** – keyboards (both ex-POPPA HOP)

Sonet Takoma

Dec 78. (lp) *(SNTF 783)* *<7066>* **THE HUMAN CONDITION** [ ] [ ]
– Strut my stuff / Hot money / House of blue lights / Just got to be there / You just got the rock / Human condition / She's lookin' good / Open up your backdoor / Wrapped up.

— (later in 70's) **BOB HITE** returned (he was to die of heart attack 4th Apr81)

— re-united + re-formed with **FITO, VESTINE,** and **TAYLOR** and others, **RAUL E. RODRIGUEZ + F.M. HALEY.**

not iss. Destiny

1982. (lp) *<10007>* **KINGS OF THE BOOGIE** [–] [ ]
– Kings of the boogie / Stoned bad street fighting man / So fine / You just can't get close to me / Hell's just on down the road / I was wrong / Little crystal / Dog house blues / Sleepy hollow baby / Chicken shack. *<re-iss. 1981 as 'DOG HOUSE BLUES' on 'Rhino'; > (re-iss. Oct85 on 'Platinum' lp/c; PLP/PMC 20)*

not iss. A.L.A.

1984. (12"ep) *<1996>* **THE HEAT BROS '84** [–] [ ]

— **JAMES THORNBERRY** – slide guitar, vocals, harmonica repl. VESTINE.

Bedrock not iss.

Dec 87. (blue-lp) *(BEDLP 5)* **THE BOOGIE ASSAULT (LIVE IN AUSTRALIA)** [ ] [ ]
– Kings of the boogie / Stoned bad street fighting man / So fine / You just can't get close to me / Hell's just on down the road / I was wrong / Little crystal / Dog house blues / Sleepy hollow baby / Chicken shack. *(cd-iss. Mar89; BEDLP 5CD)*

not iss. Chameleon

1990. (cd) <*SPV 858805*> **REHEATED**
– Looking for the party / Driftin' / I'm watching you / Bullfrog blues / Hucklebuck / Mercury blues / Gunstreet girl / I love to rock and roll / So fine (Betty Jean) / Take me to the river / Red headed woman / Built for comfort. *(UK-iss.Mar96 on 'SPV'; same)*

— new line-up; **VESTINE / DE LA PARRA / THORNBURY / + JUNIOR WATSON** – guitar, vocals / **RON SHUMAKE** – bass, vocals

Aim Topic

Sep 93. (cd)(c) *(AIM CD/C 1033)* **BURNIN' (live in Australia 1990)**
– Let's work together / Gamblin' woman / Hucklebuck / Sunnyland / Rollin' and tumblin' / Nitwit / Gunstreet girl / One way out / J.J. jump / Mercury blues.

— **TAYLOR + MANDEL** returned

Aim River Road

Jul 95. (cd) *(AIM 1044)* **INTERNAL COMBUSTION**
– I used to be bad / John Lee Hooker boogie / Remember Woodstock / (You'll have to) Come and get it / The heat in me is up / It' hot / Vision of you / Nothing at all / 24 hours / Gamblin' woman / I might be tempted. *(re-iss. Jan96 on 'Connoisseur'; FPCCD 01)*

— **ROBERT LUCAS** – (new) vocals; repl. TAYLOR + MANDEL

not iss. A&M

1996. (cd) <*161416*> **BLUES BAND**
– Stranger / Quiet woman / Iron horse / Jr.'s shuffle / Creole queen / Keep it to yourself / Boogie music / Going up the country / See these tears / One kind favor / Oh baby / Gorgo boogie.

Ruf Ruf

Sep 99. (cd) <*(RUF 1041)*> **BOOGIE 2000**
– Wait and see / Last man who'll ever have to sing the blues / World of make believe / Dark clouds / Searchin' for my baby / I got loaded / Too much goddyup (not enough whoa) / She split / 2000 reasons (Y2K blues) / Road to Rio / Can I come home / I'm so tired.

Feb 03. (cd) *(MYSCD 148)* **LIVE IN OZ featuring WALTER TROUT (live)**
– One the road again / Amphetamine Annie / Going up the country / Let's work together / Kings of the boogie / Refried hockey boogie / Hell's on down the line / Chicken shack boogie / So long.
(above issued on 'Mystic') (next with various blues guests)

May 03. (cd) <*(RUF 1066)*> **FRIENDS IN THE CAN**
– Same old games / Bad trouble / Black coffee / Getaway / It don't matter / Let's work together / 1, 2, 3, here we go again / That fat cat / Home to you / Never get out of these blues alive / Little wheel / Let's work together / Geataway.

– compilations, etc. –

Jan 70. (lp) *Pye International; (NSPL 28129) / Janus; <3009>* **VINTAGE HEAT**

Jun 70. (7") *Pye International; (7N 25513)* **SPOONFUL. / BIG ROAD BLUES**

1973. (lp; with CLARENCE GATEMOUTH BROWN) *Barclay; (80603)* **GATE'S ON HEAT** France

Jul 75. (lp; with MEMPHIS SLIM) *Barclay; (80607)* **MEMPHIS HEAT** France

Nov 76. (7"ep) *United Artists; (REM 407)* **REMEMBER CANNED HEAT**
– On the road again / Let's work together / Going up the country.

Nov 76. (lp) *D.J.M.; (DJB 26072) / Wand; <WDS 693>* **LIVE AT TOPANGA CORRAL (live)** 1971

May 84. (7") *EMI-Golden; (G45 24)* **ON THE ROAD AGAIN. / LET'S WORK TOGETHER**

1987. (d-lp) *Rhino; <RNDA 71105>* **INFINITE BOOGIE**

Feb 88. (lp)(cd) *Rhino; <RNLP 801><RNCD 75776>* **HOOKER 'N' HEAT VOL.2**

Aug 89. (7") *E.M.I.; (EM 100)* **LET'S WORK TOGETHER. / GOIN' UP THE COUNTRY**
(12"+=) *(12EM 100)* – Rollin' and tumblin'.
(cd-s+=) *(CDEM 100)* – Amphetamine Annie.

Sep 89. (lp/c)(cd) *E.M.I.; (GO/TC-GO 2026)(CDP 793114-2)* **LET'S WORK TOGETHER (THE BEST OF CANNED HEAT)**
– On the road again / Bullfrog blues / Rollin' and tumblin' / Amphetamine / Annie / Fried hockey boogie / Sic 'em pigs / Poor Moon / Let's work together / Going up the country / Boogie music / Same all over / Time was / Sugar bee / Rockin' with the king / That's alright mama / My time ain't long.

Apr 90. (d-lp)(cd) *Bear Family; (BTS 964410)(BTCD 9779 409)* **LIVE AT THE TURKU ROCK FESTIVAL (live in Finland)** German

Feb 92. (cd) *Thunderbolt; (CDTB 130)* **STRAIGHT AHEAD**
(re-iss. Apr97; same)

Oct 92. (cd) *Carlton; (SMS 053)* **ROCK LEGENDS VOL.1**

Nov 92. (3xcd-box) *Liberty; (CANNED 780275-2)* **THE BIG HEAT**

Jul 93. (cd) *Charly; (CCCD 1104)* **LIVE**

Aug 94. (d-cd) *E.M.I.; (CDEM 15431)* **UNCANNED (THE BEST OF CANNED HEAT)**

Feb 95. (cd) *In-Akustik; (INAK 8804)* **BOOGIE UP THE COUNTRY (live in West Germany 1987)**

Feb 95. (cd) *B.A.M.; (KLMCD 015)* **PEARLS OF THE PAST VOL.2 – CANNED HEAT**

Feb 96. (cd) *Prestige; (CSGSP 079)* **BIG ROAD BLUES**

Feb 97. (cd) *EMI Gold; (CDGOLD 1076)* **ON THE ROAD AGAIN**

May 97. (cd) *Disky; (DC 87865-2)* **THE BEST OF CANNED HEAT**

Mar 99. (cd) *Start; (SRH 806)* **ON THE ROAD AGAIN**

□ Jerry CANTRELL (see under ⇒ ALICE IN CHAINS)

CAPTAIN BEEFHEART

Born: DON VAN VLIET, 15 Jan'41, Glendale, Los Angeles, California, USA. Started out as a child-prodigy sculptor who, between the ages of five and thirteen, had his clay animals featured on a weekly TV show hosted by Portuguese sculptor Augustino Rodriguez. An opportunity to develop his art skills were halted when his parents declined a scholarship on his behalf to study art in Europe, preferring instead to move to Lancaster in the Mojave desert. There, he met FRANK ZAPPA at the local high school, setting up a few local bands while ZAPPA started to write a script for a B-movie 'CAPTAIN BEEFHEART MEETS THE GRUNT PEOPLE'. When FRANK went to Los Angeles to form The MOTHERS OF INVENTION, DON adopted the name CAPTAIN BEEFHEART and set about recruiting The MAGIC BAND. They signed to 'A&M' in 1964, releasing their version of BO DIDDLEY's 'DIDDY WAH DIDDY', which sold enough copies to encourage the label to buy studio time for an album. When completed, president Jerry Moss rejected the tapes, citing it too strange and anti-commercial. Undaunted, VAN VLIET and a new set of musicians, including RY COODER, re-recorded most of these masters, the album 'SAFE AS MILK' finally surfacing in 1967 on the 'Buddah' label. This was a masterpiece of its time, full of BEEFHEART on a HOWLIN' WOLF-style trip; the great tracks being 'ELECTRICITY', 'ABBA ZABA', 'AUTUMN CHILD' & 'ZIG ZAG WANDERER'. However, RY COODER departed for safer pastures when VAN VLIET/BEEFHEART left the stage halfway through their set at the 1967 Monterey Pop Festival, leaving the band to play to a bewildered but carefree hippy audience. BEEFHEART often showed signs of outlandish behaviour which split the band up as much as his personality. Late in 1968, they recorded another album, 'MIRROR MAN', although this was shelved until his popularity had grown in the early 70's. However, one album did appear that year, 'STRICTLY PERSONAL', which BEEFHEART slammed for its radical remix by producer BOB KRASNOW. This riled him so much that he signed a new contract with old friend ZAPPA who gave him complete artistic control on his new 'Straight' label. Having written about 30 songs in a day, BEEFHEART took his new bunch of weirdo musicians (ANTENNAE JIMMY SEMENS, DRUMBO,

CAPTAIN BEEFHEART

ART TRIPP III, ZOOT HORN ROLLO and THE MASCARA SNAKE) to rehearse in a house which was close-by an old friend JIMMY CARL BLACK (drummer for ZAPPA). They stayed there for a full eight months, only one of them at a time venturing out if the band was in need of food & drink, etc. This was VAN VLIET's tyrannical way of keeping the band tight, so as to establish virtuoso musicianship while he got on with the weird vocals. The resulting album (a double!) 'TROUT MASK REPLICA' was handed to ZAPPA, much to his surprise, after four and a half hours in the studio. When released at the turn of the decade, it was initially given the thumbs down by many critics and fans. Those hardy enough to give it a few tolerant spins, however, were convinced of its genius. The record surprisingly nearly made the UK Top 20, having been played to death on John Peel's Radio 1 night-time show. Its virtual insanity was literally not of this world, utilising the complex structures of jazz legend ORNETTE COLEMAN; the best tracks to break through – to the sane among us, were 'THE BLIMP', 'PENA', 'DALI'S CAR', 'ELLA GURU' & 'OLD FART AT PLAY'. It has since become regarded as a classic, although it should never be played to someone not of your generation. He returned a thank-you to ZAPPA, when he sang a track, 'WILLIE THE WIMP', on his 'Hot Rats' album, although their friendship was fraying with every meeting, two egos too big for one room. In 1970, he settled down to a more conventional avant-garde Delta-blues album 'LICK MY DECALS OFF, BABY' (compared that is, to their last). It was another excellent set; combing through the depths of his unearthly roots to find tracks such as 'DOCTOR DARK', 'I LOVE YOU, YOU BIG DUMMY' and the title track. 1972 saw another great album 'THE SPOTLIGHT KID', featuring the delights of 'CLICK CLACK', 'I'M GONNA BOOGLARIZE YOU BABY' & 'WHEN IT GROWS IT STACKS'. Their next, 'CLEAR SPOT' covered new territory on softer tracks like 'TOO MUCH TIME' & 'MY HEAD IS MY ONLY HOUSE UNLESS IT RAINS', tempting the MAGIC BAND to bail out and form their own outfit, MALLARD. The album did, however, include another powerful BEEFHEART special in the shape of 'BIG EYED BEANS FROM VENUS'. In 1974, with a new line-up, he signed to UK's 'Virgin' label but his work at this point, especially on the albums 'UNCONDITIONALLY GUARANTEED' & 'BLUEJEANS & MOONBEAMS', were just above average. He tried to escape yet another restrictive deal; it was said he would sign anything, and teamed up with his old pal FRANK ZAPPA and The MOTHERS. Their collaboration, 'BONGO FURY', set the ball rolling for a litigation battle between him and 'Virgin' UK, resulting in another deal!, this time with 'Warner Brothers' for the 1978 album 'SHINY BEAST (BAT CHAIN PULLER)', a marked return to form on some tracks. Virgin won the rights to this album, which gained a UK release in early 1980. Two other records surfaced in the next two years; 'DOC AT RADAR STATION' and the considerably better 'ICE CREAM FOR CROW', the latter containing the excellent title track, his final epitaph. He retired from the music business and set up home with his wife JAN at a trailer park in the Mojave desert. Still an avid sculptor and painter, with the help of fan Julian Schnabel, he began exhibiting his primitive canvases which made him more money than his records ever did. In the mid-80's, a host of young British indie acts including STUMP, McKENZIES, The SHRUBS, etc, took on the mantle of the BEEFHEART sound. Always asked if he would return, BEEFHEART has repeatedly refused to get back on the bandwagon (having fallen into ill-health, both physically and mentally, a return to the recording studio is unlikely to say the least). A remarkable figure of his time, DON VAN VLIET exemplified the glory of not worrying about the exploitation of the music industry, only happy with his own, and of course the MAGIC BAND's work. Let's just hope he's around for several more years to enjoy whatever he creates.

• **Trivia:** He also covered Jack Nitzsche's 'HARD WORKIN' MAN' on the 1978 film 'Blue Collar', which starred Harvey Keitel.

Album rating: SAFE AS MILK (*10) / STRICTLY PERSONAL (*6) / TROUT MASK REPLICA (*10) / LICK MY DECALS OFF, BABY (*9) / MIRROR MAN earlier recording (*7) / THE SPOTLIGHT KID (*8) / CLEAR SPOT (*8) / UNCONDITIONALLY GUARANTEED (*6) / BLUEJEANS & MOONBEAMS (*9) / BONGO FURY; with Frank Zappa (*5) / SHINY BEAST (BAT CHAIN PULLER) (*6) / DOC AT RADAR STATION (*6) / ICE CREAM FOR CROW (*7) / early collections, etc. (selective):- THE LEGENDARY A&M SESSIONS mini (*5) / I MAY BE HUNGRY BUT I SURE AIN'T WEIRD (*6) / A CARROT IS AS CLOSE AS A RABBIT GETS TO A DIAMOND (*8) / GROW FINS boxed (*8) / MERSEYTROUT – LIVE IN LIVERPOOL 1980 (*7) / THE DUST BLOWS FORWARD (*10)

CAPTAIN BEEFHEART & HIS MAGIC BAND

DON VAN VLIET – vocals, harmonica, occasional guitar, wind instruments / **ALEX ST. CLAIRE SNOUFFER** – guitar / **DOUG MOON** – guitar / **JERRY HANDLEY** – bass / **PAUL BLAKELY** – drums

A&M A&M

1966. (7") *<794>* **DIDDY WAH DIDDY. / WHO DO YOU THINK YOU'RE FOOLING** [–] [ ]

1966. (7") *<818>* **MOONCHILD. / FRYING PAN** [–] [ ]

1968. (7") *(AMS 726)* **MOONCHILD. / WHO DO YOU THINK YOU'RE FOOLING** [ ] [–]

—— **JOHN FRENCH** (DRUMBO) – drums; repl. BLAKELY (MOON also departed) / **RY COODER** guested on 2 tracks below

Pye Inter Kama Sutra

Jan 68. (7") *(7N 25443)* **YELLOW BRICK ROAD. / ABBA ZABA** [ ] [–]

Feb 68. (lp) *(NPL 28110)* *<BDS 5001>* **SAFE AS MILK** [ ] Nov67 [ ]
– Sure 'nuff 'n yes I do / Zig zag wanderer / Call on me / Dropout boogie / I'm glad / Electricity / Yellow brick road / Abba zaba / Plastic factory / Where there's woman / Plastic factory / Grown so ugly / Autumn child. *(re-iss. 1968 on 'Marble Arch' 2 tracks less; MAL 1117) (re-iss. 1970 on 'Buddha' stereo; 623 171) (re-iss. Jan82 on 'P.R.T.'; NCP 1004) (re-iss. Jul85 on 'Buddah' lp/c; 252260-1/-4) (cd-iss. May91 on 'Castle'; CLACD 234) (cd re-mast.Sep99 on 'Buddha-RCA'+=; 74321 89175-2)* – Safe as milk (take 5) / On tomorrow / Big black baby / Flower pot / Dirty blue Gene / Trust us (take 9) / Korn ring finger. *(lp re-iss. Sep99 on 'Simply Vinyl'; SVLP 122)*

—— **JEFF COTTON** (ANTENNAE JIMMY SEMENS) – guitar; repl. COODER who went solo (HERB BERMANN co-contributed several songs)

Liberty Blue Thumb

Dec 68. (lp; mono/stereo) *(LBL/LBS 83172)* *<BTS 1>* **STRICTLY PERSONAL** [ ] Oct68 [ ]
– Ah feel like ahcid / Safe as milk / Trust us / Son of Mirror Man – Mere man / On tomorrow / Beatle bones 'n' smokin' stones / Gimme dat harp boy / Kandy korn. *(re-iss. Nov79 lp/c; LBR/TCR 1006) (cd-iss. Aug94 on 'E.M.I.'; CZ 529) (lp re-iss. Dec99 on 'Simply Vinyl'; SVLP 157)*

—— **The CAPTAIN** retained **DRUMBO** and **ANTANNAE** plus new members **ZOOT HORN ROLLO** (b.BILL HARKLEROAD) – brass, narrator, guitar, flute / **ROCKETTE NORTON** (b.MARK BOSTON) – bass, narrator / **THE MASCARA SNAKE** (b.VICTOR HAYDEN) – clarinet / guest **DOUG MOON** returned

Straight Straight

Nov 69. (d-lp) *(STS 1053)* *<RS 2027>* **TROUT MASK REPLICA** [21] [ ]
– Frownland / The dust blows forward 'n dust blows back / Dachau blues / Ella guru / Hair pie: bake 1 / Moonlight on Vermont / Hair pie: bake 2 / Pena / Well / When big Joan sets up / Fallin' ditch / Sugar 'n spikes / Ant man bee / Pachuco cadaver / Bills corpse / Sweet sweet bulbs / Neon meate dream of an octafish / China pig / My human gets me blues / Dali's car / Orange claw hammer / Wild life / She's too much for my mirror / Hobo chang ba / The blimp (mousetrap replica) / Steal softly thru snow / Old fart at play / Veteran's day poppy. *(re-iss. May75 on 'Reprise'; K 64026) (re-iss. cd Sep94 & Jul00 on 'WEA'; K 927196-2)*

—— **ED MARIMBA** (ART TRIPP) – marimba (ex-MOTHERS OF INVENTION) repl. THE MASCARA SNAKE

Jan 71. (lp) *(STS 1063)* *<RS 6240>* **LICK MY DECALS OFF, BABY** [20] [ ]
– Lick my decals off, baby / Doctor Dark / I love you, you big dummy / Peon / Bellerin' plain / Woe-is-uh-me-bop / Japan in a dishpan / I wanna find a woman that'll hold my big toe till I have a go / Petrified forest / One rose that I mean / The Buggy boogie woogie / The Smithsonian Institute blues (or the big dig) / Space-age couple / The clouds are full of wine (not whiskey or rye) / Flash Gordon's ape. *(re-iss. Jul73 on 'Reprise')* *<US cd-iss. Oct90 on 'Enigma';*

CAPTAIN BEEFHEART

— **THE WINGED EEL FINGERLING** (r.n. ELLIOT INGBER) – guitar, etc. (ex-MOTHERS etc.) repl. SEMENS who had already formed MU

Reprise Reprise

Jan 72. (7") *<1068>* **CLICK CLACK. / I'M GONNA BOOGLARIZE YOU BABY** [–] [ ]

Feb 72. (lp) *(K 44162) <RS 2050>* **THE SPOTLIGHT KID** [44] [ ]
– I'm gonna booglarize you baby / White jam / Blabber 'n smoke / When it blows its stacks / Alice in Blunderland / The spotlight kid / Click clack / Grow fins / There ain't no Santa Claus on the evenin' stage / Glider.

CAPTAIN BEEFHEART and the MAGIC BAND

— **ROY 'OREJON' ESTRADA** – bass (ex-LITTLE FEAT, ex-MOTHERS OF INVENTION) repl. INGBER / augmented by backing vocals The **BLACKBERRIES / RUSS TITELMAN** – guitar (guested, as he did on "Safe as Milk")

Nov 72. (lp) *(K 54007) <MS 2115>* **CLEAR SPOT** [ ] [ ]
– Low yo yo stuff / Nowadays a woman's gotta hit a man / Too much time / Circumstances / My head is my only house unless it rains / Sun zoom sparks / Clear spot / Crazy little thing / Long neck bottles / Her eyes are a blue million miles / Big eyed beans from Venus / Golden birdies.

Mar 73. (7") *(K 14233) <1133>* **TOO MUCH TIME. / MY HEAD IS MY ONLY HOUSE UNLESS IT RAINS** [ ] [ ]

— **ALEX SAINT CLAIRE** – guitar; returned to repl. ROY

— added **MARK MARCELLINO** – keyboards

Virgin Mercury

Apr 74. (lp) *(V 2015) <SRM1 709>* **UNCONDITIONALLY GUARANTEED** [ ] [ ]
– Upon the my-o-my / Sugar bowl / New electric ride / Magic be / Happy love song / Full moon, hot sun / I got love on my mind / This is the day / Lazy music / Peaches. *(re-iss. Aug82 + Aug85 on 'Fame' lp/c; FA/TCFA 3034) (re-iss. Aug88; OVED 66) (cd-iss. Jun88; CDV 2015)*

Apr 74. (7") *(VS 110)* **UPON THE MY-O-MY. / MAGIC BE** [ ] [–]

Apr 74. (7") *<73494>* **UPON THE MY-O-MY. / I GOT LOVE ON MY MIND** [–] [ ]

— **IRA INGBER** – bass; repl. SAINT CLAIRE / added new session men **MARK GIBBONS** – keyboards / **MICHAEL SMOTHERMAN** – keyboards, vocals / **JIMMY CARAVAN** – keyboards / **DEAN SMITH** – guitar / **BOB WEST** – bass / **GENE PELLO** – drums / **TY GRIMS** – percussion

Nov 74. (lp) *(V 2123) <SRM1 1018>* **BLUEJEANS & MOONBEAMS** [ ] [ ]
– Party of special things do / Same old blues / Observatory crest / Pompadour swamp / Captain's holiday / Rock'n'roll's evil doll / Further than we've gone / Twist ah luck / Bluejeans and moonbeams. *(re-iss. Mar84; OVED 19) (cd-iss. Jun88; CDV 2023)*

— Late '75 **BEEFHEART** collaborated with **FRANK ZAPPA** on **"BONGO FURY"** album. This was a near live album with 2 studio tracks.

— His new touring band featured past members **ELLIOT, INGBER** and **JOHN FRENCH** plus **DENNY WHALLEY** – slide guitar / **BRUCE FOWLER** – trombone (both on bongos)

— His '76 band were **DRUMBO, WHALLEY, JEFF MORRIS TEPPER** – slide guitar, guitar + **JOHN THOMAS** – piano (they recorded first sessions for the next album)

— **ERIC DREW FELDMAN** – synthesizer; repl. THOMAS / **ROBERT ARTHUR WILLIAMS** – drums; repl. DRUMBO / **RICHARD REDUS** – slide guitar, guitars. accordion, fretless bass; repl. WHALLEY / **ART TRIPP III** – marimba, percussion; returned from MALLARD **BRUCE LAMBOURNE FOWLER** also returned

Virgin Warners

Feb 80. (lp) *(V 2149) <BSK 3256>* **SHINY BEAST (BAT CHAIN PULLER)** [ ] 1979 [ ]
– The floppy boot stomp / Tropical hot dog night / Ice rose / Harry Irene / You know you're a man / Bat chain puller / When I see mommy I feel like a mummy / Owed t'Alex / Candle mambo / Love lies / Suction prints / Apes-ma. *(re-iss. Aug88; OVED 67) (cd-iss. Jun87; CDV 2149)*

— **GARY LUCAS** – french horn, guitar (on 1); repl. REDUS

— **DRUMBO (JOHN FRENCH)** also returned

Virgin Virgin

Aug 80. (lp) *(V 2172) <13148>* **DOC AT RADAR STATION** [ ] [ ]
– Hot head / Ashtray heart / A carrot is as close as a rabbit gets to a diamond / Run paint run run / Sue Egypt / Brickbats / Dirty blue Gene / Best batch yet / Telephone / Flavor bud living / Sheriff of Hong Kong / Making love to a vampire with a monkey on my knee. *(re-iss. Aug88; OVED 68) (cd-iss. Jun88; CDV 2172)*

— The CAPTAIN brought in **RICHARD 'MIDNIGHT HAT SIZE' SNYDER** – guitar, bass, marimba, viola / **CLIFF R. MARTINEZ** – drums, percussion, etc / to add to **TEPPER + LUCAS** FELDMAN remained a guest

Aug 82. (12") *(VS 534-12) <03190>* **LIGHT REFLECTED OFF THE OCEANS OF THE MOON. / ICE CREAM FOR CROW** [ ] [–]

Sep 82. (lp) *(V 2237)* **ICE CREAM FOR CROW** [90] [–]
– Ice cream for crow / The host the ghost the most holy-o / Semi-multicoloured caucasian / Hey Garland, I dig your tweed coat / Evening bell / Cardboard cutout sundown / The past sure is tense / Ink mathematics / The witch doctor life / "81" poop hatch / The thousandth and tenth day of the human totem pole / Skeleton makes good. *(re-iss. Aug88; OVED 121) (cd-iss. Apr88; CDV 2237) <US cd-iss. 1990 on 'Caroline'; CAROL 1632-2>*

— BEEFHEART retired from the music business to concentrate on painting/sculpting in his recently bought Mojave desert home.

– compilations etc. –

Jul 70. (lp) *Buddah; (2349 002)* **DROPOUT BOOGIE** [ ] [–]
(a re-iss. of "SAFE AS MILK" 2 tracks less)

May 71. (lp) *Buddah; (2365 002) <BDS 5077>* **MIRROR MAN** (rec.1967; not one night in 1965 as stated on sleeve!) [49] [ ]
– Tarotplane / Kandy korn / 25th century Quaker / Mirror man. *(re-iss. May82 on 'P.R.T.'; NCP 1006) (re-iss. Apr86 on 'Edsel'; ED 184) (cd-iss. May91 on 'Castle'; CLACD 235) (cd re-iss. Sep99 as 'THE MIRROR MAN SESSIONS' on 'Buddha-RCA'+=; 74321 69174-2)* – Trust us (take 6) / Safe as milk (take 12) / Beatle bones n' smokin' stones / Moody Liz (take 8) / Gimme dat harp boy. *(lp re-iss. Nov99 on 'Simply Vinyl'; SVLP 143)*

1975. (lp) *WRMB;* **WHAT'S ALL THIS BOOGA-BOOGA MUSIC (live)** [–] [ ]

Aug 76. (d-lp) *Reprise; (K 84006)* **TWO ORIGINALS OF . . .** [ ] [ ]
– (LICK MY DECALS OFF, BABY / THE SPOTLIGHT KID)

Nov 77. (d-lp/d-c) *Pye; (FILD/ZCFILD 008)* **THE CAPTAIN BEEFHEART FILE** (first 2-lp's) [ ] [–]

1978. (d-lp) *Impossible;* **EASY TEETH** [–] [ ]

Jan 78. (7") *Buddah; (BDS 466)* **SURE 'NUFF 'N' YES I DO. / ELECTRICITY** [ ] [–]

May 78. (7") *M.C.A.; (MCA 366)* **HARD WORKIN' MAN (by Jack Nitzsche featuring Captain Beefheart). / Coke Machine (by Jack Nitzsche)** [ ] [–]
above also features RY COODER – on guitar

1978. (7"pic-ep) *Virgin; (SIXPACK 1)* **SIX-PACK / SIX TRACK** [ ] [–]
– Sugar bowl / Same old blues / Upon the my-o-my / Magic be / Rock'n'roll's evil doll / New electric ride.

Jul 83. (10"lp/c) *P.R.T.; (DOW/ZCDOW 15)* **MUSIC IN SEA MINOR** [ ] [–]

Jul 84. (lp/pic-lp) *Design; (PIL/+P 4)* **TOP SECRET** [ ] [–]

Oct 84. (m-lp) *A&M; (AMY 226)* **THE LEGENDARY SESSIONS** [ ] [–]
– Diddy wah diddy / Who do you think you're fooling / Moonchild / Frying pan / Here I am, I always am. *(re-iss. Oct86 on 'Edsel'; BLIMP 902) (cd-iss. Mar92; BLIMPCD 902)*

Jun 88. (d-lp/c/d-cd) *That's Original; (TFO LP/MC/CD 11)* **SAFE AS MILK / MIRROR MAN** [ ] [–]
(re-iss. d-cd.May91 on 'Castle')

Feb 91. (d-cd) *Reprise; (7599 26249-2)* **THE SPOTLIGHT KID / CLEAR SPOT** [ ] [–]

Jul 91. (cd) *The Collection; (ORO 146)* **ZIG ZAG WANDERER** [ ] [–]
(re-iss. Nov96 & Oct98 on 'Wooded Hill'; HILLCD 6)

Jun 92. (cd) *Sequel; (NEXCD 215)* **I MAY BE HUNGRY BUT I SURE AIN'T WEIRD – THE ALTERNATIVE CAPTAIN BEEFHEART** [ ] [–]

Jun 93. (cd) *Virgin Universal; (CDVM 9028) <88303-2>* **A CARROT IS AS CLOSE AS A RABBIT GETS TO A DIAMOND** [ ] [ ]
– Sugar bowl / The past sure is tense / Happy love song / The floppy boot stomp / Bluejeans and moonbeams / Run paint run run / This is the day / Tropical hot dog night / Observatory crest / The host the ghost the most holy o / Harry Irene / I got love on my mind / Pompadour swamp / Love

lies / Sheriff of Hong Kong / Further than we've gone / Candle mambo / Light reflected off the oceans of the Moon / A carrot is as close as a rabbit gets to a diamond.

Nov 93. (cd) *Movieplay Gold; (MPG 74025)* **LONDON 1974** (live) [ ] [-]

Jan 98. (cd) *Camden-RCA; (74321 55846-2)* **ELECTRICITY** [ ] [-]

Nov 98. (7") *Table Of Elements; <(TOE 759)>* **SPITBALL SCALPED UH BABY. /** [ ] [ ]

Nov 98. (cd+book) *Sonic Book; (SB 1)* **PEARLS BEFORE SWINE** (poems, paintings, aphorisms & discography) [ ] [-]

May 99. (5xcd-box) *Revenant; (REV 210)* **GROW FINS** (rarities 1965-1982) [ ] [ ]

May 99. (d-lp) *Xeric; <(XERLP 96)>* **GROW FINS VOL.1 – JUST GOT BACK FROM THE CITY 1965-1967 / ELECTRICITY 1968** [ ] [ ]

Sep 99. (d-lp) *Xeric; <(XERLP 97)>* **GROW FINS VOL.2 – THE TROUT MASK REPLICA HOUSE SESSIONS 1969** [ ] [ ]

Oct 00. (cd) *Ozit; <(BF 4003)>* **MERSEYTROUT – LIVE IN LIVERPOOL 1980** (rec. 29 October 1980) [ ] [ ]

– Toaster (bass solo) / Nowadays a woman's gotta hit a man / Abba zabba / Hothead / Dirty blue Jean / Best batch yet / One man sentence (poem) / Safe as milk / Flavour bud living / Her eyes are a blue million miles / One red rose that I mean / Doctor Dark / Bat chain puller / My human gets me blues / Sugar 'n' spikes / Veterans' day poppy / Dropout boogie / Sheriff of Hong Kong / Kandy korn / Suction prints / Big eyed beans from Venus.

May 01. (d-lp) *Table Of Elements; <(TOELP 52)>* **GROW FINS VOL.3** [ ] [ ]

May 02. (cd) *Ozit; <(OZITCD 6003)>* **DUST SUCKER** [ ] [ ]

May 02. (cd) *EMI Gold; (539383-2)* **THE BEST OF CAPTAIN BEEFHEART & HIS MAGIC BAND** [ ] [-]

Jun 02. (cd) *Viper; (VIPERCD 011)* **MAGNETIC HANDS** (live in the UK 1972-1980) [ ] [-]

May 03. (cd) *Viper; (VIPERCD 015)* **RAILROADISM** (live, etc.) [ ] [-]

Jul 03. (cd) *EMI; (INTROCD 3)* **INTRODUCING . . . CAPTAIN BEEFHEART** [ ] [-]

Jul 03. (cd; as the MAGIC BAND) *All Tomorrow's Parties; <(ATPCD 7)>* **BACK TO THE FRONT** [ ] [ ]

Sep 03. (cd) *Ozit; (OZIT 8003)>* **DICHOTOMY** (rarities, outtakes & demos from the 60s & 70s) [ ] [ ]

Nov 03. (d-cd) *Masterplan; (MP 42017)* **LIVE AT MY FATHER'S PLACE** (live) [ ] [ ]

Oct 04. (d-cd) *Ozit; <(OZITCD 9003)>* **LIVE 'N' RARE** (live..) [ ] [ ]

Jun 05. (cd) *Ozit; <(OZITCD 7003)>* **PRIME QUALITY BEEF** [ ] [ ]

Sep 05. (d-cd) *Buddah; (82876 71879-2)* **SAFE AS MILK / THE MIRROR MAN SESSIONS** [ ] [ ]

Feb 06. (cd) *Sony BMG; (82876 80530-2)* **THE BUDDAH YEARS** [ ] [ ]

Apr 06. (cd) *Major League; <(MLP 12CD)>* **AMSTERDAM 1980** (live) [ ] [ ]

Apr 06. (d-cd) *Ozit; <(OZITCD 9004)>* **THE CAPTAIN'S LAST CONCERT PLUS** (live) [ ] [ ]

May 06. (d-cd) *Rhino; <(8122 75863-2)>* **THE DUST BLOWS FORWARD** [ ] Aug99 [ ]

– Diddy wah diddy / Frying pan / Electricity / Abba zaba / Beatle bones 'n' smokin' stones / Safe as milk / Moonlight on Vermont / Ella Guru / Old Fart at play / Sugar 'n' spikes / Orange claw hammer / My human gets me blues / China pig / Lick my decals off baby / Woe is uh me bop / I wanna find a woman that'll hold my big toe till I have to go / Smithsonian Institute blues (or the big dig) / I'm gonna booglarize you baby / Click clack / Grow fins / When it blows it's stack / Little scratch / Nig eyed beans from Venus / Golden birdies // Nowadays a woman's gotta hit a man / Low yo yo stuff / Too much time / My head is my only house unless it rains / Clear spot / Upon the my-o-my / Party of special things to do / Sam with the showing scalp flat top (live) / Debra Cadabra (live) / Hard working man / Bat chain puller / Floppy boot stomp / Tropical hot dog night / Owed t' Alex / Hot head / Ashtray heart / Sue Egypt / Making love to a vampire with a monkey sitting on my knee / Ice cream for crow / Past sure is tense / Light reflected off the oceans of the Moon.

the CARS

Formed: Boston, Massachusetts, USA . . . 1976 by BENJAMIN ORR, GREG HAWKES and ELLIOT EASTON who started out touring as CAP 'N' SWING. Manager Fred Davis was successful in getting a demo of 'JUST WHAT I NEEDED' playlisted on US radio and they duly signed to 'Elektra', having added RIC OCASEK and DAVID ROBINSON. The track was released simultaneously with their eponymous 1978 debut album, an American new wave milestone which also caught the attention of UK hipsters eager for something a bit easier on the ear than British punk. Taking 70's Anglo art-rock as base material, The CARS combined synthesized cool with an American classic rock sensibility. This recipe was realised in irresistibly infectious style with 'MY BEST FRIEND'S GIRL', a UK Top 3 hit later that year. On subsequent albums however, the band's predeliction for moody experimentation saw the singles dry up. Though 'CANDY-O' (1979), 'PANORAMA' (1980) and 'SHAKE IT UP' (1981), all reached the US Top 10, they spawned only a couple of major hits in the former's 'LET'S GO' and the latter's title track while further success in Britain had faltered completely. After a two year break, however (during which time, OCASEK released a solo set, 'BEATITUDE' – 1983), the band returned with the commercially revved-up 'HEARTBEAT CITY' (1984). Motoring squarely for the AOR market, the group scored a sizeable Top 5 transatlantic hit with the polished atmospherics of the ORR-penned 'DRIVE'. The song would later become forever linked with images of famine-plagued Ethiopia after it was used as part of a Live Aid documentary. The album itself made the Top 5 and provided a further two major Stateside hits in 'YOU MIGHT THINK' and 'MAGIC'. After a mid-80's break during which the various members pursued solo projects, The CARS spluttered to a halt with the poorly received 'DOOR TO DOOR' in 1987. OCASEK reappeared from time to time in the following years, mainly in connection with his production work. Sadly, on October 3rd, 2000, founder member BENJAMIN ORR died of cancer.

• **Songwriters:** All written by OCASEK, ORR and EASTON, except THINK IT OVER and MAYBE BABY (Buddy Holly).

Album rating: THE CARS (*7) / CANDY-O (*5) / PANORAMA (*4) / SHAKE IT UP (*5) / HEARTBEAT CITY (*7) / THE CARS' GREATEST HITS compilation (*7) / DOOR TO DOOR (*3) / JUST WHAT I NEEDED – ANTHOLOGY compilation (*7) / Ric Ocasek: BEATITUDE (*4) / THIS SIDE OF PARADISE (*4) / FIREBALL ZONE (*4) / QUICK CHANGE WORLD (*4) / TROUBLIZING (*3) / Elliott Easton: CHANGE NO CHANGE (*4) / Benjamin Orr: THE LACE (*4) / Greg Hawkes: NIAGARA FALLS (*3)

RIC OCASEK (b. RICHARD OTCASEK, 23 Mar'49, Baltimore, Maryland) – vocals, guitar / **BENJAMIN ORR** (b. ORZECHOWSKI, in Cleveland, Ohio) – vocals, bass / **ELLIOT EASTON** (b. ELLIOT STEINBERG, 18 Dec'53, Brooklyn, N.Y.) – guitar / **GREG HAWKES** – keyboards, saxophone (ex-MILKWOOD, with ORR and OCASEK) / **DAVID ROBINSON** – drums (ex-The POP, ex-DMZ, ex-MODERN LOVERS)

Elektra Elektra

Aug 78. (7") *<45491>* **JUST WHAT I NEEDED. / I'M IN TOUCH WITH YOUR WORLD** [-] [27]

Aug 78. (lp/c) *(K/K4 52088) <135>* **THE CARS** [29] Jun78 [18]

– Good times roll / My best friend's girl / Just what I needed / I'm in touch with your world / Don't cha stop / You're all I've got tonight / Bye bye love / Moving in stereo / All mixed up. *(cd-iss. Jan84; 252 088)*

Oct 78. (7"pic-d) *(K 12301)* **MY BEST FRIEND'S GIRL. / MOVING IN STEREO** [3] [-]

Oct 78. (7") *<45537>* **MY BEST FRIEND'S GIRL. / DON'T CHA STOP** [-] [35]

Jan 79. (7"pic-d) *(K 12312)* **JUST WHAT I NEEDED. / I'M IN TOUCH WITH YOUR WORLD** [17] [-]

May 79. (7") *(K 12352) <46014>* **GOOD TIMES ROLL. / ALL MIXED UP** [ ] Mar79 [41]

Jun 79. (lp/c) *(K/K4 52088) <507>* **CANDY-O** [30] [3]

– Let's go / Since I held you / It's all can do / Double life / Shoo be doo /

Candy-O / Nightspots / You can't hold on too long / Lust for kicks / Got a lot on my head / Dangerous type. *(cd-iss. Jan84; 252 148)*

Jul 79. (7"pic-d) *(K 12371)* <46063> **LET'S GO. / THAT'S IT** 51 Jun79 14

Sep 79. (7"pic-d) *(K 12385)* **DOUBLE LIFE. / COME AROUND** –

Oct 79. (7") <46546> **IT'S ALL I CAN DO. / GOT A LOT ON MY HEAD** – 41

Jan 80. (7") <46580> **DOUBLE LIFE. / CANDY-O** –

Jan 80. (7") *(K 12416)* **IT'S ALL I CAN DO. / CANDY-O** –

Sep 80. (lp/c) *(K/K4 52240)* <514> **PANORAMA** 5

– Panorama / Touch and go / Gimme some slack / Don't tell me no / Getting through / Misfit kid / Down boys / You wear those eyes / Running to you / Up and down. *(cd-iss. 1986; 252 240)*

Sep 80. (7") <47039> **TOUCH AND GO. / DOWN BOYS** 37

Jan 81. (7") <47080> **DON'T TELL ME NO. / DON'T GO TO PIECES** –

Mar 81. (7") <47101> **GIMME SOME SLACK. / DON'T GO TO PIECES** –

Nov 81. (lp/c) *(K/K4 52330)* <567> **SHAKE IT UP** 9

– Since you're gone / Shake it up / I'm not the one / Victim of love / Cruiser / A dream away / This could be love / Think it over / Maybe baby. *(cd-iss. 1986; 252 330)*

Nov 81. 7"pic-d) *(K 12583)* <47250> **SHAKE IT UP. / CRUISER** 4

Mar 82. (7") <47433> **SINCE YOU'RE GONE. / THINK IT OVER** – 41

May 82. (7") *(K 13177)* **SINCE YOU'RE GONE. / MAYBE BABY** 37 –

Jun 82. (7") <47479> **THIS COULD BE LOVE. / VICTIM OF LOVE** –

Aug 82. (7") *(K 13187)* **THINK IT OVER. / I'M NOT THE ONE** –

Mar 84. (7") <69744> **YOU MIGHT THINK. / HEARTBEAT CITY** – 7

Mar 84. (lp/c) *(960 296-1/-4)* <60296> **HEARTBEAT CITY** 25 3

– Hello again / Magic / Stranger eyes / It's not the night / I refuse / Looking for love / Drive / You might think / Why can't I have you / Heartbeat city. *<cd-iss. Jul84>*

Apr 84. (7") *(E 9741)* **WHY CAN'T I HAVE YOU. / JACKIE** –

May 84. (7") <69724> **MAGIC. / I REFUSE** – 12

Sep 84. (7"/12") *(E 9706/+T)* <69706> **DRIVE. / STRANGER EYES** 5 Jul84 3

(re-iss. Jul85; hit UK No.4)

Oct 84. (7") <69681> **HELLO AGAIN. / ('A'dub)** – 20

Nov 84. (7") *(E 9718)* **YOU MIGHT THINK. / I REFUSE** –

(12"+=) *(E 9710T)* – Let's go.

Jan 85. (7") <69657> **WHY CAN'T I HAVE YOU. / HEARTBEAT CITY** – 33

(12"+=) *(E 9741T)* – Hello again (remix) / Moving in stereo.

Sep 85. (7") *(EKR 3)* **HEARTBEAT CITY. / WHY CAN'T I HAVE YOU** –

(12"+=) *(EKR 3T)* – Chemistry / Hello again.

Oct 85. (7") <69589> **TONIGHT SHE COMES. / JUST WHAT I NEEDED** – 7

Nov 85. (7"pic-d) *(EKR 30)* **TONIGHT SHE COMES. / BREAKAWAY** –

(12"+=) *(EKR 30T)* – Just what I needed.

Nov 85. (lp/c)(cd) *(EKT 25/+C)(960 464-2)* <60464> **THE CARS' GREATEST HITS** (compilation) 27 12

– Just what I needed / Since you're gone / You might think / Good times roll / Touch and go / Drive / Tonight she comes / My best friend's girl / Heartbeat city / Let's go / Magic / Shake it up. *(c+=/cd+=)* – I'm not the one.

Jan 86. (7") <69569> **I'M NOT THE ONE. / HEARTBEAT CITY** – 32

Mar 86. (7") *(EKR 38)* **I'M NOT THE ONE (remix). / SINCE YOU'RE GONE** –

(12"+=) *(EKR 38T)* – Shake it up.

Sep 87. (7") *(EKR 63)* <69446> **YOU ARE THE GIRL. / TA TA WAYO WAYO** Aug87 17

(12"+=/12"pic-d+=) *(EKR 63T/+P)* – Tonight she comes.

Sep 87. (lp/c)(cd) *(EKT 42/+C)(960 747-2)* <60747> **DOOR TO DOOR** 72 26

– Leave or stay / You are the girl / Double trouble / Fine line / Everything you say / Ta ta wayo wayo / Strap me in / Coming up you / Wound up on you / Go away / Door to door.

Nov 87. (7") <69427> **STRAP ME IN. / DOOR TO DOOR** – 85

Jan 88. (7") <69432> **COMING UP YOU. / DOUBLE TROUBLE** – 74

— disbanded early 1988. OCASEK married Paulina Porizkova (23 Aug'89) while continuing his solo career; ORR and EASTON also released solo sets

– compilations, etc. –

Jan 96. (d-cd) *Elektra; (0349 73506-2)* **JUST WHAT I NEEDED – ANTHOLOGY**

May 99. (d-cd) *Rhino Deluxe; <(8122 75700-2)>* **THE CARS**

Johnny CASH

Born: 26 Feb'32, Kingsland, Arkansas, USA (where a statue of "The Man in Black" now stands). The third of seven children born to poor sharecropper parents, Ray and Annie Cash, JOHNNY attended Dyess High School in Arkansas and won his first talent contest at age seventeen. In 1950, he joined the Air Force and served overseas in Germany, being discharged in 1954 as a staff sergeant (his other pre-musical jobs included salesman, assembly line worker and margarine factory operative). Young CASH, however, was destined for greater things; the birth of Rock'n'Roll, or more correctly its rockabilly predecessor, was the perfect vehicle for his budding singing and songwriting talents. After initially playing in a combo called the TENNESSEE TWO (later the TENNESSEE THREE), he was subsequently spotted and signed by Sam Phillips for his influential 'Sun' record label in 1955 as a fellow stable-mate to rockers ROY ORBISON, JERRY LEE LEWIS, CARL PERKINS and a little-known truck driver named ELVIS PRESLEY (CASH, PERKINS, LEWIS and PRESLEY were to become known as "The Million Dollar Quartet"). While the others took the rock road, CASH churned out a string of country-influenced hit singles and albums ('BIG RIVER', 'I WALK THE LINE', 'RING OF FIRE', 'SAN QUENTIN' and 'FOLSOM PRISON' being typical of his slow western, macho, half-spoken/half-sung drawl) between 1955 and 1968, his rising fame running parallel with a notorious reputation offstage as a violent, hot-headed heavy boozer and pill-popper. As his career soared, so his personal life disintegrated, ending in divorce after a stormy marriage to first wife, Vivien Liberto. Along with the infamous Folsom Prison and San Quentin Prison live albums (Grammy award winners both), this image established his blue-collar following and consolidated his position as the champion of the underdog in America. He rapidly established himself as the hottest property in country music, selling over fifty million records and even outselling the Beatles in America for a time. He married June Carter in 1968, erstwhile member of the legendary all-singing CARTER FAMILY. Her calming influence on him was to prove a major factor in the style and quality of his later recordings. As the decade turned, he became involved in TV, hosting the Johnny Cash Show and bringing many cult names, (BOB DYLAN, NEIL YOUNG, HANK WILLIAMS Jnr. et al.) to a wider audience. CASH, influenced by his new wife, turned to religion around this time, making a film 'Gospel Road', while various religious organisations and charities benefitted from the newly converted wild man of country. He continued to tour non-stop during the 70's and 80's, including shows for Vietnam draftees and tours behind the then Iron Curtain. Two books were published, 'Man in Black' in 1975 and 'Man in White' in 1987. The 80's also saw him becoming a member of "outlaw" country band, the HIGHWAYMEN alongside KRIS KRISTOFFERSON, WAYLON JENNINGS and WILLIE NELSON, with whom he toured the world to sellout concerts and more recording success. The 90's, meanwhile, saw CASH resurrected as an alternative hero (via a guest track – 'THE WANDERER' – on U2's 1993 album, 'Zooropa') by Rick Rubin and his 'American' label, who released comeback set, 'AMERICAN RECORDINGS' (1994). He garnered even more critical kudos with 1996's 'UNCHAINED', wherein he even had a

JOHNNY CASH

crack at Soundgarden's 'RUSTY CAGE' and Beck's 'ROWBOAT'. His compositions are still covered by today's up-and-coming artists while his frequent appearances on MTV have kept his popularity high, despite failing health and a less rigourous tour schedule. He's now the head of a family of five, the most famous of whom is ROSANNE CASH, a minor C&W star in her own right. He has been inducted into all of music's four Halls of Fame: Songwriters (1989), Rock'n'Roll (1992) and, of course, Country Music (1980) and Rockabilly (1994), a unique achievement among his peers as is his grand total of seven Grammys, three multi-platinum albums ('FOLSOM PRISON', 'SAN QUENTIN' and 'GREATEST HITS') and 130 (yes 130!) hits on the Billboard charts. On a more depressing note, CASH has had to contend with ongoing health problems over the last few years and has recently been diagnosed with Parkinson's disease, having to abandon a US show midway through. The man in black made a startling comeback with his album 'AMERICAN 3: SOLITARY MAN' (2000), a sort of half covers album and a musician's jamboree all in one. CASH not only covered such classics as Tom Petty's 'I WON'T BACK DOWN' and U2's 'THE ONE', but he also did a fantastic job at recreating PALACE man and fellow crooner Will Oldham's 'I SEE A DARKNESS', to much heightened effect. MERLE HAGGARD, the Bluegrass legend popped in to lend his voice to the CASH penned 'I'M LEAVING NOW' and he basically transformed his own 'FIELD OF DIAMONDS IN THE SKY' from jangling country to a heart-felt holler. But it's the lonesome guitar and theatrical piano trills on Nick Cave's 'THE MERCY SEAT' that really put things in perspective; when CASH sings, " . . .and I'm not afraid to die", you know he really feels it, shining a whole new light on the meaning behind the track. And perhaps that was the biggest compliment you could pay such a revered figure as CASH: each song he covered came into its own through his extraordinary talent and minimalistic guitar playing – not to mention RICK RUBIN's 'Live' production. That is the kind of power that JOHNNY CASH's music will always command. And so to the last chapter of his critical rebirth and sadly, the last chapter of his life. 'AMERICAN IV: THE MAN COMES AROUND' (2002) continued with the strategy of edifying contemporary songs with a lifetime's worth of hard-won experience. Again, the ones which worked best were the ones least likely to succeed on paper, such as Nine Inch Nails' 'HURT' and Depeche Mode's 'PERSONAL JESUS'. Released as a double-A single, the songs made the UK Top 40, while the compelling, revelatory video was nominated at the MTV video music awards. JOHNNY CASH finally succumbed to his ongoing health problems on the 12th of September 2003, at the age of 71, just four months after his wife. Few recording artists pushed their creative boundaries as long and as hard as JOHNNY CASH, while even fewer – if any – managed to sustain that achievement (and – for what it's worth – confound and impress contemporary critics) right up until their final days, and for that we should be grateful. In 2005, moviemakers were treated to CASH's life story via biopic, 'Walk The Line', starring Joacqin Phoenix in the main role.

• **Songwriters:** CASH penned except; THE WAYS OF A WOMAN IN LOVE (Charlie Rich) / RING OF FIRE (Merle Haggard & June Carter) / IT AIN'T ME BABE + WANTED MAN (Bob Dylan) / A BOY NAMED SUE (Shel Silverstein) / IF I WERE A CARPENTER (Tim Hardin) / SUNDAY MORNING COMING DOWN (Kris Kristopherson) / JOHNNY 99 (Bruce Springsteen) / DADDY SANG BASS (Carl Perkins) / THE HIGHWAYMAN (Jimmy Webb) / BIRD ON A WIRE (Leonard Cohen) / THIRTEEN (Glen Danzig) / THE BEAST IN ME (Nick Lowe) / THE MAN WHO COULDN'T CRY (Loudon Wainwright III). The 1964 album BITTER TEARS was written by PETER LA FARGE. • **Trivia:** In 1969, he guested on BOB DYLAN's 'Nashville Skyline' lp track, 'THE GIRL FROM NORTH COUNTRY'.

Album rating (selective): RIDE THIS TRAIN (*7) / I WALK THE LINE (*7) / AT FOLSOM PRISON (*8) / AT SAN QUENTIN (*7) / ONE PIECE AT A TIME (*6) / THE MAN IN BLACK – THE DEFINITIVE JOHNNY CASH compilation (*8) / THE MYSTERY OF LIFE (*6) / AMERICAN RECORDINGS (*7) / UNCHAINED (*7) / AMERICAN III: SOLITARY MAN (*6) / AMERICAN IV: THE MAN COMES AROUND (*5) / MAN IN BLACK – THE VERY BEST OF . . . double compilation (*8) / THE LEGEND OF JOHNNY CASH compilation (*8) / RING OF FIRE: THE LEGEND OF JOHNNY CASH compilation (*9)

JOHNNY CASH – vocals, guitar / with various backers

London | Sun

Jun 55. (7",78) *<221>* **CRY! CRY! CRY! / HEY PORTER** [–] [ ]
(UK-iss.Oct70 on 'Sun'; 6094 005)

Jan 56. (7",78) *<232>* **FOLSOM PRISON BLUES. / SO DOGGONE LONESOME** [–] [ ]

Jan 57. (7",78) *(HL 8358) <241>* **I WALK THE LINE. / GET RHYTHM** [ ] Aug56 [17]

Jun 57. (7",78) *(HLS 8427) <258>* **TRAIN OF THOUGHT. / THERE YOU GO** [ ] Nov56 [ ]

Aug 57. (7",78) *(HLS 8461) <266>* **NEXT IN LINE. / DON'T MAKE ME GO** [ ] Jun57 [99]

Oct 57. (lp) *<SLP 1220>* **JOHNNY CASH WITH HIS HOT & BLUE GUITAR** [–] [ ]
– The rock island line / I heard that lonesome whistle blow / Country boy / If the good Lord's willing and the creeks don't rise / Cry cry cry / Remember me / I'm so doggone lonesome / I was there when it happened / I walk the line / The wreck of the old 97 / Folsom Prison blues / Doin' my time. *(UK-iss.Feb81 on 'Charly'; CRM 2013)*

Dec 57. (7",78) *(HLS 8514) <279>* **HOME OF THE BLUES. / GIVE MY LOVE TO ROSE** [ ] Sep57 [88]

Apr 58. (7",78) *(HLS 8586) <283>* **BALLAD OF A TEENAGE QUEEN. / BIG RIVER** [ ] Jan58 [14]

Jul 58. (7",78) *(HLS 8656) <295>* **GUESS THINGS HAPPEN THAT WAY. / COME IN STRANGER** [ ] [11] May58 [66]

Oct 58. (7",78) *(HLS 8709) <302>* **THE WAYS OF A WOMAN IN LOVE. / YOU'RE THE NEAREST THING TO HEAVEN** [ ] Aug58 [24]

Philips | Columbia

Nov 58. (7",78) *(PB 874) <41251>* **ALL OVER AGAIN. / WHAT DO I CARE** [ ] [38] Sep58 [52]

— In Dec'58, 'Sun' and CASH had their first of a number of Top 100 successes with 'IT'S JUST ABOUT TIME'.

Jan 59. (7",78) *(PB 897) <41313>* **DON'T TAKE YOUR GUNS TO TOWN. / I STILL MISS SOMEONE** [ ] [32]

Jan 59. (lp) *(BBL 7298) <1253>* **THE FABULOUS JOHNNY CASH** [ ] [19]
– Run softly, blue river / Frankie's man, Johnny / That's all over / The troubadour / One more ride/ That's enough / I still miss someone / Don't take your guns to town / I'd rather die young / Pickin' time / Shepherd of my heart / Supper-time. *(UK re-iss. Jun62 on 'C.B.S.'; 62042)*

May 59. (7",78) *(PB 928) <41371>* **FRANKIE'S MAN, JOHNNY. / YOU DREAMER YOU** [ ] Apr59 [57]

Sep 59. (7",78) *(PB 953) <41427>* **I GOT STRIPES. / FIVE FEET HIGH AND RISING** [ ] [43] [76]

— recruited new drummer **W.S.HOLLAND** who stayed for next 30 years.

Dec 59. (7",78) *(PB 979) <41481>* **THE LITTLE DRUMMER BOY. / I'LL REMEMBER YOU** [ ] [63]

Jan 60. (lp) *(BBL 7353) <CS 8148>* **SONGS OF OUR SOIL** [ ] [ ]
– Drink to me / Five feet high and rising / Man on the hill / Hank and Joe and me / Clementine / Don't step on mother's roses / Great speckled bird / I want to go home / Caretaker / Old Apache squaw / My grandfather's clock / It could happen to you.

Apr 60. (7") *(PB 1017) <41618>* **SEASONS OF MY HEART. / SMILING BILL McCALL** [ ] [ ]

Jun 60. (lp) *(BBL 7373) <CS 8522>* **HYMNS BY JOHNNY CASH** [ ] [ ]
– It was Jesus / I saw a man / Are all the children in / The old account / Lead me gently home / Swing low, sweet chariot / Snow in his hair / Lead me, father / I called him / These things shall pass / He'll be a friend / God will.

Jul 60. (7") *<41707>* **SECOND HONEYMOON. / HONKY-TONK GIRL** [–] [ ]

Oct 60. (7") *(PB 1075) <41804>* **GOING TO MEMPHIS. / LOADING COAL** [ ] [ ]

Oct 60. (lp) *(BBL 7358) <CS 8254>* **NOW THERE WAS A SONG** [ ] [ ]
– Seasons of my heart / I couldn't keep from crying / I feel better all over /

My shoes keep walking back to you / Time changes everything / I'd just be a fool enough (to fall) / Why do you punish me / Transfusion blues / I will miss you when you go / I'm so lonesome, I could cry / Just one more / Honky-tonk girl. *(re-iss. May62 on 'C.B.S.'; 62028) (cd-iss. Feb95;)*

Dec 60. (lp) *(BBL 7417) <CS 8255>* **RIDE THIS TRAIN** [ ] [ ]
– Loading coal / Slow rider / Lumberjack / Dorraine of Ponchartrain / Going to Memphis / When papa played the dobro / Boss Jack / Old Doc Brown. *(re-iss. May62 on 'C.B.S.'; 62575)*

Jan 61. (7") *<41920>* **LOCOMOTIVE MAN. / GIRL IN SASKATOON** [–] [ ]

May 61. (7") *(PB 1148) <41995>* **THE REBEL – JOHNNY YUMA. / FORTY SHADES OF GREEN** [ ] [ ]

Nov 61. (7") *(PB 1200) <42147>* **TENNESSEE FLAT-TOP BOX. / TALL MEN** [ ] Sep61 [84]

Jan 62. (7") *<42301>* **THE BIG BATTLE. / WHEN I'VE LEARNED** [–] [ ]

May 62. (7") *<42425>* **IN THE JAILHOUSE NOW. / LITTLE AT A TIME** [–] [ ]

Aug 62. (7") *<42512>* **BONANZA! / PICK A BALE O' COTTON** [–] [94]

Nov 62. (7"; JOHNNY CASH with The CARTER FAMILY) *<42615>* **WERE YOU THERE (WHEN THEY CRUCIFIED MY LORD). / (THERE'LL BE) PEACE IN THE VALLEY (FOR ME)** [–] [ ]

C.B.S. Columbia

Mar 63. (7") *<42665>* **BUSTED. / SEND A PICTURE OF MOTHER** [–] [ ]

May 63. (lp) *(BPG 62119) <8730>* **BLOOD, SWEAT AND TEARS** [ ] Mar63 [80]
– The legend of John Henry's hammer / Tell him I'm gone / Another man done gone / Busted / Casey Jones / Nine pound hammer / Chain gang / Waiting for a train / Roughneck. *(cd-iss. Feb95;)*

Jul 63. (7") *(AAG 159) <42788>* **RING OF FIRE. / I'D STILL BE THERE** [ ] May63 [17]

Oct 63. (lp; stereo/mono) *(S+/BPG 62171) <8853>* **RING OF FIRE – THE BEST OF JOHNNY CASH** (compilation) [ ] Jul63 [26]
– Ring of fire / I'd still be there / What do I care / I still miss someone / Forty shades of green / Were you there (when they crucified my Lord) / The rebel – Johnny Yuma / Bonanza / The big battle / Remember the Alamo / Tennessee flat-top box / (There'll be) Peace in the valley (for me).

Nov 63. (7") *(AAG 173) <42880>* **THE MATADOR. / STILL IN TOWN** [ ] Oct63 [44]

Nov 63. (lp; stereo/mono) *(S+/BPG 62284)* **THE CHRISTMAS SPIRIT** (festive) [ ] [–]

Feb 64. (7") *<42964>* **UNDERSTAND YOUR MAN. / DARK AS A DUNGEON** [–] [35]

Sep 64. (lp; stereo/mono) *(S+/BPG 62371) <8990>* **I WALK THE LINE** (new versions of old recordings) [ ] [53]
– I walk the line / Bad news / Folsom Prison blues / Give my love to Rose / Hey Porter / I still miss someone / Understand your man / Wreck of old '97 / Still in town / Goodbye, little darlin' / Big river / Troublesome waters.

Dec 64. (7") *<43058>* **BAD NEWS. / THE BALLAD OF IRA HAYES** [–] [ ]

Jan 65. (lp; stereo/mono) *(S+/BPG 62463) <9048>* **BITTER TEARS (BALLADS OF THE AMERICAN INDIAN)** [ ] [47]
– As long as the grass shall grow / Apache tears / Custer / The talking leaves / The ballad of Ira Hayes / Drums / White girl / The vanishing race. *(cd-iss. Feb95;)*

Mar 65. (7") *(201741) <43206>* **ORANGE BLOSSOM SPECIAL. / ALL OF GOD'S CHILDREN AIN'T FREE** [ ] Feb65 [80]

Apr 65. (lp; stereo/mono) *(S+/BPG 62501) <9109>* **ORANGE BLOSSOM SPECIAL** [ ] Mar65 [49]
– Orange blossom special / The long black veil / It ain't me babe / The wall / Don't think twice, it's alright / You wild Colorado / Mama, you've been on my mind / When it's springtime in Alaska (it's forty below) / All of God's children ain't free / Danny boy / Wildwood flower / Amen.

May 65. (7") *(201760) <43145>* **IT AIN'T ME BABE. / TIME AND TIME AGAIN** [28] Oct64 [58]

Jun 65. (7") *<43313>* **STREETS OF LAREDO. / MISTER GARFIELD** [–] [ ]

Aug 65. (7") *(210809)* **RING OF FIRE. / STREETS OF LAREDO** [ ] [–]

Sep 65. (7") *<43342>* **THE SONS OF KATIE ELDER. / CERTAIN KINDA HURTIN'** [–] [ ]

Nov 65. (7") *<43420>* **PICKIN' TIME. / HAPPY TO BE WITH YOU** [–] [ ]

Mar 66. (7") *(202046) <43496>* **THE ONE ON THE RIGHT IS ON THE LEFT. / COTTON PICKIN' HANDS** [ ] Feb66 [46]

Jul 66. (7") *(202256) <43673>* **EVERYBODY LOVES A NUT. / AUSTIN PRISON** [ ] [96]

Jul 66. (lp; stereo/mono) *(S+/BPG 62717) <9292>* **EVERYBODY LOVES A NUT** [28] [88]
– Everybody loves a nut / The one on the right is on the left / A cup of coffee / The bug that tried to crawl around the world / The singing star's queen / Austin Prison / Dirty old egg – Sucking dog / Take me home / Please don't play / Red river valley / Boa constrictor / Joe Bean.

Oct 66. (7") *<43763>* **BOA CONSTRICTOR. / BOTTOM OF A MOUNTAIN** [–] [ ]

Nov 66. (lp; stereo/mono) *(S+/BPG 62760)* **HAPPINESS IS YOU** [ ] [–]
– Happiness is you / Guess things happen that way / Ancient history / You comb her hair / She came from the mountains / For lovin' me / No one will ever know / Is this my destiny / A wound time can't erase / Happy to be with you / Wabash cannonball.

Jan 67. (7") *(202546) <43921>* **YOU BEAT ALL I EVER SAW. / PUT THE SUGAR TO BED** [ ] [ ]

Mar 67. (lp; stereo/mono) *(S+/BPG 62972)* **FROM SEA TO SHINING SEA** [ ] [–]
– From sea to shining sea / Whirl anmd the suck / Call daddy from the mine / The frozen four-hundred-pound fair-to-middlin' cotton picker / The walls of a prison / The masterpiece / You and Tennessee / Another song to sing / The flint arrowhead / Cisco Clifton's fillin' station / Shrimpin' sailin' / From sea to shining sea (reprise). *(hit No.40 in May68)*

Jul 67. (7"; with JUNE CARTER) *<44011>* **JACKSON. / PACK UP YOUR SORROWS** [–] [ ]

Sep 67. (lp; stereo/mono) *(S+/BPG 63062) <9478>* **JOHNNY CASH'S GREATEST HITS, VOLUME 1** (compilation) [ ] Jul67 [82]
– Jackson (with JUNE CARTER) / I walk the line / Understand your man / Orange blossom special / The one on the right is on the left / Ring of fire / It ain't me babe / The balad of Ira Hayes / The rebel – Johnny Yuma / Five feet high and rising / Don't take your guns to town. *(UK hit No.23 Dec69) (cd+c.iss.Nov93 on 'Sony Europe')*

Sep 67. (7"; with JUNE CARTER) *<44158>* **YOU'LL BE ALRIGHT. / LONG-LEGGED GUITAR-PICKIN' MAN** [–] [ ]

Nov 67. (lp; stereo/mono) *(S+/BPG 63105) <9528>* **CARRYIN' ON WITH JOHNNY CASH & JUNE CARTER** [ ] Sep67 [ ]
– Long-legged guitar pickin' man / Shantytown / It ain't me babe / Fast boat to Sydney / Pack up your sorrows / I got a woman / Jackson / Oh, what a good thing we had / You'll be all right / No, no, no / What'd I say.

Nov 67. (7") *<44288>* **RED VELVET. / THE WIND CHANGES** [–] [ ]

Jan 68. (7") *<44373>* **ROSANNA'S GOING WILD. / ROLL CALL** [–] [91]

Feb 68. (7") *(CBS 3268)* **ROSANNA'S GOING WILD. / LONG-LEGGED GUITAR-PICKIN' MAN (with JUNE CARTER)** [ ] [–]

Apr 68. (7") *(CBS 3433)* **A CERTAIN KIND OF HURTIN'. / ANOTHER SONG TO SING** [ ] [–]

Jun 68. (7") *(CBS 3549) <44513>* **FOLSOM PRISON BLUES (live). / THE FOLK SINGER** [ ] May68 [32]

Jun 68. (lp) *(CBS 63308) <9639>* **JOHNNY CASH AT FOLSOM PRISON (live prison gig)** [ ] [13]
– Folsom prison blues / Dark as a dungeon / I still miss someone / Cocaine blues / 25 minutes to go / Orange blossom special / The long black veil / Send a picture of mother / The wall / Dirty old egg sucking dog / Flushed from the bathroom of your heart / Jackson (with JUNE CARTER) / Give my love to Rose / I got stripes / Green green grass of home / Greystone chapel. *(cd/c-iss.Jan95 on 'Success';)*

Jan 69. (7") *(CBS 3878) <44689>* **DADDY SANG BASS. / HE TURNED THE WATER INTO WINE** [ ] Dec68 [42]

May 69. (lp) *(CBS 63428) <KC 9726>* **THE HOLY LAND** [ ] Feb69 [54]
– Prologue / Land of Israel / A mother's love / This is Nazareth / Nazareth town of Canaan / He turned the water into wine / My wife June at the sea of Galilee / Beautiful words / Our guide Jacob at Mount Tabor / The ten commandments / Daddy sang bass / At the wailing wall / Come to the wailing wall / In Bethlehem / In garden of Gethsemane / The fourth man / On the Via Dolorosa / Church of the holy / Sepulchre / At Calvary / God is not dead.

— CASH guested on BOB DYLAN's country 1969 album 'Nashville Skyline'.

— In Jun'69, he also began own self-titled TV show, with The CARTER FAMILY, CARL PERKINS, etc.

— **BOB WOTTON** – guitar repl. LUTHER who died in a house fire.

Aug 69. (lp) *(CBS 63629) <CS 9827>* **JOHNNY CASH AT SAN QUENTIN (live prison gig)** [2] Jun69 [1]

– Wanted man / Wreck of the old 97 / I walk the line / Darling companion / Starkville city jail / San Quentin / A boy named Sue / Peace in the valley / Folsom prison blues. *(cd-iss. Mar94 on 'Sony Collectors')*

Aug 69. (7") *(CBS 4460)* *<44944>* **A BOY NAMED SUE. / SAN QUENTIN** 4 Jul69 2

Dec 69. (7") *(CBS 4638)* *<45020>* **BLISTERED. / SEE RUBY FALL** 50 Nov69 75

Feb 70. (7"; with JUNE CARTER) *<45064>* **IF I WERE A CARPENTER. / 'CAUSE I LOVE YOU** – 36

Feb 70. (lp) *(CBS 63796)* *<9943>* **HELLO, I'M JOHNNY CASH** 6 6
– Southwind / The Devil to pay / Cause I love you / See Ruby fall / If I were a carpenter / To beat the Devil / Blistered / Wrinkled, crinkled, wadded dollar bill / I've got a thing about trains / Jesus was a carpenter.

May 70. (7") *(CBS 4934)* *<45134>* **WHAT IS TRUTH. / SING A TRAVELLING SONG** 21 Apr70 19

Aug 70. (d-lp) *(CBS 66237)* *<29>* **THE WORLD OF JOHNNY CASH** (compilation) 5 May70 54
– I still miss someone / Pickin' time / My shoes keep walking back to you / I want to go home / I feel better all over / I'm so lonesome I could cry / Supper-time / In them old cotton fields back home / Delia's gone / One more ride / Accidentally on purpose / In the jailhouse now / I gorgot more than you'll ever know / Casey Jones / Frankie's man, Johnny / The legend of John Henry's hammer / When papa played the dobro / Busted / Sing it pretty, Sue / Waiting for a train.

Aug 70. (7") *<45211>* **SUNDAY MORNING COMING DOWN. / I'M GONNA TRY TO BE THAT WAY** – 46

Oct 70. (7") *(CBS 5252)* **25 MINUTES TO GO. / I'M GONNA TRY TO BE THAT WAY** –

Dec 70. (lp) *(CBS 64089)* *<30100>* **THE JOHNNY CASH SHOW (live)** 18 Nov70 44
– Sunday morning coming down / Come along and ride this train (medley): Six days on the road – There ain't no easy run – The sailor on a concrete sea / These hands / I'm gonna try to be that way / Come along and ride this train (medley): Mississippi Delta land – Detroit City – Uncloudy day – No setting sun – Mississippi Delta land / Here was a man (dialogue).

Jan 71. (7") *(CBS 5364)* *<45269>* **FLESH AND BLOOD. / THIS SIDE OF THE LAW** Dec70 54

Apr 71. (7") *(CBS 7122)* *<45339>* **MAN IN BLACK. / LITTLE BIT OF YESTERDAY** Mar71 58

Jun 71. (lp) *(CBS 70083)* *<S 30397>* **I WALK THE LINE** (soundtrack) Dec70
– Flesh and blood / I walk the line / Hungry / This town / This side of the law / Flesh and blood (instrumental) / 'Cause I love you / The world's gonna fall on you / Face of despair / Standing on the promises – Amazing grace.

Jun 71. (7") *(CBS 7300)* *<45393>* **SINGING IN VIETNAM TALKING BLUES. / YOU'VE GOT A NEW LIGHT SHINING**

Sep 71. (lp) *(CBS 70087)* *<S 30385>* **LITTLE FAUSS AND BIG HALSY** (soundtrack) Nov70
– Rollin' free / The ballad of Little Fauss and Big Halsy / The ballad of Little Fauss and Big Halsy (instrumental) / 7:06 union / The little man / The little man (instrumental) / Wanted man / Rollin' free (instrumental) / True love is greater than friendship / Movin'. *<(cd-iss. Sep99 on 'Bear Family'+=; BCD 16130)>* – I WALK THE LINE soundtrack + extra versions.

Sep 71. (lp) *(CBS 64331)* *<30550>* **THE MAN IN BLACK** 18 Jun71 56
– The preacher said Jesus said / Orphan of the road / You've got a new light shining in your eyes / If not for love / The man in black / Singin' in Vietnam talkin' blues / Ned Kelly / Look for me / Dear Mrs. / I talk to Jesus every day. *(included a duet with evangelist BILLY GRAHAM)*

Sep 71. (7"; with JUNE CARTER) *<45431>* **I'LL BE LOVING YOU. / NO NEED TO WORRY** –

Oct 71. (lp) *<30887>* **THE JOHNNY CASH COLLECTION (HIS GREATEST HITS, VOLUME II)** (compilation) – 94

Nov 71. (7") *<45460>* **I PROMISE YOU. / PAPA WAS A GOOD MAN** –

—— early '72, he appeared in the film, 'A Gunfight' and TV's 'Colombo'

Mar 72. (7") *(CBS 7797)* *<45534>* **A THING CALLED LOVE. / DADDY** 4

May 72. (lp) *(CBS 64898)* *<31332>* **A THING CALLED LOVE** 8
– Kate / Melva's wine / A thing called love / I promise you / Papa was a good man / Tear stained letter / Mississippi sand / Daddy / Arkansas lovin' man / The miracle man. *(re-iss. Dec85;)*

May 72. (7"ep) *(CBS-EP 9155)* **THE BALLAD OF LITTLE FAUSS & BIG HALSY** –

Jun 72. (7") *(CBS 8036)* *<45590>* **KATE. / THE MIRACLE MAN** May72 75

Aug 72. (7"; with JUNE CARTER) *<45631>* **IF I HAD A HAMMER. / I GOTTA BOY** –

Oct 72. (7") *<45660>* **COUNTRY TRASH. / ONEY** –

Nov 72. (lp) *(CBS 65163)* *<31645>* **JOHNNY CASH: AMERICA (A 200-YEAR SALUTE IN STORY AND SONG)**
– (Opening dialogue) / Paul Revere / Begin West movement / The road to Kaintuck / To the shining mountains / The battle of New Orleans / Southwestward / Remember the Alamo / Opening the west / Lorena / The Gettysburg address / The west / Big foot / Like a young colt / Mister Garfield / A proud land / The big battle / On wheels and wings / Come take a trip in my airship / Reaching for the stars / These are my people.

Dec 72. (7"; with others) *<45679>* **THE WORLD NEEDS A MELODY. / A BIRD WITH BROKEN WINGS CAN'T FLY** –

Mar 73. (7") *(CBS 1115)* *<45740>* **ANY OLD WIND THAT BLOWS. / KENTUCKY STRAIGHT** Feb73

Apr 73. (lp) *(CBS 65431)* *<32091>* **ANY OLD WIND THAT BLOWS** Feb73
– Any old wind that blows / Kentucky Straight / The loving gift / The good Earth / Best friend / Oney / The ballad of Annie Palmer / Too little, too late / If I had a hammer / Country trash / Welcome back Jesus.

Jun 73. (7"; with JUNE CARTER) *<45758>* **HELP ME MAKE IT THROUGH THE NIGHT. / A LOVING GIFT** –

Jun 73. (d-lp) *(CBS 68243)* **THE GOSPEL ROAD** (religious & narrations) –

Aug 73. (7") *(CBS 1490)* *<45786>* **CHILDREN. / LAST SUPPER**

Oct 73. (7"; with The CARTER FAMILY) *<45890>* **BALLAD OF BARBARA. / PRAISE THE LORD AND PASS THE SOUP** –

Oct 73. (lp) *(CBS 65689)* *<32443>* **JOHNNY CASH AND HIS WOMAN**
– The color of love / Saturday night in Hickman County / Allegheny / Life has it's ups and downs / Matthew 24 (is knocking at the door) / The city of New Orleans / Tony / The pine tree / We're for love / Godshine.

Oct 73. (7"; with JUNE CARTER CASH) *<45929>* **ALLEGHENY. / WE'RE FOR LOVE** –

Nov 73. (7"; with MOTHER MAYBELLE CARTER) *<45938>* **DIAMONDS IN THE ROUGH. / PICK THE WILDWOOD FLOWERS** –

Dec 73. (7"; with JUNE CARTER CASH) *(CBS 1994)* **JACKSON. / WE'RE FOR LOVE** –

Dec 73. (7") *<45979>* **CHRISTMAS AS I KNEW IT. / THAT CHRISTMAS FEELING (with TOMMY CASH)** –

Feb 74. (7") *<45997>* **JACOB GREEN. / ORLEANS PARISH PRISON** –

Apr 74. (7") *<46028>* **RAGGED OLD FLAG. / DON'T GO NEAR THE WATER** –

May 74. (lp) *(CBS 80113)* *<32917>* **RAGGED OLD FLAG**
– Ragged old flag / Don't go near the water / All I do is drive / Southern comfort / King of the hill / Pie in the sky / Lonesome to the bone / While I've got it on my mind / Good morning friend / I'm a worried man / Please don't let me out / What on Earth (will you do for Heaven's sake).

Jun 74. (7") *(CBS 2396)* **SOUTHERN COMFORT. / DON'T GO NEAR THE WATER** –

Aug 74. (7") *<10011>* **CRYSTAL CHANDELIERS & BURGANDY. / THE JUNKIE AND THE JUICEHEAD (MINUS ME)** –

Oct 74. (7"; with ROSIE NIX) *<10048>* **FATHER AND DAUGHTER. / DON'T TAKE YOUR GUNS TO TOWN** –

Oct 74. (lp) *(CBS 80348)* *<33086>* **THE JUNKIE AND THE JUICEHEAD MINUS ME**
– The junkie and the juicehead (minus me) / Don't take your guns to town / Broken freedom song / I do believe / Ole slewfoot / Keep on the sunny side / Father and daughter (father and son) / Crystal chandeliers and burgandy / Friendly gates / Bily & Rex & Oral & Bob / Jesus / Lay back with my woman.

Jan 75. (7") *(CBS 2900)* *<10066>* **THE LADY CAME FROM BALTIMORE. / LONESOME TO THE BONE**

May 75. (7") *<10116>* **MY OLD KENTUCKY HOME. / HARD TIMES COMIN'** –

May 75. (lp) *(CBS 80634)* *<33370>* **JOHN R. CASH**
– My old Kentucky home (turpentine and dandelion wine) / Hard times comin' / The lady came from Baltimore / Lonesome to the bone / The night they drove old Dixie down / Clean your own tables / Jesus was our

saviour (cotton was our king) / Reason to believe / Cocaine Carolina / Smokey factory blues.

Aug 75. (7") *(CBS 3499)* **SMOKEY FACTORY BLUES. / CLEAN YOUR OWN TABLES** [ ] [-]

Nov 75. (lp) *(CBS 81012)* *<34193>* **LOOK AT THEM BEANS** [ ] [ ]
– Texas 1947 / What have you got / Planned tonight, Diana / Look at them beans / No charge / I hardly ever sing / Beer drinking songs / Down the road I go / I never met a man like you before / All round cowboy / Gone / Down at Drippin' Springs.

Nov 75. (7") *<10177>* **LOOK AT THEM BEANS. / ALL AROUND COWBOY** [-] [ ]

Jan 76. (7") *<10237>* **TEXAS 1947. / I HARDLY EVER SING BEER DRINKING SONGS** [-] [ ]

Mar 76. (7") *(CBS 4096)* *<10279>* **STRAWBERRY CAKE. / I GOT STRIPES** [ ] [ ]

Mar 76. (lp) *(CBS 81211)* *<34088>* **STRAWBERRY CAKE (live)** [ ] [ ]
– Big river / Doin' my time / I still miss / Someone / I got stripes / Medley: Church in the wildwood – Lonesone valley / Strawberry cake / Rock Island Line / Navajo / Destination / Victoria Station / The fourth man.

May 76. (7"; with The TENNESSEE THREE) *(CBS 4287)* *<10321>* **ONE PIECE AT A TIME. / GO ON BLUES** [32] Apr76 [29]

Jun 76. (lp; with The TENNESSEE THREE) *(CBS 81416)* *<34193>* **ONE PIECE AT A TIME** [49] [ ]
– Let there be country / One piece at a time / In a young girl's mind / Mountain lady / Michigan city howdy do / Sold out of flagpoles / Committed to Parkview / Daughter of a railroad man / Love has lost again / Go on blues. *(re-iss. Mar81 lp/c; CBS/40 32016)*

Jul 76. (7") *<10381>* **MOUNTAIN LADY. / SOLD OUT OF FLAGPOLES** [-] [ ]

Sep 76. (7") *<10424>* **RIDIN' ON THE COTTON BELT. / IT'S ALL OVER** [-] [ ]

Nov 76. (7"; with JUNE CARTER CASH) *<10436>* **FAR SIDE BANKS OF JORDAN. / OLD TIME FEELING** [-] [ ]

Feb 77. (lp) *(CBS 81566)* *<34314>* **THE LAST GUNFIGHTER BALLAD** [ ] [ ]
– I will dance with you / The last gunfighter ballad / Far side banks of Jordan (with JUNE CARTER CASH) / Ridin' on the cotton belt / Give it away / You're so close to me / City jail / Cindy / I love you / Ballad of Barbara / That silver haired daddy of mine.

Apr 77. (7") *(CBS 5107)* *<10483>* **THE LAST GUNFIGHTER BALLAD. / CITY JAIL** [ ] [ ]

Aug 77. (lp) *(CBS 82156)* *<34833>* **THE RAMBLER** [ ] [ ]
– Hit the road and go / If it wasn't for the Wabash River / Lady / After the ball / No earthly good / A Wednesday car / My cowboy's last ride / Calilou.

Sep 77. (7") *(CBS 5564)* *<10587>* **LADY. / HIT THE ROAD AND GO** [ ] [ ]

Dec 77. (7") *<10623>* **CALILOU. / AFTER THE BALL** [-] [ ]

Apr 78. (7") *<10681>* **I WOULD LIKE TO SEE YOU AGAIN. / LATELY** [-] [ ]

Apr 78. (lp) *(CBS 82676)* *<35313>* **I WOULD LIKE TO SEE YOU AGAIN** [ ] [ ]
– I would like to see you again / Lately / I wish I was crazy again / Who's Gene Autrey / Hurt so bad / I don't think I could take you back again / Abner Brown / After taxes / There ain't no good / Chain gang / That's the way it is / I'm alright now.

Jun 78. (7"; by JOHNNY CASH & WAYLON JENNINGS) *(CBS 6401)* *<10742>* **THERE AIN'T NO GOOD CHAIN GANG. / I WISH I WAS CRAZY AGAIN** [ ] [ ]

Sep 78. (7") *<10817>* **GONE GIRL. / I'M ALRIGHT NOW** [-] [ ]

Jan 79. (7") *<10855>* **IT'LL BE HER. / IT COMES AND GOES** [-] [ ]

Mar 79. (7") *(CBS 7153)* *<10888>* **I WILL ROCK AND ROLL WITH YOU. / A SONG FOR THE LIFE** [ ] [ ]

Apr 79. (lp/c) *(CBS/40 83323)* *<35646>* **GONE GIRL** [ ] [ ]
– Gone girl / I will rock and roll with you / Diplomat / No expectations / It comes and goes / It'll be her / Gambler / Cajun born / You and me / A song for the life.

Sep 79. (lp/c) *(CBS/40 83757)* *<36086>* **SILVER** [ ] [ ]
– The L&N don't stop here anymore / Lonesome to the bone / Bull rider / I'll say it's true (with GEORGE JONES) / Ghost riders in the sky / Cocaine blues / Muddy waters / West Canterbury / Subdivision blues / Lately I been leanin' towards the blues / I'm gonna sit on the porch and pick my old guitar.

Oct 79. (7") *<10961>* **GHOST RIDERS IN THE SKY. / I'M GONNA SIT ON THE PORCH AND PICK MY OLD GUITAR** [-] [ ]

Dec 79. (7") *<11103>* **I'LL SAY IT'S TRUE. / COCAINE BLUES** [-] [ ]

Mar 80. (7") *<11237>* **BULL RIDER. / LONESOME TO THE BONE** [-] [ ]

Mar 80. (lp/c) *(CBS/40 84132)* **A BELIEVER SINGS THE TRUTH** [ ] [-]
– Wings in the morning / Gospel boogie (a wonderful time up there) / Over the next hill / He's alive / I've got Jesus in my soul / When he comes / I was there when it happened (so I guess I ought to know) / I'm a new born man / There are strange things happening every day / Children go where I send thee / I'm just an old chunk of coal (but I'll be a diamond someday) / Lay me down in Dixie / Don't take everybody for your friend / You'll get yours, I'll get mine / O come angel band / This train is bound for glory / I'm gonna try to be that way / What on earth (will you do for Heaven's sake) / That's enough / The greatest cowboy of them all.

Oct 80. (7"; with MARTY ROBBINS) *<11283>* **SONG OF THE PATRIOT. / SHE'S A GO-ER** [-] [ ]

Dec 80. (lp/c) *(CBS/40 84607)* *<36779>* **ROCKABILLY BLUES** [ ] [ ]
– Cold lonesome morning / Without love / W.O.M.A.N. / The cowboy who started the fight / The 20th century is almost over / Rockabilly blues (Texas 1955) / The last time / She's a go-er / It ain't nothin' new babe / One way rider.

Dec 80. (7") *<11340>* **COLD LONESOME MORNING. / THE COWBOY WHO STARTED TO FIGHT** [-] [ ]

Feb 81. (7") *<11399>* **THE LAST TIME. / ROCKABILLY BLUES (TEXAS 1965)** [-] [ ]

Apr 81. (7") *<11424>* **WITHOUT LOVE. / IT AIN'T NOTHIN' NEW BABE** [-] [ ]

Jun 81. (lp/c) *(CBS/40 84990)* *<37179>* **THE BARON** [ ] [ ]
– The baron / Mobile boy / Magnolia blossoms / I learned the hard way / A ceiling, four walls and a floor / Hey hey train / The reverend Mr.Black / The blues keep gettin' bluer / Chattanooga city limit sign / Thanks to you / The greatest love affair.

Oct 81. (7") *(A 1155)* *<60516>* **THE BARON. / I WILL DANCE WITH YOU** [ ] [ ]

Jan 82. (7") *<02189>* **MOBILE BOY. / THE HARD WAY** [-] [ ]

Mar 82. (7") *<02669>* **THE REVEREND MR. BLACK. / CHATTANOOGA CITY LIMIT SIGN** [-] [ ]

May 82. (lp/c; by JOHNNY CASH, JERRY LEE LEWIS & CARL PERKINS) *(CBS/40 85609)* **THE SURVIVORS** [ ] Mar82 [ ]
– Get rhythm / I forgot to remember to forget / Goin' down the road feeling bad / That silver haired daddy of mine / Matchbox / I'll fly away / Whole lotta shakin' goin' on / Rockin' my life away / Blue suede shoes / There will be peace in the valley for me / Will the circle be unbroken / I saw the light. *(re-iss. Sep85 on 'Hallmark')*

Nov 82. (7") *<03058>* **I'VE BEEN TO GEORGIA ON A FAST TRAIN. / SING A SONG** [-] [ ]

Nov 82. (lp/c) *(CBS/40 85881)* *<38094>* **THE ADVENTURES OF JOHNNY CASH** [ ] [ ]
– I've been to Georgia on a fast train / John's fair weather friends / Paradise / we must believe in magic / Only love / Good old American guest / I'll cross over Jordan some day / Sing a song / Ain't gonna hobo no more.

Jan 83. (7") *<03317>* **AIN'T GONNA HOBO NO MORE. / JOHN'S FAIR WEATHER FRIENDS** [-] [ ]

Apr 83. (7") *<03524>* **I'LL CROSS OVER JORDAN SOME DAY. / WE MUST BELIEVE IN MAGIC** [-] [ ]

Oct 83. (7"; with JUNE CARTER) *<04060>* **BRAND NEW DANCE. / I'M RAGGED BUT I'M RIGHT** [-] [ ]

Oct 83. (7"; with JUNE CARTER) *(A 3804)* **JOHNNY 99. / BRAND NEW DANCE** [ ] [-]

Nov 83. (lp/c) *(CBS/40 25471)* **JOHNNY 99** [ ] [ ]
– Highway patrolman / That's the truth / God bless Robert E.Lee / New cut road / Johnny 99 / Ballad of the ark / Joshua gone to Barbados / Girl from the canyon / Brand new dance / I'm ragged but I'm right.

Jan 84. (7") *<04227>* **JOHNNY 99. / NEW CUT ROAD** [-] [ ]

Apr 84. (7") *<04428>* **THAT'S THE TRUTH. / JOSHUA GONE TO BARBADOS** [-] [ ]

Oct 84. (7") *(A 4722)* *<04513>* **CHICKEN IN BLACK. / BATTLE OF NASHVILLE** [ ] [ ]

the HIGHWAYMAN

— were formed by country stars **JOHNNY CASH, WAYLON JENNINGS, WILLIE NELSON & KRIS KRISTOFFERSON** (same label)

Aug 85. (7") *<04881>* **THE HIGHWAYMAN. / THE HUMAN CONDITION** [-] [ ]

Sep 85. (lp/c) *(CBS/40 26466)* *<40056>* **THE HIGHWAYMAN** [ ] May85 [92]
– The highwayman / The last cowboy song / Jim, I wore a tie today / Big river / Committed to Parkview / Desperados waiting for the train /

Deportees (plane wreck at Los Gatos) / Welfare line / Against the wind / The twentieth century is almost over. *(cd-iss. 1987; CD 26466) (cd re-iss. Apr90; 902296-2)*

Apr 90. (cd/c/lp; as WILLIE NELSON, JOHNNY CASH, WAYLON JENNINGS & KRIS KRISTOFFERSON) *(466652-2/-4/-1) <45240>* **THE HIGHWAYMAN 2** Mar90 79
– Silver stallion / Born and raised in black and white / Two stories wide / We're all in the corner / American remains / Anthem '84 / Angels love bad men / Songs that made a difference / Living legend / Texas. *(d-cd-iss. Oct93 on 'Sony Europe' incl. 1985 lp)*

Apr 90. (7") *<73233>* **SILVER STALLION. / AMERICAN DREAMS** –

Jun 90. (7") *<73381>* **BORN AND RAISED IN BLACK AND WHITE. / TEXAS** –
(above singles were credited as the second album)

JOHNNY CASH

— had continued with solo career

Oct 85. (7") *<05594>* **DESPERADOES WAITING FOR A TRAIN. / THE TWENTIETH CENTURY IS ALMOST OVER** –

Dec 85. (7") *<05672>* **I'M LEAVING NOW. / EASY STREET** –

Dec 85. (lp/c) *(CBS/40 26689)* **RAINBOW**
– I'm leaving now / Here comes that rainbow again / They're all the same to me / Easy street / Have you ever seen the rain / You beat all I ever saw / Unwed fathers / Love me like you used to / Casey's last ride / Borderline (a musical whodunit).

Jun 86. (lp/c; JOHNNY CASH & WAYLON JENNINGS) *(CBS/40 26922)* **HEROES**
– Folks out on the road / I'm never gonna roam again / American by birth / Field of diamonds / Heroes / Even cowgirls get the blues / Love is the way / The ballad of forty dollars / I'll always love you in my own crazy way / One too many mornings.*(cd-iss. Nov93 on 'Sony';)*

Jun 86. (7"; by JOHNNY CASH & WAYLON JENNINGS) *<05896>* **AMERICAN BY BIRTH. / EVEN COWGIRLS GET THE BLUES** –

Sep 86. (7"; by JOHNNY CASH & WAYLON JENNINGS) *<06287>* **THE BALLAD OF FORTY DOLLARS. / FIELD OF DIAMONDS** –

Mercury Mercury

May 87. (lp/c)(cd) *(MERH/+C 108)<(832031-2)>* **JOHNNY CASH IS COMING TO TOWN**
– The big light / The ballad of Barbra / I'd rather have you / Let him roll / The night Hank Williams came to town / Sixteen tons / Letters from home / W.Lee O'Daniel and the light crust dough boys / Heavy metal (don't mean rock'n'roll to me) / My ship will sail.

Aug 87. (7"; JOHNNY CASH & WAYLON JENNINGS) *(MER 225) <888459-7>* **THE NIGHT HANK WILLIAMS CAME TO TOWN. / I'D RATHER HAVE YOU**

Jan 88. (7") *<888719-7>* **THE BALLAD OF BARBRA. / SIXTEEN TONS** –

May 88. (7") *<MER 263)* **THE BIG LIGHT. / SIXTEEN TONS** –

— next feat. daughter and son **ROSANNE + JOHN** plus other guests **HANK WILLIAMS JR., PAUL McCARTNEY, EMMYLOU HARRIS, WAYLON JENNINGS** and **The EVERLY's**

Oct 88. (lp/c/cd) *<(834778-1/-4/-2)>* **WATER FROM THE WELLS OF HOME**
– As long as I live / Ballad of a teenage queen / Last of the drifters / Where did we go right / Call me the breeze / That ole wheel / Sweeter than the flowers / Ballad of Robb MacDunn / New moon over Jamaica.

Nov 88. (7") *<874562-7>* **THAT OLE WHEEL. / THE LAST OF THE DRIFTERS** Jan89

Feb 89. (7") *<872420-7>* **BALLAD OF A TEENAGE QUEEN. / GET RHYTHM** Oct88

Feb 90. (cd/c/lp) *<(842155-2/-4/-1)>* **BOOM CHICKABOOM**
– A backstage pass / Farmer's almanac / Family bible / I love you, I love you / Monteagle mountain / Cat's in the cradle / Don't go near the water / Harley / Hidden shame / That's one you owe me.

Feb 90. (7") *<875626-7>* **CAT'S IN THE CRADLE. / I LOVE YOU, I LOVE YOU** –

Mar 91. (cd/c/lp) *<(848051-2/-4/-1)>* **THE MYSTERY OF LIFE**
– The greatest cowboy of them all / I'm an easy rider / The mystery of life / Hey porter / Beans for breakfast / Goin' by the book / Wanted man / I'll go somewhere and sing my songs again / The hobo song / The angel and the badman.

Apr 91. (7") **THE MYSTERY OF LIFE. / I'M AN EASY RIDER**
(cd-s+=) – Veterans' day.

Spirit Of America Spirit Of America

Oct 93. (cd/c) **IT AIN'T ME BABE**

American American

Oct 94. (cd/c) *(74321 23685-2/-4) <45520>* **AMERICAN RECORDINGS** May94
– Delia's gone / Let the train blow the whistle / The beast in me / Drive on / Why me / Thirteen / Oh bury me nought / Bird on a wire / Tennessee stud / Down there by the train / Like a soldier / The man who couldn't cry.

— next with backers **TOM PETTY & THE HEARTBREAKERS**

Nov 96. (cd/c) *(74321 39742-2) <43097>* **UNCHAINED**
– Rowboat / Sea of heartbreak / Rusty cage / One rose / Country boy / Memories are made of this / Spiritual / Kneeling drunkard's plea / Southern accents / Mean eyed cat / Meet me in Heaven / I never picked cotton / Unchained / I've been elsewhere.

Jun 98. (cd/c; by JOHNNY CASH & WILLIE NELSON) *(491531-2/-4) <69416>* **VH1 STORYTELLERS** (live)
– Ghost riders in the sky / Worried man / Family bible / Don't take your guns to town / Funny how time slips away / Flesh and blood / Crazy / Unchained / Night life / Drive on / Me and Paul / I still miss someone / Always on my mind / Folsom prison blues / On the road again.

Oct 00. (cd) *(500986-2) <69691>* **AMERICAN III: SOLITARY MAN** 88
– I won't back down / Solitary man / That lucky old sun (just rolls around heaven all day) / One / Nobody / I see a darkness / The mercy seat / Would you lay with me (in a field of stones) / Field of diamonds / Before my time / Country trash / Mary of the wild moor / I'm leavin' now / Wayfaring stranger.

Lost Highway Universal

Nov 02. (cd)(d-lp) *<(063339-2)><(63336-1)>* **AMERICAN IV: THE MAN COMES AROUND** 22
– The man comes around / Hurt / Give my love to Rose / Bridge over troubled water (with FIONA APPLE) / I hung my head / The first time ever I saw your face / Personal Jesus / In my life / Sam Hall / Danny boy / Desperado (with DON HENLEY) / I'm so lonesome I could cry (with NICK CAVE) / The streets of Laredo / Tear stained letter / We'll meet again. *(UK re-pro.Feb04)* – hit UK No.40

Apr 03. (cd-s) *(77998-2)* **HURT / PERSONAL JESUS / WICHITA LINEMAN / HURT (video)** 42 –
(re-iss. Nov03; same) – hit No.39

— sadly, JOHNNY was to die on the 12th September 2003

– (selective) compilations, etc. –

Jan 59. (7",78) *London; (HLS 8789) / Sun; <309>* **IT'S JUST ABOUT TIME. / I JUST THOUGHT YOU'D LIKE TO KNOW** 47 Dec58 85

Aug 59. (7",78) *London; (HLS 8928) / Sun; <321>* **KATY TOO. / I FORGOT TO REMEMBER TO FORGET** Jul59 66

Mar 60. (7") *London; (HLS 9070) / Sun; <334>* **STRAIGHT A'S IN LOVE. / I LOVE YOU BECAUSE** 84

Sep 60. (7") *London; (HLS 9182) / Sun; <343>* **DOWN THE STREET TO 301. / THE STORY OF A BROKEN HEART** Jul60 85

Mar 61. (7") *London; (HLS 9314) / Sun; <355>* **OH LONESOME ME. / LIFE GOES ON** Dec60 93

Jun 68. (lp) *C.B.S.; (CBS 63316)* **OLD GOLDEN THROAT** 37 –
(re-iss. Sep82 on 'Bear Family'; BF 15072)

Jul 69. (lp) *C.B.S.; (CBS 63521)* **MORE OF OLD GOLDEN THROAT** –
(re-iss. Sep82 on 'Bear Family'; BFX 15073)

Nov 69. (7") *Sun; <1103>* **GET RHYTHM. / HEY PORTER** – 60

Feb 70. (7") *Sun; <1111>* **ROCK ISLAND LINE. / NEXT IN LINE** – 93

Dec 70. (lp) *Sun; (6467 001) <100>* **ORIGINAL GOLDEN HITS, VOLUME 1** Sep69 95

Dec 70. (lp) *Sun; (6467 007) <101>* **ORIGINAL GOLDEN HITS, VOLUME 2** Sep69 98

Nov 71. (lp) *Hallmark; (SHM 739)* **JOHNNY CASH** 43 –

Sep 72. (d-lp) *C.B.S.; (67201)* **STAR PORTRAIT** 16 –

Oct 76. (lp) *C.B.S.; (10000)* **THE BEST OF JOHNNY CASH** 48 –

Jun 78. (lp/c) *C.B.S.; (CBS/40 10009)* **ITCHY FEET – 20 FOOT TAPPIN' GREATS** 36 –
– Folsom prison blues / I walk the line / Ring of fire / Forty shades of green / I still miss someone / There ain't no good chain gang / Busted /

Twenty five minutes to go / Orange blossom special / It ain't me babe / A boy named Sue / San Quentin / Don't take your guns to town / The one on the right is on the left / Jackson / Hey porter / Daddy sang bass / I got stripes / A thing called love / One piece at a time. *(cd-iss. Oct94 on 'Columbia'; 477504-2) (re-iss. Apr95 on 'Columbia'; 468116-2/-4)*

ug 94. (cd/c) *Columbia; (MOOD CD/C 35)* **THE MAN IN BLACK – THE DEFINITIVE COLLECTION** 15 –
– Ring of fire / I walk the line / Get rhythm (live) / It ain't me babe / I still miss someone / (Ghost) Riders in the sky / The baron / Sunday morning coming down / Daddy sang bass / Jackson (with JUNE CARTER) / One piece at a time / Orange blossom special / Folsom prison blues (live) / San Quentin (live) / A boy named Sue (live) / A thing called love / Don't take your guns to town / Wanted man / Big river / Without love / No expectations / Highway patrolman / Singin' in Vietnam talkin' blues / Man in black.

l 99. (cd) *Columbia; (494896-2)* **THE FABULOUS / THE SONGS OF OUR SOUL**

ug 99. (d-cd) *Snapper; (SMDCD 213)* **THE ESSENTIAL SUN COLLECTION** –

eb 02. (d-cd) *Sony; (506345-2) <503023>* **MAN IN BLACK – THE VERY BEST OF JOHNNY CASH** 39 Sep01

pr 04. (cd) *Mercury; (9861333) / American; <00023620-2>* **MY MOTHER'S HYMN BOOK**

ep 05. (3xcd-box) *Metro; (METRCD 805)* **WALKING THE LINE (THE LEGENDARY SUN RECORDINGS)** 25

ct 05. (cd) *American; <5288>* **THE LEGEND OF JOHNNY CASH** – 5
– Cry! cry! cry! / Hey porter / Folsom Prison blues / I walk the line / Get rhythm / Big river / Guess things happen that way / Ring of fire / Jackson / A boy named Sue (live) / Sunday morning coming down / Man in black / One piece at a time / Highwayman / The wanderer / Delia's gone / Rusty cage / I've been everywhere / Give my love to Rose / The man comes around (early take) / Hurt.

ov 05. (cd) *Universal; (9885850)* **RING OF FIRE: THE LEGEND OF JOHNNY CASH** 11 –
– Ring of fire / I walk the line / Jackson / Folsom Prison blues / A boy named Sue / Big river / Get rhythm / Cry cry cry / Hey porter / A thing called love / Guess things happen that way / San Quentin / Man in black / Highwayman / The wanderer / I've been everywhere / Rusty cage / Personal Jesus / Give my love to Rose / One / Hurt.

the CATCH (see under ⇒ EURYTHMICS)

Nick CAVE

orn: NICHOLAS EDWARD CAVE, 22 Sep'57, Warracknabeal, ustralia. He was the main man behind punk/power-pop outfit, he BOYS NEXT DOOR, completing the band with neighbours ICK HARVEY, TRACY PEW and PHIL CALVERT. Formed in aulfield, Melbourne in late '77, they issued a one-off version of ancy Sinatra's 'THESE BOOTS WERE MADE FOR WALKING', efore they added a fifth member, ROWLAND S. HOWARD. After n album, 'DOOR, DOOR', was released on 'Mushroom' records 1979, they came to England as the BIRTHDAY PARTY, taking heir name from a Harold Pinter play. The band were subsequently napped up by IVO on the (then) new indie label '4 a.d.', after a ecent 'HEE-HAW' EP was given some night time airing by John eel. About as extreme as any music ever released by the label, the IRTHDAY PARTY were more a wake than a celebration, albeit ne with more than its fair share of black humour. Their first K album, 'PRAYERS ON FIRE' (1981), featured such enduringly harp material as 'ZOO MUSIC GIRL', 'CRY', 'CAPERS' and 'NICK HE STRIPPER', although for many obsessive fans and critics like, 'RELEASE THE BATS' remains the definitive track. Issued n summer '81, the single was a gothic slice of avant-garde that ook over the territory once belonging to the likes of PERE UBU nd the POP GROUP. Later that year, TRACY PEW was jailed or drunk driving, a revolving cast of BARRY ADAMSON, CHRIS WALSH and HARRY HOWARD deputising for him on tour. Live, the BIRTHDAY PARTY were even more unhinged than on vinyl, their demented stage show setting them apart from the masses of up and coming goth-rock acts around at the time. While TRACY was behind bars, NICK, ROWLAND and MICK teamed up as the TUFF MONKS with fellow Australians, the GO-BETWEENS on a one-off 45, 'AFTER THE FIREWORKS'. A further album, 'JUNKYARD' (which hit UK Top 75 in 1982), assured the BIRTHDAY PARTY's position as cult favourites among those who favoured black as a fashion statement. Later that year, ROWLAND hooked up with mistress of soft-porn new wave, LYDIA LUNCH, for a cover of Lee Hazlewood & Nancy Sinatra's 'SOME VELVET MORNING', while The BIRTHDAY PARTY were trimmed to a quartet for 'THE BAD SEED' EP. Released in early '83, the set included the incendiary 'SONNY'S BURNING', arguably the group's finest track. Having moved to Berlin to escape the pressures of critical adulation, the party was finally over after the appropriately titled 'MUTINY' EP. CAVE, who at the time also lived in London, played a few low-key gigs in '83 backed by the CAVEMEN who subsequently became the BAD SEEDS. Including a couple of his cronies from the BIRTHDAY PARTY days, MICK HARVEY and BLIXA BARGELD (also a member of cheery industrial types, EINSTURZENDE NEUBAUTEN), the initial line-up also boasted ex-MAGAZINE man, BARRY ADAMSON, who stayed with the band for the first four albums. Released on 'Mute' (whom CAVE was still contracted to), the debut long player, 'FROM HER TO ETERNITY' (1984), introduced CAVE's preoccupation with the ELVIS myth on a cover of 'IN THE GHETTO', an obsession indulged in greater depth on 'THE FIRSTBORN IS DEAD' (1985). The spit and thrash of the BIRTHDAY PARTY had now been replaced with a skeletal, funereal musical backing to accompany CAVE's ominous crooning. Part hellfire preacher, part damned sinner, CAVE's tales of murder most foul and general debauchery were almost always set in a context (real or implied) of Old Testament morality. Yep, this crazy cat's got that old-time religion, his songs steeped in the shadowy blues of the Mississippi Delta and the lure of his namesake, Old Nick himself. While 'KICKING AGAINST THE PRICKS' (1986), an album of covers, saw the likes of 'BLACK BETTY' and 'BY THE TIME I GET TO PHOENIX', falling under CAVE's dark spell like lambs to the slaughter, the singer came into his own on 'YOUR FUNERAL ... MY TRIAL' later that year. Rich in dark, dense imagery, the compelling narratives of crime and punishment were further developed on 'TENDER PREY' (1988). In the couple of years preceding the next BAD SEEDS release, CAVE published his first novel, 'AND THE ASS SAW THE ANGEL', and appeared in the film, 'GHOSTS ...OF THE CIVIL DEAD', as well as scoring the soundtrack (along with HARVEY and BARGELD). Largely acoustic, 'THE GOOD SON' (1990) saw CAVE and his BAD SEEDS return in moodily intense style, grandiose string arrangements complementing CAVE's sombre intonations. 'HENRY'S DREAM' (1992) was somewhat more menacing with the chilling 'JACK THE RIPPER', although 'STRAIGHT TO YOU' found CAVE applying his vocal intensity in lovelorn ballad mode with impressive results. Further musings on the nature of love pervaded 'LET LOVE IN' (1994), although the apocalyptic antipode was back on familiar blood-stained ground with 'MURDER BALLADS' a couple of years later. Against a minimal musical backdrop, CAVE recounted tales of a lyrical savagery that made his earlier work read like nursery rhymes. As well as a duet with POLLY HARVEY, the record saw an unlikely, but interesting pairing with KYLIE MINOGUE (!) on 'WHERE THE WILD ROSES GROW'. In comparison, 'THE BOATMAN'S CALL' (1997) was almost evangelical, an opus that seemed to find NICK as at peace with himself and the world as he's ever been. That's not to say this was a happy record, far from it, as CAVE reflected on the redemptive power of love, and the pain of love lost. Mooted by many critics as his best work to date, it was certainly his most accessible and possessed an atmosphere of meditative grace that set it apart from much of his previous output. In a music world of MTV mediocrity, CAVE's dark, defiantly individual stance is somehow comforting, though you wouldn't necessarily want to meet the man down a dark alley late at night. Later in 1997, CAVE was rumoured to be working on a blues covers album with TIM ROSE, while he was also set to star alongside Ewan Bremner in the film, 'Rhinoceros Hunting In Budapest'. A second volume of 'King Ink' hit the book shops in March '98 although more publicity was generated via the release of a long-overdue NICK CAVE & THE BAD SEEDS best of compilation. With 'NO MORE SHALL WE PART' (2003), CAVE confirmed his position as one of popular music's truly great, visionary singer/songwriters. Although it lacked the peaceful, redemptive power of 'THE BOATMAN'S CALL', the record's hollow-eyed laments achieved a dignified grace which most writers can only dream about. Nor was the man's almost biblical narrative intensity confined to first-person pleas and ruminations; with the likes of 'GOD IS IN THE HOUSE', CAVE painted perhaps one of the most vivid portraits of small town America yet committed to disc. Perhaps one of the most revelatory CAVE moments of recent years came with a South Bank Show retrospective; the sequence with the late NINA SIMONE – featuring an uncharacteristically star-struck looking NICK – was a poignant highlight. While some critics pointed to a fall in standards with 'NOCTURAMA' (2003), CAVE had merely decided to diversify his approach and stir things up a bit, both musically and on the production front. Thus the limpid balladry of 'STILL IN LOVE' and 'ROCK OF GIBRALTAR' had their seething, polar opposites in the anarchic (if hilarious) 'DEAD MAN IN MY BED' and the epic 'BABE, I'M ON FIRE', perhaps more accurately reflecting both CAVE's career trajectory and his artistic impulse. Never ever one to rest on his lapel-suave laurels, he was back in 2004 with 'ABATTOIR BLUES / THE LYRE OF ORPHEUS', a gospel-charged double set that felled his critics in mid-sentence (and charted higher – No.11 – than any studio set since the infamous 'MURDER BALLADS'). Were it not for that fact that it was conceived as two distinct volumes, it might've been tempting to view it as CAVE's 'Exile On Main St.', although that in turn might suggest a last stand before a long, drawn-out retreat. On the evidence of 'ABATTOIR..'s blitzkrieg roots-rock, retreat was the last thing on his mind. With the BAD SEEDS firing on all cylinders and the London Community Gospel Choir as a rearguard in rude voice, the record pointed the way to a more classicist sound – condensed in the thundering single, 'THERE SHE GOES, MY BEAUTIFUL WORLD – without any backwards pedalling, and with no concession to the modern world save for undimmed irony: "I woke up this morning with a frappucino in my hand", he laments dryly on the title track. 'THE LYRE OF ORPHEUS' was the "quiet" disc, opening with 'THE GOOD SON'-esque, myth-trampling waltz of its title track, employing some INCREDIBLE STRING BAND-esque, gossiping flutes on 'BREATHLESS' (perhaps the most accessible song CAVE has ever written) and closing with gospel-gothic epic, 'O CHILDREN'. From the sublime to the big screen, CAVE's next project was 'THE PROPOSITION' (2006), another John Hillcoat film for which he both co-wrote the script and composed the soundtrack, a largely instrumental series of flinty, apocalyptic blues scored in collaboration with DIRTY THREE/BAD SEED multi-instrumentalist WARREN ELLIS.

• **Covered:** RUNNING SCARED (Roy Orbison) / BLACK BETTY (Ram Jam) / BY THE TIME I GET TO PHOENIX (Jim Webb) / MUDDY WATER (Johnny Rivers) / HEY JOE (Jimi Hendrix) / ALL TOMORROW'S PARTIES (Velvet Underground) / THE CARNIVAL IS OVER (Seekers) / SOMETHING'S GOTTEN HOLD OF MY HEART (Gene Pitney) / HELPLESS (Neil Young) / WHAT A WONDERFUL WORLD (Ray Charles) / LET IT BE + HERE COMES THE SUN (Beatles) / etc. mainly from his cove album KICKING AGAINST THE PRICKS.

Album rating: Boys Next Door: DOOR DOOR (*6) / Birthday Party: PRAYEF ON FIRE (*8) / DRUNK ON THE POPE'S BLOOD (*6) / JUNKYARD (*6) HITS compilation (*8) / LIVE 1981-1982 collection (*7) / Nick Cave & The Ba Seeds: FROM HER TO ETERNITY (*7) / THE FIRSTBORN IS DEAD (*8) KICKING AGAINST THE PRICKS (*6) / YOUR FUNERAL . . . MY TRIAL (*6) TENDER PREY (*6) / GHOSTS . . .OF THE CIVIL DEAD soundtrack (*5; by Ni Cave, Mick Harvey, Blixa Bargeld) / THE GOOD SON (*8) / HENRY'S DREA (*8) / LIVE SEEDS (*6) / LET LOVE IN (*8) / MURDER BALLADS (*7) / TH BOATMAN'S CALL (*9) / TO HAVE AND TO HOLD soundtrack (*6; by Bli Bargeld – Nick Cave – Mick Harvey) / THE BEST OF NICK CAVE & THE BA SEEDS compilation (*9) / NO MORE SHALL WE PART (*7) / NOCTURAM (*6) / ABATTOIR BLUES – THE LYRE OF ORPHEUS (*8) / B-SIDES & RARITIE collection (*6) / THE PROPOSITION soundtrack w/ Warren Ellis (*6)

BOYS NEXT DOOR

NICK CAVE – vocals / **MICK HARVEY** (b.29 Sep'58, Rochester, Australia) guitar / **TRACY PEW** – bass / **PHIL CALVERT** – drums

Suicide not i

May 78. (7") *(103140)* **THESE BOOTS ARE MADE FOR WALKING. / BOY HERO** [–] Austra [–]

—— (Dec'78) added **ROWLAND S. HOWARD** (b.24 Oct'59, Melbourne) guitar (ex-YOUNG CHARLATANS)

Mushroom not i

May 79. (7") *(K 7492)* **SHIVERS. / DIVE POSITION** [–] Austra [–]

May 79. (lp) *(L 36931)* **DOOR, DOOR** [–] Austra [–]
– The nightwatchman / Brave exhibitions / Friends of my world / T voice / Roman Roman / Somebody's watching / After a fashion / Di position / I mistake myself / Shivers. *(Australian cd-iss. 1987; D 1922 (cd-iss. Mar93 on 'Grey Area-Mute';)*

Missing Link not i

Dec 79. (12"ep) *(MLEP-3)* **HEE-HAW** [–] Austra [–]
– Catholic skin / The red clock / Faint heart / The hair shirt / Death drowning. *(Australia re-iss. Dec83; credited as BIRTHDAY PARTY; IN 008)*

Feb 80. (7"gig freebie) *(MLS 16)* **HAPPY BIRTHDAY. / THE RIDDLE HOUSE** [–] Austra [–]

the BIRTHDAY PARTY

—— (same line-up & label)

Jul 80. (7") *(MLS 18)* **MR. CLARINET. / HAPPY BIRTHDAY** [–] Austra [–]

Nov 80. (lp) *(LINK 7)* **THE FIRST ALBUM** (originally credited to BOYS NEXT DOOR) [–] Austra [–]
– Mr. clarinet / Hats on wrong / The hair shirt / Guilt parade / Ridd house / The friend catcher / Waving my arms / The red clock / Cat man Happy birthday.
(below Australian releases only are with different label mentioned)

4.a.d. not i

Oct 80. (7"m) *(AD 12)* **THE FRIEND CATCHER. / WAVING MY ARMS / CATMAN** [ ] [–]

Apr 81. (lp) *(CAD 104)* **PRAYERS ON FIRE** [ ] [–]
– Zoo music girl / Cry / Capers / Nick the stripper / Ho-ho / Figure fun / King Ink / A dead song / Yard / Dull day / Just you and me. *(cd-is Apr88+=; CAD 104CD)* – Blundertown / Kathy's kisses.

Jun 81. Missing Link; (12"m) *(MSD 479)* **NICK THE STRIPPER. / BLUNDER TOWN / KATHY'S KISSES** [–] Austra [–]

Aug 81. (7") *(AD 111)* **RELEASE THE BATS. / BLAST OFF** [ ] [–]

Oct 81. (7") *(AD 114)* **MR. CLARINET. / HAPPY BIRTHDAY** [ ] [–]

Feb 82. (m-lp) *(JAD 202)* **DRUNK ON THE POPE'S BLOOD (live)** [ ] [–]
– (Sometimes) Pleasure heads must burn / King Ink / Zoo music girl Loose / LYDIA LUNCH:- The Agony Is The Ecstasy.

—— (Dec81) while **TRACY PEW** was in jail for drunk driving he was replace on tour only by either BARRY ADAMSON, CHRIS WALSH or **HARR HOWARD**

May 82. (lp) *(CAD 207)* **JUNKYARD** [73] [–]
– She's hit / Dead Joe / Dim locator / Hamlet (pow-pow-pow) / Sever sins / Big-Jesus-trash-can / Kiss me back / 6" gold blade / Kewpie doll Junkyard. *(cd-iss. Apr88+=; CAD 207CD)* – Dead Joe (version) / Releas the bats / Blast off.

—— In Sep'82, ROLAND S. HOWARD did duet with LYDIA LUNCH on 1 'Some Velvet Morning. / I Fell In Love With A Ghost'; *BAD 210)*

Nov 82. Missing Link; (7") *(MLS 32)* **NICK THE STRIPPER. / BLUNDERTOWN** [–] Austra [–]

— Now quartet when **CALVERT** joined **PSYCHEDELIC FURS**. (HARVEY now drums)

Feb 83. (12"ep) *(BAD 301)* **THE BAD SEED** [ ] [–]
– Sonny's burning / Wild world / Fears of gun / Deep in the woods.

— **JEFFREY WEGENER** – drums (ex-LAUGHING CLOWNS) repl. HARVEY Also **BLIXA BARGELD** – guitar (of EINSTURZENDE NEUBAUTEN) repl. absent HOWARD

Mute | not iss.

Nov 83. (12"ep) *(12MUTE 29)* **MUTINY!** [ ] [–]
– Jennifer's veil / Mutiny in Heaven / Swampland / Say a spell.

— Disbanded Autumn 1983. TRACY joined The SAINTS. (He was later to die late '86 of epileptic fit aged 28). ROWLAND HOWARD formed CRIME & THE CITY SOLUTION. NICK CAVE went solo, forming his BAD SEEDS taking with him MICK HARVEY.

– compilations, etc. – (all mostly UK)

on '4 a.d.' unless otherwise stated

Jun 83. (12"ep) *(BAD 307)* **THE BIRTHDAY PARTY EP** [ ] [–]
– Release the bats / Blast off / The friend catcher / Mr. Clarinet / Happy birthday.

Apr 85. (d-lp) *Missing Link; (ING 009)* **IT'S STILL LIVING (live)** [–] Austra [–]

Dec 85. (lp) *Missing Link; (LINK 22)* **A COLLECTION – BEST AND RAREST** [–] Austra [–]

Feb 87. (12"ep) *Strange Fruit; (SFPS 020)* **THE PEEL SESSION** (21.4.81) [ ] [–]
– Release the bats / Rowland around in that stuff / (Sometimes) Pleasure heads must burn / Loose. *(re-iss. Aug88 cd-ep; SFPSCD 020)*

Oct 88. (12"ep/cd-ep) *Strange Fruit; (SFPS/+CD 058)* **THE PEEL SESSIONS** (2.12.81) [ ] [–]
– Big-Jesus-trash-can / She's hit / Bully bones / 6" gold blade.

Aug 89. (cd) *(CAD 301CD)* **MUTINY / THE BAD SEED** [ ] [–]

Aug 89. (cd) *(CAD 307CD)* **HEE-HAW** [ ] [–]
– (contains tracks from THE BIRTHDAY PARTY lp)

Oct 92. (d-lp/cd)(c) *(DAD 2016/+CD)(DADC 2016)* **HITS** [ ] 1998 [ ]
– The friend catcher / Happy birthday / Mr. Clarinet / Nick the stripper / Zoo music girl / King Ink / Release the bats / Blast off / She's hit / 6" Gold blade / Hamlet (pow, pow, pow) / Dead Joe / Junkyard / Big-Jesus-Trash-Can / Wild world / Sonny's burning / Deep in the woods / Swampland / Jennifer's veil / Mutiny in Heaven.

Jul 99. (cd) *(CAD 9005CD)* **LIVE 1981-1982 (live)** [ ] [ ]

NICK CAVE & THE BAD SEEDS

— **NICK CAVE** – vocals / **MICK HARVEY** – guitar, keyboards / **BLIXA BARGELD** (b.12 Jan'59, Berlin, Germany) – guitar (of EINSTURZENDE NEUBAUTEN) / **BARRY ADAMSON** (b. 1 Jun'58, Manchester, England) – bass, guitar (ex-MAGAZINE, ex-PETE SHELLEY) / **HUGO RACE** – drums

Mute | Restless

Jun 84. (7") *(MUTE 32)* **IN THE GHETTO. / THE MOON IS IN THE GUTTER** [ ] [–]

— added **ANITA LANE** – synthesizers (ex-solo artist)

Jun 84. (lp) *(STUMM 17)* *<71435>* **FROM HER TO ETERNITY** [40] [ ]
– Avalanche / Cabin fever / Well of misery / From her to eternity / Wings of flies / Saint Huck / A box for black Paul. *(cd-iss. 1987+=; CDSTUMM 17)* – In the ghetto / The Moon is in the gutter / From her to eternity (1987).

— **THOMAS WYDLER** (b. 9 Oct'59, Zurich, Switzerland) – drums (ex-DIE HAUT) repl. HUGO + ANITA

Mute | Homestead

Jun 85. (lp/c) *(STUMM/CSTUMM 21)* *<HMS 026>* **THE FIRSTBORN IS DEAD** [53] [ ]
– Tupelo / Say goodbye to the little girl tree / Train long suffering / Black crow king / Knockin' on Joe / Wanted man / Blind Lemon Jefferson. *(cd-iss. Apr88; CDSTUMM 21)*

Jul 85. (7") *(7MUTE 38)* **TUPELO. / THE SIX STRINGS THAT DREW BLOOD** [ ] [–]

Jun 86. (7") *(7MUTE 47)* **THE SINGER. / RUNNING SCARED** [ ] [–]
(12"+=) *(12MUTE 47)* – Black Betty.

Aug 86. (cd/c/lp) *(CD/C+/STUMM 28)* *<HMS 065>* **KICKING AGAINST THE PRICKS** [89] [ ]
– Muddy water / I'm gonna kill that woman / Sleeping Annaleah / Long black veil / Hey Joe / The singer / Black Betty * / Running scared * / All tomorrow's parties / By the time I get to Phoenix / The hammer song / Something's gotten hold of my heart / Jesus met the woman at the well / The carnival is over. *(cd+= *)*

Nov 86. (cd/c/lp) *(CD/C+/STUMM 34)* *<HMS 073>* **YOUR FUNERAL . . . MY TRIAL** [ ] [ ]
– Sad waters / The Carny / Your funeral . . . my trial / Stranger than kindness / Jack's shadow / Hard on for love / She fell away / Long time man. *(cd+=)* – Scum.

— **CAVE** retained **HARVEY, BARGELD** and **WYDLER**, bringing in **ROLAND WOLF** – bass / **KID CONGO POWERS** (b. BRIAN TRISTAN, 27 Mar'61, La Puente, Calif.) – guitar (ex-CRAMPS, ex-GUN CLUB)

Mute | Mute-Elektra

May 88. (7") *(MUTE 52)* **THE MERCY SEAT. / NEW DAY** [ ] [–]
(12"+=) *(12MUTE 52)* – ('A'video mix).
(cd-s+=) *(CDMUTE 52)* – From her to eternity (film version) / Tupelo (version).

Sep 88. (cd/c/lp) *(CD/C+STUMM 52)* *<75401>* **TENDER PREY** [67] [ ]
– The mercy seat / Up jumped the Devil / Deanna / Watching Alice / Mercy / City of refuge / Slowly goes the night / Sunday's slave / Sugar, sugar, sugar / New morning. *(cd+=)* – The mercy seat (video mix). *(free-12"ep.w/above)* **AND THE ASS SAW THE ANGEL** (narration/book) – One Autumn / Animal static / Mah sanctum / Lamentation.

Sep 88. (12") *(12MUTE 86)* **DEANNA. / THE GIRL AT THE BOTTOM OF MY GLASS** [ ] [–]

Ionic-Mute | Restless

Mar 89. (cd/c/lp; NICK CAVE, MICK HARVEY, BLIXA BARGELD) *(CD/C+/IONIC 3)* *<71433>* **GHOSTS . . .OF THE CIVIL DEAD** (soundtrack) [ ] [ ]
– The news (voice: Michelle Babbit) / Introduction – A prison in the desert / David Hale – I've been a prison guard since I was 18 years old / Glover – I was 16 when they put me in prison / David Hale – You're danglin' us like a bunch of meat on a hook / Pop mix / Glover – We were united once / David Hale – The day of the murders / Lilly's theme ("a touch of warmth") / Maynard mix / David Hale – What I'm tellin' is the truth / Outro – The free world / Glover – One man released so they can imprison the rest of the world.

— (now a 5-piece, without WOLF)

Mute | Elektra

Mar 90. (12"/cd-s/ 7") *(12/CD+/MUTE 108)* **THE SHIP SONG. / THE TRAIN SONG** [ ] [–]

Apr 90. (cd/c/lp) *(CD/C+/STUMM 76)* *<60988>* **THE GOOD SON** [47] Oct90 [ ]
– Foi na cruz / The good son / Sorrow's child / The weeping song / The ship song / The hammer song / Lament / The witness song / Lucy. *(w/-7"/cd-s)* **THE MERCY SEAT / CITY OF REFUGE / DEANNA (all acoustic)**

Sep 90. (12"/7") *(12+/MUTE 118)* **THE WEEPING SONG. / COCKS 'N' ASSES** [ ] [–]
(cd-s+=) *(12/CD MUTE 118)* – Helpless / (some with hidden track).

— **CONWAY SAVAGE** (b.27 Jul'60, Foster, Australia) – keyboards + **MARTYN P. CASEY** – 10 Jul'60, Chesterfield, England) – bass (ex-TRIFFIDS) repl. KID CONGO

Mar 92. (7") *(MUTE 140)* **STRAIGHT TO YOU. / JACK THE RIPPER (acoustic)** [68] [–]
(12"+=/cd-s+=) *(12/CD MUTE 140)* – Blue bird.

Apr 92. (cd/c/lp) *(CD/C+/STUMM 92)* *<61323>* **HENRY'S DREAM** [29] May92 [ ]
– Papa won't leave you Henry / I had a dream, Joe / Straight to you / Brother, my cup is empty / Christina the astonishing / When I first came to town / John Finn's wife / Loom of the land / Jack the ripper.

Aug 92. (7") *(LMUTE 147)* **I HAD A DREAM, JOE. / THE GOOD SON (live)** [ ] [–]
(12"/cd-s) *(12/CD MUTE 147)* – ('A'side) / The Carny (live) / The mercy seat (live) / The ship song (live).

Nov 92. (c-s/7"; by NICK CAVE & SHANE MacGOWAN) *(C+/MUTE 151)* **WHAT A WONDERFUL WORLD. / A RAINY NIGHT IN SOHO** [72] [–]
(7") *(MUTE 151D)* – ('A'side / Lucy (by SHANE MacGOWAN).
(12"/cd-s) *(12/CD MUTE 151)* – (all 3 tracks).

Sep 93. (cd) *(CDMUTE 122)* *<61554>* **LIVE SEEDS (live)** [67] [ ]
– Mercy seat / Deanna / The ship song / Papa won't leave you Henry / Plain gold ring / John Finn's wife / Tupelo / Brother my cup is empty / The weeping song / Jack the ripper / The good son / From her to eternity. *(re-iss. Sep96; LCDSTUMM 122)*

Mar 94. (12/cd-s/7"silver) *(12/CD+/MUTE 160)* **DO YOU LOVE ME? / CASSIEL'S SONG / SAIL AWAY** [68] [–]

Apr 94. (cd/c/lp) *(CD/C+/STUMM 123)* *<61645>* **LET LOVE IN** [12] [ ]

– Do you love me? / Nobody's baby now / Loverman / Jangling Jack / Red right hand / I let love in / Thirsty dog / Ain't gonna rain anymore / Lay me low / Do you love me? (part 2).

—— **JAMES JOHNSON** – guitar (of GALLON DRUNK) repl. on tour only BLIXA

Jul 94. (7"pic-d) *(MUTE 169)* **LOVERMAN. / (I'LL LOVE YOU) TILL THE END OF THE WORLD** [ ] [–]
(12"/cd-s) *(12/CD MUTE 169)* – ('A'side) / B side.

Oct 94. (7"red) *(MUTE 172)* **RED RIGHT HAND. / THAT'S WHAT JAZZ IS TO ME** [ ] [–]
(cd-s+=) *(CDMUTE 172)* – Where the action is.

Oct 95. (c-s/7"; NICK CAVE & THE BAD SEEDS featuring KYLIE MINOGUE) *(C+/MUTE 185)* **WHERE THE WILD ROSES GROW. / THE BALLAD OF ROBERT MOORE & BETTY COLTRANE** [11] [–]
(cd-s+=) *(CDMUTE 185)* – The willow garden.

Feb 96. (cd/c/lp) *(CD/C+/STUMM 138)* <46195> **MURDER BALLADS** [8] [ ]
– Song of joy / Stagger Lee / Henry Lee / Lovely creature / Where the wild roses grow (featuring KYLIE MINOGUE) / The curse of Millhaven / The kindness of strangers / Crow Jane / O'Malley's bar / Death is not the end.

Feb 96. (7"; by NICK CAVE & PJ HARVEY) *(MUTE 189)* **HENRY LEE. / KING KONG KITCHEE KITCHEE KI-MI-O** [36] [–]
(c-s+=/cd-s+=) *(C/CD MUTE 189)* – Knoxville girl.

—— <most UK singles were given a US release in 1996>

—— JOHNSON was repl. by **JIM SCLAVUNOS** + **WARREN ELLIS**

Mute Elektra

Feb 97. (7") *(MUTE 192)* **INTO MY ARMS. / LITTLE EMPTY BOAT** [53] [–]
(cd-s+=) *(CDMUTE 192)* – Right now I'm a-roaming.

Mar 97. (cd/c) *(CD/C+/STUMM 142)* <46530> **THE BOATMAN'S CALL** [22] [ ]
– Into my arms / Lime tree harbour / People ain't no good / Brompton oratory / There is a kingdom / (Are you) The one that I've been waiting for? / Where do we go now but nowhere? / West country girl / Black hair / Idiot prayer / Far from me / Green eyes.

May 97. (7") *(MUTE 206)* **(ARE YOU) THE ONE THAT I'VE BEEN WAITING FOR? / COME INTO MY SLEEP** [67] [–]
(cd-s+=) *(CDMUTE 206)* – Black hair (band version) / Babe, I got you bad.

May 98. (cd/c/d-lp) *(CD/C+/MUTEL 004)* <46960> **THE BEST OF NICK CAVE & THE BAD SEEDS** (compilation) [11] [ ]
– Deanna / Red right hand / Straight to you / Tupelo / Nobody's baby now / Stranger than kindness / Into my arms / (Are you) The one that I've been waiting for? / The Carny / Do you love me? / The mercy seat / Henry Lee (feat. PJ HARVEY) / The weeping song / The ship song / Where the wild roses grow (feat. KYLIE MINOGUE) / For her to eternity. *(special d-cd; LCDMUTEL 004)* **LIVE AT THE ROYAL ALBERT HALL** – Stranger than kindness / The ship song / Let love in / Brompton oratory / Red right hand / Lime tree arbour / The weeping song / Henry Lee / Where the wild roses grow / Deanna / Straight to you / Tupelo / Nobody's baby now / Into my arms / (Are you) The one that I've been waiting for? / The Carny / Do you love me? / The mercy seat / From her to eternity.

Aug 98. (cd; as BLIXA BARGELD – NICK CAVE – MICK HARVEY) *(IONIC 15CD)* <69031> **TO HAVE AND TO HOLD** (soundtrack) [ ] Feb97 [ ]
– To have and to hold / The jungle of love / Candlelit bedroom / Luther / A house in the jungle / Delerium / The river at night / (other artist) / Romantic theme / Snow vision / Rose / The clouds / Noah's funeral / The fight / Kate leaves / We're coming – The riot / Murder / The red dress / (other artist) / To have and to hold – end titles / (other artist).

Mar 01. (10"/cd-s) *(10/CD MUTE 249)* **AS I SAT SADLY BY HER SIDE. / LITTLE JANEY'S GONE / GOOD GOOD DAY** [42] [–]

Apr 01. (cd/c/d-lp) *(CD/C+/STUMM 164)* <48039> **NO MORE SHALL WE PART** [15] [ ]
– As I sat sadly by her side / And no more shall we part / Hallelujah / Love letter / Fifteen feet of pure white snow / God is in the house / Oh my Lord / Sweetheart come / The sorrowful wife / We came along this road / Gates to the garden / Darker with the day. *(special cd+=; LCDSTUMM 164)* – Bless his ever loving heart / Grief came riding.

May 01. (10") *(10MUTE 262)* **FIFTEEN FEET OF PURE WHITE SNOW. / GOD IS IN THE HOUSE (westside session) / AND NO MORE SHALL WE PART (westside session)** [52] [–]
(cd-s) *(CDMUTE 262)* – (first 2 tracks) / We came along this road (westside session).

Mute Anti

Feb 03. (cd/lp) *(CD+/STUMM 207)* <86668> **NOCTURAMA** [20] [ ]
– Wonderful life / He wants you / Right out of your hand / Bring it on / Dead man in my bed / Still in love / There is a town / Rock of Gibraltar / She passed by my window / Babe, I'm on fire.

Feb 03. (10") *(10MUTE 265)* **BRING IT ON. / SHOOT ME DOWN / SWING LOW** [58] [–]
(cd-s+=) *(CDMUTE 265)* – ('A'-video).

Jun 03. (10"/cd-s) *(10/CD MUTE 290)* **HE WANTS YOU / BABE, I'M ON FIRE. / LITTLE GHOST SONG / EVERYTHING MUST CONVERGE** [ ] [–]

Sep 03. (7") *(MUTE 318)* **ROCK OF GIBRALTAR. / NOCTURAMA** [ ] [–]

—— now without BARGELD

Sep 04. (cd-s/7") *(CD+/MUTE 324)* **NATURE BOY. / SHE'S LEAVING YOU (feat. vocals by the London Community Gospel Choir)** [37] [–]

Sep 04. (d-cd/d-lp) *(CD+/STUMM 233)* <86729-2> **ABATTOIR BLUES / THE LYRE OF ORPHEUS** [11] Oct04 [ ]
– Abattoir Blues:- Get ready for love / Cannibal's hymn / Hiding all away / Messiah ward / There she goes, my beautiful world / Nature boy / Abattoir blues / Let the bells ring / Fable of the brown age // The Lyre Of Orpheus:- The lyre of Orpheus / Breathless / Babe, you turn me on / Easy money / Supernaturally / Spell / Carry me / O children.

Nov 04. (cd-s/7") *(CD+/MUTE 329)* **BREATHLESS. / THERE SHE GOES, MY BEAUTIFUL WORLD / UNDER THE MOON** [45] [–]

Mar 05. (7") *(MUTE 339)* **GET READY FOR LOVE. / HIDING ALL AWAY (live at Maida Vale)** [62] [–]
(cd-s+=) *(CDMUTE 339)* – There she goes, my beautiful world (live at Maida Vale).

Mute Mute

Mar 06. (cd; by NICK CAVE & WARREN ELLIS) *(CDSTUMM 255)* <9305> **THE PROPOSITION** (soundtrack) [ ] [ ]
– Happy land / The proposition pt.1 / Road to Banyon / Down to the valley / Moan thing / The rider pt.1 / Martha's dream / Gun thing / Queenie's suite / The rider pt.2 / The proposition pt.2 / Sad violin thing / The rider pt.3 / The proposition pt.3 / The rider song / Clean hands, dirty hands.

– compilations, ethers, etc. –

Mar 05. (t-cd) *Mute; (CDMUTEL 11)* <9246> **B-SIDES & RARITIES** [74] [ ]

☐ CEE-LO (see under ⇒ GNARLS BARKLEY)

Tracy CHAPMAN

Born: 20 Mar'64, Cleveland, Ohio, USA. A budding singer/songwriter from childhood, CHAPMAN's break came while attending Medford University (Tufts) where she met Brian Koppelman, son of industry bigwig, Charles. Through this valuable contact, CHAPMAN secured a manager in Elliot Roberts and a deal with 'Elektra', an eponymous debut album following in Spring '88. Critically acclaimed upon release, its sparse, grainy yet soulful and cathartic nu-folk sketched vivid portraits of everyday suffering shot through with the desire for individual freedom and the redemptive power of love. Although the record's initial release was fairly low-key, CHAPMAN landed a support slot with 10,000 MANIACS and the rave reviews continued, so far, so good; what really kicked off her career, however, was a show-stopping performance at the Nelson Mandela 70th birthday concert in London, an event beamed around the globe via satellite. Sales of her debut went into overdrive, the album eventually topping both the UK and US charts, while 'FAST CAR' raced up the singles chart. A cliche perhaps, but CHAPMAN had literally become an international superstar almost overnight, her success especially surprising bearing in mind she was a young black woman singing about issues many people would rather ignore. She subsequently undertook a high profile Amnesty International tour, a strong follow-up set, 'CROSSROADS' (1989) giving her another UK No.1. Some felt the album had been a bit hastily recorded, the record inevitably failing to scale the commercial heights of its predecessor; while CHAPMAN was an articulate, observant voice for the dispossessed, she was also a singer who shied away from the showbiz limelight. It would be another three years before 'MATTERS OF THE HEART' (1992), a competent effort which nevertheless brought criticisms of water treading. Although CHAPMAN's profile had diminished considerably by the mid-90's, a fourth set, 'NEW BEGINNING' made the US Top 5, while 'GIVE ME ONE REASON' became her highest charting single to date. The new millennium saw TRACY's first album for four years, 'TELLING STORIES' (2000), a US Top 40 set and a return to basics courtesy of co-producer David Kershenbaum. With the John Parish-produced 'LET IT RAIN' (2002), CHAPMAN continued in her own quietly effective way, playing to her own committed band of fans and ceding little if any ground to contemporary trends of whatever genre. 'WHERE YOU LIVE' (2005) teamed her up with Tchad Blake (PEARL JAM, PETER GABRIEL, TOM WAITS, etc.), the feted American producer noted for his distinctive, compressed sound. Working with CHAPMAN, he took a more naturalistic approach, allowing the singer's quiet art to do the talking, and direct her into both the US and UK Top 50.

• **Covered:** trad song HOUSE OF THE RISING SUN (Glenn Yarborough) / GET UP STAND UP (Bob Marley).

Album rating: TRACY CHAPMAN (*9) / CROSSROADS (*5) / MATTERS OF THE HEART (*4) / NEW BEGINNING (*5) / TELLING STORIES (*6) / COLLECTION compilation (*8) / LET IT RAIN (*5) / WHERE YOU LIVE (*6)

TRACY CHAPMAN – vocals, acoustic guitar / with **JACK HOLDER** – guitar, organ / **LARRY KLEIN** – bass / **DENNY FONGHEISER** – drums

Apr 88. (lp/c)(cd) *(EKT 44/+C)<(K 960774-2)>* **TRACY CHAPMAN** [1] [1]
– Talkin' 'bout a revolution / Fast car / Across the lines / Behind the wall / Baby can I hold you / Mountains o' things / She's got her ticket / Why? / For my lover / If not now . . . / For you.

May 88. (7") *(EKR 73) <69412>* **FAST CAR. / FOR YOU** [5] [6]
(12"+=) *(EKR 73T)* – Behind the wall.

Aug 88. (7"/12") *(EKR 78/+T)* **TALKIN' BOUT A REVOLUTION. / IF NOT NOW . . .** [ ] [-]
(cd-s+=) *(EKR 78CD)* – She's got her ticket.

Sep 88. (7") *<69383>* **TALKIN' BOUT A REVOLUTION. / BEHIND THE WALL** [-] [75]

Oct 88. (7") *<69356>* **BABY CAN I HOLD YOU. / IF NOT NOW . . .** [-] [48]

Nov 88. (7") *(EKR 82)* **BABY CAN I HOLD YOU. / ACROSS THE LINES** [ ] [-]
(12"+=/cd-s+=) *(EKR 82 T/CD)* – Mountain o' things.

Sep 89. (7"/c-s) *(EKR 95/+C) <69273>* **CROSSROADS. / BORN TO FIGHT** [61] [90]
(12"+=) *(EKR 95T)* – Fast car.
(cd-s+=) *(EKR 95CD)* – Mountain o' things (live).

Oct 89. (lp/c)(cd) *(EKT 61/+C)<(K 960888-2)>* **CROSSROADS** [1] [9]
– Crossroads / Bridges / Freedom now / Material world / Be careful of my heart / Subcity / Born to fight / A hundred years / This time / All that you have is your soul.

Feb 90. (7") *(EKR 107)* **ALL THAT YOU HAVE IS YOUR SOUL. / SUBCITY** [ ] [-]
(12"+=) *(EKR 107T)* – Freedom now.

Feb 90. (7") **ALL THAT YOU HAVE IS YOUR SOUL. / MATERIAL WORLD** [-] [ ]

Apr 92. (7"/c-s) **BANG BANG BANG. / WOMAN'S WORK** [ ] [ ]
(12"+=/cd-s+=) – House of the rising Sun.

May 92. (cd)(lp/c) *<(7559 61215-2)>(EKT 98/+C)* **MATTERS OF THE HEART** [19] [ ]
– Bang bang bang / So / I used to be a sailor / The love that you had / Woman's work / These are the things / Short supply / Dreaming on a world / Open arms / Matters of the heart. *(re-iss. cd+c Nov93)*

Jul 92. (7"/c-s) **DREAMING ON A WORLD. / WOMAN'S WORK** [ ] [ ]
(cd-s+=) – ('A'extended) / House of the rising Sun.

Nov 95. (cd/c) *<(7559 61850-2/-4)>* **NEW BEGINNING** [ ] [4]
– Heaven's here on Earth / New beginning / Smoke and ashes / Cold feet / At this point in my life / the promise / The rape of the world / Tell it like it is / Give me one reason / Remember the tin man / I'm ready.

Mar 96. (c-s) *<64346>* **GIVE ME ONE REASON. / THE RAPE OF THE WORLD** [-] [3]

May 96. (cd-s) *(EKR 222CD)* **GIVE ME ONE REASON / THE RAPE OF THE WORLD / HOUSE OF THE RISING SUN** [ ] [-]

Mar 97. (c-s) *(E 3969C)* **GIVE ME ONE REASON / FAST CAR** [ ] [ ]
(cd-s+=) *(E 3969CD)* – Talking 'bout a revolution.

Feb 00. (cd/c) *<(7559 62478-2/-4)>* **TELLING STORIES** [ ] [33]
– Telling stories / Less than strangers / Speak the word / IT's ok / Wedding song / Unsung psalm / Nothing yet / Paper and ink / Devotion / The only one / First try. *(d-cd-iss. May00 +=; 7559 62541-2)* – live:- Fast car / Talkin' 'bout a revolution / Three little birds / House of the rising sun / Mountains o' things / Behind the wall / Baby can I hold you.

Sep 01. (cd/c) *(7559 62700-2/-4)* **COLLECTION** (compilation) [3] [-]
– Fast car / Subcity / Baby can I hold you / The promise / I'm ready / Crossroads / Bang bang bang / Telling stories / Smoke and ashes / Speak the word / Wedding song / Open arms / Give me one reason / Talkin' 'bout a revolution / She's got her ticket / All that you have is your soul.

Oct 02. (cd-s) *(E 7335CD)* **YOU'RE THE ONE / I AM YOURS** [ ] [-]

Oct 02. (cd) *<(7559 62836-2)>* **LET IT RAIN** [36] [25]
– Let it rain / Another sun / You're the one / In the dark / Almost / Hard wired / Say hallelujah / Broken / Happy / Goodbye / I am yours / Over in love (instrumental). *<(d-cd-iss. Mar03 +=; 7559 62861-2)>* – live:- You're the one / Give me one reason / Talkin' 'bout a revolution / I am yours / Get up stand up.

Sep 05. (cd) *<(7567 83803-2)>* **WHERE YOU LIVE** [43] [49]
– Change / Talk to you / 3000 miles / Going back / Don't dwell / Never yours / America / Love's proof / Before Easter / Taken / Be and be not afraid.

the CHARLATANS (UK)

Formed: Northwich, Cheshire, England . . . late 1989 by MARTIN BLUNT, ROB COLLINS, JON BROOKES and JON BAKER. They soon found a frontman in singer TIM BURGESS and after a few attempts at getting a record deal, they set up their own 'Dead Dead Good' label. Early in 1990, they scored a massive indie hit with the 'INDIAN ROPE' single. Following the explosion of the "Madchester" scene, the label was taken over by the Beggars Banquet subsidiary, 'Situation 2', for whom they recorded their first Top 10 hit, 'THE ONLY ONE I KNOW'. Another hammond-driven classic, 'THEN', preceded a late summer chart topping debut album, 'SOME FRIENDLY'. A relatively quiet year followed, during which MARTIN BLUNT nearly retired due to severe depression. However, it was actually BAKER who departed after playing at London's Royal Albert Hall. Come 1992, MARK COLLINS (ex-WALTONES) was drafted in and things looked brighter when the single, 'WEIRDO', gave them another Top 20 hit. Their second album, however, ('BETWEEN 10TH AND 11TH'), was given the thumbs down by the music press, hence its failure to secure a respectable chart placing. This was not the only setback that year, as ROB COLLINS was charged with aiding and abetting an armed robbery. A year later, although maintaining his innocence, he was sentenced to several months in jail, later being released in early 1994 on good behaviour. 'CAN'T GET OUT OF BED', saw them return in fine style, and was lifted from the Top 10 album 'UP TO OUR HIPS'. TIM then moonlighted on singles by SAINT ETIENNE and the CHEMICAL BROTHERS, before the group were back to their best on the eponymous 1995 album. From its retro cover art, to the 'Sympathy For The Devil'-style single, 'JUST WHEN YOU'RE THINKIN' THINGS OVER', the album was an obvious homage to The ROLLING STONES. Tragically, on 23rd of July '96, ROB COLLINS was killed when his car spun off a road in Wales. The coroners report concluded that he was the driver and also that he had twice the legal amount of alcohol in his blood. They had just recorded their fifth album, 'TELLIN' STORIES', preceded by their biggest hit singles to date, 'ONE TO ANOTHER' and 'NORTH COUNTRY BOY'. With The CHARLATANS momentum seemingly unstoppable while every other 'baggy' band fell by the wayside, BURGESS and Co celebrated their longevity with a career retrospective, 'MELTING POT' (1998). With newboy TONY ROGERS finally getting his chance to perform in the place of COLLINS and with the group signing a major deal via 'M.C.A.', The CHARLATANS were ready to take their place back in indie-rock – albeit minus a few hundred thousand admittedly stolen by their accountant, Trevor Williams. Their sixth album, 'US AND US ONLY' (1999), was a test of sorts, its subsequent No.2 peak position in the UK charts an indication that they were still wanted by their ageing fanbase; the STONE ROSES, the VERVE and OASIS, where were they now? Seven albums and still going strong, the CHARLATANS set out their stall for the 21st century with Top 3 set, 'WONDERLAND' (2001). This time around BURGESS was wielding a bit of soulpower, reaching for the skies with a hitherto unheard falsetto on hit singles such as 'LOVE IS THE KEY' and 'A MAN NEEDS TO BE TOLD'. The grooves were also slicker and sexier, hints of CURTIS MAYFIELD's funkier moments revealing themselves on the latter especially. Frontman TIM BURGESS branched out on his own in 2003 to record the brilliantly diverse solo album 'I BELIEVE IN THE SPIRIT'. Sounding nothing like his usual band, the album, laced with sugary pop melodies, strange waltzes and finely executed keyboards, you would be forgiven for thinking that you were listening to early TIM BUCKLEY fused with DONOVAN. It is just a shame, however, that the CHARLATANS never reached such a high standard of music, which makes you wonder: is it worth BURGESS going back when he's got such a good thing going? On the evidence of 'UP AT THE LAKE' (2004), the answer was well, yes. Realising where their strengths lay, the band left the edge cutting to post-punk preoccupied teenagers, returning to the hammond-grooving, BEATLES 'n' STONES sound which made them perennial festival favourites back in the late 90s. 'SIMPATICO' (2006) – their first for 'Sanctuary' – was likened again to the 'STONES, it's groovy, danceable rhythms also harking back to the days of Madchester, while it proved to be their best seller for ages.

• **Songwriters:** Group compositions except; I FEEL MUCH BETTER ROLLING OVER (Small Faces).

Album rating: SOME FRIENDLY (*8) / BETWEEN 10TH & 11TH (*5) / UP TO OUR HIPS (*7) / THE CHARLATANS (*8) / TELLIN' STORIES (*8) / MELTING POT compilation (*8) / US AND US ONLY (*7) / WONDERLAND (*5) / LIVE IT LIKE YOU LOVE IT – THE BEST OF THE CHARLATANS LIVE collection (*6) / UP AT THE LAKE (*6) / SIMPATICO (*6) / Tim Burgess: I BELIEVE (*6)

TIM BURGESS (b.30 May'68) – vocals (ex-ELECTRIC CRAYONS) repl. BAZ KETTLEY / **ROB COLLINS** (b.23 Feb'63) – organ / **JON BAKER** (b.1969) – guitar / **JON BROOKS** (b.1969) – drums / **MARTIN BLUNT** (b.1965) – bass (ex-MAKIN' TIME, ex-TOO MUCH TEXAS w / TIM)

Dead Dead Good — not iss.

Feb 90. (7") *(GOOD ONE SEVEN)* **INDIAN ROPE. / WHO WANTS TO KNOW** — 89 | –
(12"+=) *(GOOD ONE TWELVE)* – You can talk to me. *(re-iss. Jul91 12"/cd-s; GOOD 1 T/CD, hit No.57) (re-iss. cd-s Oct96)*

Situation 2 — Beggars Banquet

May 90. (7") *(SIT 70)* **THE ONLY ONE I KNOW. / EVERYTHING CHANGED** — 9 |
(12"+=) *(SIT 70T)* – Imperial 109.
(cd-s++=) *(SIT 70CD)* – You can talk to me.

Sep 90. (7"/c-s) *(SIT 74/+C)* **THEN. / TAURUS MOANER** — 12 |
(12"+=/cd-s+=) *(SIT 74 T/CD)* – ('A'-alternate take) / ('B'instrumental).

Oct 90. (lp/c/cd/s-lp) *(SITU 30/+MC/CD/R)* <2411> **SOME FRIENDLY** — 1 | 73
– You're not very well / White shirt / Opportunity / Then / 109 pt.2 / Polar bear / Believe you me / Flower / Sonic / Sproston Green. *(cd+=)* – The only one I know. *(cd re-iss. Sep95 on 'Beggars Banquet'; BBL 30CD)*

Feb 91. (7"/c-s) *(SIT 76/+CS)* **OVER RISING. / WAY UP THERE** — 15 |
(12"/c-s+=/cd-s+=) *(SIT 76 T/TC/CD)* – Happen to die / Opportunity Three (re-work).

— **MARK COLLINS** – guitar (ex-WALTONES, ex-CANDLESTICK PARK) repl. BAKER

Oct 91. (7"/c-s) *(SIT 84/+C)* **ME IN TIME. / OCCUPATION H. MONSTER** — 28 |
(12"+=/cd-s+=) *(SIT 84 T/CD)* – Subtitle.

Feb 92. (7"/c-s) *(SIT 88/+C)* **WEIRDO. / THEME FROM 'THE WISH'** — 19 | –
(12"+=/cd-s+=) *(SIT 88 T/CD)* – Sproston Green (U.S. remix) / ('A'-alternate take).

Mar 92. (lp/c/cd) *(SITU 37/+MC/CD)* <61108> **BETWEEN 10th AND 11th** — 21 |
– I don't want to see the lights / Ignition / Page one / Tremelo song / The end of everything etc / Subtitle / Can't even be bothered / Weirdo / Chewing gum weekend / (No one) Not even the rain. *(re-iss. cd Sep95 on 'Beggars Banquet'; BBL 37CD)*

Jun 92. (c-s) *(SIT 97C)* **TREMELO SONG (alternate take) / THEN (live) / CHEWING GUM WEEKEND (live) / TREMELO SONG** — 44 |
(12") *(SIT 97T)* – Happen to die (unedited) repl. last version.
(cd-s) *(SIT 97CD1)* – ('A'side) / Happen to die (unedited) / Normality swing (demo).
(cd-s) *(SIT 97CD2)* – ('A'live April '92) / Then (live) / Chewing gum weekend (live).

— ROB COLLINS was imprisoned in Sep'93 for taking part in a robbery. (see above) He had already recorded below while awaiting trial, and was free just in time to feature on Top Of The Pops.

Beggars Banquet — Beggars Banquet

Jan 94. (7"/c-s) *(BBQ 27/+C)* **CAN'T GET OUT OF BED. / WITHDRAWN** — 24 | –
(12"+=/cd-s+=) *(BBQ 27 T/CD)* – Out.

Mar 94. (cd-ep) *(BBQ 31CD)* **I NEVER WANT AN EASY LIFE IF ME AND HE WERE EVER TO GET THERE / ONLY A BOHO / SUBTERRAINEAN / CAN'T GET OUT OF BED (demo)** — 38 | –

Mar 94. (cd/c/lp) *(BBQ CD/MC/LP 147)* <92352> **UP TO OUR HIPS** — 8 |
– Come in number 21 / I never want an easy life / If me and he were ever to get there / Can't get out of bed / Feel flows / Autograph / Jesus hairdo / Up to our hips / Patrol / Another rider up in flames / Inside – looking out. *(re-iss. cd Sep95; BBL 147CD)*

Jun 94. (c-s) *(BBQ 32C)* **JESUS HAIRDO / PATROL (Dust Brothers mix)** — 48 | –
(12"+=) *(BBQ 32T)* – Feel flows (the carpet kiss mix).
(cd-s+=) *(BBQ 32CD1)* – Stir it up / Feel flows (Van Basten mix).
(cd-s) *(BBQ 32CD2)* – ('A'side) / I never want an easy life / Another rider up in flames / Up to our hips (BBC Radio 1 live sessions).

Dec 94. (7"/c-s) *(BBQ 44/+C)* **CRASHIN' IN. / BACK ROOM WINDOW** — 31 | –
(12"+=/cd-s+=) *(BBQ 44 T/CD)* – Green flashing eyes.

May 95. (7"/c-s) *(BBQ 55/+C)* **JUST LOOKIN'. / BULLET COMES** — 32 | –
(cd-s+=) *(BBQ 55CD)* – Floor nine.

Aug 95. (c-s) *(BBQ 60C)* **JUST WHEN YOU'RE THINKIN' THINGS OVER / FRINCK / YOUR SKIES ARE MINE** — 12 | –
(cd-s+=) *(BBQ 60CD)* – Chemical risk (toothache remix).
(12") *(BBQ 60T)* – (first 2 tracks) / Chemical risk dub (toothache remix) / Nine acre dust (Dust Brothers mix).

Aug 95. (cd/c/d-lp) *(BBQ CD/MC/LP 174)* <92602> **THE CHARLATANS** — 1 |
– Nine acre court / Feeling holy / Just lookin' / Crashin' in / Bullet comes / Here comes a soul saver / Just when you're thinkin' things over / Tell everyone / Toothache / No fiction / See it through / Thank you. *(d-lp+=)* – Chemical risk (toothache remix).

— On 23rd July '96, ROB COLLINS was killed in a car crash (see above).

Aug 96. (7"/c-s/cd-s) *(BBQ 301/+C/CD)* **ONE TO ANOTHER. / TWO OF US / REPUTATION** — 3 | –

— **MARTIN DUFFY** – keyboards (of PRIMAL SCREAM) augmented

Beggars Banquet — M.C.A.

Mar 97. (7"/c-s/cd-s) *(BBQ 309/+C/CD)* **NORTH COUNTRY BOY. / AREA 51 / DON'T NEED A GUN** — 4 | –

Apr 97. (cd/c/lp) *(BBQ CD/MC/LP 190)* <11622> **TELLIN' STORIES** [1] [ ]
– With no shoes / North country boy / Tellin' stories / One to another / You're a big girl now / How can you leave us / Area 51 / How high / Only teethin' / Get on it / Rob's theme / Two of us / Reputation.

Jun 97. (7"/c-s) *(BBQ 312/+C)* **HOW HIGH. / DOWN WITH THE MOOK** [6] [–]
(cd-s+=) *(BBQ 312CD)* – Title fight.

Oct 97. (7") *(BBQ 318)* **TELLIN' STORIES. / KEEP IT TO YOURSELF** [16] [–]
(c-s+=) *(BBQ 318C)* – Thank you (live).
(cd-s++=) *(BBQ 318CD)* – Clean up kid.

Beggars Banquet / Beggars Banquet

Feb 98. (cd/c/lp) *(BBQ CD/MC/LP 198)* <80198> **MELTING POT** (compilation) [4] [ ]
– The only one I know / Then / Opportunity three / Over rising / Sproston Green (U.S. version) / Weirdo / Theme from the wish / Patrol (The Chemical Brothers mix) / Can't get out of bed / I never want an easy life if me & he were ever to get there / Jesus hairdo / Crashin' in / Just lookin' / Here comes a soul saver / Just when you're thinkin' things over / One to another / North country boy. *(cd re-iss. May02; same)*

— (1997) **TONY RODGERS** was now the replacement for ROB

M.C.A. / Universal

Oct 99. (7") *(MCS 40220)* **FOREVER. / WHEN YOUR SHIP COMES IN** [12] [–]
(c-s/cd-s+=) *(MCS C/TD 40220)* – Great place to leave.
(cd-s) *(MCSXD 40220)* – ('A'side) / Sleepy little sunshine boy / ('A'-CD enhanced).

Oct 99. (cd/c/lp) *(MCD/MCC/MCA 60069)* <112058> **US AND US ONLY** [2] [ ]
– Forever / Good witch, bad witch / Impossible / The blonde waltz / A house is not a home / Senses / My beautiful friend / I don't care where you live / The blind stagger / Good witch, bad witch / Watching you.

Dec 99. (7") *(MCS 40225)* **MY BEAUTIFUL FRIEND. / SCORCHED** [31] [–]
(c-s/cd-s+=) *(MCS C/TD 40225)* – Your precious love.
(cd-s) *(MCSXD 40225)* – ('A'mixes + CD-enhanced).

May 00. (7"/cd-s) *(MCS/+XD 40231)* **IMPOSSIBLE. / YOU GOT IT I WANT IT** [15] [–]
(c-s/cd-s) *(MCS C/TD 40231)* – ('A'side) / Don't go giving it up / ('A'-video).

Aug 01. (7") *(7") (MCS 40262)* **LOVE IS THE KEY. / VIVA LA SOCIALE** [16] [–]
(cd-s+=) *(MCSTD 40262)* – It's about time.

Sep 01. (cd/d-lp) *(MCD/MCA 60076)* <014910> **WONDERLAND** [2] [ ]
– You're so pretty – we're so pretty / Judas / Love is the key / A man needs to be told / I just can't get over losing you / The bell and the butterfly / And if I fall / Wake up / Is it in you? / Ballad of the band. *(d-lp+=)* – Right on / Love to you.

Nov 01. (7") *(MCS 40271)* **A MAN NEEDS TO BE TOLD. / SHOTGUN** [31] [–]
(cd-s+=) *(MCSTD 40271)* – Ballad of the band (Ianocce remix).
(cd-s) *(MCSXD 40271)* – ('A') / All I desire / Love is the key (live) / ('A'-video).

Apr 02. (12") *(MCST 40283)* **YOU'RE SO PRETTY – WE'RE SO PRETTY. / ('A'-Lo Fidelity Allstars) / SILLY THING** [ ] [–]
(cd-s) *(MCSTD 40283)* – ('A') / ('A'-Lo Fidelity Allstars) / Room 118.

Jul 02. (cd) *(MCD 60080)* <64169-2> **LIVE IT LIKE YOU LOVE IT – THE BEST OF THE CHARLATANS LIVE** (live) [40] Oct02 [ ]
– Love is the key / Judas / Tellin' stories / The man needs to be told / One to another / The only one I know / Impossible / North country boy / You're so pretty – we're so pretty / Weirdo (with JOHNNY MARR) / How high / Forever / And if I fall / Sproston Green.

May 04. (7") *(MCS 40363)* **UP AT THE LAKE. / I'LL SING A HYMN (YOU CAME TO ME)** [23] [–]
(cd-s) *(MCSTD 40463)* – ('A') / For where there is love, there will always be miracles.

May 04. (cd/3x7"-lp) *(MCD/MCS 60093)* <9866484> **UP AT THE LAKE** [13] Jun04 [ ]
– Up at the lake / Feel the pressure / As I watch you in disbelief / Cry yourself to sleep / Bona fide treasure / High up your tree / Blue for you / I'll sing you a hymn *[3x7"-lp]* / Loving you is easy / Try again today / Apples and oranges / Dead love.

Jul 04. (7"clear) *(MCS 40370)* **TRY AGAIN TODAY. / M.I.A.** [24] [–]
(cd-s+=) *(MCS 40370)* – Give me a reason / ('A'-video).
(dvd-s) *(MCSVD 40370)* – ('A'-video) / (live from Keele University – the warm-up gig) / Try again today.

Sanctuary / Sanctuary

Apr 06. (cd/lp) *(SAN CD/LP 358)* <4778> **SIMPATICO** [10] May06 [ ]
– Blackened blue eyes / NYC (there's no need to stop) / For your entertainment / Dead mans eye / Muddy ground / City of the dead / Road to paradise / The architect / Glory glory / Sunset & vine.

May 06. (7") *(SANSE 421)* **BLACKENED BLUE EYES. / DON'T YOU WORRY** [28] [–]
(cd-s+=) *(SANXD 421)* – Cry cry cry / ('A'-video).
(cd-s) *(SANXS 421)* – ('A') / Arise arise.

– compilations, etc. –

May 02. (cd) *Beggars Banquet; (BEGL 2032CD)* **SONGS FROM THE OTHER SIDE** (B-sides) [55] [–]

TIM BURGESS

with various band members

P.I.A.S. / not iss.

Sep 03. (7") *(PIASB 109-7)* **I BELIEVE IN THE SPIRIT. / WHO THE CAP FIT** [44] [–]
(cd-s+=) *(PIASB 109CD)* – I believe in the West Coast.

Sep 03. (cd/lp) *(PIASB 099 CD/LP)* **I BELIEVE** [38] [–]
– I believe in the spirit / Held in straps / Only a boy / We all need love / Oh my corazon / Be my baby / Years ago / Say yes / Spend the night / Po' boy soul / All I ever do.

Nov 03. (7") *(PIASB 119-7)* **ONLY A BOY. / ROUGH TIME** [54] [–]
(cd-s+=) *(PIASB 119CD)* – Wait til the sun shines Irie.

Ray CHARLES

Born: RAY CHARLES ROBINSON, 23 Sep'30, Albany, Georgia, USA. While encouraged to take up the piano at an early age after his family moved to Greenville, Florida, the young ROBINSON was afflicted by glaucoma (after witnessing the death of his brother) at the age of seven and subsequently went blind. Using Braille, he studied composition at the St. Augustine School for the Deaf and the Blind as well as learning instruments such as organ and saxophone. The troubles continued to pile up, however, as both his mother and father died before he reached the age of sixteen. Leaving school, he survived by playing in various dance bands around Florida before saving enough money to move to Seattle. As R.C. ROBINSON he began playing with The McSON TRIO (alongside guitarist GOSSADY McGHEE and bassist MILTON GARRAD) before signing to Jack Lauderdale's 'Downbeat' label in 1949. To avoid confusion with boxer Sugar Ray Robinson, he began recording as RAY CHARLES (accompanied by The MAXIM TRIO) and released his debut single, 'CONFESSION BLUES', the same year; a further two singles followed before the label was taken over by 'Swingtime'. Subsequently working with JOHNNY MOORE'S THREE BLAZERS, CHARLES continued cutting sides in the 'sepia Sinatra' style of singers such as NAT 'KING' COLE and CHARLES BROWN. 1951's 'BABY LET ME HOLD YOUR HAND' and 'KISS-A-ME BABY' marked his first couple of R&B Top 10 hits, during which time he embarked on a national tour with blues man LOWELL FULSON. Starting out as a sideman, CHARLES soon advanced to musical director and the experience put him in good stead for a subsequent stint in New Orleans with GUITAR SLIM. He both arranged and played piano on SLIM's million-selling 1954 hit for 'Specialty', 'The Things That I Used To Do', CHARLES duly incorporating a more organic, gospel-influenced style into his own recordings. Adding alto sax and a quartet of horn players, the singer signed to 'Atlantic' and perfected his thrilling marriage of earthy, hollering gospel and raw R&B with 1955's 'I'VE GOT A

WOMAN'. The track narrowly missed top spot on the R&B chart and initiated a string of such hits wherein CHARLES alchemised various black music styles in what amounted to a blueprint for 60's soul. His first brush with the pop chart came in summer '59 with the classic 'WHAT'D I SAY', a raucous combination of gospel, jump-blues and rock'n'roll that made him a national star overnight. A cover of Hank Snow's 'I'M MOVIN' ON' followed into the Top 40 while 'THE GENIUS OF RAY CHARLES' (1960) album made the Top 20, its combination of sentimental balladry and big-band ebullience setting the tone for many of his future recordings. 1960 was also the year he moved to 'ABC Paramount', thrashing out a deal whereby he was given far more creative control as well as full ownership of the mastertapes (virtually unheard of in those days). Things got off to a great start with a stunning US No.1 cover of pop standard, 'GEORGIA ON MY MIND', while female backing singers, The RAELETTES, spiced up CHARLES' rasp on 'HIT THE ROAD JACK' (another No.1) and a rollicking 'UNCHAIN MY HEART'. 1962 saw him recording a set of duets with BETTY CARTER as well as making a shock move into country with the No.1 album, 'MODERN SOUNDS IN COUNTRY AND WESTERN MUSIC'. Having already cut a number of straight jazz albums at 'Atlantic', CHARLES proved there were few boundaries to his eclectic talent with unique interpretations of country standards like Don Gibson's 'I CAN'T STOP LOVING YOU' (a transatlantic No.1) and Hank Williams' 'HEY GOOD LOOKIN'. 1963's brassy Top 5 remake of Harlan Howard's 'BUSTED' proved uncannily prophetic as CHARLES was arrested for possession of heroin two years later; though he took a year out to fight his addiction, he was back in court on a second drugs rap in 1967, the judge refraining from handing out a prison sentence but fining him heavily and putting him on four years probation. By the time he'd formed his own label, 'Tangerine' (through which he released material by other artists as well as his own), in the mid-late 60's his sound was increasingly catering to the MOR market though he could still come up with funky little gems like the 1969 collaboration with JIMMY LEWIS, 'IF IT WASN'T FOR BAD LUCK' and 1971's instrumental 'BOOTY BUTT'. He also cut a couple of notable albums during the 70's, the black consciousness-centred (CHARLES was a vocal supporter of the civil rights movement and its leader, Martin Luther King) 'A MESSAGE FROM THE PEOPLE' (1972) and 1975's 'RENAISSANCE'. 1976, meanwhile, found him recording a pop interpretation of 'PORGY AND BESS' with CLEO LAINE, CHARLES going on to cut unlikely recordings with everyone from CLINT EASTWOOD! (a track from the film 'Any Which Way You Can) and BILLY JOEL to INXS. An early 80's move to 'Columbia' saw him attempt a fully fledged transformation into country on 'WISH YOU WERE HERE TONIGHT' (1983) and 'FRIENDSHIP' (1984), the latter an album of collaborations with the likes of JOHNNY CASH, MERLE HAGGARD and WILLIE NELSON. If critics weren't too enamoured with these efforts, CHARLES certainly didn't redeem himself with 1985's Xmas set, 'THE SPIRIT OF CHRISTMAS'. Nevertheless, he won a grammy for his 1990 duet with CHAKA KHAN, 'I'LL BE GOOD TO YOU' (from QUINCY JONES' 'Back On The Block' album) while he endeared himself to a whole new generation of American youth with a series of ads for Diet Pepsi. Into the new millennium, Brother RAY recorded both a solo set, 'THANKS FOR BRINGING LOVE AROUND AGAIN' (2002) and an album of duets, 'GENIUS LOVES COMPANY', the latter only released after his death from liver disease on June 10th 2004. Collaborative partners included the usual suspects (ELTON JOHN, B.B. KING, WILLIE NELSON, BONNIE RAITT, JAMES TAYLOR, JOHNNY MATHIS) and younger talent such as NORAH JONES and ELVIS COSTELLO's new wife DIANA KRALL, an all-star line-up which couldn't really fail to top the US charts. RAY CHARLES remains one of the true giants and founding fathers of modern music, his part in the development of soul especially, beyond question. His versatility and eclecticism remain unparalleled, with his influence apparent in the vocal style of everyone from STEVIE WONDER to VAN MORRISON and JOE COCKER. Although he lived long enough to oversee the first edit of his bio-pic, 'Ray', CHARLES died before the film hit the theaters and assumed blockbuster status. Not only did actor/singer, Jamie Foxx, win an Oscar in the leading role, but the soundtrack – composed of technologically enhanced original classics – went Top 10.

• **Songwriters:** RAY wrote most of material, although at times lending from others, i.e.- LET THE GOOD TIMES ROLL (Shirley & Lee) / GEORGIA ON MY MIND (Hoagy Carmichael) / HIT THE ROAD JACK (Percy Mayfield) / YOU ARE MY SUNSHINE (Jimmie Davis) / YOUR CHEATIN' HEART + TAKE THESE CHAINS FROM MY HEART (Hank Williams) / THAT LUCKY OLD SUN (?) / MAKIN' WHOOPEE (?) / CRY (Johnny Ray) / I'M A FOOL TO CARE (Joe Barry) / TOGETHER AGAIN (Buck Owens) / ELEANOR RIGBY + YESTERDAY (Beatles) / WHAT AM I LIVING FOR? (Chuck Willis) / LOOK WHAT THEY'VE DONE TO MY SONG, MA? (Melanie) / LIVING FOR THE CITY (Stevie Wonder) / etc. • **Miscellaneous:** Many didn't know at the time, but RAY was married to gospel singer DELLA REESE for 22 years, until they divorced late 1977. Also note that the Ray Charles Singers – who had US hits in the 60's – were in fact conducter Charles Ray Offenberg and not RAY himself.

Best CD compilation: THE DEFINITIVE . . . (*8)

RAY CHARLES – vocals, piano / **GISADY McGHEE** – guitar / **MILTON GARRAD** – bass

		not iss.	Downbea
1949.	(78; as the MAXIM TRIO) <171> **CONFESSION BLUES. / I LOVE YOU, I LOVE YOU**	-	
1949.	(78) <178> **BLUES BEFORE SUNRISE. / HOW LONG BLUES**	-	
1949.	(78) <179> **A SENTIMENTAL BLUES. / YOU'LL NEVER MISS THE WATER**	-	

		not iss.	Swingtim
1949.	(78; as the MAXIM TRIO) <211> **ALONE IN THIS CITY. / CAN ANYONE ASK FOR MORE**	-	
1949.	(78; as the MAXIM TRIO) <212> **LET'S HAVE A BALL. / ROCKIN' CHAIR BLUES**	-	
1949.	(78) <213> **IF I GIVE YOU MY LOVE. / unknown**	-	
1950.	(78) <215> **I'VE HAD MY FUN. / SITTIN' ON TOP OF THE WORLD**	-	
1950.	(78) <216> **AIN'T THAT FINE. / DON'T PUT YOUR DREAMS ALL IN ONE BASKET**	-	
1950.	(78) <217> **SEE SEE RIDER. / WHAT HAVE I DONE**	-	
1950.	(78) <218> **HONEY, HONEY. / SHE'S ON THE BALL**	-	
1950.	(78) <228> **LATE IN THE EVENING BLUES. / TH' EGO SONG**	-	
1950.	(78) <229> **I'LL DO ANYTHING BUT WORK. / SOMEDAY**	-	
1951.	(78) <249> **ALL TO MYSELF. / I WONDER WHO'S KISSING HER NOW**	-	
1951.	(7",78) <250> **BABY, LET ME HOLD YOUR HAND. / (I'M JUST A) LONELY BOY**	-	
1952.	(7",78) <274> **KISS-A-ME BABY (ALL NIGHT LONG). / I'M GLAD FOR YOUR SAKE**	-	
1952.	(7") <276> **CHANGEABLE WOMAN BLUES. / MOONRISE**	-	
1952.	(7",78) <297> **HEY, NOW. / BABY WON'T YOU PLEASE COME HOME**	-	
1952.	(7",78) <300> **GUITAR BLUES. / BABY LET ME HEAR YOU CALL MY NAME** *<re-iss. 1952 on 'Sittin-In-With'; 641>*	-	

—— **RAY** added sax / + **4 other horn players** / + **DAVID NEWMAN** – saxophone

		not iss.	Atlantic
Jun 52.	(7") <976> **ROLL WITH MY BABY. / THE MIDNIGHT HOUR**	-	
1953.	(7") <984> **THE SUN'S GONNA SHINE AGAIN. / JUMPIN' IN THE MORNING**	-	
1953.	(7") <999> **MESS AROUND. / FUNNY (BUT I STILL LOVE YOU)**	-	

1953. (7") <1008> **HEARTBREAKER. / FEELIN' SAD** [–] [ ]

1954. (7") <1021> **IT SHOULD'VE BEEN ME. / SINNER'S PRAYER** [–] [ ]

1954. (7") <1037> **DON'T YOU KNOW (BABY?). / LOSING HAND** [–] [ ]

1954. (7") <1050> **I'VE GOT A WOMAN. / COME BACK BABY** [–] [ ]

1955. (7") <1063> **THIS LITTLE GIRL OF MINE. / A FOOL FOR YOU** [–] [ ]

1955. (7") <1076> **BLACKJACK. / GREENBACKS** [–] [ ]

1956. (7") <1085> **I'LL DROWN IN MY OWN TEARS. / MARY ANN** [–] [ ]

1956. (7") <1096> **HALLELUJAH, I LOVE HER SO. / WHAT WOULD I DO WITHOUT YOU?** [–] [ ]

1956. (7") <1108> **LONELY AVENUE. / LEAVE MY WOMAN ALONE** [–] [ ]

1957. (7") <1124> **AIN'T THAT LOVE. / I WANT TO KNOW** [–] [ ]

1957. (7") <1143> **IT'S ALL RIGHT. / GET ON THE RIGHT TRACK BABY** [–] [ ]

Jul 57. (lp) *<8006>* **RAY CHARLES SINGS** [–] [ ]
– Ain't that love / I'll drown in my own tears / Come back baby / Sinner's prayer / Funny / Losing hand / A fool for you / Hallelujah I love her so / Mess around / This little girl of mine / Mary Ann / Greenbacks / Don't you know / I got a woman. *<UK-iss.Mar67 as 'HALLELUJAH, I LOVE HER SO'; 587 056>*

Oct 57. (7") <1154> **SWANEE RIVER ROCK (TALKIN' 'BOUT THAT RIVER). / I WANT A LITTLE GIRL** [–] [34]

1957. (lp) <1259> **THE GREAT RAY CHARLES** [–] [ ]
– The Ray / My melancholy baby / Black coffee / There's no you / Doodlin' / Sweet sixteen bars / I surrender dear / Undecided. *(UK-iss.Nov58 on 'London-Jazz'; LTZK 15134)*

1958. (7") <1172> **TALKIN' 'BOUT YOU. / THAT'S ENOUGH** [–] [ ]

1958. (lp) <1289> **RAY CHARLES AT NEWPORT (live)** [ ] [ ]
– The right time / In a little Spanish town / I got a woman / Blues waltz / Hot rod / Talkin' 'bout you / Sherry / A fool for you. *(UK-iss.Mar59 on 'London-Jazz'; LTZK 15149) (re-iss. Feb69 & Mar73 on 'Atlantic')*

1958. (lp; as RAY CHARLES & MILT JACKSON) <1279> **SOUL BROTHERS** [–] [ ]
– How long blues / Cosmic Ray / The genius after hours / Charlesville / Bags of blues / 'Deed I do / Blue funk / Soul brothers / Bags' guitar blues / Soul meeting / Hallelujah I love her so / Blue genius / X-Ray blues / Love on my mind. *(UK-iss.Feb59 on 'London-Jazz'; LTZK 15146) <re-iss. 1961 as 'SOUL MEETING'; 1360> (UK-iss.Mar64 on 'London' mono/stereo; HAK/SHK 8045) (re-iss. 1973 & Jul76 on 'Atlantic') (d-cd-iss. May93)*

1958. (7") <1180> **YES INDEED. / I HAD A DREAM** [–] [ ]

1958. (lp) <8025> **YES INDEED!** [–] [ ]
– What would I do without you / It's all right / I want to know / Yes indeed / Got on the right track baby / Talkin' 'bout you / Swanee River rock / Lonely Avenue / Blackjack / The sun's gonna shine again / I had a dream / I want a little girl / Heartbreaker / Leave my woman alone. *(UK-iss.Mar59 on 'London'; HAE 2168) (re-iss. 1968 on 'Atlantic')*

1958. (7") <1196> **YOU BE MY BABY. / MY BONNIE** [–] [ ]

London Atlantic

Dec 58. (7",78) *(HLE 8768)* <2006> **ROCKHOUSE (part 1). / ROCKHOUSE (part 2)** [ ] [79]

Feb 59. (7") <2010> **(THE NIGHT TIME IS) THE RIGHT TIME. / TELL ALL THE WORLD ABOUT YOU** [–] [95]

May 59. (7") <2022> **THAT'S ENOUGH. / TELL ME, HOW YOU FEEL?** [–] [ ]

Jul 59. (7",78) *(HLE 8917)* <2031> **WHAT'D I SAY (part 1). / WHAT'D I SAY (part 2)** [ ] Jun59 [6]

Aug 59. (lp) <8029> **WHAT'D I SAY** [–] [ ]
– What'd I say (part 1&2) / Jumping in the mornin' / You be my baby / Tell me how you feel / What kind of man are you / Rock house (part 1&2) / Roll with my baby / Tell all the world about you / My Bonnie / That's enough. *(UK-iss.Mar60 on 'London'; HAE 2226) <US re-iss. Aug61, hit No.20> (re-iss. Oct69)*

Dec 59. (7",78) *(HLE 9009)* <2043> **I'M MOVIN' ON. / I BELIEVE TO MY SOUL** [ ] Oct59 [40]

Feb 60. (7") *(HLE 9058)* <2047> **LET THE GOOD TIMES ROLL. / DON'T LET THE SUN CATCH YOU CRYIN'** [ ] [78] Jan60 [95]

Feb 60. (lp) <1312> **THE GENIUS OF RAY CHARLES** [–] [17]
– Let the good times roll / It had to be you / Alexander's ragtime band / Two years of torture / When your lover has gone / 'Deed I do / Just for a thrill / You won't let me go / Tell me you'll wait for me / Don't let the sun catch you cryin' / Am I blue? / Come rain or come shine. *(UK-iss.May60 on 'London'Jazz'; LTZK 15190) (cd-iss. Aug93)*

H.M.V. ABC Paramount

1960. (7") *<10081>* **WHO YOU GONNA LOVE? / MY BABY (I LOVE HER, YES I DO)** [–] [ ]

Aug 60. (7") *(POP 774) <10118>* **STICKS AND STONES. / WORRIED LIFE BLUES** [ ] Jun60 [40]

Oct 60. (lp) *(CLP 1387) <335>* **THE GENIUS HITS THE ROAD** [ ] Sep60 [9]
– Alabama bound / Georgia on my mind / Basin Street blues / Mississippi mud / Moonlight in Vermont / New York's my home / California, here I come / Moon over Miami / Deep in the heart of Texas / Carry me back to Old Virginny / Blue Hawaii / Chattanooga choo choo.

Oct 60. (7",78) *(POP 792) <10135>* **GEORGIA ON MY MIND. / CARRY ME BACK TO OLD VIRGINNY** [24] Sep60 [1]

Feb 61. (7") *(POP 825) <10164>* **RUBY. / HARDHEARTED HANNAH** [ ] [28] Nov60 [55]

May 61. (7") *(POP 838) <10141>* **THEM THAT GOT. / I WONDER** [ ] Jan61 [58]

H.M.V. Impulse!

Jun 61. (7") *<202>* **I'VE GOT NEWS FOR YOU. / I'M GONNA MOVE TO THE OUTSKIRTS OF TOWN** [–] [66] [84]

Jul 61. (7") *(POP 862) <200>* **ONE MINT JULEP. / LET'S GO** [ ] Feb61 [8]

Sep 61. (lp) *(CLP 1449) <355>* **DEDICATED TO YOU** [ ] Feb61 [11]
– Hardhearted Hannah / Nancy / Margie / Ruby / Rosetta / Stella by starlight / Cherry / Josephine / Candy / Marie / Diane / Sweet Georgia Brown.

Nov 61. (lp) *(CLP 1475) <2>* **GENUIS + SOUL = JAZZ** [ ] Mar61 [4]
– From the heart / I've got news for you / Moanin' / Let's go / One mint julep / I'm gonna move to the outskirts of town / Stompi' room only / Mister C / Strike up the band / Birth of the blues. *(re-iss. +c+cd.Sep89 on 'Essential') (re-iss. cd Jul95 on 'Actual Jazz')*

H.M.V. ABC Paramount

Oct 61. (7") *(POP 935) <10244>* **HIT THE ROAD JACK. / THE DANGER ZONE** [6] Sep61 [1]

Jan 62. (7") *(POP 969) <10244>* **UNCHAIN MY HEART. / BUT ON THE OTHER HAND BABY** [ ] [9] Nov61 [72]

Feb 62. (7"; by RAY CHARLES & BETTY CARTER) <10298> **BABY IT'S COLD OUTSIDE. / WE'LL BE TOGETHER AGAIN** [–] [91]

Mar 62. (lp; by RAY CHARLES and BETTY CARTER) *(CLP 1520) <385>* **RAY CHARLES AND BETTY CARTER** [ ] Sep61 [52]
– Everytime we say goodbye / You and I / Intro; Goodbye / We'll be together again / People will say we're in love / Cocktails for two / Side by side / Baby it's cold outside / Together / For all we know / It takes twoo to tango / Alone together. *(re-iss. c+cd.Nov89 on 'Essential')*

Apr 62. (7") *(POP 1017) <10314>* **HIDE NOR HAIR. / AT THE CLUB** [ ] [20] Mar62 [44]

May 62. (lp) *(CLP 1580) <410>* **MODERN SOUNDS IN COUNTRY AND WESTERN MUSIC** [6] Apr62 [1]
– Bye bye love / You don't know me / Half as much / I love you so much it hurts / Just a little lovin' / Born to lose / Worried mind / It makes no difference now / You win again / Careless love / I can't stop loving you / Hey, good lookin'.

May 62. (7") *(POP 1034) <10330>* **I CAN'T STOP LOVING YOU. / BORN TO LOSE** [1] [1] Apr62 [41]

Sep 62. (7") *(POP 1064) <10345>* **YOU DON'T KNOW ME. / CARELESS LOVE** [9] [2] Jul62 [60]

Nov 62. (7") *(POP 1099) <10375>* **YOUR CHEATING HEART. / YOU ARE MY SUNSHINE** [13] [29] [7]

Feb 63. (lp) *(CLP 1613) <435>* **MODERN SOUNDS IN COUNTRY AND WESTERN MUSIC VOL.2** [15] Oct62 [2]
– You are my sunshine / No letter today / Someday (you'll want me to want you)/ Don't tell me your troubles / Midnight / Oh, lonesome me / Take these chains from my heart / Your cheating heart / I'll never stand in your way / Making believe / Teardrops in my heart / Hang your head in shame.

Mar 63. (7") *(POP 1133)* <10405> **DON'T SET ME FREE. / THE BRIGHTEST SMILE IN TOWN** 37 20
Feb63 92

Apr 63. (lp) *(CLP 1626)* <415> **RAY CHARLES' GREATEST HITS** (compilation of hits) 16 Aug62 5

May 63. (7") *(POP 1161)* <10435> **TAKE THESE CHAINS FROM MY HEART. / NO LETTER TODAY** 5 Apr63 8

Jul 63. (7") *(POP 1202)* <10453> **NO ONE. / WITHOUT LOVE (THERE IS NOTHING)** 35 21
Jun63 29

Oct 63. (7") *(POP 1221)* <10481> **BUSTED. / MAKE BELIEVE** 21 Aug63 4

Oct 63. (lp) *(CLP 1678)* <465> **INGREDIENTS IN A RECIPE FOR SOUL** Aug63 9
– Busted / Where can I go / Born to the blue / That lucky old sun / Ol' man river / In the evening / A stranger in town / Ol' man time / Over the rainbow / You'll never walk alone. *(cd-iss. Jun95 on 'Personality') (re-iss. cd Jul95 on 'Actual Jazz')*

Jan 64. (7") <10509> **THAT LUCKY OLD SUN. / OL' MAN TIME** – 20

Jan 64. (7") *(POP 1251) THAT LUCKY OLD SUN. / MISSISSIPPI MUD* –

Mar 64. (7") *(POP 1272)* <10530> **BABY, DON'T YOU CRY. / MY HEART CRIES FOR YOU** 39
Feb64 38

May 64. (lp) *(CLP 1728)* <480> **SWEET AND SOUR TEARS** Mar64 9
– Cry / Guess I'll hang my tears out to dry / A tear fell / No one to cry to / You've got me crying again / After my laughter came tears / Teardrops from my eyes / Don't cry baby / Cry me a river / Baby, don't you cry / Willow weep for me / I cried for you.

Jun 64. (7") *(POP 1315)* <10557> **MY BABY DON'T DIG ME. / SOMETHING'S WRONG** May64 51

Sep 64. (7") *(POP 1333)* <10571> **NO ONE TO CRY TO. / A TEAR FELL** 38 50
Jul64 55

Nov 64. (lp) *(CLP 1728)* <495> **HAVE A SMILE WITH ME** Aug64 36
– Smack dab in the middle / Feudin' and fightin' / Two ton Tessie / I never see Maggie alone / Move it on over / Ma (she's making eyes at me) / The thing / The man with the weird beard / The naughty lady of Shady Lane / Who cares (for me).

Nov 64. (7") *(POP 1350)* <10588> **SMACK DAB IN THE MIDDLE. / I WAKE UP CRYING** Sep64 52

Dec 64. (7") <10609> **MAKIN' WHOOPEE. / (instrumental)** – 46

Jan 65. (7") *(POP 1383)* **MAKIN' WHOOPEE. / MOVE IT ON OVER** 42 –

Mar 65. (7") *(POP 1392)* <10615> **CRY. / TEARDROPS FROM MY EYES** 58

Apr 65. (7") *(POP 1414)* **LIGHT OUT OF DARKNESS. / PLEASE FORGIVE & FORGET** –

Apr 65. (lp) *(CLP 1872)* <500> **RAY CHARLES LIVE IN CONCERT (live)** Feb65 80
– Opening (introduction) / Swing a little taste / I gotta woman / Margie / You don't know me / Hide nor hair / Baby, don't you cry / Makin' whoopee / Hallelujah I love her so / Don't set me free / What'd I say / Finale. *(cd-iss. Aug93)*

Apr 65. (7") <10649> **I GOTTA WOMAN (part 1). / I GOTTA WOMAN (part 2)** – 79

May 65. (7") <10663> **WITHOUT A SONG (part 1) / WITHOUT A SONG (part 2)** –

Jul 65. (7") *(POP 1437)* **I GOTTA WOMAN. / WITHOUT A SONG** –

Aug 65. (7") *(POP 1457)* <10700> **I'M A FOOL TO CARE. / LOVE'S GONNA LIVE HERE** Jul65 84

Oct 65. (7") *(POP 1484)* <10720> **THE CINCINNATI KID. / THAT'S ALL I AM TO YOU**

Oct 65. (lp) *(CLP 1914)* <520> **COUNTRY AND WESTERN MEETS RHYTHM & BLUES** Aug65
– Together again / I like to hear it sometime / I've got a tiger by the tail / Please forgive and forget / I don't care / Next door to the blues / Blue moon of Kentucky / Light out of darkness / Maybe it's nothing at all / All night long / Don't let her know / Watch it baby.

Dec 65. (7") *(POP 1502)* <10739> **CRYING TIME. / WHEN MY DREAMBOAT COMES HOME** 6

Apr 66. (7") *(POP 1519)* <10785> **TOGETHER AGAIN. / YOU'RE JUST ABOUT TO LOSE YOUR CLOWN** 48 19
Mar66 91

May 66. (lp; mono/stereo) *(CLP/CSD 3533)* <544> **CRYING TIME** Mar66 15
– Crying time / No use crying / Let's go get stoned / Going down slow / Peace of mind / Tears / Drifting blues / We don't see eye to eye / You're in for a big surprise / You're just about to lose your crown / Don't you think I ought to know / You've got a problem.

H.M.V. ABC-TR

Jun 66. (7") *(POP 1537)* <10808> **LET'S GO GET STONED. / THE TRAIN** May66 31

Sep 66. (7") *(POP 1551)* <10840> **I CHOSE TO SING THE BLUES. / HOPELESSLY** Aug66 32

Nov 66. (lp; mono/stereo) *(CLP/CSD 3574)* <550> **RAY'S MOODS** Sep66 52
– What-cha doing in there (I wanna know) / Please say you're fooling / By the light of the silvery Moon / You don't understand / Maybe it's because of love / Chitlins with candied yams / Granny wasn't grinning that day / She's lonesome again / Sentimental journey / A born loser / It's a man's world / A girl I used to know.

Nov 66. (7") *(POP 1556)* <10865> **PLEASE SAY YOU'RE FOOLING. / I DON'T NEED NO DOCTOR** 64
72

—— some of the above singles were cred. to RAY CHARLES & HIS ORCHESTRA

Mar 67. (7") <10901> **I WANT TO TALK ABOUT YOU. / PLEASE SAY YOU'RE FOOLING** – 98

Apr 67. (7") *(POP 1589)* **YOU WIN AGAIN. / BYE BYE BYE** –

Jun 67. (7") *(POP 1595)* <10938> **HERE WE GO AGAIN. / SOMEBODY OUGHT TO WRITE A BOOK ABOUT IT** 38 May67 15

Sep 67. (lp; mono/stereo) *(CLP/CSD 3630)* <595> **RAY CHARLES INVITES YOU TO LISTEN** Jul67 76
– She's funny that way (I got a woman crazy for me) / How deep is the ocean (how high is the sky) / You made me love you (I didn't wanna do it) / Yesterday / I'll be seeing you / Here we go again / All for you / Love walked in / Gee, baby ain't I good to you / People.

Sep 67. (7") *(POP 1607)* <10970> **IN THE HEAT OF THE NIGHT. / SOMETHING'S GOT TO CHANGE** Aug67 33

Stateside ABC-TR

Dec 67. (7") *(SS 2071)* <11009> **YESTERDAY. / NEVER HAD ENOUGH OF NOTHING YET** 44 Nov67 25

Mar 68. (7") *(SS 2099)* <11045> **THAT'S A LIE. / GO ON HOME** Feb68 64

Jul 68. (7") *(SS 2120)* <11090> **ELEANOR RIGBY. / UNDERSTANDING** 36 35
May68 46

Nov 68. (7") *(SS 2132)* <11133> **SWEET YOUNG THING LIKE YOU. / LISTEN, THEY'RE PLAYING OUR SONG** 83
Aug68 92

Jan 69. (7"; as RAY CHARLES & JIMMY LEWIS) <11170> **IF IT WASN'T FOR BAD LUCK. / WHEN I STOP DREAMING** – 77

Feb 69. (lp; stereo/mono) *(S+/SL 10269)* <625> **A PORTRAIT OF RAY** Apr68 51
– Eleanor Rigby / Am I blue / Never say naw / Sun died / Yesterday / When I stop dreaming / I won't leave / Sweet young thing like you / Bright lights and you girl / Understanding.

Mar 69. (7") <11193> **I'LL BE YOUR SERVANT. / I DIDN'T KNOW WHAT TIME IT WAS** –

May 69. (7") <11213> **LET ME LOVE YOU. / I'M SATISFIED** – 94

Jul 69. (lp; stereo/mono) *(S+/SL 10281)* <675> **I'M ALL YOURS – BABY!** Mar69
– Yours / I didn't know what the time was / Love is here to stay / Memories of you / Till the end of time / I had the craziest dream / Someday / Indian love call / I dream of you (more than you dream I do) / Gloomy Sunday

Sep 69. (7") *(SS 2155)* <11239> **WE CAN MAKE IT. / I CAN'T STOP LOVING YOU BABY**

Nov 69. (7") <11251> **CLAUDIE MAE. / SOMEONE TO WATCH OVER ME** –

Feb 70. (lp; stereo/mono) *(S+/SL 10293)* <695> **DOING HIS THING** Jul69
– The same thing that can make you laugh (can make you cry) / Finders keepers, losers weepers / You ought to change your ways / Baby please / Come and get it / We can make it / I'm ready / That thing called love / If it wasn't for bad luck / I told you so.

Feb 70. (7") <11259> **LAUGHIN' AND CLOWNIN'. / THAT THING CALLED LOVE** – 98

Tangerine Tangerine

May 71. (7"; as RAY CHARLES ORCHESTRA) *(6121 001)* <1015> **BOOTY BUTT (instrumental). / ZIG ZAG (instrumental)** Mar71 36

Jul 71. (lp) *(6495 001)* *<1512>* **MY KIND OF JAZZ** (instrumental) [ ] Jul70 [ ]
– Golden boy / Booty butt / This here / I remember Clifford / Sidewinder / Bluesette / Pas-se-o-ne blues / Zig zag / Senior blues.

Probe | ABC-Tangerine

Oct 70. (7") *(SS 2170)* *<11271>* **TILL I CAN'T TAKE IT ANYMORE. / IF YOU WERE MINE** [ ] Sep70 [41]

Nov 70. (lp) *(SPB 1015)* *<707>* **LOVE COUNTRY STYLE** [ ] Aug70 [ ]
– f you were mine / Ring of fire / Your love is so doggone good / Don't change on me / Till I can't take it anymore / You've still got a place in my heart / I keep it hid / Sweet memories / Good morning dear / Show me the sunshine.

Mar 71. (7") *(PRO 524)* *<11219>* **DON'T CHANGE ON ME. / SWEET MEMORIES** [ ] [36]

Jul 71. (lp) *(SPB 1039)* *<726>* **VOLCANIC ACTION OF MY SOUL** [ ] May71 [52]
– See you then / What am I living for / Feel so bad / The long and winding road / The three bells / All I ever need is you / Wichita lineman / Something / I may be wrong (but I think you're wonderful) / Down in the valley.

Aug 71. (7") *<11308>* **FEEL SO BAD. / YOUR LOVE IS SO DOGGONE GOOD** [–] [68]

Oct 71. (7") *(PRO 539)* **THE LONG AND WINDING ROAD. / WICHITA LINEMAN** [ ] [–]

Dec 71. (7") *<11317>* **WHAT AM I LIVING FOR. / TIRED OF MY TEARS** [–] [54]

Jun 72. (7") *(PRO 566)* *<11329>* **LOOK WHAT THEY'VE DONE TO MY SONG, MA. / AMERICA THE BEAUTIFUL** [ ] [65]

Sep 72. (lp) *(SPB 1060)* *<755>* **A MESSAGE FROM THE PEOPLE** [ ] Apr72 [52]
– Lift every voice and sing / Seems like I gotta do wrong / Heaven help us all / There'll be no peace without all men as one / Hey mister / What have they done to my song, ma / Abraham, Martin and John / Take me home, country roads / Every Saturday night / America the beautiful.

Aug 72. (7") *<11337>* **HEY MISTER. / THERE'LL BE NO PEACE WITHOUT ALL MEN AS ONE** [–] [ ]

Jan 73. (7") *<11344>* **EVERY SATURDAY NIGHT. / TAKE ME HOME, COUNTRY ROADS** [–] [ ]

Feb 73. (lp) *(SPB 1066)* *<765>* **THROUGH THE EYES OF LOVE** [ ] Nov72 [ ]
– My first night alone without you / I can make it thru the days (but oh those lonely nights) / Someone to watch over me / A perfect love / If you wouldn't be my lady / You leave me breathless / Never ending song of love / Rainy night in Georgia.

May 73. (7") *<11351>* **I CAN MAKE IT THRU THE DAYS (BUT OH THOSE LONELY NIGHTS). / RING OF FIRE** [–] [81]

London | Crossover

Nov 73. (7") *(HLU 10432)* *<973>* **COME LIVE WITH ME. / EVERYBODY SING** [ ] [82]

Jan 74. (7") *<974>* **LOUISE. / SOMEBODY** [–] [ ]

Apr 74. (lp) *(SHU 8467)* *<9000>* **COME LIVE WITH ME** [ ] Jan74 [ ]
– Till there was you / If you go away / It takes so little time / Somebody / Come live with me / Problems, problems / Louise / Where was he / Everybody sing.

Aug 75. (lp) *(SHU 8485)* *<9005>* **RENAISSANCE** [ ] Jun75 [ ]
– Living for the city / Then I'll be home / My God and I / We're gonna make it / For mama / Sunshine / Bein' green / Sail away.

Sep 75. (7") *<981>* **LIVING FOR THE CITY. / THEN I'LL BE HOME** [–] [91]

Sep 75. (7") *(HLU 10505)* **LIVING FOR THE CITY. / FOR MAMA** [ ] [–]

Jan 76. (7") *<985>* **AMERICA THE BEAUTIFUL. / SUNSHINE** [–] [ ]

London | R.C.A.

Oct 76. (7"; by RAY CHARLES & CLEO LAINE) *(HLU 10541)* *<PB 10800>* **OH LAWD, I'M ON MY WAY. / OH BESS, WHERE'S MY BESS?** [ ] [ ]

Dec 76. (d-lp; by RAY CHARLES & CLEO LAINE) *(D 31-32)* *<1831>* **PORGY AND BESS** [ ] Nov76 [ ]
– Summertime (instrumental) / Summertime / My man's gone now / A woman is a sometimes thing / They pass by singing / What you want wild Bess / I got plenty o' nothin' (instrumental) / I got plenty o' nothing / Buzzard song / Bess, you is a woman / Oh doctor Jesus / Crab man's call / Here come de honey man / Strawberry woman's call / It ain't necessarily so (instrumental) / It ain't necessarily so / There's a boat dat's leaving for New York (instrumental) / There's a boat dat's leaving for New York / Oh Bess, oh where's my Bess? / Oh lawd I'm on my way.

London | Atlantic

Jul 77. (7") *(HLU 10554)* **I CAN SEE CLEARLY NOW. / LET IT BE** [ ] [–]

Nov 77. (7") *<3443>* **I CAN SEE CLEARLY NOW. / ANONYMOUS LOVE** [–] [ ]

Jan 78. (lp) *(SHU 8509)* *<19142>* **TRUE TO LIFE** [ ] Nov77 [78]
– I can see clearly now / The jealous kind / Oh what a beautiful morning / How long has this been goin' on / Be my love / Anonymous love / Heavenly music / Game number nine / Let it be.

1978. (7") *<3473>* **A PEACE THAT WE NEVER COULD ENJOY. / GAME NUMBER NINE** [–] [ ]

1978. (7") *<3527>* **YOU FORGET YOUR MEMORY. / RIDING THUMB** [–] [ ]

Nov 78. (lp/c) *(SHU/KSACU1 8519)* *<19199>* **LOVE AND PEACE** [ ] [ ]
– Take off that dress / She knows / You 20th century fox / Riding thumb / We had it all / A peace that we never could enjoy / No achievement showing / Is there anyone out there / Give the poor man a break.

Dec 78. (7") *<3549>* **CHRISTMAS TIME. / THERE'LL BE NO PEACE WITHOUT ALL MEN AS ONE** [–] [ ]

Aug 79. (7") *<3611>* **SOME ENCHANTED EVENING. / YOU 20TH CENTURY FOX** [–] [ ]

Sep 79. (lp/c) *(SHU/KSAC1 8537)* *<19251>* **AIN'T IT SO** [ ] [ ]
– Some enchanted evening / Blues in the night / Just because / What'll I do / One of these days / Love me or set me free / Drift away / Love me tonight.

Nov 79. (7") *<3634>* **LOVE ME OR SET ME FREE. / JUST BECAUSE** [–] [ ]

Oct 80. (7"; by RAY CHARLES & CLINT EASTWOOD) *<49608>* **BEERS TO YOU (w/CLINT EASTWOOD). / COTTON-EYED CLINT (by the TEXAS OPERA COMPANY)** [–] [ ]
(above from the movie 'Any Which Way You Can' on 'Warners')

Dec 80. (7") *(HL 10579)* *<3762>* **COMPARED TO WHAT. / NOW THAT WE'VE FOUND EACH OTHER** [ ] [ ]

— in Oct'80, he issued SHAKE YOUR TALL FEATHER. / MINNIE THE MOOCHER with "CAB CALLOWAY")

C.B.S. | Columbia

Mar 83. (7") *<03429>* **STRING BEAN. / BORN TO LOVE ME** [–] [ ]

Mar 83. (lp) *(CBS/40 25065)* *<38293>* **WISH YOU WERE HERE TONIGHT?** [ ] [ ]
– 3/4 times / Ain't your memory got no pride at all / I don't want no stranger sleepin' in my bed / Born to love me / Let your love flow / Shakin' your head / String bean / I Wish you were here tonight? / You've got the longest leaving act / You feel good all over. *(cd-iss. Apr90 on 'Pickwick')*

May 83. (7") *(CBS 3407)* **I WISH YOU WERE HERE TONIGHT. / YOU FEEL GOOD ALL OVER** [ ] [–]

1983. (7") *<03810>* **YOU FEEL GOOD ALL OVER. / 3/4 TIME** [–] [ ]

1983. (7") *<04083>* **AIN'T YOUR MEMORY GOT NO PRIDE AT ALL. / I DON'T WANT NO STRANGERS SLEEPING IN MY BED** [–] [ ]

1983. (7"; as RAY CHARLES with GEORGE JONES & CHET ATKINS) *<04297>* **I WISH YOU WERE HERE TONIGHT. / WE DIDN'T SEE A THING** [–] [ ]

1984. (7") *<04420>* **DO I EVER CROSS YOUR MIND. / THEY CALL IT LOVE** [–] [ ]

Jul 84. (lp/c) *(CBS/40 25764)* *<38990>* **DO I EVER CROSS YOUR MIND** [ ] [ ]
– I had it all / Do I ever cross your mind / Woman sensuous woman / Then I'll be over you / Lay around and love on you / Love of my life / They call it love / If I were you / Workin' man's woman / I was on Georgia time.

1984. (7") *<04500>* **WOMAN, SENSUOUS WOMAN. / I WAS ON GEORGIA TIME** [–] [ ]

Oct 84. (lp/c) *(CBS/40 26060)* *<39415>* **FRIENDSHIP** [ ] [75]
– Two old cats like us / This old heart / We didn't see a thing / Who cares / Rock and roll shoes / Friendship / It ain't gonna worry my mind / Little hotel room / Crazy old soldier / Seven Spanish angels.

1984. (7"; by RAY CHARLES with B.J. THOMAS) *<04531>* **ROCK AND ROLL SHOES. / THEN I'LL BE OVER YOU** [–] [ ]

Mar 85. (7"; by RAY CHARLES with WILLIE NELSON) *(CBS 4991)* *<04715>* **SEVEN SPANISH ANGELS. / WHO CARES (with JANE FRICKIE)** [ ] [ ]

1985. (7"; by RAY CHARLES with MICKEY GILLEY) *<04860>* **IT AIN'T GONNA WORRY MY MIND. / CRAZY OLD SOLDIER (with JOHNNY CASH)** [–] [ ]

1985. (7"; by RAY CHARLES with HANK WILLIAMS JR.) *<05575>* **TWO OLD CATS LIKE US. / LITTLE HOTEL ROOM (with MERLE HAGGARD)** [–] [ ]

Dec 85. (lp/c) *(CBS/40 26562) <40125>* **THE SPIRIT OF CHRISTMAS** [ ] [ ]
– What child is this / Little drummer boy / Santa Claus is coming to town / This time of the year / Rudolph the red-nosed reindeer / That spirit of Christmas / All I want for Christmas / Christmas in my heart / Winter wonderland / Christmas time.

Aug 86. (7") *<06172>* **THE PAGES OF MY MIND. / SLIP AWAY** [–] [ ]

Aug 86. (lp/c) *(CBS/40 26856) <40338>* **FROM THE PAGES OF MY MIND** [ ] [ ]
– The pages of my mind / Slip away / Anybody wit the blues / Class reunion / Caught a touch of your love / A little bit of Heaven / Dixie Moon / Over and over (again) / Beaucoup love / Love is worth the pain.

Nov 86. (7") *<06370>* **DIXIE MOON. / A LITTLE BIT OF HEAVEN** [–] [ ]

— RAY was credited on BILLY JOEL's 'Baby Grand' 45 (Apr'87), then semi-retired from the music biz but continued acting mainly on 'Moonlighting' and 'St. Elsewhere'.

Sep 88. (lp/c/cd) *(461183-1/-4/-2) <40703>* **JUST BETWEEN US** [ ] [ ]
– Nothing like a hundred miles / I wish I'd never loved you at all / Too hard to love you / Now I don't believe that anymore / Let's call the whole thing off / Stranger in my own hometown / Over the top / I'd walk a little more for you / If that's what cha want / Save the bones for Henry Jones.

— In the early 90's, he featured on QUINCY JONES + CHAKA KHAN's hit, 'I'll Be Good To You'.

WEA Warners

Oct 90. (cd/c/lp) *<2-/4-/1-26343>* **WOULD YOU BELIEVE?** [–] [ ]
– I'll take care of you / Your love keeps me satisfied / Ellie, my love / I can't get enough / Let's get back to where we left off / Child support, alimony / Fresh out of tears / Living without you / Where're the stairs? / Leave him!

Mar 93. (c-s) *<18611>* **A SONG FOR YOU / I CAN'T GET ENOUGH** [–] [ ]

Mar 93. (cd/c) *<(7599 26735-2/-4)>* **MY WORLD** [ ] [ ]
– My world / A song for you / None of us are free / So help me God / Let me take over / One drop of love / If I could / Love has a mind of its own / I'll be there / Still crazy after all these years.

— BILLY PRESTON featured on keyboards

— In Nov'93, RAY teamed up with INXS on their hit 'Please (You Got That . . .)'

Qwest Qwest

Feb 96. (cd) *<(9362 46107-2)>* **STRONG LOVE AFFAIR** [ ] Jan96 [ ]
– All she wants to do is love me / Say no more / No time to waste time / Angelina / Tell me what you want me to do / Strong love affair / Everybody's handsome child / Out of my life / The fever / Separate ways / I need a good woman bad / If you give me your heart.

XIII Bis Crossover

Nov 02. (cd) *(640281-2) <4000>* **THANKS FOR BRINGING LOVE AROUND AGAIN** [ ] Apr02 [ ]
– What'd I say (new version) / Can you love me like that / How did you feel the morning after / I love you more than I ever have / Really got a hold on me / Thanks for bringing love around again / Save your lovin' just for me / I just can't get enough of you / Ensemble / New Orleans / Mr. Creole / Mother.

— sadly, RAY died of liver disease on 10th June 2004

Liberty Concord

Aug 04. (cd) *(866540-2) <2248>* **GENIUS LOVES COMPANY** [29] [1]
– Here we go again (feat. NORAH JONES) / Sweet potato pie (feat. JAMES TAYLOR) / You don't know me (feat. DIANA KRALL) / Sorry seems to be the hardest word (feat. ELTON JOHN) / Fever (feat. NATALIE COLE) / Do I ever cross your mind? (feat. BONNIE RAITT) / It was a very good year (feat. WILLIE NELSON) / Hey girl (feat. MICHAEL McDONALD) / Sinner's prayer (feat. B.B. KING) / Heaven help us all (feat. GLADYS KNIGHT) / Somewhere over the rainbow (feat. JOHNNY MATHIS) / Crazy love (live feat. VAN MORRISON).

– (selective) compilations, etc. –

Nov 60. (lp) *London; (HAK 2284) / Atlantic; <8039>* **RAY CHARLES IN PERSON (live)** [ ] Jul60 [13]
(re-iss. Apr69 on 'Atlantic') (below re-iss. Jan68)

Dec 60. (7") *London; (HLK 9251) / Atlantic; <2084>* **COME RAIN OR COME SHINE. / TELL ME YOU'LL WAIT FOR ME** [ ] [83]

Nov 61. (lp) *Atlantic; <8054>* **DO THE TWIST!** [–] [11]

Aug 62. (d-lp) *Atlantic; <900>* **THE RAY CHARLES STORY** [–] [14]

Mar 62. (lp) *London-Jazz; (LTZK 15238) / Atlantic; <8052>* **THE GENIUS SINGS THE BLUES** [ ] Nov61 [73]

Feb 63. (lp) *London; (HAK 8035) / Atlantic; <1369>* **THE GENIUS AFTER HOURS** [ ] Aug61 [49]

Mar 67. (d-lp) *ABC Paramount; <590>* **A MAN AND HIS SOUL** [–] [77]

Sep 68. (lp; stereo/mono) *Stateside; (S+/SL 10241)* **GREATEST HITS VOL.2** [24] [–]

Aug 80. (lp) *London; (RAYTV 1)* **HEART TO HEART – 20 RAY CHARLES' HOTTEST HITS** [29] [–]

Mar 90. (cd/c/lp) *Arcade; (RCL D/C/P 101)* **THE COLLECTION** [36] [–]
– Your cheatin' heart / Hit the road Jack / Georgia on my mind / Unchai my heart / One mint julep / Take these chains from my heart / I can' stop loving you / Busted / You are my sunshine / Making whoopee / Let' go get stoned / My heart cries for you / Feel so bad / The lucky old Sun Smack dab in the middle / Crying time / If it wasn't for bad luck / In th heat of the night / Eleanor Rigby / Born to lose / No one / Hard hearted Hannah / Yesterday.

Mar 93. (d-cd/d-c) *Arcade; (ARC 9464-2/-4)* **THE LIVING LEGEND** [48] [–]

Sep 98. (cd) *Atlantic; (7567 80865-2)* **AT NEWPORT** (remastered) [ ] [ ]

Aug 01. (d-cd/d-c) *Warner-ESP; <(8122 73556-2/-4)>* **THE DEFINITIVE RAY CHARLES** [13] [ ]

Jan 05. (cd) *Rhino; <(8122 76540-2)>* **RAY** (soundtrack) [36] Oct04 [9]
– Mess around / I've got a woman / Hallelujah I love her so (live) / Drowr in my own tears / (Night time is) The right time / Mary Ann / Hard time (no one knows better than I) / What'd I say (live) / Georgia on my mind Hit the road Jack / Unchain my heart / I can't stop loving you (live) / Born to lose / Bye bye, love / You don't know me (live) / Let the good times ro (live) / Georgia on my mind (live). *<(re-iss. Feb05; 8122 79597-2)>*

May 05. (cd) *Rhino; <(8122 78703-2)>* **MORE MUSIC FROM RAY** (soundtrack) [ ] Jan05 [ ]
– Leave my woman alone / Lonely avenue / Rockhouse (pts.1 & 2) / believe to my soul / Losing hand / I'm movin' on / But on the othe hand baby / Baby, it's cold outside / The danger zone / Busted / Makin whoopee / Let's go get stoned / Drifting blues / Baby let me hold you hand / Drown in my own tears – You don't know me / Everyday I hav the blues / America the beautiful / *(+ dvd +=)* – Don't set me free / Carr me back to Old Virginny / (O-Genio trailer).

CHEAP TRICK

Formed: Rockford, Illinois, USA . . . 1972 by main writer RICK NIELSEN and TOM PETERSSON, who were part of The GRIM REAPERS prior to becoming FUSE. This brief early period only produced one self-titled album, before they enlisted the help of THOM MOONEY and ROBERT 'STEWKEY' ANTONI, fresh from (TODD RUNDGREN's) NAZZ. In 1972, they changed thei moniker yet again, this time to the SICK MAN OF EUROPE recruiting BUN E. CARLOS in place of the departing MOONEY This primitive incarnation of CHEAP TRICK also saw the inclusion of new vocalist RANDY 'XENO' HOGAN, although after two years of steady touring he was replaced by ROBIN ZANDER. With the classic line-up now in place, the band secured a deal with 'Epic' releasing their eponymous debut album early in '77. Coming at a time of musical turbulence (new wave/punk had just arrived), the album failed to excite an interest from either critics or rock fans More marketable was the band's highly original image, ZANDER and PETERSSEN the good-lookers, while CARLOS was the joker in the pack with his Tweedle-Dee/Dum attire (i.e. baseball cap, bow-tie and all-round eccentricity). Tours supporting KISS and QUEEN helped promote the band's off-the-wall appeal to a wider audience the follow-up, 'IN COLOR' (also in '77) gaining healthy sales and a US Top 75 placing. The album featured the excellent 45, 'I WANT YOU TO WANT ME', a flop first time around, although a live equivalent subsequently made the US Top 10 in 1979. Following on from the success of their third studio album, 'HEAVEN TONIGHT' (1978), their harder-edged live set, 'AT BUDOKAN' turned their popularity in Japan into even greater commercial heights in America. The record struck platinum, hitting Top 5 in the process and making them virtual overnight international stars over the ensuing decade. Another Top 10'er, 'DREAM POLICE' (1979), consolidated their newfound fame, although this was nearly wrecked when the BEATLES-influenced CHEAP TRICK worked with the legendary GEORGE MARTIN on the album, 'ALL SHOOK UP'. PETERSSEN felt the strain and bailed out before their next album, 'ONE ON ONE' (1982), which had seen JON BRANDT come in as a replacement for the temporary PETE COMITA. In 1983, they employed the services of TODD RUNDGREN (who didn't!?) on their album of that year, 'NEXT POSITION PLEASE', which was a relative flop compared to the lofty chart heights of its predecessors. After a near return to form with the 1985 album, 'STANDING ON THE EDGE', they trawled a creative and commercial trough with 'THE DOCTOR'. Drastic measures were needed; PETERSSEN returned and the group drafted in outside writers to make 1988's 'LAP OF LUXURY' their most successful album of the decade. Of course, this was due in no small part to CHEAP TRICK achieving their first singles chart topper, 'THE FLAME'. Their AOR formula was utilised once more on their 1990 'BUSTED', although this was to be their last taste of major chart action for some time. The 1994 'Warner Brothers' set, 'WOKE UP WITH A MONSTER' saw the band attempting to recapture their heady 70's sound. Three years later, after a one-off for the seminal cult-indie label, 'Sub Pop', CHEAP TRICK released an eponymous set which dented the US Top 100. Come the end of the decade the band were in retrospective mood for a small series of residencies in various US cities, airing one of their first three albums in whole each night. A novel idea, and one which provided the material for 1999's 'MUSIC FOR HANGOVERS', a spirited live effort which offered few surprises but revealed an enthusiasm undimmed by the passing years. Longtime fans also lapped up 'SILVER' (2001), another live affair recorded at a special 25th anniversary homecoming show. In contrast to its predecessor, the record featured more obscure treats while the likes of SMASHING PUMPKINS' BILLY CORGAN and SLASH added a dash of celebrity appeal. The power-pop deities released their first new studio material in seven years with 'SPECIAL ONE' (2004), essentially one for the fans. Going right back to basics (even the name referred their hometown), 'ROCKFORD' (2006) was hailed as the group's best work since the early 80s.

• **Covered:** AIN'T THAT A SHAME (Fats Domino) / DON'T BE CRUEL (Elvis Presley) / DANCING THE NIGHT AWAY (Motors) / SPEAK NOW (Terry Reid) / MONEY (Barrett Strong) / MAGICAL MYSTERY TOUR (Beatles).

Album rating: CHEAP TRICK (*7) / IN COLOR (*6) / HEAVEN TONIGHT (*7) / AT BUDOKAN (*7) / DREAM POLICE (*5) / ALL SHOOK UP (*4) / ONE ON ONE (*5) / NEXT POSITION PLEASE (*4) / STANDING ON THE EDGE (*5) / THE DOCTOR (*3) / LAP OF LUXURY (*5) / BUSTED (*4) / THE GREATEST HITS compilation (*6) / BUDOKAN II early live (*5) / WOKE UP WITH A MONSTER (*4) / CHEAP TRICK on 'Red Ant' 1997 (*4) / MUSIC FOR HANGOVERS (*6) / SILVER (*6) / SPECIAL ONE (*4) / ROCKFORD (*6) / Robin Zander: ROBIN ZANDER (*6)

FUSE

RICK NIELSEN (b.22 Dec'46, Rockford)– guitar / **JOE SUNBERG** – vocals / **CRAIG MYERS** – guitar / **TOM PETERSSON** (b. 9 May'50) – bass / **CHIP GREENMAN** – drums

not iss. | Epic

Jul 68. (7") <5-10514> **HOUND DOG. / CRUISIN' FOR BURGERS** [–] [ ]
<originally-iss.Jun68 as GRIM REAPERS on 'Smack'; >

Jul 69. (lp) <26502> **FUSE** [–] [ ]
– Across the skies / Permanent rresident / Show me / To your health / In a window / 4-4 3-4 / Mystery ship / Sad day. *<cd-iss. 2001 on 'Rewind'+=; 55018>* – Hound dog / Cruisin' for burgers.

—— split soon after above **NIELSEN** and **PETERSSON** teamed up invariably as NAZZ and FUSE with ex-NAZZ members **ROBERT 'STEWKEY' ANTONI** – vocals / **THOM MOONEY** – drums

—— In '72 they became **The SICK MAN OF EUROPE** and moved to Philadelphia / **BUN E. CARLOS** (b.BRAD CARLSON, 12 Jun'51) – drums (ex-PAGANS) repl. MOONEY / **XENO** (r.n. RANDY HOGAN) – vocals repl. STEWKEY / **RICK SZELUGA** – bass repl. PETERSSON for a short while, until they became in '73 . . .

CHEAP TRICK

NIELSEN, PETERSSON, CARLOS and **XENO)**

—— Oct74 **ROBIN ZANDER** (b.23 Jan'53, Loves Park, Illinois) – vocals, guitar (ex-TOONS) repl. XENO who joined STRAIGHT UP

Epic | Epic

Mar 77. (7") <50375> **OH CANDY. / DADDY SHOULD HAVE STAYED IN HIGH SCHOOL** [–] [ ]

Mar 77. (lp) *(EPC 81917)* <34400> **CHEAP TRICK** [ ] Jan77 [ ]
– Hot love / Speak now or forever hold your peace / He's a whore / Mandocello / The ballad of T.V. violence (I'm not the only boy) / Elo kiddies / Daddy should have stayed in high school / Taxman, Mr Thief / Cry cry / Oh Candy. *(re-iss. Nov81 lp/c; EPC/40 32070) <cd-iss. Jun88 on 'Collector's Choice'; EK 34400> (cd re-iss. Jul97; 487933-2) (cd re-iss. Oct98 on 'Columbia'; 491229-2)*

Nov 77. (7") *(EPC 5701)* <50435> **I WANT YOU TO WANT ME. / OH BOY (instrumental)** [ ] [ ]
(re-iss. Mar78; same)

Nov 77. (lp/c) *(EPC/40 82214)* <34884> **IN COLOR** [ ] Aug77 [73]
– Hello there / Big eyes / Downed / I want you to want me / You're all talk / Oh Caroline / Clock strikes ten / Southern girls / Come on, come on / So good to see you. *<cd-iss. Jun88 on 'Collector's Choice'; EK 34844> (cd-iss. Oct93 on 'Sony Europe'; 982833-2) (cd re-iss. Oct98 on 'Columbia'; 491230-2)*

Nov 77. (7") <50485> **SOUTHERN GIRLS. / YOU'RE ALL TALK** [–] [ ]

Mar 78. (7") *(EPC 6199)* **SO GOOD TO SEE YOU. / YOU'RE ALL TALK** [ ] [–]

May 78. (7") *(EPC 6394)* <50570> **SURRENDER. / AUF WIEDERSEHEN** [ ] [62]

May 78. (lp/c) *(EPC/40 82679)* <35312> **HEAVEN TONIGHT** [ ] [48]
– Surrender / On top of the world / California man / High roller / Auf wiedersehen / Takin' me back / On the radio / Heaven tonight / Stiff competition / How are you / Oh Claire. *(cd-iss. Sep93 on 'Sony Europe'; 982993-2) (cd re-iss. Oct98; 491231-2)*

Jul 78. (7") *(EPC 6427)* **CALIFORNIA MAN. / STIFF COMPETITION** [ ] [–]

Aug 78. (7") <50625> **CALIFORNIA MAN. / I WANT YOU TO WANT ME** [–] [ ]

Feb 79. (lp,yellow-lp/c) *(EPC/40 86083)* <35795> **AT BUDOKAN (live)** [29] [4]
– Hello there / Come on, come on / Look out / Big eyes / Need your love / Ain't that a shame / I want you to want me / Surrender / Goodnight now / Clock strikes ten. *(re-iss. as d-lp.Nov81' EPC 32595) (cd-iss. Feb86; CDEPC 86083) (re-iss. Jul91 on 'Essential' cd/c; ESS CD/MC 949)*

Feb 79. (7"; w-drawn) *(EPC 7144)* <50814> **VOICES (live). / SURRENDER (live)** [ ] Nov79 [32]

Mar 79. (7",7"orange) *(EPC 7258)* <50680> **I WANT YOU TO WANT ME (live). / CLOCK STRIKES TEN (live)** [29] [7]

Jul 79. (7") *(EPC 7724)* **SURRENDER (live). / AUF WIEDERSEHEN (live)** [ ] [–]

Sep 79. (7") *(EPC 7839)* <50743> **AIN'T THAT A SHAME (live). / ELO KIDDIES** [ ] Jul79 [35]

Sep 79. (lp/pic-lp/c) *(EPC/11/40 83522)* <35773> **DREAM POLICE** [41] [6]
– Dream police / Way of the world / The house is rockin' (with domestic problems) / Gonna raise Hell / I'll be with you tonight / Voices / Writing on the wall / I know what I want / Need your love.

Oct 79. (7") *(EPC 7880)* <50744> **DREAM POLICE. / HEAVEN TONIGHT** [ ] Sep79 [26]

Jan 80. (7") *(EPC 8114)* **WAY OF THE WORLD. / OH CANDY** [73] [–]

Mar 80. (7"ep) *(EPC 8335)* **I'LL BE WITH YOU TONIGHT. / HE'S A WHORE / SO GOOD TO SEE YOU** [ ] [–]

Apr 80. (7") *<50887>* **EVERYTHING WORKS IF YOU LET IT. / WAY OF THE WORLD** – 44
Jul 80. (7") *(EPC 8755)* **EVERYTHING WORKS IF YOU LET IT. / HEAVEN TONIGHT** –
Oct 80. (7") *(EPC 9071) <50942>* **STOP THIS GAME. / WHO D'KING** 48
Oct 80. (lp/c) *(EPC/40 86124) <36498>* **ALL SHOOK UP** 24
– Stop this game / Just got back / Baby loves to rock / Can't stop it but I'm gonna try / World's greatest lover / High Priest of rhythmic noise / Love comes a-tumblin' down / I love you honey but I hate your friends / Go for the throat (use your own imagination) / Who d'king. *<cd-iss. Jun88 on 'Collector's Choice'; EK 36498>*
Jan 81. (7") *(EPC 9502)* **WORLD'S GREATEST LOVER. / HIGH PRIEST OF RHYTHMIC NOISE**

—— **PETE COMITA** (b. Italy) – bass repl. PETERSSON who formed own group with his wife

Aug 81. (7") *<47187>* **REACH OUT. / I MUST BE DREAMING** –

—— (above single from the film 'Heavy Metal'. issued on 'Full Moon-Asylum') now alongside **NIELSEN** (some bass), **ZANDER** + **CARLOS**

—— (late '81) **JON BRANT** (b.20 Feb'54) – bass (on three songs) repl. COMITA

May 82. (7") *(EPCA 2406) <02968>* **IF YOU WANT MY LOVE. / FOUR LETTER WORD** 57 45
May 82. (lp,red-lp/pic-lp/c) *(EPC/11/40 85740) <38021>* **ONE ON ONE** 95 39
– I want you / One on one / If you want my love / Oo la la la / Lookin' out for number one / She's tight / Time is runnin' / Saturday at midnight / Love's got a hold on me / I want be man / Four letter word. *(re-iss. Jun85; EPC 32654)*
Sep 82. (7") *<03233>* **SHE'S TIGHT. / ALL I REALLY WANT TO DO** – 65
Aug 83. (7") *<04078>* **DANCING THE NIGHT AWAY. / DON'T MAKE OUR LOVE A CRIME** –
Sep 83. (lp/c) *(EPC/40 25490) <38794>* **NEXT POSITION PLEASE** 61
– I can't take it / Borderline / I don't love her anymore / Next position please / Younger girls / Dancing the night away / 3-D / You say jump / Y.O.Y.O.Y. / Won't take no for an answer / Heaven's falling / Invaders of the heart. *<US c+=/cd+=>* – You take too much / Don't make our love a crime.
Sep 83. (12"ep) *(EPCTA 3743)* **DANCING THE NIGHT AWAY / AIN'T THAT A SHAME. / I WANT YOU TO WANT ME / SURRENDER** –
Nov 83. (7") *<04216>* **I CAN'T TAKE IT. / YOU TALK TOO MUCH** –
Feb 84. (7") *<29723>* **SPRING BREAK. / GET READY** –
(above from the film 'Spring Break', issued on 'Warner Bros')
(below issued on 'Pasha' US)
1984. (7") *<04392>* **UP THE CREEK. / (other artist)** –
Sep 85. (7") *(A 6390) <05431>* **TONIGHT IT'S YOU. / WILD WILD WOMEN** Jul85 44
(12"+=) *(EPCTX 6390)* – I want you to want me / If you want my love.
Oct 85. (lp/c) *(EPC/40 26374) <39592>* **STANDING ON THE EDGE** Aug85 35
– Little sister / Tonight it's you / She's got motion / Love comes / How about you / Standing on the edge / This time around / Rock all night / Cover girl / Wild wild women.
Jun 86. (7") *<06137>* **MIGHTY WINGS. / (other artist)** –
Nov 86. (lp/c) *(EPC/40 57087) <40405>* **THE DOCTOR** Oct86
– It's up to you / Rearview mirror romance / The doctor / Are you lonely tonight / Name of the game / Kiss me red / Take me to the top / Good girls go to heaven (bad girls go everywhere) / Man-u-lip-u-later / It's only love. *(cd-iss. May87; CDEPC 57087)*
Nov 86. (7") *<06540>* **IT'S ONLY LOVE. / NAME OF THE GAME** –

—— **TOM PETERSSON** – bass, vocals returned to repl. BRANT

May 88. (7"/7"sha-pic-d) *(651466-7/-0) <07745>* **THE FLAME. / THROUGH THE NIGHT** Apr88 1
(12"+=/cd-s+=) *(EPC 651466-6/-2)* – I want you to want me / If you want my love. *<re-iss. Dec88; 73792>*
May 88. (lp/c/cd) *(460782-1/-4/-2) <40922>* **LAP OF LUXURY** 18
– Let go / No mercy/ The flame / Space / Never had a lot to lose / Don't be cruel / Wrong side of love / All we need is a dream / Ghost town / All wound up. *(re-iss. cd Oct93 on 'Sony Europe'; 982839-2)*
Aug 88. (7"/7"sha-pic-d) *(652896-7/-0) <07965>* **DON'T BE CRUEL. / I KNOW WHAT I WANT** Jul88 4
(12"+=/cd-s+=) *(652896-6/-2)* – California man / Ain't that a shame.
(3"cd-s+=) *(653005-3)* – Dream police / Way of the world.
Oct 88. (7"/c-s) *<08097>* **GHOST TOWN. / WRONG SIDE OF LOVE** – 33
Jan 89. (7"/c-s) *<68563>* **NEVER HAD A LOT TO LOSE. / ALL WE NEED IS A DREAM** – 75

—— In Feb89, ZANDER dueted with Heart's ANN WILSON on US Top 10 single 'SURRENDER TO ME'.

Aug 90. (7"/c-s) *(656148-7/-4) <73444>* **CAN'T STOP FALLIN' INTO LOVE. / YOU DRIVE, I'LL STEER** Jul90 12
(12"+=/cd-s+=) *(656148-6/-2)* – The flame.
Sep 90. (cd/c/lp) *(466876-2/-4/-1) <46013>* **BUSTED** Jul90 48
– Back 'n blue / I can't understand it / Wherever would I be / If you need me / Can't stop falling into love / Busted / Walk away / You drive, I'll steer / When you need someone / Had to make you mine / Rock'n'roll tonight.
Sep 90. (7"/c-s; w-drawn) *<73566>* **IF YOU NEED ME. / BIG BANG** –
Oct 90. (7"/c-s) *<73580>* **WHEREVER WOULD I BE. / BUSTED** – 50
Oct 91. (cd/c) *(469086-2/-4) <48681>* **THE GREATEST HITS** (compilation)
– Magical mystery tour / Dream police / Don't be cruel / Tonight it's you / She's tight / I want you to want me (live) / If you want my love / Ain't that a shame / Surrender / The flame / I can't take it / Can't stop fallin' into love / Voices *(re-iss. May94; same)*

—— ROBIN ZANDER issued an eponymous solo set in '93

Warners Warners
Mar 94. (cd/c) *<(9362 45425-2/-4)>* **WOKE UP WITH A MONSTER**
– My gang / Woke up with a monster / You're all I wanna do / Never run out of love / Didn't know I had it / Ride the pony / Girlfriends / Let her go / Tell me everything / Cry baby / Love me for a minute.
Sub Pop Sub Pop
Mar 97. (7") *<(SP 393)>* **BABY TALK. / BRONTOSAURUS**
Red Ant Red Ant
Jun 97. (cd-ep) *<(RAAX 1001)>* **SAY GOODBYE / YEAH YEAH / VOICES (live) / SURRENDER (live)**
Jun 97. (cd) *<(RAACD 002)>* **CHEAP TRICK** Apr97 99
– Anytime / Hard to tell / Carnival game / Shelter / You let a lotta people down / Baby no more / Yeah yeah / Say goodbye / Wrong all along / Eight miles low / It all comes back to you.
Cheap Trick Cheap Trick
Jul 99. (cd) *<(CTU 20001)>* **MUSIC FOR HANGOVERS (live)** Jun99
– Oh Claire / Surrender / Hot love / I can't take it / I want you to want me / Taxman, Mr. Thief / Mandocello / Oh Caroline / How are you? / If you want my love / Dream police / So good to see you / The ballad of TV violence (I'm not the . . .) / Gonna raise hell.
not iss. J.V.C.
Feb 01. (d-cd) *<2001>* **SILVER** (live August 28, 1999) – Japan –
– Ain't that a shame / I want you to want me / Oh, Candy / That 70's song / Voices / If you want my love / She's tight / Can't stop fallin' into love / Gonna raise hell / I can't take it / It all comes back to you / Tonight it's you / Time will let you know / World's greatest lover / The flame / Stop this game / Dream police / I know what I want / Woke up with a monster / Never had a lot to lose / You're all talk / I'm losin' you / Hard to tell / Oh Claire / Surrender / Just got back / Day tripper / Who d'king.
C.T.U. Big 3
Jun 04. (cd) *(CTU 333-2) <36768>* **SPECIAL ONE**
– Scent of a woman / Too much / Special one / Pop drone / My obsession / Words / Sorry boy / Best friend / If I could / Low life in high heels / Hummer. *(UK+=)* – (DVD tracks).
S.P.V. Big 3
Jun 06. (cd) *<36788>* **ROCKFORD**
– Welcome to the world / Perfect stranger / If it takes a lifetime / Come on come on come on / O Claire / This time you got it / Give it away / One more / Every night and every day / Dream the night away / All those years / Decaf.

– compilations etc. –

Apr 80. (10"m-lp) *Epic; <36453>* **FOUND ALL THE PARTS (rare '76-'79)** – 39
– Day tripper (live) / Can't hold on / Such a good girl / Take me I'm yours.
Oct 91. (cd/c) *Castle; (CCS CD/MC 309)* **THE COLLECTION** –
Feb 94. (cd) *Epic; <EK 53308>* **BUDOKAN II (live)** –

Aug 96. (4xcd-box) *Columbia; <(E4K 649384)>* **SEX, AMERICA, CHEAP TRICK**
(re-iss. Oct01 on 'Sony'; 504493-2)>
May 98. (d-cd) *Columbia; (489650-2) <65527>* **AT THE BUDOKAN – THE COMPLETE CONCERT** Apr98
Nov 98. (cd) *Sony; <2820>* **DON'T BE CRUEL** –
Sep 00. (cd) *Epic; (499660-2)* **CHEAP TRICK / IN COLOR** –
Oct 00. (cd) *Epic; (499677-2) <66015>* **THE AUTHORISED GREATEST HITS**

ROBIN ZANDER

— with numerous session people

Interscope Interscope

Aug 93. (c-s) *(A 8386C)* **I'VE ALWAYS GOT YOU / STONE COLD RHYTHM SHAKE** –
(cd-s+=) *(A 8386CD)* – Everlasting love.
Sep 93. (cd/c) *<(6544 92204-2/-4)>* **ROBIN ZANDER**
– Reactionary girl / I've always got you / Show me Heaven / Jump into the fire / Time will let you know / Boy (I'm so in love with you) / Tell it to the world / Emily / I believe in you / Secret / Everlasting love / Walkin' shoes.

the CHEMICAL BROTHERS

Formed: North London, England . . . 1989 by DJ's ED SIMONS and TOM ROWLANDS (the latter had been part of 'Deconstruction' act, ARIEL, who released one single, 'ROLLERCOASTER'). The pair had met at Manchester University, and, discovering a shared love of techno and classic hip hop, they set about creating their own club night, 'NAKED UNDER LEATHER'. The logical next step was to cut their own record and with 'SONG TO THE SIREN', they successfully blended their myriad influences into an abrasive chunk of freak-beat techno. Wildly impressed, 'Junior Boys Own' maestro ANDY WEATHERALL released the single in early 1993, the more discerning underground D.J.'s of the time caning the track at club nights across the country. The record was credited to the DUST BROTHERS, the name SIMONS and ROWLANDS assumed for their DJ work. Later the same year, they released the 'Fourteenth Century Sky' EP which included the definitive 'CHEMICAL BEATS'. 'MY MERCURY MOUTH' from the 1994 EP of the same name was equally impressive and by this point the DUST BROTHERS had become one of the hippest name-drops among the dance cognoscenti. Their seminal reworking of SAINT ETIENNE's 'Like A Motorway', together with a DJ spot on PRIMAL SCREAM's 1994 tour further increased their profile and it wasn't long before the major record labels came sniffing round. Signing to 'Virgin', they released 'LEAVE HOME' in 1995, following it up with the top ten debut album, 'EXIT PLANET DUST'. The duo were now trading under the moniker of the CHEMICAL BROTHERS following objections from the DUST BROTHERS (U.S), a highly rated hip hop production team (Responsible for the BEASTIE BOYS' classic, 'Paul's Boutique'). For the most part, the debut was an unrelenting, exhilarating, rollercoaster ride of breakbeat techno, only letting up on 'ALIVE: ALONE' (featuring a BETH ORTON vocal) and the TIM BURGESS (of CHARLATANS fame) collaboration, 'LIFE IS SWEET'. The 'LOOPS OF FURY EP' was as uncompromising as the title suggests while the 'SETTING SUN' (featuring NOEL GALLAGHER on vocals) single gave the CHEMICALS' their first No.1 later that year. The track featured a 'TOMORROW NEVER KNOWS'-style rhythm pattern, the follow-up album, 'DIG YOUR OWN HOLE' (1997), similarly psychedelic in its reach. Using samples from 60's theramin pioneers LOTHAR AND THE HAND PEOPLE, and featuring a guest spot from MERCURY REV's JONATHAN DONOHUE, the album was more thrillingly diverse than the debut. With a mindbending live show, universal critical acclaim and even a burgeoning Stateside career, the CHEMICAL BROTHERS could do no wrong. After initiating their own record label, 'Freestyle Dust' (which released DJ-styled set, 'BROTHER'S GONNA WORK IT OUT'), ROWLANDS and SIMONS were back with a third album, 'SURRENDER' (1999). Featuring guest vocals by NOEL GALLAGHER (on Top 10 hit, 'LET FOREVER BE'), BERNARD SUMNER (on 'OUT OF CONTROL'), BOBBY GILLESPIE (on 'UNDER THE INFLUENCE'), HOPE SANDOVAL (on 'ASLEEP FROM DAY') and JONATHAN DONAHUE (on 'DREAM ON'), the album crashed into the charts at No.1 and even cracked America by making the Top 40. Following in the back to basics vein of the 'MUSIC RESPONSE' EP, 2002's 'COME WITH US' was the sound of The 'BROTHERS stepping off the celebrity podium. Or at least stepping off long enough to concoct the kind of heavy duty science which made them so great in the first place. While the by now predictable guest slots from the likes of BETH ORTON and RICHARD ASHCROFT threatened to dilute the album's overall impact, the sonic momentum of tracks such as 'GALAXY BOUNCE' and 'IT BEGAN IN AFRIKA' carried it off blindingly. More interesting was the FLAMING LIPS collaboration featured on 'SINGLES 93-03' (2003), a collection which could've been more sympathetically curated. With their fourth No.1 album in succession, 'PUSH THE BUTTON' (2005), the 'BROTHERS once again proved themselves a twisted nerve centre of contemporary beat-culture, plugging into collaborators as diverse as Q-TIP (the Top 3 hip-hop arabesque of opener 'GALVANISE') and BLOC PARTY's KELE OKEREKE's (the storming disco fever and test-transmission pulse of Top 20 hit, 'BELIEVE'), and nailing punk-funk on 'THE BIG JUMP'; only 'COME INSIDE' relied on the whooshing dynamics of old.

• **Songwriters:** ROWLANDS-SIMONS except samples of Blake Baxters 'Brothers Gonna Work It Out' on 'LEAVE HOME'. Borrowed SWALLOW's; 'Peekaboo' & 'Follow Me Down'.

Album rating: EXIT PLANET DUST (*9) / DIG YOUR OWN HOLE (*9) / SURRENDER (*8) / COME WITH US (*7) / SINGLES 93-03 compilation (*8) / PUSH THE BUTTON (*6)

DUST BROTHERS

TOM ROWLANDS (b.11 Jan'71, Kingston upon Thames, Surrey, England) – keyboards / **ED SIMONS** (b. 9 Jun'70, Oxford, England) – synthesizers, etc

Junior Boys Own not iss.

1993. (12") *(JBO 10)* **SONG TO THE SIREN. / SONG TO THE SIREN (Sabres Of Paradise mixes)** –
1993. (12"ep) *(COLLECT 004)* **FOURTEENTH CENTURY SKY EP** –
– Chemical beats / One too many mornings / Dope coil / Her jazz.
(above issued on 'Boys Own')
May 94. (12"ep) *(JBO 20)* **MY MERCURY MOUTH EP** –
– My mercury mouth / If you kling to me I'll klong to you / Dust-up beats.

the CHEMICAL BROTHERS

TOM ROWLANDS + **ED SIMONS** with voices by **TIM BURGESS** (CHARLATANS) + **BETH ORTON** (solo artist)

Virgin AstralWerks

Jun 95. (12") *(CHEMST 1) <6167>* **LEAVE HOME (Sabres Of Paradise mix). / LET ME IN MATE** 17 Sep95
(12") *(CHEMSTX 1)* – ('A'-Underworld mixes).
(cd-s) *(CHEMSD 1)* – (all above except 'Let Me In Mate')
Jun 95. (cd/c/d-lp) *(XDUST CD/MC/LP 1) <6157>* **EXIT PLANET DUST** 9 Aug95
– Leave home / In dust we trust / Song to he siren / Three little birdies down beats / Fuck up beats / Chemical beats / Chico's groove / One too many mornings / Life is sweet / Playground for a wedgeless firm / Alive alone.
Aug 95. (12") *(CHEMSD 2)* **LIFE IS SWEET. / ('A'-Daft Punk remix) / ('A'-remix 1) / ('A'-remix 2)** 25 –
(cd-s) *(CHEMSD 2)* – ('A'-remix 1, repl.by) Leave home (terror drums).
(cd-s) *(CHEMSDX 2)* – ('A'remix 1) / If you kling to me I'll klong to you / Chico's groove (mix 2).

Jan 96. (12"ep/cd-ep) *(CHEMS T/D 3) <6174>* **LOOPS OF FURY EP** 13
– Chemical beats (Dave Clarke remix) / Loops of fury / (The best part of) Breaking up / Get up on it like this.

Oct 96. (c-s/12"/cd-s) *(CHEMS C/T/D 4) <6187>* **SETTING SUN. / ('A'extended & instrumental mixes) / BUZZ TRACKS** 1 Jan97 80
above featured NOEL GALLAGHER (Oasis) on vocals/ co-writer

Mar 97. (12"/cd-s) *(CHEMS T/D 5) <6195>* **BLOCK ROCKIN' BEATS. / PRESCRIPTION BEATS / MORNING LEMON** 1
(cd-s) *(CHEMSDX 5)* – ('A'mixes).

Apr 97. (cd/c/d-lp) *(XDUST CD/MC/LP 2) <6180>* **DIG YOUR OWN HOLE** 1 14
– Block rockin' beats / Dig your own hole / Elektrobank / Piku / Setting sun / It doesn't matter / Don't stop the rock / Get up on it like this / Lost in the k-hole / Where do I begin / The private psychedelic reel.

Sep 97. (12") *(CHEMST 6) <6204>* **ELEKTROBANK. / NOT ANOTHER DRUGSTORE / ('A'-Dust Brothers remix)** 17
(cd-s+=) *(CHEMSD 6)* – Don't stop the rock (electronic version).
(cd-s+=) *(CHEMSDX 6)* – These seats are made for breakin'.

Dec 97. (ltd;12"/cd-s) *(CHEMS T/DX 7)* **THE PRIVATE PSYCHEDELIC REEL. / SETTING SON (live)** –

Sep 98. (cd/c) *(XDUST CDX 101) <6243>* **BROTHER'S GONNA WORK IT OUT: A DJ REMIX ALBUM** 7 95

May 99. (c-s/12"/cd-s) *(CHEMS C/D/T 8)* **HEY BOY HEY GIRL. / FLASHBACK / SCALE** 3

Jun 99. (cd/c/lp) *(XDUST CD/MC/LP 4) <47610>* **SURRENDER** 1 32
– Music: response / Under the influence / Out of control / Orange wedge / Let forever be / The sunshine underground / Asleep from day / Got glint? / Hey boy hey girl / Surrender / Dream on.

Aug 99. (7"/c-s) *(CHEMS LH/C 9)* **LET FOREVER BE. / ('A'-album version)** 9 –
(12"/cd-s) *(CHEMS T/D 9)* – ('A'side) / Diamond sky / Studio K.

Oct 99. (c-s/cd-s) *(CHEMS C/D 10)* **OUT OF CONTROL / POWER MOVE / OUT OF CONTROL (Sasha remix)** 21 –
(12") *(CHEMST 10)* – ('A'mixes).

Nov 00. (cd-ep) *<VIR 38751>* **MUSIC: RESPONSE EP** –
– Music: response / Freak of the week / Enjoyed / Music: response / Music: response / Out of control / Got glint?

Sep 01. (c-s) *(CHEMSC 12) <ASW 38798>* **IT BEGAN IN AFRIKA / IT BEGAN IN AFRIKA (extended)** 8 Oct01
(12"+=/cd-s+=) *(CHEMS T/D 12)* – Hot acid rhythm 1.

Jan 02. (12") *(CHEMST 14)* **STAR GUITAR. / STAR GUITAR (Pete Heller expanded)** 8 –
(cd-s) *(CHEMSD 14)* – ('A'-edit) / Base 6.

Jan 02. (cd/d-lp) *(XDUST CD/LP 5) <11682>* **COME WITH US** 1 32
– Come with us / It began in Afrika / Galaxy bounce / Star guitar / Hoops / My elastic eye / The state we're in (with BETH ORTON) / Denmark / Pioneer skies / The test (with RICHARD ASHCROFT). *(extra cd; XDUSTCDX 5)*

Apr 02. (12") *(CHEMST 15)* **COME WITH US. / H.I.A.** 14 –
(cd-s) *(CHEMSD 15)* – ('A'edit) / The test (edit) / ('A'-Fatboy Slim remix).

Sep 03. (12"; by CHEMICAL BROTHERS / FLAMING LIPS) *(CHEMST 18)* **THE GOLDEN PATH. / NUDE NIGHT** 17 –
(cd-s+=) *(CHEMSD 18)* – ('A'-Ewan Pearson extended vocal mix).

Sep 03. (cd/4xlp) *(XDUST CD/LP 6) <93142>* **SINGLES 93-03** (compilation) 9
– Song to the siren / Chemical beats / Leave home / Setting sun (with NOEL GALLAGHER) / Block rockin' beats / The private psychedelic reel / Hey boy hey girl / Let forever be / Out of control / Star guitar / The test / Get yourself high / The golden path (with FLAMING LIPS). *(d-cd+=; XDUSTCDX 6)* – Not another drugstore (Planet Nine remix with ONE INCH PUNCH) / The duke / If you kling to me I'll klong to you / Otter rock / Morning lemon / Galaxy bounce / Loops of fury / Delik / Elektrobank (live from the Roxy NYC November 1996) / Under the influence (mix 2) / Piku playground (live).

Jan 05. (cd-s) *(CHEMSD 21)* **GALVANIZE / RIZE UP** 3
(12") *(CHEMST 21)* – ('A'-extended) / Electronic battle weapon 7.
(cd-s+=) *(CHEMSDX 21)* – ('A'-video).
(cd-s) *<76599>* – (UK cd tracks) / Electronic battle weapon 7.

Jan 05. (cd/lp) *(XDUST CD/LP 7) <63282/63331>* **PUSH THE BUTTON** 1 59
– Galvanize / The boxer / Believe / Hold tight London / Come inside / The big jump / Left right / Close your eyes / Shake break bounce / Marvo Ging / Surface to air.

May 05. (cd-s) *(CHEMSD 22)* **BELIEVE / GIANT** 18 –
(ext.12"+=) *(CHEMST 22)* – Galvanize (Abe Duque remix).
(ext.cd-s) *(CHEMSDX 22)* – ('A') / Spring / ('A'-Erol Aiken 'Fell Me' re-work) / ('A'-video).

Jul 05. (cd-s) *(CHEMSD 23)* **THE BOXER / SWIPER** 41
(12"+=) *(CHEMST 23)* – ('A'-DFA extended re-wiring).
(cd-s) *(CHEMSDX 23)* – ('A') / ('A'-DFA version) / Believe (live at the Milano Forum) / ('A'-video).
(cd-s+=) *<72949>* – Giant / Spring / Believe (Mathew Jonson remix) / Believe (Erol Alkan's 'Fell Me' re-work) / Galvanize (Abe Duque remix).

– collections, etc. –

Oct 02. (d-cd) *Freestyle Dust; (812901-2)* **DIG YOUR OWN HOLE / EXIT PLANET DUST** –
(re-iss. Sep04; VBX 12)

Sep 04. (d-cd) *Freestyle Dust; (VBX 11)* **COME WITH US / SURRENDER**

CHER

Born: CHERILYN SARKASIAN LA PIER, 20 May'46, El Centro, California, USA. Relocating to L.A. in her late teens, the would-be actress fell in with SONNY BONO and had her first taste of the music business singing backup on PHIL SPECTOR sessions, the production maestro subsequently issuing her BEATLES tribute, 'RINGO I LOVE YOU' on his own 'Annette' label in 1964. She married BONO the same year and the pair proceeded to cut a handful of unsuccessful duets as CAESAR & CLEO for the small 'Vault' imprint. Playing alongside British invasion acts like The DAVE CLARK FIVE and HERMAN'S HERMITS, the duo were eventually picked up by 'Reprise' for a couple of singles, 'JUST YOU' and 'BABY DON'T GO'. These flopped upon initial release and the couple (renamed SONNY and CHER) moved on to 'Atco' where they hit paydirt in summer '65 with 'I GOT YOU BABE', a transatlantic No.1 marrying the cutesy pop appeal of the SPECTOR era to the new folk-rock sensibility of hip Hollywood. Decked out in garish hippie garb, the incongruous couple became the love generation darlings of Sunset Strip and 'Imperial' signed up CHER for a solo deal. Although her debut (as CHERILYN), 'DREAM BABY' had stiffed earlier in the year, her cover of Bob Dylan's 'ALL I REALLY WANT TO DO' competed with The BYRDS' version of the same song that summer while her Top 20 (Top 10 UK) album of the same name featured yet more DYLAN material. Meanwhile, the SONNY & CHER album, 'LOOK AT US' (1965) narrowly missed the US No.1 spot and over the course of the ensuing decade or so, CHER attempted (not always successfully) to maintain a solo career in tandem with her SONNY partnership. Her predeliction for cringeing puns was revealed with 'THE SONNY SIDE OF CHER' (1966), an album that spawned one of her biggest solo hits (transatlantic No.3), 'BANG BANG (MY BABY SHOT ME DOWN). 1966-67 proved rockier but CHER was back in the Top 10 in 1968 with 'YOU BETTER SIT DOWN KIDS'. This signalled the end of her tenure with 'Imperial' and she moved on to 'Atco' for a commercially bleak couple of years before her early-mid 70's revival. Her success with SONNY followed the same pattern and after 1967's 'THE BEAT GOES ON', it'd be a further four years before the duo racked up another Top 10 hit with 'ALL I EVER NEED IS YOU'. By this point both had signed to 'Kapp' ('M.C.A.' in Britain), churning out rubbish like 'A COWBOY'S WORK IS NEVER DONE'. The latter proved to be their last Top 10 hit and after a final couple of singles on 'Warners', the couple ended both their creative and marital partnership, divorcing on the 26th of June 1974. CHER's solo career, meanwhile, had been rekindled with a 1971 US No.1 hit, 'GYPSYS, TRAMPS & THIEVES', her charismatic half-Cherokee identity melodramatically stamped over further No.1's, 'HALF-BREED' and 'DARK LADY'. A matter of days after her divorce from BONO she married GREG ALLMAN ith whom she recorded the execrable 'ALLMAN AND WOMAN: WO THE HARD WAY' (1977). Her critical stock was hardly nproved with her opportunistic disco effort, 'TAKE ME HOME' 1979) although it did put her back in the US Top 10. Newly signed) decadent disco/KISS stronghold, 'Casablanca', CHER followed p with an attempt at heavy rock/metal the following year with the 3LACK ROSE' album (also billed as BLACK ROSE). By this point ie'd divorced ALLMAN and was dating ex-STEVE MILLER BAND uitarist, LES DUDEK, who both played on and produced the latter :t. Unsurprisingly it sank without trace and CHER moved on once nore to 'Columbia' where she cut one album, 'I PARALYZE'(!), efore turning her attention to film work. Although she was a eteran of the TV chat show (having hosted both a SONNY & CHER nd solo version in the 60's/70's), a Broadway appearance in Robert ltman's 'Come Back To The Five And Dime, Jimmy Dean, Jimmy ean' led to roles in 80's movies like 'Silkwood', 'Mask', 'Witches f Eastwick', 'Moonstruck' (for which she netted an Oscar) and uspect'. With her profile sufficiently raised, the mainstream late 0's resurgence of soft rock/AOR/metal was a perfect vehicle for HER's commercial comeback; newly signed to 'Geffen', she hit ie Top 10 in 1987 with "power-ballad", 'I FOUND SOMEONE'. US Top 10 duet with PETER CETERA, 'AFTER ALL', spurred on ie success of 1989's 'HEART OF STONE' album and its US Top hit, 'IF I COULD TURN BACK TIME'. More tortuous Top 10 orch balladry followed with 'JUST LIKE JESSE JAMES' although HER saved her most cloying material 'til last; taken from the film, Aermaids' (in which she starred), 'THE SHOOP SHOOP SONG T'S IN HIS KISS)' gave CHER her first solo UK No.1 in 1991. acked onto the 'LOVE HURTS' (1991) album, the song's massive opularity even pushed the album itself to No.1 and CHER enjoyed British popularity previously unwitnessed. A 1992 greatest hits :t gave her another UK No.1 while a reworking of 'I GOT YOU ABE' with the inimitable BEAVIS & BUTT-HEAD proved she : least had a sense of humour under all the histrionics. She was ack at No.1 again in 1995 alongside CHRISSIE HYNDE, NENEH HERRY and ERIC CLAPTON with the Comic Relief charity song, OVE CAN BUILD A BRIDGE'. A year later, her comeback set, T'S A MAN'S WORLD', stalled at No.10 and faired even worse the States. Tragedy was to strike early in '98 (January 5th) when er ex-husband and recently elected politician SONNY BONO died istantly after hitting a tree during a skiing trip. Later that year, HER was to gain some consolation when she scored a massive est-selling UK No.1 with 'BELIEVE' (later to do the same in merica). If Christmas 1999's greatest hits set didn't convince you ien 'LIVING PROOF' (2001) was indeed, er, living proof that the vergreen CHER has got more than a little music biz mileage left her yet. She may have a few years on MADONNA but the club-iendly grooves confirmed her newest incarnation as dance-pop iva.

Covered: BLOWIN' IN THE WIND + LIKE A ROLLING STONE (Bob ylan) / ALFIE (hit: Cilla Black) / SONNY (Bobby Hebb) / DARK LADY ohnny Durill) / GYPSYS, TRAMPS AND THIEVES (Robert Stone) / HALF-REED (Mary Dean & Al Capps) / NEEDLES AND PINS (Searchers) / 'S NOT UNUSUAL (hit; Tom Jones) / TWELTH OF NEVER (Johnny Aathis) / ELUSIVE BUTTERFLY (Bob Lind) / UNTIL IT'S TIME FOR YOU O GO (Elvis Presley) / CATCH THE WIND (Donovan) / PIED PIPER Crispan St. Peters) / YOU DON'T HAVE TO SAY YO LOVE ME (Dusty pringfield) / GIRL FROM IPANEMA (Stan Getz) / OUR DAY WILL COME Ruby & The Romantics) / OLD MAN RIVER (Paul Robeson) / I WALK ON ILDED SPLINTERS (Dr.John) / FOR WHAT IT'S IT'S WORTH (Buffalo pringfield) / BABY I LOVE YOU (Ronettes) / LOVE HURTS (Everly rothers) / I FOUND SOMEONE (Michael Bolton-Mark Mangold) / WE LL SLEEP ALONE (Bon Jovi-Child) / OH NO NOT MY BABY (Goffin-ing) / THE SHOOP SHOOP SONG (IT'S IN HIS KISS) (Rudy Clark) / round this time in the 90's, DESMOND CHILD & DIANE WARREN wrote er material. HEART OF STONE (was originally written for BUCKS FIZZ! by Pete Sinfield & Andy Hill). • **Trivia:** In 1981, CHER dueted with MEAT LOAF on his 'Dead Ringer For Love' single. She appeared with SONNY on many TV specials in the 60's/70's.

Best CD compilation: THE VERY BEST OF CHER (*8)

CHER – vocals (with session people; no band at this time)

		Liberty	Imperial
Mar 65.	(7"; as CHERILYN) <66081> **DREAM BABY. / STAN QUETZEL**	–	
Jun 65.	(7") <(LIB 66114)> **ALL I REALLY WANT TO DO. / I'M GONNA LOVE YOU**	9	15
Sep 65.	(lp; stereo/mono) *(S+/LBY 3058)* <12292> **ALL I REALLY WANT TO DO**	7	16

– All I really want to do / I go to sleep / Needles and pins / Don't think twice / She thinks I still care / Dream baby / The bells of Rhymney / Girl don't come / See see rider / Come and stay with me / Cry myself to sleep / Blowin' in the wind.

Oct 65.	(7") <(LIB 66136)> **WHERE DO YOU GO. / SEE SEE RIDER**		25
Mar 66.	(7") <(LIB 66160)> **BANG BANG (MY BABY SHOT ME DOWN). / OUR DAY WILL COME**	3	2
May 66.	(lp; stereo/mono) *(S+/LBY 3072)* <12301> **THE SONNY SIDE OF CHER**	11	Apr66 26

– Bang bang (my baby shot me down) / Elusive butterfly / Where do you go / Our day will come / The girl from Ipanema / It's not unusual / Like a rolling stone / Time / Come to your window / Old man river / Milord / A young girl (une enfante).

Jul 66.	(7") *<LIB 66192>* **ALFIE. / SHE'S NO BETTER THAN ME**	–	32
Aug 66.	(7") *(LIB 12034)* **I FEEL SOMETHING IN THE AIR. / COME TO YOUR WINDOW**	43	–
Sep 66.	(7") *(LIB 12038)* **SUNNY. / SHE'S NO BETTER THAN ME**	32	–
Oct 66.	(lp; stereo/mono) *(S+/LBY 3081)* <12320> **CHER**		Sep66 59

– Sunny / Twelth of never / You don't have to say you love me / I feel something in the air (magic in the air) / Will you love me tomorrow / Until it's time for you to go / Cruel war / Catch the wind / Pied piper / Homeward bound / I want you / Alfie.

Nov 66.	(7") *(LIB 12038)* **MAMA (WHEN MY DOLLIES HAVE BABIES). / BEHIND THE DOOR**		–
Nov 66.	(7") <66217> **BEHIND THE DOOR. / MAGIC IN THE AIR**	–	97
Feb 67.	(7") <66223> **DREAM BABY. / MAMA (WHEN MY DOLLIES HAVE BABIES)**	–	
Aug 67.	(7") <66252> **HEY JOE. / OUR DAY WILL COME**	–	94
Oct 67.	(7") <66261> **YOU BETTER SIT DOWN KIDS. / MAMA (WHEN MY DOLLIES HAVE BABIES)**	–	9
Dec 67.	(lp; stereo/mono) *(LBS/LBL 83051)* <12358> **WITH LOVE – CHER**	47	Nov67

– You better sit down, kids / But I can't love you more / Hey Joe / Mama (when my dollies have babies) / Behind the door / Sing for your supper / Look at me / There but for fortune / I will wait for you / The times they are a-changin'.

Feb 68.	(7") *(LBF 15038)* **YOU BETTER SIT DOWN KIDS. / ELUSIVE BUTTERFLY**		9
Jun 68.	(7") <66282> **THE CLICK SONG NUMBER ONE. / BUT I CAN"T LOVE YOU MORE**	–	
Jul 68.	(lp; stereo/mono) *(LBS/LBL 83156)* <12373> **BACKSTAGE**		

– Go now / Carnival (manha de carnaval) (cancion de orfeo) / It all adds up now / Reason to believe / Masters of war / Do you believe in magic / I wasn't ready / A house is not a home / Take me for a little while / The impossible dream (the quest) / The click song number one / Song called children.

Sep 68.	(7") <66307> **TAKE ME FOR A LITTLE WHILE. / SONG CALLED CHILDREN**	–	

		Atlantic	Atco
Feb 69.	(7") <6658> **YOURS UNTIL TOMORROW. / THOUGHT OF LOVING YOU**	–	
Apr 69.	(7") <6684> **CHASTITY'S SONG (BAND OF THIEVES). / WALK ON GILDED SPLINTERS**	–	
Jun 69.	(7") *(584 278)* **WALK ON GILDED SPLINTERS. / TONIGHT I'LL BE STAYING HERE WITH YOU**		–
Jul 69.	(lp; mono/stereo) *(226/228 036)* <SD33 298> **3614 JACKSON HIGHWAY**		

– For what it's worth / (Just enough to keep me) Hangin' on / (Sittin' on) The dock of the bay / Tonight I'll be staying here with you / I threw it all away / Walk on guilded splinters / Lay baby lay / Please don't tell me / Cry like a baby / Do right woman, do right man / Save the children.

Atco — Atco

Sep 69. (7") *(226 003)* *<6704>* **FOR WHAT IT'S WORTH. / (JUST ENOUGH TO KEEP ME) HANGIN' ON** [ ] [ ]

Nov 69. (7") *<6713>* **YOU MADE ME SO VERY HAPPY. / FIRST TIME** [–] [ ]

Jun 70. (7") *<6793>* **SUPERSTAR. / FIRST TIME** [–] [ ]

Feb 71. (7") *<6868>* **LAY LADY LAY. / (JUST ENOUGH TO KEEP ME) HANGIN' ON** [–] [ ]

M.C.A. — Kapp

May 71. (7") *(MU 1137)* *<2134>* **CLASSIFIED 1A. / DON'T PUT IT ON ME** [ ] [ ]

Sep 71. (7") *(MU 1142)* *<2146>* **GYPSYS, TRAMPS AND THIEVES. / HE'LL NEVER KNOW** [4] [1]

Nov 71. (lp) *(MUPS 438)* *<3649>* **CHER** <US-title 'GYPSYS, TRAMPS & THIEVES'> [ ] [16]
– The way of love / Gypsys, tramps and thieves / He'll never know / Fire and rain / When you find out where you're goin' let me know / He ain't heavy, he's my brother / I hate to sleep alone / I'm in the middle / Touch and go / One honest man. *(re-iss. Aug81 on 'Music For Pleasure';)*

Jan 72. (7") *<2158>* **THE WAY OF LOVE. / DON'T PUT IT ON ME** [–] [7]

Feb 72. (7") *(MU 1148)* **THE WAY OF LOVE. / FIRE AND RAIN** [ ] [–]

Jun 72. (7") *(MU 1158)* *<2171>* **LIVING IN A HOUSE DIVIDED. / ONE HONEST MAN** [ ] May72 [22]

Aug 72. (lp) *(MUPS 459)* *<5514>* **FOXY LADY** [ ] Jul72 [43]
– Living in a house divided / It might as well stay Monday (from now on) / Song for you / Down, down, down / Don't try to close a rose / The first time / Let me down easy / If I knew then / Don't hide your love / Never been to Spain

Nov 72. (7") *(MU 1168)* *<2184>* **DON'T HIDE YOUR LOVE. / THE FIRST TIME** [ ] Sep72 [46]

M.C.A. — M.C.A.

May 73. (lp) *(MUPS 484)* *<2101>* **BITTERSWEET WHITE LIGHT** [ ] Apr73 [ ]
– By myself / I got it bad and that ain't good / Am I blue / How long has this been going on / The man I love / Jolson medley: Sonny boy – My mammy – Rock-a-bye your baby with a Dixie melody / More than you know / Why was I born / The man that got away.

Jun 73. (7") *(MU 1196)* *<40039>* **AM I BLUE. / HOW LONG WAS THIS BEEN GOING ON** [ ] May73 [ ]

Aug 73. (7") *(MU 1215)* *<40102>* **HALF-BREED. / MELODY** [ ] Jul73 [1]

Oct 73. (lp) *(MCF 2501)* *<2104>* **HALF-BREED** [ ] Sep73 [28]
– My love / Two people clinging to a thread / Half-breed / The greatest song I ever heard / How can you mend a broken heart / Carousel man / David's song / Melody / The long and winding road / This God-forsaken day / Ruby Jean & Billie Lee. *<US = last track repl. by>* – Chastity sun.

Jan 74. (7") *(MCA 101)* *<40161>* **DARK LADY. / TWO PEOPLE CLINGING TO A THREAD** [36] [1]

May 74. (7") *(MCA 140)* *<40245>* **TRAIN OF THOUGHT. / DIXIE GIRL** [ ] [27]

Jun 74. (lp) *(MCF 2559)* *<2113>* **DARK LADY** [ ] May74 [69]
– Train of thought / I saw a man and he danced with his wife / Make the man love me / Just what I've been lookin' for / Dark lady / Miss Subway of 1952 / Dixie girl / Rescue me / What'll I do (from The Great Gatsby) / Apples don't fall from the tree.

Aug 74. (7") *(MCA 152)* *<40273>* **I SAW A MAN AND HE DANCED WITH HIS WIFE. / I HATE TO SLEEP ALONE** [ ] [42]

Apr 75. (7") *(MCA 188)* **RESCUE ME. / DIXIE GIRL** [ ] [–]

Warners — Warners

May 75. (lp) *(K 56111)* *<2850>* **STARS** [ ] [ ]
– Love enough / Bell bottom blues / These days / Mr. Soul / Just this one time / Geronimo's Cadillac / The bigger they come the harder they fall / Love hurts / Rock and roll doctor / Stars.

Jun 75. (7") *<8096>* **GERONIMO'S CADILLAC. / THESE DAYS** [–] [ ]

Phil Spector Int. — Warner Spector

Jul 75. (7"; CHER & NILSSON) *(2010 006)* *<402>* **A LOVE LIKE YOURS (DON'T COME KNOCKING EVERY DAY). / (JUST ENOUGH TO KEEP ME) HANGIN' ON** [ ] Apr75 [ ]

Mar 76. (7") *(2010 013)* *<400>* **A WOMAN'S STORY. / BABY I LOVE YOU** [ ] Feb75 [ ]

Oct 76. (7") *<8263>* **LONG DISTANCE LOVE AFFAIR. / BORROWED TIME** [–] [ ]

Oct 76. (lp) *(K 56292)* *<BS 2898>* **I'D RATHER BELIEVE IN YOU** [ ] [ ]
– Long distance love affair / I'd rather believe in you / I know (you don love me) / Silver wings and golden rings / Flashback / It's a cryin' shame Early morning strangers / Knock on wood / Spring / Borrowed time.

Jan 77. (7") *<8311>* **PIRATE. / SEND THE MAN OVER** [–] [93]

Apr 77. (lp) *(K 56401)* *<3046>* **CHERISHED** [ ] [ ]
– Pirate / He was beautiful / War paint and soft feathers / Love the de out of ya / She loves to hear the music / L.A. plane / Again / Dixie / Ser the man over / Thunderstorm.

May 77. (7") *(8366)* **WAR PAINT AND SOFT FEATHERS. / SEND THE MAN OVER** [–] [ ]

— CHER collaborated with husband GREGG ALLMAN late '77 on lp, 'TW THE HARD WAY' and the single, 'LOVE ME' / 'MOVE ME'.

Casablanca — Casabl

Mar 79. (7") *(CAN 147)* *<965>* **TAKE ME HOME. / MY SONG (TOO FAR GONE)** [ ] Feb79 [8]

Apr 79. (lp/c) *(CAL/ACCAN 2047)* *<7133>* **TAKE ME HOME** [ ] Feb79 [25]
– Take me home / Wasn't it good / Say the word / Happy was the day w met / Git down (guitar groupie) / Pain in my heart / Let this be a lessc to you / It's too late to love me now / My song (too far gone).

Jul 79. (7") *(CAN 156)* *<987>* **WASN'T IT GOOD. / IT'S TOO LATE TO LOVE ME NOW** [ ] May79 [49]
(12") *(CANL 156)* – ('A'side) / Take me home.

Oct 79. (7"/12") *(CAN/+L 164)* *<2208>* **HELL ON WHEELS. / GIT DOWN (GUITAR GROUPIE)** [ ] Sep79 [59]

Mar 80. (lp) *<(NBLP 7184)>* **PRISONER** [ ] Oct79 [ ]
– Prisoner / Holdin' out for love / Shoppin' / Boys and girls / Mirr image / Hell on wheels / Holy smoke / Outrageous.

Mar 80. (7") *(CAN 185)* **IT'S TOO LATE TO LEAVE ME NOW. / SHOPPIN'** [ ] [–]

Mar 80. (7") *<2228>* **HOLDING OUT FOR LOVE. / BOYS AND GIRLS** [–] [ ]

Mar 82. (7") *(CAN 1009)* **HOLDIN' OUT FOR LOVE. / OUTRAGEOUS** [ ] [–]

BLACK ROSE

— **CHER** with boyfriend at the time **LES DUDEK** – guitar (ex-STEVE MILLE BAND) / **MIKE FINNEGAN** – keyboards, vocals / **GARY FURGASON** drums / **TREY THOMPSON** – bass / **RON RITCHOTTE** – guitar

Casablanca — Casabl

Nov 80. (7") *<2296>* **YOUNG AND PRETTY. / TAKE IT FROM THE BOYS** [–] [ ]

Nov 80. (lp) *<(NBLP 7234)>* **BLACK ROSE** [ ] [ ]
– Never should've started / Julie / Take it from the boys / We all fly home 88 degrees / You know it / Young and pretty / Fast company.

Feb 81. (7") *<2312>* **NEVER SHOULD'VE STARTED. / YOUNG AND PRETTY** [–] [ ]

— lack of success led the group to part

CHER

— went solo again (with various session people)

C.B.S. — Colum

Mar 82. (7") *(CBS 2227)* *<02850>* **RUDY. / DO I EVER CROSS YOUR MIND** [ ] [ ]

Aug 82. (7") *(CBS 2609)* *<03150>* **I PARALYZE. / WALK WITH ME** [ ] [ ]

Nov 82. (lp/c) *<(CBS/40 85850)>* **I PARALYZE** [ ] [ ]
– Rudy / Games / I paralyze / When the love is gone / Say what's on you mind / Back on the street again / Walks with me / The book of love / D I ever cross your mind. *(cd-iss. Jun99 on 'Varese Sarabande'; VSD 6039)*

— CHER turned to acting (full-time) and subsequently appeared i many films (see above Filmography); she was back in the charts i '87

Geffen — Geffe

Oct 87. (7"/7"pic-d) *(GEF 31/+P)* *<28191>* **I FOUND SOMEONE. / DANGEROUS TIMES** [5] [10]
(12"+=/12"pic-d+=) *(GEF 31T/+P)* – ('A'version).

Dec 87. (lp/c)(cd) *(WX 132/+C)(924164-2)* *<24164>* **CHER** [26] Nov87 [32]
– I found someone / We all sleep alone / Bang bang (my baby sh me down) / Main man / Give our love a fightin' chance / Perfection Dangerous times / Skin deep / Working girl / Hard enough getting ov

you. *(re-iss. Jan91 lp/c/cd; GEF/+C/D 24164) (re-iss. Mar93 cd/c; GFL D/C 24164) (cd re-iss. Nov96; GED 24164)*

Apr 88. (7") *(GEF 35)* *<27986>* **WE ALL SLEEP ALONE (remix). / WORKING GIRL** [47] [14]
(12"+=/12"pic-d+=/3"cd-s+=) *(GEF 35 T/TP/CD)* – I found someone.

Sep 88. (7") *(GEF 44)* *<27894>* **SKIN DEEP. / PERFECTION** [ ] Jul88 [79]
(ext-12"+=/cd-s+=) *(GEF 44 T/CD)* – ('A'dub version).

Dec 88. (7") *<27742>* **MAIN MAN. / HARD ENOUGH GETTING OVER YOU** [–] [ ]

May 89. (7"/c-s; by CHER & PETER CETERA) *(GEF 52/+C)* *<27529>* **AFTER ALL. / DANGEROUS TIMES** [ ] Mar89 [6]
(12"+=/cd-s+=) *(GEF 52 T/CD)* – I found someone / Main man.

Jul 89. (lp/c)(cd) *(WX 262/+C)(924239-2)* *<24239>* **HEART OF STONE** [7] [10]
– If I could turn back time / Just like Jesse James / You wouldn't know love / Heart of stone / Still in love with you / Love on a rooftop / Emotional fire / All because of you / Does anybody really fall in love anymore? / Starting over / Kiss to kiss / After all. *(re-iss. Jan91 lp/c/cd; GEF/+C/D 24239)*

Jul 89. (7"/c-s) *(GEF 59/+C)* *<22886>* **IF I COULD TURN BACK TIME. / SOME GUYS** [6] [3]
(12"+=) *(GEF 59T)* – Kiss to kiss.
(cd-s+=) *(GEF 59CD)* – ('A'remix) / ('A'rock guitar mix) / I found someone.

Jan 90. (7"/c-s) *(GEF 69/+C)* *<22844>* **JUST LIKE JESSE JAMES. / STARTING OVER** [11] Oct89 [8]
(12"+=/cd-s+=) *(GEF 69 T/CD)* – I found someone.

Mar 90. (7"/c-s) *(GEF 75/+C)* *<19953>* **HEART OF STONE. / ALL BECAUSE OF YOU** [43] Feb90 [20]
(12"+=/cd-s+=) *(GEF 75 T/CD)* – Working girl.

Jul 90. (7"/c-s) *(GEF 77/+C)* **YOU WOULDN'T KNOW LOVE. / KISS TO KISS** [55] [–]
(12"+=) *(GEF 77T)* – Bang bang / Heart of stone.
(7"ep/cd-ep) *(GEF 77 D/CD)* – ('A'side) / If I could turn back time / I found someone / We all sleep alone (remix).

Oct 90. (7"/c-s) *(GEF 84/+C)* **BABY I'M YOURS. / HARD ENOUGH GETTING OVER YOU** [ ] [–]
(12"+=/cd-s+=) *(GEF 84 T/CD)* – Just like Jesse James.

Nov 90. (7") *<19659>* **THE SHOOP SHOOP SONG (IT'S IN HIS KISS). / LOVE ON A ROOFTOP** [–] [33]

Apr 91. (7"/c-s) *(656673-7/-4)* **THE SHOOP SHOOP SONG (IT'S IN HIS KISS). / BABY I'M YOURS** [1] [–]
(12"+=/cd-s+=) *(656673-6/-2)* – We all sleep alone.
(above single from the film 'Mermaids' and released on 'Epic' UK & 'Geffen' US)

Jun 91. (lp/c/cd) *<(GEF/+C/CD 24427)>* **LOVE HURTS** [1] [48]
– Save up all your tears / Love hurts / Love and understanding / Fires of Eden / I'll never stop loving you / The shoop shoop song (it's in his kiss) / One small step / A world without heroes / Could've been you / When love calls your name / When lovers become strangers / Who you gonna believe. *(cd re-iss. Mar95; GFLD 19266)*

Jul 91. (7"/c-s) *(GFS 5/+C)* *<19023>* **LOVE AND UNDERSTANDING. / TRAIL OF BROKEN HEARTS** [10] Jun91 [17]
(12"+=/cd-s+=) *(GFS 5 T/CD)* – If I could turn back time.

Sep 91. (7"/c-s) *(GFS 11/+C)* *<19105>* **SAVE UP ALL YOUR TEARS. / A WORLD WITHOUT HEROES** [37] [37]
(12"+=/cd-s+=) *(GFS 11 T/CD)* – Love and understanding.

Nov 91. (7"/c-s) *(GFS 16/+C)* **LOVE HURTS. / ONE SMALL STEP** [43] [ ]
(12"+=/cd-s+=) *(GFS 16 T/CD)* – Just like Jesse James.

Mar 92. (7"/7"pic-d/c-s) *(GFS 19/+P/C)* **COULD'VE BEEN YOU. / LOVE AND UNDERSTANDING** [31] [ ]
(12"sha-pic-d+=/cd-s+=) *(GFS 19 T/CD)* – Save up all your tears.

Nov 92. (cd/c/d-lp) *<(GED/GEC/GEF 24439)>* **GREATEST HITS 1965-92** (compilation) [1] [ ]
– Oh no not my baby / Whenever you're near / Many rivers to cross (live) / Love and understanding / Save up all your tears / The shoop shoop song (it's in his kiss) / If I could turn back time / Just like Jesse James / Heart of stone / I found someone / We all sleep alone / Bang bang (my baby shot me down) (with SONNY) / Dead ringer for love (with MEAT LOAF) / Dark lady / Gypsys, tramps and thieves / I got you babe (with SONNY).

Nov 92. (7"/c-s) *(GFS 29/+C)* **OH NO NOT MY BABY. / LOVE HURTS** [33] [ ]
(cd-s+=) *(GFS 29TD)* – Love on a rooftop / Main man.

Jan 93. (7"/c-s) *(GFS 31/+C)* **MANY RIVERS TO CROSS. / WHO YOU GONNA BELIEVE** [37] [ ]
(cd-s+=) *(GFS 31TD)* –

Feb 93. (7"/c-s) *(GFS 32/+C)* **WHENEVER YOU'RE NEAR. / COULD'VE BEEN YOU** [72] [ ]
(12"pic-d+=/cd-s+=) *(GFS 32 TP/TD)* – You wouldn't know love / I'll never stop loving you.

Jan 94. (c-s/cd-s; by CHER with BEAVIS & BUTT-HEAD) *(GFS C/TD 64)* **I GOT YOU BABE. / Sonny & Cher: I GOT YOU BABE** [35] [ ]

— BEAVIS & BUTT-HEAD; cult TV cartoon characters who have already carved up a lot of parental hysteria by their use of foul language and violence. In March '95 – alongside CHRISSIE HYNDE, NENEH CHERRY and ERIC CLAPTON – she hit UK No.1 with charity Comic Relief song 'LOVE CAN BUILD A BRIDGE'.

WEA Reprise

Oct 95. (c-s) *(WEA 021C)* **WALKING IN MEMPHIS / THE FALL** [11] [ ]
(cd-s+=) *(WEA 021CD1)* – Angels running.
(cd-s) *(WEA 021CD2)* – ('A'-Shut up and dance instrumental) / ('A'mixes).

Nov 95. (cd/c) *(0630 12670-2/-4)* *<46179>* **IT'S A MAN'S WORLD** [28] [64]
– Walking in Memphis / Not enough love in the world / One by one / I wouldn't treat a dog (the way you treated me) / Angels running / Paradise is here / I'm blowin' away / Don't come around tonite / What about the moonlight / The same mistake / The gunman / The sun ain't gonna shine anymore / Shape of things to come / It's a man's, man's, man's world.

Jan 96. (c-s) *(WEA 032C)* **ONE BY ONE / WALKING IN MEMPHIS (mix)** [7] [–]
(12"+=/cd-s+=) *(WEA 032 T/CD)* – It's a man's world.

Apr 96. (c-s) *(WEA 032C)* **NOT ENOUGH LOVE IN THE WORLD / ONE BY ONE (Sam Ward mix)** [31] [ ]
(cd-s) *(WEA 032CD)* – ('A'side) / One by one (Jr. Vasquez mixes).

Jun 96. (c-s) *<17695>* **ONE BY ONE / I WOULDN'T TREAT A DOG (THE WAY YOU TREATED ME)** [–] [52]

Jul 96. (c-s) *(WEA 071C)* **THE SUN AIN'T GONNA SHINE ANYMORE / PARADISE IS HERE** [26] [ ]
(cd-s) *(WEA 071CD)* – Not enough love in the world (mix).

WEA Warners

Oct 98. (c-s/cd-s) *(WEA 175 C/CD)* *<44576>* **BELIEVE / ('A'mixes; Phat 'n' phunky / Club 69 phunk club / Almighty definitive)** [1] [1]
(12"+=/cd-s+=) *(WEA 175 T/CD2)* – ('A'mixes; Xenomania Mad Tim.. Club 69 future anthem / Grips heartbroken / + 3 dub).

Oct 98. (cd/c) *(3984 25319-2/-4)* *<47121>* **BELIEVE** [8] [4]
– Believe / The power / Runaway / All or nothing / Strong enough / Dov'e l'amore / Takin' back my heart / Taxi taxi / Love is the groove / We all sleep alone.

Feb 99. (c-s) *(WEA 201C)* *<44644>* **STRONG ENOUGH / ('A'mix)** [5] May99 [57]
(cd-s) *(WEA 201CD1)* – ('A'mixes; Club 69 / Pumpin' Dolls vocal epic / male / Club 69 phunk).
(cd-s) *(WEA 201CD2)* – ('A'mixes; Marc Andrews / Pumpin' Dolls cashmere / D-Bop melt / Club 69 phuture / Pumpin' Dolls radio).
(12") *(WEA 201T)* – ('A'mixes; some of above).

Jun 99. (c-s) *(WEA 212C)* **ALL OR NOTHING / STRONG ENOUGH (club)** [12] [–]
(cd-s+=) *(WEA 212CD1)* – ('A'-almighty mixes).
(cd-s) *(WEA 212CD2)* – ('A'-K-Klass mixes).

Oct 99. (c-s) *(WEA 230C)* **DOV'E L'AMORE / ('A'mix)** [21] [–]
(cd-s) *(WEA 230CD1)* – ('A'mixes).
(cd-s) *(WEA 230CD2)* – ('A'mixes).
(12") *(WEA 230T)* – ('A'mixes).

Nov 99. (cd/c) *(8573 80420-2/-4)* *<24509>* **GREATEST HITS** <US-title 'IF I COULD TURN BACK TIME – CHER'S GREATEST HITS'> (compilation) [7] Aug99 [57]
– Love and understanding / Save up all your tears / The shoop shoop song (it's in his kiss) / After all / If I could turn back time / Just like Jesse James / Heart of stone / I found someone / We all sleep alone / Bang bang / Take me home / Dark lady / Half-breed / The way of love / The way of love / Gypsys, tramps and thieves / I got you babe.

Nov 01. (c-s/cd-s) *(WEA 337 C/CD)* **THE MUSIC'S NO GOOD WITHOUT YOU / (extended) / DOV'A L'AMORE (Emilio Estefan Jr. extended)** [8] [ ]
(cd-s) *(WEA 337CDX)* – ('A'-extended radio) / ('A'-almighty 12" mix) / All or nothing (Danny Tenaglia international mix).

Nov 01. (cd/c) *<(0927 42463-2/-4)>* **LIVING PROOF** [46] Feb02 [ ]
– The music's no good without you / Alive again / This is a song for the lonely / Different kind of love song / Rain rain / Love so high / Body to body heart to heart / Love is a lonely place without you / Real love / Love one another / You take it all / When the money's gone.

WEA / Rhino

Nov 03. (cd) *(5046 68586-2)* *<R2 73852>* **THE VERY BEST OF CHER** (compilation) 17 Apr03 4
– Believe / If I could turn back time / Save up all your tears / Walking in Memphis / Shoop shoop song (it's in his kiss) / Love and understanding / I found someone / Just like Jesse James / One by one / Love can build a bridge (with CHRISSIE HYNDE & NENEH CHERRY) / Strong enough / All or nothing / A different kind of love song / Heart of stone / Music's no good without you / Dov'e l'amore (Emilio Estefan Jr. extended mix) / Gypsies, tramps and thieves / The beat goes on (SONNY & CHER) / I got you babe (SONNY & CHER) / All I really want to do / Bang bang (my baby shot me down) (original version).

– (selective) compilations, etc. –

Nov 68. (lp) *Liberty; (LBS 83105) / Imperial; <12406>* **CHER'S GOLDEN GREATS** [ ] [ ]
Jan 72. (d-lp) *United Artists; <88>* **CHER SUPERPAK** – 92
Nov 75. (lp) *Sunset; (SLS 50378)* **GOLDEN HITS** [ ] –
Oct 72. (d-lp) *United Artists; <94>* **CHER SUPERPAK, VOL.II** – 95
May 93. (cd/c) *Spectrum; (550038-2/-4)* **TAKE ME HOME / PRISONER** [ ] –
Apr 93. (cd) *Movieplay Gold; (MPG 74017)* **GYPSYS, TRAMPS & THIEVES** [ ] –
Jul 93. (cd/c) *M.C.A.; (MCL D/C 19208)* **CHER / FOXY LADY** [ ] –
Jul 93. (cd/c) *M.C.A.; (MCL D/C 19209)* **HALF BREED / DARK LADY** [ ] –
Nov 95. (3xcd-box) *CDOMB 005)* **ALL I REALLY WANT TO DO / SONNY SIDE OF CHER / CHER** [ ] –
Jan 96. (cd) *Disky; (SE 86567-2)* **YOU BETTER SIT DOWN KIDS** [ ] –
Apr 96. (cd) *Universal; (AA314 532320-2)* **THE CASABLANCA YEARS** [ ] [ ]
Sep 96. (cd) *E.M.I.; (CDP 792773-2)* **BANG BANG (MY BABY SHOT ME DOWN)** [ ] –
Nov 98. (cd) *Spectrum; (550038-2)* **TAKE ME HOME / PRISONER** [ ] –
Feb 99. (cd) *Magic; (497941-2)* **SUNNY** [ ] –
Apr 99. (cd) *E.M.I.; (499900-2)* **THE BEST OF CHER** [ ] –
Dec 99. (cd) *Magic; (523511-2)* **WITH LOVE** [ ] –
Jan 00. (cd) *Universal; (E 490528-2)* **UNIVERSAL MASTERS COLLECTION** [ ] [ ]
Sep 00. (cd) *Universal; (AAMCAD 11899)* **BITTERSWEET: THE LOVE SONGS** [ ] [ ]
Dec 00. (cd) *Disky; (BA 86022-2)* **BASIC ORIGINAL HITS** [ ] –
Feb 01. (cd) *M.C.A.; (MCBD 19511)* **GYPSIES TRAMPS AND THIEVES: THE BEST OF CHER** [ ] [ ]
Feb 01. (cd) *EMI Plus; (5761410)* **THE STORY** [ ] [ ]
Feb 01. (cd) *Raven; (RVCD 108)* **BEHIND THE DOOR 1964-1974** [ ] [ ]
Oct 02. (cd) *Disky; (GO 79348-2)* **ALL I REALLY WANT TO DO** [ ] –
Feb 03. (cd) *M.C.A.; (MCBD 19524)* **BLUE: ALL TIME GREAT LOVE SONGS** [ ] [ ]
Mar 03. (cd) *Universal; (AA881 12154-2)* **20THE CENTURY MASTERS** [ ] [ ]
Aug 03. (3xcd-box) *Spectrum; (9809420)* **THE CASABLANCA YEARS / LOVE SONGS / CHER** [ ] [ ]

SONNY & CHER

not iss. / Vault

1963. (7"; as CAESAR & CLEO) *<909>* **THE LETTER. / SPRING FEVER** – [ ]
<re-iss. Oct65 as SONNY & CHER; 916> – hit No.75 *(UK-iss.Oct65 on 'Vocalion'; VL 9247)*

Reprise / Reprise

1964. (7"; as CAESAR & CLEO) *<0308>* **LOVE IS STRANGE. / DO YOU WANT TO DANCE** – [ ]
1964. (7") *<0309>* **BABY DON'T GO. / LOVE IS STRANGE** – [ ]
Feb 65. (7") *(R 20309)* **BABY DON'T GO. / WALKING THE QUETZEL** [ ] –

Atlantic / Atco

Oct 64. (7") *<6345>* **JUST YOU. / SING C'EST LA VIE** – [ ]
<re-iss. Aug65> – hit No.20
Jul 65. (7") *(AT 4035)* *<6359>* **I GOT YOU BABE. / IT'S GONNA RAIN** 1 1

—— In Aug'65, SONNY had his first solo hit with 'LAUGH AT ME' which hit US No.10 and UK No.9 – the re-issue of 'BABY DON'T GO' also hit US No.8 at the same time. A month later, CHER contributed vocals to BONNIE + THE TREASURES 7", 'Home Of The Brave'

Oct 65. (7") *(AT 4047)* *<6381>* **BUT YOU'RE MINE. / HELLO** 17 15
Oct 65. (lp; mono/stereo) *(ATL/STL 5036)* *<S33 177>* **LOOK AT US** 7 Aug65 2
– I got you babe / Unchained melody / Then he kissed me / Sing c'est la vie / It's gonna rain / 500 miles / Just you / The letter / Let it be me / You don't love me / You've really got a hold on me / Why don't they let us fall in love. *<(cd-iss. Jul98 on 'Sundazed'; SC 6139)>*
Feb 66. (7") *(AT 4069)* *<6395>* **WHAT NOW MY LOVE. / I LOOK FOR YOU** 13 Jan66 16
Jun 66. (7") *(584 018)* *<6420>* **HAVE I STAYED TOO LONG. / LEAVE ME BE** 42 49
May 66. (lp; mono/stereo) *(587/588 006)* *<S33 183>* **THE WONDROUS WORLD OF SONNY & CHER** 15 Apr66 34
– Summertime / Tell him / I'm leaving it all up to you / But you're mine / Bring it on home to me baby / Set me free / What now my love / Leave me be / I look for you / Laugh at me / Turn around / So fine. *<(cd-iss. Jul98 on 'Sundazed'; SC 6140)>*
Sep 66. (7") *(584 040)* *<6440>* **LITTLE MAN. / MONDAY** 4 21
Nov 66. (7") *<6449>* **LIVING FOR YOU. / LOVE DON'T COME** – 87
Nov 66. (7") *(584 057)* **LIVING FOR YOU. / TURN AROUND** 44 –
Jan 67. (7") *(584 078)* *<6461>* **THE BEAT GOES ON. / LOVE DON'T COME** 29 6
Apr 67. (lp; mono/stereo) *(587/588 052)* *<S33 203>* **IN CASE YOU'RE IN LOVE** [ ] Mar66 45
– The beat goes on / Groovy kind of love / You baby / Monday / Love don't come / Podunk / Little man / We'll sing in the sunshine / Misty roses / Stand by me / Living for you / Cheryl's goin' home. *<(cd-iss. Jul98 on 'Sundazed'; SC 6141)>*
May 67. (7") *(584 110)* *<6480>* **A BEAUTIFUL STORY. / PODUNK** [ ] Apr67 53
May 67. (lp) *<S33 214>* **GOOD TIMES** (soundtrack) – 73
– I got you babe (instrumental) / It's the little things / Good times / Trust me / Don't talk to strangers / I'm gonna love you / Just a name / I got you babe. *<cd-iss. 1999 on 'One Way'; 35140>*
Aug 67. (7") *(584 129)* *<6486>* **PLASTIC MAN. / IT'S THE LITTLE THINGS** [ ] Jun67 74
Sep 67. (7") *<6507>* **IT'S THE LITTLE THINGS. / DON'T TALK TO STRANGERS** – 50
Dec 67. (7") *(584 162)* *<6541>* **GOOD COMBINATION. / YOU AND ME** [ ] 56
Feb 68. (7") *(584 168)* *<6555>* **CIRCUS. / Sonny Bono: I WOULD MARRY YOU TODAY** [ ] [ ]
Sep 68. (7") *(584 215)* *<6605>* **YOU GOTTA HAVE A THING OF YOUR OWN. / I GOT YOU BABE** [ ] [ ]
1969. (7") *<6683>* **YOU'RE A FRIEND OF MINE. / I WOULD MARRY YOU TODAY** – [ ]

Atco / Atco

Jul 70. (7") *(2091 021)* *<6758>* **GET IT TOGETHER. / HOLD YOU TIGHTER** [ ] [ ]

M.C.A. / Kapp

Jun 71. (7") *(MU 1139)* *<2141>* **REAL PEOPLE. / SOMEBODY** [ ] [ ]
Oct 71. (lp) *(MUPS 435)* *<3654>* **SONNY AND CHER LIVE (live)** [ ] Sep71 35
– What now my love / The beat goes on / Once in a lifetime / More today than yesterday / Gotta get you into my life / Someday (you'll want me to want you) / Danny boy / Laugh at me / Something / Hey Jude / I got you babe.
Nov 71. (7") *(MU 1145)* *<2151>* **ALL I EVER NEED IS YOU. / I GOT YOU BABE (live)** 8 Oct71 7
Jun 72. (lp) *(MUPS 452)* *<3660>* **ALL I EVER NEED IS YOU** [ ] Feb72 14
– All I ever need is you / Here comes that rainy day feeling / More today than yesterday / Crystal clear / Muddy waters / United we stand / A cowboy's work is never done / I love what you did with the love I gave you / You better sit down kids / We'll watch the sun coming up / Somebody.
Apr 72. (7") *(MU 1154)* *<2163>* **A COWBOY'S WORK IS NEVER DONE. / SOMEBODY** [ ] Feb72 8
Aug 72. (7") *(MU 1164)* *<2176>* **WHEN YOU SAY LOVE. / CRYSTAL CLEAR – MUDDY WATERS** [ ] Jul72 32

M.C.A. / M.C.A.

Feb 73. (lp) *(MCF 3672)* *<2101>* **MAMA WAS A ROCK AND ROLL SINGER, PAPA USED TO WRITE ALL HER SONGS** [ ] Jun73 [ ]
– It never rains in Southern California / I believe in you / I can see clearly

now / Rhythm of your heartbeat / Mama was a rock and roll singer, papa used to write all her songs (parts 1 & 2) / By love I mean / Brother Love's travelling salvation show / You know darn well / The greatest show on Earth / Listen to the music.

Apr 73. (7") *(MU 1194)* <40026> **MAMA WAS A ROCK AND ROLL SINGER, PAPA USED TO WRITE ALL HER SONGS. / (part 2)** ☐ Mar73 77

Jul 73. (7") *(MUS 1211)* <40083> **THE GREATEST SHOW ON EARTH. / YOU KNOW DARN WELL I DO** ☐ ☐

May 74. (d-lp) *(MCSP 257)* <8004> **LIVE IN LAS VEGAS VOL.2 (live)** ☐ Dec73 ☐
– All I ever need is you / I can see clearly now / You've got a friend / Where you lead / You'd better sit down kids / A cowboy's work is never done / I got you babe / Gypsies, tramps and thieves / Brother Love's travelling salvation show / You and I / Superstar / Bang bang (my baby shot me down).

— they decided to end partnership as they separated and divorced on 26th June 1974 (see biography above). Professionally they did re-unite in 1976-77 on US TV 'SONNY & CHER SHOW' again

not iss. Warners

1977. (7") <8341> **YOU'RE NOT RIGHT FOR ME. / WRONG NUMBER** – ☐

– (selective) compilations, etc. –

on 'Atlantic' UK, 'Atco' US unless mentioned otherwise

Aug 65. (7") *Reprise;* <0392> **BABY DON'T GO. / WALKIN' THE QUETZAL (or) LOVE IS STRANGE** – 8

Oct 65. (lp; with Various Artists) *Reprise;* <6177> **BABY DON'T GO** – 69

Oct 67. (lp) *(588 083)* <33219> **THE BEST OF SONNY & CHER** ☐ Aug67 23
– The beat goes on / What now my love / I got you babe / Little man / Just you / Let it be me / A beautiful story / It's the little things / But you're mine / Sing c'est la vie / Laugh at me / Living for you. *(re-iss. Aug72 lp/c; K/K4 40012)*

1975. (lp) <11000> **THE BEAT GOES ON – THE BEST OF SONNY & CHER** – ☐
(cd-iss. Jun93 on 'Atco'; 7567 91796-2)

Dec 90. (cd/c/lp) *W.E.A.; (9548 30152-2/-4/-1)* **THE SONNY & CHER COLLECTION** ☐ ☐

May 93. (7"/c-s) *Epic; (659240-7/-4)* **I GOT YOU BABE. / (Beavis & Butt-head intro)** 66 –
(cd-s+=) *(659240-2)* – (Beavis & Butt-head outro).

Mar 03. (cd) *Universal; (E 118231-2)* **THE HIT SINGLES COLLECTION** ☐ ☐

Feb 02. (d-cd) *BR Music; (BS 8124-2)* **THE SINGLES PLUS** ☐ ☐

☐ CINERAMA (see under ⇒ the WEDDING PRESENT)

☐ CITY (see under ⇒ KING, Carole)

Eric CLAPTON

Born: ERIC PATRICK CLAPP, 30 Mar'45, Ripley, Surrey, England. Brought up by his grandparents, CLAPTON later attended Kingston Art College where he studied stained glass design. Heavily influenced by ROBERT JOHNSON, B.B. KING and BUDDY GUY, CLAPTON was a self taught musician (he had been given a £14 guitar by his grandparents on his 14th birthday) and began playing with TOM McGUINNESS in his first band, The ROOSTERS, in January 1963. Eight months later, they left The ROOSTERS and joined CASEY JONES AND THE ENGINEERS, although this didn't last long and CLAPTON's first big break came in October 1963 when he was asked to replace TOP TOPHAM in The YARDBIRDS. The latter act had just taken over from The ROLLING STONES as the resident band at the Crawdaddy Club in Richmond; CLAPTON, nicknamed "Slowhand" by the band's manager, GIORGIO GOMELSKY, quickly outshone the singer, KEITH RELF, and became the principal focal point of the group, although he left them on the eve of their chart success in 1965, complaining that their music had become too commercial. CLAPTON had recorded only one album with The YARDBIRDS but his potential shone out on 'FIVE LONG YEARS' and 'SMOKESTACK LIGHTNING'. The highlight of the album, entitled, 'FIVE LIVE YARDBIRDS', was a rendition of Chuck Berry's 'TOO MUCH MONKEY BUSINESS'. He then joined JOHN MAYALL's BLUESBREAKERS in April 1965 and around this time the famous, although unsubstantiated phrase, 'CLAPTON IS GOD' was coined. Again, he only recorded one album although it was to be the spark for the blues boom of the sixties. That album was 'BLUESBREAKERS WITH ERIC CLAPTON', recorded over one weekend with no track laid down in more than one take. He left the BLUESBREAKERS in 1966 and immediately formed CREAM with GINGER BAKER and JACK BRUCE. CREAM broke up in November 1968 and CLAPTON played on the GEORGE HARRISON-penned BEATLES track, 'While My Guitar Gently Weeps' (under the name, L'ANGELO MYSTERIOSO), and also contributed to HARRISON's solo album, 'WONDERWALL MUSIC'. CLAPTON subsequently formed BLIND FAITH with BAKER, STEVE WINWOOD and RIC GRECH, and although they topped the charts on both sides of the Atlantic with their eponymous debut set, they couldn't cope with the high pressure expected of a "supergroup", and broke up in 1970. He was still only 24 but fame had taken its toll and he retreated into the ranks of DELANEY & BONNIE AND FRIENDS from which he formed his own, equally laid back DEREK AND THE DOMINOES. By this time CLAPTON was actively trying to shun publicity and even refused to have his name on the cover of the classic album, 'LAYLA AND OTHER ASSORTED LOVE SONGS'. Meanwhile, his debut solo lp was recorded in Los Angeles in 1970; issued shortly after, it reached the UK and US Top 20. The following year, the second DEREK AND THE DOMINOES album was scrapped due to the band's worsening drugs problem and they decided to call it a day. CLAPTON went into seclusion, only coming out for the occasional charity performance (including the Concert For Bangladesh). Ironically, 'LAYLA' (a song written about GEORGE HARRISON's wife PATTI), gave the now defunct DEREK AND THE DOMINOES a belated Top 10 hit in the UK in 1972. PETE TOWNSHEND, concerned for his friend's health, persuaded CLAPTON to take part in an all-star comeback concert in 1973 at London's Rainbow Theatre with RON WOOD, STEVE WINWOOD, JIM CAPALDI and many others. The performance was recorded and the resulting album, 'ERIC CLAPTON'S RAINBOW CONCERT' reached a respectable Top 20 slot on both sides of the Atlantic. The success of the project and the album did not, however, convince CLAPTON to step back into the limelight and he retreated once more. The guitarist underwent a course of electronically adapted acupuncture in 1974, eventually got rid of the habit and told record boss, Robert Stigwood, that he was ready to come back. TOM DOWD was brought in as producer although CLAPTON had only two songs in mind, 'PLEASE BE WITH ME' by Charles Scott Boyer and his own, 'GIVE ME STRENGTH'. A new band was assembled with CARL RADLE, JAMIE OLDAKER, DICK SIMS, GEORGE TERRY and YVONNE ELLIMAN and MARCY LEVY (LEVY would later resurface as MARCELLA DETROIT in SHAKESPEAR'S SISTER). In August 1974, the first single from the comeback sessions, a brilliant version of Bob Marley's 'I SHOT THE SHERIFF', was released and reached an unexpected UK number 9; many observers speculated that he was ill-advised in trying to cross over music boundaries. Later the same month, the accompanying album, '461 OCEAN BOULEVARD' (named after the address of the recording studio), was released to UK Top 3 success. His long guitar solos had now been trimmed down in line with his more basic approach to songwriting, apparent on subsequent hit album, 'THERE'S ONE

IN EVERY CROWD' (1975); his version of 'SWING LOW SWEET CHARIOT' reached UK Top 20. In August of the same year, he hit the charts with yet another cover, Bob Dylan's 'KNOCKIN' ON HEAVEN'S DOOR', while the live album, 'E.C. WAS HERE', kept his profile high. During this period, GEORGE TERRY was taking on most of the lead guitar work as CLAPTON was still reluctant to be in the forefront. In September 1976, 'NO REASON TO CRY' reached UK Top 10, its credibility factor enhanced by the talents of BOB DYLAN & THE BAND. CLAPTON reciprocated by performing 'FURTHER ON UP THE ROAD' (with new band member, SERGIO PASTORA, on percussion) at THE BAND's 'LAST WALTZ' farewell concert. 'SLOWHAND' released in 1977, was only kept off the US top spot by 'Saturday Night Fever', while the painfully sentimental single, 'WONDERFUL TONIGHT' (the second song written for PATTI) reached Top 20; other highlights were JJ Cale's 'COCAINE' and John Martyn's 'MAY YOU NEVER'. The following year's 'BACKLESS' followed in much the same head-nodding vein, CLAPTON obviously remaining oblivious to the energy and attitude of the burgeoning punk scene. In March 1979, he decided to embark on a world tour with an all-new UK band consisting of ALBERT LEE, CHRIS STAINTON, DAVE MARKEE and HENRY SPINETTI. The veteran troupe recorded live tracks at the Budokan in Japan (the resulting album, 'JUST ONE NIGHT' was a transatlantic Top 5 success the following year), and during the tour, CLAPTON finally married his long time love, PATTI. The 70's had not been an easy time for CLAPTON and his disciples, his heroin addiction subsequently replaced by a copious intake of cognac. In May 1980, ex-PROCOL HARUM stalwart, GARY BROOKER, replaced STAINTON for a British tour, although later in the month, CLAPTON was saddened to hear that his former bass player, CARL RADLE, had died of chronic kidney disease. CLAPTON wasn't in the best of health himself, the guitarist admitted to hospital in Minnesota during his 1980 tour of America with doctors estimating that he would have had under an hour to live had his ulcer burst. With his health restored, and with the revitalisation of the adult rock market (beginning with the early 80's introduction of the Compact Disc), CLAPTON re-emerged as a revered elder statesman of rock, although he had a further setback when he was hospitalised in April 1981 after a car accident. He recovered from this and went on to contribute to PHIL COLLINS' debut album (beginning a long standing friendship/working relationship) and also returned to live work by performing with JEFF BECK at 'The Secret Policeman's Other Ball'. CLAPTON's last album for 'R.S.O.', 'ANOTHER TICKET', reached the UK Top 20, although success was limited in the States; later that year he decided to form his own 'Duck' Records. The following year he released 'MONEY AND CIGARETTES', the album (featuring RY COODER and ALBERT LEE amongst others) seeing him back in the Top 20 on both sides of the Atlantic. In between numerous charity concerts, "God" managed to record his next album, 'BEHIND THE SUN' (1985), the Top 10 (US Top 40) set being produced by PHIL COLLINS, TED TEMPLEMAN and RUSS TITELMAN. Later that year, CLAPTON ventured into TV soundtrack work, co-writing the Ivor Novello award winning 'EDGE OF DARKNESS' theme with MICHAEL KAMEN. By this point, CLAPTON was in his slick, Armani suit-wearing period, his polished follow-up, 'AUGUST' (again produced by COLLINS), contained the semi-classic tracks, 'BEHIND THE MASK' and the TINA TURNER duet 'TEARING US APART'. In 1987 he began his first series of concerts at the Royal Albert Hall, London (they would become an annual event and by 1990, he had built up to 18 consecutive nights). Towards the end of the decade, CLAPTON completed the score for the Mickey Rourke-starring film, 'HOMEBOY', while his next album proper, 'JOURNEYMAN' (1989; Top 5), found CLAPTON rediscovering his guitar. Tragedy was to rear its ugly head again in 1990, when, on August the 27th, three members of his entourage died along with STEVIE RAY VAUGHAN in a helicopter crash following a concert in East Troy, Wisconsin. In 1991, at his annual Albert Hall residency (now up to a staggering 24 shows; the performances would subsequently be released as concert set, '24 NIGHTS'), he decided to split each show into five segments – a four piece band, a second four piece band with different percussion, a nine piece band, a blues band with guitarists ALBERT COLLINS, ROBERT CRAY, BUDDY GUY and JIMMIE VAUGHAN, and a nine piece band with orchestra conducted by MICHAEL KAMEN. Incredibly, CLAPTON underwent further emotional trauma, when in March that year, his 4-year old son, CONOR, died after falling out of a skyscraper window. Not surprisingly, CLAPTON shunned the world for some time, only reappearing in September on BUDDY GUY's first album for over a decade, 'Damn Right I've Got The Blues'. A live version of 'WONDERFUL TONIGHT' (from the '24 NIGHTS' set) reached the UK Top 30 and rounded off a year of highs and lows to match any that he'd faced previously. 1992 began with a recording of an 'MTV UNPLUGGED' show, and, backed by NATHAN EAST, ANDY FAIRWEATHER LOW, RAY COOPER and CHUCK LEAVELL, he performed new material, 'THE CIRCUS LEFT TOWN' and 'TEARS IN HEAVEN' along with standards including a drastically pared down version of 'LAYLA'. The resulting album went on to be the most successful of his career (UK No.2 and US No.1), although he allegedly didn't even want it released! It also showed CLAPTON's return to his blues roots with Big Bill Broozny's 'HEY HEY', a stunning version of Robert Johnson's 'MALTED MILK' and Muddy Waters' 'ROLLIN AND TUMBLIN'. However, it was the aforementioned heart-rending tribute to his son, 'TEARS IN HEAVEN' (lyrics by Will Jennings) that stole the show, CLAPTON's voice wracked with the pain of his bereavement (the song subsequently won him another Ivor Novello award). Following on from more film soundtrack work (i.e. 'Lethal Weapon 3' and 'Rush'), his 1994 album, 'FROM THE CRADLE', saw him completely back to his blues roots with standards like Willie Dixon's 'GROANIN THE BLUES' and Lowell Fulson's 'RECONSIDER BABY'. Although the brilliant 'MOTHERLESS CHILD' lingered in the lower regions of the charts, he finally scored his first No.1 single backing CHRISSIE HYNDE, CHER and NENEH CHERRY on the 1995 Childline single, 'LOVE CAN BUILD A BRIDGE'. CLAPTON continued to tour, play charity gigs and had even taken to giving interviews (something he wasn't exactly noted for in the past). 1998's 'PILGRIM' was an elegiac, often intensely personal set of reflections on his journey through life, the death of his son understandably still permeating his muse. The album also inaugurated his production/writing partnership with Simon Climie (once of 80's pop act CLIMIE FISHER), a pairing that remained in place – at least in terms of production – for 'RIDING WITH THE KING' (2000). A collaboration with legend B.B. KING, the record's enjoyable if predictable run-through of blues favourites provided a bit of light relief for fans and quite possibly a modicum of release and catharsis for CLAPTON himself. The guitarist continued to look to the past with 'REPTILE' (2001), his first solo studio set of the new decade. The sleeve featured CLAPTON as a grinning youngster while many of the songs were interpretations of R&B hits from his youth such as Ray Charles' 'COME BACK BABY' and John Greer's 'GOT YOU ON MY MIND'. He also paid tribute to one of his major latter day influences with a reading of 'TRAVELIN' LIGHT', one of J.J. Cale's most atmospheric 70's efforts. With his umpteenth live set, 'ONE MORE CAR, ONE MORE RIDER' (2002), it was difficult to avoid the impression that CLAPTON seems content to motor along comfortably in the middle of the road, wary of ratcheting up his muse a few gears. Long time favourites like 'KEY TO THE HIGHWAY' and 'BELL BOTTOM BLUES' made for pleasant enough listening, but fans must be tired waiting on a set which finally fires on all cylinders. 'ME AND MR. JOHNSON' (2004) wasn't it, a full blown, transatlantic Top 10 album's worth of ROBERT JOHNSON covers. Given that the man himself never made it past 30, and the most searing covers of his songs (CLAPTON's own 'CROSSROADS' and the 'STONES' 'LOVE IN VAIN' to name two) have been cut by players around the same age, there's an argument that JOHNSON's art is a young man's game, preoccupied with judgement and mortality but, ironically, charged with a mystique that escapes older players. CLAPTON didn't sound like he had a hellhound on his trail – how could he? – but he at least sounded mildly lascivious on the grinding 'MILKCOW'S CALF BLUES'. Following the excitement of the reformed CREAM's Royal Albert Hall residency in May 2005, CLAPTON's next album proper, 'BACK HOME' (2005), was a Simon Climie-assisted return to MOR, flirting with 'I SHOT THE SHERIFF'-style reggae, lashings of blue eyed soul ('RUN HOME TO ME' even recalled VAN MORRISON) and general elder statesman head nodding, and featuring a clutch of covers including the Spinners' 'LOVE DON'T LOVE NOBODY', George Harrison's 'LOVE COMES TO EVERYONE' and Stevie Wonder/Syreeta Wright's 'I'M GOING LEFT'.

• **Covered:** AFTER MIDNIGHT + I'LL MAKE LOVE TO YOU ANYTIME (J.J. Cale) / SWING LOW SWEET CHARIOT (spiritual/gospel trad.) / WILLIE AND THE HAND JIVE + CRAZY COUNTRY HOP (Johnny Otis) / HAVE YOU EVER LOVED A WOMAN (Billy Myles) / NOBODY KNOWS YOU WHEN YOU'RE DOWN AND OUT (Jimmy Cox) / KEY TO THE HIGHWAY (Sager/Broonzy) / KNOCK ON WOOD (Eddie Floyd) / BEHIND THE MASK (Michael Jackson co-wrote w/others; covered by Yellow Magic Orchestra) / WATCH YOURSELF (Buddy Guy) / WORRIED LIFE BLUES (Mecio Merryweather) / HOODOO MAN (Sonny Boy Williamson) / HOUND DOG (hit; Elvis Presley) / DOUBLE TROUBLE (Otis Rush) / SIGN LANGUAGE (Bob Dylan) / FLOATING BRIDGE and EVERYBODY OUGHTA (Sleepy John Estes) / LEAD ME ON (Womack/Womack) / BEFORE YOU ACCUSE ME (Bo Diddley) / RUNNING ON FAITH + PRETENDING (. . . Williams) / RUN SO FAR (Wilbert Harrison) / DON'T KNOW WHICH WAY TO GO (Willie Dixon) / etc. • **Trivia:** In 1966 (with JACK BRUCE, PAUL JONES, STEVE WINWOOD and PETE YORK), CLAPTON briefly formed The POWERHOUSE, who recorded three songs for 'Elektra' compilation, 'WHAT'S SHAKIN'.

Album rating: BLIND FAITH by Blind Faith (*7) / ERIC CLAPTON (*7) / LAYLA AND OTHER ASSORTED LOVE SONGS; Derek & The Dominoes (*9) / THE RAINBOW CONCERT (*5) / IN CONCERT; Derek & The Dominoes (*5) / 461 OCEAN BOULEVARD (*8) / THERE'S ONE IN EVERY CROWD (*5) / E.C. WAS HERE (*5) / NO REASON TO CRY (*6) / SLOWHAND (*7) / BACKLESS (*6) / JUST ONE NIGHT (*3) / ANOTHER TICKET (*6) / TIME PIECES: BEST OF ERIC CLAPTON compilation (*7) / MONEY AND CIGARETTES (*6) / TIME PIECES II: LIVE IN THE 70'S collection (*6) / BEHIND THE SUN (*5) / AUGUST (*6) / CROSSROADS compilation (*9) / JOURNEYMAN (*7) / 24 NIGHTS (*4) / RUSH soundtrack (*6) / UNPLUGGED (*7) / FROM THE CRADLE (*6) / THE CREAM OF ERIC CLAPTON collection (*7) / CROSSROADS 2: LIVE IN THE 70's collection (*6) / PILGRIM (*5) / THE STORY OF US soundtrack (*5) / REPTILE (*6) / ONE MORE CAR, ONE MORE RIDER (*4) / ME AND MR. JOHNSON (*6) / BACK HOME (*4)

BLIND FAITH

STEVE WINWOOD (b.12 May'48, Birmingham, England) – vocals, keyboards (ex-TRAFFIC, ex-SPENCER DAVIS GROUP) / **ERIC CLAPTON** (b.30 Mar'45, Ripley, England) – guitar, vocals (ex-CREAM, ex-JOHN MAYALL . . . , ex-YARDBIRDS, etc) / **RIC GRECH** (b. 1 Nov'46, Bordeaux, France) – bass (ex-FAMILY) / **GINGER BAKER** (b.19 Aug'39, Lewisham, England) – drums (ex-CREAM, ex-GRAHAM BOND ORGANISATION, ex-BLUES INC.)

Polydor R.S.O.

Aug 69. (lp) *(583-059)* <304> **BLIND FAITH** [1] Jul69 [1]
– Had to cry today / Can't find my way home / Well all right / Presence of the Lord / Sea of joy / Do what you like. *<US re-iss. Feb77 on 'R.S.O.'; 3016> (re-iss. Nov77 on 'R.S.O.'; 2394 142) (re-iss. Aug83 on 'R.S.O.'; SPELP 14) (cd-iss. Apr86+=; 825 094-2) (cd re-iss. Sep95)* – Exchange and mart / Spending all my days. *(lp re-iss. Aug99 on 'Simply Vinyl'; SVLP 104)*

— disbanded later 1969 – GINGER BAKER formed AIRFORCE with STEVE WINWOOD. The latter returned to TRAFFIC before carving out a solo career and RIC GRECH also went solo.

– compilations, others, etc. –

1977. (7") *R.S.O.; <873>* **CAN'T FIND MY WAY HOME. / PRESENCE OF THE LORD** [-] [ ]

ERIC CLAPTON

ERIC CLAPTON – vocals, guitar (ex-DELANEY & BONNIE, ex-BLIND FAITH ex-CREAM, ex-JOHN MAYALL'S BLUESBREAKERS, ex-YARDBIRDS, etc) featured his **DOMINOES** musicians plus **STEPHEN STILLS** – guitar

Polydor Atco

Aug 70. (lp) *(2383 021)* <329> **ERIC CLAPTON** [17] Jul70 [13]
– Slunky / Bad boy / Lonesome and a long way from home / After midnight / Easy now / Blues power / Bottle of red wine / Lovin' you lovin' me / I've told you for the last time / I don't know why / Let it rain. *(re-iss. Nov82 & Feb83)*

— In Oct 70, CLAPTON guested on KING CURTIS single 'TEASIN'. / 'SOULIN'

Nov 70. (7") *(2001 096)* <6784> **AFTER MIDNIGHT. / EASY NOW** [ ] Oct70 [18]

DEREK AND THE DOMINOES

ERIC CLAPTON – vox, guitar with **BOBBY WHITLOCK** – keyboards, vocals / **CARL RADLE** – bass / **JIM GORDON** – drums / **and guest DUANE ALLMAN** – guitar

Sep 70. (7"w-drawn) *(2058 057)* **TELL THE TRUTH. / ROLL IT OVER** [-] [-]

Dec 70. (7") *(2058 130)* <6809> **LAYLA. / BELL BOTTOM BLUES** [ ] [-]

Jan 71. (d-lp) *(2625 005)* <SD2 704> **LAYLA & OTHER ASSORTED LOVE SONGS** [ ] Nov70 [16]
– I looked away / Bell bottom blues / Keep on growing / Nobody knows you when you're down and out / I am yours / Anyday / Key to the highway / Tell the truth / Why does love got to be so sad? / Have you ever loved a woman / Little wing / It's too late / Layla / Thorn tree in the garden. *(re-iss. Aug74 & Nov77; 2671 110) (re-iss. Jan84; SPDLP 1) (cd-iss. Mar91; 823277-2) (LAYLA REMASTERED – 20th ANNIVERSARY EDITION d-cd/d-c; 847083-2/-4)*

Feb 71. (7") <6803> **BELL BOTTOM BLUES. / KEEP ON GROWING** [-] [91]

Mar 71. (7") <6809> **LAYLA. / I AM YOURS** [-] [51]
<re-iss. Apr72; 15040> – hit No.10

Jul 72. (7") *(2058 130)* **LAYLA. / I AM YOURS** [7] [-]

— split Spring '71 but left behind posthumous album below, etc

R.S.O. Polydor

Sep 72. (7") <15049> **LET IT RAIN. / EASY NOW** [-] [48]

Mar 73. (d-lp) *(2659 020)* <28800> **DEREK AND THE DOMINOES – IN CONCERT (live)** [36] Jan73 [20]
– Why does love got to be so sad? / Got to get better in a little while / Let it rain / Presence of the Lord / Tell the truth / Bottle of red wine / Roll it over / Blues power / Have you ever loved a woman. *(d-cd-iss. Jan94; 831416-2)*

Apr 73. (7") *(2090 104)* **WHY DOES LOVE GOT TO BE SO SAD? (live). / PRESENCE OF THE LORD (live)** [ ] [-]

Jun 73. (7") <15056> **BELL BOTTOM BLUES. / LITTLE WING** [-] Feb73 [78]

— In '71 ERIC had virtually retired into session work. He appeared in GEORGE HARRISON's Bangla Desh concert, 1st Aug'71.

ERIC CLAPTON

returned for a one-off concert at the Rainbow, 13Jan73 with **PETE TOWNSHEND** – guitar / **RON WOOD** – guitar / **STEVE WINWOOD** – keyboards / **JIMMY KARSTEIN & JIM CAPALDI** – drums / **REE BOP** – percussion / **RIC GRECH** – bass

Polydor R.S.O.

Sep 73. (lp) *(2479 116)* <877> **THE RAINBOW CONCERT** [19] [18]
– Badge / Roll it over / Presence of the Lord / Pearly queen / After midnight / Little wing. *(re-iss. Aug83 on 'R.S.O.' lp/c; SPE LP/MC 23) (cd-iss. 1988; 831 320-2) (re-iss. May95 cd/c; 527472-2/-4)*

Oct 73. (7") *<400>* **PRESENCE OF THE LORD (live). / WHY DOES LOVE GOT TO BE SO BAD?** [-] [ ]

— **ERIC CLAPTON** went solo again with **GEORGE TERRY** – guitar (ex-sessions) / **CARL RADDLE** – bass (ex-DEREK AND THE DOMINOES, ex-DELANEY & BONNIE) / **DICK SIMS** – keyboards (ex-BOB SEGER) / **JAMIE OLDAKER** – drums (ex-BOB SEGER) / **MARCY LEVY** – b.vocals (ex-BOB SEGER) / **YVONNE ELLIMAN**

R.S.O. R.S.O.

Jul 74. (7") *(2090 132) <409>* **I SHOT THE SHERRIF. / GIVE ME STRENGTH** [9] [1]

Aug 74. (lp/c) *(2479/ 116) <4801>* **461 OCEAN BOULEVARD** [3] Jul74 [1]
– Motherless children / Give me strength / Willie and the hand jive / Get ready / I shot the sheriff / I can't hold out / Please be with me / Steady rollin' man / Mainline Florida. *(re-iss. Aug83 lp/c; SPE LP/TC 24) (cd-iss. Nov89; 839 874-2)*

Oct 74. (7") *(2090 139) <503>* **WILLIE AND THE HAND JIVE. / MAINLINE FLORIDA** [ ] [26]

— added **MARCY LEVY** – vocals, tambourine

Apr 75. (7") *(2058 560) <509>* **SWING LOW SWEET CHARIOT. / PRETTY BLUE EYES** [19] [ ]

Apr 75. (lp/c) *(2479/ 132) <4806>* **THERE'S ONE IN EVERY CROWD** [15] [21]
– We've been told (Jesus' coming soon) / Swing low sweet chariot / Little Rachel / Don't blame me / The sky is crying / Singing the blues / Better make it through today / Pretty blue eyes / High / Opposites. *(re-iss. Mar85 lp/c; SPE LP/MC 92) (cd-iss. Nov86; 829 649-2)*

Aug 75. (7") *(2090 166) <513>* **KNOCKIN' ON HEAVEN'S DOOR. / SOMEONE LIKE YOU** [38] [ ]

Sep 75. (lp/c) *(2479 179) <4809>* **E.C. WAS HERE (live)** [14] [20]
– Have you ever loved a woman / Presence of the Lord / Drifting blues / Can't find my way home / Ramblin' on my mind / Further on up the road. *(re-iss. Aug83 lp/c; SPE LP/MC 21) (cd-iss. Jul92; 831519-2)*

— added **SERGIO PASTORA** – percussion (ex-BOB SEGER)

Aug 76. (lp/c) *(2479 179) <3801>* **NO REASON TO CRY** [8] Sep76 [15]
– Beautiful thing / Carnival / Sign language / County jail blues / All our past times / Hello old friend / Double trouble / Innocent times / Hungry / Black summer rain. *(re-iss. Aug83 lp/c; SPE LP/MC 2) (cd-iss. Dec86; 813 582-2)*

Oct 76. (7") *(2090 208) <861>* **HELLO OLD FRIEND. / ALL OUT PAST TIMES** [ ] [24]

Feb 77. (7") *(2090 284) <868>* **CARNIVAL. / HUNGRY** [ ] [ ]

— augmented by five piece when ELLIMAN then PASTORA both went solo

Nov 77. (7") *(2090 294) <886>* **LAY DOWN SALLY. / COCAINE** [39] [3]

Nov 77. (lp/c) *(2479 201) <3030>* **SLOWHAND** [23] [2]
– Cocaine / Wonderful tonight / Lay down Sally / Next time you see her / We're all the way / The core / May you never / Mean old Frisco / Peaches and diesel. *(re-iss. Aug83 lp/c)(cd; SPE LP/MC 25)(823 276-2)*

Mar 78. (7") *(2090 275) <895>* **WONDERFUL TONIGHT. / PEACHES AND DIESEL** [ ] May78 [16]

— **ERIC CLAPTON & HIS BAND**

ERIC now backed up only by **SIMS, OLDAKER** and **RADLE** when MARCY LEVY went solo and GEORGE TERRY went into sessions.

Sep 78. (7") *(RSO 21) <910>* **PROMISES. / WATCH OUT FOR LUCY** [37] [9] [40]

Nov 78. (lp/c) *(RSD/TRSD 5001) <3039>* **BACKLESS** [18] [8]
– Walk out in the rain / Watch out for Lucy / I'll make love to you anytime / Roll it / Tell me that you love me / If I don't be there by morning / Early in the morning / Promises / Golden ring / Tulsa time. *(re-iss. Aug83 lp/c; SPE LP/MC 1) (cd-iss. Jan89; 813 581-2)*

Mar 79. (7") *<928>* **TULSA TIME. / COCAINE** [-] [ ]

Mar 79. (7") *(RSO 24)* **IF I DON'T GET THERE BY MORNING. / TULSA TIME** [ ] [-]

— added **ALBERT LEE** – guitar (ex-solo artist, etc.) to complete new band, **DAVE MARKEE** – bass repl.CARL / **HENRY SPINETTI drums** repl. JAMIE

May 80. (d-lp/d-c) *(RSDX/+C 2) <4202>* **JUST ONE NIGHT (live at Budokhan)** [3] [2]
– Tulsa time / Early in the morning / Lay down Sally / Wonderful tonight / If I don't be there by morning / Worried life blues / All our past times / After midnight / Double trouble / Setting me up / Blues power / Ramblin' on my mind / Cocaine / Farther on up the road. *(d-cd-iss. Nov88; 800 093-2)*

Jul 80. (7") *<1039>* **TULSA TIME (live). / COCAINE (live)** [ ] Jun80 [30]

Oct 80. (7") *<1051>* **BLUES POWER (live). / EARLY IN THE MORNING (live)** [-] [76]

— **GARY BROOKER & CHRIS STAINTON** – keyboards repl. DICK

Feb 81. (7") *(RSO 74) <1060>* **I CAN'T STAND IT. / BLACK ROSE** [ ] [10]

Feb 81. (lp/c) *(RSD/TRSD 5008) <3095>* **ANOTHER TICKET** [18] Mar81 [7]
– Something special / Black rose / Blow wind blow / Another ticket / I can't stand it / Hold me Lord / Floating bridge / Catch me if you can / Rita Mae. *(re-iss. Apr84 lp/c; SPE LP/MC 67) (cd-iss. Feb87; 827 579-2)*

Apr 81. (7") *(RSO 75) <1064>* **ANOTHER TICKET. / RITA MAE** [ ] [78]

— **ERIC CLAPTON** retained **LEE** and recruited **RY COODER, ROGER HAWKINS, DONALD 'DUCK' DUNN** plus backing vocalists **JOHN SAMBATAO** and **CHUCK KIRKPATRICK**

Duck-Warners Duck-Warners

Feb 83. (7") *(W 9780) <29780>* **I'VE GOT A ROCK'N'ROLL HEART. / MAN OVERBOARD** [ ] Jan83 [18]
(12"+=) *(W 9780T)* – Everybody oughta make a change.

Feb 83. (lp/c) *(W 3773/+4) <23773>* **MONEY AND CIGARETTES** [13] [16]
– Everybody outta make a change / The shape you're in / Ain't going down / I've got a rock'n'roll heart / Man overboard / Pretty girl / Man in love / Crosscut saw / Slow down Linda / Crazy country hop. *(cd-iss. 1984; 923 773-2) (cd re-iss. Feb95;)*

Apr 83. (7"/7"pic-d) *(W 9701/+P)* **THE SHAPE YOU'RE IN. / CROSSCUT SAW** [75] [ ]
(12"+=) *(W 9701T)* – Pretty girl.

May 83. (7") *(W 9651)* **SLOW DOWN LINDA. / CRAZY COUNTRY HOP** [ ] [ ]
(12"+=) *(W 9651T)* – The shape you're in.

— **CLAPTON** put together a new band. **TIM RENWICK** – guitar (ex-SUTHERLAND BROTHERS & QUIVER) / **CHRIS STAINTON** – keyboards (ex-solo, ex-JOE COCKER) / **DONALD 'DUCK' DUNN** – bass (ex-BOOKER T. AND THE M.G.'s) / **JAMIE OLDAKER** – drums (returned) **MARCY LEVY** (returned) & **SHAUN MURPHY** – backing vocals

Mar 85. (7") *(W 9069) <29081>* **FOREVER MAN. / TOO BAD** [51] [26]
(12"+=) *(W 9069T)* – Something's happening.

Mar 85. (lp/c/cd) *(925166-1/-4/-2) <25166>* **BEHIND THE SUN** [8] [34]
– She's waiting / See what love can do / Same old blues / Knock on wood / Something's happening / Forever man / It all depends / Tangled in love / Never make you cry / Just like a prisoner / Behind the sun. *(re-iss. cd Feb95;)*

May 85. (7") *<28986>* **SEE WHAT LOVE CAN DO. / SHE'S WAITING** [-] [89]

Jul 85. (7") *(W 8954)* **SHE'S WAITING. / JAILBAIT** [ ] [-]

Dec 85. (7"; by ERIC CLAPTON & MICHAEL KAMEN) *(RESL 178)* **EDGE OF DARKNESS. / SHOOT OUT** [65] [-]
(c-s/12") *(Z/12 RSL 178)* – ('A'side) / Escape from Northmoor. *(re-iss. cd-ep+= Feb89; CDRSL 178)* – Obituary / Oxford circus / Northmoor.
(above from TV mini-series 'Edge Of Darkness' on 'BBC' records)

Nov 86. (lp/c)(cd) *(WX 71/+C)(925476-2) <25476>* **AUGUST** [3] Dec86 [37]
– It's in the way that you use it / Run / Tearing us apart / Bad influence / Hung up on your love / Take a chance / Hold on / Miss you / Holy mother / Behind the mask. *(cd+=)* – Grand illusion. *(re-iss. cd Feb95;)*

Jan 87. (7") *(W 8461)* **BEHIND THE MASK. / GRAND ILLUSION** [15] [ ]
(12"+=) *(W 8461T)* – Wanna make love to you.
(d7"+=) *(W 8461F)* – White room (live) / Crossroads (live).

Mar 87. (7") *(W 8397)* **IT'S IN THE WAY THAT YOU USE IT. / BAD INFLUENCE** [ ] [ ]
(d7+=/12"+=) *(W 8397 8397 F/T)* – Old ways / Pretty girl.

— **GREG PHILLINGANES** also joined

Jun 87. (7"; by ERIC CLAPTON & TINA TURNER) *(W 8299)* **TEARING US APART. / HOLD ON** [56] [ ]
(12"+=) *(W 8299T)* – Run.

— In Aug'87, CLAPTON (with MICHAEL KAMEN & DAVID SANBORN) provided the score for the first 'LETHAL WEAPON' movie; on 'Warners'

Nov 87. (7") *(W 8141)* **HOLY MOTHER. / TANGLED IN LOVE** [ ] [ ]
(12"+=) *(W 8141T)* – Behind the mask / Forever man.

Dec 88. (cd/c/lp) *(CD/TC+/V 2574) <791241-2>* **HOMEBOY** (soundtrack w/ MICHAEL KAMEN) [ ] [ ]
– Travelling east / Johnny / Call me if you need me (MAGIC SAM) / Bridge / Pretty baby (J.B. HUTTO & THE NEW HAWKS) / Dixie / Ruby's loft / I want to love you baby (PEGGY SCOTT & JO JO BENSON) / Bike ride / Ruby / Living in the real world (BRAKES) / Final

flight / Dixie / Homeboy. *(cd+=)* – Country bikin' / Party / Training / Chase.
(above issued on 'Virgin')

— In Aug'89, CLAPTON was credited with MICHAEL KAMEN (& DAVID SANBORN) on the soundtrack to 'Lethal Weapon 2'

— now with **ALLAN CLARKE, ROBERT CRAY, GEORGE HARRISON, PHIL COLLINS,** etc

Nov 89. (7") *<22732>* **PRETENDING. / BEFORE YOU ACCUSE ME** [–] [55]

Nov 89. (lp)(c/cd) *(WX 322)(926074-4/-2) <26074>* **JOURNEYMAN** [3] [16]
– Pretending / Anything for your love / Bad love / Running on faith / Hard times / Hound dog / No alibis / Run so far / Old love / Breaking point / Lead me on / Before you accuse me.

Jan 90. (7") *(W 2644)* **BAD LOVE. / BEFORE YOU ACCUSE ME** [ ] [–]
(c-s/12"/cd-s) *(W 2644 C/T/CD)* – ('A'side) / Badge (live) / Let it rain (live).

Mar 90. (7") *<19980>* **BAD LOVE. / HARD TIMES** [–] [88]

Mar 90. (7"/7"box/c-s) *(W 9981/+B/C)* **NO ALIBIS. / RUNNING ON FAITH** [53] [ ]
(12"+=) *(W 9981T)* – Behind the mask (live) / Cocaine (live).
(cd-s+=) *(W 9981CD)* – No alibis (live) / Cocaine (live).

Jun 90. (7") *(W 9970)* **PRETENDING. / HARD TIMES** [ ] [–]
(12"+=) *(W 9970T)* – Knock on wood.
(cd-s++=) *(W 9970CD)* – Behind the sun.

— with **ALAN CLARKE** – keyboards / **NATHAN EAST** – bass / **STEVE FERRONE** – drums / **PHIL PALMER** – guitar / **RAY COOPER** – guitar / **RICHARD TEE** – piano / **CRAIG PHILLINGAMES** – keyboards, synths. and The NATIONAL PHILHARMONIC ORCHESTRA.

Oct 91. (d-cd)(d-lp/d-c) *(7599 <26420-2>)(WX 373/+C)* **24 NIGHTS (live)** [17] [38]
– Badge / Running on faith / White room / Sunshine of your love / Watch yourself / Have you ever loved a woman / Worried life blues / Hoodoo man / Pretending / Bad love / Old love / Wonderful tonight / Bell bottom blues / Hard times / Edge of darkness.

Nov 91. (7") *(W 0069)* **WONDERFUL TONIGHT (live). / EDGE OF DARKNESS (live)** [30] [–]
(c-s/12"/cd-s) *(W 0069 C/T/CD)* – ('A'side) / Layla (band version) / Cocaine.

Jan 92. (cd) *(<7599 26794-2>)* **RUSH** (soundtrack) [ ] [24]
– New recruit / Tracks and lines / Realization / Kristen and Jim / Preludin fugue / Cold turkey / Will Gaines / Help me up / Don't know which way to go (with BUDDY GUY) / Tears in Heaven. *(cd re-iss. Oct94; same)*

— **CHUCK LEAVELL** – keyboards (ex-ALLMANS) repl. CRAIG and RICHARD / **ANDY FAIRWEATHER-LOW** – guitar (ex-AMEN CORNER, ex-solo) repl. PHIL backing singers **KATIE KISSOON + TESSA MILES**

Jan 92. (7"/c-s) *(W 0081/+C)* **TEARS IN HEAVEN. / WHITE ROOM (live)** [5] [–]
(12"+=/cd-s+=) *(W 0081 T/CD)* – Tracks & lines / Bad love (live).

Jan 92. (c-s) *<19038>* **TEARS IN HEAVEN / TRACKS AND LINES** [–] [2]

— In Jul'92, ERIC teamed up with ELTON JOHN on single 'RUNAWAY TRAIN'. A month later, STING was his co-collaborator on another hit 'IT'S PROBABLY ME'; both taken from the movie, 'Lethal Weapon 3'

Sep 92. (7"/c-s) *(W 0134/+C)* **LAYLA (live acoustic). / TEARS IN HEAVEN (live acoustic)** [45] [–]
(cd-s+=) *(W 0134CD)* – (MTV unplugged interview).

Sep 92. (c-s) *<18787>* **LAYLA (live acoustic) / SIGNE (live acoustic)** [–] [12]

Sep 92. (cd)(lp/c) *(9362 <45024-2>)(WX 480/+C)* **UNPLUGGED (live acoustic)** [2] [1]
– Signe / Before you accuse me / Hey hey / Tears in Heaven / Lonely stranger / Nobody knows when you're down & out / Layla / Running on faith / Walkin' blues / Alberta / San Francisco Bay blues / Malted milk / Old love / Rollin' & tumblin'.

Sep 94. (cd/c/lp) *(9362 <45737-2/-4/-1>)* **FROM THE CRADLE** [1] [1]
– Third degree / Hoochie coochie man / Standin' round cryin' / Groanin' the blues / Blues before sunrise / Reconsider baby / Five long years / I'm tore down / How long blues / Goin' away baby / Blues leave me alone / Sinner's prayer / Motherless child / It hurts me too / Someday after a while.

Oct 94. (c-s) *(W 0271C)* **MOTHERLESS CHILD. / DRIFTIN'** [63] [ ]
(12"+=/cd-s+=) *(W 0271CD)* – County jail blues / 32-20 blues.

— In Mar'95, alongside CHER, CHRISSIE HYNDE and NENEH CHERRY, he hit UK No.1 with charity Comic Relief single 'LOVE CAN BUILD A BRIDGE'.

Jul 96. (c-s) *(W 0358C) <17621>* **CHANGE THE WORLD / DANNY BOY** [18] [5]
(cd-s+=) *(W 0358CD)* – ('A'instrumental).

Mar 98. (cd/c) *(<9362 46577-2/-4>)* **PILGRIM** [6] [4]
– My father's eyes / River of tears / Pilgrim / Broken hearted / One chance / Circus / Goin' down slow / Fall like rain / Born in time / Sick and tired / Needs his woman / She's gone / You were there / Inside of me.

Mar 98. (c-s) *(W 0443C)* **MY FATHER'S EYES / THEME FROM A MOVIE THAT NEVER HAPPENED** [33] [–]
(cd-s+=) *(W 0443CD)* – Inside of me.

Jun 98. (c-s) *(W 0447C)* **CIRCUS / TEARS IN HEAVEN** [39] [–]
(cd-s+=) *(W 0447CDX)* – Wonderful tonight / Edge of darkness.
(cd-s) *(W 0447CD)* – ('A'side) / Behind the mask / Bad love / Tearing us apart.

Nov 98. (c-s) *(W 456C)* **PILGRIM / NEED HIS WOMAN** [ ] [–]
(cd-s+=) *(W 456CD)* – ('A'mix).

Oct 99. (c-s/cd-s) *(W 508 C/CD)* **BLUE EYES BLUE / CIRCUS / OLD LOVE** [ ] [–]
(cd-s+=) *(W 508CDX)* – Tearing us apart.

Oct 99. (cd/c) *(9362 47564-2/-4) <47553>* **CLAPTON CHRONICLES – THE BEST OF ERIC CLAPTON** (compilation) [6] [20]
– Blue eyes blue / Change the world / My father's eyes / Tears in Heaven / Layla / Pretending / Bad love / Before you accuse me (take a look at yourself) / It's in the way that you use it / Forever man / Running on faith / She's waiting / River of tears / I get lost / Wonderful tonight.

Apr 00. (cd; by ERIC CLAPTON & MARC SHAIMAN) *<(9362 47603-2)>* **THE STORY OF US** (soundtrack) [ ] Nov99 [ ]
– Main title – (I) Get lost / A spoon is just a spoon / The girl in the pith helmet / Fighting / Empty nest / (other artist) / Touching feet under the covers / Everything I love is in this bed / Dry cleaning – (I) Get lost / (other artist) / Family bed / Bust baby montage / Wonderful tonight / Silent drive to camp / Camp montage / (other artist) / Epiphany at the bistro / I hate the Kirbys / Love in Venice / Ben takes the apartment / Writing montage / Pictures on a wall / (other artist) / Let's go to chow fun.

— in Jun'00, ERIC collaborated with B.B. KING on the hit album, 'RIDING WITH THE KING'

Mar 01. (cd/c/d-lp) *(<9362 47966-2/-4>)* **REPTILE** [7] [5]
– Reptile / Got you on my mind / Travelin' light / Believe in life / Come back baby / Broken down / Find myself / I ain't gonna stand for it / I want a little girl / Second nature / Don't let me be lonely tonight / Modern girl / Superman inside / Son and Sylvia.

Nov 02. (d-cd) *(<9362 48397-2>)* **ONE MORE CAR, ONE MORE RIDER: LIVE ON TOUR 2001** (live) [69] [43]
– Key to the highway / Reptile / Got you on my mind / Tears in Heaven / Bell bottom blues / Change the world / My father's eyes / River of tears / Goin' down slow / She's gone / I want a little girl / Badge / (I'm your) Hoochie coochie man / Have you ever loved a woman / Cocaine / Wonderful tonight / Layla / Wonderful tonight / Layla / Sunshine of your love / Over the rainbow.

Mar 04. (cd) *(<9362 48730-2>)* **ME AND MR. JOHNSON** [10] [6]
– When you got a good friend / Little Queen of Spades / They're red hot / Me and the Devil blues / Travelling Riverside blues / Last fair deal gone down / Stop breakin' down blues / Milkcow's calf blues / Come on in my kitchen / If I had possession over judgement day / Love in vain / 32-20 blues / Hell hound on my trail.

Aug 05. (cd) *(<9362 49395-2>)* **BACK HOME** [19] [13]
– So tired / Say what you will / I'm going left / Love don't love nobody / Revolution / Love comes to everyone / Lost and found / Piece of my heart / One day / One track mind / Run home to me / Back home. *(<ltd-cd w/ dvd+=; 9362 49440-2>)* – (extra tracks).

– compilations, etc. (selective) –

issued 'Polydor' UK / 'Atco' US, unless mentioned otherwise

Aug 72. (d-lp) *(2659 012) <803>* **THE HISTORY OF ERIC CLAPTON** [20] Mar72 [6]
– I ain't got you / Hideaway / Tales of brave Ulysses / I want to discuss it / Teasin' / Blues power / Spoonful / Badge / Tell the truth / Jam / Layla.

Feb 73. (lp) *(5526>* **CLAPTON** [–] [67]

Apr 73. (lp) *(2659 025) <3503>* **AT HIS BEST** [ ] Oct72 [87]
now 'R.S.O.' UK+US until mentioned

Jan 82. (7"/12") *(RSO/+X 87)* **LAYLA (Derek & The Dominoes). / WONDERFUL TONIGHT** [4] [ ]

Mar 82. (7") *(RSO 88)* **I SHOT THE SHERIFF. / COCAINE** [64] [ ]
(12"+=) *(RSOX 88)* – Knockin' on Heaven's door (live).

Apr 82. (lp/c) *(RSD/TRSD 5010) <3099>* **TIME PIECES – THE BEST OF ERIC CLAPTON** [20] [ ]

– I shot the sheriff / After midnight / Knockin' on Heaven's door / Wonderful tonight / Layla / Cocaine / Lay down Sally / Willie and the hand jive / Promises / Swing low, sweet chariot / Let it grow. *(cd-iss. 1984; 800 014-2) (re-iss. Nov88 & Apr95; same)*

May 84. (d-lp/d-c) *Starblend; (ERIC/ERIK 1)* **BACK TRACKIN'** 29 –
– I shot the sheriff / Knockin' on Heaven's door / Lay down Sally / Promises / Swing low sweet chariot / Wonderful tonight / Sunshine of your love (CREAM) / Tales of brave Ulysses (CREAM) / Badge (CREAM) / Little wing (DEREK & THE DOMINOES) / Layla (DEREK & THE DOMINOES) / Cocaine / Strange brew (CREAM) / Spoonful (CREAM) / Let it rain / Have you ever loved a woman? (DEREK & THE DOMINOES) / Presence of the Lord (BLIND FAITH) / Crossroads (CREAM) / Roll it over (DEREK & THE DOMINOES live) / Can't find my way home (live) / Blues power (live) / Further on up the road (live). *(re-iss. Feb85 on 'Polydor' d-cd; 821 937-2) (re-iss. cd Feb91;)*

Sep 87. (d-lp/c)(cd) *(ECTV/+C 1)(833 519-2)* **THE CREAM OF ERIC CLAPTON** 9 –
– Layla / Badge / I feel free / Sunshine of your love / Crossroads / Strange brew / White room / Cocaine / I shot the sheriff / Behind the mask / Forever man / Lay down Sally / Knockin' on Heaven's door / Wonderful tonight / Let it grow / Promises / I've got a rock & roll heart. *(re-charted Sep92, hit UK No.49) (re-iss. Mar94 cd/c; 521881-2/-4) <US re-iss. Mar95; >; hit No.80)*

Apr 88. (6xlp/4xc/4xcd) *(<835 261-1/-4/-2>)* **CROSSROADS** 34
(above features all his work of past 25 years) (YARDBIRDS – solo)

Nov 95. (3xcd-box) **SLOWHAND / 461 OCEAN BOULEVARD / THERE'S ONE IN EVERY CROWD**

Mar 96. (4xcd-box) *(529 305-2)* **CROSSROADS 2 (LIVE IN THE SEVENTIES)** –

Jun 99. (d-cd/d-c) *(<547178-2/-4>)* **BLUES** 52 Jul99 52

Oct 00. (d-cd) *Universal; (E 539049-2)* **461 OCEAN BOULEVARD / SLOWHAND** –

Sep 03. (cd) *(980808-2) <7960-2>* **MARTIN SCORSESE PRESENTS . . . THE BLUES**

Jun 04. (cd) *<27590-2>* **20th CENTURY MASTERS: THE MILLENNIUM COLLECTION**

Jan 05. (cd+dvd) *Reprise; <(9362 48978-2)>* **SESSIONS FOR ROBERT J** Dec04

Oct 05. (3xcd-box) *Warners; <(9362 49493-2)>* **TRILOGY**
– (MONEY AND CIGARETTES / AUGUST / JOURNEYMAN)

the CLASH

Formed: London, England . . . early '76, by MICK JONES, PAUL SIMONON, JOE STRUMMER (ex-101'ers) and TERRY CHIMES (future PIL member, KEITH LEVENE, also had a brief spell). After a riotous tour supporting the SEX PISTOLS, their manager, BERNIE RHODES, attained a deal with major label big boys 'C.B.S.' in early '77 and subsequently unleashed the two minute classic, 'WHITE RIOT'. A driving chantalong stomp, the record smashed into the UK Top 40 and announced the arrival of a band whose influence and impact was second only to the 'PISTOLS. In contrast to LYDON and Co., The CLASH manipulated the energy of punk as a means of political protest and musical experimentation. 'THE CLASH' (1977) was a blinding statement of intent, a finely balanced masterwork of infectious hooklines and raging conviction. 'I'M SO BORED WITH THE U.S.A.' and 'CAREER OPPORTUNITIES' railed against inertia, while a cover of Junior Murvin's 'POLICE AND THIEVES' was the first of many sporadic forays into dub reggae. The album went Top 20, lauded by many critics as the definitive punk set, while a further two classic singles (not on the album), 'CLASH CITY ROCKERS' and 'WHITE MAN IN HAMMERSMITH PALAIS' made the Top 40 (the latter addressing the issue of racism, a subject never far from the band's agenda). CBS (and no doubt the band themselves) were keen to break America, subsequently enlisting the production services of BLUE OYSTER CULT guru, SANDY PERLMAN for follow-up set, 'GIVE 'EM ENOUGH ROPE' (1978). The album's more rock-based, less frenetic approach met with some criticism and despite the label's best efforts, the record just failed to crack the American Top 100. It had, however, made No.2 in Britain and spawned the band' first Top 20 hit in 'TOMMY GUN'. The CLASH subsequently se out to tour the States, while British fans lapped up 'THE COST OF LIVING' EP and its incendiary cover of Sonny Curtis's ' FOUGHT THE LAW'. Finally, in late '79, The CLASH delivere their marathon masterwork, 'LONDON CALLING'. Overseen b seasoned producer, Guy Stevens, the double set showed The CLASH at an assured creative peak, from the anthemic echo of the title tracl to the brooding 'GUNS OF BRIXTON'. A UK Top 10'er, it finall cracked the States (Top 30), its universal acclaim spurred them o to ever more ambitious endeavours. After the plangent dub of th 'BANKROBBER' and 'THE CALL-UP' singles, the band unleashe the sprawling, triple vinyl set, 'SANDINISTA!' in December 1980 The record's wildly experimental material met with critical pasting the bulk of the album's tracks failing to withstand repeated listening Its relatively poor sales (still at single vinyl price!) forced a back t basics rethink for 'COMBAT ROCK' (1982). Although the recor was a healthy seller, it sounded laboured; ironically, it became Th CLASH's biggest selling album in America, where the 'ROCK THE CASBAH' single made the Top 10. Drummer TOPPER HEADON was already long gone by this point and was replaced by CHIMES who had left after the 1977 debut; JONES too, was kicked ou the following year. The band stumbled on for a further album 'CUT THE CRAP' in 1985, before finally disbanding the followin month. While JONES enjoyed mid-80's success with BIG AUDIC DYNAMITE, STRUMMER embarked on a low key solo caree before working with his pal SHANE MacGOWAN in The POGUES The CLASH fever gripped the nation again in 1991 when 'SHOULD I STAY OR SHOULD I GO' (a Top 20 hit in 1983), hit the to of the charts after being used in a Levi jeans advert (what else!?) A best of double set, 'THE STORY OF THE CLASH VOL.1' flew off the shelves and rumours were rife of a CLASH reunio (unceremoniously quashed by STRUMMER). Come the late 90's STRUMMER was back from music biz oblivion fronting his ow band, The MESCALEROS. Debut set, 'ROCK ART & THE X-RAY STYLE' (1999) ran a gamut of genres without really assertin STRUMMER's personality on any of them. 'GLOBAL A GO-GO' (2001) was significantly more focused and cohesive, the forme CLASH man casting his witty, worldly wise perspective over a serie of ventures into off-kilter world-beat. Tragically, JOE was to die o heart failure at his home in Somerset on the 22nd of December 2002. 'STREETCORE' (2003) was STRUMMER's final musical wil and testament, reverting back to his roots with a searing vengeance resurrecting the dub-rock perfected by the CLASH. Railing agains the world's downward spiral with all the outrage and wisdom of a seasoned campaigner, the likes of 'COMA GIRL' and 'GET DOWN MOSES' burned with the kind of righteous fury only the like of STRUMMER could ignite. Among the record's few mellowe moments, 'LONG SHADOW' courted a country-roots vibe whil an emotional rendition of Bob Marley's 'REDEMPTION SONG and a reworked version of Bobby Charles' 'Before I Grow Too Old (retitled 'SILVER AND GOLD') offered solace in the face of s much corruption and chaos. Its greatest tragedy was also its drivin force, STRUMMER, who still had so much left to say and the sharp focused artistic faculties to say it.

• **Covered:** PRESSURE DROP (Maytals) / POLICE ON MY BACK (Equals) ARMAGIDEON TIME (Willie Williams) / JUNCO PARTNER + ENGLISH CIVIL WAR (unknown trad) / EVERY LITTLE BIT HURTS (Ed Cobb) BRAND NEW CADILLAC (Vince Taylor). • **Trivia:** Early in 1980, the banc featured live in the docu-film 'Rude Boy' about a fictionalised CLASH roadie JOE STRUMMER went into acting 1986 (Straight To Hell) / 1989 (Lost I Space).

Album rating: THE CLASH (*10) / GIVE 'EM ENOUGH ROPE (*8) / LONDON CALLING (*9) / SANDINISTA! (*7) / COMBAT ROCK (*6) / CUT THE CRA (*4) / THE STORY OF THE CLASH, VOL.1 compilation (*9) / CLASH ON

Joe Strummer of The CLASH

BROADWAY (*7) / SUPER BLACK MARKET CLASH (*7) / FROM HERE TO ETERNITY live collection (*8) / THE ESSENTIAL CLASH compilation (*9) / Joe Strummer: WALKER soundtrack (*6) / EARTHQUAKE WEATHER (*6) / Joe Strummer & The Mescaleros: ROCK ART AND THE X-RAY STYLE (*5) / GLOBAL A GO-GO (*6) / STREETCORE (*7)

JOE STRUMMER (b. JOHN GRAHAM MELLOR, 21 Aug'52, Ankara, Turkey / raised London) – vocals, guitar (ex-101'ers) / **PAUL SIMONON** (b.15 Dec'55, Brixton, England) – bass, vocals / **MICK JONES** (b. MICHAEL JONES, 26 Jun'55) – guitar, vocals / **TORY CRIMES** (b. TERRY CHIMES, 25 Jan'55) – drums

C.B.S. | Epic

Mar 77. (7") *(S-CBS 5058)* **WHITE RIOT. / 1977** [38] [–]

Apr 77. (lp/c) *(CBS/40 82000)* **THE CLASH** [12] [–]
– Janie Jones / Remote control / I'm so bored with the U.S.A. / White riot / Hate and war / What's my name / Deny / London's burning / Career oportunities / Cheat / Protex blue / Police and thieves / 48 hours / Garage land. *<US-iss.Aug79 on 'Epic'; 36060> (tracks differed & contained free 7")* – GROOVY TIMES. / GATES OF THE WEST *(this lp version UK-iss.Jan91 on cd) (re-iss. Nov82 lp/c; CBS/40 32232) (cd-iss. Apr89 on 'Columbia'; CD 32232) (cd re-iss. Aug91 on 'Columbia'; 468783-2) (cd re-iss. Oct99 on 'Columbia' cd/lp; 495344-2/-1; US version; 495345-2/-1) (lp re-iss. Oct99 on 'Simply Vinyl'; SVLP 131)*

— (Jan'77) (NICKY) **TOPPER HEADON** (b.30 May'55, Bromley, Kent, England) – drums; repl. CHIMES who later joined COWBOYS INTERNATIONAL and GENERATION X

May 77. (7") *(S-CBS 5293)* **REMOTE CONTROL. / LONDON'S BURNING (live)** [ ] [–]

Sep 77. (7") *(S-CBS 5664)* **COMPLETE CONTROL. / THE CITY OF THE DEAD** [28] [–]

Feb 78. (7") *(S-CBS 5834)* **CLASH CITY ROCKERS. / JAIL GUITAR DOORS** [35] [–]

Jun 78. (7") *(S-CBS 6383)* **(WHITE MAN) IN HAMMERSMITH PALAIS. / THE PRISONER** [32] [–]

Nov 78. (lp/c) *(CBS/40 82431)* *<35543>* **GIVE 'EM ENOUGH ROPE** [2] Feb79 [ ]
– Safe European home / English civil war / Tommy gun / Julie's been working for the drug squad / Guns on the roof / Drug-stabbing time / Stay free / Cheapstakes / All the young punks (new boots and contracts). *(re-iss. 1984 lp/c; CBS/40 32444) (cd-iss. Jan91; CD 32444) (re-iss. Oct99 on 'Columbia' cd/lp; 495346-2/-1)*

Nov 78. (7") *(S-CBS 6788)* **TOMMY GUN. / 1, 2, CRUSH ON YOU** [19] [–]

Feb 79. (7") *(S-CBS 7082)* **ENGLISH CIVIL WAR. / PRESSURE DROP** [25] [–]

May 79. (7"ep) *(S-CBS 7324)* **THE COST OF LIVING** [22] [–]
– I fought the law / Groovy times / Gates of the west / Capital radio.

Jul 79. (7") *<50738>* **I FOUGHT THE LAW. / (WHITE MAN) IN HAMMERSMITH PALAIS** [–] [ ]

— added on tour MICKEY GALLAGHER – keyboards (ex-IAN DURY)

Dec 79. (7") *(S-CBS 8087)* **LONDON CALLING. / ARMAGIDEON TIME** [11] [–]
(12"+=) *(CBS12 8087)* – Justice tonight (version) / Kick it over (version).

Dec 79. (d-lp/c) *(CLASH/+C 3)* *<36328>* **LONDON CALLING** [9] Jan80 [27]
– London calling / Brand new Cadillac / Jimmy Jazz / Hateful / Rudie can't fail / Wrong 'em boyo / Death or glory / Koka Kola / The card cheat / Spanish bombs / The right profile / Lost in the supermarket / The guns of Brixton / Lover's rock / Four horsemen / I'm not down / Revolution rock / Train in vain. *(re-iss. Feb88 on 'Columbia' d-lp/c; 460114-1/-4) (cd-iss. Apr89 on 'Columbia'; 460114-2) (re-iss. Oct99 on 'Columbia' cd/d-lp; 495347-2/-1) (d-lp re-iss. Oct99 on 'Simply Vinyl'; SVLP 133) (d-cd iss.Sep04 'Anniversary Edition'+=; 517928-3)* – (extra tracks, etc) (hit UK No.26)

Mar 80. (7") *<50851>* **TRAIN IN VAIN (STAND BY ME). / LONDON CALLING** [–] [27]

Aug 80. (7") *(S-CBS 8323)* **BANKROBBER. / Mickey Dread: ROCKERS GALORE . . . UK TOUR** [12] [–]

Nov 80. (7") *(S-CBS 9339)* **THE CALL-UP. / STOP THE WORLD** [40] [–]

Nov 80. (10"m-lp) *<36846>* **BLACK MARKET CLASH** [–] [74]
– Time is tight / Capital radio / Bankrobber / Pressure drop / The prisoner / City of the dead / Justice tonight – kick it over (version). *(UK-iss.Sep91 on 'Columbia' cd/c; 468763-2/-4)*

Dec 80. (t-lp/d-c) *(CBS/40 FSLN 1)* *<37037>* **SANDINISTA!** [19] [24]
– The magnificent seven / Hitsville U.K. / Junco partner / Ivan meets G.I. Joe / The leader / Something about England / Rebel waltz / Look here / The crooked beat / Somebody got murdered / One more time / One more dub / Lightning strikes (not once but twice) / Up in Heaven (not only here) / Corner soul / Let's go crazy / If music could talk / Th sound of the sinners / Police on my back / Midnight log / The equaliser The call up / Washington bullets / Broadway / Lose this skin / Charli don't surf / Mensforth Hill / Junkie slip / Kingston advice / The stree parade / Version city / Living in fame / Silicone on sapphire / Versio pardner / Career opportunites (version) / Shepherds delight. *(d-cd-is Apr89 on 'Columbia'; 463364-2) (re-iss. Oct99 on 'Columbia' d-cd/d-lp 495348-2/-1)*

Jan 81. (7") *(S-CBS 9480)* **HITSVILLE U.K. / RADIO ONE** [56] [–]

Feb 81. (7") *<51013>* **HITSVILLE U.K. / POLICE ON MY BACK** [–] [ ]

Apr 81. (12"ep) *<02036>* **THE CALL-UP / THE COOL-OUT. / THE MAGNIFICENT SEVEN / THE MAGNIFICENT DANCE** [–] [ ]

Apr 81. (7"/12") *(A/+12 1133)* **THE MAGNIFICENT SEVEN. / THE MAGNIFICENT DANCE** [34] [–]

Nov 81. (7") *(A 1797)* **THIS IS RADIO CLASH. / RADIO CLASH** [47] [–]
(12"+=) *(A12 1797)* – Outside broadcast / Radio 5.

— **TERRY CHIMES** returned to repl. HEADON who later went solo (signe to 'Mercury', released a couple of singles – 'DRUMMIN' MAN', LEAV IT TO LUCK' and 'I'LL GIVE YOU EVERYTHING' – all from th 1986 album, 'WAKING UP', which featured 60's soul singer, JIMMY HELMS)

Apr 82. (7") *(A 2309)* **KNOW YOUR RIGHTS. / FIRST NIGHT BACK IN LONDON** [43] [–]

May 82. (lp/c) *(CBS/40 FMLN 2)* *<37689>* **COMBAT ROCK** [2] [7]
– Know your rights / Car jamming / Should I stay or should I go / Rock the Casbah / Red angel dragnet / Straight to Hell / Overpowered by funk Atom tan / Sean Flynn / Ghetto defendant / Inoculated city / Death i a star. *(re-iss. Nov86 lp/c; CBS/40 32787) (cd-iss. Jan91 on 'Columbia'; C 32787) (re-iss. Oct99 on 'Columbia' cd/lp; 495349-2/-1) (lp re-iss. Oct99 o 'Simply Vinyl'; SVLP 132)*

May 82. (7") *<03006>* **SHOULD I STAY OR SHOULD I GO. / INNOCULATED CITY** [–] [ ]

Jun 82. (7"/7"pic-d) *(A/+11 2479)* *<03245>* **ROCK THE CASBAH. / LONG TIME JERK** [30] Sep82 [8]
(12") *(A12 2479)* – ('A'side) / Mustapha dance.

Jul 82. (7") *<03061>* **SHOULD I STAY OR SHOULD I GO. / FIRST NIGHT BACK IN LONDON** [–] [45]

Sep 82. (7"/7"pic-d/12") *(A/+11/12 2646)* **SHOULD I STAY OR SHOULD I GO. / STRAIGHT TO HELL** [17] [–]

Feb 83. (7") *<03547>* **SHOULD I STAY OR SHOULD I GO? / COOL CONFUSION** [–] [50]

— (Feb83-Jan84) **STRUMMER & SIMONON** brought in new musician **PETE HOWARD** – drums (ex-COLD FISH),repl. CHIMES who late joined HANOI ROCKS / **NICK SHEPHERD** – guitar (ex-CORTINAS + **VINCE WHITE** – guitar; repl. JONES who formed BIG AUDIO DYNAMITE

Sep 85. (7") *(A 6122)* **THIS IS ENGLAND. / DO IT NOW** [24] [–]
(12"+=) *(A12 6122)* – Sex mad roar.

Nov 85. (lp/c) *(CBS/40 26601)* *<40017>* **CUT THE CRAP** [16] [88]
– Dictator / Dirty punk / We are The Clash / Are you red.. Y Cool under heat / Movers and shakers / This is England / Three car trick / Play to win / Fingerpoppin' / North and south / Life is wild *(cd-iss. Apr89 on 'Columbia'; CD 465110-2) (cd-iss. Dec92 on 'Columbia';*

— disbanded Dec'85 and STRUMMER went solo (see below). SHEPHERI formed HEAD. In the early 90's, SIMONON formed HAVANA 3 A.M who comprised NIGEL DIXON (ex-WHIRLWIND), GARY MYRICK an TRAVIS WILLIAMS. Signing to 'I.R.S.', they released only one 50's styl eponymous rock album in 1991 before splitting their quiffs.

– compilations, others, etc. –

on 'C.B.S.' unless mentioned otherwise

Nov 82. (c-ep) *(A40 2907)* **COMPLETE CONTROL / LONDON CALLING / BANKROBBER / CLASH CITY ROCKERS** [ ] [–]

Sep 86. (c-ep) *(450 123-4)* **THE 12" TAPE** [ ] [–]
– London calling / The magnificent dance / This is Radio Clash Rock the Casbah / This is England. *(cd-iss. Nov92 on 'Columbia 450123-2)*

Mar 88. (7") *(CLASH 1)* **I FOUGHT THE LAW. / THE CITY OF THE DEAD / 1977** [29] [–]
(12"+=/cd-s+=) *(CLASH T/C 1)* – Police on my back / 48 hours.

Mar 88. (d-lp/c/cd) *(460244-1/-4/-2)* <44035> **THE STORY OF THE CLASH** [7] [ ]
– The magnificent seven / Rock the Casbah / This is Radio Clash / Should I stay or should I go / Straight to Hell / Armagideon time / Clampdown / Train in vain / Guns of Brixton / I fought the law / Somebody got murdered / Lost in the supermarket / Bank robber / White man in Hammersmith Palais / London's burning / Janie Jones / Tommy gun / Complete control / Capital radio / White riot / Career opportunities / Clash city rockers / Safe European home / Stay free / London calling / Spanish bombs / English civil war / Police and thieves. *(re-iss. Mar91 as THE STORY OF THE CLASH VOL.1, on 'Columbia'; same)* – (hit UK 13) *(re-iss. Oct95 on 'Columbia'; same) (re-iss. Oct99 on 'Columbia' cd/d-lp; 495351-2/-4)*

Apr 88. (7"/7"box) *(CLASH/+B 2)* **LONDON CALLING. / BRAND NEW CADILLAC** [46] [–]
(12"+=) *(CLASHT 2)* – Rudie can't fail.
(cd-s+=) *(CLASHC 2)* – The street parade.

Jul 90. (7"/c-s) *(656072-7/-4)* **RETURN TO BRIXTON (remix). / ('A'-SW2 mix)** [57] [–]
(12"+=/cd-s+=) *(656072-6/-2)* – The guns of Brixton.

Feb 91. (7"/c-s) *Columbia; (656667-7/-4)* **SHOULD I STAY OR SHOULD I GO. / B.A.D. II: Rush** [1] [–]
(12"+=/cd-s+=) *(656667-6/-2)* – ('B'dance mix) / Protex blue.
(cd-s) *(656667-5)* – ('A'side) / London calling / Train in vain / I fought the law.

Apr 91. (7"/c-s) *Columbia; (656814-7/-4)* **ROCK THE CASBAH. / MUSTAPHA DANCE** [15] [–]
(12"+=/cd-s+=) *(656814-6/-2)* – The magnificent dance / This is Radio Clash.
(cd-s) *(656814-5)* – ('A'side) / Tommy gun / (White man) In Hammersmith Palais / Straight to Hell.

Jun 91. (7"/c-s) *Columbia; (656946-7/-4)* **LONDON CALLING. / BRAND NEW CADILLAC** [64] [ ]
(12"+=) *(656946-6)* – Return to Brixton (remix).
(cd-s++=) *(656946-2)* – The call-up.

Oct 91. (7"/c-s) *Columbia; (656-7/-4)* **TRAIN IN VAIN (STAND BY ME). / THE RIGHT PROFILE** [ ] [–]
(cd-s+=) *(656-2)* – Groovy times / Gates to the west.
(pic-cd-s+=) *(656-5)* – ('A'remix) / Death or glory.

Nov 91. (cd/c) *Columbia; (468946-2/-4)* **THE SINGLES COLLECTION** [68] [ ]

Nov 93. (cd/d-lp) *Columbia; (474546-2)* <63895> **SUPER BLACK MARKET CLASH** [ ] [ ]
(re-iss. Oct99 cd/d-lp; 495352-2/-1)

May 94. (3xcd-box/3xc-box) *Columbia; (469308-2/-4)* **THE CLASH ON BROADWAY** [ ] [ ]
(re-iss. Feb00 on 'Legacy'; 497453-2)

Oct 99. (cd/c/d-lp) *Columbia; (496183-2/-4/-1)* <65747> **FROM HERE TO ETERNITY (live)** [13] [ ]
– Complete control / London's burning / What's my name / Clash city rockers / Career opportunities / White man in Hammersmith Palais / Capitol radio / City of the dead / I fought the law / London calling / Armagideon time / Train in vain / Guns of Brixton / The magnificent seven / Know your rights / Should I stay or should I go / Straight to Hell. *(cd re-iss. Dec01; same)*

Oct 02. (3xcd-box) *Epic; (509662-2)* **THE CLASH (US version) / LONDON CALLING / COMBAT ROCK** [ ] [ ]

Oct 02. (12") *Columbia; (VJAY 26)* **ROCK THE CASBAH. / THE MAGNIFICENT SEVEN** [ ] [–]

Mar 03. (d-cd) *Sony TV; (510998-2)* <89056> **THE ESSENTIAL CLASH** [18] [99]
– White riot / 1977 / London's burning / Complete control / Clash city rockers / I'm so bored with the U.S.A. / Career opportunities / Hate and war / Cheat / Police and thieves / Janie Jones / Garageland / Capital Radio One / White man in Hammersmith Palais / English civil war / Tommy gun / Safe European home / Julie's been working for the drug squad / Stay free / Groovy times / I fought the law / London calling / Guns of Brixton / Clampdown / Rudie can't fail / Lost in the supermarket / Jimmy Jazz / Train in vain / Bankrobber / The magnificent seven / Ivan meets GI Joe / Stop the world / Somebody got murdered / Street parade / Broadway / This is Radio Clash / Ghetto defendant / Rock the casbah / Straight to hell / Should I stay or should I go / This is England.

— The CLASH also appeared under different guises for singles below

May 83. (12"; FUTURA 2000 with The Clash) *Celluloid; (CYZ 104)* **ESCAPADES OF FUTURA 2000** [ ] [–]

Dec 83. (7"; JANIE JONES & THE LASH) *Big Beat; (NS 91)* **HOUSE OF THE JU-JU QUEEN. / SEX MACHINE** [ ] [–]

— They can also be heard on TYMON DOGG's 45; 'Lose This Skin' (May80)

JOE STRUMMER

C.B.S. / Epic

Oct 86. (7"/12") *(A/TA 7244)* **LOVE KILLS. / DUM DUM CLUB** [69] [–]

Virgin / Virgin

Feb 88. (cd/c/lp) *(CD/TC+/V 2497)* <90686-2/-4/-1> **WALKER** (soundtrack) [ ] [ ]
– Filibustero / Omotepe / Sandstorm / Machete / Viperland / Nica libre / Latin romance / The unknown immortal / Musket waltz / The brooding side of madness / Tennessee rain / Smash everything / Tropic of no return / Tropic of Pico. *<cd-iss. Jul05 on 'Astralwerks'+=; 7763-2>* – Brooding side of madness – new extended Outer Limits mix / Straight shooter / Filibustero – Freestyle mix.

Epic / Epic

Jun 88. (7"/7"s) *(TRASH/+P 1)* **TRASH CITY. / THEME FROM A PERMANENT RECORD** [ ] [–]
(12"+=/pic-cd-s+=) *(TRASH T/C 1)* – Nerfititi rock.

— STRUMMER was augmented by new band **JACK IRONS** – drums (of RED HOT CHILI PEPPERS) **ZANDON SCHLOSS** – guitar (ex-CIRCLE JERKS) / **RONNIE MARSHALL** – bass (of TONE LOC)

Aug 89. (7"/c-s) *(STRUM/+M 1)* **GANGSTERVILLE. / JEWELLERS AND BUMS** [ ] [–]
(7"ep+=) *(STRUME 1)* – Passport to Detroit / Punk rock blues.
(12"+=/cd-s+=) *(STRUM T/C 1)* – Don't tango with my django.

Sep 89. (lp/c/cd) *(465347-1/-4/-2)* <45372> **EARTHQUAKE WEATHER** [58] [ ]
– Gangsterville / King of the bayou / Island hopping / Slant six / Dizzy's goatee / Shouting street / Boogie with your children / Leopardskin limousines / Sikorsky parts / Jewellers and bums / Highway on zero street / Ride your donkey / Passport to Detroit / Sleepwalk.

Oct 89. (7") *(STRUM 2)* **ISLAND HOPPING. / CHOLO VEST** [ ] [–]
(12"+=/cd-s+=/7"ep+=) *(STRUM T/C/E 2)* – Mango street / Baby o' boogie.

— STRUMMER joined The POGUES on tour, deputising when SHANE McGOWAN was under the bottle. At the start of 1992, he had begun writing with them, so who knows? At least it will quell the dogged persistent rumours of a CLASH reformation.

JOE STRUMMER & THE MESCALEROS

— **STRUMMER** with **RICHARD NORRIS** – keyboards / **GED DYSON** – drums / **SCOTT SHIELDS** – bass / **ANTHONY GENN** – strings

Mercury / Epitaph

Aug 99. (12"/cd-s) *(MER/+CD 523)* **YALLA YALLA. / X-RAY STYLE / TIME AND THE TIDE** [ ] [–]

Oct 99. (cd/c/lp) *(546654-2/-4/-1)* <80424> **ROCK ART & THE X-RAY STYLE** [71] [ ]
– Tony Adams / Sandpaper blues / X-ray style / Techno D-day / The road to rock'n'roll / Nitcomb / Diggin' the new / Forbidden city / Yalla yalla / Willesden to Cricklewood.

— **STRUMMER, SHIELDS + GENN** recruited **MARTIN SLATTERY** – bass, flute, synthesizers, etc + **TYMON DOGG** – guitars, etc.

Hellcat / Hellcat

Jul 01. (7") *(1057-7)* **JOHNNY APPLESEED. / COOL 'N OUT** [ ] [–]

Jul 01. (cd/lp) *(<8 0440-2/-1>)* **GLOBAL A GO-GO** [68] [ ]
– Johnny Appleseed / Cool 'n' out / Global a go-go / Bhindi bhagee / Gamma ray / Mega bottle ride / Shaktar Donetsk / Mondo bongo / Bummed out city / At the border, guy / Minstrel boy.

— on 22 Dec'02, JOE died of a heart attack

Oct 03. (7") *(1137-7)* **COMA GIRL. / YALLA YALLA (live)** [33] [–]
(cd-s+=) *(1136-2)* – Blitzkrieg bop (live).
(cd-s) *(1135-2)* – ('A'side) / The harder they come (live) / Rudi, a message to you (live).

Oct 03. (cd/lp) *(0454-2/-1)* <80454> **STREETCORE** [50] [ ]
– Coma girl / Get down Moses / Long shadow / Arms aloft / Ramshackle day parade / Redemption song / All in a day / Burnin' streets / Midnight jam / Silver and gold.

Dec 03. (7"pic-d) *(1149-7)* **REDEMPTION SONG. / ARMS ALOFT / JUNCO PARTNER (live)** [46] [ ]
(cd-s) *(1148-2)* – (first 2 tracks) / Armageddon time (live).
(cd-s) *(1147-2)* – (first 2 tracks) / Pressure drop (live).

Jimmy CLIFF

Born: JAMES CHAMBERS, 1 Apr'48, St. Catherine, Jamaica, his earliest musical influences stemmed from Trinidad, the birthplace of Calypso. However, by the time JIMMY left home for Kingston in '62, his real interest lay in the imported sounds of boogie and blues from the States. As the boogie sound blended with calypso, mento and Jamaican folk music, so "Ska" was born. CLIFF cut his first track at Federal studio (owned at the time by the dominant force in Jamaican recording, Ken Khouri) for Count Boysie's sound system, who, in turn, would air the track at dances. The single was never released, although after a few more attempts with various systems, 'HURRICANE HATTIE' delivered CLIFF's first hit, produced by Leslie Kong, who at the time had little knowledge of the music business, but plenty of money to hire the best musicians on the islands, and was to be involved in CLIFF's finest work. By '63, CLIFF had his second hit with 'MISS JAMAICA', going on to score with 'MY LUCKY DAY' and 'MISS UNIVERSE', although he was barely earning a decent living. A brief attempt to break "Ska" in the States led to CLIFF meeting Chris Blackwell (head of 'Island' records), who persuaded him to try his luck in England, CLIFF moving over in '65. The trip to America had opened the singer's eyes to soul music, this influence subsequently coming to the fore in both his gigs and recordings of the mid-'60s. After a couple of near misses with Island, the album, 'HARD ROAD TO TRAVEL', was released in '67, amongst the tracks a poppy version of Procol Harum's 'WHITER SHADE OF PALE'. During this period, he built up a strong fanbase in Britain without the hits and cash to go with it; unsurprisingly, his spirits were low, made apparent in his classic track, 'MANY RIVERS TO CROSS', which he wrote in '68. A trip to Brazil the same year to attend an international song contest saw CLIFF pulling off a hit in the country with 'WATERFALL', as well as inspiring him to write 'WONDERFUL WORLD, BEAUTIFUL PEOPLE'. On the way back from Brazil, CLIFF stopped off in Jamaica for the first time since '65, recording material for his subsequent debut LP for Trojan, 'JIMMY CLIFF', and catching up with the sounds of rock-steady and reggae, the new style coming to the fore on the LP. Released in England at a time when Trojan scored the majority of their hits, the LP proved the pinnacle of CLIFF's recording career, listing 'MANY RIVERS TO CROSS' and the sublime 'USE WHAT I GOT', as well as the melancholy sounds of a rare ballad, 'COME INTO MY LIFE'. After the international success of 'WONDERFUL WORLD, BEAUTIFUL PEOPLE', CLIFF recorded the inspired protest song, 'VIETNAM', although the major success he craved continued to evade him with the record being rejected for US release as it was considered "too upbeat". 'WILD WORLD', penned by CAT STEVENS, gave CLIFF a glimmer of success, in the meantime producing DESMOND DEKKER's 'You Can Get It If You Really Want' and the PIONEERS' hit 'Let Your Yeah Be Yeah', before launching his second set, the unforgettable 'ANOTHER CYCLE' in '71. Superstar status was eventually achieved through an unforseen medium; film. 'THE HARDER THEY COME' not only starred CLIFF but used four of his songs, including the title track, as well as the infectious 'YOU CAN GET IT IF YOU REALLY WANT'. Incredibly, when 'THE HARDER THEY COME' was released in '72, it failed to chart, CLIFF becoming disillusioned with Island and moving to 'E.M.I.' in '73. From this point onwards, his 70s output (including 'UMLIMITED', 'STRUGGLING MAN', 'HOUSE OF EXILE' 'BRAVE WARRIOR', 'FOLLOW MY MIND and 'GIVE THANX') failed to match the high standards he had previously set for himself, his style shifting away from the reggae sound that had formed the basis of his fame. Having moved to 'Columbia' records in the early 80s, JC's profile was never huge although he continued to record both solo and with help from other artists; both the KOOL & THE GANG assisted 'THE POWER AND THE GLORY' (1983) and its follow-up 'CLIFF HANGER' (1985) were nominated for Grammys, with the latter actually taking home the prize. The same year, he wrote 'TRAPPED' for BRUCE SPRINGSTEEN, who sang it on the charity album, 'USA For Africa'. The Jamaican icon subsequently resumed his relationship with film, both starring in, and composing the soundtrack to, Caribbean comedy, 'CLUB PARADISE' (1986). His cinematic endeavours overshadowed his solo material once again when, in 1993, his cover of Johnny Nash's 'I CAN SEE CLEARLY NOW' (from the soundtrack to 'Cool Runnings') made the US Top 20. Following a couple of late 90s sets, 'HIGHER AND HIGHER (1998) and 'HUMANITARIAN' (1999), JIMMY was joined by a roll call of rock royalty (including ANNIE LENNOX, STING, WYCLEF JEAN and the late JOE STRUMMER) on the DAVE STEWART produced 'BLACK MAGIC' (2004).

Album rating: JIMMY CLIFF (*6) / WONDERFUL WORLD, BEAUTIFU PEOPLE (*7) / HARD ROAD TO TRAVEL (*5) / ANOTHER CYCLE (*6) / TH HARDER THEY COME soundtrack (*9) / UNLIMITED (*5) / STRUGGLIN MAN (*5) / THE BEST OF JIMMY CLIFF compilation (*7) / BRAVE WARRIO (*5) / FOLLOW MY MIND (*4) / GIVE THANX (*4) / I AM THE LIVIN (*4) / GIVE THE PEOPLE WHAT THEY WANT (*4) / HOUSE OF EXILE (*4) SPECIAL (*4) / THE POWER AND THE GLORY (*5) / CAN'T GET ENOUG OF IT (*4) / CLIFF HANGER (*4) / SENSE OF DIRECTION (*5) / HANG FIR (*5) / IMAGES (*5) / SAVE OUR PLANET EARTH (*4) / BREAKOUT (*5) THE COOL RUNNER LIVE IN LONDON (*3) / HIGHER AND HIGHER (*5) HUMANITARIAN (*5) / BLACK MAGIC (*5)

JIMMY CLIFF – vocals / with various session people

		Blue Beat	not iss
1962.	(7"; JIMMY CLIFF with CAVALIERS COMBO) *(BB 78)* **I'M SORRY. / The BLUE BEATS with RED PRICE: Roarin'**		–
		Island	not iss
1962.	(7") *(WI 012)* **HURRICANE HATTY. / DEAREST BEVERLEY**		–
1962.	(7") *(WI 016)* **MISS JAMAICA. / GOLD DIGGER**		–
1962.	(7") *(WI 025)* **SINCE LATELY. / I'M FREE**		–
1963.	(7") *(WI 062)* **MY LUCKY DAY. / ONE EYED JACKS**		–
1963.	(7") *(WI 070)* **KING OF KINGS. / Sir Percy: OH YEAH**		–
1963.	(7") *(WI 112)* **MISS UNIVERSE. / THE PRODIGAL**		–
		Black Swan	not iss
1963.	(7") *(WI 403)* **THE MAN. / YOU ARE NEVER TOO OLD**		–
		Stateside	not iss
Sep 64.	(7") *(SS 342)* **ONE EYED JACKS. / KING OF KINGS**		–
		Fontana	not iss
Jan 66.	(7") *(TF 641)* **CALL ON ME. / PRIDE AND PASSION**		–
		Island	not iss
Feb 67.	(7") *(WIP 6004)* **AIM AND AMBITION. / GIVE AND TAKE**		–
May 67.	(7") *(WIP 6011)* **I GOT A FEELING. / HARD ROAD TO TRAVEL**		–
Oct 67.	(7") *(WIP 6024)* **THAT'S THE WAY LIFE GOES. / THANK YOU**		–
Jan 68.	(lp) *(ILP 962)* **HARD ROAD TO TRAVEL** – Reward / Let's dance / Can't get enough of it / I've got a feeling / All know about you / Give and take / Pride and passion / Searchin' for my baby / Hard road to travel / A whiter shade of pale / Call on me / Aim and ambition.		–
Jun 68.	(7"; JACKIE EDWARDS & JIMMY CLIFF) *(WIP 6036)* **SET ME FREE. / HERE I COME**		–
Jul 68.	(7") *(WIP 6039)* **WATERFALL. / REWARD**		–
		Trojan	A&M
Oct 69.	(7") *(TR 690)* **WONDERFUL WORLD, BEAUTIFUL PEOPLE. / HARD ROAD TO TRAVEL**	6	–
Nov 69.	(7") *<1146>* **WONDERFUL WORLD, BEAUTIFUL PEOPLE. / WATERFALL**	–	25
Dec 69.	(lp) *(TRLS 16) <4251>* **JIMMY CLIFF** <US-title 'WONDERFUL WORLD'> – Many rivers to cross / Vietnam / My ancestors / Hard road to travel / Hello sunshine / Wonderful world, beautiful people / Sufferin' in the land		

Use what I got / That's the way it goes / Come into my life. *(re-iss. 1983 lp/c; TRLS/ZCTRLS 16) (cd-iss. Mar94 on 'Trojan'; CDTRL 16)*

Jan 70. (7") *(TR 7722)* **VIETNAM. / SHE DOES IT RIGHT** 46 –

Feb 70. (7") *<1167>* **COME INTO MY LIFE. / VIETNAM** – 89

Mar 70. (7") *(TR 7745)* **SUFFERING. / COME INTO MY LIFE** –

May 70. (7") *(TR 7767) <1201>* **YOU CAN GET IT IF YOU REALLY WANT. / BE AWARE**

Island A&M

Jul 70. (7") *(WIP 6087)* **WILD WORLD. / BE AWARE** 8 –

Nov 70. (7") *(WIP 6097)* **SYNTHETIC WORLD. / I GO TO PIECES** –

Feb 71. (7") *(WIP 6103)* **GOODBYE YESTERDAY. / BREAKDOWN** –

May 71. (7") *<1270>* **GOODBYE YESTERDAY. / LET'S SEIZE THE TIME** –

Aug 71. (7") *(WIP 6110)* **SITTING IN LIMBO. / THE BIGGER THEY COME** –

Sep 71. (lp) *(ILPS 9159)* **ANOTHER CYCLE** –
– Take a look at yourself / Please tell me why / Rap / Opportunity only knocks once / My friend's wife / Another cycle / Sitting in limbo / Oh, how I miss you / Inside out, upside down / One thing is over.

Jul 72. (7") *(WIP 6132)* **TRAPPED. / STRUGGLIN' MAN** –

Oct 72. (7") *(WIP 6139)* **THE HARDER THEY COME. / MANY RIVERS TO CROSS**

Nov 72. (lp) *(<ILPS 9202>)* **THE HARDER THEY COME** (soundtrack w/ other artists) Mar75
– You can get it if you really want / Draw your breaks (SCOTTY) / Rivers of Babylon (MELODIANS) / Many rivers to cross / Sweet and dandy (MAYTALS) / The harder they come / Johnny too bad (SLICKERS) / Shanty town (DESMOND DEKKER) / Pressure drop (MAYTALS) / Sitting in limbo. *(re-iss. Sep86 lp/c/cd; ILPM/ICM/CCD 9202) (re-iss. Oct90 on 'Reggae Refreshers' cd/c; RRCD/RRCT 11) (cd re-iss. Jul01; RRCD 61) (d-cd-iss. Aug03 on 'Island'+=; 6949529)* – You can get it if you really want / The harder they come.

E.M.I. Reprise

May 73. (7") *<1177>* **BORN TO WIN. / BLACK QUEEN** –

Jul 73. (7") *(EMI 2042)* **OH MY LOVE. / OH JAMAICA**

Aug 73. (lp) *(EMA 757) <2147>* **UNLIMITED**
– Under the Sun, Moon and stars / Fundamental reggay / World of peace / Black queen / Be true / Oh Jamaica / Commercialization / The price of peace / On my life / I see the light / Rip off / Poor slave / Born to win. *(re-iss. Oct90 lp/c/cd; CDTRJ/ZCTRJ/TRJC 100)*

Oct 73. (7") *(EMI 2065)* **FUNDAMENTAL REGGAY. / THE MONEY VERSION** –

May 74. (7") *(EMI 2160)* **LOOK WHAT YOU DONE TO MY LIFE. / I'VE BEEN DEAD 400 YEARS** –

Jun 74. (lp) *(ILPS 9235)* **STRUGGLING MAN** –
– Struggling man / When you're young / Better days are coming / Sooner or later / Those good old days / Can't stop worrying, can't stop loving you / Let's seize the time / I can't live without you / Going back west / Come on people.

Jul 74. (7") *(EMI 2189)* **MONEY WON'T SAVE YOU. / YOU CAN'T BE WRONG AND GET IT RIGHT** –

Nov 74. (7") *(EMI 2244)* **DON'T LET IT DIE. / ACTIONS SPEAK LOUDER THAN WORDS** –

Dec 74. (lp) *(EMC 3035) <2188>* **HOUSE OF EXILE** <US-title 'MUSIC MAKER'>
– Brother / I want to know / House of exile / Foolish pride / No.1 rip-off man / Long time no see / Music maker / My love is solid as a rock / You can't be wrong and get it right / Look what you do to my life, devil woman / Money won't save you / I've been dead 400 years. *(cd-iss. Dec95 on 'EMI Europe')*

Dec 74. (7") *<1315>* **MUSIC MAKER. / YOU CAN'T BE WRONG AND GET RIGHT** –

1975. (lp) *(EMC 3078)* **BRAVE WARRIOR** –
– My people / Bandwagon / Every tub / Don't let it die / Actions speak louder than words / A million teardrops / Brave warrior / Save a little loving / My people (reprise).

Sep 75. (7") *(EMI 2346)* **OH JAMAICA. / MILLION TEARDROPS** –

Reprise Reprise

Nov 75. (lp) *(K 54061) <2218>* **FOLLOW MY MIND**
– Look at the mountains / The news / I'm gonna live, I'm gonna love / Going mad / Dear mother / Who feels it, knows it / Remake the world / No woman no cry / Wahjahka man / Hypocrite / If I follow my mind / You're the only one. *(cd-iss. Jan96; 7599 26311-2)*

Apr 76. (7") *(K 14423)* **LOOK AT MY MOUNTAINS. / NO WOMAN NO CRY** –

1976. (lp) *(K 54086) <2256>* **LIVE IN CONCERT (live)**
– You can get it if you really want / Vietnam / Fountain of life / Many rivers to cross / Wonderful world, beautiful people / Under the Sun, Moon and stars / Wild world / Sitting in limbo / Struggling man / The harder they come. *(cd-iss. Feb92 on 'WEA'; 759927232-2)*

1976. (7") *<1383>* **HARDER THEY COME (live). / VIETNAM (live)** –

Warners Warners

1978. (lp) *(K 56558) <3240>* **GIVE THANX**
– Bongo man / Stand up and fight back / She is a woman / You left me standing by the door / Footprints / Medley in Afrika / Wanted man / Lonely street / Love I need / Universal love (beyond the boundaries).

Jan 79. (7") *(K 17295)* **STAND UP AND FIGHT BACK. / FOOTPRINTS**

Jun 80. (7") *(K 79135)* **ALL THE STRENGTH WE GOT. / LOVE AGAIN**

Jul 80. (lp) *(K 99089) <5153>* **I AM THE LIVING**
– I am the living / Another summer / All the strength we got / It's the beginning of the end / Gone clear / Love again / Morning train / Satan's kingdom. *(cd-iss. Jan96; 0630 12991-2)*

Oct 80. (7") *(K 79182)* **ANOTHER SUMMER. / SATAN'S KINGDOM** –

Jan 81. (7") **ANOTHER SUMMER. / IT'S THE BEGINNING OF THE END** –

Sep 81. (lp) *(K 99160) <5153>* **GIVE THE PEOPLE WHAT THEY WANT**
– Son of man / Give the people what they want / Experience / Shelter of your love / Majority rule / Let's turn the tables / Material world / World in trap / What are you doing with your life / My philosophy. *(cd-iss. Jan96; 9031 74825-2)*

Sep 81. (7") **MY PHILOSOPHY. / SHELTER OF YOUR LOVE** –

— 1982 with backing group ONENESS

C.B.S. Columbia

Jul 82. (7") *(A 2605)* **ROOTS RADICAL. / RUB-A-DUB PARTNER** –

Jul 82. (7") **PEACE OFFICER. / SPECIAL** –

Jul 82. (lp/c) *(CBS/40 85878)* **SPECIAL** –
– Special / Love is all / Peace officer / Treat the youths right / Keep on dancing / Rub-a-dub partner / Roots radical / Love heights / Originator / Rock children / Where there is love.

Sep 82. (7") *(A 2825)* **SPECIAL. / KEEP ON DANCING (dub)** –

Jan 83. (7") *(A 3037)* **LOVE IS ALL. / ORIGINATOR / ROOTS RADICAL** –

Oct 83. (7") *(A 3849)* **REGGAE NIGHTS. / LOVE HEIGHTS** –
(12"+=) *(TA 3849)* – ('A'instrumental).

Oct 83. (lp/c) *(CBS/40 25761)* **THE POWER AND THE GLORY**
– We all are one / Sunshine in the music / Reggae nights / Piece of the pie / American dream / Roots woman / Love solution / The power and the glory / Journey. *(cd-iss. 1988; CD 25761)*

Jan 84. (7") *<04335>* **WE ALL ARE ONE. / ROOTS WOMAN** –

Jan 84. (7") *(A 4056)* **WE ARE ALL ONE. / NO APOLOGY** –
(12"+=) *(TA 4056)* – Piece of the pie.

Aug 84. (7") *(A 4636)* **REGGAE MOVEMENT. / TREAT THE YOUTHS RIGHT** –
(12"+=) *(TA 4636)* – ('A'dub movement).

Jul 85. (7") *(A 6370) <05396>* **HOTSHOT. / MODERN WORLD**
(12"+=) *(TA 6370)* – Reggae night / ('A'instrumental).

Aug 85. (lp/c/cd) *(CBS/40/CD 26528)* **CLIFF HANGER**
– Hitting with music / American sweet / Arrival / Brown eyes / Reggae street / Hot shot / Sunrise / Dead and awake / Now and forever / Nuclear war. *(cd re-iss. Feb97 on 'Columbia'; 471220-2)*

Aug 85. (7") *<05716>* **AMERICAN SWEET. / REGGAE MOVEMENT** –

Jul 86. (7"; with ELVIS COSTELLO) *<06135>* **SEVEN DAY WEEKEND. / BRIGHTEST STAR** –

Jul 86. (lp/c) *(CBS/40 70298) <PK/PCT 40404>* **CLUB PARADISE** (soundtrack w/ other artists)
– Club Paradise / American plan / Brightest star / The lion awakes / Third World people / You can't keep a good man down / Seven day weekend

(with ELVIS COSTELLO) / Grenada (MIGHTY SPARROW) / Love people (BLUE RIDDIM BAND) / Sweetie come from America (WELL PLEASED & SATISFIED).

Sep 86. (7") *<06235>* **CLUB PARADISE. / THIRD WORLD PEOPLE** [-] [ ]

Mar 88. (lp/c/cd) *(460139-1/-4/-2)* **HANGING FIRE** [ ] [ ]
– Love me love me / Hanging fire / Girls and cars / She was so right for me / It's time / Reggae down Babylon / Hold tight (eye for an eye) / Soar like an angel.

Mar 88. (7") **LOVE ME LOVE ME. / SUNSHINE IN THE MUSIC** [-] [ ]

not iss. — Cliff

Oct 89. (lp/c/cd) *<3312-1/-4/-2>* **IMAGES** [-] [ ]
– Turning point / Rebel in me / First love / Everliving love / Trapped / Pressure / Image of the beast / Save our Planet Earth / No justice / Johnny too bad / Dance reggae dance / The grass is greener.

Musidisc — not iss.

Oct 90. (cd/c/lp) *(10655-2/-4/-1)* **SAVE OUR PLANET EARTH** [ ] [-]
– Turning point / Rebel in me / First love / Everliving love / Trapped / Pressure / Image of the beast / Save our Planet Earth / No justice / Johnny too bad.

Columbia — Chaos

Mar 94. (7"/c-s) *(660 198-7/-4) <77207>* **I CAN SEE CLEARLY NOW. / (track by Tony Rebel)** [23] Oct93 [18]
(cd-s+=) *(660 198-2)* – (track by the Wailing Souls).
(above from the film 'Cool Runnings')

not iss. — Island

May 98. (cd) *<524471>* **HIGHER AND HIGHER** [-] [ ]
– Higher and higher / You can get it if you really want / Wonderful world / Many rivers to cross / I can see clearly now / Soul mate / Ashe music / Crime / Save our planet earth / Rebel in me / Bob yu did yu job / Melody tempo harmony. *(UK-iss.Mar03 on 'Universal'; E 524258-2)*

not iss. — Eureka

Jun 99. (cd) *<970236>* **HUMANATARIAN** [-] [ ]
– Humanitarian / Rise up / Giants / Come up to my love / How long / Let's jam / Keep the family / Drifters / The hill / I walk with love / I'm in all / Humanitarian (slow). *<bonus +=>* – Ob-la-di, ob-la-da / You've got a friend.

Unique — Artemis

Aug 04. (cd) *(UNIQUECD 116) <51564>* **BLACK MAGIC** [ ] [ ]
– I want I do I get / Dance / Jamaica time / People / Fantastic plastic people / Love comes / Black magic / The world is yours (positive mid) / Terror (September 11th) / Over the border / War in Jerusalem / Let's go dancin' (ooh, la, la, la) / The city / Take your time / No problems only solutions / Good life.

– (selective) compilations, etc. –

note; on 'Island' unless mentioned otherwise

Mar 76. (lp) *(ICD 6)* **THE BEST OF JIMMY CLIFF** [ ] [-]
– Hard road to travel / Sooner or later / Sufferin' in the land / Keep your eye on the sparrow / Struggling man / Wild world / Vietnam / Another cycle / Wonderful world, beautiful people / The harder they come / Let your yeah be yeah / Synthetic world / I'm no immigrant / Give and take / Many rivers to cross / Going back west / Sitting in limbo / Come into my life / You can get it if you really want / Goodbye yesterday. *(cd-iss. 1988 on 'Mango'; CICD 6) (cd re-iss. Mar96 on 'Reggae Refreshers'; RRCD 50)*

Feb 87. (lp) *See For Miles; (SEE 83)* **FUNDAMENTAL REGGAY** [ ] [-]
(cd-iss. Jan91 +=; SEECD 83) – (extra tracks).

Jun 94. (d-cd) *Trojan; (CDTRL 342)* **MANY RIVERS TO CROSS** [ ] [-]

Aug 99. (cd) *Castle Pie; PIESCD 027)* **WONDERFUL WORLD BEAUTIFUL PEOPLE** [ ] [-]

May 01. (cd) *Music Club; (MCCD 458)* **YOU CAN GET IT IF YOU REALLY WANT: THE BEST OF JIMMY CLIFF** [ ] [-]

Aug 03. (cd) *EMI Gold; (591557-2)* **THE E.M.I. YEARS 1973-1975** [ ] [-]

Aug 03. (cd) *Columbia; <(511386-2)>* **SUNSHINE IN THE MUSIC** [ ] [ ]

George CLINTON

Born:22 Jul'40, Kannapolis, North Carolina, USA. Raised in Newark, New Jersey, CLINTON's love of doo-wop inspired him to form The PARLIAMENTS. They released a couple of singles in 1955, before moving to Detroit and recording for 'Gordy (Tamla Motown)' in 1962. The band made little progress, although GEORGE wrote songs for Motown artists such as The JACKSON 5 and DIANA ROSS. In 1965, unsuccessful in their attempts to land a deal, they issued a one-off 45, 'THAT WAS MY GIRL', for 'Golden World'. In 1967, he created the earliest incarnations of his future psychedelic image and added new musicians such as EDDIE HAZEL and BERNIE WORRELL. Signing to 'Revilot' in the States, they then hit Top 20 with single '(I WANNA) TESTIFY'. After a series of flops, he was stopped temporarily by Motown writers HOLLAND-DOZIER-HOLLAND from using PARLIAMENT'S name. Meanwhile, CLINTON was being heavily influenced by The MC5, JIMI HENDRIX, SLY & THE FAMILY STONE, the primal throb of The STOOGES and radical politics, not to mention a hefty dose of LSD. By the late 60's, his group had evolved into FUNKADELIC and signed to 'Westbound'. The eponymous debut album of 1970 set the scene with its marriage of skintight rhythm, slow burning vocals and searing psychedelic guitar freakouts. Meanwhile, CLINTON had been given back the rights to The PARLIAMENTS moniker, changing it simply to PARLIAMENT, and signing to 'Invictus'. More or less the same line-up that'd recorded 'FUNKADELIC', worked on 'OSMIUM', PARLIAMENT's 1971 debut. While this album was more in keeping with the free range psychedelia of FUNKADELIC, PARLIAMENT became a vehicle for the more groove-orientated instalments in the P-FUNK saga. The 'PARLIAFUNKADELICAMENT THANG' effect was akin to a mind-bending 60's trip put through the blender of 70's excess with a soundtrack that combined soul, blues, gospel, psychedelic rock, sex and politics to create P-FUNK. Over the coming years the collective would grow into a large musical corporation which featured over 35 members, releasing such classic albums as FUNKADELIC's 'MAGGOT BRAIN' (1971) and 'COSMIC SLOP' (1973), while PARLIAMENT's first two dancefloor friendly albums, 'UP FOR THE DOWN STROKE' (1974) and 'CHOCOLATE CITY' (1975), set the scene for the landmark 'MOTHERSHIP CONNECTION', an interstellar concept piece from the inner galaxy of CLINTON's fevered mind. His re-definition of the black man's past and sci-fi vision of the future was underpinned by the precocious instrumental precision of former JB's trio BOOTSY COLLINS, BERNIE WORRELL and FRED WESLEY. CLINTON furthered his conceptual reach with 1977's 'FUNKENTELECHY VS THE PLACEBO SYNDROME', in which he presented his ideas of the Man keeping the kids oppressed through material dependency. In the meantime, FUNKADELIC had signed to 'Warners' and 1978's anthemic celebration of P-Funk, 'ONE NATION UNDER A GROOVE,' saw them reach a commercial and artistic peak, having already hit the US Top 30 two years previously with 'TEAR THE ROOF OFF THE SUCKER'. By the turn of the decade, there were so many side projects taking up the creative energy of the P-FUNK posse (BOOTSY'S RUBBER BAND, PARLET, HORNY HORNS, etc), that both PARLIAMENT and FUNKADELIC fizzled out, the latter releasing the last decent effort in 1981's 'ELECTRIC SPANKING OF WAR BABIES'. CLINTON went on to a solo career, offering the excellent 'COMPUTER GAMES' album and accompanying canine madness of the 'ATOMIC DOG' single. The rest of the 80s weren't so pretty for the funk kingpin as he wrestled with legal/royalty problems accumulated from his 70's supergroups. While his solo recordings –

including 'YOU SHOULDN'T NUF BIT FISH' (1984) and 'SOME OF MY BEST JOKES ARE FRIENDS' (1985) – became more digitised and less convicing as the decade wore on, his willingness to experiment still resulted in the odd – very odd – hit; witness the reversed bassline in his last gasp hit (Top 60 in spring '86), 'DO FRIES GO WITH THAT SHAKE'. Going on to sign with PRINCE's 'Paisley Park' in the late 80's, he released 'THE CINDERELLA THEORY' (1989) and 'HEY MAN, SMELL MY FINGER' (1993) to generally positive reviews, even if the latter's title was nastier than much of the funk. He also guested on PRINCE's pallid soundtrack, 'Graffiti Bridge' (1990), a link-up which should've stank to high heaven but which went off with barely a whiff. Hardly oblivious to the rise of hip-hop culture (he'd already begun to try out his rapping chops), CLINTON hit upon the idea of a series of samplers entitled 'SAMPLE SOME OF DISC, SAMPLE SOME OF D.A.T.', offering would-be samplers a pricey array of back catalogue snippets. His next couple of offerings, 'DOPE DOGS' (1995) and 'T.A.P.O.A.F.O.M.' (1996) were co-credited to the P-FUNK ALL STARS, while most of his latter-day releases have been extended-jam live efforts also featuring variations on the revolving ALL STAR line-up, most recently 'HOW LATE DO U HAVE 2 B B 4 U R ABSENT' (2005). The ageing, dayglo warrior had guested on records by PRIMAL SCREAM and ICE CUBE, as well as playing to sold out shows worldwide with the P-FUNK ALLSTARS. CLINTON's unswerving belief in the power of the funk to set people free (in every sense) lends his music a delirious, hedonistic quality, which, together with his synthesis of disparate musical styles and technology, is an ever present influence on a diverse range of artists, not least the P-FUNK sampling hip-hop community.

• **Covered:** SUNSHINE OF YOUR LOVE (Cream). • **Trivia:** In 1985, he collaborated with THOMAS DOLBY on 'DOLBY'S CUBE' single 'May The Cube Be With You'. Note: – An entirely different George Clinton surprised us with 'ABC' release 'Please Don't Run From Me'.

Album rating: Parliament: OSMIUM (*5) / UP FOR THE DOWN STROKE (*6) / CHOCOLATE CITY (*6) / MOTHERSHIP CONNECTION (*8) / CLONES OF DR. FUNKENSTEIN (*7) / LIVE – P FUNK EARTH TOUR (*6) / FUNKENTELECHY VS. THE PLACEBO SYNDROME (*8) / MOTOR BOOTY AFFAIR (*7) / GLORYHALLASTOOPID (*6) / TROMBIPULATION (*5) / GREATEST HITS (THE BOMB) compilation (*7) / TEAR THE ROOF OFF compilation (*8) / DOPE DOGS (*6) / THE BEST OF PARLIAMENT: GIVE UP THE FUNK compilation (*9) / Funkadelic: FUNKADELIC (*7) / FREE YOUR MIND . . . AND YOUR ASS WILL FOLLOW (*6) / MAGGOT BRAIN (*8) / AMERICA EATS ITS YOUNG (*6) / COSMIC SLOP (*7) / STANDING ON THE EDGE OF GETTING IT ON (*6) / LET'S TAKE IT TO THE STAGE (*7) / FUNKADELIC'S GREATEST HITS compilation (*6) / TALES OF KIDD FUNKADELIC (*6) / HARDCORE JOLLIES (*6) / ONE NATION UNDER A GROOVE (*8) / UNCLE JAM WANTS YOU (*6) / THE ELECTRIC SPANKING OF WAR BABIES (*7) / MUSIC FOR YOUR MOTHER compilation (*8) / George Clinton: COMPUTER GAMES (*6) / YOU SHOULDN'T-NUF BIT FISH (*6) / SOME OF MY BEST FRIENDS ARE JOKES (*7) / R&B SKELETONS IN THE CLOSET (*7) / THE CINDERELLA THEORY (*6) / HEY MAN . . . SMELL MY FINGER (*6) / THE AWESOME POWER OF A FULLY OPERATIONAL MOTHERSHIP (*5) / GREATEST FUNKIN' HITS (*6) / 500,000 KILOWATTS OF P-FUNK POWER (*5) / HOW LATE DO U HAVE 2 B B 4 U R ABSENT? (*6)

the PARLIAMENTS

GEORGE CLINTON – vox / **CHARLES BUTCH DAVIS** – vocals / **CALVIN SIMON** – vocals repl. GENE BOYKIN / **ROBERT LAMBERT** – vocals repl. HERBIE JENKINS / **GRADY THOMAS** – vocals repl. DANNY MITCHELL

not iss. | Hull-/Apt

May 59. (7") *<25036>* **POOR WILLIE. / PARTY BOYS** | – |

—— **JOHNNY MURRAY** repl. LAMBERT

not iss. | Flip

1959. (7") *<100>* **LONELY ISLAND. / (YOU MAKE ME WANNA) CRY** | – |

not iss. | Symbol

1961. (7") *<917>* **I'LL GET YOU YET. / YOU'RE CUTE** | – |

not iss. | U.S.A.

1961. (7") *<719>* **MY ONLY LOVE. / TO BE ALONE** | – |

—— Spent 4 years writing for Motown . . . then sign to (see below)

—— **CLARENCE 'Fuzzy' HASKINS** – vocals repl. JOHNNY MURRAY + CALVIN SIMON **RAYMOND DAVIS** – vocals repl. BUTCH DAVIS

not iss. | Golden World

1966. (7") *<46>* **HEART TROUBLE. / THAT WAS MY GIRL** | – |

—— added **EDDIE HAZEL** – lead guitar / **TAWL ROSS** – rhythm guitar / **BILLY NELSON** – bass / **MICKEY ATKINS** – organ (on some) / **TIKI FULWOOD** – drums

not iss. | Revilot

Jun 67. (7") *<207>* **(I WANNA) TESTIFY. / I CAN FEEL THE ICE MELTING** | – | 20

Sep 67. (7") *<211>* **ALL YOUR GOODIES ARE GONE (THE LOSER'S SEAT). / DON'T BE SORE AT ME** | – | 80

Nov 67. (7") *<214>* **THE GOOSE (THAT LAID THE GOLDEN EGG). / LITTLE MAN** | – |

Jan 68. (7") *<217>* **LOOK AT WHAT I ALMOST MISSED. / WHAT YOU BEEN GROWING** | – |

Nov 68. (7") *<228>* **A NEW DAY BEGINS. / I'LL WAIT** | – |
<re-iss. Jan69 on 'Atco'; 6675>; hit No.44>

—— 12 years later, this song was to give CLINTON rights to group name.

not iss. | Funkedelic

1969. (7"; ROSE WILLIAMS with GEORGE CLINTON & FUNKADELICS) *<6709>* **WHATEVER MAKES MY BABY FEEL GOOD. / ('A'instrumental)** | – |

FUNKADELIC

—— **CLINTON** + **RAYMOND DAVIS** – vocals / **CLARENCE 'Fuzzy' HASKINS** – vocals / **EDDIE HAZEL** – lead guitar / **TAWL ROSS** – rhythm guitar / **TKI FULTON** – drums / **MICKEY ATKINS** – some organ

BERNIE WORRELL – keyboards repl. ATKINS

Pye Int. | Westbound

1969. (7") *<148>* **MUSIC FOR MY MOTHER. / ('A'instrumental)** | – |

Sep 69. (7") *<150>* **I'LL BET YOU. / QUALIFY AND SATISFY** | – | 63

Apr 70. (7") *(7N 25519) <158>* **I GOT A THING, YOU GOT A THING, EVERYBODY'S GOT A THING. / FISH, CHIPS & SWEAT** | Feb70 | 80

Sep 70. (lp) *(NSPL 28137) <2000>* **FUNKADELIC** | Mar70 |
– Mommy, what's a Funkadelic? / I'll bet you / Music for my mother / I got a thing, you got a thing, everybody's got a thing / Good old music / Quality and satisfaction / What is soul?. *(re-iss. Aug89 on 'Westbound' lp/c/cd; SEW/SEWC/CDSEW 010)*

Dec 70. (7") *<167>* **I WANNA KNOW IF IT'S GOOD TO YOU. / ('A'instrumental)** | – | 81

1971. (lp) *(NSPL 28137) <2001>* **FREE YOUR MIND . . . AND YOUR ASS WILL FOLLOW** | Oct70 | 92
– Free your mind and your ass will follow / Friday night, August 14th / Funky dollar bill / I wanna know if it's good to you / Some more / Eulogy and light. *(re-iss. Feb90 on 'Westbound' lp/c/cd; SEW/SEWC/CDSEW 012)*

Apr 71. (7") *(7N 25548) <175>* **YOU & YOUR FOLKS, ME & MINE. / FUNKY DOLLAR BILL** | Feb71 | 91

PARLIAMENT

(i.e. **CLINTON & FUNKADELIC** musicians) + **R.DAVIS / G.THOMAS / F.HASKINS / C.SIMON**

Invictus | Invictus

Dec 70. (7") *<9077>* **I CALL MY BABY PUSSYCAT. / LITTLE OLE COUNTRY BOY** | – |
(UK-iss.Dec84 on 'H.D.H.'; HDH 457)

Feb 71. (7") *<9091>* **RED HOT MAMA. / LITTLE OLE COUNTRY BOY** | – |

Jul 71. (lp) *(SVT 1004) <7302>* **OSMIUM** | Dec70 |
– The breakdown / Call my baby Pussycat / Little ole country boy / Moonshine Heather / Oh Lord – why Lord – prayer / Red hot mama / My automobile / Nothing before me but thang / Funky woman / Come on in out of the rain / The silent boatman. *(re-iss. Feb90 as 'RHENIUM' on 'H.D.H.' cd/c/lp; HDH CD/MC/LP 008)* – (extra tracks) *(cd-iss. Jul93;)*

Jul 71. (7") *(INV 513)* **LIVIN' THE LIFE. / THE SILENT BOATMAN** | | –

Jul 71. (7") *<9095>* **THE BREAKDOWN. / LITTLE OLE COUNTRY BOY** –
Sep 71. (7") *<9123>* **COME IN OUT OF THE RAIN. / LITTLE OLE COUNTRY BOY**

FUNKADELIC

Now without NELSON + ROSS. Replaced by **GARY SHIDER** – guitar

Westbound Westbound

Sep 71. (7") *<185>* **CAN YOU GET TO THAT. / BACK IN OUR MINDS** – 93
Sep 71. (lp) *(6310 200) <2007>* **MAGGOT BRAIN** Aug71
– Maggot brain / Can you get to that / Hit it and quit it / You and your folks, me and mine / Super stupid / Back in our minds / Wars of armageddon. *(re-iss. Aug89 lp/c/cd; SEW/SEWC/CDSEW 002)*

—— added **WILLIAM BOOTSY COLLINS** – bass / **CATFISH COLLINS** – guitar / **FRANKIE 'Kash' WADDY** – drums (all of The J.B.'s, ex-JAMES BROWN)

Jul 72. (d-lp) *<2020>* **AMERICA EATS IT'S YOUNG** –
– You hit the nail on the head / If you don't like the effects / Don't produce the cause / Everybody is going to make it this time / A joyful process / We hurt too / Loose booty / Philmore / I call my baby Pussycat / America eats its young / Biological speculation / That was my girl / Balance / Miss Lucifer's love / Wake up. *(UK cd-iss. Jul90 cd/c/lp; CDSEWD/SEWC2/SEW2 029)*
1972. (7") *<197>* **I MISS MY BABY. / BABY I OWE YOU SOMETHING GOOD** –
1972. (7") *<198>* **HIT AND QUIT IT. / A WHOLE LOT OF BS** –
1973. (7") *<205>* **LOOSE BOOTY. / A JOYFUL PROCESS** –
Jul 73. (lp) *<2022>* **COSMIC SLOP** –
– Happy dug out / You can't miss what you can't measure / March to the witches castle / Let's make it last / Cosmic slop / No compute (alias spit don't make no babies) / Broken heart / Trash a go-go / Can't stand the strain. *(UK-iss.Feb91 cd/c/lp; CDSEW/SEWC/SEWA 035)*
1973. (7") *<218>* **COSMIC SLOP. / YOU DON'T LIKE THE EFFECTS, DON'T PRODUCE THE CAUSE** –

—— added **FRED WESLEY & MACEO PARKER** – horns (both of J.B.'s)

Nov 74. (lp) *<1001>* **STANDING ON THE VERGE OF GETTING IT ON** – Sep74
– Red hot mama / Alice in my fantasies / I'll stay / Sexy ways / Standing on the verge of getting it on / Jimmy's got a little bit of bitch in him / Good thoughts, bad thoughts. *(re-iss. Aug91 cd/c/lp; CDSEW/SEWC/SEWA 040)*
Nov 74. (7") *<224>* **(STANDING) ON THE VERGE OF GETTING IT ON. / JIMMY'S GOT A LITTLE BIT OF BITCH IN HIM** –
1975. (7") *<5000>* **RED HOT MAMA. / VITAL JUICES** –
1975. (lp) *<1004>* **FUNKADELIC'S GREATEST HITS** (compilation) – Jul74

20th Century Westbound

Jun 75. (lp) *(215)* **LET'S TAKE IT TO THE STAGE** –
– Good to your earhole / Better by the pound / Be my beach / No head no backstage pass / Let's take it to the stage / Get off your ass and jam / Baby I owe you something good / Stuffs & things / The song is familiar / Atmosphere. *(UK re-iss. Mar92 cd/c/lp; CDSEW/SEWC/SEWA 044)*
Oct 75. (7") *<5014>* **BETTER BY THE POUND. / STUFFS AND THINGS** – 99
Jan 76. (7") *<5026>* **LET'S TAKE IT TO THE STAGE. / BIOLOGICAL SPECULATION** –

—— **MIKE HAMPTON** – guitar repl. EDDIE HAZEL who went solo

1976. (lp) *<227>* **TALES OF KIDD FUNKADELIC** –
– Butt to butt resuscitation / Let's take it to the people / Undisco kid / Take your dead ass home / I'm never gonna tell it / Takes of Kidd Funkadelic / How do yeaw view you. *(UK re-iss. Mar93 cd/lp; CDSEW/SEWA 054)*
1976. (7") *<5029>* **UNDISCO KIDD. / HOW DO YEAW VIEW YOU** –

—— After one more compilation 'THE BEST OF FUNKADELIC EARLY YEARS, VOL.1' in 1977, COLLINS continued with BOOTSY'S RUBBER BAND. Also leaving were HASKINS, SIMON and DAVIS who were to form own FUNKADELIC in the early 80's. They and 'Lax' label issued album CONNECTIONS AND DISCONNECTIONS (without CLINTON).

—— Meanwhile in the mid-70's,

PARLIAMENT

(**CLINTON, etc.**) were signed to . . .

Casablanca Casablan

Dec 74. (7") *<0003>* **THE GOOSE (pt.1). / (pt.2)** –
Dec 74. (lp) *(CAL 2011) <7002>* **UP FOR THE DOWN STROKE** Aug74
– Up for the down stroke / Testify / The goose / I can move you (if you le me) / I just got back / All your goodies are gone / Whatever makes bab feel good / Presence of a brain. *(re-iss. May77 & Nov78; same)*
Feb 75. (7") *(CBX 505) <0013>* **UP FOR THE DOWN STROKE. / PRESENCE OF A BRAIN** Aug74 63
Feb 75. (7") *<811>* **TESTIFY. / I CAN MOVE YOU (IF YOU LET ME)** –
May 75. (7") *<831>* **CHOCOLATE CITY. / ('A'long version)** – 94
Jun 75. (lp) *(CAL 2012) <7014>* **CHOCOLATE CITY** Apr75 91
– Chocolate city / Ride on / Together / Side effects / What comes funky Let me be / If it don't fit (don't force it) / Misjudged you / Big footin *(re-iss. May77; same)*
Nov 75. (7") *<843>* **RIDE ON. / BIG FOOTIN'** –
Jun 76. (7") *<852>* **P. FUNK (WANTS TO GET FUNKED UP). / NIGHT OF THE THUMPASORUS PEOPLES** –
Jun 76. (lp) *(CAL 2013) <7022>* **MOTHERSHIP CONNECTION** Feb76 13
– P. Funk (wants to get funked up) / Mothership connection (star child) Unfunky UFO / Supergroovalisticprosifunkstication (the thumps bump) Handcuffs / Tear the roof off the sucker (give up the funk) / Night of th thumpasorus people. *(re-iss. May77; same) (re-iss. Aug87; 824 502-1/-4)*
Jun 76. (7") *(CBX 518) <856>* **TEAR THE ROOF OFF THE SUCKER (GIVE UP THE FUNK). / P. FUNK (WANTS TO GET FUNKED UP)** May76 15
1976. (7") *<864>* **STAR CHILD. / SUPERGROOVALISTICPROSIFUNKSTACATION (THE THUMPS BUMB)** –
Oct 76. (7",12") *<871>* **DO THAT STUFF. / HANDCUFFS** –
May 77. (lp) *(CAL 2001) <7034>* **THE CLONES OF DR. FUNKENSTEIN** Oct76 20
– Prelude / Gamin' on ya / Dr. Funkenstein / Children of productions Gettin' to know you / Do that stuff / Everything is on the one / I've bee watching you (move your sexy body) / Funkin' for fun. *(re-iss. Feb9 cd/c/lp; 842620-2)*
Jan 77. (7") *<875>* **DR. FUNKENSTEIN. / CHILDREN OF PRODUCTION** –
May 77. (7"m) *(CAN 103)* **TEAR THE ROOF OFF THE SUCKER (GIVE UP THE FUNK). / DR. FUNKENSTEIN / P. FUNK (WANTS TO GET FUNKED UP)** –
Jun 77. (d-lp) *(CALD 5002) <7053>* **PARLIAMENT LIVE – P.FUNK EARTH TOUR (live)** May77 29
– P. Funk (wants to get funked up) / Dr. Funkenstein' supergroovalisticprosi-funkstication / Medley: (a) Let's take it to the stage (b) Take your dead ass home, (c) Say som'n nasty / Do that stuff / Th landing (of the holy mothership) / The undisco Kidd (the girl is bad) Children of production / Mothership connection (star child) / Swin down, sweet chariot / This is the way we funk with you (featuring Mik Hampton; lead snare) / Dr. Funkenstein / Gamin' on you / Tear the roo off the sucker medley:- (a) Give up the funk (tear the roof off the sucker (b) Get off your ass and jam / Night of the thumpasorus people / Fantas is reality.
1977. (7") *<892>* **FANTASY IS REALITY. / THE LANDING (OF THE HOLY MOTHERSHIP)** –
Dec 77. (lp) *(CALN 2021) <7084>* **FUNKENTELECHY VS. THE PLACEBO SYNDROME** 13
– Bop gun (endangered species) / Sir Nose D'voidoffunk / Pay attentio B-3M / Wizard of finance / Funkentelechy / Placebo syndrome / Flas light.
Jan 78. (7") *(CAN 115) <900>* **BOP GUN (ENDANGERED SPECIES). / I'VE BEEN WATCHING YOU (MOVE YOUR SEXY BODY)** Nov77
(12"+=) *(CANL 115)* – Do that stuff. *<US-12" has 2 'A'mixes>*
Apr 78. (7") *(CAN 123) <909>* **FLASH LIGHT. / SWING LOW, SWEET CHARIOT (live)** Feb78 16
(US-12") *<same>* – (2 'A'mixes).
1978. (7") *<921>* **FUNKENTELECHY (part 1). / (part 2)** –

—— Early '78, other PARLIAMENT / FUNKADELIC off-shoots "PARLET (vocalists MALLIA FRANKLIN, JEANETTE WASHINGTON and SHIRLE HAYDEN) released album 'THE PLEASURE PRINCIPLE'. Another albur

'INVASIONS OF THE BODY SNATCHERS' was further issued Jul 79. "The BRIDES OF FUNKENSTEIN" (vocalists LYNN MABRY and DAWN SILVA) released album 'FUNK OR WALK' on 'Atlantic' late 1978.

FUNKADELIC

meanwhile had reappeared signing to . . .

Warners Warners

1977. (7") *<8309>* **COMIN' ROUND THE MOUNTAIN. / IF YOU GOT FUNK, YOU GOT STYLE** –

Feb 78. (lp) *(K 56299) <2973>* **HARDCORE JOLLIES** Nov77 96
– Osmosis phase one / Comin' round the mountain / Smokey / If you got funk, you got style / Hardcore jollies / Terribitus phase two / Sould mate / Cosmic slop / You scared the lovin' outta me / Adolescent funk. *(re-iss. Jul93 on 'Charly' cd/lp; CDGR/LPGR 101)*

Feb 78. (7") *<8367>* **SMOKEY. / SOUL MATE** –

— add **JEROME BRAILEY** – drums (who had joined PARLIAMENT mid '76) / **WALTER 'JUNIE' MORRISON** – keyboards (ex-OHIO PLAYERS)

Nov 78. (7"/12") *(K 17246/+T) <8618>* **ONE NATION UNDER A GROOVE (part 1). / (part 2)** 9 Oct78 28

Dec 78. (lp) *(K 56539) <3209>* **ONE NATION UNDER A GROOVE** 56 Sep78 16
– One nation under a groove / Groovallegience / Who says a funk band can't play rock / Promentalashitbackwashipsychosisenema squad / Into you / Cholly (funk getting ready to roll) / Lunchmeat and phobia / P.E.squad / Doodoo chasers / Maggot brain. *(re-iss. Jul93 on 'Charly' cd/lp; CDGR/LPGR 100)*

Apr 79. (7") *(K 17321) <8735>* **CHOLLY (FUNK GETTING READY TO ROLL). / INTO YOU**
(US-12") *<same>* – (2-'A'mixes).

— drummer BRAILEY left to form own group MUTINY.

Oct 79. (lp) *(K 56712) <3371>* **UNCLE JAM WANTS YOU** 18
– Freak of the week / (Not just) Knee deep / Uncle Jam / Field manoeuvres / Cholly wants to go to California / Foot soldiers. *(re-iss. Jun93 on 'Charly' cd/lp; CDGR/LPGR 103)*

Jan 80. (7") *(K 17494) <49040>* **(NOT JUST) KNEE DEEP. / (part 2)** Oct79 77

1980. (7") *<49117>* **UNCLE JAM. / (part 2)** –

Aug 81. (7"/12") *(K 17786/+T) <49667>* **THE ELECTRIC SPANKING OF WAR BABIES. / THE ELECTRIC SPANKING (instrumental)**

Apr 81. (lp) *(K 56874) <3482>* **THE ELECTRIC SPANKING OF WAR BABIES**
– The electric spanking of war babies / Electrocuties / Funk gets stronger / Brettino's bounce / She loves you / Shockwaves / Oh, I / Laka-prick. *(re-iss. Jun93 on 'Charly' cd/lp; CDGR/LPGR 102)*

1981. (7") *<49807>* **SHOCKWAVES. / BRETTINO'S BOUNCE** –

— (above featured CLINTON's long-time friend SLY STONE)

— The FUNKADELIC project had now been abandoned, due to splinter band.

PARLIAMENT

were still around simultaneously with FUNKADELIC and continued throughout the 80's.

Casablanca Casablanca

Dec 78. (7") *(CAN 136) <950>* **AQUA BOOGIE (A PSYCHO ALPHADISCOBETABIOQUADOLOOP). / (YOU'RE A FISH AND I'M A) WATER SIGN** 89

Dec 78. (lp/pic-lp) *(CAL N/H 2043) <7125>* **MOTOR-BOOTY AFFAIR** 23
– Mr. Wiggles / Rumpopsteelskin / (You're a fish and I'm a) Water sign / Aqua boogie (a psychoalphadiscobetabioquadoloop) / One of those funky things / Liquid sunshine / Motor-booty affair / Deep. *(re-iss. Feb91 cd/c/lp; 842621-2)*

1979. (7") *<976>* **RUMPOFSTEELSKIN. / LIQUID SUNSHINE** –

Jul 79. (7"/12") *(CAN/+L 154)* **DEEP. / FLASH LIGHT** –

Dec 79. (lp) *<(NBLP 7195)>* **GLORYHALLASTOOPID – OR PIN THE TALE ON THE FUNKY** – 44
– Party people / Big bang theory / Freeze (sizzaleenmean) / Colour me funky / Theme from the black hole / May we bang you / Gloryhallastoopid (or pin the tale on the funky).

Jan 80. (12") *(CANL 188)* **THEME FROM THE BLACK HOLE. / THE BIG BANG THEORY** –

Apr 80. (7") *<(NR 2222)>* **PARTY PEOPLE. / PARTY PEOPLE (reprise)** Dec79
(12") – ('A'side) / Tear the roof off the sucker (give up the funk) / Flash light.

1980. (7") *<2235>* **THEME FROM THE BLACK HOLE. / (YOU'RE A FISH AND I'M A) WATER SIGN** –

Apr 81. (7"/12") *(CAN/+L 223) <2250>* **AGONY OF DE FEET. / THE FREEZE (SIZZALEENMEAN)**

Apr 81. (lp) *<(NBLP 7249)>* **TROMBIPULATION** Jan81 61
– Trombipulation / crush it / Long way round / Agony of de feet / Now doo review / Let's play house / Body language / Peck-a-groove. *(cd-iss. Feb91; 842623-2)*

— PARLIAMENT were also defunkt, leaving behind a few exploitation releases

1981. (12") *<NBD 20235>* **CRUSH IT. / BODY LANGUAGE** –

GEORGE CLINTON

(solo) with numerous session people and **BOOTSY COLLINS / FRED WESLEY**

— another GEORGE CLINTON issued 1979 single 'Please Don't Run From Me'

Capitol Capitol

Nov 82. (lp/c) *<(EST/TCEST 12246)>* **COMPUTER GAMES** 40
– Get dressed / Man's best friend / Loopzilla / Pot sharing tots / Computer games / Atomic dog / Free alterations / One fun at a time. *(re-iss. May95 on 'MCI' cd/c; MUS CD/MC 511) (cd-iss. Apr97 on 'E.M.I.'; REPLAYCD 45)*

Nov 82. (7") *(CL 271) <5160>* **LOOPZILLA. / POT SHARING TOTS** 57
(12"+=) *(12CL 271)* – ('A'-broadcast version).
(US-12") *<8538>* – (2-'A'versions).

Feb 83. (7")(12") *(CL 280) <5201><8556>* **ATOMIC DOG. / MAN'S BEST FRIEND**
(12"+=) *(12CL 280) <8544>* – ('A'instrumental).

1983. (7") *<5222>* **GET DRESSED. / FREE ALTERATIONS** –

Dec 83. (7"/12") *(CL 319) <5296><8572>* **NUBIAN NUT. / FREE ALTERATIONS**
(12") *<9039>* – (2-'A'versions).

Jan 84. (lp/c) *<(EST/TCEST 12308)>* **YOU SHOULDN'T NUF BIT FISH** Dec83
– Nubian nut / Quickie / Last dance / Silly millameter / Stingy / You shouldn't – Nuf bit fish. *(cd-iss. Sep91 on 'E.M.I.'; CZ 469)*

1984. (7")(12") *<5324><8580>* **QUICKIE. / LAST DANCE** –

1984. (7")(ext-12") *<5332><9065>* **LAST DANCE. / LAST DANCE (version)** –

Jul 85. (7") *(CL 365) <5473>* **DOUBLE OH-OH. / BANGLADESH**
(12") *<8642>* – (2-'A'versions).

Sep 85. (lp/c) *(CLINT/TC-CLINT 1) <12417>* **SOME OF MY BEST JOKES ARE FRIENDS** Aug85
– Some of my best jokes are friends / Double oh-oh / Bulletproof / Pleasures of exhaustion (do it till I drop) / Bodyguard / Bangladesh / Thrashin' / Some of my best jokes are friends – reprise.

Dec 85. (7")(12") *<5504><8653>* **BULLETPROOF. / SILLY MILLAMETER** –

Apr 86. (7") *(CL 402)* **DO FRIES GO WITH THAT SHAKE. / PLEASURES OF EXHAUSTION (DO IT TILL I DROP)** 57
(UK-12"+=) *(12CL 402)* – Scratch medley.
(US-12") *<15219>* – (2-'A'versions).

— Did he release IRON EAGLE (Soundtrack) album around this time?

May 86. (7") *<5602>* **HEY GOOD LOOKIN'. / ('A'mix)** –
(12"+=) *<15263>* – ('A'extended).

May 86. (lp) *<12481>* **R&B SKELETONS (IN THE CLOSET)** –
– Hey good looking / Do fries go with that shake / Mix master suite – Startin' from scratch – Counter irritant – Nothing left to burn – Electric Pygmies – Intense – Cool Joe – R&B Skeleton (in the closet). *(UK cd-iss. Sep91 on 'E.M.I.'; CZ 470)*

1986. (7") *<5642>* **R&B SKELETONS IN THE CLOSET. / NUBIAN NUT** –

1987. (lp) *<12534>* **THE BEST OF GEORGE CLINTON & THE MOTHERSHIP CONNECTION LIVE FROM HOUSTON (live)** –
– Atomic dog / R&B skeletons (in the closet) / Quickie / Do fries go with that shake / Hey good lookin' / Double oh-oh / Nubian nut / Last dance.

Paisley Park Paisley Park

Jul 89. (7"/12") *(W 7557/+T) <27557>* **WHY SHOULD I DOG U OUT (part 1). / (part 2)**

Aug 89. (lp/c/cd) *(K 925994-1/-4/-2)* <25994> **THE CINDERELLA THEORY**
– Airbound / Tweakin' / The Cinderella theory / Why should I dog you out? / Serious slammin' / There I go again / (She's got it) Goin' on / The banana boat song / French kiss / Rita bewitched / Kredit-Kard / Airbound (reprise).

1989. (7") *<22190>* **TWEAKIN'. / FRENCH KISS** –
(12") *<21337>* – ('A'side) / Hysterical / ('A'remix).

Oct 93. (cd/c) *(7599 25518-2/-4)* **HEY MAN, SMELL MY FINGER**
– Martial law / Paint the White House black / Way up / Dis beat disrupts / Get satisfied / Hollywood / Rhythm and rhyme / The big pump / If true love / High in my hello / Maximumisness / Kickback / The flag was still there / Martial law (hey man . . . smell my finger) (single version). *(re-iss. Mar95 on 'New Power Generation' cd/c; NPG 6053-2/-4)*

— CLINTON guested for PRIMAL SCREAM on their early 1994 album 'GIVE OUT BUT DON'T GIVE UP'. To start the second half of '94, he featured on ICE CUBE single 'BOP GUN (ONE NATION) ', a re-indition of his old FUNKADELIC number.

Essential / Rykodisc

Feb 95. (cd) *(ESSCD 280)* **FIFTH OF FUNK**
– Flatman and Robin / Count Funkula (I didn't know that funk was loaded) / Thumparella (Oh Kay) / Eyes of a dreamer / I found you / Ice melting in your heart / Clone ranger / Who do you love / Up up up and away / Can't get over losing you / Rat kissed the cat / Too tight for light / Every little bit hurts. *(re-iss. Apr97; ESMCD 490)*

the P-FUNK ALL STARS

— another CLINTON aggregation

not iss. / Hump

1982. (7") *<1>* **HYDRAULIC PUMP. / (part 2)** –
1982. (7") *<3>* **ONE OF THOSE SUMMERS. / IT'S TOO FUNKY IN HERE** –

not iss. / CBS

1983. (7") *<04032>* **GENERATOR POP. / (part 2)** –

not iss. / Uncle Jam

1983. (lp) *<39168>* **URBAN DANCEFLOOR GUERRILLAS** –

Westbound / Westbound

Oct 90. (d-cd/d-c/d-lp) *(CDSEW2/SEWC2/SEW2 031)* **P-FUNK ALL STARS LIVE (live at The Beverly Theater 1983)**
Jun 95. (cd/lp) *(CD+/SEWD 097)* **HYDRAULIC FUNK** (early material) –
– Pump up and down / Pumpin' it up / Copy cat / Throw your hand up in the air / Generator pop / Acupuncture / One of those summers / Catch a keeper / Pumpin' you is so easy / Generator pop (mix).

GEORGE CLINTON & THE P-FUNK ALL STARS

Hot Hands / Hot Hands

Apr 95. (12"/cd-s) *(12/CD HOTH 1)* **FOLLOW THE LEADER. / ('A'-D&S radio mix) / ('A'-Kool az phuk mix)**
May 95. (cd/c) *(HOTH CD/CD/MC/LP 1)* **DOPE DOGS** Mar95
– Dog star (fly on) / U.S. custom coast guard dope dog / Some next shit / Just say ding (databoy) / Help Scottie, help (I'm tweaking and I can't beam up!) / Pepe (the pill popper) / Back against the wall / Fifi / All sons of bitches / Sick 'em / I ain't the lady (he ain't the tramp) / Pack of wild dogs / Tales that wag the dog / My dog.

MJJ-Epic / MJJ-Epic

May 96. (c-s) *(663321-4)* **IF ANYBODY GETS FUNKED UP (IT'S GONNA BE YOU) (Colin Wolfe mix) / (album mix)**
(12"+=/cd-s+=) *(663321-6/-2)* – ('A'-Colin Wolfe instrumental).
Jun 96. (cd/c/lp) *(483833-2/-4/-1)* **T.A.P.O.A.F.O.M.**
– If anybody gets funked up (it's gonna be you) / Summer swim / Funky kind (gonna knock it down) / Mathematics / Hard as steel / New spaceship / Underground angel / Let's get funky / Flatman and Bobbin / Sloppy seconds / Rock the party / Get your funk on / T.A.P.O.A.F.O.M. (fly away).

— also P-FUNK singles on UK 'Frontline' in 1995; 'P-FUNK ERA' & 'RETURN OF THE GANGSTA'

Premier / Capitol

Mar 97. (d-lp/cd) *(PRMD/+CD 20)* <33911> **THE GREATEST FUNKIN' HITS** (remixes) Oct96

Fruit Tree / Fruit Tree

Feb 04. (cd; as GEORGE CLINTON) *<(FT 830)>* **500,000 KILOWATTS OF P-FUNK POWER (live)**
– Bop gun / Standing on the verge / Good love (instrumental) / Funkentelechy / Funk getting ready to roll / Let's take it to the stage / Cosmic slop / Maggot brain / Make my funk the P-Funk / Flashlight / Aquaboogie / Give up the funk / The Mothership connection / Atomic dog / Pepe (the pill popper) / Let's get satisfied – Dope dog / Ain't nothin' but a jam y'all / State of the nation.

Nocturne / C Kunspyru

Mar 06. (d-cd) *(GCE 009)* *<10>* **HOW LATE DO U HAVE 2 B B 4 U R ABSENT?** Sep05
– Bounce 2 this / Su, su, su / Paradigm / U can depend on me / U ain't runnin' shit / Inhale slow / Because – Last time zone / Never ending love / Sexy side of you / Saddest day / I can dance / I'll be sittin' here / Don't dance too close / More than words can say (live) / Butt-a-butt / Something stank / Our secret / Viagra / Gypsy woman / Whole lotta shakin' / Goodnight sweetheart, goodnight / Whatchamacallit / Trust in yourself / Booty.

– (GEORGE CLINTON compilations) –

Aug 92. (cd/c/lp; Various) *Essential; (ESS CD/MC/LP 185)* **GEORGE CLINTON FAMILY SERIES – VOL.1** –
(cd re-iss. Jul96; ESMCD 383)
Jan 93. (cd/c/lp; Various) *Essential; (ESS CD/MC/LP 189)* **GEORGE CLINTON FAMILY SERIES – VOL.2** –
(cd re-iss. Jul96; ESMCD 384)
Feb 93. (cd/lp) *Music Of Life; (MOL CD/LP 026)* **SAMPLE SOME OF DISC, SAMPLE SOME OF DAT** –
(re-iss. Nov94 cd/lp; MOL CD/LP 36)
Jun 93. (cd/c/lp; Various) *Essential; (ESS CD/MC/LP 190)* **GEORGE CLINTON FAMILY SERIES PART 3 – P IS THE FUNK** –
(cd re-iss. Jul96; ESMCD 385)
Sep 93. (cd/c/lp; Various) *Essential; (ESS CD/MC/LP 198)* **GEORGE CLINTON FAMILY SERIES – VOL.4** –
Oct 93. (cd/lp) *Music For Life; (MOL CD/LP 33)* **SAMPLE SOME OF DISC, SAMPLE SOME OF DAT, VOL.II** –

– (PARLIAMENT) compilations –

Sep 86. (lp/c) *Club; (JAB B/C 18)* **UNCUT FUNK – THE BOMB (THE BEST OF PARLIAMENT)** –
May 93. (d-cd) *Mercury; (514417-2)* **TEAR THE ROOF OFF: 1974-80**
(re-iss. Sep95; same)
Oct 94. (cd; PARLIAMENTS) *Goldmine; (GSCD 052)* **I WANNA TESTIFY**
Sep 95. (cd) *Mercury; (526995-2)* **GIVE UP THE FUNK** –
Jun 97. (cd) *Deepbeats; (DEEPMO 23)* **PARLIAMENT – THE EARLY YEARS** –

– (FUNKADELIC) compilations, etc –

1989. (12") *M.C.A.; <23953>* **BY THE WAY OF THE DRUM. / ('A'edit) / ('A'instrumental)** –
Aug 90. (4xpic-cd-box) *Westbound; (WBOXPD 1)* **FUNKADELIC PICTURE DISC BOX SET** –
Oct 92. (d-cd/d-c/d-lp) *Westbound; (CDSEW/SEWC/SEW 2055)* **MUSIC FOR YOUR MOTHER (the singles)**
Mar 94. (4xpic-cd-box) *Westbound; (WBOXPD 5)* **PICTURE DISC BOXED SET VOLUME 2**
– (COSMIC SLOP / TALES OF KIDD FUNKADELIC / LET'S TAKE IT TO THE STAGE / STANDING ON THE VERGE OF GETTING IT ON)
Mar 94. (cd/lp) *Charly; (CDGR/LPGR 104)* **THE BEST OF FUNKADELIC 1976-1981** –
(cd re-iss. Mar01 on 'Snapper'; SNAP 001CD)
Nov 94. (cd) *Charly; (CPCD 8064)* **HARDCORE FUNK JAM** –
Oct 94. (4xcd-box) *Sequel; (NEFCD 273)* **PARLIAMENT / FUNKADELIC LIVE (live)** –
Apr 96. (c-s/12"/cd-s) *Charly; (MC/12/CD NATION 1)* **ONE NATION UNDER A GROOVE** –
Apr 96. (cd) *Westbound; (CDSEWD 108)* **FUNKADELIC LIVE (live Rochester 1971)**
May 97. (cd/c) *Southbound; (CD+/SEWD 115)* **FINEST**

Sep 97. (cd) *Music Club; (MCCD 307)* **ULTIMATE FUNKADELIC** [ ] [–]
Mar 98. (d-cd) *Charly; (CPCD 83062)* **THE VERY BEST OF FUNKADELIC** [ ] [ ]
Sep 99. (cd) *Delta; (47004)* **FUNK GETS STRONGER** [ ] [–]
Aug 00. (cd) *Metro; (METRCD 025)* **ORIGINAL COSMIC FUNK CREW** [ ] [–]
Jan 02. (4xcd-box) *Snapper; (SNAB 909CD)* **THE COMPLETE RECORDINGS 1976-1981** [ ] [ ]

Eddie COCHRAN

Born: EDWARD RAY COCHRAN, 3 Oct'38, Oklahoma City, Oklahoma. Raised in Albert Lea, Minnesota, he later moved with his Irish parents to Bell Gardens, Los Angeles in 1951. Four years later, the young, self-taught guitarist EDDIE formed The COCHRANS with his hillbilly friend, HANK COCHRAN (no relation), the pair soon securing a deal with 'Ekko'. Songwriter JERRY CAPEHEART joined the duo early in 1956 for a single 'WALKIN' STICK BOOGIE', although HANK subsequently moved to Nashville after CAPEHEART became EDDIE's new writing partner (and later manager). Although their first collaboration, 'SKINNY JIM', flopped, CAPEHEART negotiated a deal with 'Liberty', who, in turn, released his major label debut, 'SITTIN' IN THE BALCONY'. Boosted by a cameo role in the rock'n'roll movie, 'The Girl Can't Help It' (performing 'TWENTY FLIGHT ROCK'), the single became a Top 20 hit in the Spring of '57. After a couple of flops and minor hits during the next year, he finally recorded a commercial follow-up in 'SUMMERTIME BLUES', a lip-curling, deceptively simple, all-time classic, which introduced COCHRAN the leather-clad, rebellious rocker to hordes of screaming female fans. Rock'n'roll's answer to James Dean, he eventually followed up with two more attitude-stoked nuggets, 'C'MON EVERYBODY' and 'SOMETHIN' ELSE'; twenty years on, the SEX PISTOLS – with SID VICIOUS at the helm – resurrected these hits in appropriately snotty punk style. In the interim, COCHRAN took part in the Alan Freed / Hal Roach film, 'Go, Johnny Go!', although he had to withdraw from a winter tour alongside his famous friend, BUDDY HOLLY. The tour in question was the ill-fated jaunt that claimed the lives of not just HOLLY, but RICHIE VALENS and BIG BOPPER, all three dying when their plane crashed in February '59. Early the following year, on the strength of his UK success (he was now a bigger star in Britain than he was in the States!), COCHRAN toured around England with co-headliner, GENE VINCENT, for a few months. Having accepted an extension to stay for further shows, he invited girlfriend, SHARON SHEELEY, to come over for her birthday. However, on the 17th of April 1960, COCHRAN, SHEELEY and VINCENT were involved in a car crash, when their London cab skidded off the road. While SHEELEY and VINCENT suffered a few broken bones, EDDIE COCHRAN died after being propelled through the windscreen. A month later, the poignantly titled 'THREE STEPS TO HEAVEN' hit the top of the British charts while criminally ignored in his native America. A plethora of material was posthumously issued, most selling well enough to again hit the UK charts; nearly four decades on, his best songs still retain a primal power which successive generations of musicians have strived to capture. To think that EDDIE was only twenty-one when he died, one can only speculate as to what heights he might have scaled.

Songwriters: As said above plus covers: SITTIN' IN THE BALCONY (Johnny Dee) / SOMETHIN' ELSE + LONELY (c.Sharon Sheeley) / HALLELUJAH I LOVE HER SO (Ray Charles) / MY WAY (Paul Anka) / WEEKEND (Post-Post) / CUT ACROSS SHORTY (Wilkin-Walker) / NERVOUS BREAKDOWN (. . . Roccuzzo) / etc.

Best CD compilation: LEGENDARY MASTERS (*9)

COCHRAN BROTHERS

EDDIE – guitar, vocals / **HANK COCHRAN** (no relation) – vocals, guitar / with **CONNIE 'GUMBO' SMITH** – bass / **HAROLD HENSLEY** – fiddle

not iss. | Ekko

Jul 55. (7",78) *<1003>* **MR. FIDDLE. / TWO BLUE SINGIN' STARS** [–] [ ]
Nov 55. (7",78) *<1005>* **GUILTY CONSCIENCE. / YOUR TOMORROW MAY NEVER COME** [–] [ ]

— (next 7", in Feb'56 **WALKIN' STICK BOOGIE. / ROLLIN'** was credited to **JERRY CAPEHEART with The COCHRAN BROTHERS** on 'Cash' records.

Jun 56. (7",78) *<3001>* **TIRED AND SLEEPY. / FOOL'S PARADISE** [–] [ ]

EDDIE COCHRAN

not iss. | Crest

Oct 56. (7",78) *<1026>* **SKINNY JIM. / HALF LOVED** [–] [ ]

London | Liberty

Apr 57. (7",78) *(HLU 8386)* **20 FLIGHT ROCK. / DARK LONELY STREET** [ ] [–]
Jul 57. (7",78) *(HLU 8433) <55056>* **SITTIN' IN THE BALCONY. / DARK LONELY STREET** [ ] Mar57 [18]
Jun 57. (7",78) *<55070>* **MEAN WHILE I'M MAD. / ONE KISS** [–] [ ]
Aug 57. (7",78) *<55087>* **DRIVE IN-SHOW. / AM I BLUE** [–] [82]
Nov 57. (7",78) *<55112>* **20 FLIGHT ROCK. / CRADLE BABY** [–] [ ]
Jan 58. (7",78) *<55123>* **JEANIE, JEANIE, JEANIE. / POCKET FULL OF HEARTACHES** [–] [94]
Apr 58. (7",78) *<55138>* **PRETTY GIRL. / THERESA** [–] [ ]
Aug 58. (lp) *(HA-U 2093)* **SINGIN' TO MY BABY** [ ] [–]
– Sittin' in the balcony / Completely sweet / Undying love / I'm alone because I love you / Lovin' time / Proud of you / Am I blue / Twenty flight rock / Drive-in show / Mean when I'm mad / Stockin's 'n' shoes / Tell me why / Have I told you lately that I love you / Cradle baby / One kiss. *(re-dist.Jul60, hit UK No.19) (re-iss. Sep63 on 'Liberty'; LBY 1158)* – hit No.20 *(re-iss. Nov68 on 'Liberty' mono/stereo; LBL/LBS 83152)*
Sep 58. (7",78) *(HLU 8702) <55144>* **SUMMERTIME BLUES. / LOVE AGAIN** [18] Aug58 [8]
Jan 59. (7",78) *(HLU 8792) <55166>* **C'MON EVERYBODY. / DON'T EVER LET ME GO** [6] Dec58 [35]
(re-iss. Mar84 on 'United Artists'; UP 603)

— Augmented by **The KELLY FOUR: JIM STIVERS** – piano / **MIKE HENDERSON** – sax / **DAVE SCHRIEBER** – bass / **GENE RIDGIO** – drums

Jun 59. (7",78) *(HLU 8880) <55177>* **TEENAGE HEAVEN. / I REMEMBER** [ ] Jan59 [99]
Sep 59. (7",78) *(HLU 8944) <55203>* **SOMETHIN' ELSE. / BOLL WEEVIL SONG** [22] Aug59 [58]
(re-iss. Sep79 on 'United Artists'; UP 36521)
Jan 60. (7",78) *(HLW 9022) <55217>* **HALLELUJAH I LOVE HER SO. / LITTLE ANGEL** [22] Dec59 [ ]
Tragedy struck on the 17th of April 1960 when EDDIE was killed (see above). Below release was already recorded and due out.
May 60. (7",78) *(HLG 9115) <55242>* **THREE STEPS TO HEAVEN. / CUT ACROSS SHORTY** [1] [ ]

– (selective) compilations, etc. –

on 'Liberty' unless mentioned otherwise

Sep 60. (lp) *London; (HAG 2267)* **THE EDDIE COCHRAN MEMORIAL ALBUM** [9] [–]
– C'mon everybody / Three steps to Heaven / Cut across Shorty / Jeannie, Jeannie, Jeannie / Pocketful of hearts / Hallelujah, I love her so / Don't ever let me go / Summertime blues / Teresa / Somethin' else / Pretty girl / Teenage heaven / Boll Weevil song / I remember. *(re-iss. Apr63 on 'Liberty'; LBY 1127)* – hit No.11 *(re-iss. Apr68 on 'Liberty' mono/stereo; LBL/LBS 83009)*
Sep 60. (7") *London; (HLG 9196) / Liberty; <55278>* **SWEETIE PIE. / LONELY** [38] [ ]
(above was flipped over after 3 weeks and hit UK No.41)
Jun 61. (7") *London; (HLG 9362)* **WEEKEND. / CHERISHED MEMORIES** [15] [–]
Nov 61. (7") *London; (HLG 9460)* **JEANNIE, JEANNIE, JEANNIE. / POCKETFUL OF HEARTS** [31] [–]
Dec 62. (lp) *(LBY 1109)* **CHERISHED MEMORIES** [15] [–]
– Cherished memories / I've waited so long / Never / Skinny Jim / Half loved / Weekend / Nervous breakdown / Let's go together / Rock and roll

blues / Dark lonely street / Pink pegged slacks / That's my desire / Sweetie pie / Think of me. *(re-iss. Nov68 mono/stereo; LBL/LBS 83072E) (re-iss. Feb72 on 'Sunset'; SLS 50289) (re-iss. Sep83 lp/c; LBR/TC-LBR 182701-1/-4)*

Apr 63. (7") *(LIB 10088)* **MY WAY. / ROCK AND ROLL BLUES** [23] [–]

Apr 68. (7") *(LBF 15071)* **SUMMERTIME BLUES. / LET'S GET TOGETHER** [34] [–]

Aug 68. (7") *(LBF 15109)* **MILK COW BLUES. / SOMETHIN' ELSE** [ ] [–]

Apr 70. (lp) *(LBS 83337)* **THE VERY BEST OF EDDIE COCHRAN (10th ANNIVERSARY ALBUM)** [34] [–]

Aug 70. (7") *(LBF 15366)* **C'MON EVERYBODY. / MEAN WHEN I'M MAD** [ ] [–]

Nov 70. (lp) *Sunset; (SLS 50155)* **C'MON EVERYBODY** [ ] [–]
(re-iss. Mar88 on 'Liberty' cd/c/lp with extra tracks; CD/TC+/ECR 1) – hit UK No.53

Apr 75. (lp) *United Artists; (UAG 29760) <LA 428E>* **THE VERY BEST OF EDDIE COCHRAN (15th ANNIVERSARY ALBUM)** [ ] [ ]
(re-iss. May82 on 'Fame' lp/c; FA/TC-FA 3019) (cd-iss. May90; CDFA 3019)

Aug 79. (lp/c) *United Artists; (UAK/TCK 30244)* **THE EDDIE COCHRAN SINGLES ALBUM** [39] [–]

Jan 88. (7") *(EDDIE 501)* **C'MON EVERYBODY. / DON'T EVER LET ME GO** [14] [–]
(12"+=/cd-s+=) *(12/CD EDDIE 501)* – Skinny Jim / Jeannie, Jeannie, Jeannie.

Mar 91. (4xcd-box) *(CDECB 1)* **THE EDDIE COCHRAN BOX SET** [ ] [–]

Oct 97. (cd) *Music Club; (MCCD 318)* **RARE 'N' ROCKIN': 28 GEMS FROM THE GOLDEN AGE OF ROCK'N'ROLL** [ ] [–]

Feb 98. (cd) *Disky; (TO 86095-2)* **THE ORIGINAL** [ ] [ ]

Apr 98. (cd) *Razor & Tie; (RE 2162-2)* **SOMETHIN' ELSE: THE FINE LOOKIN' HITS OF EDDIE COCHRAN** [ ] [ ]

Oct 99. (cd) *Rockstar; (RSRCD 011)* **ROCKIN' IT COUNTRY STYLE: THE LEGENDARY CHUCK FOREMAN RECORDINGS 1953-1955** [ ] [ ]

Oct 99. (cd; with GENE VINCENT) *Rockstar; (RSRCD 016)* **TOWN HALL PARTY 1958-1959** [ ] [ ]

Sep 00. (cd; with GENE VINCENT) *Rockstar; (RSRCD 018)* **ROCK'N'ROLL MEMORIES** [ ] [ ]

Feb 01. (cd) *E.M.I.; (5761430)* **THE STORY** [ ] [ ]

Jul 01. (cd) *E.M.I.; (533631-2)* **TWELVE OF HIS BIGGEST HITS – NEVER TO BE FORGOTTEN** [ ] [ ]

Joe COCKER

Born: JOHN ROBERT COCKER, 20 May'44, Sheffield, England. COCKER's first musical influence was RAY CHARLES, after hearing the track 'What'd I Say', also taking in the blues sounds of LIGHTNIN' HOPKINS, MUDDY WATERS and JOHN LEE HOOKER. Pipefitter by day and pub singer by night, his band, VANCE ARNOLD & THE AVENGERS were signed to 'Decca' in '65, cutting the BEATLES cover, 'I'LL CRY INSTEAD'. Although the single failed to achieve any real success, COCKER gave it a second bash in '67, making a demo tape for the influential Denny Cordell, the producer of Procol Harum's 'A WHITER SHADE OF PALE'. This proved a shrewd move, his subsequent single (cut by Cordell), 'MARJORINE', leading to a deal with A&M. '68 saw COCKER catapulted to fame with a cover of the Beatles' 'WITH A LITTLE HELP FROM MY FRIENDS', featuring JIMMY PAGE on guitar. Reaching No.1 in Britain, the song showcased COCKER's powerful, gravel-throated voice and his ability to make a song his own. With heavyweight fame looming large, COCKER hired manager Dee Anthony, who promptly booked him for gigs in America with his group, the GREASE BAND, and in '69, the Cordell produced album, 'WITH A LITTLE HELP FROM MY FRIENDS' was issued, featuring the talents of STEVE WINWOOD and MATTHEW FISHER, amonst others. The set received critical and commercial acclaim, featuring an inspired version of Dylan's 'I SHALL BE RELEASED' as well as the spell-binding rendition of Traffic's 'FEELIN ALRIGHT', the next single to be lifted fro the album. With the festival scene buzzing, JOE and the GREAS BAND appeared in America on a series of five gigs, the last bein the Woodstock Music and Arts Fair in Bethal, New York, where h full-on performance of 'WITH A LITTLE HELP . . .' summed u the mood of the weekend. His second long-player, 'JOE COCKER produced a Top 10 in the UK with a LEON RUSSELL-penne 'DELTA LADY', the album characterised by COCKER's primordia blasting vocals. Dismantling the GREASE BAND in 1970 after hectic two years on the road, his next outfit was assembled a matt of weeks later for a few gigs he had forgotten about. The MA DOGS band, made up of LEON RUSSELL and a full horn sectio from the recently disbanded DELANEY & BONNIE & FRIEND almost immediately created a hit with 'THE LETTER', a cover the Box Tops' 1967 pop hit. A live recording, 70's 'MAD DOGS ENGLISHMEN' (recorded at Fillmore during the tour of the sam name), solidified COCKER's fame, the album rocketing to No.2 o the Billboard chart and the tour being released as a film, premierin at Cannes in '71. Ironically, the tour left COCKER a wreck and led his withdrawal from the music business. A half-hearted comebac in '72 saw the release of 'JOE COCKER' (without the exclamatio mark, which is exactly what it was) while another comeback set i May '74, 'I CAN STAND A LITTLE RAIN' was equally disastrou Although 'YOU ARE SO BEAUTIFUL' (taken from that albun charted in March '75, the personal turmoil continued, painful illustrated by John Belushi's hilarious impersonation of COCKE on Saturday Night Live. The rest of the 70's saw the release a string of lacklustre albums and an end to his relationship wi 'A&M'. COCKER subsequently signed to 'Elektra / Asylum' in '7 before moving to 'Island' in '82, his first release for the labe 'SHEFFIELD STEEL', borrowing the talents of SLY & ROBBIE lukewarm effect. The comeback that had threatened to happen wi the release of the album actually came a year later with 'UP WHER WE BELONG', a duet sung with JENNIFER WARNES and the lo theme to the movie, 'An Officer And A Gentleman'. COCKER w on the move again in '84, signing to 'Capitol', where he released s albums, appealing largely to the AOR market, while the '90s saw JO teaming up with BRYAN ADAMS before rehashing his two mo celebrated recordings, 'WITH A LITTLE HELP . . .' and 'FEELI ALRIGHT' for the commercial re-run of Woodstock '94. Now wi Sony's '550' label, he continues to tour the globe and confound th critics with his durability – a new set, 'NO ORDINARY WORL was released towards the end of 1999. On the evidence of th 'RESPECT YOURSELF' (2002), COCKER's soulful rasp seemed be continuing to mature like a fine malt, smoky, peaty and designe to put hairs on your chest. Sure, he still went over the top fro time to time, inflating songs to bursting point, but on the likes Randy Newman's 'EVERYTIME IT RAINS', COCKER proved h still has one of the most durable voices in the business. Bringing i another raft of the usual suspects (ERIC CLAPTON, JEFF BEC and JEFF 'Skunk' BAXTER), 'E.M.I.'/COCKER targeted the adu contemporary market with a second successive 00s covers se 'HEART & SOUL' (2004).

• **Songwriters:** Pens some with band (GREASE BAND) member CHR STAINTON. Covers:- SHE CAME IN THROUGH THE BATHROO WINDOW + YOU'VE GOT TO HIDE YOUR LOVE AWAY (Beatles) YOU ARE SO BEAUTIFUL (Billy Preston) / JUST LIKE A WOMAN + SHALL BE RELEASED + WATCHING THE RIVER FLOW (Bob Dylan) DON'T LET ME BE MISUNDERSTOOD (hit; Nina Simone) / DARLING B HOME SOON (Lovin' Spoonful) / BIRD ON THE WIRE + I'M YOUR MA (Leonard Cohen) / HONKY TONK WOMEN (Rolling Stones) / I'VE BEE LOVING YOU TOO LONG (Otis Redding) / GIVE PEACE A CHANC (John Lennon) / ST.JAMES INFIRMARY (Graham Bond) / LAWDY MI CLAWDY (Little Richard) / MANY RIVERS TO CROSS (Jimmy Cliff) I HEARD IT THROUGH THE GRAPEVINE (Barrett Strong) / TALKIN BACK TO THE NIGHT (Steve Winwood) / INNER CITY BLUES (Marv

Gaye) / UNCHAIN MY HEART (Ray Charles) / UP WHERE WE BELONG Buffy Sainte Marie & Jack Nitzsche) / DON'T LET THE SUN GO DOWN ON ME (Elton John) / CAN'T FIND MY WAY HOME (Blind Faith) / THE MOON IS A HARSH MISTRESS (Jimmy Webb) / FIVE WOMEN (Prince) / TWO WRONGS DON'T MAKE A RIGHT (Bendith-Schwartz) / TEMPTED Squeeze) / I STILL CAN'T BELIEVE IT'S TRUE (. . . Cadd) / LET THE HEALING BEGIN (Tony Joe White) / HAVE A LITTLE FAITH IN ME (John Hiatt) / THE SIMPLE THINGS (Shanks-Neigher-Roy) / SUMMER IN THE CITY (Lovin' Spoonful) / THE GREAT DIVIDE (J.D. Souther) / HIGHWAY HIGHWAY (Steven Allen Davis) / TOO COOL (G.Sutton-K.Fleming) / SOUL TIME (Will Jennings-Frankie Miller) / OUT OF THE BLUE (Robbie Robertson) / HELL AND HIGHWATER (John Miles) / STANDING KNEE DEEP IN A RIVER (Bob McDill-Dickey Lee-Bucky Jones) / TAKE ME HOME (Kipner-Capek-Jordan) / and many more.

Album rating: WITH A LITTLE HELP FROM MY FRIENDS (*7) / JOE COCKER! *7) / MAD DOGS & ENGLISHMEN soundtrack (*7) / COCKER HAPPY early stuff (*5) / SOMETHING TO SAY (*4) / I CAN STAND A LITTLE RAIN (*5) / JAMAICA SAY YOU WILL (*3) / STINGRAY (*5) / LUXURY YOU CAN AFFORD *5) / SHEFFIELD STEEL (*5) / A CIVILIZED MAN (*4) / COCKER (*4) / UNCHAIN MY HEART (*5) / ONE NIGHT OF SIN (*3) / JOE COCKER LIVE! *4) / NIGHT CALLS (*4) / THE LEGEND: THE ESSENTIAL COLLECTION compilation (*7) / HAVE A LITTLE FAITH (*5) / ORGANIC (*5) / ACROSS FROM MIDNIGHT (*5) / NO ORDINARY WORLD (*4) / RESPECT YOURSELF *4) / HEART & SOUL (*5)

JOE COCKER – vocals, (touring band JOE COCKER'S BIG BLUES) with **DAVE HOPPER** – guitar / **VERNON NASH** – piano / **DAVE GREEN** – bass / **DAVE MEMMOT** – drums Record company used session men instead incl. **BIG JIM SULLIVAN** – guitar

Decca / not iss.

Oct 64. (7") *(F 11974)* **I'LL CRY INSTEAD. / PRECIOUS WORDS** — [ ] [–]

— He formed **The GREASE BAND** in '67 retaining **NASH** and **MEMMOTT** and recruited **CHRIS STAINTON** – bass, and **FRANK MYLES** – guitar. But once again opted for session musicians incl. **CLEM CATTINI** – drums / **J. PAGE & A. LEE** – guitar. Although STAINTON did appear. (JIMMY PAGE also appeared on next 45)

Regal Zonophone / A&M

Sep 68. (7") *(RZ 3006) <928>* **MARJORINE. / THE NEW AGE OF LILY** — [48] [ ]

— **JOE COCKER & THE GREASE BAND** with **STAINTON** brought in new guys **TOMMY EYRE** – keyboards / **MICKEY GEE** – guitar / **TOMMY REILLY** – drums

Sep 68. (7") *(RZ 3013) <991>* **WITH A LITTLE HELP FROM MY FRIENDS. / SOMETHING'S COMING ON** — [1] Nov68 [68]

— **MENRY McCULLOCH** – guitar repl. MICKEY GEE (he later joined SHAKIN' STEVENS) **KENNY SLADE** – drums repl. REILLY Plus of course a huge selection of session people

May 69. (lp) *(SLRZ 1006) <AM 4182>* **WITH A LITTLE HELP FROM MY FRIENDS** — [ ] [35]
– Feeling alright / Bye bye blackbird / Change in Louise / Marjorine / Just like a woman / Do I still figure in your life / Sandpaper Cadillac / Don't let me be misunderstood / With a little help from my friends / I shall be released. *(re-iss. Oct81 on 'Cube' lp/c; TOOFA/ZCTOF 1) (cd-iss. 1988 on 'Cube'; 846316) (re-iss. Feb90 on 'Castle' cd/c; CLA CD/MC 172) (cd re-iss. Oct98 on 'Polydor'; 393106-2)*

Jun 69. (7") *<1063>* **FEELING ALRIGHT. / SANDPAPER CADILLAC** — [–] [69]
<re-iss. Dec71, hit No.33>

— **JOE'S GREASE BAND** retained **STAINTON** – now keyboards and **McCULLOCH ALAN SPENNER** – bass repl. TOMMY EYRE who joines AYNSLEY DUNBAR, etc.

BRUCE ROWLANDS – drums repl. KENNY SLADE who went into sessions

Sep 69. (7") *(RZ 3024) <1112>* **DELTA LADY. / SHE'S GOOD TO ME** — [10] [69]

Nov 69. (lp) *(SLRZ 1011) <AM 4224>* **JOE COCKER!** — [ ] [11]
– Dear landlord / Bird on the wire / Lawdy Miss Clawdy / She came in through the bathroom window / Hitchcock railway / That's your business now / Something / Delta lady / Hello little friend / Darling be home soon. *(re-iss. May91 on 'Castle' cd/c; CLA CD/MC 238) (cd re-iss. Oct98 on 'Polydor'; 394224-2)*

Dec 69. (7") *<1147>* **SHE CAME IN THROUGH THE BATHROOM WINDOW. / CHANGE IN LOUISE** — [–] [30]

Jun 70. (7") *(RZ 3027) <1174>* **THE LETTER. / SPACE CAPTAIN** — [39] Apr70 [7]

— Early '70, he retained **STAINTON** and assembled his **MAD DOGS AND ENGLISHMEN** entourage which included **LEON RUSSELL & THE SHELTER PEOPLE** – guitar, piano / **DON PRESTON** – guitar CARL RADLE – bass / **BOBBY KEYS** – sax / **JIM PRICE** – trumpet / **JIM KELTNER** – drums plus even more session people, over 10, which was documented on film in '71.

A&M / A&M

Sep 70. (d-lp) *(<AMLD 6002>)* **MAD DOGS & ENGLISHMEN** (live soundtrack) — [16] [2]
– (introduction) / Honky tonk women / (introduction) / Sticks and stones / Cry me a river / Bird on the wire / Feeling alright / Superstar / (introduction) / Let's go get stoned / Blue medley: I'll drown in my own tears – When something is wrong with my baby – I've been loving you too long / (introduction) / Girl from North Country / Give peace a chance / (introduction) / She came in through the bathroom window / Space captain / The letter / Delta lady. *(re-iss. 1983 d-lp/d-c; AMLS/CDM 6002) (cd-iss. 1988; CDA 6002) <US d-cd-iss. Jan86 on 'Mobile Fidelity'; MFCD 2-824> (cd re-iss. Jan97; 396002-2) (cd re-iss. Oct98 on 'Polydor'; 540698-2) (cd re-iss. Dec98 on 'Mobile Fidelity'; UDCD 736)*

Fly / A&M

Oct 70. (7") *(BUG 3) <1200>* **CRY ME A RIVER (live). / GIVE PEACE A CHANCE (live)** — [ ] [11]

Apr 71. (lp) *(HIFLY 3)* **COCKER HAPPY** (older material) — [ ] [–]
– Hitchcock railway / She came in through the bathroom window / Marjorine / She's good to me / Hello little friend / With a little help from my friends / Delta lady / Darlin' be home soon / Do I still figure in your life / Feeling alright / Something's coming on / The letter. *(re-iss. May85 on 'Sierra' lp/c; FEDB/CFEDB 5011) (cd-iss. Oct94 on 'Disky'; CUCD 01)*

— JOE retained **STAINTON** and some of his past session men

May 71. (7") *(BUG 9) <1258>* **HIGH TIME WE WENT. / BLACK EYED BLUES** — [ ] [22]

— now with the CHRIS STAINTON BAND" (a 12-piece) retaining **KEYS, PRICE** and **KELTNER.** (also had loads of session men)

Aug 72. (7") *(BUG 25) <1370>* **MIDNIGHT RIDER. / WOMAN TO WOMAN** — [ ] [27] [56]

Dec 72. (lp) *(HIFLY 13) <AM 4368>* **SOMETHING TO SAY** <US-title 'JOE COCKER'> — [ ] [30]
– Pardon me sir / High time we went / She don't mind / Black eyed blues / Something to say / Midnight rider / Do right woman / Woman to woman / St. James infirmary blues. *(cd-iss. Oct98 on 'Polydor'; 394368-2)*

Feb 73. (7") *(BUG 28)* **PARDON ME SIR. / SHE DON'T MIND** — [ ] [–]

Feb 73. (7") *<1407>* **PARDON ME SIR. / ST. JAMES INFIRMARY BLUES** — [–] [51]

— now (complete new line-up) **STAINTON** joined TUNDRA / **HENRY McCULLOCH** – guitar / **MICK WEAVER** (aka WYNDER K. FROG) – keyboards / **BUFFALO GELBER** – bass / **JIMMY KARSTEIN** – drums

Jun 74. (7") *(BUG 47) <1539>* **PUT OUT THE LIGHT. / IF I LOVE YOU** — [ ] [46]

Aug 74. (lp/c) *(HIFLY/ZCFLY 18) <AM 3633>* **I CAN STAND A LITTLE RAIN** — [ ] [11]
– Put out the light / I can stand a little rain / I get mad / Sing me a song / The moon is a harsh mistress / Don't forget me / You are so beautiful / It's a sin when you love somebody / Performance / Guilty. *(re-iss. Apr89 on 'Castle' lp/c/cd; CLA LP/MC/CD 144) (cd re-iss. Oct98 on 'Polydor'; 393175-2)*

Dec 74. (7") *(BUG 57)* **YOU ARE SO BEAUTIFUL. / I GET MAD** — [ ] [–]

Dec 74. (7") *<1641>* **YOU ARE SO BEAUTIFUL. / IT'S A SIN WHEN YOU LOVE SOMEBODY** — [–] [5]

— He then formed **JOE COCKER & The COCK'N'BULL BAND** with **WEAVER** plus **ALBERT LEE** – guitar / **PETER GAVIN** – drums / **ANDY DENNO** – bass

JOE COCKER retained **LEE, GAVIN** plus touring band **RICHARD TEE** – keyboards / **GORDON EDWARDS** – bass / **CORNELL DUPREE** – guitar / **KENNY SLADE** – percussion and three girl backing singers

Jul 75. (7") *<1749>* **I THINK IT'S GONNA RAIN TODAY. / OH MAMA** — [–] [ ]

Aug 75. (lp/c) *(HIFLY/ZCFLY 20) <AM 4529>* **JAMAICA SAY YOU WILL** — [ ] [42]
– (That's what I like) In my woman / Where am I now / I think it's going to rain today / Forgive me now / Oh mama / Lucinda / If I love you / Jamaica say you will / It's all over but the shoutin' / Jack-a-diamonds. *(cd-iss. Oct98 on 'Polydor'; 394529-2)*

Oct 75. (7") *(BUG 61)* **IT'S ALL OVER BUT THE SHOUTIN'. / SANDPAPER CADILLAC** — [ ] [–]

Oct 75. (7") <1758> **JAMAICA SAY YOU WILL. / IT'S ALL OVER BUT THE SHOUTIN'** –

— **JOE COCKER & STUFF** retained **TEE, EDWARDS** and **DUPREE** added **ERIC GALE** – guitar repl. LEE who went solo **STEVE GADD drums** repl. GAVIN

A&M A&M

Apr 76. (7") <1805> **THE MAN IN ME. / (part 2)** –

Apr 76. (lp/c) *(AMLH/CAM 64574)* <AM 4574> **STINGRAY** 70
– The jealous kind / I broke down / You came along / Catfish / Moon dew / The man in me / She is my lady / Worrier / Born thru indifference with you / A song for you. *(cd-iss. Oct98 on 'Polydor'; 394574-2)*

Jul 76. (7") *(AMS 7243)* <1830> **THE JEALOUS KIND. / YOU CAME ALONG**

Sep 76. (7") *(AMS 7257)* <1855> **I BROKE DOWN. / YOU CAME ALONG**

— JOE then joined **KOKOMO** for a month late '76 (no recordings). Took a long time off from studio & stage. Returned with a host of session people

Asylum Asylum

Sep 78. (7") <45540> **FUN TIME. / WATCHING THE RIVER FLOW** –

Sep 78. (lp/c) *(K/K4 53087)* <6E 145> **LUXURY YOU CAN AFFORD** 76
– Fun time / Watching the river flow / Boogie baby / A white shade of pale / I can't say no / Southern lady / I know (you don't want me no more) / What you did to me last night / Lady put the light out / Wasted years / I heard it through the grapevine. *(cd-iss. Jan96 on 'WEA'; 7559 60821-2)*

Sep 78. (7") *(K 13138)* **FUN TIME. / I CAN'T SAY NO** –

Jan 79. (7") *(K 13148)* **A WHITER SHADE OF PALE. / WATCHING THE RIVER FLOW**

— In Sep'81, JOE was credited on a single 'I'm So Glad I'm Standing Here Today' and guested on 'Standing Still' by the CRUSADERS.

— **JOE COCKER** returned to solo work '82, (first w/ SLY DUNBAR + ROBBIE SHAKESPEARE)

Island Island

Jun 82. (7"/12") *(WIP/12WIP 6708)* **SWEET LITTLE WOMAN. / LOOK WHAT YOU'VE DONE**

Jul 82. (lp/c) *(ILPS/ICT 9700)* <9750> **SHEFFIELD STEEL**
– Look what you've done / Shocked / Sweet little woman / Seven days / Marie / Ruby Lee / Many rivers to cross / So good so right / Talking back to the night / Just like always. *(cd-iss. Jul92; IMCD 149) (cd re-mast.Oct02 +=; 063152-2)* – Sweet little woman (12" mix) / Look what you've done (12" mix) / Right in the middle of falling in love / Inner city blues.

Aug 82. (7") *(WIP 6802)* **MANY RIVERS TO CROSS. / TALKING BACK TO THE NIGHT**
below from the film 'An Officer and a Gentleman'

Jan 83. (7"; JOE COCKER & JENNIFER WARNES) *(WIP 6830)* <99996> **UP WHERE WE BELONG. / SWEET LITTLE WOMAN** 7 Aug82 1

Jun 83. (7") *(IS 115)* **THROW IT AWAY. / EASY RIDER** –

Capitol Capitol

Jun 84. (7") *(CL 333)* <5338> **CIVILIZED MAN. / A GIRL LIKE YOU**

Jun 84. (lp/c)(cd) *(EJ 240139-1/-4)(CDP 746038-2)* <12335> **CIVILIZED MAN** 100 May84
– Civilized / There goes my baby / Come on in / Tempted / Long drag off a cigarette / I love the night / Crazy in love / A girl like you / Hold on (I feel our love is changing) / Even a fool would let go. *(re-iss. Jul88 lp/c; ATAK/TC-ATAK 115) (cd re-iss. Apr92; EJ 240139-2)*

Aug 84. (7") <5390> **CRAZY IN LOVE. / COME ON IN** –

Nov 84. (7") *(CL 347)* <5412> **EDGE OF A DREAM (from the film 'Teachers'). / TEMPTED** Oct84 69

Feb 86. (7") <5557> **SHELTER ME. / TELL ME THERE'S A WAY** – 91

Mar 86. (7") *(CL 362)* **SHELTER ME. / ONE MORE TIME** –
(12"+=) *(12CL 362)* – If you have love, give me some.

Apr 86. (lp/c)(cd) *(EST/TC-EST 2009)(CDP 746268-2)* <12394> **COCKER** 50
– Shelter / A to Z / Don't you love me anymore / Living without your love / Don't drink the water / You can leave your hat on / Heart of the matter / Inner city blues / Love is on a fade / Heaven. *(re-iss. Oct89 on 'Fame' cd/c/lp; CD/TC+/FA 3227) (re-iss. Jul94; CDEST 2009)*

May 86. (7"/12") *(CL/12CL 404)* **DON'T YOU LOVE ME ANYMORE. / TELL ME THERE'S WAY** –

May 86. (7") <5626> **DON'T YOU LOVE ME ANYMORE. / DON'T DRINK THE WATER** –

Jun 86. (7"/12") *(CL/12CL 413)* **YOU CAN LEAVE YOUR HAT ON. / LONG DRAG OFF THE CIGARETTE** –

Oct 87. (7") *(CL 465)* **UNCHAIN MY HEART. / THE ONE** 46 –
(12") *(12CL 465)* – ('A'side) / ('A'-Rock mix) / The one.
(cd-s+=) *(CDCL 465)* – ('A'dance mix) / You can leave your hat on.

Oct 87. (7") <44072> **UNCHAIN MY HEART. / SATISFIED** –

Oct 87. (cd/c/lp) *(CD/TC+/EST 2045)* <48285> **UNCHAIN MY HEART** 89
– Unchain my heart / Two wrongs (don't make a right) / I stand i wonder / The river's rising / Isolation / All our tomorrows / A woman love a man / Trust in me / The one / Satisfied. *(re-iss. Jun89; CDP 748285-2) (re-iss. Aug92; CDEST 2045)*

Dec 87. (7") <44101> **TWO WRONGS (DON'T MAKE A RIGHT). / ISOLATION** –

Dec 87. (7"/12") *(MCA/+S 129)* <53077> **LOVE LIVES ON. / ON MY WAY TO YOU**
(above from the movie, 'Bigfoot & The Hendersons' – US title 'Harry The Hendersons', on 'M.C.A.')

May 88. (7") *(CL 493)* **DON'T YOU LOVE ME NO MORE. / ALL OUR TOMORROWS** –
(12"+=) *(12CL 493)* – Tell me there's a way.
(cd-s++=) *(CDCL 493)* – With a little help from my friends.

Jul 89. (cd/c/lp) *(CD/TC+/EST 2098)* <92861> **ONE NIGHT OF SIN** 52
– When the night comes / I will live for you / I've got to use m imagination / Letting go / Just to keep from drowning / The unforgive * / Another mind gone / Fever / You know it's gonna hurt / Bad bad sign I'm your man / One night of sin. *(cd+= *) (cd re-iss. Mar94; same)*

Oct 89. (c-s,cd-s) <44437> **WHEN THE NIGHT COMES. / ONE NIGHT OF SIN** – 11

Nov 89. (7") *(CL 535)* **WHEN THE NIGHT COMES. / RUBY LEE** 65 –
(12"+=/cd-s+=) *(12/CD CL 535)* – ('A'extended).

— **JOE COCKER BAND** is **DERIC DYER** – sax, keys, perc. / **STEVE HOLLE** – drums / **PHIL GRANDE** – lead guitar / **JEFF LEVINE** – keyboards **KEITH MACK** – rhythm guitar / **CHRIS STAINTON** – keyboards / **T.M STEVENS** – bass, vocals / **DOREEN CHANTER** – vocals / **MAXINE GREE** – vocals / **CRYSTAL TALIEFERO** – vocals, percussion / **The MEMPHI HORNS:- WAYNE JACKSON, ANDREW LOVE, GARY GAZAWAY**

Jun 90. (cd/c/d-lp) *(CD/TC+/ESTSP 25)* <93416> **JOE COCKER LIVE (live)** 95
– Feeling alright? / Shelter me / Hitchcock railway / Up where we belong You can leave your hat on / Guilty / When the night comes / Uncha my heart / With a little help from my friends / You are so beautiful / Th letter / She came in through the bathroom window / High time we went What are you doing with a fool like me (studio) / Living in the promis land (studio).

May 90. (c-s,cd-s) <44543> **WHAT ARE YOU DOING WITH A FOOL LIKE ME? / ANOTHER MIND GONE** – 96
(studio:- **KENNY RICHARDS** – drums / **EARL SLICK** – guitar **BASHARI JOHNSON** – percussion, b.vocals – **TAWATHA AGE VANEESE THOMAS & FONZI THORNTON.**)

Capitol Allian

Oct 91. (cd/c/lp) *(CD/TC+/ESTU 2167)* <97801> **NIGHT CALLS** 25 Jul92
– Love is alive / Little bit of love / Please no more / There's a storm coming You've got to hide your love away / I can hear the river / Don't let the Su go down on me / Night calls / Five women / Can't find my way home Not too young to die of a broken heart / Out of the rain.

Oct 91. (c-s/7") **NIGHT CALLS. / OUT OF THE RAIN** –
(12"+=/cd-s+=) – Not too young to die of a broken heart.

Mar 92. (c-s/7") *(TC+/CL 645)* **(ALL I KNOW) FEELS LIKE FOREVER. / WHEN THE NIGHT COMES** 25 –
(cd-s+=) *(CDCL 645)* – Up where we belong / With a little help from m friends.

May 92. (c-s/7") *(TC+/CL 657)* **NOW THAT THE MAGIC HAS GONE. / FIVE WOMEN** 28 –
(12"+=/cd-s+=) *(12/CD CL 657)* – Two wrongs don't make a right / Th letter.

Jun 92. (c-s/7") *(TC+/CL 664)* **UNCHAIN MY HEART. / YOU CAN LEAVE YOUR HAT ON** 17 –
(12"+=/cd-s+=) *(12/CD CL 664)* – The one / ('A'-Rock mix).

Nov 92. (c-s/7") *(TC+/CL 674)* **WHEN THE NIGHT COMES. / YOU'VE GOT TO HIDE YOUR LOVE AWAY** 61
(cd-s+=) *(CDCL 674)* – Tempted / I still can't believe it's true.
(cd-s) *(CDCLS 674)* – ('A'side) / The Moon is a harsh mistress / I'm you man / She came in through the bathroom window.

— now w / **JACK BRUNO** – drums / **BOB FEIT** + **TONY JOE WHITE** + **TIM PIERCE** – guitar / **CHRIS STAINTON** – keyboards / **LENNY CASTRO** – percussion / **C.J. VANSTON** – organ

Capitol 550 Music

Aug 94. (c-s) *(TCCL 722)* **THE SIMPLE THINGS / SUMMER IN THE CITY** [17] [–]
(cd-s+=) *(CDCL 722)* – With a little help from my friends (live).
(cd-s) *(CDCLS 722)* – ('A'side) / Angeline / My strongest weakness.

Sep 94. (cd/c/lp) *(CD/TC+/EST 2233)* <66460> **HAVE A LITTLE FAITH** [9] [ ]
– Let the healing begin / Have a little faith in me / The simple things / Summer in the city / The great divide / Highway highway / Too cool / Soul time / Out of the blue / Angeline / Hell and highwater / Standing knee deep in a river / Take me home.

Oct 94. (c-s/cd-s) *(TC/CD CL 729)* **TAKE ME HOME. (featuring BEKKA BRAMBLETT) / TEMPTED / UNCHAIN MY HEART (90's version)** [41] [–]
(cd-s) *(CDCLS 729)* – ('A'side) / Up where we belong / You can leave your hat on.

Dec 94. (c-s/cd-s) *(TC/CD CL 727)* **LET THE HEALING BEGIN / SUMMER IN THE CITY (2-mixes)** [32] [–]
(cd-s) *(CDCLS 727)* – ('A'side) / You are so beautiful (live) / The letter (live).

Sep 95. (c-s) *(TCCL 744)* **HAVE A LITTLE FAITH / THE SIMPLE THINGS (live) / LET THE HEALING BEGIN (live)** [67] [–]
(cd-s) *(CDCLS 744)* – ('A'side) / Summer in the city (live) / Angeline (live).

Oct 96. (c-s) *(TCCL 779)* **DON'T LET ME BE MISUNDERSTOOD / SOMETHING / HIGH LONESOME BLUE** [53] [–]
(cd-s) *(CDCLS 779)* – ('A'side) / Human touch / Anybody seen my girl.

Oct 96. (cd/c/lp) *(CD/TC+/ESTD 6)* <67880> **ORGANIC** [49] [ ]
– Into the mystic / Bye bye blackbird / Delta lady / Heartful of rain / Don't let me be misunderstood / Many rivers to cross / High lonesome blue / Sail away / You and I / Darlin' be home soon / Dignity / You can leave your hat on / You are so beautiful / Can't find my way home.

Capitol C.M.C.

Aug 97. (c-s) *(TCCL 793)* **COULD YOU BE LOVED / THAT'S THE WAY HER LOVE IS** [ ] [–]
(cd-s+=) *(CDCLS 793)* – ('A'-Catania mix) / Summer in the city.

Sep 97. (cd/c/lp) *(CD/TC+/EST 2301)* <86245> **ACROSS FROM MIDNIGHT** [ ] [ ]
– Tonight / Could you be loved / That's all I need to know / N'oubliez jamais / What do I tell my heart / Wayward soul / Loving you tonight / Across from midnight / What do you say / Last one to know / That's the way love is / Need your love so bad.

Parlophone Red Ink

Oct 99. (cd-s) *(CDR 6526)* **DIFFERENT ROADS / YOU CAN LEAVE YOUR HAT ON (live) / WHEN THE NIGHT COMES (live)** [ ] [–]

Oct 99. (cd/c) *(523091-2/-4)* <13601> **NO ORDINARY WORLD** [63] Aug00 [ ]
– First we take Manhattan / Different roads / My father's son / While you see a chance / She believes in me / No ordinary world / Where would I be now / Ain't gonna cry again / Soul rising / Naked without you / Love to lean on / On my way home. <*US*+=> – Lied to me / Love made me a promise.

May 02. (cd-s) *(CDR 6579)* **NEVER TEAR US APART / YOU ARE SO BEAUTIFUL (live) / YOU CAN LEAVE YOUR HAT ON (live)** [ ] [–]

Jun 02. (cd) *(539643-2)* <59480> **RESPECT YOURSELF** [51] Jul02 [ ]
– You can have my heart / Love not war / You took it so hard / Never tear us apart / This is your life / Respect yourself / I'm listening now / Leave a light on / It's only love / Every time it rains / Midnight without you.

E.M.I. E.M.I.

Sep 04. (cd) *(<866401-2>)* **HEART & SOUL** [ ] Oct04 [61]
– What's goin' on / Chain of fools / One / I who have nothing / Maybe I'm amazed / I keep forgetting / I put a spell on you / Every kind of people / Love don't live here any more / Don't let me be lonely / Jealous guy / Everybody hurts.

– (selective) compilations, etc. –

Apr 72. (d-lp) *Cube; (TOOFA 1-2)* **WITH A LITTLE HELP FROM MY FRIENDS / JOE COCKER!** [29] [–]

Mar 88. (d-lp/c/d-cd) *That's Original; (TFO LP/MC/CD 4)* **JAMAICA SAY YOU WILL / COCKER HAPPY** [ ] [–]
(d-cd.iss-Sep91)

Feb 92. (3xcd-box) *Castle; (CLABX 902)* **3 ORIGINALS** [ ] [–]
– (COCKER HAPPY / SOMETHING TO SAY / WITH A LITTLE HELP FROM MY FRIENDS)

Jun 92. (cd/c) *Polygram TV; (515411-2/-4)* **THE LEGEND** [4] [–]
– Up where we belong (with JENNIFER WARNES) / With a little help from my friends / Delta lady / The letter / She came in through the bathroom window / A whiter shade of pale / Love the one you're with (live) / You are so beautiful / Let it be / Just like a woman / Many rivers to cross / Talking back to the night / Fun time / I heard it through the grapevine / Please give peace a chance (live) / Don't let me be misunderstood / Honky tonk woman (live) / Cry me a river (live).

Dec 95. (4xcd-box) *A&M; (540236-2)* **THE LONG VOYAGE HOME** [ ] [–]

Mar 97. (3xcd-box) *E.M.I.; (CDOMB 024)* **CIVILIZED MAN / COCKER / UNCHAIN MY HEART** [ ] [–]

Jul 97. (cd; JOE COCKER & THE GREASE BAND) *Strange Fruit; (SFRSCD 036)* **ON AIR** [ ] [–]

Feb 99. (cd/c) *Parlophone; (497719-2/-4) / Mushroom; <33120>* **THE BEST OF JOE COCKER** [24] [ ]
– Unchain my heart / You can leave your hat on / When the night comes / Now that the magic has gone / Shelter me / Many rivers to cross / Feels like forever / Night calls / Tempted / Summer in the city / Have a little faith in me / Don't let me be misunderstood / One night of sin / You've got to hide your love away / You are so beautiful / Let the healing begin / Civilized man.

Apr 00. (cd) *Voiceprint; (VP 214CD)* **VANCE ARCHER & THE AVENGERS LIVE** [ ] [ ]

Mar 03. (d-cd) *Capitol; <(582351-2)>* **CIVILIZED MAN / ONE NIGHT OF SIN** [ ] [ ]

COCTEAU TWINS

Formed: Grangemouth, Scotland . . . late 1981 when the (then) trio of ELIZABETH FRASER, ROBIN GUTHRIE and WILL HEGGIE visited London to hand DJ John Peel a demo tape. He booked them for sessions on his Radio One night time show and they subsequently signed to IVO WATT-RUSSELL's indie label, '4 a.d.'. The COCTEAUS' debut offering, 'GARLANDS', was hastily recorded, hitting the shops just over a week later and giving a hint of things to come with an interesting fusion of monochromatic rhythms, textured guitar distortion and sampling technology. Resisting many offers from the majors, they were back in the studio again for 1983's 'LULLABIES' EP and 'HEAD OVER HEELS' album. A mesmerising collage of irridescent guitar soundscapes and sheets of feedback perforated with FRASER's unintelligible but highly emotive warbling, the latter record was a blueprint for the best of COCTEAU TWINS' work. After a support slot to OMD, WILL HEGGIE departed, making the long trip back north to set up his own outfit, LOWLIFE. Around the same time ROBIN and LIZ hit No.1 in the indie charts when guesting for 'IVO/4 a.d.' ensemble, THIS MORTAL COIL on 'SONG TO THE SIREN'; it was mistakenly thought by many to be a COCTEAU TWINS off-shoot, rather than IVO's project. That idea was laid to rest after the album, 'IT'LL END IN TEARS', was issued in '84. Meanwhile, COCTEAU TWINS were back with another blissed out masterpiece, 'TREASURE', introducing newcomer, SIMON RAYMONDE on bass and seeing LIZ explore hitherto uncharted vocal territory in a fascinating, enigmatic and occasionally unsettling language that communicated everything and nothing. It also marked their first taste of Top 30 success although they surpassed this with 1986's more inscrutably minimalist Top 10 effort, 'VICTORIALAND'. An abortive film project collaboration with HAROLD BUDD was issued at the end of the year as they headed towards an increasingly "New Age"-style sound. Two more classics, 'BLUE BELL KNOLL' and 'HEAVEN OR LAS VEGAS' were released over the next half decade, both finding a home in the US charts for 'Capitol' records. In 1992, they finally succumbed to signing for 'Fontana' in the UK, leading to a comeback album, 'FOUR-CALENDAR CAFE' in

'93. Many longtime fans were disappointed with what was surely the duo's most accessible, grounded album to date yet devoid of much of the mystery that made their earlier work so alluring. The following year saw LIZ guest on FUTURE SOUND OF LONDON's ambient venture, 'Lifeforms'; she would subsequently go on to perform on MASSIVE ATTACK's 'Teardrops' single in '98. After another 3-year hiatus, FRASER and GUTHRIE returned with 'MILK & KISSES' (1996), a typically COCTEAU-esque affair that moved some critics to suggest the band were treading water; it was to be their epitaph as the band dissolved along with FRASER and GUTHRIE's marriage. ROBIN resurfaced towards the end of 2000 via VIOLET INDIANA. His working partner on this collaboration was former MONO diva, SIOBHAN DE MARE, a slightly less ethereal vocalist than FRASER, witnessed on their debut EP, 'CHOKE'. The material on the EP, and especially on the debut album 'ROULETTE' (2001), evoked a laid-back GALAXIE 500-esque wig-out with GUTHRIE's instrumentation quite similar to the spacey hypnotics of TRANSIENT WAVES or PIANO MAGIC. DE MARE's whispering vocals on 'ROULETTE' were awesome and she did manage to completely re-invent her voice on the stand-out track 'SUNDANCE' where she soars while GUTHRIE's guitar spirals out of control. The pair issued a single 'KILLER EYES' at the end of 2001, which featured some fantastic B-sides such as the sparse 'STORM' and the free-jazz influenced 'SAFE WORLD'. GUTHRIE's debut solo album, 'IMPERIAL' (2003), meanwhile, returned to the impressionistic soundscapes formerly expored by the COCTEAU's, swathing his guitar playing in miasmic effects and only occasionally grounding himself with the most basic of percussive structures. GUTHRIE revived his partnership with SIOBHAN on a second VIOLET INDIANA set, 'RUSSIAN DOLL' (2004), filmic feng-shui sonics which prefigured a bonafide move into soundtracks with HAROLD BUDD collaboration 'MYSTERIOUS SKIN' (2005). FRASER had already been busy on the cinema front, contributing to the first part of the 'Lord Of The Rings' trilogy, 'The Fellowship Of The Ring' as well as its follow-up, 'The Two Towers'. While her solo debut was forever on the cards, GUTHRIE was onto his second, releasing 'CONTINENTAL' in 2006.

• **Trivia:** ROBIN has produced many '4.a.d.' outfits in addition to the GUN CLUB (1987).

Album rating: GARLANDS (*7) / HEAD OVER HEELS (*8) / TREASURE (*9) / VICTORIALAND (*8) / THE MOON AND THE MELODIES with Harold Budd (*5) / THE PINK OPAQUE compilation (*8) / BLUE BELL KNOLL (*7) / HEAVEN OR LAS VEGAS (*7) / FOUR-CALENDAR CAFE (*6) / MILK & KISSES (*7) / THE BBC SESSIONS collection (*7) / STARS AND TOPSOIL compilation (*9) / LULLABIES TO VIOLAINE VOL.1/2 compilations (*8/*7) / Violet Indiana: ROULETTE (*7) / RUSSIAN DOLL (*6) / Robin Guthrie: IMPERIAL (*6) / MYSTERIOUS SKIN soundtrack w/ Harold Budd (*7) / CONTINENTAL (*6)

ELIZABETH FRASER (b.29 Aug'63) – vocals / **ROBIN GUTHRIE** (b. 4 Jan'62) – guitar, drum programming, keyboards / **WILL HEGGIE** – bass

4 a.d. not iss.

Jul 82. (lp) *(CAD 211)* **GARLANDS** [ ] [–]
– Blood bitch / Wax and wane / But I'm not / Blind dumb deaf / Grail overfloweth / Shallow than halo / The hollow men / Garlands. *(c-iss.Apr84 +=; CADC 211)* – Dear heart / Blind dumb deaf / Hearsay please / Hazel. *(cd-iss. 1986 ++=; CAD 211CD)* – Speak no evil / Perhaps some other acorn. *<US cd-iss. 1991 on 'Alliance'; 96415>*

Sep 82. (12"ep) *(BAD 213)* **LULLABIES** [ ] [–]
– It's all but an ark lark / Alas dies laughing / Feathers-Oar-Blades.

Mar 83. (7") *(AD 303)* **PEPPERMINT PIG. / LAUGH LINES** [ ] [–]
(12"+=) *(BAD 303)* – Hazel.

— Trimmed to a duo when HEGGIE left to form LOWLIFE

Oct 83. (lp) *(CAD 313)* **HEAD OVER HEELS** [51] [–]
– When mama was moth / Sugar hiccup / In our anglehood / Glass candle grenades / Multifoiled / In the gold dust rush / The tinderbox (of a heart) / My love paramour / Musette and drums / Five ten fiftyfold. *(c-iss.Apr84 +=; CADC 313) (cd-iss. 1986 +=; CAD 313CD)* – SUNBURST AND SNOWBLIND EP *<US cd-iss. 1991 on 'Alliance'; 96416>*

Oct 83. (12"ep) *(BAD 314)* **SUNBURST AND SNOWBLIND** [ ] [–]
– Sugar hiccup / From the flagstones / Because of whirl-Jack / Hitherto.

— added **SIMON RAYMONDE** (b. 3 Apr'62, London, England) – bass, keyboards, guitar (ex-DROWNING CRAZE)

Apr 84. (7") *(AD 405)* **PEARLY DEWDROPS DROP. / PEPPER-TREE** [29] [–]
(12"+=) *(BAD 405)* – The spangle maker.

Nov 84. (lp/c) *(CAD/+C 412)* **TREASURE** [29] [–]
– Ivo / Lorelei / Beatrix / Persephone / Pandora – for Cindy / Amelia / Aloysius / Cicely / Otterley / Donimo. *(cd-iss. 1986; CAD 412CD) <US cd-iss. 1991 on 'Alliance'; 96418>*

Mar 85. (7") *(AD 501)* **AIKEA-GUINEA. / KOOKABURRA** [41] [–]
(12"+=) *(BAD 501)* – Rococo / Quiquose.

Nov 85. (12"ep) *(BAD 510)* **TINY DYNAMITE** [52] [–]
– Pink orange red / Ribbed and veined / Sultitan Itan / Plain tiger.

Nov 85. (12"ep) *(BAD 511)* **ECHOES IN A SHALLOW BAY** [65] [–]
– Great spangled fritillary / Melonella / Pale clouded white / Eggs and their shells *(cd-iss. Oct86 +=; BAD 510/511)* – TINY DYNAMITE

— **RICHARD THOMAS** – saxophone, bass (of DIF JUZ) repl. SIMON who fell ill

Apr 86. (lp/c)(cd) *(CAD/+C 602)(CAD 602CD)* **VICTORIALAND** [10] [ ]
– Lazy calm / Fluffy tufts / Throughout the dark months of April and May / Whales tales / Oomingmak / Little Spacey / Feet-like fins / How to bring a blush to the snow / The thinner the air. *<US cd-iss. 1991 on 'Alliance' 96417>*

— **SIMON RAYMONDE** returned repl.temp. RICHARD (back to DIF JUZ)

Oct 86. (7") *(AD 610)* **LOVE'S EASY TEARS. / THOSE EYES, THAT MOUTH** [53] [–]
(12"+=) *(BAD 610)* – Sigh's smell of farewell.

— next was a one-off collaboration with label new signing **HAROLD BUDD** – piano

4 a.d. Relativi

Nov 86. (lp/c)(cd; by HAROLD BUDD, ELIZABETH FRASER, ROBIN GUTHRIE, SIMON RAYMONDE) *(CAD/+C 611)(CAD 611CD) <8143>* **THE MOON AND THE MELODIES** [46] [ ]
– Sea, swallow me / Memory gongs / Why do you love me? / Eyes are mosaics / She will destroy you / The ghost has no home / Bloody and blunt / Ooze out and away, one how.

4 a.d. Capitol

Sep 88. (lp/c/dat)(cd) *(CAD/+C/T 807)(CAD 807CD) <90892>* **BLUE BELL KNOLL** [15] [ ]
– Blue bell knoll / Athol-brose / Carolyn's fingers / For Phoebe still a baby / The itchy glowbo blow / Cico buff / Suckling the mender / Spooning good singing gum / A kissed out red floatboat / Ella megablast burls forever.

Oct 88. (7") **CAROLYN'S FINGERS. / BLUE BELL KNOLL** [–] [ ]

— In Apr'90, LIZ was heard on Ian McCulloch's (ex-ECHO & THE BUNNYMEN) 'Candleland' single.

Aug 90. (7"/c-s) *(AD 0011/+C)* **ICEBLINK LUCK. / MIZAKE THE MIZAN** [38] [–]
(12"+=/cd-s+=) *(AD 0011 T/CD)* – Watchiar.

Sep 90. (cd)(lp/c) *(CAD 0012CD)(CAD/+C 0012) <C2/C1/C4 93669>* **HEAVEN OR LAS VEGAS** [7] [99]
– Cherry coloured funk / Pitch the baby / Iceblink luck / Fifty-fifty clown / Heaven or Las Vegas / I wear your ring / Fotzepolitic / Wolf in the breast / Road, river and rail / Frou-frou foxes in midsummer fires.

— on U.S. tour, augmented by **MITSUO TATE + BEN BLAKEMAN** – guitars

Fontana Capitol

Sep 93. (7"/c-s) *(CT/+C 1)* **EVANGELINE. / MUD AND LARK** [34] [–]
(12"pic-d+=/cd-s+=) *(CT X/CD 1)* – Summer-blink.

Oct 93. (cd/c/lp) *(518259-2/-4/-1) <C2/C4/C1 99375>* **FOUR-CALENDAR CAFE** [13] [78]
– Know who you are ate every age / Evangeline / Blue beard / Theft and wandering around lost / Oil of angels / Squeeze-wax / My truth / Essence / Summerhead / Pur.

Dec 93. (cd-s) *(COCCD 1)* **WINTER WONDERLAND. / FROSTY THE SNOWMAN** [58] [–]
(above festive tracks, deleted after a week in UK Top 60)

Feb 94. (7"/c-s) *(CT/+C 2)* **BLUEBEARD. / THREE SWEPT** [33] [–]
(12"+=) *(CTX 2)* – Ice-pulse.
(cd-s++=) *(CTCD 2)* – ('A'acoustic).

Sep 95. (7"//7"/cd-ep) *(CCT//CTT/CTCD 3) <30548>* **TWINLIGHTS** [59] Dec95 [ ]
– Rilkean heart / Golden-vein // Pink orange red / Half-gifts.

Oct 95. (12"ep/cd-ep) *(CT X/CD 4)* *<36240>* **OTHERNESS** (An Ambient EP) [59] Dec95 [ ]
– Feet like fins / Seekers who are lovers / Violaine / Cherry coloured funk.

Mar 96. (cd-ep) *(CTCD 5)* **TISHBITE / PRIMITIVE HEART / FLOCK OF SOUL** [34] [–]
(12"ep/cd-ep) *(CT X/DDD 5)* – (title track) / Round / An Elan.

Apr 96. (cd/c/lp) *(514 501-2/4/-1) <37049-2/-4/-1>* **MILK & KISSES** [17] [99]
– Violaine / Serpent skirt / Tishbite / Half-gifts / Calfskin smack / Rilkean heart / Ups / Eperdu / Treasure hiding / Seekers who are lovers. *(also ltd.cd; 532 363-2)*

Jul 96. (12") *(CTX 6)* **VIOLAINE. / ALICE** [56] [–]
(cd-s+=) *(CTDD 6)* – Circling girl.
(cd-s) *(CTCD 6)* – ('A'side) / Tranquil eye / Smile.

—— towards the end of 2000, GUTHRIE worked as the duo VIOLET INDIANA (alongside SIOBHAN DE MARE, ex-MONO), releasing the 'CHOKE' EP for his 'Bella Union' imprint

– compilations, others, etc. –

Dec 85. (cd) *4 a.d.; (CAD 513CD) / Relativity; <ENC 8040>* **THE PINK OPAQUE** [ ] Sep85 [ ]
– The spangle maker / Millimillenary / Wax and wane / Hitherto / Pearly-dewdrops' drops (12" Version) / From the flagstones / Aikea-Guinea / Lorelei / Pepper-tree / Musette and drums.

Nov 91. (10xcd-ep-box) *Capitol; (CTBOX 1)* **THE SINGLES COLLECTION** [ ] [–]
– (above featured previous 9 singles + new 1) (sold separately Mar92)

Sep 99. (d-cd) *Bella Union; (BELLACD 14)* **THE BBC SESSIONS** [ ] [ ]

Oct 00. (cd) *4 a.d.; (CAD2K 019CD) <370019>* **STARS AND TOPSOIL 1982-1990** [ ] [ ]
– Blind dumb deaf / Sugar hiccup / My love paramour / Pearly dewdrops drop / Lorelei / Pandora / Aikea guinea / Pink orange red / Pale clouded white / Lazy calm / Thinner the air / Orange appled / Cico buff / Carolyn's fingers / Fifty fifty clown / Iceblink luck / Heaven or Las Vegas / Watchiar.

Nov 05. (4xcd-box) *4 a.d.; (<CTBOX 2>)* **LULLABIES TO VIOLAINE** (the EP's) [ ] Mar06 [ ]
(<re-iss. Mar06 d-cd 'VOL.1'; DAD 2513CD>) (<re-iss. Mar06 d-cd 'VOL.2'; DAD 2514CD>)

VIOLET INDIANA

ROBIN GUTHRIE – guitars, etc. / **SIOBHAN DE MARE** – vocals (ex-MONO)

Bella Union Instinct

Nov 00. (cd-ep) *(BELLACD 22)* **CHOKE EP** [ ] [–]
– Purr la perla / Busted / Silent / Torn up.

Apr 01. (cd) *(BELLACD 24) <571>* **ROULETTE** [ ] May01 [ ]
– Air kissing / Busted / Sundance / Powder river / Little echo / Angel / Poison gorgeous / Hiding / Rage days / Liar / Feline or famine / Killer eyes.

May 01. (cd-ep) *(BELLACD 26)* **KILLER EYES EP** [ ] [–]
– Killer eyes / Storm / Safe word / Killer eyes (CD-Rom).

Oct 01. (cd-ep) *(BELLACD 28)* **SPECIAL EP** [ ] [–]
– Jailbird / Poppy / Sky / Chapter 3.

Bella Union Bella Union

May 04. (cd) *(<BELLA 66CD>)* **RUSSIAN DOLL** [ ] Jun04 [ ]
– Never enough / Quelque jour / (My baby was a) Cheat / New girl / The visit / You / Touch me / Innocent / Beyond the furr / Close the world.

May 04. (cd-ep) *(<BELLA 67CD>)* **BEYOND THE FURR / CRYSTAL MOUNTAIN / PERFECT DAY** [ ] Jul04 [ ]

ROBIN GUTHRIE

Bella Union Bella Union

Mar 03. (cd) *(BELLACD 48) <69969>* **IMPERIAL** [ ] [ ]
– Imperial / Freefall / Thunderbird road / Tera / Crossing the line / Into Stressa / Music for labour / Falling from grace / Elemental / Drift.

Rykodisc Commotion

Jul 05. (cd; ROBIN GUTHRIE / HAROLD BUDD) *(RCD 16058) <CR 008>* **MYSTERIOUS SKIN** (soundtrack) [ ] May05 [ ]
– Neil's theme / The memories returning / Snowfall / Neil's farewell / Childhood lost / Halloween / A silhouette approaches / Goodbye to Wendy / Brian's nightmare – The unknown, part one / Twilight / The unknown, part two / The discovery / Loitering / The writing on the wall / One true love.

Rocket Girl Darla

Jun 06. (cd) *(RGIRL 44) <DAR 174>* **CONTINENTAL** [ ] May06 [ ]
– Continental / Conquering the romantic / Crescent / Monument / Amphora / The day star / Radiance / As I breathe / Last exit / Pale.

Leonard COHEN

Born: 21 Sep'34, Montreal, Canada. Emerging from the tail end of the beatnik scene in the early 60's, COHEN was nearing his mid thirties and had already published several volumes of poetry as well as two novels when he came to record his debut album, 'SONGS OF LEONARD COHEN'. Released in 1968, the record is still regarded by many as his finest work and includes two of his best loved and well known songs in 'SUZANNE' and 'SISTERS OF MERCY'. Musically, the album was sparse, fragile acoustic guitar accompanying COHEN's highly distinctive, tortured sliver of a voice. All ravaged sophistication and doomed romance, COHEN was inevitably compared with the likes of JACQUES BREL, although the richness of the imagery he employed immediately set him apart. While the seemingly self-pitying, bedsit-friendly image saw him panned and parodied by critics, he found an appreciative audience among disillusioned hippies as the singer/songwriter movement began to gather strength. Always more popular in Britain and Europe than America, his debut album reached No.13 in the UK charts. The follow-up, 'SONGS FROM A ROOM' (1969) was almost as good, another opus cloaked in a melancholic intensity and an aching sense of loss, boasting such timeless COHEN fare as 'BIRD ON A WIRE', 'THE PARTISAN' and 'LADY MIDNIGHT'. The record reached No.2 in Britain and COHEN set off for Europe on an extensive round of touring that included an appearance at the Isle Of Wight festival in 1970. Following the release of 'SONGS OF LOVE AND HATE' (1971), the singer embarked on another sojourn to foreign shores, even playing for Israeli soldiers at various military bases, an experience that informed a large part of the lyrical themes on 'NEW SKIN FOR THE OLD CEREMONY' (1974). It was to be another three years before the next studio release and in the interim, 'Columbia' issued a fairly representative best of package. Upon its release, 'DEATH OF A LADIES MAN' (1977) was met with puzzlement and derision, COHEN's subtle, quasi-mystical lyricism suffocated under a typically high powered PHIL SPECTOR production. Vocal in his embarrassment over the album, COHEN returned to more complementary arrangements and structures on 'RECENT SONGS' (1979). The early 80's saw COHEN concentrate on poetry and prose, even making a film, 'I Am A Hotel', in 1983. Returning to the music scene in 1985 with 'VARIOUS POSITIONS', COHEN still had a cult audience in Europe, one that mushroomed with the release of 'I'M YOUR MAN' in 1988. As a purveyor of effortlessly cool urban existentialism on the likes of 'FIRST WE TAKE MANHATTAN', COHEN attracted a new generation of disaffected music fans. It seems he was also held in high regard by the younger generation of fellow artists who showed their appreciation with a 1991 tribute album, 'I'M YOUR FAN'. Among those interpreting COHEN's finer moments (with mixed results) were NICK CAVE, R.E.M., IAN McCULLOCH and PIXIES. 'THE FUTURE' (1992) saw COHEN achieve his biggest commercial success since the 70's; although never the most prolific of artists, the record was his sole studio release of the 90's. As he came out of the monastery and down from the mountain, COHEN must have still thought it was the 1980's judging by the use of synth and programming on his subsequent album, the boringly-titled 'TEN NEW SONGS' (2001). Aided by long-time collaborator SHARON ROBINSON (who co-wrote 'EVERYBODY KNOWS' on the album 'I'M YOUR MAN' and scoops all of the musical and production credits here), COHEN still managed to uphold his poetic visions

LEONARD COHEN

nd bedsit romanticism. The songs (there's ten of them, you now) still had that "LEONARD COHEN afterworld" that KURT :OBAIN sang about, but musically the set disappoints. 'A :HOUSAND KISSES DEEP' re-vamps Robert Frost's classic poem Stopping By The Woods On A Snowy Evening' and COHEN's leep, almost whispering vocals in 'HERE IT IS' was indeed spine-ingling. The release of 'DEAR HEATHER' (2004) coincided with .is 70th birthday, something that the newly septuagenarian bard ounded pretty at ease with on this jazzy, relatively uplifting UK 'op 40 album; at times COHEN came across like a saner, more oporific TOM WAITS or a less profane SERGE GAINSBOURG, ven covering country standard 'TENNESSEE WALTZ' for good neasure.

Covered: ALWAYS (Irving Berlin) / THE PARTISAN (A.Marly/ H.Zaret-ernard) / BE FOR REAL (Frederick Knight). • **Trivia:** His long-time ual backing singer and solo artist JENNIFER WARNES released album 'AMOUS BLUE RAINCOAT' which contained all songs written by COHEN.

lbum rating: THE SONGS OF LEONARD COHEN (*8) / SONGS FROM A OOM (*6) / SONGS OF LOVE AND HATE (*6) / LIVE SONGS (*4) / NEW SKIN OR THE OLD CEREMONY (*5) / GREATEST HITS compilation (*9) / DEATH F A LADIES' MAN (*4) / RECENT SONGS (*5) / VARIOUS POSITIONS (*5) / M YOUR MAN (*7) / THE FUTURE (*7) / COHEN LIVE (*4) / TEN NEW ONGS (*6) / THE ESSENTIAL double compilation (*9) / MOJO PRESENTS . . . N INTRODUCTION TO . . . compilation (*7) / DEAR HEATHER (*6)

EONARD COHEN – vocals, guitar (with various session people)

C.B.S. Columbia

eb 68. (lp) *(CBS 63241)* *<9533>* **SONGS OF LEONARD COHEN** 13 83
– Suzanne / Master song / Winter lady / The stranger song / Sisters of mercy / So long, Marianne / Hey, that's no way to say goodbye / Stories of the street / Teachers / One of us cannot be wrong. *(cd-iss. Nov91; 468600-2) (cd re-iss. Apr03; 505136-2)*

.pr 68. (7") *<44439>* **SUZANNE. / HEY, THAT'S NO WAY TO SAY GOODBYE** –

lay 68. (7") *(CBS 3337)* **SUZANNE. / SO LONG, MARIANNE** –

.pr 69. (lp) *(CBS 63587)* *<9767>* **SONGS FROM A ROOM** 2 63
– Bird on the wire / Story of Isaac / Bunch of lonesome heroes / The partisan / Seems so long ago, Nancy / Old revolution / The butcher / You know who I am / Lady midnight / Tonight will be fine. *(re-iss. Nov81; CBS 32074) (cd-iss. Feb88; CDCBS 63587) (re-iss. cd Jun90 & Nov02; CD 32074)*

lay 69. (7") *(CBS 4245)* *<44827>* **BIRD ON THE WIRE. / SEEMS SO LONG AGO, NANCY**

lar 71. (lp) *(CBS 69004)* *<30103>* **SONGS OF LOVE AND HATE** 4
– Avalanche / Last year's man / Dress rehearsal rag / Diamonds in the mine / Love call you by your first name / Famous blue raincoat / Sing another song / Boys / Joan of Arc. *(re-iss. Sep82 lp/c; CBS/40 32219) (re-iss. Jun94 on 'Columbia' cd/c; 476799-2/-4)*

ıl 71. (7") *(CBS 7292)* **JOAN OF ARC. / DIAMONDS IN THE MINE** –

ıl 72. (7"ep) *(CBS 9162)* *<7684>* **McCABE & MRS. MILLER** (soundtrack)
– Sisters of mercy / Winter lady / The stranger song.

— w / **RON CORNELIUS** – guitar / **BOB JOHNSTON** – organ, guitar, harmonica / **CHARLIE DANIELS** – bass, fiddle / **ELKIN FOWLER** – banjo, guitar / **JENNIFER WARNES** – vocals / **PETER MARSHALL** – bass / **DAVID O'CONNOR** – guitar

.pr 73. (lp) *(CBS 65224)* *<31724>* **LIVE SONGS (live)**
– (minute prologue) / Passing through / You know who I am / Bird on the wire / Nancy / Improvisation / Story of Isaac / Please don't pass me by (a disgrace) / Tonight will be fine / Queen Victoria. *(re-iss. Mar84 lp/c; CBS/40 32272) (cd-iss. May88; CDCBS 65224)*

.pr 73. (7") *<45852>* **NANCY (live). / PASSING THROUGH (live)** –

ıl 74. (7") *(CBS 2494)* **BIRD ON THE WIRE (live). / TONIGHT WILL BE FINE (live)**

— now w/ loads of sessioners

.ug 74. (lp) *(CBS 69087)* *<33167>* **NEW SKIN FOR THE OLD CEREMONY** 24
– Is this what you wanted / Chelsea hotel No.2 / Lover lover lover / Field Commander Cohen / Why don't you try / There is a war / A singer must die / I tried to leave you / Who by fire / Take this longing / Leaving Green sleeves. *(c-iss.Jun86; CBS40 32660) (cd-iss. Jun88; CDCBS 69087) (cd re-iss. Apr96; CD 32660)*

Nov 74. (7") *(CBS 2699)* **LOVER LOVER LOVER. / WHO BY FIRE**

Nov 75. (lp) *(CBS 69161)* *<34077>* **GREATEST HITS** (compilation)
– Suzanne / Sisters of mercy / So long, Marianne / Bird on the wire / Lady Midnight / The partisan / Hey, that's no way to say goodbye / Famous blue raincoat / Last year's man / Chelsea hotel No.2 / Who by fire / Take this longing. *(re-iss. Apr85 lp/c; CBS/40 32644) (cd-iss. Jun88; CDCBS 69161); hit UK No.99) (re-iss. cd Jun89; CDCBS 32644)*

Nov 77. (lp/c) *(CBS/40 86042)* *<3125>* **DEATH OF A LADIES MAN** 35
– True love leaves no traces / Iodine / Paper thin hotel / Memories / I left a woman waiting / Don't go home with your hard-on / Fingerprints / Death of a ladies man. *(cd-iss. Jun88; CDCBS 86042) (re-iss. cd May95; CD 86042)*

Dec 77. (7") *(CBS 5882)* **MEMORIES. / DON'T GO HOME WITH YOUR HARD-ON**

Mar 78. (7") *(CBS 6095)* **TRUE LOVE LEAVES NO TRACES. / I LEFT A WOMAN WAITING**

Sep 79. (lp/c) *(CBS/40 86097)* *<36364>* **RECENT SONGS**
– The guests / Humbled in love / The window / Came so far for beauty / The lost Canadian (un Canadien errant) / The traitor / Our lady of solitude / The gypsy's wife / The smokey life / The ballad of absent mare. *(cd-iss. Jun88; CDCBS 86097) <US cd-iss. May88; CK 36264> (re-iss. cd.Dec93 on 'Sony Europe';) (re-iss. May94 on 'Columbia' cd/c; 474750-2/-4)*

C.B.S. Passport

Feb 85. (lp/c) *(CBS/40 26222)* *<6045>* **VARIOUS POSITIONS** 52
– Dance me to the end of love / Come back to you / The law / Night comes on / Hallelujah / The captain / Hunter's lullaby / Heart with no companion / If it be your will. *(cd-iss. May87; CDCBS 26222) (re-iss. Oct89 lp/c; 465 569-1/-4)*

Feb 85. (7") *(A 6052)* **DANCE ME TO THE END OF LOVE. / THE LAW** –

C.B.S. Columbia

Jan 88. (7") *(651 352-7)* **FIRST WE TAKE MANHATTAN. / SISTERS OF MERCY** –
(12"+=/cd-s+=) *(651 352-6/-2)* – Bird on the wire / Suzanne.

Feb 88. (lp/c/cd) *(460642-1/-4/-2)* *<44191>* **I'M YOUR MAN** 48
– First we take Manhattan / Ain't no cure for love / Everybody knows / I'm your man / Take this waltz / Jazz police / I can't forget / Tower of song. *(re-iss. Jul90 lp/c; same) (re-iss. cd Dec95; 460642-9)*

May 88. (7") *(651 599-7)* **AIN'T NO CURE FOR LOVE. / JAZZ POLICE**
(12"+=/cd-s+=) *(651 599-6/-2)* – Hey that's no way to say goodbye / So long, Marianne.

Columbia Columbia

Nov 92. (cd/c/lp) *(472498-2/-4/-1)* *<53226>* **THE FUTURE** 36
– The future / Waiting for the miracle / Be for real / Closing time / Anthem / Democracy / Light as the breeze / Always / Tacoma trailer. *(d-cd-iss. Feb93; 472498-2D)* – SONGS OF LEONARD COHEN

May 93. (cd-ep) *(658942-2)* **CLOSING TIME / FIRST WE TAKE MANHATTAN / FAMOUS BLUE RAINCOAT / WINTER LADY** –

Jul 94. (cd) *(477171-2)* *<66327>* **COHEN LIVE (live)**
– Dance me to the end of love / Bird on the wire / Everybody knows / Joan Of Arc / There is a war / Sisters of mercy / Hallelujah / I'm your man / Who by fire / One of us cannot be wrong / If it be your will / Heart with no companion / Suzanne. *(cd re-iss. Jan99; same)*

Oct 01. (cd) *(501202-2)* *<85953>* **TEN NEW SONGS** 26
– In my secret life / A thousand kisses deep / That don't make it junk / Here it is / Love itself / By the rivers dark / Alexandra leaving / You have loved enough / Boogie street / The land of plenty.

Oct 04. (cd) *(514768-2)* *<92891>* **DEAR HEATHER** 34
– Go no more a-roving / Because of / The letters / Undertow / Morning glory / On that day / Villanelle for our time / There for you / Dear Heather / Nightingale / To a teacher / The faith / Tennessee waltz (live).

– compilations, others, etc. –

on 'CBS' (later 'Columbia') UK / 'Columbia' US unless stated.

Mar 73. (7") *(CBS 8353)* **SUZANNE. / BIRD ON THE WIRE**

May 76. (7") *(CBS 4306)* **SUZANNE. / TAKE THIS LONGING**

Aug 83. (7"ep/c-ep) *Pickwick; (7SR/7SC 5022)* **SCOOP 33** –
– Suzanne / Hey, that's no way to say goodbye / Joan of Arc / Bird on the wire / Paper thin hotel / Lady midnight.

May 88. (cd) *<CK 34077>* **THE BEST OF LEONARD COHEN** –
(UK-iss.Oct94; 32644)

Apr 90. (cd) *Collectors Choice; (902 297-2)* **SO LONG, MARIANNE** –
(re-iss. Nov93; same) (re-iss. Dec95 on 'Columbia' cd/c; 460500-2/-4)

Sep 92. (d-cd) *(461012-2)* **NEW SKIN FOR THE OLD CEREMONY / SONGS FROM A ROOM**

Oct 92. (3xcd-box) *(472268-2)* **SONGS FROM A ROOM / VARIOUS POSITIONS / I'M YOUR MAN**

Oct 93. (3xcd-box) *(474146-2)* **SONGS OF LEONARD COHEN / SONGS OF LOVE & HATE / LIVE SONGS**

Feb 95. (d-cd) *(478480-2)* **SONGS FROM A ROOM / SONGS OF LOVE & HATE** –

Sep 01. (3xcd-box) *(499919-2)* **SONGS OF LEONARD COHEN / SONGS OF LOVE AND HATE / NEW SKIN FOR THE OLD CEREMONY**

Sep 01. (3xcd-box) *(504558-9)* **DEATH OF A LADIES MAN / RECENT SONGS / THE FUTURE**

Jan 03. (d-cd) *Sony TV; (497995-2) <86884>* **THE ESSENTIAL** 70 Oct02
– Suzanne / The stranger song / Sisters of mercy / Hey, that's no way to say goodbye / So long, Marianne / Bird on a wire / The partisan / Famous blue raincoat / Chelsea hotel No.2 / Take this longing / Who by fire / The guests / Hallelujah / If it be your will / Night comes on / I'm your man / Everybody knows / Tower of song / Ain't no cure for love / Take this waltz / First we take Manhattan / Dance me to the end of love (live) / The future / Democracy / Waiting for the miracle / Closing time / Anthem / In my secret life / Alexandra leaving / A thousand kisses deep / Love itself.

Sep 03. (d-cd) *(512852-2)* **MOJO PRESENTS . . . AN INTRODUCTION TO LEONARD COHEN** –

Sep 04. (d-cd) *(5175949)* **TEN NEW SONGS / THE FUTURE** –

COLDPLAY

Formed: London, England . . . early 1998 by CHRIS MARTIN and PHIL HARVEY, the latter would become their manager/financer/5th member after CHRIS found new pals/musicians – JON BUCKLAND, Edinburgh-born GUY BERRYMAN and WILL CHAMPION – while at university. These VERVE inspired mellow-ites issued a limited pressing of 500 copies of their self-financed debut, 'THE SAFETY' EP. After interest from 'Fierce Panda' (who released their single 'BROTHERS AND SISTERS'), the group looked set to conquer the indie charts with their new style of JEFF BUCKLEY-esque melancholia. 'BLUE ROOM' EP (1999) – and their first for 'Parlophone' – featured the classy Chris Alison-produced track 'HIGH SPEED', a dreamy "psychefeelia" song; touching, moody and soft, oh so soft! Supporting tortured HEAD brothers SHACK, enabled the band to delve further into the twisted world of moving rock and reach deeper into the minds of fans who had not yet overcome the departure of Brit pop. Come in Mr. ASHCROFT . . . your time is up! A second single, 'SHIVER', was their first to break into the UK Top 40, however, this would be well surpassed when summer 2000 follow-up, 'YELLOW', slid into the Top 5. The album, 'PARACHUTES' (2000), received rave reviews from all and sundry and shot into the UK charts at No.1 – it would subsequently touch American hearts and souls not long after. Warm, melancholy and passionate were a few select words to describe this Mercury Prize nomination which also featured a further Top 10 hit and Virgin playlist fave, 'TROUBLE'. The boys were back on top form (and No.1) in 2002, come the release of their second full-length album, 'A RUSH OF BLOOD TO THE HEAD'. It displayed all of the same qualities of the first, although the songs seemed to sit with the listener longer. An example of this was the single 'IN MY PLACE', a poignant but uplifting track that showed-off MARTIN's voice well, not to mention the rest of the group's excellent musicianship. The album glided from one song to the next, like a paper aeroplane in the breeze. At times, sounding almost identical to old ECHO AND THE BUNNYMEN, MARTIN must've taken notes from the old post-New Wave romantics, as at the end of 2002 he began dating a certain actress named Gwyneth Paltrow (he married her on 5th December 2003). Turn on the TV and you will probably hear som commercial or cult programme use 'THE SCIENTIST' as a theme the world was indeed progressing and COLDPLAY were winnir Grammys. Love 'em or hate 'em, COLDPLAY's lugubrious, song for-the-common-man graft was everyhwere in 2005, especially th summer of 2005 with the simultaneous release of Top 3 singl 'SPEED OF SOUND', and transatlantic chart-topping third albun 'X&Y' (2005). It was the 80s all over again as younger bands ape Thatcher-era post-punk desolation (in a wealthy Blairite presen and CHRIS MARTIN became a BONO for the Ikea generatio minus the politics and plus a barrowload of pained platitudes. RICHARD ASHCROFT-guesting appearance at July's Live8 furthe endeared them to the masses, while another couple of singles, 'FI YOU', and 'TALK', both went Top 10.

Album rating: PARACHUTES (*9) / A RUSH OF BLOOD TO THE HEAD (*9) X&Y (*8)

CHRIS MARTIN (b. 2 Mar'77, Devon, England) – vocals, piano, rhyth guitar / **JON BUCKLAND** (b.11 Sep'77) – guitar, harmonica, vocals / **GU BERRYMAN** (b.12 Apr'78, Kirkcaldy, Scotland) – bass / **WILL CHAMPIO** (b.31 Jul'78, Southampton, England) – drums, percussion, vocals

own label / not i

Apr 98. (7"ep) *(none)* **THE SAFETY ep** –
– Bigger stronger / No more keeping my feet on the ground / Such a rus

Fierce Panda / not i

Apr 99. (7") *(NING 068)* **BROTHERS AND SISTERS. / EASY TO PIECES** –
(cd-s+=) *(NING 068CD)* – Only superstition.

Parlophone / Capi

Oct 99. (12"ep/cd-ep) *(12R/CDR 6528)* **BLUE ROOM EP** –
– Bigger stronger / Don't panic / See you soon / High speed / Such a rus

Mar 00. (7") *(R 6536)* **SHIVER. / FOR YOU** 35 –
(cd-s+=) *(CDR 6536)* – Careful where you stand.

Jun 00. (c-s/7") *(TC+/R 6538) <radio cut>* **YELLOW. / HELP IS ROUND THE CORNER** 4 Feb01 48
(cd-s+=) *(CDR 6538)* – No more keeping my feet on the ground.

Jul 00. (cd/c/lp) *(527783-2/-4/-1) <30162>* **PARACHUTES** 1 Dec00 51
– Don't panic / Shiver / Spies / Sparks / Yellow / Trouble / Parachutes High speed / We never change / Everything's not lost.

Oct 00. (c-s/cd-s/7") *(TC/CD+/R 6549)* **TROUBLE. / BROTHERS AND SISTERS / SHIVER (Jo Whiley lunchtime social)** 10 –

Aug 02. (c-ep/12"ep/cd-ep) *(TCR/12R/CDR 6579)* **IN MY PLACE / ONE I LOVE / I BLOOM BLAUM** 2 –

Aug 02. (cd/c/lp) *(5405-4-2/-4/-1) <40504>* **A RUSH OF BLOOD TO THE HEAD** 1 5
– Politik / In my place / God put a smile upon your face / The scientist Clocks / Daylight / Green eyes / Warning sign / A whisper / A rush of bloo to the head / Amsterdam.

Nov 02. (7") *(R 6588)* **THE SCIENTIST. / 1.36 (featuring Tim Wheeler & Simon Pegg)** 10 –
(cd-s+=) *(CDR 6588)* – I ran away.

—— in Feb'03, CHRIS MARTIN was credited on RON SEXSMITH's single, 'Go In Them Hills'

Mar 03. (7") *(R 6594)* **CLOCKS. / CRESTS OF WAVES** 9 –
(cd-s+=) *(CDR 6594)* – Animals.

Jun 03. (cd-s) *<52608>* **CLOCKS / YELLOW** – 29

May 05. (7") *(R 6664) <radio>* **SPEED OF SOUND. / THING I DON'T UNDERSTAND** 2 8
(10"clear+=/cd-s+=) *(10R/CDR 6664)* – Proof.

Jun 05. (cd) *(474786-2) <42427>* **X&Y** 1 1
– Square one / What if / White shadows / Fix you / Talk X&Y / Speed of sound / A message / Low / The hardest part Swallowed in the sea / Twisted logic. *(hidden track+=)* – Til kingdo come.

Sep 05. (7") *(R 6671) <radio>* **FIX YOU. / THE WORLD TURNED** 4 59
(cd-s+=) *(CDR 6671)* – Poor me (live) / ('A'-CD-Rom video).

Dec 05. (7") *(R 6679) <radio>* **TALK. / GRAVITY** 10 Jan06 86
(dvd-s+=) *(DVDR 6679)* – ('A'-video) / Speed of sound (video) / ('A making of the video).
(cd-s) *(CDR 6679)* – ('A') / Sleeping sun.
(12") *(12RX 6679)* – ('A'-Thin White Duke mix) / ('A'-FK dub) / ('A Junkie XL mix).

Apr 06. (ltd-12") *(12R 6687)* **THE HARDEST PART** – –

COLDPLAY

☐ Allen COLLINS BAND (see under ⇒ LYNYRD SKYNYRD)

Edwyn COLLINS

Born: 23 Aug'59, Edinburgh, Scotland. COLLINS formed ORANGE JUICE in Glasgow, Scotland . . . 1977 initially as the NU-SONICS with JAMES KIRK, STEPHEN DALY and ALAN DUNCAN, who was subsequently replaced by DAVID McCLYMONT. In 1979, ORANGE JUICE signed to local indie label 'Postcard', the hub of the burgeoning Glasgow indie scene masterminded by ALAN HORNE. In contrast to the post-punk miserabilism coming out of England, ORANGE JUICE were purveyors of studiedly naive, wide-eyed indie pop as best sampled on the brace of early 45's, 'FALLING AND LAUGHING', 'BLUE BOY', 'SIMPLY THRILLED HONEY' and 'POOR OLD SOUL' (later collected on 1993's retrospective, 'THE HEATHER'S ON FIRE'). They subsequently signed to 'Polydor' in 1981, releasing a debut album, 'YOU CAN'T HIDE YOUR LOVE FOREVER', early the following year. Though some of their die-hard fans inevitably accused them of selling out, the set almost made the UK Top 20, its charming guitar pop auguring well for the future. The band suffered internal ruction soon after the album's release, however, MALCOLM ROSS and ZEKE MANYIKA replacing KIRK and DALY respectively. The Nigerian-born MANYIKA injected a newfound rhythmic thrust into the follow-up album, 'RIP IT UP' (1982), the clipped funk of the title track providing the band with their only Top 40 hit, albeit a sizeable one. Despite this belated success, further tensions reduced the band to a duo of COLLINS and MANYIKA who recorded an impressive mini-set, 'TEXAS FEVER' (1984) under the production auspices of reggae veteran, DENNIS BOVELL. Later that year saw the release of swansong set, 'THE ORANGE JUICE – THE THIRD ALBUM', a far more introspective affair which found COLLINS at a low ebb. The singer had already released a cover of The Velvet Underground's 'PALE BLUE EYES', with PAUL QUINN and subsequently embarked on a solo career which remained low key for the ensuing decade. Initially signed to ALAN McGEE's "side" label, 'Elevation', his first two solo singles flopped and as the label went belly-up, COLLINS opted for 'Demon' records. He finally issued a long-awaited album, 'HOPE AND DESPAIR' in summer '89. An eclectic, rootsy affair borne of COLLINS' troubled wilderness years, the record was hailed by the same critics who so vehemently supported ORANGE JUICE. Yet despite the praise, it seemed COLLINS was destined for cult appeal; a second 'Demon' set, 'HELLBENT ON COMPROMISE' (1990) failed to lift his profile and COLLINS went to ground. Well, not completely, the singer honing his production skills for indie outfits such as A HOUSE and The ROCKINGBIRDS. The throaty-voxed singer finally re-emerged in 1994 with 'GORGEOUS GEORGE', the record he'd been threatening to make for years. Recorded on classic studio equipment, the record's organic feel coupled with COLLIN's mordant cynicism and razor sharp songwriting resulted in a massive worldwide hit, 'A GIRL LIKE YOU'. With its crunching, NEIL YOUNG-like riffing and infectious delivery, the record was initially released in Europe and Australia before eventually hitting the Top 5 in the UK a year on. Though 1997's 'THE MAGIC PIPER' (from the album 'I'M NOT FOLLOWING YOU') didn't quite match this commercial feat, COLLINS remains one of Scotland's most accomplished songwriters with a reliable line in caustic wit. In 2002, his brand of humour was taken a step further via the release of 'DOCTOR SYNTAX', an album which saw COLLINS, for the first time, use beats and samples courtesy of SEBASTIAN LEWSLEY. The set comprised COLLINS' trademark guitar-led love songs, but with an edgier, personalised production. 'THE BEATLE was obviously a direct ode to his peers, although 'SPLITTIN UP' exemplified COLLINS' songwriting abilities by ten. '20 YEAR TOO LATE' employed a retro-electro-synth feel accompanied b some strange rapping never before encountered on an EDWY COLLINS record.

• **Songwriters:** ORANGE JUICE: most written by COLLINS, some wi MANYIKA. Note that KIRK was the writer of FELICITY, and ROSS provid PUNCH DRUNK. • **Covered:** L.O.V.E. (Al Green), while COLLINS solo tri his hand at MY GIRL HAS GONE (Smokey Robinson) + TIME OF TH PREACHER (Willie Nelson) / WON'T TURN BACK (Vic Godard).

Album rating: Orange Juice: YOU CAN'T HIDE YOUR LOVE FOREVER (*7 RIP IT UP (*6) / TEXAS FEVER mini (*5) / THE ORANGE JUICE (*5) THE ESTEEMED ORANGE JUICE (THE VERY BEST OF ORANGE JUIC compilation (*9) / Edwyn Collins: HOPE AND DESPAIR (*6) / HELLBENT O COMPROMISE (*6) / GORGEOUS GEORGE (*8) / I'M NOT FOLLOWIN YOU (*6) / DOCTOR SYNTAX (*6) / A CASUAL INTRODUCTION 1981-20 compilation (*8)

ORANGE JUICE

EDWYN COLLINS – vocals, guitar, occasional violin / **JAMES KIRK** – guita vocals / **DAVID McCLYMONT** – bass, synths; repl. ALAN DUNCAN **STEPHEN DALY** – drums

Postcard / not

Feb 80. (7") *(80-1)* **FALLING AND LAUGHING. / MOSCOW** ☐ –
(free 7"flexi) *(LYN 7609)* – FELICITY (live).

Aug 80. (7") *(80-2)* **BLUE BOY. / LOVE SICK** ☐ –

Dec 80. (7") *(80-6)* **SIMPLY THRILLED HONEY. / BREAKFAST TIME** ☐ –

Mar 81. (7") *(81-2)* **POOR OLD SOUL. / (part 2)** ☐ –

Jun 81. (7"; w-drawn) *(81-6)* **WAN LIGHT. / YOU OLD ECCENTRIC** – –

Polydor / Poly

Oct 81. (7") *(POSP 357)* **L.O.V.E. LOVE. / INTUITION TOLD ME PT.2** 65 –
(12"+=) *(POSPX 357)* – Moscow.

Jan 82. (7") *(POSP 386)* **FELICITY. / IN A NUTSHELL** 63 –
(12"+=) *(POSPX 386)* – You old eccentric.

Feb 82. (lp/c) *(POLS/+C 1057)* **YOU CAN'T HIDE YOUR LOVE FOREVER** 21 ☐
– Falling and laughing / Untitled melody / Wan light / Tender objec Dying day / L.O.V.E. love / Intuition told me (part 1) / Upwards ar onwards / Satellite city / Three cheers for our side / Consolation priz Felicity / In a nutshell.

— **MALCOLM ROSS** – guitar (ex-JOSEF K) + **ZEKE MANYIKA** (b. Nigeri – percussion, vocals, synths; repl. KIRK DALY who subsequently form MEMPHIS, releasing only one single for 'Swamplands', 'YOU SUPPLY TH ROSES', early 1985

Jul 82. (7"/10") *(POSP/+T 470)* **TWO HEARTS TOGETHER. / HOKOYO** 60 –

Oct 82. (7") *(POSP 522)* **I CAN'T HELP MYSELF. / TONGUES BEGIN TO WAG** 42 ☐
(12"+=) *(POSPX 522)* – Barbeque.

Nov 82. (lp/c) *(POLS/+C 1076)* **RIP IT UP** 39 ☐
– Rip it up / Breakfast time / A million pleading faces / Mud in yo eye / Turn away / I can't help myself / Flesh of my flesh / Louise Louis Hokoyo / Tenter hook. *(cd-iss. Jul89; 839768-2)*

Feb 83. (7") *(POSP 547)* **RIP IT UP (remix). / SNAKE CHARMER** 8 ☐
(some w/ live c-s+=) – The Felicity Flexi Session: The formative years Simply thrilled honey / Botswana / Time to develop / Blue boy.
(d7"+=) *(POSPD 547)* – Sad lament / Lovesick.
(12") *(POSPX 547)* – ('A'side) / Sad lament / ('A'long version).

May 83. (7"/7"pic-d/ext.12") *(OJ/OJP/OJX 4)* **FLESH OF MY FLESH. / LORD JOHN WHITE AND THE BOTTLENECK TRAIN** 41 –

— basically now a duo of **COLLINS** + **MANYIKA** with session peo replacing ROSS (who joined AZTEC CAMERA) and McCLYMONT (to T MOODISTS)

Feb 84. (7") *(OJ 5)* **BRIDGE. / OUT FOR THE COUNT** 67 –
(free 7"flexi w/ above) *(JUICE 1)* – Poor old soul (live).
(12"+=) *(OJX 5)* – ('A'-Summer '83 mix).

EDWYN COLLINS

Feb 84. (m-lp/c) *(OJM LP/MC 1)* **TEXAS FEVER** [34] [–]
– Bridge / Craziest feeling / Punch drunk / The day I went down to Texas / A place in my heart / A sad feeling. *(cd-iss. Mar98 +=; 539982-2)* – Leaner period / Out for the count / Move yourself.

Apr 84. (7") *(OJ 6)* **WHAT PRESENCE?! / A PLACE IN MY HEART (dub)** [47] [ ]
(free c-s w/ above) *(OJC 6)* – In a nutshell (live) / Simply thrilled honey (live) / Dying day (live).
(12"+=) *(OJX 6)* – ('A'extended).

Oct 84. (7") *(OJ 7)* **LEAN PERIOD. / BURY MY HEAD IN MY HANDS** [74] [–]
(free 7"flexi w/ above) *(JUICE 3)* – Rip it up / What presence?!
(12"+=) *(OJX 7)* – ('A'extended).

Nov 84. (lp/c) *(OJ LP/MC 1)* **THE ORANGE JUICE – THE THIRD ALBUM** [ ] [–]
– Get while the goings good / Salmon fishing in New York / I guess I'm just a little sensitive / Burning desire / The artisan / Lean period / What presence?! / Out for the count / All that mattered / Seacharger. *(re-iss. Aug86 lp/c; SPE LP/MC 102) (c+=remixes)* – I can't help myself / Rip it up / Love struck / Flesh of my flesh / Out for the count / What presence?! / Lean period.

— disbanded after above album; MANYIKA went solo, as did EDWYN COLLINS. He'd already (in Aug'84) hit UK No.72 with PAUL QUINN on 7"/12" 'PALE BLUES EYES' (a Velvet Underground cover) released on 'Swamplands'.

– compilations, others, etc. –

Jul 85. (lp/c) *Polydor; (OJ LP/MC 3)* **IN A NUTSHELL** [ ] [–]
– Falling and laughing / Poor old soul (live) / L.O.V.E. / In a nutshell / Felicity / I can't help myself / Hokoyo / Rip it up / Flesh of my flesh / A place in my heart / Bridge / Out for the count / The artisans / What presence?! *(w/free 7"flexi)* – Felicity.

Jan 91. (cd/c) *Polydor; (847 727-2/-4)* **THE ORANGE JUICE / YOU CAN'T HIDE YOUR LOVE FOREVER** [ ] [–]

Jul 92. (cd) *Polydor; (513618)* **THE VERY BEST OF ORANGE JUICE (THE ESTEEMED ORANGE JUICE)** [ ] Oct95 [ ]
– Falling and laughing / Consolation prize (live) / Old encentric / L.O.V.E. love / Felicity / In a nutshell / Rip it up / I can't help myself / Flesh of my flesh / Tenterhook / Bridge / The day I went down to Texas / Punch drunk / A place in my heart / A sad lament / Lean period / I guess I'm just a little too sensitive / The artisans / Salmon fishing in New York / What presence?! / Out for the count. *(re-iss. cd Sep95; same)* – (extra track).

Jul 92. (lp/c/cd) *Postcard; (DUBH 922/+MC/CD)* **OSTRICH CHURCHYARD (live in Glasgow)** [ ] [–]
– Louise Louise / Three cheers for our side / To put it in a nutshell / Satellite city / Consolation prize / Holiday hymn / Intuition told me (parts 1 & 2) / Wan light / Dying day / Texas fever / Tender object. *(cd+=/c+=)* – Falling and laughing / Lovesick / Poor old soul / You old eccentric. *(cd re-iss. Oct95; DUBH 954CD)*

May 93. (7") *Postcard; (DUBH 934)* **BLUEBOY. / LOVESICK** [ ] [–]
(cd-s+=) *(DUBH 934CD)* – Poor old soul (French version) / Poor old soul (instrumental).

Jul 93. (lp/cd) *Postcard; (DUBH 932/+CD)* **THE HEATHER'S ON FIRE** [ ] [–]
– Falling and laughing / Moscow / Moscow Olympics / Blue boy / Love sick / Simply thrilled honey / Breakfast time / Poor old soul / Poor old soul pt.2 / Felicity / Upwards and onwards / Dying day / Holiday hymn. *(re-iss. cd Oct95; DUBH 955CD)*

EDWYN COLLINS

solo, with **DENNIS BOVELL, MALCOLM ROSS, ALEX GRAY + CHRIS TAYLOR**

Elevation — not iss.

May 87. (7") *(ACID 4)* **DON'T SHILLY SHALLY. / IF EVER YOU'RE READY** [ ] [–]
(12"+=) *(ACID 4T)* – Queer fish.

Elevation — not iss.

Nov 87. (7") *(ACID 6)* **MY BELOVED GIRL. / CLOUDS (FOGGING UP MY MIND)** [ ] [–]
(12"+=) *(ACID 6T)* – My (long time) beloved girl.
(7"box+=) *(ACID 6B)* – 50 shades of blue (acoustic) / What's the big idea.

— now with **BERNARD CLARKE** – keyboards / **DENNIS BOVELL** – bass / **DAVE RUFFY** – drums

Demon — not iss.

Jun 89. (lp/c/cd) *(FIEND/+C/CD 144)* **HOPE AND DESPAIR** [ ] [–]
– Coffee table song / 50 shades of blue / You're better than you know / Pushing it to the back of my mind / The wheels of love / Darling, they want it all / The beginning of the end / The measure of the man / Testing time / Let me put my arms around you / The wide eyed child in me / Ghost of a chance. *(c+=/cd+=)* – If ever you're ready. *(re-iss. cd Sep95)*

Jul 89. (7") *(D 1064)* **THE COFFEE TABLE SONG. / JUDAS IN BLUE JEANS** [ ] [–]
(12"+=) *(D 1064T)* – Out there.

Oct 89. (7") *(D 1065)* **50 SHADES OF BLUE (new mix). / IF EVER YOU'RE READY** [ ] [–]
(12") *(D 1065T)* – ('A'extended) / Kindred spirit / Just call her name / Ain't that always the way.
(cd-s) *(D 1065CD)* – ('A'side) / Judas in blue jeans / Kindred spirit / Just call her name.

Oct 90. (lp/c/cd) *(FIEND/+C/CD 195)* **HELLBENT ON COMPROMISE** [ ] [–]
– Means to an end / You poor deluded fool / It might as well be you / Take care of yourself / Graciously / Someone else besides / My girl has gone / Everything and more / What's the big idea? / Hellbent medley:- Time of the preacher – Long time gone. *(re-iss. cd Oct95; same)*

— now with **STEVEN SKINNER** – guitar / **PHIL THORNALLEY** – bass / **PAUL COOK** – drums

Setanta — Bar None

Aug 94. (cd/c/lp) *(SET CD/MC/LP 014) <058>* **GEORGEOUS GEORGE** [ ] Sep95 [ ]
– The campaign for real rock / A girl like you / Low expectations / Out of this world / If you could love me / North of Heaven / Georgeous George / It's right in front of you / Make me feel again / You got it all / Subsidence / Occupy your mind. *(re-iss. Jul95, hit UK No.8)*

Oct 94. (c-ep) *(ZOP 001C)* **EXPRESSLY EP** [42] [–]
– A girl like you / A girl like you (Macrame remix by Youth).
(cd-ep+=) *(ZOP 001CD1)* – Out of this world (I hear a new world) (St.Etienne remix) / Occupy your mind.
(cd-ep) *(ZOP 001CD2)* – ('A'side) / Don't shilly shally (Spotters'86 demo) / Something's brewing / Bring it on back.

Mar 95. (12"ep) *(ZOP 002CD1)* **IF YOU COULD LOVE ME (radio edit). / IN A BROKEN DREAM / INSIDER DEALING / ('A'-MC Esher mix)** [ ] [ ]
(cd-ep) *(ZOP 002CD1)* – (first 3 tracks) / Hope and despair.
(cd-ep) *(ZOP 002CD2)* – ('A'side) / If ever you're ready / Come to your senses / A girl like you (the Victoria Spaceman mix).

Jun 95. (7") *(ZOP 0037)* **A GIRL LIKE YOU. / YOU'RE ON YOUR OWN** [4] [–]
(c-s+=) *(ZOP 003C)* – If you could love me (acoustic version).
(cd-s++=) *(ZOP 003CD)* – Don't shilly shally (Spotters '86 demo).

Oct 95. (c-s) *<58-1234>* **A GIRL LIKE YOU / IF YOU COULD LOVE ME** [–] [32]
(above used on the film 'Empire Records')

Feb 96. (c-s) *(ZOP 004C)* **KEEP ON BURNING / IF YOU COULD LOVE ME (IN TIME AND SPACE)** [45] [–]
(cd-s+=) *(ZOP 004CD1)* – Lava lamp / The campaign for real rock.
(cd-s) *(ZOP 004CD2)* – Won't turn back / You've grown a beard / A girl like you (live) / White room.

Setanta — Sony

Jul 97. (12") *(SET 041T)* **THE MAGIC PIPER. / A GIRL LIKE YOU (Makrame mix) / WELWYN GARDEN CITY** [32] [–]
(cd-s) *(SETCDA 041)* – ('A'side) / More than you bargained for / Red menace / It takes a little time.
(cd-s) *(SETCDB 041)* – ('A'side) / Who is it? / Who is it? (halterbacked by the Victorian spaceman / Welwyn Garden City.

Sep 97. (cd/c/lp) *(SET CD/MC/LP 039) <68716>* **I'M NOT FOLLOWING YOU** [55] Oct97 [ ]
– It's a steal / The magic piper (of love) / Seventies night / No one waved goodbye / Downer / Keep on burning / Running away with myself / Country rock / For the rest of my life / Superficial cat / Adidas world / I'm not following you.

Oct 97. (7") *(SET 045)* **ADIDAS WORLD. / HIGH FASHION** [71] [–]
(cd-s+=) *(SETCDA 045)* – Mr. Bojangles / Talking 'bout the times.
(cd-s) *(SETCDB 045)* – ('A'side) / Episode 3 / Episode 5 / Episode 10 (no, no, no Adidas – Adilated by . . .).

Nov 97. (d12") *(ZOPPR 005)* **I HEAR A NEW WORLD** [ ] [–]
– (mixes; Red Snapper / Deadly Avenger Supershine / Red Snapper vocal / DOWNER (James Lavelle mix) // THE MAGIC PIPER (the Wiseguys sniper mix) / ADIDAS WORLD (adilated by Sebastian Lawsely) / DOWNER (James Lavelle vocal).

— in Apr'01, EDWYN collaborated with BERNARD BUTLER on the 'Setanta' single 'MESSAGE FOR JOJO'

Apr 02. (cd) *(SETCD 098)* **DOCTOR SYNTAX** –
– Never felt like this / Should've done that / Mine is at / No idea / The Beathes / Back to the back room / Splitting up / Johnny Teardrop / 20 years too late / It's a funny thing / Calling on you.

Sep 02. (cd-s) *(SETCD 112)* **JOHNNY TEARDROP / NEVER FELT LIKE THIS / POSTER** –

Oct 02. (cd) *(SETCD 113)* **A CASUAL INTRODUCTION 1981-2001** (compilation) –
– A girl like you / What presence? (ORANGE JUICE) / Magic piper (of love) / Rip it up (ORANGE JUICE) / A sad lament (ORANGE JUICE) / Witch queen of New Orleans / Johnny teardrop / Gorgeous George / Ghost of a chance / Campaign for real rock / Hope and despair / Falling and laughing (ORANGE JUICE) / Keep on burning / Adidas world / Felicity (ORANGE JUICE) / Tenterhook (ORANGE JUICE) / Witchcraft / Graciously.

□ COMMANDER VENUS (see under ⇒ BRIGHT EYES)

Ry COODER

Born: RYLAND PETER COODER, 15 Mar'47, Los Angeles, California, USA. He sessioned for the likes of JACKIE DE SHANNON and TAJ MAHAL, before moving on to CAPTAIN BEEFHEART in 1967. He nearly replaced BRIAN JONES in The ROLLING STONES, although he chose to only guest on their 'Let It Bleed' album, contributing searing bottleneck slide work to a number of songs, most effectively on the classic title track. By the time COODER was offered a solo deal by 'Reprise' in 1970, he was already one of the most adaptable, respected and gifted guitarists in the world, equally adept at playing other instruments such as the banjo and mandolin. Guesting on LITTLE FEAT's eponymous 1970 debut, COODER released his own self-titled solo set the following year. An impressive start, the record was largely made up of cover material, including an abrasive cover of Woody Guthrie's 'DO RE MI', a mandolin rendition of Sleepy John Este's 'GOIN' TO BROWNSVILLE' and a brilliantly drawling version of Randy Newman's biting 'OLD KENTUCKY HOME'. A follow-up long-player, 'INTO THE PURPLE VALLEY' (1972) was a more stripped down affair, highlighting his slide work, most notably on another Woody Guthrie number, 'VIGILANTE MAN'. Subsequent albums, 'BOOMER'S STORY' (1972) and PARADISE AND LUNCH' (1974), covered similar territory, jazz pianist EARL HINES guesting on the latter. It was 1978's 'CHICKEN SKIN MUSIC', that had the critics in rapture, however, its Hawaiian slack guitar and Tex-Mex stylings lent genuine authenticity by the contributions of star players GABBY PAHINUI and FLACO JIMENEZ together with the gospel vocals of BOBBY KING. These collaborations with respected players in the field of world music were a blueprint for much of COODER's subsequent output. In the meantime, he dabbled in ragtime and vaudeville with 'JAZZ' (1978), while 1979's 'BOP TILL YOU DROP' signalled a move away from traditional music to rock'n'roll and R&B. The latter album also saw COODER make a rare entry into the UK Top 40, something he only repeated with 1982's 'THE SLIDE AREA'. During the 80's, COODER moved sideways into soundtrack work, his atmospheric slide work fitting the bill for a number of Hollywood studios. Having already worked on 'Performance' in the late 60's, COODER proceeded to turn in impressive scores including 'THE LONG RIDERS' (1980), 'THE BORDER' (1982), 'JOHNNY HANDSOME' (1989) and most famously (and effectively) 'PARIS, TEXAS' (1985). The 90's saw the irrepressible guitarist team up with Indian musician, VISHANA MOHAN BHATT, for 'A MEETING BY THE RIVER' (1993), a magical, hypnotic fusion of Delta blues and Eastern classical/folk. Around the same time as soundtrack score for 'GEROMINO: AN AMERICAN LEGEND', another groundbreaking set was released the following year in 'TALKING TIMBUKTU' (1994), a Grammy winning piece upon which COODER sparred with African guitarist ALI FARKA TOURE. The greatest critical praise, however, was probably reserved for the celebrated 'BUENA VISTA SOCIAL CLUB' (1997), a benchmark recording which saw COODER jam with some of Cuba's oldest (we're talking in their 80's and 90's here!) and most accomplished musicians. Contemporary music's most talented curator was back (from further soundtrack work) in 2003 with another imaginatively conceived collaboration, this time in tandem with Cuban guitar maestro MANUEL GALBAN. A strange beast, 'MAMBO SINUENDO' was a largely instrumental amalgam of classic mambo and vintage easy listening sophistication, all sown up with hints of the Hawaiian, slack-keyed whinny which COODER has proved himself so adept at in the past. That America's greatest living curator continues to be more appreciated outside of his homeland was reflected in the chart positions of the dazzling 'CHAVEZ RAVINE' (2005): UK Top 40; US Top 200. This universally acclaimed, 'Songs From The Capeman'-esque concept set might've been billed as a solo record – the man's first since the late 80's – but the raft of hand-picked collaborators told its own story. Alongside regular partners like FLACO JIMENEZ and JIM KELTNER, COODER recruited Pachuco legends DON TOSTI and LALO GUERRERO as well as the Midniters' LITTLE WILLIE G for an ambitious narration of yet another unsavoury – and until now largely forgotten – episode in American history. The iconically apocalyptic cover art likewise told its own story, one which – as neighborhoods are regularly bulldozed from Palestine to Zimbabwe – is still being played out fifty years later. Against a post-WWII backdrop of both alien and terrestrial paranoia, COODER reanimated the sepia memories of predominantly Chicano-populated L.A. barrio, Chavez Ravine, the victim of dodgy politics and rapacious redevelopment. No white musician straddles the Latino divide as comfortably as COODER, and much on the material on here – not least GUERRERO's glorious 'LOS CHUCOS SUAVES' – matched his BUENA VISTA high water mark. Longtime fans could also feast on some bonafide COODER vocals, as wry and resonant as they ever were.

• **Covered:** VIGILANTE MAN (Woody Guthrie) / GET RHYTHM (Johnny Cash) / HE'LL HAVE TO GO (hit; Jim Reeves) / LITTLE SISTER (Pomus-Shuman) / 13 QUESTION METHOD (Chuck Berry) / MONEY HONEY (hit; Drifters) / STAND BY ME (Ben E. King) / IT'S ALL OVER NOW (Bobby Womack) / GOODNIGHT IRENE (Leadbelly) / NEED A WOMAN (Bob Dylan) / BLUE SUEDE SHOES (Carl Perkins) / ALL SHOOK UP (Elvis Presley) / and loads more. The JAZZ album had early 1940's covers, etc.

Album rating: RY COODER (*6) / INTO THE PURPLE VALLEY (*7) / BOOMER'S STORY (*7) / PARADISE AND LUNCH (*7) / CHICKEN SKIN MUSIC (*8) / SHOWTIME (*5) / JAZZ (*6) / BOP TILL YOU DROP (*5) / BORDERLINE (*6) / THE LONG RIDERS soundtrack (*6) / THE BORDER soundtrack (*5) / RY COODER LIVE (*5) / THE SLIDE AREA (*4) / PARIS, TEXAS soundtrack (*8) / ALAMO BAY soundtrack (*7) / WHY DON'T YOU TRY ME TONIGHT compilation (*7) / BLUE CITY soundtrack (*4) / CROSSROADS soundtrack (*6) / GET RHYTHM (*5) / JOHNNY HANDSOME soundtrack (*5) / TRESPASS soundtrack (*5) / A MEETING BY THE RIVER with V.M. Bhatt (*5) / TALKING TIMBUKTU with Ali Farka Toure (*8) / GERONIMO: AN AMERICAN LEGEND soundtrack (*5) / MUSIC BY RY COODER compilation/soundtracks (*7) / THE BEST OF RY COODER compilation (*8) / LAST MAN STANDING soundtrack (*4) / BUENA VISTA SOCIAL CLUB soundtrack by Buena Vista Social Club (*9) / THE END OF VIOLENCE soundtrack (*6) / PRIMARY COLORS soundtrack (*6) / MAMBO SINUENDO with Manuel Galban (*7) / CHAVEZ RAVINE (*7)

RY COODER – vocals, guitar (ex-CAPTAIN BEEFHEART & HIS MAGIC BAND) plus session people too numerous to mention

Reprise Reprise

Oct 70. (7") *<0910>* **GOIN' TO BROWNSVILLE. / AVAILABLE SPACE** –

Dec 70. (7") *<0940>* **ALIMONY. / PIGMEAT** –

Jan 71. (lp) *(K 44093) <RSLP 6402>* **RY COODER** Dec70

– Alimony / France chance / One meat ball / Do re mi / Old Kentucky home (turpentine & dandelion wine) / How can a poor man stand such times and live? / Available space / Pig meat / Police dog blues / Goin' to Brownsville / Dark is the night. *(cd-iss. May95 on 'Warners'; 7599-27510-2)*

May 71. (7") *(RS 23497)* **HOW CAN A POOR MAN STAND SUCH TIMES AND LIVE. / GOIN' TO BROWNSVILLE** –

Feb 72. (7") *<1009>* **ON A MONDAY. / DARK IS THE NIGHT** –

Feb 72. (lp) *(K 44142) <2052>* **INTO THE PURPLE VALLEY**

– How can you keep on moving / Billy the kid / Money honey / F.D.R. in Trinidad / Teardrops will fall / Denomination blues / On a Monday / Hey porter / Great dreams from heaven / Taxes on the farmer feeds us all / Vigilante man. *(cd-iss. 1988; K2 44142)*

Feb 72. (7") *(K 14151)* **MONEY HONEY. / ON A MONDAY** –

Apr 72. (7") *<1071>* **MONEY MONEY. / BILLY THE KID** –

Oct 72. (7") *<1167>* **BOOMER'S STORY. / BILLY THE KID** –

Nov 72. (lp) *(K 44224) <2117>* **BOOMER'S STORY**

– Boomer's story / Cherry ball blues / Crow black children / Axe sweet mama / Maria Elena / Dark end of the street / Rally 'round the flag / Comin' in on a wing and a prayer / President Kennedy / Good morning Mr. Railroad man. *(cd-iss. Jan93 on 'WEA'; 7599 26398-2)*

May 74. (lp) *(K 44260) <2179>* **PARADISE AND LUNCH**

– Tamp 'em up solid / Tattler / Married man's a fool / Jesus on the mainline / It's all over now / Fool about a cigarette – Feelin' good / If walls could talk / Mexican divorce / Ditty wa ditty. *(cd-iss. 1988; K2 44260)*

— next with **FLACO JIMENEZ** – accordion / **GABBY PAHINUI** – steel guitar / **BOBBY KING** – gospel vocals

Oct 76. (lp/c) *(K/K4 54083) <2254>* **CHICKEN SKIN MUSIC**

– The bourgeois blues / I got mine / Always lift him up / He'll have to go / Smack dab in the middle / Stand by me / Yellow roses / Chloe / Goodnight Irene. *(cd-iss. 1988; 254083)*

Mar 77. (7") *(K 14457)* **HE'LL HAVE TO GO. / THE BOURGEOIS BLUES** –

Warners Warners

Aug 77. (lp/c) *(K/K4 56386) <3059>* **SHOW TIME (live)**

– School is out / Alimony / Jesus on the mainline / ark end of the street / Viva sequin – Do re mi / Volver, volver / How can a poor man stand such times and live? / Smack dab in the middle. *(cd-iss. Nov93; 7599 27319-2)*

Aug 77. (7") *<8384>* **SCHOOL IS OUT (live). / JESUS ON THE MAINLINE (live)** –

Jun 78. (lp/c) *(K/K4 56488) <3197>* **JAZZ**

– Face to face I shall meet him / Davenport blues / In a mist / Big bad Bill is sweet William now / Happy meeting in glory / We shall be happy / Nobody / Shine / Flashes / Dream / Pearls / Tia Juana. *(cd-iss. 1988; K2 25688)*

Jun 79. (7") *<49055>* **LITTLE SISTER. / DOWN IN HOLLYWOOD** –

Aug 79. (lp/c) *(K/K4 56691) <3358>* **BOP TILL YOU DROP** 36 62

– Little sister / Go home girl / The very thing that makes you rich (makes me poor) / I think it's gonna work out fine / Down in Hollywood / Look at granny run run / Trouble, you can't fool me / Don't mess up a good thing / I can't win. *(cd-iss. 1983; K2 56691)*

Aug 79. (7") *(K 17460)* **LITTLE SISTER. / GO HOME GIRL** –

Oct 79. (7") *<49081>* **THE VERY THING THAT MAKES YOU RICH (MAKES ME POOR). / LITTLE SISTER** –

Jun 80. (lp/c) *(K/K4 56826) <HS 3448>* **THE LONG RIDERS** (soundtrack)

– The long riders / I'm a good old rebel / Seneca square dance / Archie's funeral (hold to God's unchanging hand) / I always knew that you were the one / Rally 'round the flag / Wildwood boys / Better things to think about / Jesse James / Cole Younger polka / Escape from Northfield / Leaving Missouri / Jesse James. *<(cd-iss. Jan96 on 'WEA'; 7599 23448-2)>*

Oct 80. (lp/c) *(K/K4 56864) <3489>* **BORDERLINE** 35 Jan81 43

– 634-5789 / Speedo / Why don't you try me / Down in the Boondocks / Johnny Porter / The way we make a broken heart / Crazy 'bout an automobile (every woman I know) / The girls from Texas / Borderline / Never make a move too soon. *(cd-iss. 1988; 25686-2)*

Oct 80. (7") *<49677>* **BORDERLINE. / THE GIRLS FROM TEXAS** –

Oct 80. (7") *(K 17713)* **634-5789. / THE GIRLS FROM TEXAS** –

Dec 80. (7") **CRAZY 'BOUT AN AUTOMOBILE. / BORDERLINE** –

Aug 81. (7") *(K 17844)* **CRAZY 'BOUT AN AUTOMOBILE (EVERY WOMAN I KNOW). / THE VERY THING THAT MAKES YOU RICH (MAKES ME POOR)** –

(12"+=) *(K 17844T)* – If walls could talk / Look at granny run run.

Apr 82. (lp/c) *(K/K4 56976) <3651>* **THE SLIDE AREA** 18

– UFO has landed in the ghetto / I need a woman / Gypsy woman / Blu suede shoes / Mama, don't treat your daughter mean / I'm drinking again Which came first / That's the way love turned out for me. *(cd-iss. Jul88 K2 56976)*

May 82. (d7") *(K 17952)* **GYSPY WOMAN. / ALIMONY** –

(with free 7") *(SAM 149)* – TEARDROPS WILL FALL / IT'S ALL OVE NOW

May 82. (lp) *(MCF 3133) <BSR 6105>* **THE BORDER (soundtrack)** Mar82

– Earthquake / Across the borderline (vocal: FREDDIE FENDER) Maria / Texas bop (JIM DICKINSON) / Highway 23 / Palomita (SAM SAMUDIO) / Rio Grande / Too late (vocal: JOHN HIATT) / No quier (SAM SAMUDIO) / Skin game (vocal: JOHN HIATT) / El scorcho Building fires (vocal: BRENDA PATTERSON) / Nino.

above issued on 'M.C.A.' + 'Backstreet' US

Feb 85. (lp) *(925270-1) <25270>* **PARIS, TEXAS** (soundtrack)

– Paris, Texas / Brothers / Nothing out there / A cancion Mixteca / N safety zone / Houston in two seconds / She's leaving the bank / On th couch / I knew these people / Dark was the night. *<(cd-iss. May01; 936 48088-2)>*

— RY provided the unreleased score for 'Brewster's Millions' (1985)

Feb 86. (lp/c) *(SLA P/C 7) <SLASH 3>* **ALAMO BAY** (soundtrack) Jan85

– Theme from Alamo Bay / Gooks on Main Street / Too close / Kla meeting / Sailfish evening / The last stand (Alamo Bay) / Quatro vicios Search & destroy / Glory.

(above issued on 'Slash' UK/US)

Mar 86. (lp/c)(cd) *(WX 37/+C)(40864-2)* **WHY DON'T YOU TRY ME TONIGHT (THE BEST OF RY COODER)** (compilation) –

– How can a poor man stand such times and live? / Available space / Mone honey / Tattler / He'll have to go / Smack dab in the middle / Dark en of the street / Down in Hollywood / Little sister / I think it's gonna wor out fine / Crazy 'bout an automobile (every woman I know) / 634-5789 Why don't you try me tonight.

Jul 86. (lp/c) *(925386-1/-4) <25386>* **BLUE CITY** (soundtrack)

– Blue city down / Elevation 13 feet / Marianne (TRUE BELIEVERS) / Nic bike / Greenhouse / Billy and Annie / Tell me something slick (POPS AN TIMER) / Blue city / Don't take your guns to town / A leader of men / No even Key West.

Jul 86. (7") **BILLY AND ANNIE. / TELL ME SOMETHING SLICK** –

Jul 86. (7") *<28723>* **CROSSROADS. / FEEL IT (BAD BLUES)** –

Jul 86. (lp/c) *<(9 25399-1/-4)>* **CROSSROADS** (soundtrack) May86 85

– Crossroads / Down in Mississippi / Cotton needs pickin' / Viola Le blues / See you in Hell, blind boy / Nitty gritty Mississippi / He made woman out of me / Feelin' bad blues / Somebody's callin' my name / Willi Brown blues / Walkin' away blues. *<(cd-iss. Oct91; 9 25399-2)>*

Dec 87. (lp/c)(cd) *(WX 121/+C)(925639-2) <25639>* **GET RHYTHM** 75 Nov87

– Get rhythm / Low-commotion / Going back to Okinawa / 13 questio method / Women will rule the world / All shook up / I can tell by the wa you smell / Across the borderline / Let's have a ball.

Jan 88. (7") **GET RHYTHM. / GOING BACK TO OKINAWA** –

Apr 88. (7") **ALL SHOOK UP. / GET YOUR LIES STRAIGHT** –

Apr 88. (7"/10") *(WB/WTE 8107)* **GET RHYTHM. / GET YOUR LIES STRAIGHT** –

(12"+=/3"cd-s+=) *(WT/WCD 8107)* – Down in Hollywood.

— in 1988, RY provided the score for short animation film, 'Pecos Bill'

Oct 89. (lp/c)(cd) *(WX 307/+C)<(9 25886-2)>* **JOHNNY HANDSOME** (soundtrack)

– Main theme / I can't walk this time – The prestige / Angola / Clip join rhumba / Sad story / Fountain walk / Cajun metal / First week at work Greasy oysters / Smells like money / Sunny's tune / I like your eyes / Adio Donna / Cruising with Rafe / How's my face / End theme. *<(cd re-iss Feb95; same)>*

— In 1991, he recorded soundtrack for Robin Williams film 'Pecos Bill'. H also teamed up with NICK LOWE, JOHN HIATT and JIM KELTNER i band LITTLE VILLAGE. In 1992, he and DAVID LINDLEY were part of Th PAHINUI BROTHERS who released Aug'92 eponymous album for 'Privat Music'.

WEA Warne

Jan 93. (cd/c) *(9362 45220-2/-4) <25399>* **TRESPASS** (soundtrack) Dec92

– Video drive-by / Trespass (main title) / East St. Louis toodle-o / Orgi

Bros. / Goose and lucky / You think it's on now / Solid gold / Heroin / Totally boxed in / Give 'em cops / Lucy in the trunk / We're rich / King of the street / Party lights. *(re-iss. Feb95; same)*
(above not to be confused with V/A s/t which hit US Top 100)

— **RY** – bottle neck guitar; with **VISHWA MOHAN BHATT** – mohan vina / **JOACHIM COODER** (his 14 year old son) / **SUKHVINDER** – tabla

Topic Water Lily

Apr 93. (cd; RY COODER & V.M. BHATT) *(WLACS 029)* **A MEETING BY THE RIVER** ☐ ☐
– A meeting by the river / Longing / Ganges Delta blues / Isa Lei. *(re-iss. Aug98; same)*

— in Mar'94, COODER collaborated with ALI FARKA TOURE on the 'World Circuit' album, 'TALKING TIMBUKTU'

Columbia Columbia

Apr 94. (cd/c) *(475654-2/-4) <CK/CT 57760>* **GERONIMO: AN AMERICAN LEGEND** (soundtrack) ☐ Jan94 ☐
– Geronimo: main title / Restoration / Goyakla is coming / Bound for Canaan (Sieber & Davis) (the 6th Cavalry) / Cibecue / The governor's ball: Get off the track – Danza – Battle cry of freedom / Wayfaring stranger / Judgement day / Bound for Canaan (Sieber & Davis) / Embudos / Sand fight / Army brass band: The young recruit – The girl I left behind me – Come come away / Yaqui village / I have seen my power / La vista / Davis / Train to Florida.

Verve Verve

Oct 96. (cd) *<(533415-2)>* **LAST MAN STANDING** (soundtrack) ☐ Sep96 ☐
– Last man standing / Wanda / Jericho blues / Mexican highjack / Just between you and me / Hickey's back / Gorgio leaves town / Felina / We're quits – This is Hickey / Church – Ranger Tom Pickett / Five mile road / Jericho two-step / Smoke bath – Girl upstairs? / Felina drives / Gotta get her back / Lucy's ear / Bathtub / Where's the girl? / Find him / Icebox – Drive to Slim's – Slim's on fire / Hideout / This town is finished / Sunrise / I don't want to die in Texas / Somewhere in the desert (end title) / Sanctuary.

— now **COODER** with **ELIADES OCHOA** – vocals, guitar / **COMPAY SEGUNDO** – vocals, guitar / **IBRAHIM FERRER** – vocals / **RUBEN GONZALEZ** – piano, etc.

World Circuit Nonesuch

Jun 97. (cd; as the BUENA VISTA SOCIAL CLUB) *(WCD 050) <79478-2>* **BUENA VISTA SOCIAL CLUB** (soundtrack) 44 Sep97 80
– Chan chan / De camino a la vereda / El cuarto de tula / Pueblo nuevo / Dos gardenias / Y tu que has hecho? / Viente anos / El carretero / Candela / Amor de loca juventud / Orgullecida / Murmullo / Buena Vista social club / La bayamesa. *(lp-iss.Dec98 on 'Rock The House'; RTH 79468)*

Outpost Outpost

Sep 97. (cd) *<(OPD 30007)>* **THE END OF VIOLENCE** (soundtrack) ☐ ☐
– Define violence / I'm leaving you / Seeds of violence / Observatory / I'm losing you / You shoot him! / Four weeks later / Mathilda / Six by numbers / Kinko's / Vamos Empezar / A night in L.A. / Pourquoi? / E-mail / Don't even know she got one (echoplex mix) / What a city! / Paige / The end of violence (end title).

M.C.A. M.C.A.

Nov 98. (cd) *<(MCD 11775)>* **PRIMARY COLOURS** (soundtrack) ☐ Apr98 ☐
– Camptown races / Not the best people / There will be a happy meeting in glory / Our position / (other artist) / I like this porch / Wide sky (with JON HASSELL) / See that moon / Very close friend of mine / Long trip / Tennessee waltz / Don't break our hearts / Camptown races / You are my sunshine.

Nonesuch Nonesuch

Jan 03. (cd; by RY COODER & MANUEL GALBAN) *<(7559 79691-2)>* **MAMBO SINUENDO** 40 52
– Drume negrita / Monte adentro / Los twangueros / Patricia / Caballo viejo / Mambo sinuendo / Bodas de oro / Echale salsita / La luna en tu Mirada / Secret love / Bolero sonambulo / Maria la lo.

Jun 05. (cd) *<(7559 79877-2)>* **CHAVEZ RAVINE** 35 ☐
– Poor man's shangri-la / Onda callejera / Don't call me red / Corrido de boxeo / Muy Fifi / Los chucos suaves / Chinito chinito / 3 cool cats / El U.F.O. cayo / It's just work for me / In my town / Ejercito militar / Barrio viejo / 3rd base, Dodger Stadium / Soy luz y sombra.

– compilations, etc. –

May 93. (cd; by the RISING SONS featuring RY COODER & TAJ MAHAL) *Columbia; (472865-2)* **THE RISING SONS** ☐ ☐

1994. (cd) *Reprise; <45599>* **RIVER RESCUE: THE VERY BEST OF . . .** – ☐

Jun 95. (d-cd) *WEA; <(9362 45987-2)>* **MUSIC BY RY COODER** ☐ ☐

Norman COOK

Born: QUENTIN COOK, 31 Jul'63, London, England. Following the demise of sunny agit-prop popsters, The HOUSEMARTINS, bassist COOK returned to his Brighton base and pursued his interest in the burgeoning dance culture. Already a budding DJ by the time HEATON & Co. split, the future man of many pseudonyms initially began recording club orientated music under his own name. Signed to 'Go! Beat', the dance arm of his previous band's now defunct label, 'Go! Discs', COOK enjoyed his debut hit via a collaboration with labelmate BILLY BRAGG on 'WON'T TALK ABOUT IT'. After a further minor solo hit, COOK initiated the BEATS INTERNATIONAL project with the classic 'DUB BE GOOD TO ME' single. Splicing the bassline from The CLASH's 'Guns Of Brixton' with the S.O.S BAND's 'Just Be Good To Me' proved a masterstroke, LINDY LAYTON's (soon to be a solo star in her own right) teasing, girlish vocal the icing on a vinyl cake which furnished COOK with a massive selling No.1 record in 1990. Also on board for the new venture were LESTER NOEL, keyboardist ANDY BOUCHER and percussionist LUKE CRESSWELL, the attendant Top 20 album 'LET THEM EAT BINGO' (1990) in addition finding COOK collaborating with a diverse cast of names including hip hop'ers DOUBLE TROUBLE and ex-DAMNED man, CAPTAIN SENSIBLE. A follow-up single revamping 'WON'T TALK..' with LAYTON on vocals made the Top 10 while the album's pot-pourri of rhythmic styles provided a further minor single in the innovative 'BURUNDI BLUES'. 1991's follow-up album, 'EXCURSION ON THE VERSION' followed in a more dub-centric vein, evidenced by the 'ECHO CHAMBER' single. A willingness to experiment was nevertheless the record's enduring characteristic, with further attempts at COOK-style soul and hip-hop. Although he failed to repeat the success of the debut single, his kudos as a remixer and producer were now firmly established. By 1992, BEATS INTERNATIONAL had run its natural course and COOK secured a new outlet for his rapidly improving songwriting talents through FREAK POWER, a more conventional band comprising bonafide musicians and dealing in sounds of a decidedly acid-jazzy persuasion. Signed to 'Island' subsidiary, '4th & Broadway', the tongue-in-cheek, smokily laid-back grooves of the group's debut single, 'TURN ON, TUNE IN, COP OUT' furnished them with a minor Top 30 hit upon its initial release in 1993. A highlight of the fine album, 'DRIVE-THRU BOOTY' (1995) alongside rump-shaking follow-up single, 'RUSH', the track was subsequently used on a Levi's 501 commercial, becoming one of '95's biggest hits. Like many other acts given the Levi's treatment, however, it eventually proved to be the kiss of death for the outfit, a second album, 'MORE OF EVERYTHING FOR EVERYBODY' (1997) failing to chart and subsequent releases flopping amid drug-related touring problems. By this point, however, the industrious COOK had already notched up a series of massive club smashes under his PIZZAMAN alias, many of his anthemic house monsters crossing over into the pop charts with 'TRIPPIN' ON SUNSHINE' becoming a Top 20 hit second time around in Spring '96. Concurrent with the rise of The CHEMICAL BROTHERS, The Heavenly Social club and all things "Big Beat", the chameleon-like COOK then turned his hand to some block rockin' beats and came up with one of 1997's most critically acclaimed albums, 'BETTER LIVING THROUGH CHEMISTRY'. Released under the FATBOY SLIM moniker and preceded by a clutch of blistering breakbeat 12"ers including 'SANTA CRUZ' (featured on the seminal 'BRIT HOP AND AMYL HOUSE' compilation) and 'EVERYBODY LOVES A 303', the record proved to be COOK's most cohesive and thrilling dalliance with dance music to date. A year later, FATBOY SLIM's 'ROCKAFELLER SKANK' (a take-off from a FALL tune) was racing up the charts and even broke this unusual set-up into the American Hot 100. Incredibly, COOK almost made No.1 yet again with a follow-up FATBOY SLIM album, 'YOU'VE COME A LONG WAY, BABY', possibly his most contagious, outrageous release to date. However, it was 'PRAISE YOU' indeed, after the single of that name topped the UK chart early in 1999 and eventually gave him a US Top 40 entry later in the year. COOK subsequently married "hyper" TV presenter/radio DJ, Zoe Ball, ah! showbiz couples, aren't they just worth reading about every day in the tabloids. MR. NORMAN COOK followed up his breakthrough masterpiece with a cross-over mix of dance, big beat techno, soul, funk, jive and R&B that he cleverly titled 'HALFWAY BETWEEN THE GUTTER AND THE STARS' (2001), a blistering brew that begins with a cheesy piece of funk narration and never ceases to quieten until the final 'SONG FOR SHELTER'. In retrospect, it's fair to say that 'HALFWAY . . .' was a much more accomplished album than 'YOU'VE COME A LONG WAY BABY'; the JIM MORRISON-sampled 'BIRD OF PREY' is truly excellent, with its trance-enducing drone imitating MORRISON's baritone vocals perfectly. Elsewhere on the album, 'YA MAMA' cooks up some seriously hard-hitting techno dance (with a psychotic and disturbingly insane video to go along with it), while 'WEAPON OF CHOICE' was just an excuse to watch Christopher Walken dance around a hotel lobby for four-and-half minutes. MACY GRAY lent her vocals to 'DEMONS' and 'LOVE LIFE', wailing along with COOK's funked-out Trip-Hop. So, the ex-HOUSEMARTINS' bassist had indeed come a long way! COOK had another good trawl through his beloved 70s vinyl for 'PALOOKAVILLE' (2004), both in terms of crafty samples and as base material for what – at least on 'NORTH WEST THREE' – was pretty much an out and out cover (of John & Beverley Martyn's 'Primrose Hill'); at least 'JIN-GO-LO-BA' and 'THE JOKER' identified themselves as straight interpretations (of the Babatunde Olatungi / Steve Miller classics respectively), or at least as straight as BOOTSY COLLINS could render the latter. With so many definitive floorfillers, 'WHY TRY HARDER – THE GREATEST HITS' (2006), couldn't fail to hit the UK Top 3, although it wasn't strictly a compilation with two new closing tracks, 'CHAMPION SOUND' and 'THAT OLD PAIR OF JEANS' (featuring BLACKALICIOUS' LATEEF).

• **Songwriters:** COOK, and some with ASHLEY SLATER in FREAK POWER. Covered RUNNING AWAY (Sly & The Family Stone).

Album rating: Beats International: LET THEM EAT BINGO (*6) / EXCURSION OF THE VERSION (*4) / Freak Power: DRIVE THRU BOOTY (*5) / MORE OF EVERYTHING FOR EVERYBODY (*4) / Fatboy Slim: BETTER LIVING THROUGH CHEMISTRY (*8) / YOU'VE COME A LONG WAY, BABY (*8) / HALFWAY BETWEEN THE GUTTER AND THE STARS (*7) / PALOOKAVILLE (*6) / WHY TRY HARDER – THE GREATEST HITS compilation (*8)

NORMAN COOK – multi (solo) with various people

Go! Discs / Elektra

Jun 89. (7"/c-s; NORMAN COOK featuring BILLY BRAGG. / NORMAN COOK featuring MC WILDSKI) *(GOD/+MC 33)* **WON'T TALK ABOUT IT. / BLAME IT ON THE BASSLINE** [29] [ ]
(12"+=/cd-s+=) *(GOD X/CD 33)* – Blame it on the bonus beats / Blame it on the acappella.
(12"+=) *(GODXR 33)* – Blame it on the bonus beats / ('B'dub).

Oct 89. (7"/c-s; NORMAN COOK featuring LESTER) *(GOD/+MC 37)* **FOR SPACIOUS LIES. / FOR SPACIOUS LIES (dance mix) / THE INVASION OF THE ESTATE AGENTS** [48] [ ]
(12"+=/cd-s+=) *(GOD X/CD 37)* – For spacious ballad.

BEATS INTERNATIONAL

NORMAN COOK with **LINDY LAYTON & LESTER NOEL** – vocals / **ANDY BOUCHER** – keyboards / **LUKE CRESSWELL** – percussion

Feb 90. (7"/c-s; BEATS INTERNATIONAL featuring LINDY LAYTON) *(GOD/+MC 39) <64970>* **DUB BE GOOD TO ME. / THE INVASION OF THE ESTATE AGENTS** [1] Mar90 [76]
(12"+=/cd-s+=) *(GOD X/CD 39)* – Just be good to me (acappella) / The invasion of the freestyle – Discuss.
(12") *(GODXR 39)* – ('A'-Smith & Mighty mix) / Before I go too dub / ('A'-Norman Cook's excursion on the version) / ('A'-Smith & Mighty mellow mix).

Mar 90. (cd/c/lp) *(842 196-2/-4/-1) <60921>* **LET THEM EAT BINGO** [17] [ ]
– Burundi blues / Dub be good to me / Before I grow too old / The ragged trousered percussionists / For spacious lies / Blame it on the bassline / Won't talk about it / Dance to the drummer's beat / Babies makin' babies (stoop rap) / The whole world's down on me / Tribute to King Tubby. *(some lp's cont. 12"ep)* – BINGO BEATS *(cd+=)* – For spacious lies.

May 90. (7"/c-s) *(GOD/+MC 43) <64948>* **WON'T TALK ABOUT IT. / BEATS INTERNATIONAL THEME** [9] Aug90 [76]
(12"+=/cd-s+=) *(GOD X/CD 43)* – ('A'extended).
(12") *(GODXR 43)* – ('A'-Frankie Foncett mix) / ('A'-Chad Jackson mix) / (bonus beats).

Sep 90. (7"/c-s) *(GOD/+MC 45)* **BURUNDI BLUES. / THEME FROM THE DEERSTALKER** [51] [–]
(12"+=/cd-s+=) *(GOD X/CD 45)* – Burundi dub.
(12") *(GODXR 45)* – ('A'-Boilerhouse mix) / ('A'-Boilerhouse guitar & vocal mix) / ('A'-Traditional version).

Feb 91. (7"/c-s) *(GOD/+MC 51)* **ECHO CHAMBER. / INCH BY INCH** [60] [–]
(12"+=) *(GODX 51)* – Daddy Freddy's echo chamber.
(cd-s++=) *(GODCD 51)* – ('A'-extended).
(12") *(GODXR 51)* – ('A'-Boilerhouse mix) / ('A'-instrumental) / ('A'-Boilerhouse instrumental).

Sep 91. (7"/c-s) *(GOD/+MC 59)* **THE SUN DOESN'T SHINE. / WAKE THE DEAD** [66] [–]
(12"+=/cd-s+=) *(GOD X/CD 59)* – Crazy for you / ('A'-extended).

Oct 91. (cd/c/lp) *(828 290-2/-4/-1)* **EXCURSION OF THE VERSION** [ ] [ ]
– Brand new beat / Change your mind / Love is green / Echo chamber / The sun doesn't shine / Herman / Three foot skank / No more Mr. Nice guy / Eyes on the prize / Ten long years / In the ghetto. *(cd+=/c+=)* – Come home.

Nov 91. (7"/c-s) *(GOD/+MC 64)* **IN THE GHETTO (version one). / OH, THAT'S DEEP** [44] [–]
(12"+=/cd-s+=) *(GOD X/CD 64)* – (version two) / (version three).

FREAK POWER

NORMAN COOK – guitar, vox / **ASHLEY SLATER** – vocals, trombone / **CYRIL McCAMMON** – keyboards, vox / **DALE DAVIES** – bass / **PETE ECKFORD** – percussion / **JIM CARMICHAEL** – drums

Fourth & Broadway / Fourth & Broadway

Oct 93. (7"/c-s) *(BRW/BRCA 284)* **TURN ON, TUNE IN, COP OUT. / GETTING OVER THE HUMP** [29] [ ]
(12"+=/cd-s+=) *(12BRW/BRCD 284)* – (2-'A'mixes).

Feb 94. (7"/c-s) *(BRW/BRCA 291)* **RUSH. / PARTY TILL WE PART** [62] [ ]
(12"+=/cd-s+=) *(12BRW/BRCD 291)* – (2-'A'mixes).

Oct 94. (c-s/12"/cd-s) *(BRCA/12BRW/BRCD 298)* **GET IN TOUCH / (Colonel Kurtz mix) / CHEW THE BONE / (uptight vocal mix)** [ ] [–]

Mar 95. (7"/c-s) *(BRW/BRCA 317)* **TURN ON, TUNE IN, COP OUT. / GETTING OVER THE HUMP** [3] [ ]
(12"+=) *(12BRW 317)* – (2-'A'mixes).
(cd-s++=) *(BRCD 317)* – ('A'mix).

Apr 95. (cd/lp) *(BRCD/BRLP 606)* **DRIVE-THRU BOOTY** [11] [ ]
– Moonbeam woman / Turn on, tune in, cop out / Get in touch / Freak

power / Running away / Change my mind / What it is? / Waiting for the story to end / Rush / Big time / The whip. *(re-iss. Oct95 d-cd+=/d-lp+=; BRCDX/BRLPX 606)* – IN DUB

May 96. (c-s) *(BRCA 331)* **NEW DIRECTION / ('A'-Fila Brazillia mix)** [60] [–]
(12"+=/cd-s+=) *(12BRW/BRCD 331)* – ('A'mixes incl. Way out west).

Jun 96. (cd/c/lp) *(BRCD/BRCA/BRLP 619)* **MORE OF EVERYTHING FOR EVERYBODY** [ ] [ ]

Aug 96. (c-s) *(BRCA 335)* **CAN YOU FEEL IT / ('A'-Matty's mix)** [ ] [–]
(12"+=/cd-s+=) *(12BRW/BRCD 335)* – ('A'mixes; Todd's rubber room + Bass bin twins mix).

Southern — not iss.

Dec 97. (12") *(ECB 14)* **NO WAY. / ('A'mixes)** [ ] [–]

DeConstruct — not iss.

Apr 98. (c-s) *(74321 57857-4)* **NO WAY / ('A'-Norman Cook's dub mix)** [29] [ ]
(12"+=/cd-s+=) *(74321 57857-1/-2)* – ('A'mixes; full + Dee Jay Delite).

PIZZAMAN

— aka **NORMAN COOK** with various members

Loaded — not iss.

Apr 94. (12") *(12LOAD 8)* **BABY LOOP. / SANS BATEAUX** [ ] [–]

Aug 94. (7") *(LOAD 16)* **TRIPPIN' ON SUNSHINE. / ('A'-Play boy's mixing thing)** [33] [–]
(12"+=/cd-s+=) *(LOAD 16 12/CD)* – ('A'mixes; Californian sunshine / Play boy's fully loaded).

Jun 95. (c-s) *(CALOAD 24)* **SEX ON THE STREETS / SEX ON THE STREETS (Play boy's fully loaded dub)** [24] [–]
(12"+=/cd-s+=) *(12/CD LOAD 24)* – ('A'mixes; Goodfello's / Red Jerry / Wildchild 0703 dub).
(re-entered the chart Jan96 and hit No.23)

Nov 95. (c-s) *(CALOAD 29)* **HAPPINESS / ('A'club mix)** [19] [–]
(12"+=/cd-s+=) *(12/CD LOAD 29)* – ('A'mixes; club / Euro).

May 96. (c-s) *(CALOAD 32)* **TRIPPIN' ON SUNSHINE / ('A'mixes; Impulsion big pizza II / Biff And Memphis)** [18] [ ]
(12"+=/cd-s+=) *(12/CD LOAD 32)* – ('A'-Californian mix).

Sep 96. (c-s) *(CALOAD 39)* **HELLO HONKY TONKS (ROCK YOUR BODY) / ('A'-Pizzaman mix)** [41] [ ]
(12"+=/cd-s+=) *(12/CD LOAD 39)* – ('A'mixes; Cotton club).

Jul 97. (c-s) *(MCRODEO 956)* **GOTTAMAN / (Distant drum mix)** [ ] [–]
(12") *(RODEO 956-12)* – ('A'-Pizzaman) / (Distant drum mix).
(cd-s+=) *(CDRODEO 956)* – ('A'-Gregario mix).

FATBOY SLIM

aka **NORMAN COOK** with the Skint crew, etc

Skint — Astralwerks

Mar 96. (12") *(SKINT 1)* **SANTA CRUZ / THE WEEKEND BONUS BEATS. / THE WEEKEND STARTS HERE / NEAL CASSADY STARTS HERE** [ ] [–]

Mar 96. (12"/cd-s) *(SKINT 6/+CD)* **EVERYBODY LOVES A 303. / LINCOLN MEMORIAL / WE REALLY WANT TO SEE THOSE FINGERS** [ ] [–]

Sep 96. (12"/cd-s) *(SKINT 12/+CD)* **PUNK TO FUNK. / KNUF OT KNUP / BIG BEAT SOUFFLE** [ ] [–]

Apr 97. (12"/cd-s) *(SKINT 19/+CD)* **GOING OUT OF MY HEAD. / MICHAEL JACKSON / NEXT TO NOTHING** [57] [–]

Oct 97. (12"/cd-s) *(SKINT 31/+CD)* **EVERYBODY NEEDS A 303 / (original 12"). / EVERYBODY LOVES A CARNIVAL / NEAL CASSADY STARTS HERE** [34] [–]
(cd-s) *(SKINT 31XCD)* – Everybody loves a carnival / Everybody loves a filter / Es paradis / Where you're at.

Nov 97. (cd/c/d-lp) *(BRASSIC 2 CD/MC/LP)* **BETTER LIVING THROUGH CHEMISTRY** [ ] [ ]
– Song for Lindy / Santa Cruz / Going out of my head / The weekend starts here / Everybody needs a 303 / Give the po' man a break / 10th & Crenshaw / First down / Punk to funk / The sound of Milwaukee. *(d-lp+=)* – Michael Jackson / Next to nothing.

Jun 98. (c-s) *(SKINT 35MC)* *<6 6242>* **THE ROCKAFELLER SKANK / THE ROCKAFELLER SKANK (long version)** [6] Nov98 [76]
(12"+=/cd-s+=) *(SKINT 35/+CD)* – Always read the label / Tweakers delight.

Jul 98. (cd/c; FATBOY SLIM mixes Various Artists) *(BRASSIC 9 CD/MC)* **ON THE FLOOR AT THE BIG BEAT BOUTIQUE** [ ] [–]
<US-iss.Apr00; 49130>

Oct 98. (c-s) *(SKINT 39MC)* **GANGSTER TRIPPIN' / THE WORLD WENT DOWN** [3] [ ]
(12"+=/cd-s+=) *(SKINT 39/+CD)* – Jack it up (DJ Delite).

Oct 98. (cd/c/d-lp) *(BRASSIC 11 CD/MC/LP)* *<ASW 66247>* **YOU'VE COME A LONG WAY, BABY** [1] [34]
– Right here, right now / The Rockafeller skank / In Heaven / Gangster tripping / Build it up – Tear it down / Kalifornia / Soul surfing / You're not from Brighton / Praise you / Love island / Acid 8000.

Jan 99. (c-s) *(SKINT 42MC)* *<66254>* **PRAISE YOU / THE ROCKAFELLER SKANK (Mulder's Urban takeover remix)** [1] Feb99 [36]
(12"+=/cd-s+=) *(SKINT 42/+CD)* – Sho nuff.

Apr 99. (c-s) *(SKINT 46MC)* **RIGHT HERE, RIGHT NOW / DON'T FORGET YOUR TEETH** [2] [–]
(12"+=/cd-s+=) *(SKINT 46/+CD)* – Praise you (original).

— FATBOY SLIM was also credited on FREDDY FRESH's hit, 'Badder Badder Schwing'

Oct 00. (c-s) *(SKINT 58MC)* **SUNSET (BIRD OF PREY) / MY GAME** [9] [–]
(12"+=/cd-s+=) *(SKINT 58/+CD)* – ('A'-Darren Emerson remix).

Nov 00. (cd/c/d-lp) *(BRASSIC 20 CD/MC/LP)* *<50460>* **HALFWAY BETWEEN THE GUTTER AND THE STARS** [8] [51]
– Talking bout my baby / Star 69 / Sunset (bird of prey) / Love life (feat. MACY GRAY) / Ya mama / Mad flava / Retox (feat. ASHLEY SLATER) / Weapon of choice (feat. BOOTSY COLLINS) / Drop the hate / Demons (feat. MACY GRAY) / Song for shelter (feat. ROLAND CLARK & ROGER SANCHEZ).

Jan 01. (c-s; by FATBOY SLIM & MACY GRAY) *(SKINT 60MC)* **DEMONS** [16] [–]
(12"+=/cd-s+=) *(SKINT 60/+CD)* – ('A'mixes).

Apr 01. (c-s) *(SKINT 64MC)* **STAR 69 / (Timo Mass remix)** [10] [–]
(12"+=/cd-s+=) *(SKINT 64/+CD)* – ('A'-X-Press 2 remix).

Sep 01. (c-s) *(12"/cd-s) (SKINT 71/+CD)* **YA MAMA. / SONG FOR SHELTER** [30] [–]
(cd-s) *(SKINT 71XCD)* – ('A'mixes).

Jan 02. (12") *(FAT 18)* **RETOX (remixes)** [73] [–]

Sep 04. (cd-s) *(SKINT 100CD)* **SLASH DOT DASH / CLOSE TO HOME** [12] [–]
(12"+=) *(SKINT 100)* – ('A'-DeJay Delite) / Jin-go-la-ba (Jon Carter remix) / Jin-go-la-ba (DeJay Delite mix).
(cd-s) *(SKINT 100CDX)* – ('A'-Dylan edit) / Jin-go-la-ba (Jon Carter mix) / What they looking for / ('A'-video).

Oct 04. (cd) *(BRASSIC 29CD)* *<64748>* **PALOOKAVILLE** [14] [ ]
– Don't let the man get you down / Slash dot dash / Wonderful night (feat. LATEEF) / Long way from home (feat. JOHNNY QUALITY) / Put it back together (feat. DAMON ALBARN) / Mi bebe masoquista / Push and shove (feat. JUSTIN ROBERTSON) / North West three / The journey (feat. LATEEF) / Jin-go-lo-ba / Song for Chesh / The joker (feat. BOOTSY COLLINS).

Nov 04. (cd-s) *(SKINT 104CD)* **WONDERFUL NIGHT (mixes; album / Thrash / nightclub / Chief Xcel / video)** [51] [–]
(12") *(SKINT 104)* – (mixes; original / Thrash / DJ Delite / club / Chief Xcel world wide).

Mar 05. (cd-s) *(SKINT 106CD)* **THE JOKER / THE RIVER CARD / THE JOKER (ATFC's Aces High remix) / THE JOKER (Lazyboy remix)** [32] [–]
(dvd-s) *(SKINT 106DVD)* – ('A') / (photos w/ 'A'-Kid Carpet remix).
(12") *(SKINT 106)* – ('A'-mixes; ATFC / ATFC acapella / Yousef / Yousef instrumental).
(12") *(SKINT 106T)* – ('A'-mixes; original / Lazyboy / Kid Carpet / Justin Robertson dancehall dub).

Jun 06. (cd) *(BRASSIC 40CD)* *<56814>* **WHY TRY HARDER – THE GREATEST HITS** (compilation) [2] [ ]
– The Rockafeller skank / Praise you / Brimful of Asha / Weapon of choice / Gangster trippin' / I see you baby / Wonderful night / Right here, right now / Going out of my head / Sunset (bird of prey) / Everybody loves a carnival / Don't let the man get you down / Demons / Sho nuff / Slash dot dash / Santa Cruz / Champion sound / That old pair of jeans.

Jun 06. (7") *(SKINT 123X)* **THAT OLD PAIR OF JEANS. / PRAISE YOU (Mike D & Ad Rock mix)** [39] [–]

(cd-s+=) *(SKINT 123CD)* – Right here, right now (Redanka remix) / Right here, right now (Freemasons remix).

(12") *(SKINT 123)* – ('A') / Right here, right now (Freemasons remix) / Everybody needs a 303 (Plump DJ's remix) / Right here, right now (Redanka edit).

– others, etc. –

Mar 00. (cd) *Hip-O; <564787>* **THE FATBOY SLIM / NORMAN COOK COLLECTION** [–] [ ]

Alice COOPER

Formed: Initially as a group by VINCENT FURNIER (son of a preacher), Phoenix, Arizona . . . 1965 as The EARWIGS. Together with his partners in musical crime, GLEN BUXTON, MICHAEL BRUCE, DENNIS DUNAWAY and NEAL SMITH, FURNIER relocated to L.A., becoming The SPIDERS and enjoying healthy airplay for their debut single, 'DON"T BLOW YOUR MIND', released on the local 'Santa Cruz' label. After another low key single and a brief name change to NAZZ, the band adopted the improbable moniker of ALICE COOPER (a 17th Century witch, apparently), signing to FRANK ZAPPA's 'Straight' records. Turgid, clumsy cod-psychedelia, the debut album, 'PRETTIES FOR YOU' (1969) didn't bode well, while 'EASY ACTION' (1970) fared little better. Moving to Detroit in 1970, the band were inspired by the Motor City madness of MC5 and The STOOGES, tightening up their sound and developing their theatrical shock tactics. FURNIER simultaneously used the band name for his ghoulish, androgynous alter-ego, infamously embellishing the band's stage show with all manner of sick trickery: simulated hangings, mangled baby dolls, a live snake, mmm . . . nice. Signing to 'Warners' and drafting in BOB EZRIN on production, the band actually started writing material to match the effectiveness of their live shows. This wasn't gloomy, horror soundtrack minimalism, however, it was freewheeling, revved-up rock'n'roll, often with more than a touch of tongue-in-cheek humour. While 'KILLER' probably stands as COOPER's peak achievement, with the hilarious 'UNDER MY WHEELS' and the classic 'BE MY LOVER', the band really hit big with 'SCHOOL'S OUT' (1972). The title track was an irrepressible blast of adolescent-style attitude that made the UK No.1 spot and propelled the album to the upper reaches of the charts on both sides of the Atlantic. The 'ELECTED' single was another hit and the accompanying 'BILLION DOLLAR BABIES' (1973) album made UK and US No.1. 'MUSCLE OF LOVE' (1974) didn't fare quite so well and cracks were beginning to show in the songwriting armoury. COOPER subsequently sacked the rest of the band in the Summer of '74, hiring a cast of musicians that had previously backed up LOU REED. 'WELCOME TO MY NIGHTMARE' (1975; complete with eerie narration by the legendary VINCENT PRICE) was the last great vintage COOPER effort, a macabre concept album that spawned the hit single, 'ONLY WOMEN BLEED'. In contrast to his superfreak, anti-hero stage character, offstage COOPER was becoming something of a celebrity, hobnobbing with the Hollywood elite and even hosting his own TV show, wherein the band shamelessly retrod past glories. By the end of the decade, his musical output had degenerated into AOR mush and he spent time in rehab for alcohol addiction. His early 80's work was hardly inspiring and even after a new deal with 'M.C.A.', the subsequent albums, 'CONSTRICTOR' and 'RAISE YOUR FIST AND YELL' failed to resurrect the (unclean) spirit of old. The latter did contain the anthemic 'FREEDOM' and the records were an attempt at the heady rock'n'roll of yore, COOPER even resuming the schlock shock for the subsequent tour. However, it was only with the help of hair-rock writer, DESMOND CHILD, that ALICE once again became a major player on the metal scene, the 'POISON' single seeing COOPER return to the Top 10 for the first time since his 70's heyday. The accompanying album, 'TRASH', fared almost as well, although it sounded about as menacing as BON JOVI. 'HEY STOOPID' (1989) consolidated COOPER's newfound success, as did 'THE LAST TEMPTATION' (1994). Things went quiet on the recording for a while, although the pro-am golfer COOPER continued to pop up in places where you'd least expect him, 'Wayne's World' (1992 movie), US chat shows etc. With appearances from the likes of ROB ZOMBIE and SLASH, 1997's 'A FISTFUL OF ALICE' album was one of the man's better live efforts while 'BRUTAL PLANET' (2000) finally found the grandaddy of gore back in the studio. More streetwise than schlock, the album delivered a sharp poke in the eye to those who'd already written him off for the umpteenth time. With the millennial 'DRAGONTOWN' (2001), COOPER proved that middle age hasn't mellowed him just yet. A half decent attempt at teaching the young upstarts a thing or two about being bad, COOPER proved that, lyrically at least, he still has few challengers when it comes to twisted humour. No prizes for guessing the subject matter of 'DISGRACELAND', a PRESLEY "tribute" that doesn't quite match The CRAMPS' 'A Date With Elvis' but tries hard. 'EYES OF ALICE COOPER' (2003) marked a return to the man's natural environs of sleazy hard-rock, leaving behind his half-realised attempts at getting hip to nu-metal. Lyrically, he was still outsmarting almost any other writer in his peergroup (and most of the young bucks as well), with pinpoint portraits like 'MAN OF THE YEAR'; COOPER could also be seen opposite wee Ronnie Corbett in a TV ad for Sky. Taking time out from his golfing sojourns, ALICE cut another warped back-to-basics effort, 'DIRTY DIAMONDS' (2005), right back to his 60s psych beginnings with a cover of the Left Banke's 'PRETTY BALLERINA'.

• **Songwriters:** ALICE wrote/co-wrote with band most of material, also using producer BOB EZRIN. DICK WAGNER to BERNIE TAUPIN also contributed in the 70's. On 'CONSTRICTOR' album, ALICE co-wrote with ROBERTS, some with KELLY and WEGENER. Collaborated with DESMOND CHILD in '89 and JACK PONTI, VIC PEPE, BOB PFEIFER in 1991. Covered:- SUN ARISE (trad.; a Rolf Harris hit) / SEVEN AND SEVEN IS (Love) / FIRE (Jimi Hendrix). • **Trivia:** Film cameo appearances have been:- DIARY OF A HOUSEWIFE (1970) / SGT. PEPPER'S LONELY HEARTS CLUB BAND (1978) / ROADIE (1980) / PRINCE OF DARKNESS (1987) / FREDDIE'S DEAD: THE FINAL NIGHTMARE (1991' he also acted!). In 1975 he sang 'I'M FLASH' on the Various Artists concept album 'FLASH FEARLESS VS.THE ZORG WOMEN Pts.5 & 6'.

Album rating: PRETTIES FOR YOU (*5) / EASY ACTION (*5) / LOVE IT TO DEATH (*8) / KILLER (*8) / SCHOOL'S OUT (*7) / BILLION DOLLAR BABIES (*8) / MUSCLE OF LOVE (*6) / WELCOME TO MY NIGHTMARE (*8) / ALICE COOPER GOES TO HELL (*6) / LACE AND WHISKEY (*5) / THE ALICE COOPER SHOW (*6) / FROM THE INSIDE (*6) / FLUSH THE FASHION (*6) / SPECIAL FORCES (*6) / ZIPPER CATCHES SKIN (*6) / DA DA (*6) / CONSTRICTOR (*5) / RAISE YOUR FIST AND YELL (*5) / TRASH (*5) / HEY STOOPID (*5) / BEAST OF ALICE COOPER compilation (*8) / THE LAST TEMPTATION (*5) / CLASSICKS compilation (*8) / A FISTFUL OF ALICE (*5) / BRUTAL PLANET (*6) / THE DEFINITIVE compilation (*8) / DRAGONTOWN (*5) / THE EYES OF ALICE COOPER (*5) / DIRTY DIAMONDS (*5)

the SPIDERS

ALICE COOPER (b.VINCENT DAMON FURNIER, 4 Feb'48, Detroit) – vocals / **GLEN BUXTON** (b.17 Jun'47, Washington DC) – lead guitar / **MICHAEL BRUCE** (b.21 Nov'48, California) – rhythm guitar, keyboards / **DENNIS DUNAWAY** (b.15 Mar'46, California) – bass / **NEAL SMITH** (b.10 Jan'48, Washington DC) – drums

not iss. Santa Cru

1967. (7") *<SCR 10.003>* **DON'T BLOW YOUR MIND. / NO PRICE TAG** [–] [ ]

not iss. Very

1967. (7") *<001>* **WONDER WHO'S LOVING HER NOW. / LAY DOWN AND DIE, GOODBYE** [–] [ ]

ALICE COOPER

Straight Straight

Dec 69. (lp) <(STS 1051)> **PRETTIES FOR YOU** Jun69
– Titanic overture / 10 minutes before the worm / Sing low sweet cheerio / Today Mueller / Living / Fields of regret / No longer umpire / Levity ball / B.B. on Mars / Reflected / Apple bush / Earwigs to eternity / Changing, arranging.

Jan 70. (7") *<101>* **LIVING. / REFLECTED** –

Jun 70. (lp) *<(STS 1061)>* **EASY ACTION**
– Mr. and Misdemeaner / Shoe salesman / Still no air / Below your means / Return of the spiders / Laughing at me / Refridgerator heaven / Beautiful flyaway / Lay down and die, goodbye.

Jun 70. (7") *<7141>* **CAUGHT IN A DREAM. / EIGHTEEN** –

Nov 70. (7") *<7398>* **RETURN OF THE SPIDERS. / SHOE SALESMAN** –

Straight Warners

Apr 71. (7") *(S 7209) <7499>* **EIGHTEEN. / IS IT MY BODY** Feb71 21

Jun 71. (lp) *(STS 1065) <1883>* **LOVE IT TO DEATH** Mar71 35
– Caught in a dream / Eighteen / Long way to go / Black Juju / Is it my body / Hallowed be my name / Second coming / Ballad of Dwight Fry / Sun arise. *(re-iss. Dec71 on 'Warners' lp/c; K/K4 46177)* – hit UK No.28 in Sep'72.

Warners Warners

Jun 71. (7") *<7490>* **CAUGHT IN A DREAM. / HALLOWED BE THY NAME** – 94

Dec 71. (7") *(K 16127) <7529>* **UNDER MY WHEELS. / DESPERADO** 59
(re-iss. Aug74; same)

Dec 71. (lp/c) *(K/K4 56005) <2567>* **KILLER** 27 Nov71 21
– Under my wheels / Be my lover / Halo of flies / Desperado / You drive me nervous / Yeah yeah yeah / Dead babies / Killer. *(cd-iss. Sep89 on 'WEA'; 927255-2)*

Jan 72. (7") *<7568>* **BE MY LOVER. / YEAH YEAH YEAH** – 49

Feb 72. (7") *(K 16154)* **BE MY LOVER. / YOU DRIVE ME NERVOUS** –

Jul 72. (7") *(K 16188) <7596>* **SCHOOL'S OUT. / GUTTER CAT** 1 May72 7

Jul 72. (lp/c) *(K/K4 56007) <2623>* **SCHOOL'S OUT** 4 Jun72 2
– School's out / Luney tune / Gutter cat vs. the jets / Street fight / Blue Turk / My stars / Public animal No.9 / Alma mater / Grande finale. *(cd-iss. Sep89 on 'WEA'; 927260-2)*

Oct 72. (7") *(K 16214) <7631>* **ELECTED. / LUNEY TUNE** 4 26

Feb 73. (7") *(K 16248) <7673>* **HELLO HURRAY. / GENERATION LANDSLIDE** 6 Jan73 35

Mar 73. (lp/c) *(K/K4 56013) <2685>* **BILLION DOLLAR BABIES** 1 1
– Hello hurray / Raped and freezin' / Elected / Billion dollar babies / Unfinished sweet / No more Mr. Nice guy / Generation landslide / Sick things / Mary Ann / I love the dead. *(cd-iss. Jan93 on 'WEA'; 7599 27269-2) (d-cd-iss. Mar01; 8122 79791-2)* – (with extra tracks).

Apr 73. (7") *(K 16262) <7691>* **NO MORE MR. NICE GUY. / RAPED AND FREEZIN'** 10 25

Jul 73. (7") *<7724>* **BILLION DOLLAR BABIES. / MARY ANN** – 57

Jan 74. (lp/c) *(K/K4 56018) <2748>* **MUSCLE OF LOVE** 34 Dec73 10
– Muscle of love / Woman machine / Hard hearted Alice / Man with the golden gun / Big apple dreamin' (hippo) / Never been sold before / Working up a sweat / Crazy little child / Teenage lament '74. *(cd-iss. Nov99; 7599 26226-2)*

Jan 74. (7") *(K 16345) <7762>* **TEENAGE LAMENT '74. / HARD HEARTED ALICE** 12 Dec73 48

Mar 74. (7") *<7783>* **MUSCLE OF LOVE. / CRAZY LITTLE CHILD** –

Jun 74. (7") *<8023>* **MUSCLE OF LOVE. / I'M EIGHTEEN** –

Sep 74. (lp/c) *(K/K4 56043) <2803>* **ALICE COOPER'S GREATEST HITS** (compilation) Aug74 8
– I'm eighteen / Is it my body / Desperado / Under my wheels / Be my lover / School's out / Hello hurray / Elected / No more Mr. Nice guy / Billion dollar babies / Teenage lament '74 / Muscle of love. *(cd-iss. Jun89; K2 56045)*

— **ALICE** sacked rest of band, who became BILLION DOLLAR BABIES. He brought in **DICK WAGNER** – guitar, vocals / **STEVE** (DEACON) **HUNTER** – guitars / **PRAKASH JOHN** – bass / **PENTII 'Whitey' GLAN** – drums / **JOSEF CHIROWSKI** – drums (all ex-LOU REED band)

Anchor Atlantic

Feb 75. (7") *(1012) <3280>* **DEPARTMENT OF YOUTH. / COLD ETHYL** –

Mar 75. (lp/c) *(ANC L/K 2011) <18130>* **WELCOME TO MY NIGHTMARE** 19 5
– Welcome to my nightmare / Devil's food / The black widow / Some folks / Only women bleed / Department of youth / Cold Ethyl / Years ago / Steven / The awakening / Escape. *<cd-iss. Sep87 on 'Atlantic'; SD 19157>*

Apr 75. (7") *<3254>* **ONLY WOMEN BLEED. / COLD ETHYL** – 12

Jun 75. (7") *(1018)* **ONLY WOMEN BLEED. / DEVIL'S FOOD** –

Aug 75. (7") *<3280>* **DEPARTMENT OF YOUTH. / SOME FOLKS** – 67

Oct 75. (7") *<3298>* **WELCOME TO MY NIGHTMARE. / COLD ETHYL** – 45

Nov 75. (7") *(1025)* **WELCOME TO MY NIGHTMARE. / BLACK WIDOW** –

Warners Warners

Jun 76. (lp/c) *(K/K4 56171) <2896>* **ALICE COOPER GOES TO HELL** 23 27
– Go to Hell / You gotta dance / I'm the coolest / Didn't we meet / I never cry / Give the kid a break / Guilty / Wake me gently / Wish you were here / I'm always chasing rainbows / Going home. *(cd-iss. May94; 7599 27299-2)*

Jun 76. (7") *(K 16792) <8228>* **I NEVER CRY. / GO TO HELL** 12

Apr 77. (7") *<8349>* **YOU AND ME. / IT'S HOT TONIGHT** – 9

Apr 77. (7") *(K 16935)* **(NO MORE) LOVE AT YOUR CONVENIENCE. / IT'S HOT TONIGHT** 44 –

May 77. (lp/c) *(K/K4 56365) <3027>* **LACE AND WHISKEY** 33 42
– It's hot tonight / Lace and whiskey / Road rats / Damned if you do / You and me / King of the silver screen / Ubangi stomp / (No more) Love at your convenience / I never wrote those songs / My God.

Jul 77. (7") *(K 16984)* **YOU AND ME. / MY GOD** –

Jul 77. (7") *<8448>* **(NO MORE) LOVE AT YOUR CONVENIENCE. / I NEVER WROTE THOSE SONGS** –

— **FRED MANDEL** – keyboards repl. JOSEF

Dec 77. (lp/c) *(K/K4 56439) <3138>* **THE ALICE COOPER SHOW (live)**
– Under my wheels / I'm eighteen / Only women / Sick things / Is it my body / I never cry / Billion dollar babies / Devil's food – The black widow / You and me / a. I love the dead – b. Go to hell – c. Wish you were here / School's out.

— **Alice COOPER** now basically a solo artist with session people, which retaining **MANDEL, DAVEY JOHNSTONE** – guitar (ex-ELTON JOHN) / **MARK VOLMAN + HOWARD KAYLAN** – backing vocals (ex-TURTLES)

Dec 78. (7") *(K 17270) <8695>* **HOW YOU GONNA SEE ME NOW. / NO TRICKS** 61 Oct78 12

Dec 78. (lp/c) *(K/K4 56577) <3263>* **FROM THE INSIDE** 68 60
– From the inside / Wish I were born in Beverly Hills / The quiet room / Nurse Rozetta / Millie and Billie / Serious / How you gonna see me now / For Veronica's sake / Jacknife Johnny / Inmates (we're all crazy). *(cd-iss. Jun99; 7599 26064-2)*

Jan 79. (7") *<8760>* **FROM THE INSIDE. / NURSE ROZETTA** –

above w / **JOHN LO PRESTI** – bass / **DENNIS CONWAY** – drums

May 80. (lp/c) *(K/K4 56805) <3436>* **FLUSH THE FASHION** 56 44
– Talk talk / Clones (we're all) / Pain / Leather boots / Aspirin damage / Nuclear infected / Grim facts / Model citizen / Dance yourself to death / Headlines. *(cd-iss. Jun99; 7599 26229-2)*

Jun 80. (7") *(K 17598) <49204>* **CLONES (WE'RE ALL). / MODEL CITIZEN** May80 40

Sep 80. (7") *<49526>* **DANCE YOURSELF TO DEATH. / TALK TALK** –

— now w / **MIKE PINERA + DAVEY JOHNSTONE** – guitar / **DUANE HITCHINGS** – keyboards / **ERIC SCOTT** – bass / **CRAIG KRAMPF** – drums

Sep 81. (7") *<49780>* **WHO DO YOU THINK WE ARE. / YOU WANT IT, YOU GOT IT** –

Sep 81. (lp/c) *(K/K4 56927) <3581>* **SPECIAL FORCES** 96
– Who do you think we are / Seven and seven is / Prettiest cop in the block / Don't talk old to me / Generation landslide '81 / Skeletons in the closet / You want it, you got it / You look good in rags / You're a movie / Vicious rumours. *(cd-iss. Jun99; 7599 26230-2)*

Feb 82. (7") *(K 17924) <49848>* **SEVEN AND SEVEN IS (live). / GENERATION LANDSLIDE '81 (live)** 62

May 82. (7"/7"pic-d) *(K 17940/+M)* **FOR BRITAIN ONLY. / UNDER MY WHEELS (live)** [66] [–]
(12"+=) *(K 17940T)* – Who do you think we are (live) / Model citizen (live).

— now w / **MIKE PINERA + DAVEY JOHNSTONE** – guitar / **DUANE HITCHINGS** – keyboards / **ERIC SCOTT** – bass / **CRAIG KRAMPF** – drums

Oct 82. (7") *<29928>* **I LIKE GIRLS. / ZORRO'S ASCENT** [–] [ ]
Oct 82. (lp/c) *(K/K4 57021) <23719-1/-4>* **ZIPPER CATCHES SKIN** [ ] [ ]
– Zorro's ascent / Make that money (Scrooge's song) / I am the future / No baloney homosapiens / Adaptable (anything for you) / I like girls / Remarkably insincere / Tag, you're it / I better be good / I'm alive (that was the day my dead pet returned to save my life). *(cd-iss. Jun99; 7599 23719-2)*

— **COOPER + WAGNER** re-united w / **EZRIN + PRAKASH** and recruited **GRAHAN SHAW** – synth / **JOHN ANDERSON + RICHARD KOLINGA** – drums

Mar 83. (7") *(K 15004)* **I AM THE FUTURE (remix). / ZORRO'S ASCENT** [ ] [–]
Mar 83. (7") *<29828>* **I AM THE FUTURE (remix). / TAG, YOU'RE IT** [–] [ ]
Nov 83. (lp/c) *(923969-1/-4) <23969-1/-4>* **DA DA** [93] [ ]
– Da da / Enough's enough / Former Lee Warner / No man's land / Dyslexia / Scarlet and Sheba / I love America / Fresh blood / Pass the gun around. *(cd-iss. Jun99; 7599 23969-2)*
Nov 83. (12"m) *(ALICE 1T)* **I LOVE AMERICA. / FRESH BLOOD / PASS THE GUN AROUND** [ ] [ ]

— band now consisted of **KANE ROBERTS** (b.16 Jan'59) – guitar, vocals / **DAVID ROSENBERG** – drums / **PAUL DELPH** – keyboards, vocals / **DONNIE KISSELBACK** – bass, vocals / **KIP WINGER**

M.C.A. M.C.A.

Oct 86. (7") *(MCA 1090) <52904>* **HE'S BACK (THE MAN BEHIND THE MASK). / BILLION DOLLAR BABIES** [61] [ ]
(12"+=) *(MCAT 1090)* – I'm eighteen.
Oct 86. (lp/c) *(MCF/+C 3341) <5761>* **CONSTRICTOR** [41] [59]
– Teenage Frankenstein / Give it up / Thrill my gorilla / Life and death of the party / Simple disobedience / The world needs guts / Trick bag / Crawlin' / The great American success story / He's back (the man behind the mask).
Apr 87. (7") *(MCA 1113)* **TEENAGE FRANKENSTEIN. / SCHOOL'S OUT (live)** [ ] [–]
(12"+=) *(MCAT 1113)* – Only women bleed.

— **KEN K. MARY** – drums repl.ROSENBERG / **PAUL HOROWITZ** – keyboards, repl. DELPH + KISSELBACH.

Oct 87. (lp/pic-lp/c) *(MCF/+P/C 3392) <42091>* **RAISE YOUR FIST AND YELL** [48] [73]
– Freedom / Lock me up / Give the radio back / Step on you / Not that kind of love / Prince of darkness / Time to kill / Chop, chop, chop / Gail / Roses on white lace. *(cd-iss. May88; DMCF 3392)*
Mar 88. (7") *(MCA 1241) <53212>* **FREEDOM. / TIME TO KILL** [50] [ ]
(12"+=/12"s+=) *(MCA T/X 1241)* – School's out (live).

— retained **KIP WINGER** bringing in guests **JON BON JOVI, RICHIE SAMBORA** plus **JOE PERRY, TOM HAMILTON, JOEY KRAMER** etc.

— **COOPER + WAGNER** re-united w / **EZRIN + PRAKASH** and recruited **GRAHAN SHAW** – synth / **JOHN ANDERSON + RICHARD KOLINGA** – drums

Epic Epic

1988. (7") *<08114>* **I GOT A LINE ON YOU. / LIVIN' ON THE EDGE** [–] [ ]
Jul 89. (7") *(655061-7) <68958>* **POISON. / TRASH** [2] Sep89 [7]
(12"+=) *(655061-8)* – The ballad of Dwight Fry.
(cd-s++=) *(655061-2)* – I got a line on you (live).
(12"+=) *(655061-9)* – Cold Ethyl (live).
Aug 89. (lp/c/cd) *(465130-1/-4/-2) <45137>* **TRASH** [2] [20]
– Poison / Spark in the dark / House of fire / Why trust you / Only my heart talkin' / Bed of nails / This maniac's in love with you / Trash / Hell is living without you / I'm your gun. *(re-iss. Sep93 cd/c; same)*
Sep 89. (7"/7"green/7"red/7"blue/c-s) *(ALICE/+G/R/B/M 3)* **BED OF NAILS. / I'M YOUR GUN** [38] [–]
(12"+=/12"w-poster/12"pic-d+=) *(ALICE T/Q/P 3)* – Go to Hell (live).
(cd-s++=) *(ALICEC 3)* – Only women bleed (live).
Dec 89. (7"/7"sha-pic-d/c-s) *(ALICE/+P/M 4)* **HOUSE OF FIRE. / THIS MANIAC'S IN LOVE WITH YOU** [65] [–]
(12"+=/cd-s+=) *(ALICE T/C 4)* – Billion dollar babies (live) / Under my wheels (live).
(7"sha-pic-d) *(ALICEX 4)* – ('A'side) / POISON (live).
(12"pic-d+=/12"w-poster+=) *(ALICE S/Q 4)* – Spark in the dark (live) / Under my wheels (live).
Jan 90. (c-s) *<73085>* **HOUSE OF FIRE / BALLAD OF DWIGHT FRY** [–] [56]
Apr 90. (cd-s) *<73268>* **ONLY MY HEART TALKIN'. / UNDER MY WHEELS (live)** [–] [89]

— (Mar'90) touring band **PETE FRIEZZEN** – guitar / **AL PITRELLI** – guitar / **TOMMY CARADONNA** – bass / **DEREK SHERINIAN** – keyboards / **JONATHAN MOVER** – drums

— (1991 sessions) **STEVE VAI, JOE SATRIANI, STEF BURNS** (on tour), **VINNIE MOORE, MICK MARS, SLASH** – guitars / **HUGH McDONALD, NIKKI SIXX** – bass / **MICKEY CURRY** – drums / **ROBERT SALLEY, JOHN WEBSTER** – keyboards / **STEVE CROES** – synclaiver

Jun 91. (7"/c-s) *(656983-7/-4)* **HEY STOOPID. / WIND-UP TOY** [21] [–]
(12"+=/12"pic-d+=/cd-s+=) *(656983-6/-8/-9)* – It rained all night.
Jun 91. (cd/c/lp) *(468416-2/-4/-1) <46786>* **HEY STOOPID** [4] [47]
– Hey stoopid / Love's a loaded gun / Snakebite / Burning our bed / Dangerous tonight / Might as well be on Mars / Feed me Frankenstein / Hurricane years / Little by little / Die for you / Dirty dreams / Wind-up toy. *(cd re-iss. Mar96; same)*
Jul 91. (cd-s) *<73845>* **HEY STOOPID. / IT RAINED ALL NIGHT** [–] [78]
Sep 91. (7"/c-s) *(657438-7/-4)* **LOVE'S A LOADED GUN. / FIRE** [38] [ ]
(12"+=/12"pic-d+=/sha-pic-cd-s+=) *(657438-6/-8/-9)* – Eighteen (live '91).
Jun 92. (7"/c-s) *(658092-7/-4)* **FEED MY FRANKENSTEIN. / BURNING OUR BED** [27] [ ]
(12"pic-d+=/cd-s+=) *(658092-6/-2)* – Poison / Only my heart talkin'.
(cd-s+=) *(658092-5)* – Hey stoopid / Bed of nails.

— w / **STEF BURNS** – guitar, vocals / **GREG SMITH** – bass, vocals / **DEREK SHERINIAN** – keyboards, vocals / **DAVID VOSIKKINEN** – drums

May 94. (c-s) *(660347-4)* **LOST IN AMERICA. / HEY STOOPID (live)** [22] [ ]
(12"pic-d+=/pic-cd-s+=) *(660347-2)* – Billion dollar babies (live) / No more Mr.Nice Guy (live).
Jun 94. (cd/c/lp) *(476594-2/-4/-1) <52771>* **THE LAST TEMPTATION** (w /free comic) [6] [68]
– Sideshow / Nothing's free / Lost in America / Bad place alone / You're my temptation / Stolen prayer / Unholy war / Lullaby / It's me / Cleansed by fire.
Jul 94. (c-s) *(660563-4)* **IT'S ME. / BAD PLACE ALONE** [34] [ ]
(12"pic-d+=/pic-cd-s+=) *(660563-2)* – Poison / Sick things.
Oct 95. (cd/c) *(480845-2/-4) <67219>* **CLASSICKS** (compilation) [ ] [ ]
– Poison / Hey stoopid / Feed my Frankenstein / Love's a loaded gun / Stolen prayer / House of fire / Lost in America / It's me / Under my wheels (live) / Billion dollar babies (live) / I'm eighteen (live) / No more Mr. Nice guy (live) / Only women bleed (live) / School's out (live) / Fire.

— now with **REB BEACH** – guitar / **RYAN ROXIE** – guitar / **PAUL TAYLOR** – keyboards / **TODD JENSEN** – bass / **JIMMT DeGRASSO** – drums / guests; SAMMY HAGAR, BOB ZOMBIE + SLASH

E.M.I. Capitol

Jun 97. (cd) *(CTM CD/MC 331) <33080>* **A FISTFUL OF ALICE (live)** [ ] [ ]
– School's out / Under my wheels / I'm eighteen / Desperado / Lost in America / Teenage lament '74 / I never cry / Poison / No more Mr. Nice guy / Welcome to my nightmare / Only women bleed / Feed my Frankenstein / Elected / Is anyone home? (studio).

Eagle Spitfire

Jun 00. (cd) *(EAGCD 115) <15038>* **BRUTAL PLANET** [38] [ ]
– Brutal planet / Wicked young man / Sanctuary / Blow me a kiss / Eat some more / Pick up the bones / Pessi-mystic / Gimme / It's the little things / Take it like a woman / Cold machines.
Aug 00. (cd-s) *(EAGXS 157)* **GIMME / BRUTAL PLANET / GIMME (CD-Rom video)** [ ] [–]
Oct 01. (cd) *(EAGCD 181) <15200>* **DRAGONTOWN** [ ] Sep01 [ ]
– Triggerman / Deeper / Dragontown / Sex, death and money / Fantasy man / Somewhere in the jungle / Dusgraceland / Sister Sara / Every woman has a name / I just wanna be God / It's much too late / The sentinel.

— now with **RYAN ROXIE** – guitar / **ERIC DOVER** – guitar / **ERIC SINGER** – drums / **CHUCK GARRIC** – bass / **TED ANDREADIS** – percussion, keyboards / **SCOTT GILMAN** – clarinet, sax / **WAYNE KRAMER** – guitar

Spitfire Eagle Red

Sep 03. (cd) *(SPIT 090)* <20028> **THE EYES OF ALICE COOPER** ☐ ☐
– What do you want from me? / Between high school & old school / Man of the year / Novocaine / Bye bye, baby / Be with you awhile / Detroit city / Spirits rebellious / This house is haunted / Love should never feel like this / The song that didn't rhyme / I'm so angry / Backyard brawl. *(lp-iss.Oct03 on '5160'; 5160 018)*

Spitfire New West

Jul 05. (cd) *(SPITCD 257)* <6078> **DIRTY DIAMONDS** ☐ Aug05 ☐
– Woman of mass distraction / Perfect / You make me wanna . . . / Dirty diamonds / The saga of Jesse Jane / Sunset babies (all got rabies) / Pretty ballerina / Run down the Devil / Steal that car / Six hours / Your own worst enemy / Zombie dance. *(bonus+=)* – Stand.

– compilations, others, etc. –

on 'Warners' unless otherwise stated

Mar 73. (7") **BE MY LOVER. / UNDER MY WHEELS** – ☐
Jun 73. (d-lp) *(K 66021)* **SCHOOLDAYS** (1st-2 lp's) ☐ ☐
Feb 75. (7"ep) *(K 16409)* **SCHOOL'S OUT / NO MORE MR.NICE GUY. / BILLION DOLLAR BABIES / ELECTED** ☐ –
Feb 76. (7") *(K 16287)* **SCHOOL'S OUT. / ELECTED** ☐ –
(re-iss. Dec80; same) (re-iss. Sep85 on 'Old Gold'; OG 9519)
Dec 77. (7"ep/12"ep) *Anchor; (ANE 7/12 001)* **DEPARTMENT OF YOUTH EP** ☐ –
– Department of youth / Welcome to my nightmare / Black widow / Only women bleed.
1978. (7") **I'M EIGHTEEN. / SCHOOL'S OUT** – ☐
Apr 84. (pic-lp) *Design; (PXLP 3)* **ROCK'N'ROLL REVIVAL: TORONTO LIVE '69 (live)** ☐ –
(re-iss. Apr86 as 'FREAKOUT SONG' on 'Showcase'; SHLP 115)
Apr 87. (m-lp/c) *Thunderbolt; (THBM/+C 005)* **LADIES MAN (live'69)** ☐ –
(cd-iss. Aug88; CDTHBM 005) (re-iss cd.Jun91; same) (cd re-iss. Aug98 on 'MagMid'; MM 011)
Dec 89. (lp/c)(cd) *W.E.A.; (WX 331/+C)(241781-2)* **THE BEAST OF ALICE COOPER** ☐ ☐
– School's out / Under my wheels / Billion dollar babies / Be my lover / Desperado / Is it my body? / Only women bleed / Elected / I'm eighteen / Hello hurray / No more Mr. Nice guy / Teenage lament '74 / Muscle of love / Department of youth.
Jul 90. (cd-box) *Enigma; (773 362-2)* **PRETTIES FOR YOU** ☐ –
Jul 90. (cd-box) *Enigma; (773 391-2)* **EASY ACTION** ☐ –
May 92. (lp/cd) *Edsel; (NEST/+CD 903)* **LIVE AT THE WHISKEY A GO GO, 1969 (live)** ☐ –
Oct 92. (cd) *Pickwick; (SMA 054)* **ROCK LEGENDS VOL.2** ☐ –
Apr 93. (cd) *Pulsar; (PULS 010)* **NOBODY LIKES ME** ☐ –
Sep 94. (cd) *Wisepack; (LECD 085)* **LEGENDS IN MUSIC** ☐ –
Jul 97. (cd) *Going For A Song; (GFS 071)* **ALICE COOPER** ☐ –
May 98. (cd) *Dressed To Kill; (DRESS 603)* **SNORTING ANTHRAX** ☐ –
Jun 98. (cd) *Raven; (RVCD 69)* **FREEDOM FOR FRANKENSTEIN: HITS AND PIECES 1984-1994** ☐ ☐
Apr 99. (4xcd-box) *Rhino;* <*(8122 75680-2)*> **THE LIFE AND CRIMES OF ALICE COOPER** ☐ ☐
Jul 00. (cd) *Epic; (498788-2)* **SUPER HITS** ☐ –
Feb 01. (cd/c) *Warners;* <*(8122 73534-2/-4)*> **THE DEFINITIVE ALICE COOPER** 33 ☐
– I'm eighteen / Desperado / Under my wheels / Halo of flies / School's out / Elected / Hello hooray / Generation landslide / No more Mr. Nice Guy / Billion dollar babies / Teenage lament '74 / Muscle of love / Only women bleed / Welcome to my nightmare / Department of love / I never cry / You and me / How you gonna see me now / From the inside / Poison / Hey stoopid.
Oct 01. (4xcd-box) *Rhino;* <*(8122 73573-2)*< **THE LIFE AND CRIMES OF ALICE COOPER** ☐ ☐
Aug 03. (cd) *Epic; (511385-2)* **HELL IS** ☐ –

the COOPER TEMPLE CLAUSE

Formed: Reading, England . . . 1999 by vocalist BEN GAUTREY, TOM BELLAMY, DAN FISHER, DIDZ HAMMOND, KIERAN MAHON and JOHN HARPER. Like a mad hybrid between KULA SHAKER and GAY DAD, the COOPER TEMPLE CLAUSE were rocking out in a bad/good way, while slyly winking at their newly composed fanbase. We can imagine it: six geezers (with deliberately 'ironic' mullet hair-cuts) from Reading, playing trash glam Brit-rock and being crowned as NME darlings. Yet for a band that were supposed to be christening a new type of Brit-rock, the COOPER TEMPLE CLAUSE's debut EP 'THE HARDWARE' (in March 2001) recycled the old GAY DAD, WARM JETS, DANDY WARHOLS vibe that simply made them look like stringent copycats. However, after the guitar strumming pop-rock double-A single 'FILM-MAKER' / 'BEEN TRAINING DOGS' (a Top 20 hit early 2002), CTC came of age through their debut UK Top 30 album 'SEE THIS THROUGH AND LEAVE'. Featuring hit-to-be, 'WHO NEEDS ENEMIES?', the album was relentless to the end; if you were sick of OASIS and the Brit-rock crew, this was for you. The COOPER TEMPLE CLAUSE were back with their sophomore album 'KICK UP THE FIRE AND LET THE FLAMES BREAK LOOSE' (2003). Much of the same mix of rock and experimental programmed beats as seen on their debut, the band had a winner in the explosive, emotionally raw single 'THE SAME MISTAKES' (with a great video to boot). Elsewhere the album was as ferocious as the title suggested, making the 'CLAUSE one of the most exciting British bands in the post-RADIOHEAD slump.

Album rating: SEE THIS THROUGH AND LEAVE (*7) / KICK UP THE FIRE AND LET THE FLAMES BREAK LOOSE (*7)

BEN GAUTREY – vocals, guitar, bass / **DAN FISHER** – guitar / **TOM BELLAMY** – guitar, effects, keyboards, etc. / **KIERAN MAHON** – keyboards, guitar, synths, vocals / **DIDZ HAMMOND** (b. DAVID JONATHAN HAMMOND, 19 Jul'81) – bass / **JON HARPER** – drums

Morning-BMG BMG Inter..

Mar 01. (d7"ep; 1 white) *(MORNING 2)* **THE HARDWARE EP** ☐ –
– The Devil walks in the sand / Solitude / Way out west / Sister soul.
May 01. (cd-ep) *(MORNING 5)* **THE WARFARE EP** ☐ –
– Panzer attack / I'll still write / Mansell.
(d7"ep; 1 white+=) *(MORNING 6)* – Panzer attack (acoustic).
Sep 01. (7") *(MORNING 11)* **LET'S KILL MUSIC. / GIRL INK AGE** 41 –
(cd-s) *(MORNING 9)* – ('A') / Panzer attack (Dirty Sanchez remix) / ('A'-video).
(cd-s) *(MORNING 10)* – ('A') / My darling (nasty angel) / ('A'-Dirty Sanchez remix).
Dec 01. (cd-ep) <29903> **THE HARDWARE EP + THE WARFARE EP** – ☐
Jan 02. (7"/cd-s) *(MORNING 17/15)* **FILM-MAKER. / BEEN TRAINING DOGS** 20 –
(cd-s+=) *(MORNING 16)* – Safe enough distance away.
Feb 02. (cd/d-lp) *(MORNING 18/20)* <92034> **SEE THIS THROUGH AND LEAVE** 27 ☐
– Did you miss me? / Film-maker / Panzer attack / Who needs enemies? / Amber / Digital observations / Let's kill music / 555-4823 / Been training dogs / The lake / Murder song. *(d-cd-iss. +=; MORNING 19)* – The Devil walks in the sand / Way out west / I'll still write / Panzer attack (live) / Let's kill music (live) / Film-maker (video) / Let's kill music (video) / Been training dogs (live).
May 02. (cd-s) *(MORNING 23)* **WHO NEEDS ENEMIES? / BEFORE THE MOOR / ONE QUICK FIX** 22 –
(cd-s) *(MORNING 24)* – ('A') / Lapitu (bedtime story) / Not quite enough.
(cd-s) *(MORNING 25)* – ('A') / Jesus, you smoke too / ('A'-video).
Sep 03. (7") *(MORNING 32)* **PROMISES PROMISES. / OUR EYES ARE BRIGHT** 19 –
(cd-s) *(MORNING 30)* – ('A') / On. off. on / I know.

(dvd-s) *(MORNING 31)* – ('A') / Resident writer / ('A'-video) / (making of.. video).

Sep 03. (cd/d-lp) *(MORNING 33/34)* <59573> **KICK UP THE FIRE AND LET THE FLAMES BREAK LOOSE** | 5 | Feb04 | |
– The same mistakes / Promises promises / New toys / Talking to a brick wall / Into my arms / Blind pilots / A.I.M. / Music box / In your prime / Written apology. *(dvd+=; MORNING 36)* – (videos).

Nov 03. (7") *(MORNING 40)* **BLIND PILOTS. / HABIT OF A LIFETIME** | 37 | – |
(cd-s) *(MORNING 38)* – ('A') / Derelict / I want you to think I could be / ('A'-x-rated video).
(dvd-s) *(MORNING 39)* – ('A') / (making of . . . video 15 min) / (clips from x-rated video).

— with the band inactive (until autumn 06), DIDZ joined DIRTY PRETTY THINGS (the band of ex-LIBERTINES singer/guitarist, CARL BARAT)

Julian COPE

Born: 21 Oct'57, Deri, Caerphilly, Wales, although he was raised in Liverpool, England. His first foray into the music business was with the CRUCIAL THREE, alongside IAN McCULLOCH and PETE WYLIE. During the autumn of '78, COPE formed the TEARDROP EXPLODES (originally named A SHALLOW MADNESS), with MICK FINKLER and PAUL SIMPSON. In late '78, a deal was inked with local UK indie label, 'Zoo', and after three critically acclaimed singles, they transferred to the major label, 'Mercury,' in July 1980. Keyboard-biased TEARDROP EXPLODES were mostly influenced by 60's pop psychedelia, COPE sounding distinctly like a modern, post-new wave SCOTT WALKER. Their first hit came about via 'WHEN I DREAM', a classic lifted from their classic album, Top 30 'KILIMANJARO' (1980); early in 1981, they cashed-in when 'REWARD' delivered them a Top tenner. 'TREASON', the next 45, didn't emulate this feat, although it still managed a Top 20 placing. Their second album, 'WILDER' (1981), was another commercial success, although it lacked the bite of its predecessor. A few minor hits followed over the next year and a bit, but it was clear JULIAN was gearing up for a solo career. Remaining with 'Mercury' records, he released two albums in 1984, 'WORLD SHUT YOUR MOUTH' and 'FRIED', both receiving a lukewarm response from the music press. On-stage antics such as cutting his stomach (IGGY POP-like) and singing perched on a high pole, saw him develop a weird new character; often he perfomed through his alter-ego (SQWUBBSY a seven foot giant). COPE subsequently signed for 'Island' in 1985, leaving behind the unissued (until 1990) 'SKELLINGTON' LP. Around the same time he suffered a marriage break-up and drug problems, although he re-married in 1986. Re-emerging triumphantly in 1986, he charted with the Top 20 hit 45, 'WORLD SHUT YOUR MOUTH' (curiously enough, the song wasn't included on the 1984 album of the same name). The single was a taster for the following year's comeback album 'SAINT JULIAN', a record which almost gave him his first solo top ten hit. A disappointing pop album, 'MY NATION UNDERGROUND', dealt his street cred a bitter blow and he retreated somewhat with two (meant for mail-order) 1990 albums, the aforementioned 'SKELLINGTON' and 'DROOLIAN'. He returned in fine fashion a year later with the splendid double-set, 'PEGGY SUICIDE', a record that targeted pollution and even the dreadful Tory poll tax (something he protested against vehemently). In 1992, he brought back his old influences (CAN, FAUST, "Kraut-rock") with 'JEHOVAKILL'. Creatively, the album was an admirable effort although it bombed both commercially and critically. This was his last for 'Island', who dropped him unceremoniously after he recorded the 'RITE' CD-album for German release. In 1994, he signed with 'Echo' and returned with three varying albums, 'AUTOGEDDON' (1994), '20 MOTHERS' (1995) and 'INTERPRETER' (1996). With a much needed direction change, COPE opted to form a fresh post-millennium outfit, BLOOD DONOR (along loyal sidekick, THIGHPAULSANDRA). Their album 'LOVE, PEACE & FUCK' (2001), was Krautrock centered around lyrics inspired by Celtic, Viking and Druid folklore. The punningly-titled 'CITIZEN CAIN'D' (2005) was a surprising and unheralded return to the Stateside garage-fuzz that first inspired him; a by-product of this was a simultaneous return to more conventional songwriting. Once again COPE performed a stylistic volte-face via his 'DARK ORGASM' (2005), the critical jury out on his murky mid-70s dalliances.

• **Songwriters:** COPE penned except; READ IT IN BOOKS (co-with; Ian McCulloch). He wrote all material, except NON-ALIGNMENT PACT (Pere Ubu) / COPE covered FREE YOUR MIND AND YOUR ASS WILL FOLLOW (Funkadelic) / ARE YOU HUNG UP? (Mothers Of Invention). • **Trivia:** The album, 'DROOLIAN', was released as part of a campaign to free from jail, ROKY ERICKSON (ex-13th FLOOR ELEVATORS). In 1990, COPE took part in the Anti-Poll tax march from Brixton to Trafalgar Square.

Album rating: Teardrop Explodes: KILIMANJARO (*9) / WILDER (*7) / EVERYBODY WANTS TO SHAG THE TEARDROP EXPLODES posthumous (*7) / PIANO (*6) / THE GREATEST HIT compilation (*7) / Julian Cope: WORLD SHUT YOUR MOUTH (*7) / FRIED (*7) / SAINT JULIAN (*7) / MY NATION UNDERGROUND (*8) / SKELLINGTON (*7) / DROOLIAN (*7) / PEGGY SUICIDE (*8) / JEHOVAHKILL (*5) / AUTOGEDDON (*6) / 20 MOTHERS (*8) / INTERPRETER (*5) / FLOORED GENIUS: THE BEST OF JULIAN COPE & THE TEARDROP EXPLODES 1979-1991 compilation (*8) / FLOORED GENIUS VOL.2 (1983-91) compilation (*7) / Brain Donor: LOVE, PEACE & FUCK (*6) / Julian Cope: CITIZEN CAIN'D (*7) / DARK ORGASM (*4)

the TEARDROP EXPLODES

JULIAN COPE – vocals, bass / **PAUL SIMPSON** – keyboards / **MICK FINKLER** – guitar / **GARY DWYER** – drums

Zoo | not iss

Feb 79. (7"m) *(CAGE 003)* **SLEEPING GAS. / CAMERA CAMERA / KIRBY WORKERS' DREAM FADES** | | – |

— **GERARD QUINN** – keyboards; repl. SIMPSON who formed WILD SWANS

May 79. (7") *(CAGE 005)* **BOUNCING BABIES. / ALL I AM IS LOVING YOU** | | – |

— **DAVID BALFE** – keyboards (ex-LORI & THE CHAMELEONS, ex-BIG IN JAPAN, ex-THOSE NAUGHTY LUMPS) repl. QUINN who joined The WILD SWANS

Mar 80. (7") *(CAGE 008)* **TREASON (IT'S JUST A STORY). / READ IT IN BOOKS** | | – |

— **ALAN GILL** – guitar (ex-DALEK I) repl. FINKLER now (COPE, DWYER, BALFE + GILL)

Mercury | Mercury

Sep 80. (7") *(TEAR 1)* **WHEN I DREAM. / KILIMANJARO** | 47 | – |

Oct 80. (lp) *(6359 035)* <4016> **KILIMANJARO** | 24 | |
– Ha ha I'm drowning / Sleeping gas / Treason (it's just a story) / Second head / Poppies in the field / Went crazy / Brave boys keep their promises / Bouncing babies / Books / Thief of Baghdad / When I dream. *(re-iss Mar81 lp/c +=; 6359/7150 035)* – Reward. *(re-iss. Jul84 lp/c; PRICE/PRIMC 59) (re-iss. May89 & Jan96 lp/c/cd; 836 897-1/-4/-2) (cd re-mast.Nov00 ++= 548322-2)* – Kilimanjaro / Strange house in the snow / Use me / Traison / Sleeping gas (live).
(below trumpet by RAY MARTINEZ)

Jan 81. (7") *(TEAR 2)* **REWARD. / STRANGE HOUSE IN THE SNOW** | 6 | – |

Apr 81. (7") *(TEAR 3)* **TREASON (IT'S JUST A STORY). / USE ME** | 18 | – |
(12"+=) *(TEAR 3-12)* – Traison (c'est juste une histoire).

Jun 81. (7") *(TEAR 4)* **POPPIES IN THE FIELD. / HA HA I'M DROWNING** | | – |
(d7"+=) *(TEAR 44)* – Bouncing babies / Read it in books.

— **TROY TATE** – guitar, vocals (ex-INDEX, ex-SHAKE) repl. GILL

Sep 81. (7") *(TEAR 5)* **PASSIONATE FRIEND. / CHRIST VS. WARHOL** | 25 | – |

— on session/gigs **ALFIE ALGIUS** (b. Malta) – bass / **JEFF HAMMER** – keyboards

Nov 81. (lp/c) *(6359/7150 056)* <4035> **WILDER** | 29 | |
– Bent out of shape / Colours fly away / Seven views of Jerusalem / Pure joy / Falling down around me / The culture bunker / Passionate

friend / Tiny children / Like Leila Khaled said / . . .And the fighting takes over / The great dominions. *(re-iss. Jun87 lp/c; PRICE/PRIMC 112) (re-iss. May89 & Jan96 lp/c/cd; 836 896-1/-4/-2) (cd re-mast.Nov00 +=; 548284-2)* – Window shopping for a new crown of thorns / East of the equator / Rachael built a steamboat / You disappear from view / Suffocate / Ouch monkeys / Soft enough for you / The in-psychlopedia.

Nov 81. (7") *(TEAR 6)* **COLOURS FLY AWAY. / WINDOW SHOPPING FOR A NEW CROWN OF THORNS** [54] [–]
(12"+=) *(TEAR 6-12)* – East of the equator.

— **DAVID BALFE** returned

— **RON FRANCOIS** – bass (ex-SINCEROS) repl. guests

Jun 82. (7"/7"g-f) *(TEAR 7/+G)* **TINY CHILDREN. / RACHAEL BUILT A STEAMBOAT** [44] [–]
(12"+=) *(TEAR 7-12)* – Sleeping gas (live).

— now trio of **COPE, DWYER + BALFE** plus session man **FRANCOIS**

— TROY TATE went solo and joined FASHION

Mar 83. (7") *(TEAR 8)* **YOU DISAPPEAR FROM VIEW. / SUFFOCATE** [41] [–]
(d7"+=/12"+=) *(TEAR 88/8-12)* – Soft enough for you / Ouch monkeys / The in-psychlopedia.

— disbanded early '83; BALFE went into producing films and music; JULIAN COPE went solo augmented by DWYER

– compilations, others, etc. –

Jun 85. (7") *Mercury; (TEAR 9)* **REWARD (remix). / TREASON (IT'S JUST A STORY)** [ ] [–]
(12"+=) *(TEAR 9-12)* – Strange house in the snow / Use me.

Jan 90. (7") *Fontana; (DROP 1)* **SERIOUS DANGER. / SLEEPING GAS** [ ] [–]
(12"+=)(c-s+=/cd-s+=) *(DROP 1-12)(DRO MC/CD 1)* – Seven views of Jerusalem.

Mar 90. (cd/c/lp) *Fontana; (842 439-2/-4/-1)* **EVERYBODY WANTS TO SHAG THE TEARDROP EXPLODES** (long lost 3rd album) [72] [–]
– Ouch monkey's / Serious danger / Metranil Vavin / Count to ten and run forever / In-psychlopaedia / Soft enough for you / You disappear from view / The challenger / Not only my friend / Sex / Terrorist / Strange house in the snow.

Apr 90. (7") *Fontana; (DROP 2)* **COUNT TO TEN AND RUN FOR COVER. / REWARD** [ ] [–]
(12"+=)(cd-s+=) *(DROP 2-12)(DROCD 2)* – Poppies / Khaled said.

Nov 90. (cd/c/lp) *Document; (DCD/DMC/DLP 004)* **PIANO** (early material) [ ] [–]
– Sleeping gas / Camera camera / Kirkby workers dream fades / Bouncing babies / All I am is loving you / Treason / Books / Take a chance / When I dream / Kwalo Klobinsky's lullaby.

Dec 93. (cd/lp) *Windsong; (<WIN CD/LP 050>)* **BBC LIVE IN CONCERT (live)** [ ] Jan95 [ ]

Aug 95. (d-cd) *Mercury; (528601-2)* **WILDER / KILIMANJARO** [ ] [–]

Oct 01. (cd) *Mercury; (586391-2)* **THE GREATEST HIT – THE BEST OF THE TEARDROP EXPLODES** [ ] [–]
– Reward / Passionate friend / Treason (it's just a story) / Ha ha I'm drowning / The culture bunker / Colours fly away / Sleeping gas / Suffocate / When I dream / Tiny children / . . .And the fighting takes over / The in-psychlopedia / Christ vs. Warhol / You disappear from view / The great dominions.

Aug 02. (cd) *Spectrum; (544616-2)* **THE COLLECTION** [ ] [–]

JULIAN COPE

JULIAN COPE – vocals, guitar, keyboards / with **GARY DWYER** / **STEVE CREASE + ANDREW EDGE** – drums / **STEPHEN LOWELL** – lead guitar / **RON FRANCOIS** – bass / **KATE ST. JOHN** – oboe

Mercury / not iss.

Nov 83. (7") *(COPE 1)* **SUNSHINE PLAYROOM. / HEY HIGH CLASS BUTCHER** [64] [–]
(12"+=) *(COPE 1-12)* – Wreck my car / Eat the poor.

Feb 84. (lp/c) *(MERL/+C 37)* **WORLD SHUT YOUR MOUTH** [40] [–]
– Bandy's first jump / Metranil Vavin / Strasbourg / An elegant chaos / Quizmaster / Kolly Kibber's birthday / Sunshine playroom / Head hang low / Pussy face / The greatness and perfection of love / Lunatic and fire pistol. *(cd-iss. 1986; 818 365-2)*

Mar 84. (7") *(MER 155)* **THE GREATNESS AND PERFECTION OF LOVE. / 24a VELOCITY CRESCENT** [52] [–]
(12"+=) *(MERX 155)* – Pussyface.

Nov 84. (lp/c) *(MERL/+C 48)* **FRIED** [87] [–]
– Reynard the fox / Bill Drummond said / Laughing boy / Me singing / Sunspots / Me singing / Bloody Assizes / Search party / O king of chaos / Holy love / Torpedo. *(cd-iss. 1986; 822 832-2) (cd re-iss. Sep98 +=; 532370-2)* – I went on a chourney / Mik mak mok / Land of fear.

Feb 85. (7") *(MER 182)* **SUNSPOTS. / I WENT ON A CHOURNEY** [ ] [–]
(d7"+=) *(MER 182-2)* – Mik mak mok / Land of fear.

— **COPE** recruited Americans **DONALD ROSS SKINNER** – guitar / **JAMES ELLER** – bass / **DOUBLE DE HARRISON** – keyboards / **CHRIS WHITTEN** – drums

Island / Island

Sep 86. (7") *(IS 290)* <99479> **WORLD SHUT YOUR MOUTH. / UMPTEENTH UNNATURAL BLUES** [19] Feb87 [84]
(d7"+=) *(ISB 290)* – ('A'-Trouble Funk remix) / Transportation.
(c-s+=) *(CIS 290)* – I've got levitation / Non-alignment pact.
(12"++=) *(12IS 290)* – (all extra above).

Jan 87. (7") *(IS 305)* **TRAMPOLENE. / DISASTER** [ ] [–]
(7"ep+=/12"ep+=) *(ISW/12IS 305)* – Mock Turtle / Warwick the kingmaker.

Feb 87. (m-lp) *<90560>* **JULIAN COPE** [–] [ ]
– World shut your mouth / Transportation / Umpteenth unnatural blues / Non-alignment pact / I've got levitation.

Mar 87. (lp/c/cd) *(ILPS/ICT/CID 9861) <90571>* **SAINT JULIAN** [11] [ ]
– Trampolene / Shot down / Eve's volcano (covered in sin) / Spacehopper / Planet ride / Trampolene / World shut your mouth / Saint Julian / Pulsar NX / Space hopper / Screaming secrets / A crack in the clouds. *(re-iss. Aug91 cd)(c; IMCD 137)(ICM 2023)*

Apr 87. (7") *(IS 318)* **EVE'S VOLCANO (COVERED IN SIN). / ALMOST BEAUTIFUL CHILD** [ ] [–]
(12"+=) *(12IS 318)* – Pulsar NX (live) / Shot down (live).
(12"+=) *(12ISX 318)* – Spacehopper – Annexe / ('B'side; pt.II).
(cd-s++=) *(CID 318)* – (all 3 extra above).

— **DAVE PALMER** – drums (studio) / **MIKE JOYCE** – drums (tour) repl. WHITTEN / added **RON FAIR** – keyboards / **ROOSTER COSBY** – percussion, some drums

Sep 88. (7") *(IS 380)* **CHARLOTTE ANNE. / CHRISTMAS MOURNING** [35] [–]
(12"+=/12"pic-d+=/pic-cd-s+=) *(12IS/12ISP/CIDP 380)* – Books / A question of temptation.

Oct 88. (lp/c/cd) *(ILPS/ICT/CID 9918) <91025>* **MY NATION UNDERGROUND** [42] [ ]
– 5 o'clock world / Vegetation / Charlotte Anne / My nation underground / China doll / Someone like me / Easter everywhere / I'm not losing sleep / The great white hoax. *(re-iss. Aug91 cd)(c; IMCD 138)(ICM 9918)*

Nov 88. (7") *(IS 399)* **5 O'CLOCK WORLD. / S.P.Q.R.** [42] [–]
(10"+=/12"+=/pic-cd-s+=) *(10IS/12IS/CIDP 399)* – Reynard in Tokyo (extended live).

Jun 89. (7") *(IS 406)* **CHINA DOLL. / CRAZY FARM ANIMAL** [53] [–]
(10"+=/10"pic-d+=/12"+=) *(10IS/10ISP/12IS 406)* – Desi.
(cd-s++=) *(CID 406)* – Rail on.

— **COPE** retained **SKINNER & COSBY** plus **J.D. HASSINGER** – drums / **TIM** – keyboards / **BRAN** – bass (both of Guernsey)

Jan 91. (7"/c-s) *(IS/CIS 483)* **BEAUTIFUL LOVE. / PORT OF SAINTS** [32] [–]
(12"+=/cd-s+=) *(12IS/CID 483)* – Love L.U.V. / Unisex cathedral.
(12"pink+=) *(12ISX 483)* – Love L.U.V. / Dragonfly.

Mar 91. (cd/c/d-lp) *(CID/ICT/ILPSD 9977) <848338-2/-4>* **PEGGY SUICIDE** [23] [ ]
– Pristeen / Double vegetation / East easy rider / Promised land / Hanging out & hung up on the line / Safesurfer / If you loved me at all / Drive, she said / Soldier blue / You . . . / Not raving but drowning / Head / Leperskin / Beautiful love / Uptight / Western Front 1992 CE / Hung up & hanging out to dry / The American Lite / Las Vegas basement. *(cd re-iss. Aug94 & Apr02; IMCD 188)*

Apr 91. (7"/c-s) *(IS/CIS 492)* **EAST EASY RIDER. / BUTTERFLY E** [51] [–]
(12"+=/cd-s+=) *(12IS/CID 492)* – Almost live / Little donkey.
(12"pic-d+=) *(12ISX 492)* – Easty Risin' / Ravebury stones.

Jul 91. (7"/c-s) *(IS/CIS 497)* **HEAD. / BAGGED – OUT KEN** [57] [–]
(12"+=/cd-s+=) *(12IS/CID 497)* – Straw dogs / Animals at all.

Oct 92. (7"/c-s) *(IS/CIS 545)* **FEAR LOVES THE SPACE. / SIZEWELL B.** [42] [-]
(12"pic-d+=) *(12ISX 545)* – I have always been here before / Gogmagog.

Oct 92. (cd/c/d-lp) *(<514052-2/-4/-1>)* **JEHOVAHKILL** [20] Dec92 [ ]
– Soul desert / No harder shoulder to cry on / Akhenaten / The mystery trend / Upwards at 45° / Cut my friends down / Necropolis / Slow rider / Gimme back my flag / Poet is priest / Julian H Cope / The subtle energies commission / Fa-fa-fa-fine / Fear loves this place / Peggy Suicide is missing. *(cd re-iss. Aug94; IMCD 189)*

— Next was last in the 90's album trilogy about pollution. Its theme this time was the car, (coincidentally he had just passed his driving test). It featured usual musicians.

Echo American

Jul 94. (cd/c/lp) *(ECH CD/MC/LP 001) <45705>* **AUTOGEDDON** [16] Aug94 [ ]
– Autogeddon blues / Madmax / Don't call me Mark Chapman / I gotta walk / Ain't no gettin' round gettin' round / Paranormal in the West Country (medley): i) Paranormal pt.1, ii) Archdrude's roadtrip. iii) Kar-ma-kanik / Ain't but the one way / S.t.a.r.c.a.r. *(cd re-iss. Mar99; same)*

Aug 95. (7"yellow/c-s) *(ECS/+MC 11)* **TRY TRY TRY. / WESSEXY** [24] [-]
(cd-s+=) *(ECSCD 11)* – Baby, let's play vet / Don't jump me, mother.

Aug 95. (cd/c/d-lp) *(ECH CD/MC/LP 005)* **20 MOTHERS** [20] [-]
– Wheelbarrow man / I wandered lonely as a child / Try try try / Stone circles 'n' you / Queen – Mother / I'm your daddy / Highway to the sun / 1995 / By the light of the Silbury moon / Adam and Eve hit the road / Just like Pooh Bear / Girl-call / Greedhead detector / Don't take roots / Senile get / The lonely guy / Cryingbabiessleeplessnights / Leli B. / Road of dreams / When I walk through the land of fear.

Echo Cooking Vinyl

Jul 96. (7"white-ep/cd-ep) *(ECS/+CDX 022)* **I COME FROM ANOTHER PLANET, BABY. / HOW DO I UNDERSTAND MY MOTORMAN? / IF I COULD DO IT ALL OVER AGAIN, I'D DO IT OVER YOU** [34] [-]
(cd-s) *(ECSCD 022)* – Ambulance: Weesex post-ambient therapy.

Sep 96. (7"white) *(ECS 025)* **PLANETARY SIT-IN. / CUMMER IN SUMMERTIME / TORCH** [34] [-]
(cd-s) *(ECSCX 025)* – ('A'-Radio sit-in mixes).

Oct 96. (cd/c/lp) *(ECH CD/MC/LP 12) <9007>* **INTERPRETER** [39] Feb97 [ ]
– I come from another planet, baby / I've got my TV and my pills / Planetary sit-in / Since I lost my head, it's awl-right / Cheap new age fix / Battle for the trees / Arthur / Spacerock with me / Re-directed male / Maid of constant sorrow / Loveboat / Dust.

— look out for 'DISCOVER ODIN: JULIAN COPE AT THE BRITISH MUSEUM' a partly spoken-word CD on 'Head Heritage' released in US 2001

BRAIN DONOR

— aka **JULIAN COPE** with **THIGHPAULSANDRA** – synths

Impresario not iss.

Apr 01. (7"/cd-s) *(IMP/+CD 007)* **SHE SAW ME COMING. / SHAMAN UFO** [ ] [-]

Jul 01. (7"/cd-s) *(IMP/+CD 009)* **GET OFF YOUR PRETTY FACE. / WHO WILL ENTERTAIN YOUR MORON** [ ] [-]

Sep 01. (cd/lp) *(IMPODD CD/LP 001)* **LOVE, PEACE & FUCK** [ ] [-]
– She saw me coming / Get off your pretty face / Pagan dawn / Odin's gift to his mother (theme from speed kills) / Hairy music / U-know! – You take the credit / Laghnasad / She's gotta have it. *(lp re-iss. Jul02; same)*

JULIAN COPE

Head Heritage not iss.

Jan 05. (d-cd) *(none)* **CITIZEN CAIN'D** [ ] [-]
– Hell is wicked / I can't hardly stand it / I'm living in the room they found Saddam in / Gimme head / Dying to meet you / I will be absorbed / Feels like a crying shame / World War pigs / Stomping dionysus / Homeless strangers / Living dead / Edge of death.

Bertus not iss.

Nov 05. (cd) *(none)* **DARK ORGASM** [ ] [-]
– Zoroaster / White bitch comes good / She's got a ring on her finger (& another through her nose) / Mr. Invasion / Nothing to lose except my mind / I've found a new way to love her / I don't wanna grow back / Death & resurrection show.

– (COPE) compilations, others, etc. –

Feb 85. (7"; as RABBI JOSEPH GORDON) *Bam Caruso; (NRICO 30)* **COMPETITION. / BELIEF IN HIM** [ ] [-]

May 90. (cd/lp) *Copeco-Zippo; (JUCD/JULP 89)* **SKELLINGTON** (1985 lost lp) [ ] [-]
– Doomed / Beaver / Me & Jimmy Jones / Robert Mitchum / Out of my mind on dope and speed / Don't crash here / Everything playing at once / Little donkey / Great white wonder / Incredibly ugly girl / No how, no why, no way, no where, no when / Comin' soon.

Jul 90. (cd/lp) *Mofo-Zippo; (MOFOCO CD/LP 90)* **DROOLIAN** [ ] [-]

Jul 92. (c-s/7") *Island; (C+/IS 534)* **WORLD SHUT YOUR MOUTH (remix). / DOOMED** [44] [-]
(12"+=/cd-s+=) *(12/CD IS 534)* – Reynard the fox / The elevators / Levitation.

Aug 92. (cd/c/d-lp) *Island; (CID/ICT/ILPSD 8000) <512788>* **FLOORED GENIUS – THE BEST OF JULIAN COPE AND THE TEARDROP EXPLODES 1981-1991** [22] Oct92 [ ]
– Reward / Treason / Sleeping gas / Bouncing babies / Passionate friend / The great dominions (; all TEARDROP EXPLODES) / The greatness & perfection of love / An elegant chaos / Sunspots / Reynard the fox / World shut your mouth / Trampolene / Spacehopper / Charlotte Anne / China doll / Out of my mind on dope & speed / Jellypop perky Jean / Beautiful love / East easy rider / Safesurfer.

Nov 92. (d-cd) *Island; (ITSCD 11)* **SAINT JULIAN / MY NATION UNDERGROUND** [ ] [-]

Nov 93. (cd/lp) *Nighttracks; (CD/LP NT 003) / Dutch East India; <DEI 8124>* **BEST OF THE BBC SESSIONS 1983-91 (FLOORED GENIUS VOL.2)** [ ] Feb94 [ ]
– The greatness and perfection of love / Head hang low / Hey, hey high class butcher / Sunspots / Me singing / Hobby / 24a Velocity Crescent / Laughing boy / O king of chaos / Reynard the fox / Pulsar / Crazy farm animal / Christmas mourning / Planet rider: transmitting / Soul medley: Free your mind and your ass will follow – Are you hung up? / You think it's love / Double vegetation. *(cd re-iss. May98 on 'Strange Fruit'; SFRSCD 61)*

Jun 97. (cd) *Island; (IMCD 251)* **THE FOLLOWERS OF SAINT JULIAN** [ ] [-]

Feb 99. (cd) *Island; (IMCD 260) <524636>* **LEPER SKIN (AN INTRODUCTION TO JULIAN COPE)** [ ] May99 [ ]
– Shot down / World shut your mouth / Trampolene / Planet ride / Transporting / Books / Charlotte Anne / Crazy farm animal / Hanging out and hung up on the line / Soul desert / The mystery trend / Pristeen / Double vegetation / Upwards at 45 degrees / Safesurfer.

Sep 01. (cd) *Spectrum; (544586-2)* **THE COLLECTION** [ ] [-]

the CORAL

Formed: Hoylake, Wirral, England ... 1996 by neighbourhood friends JAMES SKELLY, IAN SKELLY, PAUL DUFFY, LEE SOUTHALL, BILL RYDER-JONES and finally NICK POWER on organ. Picking up where the LA'S left off, fellow scousers, The CORAL unleashed their Mersey-flavoured debut single 'SHADOWS FALL' in 2001 and were, instantly, hailed by NME as the best new band in England. 'THE OLDEST PATH' EP was released in the same year, as hype surrounding the band began to reach fever pitch. The momentum was carried into 2002 which saw the release of the 'SKELETON KEY' EP and also their self-titled UK Top 5 debut album. A joyous, neo-psychedelic record, the eponymous 'THE CORAL', established the group as natural successors to the long line of great Liverpudlian bands and, no, that does not include SPACE. Exactly a year on, summer 2003 produced yet another fantastic set of songs via their sophomore set, 'MAGIC AND MEDICINE'. Featuring major UK hits, 'DON'T THINK YOU'RE THE FIRST' and 'PASS IT ON', the sextet came of age, recreating a feel for the past (LOVE, the LA's, etc.) while still having twelve feet firmly set in the present/future. IAN BROUDIE remained on board for mini-set, 'NIGHTFREAK AND THE SONS OF BECKER' (2004), a UK Top 5 entry which plugged the gap until the release of third album proper, 'THE INVISIBLE INVASION' (2005). With BROUDIE making way for PORTISHEAD duo GEOFF BARROW and ADRIAN UTLEY, the ound was darker and more direct, the most impressive DOORS-f-perception production since the INSPIRAL CARPETS heyday. Highlights on the UK Top 3 set included JIM MORRISON-Paints t Black opener 'SHE SINGS THE MOURNING' and even more DOORS-ish 'THE OPERATOR'. The mid-60s were still floating round in the mix, especially on the pristine pop of Top 10 hit, 'IN THE MORNING'.

lbum rating: THE CORAL (*8) / MAGIC AND MEDICINE (*8) / NIGHTFREAK AND THE SONS OF BECKER mini (*6) / THE INVISIBLE NVASION (*7)

AMES SKELLY – vocals, guitar / **LEE SOUTHALL** – guitar, vocals / **NICK POWER** – organ / **BILL RYDER-JONES** – guitar, trumpet / **PAUL DUFFY** – bass, saxophone / **IAN SKELLY** – drums

Deltasonic not iss.

ul 01. (cd-ep) *(DLTCD 1)* **SHADOWS FALL EP** [ ] [–]
– Shadows fall / The ballad of Simon Diamond / A sparrow's song.

ec 01. (cd-ep) *(DLTCD 3)* **THE OLDEST PATH EP** [ ] [–]
– The oldest path / God knows / Short balled / Flys.

Deltasonic Sony

pr 02. (cd-ep) *(672522-2) <87023>* **SKELETON KEY EP** [ ] [ ]
– Skeleton key / Dressed like a cow / Darkness / Sheriff John Brown / Skeleton key (video). *<US-only+=>* – The oldest path.

ul 02. (7"m) *(DLT 005)* **GOODBYE. / GOOD FORTUNE / TRAVELLING CIRCUS** [21] [–]
(cd-s+=) *(DLTCD 005)* – ('A'-CD rom).
(cd-s) *(DLTCD2 005)* – ('A') / Dressed like a cow (live) / Goodbye (live) / The Coral mini movie (video).

ul 02. (cd/lp) *(DLT CD/LP 006) <508478>* **THE CORAL** [5] Feb03 [ ]
– Spanish man / I remember when / Shadows fall / Dreaming of you / Simon Diamond / Goodbye / Waiting for the heartaches / Skeleton key / Wildfire / Badman / Calenders and clocks. *(lp+=)* – Simian technology. *(hidden cd track+=)* – Time travel.

Oct 02. (7"m) *(DLT 008)* **DREAMING OF YOU. / ANSWER ME / FOLLOW THE SUN** [13] [–]
(cd-s+=) *(DLTCD 008)* – ('A'-video).
(cd-s) *(DLTCD2 008)* – ('A') / Sweet Sue / Another turn in the lock / ('A'-acoustic video version).

Mar 03. (7") *(DLT 010)* **DON'T THINK YOU'RE THE FIRST. / SEE THROUGH BERGERAC** [10] [–]
(cd-s+=) *(DLTCDC 010)* – Witchcraft / ('A'-video).
(cd-s) *(DLTCDC2 010)* – ('A') / Tiger lily / Teenage machine age.

ul 03. (7") *(DLT 013)* **PASS IT ON. / SHADOWS FALL (acoustic)** [5] [–]
(cd-s+=) *(DLTCD 013)* – Run run.

ul 03. (cd/lp) *(DLT CD/LP 014) <512560>* **MAGIC AND MEDICINE** [5] Sep03 [ ]
– In the forest / Don't think you're the first / Liezah / Talkin' gypsy market blues / Secret kiss / Milkwood blues / Bill McCai / Eskimo lament / Careless hands / Pass it on / All of our love / Confessions of A.D.D.D.

Oct 03. (7") *(DLT 015)* **SECRET KISS. / GOD KNOWS (new mix)** [25] [–]
(cd-s+=) *(DLTCD2 015)* – Not the girl.
(cd-s) *(DLTCD 015)* – ('A') / Who's that knockin' / See my love / ('A'video).

Nov 03. (7"pic-d) *(DLT 017)* **BILL McCAI. / BOY AT THE WINDOW** [23] [–]
(cd-s+=) *(DLTCD 017)* – Nosferatu / ('A'-video).
(cd-s) *(DLTCD2 017)* – ('A') / When good times go bad / From a leaf to a tree.

an 04. (m-cd/m-lp) *(DLT CD/LP 018) <691889>* **NIGHTFREAK AND THE SONS OF BECKER** [5] Feb04 [ ]
– Precious eyes / Venom cable / I forgot my name / Song of the corn / Sorrow or the song / Auntie's operation / Why does the sun come up? / Grey harpoon / Keep me company / Migraine / Lovers paradise.

May 05. (7") *(DLT 033)* **IN THE MORNING. / GINA JONES** [6] [–]
(cd-s+=) *(DLTCD 033)* – The image of Richard Burton as Crom / ('A'-video).
(cd-s) *(DLTCD2 033)* – ('A') / Leeslunchboxbyblueleadandthevelcrounderpants.

May 05. (cd/d-lp) *(DLT CD/LP 036) <77898>* **THE INVISIBLE INVASION** [3] [ ]
– She sings the mourning / Cripples crown / So long ago / The operator / A warning to the curious / In the morning / Something inside of me / Come home / Far from the crowd / Leaving today / Arabian sand / Late afternoon. *(ltd-d-cd+=; DLTCDLE 036)* – live:- Pass it on / Shadows fall / Don't think you're the first / Dreaming of you / A warning to the curious / She sings the mourning / Something inside of me / Arabian sand.

Aug 05. (7") *(DLT 039)* **SOMETHING INSIDE OF ME. / THE CASE OF ARTHUR TANNEN** [41] [–]
(cd-s+=) *(DLTCD2 039)* – The box / ('A'-video).
(cd-s) *(DLTCD 039)* – ('A') / The conjuror.

☐ Billy CORGAN (see under ⇒ SMASHING PUMPKINS)

☐ Chris CORNELL (see under ⇒ SOUNDGARDEN)

Elvis COSTELLO

Born: DECLAN PATRICK MacMANUS, 25 Aug'54, Paddington, London, England. The son of a jazz bandleader, he grew up listening to the sounds of the day; the BEATLES (he was a member of their fanclub), the KINKS, the WHO and the sounds of Motown were all to instil in him a love of rock'n'roll and help shape his own musical style. Dividing his time between playing clubs at night and working as a computer operator during working hours (the strain on his eyes leading to the wearing of his now trademark glasses), he subsequently moved to London in 1974 to become frontman and songwriter for a country-rock group called Flip City. Flogging his demos far and wide, the newly formed 'Stiff' label duly took on his talent, McMANUS changing his name to ELVIS COSTELLO; 'Elvis', a challenge to the rock establishment, and 'Costello', his mother's maiden name. While at Stiff he met his long time collaborators NICK LOWE and Jake Rivera, who would in turn become producer and manager to COSTELLO. His first album was recorded in 24 hours, backed by CLOVER, a country and western bar band with a certain HUEY LEWIS at the helm (although he did not participate in the sessions). After little success with the first two singles, 'ALISON' and 'LESS THAN ZERO', the man resorted to playing outside a CBS Records international convention taking place at the Hilton in London. Although arrested, the stunt worked, and in '77 his first album, 'MY AIM IS TRUE' was released by 'Columbia' (US), stand out tracks including the aforementioned singles and 'WATCHING THE DETECTIVES'. Produced by LOWE, the record was hailed as one of the finest debuts in rock history, blending the Stiff sound of punk and new wave with COSTELLO's cynical observations on life. Voted Album of the Year in Rolling Stone's annual poll, COSTELLO toured the States with his newly assembled backing band, The ATTRACTIONS. America got its first taste of COSTELLO's independent stance when his appearance on Saturday Night Live turned into a scathing attack on the media. His next two albums, 'THIS YEARS MODEL' and 'ARMED FORCES' (originally titled Emotional Fascism) were to prove an artistic peak, as well as being commercially successful, the latter charting in the Top 10. Released in 1980, 'GET HAPPY' abandoned the new wave sound for a more 60's Motown approach. With 20 songs on the original LP (and 10 more on the CD reissue), it proved COSTELLO was in prime songwriting mode, the record swiftly followed by his fifth set, 'TRUST' (1981), sounding as captivating and twisted as its predecessor was fast and loose. In between these two sets was the Nashville covers album, 'ALMOST BLUE' more a curiosity than a stand out success. 'IMPERIAL BEDROOM', released in '82, is often cited as COSTELLO's best album, and was produced by the Beatles engineer, Geoff Emerick (who would later go on to produce the '96 effort 'ALL THIS USELESS BEAUTY'). Not surprisingly then, it was compared to the masterpieces of the BEATLES and the BEACH BOYS, and included such fan favourites as 'MAN OUT OF TIME' and 'THE LONG HONEYMOON'. 'PUNCH THE CLOCK', released in '83, and featuring CHET BAKER on the track 'SHIPBUILDING', was less ambitious than the previous album,

ELVIS COSTELLO

while 'GOODBYE CRUEL WORLD', released the following year, was his worst record by some margin, starting out as an attempt at folk-rock, but ending up as an example of the '80s sound gone wrong. By this time, a split had developed between COSTELLO and the ATTRACTIONS, and 'KING OF AMERICA' was the penultimate album recorded with this combination until 'BRUTAL YOUTH' in '94. With backing from The CONFEDERATES and co-production by T-BONE BURNETT, it featured a mixture of country and folk with a fair splattering of rockabilly with varied success. 'BLOOD & CHOCOLATE' (1986) was notable both for the return of NICK LOWE as producer and the man's split from the ATTRACTIONS. With LOWE at the helm, the record was far removed from his '84 effort, featuring a nastier, meatier version of 'THIS YEARS MODEL' plus 'POISONED ROSE', the latter track boasting the bass playing of the legendary jazz bassist RAY BROWN. Subsequently signing to 'Warners', his first release was the darkly comic and commercially successful 'SPIKE' (1989), its considerable sales due largely to the hit single, 'VERONICA', although it also featured songs of genuine outrage such as 'TRAMP THE DIRT DOWN' and 'LET HIM DANGLE'. The next few years saw COSTELLO become more adventurous in an attempt to break away from the past, symbolised by a change of image. 'MIGHTY LIKE A ROSE' remains arguably his most underrated album, while the follow up, 'THE JULIET LETTERS' (featuring The Brodsky Quartet), mixed pop with chamber music to commercial failure but critical praise. 'BRUTAL YOUTH' in '94 saw the reunion of COSTELLO and the ATTRACTIONS (dubbed the Distractions) and included one of the most beautiful recordings of his career in 'ROCKING HORSE ROAD', while the follow up, 'ALL THIS USELESS BEAUTY', was the ATTRACTIONS' swansong and inexplicably a commercial failure. Collaborations outside of his albums for 'Columbia' and 'Warners' are numerous, COSTELLO winning a BAFTA with RICHARD HARVEY for the soundtrack to 'G.B.H.' and also contributing the track, 'MY MOOD SWINGS' to the Cohen Brothers film, 'The Big Lebowski'. Perhaps the most intriguing partnership never to see the light of day, save for three releases as obscure B-Sides, was his collaboration with country legend, GEORGE JONES, singing 'non-country' songs such as Hoagy Carmichael's 'MY RESISTANCE IS LOW' and Bruce Springsteen's 'BRILLIANT SURPRISE'. A collaboration was released at the back end of '98 featuring an album's worth of COSTELLO and BURT BACHARACH material, 'PAINTED FROM MEMORY', together again after the magnificent 'God Give Me Strength' (which was originally recorded on the 'Grace Of My Heart' soundtrack). A subsequent tribute album of COSTELLO's songs by the likes of JOHNNY CASH, JUNE TABOR, NICK LOWE and ROBERT WYATT demonstrated both the man's musical versatility and the songwriting skills which have made him such an integral part of the last 25 years of popular music. Solo once again, ELVIS COSTELLO was back in chart land courtesy of stripped-down, bare-bones set, 'WHEN I WAS CRUEL' (2002). Possibly short of production techniques, once provided by Mitchell Froom or Marc Ribot, the record still managed to encompass all of ELVIS's songwriting craft. It was exactly that craft which COSTELLO strived to chisel and refine with 'NORTH' (2003), yet another career diversion in which the restless songwriter looked once again to the fields of classical, easy listening and jazz for his inspiration (he had recently found a new love in jazz singer DIANA KRALL having split with CAIT O'RIORDON after 16 years of marriage). The result was a hushed set of elegant balladry and restrained, sophisticated pop, perhaps the most "adult"-sounding set of songs he's yet come up with. If 'IL SOGNO' (2004) was another polite and hugely ambitious foray into classical – a score for an an adaptation of Shakespeare's 'A Midsummer Night's Dream', commissioned by Italian ballet company Aterballeto and performed by the London Symphony Orchestra – COSTELLO (and the IMPOSTERS; pretty much a tweaked ATTRACTIONS) got seriously back to his roots with 'THE DELIVERY MAN' (2004). Touted as a concept set narrating the murderous love life of a Southern delivery dude, the record was more a reacquaintance with vintage Americana. The fact that it was released on 'Universal' subsidiary 'Lost Highway', featured guest spots from EMMYLOU HARRIS and LUCINDA WILLIAMS, as well as his Oscar nominated, T-BONE BURNETT-partnered contribution to the 'COLD MOUNTAIN' soundtrack, 'THE SCARLET TIDE', wasn't the whole story; lead track 'BUTTON MY LIP' ranked as the fiercest missive from rock's renaissance bard in many a year. A US Top 40 placing reflected its populist appeal, unlike the more specialist 'MY FLAME BURNS BLUE' (2006), another 'Deutsche Grammophon' job which barely scraped the charts. Co-credited to jazz-classical ensemble, the METROPOLE ORKEST, and recorded live at Holland's trendy North Sea Jazz Festival, the album was an unexpected delight for more discerning COSTELLO buffs, showcasing specially composed lyrics for both Charles Mingus' 'HORA DECUBITUS' (commissioned by Mingus' widow) and Billy Strayhorn's 'BLOOD COUNT', as well as hard swinging reworkings of his own past classics. The same year, COSTELLO performed the material of another black music legend, ALLEN TOUSSAINT, recording an album of duets with the New Orleans figurehead after appearing alongside him at various Hurricane Katrina benefits. More than half the songs on 'THE RIVER IN REVERSE', were TOUSSAINT originals although COSTELLO penned the title track.

• **Songwriters:** All penned by COSTELLO, bar NEAT NEAT NEAT (Damned) / I CAN'T STAND UP FOR FALLING DOWN (Sam & Dave) / SWEET DREAMS (Patsy Cline) / A GOOD YEAR FOR THE ROSES (Jerry Chestnut) / DON'T LET ME BE MISUNDERSTOOD (Nina Simone) / I WANNA BE LOVED (Farnell Jenkins) / THE UGLY THINGS (Nick Lowe) / YOU'RE NO GOOD (Swinging Blue Jeans) / FULL FORCE GALE (Van Morrison) / YOU'VE GOT TO HIDE YOUR LOVE AWAY (Beatles) / STEP INSIDE LOVE (Cilla Black) / STICKS & STONES (Ray Charles) / FROM HEAD TO TOE (Smokey Robinson) / CONGRATULATIONS (Paul Simon) / STRANGE (Screaming Jay Hawkins) / HIDDEN CHARMS (Willie Dixon) / REMOVE THIS DOUBT (Supremes) / I THREW IT ALL AWAY (Bob Dylan) / LEAVE MY KITTEN ALONE (Little Willie John) / EVERYBODY'S CRYIN' MERCY (Mose Allison) / I'VE BEEN WRONG BEFORE (Randy Newman) / BAMA LAMA BAMA LOO (Little Richard) / MUST YOU THROW DIRT IN MY FACE (Louvin Bros.) / POURING WATER ON A DROWNING MAN (James Carr) / THE VERY THOUGHT OF YOU (Ray Noble) / PAYDAY (Jesse Winchester) / PLEASE STAY (Bacharach-David) / RUNNING OUT OF FOOLS (Jerry Ragavoy) / DAYS (Kinks) / SHE (hit; Charles Aznavour) / etc. • **Trivia:** He has also produced The SPECIALS (1979) / SQUEEZE (1981) / POGUES (1985).

Album rating: MY AIM IS TRUE (*9) / THIS YEAR'S MODEL (*9) / ARMED FORCES (*9) / GET HAPPY!! (*8) / TRUST (*8) / ALMOST BLUE (*5) / IMPERIAL BEDROOM (*8) / PUNCH THE CLOCK (*7) / GOODBYE CRUEL WORLD (*5) / KING OF AMERICA (*7) / BLOOD & CHOCOLATE (*7) / OUT OF OUR IDIOT collection (*5) / THE COURIER soundtrack as Declan McManus w/ V/A (*4) / SPIKE (*5) / MIGHTY LIKE A ROSE (*5) / THE JULIET LETTERS with Brodsky Quartet (*5) / BRUTAL YOUTH (*6) / KOJAK VARIETY (*4) / ALL THIS USELESS BEAUTY (*5) / EXTREME HONEY compilation (*6) / PAINTED FROM MEMORY with Burt Bacharach (*5) / THE SWEETEST PUNCH re-working (*4) / THE VERY BEST OF ELVIS COSTELLO & THE ATTRACTIONS compilation (*8) / WHEN I WAS CRUEL (*5) / NORTH (*6) / IL SOGNO (*5) / THE DELIVERY MAN (*6) / MY FLAME BURNS BLUE (*6) / THE RIVER IN REVERSE w/ Allen Toussaint (*7)

ELVIS COSTELLO

(solo) – vocals, guitar with backing band The **SHAMROCKS,** (alias CLOVER) / **JOHN McFEE** – guitar / **ALEX CALL** – guitar, vocals / **SEAN HOPPER** – keyboards / **JOHN CIAMBOTTI** – bass / **MICHAEL SHINE** – drums

	Stiff	Columbia
Mar 77. (7") *(BUY 11)* **LESS THAN ZERO. / RADIO SWEETHEART**	☐	–

May 77. (7") *(BUY 14)* **ALISON. / WELCOME TO THE WORKING WEEK** [ ] [ ]
Jun 77. (7") *<3-10641>* **ALISON. / MIRACLE MAN** [–] [ ]
Jul 77. (7") *(BUY 15)* **(THE ANGELS WANNA WEAR MY) RED SHOES. / MYSTERY DANCE** [ ] [–]
Jul 77. (lp/c) *(SEEZ/ZSEEZ 3) <JC 35037>* **MY AIM IS TRUE** [14] Nov77 [32]
– Welcome to the working week / Miracle man / No dancing / Blame it on Cain / Alison / Sneaky feelings / (The angels wanna wear my) Red shoes / Less than zero / Mystery dance / Pay it back / I'm not angry / Waiting for the end of the world. *<re-iss. US Mar78 +=> (AL 35037>* – Watching the detectives. *(re-iss. Jul86 on 'Imp' lp/c/cd; FIEND/+CASS/CD 13) (re-mast.Mar93 & Aug99 on 'Demon'++=; DPAM 1)* – Radio sweetheart / Stranger in the house / Imagination (is a powerful deceiver) / Mystery dance / Cheap reward / Jump up / Wave a white flag / Blame it on Cain / Poison moon. *(d-cd iss.Sep01 on 'Demon' MANUS 101)*

ELVIS COSTELLO & THE ATTRACTIONS

— **STEVE NIEVE** (b.NASON)– keyboards repl. HOPPER to HUEY LEWIS & THE NEWS **BRUCE THOMAS** – bass, vocals (ex-QUIVER)repl. CIAMBOTTI, CALL + McFEE / **PETE THOMAS** (b.9 Aug'54, Sheffield, England)– drums (ex-CILLI WILLI, ex-WILKO JOHNSON)repl. SHINE

Oct 77. (7"m) *(BUY 20)* **WATCHING THE DETECTIVES. / BLAME IT ON CAIN (live) / MYSTERY DANCE (live)** [15] [–]
Nov 77. (7" *<3-10705>* **WATCHING THE DETECTIVES. / ALISON** [–] [ ]

Radar Columbia

Mar 78. (7") *(ADA 3)* **(I DON'T WANT TO GO TO) CHELSEA. / YOU BELONG TO ME** [16] [–]
Mar 78. (lp/c) *(XX LP/C 11) <35331>* **THIS YEAR'S MODEL** [4] [30]
– No action / This year's girl / The beat / Pump it up / Little Triggers / You belong to me / Hand in hand / (I don't want to go to) Chelsea * / Lip service / Living in Paradise / Lipstick vogue / Night rally *. *(free-7"w/ above) (SAM 83)* – STRANGER IN THE HOUSE. / NEAT NEAT NEAT *<tracks * repl. by* 'Radio Radio' *on US version> (re-iss. May80 on 'F-Beat'; XXLP 4) (re-iss. Apr84 on 'Imp'; FIEND/+CASS 18) (cd-iss. Jan86; FIENDCD 18) (re-mast.Mar93 & Aug99 on 'Demon'++=; DPAM 2)* – Big tears / Crawling to the USA / Running out of angels / Green shirt / Big boys.
May 78. (7") *(ADA 10)* **PUMP IT UP. / BIG TEARS** [24] [–]
Jul 78. (7") *<3-10762>* **THIS YEAR'S GIRL. / BIG TEARS** [–] [ ]
Oct 78. (7") *(ADA 24)* **RADIO RADIO. / TINY STEPS** [29] [ ]
Jan 79. (lp/c) *(RAD/RAC 14) <35709>* **ARMED FORCES** [2] [10]
– Accidents will happen / Senior service / Oliver's army / Big boys / Green shirt / Party girl / Goon squad / Busy bodies / Sunday's best * / Moods for moderns / Chemistry class / Two little Hitlers. *(free 7"w/ above) (SAM 90) <AE 71171>* LIVE AT HOLLYWOOD HIGH EP:- Accidents Will Happen / Alison / Watching The Detectives. *<track * repl. by* '(What's So Funny 'Bout) Peace, Love And Understanding' *on US version + re-issue> (re-iss. May80 on 'F-Beat'; XXLP 5) (re-iss. Apr84 on 'Imp' lp/c; FIEND/+CASS 21) (cd-iss. Jan86; FIENDCD 21) (re-mast.Mar93 & Aug99 on 'Demon'+=; DPAM 3)* – My funny valentine / Tiny steps / Clean money / Talking in the dark / Wednesday week / (above EP). *(d-cd re-iss. Oct02 on 'Demon'+=; MANUS 103)* – (live tracks).
Feb 79. (7") *(ADA 31)* **OLIVER'S ARMY. / MY FUNNY VALENTINE** [2] [ ]
May 79. (7"m) *(ADA 35)* **ACCIDENTS WILL HAPPEN. / TALKING IN THE DARK / WEDNESDAY WEEK** [28] [ ]

ELVIS COSTELLO

solo, but still used ATTRACTIONS

F-Beat Columbia

Feb 80. (7") *(XX 1)* **I CAN'T STAND UP FOR FALLING DOWN. / GIRLS TALK** [4] [ ]
Feb 80. (lp/c) *(XX LP/C 1) <36347>* **GET HAPPY!!** [2] [11]
– Love for tender / Opportunity / The imposter / Secondary modern / King Horse / Possession / Man called Uncle / Clowntime is over / New Amsterdam / High fidelity / I can't stand up for falling down / Black and white world / Five years in reverse / B movie / Motel matches / Human touch / Beaten to the punch / Temptation / I stand accused / Riot act. *(re-iss. Apr84 on 'Imp' lp/c; FIEND/+CASS 24) (cd-iss. Jan86; FIENDCD 24) (re-mast.May94 & Aug99 on 'Demon'+=; DPAM 5)* – Girls talk / Clowntime is over No.2 / Getting mighty crowded So young / Just a memory / Hoover factory / Ghost train / Dr. Luther's assistant / Black & white world / Riot act.
Apr 80. (7") *(XX 3)* **HIGH FIDELITY. / GETTING MIGHTY CROWDED** [30] [ ]
(12"+=) *(XX 3T)* – Clowntime is over (version 2).
Jun 80. (7") *(XX5)* **NEW AMSTERDAM. / DR. LUTHER'S ASSISTANT** [36] [ ]
(7"ep+=) *(XX 5E)* – Ghost train / Just a memory.

ELVIS COSTELLO & THE ATTRACTIONS

(same line-up)

Dec 80. (7"m) *(XX 12)* **CLUBLAND. / CLEAN MONEY / HOOVER FACTORY** [60] [ ]
Jan 81. (lp/c) *(XX LP/C 11) <37051>* **TRUST** [9] [28]
– Clubland / Lovers walk / You'll never be a man / Pretty words / Strict time / Luxembourg / Watch your step / New lace sleeves / From a whisper to a scream / Different finger / White knuckles / Shot with his own gun / Fish 'n' chip paper / Big sister's clothes. *(re-iss. Apr84 on 'Imp'; lp/c; FIEND/+CASS 30) (cd-iss. Jan86; FIENDCD 30) (re-mast.May94 & Aug99 on 'Demon'+=; DPAM 6)* – Black sails in the sunset / Big sister / Sad about girls / Twenty-five to twelve / Love for sale / Weeper's dream / Gloomy Sunday / Boy with a problem / Seconds of pleasure.
Feb 81. (7") *(XX 14)* **FROM A WHISPER TO A SCREAM. / LUXEMBOURG** [ ] [ ]
Sep 81. (7") *(XX 17)* **GOOD YEAR FOR THE ROSES. / YOUR ANGEL STEPS OUT OF HEAVEN** [6] [ ]
Oct 81. (lp/c) *(XX LP/C 13) <37562>* **ALMOST BLUE** [7] [50]
– Why don't you love me (like you used to do) / Sweet dreams / Sucess / I'm your toy / Tonight the bottle let me down / Brown to blue / Good year for the roses / Sittin' and thinkin' / Colour of the blues / Too far gone / Honey hush / How much I lied. *(re-iss. Apr84 on 'Imp' lp/c; FIEND/+CASS 33) (cd-iss. Jan86; FIENDCD 33) (re-mast.Oct94 & Aug99 on 'Demon'+=; DPAM 7)* – He's got you (live) / Cry cry (live) / There won't be me anymore (live) / Sittin' and thinkin' (live) / Honey hush (live) / Psycho (live) / Your angel steps out of Heaven / Darling, you know I wouldn't lie / My shoes keep walking back to you / Tears before bedtime / I'm your toy (live).
Dec 81. (7") *(XX 19)* **SWEET DREAMS. / PSYCHO (live)** [42] [ ]
Apr 82. (7"m) *(XX 21)* **I'M YOUR TOY (live). / CRY CRY CRY / WONDERING** [51] [ ]
(12"ep) *(XX 21T)* – ('A'side) / My shoes keep walking back to you / Blues keep calling / Honky tonk girl. (w/ The ROYAL PHILHARMONIC)
Jun 82. (7"m) *(XX 26)* **YOU LITTLE FOOL. / BIG SISTER / THE STAMPING GROUND (The Emotional Toothpaste)** [52] [ ]
Jul 82. (lp/c) *(XX LP/C 17) <38157>* **IMPERIAL BEDROOM** [6] [30]
– Beyond belief / Tears before bedtime / Shabby doll / The long honeymoon / Man out of time / Almost blue / . . .And in every home / The loved ones / Human hands / Kid about it / Little savage / Boy with a problem / Pidgin English / You little fool / Town cryer. *(re-iss. Apr84 on 'Imp' lp/c; FIEND/+CASS 36) (cd-iss. Jan86; FIENDCD 36) (re-mast.Oct94 & Aug99 on 'Demon'+=; DPAM 8)* – From head to toe / The world of broken hearts / Night time / Really mystified / I turn around / Seconds of pleasure / The stamping ground / Shabby doll / Imperial bedroom. *(d-cd iss.Oct02 on 'Demon'+=; MANUS 108)* – (alt. & live tracks).
Jul 82. (7") *(XX 28)* **MAN OUT OF TIME. / TOWN CRYER (alt.take)** [58] [–]
Jul 82. (7") *<CNR 03269>* **MAN OUT OF TIME. / (one-side)** [–] [ ]
(12"+=) *(XX 28T)* – Imperial bedroom.
Sep 82. (7") *(XX 30)* **FROM HEAD TO TOE. / THE WORLD OF BROKEN HEARTS** [43] [ ]
(below from the film 'Party Party' and released on 'A&M')
Nov 82. (7") *(AMS 8267)* **PARTY PARTY. / IMPERIAL BEDROOM** [48] [ ]
(below ELVIS as "The IMPOSTER" and issued on 'Imp-Demon')
May 83. (7") *(IMP 001)* **PILLS AND SOAP. / ('A'extended)** [16] [ ]
Jul 83. (7") *(XX 32) <04045>* **EVERYDAY I WRITE THE BOOK. / HEATHEN TOWN** [28] [36]
(12"+=) *(XX 32T) <44-04115>* – Night time.
Jul 83. (lp/c) *(XX LP/C 19) <38897>* **PUNCH THE CLOCK** [3] [24]
– Let them all talk / Everyday I write the book / The greatest thing / The element within her / Love went mad / Shipbuilding / T.K.O. (boxing day) / Charm school / The invisible man / Mouth almighty / King of thieves / Pills and soap / The world and his wife. *(re-iss. Sep84 lp/c/cd; ZL/ZK/ZD 70026) (re-iss. Jan88 on 'Demon' lp/c/cd; FIEND/+CASS/CD 72) (re-mast.Feb95 & Aug99 on 'Demon'+=; DPAM 9)* – Heathen town / The flirting kind / Walking on thin ice / Town where time stood still / Shatterproof / The world and his wife (live) / Everyday I write the book (live).
Sep 83. (7"/ext.12") *(XX 33/+T) <04266>* **LET THEM ALL TALK. / KEEP IT CONFIDENTIAL** [59] [ ]

(below also as "The IMPOSTER" and issued on 'Imp')

Apr 84. (7") *(TRUCE 1)* **PEACE IN OUR TIME. / WITHERED AND DEAD** 48

Jun 84. (7") *(XX 35)* *<05625>* **I WANNA BE LOVED. / TURNING THE TOWN RED** 25
(12"+=) *(XX 35T)* – ('A'extended smoochy'n'runny mix).
(12"+=) *(XX 35Z)* – ('A'discotheque version).

Jun 84. (lp/c) *(ZL/ZK 70317)* *<39429>* **GOODBYE CRUEL WORLD** 10 35
– The only flame in town / Home truth / Room with no number / Inch by inch / Worthless thing / Love field / I wanna be loved / The comedians / Joe Porterhouse / Sour milk cow blues / The great unknown / The deportees club / Peace in our time. *(cd-iss. Mar86; ZD 70317) (re-iss. Jan88 on 'Demon' lp/c/cd; FIEND/+CASS/CD 75) (cd re-mast.Feb95 & Aug99 on 'Demon'+=; DPAM 10)* – Turning the town red / Baby it's you / Get yourself another fool / I hope you're happy now / The only flame in town (live) / Worthless thing (live) / Motel matches (live) / Sleepless nights (live) / Deportee.

Aug 84. (7"/'A'disco-12") *(XX 37/+T)* *<04502>* **THE ONLY FLAME IN TOWN. / THE COMEDIANS** 71 Jul84 56
('A'disco-12"+=) *(XX 37Z)* *<44-05081>* – Pump it up (1984 dance mix).

— (In May'85, guested on JOHN HIATT single 'Living A Little')
(below as The COWARD BROTHERS (w/ T-BONE BURNETT) + issued on 'Imp')

Jul 85. (7") *(IMP 006)* **THE PEOPLE'S LIMOUSINE. / THEY'LL NEVER TAKE THEIR LOVE FROM ME**

the COSTELLO SHOW

featuring The ATTRACTIONS and The CONFEDERATES
Zadded **JAMES BURTON** – guitar / **MITCHELL FROOM** – keyboards / **JERRY SCHEFF** – bass / **JIM KELTNER** – drums / **RON TUTT** – drums (i.e. The CONFEDERATES)

F-Beat Columbia

Jan 86. (7") *(ZB 40555)* *<05809>* **DON'T LET ME BE MISUNDERSTOOD. / BABY'S GOT A BRAND NEW HAIRDO** 33
(12"+=) *(ZT 40556)* – Get yourself another fool.

Feb 86. (lp/c/cd) *(ZL/ZK/ZD 70946)* *<40173>* **KING OF AMERICA** 11 39
– Brilliant mistake / Lovable / Our little angel / Don't let me be misunderstood / Glitter gulch / Indoor fireworks / Little palaces / I'll wear it proudly / American without tears / Eisenhower blues / Poisoned rose / The big light / Jack of all parades / Suit of lights / Sleep of the just. *(re-iss. Jan88 on 'Demon' lp/c/cd; FIEND/+CASS/CD 78) (re-mast.Jul95 & Aug99 on 'Demon' cd+=/d-lp+=; DPAM/+LP 11)* – LIVE ON BROADWAY – Coward Brothers:- The people's limousine / They'll never take her love from me / Suffering face / Shoes without heels / King of confidence.

ELVIS COSTELLO & THE ATTRACTIONS

ELVIS, BRUCE, STEVE & PETE plus guest **NICK LOWE** – guitar

Imp-Demon Columbia

Aug 86. (7") *(IMP 007)* *<06326>* **TOKYO STORM WARNING. / (part 2)** 73
(12"+=) *(IMP 007T)* – Black sails in the sunset.

Sep 86. (lp/c/cd) *(FIEND/+CASS/CD 80)* *<40518>* **BLOOD & CHOCOLATE** 16 84
– Uncomplicated / I hope you're happy now / Tokyo storm warning / Home is anywhere you hang your head / I want you / Honey are you straight or are you blind? / Blue chair / Battered old bird / Crimes of Paris / Poor Napoleon / Next time around. *(cd re-mast.Sep95 & Aug99 on 'Demon'+=; DPAM 12)* – Seven day weekend / Forgive her anything / Blue chair / Baby's got a brand new hairdo / American without tears No.2 / A town called big nothing (really big nothing). *(cd w/ bonus interview disc) (d-cd iss.Feb02 on 'Demon' +=; MANUS 112) <US-iss on 'Rhino'; 78355>* – Leave my kitten alone / New rhythm method / Forgive her anything / Crimes of Paris / Uncomplicated / Battered old bird / Seven day weekend / Blue chair / Baby's got a brand new hairdo (live) / American without tears No.2 / All these things / Pouring water on a drowning man / Running out of fools / Tell me right now / Lonely blue boy.

Nov 86. (7") *(IMP 008)* **I WANT YOU. / (part 2)**
(12"+=) *(IMP 008T)* – I hope you say you're happy.

Demon Columbia

Jan 87. (7") *(D 1047)* **BLUE CHAIR. / AMERICA WITHOUT TEARS NO.2 (Twilight version)**
(12"+=) *(D 1047T)* – Shoes without heels.

May 87. (7"/12") *(D 1052/+T)* **A TOWN CALLED BIG NOTHING. / RETURN TO BIG NOTHING** –
(above as "McMANUS GANG" featuring SY RICHARDSON)

DECLAN McMANUS

aka COSTELLO, of course!

Virgin Virgin

Feb 88. (cd/c/lp) *(CD/TC+/V 2517)* *<90954-2/-4/-1>* **THE COURIER** (soundtrack)
– (other artists) / Painted villain / Stalkin' / Funeral music / Rat poison / Unpainted villain / Last boat leaving. *<US cd+=>* – Mad Dog / (+ other artists).

ELVIS COSTELLO

solo, with mostly **FROOM, KELTNER, PETE THOMAS** (2), **MICHAEL BLAIR** – percussion / **MARC RIBOT** – guitar / **JERRY MAROTTA** – drums / **PAUL McCARTNEY, ROGER McGUINN, CAIT O'RIORDAN, T-BONE BURNETT, CHRISSIE HYNDE** on 1 or 2, plus The DIRTY DOZEN BRASS BAND (GREGORY DAVIS, EFREM TOWNS, ROGER LEWIS, KEVIN HARRIS, KIRK JOSEPH, C. JOSEPH, plus loads more)

Warners Warners

Feb 89. (lp/c)(cd) *(WX 238/+C)(925848-2)* *<25848>* **SPIKE** 5 32
– ...This town ... / Let him dangle / Deep dark truthful mirror / Veronica / God's comic / Chewing gum / Tramp the dirt town / Stalin Malone / Satellite / Pads, paws and claws / Baby plays around / Miss Macbeth / Any king's shilling / Coal train robberies * / Last boat leaving. *(cd+= *) (<d-cd iss.Sep01 on 'Rhino'+=; 8122 74286-2>)* – demos:- Miss Macbeth / This town / Deep dark truthful mirror / Coal train robberies / Satellite / Pads, paws and claws / Let him dangle / Veronica / Tramp the dirt down / Baby plays around / Put your big toe in the milk of human kindness / Last boat leaving / Ugly things / You're no good / Point of no return / Room nobody lives in / Stalin Malone (vocal version).

Feb 89. (7") *(W 7558)* *<22981>* **VERONICA. / YOU'RE NO GOOD** 31 19
(12"+=/12"poster+=/cd-s+=/pic-cd-s) *(W 7558 T/TW/CD/CDX)* – The room nobody lives in / Coal train robberies.

May 89. (7"ep/10"ep) *(W 2949/+TE)* **BABY PLAYS AROUND / POISONED ROSE. / ALMOST BLUE / MY FUNNY VALENTINE** 65
(c-ep/12"ep/cd-ep) *(W 2949 C/T/CD)* – (2nd track repl. by) Point of no return.

Apr 91. (7"/c-s) *(W 0025/+C)* **THE OTHER SIDE OF SUMMER. / COULDN'T CALL IT UNEXPECTED #4** 43
(12"+=/cd-s+=) *(W 0025 T/CD)* – The ugly things.

May 91. (lp/c/cd) *(WX 419/+C/CD)* *<26575>* **MIGHTY LIKE A ROSE** 5 55
– The other side of summer / How to be dumb / All grown up / Invasion hit parade / Harpers bizarre / Hurry down doomsday (the bugs are taking over) / After the fall / Georgie and her rival / So like Candy / Interlude: Couldn't call it unexpected #2 / Playboy to a man / Sweet pear / Broken / Couldn't call it unexpected #4. *(re-iss. cd Feb95; 7599 26675-2) (<d-cd-iss. Nov02 on 'Rhino'+=;8122 78189-2>)* – Mischievous ghost / St. Stephen's day murders / The other side of summer / Deep dark truthful mirror / Hurry down doomsday / All growing up / Georgia and her rival / Forgive her anything / It started to come to me / I still miss someone / The last town I painted / Put your big toe in the milk of human kindness / Invasion hit parade / Just another mystery train / Broken.

— in Jul'91, ELVIS COSTELLO & RICHARD HARVEY issued the TV soundtrack for 'G.B.H.'; they later teamed up for 'JAKE'S PROGRESS'

Oct 91. (7") *(W 0068)* **SO LIKE CANDY. / VERONICA (demo)**
(12"+=/cd-s+=) *(W 0068 T/CD)* – Couldn't call it unexpected (live) / Hurry down doomsday (the blues are taking over).

— In 1992, he wrote material for WENDY JAMES (Transvision Vamp)

ELVIS COSTELLO / the BRODSKY QUARTET

with **MICHAEL THOMAS + IAN BELTON** – violins / **PAUL CASSIDY** – viola / **JACQUELINE THOMAS** – violincello (all co-wrote music with him)

Jan 93. (cd/c) *(<9362 45180-2/-4>)* **THE JULIET LETTERS** 18
– Deliver us / For other eyes / Swine / Expert rites / Dead letter / I almost had a weakness / Why? / Who do you think you are? / Taking my life in your hands / This offer is unrepeatable / Dear sweet filthy world / The letter home / Jacksons, Monk and Rowe / This sad burlesque / Romeo's seance / I thought I'd write to Juliet / Last post / The first to leave / Damnation's cellar / The birds will still be singing. *(cd re-iss. Dec96; same)*

Feb 93. (c-s) *(W 0159)* **JACKSONS, MONK AND ROWE / THIS SAD BURLESQUE** [ ] [–]
(cd-s+=) *(W 0159CDX)* – (interviews).

ELVIS COSTELLO

Mar 94. (7"/c-s) *(W 0234/+C)* **SULKY GIRL. / A DRUNKEN MAN'S PRAISE OF SOBRIETY** [22] [ ]
(cd-s+=) *(W 0234CD)* – Idiophone / ('A'album version).

Mar 94. (cd/c) *(<9362 45535-2/-4>)* **BRUTAL YOUTH** [2] [34]
– Pony St. / Kinder murder / 13 steps lead down / This is Hell / Clown strike / You tripped at every step / Still too soon to know / 20% amnesia / Sulky girl / London's brilliant parade / My science fiction twin / Rocking horse road / Just about glad / All the rage / Favourite hour. *(<d-cd iss.Feb02 on 'Rhino'+=; 8122 78390-2)>* – This is Hell (alt.) / Idiophone / Abandon words / Poisoned letter / A drunken man's praise of sobriety / Pony St. / Just about glad / Clown strike / Rocking horse road (demo) / 13 steps lead down (demo) / All the rage (demo) / Sulky girl (demo) / You tripped at every step (alt.)

Apr 94. (7"/c-s) *(W 0245/+C)* **13 STEPS LEAD DOWN. / DO YOU KNOW WHAT I'M SAYING?** [59] [ ]
(cd-s) *(W 0245CD)* – ('A'side) / Puppet girl / Basement kiss / We despise you.

Jul 94. (7"/c-s) *(W 0251/+C)* **YOU TRIPPED AT EVERY STEP. / YOU'VE GOT TO HIDE YOUR LOVE AWAY** [ ] [ ]
(cd-s+=) *(W 0251CD)* – Step inside love / Sticks & stones.

Nov 94. (c-s) *(W 0270C)* **LONDON'S BRILLIANT PARADE / LONDON'S BRILLIANT** [48] [ ]
(12"+=) *(W 0270T)* – My resistance is low / Congratulations.
(cd-s) *(W 270CD1)* – ('A'side) / Sweet dreams / The loved ones / From head to toe.
(cd-s) *(W 270CD2)* – ('A'side) / New Amsterdam / Beyond belief / Shipbuilding.

May 95. (cd/c) *(<9362 45903-2/-4>)* **KOJAK VARIETY** [21] [ ]
– Strange / Hidden charms / Remove this doubt / I threw it all way / Leave my kitten alone / Everybody's cryin' mercy / I've been wrong before / Bama lama bama loo / Must you throw dirt in my face / Pouring water on a drowning man / The very thought of you / Payday / Please stay / Running out of fools / Days. *(cd re-iss. Dec96; same)*

Aug 95. (cd; by ELVIS COSTELLO & BILL FRISELL) *(<9362 46073-2>)* **DEEP DEAD BLUE** [ ] Nov95 [ ]
– Weird nightmare / Love field / Shamed into love / Gigi / Poor Napoleon / Baby plays around / Deep dead blue.

ELVIS COSTELLO & THE ATTRACTIONS

Apr 96. (c-s) *(W 0348C)* **IT'S TIME / LIFE SHRINKS** [58] [ ]
(cd-s+=) *(W 0348CD)* – Brilliant disguise.

May 96. (cd/c) *(<9362 46198-2/-4>)* **ALL THIS USELESS BEAUTY** [28] [53]
– The other end of the telescope / Little atoms / All this useless beauty / Complicated shadows / Why can't a man stand alone / Distorted angel / Shallow grave / Poor fractured atlas. *(cd re-iss. Jul00; same)* *(<d-cd iss.Sep01 on 'Rhino'+=; 8122 74284-2>)* Starting to come with me / You bowed down / It's time / I want to vanish / Almost ideal eyes / My dark life (with BRIAN ENO) / The day is done (with FAIRFIELD FOUR) / What do I do now / The bridge I burned / demos:- It's time / Complicated shadows / You bowed down / Mistress and maid / Distorted angel / The world's greatest optimist / The only flame in town / The comedians (demo) / Days take care of everything / Hidden shame / Why can't a man stand alone.

Jul 96. (cd-s) *(W 0364CD)* **LITTLE ATOMS / WHY CAN'T A MAN STAND ALONE / ALMOST IDEAL EYES / JUST ABOUT GLAD** [ ] [ ]

Jul 96. (cd-s) *(W 0365CD)* **THE OTHER END OF THE TELESCOPE / ALMOST IDEAL EYES / BASEMENT KISS (live) / COMPLICATED SHADOWS (demo)** [ ] [ ]

Jul 96. (cd-s) *(W 0366CD)* **DISTORTED ANGEL / ALMOST IDEAL EYES / LITTLE ATOMS (DJ Food mix) / Lush: ALL THIS USELESS BEAUTY** [ ] [ ]

Jul 96. (cd-s) *(W 0367CD)* **ALL THIS USELESS BEAUTY / ALMOST IDEAL EYES / Sleeper: THE OTHER END OF THE TELESCOPE / DISTORTED ANGEL (Tricky mix)** [ ] [ ]

ELVIS COSTELLO with BURT BACHARACH

Mercury Mercury

Sep 98. (cd/c) *(<538002-2/-4>)* **PAINTED FROM MEMORY** [32] [78]
– In the darkest place / Toledo / I still have that other girl / This house is empty now / Tears at the birthday party / Such unlikely lovers / My thief / Long division / Painted from memory / The sweetest punch / What's her name today? / God give me strength. *(special iss.Apr99; 546165-2)*

Apr 99. (cd-s) *(870965-2)* **TOLEDO / TEARS AT THE BIRTHDAY PARTY (live) / INCH BY INCH (live)** [72] [ ]
(cd-s) *(870967-2)* – ('A'side) / Such unlikely lovers (live) / Baby plays around (live).

Jul 99. (c-s) *(MERMC 521)* **SHE / THE HOUSE IS EMPTY NOW** [19] [ ]
(cd-s+=) *(MERDD 521)* – What's her name today.
(cd-s) *(MERCD 521)* – ('A'side) / Painted from memory / Sweetest punch.

Sep 99. (cd; ELVIS COSTELLO / BURT BACHARACH / BILL FRISELL) *(<559865-2>)* **THE SWEETEST PUNCH** (re-workings of above) [ ] [ ]

ELVIS COSTELLO

Mercury Mercury

Apr 02. (7") *(582887-7)* **TEAR OFF YOUR OWN HEAD (IT'S A DOLL'S REVOLUTION). / WHEN I WAS CRUEL** [58] [–]
(cd-s) *(582887-2)* – ('A'side) / The Imposter vs. the floodtide (dust and petals) / Revolution doll.

Apr 02. (cd)(d-lp) *(<586 829-2>)(586 775-1)* **WHEN I WAS CRUEL** [17] [20]
– 45 / Spooky girlfriend / Tear off your own head (it's a doll's revolution) / When I was cruel No.2 / Soul for hire / 15 petals / Tart / Dust 2 . . . / Dissolve / Alibi / . . .Dust / Daddy can I turn this? / My little blue window / Episode of blonde / Radio silence. *(d-cd iss.Sep02 +=; 63894-2)* – Smile (New York sudio version) / When I was cruel (studio) / 15 petals (live) / Spooky girlfriend (live) / Honeyhouse (Imposter mix) / Watching the detectives / My funny valentine (live) / Dust (live) / Uncomplicated (live) / Smile (live).

Sep 02. (7") *(063915-7)* **45. / MY MOOD SWINGS** [ ] [–]
(cd-s+=) *(063915-2)* – Peroxide side (blunt cut).

Deutsche Grammophon Deutsche Grammophon

Sep 03. (cd) *(9809165)* *<99902>* **NORTH** [44] [57]
– You left me in the dark / Someone took the words away / When did I stop dreaming? / You turned to me / Fallen / When it sings / Still / Let me tell you about her / Can you be true? / When green eyes turn blue / I'm in the mood again.

—— next with London Symphony Orchestra

Sep 04. (cd) *(471577-2)* *<32840-2>* **IL SOGNO** (ballet soundtrack) [ ] [ ]
– Prelude / Overture / Puck 1 / Act One:- The court / The state of affairs / Hermia and Lysander / The jealousy of Helena / Worker's playtime / Act Two:- Oberon and Titania / The conspiracy of Oberon and Puck / Slumber / Puck 2 / The identity parade / The face of Bottom / The spark of love / Tormentress / Oberon humbled / Twisted – Entangled – Transform and exchange / The fairy and the ass / Sleep / Bottom awakes / Lovers arise / Act Three:- The play / The wedding.

ELVIS COSTELLO & THE IMPOSTERS

Universal Lost Highway

Sep 04. (cd/d-lp) *(9863727)* *<259302/B0000616-OT-ST01>* **THE DELIVERY MAN** [73] [40]
– Button my lip / Country darkness / There's a story in your voice (feat. LUCINDA WILLIAMS) / Either side of the town / Bedlam / The delivery man / Monkey to man / Nothing clings like ivy (feat. EMMYLOU HARRIS) / The name of this thing is not love / Heart shaped bruise (feat. EMMYLOU HARRIS) / She's pulling out the pin *[UK-only]* / Needle time / The judgement / The scarlet tide (feat. EMMYLOU HARRIS). *(cd re-iss. Feb05 on 'Lost Highway'+=; 2103601)* – Bedlam (live in Memphis video). *(d-cd+=)*– The Clarksdale Sessions:- The monkey / Country darkness / Needle time / The scarlet tide / In another room / The delivery man / The dark end of the street.

ELVIS COSTELLO with the METROPOLE ORKEST

Deutsche Grammophon Deutsche Grammophon

Mar 06. (d-cd) *(4775961)* *<5994>* **MY FLAME BURNS BLUE** (live mid 2004) [ ] [ ]

– Hora decubitus / Favourite hour / That's how you got killed before / Upon a veil of midnight blue / Clubland / Almost blue / Speak darkly, my angel / Almost ideal eyes / Can you be true? / Put away forbidden playthings / Episode of blonde / My flame burns blue (blood count) / Watching the detectives / God gave me strength / Prelude / Overture / Puck one / The court / Workers' playtime / Oberon and Titania / The conspiracy of Oberon and Puck / Puck two / The identity parade / The face of Bottom / The spark of love / Tormentress / Oberon humbled / Twisted – Entangled – Transform and exchange / The fairy and the ass / Sleep / The play / The wedding.

ELVIS COSTELLO / ALLEN TOUSSAINT

Verve Forecast — Verve Forecast

May 06. (cd)(lp) *(9856057)(9856454) <6660><683901>* **THE RIVER IN REVERSE** ☐ Jun06 ☐
– On your way down / Nearer to you / Tears, tears and more tears / The sharpest thorn / Who's gonna help brother get further? / The river in reverse / Freedom for the stallion / Broken promise land / Ascension day / International echo / All these things / Wonder woman / Six-fingered man.

– compilations, others, etc. –

Mar 80. (c) *F-Beat; (XXC 6)* **TEN BLOODY MARYS & TEN HOW'S YOUR FATHERS** ☐ –
– Clean money / Girls talk / Talking in the dark / Radio sweetheart / Big tears / Crawling to the USA / Just a memory / Watching the detectives / Stranger in the house / Clowntime is over (N.2) / Getting mighty crowded / Hoover factory / Tiny steps / (What's so funny 'bout) Peace, love and understanding / Dr. Luther's assistant / Radio radio / Black and white world (No.2) / Wednesday week / My funny valentine / Ghost train. *(re-iss. Apr84 on 'Imp' lp/c; FIEND/+CASS 27) (cd-iss. Jan86; FIENDCD 27) (re-iss. cd Mar93; FIENDCD 27X)*

Oct 80. (lp) *Columbia; <JC 36839>* **TAKING LIBERTIES** (virtually 'TEN BLOODY MARYS') – 28

Apr 85. (lp/c/cd) *Telstar; (STAR/STAC/TCD 2247)* **THE BEST OF ELVIS COSTELLO – THE MAN** 8 –
– Watching the detectives / Oliver's army / Alison / Accidents will happen / Pump it up / High fidelity / Pills and soap (THE IMPOSTER) / (I don't want to go to) Chelsea / New lace sleeves / A good year for the roses / I can't stand up for falling down / Clubland / Beyond belief / New Amsterdam / Green shirt / Everyday I write the book / I wanna be loved / Shipbuilding (THE IMPOSTER). *(re-iss. May86 on 'Imp' lp/c/cd; FIEND/+CASS/CD 52) (re-iss. cd Mar93 on 'Demon'; FIENDCD 52X)*

Apr 85. (7",7"green) *F-Beat; (ZB 40086)* **GREEN SHIRT. / BEYOND BELIEF** 68 –
(12"+=,12"green+=) *(ZT 40086)* – ('A'extended).
(d7"+=) *(ZB 40085-7)* – Oliver's army / A good year for the roses.
(Nov85; d7"+=) *(same)* – The people's limousine / They'll never take her love away from me.

Nov 85. (12"ep) *Stiff; (BUYIT 239)* **WATCHING THE DETECTIVES / RADIO SWEETHEART. / LESS THAN ZERO / ALISON** ☐ –

Oct 87. (lp/c/cd; under various pseudonyms) *Demon; (<FIEND/+CASS/CD 67>)* **OUT OF OUR IDIOT** ☐ ☐
– Seven day weekend / Turning the town red / Heathen town / The people's limousine / So young / American without tears No.2 / Get yourself another fool / Walking on thin ice / Blue chair / Baby it's you / From head to toe / Shoes without heels / Baby's got a brand new hairdo / The flirting kind / Black sails in the sunset / Imperial bedroom / The stamping ground / Little goody two shoes / Withered and died / A town called big nothing / Big sister. *(re-iss. cd Mar93; FIENDCD 67X)*

Oct 89. (d-lp/c/d-cd/dat) *Demon; (D-)FIEND CASS/CD/DAT 160)* **GIRLS, GIRLS, GIRLS** 67 –
– Watching the detectives / I hope you're happy now / This year's girl / Lover's walk / Pump it up / Strict time / Temptation / (I don't want to go to) Chelsea / High fidelity / Lovable / Mystery dance / Big tears / Uncomplicated / Lipstick vogue / Man out of time / Brilliant mistake / New lace sleeves / Accidents will happen / Beyond belief / Black and white world / Green shirt / The loved ones / New Amsterdam / Red shoes / King horse / Big sister's clothes // Alison / Men called uncle / Party girl / Shabby doll / Motel matches / Tiny steps / Almost blue / Riot act / Loved filed / Possession / Poisoned rose / Indoor fireworks / I want you / Oliver's army / Pills and soap / Sunday's best / Watch your step / Less than zero / Clubland / Tokyo storm warning / Shipbuilding. *(d-cd iss.Sep96 & Oct99; same)*

Nov 89. (c) *Demon; (FIENDCASS 161)* **GIRLS, GIRLS, GIRLS, VOL.2** (see above) ☐ –

Nov 93. (4xcd-box) *Demon; (DPAM BOX1)* **THE FIRST 2 1/2 YEARS** ☐ –
– (MY AIM IS TRUE / THIS YEAR'S MODEL / ARMED FORCES / LIVE AT EL MOCAMBO).

Nov 94. (cd/c/lp) *Demon; (DPAM CD/MC/LP 13) / Rykodisc; <40203>* **THE VERY BEST OF ELVIS COSTELLO** 57 Oct94 ☐
– Alison / Watching the detectives / (I don't want to go to) Chelsea / Pump it up / Radio, radio / (What's so funny 'bout) Peace, love and understanding / Oliver's army / Accidents will happen / I can't stand up for falling down / New Amsterdam / High fidelity / Clubland / Watch your step / Good year for the roses / Beyond belief / Man out of time / Everyday I write the book / Shipbuilding / Love field / Brilliant mistake / Indoor fireworks / I want you. *(cd re-iss. Oct99; same)*

Oct 97. (cd) *Warners; (9362 46801-2)* **EXTREME HONEY: THE VERY BEST OF THE WARNER BROS. YEARS** ☐ ☐
– The bridge I burned / Veronica / Sulky girl / So like candy / 13 steps lead down / All this useless beauty / My dark life / Other side of summer / Kinder murder / Deep dark truthful mirror / Hurry down doomsday (the bugs are taking over) / Poor fractured atlas / Birds will still be singing / London's brilliant parade / Tramp the dirt down / Couldn't call it unexpected, No.4 / I want to vanish / All the rage.

Aug 99. (d-cd/d-c) *Universal TV; (546490-2/-4)* **THE VERY BEST OF ELVIS COSTELLO** 4 –
– (What's so funny 'bout) Peace, love and understanding / Oliver's army / Watching the detectives / Alison / (I don't want to go to) Chelsea / Accidents will happen / Pump it up / I can't stand up for falling down / Radio, radio / Clubland / Good year for the roses / Man out of time / I wanna be loved / Everyday I write the book / Brilliant mistake / The other side of summer / Tokyo storm warning / Sulky girl / So like candy / Veronica / She / Big tears / Beyond belief / Lipstick vogue / Green shirt / Pills and soap / Tramp the dirt down / Shipbuilding / High fidelity / New lace sleeves / (The angels wanna wear my) Red shoes / Talking in the dark / New Amsterdam / I hope you're happy now / Riot act / My funny valentine / Indoor fireworks / Almost blue / I want you / God give me strength / That day is done / I want to vanish.

— his first 4 singles were also re-issued together around 1980 and could be found on 'Stiff' 10-pack Nos.11-20).

— The ATTRACTIONS released two singles and an album (Aug80) 'MAD ABOUT THE WRONG BOY' on 'F-Beat'.

ELVIS COSTELLO & RICHARD HARVEY

Demon — Demon

Jul 91. (cd/c/lp) *(DS CD/MC/LP 4)* **G.B.H.** (TV soundtrack) ☐ –
– G.B.H. opening titles: The life and times of Michael Murray / "It wasn't me" / Men of alloy / Lambs to the slaughter / Bubbles / The 'Goldilocks' theme / Perfume – the odour of money / Assassin (BARBARA DOUGLAS) / Pursuit suite / The roaring boy (PRUFROCK QUARTET) / " . . .So I used five!" / Love from a cold land / In a cemetary garden / "Smack 'im!" / Woodlands – oh joy! / "It's cold up there" / Going home service / Grave music / The puppet masters' work / "He's so easy" / Another time, another place / Closing titles. *<US-iss.Feb94 on 'Rykodisc'; RCD 20284>*

Nov 95. (cd) *(<DSCD 14>)* **JAKE'S PROGRESS** (TV soundtrack) ☐ Feb96 ☐
– Jake's Progress opening sequence / Map of Africa / Julie's pregnant pause / Monica's fortune telling / 'Cisco kid / Graveyard waltz / Housewarming / Moving in / Howling at the Moon / Unhappy home service / Ursine variations / Mrs. Rampton reminisces / A friend in need / Death of Alex – Closing titles / Remembering Alex / Leaving home / Eliot's heartbreak and flashback / Kate's abuse / Grave dance / Banquo / Fall from grace / Play with me, mummy.

☐ John COUGAR
(see under ⇒ MELLENCAMP, John Cougar)

COUNTING CROWS

Formed: Bay Area, San Francisco, California, USA . . . August '91 out of early 90's outfit, SORDID HUMOR (along with TOM BARNES on vocals and guitar plus bassist JIM GORDON). 'CROWS vocalist/songwriter ADAM DURITZ and guitarist DAVID BRYSON (on production only) had both been members of this folky outfit, 'Capricorn' releasing the album 'LIGHT MUSIC FOR DYING PEOPLE' after they were famous. COUNTING CROWS' success was mainly due to 'MR JONES', a highly melodic slice of laid-back rock that was caned by both MTV and radio, resulting in the T-BONE BURNETT-produced album, 'AUGUST AND EVERYTHING AFTER' (1993), selling by the million. The record (which featured MARIA McKEE on backing vocals) was a professional, coffee table-friendly package of Roots rock that at times came across like a more polished JAYHAWKS. Two further singles, 'ROUND HERE' and 'RAIN KING' were issued, although they failed to dent the Top 40, by which time BEN MIZE had been drafted in to replace BOWMAN. Their long-awaited GIL NORTON-produced sophomore set, 'RECOVERING OF THE SATELLITES' (1996), disappointed no one and duly climbed to No.1 (UK Top 5), minor British hits such as 'ANGEL OF THE SILENCES', 'A LONG DECEMBER' and 'DAYLIGHT FADING', obvious highlights. A tad ambitious was their next album (a double live set!), 'ACROSS THE WIRE' (1998), all the best tunes were there of course although it was only a moderate seller peaking at No.19 in the US chart. That three year long wait for a studio album was up in November '99, 'THIS DESERT LIFE' finally making it to the shelves and returning the reclusive COUNTING CROWS to the Top 10. Something of a departure from their downbeat recent efforts, 'HARD CANDY' (2002) was a bold, robust, meticulously crafted pop record. Rootsy, lovelorn, with the sad-eyed soul of an ageing poet, but a pop record nonetheless. DURITZ offered up his hard-won wisdom more engagingly than on previous outings while the dense weave of instrumentation added to an atmosphere of careworn joy. With its unconventional sequencing and inclusion of some filler, 'FILMS ABOUT GHOSTS: THE BEST OF' (2003) wasn't a great best of, although casual fans could find all the hits including the UK Top 20 cover of Joni Mitchell's 'BIG YELLOW TAXI'.

• **Songwriters:** DURITZ; some w /BRYSON, except ROUND HERE (Himalyans) / THE GHOST IN YOU (Psychedelic Furs) / OOH LA LA (Faces) / FRIEND OF THE DEVIL (Grateful Dead) / YOU AIN'T GOIN' NOWHERE (Bob Dylan) / START AGAIN (Teenage Fanclub) / RETURN OF THE GREVIOUS ANGEL (Gram Parsons) / etc.

Album rating: AUGUST AND EVERYTHING AFTER (*8) / RECOVERING THE SATELLITES (*7) / ACROSS THE WIRE – ALIVE IN NEW YORK (*6) / THIS DESERT LIFE (*7) / HARD CANDY (*7) / FILMS ABOUT GHOSTS: THE BEST OF . . . compilation (*8) / NEW AMSTERDAM (*6)

ADAM DURITZ (b. 1 Aug'64, Baltimore, Maryland) – vocals, piano, harmonica / **DAVID BRYSON** (b. 5 Nov'61) – guitar, vocals / **DAN VICKREY** (b.26 Aug'66, Walnut Creek, Calif.) – guitar / **MATT MALLEY** (b. 4 Jul'63) – bass, vocals / **CHARLIE GILLINGHAM** (b.12 Jan'60, Torrance, Calif.) – piano, organ, accordion, chamberlain, vocals / **STEVE BOWMAN** (b.14 Jan'67) – drums, vocals

Geffen Geffen

Oct 93. (cd/c) *<(GED/GEC 24528)>* **AUGUST AND EVERYTHING AFTER** 16 4
– Round here / Omaha / Mr. Jones / Perfect blue buildings / Anna begins / Time and time again / Rain king / Sullivan Street / Ghost train / Raining in Baltimore / A murder of one.

Apr 94. (7"/c-s) *(GFS/+C 69)* **MR. JONES. / RAINING IN BALTIMORE** 28 –
(cd-s+=) *(GFSTD 69)* – Rain king / ('A'acoustic).

Jun 94. (7"/c-s) *(GFS/+C 74)* **ROUND HERE. / GHOST TRAIN** 70 –
(cd-s+=) *(GFSTD 74)* – The ghost in you (live).

Oct 94. (c-s) *(GFSC 82)* **RAIN KING / A MURDER OF ONE** 49
(cd-s+=) *(GFSTD 82)* – Mr. Jones (acoustic live).

—— **BEN MIZE** (b. 2 Feb'71) – drums, vocals; repl. BOWMAN

Oct 96. (c-s) *(GFSC 22182)* **ANGEL OF THE SILENCES / ROUND HERE (live)** 41 –
(cd-s+=) *(GFSTD 22182)* – Recovering the satellites.

Oct 96. (cd/c) *<(GED/GEC 24975)>* **RECOVERING OF THE SATELLITES** 4 1
– Catapult / Angel of the silences / Daylight fading / Goodnight Elisabeth Children in bloom / Have you seen me lately? / Miller's angels / Anothe horsedreamer's blues / Recovering the satellites / Monkey / Mercury / long December / Walkaways.

Dec 96. (c-s) *(GFSC 22190)* **A LONG DECEMBER. / GHOST TRAIN (live)** 62 –
(cd-s+=) *(GFSTD 22190)* – Sullivan Street (live).

May 97. (c-s) *(GFSC 22247)* **DAYLIGHT FADING / DAYLIGHT FADING (live)** 54 –
(cd-s+=) *(GFSTD 22247)* – Rain king (live).
(cd-s) *(GFSXD 22247)* – ('A'side) / Time and time again (live) / Miller' angels (demo).

Dec 97. (cd-s) *(GFSTD 21910)* **A LONG DECEMBER / GHOST TRAIN (live)** 68 –
(cd-s) *(GFSXD 21910)* – Sullivan Street (live).

Jul 98. (d-cd) *<(GED 25226)>* **ACROSS THE WIRE – LIVE IN NEW YORK** (VH1 storytellers // MTV live from the 10 spot) 27 19
– Round here / Have you seen me lately? / Angels of the silences / Catapult Mr. Jones / Rain king / Mercury / Ghost train / Anna begins // Recoverin the satellites / Angels of the silences / Rain king / Sullivan Street / Childre in bloom / Have you seen me lately? / Raining in Baltimore / Round here I'm not sleeping / A murder of one / A long December / Walkaways.

—— disc 1 rec. live at Chelsea Studios, New York, August 12, 1997 // disc 2 re live at Hammersmith Ballroom, New York, November 6th, 1997

Oct 99. (cd-s) *(497188-2) <album cut>* **HANGINAROUND / MERCURY / GOODNIGHT ELIZABETH** 46 28
(cd-s) *(497184-2)* – ('A'side) / Baby I'm a big star / Omaha.

Nov 99. (cd/c) *<(490415-2/-4)>* **THIS DESERT LIFE** 19 8
– Hanginaround / Mrs. Potter's lullaby / Amy hit the atmosphere Four days / All my friends / High life / Colorblind / I wish I was girl / Speedway / St. Robinson in his Cadillac dream. *(lp-iss.Mar03 o 'Universal'; AA69490415-1)*

Jun 02. (c-s) *(497741-4)* **AMERICAN GIRLS / START AGAIN** 33
(cd-s+=) *(497745-2)* – Someday / ('A'-video).
(cd-s) *(497740-2)* – ('A') / Blues run the game / Mercy.

Jul 02. (cd) *<(493366-2)>* **HARD CANDY** 9 5
– Hard candy / American girls / Good time / If I could give all my lo (Richard Manuel is dead) / Goodnight L.A. / Butterfly in reverse / Miami New frontier / Carriage / Black and blue / Why should you come when call? / Up all night (Frankie Miller goes to Hollywood) / Holiday in Spai *(UK re-iss. Jan03 +=; 493560-2)(hit No.40)* – 4 white stallions / You ain going nowhere / Big yellow taxi.

Feb 03. (c-s; by COUNTING CROWS & VANESSA CARLTON) *(497831-4)* **BIG YELLOW TAXI / AMERICAN GIRLS (live acoustic)** 16 –
(cd-s) *(497849-2)* – ('A'side) / If I could give all my love (Richard Manu is dead) (live acoustic) / Hard candy (live acoustic) / ('A'-video).
(cd-s) *(497830-2)* – ('A'side) / Amie / Miami (live acoustic).

Jun 03. (cd-s) *(980683-0)* **IF I COULD GIVE ALL MY LOVE / BIG YELLOW TAXI (live) / Ooh la la (live)** 50 –
(cd-s) *(980683-1)* – ('A'side) / Long December (live) / Return of th grevious angel.

Jan 04. (cd) *(986179-0) <00016761-2>* **FILMS ABOUT GHOSTS: THE BEST OF . . .** (compilation) 15 Nov03 32
– Angels of the silences / Round here / Rain king / A long December Hanginaround / Mrs. Potter's lullaby / Mr. Jones / Recovering th satellites / American girls / Big yellow taxi / Omaha / Friend of the Devil Einstein on the beach (for an eggman) / Anna begins / Holiday in Spain She don't want nobody near.

Mar 04. (cd-s) *(9861994)* **HANGINAROUND '04 (rock mix) / FRIEND OF THE DEVIL (live in San Francisco) / AUGUST AND EVERYTHING AFTER (live in SAn Francisco)** 68 –

Jul 04. (7"pic-d) *(9862882)* **ACCIDENTALLY IN LOVE. / AMERICAN GIRLS (live in Oslo) / IF I COULD GIVE ALL MY LOVE – or – RICHARD MANUEL IS DEAD (live in Oslo)** 28 39

(cd-s+=) *<(9862881)>* – ('A'-video).
(above from the film, 'Shrek 2')

Jun 06. (cd) *(INTW 33101) <B00069690-2>* **NEW AMSTERDAM** (live at Heineken Music Hall February 4-6, 2003) [ ] [52]
– Rain king / Richard Manuel is dead / Catapult / Goodnight L.A. / 4 white stallions / Omaha / Miami / Hazy / Good time / St. Robinson in his cadillac dream / Perfect blue buildings / Hanginaround / Goodnight Elizabeth / Hard candy / Holiday in Spain. *(UK+=)* – Mr. Jones (live at the Ahoy Holland).

□ COVERDALE ° PAGE (see under ⇒ WHITESNAKE)

Graham COXON

Born: 12 Mar'69, Hanover, West Germany. Raised in London, guitarist COXON first hooked up with DAMON ALBARN at Goldsmith's College where they formed Brit-pop legends, BLUR. Following the worldwide success of 'Parklife' (1994) and the more experimental 'Blur' (1997), both songwriters took time out to work on various projects. While ALBARN undertook unconventional forays into soundtrack work and animated electro-pop (GORILLAZ), COXON released a straightforward solo album, 'THE SKY IS TOO HIGH' (1998), on his own 'Transcopic' imprint. Inspired by mavericks both homegrown and Stateside (SYD BARRETT, LOU BARLOW, JOHN FAHEY, etc.), this largely acoustic try-out was the beginning of an unexpectedly prolific solo career. Turning up the volume for the stacatto thrash and London versus New York noise of 'THE GOLDEN D' (2000), COXON revealed his love of vintage SONIC YOUTH more overtly than ever. 'CROW SIT ON BLOOD TREE' (2001) had a BEEFHEART-ed title and a blues-meets-BARRETT-meets-BUZZCOCKS agenda which charted his journey ever further from the BLUR blueprint. It came as no surprise then when COXON announced his departure from the band which had pretty much defined his career thus far. Fourth solo set (in as many years), 'THE KISS OF MORNING' (2002), was the troubadour's folk/country statement, even – like DYLAN before him – adapting and toning down his nasal sneer for the occasion, and inviting pedal-steel legend BJ COLE to play on the mellow-core 'MOUNTAIN OF REGRET'. Having got the Americana out of his system (and using the corporate muscle of 'Parlophone'), COXON finally came good with the Stephen Street-produced 'HAPPINESS IN MAGAZINES' (2004), a record that boasted a cleaner, classic BUZZ-punk sound and no less than three hits in comparison with his usual zero: 'FREAKIN' OUT' (twice!), 'BITTERSWEET BUNDLE OF MISERY', and 'SPECTACULAR'. Despite rumours of a BLUR reunion, the bespectacled songsmith kept up his punishing schedule with sixth album, 'LOVE TRAVELS AT ILLEGAL SPEEDS' (2006), another UK Top 30 entry and the source of COXON's second Top 20 hit, 'STANDING ON MY OWN AGAIN'.

Covers: THAT'S WHEN I REACH FOR MY REVOLVER (Mission Of Burma) / BILLY HUNT (Jam).

Album rating: THE SKY IS TOO HIGH (*7) / THE GOLDEN D (*5) / CROW SIT ON BLOOD TREE (*5) / THE KISS OF MORNING (*8) / HAPPINESS IN MAGAZINES (*8) / LOVE TRAVELS AT ILLEGAL SPEEDS (*8)

GRAHAM COXON – vocals, guitar / with various others

Transcopic — Caroline

Aug 98. (cd/lp) *(TRAN 005 CD/LP) <7560>* **THE SKY IS TOO HIGH** [31] [ ]
– That's all I wanna do / Where'd you go? / In a salty sea / A day is far too long / R U lonely? / I wish / Hard and slow / Me you, we two / Waiting / Who the fuck? / Morning blues. *(cd re-iss. Dec01 & Oct02; same)*

E.M.I. — E.M.I.

Jun 00. (cd/lp) *(<5 27024-2/-1>)* **THE GOLDEN D** [ ] [ ]
– Jamie Thomas / The fear / Satan I gatan / Fame and fortune / My idea of hell / Lake / Fags and failure / Leave me alone / Keep hope alive / Oochy woochy / That's when I reach for my revolver / Don't think about always. *(cd re-iss. Oct02; same)*

Transcopic — not iss.

Jul 01. (7"/cd-s) *(TRAN 011/+CD)* **THANK GOD FOR THE RAIN. / YOU WILL NEVER BE** [ ] [–]

Aug 01. (cd/d-lp) *(TRAN 010 CD/LP) <863151>* **CROW SIT ON BLOOD TREE** [ ] [–]
– Empty word / I'm goin' away / All has gone / Burn it down / Too uptight / Big bird / Tired / Hurt prone / Bonfires / Thank God for the rain / You never will be / A place for grief. *(re-iss. Oct02; same)*

— he'd now split from BLUR

Oct 02. (7") *(TRAN 020)* **ESCAPE SONG. / MOUNTAIN OF REGRET** [ ] [–]

Oct 02. (cd/d-lp) *(TRAN CD/LP 018)* **THE KISS OF MORNING** [ ] [–]
– Bitter tears / Escape song / Locked doors / Baby, you're out of your mind / It ain't no lie / Live line / Just be mine / Do what you're told to / Mountain of regret / Latte / Walking down the highway / Song for the sick / Good times.

Parlophone — E.M.I.

Mar 04. (7") *(R 6632)* **FREAKIN' OUT. / FEEL RIGHT** [37] [–]
(cd-s) *(CDR 6632)* – ('A') / All over me.
(cd-s+=) *(CDRS 6632)* – Singin' in the morning / ('A'-video).

May 04. (7") *(R 6637)* **BITTERSWEET BUNDLE OF MISERY. / MY LITTLE GIRL** [22] [–]
(cd-s) *(CDR 6637)* – ('A') / Right to pop!
(cd-s+=) *(CDRS 6637)* – All I wanna do is listen to the Yuz / ('A'-video).

May 04. (cd) *(<577519-2>)* **HAPPINESS IN MAGAZINES** [19] [ ]
– Spectacular / No good time / Girl done gone / Bittersweet bundle of misery / All over me / Freakin' out / People of the earth / Hopeless friend / Are you ready? / Bottom bunk / Don't be a stranger / Ribbons and leaves.

Jul 04. (7") *(R 6643)* **SPECTACULAR. / BILLY HUNT** [32] [–]
(cd-s) *(CDR 6643)* – ('A') / Life it sucks / I wish (live) / ('A'-video).

Oct 04. (cd-s) *(CDR 6652)* **FREAKIN' OUT / ALL OVER ME** [17] [–]
(cd-s+=) *(CDRS 6652)* – Singing in the morning / ('A'-video).

Feb 06. (7") *(R 6681)* **STANDING ON MY OWN AGAIN. / SAY SO WHAT** [20] [–]
(7"white) *(R 6681X)* – ('A') / Livin'.
(cd-s+=) *(CDR 6681)* – Right to pop! (Peel session) / ('A'-video) / (making of the video).

Mar 06. (cd)(d-lp) *(350519-2)(519135-0) <5568127>* **LOVE TRAVELS AT ILLEGAL SPEEDS** [24] [ ]
– Standing on my own again / I can't look at your skin / Don't let your man know / Just a state of mind / You & I / Gimme some love / I don't wanna go out / Don't believe anything I say / Tell it like it is / Flights to the sea (lovely rain) / What's he got? / You always let me down / See a better day. *(ltd-cd w/dvd+=; 354134-2)* – (DVD tracks).

May 06. (7") *(R 6691)* **YOU & I. / SEE-SAW** [39] [–]
(cd-s) *(CDR 6691)* – ('A') / Click click click.
(cd-s+=) *(CDRS 6691)* – Light up your candles / ('A'-video).

the CRAMPS

Formed: New York City, New York, USA ... 1975 by LUX INTERIOR and POISON IVY, who recruited fellow weirdos BRYAN GREGORY and PAM 'BALAM' GREGORY (the latter was replaced by MIRIAM LINNA, who in turn was superseded by NICK KNOX). The trashiest, sleaziest 50's throwbacks to ever besmirch the good name of rock'n'roll, The CRAMPS took the genre's inherit debauchery to its thrilling (and often hilarious) conclusion. Crawling from the mire of CBGB's punk scene like the proverbial Swamp Thing in one of their beloved B-movies, The CRAMPS started as they meant to go on, initiating their vinyl career in 1978 with an obscure cover, 'THE WAY I WALK'. The single was backed with a riotous mangling of The Trashmen's 'SURFIN' BIRD', as close to a theme tune as the band came. A follow-up, 'HUMAN FLY', introduced LUX's impressive capacity for disturbingly accurate animal (and insect!) noises, its voodoo surf twang and creeping tempo scarier than the frontman's skintight leotard. Subsequently signed to Miles Copeland's 'I.R.S.' label, The CRAMPS set up shop in Sun Studios, Memphis (where else?!) with producer ALEX CHILTON at the production helm, working on the material for their acclaimed debut set, 'SONGS THE LORD TAUGHT US' (1980). Featuring such bad taste gems as 'GARBAGEMAN' (more animal noises!), 'I WAS A TEENAGE WEREWOLF' and 'STRYCHNINE', the record further boosted the band's cult following. The departure of GREGORY after the 'DRUG TRAIN' single was the first in a long series of line-up changes through which IVY (the sexiest thing in stockings!) and INTERIOR were the only constants. With KID CONGO POWERS as a replacement, the band cut the less convincing 'PSYCHEDELIC JUNGLE' (1981), their final release for Copeland whom they later sued. A short spell with the French 'New Rose' label and then 'Big Beat' saw the release of the live mini 'SMELL OF FEMALE' (1983). This went at least some way to capturing the cheap thrills of a CRAMPS gig, though readers are advised to experience the real thing; if the primeval spirit of raw rock'n'roll doesn't move you, then the sight of a grown man in a leather thong and and high heels just might! INTERIOR had always modelled himself on a kind of ELVIS-from-the-crypt and in 1986, The CRAMPS met their maker, so to speak, on the classic 'A DATE WITH ELVIS'. The likes of 'THE HOT PEARL SNATCH', 'CAN YOUR PUSSY DO THE DOG?' and 'WHAT'S INSIDE A GIRL?', need no further explanation save that THE KING was no doubt turning in his grave. Though this marked a creative and commercial peak of sorts, The CRAMPS continued to think up the best song titles in the Western World over a string of late 80's/90's albums, including 'STAY SICK' (1990), 'LOOK MOM, NO HEAD' (1991; essential if only for the IGGY POP collaboration, 'MINISKIRT BLUES'), 'FLAME JOB' (1994) and 'BIG BEAT FROM BADSVILLE' (1997). Though they've hardly pushed back the boundaries of music, The CRAMPS are arguably even more essential now than in their heyday, if only to remind the current crop of indie dullards what it REALLY means to play "The Devil's Music". Now in their fifties (well, LUX, at any rate), the CRAMPS showed no signs of ageing gracefully with their first album of new material in over five years, 'FIENDS OF DOPE ISLAND' (2003). The most interesting titles of the album, and perhaps the year, had to be 'PAPA SATAN SANG LOUIE' and 'ELVIS FUCKS CHRIST', as good an indicator as any of the band's reliably static musical development.

• **Songwriters:** Most written by LUX and IVY except SURFIN' BIRD (Trashmen) / FEVER (Little Willie John) / THE WAY I WALK (Robert Gordon) / GREEN DOOR (Jim Lowe) / SHE SAID (Hasil Adkins) / JAILHOUSE ROCK (Elvis Presley) / MULESKINNER BLUES (Fendermen) / PSYCHOTIC REACTION (Count Five) / LONESOME TOWN (Ricky Nelson) / HARD WORKIN' MAN (Jack Nitzche) / HITSVILLE 29 B.C. (Turnbow) / WHEN I GET THE BLUES (Larry Mize) / HOW COME YOU DO ME? (. . .Joiner) / STRANGE LOVE (. . .West) / BLUES BLUES BLUES (. . .Thompson) / TRAPPED LOVE (Kohler-Fana) / SINNERS (Freddie & The Hitchhikers) / ROUTE 66 (Bobby Troup) / etc. • **Trivia:** Their fan club was surprisingly based in Grangemouth, Scotland (wee Marty fi the Nash ran it!)

Album rating: SONGS THE LORD TAUGHT US (*7) / PSYCHEDELIC JUNGLE (*7) / OFF THE BONE compilation (*8) / SMELL OF FEMALE (*6) / A DATE WITH ELVIS (*7) / STAY SICK (*6) / LOOK MOM, NO HEAD! (*5) / FLAMEJOB (*6) / BIG BEAT FROM BADSVILLE (*5) / FIENDS OF DOPE ISLAND (*5)

LUX INTERIOR (b. ERICK LEE PURKHISER, 21 Oct'46, Akron, Ohio) – vocals / **POISON IVY RORSCHACH** (b. KIRSTY MARLANA WALLACE, 1954, Sacramento, Calif.) – guitar / **BRYAN GREGORY** (b. Detroit, Mich.) – guitar / **NICK KNOX** (b. NICHOLAS STEPHANOFF) – drums repl. MIRIAM LINNA (later to The ZANTEES & The A-BONES) who had repl. PAM 'BALAM' GREGORY

not iss. Vengeance

Apr 78. (7") <666> **THE WAY I WALK. / SURFIN' BIRD** –
Nov 78. (7") <668> **HUMAN FLY. / DOMINO** –

Illegal I.R.S

Jun 79. (12"ep) *(ILS 12-013)* **GRAVEST HITS** –
– Human fly / The way I walk / Domino / Surfin' bird / Lonesome town *(re-iss. Sep82 – 7"blue-ep / re-iss. Mar83- 7"red-ep; same)*

Mar 80. (7") *(ILS 0017)* **FEVER. / GARBAGEMAN** –

Apr 80. (lp) *(ILP 005)* <SP 007> **SONGS THE LORD TAUGHT US**
– TV set / Rock on the Moon / Garbageman / I was a teenage werewolf Sunglasses after dark / The mad daddy / Mystery plane / Zombie dance What's behind the mask / Strychnine / I'm cramped / Tear it up / Fever *(cd-iss. Jul98 on 'E.M.I.'; 493836-2)*

May 80. (7") <IR 9014> **DRUG TRAIN. / GARAGEMAN** –

Jul 80. (7"m) *(ILS 021)* **DRUG TRAIN. / LOVE ME / I CAN HARDLY STAND IT** –

— **KID CONGO POWERS** (b. BRIAN TRISTAN, 27 Mar'61, La Puente, Calif. – guitar; repl. JULIEN BOND, who had repl. GREGORY for two month mid 1980 (BRYAN was to die on 10th January, 2001)

I.R.S. I.R.S

May 81. (7"yellow) *(PFS 1003)* <IR 9021> **GOO GOO MUCK. / SHE SAID** Aug81

May 81. (lp) <(SP 70016)> **PSYCHEDELIC JUNGLE** Jul81
– Green fuzz / Goo goo muck / Rockin' bones / Voodoo idol Primitive / Caveman / The crusher / Don't eat stuff off the sidewalk Can't find my mind / Jungle hop / The natives are restless / Unde the wires / Beautiful gardens / Green door. *(cd-iss. Sep98 on 'E.M.I. 496504-2)*

Oct 81. (12"m) *(PFSX 1008)* **THE CRUSHER. / SAVE IT / NEW KIND OF KICK** –

— (LUX, IVY & NICK were joined by **IKE KNOX** (Nick's cousin) – guitar repl. KID CONGO who returned to GUN CLUB (appeared on live track 83-84)

Big Beat not iss

Nov 83. (red-m-lp) *(NED 6)* **SMELL OF FEMALE (live)** 74 –
– Faster pussycat / I ain't nuthin' but a gorehound / Psychotic reaction The most exhalted potentate of love / You got good taste / Call of th wig hat. *(pic-lp Jun84; NEDP 6) (re-iss. Feb91 cd+=/c+=; CDWIKM/WIKM 95)* – Beautiful gardens / She said / Surfin' dead. *(lp re-mast.Nov01 o 'Vengeance'; VENG 670)*

— (signed to below label in France)

New Rose New R

Mar 84. (7"/7"pic-d) *(NEW 28/+P)* **FASTER PUSSYCAT. / YOU GOT GOOD TASTE** – French –

Mar 84. (7"colrd;various) *(NEW 33)* **I AIN'T NUTHIN' BUT A GOREHOUND. / WEEKEND ON MARS** – French –

— **CANDY FUR** (DEL-MAR) – guitar; repl. IKE

Big Beat not is

Nov 85. (7"orange) *(NS 110)* **CAN YOUR PUSSY DO THE DOG? / BLUE MOON BABY** 68 –
(12"blue+=) *(NST 110)* – Georgia Lee Brown.

Feb 86. (blue-lp/c/cd) *(WIKA/WIKC/CDWIK 46)* **A DATE WITH ELVIS** 34 –
– How far can too far go / The hot pearl snatch / People ain't too good What's inside a girl? / Can your pussy do the dog? / Kizmiaz / Cornfe dames / Chicken / (Hot pool of) Woman need / Aloha from Hell / It' just that song. *<US-iss.1994 on 'Capitol'; 73579> (lp re-mast.Nov01 o 'Vengeance'; VENG 671)*

May 86. (7") *(NS 115)* **WHAT'S INSIDE A GIRL? / GET OFF THE ROAD** –
(12"+=) *(NST 115)* – Give me a woman.
(Mar87; cd-s++=) *(CRAMP 1)* – Scene / Heart of darkness.

Enigma Enign

Jan 90. (7"/7"sha-pic-d/c-s) *(ENV/+PD/TC 17)* **BIKINI GIRLS WITH MACHINE GUNS. / JACKYARD BACKOFF** 35
(12"+=/cd-s+=) *(12ENV/ENVCD 17)* – Her love rubbed off.

Feb 90. (cd/c/lp) *(CDENV/TCENV/ENVLP 1001)* <73543> **STAY SICK** 62
– Bop pills / Goddam rock'n'roll / Bikini girls with machine guns / A women are bad / Creature from the black leather lagoon / Shortenin bread / Daisy's up your butterfly / Everything goes / Journey to the centr of a girl / Mama oo pow pow / Saddle up a buzz buzz / Muleskinne blues. *(cd+=)* – Her love rubbed off. *(pic-lp Nov90; ENVLPPD 101) (re iss. Feb94 cd/lp; CD+/WIKD 126) (lp re-mast.Nov01 on 'Vengeance'; VEN 672)*

Apr 90. (7"/c-s) *(ENV/+TC 19)* **ALL WOMEN ARE BAD. / TEENAGE RAGE (live)** –

(12"+=/12"pic-d+=/cd-s+=) *(12ENV/12ENVPD/ENVCD 19)* – King of the drapes (live) / High school hellcats (live).

Aug 90. (7") *(ENV 22)* **CREATURE FROM THE BLACK LEATHER LAGOON. / JAILHOUSE ROCK** [ ] [–]
(12"+=/12"pic-d+=/cd-s+=) *(12ENV/12ENVPD/CDENV 22)* – Beat out my love.

Sep 90. (cd-ep) *<773617-2>* **CREATURE FROM THE BLACK LEATHER LAGOON / JAILHOUSE ROCK / JACKYARD BACKOFF / BEAT OUT MY LOVE / HER LOVE RUBBED OFF** [–] [ ]

— **LUX & IVY** were joined by **SLIM CHANCE** – guitar (ex-PANTHER BURNS) / **JIM SCLAVUNOS** – drums

Big Beat | Restless

Sep 91. (7") *(NST 135)* **EYEBALL IN MY MARTINI. / WILDER WILDER FASTER FASTER** [ ] [–]
(12"+=/cd-s+=) *(12/CD NST 135)* – Wilder wilder faster faster.

Sep 91. (cd/c/lp) *(CDWIK/WIKDC/WIKAD 101) <72586>* **LOOK MOM, NO HEAD!** [ ] [ ]
– Dames, booze, chains and boots / Two headed sex change / Blow up your mind / Hard workin' man / Miniskirt blues / Alligator stomp / I wanna get in your pants Bend over, I'll drive / Don't get funny with me / Eyeball in my Martini / Hipsville 29 B.C. / When I get the blues (the strangeness in me). *(also pic-lp/pic-cd; WIKDP/CDWIKD 101) (lp re-mast.Nov01 on 'Vengeance'; VENG 673)*

— **NICKY ALEXANDER** – drums (ex-WEIRDOS); repl. JIM

Sep 92. (cd-ep) *(CDNST 136)* **BLUES FIX EP** [ ] [–]
– Hard workin' man / It's mighty crazy / Jelly roll rock / Shombalor.

— **HARRY DRUMDINI** – drums; repl. NICKY

Creation | Medicine – Warners

Oct 94. (7") *(CRE 180)* **ULTRA TWIST! / CONFESSIONS OF A PSYCHO CAT** [ ] [–]
(12"+=)(cd-s+=) *(CRE 180T)(CRESCD 180)* – No club love wolf.

Oct 94. (cd/c/lp) *(CRECD/C-CRE/CRELP 170) <24592>* **FLAMEJOB** [ ] [ ]
– Mean machine / Ultra twist / Let's get f*cked up / Nest of the cuckoo bird / I'm customized / Sado country auto show / Naked girl falling down the stairs / How come you do me? / Inside out and upside down (with you) / Trapped love / Swing the big eyed rabbit / Strange love / Blues blues blues / Sinners / Route 66 (get your kicks on). *(cd re-iss. Jan01; same)*

Feb 95. (7") *(CRE 196)* **NAKED GIRL FALLING DOWN THE STAIRS. / LET'S GET F*CKED UP** [ ] [–]
(cd-s+=) *(CRESCD 196)* – Surfin' bird.

Epitaph | Epitaph

Oct 97. (cd/c/lp) *<(6516-2/-4/-1)>* **BIG BEAT FROM BADSVILLE** [ ] [ ]
– Cramp stomp / God monster / It thing hard on / Like a bad girl should / Sheena's in a goth gang / Queen of pain / Monkey with your tail / Devil behind that bush / Super goo / Hypno sex ray / Burn she devil, burn / Wet nightmare / Badass bug / Haulass hyena. *(lp re-mast.Nov01 on 'Vengeance'; VENG 674)*

Dec 97. (7") *(6527-7)* **LIKE A BAD GIRL SHOULD. / WET NIGHTMARE** [ ] [–]
(cd-s+=) *(6527-2)* – I walked all night.

Vengeance | Vengeance

Mar 03. (7") *(VENG 676)* **BIG BLACK WITCHCRAFT ROCK. / BUTCHER PETE** [ ] [–]

Apr 03. (lp/cd) *<(VENG 675/+CD)>* **FIENDS OF DOPE ISLAND** [ ] [ ]
– Big black witchcraft rock / Papa Satan sang Louie / Hang up / Fissure of Rolando / Dr. Fucker M.D. (Musical Deviant) / Dopefiend boogie / Taboo / Elvis fucking Christ! / She's got balls / Oowee baby / Mojo man from Mars / Color me black / Wrong way ticket.

– compilations, others, etc. –

May 83. (lp) *Illegal; (ILP 012) / I.R.S.; <SP 70042>* **OFF THE BONE** <US-title 'BAD MUSIC FOR BAD PEOPLE'> [44] Feb84 [ ]
– Human fly / The way I walk / Domino / Surfin' bird / Lonesome town / Garbageman / Fever / Drug train / Love me / I can't hardly stand it / Goo goo muck / She said / The crusher / Save it / New kind of kick. *(cd-iss. Jan87; ILPCD 012) (cd re-iss. 1992 on 'Castle'+=;)* – Uranium Rock / Good taste (live). *(cd re-iss. Apr98 on 'E.M.I.'; 493837-2) (lp re-iss. May01 on 'Simply Vinyl'; SVLP 327)*

1984. (4x7"box) *New Rose;* **I AIN'T NUTHIN' BUT A GOREHOUND. / WEEKEND ON MARS // FASTER PUSSYCAT. / YOU GOT GOOD TASTE // CALL OF THE WIG HAT. / THE MOST EXHALTED POTENTATE OF LOVE // PSYCHOTIC REACTION. / (one sided)** [–] French [–]
(all 4 either blue/white/black/green)

May 86. (7") *New Rose; (NEW 71)* **KIZMIAZ. / GET OFF THE ROAD** [–] [–]
(12"+=) *(NEW 70)* – Give me a woman.

Nov 87. (lp) *Vengeance;* **ROCKIN' AND REELIN' IN AUCKLAND, NEW ZEALAND (live)** [–] [ ]
(UK cd-iss. Sep94 on 'Big Beat'; CDWIKD 132) (lp re-mast.Nov01 on 'Vengeance'; VENG 669)

Sep 00. (3xcd-box) *EMI; (528345-2)* **SONGS THE LORD TAUGHT US / OFF THE BONE / PSYCHEDELIC JUNGLE** [ ] [–]

CREAM

Formed: London, England . . . mid '66 as the first ever supergroup, by ERIC CLAPTON, GINGER BAKER and JACK BRUCE, who'd all cut their teeth with top-flight R&B outfits earlier in the decade. This fine pedigree led to Robert Stigwood signing them to his newly-founded 'Reaction' label, after their lauded debut at The National Jazz & Blues Festival in Windsor on the 3rd of July '66. Their initial 45, 'WRAPPING PAPER', gave them the first of many Top 40 hits, a track that didn't inspire much critical praise. To end the year, they issued a debut album, 'FRESH CREAM', lifting from it the breezy psychedelic single, 'I FEEL FREE', a number which united BRUCE and poet/lyricist PETE BROWN in a new songwriting partnership. It also gave CREAM their biggest hit to date, reaching No.11 in the UK. Alongside original material, the album featured updated blues standards, 'SPOONFUL' (Willie Dixon), 'ROLLIN' & TUMBLIN' (Muddy Waters) and 'I'M SO GLAD' (Skip James). Over the course of the next six months, they became increasingly influenced by the pioneering psychedelic blues of JIMI HENDRIX. This was much in evidence on the next 45, 'STRANGE BREW', a slow-burning piece of sinister psych-blues. One of the highlights of their second album, 'DISRAELI GEARS', this record also featured such enduring CREAM classics as, 'SUNSHINE OF YOUR LOVE' (a US-only Top 5 hit), 'TALES OF BRAVE ULYSSES' & 'WORLD OF PAIN'. In fact every track was fantastic and the album remains an essential purchase for any self-respecting record collector. Their third set, 'WHEELS OF FIRE', recorded in San Francisco and New York, consisted of two records – one studio, one live. The former featured an ominous cover of BOOKER T's 'BORN UNDER A BAD SIGN', while the live disc included a definitive re-working of ROBERT JOHNSON's 'CROSSROADS'. However, the album (which was soon split into two single lp's) failed to garner the same critical praise as its predecessor, pandering too heavily to commerciality. They played their farewell tour in November '68, culminating in a legendary sell-out show on the 26th at the Royal Albert Hall. They were already in the charts with 'WHITE ROOM', yet it was the GEORGE HARRISON/CLAPTON-penned 'BADGE', which was to become a fitting epitaph upon its posthumous release in early '69. All went on to high-profile solo careers, the most obvious being ERIC 'God' CLAPTON. Like almost every other major 60s/70s rock act, CREAM finally succumbed to reformation temptation in 2005, announcing a four-night spring residence at London's Royal Albert Hall, the same place they signed off over 37 years earlier. A commemorative double-set was released later in the year, a cheaper alternative to the outrageous prices tickets were changing hands for at the time.

Album rating: FRESH CREAM (*6) / DISRAELI GEARS (*9) / WHEELS OF FIRE (*8) / GOODBYE (*5) / THE BEST OF CREAM compilation (*7) / LIVE

CREAM

CREAM collection (*5) / LIVE CREAM VOL.2 collection (*5) / HEAVY CREAM compilation (*6) / STRANGE BREW – THE VERY BEST OF CREAM compilation (*9) / I FEEL FREE – ULTIMATE CREAM compilation (*8) / ROYAL ALBERT HALL: LONDON MAY 2-3-5-6 2005 reunion (*6)

ERIC CLAPTON (b. ERIC PATRICK CLAPP, 30 May'45, Ripley, Surrey, England) – guitar, vocals (ex-YARDBIRDS, ex-JOHN MAYALL'S BLUESBREAKERS) / **JACK BRUCE** (b. JOHN BRUCE, 14 May'43, Glasgow, Scotland) – vocals, bass (ex-GRAHAM BOND, ex-JOHN MAYALL'S BLUESBREAKERS, ex-MANFRED MANN) / **GINGER BAKER** (b. PETER BAKER, 19 Aug'39, Lewisham, London, England) – drums (ex-GRAHAM BOND ORGANISATION, ex-ALEXIS KORNER'S BLUES INCORPORATED)

Reaction Atco

Oct 66. (7") *(591 007)* **WRAPPING PAPER. / CAT'S SQUIRREL** [34] [–]

Dec 66. (lp; mono/stereo) *(593/594 001)* *<33206>* **FRESH CREAM** [6] [39]
– N.S.U. / Sleepy time time / Dreaming / Sweet wine / Spoonful / Cat's squirrel / Four until late / Rollin' and tumblin' / I'm so glad / Toad. *(re-iss. Feb69; stereo); reached No.7 UK. (re-iss Oct70 as 'FULL CREAM'; 2447 010) (re-iss. Mar75 as 'CREAM' on 'Polydor'+=; 2384 067); 2 tracks) (cd-iss. Jan84+=; 827 576-2)* – Wrapping paper / The coffee song. *(cd re-iss. Mar98; 531810-2) (lp re-iss. Aug99 on 'Simply Vinyl'; SVLP 106)*

Dec 66. (7") *(591 011)* *<6462>* **I FEEL FREE. / N.S.U.** [11] [ ]

Jun 67. (7") *(591 015)* *<6488>* **STRANGE BREW. / TALES OF BRAVE ULYSSES** [17] [ ]

Nov 67. (7") *<6522>* **SPOONFUL. / (part 2)** [–] [ ]

Nov 67. (lp; mono/stereo) *(593/594 003)* *<33232>* **DISRAELI GEARS** [5] [4]
– Strange brew / Sunshine of your love / World of pain / Dance the night away / Blue condition / Tales of brave Ulysses / S.W.L.A.B.R. / We're going wrong / Outside woman blues / Take it back / Mother's lament. *<US re-iss. Feb77 on 'R.S.O.'; 3010> (re-iss. Nov77 on 'R.S.O.'; 239 412-2) (cd-iss. Jan84 on 'Track'; 823 636-2) (cd re-iss. Mar98; 531811-2) (lp re-iss. Jun99 on 'Simply Vinyl'; SVLP 87)*

Polydor Atco

Jan 68. (7") *<6544>* **SUNSHINE OF YOUR LOVE. / S.W.L.A.B.R.** [–] [5]
(UK-iss.Sep68; 56286); hit No.25)

May 68. (7") *(56258)* *<6575>* **ANYONE FOR TENNIS. / PRESSED RAT AND WARTHOG** [40] [64]

— **FELIX PAPPALARDI** – producer, instruments guested as 4th p/t member

Aug 68. (d-lp; mono/stereo) *(582/583 031-2)* *<2-700>* **WHEELS OF FIRE** [3] Jul68 [1]
(re-iss. 1972; 2612 001) <US re-iss. Feb77 on 'R.S.O.'; 3802> (re-iss. Jan84 on 'R.S.O.'; 3216 036) (cd-iss. Jan84; 8254 142) (cd re-iss. Feb89; 827 658-2) (cd re-iss. Mar98; 531812-2) (d-lp re-iss. Apr00 on 'Simply Vinyl'; SVLP 202)

Aug 68. (lp; mono/stereo) *(582/583 033)* **WHEELS OF FIRE – IN THE STUDIO** [7] [–]
– White room / Sitting on top of the world / Passing the time / As you said / Pressed rat and warthog / Politician / Those were the days / Born under a bad sign / Deserted cities of the heart. *(re-iss. Nov77 on 'R.S.O.'; 2394 136)*

Aug 68. (lp; mono/stereo) *(582/583 040)* **WHEELS OF FIRE – LIVE AT THE FILLMORE (live)** [ ] [–]
– Crossroads / Spoonful / Traintime / Toad. *(re-iss. Nov77 on 'R.S.O.'; 2394 137)*

Jan 69. (7") *(65300)* *<6617>* **WHITE ROOM. / THOSE WERE THE DAYS** [28] Sep68 [6]

— they split around mid-'68. The rest of their releases were posthumous and CLAPTON went solo after forming BLIND FAITH with BAKER. He also went solo. JACK BRUCE went solo, etc.

CREAM

originals re-formed in spring 2005

Reprise Reprise

Oct 05. (d-cd/t-lp) *(<9362 49416-2/-1>)* **ROYAL ALBERT HALL: LONDON MAY 2-3-5-6 2005** (live) [61] [59]
– I'm so glad / Spoonful / Outside woman blues / Pressed rat & warthog / Sleepy time time / N.S.U. / Badge / Politician / Sweet wine / Rollin' and tumblin' / Stormy Monday / Deserted cities of the heart / Born under a bad sign / We're going wrong / Crossroads / White room / Toad / Sunshine of your love / Sleepy time time (alt. take).
in Nov'05, CREAMS vs. the HOXTONS had a UK Top 50 hit with 'SUNSHINE OF YOUR LOVE'

– compilations, others, etc. –

either 'Polydor' in UK and 'Atco' in the US

Jan 69. (7") *<6646>* **CROSSROADS. / PASSING THE TIME** [–] [28]

Mar 69. (lp) *(583 053)* *<7001>* **GOODBYE** [1] [2]
– I'm so glad (live) / Politician (live) / Sitting on top of the world (live) / Badge / Doing that scrapyard thing / What a bringdown. *(re-iss. Nov77 & Aug84 on 'R.S.O.'; 2394 178) (cd-iss. Jan84.+=; 823 660-2)* – Anyone for tennis. *(cd re-iss. Mar98; 531815-2) (lp re-iss. May00 on 'Simply Vinyl'; SVLP 211)*

Apr 69. (7") *(56315)* *<6668>* **BADGE. / WHAT A BRINGDOWN** [18] Mar69 [60]
(re-iss. Oct72; 2058 285)

Nov 69. (lp) *(583 060)* *<291>* **BEST OF CREAM** [6] Jul69 [3]
– Sunshine of your love / Badge / Crossroads / White room / Swlabr / Born under a bad sign / Tales of brave Ulysses / Strange brew / I feel free. *(re-iss. Nov77 on 'R.S.O.'; 3216 031) (re-iss. Apr86 on 'Arcade'; ADAH 429)*

Jun 70. (lp) *(2383 016)* *<33-328>* **LIVE CREAM (live)** [4] Apr70 [15]
– N.S.U. / Sleepy time time / Lawdy mama / Sweet wine / Rollin' and tumblin'. *(re-iss. Nov77 & Mar85 on 'R.S.O.' lp/c; SPE LP/MC 93) (cd-iss. May88; 827 577-2) (cd re-iss. Mar98; 531816-2)*

Jun 72. (lp) *(2383 119)* *<7005>* **LIVE CREAM VOL.2** [15] Mar72 [27]
– Deserted cities of the heart / White room / Politician / Tales of brave Ulysses / Sunshine of your love / Steppin' out. *(re-iss. Nov77 on 'R.S.O.';) (cd-iss. May88; 823 661-2) (cd re-iss. Mar98; 531817-2)*

Apr 73. (d-lp) *(2659 022)* *<3502>* **HEAVY CREAM** [ ] Oct72 [ ]

Aug 82. (7") *R.S.O.; (RSO 91)* **BADGE. / TALES OF BRAVE ULYSSES** [ ] [ ]
(12"+=) *(RSOX 91)* – White room.

Feb 83. (lp/c) *R.S.O.; (RSD/TRSD 5021)* **STRANGE BREW – THE VERY BEST OF CREAM** [ ] [ ]
– Badge / Sunshine of your love / Crossroads / White room / Born under a bad sign / Swlabr / Strange brew / Anyone for tennis / I feel free / Tales of brave Ulysses / Politician / Spoonful. *(cd-iss. Nov87 on 'Polydor';)*

Nov 92. (cd) *I.T.M.; (ITM 960002)* **THE ALTERNATIVE ALBUM** [ ] [–]
(re-iss. Jan97 & Dec99 on 'Masterplan'; MP 42009)

Feb 95. (cd/c) *(523 752-2/-4)* **THE VERY BEST OF CREAM** [ ] [ ]
– White room / I feel free / Tales of brave Ulysses / I'm so glad / Toad / Sunshine of your love / Strange brew / N.S.U. / Born under a bad sign / Badge / Crossroads.

Sep 97. (4xcd-box) *(539000-2)* **THOSE WERE THE DAYS** [ ] [ ]

Apr 03. (cd) *(76048-2)* *<0000069>* **AT THE BBC** [ ] [ ]

May 05. (cd) *(987136-2)* **I FEEL FREE – ULTIMATE CREAM** [6] [–]
– Wrapping paper / I feel free / N.S.U. / Sweet wine / I'm so glad / Strange brew / Sunshine of your love / World of pain / Tales of brave Ulysses / Swalbr / We're going wrong / White room / Sittin' on top of the world / Passing the time / Politician / Those were the days / Deserted cities of the heart / Crossroads (live) / Anyone for tennis / Badge / Doing the scrapyard thing / What a bringdown. *(d-cd+=; 9871106)* – live:- N.S.U. / Sleepy time time / Rollin' and tumblin' / Steppin' out / Crossroads / Sunshine of your love / I'm so glad / Toad. *(3xcd-box+=; 9871430)* – (BBC sessions).

Sep 05. (d-cd) *(9880146)* *<4193>* **GOLD** [ ] [ ]

☐ the CREATURES
(see under ⇒ SIOUXSIE & THE BANSHEES)

CREED

Formed: Tallahassee, Florida, USA . . . 1994 by singer SCOTT STAPP and guitarist MARK TREMONTI, who hooked up with rhythm section BRIAN MARSHALL and SCOTT PHILLIPS. Another band to emerge from the post-Grunge scene, although EDDIE VEDDER and LAYNE STALEY have no fears here about their mantle being taken by these lads. A year or two into their career, CREED released a self-financed debut set, 'MY OWN PRISON', which sold its initial batch and made major labels take note. 'Epic' (through subsidiary 'Wind-Up') finally won the battle for their signatures early in '97 and with a new producer, Ron St. Germain, remixed and re-issued the album later in the year. "Grunge was not dead!" was the claim of their teen-metal followers, although CREED themselves denied they were part of that genre and were just a basic rock'n'roll band – basic being the key word. 'MY OWN PRISON' started a steady rise up the American charts finally peaking at No.22 a year later, although Britain had to wait until early '99 to get its first taste of million-sellers CREED. By which point, Grunge had certainly been well and truly buried. Meanwhile, back in the States, the glum-rockers were just about to serve up a second helping in the shape of 'HUMAN CLAY' (1999) – a difficult second album indeed that nevertheless topped the chart. Proving that earnestness will indeed get you everywhere, CREED were back with another helping of stadium dirge in the form of 'WEATHERED' (2001). Indicating that their inimitably American rawk might be twisting the arm of angst-ridden Brit youth, the record nudged into the UK Top 50, while, of course, cleaning up in the States (No.1). By 2004, CREED (without STAPP) had evolved into the more overtly metallic ALTER BRIDGE, fronted by ex-MAYFIELD FOUR bellower MYLES KENNEDY. Not abandoning their grunge heritage completely, the album 'ONE DAY REMAINS' (2004) made the US Top 5, while the solo SCOTT STAPP bided his time before the release of his own US Top 20 debut, 'THE GREAT DIVIDE' (2005). The record's simplistic approach suggested that STAPP was less willing to abandon his CREED of old.

• **Covered:** I'M EIGHTEEN (Alice Cooper) / RIDERS ON THE STORM (Doors). • **Note:** not to be confused with mid-90's act who issued 12" singles on 'Rectory'.

Album rating: MY OWN PRISON (*6) / HUMAN CLAY (*5) / WEATHERED (*4) / Alter Bridge: ONE DAY REMAINS (*4) / Scott Stapp: THE GREAT DIVIDE (*4)

SCOTT STAPP (b. ANTHONY SCOTT FLIPPEN, 8 Aug'73, Orlando, Florida) – vocals / **MARK TREMONTI** (b.18 Apr'74, Detroit, Michigan) – guitar, vocals / **BRIAN MARSHALL** (b.24 Apr'74) – bass / **SCOTT PHILLIPS** (b.22 Feb'73, Madison, Florida) – drums

Wind Up-Epic | Wind Up-Epic

Oct 97. (cd) *<13049>* **MY OWN PRISON** [–] [22]
– Torn / Ode / My own prison / Pity for a dime / In America / Illusion / Unforgiven / Sister / What's this life for / One. *<US originally iss.1997 on 'Blue Collar'; 5066> (UK-iss.Feb99 on 'Wind-Up – Epic'; 493072)*

Feb 99. (-) *<radio cut>* **ONE** [–] [70]

Sep 99. (cd/c) *(495027-2/-4) <13053>* **HUMAN CLAY** [ ] [1]
– Are you ready / What if / Beautiful / Say I / Wrong way / Faceless man / Never die / With arms wide open / Higher / Wash away those years / Inside us all. *(re-dist.Jan01)* – hit UK No.29

Jan 00. (7"/cd-s) *(668315-7/-2) <radio cut>* **HIGHER / I'M EIGHTEEN / ROADSIDE BLUES (live)** [47] Aug99 [7]

Jan 01. (7"maroon) *(670695-7) <album cut>* **WITH ARMS WIDE OPEN. / WITH ARMS WIDE OPEN (acoustic)** [13] Mar00 [1]
(c-s+=) *(670695-4)* – Wash away those tears.
(cd-s+=) *(670695-2)* – ('A'-new version / Strings / CD-ROM).

Sep 01. (7") *(671064-7)* **HIGHER. / I'M EIGHTEEN** [64] [–]
(c-s) *(671064-4)* – ('A'side) / To whom it may concern.
(cd-s) *(671064-2)* – ('A'side) / Is this the end / Roadhouse blues (live).

Nov 01. (cd) *(504979-2) <13075>* **WEATHERED** [44] [1]
– Bullets / Freedom fighter / Who's got my back? / Signs / One last breath / My sacrifice / Stand here with me / Weathered / Hide / Don't stop dancing / Lullaby.

Mar 02. (7") *(672316-7) <radio>* **MY SACRIFICE. / RIDERS ON THE STORM (with Robbie Kreiger)** [18] Oct01 [4]
(cd-s+=) *(672316-2)* – With arms wide open (strings version) / ('A'-video).

Jul 02. (cd-s) *(672826-2)* **ONE LAST BREATH / BULLETS / I'M EIGHTEEN / ('A'video)** [47] [–]

Sep 02. (cd-s) *<672984>* **ONE LAST BREATH / IS THIS THE END / MY OWN PRISON / ONE LAST BREATH (dub)** [–] [6]

—— disbanded in 2004

ALTER BRIDGE

MYLES KENNEDY – vocals (ex-MAYFIELD FOUR) / **MARK TREMONTI** – guitar / **BRIAN MARSHALL** – bass / **SCOTT PHILLIPS** – drums

Wind-Up Epic | Wind-Up Epic

Sep 04. (cd) *(517886-2) <13097>* **ONE DAY REMAINS** [ ] [5]
– Find the real / One day remains / Open your eyes / Burn your eyes / Burn it down / Metalingus / Broken wings / In loving memory / Down to my last / Watch your words / Shed my skin / The end is here.

SCOTT STAPP

Sony | Wind-Up Epic

May 06. (cd) *(82876 75390-2) <13099>* **THE GREAT DIVIDE** [ ] Nov05 [19]
– Reach out / Fight song / Hard way / Justify / Let me go / Surround me / The great divide / Sublime / You will soar / Broken.

CREEDENCE CLEARWATER REVIVAL

Formed: El Cerrito, California, USA . . . late 1959 as school group The BLUE VELVETS by JOHN FOGERTY, STU COOK and DOUG CLIFFORD. JOHN soon invited other multi-instrumentalist and brother TOM. After one 45 on a local label, they became The GOLLIWOGS in 1964 and signed to label 'Fantasy' where TOM was working as a clerk. The 'BROWN EYED GIRL' single was a moderate success although subsequent releases stiffed. Following DOUG and JOHN's compulsory spell in the forces (no hippy draft dodging for these guys!) the group became CREEDENCE CLEARWATER REVIVAL, releasing their debut single, an inspired cover of 'SUZIE Q,' in September '68. A top 20 hit, it was closely followed by another cover, SCREAMIN' JAY HAWKINS' 'I PUT A SPELL ON YOU' (1968) and a self-titled debut album the following year. Despite hailing from Berkeley in California, CREEDENCE, or at least JOHN FOGERTY lived and breathed a Southern fantasy of "Backwood Bayous", "Cajun Queens" and "Hoodoos" (eh?!). This was swamp R&B of the rootsiest pedigree, utilising a simple but stunningly effective hybrid of raw rock'n'roll, country and blues. FOGERTY's voice was an instrument in its own right, a life-affirming bellow that equalled MARVIN GAYE and OTIS REDDING for soulfulness and if his early classics fail to send a shiver up your spine, it'd be an idea to check your pulse. The man was also blessed with the ability to write insanely catchy songs which were nevertheless steeped in Southern authenticity. 'PROUD MARY' / 'BORN ON THE BAYOU' (1969) was the first in an avalanche of hits that saw CREEDENCE become one of the world's biggest selling bands during their heyday of '69-70. The classic 'GREEN RIVER' (1969) spawned perhaps their best known track, the apocalyptic swamp-pop of 'BAD MOON RISING' as well as the poignant country soul of 'LODI' and the blistering title track. 'DOWN ON THE CORNER' (1970) kept up the run of hit singles while 'WILLY AND THE POOR BOYS' (1970) remains the definitive CCR album. From the passionate politicism of 'FORTUNATE SON' to the desolate strangeness of 'EFFIGY', the album ran the gamut of the band's influences. There was no stopping the prolific FOGERTY at this point and a mere six months later the band released 'COSMO'S FACTORY' (1970). Coming within a whisker of its predecessor, the album produced the top ten hits 'TRAVELLIN' MAN' (1970), 'UP AROUND THE BEND' (1970) and 'LONG AS I CAN SEE THE LIGHT' (1970) as well as their driving cover of MARVIN GAYE's 'I HEARD IT THROUGH THE GRAPEVINE'. While 'PENDULUM' (1971) was slated as a disappointment, it nevertheless held nuggets like the gorgeous 'HAVE YOU EVER SEEN THE RAIN' and the rousing 'HEY TONIGHT'. By this point, however, internal disputes were rife and TOM left for a solo career a month after the album's release. Pared down to a trio, CCR cut a final studio album, 'MARDI GRAS' (1971) before splitting in 1973. JOHN released his first solo outing the same year, a collection of purist 'ountry under the BLUE RIDGE RANGERS moniker, following it ıp with 'JOHN FOGERTY' in 1975. While the album contained he FOGERTY classics, 'ROCKIN' ALL OVER THE WORLD' and ALMOST SATURDAY NIGHT', and his voice was still incredible, ıis earlier songwriting sharpness sounded blunted. Retreating to a 'arm for a life of rural bliss with his family, it was 10 years before 'OGERTY returned with 'CENTERFIELD' (1985). Although it sold wo million copies, the album was again slightly disappointing ınd led to FOGERTY gaining a place in the history books for eing possibly the only artist ever to be sued (by 'Fantasy' owner AUL ZAENTZ) for plagiarising his own material. 'EYE OF THE :OMBIE' (1986) was average while 'BLUE MOON SWAMP' (1997) vas hardly worth waiting a decade for. If the title of 'DEJA VU ALL OVER AGAIN' (2004), laid FOGERTY wide open for quips n his musical conservatism, the title track itself was actually one f his finest, most sharpely observed (and yes, most CREEDENCE-ke) in years, an inevitable comment on Iraq from a songwriter ld enough to remember Vietnam. And amid the usual quota of eneration-yawning missteps (see the DIRE STRAITS-grumpiness f 'NOBODY'S HERE ANYMORE'), there was enough homespun ock'n'roll to make the album worthwhile for CCR diehards, a UK 'op10/US Top 30 placing making it his highest charting release ince the mid-80's. A year later, 'THE LONG ROAD HOME: 'HE ULTIMATE JOHN FOGERTY/CREEDENCE COLLECTION' 2005), saw FOGERTY make a belated peace with 'Fantasy', as he label drew a line from his Bayou beginnings right through to DEJA VU..', illuminating the defiantly unpretentious, common-ıan dignity at the heart of his writing. Despite being the driving orce behind a band that has influenced artists as diverse as 'ONIC YOUTH, HANOI ROCKS and STATUS QUO (!), it seems ncreasingly unlikely that FOGERTY is going to come up with omething that does his legend justice.

Covered: SUZIE Q (Dale Hawkins) / OOBY DOOBY (Roy Orbison) / IELLO MARY LOU (Ricky Nelson) / etc. • **Miscellaneous:** TOM FOGERTY vas to die of tuberculosis on the 6th September '90.

lbum rating: CREEDENCE CLEARWATER REVIVAL (*5) / BAYOU :OUNTRY (*6) / GREEN RIVER (*8) / WILLY AND THE POOR BOYS *9) / COSMO'S FACTORY (*7) / PENDULUM (*6) / MARDI GRAS (*4) / :REEDENCE GOLD compilation (*8) / MORE CREEDENCE GOLD compilation *7) / LIVE IN EUROPE (*4) / THE ROYAL ALBERT HALL CONCERT *4) / THE COLLECTION double compilation (*9) / John Fogerty: THE BLUE IDGE RANGERS (*5) / JOHN FOGERTY (*4) / CENTERFIELD (*7) / EYE F THE ZOMBIE (*4) / BLUE MOON SWAMP (*7) / PREMONITION (*6) /)EJA VU ALL OVER AGAIN (*5) / THE LONG ROAD HOME compilation *8)

he BLUE VELVETS

OHN FOGERTY (b.28 May'45, Berkeley, Calif.)– vocals, guitar / **TOM OGERTY** (b. 9 Nov'41, Berkeley)– rhythm guitar, piano / **STU COOK** (b.25 pr'45, Portland, Calif.)– bass / **DOUG 'COSMO' CLIFFORD** (b.24 Apr'45, alo Alto, Calif.)- **drums**

not iss. — Orkhestra

962. (7") *<1010>* **HAVE YOU EVER BEEN LONELY. / BONITA** [–] [ ]

he GOLLIWOGS

ıme line-up (TOM sang lead on first)

not iss. — Fantasy

Iov 64. (7") *<590>* **DON'T TELL ME NO LIES. / LITTLE GIRL** [–] [ ]

ın 65. (7") *<597>* **YOU CAME WALKING. / WHERE YOU BEEN** [–] [ ]

ug 65. (7") *<599>* **YOU CAN'T BE TRUE. / YOU GOT NOTHIN' ON ME** [–] [ ]

Vocalion — Scorpio

ın 66. (7") *(VF 9266) <404>* **BROWN-EYED GIRL. / YOU BETTER BE CAREFUL** [ ] [ ]

Mar 66. (7") *(VF 9283) <405>* **FRAGILE CHILD. / FIGHT FIRE** [ ] [ ]

Dec 66. (7") *<408>* **WALKING ON THE WATER. / YOU BETTER GET IT** [–] [ ]

Nov 67. (7") *<412>* **PORTERVILLE. / CALL IT PRETENDING** [–] [ ]

(above single was soon later credited to below group name) *(also, a compilation album of some singles above was released in '74 on 'Fantasy')*

CREEDENCE CLEARWATER REVIVAL

same line-up

Liberty — Fantasy

Sep 68. (7") *<616>* **SUZIE Q. (part 1). / SUZIE Q. (part 2)** [–] [11]

Nov 68. (7") *<617>* **I PUT A SPELL ON YOU. / WALK ON THE WATER** [–] [ ]

Apr 69. (lp) *(LBS 83259) <8382>* **CREEDENCE CLEARWATER REVIVAL** [ ] Jul68 [52]
– I put a spell on you / Suzie Q. / The working man / Ninety-nine and a half (won't do) / Get down woman / Porterville / Gloomy / Walk on the water. *(re-iss. Mar73 on 'Fantasy'; FT 506) (re-iss. Jul84 on 'Fantasy' lp/c; FAS LP/K 5002) (re-iss. Aug87 on 'Fantasy' lp/c/cd; FACE/FACC/CDFE 501)*

May 69. (7") *(LBF 15223) <619>* **PROUD MARY. / BORN ON THE BAYOU** [8] Jan69 [2]

Jun 69. (lp) *(LBS 83261) <8387>* **BAYOU COUNTRY** [ ] Feb69 [7]
– Born on the bayou / Bootleg / Graveyard train / Good golly Miss Molly / Penthouse pauper / Keep on chooglin' / Proud Mary. *(hit UK No.62 in May'70) (re-iss. Mar73 on 'Fantasy'; FT 507) (re-iss. Jul84 on 'Fantasy' lp/c; FAS LP/K 5003) (re-iss. Aug87 on 'Fantasy' lp/c/cd; FACE/FACC/CDFE 502)*

Aug 69. (7") *(LBF 15230) <622>* **BAD MOON RISING. / LODI** [1] [2]
May69 [52]

Nov 69. (7") *(LBF 15250) <625>* **GREEN RIVER. / COMMOTION** [19] [2]
Jul69 [30]

Dec 69. (lp) *(LBS 83273) <8393>* **GREEN RIVER** [20] Sep69 [1]
– Green river / Commotion / Tombstone shadow / Wrote a song for everyone / Bad moon rising / Lodi / Cross-tie walker / Sinister purpose / Lodi / Wrote a song for everyone / Night time is the right time. *(re-iss. Mar73 on 'Fantasy'; FT 504) (re-iss. Jul84 on 'Fantasy' lp/c; FAS LP/K 5004) (re-iss. Aug87 on 'Fantasy' lp/c/cd; FACE/FACC/CDFE 503)*

Feb 70. (7") *(LBF 15283) <634>* **DOWN ON THE CORNER. / FORTUNATE SON** [31] Oct 69 [3]
[14]

Mar 70. (lp) *(LBS 83338) <8397>* **WILLY AND THE POOR BOYS** [10] Dec69 [3]
– Down on the corner / It came out of the sky / Cotton fields / Poor boy shuffle / Feelin' blue / Fortunate son / Don't look now (it ain't you or me) / The midnight special / Side of the road / Effigy. *(re-iss. Mar73 on 'Fantasy'; FT 503) (re-iss. Jul84 on 'Fantasy' lp/c; FAS LP/K 5005) (re-iss. Aug87 on 'Fantasy' lp/c/cd; FACE/FACC/CDFE 504)*

Mar 70. (7") *(LBF 15310) <637>* **TRAVELIN' BAND. / WHO'LL STOP THE RAIN** [8] Jan70 [2]

Jun 70. (7") *(LBF 15354) <641>* **UP AROUND THE BEND. / RUN THROUGH THE JUNGLE** [3] Apr70 [4]

Aug 70. (7") *(LBF 15384) <645>* **LONG AS I CAN SEE THE LIGHT. / LOOKIN' OUT MY BACK DOOR** [20] B-side [2]

Sep 70. (lp) *(LBS 83388) <8402>* **COSMO'S FACTORY** [1] Jul70 [1]
– Ramble tamble / Before you accuse me / Travelin' band / Ooby dooby / Lookin' out my back door / Run through the jungle / Up around the bend / My baby left me / Who'll stop the rain / I heard it through the grapevine / Long as I can see the light. *(re-iss. Mar73 on 'Fantasy'; FT 502) (re-iss. Jul84 lp/c; FAS LP/K 506) (re-iss. Aug87 on 'Fantasy' lp/c/cd; FACE/FACC/CDFE 505)*

Jan 71. (lp) *(LBG 83400) <8410>* **PENDULUM** [23] Dec70 [5]
– Pagan baby / Sailor's lament / Chameleon / Have you ever seen the rain / (Wish I could) Hideaway / Born to move / Hey tonight / It's just a thought / Molina / Rude awakening No.2. *(re-iss. Mar73 on 'Fantasy'; FT 508) (re-iss. Jul84 on 'Fantasy' lp/c; FAS LP/K 5007) (re-iss. Nov89 on 'Fantasy' lp/c/cd; FACE/FACC/CDFE 512) (cd re-iss. Jan99 on 'Akarma'; 8410)*

Mar 71. (7") *(LBF 15440) <655>* **HAVE YOU EVER SEEN THE RAIN. / HEY TONIGHT** [36] Jan71 [8]
(re-iss. Apr71 on 'United Artists'; UP 35210)

— now a trio when TOM FOGERTY departed to go solo (Feb'71)

U.A. — Fantasy

Jul 71. (7") *(UP 35261) <665>* **SWEET HITCH-HIKER. / DOOR TO DOOR** [36] [6]

Fantasy Fantasy

Apr 72. (7") <676> **SOMEDAY NEVER COMES. / TEARIN' UP THE COUNTRY** [–] [25]

Jul 72. (lp) <(FAN 9404)> **MARDI GRAS** [ ] Apr72 [12]
– Lookin' for a reason / Take it like a friend / Need someone to hold / Tearin' up the country / Hello Mary Lou / Someday never comes / What are you gonna do / Hello Mary Lou / Door to door / Sweet hitch-hiker. *(re-iss. Mar73; FT 505) (re-iss. Jul84 lp/c; FAS LP/K 5008) (re-iss. Nov89 lp/c/cd; FACE/FACC/CDFE 513)*

—— split Oct'72

– compilations etc. –

on 'Fantasy' unless mentioned otherwise

Dec 72. (7") *(FRC 101)* **BORN ON THE BAYOU. / I PUT A SPELL ON YOU** [ ] [–]

Jan 73. (lp) *(501)* <9418> **CREEDENCE GOLD** [ ] Nov72 [15]
– Proud Mary / Down on the corner / Bad Moon rising / I heard it through the grapevine / Midnight special / Have you ever seen the rain / Born on the bayou / Suzie Q. *(cd-iss. Sep91; CDFE 515)*

Mar 73. (7") *(FRC 104)* **IT CAME OUT OF THE SKY. / SIDE O' THE ROAD** [ ] [–]

Sep 73. (lp) *(512)* <9430> **MORE CREEDENCE GOLD** [ ] Jul73 [61]
– Hey tonight / Run through the jungle / Fortunate son / Bootleg / Lookin' out my back door / Molina / Who'll stop the rain / Sweet hitch-hiker / Good golly Miss Molly / I put a spell on you / Don't look now / Lodi / Porterville / Up around the bend. *(cd-iss. Sep91; CDFE 516)*

May 74. (d-lp) *(520)* <FCCR 1> **LIVE IN EUROPE (live 1971)** [ ] Nov73 [ ]
– Born on the bayou / Green river / It came out of the sky / Door to door / Travellin' band / Fortunate son / Porterville / Up around the bend / Suzie Q / Commotion / Lodi. *(re-iss. Feb90 lp/c/cd; FACE/FACC/CDFE 514)*

Mar 76. (d-lp) *(528)* <FCCR 2> **CHRONICLE (THE 20 GREATEST HITS)** [ ] Feb76 [100]
– Suzie Q. / I put a spell on you / Proud Mary / Bad Moon rising / Lodi / Green river / Commotion / Down on the corner / Fortunate son / Travellin' band / Who'll stop the rain / Up around the bend / Run through the jungle / Lookin' out my back door / Long as I can see the light / I heard it through the grapevine / Have you ever seen the rain? / Hey tonight / Sweet hitch-hiker / Someday never comes. *(cd-iss. Jun87 on 'Polydor'+=; 821 742-2)* – I heard it through the grapevine.

Mar 76. (7") *(FTC 128)* <759> **I HEARD IT THROUGH THE GRAPEVINE. / GOOD GOLLY MISS MOLLY** [ ] Dec75 [43]

Jul 77. (7"m) *(FTC 142)* **BAD MOON RISING. / PROUD MARY / GREEN RIVER** [ ] [–]

Nov 78. (7"m) *(FTC 164)* **WHO'LL STOP THE RAIN. / PROUD MARY / HEY TONIGHT** [ ] [–]

Jun 79. (lp) *(FT 558)* **GREATEST HITS (20 GOLDEN)** [35] [ ]

Jul 79. (7") *(FRC 178)* **I HEARD IT THROUGH THE GRAPEVINE. / John Fogerty: ROCKIN' ALL OVER THE WORLD** [ ] [–]
(12") *(12FTC 178)* – ('A'side) / Keep on chooglin' (extended).

1979. (7") <908> **COMMOTION. / TOMBSTONE SHADOW** [–] [ ]

1979. (7") <917> **BAD MOON RISING. / MEDLEY U.S.A.** [–] [ ]

1979. (7") <920> **LODI. / COTTON FIELDS** [–] [ ]

1979. (7") <957> **I HEARD IT THROUGH THE GRAPEVINE – UP AROUND THE BEND (medley). / PROUD MARY – LODI (medley)** [–] [ ]

Feb 81. (lp/c) *Music For Pleasure-Fantasy;* <(MPF/+5 4501)> **LIVE AT THE ROYAL ALBERT HALL (live)**
<US-title 'THE CONCERT'> [ ] Dec80 [62]
(re-iss. Jul89 as 'THE CONCERT' on 'Fantasy' lp/c/cd; FACE/FACC/CDFE 511)

Aug 81. (7") *Golden Grooves; (GOLD 521)* **PROUD MARY. / UP AROUND THE BEND** [ ] [–]

Oct 81. (7") *Golden Grooves; (GOLD 530)* **BAD MOON RISING. / GOOD GOLLY MISS MOLLY** [ ] [–]

Feb 82. (lp/c) *Music For Pleasure-Fantasy; (MPF/+5 4500)* **THE HITS ALBUM** [ ] [–]

Sep 85. (7") *Old Gold; (OG 9569)* **BAD MOON RISING. / LONG AS I SEE THE LIGHT** [ ] [–]

Sep 85. (7") *Old Gold; (OG 9570)* **PROUD MARY. / TRAVELLIN' BAND** [ ] [–]

Oct 85. (d-lp/c) *Impression; (IMD P/K 3)* **THE CREEDENCE COLLECTION** [68] [–]

Jun 87. (cd) <(CDCCR 3)> **CHRONICLE VOL.2** [ ] [ ]

May 88. (cd) *Arcade; (01279161)* **THE COMPLETE HITS ALBUM VOL.1** [ ] [–]

May 88. (cd) *Arcade; (01279261)* **THE COMPLETE HITS ALBUM VOL.2** [ ] [–]

Jun 88. (7") *Ace; (NS 124)* **BAD MOON RISING. / HAVE YOU EVER SEEN THE RAIN?** [ ] [–]
(12"+=) *(NST 124)* – Keep on chooglin'.

Jun 88. (lp/c/cd) *(FACE/FACC/FAX 509)* **THE BEST OF – VOLUME 1** [ ] [ ]

Aug 88. (lp/c) *(FACE/FACC 510)* **THE BEST OF – VOLUME 2** [ ] [ ]

Dec 88. (cd) <8029 852-2> **CHOOGLIN'** [–] [ ]
(UK-iss.Nov92; CDFE 517)

Apr 92. (7") *Epic; (658004-7)* **BAD MOON RISING. / AS LONG AS I CAN SEE THE LIGHT** [71] [–]
(cd-s+=) *(658004-2)* –

Dec 92. (cd) *(CDFE 518)* **CREEDENCE COUNTRY** [ ] [ ]

Aug 95. (cd-s) *Old Gold; (OG 6306)* **TRAVELLIN' BAND. / WHO'LL STOP THE RAIN** [ ] [–]

Sep 95. (cd-s) *Old Gold; (12623 6326-2)* **UP AROUND THE BEND / RUN THROUGH THE JUNGLE** [ ] [–]

the BLUE RIDGE RANGERS

—— was JOHN FOGERTY's first total solo venture

Fantasy Fanta

Dec 72. (7") <689> **JAMBALAYA (ON THE BAYOU). / WORKING ON A BUILDING** [–] [16]

Apr 73. (lp) *(F 1511)* <9415> **BLUE RIDGE RANGERS** [ ] [47]
– Blue ridge mountain blues / Somewhere listening (for my name) You're the reason / Jambalaya (on the bayou) / She thinks I still care California blues (blue yodel #4) / Workin' on a building / Please help m I'm falling / Have thine own way, Lord / I ain't never / Hearts of stone Today I started loving you. *<re-iss. Aug86; 1061150> (re-iss. Sep87 lp/c/c FACE/FACC/CDFA 506)*

May 73. (7") *(FRC 105)* <700> **HEARTS OF STONE. / SOMEWHERE LISTENING (FOR MY NAME)** [ ] Mar73 [37]

Oct 73. (7") *(FRC 110)* <710> **BACK IN THE HILLS. / YOU DON'T OWN ME** [ ] Jul73 [ ]

JOHN FOGERTY

solo, plays / sings everything

Fantasy Fanta

Mar 74. (7") *(FTC 111)* <717> **COMING DOWN THE ROAD. / RICOCHET** [ ] [ ]

Fantasy Asylu

Sep 75. (7") *(FTC 119)* <45274> **ROCKIN' ALL OVER THE WORLD. / THE WALL** [ ] [27]

Oct 75. (lp) *(FT 526)* <1046> **JOHN FOGERTY** [ ] [78]
– Rockin' all over the world / You rascal you / The wall / Traveli high / Lonely teardrops / Almost Saturday night / Where the riv flows / Sea cruise / Dream – Song / Flyin' away. *(re-iss. Sep87 lp/c/c FACE/FACC/CDFE 507)*

Dec 75. (7") <45291> **ALMOST SATURDAY NIGHT. / SEA CRUISE** [–] [78]

May 76. (7") *(FTC 133)* <45309> **YOU GOT THE MAGIC. / EVIL THING** [ ] [87]

—— JOHN FOGERTY returned after 9 years complete with new session peopl

Warners Warn

Feb 85. (7") *(W 9100)* <29100> **THE OLD MAN DOWN THE ROAD. / BIG TRAIN (FROM MEMPHIS)** [ ] Dec84 [10]

Feb 85. (lp/c/cd) *(925203-1/-4/-2)* <25203> **CENTERFIELD** [48] Jan85 [1]
– The old man down the road / Rock and roll girls / Big train (fro Memphis) / I saw it on T.V. / Mr. Greed / Searchlight / Centerfield / I can help myself / Zant Kant danz. *(cd re-iss. Nov93; same)*

Jun 85. (7") *(W 9053)* <29053> **ROCK AND ROLL GIRLS. / CENTERFIELD** [ ] [20]
Mar85 [44]

—— now with **JOHN ROBINSON** – drums / **NEIL STUBENHAUS** – bass

Oct 86. (lp/c/cd) *(925449-1/-4/-2)* <25449> **EYE OF THE ZOMBIE** [44] [26]
– Goin' back home / Eye of the zombie / Headlines / Knockin' on yo door / Change in the weather / Violence is golden / Wasn't that a womar Soda pop / Sail away.

Oct 86. (7") *(W 8657)* <28657> **EYE OF THE ZOMBIE. / I CONFESS (with Bobby King)** [ ] [81]
(12"+=) *(W 8657T)* – I can't help myself.

Dec 86. (7") *<28535>* **CHANGE IN THE WEATHER. / MY TOOT TOOT** [-] [ ]

— returned after another 10 years in the proverbial wilderness

Warners Warners

Jun 97. (cd/c) *<(9362 45426-2/-4)>* **BLUE MOON SWAMP** [ ] May97 [37]
– Southern streamline / Hot rod heart / Blueboy / Hundred and ten in the shade / Rattlesnake highway / Bring it down to Jelly Roll / Walking in a hurricane / Swamp river days / Rambunctions boy / Joy of my life / Blue moon nights / Bad bad boy.

Oct 97. (cd-d) *<17283>* **BLUEBOY / BAD BAD BOY** [-] [ ]

— his live band were basically **KENNY ARONOFF** – drums / **BOB GLAUB** – bass / **MIKE CANIPE** – guitar

Jun 98. (cd) *<(9362 46908-2)>* **PREMONITION (live)** [ ] [29]
– Born on the bayou / Green river / Susie Q. / I put a spell on you / Who'll stop the rain / Premonition / Almost Saturday night / Rockin' all over the world / Joy of my life / Down on the corner / Centerfield / Swamp river days / Hot rod heart / The old man down the road / Bad moon rising / Fortunate son / Proud Mary / Travelin' band.

Geffen Geffen

Nov 04. (cd) *<(32570-2)>* **DEJA VU ALL OVER AGAIN** [ ] Sep04 [23]
– Deja vu (all over again) / Sugar-sugar (in my life) / She's got baggage / Radar / Honey do / Nobody's here anymore / I will walk with you / Rhubarb pie / Wicked old witch / In the garden.

– compilation –

Nov 05. (d-cd) *Concord; (189690-2) / Fantasy; <6989>* **THE LONG ROAD HOME: THE ULTIMATE JOHN FOGERTY / CREEDENCE COLLECTION** [ ] [ ]
– Born on the bayou / Bad moon rising / Centerfield / Who'll stop the rain / Rambunctious boy / Fortunate son / Lookin' out my back door / Up around the bend / Almost SAturday night (live) / Down on the corner / Bootleg (live) / Have you ever seen the rain? / Sweet hitch-hiker / Hey tonight (live) / The old man down the road / Rockin' all over the world (live) / Lodi / Keep on chooglin' (live) / Green river / Deja vu (all over again) / Run through the jungle / Hot road heart / Travelin' band / Proud Mary / Fortunate son (live).

□ Peter CRISS (see under ⇒ KISS)

CROSBY, STILLS, NASH (& YOUNG)

Formed: Los Angeles, California, USA ... summer 1968 as a superband trio (DAVID) CROSBY, (STEPHEN) STILLS and (GRAHAM) NASH. Their eponymous first offering was released in Summer '69 and soon broke into the US Top 10. Featuring the distinctive songwriting talent of each member respectively on 'GUINNEVERE', 'SUITE: JUDY BLUE EYES' and 'MARRAKESH EXPRESS', the album introduced the close harmonising that would come to characterise the band. Later that year the trio recruited NEIL YOUNG (ex-BUFFALO SPRINGFIELD) who'd played an electric set on their mid-'69 gigs and who'd already embarked on his successful solo career. The newly augmented line-up played Woodstock as well as supporting The ROLLING STONES at their ill-fated Altamont concert which, ironically, saw the dreams of the Woodstock generation shatter. Nevertheless the band were adopted as hippy flagbearers and after lifting the coveted 'Best Newcomers' award at The Grammys, they released their magnum opus, 'DEJA VU' (1970). With YOUNG contributing the achingly gorgeous 'HELPLESS' and the sublime 'COUNTRY GIRL' suite, his intensity, both vocal and instrumental was a towering influence although STILLS offered a powerful cover of JONI MITCHELL's 'WOODSTOCK'. NASH's 'TEACH YOUR CHILDREN' and 'OUR HOUSE' were slighter in comparison but rounded out the record perfectly. Blighted by ego problems with drug habits to match, the band split the same month as YOUNG's ominous 'OHIO' single was released, an inspired protest against the killing of four students by the National Guard during an anti-war demo at Kent State University. The patchy, posthumous live album 'FOUR-WAY STREET' (1971) was hardly a fitting epitaph although predictably it sold in bucketloads. While YOUNG continued with his mercurial solo career, STILLS released a follow-up to his well-received debut solo album and later recorded with the country-inflected MANASSAS. CROSBY and NASH, meanwhile, worked as a duo, releasing their eponymous debut in 1972. Minus STILLS and YOUNG, the record was pleasant if hardly essential, lacking the tension that had made CSN&Y so compelling. The inevitable reunion took place in 1974 and the biggest personality clash in rock toured the world to ecstatic audiences although the band couldn't keep it together long enough to record anything concrete in the studio (the fact that YOUNG travelled in his own tourbus didn't bode too well). STILLS and YOUNG recorded the 'LONG MAY YOU RUN' album in 1976 which boasted the wistful charm of the title track and the exquisite 'FONTAINEBLEU' but was otherwise fairly lacklustre. The following year CROSBY, STILLS and NASH reformed and recorded the million selling 'CSN', again another inoffensive collection which lacked the focus YOUNG had brought to the group in the past. Indeed, while CSN were touring their particular brand of polite folk-Pop, YOUNG was interpreting punk with his 'LIVE RUST' and 'RUST NEVER SLEEPS' albums, outstripping CSN creatively and commercially. 'DAYLIGHT AGAIN' (1982) spawned the American singles 'WASTED ON THE WAY' and 'SOUTHERN CROSS' while the band split later the same year as CROSBY was sentenced to five years for drugs and firearms offences. In the event, he was allowed to attend a rehabilitation program as an alternative which he later reneged on and did actually serve some time during the mid-80's. Out on bail, he appeared live with STILLS, NASH and YOUNG at Live Aid and the quartet made a long-awaited second album in 1988, 'AMERICAN DREAM'. Although it eclipsed most of the YOUNG-less CSN material, it was hardly the masterpiece people had waited almost two decades for. The standout track was CROSBY's 'COMPASS', a song borne of his drug-induced hardships. NEIL YOUNG subsequently refused to tour the record and that, more or less, was that. CSN continued unbowed, even after CROSBY underwent a liver transplant following the release of the 'AFTER THE STORM' (1994) album. With YOUNG now almost in the 30th year of a solo career which showed no sign of letting up (even if his recent output has been under par), it didn't appear likely that he would ever re-unite with his old sparring partners. However, the er, 'LOOKING FORWARD' (1999) set (was it?) heralded the one-off return of CSN&Y. NASH was also back in his own right with 2002's 'SONGS FOR SURVIVORS', one of the better releases to come from the CSN&Y camp over the last decade. Unassuming and largely acoustic, the record showcased a voice which has weathered nicely with the years, furnishing the harmonies with a warm, burnished veneer. CROSBY supplied guest vocals while veteran drummer RUSS KUNKEL played, co-produced and co-wrote opener 'DIRTY LITTLE SECRET'. Musically reclusive over the last 14 years, STILLS finally re-emerged with the long-awaited 'MAN ALIVE' (2005), an album that inevitably featured NASH, YOUNG and an unlikely guest, HERBIE HANCOCK. Critics hailed it as one of his best since the early 70s, STILLS singing the acoustic wisdom of his years and covering Booker T. Jones' 'OLD MAN TROUBLE'.

• **Songwriters:** All 4 took a hand individually and later together in all songs. Also covered; WOODSTOCK (Joni Mitchell) / DEAR MR. FANTASY (Traffic) / and a few more.

Album rating: CROSBY, STILLS & NASH (*8) / DEJA VU (*9; & Young) / FOUR-WAY STREET (*7; & Young) / SO FAR compilation (*7; & Young) / CSN (*7) / REPLAY compilation (*7) / DAYLIGHT AGAIN (*6) / ALLIES (*5) / AMERICAN DREAM (*5; & Young) / LIVE IT UP (*4) / AFTER THE STORM (*4) / LOOKING FORWARD (*4; & Young) / GREATEST HITS compilation (*8) /

ATLANTIC

David Crosby: IF I COULD ONLY REMEMBER MY NAME (*8) / GRAHAM NASH & DAVID CROSBY (*5; with Graham Nash) / WIND ON THE WATER (*5; with Graham Nash) / WHISTLING DOWN THE WIRE (*4; with Graham Nash) / CROSBY/NASH LIVE (*4; with Graham Nash) / THE BEST OF CROSBY/NASH compilation (*5; with Graham Nash) / OH YES I CAN (*5) / THOUSAND ROADS (*5) / IT'S ALL COMING BACK TO ME NOW (*4) / Stephen Stills: STEPHEN STILLS (*8) / STEPHEN STILLS 2 (*6) / MANASSAS (*6) / DOWN THE ROAD (*4; with Manassas) / STILLS (*5) / STEPHEN STILLS LIVE (*4) / ILLEGAL STILLS (*5) / LONG MAY YOU RUN (*5; as Stills-Young Band) / STILL STILLS – THE BEST OF STEPHEN STILLS compilation (*6) / THOROUGHFARE GAP (*3) / RIGHT BY YOU (*5) / STILLS ALONE (*5) / TURN BACK THE PAGES compilation (*6) / MAN ALIVE (*5) / Graham Nash: SONGS FOR BEGINNERS (*7) / WILD TALES (*5) / EARTH AND SKY (*4) / INNOCENT EYES (*4) / SONGS FOR SURVIVORS (*5)

CROSBY, STILLS & NASH

DAVID CROSBY (b. DAVID VAN CORTLAND, 14 Aug'41, Los Angeles, Calif.) – vocals, guitar (ex-BYRDS) / **STEPHEN STILLS** (b. 3 Jan'45, Dallas, Texas)– vocals, guitar, bass, keyboards (ex-BUFFALO SPRINGFIELD) / **GRAHAM NASH** (b. 2 Feb'42, Blackpool, England)– vocals, guitar (ex-HOLLIES)
with **DALLAS TAYLOR** – drums

Atlantic Atlantic

Jun 69. (lp) *(588 189)* *<8229>* **CROSBY, STILLS & NASH** [25] [6]
– Suite: Judy blue eyes / Marrakesh express / Guinnevere / You don't have to cry / Pre-road downs / Wooden ships / Lady of the island / Helplessly hoping / Long time gone / 49 bye-byes. *(re-iss. 1972; K 40033) (cd-iss. Jul87; K2 40033)*

Jul 69. (7") *(584 283)* *<2652>* **MARRAKESH EXPRESS. / HELPLESSLY HOPING** [17] [28]

Oct 69. (7") *(584 304)* *<2676>* **SUITE: JUDY BLUE EYES. / LONG TIME GONE** [ ] Sep69 [21]

CROSBY, STILLS, NASH & YOUNG

— added **NEIL YOUNG** (b.12 Nov'45, Toronto, Canada) – guitar, vocals (ex-BUFFALO SPRINGFIELD) also **GREG REEVES** – bass

Mar 70. (lp) *(2401 001)* *<7200>* **DEJA VU** [5] [1]
– Carry on / Teach your children / Almost cut my hair / Helpless / Woodstock / Deja vu / Our house / 4 + 20 / Country girl: Whiskey boot hill – Down, down, down – Country girl / Everybody I love you. *(re-iss. 1972 lp/c; K/K4 50001) (cd-iss. May87; K2 50001)*

Apr 70. (7") *(2091 002)* **TEACH YOUR CHILDREN. / COUNTRY GIRL** [ ] [–]

May 70. (7") *(2091 010)* *<2723>* **WOODSTOCK. / HELPLESS** [ ] Mar70 [11]

May 70. (7") *<2735>* **TEACH YOUR CHILDREN. / CARRY ON** [–] [16]

Aug 70. (7") *(2091 023)* *<2740>* **OHIO. / FIND THE COST OF FREEDOM** [ ] Jun70 [14]

Nov 70. (7") *(2091 039)* *<2760>* **OUR HOUSE. / DEJA VU** [ ] Sep70 [30]

— (May'70) **CALVIN 'FUZZY' SAMUELS** – bass repl. REEVES **JOHN BARBATA** – drums (ex-TURTLES) repl. TAYLOR

— (Aug'70) split before release of posthumous album below with last line-up

Apr 71. (d-lp) *(2657 007)* *<2-902>* **FOUR-WAY STREET (live)** [5] [1]
– On the way home / Teach your children / Triad / The Lee shore / Chicago / Right between the eyes / Cowgirl in the sand / Don't let it bring you down / 49 bye-byes / Love the one you're with / Pre-road downs / Long time gone / Southern man / Ohio / Carry on / Find the cost of freedom. *(re-iss. 1972 lp/c; K/K4 60003) (cd-iss. Jul87; K2 60003) (d-cd re-iss. Aug92)*

— Their solo recordings, excluding NEIL YOUNG's, are below

STEPHEN STILLS

— - vocals, guitar with **STEPHEN FROMHOLTZ** – guitar / **PAUL HARRIS** – keyboards / **DALLAS TAYLOR** – drums / **CALVIN SAMUELS** – bass / plus Memphis Horns

Atlantic Atlantic

Nov 70. (lp) *(2401 004)* *<7202>* **STEPHEN STILLS** [30] [3]
– Love the one you're with / Do for the others / Church (part of someone) / Old times, good times / Go back home / Sit yourself down / To a flame / Black queen / Cheroke / We are not helpless. *(cd-iss. Oct95; 7567 82809-2)*

Dec 70. (7") *(2091 046)* *<2778>* **LOVE THE ONE YOU'RE WITH. / TO A FLAME** [37] [14]

May 71. (7") *(2091 069)* *<2790>* **SIT YOURSELF DOWN. / WE ARE NOT HELPLESS** [ ] Mar71 [37]

Jul 71. (lp) *(2401 013)* *<7206>* **STEPHEN STILLS 2** [22] [8]
– Change partners / Nothin' to do but today / Fishes and scorpions / Sugar babe / Know you got to run / Open secret / Relaxing town / Singin' call / Ecology song / Word game / Marianne / Bluebird revisited. *(re-iss. 1978;) (cd-iss. 1991; 7567-82389-2)*

Jul 71. (7") *(2091 117)* *<2806>* **CHANGE PARTNERS. / RELAXING TOWN** [ ] Jun71 [43]

Sep 71. (7") *(2091 141)* *<2820>* **MARIANNE. / NOTHIN' TO DO BUT TODAY** [ ] Aug71 [42]

STEPHEN STILLS & MANASSAS

STILLS retained **SAMUELS, HARRIS** and **TAYLOR,** brought in **CHRIS HILLMAN** – guitar, vocals / **AL PERKINS** – steel guitar, guitar / **JOE LALA** – percussion / **KENNY PASSARELLI** – bass (ex-JOE WALSH) repl. SAMUELS

Atlantic Atlantic

May 72. (d-lp/c) *(K/K4 60021)* *<2-903>* **MANASSAS** [30] Apr72 [4]
– Fallen eagle / Jesus gave love away for free / Colorado / So begins the task / Hide to the deep / Don't look at my shadow / It doesn't matter / Johnny's garden / Bound to fall / How far / Move around / The love gangster / Song of love / Rock'n'roll crazies – Cuban bluegrass / Jet set (sigh) / Anyway / Both of us (bound to lose) / What to do / Right now / The treasure (take one) / Blues man. *(cd-iss. Feb93 & Oct95; 7567 82808-2)*

May 72. (7") *<2876>* **IT DOESN'T MATTER. / ROCK'N'ROLL CRAZIES – CUBAN BLUEGRASS** [–] [61]

Aug 72. (7") *(K 10147)* **IT DOESN'T MATTER. / FALLEN ANGEL** [ ] [–]

Nov 72. (7") *<2888>* **ROCK'N'ROLL CRAZIES. / COLORADO** [–] [92]

May 73. (lp/c) *(K/K4 40440)* *<7250>* **DOWN THE ROAD** [33] [26]
– Isn't it about time / Lies / Pensamiento / So many times / Business on the street / Do you remember the Americans / Down the road / City junkies / Guaguanco de Vero / Rollin' my stone. *(cd-iss. Nov93; 7567 81424-2)*

May 73. (7") *(K 10306)* *<2959>* **ISN'T IT ABOUT TIME. / SO MANY TIMES** [ ] Apr73 [56]

Jul 73. (7") *(K 10340)* *<2917>* **GUAGUANCO DE VERO. / DOWN THE ROAD** [ ] Feb73 [ ]

— (Sep73) **HARRIS, PERKINS and HILLMAN joined SOUTHERN HILLMAN FURAY BAND. STEPHEN STILLS** formed his own band, retaining **PASSARELLI** and **LALA** plus **DONNIE DACUS** – guitar / **JERRY AIELLO** – keyboards / **HUSS KUNKEL** – drums

CROSBY, STILLS NASH & YOUNG

— (May'74) re-formed, mainly for concerts. Augmented by **TIM DRUMMOND** – bass / **RUSS KUNKEL** – drums / **JOE LALA** – percussion

STEPHEN STILLS

— went solo again (Feb75) with new band **LALA, DACUS, AIELLO** plus **GEORGE PERRY** – bass / **RONNIE ZIEGLER** – drums

C.B.S. Columbia

Jun 75. (lp/c) *(69146)* *<33575>* **STILLS** [31] [19]
– Turn back the pages / My favorite changes / My angel / In the way / Love story / To mama Christopher and the old man / First things first / New mama / As I come of age / Shuffle just as bad / Cold cold world / Myth of Sisyphus.

Jul 75. (7") *(3497)* *<10179>* **TURN BACK THE PAGES. / SHUFFLE JUST AS BAD** [ ] [84]

— added **RICK ROBERTS** – guitar, vocals (of FIREFALL)

Apr 76. (7") *<10369>* **BUYIN' TIME. / SOLDIER** [–] [ ]

May 76. (lp/c) *(81330)* *<34148>* **ILLEGAL STILLS** [54] [30]
– Buyin' time / Midnight in Paris / Different tongues / Closer to you / Soldier / The loner / Stateline blues / No me nieges / Ring of love / Circlin'.

Jul 76. (7") *(4416)* **THE LONER. / STATELINE BLUES** [ ] [–]

STILLS-YOUNG BAND

STEPHEN STILLS – vocals, guitar / **NEIL YOUNG** – vocals, guitar with **AIELLO, PERRY, VITALE + LALA**

Reprise Reprise

Sep 76. (7") *(K 14446)* *<1365>* **LONG MAY YOU RUN. / 12:8 BLUES** [ ] [ ]

Oct 76. (lp/c) *(K/K4 54081)* *<2253>* **LONG MAY YOU RUN** [12] [26]
– Long may you run / Make love to you / Midnight on the bay / Black

coral / Ocean girl / Let it shine / 12/8 blues (all the same) / Fontainebleau / Guardian angel. *(cd-iss. Jul93; K2 54081)*

Dec 76. (7") *<1370>* **MIDNIGHT ON THE BAY. / BLACK CORAL** –

— CROSBY, STILLS & NASH re-formed in '77 (see further on for more solo STILLS)

DAVID CROSBY

with loads of session people, too numerous to mention.

Atlantic Atlantic

Feb 71. (lp) *(2401 005) <SD 7203>* **IF I COULD ONLY REMEMBER MY NAME** 12 12
– Music is love / Cowboy movie / Tamalpais High (at about 3) / Laughing / What are their names / Traction in the rain / Song with no name (tree with no leaves) / Orleans / I'd swear there was somebody here. *(re-iss. 1972 lp/c; K/K4 40320) (cd-iss. Nov93; 56781415-2)*

Apr 71. (7") *<2792>* **MUSIC IS LOVE. / LAUGHING** – 95

Jul 71. (7") *<2809>* **ORLEANS. / TRACTION IN THE RAIN** –

GRAHAM NASH & DAVID CROSBY

duo (DAVID & GRAHAM) with more sessioners and left over GRATEFUL DEAD members which were included on DAVID's debut solo album.

May 72. (lp/c) *(K/K4 50011) <7220>* **GRAHAM NASH & DAVID CROSBY** 13 Apr72 4
– Southbound train / Whole cloth / Black notes / Strangers room / Where will I be / Page 43 / Frozen smiles / Games / Girl to be on my mind / The wall song / Immigration man.

May 72. (7") *<2873>* **IMMIGRATION MAN. / WHOLE CLOTH** – 36

Jul 72. (7") **SOUTHBOUND TRAIN. / WHOLE CLOTH** –

Jul 72. (7") *<2892>* **SOUTHBOUND TRAIN. / THE WALL SONG** – 99

— after CROSBY, STILLS, NASH & YOUNG reunion May74-Feb75

— resurrected partnership, with steady band members **CRAIG DOERGE** – keyboards / **LEE SKLAR** + **TIM DRUMMOND** – bass / **DANNY KOOTCH** & **RUSS KUNKEL** – drums / **DAVID LINDLEY** – guitar, violin.

Polydor A.B.C.

Jan 76. (lp) *(2310 428) <902>* **WIND ON THE WATER** Oct75 6
– Carry me / Mama lion / Bittersweet / Take the money and run / Naked in the rain / Love work out / Low down payment / Cowboy of dreams / Homeward through the haze / Fieldworker / To the last whale. *(cd-iss. Nov91 on 'Thunderbolt'; CDTB 128) (cd re-iss. Mar97 on 'Nectar'; NTMCD 550)*

Nov 75. (7") *(2001 615) <12140>* **CARRY ME. / MAMA LION** 52

Mar 76. (7") *<12165>* **TAKE THE MONEY AND RUN. / BITTERSWEET** –

May 76. (7") *(2001 660) <12185>* **LOVE WORK OUT. / BITTERSWEET**

Jul 76. (lp) *(2319 468) <956>* **WHISTLING DOWN THE WIRE** 26
– Spotlight / Broken bird / Time after time / Dancer / Mutiny / J.B.'s blues / Marguerita / Taken at all / Foolish man / Out of the darkness.

Aug 76. (7") **OUT OF THE DARKNESS. / LOVE WORK OUT** –

Aug 76. (7") *<12199>* **OUT OF THE DARKNESS. / BROKEN BIRD** – 89

Oct 76. (7") *<12217>* **SPOTLIGHT. / FOOLISH MAN** –

— CROSBY STILLS & NASH re-formed '77 (see further on)

GRAHAM NASH

solo using C,S & N past members plus GRATEFUL DEAD main men

Atlantic Atlantic

Jun 71. (lp) *(2401 011) <SD 7204>* **SONGS FOR BEGINNERS** 13 15
– Military madness / Better days / Wounded bird / I used to be a king / Be yourself / Simple man / Man in the mirror / There's only one / Sleep song / Chicago / We can change the world. *<(cd-iss. Feb93; 7567 81416-2)> (cd re-iss. Feb00; 72042)*

Jun 71. (7") *(2091 096) <2804>* **CHICAGO. / SIMPLE MAN** May71 35

Aug 71. (7") *<2827>* **MILITARY MADNESS. / SLEEP SONG** – 73

Sep 71. (7") *(2091 135)* **MILITARY MADNESS. / I USED TO BE A KING** –

Nov 71. (7") *<2840>* **I USED TO BE A KING. / WOUNDED BIRD** –

Nov 73. (7") *<2990>* **PRISON SONG. / HEY YOU (LOOKING AT HTE MOON)** –

Mar 74. (lp/c) *(K/K4 50025) <SD 7288>* **WILD TALES** Dec73 34
– Wild tales / Hey you (looking at the Moon) / Prison song / You'll never be the same / And so it goes / Oh! Camil (the winter soldier) / I miss you / On the line / Another sleep song.

Mar 74. (7") *(K 10425)* **ON THE LINE. / I MISS YOU** –

Aug 74. (7") *(K 10470)* **GRAVE CONCERN. / ANOTHER SLEEP SONG** –

— GRAHAM rejoined below and had more solo releases later.

CROSBY, STILLS & NASH

reformed in '77, with various session men.

Atlantic Atlantic

Jun 77. (lp/c) *(K 50369) <19104>* **CSN** 23 2
– Shadow captain / See the changes / Carried away / Fair game / Anything at all / Cathedral / Dark star / Just a song before I go / Cold rain / In my dreams / I give you give blind.

Jun 77. (7") *(K 10947) <3401>* **JUST A SONG BEFORE I GO. / DARK STAR** May77 7

Oct 77. (7") *(K 11024) <3432>* **FAIR GAME. / ANYTHING AT ALL** Sep77 43

Dec 77. (7") *<3453>* **CARRIED AWAY. / I GIVE YOU GIVE BLIND** –

STEPHEN STILLS

more solo releases with session people & his tour band **DALLAS TAYLOR** – drums / **GEORGE PERRY** – bass / **MIKE FINNEGAN** – keyboards / **JERRY TOLMAN** & **BONNIE BRAMLETT** – b.vocals

C.B.S. Columbia

Sep 78. (7") *(6662) <10804>* **CAN'T GET NO BOOTY. / LOWDOWN**

Oct 78. (lp) *(82859) <35380>* **THOROUGHFARE GAP** 83
– You can't dance alone / Thoroughfare gap / We will go / Beaucoup yumbo / What's the game / Midnight rider / Woman Lleva / Lowdown / Not fade away / Can't get no booty.

Nov 78. (7") *<10872>* **THOROUGHFARE GAP. / LOWDOWN** –

GRAHAM NASH

solo, with usual and past session people + CROSBY, STILLS & YOUNG

Capitol Capitol

Jan 80. (7") *<4812>* **IN THE 80'S. / T.V. GUIDE** –

Mar 80. (7") *<4849>* **OUT ON THE ISLAND. / HELICOPTER SONG** –

Mar 80. (lp) *(12014)* **EARTH & SKY**
– Earth & sky / Love has come / Out on the island / Skychild / Helicopter song / Barrel of pain / T.V. guide / It's alright / Magical child / In the 80's.

May 80. (7") *<4879>* **EARTH & SKY. / MAGICAL CHILD** –

CROSBY, STILLS & NASH

re-formed mid '82, with session men

Atlantic Atlantic

Jul 82. (lp/c) *(K/K4 50896) <19360>* **DAYLIGHT AGAIN** 8
– Turn your back on love / Wasted on the way / Southern cross / Into the darkness / Delta / Since I met you / Too much love to hide / Song for Susan / You are alive / Might as well have a good time / Daylight again. *(cd-iss. Oct94; 7567 82672-2)*

Nov 82. (7") *(K 11747) <4058>* **WASTED ON THE WAY. / DELTA** Jul82 9

Nov 82. (7") *(K 11749) <89969>* **SOUTHERN CROSS. / INTO THE DARKNESS** Sep82 18

Jan 83. (7") *<89888>* **TOO MUCH LOVE TO HIDE. / SONG FOR SUSAN** – 69

Jun 83. (lp) *(78-0075-1) <80075>* **ALLIES (live)** 43
– War games / Raise a voice / Turn your back on love / Barrel of pain / Shadow captain / Dark star / Blackbird / He played real good for free / Wasted on my way / For what it's worth. *(cd-iss. 1984; 780 075-2)*

Jul 83. (7") *(A 9818) <89812>* **WAR GAMES (live). / SHADOW CAPTAIN (live)** Jun83 45
(12") *(A 9818T)* – ('A'side) / Dark Star (live) / Keep your . . .

Sep 83. (7") *<89775>* **RAISE A VOICE (live). / FOR WHAT IT'S WORTH (live)** –

— split Aug'82, when CROSBY was sentenced to 5 years for drugs. He got leniency, when he agreed to rehabilitate himself in a drug hospital Dec'84.

STEPHEN STILLS

solo again (2nd single featured WALTER FINNEGAN)

W.E.A. Atlantic

Aug 84. (7") *<89633>* **STRANGER. / NO HIDING PLACE** [–] [61]

Sep 84. (lp/c) *(780 177-1) <80177>* **RIGHT BY YOU** [ ] Aug84 [75]
– 50/50 / Stranger / Flaming heart / Love again / No problem / Can't let go / Grey to green / Only love can break your heart / No hiding place / Right by you. *(cd-iss. Nov93; 7567 80177-2)*

Oct 84. (7") *<89611>* **CAN'T LET GO. / GREY TO GREEN** [–] [67]
(above as STEPHEN STILLS featuring MICHAEL FINNIGAN)

Dec 84. (7") *<89597>* **ONLY LOVE CAN BREAK YOUR HEART. / LOVE AGAIN** [–] [ ]

not iss. Vision

Sep 91. (cd/c/lp) *<3323>* **STILLS ALONE** [–] [ ]
– Isn't it so / Everybody's talkin' / Just isn't like you / In my life / Ballad of Hollis Brown / Singin call / The right girl / Blind fiddler medley / Amazonia / Treetop flyer.

Talking Elephant Titan – Pyramid

Aug 05. (cd) *(TECD 077) <50102-2>* **MAN ALIVE** [ ] [ ]
– Ain't it always / Feed the people / Hearts gate / Round the bend / I don't get it / Around us / Ole man trouble / Different man / Piece of me / Wounded world / Drivin' thunder / Acadienne / Spanish suite.

– compilations, etc. –

Apr 03. (cd) *Columbia; (507881-2)* **TURN BACK THE PAGES – THE BEST OF STEPHEN STILLS** [ ] [–]

Nov 03. (cd) *Raven; <(RVCD 179)>* **TURNIN' BACK THE PAGES – THE COLUMBIA RECORDINGS 1975-1978** [ ] [ ]

GRAHAM NASH

solo, he had rejoined The HOLLIES between Sep81-Apr83

Atlantic Atlantic

Apr 86. (7") *(A 9434) <89434>* **INNOCENT EYES. / I GOT A ROCK** [ ] [84]

Apr 86. (lp/c) *(781-633-1/-4) <81633>* **INNOCENT EYES** [ ] [ ]
– See you in Prague / Keep away from me / Innocent eyes / Chippin' away / Over the wall / Don't listen to the rumours / Sad eyes / Newday / Glass and steel / I got a rock.

Jul 86. (7") *<89396>* **SAD EYES. / NEWDAY** [–] [ ]

Oct 86. (7") *<89373>* **CHIPPIN' AWAY. / NEWDAY** [–] [ ]

CROSBY, STILLS, NASH & YOUNG

re-formed yet again

Atlantic Atlantic

Nov 88. (7") *<88966>* **GOT IT MADE. / THIS OLD HOUSE** [–] [69]

Nov 88. (lp/c)(cd) *(WX 233/+C)(781 886-2) <81888>* **AMERICAN DREAM** [ ] [16]
– American dream / Got it made / Name of love / Don't say goodbye / This old house / Nighttime for the generals / Shadowland / Drivin' thunder / Clear blue skies / That girl / Compass / Soldiers of peace / Feel your love / Night song.

Jan 89. (7") *(A 9003) <88966>* **AMERICAN DREAM. / COMPASS** [55] [ ]
(12"+=) *(A 9003T)* – Soldiers of peace.
(12"g-f++=) *(A 9003TX)* – Ohio.

DAVID CROSBY

solo again

A&M A&M

Feb 89. (lp/c/cd) *<(AMA/AMC/CDA 5232)>* **OH YES I CAN** [ ] [ ]
– Drive my car / Melody / Monkey and the underdog / In the wide ruin / Tracks in the dust / Drop down mama / Lady of the harbour / Distances / Flying man / Oh yes I can / My country 'tis of thee.

Feb 89. (7") *(AM 500)* **DRIVE MY CAR. / TRACKS IN THE DUST** [ ] [ ]
(12"+=) *(AMY 500)* – Flying men.

Apr 89. (7"/12") *(AM/+Y 502)* **LADY OF THE HARBOR. / DROP DOWN MAMA** [ ] [ ]

— with band **LELAND SKLAR** – bass / **RUSSELL KUNKEL** + **JEFF PORCARO** – drums / **CRAIG DOERGE** – keyboards / **ANDY FAIRWEATHER-LOWE** – guitar / **DEAN PARKS** – guitar, flute / **BERNIE LEADON** – acoustic guitar / **C.J. VANSTON** – keyboards / with many guests **JACKSON BROWNE** + **DON WAS** plus outside writers + on session **PHIL COLLINS, JONI MITCHELL, MARC COHN, JIMMY WEBB, PAUL BRADY, STEPHEN BISHOP, JOHN HIATT, BONNIE HAYES** + **NOEL BRAZIL.**

Atlantic Atlantic

May 93. (7"/c-s; by DAVID CROSBY featuring PHIL COLLINS) *<87360>* **HERO. / COVERAGE** [ ] [44]
(cd-s+=) – Fare thee well.

Jun 93. (cd/c) *<(7567 82484-2/-4)>* **THOUSAND ROADS** [ ] [ ]
– Hero / Too young to die / Old soldier / Through your hands / Yvette in English / Thousand roads / Columbus / Helpless heart / Coverage / Natalie.

Mar 95. (cd/c) *<(7567 82620-2/-4)>* **IT'S ALL COMING BACK TO ME NOW (live '93)** [ ] [ ]
– In my dreams / Rusty and blue / Hero / Till it shines on you / 1000 roads / Cowboy movie / Almosy cut my hair / Deja vu / Long time gone / Wooden ships.

Sams Sams

Sep 98. (cd) *(145)* **CPR** [ ] [ ]

CROSBY, STILLS & NASH

with **JOE VITALE** – drums, organ, synth bass / **LELAND SKLAR** – bass / **CRAIG DOERGE** – keyboards / **MIKE LANDAU** – guitar / **MIKE FISHER** – percussion

East West Atlantic

Jun 90. (cd/c/lp) *<(7567 82101-2/-4/-1)>* **LIVE IT UP** [ ] [57]
– Live it up / If anybody had a heart / Tomboy / Haven't we lost enough / Yours and mine / (Got to keep) Open / Straight line / House of broken dreams / Arrows / After the dolphin.

Jul 90. (7") *<87909>* **LIVE IT UP. / CHUCK'S LAMENT** [–] [ ]

Aug 94. (cd/c) *<(7567 82654-2/-4)>* **AFTER THE STORM** [ ] [98]
– Only waiting for you / Find a dream / Camera / Unequal love / Till it shines / It won't go away / These empty days / In my life / Street to lean on / Bad boyz / After the storm / Panama.

CROSBY, STILLS, NASH & YOUNG

Nov 99. (cd/c) *<(9362 47436-2/-4)>* **LOOKING FORWARD** [54] [26]
– Faith in me / Looking forward / Stand and be counted / Heartland / Seen enough / Slowpoke / Dream for him / No tears left / Out of control / Someday soon / Queen of them all / Sanibel.

– their compilations etc. –

on 'Atlantic' unless mentioned otherwise

Aug 74. (lp/c) *(K/K4 50023) <18100>* **SO FAR – THE BEST OF . . .** [25] [1]
– Woodstock / Marrakesh express / You don't have to cry / Teach your children / Love the one you're with / Almost cut my hair / Wooden ships / Dark star / Helpless / Chicago – We can change the world / Cathedral / 4 + 20 / Our house / Change partners / Just a song before I go / Ohio / Wasted on the way / Southern cross / Suite: Judy blue eyes / Carry on – Questions / Horses through a rainstorm / Johnny's garden / Guinnevere / Helplessly hoping / The Lee Shore / Taken it all / Shadow captain / As I come of age / Drive my car / Dear Mr. Fantasy / In my dreams / Yours and mine / Haven't we lost enough? / After the dolphin / Find the cost of freedom. *(cd-iss. Jan87; K2 50023) (cd re-iss. Oct94; 7567 82648-2)*

Oct 75. (d-lp) *(K 60063)* **TWO ORIGINALS OF STEPHEN STILLS (1st 2 lp's)** [ ] [–]

Dec 75. (lp) *(K 50214) <18156>* **STEPHEN STILLS – LIVE (live)** [ ] [ ]

Jan 77. (lp) *(K 50327) <18201>* **STEPHEN STILLS – THE BEST OF STEPHEN STILLS** [ ] [ ]
– Love the one you're with / It doesn't matter / We are not helpless / Marianne / Bound to fall / Isn't it about time / Change partners / Go back home / Johnny's garden / Rock and roll crazies – Cuban bluegrass / Sit yourself down.

Nov 77. (lp; CROSBY & NASH) *Polydor; (2310 565) / A.B.C.; <1042>* **LIVE (live)** [ ] [52]

Jan 79. (lp; CROSBY & NASH) *Polydor; (2310 626) / A.B.C.; <1102>* **THE BEST OF CROSBY & NASH** [ ] Oct78 [ ]
(re-iss. Nov80)

Nov 80. (lp/c) *Atlantic; (K/K4 50766)* <16026> **REPLAY** [ ] Sep80 [ ]
– Carry on / Marrakesh express / Just a song before I go / First things first / Shadow captain / To the last whale / Love the one you're with / Pre-road downs / Change partners / I give you give blind / Cathedral. *(cd-iss. Oct94; 7567 82648-2)*

Dec 91. (d-cd/d-c) *(7567 80487-2/-4)* **CARRY ON** [ ] [ ]

Dec 91. (4xcd-box/4xc-box) *East West; (7567 82319-2/-4)* **THE BEST OF CROSBY, STILLS & NASH** [ ] [-]

Feb 92. (7"/c-s) *East West;* **OUR HOUSE. / MARRAKESH EXPRESS** [ ] [ ]
(12"+=/cd-s+=) – Carry on / Dear Mr. Fantasy (STEPHEN STILLS / GRAHAM NASH).
(above A-side was re-actified on a famous building society TV ad)

Mar 05. (cd) *Rhino;* <*(8122 76537-2)*> **GREATEST HITS** [38] [24]
– Suite: Judy blue eyes / Long time gone / Just a song before I go / Southern cross / Marrakesh express / Helplessly hoping / Shadow captain / Our house / Guinnevere / See the changes / Teach your children / Wooden ships / Delta / 49 bye-byes / Wasted on the way / Carry on – Questions / In my dreams / Cathedral / Daylight again.

GRAHAM NASH

not iss. Artemis

Jul 02. (cd) <*751130*> **SONGS FOR SURVIVORS** [-] [ ]
– Dirty little secret / Blizzard of lies / Lost another one / The Chelsea hotel / I'll be there for you / Nothing in the world / Where love lies tonight / Pavanne / Liar's nightmare / Come with me. *(UK-dvda-iss.Jul03; 69286010929-2)*

Sheryl CROW

Born: 11 Feb'62, Kennett, Missouri, USA. She left university after studying classical music before subsequently relocating to St. Louis. In the mid-80's, SHERYL set off to L.A. and finally cut her teeth as SHIRLEY CROW on MICHAEL JACKSON's 1988 'Bad' tour. The singer/songwriter then earned her crust by singing back-up for ROD STEWART, DON HENLEY and JOE COCKER. With ambitions of becoming a solo singer, she handed a demo tape to producer, Hugh Padgham, who, with a recommendation from STING, got her signed to 'A&M' in '91. An album of unproductive songs was shelved but with the help of a second producer, Bill Bottrill, she emerged late in 1993 with debut set, 'TUESDAY NIGHT MUSIC CLUB'. Although it didn't sell immediately, it became a deserved smash a year later after a support slot to the re-formed EAGLES and a well-received appearance at WOODSTOCK II. Suddenly her album turned gold and a single, 'ALL I WANNA DO', almost hit No.1. Its easy-going swing was characteristic of the album as a whole and the singer's EDIE BRICKELL / ROSIE VELA-esque narratives translated into further hits with 'CAN'T CRY ANYMORE' and the evocative 'RUN BABY RUN'. Now as much of a female role model as ALANIS MORISSETTE, SHERYL scored a second UK Top 10 with 'IF IT MAKES YOU HAPPY'. Arguably her finest moment to date, the song had a gritty passion missing from her earlier work and the rootsier, harder hitting sound indicated the direction of the new album. Simply titled, 'SHERYL CROW' (1996), the record saw her paying homage to her musical heroes, primarily the ROLLING STONES but also BOB DYLAN. A second transatlantic success, the album spawned further hits in 'EVERYDAY IS A WINDING ROAD', 'HARD TO MAKE A STAND' and 'A CHANGE WOULD DO YOU GOOD'. Yet despite the promise of the first single, the bulk of the album sounded as though she was merely going through the motions, especially on the lacklustre 'A CHANGE . . .'. A crowd-buoying performance at a mud caked Glastonbury Festival proved she's made of sterner stuff than her glossy image might suggest. SHERYL undoubtably has the potential, it's just a shame she doesn't harness it more often. By the time her third album, 'THE GLOBE SESSIONS' (1998) was issued, SHERYL CROW had a hard time maintaining her rockier, rootsy edge while also trying to take the album in a different direction. Songs such as 'THERE GOES THE NEIGHBORHOOD' displayed CROW's usual pop rock motif, albeit with jangling STONES-like guitars used to almost overkill. Standout tracks on the album came from her ability to create beautiful and unrestrained ballads; 'RIVERWIDE' was a lush, sweeping track that oozed Celtic overtones, while 'MISSISSIPPI', an actual outtake from Dylan's 'TIME OUT OF MIND', was perhaps the strongest song on the whole set. CROW took her show on the road one year later and most memorably performed her final concert of the year at Central Park, as the live album 'SHERYL CROW AND FRIENDS: LIVE IN CENTRAL PARK' (1999) testified. KEITH RICHARDS, CHRISSIE HYNDE, ERIC CLAPTON and the DIXIE CHICKS all participated, although it didn't translate as well on record. With 2002's 'C'MON C'MON', it seemed as if the singer had finally hit upon the right balance of roots revival, pop nous, confident writing and rock star guts which she had always seemed capable of. The rest of the album carried on where hit single 'SOAK UP THE SUN' left off, the sound of an artist in her element at last. CROW seemed an unlikely candidate for celebrity couple status, but her relationship with Tour De France cyclist (and 7-times winner) Lance Armstrong, generated a fair amount of press coverage. 'WILDFLOWER' (2005) replicated the chart positions (US/UK No.2) of its predecessor, while the music/lyrics didn't quite remain the same, influenced as they were by SHERYL's surprise romance. Touted as a BRUCE SPRINGSTEEN-style double-whammy, the record eventually appeared as a single disc, bearing the kind of svelte production and mooning, homespun melody that suggested a lost Laurel Canyon classic. The singer's life entered a period of turmoil early in 2006 as the announcement of her separation from Armstrong was closely followed by the revelation that she had been diagnosed with breast cancer.

• **Songwriters:** Writes lyrics mainly / songs by BILL BOTTRELL or BAERWALD-GILBERT-McLEOD, etc. except I'M GONNA BE A WHEEL SOMEDAY (Fats Domino) / D'YER MAKER (Led Zeppelin) / MISSISSIPPI (Bob Dylan) / THE FIRST CUT IS THE DEEPEST (Cat Stevens). • **Trivia:** The track, 'HUNDREDS OF TEARS', featured on 'Pointbreak' movie soundtrack. Another two, 'STRONG ENOUGH' and 'NO ONE SAID IT WOULD BE EASY', were heard in the 1994 film 'Kalifornia'.

Album rating: TUESDAY NIGHT MUSIC CLUB (*7) / SHERYL CROW (*8) / THE GLOBE SESSIONS (*6) / . . . AND FRIENDS: LIVE AT CENTRAL PARK (*5) / C'MON, C'MON (*7) / THE VERY BEST OF SHERYL CROW compilation (*7) / WILDFLOWER (*6)

SHERYL CROW – vocals + sessioners incl. BILL BOTTRILL

A&M A&M

Sep 93. (7"/c-s) *(580 380-7/-4)* **RUN, BABY, RUN. / ALL BY MYSELF** [ ] [ ]
(cd-s+=) *(580 381-2)* – The na-na song / Reach around jerk.

Oct 93. (cd/c) *(540 126-2/-4)* <*0126*> **TUESDAY NIGHT MUSIC CLUB** [68] [3]
– Run, baby, run / Leaving Las Vegas / Strong enough / Can't cry anymore / Solidify / The na-na song / No one said it would be easy / What I can do for you / All I wanna do / We do what we can / I shall believe. *<re-dist.US Feb94> (re-dist.Sep94; hit UK No.22 + No.8 early '95) (re-iss. cd May95; 540 368-2)* – (w/ free cd '6 TRACK LIVE MINI-ALBUM'; *540 126-18)*

Feb 94. (7"/c-s) *(580 462-7/-4)* **WHAT I CAN DO FOR YOU. / VOLVO COWGIRL 99** [ ] [ ]
(cd-s+=) *(580 463-2)* – ('A'version) / I shall believe.

Apr 94. (7"/c-s) *(580 568-7/-4)* **RUN, BABY, RUN. / LEAVING LAS VEGAS (acoustic)** [ ] [ ]
(cd-s+=) *(580 569-2)* – All by myself / Reach around jerk.

Apr 94. (c-s) <*0582*> **LEAVING LAS VEGAS / THE NA-NA SONG** [-] [60]

Jun 94. (7"/c-s) *(580 644-7/-4)* **LEAVING LAS VEGAS. / LEAVING LAS VEGAS (live)** [66] [-]
(cd-s) *(580 645-2)* – ('A'side) / I shall believe (live) / What I can do for you (live).
(cd-s) *(580 647-2)* – ('A'side) / No one said it would be easy (live) / The na-na song (live).

Oct 94. (7"/c-s) *(580 842-7/-4)* <0702> **ALL I WANNA DO (remix). / SOLIDIFY** 5 Jul94 2
(cd-s+=) *(580 843-2)* – I'm gonna be a wheel someday.
(cd-s) *(580 845-2)* – ('A'acoustic live) / Run, baby, run (acoustic live) / Leaving Las Vegas (acoustic live).

Dec 94. (c-s) *<0798>* **STRONG ENOUGH / WHAT I CAN DO FOR YOU** – 5

Jan 95. (7"/c-s) *(580 918-7/-4)* **STRONG ENOUGH. / NO ONE SAID IT WOULD BE EASY** 33 –
(cd-s+=) *(580 919-2)* – All I wanna do (live).
(cd-s) *(580 921-2)* – ('A'side) / All by myself / ('A'live) / Reach around jerk.

May 95. (c-s/cd-s) *(581 055-4/-2)* **CAN'T CRY ANYMORE / ALL I WANNA DO / STRONG ENOUGH (US version) / WE DO WHAT WE CAN** 33 –
(cd-ep) *(581 057-2)* – ('A'side) / What I can do for you (live) / No one said it would be easy (live) / I shall believe (live).

Jun 95. (c-s) *<0798>* **CAN'T CRY ANYMORE / WE DO WHAT WE CAN** – 36

Jul 95. (c-s) *(581 146-4)* **RUN, BABY, RUN / LEAVING LAS VEGAS** 24 –
(cd-s) *(581 147-2)* – ('A'side) / Can't cry anymore (live) / Reach around jerk (live) / I shall believe (live).
(cd-s) *(581 149-2)* – ('A'side) / Strong enough (live) / No one said it would be easy (live) / The na-na song (live).

Oct 95. (c-s) *(581 220-4)* **WHAT I CAN DO FOR YOU / LEAVING LAS VEGAS (live)** 43 –
(cd-s) *(581 221-2)* – ('A'side) / D'yer maker / I'm gonna be a wheel someday / No one said it would be easy.
(cd-s) *(581 229-2)* – ('A'live) / All I wanna do (live) / Strong enough (live) / Can't cry anymore (live).

Sep 96. (c-s) *<1874>* **IF IT MAKES YOU HAPPY / KEEP ON GROWING** – 10

Sep 96. (7") *(581 902-7)* **IF IT MAKES YOU HAPPY. / ALL I WANNA DO** 9 –
(c-s+=/cd-s+=) *(581 903-4/-2)* – Run, baby, run / Leaving Las Vegas.
(cd-s) *(581 885-2)* – ('A'side) / On the outside / Keep on growing / The book.

Oct 96. (cd/c) *(540 590-2/-4)* *<540587>* **SHERYL CROW** 5 6
– Maybe angels / A change / Home / Sweet Rosalyn / If it makes you happy / Redemption day / Hard to make a stand / Everyday is a winding road / Love is a good thing / Oh Marie / Superstar / The book / Ordinary morning / Free man. *(d-cd-iss. Nov97; 540719-2)*

Nov 96. (c-s/cd-s) *(582 021-4/-2)* **EVERYDAY IS A WINDING ROAD / STRONG ENOUGH / CAN'T CRY ANYMORE / WHAT I CAN DO FOR YOU** 12 Mar97 11
(cd-s) *(582 023-2)* – ('A'side) / If it makes you hapy (live BBC) / All I wanna do (live BBC) / Run, baby, run (live BBC).

Mar 97. (c-s/cd-s) *(582 147-4/-2)* **HARD TO MAKE A STAND / HARD TO MAKE A STAND (alt.) / HARD TO MAKE A STAND (live) / IN NEED** 22
(cd-s) *(582 149-2)* – ('A'side) / Sad sad world / No one said it would be easy (live) / If it makes you hapy (live).

Jul 97. (c-s) *(582 217-4)* **A CHANGE WOULD DO YOU GOOD / EVERYDAY IS A WINDING ROAD (live) / CAN'T CRY ANYMORE (live) / LEAVING LAS VEGAS (live)** 8
(cd-s) *(582 271-2)* – (first 2 tracks) / If it makes you happy / Hard to make a stand.
(cd-s) *(582 209-2)* – ('A'track) / Hard to make a stand (live) / On the outside (live) / ('A'live).

Oct 97. (cd-s) *(582399-2)* **HOME / STRONG ENOUGH / SWEET ROSALYN / I SHALL BELIEVE** 25
(cd-s) *(582401-2)* – ('A'side) / Hard to make a stand / Can't cry anymore / Redemption day.

Dec 97. (c-s) *(582456-4)* **TOMORROW NEVER DIES / ORDINARY MORNING** 12
(cd-s+=) *(582457-2)* – The book / No one said it would be easy.
(cd-rom) *(044067-2)* – ('A'mixes + CD-Rom).

Aug 98. (c-s) *(582761-4/-2)* *<radio play>* **MY FAVOURITE MISTAKE / SUBWAY RIDE / CRASH & BURN** 9 20
(cd-s) *(582763-2)* – ('A'side) / In need (new remix) / Carolina.

Sep 98. (cd/c) *(540974-2/-4)* *<540959>* **THE GLOBE SESSIONS** 2 5
– My favourite mistake / There goes the neighbourhood / Riverwide / It don't hurt / Maybe that's something / Am I getting through (part I & II) / Anything but down / The difficult kind / Mississippi / Members only / Crash & burn / Resuscitation. *(special d-cd Mar99 +=; 541025-2)* – A change would do you good / Riverwide / It don't hurt / Strong enough / The difficult kind / Everyday is a winding road.

Nov 98. (c-s) *(582806-4)* **THERE GOES THE NEIGHBOURHOOD / STRAIGHT TO THE MOON** 19
(cd-s+=) *(582807-2)* – My favourite mistake (live).
(cd-s) *(582809-2)* – ('A'live) / You always get your way / Hard to make a stand (live).

Feb 99. (c-s) *(582826-4)* *<radio cut>* **ANYTHING BUT DOWN / RUN BABY RUN (live)** 19 Mar99 49
(cd-s+=) *(582829-2)* – Riverwide (live).
(cd-s) *(582827-2)* – ('A'side) / Leaving Las Vegas (live) / Mississippi (live).

Aug 99. (c-s) *(667888-4)* **SWEET CHILD O' MINE / (pop mix)** 30 –
(cd-s) *(667888-2)* – ('A'side) / If it makes you happy / A change would do you good / ('A'-CD-Rom).
(above issued on 'Columbia')

Dec 99. (cd/c) *<(490574-2/-4)>* **SHERYL CROW AND FRIENDS LIVE FROM CENTRAL PARK (live)**
– Everyday is a winding road / My favourite mistake / Leaving Las Vegas / Strong enough (w/ DIXIE CHICKS) / It don't hurt / A change would do you good / Gold dust woman (w/ STEVIE NICKS) / If it makes you happy (w/ CHRISSIE HYNDE) / All I wanna do / Happy (w/ KEITH RICHARDS & CHRISSIE HYNDE) / The difficult kind (w/ SARAH McLACHLAN) / White room / There goes the neighbourhood / Tombstone blues (w/ KEITH RICHARDS & DIXIE CHICKS).

Apr 02. (c-s) *(497705-4)* **SOAK UP THE SUN / EVERYDAY IS A WINDING ROAD / IF IT MAKES YOU HAPPY** 16 17
(cd-s) *(497704-2)* – ('A'side) / Chances are / You're not the one / ('A'-video).
(cd-s) *(497705-2)* – ('A'side) / My favourite mistake (live) / A change would do you good (live).

Apr 02. (cd) *<(493262-2)>* **C'MON, C'MON** 2 2
– Steve McQueen / Soak up the sun / You're an original / Safe and sound / C'mon, c'mon / It's so easy / Over you / Lucky kid / Diamond road / It's only love / Abilene / Hole in my pocket / Weather channel. *(UK+=)* – Missing / I want you.

Jun 02. (c-s) *(497742-4)* **STEVE McQUEEN / IF IT MAKES YOU HAPPY (live)** 44 –
(cd-s+=) *(497742-2)* – My favourite mistake (live).

Oct 03. (cd) *(986109-2)* *<52102-2>* **THE VERY BEST OF SHERYL CROW** (compilation) 2 Nov03 2
– All I wanna do / Soak up the sun / My favourite mistake / The first cut is the deepest / Everyday is a winding road / Leaving Las Vegas / Strong enough / Light in your eyes / If it makes you happy / The difficult kind / Picture (with KID ROCK) / Steve McQueen / A change would do you good / Home / There goes the neighbourhood / I shall believe / Let's get free.

Oct 03. (cd-s) *<(9813556)>* **THE FIRST CUT IS THE DEEPEST / EVERYDAY IS A WINDING ROAD (live at Central Park) / MY FAVOURITE MISTAKE (live at Central Park)** 37 17

Jun 04. (cd-s) *(986270-0)* **LIGHT IN YOUR EYES / YOU'RE NOT THE ONE / MY FAVOURITE MISTAKE (live from Abbey Road studios)** 73 –

Sep 05. (cd-s) *<(9885348)>* **GOOD IS GOOD / WILDFLOWER (acoustic) / I KNOW WHY (acoustic) / ('A'-video)** 75 64

Sep 05. (cd) *(9884801)* *<52290-2>* **WILDFLOWER** 25 2
– I know why / Perfect lie / Good is good / Chances are / Wildflower / Lifetimes / Letter to God / Live it up / I don't wanna know / Always on your side / Where has all the love gone. *(UK+=)* – Wildflower (acoustic) / Where has all the love gone (acoustic). *(ltd-cd w/dvd+=; 9884810)* – (DVD tracks).

Dec 05. (-) *<radio>* **ALWAYS ON YOUR SIDE** – 33

CROWDED HOUSE

Formed: New Zealand ... virtually as SPLIT ENDS in October '72 by TIM FINN and PHIL JUDD. They slightly altered their name to SPLIT ENZ, stylising their own brand of tongue-in-cheek pop, inspired no doubt, by SPARKS and ROXY MUSIC. In fact, PHIL MANZANERA, guitarist of the latter, produced and remixed their 'SECOND THOUGHTS' album in 1976. They were subsequently joined by TIM's brother NEIL, as a replacement for chief songwriter, JUDD. With TIM's more melodic sensibilities increasingly to the fore, the band enjoyed some belated success with the 'TRUE COLOURS' (1980) album. A single, 'I GOT YOU', even hit the British Top 20, topping the Australian charts for over two months. Despite their pop charm, the band's latter day albums such as 'TIME AND TIDE' (1982) and 'CONFLICTING EMOTIONS' (1984) sold relatively poorly outside Australia/NZ. They finally split for good in 1985, with NEIL forming CROWDED HOUSE alongside PAUL HESTER and NICK SEYMOUR. Relocating to L.A., the band signed to 'Capitol' and enjoyed massive Stateside success with their eponymous debut album in 1986/87. Taking the popcraft of SPLIT ENZ and injecting it with an aching melody, NEIL FINN proved himself an exquisite songwriter. The standout track was the bittersweet 'DON'T DREAM IT'S OVER' (later a UK hit for PAUL YOUNG), while other near misses were 'SOMETHING SO STRONG' and 'WORLD WHERE YOU LIVE'. Yet they couldn't repeat the formula on follow-up, 'TEMPLE OF LOW MEN' (1988), the album just scraping into the American Top 40 and failing miserably in Britain. There was only one thing for it, TIM had to return; with his additional songwriting and harmony vocals, 'WOODFACE' (1991) was a near masterpiece. If 'WEATHER WITH YOU' was perhaps a little sugary and 'CHOCOLATE CAKE' a mite leaden, there was no denying the swoonsome beauty of 'FALL AT YOUR FEET' and the almost spiritual reverence of 'FOUR SEASONS IN ONE DAY'. The trademark offbeat humour was still bubbling under the surface, rising to the top on the likes of 'THERE GOES GOD'. Although the set was slow to pick up, it deservedly spent more than two years in the British charts, although incredibly it failed to take off in the States. An unlikely pairing with former KILLING JOKE bassist/dance guru, YOUTH, led to CROWDED HOUSE's most experimental, profound and possibly finest effort in 'TOGETHER ALONE' (1993). Recorded at Kare Kare (a remote coastal area in their native New Zealand), the album was shrouded in an atmosphere of mystical calm and resolve, even on the rockier tracks such as 'LOCKED OUT'. 'DISTANT SUN' was a glorious burst of life-affirming, semi-acoustic melody, although it was the hypnotic grace of 'FINGERS OF LOVE' and 'PRIVATE UNIVERSE' which really carried the essence of this masterpiece. Enjoying another extended residence in the UK charts and spawning another string of hit singles, few could have predicted it would be the band's swansong. Yet after a further bout of touring and a UK No.1 compilation, 'RECURRING DREAM' (1996), the band announced a split amid tearful farewell shows. TIM FINN (husband of actress, Greta Scacchi), who had combined a solo career that encompassed a handful of albums (the last of which was the UK Top 30 'BEFORE AND AFTER' in 1993), formed one-off trio, ALT, with ANDY WHITE and LIAM O'MAONLAI. The FINN brothers were awarded OBE's for their services to New Zealand's music industry. With 'SAY IT IS SO' (2000), TIM FINN completed another chapter in his long but frustratingly sporadic solo career. Not that it wasn't worth waiting for, especially with the tantalising prospect of the pop songsmith having decamped to Nashville. Unsurprisingly, the record's homespun atmospherics and oblique lyrics preclude any CROWDED HOUSE polish. Instead, FINN was revealed as having matured into a singer/songwriter of considerable depth, alive to the possibility that less is, more often than not, more. In an unprecedented burst of solo creativity, the CROWDED HOUSE founder released another fine set, 'FEEDING THE GODS', in 2001, the same year his brother NEIL got in on the act with 'ONE NIL', his own solo follow-up to 1998's Top 5 (UK) 'TRY WHISTLING THIS'. While that album was all about realising experimental, if still unerringly melodic, ideas extraneous to the CROWDED HOUSE formula, the Top 20 'ONE NIL' stuck to the singing/songwriting tools of his trade. No surprises then, but a solid effort with guest appearances by the likes of SHERYL CROW and LISA GERMANO.

• **Songwriters:** NEIL FINN penned except MR. TAMBOURINE MAN (Bob Dylan) + EIGHT MILES HIGH + SO YOU WANT TO BE A ROCK'N'ROLL STAR (Byrds). SPLIT ENZ; either NEIL or TIM. • **Trivia:** SIX MONTHS IN A LEAKY BOAT was banned by the BBC in 1982, due to the Argentian / Falklands conflict. NICK is the brother of HUNTER + COLLECTORS' frontman, MARK SEYMOUR.

Album rating: Split Enz: MENTAL NOTES (*6) / SECOND THOUGHTS (*5) / DIZRHYTHMIA (*7) / FRENZY (*5) / TRUE COLOURS (*7) / WAIATA (*5) / TIME AND TIDE (*6) / SEE YA 'ROUND (*4) / HISTORY NEVER REPEATS compilation (*7) / Crowded House: CROWDED HOUSE (*5) / TEMPLE OF LOW MEN (*6) / WOODFACE (*8) / TOGETHER ALONE (*7) / RECURRING DREAM – THE VERY BEST OF CROWDED HOUSE compilation (*9) / AFTERGLOW collection (*6) / Tim Finn: ESCAPADE (*5) / BIG CANOE (*5) / TIM FINN (*7) / BEFORE AND AFTER (*6) / SAY IT IS SO (*6) / FEEDING THE GODS (*5) / ALTITUDE (*6; with Alt:= with Andy White & Liam O'Maonlai) / FINN (*5; as Finn:= Tim & Neil) / Neil Finn: TRY WHISTLING THIS (*6) / ONE NIL (*6) / RAIN soundtrack (*6) / 7 WORLDS COLLIDE (*5)

SPLIT ENZ

TIM FINN (b. BRIAN TIMOTHY FINN, 25 Jun'52, Te Awamutu, New Zealand) – vocals, piano / **PHIL JUDD** – vocals, guitar / **JONATHAN CHUNN** – bass / **MILES GOLDING** – violin / **MICHAEL HOWARD** – drums

Vertigo not iss.

Apr 73. (7"; as SPLIT ENDS) **FOR YOU. /** [ ] [–]

—— **EDDIE RAYNOR** – keyboards repl. MILES / **WALLY WILKINSON** – guitar + **NOEL CROMBIE** – percussion repl. HOWARD

Mushroom not iss.

Jun 75. (lp) *(L 35588)* **MENTAL NOTES** [–] Austra [–]
– Late last night / Walking down a road / Titus / Lovey dovey / Sweet dreams / Stranger than fiction / Time for a change / Matinee idyll / The woman who loves you / Mental notes. *(UK-iss.Aug76 on 'Chrysalis' lp/c; CHR/ZCHR 1131)*

Jun 75. (7") **TITUS. /** [–] Austra [–]

Sep 75. (7") **LOVEY DOVEY. /** [–] Austra [–]

May 76. (lp) *(L 35981)* **SECOND THOUGHTS** (re-mixes of debut) [–] Austra [–]

—— **NEIL FINN** (b.27 May'58, Te Awamutu, New Zealand) – vocals, guitar repl. JUDD / JON and drummer EMLYN CROWTHER were repl. by Englishmen **NIGEL GRIGGS** (b.18 Aug'49) – bass / **MALCOLM GREEN** (b.25 Jan'53) – drums / **ROBERT GILLIE** – saxophone
(next iss. Australia; May77 on 'Mushroom')

Chrysalis Mushroom

Nov 76. (7") *(CHS 2120)* **LATE LAST NIGHT. / WALKING DOWN THE ROAD** [ ] [ ]

Feb 77. (7") *(CHS 2131)* **ANOTHER GREAT DIVIDE. / STRANGER THAN FICTION** [ ] [–]

Oct 77. (7") *(CHS 2170)* **MY MISTAKE. / CROSSWORDS** [ ] [ ]
(12"+=) *(CHS 2170-12)* – The woman who loves you.

Oct 77. (lp/c) *(CHR/ZCHR 1145)* **DIZRHYTHMIA** [ ] [ ]
– Bold as brass / My mistake / Parrot fashion love / Sugar and spice / Without a doubt / Crosswords / Charley / Nice to know / Jambouree. *(Aus-iss.; 36347)*

—— JUDD re-joined but quit again, while GILLIE also quit

Mushroom not iss.

1978. (lp) *(L 36921)* **FRENZY** [–] Austra [–]
– I see red / Give it a whirl / Master plan / Famous plan / Hermit McDermitt / Stuff and nonsense / Marooned / Frenzy / The roughest toughest game in the world / She got body she got soul / Betty / Abu Dhabi / Mind over matter.

—— now without WILKINSON

Illegal not iss.

Nov 79. (7"m) *(ILS 0019)* **I SEE RED. / GIVE IT A WHIRL / HERMIT McDERMITT** [ ] [–]

—— Issued earlier in Australia

—— Initial A&M material iss.Australia 1979 'Mushroom'.

A&M A&M

Aug 80. (lp/c) *(AMLH/CAM 64822)* <4822> **TRUE COLOURS** [42] [40]
– Shark attack / I got you / What's the matter with you / I hope I never /

Nobody takes me seriously / Missing persons / Poor boy / How can I resist her / The choral sea. *(cd-iss. 1988; CDA 3235) (re-iss. Oct92 cd/c; CD/C MID 130)*

Aug 80. (7") *(AMS 7546) <2252>* **I GOT YOU. / DOUBLE HAPPY** 12 53

Nov 80. (7") *(AMS 7574)* **NOBODY TAKES ME SERIOUSLY. / THE CHORAL SEA** –

Jan 81. (7") *(AMS 8101)* **POOR BOY. / MISSING PERSON**

Jan 81. (7") *<2285>* **I HOPE I NEVER. / THE CHORAL SEA** –

Mar 81. (7") *<2293>* **NOBODY TAKES ME SERIOUSLY. / WHAT'S THE MATTER WITH YOU** –

Mar 81. (lp/c) *(AMLH/CAM 64848) <4848>* **WAIATA** May81 45
– Hard act to follow / One step ahead / I don't wanna dance / Iris / Whale / Clumsby / History never repeats / Walking through the ruins / Ships / Ghost girl / Albert of India.

Apr 81. (7"m) *(AMS 8128)* **HISTORY NEVER REPEATS. / SHARK ATTACK / WHAT'S THE MATTER WITH YOU** 63 –

Jun 81. (7") *(AMS 8146) <2339>* **ONE STEP AHEAD. / IN THE WARS**

— MALCOLM GREEN left and NOEL now on drums

Apr 82. (7") *(AMS 8216) <2411>* **SIX MONTHS IN A LEAKY BOAT. / MAKE SOME SENSE OF IT**

Apr 82. (lp/c) *(AMLH/CAM 64894) <4894>* **TIME AND TIDE** 71 58
– Dirty creature / Giant heartbeat / Hello Sandy Allen / Never ceases to amaze me / Lost for words / Small world / Take a walk / Pioneer / Six months in a leaky boat / Haul away / Log cabin fever / Make some sense of it.

Aug 84. (7") *(AMS 203) <2652>* **MESSAGE TO THE GIRL. / BON VOYAGE (KIAKATIA)**

Aug 84. (lp/c) *(AMLH/CAM 64963) <4963>* **CONFLICTING EMOTIONS** Jul84
– Strait old line / Bullett brain and cactus head / Message to my girl / Working up an appetite / Our day / No mischief / The devil you know / I wake up every night / Conflicting emotions / Bon voyage. *(cd-iss. 1988)*

— Now a quartet (**EDDIE RAYNOR, NEIL FINN, NIGEL GRIGGS + NOEL CROMBIE**) when TIM FINN married actress Greta Saatchi and went solo

Jan 85. (m-lp) **SEE YA 'ROUND (live)** – NZ –
– Breakin' my back / I walk away / Doctor love / One mouth is fed / Years go by / Voices / The lost cat / Adz / This is massive / Kia kaha / Ninnie knees up.

— disbanded 1985; NEIL formed CROWDED HOUSE, which later included TIM. A year later, PHIL JUDD, NOEL CROMBIE, NIGEL GRIGGS and MICHAEL DEN ELZEN formed their own outfit, SCHNELL FENSTER, who released two quirky-funk/jazz sets, 'SOUND OF TREES' (1988) and 'OK ALRIGHT A HUH OH YEAH' (1991).

– compilations, etc. –

Dec 80. (lp) *Chrysalis; (CHR 1329)* **BEGINNING OF THE ENZ** –

Sep 87. (d-lp) *Concept; (CCQ 050)* **COLLECTION: 1973-1984 . . . THE BEST OF SPLIT ENZ** – Austra –

Oct 92. (cd) *Chrysalis; (CDMID 175)* **HISTORY NEVER REPEATS (THE BEST OF SPLIT ENZ)**
– I got you / Hard act to follow / Six months in a leaky boat / What's the matter with you / One step ahead / I see red / Message to my girl / History never repeats / I hope I never / Dirty creature / Poor boy.

Feb 94. (cd/c) *Chrysalis; (CD/TC CHR 6059)* **THE BEST OF SPLIT ENZ**

Apr 95. (cd) *Mushroom; (D 98010)* **ANNIVERSARY** –

CROWDED HOUSE

NEIL FINN – vocals, guitar, piano / **NICK SEYMOUR** (b. 9 Dec'58, Benella, Australia) – bass / **PAUL HESTER** (b. 8 Jan'59, Melbourne) – drums, vocals with many guests **TIM PIERCE** – guitar / **MITCHELL FROOM** – keyboards, producer / **JOE SATRIANI** – b.vox / **JORGE BERMUDEZ** – percussion etc.

Capitol Capitol

Aug 86. (7") *(CL 416)* **WORLD WHERE YOU LIVE. / THAT'S WHAT I CALL LOVE**
(ext.12"+=) *(12CL 416)* – Can't carry on.
(ext.c-s+=/ext.cd-s+=) *(TC/CD CL 416)* – Something so strong / Don't dream it's over.

Mar 87. (7") *(CL 438) <5614>* **DON'T DREAM IT'S OVER. / THAT'S WHAT I CALL LOVE** 27 Jan87 2
(c-s+=/12"+=) *(TC/12 CL 438)* – ('A'extended).

Mar 87. (7") *<5634>* **LOVE YOU 'TIL I DIE. / MEAN TO ME** –

Mar 87. (lp/c)(cd) *(EST/TC-EST 2016)(CDP 746693-2) <12485>* **CROWDED HOUSE** Aug86 12
– World where you live / Now we're getting somewhere / Don't dream it's over / Mean to me / Love you 'til the day I die / Something so strong / Hole in the river / I walk away / Tombstone / That's what I call love. *(cd+=)* – Can't carry on. *(re-iss. Mar94 cd/c; same)*

Jun 87. (7") *(CL 456) <5695>* **SOMETHING SO STRONG. / I WALK AWAY** Apr87 7
(12"+=) *(12CL 456)* – Don't dream it's over (live).

Aug 87. (7") *<44033>* **WORLD WHERE YOU LIVE. / HOLE IN THE RIVER** – 65

Nov 87. (7") *<44083>* **NOW WE'RE GETTING SOMEWHERE. / TOMBSTONE** –

Jun 88. (7") *(CL 498) <44164>* **BETTER BE HOME SOON. / KILL EYE** 42
(12"+=/cd-s+=) *(12/CD CL 498)* – Don't dream it's over (live).

Jul 88. (lp/c)(cd) *(EST/TC-EST 2064)(CDP 748763-2) <48763>* **TEMPLE OF LOW MEN** 40
– I feel possessed / Kill eye / Into temptation / Mansion in the slums / When you come / Never be the same / Love this life / Sister madly / In the lowlands / Better be home soon.

Aug 88. (7") *<44226>* **INTO TEMPTATION. / BETTER BE HOME SOON** –

Aug 88. (7") *(CL 509)* **SISTER MADLY. / MANSION IN THE SLUMS**
(12"+=/cd-s+=) *(12/CD CL 509)* – Something so strong (live).

Nov 88. (12"ep) *<44406>* **I FEEL POSSESSED. /** –

— added **TIM FINN** – vocals, piano, keyboards

Jun 91. (cd)(c/lp) *(CDP 793559-2)(TC+/EST 2144) <93559>* **WOODFACE** 34 83
– Chocolate cake / It's only natural / Fall at your feet / Tall trees / Four seasons in one day / Weather with you / Whispers and moans / There goes God / Fame is / All I ask / As sure as I am / Italian plastic / She goes on / How will you go. *(album hit UK No.6 in Feb92)*

Jun 91. (c-s/7") *(TC+/CL 618)* **CHOCOLATE CAKE. / AS SURE AS I AM** 69
(12"+=/cd-s+=) *(12/CD CL 618)* – Anyone can tell.

Oct 91. (c-s) *<44747>* **FALL AT YOUR FEET / WHISPERS AND MOANS** – 75

Oct 91. (c-s/7") *(TC+/CL 626)* **FALL AT YOUR FEET. / DON'T DREAM IT'S OVER** 17 –
(cd-s+=) *(CDCL 626)* – Sister madly / Better be home soon.
(cd-s) *(CDCLX 626)* – ('A'side) / Six months in a leaky boat (live) / Now we're getting somewhere (live) / Something so strong (lp version).

— reverted to a trio again, when TIM departed Autumn '91. He was replaced on tour in 1993 by US session keyboard player **MARK HART** (b. 2 Jul'53, Fort Scott, Kansas)

Feb 92. (c-s/7") *(TC+/CL 643)* **WEATHER WITH YOU. / INTO TEMPTATION** 7
(cd-s) *(CDCL 643)* – ('A'side) / Mr. Tambourine man (live) / Eight miles high (live) / So you want to be a rock'n'roll star (live).
(cd-s) *(CDCLS 643)* – ('A'side) / Fall at your feet (live) / When you come (live) / Walking on the spot (live).

Jun 92. (c-s/7") *(TC+/CL 655)* **FOUR SEASONS IN ONE DAY. / THERE GOES GOD** 26
(cd-s) *(CDCL 655)* – ('A'side) / Dr. Livingstone (live) / Recurring dream (live) / Anyone can tell (live).
(cd-s) *(CDCLS 655)* – ('A'side) / Weather with you (live) / Italian plastic (live) / Message to my girl (live).

Sep 92. (c-s/7") *(TC+/CL 661)* **IT'S ONLY NATURAL. / CHOCOLATE CAKE** 24
(cd-s+=) *(CDCL 661)* – Medley:- It's only natural – Six months in a leaky boat – Hole in the river / The burglar's song.

Sep 93. (c-s/7") *(TC+/CL 697)* **DISTANT SUN. / WALKING ON THE SPOT** 19
(cd-s+=) *(CDCL 697)* – Throw your arms around me (live) / One step ahead (live).
(cd-s) *(CDCLS 697)* – ('A'side) / This is massive (live) / When you come (live).

Oct 93. (cd/c/lp) *(CD/TC+/EST-U 2215) <27048>* **TOGETHER ALONE** 4 73
– Kare Kare / In my command / Nails in my feet / Black & white boy / Fingers of love / Pineapple head / Locked out / Private universe / Walking on the spot / Distant sun / Catherine wheels / Skin feeling / Together alone.

Nov 93. (c-s/7") *(TC+/CL 701)* **NAILS IN MY FEET. / ZEN ROXY** 22
(cd-s+=) *(CDCL 701)* – Don't dream it's over (live).

Feb 94. (c-s) *(TCCL 707)* **LOCKED OUT. / DISTANT SUN (live)** 12
(cd-s+=) *(CDCL 707)* – Hole in the river (live) / Sister Madly (live).
(10"+=) *(10CL 707)* – Private universe (live) / Fall at your feet (live).
(cd-s) *(CDCLS 707)* – ('A'side) / Private universe (live) / Fall at your feet (live) / Better be home soon (live).

Jun 94. (c-s) *(TCCL 715)* **FINGERS OF LOVE (live). / NAILS IN MY FEET (live)** 25
(cd-s) *(CDCL 715)* – ('A'side) / Skin feeling / Kare Kare (live) / In my command (live).
(10") *(10CL 715)* – ('A'side) / Love u till the day I die (live) / Whispers and moans (live) / It's only natural (live).
(cd-s) *(CDCLS 715)* – ('A'side) / Catherine wheels / Pineapple head (live) / Something so strong (live).

Sep 94. (c-s) *(TCCL 723)* **PINEAPPLE HEAD (live). / WEATHER WITH YOU** 27
(10"+=/cd-s+=) *(10/CD CL 723)* – Don't dream it's over / Together alone.

— NEIL and TIM were awarded O.B.E.'s in Queen's birthday honours.

Jun 96. (c-s) *(TCCL 774)* **INSTINCT / RECURRING DREAM** 12
(cd-s+=) *(CDCL 774)* – Weather with you (live) / Chocolate cake (live).
(cd-s) *(CDCLS 774)* – ('A'side) / World where you live (live) / In the lowlands (live) / Into temptation (live).

Jun 96. (cd/c/lp) *(CD/TC+/EST 2283)* <38250> **RECURRING DREAM – THE VERY BEST OF CROWDED HOUSE** (compilation) 1
– Weather with you / World where you live / Fall at your feet / Locked out / Don't dream it's over / Into temptation / Pineapple head / When you come / Private universe / Not the girl you think you are / Instinct / I feel possessed / Four seasons in one day / It's only natural / Distant sun / Something so strong / Mean to me / Better be home soon / Everything is good for you. *(cd w/extra live-cd; CDESTX 2283)* – There goes God / Newcastle jam / Love u till the day I die / Hole in the river / Pineapple head / Private universe / How will you go / Left hand / Whispers and moans / Kill eye / Fingers of love / Don't dream it's over / When you come / Sister madly / In my command.

Aug 96. (c-s) *(TCCL 776)* **NOT THE GIRL YOU THINK YOU ARE. / BETTER BE HOME SOON (live)** 20
(cd-s+=) *(CDCL 776)* – Private universe (live) / Fingers of love (live).
(cd-s) *(CDCLS 776)* – ('A'side) / Instinct (live) / Distant sun (live) / Fall at your feet (live).

Oct 96. (7") *(CL 780)* **DON'T DREAM IT'S OVER. / WEATHER WITH YOU (live)** 25
(cd-s+=) *(CDCLS 780)* – Into temptation (live) / Locked out (live).
(cd-s) *(CDCL 780)* – ('A'side) / Four seasons in one day (live) / In my command (live) / Pineapple head (live).

— they were now no longer, having disbanded June '96

– compilations, etc. –

Nov 95. (3xcd-box) *E.M.I.; (CDOMB 001)* **CROWDED HOUSE / TEMPLE OF LOW MEN / WOODFACE**

Feb 00. (cd) *Capitol; (533722-2) <650011>* **AFTERGLOW** (leftovers) 18
– I am in love / Sacred cow / You can touch / Help is coming / I love you Dawn / Dr. Livingstone / My telly's gone bung / Private universe / Lester / Anyone can tell / Recurring dream / Left hand / Time immemorial.

May 02. (cd) *EMI Gold; (538945-2)* **IT'S ONLY NATURAL – THE COLLECTION** –

Jun 03. (cd) *Capitol; <82678>* **CLASSIC MASTERS** –

Sep 03. (d-cd) *Capitol; (592024-2)* **CROWDED HOUSE / WOODFACE** –

TIM FINN

— (solo with some SPLIT ENZ members)

Epic A&M

Nov 83. (7") *<2572>* **GRAND ADVENTURE. / THROUGH THE YEARS** –

Nov 83. (7") *(A 3932)* **FRACTION TOO MUCH FRICTION. / BELOW THE PAST** Apr84

Jan 84. (7") *<2597>* **MADE MY DAY. / GRAND ADVENTURE** –

Jun 84. (lp/c) *(EPC/40 25812)* <4972> **ESCAPADE** Sep83
– Fraction too much friction / Staring at the embers / Through the years / Not for nothing / In a minor key / Made my day / Wait and see / Below the belt / I only want to know / Growing pains. *(cd-iss. Oct93 on 'Sony Europe';) (re-iss. Jun94 cd/c; 474610-2/-4)*

Virgin Virgin

Mar 86. (7") *(VS 849)* **NO THUNDER NO FIRE NO CAR. / SEARCHING FOR THE STREETS** –

Apr 86. (lp/c/cd) *(V/TCV/CDV 2369)* <90879> **THE BIG CANOE**
– Are we one or are we two? / Searching the streets / Hole in my heart / Spiritual hung / Don't bury my heart / Timmy / So into wine / Hyacinth / Big canoe. *(re-iss. cd Mar94; OVED 221)*

Jun 86. (7"/12") *(VS 866/+12)* **CARVE YOU IN MARBLE. / HOLE IN MY HEART** –

Capitol Capitol

Apr 89. (lp/c/cd) *(EST/TC-EST/CD-EST 2088)* <48735> **TIM FINN**
– Young mountain / Not even close / How'm I gonna sleep / Parihaka / Tears inside / Birds swim fish fly / Suicide on Downing Street / Show a little mercy / Crescendo / Been there, done that. *(re-iss. Oct92; same)*

Jul 89. (7") *(CL 542)* <44339> **HOW'M I GONNA SLEEP. / CRUEL BLACK CROW**
(12"+=/cd-s+=) *(12/CD CL 542)* – Six months in a leaky boat.

— with **RICHARD THOMPSON / ANDY WHITE / LIAM O'MAONLAI**

Jun 93. (c-s) *(659248-4)* **PERSUASION. / STRANGENESS AND CHARM (version)** 43
(cd-s) *(659248-2)* – ('A'side) / Parihaka / Secret heart / ('A'acoustic).
(cd-s) *(659248-5)* – ('A'side) / Six months in a leaky boat (live) / Not even close (live) / Protected (live).

Jun 93. (cd/c) *(CD/TC EST 2202)* <94904> **BEFORE AND AFTER** 29
– Hit the ground running / Protected / In love with it all / Persuasion / Many's the time (in Dublin) / Funny way / Can't do both / In your sway / Strangness in charm / Always never now / Walk you home / I found it *(cd re-iss. Sep94; same)*

Sep 93. (c-s) *(TCCL 694)* **HIT THE GROUND RUNNING. / NO MORE TEARS** 50
(cd-s+=) *(CDCL 694)* – Not made of stone / You've changed.
(cd-s) *(CDCLS 694)* – ('A'side) / Walk you home (live) / Charlie (live w / PHIL MANZANERA) / ('A'live).

ALT

TIM FINN / + **ANDY WHITE** – vocals, guitar (former solo artist) / **LIAM O'MAONLAI** – vocals, guitar (ex-HOTHOUSE FLOWERS). ALT (ANDY, LIAM & TIM) recorded in Australia, although initiated in Dublin.

Parlophone Cooking Vinyl

Jun 95. (cd/c) *(CD/TC PCS 7377)* <9001> **ALTITUDE** 67 Oct95
– We're all men / Penelope tree / When the winter comes / Favourite girl / Swim / The refugee tree / What you've done / Second swim / Girlfriend guru / Mandala / I decided to fly / The day you were born / Halfway round the world.

FINN

TIM + NEIL duo

Parlophone not iss.

Oct 95. (c-s) *(TCR 6417)* **SUFFER NEVER / WEATHER WITH YOU (demo)** 29 –
(cd-s+=) *(CDRS 6417)* – Prodigal son (demo) / Catherine wheel (demo).
(cd-s) *(CDR 6417)* – ('A'side) / Strangeness and charm (demo) / In love with it all (demo) / Four seasons in one day.

Oct 95. (cd/c) *(CD/TC FINN 1)* **FINN** 15 –
– Only talking sense / Eyes of the world / Mood swinging man / Last day of June / Suffer never / Angels heap / Niwhai / Where is my soul / Bullets in my hairdo / Paradise ((wherever you are) / Kiss the road of Rarotonga.

Nov 95. (c-s/cd-s) *(TCR/CDR 6421)* **ANGELS HEAP / IT'S ONLY NATURAL (demo) / CHOCOLATE CAKE (demo)** 41 –
(cd-s) *(CDRS 6421)* – ('A'side) / There goes God (demo) / How will you go (demo).

— in '96, TIM collaborated with ANNA PACQUIN on a children's project EP, 'MAGNIFICENT NOSE & OTHER STORIES'

NEIL FINN

— with augmentation from a host of musicians on a few tracks each

Jun 98. (c-s) *(TCR 6495)* **SHE WILL HAVE HER WAY / ASTRO** 26
(cd-s+=) *(CDRS 6495)* – 808 song.
(c-s) *(CDR 6495)* – ('A'side) / Faster than light / Identical twin.

Jun 98. (cd/c/lp) *(72434 95139-2/-4/-1)* *<69372>* **TRY WHISTLING THIS** 5
– Last one standing / Souvenir / King tide / Try whistling this / She will have her way / Sinner / Twisty bass / Loose tongue / Truth / Astro / Dream date / Faster than light / Addicted.

Oct 98. (c-s/cd-s) *(TCR/CDRS 6505)* **SINNER / TOKYO / SHE COMES SCATTERED** 39 –
(cd-s) *(CDR 6505)* – ('A'live) / Not the girl you think you are (live) / Last one standing (live).

Mar 01. (cd-s) *(CDR 6557)* **WHEREVER YOU ARE / DRIVING ME MAD (web) / THE LAST TO KNOW (web)** 32 –
(cd-s) *(CDRS 6557)* – ('A'side) / Underestimated / Now I get it.

Apr 01. (cd) *(532039-2)* *<532112>* **ONE NIL** 14 Mar01
– The climber / Rest of the day off / Hole in the ice / Wherever you are / Last to know / Don't ask why / Secret god / Turn and run / Elastic heart / Anytime / Driving me mad / Into the sunset.

Jun 01. (cd-s) *(CDRS 6560)* **THE LAST TO KNOW / TRY WHISTLING THIS (live) / DISTANT SUN (live)** –
(cd-s) *(CDR 6560)* – ('A'live) / Loose tongue (live) / Not the girl you think you are (live).

Sep 01. (cd-s) *(CDR 6563)* **HOLE IN THE ICE / LOOSE TONGUE (live) / NOT THE GIRL YOU THINK YOU ARE (live)** 43 –
(cd-s) *(CDRS 6563)* – ('A'live) / Try whistling this (live) / Distant sun (live) / ('A'video).

E.M.I. not iss.

Oct 01. (cd) *(536964-2)* **RAIN** (Soundtrack w/ Various Artists) – NewZ –
– You don't know / (track by EDMUND McWILLIAMS) / Summer of love (w/ EDMUND McWILLIAMS) / Mum in bed / Orange and blue / Red room / (track by LISA GERMANO) / The affair / (track by HUMAN INSTINCT) / Boat dawn / Boat joyride / Kids floating / Batman / Shower / (track by LISA GERMANO) / Drive home (w/ EDMUND McWILLIAMS) / (track by LIAM FINN).

— Friends below:- JOHNNY MARR, ED O'BRIEN, EDDIE VEDDER, LISA GERMANO, SEBASTIAN STEINBERG, PHIL SELWAY, PAUL JEFFREY, etc.

Parlophone Nettwerk

Nov 01. (cd; by NEIL FINN & FRIENDS) *(536645-2)* *<30258>* **7 WORLDS COLLIDE (live at the St. James)** Feb02
– Anytime / Take a walk / The climber / Loose tongue / Down on the corner / There is a light that never goes out / Paper doll / Turn and run / Angels heap / Edible flowers / Stuff and nonsense / I see red / She will have her way / Parting ways / Weather with you / Paradise (wherever you are) / Don't dream it's over.

Apr 02. (cd) *<30265>* **ONE ALL** (remixes) –

TIM FINN

Frenz Of The Enz not iss.

Jun 99. (cd-ep) **FAR OUT** – NewZ –
– Roadtrip / Currents / Need to be right / Death of a popular song / Some dumb reason.

Hypertension What Are?

Dec 00. (cd) *(HYP 0202)* *<60039>* **SAY IT IS SO** Feb00
– Underwater mountain / Shiver / Good together / Roadtrip / Currents / Need to be right / Twinkle / Big wave rider / Death of a popular song / Some dumb reason / Rest.

Sep 01. (cd) *<60052>* **FEEDING THE GODS** –
– Songline / I'll never know / Subway dreaming / Say it is so / What you've done / Sawdust and splinters / Dead man / Commonplace / Waiting for your moment / Party was you / Incognito in California.

the CULT

Formed: Bradford, England . . . 1982 as the SOUTHERN DEATH CULT for whom IAN ASTBURY (then going under the name IAN LINDSAY) took on vocal duties. Having spent time in Canada as a kid, ASTBURY had been profoundly influenced by Native American culture and problems soon arose when the singer felt his pseudo hippy/Red Indian philosophy was being compromised by the band set-up. The group split the following year, ASTBURY keeping the name but shortening it to DEATH CULT. Relocating to London, ASTBURY duly recruited a new band (all seasoned hands on the post-punk circuit) and released an eponymous, 4-track 12" single. The band released a further solitary single, 'GOD'S ZOO', before trimming the name further to The CULT. While the band's music still betrayed slight indie/goth tendencies, they were eager to lose the 'gothic' tag. 'DREAMTIME' (1984) sounded confused and directionless, and it wasn't until 'LOVE', the following year, that the band fashioned some kind of distinct identity. Veering from the cascading bombast of the classic singles, 'RAIN' and 'SHE SELLS SANCTUARY' to the mystic schtick of 'BROTHER WOLF, SISTER MOON', the album semi-successfully ploughed a deeper retro furrow than the myriad BYRDS clones of the day. ASTBURY's flowing locks were also something of an anomaly for an 'alternative' band in those dark 80's days, and the band were derided in some areas of the music press. The CULT's response was to throw caution to the wind and do what they'd probably always secretly dreamed of doing, writing massive, anthemic heavy rock songs. With metal guru RICK RUBIN at the production helm, DUFFY's guitar was pushed way up in the mix and the sound generally tightened. The result: any fans clinging to gothic pretensions were aghast while Kerrang readers loved it. Possibly The CULT's finest moment, it spawned the booty-shaking singles 'LOVE REMOVAL MACHINE', 'LI'L DEVIL' and 'WILDFLOWER', hell, it even had a cover of 'BORN TO BE WILD'! 'SONIC TEMPLE' (1989) was another heavy rock effort, if a bit more grandiose in its reach, featuring their tribute to doomed 60's child, EDIE SEDGEWICK, 'EDIE (CIAO BABY)'. This album saw The CULT finally gain major success in America, the US 'big rock' sound evident in the record's grooves. Line-up changes had dogged The CULT throughout their career and by 1991, ASTBURY and DUFFY were the only remaining members from the original line-up. That year's album, 'CEREMONY', sounded somewhat listless, although it was a relative success. 1993 saw a No.1 compilation album, 'PURE CULT' selling like hotcakes, although people weren't quite so eager to shell out for '94's 'THE CULT' album. Their glory days were clearly over, the band remaining a cult (!) phenomenon. In 1996, ASTBURY was in full flight again, fronting a new rock outfit, The HOLY BARBARIANS, although the album, 'CREAM' didn't shift many copies. The ageing rock warrior finally released a bonafide solo album in the shape of 1999's 'SPIRIT/LIGHT/SPEED', enlisting former MASTERS OF REALITY man, CHRIS GOSS, on guitar and production duties. While the lyrical sentiments and mystic overtones remained the same – check out the Che Guevara-style sleeve – the music made a concerted effort to get hip with some pre-millennial industrial angst. When the long awaited new CULT album, 'BEYOND GOOD AND EVIL' finally arrived in summer 2001, it came as little surprise that the new noised-up approach remained intact. Save for a few nods to their classic late 80's/early 90's heyday, the band embraced the harsher sonic climate of post-metal with DUFFY giving it laldy on the distortion pedal. Having said that, oldtime CULT fans were placated to a certain degree with the reliable ASTBURY wail and an obvious reluctance to completely forego the killer hooks which made them so compelling in the first place. Of late, ASTBURY was fronting a revitalised DOORS (OF THE 21st CENTURY) on major global concerts.

• **Songwriters:** From '83 onwards, all by ASTBURY / DUFFY. Covered WILD THING (Troggs) / LOUIE LOUIE (Kingsmen) / CONQUISTADOR (Theatre Of Hate) / FAITH HEALER (Alex Harvey).

Album rating: THE SOUTHERN DEATH CULT (*6; as the Southern Death Cult) / DREAMTIME (*7) / LOVE (*8) / ELECTRIC (*6) / SONIC TEMPLE (*8) / CEREMONY (*6) / PURE CULT compilation (*7) / THE CULT (*5) / BEYOND GOOD AND EVIL (*6) / Holy Barbarians: CREAM (*6) / Ian Astbury: SPIRIT/LIGHT/SPEED (*5)

the SOUTHERN DEATH CULT

IAN LINDSAY (b. ASTBURY, 14 May'62, Heswell, Cheshire, England)– vocals / **BUZZ BURROWS** – guitar / **BARRY JEPSON** – bass / **AKY (NAWAZ QUERESHI)** – drums

Situation2 | not iss.

Dec 82. (7") *(SIT 19)* **FATMAN. / MOYA** [ ] [–]
(12"+=) *(SIT 19T)* – The girl.

Beggars Banquet | not iss.

Jun 83. (lp) *(BEGA 46)* **THE SOUTHERN DEATH CULT** [43] [–]
– All glory / Fatman / Today / False faces / The crypt / Crow / Faith / Vivisection / Apache / Moya. *(re-iss. Jul88 lp/c/cd; BBL/+C 46/+CD) (cd re-iss. Sep96; BBL 2009CD)*

— (Apr'83) (as BUZZ, AKY and BARRY formed GETTING THE FEAR)

— **IAN ASTBURY** recruited new people– BILLY DUFFY (b.12 May'61)– lead guitar (ex-THEATRE OF HATE, ex-NOSEBLEEDS) / **JAMIE STUART** – bass (ex-RITUAL, ex-CRISIS) / **RAY MONDO** (r.n. SMITH)– drums (ex-RITUAL)

Situation2 | not iss.

Jul 83. (12"ep; as DEATH CULT) *(SIT 23T)* **BROTHERS GRIMM / HORSE NATION. / GHOST DANCE / CHRISTIANS** [ ] [–]

— **NIGEL PRESTON** – drums (ex-SEX GANG CHILDREN) repl. MONDO

Nov 83. (7"/12"; as DEATH CULT) *(SIT 29/+T)* **GOD'S ZOO. / GOD'S ZOO (THESE TIMES)** [ ] [–]
(re-iss. Nov88)

the CULT

— (same line-up)

Situation2 | not iss.

May 84. (7") *(SIT 33)* **SPIRITWALKER. / A FLOWER IN THE DESERT** [ ] [–]
(12"+=) *(SIT 33T)* – Bone rag.

Beggars Banquet | Sire

Aug 84. (lp/c) *(BEG A/C 57)* **DREAMTIME** [21] [ ]
– Horse nation / Spiritwalker / 83rd dream / Butterflies / Go west (crazy spinning circles) / Gimmick / A flower in the desert / Dreamtime / Rider in the snow / Bad medicine waltz. *(free live-lp w/ above, also on c)* **DREAMTIME AT THE LYCEUM** *(CULT 1)* – 83rd dream / God's zoo / Bad medicine / A flower in the desert / Dreamtime / Christians / Horse nation / Bone rag / Ghost dance / Moya. *(pic-lp iss.Dec84; BEGA 57P) (re-iss. Oct88 lp/c/cd; BBL/+C 57/+CD)* – Bone rag / Sea and sky / Resurrection Joe.

Sep 84. (7"/7"poster) *(BEG 115/+P)* **GO WEST. / SEA AND SKY** [ ] [–]
(12"+=) *(BEG 115T)* – Brothers Grimm (live).

Dec 84. (7") *(BEG 122)* **RESURRECTION JOE. / ('A'-Hep cat mix)** [74] [–]
(12"+=) *(BEG 122T)* – ('A'extended).

May 85. (7") *(BEG 135)* **SHE SELLS SANCTUARY. / NO.13** [15] [–]
(12"+=) *(BEG 135T)* – The snake.
(12") *(BEG 135TP)* – ('A'-Howling mix) / Assault on sanctuary.
(c-s) *(BEG 135C)* – ('A'extended) / ('A'-Howling mix) / The snake / Assault on sanctuary.

Jul 85. (7") <28820> **SHE SELLS SANCTUARY. / LITTLE FACE** [–] [ ]

— **MARK BRZEZICKI** – drums (of BIG COUNTRY) deputised repl. PRESTON

Sep 85. (7") *(BEG 147)* **RAIN. / LITTLE FACE** [17] [–]
(12"+=) *(BEG 147T)* – (Here comes the) Rain.

Oct 85. (lp/c)(cd) *(BEGA/BEGC 65)(BEGA 65CD)* <25359> **LOVE** [4] [87]
– Nirvana / Big neon gliter / Love / Brother Wolf, Sister Moon / Rain / The phoenix / The hollow man / Revolution / She sells sanctuary / Black angel. *(cd+=)* – Judith / Little face. *(cd re-iss. Apr97; BBL 65)*

— **LES WARNER** (b.13 Feb'61) – drums (ex-JOHNNY THUNDERS, etc) repl. MARK

Nov 85. (7") *(BEG 152)* **REVOLUTION. / ALL SOULS AVENUE** [30] [–]
(d7"+=/c-s+=/12"+=) *(BEG D/C/T 152)* – Judith / Sunrise.

Feb 87. (7") *(BEG 182)* **LOVE REMOVAL MACHINE. / WOLF CHILD'S BLUES** [18] [–]
(12"+=) *(BEG 182T)* – ('A'extended).
(d7"+=) *(BEG 182D)* – Conquistador / Groove Co.
(c-s++=) *(BEG 182C)* – (all above).

Apr 87. (lp/c)(cd) *(BEGA/BEGC 80)(BEGA 80CD)* <25555> **ELECTRIC** [4] [38]
– Wild flower / Peace dog / Lil' devil / Aphrodisiac jacket / Electric ocean / Bad fun / King contrary man / Love removal machine / Born to be wild / Outlaw / Memphis hip shake. *(gold-pic-lp Aug87; BEGA 80G) (cd re-iss. Apr97; BBL 80CD)*

Apr 87. (7") *(BEG 188)* **LIL' DEVIL. / ZAP CITY** [11] [–]
(12"+=) *(BEG 188T)* – She sells sanctuary (live) / Bonebag (live).
(d12"+=/c-s+=) *(BEG 188 TD/C)* – She sells sanctuary (live) / The phoenix (live) / Wild thing . . .Louie Louie (live).
(cd-s+=) *(BEG 188CD)* – Love removal machine (live) / The phoenix (live) / She sells sanctuary (live).

May 87. (7") <29290> **LIL' DEVIL. / MEMPHIS HIPSHAKE** [–] [ ]

Aug 87. (7"/7"pic-d) *(BEG 195/+P)* <28213> **WILD FLOWER. / LOVE TROOPER** [24] [ ]
(12"+=) *(BEG 195T)* – ('A'extended rock mix).
(c-s++=) *(BEG 195C)* – Horse nation (live).
(d7"+=) *(BEG 195D)* – Outlaw (live) / Horse nation (live).
(cd-s+=) *(BEG 195CD)* – (all 5 above) / She sells sanctuary (live).
(12") *(BEG 195TR)* – ('A'ext.) / ('A'-Guitar dub) / ('B'side).

— **MICKEY CURRY** – (on session) drums repl. WARNER + KID CHAOS

Mar 89. (7"/c-s) *(BEG 228/+C)* <27543> **FIRE WOMAN. / AUTOMATIC BLUES** [15] May89 [46]
(12"+=/3"cd-s+=) *(BEG 228 T/CD)* – Messin' up the blues.
(12") *(BEG 228TR)* – ('A'-L.A. rock mix) / ('A'-N.Y.C. rock mix).

Apr 89. (lp/c)(cd) *(BEGA/BEGC 98)(BEGA 98CD)* <25871> **SONIC TEMPLE** [3] [10]
– Sun king / Fire woman / American horse / Edie (ciao baby) / Sweet soul sister / Soul asylum / New York City / Automatic blues / Soldier blue / Wake up time for freedom. *(c+=/cd+=)* – Medicine train. *(cd re-iss. Apr97; BBL 98CD)*

— **ASTBURY, DUFFY + STUART** were joined by **MATT SORUM** – drums / **MARK TAYLOR** – keyboards (on tour)

Jun 89. (7"/7"gf/c-s) *(BEG 230/+G/C)* **EDIE (CIAO BABY). / BLEEDING HEART GRAFFITI** [32] [–]
(pic-cd+=) *(BEG 230CP)* – Lil' devil (live) / Love removal machine (live).
(12"/12"poster) *(BEG 230 T/TP)* – ('A'side) / Medicine train / Love removal machine (live).
(3"cd-s) *(BEG 230CD)* – ('A'side) / Love removal machine (live) / Revolution (live).

Sep 89. (7") <22873> **EDIE (CIAO BABY). / LOVE REMOVAL MACHINE** [–] [93]

Nov 89. (7"/c-s) *(BEG 235/+C)* **SUN KING. / EDIE (CIAO BABY)** [39] [–]
(12"+=/12"hologram+=) *(BEG 235T/+H)* – She sells sanctuary.
(cd-s++=) *(BEG 235CD)* – ('A'extended).

Feb 90. (7"/c-s) *(BEG 241/+C)* **SWEET SOUL SISTER. / THE RIVER** [42] [–]
(12"gf+=) *(BEG 241TG)* – American horse (live).
(cd-s+=) *(BEG 241CG)* – Soul asylum (live).
(cd-s) *(BEG 241CD)* – ('A'rock mix) / American horse (live) / ('A'live).
(12") *(BEG 241TR)* – ('A'rock's mix) / Soul asylum (live).
(12") *(BEG 241TP)* – ('A'rock's mix) / ('A'side) / ('A'live).

Mar 90. (c-s) <19926> **SWEET SOUL SISTER. / SOLDIER BLUE** [–] [ ]

— (Apr-Oct90) **MARK MORRIS** – bass (ex-BALAAM AND THE ANGEL) repl. STUART

— (1991) **ASTBURY and DUFFY** brought in **CHARLIE DRAYTON** – bass / **MICKEY CURRY** – drums / **RICHIE ZITO** – keyboards, producer / **BELMONT TENCH** – piano, mellotron / **TOMMY FUNDERBUCK** – backing vocals

Sep 91. (7"/c-s) *(BEG 255/+C)* **WILD HEARTED SON. / INDIAN** [40] [–]
('A'ext.12"+=) *(BEG 255T)* – Red Jesus.
(cd-s++=) *(BEG 255CD)* – ('A'extended version).

Sep 91. (cd)(c/lp) *(BEGA 122CD)(BEGC/BEGA 122)* <26673> **CEREMONY** [9] [25]
– Ceremony / Wild hearted son / Earth mofo / White / If / Full tilt / Heart of soul / Bangkok rain / Indian / Sweet salvation / Wonderland.

Feb 92. (7"/c-s) *(BEG 260/+C)* **HEART OF SOUL. / EARTH MOFO** [51] [–]
(12"+=/cd-s+=) *(BEG 260 T/CD)* – Edie (ciao baby) (acoustic) / Heart of soul (acoustic).

Beggars Banquet — Alex

Jan 93. (12"ep) *(BEG 263T)* **SANCTUARY 1993 MIXES** [15] [–]
– She sells sanctuary / ('A'-Dog Star Rising) / ('A'-Slutnostic mix) / ('A'-Sundance mix).
(cd-ep) *(BEG 263CD2)* – ('A'live) repl. above original.
(cd-ep) *(BEG 263CD1)* – (first 2 tracks) / ('A'-Phlegmatic mix) / ('A'-Flusteresqueish mix).

Feb 93. (d-lp/c)(cd/4x12") *(BEGA/BEGC 130)(BEGA 130 CD/B)* *<3246>* **PURE CULT** compilation) [1] [ ]
– She sells sanctuary / Fire woman / Lil' devil / Spiritwalker / The witch / Revolution / Wild hearted Sun / Love removal machine / Rain / Edie (ciao baby) / Heart of soul / Love / Wildflower / Go west / Ressurection Joe / Sun king / Sweet soul ister / Earth mofo. *(d-lp w/ other d-lp)* LIVE AT THE MARQUEE '91 *(cd re-iss. Jun00; BEGA 2026CD)*

— **ASTBURY** + **DUFFY** now with **CRAIG ADAMS** (b. 4 Apr'62, Otley, England) – bass (ex-MISSION, ex-SISTERS OF MERCY) + **SCOTT GARRETT** (b.14 Mar'66, Washington, D.C.) – drums

Sep 94. (c-s) *(BBQ 40C)* **COMING DOWN. / ('A'remix)** [50] [–]
(12"+=/cd-s+=) *(BBQ 40 T/CD)* – Gone.

Oct 94. (cd/c/lp) *(BBQ CD/MC/LP 164)* *<45673>* **THE CULT** [21] [69]
– Gone / Coming down / Real grrrl / Black Sun / Naturally high / Joy / Star / Sacred life / Be free / Universal you / Emperor's new horse / Saints are down. *(cd re-iss. Apr97; BBL 164CD)*

Dec 94. (c-s) *(BBQ 45C)* **STAR. / BREATHING OUT** [65] [–]
(12"+=/cd-s+=) *(BBQ 45 T/CD)* – The witch (extended).

— In Apr'95, they cancelled tour, due to new guitarist JAMES STEVENSON returning to the re-formed GENE LOVES JEZEBEL.

HOLY BARBARIANS

— **IAN ASTBURY** plus **PATRICK SUGG** – guitar, vocals (ex-LUCIFER WONG) / **SCOTT GARRETT** – drums / **MATT GARRETT** – bass

Beggars Banquet — Warners

Apr 96. (7") *(BBQ 65)* **SPACE JUNKIE. / DOLLY BIRD** [ ] [–]
(cd-s+=) *(BBQ 65CD)* – Hate you.

May 96. (cd/c/lp) *(BBQ CD/MC/LP 182)* *<46223>* **CREAM** [ ] [ ]
– Brothers fights / Dolly bird / Cream / Blind / Opium / Space junkie / She / You are there / Magick Christian / Bodhisattva.

IAN ASTBURY

— with **WITCHMAN (JOHN ROOME)** + **CHRIS GOSS**

Jun 00. (7") *(BBQ 344)* **HIGH TIME AMPLIFIER. / TYGER** [ ] [–]
(cd-s+=) *(BBQ 344CD)* – ('A'-Witchman mix).

Jul 00. (cd/lp) *(BBQ CD/LP 208)* *<80208>* **SPIRIT/LIGHT/SPEED** [ ] [ ]
– Back on Earth / High time amplifier / Devil's mouth / Tonight (illuminated) / Metaphysical pistol / The witch (SLT return) / It's over / El che – Wild like a horse / Tyger / Shambala (R.F.L.).

the CULT

— re-formed with **ASTBURY** + **DUFFY** + **SORUM**

Atlantic — Atlantic

Jun 01. (cd/c) *(<7567 83440-2/-4>)* **BEYOND GOOD AND EVIL** [69] [37]
– War (the process) / The saint / Rise / Take the power / Breathe / Nico / American gothic / Ashes and ghosts / Shape the sky / Speed of light / True believers / My bridges burn.

– compilations, others, etc. –

all on 'Beggars Banquet'

Dec 88. (pic-cd-ep) *(BBP 1CD)* **THE MANOR SESSIONS** [ ] [–]
Dec 89. (pic-cd-ep) *(BBP 2CD)* **THE LOVE MIXES** [ ] [ ]
Dec 89. (pic-cd-ep) *(BBP 3CD)* **THE ELECTRIC MIXES** [ ] [ ]
Aug 91. (pic-cd-ep) *(BBP 6CD)* **SPIRITWALKER / A FLOWER IN THE DESERT / BONE BAG / GO WEST / SEA AND SKY / BROTHERS GRIMM (live)** [–] [–]
Aug 91. (pic-cd-ep) *(BBP 7CD)* **RESURRECTION JOE / SHE SELLS SANCTUARY / THE SNAKE / NO.13 / ASSAULT ON SANCTUARY / RESURRECTION JOE (Hep Cat mix)** [–] [–]
Aug 91. (pic-cd-ep) *(BBP 8CD)* **RAIN / LITTLE FACE / REVOLUTION / ALL SOULS AVENUE / JUDITH / SUNRISE** [–] [–]
Aug 91. (pic-cd-ep) *(BBP 9CD)* **LOVE REMOVAL MACHINE / CONQUISTADOR / GROOVE CO. / ZAP CITY / LOVE TROOPER / WOLF CHILD'S BLUES / LIL' DEVIL** [–] [–]
Aug 91. (pic-cd-ep) *(BBP 10CD)* **WILD FLOWER / WILD FLOWER (guitar dub) / HORSE NATION (live) / OUTLAW (live) / SHE SELLS SANCTUARY (live) / BONE BAG (live) / PHOENIX (live) / WILD THING . . . LOUIE LOUIE** [–] [–]
Aug 91. (pic-cd-ep) *(BBP 11CD)* **FIRE WOMAN / AUTOMATIC BLUES / MESSIN' UP THE BLUES / EDIE)CIAO BABY) / BLEEDING HEART GRAFFITI / SUN KING / FIRE WOMAN (L.A. rock mix) / FIRE WOMAN (N.Y.C. rock mix)** [–] [–]
Aug 91. (pic-cd-ep) *(BBP 12CD)* **SWEET SOUL SISTER / THE RIVER / LOVE REMOVAL MACHINE (live) / LIL' DEVIL (live) / REVOLUTION (live) / SWEET SOUL SISTER (live) / AMERICAN HORSE (live) / SOUL ASYLUM (live) / SWEET SOUL SISTER (Rock's mix)** [–] [–]
Aug 91. (10x pic-cd-ep) *(CBOX 1)* **SINGLES COLLECTION 1984-1990** [ ] [–]
– (all above)
Jun 92. (video w/free cd-ep) **FAITH HEALER / FULL TILT (live) / LOVE REMOVAL MACHINE (live)** [ ] [ ]
Sep 96. (cd; as DEATH CULT) *(BBL 2008CD)* **GHOST DANCE** [ ] [ ]
Nov 00. (6xcd-box) *(RCBOX 1CD)* *<82030>* **RARE CULT** [ ] [ ]
Nov 00. (cd) *(BBL 2029CD)* *<82029>* **THE BEST OF RARE CULT** [ ] [ ]

the CURE

Formed: Crawley, Sussex, England ... 1976 initially as the EASY CURE by ROBERT SMITH, LAWRENCE TOLHURST and MICHAEL DEMPSEY. In 1978, following a brief liaison with the small 'Hansa' label the previous year, the band recorded a one-off '45, 'KILLING AN ARAB', for indie operation, 'Small Wonder'. Although actually inspired by classic Albert Camus novel, 'The Outsider', the track was met with its fair share of controversy upon its early '79 re-release by Chris Parry's new 'Fiction' imprint. A subsequent debut album, 'THREE IMAGINARY BOYS' (1979) remains among the CURE's finest work, their strangely accessible post-punk snippets lent an air of suppressed melancholy by SMITH's plangent whine. The record almost scraped into the Top 40, while the pop brilliance of accompanying single, 'BOYS DON'T CRY', saw the CURE lauded as one of the UK's most promising young bands. With SIMON GALLUP replacing DEMPSEY (who joined ASSOCIATES), the group again drew critical plaudits for the insidious 'JUMPING SOMEONE ELSE'S TRAIN'. A track railing against fashion victims, the CURE carved out their own solitary path over the course of the next three albums. Claustrophobic is normally the favoured critical bon mot in getting to grips with the CURE's sound and few would argue that the spiralling disorientation of 'A FOREST' was easy listening. SMITH and co's first Top 40 hit, the track previewed follow-up set, 'SEVENTEEN SECONDS' (1980), an album which took them into the UK Top 20 despite its gloomy sound. Revered by the more pasty faced among the group's fanbase, 'FAITH' (1981) and 'PORNOGRAPHY' (1982) ploughed a similarly grim furrow, although the latter set went Top 10. Internal feuding subsequently led to the departure of GALLUP, SMITH and TOLHURST taking charge and effecting a bit of a stylistic departure on the more flippantly pop-friendly 'LET'S GO TO BED' (not before you take that eyeliner off, BOB) single. Finally, in summer of the following year, the CURE scored a long awaited breakthrough hit with 'THE WALK', the track narrowly missing the Top 10. Nevertheless, SMITH was simultaneously busying himself with SIOUXSIE AND THE BANSHEES, contributing guitar to their Top 5 cover of the Beatles' 'Dear Prudence' and playing on the 'Hyaena' album as well as hooking up with BANSHEES man, STEVE SEVERIN, for side project, the GLOVE. Meanwhile, the flouncing 'LOVECATS' single introduced the group to a whole new audience, a song with an alarmingly high irritability factor that still gets played to death by radio. With SMITH back on board in a full-time capacity by spring '84, the CURE again managed to take their skewered pop vision into the pop charts with 'THE CATERPILLAR', a track lifted from bizarre new album, 'THE TOP' (1984). More line-up changes occurred prior to the recording of the band's breakthrough set, 'HEAD ON THE DOOR' (1985), including the return of SIMON GALLUP. Trailed by the classic 'IN BETWEEN DAYS', the record spawned a further major hit in the glockenspiel weirdness of 'CLOSE TO ME', its breathy claustrophobia segueing into a sassy, brassy finale. The track was also accompanied by a celebrated video (directed by long standing associate Tim Pope), featuring the whole band, erm, playing inside a wardrobe (honestly!). A subsequent two year lull was punctuated by an impressive singles retrospective, 'STANDING ON A BEACH' (1986), before the band returned with the sprawling 'KISS ME, KISS ME KISS ME' (1987) double set. Hardly an easy ride, the record showcased the many strange faces of the CURE and more, incredibly making the US Top 40 where they'd slowly been building up a cult following. This time around there was no stellar pop to liven up the Stock, Aitken & Waterman-clogged Top 10 although the record did spawn a trio of minor hits in 'WHY CAN'T I BE YOU', 'CATCH' and 'JUST LIKE HEAVEN'. The latter track was later privy to a genius fuzz-pop mangling courtesy of DINOSAUR JR., an interpretation that reportedly impressed SMITH no end. The CURE were now a formidable commercial proposition on both sides of the Atlantic, which probably explains why the ponderous 'DISINTEGRATION' (1989) album made the UK Top 3 and the 'LOVESONG' single almost topped the American Hot 100. The turn of the decade saw major upheaval as TOLHURST finally bailed out after clashing with SMITH, a pared down line up of SMITH, GALLUP, PORL THOMPSON, BORIS WILLIAMS and PERRY BAMONTE seeing the group through most of the following decade. A remix album, 'MIXED UP', appeared in 1990, its sensual dancefloor appeal illustrating just how adaptable the band's music was, bearing in mind that SMITH and Co. were sometimes dismissed as whimsical, goth-pop throwbacks. New material finally arrived in spring '92 with the 'WISH' album, the huge hit 'FRIDAY I'M IN LOVE' following in their occasional tradition of jangling dreaminess. The album itself became the CURE's first UK No.1, missing the top of the American charts by a whisker; the band were now sufficiently world dominating that they could almost get away with two double live albums, 'SHOW' and 'PARIS', released simultaneously in late '93. The remainder of the decade saw the band's profile at its lowest since their shadowy beginnings, a low-key 1996 set, 'WILD MOOD SWINGS' their sole studio output in almost five years. While that album flirted with pop stylings, the CURE resorted to navel-gazing type with 'BLOODFLOWERS' (2000), presented as the third and final part of a trilogy that already featured 'PORNOGRAPHY' and 'DISINTEGRATION'. While the record undoubtedly qualified as classic CURE, there were few glimpses of the maverick streak which made their mid-period work so interesting. Much was made of the fact that 'THE CURE' (2004) came unaccompanied by the usual pronouncements of imminent immolation; nor was it part of any thematic trilogy, or even possessed of a theme in its own right. But – as the transatlantic Top 10 placings suggested – it did arrive at the right time, as assorted British and American debutantes defiantly resurrected the early 80's; haircuts, basslines, CURE namechecks and all. As if to prove that he really was as lugubrious an inspiration as his admirers would have it, he put extra welly into the wailing this time round, dividing fans and critics on the extent of their continuing relevance.

• **Songwriters:** Group compositions, except covers of FOXY LADY + PURPLE HAZE (Jimi Hendrix), HELLO I LOVE YOU (Doors). • **Trivia:** SMITH married childhood sweetheart Mary Poole on the 13th of August '88.

Album rating: THREE IMAGINARY BOYS (*8) / BOYS DON'T CRY exploitation (*7) / SEVENTEEN SECONDS (*6) / FAITH (*6) / PORNOGRAPHY (*6) / JAPANESE WHISPERS mini (*6) / THE TOP (*7) / CONCERT: LIVE (*5) / THE HEAD ON THE DOOR (*7) / STANDING ON THE BEACH / STARING AT THE SEA: THE SINGLES compilation (*9) / KISS ME, KISS ME, KISS ME (*7) / DISINTEGRATION (*8) / MIXED UP (*4) / WISH (*6) / PARIS (*4) / SHOW (*4) / WILD MOOD SWINGS (*5) / GALORE – THE SINGLES 1987-1997 compilation (*6) / BLOODFLOWERS (*6) / GREATEST HITS compilation (*8) / THE CURE (*6)

ROBERT SMITH (b.21 Apr'59, Blackpool, England) – vocals, lead guitar / **LAWRENCE TOLHURST** (b. 3 Feb'59) – drums, keyboards / **MICHAEL DEMPSEY** – bass

Small Wonder — not iss.

Aug 78. (7") *(SMALL 11)* **KILLING AN ARAB. / 10.15 SATURDAY NIGHT** [ ] [–]

Fiction — not iss.

Jan 79. (7") *(FICS 001)* **KILLING AN ARAB. / 10.15 SATURDAY NIGHT** [ ] [–]

May 79. (lp/c) *(FIX/+C 1)* **THREE IMAGINARY BOYS** [44] [–]
– 10.15 Saturday night / Accuracy / Grinding halt / Another day / Object / Subway song / Foxy lady / Meat hook / So what / Fire in Cairo / It's not you / Three imaginary boys. *(cd-iss. Apr90; 827 686-2)*

May 79. (7") *(FICS 002)* **BOYS DON'T CRY. / PLASTIC PASSION** [ ] [–]

— **SIMON GALLUP** (b. 1 Jun'60, Surrey, England) – bass, keyboards (ex-MAG-SPYS, ex-LOCKJAW) repl. DEMPSEY who joined The ASSOCIATES

Oct 79. (7") *(FICS 005)* **JUMPING SOMEONE ELSE'S TRAIN. / I'M COLD** [ ] [–]

— added **MATHIEU HARTLEY** – keyboards, synthesizers

Nov 79. (7") *(FICS 006)* **I'M A CULT HERO (as "CULT HERO"). / I DIG YOU** [ ] [–]

— (on above they backed FRANK BELL)

Mar 80. (7"/ext.12") *(FICS/+X 10)* **A FOREST. / ANOTHER JOURNEY BY TRAIN** [31] [–]

Apr 80. (lp/c) *(FIX/+C 004)* **SEVENTEEN SECONDS** [20] [–]
– A reflection / Play for today / Secrets / In your house / Three . . . / The final sound / A forest / M / At night / Seventen seconds. *(cd-iss. Jan86; 825 354-2)*

— reverted to trio of **SMITH, TOLHURST & GALLUP** when HARTLEY left to form CRY.

Mar 81. (7"/ext.12") *(FICS/+X 12)* **PRIMARY. / DESCENT** [43] [–]

Fiction — P.V.C.

Apr 81. (lp/c) *(FIX/+C 6)* *<2383 605>* **FAITH** [14] [ ]
– The holy hour / Primary / Other voices / All cats are grey / The funeral party / Doubt / The drowning man / Faith. *(cd-iss. Jan86; 827 687-2) (c+=)* **CARNAGE VISORS** (film soundtrack)

Oct 81. (7") *(FICS 14)* **CHARLOTTE SOMETIMES. / SPLINTERED IN HER HEAD** [44] [–]
(12"+=) *(FICSX 14)* – Faith (live).

Fiction — A&M

Apr 82. (lp/c) *(FIX D/C 7)* *<4902>* **PORNOGRAPHY** [8] [ ]
– One hundred years / A short term effect / The hanging garden / Siamese twins / The figurehead / A strange day / Cold / Pornography. *(cd-iss. Jan86; 827 688-2)*

Jul 82. (7") *(FICS 15)* **THE HANGING GARDEN. / KILLING AN ARAB (live)** [34] [–]
(d7"+=) *(FICG 15)* – One hundred years (live) / A forest (live).

— **STEVE GOULDING** – bass repl. GALLUP who later joined FOOLS DANCE (LOL now keyboards)

Nov 82. (7"/ext.12") *(FICS/+X 17)* **LET'S GO TO BED. / JUST ONE KISS** [44] [–]

— trimmed to duo of **SMITH + TOLHURST**

Jul 83. (7"/7"pic-d) *(FICS/+P 18)* **THE WALK. / THE DREAM** [12] [–]
(12"+=) *(FICXT 18)* *<23928>* – The upstairs room / Lament.
(free 12"w/ free 12") *(FICSX 17)* – Let's go to bed / Just one kiss.

— added **PHIL THORNALLEY** – bass / **ANDY ANDERSON**-**drums** (ex-BRILLIANT)

Oct 83. (7"/7"pic-d) *(FICS/+P 19)* **THE LOVECATS. / SPEAK MY LANGUAGE** [7] [–]
(ext.12"+=) *(FICSX 19)* – Mr. Pink eyes.

Dec 83. (m-lp/c) *(FIXM/+C 8)* <25076> **JAPANESE WHISPERS** 26 |
– Let's go to bed / The dream / Just one kiss / The upstair's room / The walk / Speak my language / Lament / The lovecats. *(cd-iss. Apr87; 817 470-2)*

Mar 84. (7"/7"pic-d) *(FICS/+P 20)* **THE CATERPILLAR. / HAPPY THE MAN** 14 | –
(12"+=) *(FICSX 20)* – Throw your foot.

Apr 84. (lp/c)(cd) *(FIXS/+C 9)(821 136-2)* <25086> **THE TOP** 10 |
– Shake dog shake / Birdmad girl / Wailing wall / Give me it / Dressing up / The caterpillar / Piggy in the mirror / The empty world / Bananafishbones / The top.

— added **PORL THOMPSON** (b.8 Nov'57, London, England) – guitar, saxophone, keyboards (a member in '77)

Oct 84. (lp/d-c)(cd) *(FIXH/+C 10)(823 682-2)* **CONCERT – THE CURE LIVE (live)** 26 | –
– Shake dog shake / Primary / Charlotte sometimes / The hanging garden / Give me it / The walk / One hundred years / A forest / 10.15 Saturday night / Killing an Arab. *(d-c+=)* **CURIOSITY: CURE ANOMALIES 1977-1984** – Heroin face / Boys don't cry / Subway song / At night / In your house / The drowning man / Other voices / The funeral party / All mine / Forever.

— **SIMON GALLUP** returned to repl. PORL. **BORIS WILLIAMS** (b.24 Apr'57, Versailles, France) – drums (ex-THOMPSON TWINS) repl. ANDERSON who joined JEFFREY LEE PIERCE (of The GUN CLUB)

Fiction | Elektra

Jul 85. (7") *(FICS 22)* **IN BETWEEN DAYS. / EXPLODING BODY** 15 | –
(12"+=) *(FICSX 22)* – A few hours after this.

Aug 85. (lp/c)(cd) *(FIXH/+C 11)(827 231-2)* <60435> **THE HEAD ON THE DOOR** 7 | 59
– In between days / Kyoto song / The blood / Six different ways / Push / The baby screams / Close to me / A night like this / Screw / Sinking.

Sep 85. (7"/7"poster) *(FICS/+G 23)* **CLOSE TO ME (remix). / A MAN INSIDE MY MOUTH** 24 | –
(12"+=) *(FICSX 23)* – Stop dead.
(10"++=) *(FICST 23)* – New day.

Jan 86. (7") <69604> **IN BETWEEN DAYS. / STOP DEAD** – | 99

Mar 86. (7") <69551> **CLOSE TO ME. / SINKING** – |

Apr 86. (7") *(FICS 24)* **BOYS DON'T CRY (new mix). / PILLBOX BLUES** 22 | –
(club-12"+=) *(FICSX 24)* – Do the Hansa.

May 86. (lp/d-c)(cd) *(FIXH/+C 12)(829 239-2)* <60477> **STANDING ON THE BEACH / STARING AT THE SEA** (compilation of A's & B's) 4 | 48
– Killing an Arab / Boys don't cry / Jumping someone else's train / A forest / Primary / Charlotte sometimes / The hanging garden / Let's go to bed / The walk / The lovecats / The caterpillar / In between days / Close to me. *(cd+=)* – 10.15 Saturday night / Play for today / Other voices / A night like this. *(re-iss. Feb91; same)*

Apr 87. (7"/ext.12") *(FICS/+X 25)* <69474> **WHY CAN'T I BE YOU? / A JAPANESE DREAM** 21 | Jun87 54
(d7"+=) *(FIGSG 25)* – Six different ways (live) / Push (live).

May 87. (d-lp/c)(cd) *(FIXH/+C 13)(832 130-2)* <60737> **KISS ME KISS ME KISS ME** 6 | 35
– The kiss / Catch / Torture / If only tonight we could sleep / Why can't I be you? / How beautiful you are / Snakepit / Hey you / Just like heaven / All I want / Hot hot hot!!! / One more time / Like cockatoos / Icing sugar / The perfect girl / A thousand hours / Shiver and shake / Fight. *(pic-lp.Dec87; FIXP 13) (free-ltd.12"orange / or green,w/cd) – A Japanese dream / Breathe / Chain of flowers / Sugar girl / Snow in summer / Icing sugar (remix).*

— added on tour **ROBERT O'CONNELL** – keyboards (ex-PSYCHEDELIC FURS)

Jul 87. (7"/7"clear) *(FICS/+P 26)* **CATCH. / BREATHE** 27 |
(c-s+=/12"+=) *(FICS C/X 26)* – A chain of flowers.
(7"ep+=) *(FICSE 26)* – Kyoto song (live) / A night like this (live).

Oct 87. (7",7"white/7"pic-d) *(FICS/+P 27)* **JUST LIKE HEAVEN. / SNOW IN SUMMER** 29 | –
(12"+=/cd-s+=) *(FICSX/FIXCD 27)* – Sugar girl.

Oct 87. (7") <69443> **JUST LIKE HEAVEN. / BREATHE** – | 40

Feb 88. (12"/cd-s) *(FICSX/FIXCD 28)* <69424> **HOT HOT HOT!!! (extended remix). / HOT HOT HOT!!! (remix) / HEY YOU!!! (extended remix)** 45 | 65

Apr 89. (7"/7"gf/7"clear) *(FICS/+G/P 29)* **LULLABY (remix). / BABBLE** 5 | –
(ext.12"+=/ext.12"pink+=) *(FIC SX/VX 29)* – Out of mind. (3"cd-s++=) *(FICCD 29)* – ('A'extended).

May 89. (lp/c)(cd) *(FIXH/+C 14)(839 353-2)* <60855> **DISINTEGRATION** 3 | 12
– Plainsong / Pictures of you / Closedown / Lovesong / Lullaby / Fascination street / Prayers for rain / The same deep water as you / Disintegration / Untitled. *(cd+=)* – Last dance / Homesick. *(pic-lp Apr90; FIXHP 14)*

May 89. (7") <69300> **FASCINATION STREET. / BABBLE** – | 46

Aug 89. (7"/7"box/c-s) *(FIC S/SG/CD 30)* <69280> **LOVESONG. / 2 LATE** 18 | 2
(ext.12"+=) *(FICSX 30)* – Fear of ghosts.
(cd-s++=)(cd-vid++=) *(FICCD 30)(081398-2)* – ('A'-12"mix).

Nov 89. (c-s) <69249> **LULLABY / HOMESICK** – | 74

— (Mar'89) reverted to a quintet when TOLHURST left **SMITH, GALLUP, THOMPSON, WILLIAMS + PERRY BAMONTE** (b. 6 Sep'60, London, England) – keyboards

Mar 90. (7"/7"green/c-s) *(FIC A/PA/CA 34)* **PICTURES OF YOU (remix). /** 24 | 71
(ext.12"+=/ext.12"green+=/cd-s+=) *(FICXA/FIXPA/FICDA 34)* – Fascination Street (live).
(7"/7"purple/c-s) *(FIC B/PB/CB 34)* <64974> – PICTURES OF YOU (remix). / PRAYERS FOR RAIN (live)
(12"+=/12"purple+=/cd-s+=) *(FICXB/FIXPB/FICDB 34)* – Disintigration (live).

— (W.H. Smith's released ENTREAT (May90) a live EP, which featured the 5 tracks +=) – Closedown / Homesick / Untitled.

Sep 90. (7"/c-s) *(FIC S/CS 35)* **NEVER ENOUGH. / HAROLD AND JOE** 13 | Oct90 72
(12"+=/cd-s+=/pic-cd-s+=) *(FICSX/FICCD/FICDP 35)* – Let's go to bed (milk mix).

Oct 90. (7"/c-s) *(FIC S/CS 36)* <64911> **CLOSE TO ME (closet remix). / JUST LIKE HEAVEN (dizzy mix)** 13 | Jan91 97
(12"+=/cd-s+=) *(FIC SX/CD 36)* – Primary (red mix).
(cd-s+=) *(FICDR 36)* – Why can't I be you? (extended).

Nov 90. (cd)(d-lp/c) *(847 009-2)(FIXH/+C 18)* <60978> **MIXED UP** (remix album) 8 | 14
– Lullaby (extended mix) / Close to me (closer mix) / Fascination Street (extended mix) / The walk (everything mix) / Lovesong (extended mix) / A forest (tree mix) / Pictures of you (extended dub mix) / Hot hot hot!!! (extended mix) / The caterpillar (flicker mix) / Inbetween days (shiver mix) / Never enough (big mix).

Apr 91. (cd)(lp/c) *(843 359-2)(FIXH/+C 17)* **ENTREAT (live)** 10 |
– (finally nationally released; see above)

Mar 92. (7"/c-s) *(FIC S/CS 39)* <64766> **HIGH. / THIS TWILIGHT GARDEN** 8 | 42
('A'-Higher mix-12"+=) *(FICSX 39)* – Play.
(cd-s+=) *(FICCD 39)* – (all above).

Apr 92. (12"clear) *(FICSX 41)* **HIGH (trip mix). / OPEN (fix mix)** 44 | 43
(cd-s) *(FICCD 41)* – (see last cd-s for 4 tracks).

Apr 92. (cd)(d-lp/c) *(513 261-2)(FIXH/+C 20)* <61309> **WISH** 1 | 2
– Open / High / Apart / From the edge of the deep green sea / Wendy time / Doing the unstuck / Friday I'm in love / Trust / A letter to Elise / Cut / To wish impossible things / End.

May 92. (7"/c-s) *(FIC S/CS 42)* <64742> **FRIDAY I'M IN LOVE. / HALO** 6 | 18
('A'-Strangelove mix-12"colrd+=) *(FICSX 42)* – Scared as you.
(cd-s+=) *(FICCD 42)* – (all above).

Oct 92. (7"/c-s) *(FIC S/CS 46)* **A LETTER TO ELISE. / THE BIG HAND** 28 |
(Blue mix-12"+=) *(FICSX 46)* – A foolish arrangement.
(cd-s+) *(FICCD 46)* – (all above).

Sep 93. (d-cd/d-c/d-lp) *(FIX CD/MC/LP 25)* <61551> **SHOW (live)** 29 | 42
– Tape / Open / High / Pictures of you / Lullaby / Just like Heaven / Fascination Street / A night like this / Trust / Doing the unstuck / The walk / Let's go to bed / Friday I'm in love / In between days / From the edge of the deep green sea / Never enough / Cut / End.

— PORL departed after the above.

Oct 93. (cd/c/d-lp) *(FIX CD/MC/LP 26)* <61552> **PARIS (live)** 56 |
– The figurehead / One hundred years / At night / Play for today / Apart / In your house / Lovesong / Catch / A letter to Elise / Dressing up / Charlotte sometimes / Close to me.

Apr 96. (c-s) *(576468-4)* **THE 13TH (swing radio mix) / IT USED TO BE ME** 15 | –
(cd-s+=) *(576469-2)* – ('A'-Killer bee mix).
(cd-s) *(576493-2)* – ('A'-Two chord cool mix) / Ocean / Adonais.

Apr 96. (c-s) <64292> **THE 13TH / ADONAIS** – | 44

May 96. (cd/c/lp) *(FIX CD/MC/LP 28)* <61744> **WILD MOOD SWINGS** [9] [12]
– Want / Club America / This is a lie / The 13th / Strange attraction / Mint car / Jupiter crash / Round & round & round / Gone! / Numb / Trap / Treasure / Bare.

Jun 96. (c-s) *(FICCS 52)* <64275> **MINT CAR / HOME** [31] [58]
(cd-s+=) *(FICCD 52)* – ('A'-buskers mix).
(cd-s) *(FISCD 52)* – ('A'-electric mix) / Waiting / A pink dream.

Nov 96. (c-s) *(FICCS 53)* **GONE! / THIS IS A LIE (ambient mix)** [60] [ ]
(cd-s+=) *(FICD 53)* – Strange attraction (strange mix) / The 13th (feels good mix).

Nov 97. (cd/c/lp) *(FIX CD/MC/LP 30)* <62117> **GALORE – THE SINGLES 1987-1997** (compilation) [37] [32]
– Why can't I be you / Catch / Just like Heaven / Hot, hot, hot / Lullaby / Fascination Street / Love song / Pictures of you / Never enough / Close to me / High / Friday I'm in love / Letter to Elise / The 13th / Mint car / Strange attraction / Gone / Wrong number.

Nov 97. (c-s) *(FICMC 54)* **WRONG NUMBER / ('A'-radio mix mix)** [62] [–]
(12"/cd-s+=) *(FIC SX/D 54)* – ('A'mixes).

Feb 00. (d-lp/cd) *(FIX/+CD 31)* <62236> **BLOODFLOWERS** [14] [16]
– Out of this world / Watching me fall / Where the birds always sing / Maybe someday / The last day of summer / There is no if . . . / The loudest sound / 39 / Bloodflowers.

Oct 01. (cd-s) *(587389-2)* **CUT HERE / SIGNAL TO NOISE / CUT HERE (missing mix) / CUT HERE (video)** [54] [–]

Nov 01. (cd) *(589435-2)* <62726> **GREATEST HITS** (compilation) [33] [58]
– Boys don't cry / A forest / Let's go to bed / The walk *[US-only]* / The lovecats / Caterpillar *[UK-only]* / Inbetween days / Close to me / Why can't I be you? / Just like Heaven / Lullaby / Lovesong / Pictures of you *[UK-only]* / Never enough / High / Friday I'm in love / Mint car / Wrong number / Cut here / Just say yes. *(d-cd-iss. +=; 589434-2)* – (acoustic versions).

Geffen Geffen

Jun 04. (cd) *(9862886)* <28700-2> **THE CURE** [8] [7]
– Lost / Labyrinth / Before time / The end of the world / Anniversary / Us or them / Alt.end / (I don't know what's going) On / Taking off / Never / The promise. *(CD-Rom+=)* – Going nowhere.

Jul 04. (7"pic-d) *(9863250)* **THE END OF THE WORLD. / FAKE** [25] [–]
(cd-s+=) *(9862976)* – This morning / ('A'-video).

Oct 04. (7"pic-d) *(9864601)* **TAKING OFF. / WHY CAN'T I BE ME** [39] [–]
(cd-s+=) *(9864491)* – Your god is fear / ('A'-video).

– compilations, etc. –

Aug 83. (lp/c) *Fiction; (SPE LP/MC 26) / P.V.C.; <7916>* **BOYS DON'T CRY** [71] Aug80 [ ]
– Boys don't cry / Plastic passion / 10.15 Saturday night / Accuracy / Object * / Jumping someone else's train / Subway song / Killing an Arab / Fire in Cairo / Another day / Grinding halt / World war * / Three imaginary boys. *(cd-iss. Nov86; 815 011-2) (w/ out tracks * +=)* – So what.

May 86. (7") *P.V.C.;* **BOYS DON'T CRY. / LET'S GO TO BED** [–] [ ]

May 88. (12"ep/cd-ep) *Strange Fruit; (SFPS/+CD 050)* **PEEL SESSIONS** [ ] [–]
– Killing an Arab / Boys don't cry / 10:15 Saturday night / Fire in Cairo.

Oct 88. (vid-cd) *Fiction; (080184-2)* **WHY CAN'T I BE YOU (video) / JAPANESE DREAM / HEY YOU / WHY CAN'T I BE YOU** [ ] [–]

Oct 88. (vid-cd) *Fiction; (080182-2)* **IN BETWEEN DAYS (video) / SIX DIFFERENT WAYS (live) / PUSH (live)** [ ] [–]

Oct 88. (vid-cd) *Fiction; (080186-2)* **CATCH (video) / CATCH / BREATHE / A CHAIN OF FLOWERS / ICING SUGAR (new mix)** [ ] [–]

CYPRESS HILL

Formed: Los Angeles, California, USA ... 1988 by DJ MUGGS, B-REAL and SEN DOG. In the early 90's, after signing to US 'Columbia' label through their own 'Ruffhouse' label, the hard-core rappers cracked the Top 40 with their eponymous debut. The album contained the single, 'I COULD JUST KILL A MAN', alongside the dirty, trippy narcotica of tracks like 'ULTRAVIOLET DREAMS' and 'SOMETHING FOR THE BLUNTED'. With B-REAL's sneering intonation and the bass-heavy production, CYPRESS HILL were instantly recognisable. Tireless advocators of marijuana use (and legalisation), most of the band's music was so claustrophobically heavy it sounded like they'd been stoned since birth. Influenced by the infamous 'Rodney King' incident in L.A., the follow-up album, 'BLACK SUNDAY' (1993) took a decidedly darker turn, gangsta-like bravado ('LICK A SHOT', 'COCK THE HAMMER', 'A TO THE K') interspersing the trademark homages to hash. 'INSANE IN THE BRAIN' (1993) was the first in a string of U.K. hit singles and the band consolidated their success in Britain by playing at a number of predominantly white rock festivals, proving their crossover appeal. 'CYPRESS HILL III (TEMPLES OF BOOM)' (1996) upped the gangsta ante with such subtle fare as 'KILLAFORNIA' and 'KILLA HILL NIGGAS' although the hopelessly stoned vibe was still sufficiently alive and kicking (or head bowed and nodding) to satisfy fans. The subsequent departure of SEN DOG hit CYPRESS HILL hard and although they attempted to regroup with replacement BARRON RICKS, 'IV' (1998) was the closest they'd yet come to self-parody. Their UK stock nevertheless remained high, hovering around the Top 20 with 'TEQUILA SUNRISE' and a RUN DMC-style JASON NEVINS revamp of 'INSANE IN THE BRAIN'. CYPRESS HILL also followed the ailing East Coast rappers in their unadvised stab at rap-metal hokum, devoting one whole side of 'SKULL & BONES' (2000) to such time wasting. Needless to say LIMP BIZKIT were involved; when, oh, when are any of these bands going to realise that it's been done before (years ago) and sounded so much better the first time. While the return of SEN DOG had revitalised their dope-induced sonic doomscapes, the trio's rock fetishism was encapsulated with 'LIVE AT THE FILLMORE' (2000). From the cover art to the riffed-up reinvention of their classic early 90's material, the album oozed testosterone. Sure, it was high adrenaline stuff, thrilling enough in its own way but lacking in the spooked-out paranoia which defined their sound. 'STONED RAIDERS' (2001) doggedly continued with the riff-rap albeit with occasionally more playful results. Much more easy to digest were MUGGS' two chapters of ' . . .PRESENTS THE SOUL ASSASSINS', released in 1997 and 2000 respectively. Left to his own devices, the quicksilver producer created a vapourous, filmic epic with walk-on parts from the great and the good of hip hop: WYCLEF JEAN, KRS-ONE, DR DRE, RZA and MOBB DEEP amongst others. While the follow-up wasn't graced with quite as much talent, MUGGS' haunted, twilight-zone musical vision once again hypnotized and confounded in equal measure. As did his detour into sweeping, cinematic electronica, 2003's 'DUST'. While guests GREG DULLI and JOSH TODD were plucked from the confines of alternative rock, their presence fleshed out MUGGS' ambitious soundscapes amid careening string parts and distended synth washes. Straining not to sound like an anachronism in the glib, high-stakes game of post-millennial hip-hop, CYPRESS HILL subsequently ironed out the guitars and worked a few changes: 'TIL DEATH DO US PART' (2004) found B-REAL modifying his whippet yelp into a more digestible flow, while DJ MUGGS looked to the Caribbean. His dub flirtations weren't entirely successful but on the likes of the Alchemist-produced 'LATIN THUGS' at least, he'd hit on something worth pursuing: Anglo-Hispanic wordplay (courtesy of Puerto Rican face, TEGO CALDERON) locked into a balmy Latin brass loop.

• **Songwriters:** Group penned. WE AIN'T GOIN' OUT LIKE THAT sampled; THE WIZARD (Black Sabbath) / WHEN THE SH-- GOES DOWN sampled; DEEP GULLY (Outlaw Blues Band) / LIL' PUTOS sampled; ODE TO BILLY JOE (Bobbie Gentry) / etc. • **Trivia:** MUGGS also produced HOUSE OF PAIN, BEASTIE BOYS and ICE CUBE.

Album rating: CYPRESS HILL (*9) / BLACK SUNDAY (*8) / CYPRESS HILL III – TEMPLES OF BOOM (*6) / IV (*6) / SKULL & BONES (*7) / LIVE AT

HE FILLMORE (*5) / STONED RAIDERS (*7) / TILL DEATH US DO PART *4) / Muggs: PRESENTS THE SOUL ASSASSINS, CHAPTER I (*6) / MUGGS RESENTS THE SOUL ASSASSINS, CHAPTER II (*5) / DUST (*7)

-REAL (b. LOUIS FREESE, 2 Jun'70) – vocals (ex-DVX) / **SEN DOG** b. SENEN REYES, 20 Nov'65, Cuba) – vocals (ex-DVX) / **DJ MUGGS** o. LAWRENCE MUGGERUD, 28 Jan'68, Queens, N.Y.) – DJ, producer ex-7A3)

Ruffhouse Ruffhouse

an 92. (cd/c/lp) *(468893-2/-4/-1) <47889>* **CYPRESS HILL** [ ] Nov91 [31]
– Pigs / How I could just kill a man / Hand on the pump / Hole in the head / Ultraviolet dreams / Light another / The phuncky feel one / Break it up / Real estate / Stoned is the way of the walk / Psycobetabuckdown / Something for the blunted / Latin lingo / The funky Cypress Hill shit / Tres equis / Born to get busy. *(cd re-iss. May94 & Feb97; same) (lp re-iss. Jan00 on 'Simply Vinyl'; SVLP 170)*

eb 92. (7") *<73930>* **HOW I COULD JUST KILL A MAN. / THE PHUNKY FEEL ONE** [–] [77] [94]

pr 92. (c-s) *<74105>* **HAND ON THE PUMP / REAL ESTATE** [–] [ ]
(cd-s) *<74332>* – ('A'-Mugg's Blunted mix) / ('A'extended mix) / ('A'-instrumental) / Hand on the glock.

ın 92. (12"ep/cd-ep) *<74478>* **LATIN LINGO (Prince Paul mix) / STONED IS THE WAY OF THE WALK (reprise) / HAND ON THE GLOCK** [–] [ ]

ıl 93. (c-s) *<77135>* **INSANE IN THE BRAIN / STONED IS THE WAY OF THE WALK** [–] [19]

ıl 93. (c-s) *(659533-4)* **INSANE IN THE BRAIN (radio version). / WHEN THE SH-- GOES DOWN (radio version)** [32] [–]
(12"+=/cd-s+=) *(659533-6/-2)* – ('A'instrumental).
(re-iss. May00; same)

ıl 93. (cd/c/lp) *(474075-2/-4/-1) <53931>* **BLACK SUNDAY** [13] [1]
– I wanna get high / I ain't goin' out like that / Insane in the brain / When the sh-- goes down / Lick a shot / Cock the hammer / Interlude / Lil' putos / Legalize it / Hits from the bong / What go around come around, kid / A to the K / Hand on the glock / Break 'em off some.

ep 93. (c-s) *(659670-8)* **WHEN THE SH-- GOES DOWN (extended). / LATIN LINGO / HOW COULD I JUST KILL A MAN (the Killer mix)** [19] [–]
(12"+=/cd-s+=) *(659670-6/-2)* – ('A'instrumental) / The phunky feel one (extended).

ec 93. (c-s) *(659690-4) <77307>* **I AIN'T GOIN' OUT LIKE THAT. / HITS FROM THE BONG** [15] [65]
(12"+=/cd-s+=) *(659690-6/-2)* – When the sh-- goes down (Diamond D mix).
(re-iss. May00; same)

eb 94. (c-s) *(660176-4)* **INSANE IN THE BRAIN. / STONED IS THE WAY OF THE WALK** [21] [–]
(12"+=) *(660176-6)* – Latin lingo (Prince Paul mix).
(cd-s) *(660176-2)* – ('A'side) / Something for the blunted.
(re-iss. May00; same)

pr 94. (c-s) *(660319-4)* **LICK A SHOT (Baka Boys remix). / I WANNA GET HIGH** [20] [ ]
(12"+=/cd-s+=) *(660319-6/-2)* – Scooby Doo.
(re-iss. May00; same)

ep 95. (c-s) *(662354-4) <78042>* **THROW YOUR SET IN THE AIR / KILLA HILL NIGGAS** [15] [45]
(12"+=/cd-s+=) *(662354-6/-2)* – ('A'-Slow roll remix) / ('B'instrumental).
(re-iss. May00; same)

ct 95. (cd/c/d-lp) *(478127-2/-4/-1) <66991>* **CYPRESS HILL III / TEMPLES OF BOOM** [11] [3]
– Spark another owl / Throw your set in the air / Stoned raiders / Illusions / Killa hill niggas / Boom biddy bye bye / No rest for the wicked / Make a move / Killafornia / Funk freakers / Locotes / Red light visions / Strictly hip hop / Let it rain / Everybody must get stoned. *(d-cd+=/t-lp+=; 478127-9/-0)* – DJ MUGGS BUDDHA MIX:- Hole in the head – How could I just kill a man – Insane in the brain – Stoned is the way of the walk – Hits from the bong – Hand on the pump – Real estate – I wanna get high. *(cd re-iss. Jan99; same)*

eb 96. (12"ep) *(662905-6)* **ILLUSIONS / THROW YOUR SET IN THE AIR (radio version). / ILLUSIONS (harpsicord mix) / ILLUSIONS (harpsicord instrumental)** [23] [ ]
(cd-ep) *(662905-2)* – ('A'mixes).
(re-iss. May00; same)

—— SEN DOG went solo (DOGWOOD) and was repl. by DJ SCANDALOUS

Jun 96. (c-s) *<78339>* **BOOM BIDDY BYE BYE / ('A'version)** [–] [87]

Aug 96. (m-cd/m-c/m-lp) *(485230-2/-4/-1) <67780>* **UNRELEASED & REVAMPED EP** [29] [21]
– Boom biddy bye bye (Fugees remix) / Throw your hands in the air / Intellectual dons (featuring Call O Da Wild) / Hand on the pump (Muggs' blunted mix) / Whatta you know / Hits from the bong (T-Ray's mix) / Illusions (Q-Tip remix) / Latin lingo (Prince Paul mix) / When the ship goes down (Diamond D remix).

—— **MUGGS and B-REAL** recruited **BARON** – rapper / **ERIC BOBO** – percussion

Sep 98. (12"/cd-s) *(666493-6/-2)* **TEQUILA SUNRISE (mixes' radio / clean / radio edit featuring Fat Joe / Spanish)** [23] [ ]
(cd-s) *(666493-5)* – ('A'side) / Champions (featuring PMD) / Can you handle this.
(re-iss. May00; same)

Oct 98. (cd/c/lp) *(491604-2/-4/-1) <69037>* **IV** [25] [11]
– Looking through the eye of a pig / Checkmate / From the window of my room / Prelude to a come up (featuring Mc EIHT) / Riot starter / Audio X (featuring BARRON RICKS) / Steel magnolia (featuring BARRON RICKS) / I remember that freak bitch (from the club) (featuring BARRON RICKS – interlude part 2) / (Goin' all out) Nothin' to lose / Tequila sunrise (featuring BARRON RICKS) / Dead men tell no tales / Feature presentation (featuring BARRON RICKS) / Chance infinite / Dr. Greenthumb / 16 men till there's no men left / High times / Clash of the Titans / Lightning strikes. *(cd re-iss. Aug01; same)*

Mar 99. (c-s/cd-s) *(667120-4/-2) <79024>* **DR. GREENTHUMB (clean radio mix) / DR. GREENTHUMB (Fun Lovin' Criminals clean remix)** [34] Sep98 [70]
(12") *(667120-2)* – ('A'-version) / ('A'-Fun Lovin' Criminals instrumental remix) / ('A'-Fun Lovin' Criminals remix).
(re-iss. May00; same)

Jun 99. (c-s; JASON NEVINS vs CYPRESS HILL) *(INCRL 17MC)* **INSANE IN THE BRAIN / ('A'mix)** [19] [ ]
(cd-s) *(INCRL 17CD)* – ('A'mixes).
(cd-s) *(INCRL 17CDX)* – ('A'mixes).
(above issued on 'Incredible')

—— **SEN DOG** returned to repl. BARRON

Apr 00. (c-s) *(669264-4)* **RAP SUPERSTAR / ROCK SUPERSTAR** [13] [ ]
(cd-s) *(669264-2)* – ('A'side) / ('A'instrumental) / Loco en el cocoa (Insane In The Brain).
(cd-s+=) *(669264-5)* – ('B'side) / Checkmate (Hang 'Em High remix) / Fistful.

Apr 00. (cd/c) *(495183-2/-8/-4) <69990>* **SKULL & BONES** [6] May00 [5]
– Intro / Another victory / Rap superstar / Cuban necktie / What U want from me / Stank ass hoe / Highlife / Certified bomb / Can I get a hit / We live this shit / Worldwide / Rock superstar. *(d-cd; 495183-2)* – Valley of chrome / Get out of my head / Can't get the best of me / Man / Dust.

Sep 00. (c-s) *(669789-4)* **CAN'T GET THE BEST OF ME / HIGHLIFE** [35] [ ]
(cd-s+=) *(669789-2)* – Do you know who I am / ('A'-CD-ROM).
(cd-s) *(669789-5)* – ('A'side) / Highlife (Fredwreck mix) / Rap superstar (Alchemist remix).

Dec 00. (cd/c) *(500558-2/-4) <85184>* **LIVE AT THE FILLMORE (live)** [ ] [ ]
– Hand on the pump / Real estate / How I could just kill a man / Insane in the brain / Pigs / Looking through the eye of a pig / Cock the hammer / Checkmate / Can't get the best of me / Lick a shot / A to the K / I ain't goin' out like that / I wanna get high / Stoned is the way of the walk / Hits from the bong / Riot starter / (Rock) Superstar.

Nov 01. (c-s) *(672166-4)* **TROUBLE / LOWRIDER (explicit) / TROUBLE (explicit)** [33] [ ]
(cd-s) *(672166-2)* – (first 2 tracks) / Rock superstar.
(cd-s) *(672166-5)* – (first 2 tracks) / Jack you back (live).

Dec 01. (cd/c/lp) *(504171-2/-4/-1) <85740>* **STONED RAIDERS** [71] [64]
– (intro) / Trouble / Kronologik (with KURUPT) / Southland killers (with MC REN & KING TEE) / Bitter / Amplified / It ain't easy / Memories / Psychodelic vision / Red meth & B (with REDMAN & METHOD MAN) / Lowrider / Catastrophe / L.I.F.E. (with KOCANE) / Here is something you can't understand (with KURUPT).

Mar 04. (cd-s) *(674617-2)* **WHAT'S YOUR NUMBER? / READY TO DIE / ROLL IT UP AGAIN / ('A'-video)** [44] [ ]
(12") *(674617-6)* – ('A') / Roll it up again / I ain't going out like that.

Mar 04. (cd) *(COL 515029-2)* <*90781*> **TILL DEATH US DO PART** 53 21
– Another body drops / Till death comes / Latin thugs / Ganja bus / Busted in the hood / Money / Never know / Last laugh / Bong hit / What's your number? / Once again / Number seven / One last cigarette / Street wars / Till death us do part / Eulogy.

– compilations, etc. –

on 'Ruffhouse' unless mentioned otherwise

May 00. (3xcd-box) *(498283-2)* **CYPRESS HILL / BLACK SUNDAY / TEMPLES OF BOOM** ☐ ☐
(re-iss. Nov00 & Sep01; same)

May 00. (cd) *(496287-2)* **LOS GRANDES EXITOS EN ESPANOL** ☐ ☐

MUGGS

not iss. Columbia

Feb 97. (12"; with The SOUL ASSASSINS featuring DR. DRE & B REAL) <*78518*> **PUPPET MASTER. / (version)** – ☐

Mar 97. (cd/lp) <*66820*> **MUGGS PRESENTS THE SOUL ASSASSINS, CHAPTER I** ☐ 20
– The time has come / Puppet master (DR. DRE & B REAL) / Decisions, decisions (GOODIE MOB) / Third world (RZA & GENIUS GZA) / Battle of 2001 (CYPRESS HILL) / Devil in a blue dress (LA THE DARKMAN) / Heavy weights (MC EIHT) / Move ahead (KRS-ONE) / It could happen to you (MOBB DEEP) / Life is tragic (INFAMOUS MOBB) / New York undercover (CALL O' DA WILD) / John 3:16 (WYCLEF FROM THE REFUGEE CAMP).

Ruff Life Ruff Life

Oct 00. (cd/d-lp) <*(RLCD/RLLP 02)*> **MUGGS PRESENTS THE SOUL ASSASSINS, CHAPTER II** ☐ ☐
– Real life (KOOL G. RAP) / We will survive (G.O.D. PT.III) / You better believe it (XZIBIT & KING LEE) / When the fat lady sings (GZA) / This some 'n to (GOODIE MOB) / Armageddon (interlude) (KURUPT) / Victory or defeat (HOSTYLE OF SCREWBALL) / Heart of the assassin (CHACE INFINITE, KRONDON & PHENAM aka DON KRISIS) / Suckers are hidin' (DILATED PEOPLES) / When the pain inflict (KURUPT & ROSCOE) / Don't trip (CYPRESS HILL & JESSIE MOSS) / Razor to your throat (EVERLAST) / Millennium thrust (SELF-SCIENTIFIC).

Anti Anti

Mar 03. (cd) <*(6636-2)*> **DUST** ☐ ☐
– I know / Rain / Niente / Morta / Faded / Chasing shadows / Tears / Cloudy days / Fat city / Believer / Gone for good / Blip / Dead flowers / Far away.

May 03. (cd-s) *(ANTI 1117-2)* **RAIN** ☐ ☐

☐ Chuck D (see under ⇒ PUBLIC ENEMY)

☐ D-12 (see under ⇒ EMINEM)

DAFT PUNK

Formed: Paris, France ... 1992 originally as DARLING, by THOMAS BANGALTER (his father was the man behind such disco gems as 'CUBA' by the GIBSON BROTHERS and 'D.I.S.C.O.' by OTTOWAN) and GUY-MANUEL DE HOMEM CHRISTO. The duo had one track included on a STEREOLAB-compiled various artists album, described as "Daft Punk" by one daft critic. The lads were then daft enough to adopt this moniker as a full-time concern, releasing a clutch of 12"ers in the mid 90's on the Scottish dance label, 'Soma'. The grunge disco classic, 'DA FUNK', was a massive underground club hit, creating a buzz that eventually led to a major label signing race. 'Virgin' subsequently came out on top (oo er!), securing the pleasure of releasing their soon-to-be widely acclaimed debut long player, 'HOMEWORK'. Issued in early '97, it hit the UK Top 10 as well as surprisingly breaking new ground in the States on the back of the minimalist 70's trance-funk oddity 'AROUND THE WORLD', which was their second UK Top 10 smash. While 1977 was the year of punk, 1997 was most definitely the year of DAFT PUNK, the duo wowing fans at sold out venues and bulging festival dance tents up and down the country. Come 1998, BANGALTER was riding even higher in the charts with the irresistible disco-house shimmy of STARDUST's 'MUSIC SOUNDS BETTER WITH YOU'. This served as a taster for DP's first single of the new millennium, 'ONE MORE TIME', a digi-pop classic featuring a treated vocal by NY garage star, ROMANTHONY. The accompanying album, 'DISCOVERY' (2001), confirmed DAFT PUNK's maturation from acid-house pranksters to masters of seamlessly updated electro-pop cum 70's/80's retro chic, drawing inspiration from the obvious (GIORGIO MORODER, BUGGLES) to the not so obvious (STEVE MILLER, VANGELIS). With everyone from BASEMENT JAXX to MOGWAI releasing full-length remix sets, DAFT PUNK delivered their own take on the format, 'DAFT CLUB' (2003); earlier that year BANGALTER diversified into French cinema courtesy of the soundtrack to controversial movie, 'IRREVERSIBLE'. Back to the piston-packing electro-grunge of old and – on the likes of 'MAKE LOVE' at least – taking a deep gulp of melodic AIR, 'HUMAN AFTER ALL' (2005) was once again worth the wait, and once again reached the UK Top 10. Singles, 'ROBOT ROCK' and 'TECHNOLOGIC' probably deserved higher placings than Top 40, although they still shifted into gear nicely alongside the monster hits on 2006 anthology, 'MUSIQUE VOL.1: 1993-2005'.

Album rating: HOMEWORK (*8) / DISCOVERY (*7) / DAFT CLUB remixes (*5) / HUMAN AFTER ALL (*7) / MUSIQUE VOL.1: 1993-2005 compilation (*8) / Thomas Bangalter: IRREVERSIBLE soundtrack (*5)

THOMAS BANGALTER (b. 3 Jan'75) – electronics / **GUY-MANUEL DE HOMEM CHRISTO** (b. 8 Feb'74) – electronics

Soma — not iss.

Apr 94. (12"ep) *(SOMA 014)* **NEW WAVE EP** [ ] [–]
– French teen / New wave / Alive (the new wave finale) / +1 .

May 95. (12"ep) *(SOMA 025)* **DA FUNK / DA FUNK (version) / MUSIQUE** [ ] [–]

Virgin — Virgin

Jan 97. (cd/c/d-lp) *(CD/TC+/V 2821)* **HOMEWORK** [8] Mar97 [ ]
– Daftendirekt / Wdpk 83.7 fm / Revolution 909 / Da funk / Phoenix / Fresh / Around the world / Rollin' & scratchin' / Teachers / High fidelity / Rock'n roll / Oh yeah / Burnin' / Indo silver club / Alive / Funk Ad.

Feb 97. (7"/c-s) *(VS LH/C 1625)* **DA FUNK. / MUSIQUE** [7] [ ]
(12"+=/cd-s+=) *(VS T/CD 1625)* – ('A'original).

Apr 97. (7"/c-s) *(VS LH/C 1633)* *<8950116-2>* **AROUND THE WORLD. / TEACHERS** [5] Aug97 [61]
(12"+=/cd-s+=) *(VS T/CD 1633)* – ('A'-Motorbass remix).

Sep 97. (c-s/cd-s) *(VS C/CD 1649)* **BURNIN' / (mixes by Slam & Ian Pooley)** [30] [ ]
(12"+=) *(VST 1649)* – ('A'remixes by DJ Sneak).

Feb 98. (c-s/12"/cd-s) *(VS C/T/CDT 1682)* **REVOLUTION 909. / ('A'-Roger Sanchez mix) / ('A'-acappella)** [47] [–]

Nov 00. (c-s/cd-s) *(VSC/+DT 1791)* *<38758>* **ONE MORE TIME / (radio mix)** [2] Jan01 [61]
(12") *(VST 1791)* – ('A'mixes).

Mar 01. (cd/c/d-lp) *(CDVX/TCV/VX 2940)* *<49606>* **DISCOVERY** [2] [44]
– One more time / Aerodynamic / Digital love / Harder, better, faster, stronger / Crescendolls / Nightvision / Superheroes / High life / Something about us / Voyager / Veridis quo / Short circuit / Face to face / Too long.

Mar 01. (12") *(VST 1799)* **AERODYNAMIC. / AERODYNAMITE** [ ] [–]

Jun 01. (c-s/cd-s) *(VSC/+DT 1810)* **DIGITAL LOVE (mixes)** [14] [ ]
(12") *(VST 1810)* – ('A'side) / Digital dub.

Nov 01. (12"/cd-s) *(VST/VSCDT 1822)* **HARDER, BETTER, FASTER, STRONGER. / (mixes; Breakers break / Pete Heller's stylus)** [25] [–]
(12") *(VSTX 1822)* – ('A'-Neptunes remix) / Aerodynamic (Slum Village remix).

Dec 03. (cd-s) *<547645>* **SOMETHING ABOUT US – LOVE THEME FROM INTERSTELLA 5555 / VERIDIS QUO / VOYAGER / ('A'-mix & video)** [–] [ ]

Mar 05. (cd) *<CDV 2996>* *<63562>* **HUMAN AFTER ALL** [10] [98]
– Human after all / The prime time of your life / Robot rock / Steam machine / Make love / The brainwasher / On/off / Television rules the nation / Technologic / Emotion.

Apr 05. (12") *(VST 1897)* **ROBOT ROCK (mixes; edit / Soulwax / Maximum overdrive)** [32] [ ]
(cd-s+=) *(VSCDX 1897)* *<68769>* – ('A'-video).

Jul 05. (cd-s) *(VSCDT 1900)* **TECHNOLOGIC / (Basement Jaxx Kontrol mix)** [40] [–]
(12"+=) *(VST 1900)* – ('A'-Vitalic remix).
(cd-s) *(VSCDX 1900)* – (above extra) / ('A'-Peaches no lgic remix) / ('A'-video).

– compilations, others, etc. –

on 'Virgin' / US 'Astralwerks' unless mentioned otherwise

Oct 01. (cd/lp) *(CD+/V 2952)* *<11139>* **ALIVE 1997 (live)** [ ] Nov01 [ ]

Oct 01. (d-cd) *(810847-2)* **DISCOVERY / HOMEWORK** [ ] [–]

Dec 03. (cd) *(CDV 2982)* *<596389>* **DAFT CLUB** (remixes) [ ] [ ]

Sep 04. (3xcd-box) *(VBX 27)* **HOMEWORK / DISCOVEDRY / DAFT CLUB** [ ] [–]

Apr 06. (cd) *(CDV 3019)* *<58405-2>* **MUSIQUE VOL.1: 1993-2005** [34] [ ]
– Musique / Da funk / Around the world / Revolution 909 / Alive / One

more time / Harder better faster stronger / Something about us / Robot rock / Techologic / Human after all / Rollin' & scratchin' (live) / Chord memory – Ian Pooley remix / Mothership reconnection (Scott Groove remix). *(ltd-cd w/dvd+=; DCVX 3019)* – (videos).

THOMAS BANGALTER

		Roule	Virgin
Mar 97.	(12"ep) *(ROULE 301ST)* **TRAX ON DA ROCKS EP** – Trax on da rocks / Roule boule / What to do / Outrun / Ventura. *(re-iss. Jan02; same)*	☐	–
Mar 97.	(12") *(ROULE 302ST)* **SPINAL SCRATCH. / SPINAL BEATS** *(re-iss. May98 & Jan02; same)*	☐	–
Nov 97.	(12"; as THOMAS BANGALTER & ALAN BRAXE) *(ROULE 303)* **VELOCITY EP**	☐	–
Jul 98.	(12"; as STARDUST) *(ROULE 305ST)* <38651> **MUSIC SOUNDS BETTER WITH YOU (club mix). / ('A'-Bob Sinclair remix)** *(re-dist.Aug98 on 'Virgin'; DINSD 175)* – hit UK No.2 above with **ALAN 'BRAXE' QUEME + BENJAMIN 'DIAMOND' COHEN**	55	Sep98 62
Oct 98.	(12"ep) *(ROULE 306ST)* **TRACKS ON DA ROCKS VOL.2** – Club soda / Extra dry / Shuffle / Colossus / Turbo. *(re-iss. Jan02; same)*	☐	☐
Jul 00.	(12"; as THOMAS BANGALTER & DJ FALCON) *(ROULE 309-12)* **TOGETHER. / OUTRAGE** *(re-iss. Jan02; same)*	☐	–
Dec 02.	(12"; by THOMAS BANGALTER & DJ FALCON) **SO MUCH LOVE TO GIVE**	71	–
Feb 03.	(cd) *(ROULE 001CD)* *<90705>* **IRREVERSIBLE** (soundtrack) – Irreversible / Tempus edax rerum / Rectum / Night beats / Stress / Paris by night / Outrage / Outrun / Spinal scratch / Extra dry / Desaccords / Ventura – Into the tunnel / The end. *<re-cd; 826011>* – (other artists).	☐	☐

□ Roger DALTREY (see under ⇒ the WHO)

□ DAMAGEPLAN (see under ⇒ PANTERA)

the DAMNED

Formed: London, England ... May 1976 by BRIAN JAMES and RAT SCABIES who soon found the CAPTAIN and former undertaker, DAVE VANIAN. Signed to new UK indie label, 'Stiff', by JAKE RIVERA, they released the classic track, 'NEW ROSE', produced by stablemate, NICK LOWE. The DAMNED became the first "New Wave Punks" to release and chart with an album, namely the enduring 'DAMNED DAMNED DAMNED' (1977). One of the classic punk debuts, the album pogo'd and thrashed its way through a frenetic set of three-chord wonders, LOWE's garden shed production underlining the riotous pandemonium. The band had also broken into the Top 40, although ironically enough, prolonged chart success would come later in the 80's when the DAMNED had changed almost beyond recognition. Live, the band were also one of the major attractions on the London scene; with VANIAN's proto-goth affectations, SENSIBLE's beret-topped antics and SCABIES' demented-drummer persona all competing against each other, The DAMNED were indeed a motley crew. Their musical assault was bolstered later that year by a second guitarist, LU EDMONDS, who debuted on the flaccid 'MUSIC FOR PLEASURE' (1977). The album was universally derided and SCABIES soon left for pastures new. Although future CULTURE CLUB man, JOHN MOSS was drafted in briefly as a replacement, the band splintered early the following year. After a period of solo work, VANIAN, SENSIBLE and SCABIES regrouped as the DAMNED early in '79 and emerged rejuvenated into the UK Top 20 via the impressive 'LOVE SONG'. With ALGY WARD completing the line-up, the band scored a second chart hit with 'SMASH IT UP', releasing their lauded 'MACHINE GUN ETIQUETTE' album later that year. Sure, they were still as swift and deadly as the title might suggest, but somehow they'd acquired a mastery of pop dynamics; a third single, 'I JUST CAN'T BE HAPPY TODAY', was the closest they'd yet come to a rock-solid tune. PAUL GRAY replaced WARD for 1980's 'UNTITLED (THE BLACK ALBUM)', an even more surprising, ambitious double set which flew in the face of punk convention with its rampant experimentalism. The poppy 'STRAWBERRIES' (1982) marked the last stand of CAPTAIN SENSIBLE, who'd scored with the annoying 'HAPPY TALK' earlier that summer, the first fruits of his solo deal with 'A&M'. VANIAN and SCABIES lumbered on with new members ROMAN JUGG and BRYN MERRICK, suprisingly enough enjoying major chart success with a string of overtly commercial, pseudo-goth rockers, the biggest of which, a cover of BARRY RYAN's 'ELOISE', made the Top 3. 'PHANTASMAGORIA' (1985) became their biggest selling album to date, catering to a whole new generation of fans. Most critics were agreed, however, that it paled in comparison to their earlier work, the DAMNED finally fading in the late 80's. For any interested parties, the band periodically get together with an amorphous line-up for all-dayers and one-off gigs; old punks never die, they just tour with The DAMNED. With the horsemen of the apocalypse holding fire just yet, The DAMNED made an unlikely return from the recording grave with 'GRAVE DISORDER' (2001). Boasting a line-up of VANIAN and SENSIBLE alongside newcomers PATRICIA MORRISON, MONTY OXY MORON and PINCH, the interminably resurrected rockers trawled familiar, if never exactly predictable, musical and lyrical territory with customary disregard for current trends.

• **Songwriters:** Most written by JAMES, until he left, when group took over. Covered:- HELP! (Beatles) / I FEEL ALRIGHT (Stooges / Iggy Pop) / JET BOY JET GIRL (New York Dolls) / CITADEL (Rolling Stones) / ELOISE (Paul & Barry Ryan) / WHITE RABBIT (Jefferson Airplane) / ALONE AGAIN OR (Love) / WILD THING (Troggs) / LET THERE BE RATS (aka DRUMS) (Sandy Nelson). • **Trivia:** NICK MASON (Pink Floyd drummer) produced disappointing 2nd album MUSIC FOR PLEASURE. CAPTAIN SENSIBLE had UK-No.1 in 1982 with (Rogers-Hammerstein's) HAPPY TALK, and although briefly, became a top disco/pop act abroad.

Album rating: DAMNED DAMNED DAMNED (*8) / MUSIC FOR PLEASURE (*5) / MACHINE GUN ETIQUETTE (*7) / BLACK ALBUM (*6) / BEST OF THE DAMNED compilation (*8) / STRAWBERRIES (*5) / PHANTASMAGORIA (*5) / ANYTHING (*3) THE LIGHT AT THE END OF THE TUNNEL compilation (*7) / FINAL DAMNATION exploitation (*4) / I'M ALRIGHT JACK AND THE BEANSTALK (*4) / GRAVE DISORDER (*5)

DAVE VANIAN (b. DAVE LETTS) – vocals / **BRIAN JAMES** (b. BRIAN ROBERTSON) – guitar (ex-LONDON S.S.) / **CAPTAIN SENSIBLE** (b. RAY BURNS, 23 Apr'55) – bass, vocals / **RAT SCABIES** (b. CHRIS MILLER, 30 Jul'57) – drums (ex-LONDON S.S.)

		Stiff	Frontier
Nov 76.	(7") *(BUY 6)* **NEW ROSE. / HELP!**	☐	–
Feb 77.	(7") *(BUY 10)* **NEAT NEAT NEAT. / STAB YOR BACK / SINGALONGASCABIES**	☐	–
Feb 77.	(lp) *(SEEZ 1)* **DAMNED DAMNED DAMNED** – Neat neat neat / Fan club / I fall / Born to kill / Stab yor back / Feel the pain / New rose / Fish / See her tonite / 1 of the 2 / So messed up / I feel alright. *(re-iss. Apr87 on 'Demon' lp/c/cd; FIEND/+CASS/CD 91) (pic lp 1988; PFIEND 91) (<cd re-iss. Nov97 on 'Frontier'; 31033-2>) (cd re-iss. Aug00 on 'Edsel'; EDCD 677)*	36	Apr77 ☐

— added (ROBERT) **LU EDMUNDS** – guitar

Sep 77.	(7") *(BUY 18)* **PROBLEM CHILD. / YOU TAKE MY MONEY**	☐	–
Nov 77.	(lp) *(SEEZ 5)* **MUSIC FOR PLEASURE** – Problem child / Don't cry wolf / One way love / Politics / Stretcher case / Idiot box / You take my money / Alone / Your eyes / Creep (you can't fool me) / You know. *(re-iss. Apr88 on 'Demon' lp/c/cd; FIEND/+CASS/CD 108*	☐	☐
Dec 77.	(7",7"purple) *(BUY 24)* **DON'T CRY WOLF. / ONE WAY LOVE**	☐	–

— **DAVE BERK** – drums (ex-JOHNNY MOPED) repl. SCABIES who formed various bands

— **JOHN MOSS** – drums replaced BERK. They split Feb 78. VANIAN joined DOCTORS OF MADNESS. SENSIBLE formed SOFTIES then KING. EDMUNDS & MOSS formed THE EDGE. MOSS later joined ADAM & THE ANTS then CULTURE CLUB. EDMUNDS became part of ATHLETICO SPIZZ 80, The MEKONS, SHRIEKBACK, PIL. etc. BRIAN JAMES formed TANZ DER YOUTH, who released one single, 'I'M SORRY I'M SORRY' for 'Radar', before going solo the following year (1979) to issue his version of 'AIN'T THAT A SHAME'. He subsequently formed another punk supergroup, The HELLIONS, issuing one 1981 single for 'Illegal', 'WHY WHY WHY', before he jointly formed The LORDS OF THE NEW CHURCH. The DAMNED re-formed in Autumn '78 as The **DOOMED** with LEMMY of MOTORHEAD on bass. (1 gig) **HENRY BADOWSKI** – bass (ex-CHELSEA) replaced LEMMY. The group reverted to name The **DAMNED** with originals VANIAN, SENSIBLE (now guitar & keyboards) and **SCABIES**

— **ALGY WARD** – bass (ex-SAINTS) replaced BADOWSKI who went solo

Chiswick — Roadrunner

Apr 79. (7",7"red) *(CHIS 112)* **LOVE SONG. / NOISE NOISE NOISE / SUICIDE** — 20 — –
(re-iss. 7"blue Feb82 on 'Big Beat'; NS 75)

Oct 79. (7") *(CHIS 116)* **SMASH IT UP. / BURGLAR** — 35 — –
(re-iss. 7"red Mar82 on 'Big Beat'; NS 76)

Nov 79. (lp) *(CWK 3011)* **MACHINE GUN ETIQUETTE** — 31 — Dec79
– Love song / Machine gun etiquette / I just can't be happy today / Melody Lee / Anti-Pope / These hands / Plan 9 channel 7 / Noise noise noise / Looking at you / Smash it up (parts 1 & 2). *(re-iss. Jun85 on 'Ace' lp/c; DAM/+MC 3) (cd-iss. 1986 +=; CDWIK 905)* – Ballroom blitz / Suicide / Rabid (over you) / White rabbit.

Nov 79. (7") *(CHIS 120)* **I JUST CAN'T BE HAPPY TODAY. / BALLROOM BLITZ / TURKEY SONG** — 46 — –

— **PAUL GRAY** – bass, vocals (ex-EDDIE AND THE HOT RODS) repl. WARD who formed TANK

Jun 80. (7";w-drawn) *(CHIS 130)* **WHITE RABBIT. / RABID (OVER YOU) / SEAGULLS** — — –

Sep 80. (7"m/12"m) *(CHIS/+12 135)* **THE HISTORY OF THE WORLD (part 1). / I BELIEVE THE IMPOSSIBLE / SUGAR AND SPITE** — — –

Nov 80. (d-lp) *(CWK 3015)* **UNTITLED** (THE BLACK ALBUM) (1/2 studio, 1/4 live, 1/4 concept) — 29 — –
– Wait for the blackout / Lively arts / Silly kids games / Drinking about my baby / Hit and miss / Doctor Jekyll and Mr. Hyde / 13th floor vendetta / Twisted nerve / Sick of this and that / History of the world (part 1) / Therapy // Curtain call / live side:- Love song / Second time around / Smash it up (parts 1 & 2) / New rose / I just can't be happy today / Plan 9 Channel 7. *(re-iss. Aug82 on 'Ace' as one-lp/d-c; DAM/+MC 3) (c-iss.Jun85; TCWIK 3015) (cd-iss. Mar90; CDWIK 906)* – (omits live tracks)

Nov 80. (7"m) *(CHIS 139)* **THERE AINT NO SANITY CLAUS. / HIT OR MISS / LOOKING AT YOU (live)** — — –

N.E.M.S. — not iss.

Nov 81. (d7"ep) *(TRY 1)* **FRIDAY THE 13th** — 50 — –
– Disco man / The limit club / Citadel / Billy bad breaks.

Bronze — not iss.

Jul 82. (7"m/7"pic-d) *(BRO/+P 149)* **LOVELY MONEY. / LOVELY MONEY (disco) / I THINK I'M WONDERFUL** — 42 — –

Sep 82. (7"ep) *(BRO 156)* **DOZEN GIRLS. / TAKE THAT / MINE'S A LARGE ONE, LANDLORD / TORTURE ME** — — –

Oct 82. (lp/c) *(BRON 542)* **STRAWBERRIES** — 15 — –
– Ignite / Generals / Stranger on the town / Dozen girls / The dog / Gun fury / Pleasure and the pain / Life goes on / Bad time for Bonzo / Under the floor again / Don't bother me. *(re-iss. Mar86 on 'Legacy' red-lp/c; LLM/+K 3000) (re-iss. Dec86 on 'Dojo' lp/cd; DOJO LP/CD 46) (cd re-iss. Nov92 on 'Dojo'; DOJOCD 46) (cd-iss. Apr94 on 'Cleopatra'; CLEO 1029-2) (cd re-iss. Mar97 on 'Essential'; ESMCD 473) (cd re-iss. JUn01 on 'Castle'; CMRCD 246)*

Nov 82. (7"m) *(BRO 159)* **GENERALS. / DISGUISE / CITADEL ZOMBIES** — — –

Damned — not iss.

Nov 83. (pic-lp/lp) *(P+/DAMU 2)* **LIVE IN NEWCASTLE (live)** — – — mail-o –
(cd-iss. Jan94 on 'Receiver'; RRCD 181)

Plus One — not iss.

May 84. (7"colrd/7"pic-d) *(DAMNED 1/+P)* **THANKS FOR THE NIGHT. / NASTY** — — –
(re-iss. 12"-ltd.1985 +=; DAMNED 1T) – Do the blitz.

— **VANIAN** and **SCABIES** recruited new guys **ROMAN JUGG** (b. Barry, Wales) – guitar, keyboards / who replaced the CAPTAIN who carried on with solo career. **BRYN MERRICK** (b. Barry, Wales) – bass; repl. GRAY

M.C.A. — Off Beat

Mar 85. (7"/7"pic-d/'A'-Spic'n'Spec mix-12") *(GRIM/+P/T 1)* **GRIMLY FIENDISH. / EDWARD THE BEAR** — 21 — –
(12"white+=) *(GRIMX 1)* – ('A'-Bad Trip mix).

Jun 85. (7") *(GRIM 2)* **SHADOW OF LOVE. / NIGHTSHIFT** — 25 —
('A'-Ten Inches Of Hell mix-10"+=) *(GRIMX 2)* – Would you.
(12"+=) *(GRIMT 2)* – Would you.
(d7"+=) *(GRIMY 2)* – Let there be Rats / Wiped out.

Jul 85. (lp/c/pic-lp/white-lp/blue-lp) *(MCF/+C/P/W/B 3275)* **PHANTASMAGORIA** — 11 —
– Street of dreams / Shadow of love / There'll come a day / Sanctum sanctorium / Is it a dream / Grimly fiendish / Edward the bear / The eighth day / Trojans. *(free 7" w.a.)* I JUST CAN'T BE HAPPY TODAY *(re-iss. 1986; same)* – (contains free 12"blue ELOISE) *(cd-iss. Aug89; DMCL 1887)*

Sep 85. (7") *(GRIM 3)* **IS IT A DREAM (Wild West End mix) / STREET OF DREAMS (live)** — 34 —
(12"+=) *(GRIMT 3)* – Curtain call (live) / Pretty vacant (live) / Wild thing (live).

Jan 86. (7") *(GRIM 4)* **ELOISE. / TEMPTATION** — 3 —
(12"blue+=/'A'-No Sleep Until Wednesday mix-12") *(GRIM T/X 4)* – Beat girl.

Nov 86. (7") *(GRIM 5)* **ANYTHING. / THE YEAR OF THE JACKAL** — 32 —
(10"blue+=,10"yellow+=) *(GRIMX 5)* – ('A'mixes).
(12"+=) *(GRIMT 5)* – Thanks for the night.

Nov 86. (lp/c/cd) *(MCG/MCGC/DMCG 6015)* *<5966>* **ANYTHING** — 40 —
– Anything / Alone again or / The portrait / Restless / In dulce decorum / Gigolo / The girl goes down / Tightrope walk / Psychomania.

Feb 87. (7"colrd/12"clear) *(GRIM/+T 6)* **GIGOLO. / THE PORTRAIT** — 29 — –

Apr 87. (7") *(GRIM 7)* **ALONE AGAIN OR. / IN DULCE DECORUM** — 27 — –
(12"+=) *(GRIMT 7)* – Psychomania.
(d7"++=) *(DGRIM 7)* – Eloise.

Nov 87. (7") *(GRIM 8)* **IN DULCE DECORUM. / PSYCHOMANIA** — 72 — –
(12"+=) *(GRIMT 8)* – ('A'dub).

— disbanded in the late 80's (ROMAN + BRYN formed The MISSING MEN) although re-union gigs were forthcoming

Essential — Restless

Aug 89. (green-lp) *(ESCLP 008)* *<72385>* **FINAL DAMNATION** (live '88 reunion) — —
– See her tonite / Neat neat neat / Born to kill / I fall / Fan club / Fish / Help / New rose / I feel alright / I just can't be happy today / Wait for the blackout / Melody Lee / Noise noise noise / Love song / Smash it up (parts 1 & 2) / Looking at you / The last time. *(cd-iss. Apr94 on 'Castle'; CLACD 338) (cd re-iss. Jun01 on 'Castle'; CMRCD 247)*

— **VANIAN** + **SCABIES** re-formed er, **The DAMNED** alongside **ALAN LEE SHAW** – guitar (ex-RINGS, ex-MANIACS), **KRIS DOLLIMORE** – guitar (ex-GODFATHERS) + **MOOSE** – bass (ex-NEW MODEL ARMY)

Seadog — not iss.

Dec 96. (lp) *(SEALLP 102)* **I'M ALRIGHT JACK AND THE BEANSTALK** — — –
– I need a life / Testify / Shut it / Tailspin / Not of this earth / Running man / My desire / Never could believe / Heaven . . . can take your lies / Shadow to fall / No more tears / Prokofiev. *(re-iss. Apr97 on 'The Record Label' cd/c; MOCDR/MOMC 1) (cd re-iss. Sep02 on 'Castle'+=; CMRCD 543)* – BBC sessions:- Testify / I need a life / Never could believe / Neat neat neat. *<US cd-iss. Oct02 on 'Sanctuary'; 81231>*

— the real DAMNED re-formed in 2001 with **VANIAN, SENSIBLE,** plus **PATRICIA MORRISON** – bass (ex-SISTERS OF MERCY) / **MONTY OXY MORON** – keyboards / **PINCH** – drums (ex-ENGLISH DOGS)

Nitro — Nitro

Aug 01. (cd/lp) *(<15844-2/-1>)* **GRAVE DISORDER** — —
– Democracy / Song.com / Thrill kill / She / Looking for action / Would you be so hot (if you weren't dead?) / Absinthe / Amen / Neverland / 'Til the end of time / Obscene. *<US+=>* – W / Beauty of the beast.

– compilations, etc. (selective) –

1981. (4x7"box) *Stiff; (GRAB 2)* **FOUR PACK** — — –
– (NEW ROSE / NEAT NEAT NEAT / PROBLEM CHILD / DON'T CRY WOLF)

Nov 81. (lp/c) *Ace; (DAM/+C 1)* **THE BEST OF THE DAMNED** 43 –
– New rose / Neat neat neat / I just can't be happy today / Jet boy jet girl / Hit or miss / There ain't no sanity claus / Smash it up (parts 1 & 2) / Plan 9 channel 7 / Rabid (over you) / Wait for the blackout / History of the world (part 1). *(cd-iss. Oct87; CDDAM 1)*

May 82. (7"/7"pic-d) *Big Beat; (NS/+P 77)* **WAIT FOR THE BLACKOUT. / Captain Sensible & The Softies: JET BOY, JET GIRL** –

Oct 82. (7"green) *Big Beat; (NS 80)* **LIVELY ARTS. / TEENAGE DREAM** –
(10"+=) *(NST 80)* – I'm so bored.

Nov 82. (lp) *Ace; (NED 1)* **LIVE SHEPPERTON 1980** (live) –
– Love song / Second time around / I just can't be happy today / Melody Lee / Help / Neat neat neat / Looking at you / Smash it up (parts 1 & 2) / New rose / Plan 9 channel 7. *(also iss.Nov82 on 'Big Beat'; WIKM 27) (c-iss.Jun85; WIKC 27) (cd-iss. Jun88; CDWIKM 27)*

Nov 85. (12"ep) *Stiff; (BUYIT 238)* **NEW ROSE / NEAT NEAT NEAT. / STRETCHER CASE / SICK OF BEING SICK** –

Jan 86. (lp/c/cd) *Dojo; (DOJO LP/TC/CD 21)* **DAMNED BUT NOT FORGOTTEN** –
(cd re-iss. Nov92; same) (cd re-iss. Feb97 on 'Essential'; ESMCD 472) (cd re-iss. Jun01 on 'Castle'; CMRCD 245)

Jun 86. (12"ep) *Strange Fruit; (SFPS 002)* **THE PEEL SESSIONS** (10.5.77) –
– Sick of being sick / Stretcher case / Feel the pain / Fan club. *(c-ep.1987; SFPSC 002) (cd-ep.May88; SFPSCD 002)*

Jul 86. (blue-m-lp) *Stiff; (GET 4)* **THE CAPTAIN'S BIRTHDAY PARTY – LIVE AT THE ROUNDHOUSE** –
(cd-iss. Nov91 on 'Demon'; VEXCD 7)

Jul 87. (12"ep) *Strange Fruit; (SFPS 040)* **THE PEEL SESSIONS** (30.11.76) –
– Stab yor back / Neat neat neat / New rose / So messed up / I fall.

Oct 87. (cd/lp) *I.D.; (C+/NOSE 18)* **MINDLESS, DIRECTIONLESS, ENEMY** (live) –
(re-iss. Jun89 cd/c/lp; CDOSE/KOSE/NOSE 18X)

Dec 87. (d-lp) *M.C.A.; (MCSP 312)* **THE LIGHT AT THE END OF THE TUNNEL** 87 –
(d-cd-iss. Apr92; MCLDD 19007)

Dec 99. (cd) *Chiswick; (CDWIKK 198)* **MARVELLOUS: THE BEST OF THE DAMNED** –

Oct 01. (d-cd) *Castle; (CMDDD 357)* **LIVE ANTHOLOGY**
– (BALLROOM BLITZ / LIVE IN NEWCASTLE / SCHOOL BULLIES)

May 02. (d-cd) *Castle; (CMEDD 476)* **SMASH IT UP: THE ANTHOLOGY 1976-1987**

Jan 03. (5xcd-s) *Earmark; (CMMBX 644)* **THE STIFF SINGLES 1976-1977**

Oct 04. (3xcd-box) *Sanctuary; (SMETD 128)* **NEAT NEAT NEAT: THE COLLECTION**

☐ Evan DANDO (see under ⇒ LEMONHEADS)

the DANDY WARHOLS

Formed: Portland, Oregon, USA . . . mid 90's by buzzed-up guys, COURTNEY TAYLOR-TAYLOR and PETER HOLMSTROM, who, with rhythm section, ERIC HEDFORD and feisty babe, ZIA McCABE, emerged from their recording basement in 1996. After a one-off double mini-CD, the harmony-fuelled psychedelia of 'DANDYS RULE OK', they inked a deal with 'Capitol', although they riled their bosses by failing to deliver on a promised set of songs; exposure in the Rolling Stone was subsequently mis-timed. Unsurprisingly the band gave themselves a proverbial kick up the ass and rose from their drug ashes with a fine set of songs, two of which ('EVERYDAY SHOULD BE A HOLIDAY' and 'NOT IF YOU WERE THE LAST JUNKIE ON EARTH') were UK Top 30 singles and preceded their Top 20 album, ' . . .THE DANDY WARHOLS COME DOWN' (1998). Spending just over a year in the studio – HEDFORD being replaced by BRENT DeBOER – the DANDY WARHOLS emerged with the most accomplished set to date, 'THIRTEEN TALES FROM URBAN BOHEMIA' (2000). It took a little while for audiences to catch on to its excellent pop sensibilities, as the album didn't really become a hit for the band until their notoriously catchy single 'BOHEMIAN LIKE YOU' (virtually ignored on its initial release) was used to great effect in a mobile phone ad. Surprisingly, on its second outing, the song crashed into the UK Top 5 and suddenly people had forgotten that the DANDY WARHOLS were perhaps the coolest band around. The final outcome of the set was more focused on creating an atmosphere, or a feeling instead of ten drugged-up love songs and three great singles (as was the case on 'COME DOWN'). Hippy cowboy anthem 'GET OFF' served as proverbial candy for the ear, while 'COUNTRY LEVER' and the strange musings on 'HORSE PILLS' really set the tone for one of the fullest and freshest albums of the year. After the massive success of 'BOHEMIAN LIKE YOU', the band followed it up quickly (almost too quickly) with a disappointing set in the same vein as 'COME DOWN', but a tad less ambitious. With DURAN DURAN's NICK RHODES manning the engineering desk for 'WELCOME TO THE MONKEY HOUSE' (2003), and HOLMSTROM becoming PETER LOEW (after marrying MICHELLE LOEW), the DANDY's started to dabble in electronic machinery such as synths, drum machines and a whole host of other gadgets. What it really displayed was a lost sense of irony on the band's part; from the empty, drug-inspired downers that have always plagued their albums to the speedball cocktails of throbbing pop-rock such as 'THE DANDY WARHOLS LOVE ALMOST EVERYONE', even down to the VELVETS/WARHOL pastiche of the banana cover by feted artist Ron English. 'DiG!' was an unlikely Grand Jury winner at the Sundance Film Festival in 2004, a neo-rockumentary drawing its energy from the rivalry between the DANDYs and the BRIAN JONESTOWN MASSACRE. Its unexpected success raised the band's profile ahead of fifth long-player, 'ODDITORIUM OR WARLORDS OF MARS' (2005), even if the chart positions weren't at all healthy. Once beyond the convoluted title, there was the usual blend of degenerate rock, psychedelia and pop cynicism.

• **Covers:** THE WRECK OF THE EDMUND FITZGERALD (Gordon Lightfoot) / FREE FOR ALL (Ted Nugent) / HELLS BELLS (Ac/Dc) / EIGHT DAYS A WEEK (Beatles) / CALL ME (Blondie) / RELAX (Frankie Goes To Hollywood) / THE JEAN GENIE (David Bowie) / MY SHARONA (Knack) / etc.

Album rating: DANDYS RULE OK (*6) / . . .THE DANDY WARHOLS COME DOWN (*7) / THIRTEEN TALES FROM URBAN BOHEMIA (*8) / WELCOME TO THE MONKEY HOUSE (*6) / ODDITORIUM OR WARLORDS OF MARS (*6)

COURTNEY TAYLOR-TAYLOR (b.16 Jul'67) – vocals, guitar / **PETER HOLMSTROM** – guitar / **ERIC HEDFORD** – drums / **ZIA McCABE** – bass, keyboards, vocals

Tim/Kerr Tim/Ker

Sep 95. (cd-s) <*TK 0088*> **THE LITTLE DRUMMER BOY / DICK / (IT DOESN'T TAKE A GENIUS)** –

Dec 95. (2xm-cd) <*(TK95CD 0091)*> **DANDYS RULE OK**
– Introduction by young Tom / Dandy Warhol's T.V. theme song / Ride / Best friend / Not your bottle / (Tony, this song is called) Lou Weed / Nothin' to do / Coffee and tea wrecks / Genius / Dick / Just try / Nothing (lifestyle of a tortured artist for sale) / Grunge Betty / Prelude – It's a fast-driving rave-up with the Dandy Warhols sixteen minutes – Finale // Little drummer boy / Dick / (It doesn't take a) Genius / Untitled. *(re-iss. Sep98 on 'Capitol'; 496409-2) (re-iss. Sep00 on 'Dandy'; DR 001)*

Jan 96. (pic-d-cd) <*(TK 95PD 104)*> **RIDE / WE LOVE YOU DICK**

Capitol Capitol

Feb 98. (c-s/7"purple) *(TC+/CL 797)* **EVERYDAY SHOULD BE A HOLIDAY. / ONE (ULTRA LAM WHITE BOY)** 29 –
(cd-s+=) *(CDCL 797)* – Head.

Apr 98. (7"orange) *(CL 800)* **NOT IF YOU WERE THE LAST JUNKIE ON EARTH. / GENIUS (live)** 13 –
(cd-s+=) *(CDCLS 800)* – Ride (live).
(cd-s) *(CDCL 800)* – ('A') / ('A'-live) / It's a fast drivin' rave up with the Dandy Warhols sixteen minutes (live).

May 98. (cd/c) <(8 36505-2/-4)> **. . .THE DANDY WARHOLS COME DOWN** [16] [ ]
– Be-in / Boys better / Minnesoter / Orange / I love you / Not if you were the last junkie on earth / Every day should be a holiday / Good morning / Whipping tree / Green / Cool as Kim Deal / Hard on for Jesus / Pete International airport / The creep out. *(d-lp iss.Mar98 on 'Tim/Kerr'; TK 1671)*

Jul 98. (7"green) *(CL 805)* **BOYS BETTER. / NOTHIN' TO DO** [36] [–]
(cd-s+=) *(CDCL 805)* – Grunge Betty.
(cd-s) *(CDCLS 805)* – ('A') / The wreck of the Edmund Fitzgerald / Free for all.

— **BRENT DeBOER** – drums, vocals; repl. HEDFORD

May 00. (7") *(CL 821)* **GET OFF. / PHONE CALL** [38] [–]
(cd-s+=) *(CDCLS 821)* – White gold.
(cd-s) *(CDCL 821)* – ('A') / Not if you were the last junkie on earth (live) / I love you (live).

Jun 00. (cd) *(857787-2)* <CDP 5778> **THIRTEEN TALES FROM URBAN BOHEMIA** [51] Aug00 [ ]
– Godless / Mohammed / Nietzsche / Country leaver / Solid / Horse pills / Get off / Sleep / Cool scene / Bohemian like you / Retarded / Shakin' / Big Indian / The gospel. *(d-lp iss.Oct00; SCZ 787) (re-iss. Nov01; same)* – hit UK No.32

Aug 00. (7") *(CL 823)* **BOHEMIAN LIKE YOU. / HELLS BELLS** [42] [–]
(cd-s+=) *(CDCLS 823)* – Lance.
(cd-s) *(CDCL 823)* – ('A') / Retarded / Dub song.

Jul 01. (12") *(12CL 829)* **GODLESS / ('A'-Massive Attack remix / dub / instrumental)** [66] [–]
(cd-s+=) *(CDCL 829)* – ('A'-video).

Oct 01. (c-s) *(TCCL 829)* **BOHEMIAN LIKE YOU / HELLS BELLS / LANCE** [5] [–]
(cd-s) *(CDCL 829)* – ('A') / Retarded / Dub song.

Mar 02. (c-s) *(TCCL 835)* **GET OFF / STARS (acoustic)** [34] [–]
(cd-s+=) *(CDCL 835)* – Eight days a week (acoustic) / ('A'-video).

— **PETER** officially became **PETER LOEW**

May 03. (7"yellow) *(CL 843)* **WE USED TO BE FRIENDS. / MINNESOTER (thee slayer hippie mix)** [18] [–]
(cd-s) *(CDCL 843)* – Call me / Relax.

May 03. (cd/lp) *(590123-2/-1)* <84368> **WELCOME TO THE MONKEY HOUSE** [20] [ ]
– Welcome to the monkey house / We used to be friends / Plan A / Dope (wonderful you) / I am a scientist / I am over it / The Dandy Warhols love almost everyone / Insincere because I / You were the last high / Heavenly / I am sound / Hit rock bottom / (You come in) Burned.

Jul 03. (7"white) *(CL 845)* **YOU WERE THE LAST HIGH. / WE USED TO BE FRIENDS (Kenn Richards mix)** [34] [–]
(cd-s) *(CDCL 845)* – ('A') / We used to be friends (Coates & Stiles mix) / Everyday should be a holiday (Tony Lash mix).
(cd-s) *(CDCLX 845)* – ('A') / Sun / Dye.

Nov 03. (7"blue) *(CL 851)* **PLAN A. / THE JEAN GENIE** [66] [–]
(cd-s+=) *(CDCL 851)* – You were the last high (Dirty Vegas dub) / ('A'-video).

Sep 05. (7") *(CL 871)* **SMOKE IT. / 11CC** [59] [–]
(cd-s) *(CDCLS 871)* – ('A') / Throaty Numan / Wie gehts / ('A'-video).

Sep 05. (cd) <(8 74590-2)> **ODDITORIUM OR WARLORDS OF MARS** [67] [89]
– Colder than the coldest winter was cold / Love is the new feel awful / Easy / All the money or the simple life honey / The new country / Holding me up / Did you make a song with Otis / Everyone is totally insane / Smoke it / Down like disco / There is only this time / A loan tonight. *(ltd-cd w/dvd+=; 337543-2)* – (DVD tracks).

Dec 05. (cd-s/7") *(CD+/CL 874)* **ALL THE MONEY OR THE SIMPLE LIFE HONEY. / SMOKE IT (trippy vox)** [ ] [–]
(cd-s) *(CDCLS 874)* – ('A') / My Sharona / Snuggly.

– compilations, etc. –

Oct 02. (d-cd) *E.M.I.; (541130-2)* **DANDY'S RULE OK / THIRTEEN TALES FROM URBAN BOHEMIA** [ ] [–]

☐ DANGER MOUSE (see under ⇒ GNARLS BARKLEY)

the DARKNESS

Formed: Lowestoft, Suffolk, England ... late 90's as EMPIRE by brothers JUSTIN and DAN HAWKINS, Scotsman FRANKIE POULLAIN (who claimed to be five years younger to the press!) and ED GRAHAM. The revenge of 80's hair-metal in all its spandex-clad, critic-baiting, monster hook glory, the DARKNESS were perhaps an inevitable cultural blip on an otherwise insufferably uber-cool and irony-saturated music scene. That they emerged from the ruins of a bonafide prog rock outfit (the EMPIRE mentioned above) only made their unselfconsciously unfashionable stance all the more er.. unselfconsciously unfashionable. With JUSTIN HAWKINS famously taking up the vacant lead singer role after a show-stopping karaoke performance of Queen's 'BOHEMIAN RHAPSODY', the band's championing of flamboyance over fakery seemed written in the cards. Or, in more heavy metal terms, glimpsed in the crystal ball. A series of London gigs allowed JUSTIN all the exposure he needed to prove that good old rock'n'roll props like skintight strides, acrobatic stage antics and ridiculous falsetto squealing were what the kids really wanted. A sneering music press be damned, the DARKNESS released their debut EP, 'I BELIEVE IN A THING CALLED LOVE', on indie label, 'Must Destroy Music', in summer 2002. Support slots with the likes of DEF LEPPARD and DEEP PURPLE followed before single 'KEEP YOUR HANDS OFF MY WOMAN', edged into the UK Top 50 early the following year. The hype only accelerated as 'Atlantic' signed them up. A further single, 'GROWING ON ME', just missed the Top 10 while debut album, 'PERMISSION TO LAND' (2003), hit UK No.1 soon afterwards. From its disturbingly BOSTON-esque sleeve to its meaty power ballads and cod-metal lyrics, the album could've been plucked ripe from the late 70's or the 80's. It was unreconstructed for sure, utterly decadent, certainly, but there was also an undercurrent of humour (if stopping short of irony) and more importantly, a killer instinct for huge melodies and chest-beating choruses. In other words, it wasn't rocket science; and in these days of regulation post-rock glumness, maybe that was a blessing. Towards the end of 2003, a re-release of ' . . .A THING CALLED LOVE' and the festive-baiting, 'CHRISTMAS TIME (DON'T LET THE BELLS END)' both narrowly missed the No.1 spot – we had finally seen the light. POULLAIN left all the spandex-splintering shenanigans behind in May 2005, when – amid claims he was "frozen out" – the band replaced him with one of their roadies, RICHIE EDWARDS. JUSTIN indulged his incurable 70s fixation with his Top 10 cover of Sparks' 'THIS TOWN AIN'T BIG ENOUGH FOR THE BOTH OF US', under the unlikely and very un-rock'n'roll pseudonym, BRITISH WHALE. Employing the services of vintage QUEEN producer, Roy Thomas Baker, the DARKNESS were finally re-animated later in the year with sophomore set, 'ONE WAY TICKET TO HELL . . . AND BACK'. Managing to reference both AC/DC and ELO in one fell swoop, the album's title was truncated for lead Top 10 single, 'ONE WAY TICKET'. Lacking the exploding choruses of yore, the record failed to take off never mind getting permission to land; its best shot at a Top 10 hook was 'IS IT JUST ME?'.

Album rating: PERMISSION TO LAND (*8) / ONE WAY TICKET TO HELL . . . AND BACK (*5)

JUSTIN HAWKINS (b.17 Mar'75, Chertsey, Surrey, England) – vocals, guitar, keyboards / **DAN HAWKINS** (b.12 Dec'76) – guitar, vocals / **FRANKIE POULLAIN** (b. FRANCIS GILES PATTERSON, 15 Apr'67, Edinburgh, Scotland) – bass / **ED GRAHAM** (b.20 Feb'76, Great Yarmouth, England) – drums

Must Destroy Atlantic

Aug 02. (cd-ep) *(DUSTY 001CD)* **I BELIEVE IN A THING CALLED LOVE EP** [ ] [–]

– I believe in a thing called love / Love on the rocks with no ice / Love is only a feeling.

Feb 03. (7") *(DESTROYER 6)* **GET YOUR HANDS OFF MY WOMAN. / THE BEST OF ME** [43] [–]
(cd-s+=) *(DUSTY 006CD)* – ('A'-Profane version).

Jun 03. (7") *(DESTROYER 10)* **GROWING ON ME. / HOW DARE YOU CALL THIS LOVE?** [11] [–]
(cd-s+=) *(DUSTY 010CD)* – Bareback.

Jul 03. (cd/lp) *(5046 67452-2/-1) <60817>* **PERMISSION TO LAND** [1] Aug03 [39]
– Black shuck / Get your hands off my woman / Growing on me / I believe in a thing called love / Love is only a feeling / Givin' up / Stuck in a rut / Friday night / Love on the rocks with no ice / Holding my own.

Sep 03. (7"pic-d/cd-s) *(DARK 01/+CD)* **I BELIEVE IN A THING CALLED LOVE. / MAKIN' OUT / PHYSICAL SEX** [2] [–]

Dec 03. (7"sha-pic-d/cd-s) *(DARK 02/+CD)* **CHRISTMAS TIME (DON'T LET THE BELLS ENDS). / I LOVE YOU 5 TIMES** [2] [–]

Mar 04. (7"pic-d) *(DARK 03)* **LOVE IS ONLY A FEELING. / PLANNING PERMISSION** [5] [–]
(cd-s+=) *(DARK 03CD)* – The curse of the Tolland man.
(dvd-s) *(DARK 03DVCD)* – ('A'-video) / (behind the scenes footage) / Get your hands off my woman (live at the Astoria).

Jul 05. (7"clear/cd-s; as BRITISH WHALE) *(ATUK 011/+CD)* **THIS TOWN AIN'T BIG ENOUGH FOR THE BOTH OF US. / AMERICA** [6] [–]
(dvd-s) *(ATUK 011DVD)* – ('A') / ('A'-video) / ('A'-making of..)

— **RICHIE EDWARDS** (b.25 Sep'74, Lichfield, England) – bass; repl. POULLAIN

Nov 05. (7") *(DARK 04)* **ONE WAY TICKET. / GRIEF HAMMER** [8] [ ]
(dvd-s+=) *(DARK 04DVD)* – ('A'-video) / (making of the video).
(cd-s) *(DARK 04CD) <11132>* – ('A') / Wanker.

Nov 05. (cd/d-lp) *(5101 11218-2/-1) <62838>* **ONE WAY TICKET TO HELL . . . AND BACK** [11] [58]
– One way ticket / Knockers / Is it just me? / Dinner lady arms / Seemed like a good idea at the time / Hazel eyes / Bald / Girlfriend / English country garden / Blind man.

Feb 06. (7"pic-d) *(DARK 05)* **IS IT JUST ME? / SHIT GHOST** [8] [–]
(dvd-s+=) *(DARK 05DVD)* – ('A'-video) / (making of the video).
(cd-s) *(DARK 05CD)* – ('A') / Shake (like a lettuce leaf).

May 06. (cd-s) *(DARK 06CD)* **GIRLFRIEND / (Richie Edwards mix featuring DJ Tidy Brine)** [39] [–]
(dvd-s) *(DARK 06DVD)* – ('A'-video) / (making of the video) / ('A') / ('A'-British Whale mix) / ('A'-Space Cowboy house mix).
(12"pic-d) *(DARK 06T)* –

DASHBOARD CONFESSIONAL

Formed: Boca Raton, Florida, USA . . . 2000 by singer, songwriter, and driving force CHRISTOPHER CARRABA. CARRABA had fronted bands like the VACANT ANDIES and FURTHER SEEMS FOREVER, but found the solo process to be more receptive and gainful to the material he was writing. As DASHBOARD CONFESSIONAL he released debut LP, 'THE SWISS ARMY ROMANCE', in late 2000 on 'Drive-Thru' records. A solid first effort, it contained finely composed indie acoustic songs like 'LIVING IN YOUR LETTERS', although there wasn't much to distinguish it from similar indie releases. In 2001, now on 'Vagrant' records, he released the 'DROWNING' EP, and second full-set, 'THE PLACES YOU HAVE COME TO FEAR THE MOST'. CARRABA's heartfelt musings occasionally weighed heavy with naivety, but then they did appear to target the teen market. 'SCREAMING INFIDELITIES' became a Modern Rock hit, adopted by many US indie/pop kids. In a busy (and successful) year for DASHBOARD CONFESSIONAL, CARRABA also hit the road, firstly a joint tour with the WEAKERTHANS, then as part of the 'Vagrant Across America' tour with labelmates including HOT ROD CIRCUIT. Maintaining the momentum, the melancholic 'SC IMPOSSIBLE' EP was released in late 2001, and DASHBOARI CONFESSIONAL became a duo with the recruitment of SUNNY DAY REAL ESTATE's DAN HOERNER. With CARRABA's largel acoustic ditties being tailor made for MTV's 'UNPLUGGED', i came as no big surprise when DASHBOARD CONFESSIONAI made their contribution to the veteran series in 2002. With the Gi Norton-produced 'A MARK, A MISSION, A BRAND, A SCAR (2003), meanwhile, CARRABA took his unashamedly teenage orientated angst-odyssey to new artistic heights, with Norto coaxing out the most accessible aspects of the lad's painfull sensitive songwriting. Unsurprisingly, it was a recipe for critical an commercial success, coming within a hair's breadth of the US No. position.

Album rating: THE SWISS ARMY ROMANCE (*5) / THE PLACES YOU HAV COME TO FEAR THE MOST (*6) / MTV UNPLUGGED (*5) / A MARK, MISSION, A BRAND, A SCAR (*8)

CHRISTOPHER CARRABA (b.10 Apr'75, West Hartford, Connecticu USA) – vocals, guitars, etc. (ex-FURTHER SEEMS FOREVER)

not iss. Drive-T

Nov 00. (cd) *<DRIVETHRU 22CD>* **THE SWISS ARMY ROMANCE** [–] [ ]
– Screaming infidelities / The sharp hint of new tears / Living in you letters / The Swiss Army romance / Turpentine chaser / A plain morning Age six racer / Again I go unnoticed / Ender will save us all / Shir and gloves / (untitled). *(UK-iss.Jul01; same as US) <re-iss. Apr03 o 'Vagrant'+=; VR 380CD>* – Hold on / This is a forgery.

not iss. Fiddl

Mar 01. (cd-ep) *<12>* **THE DROWNING EP** [–] [ ]
– Drowning / Anyone anyone? / For Justin.

Vagrant Vagra

Mar 01. (cd) *<(VR 354CD)>* **THE PLACES YOU HAVE COME TO FEAR THE MOST** [ ] [ ]
– The brilliant dance / Screaming infidelities / The best deceptions / Th ruined puzzle / Saints and sailors / The good fight / Standard lines / Agai I go unnoticed / The places you have come to fear the most / This bitte pill. *(re-iss. Mar02 on 'B-Unique'; BUN 018) (re-iss. Aug02 on 'Universal 910354-2)*

— added **DAVE HOERNER** – guitar (of SUNNY DAY REAL ESTATE)

Dec 01. (cd-ep) *<VR 362>* **SO IMPOSSIBLE** [–] [ ]
– For you to notice . . . / So impossible / Remember to breathe / Hand down. *(UK-iss.Mar03; same as US)*

Apr 02. (cd-ep) *<36>* **SUMMER'S KISS EP** [–] [ ]
– Living in your letters / The sharp hint of new tears / Turpentine chaser Ender will save us all.

— <above issued on 'Eulogy'>

— **CARRABA** added **DAN BONEBRAKE** – bass / **MIKE MARSH** – drums

Dec 02. (cd) *<(VR 378CD)>* **MTV UNPLUGGED** (live) [ ] [ ]
– Swiss army romance / The best deceptions / Remember to breathe / Th good fight / The sharp hint of new tears / So impossible / The places yo have come to fear the most / Turpentine chaser / Living in your letters For you to notice / The brilliant dance / Screaming infidelities / Saints an sailors / Again I go unnoticed / Hands down. *<re-iss. Apr03 += w/dv 493692-0>*

— **SCOTT SCHOENBECK** – bass; repl. DAN

Jul 03. (cd) *<(VR 385CD)>* **A MARK, A MISSION, A BRAND, A SCAR** [ ] [ ]
– Hands down / Rapid hope loss / As lovers go / Carry this picture / Ben and not break / Ghost of a good thing / Am I missing / Morning calls Carve your heart out yourself / So beautiful / Hey girl / If you can't lea it be, might as well make it bleed / Several ways to die trying.

Universal Unive

Aug 03. (re-cd+=) *<(9810554-2)>* **A MARK, A MISSION, A BRAND, A SCAR** [ ] [2]
– (+=) / This old wound / The end of an anchor. *<re-iss. Nov03 w/ dvd+ 9810554>*

Oct 03. (7") *(9813791)* **HANDS DOWN. / I DO** [60] [–]
(cd-s+=) *(9813790)* – Saints and sailors (MTV unplugged version) ('A'-video).

Mar 04. (7") *(9861991)* **RAPID HOPE LOSS. / THIS IS A FORGERY** [75] [–]
(cd-s+=) *(9861991)* – Hold on.

Aug 04. (cd-ep) *<(TVT 3510)>* **VINDICATED / THE WARMTH OF THE SAND / HANDS DOWN (acoustic)** □ □
above feat. in movie, 'Spider-Man 2' on 'TVT' records
Jul'06, DASHBOARD.. will release album, 'DUSK AND SUMMER'

the DATSUNS

Formed: Cambridge, New Zealand . . . 1997 by DOLF DE BORST, CHRISTIAN LIVINGSTONE, PHIL SOMERVELL and MATT OSMENT, calling themselves the TRINKETS and dominating the college rock scene until their mighty rise in 2002. Winning battle of the bands competitions in and around Cambridge, the four-piece garage rock collective issued minor singles on their own 'Hell Squad' imprint, before embarking on a whirlwind tour of Australia, which ultimately gave them the confidence to venture into the cut-throat world of the British music scene. They were in luck, however, thanks to the garage rock revival of the WHITE STRIPES et al, and were hailed by many a music rag as "the best new band since the last best new band" (joke). 'Virgin' offshoot label 'V2' stepped in and offered the DATSUNS – whose live performances got almost as messy as . . . TRAIL OF DEAD's – a record contract, thrusting the floppy-haired foursome into the limelight. A single 'IN LOVE' was issued in 2002 and made John Peel's revolving playlist, not to mention an addition to his 'Live At Fabric' compilation. The group successfully lived up to the hype by releasing their self-titled debut at the close of the year, reaching the UK Top 20 aided by hits, 'IN LOVE' and 'HARMONIC GENERATOR'. By 2004, and with JOHN PAUL JONES on production duties, the DATSUNS veered into a hard-rock shoulder of LED ZEPPELIN comparisons (amongst other 70s heavyweights) on sophomore set, 'OUTTA SIGHT / OUTTA MIND'. The critics had heard it all before of course, sending the LP (and lead single, 'BLACKEN MY THUMB') into a proverbial chart lay-by (Top 60).

Album rating: THE DATSUNS (*8) / OUTTA SIGHT – OUTTA MIND (*4)

DOLF DE BORST – vocals, bass / **CHRISTIAN LIVINGSTONE** – guitar, vocals / **PHIL SOMERVELL** – guitar, vocals / **MATT OSMENT** – drums

Hellsquad / not iss.

2000. (ltd-7") *(HS 002)* **SUPER GYRATION! / HOOTCHIE MAMA** □ –
2001. (7"purple) *(HS 003)* **FINK FOR THE MAN. / TRANSISTOR** □ –
May 02. (7") *(HS 005)* **LADY. / MF FROM HELL** □ –
Sep 02. (ltd-7") *(HS 007)* **IN LOVE. / LITTLE BRUISE** – tour –
Sep 02. (ltd-7") *(HS 008)* **SITTIN' PRETTY. / THE TERRIBLE POWER** – tour –

V2 / V2

Sep 02. (7") *(VVR 502095-3)* **IN LOVE. / LITTLE BRUISE** 25 –
(cd-s) *(VVR 502095-3)* – ('A') / Supergyration.
Oct 02. (cd) *(VVR 102096-2)* *<27149>* **THE DATSUNS** 17 Feb03 □
– Sittin' pretty / MF from Hell / Lady / Harmonic generator / What would I know / At your touch / Fink for the man / In love / You build me up / Freeze sucker. *(lp-iss. on 'Sweet Nothing'; SNLP 019) <US cd w/dvd+=; 714923>* – (DVD tracks).
Feb 03. (7") *(VVR 502122-7)* **HARMONIC GENERATOR. / FREEZE SUCKER** 33 –
(cd-s) *(VVR 502122-3)* – ('A') / Transistor / O woe is me / ('A'-video).
(cd-s) *(VVR 502122-8)* – ('A') / Sittin' pretty (live session) / Fink for the man (live session).
Aug 03. (cd-s) *(VVR 502175-3)* **MF FROM HELL / AIN'T GOT TIME FOR LOVE / IN LOVE (toe rag demo)** 55 –
(cd-s) *(VVR 502175-8)* – ('A'-live) / What would I know (live) / At your touch (SBN session) / ('A'-video).
Jun 04. (7") *(VVR 502695-7)* **BLACKEN MY THUMB. / NOT COMING BACK** 48 –
(cd-s) *(VVR 502695-3)* – ('A') / Good luck . . . you're gonna need it / Burst your bubble.
Jun 04. (cd) *(VVR 102694-2)* *<27202>* **OUUTA SIGHT – OUTTA MIND** 58 Jul04 □
– Blacken my thumb / That sure ain't right / Girls best friend / Messin' around / Cherry lane / Get up! (don't fight it) / Hong Kong fury / What I've lost / You can't find me / Don't come knocking / Lucille / I got no words.
Oct 04. (7") *(VVR 502889-7)* **GIRLS BEST FRIEND. / ATOM BOMB** 71 –
(cd-s) *(VVR 502889-3)* – ('A') / Charging rhino / Conversation killer.
May 06. (10"ep) *(VVR 504034-0)* **STUCK HERE FOR DAYS** □ –
– Stuck here for days / Kick and a bang / Sky is falling / One eye open.

□ Dave DAVIES (see under ⇒ KINKS)

□ Ray DAVIES (see under ⇒ KINKS)

the Spencer DAVIS GROUP

Formed: Birmingham, England . . . August 1963, SPENCER DAVIS meeting PETER YORK and the WINWOOD brothers STEVE and MUFF at a local jazz club. It was soon apparent that the veterans (in the early 20's), were being overshadowed by the precocious 15-year old multi-talented STEVE. After a year on the circuit, they signed to 'Fontana' records with the aid of 'Island' owner CHRIS BLACKWELL, who had recommended the act. Their early 45's failed to distinguish them from the R&B pack (having only achieved minor placings) and it was only with the release of JACKIE EDWARDS' 'KEEP ON RUNNING' that the band exploded onto the scene. It topped the chart for one week in January 1966, a year that also saw the rejuvenation of 'THE FIRST LP' (which hit Top 10), a follow-up 45, 'SOMEBODY HELP ME' (another No.1) and STEVE's first self-penned hit, 'WHEN I COME HOME'. A prolific period for the band, they ended the year on a high, having scored with another Top 10 album and their third slice of genius, 'GIMME SOME LOVIN' (denied pole position by The Four Tops' 'Reach Out I'll Be There'). Still only 17, STEVE's 'Motown'-influenced vocal talent increasingly began to outlive the basic R&B backing the rest of the band were providing. Breaking away from the group, he took a more psychedelic approach with his new outfit, TRAFFIC. SPENCER DAVIS soldiered on with a new line-up, but it was clear the spark had been extinguished and the hits soon dried up.

• **Other covers:** DIMPLES (John Lee Hooker) / EVERY LITTLE BIT HURTS (Brenda Holloway) / etc. • **Trivia:** Late in 1967, they made a small cameo appearance in the film 'HERE WE GO ROUND THE MULBERRY BUSH'.

Best CD compilation: EIGHT GIGS A WEEK: THE STEVE WINWOOD YEARS (*7)

SPENCER DAVIS (b.17 Jul'41, Swansea, Wales) – guitar, vocals, harmonica (ex-SAINTS) / **STEVE WINWOOD** (b.12 May'48, Birmingham) – vocals, keyboards, guitar / **MUFF WINWOOD** (b.MERVYN, 14 Jun'43) – bass, vocals / **PETER YORK** (b.15 Aug'42, Middlesborough, England) – drums

Fontana / Fontana

Aug 64. (7") *(TF 471)* **DIMPLES. / SITTIN' AND THINKIN'** □ –
Oct 64. (7") *(TF 499)* *<1960>* **I CAN'T STAND IT. / MIDNIGHT TRAIN** 47 Mar65 □
Jan 65. (7") *(TF 530)* **EVERY LITTLE BIT HURTS. / IT HURTS ME SO** 41 –
May 65. (7") *(TF 571)* **STRONG LOVE. / THIS HAMMER** 44 –
Jul 65. (lp) *(TL 5242)* **THEIR FIRST LP** (hit-Jan66) 6 –
– My babe / Dimples / Searchin' / Every little bit hurts / I'm blue (gong gong song) / Sittin' and thinkin' / I can't stand it / Here right now / Jump back / It's gonna work out fine / Midnight train / It hurts me so. *(re-iss. 1968 as 'EVERY LITTLE BIT HURTS' on 'Wing'; WL 1165)*

Fontana / Atco

Nov 65. (7") *(TF 632)* *<6400>* **KEEP ON RUNNING. / HIGH TIME BABY** 1 76
Jan 66. (lp) *(TL 5295)* **THE SECOND ALBUM** 2 –
– Look away / Keep on running / This hammer / Georgia on my mind / Please do something / Let me down easy / Strong love / I washed my hands in muddy water / Since I met you baby / You must believe me / Hey darling / Watch your step.

Mar 66. (7") *(TF 679)* *<6416>* **SOMEBODY HELP ME. / STEVIE'S BLUES** [1] [ ]
Aug 66. (7") *(TF 739)* **WHEN I COME HOME. / TRAMPOLINE** [12] [–]
Sep 66. (lp) *(TL 5359)* **AUTUMN '66** [4] [–]
– Together till the end of time / Take this hurt off me / Nobody knows you when you're down and out / Midnight special / When a man loves a woman / When I come home / Mean woman blues / Dust my blues / On the green light / Neighbour, neighbour / High time baby / Somebody help me.

Fontana U.A.

Oct 66. (7") *(TF 762)* *<50108>* **GIMME SOME LOVING. / BLUES IN F** [2] Jan67 [7]
(above 'A'side was different remix in the States)
Jan 67. (7") *(TF 785)* *<50144>* **I'M A MAN. / CAN'T GET ENOUGH OF IT** [9] Mar67 [10]
Mar 67. (lp; mono/stereo) *<UAL3/UAS6 578>* **GIMME SOME LOVIN'** [–] [54]
– Gimme some lovin' / Keep on running / This hammer (the hammer song) / Nobody knows you when you're down and out / When I come home / It hurts me so / Somebody help me / Midnight special / Here right now / Trampoline / Sittin' and thinkin' / Goodbye Stevie. *<(cd-iss. Jul01 on 'Sundazed'+=; SC 11103)>* – Jump back / It's gonna work out fine / I'm blue (gong gong song) / I'm getting better / She put the hurt on me / Blues in F / High time baby / Drown in my tears.
Jun 67. (7") *<50162>* **SOMEBODY HELP ME. / ON THE GREEN LIGHT** [–] [47]

—— **EDDIE HARDIN** (b. EDWARD HARDING, 19 Feb'49) – organ, vocals replaced STEVE who joined TRAFFIC and later BLIND FAITH then solo. / **PHIL SAWYER** (b.8 Mar'47) – lead guitar replaced MUFF who became A&R man, / also **CHARLIE McCRACKEN** – bass (guest)

Jul 67. (lp; mono/stereo) *<UAL3/UAS6 589>* **I'M A MAN** [–] [83]
– I'm a man / Every little bit hurts / Searchin' / I can't stand it / Dimples / Look away / Georgia on my mind / My babe / I can't get enough of it / On the green light / Stevie's blues / Midnight train. *<(cd-iss. Jul01 on 'Sundazed'+=; SC 11104)>* – Watch your step / You must believe me / Strong love / Hey darling / Waltz for Lumumba / Please do something / Let me down easy / Stevie's groove.
Jul 67. (7") *(TF 854)* *<50202>* **TIME SELLER. / DON'T WANT YOU NO MORE** [30] [100]

U.A. U.A.

Dec 67. (7") *(UP 1203)* **MR. SECOND CLASS. / SANITY INSPECTOR** [35] [–]
Dec 67. (7") *<50286>* **AFTER TEA. / LOOKING BACK** [–] [ ]
Mar 68. (7") *(UP 2213)* **AFTER TEA. / MOONSHINE** [ ] [–]
Apr 68. (lp; stereo/mono) *(S+/ULP 1192)* **WITH THEIR NEW FACE ON** [ ] [–]
– With his new face on / Mr. Second class / Alec in transitland / Sanity inspector / Feel your way / Morning sun / Moonshine / Don't want you no more / Time seller / Stop me, I'm fallin'. *(cd-iss. Nov97 on 'Repertoire'+=; REP 4648)* – After tea / Aquarius der wassermann / Let the sunshine / Feel your way / I'm lost / Pools winner / Morning sun.

—— (Nov'68) **DEE MURRAY** – bass / **NIGEL OLSSON** – drums repl. HARDIN & YORK who formed self named duo.

1969. (lp) *<UAS 6691>* **HEAVIES** [–] [ ]
– Please do something / Waltz for lum umba / I'm blue (gong gong song) / Hey darling / Mean woman blues / Watch your step / Drown in my own tears / Together til' the end of time / Take this hurt off me / Back into my life again.

—— (signed to 'Date-Columbia' and copies of album 'LETTERS FROM EDITH' surfaced; US title 'FUNKY')

—— split mid '69. MURRAY and OLSSON joined ELTON JOHN's Band.

1971. (lp; by SPENCER DAVIS & PETER JAMESON) *(UAS 29177)* **IT'S BEEN SO LONG** [ ] [ ]
– It's been so long / Crystal river / One hundred years ago / Balkan blues / Brother can you make up your mind / Mountain lick / Jav's tune / King of her / It's too late now.
1972. (lp; by SPENCER DAVIS) *(UAS 29361)* **MOUSETRAP** [ ] [ ]
– Rainy season / Listen to the rhythm / What can I be / Tried / Easy rider / Tumbledown tenement row / Sunday walk in the rain / I washed my hands in muddy water / Sailor's lament / Hollywood Joe / In the hills of Tennessee / Ella speed.
1972. (7"; by SPENCER DAVIS) *<50922>* **LISTEN TO THE RHYTHM. / SUNDAY WALK IN THE RAIN** [–] [ ]
1972. (7"; by SPENCER DAVIS) *<50993>* **RAINY SEASON. / TUMBLE-DOWN TENEMENT ROW** [–] [ ]

—— now group re-united w / **HARDIN, YORK, FENWICK + CHARLIE McCRACKEN** – bass

Vertigo Vertig

Mar 73. (7") *(6059 076)* **CATCH YOU ON THE REBOB. / THE EDGE** [ ] [–]
May 73. (lp) *(6360 088)* **GLUGGO** [ ] [–]
– Catch you on the Moon / Don't it let it bring you down / Alone / Today Gluggo, tomorrow the world / Feeling rude / Legal eagle shuffle / Trouble in mind / Mr.Operator / Tumbledown tenement row.
May 73. (7") *<110>* **DON'T LET IT BRING YOU DOWN. / TODAY GLUGGO, TOMORROW THE WORLD** [–] [ ]
Jun 73. (7") *(6059 082)* **MR. OPERATOR. / TOUCHING CLOTH** [ ] [–]
Oct 73. (7") *(6059 087)* *<112>* **LIVIN' IN A BACK STREET. / SURE NEED A HELPING HAND** [ ] [ ]
Jun 74. (lp) *(6360 105)* **LIVIN' IN A BACK STREET** [ ] [ ]
– Living in a backstreet / One night / Hanging around / No reason / Fastec thing / On four wheels / Backstreet boys / Another day / Sure need a helping hand / We can give it a try / Let's have a party. *(cd-iss. Nov97 on 'Repertoire'; REP 4682)*

—— SPENCER retired from solo work until 1983.

Allegience not iss

Apr 84. (lp/c) *(ALE/+C 5603)* **CROSSFIRE** [ ] [–]
– Blood runs hot / Don't want you no more / Love is on a roll / Crossfire / Private number / Just a gigolo / Careless love / A pretty girl is like a melody / When the day is done / Hush-a-bye. *(cd-iss. Dec92 as 'NOW' on 'Kenwest'; SPCD 352)*
May 84. (7"; by SPENCER DAVIS & DUSTY SPRINGFIELD) *(ALES 3)* **PRIVATE NUMBER. / DON'T WANT YOU NO MORE** [ ] [–]

—— SPENCER became an executive at Island records in the mid 70's. In mid 80's, **SPENCER DAVIS BAND** reformed with others **DON KIRKPATRICK** / **EDDIE TREE** – guitars / **RICK SERATTE** – keys / **CHARLIE HARRISON** – bass / **BRYAN HITT** – drums (ex-WANG CHUNG)

In Akustik not iss

1988. (cd; as SPENCER DAVIS with PETE YORK & COLIN HODGKINSON) *(INAK 8410)* **LIVE TOGETHER** (rec.1984) [ ] [–]
– Keep on running / Midnight special / Walking blue / Mistakes / Sliding delta / I'm a man / Crossfire / Blood runs hot / Trouble in mind / Somebody help me / Don't leave me / Tulsa time / Gimme some lovin' / Muddy waters. *(re-iss. Mar95 & Jul00; same)*
1988. (cd) *(INAK 8590CD)* **24 HOURS – LIVE IN GERMANY** (rec.1985) [ ] [–]
– Twenty four hours / Lady cop / Sensitive kind / The Moon is a harsh mistress / On the green line / Pockey way / I'll take your love / Don't want you no more / Strong love / Route 66 / Easy rider / Knock on your door / Spiral times. *(re-iss. Mar95 & Jul00; same)*

– (selective) compilations, etc. –

Mar 68. (lp; mono/stereo) *Island; (ILP/+S 9070)* **THE BEST OF THE SPENCER DAVIS GROUP FEATURING STEVIE WINWOOD** [ ] [–]
(re-iss. Oct86; same) (cd-iss. May88; CID 9070) (re-iss. cd Mar93; IMCD 15
Mar 68. (lp) *United Artists; <UAS 6641>* **SPENCER DAVIS' GREATEST HITS** [–] [ ]
1971. (lp) *Date; <4021>* **FUNKY** (US shelved LP) [–] [ ]
– I met a woman / Letter from Edith / Raintree river / What a way to die / Funky / Magical day / I guess I'm wasting my time / Poor misguided woman / And the gods came down / New Jersey turnpike. *(cd-iss. Jul0 on 'Angel Air'+=; SJPCD 021)* – With their new face on / Time seller / Fee your way / Taking out time / Mr. Second class / After tea / Groove extra / Moonshine / The girls song / Aquarius – Let the sunshine in / Dust m blues (live).
Jun 94. (cd) *R.P.M.; (RPMCD 127)* **TAKING OUT TIME 1967-69** [ ] [–]
Jun 95. (cd) *R.P.M.; (RPMCD 150)* **CATCH YOU ON THE REBOP – LIVE IN EUROPE 1973** [ ] [–]
Mar 96. (d-cd) *Island Chronicles; (CRNCD 5)* **EIGHT GIGS A WEEK – THE STEVE WINWOOD YEARS** [ ] [–]
Jun 99. (d-cd) *Eagle; (EDMCD 88)* **THE MASTERS** [ ] [–]
Jan 00. (cd) *Universal; (E 546252-2)* **UNIVERSAL MASTERS COLLECTION** [ ] [ ]
Aug 00. (cd) *R.P.M.; (RPM 207)* **MOJO RHYTHMS & MIDNIGHT BLUES – THE LIVE ALBUM VOL.1: SESSIONS 1965-1968** [ ] [ ]

Nov 00. (cd) *R.P.M.; (RPM 216)* **MOJO RHYTHMS & MIDNIGHT BLUES – THE LIVE ALBUM VOL.2: SHOWS 1965-1968** [ ] [ ]
May 02. (cd+cd-rom) *R.P.M.; (RPM 508)* **TIME SELLER** [ ] [ ]
Nov 02. (cd) *Purple; (PUR 329)* **LIVE IN EUROPE 1973** [ ] [ ]
Feb 03. (cd) *R.P.M.; (RPM 188)* **MULBURRY BUSH** [ ] [ ]
Mar 03. (cd) *Spectrum; (544974-2)* **THE COLLECTION** [ ] [ ]

DE LA SOUL

Formed: Amityville, Long Island, New York, USA . . . 1987 by DAVID JOLICOEUR (TRUGOY THE DOVE), KELVIN MERCER (POSDNOUS) & VINCENT MASON (PACEMASTER MASE). They quickly set about writing their soon-to-be critically acclaimed cross-Atlantic debut album, '3 FEET HIGH AND RISING', which made the Top 30 in the spring of '89. Psychedelic hip-hop rappers, influenced a little by the mid 80's urban scene, they dressed mostly in baggy sportswear, infusing their lyrics with a pseudo flower-power, visionary attitude, termed as 'daisy-age'. These hip hop gypsies sampled everything from JAMES BROWN (again!) to STEELY DAN, the latter on debut hit 'ME MYSELF AND I'. Produced by STETSASONIC's PRINCE PAUL, it featured cameos from A TRIBE CALLED QUEST, JUNGLE BROTHERS (their inspiration) and QUEEN LATIFAH. Their much-anticipated but disappointing 1991 follow-up, 'DE LA SOUL IS DEAD,' accurately predicted their fate. Nevertheless, the album sold respectably and on reflection, many critics acknowledged that it contained some disturbing but poignant messages. On '93's 'BUHLOONE MINDSTATE', DE LA SOUL were back on top form once again, firing subtly subversive broadsides at the white middle class ruling system. Following 1996's 'STAKES IS HIGH', the trio took an extended break before coming back with the first installment in a proposed trio of albums billed as 'ART OFFICIAL INTELLIGENCE'. Unfortunately, this first volume, 'MOSAIC THUMP' (2000), proved as weak as the pun of the series' title. Like many old school crews, DE LA SOUL have obviously found it difficult to square their refined sensibilities with the more aggressive climate of current day hip hop. Despite the contributions of JAYDEE and BUSTA RHYMES amongst others, DE LA SOUL's attempts at sounding contemporary sound forced at best. Not so the second volume in the series, 'AIO: BIONIX' (2001), a belated return to form revelling in the kind of irreverent playfulness they seemed to have consigned to history more than a decade ago. Catalysed by producer Dave West's winning sonic backdrop, the veteran trio turned in some of the best lyrical smarts since their celebrated debut. Throwing in their 'AOI' label with veteran stronghold 'Sanctuary', DE LA SOUL delivered their seventh set, 'THE GRIND DATE' (2004), with production cameos from the likes of MADLIB and even an appearance by FLAVA FLAV. More high profile was the trio's own cameo on GORILLAZ hit, 'Feel Good Inc.', a 2005 link up which netted them a Grammy.

Album rating: 3 FEET HIGH AND RISING (*9) / DE LA SOUL IS DEAD (*6) / BUHLOONE MINDSTATE (*6) / STAKES IS HIGH (*7) / ART OFFICIAL INTELLIGENCE: MOSAIC THUMP (*7) / AOI: BIONIX (*6) / THE BEST OF DE LA SOUL or TIMELESS: THE SINGLES COLLECTION compilation (*7) / THE GRIND DATE (*6)

TRUGOY THE DOVE (b. DAVID JOLICOEUR, 21 Sep'68, Brooklyn) – vocals / **POSDNOUS** (b. KELVIN MERCER, 17 Aug'69, Bronx) – vocals / **PACEMASTER MASE** (b. VINCENT MASON, 24 Mar'70, Brooklyn) – DJ

Tommy Boy Tommy Boy

Jul 88. (7") **PLUG TUNIN'. / FREEDOM OF SPEAK** [–] [ ]
Oct 88. (7") *<(TB 917)>* **JENIFA (TAUGHT ME). /** [ ] [ ]

Big Life Tommy Boy

Mar 89. (lp/c/cd) *(DLS LP/MC/CD 1) <TB/+C/CD 1019>* **3 FEET HIGH AND RISING** 13 24
– Intro / The magic number / Change in speak / Cool breeze on the rocks / Can you kep a secret / Jenifa (taught me) / Ghetto thang / Transmitting live from Mars / Eye know / Take it off / A little bit of soap / Tread water / Say no go / Do as De La does / Plug tunin' / De La orgee / Buddy / Description / Me myself and I / This is a recording for living in a fulltime era I can do anything / D.A.I.S.Y. age / Potholes in my lawn. *(cd re-iss. Jan96; DLSCD 1) (cd re-iss. Jun97 +=; TBCD 1019)* – Plug tunin' (12"mix). *(re-iss. Sep99, hit UK No.17)*
Mar 89. (7") *(BLR 7) <7926>* **ME MYSELF AND I. / BRAIN WASHED FOLLOWER** 22 Feb89 34
(12"+=) *(BLR 7T)* – Ain't hip to be labelled a hippie / What's more. *(re-iss. Sep99 on 'B.C.M.'; BCM 14232)*
(cd-s+=) *(BLR 7CD)* – Ain't hip to be labelled a hippie / ('A'version).
(12"+=) *(BLR 7R)* – ('A'remixes).
Jun 89. (7"/7"pic-d) *(BLR 10/+P)* **SAY NO GO. / THEY DON'T KNOW THAT THE SOUL DON'T GO FOR THAT** 18 [ ]
(12"+=/cd-s+=) *(BLR 10 T/CD)* – ('A'versions).
(12"+=) *(BLR 10R)* – ('A'remixes). *(re-iss. Sep99 on 'B.C.M.'; BCM 12295)*
Sep 89. (7"/7"pic-d/c-s) *(BLR 13/+P/C)* **EYE KNOW. / THE MACK DADDY ON THE LEFT** 14 [ ]
(12"+=/cd-s+=) *(BLR 13 T/CD)* – ('A'versions).
Dec 89. (7"/c-s) *(BLR 14/+MC)* **THE MAGIC NUMBER. / BUDDY** 7 [ ]
(12"+=/cd-s+=) *(BLR 14 T/CD)* – Ghetto thang.
(12"+=) *(BLR 14R)* – ('A'remixes). *(re-iss. Sep99 on 'B.C.M.'; BCM 12387)*

— In Mar'90, DE LA SOUL were credited on QUEEN LATIFAH's UK Top 20 single 'MAMA GAVE BIRTH TO THE SOUL CHILDREN' *(Gee Street; GEE 26)*

Apr 91. (7"/c-s) *(BLR 42/+MC)* **RING RING RING (HA HA HEY). / PILES AND PILES OF DEMO TAPES BI DA MILES** 10 [ ]
(12") *(BLR 42T)* – ('A'extended) / Afro connection of a mis / ('A'-sax version).
(cd-s+=) *(BLR 42CD)* – ('A'-party mix).
May 91. (cd/c/d-lp) *(BLR CD/MC/LP 8) <TB/+C/CD 1029>* **DE LA SOUL IS DEAD** 7 26
– Intro / Oodles of O's / Talkin' bout hey love / Pease porridge / (skit 1) / Johnny's dead aka Vincent Mason (live from the BK lounge) / A roller skating jam named 'Saturdays' (disco fever edit) / WRMS' dedication to the bitty / Bitties in the BK lounge / (skit 2) / Let, let me in / Rap de rap show / Millie pulled a pistol on Santa / (skit 3) / Pass the plugs / Ring ring ring (ha ha hey) / WRMS: Cat's in control / (skit 4) / Shwingalokate / Fanatic of the B word / Keepin' the faith / (skit 5). *(cd re-iss. Jan96; DLSCD 8)*
Jul 91. (7"/c-s) *(BLR 55/+MC)* **A ROLLER SKATING JAM CALLED 'SATURDAYS'. / WHAT YOUR LIFE CAN TRULY BE** 22 [ ]
(12"+=/cd-s+=) *(BLR 55 T/CD)* – ('A'-disco mix) / Who's skatin'.
Nov 91. (7"/c-s) *(BLR 64/+MC)* **KEEPIN' THE FAITH (remix). / ('A'instrumental)** 50 [ ]
(12"+=) *(BLR 64T)* – Roller skating jam called 'Saturdays' / Ring ring ring (ha ha hey).
(cd-s) *(BLR 64CD)* – (2 'A'versions) / ('A'instrumental) / ('A' funky mix).
Sep 93. (7"/c-s) *(BLR/+C 103) <7586>* **BREAKADAWN. / EN FOCUS (vocal version)** 39 76
(12"+=/cd-s+=) *(BLR T/CD 103)* – ('A'mixes).
Oct 93. (cd/c/lp) *(BLR CD/MC/LP 25) <1063>* **BUHLOONE MIND STATE** 37 Sep93 40
– Intro / Eye patch / En focus / Patti Dooke / I be blowin' / Long Island wildin' / Ego trippin' / Paul Revere / Three days later / Area / I am I be / In the woods / Breakadawn / Dave has a problem . . . seriously / Stone age / Lonely days.

— In Mar'94. they teamed up with TEENAGE FANCLUB on the single 'FALLIN' *(Epic 660262-4/-2)*. From the rap-rock film 'Judgement Night'.

Nov 95. (12"/cd-s) *(BLR T/D 132)* **ME MYSELF & I (radio mix) / AIN'T HIP TO BE LABELED A HIPPIE (vocal) / ME MYSELF AND I (instrumental). / WHAT'S MORE / ME MYSELF AND I (oblapos mode) / BRAIN WASHED FOLLOWER (vocal) / ME MYSELF AND I (oblapos instrumental)** [ ] [–]

Tommy Boy Tommy Boy

Jun 96. (c-s) *(TBC 7730)* **STAKES IS HIGH / ('A'-UK clean version)** 55 [ ]
(cd-s) *<(TBCD 7730)>* – ('A'side) / ('A'extended) / ('A'-DJ original) / The bizness.
(12") *(TBV 7730)* – ('A'extended) / ('A'-DJ original) / ('A'-album version) / ('A'-acapella).
Jul 96. (cd/c/d-lp) *<(TB CD/C/V 1149)>* **STAKES IS HIGH** 42 13

– Intro / Supa emcees / The bizness (featuring COMMON SENSE) / Wonce again Long Island / Dinninit / Brakes / Dog eat dog / Baby baby baby ooh baby / Long Island degrees / Betta listen / Itsoweezee (featuring HOT) / 4 more (featuring ZHANE) / Big brother beat (featuring MOS DEF) / Down syndrome / Pony ride (featuring TRUTH ENOLA) / Stakes is high / Sunshine. *(cd re-iss. Feb97; same)*

Mar 97. (c-ep/12"ep/cd-ep) *(TB C/V/CD 7779)* **4 MORE / BABY BABY BABY BABY OOH BABY. / ITZSOWEEZEE / SWEET DREAMS** [52] [ ]

Jul 00. (12"/cd-s; by DE LA SOUL featuring REDMAN) *(TBV/TBCD 2102/+A)* **OOOH. / WORDS AND VERBS** [29] [ ]
(cd-s) *(TBCD 2102B)* – ('A'side) / So good.

Aug 00. (cd/d-lp) *(TBCD/TBV 1348)* *<1361>* **ART OFFICIAL INTELLIGENCE: MOSAIC THUMP** [22] [9]
– Spitkicker.com – Say R / U can do (life) / My writes (with RASH / J-RO OF THA LIKS / XZIBIT) / Oooh. (with REDMAN) / Thru ya city (with DV ALIAS KHRIST) / I.C. y'all (with BUSTA RHYMES) / View / Set the mood (with INDEED) / All good (with CHAKA KHAN) / Declaration / Squat! (with MIKE D & AD ROCK) / Words from the chief rocker (with BUSY BEE) / With me / Copa (cabanga) / Foolin' / The art of getting jumped / U don't wanna B.D.S. (with FREDDIE FOX).

Oct 00. (12"/cd-s; by DE LA SOUL featuring CHAKA KHAN) *(TBV/TBCD 2154/+A)* *<2178>* **ALL GOOD / (MJ Cole mix) / (original instrumental)** [33] [96]
(cd-s) *(TBCD 2154B)* – ('A'mixes).

Dec 01. (cd/lp) *<(TBCD/TBV 1362)>* **AOI: BIONIX** [ ] [ ]
– Intro / Bionix / Baby phat (featuring DEVIN THE DUDE + ELIZABETH "YUMMY" BINGHAM) / Simply / Simply havin / Held down / Reverend Do Good #1 / Watch out (with JOSE "PERICO" HERNANDEZ) / Special (with ELIZABETH "YUMMY" BINGHAM) / Reverend Do Good #2 / The sauce (with PHILLY BLACK & SMILES PATRON) / Am I worth you? / Pawn star (with SHELL COUNCIL & JASON SPEARS) / What we do (for love) (with SOULSTICE, CLAUDIA & SLICK RICK) / Reverend Do Good #3 / Peer pressure (with B-REAL) / It's American / Trying people.

Feb 02. (12"/; as DE LA SOUL featuring DEVIN THE DUDE & ELIZABETH "YUMMY" BINGHAM) *(TBV 2395)* **BABY PHAT / (instrumental)** [55] [–]
(cd-s+=) *(TBCD 2395A)* – Watch out (clean + instrumental).
(cd-s) *(TBCD 2395B)* – ('A'side) / Watch out / All good? (can 7 supermarket mix).

Sanctuary Sanctuary

Oct 04. (cd) *(SANCD 296)* *<87512>* **THE GRIND DATE** [ ] [87]
– The future / Verbal clap / Much more / Shopping bags (she got from you) / The grind date / Church / It's like that / He comes / Days of our lives / Come on down / No / Rock Co. Kane flow.

– compilations, etc. –

May 03. (cd) *Rhino; <73860>* **TIMELESS: THE SINGLES COLLECTION** [–] [ ]

Jun 03. (cd/d-lp) *Warners; (8122 73665-2/-1)* **THE BEST OF DE LA SOUL** [17] [–]
– Me myself and I / Say no go / Eye know / Magic number / Potholes in my lawn (12" vocal version) / Buddy (with JUNGLE BROTHERS, Q-TIP & PHIFE) / Ring ring ring (ha ha hey) / Roller skating jam named Saturdays / Keepin' the faith / Breakadawn / Stakes is high / 4 more (with ZHANE) / Oooh (with REDMAN) / All good (with CHAKA KHAN) / Thru ya city (with DV ALIAS KHRIST) / Baby phat (with DEVIN THE DUDE & ELIZABETH "YUMMY" BINGHAM) / Watch out.

DEAD KENNEDYS

Formed: San Francisco, California, USA . . . early 1978 by JELLO BIAFRA and EAST BAY RAY, who recruited KLAUS FLOURIDE, TED and briefly, the mysterious 6025. Inspired by British punk rock, BIAFRA formed The DEAD KENNEDYS primarily as a vehicle for his raging, razor-sharp satire of America and everything it stood for. Public enemy #1 from the off, major labels steered well clear of the band, BIAFRA and Co. subsequently forming their own label, the legendary 'Alternative Tentacles', releasing 'CALIFORNIA UBER ALLES' as their debut 45 in late '79. A scathing critique of California governor, Jerry Brown, the record introduced the singer's near-hysterical vocal undulations set against a pulverising punk/hardcore musical backdrop. Released on the independent 'Fast' imprint in Britain, the record's initial batch of copies sold like proverbial hotcakes. The 1980 follow-up, 'HOLIDAY IN CAMBODIA' (released on Miles Copeland's 'Faulty' label; 'Cherry Red' in the UK), remains The DEAD KENNEDYS' most viciously realised moment, a dark, twisting diatribe on American middle-class liberal trendies. Later in the year, the group kept up their aural assault with a debut album, 'FRESH FRUIT FOR ROTTING VEGETABLES', an unexpected Top 40 entry in the seemingly "Punk Is Dead" Britain, which contained the aforesaid 45's plus perennial favourites, 'LET'S LYNCH THE LANDLORD', 'DRUG ME' and the forthcoming UK hit, 'KILL THE POOR'. The record also offered a glimpse of BIAFRA's reassuringly twisted sense of humour in such surreal cuts as 'STEALING PEOPLE'S MAIL' and 'VIVA LAS VEGAS' (the latter was a hit for Elvis!). In 1981, drummer D.H. PELIGRO replaced TED, making his debut on the bluntly-titled 'TOO DRUNK TO FUCK', the only UK Top 40 charting single in musical history (up to that point!) to utilise the "f***" word. Once again mocking the inherent hypocrisy of corporate America, The DEAD KENNEDYS released a frenetic 10" mini-set, 'IN GOD WE TRUST INC.' (1981), highlights being the self-explanatory 'NAZI PUNKS FUCK OFF' (a US-only single) and a deadpan version of 'RAWHIDE'. The band then took a brief hiatus, busying themselves with an 'Alternative Tentacles' compilation of promising unsigned American bands, entitled 'Let Them Eat Jellybeans'. That same year (1982), the group released their second album proper, 'PLASTIC SURGERY DISASTERS'; issued on 'Statik' in the UK, it featured the singles 'BLEED FOR ME' and 'HALLOWEEN'. Spending the ensuing few years touring, the band resurfaced in 1985 with 'FRANKENCHRIST', an album that finally saw BIAFRA's upstanding enemies closing in (ie. the PMRC, the US government, etc) due to the album's free "penis landscape" poster by Swiss artist H.R. Giger. Although BIAFRA and Co. (including some senior label staff) were tried in court for distributing harmful material to minors (a revised obscenity law), the case was subsequently thrown out after a hung jury. Nevertheless, the cost of the trial effectively put the band out of business, The DEAD KENNEDYS poignantly-titled finale, 'BEDTIME FOR DEMOCRACY' being issued late in 1986. Although KLAUS and RAY followed low-key solo careers, the ever-prolific BIAFRA vociferously protested against his treatment on spoken-word sets, 'NO MORE COCOONS' (1987) and 'THE HIGH PRIEST OF HARMFUL MATTER' (1989). He subsequently collaborated with a wide range of hardcore/industrial acts such as D.O.A., NO MEANS NO and TUMOR CIRCUS, although it was with LARD (a project with MINISTRY mainmen, AL JOURGENSEN and PAUL BARKER) that BIAFRA really came into his own. A late 80's mini-set, 'THE POWER OF LARD' preceded a full-length album, 'THE LAST TEMPTATION OF LARD', a minor UK hit early in 1990. This demented set included such hilarious BIAFRA monologues as 'CAN GOD FILL TEETH?' and even a rendition of Napolean XIV's 'THEY'RE COMING TO TAKE ME AWAY'. In 1994, he hooked up with another likeminded soul in hillbilly punk, MOJO NIXON, releasing one album, 'PRAIRIE HOME INVASION' (the title possibly a parody of an ICE-T album). BIAFRA continues to work at 'Alternative Tentacles', supplying the country with suitably deranged hardcore and occasionally taking time out for other projects, most recently a second LARD set, 'PURE CHEWING SATISFACTION' (1997).

• **Trivia:** In 1979, BIAFRA stood in the elections for Mayor of San Francisco (he came 4th!).

Album rating: FRESH FRUIT FOR ROTTING VEGETABLES (*9) / IN GOD WE TRUST INC. mini (*5) / PLASTIC SURGERY DISASTERS (*6) / FRANKENCHRIST (*6) / BEDTIME FOR DEMOCRACY (*5) / GIVE ME CONVENIENCE OR GIVE ME DEATH compilation (*8) / Jello Biafra: NO MORE COCOONS spoken (*5) / HIGH PRIEST OF HARMFUL MATTER spoken (*5) /

THE LAST TEMPTATION OF LARD with Lard (*6) / THE LAST SCREAM OF THE MISSING NEIGHBORS with D.O.A. (*6) / THE SKY IS FALLING AND I WANT MY MOMMY with No Means No (*5) / I BLOW MINDS FOR A LIVING (*6) / HIGH VOLTAGE CONSPIRACY FOR RADICAL FREEDOM with Tumor Circus (*5) / PRAIRIE HOME INVASION with Mojo Nixon (*6) / BEYOND THE VALLEY OF THE GIFT POLICE (*5) / PURE CHEWING SATISFACTION with Lard (*5) / BECOME THE MEDIA (*4) / IF EVOLUTION IS OUTLAWED, ONLY OUTLAWS WILL EVOLVE compilation (*6) / MACHINE GUN IN THE CLOWN'S HAND (*3)

JELLO BIAFRA (b. ERIC BOUCHER, 17 Jun'58, Boulder, Colorado) – vocals / **EAST BAY RAY** (b. RAY GLASSER, Castro Valley, California) – guitar, (synthesisers-later 80's) / **KLAUS FLUORIDE** (b. Detroit, Michigan) – bass, vocals / **BRUCE SLESINGER** (aka TED) – drums

Fast — Alternative Tentacles

Oct 79. (7") *(FAST 12)* *<AT 95-41>* **CALIFORNIA UBER ALLES. / MAN WITH THE DOGS**

Cherry Red — Faulty-IRS

Jun 80. (7")12" *(CHERRY/12CHERRY 13)* *<IR 9016>* **HOLIDAY IN CAMBODIA. / POLICE TRUCK**
(re-iss. 7"/cd-s Jun88 & Mar95; same)

Sep 80. (lp) *(B-RED 10)* *<SP 70014>* **FRESH FRUIT FOR ROTTING VEGETABLES** — 33 — Nov80
– Kill the poor / Forward to death / When ya get drafted / Let's lynch the landlord / Drug me / Your emotions / Chemical warfare / Calilfornia uber alles / I kill children / Stealing people's mail / Funland at the beach / Ill in my head / Holiday in Cambodia / Viva Las Vegas. *(cd-iss. Nov87 & Mar95 & Sep01; CDBRED 10) (d-cd-iss. Sep01 +=; CDSBRED 155)* – (bonus tracks).

Oct 80. (7") *(CHERRY 16)* **KILL THE POOR. / IN SIGHT** — 49 — –
(re-iss. Nov87 & Mar95; CDCHERRY 16)

— D.H. PELIGRO (b. DARREN, East St.Louis, Illinois) – drums; repl. BRUCE/TED

Cherry Red — Alternative Tentacles

May 81. (7"/12") *(CHERRY/12CHERRY 24)* *<VIRUS 2>* **TOO DRUNK TO FUCK. / THE PREY** — 36
(re-iss. May88 & Mar95 cd-s; CDCHERRY 24)

Statik — Alternative Tentacles

Nov 81. (10"ep) *(STATEP 2)* *<VIRUS 5>* **IN GOD WE TRUST INC.**
– Religious vomit / Moral majority / Kepone factory / Dog bite / Nazi punks fuck off / We've got a bigger problem now / Rawhide. *<US c-ep+=; VIRUS 5C>* – Too drunk to fuck / The prey / Holiday in Cambodia. *(re-iss. Jun92 cd-ep; STATEP 2CD)*

Dec 81. (7") *<VIRUS 6>* **NAZI PUNKS FUCK OFF. / MORAL MAJORITY** — –

Jul 82. (7"/12") *(STAT/+12 22)* *<VIRUS 23>* **BLEED FOR ME. / LIFE SENTENCE**
(cd-s Jun92; STAT 22CD)

Nov 82. (lp) *(STATLP 11)* **PLASTIC SURGERY DISASTERS** — — –
– Government flu / Terminal preppie / Trust your mechanic / Well paid scientist / Buzzbomb / Forest fire / Halloween / Winnebago warrior / Riot / Bleed for me / I am the owl / Dead end / Moon over Marin. *(re-iss. Oct85; same) (cd-iss. Nov86 & Jun92 & Jun98 +=; same)* – IN GOD WE TRUST INC. *(cd re-iss. Feb01 on 'Decay'+=; DKS 6/9CD)* – IN GOD WE TRUST INC.

Nov 82. (7"/12") *(STAT/+12 27)* *<VIRUS 28>* **HALLOWEEN. / SATURDAY NIGHT HOLOCAUST**
(cd-s Jun92; STAT 27CD)

— meanwhile KLAUS and EAST BAY released solo singles (see below)

Alternative Tentacles — Alternative Tentacles

May 82. (12"; KLAUS FLUORIDE) *<(VIRUS 12)>* **SHORTNING BREAD. / DROWNING COWBOY**

Jun 84. (7"; EAST BAY RAY) *<(VIRUS 34)>* **TROUBLE IN TOWN. / POISON HEART**
(12 re-iss. Apr89 on 'New Rose' France; GMO 40)

Aug 84. (12"ep; KLAUS FLUORIDE) **CHA CHA CHA WITH MR. FLUORIDE** — — –
– Ghost riders / etc.

Dec 85. (lp) *<(VIRUS 45)>* **FRANKENCHRIST**
– Soup is good food / Hellnation / This could be anywhere (this could be everywhere) / A growing boy needs his lunch / Chicken farm / Macho-rama (invasion of the beef-patrol) / Goons of Hazzard / At my job / M.T.V. – Get off the air / Stars and stripes of corruption. *(cd-iss. 1986 & Jun98; VIRUS 45CD) (cd re-iss. Feb01 on 'Decay'; DKS 11CD)*

Dec 86. (lp/c/cd) *<(VIRUS 50/+C/CD)>* **BEDTIME FOR DEMOCRACY**
– Take this job and shove it / Hop with the jet set / Dear Abby / Rambozo the clown / Fleshdunce / The great wall / Shrink / Triumph of the swill / I spy / Macho insecurity / Cesspools in Eden / One-way ticket to Pluto / Do the slag / Gone with the wind / A commercial / Anarchy for sale / Chickenshit conformist / Where do ya draw the line / Potshot heard round the world / D.M.S.O. / Lie detector. *(cd re-iss. Jun98; same) (cd re-iss. Feb01 on 'Decay'; DKS 12CD)*

— split December '86 when RAY departed (he subsequently turned up in SKRAPYARD). KLAUS FLUORIDE went solo, releasing albums 'BECAUSE I SAY SO' (1988) and 'THE LIGHT IS FLICKERING' (1991) and forming acoustic outfit FIVE YEAR PLAN

– compilations, etc. –

on 'Alternative Tentacles' unless mentioned otherwise

Jun 87. (lp/cd) *<(VIRUS 57/+CD)>* **GIVE ME CONVENIENCE OR GIVE ME DEATH** — 84
– Police truck / Too drunk to f*** / California uber alles / Man with the dogs / In sight / Life sentence / A child and his lawnmower / Holiday in Cambodia / Night of the living rednecks / I fought the law / Saturday night holocaust / Pull my strings / Short songs / Straight A's / Kinky sex makes the world go round / The prey. *(cd+=/free flexi-disc)* – BUZZBOMB FROM PASADENA *(cd re-iss. Feb01 on 'Decay'; DKS 13CD)*

Jun 93. (7"ep) *Subterranean; (SUB 24)* **NAZI PUNKS **** OFF / ARYANISMS. / ('A'live) / CONTEMPTUOUS** — — –
(re-iss. Dec97 & Jul00; same)

Feb 01. (cd) *Decay; (DKS 14CD) / Manifesto; <42905>* **MUTINY ON THE BAY (live)** — — Apr01

the DEAD 60s

Formed: Liverpool, England ... 2002 as RESTHOLME, then PINHOLE by MATT McMANAMON, BEN GORDON, CHARLIE TURNER and BRYAN JOHNSON. Encoding their proto-punk ethos in their new moniker, the DEAD 60s, they synthesized a raft of neo-dub and post-punk/Two-Tone influences instead: to a man critics came to the same conclusions, the CLASH, the SPECIALS, early MEKONS and vintage KING TUBBY/LEE PERRY. Another period touch was the release of luridly coloured 7-inchers such as 'YOU'RE NOT THE LAW', 'RIOT RADIO', 'THE LAST RESORT' and 'LOADED GUN' – the best titles the CLASH never used, and all delivered on Scouse indie central, 'Deltasonic' (also home, ironically perhaps, of the CORAL and the ZUTONS, to both of whom the 60s are presumably very much alive). Inking a deal with major conglomerate, 'Epic' (in the States only), the Liverpudlians went through with the unusual step of issuing their eponymous debut on the American market four months prior to its September 2005 release in Blighty. Both the album and two further UK singles, a re-issue of 'RIOT RADIO' and non-LP track 'GHOSTFACED KILLER', hit the Top 30. With all the hassle over Sony/BMG's problematic XCP anti-piracy software (the CD was withdrawn in the US and subsequently re-released), Stateside fans must have wished audio technology was as stunted as the band's musical horizons.

• **Covers:** 7 NATION ARMY (White Stripes).

Album rating: THE DEAD 60s (*7)

MATT McMANAMON – vocals, guitar / **BEN GORDON** – guitar, organ / **CHARLIE TURNER** – bass, vocals / **BRYAN JOHNSON** – drums

Deltasonic — Epic

May 04. (7"red/cd-s) *(DLT/+CD 021)* **YOU'RE NOT THE LAW. / TOO MUCH TV (dub)** — — –

Oct 04. (7"yellow) *(DLT 025)* **RIOT RADIO. / NO GOOD TOWN (dub)** — 30 — –
(cd-s+=) *(DLTCD 025)* – Soul survivor / ('A'-video).

Mar 05. (7"pink) *(DLT 032)* **THE LAST RESORT. / LAWNMOWER (dub)** — 24 — –
(cd-s) *(DLTCD 032)* – ('A') / Invader (dub).

(cd-s) *(DLTCD2 032)* – ('A') / Saturday night (dub) / Do you receive me (dub) / ('A'-video).

Jun 05. (7"green) *(DLT 037)* **LOADED GUN. / CONTROL THIS DUB** 28 –

(cd-s) *(DLTCD 037)* – ('A') / 7 nation army.

(cd-s) *(DLTCD2 037)* – ('A') / TV & magazines / Cold soul / ('A'-video).

Sep 05. (7"white) *(DLT 041)* **RIOT RADIO. / NEW TOWN DISASTER** 30 –

(cd-s+=) *(DLTCD2 041)* – Satellite receiver dub / ('A'-video).

(cd-s) *(DLTCD 041)* – ('A') / Car crash party.

Sep 05. (cd) *(DLTCD 038)* *<EK 94453>* **THE DEAD 60s** 23 May05

– Riot radio / A different age / Nowhere / Red light / Just another love song / Control this / Loaded gun / Nationwide / We get low / Horizontal / New town disaster / The last resort / You're not the law. *(ltd d-cd+=/d-lp+=; DLT CDLE/LPLE 038)* – Too much TV dub / Invader dub / D-60 fights the evil force / No control dub / Tower block dub / CNS lazer attack D-60 / Police radio dub / Flight mission dub / No good town dub / Game over. *<US re-iss. Nov05 w/out XCP; 82876 77675-2)*

Nov 05. (7"luminous) *(DLT1 042)* **GHOSTFACED KILLER. / (CNS hip hop remix)** 25 –

(7"light green) – ('A') / D-60 fights the evil force.

(cd-s) *(DLTCD 042)* – ('A') / Riot radio (live in NY) / You're not the law (live 2004) / ('A'-CNS horrorcore remix) / ('A'-video).

DEATH CAB FOR CUTIE

Formed: Bellingham, Washington, USA . . . late 1996 by frontman, singer/songwriter and all around innovator BEN GIBBARD, who began his career in the strange world of Lo-Fi casio pop – The ALL-TIME QUARTERBACK!. After writing a handful of songs he recruited guitarist CHRISTOPHER WALLA, NICK HARMER and drummer NATHAN GOOD, to form the devilishly-titled DEATH CAB FOR CUTIE. An amalgamation of MODEST MOUSE's tripped-out guitar hooks and BUILT TO SPILL's solid indie rock sensibility, their debut album 'SOMETHING ABOUT AEROPLANES' (1999), caught the ears of the indie sect and left them crying out for more. Well, in between re-issuing the aforementioned ALL-TIME QUARTERBACK! eponymous set (1999), GIBBARD and Co started work on what was to become 'WE HAVE THE FACTS AND WE'RE VOTING YES' (2000), possibly the outfit's greatest achievement to date. GIBBARD's voice soared in songs such as 'SCIENTIST STUDIES' and the title track, but seems fractured and poignant on the romantic 'THE EMPLOYMENT PAGES'. DCFC delivered a modest EP, 'FORBIDDEN LOVE' in the same year, which contained three new cuts and two alternative arrangements of '405' and 'COMPANY CALLS (EPILOGUE)' (both on 'WE HAVE THE FACTS . . .'). They followed this with 'THE PHOTO ALBUM' (2001), which seemed to be taking the group in a new direction, namely that of PREFAB SPROUT and assorted Scottish, Postcard-esque janglers. 'YOU CAN PLAY THESE SONGS WITH CHORDS' (2002) was originally intended as a demo-only cassette, but was released including the collective's earlier singles 'PROVE MY HYPOTHESIS' and 'SONG FOR HUCKABLY'. Even softer and more solitary than its predecessor, 'TRANSATLANTICISM' (2003), marked a belated entry into the US Top 100, carrying the torch for sophisti-indie in the abrasive neo-New Wave era. With a name summing up the post-millennial craze for side-projects, the POSTAL SERVICE delivered the joint labours of GIBBARD and electro technician JIMMY TAMBORELLO (as well as up and coming indie face JENNY LEWIS – of RILO KILEY – and JEN WOODS) on a one-off 'Sub Pop' long-player, 'GIVE UP' (2003). Taking unashamedly 80s pointers from vintage VINCE CLARKE and CHRIS LOWE as well as spiritual support from '99 Luft Balloons' NENA, the snail-mail synth-poppers drew more attention than they bargained for: corporations Mars, Honda and insurance company Kaiser Permanente were sold on songs such as lead single 'SUCH GREAT HEIGHTS' (as covered by IRON & WINE) and future US minor hit, 'WE WILL BECOME SILHOUETTES', while the "real" US postal service were interested in the band for other, more litigious reasons, taking exception to the use of their moniker. A mutual agreement obviated any cash claims and left the POSTAL SERVICE free for future sorties. DCFC were back in circulation mid 2005 via a fresh contract with 'Atlantic' and a less-controversial, more staid follow-up set, 'PLANS'. Finally transcending many of their more obvious influences (and adding some new ones, imagine Lennon, say say say McCartney), the album's made to measure maturity was obvious from minor hits, 'SOUL MEETS BODY' and 'CROOKED TEETH', effortlessly buoying them into the US Top 5.

• **Covered:** THIS CHARMING MAN (Smiths) / WAIT (Secret Stars) / WHY I CRY (Magnetic Fields) / ALL IS FULL OF LOVE (Bjork) / the POSTAL SERVICE covered SUDDENLY EVERYTHING HAS CHANGED (Flaming Lips) / AGAINST ALL ODDS (Phil Collins).

Album rating: SOMETHING ABOUT AIRPLANES (*7) / ALL-TIME QUARTERBACK! by All-Time Quarterback! (*6) / WE HAVE THE FACTS AND WE'RE VOTING YES (*7) / THE PHOTO ALBUM (*8) / YOU CAN PLAY THESE SONGS WITH CHORDS early collection (*5) / TRANSATLANTICISM (*8) / PLANS (*7) / the Postal Service: GIVE UP (*7)

BEN GIBBARD (b.11 Aug'76, Bremerton, Washington) – vocals, guitars, organ / **CHRISTOPHER WALLA** (b. 2 Nov'75, Bothell, Washington) – guitar, organ, etc. / + **ABIGAIL HALL** – (guest vocals)

Elsinor Elsinor

Nov 97. (c) *<els 012>* **YOU CAN PLAY THESE SONGS WITH CHORDS** –

– President of what? / Champagne from a paper cup / Pictures in an exhibition / Hindsight / That's incentive / Amputations / Two cars / Line of best fit. *<cd-iss. Oct02 on 'Barsuk'+=; BARK 28>* – This charming man / TV trays / New candles / Tomorrow / Flustered – Hey tomcat! / State street residential / Wait / Prove my hypothesis / Song for Kelly Huckaby / Army corps of architects. *<(re-iss. cd Aug05; same)>*

— added **NICK HARMER** (b.23 Jan'75, Germany) – bass, keyboards / **NATHAN GOOD** – drums

Oct 98. (7"ep) *<els 014>* **YOUR BRUISE. / Revolutionary Hydra: LINEAR TIME / ANACORTES TYPE WRITER / CRUEL OCEANOGRAPHY** –

— BEN plays bass for REVOLUTIONARY HYDRA

Jun 99. (cd) *<(els 017cd)>* **SOMETHING ABOUT AIRPLANES** Mar99

– Bend to squares / President of what? / Champagne from a paper cup / Your bruise / Pictures in an exhibition / Sleep spent / The face that launched 1000 ships / Amputations / Fake frowns / Line of best fit. *<blue-lp iss.2002 on 'Sonic Boom'; SBR 002>* *<(re-iss. Aug05 on 'Barsuk'; KRANG 5)>*

Sep 99. (cd; as ALL-TIME QUARTERBACK!) *<els 025cd>* **ALL-TIME QUARTERBACK!** –

– Plans get complex / Dinner at eight in the suburbs / Cleveland (live) / Empire state (live) / Rules broken / Untitled / Factory direct (live) / Why I cry / Underwater (live) / Sock hop (live) / Send packing. *(UK-iss.Jul02 on 'Barsuk'+=; BARK 26)* – Plans get complex (video).

above record was down to GIBBARD on his own

not iss. Sonic Boo

Sep 99. (7"clear) *<SBR 003>* **PROVE MY HYPOTHESIS. / WAIT** –

(UK-iss.Aug00; same)

Barsuk Barsuk

Feb 00. (7") *<BARK 9>* **DEATH CAB FOR FIVER** –

– Spring break broke / Sleep tight.

Mar 00. (cd) *<BARK 11>* **WE HAVE THE FACTS AND WE'RE VOTING YES** –

– We have all the facts and we're voting yes / The employment pages / For what reason / Lowell, MA / Little fury bugs / 405 / Company calls / Company calls (epilogue) / No joy in mudville / Scientist studies. *(UK-iss.Aug02 on 'Fierce Panda'+=; NONG 26CD)* – Song for Kelly Huckaby / Prove my hypothesis / Wait. *<(re-iss. Aug05; same)>*

Mar 00. (7") *<SP 496>* **UNDERWATER! / THE ARMY CORPS OF ARCHITECTS** –

(above issued on 'Sub Pop Singles Club')

— **MICHAEL SCHORR** – drums; repl. GOOD

Nov 00. (cd-ep) *<(BARK 15)>* **THE FORBIDDEN LOVE** Oct00

– Photobooth / Technicolor girls / Song for Kelly Huckaby / 405 (acoustic) / Company calls epilogue (alternate take).

Fierce Panda | Barsuk

'eb 02. (cd-s) *(NING 115CD)* **A MOVIE SCRIPT ENDING / PHOTO BOOTH / TECHNICOLOR GIRLS** [ ] [-]

'eb 02. (cd) *(NONG 24CD)* *<BARK 21>* **THE PHOTO ALBUM** [ ] Oct01 [ ]
– Steadier footing / A movie script ending / We laugh indoors / Information travels faster / Why you'd want to live here / Blacking out the friction / I was a kaleidoscope / Styrofoam plates / Coney Island / Debate exposes doubt. *(UK+=)* – Gridlock caravans / 20th century towers / All is full of love. *(lp-iss.Apr02 on 'Barsuk'+=; BARK 21LP)* – Gridlock caravans. *<(cd re-iss. Aug05; same)>*

'eb 02. (ltd;cd-ep) *<BARK 23>* **THE STABILITY EP** [-] [ ]
– 20th Century towers / All is full of love / Stability / Gridlock caravans.

4ay 02. (7") *(NING 116)* **I WAS A KALEIDOSCOPE. / 405 (acoustic)** [ ] [-]
(cd-s) *(NING 116CD)* – ('A') / We laugh indoors (dub) / Stability.

Aug 02. (7") *(NING 126)* **WE LAUGH INDOORS. / DEBATE EXPOSES DOUBT (acoustic session)** [ ] [-]
(cd-s) *(NING 126CD)* – ('A') / For what reason (alternate) / I was a kaleidoscope (live).

— **JASON McGERR** – drums (ex-EUREKA FARM) repl. SCHORR

)ct 03. (cd) *(NONG 32CD)* *<BARK 32>* **TRANSATLANTICISM** [ ] [97]
– The new year / Lightness / Title and registration / Expo '86 / The sound of settling / Tiny vessels / Transatlanticism / Passenger seat / Death of an interior decorator / We looked like giants / A lack of color.

eb 04. (7") *(NING 149)* **THE NEW YEAR. / TV TRAYS** [ ] [-]
(cd-s) *(NONG 149CD)* – ('A') / Blacking out the friction (demo) / Rustered / Hey tomcat!

Aug 04. (cd-ep) *<BARK 39>* **STUDIO X SESSIONS EP** [-] [ ]
– The new year / Blacking out the friction / Bend to squares / Army corps of architects.

Aug 04. (7") *(NING 158)* **THE SOUND OF SETTLING. / THIS CHARMING MAN** [ ] [-]
(cd-s) *(NONG 158CD)* – ('A') / Lightness (live at Studio X) / That's incentive.

4ar 05. (m-cd) *<BARK 43>* **THE JOHN BYRD E.P.** [-] [ ]
– We laugh indoors / Why you'd want to live here / Lightness / Photobooth / We looked like giants / 405 / Blacking out the friction – Brand new love. *(UK-iss.Feb06; same as US)*

Atlantic | Atlantic

Aug 05. (cd) *<(7567 83834-2)>* **PLANS** [ ] [4]
– Marching bands of Manhattan / Soul meets body / Summer skin / Different names for the same thing / I will follow you into the dark / Your heart is an empty room / Someday you will be loved / Crooked teeth / What Sarah said / Brothers on a hotel bed / Stable song. *<US lp-iss.Sep05 on 'Barsuk'; BARK 47>* – Talking like turnstiles.

)ct 05. (7") *(AT AT 0217)* *<radio>* **SOUL MEETS BODY. / JEALOUSY RIDES WITH ME** [ ] [60]

pr 06. (7"green) *(AT 0232)* **CROOKED TEETH. / WORLD SHUT YOUR MOUTH** [69] Feb06 [ ]
(7"red) *(AT 0232X)* – ('A') / Talking like turnstiles.
(cd-s+=) *(AT 232CD)* – ('A'-video) / (making of Plans video).

he POSTAL SERVICE

EN GIBBARD, JIMMY TAMBORELLO (latter of DNTEL & FIGURINE)

Sub Pop | Sub Pop

an 03. (cd-ep) *<SPCD 609>* **SUCH GREAT HEIGHTS** [-] [ ]
– Such great heights / There's never enough time / We will become silhouettes (by SHINS) / Such great heights (by IRON & WINE).

pr 03. (cd) *<(SPCD 595)>* **GIVE UP** [ ] Feb03 [ ]
– The district sleeps alone tonight / Such great heights / Sleeping in / Nothing better / Recycled air / Clark Gable / We will become silhouettes / This place is a prison / Brand new colony / Natural anthem. *<d-lp iss.Nov04 +=; There's never enough time / We will become silhouettes (by SHINS) / Such great heights (by IRON & WINE) / Suddenly everything has changed / The district sleeps alone tonight (DJ Downfall persistent beat mix) / Such great heights (John Tejada mix).*

ıl 03. (cd-ep) *<SPCD 614>* **THE DISTRICT SLEEPS ALONE TONIGHT** [-] [ ]
– The district sleeps alone tonight / The district sleeps alone tonight (remix by DJ Downfall) / Such great heights (remix by John Tejada) / Suddenly everything has changed.

Feb 05. (12"/cd-s) *<SP/+CD 656>* **WE WILL BECOME SILHOUETTES** [-] [82]
– We will become silhouettes / Be still my heart / Nothing better (Styrofoam remix) / We will become silhouettes (Matthew Dear's not so scared mix).

DEEP PURPLE

Formed: London, England . . . 1968 intially as ROUNDABOUT, by former Searchers sticksman, CHRIS CURTIS. He duly recruited classically-trained organist, JON LORD and guitar maestro, RITCHIE BLACKMORE, who was living in Germany at the time. By Spring of that year, the band had become DEEP PURPLE with NICK SIMPER on bass and ROD EVANS on vocals. Their debut single, a cover of JOE SOUTH's 'HUSH', reached the US Top 5 and the band were subsequently furnished with a three album contract, signing with 'Tentagramme' in America (a label run by US comedian Bill Cosby!), 'Parlophone'in Britain. This line-up (known as Mk.I in DEEP PURPLE parlance) recorded three albums, 'SHADES OF DEEP PURPLE' (1968), 'BOOK OF TALIESYN' (1969) and the eponymous 'DEEP PURPLE' (1969), littered with chugging, proto-metal covers of the era's pop hits a la VANILLA FUDGE. Following the collapse of 'Tentagramme', the band signed with 'Warners', drafting in IAN GILLAN and ROGER GLOVER (both ex-EPISODE SIX) to replace EVANS and SIMPER respectively. The revamped line-up's first release was the pseudo-classical drivel of the live 'CONCERTO FOR GROUP AND ORCHESTRA WITH THE ROYAL PHILHARMONIC ORCHESTRA' (1970). Thankfully, after the record failed to sell in any great quantity, common sense prevailed and BLACKMORE steered the group in a heavier direction. 'IN ROCK', released later the same year, announced the arrival of a major contender in the heavyweight arena alongside the likes of BLACK SABBATH and LED ZEPPELIN. Preceded by the lumbering 'BLACK NIGHT' (No.2 in the UK) single, the album was dinosaur rock before the phrase was even coined; the pummelling rhythm section of GLOVER and PAICE driving the beast ever onward while BLACKMORE's razor sharp guitar solos clawed mercilessly at LORD's shuddering organ. 'CHILD IN TIME' was the ballad, the full range of GILLAN's talent on show as he progressed from mellow musings to his trademark glass-shattering shriek. While 'FIREBALL' (1971) was competent, if lacking in the songs department, 'MACHINE HEAD' (1972) was the DEEP PURPLE tour de force, the classic album from the classic Mk.II line-up. Cuts like 'HIGHWAY STAR' and 'SPACE TRUCKIN' were relentless, high-octane metal riff-athons which became staples in the DP live set for years to come. 'SMOKE ON THE WATER' probably stands as the band's most famous track, its classic three chord bludgeon and tale of disaster averted, reaching No.4 in America upon its release as a single a year later. This further boosted 'MACHINE HEAD's sales into the millions, DEEP PURPLE now firmly established as a world class act. The band also had a stellar live reputation, the concert double set, 'MADE IN JAPAN' (1972), going on to achieve cult status among metal afficiondos and earning the group a place in the Guinness Book Of Records as loudest band, woaargh!! As the heavy touring and recording schedule ground on, the beast began to stumble, however, recording a further, fairly lacklustre album, 'WHO DO WE THINK WE ARE' (1973), before disintegrating later that summer among constant in-fighting and personality clashes. BLACKMORE, LORD and PAICE remained, enlisting future WHITESNAKE vocalist DAVID COVERDALE on vocals and GLENN HUGHES (ex-TRAPEZE) in place of GLOVER to create DEEP PURPLE Mk.III. 'BURN' (1974) and 'STORMBRINGER' (1974) were characterised by COVERDALE's bluesy voice, although the new boy and BLACKMORE were not exactly fond of each other, the latter eventually quitting in 1975. His replacement was semi-legendary guitarist TOMMY BOLIN, who graced 'COME TASTE THE BAND' (1975). Less than a year later, however, DEEP PURPLE were no more, the behemoth finally going belly up after the perils of rock'n'roll had finally taken their toll. While BOLIN overdosed on heroin, of the remaining members, GLENN HUGHES reformed TRAPEZE while COVERDALE formed WHITESNAKE. BLACKMORE, meanwhile, had not been simply sitting around stuffing cucumbers down his pants and turning his amp up to 11, he had formed the rather grandiose-sounding RITCHIE BLACKMORE'S RAINBOW. The other key member of DEEP PURPLE, IAN GILLAN, had also been equally prolific during the 70's, initially with the IAN GILLAN BAND. A revamped DEEP PURPLE is where the paths of messrs. BLACKMORE, GILLAN, GLOVER, LORD and PAICE (the latter two had dabbled in solo and group work throughout the 70's – see discography) crossed once more. While the comeback album, 'PERFECT STRANGERS' (1984), was welcomed by fans, it became clear that the ever-dominant BLACKMORE was being as dominant as ever. After another relatively successful studio effort, 'HOUSE OF BLUE LIGHT' (1987), and a live album, GILLAN was given the order of the boot. Typically incestuous, DEEP PURPLE then recruited ex-RAINBOW man, JOE LYNN TURNER, for the awful 'SLAVES AND MASTERS' (1990) album. In an increasingly absurd round of musical chairs, GILLAN was then reinstated, consequently clashing once more with BLACKMORE who eventually stomped off to reform RAINBOW. DEEP PURPLE lumbered on, recruiting STEVE MORSE for their 1996 album, 'PURPENDICULAR'. 'ABANDON' (1998) was another to disappoint their ever faithful support who were literally growing old and grey waiting for them to retire. Following on from the conceit of 1971's 'CONCERTO FOR GROUP AND ORCHESTRA', DP decided to bring the dreaded rock-meets-classical concept into the 21st Century. 'LIVE AT THE ROYAL ALBERT HALL' (2000) found the lads backed up by the London Symphony Orchestra, dredging up past classics and rendering them so far out of context it was hard to ascertain exactly who this album was aimed at. Nevertheless, guest appearances by the likes of RONNIE JAMES DIO and strangely, SAM BROWN, made for at least minor diversions from the muddled ambitions of the main programme. On a completely different note, in all senses of the term, 'BANANAS' (2003), was a back-to-the-roots kind of affair, or at least it would have been if DEEP PURPLE had started out sounding this relaxed. Less bombast, self indulgence and ego made for one of the better DP sets of recent years with a really quite surprising suppleness to the blues-boogie on offer. The absence of LORD wasn't felt too badly either, with veteran DON AIREY doing a fine job and earning a couple of writing credits on the better tracks. The same line-up remained remarkably intact on 2005's 'RAPTURE OF THE DEEP', berating the ageist attitudes of corporate music media on the corrosive 'MTV'.

• **Songwriters:** Mk.I:-Mostly BLACKMORE / EVANS / LORD. Mk.II:- Group. Mk.III:- BLACKMORE / COVERDALE, adding at times LORD and PAICE. Mk.IV:- Permutate any two of COVERDALE, BOLIN or HUGHES. Covered HUSH (Joe South) / WE CAN WORK IT OUT + HELP (Beatles) / KENTUCKY WOMAN (Neil Diamond) / RIVER DEEP MOUNTAIN HIGH (Ike & Tina Turner) / HEY JOE (Jimi Hendrix) / I'M SO GLAD (Cream).
• **Trivia:** To obtain charity monies for the Armenian earthquake disaster late 1989, BLACKMORE, GILLAN and others (i.e. BRUCE DICKINSON, ROBERT PLANT, BRIAN MAY etc.) contributed to Top 40 new version of SMOKE ON THE WATER.

Album rating: SHADES OF DEEP PURPLE (*5) / THE BOOK OF TALIESYN (*4) / DEEP PURPLE (*4) / CONCERTO FOR GROUP AND ORCHESTRA (*1) / IN ROCK (*8) / FIREBALL (*7) / MACHINE HEAD (*9) / MADE IN JAPAN (*8) / WHO DO WE THINK WE ARE (*6) / BURN (*7) / STORMBRINGER (*5) / COME TASTE THE BAND (*6) / DEEPEST PURPLE compilation (*9) / PERFECT STRANGERS (*6) / HOUSE OF BLUE LIGHT (*5) / NOBODY' PERFECT (*5) / SLAVES AND MASTERS (*4) / COME HELL OR HIGH WATE (*7) / PURPENDICULAR (*5) / ABANDON (*4) / LIVE AT THE ROYAL ALBER HALL (*5) / BANANAS (*5) / THE PLATINUM COLLECTION compilation (*8) RAPTURE OF THE DEEP (*6)

RITCHIE BLACKMORE (b.14 Apr'45, Weston-Super-Mare, Avor England) – guitar (ex-MANDRAKE ROOT, ex-OUTLAWS, ex SCREAMING LORD SUTCH, etc.) / **JON LORD** (b.9 Jun'41, Leiceste England) – keyboards (ex-FLOWERPOT MEN) / **NICK SIMPER** (b. 194 Southall, London) – bass (ex-JOHNNY KIDD & PIRATES) / **ROD EVAN** (b.19 Jan'45, Edinburgh, Scotland) – vocals (ex-MAZE, ex-M.I.FIVE) **IAN PAICE** (b.29 Jun'48, Nottingham, England) – drums (ex-MAZE, ex M.I.FIVE)

Parlophone Tetragr

Jun 68. (7") *(R 5708) <1503>* **HUSH. / ONE MORE RAINY DAY** [ ] [4]

Sep 68. (lp) *(PCS 7055) <102>* **SHADES OF DEEP PURPLE** [ ] [24]
– And the address / Hush / One more rainy day / (prelude) Happiness I'm so glad / Mandrake root / Help / Love help me / Hey Joe. *(r iss. Feb77 on 'EMI Harvest'; SHSM 2016) (cd-iss. Mar89; CZ 170) (cd-is Feb95 on 'Fame'; CDFA 3314) (lp re-iss. Nov97 on 'E.M.I.'; LPCENT 25) (re-mast.Feb00 on 'Liberty'; 498336-2)*

Nov 68. (7") *<1508>* **KENTUCKY WOMAN. / HARD ROAD** [–] [38]

Nov 68. (7") *(R 5745)* **KENTUCKY WOMAN. / WRING THAT NECK** [ ] [–]

Jan 69. (7") *<1514>* **RIVER DEEP – MOUNTAIN HIGH. / LISTEN, LEARN, READ ON** [–] [53]

Feb 69. (7") *(R 5763)* **EMMARETTA. / WRING THAT NECK** [ ] [–]

Apr 69. (7") *<1519>* **EMMARETTA. / THE BIRD HAS FLOWN** [–] [ ]

Harvest Tetragr

Jun 69. (lp/c) *(SHVL/TC-SHVL 751) <107>* **BOOK OF TALIESYN** [ ] Jan69 [54]
– Listen, learn, read on / Wring that neck / Kentucky woman / Shield / Exposition – b) We can work it out / The shield / Anthem / River dee mountain high. *(re-iss. Jun85 on 'EMI';) (cd-iss. Aug89; CDP 792408-2) (re-iss. Feb96 on 'Premier'; CZ 171) (cd re-mast.Feb00 on 'Liberty'; 521608-*

Nov 69. (lp) *(SHVL 759) <119>* **DEEP PURPLE** [ ] Jul69 [ ]
– Chasing shadows / Blind / Lalena: (a) Faultline, (b) The painter / W didn't Rosemary? / The bird has flown / April. *(re-iss. Jun85 on 'EM) (cd-iss. Mar89; CZ 172) (re-iss. cd May95 on 'Fame'; CDFA 3317) (re-mast.Feb00 on 'Liberty'; 521597-2)*

—— (In Jun'69 below two were used on session for 'HALLELUJAH'. They becam regular members after the recording of 'DEEP PURPLE' album.) / **IA GILLAN** (b.19 Aug'45, Hounslow, London) – vocals (ex-EPISODE SI replaced EVANS who joined CAPTAIN BEYOND. / **ROGER GLOVER** (b. Nov'45, Brecon, Wales) – bass (ex-EPISODE SIX) replaced SIMPER wh later formed WARHORSE

Jul 69. (7") *(HAR 5006) <1537>* **HALLELUJAH (I AM THE PREACHER). / APRIL (part 1)** [ ] [ ]

Harvest Warn

Jan 70. (lp/c) *(SHVL/TC-SHVL 767) <1860>* **CONCERTO FOR GROUP AND ORCHESTRA WITH THE ROYAL PHILHARMONIC ORCHESTRA (live)** [26] May70 [ ]
– First Movement: Moderato – Allegro / Second Movement: Anda (part 1) – Andante conclusion / Third Movement: Vivace – Presto. *(cd-i Aug90 on 'E.M.I.'+=; CZ 342)* – Wring that neck / Child in time.

Jun 70. (7") *(HAR 5020)* **BLACK NIGHT. / SPEED KING** [2] [–]

Jun 70. (lp/c) *(SHVL/TC-SHVL 777) <1877>* **DEEP PURPLE IN ROCK** [4] Sep70 [ ]
– Speed king / Blood sucker / Child in time / Flight of the rat / Into t fire / Living wreck / Hard lovin' man. *(re-iss. May82 on 'Fame' lp/c; FA/T FA 3011) (cd-iss. Apr88; CDFA 3011) (pic-lp.Jun85; EJ 2603430) (purple- iss.1995 on 'E.M.I.'; 7243-8-34019-8) (with free-lp)* – Black night / Spe king (piano version) / Cry free (Roger Glover remix) / Jam stew / Flig of the rat (Roger Glover remix) / Speed king (Roger Glover remix) / Bla night (Roger Glover remix).

Jul 70. (7") *<7405>* **BLACK NIGHT. / INTO THE FIRE** [–] [66]

Feb 71. (7") *(HAR 5033) <7493>* **STRANGE KIND OF WOMAN. / I'M ALONE** [6] [ ]

Sep 71. (lp/c) *(SHVL/TC-SHVL 793) <2564>* **FIREBALL** [1] Aug71 [32]
– Fireball / No no no / Demon's eye / Anyone's daughter / The mul Fools / No one came. *(re-iss. Mar84 on 'Fame' lp/c; FA/TC-FA 41-30 1/-4) (re-iss. Aug87 lp/c; ATAK/TC-ATAK 105) (re-iss. Oct87 on 'E.M lp/c; EMS/TC-EMS 1255) (cd-iss. Jan88 on 'E.M.I.'; CZ 30) (pic-lp.Jun85 'E.M.I.'; EJ 2403440) (lp re-iss. 1996 on 'E.M.I.'; 7243-8-53711-0) (with f*

lp) – Strange kind of woman (remix '96) / I'm alone / Freedom (session out-take) / Slow train (session out-take) / Midnight in Moscow – Robin Hood – William Tell – Fireball (the noise abatement) / Backwards piano / No one came (remix '96).

Oct 71. (7") *(HAR 5045)* **FIREBALL. / DEMON'S EYE** [15] [–]

Nov 71. (7") *<7528>* **FIREBALL. / I'M ALONE** [–] [ ]

Purple Warners

Mar 72. (7") *(PUR 102) <7572>* **NEVER BEFORE. / WHEN A BLIND MAN CRIES** [35] [ ]

Apr 72. (lp/c) *(TPSA/TC-TPSA 7504) <2607>* **MACHINE HEAD** [1] [7]
– Highway star / Maybe I'm a Leo / Pictures of home / Never before / Smoke on the water / Lazy / Space truckin'. *(re-iss. Jun85 on 'E.M.I.' lp/c; ATAK/TC-ATAK 39) (re-iss. Oct86 on 'Fame' lp/c; FA/TC-FA 3158) (cd-iss. Mar87 on 'E.M.I.'; CZ 83) (cd re-iss. Mar89; CDFA 3158) (re-iss. Sep97 on 'E.M.I.' d-cd/d-lp; CD+/DEEPP 3)*

Jun 72. (7") *<7595>* **LAZY. / WHEN A BLIND MAN CRIES** [–] [ ]

Oct 72. (7") *<7634>* **HIGHWAY STAR. / (part 2)** [–] [ ]

Dec 72. (d-lp/d-c) *(TPSP/TC2-TPSP 351) <2701>* **MADE IN JAPAN (live)** [16] Apr73 [6]
– Highway star / Child in time / Smoke on the water / The mule / Strange kind of woman / Lazy / Space truckin'. *(cd-iss. Sep88 on 'E.M.I.'; CDTPS 351) (re-iss. Oct92 on 'Fame' cd/c; CD/TC FA 3268) (re-iss. Jan98 on 'E.M.I.' cd/lp; 857864-2/-4)* – hit No.73

Feb 73. (lp/c) *(TPSA/TC-TPSA 7508) <2678>* **WHO DO YOU THINK WE ARE!** [4] Jan73 [15]
– Woman from Tokyo / Mary Long / Super trouper / Smooth dancer / Rat bat blue / Place in line / Our lady. *(re-iss. Jun85 on 'E.M.I.' lp/c; ATAK/TC-ATAK 127) (cd-iss. Oct87 on 'E.M.I.'; CZ 6) (cd re-iss. Dec94 on 'Fame'; CDFA 3311) (cd re-iss. Jul00 on 'E.M.I.'+=; 521607-2)* – (the 1999 remixes).

Apr 73. (7") *<7672>* **WOMAN FROM TOKYO. / SUPER TROUPER** [–] [80]

May 73. (7") *<7710>* **SMOKE ON THE WATER. / (part 2)** [–] [4]

Sep 73. (7") *<7737>* **WOMAN FROM TOKYO. / SUPER TROOPER** [–] [60]

— **BLACKMORE, LORD** and **PAICE** brought in new members / **DAVID COVERDALE** (b.22 Sep'49, Saltburn-by-the-sea, Cleveland, England) – vocals replaced GILLAN who later formed own band. / **GLENN HUGHES** (b.Penkridge, England) – bass (ex-TRAPEZE) repl. GLOVER who became top producer.

Feb 74. (lp/c) *(TPS/TC-TPS 3505) <2766>* **BURN** [3] [9]
– Burn / Might just take your life / Lay down stay down / Sail away / You fool no one / What's goin' on here / Mistreated / "A" 200. *(re-iss. Mar84 on 'E.M.I.' lp/c; ATAK/TC-ATAK 11) (cd-iss. Jul89; CZ 203)*

Mar 74. (7") *(PUR 117) <7784>* **MIGHT JUST TAKE YOUR LIFE. / CORONARIAS REDIG** [ ] [91]

May 74. (7") *<7809>* **BURN. / CORONARIAS REDIG** [–] [ ]

Nov 74. (lp/c) *(TPS/TC-TPS 3508) <2832>* **STORMBRINGER** [6] [20]
– Stormbringer / Love don't mean a thing / Holy man / Hold on / Lady double dealer / You can't do it right (with the one you love) / High ball shooter / The gypsy / Soldier of fortune. *(re-iss. Jun85 on 'E.M.I.' lp/c; ATAK/TC-ATAK 70) (cd-iss. Oct88 on 'E.M.I.'; CZ 142)*

Nov 74. (7") *<8049>* **HIGH BALL SHOOTER. / YOU CAN'T DO IT RIGHT** [–] [ ]

Jan 75. (7") *<8069>* **STORMBRINGER. / LOVE DON'T MEAN A THING** [–] [ ]

— **TOMMY BOLIN** (b.1951, Sioux City, Iowa, USA) – guitar (ex-JAMES GANG, ex-ZEPHYR) repl. BLACKMORE who formed RAINBOW. (see further below)

Oct 75. (lp/c) *(TPSA/TC-TPSA 7515) <2895>* **COME TASTE THE BAND** [19] [43]
– Comin' home / Lady luck / Gettin' together / Dealer / I need love / Drifter / Love child / This time around – Owed to the 'G' / You keep on moving. *(re-iss. Jun85 on 'E.M.I.' lp/c;) (cd-iss. Jul90 on 'E.M.I.'; CZ 343) (cd re-iss. Jul95 on 'Fame'; CDFA 3318)*

Mar 76. (7") *(PUR 130)* **YOU KEEP ON MOVING. / LOVE CHILD** [ ] [–]

Mar 76. (7") *<8182>* **GETTIN' TIGHTER. / LOVE CHILD** [–] [ ]

Nov 76. (lp/c) *(TPSA/TC-TPSA 7517) <2995>* **MADE IN EUROPE (live)** <US title 'DEEP PURPLE LIVE'> [12] [ ]
– Burn / Mistreated (interpolating 'Rock me baby') / Lady double dealer / You fool no one / Stormbringer. *(cd-iss. Jul90 on 'E.M.I.'; CZ 344)*

— split Spring 76, TOMMY BOLIN went solo. He died (of an overdose) 4th Dec'76. HUGHES reformed TRAPEZE. COVERDALE formed WHITESNAKE, he was later joined by LORD and PAICE, after they had been in PAICE, ASHTON and LORD. Remarkably **DEEP PURPLE** reformed 8 years later with early 70's line-up. **GILLAN, BLACKMORE, LORD, PAICE** and **GLOVER.**

Polydor Mercury

Nov 84. (lp/pic-lp/c) *(POLH/+P/C 16) <824003>* **PERFECT STRANGERS** [5] [17]
– Knocking at your back door / Under the gun / Nobody's home / Mean streak / Perfect strangers / A gypsy's kiss / Wasted sunsets / Hungry daze. *(c+=)* – Not responsible. *(re-iss. Mar91 cd/c/lp; 823777-2/-4/-1) (cd re-mast.Aug99; 546045-2)*

Jan 85. (7"/7"pic-d) *(POSP/+P 719)* **PERFECT STRANGERS. / SON OF ALERIK** [48] Mar85 [ ]
(12"+=) *(POSPX 719)* – Wasted sunsets / Hungry daze.

Jun 85. (7"/12") *(POSP/+X 749) <880477>* **KNOCKING AT YOUR BACK DOOR. / PERFECT STRANGERS** [68] Jan85 [61]

Jan 87. (lp/c)(cd) *(POLH/+C 32)(<831318-2>)* **THE HOUSE OF BLUE LIGHT** [10] [34]
– Bad attitude / The unwritten law / Call of the wild / Mad dog / Black and white / Hard lovin' woman / The Spanish archer / Strangeways / Mitzi Dupree / Dead or alive. *(re-iss. Mar91 lp/c; 831318-1/-4) (cd re-mast.Aug99; 546162-2)*

Jan 87. (7"/7"pic-d) *(POSP/+P 843)* **CALL OF THE WILD. / STRANGEWAYS** [ ] [ ]
(12") *(POSPX 843)* – ('A'side) / ('B'-long version).

Jun 88. (7") *(PO 4)* **HUSH (live). / DEAD OR ALIVE (live)** [62] [ ]
(12"+=/cd-s+=) *(PZ/+CD 4)* – Bad attitude (live).

Jun 88. (d-lp/d-c)(cd) *(PODV/+C 10)(<835897-2>)* **NOBODY'S PERFECT (live)** [38] [ ]
– Highway star / Strange kind of woman / Perfect strangers / Hard lovin' woman / Knocking at your back door / Child in time / Lazy / Black night / Woman from Tokyo / Smoke on the water / Hush. *(d-lp has extra tracks) (re-iss. Mar91 d-lp/d-c; 835897-1/-4) (cd re-mast.Aug99; 546128-2)*

— **JOE LYNN TURNER** – vocals (ex-RAINBOW, ex-YNGWIE MALMSTEEN'S RISING FORCE) repl. GILLAN who continued solo.

R.C.A. R.C.A.

Oct 90. (7") <c-s> *(PB 49247) <2703>* **KING OF DREAMS. / FIRE IN THE BASEMENT** [70] [ ]
(12"+=/cd-s+=) *(PT/PD 49248)* – ('A'-album version).

Nov 90. (cd/c/lp) *(PD/PK/PL 90535) <2421>* **SLAVES AND MASTERS** [45] [87]
– King of dreams / The cut runs deep / Fire in the basement / Truth hurts / Breakfast in bed / Love conquers all / Fortuneteller / Too much is not enough / Wicked ways. *(re-iss. cd Apr94; 74321 18719-2)*

Feb 91. (7"/c-s) *(PB/PK 49225)* **LOVE CONQUERS ALL. / TRUTH HURTS** [57] [ ]
(12"+=)(12"pic-d+=)(cd-s+=) *(PT 49212)(PT 49224)(PD 49226)* – Slow down sister.

— early 70s line-up again after TURNER was sacked.

R.C.A. Giant

Jul 93. (cd/c/lp) *(74321 15240-2/-4/-1) <24517>* **THE BATTLE RAGES ON** [21] [ ]
– The battle rages on / Lick it up / Anya / Talk about love / Time to kill / Ramshackle man / A twist in the tale / Nasty piece of work / Solitaire / One man's meat. *(re-iss. cd Oct95; same)*

Arista Arista

Nov 94. (cd/c/d-lp) *(<74321 23416-2/-4/-1>)* **COME HELL OR HIGH WATER (live mid-93)** [ ] [ ]
– Highway star / Black night / Twist in the tail / Perfect strangers / Anyone's daughter / Child in time / Anya / Speed king / Smoke on the water.

— **STEVE MORSE** – guitar (ex-DIXIE DREGS) repl. JOE SATRIANI who repl. BLACKMORE on European tour late '93-mid '94

R.C.A. C.M.C.

Feb 96. (cd/c) *(74321 33802-2/-4) <86201>* **PURPENDICULAR** [58] [ ]
– Vavoom: Ted the mechanic / Loosen my strings / Soon forgotten / Sometimes I feel like screaming / Cascades: I'm not your lover / The aviator / Rosa's cantina / A castle full of rascals / A touch away / Hey Cisco / Somebody stole my guitar / The purpendicular waltz.

May 98. (cd) *(495306-2) <86250>* **ABANDON** [ ] [ ]
– Any fule kno that / Almost human / Don't make me happy / Seventh heaven / Watching the sky / Fingers to the bone / Jack Ruby / She was / Whatsername / 69 / Evil Louie / Bludsucker.

— next with The LONDON SYMPHONY ORCHESTRA

Eagle Spitfire

Jan 00. (d-cd) *(EDGCD 124) <15068>* **LIVE AT THE ROYAL ALBERT HALL (live 1999)** [ ] Feb00 [ ]
– Pictured within / Wait a while / Sitting in a dream / Love is all / Via

Miami / That's why God is singing the blues / Take it off the top / Hard road (wring that neck) / Pictures of home / Concerto for group and orchestra / Ted the mechanic / Watching the sky / Sometimes I feel like screaming / Smoke on the water.

— **DON AIREY** – keyboards (ex-RAINBOW) repl. LORD

Capitol Sanctuary

Aug 03. (cd) *(591049-2) <86351>* **BANANAS** [ ] Sep03 [ ]
– House of pain / Sun goes down / Haunted / Razzle dazzle / Silver tongue / Walk on / Pictures of innocence / I got your number / Never a word / Bananas / Doing it tonight / Contact lost.

Edel Eagle

Oct 05. (cd/d-lp) *(0165554 2/1 ERE) <20083>* **RAPTURE OF THE DEEP** [ ] Nov05 [ ]
– Money talks / Girls like that / Wrong man / Rapture of the deep / Clearly quite absurd / Don't let go / Back to back / Kiss tomorrow goodbye / MTV (*) / Junktard blues / Before time began. *(d-lp + ltd-cd+= *; 0165762ERE) (cd re-iss. Mar06; 0169352ERE)*

– compilations, etc. (selective) –

Sep 72. (d-lp) *Warners; <2644>* **PURPLE PASSAGES** [–] [57]

Jun 75. (lp/c) *Purple; (TPSM/TC-TPSM 2002)* **24 CARAT PURPLE (1970-73)** [14] [–]
– Woman from Tokyo / Fireball / Strange kind of woman / Never before / Black night / Speed king / Smoke on the water / Child in time. *(re-iss. Sep85 on 'Fame' lp/c; FA41 3132-1/-4) (cd-iss. Oct87; CDFA 3132)*

Mar 77. (7"m,7"purple) *Purple; (PUR 132)* **SMOKE ON THE WATER. / CHILD IN TIME / WOMAN FROM TOKYO** [21] [ ]

Sep 77. (7"ep) *Purple; (PUR 135)* **NEW LIVE & RARE** [31] [ ]
– Black night (live) / Painted horse / When a blind man cries.

Jan 78. (lp/c) *Purple; (TPS 3510)* **POWERHOUSE** (early 70's line-up) [ ] [–]

Sep 78. (7"ep) *Purple; (PUR 137)* **NEW LIVE & RARE VOL.2** [45] [ ]
– Burn (edit) / Coronarias redig / Mistreated (live).

Oct 78. (lp/c) *Harvest; (SHSM 2026)* **THE SINGLES A's & B's** [ ] [–]
(re-iss. Nov88 on 'Fame' cd/c/lp; CD/TC+/FA 3212) (cd-iss. Jan93 on 'E.M.I.'; TCEMC 3658)

Apr 79. (lp/c) *Purple; (TPS/TC-TPS 3514)* **THE MARK II PURPLE SINGLES** [24] [ ]

Apr 79. (7"/12") *Harvest; (HAR 5178)* **BLACK NIGHT. / STRANGE KIND OF WOMAN** [ ] [ ]

Jul 80. (lp/c) *E.M.I.; (EMTV/TC-EMTV 25) / Warners; <3486>* **DEEPEST PURPLE** [1] Oct80 [ ]
– Black night / Speed king / Fireball / Strange kind of woman / Child in time / Woman from Tokyo / Highway star / Space truckin' / Burn / Demon's eye / Stormbringer / Smoke on the water. *(cd-iss. Aug84; CDP 746032-2) (re-iss. 1989 lp/c; ATAK/TC-ATAK 138) (re-iss. Jul90 on 'Fame' cd/c/lp; CD/TC+/FA 3239) (cd re-iss. Aug00 on 'Harvest'; CDP 746032-2)*

Jul 80. (7") *Harvest; (HAR 5210)* **BLACK NIGHT. / SPEED KING (live)** [43] [–]

Oct 80. (7"ep) *Harvest; (SHEP 101)* **NEW LIVE & RARE VOL.3** [48] [ ]
– Smoke on the water (live) / The bird has flown / Grabsplatter.

Dec 80. (lp/c) *Harvest; (SHDW 412)* **IN CONCERT 1970-1972** (live) [30] [ ]
– Speed king / Wring that neck / Child in time / Mandrake root / Highway star / Strange kind of woman / Lazy / Never before / Space truckin' / Lucille. *(cd-iss. May92;)*

Aug 82. (lp/c) *Harvest; (SHSP/TC-SHSP 4124)* **DEEP PURPLE LIVE IN LONDON** (live '74) [23] [ ]
– Burn / Might just take your life / Lay down, stay down / Mistreated / Smoke on the water / You fool no one.

Jun 85. (d-lp/d-c) *Harvest; (PUR/TC-PUR 1)* **THE ANTHOLOGY** [50] [ ]
(d-cd iss.Mar91 on 'E.M.I.'; CDEM 1374)

Jun 95. (12"/cd-s) *E.M.I.; (CD/12 EM 382)* **BLACK NIGHT (remix). / SPEED KING (remix)** [66] [–]

Nov 95. (3xcd-box) *E.M.I.; (CDOMB 002)* **BOOK OF TALIESYN / SHADES OF DEEP PURPLE / DEEP PURPLE IN CONCERT** [ ] [–]

Oct 98. (cd/c/d-lp) *E.M.I.; (496807-2/-4/-1)* **THE VERY BEST OF** [39] [ ]
– Hush / Black night / Speed king / Child in time / Strange kind of woman / Fireball / Demon's eye / Smoke on the water / Highway star / When a blind man cries / Never before / Woman from Tokyo / Burn / Stormbringer / You keep on moving / Perfect strangers / Ted the mechanic / Any fule know that. *(d-cd-iss. ; 496808-2)*

Nov 98. (4xcd-box) *Connoisseur; (DPBOX 400)* **ON THE ROAD** (live) [ ] [–]

Jan 00. (d-cd) *Eagle; (EDGCD 124) / Spitfire; <15068>* **LIVE AT THE ROYAL ALBERT HALL with The London Symphony Orchestra** [ ] [ ]

Apr 00. (cd) *Purple; (PUR 303)* **DAYS MAY COME AND DAYS MAY GO (THE CALIFORNIA REHEARSALS JUNE 1975)** [ ] [ ]

Sep 00. (3xcd-box) *E.M.I.; 528344-2)* **SHADES OF / BOOK OF TALIESYN / DEEP PURPLE** [ ] [–]

Sep 00. (cd) *EMI Gold; (528512-2)* **ANTHEMS** [ ] [–]

Jun 05. (t-cd) *E.M.I.; (578591-2)* **THE PLATINUM COLLECTION** [39] [–]

DEF LEPPARD

Formed: Sheffield, England . . . 1977 as ATOMIC MASS by RICI SAVAGE, PETE WILLIS and TONY KENNING. Frontman JO ELLIOT came into the picture not long after and the band adopte the name DEAF LEOPARD, soon altering it to the more rock'n'ro DEF LEPPARD. Additional guitarist STEVE CLARK joined i time for the band's first gigs in July 1978, while FRANK NOO replaced KENNING on drums prior to the band recording thei first single. With finance provided by ELLIOT's father, the grou issued a debut EP on their own label, 'Bludgeon Riffola', entitle 'GETCHA ROCKS OFF' (was the young BOBBY GILLESPIE fan, perchance?). Later that year (1979), with RICK ALLEN takin up permanent residence on the drum stool, and following tour supporting AC/DC etc., the band were signed to 'Vertigo'. Thi prompted a move to London and in 1980, their debut albun 'ON THROUGH THE NIGHT', broke the UK Top 20 althoug it would be America that would initially embrace the band. The were certainly metal, albeit metal of the most easy listening variet and while the critics hated them, their growing army of fans lappe up their every release. Although 'HIGH 'N' DRY' (1981) marke the beginning of their association with MUTT LANGE and wa far more assured in terms of songwriting, DEF LEPPARD's bi break came with 1983's 'PYROMANIA'. Legendary for its use c all manner of studio special effects and state-of-the-art technolog the record revolutionised heavy metal and became the benchmar by which subsequent 80's albums were measured. Yet it wasn't case (as it so often is) of studio flash masking a dearth of genuin talent, DEF LEPPARD were actually capable of turning out finel crafted songs over the course of a whole album. Highly melodic an relentlessly hook-laden, the Americans loved 'PYROMANIA' an its attendant singles, 'PHOTOGRAPH', and 'ROCK OF AGES', th album selling over 7 million copies. Tragedy struck, however, whe RICK ALLEN lost his arm in a car crash on New Year's Eve 1984. true metal warrior, ALLEN soldiered bravely on using a customise drum kit with programmable drum pads and foot pedals. Bearin in mind ALLEN's accident and the band's perfectionist nature, fou years wasn't too long to wait for a new album, and for the majorit of fans the delay was well worth it. A melodic rock tour de force, th album finally broke the band in their home country with three c its attendant singles reaching the UK Top 10, 'LOVE BITES' givin the band their first No.1. Similarly successful across the Atlantic an worldwide, the album sold a staggering amount, DEF LEPPAR staking their claim as the biggest heavy metal act on the plane Ironically, just as the group were entering the big league, trage struck again as STEVE CLARK was found dead in January 1991 aft a prolonged drink/drugs binge. The band recruited elder statesma of rock, VIVIAN CAMPBELL, as a replacement and began wor on the 'ADRENALIZE' (1992) album. While the likes of singl 'LET'S GET ROCKED' bordered on the cringeworthy (if only fc the awful title), the album's glossy pop-metal once again pulled i the punters in their millions. The next few years saw the release c a B-sides/rareties affair, 'RETRO ACTIVE' (1993) and greatest hits collection, 'VAULT' (1995). A new studio set, 'SLANG', eventually graced the racks in 1996, showcasing a more modern sound (ELLIOT had even traded in his poodle mane for a relatively trendy bobbed haircut). A record executive's wet dream, DEF LEPPARD remain radio friendly unit shifters in the true sense of the phrase. Very much a product of their era, and that era being hair metal's late 80's pre-grunge heyday, DEF LEPPARD seemed something of an anachronism come the dawn of the new millennium. Especially with a record as true to form as 'EUPHORIA' (1999), as musuclar and as charismatic a set as the band have recorded yet completely out of sync with trends in music in general and in the rock/metal world especially. While the likes of BON JOVI seem to be able to adapt much more easily, Sheffield's veterans looked to be either unwilling or unable to do so. 'X' (2002) didn't exactly remedy the situation, with the band sounding more and more like candidates for a safe, unchallenging musical middle age. Titled after one of their early classics, 'ROCK OF AGES' (UK variation 'BEST OF'), marked time by consolidating their earlier greatest hits. By May 2006, DL had succumbed to the fatal middle-aged temptation of a full-blown covers set, 'YEAH!'; see below for some eyebrow-raising selections.

• **Songwriters:** Group compositions, except ONLY AFTER DARK (Mick Ronson) / ACTION + HELLRAISER (Sweet) / YOU CAN'T ALWAYS GET WHAT YOU WANT (Rolling Stones) / LITTLE WING (Jimi Hendrix) / ELECTED + UNDER MY WHEELS (Alice Cooper) / ZIGGY STARDUST + REBEL REBEL + DRIVE-IN SATURDAY (David Bowie) / NOW I'M HERE (Queen) / STAY WITH ME (Rod Stewart & The Faces) / 'CAUSE WE ENDED AS LOVERS + LED BOOTS (Jeff Beck) / NO MATTER WHAT (Badfinger) / WATERLOO SUNSET (Kinks) / 20th CENTURY BOY (T. Rex) / ROCK ON (David Essex) / HANGING ON THE TELEPHONE (hit; Blondie) / 10538 OVERTURE (Electric Light Orchestra) / STREET LIFE (Roxy Music) / LITTLE BIT OF LOVE (Free) / THE GOLDEN AGE OF ROCK'N'ROLL (Mott The Hoople) / HE'S GONNA STEP ON YOU AGAIN (John Kongos) / DON'T BELIEVE A WORD (Thin LIzzy). Roadie STUMPUS MAXIMUS covered; PLEASE RELEASE ME (Engelbert Humperdinck).

Album rating: ON THROUGH THE NIGHT (*5) / HIGH 'N' DRY (*6) / PYROMANIA (*7) / HYSTERIA (*7) / ADRENALIZE (*6) / RETROACTIVE compilation (*5) / VAULT 1980-1995 – DEF LEPPARD'S GREATEST HITS compilation (*8) / SLANG (*5) / EUPHORIA (*6) / X (*4) / BEST OF compilation UK (*7) / ROCK OF AGES: THE DEFINITIVE COLLECTION compilation US (*8) / YEAH! (*3)

JOE ELLIOT (b. 1 Aug'59) – vocals / **PETE WILLIS** – lead guitar / **STEVE CLARK** (b.23 Apr'60) – guitar / **RICK SAVAGE** (b. 2 Dec'60) – bass / **FRANK NOON** – drums

Bludgeon Riffola / not iss.

Jan 79. (7"ep) *(SRT-CUS 232)* **THE DEF LEPPARD EP** [ ] [–]
– Ride into the sun / Getcha rocks off / The overture.

Feb 79. (7"m) *(MSB 001)* **RIDE INTO THE SUN / GETCHA ROCKS OFF / THE OVERTURE** [ ] [–]

—— **RICK ALLEN** (b. 1 Nov'63) – drums; repl. FRANK who later joined LIONHEART, then WAYSTED

Vertigo / Mercury

Aug 79. (7"m) *(6059 240)* **GETCHA ROCKS OFF. / RIDE INTO THE SUN / THE OVERTURE** [ ] [–]

Nov 79. (7") *(6059 247)* **WASTED. / HELLO AMERICA** [61] [ ]

Feb 80. (7") *(LEPP 1)* **HELLO AMERICA. / GOOD MORNING FREEDOM** [45] [ ]

Mar 80. (lp)(c) *(9102 040)(7231 028) <3828>* **ON THROUGH THE NIGHT** [15] [51]
– Rock brigade / Hello America / Sorrow is a woman / It could be you / Satellite / When the walls come tumblin' down / Wasted / Rocks off / It don't matter / Answer to the master / Overture. *(re-iss. Jan89 lp/c/cd; 822533-1/-4/-2)*

Jun 80. (7") *<76064>* **ROCK BRIGADE. / WHEN THE WALLS COME TUMBLIN' DOWN** [–] [ ]

Jul 81. (lp/c) *(6359/7150 045) <4021>* **HIGH 'N' DRY** [26] [38]
– High 'n' dry (Saturday night) / You got me runnin' / Let it go / Another hit and run / Lady Strange / Mirror, mirror (look into my eyes) / No no no / Bringin' on the heartbreak / Switch 625. *<US re-iss. May84 +=; 818836>* – Bringin' on the heartbreak (remix) / Me and my wine. *(re-iss. Jan89 lp/c/cd+=; 818836-1/-4/-2)* – You got me runnin' (remix) / Me and my wine.

Aug 81. (7") *(LEPP 2) <76120>* **LET IT GO. / SWITCH 625** [ ] [ ]

Jan 82. (7") *(LEPP 3)* **BRINGIN' ON THE HEARTACHE (remix). / ME AND MY WINE** [ ] [–]
(12"+=) *(LEPP 3-12)* – You got me runnin'.

—— **PHIL COLLEN** (b. 8 Dec'57) – lead guitar (ex-GIRL) repl. PETE

Jan 83. (7") *(VER 5) <811215>* **PHOTOGRAPH. / BRINGIN' ON THE HEARTBREAK** [66] [–]
(12"+=) *(VERX 5)* – Mirror, Mirror (look into my eyes).

Feb 83. (7") *<811215>* **PHOTOGRAPH. / ACTION! NOT WORDS** [–] [12]

Mar 83. (lp/c) *(VERS/+C 2) <810308>* **PYROMANIA** [18] Jan83 [2]
– Rock! rock! (till you drop) / Photograph / Stagefright / Too late for love / Die hard the hunter / Foolin around / Rock of ages / Comin' under fire / Action! not words / Billy's got a gun. *(cd-iss. 1988; 810308-2)*

Jun 83. (7") *<812604>* **ROCK OF AGES. / BILLY'S GOT A GUN** [–] [16]

Aug 83. (7"/7"s/ 7"sha-pic-d/12") *(VER/+Q/P/X 6)* **ROCK OF AGES. / ACTION! NOT WORDS** [41] [–]

Aug 83. (7") *<814178>* **FOOLIN'. / COMIN' UNDER FIRE** [–] [28]

Nov 83. (7") *(VER 8) <814178>* **FOOLIN'. / TOO LATE FOR LOVE** [ ] [–]
(12"+=) *(VERX 8)* – High'n'dry.

Jun 84. (7") *<818779>* **BRINGIN' ON THE HEARTBREAK (remix). / ME AND MY WINE** [–] [61]

Aug 85. (7"/7"g-f) *(VER/+G 9)* **PHOTOGRAPH. / BRINGIN' ON THE HEARTBREAK** [ ] [–]
(12"+=) *(VERX 9)* – Mirror, mirror.

—— Remained a 5-piece although RICK ALLEN lost an arm in a car crash (31st December '84). He now used a specially adapted programmable drum pads and foot pedals.

Jul 87. (7") *(LEP 1)* **ANIMAL. / TEAR IT DOWN** [6] [–]
(12"+=/12"red+=) *(LEP X/C 1)* – ('A'extended).
(cd-s++=) *(LEPCD 1)* – Women.

Aug 87. (lp/pic-lp/c)(cd) *(HYS LP/PD/MC 1)(<830675>)* **HYSTERIA** [2] [1]
– Women / Rocket / Animal / Love bites / Pour some sugar on me / Armageddon it / Gods of war / Don't shoot shotgun / Run riot / Hysteria / Excitable / Love and affection. *(cd+=)* – I can't let you be a memory.

Aug 87. (7") *<888757>* **WOMEN. / TEAR IT DOWN** [–] [80]

Sep 87. (7"/7"sha-pic-d/c-s) *(LEP/+S/MC 2)* **POUR SOME SUGAR ON ME. / I WANNA BE YOUR HERO** [18] [–]
(12"+=) *(LEPX 2)* – ('A'extended mix).

Oct 87. (7") *<888832>* **ANIMAL. / I WANNA BE YOUR HERO** [–] [19]

Nov 87. (7"/7"s/c-s) *(LEP/+S/MC 3) <870004>* **HYSTERIA. / RIDE INTO THE SUN ('87 version)** [26] Jan88 [10]
(12"+=/12"s+=) *(LEPX 3/+13)* – Love and affection (live).
(cd-s++=) *(LEPCD 3)* – I wanna be your hero.

Apr 88. (7") *<870298>* **POUR SOME SUGAR ON ME. / RING OF FIRE** [–] [2]

Apr 88. (7"/7"s) *(LEP/+P 4)* **ARMAGEDDON IT! (The Atomic mix). / RING OF FIRE** [20] [–]
(12"+=/12"s+=) *(LEPX/+B 4)* – ('A'version).
(pic-cd-s++=) *(LEPCD 4)* – Animal / Pour some sugar on me.

Jul 88. (7"g-f) *(LEPG 5) <870402>* **LOVE BITES. / BILLY'S GOT A GUN (live)** [11] [1]
(12"+=/12"box+=/cd-s+=) *(LEP X/XB/CD 5)* – Excitable (orgasmic mix).

Nov 88. (7") *<870692>* **ARMAGEDDON IT. / RELEASE ME (STUMPUS MAXIMUS & THE GOOD OL' BOYS)** [–] [3]

Jan 89. (7"/7"s) *(LEP/+C 6)* **ROCKET. / RELEASE ME (STUMPUS MAXIMUS & THE GOOD OL' BOYS)** [15] [–]
('A'-Lunar mix; 12"+=/12"s+=/12"pic-d+=/cd-s+=) *(LEP X/XC/XP/CD 6)* – Rock of ages (live).

Feb 89. (7") *<872614>* **ROCKET. / WOMEN (live)** [–] [12]

—— STEVE CLARK was found dead on the 8th of January '91 after drinking/drugs session. Replaced by **VIVIAN CAMPBELL** (b.25 Aug'62, Belfast, N.Ireland) – guitar (ex-DIO, ex-WHITESNAKE, ex-SHADOWKING)

Mar 92. (7"/c-s) *(DEF/+MC 7) <866568>* **LET'S GET ROCKED. / ONLY AFTER DARK** [2] [15]
(12"pic-d+=) *(DEFXP 7)* – Too late for love (live).
(pic-cd-s+=) *(DEFCD 7)* – Women (live).

Apr 92. (cd/c/lp) *(510978-2/-4/-1) <512185>* **ADRENALIZE** [1] [1]
– Let's get rocked / Heaven is / Make love like a man / Tonight / White lightning / Stand up (kick love into motion) / Personal property / Have

you ever needed someone so bad / I wanna touch you / Tear it down. *(pic-lp iss.Dec92, w / 2 extra tracks; 510978-0) (lp re-iss. Nov99 on 'Simply Vinyl'; SVLP 148)*

Jun 92. (7"/c-s) *(LEP/+MC 7)* *<864038>* **MAKE LOVE LIKE A MAN. / MISS YOU IN A HEARTBEAT** [12] [36]
(12"+=) *(LEPXP 7)* – Two steps behind (acoustic).
(cd-s++=) *(LEPCD 5)* – Action.

Aug 92. (c-s) *<864136>* **HAVE YOU EVER NEEDED SOMEONE SO BAD / ELECTED (live)** [–] [12]

Sep 92. (7"/c-s) *(LEP/+MC 8)* **HAVE YOU EVER NEEDED SOMEONE SO BAD. / FROM THE INSIDE** [16] [–]
(12"pic-d+=) *(LEPXP 8)* – You can't always get what you want.
(cd-s++=) *(LEPCD 8)* – Little wing.

Dec 92. (c-s) *<864604>* **STAND UP (KICK LOVE INTO MOTION) / FROM THE INSIDE (THE ACOUSTIC HIPPIES FROM HELL)** [–] [34]

Jan 93. (7"etched/c-s) *(LEP/+MC 9)* **HEAVEN IS. / SHE'S TOO TOUGH** [13] [–]
(pic-cd-s+=) *(LEPCD 9)* – Let's get rocked (live) / Elected (live).
(12"pic-d) *(LEPX 9)* – ('A'side) / Let's get rocked (live) / Tokyo road (live).

Mar 93. (c-s) *<862016>* **TONIGHT / SHE'S TOO TOUGH** [–] [62]

Apr 93. (7"/c-s) *(LEP/+MC 10)* **TONIGHT. / NOW I'M HERE (live)** [34] [–]
(12"pic-d+=) *(LEPX 10)* – Hysteria (live).
(cd-s+=) *(LEPCD 10)* – Photograph (live).
(cd-s) *(LEPCB 10)* – ('A'side) / Pour some sugar on me / ('A'demo).

Sep 93. (7"/c-s) *(LEP/+MC 12)* *<77116>* **TWO STEPS BEHIND. / TONIGHT (acoustic demo)** [32] Aug93 [12]
(cd-s+=) *(LEPCD 12)* – S.M.C.

— <above single from the film 'Last Action Hero' on 'Columbia' US>

Oct 93. (cd/c/lp) *(<518305-2/-4/-1>)* **RETRO ACTIVE** [6] [9]
– Desert song / Fractured love / Two steps behind (acoustic) / Only after dark / Action / She's too tough / Miss you in a heartbeat (acoustic) / Only after dark (acoustic) / Ride into the sun / From the inside / Ring of fire / I wanna be your hero / Miss you in a heartbeat / Two steps behind.

Nov 93. (c-s,cd-s) *<858080>* **MISS YOU IN A HEARTBEAT (acoustic version) / LET'S GET ROCKED (live)** [–] [39]

Jan 94. (7"/c-s) *(LEP/+MC 13)* **ACTION. / MISS YOU IN A HEARTBEAT (demo)** [14] [–]
(cd-s+=) *(LEPCD 13)* – She's too tough (demo).
(cd-s+=) *(LEPCX 13)* – Two steps behind (demo) / Love bites (live).

Oct 95. (c-s) *(LEPMC 14)* **WHEN LOVE & HATE COLLIDE / POUR SOME SUGAR ON ME (remix)** [2] [–]
(cd-s+=) *(LEPCD 14)* – Armageddon it! (remix).
(cd-s++=) *(LEPDD 14)* – ('A'demo).
(cd-s) *(LEP 14)* – ('A'side) / Rocket (remix) / Excitable (remix).
(cd-s) *(LEP 14)* – ('A'side) / Excitable (remix) / ('A'demo).

Oct 95. (cd/c/lp) *(528656-2/-4/-1)* *<528815>* **VAULT 1980-1995 DEF LEPPARD GREATEST HITS** (compilation) [3] [15]
– Pour some sugar on me / Photograph / Love bites / Let's get rocked / Two steps behind / Animal / Heaven is / Rocket / When love & hate collide / Action / Make love like a man / Armageddon it / Have you ever needed someone / So bad / Rock of ages / Hysteria / Bringin' on the heartbreak. *(cd w/free cd)* – LIVE AT DON VALLEY, SHEFFIELD

Nov 95. (c-s) *<852424>* **WHEN LOVE AND HATE COLLIDE / CAN'T KEEP AWAY FROM THE FLAME** [–] [58]

Apr 96. (c-s) *(LEPMC 15)* **SLANG / ANIMAL (live acoustic)** [17] [–]
(cd-s+=) *(LEPCD 15)* – Ziggy Stardust (live acoustic) / Pour some sugar on me (live acoustic).
(cd-s) *(LEPDD 15)* – ('A'side) / Can't keep the flame away / When love and hate collide (strings and piano version).

May 96. (cd/c/lp) *(<532486-2/-4/-1>)* **SLANG** [5] [14]
– Truth / Turn to dust / Slang / All I want is everything / Work it out / Breathe a sigh / Deliver me / Gift of flesh / Blood runs cold / Where does love go when it dies / Pearl of euphoria. *(cd w/ free cd rec. live in Singapore)* – Armageddon it / Two steps behind / From the inside / Animal / When love & hate collide / Pour some sugar on me.

Jun 96. (c-s) *(LEPMC 16)* **WORK IT OUT / TWO STEPS BEHIND** [22] [–]
(cd-s+=) *(LEPCD 16)* – Move with me slowly.
(cd-s) *(LEPDD 16)* – ('A'side) / ('A'demo) / Truth?

Sep 96. (c-s) *(LEPMC 17)* **ALL I WANT IS EVERYTHING / WHEN SATURDAY COMES** [38] [–]
(cd-s+=) *(LEPCD 17)* – Jimmy's theme / ('A'radio edit).
(cd-s) *(LEPDD 17)* – ('A'side) / 'Cause we ended as lovers / Led boots / ('A'radio edit).

Nov 96. (c-s) *(578838-4)* **BREATHE A SIGH / ROCK! ROCK! (TILL YOU DROP)** [43] [–]
(cd-s+=) *(578839-2)* – Deliver me (live) / Slang (live).
(cd-s) *(578841-2)* – ('A'side) / Another hit and run (live) / All I want is everything (live) / Work it out (live).

Jun 99. (cd/c) *(<546 244-2/212-4>)* **EUPHORIA** [11] [11]
– Demolition man / Promises / Back in your face / Goodbye / All night / Paper sun / It's only love / 21st century sha la la girl / To be alive / Disintigrate / Guilty / Day after day / Kings of oblivion.

Jul 99. (c-s) *(562136-4)* **PROMISES / BACK IN YOUR FACE – GOODBYE – ALL NIGHT (excerpts)** [41] [ ]
(cd-s+=) *(562137-2)* – Under my wheels.
(cd-s) *(562136-2)* – ('A'side) / World's collide / Immortal.

Sep 99. (c-s) *(562288-4)* **GOODBYE / IMMORTAL** [ ] [ ]
(cd-s+=) *(562288-2)* – Burnout.
(cd-s) *(562289-2)* – ('A'side) / Who do you love? / When love and hate collide.

Aug 02. (cd-s) *(063969-2)* **NOW / LET ME BE THE ONE (acoustic) / SNIPPETS / ('A'-video)** [23] [–]
(cd-s) *(063968-2)* – ('A'side) / Stay with me / Rebel rebel.
(cd-s) *(063967-2)* – ('A'side) / Pour some sugar on me (live) / Let's get rocked (live).

Aug 02. (cd) *(<063120-2>)* **X** [14] [11]
– Now / Unbelievable / You're so beautiful / Everyday / Long long way to go / Four letter word / Torn to shreds / Love don't lie / Gravity / Cry / Girl like you / Let me be the one / Scar.

Apr 03. (cd-s) *(9800024)* **LONG LONG WAY TO GO / 10 TIMES BIGGAR THAN LOVE / NOW (acoustic) / ('A'-video)** [40] [–]

Oct 04. (cd) *(9868512)* *<00046470-2>* **BEST OF** (compilation) [6] [–]
– Pour some sugar on me / Photograph / Love bites / Let's get rocked / Two steps behind / Animal / Heaven is / Rocket / When love & hate collide / Action / Long, long way to go / Make love like a man / Armageddon it / Have you ever needed someone so bad / Rock of ages / Hysteria / Bringin' on the heartbreak. *(ltd d-cd+=; 9868511)* – Rock rock (till you drop) / Waterloo sunset / Promises / Slang / Foolin' / Now / Rock brigade / Women / Let it go / Too late for love / High 'n' dry (Saturday night) / Work it out / Billy's got a gun / Another hit and run / Stand up (kick love into motion) / Wasted / Die hard the hunter.

May 05. (d-cd) *<B00046470-2>* **ROCK OF AGES: THE DEFINITIVE COLLECTION** (compilation) [–] [10]
– Pour some sugar on me / Photograph / Love bites / Let's get rocked / TWo steps behind / Animal / Heaven is / Foolin' / Rocket / When love & hate collide / Armageddon it / Have you ever needed someone so bad / Rock of ages / Hysteria / Miss you in a heartbeat / Bringin' on the heartbreak / Switch 625 // Rock rock (till you drop) / Let it go / High 'n' dry (Saturday night) / Too late for love / No matter what / Promises / Mirror, mirror (look into my eyes) / Women / Another hit and run / Slang / Stand up (kick love into motion) / Rock brigade / Now / Paper sun / Work it out / Die hard the hunter / Wasted / Billy's got a gun.

May 06. (cd) *(9857885)* *<5340>* **YEAH!** [ ] [16]
– 20th Century boy / Rock on / Hanging on the telephone / Waterloo sunset / Hell raiser / 10538 overture / Street life / Drive-in Saturday / Little bit of love / The golden age of rock'n'roll / No matter what / He's gonna step on you again / Don't believe a word / Stay with me.

DEFTONES

Formed: Sacramento, California, USA ... 1989, by magnetic frontman CHINO MORENO, plus STEPHEN CARPENTER, CHI CHENG and ABE CUNNINGHAM. One of the more promising acts to have signed to MADONNA's 'Maverick' label (through 'Warners'), DEFTONES released their debut album, 'ADRENALINE' in 1995. Like a gonzoid cross between JONATHAN DAVIS and ZACK DE LA ROCHA, CHINO's incendiary live presence helped the group build up a loyal following. By the release of their next set, 'AROUND THE FUR' (1997), their post-metal noise (with DJ support from 5th member, FRANK DELGADO) had reached fruition, from the sonic assault of the album's opener, 'MY OWN SUMMER (SHOVE IT)' to 'HEADUP' (a collaboration with Sepultura's MAX CAVALERA). After much soul searching and turmoil, the veteran – at least in terms of today's high turnover music scene – Cali noise abusers returned with that difficult third album, 'WHITE PONY' (2000). Older and wiser if no more content with his lot, the perennially pissed off MORENO reflects on his lost youth in 'TEENAGER' while TOOL frontman MAYNARD JAMES KEENAN joins the fray on the poignant 'PASSENGER'. Leaving the rap-metal posturing to the young pretenders, DEFTONES took their foot off the gas while still maintaining a head of steam. With its stark, eponymous title and skull adorned cover, 2003's 'DEFTONES' suggested a statement of intent recorded to claim back territory lost during their lengthy sabbatical. MORENO certainly sounded more aggrieved than ever, and the band had rarely played with so much feral aggression, although it was tempting to lament possibilities opened up on 'WHITE PONY' and left unexplored here. Perhaps MORENO had exhausted his more abstruse creative impulses on the TEAM SLEEP project, a collaboration with DJ CROOK and guitarist TOM WILKINSON. Just when it seemed as if the trio had taken a terminal forty winks, they finally surfaced from hibernation with an eponymous debut album in May 2005. Adjectives like narcoleptic and soporific were on hand as MORENO jettisoned the DEFTONES crunch, layering sheets of undistorted sound in apparent homage to shoegazing trailblazers MY BLOODY VALENTINE, the CATHERINE WHEEL and SLOWDIVE. At least some of these influences were made clear on DEFTONES 'B-SIDES & RARITIES' (2005) collection, which featured a raft of mostly 80s covers.

• **Covered:** THE CHAUFFEUR (Duran Duran) / TO HAVE AND TO HOLD (Depeche Mode) / SAVORY (Jawbox) / WAX AND WANE (Cocteau Twins) / SIMPLE MAN (Lynyrd Skynyrd) / SINATRA (Helmet) / NO ORDINARY LOVE (Sade) / IF ONLY TONIGHT WE COULD SLEEP (Cure) / PLEASE PLEASE PLEASE LET ME GET WHAT I WANT (Smiths).

Album rating: ADRENALINE (*9) / AROUND THE FUR (*8) / WHITE PONY (*6) / BACK TO SCHOOL (MINI MAGGIT) (*6) / DEFTONES (*5) / B-SIDES & RARITIES collection (*5) / Team Sleep: TEAM SLEEP (*6)

CHINO MORENO (b. CAMILO WONG MORENO, 20 Jun'73) – vocals / **STEPHEN CARPENTER** (b. 3 Aug'75) – guitar / **CHI CHENG** (b.15 Jul'70) – bass, vocals / **ABE CUNNINGHAM** (b.27 Jul'73, Long Beach, Calif.) – drums

Maverick Maverick

Oct 95. (cd/c) *<(9362 46054-2/-4)>* **ADRENALINE** [ ] [ ]
– Bored / Minus blindfold / One weak / Nosebleed / Lifter / Root / 7 words / Birthmark / Engine No.9 / Fireal.

— added **FRANK DELGADO** – turntablist

Nov 97. (cd/c) *<(9362 46810-2/-4)>* **AROUND THE FUR** [56] [29]
– My own summer (shove it) / Lhabia / Mascara / Around the fur / Be quiet and drive / Lotion / Dai the flu / Headup / MX.

Mar 98. (7"/c-s) *(W 0432/+C)* **MY OWN SUMMER (SHOVE IT). / ROOT (live)** [29] [ ]
(cd-s+=) *(W 0432CD)* – Nosebleed (live) / Lifter (live).
(cd-s) *(W 0432CDX)* – ('A'side) / Lotion (live) / Fireal swords (live) / Bored (live).

Jun 98. (7") *(W 0445)* **BE QUIET AND DRIVE (FAR AWAY). / ('A'acoustic)** [50] [ ]
(cd-s+=) *(W 0445CD)* – Birthmark (live).
(cd-s) *(W 0445CDX)* – ('A'side) / Engine No.9 (live) / Teething (live).

Jun 00. (cd/lp) *<(9362 47799-2/-1)>* **WHITE PONY** [13] [3]
– Fleticeria / Digital bath / Elite / RX queen / Street carp / Teenager / Knife party / Korea / Passenger / Change (in the house of flies) / Pink maggit. *<US-iss.+=>* – The boy's republic.

Aug 00. (cd-s) *(W 531CDX)* **CHANGE (IN THE HOUSE OF FLIES) / (+ 2 similar versions)** [53] [–]

Mar 01. (m-cd) *<(9362 48082-2)>* **BACK TO SCHOOL (MINI MAGGIT)** [35] [ ]
– Back to school (mini maggit) / Falticeira (live) / Back to school (live) / Nosebleed (live) / Teething (live) / Change (in the house of flies) (live acoustic) / Pink maggit / White pony EPK (short version).

May 03. (7") *(W 605)* **MINERVA. / SINATRA** [15] [–]
(cd-s+=) *(W 605CD)* – Sleep walk.

May 03. (cd) *(9362 48391-2) <48350>* **DEFTONES** [7] [2]
– Hexagram / Needles and pins / Minerva / Good morning beautiful / Deathblow / When girls telephone boys / Battle-axe / Lucky you / Bloody cape / Anniversary of an uninteresting event / Moana.

Sep 03. (7") *(W 623)* **HEXAGRAM. / BLOODY CAPE** [68] Dec03 [ ]
(cd-s+=) *(W 623CD) <42666>* – Lovers / ('A'-video).

Nov 05. (cd) *(8122 73267-2) <76460>* **B-SIDES & RARITIES** (compilation) [ ] Oct05 [43]
– Savory / Wax and wane / Change (in the house of flies) – acoustic / Simple man / Sinatra / No ordinary love / Teenager / Crenshaw punch – I'll throw rocks at you / Black moon / If only tonight we could sleep (live) / Please please please let me get what I want / Digital bath (live) / The chauffeur / Be quiet and drive (far away) – acoustic. *(ltd-cd w/dvd+=; 8122 76460-2)* – (videos).

TEAM SLEEP

CHINO MORENO – vocals / **TODD WILKINSON** – guitar / **DJ CROOK** – programming, DJ / + guests

Maverick Maverick

May 05. (cd) *<(9362 48160-2)>* **TEAM SLEEP** [ ] [52]
– Ataraxia / Ever (foreign flag) / Your skull is red / Princeton review / Blvd. nights / Delorian / Our ride to the rectory / Tomb of Liegia / Elizabeth / Staring at the queen / Ever since WWI / King Diamond / Live from the stage / Paris arm / 11/11.

DELAYS

Formed: Southampton, England . . . 2001 as CORKY by band of brothers GREG and AARON GILBERT, and COLIN and ROWLY FOX. After a one-off single, 'SAFETY IN NUMBERS' as IDORU, Geoff Travis promoted them from 'Blanco Y Negro' to 'Rough Trade', albeit with new moniker, DELAYS. Over a series of progressively higher profile 45's (most memorably the UK Top 20 hit 'LONG TIME COMING'), the band swapped the South Coast of Blighty for West Coast Pacific, mimicking FLEETWOOD MAC's transition from Brit-rockers to L.A. FM staples. Critics fell over themselves to point out the striking STEVIE NICKS connection, marvelling over how an English geezer could sound so much like a 70s soft-rock siren. 'FADED SEASIDE GLAMOUR' (2004) wasn't exactly 'Rumours' but it was a minor, UK Top 20 pop masterpiece, distinguishing itself from the New Wave of New Wave of New Wave (KAISER CHIEFS, the KILLERS, et al), with more melodious references to the LA's, the HOLLIES or even the BYRDS. Unusually for a British indie band, DELAYS recorded their UK Top 30 follow-up, 'YOU SEE COLOURS' (2006), at PETER GABRIEL's distinguished 'Real World' studios, creating another laboriously crafted homage to unchained melody.

• **Covers:** RIDE IT ON (Mazzy Star) / BEAUTIFUL BOY (John Lennon).

Album rating: FADED SEASIDE GLAMOUR (*8) / YOU SEE COLOURS (*7)

GREG GILBERT – vocals, guitar / **AARON GILBERT** – keyboards, vocals / **COLIN FOX** – bass, vocals / **ROWLY FOX** – drums

Blanco Y Negro not iss.

Nov 01. (cd-s; as IDORU) *(NEG 139)* **SAFETY IN NUMBERS. / STARK DEVOTION** [ ] [–]
(cd-s+=) *(NEG 139CD)* – Overlover.

Rough Trade Rough Trade

Apr 03. (cd-s) *(RTRADESCD 085)* **NEARER THAN HEAVEN / WAY SMOOTH / OVER AND OUT** [ ] [–]

Jul 03. (7") *(RTRADES 103)* **HEY GIRL. / ZERO ZERO ONE** [40] [–]
(cd-s+=) *(RTRADESCD 102)* – Overlover.
(cd-s) *(RTRADESCD 103)* – ('A') / Whenever you fall I die / ('A'-video).

Nov 03. (7") *(RTRADES 153)* **RIDE IT ON. / (other by the VEILS)** [ ] [–]

Jan 04. (7"mustard) *(RTRADES 136)* **LONG TIME COMING. / HAND ME DOWNS** [16] [–]
(dvd-s+=) *(RTRADESDV 136)* – ('A'-video) / Swallowing the silence.
(cd-s) *(RTRADESCD 136)* – ('A') / Chicago.

Mar 04. (7") *(RTRADS 175)* **NEARER THAN HEAVEN. / WHEN YOU FALL I DIE (acoustic)** [21] [–]
(cd-s) *(RTRADSCD 175)* – ('A') / Quiet / Long time coming (live).
(dvd-s) *(RTRADSDVD 175)* – ('A'-video) / Waysmooth / Over and out (acoustic demo) / ('A').

Apr 04. (cd) *(RTRADCD 114)* <83238> **FADED SEASIDE GLAMOUR** 17 May04
– Wanderlust / Nearer than Heaven / Long time coming / Bedroom scene / No ending / You wear the sun / Hey girl / Stay where you are / There's water here / Satellites lost / One night away / On. *(ltd-cd w/dvd+=; RTRADDVCD 114)* – (DVD tracks).

Nov 04. (7") *(RTRADS 197)* **LOST IN A MELODY. / ONE NIGHT AWAY (live acoustic)** 28 –
(cd-s) *(RTRADSCD 197)* – ('A') / Wanderlust / ('A'-Tom Middleton cosmos remix).
(dvd-s) *(RTRADSDVD 197)* – ('A'-video) / Wanderlust (live) / Osaka blades.

Feb 06. (7") *(RTRADS 265)* **VALENTINE. / TALKING ME DOWN** 23 –
(cd-s) *(RTRADSCD 265)* – ('A') / Someday soon you're gonna happen.
(cd-s) *(RTRADSCDX 265)* – ('A') / Shadows on our school / ('A'-Freeform 5 remix) / ('A'-video).

Mar 06. (cd/lp) *(RTRAD CD/LP 214)* **YOU SEE COLOURS** 24 –
– You and me / Valentine / This towns religion / Sink like a stone / Too much in your life / Winters memory of summer / Given away / Hideaway / Lillian / Out of nowhere / Waste of space.

May 06. (7") *(RTRADS 336)* **HIDEAWAY. / BEAUTIFUL BOY** 35 –
(cd-s) *(RTRADSCD 336)* – ('A') / Broken pylons.
(cd-s) *(RTRADSCDX 336)* – ('A') / Valentine (Torch Team remix) / A glow like honey / ('A'-video).

the DELGADOS

Formed: Glasgow, Scotland ... late 1994 by ex-university graduates, ALUN WOODWARD, EMMA POLLOCK, STEWART HENDERSON and PAUL SAVAGE. Not only did they kickstart Scotland's flagging (nae, virtually dead) indie scene, they did it by initiating their own imprint, 'Chemikal Underground'. The label's debut, 'MONICA WEBSTER', was greatly received by the music press and of course, who else? DJ John Peel, their angular guitar reminiscent of PAVEMENT, although ALUN and EMMA's twee vocal touches called to mind BELLE & SEBASTIAN. Single after single continued to impress until the excellent debut album, 'DOMESTIQUES', surfaced in late '96. Their "difficult" second album, 'PELOTON' (1998), managed to crack the UK Top 60, spurred on by indie hits, 'PULL THE WIRES FROM THE WALL' and 'THE WEAKER ARGUMENT DEFEATS THE STRONGER'. But perhaps it was their third and most accomplished set, 'The GREAT EASTERN' (named after a shelter in Glasgow's East end) which secured the group's ever growing reputation. For one, the album itself had not one weak point among the ten-or-so tracks, which segued like needle into thread. The DELGADOS – or "slim ones" to Spanish speaking GRD readers – owe much of this feat to the whistling flutes, assortment of horns and ambiguous use of orchestration which popped up throughout the set's dizzying array of songs. Stand out tracks included 'AMERICAN TRILOGY', 'AYE TODAY' and the frail accompaniment of closing number, 'MAKE YOUR MOVE'. Although the album failed to crack the mainstream, it did reach the minor regions of the charts, as did aforementioned single 'AMERICAN TRILOGY'. Battening down once again in the 'Chemikal Underground' bunker, the DELGADOS worked alongside DAVID FRIDMANN (original MERCURY REV-er) on 'UNIVERSAL AUDIO' (2004), shifting the emphasis to the melodies and drawing critical comparisons with mid-period XTC. The many and varied sessions recorded with the late great John Peel were anthologised on 'THE COMPLETE BBC PEEL SESSIONS' (2006), the nearest thing to a career overview they've yet released.

• **Covers:** THE DIRGE (New Bad Things) / SACRE CHARLEMAGNE (France Gall) / A VERY CELLULAR SONG (Incredible String Band) / HOW CAN WE HANG ON TO A DREAM? (Tim Hardin) / MR. BLUE SKY (Electric Light Orchestra) / CALIFORNIA UBER ALLES (Dead Kennedys) / LAST ROSE OF SUMMER (Ewan MacColl) / PARCEL OF ROGUES (Robert Burns; trad).

Album rating: DOMESTIQUES (*9) / PELOTON (*8) / THE GREAT EASTERN (*8) / HATE (*8) / UNIVERSAL AUDIO (*7) / THE COMPLETE BBC PEEL SESSIONS compilation (*8)

ALUN WOODWARD – vocals, guitar / **EMMA POLLOCK** – vocals, guitar / **STEWART HENDERSON** – bass / **PAUL SAVAGE** – drums

Chemikal Underground / March

Jul 95. (7") *(chem 001)* **MONICA WEBSTER. / BRAND NEW CAR** –

Aug 95. (7"ep/cd-ep) *(SCAN/+CS 07)* **THE LAZARWALKER EP** –
– Primary alternative / Lazarwalker / Buttonhole / Blackwell.
(above iss. on 'Radarscope') (below iss. on 'Boa'; B-side alter-ego)

Dec 95. (ltd-7") *(HISS 4)* **LIQUIDATION GIRL. / Van Impe: unknown** –

Dec 95. (7"; various artists) *<che 47>* **I've Only Just Started To Breathe** –

Mar 96. (7"ep/cd-ep) *(chem 004/+cd)* **CINECENTRE. / THIRTEEN GLIDING PRINCIPLES / M. EMULATOR** –

Aug 96. (7"ep/cd-ep) *(chem 006/+cd)* **UNDER CANVAS / EEN TELF. / BEAR CLUB / STRATHCONA** –

Oct 96. (7") *(100gm 18)* **BOOKER T JONES. / (other track by URUSEI YATSURA)** – Japan –
– Booker T Jones / (other track by URUSEI YATSURA).
(above on Japanese '100 Guitar Mania' via 'Stolen Ecstasy' series)

Oct 96. (7"ep/cd-ep) *(chem 008/+cd)* **SUCROSE / CHALK. / EUROSPRINT / THE DIRGE** –

Nov 96. (lp/cd) *(chem 009/+CD)* <MAR 027> **DOMESTIQUES**
– Under canvas under wraps / Leaning on a cane / Strathcona slung / Tempered; not tamed / One more question / Big business in Europe / Falling & landing / Akumulator / Sucrose / Pinky / Friendly conventions / Smaller mammals / 4th channel / d'Estus morte.

Jun 97. (7") *(LISS 20)* **SACRE CHARLEMAGNE. / (other by The NEW BAD THINGS)** –
(above release on 'Lissys')

Mar 98. (d7"/cd-s) *(chem 022/+cd)* **EVERYTHING GOES AROUND THE WATER. / BLACKPOOL / THE DROWNED AND THE SAVED** –

May 98. (7") *(chem 023)* **PULL THE WIRES FROM THE WALL. / MAURON CHANSON** 69 –
(cd-s+=) *(chem 023cd)* – Mark the day.

Jun 98. (cd) *(chem 024cd)* **PELOTON** 56 –
– Everything goes around the water / The arcane model / The actress / Clarinet / Pull the wires from the wall / Repeat failure / And so the talking stopped / Don't stop / Blackpool / Russian orthodox / The weaker argument defeats the stronger.

Sep 98. (7") *(chem 029)* **THE WEAKER ARGUMENT DEFEATS THE STRONGER. / A VERY CELLULAR SONG** –
(cd-s+=) *(chem 029cd)* – The actress – Irian Jaya remix.

Chemikal Underground / Beggar Banquet

Apr 00. (lp/cd) *(chem 040/+cd)* <81021> **THE GREAT EASTERN** 72 May00
– The past that suits you best / Accused of stealing / American trilogy / Reasons for silence / Thirteen gliding principles / No danger / Aye today / Witness / Knowing when to run / Make your move.

May 00. (7") *(chem 039)* **AMERICAN TRILOGY. / EUPHORIA HEIGHTS** 61 –
(cd-s+=) *(chem 039cd)* – How can we hang on to a dream?
(cd-s+=) *(chem 039cdx)* – ('A'-CD rom) / Make your move.

Sep 00. (7") *(chem 044)* **NO DANGER. / THE CHOICES YOU'VE MADE** –
(cd-s+=) *(chem 044cd)* – Don't sleep.

Mantra / Mantra

Sep 02. (7") *(MNT 75)* **COMING IN FROM THE COLD. / COALMAN** –
(cd-s+=) *(MNT 75CD)* – Crutches.

Oct 02. (cd/lp) *(MNT CD/LP 1031)* <81034> **HATE** 57 Jan03
– The light before we land / All you need is hate / Woke from dreaming / The drowning years / Coming in from the cold / Child killers / Favours / All rise / Never look at the sun / If this is a plan. *<US cd+=>* – Coalman / Mad drums / Coming in from the cold (video). *(cd re-iss. Jan04; MNTCD 1031)*

Feb 03. (7") *(MNT 79)* **ALL YOU NEED IS HATE. / MAD DRUMS** 72 –
(cd-s+=) *(MNT 79CD)* – Mr Blue Sky.

		Chemikal Underground	Chemikal Underground
Sep 04.	(7"/cd-s) *(Chem 073/+cd)* **EVERYBODY COME DOWN. / DON'T LEAVE CLEAN / I SEE SECRETS**	67	-
Sep 04.	(cd/lp) *(Chem 075 cd/lp)* <860206> **UNIVERSAL AUDIO**		

– I fought the angels / Is this all that I came for? / Come undone / Get action! / Sink or swim / Bits of bone / The city consumes us / Girls of valour / Keep on breathing / Now and forever.

– compilations, etc. –

Sep 97.	(cd) *Strange Fruit; (SFRSCD 037)* **THE BBC SESSIONS**		-

– Primary alternative / I've only just started to breathe / Lazarwalker / Indian fables / Under canvas under wraps / Sucrose / Teen elf / Thirteen gliding principles / Friendly conventions / Tempered; not tamed / Falling and landing. *(re-iss. May00; same)*

Jun 06.	(d-cd) *Chemikal Underground; (Chem 088cd)* **THE COMPLETE BBC PEEL SESSIONS**		-

– Lazarwalker / Blackwell / I've only just started to breathe / Primary alternative / Under canvas under wraps / 4th channel / Teen elf / Sucrose / Everything goes around the water / The Arvane motel / Pull the wires from the wall / Mauron chanson / Repeat failure / Don't stop / Blackpool / The weaker argument defeats the stronger // No danger / Make your move / Accused of stealing / Aye today / Mr. Blue sky / California uber alles / Matthew and son / Last rose of summer / Parcel of rogues / I fought the angels / Ballad of accounting / Is this all that I came for? / Everybody come down.

DEPECHE MODE

Formed: Basildon, Essex, England . . . 1976 by VINCE CLARKE, MARTIN GORE and ANDY FLETCHER while still at school. The line-up was completed by frontman DAVE GAHAN, and by 1980 they had adopted the DEPECHE MODE moniker, immersing themselves in the London 'New Romantic' scene which spawned the likes of SPANDAU BALLET and VISAGE. After gigging around the capital and having a track, 'PHOTOGRAPHIC', included on the 'Some Bizzare Album' various artists collection, the band were picked up by the fledgling 'Mute' label. While their debut single, 'DREAMING OF ME', scraped the lower regions of the chart in 1981, a follow-up, 'NEW LIFE', almost made the Top 10. Dominated by synthesizers and drum machines, yet retaining a keen sense of melody, the band initially took their cue from KRAFTWERK. As evidenced on their insanely catchy Top 10 breakthrough, 'JUST CAN'T GET ENOUGH' (the first of 24 consecutive Top 30 hits), their lyrics weren't quite as enigmatic as their Teutonic heroes, although they improved with time. The success of the single (which no doubt still gets played ten times a night in French discos!) paved the way for the debut album, 'SPEAK AND SPELL' (1981), a promising collection of catchy synth-pop fare which made the UK Top 10. Chief songwriter VINCE CLARKE quit shortly after, going on to pastures new with YAZOO and then ERASURE, GORE taking up the pensmith chores for the follow-up album, 'A BROKEN FRAME' (1982). Shortly after its release, ALAN WILDER, who had previously toured with the band, was recruited as a full time replacement for CLARKE. Like its predecessor, 'CONSTRUCTION TIME AGAIN' (1983) failed to make any significant leap forward from the debut, musically at least, although it did contain the classic 'EVERYTHING COUNTS', GAHAN's voice summoning up as much portentous doom as he could muster. While the 'PEOPLE ARE PEOPLE' single gave the band valuable exposure in America, their real breakthrough came with 1984's 'SOME GREAT REWARD'. Featuring the likes of 'BLASPHEMOUS RUMOURS' and 'MASTER AND SERVANT', the album was palpably darker, the music more satisfyingly varied. 'BLACK CELEBRATION' (1986) was deliberately darker still, much of the material creeping along at a funereal pace. 'MUSIC FOR THE MASSES' (1987) was the band's biggest Stateside success to date, the material for the live album, '101' (1989) coming from the American leg of their 1988 sell-out world tour. 'VIOLATOR' (1990) was heralded as DEPECHE MODE's best work since 'SOME GREAT REWARD', spawning two of their better singles in 'PERSONAL JESUS' and the uncharacteristically emotional 'ENJOY THE SILENCE'. Never the warmest sounding band, with 'SONGS OF FAITH AND DEVOTION' (1993) their clinical sound was softened somewhat with a move towards more rock-centric territory. That's not to say the music was soft, at least not on the single, 'I FEEL YOU', a dirty great guitar riff grinding away relentlessly. Elsewhere, the album had something of a transcendent, redemptive quality about it on such powerful tracks as 'MERCY IN YOU' and 'ONE CARESS'. The record gave the band their first No.1, UK and US, although some longtime fans were understandably miffed at the band's new direction. The mid-90's brought the most turbulent period in the band's long career as GAHAN reportedly attempted suicide amid his battle with drug addiction. Add to that the departure of WILDER (who went to work on solo project RECOIL) and it seemed DEPECHE MODE had reached the end of the line. If nothing else, though, this band are doggedly determined, GAHAN beating his drug problem and enlisting BOMB THE BASS guru TIM SIMENON to help create an enticingly different sound on 1997's 'ULTRA'. No doubt overjoyed that their heroes had been resurrected, the group's staunch fanbase ensured the album would once again top the UK chart. The record was also a blueprint of sorts for 'EXCITER' (2001), maverick production touches supplied this time around by LFO man, MARK BELL. GAHAN's ongoing singing tuition reaped darkly alluring rewards, drawing the listener in to a late-night vigil of brooding acoustica and stained velour romance. This singular atmosphere was carried over, to some extent, with 2003's 'PAPER MONSTERS', GAHAN's tentative solo debut. Unsurprisingly, much of the subject matter concerned the man's not so distant descent into personal chaos, with the likes of 'HIDDEN HOUSES' making emotionally brave attempts to work through his experiences with a clear pen rather than burying it all in metaphor. GORE, meanwhile, had actually beaten GAHAN's release schedule by a few months, making his own solo debut with 'COUNTERFEIT 2' (2003). A belated follow-up to his 1989 mini-set, the album found GORE tackling a range of material with more reverence than originality although the selection was interesting enough in its own right. Back on DEPECHE MODE business, 'REMIXES 81-04', did exactly what it said on the tin, celebrating their pioneering work on twelve inch. Top 10 set, 'PLAYING THE ANGEL' (2005), meanwhile, continued the band's latter day renaissance, taking full advantage of an 80s-amenable climate to create what was roundly acclaimed as their most authentic, claustrophobic album since their heyday. While the very MATT JOHNSON-esque phrasing of 'JOHN THE REVELATOR' would've arguably made a fine lead single, the seasoned synth merchants went with the obvious 'PRECIOUS', which – along with 'A PAIN THAT I'M USED TO' and 'SUFFER WELL' – hit the UK Top 20.

• **Covered:** ROUTE 66 (Chuck Berry) / DIRT (Stooges) / MARTIN L. GORE's covered NEVER TURN YOUR BACK ON MOTHER EARTH (Sparks) / MOTHERLESS CHILD (John Lennon) / COMPULSION (Joe Crow) / IN A MANNER OF SPEAKING (Tuxedomoon) / GONE GONE GONE (Comsat Angels) / SMILE IN THE CROWD (Durutti Column) / COMING BACK TO YOU (Leonard Cohen) / IN MY TIME OF DYING (trad.) / STARDUST (David Essex) / I CAST A LONESOME SHADOW (Russwurm – Thompson) / IN MY OTHER WORLD (Julee Cruise) / LOVERMAN (Nick Cave) / BY THIS RIVER (Eno & Cluster) / LOST IN THE STARS (Anderson – Weill) / DAS LIED VOM EINSAMEN MADCHEN (Gilbert – Heymann) / TINY GIRLS (Iggy Pop) / CANDY SAYS (Lou Reed).

Album rating: SPEAK & SPELL (*6) / A BROKEN FRAME (*6) / CONSTRUCTION TIME AGAIN (*7) / SOME GREAT REWARD (*7) / THE SINGLES 1981-1985 compilation (*9) / BLACK CELEBRATION (*8) / MUSIC FOR THE MASSES (*7) / 101 live soundtrack (*5) / VIOLATOR (*7) / SONGS OF

FAITH & DEVOTION (*7) / SONGS OF LOVE & DEVOTION LIVE (*3) / ULTRA (*6) / THE SINGLES 86>98 compilation (*7) / EXCITER (*6) / REMIXES 81-04 collection (*5) / PLAYING THE ANGEL (*7) / Martin L. Gore: COUNTERFEIT mini (*4) / COUNTERFEIT 2 (*5) / Dave Gahan: PAPER MONSTERS (*6)

VINCE CLARKE (b. 3 Jul'60, South Woodford, England) – keyboards, synthesiser / **DAVID GAHAN** (b. 9 May'62, Epping, England) – vocals / **MARTIN GORE** (b.23 Jul'61) – keyboards, synthesizer, vocals / **ANDY FLETCHER** (b. 8 Jul'61, Nottingham, England) – guitar, synthesiser, drum machine

Mute Sire

Mar 81. (7") *(MUTE 013)* **DREAMING OF ME. / ICE MACHINE** 57
Jun 81. (7") *(MUTE 014)* **NEW LIFE. / SHOUT!** 11
(12") *(12MUTE 014)* – ('A'extended) / ('B'-Rio mix).
Sep 81. (7") *(MUTE 016)* **JUST CAN'T GET ENOUGH. / ANY SECOND NOW** 8 –
(12") *(12MUTE 016)* – ('A'-Schizo mix) / ('B'-altered).
Oct 81. (lp/c) *(STUMM/CSTUMM 5)* <3642> **SPEAK & SPELL** 10
– New life / Just can't get enough / I sometimes I wish I was dead / Puppets / Boys say go / No disco / What's your name / Photographic / Tora! Tora! Tora! / Big Muff / Any second now. *(cd-iss. Apr88 +=; CDSTUMM 5)* – Dreaming of me / New life (extended) / Shout! (Rio mix) / Any second now (altered mix).
Nov 81. (7") **JUST CAN'T GET ENOUGH. / TORA! TORA! TORA!** –

— **ALAN WILDER** (b. 1 Jun'59, London, England) – electronics (ex-HITMEN) repl. VINCE who formed YAZOO

Jan 82. (7"/ext.12") *(MUTE/12MUTE 018)* **SEE YOU. / NOW, THIS IS FUN** 6 Aug82
Apr 82. (7") *(MUTE 022)* **THE MEANING OF LOVE. / OBERKORN (IT'S A SMALL TOWN)** 12
(12") *(12MUTE 022)* – ('A'extended) / ('B'-Fairly odd mix).
Aug 82. (7") *(7BONG 1)* **LEAVE IN SILENCE. / EXCERPT FROM MY SECRET GARDEN** 18
(ext.12"+=) *(12BONG 1)* – ('A'quieter version).
Sep 82. (lp/c) *(STUMM/CSTUMM 9)* <23751> **A BROKEN FRAME** 8
– Leave in silence / My secret garden / Monument / Nothing to fear / See you / Satellite / The meaning of love / A photograph of you / Shouldn't have done that / The sun and the rainfall. *(cd-iss. Jul88; CDSTUMM 13)*
Feb 83. (7"/ext.12") *(7/12 BONG 2)* **GET THE BALANCE RIGHT. / THE GREAT OUTDOORS** 13
(12") *(L12BONG 2)* – ('A'side) / My secret garden (live) / See you (live) / Satellite (live) / Tora! Tora! Tora! (live).
Jul 83. (7") *(7BONG 3)* **EVERYTHING COUNTS. / WORK HARD** 6
(12") *(12BONG 3)* – ('A'-larger amounts) / ('B'-East End mix).
(12") *(L12BONG 3)* – ('A'side) / Boys say go (live) / New life (live) / Nothing to fear (live) / The meaning of love (live).
Aug 83. (lp/c) *(STUMM/CSTUMM 13)* **CONSTRUCTION TIME AGAIN** 6 –
– Love in itself / More than a party / Pipeline / Everything counts / Two minute warning / Shame / The landscape is changing / Told you so / And then . . . *(cd-iss. Jul88; CDSTUMM 13)*
Sep 83. (7") *(BONG 4)* **LOVE IN ITSELF. / FOOLS** 21
(12") *(12BONG 4)* – Love in itself (3) / (4) / Fools (bigger).
(12") *(L12BONG 4)* – ('A'side) / Just can't get enough (live) / Photograph (live) / A photograph of you (live) / Shout! (live).
Mar 84. (7") *(7BONG 5)* <29221> **PEOPLE ARE PEOPLE. / IN YOUR MEMORY** 4 May85 13
(12"+=) *(L12BONG 5)* – ('A'-On-U-Sound remix).
(12") *(12BONG 5)* – ('A'different mix) / ('B'-Slik mix).
Jul 84. (lp) <25124> **PEOPLE ARE PEOPLE** – 71
– People are people / Everything counts / Get the balance right / Love in itself / Now this is fun / Leave in silence / Told you so / Work hard.
Aug 84. (7") *(7BONG 6)* <28918> **MASTER AND SERVANT. / SET ME FREE (RENOVATE ME)** 9 Aug85
('A'-Slavery whip mix-12"+=) *(12BONG 6)* – ('A'voxless).
('A'-On-U-Sound mix-12"+=) *(L12BONG 6)* – Are people people?.
Sep 84. (lp/c) *(STUMM/CSTUMM 19)* <25194> **SOME GREAT REWARD** 5 Jan85 51
– Something to do / Lie to me / People are people / It doesn't matter / Stories of old / Somebody / Master and servant / If you want to / Blasphemous rumours. *(cd-iss. Sep87; CDSTUMM 19)*
Nov 84. (7") *(7BONG 7)* **BLASPHEMOUS RUMOURS. / SOMEBODY** 16
(7"ep+=) *(7BONG 7E)* – Told you so (live) / Everything counts (live).
(12"+=) *(12BONG 7)* – Ice machine / Two minute warning / Everything counts (live).
May 85. (7"/remix-12") *(7/12 BONG 8)* **SHAKE THE DISEASE. / FLEXIBLE** 18
(12") *(L12BONG 8)* – Edit the shake / Master and servant (live) / Flexible (deportation mix) / Something to do (metal mix).
Sep 85. (7"/remix-12") *(7/12 BONG 9)* **IT'S CALLED A HEART. / FLY ON THE WINDSCREEN** 18
(ext.d12"+=) *(D12BONG 9)* – ('A'-slow mix) / ('A'-death mix).
Oct 85. (lp/c) *(MUTEL/CMUTEL 1)* <25346> **THE SINGLES 1981-1985** (compilation) <US-title 'CATCHING UP WITH DEPECHE MODE'> 6
– People are people / Master and servant / It's called a heart / Just can't get enough / See you / Shake the disease / Everything counts / New life / Blasphemous rumours / Leave in silence / Get the balance right / Love in itself / Dreaming of me. *(c+=)* – (2 extra). *(cd-iss. Sep87; CDMUTEL 1)*
Feb 86. (7") *(7BONG 10)* **STRIPPED. / BUT NOT TONIGHT** 15
(ext.12"+=) *(12BONG 10)* – Breathing in fumes / Fly on the windscreen (quiet mix) / Black day.
Mar 86. (lp/c) *(STUMM/CSTUMM 26)* <25429> **BLACK CELEBRATION** 4 90
– Black celebration / Fly on the windscreen – final / A question of tlust / Sometimes / It doesn't matter two / A question of time / Stripped / Here is the house / World full of nothing / Dressed in black / New dress. *(cd-iss. Sep87+=; CDSTUMM 26)* – But not tonight / Breathing in fumes / Black day.
Apr 86. (7") *(7BONG 11)* **A QUESTION OF LUST. / CHRISTMAS ISLAND** 28
(free c-s. w/7") *(CBONG 11)* – ('A'-Flood mix) / If you want (live) / Shame (live) / Blasphemous rumours (live).
(ext.12"+=) *(12BONG 11)* – It doesn't matter (instrumental) / People are people (live) / A question of lust (minimal).
Aug 86. (7") *(7BONG 12)* **A QUESTION OF TIME. / BLACK CELEBRATION** 17
(ext.12"+=) *(12BONG 12)* – Stripped (live) / Something to do (live).
(12") *(L12BONG 12)* – ('A'-Newtown mix) / ('A'live) / ('B'-Black tulip mix) / More than a party (live).
Apr 87. (7") *(7BONG 13)* <28366> **STRANGELOVE. / PIMPF** 16 76
('A'-Maximix-12"+=) *(12BONG 13)* – ('A'Midimix).
(cd-s++=) *(CDBONG 13)* – Agent orange.
('A'-Blind mix-12"+=) *(L12BONG 13)* – ('A'-Pain mix) / Agent orange.
Aug 87. (7") *(7BONG 14)* <28189> **NEVER LET ME DOWN AGAIN. / PLEASURE, LITTLE PLEASURE** 22 63
(12"/c-s) *(12/C BONG 14)* – ('A'-split mix) / ('B'-glitter mix) / ('A'-aggro mix).
(cd-s++=) *(CDBONG 14)* – To have and to hold (Spanish taster).
(12") *(L12BONG 14)* – ('A'-Tsangarides mix) / ('B'-join mix) / To have and to hold (Spanish taster).
Sep 87. (cd/d-c/lp,clear-lp) *(CD/C+/STUMM 47)* <25614> **MUSIC FOR THE MASSES** 10 35
– Never let me down again / The things you said / Strangelove / Sacred / Little 15 / Behind the wheel / I want you now / To have to hold / Nothing / Pimpf. *(cd+=)* – Agent orange / Never let me down again (aggro mix) / To have and to hold (Spanish) / Pleasure the treasure (glitter mix). *(d-c+=)* – BLACK CELEBRATION (album)
Dec 87. (7") *(7BONG 15)* <27991> **BEHIND THE WHEEL. / ROUTE 66** 21 61
(c-s+=/cd-s+=) *(C/CD BONG 15)* – ('A'-Shep Pettibone mix) / ('A'-lp version).
(12") *(12BONG 15)* – ('A'-Shep Pettibone mix) / ('B'-Beatmasters mix).
(12") *(L12BONG 15)* – ('A'-Beatmasters mix) / ('B'-Casualty mix).
May 88. (7"import) *(LITTLE 15)* **LITTLE 15. /** 60
Sep 88. (7") <27777> **STRANGELOVE. / NOTHING** – 50
Feb 89. (7") *(7BONG 16)* <40296> **EVERYTHING COUNTS (live). / NOTHING (live)** 22
(12"+=/cd-s+=) *(12/CD BONG 16)* – Sacred (live) / A question of lust (live).
(remix-cd-s) *(CDLBONG 16)* – Strangelove (remix).
(3"cd-s) *(LCDBONG 16)* – ('A'-Tim Simenon & M. Saunders remix) / ('B'-Justin Strauss remix) / Strangelove (Tim Simenon & M. Saunders remix).
(12") *(L12BONG 16)* - **('A'-Bomb The Bass mix) / ('B'-Hijack mix).**
(10") *(10BONG 16)* – ('A'-Absolute mix) / ('B'-US mix) / ('A'-1983 mix).
Mar 89. (d-cd/d-c/d-lp) *(CD/C+/STUMM 101)* <25853> **101** (live soundtrack) 5 45
– Pimpf / Behind the wheel / Strangelove / Sacred * / Something to do / Blasphemous rumours / Stripped / Somebody / Things you said / Black

generation / Shake the disease / Nothing * / Pleasure little treasure / People are people / A question of time / Never let me down again / A question of lust * / Master and servant / Just can't get enough / Everything counts *. *(c+=*/cd+=*)*

Aug 89. (7")<US-c-s> *(BONG 17) <19941>* **PERSONAL JESUS. / DANGEROUS** 13 Nov89 28
(7"g-f+=/12"+=/c-s+=/cd-s+=) *(G/12/C/CD BONG 17)* – ('A'acoustic mix).
('A'pump mix-3"cd-s) *(LCDBONG 17)* – ('A'-Telephone stomp mix).

Feb 90. (c-s/7") *(C+/BONG 18) <19885>* **ENJOY THE SILENCE. / MEMPHISTO** 6 Mar90 8
(cd-s+=) *(LCDBONG 18)* – ('A'-Bassline):- Bassline / Harmonium / Rikki Tick Tick / Memphesto.
(etched-12"/3"cd-s) *(XL12/XLCD BONG 18)* – ('A'-The quad: Final mix).

Mar 90. (cd/c/lp) *(CD/C+/STUMM 64) <26081>* **VIOLATOR** 2 7
– World in my eyes / Sweetest perfection / Personal Jesus / Halo / Waiting for the night / Enjoy the silence / Policy of truth / Blue dress / Clean.

May 90. (c-s/7") *(C+/BONG 19) <19842>* **POLICY OF TRUTH. / KALEID (remix)** 16 Aug90 15
('A'-Trancentral mix; 12"+=/cd-s+=) *(LCDBONG 19)* – ('A'-Pavlov's dub mix).

Sep 90. (12"/cd-s/7") *(12/CD+/BONG 20) <19580>* **WORLD IN MY EYES. / HAPPIEST GIRL / SEA OF SIN** 17 Nov90 52
(12") *(L12BONG 20)* – (first 2 tracks) / ('A'remix).
(c-s+=)(cd-s+=) *(CDLBONG 20)* – Meaning of love / Somebody.

Feb 93. (c-s/7") *(C+/BONG 21) <18600>* **I FEEL YOU. / ONE CARESS** 8 37
(12"+=)(cd-s+=) *(12/CD BONG 21)* – ('A'-Throb mix) / ('A'-Babylon mix).
(12"/cd-s) *(12L/CDL BONG 21)* – ('A'side) / ('A'swamp mix) / ('A'-Renegade Soundwave mix) / ('A'-Helmut mix).

Mar 93. (cd/c/lp) *(CD/C+/STUMM 106) <45243>* **SONGS OF FAITH AND DEVOTION** 1 1
– I feel you / Walking in my shoes / Condemnation / Mercy in you / Judas / In your room / Get right with me / Rush / One caress / Higher love. *(live version of album iss.Dec93; same)*

May 93. (7"/c-s) *(7/C BONG 22) <18506>* **WALKING IN MY SHOES. / MY JOY** 14 69
(12"+=/cd-s+=) *(12/CD BONG 22)* – ('A'-Grungy Gonads mix).
(ext;12"/cd-s) *(L12/LCD BONG 22)* – ('A'-Random Carpet mix) / ('A'-Anandamidic mix) / ('A'-Mark Stent 12" Ambient Whale mix).

Sep 93. (7"/c-s) *(7/C BONG 23)* **CONDEMNATION. / DEATH'S DOOR (jazz mix)** 9
(cd-s+=) *(CDBONG 23)* – Rush (spiritual mix) / Rush (amylnitrate mix).
(12"+=) *(12BONG 23)* – Rush (mixes).
(12"/cd-s) *(L12/LCD 23)* – ('A'live) / Personal Jesus (live) / Enjoy the silence (live) / Halo (live).

Dec 93. (cd) *<45505>* **SONGS OF FAITH AND DEVOTION – LIVE (live)** –

Jan 94. (c-s) *(CBONG 24)* **IN YOUR ROOM (Zephyr mix) / HIGHER LOVE (Adrenaline mix)** 8
('A'-Jeep Rock mix; cd-s+=) *(XLCDBONG 24)* – ('A'-Apex mix).
(12"++=) *(12BONG 24)* – ('A'-extended Zephyr mix).
(cd-s) *(CDBONG 24)* – ('A'-Zephyr mix) / ('A'extended Zephyr mix) / Never let me down again / Death's door.
(cd-s) *(LCDBONG 24)* – ('A'side) / Policy of truth / World in my eyes / Fly on the windscreen (final).
(12"++=) *(L12BONG 24)* – Never let me down again / Death's door.

— ANDREW FLETCHER departed to take over groups' business affairs.

— On the 17th August '95, GAHAN was thought by the music press to have attempted suicide by cutting at his wrists after his wife left him. His record company however said this had been an accident and was over-hyped by the media.

Feb 97. (cd-s) *(12BONG 25) <17409>* **BARREL OF A GUN / PAINKILLER / ('A'-Underworld soft mix) / ('A'-One Inch Punch mix)** 4 47
(12") *(L12BONG 25)* – ('A'-One Inch Punch mix) / ('A'-United mix) / Painkiller (Plastikman mix) / Painkiller.
(cd-s) *(LCDBONG 25)* – ('A'-Underworld hard mix) / ('A'-United mix) / Painkiller (Plastikman mix).
(12") *(12BONG 25)* – ('A'-Underworld hard mix) / ('A'-3 Phase mix) / ('A'-One Inch Punch mix) / ('A'-United mix).

Apr 97. (c-s) *(CBONG 26) <43845>* **IT'S NO GOOD / SLOWBLOW** 5 38
(cd-s+=) *(CDBONG 26)* – ('A'-Bass bounce mix) / ('A'-Speedy J mix).
('A'-Hardfloor mix; cd-s+=) *(LCDBONG 26)* – ('A'-Andrea Parker mix) / ('A'-Motor bass mix).
(12") *(12BONG 26)* – ('A'-Hardfloor mix) / ('A'-Speedy J mix) / ('A'-Motor bass mix) / ('A'-Andrea Parker mix) / ('A'-Dom T mix).

Apr 97. (cd/c/lp) *(CD/C+/Stumm 148) <46522>* **ULTRA** 1 5
– Barrel of a gun / The love thieves / Home / It's no good / Uselink / Useless / Sister of night / Jazz thieves / Freestate / The bottom line / Insight.

Jun 97. (c-s) *(CBONG 27) <17314>* **HOME / IT'S NO GOOD** 23 Nov97 88
('A'-Grantby mix; cd-s+=) *(LCDBONG 27)* – ('A'-Jedi Knights remix: Drowning in time) / Barrel of a gun.
(12") *(12BONG 27)* – ('A'-Jedi Knights remix: Drowning in time) / ('A'-Grantby mix) / ('A'-Air around the golf remix) / ('A'-LFO mix).
(cd-s) *(CDBONG 27)* – ('A'side) / ('A'-LFO mix) / ('A'-The Noodles and the damage done mix).

Oct 97. (cd-s) *(CDBONG 28)* **USELESS / ('A'-Escape From Wherever parts 1&2) / ('A'-Cosmic Blues mix) / BARREL OF A GUN (video)** 28
(12") *(12BONG 28)* – ('A'-The Kruder & Dorfmeister session) / ('A'-CJ Bolland funky sub mix) / ('A-Air 20 mix).
(cd-s) *(LCDBONG 28)* – ('A'-CJ Bolland ultrasonar mix) / ('A'-The Kruder & Dorfmaister session) / ('A'live) / It's no good (CD-rom).

Sep 98. (cd-s) *(CDBONG 29) <44546>* **ONLY WHEN I LOSE MYSELF / SURRENDER / HEADSTAR** 17 61
(12"/cd-s) *(12/LCD BONG 29)* – ('A'-Subsonic legacy remix) / ('A'-Dan The Automator remix) / Headstar (Luke Slater remix).
(12") *(L12BONG 29)* – ('A'remixes) / Painkiller / Surrender.
(cd-s+=) *(XLCDBONG 29)* – World in my eyes.

Sep 98. (d-cd/c/3x12") *(CD/C+/MUTEL 5) <47110>* **THE SINGLES 86>98** (compilation) 5 Oct98 38
– Stripped / A question of lust / A question of time / Strangelove / Never let me down again / Behind the wheel / Personal Jesus / Enjoy the silence / Policy of truth / World in my eyes / I feel you / Walking in my shoes / Condemnation / In your room / Barrel of a gun / It's no good / Home / Useless / Only when I lose myself / Little 15 / Everything counts (live).

Apr 01. (cd-s) *(CDBONG 30) <44982>* **DREAM ON / DREAM ON (Easy Tiger Bertrand Burgalat mix) / DREAM ON (A.S. Dragon version)** 6 85
(12") *(12BONG 30)* – ('A'-Bushwacka tough guy mix) / ('A'-Dave Clarke remix) / ('A'-Bushwacka blunt mix).
(cd-s) *(LCDBONG 30)* – ('A'-Bushwacka tough guy mix) / ('A'-Dave Clarke acoustic) / ('A'-Octagon Man mix) / ('A'-Kid 606 mix).

May 01. (cd/c/lp) *(CD/C+/STUMM 190) <47960>* **EXCITER** 9 8
– Dream on / Shine / The sweetest condition / When the body speaks / The dead of night / Lovetheme / Freelove / Comatose / I feel loved / Breathe / Easy tiger / I am you / Goodnight lovers.

Jul 01. (cd-s) *(CDBONG 31)* **I FEEL LOVED / DIRT / I FEEL LOVED (extended instrumental)** 12 –
(12"+=/cd-s+=) *(12/LCD BONG 31)* – ('A'-Tenaglia's labour of love mix) / ('A'-Thomas Brickman mix) / ('A'-Chamber's remix).

Nov 01. (cd-s) *(CDBONG 32)* **FREELOVE / ZENSTATION / STEREONERD** 19 –
(12") *(12BONG 32)* – (first & third tracks) / ('A'-Console remix) / ('A'-DJ Muggs remix) / ('A'versions).
(cd-s) *(CDLBONG 32)* – ('A'versions).

Feb 02. (12"/cd-s) *(12/CD BONG 33)* **GOODNIGHT LOVERS / WHEN THE BODY SPEAKS (acoustic). / THE DEAD OF NIGHT (Electronicat remix) / GOODNIGHT LOVERS (Isan Falling Leaf mix)** – –

Oct 04. (cd-s) *(CDBONG 34)* **ENJOY THE SILENCE (Timo Maas extended remix) / HALO (Goldfrapp remix)** 7 –
(12") *(12BONG 34)* – ('A') / ('A'-Ewan Pearson remix).
(cd-s+=) *(LCDBONG 34)* – Something to do (Black Strobe remix).
(above extra track actually hit UK 75 in its own right Dec04)

Oct 04. (cd) *(LCDMUTEL 8) <48781>* **REMIXES 81-04** (compilation w/ other artists) 24
(ltd d-cd w/ bonus cd+=; CDMUTEL 8)

Oct 05. (cd-s) *(CDBONG 35)* **PRECIOUS / (Sasha's spooky mix)** 4 71
(12") *(12BONG 35)* – (Sasha's spooky mix – extended) / (Sasha's gargantuan vocal mix – extended).
(12"/cd-s) *(L12/LCD BONG 35) <42831-0>* – (Misc. full vocal mix) / (Michael Mayer Balearic mix) / (Motor remix) / (Misc. crunch mix).
(dvd-s) *(DVDBONG 35)* – (video) / (Motor remix) / (Michael Mayer ambient mix).

Oct 05. (cd/d-lp) *(CD+/STUMM 260) <49348>* **PLAYING THE ANGEL** 6 7
– A pain that I'm used to / John the revelator / Suffer well / The sinner in me / Precious / Macro / I want it all / Nothing's impossible / Introspectre / Damaged people / Lillian / The darkest star. *(ltd-cd w/dvd; LCDSTUMM 260)* – (documentaries & videos).

Dec 05. (cd-s/7"pic-d) *(CD+/BONG 36)* **A PAIN THAT I'M USED TO. / NEWBORN** 15 –
(dvd-s+=) *(DVDBONG 36)* – (making the video).
(12") *(12BONG 36)* – (Jacques Lu Cont mix + dub).
(cd-s+=) *(LCDBONG 36)* – ('A'-mixes; Goldfrapp / Bitstream Spansule / Telex).
(12") *(L12BONG 36)* – (Bitstream Threshold + Spansule mixes).

Mar 06. (7"pic-d) *(BONG 37)* **SUFFER WELL. / THE DARKEST STAR (Monolake remix)** 12 –
(cd-s) *(CDBONG 37)* – ('A') / Better days.
(12") *(12BONG 37)* – ('A'-Tiga remix) / ('A'-Tiga dub) / ('A'-Narcotic THrust vocal dub).
(12") *(L12BONG 37)* – ('A'-Metope remix) / ('A'-Metope vocal) / ('A'-M83 remix) / ('A'-Basteroid 'Dance Is Gone' vocal mix).
(cd-s) *(LCDBONG 37)* – ('A'-remixes; Tiga / Narcotic Thrust vocal dub / Alter Ego / M83 / Metope vocal / Metope).
(dvd-s) *(DVDBONG 37)* – ('A'-video) / ('A'-Alter Ego dub) / Better days (Basteroid 'Dance Is Gone' vocal mix).

Jun 06. (cd-s) *(CDBONG 38)* **JOHN THE REVELATOR / LILIAN** 18 –
(7"pic-d) *(BONG 38)* – ('A'-UNKLE dub) / ('B'-Robag Wruhme Slomoschen kikker).
(12") *(12BONG 38)* – ('A'-Dave is in the disco Tiefschwarz remix) / ('A'-Tiefschwarz dub) / ('B'-Chab dub).
(12") *(L12BONG 38)* – ('A'-Murk mode dub) / ('A'-Boosta club remix) / ('A'-Chab vocal remix).
(cd-s) *(LCDBONG 38)* – ('A'-remixes; Dave is in the disco Tiefschwarz / Murk mode / UNKLE re-construction / Boosta club / Tiefschwarz dub).

– compilations, others, etc. –

on 'Mute' unless otherwise mentioned

Nov 91. (6xcd-ep-box) *(DMBX 1CD)* **SINGLES BOX SET** ☐ –
Nov 91. (6xcd-ep-box) *(DMBX 2CD)* **SINGLES BOX SET** ☐ –
Nov 91. (6xcd-ep-box) *(DMBX 3CD)* **SINGLES BOX SET** ☐ –

MARTIN L. GORE

Mute Sire

Jun 89. (m-cd/m-c/m-lp) *(CD/C+/STUMM 67)* <25980> **COUNTERFEIT** 51 ☐
– Smile in the crowd / Never turn your back on Mother Earth / Gone / Motherless child / Compulsion / In a manner of speaking.

Mute Reprise

Apr 03. (cd-s) *(CDMUTE 296)* **STARDUST / I CAST A LONESOME SHADOW (Stewart Walker remix) / LIFE IS STRANGE** 44 –
(12") *(12MUTE 296)* – ('A'-Atom remix) / ('A'-Atom instrumental) / I cast a lonesome shadow (Stewart Walker instrumental).

Apr 03. (cd/lp) *(CD+/STUMM 214)* <48469> **COUNTERFEIT VOL.2** ☐ ☐
– In my time of dying / Stardust / I cast a lonesome shadow / In my other world / Loverman / By this river / Oh my love / Das lied vom einsamen madchen / Tiny girls / Candy says.

DAVE GAHAN

with various backing

Mute Reprise

May 03. (cd-s) *(CDMUTE 294)* <WB 42620> **DIRTY STICKY FLOORS / STAND UP / MAYBE** 18 Jul03 ☐
(cd-s) *(LCDMUTE 294)* – ('A'mixes).
(12") *(12MUTE 294)* – ('A'-Junkie XL vocal) / ('A'-Junkie XL dub).
(12") *(L12MUTE 294)* – ('A'-Lexicon Avenue vocal) / ('A'-silencerz remix).

Jun 03. (cd/lp) *(CD+/STUMM 216)* <48471> **PAPER MONSTERS** 36 ☐
– Dirty sticky floors / Hold on / A little piece / Bottle living / Black and blue again / Stay / I need you / Bitter apple / Hidden houses / Goodbye.

Aug 03. (cd-s) *(CDMUTE 301)* **I NEED YOU / CLOSER / BREATHE** 27 –
(cd-s) *(LCDMUTE 301)* – ('A'-Ladytronic detoxxmix) / ('A'-Gabriel & Dresden unplugged mix) / ('A'-Jay's summer dub).
(12") *(12MUTE 301)* – ('A'-Gabriel & Dresden unplugged) / ('A'-Jay's summer dub).
(12") *(L12MUTE 301)* – ('A'-Ladtronic detoxxmix) / ('A'-Ladytron detoxxmix intrumental).

Oct 03. (cd-s) *(CDMUTE 310)* **BOTTLE LIVING / HOLD ON / BOTTLE LIVING (Tomcraft vocal)** 36 ☐
(cd-s) *(LCDMUTE 310)* – ('A'-Machinehead lyric mix) / ('A'-Raumschmiere vocal mix) / Hidden houses (Alexander Kowalski remix).
(cd-s) *<42671-2>* – (all tracks above).

□ DEREK & THE DOMINOES
(see under ⇒ CLAPTON, Eric)

□ DESAPARECIDOS (see under ⇒ BRIGHT EYES)

□ DESERT SESSIONS
(see under ⇒ QUEENS OF THE STONE AGE)

DEVO

Formed: Akron, Ohio, USA ... 1972 by two sets of brothers, MARK and BOB MOTHERSBAUGH together with GERALD and BOB CASALE (drummer, ALAN MYERS completed the line-up). From the early 70's, they had been known as The DE-EVOLUTION BAND, before sensibly abbreviating the name to DEVO. This bunch of lab-coated weirdos (taking up The RESIDENTS terminally skewed vision) issued two obscure 45's on their own indie label, 'Booji Boy', which were heavily imported into Britain through leading indie outlet, 'Stiff,' late in 1977. Early the following year, both the double A-sided 'MONGOLOID' / 'JOCKO HOMO' and a hilarious electro-fied rendition of The Rolling Stones' '(I CAN'T GET NO) SATISFACTION', were repressed due to popular demand, the singles subsequently becoming minor chart entries. After a third classic, 'BE STIFF' also hit UK Top 75, the flowerpot-headed, potato-faced futurists secured a deal with 'Virgin' ('Warners' in the US) and continued to inject a quirky humour into the po-faced New Wave movement with a fourth hit, 'COME BACK JONEE'. A debut album, inspiringly titled 'Q: ARE WE NOT MEN? A: WE ARE DEVO!' (produced by BRIAN ENO, who else!?), was released a month later to a confused but appreciative audience who helped propel the record into the Top 20 (Top 100 US). However, their follow-up set, 'DUTY NOW FOR THE FUTURE' (1979), suffered a slight backlash, the novelty wearing thin without the impact of a hit single. 1980's 'FREEDOM OF CHOICE' would have suffered a similar fate, but for a freak US Top 20 single, 'WHIP IT'. The rest of their 80's output lacked their early wit, although America embraced such albums as 'DEV-O LIVE' (1981), 'NEW TRADITIONALISTS' (1981), 'OH NO, IT'S DEVO' (1982) and 'SHOUT' (1984). Having disbanded in the middle of the decade, DEVO (with new drummer, DAVID KENDRICK) reformed in 1988, signing to 'Enigma' and releasing one non-event of an album after another. Their days of inspired innovation now behind them, the legacy of DEVO was nevertheless plundered to unusual effect when SOUNDGARDEN, SUPERCHUNK and even ROBERT PALMER!!! covered their 1980 classic, 'GIRL U WANT'.

• **Songwriters:** GERALD and MARK wrote most of material, SECRET AGENT MAN (Johnny Rivers) / ARE U EXPERIENCED (Jimi Hendrix) / WORKING IN THE COAL MINE (Lee Dorsey). • **Trivia:** In 1982, DEVO had contributed services to choreographer TONI BASIL on her debut solo album 'WORD OF MOUTH'. In the late 70's, MARK had appeared on HUGH CORNWALL (of The STRANGLERS) and ROBERT WILLIAMS collaboration 'Nosferatu'.

Album rating: Q: ARE WE NOT MEN? A: WE ARE DEVO! (*8) / DUTY NOW FOR THE FUTURE (*7) / FREEDOM OF CHOICE (*7) / DEV-O LIVE mini (*2) / NEW TRADITIONALISTS (*6) / OH NO! IT'S DEVO (*6) / SHOUT (*4) / E-Z LISTENING DISC collection (*4) / TOTAL DEVO (*4) / NOW IT CAN BE TOLD (DEVO AT THE PALACE 12/9/88) live (*5) / SMOOTH NOODLE MAPS (*4) / HARDCORE DEVO, VOL.1 compilation (*6) / THE GREATEST HITS compilation (*7) / HARDCORE DEVO, VOL.2 compilation (*5) / DEVO LIVE: THE MONGOLOID YEARS compilation (*4) / HOT POTATOES: THE BEST OF DEVO compilation (*8)

BOB MOTHERSBAUGH – vocals, guitar / **MARK MOTHERSBAUGH** – keyboards, synthesizers / **BOB CASALE** – guitar / **JERRY CASALE** – bass, vocals / **ALAN MYERS** – drums repl. JIM MOTHERSBAUGH

Stiff Booji Boy

Feb 78. (7") *(DEV 1) <7033-14>* **MONGOLOID. / JOCKO HOMO** 62 1977

Apr 78. (7")(12") *(DEV 2)(BOY 1)* **(I CAN'T GET ME NO) SATISFACTION. / SLOPPY (I SAW MY BABY GETTING)** 41 1977
<re-iss. 1978 on 'Bomp'; 72843>

Stiff not iss.

Jul 78. (7"clear,7"lemon) *(BOY 2)* **BE STIFF. / SOCIAL FOOLS** 71 –

Virgin Warners

Aug 78. (7"grey) *(VS 223)* **COME BACK JONEE. / SOCIAL FOOLS** 60 –

Sep 78. (lp/c) *(V/TCV 2106) <3239>* **Q: ARE WE NOT MEN? A: WE ARE DEVO!** 12 78
– Uncontrollable urge / (I can't get no) Satisfaction / Praying hands / Space junk / Mongoloid / Jocko homo / Too much paranoias / Gut feeling – (slap your mammy) / Come back Jonee / Sloppy (I saw my baby getting) / Shrivel-up. *(w/free flexi-7"; VDJ 27) (pic-lp; VP 2106) (re-iss. Mar84 lp/c; OVED/+C 37)*

Jan 79. (7") *<WB 8745>* **COME BACK JONEE. / PRAYING HANDS** –

Jun 79. (7") *(VS 265)* **THE DAY MY BABY GAVE ME A SURPRIZE. / PENETRATION IN THE CENTREFOLD** –

Jun 79. (lp/c) *(V/TCV 2125) <3337>* **DUTY NOW FOR THE FUTURE** 49 73
– Devo corporate anthem / Clockout / Timing X / Wiggly world / Blockhead / Strange pursuit / S.I.B. (Swelling Itching Brain) / Triumph of the will / The day my baby gave me a surprize / Pink pussycat / Secret agent man / Smart patrol – Mr. DNA / Red eye. *(re-iss. Mar84 lp/c; OVED/+C 38)*

Jul 79. (7") *<WBS 49028>* **SECRET AGENT MAN. / RED EYE EXPRESS** –

Aug 79. (7") *(VS 280)* **SECRET AGENT MAN. / SOO BAWLS** –

May 80. (7") *(VS 350)* **GIRL U WANT. / TURN AROUND** –

May 80. (lp/c) *(V/TCV 2162) <3435>* **FREEDOM OF CHOICE** 47 22
– Girl u want / It's not right / Whip it / Snowball / Ton o' luv / Freedom of choice / Gates of steel / Cold war / Don't you know / That's Pep! / Mr. B's ballroom / Planet Earth. *(re-iss. Mar84 lp/c; OVED/+C 39)*

Jul 80. (7") *<WBS 49524>* **GIRL U WANT. / MR. B'S BALLROOM** –

Aug 80. (7") *<WBS 49550>* **WHIP IT. / TURN AROUND** – 14

Nov 80. (7") *(VS 383)* **WHIP IT. / SNOWBALL** 51 –
(12"+=) *(VS 383-12)* – Gates of steel.

Nov 80. (7") *<WBS 49621>* **FREEDOM OF CHOICE. / SNOWBALL** –

Mar 81. (7") *<WBS 49711>* **GATES OF STEEL. / BE STIFF (live)** –

May 81. (m-lp/m-c) *(OVED 1) <3548>* **DEV-O LIVE (live)** Apr81 49
– Freedom of choice (theme song) / Whip it / Girl u want / Gates of steel / Be stiff / Planet Earth.

Jun 81. (7") *<WBS >* **THROUGH BEING COOL. / GOING UNDER** –

Aug 81. (7") *(VS 450)* **THROUGH BEING COOL. / RACE OF DOOM** –

Aug 81. (lp/c) *(V/TCV 2191) <3595>* **NEW TRADITIONALISTS** 50 24
– Through being cool / Jerkin' back 'n' forth / Pity you / Soft things / Going under / Race of doom / Love without anger / The super thing / Beautiful world / Enough said. *(re-iss. Aug87 lp/c; OVED/+C 73)*

Aug 81. (7") *<WBS 47204>* **WORKING IN THE COAL MINE. / PLANET EARTH** – 43
<above & below issued on 'Full Moon' US>

Oct 81. (7") *<WBS 49834>* **BEAUTIFUL WORLD. / ENOUGH SAID** –

Oct 81. (7") *(VS 457)* **WORKING IN THE COAL MINE. / ENOUGH SAID** –

Jan 82. (7") *(VS 470)* **BEAUTIFUL WORLD. / THE SUPER THING** –

Mar 82. (7") *<WBS 50010>* **JERKIN' BACK 'N' FORTH. / MECHA MANIA BOY** –

Oct 82. (7")<US-7"/12"> *(VS 536) <WBS 29931/29906>* **PEEK-A-BOO. / FIND OUT**

Oct 82. (lp/c) *(V/TCV 2241) <23741>* **OH NO! IT'S DEVO!** 47
– Time out for fun / Peek-a-boo / Out of synch / Explosions / That's good / Patterns / Big mess / Speed racer / What I must do / I desire / Deep sleep. *(re-iss. Aug88 lp/c; OVED/+C 122)*

Jan 83. (7") *<WBS 29811>* **THAT'S GOOD. / WHAT MUST I DO** –

Jun 83. (7"/12") *(MCA/+T 822) <52215>* **THEME FROM DOCTOR DETROIT. / (track by James Brown)** May83 59
(above issued on 'M.C.A.' UK / 'Backstreet' US>

Warners Warners

Oct 84. (7") *<29133>* **ARE YOU EXPERIENCED?. / GROWING PAINS** –

Oct 84. (lp/c) *(925 097-1/-4) <25097>* **SHOUT!** 83
– Shout / The satisfied mind / Don't rescue me / The 4th dimension / C'mon / Here to go / Jurisdiction of love / Puppet boy / Please please / Are you experienced?

Mar 85. (7") *(W 9119)* **SHOUT. / C'MON** –
(d7"+=) *(W 9119F)* – Mongoloid / Jocko homo.

—— **DAVID KENDRICK** – drums; repl. MYERS

Enigma Enigma

Jul 88. (lp/c/cd) *(ENVLP/TCENV/CDENV 503) <73303>* **TOTAL DEVO** Jun88
– Baby doll / Disco dancer / Some things never change / Plain truth / Happy guy / Don't be cruel / I'd cry if you died / Agitated / Man turned inside out / Blow up. *(cd re-iss. Mar95 on 'Restless'; 72756-2)*

Jul 89. (3 sided-lp/cd) *(ENVLP/CDENV 532)* **NOW IT CAN BE TOLD (DEVO AT THE PALACE 12/9/88) (live)**
(cd re-iss. Mar95 on 'Restless'; REST 72755-2)

Oct 90. (7") **POST-POST MODERN MAN. / WHIP IT (live)**
(12"+=) – ('A'-Ultra post mix).
(cd-s++=) – Baby doll (mix).

Oct 90. (cd/c/lp) *(CDENV/TVENV/ENVLP 1006) <73526>* **SMOOTH NOODLE MAPS** Jun90
– Stuck in a loop / Post-post modern man / When we do it / Spin the wheel / Morning dew / A chance is gonna cum / The big picture / Pink jazz trancers / Devo has feelings too / Jimmy / Danghaus. *(re-iss. cd Mar95 on 'Restless'; REST 72757-2)*

– compilations, etc. –

Jan 79. (m-lp) *Stiff; (ODD 1)* **BE STIFF** (first 3 singles) –

May 83. (12"ep) *Virgin; (VS 594-12)* **COME BACK JONEE. / WHIP IT / + 2** –

Aug 87. (cd) *Rykodisc; <RCD2 0031>* **E-Z LISTENING DISC** –
(UK-iss.Nov91; same as US)

Oct 90. (cd) *Fan Club; (FC 065) / Rykodisc; <RCD/RLP 10188>* **HARDCORE DEVO, VOL.1** (demos 74-77) Aug90
(re-iss. c Mar94 on 'New Rose'; 422105)

Dec 90. (cd) *Warners; <26449>* **THE GREATEST HITS** –

Dec 90. (cd) *Warners; <26450>* **THE REST: GREATEST MISSES** –

Dec 91. (cd) *Rykodisc; <(RCD 20208)>* **HARDCORE DEVO, VOL.2: 1974-1977** Aug91
(re-iss. c Mar94; RACS 0208)

Oct 92. (cd) *Rykodisc; <(RCD 20209)>* **DEVO LIVE: THE MONGOLOID YEARS (live)**

Jun 93. (cd) *Virgin; (CDV 2106)* **Q: ARE WE NOT MEN? A: WE ARE DEVO / DEV-O LIVE**

Jun 93. (cd) *Virgin; (CDV 2125)* **DUTY NOW FOR THE FUTURE / NEW TRADITIONALISTS**

Jun 93. (cd) *Virgin; (CDV 2241)* **OH NO! IT'S DEVO / FREEDOM OF CHOICE**

Sep 93. (cd/c) *Virgin; (CDVM/TCVM 9016)* **HOT POTATOES: THE BEST OF DEVO** –
– Jocko homo / Mongoloid / Satisfaction (I can't get me no) / Whip it / Girl u want / Freedom of choice / Peek-a-boo / Thru being cool / That's good / Working in a coalmine / Devo corporate anthem / Be stiff / Gates of steel / Come back Jonee / Secret agent man / The day my baby gave me a surprise / Beautiful world / Big mess / Whip it (HMS & M remix). *(lp-iss.Apr01 on 'Simply Vinyl'; SVLP 320)*

Oct 94. (3xcd-box) *Virgin; (TPAK 38)* **THE COMPACT COLLECTION** –
– (Q: ARE WE NOT MEN / DUTY NOW FOR THE FUTURE / OH NO IT'S DEVO!)

Aug 96. (cd-rom) *Discovery: <none>* **ADVENTURES OF SMART PATROL** –

May 00. (d-cd) *Rhino; <(8122 75967-2)>* **PIONEERS WHO GOT SCALPED: THE ANTHOLOGY**

Apr 02. (cd) *Rhino; <76037>* **THE ESSENTIALS** –

DEXYS MIDNIGHT RUNNERS

Formed: Birmingham, England . . . July '78 by ex-KILLJOYS members, KEVIN ROWLAND and AL ARCHER, taking the name from pep pill, 'dexedrine'. With a cast of players including PETE SAUNDERS, PETE WILLIAMS, BOBBY JUNIOR (soon replaced with ANDY 'STOKER' GROWCOTT) and the brass section of Scottish-born "Big" JIM PATTERSON, J.B. BLYTE and STEVE 'BABYFACE' SPOONER, the band set out to emulate their heroes of the mid-60's soul scene. After a minor debut hit with 'DANCE STANCE' (and the replacement of SAUNDERS with ex-MERTON PARKAS/future STYLE COUNCIL man, MICK TALBOT), a brilliant tribute to one such hero, 'GENO' (Washington), saw DEXYS topping the UK charts in Spring 1980. A third single, 'THERE THERE MY DEAR', was issued later that summer, with a debut album, 'SEARCHING FOR THE YOUNG SOUL REBELS', following into the Top 10. Sporting an image inspired by Martin Scorcese's classic 'Mean Streets' movie (i.e. New York dockers) and coupling it with their idiosyncratic 80's take on classic soul, DEXY's were initially the toast of the UK music press. There was dissension in the ranks, however, the bulk of the band leaving in early '81 to form BUREAU; with ROWLAND and PATERSON the only remaining members, they bolstered the line-up with new recruits, BILLY ADAMS, MICKEY BILLINGHAM, PAUL SPEARE, BRIAN MAURICE, SEB SHELTON and STEVE WYNNE. The resulting single, 'SHOW ME', hit the Top 20 later that summer, although a follow-up, 'LIARS A TO E', failed to chart and the group retired to reconsider their approach. Augmenting the group with The EMERALD EXPRESS (that is, fiddlers HELEN O'HARA, STEVE BRENNAN and ROGER MacDUFF), DEXYS re-emerged in Spring '82 with a revamped Irish folk/soul hybrid (not too dissimilar to 'His Band And The Street Choir'-era VAN MORRISON, a rousing cover of Van The Man's 'JACKIE WILSON SAID' making the Top 5 later that year) and a suitably dishevelled gypsy/romantic vagabond image. 'THE CELTIC SOUL BROTHERS' introduced this new approach and although the track just missed the Top 40, a classic follow-up, 'COME ON EILEEN', was a massive transatlantic No.1 smash; not only were DEXYS big news again in Britain, they'd cracked America (albeit briefly) and the subsequent album, 'TOO-RYE-AY (1982) was the most successful of their career. Yet again, however, the line-up splintered and the momentum faltered, the brass section of PATTERSON, MAURICE and SPEAR departing in summer '82. It would be a further three years before the release of 'DON'T STAND ME DOWN', a considerably lower-key effort which enjoyed only a brief sojourn in the charts. A solitary hit single, 'BECAUSE OF YOU' (used as a theme for TV sitcom, 'Brush Strokes') followed in 1986, before DEXYS were consigned to history and ROWLAND faded into musical folklore. Despite his revered talent, the maverick Celtic minstrel had only release one solo set, 'THE WANDERER' in 10 years, with live performances a rarity. However in early 1997, ROWLAND inked a deal with 'Creation' records and finally came up with some new material (including the wearing of kinky lingerie!) for his er, cumback covers set, 'MY BEAUTY' (1999). Actually, apart from his embarrassing OTT attire, the album might've done quite well, although only the appropriately titled 'I CAN'T TELL THE BOTTOM FROM THE TOP' made it worthwhile.

• **Songwriters:** All penned by ROWLAND, except BURNING DOWN THE WALLS OF HEARTACHE (Johnny Johnson & The Bandwagon) / ONE WAY LOVE (Russell-Meade) / SOUL FINGER (Bar-Kays).

Album rating: SEARCHING FOR THE YOUNG SOUL REBELS (*8) / TOO-RYE-AYE (*7) / DON'T STAND ME DOWN (*5) / THE VERY BEST OF DEXYS MIDNIGHT RUNNERS compilation (*8) / Kevin Rowland: THE WANDERER (*4) / MY BEAUTY (*5) / Dexys Midnight Runners: LET'S MAKE THIS PRECIOUS compilation (*7)

KEVIN ROWLAND – vocals, guitar (b.17 Aug'53, Wolverhampton, England) (ex-KILLJOYS, as **KEVIN ROLAND**) / **AL ARCHER** – guitar, vocals (ex-KILLJOYS) / **PETE SAUNDERS** – keyboards / **PETE WILLIAMS** – bass, vocals / **JIMMY PATTERSON** (b. Scotland) – trombone / **J.B. BLYTE** – tenor, saxophone / **STEVE 'BABYFACE' SPOONER** – alto sax / **ANDY 'STOKER' GROWCOTT** – drums; repl. BOBBY JUNIOR

Parlophone | not iss.

Nov 79. (7") *(R 6028)* **DANCE STANCE. / I'M JUST LOOKING** [40] [–]

— **MICK TALBOT** – keyboards (ex-MERTON PARKAS) repl. SAUNDERS

Mar 80. (7") *(R 6033)* **GENO. / BREAKING DOWN THE WALLS OF HEARTACHE** [1] [–]

Jun 80. (7") *(R 6038)* **THERE THERE MY DEAR. / THE HORSE** [7] [–]

Jul 80. (lp/c) *(PCS/TCPCS 7213)* **SEARCHING FOR THE YOUNG SOUL REBELS** [6] [–]
– Burn it down / Tell me when my light turns green / The teams that meet in caffs / I'm just looking / Geno / Seven days too long / I couldn't help it if I tried / Thankfully not living in Yorkshire, it doesn't apply / Keep it / Love (pt.1) / There, there my dear. *(re-iss. 1982 on 'Fame' lp/c;) (cd-iss. Jan88; CZ 31) (lp re-iss. Dec99 on 'Simply Vinyl'; SVLP 154) (cd re-mast.Sep00 on 'E.M.I.'+=; 525600-0)* – Geno (video) / There, there my dear (video).

Nov 80. (7") *(R 6042)* **KEEP IT PART TWO . / ONE WAY LOVE** [ ] [–]

Mar 81. (7") *(R 6046)* **PLAN B. / SOUL FINGER** [58] [–]

— **ROWLAND** + **PATERSON** recruited new guys **BILLY ADAMS** – guitar / **MICKEY BILLINGHAM** – keyboards / **PAUL SPEARE** – tenor sax / **BRIAN MAURICE** – alto sax / **SEB SHELTON** – drums (ex-SECRET AFFAIR) / **STEVE WYNNE** – bass (replaced ARCHER, GROWCOTT and TALBOT who formed BUREAU)

Mercury | Mercury

Jun 81. (7") *(DEXYS 6)* **SHOW ME. / SOON** [16] [ ]

Nov 81. (7") *(DEXYS 7)* **LIARS A TO E. / . . . AND YES, WE MUST REMAIN THE WILDHEARTED OUTSIDERS** [ ] [ ]

— retained **ADAMS, SHELTON, PATTERSON** / + **GIORGIO KILKENNY** – bass repl. WYNNE

DEXYS MIDNIGHT RUNNERS & The EMERALD EXPRESS

— added **HELEN O'HARA** – violin, vocals repl. BILLINGHAM / **STEVE BRENNAN** – violin / **ROGER MacDUFF** – violin

Mar 82. (7") *(DEXYS 8)* **THE CELTIC SOUL BROTHERS. / LOVE (part 2)** [45] [ ]

Jun 82. (7") *(DEXYS 9) <76189>* **COME ON EILEEN. / DUBIOUS** [1] Jan83 [1]
(12"+=) *(DEXYS 9-12)* – Liars A to E (remix).

Jul 82. (lp/c) *(MERS/+C 8) <4069>* **TOO-RYE-AY** [2] Feb83 [14]
– The Celtic soul brothers / Let's make this precious / All in all / Jackie Wilson said (I'm in Heaven when you smile) / Old / Plan B – I'll show you / Liars A to E / Until I believe in my soul / Come on Eileen. *(cd-iss. Jan83; 810054-2) (re-iss. Jul86 lp/c; PRICE/PRIMC 89) (cd re-mast.Mar96; 514839-2) (cd re-iss. Aug00 +=; 542961-2)* – The Celtic soul brothers (video) / Come on Eileen (video).

KEVIN ROWLAND & DEXYS MIDNIGHT RUNNERS

— PATTERSON left June '82, MAURICE and SPEARE left July '82

Sep 82. (7") *(DEXYS 10)* **JACKIE WILSON SAID. / LET'S MAKE THIS PRECIOUS** [5] [ ]
(12"+=) *(DEXYS 10-12)* – T.S.O.P.

Nov 82. (7") *(DEXYS 11)* **LET'S GET THIS STRAIGHT FROM THE START. / OLD (live)** [17] [ ]
(12"+=) *(DEXYS 11-12)* – Respect (live).

Mar 83. (7"/7"s) *(DEXY S/P 12) <811142>* **THE CELTIC SOUL BROTHERS. / REMINISCE PART ONE** [20] May83 [86]
(12"+=) *(DEXYS 12-12)* – Show me.

DEXYS MIDNIGHT RUNNERS

DEXYS MIDNIGHT RUNNERS

—— line-up **ROWLAND, O'HARA & ADAMS / JIMMY PATTERSON** – trombone (returned) + new part-time sessioners / **NICKY GATFIELD** – saxophone / **JULIAN LITTMAN** – mandolin / **JOHN EDWARDS** – bass / **TOMMY EVANS** – steel guitar / **TIM DANCY** – drums / **ROBERT NOBLE** – keyboards, synth / and special guest star **VINCENT CRANE** – piano (ex-ATOMIC ROOSTER)

Sep 85. (lp/c)(cd) *(MERH/+C 56)(822989-2)* **DON'T STAND ME DOWN** [22] [–]
– The occasional flicker / This is what she's like / Knowledge of beauty / One of those things / Reminisce part two / Listen to this / The waltz. *(cd+=)* – This is what she's like (instrumental). *(cd re-iss. Jun97 on 'Creation'; CRECD 154) (cd re-iss. Feb03 on 'E.M.I.'; 530803-2)*

Nov 85. (7") *(DEXYS 13)* **THIS IS WHAT SHE'S LIKE. / ('A'instrumental)** [ ] [–]
(12"+=) *(DEXYS 13-12)* – Reminisce (part 1).
(10") *(DEXYS 13-10)* – ('A'side) / Marguerita time.
(d7"++=) *(DEXYD 13)* – ('A'&'B'versions).

Oct 86. (7") *(BRUSH 1)* **BECAUSE OF YOU. / KATHLEEN MAVOUREEN** [13] [–]
(12"+=) *(BRUSH 1-12)* – Sometimes theme.

KEVIN ROWLAND

Mercury / not iss.

Apr 88. (7") *(DEXYS 14)* **WALK AWAY. / EVEN WHEN I HOLD YOU** [ ] [–]
(12"+=/12"box+=) *(DEXY S/B 14-12)* – ('A'version) / The way you look tonight.
(cd-s+=) *(DEXCD 14)* – The way you look tonight / Because of you.

Jun 88. (lp/c)(cd) *(MERH/+C 121)(834488-2)* **THE WANDERER** [ ] [–]
– Young man / Walk away / You'll be the one for me / Heartaches by the number / I am a wanderer / Tonight / When you walk alone / Age can't wither you / I want / Remember me.

Jul 88. (7") *(ROW 1)* **TONIGHT. / KEVIN ROWLAND'S BAND** [ ] [–]
(12"+=) *(ROW 1T)* – Come on Eileen.

Oct 88. (7") *(ROW 2)* **YOUNG MAN. / ONE WAY TICKET TO PALOOKAHVILLE** [ ] [–]
(12"+=) *(ROW 2-12)* – Jackie Wilson said (I'm in heaven when you smile).
(cd-s++=) *(ROWCD 2)* – Show me.

Creation / not iss.

Sep 99. (c-s/cd-s) *(CRE CS/SCD 332)* **CONCRETE AND CLAY / I CAN'T TELL THE BOTTOM FROM THE TOP** [ ] [–]

Oct 99. (cd) *(CRECD 216)* **MY BEAUTY** [ ] [–]
– The greatest love of all / Rag doll / Concrete and clay / Daydream believer / This guy's in love with you / The long and winding road / It's getting better / I can't tell the bottom from the top / Labelled with love (I'll stay with my dreams) / Reflections of my life / You'll never walk alone.

– DEXYS compilations, others, etc. –

Mar 83. (lp) *E.M.I.; (EMS 1007)* **GENO** [79] [ ]
(re-iss. Oct87 lp/c; ATAK/TC-ATAK 72) (cd-iss. Jun88 on 'Fame'; CDFA 3189)

Mar 84. (7") *EMI Gold; (G 455)* **DANCE STANCE. / THERE THERE MY DEAR** [ ] [–]

1989. (cd-video) *Mercury; (080 628-2)* **COME ON EILEEN / THE CELTIC SOUL BROTHERS / JACKIE WILSON SAID (I'M IN HEAVEN WHEN YOU SMILE) / LIARS TO E** [ ] [–]

Mar 90. (7") *Old Gold; (OG 9900)* **COME ON EILEEN. / JACKIE WILSON SAID (I'M IN HEAVEN WHEN YOU SMILE)** [ ] [–]

Sep 92. (cd-s) *Old Gold; (126238342-2)* **GENO / THERE THERE MY DEAR / DANCE STANCE** [ ] [–]

Jun 91. (cd/c/lp) *Mercury; (846460-2/-4/-1)* **THE VERY BEST OF DEXYS MIDNIGHT RUNNERS** [12] [ ]
– Come on Eileen / Jackie Wilson said (I'm in heaven when you smile) / Let's get this straight (from the start) / Because of you / Show me / The Celtic soul brothers (more, please, thank you) / Liars a to e / One way love / Old / Geno / There there my dear / Breakin' down the walls of heartache / Dance stance / Plan b / Keep it / I'm just looking / Soon / This is what she's like / Soul finger. (cd+=) – (5 extra tracks) *(re-iss. Jul92)*

Jun 91. (7") *Mercury;* **COME ON EILEEN. / BECAUSE OF YOU** [ ] [–]
(12"+=/cd-s+=) – Let's get this straight (from the start).

May 93. (cd/c) *Spectrum; (550 003-2/-4)* **BECAUSE OF YOU** [ ] [–]

Nov 93. (cd) *Windsong; (WINCD 047)* **BBC RADIO 1 LIVE IN CONCERT – NEWCASTLE (live)** [ ] [–]

Jul 95. (cd) *Nighttracks; (CDNT 009)* **1980-1982 – THE RADIO SESSIONS** [ ] [–]

Aug 95. (d-cd) *Mercury; (528608-2)* **TOO RYE AYE / DON'T STAND ME DOWN** [ ] [–]

May 96. (cd) *Premier; (PRMUCD 1)* **IT WAS LIKE THIS** [ ] [–]

Sep 03. (cd-s) *E.M.I.; (CDDEXYS 2003)* **MANHOOD / MANHOOD (radio) / REMINISCE (part two) / I'LL STAY FOREVER MY LOVE** [ ] [–]

Sep 03. (cd) *E.M.I.; (592680-2)* **LET'S MAKE THIS PRECIOUS – THE BEST OF DEXYS MIDNIGHT RUNNERS** [75] [–]
– Geno / The Celtic soul brothers (more please thank you) / Come on Eileen / Jackie Wilson said (I'm in Heaven when you smile) / Manhood / Because of you / I love you / Show me / There, there my dear / Tell me when my light turns green / Breaking down the walls of heartache / Plan B / Let's get this straight (from the start) / This is what she's like / Let's make this precious / My national pride / Until I believe in my soul / My life in New England.

Neil DIAMOND

Born: NEIL LESLIE DIAMOND, 24 Jan'41, Brooklyn, New York, USA. By the time he'd graduated from Brooklyn's Erasmus high school and embarked upon a degree at New York University, DIAMOND had already begun writing and recording. As one-half of the duo NEIL & JACK (with Jack Parker), he released a couple of early singles on the small 'Duel' label before cutting a one-off solo track for 'Columbia' in 1963. Upon dropping out of university he began working full-time as a staff writer for various publishers (while toying with the name of Noah Kaminsky), providing material for the likes of CLIFF RICHARD, JAY & THE AMERICANS and most successfully, The MONKEES, for whom he wrote the 1967 US No.1, 'I'm A Believer'. A year previous, DIAMOND had signed a new recording contract with 'Bang' records and had already scored a Top 10 hit with 'CHERRY, CHERRY' following on from the minor chart success of his definitive 'SOLITARY MAN'. A string of moderate Jeff Barry/Ellie Greenwich-produced hits ensued over the next two years including the classics, 'GIRL, YOU'LL BE A WOMAN SOON' and 'KENTUCKY WOMAN'. Wrapping his ominous baritone around hook-driven, rootsy pop-rock DIAMOND had created a songwriting formula that was irresistibly populist yet enduring, his success encouraging him to push for full creative control and make it as a credible singer/songriter in his own right. 'Uni' subsequently offered him the deal he was looking for and despite the relative failure of the experimental 'VELVET GLOVES AND SPIT' (1968) album, the hits began rolling in at the turn of the decade as the anthemic 'SWEET CAROLINE' became his biggest hit to date (US Top 5) in summer '69. The accompanying album, 'TOUCHING YOU TOUCHING ME' (1970), established his credentials/ambitions with a tasteful selection of covers from the likes of FRED NEIL and JONI MITCHELL while also spawning a second major hit in 'HOLLY HOLY'. Later that year he scored his first US No.1 (UK No.3) with 'CRACKLIN' ROSIE', a highlight of the 'TAPROOT MANUSCRIPT' (1971) set wherein he even attempted an ambitious suite, 'THE AFRICAN TRILOGY'. Despite his wish to be recognised as a "serious" singer/songwriter DIAMOND just couldn't help penning gloriously catchy, future karaoke classics like 'I AM . . . I SAID' (transatlantic Top 5) and 'SONG SUNG BLUE' (US No.1) while late 1973's 'HOT AUGUST NIGHT' live set captured his lavish showmanship on vinyl and cemented his superstar status. 'Columbia' were so impressed they stumped up five million dollars for his record-breaking signing later that year, their investment paying off as the 'JONATHAN

LIVINGSTON SEAGULL' (1973) soundtrack ended up coining in more cash than the film itself. The BAND's ROBBIE ROBERTSON lent DIAMOND a modicum of street cred by producing 1976's 'BEAUTIFUL NOISE', a concept effort based on NEIL's formative years as a Brill Building protoge. Even through the punk era, DIAMOND kept racking up the hits, scoring another US No.1 in 1978 via the BARBRA STREISAND duet, 'YOU DON'T BRING ME FLOWERS'. The album of the same name also spawned another karaoke fave in the shape of country-tinged singalong, 'FOREVER IN BLUE JEANS' (Top 20), cheesy MOR maybe but great stuff all the same. Surprisingly perhaps, the man's biggest success was yet to come, arriving in the shape of his soundtrack to a remake of 1920's movie, 'The Jazz Singer' in which DIAMOND himself starred alongside Laurence Olivier. Released in late 1980, the record went multi-platinum and spawned three US Top 10 singles, 'LOVE ON THE ROCKS', 'HELLO AGAIN' and 'AMERICA'. The polished balladry of 'HEARTLIGHT' (1982) brought further success in the States with its title track becoming an MOR radio staple. Despite a surprise Top 10 placing in the UK, 'PRIMITIVE' (1984) found DIAMOND treading water if not drowning in a stagnant pond of romantic mush. 'HEADED FOR THE FUTURE' (1986) attempted to bring him up to date without much success while 'HOT AUGUST NIGHT II' (1987) was a pale reflection of its predecessor. Signing to 'Columbia' at the dawn of the 90's, DIAMOND revisited the era of the 60's songwriter with the critically mauled 'ON THE ROOF – SONGS OF THE BRILL BUILDING' (1993). More successful was 'TENNESSEE MOON' (1996), DIAMOND's Nashville record. Essentially a singles artist, the man's various greatest hits sets are a worthy addition to even the hippest of record collections and while the likes of UB40 have covered his work to great success in the past, alt-rockers URGE OVERKILL demonstrated his kitsch appeal to brilliant effect with their 'Pulp Fiction' performance of 'GIRL, YOU'LL BE A WOMAN SOON'. DIAMOND had his own shot at celluloid interpretation on 1998's 'AS TIME GOES BY – THE MOVIE ALBUM', labouring over the likes of 'UNCHAINED MELODY' and 'MOON RIVER'. Into the new millennium, DIAMOND decided to reconfirm his identity as a singer/songwriter with 'THREE CHORD OPERA' (2001), his first album of wholly original, self-penned material in over 30 years. Having midwifed some of the starkest music of the late JOHNNY CASH's career, Rick Rubin proved why he remains the most perceptive, far-sighted and disciplined producer in the business; pushing DIAMOND into similar self-restraint, he finally steered him in the right direction, stripping away decades of studio flab. '12 SONGS' (2005) was the result, more of a piece than any long player he'd ever recorded, and received in the press as something akin to the holy grail, the album DIAMOND had threatened to make his whole career. The arrangements were typically sparse: acoustic guitar fitfully allied with sombre organ lines, and on 'WE' – one of the record's sole breezy moments, some clownish brass. Chart wise, DIAMOND achieved his highest UK/US placing (both Top 5) since 'LOVE AT THE GREEK' (1977) / 'THE JAZZ SINGER' (1981) a generation earlier, decades during which his voice had scarcely changed, losing none of its gravelly suave, and finally gracing an album built to last.

• **Covered:** NEW ORLEANS (Gary U.S. Bonds) / UNTIL IT'S TIME FOR YOU TO GO (Buffy Sainte-Marie) / HE AIN'T HEAVY, HE'S MY BROTHER (Hollies) / HEARTLIGHT + FRONT PAGE STORY (Bacharach/Bayer-Sager) / I'M ALIVE (co-with David Foster) / MORNING HAS BROKEN (Cat Stevens) / etc, etc, etc

Album rating: JUST FOR YOU (*5) / VELVET GLOVES AND SPIT (*5) / TOUCHING YOU, TOUCHING ME (*6) / TAPROOT MANUSCRIPT (*6) / STONES (*4) / MOODS (*5) / HOT AUGUST NIGHT (*7) / DOUBLE GOLD compilation (*7) / RAINBOW collection (*5) / JONATHAN LIVINGSTON SEAGULL soundtrack (*6) / HIS 12 GREATEST HITS compilation (*8) / SERENADE (*4) / BEAUTIFUL NOISE (*6) / LOVE AT THE GREEK (*4) / I'M GLAD YOU'RE HERE WITH ME TONIGHT (*4) / YOU DON'T BRING ME FLOWERS (*5) / SEPTEMBER MORN (*4) / THE JAZZ SINGER soundtrack (*6) / ON THE WAY TO THE SKY (*3) / 12 GREATEST HITS, VOL.II compilation (*6) / HEARTLIGHT (*3) / PRIMITIVE (*3) / HEADED FOR THE FUTURE (*3) / HOT AUGUST NIGHT II (*4) / THE BEST YEARS OF OUR LIVES (*5) / LOVESCAPE (*3) / THE GREATEST HITS 1966-1992 compilation (*8) / THE CHRISTMAS ALBUM (*2) / UP ON THE ROOF – SONGS FROM THE BRILL BUILDING (*4) / LIVE IN AMERICA (*4) / TENNESSEE MOON (*4) / AS TIME GOES BY – THE MOVIE ALBUM (*3) / THREE CHORD OPERA (*5) / THE ESSENTIAL . . . compilation (*8) / 12 SONGS (*7)

NEIL DIAMOND – vocals, acoustic guitar / **JACK PACKER** – vocals, acoustic guitar

not iss. — Duel

1960. (7"; as NEIL & JACK) *<508>* **YOU ARE MY LOVE AT LAST. / WHAT WILL I DO** — [-] []

1961. (7"; as NEIL & JACK) **I'M AFRAID. / TILL YOU'VE TRIED LOVE** — [-] []

— NEIL now used various session people

not iss. — Columbia

1963. (7") *<42809>* **CLOWN TOWN. / AT NIGHT** — [-] []

— He then began writing for JAY & THE AMERICANS, CLIFF RICHARD and later The MONKEES. He returned to the studio early 1966.

London — Bang

May 66. (7") *(HLZ 10049) <519>* **SOLITARY MAN. / DO IT** — [] [55]

Sep 66. (7") *(HLZ 10072) <528>* **CHERRY, CHERRY. / I'LL COME RUNNING** — [] Aug66 [6]

Nov 66. (7") *(HLZ 10092) <536>* **I GOT THE FEELIN' (OH NO NO). / THE BOAT THAT I ROW** — [] [16]

Jan 67. (lp; mono/stereo) *(HAZ 8307) <BLP/+S 214>* **THE FEEL OF NEIL DIAMOND** — [] Oct66 []
– Solitary man / Red rubber ball / La bamba / Do it / Hanky panky / Monday Monday / New Orleans / Someday baby / I got the feelin' / I'll come running / Love to love / Cherry, Cherry.

Feb 67. (7") *(HLZ 10111) <540>* **YOU GOT TO ME. / SOMEDAY BABY** — [] Jan67 [18]

Apr 67. (7") *(HLZ 10126) <542>* **GIRL, YOU'LL BE A WOMAN SOON. / YOU'LL FORGET** — [] [10]

Jul 67. (7") *(HLZ 10151) <547>* **I THANK THE LORD FOR THE NIGHT. / LONG WAY HOME** — [] [13]

Sep 67. (lp; mono/stereo) *<BLP/+S 217>* **JUST FOR YOU** — [-] [80]
– Girl, you'll be a woman soon / The long way home / Red red wine / You'll forget / The boat that I row / Cherry, Cherry / I'm a believer / Shilo / You got to me / Solitary man / Thank the Lord for the night time.

Nov 67. (7") *(HLZ 10161) <551>* **KENTUCKY WOMAN. / THE TIME IS NOW** — [] Oct67 [22]

Jan 68. (7") *(HLZ 10177) <554>* **NEW ORLEANS. / HANKY PANKY** — [] Dec67 [51]

Apr 68. (7") *(HLZ 10187) <556>* **RED RED WINE. / RED RUBBER BALL** — [] [62]

Uni — Uni

May 68. (7") *(UN 503) <55065>* **BROOKLYN ROADS. / HOLIDAY INN BLUES** — [] [58]

M.C.A. — Uni

Jun 68. (lp) *(MUPS 365) <73030>* **VELVET GLOVES AND SPIT** — [] []
– Two-bit manchild / A modern day version of love / Honey dripping times / The pot smoker's song / Brooklyn roads / Shilo / Sunday sun / Holiday inn blues / Practically newborn / Knackerffeng / Merry-go-round. *(re-iss. 1970 on 'Uni'; UNLS 106) (re-iss. 1974; MCF 2512) (re-iss. Feb82 lp/c; MCL/+C 1640) (re-iss. Apr92 cd/c; MCL D/C 1904-2/-4)*

Jul 68. (7") *(MU 1033) <55075>* **TWO-BIT MANCHILD. / BROAD OLD WOMAN (9 a.m. INSANITY)** — [] [66]

Sep 68. (7") *<55084>* **SUNDAY SUN. / HONEY DRIPPING TIMES** — [-] [68]

Apr 69. (7") *(MU 1070) <55109>* **BROTHER LOVE'S TRAVELLING SALVATION SHOW. / A MODERN DAY VERSION OF LOVE** — [] Mar69 [22]

Apr 69. (lp) *(MUPS 382) <73047>* **BROTHER LOVE'S TRAVELLING SALVATION SHOW** — [] Mar69 [82]
– Brother Love's travelling salvation show / Dig in / River runs, newgrown plums / Juliet / Long gone / And the grass won't pay you no mind / Memphis street / Glory road / Deep in the morning / If I ever knew your name / You're so sweet horseflies keep hanging round your face / Hurtin' / You don't come easy. *(re-iss. 1970 on 'Uni'+=; UNLS 107)* – Sweet Caroline. *(re-iss. 1974; MCF 2536)*

Jul 69. (7") *(MU 198)* *<55136>* **SWEET CAROLINE (GOOD TIMES NEVER SEEMED SO GOOD). / DIG IN** [ ] [4]
Uni Uni

Nov 69. (7") *(UN 512)* *<55175>* **HOLLY HOLY. / HURTIN' YOU DON'T COME EASY** [ ] Oct69 [6]

Jan 70. (lp) *(UNLS 110)* *<73071>* **TOUCHING YOU TOUCHING ME** [ ] Dec69 [30]
– Sweet Caroline (good times never seemed so good) / Until it's time for you to go / Everybody's talkin' / Mr. Bojangles / Smokey lady / Holly holy / Both sides now / And the singer sings his song / Ain't no way / New York boy.

Feb 70. (7") *<55204>* **UNTIL IT'S TIME FOR YOU TO GO. / AND THE SINGER SINGS HIS SONG** [–] [53]

May 70. (7") *(UN 522)* *<55224>* **SOOLAIMON (AFRICAN TRILOGY II). / AND THE GRASS WON'T PAY YOU NO MIND** [ ] [30]

Aug 70. (7") *(UN 529)* *<55250>* **CRACKLIN' ROSIE. / LORDY** [3] [1]
(re-iss. Feb74 on 'M.C.A.'; MCA 113)

Sep 70. (lp) *(UNLS 116)* *<73084>* **GOLD (live at Troubador)** [23] [10]
– Lordy / Both sides now / Solitary man / Holly holy / Cherry, cherry / Kentucky woman / Sweet Caroline / Thank the Lord for the night time / And the singer sings his songs / Brother Love's travelling salvation show. *(re-iss. 1974 on 'M.C.A.'; MCF 2515) (re-iss. Oct87 on 'Music For Pleasure'; MFP 5815)*

Nov 70. (7") *<55264>* **HE AIN'T HEAVY HE'S MY BROTHER. / FREE LIFE** [–] [20]

Feb 71. (7") *(UNS 531)* **SWEET CAROLINE. / BROTHER LOVE'S TRAVELLING SALVATION SHOW** [8] [–]
(re-iss. Jan74 on 'M.C.A.'; MCA 106)

Mar 71. (lp) *(UNLS 117)* *<73092>* **TAPROOT MANUSCRIPT** [19] Nov70 [13]
– Cracklin' Rosie / Free life / Coldwater morning / Done too soon / He ain't heavy he's my brother / The African trilogy (a folk ballet: I am the lion / Madrigal / Soolamain / Missa / African smile / Childsong (reprise). *(re-iss. 1974 on 'M.C.A.'; MCF 2509) (re-iss. Sep86 lp/c; MCL/+C 1707) (cd-iss. 1987 on 'M.C.A.'; DIDX 273) (cd re-iss. Aug92; MCLD 19119)*

Apr 71. (7") *(UN 532)* *<55278>* **I AM . . . I SAID. / DONE TOO SOON** [4] [4]
Mar71 [65]

Nov 71. (7") *(UN 536)* *<55310>* **STONES. / CRUNCHY GRANOLA SUITE** [ ] [14]

Nov 71. (lp) *(UNLS 121)* *<93106>* **STONES** [18] [11]
– I am . . . I said / The last thing on my mind / Husbands and wives / Chelsea morning / Crunchy granola suite / Stones / If you go away / Suzanne / I think it's going to rain today / I am . . . I said (reprise). *(re-iss. 1974 on 'M.C.A.'; MCF 2530) (cd-iss. Aug90; DMCL 1908) (cd re-iss. Apr92; MCLD 19118)*

Apr 72. (7") *(UN 538)* *<55326>* **SONG SUNG BLUE. / GITCHY GOOMY** [14] [1]

Jul 72. (lp) *(UNLS 128)* *<93136>* **MOODS** [7] [5]
– Walk on water / Song sung blue / Porcupine pie / High rolling man / Canta libre / Captain Sunshine / Play me / Gitchy goomy / Theme / Prelude in E major / Morningside. *(cd-iss. 1985 on 'M.C.A.'; DMCA 115) (cd re-iss. Jul87 on 'M.C.A.'; CDCAD 31061) (cd re-iss. 1988 on 'M.C.A.'; DIDX 272) (re-iss. Sep91 on 'M.C.A.' cd/c; DMCL/MCLC 1759) (re-iss. Apr92 on 'M.C.A.' cd/c; MCL D/C 19043)*

Aug 72. (7") *(UNS 546)* *<55346>* **PLAY ME. / PORCUPINE PIE** [ ] [11]

Nov 72. (7") *(UNS 551)* *<55352>* **WALK ON WATER. / HIGH ROLLING MAN** [ ] [17]
Uni M.C.A.

Mar 73. (7") *(UNS 556)* *<40017>* **CHERRY CHERRY (live). / MORNINGSIDE** [ ] [31]

Dec 73. (d-lp) *(ULD 1-2)* *<2-8000>* **HOT AUGUST NIGHT (live)** [32] Dec72 [5]
– Prologue / Crunchy granola suite / Done too soon / Dialogue / Solitary man / Cherry cherry / Sweet Caroline / Porcupine pie / You're so sweet / Red red wine / Soggy pretzels / And the grass won't pay you no mind / Shilo / Girl you'll be a woman soon / Play me / Canta libre / Morningside / Song sung blue / Cracklin' Rosie / Holly holy / I am . . . I said / Soolamain / Brother Love's travelling salvation show / Encore. *(re-iss. 1975 on 'M.C.A.'; MCSP 255)*

C.B.S. Columbia

Nov 73. (7") *(CBS 1843)* *<45942>* **BE. / FLIGHT OF THE GULL** [ ] [ ]

Jan 74. (lp/c) *(CBS/40 69047)* *<KS 32550>* **JONATHAN LIVINGSTON SEAGULL** (soundtrack) [35] Oct73 [2]
– Prologue / Be / Flight of the gull / Dear father / Skybird / Lonely looking sky / The odyssey: Be – Lonely looking sky – Dear father / Anthem / Be / Skybird / Dear father / Be. *(cd-iss. 1986; CD 69047) <re-iss. Dec90 on 'Columbia' cd/c/lp; 467607-2/-4/-1)>*

Apr 74. (7") *(CBS 2191)* *<45998>* **SKYBIRD. / LONELY LOOKING SKY** [ ] Feb74 [75]

Oct 74. (lp/c) *(CBS/40 69067)* *<PC 32919>* **SERENADE** [11] [3]
– I've been this way before / Rosemary's wine / Lady Magdalene / The last Picasso / Longfellow serenade / Yes I will / Reggae strut / The gift of song. *(re-iss. Jun81; CBS 32050) (cd-iss. May87; CD 69067) (re-iss. Sep89 on 'Pickwick' lp/c/cd; 982195-1/-4/-2) (re-iss. Dec95 on 'Columbia' cd/c; 465012-2/-4)*

Nov 74. (7") *(CBS 2769)* *<10043>* **LONGFELLOW SERENADE. / ROSEMARY'S WINE** [ ] [5]

Feb 75. (7") *(CBS 3058)* *<10084>* **I'VE BEEN THIS WAY BEFORE. / REGGAE STRUT** [ ] [34]

Jun 75. (7") *(CBS 3350)* *<10138>* **THE LAST PICASSO. / THE GIFT OF SONG** [ ] [ ]

Jun 76. (7") *(CBS 4398)* *<10366>* **IF YOU KNOW WHAT I MEAN. / STREET LIFE** [35] [11]

Jul 76. (lp/c) *(CBS/40 86004)* *<PC 33935>* **BEAUTIFUL NOISE** [10] [4]
– Beautiful noise / Stargazer / Lady oh / Don't think . . . feel / Surviving the life / If you know what I mean / Street life / Home is a wounded heart / Jungletime / Signs / Dry your eyes. *(re-iss. Apr87 lp/c; 450452-1/-4) (cd-iss. May87; CD 86004) (re-iss. Mar91; 450452-2)*

Sep 76. (7") *<10405>* **DON'T THINK . . . FEEL. / HOME IS A WOUNDED HEART** [–] [43]

Sep 76. (7") *(CBS 4601)* **BEAUTIFUL NOISE. / HOME IS A WOUNDED HEART** [13] [–]

Feb 77. (d-lp/d-c) *(CBS/40 95001)* *<34402>* **LOVE AT THE GREEK (live)** [3] [8]
– Street life / Kentucky woman / Sweet Caroline (good times never seem so good) / The last Picasso / Longfellow serenade / Beautiful noise / Lady-oh / Stargazer / If you know what I mean / Surviving the life / Glory road / Song sung blue / Holly holy / Brother Love's travelling salvation show / Jonathan Livingstone Seagull / Be / Dear father / Lonely looking sky / Sanctus / Skybird / Be (encore) / I've been this way before. *(cd-iss. May87) (re-iss. cd+c Apr93 on 'Columbia')*

Dec 76. (7") *<10452>* **BEAUTIFUL NOISE. / SIGNS** [–] [ ]

Mar 77. (7") *(CBS 5115)* **STARGAZER (live). / STREET LIFE (live)** [ ] [–]

Jun 77. (7") *(CBS 5350)* **I'VE BEEN THIS WAY BEFORE (live). / SURVIVING THE LIFE (live)** [ ] [–]

Jul 77. (7") *(CBS 5440)* **DON'T THINK . . . FEEL. / SIGNS** [ ] [–]

Dec 77. (7") *(CBS 5869)* *<10657>* **DESIREE. / ONCE IN A WHILE** [39] [16]

Dec 77. (lp/c) *(CBS/40 86044)* *<34990>* **I'M GLAD YOU'RE HERE WITH ME TONIGHT** [16] [6]
– God only knows / Let me take you in my arms / Once in a while / Let the little boy sing / I'm glad you're here with me tonight / Lament in D minor / Dance of the sabres / Desiree / As if / Free man in Paris. *(cd-iss. May87; CD 86044) (re-iss. Oct90 cd/c/lp; CD/40CBS 32395)*

Feb 78. (7") *(CBS 6064)* **GOD ONLY KNOWS. / ONCE IN A WHILE** [ ] [–]

Mar 78. (7") *<10720>* **I'M GLAD YOU'RE HERE WITH ME TONIGHT. / DANCE OF SABRES** [–] [ ]

Apr 78. (7") *(CBS 6288)* **I'M GLAD YOU'RE HERE WITH ME TONIGHT. / AS IF** [ ] [–]

Sep 78. (7") *(CBS 6207)* **LET ME TAKE YOU IN MY ARMS. / AS IF** [ ] [–]

Nov 78. (7"; NEIL DIAMOND & BARBRA STREISAND) *(CBS 6803)* *<10840>* **YOU DON'T BRING ME FLOWERS. / (instrumental)** [5] [1]

Dec 78. (lp/c) *(CBS/40 86077)* *<35625>* **YOU DON'T BRING ME FLOWERS** [15] [4]
– The American popular song / Forever in blue jeans / Remember me / You've got your troubles / You don't bring me flowers / The dancing bumble-bee-bumble boogie / Mothers and daughters, fathers and sons / Memphis flyer / Say maybe / Diamond girls. *(cd-iss. May87; CD 86077) (re-iss. Aug91 on 'Columbia' cd/c; 468782-2/-4)*

Feb 79. (7") *(CBS 7047)* *<10897>* **FOREVER IN BLUE JEANS. / REMEMBER ME** [16] [20]

May 79. (7") *<10945>* **SAY MAYBE. / DIAMOND GIRLS** [–] [55]

May 79. (7") *(CBS 7408)* **THE AMERICAN POPULAR SONG. / DIAMOND GIRLS** [ ] [–]

Jan 80. (7") *(CBS 8130)* *<11175>* **SEPTEMBER MORN. / I'M A BELIEVER** [ ] [17]

Jan 80. (lp/c) *(CBS/40 86096)* *<36121>* **SEPTEMBER MORN** [14] Dec79 [10]
– September morn / Mama don't know / That kind / Jazz time / The good Lord loves you / Dancing in the street / The shelter of your arms / I'm a

believer / The sun ain't gonna shine anymore / Stagger Lee. *(cd-iss. May87; CD 86096) (cd re-iss. Feb97 on 'Columbia'; 484455-2)*

Mar 80. (7") <11232> **THE GOOD LORD LOVES YOU. / JAZZ TIME** [–] [67]

Mar 80. (7") *(CBS 8322)* **DANCING IN THE STREET. / JAZZ TIME** [ ] [–]

Capitol Capitol

Oct 80. (7") *(CL 16173) <4939>* **LOVE ON THE ROCKS. / ACAPULCO** [17] [2]

Nov 80. (lp/c) *<(EAST/TCEAST 12120)>* **THE JAZZ SINGER** (soundtrack) [14] [3]
– America / Adon olom / You baby / Love on the rocks / Amazed and confused / On the Robert E. Lee / Summerlove / Hello again / Acapulco / Hey Louise / Songs of life / Jerusalem / Kol nidre – My name is Yussel / America (reprise). *(cd-iss. Jul84; CDEAST 12120) <US cd-iss. 1992 on 'Capitol'; 46026> <US cd-iss. 1996 on 'Columbia'; 67569> (re-iss. Jul98 on 'Columbia' cd/c; 483927-2/-4)*

Jan 81. (7") *(CL 16176) <4960>* **HELLO AGAIN. / AMAZED AND CONFUSED** [51] [6]

Apr 81. (7") *(CL 16197) <4994>* **AMERICA. / SONGS OF LIFE** [ ] [8]

C.B.S. Columbia

Oct 81. (lp/c) *(CBS/40 85343) <37628>* **ON THE WAY TO THE SKY** [39] [17]
– Yesterday's songs / On the way to the sky / Right by you / Only you / Save me / Be mine / The drifter / Fear of the market place / Rainy day song / Guitar Heaven / Love burns. *(cd-iss. Jul87; CD 85343)*

Nov 81. (7") *(CBS 1755) <02604>* **YESTERDAY'S SONGS. / GUITAR HEAVEN** [ ] [11]

Jan 82. (7") *(CBS 2033)* **RAINY DAY SONGS. / BE MINE TONIGHT** [ ] [–]

Feb 82. (7") *<02712>* **ON THE WAY TO THE SKY. / SAVE ME** [–] [27]

Jun 82. (7") *(CBS 2580) <02928>* **BE MINE TONIGHT. / RIGHT BY YOU** [ ] [35]

Sep 82. (7") *(CBS 2814) <03219>* **HEARTLIGHT. / YOU DON'T KNOW ME** [47] [5]

Oct 82. (lp/c) *(CBS/40 25073) <38359>* **HEARTLIGHT** [43] [9]
– Heartlight / I'm alive / I'm guilty / Hurricane / Lost amongst the stars / A fool for you / In enserada / Star flight / Front page story / Comin' home / First you have to say you love me. *(cd-iss. May87; CD 25073) (re-iss. cd Mar94 on 'Sony'; 982835-2)*

Jan 83. (7") *(CBS 3050)* **FRONT PAGE STORY. / LOVE AMONG THE STARS** [ ] [–]

Feb 83. (7") *<03503>* **I'M ALIVE. / LOST AMONGST THE STARS** [–] [35]

Apr 83. (7") *<03801>* **FRONT PAGE STORY. / I'M GUILTY** [–] [65]

Jul 84. (7") *(CBS 4458) <04541>* **TURN AROUND. / BROOKLYN ON A SATURDAY NIGHT** [ ] [62]

Aug 84. (lp/c) *(CBS/40 86036) <39199>* **PRIMITIVE** [7] [35]
– Turn around / Primitive / Fire on the tracks / Brooklyn on a Saturday night / Sleep with me tonight / Crazy / My time with you / Love's own song / It's a trip (go for the moon) / You make it feel like Christmas / One by one. *(cd-iss. May87; CD 86036) (re-iss. Aug91 on 'Sony' cd/c; 982636-2/-4)*

Sep 84. (7") *(CBS 4673)* **PRIMITIVE. / IT'S A TRIP** [ ] [–]

Sep 84. (7") *<04646>* **SLEEP WITH ME TONIGHT. / ONE BY ONE** [–] [ ]

Nov 84. (7") *<04719>* **YOU MAKE IT FEEL LIKE CHRISTMAS. / CRAZY** [–] [ ]

Nov 84. (7") *(CBS 4888)* **YOU MAKE IT FEEL LIKE CHRISTMAS. / ONE BY ONE** [ ] [–]

May 86. (7") *<05889>* **HEADED FOR THE FUTURE. / ANGEL** [–] [53]

May 86. (lp/c/cd) *(CBS/40/CD 26952) <40368>* **HEADED FOR THE FUTURE** [36] [20]
– Headed for the future / The man you need / I'll see you in the radio (Laura / Stand up for love / It should have been me / Lost in Hollywood / The story of my life / Angel / Me beside you / Love doesn't live here anymore. *(cd re-iss. Feb98 on 'Columbia'; 489453-2)*

Jul 86. (7"/12") *(A/TA 7225)* **STAND UP FOR LOVE. / THE STORY OF MY LIFE** [ ] [–]

Jul 86. (7") *<06136>* **THE STORY OF MY LIFE. / LOVE DOESN'T LIVE HERE ANYMORE** [–] [ ]

Nov 87. (7"/cd-s) *(651201-7/-2) <07614>* **I DREAMED A DREAM. / SWEET CAROLINE** [ ] [ ]

Dec 87. (d-lp/c/cd) *(460406-1/-4/-2) <40990>* **HOT AUGUST NIGHT II (live)** [74] Nov87 [59]
– Song of the whales (fanfare) / Headed for the future / September morn / Thank the Lord for the night time / Cherry cherry / Sweet Caroline / Hello again / Love on the rocks / America / Forever in blue jeans / You don't bring me flowers / I dreamed a dream / Back in L.A. / Song sung blue / Crackling Rosie / I am . . . I said / Holly holy / Soolamain / Brother Love's travelling salvation show / Heartlight. *(re-iss. Sep93 on 'Columbia')*

Jan 88. (7") *<07751>* **CHERRY CHERRY (live). / AMERICA (live)** [–] [ ]

Feb 89. (lp/c/cd) *(463201-1/-4/-2) <45025>* **THE BEST YEARS OF OUR LIVES** [42] Jan89 [46]
– The best years of our lives / Hard times for young lovers / This time / Everything's gonna be fine / Hooked on a memory of you / Take care of me / Baby can I hold you / Carmelita's eyes / Courtin' disaster / If I couldn't see you again / Long hard climb.

May 89. (7") *<08514>* **THIS TIME. / IF I COULDN'T SEE YOU AGAIN** [–] [ ]

May 89. (7"/c-s) *(654518-7/-4)* **THIS TIME. / BABY CAN I HOLD YOU** [ ] [–]
(12"+=) *(654518-6)* – Hooked on the morning of you.
(cd-s+=) *(654518-2)* – Beautiful noise / If you know what I mean.

Sep 89. (7") *<08741>* **THE BEST YEARS OF OUR LIVES. / CARMELITA'S EYES** [–] [ ]

Columbia Columbia

Oct 91. (cd/c/lp) *(468890-2/-4/-1) <48610>* **LOVESCAPE** [36] Sep91 [44]
– If there were no dreams / Mountains of love / Don't turn around / Someone who believes in you / When you miss your love / Fortune of the night / One hand, one heart / Hooked on the memory of you / Wish everything was alright / The way / Sweet L.A. days / All I really need is you / Lonely lady 17 / I feel you / Common ground. *(cd re-iss. Apr99; 468890-2)*

Jun 92. (cd/c/d-lp) *(471502/-2/-4) <52703>* **THE GREATEST HITS 1966-1992** (compilation) [1] May92 [90]
– Solitary man / Cherry, Cherry / I get the feelin' (oh no, no) / Thank you Lord for the night time / Girl, you'll be a woman soon / Kentucky woman / Shilo / You got to me / Brooklyn roads / Red, red wine / I'm a believer / Sweet Caroline / Soolaimon / Cracklin' Rose / Song sung blue / lay me / Holly holy / Morningside / Crunchy granola suite/ / Brother Love's travelling salvation show / I am . . . I said / Be / Longfellow serenade / Beautiful noise / If you know what I mean / Desiree / September morn / You don't bring me flowers (w / BARBRA STREISAND) / Forever in blue jeans / Hello America / Love on the rocks / Yesterday's songs / Heartlight / Headed for the future / Heartbreak Hotel (w / KIM CARNES) / All I really need is you. *(re-iss. Aug98; same)*

Nov 92. (7"/c-s) *(658826-7/-4)* **MORNING HAS BROKEN. / SANTA CLAUS IS COMING TO TOWN** [36] [ ]
(cd-s) *(658826-2)*– ('A'side) / Happy xmas (war is over) / Silver bells / Love on the rocks.

Nov 92. (cd/c/lp) *(472410-2/-4/-1) <52914>* **THE CHRISTMAS ALBUM** [50] [8]
– O come o come Emmanuel / We three kings of Orient are / Silent night / Little drummer boy / Santa Claus is coming to town / Christmas song / Morning has broken / Happy Xmas (war is over) / White Christmas / God rest ye merry gentlemen / Jingle bells rock / Hark the herald angels sing / Silver bells / You make it feel like Christmas / Holy night.

Sep 93. (cd/c/lp) *(474356-2/-4/-1) <57529>* **ON THE ROOF – SONGS FROM THE BRILL BUILDING** [28] [28]
– You've lost that lovin' feelin' (duet with DOLLY PARTON) / Up on the roof / Love potion number nine / Will you love me tomorrow/ Don't be cruel / Do wah diddy diddy (with MARY'S DANISH) / I (who have nothing) / Do you know the way to San Jose? / Don't make me over / River deep mountain high / A groovy kind of love / Spanish Harlem / Sweets for my sweet / Happy birthday sweet sixteen / Ten lonely guys / Save the last dance for me.

Aug 94. (d-cd/d-c) *(477211-2/-4) <66321>* **LIVE IN AMERICA (live)** [ ] [93]
– America / Hello again / Kentucky woman / You got to me / Cherry cherry / I'm a believer / Sweet Caroline / Love on the rocks / Hooked on the memory of you (with LINDA PRESS) / Lady oh / Beautiful noise / Play me / Up on the roof / You've lost that lovin' feelin' (with RAVEN KANE) / River deep, mountain high / I (who have nothing) / Missa / Soolaimon / Holly holy / And the grass won't pay you no mind / You don't bring me flowers (with RAVEN KANE) / September morn / Havah nagilah / Solitary man / Red red wine / Song sung blue / Forever in blue jeans / Heartlight / Cracklin' Rose / I am . . .I said / Crunchy Granola suite / Brother Love's traveling salvation show.

Nov 94. (cd/c) *(477598-2/-4) <66465>* **THE CHRISTMAS ALBUM VOLUME II** [ ] [51]
– Joy to the world / Mary's boy child / Deck the halls / We wish you a merry Christmas / Winter wonderland / Have yourself a merry little Christmas / I'll be home for Christmas / Rudolph the red nosed reindeer / Sleigh ride /

Candlelight carol / Away in a manger / O come all ye faithful (adesta Fidells) / O little town of Bethlehem / Angels we have heard on high / The first noel / Hallelujah chorus.

Feb 96. (cd/c) *(481378-2/-4)* <67382> **TENNESSEE MOON** [12] [14]
– Tennessee moon / One good love / Shame / A matter of love / Marry me / Deep inside of you / Gold don't rush / Like you do / Can anybody hear me / Win the world / No limit / Reminisce for a while / Kentucky woman / If I lost my way / Everybody / Talking optimist blues (good day today) / Open wide these prison doors / Blue highway. *(cd re-iss. Jan99; same)*

Nov 98. (d-cd/d-c) *(491655-2/-4)* <69540> **AS TIME GOES BY – THE MOVIE ALBUM** [68] [31]
– As time goes by / Secret love / Unchained melody / Can you feel the love tonight / The way you look / Love with the proper stranger / Puttin' on the Ritz / When you wish upon a star / Windmills of your mind / Ebb tide / True love / My heart will go on / The look of love / Can't help falling in love / Ruby / I've got you under my skin / One for my baby / And I love her / Moon river / In the still of the night / As time goes by (reprise).

Sep 01. (cd) *(502493-2)* <85500> **THREE CHORD OPERA** [49] Jul01 [15]
– I haven't played this song in years / Don't look down / I believe in happy endings / At the movies / Midnight dream / You are the best part of me / Baby let's drive / My special someone / A mission of love / Elijah's song / Leave a little room for God / Turn down the lights.

Sony Columbia

Feb 06. (cd) *(82876 76131-2)* <77508-2> **12 SONGS** [5] Nov05 [4]
– Oh Mary / Hell yeah / Captain of a shipwreck / Evermore / Save me a Saturday night / Delirious love / I'm on to you / What's it gonna be / Man of God / Create me / Face me / We.

– (selective) compilations, etc. –

1968. (7") *Bang;* <561> **SHILO. / LA BAMBA** [–] [ ]
<re-iss. Jan70; 575> – hit No.24

Jul 68. (lp) *Bang;* <219> **NEIL DIAMOND'S GREATEST HITS** [–] [100]

Jul 70. (7") *Bang;* <578> **SOLITARY MAN. / THE TIME IS NOW** [–] [21]

Sep 70. (lp) *Bang;* <221> **SHILO** [–] [52]

Dec 70. (7") *Bang;* <580> **DO IT! / HANKY PANKY** [–] [36]

Feb 71. (lp) *Bang;* <224> **DO IT!** [–] [100]

Jun 71. (7") *President; (PT 342) / Bang;* <586> **I'M A BELIEVER. / CROOKED STREET** [ ] [51]

Jan 73. (d-lp) *Bang;* <227> **DOUBLE GOLD** [–] [36]

Aug 73. (7") *London; (HLM 10427) / Bang;* <703> **THE LONG WAY HOME. / MONDAY, MONDAY** [ ] [91]

Aug 73. (7") *M.C.A.;* <40092> **THE LAST THING ON MY MIND. / CANTA LIBRE** [–] [56]

Feb 74. (lp/c) *M.C.A.; (MCF/+C 2529)* <2103> **RAINBOW** [39] Dec73 [35]

Jun 74. (lp/c) *M.C.A.; (MCF/+C 2550)* <2106> **HIS 12 GREATEST HITS** [13] May74 [29]
(cd-iss. May87; DMCA 114)

Nov 78. (lp/c) *M.C.A.; (MCTV 2)* **20 GOLDEN GREATS** [2] [–]
(re-iss. Feb91 cd/c; D+/MCTV 2) (re-iss. May96 cd/c; MCD/MCC 11452)

Jan 81. (lp/c) *M.C.A.; (MCF/+C 3092)* **LOVE SONGS** [43] [ ]
(re-iss. Apr97 cd/c; MCB D/C 19525)

Jun 82. (lp/c) *C.B.S.; (CBS/40 85844) / Columbia;* <38068> **12 GREATEST HITS VOLUME 2** [32] May82 [48]
(cd-iss. May87; CD 85844)

Dec 83. (lp) *K-Tel; (NE 1262)* **THE VERY BEST OF NEIL DIAMOND** [33] [–]

Aug 93. (3xcd-box) *Columbia; (474143-2)* **I'M GLAD YOU'RE HERE WITH ME TONIGHT / BEAUTIFUL NOISE / YOU DON'T SEND ME FLOWERS** [ ] [ ]

Jul 96. (d-cd) *M.C.A.; (MCD 33005)* **SWEET CAROLINE / MOODS** [ ] [ ]

Aug 96. (cd/c) *Sony TV – MCA; (MOOD CD/C 45)* **THE ULTIMATE COLLECTION** [5] [–]

Oct 96. (3xcd-box) *Columbia; (C3K 65013)* **IN MY LIFETIME** [ ] [–]

Nov 97. (3xcd-box) *Columbia; (488676-2)* **BEAUTIFUL NOISE / JONATHAN LIVINGSTONE SEAGULL / THE JAZZ SINGER** [ ] [–]

Sep 00. (cd) *Universal; (AA88 112119-2)* **THE NEIL DIAMOND COLLECTION** [ ] [ ]

Mar 02. (d-cd) *Sony TV; (501066-2) / Legacy;* <85681> **THE ESSENTIAL . . .** [11] Dec01 [90]
– Solitary man / Cherry cherry / I got the feelin' (oh no no) / Kentucky woman / Girl, you'll be a woman soon / You got to me / Red red wine / Thank the Lord for the night time / I'm a believer / Sweet Caroline / Song sung blue / Holly holy / I am I said / Crackin' Rosie / Play m (live) / Morningside (live) / Crunchy granola suite (live) / Brooklyn road (live) / Soolaimon (live) / America / Hello again / Love on the rocks Captain Sunshine (live) / He ain't heavy (he's my brother) / Yes I will Lady Magdalene (live) / Shilo (live) / Brother Love's travelling salvatio show (live) / If you know what I mean / Beautiful noise / You don bring me flowers (with BARBRA STREISAND) / Desiree / Forever in blu jeans / September morn / I've been this way before / Yesterday's songs Heartlight / Headed for the future / You are the best part of me.

Apr 02. (3xcd-box) *M.C.A.; (112824-2)* **PLAY ME: THE COMPLETE UNI STUDIO RECORDINGS** [ ] [ ]

Mar 03. (cd) *Universal; (AAMCAD 11947)* **20TH CENTURY MASTERS** [ ] [ ]

Mar 03. (d-cd) *Universal; (AAMCAD 211050-2)* **GLORY ROAD** [ ] [ ]

□ P. DIDDY (see under ⇒ PUFF DADDY)

□ Chris DIFFORD / DIFFORD & TILBROOK (see under ⇒ SQUEEZE)

DINOSAUR JR.

Formed: Amherst, Massachusetts, USA . . . 1983 by J. MASCIS Initially recording hardcore punk under the DEEP WOUNI moniker, the band recruited PATRICK MURPHY an metamorphosed into DINOSAUR. Their self-titled debut albur appeared in 1985, a raw blueprint for their distinctive candy coated noise rock that was good enough to secure an America tour support slot with SONIC YOUTH. After protestations fron aging West Coast rockers DINOSAUR, J. MASCIS' crew adde the JR. to their name. Subsequently recording one album fo 'S.S.T.', 'YOU'RE LIVING ALL OVER ME' (1987), the ban further developed their melodic distortion although it was th 'FREAK SCENE' (1988) single, their debut for 'Blast First', whic saw DINOSAUR JR. pressed to the cardigan-clad bosoms c the nation's pre-baggy indie kids. A wildly exhilarating piece c pristine pop replete with copious amounts of intoxicating nois pollution, MASCIS' go-on-impress-me vocals epitomised the wor slacker when that dubious cliche was still gestating in some hack' subconscious. The follow-up album, 'BUG' (1988) was arguabl the band's finest moment, perfectly crafted pop spiked wit scathing slivers of guitar squall. BARLOW departed soon afte the album's release, going off to form SEBADOH while MASCIS mob came up with a wonderfully skewed cover of The CURE' 'JUST LIKE HEAVEN'. DON FLEMING (of GUMBALL fame and JAY SPIEGEL featured on DINOSAUR JR.'s major label debu for 'WEA' subsidiary 'Blanco Y Negro', 'THE WAGON' (1991) Another slice of cascading noise-pop, the single raised expectation for the follow-up album 'GREEN MIND' (1991). More or less MASCIS solo album, it failed to live up to its promise althoug by the release of 1993's 'WHERE YOU BEEN', MASCIS had foun a permanent bassist in MIKE JOHNSON. Their most successfu album to date, DINOSAUR JR. at last reaped some rewards fror the grunge scene they'd played a major role in creating. With bot JOHNSON and MASCIS releasing solo albums in 1996, the latte finally re-emerged late 2000 with the KEVIN SHIELDS-produce 'MORE LIGHT' (issued under J MASCIS & THE FOG billing) Anyone expecting some kind of artistic rebirth or millennia rejuvenation was to be sorely disappointed as J delivered anothe set of ragged, tumbledown fuzz-pop. The slacker's slacker, MASCI makes music that seemingly hangs together by only the seare threads of his own beleaguered vocal chords and he isn't likely t change anytime soon. Not on 'FEEL SO FREE' (2002) anyhow, a album again billed to J MASCIS + THE FOG wherein MASCIS, i anything, loosened things up even further. There was certainly les noise for noise's sake as J signalled a move towards a more groove-orientated sound right from the opening bar of 'FREEDOM'. Perhaps it was no coincidence that the word "free" cropped up more than once throughout this record and it was difficult to avoid the impression that the ageing indie-rocker was perhaps shedding some excess sonic skin. DINOSAUR JR. returned (at least to the stage) in April 2005, while MASCIS himself continued his unpredictable solo career with an album's worth of songs in praise of Hindu figurehead, Sri Mata Amritanandarrayi (or Amma to her followers). From the sublime to the occult, MASCIS (together with KYLE THOMAS, DAVE SWEETAPPLE and ASA IRONS) then went and recorded an eponymous SABBATH-esque mini-opus under the WITCH moniker, returning to the drum-stool for the first time in years.

• **Songwriters:** MASCIS wrote all, except LOTTA LOVE (Neil Young) / QUICKSAND (David Bowie) / I FEEL A WHOLE LOT BETTER (Byrds) / GOIN' BLIND (Kiss) / HOT BURRITO 2 (Gram Parsons). J MASCIS solo:- EVERY MOTHER'S SON (Lynyrd Skynyrd) / THE BOY WITH THE THORN IN HIS SIDE (Smiths) / ON THE RUN (Wipers) / ANTICIPATION (Carly Simon) / LEAVING ON A JET PLANE (John Denver). • **Trivia:** In Jun'91, MASCIS moonlighted as a drummer with Boston satanic hard-core group UPSIDE DOWN CROSS, who made one self-titled album Autumn '91 on 'Taang!'.

Album rating: DINOSAUR (*6) / YOU'RE LIVING ALL OVER ME mini (*7) / BUG (*8) / GREEN MIND (*7) / WHERE YOU BEEN (*8) / WITHOUT A SOUND (*5) / HAND IT OVER (*7) / EAR-BLEEDING COUNTRY: THE BEST OF DINOSAUR JR. compilation (*8) / J Mascis: GAS FOOD LODGING w/ Barry Adamson (*7) / MARTIN AND ME (*6) / J Mascis & The Fog: MORE LIGHT (*6) / FREE SO FREE (*7) / J Mascis: J AND FRIENDS SING AND CHANT FOR AMMA (*6) / Witch: WITCH (*6)

LOU BARLOW (b.17 Jul'66, Northampton, Mass.) – guitar / **J. MASCIS** (b. JOSEPH, 10 Dec'65) – drums / **CHARLIE NAKAJIMA** – vocals / **SCOTT HELLAND** – bass

not iss. Radiobeat

Dec 83. (7"ep; as DEEP WOUND) <RB 002> **I SAW IT** [–] [ ]
– I saw it / Sisters / In my room / Don't need / Lou's anxiety song / Video prick / Sick of fun / Deep wound / Dead babies.

— **J. MASCIS** – vocals, guitar, percussion / **LOU BARLOW** – bass, ukelele, vocals / added **MURPH** (b. EMMETT "PATRICK" MURPHY, 21 Dec'64) – drums (ex-ALL WHITE JURY)

not iss. Homestead

Jun 85. (lp; as DINOSAUR) <*HMS 015*> **DINOSAUR** [–] [ ]
– Forget the swan / Cats in a bowl / The leper / Does it float / Pointless / Repulsion / Gargoyle / Several lips / Mountain man / Quest / Bulbs of passion.

Mar 86. (7"; as DINOSAUR) <*HMS 032*> **REPULSION. / BULBS OF PASSION** [–] [ ]
(UK-iss.Apr97; same)

S.S.T. S.S.T.

Mar 87. (12"ep) <*SST 152*> **DINOSAUR JR.** [–] [ ]
– Little fury things / In a jar / Show me the way. *(cd-ep iss.Dec88; SSTCD 152)*

Jul 87. (m-lp/c) <*(SST/+C 130)*> **YOU'RE LIVING ALL OVER ME** [ ] [ ]
– Little fury things / Kracked / Sludgefeast / The lung / Raisans / Tarpit / In a jar / Lose / Poledo / Show me the way. *(cd-iss. Oct95; same)*

Blast First S.S.T.

Sep 88. (7") *(BFFP 30)* **FREAK SCENE. / KEEP THE GLOVE** [ ] [ ]
(US-iss.7",7"green; SST 220)

Oct 88. (lp/c/cd) *(BFFP 31/+C/CD)* <*SST/+C/CD 216*> **BUG** [ ] [ ]
– Freak scene / No bones / They always come / Yeah we know / Let it ride / Pond song / Budge / The post / Don't. *(cd re-iss. Feb99; SST 216CD)*

— **DONNA BIDDELL** – bass (ex-SCREAMING TREES) repl. BARLOW who formed SEBADOH

Apr 89. (7"/etched-12"/cd-s) *(BFFP 47 S/T/CD)* <*SST 244*> **JUST LIKE HEAVEN. / THROW DOWN / CHUNKS (A Last Rights Tune)** [78] Feb 90 [ ]
(US version 12"ep+=/c-ep+=/cd-ep+=) (SST/+C/CD 244) – Freak scene / Keep the glove.

— DONNA left and was repl. by **DON FLEMING** – guitar + **JAY SPIEGEL** – drums (both B.A.L.L.)

Glitterhouse Sub Pop

Jun 90. (7"/7"white) *(GR 0097)* <*SP 68*> **THE WAGON. / BETTER THAN GONE** [ ] [ ]

— In Oct 90, J.MASCIS and other ex-DINOSAUR JR member FLEMING + SPIEGEL, made an album 'RAKE' as VELVET MONKEYS (aka B.A.L.L. + friends).

Blanco Y Negro Sire

Jan 91. (7"/c-s) *(NEG 48/+C)* **THE WAGON. / THE LITTLE BABY** [49] [–]
(12"+=/cd-s+=) *(NEG 48 T/CD)* – Pebbles + weeds / Quicksand.

Feb 91. (lp/c/cd) *(BYN 24/+C/CD)* <*26479*> **GREEN MIND** [36] [ ]
– The wagon / Puke + cry / Blowing it / I live for that look / Flying cloud / How'd you pin that one on me / Water / Muck / Thumb / Green mind.

Aug 91. (7"/c-s) *(NEG 52/+C)* **WHATEVER'S COOL WITH ME. / SIDEWAYS** [ ] [–]
(12"+=/cd-s+=) *(NEG 52 T/CD)* – Thumb (live) / Keep the glove (live).

— **MASCIS** + **MURPH** introduced new member **MIKE JOHNSON** (b.27 Aug'65, Grant's Pass, Oregon, USA) – bass (ex-MARK LANEGAN, ex-GEORGE LANE, ex-SNAKEPIT)

Nov 92. (7") *(NEG 60)* **GET ME. / HOT BURRITO #2** [44] [–]
(c-s+=/12"+=/cd-s+=) *(NEG 60 C/T/CD)* – Qwest (live).

Jan 93. (7") *(NEG 61)* **START CHOPPIN'. / TURNIP FARM** [20] [–]
(10"+=/12"+=/cd-s+=) *(NEG 61 TEP/T/CD)* – Forget it.

Feb 93. (lp/c/cd) *(BYN 28/+C/CD)* <*45108*> **WHERE YOU BEEN?** [10] [50]
– Out there / Start choppin' / What else is new? / On the way / Not the same / Get me / Drawerings / Hide / Goin' home / I ain't sayin'.

Jun 93. (7"/c-s/12") *(NEG 63/+C/T)* **OUT THERE. / KEEBLIN' (live) / KRACKED (live)** [44] [ ]
(10"+=) *(NEG 63TE)* – Post.
(cd-s++=) *(NEG 63CD)* – Quest (live).
(cd-s) *(NEG 63CDX)* – ('A'side) / Get me / Severed lips / Thumb (radio sessions).

— now without MURPH

Aug 94. (7"/c-s) *(NEG 74/+C)* **FEEL THE PAIN. / GET OUT OF THIS** [25] [ ]
(10"etched+=/cd-s+=) *(NEG 74 TE/CD)* – Repulsion (acoustic).

Sep 94. (cd/c/lp) *(4509 96933-2/-4/-1)* <*45719*> **WITHOUT A SOUND** [24] [44]
– Feel the pain / I don't think so / Yeah right / Outta hand / Grab it / Even you / Mind glow / Get out of this / On the brink / Seemed like the thing to do / Over your shoulder.

Feb 95. (7"green/c-s) *(NEG 77 X/C)* **I DON'T THINK SO. / GET ME (live)** [67] [ ]
(cd-s+=) *(NEG 77CD)* – What else is new? / Sludge.

Mar 97. (c-s/12"/cd-s) *(NEG 103 C/T/CD)* **TAKE A RUN AT THE SUN. / DON'T YOU THINK IT'S TIME / THE PICKLE SONG** [53] [ ]

Mar 97. (cd/c/lp) *(0630 18312-2/-4/-1)* <*46506*> **HAND IT OVER** [ ] [ ]
– Take a run at the sun / Never bought it / Nothin's goin' on / I'm insane / Can't we move this alone / Sure not over you / Loaded / Mick / I know yer insane / Gettin' rough / Gotta know.

Trade 2 not iss.

Sep 97. (7") *(TRDSC 009)* **I'M INSANE. / I MISUNDERSTOOD** [ ] [–]

– compilations, etc. –

Aug 91. (10"m-lp) *S.S.T.; (SST 275)* **FOSSILS** [–] [ ]
– Little fury things / In a jar / Show me the way / Freak scene / Keep the glove / Just like heaven / Throw down / Chunks. <*(cd-iss. +UK May93 & Oct96; SST 276CD)*>

Feb 99. (cd) *Strange Fruit; (SFRSCD 078) / Varese Sarabande;* <*061049*> **THE BBC SESSIONS** [ ] Feb00 [ ]
– Raisins / Does it float / Leper / Bulbs of passion / Keep the glove / In a jar / Get me / Keeblin / Budge / No bones.

Oct 01. (cd) *Rhino;* <*8122 78395-2*> **EAR-BLEEDING COUNTRY: THE BEST OF DINOSAUR JR.** [–] [ ]
– Repulsion / Little fury things / In a jar / Freak scene / Budge / Just like Heaven / The wagon / Thumb / Whatever's cool with me / Not you again / Out there / Start choppin' / Get me / Feel the pain / I don't think so / Take a run at the sun / Nothin's goin' on / I'm insane / Where'd you go.

J MASCIS

		Ionic-Mute	Mute-Elektra
Oct 92.	(cd; by J. MASCIS & BARRY ADAMSON) *(IONIC 9CD)* <61424> **GAS FOOD LODGING** (soundtrack w/ Various Artists)	☐	☐

– Untitled (tracks) / Flying clouds (instrumental with BARRY ADAMSON) / (other artists).

		WEA	Warners
May 96.	(cd/c) <*(46177)*> **MARTIN + ME**	☐	Apr96 ☐

– Thumb / So what else is new / Get me / Blowin' it / Repulsion / Goin' home / The boy with the thorn in his side / Not you again / On the run / Keeblin / Flying cloud / Anticipation / Drawerings / Every mother's son.

J MASCIS + THE FOG

with guest **KEVIN SHIELDS**

		City Slang	Artemis
Sep 00.	(cd-s) *(20171-2)* **WHERE'D YOU GO / CAN I TELL U STORIES / TOO HARD**	☐	–
Oct 00.	(cd/lp) *(20168-2/-1)* <76665> **MORE LIGHT**	☐	☐

– Same day / Waistin' / Where'd you go / Back before you go / Grand me to you / Anmaring / All the girls / I not fine / Can I take this on / Does the kiss fit / More light.

Jun 01.	(cd-s) *(97745)* **WAISTIN' / LEAVING ON A JET PLANE**	☐	–

		City Slang	Ultimatum
Oct 02.	(cd/lp) *(20205-2/-1)* <76685> **FREE SO FREE**	☐	☐

– Freedom / If that's how its gotta be / Set us free / Bobbin / Free so free / Tell the truth / Someone said / Everybody lets me down / Say the word / Outside. *(UK re-iss. Jan03 on 'Ultimatum'; ULT 685LP)*

		Baked Goods	Baked Goods
Jan 06.	(cd) <*(BG 07)*> **J AND FRIENDS SING AND CHANT FOR AMMA**	☐	Aug05 ☐

– Please remember that I'm here / Help me Amma / Lokah / Take me home / Amma what now / Heavy metal ai giri nandini.

– (MASCIS) compilations, etc. –

Aug 03.	(cd) *Strange Fruit; (SFRSCD 122)* **THE BBC SESSIONS**	☐	–

WITCH

J MASCIS – drums / **KYLE THOMAS** – vocals (of FEATHERS) / **ASA IRONS** – guitar (of FEATHERS) / **DAVE SWEETAPPLE** – bass

		TeePee	TeePee
Mar 06.	(cd) <*(TP 65)*> **WITCH**	☐	☐

– Seer / Soul of fire / Black saint / Changing / Rip Van Winkle / Hand of glory / Isadora.

DIRE STRAITS

Formed: Deptford, London, England . . . mid-'77 by ex-teacher and journalist MARK KNOPFLER alongside brother DAVID, JOHN ILLSLEY and PICK WITHERS. After Radio 1 DJ, Charlie Gillett gave their demo an airing later the same year, they were signed to 'Vertigo' by A&R man, John Stainze, releasing a classic debut single, 'SULTANS OF SWING', in Spring '78. A driving but subtle slice of rootsy, bluesy R&B, the song was a wonderfully observed snapshot of the London pub rock scene where they'd initially plied their trade. Although it failed to chart, their eponymous debut album (released later that summer) made the UK Top 40 after rave live reviews and a major deal with 'Warners' in the States. Comparisons with BOB DYLAN's easier going material and the laidback (horizontal, even!) country-blues grooves of J.J. CALE were the favoured choice of salivating critics although KNOPFLER's dry wit and unmistakable guitar lines gave DIRE STRAITS the stamp of authenticity. In fact, DYLAN was so impressed he invited KNOPFLER to augment him on his 1979 set, 'SLOW TRAIN COMING'; by this point, both the debut single and album had amassed transatlantic Top 10 sales with the help of a sell-out US tour while a follow-up set, 'COMMUNIQUE' (1979), further developed KNOPFLER's narrative skills on the likes of the epic 'ONCE UPON A TIME IN THE WEST'. With HAL LINDES replacing the departing DAVID and ex-E STREET BAND man, ROY BITTAN drafted in on keyboards, 'MAKING MOVIES' (1980) took a harder-edged yet more melodic, accessible and expansive approach; vivid story-songs such as the bittersweet 'ROMEO AND JULIET' saw KNOPFLER compared to SPRINGSTEEN while the heady momentum of 'TUNNEL OF LOVE' effortlessly conjured up the giddy thrills and spills of a trip to the fairground. Opening with another compelling narrative in 'TELEGRAPH ROAD' and boasting the moody 'PRIVATE INVESTIGATIONS', 'LOVE OVER GOLD' (1982) became DIRE STRAITS' first UK No.1 album, the band flying in the face of fashion and selling millions. This was nothing, however compared to the global phenomenon that was 'BROTHERS IN ARMS'; released in 1985 following the lengthy double live set 'ALCHEMY' (1984), the record's glossy production and more focused pop-friendly approach saw it breaking UK sales records. Its biggest hit, 'MONEY FOR NOTHING', was an acerbic comment on US MTV domination, the accompanying video ironically caned by the channel in all its innovative, technology-enhanced glory. It was also the closest DIRE STRAITS ever veered towards heavy rock, the bulk of the material going in for coffee table, ear-massaging atmospherics and acoustic textures. The soft-focus minimalism of the title track is arguably DIRE STRAITS' finest moment and, despite the stigma surrounding the album, 'BROTHERS IN ARMS' remains an essential 80's release. Following the attendant mammoth touring commitments, DIRE STRAITS/KNOPFLER took an extended sabbatical with only a 1988 best of to keep fans happy. Having already scored soundtracks for 'LOCAL HERO' (1983), 'COMFORT AND JOY' (1984) and 'CAL' (1984), KNOPFLER was commissioned for both 'THE PRINCESS BRIDE' (1987) and 'LAST EXIT TO BROOKLYN' (1989). He also got back to his pub-rock roots with The NOTTING HILLBILLIES, releasing an album, 'MISSING . . . PRESUMED HAVING A GOOD TIME' in 1990. Later that year, he hooked up with country picker, CHET ATKINS, for the 'NECK AND NECK' album. DIRE STRAITS eventually returned in 1991 with 'ON EVERY STREET', an album which couldn't hope to emulate 'BROTHERS . . .' and didn't even try. It made No.1 all the same and sold enough to keep their record company happy in the meantime. With KNOPFLER actually recording a solo set proper, 'GOLDEN HEART', in 1996, the chances of a further DIRE STRAITS release seemed slim although a split had yet to be confirmed. This was obvious to the record buying public when KNOPFLER delivered another chart-busting album, 'SAILING TO PHILADELPHIA' in 2000. If KNOPFLER fans must've wondered what was going on with another studio set so soon after the last, they wouldn't have been disappointed. 'THE RAGPICKER'S DREAM' (2002) inhabited that singular musical landscape sacred to KNOPFLER, where northern English tradition stalks the prairies and backwoods of rural America. It's a land far removed from DIRE STRAITS but one where the fleet-fingered singer moves with tranquil – if always strangely restless – ease, content to rein in his guitar prowess to the confines of acoustic roots music. Finally recovered after a rib-splintering motorbike crash (and months of physio), KNOPFLER returned with 'SHANGRI-LA' (2004), his flat cap charm, burnished guitar and beady narrator's eye intact. Only the latter day Celtic folk-isms were absent, as he concentrated on a perennial penchant for American roots music, even penning a wake for skiffle pioneer LONNIE DONEGAN. The soberly recounted '5.15 A.M.' ranked as one of his most compelling yarns in years, while 'The TRAWLERMAN'S SONG' dished out the kind of rippling stratocaster scraps that keep DIRE STRAITS fans on board. While the record didn't quite make the UK Top

10 (US Top 75), he was back there – and in the US Top 20 – with 'ALL THE ROADRUNNING' (2006), an extended duet with EMMYLOU HARRIS. Released on the back of the 2005 DIRE STRAITS/solo anthology, 'PRIVATE INVESTIGATIONS..' (which previewed standout track 'ALL THE ROADRUNNING'), the HARRIS collaborations had actually undergone a lengthy gestation period dating back to the late 90s.

• **Songwriters:** KNOPFLER compositions, except the NOTTING HILLBILLIES cover of FEEL LIKE GOING HOME (Charlie Rich). • **Trivia:** MARK penned 'PRIVATE DANCER' for TINA TURNER in 1983, and also produced to name but a few; 'Infidels' for BOB DYLAN and 'Knife' for AZTEC CAMERA.

Album rating: DIRE STRAITS (*8) / COMMUNIQUE (*5) / MAKING MOVIES (*6) / LOVE OVER GOLD (*6) / ALCHEMY – LIVE (*7) / BROTHERS IN ARMS (*8) / MONEY FOR NOTHING compilation (*8) / ON EVERY STREET (*5) / ON THE NIGHT (*5) / PRIVATE INVESTIGATIONS: THE BEST OF DIRE STRAITS & MARK KNOPFLER compilation (*7) / Mark Knopfler: LOCAL HERO soundtrack (*7) / CAL soundtrack (*7) / THE PRINCESS BRIDE soundtrack (*7) / LAST EXIT TO BROOKLYN soundtrack (*5) / NECK AND NECK with Chet Atkins (*6) / SCREENPLAYING compilation (*7) / GOLDEN HEART (*4) / WAG THE DOG soundtrack (*6) / METROLAND soundtrack (*6) / SAILING TO PHILADELPHIA (*6) / A SHOT AT GLORY soundtrack (*5) / THE RAGPICKER'S DREAM (*6) / SHANGRI-LA (*6) / ALL THE ROADRUNNING with Emmylou Harris (*6)

MARK KNOPFLER (b.12 Aug'49, Glasgow, Scotland) – vocals, lead guitar / **DAVID KNOPFLER** (b.1951, Glasgow) – guitar / **JOHN ILLSLEY** (b.24 Jun'49, Leicester, England) – bass / **PICK WITHERS** – drums

Vertigo Warners

May 78. (7") *(6059 206)* *<8736>* **SULTANS OF SWING. / EASTBOUND TRAIN** [ ] Jan79 [4]
(re-iss. Feb79; same) – (hit No.8)

Jun 78. (lp)(c) *(9102 021)(723 1015)* *<3266>* **DIRE STRAITS** [5] Oct78 [2]
– Down to the waterline / Water of love / Setting me up / Six blade knife / Southbound train / Sultans of swing / Wild west end / Lions / In the gallery. *(master edition Apr82; HS 9102 021) (cd-iss. 1987; 800 051-2) (cd re-iss. Jun96; same)*

Jul 79. (7") *(6059 230)* *<49006>* **LADY WRITER. / WHERE DO YOU THINK YOU'RE GOING** [ ] [45]

Aug 79. (lp)(c) *(9102 031)(723 1021)* *<3330>* **COMMUNIQUE** [5] Jun79 [11]
– Once upon a time in the west / News / Where do you think you're going / Communique / Lady writer / Angel of mercy / Portobello belle / Single-handed sailor / Follow me home. *(cd-iss. 1987; 800 052-2) (re-iss. Jun96; same)*

Oct 79. (7") *<49082>* **ONCE UPON A TIME IN THE WEST. / NEWS** [–] [ ]

— **HAL LINDES** (b.30 Jun'53, Monterey, Calif.) – guitar repl. DAVID who later went solo, also added **ROY BITTAN** – keyboards / (ex-E-STREET BAND BRUCE SPRINGSTEEN)

Oct 80. (lp/c) *(6359/7150 034)* *<3480>* **MAKING MOVIES** [4] Nov80 [19]
– Tunnel of love / Romeo and Juliet / Skateaway / Expresso love / Hand in hand / Solid rock / Les boys. *(master edition Apr82; HS 6359 034) (cd-iss. 1987; 800 050-2) (cd re-iss. Jun96; same)*

Nov 80. (7") *(MOVIE 1)* *<49688>* **ROMEO AND JULIET / SOLID ROCK** [8] Mar81 [ ]

Dec 80. (7") *<49632>* **SKATEAWAY. / SOLID ROCK** [–] [58]

Mar 81. (7") *(MOVIE 2)* **SKATEAWAY. / EXPRESSO LOVE** [37] [–]

Sep 81. (7") *(MOVIE 3)* **TUNNEL OF LOVE. / TUNNEL OF LOVE (part 2)** [54] [–]

— **ALAN CLARK** (b. 5 Mar'52, Durham, England) – keyboards repl ROY.

Aug 82. (7"/10") *(DSTR 1/+10)* **PRIVATE INVESTIGATIONS. / BADGES POSTERS STICKERS T-SHIRTS** [2] [–]

Sep 82. (lp/c) *(6359/7150 109)* *<23728>* **LOVE OVER GOLD** [1] [19]
– Telegraph road / Private investigations / Industrial disease / Love over gold / It never rains / If I had you / Twisting by the pool / Two young lovers / Badges, posters, stickers, T-shirts. *(cd-iss. 1984; 800 088-2) (cd re-iss. Jun96; same)*

Dec 82. (7") *<29880>* **INDUSTRIAL DISEASE. / BADGES POSTERS STICKERS T-SHIRT** [–] [75]

Jan 83. (7"/10"/12") *(DSTR 2/+10/12)* **TWISTING BY THE POOL. / TWO YOUNG LOVERS / IF I HAD YOU** [14] [–]

Mar 83. (m-lp) *<29800>* **TWISTING BY THE POOL** [–] [53]
– Twisting by the pool / Two young lovers / If I had you / Badges posters stickers T-shirts.

May 83. (7") *<29706>* **TWISTING BY THE POOL. / BADGES POSTERS STICKERS T-SHIRTS** [–] [ ]

— **IOMAR HAKIM** – drums, percussion repl. PICK
above was replaced by **TERRY WILLIAMS** (b.11 Jan'48, Swansea, Wales) – drums (ex-MAN, ex-MOTORS, ex-ROCKPILE) / (both played on album below alongside **MARK, JOHN, HAL + ALAN**)

Feb 84. (7"/10"/12") *(DSRT 6/+10/12)* **LOVE OVER GOLD (live). / SOLID GOLD (live)** [50] [ ]

Mar 84. (d-lp/c)(cd) *(VERY/+C 11)(810243-2)* *<25085>* **ALCHEMY – LIVE (live)** [3] Apr84 [46]
– Once upon a time in the west / Romeo and Juliet / Expresso love / Private investigations / Sultans of swing / Two young lovers / Tunnel of love / Telegraph road / Solid rock / Going home (theme from 'Local Hero'). *(c+=/cd+=)* – Love over gold (live). *(cd re-iss. Jun96; same)*

— added **GUY FLETCHER** – keyboards / also **JACK SONNI** – guitar (on tour)

Apr 85. (7"/10"/12") *(DSRT 9/+10/12)* **SO FAR AWAY. / WALK OF LIFE** [20] [–]

May 85. (lp/c)(cd) *(VERH/+C 25)(824499-2)* *<25264>* **BROTHERS IN ARMS** [1] [1]
– So far away / Money for nothing / Walk of life / Your latest trick / Why worry? / Ride across the river / The man's too strong / One world / Money for nothing / Brothers in arms. *(c+=/cd+=; extended versions)* – So far away / Money for nothing / Your latest trick / Why worry? *(cd re-iss. Jun96; ame)*

Jun 85. (7"/10"/12")(7"sha-pic-d) *(DSRT 10/+10/12)(DSPIC 10)* *<28950>* **MONEY FOR NOTHING. / LOVE OVER GOLD (live)** [4] [1]

Oct 85. (7") *<28878>* **WALK OF LIFE. / ONE WORLD** [–] [7]

Oct 85. (7"sha-pic-d)(10") *(DSPIC 11)(DSTR 11-10)* **BROTHERS IN ARMS. / GOING HOME – THEME FROM 'LOCAL HERO' (live)** [16] [ ]
(12"+=) *(DSTR 11-12)* – Why worry.
(d7"++=) *(DSTRD 11)* – Sultans of swing / Eastbound train.

Jan 86. (7") *(DSRT 12)* **WALK OF LIFE. / TWO YOUNG LOVERS (live)** [2] [–]
(12"+=) *(DSRT 12-12)* – Sultans of swing.
(d7"++=) *(DSTRD 12)* – Eastbound train (live).

Feb 86. (7") *<28789>* **SO FAR AWAY. / IF I HAD YOU** [–] [19]

Apr 86. (7") *(DSTR 13)* **YOUR LATEST TRICK. / IRISH BOY** [26] [ ]
(12"+=) *(DSTR 13-12)* – The long road.

Oct 88. (lp/c)(cd) *(VERH/+C 64)(836419-2)* *<25794>* **MONEY FOR NOTHING** (compilation) [1] Nov88 [62]
– Sultans of swing / Down to the waterline / Portobello belle (live) / Twisting by the pool / Tunnel of love / Romeo and Juliet / Where do you think you're going / Walk of life / Private investigations / Telegraph Road (live) / Money for nothing / Brothers in arms.

Nov 88. (7") *(DSTR 15)* **SULTANS OF SWING. / PORTOBELLO BELLE (live)** [62] [ ]
(12"+=)(cd-s+=) *(DSTR 15-12)(DSCD 15)* – Romeo and Juliet / Money for nothing.

Aug 91. (7"/c-s) *(DSTR/+C 16)* **CALLING ELVIS. / IRON HAND** [21] [ ]
(12"+=)(cd-s+=) *(DSTR 16-12)(DSCD 16)* – Millionaire blues.

Sep 91. (cd/c/lp) *(510160-2/-4/-1)* *<26680>* **ON EVERY STREET** [1] [12]
– Calling Elvis / On every street / When it comes to you / Fade to black / The bug / You and your friend / Heavy fuel / Iron hand / Ticket to Heaven / My parties / Planet of New Orleans / How long.

Oct 91. (7"/c-s) *(DSTR/+C 17)* *<19094>* **HEAVY FUEL. / PLANET OF NEW ORLEANS** [55] [ ]
(12"+=)(cd-s+=) *(DSTR 17-12)(DSCD 17)* – Kingdom come.

Feb 92. (7"/c-s) *(DSTR/+C 18)* **ON EVERY STREET. / ROMEO AND JULIET** [42] [–]
(cd-s+=) *(DSCD 18)* – Private investigations / Sultans of swing.

Jun 92. (7"/c-s) *(DSTR/+C 19)* **THE BUG. / TWISTING BY THE POOL** [67] [ ]
(cd-s+=) *(DSCD 19)* – ('A'version).

— added touring band 91-93 **DANNY CUMMINGS** – percussion / **PHIL PALMER** – guitar / **PAUL FRANKLIN** – pedal steel / **CHRIS WHITE** – sax, flute / **CHRIS WHITTEN** – drums

May 93. (cd/c/lp) *(514766-2/-4/-1)* *<45259>* **ON THE NIGHT (live)** [4] [ ]
– Calling Elvis / Walk of life / Heavy fuel / Romeo & Juliet / Your latest trick / Private investigations / On every street / You and your friend / Money for nothing / Brothers in arms.

May 93. (c-ep/12"ep/cd-ep) *(DSTRC/DSTR12/DSCD 20)* **ENCORES LIVE EP (live)** 31
– Your latest trick / The bug / Solid rock / Local hero (wild theme).

— Oct'93; MARK was credited on HANK MARVIN's single 'Wonderful Land'.

— DIRE STRAITS looked to have disbanded since it's been five years since a recording.

– compilations, etc. –

Oct 88. (cd-video) *Vertigo; (080 128-2)* **SULTANS OF SWING / WILD WEST END / DOWN THE WATERLINE** –
Oct 88. (cd-video) *Vertigo; (080 130-2)* **MONEY FOR NOTHING (extended) / ONE WORLD / SO FAR AWAY** –
Oct 88. (cd-video) *Vertigo; (080 132-2)* **BROTHERS IN ARMS (extended) / YOUR LATEST TRICK / RIDE ACROSS THE RIVER** –
Oct 88. (cd-video) *Vertigo; (080 134-2)* **WALK OF LIFE / WHY WORRY / RIDE ACROSS THE RIVER** –
Oct 88. (cd-video) *Vertigo; (080 136-2)* **TWISTING BY THE POOL / TWO YOUNG LOVERS / IF I HAD YOU / TWISTING BY THE POOL** –
Jul 95. (cd/c/lp) *Windsong; (WIN CD/MC/LP 072)* **LIVE AT THE BBC (live)** 71 –
Oct 98. (cd/c) *Warners; (558658-2/-4) <47130>* **SULTANS OF SWING – THE VERY BEST OF DIRE STRAITS** 6
– Sultans of swing / Lady writer / Romeo and Juliet / Tunnel of love / Private investigations / Twisting by the pool / Love over gold / So far away / Money for nothing / Brothers in arms / Walk of life / Calling Elvis / Heavy fuel / On every street / Your latest trick / Local hero – Wild theme. *(also d-cd; 538003-2)*
Nov 05. (cd) *Mercury; (9872936) <49891>* **PRIVATE INVESTIGATIONS: THE BEST OF DIRE STRAITS & MARK KNOPFLER** 20
– Sultans of swing / Love over gold / Romeo and Juliet / Tunnel of love – Intro: The Carousel waltz / Private investigations / Money for nothing / Brothers in arms / Walk of life / On every street / Going home (theme from 'Local Hero') / Why aye man / Boom, like that / What it is / All the roadrunning (w/ EMMYLOU HARRIS). *(d-cd+=; 9873054)* – Calling Elvis / Telegraph road / Darling pretty / Long road / Sailing to Philadelphia / So far away / Trawlerman's song / Your latest trick.

MARK KNOPFLER

(first with **ALAN CLARK, LINDES** plus **MIKE BRECKER** – sax)

Vertigo Warners

Feb 83. (7"/12") *(DSTR 4/+12) <29725>* **GOING HOME (THEME FROM 'LOCAL HERO'). / SMOOCHING** 56
Apr 83. (lp/c) *(VERL/+C 4) <1/-4-23827>* **LOCAL HERO** 14
– The rocks and the water / Wild theme / Freeway flyer / Boomtown / The way it always starts / The rocks and the thunder / The ceilidh and the northern lights / The mist covered mountains / The ceilidh: Louis' favourite Billy's tune / Whistle theme / Smooching / The rocks and the thunder / Going home (theme from 'Local Hero'). *(cd-iss. Jul84; 811 038-2) <US cd-iss. 1988; 2-23827>*
Jul 83. (7") *(DSTR 5)* **WILD THEME. / GOING HOME (THEME FROM LOCAL HERO)** –
Jul 84. (lp) *(880122-1)* **COMFORT AND JOY** (soundtrack) – w-drawn –
Jul 84. (12") *(DSTR 7-12)* **COMFORT / JOY. / A FISTFUL OF ICE CREAM** –
Sep 84. (7"/ext.12") *(DSTR 8/+12)* **THE LONG ROAD – THEME FROM 'CAL'. / IRISH BOY** –
Oct 84. (lp/c)(cd) *(VERH/+C 17)(<822769-2>)* **CAL (MUSIC FROM THE FILM)** 65
– Irish boy / The road / Waiting for her / Irish love / Secret place – Where will you go? / Father and son / Meeting under the trees / Potato picking / In a secret place / Fear and hatred / Love and guilt / The long road.
Oct 86. (7") *(DSTR 14)* **GOING HOME (THEME OF THE CRUSADER CHALLENGE). / WILD THEME** –
(12"+=) *(DSTR 14-12)* – Smooching.
(cd-s+=) *(DSCD 14)* – Comfort (from 'Comfort And Joy').
Nov 87. (lp/c)(cd) *(VERH/+C 53)(832 864-2) <25610>* **MUSIC FROM THE FILM SOUNDTRACK 'THE PRINCESS BRIDE'**
– Once upon a time ... Storybook love / I will never love again / Florin dance / Morning ride / The friends' song / The cliffs of insanity / The swordfight / Guide my sword / The fireswamp and the rodents of unusual size / Revenge / A happy ending / Storybook love (with WILLY DeVILLE).
Mar 88. (7"/c-s; with WILLY DeVILLE) *(VER/+MC 37)* **THEME FROM 'THE PRINCESS BRIDE': STORYBOOK LOVE. / THE FRIENDS' SONG (with GUY FLETCHER)** –
(cd-s+=) *(VERCD 37)* – Once upon a time . . . Storybook love.
Nov 89. (lp/c/cd) *(838725-1/-4/-2) <25986>* **LAST EXIT TO BROOKLYN (soundtrack)**
– Last exit to Brooklyn / Victims / Think fast / A love idea / Tralala / Riot / The reckoning / As low as it gets / Finale: Last exit to Brooklyn.

the NOTTING HILLBILLIES

MARK KNOPFLER – guitar, vocals, producer / **GUY FLETCHER** – guitar, vocals, producer / **BRENDAN CROKER** – guitar, vocals / **STEVE PHILLIPS** – guitar, vocals / with **PAUL FRANKLIN** – pedal steel guitar

Vertigo Warner

Feb 90. (7"/c-s) *(NHB/+MC 1)* **YOUR OWN SWEET WAY. / BEWILDERED** –
(12"+=)(cd-s+=) *(NHB 1-12)(NHBCD 1)* – That's where I belong.
Mar 90. (cd/c/lp) *(842 671-2/-4/-1) <26147>* **MISSING . . . PRESUMED HAVING A GOOD TIME** 2 52
– Railroad worksong / Bewildered / Your own sweet way / Run me down / One way gal / Blues stay away from me / Will you miss me / Please baby / Weapon of prayer / That's where I belong / Feel like going home.
Apr 90. (7"/c-s) *(NHB/+MC 2)* **FEEL LIKE GOING HOME. / LONESOME WIND BLUES** –
(12"+=)(cd-s+=) *(NHB 2-12)(NHBCD 2)* – One way gal.
Jun 90. (7"/c-s) *(NHB/+MC 3)* **WILL YOU MISS ME. / THAT'S WHERE I BELONG** –
(12"+=)(cd-s+=) *(NHB 3-12)(NHBCD 3)* – Lonesome wind blues.

CHET ATKINS & MARK KNOPFLER

C.B.S. Columbia

Oct 90. (7"/c-s) *(656 373-7/-4)* **POOR BOY BLUES. / SO SOFT YOUR GOODBYE**
(cd-s+=) *(656 373-2)* – There'll be some changes made.
Nov 90. (cd/c/lp) *(467435-2/-4/-1) <45307>* **NECK AND NECK** 41 Oct90
– Poor boy blues / Sweet dreams / There'll be some changes made / Just one time / So soft / Your goodbye / Yakety axe / Tahitian skies / Tears / I'll see you in my dreams / The next time I'm in town.

MARK KNOPFLER

— MARK featured on HANK MARVIN's new version of 'Wonderful Land' released Oct'93

Vertigo Warner

Mar 96. (c-s/cd-s) *(VER MC/CD 88)* **DARLING PRETTY / GRAVY TRAIN** 33 –
(cd-s+=) *(VERDD 88)* – My claim to fame.
Apr 96. (cd/c) *(514732-2/-4) <46026>* **GOLDEN HEART** 9
– Darling pretty / Imelda / Golden heart / No can do / Vic and Ray / Don't you get it / A night in summer long ago / Cannibals / I'm the fool / Je suis desole / Rudiger / Nobody's got the gun / Done with Bonaparte / Are we in trouble now.
May 96. (c-s/cd-s) *(VER MC/CD 89)* **CANNIBAL / TALL ORDER** 42 –
(cd-s+=) *(VERDD 89)* – What have I got to do.

— In 1996, a collaborative CD with STEVE PHILIPS, 'JUST PICKIN' was issued by 'Buried Treasure' *(TROV 2)*

Mercury Mercury

Jan 98. (cd/c) *(<536864-2/-4>)* **WAG THE DOG** (soundtrack)
– Wag the dog / Working on it / In the heartland / An American hero / Just instinct / Stretching out / Drooling national / We're going to war.

Mercury Warner

May 98. (cd/c) *(536912-2/-4) <47006>* **METROLAND** (soundtrack w/ Various Artists) Mar99
– Metroland theme / Annick / Tous les garcons et les filles (FRANCOISE HARDY) / Brats / Blues Clair (DJANGO REINHARDT) / Down day / A walk in Paris / She's gone / Minor swing (DJANGO REINHARDT) / Peaches (STRANGLERS) / SULTANS OF SWING (DIRE STRAITS) / So you win again (HOT CHOCOLATE) / Alison (ELVIS COSTELLO) / Metroland.
Sep 00. (c-s) *(562866-4)* **WHAT IT IS / LONG HIGHWAY** –
(cd-s+=) *(562866-2)* – Let's see you.
Sep 00. (cd/c) *(542981-2/-4) <47753>* **SAILING TO PHILADELPHIA** 4 Oct00 60

– What it is / Sailing to Philadelphia / Who's your baby now / Baloney again / The last laugh / Do America / Silvertown blues / El macho / Prairie wedding / Wanderlust / Speedway at Nazareth / Junkie doll / Sands of Nevada / One more matinee.

)ct 01. (cd) *(548127-2)* *<48324>* **A SHOT AT GLORY** (soundtrack) ☐ Apr02 ☐
– Sons of Scotland / Hard cases / He's the man / Training / The new laird / Say too much / Four in a row / All that I have in the world / Sons of Scotland – quiet theme / It's over / Wild mountain thyme.

Mercury Warners

ep 02. (cd-s) *(63913-2)* **WHY AYE MAN / SMALL POTATOES / SO FAR AWAY (live at Shepherd's Bush Empire)** ☐ –

ep 02. (cd/c/lp) *(63292-2/-4/-1)* *<48318>* **THE RAGPICKER'S DREAM** 7 Oct02 38
– Why aye man / Devil baby / Hill farmer's blues / A place where we used to live / Quality shoe / Fare thee well Northumberland / Marbletown / You don't know you're born / Coyote / The ragpicker's dream / Daddy's gone to Knoxville / Old Pigweed. *(ltd-cd+=; 63293-2)* – live:- Why aye man / Quality shoe / Sailing to Philadelphia / Brothers in arms / Why aye man (video).

ep 04. (7") *(9867836)* **BOOM, LIKE THAT. / WHO'S YOUR BABY NOW (live at the Massey Hall, Toronto)** 34 –
(cd-s) *(9867839)* – ('A') / Summer of love.

ep 04. (cd/d-lp) *(986726-0/-2)* *<48858>* **SHANGRI-LA** 11 66
– 5.15am / Boom, like that / Sucker row / The trawlerman's song / Back to Tupelo / Our shangri-la / Everybody pays / Song for Sonny Liston / Whoop de doo / Postcards from Paraguay / All that matters / Stand up guy / Donegan's gone / Don't crash the ambulance. *(ltd-cd+=; 9867259)* – (interviews + live footage).

Polydor Warners

pr 06. (cd; by MARK KNOPFLER & EMMYLOU HARRIS) *(9877385)* *<44154>* **ALL THE ROADRUNNING** 8 17
– Beachcombing / I dug up a diamond / This is us / Red staggerwing / Rollin' on / Love and happiness / Right now / Donkey town / Belle Starr / Beyond my wildest dreams / All the roadrunning / If this is goodbye.

– compilations, etc. –

'ct 93. (7"/c-s) *Vertigo; (VER/+MC 81)* **THEMES FROM LOCAL HERO: GOING HOME. / WILD THEME** ☐ –
(cd-s+=) *(VERCD 81)* – Comfort (from 'Comfort And Joy')

ov 93. (cd/c/lp) *Vertigo; (518327-2/-4/-1) / Warners; <45457-2/-4>* **SCREENPLAYING** (solo film work) ☐ ☐
– Irish boy / Irish love / Father and son / Potato picking / The long road / A love idea / Victims / Finale – Last Exit To Brooklyn / Once upon a time . . . Storybook love / Morning ride / The friends' song / Guide my sword / A happy ending / Wild theme / Boomtown / The mist covered mountains / Smooching / Going home: theme from Local Hero.

ct 00. (d-cd) *Universal; (E 546601-2)* **MISSING . . . PRESUMED HAVING A GOOD TIME (with the NOTTING HILLBILLIES) / SCREENPLAYING** ☐ ☐

DIRTY PRETTY THINGS

(see under ⇒ LIBERTINES)

he DISTILLERS

ormed: Detroit, Michigan, USA . . . 1998 by Aussie expat RODY DALLE and KIM CHI, who subsequently recruited ROSE CASPER" MAZZOLA and MAT YOUNG. After inking a deal with Hellcat / Epitaph', the band laid bare their raw, unadulterated punk nfluences on 'THE DISTILLERS' (2000), as uncompromising a elease as any amid the so-called punk revival of the late 90's. There as certainly nothing new or even particularly notable in their pproach although DALLE's demented shrieking spoke of a deeper nrest than the usual rock star posturing, while a version of Patti mith's 'ASK THE ANGELS' was more promising than the side-litting pop covers of some nu-punk acts. Given the urgency of eir sound, it was no surprise when follow-up 'SING SING DEATH OUSE' was released later the same year, another discordant, iscomfiting window on DALLE's troubled soul and even more troubled (at least judging by her lyrics) upbringing; she had also recently split from hubby TIM ARMSTRONG (of RANCID). By the time of the album's re-release in 2002 (to cash in on the interest in the feminist themed 'SENECA FALLS'), the line-up had been reduced to DALLE alongside new members RYAN SINN and ANDY OUTBREAK/GRANELLI, while TONY BRADLEY had stepped into the breach for the recording of 'CORAL FANG' (2003), the DISTILLERS' Gil Norton-produced major label debut (for 'Sire'). Appropriately perhaps, the album dispensed with the trashy quality of the earlier records, replacing it with a more composed, more intense and occasionally even a slightly theatrical dissection of shattered relationships and bruised emotions. Nevertheless, from the explicit cover art to the epic blitz of 'DEATH SEX', there was still enough subversion to please longtime fans (and 'Kerrang!') despite the corporate makeover. The release of a fourth album was held up as BRODY took time out for maternity leave, the father of her little 'un being noneother than JOSH HOMME of QUEENS OF THE STONE AGE.

Album rating: THE DISTILLERS (*6) / SING SING DEATH HOUSE (*7) / CORAL FANG (*6)

BRODY ARMSTRONG (b. BRODY DALLE, 1 Jan'79, Melbourne, Australia) – vocals, guitar / **ROSE "CASPER" MAZZOLA** – guitar / **KIM CHI** (b. FUELMAN) – bass / **MAT YOUNG** – drums

Hellcat Hellcat

Nov 99. (7"ep) **THE DISTILLERS** – ☐
– Old Scratch / L.A. girl / Colossus U.S.A. / Blackheart.

Jun 00. (cd/lp) *<(80422-2/-1)>* **THE DISTILLERS** ☐ Apr00 ☐
– Oh Serena / Idoless / The world comes tumblin' / L.A. girl / Distilla truant / Ask the angels / Old Scratch / Girlfixer / Open sky / Red carpet and rebellion / Colossus U.S.A. / Blackheart / Gypsy Rose Lee / The blackest years.

—— **RYAN SINN** – bass; repl. KIM who joined the ORIGINAL SINNERS

—— **ANDY OUTBREAK** (b. GRANELLI) – drums; repl. MAT

Feb 02. (cd/lp) *<(80441-2/-1)>* **SING SING DEATH HOUSE** ☐ ☐
– Sick of it all / I am revenant / Seneca falls / The young crazed peeling / Sing sing death house / Bullet and the bullseye / City of angels / Young girl / Hate me / Desperate / I understand / Lordy lordy.

Nov 02. (cd-s) *(1089-2)* **CITY OF ANGELS / SOLVENT / SING SING DEATH HOUSE** ☐ –

—— **BRODY DALLE** + **SINN** brought in **TONY BRADLEY** – guitar, vocals (GRANELLI formed DARKER MY LOVE)

WEA Sire

Oct 03. (cd) *(9362 48586-2)* *<48420>* **CORAL FANG** 46 97
– Drain the blood / Dismantle me / Die on a rope / The gallow is God / Coral fang / The hunger / Hall of mirrors / Beat your heart out / Love is paranoid / For tonight you're only here to know / Death sex.

Nov 03. (cd-s) *(W 628CD)* **DRAIN THE BLOOD / DISMANTLE ME (acoustic version) / CINCINNATI** 51 –

Mar 04. (cd-s) *(W 636CD1)* **THE HUNGER / DRAIN THE BLOOD (XFM session)** 48 –
(cd-s) *(W 636CD2)* – ('A') / Dismantle me (XFM session) / ('A'-XFM session).

Jun 04. (cd-s) *(W 644CD)* **BEAT YOUR HEART OUT / THE GALLOW IS GOD (acoustic) / ('A'-video)** 74 –

—— the group's in hiatus; BRODY had a baby in 2006 – RYAN joined ANGELS AND AIRWAVES (the band of TOM DeLONGE, ex-BLINK-182)

DISTURBED

Formed: Chicago, Illinois, USA . . . early 90's by DAN DONEGAN, MIKE WENGREN and FUZZ. With the addition of severely angry young man DAVID DRAIMAN in 1997, DISTURBED's bandwagon began rolling with a vengeance as they built up a grassroots following from Chicago's mean streets. Subsequently signed to 'Giant' on the strength of a demo, the band joined the nu-metal melee in 2000 with debut album, 'THE SICKNESS'. Equal parts Big Rock chorus and itchy, rap-metal chops, naggingly addictive opening track 'VOICES' was as good a place as any to enter the unforgiving world of DISTURBED. The track was subsequently released as a single while the album itself made the US Top 75, a highlight being an updated 2000 version of Tear For Fears' 'SHOUT'. While few would've predicted a US No.1 placing for only their sophomore album, that's exactly what those DISTURBED boys enjoyed with 'BELIEVE' (2002). It might've been graced with a sleeve which wouldn't have looked out of place on a VENOM album back in the 80's, but its epic, much developed metal chops were tailor-made for a market that can't seem to get enough heavy music. Although there was a shared live album, 'Music As A Weapon II' (2004), to disturb the silence between releases, metallers were really waiting for long-time-comin' third set, 'TEN THOUSAND FISTS' (2005), by which time FUZZ had been replaced by JOHN MOYER. Once again it punched its way to the top of the charts, even if there was another baffling 80s cover among the chest-thumping riffs; it's highly likely that many of their fans were probably still in short trousers when Genesis' 'LAND OF CONFUSION' first did the rounds.

Album rating: THE SICKNESS (*5) / BELIEVE (*7) / TEN THOUSAND FISTS (*6)

DAVID DRAIMAN (b.13 Mar'73, Flatbush, Brooklyn, NY) – vocals / **DAN DONEGAN** (b. 1 Aug'68, Oak Lawn, Illinois) – guitar / **FUZZ** (b. STEVE KMAK, Covington, Kentucky) – bass / **MIKE WENGREN** – drums

R.C.A. Giant – Warners

Jul 00. (cd) *(74321 70267-2)* <24738> **THE SICKNESS** [ ] Mar00 [29]
– Voices / The game / Stupify / Down with the sickness / Violence fetish / Fear / Numb / Want / Conflict / Shout 2000 / Droppin' plates / Meaning of life. *(re-iss. Jul02 on 'Warners'+=; 9362 48315-2)* – God of the mind (Valentine soundtrack version) / Stupify (live) / The game (live) / Voices (live) / Down with the sickness (live).

Mar 01. (7"red) *(74321 84896-7)* <100410> **VOICES. / VOICES (live)** [52] Nov00 [ ]
(cd-s) *(74321 84641-2)* – ('A') / Stupify (live) / The games (live).
(cd-s) *(74321 84896-2)* – ('A') / Down with the sickness (live) / ('A'-CD-ROM).

Warners Warners

Sep 02. (7") *(W 591)* **PRAYER. / FEAR (live)** [31] [58]
(cd-s+=) *(W 591CD1)* <93266> – Conflict (live).
(cd-s) *(W 591CD2)* – ('A') / Droppin' plates (live) / Shout 2000 (live).

Sep 02. (cd/lp/c) *<(9362 48320-2/-1/-4)>* **BELIEVE** [41] [1]
– Prayer / Liberate / Awaken / Believe / Remember / Intoxication / Rise / Mistress / Breathe / Bound / Devour / Darkness.

Dec 02. (7"purple) *(W 596)* **REMEMBER. / REMEMBER (live)** [56] [–]
(cd-s+=) *(W 596CD1)* – Rise (live).
(cd-s) *(W 596CD2)* – ('A') / Bound (live) / Mistress (live).

—— (late 2003) FUZZ departed; **JOHN MOYER** repl. him

—— early in 2004, DISTURBED were part of Various Artists live album, 'Music As A Weapon II', alongside CHEVELLE, TAPROOT & UNLOCO

Sep 05. (7"red/cd-s) *(W 685/+CD1)* *<radio>* **STRICKEN. / DEHUMANIZED** [ ] [95]
(cd-s) *(W 685CD2)* – ('A') / Hell / Darkness (live from Music As A Weapon II).

Sep 05. (cd) *<(9362 49433-2)>* **TEN THOUSAND FISTS** [59] [1]
– Ten thousand fists / Just stop / Guarded / Deify / Stricken / I'm alive / Sons of plunder / Overburdened / Decadence / Forgiven / Land of confusion / Sacred lie / Pain redefined / Avarice. *(ltd-cd w/book+=; 9362 49457-2)*

the DIVINE COMEDY

Formed: Londonderry, Northern Ireland . . . 1990 by bishop's son, NEIL HANNON, JOHN McCULLAGH and KEVIN TRAYNOR. Moving across the water to London, the three signed to maverick indie label, 'Setanta', releasing a SEAN O'NEILL (That Petrol Emotion)-produced debut, 'FANFARE FOR THE COMIC MUSE' (1990). A mini-set, it was followed by two further EP's, before the extroverted HANNON took over the reins as McCULLAGH and TRAYNOR bailed out. Free to pursue his ow eccentric muse, HANNON steered the DIVINE COMEDY awa from trad indie-rock towards a more self-consciously culture approach which suggested the influence of everyone from SCOT WALKER to JARVIS COCKER, in a cod-romantic ANDREV LLOYD-WEBBER-esque fashion of course! His first step toward educating the alternative pop scene came in the shape of 1993 'LIBERATION' album, his debonair charisma in full effect o tracks such as 'EUROPOP', 'BERNICE BOBS HER HAIR' and ' WAS BORN YESTERDAY'. His next set of songs, 'PROMENADE (1994), was a loose concept affair and featured the Irish comedian SEAN HUGHES, who provided verbal support on the track, 'TH BOOKLOVERS'. The name, the DIVINE COMEDY, came to th attention of 'Father Ted' loving music fans after the instrumenta 'SONGS OF LOVE', was used as the theme tune to the popula Channel 4 programme. HANNON also co-wrote another ditty fc the second series of the show; the downright silly 'My Beautif Horse' was the singing priests' (Ted and Dougal) entry for th Eurovision Song Contest!!! In 1996, HANNON (together wi his new DIVINE COMEDY recruits including JOBY TALBOT released his most perfectly conceived pop masterpiece to date i 'CASANOVA', the Roger Moore of rock crooning his way through dapper set of richly orchestrated diamonds. Duly encrusted into th Top 50, the album contained such memorably tongue-in-cheek hi as 'SOMETHING FOR THE WEEKEND', 'BECOMING MOR LIKE ALFIE' and 'THE FROG PRINCESS'. Now a firm critic fave, the DIVINE COMEDY (well, HANNON) had two more To 20 successes with 'A SHORT ALBUM ABOUT LOVE' (a mini-se and 'EVERYBODY KNOWS (EXCEPT YOU)' (a single). In Augu '98, "the Leslie Thomas" of indie-pop/rock, HANNON/the DIVIN COMEDY had his first Top 10 album, 'FIN DE SIECLE', a recor that boasted three further hits including 'GENERATION SEX' an 'NATIONAL EXPRESS'; a stop-gap UK Top 3 'best of' packag 'A SECRET HISTORY', was delivered the following year. The apt titled 'REGENERATION' (2001) displayed a wholesale change tack as HANNON and Co employed RADIOHEAD producer Nig Godrich and ditched the arch theatricality of old for a mo forthright, if not exactly earnest, musical and lyrical approach. A U Top 20 success bolstered by the hit singles 'BAD AMBASSADO and 'LOVE WHAT YOU DO', the album suggested that the impis Irish chameleon was sufficiently savvy to carry the whole thir off. HANNON returned to more familiar territory on the sel produced 'ABSENT FRIENDS' (2004), a record that generated a fe middling hits in 'COME HOME BILLY BIRD' and the title trac While hardly one to congratulate himself, the title of the man 9th set, 'VICTORY FOR THE COMIC MUSE' (2006), summe up the longevity of his highly original style, one which isn't afra to channel the past into the future: as well as covering Associate 'PARTY FEARS TWO', he kickstarted supernatural nostalgia wi the track, 'ARTHUR C. CLARKE'S MYSTERIOUS WORLD'.

• **Covered:** THERE IS A LIGHT THAT NEVER GOES OUT (Smiths) MIRANDA + LAST STAND IN METROLAND (Michael Nyman).

Album rating: FANFARE FOR THE COMIC MUSE mini (*4) / LIBERATIC (*6) / PROMENADE (*7) / CASANOVA (*8) / A SHORT ALBUM ABOUT LOV (*7) / FIN DE SIECLE (*7) / A SECRET HISTORY – THE BEST OF THE DIVIN COMEDY compilation (*7) / REGENERATION (*6) / ABSENT FRIENDS (*7 VICTORY FOR THE COMIC MUSE (*6)

NEIL HANNON (b. 7 Nov'70) – vocals, guitar, bass, piano, etc. / **JOH McCULLAGH** – bass, vocals / **KEVIN TRAYNOR** – drums

Setanta Seta

Aug 90. (m-cd/m-lp) *(SET CDM/LPM 002)* **FANFARE FOR THE COMIC MUSE** [ ] [–]
– Ignorance is bliss / Indian rain / Bleak landscape / Tailspin / Rise a fall / Logic vs. emotion / Secret garden.

Nov 91. (12"ep) *(SET 008)* **TIMEWATCH. / JERUSALEM / THE RISE AND FALL** [ ] [–]

Feb 92. (12"ep) *(SET 011)* **EUROPOP EP** [ ] [–]
– New wave / Intifada / Monitor.
(cd-ep+=) *(SET 011CD)* – Timewatch / Jerusalem / The rise and fall.

— now **HANNON** solo after the other two departed

Jul 93. (7"ep) *(CAO 008)* **LUCY. / THE POP SINGER'S FEAR OF THE POLLEN COUNT / I WAS BORN YESTERDAY** [ ] [–]

Aug 93. (cd/c/lp) *(SET CD/MC/LP 011)* **LIBERATION** [ ] [–]
– Festive road / Death of a supernaturalist / Bernice bobs her hair / I was born yesterday / Your daddy's car / Europop / Timewatching / The singer's fear of the pollen count / Queen of the south / Victoria Falls / Three sisters / Europe by train / Lucy. *(re-iss. Aug96; same)*

Oct 93. (7"pic-d-ep) *(DC 001)* **INDULGENCE No.1** [ ] [–]
– Untitled melody / Hate my way / Europe by train.

Mar 94. (cd/c/lp) *(SET CD/MC/LP 013)* **PROMENADE** [ ] [–]
– Bath / Going downhill / The booklovers / A seafood song / Geronimo / Don't look down / When the lights go out all over Europe / The summerhouse / Neptune's daughter / A drinking song / Ten seconds to midnight / Tonight we fly. *(re-iss. Aug96 & Aug97; same)*

Aug 94. (7"ep) *(DC 002)* **INDULGENCE No.2** [ ] [–]
– A drinking song / Tonight we fly (live) / When the lights go out all over Europe.

— now one-man band **NEIL HANNON** and a large ensemble of musicians including main band; **STUART 'PINKIE' BATES** – hammond organ / **JOBY TALBOT** (b. 1971, Wimbledon, England) – piano, arranger / **IVOR TALBOT** – guitar / **BRYAN MILLS** – bass / **MIGUEL 'MIGGY' BARRADAS** – drums

Apr 96. (cd/c/lp) *(SET CD/MC/LP 025) <36863>* **CASANOVA** [48] [ ]
– Something for the weekend / Becoming more like Alfie / Middle-class heroes / In & out of Paris & London / Charge / Songs of love / The frog princess / A woman of the world / Through a long & sleepless night / Theme from Casanova / The dogs & the horses.

— <above issued on 'Tristar' in the US>

Jun 96. (c-s) *(SETMC 026)* **SOMETHING FOR THE WEEKEND / SONGS OF LOVE (theme from 'Father Ted')** [14] [–]
(cd-s+=) *(SETCD 026)* – Birds of Paradise farm / Love is lighter than air.

Aug 96. (7"/c-s) *(SET/+MC 027)* **BECOMING MORE LIKE ALFIE. / YOUR DADDY'S CAR (live)** [27] [–]
(cd-s+=) *(SETCD 027)* – Untitled melody (acoustic) / The dogs & the horses (acoustic).

Nov 96. (c-s) *(SETMC 032)* **THE FROG PRINCESS / MOTORWAY TO DAMASCUS** [15] [–]
(cd-s+=) *(SETCD 032)* – A woman of the world / Lucy (demo).
(cd-s) *(SETCDL 032)* – ('A'side) / Something before the weekend / Neptune's daughter / Tonight we fly.

Feb 97. (m-cd/m-c) *(<SET CD/MC 036>)* **A SHORT ALBUM ABOUT LOVE** [13] [ ]
– In pursuit of happiness / Everybody knows (except you) / Someone / If . . . / If I were you (I'd be through with me) / Timewatching / I'm all you need.

Mar 97. (cd-ep) *(SETCDA 038)* **EVERYBODY KNOWS (EXCEPT YOU) / MAKE IT EASY ON YOURSELF (live) / A DRINKING SONG (live) / SOMETHING FOR THE WEEKEND (live)** [14] [ ]
(cd-ep) *(SETCDB 038)* – ('A'side) / Johnny Mathis' feet (live) / Your daddy's car (live) / Europe by train (live).
(cd-ep) *(SETCDC 038)* – ('A'side) / Bath (live) / Tonight we fly (live) / Middle class heroes (live).

— In April '98, The DIVINE COMEDY were part of a NOEL COWARD tribute album in which a single, 'I'VE BEEN TO A MARVELLOUS PARTY' was taken. It hit No.28 and was backed with a Shola Ama & Craig Armstrong track

— added **ROB FARRER** – percussion

Setanta Imprint

Aug 98. (cd/c) *(SET CD/MC 057) <111813>* **FIN DE SIECLE** [9] Dec98 [ ]
– Generation sex / Thrillseeker / Commuter love / Sweden / Eric the gardener / National express / Life on Earth / The certainty of chance / Here comes the flood / Sunrise. *(also ltd-cd; SETCDL 057)*

Sep 98. (7") *(SET 050)* **GENERATION SEX. / POSTCARD TO ROSIE** [19] Nov98 [ ]
(cd-s) *(SETCDA 050) <114195>* – ('A') / London Irish / Time lapse.
(cd-s) *(SETCDB 050) <114197>* – ('A') / Chasing sheep is best left to shepherds / Little acts of kindness.

Setanta Tristar

Nov 98. (c-s) *(SETMC 067)* **THE CERTAINTY OF CHANCE / MARYLAND ELECTRIC RAINSTORM** [49] Mar99 [ ]
(cd-s) *(<SETCDA 067>)* – ('A') / Last stand in Metroland / Miranda.
(cd-s) *(<SETCDB 067>)* – ('A') / Dead only quickly / Knowing the ropes.

Jan 99. (c-s) *(SETMC 069)* **NATIONAL EXPRESS / THE HEART OF ROCK AND ROLL** [8] [–]
(cd-s) *(SETCDA 069)* – ('A') / Going downhill fast / Radioactivity.
(cd-s) *(SETCDB 069)* – ('A') / Famous / Overstrand.

Aug 99. (c-s) *(SETMC 070)* **THE POP SINGER'S FEAR OF THE POLLEN COUNT / JACKIE** [17] [–]
(cd-s) *(SETCDA 070)* – ('A') / With whom to dance / Eric the gardener.
(cd-s) *(SETCDB 070)* – ('A') / This side of paradise / Vapour trail.

Aug 99. (cd/c) *(SET CD/MC 100) <51080>* **A SECRET HISTORY – THE BEST OF THE DIVINE COMEDY** (compilation) [3] Sep99 [ ]
– National express / Something for the weekend / Everybody knows (except you) / Generation sex / Becoming more like Alfie / The summerhouse / Your daddy's car / The pop singer's fear of the pollen count / The frog princess / Gin soaked boy / Lucy / Songs of love / In pursuit of happiness / I've been to a marvellous city / The certainty of chance / Too young to die / Tonight we fly.

Nov 99. (c-s) *(SETMC 071)* **GIN SOAKED BOY / EUROPOP (live)** [38] [–]
(cd-s) *(SETCDA 071)* – ('A') / Songs of love / I am.
(cd-s) *(SETCDB 071)* – ('A') / Geronimo (livd) / My lovely horse.

Parlophone Nettwerk

Feb 01. (c-s) *(TCR 6554)* **LOVE WHAT YOU DO / SOUL TRADER / GET ME TO A MONASTERY** [26] [–]
(cd-s) *(CDRS 6554)* – (first 2 tracks) / You / ('A'-video).
(cd-s) *(CDR 6554)* – (first & third tracks) / ('A'-Deadly Avenger mix).

Mar 01. (cd/c) *(531761-2/-4) <30237>* **REGENERATION** [14] [ ]
– Timestretched / Bad ambassador / Perfect lovesong / Note to self / Lost property / Eye of the needle / Love what you do / Dumb it down / Mastermind / Regeneration / The beauty regime.

May 01. (7") *(R 6558)* **BAD AMBASSADOR. / LIFE ON EARTH (live)** [34] [–]
(cd-s) *(CDRS 6558)* – ('A') / Edward the confessor / U.S.E. / ('A'video).
(cd-s) *(CDR 6558)* – ('A'-live) / Sweden (live) / Pictures of matchstick men (live).

Oct 01. (cd-s) *(CDRS 6561)* **PERFECT LOVESONG / NO EXCUSES / LES JOURS TRISTES** [42] [–]
(cd-s) *(CDR 6561)* – ('A') / Thinking the unthinkable / Oh yeah.

Mar 04. (7") *(R 6630)* **COME HOME BILLY BIRD. / ALL THINGS** [25] [–]
(cd-s) *(CDR 6630)* – ('A') / Idaho.
(cd-s) *(CDRS 6630)* – ('A') / Girl least likely / ('A'-demo) / ('A'-video).

Mar 04. (cd) *(596280-2) <30363>* **ABSENT FRIENDS** [23] May04 [ ]
– Absent friends / Sticks and stones / Leaving today / Come home Billy Bird / My imaginary friend / The wreck of the beautiful / Our mutual friend / The happy goth / Freedom road / Laika's theme / Charmed life.

Jun 04. (7") *(R 6641)* **ABSENT FRIENDS. / ANTHEM FOR BORED YOUTH** [38] [–]
(cd-s) *(CDR 6641)* – ('A') / Mr. Right.
(cd-s) *(CDRS 6641)* – ('A') / Something for the weekend (Radio 2 session) / ('A'-Radio 2 session) / ('A'-video).

Jun 06. (7") *(R 6698)* **DIVA LADY. / ELAINE (demo)** [52] [–]
(cd-s) *(CDR 6698)* – ('A') / Don't blame the young.
(cd-s) *(CDRS 6698)* – ('A') / Premonition of love / Births, deaths & marriages / ('A'-video).

Jun 06. (cd) *(365372-2)* **VICTORY FOR THE COMIC MUSE** [ ] [–]
– To die a virgin / Mother dear / Diva lady / Lady of a certain age / Light of day / Threesome / Party fears two / Arthur C. Clarke's mysterious world / Plough / Count Grassi's passage over Piedmont / Snowball in negative. *(ltd-cd w/dvd+=; 367796-2)* – (DVD tracks).

DMX

Born: EARL SIMMONS, 18 Dec'70, Yonkers, New York, USA. As a troubled teen, with a chequered past, the apprehensive MC began his quest from the gutter and into rap stardom when he struck a deal with 'Columbia'; an unsigned talent show had panned the spotlight on the unknown 21-year-old. His debut, 'BORN LOSER' (1996), flopped unceremoniously when released in the States, most likely due to the fact that 2PAC and NOTORIOUS B.I.G. were stealing the show with their very own brand of humourless hardcore rap. It wasn't until 'Def Jam' were dumbfounded by a lost demo tape and the aforementioned rap martyrs were all dead that DMX and his RUFF RYDERS (a collection of friends and producers from his hood) could stand alone as the most outstanding artists of their generation. He cameo'd on songs by MA$E, LL COOL J and JAY-Z before issuing the haunting 'IT'S DARK AND HELL IS HOT' in 1998. Through subsequent months, the set began to slowly climb its way up the American Billboard charts before selling a whopping 3 million copies, gaining the talented gothic rapper the title "The Dawg". From its outset, the album was a bleak study into the underworld of hopelessness in the ghettos and the forgotten suburban neighbourhoods, where anything could and would happen. 'DAMIEN', the album's strongest moment, was a reflection from the point of view of a crazy murderer, commanded by his alter-ego to kill. The track began with a sinister orchestral riff accompanied by a beatbox before DMX began with the line: "Why is it that every move I make turns out to be a bad one, where's my guardian angel, need one, wish I had one . . ." which then segued into a biblical chorus: it was the most disturbing rap song since 2PAC's enraged 'HIT 'EM UP'. Other tracks induced DMX's disturbed imagery: in 'PRAYER', he pleads with God, questioning him about the decisions he could have helped the rapper make in his vexatious years; in 'X IS COMING' he fantasises about the rape and subsequent murder of a 15-year-old (and to think that he's MARIAH CAREY's favourite rapper!). SIMPSON surfaced again in the same year with the major label sophomore set, 'FLESH OF MY FLESH, BLOOD OF MY BLOOD' and it was much weaker than its heavyweight contender. DMX, "The Dawg", seemed to be barking phrases instead of rapping, loosening false pretentions with his overpowering ego. MARILYN MANSON and MARY J BLIGE were among the performers included on the album which had our anti-hero soaked in blood on the cover. His worst came in the form of '. . .AND THEN THERE WAS X' (1999), a sloppy, inadequate fourth album, where The 'X droned on about his reign as the best rapper in the world. However, he was the most successful having had three US No.1 chartbusters. Things just began to get worse for the man when he issued his feeble shot at tough-love hip-hop with 'THE GREAT DEPRESSION' (2001). The album, which went number 1 in the US, drew on DMX's own personal conflicts within his life. But what personal conflicts did a millionaire rap artist have (apart from coming up with some original beats) and why did he have to share them with an entourage of producers like BINK, JUST BLAZE, BLACK KEY, KIDD KODD and SWIZZ BEATZ? 'WE RIGHT HERE' is a stonking, uptempo number that could have been a potential single, but the majority of the mood on '. . . DEPRESSION' is dark with DMX's biblical good-versus-evil charade – that made his first two albums worth recommending in the first place – just repeated over and over. In the rap world it was already becoming clear that underground artists such as AESOP ROCK, CANNIBAL OX and The ANTI POP CONSORTIUM had a lot more to offer in terms of style, character, beats and rhythms. DMX was just becoming a tadpole swimming around in the stagnant pond of mainstream rap, when really he should have sprouted legs and leaped into the garden. The prolific DMX returned in 2003, with his overtly misogynistic 'GRAND CHAMP', a record which boasted the usual major label shout-outs, thug raps and cocaine party songs, with a few dark tunes to boot. Featuring a picture of a really mean looking dog (or should we say, "dawg") on the front cover, it was quite evident that DMX, with his polished production and slick beats was probably going to stay consistent with every album that he made.

• **Note:** Not to be confused with the DMX CREW.

Album rating: IT'S DARK AND HELL IS NOT (*8) / FLESH OF MY FLES[H] BLOOD OF MY BLOOD (*7) / . . .AND THEN THERE WAS X (*6) / THE GREA[T] DEPRESSION (*5) / GRAND CHAMP (*6)

EARL SIMMONS – rapper, etc

not iss. Son[y]

Jul 93. (c-s/12"/cd-s) *<74908>* **BORN LOSER (mixes)** [–] [ ]

not iss. Metrop[o]

Nov 94. (12"; by DMX & STEPHANIE MARANO) *<1034>* **SECRET GARDEN. / (version)** [–] [ ]

Def Jam Def Ja[m]

Feb 98. (c-s/12"/cd-s; DMX featuring SHEEK of The LOX) *<568523>* **GET AT ME DOG (intro / street / instrumental / freestyle) / (interview) / STOP BEING GREEDY (street / instrumental)** [–] [39]

Jun 98. (cd/lp) *<(558227-2/-1)>* **IT'S DARK AND HELL IS NOT** [ ] May98 [1]
– Intro / Ruff Ryders' anthem / Fuckin' wit D / Storm / Look thru m[y] eyes / Get at me dog / Let me fly / X-is coming / Damien / How's it goi[n] down / Mickey / Crime story / Stop being greedy / Ate / For my dogs / can feel it / Prayer / Convo / Niggaz done started something.

—— DMX also featured on two V/A 12"ep's, 'SURVIVAL OF THE ILLEST' (Vol[s] 1 & 2) along with FAITH EVANS, ONYX and The DEF SQUAD

Aug 98. (cd-s) **STOP BEING GREEDY / (mixes)** [–] [79]

Oct 98. (12"/cd-s; by DMX featuring FAITH EVANS) *<566217>* **HOW'S IT GOIN' DOWN. / RUFF RYDERS' ANTHEM (radio)** [–] [70]

Jan 99. (cd/d-lp) *<(538640-2/-1)>* **FLESH OF MY FLESH BLOOD OF MY BLOOD** [ ] Dec98 [1]
– My niggas / Bring your whole crew / Pac man / Ain't no way / We don give a fuck / Keep your shit the hardest / Coming from / It's all good Omen / Slippin' / No love 4 me / Dogs for life / Blackout / Flesh of m[y] flesh blood of my blood / Heat / Ready to meet him.

Feb 99. (c-s/cd-s) *<566217>* **RUFF RYDERS' ANTHEM (mixes)** [–] [94]

May 99. (12") *(563867-1) <870755>* **SLIPPIN'. / RUFF RYDERS' ANTHEM / STOP BEING GREEDY** [30] Apr99 [ ]
(cd-s) *(870755-2)* – (first 2 tracks) / How's it goin' down.
(cd-s) *(870753-2)* – ('A'side) / No love for me / Get at me dog (2 versions

Nov 99. (12") *<562540>* **WHAT'S MY NAME (mixes)** [–] [67]

Dec 99. (cd/lp) *<(546933-2/-1)* **. . .AND THEN THERE WAS X** [ ] [1]
– Kennel / One more road to cross / The professional / Fame / Alot [t] learn / Here we go again / Party up (up in here) / Make a move / Wh[a] these bastards want / What's my name? / More 2 a song / Don't you ever Shakedown / D-X-L / Comin' for ya / Prayer III / Angel / Good girls, ba[d] guys.

Feb 00. (cd-s) *<562605>* **PARTY UP (UP IN HERE) / PARTY UP (instrumental) / SLIPPIN' / PARTY (video)** [–] [27]

Jun 00. (cd-s; by DMX featuring SISQO) *<562808>* **WHAT YOU WANT / WHAT THESE BASTARDS WANT (explicit) / RUFF RYDERS ANTHEM / (CD-Rom)** [–] [52]

Oct 01. (cd/d-lp) *<(586450-2/-1)>* **THE GREAT DEPRESSION** [20] [1]
– Sometimes / School street / Who we be / Trina Moe / We right here Bloodline anthem / Shorty was da bomb / Damien III / When I'm nothi[n] (with STEPHANIE MILLS) / I miss you (with FAITH EVANS) / Numb[er] 11 (with FAITH EVANS) / Pull up (skit) / I'm a bang / Pull out (skit) You could be blind (with MaSHONDA) / The prayer IV / A minute f[or] your son / Kennel (with JINX) / Loose / Big Stan / Problem child (wi[th] MYSONNE) / Drag-on / Shit's still real (with MIC GERONIMO) / B[ig] Stan.

Dec 01. (12"/c-s) *(588851-1/-4) <572720>* **WHO WE BE. / WE RIGHT HERE** [34] Sep01 [60]
(cd-s+=) *(588851-2)* – ('A'-radio & video mixes).

2002. (-; w/ FAITH EVANS) *<radio>* **I MISS YOU** [–] [86]

Apr 03. (12") *(077904-1)* **X GON' GIVE IT TO YA. / (instrumental) / PARTY UP (UP IN HERE)** [6] [60]
(cd-s) *(077904-2)* – ('A'side) / Get at me dog (with SHEEK) / Make a mov[e]

Sep 03. (cd)(d-lp) *(9861021)<(633691)>* **GRAND CHAMP** [6] [1]
– Dog intro / My life (with CHINKY) / Where the hood at? / Dogs out / G[et] it on the floor (with SWIZZ BEATZ) / Come prepared / Shot down (wi[th] 50 CENT & STYLES P) / Bring the noize / Untouchable (with SHEE[K] SYLEENA JOHNSON, INFA-RED & CROSS) / Fuck y'all / Ruff radio We're back (with EVE & JADAKISS) / Ruff radio 2 / Rob all night (if I'[m] gonna rob) / We go hard (with CAM'RON) / We 'bout to blow (with BI[G] STAN) / The rain / Gotta go / Don't gotta go home (with MONICA) A'yo kato (with MAGIC & VAL) / Thank you (with PATTI LaBELLE) The prayer V. *(d-lp+=)* – On top (with BIG STAN).

Sep 03.	(12") *(9811390)* **WHERE THE HOOD AT? / (Ruff Ryders anthem) / (instrumental)**	16	68
	(cd-s) *(9811251)* – ('A'side) / Who we be / ('A'-video).		
Jan 04.	(cd-s; DMX feat. SWIZZ BEATZ) *(9815206)* **GET IT ON THE FLOOR (mixes)**	34	-

☐ DR. DRE (see under ⇒ N.W.A.)

Fats DOMINO

Born: ANTOINE DOMINO, 26 Feb'28, New Orleans, Louisiana, USA. Growing up in a musical family, FATS began playing local honky tonk clubs before he even reached his teens. Nicknamed 'FATS' – for his 16 stone stature – by his bass player, BILLY DIAMOND, he was soon tinkling the ivories alongside Crescent City masters like PROFESSOR LONGHAIR and CHAMPION JACK DUPREE while digging the records of FATS WALLER and LOUIS JORDAN. DOMINO was barely over sixteen when he joined the band of trumpeter/producer/composer extrordinaire, Dave Bartholomew, although the pair would subsequently strike up a long and fruitful partnership. Also working as an A&R man for 'Imperial', Bartholomew helped the youngster sign to the label in 1949, the same year the pair co-penned what would become DOMINO's debut single, 'THE FAT MAN'. A rollicking piano groove oft cited as the first rock'n'roll record (alongside a host of others), the track was release by 'Imperial' in the Spring of 1950 and went on to sell a million copies over the ensuing three years. More importantly, it created a sizeable market for FATS' laid-back, free-rolling take on classic New Orleans R&B and with a crack band consisting of BARTHOLOMEW, RED TYLER and EARL PALMER, DOMINO cut a further succession of R&B hits over the next five years while touring almost constantly. It was only a matter of time before he crossed over to the mainstream pop charts and in summer 1955 FATS took his propulsive boogie-woogie to the masses with 'AIN'T THAT A SHAME', a US Top 10. Along with his appearance in two teen movies, 'Shake, Rattle & Roll' and 'The Girl Can't Help It', this success initiated almost a decade of regular chart action, his best-loved and most well known song, 'BLUEBERRY HILL', making the Top 10 on both sides of the pond in Autumn '56 (another classic 'IT'S KEEPS RAININ', has been cited as a precursor to Jamaican ska/reggae after import copies caused a musical storm – BITTY McLEAN took it to UK No.2 in 1993). This consolidated FATS as one of the most popular and respected performers of the rock'n'roll era, his unique encapsulation of his native city's multicultural musical heritage seeing him rack up more sales than any other American artist save ELVIS PRESLEY. Among the best and biggest of his hits were 'BLUE MONDAY' (sadly not an early version of NEW ORDER's electro classic), 'I'M WALKIN', 'WHOLE LOTTA LOVING' and 'WALKING TO NEW ORLEANS', all million-selling US Top 10's. By the time of FATS' move to 'ABC Paramount' in 1963, the hits were becoming thinner on the ground as the British Invasion heated up. Ironically, the BEATLES were big DOMINO fans and were no doubt both thrilled and amused when the Big Man covered 'LADY MADONNA' in 1968, one of his first singles for 'Reprise' and his last chart entry. Nevertheless, he continued to tour and record right up until the early 80's, when he finally retired from the music business. DOMINO was back in the news in August 2005, when it was thought the New Orleans giant might be one of the casualties of Hurricane Katrina. However, after a day or two he was lifted to safety, and was even planning to get back on the road.

• **Covered:** WHEN THE SAINTS GO MARCHING IN (trad.) / JAMBALAYA + YOU WIN AGAIN (Hank Williams) / I HEAR YOU KNOCKIN' (Smiley Lewis) / DID YOU EVER SEE A DREAM WALKIN' (Eddy Duchin) / RED SAILS IN THE SUNSET (Platters) / I CAN'T STOP LOVING YOU (Ray Charles) / I LEFT MY HEART IN SAN FRANCISCO (Tony Bennett) / LOVELY RITA + EVERYBODY'S GOT SOMETHING TO HIDE EXCEPT ME AND THE MONKEY (Beatles) / etc. • **Trivia:** He married childhood sweetheart Rosemary in the late 40's, bringing up 8 children in homeland New Orleans.

Best CD compilation: THE BEST OF FATS DOMINO (*7)

FATS DOMINO – vocals, piano with **DAVE BARTHOLOMEW** – trumpet / **RED TYLER** – bass / **EARL PALMER** – drums

		not iss.	Imperial
Apr 50.	(78) *<5058>* **THE FAT MAN. / DETROIT CITY BLUES**	-	
May 50.	(78) *<5065>* **BOOGIE WOOGIE BABY. / LITTLE BEE**	-	
Jul 50.	(78) *<5077>* **SHE'S MY BABY. / HIDE AWAY BLUES**	-	
Sep 50.	(78) *<5085>* **HEY LA BAS BOOGIE. / BRAND NEW BABY**	-	
Nov 50.	(7",78) *<5099>* **KOREA BLUES. / EVERY NIGHT ABOUT THIS TIME**	-	

—— FATS now finds own musicians

Feb 51.	(7",78) *<5114>* **TIRED OF CRYING. / WHAT'S THE MATTER BABY**	-	
May 51.	(7",78) *<5123>* **DON'T LIE TO ME BABY. / SOMETIMES I WONDER**	-	
Aug 51.	(7",78) *<5138>* **NO NO BABY. / RIGHT FROM WRONG**	-	
Nov 51.	(7",78) *<5145>* **ROCKIN' CHAIR. / CARELESS LOVE**	-	
Jan 52.	(7",78) *<5167>* **YOU KNOW I MISS YOU. / I'LL BE GONE**	-	
Mar 52.	(7",78) *<5180>* **GOIN' HOME. / REELIN' AND ROCKIN'**	-	
Jun 52.	(7",78) *<5197>* **POOR POOR ME. / TRUST IN ME**	-	
Sep 52.	(7"red,78) *<5209>* **HOW LONG. / DREAMING**	-	
Jan 53.	(7"red,78) *<5220>* **NOBODY LOVES ME. / CHEATIN'**	-	
May 53.	(7"red,78) *<5231>* **GOING TO THE RIVER. / MARDI GRAS IN NEW ORLEANS**	-	
Jul 53.	(7",78) *<5240>* **PLEASE DON'T LEAVE ME. / THE GIRL I LOVE**	-	

—— added **LEE ALLEN** – saxophone

		London	Imperial
Feb 54.	(7",78) *(HL 8007) <5251>* **ROSE MARY. / YOU SAID YOU LOVED ME**		Oct53
Jul 54.	(7",78) *(HL 8063) <5272>* **YOU DONE ME WRONG. / (HEY) LITTLE SCHOOL GIRL**		Feb54
Nov 54.	(7",78) *(HL 8096) <5262>* **DON'T LEAVE ME THIS WAY. / SOMETHING'S WRONG**		Dec53
Jun 54.	(7",78) *<5283>* **BABY PLEASE. / WHERE DID YOU STAY**	-	
Nov 54.	(7",78) *<5301>* **YOU CAN PACK YOUR SUITCASE. / I LIVED MY LIFE**	-	
Feb 55.	(7",78) *(HL 8124) <5313>* **LOVE ME. / DON'T YOU HEAR ME CALLIN' YOU**		1954
Apr 55.	(7",78) *(HL 8133) <5323>* **I KNOW. / THINKIN' OF YOU**		Jan55
Apr 55.	(7",78) *<5340>* **DON'T YOU KNOW. / HELPING HAND**	-	

—— now with **WALTER NELSON** – guitar / **CORNELIUS COLEMAN** – drums.

Sep 55.	(7",78) *(HLU 8173) <5348>* **AIN'T THAT A SHAME. / LA-LA-LA** *(above single hit UK chart No.23 in Jan57)*		Jun55 10
Nov 55.	(lp) *<9004>* **CARRY ON ROCKIN'** – The fat man / Tired of crying / Goin' home / You said you love me / Going to the river / Please don't leave me / Rose Mary / All by myself / Ain't that a shame / Poor me / Bo Weevil / Don't blame it on me. *<re-iss. Mar57 as 'ROCK AND ROLLIN' WITH FATS DOMINO'; same> (UK-iss.Apr57; HA-P 2041)*	-	
Sep 55.	(7",78) *<5357>* **ALL BY MYSELF. / TROUBLES OF MY OWN**	-	
Nov 55.	(7",78) *<5369>* **POOR ME. / I CAN'T GO ON (ROSALIE)**	-	
Mar 56.	(7",78) *(HLU 8256) <5375>* **BO WEEVIL. / DON'T BLAME IT ON ME**		Feb56 35
Jul 56.	(7",78) *(HLU 8280) <5386>* **I'M IN LOVE AGAIN. / MY BLUE HEAVEN**	12	3 / 19

Aug 56. (7",78) *(HLU 8309) <5396>* **WHEN MY DREAMBOAT COMES HOME. / SO-LONG** [ ] [14] Jul56 [44]

Sep 56. (7",78) *<5407>* **BLUEBERRY HILL. / HONEY CHILE** [–] [5]

Oct 56. (7",78) *(HLU 8330)* **BLUEBERRY HILL. / I CAN'T GO ON (ROSALIE)** [6] [–]

Oct 56. (lp) *(HA-U 2028) <9009>* **FATS DOMINO – ROCK AND ROLLIN'** [ ] [18]
– The fat man / Tired of crying / Goin' home / You said you love me / Going to the river / Please don't leave me / Rose Mary / All by myself / Ain't that a shame / Poor me / Bo Weevil / Don't blame it on me.

Jan 57. (7",78) *(HLU 8356)* **HONEY CHILE. / DON'T YOU KNOW** [29] [–]

Feb 57. (lp) *(HA-P 2073) <9028>* **THIS IS FATS DOMINO!** [19]
– Blueberry hill / Honey chile / What's the reason I'm not pleasing you / Blue Monday / So long / La la / Troubles of my own / You done me wrong / Reeling and rocking / The fat man's hop / Poor poor me / Trust in me.

Mar 57. (7",78) *(HLP 8377) <5417>* **BLUE MONDAY. / WHAT'S THE REASON I'M NOT PLEASING YOU** [23] [5] Dec56 [50]

Apr 57. (7",78) *(HLP 8407) <5428>* **I'M WALKIN'. / I'M IN THE MOOD FOR LOVE** [19] Feb57 [4]

Jul 57. (7",78) *(HLP 8449) <5442>* **VALLEY OF TEARS. / IT'S YOU I LOVE** [25] [8] May58 [6]

Aug 57. (7",78) *(HLP 8471) <5454>* **WHEN I SEE YOU. / WHAT WILL I TELL MY HEART** [ ] [29] [64]

Nov 57. (7",78) *(HLP 8519) <5467>* **WAIT AND SEE. / I STILL LOVE YOU** [ ] [23] Oct57 [79]

—— sessions incl. **ALLEN TOUSSAINT** – piano

Mar 58. (7",78) *(HLP 8575) <5477>* **THE BIG BEAT. / I WANT YOU TO KNOW** [20] [26] Dec57 [32]

Feb 58. (7",78) *<5492>* **YES, MY DARLING. / DON'T YOU KNOW I LOVE YOU** [–] [55]

May 58. (lp) *(HA-P 2052) <9038>* **HERE STANDS FATS DOMINO** [ ] [ ]
– Detroit City blues / Hide away blues / She's my baby / New baby / Little bee / Every night about this time / I'm walkin' / I'm in the mood for love / Cheatin' / You can pack your suitcase / Hey fat man / I'll be gone.

Jun 58. (7") *(HLP 8628) <5515>* **SICK AND TIRED. / NO, NO** [26] [22] Apr58 [55]

Jun 58. (lp) *(HA-P 2087) <9040>* **THIS IS FATS** [ ] [ ]
– The rooster song / My happiness / As time goes by / Hey la bas / ove me / Don't you hear me calling you / It's you I love / Valley of tears / Where did you stay / Baby please / Thinking of you / You know I miss you. *(re-iss. Apr79 on 'Flyover') (re-iss. US Jan83)*

Jul 58. (7",78) *(HLP 8663) <5526>* **LITTLE MARY. / PRISONER'S SONG** [ ] Jun58 [48]

Oct 58. (7",78) *(HLP 8727) <5537>* **YOUNG SCHOOL GIRL. / IT MUST BE LOVE** [ ] Sep58 [92]

Nov 58. (7",78) *(HLP 8759) <5553>* **WHOLE LOTTA LOVING. / COQUETTE** [ ] [6] [92]

Sep 58. (lp) *(HA-P 2135) <9055>* **THE FABULOUS "MR.D"** [ ] [ ]
– The big beat / I'll be glad when you're dead you rascal you / What will I tell my heart / Barrelhouse / Little Mary / Sick and tired / I want you to know / "44" / Mardi Gras in New Orleans / I can't go on / Long lonesome journey / Young school girl *(re-iss. US Jan83)*

Mar 59. (7",78) *(HLP 8822) <5569>* **WHEN THE SAINTS GO MARCHING IN. / TELLING LIES** [ ] Feb59 [50]

May 59. (7",78) *(HLP 8865) <5585>* **MARGIE. / I'M READY** [18] [51] [16]
(re-iss. Jul76 on 'United Artists')

Jun 59. (lp) *(HA-P 2223) <9065>* **LET'S PLAY FATS DOMINO** [ ] [ ]
– You left me / Ain't it good / Howdy podner / Stack & Billy / Would you / Margie / Hands across the table / When the saints go marching in / Ida Jane / Lil' Liza Jane / I'm gonna be a wheel some day / I want to walk you home.

Sep 59. (7",78) *(HLP 8942) <5606>* **I WANT TO WALK YOU HOME. / I'M GONNA BE A WHEEL SOMEDAY** [14] [8] Jul59 [17]

Dec 59. (7",78) *(HLP 9005) <5629>* **BE MY GUEST. / I'VE BEEN AROUND** [11] [8] Oct59 [33]

Dec 59. (lp) *<9062>* **FATS DOMINO SWINGS** [–] [ ]
– The fat man / Blue Monday / Blueberry Hill / I'm in love again / Going to the river / My blue Heaven / Bo Weevil / Goin' home / Please don't leave me / Ain't that a shame / I'm walkin' / Whole lotta lovin'. *(cd-iss. Nov99 on 'Magic'; 523017-2)*

Mar 60. (7",78) *(HLP 9073) <5645>* **COUNTRY BOY. / IF YOU NEED ME** [19] [25] Jan60 [98]

Jun 60. (7",78) *(HLP 9133) <5660>* **TELL ME THAT YOU LOVE ME. / BEFORE I GROW TOO OLD** [ ] [51] Apr60 [84]

Jul 60. (7",78) *(HLP 9163) <5675>* **WALKING TO NEW ORLEANS. / DON'T COME KNOCKIN'** [19] [6] Jun60 [21]

Oct 60. (7") *(HLP 9198) <5687>* **THREE NIGHTS A WEEK. / PUT YOUR ARMS AROUND ME HONEY** [45] [15] Aug60 [58]

Nov 60. (lp) *(HA-P 2312) <9127>* **A LOT OF DOMINOES** [ ] [ ]
– Put your arms around me honey / Three nights a week / Shu rah / Rising sun / My girl Josephine / The sheik of Araby / Walking to New Orleans / Don't come knockin' / Magic isles / You always hurt the one you love / It's the talk of the town / Natural born lover.

Dec 60. (7") *(HLP 9244) <5704>* **MY GIRL JOSEPHINE. / NATURAL BORN LOVER** [32] [14] Oct60 [38]

Mar 61. (7") *(HLP 9301) <5723>* **WHAT A PRICE. / AIN'T THAT JUST LIKE A WOMAN** [ ] [22] Jan61 [33]

Apr 61. (7") *(HLP 9327) <5734>* **SHU RAH. / FELL IN LOVE ON MONDAY** [ ] Mar61 [32]

Apr 61. (lp) *(HA-P 2364) <9138>* **I MISS YOU SO** [ ] [ ]
– I miss you so / It keeps rainin' / Ain't that just like a woman / Once in a while / I hear you knockin' / Isle of Capri / What a price / When I was young / Fell in love on Monday / My bleeding heart / Easter parade / I'll always be in love with you.

Jun 61. (7") *(HLP 9374) <5753>* **IT KEEPS RAININ'. / I JUST CRY** [49] May61 [23]

Sep 61. (7") *(HLP 9415) <5764>* **LET THE FOUR WINDS BLOW. / GOOD HEARTED MAN** [ ] Jul61 [15]

Sep 61. (lp) *(HA-P 2420) <9153>* **LET THE FOUR WINDS BLOW** [ ] [ ]
– Along the Navajo trail / You win again / One night / I'm alone because I love you / Won't you come on back / Trouble blues / I can't give you anything but love / Good hearted man / Your cheating heart / Let the four winds blow / In a shanty in Old Shanty Town / Am I blue.

Nov 61. (7") *(HLP 9456) <5779>* **WHAT A PARTY. / ROCKIN' BICYCLE** [ ] [22] Sep61 [83]

Nov 61. (lp) *(HA-P 2426) <9164>* **WHAT A PARTY** [ ] [ ]
– Did you ever see a dream / Walking rockin' bicycle / Before I grow too old ain't gonna do it / Bad luck and trouble / Hold hands / Trouble in mind / Coquette / What a party / I just cry / I've been calling / Tell me that you love me.

Nov 61. (7") *<5796>* **JAMBALAYA (ON THE BAYOU). / I HEAR YOU KNOCKIN'** [–] [30] [67]

Feb 62. (7") *<5816>* **YOU WIN AGAIN. / IDA JANE** [–] [22] [90]

Mar 62. (7") *(HLP 9520)* **JAMBALAYA. / YOU WIN AGAIN** [41] [–]

Apr 62. (lp) *(HA-P 2447) <9170>* **TWISTIN' THE STOMP** [ ] [ ]
– Twistin' the spots / The twist set me free / I know / Every night / Town talk / Wait and see / Twistin' the stomp / Don't deceive me / A long way from home / The girl I love / Do you know what it means to miss New Orleans / South of the border.

Jun 62. (7") *(HLP 9557) <5833>* **MY REAL NAME. / MY HEART IS BLEEDING** [ ] May62 [59]

Jul 62. (lp) *<9195>* **MILLION SELLERS BY FATS** (compilation) [–] [ ]
– You said you love me / I still love you / Be my guest / Country boy / If you need me / I want to walk you home / It's you I love / I've been around / I'm gonna be a wheel some day / I'm ready / Margie / I want you to know.

Aug 62. (7") *(HLP 9590) <5863>* **DANCE WITH MR.DOMINO. / NOTHING NEW (SAME OLD THING)** [ ] [98] Jun62 [77]

Oct 62. (7") *(HLP 9616) <5875>* **STOP THE CLOCK. / DID YOU EVER SEE A DREAM WALKING** Sep62 79

Dec 62. (7") *<5895>* **WON'T YOU COME ON BACK. / HANDS ACROSS THE TABLE** –

Jan 63. (7") *<5909>* **THOSE EYES. / HUM-DIDDY-DOO** –

H.M.V. ABC Paramount

May 63. (7") *(POP 1164) <10444>* **THERE GOES (MY HEART AGAIN). / CAN'T GO ON WITHOUT YOU** 59

Jul 63. (7") *(POP 1917) <10475>* **WHEN I'M WALKING (LET ME WALK). / I'VE GOT A RIGHT TO CRY**

Sep 63. (7") *(POP 1219) <10484>* **RED SAILS IN THE SUNSET. / SONG FOR ROSEMARY** 34 35

Sep 63. (lp) *(CLP 1690) <455>* **HERE COMES . . . FATS DOMINO**

– When I'm walking / I got a right to cry / There goes (my heart again) / Just a lonely man / Red sails in the sunset / Bye baby, bye, bye / Forever, forever / I'm livin' right / Can't go on without you / Land of 1000 dances / Song for Rosemary / Tell me the truth, baby. *(cd-iss. Sep92 + Jul93 on 'Repertoire'; REP 4161)*

Jan 64. (7") *(POP 1265) <10512>* **WHO CARES. / JUST A LONELY MAN** Dec63 63

Feb 64. (lp) *(CLP 1740) <479>* **FATS ON FIRE**

– I don't want to set the world on fire / You know I miss you / Fats on fire / Land of make believe / Old man trouble / Love me / Mary, oh Mary / Gotta get a job / The fat man / Valley of tears / Fats shuffle / I'm a fool to care. *(cd-iss. Apr98 on 'Disky'; CDBB 9616)*

Mar 64. (7") *(POP 1281) <10531>* **LAZY LADY. / DON'T WANT TO SET THE WORLD ON FIRE** Feb64 86

May 64. (7") *(POP 1303) <10545>* **SOMETHING YOU GOT BABY. / IF YOU DON'T KNOW WHAT LOVE IS** Apr64

Jul 64. (7") *(POP 1324) <10567>* **MARY OH MARY. / PACKIN' UP** Jun64

Aug 64. (7") *<10584>* **SALLY WAS A GOOD OLD GIRL. / FOR YOU** – 99

Nov 64. (7") *(POP 1370) <10596>* **HEARTBREAK HILL. / KANSAS CITY** Oct64 99

Apr 65. (7") *(POP 1421) <10631>* **WHY DON'T YOU DO RIGHT. / WIGS**

Jun 65. (lp) *(CLP 1821) <510>* **GETAWAY WITH FATS DOMINO**

– When the dreamboat comes home / Wigs / Trouble in mind / Man that's all / Kansas City / Reelin' and rockin' / On a slow boat to China / Monkey business / Heartbreak hill / Girl I'm gonna marry you / Why don't you do right / Ballin' the jack. *(re-iss. Dec83 on 'Ace-Charly'; CH 90)*

Jul 65. (7") *<10644>* **LET ME CALL YOU SWEETHEART. / GOODNIGHT SWEETHEART** –

Mercury Mercury

Sep 65. (7") *(MF 896) <72463>* **I LEFT MY HEART IN SAN FRANCISCO. / I DONE GOT FOR YOU**

Nov 65. (7") *(MF 873) <72485>* **WHAT'S THAT YOU GOT. / IT'S NEVER TOO LATE**

Dec 65. (lp; stereo/mono) *(S+/MCL 20070) <62039>* **DOMINO '65 (live)**

– (Introduction) / Blueberry hill / Please don't leave me / Domino twist / Let the four winds blow / I'm gonna be a wheel someday / I'm in the mood for love / Jambalaya (on the bayou) / Oh, what a price / Ain't that a shame / So long.

not iss. Broadmoor

Dec 67. (7") *<104>* **THE LADY IN BLACK. / WORK MY WAY UP STEADY** –

Feb 68. (7") *<105>* **BIG MOUTH. / WAIT TILL IT HAPPENS TO YOU** –

Reprise Reprise

Jun 68. (7"; UK w-drawn) *(RS 20696) <0696>* **ONE FOR THE HIGHWAY. / HONEST PAPAS LOVE THEIR MAMAS BETTER** –

Aug 68. (7") *(RS 20763) <0763>* **LADY MADONNA. / ONE FOR THE HIGHWAY** 100

Sep 68. (lp) *(RSLP 107) <6304>* **FATS IS BACK**

– My old friends / I'm ready / So swell when you're well / Wait till it happens to you / I know / Lady Madonna / Honest papas love their mamas better / Make me belong to you / One for the highway / Lovely Rita / One more song for you. *(re-iss. Nov81 on 'Mercury' lp/c; 6463/7145 043) (cd-iss. Apr99 on 'Bullseye'; CDBB 9616)*

Nov 68. (7") *<0775>* **LOVEY RITA. / WAIT TILL IT HAPPENS TO YOU** –

1969. (7") *(RS 20810)* **EVERYBODY'S GOT SOMETHING TO HIDE EXCEPT ME AND THE DONKEY. / SO SWELL WHEN YOU'RE WELL** –

1970. (7") *<0891>* **MAKE ME BELONG TO YOU. / HAVE YOU SEEN MY BABY** –

1970. (lp) *<6439>* **FATS** –

– I'm going to cross that river / Big mouth / It's a sin to tell a lie / Wait till it happens to you / I'm going to help a friend / The lady in black / Another mule / When you're smiling (the whole world smiles with you) / These old shoes / Lawdy Miss Clawdy / Work my way up steady.

1970. (7") *<0944>* **NEW ORLEANS AIN'T THE SAME. / SWEET PATOOTIE** –

Atlantic not iss.

Jun 74. (lp) *(K 50107)* **LIVE AT MONTREAUX – HELLO JOSEPHINE (live '73)** –

– Hello Josephine / I'm in love again / Blueberry hill / Jambalaya / Walking to New Orleans / I'm gonna be a wheel someday / Blue Monday / Mardi Gras in New Orleans / Stagger Lee / I want to walk you home / Let the four winds blow / I'm walking / When the saints go marching in / Sentimental journey.

Sonet Polydor

May 79. (lp) *(SNTF 793) <PD 3215>* **SLEEPING ON THE JOB**

– Sleeping on the job / After hours / When I lost my baby / Something about you baby / Move with the groove / Any old time / Shame on you / I just can't get the girl I love / Love me.

Nov 78. (7") *(SON 2168)* **SLEEPING ON THE JOB. / AFTER HOURS** –

not iss. Warners

Jan 81. (7") *<49610>* **WHISKEY HEAVEN. / BEERS TO YOU (by the Texas Opera Company)** –

—— FATS retired from music to spend time with his family, although he made a comeback album (see below)

Magnum Force Toot Toot

1985. (7"; with DOUG KERSHAW) *<1>* **MY TOOT TOOT. / MY TOOT TOOT-THREE** –

Aug 85. (7"; with DOUG KERSHAW) *(MFS 4)* **MY TOOT TOOT. / DIGGY IGGY TO** –

—— he was now backed by many session men

not iss. M.C.A.

1986. (lp) **HIS GREATEST HITS (live)** –

– My girl Josephine / The fat man / I'm gonna be a wheel someday / Blue Monday / Jambalaya (on the bayou) / Blueberry Hill / Going to the river / I'm ready / I want to walk you home / Whole lotta loving / Poor me / Ain't that a shame / I almost lost my mind / I'm in love again / I'm walkin' / Walking to New Orleans / Let the four winds blow / Shake, rattle and roll / My toot toot / I can't go on.

– (selective) compilations, etc. –

Apr 65. (lp) *Liberty; (LBY 3033)* **MILLION SELLERS BY FATS VOL.1** –

(re-iss. 1967; LBL 83023)

Jul 65. (lp) *Liberty; (LBY 3046)* **MILLION SELLERS BY FATS VOL.2** –

(re-iss. 1967; LBL 83024)

1968. (lp) *Liberty; (LBL 83101)* **MILLION SELLERS BY FATS VOL.3** –

Apr 70. (lp) *Liberty; (LBS 83331)* **THE VERY BEST OF FATS DOMINO: PLAY IT AGAIN FATS** 56 –

Feb 91. (cd/c) *E.M.I.; (CD/TC EMS 1381)* **MY BLUE HEAVEN: THE BEST OF FATS DOMINO** –

– My blue Heaven / The fat man / Please don't leave me / Ain't that a shame / I'm in love again / When my dreamboat comes home / Blueberry hill / Blue Monday / I'm walkin' / Valley of tears / Big beat / Yes my darling / Whole lotta loving / I'm ready / I'm gonna be a wheel someday / I want to walk you home / Be my guest / Walking to New Orleans (undubbed) / Let the four winds blow / What a party.

Jun 96. (cd) *Ace-Charly; (CDCHD 597)* **THE EARLY IMPERIAL SINGLES (1950-1952)** –

Apr 97. (cd) *Ace-Charly; (CDCHD 649)* **THE IMPERIAL SINGLES VOL.2 (1953-1956)** –

Jun 98. (cd) *Ace-Charly; (CDCHD 689)* **THE IMPERIAL SINGLES VOL.3: 1956-1958** –

Mar 02. (4xcd-box) *537374-2)* **WALKING TO NEW ORLEANS**

Apr 02. (cd) *Indigo; (IGOCD 2513)* **THE FAT MAN: THE ESSENTIAL EARLY FATS DOMINO**

May 02. (cd) *E.M.I.; (537600-2)* **THE FATS DOMINO JUKEBOX – 20 GREATEST HITS** ☐ ☐

Feb 03. (d-cd) *Proper Pairs; (PVCD 120)* **ROCKIN' ON RAMPART** ☐ ☐

Feb 03. (8xcd-box+book) *Bear Family; (BCD 15541)* **OUT OF NEW ORLEANS** ☐ ☐

Mar 03. (cd) *E.M.I.; (582212-2)* **THE ESSENTIAL FATS DOMINO** ☐ ☐

Feb 04. (cd) *E.M.I.; (596497-2)* **THE BEST OF FATS DOMINO** 58 2006 ☐
– Blueberry hill / Ain't that a shame / I'm walkin' / Jambalaya (on the bayou) / I'm in love again / Blue Monday / The fat man / Be my guest / The big beat / What a party / I'm ready / Sick and tired / Poor me / My girl Josephine (aka Hello Josephine) / I want to walk you home / Margie / Country boy / I'm gonna be a wheel someday / Let the four winds blow / Whole lotta loving / Please don't leave me / Goin' home / Walking to New Orleans / Going to the river / When my dreamboat comes home / Wait and see / It keeps rainin' / I hear you knocking / Valley of tears.

Lonnie DONEGAN

Born: ANTHONY JAMES DONEGAN, 29 Apr'31, Glasgow, Scotland. The son of a classical violinist who played with the Scottish National Orchestra, DONEGAN began playing guitar in his teens. He was also an avid fan of folk, country, blues and jazz, immersing himself in the sounds of FRANK CRUMIT, JOSH WHITE, HANK WILLIAMS, LOUIS ARMSTRONG, LEADBELLY, WOODY GUTHRIE, etc. His musical ambitions eventually led him to London where he auditioned for CHRIS BARBER's band; the pair hit it off immediately and became lifelong friends. Following a stint of national service in Europe (where he was introduced to the musical delights of the American Forces Radio Network), DONEGAN returned to form The KEN COLYER JAZZMEN with BARBER and KEN COLYER. Between sets, DONEGAN took the spotlight and began developing the frantic hybrid of blues, jazz, folk and country that would come to be known as 'Skiffle'. Named – by COLYER's brother – after an old blues combo, the DAN BURLEY SKIFFLE GROUP, this unique sound kicked off a musical revolution almost as far reaching as ELVIS PRESLEY's lip-curling cross of rockabilly, gospel and jump-blues. When COLYER departed the group in 1954, BARBER took the helm and the band soon found themselves in the studio courtesy of 'Decca'. DONEGAN (who now took the stage name LONNIE after a compere confused him with guitarist LONNIE JOHNSON) persuaded the A&R man to let them cut a couple of tracks in his skiffle style, subsequently included on the 10" album, 'NEW ORLEANS JOY' (1955). One of them, 'ROCK ISLAND LINE' (a trad folk song cut by LEADBELLY amongst others), was released as a single – under the LONNIE DONEGAN SKIFFLE GROUP moniker – and proceeded to tear up the charts as well as the musical rule book; six months later it had sold an incredible three million copies, staying on the UK chart for 22 weeks and even making the US Top 10, a feat previously unheard of for a British act. Follow-up track, 'DIGGIN' MY POTATOES', was banned by the BBC for its suggestive title (hmmm . . .), giving old LONNIE (who duly signed to 'Pye') one of the first 'rebel' tags of the era. The ban only served to increase his popularity and over the next decade, an avalanche of hit singles buried the UK chart including No.1's 'CUMBERLAND GAP', 'PUTTING ON THE STYLE' (both 1957) and comic novelty track, 'MY OLD MAN'S A DUSTMAN' (1960). The latter track became the first ever single to go straight in at No.1, reflecting DONEGAN's 'King Of Skiffle' status. Imitators were ten a penny, utilising any DIY instruments they could lay their hands on i.e. washboards, soup spoons, etc. In fact, a young PAUL McCARTNEY was one particularly mad keen fan, an early incarnation of The BEATLES playing at one of DONEGAN's folk appreciation society gigs in 1958. Ironically, though, the fab four's own adaptation of rock's roots steered the course of pop music in a different direction and skiffle mania was all but over by the early 60's. LONNIE's last Top 20 hit came in 1962 with 'PICK A BALE O' COTTON' and after 'THE FOLK ALBUM' (1965) failed to capture the imagination of the new folkies on the block, DONEGAN concentrated on production work for 'Pye'. 1970's flop 'LONNIEPOPS' album marked the end of his tenure with the label and he subsequently worked in Germany where there was a brief skiffle mini-revival. The man's curious brand of humour was showcased once more in 1976 with a one-off single, 'I'VE LOST MY LITTLE WILLIE'. Unfortunately he suffered a heart attack the same year and relocated to California to recuperate in the West Coast sun. 1978 saw the release of 'PUTTING ON THE STYLE', an all-star skiffle affair featuring the likes of RINGO STARR, RON WOOD and ELTON JOHN, all long time fans. The album actually made the UK Top 60 although the C&W follow-up, 'SUNDOWN' (1979) made little headway. 1981, meanwhile found him teaming up with Scots group, SHAKIN' PYRAMIDS for a one-off single although continuing heart problems curtailed him for much of the early-mid 80's. A further one-off single, 'DONEGAN'S DANCING SUNSHINE BAND', appeared in summer '87. In 1995, DONEGAN was presented with an Ivor Novello award, an occasion which saw him singing with longtime fan VAN MORRISON. The pair discussed cutting some tracks together, the results finally emerging in 1999 on 'MULESKINNER BLUES', an 'R.C.A.' set combining old and new material with contributions from the likes of ALBERT LEE, JACQUI McSHEE and even SAM BROWN. Standout tracks, though, were the two pairings with VAN the MAN, on the rabble-rousing title track and the brilliant remake of 'I'M ALABAMMY BOUND'. Clearly, DONEGAN (or VAN for that matter) hasn't reached the end of the rock island line just yet; he subsequently added Glastonbury to his already packed gig diary while his fans straddle both the generation gap and geographical boundaries. Sadly, LONNIE was to die of heart problems on the 3rd November, 2002.

Best CD collection: TALKING GUITAR BLUES – THE VERY BEST OF.. (*7)

LONNIE DONEGAN – vocals, guitar, banjo with his Skiffle Group: **DENNY WRIGHT** – lead guitar / **MICKY ASHMAN** – upright bass / **NICK NICHOLS** – drums

Decca London

Nov 55. (7"/78; as The LONNIE DONEGAN SKIFFLE GROUP) *(F/FJ 10647) <1650>* **ROCK ISLAND LINE. / JOHN HENRY** 8 Feb56 8

Feb 56. (7"/78; as The LONNIE DONEGAN SKIFFLE GROUP) *(F/FJ 10695)* **DIGGIN' MY POTATOES. / BURY MY BODY** ☐ –

Pye Nixa Mercury

Apr 56. (7"/78) *(7N/N 15036) <70872>* **LOST JOHN. / STEWBALL** 2 May56 58

Jun 56. (7"ep) *(NJE 1017)* **SKIFFLE SESSION EP** 20 –
– Railroad Bill / Stackalee / Ballad of Jessie James / Ol' Riley.

Aug 56. (7"/78) *(7N/N 15071)* **BRING A LITTLE WATER, SYLVIE. / DEAD OR ALIVE** 7 ☐
(below lp hit the singles chart due to non-existence of UK lp chart)

Dec 56. (10"lp) *(NPT 19012)* **LONNIE DONEGAN SHOWCASE LP** 26 –
– Wabash cannonball / How long how long blues / Nobody's child / I shall not be moved / I'm Alabammy bound / I'm a rambling man / Wreck of the old '97 / Frankie and Johnny. *(re-iss. 1968 on 'Marble Arch'; MAL 797)*

Dec 56. (lp) *<M 920229>* **AN ENGLISHMAN SINGS AMERICAN FOLK SONGS** – ☐

Jan 57. (7"/78) *(7N/N 15080)* **DON'T YOU ROCK ME, DADDY-O. / I'M ALABAMMY BOUND** 4 ☐

Mar 57. (7"/78) *(7N/N 15087)* **CUMBERLAND GAP. / LOVE IS STRANGE** 1 ☐

May 57. (7"/78) *(7N/N 15093)* **GAMBLIN' MAN. / PUTTING ON THE STYLE (live)** 1 ☐

Sep 57. (7"/78) *(7N/N 15108)* **MY DIXIE DARLING. / I'M JUST A ROLLING STONE** 10 ☐

ov 57. (10"lp) *(NPT 19027)* **LONNIE** [ ] [–]
– Lonesome traveller / The sunshine of his love / Ain't no more cane on the Brazos / Ain't you glad you've got religion / Times are getting hard, boys / Lazy John / Light from the lighthouse / I've got my rocks in my bed / Long summer day. *(cd-iss. Feb00 on 'Sequel'+=; NEMCD 343)* – (extra tracks).

ec 57. (7"/78) *(7N/N 15116)* **JACK O'DIAMONDS. / HAM 'N' EGGS** [14] [ ]

pr 58. (7"/78) *(7N/N 15129)* **THE GRAND COOLEE DAM. / NOBODY LOVES LIKE AN IRISHMAN** [6] [ ]

in 58. (7"/78) *(7N/N 15148)* **SALLY, DON'T YOU GRIEVE. / BETTY, BETTY, BETTY** [11] [ ]

ep 58. (7"/78) *(7N/N 15158)* **LONESOME TRAVELLER. / TIMES ARE GETTING HARD BOYS** [28] [ ]

ep 58. (lp) *(NPL 18034)* **TOPS WITH LONNIE** [ ] [–]
– Don't you rock me, daddy-o / Putting on the style / Gamblin' man / My Dixie darling / Bring a little water, Sylvie / Cumberland gap / Grand Coulee Dam / Saly, don't you grieve / Nobody loves likes an Irishman / Lost John / Does your chewing gum lose it's flavour / Tom Dooley.

ov 58. (7"/78) *(7N/N 15165)* **LONNIE'S SKIFFLE PARTY (medley part 1: LITTLE LIZA JANE – PUTTING ON THE STYLE – CAMPTOWN RACES – KNEES UP MOTHER BROWN. / (medley part 2: SO LONG – ON TOP OF OLD SMOKEY – DOWN IN THE VALLEY – SO LONG** [23] [–]

ov 58. (7"/78) *(7N/N 15172)* **TOM DOOLEY. / ROCK O' MY SOUL** [3] [ ]

Pye-Nixa Dot

ec 58. (lp) *<DLP 3159>* **LONNIE DONEGAN** [–] [ ]

in 59. (7"/78) *(7N/N 15181)* *<15911>* **DOES YOUR CHEWING GUM LOSE ITS FLAVOUR. / AUNT RILEY** [3] Feb59 [ ]
<US re-iss. Jul61; same> – hit No.5

pr 59. (7"/78) *(7N/N 15198)* **FORT WORTH JAIL. / WHOA BUCK** [14] [ ]

lay 59. (lp) *(NPL 18043)* **LONNIE RIDES AGAIN** [ ] [ ]
– Fancy talking tinker / Miss Otis regrets / Jimmie Brown the newsboy / Mr. Froggy / Take this hammer / The gold rush is over / You pass me by / Talking guitar blues / John Hardy / House of the rising sun / San Miguel. *(re-iss. 1969 on 'Marble Arch'; MAL 1153) (cd-iss. Feb00 on 'Sequel'+=; NEMCD 344)* – (extra tracks).

Pye Atlantic

in 59. (7"/78) *(7N/N 15206)* **BATTLE OF NEW ORLEANS. / DARLING COREY** [2] [ ]

ug 59. (7"/78; Irish-only) *(7N/N 15219)* **KEVIN BARRY. / MY LAGAN LOVE** [–] [–]

ep 59. (7"/78) *(7N/N 15223)* **SAL'S GOT A SUGAR LIP. / CHESAPEAKE BAY** [13] [ ]

ov 59. (7"/78) *(7N/N 15237)* **SAN MIGUEL. / TALKING GUITAR BLUES** [19] [ ]

ec 59. (lp) *<8038>* **SKIFFLE FOLK MUSIC** [–] [ ]

ar 60. (7"/78) *(7N/N 15256)* **MY OLD MAN'S A DUSTMAN. / THE GOLDEN VANITY** [1] [ ]

ay 60. (7"/78) *(7N/N 15267)* **I WANNA GO HOME (THE WRECK THE THE JOHN). / JIMMY BROWN THE NEWSBOY** [5] [ ]

ug 60. (7"/78) *(7N/N 15275)* **LORELEI. / IN ALL MY WILDEST DREAMS** [10] [ ]

ov 60. (7") *(7N 15312)* **LIVELY. / BLACK CAT (CROSS MY PATH TODAY)** [13] [ ]

ec 60. (7") *(7N 15315)* **VIRGIN MARY. / BEYOND THE SUNSET** [27] [ ]

ar 61. (7") *(7N 15330)* **(BURY ME) BENEATH THE WILLOW. / LEAVE MY WOMAN ALONE** [ ] [ ]

pr 61. (lp) *(NPL 18063)* **MORE! TOPS WITH LONNIE** [ ] [–]
– Battle of New Orleans / Lorelei / Lively! / Sal's got a sugar lip / I wanna go home / Leave my woman alone / My old man's a dustman / Fort Worth jail / Have a drink on me / (Bury me) Beneath the willow / Little Liza Jane / Puttin' on the style / Camptown races / Knees up, Mother Brown / On top of Old Smokey / Down in the valley / So long.

ay 61. (7") *(7N 15354)* **HAVE A DRINK ON ME. / SEVEN DAFFODILS** [8] [ ]

ug 61. (7") *(7N 15371)* **MICHAEL ROW THE BOAT. / LUMBERED** [6] [ ]

n 62. (7") *(7N 15410)* **THE COMMANCHEROS. / RAMBLIN' ROUND** [14] [ ]

ar 62. (7") *(7N 15424)* **THE PARTY'S OVER. / OVER THE RAINBOW** [9] [ ]

Jun 62. (7") *(7N 15446)* **I'LL NEVER FALL IN LOVE AGAIN. / KEEP ON THE SUNNYSIDE** [ ] [–]

Aug 62. (7") *(7N 15455)* **PICK A BALE OF COTTON. / STEAL AWAY** [11] [ ]

Dec 62. (7") **THE MARKET SONG. / TIT-BITS (with MAX MILLER & The LONNIE DONEGAN GROUP)** [ ] [–]

Pye A.B.C.

Dec 62. (lp) *(NPL 18073)* **SING HALLELUJAH** [ ] [ ]
– Sing hallelujah / We shall walk through the valley / No hiding place / Good news, chariot's a-comin' / Noah found grace in the eyes of the Lord / Joshua fit the battle of Jericho / His eye is on the sparrow / Born in Bethlehem / This train / New burying ground / Steal away / Nobody knows the trouble I've seen. *(cd-iss. Feb00 on 'Sequel'+=; NEMCD 345)* – (extra tracks).

Apr 63. (7") *(7N 15514)* **LOSING BY A HAIR. / TRUMPET SOUNDS** [ ] [–]

Jun 63. (7") *(7N 15530)* **IT WAS A VERY GOOD YEAR. / RISE UP** [ ] [–]

Sep 63. (7") *(7N 15564)* **LEMON TREE. / I'VE GOTTA GIRL SO FINE** [ ] [–]

Nov 63. (7") *(7N 15579)* **500 MILES AWAY FROM HOME. / THIS TRAIN** [ ] [–]

Jul 64. (7") *(7N 15669)* **BEANS IN MY EARS. / IT'S A LONG ROAD TO TRAVEL** [ ] [–]

Sep 64. (7") *(7N 15679)* **FISHERMAN'S LUCK. / THERE'S A BIG WHEEL** [ ] [–]

Mar 65. (7") *(7N 15803)* **GET OUT OF MY LIFE. / WON'T YOU TELL ME** [ ] [–]

Jul 65. (7") *(7N 15893)* **LOUISIANA MAN. / BOUND FOR ZION** [ ] [–]

Aug 65. (lp) *(NPL 18126)* **THE LONNIE DONEGAN FOLK ALBUM** [ ] [–]
– I'm gonna be a bachelor / Interstate forty / After taxes / Where in the world are we going / Diamonds of dew / Bound for Zion / She was T-bone talking woman / Wedding bells / Reverend Mr. Black / The doctor's daughter / Blistered / Farewell. *(re-iss. 1967 on 'Golden Guinea'; GGL 0382) (cd-iss. Feb00 on 'Sequel'+=; NEMCD 346)* – (extra tracks).

Jan 66. (7") *(7N 15993)* **WORLD CUP WILLIE. / WHERE IN THIS WORLD ARE WE GOING** [ ] [–]

May 66. (7") *(7N 17109)* **I WANNA GO HOME. / BLACK CAT (CROSS MY PATH TODAY)** [ ] [–]

Jan 67. (7") *(7N 17232)* **AUNT MAGGIE'S REMEDY. / MY SWEET MARIE** [ ] [–]

Columbia not iss.

Mar 68. (7") *(DB 8371)* **TOYS. / RELAX YOUR MIND** [ ] [–]

Decca not iss.

Nov 69. (7") *(F 12984)* **MY LOVELY JUANITA. / WHO KNOWS WHERE THE TIME GOES** [ ] [–]

1970. (lp) *(SKL 5068)* **LONNIEPOPS – LONNIE DONEGAN TODAY** [ ] [–]
– Little green apples / Hey! hey! / First of May / Both sides now / If you go away / Love song to a princess / Who knows where the times goes / What the world needs now is love / My lovely Juanita / Windmills of your mind / Long haired lover from Liverpool / And you need me.

Pye not iss.

Nov 70. (7") *(7N 45009)* **BURNING BRIDGES. / I CAN'T TAKE IT ANY MORE** [ ] [–]

R.C.A. not iss.

Oct 71. (7") *(RCA 2128)* **COME TO AUSTRALIA. / DON'T BLAME THE CHILD** [ ] [–]

Pye not iss.

Oct 72. (7") *(7N 45184)* **SPEAK TO THE SKY. / GET OUT OF MY LIFE** [ ] [–]

Jun 73. (7"; by LONNIE DONEGAN & KENNY BALL) *(7N 45252)* **WHO'S GONNA PLAY THIS OLD PIANO. / SOUTH** [ ] [–]

Philips not iss.

1974. (lp) *(6305 227)* **LONNIE DONEGAN MEETS LEINEMANN** [–] German [–]
– Casey's last ride / Bottle of wine / Dixie darling / Frankie and Johnny / Tops at loving you / Gloryland / Leinemann's potatoes / Me and Bobby McGee / Does your chewing gum lose its flavour / Becky Deen / Jack o' diamonds.

1976. (lp) *(6305 288)* **COUNTRY ROADS** [–] German [–]
– Country roads / Rock island line / Keep on the sunny side / Dixie Lily / Louisiana man / Dead or alive / Midnight special / Muleskinner blues / Roll in my sweet baby's arms / Lost John / Have a drink on me / Dublin O'Shea.

Black Lion — not iss.

Jul 76. (7") *(BSP 45105)* **LOST JOHN. / JENNY'S BALL** [ ] [–]

Decca — not iss.

Aug 76. (7") *(FR 13669)* **I'VE LOST MY LITTLE WILLIE. / CENSORED** [ ] [–]

Chrysalis — U.A.

Jan 78. (7") *(CHS 2205)* **ROCK ISLAND LINE. / HAM 'N' EGGS** [ ] [–]

Feb 78. (lp/c) *(CHR/ZCHR 1158)* *<UALA 827>* **PUTTIN' ON THE STYLE** [51] [ ]
– Rock Island line / Have a drink on me / Ham 'n' eggs / I wanna go home / Diggin' my potatoes / Nobody's child / Puttin' on the style / Frankie and Johnny / Drop down baby / Lost John.

Apr 78. (7") *(CHS 2211)* **PUTTIN' ON THE STYLE. / DROP DOWN BABY** [ ] [–]

May 79. (lp/c) *(CHR/ZCHR 1205)* **SUNDOWN** [ ] [–]
– I'm all out and down / Home / Streamline train / Sundown / Mama's got the know how / Morning light / Louisiana sun / The battle of New Orleans / Cajun / Dreaming my dreams with you.

Virgin — not iss.

Nov 81. (7"ep; with the SHAKIN' PYRAMIDS) *(VS 460)* **CUMBERLAND GAP / WABASH CANNONBALL. / DON'T YOU ROCK ME DADDY-O / ONLY MY PILLOW / GRAB IT AND GROWL** [ ] [–]

—— next with guests MONTY SUNSHINE, CHRIS BARBER, KEN COLYER, etc

Dakota — not iss.

Dec 81. (d-lp/d-c) *(ICSD/ZCICSD 2001)* **JUBILEE CONCERT (live Autumn 1981)** [ ] [–]
– Ace in the hole / Isle Of Capri / Going home / Shine / Jenny's ball / One sweet letter from you / Hush-a-bye / Bugle call march / Ice cream / John Henry / Take this hammer / Railroad Bill / Tom Dooley / New burying ground / Grand Coulee Dam / New York town / Miss Otis Regrets / Does your chewing gum lose its flavour on the bedpost overnight / One night of love / Rock island line / Gloryland / Corrina Corrina / Goodnight Irene.

Rosie's Records — not iss.

Jul 87. (7"; with MONTY SUNSHINE) *(RR 015)* **DONEGAN'S DANCING SUNSHINE BAND. / LEAVING BLUES** [ ] [–]

—— In 1987 he turned actor, noteably in TV series 'Rockcliffe's Babies'

—— LONNIE returned with more stars as backing

Capo-RCA — Capo-RCA

Jan 99. (cd) *(<CAPO 501>)* **MULESKINNER BLUES** [ ] [ ]
– Muleskinner blues (with VAN MORRISON) / Please don't call me in the morning / Rock island line / When I get off this feeling / Fancy talking tinker / I'm Alabammy bound (with VAN MORRISON) / Stewball / Skiffle / Welfare line / All together now / I don't wanna lose you / Poker club / Spanish nights / Always from the heart.

—— in Jan'00, LONNIE hit the UK Top 20 (No.14) with VAN MORRISON and CHRIS BARBER on their album, 'THE SKIFFLE SESSIONS, LIVE IN BELFAST'

—— LONNIE died on 3rd November 2002

– (selective) compilations, etc. –

Aug 62. (lp) *Golden Guinea; (GGL 0135)* **A GOLDEN AGE OF DONEGAN** [3] [–]
(re-iss. 1966 on 'Marble Arch'; MAL 636)

Jan 63. (lp) *Golden Guinea; (GGL 0170)* **A GOLDEN AGE OF DONEGAN VOL.2** [15] [–]
(re-iss. 1967 on 'Marble Arch'; MAL 698)

Apr 92. (cd) *See For Miles; (SEECD 331)* **LONNIE DONEGAN – THE ORIGINALS** [ ] [–]

May 92. (cd/c) *See For Miles; (SEE CD/K 346)* **THE EP COLLECTION** [ ] [–]

Jul 92. (cd) *Kaz; (KAZCD 21)* **BEST OF LONNIE DONEGAN** [ ] [–]

Dec 92. (3xcd-box) *Sequel; (NXTCD 233)* **PUTTIN' ON THE STYLES** [ ] [–]

Oct 93. (cd) *See For Miles; (SEECD 382)* **THE EP COLLECTION VOL.2** [ ] [–]

Oct 93. (8xcd-box) *Bear Family; (BCD 15700)* **MORE THAN PIE IN THE SKY** [ ] [–]

Jun 99. (d-cd) *Jasmine; (JASCD 352/3)* **LONNIE DONEGAN MEETS LEINEMANN / COUNTRY ROADS** [ ] [–]

Aug 99. (cd) *Castle Pie; (PIESD 121)* **KING OF SKIFFLE** [ ] [–]

Sep 99. (d-cd) *Sequel; (NEECD 325)* **TALKING GUITAR BLUES – THE VERY BEST OF LONNIE DONEGAN** [ ] [–]
– Lost John / Stewball / Railroad Bill / Bring a little water, Sylvie / Dead o alive / Wabash cannonball / Nobody's child / Frankie and Johnny / Don you rock me, daddy-o / Cumberland gap / Gamblin' man / Putting on th style / My Dixie darling / Jack O'Diamonds / On a Monday / Muleskinne blues / Grand Coulle Dam / Sally don't you grieve / Lonnie's skiffle (Littl Liza Jane – Putting on the style – Camptown races – Little Liza Jane Knees up mother Brown) / Tom Dooley / Does your chewing gum lose i flavour / Fort Worth jail / Battle of New Orleans / Sal's got a sugar lip Take this hammer / You pass me by / San Miguel / Talking guitar blues My old man's a dustman / I wanna go home / Lorelei / Sorry but I'm gonn have to pass / Lively / Virgin Mary / Have a drink on me / Michael ro the boat ashore / Lumbered / The commancheros / The party's over / I never fall in love again / Pick a bale of cotton / This train / Noah foun grace in the eyes of the Lord / Beans in my ears / She was T-bone talkin woman / Farewell (fare thee well) / World Cup Willie.

Feb 00. (cd) *Sequel; (NEMCD 342)* **THE ORIGINAL ALBUMS REVISITED** [ ] [–]

Sep 00. (cd) *Delta; (47040)* **PUTTING ON THE STYLE** [ ] [–]

Sep 02. (3xcd-box) *Castle; (CMETD 580)* **ROCK ISLAND LINE: THE SINGLES ANTHOLOGY** [ ] [ ]

Feb 03. (cd) *Sanctuary; (TYSAN 002)* **PUTTIN' ON THE STYLE – THE GREATEST HITS** [45] [–]
– Rock island line / Lost John / Bring a little water, Sylvie / Don't you ro me daddy-o / Cumberland gap / Gamblin' man / Puttin' on the style My dixie darling / Jack o'Diamonds / The Grand Coolie dam / Sally dor you grieve / Tom Dooley / Does your chewing gum lose its flavour on th bedpost overnight / The battle of New Orleans / Sal's got a sugar lip / M old man's a dustman / I wanna go home / Lorelei / Lively! / Have a drink o me / Michael row the boat / Lumbered / The Comancheros / The party over / Pick a bale o' cotton.

DONOVAN

Born: DONOVAN PHILIP LEITCH, 10 May'46, Maryhi Glasgow, Scotland. At the age of 10, his family moved to Hatfiel England. In 1964, while playing small gigs in Southend, he wa spotted by Geoff Stephens and Peter Eden, who became h managers. Later that year, after performing on the 'Ready Stead Go!' pop show over three consecutive weeks, the denim-cla beatnik signed to 'Pye'. His debut single, 'CATCH THE WINI (issued the same time as DYLAN's 'The Times They Are A Changin'), saw him break into the Top 5, later reaching Top 30 i America where he was enjoying the fruits of a burgeoning caree His follow-up, 'COLOURS', also made the Top 5 in the summ of '65, as did the debut album, 'WHAT'S BIN DID AND WHAT' BIN HID'. Later in the year, the 'UNIVERSAL SOLDIER' EP sa DONOVAN begin to develop his uncompromising anti-war stanc a theme which he touched on with his second album, 'FAIRYTALE Initially heralded as Britain's answer to BOB DYLAN, he began t build on his folk/pop roots, progressing into flower-power wi 'SUNSHINE SUPERMAN' in 1966. The album of the same nam (issued only in the States) saw DONOVAN hit a creative high poi and included the much revered, 'SEASON OF THE WITCH'. At th beginning of '67, the single 'MELLOW YELLOW' was riding high i the American hit parade, and 'EPISTLE TO DIPPY' soon followe suit. In the meantime, 'MELLOW YELLOW', was given a belate UK release (making Top 10), while its similarly titled parent albu (again only issued in the US), hit No.14. 'SUNSHINE SUPERMAN a UK compilation lp of both aforementioned albums, made th Top 30 in the middle of '67. His label, 'Pye', followed the sam marketing strategy with his next UK album, the double 'A GIF FROM A FLOWER TO A GARDEN', which was in actual fact, tw US-only lp's in one. During this highly prolific period, which sa him inspired by the transcendental meditation of guru Maharis Mahesh Yogi, he released two sublime pieces of acid-pop in 'THER IS A MOUNTAIN' and 'JENNIFER JUNIPER'. The momentu

·ontinued with, 'HURDY GURDY MAN', another classic sojourn nto psychedelia which hit Top 5 on both sides of the Atlantic. In .969, he collaborated with The JEFF BECK GROUP on 'GOO GOO ƺARABAJAGAL', although this was his final 45 to make a major hart appearance. An album, 'OPEN ROAD' (1970), named after ıis new band, surprised many by cracking the US & UK charts. ı 1971, he recorded a double album of children's songs 'H.M.S.)ONOVAN', which led to a critical backlash from the music press. \fter a 3-year exile in Ireland for tax reasons, he set up home in Ɔalifornia with his wife Linda Lawrence and daughters Astrella and)riole. He has fathered two other children with his new American ʋife, Enid; DONOVAN LEITCH JNR. (star of the film 'Gas, Food, .odging') and IONE SKYE, the latter said to be none too bothered bout her famous father. DONOVAN enjoyed something of a enaissance in the early 90's when HAPPY MONDAYS' mainman HAUN RYDER (now of BLACK GRAPE) sang his praises, leading o a comeback album, 'DONOVAN RISING'. He was still going trong in '96, releasing a well-received Rick Rubin-produced album, SUTRAS', for the RCA affiliated 'American' label. Nigh on a decade ıter, a near 60-year old DONOVAN returned with 'BEAT CAFE' 2004), sprung with the upright bass of DANNY THOMPSON, ·roduced by John Chelew and spiritually indebted to the original ieats i.e. JACK KEROUAC, ALLEN GINSBERG, et al and the cellar ızz they themselves dug.

Songwriters: Self-penned except, UNIVERSAL SOLDIER (Buffy Sainte-1arie) / LONDON TOWN (Tim Hardin) / REMEMBER THE ALAMO ane Bowes) / CAR CAR (Woody Guthrie) / GOLDWATCH BLUES (Mick oftley) / DONNA DONNA (Kevess-Secunda-Secanta-Schwartz-Zeitlin) /)H DEED I DO+ DO YOU HEAR ME NOW (Bert Jansch) / CIRCUS F SOUR (Paul Bernath) / LITTLE TIN SOLDIER (Shawn Phillips / ORD OF THE DANCE (Sydney Carter) / ROCK'N'ROLL WITH ME)avid Bowie-Warren Peace) / MY SONG IS TRUE (Darell Adams) / NO 1AN'S LAND (Eric Bogle) / WIND IN THE WILLOWS (Eddie Hardin) / IEWEST BATH GUIDE + MOIRA McCAVENDISH (John Betjeman) / 'HE SENSITIVE KIND (J. J. Cale) / traditional:- KEEP ON TRUCKIN' + 'OU'RE GONNA NEED SOMEBODY + CANDY MAN + THE STAR + OULTER'S CANDY + HENRY MARTIN + THE HEIGHTS OF ALMA + OUNG BUT GROWING + STEALIN'. He also put music to words/poetry y; William Shakespeare (UNDER THE GREENWOOD TREE) / Gypsy)ave (A SUNNY DAY) / Lewis Carroll (WALRUS AND THE CARPENTER JABBERWOCKY) / Thora Stowell (THE SELLER OF STARS + THE ITTLE WHITE ROAD) / Fifida Wolfe (LOST TIME) / Lucy Diamond (THE OAD) / Agnes Herbertson (THINGS TO WEAR) / Edward Lear (THE WL AND THE PUSSYCAT) / Eugene Field (WYNKEN, BLYNKEN AND 'OD) / W. B. Yeats (THE SONG OF WANDERING AENGUS) / Natalie Joan \ FUNNY MAN) / Thomas Hood (QUEEN MAB) / Astella Leitch (MEE IEE I LOVE YOU) / Warwick Embury (ONE NIGHT IN TIME) / Note; URLEY GURLEY MAN originally had a verse by GEORGE HARRISON but ıis was not recorded and he only added this for live appearances. • **Trivia:**)ONOVAN sang co-lead on the title track from ALICE COOPER's 1973 lp 3illion Dollar Babies'.

lbum rating: WHAT'S BIN DID AND WHAT'S BIN HID (*7) / CATCH THE ʋIND (*6) / FAIRYTALE (*7) / SUNSHINE SUPERMAN (US version; *7) / IELLOW YELLOW (*6) / A GIFT FROM A FLOWER TO A GARDEN (*7; WEAR OUR LOVE LIKE HEAVEN; *5 – FOR LITTLE ONES; *4) / DONOVAN IN ONCERT (*4) / HURDY GURDY MAN (*6) / DONOVAN'S GREATEST HITS ·mpilation (*7) / BARABAJAGAL (*7) / OPEN ROAD (*5) / H.M.S. DONOVAN 5) / COSMIC WHEELS (*5) / ESSENCE TO ESSENCE (*5) / 7-TEASE (*5) / .OW DOWN WORLD (*4) / DONOVAN (*4) / NEUTRONICA (*4) / LADY F THE STARS (*4) / GREATEST HITS AND MORE compilation (*8) / ROUBADOUR: THE DEFINITIVE COLLECTION compilation (*8) / SUTRAS 5) / BEAT CAFE (*6)

ONOVAN – vocals, acoustic guitar, harmonica with **BRIAN LOCKING** – ıss / **SKIP ALLEN** – drums / **GYPSY DAVE** (b. DAVID MILLS) – kazoo, etc.

Pye Hickory

1ar 65. (7") *(7N 15801)* <1309> **CATCH THE WIND. / WHY DO YOU TREAT ME LIKE YOU DO** 4 Apr65 23

1ay 65. (7") *(7N 15866)* <1324> **COLOURS. / TO SING FOR YOU** 4 Jun65 61

May 65. (lp) *(NPL 18117)* <123> **WHAT'S BIN DID AND WHAT'S BIN HID** <US title 'CATCH THE WIND'> 3 30
– Josie / Catch the wind / Remember the Alamo / Cuttin' out / Car car * (riding in my car) / Keep on truckin' / Goldwatch blues / To sing for you / You're gonna need somebody on your bond / Tangerine puppet / Donna Donna * / Ramblin' boy *(re-iss. Jul68 on 'Marble Arch';)* – (omitted *)

Sep 65. (7") *<1338>* **UNIVERSAL SOLDIER. / DO YOU HEAR ME** – 53

Sep 65. (7"ep) *(NEP 24219)* **THE UNIVERSAL SOLDIER EP** 13 –
– Universal soldier / The ballad of a crystal man / Do you hear me now* / The war drags on.

Oct 65. (lp) *(NPL 18128)* **FAIRYTALE** 20 Dec 65 85
– Colours * / To try for the sun / Sunny Goodge street / Oh deed I do / Circus of sour / The summer day reflection song / Candy man / Jersey Thursday / Belated forgiveness plea / Ballad of a crystal man / Little tin soldier * / Ballad of Geraldine. *(re-iss. Mar69 on 'Marble Arch';)* – (omitted *). *(re-iss. Feb91 on 'Castle' cd/c; CLA CD/MC 226)*

Nov 65. (7") *(7N 15984)* **TURQUOISE. / HEY GYP (DIG THE SLOWNESS)** 30 –

Nov 65. (7") *<1375>* **YOU'RE GONNA NEED SOMEBODY ON YOUR BOND. / THE LITTLE TIN SOLDIER** –

Jan 66. (7") *<1402>* **TO TRY FOR THE SUN. / TURQUOISE** –

Feb 66. (7") *(7N 17067)* **JOSIE. / LITTLE TIN SOLDIER** –

Apr 66. (7") *(7N 17088)* **REMEMBER THE ALAMO. / THE BALLAD OF A CRYSTAL MAN** –

—— **DONOVAN** plus **JOHN CAMERON** – piano, harpsicord / **HAROLD McNAIR** – flute

Pye Epic

Jul 66. (7") *(7N 17241)* *<10045>* **SUNSHINE SUPERMAN. / THE TRIP** 2 Jun66 1

Sep 66. (lp; mono><stereo) *<LN 24217><BN 26217>* **SUNSHINE SUPERMAN** – 11
– Sunshine Superman / Legend of a girl child Linda / The observation / Guinevere / Celeste / Writer in the Sun / Season of the witch / Hampstead incident / Sand and foam / Young girl blues / Three kingfishers / Bert's blues. *(UK-iss.Feb91 on 'Beat Goes On' cd/c; BGO CD/MC 68) (cd re-iss. Oct96 on 'EMI Gold'; CDGOLD 1066)*

Nov 66. (7") *<10098>* **MELLOW YELLOW. / SUNNY SOUTH KENSINGTON** – 2

Jan 67. (7") *<10127>* **EPISTLE TO DIPPY. / PREACHIN' LOVE** – 19

Feb 67. (7") *(7N 17267)* **MELLOW YELLOW. / PREACHIN' LOVE** 8 –

Feb 67. (lp; mono><stereo) *<LN 24239><BN 26239>* **MELLOW YELLOW** – 14
– Mellow yellow / Writer in the Sun / Sand and foam / The observation / Bleak city woman / House of Jansch / Young girl blues / Museum / Hampstead incident / Sunny South Kensington. *(cd-iss. Oct93 on 'Sony Europe';)*

Jun 67. (lp) *(NPL 18181)* **SUNSHINE SUPERMAN** 25 –
-(compilation of last 2 US albums)

Oct 67. (7") *(7N 17403)* *<10212>* **THERE IS A MOUNTAIN. / SAND AND FOAM** 8 Sep67 11

—— **DONOVAN** retained **HAROLD** and in came **TONY CARR** – percussion / **CANDY JOHN CARR** – bongos **CLIFF BARTON** – bass / **KEITH WEBB** – drums / **MIKE O'NEIL** – keyboards / **MIKE CARR** – vibraphone / **ERIC LEESE** – electric guitar

Dec 67. (7") *<10253>* **WEAR YOUR LOVE LIKE HEAVEN. / OH GOSH** – 23

Dec 67. (lp; mono><stereo) *<LN 24349><BN 26349>* **WEAR YOUR LOVE LIKE HEAVEN** – 60
– Wear your love like Heaven / Mad John's escape / Skip-a-long Sam / Sun / There was a time / Oh gosh / Little boy in corduroy / Under the greenwood tree / The land of doesn't have to be / Someone's singing / Song of the naturalist's wife / The enchanted gypsy.

—— **KEN BALDOCK** – bass repl. BARTON, LEESE, WEBB, O'NEIL + MIKE CARR

Dec 67. (lp; mono><stereo) *<LN 24350><BN 26350>* **FOR LITTLE ONES** –
– Voyage into the golden screen / Isle of Islay / The mandolin man and his secret / Lay of the last tinker / The tinker and the crab / Widow with shawl (a portrait) / The lullaby of spring / The magpie / Starfish-on-the-toast / Epistle to Derroll.

Feb 68. (7") *(7N 17457)* *<10300>* **JENNIFER JUNIPER. / POOR COW** 5 26

Apr 68. (d-lp-box; mono/stereo) *(NPL/NSPL 20000)* *<L2N6/B2N 171>* **A GIFT FROM A FLOWER TO A GARDEN** 13 19
– (contains 2 US Dec67 albums boxed) *(cd-iss. Jul93 & Jun97 on 'Beat Goes On'; BGOCD 194)*

May 68. (7") *(7N 17537)* *<10345>* **HURDY GURDY MAN. / TEEN ANGEL** 4 5

Sep 68. (lp; mono/stereo) *(NPL/NSPL 18237)* *<BN 26420>* **DONOVAN IN CONCERT (live)** Jul68 18
– Isle of Islay / Young girl blues / There is a mountain / Poor cow / Celeste / The fat angel / Guinevere / Widow with shawl (a portrait) / Preachin' love / The lullaby of Spring / Writer in the Sun / Rules and regulations / Pebble and the man / Mellow yellow. *(re-iss. May91 & Apr97 on 'Beat Goes On' cd/c/lp; BGO CD/MC/LP 90) (cd-iss. Nov94 on 'Start';) (re-iss. cd Jan96 on 'Happy Price'; HP 93432)*

Oct 68. (7") *<10393>* **LALENA. / AYE, MY LOVE** – 33

Oct 68. (lp) *<BN 26420>* **HURDY GURDY MAN** – 20
– Jennifer Juniper / Hurdy gurdy man / Hi, it's been a long time / Peregrine / The entertaining of a shy girl / Tangier / As I recall it / Get thy bearings / West Indian lady / Teas / The river song / The Sun is a very magic fellow / A sunny day.

Nov 68. (7") *(7N 17660)* **ATLANTIS. / I LOVE MY SHIRT** 23 –

Feb 69. (7") *<10434>* **ATLANTIS. / TO SUSAN ON THE WEST COAST WAITING** – 7 35

Mar 69. (lp) *(NPL/NSPL 18283)* *<BXN 26439>* **DONOVAN'S GREATEST HITS** (compilation) 4
– Epistle to Dippy / Sunshine Superman / There is a mountain / Jennifer Juniper / Wear your love like Heaven / Season of the witch / Mellow yellow / Colours / Hurdy gurdy man / Catch the wind / Lalena. *<re-iss. 1972; PE 26439> <re-iss. 1973; BN 26836> (re-iss. Sep79 on 'CBS-Embassy' lp/c; CBS/40 31759) (cd-iss. Aug90 on 'Epic';)*

Jun 69. (7"; DONOVAN with The JEFF BECK GROUP) *(7N 17778)* **GOO GOO BARABAJAGAL (LOVE IS HOT). / BED WITH ME** 12 –

Sep 69. (7"; DONOVAN with The JEFF BECK GROUP) *<10510>* **GOO GOO BARABAJAGAL (LOVE IS HOT). / TRUDI** – 36

Sep 69. (lp; DONOVAN with The JEFF BECK GROUP) *<BN 26481>* **BARABAJAGAL** –
– Barabajagal / Superlungs my supergirl / I love my shirt / The love song / To Susan on the West Coast waiting / Atlantis / Trudi / Pamela Jo / Happiness runs. *(cd-iss. Oct93 on 'Sony Europe';)*

—— with **JOHN CARR** – drums, vocals / **MIKE THOMPSON** – bass, vocals / **MIKE O'NEILL** – piano

Dawn Epic

Sep 70. (lp) *(DNLS 3009)* *<30125>* **OPEN ROAD** 30 Jul70 16
– Changes / Song for John / Curry land / Joe Bean's theme / People used to / Celtic rock / Riki tiki tavi / Clara clairvoyant / Roots of oak / Season of farewell / Poke at the Pope / New Year's resovolution. *(cd-iss. Sep00 on 'Repertoire'; REP 4880)*

Sep 70. (7"; DONOVAN with OPEN ROAD) *(DNS 1006)* *<10649>* **RIKI TIKI TAVI. / ROOTS OF OAK** 55

—— (DANNY – double bass)

Dec 70. (7"; DONOVAN with DANNY THOMPSON) *(DNA 1007)* **CELIA OF THE SEALS. / MR.WIND** –

Feb 71. (7") *(10694)* **CELIA OF THE SEAS. / THE SONG OF THE WANDERING AENGUS** – 84

Jul 71. (d-lp) *(DNLD 4001)* **H.M.S. DONOVAN** –
– The walrus and the carpenter / Jabberwocky / The seller of the stars / Lost time / The little white road / The star / Coulter's candy / The road / Things to wear / The owl and the pussycat / Homesickness / Fishes in love / Mr.Wind / Wynken, Bylnken and Nod / Celia of the seas / The pee song / The voyage to the Moon / The unicorn / Lord of dance / Little Ben / Can ye dance / In an old fashioned picture book / The song of the wandering Aengus / A funny man / Lord of the reedy river / Henry Martin / Queen Mab / La moor. *(cd-iss. Jan98 on 'Beat Goes On'; BGOCD 372)*

—— with guests **CHRIS SPEDDING** – guitar / **JOHN 'RABBIT' BUNDRICK** – keyboards / **JIM HORN** – bass / **COZY POWELL** – drums

Epic Epic

Mar 73. (lp) *(SEPC 65450)* *<32156>* **COSMIC WHEELS** 15 25
– Cosmic wheels / Earth sign man / Sleep / Maria Magenta / Wild witch lady / Sleep / The music makers / The intergallactic laxative / I like you / Only the blues / Appearances. *(cd-iss. Sep94 on 'Epic-Rewind'; 477378-2)*

Apr 73. (7") *(EPC 1471)* *<10983>* **I LIKE YOU. / EARTH SIGN MAN** 66

Jun 73. (7") *(EPC 1644)* *<11023>* **MARIA MAGENTA. / THE INTERGALLACTIC LAXATIVE**

—— now with **STEVE MARRIOT, PETER FRAMPTON** and **NICKY HOPKIN**

Nov 73. (7") *(EPC 1960)* **SAILING HOMEWARD. / LAZY DAZE** –

Dec 73. (lp) *(SEPC 69050)* *<32800>* **ESSENCE TO ESSENCE**
– Operating manual for spaceship Earth / Lazy daze / Life goes on / There i an ocean / Dignity of man / Yellow star / Divine daze of deathless delight Boy for every girl / Saint Valentine's angel / Life is a merry-go-round Sailing homeward. *(cd-iss. Jan98; 489443-2)*

Jan 74. (7") *<11108>* **SAILING HOMEWARD. / YELLOW STAR** –

—— Mainly used session musicians from now on.

Sep 74. (7") *(EPC 2661)* *<50016>* **ROCK'N'ROLL WITH ME. / THE DIVINE DAZE OF DEATHLESS DELIGHT** Nov74

Nov 74. (lp) *(SEPC 69104)* *<33245>* **7-TEASE**
– Rock and roll souljer / Your broken heart / Salvation stomp / Th ordinary family / Ride-a-mile / Sadness / Moon rok / Love of my life / Th voice of protest / How silly / The great song of the sky / The quest.

Jan 75. (7") *<50077>* **ROCK AND ROLL SOULJER. / HOW SILLY** –

Feb 75. (7") *(EPC 3037)* **ROCK AND ROLL SOULJER. / LOVE OF MY LIFE** –

Jun 76. (lp) *(SEPC 86011)* *<33945>* **SLOW DOWN WORLD**
– Dark-eyed blue jean angel / Cryin' shame / The mountain / Children o the world / My love is true (love song) / A well known has-been / Blac widow / Slow down world / Liberation rag.

Jun 76. (7") *<50237>* **A WELL-KNOWN HAS-BEEN. / DARK EYED BLUE JEAN ANGEL** –

Rak Aris

Aug 77. (7") *<0280>* **DARE TO BE DIFFERENT. / THE INTERNATIONAL MAN** –

Oct 77. (lp) *(SRAK 528)* **DONOVAN** –
– Local boy chops wood / Astral angel / The light / Dare to be different Brave new world / Lady of the stars / International man / Sing my song Maya's dance / Kalifornia kids. *(cd-iss. Jun98 on 'Beat Goes On'; BGOC 375)*

Nov 77. (7") *(RAK 265)* **THE LIGHT. / THE INTERNATIONAL MAN** –

Feb 78. (7") *(RAK 269)* **DARE TO BE DIFFERENT. / SING MY SONG** –

—— (note:- on above US singles [Jan 73, Jan 75, Jun 76, Aug 77] the 'B' side wa mono version on 'A').

Luggage-R.C.A. Allegia

Aug 80. (lp) *(PL 28429)* **NEUTRONICA** –
– Shipwreck / Only to be expected / Comin' to you / No hunger / Neutror Mee Mee I love you / The heights of Alma / No man's land / We are one Madrigalinda / Harmony. *(cd-iss. May01 on 'Burning Airlines'+=; PILO 089)* – (acoustic versions +).

—— with **DANNY THOMPSON** – double bass / **JOHN STEPHENS** – drums **TONY ROBERTS** – multi-wind instruments / and his 9 year-old daught **ASTELLA** – dual vocals

Oct 81. (lp) *(PL 28472)* **LOVE IS ONLY FEELING** –
– Lady of the flowers / Lover o lover / The actor / Half Moon bay / The hi of Tuscany / Lay down Lassie / She / Johnny Tuff / Love is only feeling Marjorie Margerine.

Oct 81. (7") *(7-LUG 03)* **LAY DOWN LASSIE. / LOVE IS ONLY FEELING** –

Jan 84. (lp) *(PL 70060)* *<72857>* **LADY OF THE STARS**
– Lady of the stars / I love you baby / Seasons of the witch / Bye b girl / Every reason / Boy for every girl / Local boy chops wood / Sunshi superman / Til I see you again / Living for the lovelight.
After nearly 7 years in the wilderness, he returned on new label

Permanent Perma

Nov 90. (cd/c/lp) *(PERM CD/MC/LP 2)* **DONOVAN RISING**
– Jennifer Juniper / Catch the wind / The hurdy gurdy man / Sunshi superman / Sadness / Universal soldier / Cosmic wheels / Atlantis / We your love like heaven / Colours / To Susan on the west coast waiting Young girl blues / Young but growing / Stealing / Sailing homeward / Lo will find a way / Lalena. *(d-cd-iss. Jul00 on 'Burning Airlines'; PILOT 05*

—— He had also credited on The SINGING CORNER's (Nov90) single versic of his JENNIFER JUNIPER.

Silhouette not i

Apr 92. (cd-ep) *(MDCDKR 3)* **NEW BATH GUIDE / MOIRA McCAVENDISH / BROTHER SUN, SISTER MOON** –

American-RCA / American

Oct 96. (cd) *(74321 39743-2)* **SUTRAS** [ ] [ ]
– Please don't bend / Give it all up / Sleep / Everlasting sea / High your love / The clear-browed one / The way / Deep peace / Nirvana / Eldorado / Be mine / Lady of the lamp / The evernow / Universe am I.

— with **JOHN CHELEW** – keyboards / **DANNY THOMPSON** – upright bass / **JIM KELTNER** – drums

Appleseed / Appleseed

Aug 04. (cd) *(<APRCD 1081>)* **BEAT CAFE** [ ] [ ]
– Love floats / Poorman's sunshine / Beat cafe / Yin my yang / Whirlwind / Two lovers / The question / Lord of the universe / Lover O lover / The cuckoo / Do not go gentle / Shambala.

– (selective) compilations, etc. –

on 'Pye' UK / 'Hickory' (70's 'Epic') US unless otherwise mentioned

Sep 66. (lp) *<135>* **THE REAL DONOVAN** [–] [96]
Oct 67. (lp) *Marble Arch; (MAL 718)* **UNIVERSAL SOLDIER** [5] [–]
(re-iss. Feb83 on 'Spot'; SPR/SPC 8514)
Apr 68. (lp) *<143>* **LIKE IT IS, WAS AND EVERMORE SHALL BE** [–] [ ]
Jun 69. (lp) *United Artists; (UAS 29044)* **IF IT'S TUESDAY IT MUST BE BELGIUM** (soundtrack w/ Various) [ ] [–]
Sep 89. (cd)(c/lp) *E.M.I.; (CZ 193)(TC+/EMS 1333)* **GREATEST HITS AND MORE** [ ] [–]
– Sunshine Superman / Wear your love like Heaven / Jennifer Juniper / Barabajagal (love is hot) / Hurdy gurdy man / Epistle to Dippy / To Susan on the West Coast waiting / Catch the wind / Mellow yellow / There is a mountain / Happiness runs / Season of the witch / Colours / Superlungs – My Supergirl / Lalena / Atlantis. *(cd+=)* – Preachin' love / Poor cow / Teen angel / Aye my love. *(lp re-iss. Dec99 on 'Simply Vinyl'; SVLP 155)*
Oct 90. (lp/c/cd) *See For Miles; (SEE/+K/CD 300)* **THE EP COLLECTION** [ ] [–]
Dec 90. (cd/c) *Castle; (CCS CD/MC 276)* **THE COLLECTION** [ ] [–]
Feb 91. (d-cd/d-c/d-lp) *E.M.I.; (CD/TC+/EM 1385)* **THE TRIP** (1964-1968 material) [ ] [ ]
Jul 98. (cd) *Epic; (480552-2)* **THE DEFINITE COLLECTION** [ ] [–]
Mar 00. (d-cd) *Essential; (ESDCD 861)* **ANTHOLOGY: SUMMER DAY REFLECTION SONGS** [ ] [ ]
Mar 99. (cd/c) *Platinum; (PLA TCD/C 435)* **THE TROUBADOUR** [ ] [ ]
Mar 02. (cd) *Rhino-Atlantic; <78290>* **PIED PIPER** [–] [ ]
Jul 02. (cd) *Sanctuary; <81184>* **THE VERY BEST OF . . . DONOVAN: HIS EARLY YEARS** [–] [ ]
Sep 02. (cd) *E.M.I.; (540777-2)* **SUNSHINE SUPERMAN: THE VERY BEST OF DONOVAN** [ ] [ ]
Jan 03. (d-cd) *Sony France; (487481-2)* **TROUBADOUR – THE DEFINITIVE COLLECTION 1964-1976** [ ] [ ]
May 03. (d-cd) *Superior; (SU 2950-2)* **ATLANTIS: LIVE 1984-1986** [ ] [ ]
Sep 05. (3xcd-box) *Legacy; <93919-2>* **TRY FOR THE SUN: THE JOURNEY OF DONOVAN** [–] [ ]
Oct 05. (cd) *Metro; (METRCD 155)* **THE VERY BEST OF THE EARLY YEARS** [ ] [–]

the DOOBIE BROTHERS

Formed: San Jose, California, USA . . . 1970 by JOHN HARTMAN, TOM JOHNSTON (who had both played in an earlier incarnation of The DOOBIE BROTHERS, PUD, along with GREGG MURPHY) and DAVE SHOGREN. Starting out playing bar room boogie that was popular with local bikers, they signed to 'Warners' in 1971 and released an unsuccessful eponymous Ted Templeman produced album. Their second effort, 'TOULOUSE STREET', gave them their first gold disc and set the musical blueprint for the first half of their career. Coming on like an easy-listening ALLMANS, all crystal clear harmonies and laidback strumming, the band were quintessential Californian 70's rock. 'LISTEN TO THE MUSIC' was akin to an aural massage, while 'LONG TRAIN RUNNIN' from 'THE CAPTAIN AND ME' (1973) repeated the formula, its insidious chorus and foot shuffling groove taking it into the US Top 10. By now the DOOBIE's were selling millions, the country-rock of 'BLACK WATER', giving the band their No.1 in 1974. Its parent album, 'WHAT WERE ONCE VICES ARE NOW HABITS', and the follow-up, 'STAMPEDE' (1975) showed, however, that the sound was becoming tired. Thanks to JEFF BAXTER and MICHAEL McDONALD (both ex-STEELY DAN), the band underwent a timely, if subtle transformation from country boogie to polished, AOR funk. The former had joined before the band recorded 'STAMPEDE' while McDONALD arrived in late '75, initially to fill JOHNSTON's place on tour, the frontman giving up live commitments due to medical problems. McDONALD subsequently reworked the DOOBIE's back catalogue on stage, while writing most of the band's new material. Although many old fans were probably none too happy with the change, it certainly breathed new life into the band and while 'TAKIN' IT TO THE STREETS' (1976) was a marked improvement, the band were back at the top of the charts in 1978 with the multimillion selling 'MINUTE BY MINUTE'. The album also spawned a No.1 single in 'WHAT A FOOL BELIEVES', McDONALD's rich baritone now the essential ingredient in the DOOBIE BROTHERS sound (JOHNSTON having eventually left the previous year). The band then underwent a number of line-up changes before their final studio effort, 'ONE STEP CLOSER' (1980), although by this point McDONALD basically was the DOOBIE BROTHERS and it was inevitable he'd pack the band in for a solo career. The group officially split in March '82, recording a final farewell live album later that year. While McDONALD went on to a major solo success, The DOOBIE BROTHERS reformed in 1988 with a near-original line-up, JOHNSTON back in his role as frontman. The comeback album, 'CYCLES' (1989) went gold, spawning a Top 10 single with 'THE DOCTOR', although the follow-up set, 'BROTHERHOOD' (1991) was virtually ignored. Almost a decade on from that false re-start, the 'BROTHERS were back with the cheesily titled 'SIBLING RIVALRY' (2000). Again, the regrouped band attempted to relive that loose-hipped, harmony roots-rock of old and although they were never quite going to capture the heady atmosphere of those bearded, early 70's classics, they at least manage an enjoyably updated interpretation of it. 'LIVE AT WOLF TRAP' (2004), was another testament to their staying power.

• **Songwriters:** JOHNSTON or SIMMONS penned until MICHAEL McDONALD contributed on his 1975 arrival. JESUS IS JUST ALRIGHT (Byrds) / TAKE ME IN YOUR ARMS (Holland-Dozier-Holland) / LITTLE DARLIN' (I NEED YOU) (Marvin Gaye) / etc. WHAT A FOOL BELIEVES was co-written by McDONALD and KENNY LOGGINS. • **Trivia:** They took the name 'DOOBIE' from the slang for a joint.

Album rating: THE DOOBIE BROTHERS (*5) / TOULOUSE STREET (*6) / THE CAPTAIN AND ME (*7) / WHAT WERE ONCE VICES ARE NOW HABITS (*6) / STAMPEDE (*5) / TAKIN' IT TO THE STREETS (*7) / BEST OF THE DOOBIES compilation (*8) / LIVIN' ON THE FAULT LINE (*5) / MINUTE BY MINUTE (*7) / ONE STEP CLOSER (*4) / BEST OF THE DOOBIES, VOLUME II compilation (*6) / THE DOOBIE BROTHERS FAREWELL TOUR (*4) / CYCLES (*3) / BROTHERHOOD (*3) / LISTEN TO THE MUSIC – THE VERY BEST OF THE DOOBIES compilation (*7) / ROCKIN' DOWN THE HIGHWAY – THE WILDLIFE CONCERT (*4) / SIBLING RIVALRY (*4) / GREATEST HITS compilation (*8) / LIVE AT WOLF TRAP (*4)

TOM JOHNSTON (b. Visalia, California) – vocals, guitar / **PAT SIMMONS** (b.23 Jan'50, Aberdeen, Washington) – guitar, vocals / **DAVE SHOGREN** (b. San Francisco, California) – bass / **JOHN HARTMAN** (b.18 Mar'50, Falls Church, Virginia) – drums

Warners / Warners

Apr 71. (lp) *(K 46090) <1919>* **THE DOOBIE BROTHERS** [ ] [ ]
– Nobody / Slippery St. Paul / Greenwood creek / It won't be right / Travellin' man / Feelin' down farther / The master / rowin' a litle each day / Beehive state / Closer every day / Chicago. *(cd-iss. May95; 7599 26215-2)*
Apr 71. (7") *<7495>* **NOBODY. / SLIPPERY ST. PAUL** [–] [ ]
Jul 71. (7") *<7527>* **TRAVELIN' MAN. / FEELIN' DOWN FARTHER** [–] [ ]
Sep 71. (7") *<7544>* **BEEHIVE STATE. / CLOSER EVERY DAY** [–] [ ]

— **TIRAN PORTER** (b. Los Angeles) – bass, vocals repl. SHOGREN.

— added 2nd drummer **MICHAEL HOSSACK** (b.18 Sep'50, Paterson, New York, USA)

Jul 72. (lp) *(K 46183)* *<2634>* **TOULOUSE STREET** [ ] [21]
– Listen to the music / Don't start me talkin' / Mamaloi / Toulouse Street / Rockin' down the highway / Jesus is just alright / White sun / Cotton mouth / Disciple / Snake man. *(quad-lp 1976) (cd-iss. Jul88; K2 46183) (cd-iss. May93; 7599 27263-2)*

Aug 72. (7") *<7619>* **LISTEN TO THE MUSIC. / TOULOUSE STREET** [–] [11]
(UK-iss.Feb74; K 16208) – hit No.29

Dec 72. (7") *<7661>* **JESUS IS JUST ALRIGHT. / ROCKIN' DOWN THE HIGHWAY** [–] [35]

Mar 73. (lp) *(K 46217)* *<2694>* **THE CAPTAIN AND ME** [ ] [7]
– Natural thing / Long train runnin' / China Grove / Dark-eyed Cajun woman / Clear as the driven snow / Without you / South city midnight lady / Evil woman / Busted down around O'Connelly corners / Ukiah / The captain and me. *(cd-iss. Oct87 & Feb95; K2 46217)*

Apr 73. (7") *<7698>* **LONG TRAIN RUNNIN'. / WITHOUT YOU** [–] [8]
(UK-iss.Apr74; K 16267)

Aug 73. (7") *<7728>* **CHINA GROVE. / EVIL WOMAN** [–] [15]
(UK-iss.Aug74; K 16310)

— **KEITH KNUDSON** (b.18 Oct'52, Ames, Iowa) – drums (ex-MANDELBAUM); repl. HOSSACK / added **BILL PAYNE** – keyboards (ex-LITTLE FEAT)

Feb 74. (lp/c) *(K/K4 56026)* *<2750>* **WHAT WERE ONCE VICES ARE NOW HABITS** [19] [4]
– Song to see you through / Spirit / Pursuit on 53rd street / Black water / Eyes of silver / Road angel / You just can't stop it / Tell me what you want / Down in the track / Another park, another Sunday / Flying cloud. *(quad-lp US 1976) (cd-iss. Jul88; K2 56026) (cd re-iss. May93; 7599 2780-2)*

Apr 74. (7") *<7795>* **ANOTHER PARK, ANOTHER SUNDAY. / BLACK WATER** [–] [32]

Aug 74. (7") *(K 16450)* *<7832>* **EYES OF SILVER. / YOU JUST CAN'T STOP IT** [ ] Jul74 [52]

Oct 74. (7") *<8041>* **NOBODY. / FLYING CLOUD** [–] [58]

Dec 74. (7") *<8062>* **BLACK WATER. / SONG TO SEE YOU THROUGH** [–] [1]

— **JEFF BAXTER** (b.13 Dec'48, Washington, D.C.) – guitar (ex-STEELY DAN) repl. PAYNE who rejoined LITTLE FEAT

Apr 75. (lp/c) *(K/K4 56094)* *<2835>* **STAMPEDE** [14] [4]
– Sweet Maxine / Neal's fandango / Texas lullaby / Music man / Slat key sequel rag / Take me in your arms / I cheat the hangman / Precis / Rainy day crossroad blues / I've been workin' on you / Double dealin' four flusher. *(cd-iss. Jun89; 927289-2) (cd-iss. May93; 7599 27289-2)*

Apr 75. (7") *(K 16559)* *<8092>* **TAKE ME IN YOUR ARMS. / SLAT KEY SEQUEL RAG** [29] [ ]

Jul 75. (7") *(K 16601)* *<8126>* **SWEET MAXINE. / DOUBLE DEALIN' FOUR FLUSHER** [ ] [40]

Nov 75. (7") *<8161>* **I CHEAT THE HANGMAN. / MUSIC MAN** [–] [60]

— **MICHAEL McDONALD** (b.12 Feb'52, St.Louis, Missouri) – keyboards, vocals (ex-STEELY DAN) repl. JOHNSTON who fell ill

Mar 76. (lp/c) *(K/K4 56196)* *<2899>* **TAKIN' IT TO THE STREETS** [42] [8]
– Wheels of fortune / Takin' it to the streets / 8th Avenue shuffle / Losin' end / Rio / For someone special / It keeps you runnin' / Turn it loose / Carry me away. *(cd-iss. Jun89 & Jul93; 927289-2)*

Mar 76. (7") *(K 16559)* *<8196>* **TAKIN' IT TO THE STREETS. / FOR SOMEONE SPECIAL** [ ] [13]

Aug 76. (7") *<8233>* **WHEELS OF FORTUNE. / SLAT KEY SEQUEL RAG** [–] [87]

Nov 76. (7") *<8282>* **IT KEEPS YOU RUNNIN'. / TURN IT LOOSE** [–] [37]

Nov 76. (lp/c) *(K/K4 56308)* *<2978>* **THE BEST OF THE DOOBIES** (compilation) [ ] [5]
– China Grove / Long train runnin' / Takin' it to the streets / Listen to the music / Black water / Rockin' down the highway / Jesus is just alright / It keeps you runnin' / South city midnight lady / Take me in your arms (rock me a little while) / Without you. *(cd-iss. 1988; K2 56308)*

Jan 77. (7") *(K 16835)* **LISTEN TO THE MUSIC. / LONG TRAIN RUNNIN'** [ ] [–]

— **TOM JOHNSTON** returned but left again early '77 to go solo

Jul 77. (7") *(K 16989)* *<8408>* **LITTLE DARLING (I NEED YOU). / LOSING END** [ ] [48]

Aug 77. (lp/c) *(K/K4 56383)* *<3045>* **LIVIN' ON THE FAULT LINE** [25] [10]
– You're made that way / Echoes of love / Little darling (I need you) / You belong to me / Livin' on the fault line / Nothin' but a heartache / Chinatown / There's a light / Need a lady / Larry the logger two-step. *(cd-iss. Jun89; 927315-2)*

Sep 77. (7") *(K 17044)* *<8471>* **ECHOES OF LOVE. / THERE'S A LIGHT** [ ] [66]

Mar 78. (7") *<8500>* **LIVIN' ON THE FAULT LINE. / NOTHIN' BUT A HEARTACHE** [–] [ ]

Dec 78. (lp/c) *(K/K4 56486)* *<3193>* **MINUTE BY MINUTE** [ ] [1]
– Sweet feelin' / Open your eyes / Dependin' on you / Here to love you / Minute by minute / You never change / What a fool believes / Steamer lane breakdown / How do the fools survive? / Don't stop to watch the wheels. *(cd-iss. 1988; K2 56486)*

Feb 79. (7") *(K 17314)* *<8725>* **WHAT A FOOL BELIEVES. / DON'T STOP TO WATCH THE WHEELS** [31] Jan79 [1]

Apr 79. (12") *(K 17362)* **WHAT A FOOL BELIEVES. / DON'T STOP TO WATCH THE WHEELS / IT KEEPS YOU RUNNIN'** [72] [–]

Apr 79. (7") *<8828>* **MINUTE BY MINUTE. / SWEET FEELIN'** [–] [14]

Jul 79. (7") *(K 17411)* **MINUTE BY MINUTE. / HOW DO THE FOOLS SURVIVE?** [47] [–]

Jul 79. (7") *<49029>* **DEPENDIN' ON YOU. / HOW DO THE FOOLS SURVIVE?** [–] [25]

Aug 79. (7") *(K 17461)* **OPEN YOUR EYES. / STEAMER LANE BREAKDOWN** [ ] [–]

— **JOHN McFEE** (b.18 Nov'53, Santa Cruz, California) – guitar, vocals; repl. BAXTER / **CHET McCRACKEN** (b.17 Jul'52, Seattle, Washington) – drums, vibes (ex-session man) repl. HARTMAN / added **CORNELIUS BUMPUS** (b.13 Jan'52) – keyboards, sax (ex-MOBY GRAPE) / (now septet alongside **SIMMONS, McDONALD, PORTER + KNUDSEN**)

Aug 80. (7") *<49503>* **REAL LOVE. / THANK YOU LOVE** [–] [5]

Oct 80. (lp/c) *(K/K4 56824)* *<3452>* **ONE STEP CLOSER** [53] [3]
– Dedicate this heart / Real love / No stoppin' us now / Thank you love / One step closer / Keep this train a-rollin' / Just in time / South bay strut / One by one. *(cd re-iss. Jan96; 7599 26628-2)*

Nov 80. (7") *(K 17707)* *<49622>* **ONE STEP CLOSER. / SOUTH BAY STRUT** [ ] [24]

Jan 81. (7") *<49642>* **WYNKEN, BLYNKEN AND NOD. / IN HARMONY** [–] [76]
(above credited w/ KATE + SIMON TAYLOR)

Jan 81. (7") *<49642>* **KEEP THIS TRAIN A-ROLLIN'. / JUST IN TIME** [–] [62]

Nov 81. (lp/c) *(K/K4 56956)* *<3612>* **THE BEST OF THE DOOBIES VOLUME II** (compilation) [ ] [39]
– Little darlin' / Echoes of love / You belong to me / One step closer / What a fool believes / Dependin' on you / Here to love you / One by one / Real love / Minute by minute.

Jan 82. (7") *<50001>* **HERE TO LOVE YOU. / WYNKEN, BLYNKEN AND NOD** [–] [65]

— **WILLIE WEEKS** – bass repl. PORTER

— split Mar'82, recorded final concert album Sep'82

WEA WEA

Jun 83. (d-lp/d-c) *(923 772-1/-4)* *<23772>* **THE DOOBIE BROTHERS FAREWELL TOUR (live)** [ ] [79]
– Slippery St. Paul / Takin it to the streets / Jesus is just alright / Minute by minute / Can't let it get away / Listen to the music / Echoes of love / What a fool believes / Black water / You belong to me / Slat key sequel rag / Streamer lane breakdown / South city / Midnight lady / Olana / Don't start me to talking / Long train runnin' / China grove.

Jul 83. (7") *<29552>* **YOU BELONG TO ME (live). / SOUTH CITY MIDNIGHT LADY (live)** [–] [79]

— by this time MICHAEL McDONALD had gone solo, as did PATRICK SIMMONS. **DOOBIE BROTHERS** reformed mid'88. (JOHNSTON, HARTMAN, SIMMONS, PORTER) plus **MICHAEL HOSSACK** – drums / **BOBBY LaKIND** (b.1945) – percussion

Capitol Capitol

Jul 89. (7") *(CL 536)* *<44376>* **THE DOCTOR. / TOO HIGH A PRICE** [73] May89 [9]
(12"+=/cd-s+=) *(12/CD CL 536)* – Anything for love.

Jul 89. (cd/c/lp) *(CD/TC+/EST 2100)* *<90371>* **CYCLES** [ ] Jun89 [17]
– The doctor / One chain (don't make no prison) / Take me to the highway / South of the border / Time is here and gone / Need a little taste of love / I can read your mind / Wrong number / Tonight I'm coming through (the border) / Too high a price.

Sep 89. (7") *(CL 552)* *<44441>* **NEED A LITTLE TASTE OF LOVE. / I CAN READ YOUR MIND** Aug89 45
(12"+=/cd-s+=) *(12/CD CL 552)* – The doctor.

May 91. (cd/c/lp) *(CD/TC+/EST 2141)* *<94623>* **BROTHERHOOD** 82
– Something you said / Is love enough / Dangerous / Our love / Divided highway / Under the spell / Excited / This train I'm on / Showdown / Rollin' on.

— on the 24th December '92, LaKIND died of cancer

— vocalists now **TOM JOHNSTON, MICHAEL McDONALD + PATRICK SIMMONS**

Columbia Sony

Aug 96. (d-cd) *(484452-2)* **ROCKIN' DOWN THE HIGHWAY – THE WILDLIFE CONCERT** (live) Jul96
– China grove / What a fool believes / Dangerous / Jesus is just alright / Rockin' down the highway / Dependin' on you / Eyes of silver / Another park another Sunday / Slack key sequel rag (instrumental) / South city midnight lady / Clear as the driven snow / Black water / Wild ride / Slow burn / The doctor / Take me in your arms (rock me) / Long train runnin' / Without you / Excited / Dark eyed Cajun woman / Neal's fandango / Listen to the music / Minute by minute / Takin' it to the streets.

— **JOHNSTON + SIMMONS** with **KEITH KNUDSEN** – drums

Eagle Rhino

Oct 00. (cd) *(EAGCD 049)* *<8122 75809-2>* **SIBLING RIVALRY**
– People gotta love again / Leave my heartache behind / Ordinary man / Jericho / On every corner / Angels of madness / 45th floor / Can't stand to lose / Higher ground / Gates of Eden / Don't be afraid / Rocking horse / Five corners.

Sanctuary Sanctuary

Nov 04. (cd) *(SANCD 321)* *<84725>* **LIVE AT WOLF TRAP** (live)
– Rockin' down the highway / Jesus is just alright / DAngerous / Another park, another Sunday / Steamer lane / South city midnight lady / Snake man / Five corners / Rainy day crossroad blues / Clear as the driven snow / Don't start me talkin' / Take me in your arms / Little bitty / Black water / Long train runnin' / China grove / LIsten to the music.

– compilations etc. –

on 'Warners' unless mentioned otherwise

Nov 84. (d-c) *(K4 66117)* **TAKIN' IT TO THE STREETS / LIVIN' ON THE FAULT LINE** –

Mar 86. (7") *Old Gold; (OG 9573)* **LISTEN TO THE MUSIC. / WHAT A FOOL BELIEVES** –

Jan 87. (7") *(W 8451)* **WHAT A FOOL BELIEVES. / MINUTE BY MINUTE** 57 –
(12"+=) *(W 8451T)* – Real love.

May 93. (cd) *F.N.A.C.;* **INTRODUCING . . .** –

May 93. (cd/c) *(9548 31094-2/-4)* **LISTEN TO THE MUSIC – THE VERY BEST OF THE DOOBIE BROTHERS**
(re-iss. May94 cd/c; 9548 32803-2/-4)

Nov 93. (7"/c-s) *(W 0217/+C)* **LONG TRAIN RUNNIN'. / ('A'-mix)** 7 –
(12"+=/cd-s+=) *(W 0217 T/CD)* – ('A'-mix).

Apr 94. (7"/c-s) *(W 0228/+C)* **LISTEN TO THE MUSIC ('94 remix). / ('A'mix)** 37 –
(12"+=/cd-s+=) *(W 0228 T/CD)* – ('A'-remixes by MOTIV8 / RAMP . . . / DEVELOPMENT CORPORATION).

Feb 96. (cd) *B.A.M.; (KLMCD 055)* **THE EARLY YEARS** –

May 97. (cd) *Experience; (EXP 014)* **THE DOOBIE BROTHERS** –

Nov 98. (cd) *Laserlight; (21154)* **ON OUR WAY UP** –

Feb 00. (cd) *Brilliant; (BT 33018)* **LISTEN TO THE MUSIC** –

Oct 01. (4xcd-box) *Rhino; (8122 73574-2)* *<75876-2>* **LONG TIME RUNNIN' 1970-2000** Sep99

Feb 02. (cd) *Rhino; <8122 78298-2>* **DOOBIES' CHOICE** –

Nov 02. (cd) *Disky; (SI 905176)* **DIVIDED HIGHWAY** –

Jun 04. (cd) *Rhino; <(8122 76511-2)>* **GREATEST HITS** 45 Sep01
– Listen to the music / Jesus is just alright / Rockin' down the highway / Long train runnin' / Without you / China grove / Nobody / Black water / Take me in your arms (rock me) / It keeps you runnin' / Takin' it to the streets / You belong to me / Echoes of love / What a fool believes / Minute by minute / Dependin' on you / One step closer / Real love / The doctor / Dangerous.

— JOHN HARTMAN who was a reserve fireman /policeman was refused promotion by his home state court, due to his alleged drug-taking past

the DOORS

Formed: Los Angeles, California, USA . . . July 1965 by RAY MANZAREK and JIM MORRISON. In 1966, after some personnel changes, they soon settled with JOHN DENSMORE and ROBBY KRIEGER and became The DOORS, taking their name from Aldous Huxley's work 'The Doors Of Perception'. They were released from a 'Columbia' recording contract, when ARTHUR LEE (of LOVE), recommended them to his 'Elektra' label boss Jac Holzman. Early in 1967, their eponymous debut album was issued, which soon climbed to US No.2 after an edited version of 'LIGHT MY FIRE' hit No.1 in July '67. The single and album showcased MORRISON's overtly sexual vocal theatrics against a backdrop of organ-dominated, avant-garde blues. The classic debut also contained two cover versions (see below), the lucid psychedelia of 'THE CRYSTAL SHIP', plus the extremely disturbing 11-minute epic, 'THE END' (which was later used on the soundtrack for the 1979 Francis Ford Coppola film, 'Apocalypse Now'). While other bands of the era were into peace and love, The DOORS found their salvation in a much darker vision, again in evidence on the follow-up (also in '67), 'STRANGE DAYS'. This was another classic, tracks like, 'LOVE ME TWO TIMES', 'YOU'RE LOST LITTLE GIRL' and 'PEOPLE ARE STRANGE' further enhancing the band's powerful mystique. As MORRISON's drink and drugs antics became increasingly problematic, he was arrested many times (on stage and off), mostly for lewd simulation of sexual acts and indecent exposure. Nevertheless, in the late summer of '68, they found themselves at the top of the US charts again with the 45, 'HELLO I LOVE YOU' and the album, 'WAITING FOR THE SUN'. A disappointing 4th album, 'THE SOFT PARADE' (1969), did, however, contain a classic US Top 3 hit, 'TOUCH ME'. More controversy was generated, when, in November '69, MORRISON was accused of interfering with an airline stewardess while a flight was in progress. He was later acquitted, but the following year, was given eight months hard labour after being found guilty of indecent exposure and profanity. He was freed on appeal and began work on 1970's, 'MORRISON HOTEL / HARD ROCK CAFE', a return to rawer, more basic rock'n'roll. After the recording of 'L.A. WOMAN', he relocated to Paris in the Spring of '71 with his girlfriend Pamela, amid rumours of an imminent split from the group. The aforementioned album was delivered in June, a masterpiece that carried on the re-evaluation of their blues roots. His over-indulgence in drugs and booze, had given his vocal chords a deeper resonance, showcased on such classics as, 'RIDERS ON THE STORM' (a Top 30 hit), 'LOVE HER MADLY', the JOHN LEE HOOKER cover 'CRAWLING KING SNAKE' and the freewheeling title track. Ironically, just as the band seemed to have found their feet again, JIM MORRISON was found dead in his bathtub on the 3rd of July 1971. Speculation was rife at the time, but it later became apparent he had died from a drugs/drink induced heart attack. He was also buried in Paris, his grave becoming a shrine to all but his parents, who disowned him in 1967. The others continued as a trio for the next two years, but sadly the public refused to acknowledge them as the real DOORS. The "god-like" cult of MORRISON has mushroomed to incredible proportions in the years following his death, rumours continuing, Elvis-like, to circulate that he was still alive. There have been many imitators over the last quarter of a century, although none have matched his/their dark majesty. MANZAREK and KRIEGER re-actified a new post-millennium version of the group in 2003 (The DOORS OF THE 21st CENTURY), choosing ex-CULT man IAN ASTBURY(!) to front them.

• **Songwriters:** MORRISON – words/poetry (under the influence of explorative narcotics), Group/MANZAREK compositions. Covered; ALABAMA SONG (Brecht-Weill) / BACK DOOR MAN (Howlin' Wolf) / WHO DO YOU LOVE (Bo Diddley) / LITTLE RED ROOSTER (Willie Dixon) / BEEN DOWN SO LONG (J.B. Lenoir). • **Trivia:** In 1968, they featured on a UK TV documentary 'The Doors Are Open', which was later issued on video. In 1991, Oliver Stone released a feature film 'THE DOORS', with Val Kilmer playing the role of MORRISON.

Album rating: THE DOORS (*9) / STRANGE DAYS (*8) / WAITING FOR THE SUN (*6) / THE SOFT PARADE (*5) / MORRISON HOTEL – HARD ROCK CAFE (*8) / ABSOLUTELY LIVE (*6) / 13 compilation (*8) / L.A. WOMAN (*9) / OTHER VOICES (*4) / WEIRD SCENES INSIDE THE GOLDMINE compilation (*8) / FULL CIRCLE (*4) / AN AMERICAN PRAYER – JIM MORRISON exploitation (*4) / GREATEST HITS compilation (*8) / ALIVE, SHE CRIED exploitation (*4) / BEST OF THE DOORS compilation (*8) / LIVE AT THE HOLLYWOOD BOWL exploitation (*4) / THE DOORS soundtrack (*5) / IN CONCERT exploitation (*5) / GREATEST HITS compilation (*9) / THE COMPLETE STUDIO RECORDINGS boxed-set (*8)

JIM MORRISON (b. JAMES DOUGLAS MORRISON, 8 Dec'43, Melbourne, Florida) – vocals / **RAY MANZAREK** (b.12 Feb'35, Chicago, Illinois) – keyboards, bass pedal / **ROBBY KRIEGER** (b. 8 Jan'46) – guitar / **JOHN DENSMORE** (b. 1 Dec'45) – drums / also guest **DOUG LUBAHN** – bass (of CLEAR LIGHT)

Elektra Elektra

Feb 67. (7") *(EKSN 45009)* <45611> **BREAK ON THROUGH (TO THE OTHER SIDE). / END OF THE NIGHT** [ ] Jan67 [ ]

Mar 67. (lp; mono/stereo) *<(EKL/EKS 74007)>* **THE DOORS** [ ] Jan67 [1]
– Break on through (to the other side) / Soul kitchen / The crystal ship / Twentieth century fox / Alabama song (whiskey song) / Light my fire / Back door man / I looked at you / End of the night / Take it as it comes / The end. *(re-iss. Nov71 lp/c; K/K4 42012) (cd-iss. Jan84; K2 42012) (re-iss. cd Feb89; 974007-2) (re-hit UK No.43 in Apr91)*

Apr 67. (7") *(EKSN 45012)* **ALABAMA SONG (WHISKEY BAR). / TAKE IT AS IT COMES** [ ] [–]

Jul 67. (7") *(EKSN 45014)* <45615> **LIGHT MY FIRE (edit). / THE CRYSTAL SHIP** [49] Jun67 [1]
(re-iss. Jul71; same)

Sep 67. (7") *(EKSN 45017)* <45621> **PEOPLE ARE STRANGE. / UNHAPPY GIRL** [ ] [12]

Dec 67. (lp; mono/stereo) *<(EKL/EKS 74014)>* **STRANGE DAYS** [ ] Nov67 [3]
– Strange days / You're lost little girl / Love me two times / Unhappy girl / Horse latitudes / Moonlight drive / People are strange / My eyes have seen you / I can't see your face in my mind / When the music's over. *(re-iss. Nov71 lp/c; K/K4 42016) (cd-iss. Jan86; K2 42016) (cd re-iss. Feb89; 974014-2)*

Dec 67. (7") *(EKSN 45022)* <45624> **LOVE ME TWO TIMES. / MOONLIGHT DRIVE** [ ] [25]

Apr 68. (7") *(EKSN 45030)* <45628> **THE UNKNOWN SOLDIER. / WE COULD BE SO GOOD TOGETHER** [ ] Mar68 [39]
(re-iss. Jun71; K 12004)

Aug 68. (7") *(EKSN 45037)* <45635> **HELLO, I LOVE YOU. / LOVE STREET** [15] Jul68 [1]

—— **LEROY VINEGAR** – acoustic bass repl. LABAHN

Sep 68. (lp; mono/stereo) *<(EKL/EKS 74024)>* **WAITING FOR THE SUN** [16] Aug68 [1]
– Hello I love you / Love street / Not to touch the Earth / Summer's almost gone / Wintertime love / The unknown soldier / Spanish caravan / My wild love / We could be so good together / Yes, the river flows / Five to one. *(re-iss. Nov71 lp/c; K/K4 42041) (cd-iss. Jan86; K2 42041) (cd re-iss. Feb89; 974024-2)*

Dec 68. (7") *(EKSN 45050)* <45646> **TOUCH ME. / WILD CHILD** [ ] [3]

May 69. (7") *(EKSN 45059)* <45656> **WISHFUL SINFUL. / WHO SCARED YOU** [ ] Mar69 [44]

Aug 69. (7") *(EKSN 45065)* <45663> **TELL ALL THE PEOPLE. / EASY RIDE** [ ] Jun69 [57]

Sep 69. (lp) *<(EKS 75005)>* **THE SOFT PARADE** [ ] Aug69 [6]
– Tell all the people / Touch me / Shaman's blues / Do it / Easy ride / Wild child / Runnin' blue / Wishful sinful / The soft parade. *(re-iss. Nov71 lp/c; K/K4 42079) (cd-iss. Feb89; 975005-2)*

Sep 69. (7") <45675> **RUNNIN' BLUE. / DO IT** [–] [64]

—— guest **LONNIE MACK** – bass repl. LUBAHN

Apr 70. (7") <45685> **YOU MAKE ME REAL. / ROADHOUSE BLUES** [–] [50]

Apr 70. (7") *(2101 004)* **YOU MAKE ME REAL. / THE SPY** [ ] [–]

Apr 70. (lp) *<(EKS 75007)>* **MORRISON HOTEL / HARD ROCK CAFE** [12] Mar70 [4]
– Land ho! / The spy / Queen of the highway / Indian summer / Maggie McGill / Roadhouse blues / Waiting for the sun / You make me real / Peace frog / Blue Sunday / Ship of fools. *(re-iss. Nov71 lp/c; K/K4 42080) (cd-iss. Apr86; K2 42080) (re-iss. cd.Feb89; 975007-2)*

Jul 70. (7") *(2101 008)* **ROADHOUSE BLUES. / BLUE SUNDAY** [ ] [–]

Sep 70. (d-lp) *(2665 002)* *<9002>* **ABSOLUTELY LIVE (live)** [69] Aug70 [8]
– Who do you love medley: Alabama song – Back door man – Love hides – Five to one / Build me a woman / When the music's over / Close to you / Universal mind / Break on through (to the other side) / The celebration of the lizard / Soul kitchen. *(re-iss. Nov71 d-lp; K 62005) (d-cd-iss. Mar87 w-drawn; 2665 002)*

Oct 70. (7") <45708> **UNIVERSAL MIND. / THE ICEWAGON FLEW** [–] [ ]

Mar 71. (lp/c) *(K/K4 42062)* *<74079>* **13** (compilation) [ ] Dec70 [25]
– Light my fire / People are strange / Back door man / Moonlight drive / The crystal ship / Roadhouse blues / Touch me / Love me two times / You're lost little girl / Hello, I love you / Land ho / Wild child / The unknown soldier.

—— guest **JERRY SCHEFF** – bass repl. MACK

May 71. (7") *<(EK 45726)>* **LOVE HER MADLY. / (YOU NEED MEAT) DON'T GO NO FURTHER** [ ] Apr71 [11]

Jun 71. (lp/c) *(K/K4 42090)* *<75011>* **L.A. WOMAN** [26] May71 [9]
– The changeling / Love her madly / Been down so long / Cars hiss by my window / L.A. woman / L'America / Hyacinth house / Crawling King Snake / The wasp (Texas radio and the big beat) / Riders on the storm *(cd-iss. 1984; K2 42090) (cd re-iss. Feb89 & Apr91; 975011-2)*

Jul 71. (7") *(K 12021)* <45738> **RIDERS ON THE STORM (edit). / THE CHANGELING** [22] [14]

—— **RAY** – vocals, ROBBIE and JOHN carried on when JIM MORRISON died 3rd Jul'71 of a mysterious heart attack. The trio continued on

—— (MANZAREK now on vox). Used guest session bassmen **WILLIE RUFF**, **WOLFGANG MERTZ** and **JACK CONRAD**

Nov 71. (7") *(K 12036)* <45757> **TIGHTROPE RIDE. / VARIETY IS THE SPICE OF LIFE** [ ] [71]

Dec 71. (lp/c) *(K/K4 42104)* *<75017>* **OTHER VOICES** [ ] Nov71 [31]
– In the eye of the sun / Variety is the spice of life / Ships w.sails / Tightrope ride / Down on the farm / I'm horny, I'm stoned / Wandering musician / Hang on to your life

May 72. (7") *(K 12048)* <45768> **SHIP W. SAILS. / IN THE EYE OF THE SUN** [ ] [ ]

—— bass sessions **J. CONRAD, CHARLES LARKEY, LEE SKLAR and CHRIS ETHRIDGE.**

Aug 72. (7") *(K 12059)* <45793> **GET UP AND DANCE. / TREETRUNK** [ ] [ ]

Aug 72. (lp/c) *(K/K4 42116)* *<75038>* **FULL CIRCLE** [ ] [68]
– Get up and dance / Four billion souls / Verdilac / Hardwod floor / Good rockin' / The mosquito / The piano bird / It slipped my mind / The Peking king and the New York queen.

Sep 72. (7") <45807> **THE MOSQUITO. / IT SLIPPED MY MIND** [–] [85]

Dec 72. (7"w-drawn) **THE PIANO BIRD. / GOOD ROCKIN'** [–] [–]

—— They finally split 1973. MANZAREK went solo and KRIEGER & DENSMORE formed The BUTTS BAND. With JESS RODEN as lead singer / **PHILIP CHEN** – bass / **ROY DAVIS** – keyboards, they made 2 albums for 'Blue Thumb' records; 'THE BUTTS BAND' (1974) / 'HEAR AND NOW' (1975).

– compilations, etc. –

Note; All on 'Elektra' until mentioned otherwise

Mar 72. (d-lp/d-c) *(K/K4 62009)* *<6001>* **WEIRD SCENES INSIDE THE GOLD MINE** [50] Feb72 [55]
– Break on through (to the other side) / Strange days / Shaman's blues / Love street / Peace frog / Blue Sunday / The wasp (Texas radio and the big beat) / End of the night / Love her madly / Ship of fools / The spy / The end / Take it as it comes / Running blue / L.A. woman / Five to one / Who scared you? / Don't go no further / Riders on the storm / Maggie McGill / Horse latitudes / When the music's over.

Sep 74. (lp/c) *(K/K4 42143)* *<5035>* **THE BEST OF THE DOORS** [ ] [ ]

Feb 76. (7") *(K 12203)* **RIDERS ON THE STORM. / L.A. WOMAN** [33] [–]

Sep 76. (7") *(K 12227)* **LIGHT MY FIRE. / THE UNKNOWN SOLDIER** [ ] [–]

Sep 76. (7") *(K 12228)* **LOVE HER MADLY. / TOUCH ME** [ ] [–]

Nov 78. (lp/c; by JIM MORRISON) *(K/K4 52111)* <502> **AN AMERICAN PRAYER** (poetry recorded 8 Nov'70 with some DOORS tapes) [ ] [54]
– Awake / Ghost song / Dawn's highway / Newborn awakening / To come of age / Black polished chrome / Latino chrome / Angels and sailors / Stoned immaculate / The poet's dreams / The movie / Curses invocations / World on fire / American night / Roadhouse blues / Lament / The hitchhiker / An American prayer. *(re-iss. May95 cd/c/lp;)*

Jan 79. (7") *(K 12215)* **LOVE ME TWO TIMES. / HELLO I LOVE YOU** [ ] [–]
(w/ free 7"+=) *(SAM 94)* – GHOST SONG. / ROADHOUSE BLUES

Jan 79. (7") **ROADHOUSE BLUES. / AN AMERICAN PRAYER** [–] [ ]

Jan 80. (7")<12"> *(K 12400)* <ELK 22032> **THE END. / (b-side 'Delta' not by The DOORS)** [ ] [–]

Oct 80. (lp/c) *(K/K4 52254)* <515> **GREATEST HITS** [ ] [17]
– Hello, I love you / Light my fire / People are strange / Love me two times / Riders on the storm / Break on through / Roadhouse blues / Touch me / L.A. woman / Love her madly / The ghost song / The end. *(cd-iss. Oct95 cd/c; 7559 61860-2/-4)*

Oct 80. (7") **PEOPLE ARE STRANGE. / NOT TO TOUCH THE EARTH** [–] [ ]

Oct 82. (d-c) *(K4 62034)* **MORRISON HOTEL / L.A. WOMAN** [ ] [–]

Oct 83. (7") <60269> **GLORIA (live). / MOONLIGHT DRIVE (live)** [–] [71]

Oct 83. (12") *(E 9774T)* **GLORIA (live). / LOVE ME TWO TIMES (live)** [ ] [–]

Oct 83. (lp/c) *(960269-1/-4)* <60269> **ALIVE SHE CRIED (live)** [36] [23]
– Gloria / Light my fire / You make me real / The wasp (Texas radio and the big beat) / Love me two times / Little red rooster / Moonlight drive. *(cd-iss. Jul84; 960269-2)*

Aug 84. (d-c) *(K4 62040)* **THE SOFT PARADE / AN AMERICAN PRAYER** [ ] [ ]

Jun 85. (lp/c) *(EKT 9/+C)* <60417> **CLASSICS** [ ] [ ]

Sep 85. (7") *Old Gold; (OG 9520)* **RIDERS ON THE STORM. / LIGHT MY FIRE** [ ] [–]

Nov 85. (d-lp/c/cd) *(EKT 21/+C/CD)* <60345> **BEST OF THE DOORS** [ ] [ ]
– Break on through (to the other side) / Light my fire / The crystal ship / People are strange / Strange days / Love me two times / Five to one / Waiting for the Sun / Spanish caravan / When the music's over / Hello, I love you / Roadhouse blues / L.A. woman / Riders on the storm / Touch me / Love her madly / The unknown soldier / The end. (cd+=) – Alabama song (whiskey bar). *(re-iss. Apr91 hit UK No.17 & US No.32) (re-iss. Mar98, hit UK No.37)*

Jun 87. (m-lp/c)(cd) *(EKT 40/+C)(960741-2)* <60741> **LIVE AT THE HOLLYWOOD BOWL (live)** [ ] [ ]
– Wake up / Light my fire / The unknown soldier / A little game / The hill dwellers / Spanish caravan.

Mar 91. (lp/c)(cd) *(EKT 85/+C)(961047)* <61047> **THE DOORS** (soundtrack) [11] [8]
– The movie / Riders on the storm / Love street / Break on through (to the other side) / The end / Light my fire / Ghost song / Roadhouse blues / Heroin (VELVET UNDERGROUND) / Carmina Burana (introduction; ATLANTA SYMPHONY ORCHESTRA & CHORUS) / Stoned immaculate / When the music's over / The severed garden (adagio) / L.A. woman.

Apr 91. (7") *(EKR 121)* **BREAK ON THROUGH. / LOVE STREET** [64] [ ]
(12"+=/cd-s+=) *(EKR 125 TW/CD)* – Hello I love you / Touch me.

May 91. (7") *(EKR 125)* **LIGHT MY FIRE. / PEOPLE ARE STRANGE** [7] [ ]
(ext; 12"+=/cd-s+=) *(EKR 125 TW/CD)* – Soul kitchen.

May 91. (t-lp/d-c)(d-cd) *(EKT 88/+C)(7559 61082)* <61082> **THE DOORS: IN CONCERT (live)** [24] [50]

Jul 91. (7") *(EKR 131)* **RIDERS ON THE STORM. / LOVE ME TWO TIMES (live)** [68] [ ]
(12"+=/cd-s+=) *(EKR 131 TW/CD)* – Roadhouse blues (live).

Jun 95. (c-s; by JIM MORRISON & THE DOORS) *(EKR 205C)* **THE GHOST SONG. / (interview)** [ ] [ ]
(cd-s+=) *(EKR 205CD)* – Love me two times (live) / Roadhouse blues (live).

Oct 97. (4xcd-box) <*(7559 62123-2)*> **THE DOORS BOX SET** [ ] [65]

Nov 99. (cd) <*(7559 62475-2)*> **STONED IMMACULATE** [ ] [ ]

Nov 99. (7xcd-box) <*(7559 62434-2)*> **THE COMPLETE STUDIO RECORDINGS** [ ] [ ]

Sep 00. (cd/c) <*(7559 62468-2/-4)*> **THE BEST OF THE DOORS** [9] [ ]
– Riders on the storm / Light my fire / Love me two times / Roadhouse blues (live) / Strange days / Break on through / Five to one / Moonlight drive / Alabama song / Love her madly / People are strange / Touch me / Backdoor man / The unknown soldier / L.A. woman / Hello I love you / The end. <*(d-cd+=; 7559 62569-2)*>

Sep 01. (cd) *<79376-2>* **THE VERY BEST OF THE DOORS** [–] [92]

Oct 01. (4xcd-box) *(7559 62716-2)* **THE DOORS BOX SET** [ ] [–]

Aug 03. (d-cd) *<73889-2>* **LEGACY: THE ABSOLUTE BEST** [–] [63]

DOVES

Formed: Manchester, England . . . 1998 out of dance/rave outfit, SUB SUB, by JIMI GOODWIN, along with brothers JEZ and ANDY WILLIAMS. After the hectic turbulence of the house scene in the late 80's/early 90's, SUB SUB protagonist GOODWIN rocketed straight into the number 5 spot with 'AIN'T NO USE (AIN'T NO LOVE)', which predictably ruined any future respect given to the man. A shambolic, rushed released debut album, 'FULL FATHOM FIVE' (1993), sent GOODWIN into hiding for four years (during which he cropped up on various material by TRICKY and BERNARD SUMNER). In 1998, a new direction forced out the 'CEDAR' EP, which The DOVES issued on their own 'Casino' label. Sounding similar to OASIS and heavy rivals SHACK, frontman GOODWIN did his best to capture the essence and mad-for-it-ness that he'd experienced during the early 1990's. However, the music lacked interest, and, although long drawn and enterprising at times, the tired trio sounded as magnificent as RADIOHEAD without any transmitter. With two further singles under their belt, 'Heavenly' records ('Astralwerks' in the US) gave DOVES a lucrative signing-on deal, the single 'THE CEDAR ROOM' and its parent debut album, 'LOST SOULS', both making healthy chart positions in spring 2000. The feted DOVES were now darlings of Britain's emotional indie scene, ranking alongside major players such as COLDPLAY, STARSAILOR and troubadour DAVID GRAY. However, come the release of their sophomore album 'THE LAST BROADCAST' (2002), the bearded troupe of musing musicians had formally eclipsed any of the above in terms of musical and lyrical integrity. Taking its name from the 1998 "mockumentary", which was said to have inspired 'The Blair Witch Project', ' . . .BROADCAST' generated emotional intensity from its dreamlike artwork to GOODWIN's vocals. The single, 'THERE GOES THE FEAR', used child-like guitar melodies and striking orchestral accompaniment courtesy of SEAN O'HAGAN (the HIGH LLAMAS), not to mention a tripped-out video to boot. Where most bands fall flat on their face come album Number deux, DOVES had simply evolved into something splendid and sublime – well, like a pristine dove, walking amongst a flock of dirty pigeons that currently litter Britain's indie scene. A 'LOST SIDES' (2003) B-sides collection showed up in the three-year gap between albums, as DOVES continued to court their massive fanbase on the festival circuit. Early 2005, their first Top 10 single for two years, 'BLACK AND WHITE TOWN', preceded a UK No.1 album, 'SOME CITIES', a record that refined their emotionally accute take on potted Manc-sonic history.

• **Covers:** HIT THE GROUND RUNNING (Warren Zevon) / WILLOW'S SONG (trad.) / MOONCHILD melody (King Crimson). • **Note:** Not to be confused with an early 90's DOVES who issued one album, 'Affinity', in 1991.

Album rating: Sub Sub: FULL FATHOM FIVE (*5) / Doves: LOST SOULS (*8) / THE LAST BROADCAST (*8) / LOST SIDES collection (*6) / SOME CITIES (*7)

SUB SUB

JIMI GOODWIN – vocals, guitar / **JEZ WILLIAMS** – vocals, guitar / **ANDY WILLIAMS** – vocals, drums

Rob's not iss.

Jun 92. (12"ep) *(12ROB 7)* **COAST EP** [ ] [–]
– Coast / Inside of this / Inside out / Past.

Mar 93. (7"/c-s; as SUB SUB featuring MELANIE WILLIAMS) *(7/C ROB 9)* **AIN'T NO LOVE (AIN'T NO USE. / (parkside mix)** [3] [–]
(12"+=/cd-s+=) *(12/CD ROB 9)* – ('A'mixes; piano / on the house).

Feb 94. (7"/c-s) *(7/C ROB 19)* **RESPECT. / (original)** [49] [–]
(12"+=/cd-s+=) *(12/CD ROB 19)* – ('A'-DaSilva – McCreedy + acid) / ('A'-primetime).

Aug 94. (c-s) *(CROB 29)* **ANGEL / SOUTHERN TREES (instrumental)** [ ] [–]
(12"+=/cd-s+=) *(12/CD ROB 29)* – ('A'-Deep love + Primetime).
(12") *(12ROB 29X)* – ('A'mixes).

Sep 94. (cd/c/lp) *(CD/C/LP ROB 30)* **FULL FATHOM FIVE** [ ] [ ]
– Coast / Angel / Valium jazz / Southern trees / Inside of this / Ain't no love (ain't no use) / Flute / Swamp / Respect / Past.

Jan 95. (12"/cd-s) *(12/CD ROB 39)* **SOUTHERN TREES (7" + 12" mixes). / JAGGERNATH / NORTHERN TREES** [ ] [–]

—— wisely decided to take some time out

DOVES

—— same line-up

Casino not iss.

Nov 98. (10"ep) *(CHIP 001)* **CEDAR EP** [ ] [–]
– The cedar room / Rise / Zither.

—— the track, 'GUTTER GIRL', featured on the V/A Manchester compilation EP, 'Everyone Knows Everyone Else' alongside JANE WEAVER and ANDY VOTEL

May 99. (cd-ep) *(CHIP 002CD)* **SEA EP** [ ] [–]
– Sea song / Breakmegently (incidently) / Darker.

Aug 99. (10"/cd-s) *(CHIP 003/+CD)* **HERE IT COMES. / MEET ME AT THE PIER / ACOUSTIC NO.1** [73] [–]

Heavenly Astralwerks

Mar 00. (10"/cd-s) *(HVN 95 10/CD)* **THE CEDAR ROOM. / ZITHER / KAREN** [33] [–]

Apr 00. (d-lp/cd) *(HVNLP 26/+CD)* *<ASW 50248 LP/CD>* **LOST SOULS** [16] Oct00 [ ]
– Firesuite / Here it comes / Break me gently / Sea song / Rise / Lost souls / Melody calls / Catch the sun / The man who told everything / The cedar room / Reprise / A house.

May 00. (10"/cd-s) *(HVN 96 10/CDS)* **CATCH THE SUN. / VALLEY / DOWN TO SEA** [32] [–]
(cd-s) *(HVN 96CD)* – ('A'side) / Crunch / Lost in watts.

Oct 00. (7") *(HVN 98)* **THE MAN WHO TOLD EVERYTHING. / YOUR SHADOW LAY ACROSS MY LIFE** [32] [–]
(c-s+=/cd-s+=) *(HVN 98 CS/CD)* – Firesuite.
(cd-s) *(HVN 98CDS)* – ('A'side) / Rise (live) / Suitnoise.

Heavenly Capitol

Apr 02. (10") *(HVN 111-10)* **THERE GOES THE FEAR. / HIT THE GROUND RUNNING** [3] [–]
(cd-s) *(HVN 111CD)* – ('A'side) / ('A'-video).

Apr 02. (d-lp/cd) *(HVNLP 35/+CD)* *<12232>* **THE LAST BROADCAST** [1] [83]
– Intro / Words / There goes the fear / M62 song / Where we're calling from / N.Y. / Satellites / Friday's dust / Pounding / The last broadcast / The sulphur man / Caught by the river.

Jul 02. (10") *(HVN 116-10)* **POUNDING. / SATELLITES (Soulsavers remix) / M62 SONG (Four Tet remix)** [21] [–]
(cd-s) *(HVN 116CD)* – ('A'side) / Far from grace / Northenden / ('A'-video).

Oct 02. (10") *(HVN 126-10)* **CAUGHT BY THE RIVER. / THE SULPHUR MAN (Rebelski remix) / WHERE WE'RE CALLING FROM (Hebden Bridge remix)** [29] [–]
(cd-s) *(HVN 126CD)* – ('A'side) / Hit the ground running / Willow's song / ('A'-video).

Sep 03. (cd) *(HVNLP 46CD)* *<593179>* **LOST SIDES** (collection) [50] Oct03 [ ]
– Break me gently (incidental) / Darker / Your shadow lay across my life / Meet me at the pier / Down to sea / Crunch / Zither / Valley / Northenden / Hit the ground running / Willow's song / Far from grace. *(ltd d-cd+=; HVNLP 46CDX)* – Words (Echoboy remix) / N.Y. (Chris Coco remix) / M62 song (Four Tet remix) / The sulphur man (Rebelski remix) / The last broadcast (Magnet remix) / Where we're calling from (Hebden Bridge remix) / Satellites (Soulsavers remix).

Feb 05. (7") *(HVN 145)* **BLACK AND WHITE TOWN. / 45** [6] [–]
(cd-s+=) *(HVN 145CDS)* – Eleven miles out / ('A'-video).
(cd-s) *(HVN 145CD)* – ('A') / At the tower.

Feb 05. (lp/cd) *(HVNLP 50/+CD)* *<74609>* **SOME CITIES** [1] Mar05 [ ]
– Some cities / Black and white town / Almost forgot myself / Snowden / The storm / Walk in fire / One of these days / Someday soon / Shadows of Salford / Sky starts falling / Ambition. *(ltd-cd+=; HVNLP 50CDX)* – (videos, etc).

May 05. (7") *(HVN 150)* **SNOWDEN. / BLACK CIRCUS OF PRAGUE** [17] [–]
(cd-s) *(HVN 150CD)* – ('A') / Son of a builder.
(cd-s) *(HVN 150CDS)* – ('A') / Black and white town (David Holmes remix) / Almost forgot myself (69 Corp remix).

Sep 05. (7") *(HVN 152)* **SKY STARTS FALLING. / THE STORM (Rebelski remix)** [45] [–]
(cd-s) *(HVN 152CD)* – ('A') / Some cities (Love Will Never Sever mix by Echoboy).
(dvd-s+=) *(HVN 152DVD)* – (all 3 tracks).

Nick DRAKE

Born: NICHOLAS RODNEY DRAKE, 19 Jun'48, Rangoon, Burma, South East Asia. He moved to Britain in the mid 50's, first to Tamworth-in-Ardon then Stratford. Already a budding singer-songwriter by the time he reached Cambridge University, he was discovered playing a gig by ASHLEY HUTCHINGS of Fairport Convention, who, in turn, introduced him to Witchseason Productions head JOE BOYD. Bowled over by his talent, BOYD helped him sign to 'Island', who released debut album 'FIVE LEAVES LEFT' in '69. The album highlighted his precocious talent and painful sensitivity, the music possessing a remarkable maturity not in keeping with DRAKE's young years. The melancholic resonance of DRAKE's voice and his crystalline guitar playing were complemented by delicate string arrangements, the effect one of understated intensity. After moving to London, DRAKE recorded the classic 'BRYTER LAYTER' in 1970 with BOYD again producing a cast of musicians that included RICHARD THOMPSON and JOHN CALE. The album boasted a jazzier flavour which saw DRAKE in a slightly more positive frame of mind. Ironically, like its predecessor, the album failed to sell in any great quantity. Due to his crippling shyness, DRAKE found live work too difficult, passing up the opportunity to promote his music. He fell into a deep depression, no doubt frustrated at his lack of success and inability to do something about it. After a spell in Europe he returned to record his tortured masterpiece, 'PINK MOON'. Recorded in just two nights, its spare, haunting songs were cloaked in regret and disillusionment. The bleak tone only let up occasionally as DRAKE attemted to exorcise his demons over a skeletal acoustic backing. Once again, the album was a commercial failure and DRAKE's mood blackened further, although he did begin work on a new album in 1973. He spent time in France with singer/friend FRANCOISE HARDY and his bouts of depression diminished when he decided to live there permanently. However, this didn't last long and he sadly overdosed on anti-depressants on 25th November 1974, a tragic end to a troubled but brilliant career. A questionable coroner's verdict was "Death By Suicide". The subsequent interest in DRAKE's work led to various compilations being released, including the excellent 'FRUIT TREE' boxed set. With more fans coming on board every year (and Volkswagen using the song 'PINK MOON' in a millennium TV ad), DRAKE fever reached boiling point in 2004 as Brad Pitt no less, narrated a BBC Radio documentary and 'Island' fed the market via two collections,

NICK DRAKE

the first of which 'MADE TO LOVE MAGIC' was an odds'n'sods resume that made history by furnishing the long dead songwriter with a couple of posthumous hits, 'MAGIC' and the evergreen 'RIVER MAN'.

• **Trivia:** His sister Gabrielle was a TV actress in the 70's/80's 'Crossroads' soap.

Album rating: FIVE LEAVES LEFT (*8) / BRYTER LAYTER (*9) / PINK MOON (*9) / posthumous: HEAVEN IN A WILD FLOWER (*7) / FRUIT TREE – THE COMPLETE RECORDED WORKS (*9) / TIME OF NO REPLY (*7) / WAY TO BLUE – AN INTRODUCTION TO NICK DRAKE (*9) / MADE TO LOVE MAGIC (*6) / A TREASURY (*6)

NICK DRAKE – vocals, guitar, piano with **RICHARD THOMPSON** – guitar / **DANNY THOMPSON** – double bass / **PAUL HARRIS** – keyboards / **CLAIRE LOWTHER** and **ROCKY DZIDZORNU,** plus 15-piece orchestra.

Island Antilles

Sep 69. (lp) *(ILPS 9105) <AN 7010>* **FIVE LEAVES LEFT** [ ] [ ]
– Time has told me / River man / Three hours / Day is done / Way to blue / Cello song / The thoughts of Mary Jane / Man in a shed / Fruit tree / Saturday sun. *(cd-iss. Feb87; CID 9195) (re-iss. cd May89 & Jun00; IMCD 8) (lp re-iss. Jan00 on 'Simply Vinyl'; SVLP 163)*

— retained **RICHARD** bringing in other (FAIRPORT CONVENTION members: **DAVE PEGG** – drums / **DAVE MATTACKS** – bass. Also sessioned **PAUL HARRIS, RAY WARLEIGH, CHRIS McGREGOR.**

Nov 70. (lp) *(ILPS 9134) <7028>* **BRYTER LAYTER** [ ] [ ]
– Introduction / Hazey Jane II / At the chime of a city clock / One of these things first / Hazey Jane I / Bryter layter / Fly / Poor boy / Northern sky / Sunday. *(cd-iss. May87; CID 9134) (re-iss. cd Oct89 & Jun00; IMCD 71) (lp re-iss. Jun99 on 'Simply Vinyl'; SVLP 94)*

— **NICK DRAKE** – vocals, guitar (totally solo)

Feb 72. (lp) *(ILPS 9184)* **PINK MOON** [ ] [–]
– Pink moon / Place to be / Road / Which will / Horn / Things behind the sun / Know / Parasite / Ride / Harvest breed / From the morning / Voice from the mountain / Rider on the wheel / Black eyed dog / Hanging on a star. *(cd-iss. Apr90 & Jun00; IMCD 94) (lp re-iss. Feb00 on 'Simply Vinyl'; SVLP 172)*

— NICK had put down some tracks for new album, when on 25th Nov'74, he overdosed on medication/drugs.

– compilations, others, etc. –

on 'Island' unless mentioned otherwise

1972. (lp) *<9307>* **NICK DRAKE** (69-70 material) [–] [ ]

Apr 79. (3xlp-box) *(NDSP 100)* **FRUIT TREE – THE COMPLETE RECORDED WORKS** [ ] [–]
– (contains all 3 albums)

May 85. (lp/c) *(ILPS 9826)* **HEAVEN IN A WILD FLOWER** [ ] [ ]
– Fruit tree / Cello song / Thoughts of Mary Jane / Northern sky / River man / At the chime of the city clock / Introduction / Hazey Jane I / Hazey Jane II / Pink moon / Road / Which will / Things behind the sun / Time has told me. *(cd-iss. Apr90; IMCD 91)*

Aug 86. (4xlp-box) *Hannibal / Rykodisc; (HNBX 5302)* **FRUIT TREE** [ ] [ ]
– (all 3 lp's, plus 1987 album) *(4xcd-box-iss.Dec91; HNCD 5402)(+=)* – TIME OF NO REPLY / Fruit tree / Fly / Man in a shed / Thoughts of Mary Jane.

Mar 87. (lp/cd) *Hannibal; (<HNBL/HNCD 1318>)* **TIME OF NO REPLY** [ ] [ ]
– Time of no reply / I was made to love magic / Joey / Clothes of sand / Man in a shed / Mayfair / Fly / The thoughts of Mary Jane / Been smoking too long / Strange meeting II / Rider on the wheel / Black eyed dog / Hanging on a star / Voice from the mountain.

Jun 94. (cd)(c/lp) *(IMCD 196)(ICM/ILPM 2082) <1386>* **WAY TO BLUE – AN INTRODUCTION TO NICK DRAKE** [ ] [ ]
– Cello song / Hazey Jane I / Way to blue / Things behind the sun / River man / Poor boy / Time of no reply / From the morning / One of these things first / Northern sky / Which will / Hazey Jane II / Time has told me / Pink moon / Black eyed dog / Fruit tree. *(cd re-iss. May03; IMCD 299)*

Nov 99. (cd-ep) *Sonic Book; <SB 20>* **THE SWEET SUGGESTIONS OF THE PINK MOON** [ ] [–]
– When day is done / Saturday sun / Way to blue / Time has told me.

Jun 00. (lp) *Anthology; (ANT 1521)* **TAMWORTH IN ARDEN** [ ] [–]
(cd-iss. Jan02; ANT 1500)

Nov 02. (lp) *N.R.D.; (1)* **TIME HAS TOLD ME** [ ] [–]

May 04. (7"/cd-s) *(IS/CID 854)* **MAGIC. / NORTHERN SKY** [32] [–]

May 04. (cd) *(CID 8141) <2812>* **MADE TO LOVE MAGIC** [27] Jun04 [ ]
– Rider on the wheel / Magic / River man / Joey / Thoughts of Mary Jane / Mayfair / Hanging on a star / Three hours / Clothes of sand / Voices / Time of no reply / Black eyed dog / Tow the line.

Sep 04. (7") *(IS 871)* **RIVER MAN. / RIVER MAN (demo)** [48] [–]
(cd-s) *(CID 871)* – ('A') / Day is done (feat. NORAH JONES & THE CHARLIE HUNTER BAND) / ('A'-video by Tim Pope).

Sep 04. (cd) *(CID 8149) <351836>* **A TREASURY** [ ] Oct04 [ ]
– Introduction / Hazey Jane II / River man / Cello song / Hazey Jane I / Pink moon / Poor boy / Magic (mix) / Place to be / Northern sky / Road / Fruit tree / Black eyed dog / Way to blue / From the morning.

DROWNING POOL

Formed: Dallas, Texas, USA . . . 1999 by DAVE WILLIAMS, C.J. PIERCE, STEVIE BENTON and percussionist MIKE LUCE. After snatching their name from the Paul Newman movie, this band of prog-metallers smashed onto the scene in late 1999 when their demo tape was picked up by rockers SEVENDUST, who subsequently took the group on tour as a supporting act. With still no record contract, the quartet were signed after a song from their sophomore demo wound up in a local radio station's Top 10 rock chart. DROWNING POOL signed with the 'Wind Up' imprint (home to CREED, etc) and issued their debut album 'SINNER' (2001) to rave reviews. Produced by nu-metal honcho Jay Baumgardner, the record played out like a sports metal version of TOOL, with a hint of FEAR FACTORY thrown in for good measure. The effect was slightly better than the usual rock action, with WILLIAMS' vocals being a particular highlight. The ensemble went on to tour with acts such as KITTIE and old friends SEVENDUST, as well as having the honour of sharing OZZY OSBOURNE's stage at his annual 'Ozzfest' festival . . . poor buggers. Tragically, lead singer DAVE WILLIAMS was found dead in the band's tour bus on the 14th of August 2002; the coroner later reported that he'd been afflicted with heart disease, or more specifically, cardiomyopathy. After many false starts and rumours (MACHINE HEAD's ROB FLYNN was apparently asked to join), the band finally recruited a new frontman, JASON 'Gong' JONES for second album proper, 'DESENSITIZED' (2004). Despite a tasteless sleeve featuring a baseball bat-wielding porn star, Jesse Jane, the album was overcast by the shadow of their former frontman; the new kid wasn't long for the chopping block, departing mid-2005, and leaving a vacuum eventually filled by ex-SOIL man, RYAN McCOMBS.

Album rating: SINNER (*6) / DESENSITIZED (*5)

DAVE WILLIAMS (b.29 Feb'72, Princeton, Texas) – vocals / **C.J. PIERCE** – guitar / **STEVIE BENTON** – bass / **MIKE LUCE** – drums

not iss. own labe

Nov 99. (cd) *<none>* **DROWNING POOL** [–] [ ]
– Bodies / Tear away / I am / Less than zero / Sermon / Care not / Let me go / Mask / Drama / Told you so / You made me / Chemicals / Soul / Break you / The game (Triple H theme).

2000. (cd-ep) *<none>* **PIECES OF NOTHING** [–] [ ]
– Tear away / Bodies / I am / Told you so / Follow / Less than zero.

Wind-Up Wind-U

Feb 02. (cd) *(504091-2) <13065-2>* **SINNER** [70] Jun01 [14]
– Sinner / Bodies / Tear away / All over me / Reminded / Pity / Mute / I am / Follow / Told you so / Sermon.

Apr 02. (7"blue) *(672317-7)* **BODIES. / BODIES (live)** [34] [–]
(cd-s+=) *(672317-2)* – Sermon (session) / ('A'-uncensored video).

Jul 02. (7") *(672983-7)* **TEAR AWAY. / BREAK YOU** [65] [–]
(cd-s+=) *(672983-2)* – Game / ('A'video).

— (2003) **JASON 'Gong' JONES** – vocals; repl. WILLIAMS who died 14th August 2002

Apr 04. (cd-s) *(674899-2)* **STEP UP / WALLS / (in the studio and on set) / ('A'-video)** [ ] [–]

Apr 04. (cd) *(515411-2) <13080-2>* **DESENSITIZED** [66] [17]
– Think / Step up / Numb / This life / Nothingness / Bringing me down / Love and war / Forget / Cast me aside / Killin' me / Hate.

— (Jun'05) **RYAN McCOMBS** – vocals (ex-SOIL) repl. JONES who formed A.M. CONSPIRACY

□ the DUKES OF STRATOSPHEAR (see under ⇒ XTC)

DURAN DURAN

Formed: Birmingham, England . . . 1978 by NICK RHODES, JOHN TAYLOR, STEPHEN DUFFY and clarinet player, SIMON COLLEY, taking their name from a character in cult space-kitsch movie, 'Barbarella'. The following year, ANDY WICKETT and ROGER TAYLOR replaced DUFFY (who went on to a briefly successful solo career as STEPHEN 'TIN TIN' DUFFY) and COLLEY respectively, while SIMON LE BON finally entered the fray as frontman in Spring '80. After a UK tour supporting HAZEL 'Breaking Glass' O'CONNOR, the band were snapped up by 'E.M.I.', initiating their manicured career in early '81 with 'PLANET EARTH'. The toast of the London cognoscenti, extravagantly coiffured (and even more outlandishly attired) poseurs ensured DURAN DURAN a near Top 10 hit as the scene that perpetrated one of the worst fashion crimes in history (i.e. legwarmers) was stepped up a gear. Later that summer, an eponymous debut album and a suitably po-faced follow-up single, 'GIRLS ON FILM', confirmed the band's synth-powered, post-ROXY MUSIC/BOWIE pretensions with lashings of attitude and mascara. Riding in on the floppy fringe of the New Romantic zeitgeist, the album made the UK Top 3 and, with help of heavy MTV rotation for the 'HUNGRY LIKE THE WOLF' video, eventually the US Top 10. The latter track was a transatlantic Top 5 and previewed the follow-up set, 'RIO' (1982). By this point the band's fanbase had grown from an arty clique to hordes of screaming girlies, ensuring massive success for the sub-panoramic warbling of 'SAVE A PRAYER', the streamlined aquatic rush of the title track and the whining 'IS THERE SOMETHING I SHOULD KNOW', youth centre dancefloor fillers the lot. Although the latter track wasn't included on the album, it did give the band their first UK No.1; with continuing support from MTV in the States, DURAN DURAN were also churning out ever more flamboyant videos to keep the Americans happy. A vague concept affair, 'SEVEN AND THE RAGGED TIGER' (1983) came in for a bit of a critical pasting, although the hits continued apace with the dodgy 'UNION OF THE SNAKE' and transatlantic No.1, 'THE REFLEX' (a quintessentially 80's effort complete with stuttering vocals, while the video was famous for five minutes with its water-coming-out-of-the-screen trickery, brilliant!). The zenith of DURAN DURAN's bombastic heyday came with 'THE WILD BOYS', a classic slice of white nouveau-funk with added rhythmic oomph courtesy of ex-CHIC man/producer in demand, NILE RODGERS, the accompanying video setting the boys in a storm-drenched, sub-Mad Max style netherworld. The single made No.2 in Britain and America, preceding the universally panned live effort, 'ARENA' (1984). A James Bond theme tune, 'VIEW TO A KILL' (another US No.1) nicely rounded off the first chapter in the band's career as the various members took time out to indulge themselves in solo projects. The less said about ARCADIA (LeBON, NICK RHODES and ROGER TAYLOR) the better, while the marginally more entertaining POWER STATION (ANDY/JOHN TAYLOR, ROBERT PALMER and ex-CHIC sticksman, TONY THOMPSON) released an eponymous album (1985) of sterile funk-rock, hitting the UK Top 10 with 'SOME LIKE IT HOT' and a cover of T.Rex's 'GET IT ON'. DURAN DURAN eventually returned in late '86 (minus ANDY and ROGER, the former setting out on a solo career while the latter quit the music business) with 'NOTORIOUS' (1986), the RODGERS-masterminded title track narrowly missing the top of the American charts. Gone were the hedonistic pop thrills of old, however, successive albums, 'BIG THING' (1988) and 'LIBERTY' (1990) indescribably bland. Nevertheless, ageing fans ensured continuing chart action, the latter album still making the UK Top 10, while 1993 saw them make something of a mini-comeback with 'ORDINARY WORLD', their best single for years and US Top 5 to boot. A second single, 'COME UNDONE', also made the grade, while the accompanying eponymous album gave a hint as to what was in store with an unlikely cover of the Velvet Underground's 'FEMME FATALE'. Even more unlikely was a cover of hip hop/electro landmark, 'WHITE LINES (DON'T DO IT)', just one of the many erm, "interpretations" on the 'THANK YOU' (1995) album. Incredibly, GRANDMASTER FLASH actually had a hand in this sacrilege, although what CHUCK D thought of the ridiculous rendition of '911 IS A JOKE' is anyone's guess. A well meant attempt at reinventing their heroes perhaps, but please, a cover of 'LAY LADY LAY'?! Of late, DURAN DURAN have plundered the past to regain some cred, a new (but old-sounding) American-only set, 'MEDAZZALAND' (1997) followed by a 'GREATEST HITS' package (again!) and worse still, a remix album in '99, entitled 'STRANGE BEHAVIOUR' (strange behaviour, indeed!). The millennial 'POP TRASH' (2000) proved that they couldn't even name an album title without resorting to cliche while the record's contents were hardly more adventurous. By this point, LE BON and RHODES were the only survivors from the classic line-up, WARREN CUCCURULLO (once again) completing the trio for a singularly uninspired set of overproduced, dinosaur pop. Four years on, with most of the original line-up back on board and with the 80s revival in full swing, DURAN DURAN took the opportunity to revisit their glory days with a Top 5 single, '(REACH UP FOR THE) SUNRISE'. Their biggest hit for decades, the song opened their similarly successful album, 'ASTRONAUT' (2004).

• **Songwriters:** LE BON – lyrics / RHODES – music. Covered; MAKE ME SMILE (Steve Harley & Cockney Rebel) / I WANNA TAKE YOU HIGHER (Sly & The Family Stone) / PERFECT DAY (Lou Reed) / WATCHING THE DETECTIVES (Elvis Costello) / SUCCESS (Iggy Pop) / CRYSTAL SHIP (Doors) / BALL OF CONFUSION (Temptations) / THANK YOU (Led Zeppelin). • **Trivia:** SIMON LE BON married top model, Yasmin Parvanah, on the 27th of December '85, while a year previously, the other two, ROGER and NICK, had also married Cosmopolitan models.

Album rating: DURAN DURAN (*7) / RIO (*7) / SEVEN AND THE RAGGED TIGER (*5) / ARENA (*4) / NOTORIOUS (*6) / BIG THING (*4) / DECADE compilation (*8) / LIBERTY (*2) / DURAN DURAN (THE WEDDING ALBUM) (*5) / THANK YOU (*4) / MEDAZZALAND (*3) / GREATEST compilation (*7) / STRANGE BEHAVIOUR (*2) / ASTRONAUT (*4) / the Power Station: THE POWER STATION (*5) / Arcadia: SO RED THE ROSE (*4)

SIMON LE BON (b.27 Oct'58, Bushley, Hertfordshire, England) – vocals / **ANDY TAYLOR** (b.16 Feb'61, Newcastle, England) – guitar / **NICK RHODES** (b. NICHOLAS BATES, 8 Jun'62) – keyboards / **JOHN TAYLOR** (b.20 Jul'60, Solihull, England) – bass / **ROGER TAYLOR** (b.26 Apr'60) – drums

		E.M.I.	Harvest
Jan 81.	(7") *(EMI 5137)* **PLANET EARTH. / LATE BAR**	12	
	(12"+=) *(12EMI 5137)* – Planet earth (night version).		
	(re-iss. Aug83; same)		
Apr 81.	(7"/12") *(EMI/12EMI 5168)* **CARELESS MEMORIES. / KHANDA**	37	
	(re-iss. Aug83, 7"+=/12"+=; same) – Fame.		
Jun 81.	(lp/c) *(EMC/TC-EMC 3372)* <12158> **DURAN DURAN**	3	
	– Girls on film / Planet Earth / Anyone out there / To the shore / Careless memories / (Waiting for the) Night boat / Sound of thunder / Friends of mine / Tel Aviv. *<re-dist.Feb83, hit US No.10> (re-iss. Aug83; same) (cd-iss. Oct84; CZ) (re-iss. Sep87 on 'Fame' cd/c/lp; CD/TC+/FA 3185) (re-iss. Aug95 cd/c; CD/TC PRG 1003)*		
Jul 81.	(7") *(EMI 5206)* **GIRLS ON FILM. / FASTER THAN LIGHT**	5	
	(12"+=) *(12EMI 5206)* – ('A'instrumental).		
	(re-iss. Aug83, 7"/12"; same)		
Nov 81.	(7") *(EMI 5254)* **MY OWN WAY. / LIKE AN ANGEL**	14	
	(12"+=) *(12EMI 5254)* – ('A'night version).		
	(re-iss. Aug83, 7"/12"; same)		

May 82. (7"/12") *(EMI/12EMI 5295)* <5134> **HUNGRY LIKE THE WOLF. / CARELESS MEMORIES (live)** [5] [ ]
(re-iss. Aug83, 7"/12"; same)
<re-iss. Dec82 with diff.B-side; 5195> – hit No.3.

E.M.I. Capitol

May 82. (lp/c) *(EMC/TC-EMC 3411)* <12211> **RIO** [2] Jan83 [6]
– Rio / My own way / Lonely in your nightmare / Hungry like the wolf / Hold back the rain / New religion / Last chance on the stairway / Save a prayer / The chauffeur. *(cd-iss. Aug83; CZ 291) (re-iss. Mar90 lp/c; ATAK/TC-ATAK 149) (re-iss. Sep93 cd/c; CD/TC PRG 1004)*

Aug 82. (7"/12") *(EMI/12EMI 5327)* **SAVE A PRAYER. / HOLD BACK THE RAIN (remix)** [2] [–]
(re-iss. Aug83, 7"/12"; same)

Sep 82. (m-lp) *Harvest;* <15006> **CARNIVAL** [–] [98]
– My own way / Hold back the rain / Girls on film / Hungry like the wolf.

Nov 82. (7") *(EMI 5346)* <5175> **RIO. / THE CHAUFFEUR (BLUE SILVER)** [9] [–]
(12") *(12EMI 5346)* – ('A'side) / Rio / (pt.2) / My own way. *(re-iss. Aug83, 7"/12"; same)*

Mar 83. (7") <5215> **RIO. / HOLD BACK THE RAIN** [–] [2]

Mar 83. (7"/12") *(EMI/12EMI 5371)* **IS THERE SOMETHING I SHOULD KNOW. / FAITH IN THIS COLOUR** [1] [–]
(re-iss. Aug83, 7"/12"; same)

May 83. (7") <5233> **IS THERE SOMETHING I SHOULD KNOW. / CARELESS MEMORIES** [–] [4]

Oct 83. (7") *(EMI 5429)* <5290> **UNION OF THE SNAKE. / SECRET OKTOBER** [3] [3]
(12"+=) *(12EMI 5429)* – ('A'-Monkey remix).

Nov 83. (lp/c) *(EMC/TC-EMC 1654)* <12310> **SEVEN AND THE RAGGED TIGER** [1] [8]
– The reflex / New Moon on Monday / (I'm looking for) Cracks in the pavement / I take the dice / Of crime and passion / Union of the snake / Shadows on your side / Tiger tiger / The seventh stranger. *(cd-iss. Mar84; CZ 36) (re-iss. Aug88 on 'Fame' cd/c/lp; CD/TC+/FA 3205) (re-iss. Sep93 cd/c; CD/TC PRG 1005)*

Jan 84. (7"/12") *(DURAN/12DURAN 1)* <5309> **NEW MOON ON MONDAY. / TIGER TIGER** [9] [10]

Apr 84. (7"/7"s) *(DURAN/+P 2)* **THE REFLEX. / MAKE ME SMILE (COME UP AND SEE ME) (live)** [1] [–]
(12"+=/12"pic-d+=) *(12DURAN/+P 2)* – ('A'dance mix).

Apr 84. (7") <5345> **THE REFLEX. / NEW RELIGION** [–] [1]

Oct 84. (7"/12") *(DURANC/12DURANC 3)* <5417> **THE WILD BOYS. / (I'M LOOKING FOR) CRACKS IN THE PAVEMENT** [2] [2]

Nov 84. (lp/c) *(DD/TC-DD 2)* <12374> **ARENA (live)** [6] [4]
– Is there something I should know / Hungry like the wolf / New religion / Save a prayer / The wild boys / The seventh stranger / The chauffeur / Union of the snake / Planet Earth / Careless memories. *(cd-iss. Dec84; CZ 79) (re-iss. Oct89 on 'Fame' cd/c/lp; CD/TC+/FA 3225)*

Jan 85. (7") <5438> **SAVE A PRAYER. / ('A'live version)** [–] [16]

Parlophone Capitol

May 85. (7"/7"white) *(DURAN/+G 007)* <5475> **A VIEW TO A KILL. / ('A'instrumental)** [2] [1]

—— took time off for own solo projects

the POWER STATION

(ANDY & JOHN TAYLOR) / **ROBERT PALMER** – vocals (solo artist see under own listing) / **TONY THOMPSON** – drums (ex-CHIC)

Parlophone Capitol

Mar 85. (7"/7"pic-d) *(R/+P 6091)* <5444> **SOME LIKE IT HOT. / THE HEAT IS ON** [14] [6]
(12"+=/12"pic-d+=) *(12R/+P 6091)* – ('A'extended).

Apr 85. (lp/c) *(POST/TC-POST 1)* <12380> **THE POWER STATION** [12] [6]
– Some like it hot / Murderess / Lonely tonight / Communication / Get it on (bang a gong) / Go to zero / Harvest for the world / Still in your heart. *(cd-iss. Jul85; CDP 746127-2) (re-iss. Sep88 on 'Fame' cd/c/lp; CD/TC+/FA 3206) (cd re-iss. Aug93; CDPRG 1011)*

May 85. (7")(12") <5479> **GET IT ON. / GO TO ZERO** [22] [9]

Nov 85. (7")(12") <5511> **COMMUNICATION. / MURDERESS** [75] [34]

—— **MICHAEL DES BARNES** – vocals; repl. PALMER on tour

ARCADIA

SIMON LE BON – vocals / **NICK RHODES** – keyboards / **ROGER TAYLOR** – drums / with session people

Oct 85. (7") *(NSR 1)* <5501> **ELECTION DAY. / SHE'S MOODY AND GREY SHE'S MEAN AND SHE'S RESTLESS** [7] [6]
(12"+=) *(12NSR 1)* – ('A'-Consensus mix).
(12") *(12NSRA 1)* – ('A'-Cryptic Cut No Voice mix) / ('A'mix) / ('A'-Consensus mix).

Dec 85. (lp/c) *(PCSD/TC-PCSD 101)* <12428> **SO RED THE ROSE** [30] [23]
– Election day / Keep me in the dark / Goodbye is forever / The flame / Missing / Rose Arcana / The promise / El Diablo / Lady Ice. *(re-iss. Aug93 cd/c; CD/TC PRG 1010)*

Dec 85. (7") <5542> **GOODBYE IS FOREVER. / MISSING** [–] [33]

Feb 86. (7") *(NSR 2)* **THE PROMISE. / ROSE ARCANE** [37] [ ]
(12"+=) *(12NSR 2)* – ('A'extended).

Jul 86. (7") *(NSR 3)* **THE FLAME. / FLAME AGAIN** [58] [ ]
(12") *(12NSR 3)* – ('A'extended) / ('B'-Homeboy mix) / Election day (Early Rough mix).

JOHN TAYLOR

Mar 86. (7") *(R 6125)* <5551> **I DO WHAT I DO . . . (theme from 9 1/2 weeks). / JAZZ (instrumental)** [42] [23]
(12"+=) *(12R 6125)* – ('A'-Film mix).

DURAN DURAN

—— ANDY went solo and subsequently released a handful of singles including a US Top 30 smash, 'TAKE IT EASY' (from the movie, 'American Anthem') and an album, 'THUNDER', a US Top 50 breaker in '87). (ROGER quit the music business)

—— now down to **SIMON, NICK + JOHN**

Oct 86. (7") *(DDN 45)* <5648> **NOTORIOUS. / WINTER MARCHES ON** [7] [2]
(c-s+=/12"+=) *(TC/12 DDNX 45)* – ('A'-Latin Rascals mix).

Nov 86. (lp/c)(cd) *(DDN/TCDDN 331)(CDP 746 415-2)* <12540> **NOTORIOUS** [16] [12]
– Notorious / American science / Skin trade / A matter of feeling / Hold me / Vertigo (do the demolition) / So misled / Meet el Presidente / Winter marches on / Proposition. *(re-iss. Sep93 cd/c; CD/TC PRG 1004)*

Feb 87. (7"/7"w-poster) *(TRADE/+X 1)* <5670> **SKIN TRADE. / WE NEED YOU** [22] [39]
(c-s+=) *(TCTRADE 1)* – ('A'-Stretch mix).

Apr 87. (7") *(TOUR 1)* **MEET EL PRESIDENTE. / VERTIGO (DO THE DEMOLITION)** [24] [70]
(ext.cd-s+=) *(CDTOUR 1)* – ('A'-Meet el Beat mix).

—— added **WARREN CUCCURULLO** – guitar (ex-FRANK ZAPPA, ex-MISSING PERSONS) / **STEVE FERRONE** – drums (ex-BRIAN AUGER, ex-AVERAGE WHITE BAND) (both on last lp

Sep 88. (7") *(YOUR 1)* <44237> **I DON'T WANT YOUR LOVE. / ('A'-lp version)** [14] [4]
(etched-12"+=/cd-s+=) *(12/CD YOURS 1)* – ('A'Big Mix version).

Oct 88. (cd/c/lp) *(CD/TC+/DDB 33)* <90958> **BIG THING** [15] [24]
– Big thing / I don't want your love / All she wants is / Too late Marlene / Drug (it's just a state of mind) / Do you believe in shame? / Palomino / Interlude one / Land / Flute interlude / The edge of America / Lake shore driving. *(re-iss. Mar90 on 'E.M.I.' lp/c; ATAK/TC-ATAK 148) (cd-iss. Mar90 on 'E.M.I'; CZ 290) (re-iss. Sep93 cd/c; CD/TC PRG 1007)*

Dec 88. (7") *(DD 11)* <44287> **ALL SHE WANTS IS. / I BELIEVE – ALL I NEED TO KNOW (medley)** [ ] [22]
(12"+=) *(12DDX 11)* <44287> – ('A'-US master mix).
(3"cd-s+=) *(CDDD 11)* – Skin trade (Parisian mix).

Apr 89. (7"/7"pic-d) *(DD/+PD 12)* <44337> **DO YOU BELIEVE IN SHAME? / ('A'-Krush Brothers LSD mix)** [30] Mar89 [72]
(10"+=) *(10DD 12)* – Notorious (live).
(3"cd-s++=) *(CDDD 12)* – God (London) / This is how a road gets made
(3x7"box) *(DD A/B/C 12) – Do you believe in shame? / God (London) // Palomino (edit). / This is how a road gets made // Do you believe in shame? / Drugs – it's just a state of mind.*

Nov 89. (cd/c/lp) *(CD/TC+/DDX 10)* <93178> **DECADE** [5] [67]
– Planet Earth / Girls on film / Hungry like the wolf / Rio / Save a prayer / Is there something I should know / Union of the snake / The reflex / Wild boys / A view to a kill / Notorious / Skin trade / I don't want your love / All she wants is.

Dec 89. (c-s/7") *(TC+/DD 13)* **BURNING THE GROUND. / DECADENCE** [31] [–]
(12"+=/cd-s+=) *(12/CD DD 13)* – Decadence (extended).

— **STERLING CAMPBELL** – drums repl. FERRONE

Jul 90. (c-s/7") *(TC+/DD 14)* **VIOLENCE OF SUMMER (LOVE'S TAKING OVER). / ('A'mix)** [20] [–]
(12"+=) *(12DD 14)* – ('A'extended).
(cd-s+=) *(CDDD 14)* – Throb.

Aug 90. (c-s) *<44608>* **VIOLENCE OF SUMMER (LOVE'S TAKING OVER) / YO BAD AZIZI** [–] [64]

Aug 90. (cd/c/lp) *(CD/TC+/PCSD 112) <94292>* **LIBERTY** [8] [46]
– Violence of summer (love's taking over) / Liberty / Hothead / Serious / All along the water / My Antartica / Read my lips / First impression / Can you deal with it / Venice drowning / Downtown. *(re-iss. Sep93 cd/c; CD/TC RG 1009)*

Nov 90. (c-s/7") *(TC+/DD 15)* **SERIOUS. / YO BAD AZIZI** [48] [–]
(12"+=/cd-s+=) *(12/CD DD 15)* – Water babies.

Jan 93. (c-s) *<44908>* **ORDINARY WORLD / ('A'acoustic) / SAVE A PRAYER (live)** [–] [3]

Jan 93. (c-s/7")(7"pic-d) *(TC+/DD 16)(DDP 16)* **ORDINARY WORLD. / MY ANTARTICA** [6] [–]
(cd-s+=) *(CDDDS 16)* – Save a prayer / Skin trade.
(cd-s) *(CDDDP 16)* – ('A'side) / The reflex / Hungry like the wolf / Girls on film.

Feb 93. (cd/c/lp) *(CD/TC+/DDB 34) <98876>* **DURAN DURAN** (THE WEDDING ALBUM) [4] [7]
– Too much information / Ordinary world / Love voodoo / Drowning man / Shotgun / Come undone / Breath after breath / UMF / Home of the above / Femme fatale / Shelter / To whom it may concern. *(cd-box Jan94; CDDDB 35)*

Mar 93. (c-s/7") *(TC+/DD 17)* **COME UNDONE. / ORDINARY WORLD (acoustic)** [13] [–]
(cd-s+=) *(CDDD 17)* – ('A'mixes).
(cd-s) *(CDDDS 17)* – ('A'side) / ('A'version) / Rio / Is there something I should know / A view to a kill.

Apr 93. (c-s) *<44918>* **COME UNDONE / ('A'-mix 2 master) / TIME FOR TEMPTATION** [–] [7]

Aug 93. (c-s/12") *(TC/12 DD 18)* **TOO MUCH INFORMATION. / COME UNDONE (live)** [35] [–]
(12"+=) *(12DD 18) – Come undone (12"mix Coming together) / Notorious (live).*
(cd-s) *(CDDD 18)* – ('A'side) / Drowning man.

Aug 93. (cd-s) *<44955>* **TOO MUCH INFORMATION / FIRST IMPRESSION / COME UNDONE (new mix)** [–] [45]
(with live free c-ep) **NO ORDINARY EP** – Hungry like the wolf / Notorious / Come undone.

Mar 95. (c-s/7") *(TC+/DD 20)* **PERFECT DAY. / FEMME FATALE (alt.mix)** [28] [ ]
(cd-s+=) *(CDDDS 20)* – Make me smile (come up and see me) / Perfect day (acoustic).
(cd-s) *(CDDDP 20)* – ('A'side) / Love voodoo / Needle and the damage done / 911 is a joke (alternative mix).

Mar 95. (cd/c) *(CD/TC DDB 36) <29419>* **THANK YOU** [12] [19]
– White lines / I wanna take you higher / Perfect day / Watching the detectives / Lay lady lay / 911 is a joke / Success / Crystal ship / Ball of confusion / Thank you / Drive by / I wanna take you higher again.

below actually featured GRANDMASTER FLASH

Jun 95. (c-s) *(TCDD 19)* **WHITE LINES (DON'T DO IT) / SAVE A PRAYER / NONE OF THE ABOVE (Drizabone mix)** [17] [ ]
(cd-s+=) *(CDDD 19)* – Ordinary world (acoustic).
(12") *(12DD 19)* – ('A'side) / ('A'-Junior Vasquez mix) / ('A'-Oakland fonk mix) / ('A'-70's club mix).

Virgin Capitol

May 97. (7"/c-s/cd-s) *(VS LH/C/CDT 1639)* **OUT OF MY MIND / SILVA HALO** [21] [–]
(cd-s+=) *(VSCDX 1639)* – Sinner or saint / ('A'remix).

Sep 97. (c-s,cd-s) *<58674>* **ELECTRIC BARBARELLA /** [–] [52]

Oct 97. (cd,c) *<33876>* **MEDAZZALAND** [–] [58]
– Medazzaland / Big bang generation / Electric Barbarella / Out of my mind / Who do you think you are? / Silva halo / Be my icon / Buried in the sand / Michael you've got a lot to answer for / Midnight sun / So long suicide / Undergoing treatment.

E.M.I. not iss.

Jan 99. (c-s) *(TCELEC 2000)* **ELECTRIC BARBARELLA / GIRLS ON FILM (Tin Tin Out mix)** [23] [–]
(cd-s+=) *(CDELEC 2000)* – ('A'-Tee's club mix).
(12"+=) *(12ELEC 2000)* – ('A'-Electric sex mix).

Hollywood Hollywood

May 00. (c-s) *(0108845 HWR)* **SOMEONE ELSE NOT ME / (album version)** [53] [–]
(cd-s+=) *(0100849 HWR)* – Starting to remember.

Jun 00. (cd) *(0107512 HWR) <62266>* **POP TRASH** [53] [ ]
– Someone else not me / Lava lamp / Playing with uranium / Hallucinating Elvis / Starting to remember / Pop trash movie / Fragment / Mars meets Venus / Lady Xanax / The sun doesn't shine forever / Kiss goodbye / The last day on Earth. <US+=> – Someone else not me (en Espanol).

— in 2002, NICK teamed up with STEPHEN DUFFY (again!) to form The DEVILS; one set 'DARK CIRCLES'

— added the returning **ANDY TAYLOR + JOHN TAYLOR**

Epic Epic

Sep 04. (cd-s) *(6753531)* **(REACH UP FOR THE) SUNRISE / (Alex G Cosmic mix)** [5] [–]
(cd-s) *(6753532)* – ('A') / ('A'-Jason Nevins radio mix) / ('A'-Ferry Costen dub) / Know it all / ('A'-video).

Sep 04. (cd-s) *<71976>* **(REACH UP FOR THE) SUNRISE / KNOW IT ALL** [–] [ ]

Oct 04. (cd/d-lp) *(5179202) <92900 S2/-S1>* **ASTRONAUT** [3] [17]
– (Reach up for the) Sunrise / Want you more! / What happens tomorrow / Astronaut / Bedroom toys / Nice / Taste the summer / Finest hour / Chains / One of those days / Point of no return / Still breathing.

Jan 05. (cd-s) *(6756501)* **WHAT HAPPENS TOMORROW / (REACH UP FOR THE) SUNRISE (Eric Prydz mix)** [11] [–]
(cd-s) *(6756502)* – ('A') / Silent icy river / ('A'-Harry Peat mix) / ('A'-video).

– compilations, etc. –

Nov 98. (cd/c) *E.M.I.; (496239-2/-4) / Capitol; <96239>* **GREATEST** [15] Apr99 [ ]
– Is there something I should know? / The reflex / A view to a kill / Ordinary world / Save a prayer / Rio / Hungry like the wolf / Girls on film / Planet Earth / Union of the snake / New moon on Monday / Wild boys / Notorious / I don't want your love / All she wants is / Electric Barbarella / Serious / Skin trade / Come undone.

Mar 99. (d-cd) *E.M.I.; (493972-2)* **STRANGE BEHAVOIR** (remixes) [70] [ ]

the POWER STATION

— re-grouped (**PALMER / TAYLOR / TAYLOR / THOMPSON**)

Chrysalis Chrysalis

Oct 96. (c-s) *(TCCHS 5039)* **SHE CAN ROCK IT / ('A'mix)** [63] [ ]
(cd-s+=) *(CDCHS 5039)* – Power trippin' / Charanga.

Oct 96. (cd/c) *(CD/TC CHR 6117)* **LIVING IN FEAR** [ ] [ ]
– Notoriety / Scarred / She can rock it / Let's get it on / Life forces / Fancy that / Living in fear / Shut up / Dope / Love conquers all / Taxman.

Ian DURY

Born: 12 May'42, Upminster, Essex, England. At age seven he became partially crippled from contracting polio. In 1970, he was employed as a teacher / lecturer at Canterbury College. The following year, he formed KILBURN & THE HIGH ROADS, who embarked on pub/college circuit in London. After 1 album in the mid-70's and many line-up changes, they disbanded, leaving DURY and manager DAVE ROBINSON to create solo deal for the singer. Signing to Jake Riviera's new indie label, 'Stiff', he soon raced up album charts in 1977 with the new wave favourite 'NEW BOOTS AND PANTIES!!!'. DURY's articulate patter and intelligent lyrics fused well with funky/jerky group backing which alternated between rock'n'roll and disco. He also developed many areas of Cockney rhyme-slang into rude but clever lyrics. The album made the UK Top 5, preceded by the brilliant 'SEX AND DRUGS AND ROCK AND ROLL', DURY's typically wry comment on the excesses of the music business. The following year, the singer's cast of sidemen became The BLOCKHEADS, the line-up of CHAZ JANKEL, NORMAN WATT-ROY, CHARLEY CHARLES, MICKEY GALLAGHER, JOHN TURNBULL and DAVY PAYNE playing on DURY's first hit single, 'WHAT A WASTE'. However, it was the follow-up, 'HIT ME WITH YOUR RHYTHM STICK' which really earned DURY a smutty place in the annals of pop history, its half-spoken narrative style breaking into a gloriously demented chorus. The track sat astride the UK singles chart for a few weeks, while the attendant album, 'DO IT YOURSELF' (1979) made No.2. The DURY/JANKEL writing partnership was to end soon after, however, the latter embarking on solo work and freeing up a position for ex-DR. FEELGOOD guitarist, WILKO JOHNSON. The resulting album, 'LAUGHTER' (1980), met with limited success, prompting a musical Spring clean from DURY; signing to 'Polydor', securing the esteemed services of SLY & ROBBIE and reuniting with JANKEL, the cheeky cockney released the acclaimed 'LORD UPMINSTER'. Commercial success continued to elude him, however, and DURY semi-retired in the mid-80's following the '4,000 WEEKS HOLIDAY' (1984) opus. He eventually resurfaced in 1989 with the 'APPLES' soundtrack, although he proved his inimitable sense of humour hadn't deserted him on 1992's 'THE BUS DRIVERS PRAYER & OTHER STORIES'. Having been diagnosed with cancer of the colon in 1995 (it was soon to spread into his liver), IAN DURY wanted to bow out with a bang not a whimper. In the summer of '98, the man did just that (with the help from his ever faithful BLOCKHEADS). His comeback album, 'Mr LOVE PANTS', even returned him back into the charts, but sadly, this was IAN's last lyrical message – he died on the 27th March, 2000; they said he died with a smile on his face. A posthumous final recording, the LP 'TEN MORE TURNIPS FROM THE TIP' (2002), kept the man on a high note.

• **Songwriters:** DURY – words / JANKEL – music, until his departure from The BLOCKHEADS. • **Trivia:** After he semi-retired in the mid-80's, he started an acting career in films:- NUMBER ONE (1985) / PIRATES (1986) / HEARTS OF FIRE (1987), and TV plays:- KING OF THE GHETTOS (1986) / TALK OF THE DEVIL (1986) / NIGHT MOVES (1987). His other work on TV was mainly for commercials, etc.

Album rating: NEW BOOTS AND PANTIES!! (*8) / DO IT YOURSELF (*7) / LAUGHTER (*6) / JUKEBOX DURY compilation (*6) / LORD UPMINSTER (*6) / 400 WEEKS HOLIDAY (*5) / SEX AND DRUGS AND ROCK AND ROLL compilation (*7) / APPLES (*5) / THE BUS DRIVER'S PRAYER AND OTHER STORIES (*6) / Mr LOVE PANTS (*6) / TEN MORE TURNIPS FROM THE TIP (*6)

KILBURN & THE HIGH ROADS

IAN DURY – vocals / **KEITH LUCAS** – guitar / **DAVEY PAYNE** – sax / **CHARLIE SINCLAIR** – bass repl. HUMPHREY OCEAN who had repl. CHARLIE HART / **LOUIS LAROSE** then **GEORGE BUTLER** – drums

—— Early 1974, recorded lp for 'Raft', which was shelved after 'Warners' took over label. It was later issued by them in Oct'78 as 'WOTABUNCH', after DURY was top of the charts.

—— (mid-74) **DAVID ROHOMAN** – drums repl. BUTLER / **ROD MELVIN** – piano repl. HARDY

Dawn / not iss.

Nov 74. (7") *(DNS 1090)* **ROUGH KIDS. / BILLY BENTLEY** [ ] [–]

Feb 75. (7") *(DNS 1102)* **CRIPPLED WITH NERVES. / HUFFETY PUFF** [ ] [–]

Jun 75. (lp) *(DNLS 3065)* **HANDSOME** [ ] [–]
– The roadette song / Pam's mood / Crippled with nerves / Broken skin / Upminster kid / Patience / Father / Thank you mum / Rough kids / The badger and the rabbit / The mumble rumble and the cocktail rock / The call up. *(re-iss. Nov85 on 'Flashback' lp/c; FBLP/ZCFBL 8094)*

—— Disbanded mid-75, although IAN gigged at times with a new line-up as IAN DURY & THE KILBURNS. KEITH LUCAS was later to become NICK CASH and form 999. There were also other KILBURN material re-released after DURY's success.

1977. (lp) *Warners; (K 56513)* **WOTABUNCH** [ ] [–]

Sep 78. (7") *Warners; (K 17225)* **BENTLEY. / PAM'S MOODS** [ ] [–]

Jul 83. (lp/c) *P.R.T.; (DOW/ZCDOW 17)* **UPMINSTER KIDS** [ ] [–]

IAN DURY

—— - vocals solo with **CHAZ JANKEL** – guitar, keyboards (ex-BYZANTIUM) plus session men that became The BLOCKHEADS (see below)

Stiff / Stiff

Aug 77. (7",7"orange) *(BUY 17)* **SEX AND DRUGS AND ROCK AND ROLL. / RAZZLE IN MY POCKET** [ ] [–]

Sep 77. (lp/gold-lp/c) *(SEEZ/SEEZG/ZSEEZ 4)* <0002> **NEW BOOTS AND PANTIES!!!** [5] Apr78 [ ]
– Sweet Gene Vincent / ake up and make love with me / I'm partial to your abracadabra / My old man / Billericay Dickie / Clevor Trever / If I was with a woman / Plainstow Patricia / Blockheads / Blackmail man. *(re-iss. Sep86 on 'Demon' lp/c/cd+=; FIEND/+CASS/CD 63)* – (interview). *(re-iss. cd May95 on 'Disky';) (cd re-iss. Aug98 & Apr00 on 'A Hit Label'; AHLCD 57) (cd re-iss. Jun00 on 'REpertoire'; REP 4546)*

Nov 77. (7") *(BUY 23)* **SWEET GENE VINCENT. / YOU'RE MORE THAN FAIR** [ ] [–]

IAN DURY AND THE BLOCKHEADS

—— with **JANKEL** plus **NORMAN WATT-ROY** – bass (ex-LOVING AWARENESS, ex-GLENCOE) / **CHARLEY CHARLES** – drums (ex-LOVING AWARENESS, ex-GLENCOE) / **MICKEY GALLAGHER** – keyboards (ex-LOVING AWARENESS, ex-FRAMPTON'S CAMEL) / **JOHN TURNBULL** – guitar (ex-LOVING AWARENESS) / **DAVEY PAYNE** – saxophone (ex-WRECKLESS ERIC)

Apr 78. (7"/12") *(BUY 27/+12)* **WHAT A WASTE. / WAKE UP AND MAKE LOVE WITH ME** [11] [ ]

Nov 78. (7"; as IAN & THE BLOCKHEADS) *(BUY 38)* **HIT ME WITH YOUR RHYTHM STICK. / THERE AIN'T HALF BEEN SOME CLEVER BASTARDS** [1] [ ]

May 79. (lp/c) *(SEEZ/ZSEEZ 14)* <36104> **DO IT YOURSELF** [2] Jul79 [ ]
– Inbetweenies / Quiet / Don't ask me / Sink my boats / Waiting for your taxi / This is what we find / Uneasy sunny hotsy totsy / Mischief / Dance of the screamers / Lullaby for Francies. *(re-iss. Feb90 on 'Demon' lp/c/cd; FIEND/+CASS/CD 133) (re-iss. cd May95 on 'Disky';) (cd re-iss. Sep98 on 'Repertoire'; REP 4547) (cd re-iss. Apr00 on 'A Hit Label'; AHLCD 58)*

Jul 79. (7") *(BUY 50)* **REASONS TO CHEERFUL (pt.3). / COMMON AS MUCK** [3] [ ]

Aug 80. (7") *(BUY 90)* **I WANT TO BE STRAIGHT. / THAT'S NOT ALL HE WANTS** [22] [ ]

—— **WILKO JOHNSON** – guitar (ex-DR. FEELGOOD, solo artist) repl. JANKEL who went solo

Oct 80. (7") *(BUY 100)* **SUEPERMAN'S BIG SISTER. / F***ING ADA** [51] [ ]
(12"+=) *(BUYIT 100)* – You'll see glimpses.

Nov 80. (lp/c) *(SEEZ/ZSEEZ 30)* <36998> **LAUGHTER** [48] Jan81 [ ]
– Sueperman's big sister / Pardon / Delusions of grandeur / Yes and no (Paula) / Dance of the crackpots / Over the points / (Take your elbow out of the soup you're sitting on the chicken) / Uncoolohol / Hey, hey, take me away / Manic depression / Oh, Mr. Peanut / F***ing Ada. *(cd-iss. May95 on 'Disky';) (cd re-iss. Aug98 & Apr00 on 'A Hit Label'; AHLCD 59)*

—— IAN DURY now brought in the services of rhythm boys **SLY & ROBBIE** plus **JANKEL** + **TYRONE DOWNIE** – keyboards

Polydor / Polydor

Aug 81. (7"/12") *(POSP/+X 285)* **SPASTICUS AUSTICIOUS. / ('A'instrumental)** [ ] [ ]

Sep 81. (lp/c) *(POLD/+C 5042)* <16337> **LORD UPMINSTER** [53] [ ]
– Funky disco pops / Red letter / Girls watching / Wait for me / The body song / Lonely town / Trust is a must / Spasticus austicious. *(re-iss. Dec89 on 'Great Expectations' lp/cd; PIP LP/CD 005)*

IAN DURY & THE MUSIC STUDENTS

—— with many musicians including **JANKEL, PAYNE** + **RAY COOPER**

Nov 83. (7"/12") *(POSP/+C 646)* **REALLY GLAD YOU CAME. / INSPIRATION** [ ] [ ]

Jan 84. (lp/c) *(POLD/+C 5112)* **4,000 WEEKS HOLIDAY** [54] [–]
– (You're my) Inspiration / Friends / Tell your daddy / Peter the painter / Ban the bomb / Percy the poet / Very personal / Take me to the cleaners / The man with no face / Really glad you came. *(re-iss. Dec89 on 'Great Expectations' lp/cd; PIP LP/CD 004)*

Feb 84. (7") *(POSP 673)* **VERY PERSONAL. / BAN THE BOMB** [ ] [ ]
(12"+=) *(POSPX 673)* – The sky's the limit.

IAN DURY

— solo, with **PAYNE, GALLAGHER, COOPER** plus **STEVE WHITE** – drums / **MICHAEL McEVOY** – bass, synth / **MERLIN RHYS-JONES** – guitar / **FRANCES RUFELLE** – vocals / etc.

E.M.I. not iss.

Oct 89. (7"/7"pic-d) *(EMI/+P 5534)* **PROFOUNDLY IN LOVE WITH PANDORA. / EUGENIUS (YOU'RE A GENIUS)** [45] [–]
(above from the TV series, 'Adrian Mole')

WEA not iss.

Oct 89. (7") *(YZ 437)* **APPLES. / BYLINE BROWN** [ ] [–]
Oct 89. (lp/c)(cd) *(WX 326/+C)(246355-2)* **APPLES** (soundtrack) [ ] [–]
– Apples / Love is all / Byline Browne / Bit of kit / Game on / Looking for Harry / England's glory / Bus driver's prayer / P.C. Honey / The right people / All those who say okay / Riding the outskirts of fantasy.

— In Sep'90 he reformed IAN DURY & THE BLOCKHEADS for two reunion gigs

IAN DURY

Demon not iss.

Apr 91. (lp/cd) *(FIEND/+CD 777)* **WARTS 'N' AUDIENCE (live 22 December 1990)** [ ] [–]
– Wake up / Clever Trevor / If I was with a woman *[cd-only]* Billericay Dickie / Quiet / My old man / Spasticus autisticus / Plaistow Patricia / Clever bastards / Sweet Gene Vincent / What a waste / Hit me with your rhythm stick / Blockheads. *(cd re-iss. Sep00 on 'Diablo'+=; DIAB 8037)* – Inbetweenies / Reasons to be cheerful (part 3).
Nov 92. (cd/c) *(FIEND CD/CASS 702)* **THE BUS DRIVERS PRAYER & OTHER STORIES** [ ] [–]
– That's enough of that / Bill Haley's last words / Poor Joey / Quick quick slow / Fly in the ointment / O'Donegal / Poo-poo in the prawn / Ave a word / London talking / D'orine the cow / Your horoscope / No such thing as love / Two old dogs without a name / Bus driver's prayer.

IAN DURY & THE BLOCKHEADS

— with **CHAZ JANKEL, MICKEY GALLAGHER, DAVEY PAYNE, JOHN TURNBULL, NORMAN WATT-ROY, STEVEN MONTI** (drums) / **The BREEZEBLOCKS** – backing vocals

Ronnie Harris Ronnie Harris

Jun 98. (cd) *(DUR 1)* <61863> **Mr LOVE PANTS** [57] [ ]
– Jack shit George / The passing show / You're my baby / Honeysuckle highway / Itinerant / Geraldine / Cacka boom / Bed 'o' roses No.9 / Heavy living / Mash it up Harry.

— sadly, IAN was to die on the 27th of March, 2000; his last recording was left for a few years . . .

Mar 02. (cd) *(DUR 002)* <63145> **TEN MORE TURNIPS FROM THE TIP** [60] Apr02 [ ]
– Dance little rude boy / I believe / It ain't cool / Cowboys / Ballad of the sulphate strangler / I could lie / One love / Happy hippy / Books and water / You're the why (with ROBBIE WILLIAMS).
May 02. (cd-s) *(DUR 004)* **ONE LOVE / JOCK'S POEM / BALLAD OF THE SULPHATE STRANGLER** [ ] [–]

– compilations etc. –

Nov 81. (lp/c) *Stiff; (SEEZ/ZSEEZ 41)* **JUKE BOX DURY** [ ] [–]
(re-iss. Sep82 as 'GREATEST HITS' on 'Fame' lp/c; FA/TC-FA 3031)
May 85. (7") *Stiff; (BUY 214)* **HIT ME WITH YOUR RHYTHM STICK (Paul Hardcastle mix). / SEX AND DRUGS AND ROCK AND ROLL** [55] [–]
(12"+=) *(BUYIT 214)* – Reasons to be cheerful / Wake up and make love to me (Paul Hardcastle mix).
Apr 87. (lp/c/cd) *Demon; (FIEND/+CASS/CD 69)* **SEX AND DRUGS AND ROCK AND ROLL** [ ] [–]
– Hit me with your rhythm stick / I want to be straight / There ain't half been some clever bastards / What a waste! / Common as muck / Reasons to be cheerful (pt.3) / Sex and drugs and rock and roll / Sueperman's big sister / Razzle in my pocket / You're more than fair / Inbetweenies / You'll see glimpses.
Jul 91. (7"/c-s) *Flying; (FLYR 1/+C)* **HIT ME WITH YOUR RHYTHM STICK '91 (The Flying Remix Version) / HIT ME WITH YOUR RHYTHM STICK** [73] [–]
(12"+=/cd-s+=) *(FLYR 1 T/CD)* – ('A'mix).
Aug 91. (3xcd-box) *Demon; (IAN 1)* **IAN DURY & THE BLOCKHEADS** [ ] [–]
– (NEW BOOTS AND PANTIES / DO IT YOURSELF / SEX AND DRUGS AND ROCK AND ROLL)
Aug 96. (cd) *Disky; (DC 88975-2)* **THE BEST OF IAN DURY** [ ] [–]
Sep 99. (cd) *E.M.I.; (522888-2)* **REASONS TO BE CHEERFUL – THE VERY BEST OF IAN DURY & THE BLOCKHEADS** [40] [–]
– Reasons to be cheerful / Wake up and make love with me / Hit me with your rhythm stick / Clevor Trever / What a waste / Sex and drugs and rock and roll / This is what we find / Itinerant child / Sweet Gene Vincent / I want to be straight / Blockheads / Mash it up Harry / There ain't half been some clever bastards / Billericay Dickie / Inbetweenies / Sparticus (autisticus) / My old man / Lullaby for Francis.
Apr 00. (d-cd) *Repertoire; (REP 4592)* **REASONS TO BE CHEERFUL** [ ] [–]
May 00. (cd) *Repertoire; (REP 4507)* **THE BEST OF IAN DURY** [ ] [–]

— The BLOCKHEADS also released their own singles and lp early 80's

□ DUST BROTHERS
(see under ⇒ CHEMICAL BROTHERS)

Bob DYLAN

Born: ROBERT ALLAN ZIMMERMAN, 24 May'41, Duluth, Minnesota, USA. In 1960 he left his local university, changing his name to BOB DYLAN. He also began a trek to New York where he played his first gig supporting JOHN LEE HOOKER on 11 April '61 at Gerde's Folk City. Soon after, he enjoyed harmonica session work for folk songstress Caroline Hester. Her employers 'Columbia' records, through John Hammond Snr., signed him in October '61. His eponymous debut album in 1962 gained sparse attention, although his live work created critical appraisal. In 1963 he unleashed 'THE FREEWHEELIN' BOB DYLAN', and after PETER, PAUL & MARY lifted a million seller from it, 'BLOWIN' IN THE WIND', the record gained enough respect to give him a US Top 30 album. The record also saw a pronounced development in DYLAN's songwriting dexterity on tracks like the cutting 'MASTERS OF WAR'. While his untrained, nasal vocals could be something of an acquired taste, they communicated the lyrics in a way that lent them greater depth and resonance. But DYLAN really hit his stride with 'THE TIMES THEY ARE A-CHANGIN' the following year, an album that represented his most pointed protest writing. On subsequent albums, DYLAN shied away from direct missives like 'WITH GOD ON OUR SIDE' and 'ONLY A PAWN IN THEIR GAME'. 'ANOTHER SIDE OF BOB DYLAN' (1964) was contrastingly personal in tone, 'I DON'T BELIEVE IN YOU' and 'IT AIN'T ME BABE' venting DYLAN's spleen on matters of the heart rather than the soapbox. The lyrics also began to assume an air of enigmatic suggestiveness, 'MY BACK PAGES' and 'CHIMES OF FREEDOM' boasting striking, lucid imagery which The BYRDS would later complement with their incandescent, chiming guitars and ringing harmonies. Influenced by the British R&B boom (especially The BEATLES), DYLAN stunned folk purists with the half electric/half acoustic 'BRINGING IT ALL BACK HOME' (1965). The newly plugged in DYLAN was a revelation and with the likes of the stream-of-consciousness 'SUBTERRANEAN HOMESICK BLUES', the album influenced in turn the bands DYLAN had taken his cue from. The acoustic tracks on the second side such as 'MR. TAMBOURINE MAN' and 'IT'S ALL OVER NOW BABY BLUE' rank among DYLAN's finest, the former giving The BYRDS their breakthrough hit. While the folk faithful dissed DYLAN at that summer's Newport Festival, he wowed the rock world with the masterful 'LIKE A ROLLING STONE' single and followed it up with the seminal 'HIGHWAY 61 REVISITED'

(1965). A free flowing hybrid of blues, folk and R&B that used such esteemed musicians as AL KOOPER and PAUL BUTTERFIELD, rock music had never been graced with such complex, expansive lyrics. Backed by members of The HAWKS (who'd supported DYLAN on his recent tour and later become The BAND) and a posse of crack Nashville sessioneers, DYLAN recorded another rock milestone with 'BLONDE ON BLONDE' (1966). 'VISIONS OF JOHANNA' was DYLAN at his most lysergic, casting surreal lyrical spells with hypnotic ease. After a motorcycle accident that summer he sustained severe neck injuries and went into semi-retirement, looking after his family and holing up in Woodstock with The BAND. These sessions eventually saw the light of day in 1975 as 'THE BASEMENT TAPES', a classic double album of experimental roots rock. Upon his return to the music scene, DYLAN's vocals were slightly altered and his music had taken a distinct turn towards country-rock on 'JOHN WESLEY HARDING' (1968). The following year's 'NASHVILLE SKYLINE' was stone country, even featuring a bittersweet duet with JOHNNY CASH. After a lean spell, DYLAN returned with two harder-edged rock classics, 'BLOOD ON THE TRACKS' (1975) and 'DESIRE' (1975), providing him with a much needed boost in credibility both with the critics and the buying public. From 1979's 'SLOW TRAIN COMING' on through to his 80's work, he mellowed into more spiritual themes as a result of his new found Christianity; example 'SAVED' (1980), 'SHOT OF LOVE' (1981), 'INFIDELS' (1983), 'EMPIRE BURLESQUE' (1985), 'KNOCKED OUT LOADED' (1986) and 'DOWN IN THE GROOVE' (1988). Only the DANIEL LANOIS produced 'OH MERCY' (1989) came close to capturing the magic of old, the outtakes/rarities compilations 'BIOGRAPH' (1985) and 'THE BOOTLEG SERIES' (1991) of more interest to DYLAN fans than much of his new material. His first release of the new decade, the featherweight 'UNDER THE RED SKY' (1990) was roundly lambasted as his weakest effort since 'SELF PORTRAIT', while with 'GOOD AS I BEEN TO YOU' (1992), DYLAN again confounded fans and critics (and maybe even himself) by cutting a whole album of grizzled if endearing public domain folk songs. He then confounded fans and critics all over again with another volume, released almost a year to the day since the last one. 'WORLD GONE WRONG' (1993) was more than just a replay however, with a carefully chosen – if largely obscure – setlist interpreted with craft and obvious devotion. For fans of the man's rockier material, it seemed there was little respite as DYLAN released his own, inevitable chapter of 'MTV UNPLUGGED' (1995). There were few surprises, with most of the material drawn from his mid-60's golden period, although a few more 70's classics wouldn't have gone unwelcome. He finally emerged with a collection of original songs in 1997: 'TIME OUT OF MIND' (1997) marked the first chapter in one of his sporadic (in fact one of the most significant) periods of creative rebirth. Dark, disillusioned pre-millennial blues shot through with portentous, burbling hammond organ and a lingering sense of emotional impasse and encroaching old age, the record contained DYLAN's most naked songwriting in years; example the 16 min+ 'HIGHLANDS'. 'LOVE AND THEFT' (2001) was even more rapturously received although it was a completely different beast altogether. For the first time in decades – certainly since the 70's – rock's greatest living songwriter sounded liberated, inspired to stretch out and kick back in terms of both writing and performance. 'SUMMER DAYS' was possibly his most effervescent, carefree song since 'MOZAMBIQUE', while closer 'SUGAR BABY' was in the tradition of his finest album bookends. Following on from the revelatory Vol's 4 and 5 ('LIVE AT THE ALBERT HALL' and 'THE ROLLING THUNDER REVUE' respectively), more bootlegged BOB finally made the official discography with the release of Vol.6: 'BOB DYLAN LIVE 1964 – CONCERT AT PHILHARMONIC HALL' (2004). The concert in question – bootlegged as 'Halloween Masque' – was his Halloween acoustic concert at Carnegie Hall. As a context for fans who'd never heard the unofficial version, it would've more usefully been dug up prior to the Royal Albert Hall disc (the aforementioned Vol. 4), predicting that show's iconic break with tradition, and roughly split between material from 'ANOTHER SIDE..' and 'BRINGING IT ALL BACK HOME'. Still, it was another painstakingly presented package, and another vital archival document given its due and its rightful place in the UK Top 40/US Top 30.

• **Songwriters:** 99% DYLAN compositions except; HOUSE OF THE RISING SUN + IN MY TIME OF DYIN' (trad.) / TAKE A MESSAGE TO MARY (Everly Brothers) / THE BOXER (Simon & Garfunkel) / EARLY MORNIN' RAIN (Gordon Lightfoot) / A FOOL SUCH AS I + CAN'T HELP FALLING IN LOVE (hits; Elvis Presley) / BIG YELLOW TAXI (Joni Mitchell) / MR.BOJANGLES (Jerry Jeff Walker) / LET'S STICK TOGETHER (Wilbert Harrison) / SPANISH IS THE LOVING TONGUE + SHENANDOAH (trad.) / ANGELS FLYING TOO CLOSE TO THE GROUND (Willie Nelson) / etc. **Writing credits/hits:** BLOWIN' IN THE WIND + DON'T THINK TWICE, IT'S ALRIGHT (Peter, Paul & Mary; 1963) / ALL I REALLY WANT TO DO (Cher; 1965) / IT AIN'T ME BABE (Turtles; 1965) / MR. TAMBOURINE MAN + ALL I REALLY WANT TO DO + MY BACK PAGES (Byrds; 1965-1967) / IT'S ALL OVER NOW, BABY BLUE + FAREWELL ANGELINA (Joan Baez; 1965) / IF YOU GOTTA GO, GO NOW + JUST LIKE A WOMAN + MIGHTY QUINN (Manfred Mann; 1965/66/68) / TOO MUCH OF NOTHING (Peter, Paul & Mary; 1967) / THIS WHEEL'S ON FIRE (Julie Driscoll, Brian Auger & The Trinity; 1968) / ALL ALONG THE WATCHTOWER (Jimi Hendrix; 1968) / IF NOT FOR YOU (Olivia Newton-John; 1971) / A HARD RAIN'S A-GONNA FALL (Bryan Ferry; 1973) / KNOCKIN' ON HEAVEN'S DOOR (Eric Clapton; 1975 / Guns n' Roses; 1992) / I'LL BE YOUR BABY TONIGHT (UB40 & Robert Palmer; 1990) / & some minor hits. **Filmography:** DON'T LOOK BACK (1965 documentary) / EAT THE DOCUMENTARY (1971 docu-film) / PAT GARRETT & BILLY THE KID (1973) / RENALDO AND CLARA (1978) / HEARTS OF FIRE (1987). • **Trivia:** On the 22 Nov'65, BOB married Sara Lowndes, but she divorced him in 1977. (Band members in discography are selective)

Album rating: BOB DYLAN (*7) / THE FREEWHEELIN' BOB DYLAN (*9) / THE TIMES THEY ARE A-CHANGIN' (*7) / ANOTHER SIDE OF BOB DYLAN (*8) / BRINGING IT ALL BACK HOME (*9) / HIGHWAY 61 REVISITED (*10) / BLONDE ON BLONDE (*10) / GREATEST HITS compilation (*10) / JOHN WESLEY HARDING (*6) / NASHVILLE SKYLINE (*6) / SELF PORTRAIT (*4) / NEW MORNING (*4) / MORE GREATEST HITS compilation (*7) / PAT GARRETT & BILLY THE KID soundtrack (*5) / PLANET WAVES (*6) / BEFORE THE FLOOD (*7) / BLOOD ON THE TRACKS (*10) / DESIRE (*10) / THE BASEMENT TAPES early recordings (*9) / HARD RAIN (*6) / STREET LEGAL (*7) / AT BUDOKAN (*4) / SLOW TRAIN COMING (*6) / SAVED (*4) / SHOT OF LOVE (*4) / INFIDELS (*6) / REAL LIVE (*5) / EMPIRE BURLESQUE (*6) / BIOGRAPH boxed-set (*9) / KNOCKED OUT LOADED (*4) / DOWN IN THE GROOVE (*5) / DYLAN AND THE DEAD with Grateful Dead (*3) / OH MERCY (*6) / UNDER THE RED SKY (*5) / GOOD AS I BEEN TO YOU (*5) / WORLD GONE WRONG (*5) / 30th ANNIVERSARY CONCERT (*5) / GREATEST HITS VOL.3 compilation (*6) / MTV UNPLUGGED (*5) / TIME OUT OF MIND (*7) / LOVE AND THEFT (*8) / BOB DYLAN LIVE 1975: THE ROLLING THUNDER REVUE exploitation (*7) / MASKED AND ANONYMOUS soundtrack w/ Various Artists (*5) / BOB DYLAN LIVE 1964: CONCERT AT PHILHARMONIC HALL exploitation (*8) / NO DIRECTION HOME – THE SOUNDTRACK exploitation (*7)

BOB DYLAN – vocals, guitar, harmonica

C.B.S. Columb

Mar 62. (7") *<42656>* **MIXED UP CONFUSION. / CORRINA CORRINA** [–] [ ]

Jun 62. (lp; stereo/mono) *(S+/BPG 62022) <8579>* **BOB DYLAN** [ ] Mar62 [ ]
– She's no good / Talkin' New York / In my time of dyin' / Man of constant sorrow / Fixin' to die blues / Pretty Peggy-o / Highway 51 blues / Gospel plow / Baby, let me follow you down / House of the risin' sun / Freight train blues / Song to Woody / See that grave is kept clean. *(re-dist.May65 hit No.13) (re-iss. Mar81 lp/c; CBS/40 32001) (cd-iss. Nov89; CD 32001)*

—— added musicians **HOWARD COLLINS** – guitar / **GEORGE BARNES** – bass / **HERB LOVELL** – drums / **LEONARD GASKIN** – bass / etc.

Nov 63. (lp; stereo/mono) *(S+/BPG 62193) <8786>* **THE FREEWHEELIN' BOB DYLAN** [16] May63 [22]
– Blowin' in the wind / Girl from the North Country / Masters of war /

BOB DYLAN

Down the highway / Bob Dylan's blues / A hard rains a-gonna fall / Don't think twice, it's all right / Bob Dylan's dream / Oxford Town / / Talking World War III blues / Corrina, Corrina / Honey, just allow me one more chance / I shall be free. *(re-dist.Apr65, hit No.1) (re-iss. Mar81 lp/c; CBS/40 62193) (cd-iss. Nov89; 32390)*

Jan 64. (7") *<42856>* **BLOWIN' IN THE WIND. / DON'T THINK TWICE IT'S ALRIGHT** – [ ]

Jun 64. (lp; stereo/mono) *(S+/BPG 62251) <8905>* **THE TIMES THEY ARE A-CHANGIN'** 20 Mar64 20
– The times they are a-changin' / Ballad of Hollis Brown / With God on our side / One too many mornings / North country blues / Only a pawn in their game / Boots of Spanish leather / When the ship comes in / The lonesome death of Hattie Carroll / Restless farewell. *(re-dist.Apr65, hit No.4) (re-iss. Mar81 lp/c; CBS/40 32021) (cd-iss. Nov89; CD 32021)*

Nov 64. (lp; stereo/mono) *(S+/BPG 62429) <8993>* **ANOTHER SIDE OF BOB DYLAN** 8 Sep64 43
– All I really want to do / Black crow blues / Spanish Harlem incident / Chimes of freedom / I shall be free No.10 / To Ramona / Motorpsycho nitemare / I don't believe you / Ballad in plain D / It ain't me babe. *(re-iss. Mar81 lp/c; CBS/40 32034) (cd-iss. Nov89; CD 32034)*

Mar 65. (7") *(201751)* **THE TIMES THEY ARE A-CHANGIN'. / HONEY, JUST ALLOW ME ONE MORE CHANCE** 9 –
(re-iss. May82; 1751)

—— with **BOBBY GREGG** – drums / **JOHN SEBASTIAN** – bass / **BRUCE LANGHORNE** – guitar

Apr 65. (7") *(201753) <43242>* **SUBTERRANEAN HOMESICK BLUES. / SHE BELONGS TO ME** 9 Mar65 39

May 65. (lp; stereo/mono) *(S+/BPG 62515) <9128>* **BRINGING IT ALL BACK HOME** 1 Apr65 6
– Subterranean homesick blues / She belongs to me / Maggie's farm / Love minus zero – No limit / Outlaw blues / On the road again / Bob Dylan's 115th dream / Mr. Tambourine man / Gates of Eden / It's alright, ma (I'm only bleeding) / It's all over now, baby blue. *(re-iss. Jul83 lp/c; CBS/40 32344) (cd-iss. Jul87; CD 62515) (cd re-iss. Jul89 as 'SUBTERRANEAN HOMESICK BLUES'; CD 32344)*

Jun 65. (7") *(201781)* **MAGGIE'S FARM. / ON THE ROAD AGAIN** 22 –

—— now with **AL KOOPER** – organ / **PAUL BUTTERFIELD** – guitar / **PAUL GRIFFIN** – keyboards / **CHARLIE McCOY** – guitar / **RUSS SAVAKUS** – bass

Aug 65. (7") *(201811) <43346>* **LIKE A ROLLING STONE. / GATES OF EDEN** 4 Jul65 2
(re-iss. May82; 1811)

Sep 65. (lp; stereo/mono) *(S+/BPG 62572) <9189>* **HIGHWAY 61 REVISITED** 4 3
– Like a rolling stone / Tombstone blues / It takes a lot to laugh, it takes a train to cry / From a Buick 6 / Ballad of a thin man / Queen Jane approximately / Highway 61 revisited / Just like Tom Thumb's blues / Desolation row. *(re-iss. Dec85 lp/c; CBS/40 62572) (cd-iss. Nov89; CD 62572)*

Oct 65. (7") *(201824) <43389>* **POSITIVELY 4th STREET. / FROM A BUICK 6** 8 Sep65 7

Jan 66. (7") *(201900) <43477>* **CAN YOU PLEASE CRAWL OUT YOUR WINDOW? / HIGHWAY 61 REVISITED** 17 Dec65 58

Apr 66. (7") *(202053) <43541>* **ONE OF US MUST KNOW (SOONER OR LATER). / QUEEN JANE APPROXIMATELY** 33 Feb66 [ ]

—— Now augmented by members of The **BAND:- ROBBIE ROBERTSON** – guitar / **RICHARD MANUEL** – keyboards / **LEVON HELM** – drums / **RICK DANKO** – bass / **GARTH HUDSON** – keyboards plus also **KENNY BUTTREY** – drums

May 66. (7") *(202307) <43592>* **RAINY DAY WOMEN NOS.12 & 35. / PLEDGING MY TIME** 7 Apr66 2

Jul 66. (7") *(202258) <43683>* **I WANT YOU. / JUST LIKE TOM THUMB'S BLUES (live)** 16 Jun66 20

Aug 66. (d-lp; stereo/mono) *(S+/66012) <841>* **BLONDE ON BLONDE** 3 Jul66 9
– Rainy day women Nos.12 & 35 / Pledging my time / Visions of Johanna / One of us must know (sooner or later) / Most likely you go your way (and I'll go mine) / Temporary like Achilles / Absolutely sweet Marie / 4th time around / Obviously 5 believers / I want you / Stuck inside of Mobile with the Memphis blues again / Leopard-skin pill-box hat / Just like a woman / Sad eyed lady of the lowlands. *(re-iss. May82 d-lp/d-c; CBS/40 22130) (d-cd-iss. Jul87; CD 66012) (d-cd re-iss. Jun89; CD 22130) (d-cd re-iss. Feb95; CK 64411)*

Sep 66. (7") *<43792>* **JUST LIKE A WOMAN. / OBVIOUSLY 5 BELIEVERS** – 33

Jan 67. (lp; stereo/mono) *(S+/BPG 62847) <9463>* **BOB DYLAN'S GREATEST HITS** (compilation) <US diff.tracks> 6 Apr67 10
– Blowin' in the wind / It ain't me babe / The times they are a-changin' Mr. Tambourine man / She belongs to me / It's all over now, baby blue Subterranean homesick blues / One of us must know (sooner or later) Like a rolling stone / Just like a woman / Rainy day women Nos. 12 & 3 *(re-iss. Mar88; 460907) (cd-iss. Nov89; 450882-2) (re-iss. Feb91 & Apr97 o 'Columbia'; 460907-2) (re-iss. cd Oct94 as 'BEST OF . . .';)*

May 67. (7") *(202700) <44069>* **LEOPARD-SKIN PILL-BOX HAT. / MOST LIKELY YOU GO YOUR WAY (AND I'LL GO MINE)** [ ] 81

—— now with **BUTTREY, McCOY** and **PETE DRAKE** – sitar, guitar

Feb 68. (lp; stereo/mono) *(S+/BPG 63252) <9604>* **JOHN WESLEY HARDING** 1 Jan68 2
– John Wesley Harding / As I went out one morning / I dreamed I sa St. Augustine / All along the watchtower / The ballad of Frankie L and Judas Priest / Drifter's escape / Dear landlord / I am a lonesom hobo / I pity the poor immigrant / The wicked messenger / Down alon the cove / I'll be your baby tonight. *(re-iss. Nov89 lp/c/cd; 463359-1 4/-2)*

—— next featured **CHARLIE DANIELS** – bass, guitar / etc.

May 69. (7") *(4219) <44826>* **I THREW IT ALL AWAY. / DRIFTER'S ESCAPE** 30 85

May 69. (lp) *(63601) <9825>* **NASHVILLE SKYLINE** 1 Apr69 3
– Girl from the North country (with JOHNNY CASH) / Nashville skylin rag / To be alone with you / I threw it all away / Pegy Day / Lady lady lay One more night / Tell me that it isn't true / Country pie / Tonight I'll b staying here with you. *(re-iss. May87 lp/c; CBS/40 32675) (cd-iss. Jan86; C 63601)*

Sep 69. (7") *(4434) <44926>* **LAY LADY LAY. / PEGGY DAY** 5 Jul69 7

Dec 69. (7") *(4611) <45004>* **TONIGHT I'LL BE STAYING HERE WITH YOU. / COUNTRY PIE** [ ] Oct69 50

Jul 70. (d-lp) *(66250) <30050>* **SELF PORTRAIT** 1 Jun70 4
– All the tired horses / Alberta #1 / I forgot more than you'll ever know Days of 49 / Early mornin' rain / In search of little Sadie / Let it be me Little Sadie / Woogie boogie / Belle isle / Living the blues / Like a rollir stone (version) / Copper kettle (the pale moonlight) / Gotta travel on Blue Moon / The boxer / The mighty Quinn (Quinn, the eskimo) / Tak me as I am / Take a message to Mary / It hurts me too / Minstrel boy / Sh belongs to me / Wigwam / Alberta #2. *(re-iss. Sep87 d-lp/c; 460112-1/- (re-iss. Feb91 on 'Columbia' cd/c; 460112-2/-4)*

Jul 70. (7") *(5122) <45199>* **WIGWAM. / COPPER KETTLE (THE PALE MOONLIGHT)** [ ] 41

Nov 70. (lp) *(69001) <30290>* **NEW MORNING** 1 7
– If not for you / Day of the locusts / Time passes slowly / Went to see th gypsy / Winterlude / If dogs ran free / New morning / Sign on the window One more weekend / The man in me / Three angels / Father of the nigh *(re-iss. Sep83 lp/c; CBS/40 32267) (re-iss. Feb91 & Feb94 on 'Columbia' cd CD 32267)*

Mar 71. (7") *(7092)* **IF NOT FOR YOU. / NEW MORNING** [ ] –

Jun 71. (7") *(7329) <45409>* **WATCHING THE RIVER FLOW. / SPANISH IS THE LOVING TONGUE** 24 41

Dec 71. (7") *(7688) <45516>* **GEORGE JACKSON (acoustic). / GEORGE JACKSON (big band version)** [ ] Nov71 33

Dec 71. (d-lp/c) *(CBS/40 67239) <31120>* **MORE BOB DYLAN GREATEST HITS** <US-title 'BOB DYLAN'S GREATEST HITS, VOL.II'> (compilation) 12 14
– Watching the river flow / Don't think twice, it's alright / Lay la lay / Stuck inside Mobile with the Memphis blues again / I'll be yo baby tonight / All I really want to do / My back pages / Maggie's farm Tonight I'll be staying here with you / Positively 4th Street / All alor the watchtower / The mighty Quinn (Quinn, the eskimo) / Just li Tom Thumb's blues / A hard rain's a-gonna fall / If not for you / Ne morning / Tomorrow is a long time / When I paint my masterpiece / shall be released / You ain't goin' nowhere / Down in the flood. *(cd-i Oct87; CD 67239) (cd re-iss. Aug92 on 'Columbia'; 467851-2) (re-iss. Mar on 'Columbia' cd/c; 471243-2/-4)*

Sep 73. (lp/c) *(CBS/40 69042) <32460>* **PAT GARRETT & BILLY THE KID** (soundtrack) 29 Jul73 16
– Main title theme (Billy) / Cantina theme (workin' for the law) / Billy Bunkhouse theme / River theme / Turkey chase / Knockin' on Heaver door / Final theme / Billy 4 / Billy 7. *(re-iss. Mar82 lp/c; CBS/40 3209 (cd-iss. Feb91 & Nov02 on 'Columbia'; CD 32098)*

Sep 73. (7") *(1762) <45913>* **KNOCKIN' ON HEAVEN'S DOOR. / TURKEY CHASE** 14 Aug73 12

Dec 73. (lp/c) *(CBS/40 69049) <32747>* **DYLAN** (rec.1970) [ ] 17

– Lily of the west / Can't help falling in love / Sarah Jane / The ballad of Ira Hayes / Mr. Bojangles / Mary Ann / Big yellow taxi / A fool such as I / Spanish is the loving tongue. *(re-iss. Mar83) (cd+c-iss.Feb91 on 'Columbia')*

Jan 74. (7") *(2006) <45982>* **A FOOL SUCH AS I. / LILY OF THE WEST** [ ] Dec73 [55]

Island Asylum

Feb 74. (lp/c) *(ILPS/ICT 9261) <1003>* **PLANET WAVES** [7] [1]
– On a night like this / Going going gone / Tough mama / Hazel / Something there is about you / Forever young / Dirge / You angel you / Never say goodbye / Wedding song. *(re-iss. Sep82 lp/c; CBS/40 32154) (cd-iss. Nov89 on 'C.B.S.'; CD 21154)*

Feb 74. (7") *<11033>* **ON A NIGHT LIKE THIS. / YOU ANGEL YOU** [–] [44]

Feb 74. (7") *(WIP 6168)* **ON A NIGHT LIKE THIS. / FOREVER YOUNG** [ ] [–]

Apr 74. (7") **SOMETHING THERE IS ABOUT YOU. / GOING GOING GONE** [–] [ ]

Asylum Asylum

Jul 74. (d-lp/d-c; as BOB DYLAN & THE BAND) *(IBD 1) <201>* **BEFORE THE FLOOD** (tracks by The BAND) [8] [3]
– Most likely you go your way (and I'll go mine) / Lay lady lay / Rainy day women Nos.12 & 35 / Knockin' on Heaven's door / It ain't me babe / The ballad of a thin man / Up on Cripple Creek * / I shall be released / Endless highway * / The night they drove old Dixie down * / Stage fright * / Don't think twice, it's all right / Just like a woman / It's alright ma (I'm only bleeding) / The shape I'm in * / When you awake * / The weight * / All along the watchtower / Highway 61 revisited / Like a rolling stone / Blowin' in the wind. *(re-iss. Sep82 on 'C.B.S.' d-lp/d-c; CBS/40 22137) (cd-iss. Jul87 + Nov89 + Jun96; CD 22137)*

— The BAND had been his backing group from the mid '60's.

Aug 74. (7") *<11043>* **MOST LIKELY YOU GO YOUR WAY (AND I'LL GO MINE) (live). / STAGE FRIGHT (The BAND live)** [–] [66]

Nov 74. (7") **ALL ALONG THE WATCHTOWER (live). / IT AIN'T ME BABE (live)** [–] [ ]

C.B.S. Columbia

Feb 75. (lp/c) *(CBS/40 69097) <32235>* **BLOOD ON THE TRACKS** [4] [1]
– Tangled up in blue / Simple twist of fate / You're a big girl now / Idiot wind / You're gonna make me lonesome when you go / Meet me in the morning / Lily, Rosemary and the Jack of Hearts / If you see her, say hello / Shelter from the storm / Buckets of rain. *((cd-iss. Dec85; CD 69097) (re-iss. Sep93 on 'Columbia' cd/c; 467842-2/-4)*

Mar 75. (7") *(3160) <10106>* **TANGLED UP IN BLUE. / IF YOU SEE HER, SAY HELLO** [ ] [31]

Jul 75. (d-lp/c) *(CBS/40 88147) <33682>* **THE BASEMENT TAPES** (rec.1967) [8] [7]
– Odds and ends / Orange juice blues (blues for breakfast) / Million dollar bash / Yazoo street scandal / Goin' to Acapulco / Katie's been gone / Lo and behold / Bessie Smith / Clothes line saga / Apple suckling tree / Please Mrs. Henry / Tears of rage / Too much of nothing / Yea! heavy and a bottle of wine / Ain't no more Cane / Crash on the levee (down in the flood) / Ruben Remus / Tiny Montgomery / You ain't goin' nowhere / Don't ya tell Henry / Nothing was delivered / Open the doors, Homer / Long distance operator. *(cd-iss. Nov89; 466137-2)*

Oct 75. (7") *(3665)* **MILLION DOLLAR BASH. / TEARS OF RAGE** [ ] [ ]

— next featured **EMMYLOU HARRIS** – vocals / **SCARLET RIVIERA** – violin / **RONNE BLAKELY** – vocals / **HOWIE WYTHE** – drums / **ROB STONER** – bass / **STEVEN SOLES** – guitar

Jan 76. (7") *(3879) <10245>* **HURRICANE (part 1). / HURRICANE (full version)** [43] Nov75 [33]

Jan 76. (lp/c) *(CBS/40 86003) <33893>* **DESIRE** [3] [1]
– Hurricane / Isis / Mozambique / One more cup of coffee / Oh, sister / Joey / Romance in Durango / Black diamond bay / Sara. *(re-iss. Apr85 lp/c; CBS/40 32570) (cd-iss. Jul87; 86003) (cd re-iss. Jun89; CD 32470)*

Apr 76. (7") *(4113) <10298>* **MOZAMBIQUE. / OH, SISTER** [ ] Mar76 [54]

— His HARD RAIN tour added **MICK RONSON** – guitar / **DAVID MANSFIELD** – keyboards

Sep 76. (lp/c) *(CBS/40 86016) <34349>* **HARD RAIN (live)** [3] [17]
– Maggie's farm / One too many mornings / Stuck inside of Mobile with the Memphis blues again / Lay lady lay / Shelter from the storm / You're a big girl now / I threw it all away / Idiot wind. *(re-iss. Apr83 lp/c; CBS/40 32308) (cd-iss. Nov89; CD 32308)*

Feb 77. (7") *(4859) <10454>* **RITA MAY. / STUCK INSIDE OF MOBILE WITH THE MEMPHIS BLUES AGAIN (live)** [ ] [ ]

May 78. (7"/12") *(7/12 6499) <10805>* **BABY STOP CRYING. / NEW PONY** [13] [ ]

Jun 78. (lp/c) *(CBS/40 86067) <35453>* **STREET-LEGAL** [2] [11]
– Changing of the guards / New pony / No time to think / Baby stop crying / Is your love in vain / Senor (tales of Yankee power) / True love tends to forget / We better talk this over / Where are you tonight (journey through dark heat). *(cd-iss. Mar86; CD 86087) (re-iss. May95 cd/c; 403289)*

Oct 78. (7"/12") *(7/12 6718)* **IS YOUR LOVE IN VAIN. / WE BETTER TALK THIS OVER** [56] [–]

Dec 78. (7") *(6935) <10851>* **CHANGING OF THE GUARDS. / SENOR (TALES OF YANKEE POWER)** [ ] [ ]

1978. (7"ep) **4 SONGS FROM "RENALDO AND CLARA"** [–] [ ]
– People get ready / Never let me go / Isis / It ain't me babe.

May 79. (d-lp/d-c) *(CBS/40 96004) <36067>* **BOB DYLAN AT BUDOKAN (live)** [4] [13]
– Mr. Tambourine man / Shelter from the storm / Love minus zero – No limit / Ballad of a thin man / Don't think twice, it's all right / Maggie's farm / One more cup of coffee / Like a rolling stone / I shall be released / Oh sister / Is your love in vain? / Going going gone / Blowin' in the wind / Just like a woman / Simple twist of fate / All along the watchtower / I want you / All I really want to do / Knockin' on Heaven's door / It's alright ma (I'm only bleeding) / Forever young / The times they are a-changin'. *(cd-iss. Jul87; CD 96004)*

Jun 79. (7"m) *(7473)* **FOREVER YOUNG (live). / ALL ALONG THE WATCHTOWER (live) / I WANT YOU (live)** [ ] [–]

Aug 79. (7") *(7828)* **PRECIOUS ANGEL. / TROUBLE IN MIND** [ ] [–]

Sep 79. (lp/c) *(CBS/40 86095) <36120>* **SLOW TRAIN COMING** [2] [3]
– Gotta serve somebody / Precious angel / I believe in you / Slow train / Gonna change my way of thinking / Do right to me baby (do unto others) / When you gonna wake up / Man gave names to all the animals / When he returns. *(re-iss. Nov85 lp/c; CBS/40 32524) (cd-iss. Mar86; CD 86095) (cd re-iss. Apr89; CD 32524)*

Sep 79. (7") *<11072>* **GOTTA SERVE SOMEBODY. / TROUBLE IN MIND** [–] [24]

Oct 79. (7") *(7970)* **MAN GAVE NAMES TO ALL THE ANIMALS. / WHEN HE RETURNS** [ ] [–]

Jan 80. (7") *<11168>* **MAN GAVE NAMES TO THE ANIMALS. / WHEN YOU GONNA WAKE UP** [–] [ ]

Jan 80. (7") *(8134)* **GOTTA SERVE SOMEBODY. / GONNA CHANGE MY WAY OF THINKING** [ ] [–]

Mar 80. (7") *<11235>* **SLOW TRAIN. / DO RIGHT TO ME BABY (DO UNTO OTHERS)** [–] [ ]

May 80. (7") *<11318>* **SOLID ROCK. / COVENANT WOMAN** [–] [ ]

Jun 80. (lp/c) *(CBS/40 83113) <36553>* **SAVED** [3] [24]
– A satisfied mind / Saved / Covenant woman / What can I do for you? / Solid rock / Pressing on / In the garden / Saving Grace / Are you ready. *(reiss.Sep86 lp/c; CBS/40 32742) (re-iss. Feb91 & Mar93 on 'Columbia' cd/c; 403274-2/-4)*

Jun 80. (7") *(8743) <11370>* **SAVED. / ARE YOU READY** [ ] [ ]

Jun 81. (7") *<02510>* **HEART OF MINE. / THE GROOM'S STILL WAITING AT THE ALTAR** [–] [ ]

Jul 81. (7") *(A 1406)* **HEART OF MINE. / LET IT BE ME** [ ] [–]

Aug 81. (lp/c) *(CBS/40 85178) <37496>* **SHOT OF LOVE** [6] [33]
– Shot of love / Heart of mine / Property of Jesus / Lenny Bruce / Watered down love / Dead man, dead man / In the summertime / Trouble / Every grain of sand. *(re-iss. Feb91 on 'Columbia' cd+=/c+=; 467839-2/-4)*
– The groom's still waiting at the altar. *(re-iss. cd Jun94 on 'Sony Europe'; 983338-2)*

Sep 81. (7") *(A 1460)* **LENNY BRUCE. / DEAD MAN, DEAD MAN** [ ] [–]

Oct 83. (7") *(A 3916)* **UNION SUNDOWN. / I AND I** [ ] [ ]

Nov 83. (lp/c) *(CBS/40 25539) <38819>* **INFIDELS** [9] [20]
– Jokerman / Sweetheart like you / Neighbourhood bully / License to kill / Man of peace / Union sundown / I and I / Don't fall apart on me tonight. *(cd-iss. Jul87; Cd 25539) (re-iss. Dec89 lp/c/cd; 460727-1/-4/-2)*

Dec 83. (7") *<04301>* **SWEETHEART LIKE YOU. / UNION SUNDOWN** [–] [55]

May 84. (7") *<04425>* **JOKERMAN. / ISIS** [–] [ ]

Jun 84. (7") *(A 4055)* **JOKERMAN. / LICENSE TO KILL** [ ] [–]

Dec 84. (lp/c/cd) *(CBS/40/CD 26334) <39944>* **REAL LIVE (live)** [54] [ ]
– Highway 61 revisited / Maggie's farm / I and I / License to kill / It ain't me babe / Tangled up in blue / Masters of war / Ballad of a thin man / Girl

from the North country / Tombstone blues. *(re-iss. Feb91 on 'Columbia' cd/c; 467841-2/-4)*

Jan 85. (7"/7"g-f) *(A/GA 5020)* **HIGHWAY 61 REVISITED (live). / IT AIN'T ME BABE (live)**

Jun 85. (7") *(A 6303)* *<04933>* **TIGHT CONNECTION TO MY HEART. / WE'D BETTER TALK THIS OVER**

Jun 85. (lp/c/cd) *(CBS/40/CD 86313)* *<40110>* **EMPIRE BURLESQUE** 11 33
– Tight connection to my heart (has anybody seen my love) / Seeing the real you at last / I'll remember you / Clean cut kid / Never gonna be the same again / Trust yourself / Emotionally yours / When the night comes falling from the sky / Something's burning, baby / Dark eyes. *(re-iss. cd.1988; Cd 86313) (re-iss. Feb91 on 'Columbia' cd/c; 467840-2/-4)*

Aug 85. (7"/ext.12") *(A/TA 6469)* **WHEN THE NIGHT COMES FALLING FROM THE SKY. / DARK EYES** –

—— In Apr'86, he was credited next on the TOM PETTY ⇒ single 'BAND OF THE HAND'.

Oct 85. (7") *<05697>* **WHEN THE NIGHT COMES FALLING FROM THE SKY. / EMOTIONALLY YOURS** –

Jul 86. (lp/c/cd) *(CBS/40/CD 86326)* *<40439>* **KNOCKED OUT LOADED** 35 53
– You wanna ramble / They killed him / Driftin' too far from shore / Precious memories / Maybe someday / Brownsville girl / Got my mind made up / Under your spell. *(re-iss. Feb91 & Mar93 on 'Columbia' cd/c; 467040-2/-4)*

Oct 86. (7") *(651148-7)* **THE USUAL. / GOT MY MIND MADE UP**
(12"+=) *(651148-6)* – Precious memories / Driftin' too far from shore.

Jun 88. (lp/c/cd) *(460267-1/-4/-2)* *<40957>* **DOWN IN THE GROOVE** 32 61
– Let's stick together / When did you leave Heaven? / Sally Sue Brown / Death is not the end / Had a dream about you, baby / Ugliest girl in the world / Silvio / Ninety miles an hour (down a dead end street) / Shenandoah / Rank strangers to me.

Jul 88. (7") **SILVIO. / DRIFTIN' TOO FAR FROM SHORE** –

Jul 88. (7") *(651406-7)* **SILVIO. / WHEN DID YOU LEAVE HEAVEN?** –
(12"+=) *(651406-6)* – Driftin' too far from shore.

—— Later in '88 & onwards, he was also part of supergroup TRAVELING WILBURYS

Feb 89. (lp/c/cd; BOB DYLAN & GRATEFUL DEAD) *(463381/-1/-4/-2)* *<45056>* **DYLAN & THE DEAD (live July'87)** 38 37
– Slow train / I want you / Gotta serve somebody / Queen Jane approximately / Joey / All along the watchtower / Knockin' on Heaven's door. *(re-iss. May94 on 'Columbia' cd/c; 463381-2/-4)*

Oct 89. (lp/c/cd) *(465800-1/-4/-2)* *<45281>* **OH MERCY** 6 30
– Political world / Where teardrops fall / Everything is broken / Ring them bells / Man in the long black coat / Most of the time / What good am I? / Disease of conceit / What was it you wanted / Shooting star.

Oct 89. (7") **EVERYTHING IS BROKEN. / DEAD MAN, DEAD MAN** –

Oct 89. (7") *(655358-7)* **EVERYTHING IS BROKEN. / DEATH IS NOT THE END** –
(12"/12"w-print) *(655358-6/-8)* – ('A'side) / Dead man, dead man / I want you (live).
(cd-s) *(655358-2)* – ('A'side) / Where the teardrops fall / Dead man, dead man (live) / Ugliest girl in the world (live).

Feb 90. (7") *(655643-7)* **POLITICAL WORLD. / RING THEM BELLS**
(12"+=/cd-s+=) *(655643-6/-2)* – Silvio / All along the watchtower (live).
(cd-s) *(655643-5)* – ('A'side) / Caribbean wind / You're a big girl now / It's all over now, baby blue.

Sep 90. (cd/c/lp) *(467188-2/-4/-1)* *<46794>* **UNDER THE RED SKY** 13 38
– Wiggle wiggle / Under the red sky / Unbelievable / Born in time / TV talkin' time / 10,000 men / 2x2 / God knows / Handy Dandy / Cat's in the well.

Sep 90. (7") *(656304-7)* **UNBELIEVABLE. / 10,000 MEN**
(cd-s+=) *(656304-2)* – In the summertime / Jokerman.

Feb 91. (7"/c-s) *(656707-7/-4)* **SERIES OF DREAMS. / SEVEN CURSES**
(cd-s+=) *(656707-5)* – Tangled up in blue / Like a rolling stone.

—— totally solo DYLAN

Columbia Columb

Nov 92. (cd/c/lp) *(472710-2/-4/-1)* *<53200>* **GOOD AS I BEEN TO YOU** 18 51
– Frankie & Albert / Jim Jones / Blackjack Davey / Canadee-i-o / Sittin on top of the world / Little Maggie / Hard times / Step it up and go Tomorrow night / Arthur McBride / You're gonna quit me / Diamonc Joe / Froggie went a courtin'.

—— In Aug93, a host of artists released a live tribute d-cd,d-c 'ANNIVERSARY CONCERT', which hit US No.30. Below all traditional tunes.

Nov 93. (cd/c) *(474857-2/-4)* *<57590>* **WORLD GONE WRONG** 35 70
– World gone wrong / Ragged and dirty / Love Henry / Blood in my eyes Delia / Broke down engine / Two soldiers / Stack A Lee / Jack A Roe / Love pilgrim.

—— with **TONY GARNIER** – bass / **JOHN JACKSON** – guitar / **BUCKY BAXTER** – pedal steel, dobro / **WINSTON WATSON** – drums / **BRENDAN O'BRIEN** – hammond organ

Apr 95. (cd/c/lp) *(478374-2/-4/-1)* *<67000>* **MTV UNPLUGGED** 10 May95 23
– Tombstone blues / Shooting star / All along the watchtower / The time they are a-changin' / John Brown / Desolation row / Rainy day women #12 & 35 / Love minus zero – No limit / Dignity / Knockin' on Heaven's door / Like a rolling stone / With God on our side.

May 95. (c-s) *(662076-4)* **DIGNITY / JOHN BROWN** 33
(cd-s+=) *(662076-5)* – It ain't me babe (live).
(cd-s) *(662076-2)* – ('A'side) / A hard rain's a-gonna fall.

—— To end '96, a version of 'KNOCKIN' ON HEAVEN'S DOOR' hit UK No. for DUNBLANE; Scottish musicians and children from the town hit shooting tragedy

Oct 97. (cd/c) *(486936-2/-4)* *<68556>* **TIME OUT OF MIND** 10 10
– Love sick / Dirt road blues / Standing in the doorway / Million miles Tryin' to get to Heaven / 'Til I fell in love with you / Not dark yet / Col irons bound / Make you feel my love / Can't wait / Highlands.

Jun 98. (cd-s) *(665997-2)* **LOVE SICK / COLD IRONS BOUND (live) / COCAINE (live) / BORN IN TIME (live)** 64 –
(cd-s) *(665997-5)* – ('A'side) / Can't wait (live) / Roving gambler (live) Blind Willie McTell (live).

Oct 00. (cd-s) *(669379-2)* **THINGS HAVE CHANGED / TO MAKE YOU FEEL MY LOVE / HURRICANE / SONG TO WOODY** 58 –

Sep 01. (cd) *(504364-2)* *<85975>* **LOVE AND THEFT** 3 5
– Tweedle dee and tweedle dum / Mississippi / Summer days / Bye an bye / Lonesome day blues / Floater (too much to ask) / High water (fo Charlie Patton) / Moonlight / Honest with me / Po' boy / Cry a while Sugar baby. *(special cd+=; 504364-9)* – I was young when I left home / Th times they are a-changin' (alternate version).

Jul 03. (cd; w/ Various Artists) *(512556-2)* *<90336>* **MASKED AND ANONYMOUS** (soundtrack) 94
– My back pages (MAGOKORO BROTHERS) / Gotta serve somebod (SHIRLEY CAESAR) / Down in the flood (new version) / It's all over now baby blue (GRATEFUL DEAD) / Most of the time (SOPHIE ZELMANI) On a night like this (LOS LOBOS) / Diamond Joe / Come una pietr scalciata (like a rolling stone) (ARTICOLO 31) / One more cup o coffee (SERTAB) / Non dirle che non e' cosi' (If you see her, say hello (FRANCESCO DE GREGORI) / Dixie / Senor (tales of Yankee power (JERRY GARCIA) / Cold irons bound (new version) / City of gold (DIXI HUMMINGBIRDS). *<(special d-cd+=; 512556-6)>* – All I really want t do / Love minus zero – No limit / Stuck inside of Mobile with the Memphi blues again / Tangled up in blue / Gotta serve somebody / Moonlight Cold irons bound.

– (selective) compilations, etc. –

on 'CBS / Columbia' unless otherwise mentioned

Nov 85. (5xlp-box/3xc-box/3xcd-box) *(CBS/40/CD 66509)* *<38830>* **BIOGRAPH** 33
– (above contains 16 unreleased tracks)

Apr 91. (3xcd/3xc/6xlp) *(468086-2/-4/-1)* *<47382>* **THE BOOTLEG SERIES VOLUMES 1-3 (RARE & UNRELEASED) 1961-1991** 32 49

Aug 92. (d-cd) *(466831-2)* **HIGHWAY 61 REVISITED / JOHN WESLEY HARDING** –

Oct 93. (3xcd-box) *(471621-2)* **BLONDE ON BLONDE / JOHN WESLEY HARDING / SELF PORTRAIT** –

Nov 94. (cd/c/d-lp) *(477805-2/-4/-1)* *<66783>* **GREATEST HITS VOLUME III**

– Tangled up in blue / Changing the guards / The groom's still waiting at the altar / Hurricane / Forever young / Jokerman / Dignity / Silvio / Ring them bells / Gotta serve somebody / Series of dream / Brownsville girl / Under the red sky / Knockin' on Heaven's door.

Jun 97. (d-cd/d-c) *Sony; (SONYTV 28 CD/MC)* **THE BEST OF BOB DYLAN** 8 –
– Blowin' in the wind / The times they are a-changin' / Don't think twice, it's alright / Mr. Tambourine man / Like a rolling stone / Just like a woman / All along the watchtower / Lay lady lay / If not for you / Knockin' on Heaven's door / Forever young / Tangled up in blue / Shelter from the storm / I shall be released / Oh sister / Gotta serve somebody / Jokerman / Everything is broken.

Oct 98. (d-cd/d-c) *Legacy-Columbia; (491485-2/-4) <65759>* **LIVE AT THE ROYAL ALBERT HALL: THE BOOTLEG SERIES VOL.4** <US title 'BOB DYLAN LIVE 1966: THE 'ROYAL ALBERT HALL' CONCERT 19 31
– She belongs to me / Fourth time around / Visions of Johanna / It's all over now, baby blue / Desolation row / Just like a woman / Mr. Tambourine man / Tell me, momma / I don't believe you (she acts like we never met) / Baby, let me follow you down / Just like Tom Thumb's blues / Leopard-skin pillbox hat / One too many mornings / Ballad of a thin man / Like a rolling stone.

May 00. (cd/c) *(498361-2/-4)* **THE BEST OF BOB DYLAN VOL.2** 22 –
– Things have changed / A hard rain's a-gonna fall / It ain't me babe / Subterranean homesick blues / Positively 4th street / Highway 61 revisited / Rainy day women Nos.12 & 35 / I want you / I'll be your baby tonight / Quinn the eskimo / Simple twist of fate / Hurricane / Changing the guards / License to kill / Silvio / Dignity / Not yet dark / Blowin' in the wind (live) / Highlander (live).

May 01. (d-cd/d-c) *Sony TV; (STV CD/MC 116) / Columbia; <85168>* **THE ESSENTIAL BOB DYLAN** 9 Nov00 67
– Blowin' in the wind / Don't think twice, it's all right / The times they are a-changin' / It ain't me babe / Maggie's farm / It's all over now, baby blue / Mr. Tambourine man / Subterranean homesick blues / Like a rolling stone / Positively 4th Street / Just like a woman / Rainy day women #12 & 35 / All along the watchtower / The mighty Quinn (Quinn, the eskimo) / I'll be your baby tonight / Lay lady lay / If not for you / I shall be released / You ain't goin' nowhere / Knockin' on Heaven's door / Forever young / Tangled up in blue / Shelter from the storm / Hurricane / Gotta serve somebody / Jokerman / Silvio / Everything is broken / Not dark yet / Things have changed.

Sep 01. (3xcd-box) *(501621-2)* **Q 5 STAR REVIEWS VOL.1**
– (THE FREEWHEELIN' . . . / BRINGING IT ALL BACK HOME / HIGHWAY 61 . . .)

Sep 01. (4xcd-box) *(501622-2)* **Q 5 STAR REVIEWS VOL.2**
– (BLONDE ON BLONDE / BLOOD ON THE TRACKS / THE BASEMENT TAPES)

Sep 01. (3xcd-box) *(501623-2)* **Q 5 STAR REVIEWS VOL.3**
– (DESIRE / OH MERCY / TIME OUT OF MIND)

Oct 02. (3xcd-box) *(509636-2)* **INFIDELS / OH MERCY / TIME OUT OF MIND**

Oct 02. (3xcd-box) *(509637-2)* **BRINGING IT ALL BACK HOME / HIGHWAY 61 REVISITED / BLONDE ON BLONDE**

Oct 02. (3xcd-box) *(509638-2)* **DESIRE / BLOOD ON THE TRACKS / STREET LEGAL**

Oct 02. (3xcd-box) *(509639-2)* **ANOTHER SIDE OF BOB DYLAN / THE TIMES THEY ARE A-CHANGIN' / THE FREEWHEELIN' BOB DYLAN**

Nov 02. (d-cd) *Columbia; (510140-2) / Sony; <87047>* **BOB DYLAN LIVE 1975 – THE ROLLING THUNDER REVUE (THE BOOTLEG SERIES VOL.5)** 69 56
– Tonight I'll be staying here with you / It ain't me babe / A hard rain's a-gonna fall / The lonesome death of Hattie Carroll / Romance in Durango / Isis / Mr. Tambourine man / Simple twist of fate / Blowin' in the wind (with JOAN BAEZ) / Mama, you been on my mind / I shall be released (with JOAN BAEZ) / It's all over now, baby blue / Love minus zero – No limit / Tangled up in blue / The water is wide / It takes a lot to laugh, it takes a train to cry / Oh, sister / Hurricane / One more cup of coffee / Sara / Just like a woman / Knockin' on Heaven's door (with ROGER McGUINN).

Dec 02. (d-cd) *(499858-2)* **BOB DYLAN / THE FREEWHEELIN' BOB DYLAN**

Dec 02. (d-cd) *(499859-2)* **THE TIMES THEY ARE A-CHANGIN' / ANOTHER SIDE OF BOB DYLAN**

Mar 04. (d-cd) *Columbia; (512358-2)* **BOB DYLAN LIVE 1964: CONCERT AT PHILHARMONIC HALL – THE BOOTLEG SERIES VOL.6** 33 28
– The times they are a-changin' / Spanish Harlem incident / Talkin' John Birch paranoid blues / To Ramona / Who killed Davey Moore? / Gates of Eden / If you gotta go, go now (or else you gotta stay all night) / It's alright, ma (I'm only bleeding) / I don't believe you / Mr. Tambourine man / A hard rain's a-gonna fall // Talkin' World War III blues / Don't think twice, it's all right / The lonesome death of Hattie Carroll / Mama, you been on my mind (w/ JOAN BAEZ) / Silver dagger (w/ JOAN BAEZ) / With God on our side (w/ JOAN BAEZ) / It ain't me, babe (w/ JOAN BAEZ) / All I really want to do.

Sep 05. (d-cd) *Sony; (520358-2) / Columbia; <93937-2>* **NO DIRECTION HOME: THE SOUNDTRACK – THE BOOTLEG SERIES VOL.7** 21 16
– When I got troubles / Rambler, gambler (demo) / This land is your land (live) / Song to Woody / Dink's song (demo) / I was young when I left home (demo) / Sally gal (alt. take) / Don't think twice, it's alright (demo) / Man of constant sorrow / Blowin' in the wind (live) / Masters of war (live) / A hard rain's a-gonna fall (live) / When the ship comes in (live) / Mr. Tambourine man (alt. take) / Chimes of freedom (live) / It's all over now, baby blue (alt. take) // She belongs to me (alt. take) / Maggie's farm (live) / It takes a lot to laugh, it takes a train to cry (alt. take) / Tombstone blues (alt. take) / Just like Tom Thumb's blues (alt. take) / Desolation row (alt. take) / Highway 61 revisited (alt. take) / Leopard-skin pill-box hat (alt. take) / Stuck inside of Mobile with the Memphis blues again (alt. take) / Visions of Johanna (alt. take) / Ballad of a thin man (live) / Like a rolling stone (live).

EAGLES

Formed: Los Angeles, California, USA . . . 1971, by GLENN FREY and DON HENLEY who had previously been part of LINDA RONSTADT's backing band on her 'SILK PURSE' (1970) album. They duly recruited BERNIE LEADON and RANDY MEISNER (both seasoned hands; see discography) and gave birth to the EAGLES. The very name spelled out their musical ambitions; like The BYRDS they wanted to fly high with heavenly country harmonies although they wanted a tougher, more predatory sound. Signed to 'Asylum' records that year, they stormed the charts from the off with the FREY / JACKSON BROWNE-penned, open-road classic, 'TAKE IT EASY'. The eponymous debut album followed soon after, hitting the US Top 30. Not exactly groundbreaking, it contained more than a few duffers although 'PEACEFUL EASY FEELING' still sounds gorgeous. Considered by many to be the band's finest hour, 'DESPERADO' (1973) was a Wild West concept album. While the idea sounds too awful to contemplate on paper, they somehow managed to pull it off. Amid the twists and turns of the plot lay such goose-bump masterpieces as 'TEQUILA SUNRISE' and the elegiac title track, although no major hit singles were forthcoming. With the addition of guitarist DON FELDER and BILL SZYMCZYK on production duties, 'ON THE BORDER' (1974) introduced a more robust sound, spawning the US No.1, 'BEST OF MY LOVE'. The breakthrough came with 'ONE OF THESE NIGHTS' (1975), featuring three Top 5 hits in 'LYIN' EYES', 'TAKE IT TO THE LIMIT' and the hard-edged title track. LEADON was not a happy chappy however, his country boy sensibilities displeased at the EAGLES' increasing prediliction for "rawk". Maybe it was for the best, however, as he'd no doubt have been horrified by 'HOTEL CALIFORNIA' (1976), a decidedly harder affair with nary a hint of country to be found. In its place was a set of immaculately crafted, quintessentially Californian soft rock that was the stuff of radio programmer's dreams. Up there with 'Rumours' and 'Thriller' in terms of legendary and commercial status, its slow burning title track was an epic metaphor for that crazy, frozen-nosed Californian lifestyle that mere mortals could only dream of. Even punk champion JOHN PEEL was a fan (hipper-than-thou detractors take note!), playing the classic closing track, 'THE LAST RESORT', another song dealing with the jaded, faded City Of Angels. Guitarist JOE WALSH was partly responsible for the heavier sound, having replaced LEADON, while 1977 saw another line-up change with TIMOTHY B. SCHMIT taking the place of the departing MEISNER. The band's parting shot, 'THE LONG RUN' (1979) was another massive seller although it lacked the staying power of their previous efforts. After a live album in 1980, the band drifted apart with solo careers beckoning. HENLEY's career was set back somewhat in Nov'80, however, when a 16 year-old female was found naked and drugged in his Californian home (he was fined and ordered to attend a drug counselling scheme). The following year, he recorded his debut album, 'I CAN'T STAND STILL', with DANNY KORTCHMAR and GREG LADANYI, although this lay dormant until late 1982. In the meantime, he was credited on a US Top 10 single by STEVIE NICKS 'Leather And Lace'. Upon its release, his debut hit the US Top 30, helped by an appropriately titled Top 3 single, 'DIRTY LAUNDRY'. In '84, he moved to the 'Geffen' label, and secured a cross-Atlantic Top 20 single with the atmospheric 'THE BOYS OF SUMMER' and subsequent album, 'BUILDING THE PERFECT BEAST' (1985). Four years later, HENLEY garnered further critical acclaim with 'THE END OF THE INNOCENCE' album, his last solo work to date. FREY meanwhile, still contracted to 'Asylum' records, issued the US Top 40 album, 'NO FUN ALOUD', a easy-going set that found little sympathy with the British buying public. In 1984, his next Top 40 effort, 'THE ALLNIGHTER', prompted NBC TV to feature the sax-driven 'SMUGGLER'S BLUES' and FREY himself, on their 'Miami Vice' cop series. This gave him a cross-Atlantic Top 30 hit in 1985, and was followed by another hit song from the series, 'YOU BELONG TO THE CITY'. After a quiet two years, FREY returned to business with 1988's 'SOUL SEARCHIN' album. They had always insisted it would never happen, yet in 1994 a line-up of HENLEY, FREY, WALSH, FELDER and SCHMITT reformed for an MTV performance and tour. They even released an album, 'HELL FREEZES OVER', featuring material culled from the MTV show, together with four new cuts. Their Wembley Stadium show was eagerly anticipated although some of the new material was dodgy, 'ORDINARY AVERAGE GUY' springs to mind. The EAGLES have always been an easy and predictable target for the fashion police, yet their back catalogue contains some of the finest harmonies in rock history. With HENLEY unwilling to record any new material, 'Geffen' had to make do with a greatest hits set, 'ACTUAL MILES' (1995) and a re-released 'BOYS OF SUMMER' (a UK Top 20 hit in 1998) to see them through the final years of his contract. Eager for more creative control, HENLEY signed with 'Warners' and wasted no time in cutting his first album for over a decade, 'INSIDE JOB' (2000). Given how radically the music scene had changed since the late 80's, it was strangely heartening to hear the former EAGLE more or less taking up where he left off. So, no poorly judged trip hop experiments or Tom Jones covers, merely the pleasant sound of a singer/songwriter settling into middle age with only the occasional rant at society's downward spiral. To accompany yet another anthology (2003's double disc 'VERY BEST OF'), the EAGLES released their first new material in years in the shape of the 'HOLE IN THE WORLD' single. A stab of social conscience in the wake of 9/11, the single was typical harmony-rock fare with HENLEY in comfortably weathered vocal form.

• **Songwriters:** All took turns writing and also covered; OL' 55 (Tom Waits) / OUTLAW MAN (David Blue) / PLEASE COME HOME FOR CHRISTMAS (Charles Brown) / SEVEN BRIDGES ROAD (Steve Young). HENLEY covered EVERYBODY KNOWS (Leonard Cohen). • **Trivia:** In 1979, FREY, HENLEY and WALSH appeared on RANDY NEWMAN's 'Little Criminals'. In 1990, FREY was honoured by the Rock'n'charity foundation for his work to prevent against AIDS and cancer.

Album rating: EAGLES (*5) / DESPERADO (*8) / ON THE BORDER (*6) / ONE OF THESE NIGHTS (*8) / THEIR GREATEST HITS 1971-1975 compilation

*10) / HOTEL CALIFORNIA (*10) / THE LONG RUN (*6) / THE EAGLES .IVE (*4) / EAGLES GREATEST HITS, VOL.2 compilation (*6) / BEST OF THE EAGLES compilation (*7) / HELL FREEZES OVER (*5) / THE COMPLETE GREATEST HITS or THE VERY BEST OF . . . compilation (*8) / Glenn Frey: NO FUN ALOUD (*5) / THE ALLNIGHTER (*6) / SOUL SEARCHIN' (*5) / Don Henley: I CAN'T STAND STILL (*6) / BUILDING THE PERFECT BEAST (*7) / THE END OF THE INNOCENCE (*6) / ACTUAL MILES: HENLEY'S GREATEST HITS compilation (*6) / INSIDE JOB (*6) / ONE OF THESE NIGHTS (*6)

GLENN FREY (b. 6 Nov'48, Detroit, Mich.) – guitar, vocals (ex-LINDA RONSTADT Band, ex-LONGBRANCH PENWHISTLE) / **BERNIE LEADON** (b.19 Jul'47, Minneapolis, Minnesota) – guitar, vocals (ex-LINDA RONSTADT Band, ex-FLYING BURRITO BROTHERS) / **RANDY MEISNER** (b. 8 Mar'47, Scottsbluff, Nebraska) – bass, vocals (ex-LINDA RONSTADT Band, ex-POCO, ex-RICK NELSON) / **DON HENLEY** (b.22 Jul'47, Gilmer, Texas) – drums, vocals (ex-LINDA RONSTADT Band, ex-SHILOH)

Asylum Asylum

un 72. (7") *(AYM 505)* <11005> **TAKE IT EASY. / GET YOU IN THE MOOD** [ ] May72 [12]

ep 72. (7") *(AYM 508)* <11008> **WITCHY WOMAN. / EARLY BIRD** [ ] [9]

Oct 72. (lp/c) *(SYLA/SYTC 101)* <5054> **EAGLES** [ ] Jun 72 [22]
– Take it easy / Witchy woman / Chug all night / Most of us are sad / Nightingale / Train leaves here this morning / Take the Devil / Early bird / Peaceful easy feeling / Tryin'. *(re-iss. Jun76 lp/c; K/K4 53009) (cd-iss. Feb87; K2 53009)*

Dec 72. (7") <11013> **PEACEFUL EASY FEELING. / TRYIN'** [–] [22]

eb 73. (7") *(AYM 512)* **TRYIN'. / CHUG ALL NIGHT** [ ] [–]

Apr 73. (lp/c) *(SYLA/SYTC 9011)* <5068> **DESPERADO** [ ] [41]
– Doolin-Dalton / Twenty-one / Out of control / Tequila sunrise / Desperado / Certain kind of fool / Outlaw man / Saturday night / Bitter creek. *(re-iss. Aug75 lp/c; K/K4 53008)* – hit UK No.39 *(re-iss. Jun76; K/K4 53008) (cd-iss. 1989; K 253008)*

ul 73. (7") <11017> **TEQUILA SUNRISE. / TWENTY-ONE** [ ] Jun73 [64]

Oct 73. (7") *(AYM 523)* <11025> **OUTLAW MAN. / CERTAIN KIND OF FOOL** [ ] Sep73 [59]

— added **DON FELDER** (b.21 Sep'47, Gainsville, Florida) – guitar, vocals (ex-FLOW)

Apr 74. (lp/c) *(SYLA/SYTC 9016)* <7E 1004> **ON THE BORDER** [28] [17]
– Already gone / You never cry like a lover / Midnight flyer / My man / On the border / James Dean / Ol' 55 / Is it true / Good day in Hell / Best of my love. *(re-iss. Jun76 lp/c; K/K4 43005) (quad-lp 1977) (cd-iss. 1989; K2 43005)*

Apr 74. (7") <11036> **ALREADY GONE. / IS IT TRUE** [–] [32]

May 74. (7") *(AYM 527)* **JAMES DEAN. / IS IT TRUE** [ ] [–]

ul 74. (7") *(AYM 530)* **ALREADY GONE. / OL' 55** [ ] [–]

ep 74. (7") <45202> **JAMES DEAN. / GOOD DAY IN HELL** [–] [77]

Nov 74. (7") <45218> **BEST OF MY LOVE. / OL' 55** [–] [1]

Dec 74. (7") *(AYM 538)* **BEST OF MY LOVE. / MIDNIGHT FLYER** [ ] [–]

May 75. (7"m) *(AYM 542)* **MY MAN. / TAKE IT EASY / TEQUILA SUNRISE** [ ] [–]

un 75. (lp/c) *(SYLA/SYTC 8759)* <1039> **ONE OF THESE NIGHTS** [8] [1]
– One of these nights / Too many hands / Hollywood waltz / Journey of the sorceror / Lyin' eyes / Take it to the limit / Visions / After the thrill is gone / I wish you peace. *(re-iss. Jun76 lp/c; K/K4 53014) (quad-lp 1977) (cd-iss. 1989; K2 53014)*

un 75. (7") *(AYM 543)* <45257> **ONE OF THESE NIGHTS. / VISIONS** [23] May75 [1]

Oct 75. (7") *(AYM 548)* **LYIN' EYES. / JAMES DEAN** [23] [–]

Dec 75. (7") *(K 13025)* <45279> **LYIN' EYES. / TOO MANY HANDS** [ ] Sep75 [2]

Dec 75. (7") <45293> **TAKE IT TO THE LIMIT. / AFTER THE THRILL IS GONE** [–] [4]

eb 76. (7") *(K 13029)* **TAKE IT TO THE LIMIT. / TOO MANY HANDS** [12] [–]

eb 76. (lp/c) *(K/K4 53017)* <1052> **THEIR GREATEST HITS 1971-1975** (compilation) [2] [1]
– Take it easy / Witchy woman / Lyin' eyes / Already gone / Desperado / One of these nights / Tequila sunrise / Take it to the limit / Peaceful easy feeling / Best of my love. *(cd-iss. May87; 253 017-2)*

— **JOE WALSH** (b.20 Nov'47, Wichita, Kansas) – guitar, vocals (ex-Solo artist, ex-JAMES GANG),repl. LEADON who formed own duo band

Dec 76. (lp/c) *(K/K4 53051)* <1084> **HOTEL CALIFORNIA** [2] [1]
– Hotel California / New kid in town / Life in the fast lane / Wasted time / Wasted time (reprise) / Victim of love / Pretty maids all in a row / Try and love again / The last resort. *(cd-iss. May87; 253 051)*

Jan 77. (7") *(K 13069)* <45373> **NEW KID IN TOWN. / VICTIM OF LOVE** [20] Dec76 [1]

Apr 77. (7") *(K 13079)* <45386> **HOTEL CALIFORNIA. / PRETTY MAIDS ALL IN A ROW** [8] Feb77 [1]

Jun 77. (7") *(K 13085)* <45403> **LIFE IN THE FAST LANE. / THE LAST RESORT** [ ] May77 [11]

— **TIMOTHY B. SCHMIT** (b.30 Oct'47, Sacramento, Calif.) – bass, vocals (ex-POCO) repl. MEISNER who went solo.

— (SCHMIT now alongside FREY, HENLEY, WALSH and FELDER)

Dec 78. (7") *(K 13415)* <45555> **PLEASE COME HOME FOR CHRISTMAS. / FUNKY NEW YEAR** [30] [18]

— added p/t **JOE VITALE** – keyboards

Sep 79. (7") *(K 12394)* <46545> **HEARTACHE TONIGHT. / TEENAGE JAIL** [40] [1]

Sep 79. (lp/c) *(K/K4 52181)* <508> **THE LONG RUN** [4] [1]
– The long run / I can't tell you why / In the city / The disco strangler / King of Hollywood / Heartache tonight / Those shoes / Teenage jail / The Greeks don't want no freaks / The sad cafe. *(cd-iss. 1986; 252 181)*

Nov 79. (7") *(K 12404)* <46569> **THE LONG RUN. / THE DISCO STRANGLER** [66] [8]

Jan 80. (7") *(K 12418)* <46608> **I CAN'T TELL YOU WHY. / THE GREEKS DON'T WANT NO FREAKS** [ ] [8]

May 80. (7") *(K 12424)* **THE SAD CAFE. / THOSE SHOES** [ ] [–]

Jul 80. (7") <47004> **LYIN' EYES. / Johhny Lee: LOOKIN' FOR LOVE** [–] [ ]

Sep 80. (7") <47073> **LYIN' EYES. / Jimmy Buffet: HELLO TEXAS** [–] [ ]

Nov 80. (d-lp/d-c) *(K/K4 62032)* <705> **EAGLES LIVE (live)** [24] [6]
– Hotel California / Heartache tonight / I can't tell you why / The long run / New kid in town / Life's been good / Seven bridges road / Wasted time / Take it to the limit / Doolin-Dalton / Desperado / Saturday night / All night long / Life in the fast lane / Take it easy. *(d-cd-iss. Feb93; 7559 60591-2)*

Dec 80. (7") <47100> **SEVEN BRIDGES ROAD (live). / THE LONG RUN (live)** [–] [21]

Jan 81. (7") *(K 12504)* **TAKE IT TO THE LIMIT (live). / SEVEN BRIDGES ROAD (live) / TAKE IT EASY (live)** [ ] [–]

not iss. Full Moon

Mar 81. (7") <49654> **I CAN'T TELL YOU WHY. / Ambrosia: OUTSIDE** [–] [ ]

— By this time they had all mutually agreed to disband. All five went on to individual solo careers.

DON HENLEY

WEA Asylum

Sep 82. (7") *(K 13200)* <69971> **JOHNNY CAN'T READ. / LONG WAY HOME** [ ] Aug82 [42]

Elektra Asylum

Dec 82. (7") *(E 9849)* <69894> **DIRTY LAUNDRY. / LILAH** [59] Oct82 [3]
(12"+=) *(E 9849T)* – Them and us.
(re-iss. Jun85, 7"/12"; EKR 4/+T)

Jan 83. (7") <69931> **I CAN'T STAND STILL. / THEM AND US** [–] [48]

Asylum Asylum

Feb 83. (lp/c) *(K/K4 52365)* <60048> **I CAN'T STAND STILL** [ ] Aug82 [24]
– I can't stand still / You better hang up / Long way home / Nobody's business / Talking to the Moon / Dirty laundry / Johnny can't read / Them and us / La Eile / Lilah / The uncloudy day. *(cd-iss. Jun89; 960 048-2)*

May 83. (7") *(E 9876)* **THE UNCLOUDED DAY. / LONG WAY HOME** [ ] [–]
(12"+=) *(E 9876T)* – I can't stand still.

Jul 83. (7") <69831> **NOBODY'S BUSINESS. / LONG WAY HOME** [–] [ ]

Geffen Geffen

Dec 84. (7"/12") *(A/TA 4945)* <29141> **THE BOYS OF SUMMER. / A MONTH OF SUNDAYS** [12] Nov84 [5]

Feb 85. (lp/c) *(GEF/GEC 25939)* <24026> **BUILDING THE PERFECT BEAST** [14] Dec84 [13]
– The boys of summer / You can't make love / Man with a mission / You're not drinking enough / Not enough love in the world / Building the perfect beast / All she wants to do is dance / Sunset grill / Drivin' with your eyes closed / Land of the living. *(cd+=)* – A month of Sundays. *(re-iss. Sep86 lp/c; 924026-1/-4) (cd-iss. Feb87; 924026-2) (cd re-iss. 1988; CD 25939) (re-iss. Jan91 lp/c/cd; GEF/+C/D 24026) (cd re-iss. Mar95; GFLD 19267)*

Feb 85. (7") *<29065>* **ALL SHE WANTS TO DO IS DANCE. / BUILDING THE PERFECT BEAST** [–] [9]

Apr 85. (7") *(A 6161)* **SUNSET GRILL. / BUILDING THE PERFECT BEAST** [ ] [–]

Jul 85. (7") *(A 6419) <29012>* **NOT ENOUGH LOVE IN THE WORLD. / MAN WITH A MISSION** [ ] May85 [34]

Aug 85. (7") *<28906>* **SUNSET GRILL. / MAN WITH A MISSION** [–] [22]

— his basic back-up consisted of **DANNY KORTCHMAR** – guitar, keyboards / **STAN LYNCH** – drums / **PINO PALLADINO** – bass / **JAI WINDING** – keyboards / **MIKE CAMPBELL** – keyboards

Jun 89. (lp/c)(cd) *(WX 253/+C)(924217-2) <24217>* **THE END OF THE INNOCENCE** [17] [8]
– The end of the innocence / How bad do you want it? / I will not go quietly / The last worthless evening / New York minute / Shangri-la / Little tin god / Gimme what you got / If dirt were dollars / The heart of the matter. *(re-iss. Jan91 lp/c/cd; GEF/+C/D 24217) (cd re-iss. Oct95; GFLD 19285)*

Jul 89. (7"/c-s) *(GEF/+C 57) <22925>* **THE END OF THE INNOCENCE. / IF DIRT WERE DOLLARS** [48] Jun89 [8]
(12"+=/cd-s+=) *(GEF 57 T/CD)* – The boys of summer.

Oct 89. (7"/c-s) *(GEF 66)* **NEW YORK MINUTE. / GIMME WHAT YOU GOT** [ ] [–]
(10"+=/12"+=/cd-s+=) *(GEF 66 TE/T/CD)* – Sunset grill (live).

Oct 89. (7") *<22771>* **THE LAST WORTHLESS EVENING. / GIMME WHAT YOU GOT** [–] [21]

Feb 90. (7"/c-s) *(GEF 71)* **THE LAST WORTHLESS EVENING. / ALL SHE WANTS TO DO IS DANCE** [ ] [–]
(12"+=) *(GEF 71T)* – You can't make love.
(cd-s++=) *(GEF 71CD)* – ('A'version).

Feb 90. (c-s) *<19898>* **THE HEART OF THE MATTER / LITTLE TIN GOD** [–] [21]

Jun 90. (c-s) *<19699>* **HOW BAD DO YOU WANT IT? / NEW YORK MINUTE** [–] [48]

Oct 90. (c-s) *<19660>* **NEW YORK MINUTE / THE HEART OF THE MATTER (acoustic)** [–] [48]

— In Sep'92, HENLEY and PATTY SMYTH charted US No.2 / UK No.22 with 'SOMETIMES LOVE JUST AIN'T ENOUGH' on 'M.C.A.' <54403>

— In Mar'93, DON featured on TRISH YEARWOOD's single 'Walkaway Joe'.

Nov 95. (cd/c) *<(GED/GEC 24834)>* **ACTUAL MILES: HENLEY'S GREATEST HITS** (compilation + 2 new *) [ ] [48]
– Dirty laundry / The boys of summer / All she wants to do is dance / Not enough love in the world / Sunset grill / The end of the innocence / The last worthless evening / New York minute / The heart of the matter / The garden of Allah * / You don't know me at all *. *(cd+=)* – I get the message.

Jul 98. (c-s/cd-s) *(GFS C/TD 22350)* **THE BOYS OF SUMMER / ALL SHE WANTS TO DO IS DANCE / SOMETIMES LOVE JUST AIN'T ENOUGH** [12] [–]

Warners Warners

May 00. (cd/c) *<(9362 47083-2/-4)>* **INSIDE JOB** [25] [7]
– Nobody else in the world but you / Taking you home / For my wedding / Everything is different now / Workin' it / Goodbye to a river / Inside job / They're not here, they're not coming / Damn it, Rose / Miss ghost / The genie / Annabel / My thanksgiving.

Jun 00. (-) *<radio cut>* **TAKING YOU HOME** [–] [58]

– compilations, etc. –

Jul 02. (cd) *Traditional Line; <(TL 1350)>* **ONE OF THESE NIGHTS** (live 1993 Labor Day benefit concert) [ ] [ ]
– Hotel California / One of these nights / Desperado / End of innocence / Sunset grill / Boys of summer / Life in the fast lane / Volcano (with JIMMY BUFFET) / All she wants to do is dance / Margaritaville (with JIMMY BUFFET) / Dirty laundry / Well, well, well / The heart of the matter.

GLENN FREY

Asylum Asylum

Jun 82. (lp/c) *(K/K4 52395) <60129>* **NO FUN ALOUD** [ ] [32]
– I found somebody / The one you love / Party town / I volunteer / I've been born again / Sea cruise / That girl / All those lies / She can't let go / Don't give up.

Jul 82. (7") *(K 13812) <47466>* **I FOUND SOMEBODY. / SHE CAN'T LET GO** [ ] Jun82 [31]

Oct 82. (7") *<69974>* **THE ONE YOU LOVE. / ALL THOSE LIES** [–] [15]

Jan 83. (7") *<69857>* **ALL THOSE LIES. / THAT GIRL** [–] [41]

M.C.A. M.C.A

Jul 84. (lp/c) *(MCF/+C 3232) <5501>* **THE ALLNIGHTER** [ ] [37]
– The allnighter / Sexy girl / I got love / Somebody else / Lover's moon Smuggler's blues / Let's go home / Better in the U.S.A. / The heat is on New love. *(re-act.Jun85, hit UK No.31) (cd-iss. Jul85; DMCF 3232) (cd re-is Aug89; DMCL 1893) (re-iss. Apr92 cd/c; MCL D/C 19009)*

Sep 84. (7") *(MCA 911) <52413>* **SEXY GIRL. / BETTER IN THE U.S.A.** [ ] Aug84 [20]

Oct 84. (7") *<52461>* **THE ALLNIGHTER. / SMUGGLER'S BLUES** [–] [54]

Feb 85. (7"/12") *(MCA/+T 941) <52513>* **THE HEAT IS ON. / (other by Harold Faltermeyer)** [12] Nov84 [2]
above was taken from the film, 'Beverly Hills Cop'

Mar 85. (7") *<52546>* **SMUGGLER'S BLUES. / NEW LOVE** [–] [12]
below was issued on 'BBC' records in Britain only.

Jun 85. (7") *(RESL 170)* **SMUGGLER'S BLUES. / NEW LOVE** [22] [–]
(12"+=) *(12RSL 170)* – Living in darkness.

Jul 85. (7") *(MCA 965)* **SEXY GIRL. / BETTER IN THE U.S.A.** [ ] [–]
(12"+=) *(MCAT 965)* – The heat is on (dub) / New love.

Sep 85. (7") *<52651>* **YOU BELONG TO THE CITY. / SMUGGLER'S BLUES** [–] [2]

Oct 85. (7") *(MCA 1008)* **YOU BELONG TO THE CITY. / I GOT LOVE** [ ] [–]
(12"+=) *(MCAT 1008)* – ('A'version).

Sep 88. (7") *(MCA 1284) <53363>* **TRUE LOVE. / WORKING MAN** [ ] Aug88 [13]
(12"+=/cd-s+=) *(MCAT/DMCA 1284)* – The heat is on.

Oct 88. (lp/c/cd) *(MCF/MCFC/DMCF 3429) <6239>* **SOUL SEARCHIN'** [ ] Aug88 [36]
– Soul searchin' / Livin' right / True love / I did it for your love / Workin man / Two hearts / Some kind of blue / Can't put out this fire / Let pretend we're still in love / It's your life.

Jan 89. (7") *(MCA 1294) <53452>* **SOUL SEARCHIN'. / IT'S COLD DOWN HERE** [ ] [ ]
(12"+=/cd-s+=) *(MCAT/DMCA 1294)* – True love.

Mar 89. (7") *<53497>* **LIVIN' RIGHT. / SOUL SEARCHIN'** [–] [90]

May 89. (7") *<53684>* **TWO HEARTS. / SOME KIND OF BLUE** [–] [ ]

— now writes with keyboard player **JAY OLIVER** or **JACK TEMPCHIN**

Apr 91. (c-s) *<54060>* **PART OF ME, PART OF YOU** [–] [55]
above taken from the film 'Thelma And Louise'

Jul 92. (c-s) *<54429>* **I'VE GOT MINE / A WALK IN THE DARK** [–] [91]

Jul 92. (7"/c-s) **I'VE GOT MINE. / PART OF ME, PART OF YOU** [ ] [–]
(cd-s+=) – A walk in the dark.

Aug 92. (cd/c) *<(MCA D/C 10599)>* **STRANGE WEATHER** [ ] Jul92 [ ]
– Silent spring / Long hot summer / Strange weather / Agua tranquillo Love in the 21st century / He took advantage / River of dreams / Before th ship goes down / I've got mine / Rising sun / Brave new world / Delicious A walk in the dark / Big life / Part of me, part of you.

Sep 92. (c-s) *<54461>* **RIVER OF DREAMS / HE TOOK ADVANTAGE** [–] [ ]

Mar 93. (c-s) *<54564>* **LOVE IN THE 21st CENTURY** [–] [ ]

May 93. (cd/c) *<(MCD/MCC 10826)>* **LIVE (live)** [ ] Jul93 [ ]
– Peaceful easy feeling / New kid in town / The one you love / Wi mountain thyme / Strange weather / I've got mine / Lyin' eyes – Take easy (medley) / River of dreams / True love / Love in the 21st century Smuggler's blues / The heat is on / Heartache tonight / Desperado. *(c re-iss. Mar03; AAMCAD 10826)*

Jul 93. (c-s) *<54699>* **STRANGE WEATHER (live)** [–] [ ]

– compilations, etc. –

Apr 95. (cd) *M.C.A.; <(MCD 11227)>* **SOLO CONNECTION** [ ] [ ]
– This way to happiness / Who's been sleeping in my bed / Commo ground / Call on me / The one you love / Sexy girl / Smuggler's blues The heat is on / You belong to the city / True love / Soul searchin' / Pa of me, part of you / I've got mine / River of dreams / Brave new world.

Jul 96. (d-cd) *M.C.A.; (MCD 33727)* **SOUL SEARCHIN' / STRANGE WEATHER** [ ] [ ]

Sep 00. (cd) *M.C.A.; <112359>* **THE BEST OF GLENN FREY – THE MILLENNIUM COLLECTION** [–] [ ]

Jul 01. (cd) *Universal; (E 112497-2)* **UNIVERSAL MASTERS COLLECTION** [ ] [–]

Jan 02. (cd) *Universal; <1073>* **THE BEST OF GLENN FREY** [–] [ ]

EAGLES

re-formed **HENLEY / FREY / WALSH / FELDER + SCHMIDT**

Geffen Geffen

Nov 94. (cd/c) <*(GED/GEC 24725)*> **HELL FREEZES OVER** [28] [1]
– Get over it / Love will keep us alive / The girl from yesterday / Learn to be still / Tequila sunrise / Hotel California / Wasted time / Pretty maids all in a row / I can't tell you why / New York minute / The last resort / Take it easy / In the city / Life in the fast lane / Desperado.

Nov 94. (c-s) <*19376*> **GET OVER IT / ('A'live version)** [–] [31]

Jul 96. (c-s) *(GFSC 21980)* **LOVE WILL KEEP US ALIVE / NEW YORK MINUTE** [52] [–]
(cd-s+=) *(GFSTD 21980)* – Help me through the night.

— the EAGLES were back (**HENLEY, FREY, WALSH + SCHMIDT**)

Oct 03. (cd-s) *(8122 74547-2)* **HOLE IN THE WORLD / HOLE IN THE WORLD (live)** [69] [ ]

– compilations etc. –

Note; All releases on 'Asylum' unless mentioned otherwise

Sep 76. (7") *(K 13044)* **TAKE IT EASY. / WITCHY WOMAN** [ ] [–]

Sep 76. (7") *(K 13045)* **PEACEFUL EASY FEELING. / OL' 55** [ ] [–]

Sep 76. (7") *(K 13046)* **TEQUILA SUNRISE. / ON THE BORDER** [ ] [–]

Oct 82. (lp/c) *Elektra; (E 205-1/-4) / Asylum; <60205>* **EAGLES GREATEST HITS – VOLUME 2** [ ] [52]
– Hotel California / Heartache tonight / Life in the fast lane / Seven bridges road / The sad cafe / I can't tell you why / New kid in town / The long run / Victim of love / After the thrill is gone. *(cd-iss. Dec82; 960 205-2)*

Oct 83. (d-c) *(K4 62033)* **DESPERADO / ONE OF THESE NIGHTS** [ ] [–]

Nov 83. (d-c) *(960 275-4)* **HOTEL CALIFORNIA / THE LONG RUN** [ ] [–]

May 85. (lp/c) *Elektra; (EKT 5/+C)* **THE BEST OF THE EAGLES** [10] [–]
– Tequila sunrise / Lyin' eyes / Take it to the limit / Hotel California / Life in the fast lane / Heartache tonight / The long run / Take it easy / Peaceful easy feeling / Desperado / Best of my love / One of these nights / New kid in town. *(re-hit.Aug88 made UK No.8)*

Sep 85. (7") *Old Gold; (OG 9510)* **TAKE IT TO THE LIMIT. / BEST OF MY LOVE** [ ] [–]

Sep 85. (7") *Old Gold; (OG 9511)* **HOTEL CALIFORNIA. / DESPERADO** [ ] [–]

Oct 85. (7") *Old Gold; (OG 9526)* **LYIN' EYES. / ONE OF THESE NIGHTS** [ ] [–]

Jun 88. (7") *(EKR 10)* **HOTEL CALIFORNIA. / PRETTY MAIDS ALL IN A ROW** [ ] [–]
(12"+=) *(EKRT 10)* – The sad cafe.
(cd-s++=) *(EKRCD 10)* – Hotel California (live).

Jun 89. (cd-ep) **TAKE IT EASY / ONE OF THESE NIGHTS / DESPERADO / LYIN' EYES** [ ] [–]

Jul 94. (cd/c) *(9548 32375-2/-4)* **THE VERY BEST OF EAGLES** [5] [–]
– Take it easy / Witchy woman / Peaceful easy feeling / Doolin-Dalton / Desperado / Tequila sunrise / The best of my love / James Dean / I can't tell you why / Lyin' eyes / Take it to the limit / One of these nights / Hotel California / New kid in town / Life in the fast lane / Heartache tonight / The long run.

Nov 00. (4xcd-box) <*(7559 62575-2)*> **SELECTED WORKS: 1972-1999** [ ] [ ]

May 01. (cd/c) *Elektra; (7559 62680-2/-4)* **THE VERY BEST OF EAGLES** (diff. tracks) [3] [–]

Oct 03. (d-cd) *W.S.M.; (8122 73731-2) <73971>* **THE COMPLETE GREATEST HITS** <US title 'THE VERY BEST OF . . .'> [27] [3]
– Take it easy / Witchy woman / Peaceful easy feeling / Desperado / Tequila sunrise / Doolin-Dalton / Already gone / The best of my love / James Dean / Ol' 55 / Midnight flyer / On the border / Lyin' eyes / One of these nights / Take it to the limit / After the thrill is gone / Hotel California / Life in the fast lane / Wasted time / Victim of love / The last resort / New kid in town / Please come home for Christmas / Heartache tonight / The sad cafe / I can't tell you why / The long run / In the city / Those shoes / Seven bridges road (live) / Love will keep us alive / Get over it / Hole in the world.

Jun 06. (re; d-cd) *(as prev.)* **THE COMPLETE EAGLES** [9] [–]

EAGLES OF DEATH METAL

(see under ⇒ QUEENS OF THE STONE AGE)

EARTH, WIND & FIRE

Formed: Chicago, Illinois, USA . . . 1969 as the SALTY PEPPERS by ex-'Chess' session man, MAURICE WHITE, who gathered together a jazz/fusion/funk ensemble of VERDINE WHITE, WADE FLEMONS, DON WHITEHEAD, MICHAEL BEAL, SHERRY SCOTT, YACKOV BEN ISRAEL, CHET WASHINGTON and ALEX THOMAS. Changing their name to EARTH, WIND & FIRE the following year, the band (who'd moonlighted on Melvin Van Peebles' blaxploitation bodyshock 'Sweet Sweetback's Baadasssss Song') signed to 'Warners' and released their eponymous debut set in spring '71. A further set, 'THE NEED OF LOVE', appeared in early '72, prior to a major personnel upheaval (and a change of labels to 'Columbia') which saw the induction of the silky voiced PHILIP BAILEY as frontman; by the release of 1973's 'HEAD TO THE SKY', the line-up had stabilised around VERDINE, LARRY DUNN, RALPH JOHNSON, AL McKAY, ANDREW WOODFOLK, JESSICA CLEAVES and JOHNNY GRAHAM. While that album gave the group their first major US chart success, it was 'OPEN OUR EYES' (1974), which began to encompass WHITE's pseudo mystical concepts into a more commercially viable proposition. A laidback, creamy rich blend of soul/funk with a finely polished pop sensibiltiy, 'THAT'S THE WAY OF THE WORLD' (1975) and its flagship single, 'SHINING STAR' both topped the US charts, beginning an extended run of chart success. 'GRATITUDE' (1975), 'SPIRIT' (1976) and 'ALL 'N' ALL' (1978) made the American Top 3 while EARTH, WIND & FIRE got to grips with disco on the enduring glitter ball favourite, 'BOOGIE WONDERLAND'. Recorded with female backing group, The EMOTIONS, the track was one of their bigger British hits, culled from 1979 album, 'I AM' (1979). Though their success continued into the early 80's, the group's creative and commercial flame began to dampen and they split in '84. Three years later, a core of the WHITE brothers, BAILEY and WOODFOLK reformed the band and continued to release and record material into the 90's (including 'HERITAGE' and 'MILLENNIUM') with mixed results. Into the millennium itself, EW&F finally came in from the cold with US Top 100 album, 'THE PROMISE' (2003). Better still was their 2005 effort, 'ILLUMINATION', a US Top 40 record with a contemporary production and guest appearances by hip-hop/R&B luminaries OUTKAST and the BLACK EYED PEAS, artists whose smoove grooves owe at least a little to the WHITE dynasty.

• **Songwriters:** WHITE penned with others, except covers MAKE IT WITH YOU (Bread) / WHERE HAVE ALL THE FLOWERS GONE (Pete Seeger) / GOT TO GET YOU INTO MY LIFE (Beatles) / AFTER THE LOVE HAS GONE (c.David Foster, Bill Champlin + Jay Graydon).

Album rating: EARTH, WIND & FIRE (*4) / THE NEED OF LOVE (*4) / LAST DAYS AND TIME (*4) / HEAD TO THE SKY (*6) / OPEN OUR EYES (*6) / THAT'S THE WAY OF THE WORLD (*7) / GRATITUDE (*6) / SPIRIT (*7) / ALL 'N ALL (*6) / THE BEST OF EARTH, WIND & FIRE, VOL.1 compilation (*8) / I AM (*6) / FACES (*6) / RAISE! (*5) / POWERLIGHT (*4) / ELECTRIC UNIVERSE (*4) / TOUCH THE WORLD (*5) / THE BEST OF EARTH, WIND & FIRE, VOL.II compilation (*6) / HERITAGE (*3) / MILLENNIUM (*4) / PLUGGED IN AND LIVE (*3) / IN THE NAME OF LOVE (*4) / THE PROMISE (*5) / ILLUMINATION (*6)

MAURICE WHITE (b.19 Dec'41, Memphis, USA) – vocals, drums, percussion, etc (ex-RAMSEY LEWIS TRIO, also sessioned for IMPRESSIONS / JACKIE WILSON / etc.) / **VERDINE WHITE** (b.25 Jul'51) – bass / **WADE FLEMONS** – keyboards, vocals / **DON WHITEHEAD** – piano, vocals / **MICHAEL BEAL** – guitar, etc. / **SHERRY SCOTT** – vocals / **YACKOV BEN ISRAEL** – congas, etc. / **CHET WASHINGTON** – tenor sax / **ALEX THOMAS** – trombone

not iss. Capitol

Feb 69. (7"; as the SALTY PEPPERS) <*2433*> **LA LA TIME. / (part II)** [–] [ ]

Sep 69. (7"; as the SALTY PEPPERS) *<2568>* **YOUR LOVE IS LIFE. / UH HUH YEAH** – [ ]
Warners Warners

Jan 71. (7") *<7480>* **THIS WORLD TODAY. / FAN THE FIRE** – [ ]

Mar 71. (7") *<7492>* **LOVE IS LIFE. / THIS WORLD TODAY** – 93

Mar 71. (lp) *<(WS 1905)>* **EARTH, WIND AND FIRE** [ ] [ ]
– Help somebody / Moment of truth / Love is life / Fan the fire / C'mon children / The world today / Bad tune. *(cd-iss. Jan96; 7599 26861-2)*

May 71. (7") *(WB 6125)* **HELP SOMEBODY. / LOVE IS LIFE** [ ] –

Nov 71. (7") *<7549>* **C'MON CHILDREN. / I THINK ABOUT LOVIN' YOU** – [ ]

Jan 72. (lp) *<WS 1958>* **THE NEED OF LOVE** – 89
– Energy / Beauty / I can feel it in my bones / I think about lovin' you / Everything is everything. *(cd-iss. Jan96; 7599 26862-2)*

— **WHITE** retains only brother **VERDINE,** and recruited/**employed new line-up PHILIP BAILEY** (b. 8 May'51, Denver, Colorado) – vocals, percussion / **LARRY DUNN** (b.19 Jun'53, Colorado) – keyboards, clavinet /**RALPH JOHNSON** (b. 4 Jul'51, California) – drums, percussion / **ROLAND BAUTISTA** – guitar / **RONALD LAWS** – saxophone, flute / **JESSICA CLEAVES** (b.1943) – vocals

C.B.S. Columbia

Oct 72. (lp/c) *(CBS/40 65208) <31702>* **LAST DAYS AND TIME** [ ] 87
– Time is on your side / They don't see / Make it with you / Power / Remember the children / Where have all the flowers gone / I'd rather have you / Mom. *(re-iss. Oct79 lp/c; CBS/40 31761) (cd-iss. Feb92 on 'Columbia'; 982736-2)*

— **AL McKAY** (b. 2 Feb'48, Louisiana) – guitar repl. BAUTISTA / **ANDREW WOODFOLK** (b.11 Oct'50, Texas) – horns repl. LAWS who went solo / added **JOHNNY GRAHAM** (b. 3 Aug'51, Kentucky)

May 73. (lp/c) *(CBS/40 65604) <32194>* **HEAD TO THE SKY** [ ] 27
– Evil / Keep your head to the sky / Build your nest / The world's masquerade / Clover / Zanzibar. *(quad-lp 1975; CBSQ 65604) (re-iss. Mar81 lp/c; CBS/40 32017) (cd-iss. Sep93 on 'Sony Collectors'; 982997-2)*

Oct 73. (7") *(CBS 1792) <45888>* **EVIL. / CLOVER** [ ] Jul73 50

Feb 74. (7") *(CBS 2033) <45953>* **KEEP YOUR HEAD TO THE SKY. / BUILD YOUR NEST** [ ] Nov73 53

— now w/out JESSICA

May 74. (7") *(CBS 2284) <46007>* **MIGHTY MIGHTY. / DRUM SONG** [ ] Mar74 29

Jun 74. (lp/c) *(CBS/40 65844) <32712>* **OPEN OUR EYES** [ ] Mar74 15
– Mighty mighty / Devotion / Fair but so uncool / Feelin' blue / Kalimba story / Drum song / Tee nine chee bit / Spasmodic mood / Caribou / Open our eyes. *(re-iss. Mar81; 32033)*

Sep 74. (7") *<10026>* **DEVOTION. / FAIR BUT SO UNCOOL** – 33

Nov 74. (7") *(CBS 2782) <46070>* **KALIMBA STORY. / TEE NINE CHEE BIT** [ ] Jul74 55

— added other brother **FRED WHITE** (b.13 Jan'55, Chicago) – drums

— Early 1975, EARTH WIND & FIRE were credited on two US Top 50 singles by RAMSEY LEWIS; 'Hot Dawgit' <10056> and 'Sun Goddess' <10103>.

Apr 75. (lp/c) *(CBS/40 80575) <33280>* **THAT'S THE WAY OF THE WORLD** [ ] Mar75 1
– Shining star / That's the way of the world / Happy feelin' / All about love / Yearnin', learnin' / Reasons / Africano / See the light. *(re-iss. Nov81 on 'CBS-Embassy'; 32054) (cd-iss. May87; CD 80575) (cd re-iss. Feb97 on 'Columbia'; 484467-2) <US cd-iss. 1999 on 'Legacy'+=; 65920>* – (extra mixes).

Apr 75. (7") *(CBS 3137) <10090>* **SHINING STAR. / YEARNIN', LEARNIN'** [ ] Feb75 1

Jul 75. (7") *(CBS 3519) <10172>* **THAT'S THE WAY OF THE WORLD. / AFRICANO** [ ] Jun75 12

Nov 75. (7") *(CBS 3847)* **SHININ' STAR (live). / HAPPY FEELIN'** [ ] –

Dec 75. (d-lp) *(CBS 88160) <33694>* **GRATITUDE (most live)** [ ] Nov75 1
– (introduction) / Sing a song / Gratitude / Celebrate / Can't hide love / Sunshine / Shining star / Sun Goddess / reasons / Sing a message to you / Devotion / Medley: Africano – Power / Yearnin', learnin'. *(re-iss. May82; CBS 22129) (cd-iss. 1987; CD 88160)*

Feb 76. (7") *(CBS 3859) <10251>* **SING A SONG (live). / (instrumental)** [ ] Nov75 5

Mar 76. (7") *<10309>* **CAN'T HIDE LOVE. / GRATITUDE** – 39

May 76. (7") *(CBS 4240)* **REASONS (live). / GRATITUDE** [ ] –

Aug 76. (7") *(CBS 4532) <10373>* **GETAWAY. / (instrumental)** [ ] Jul76 12

Nov 76. (lp/c) *(CBS/40 81451) <34241>* **SPIRIT** [ ] Sep76 2
– Getaway / On your face / Imagination / Spirit / Saturday nite / Earth wind and fire / Departure / Biyo / Burnin' bush. *(re-iss. Apr84 o[n] 'Pickwick'; SHM 3133)*

Jan 77. (7") *(CBS 4835) <10439>* **SATURDAY NITE. / DEPARTURE** 17 Nov76 21

Apr 77. (7") *<10492>* **BIYO. / ON YOUR FACE** – [ ]

Jun 77. (7") *<10512>* **ON YOUR FACE. / SATURDAY NITE (live)** – [ ]

Dec 77. (7") *(CBS 5778) <10625>* **SERPENTINE FIRE. / (instrumental)** [ ] Oct77 13

Jan 78. (lp/c) *(CBS/40 86051) <34905>* **ALL 'N' ALL** 13 Nov77 3
– Serpentine fire / Fantasy / In the market place / Jupiter / Love's holiday / Brazillian rhyme / I'll write a song for you / Master mind / Runnin' / Be ever wonderful. *(re-iss. Mar83 lp/c; CBS/40 32266) (cd-iss. May87; C[D] 82238) (re-iss. Apr94 on 'Sony Collectors' cd/c; 982842-2/-4)*

Jan 78. (7") *<10688>* **FANTASY. / RUNNIN'** – 32

Feb 78. (7") *(CBS 6056)* **FANTASY. / BOOGIE WONDERLAND** 14 –

Apr 78. (7") *(CBS 6267)* **JUPITER. / RUNNIN'** 41 –

Jul 78. (7") *(CBS 6490)* **MAGIC MIND. / LOVE'S HOLIDAY** 54 –

Sep 78. (7") *(CBS 6553) <10796>* **GOT TO GET YOU INTO MY LIFE. / I'LL WRITE A SONG FOR YOU** 33 Jul78 9

Oct 78. (7") *<10854>* **SEPTEMBER. / LOVE'S HOLIDAY** – 8

Nov 78. (7") *(CBS 6922)* **SEPTEMBER. / CAN'T HAVE LOVE** 3 –

Dec 78. (lp/c) *(CBS/40 83284) <35647>* **THE BEST OF EARTH, WIND & FIRE, VOL.1** (compilation) 6 Nov78 6
– Got to get you into my life / Fantasy / Can't hide love / Saturday night / Love music / Getaway / That's the way of the world / September / Shinin[g] star / Reasons / Sing a song. *(re-iss. Nov84 lp/c; CBS/40 32536) (cd-iss. Jun8[9]; CD 32536) (cd re-iss. Oct94 on 'Columbia'; 477508-2)*

May 79. (7"/12"; EARTH, WIND & FIRE WITH THE EMOTIONS) *(CBS 7292) <10956>* **BOOGIE WONDERLAND. / (instrumental)** 4 6

Jun 79. (lp/c) *(CBS/40 86084) <35730>* **I AM** 5 3
– In the stone / Can't let go / After the love has gone / Let your feeling show / Boogie wonderland / Star / Wait / Rock that / You and I. *(re-is[s]. Jun85 lp/c; CBS/40 32656) (cd-iss. May87; CD 86084)*

Jul 79. (7") *(CBS 7721) <11033>* **AFTER THE LOVE HAS GONE. / ROCK THAT** 4 2

Sep 79. (7") *(CBS 7902) <11165>* **STAR. / YOU AND I** 16 Dec79 64

Oct 79. (7") *<11093>* **IN THE STONE. / YOU AND I** – 58

Dec 79. (7") *(CBS 8077)* **CAN'T LET GO. / LOVE MUSIC** 46 –

Feb 80. (7") *(CBS 8252)* **IN THE STONE. / AFRICAN BIYO** 53 –

Sep 80. (7") *(CBS 8982) <11366>* **LET ME TALK. / (instrumental)** 29 44

Oct 80. (d-lp/c) *(CBS/40 88498) <36795>* **FACES** 10 10
– Let me talk / Turn it into something good / Pride / You / Sparkle / Bac[k] on the road / Song in my heart / You went away / And love goes on / Sa[il] away / Take it to the sky / Win or lose / Share your love / In time / Faces. *(cd-iss. Mar94 on 'Sony Collectors'; 983316-2) (cd-iss. Feb97 on 'Columbia'; 474679-2)*

Nov 80. (7") *<11407>* **YOU. / SHARE YOUR LOVE** – [ ]

Dec 80. (7") *(CBS 9377)* **BACK ON THE ROAD. / TAKE IT TO THE SKY** 63 –

Jan 80. (7") *<11434>* **AND LOVE GOES ON. / WIN OR LOSE** – 59

Feb 81. (7") *(CBS 9521)* **AND LOVE GOES ON. / FACES** [ ] –

May 81. (7") *(A 1204)* **YOU. / PRIDE** [ ] –

— **ROLAND BAUTISTA** – guitar rejoined repl. McKAY who went int[o] production.

Oct 81. (7") *(A 1679) <02536>* **LET'S GROOVE. / (instrumental)** 3 3

Nov 81. (lp/c) *(CBS/40 85272) <37548>* **RAISE!** 14 5
– Let's groove / Lady Sun / My love / Evolution orange / Kalimba tree / You are a winner / I've had enough / Wanna be with you / The changin[g] times. *(cd-iss. Aug86; CD 85272)*

Jan 82. (7") *(A 1959)* **I'VE HAD ENOUGH. / KALIMBA TREE (instrumental)** 29 –

Jan 82. (7") *<02688>* **WANNA BE WITH YOU. / KALIMBA TREE (instrumental)** – 51

Mar 82. (7") *(A 2074)* **WANNA BE WITH YOU. / MY LOVE** [ ] –

Jan 83. (7"/12") *(A/+12 2927) <03375>* **FALL IN LOVE WITH ME. / LADY SUN** 47 17

Feb 83. (lp/c) *(CBS/40 25120) <38367>* **POWERLIGHT** 22 12
– Fall in love with me / Spread your love / Side by side / Straight fro[m] the heart / The speed of love / Freedom of choice / Something special / Heart to heart / Miracles. *(cd-iss. 1988; CD 25120) (cd re-iss. Oct93 on 'Son[y] Europe')*

Mar 83. (7") *(A 3211)* **SPREAD YOUR LOVE. / HEART TO HEART** [ ] [–]
May 83. (7") *<03814>* **SIDE BY SIDE. / SOMETHING SPECIAL** [–] [76]
Jul 83. (7"/12") *<04002/04008>* **SPREAD YOUR LOVE. / FREEDOM OF CHOICE** [–] [ ]

— Still a member, PHIL BAILEY also takes on solo career.

Nov 83. (7"/12") *(A/TA 3887) <04210/04211>* **MAGNETIC. / SPEED OF LOVE** [ ] [57]
Dec 83. (lp/c) *(CBS/40 25775) <38980>* **ELECTRIC UNIVERSE** [ ] [40]
– Magnetic / Touch / Moonwalk / Could it be right / Spirit of a new world / Sweet sassy lady / We're living in our own time / Electic nation. *(cd-iss. 1988; CD 25772)*
Feb 84. (7") *(A 4164)* **TOUCH. / SEPTEMBER** [ ] [–]
(12"+=) *(TA 4164)* – After the love has gone / Boogie wonderland.
Feb 84. (7") *<04329>* **TOUCH. / SWEET SASSY LADY** [–] [ ]
May 84. (7") *<04427>* **MOONWALK. / WE'RE LIVING IN OUR OWN TIME** [–] [ ]

— disbanded March '84; both MAURICE and PHILIP continued solo

— they re-formed with (**MAURICE WHITE, VERDINE WHITE, PHILIP BAILEY, ANDREW WOODFOLK**)plus new man **SHELDON REYNOLDS** – guitar + loads of session people

Oct 87. (7") *(EWF 1) <07608>* **SYSTEM OF SURVIVAL. / WRITING ON THE WALL** [54] [60]
(12"+=) *(EWFT 1)* – ('A'acappella) / ('A'dub).
(12"+=/cd-s+=) *(EWFQT/CDEWF 1)* – ('A'-12"version).
Nov 87. (lp/c/cd) *(460409-1/-4/-2) <40596>* **TOUCH THE WORLD** [ ] [33]
– System of survival / Evil boy / Thinking of you / You and I / Musical interlude: new horizons / Money tight / Every now and then / Touch the world / Here today and gone tomorrow / Victim of the modern heart.
Dec 87. (7") *<07687>* **MUSICAL INTERLUDE: NEW HORIZONS. / YOU AND I** [–] [ ]
Feb 88. (7") *(EWF 2) <07695>* **THINKING OF YOU. / MONEY TIGHT** [ ] [67]
(12"+=) *(EWFT 2)* – ('A'version).
(12"+=/cd-s+=) *(EWFQT/CDEWF 2)* – ('A'-House mix).
Feb 88. (7") *<07687>* **EVIL BOY. / (part 2)** [–] [ ]
Nov 88. (7") *<08107>* **TURN ON (THE BEAT BOX). / (part 2)** [–] [ ]
Dec 88. (lp/c/cd) *<45013>* **THE BEST OF EARTH, WIND & FIRE, VOL.1** (compilation) [–] [ ]
– Turn on (the beat box) / Let's groove / After the love has gone / Fantasy / Devotion / Serpentine fire / Love's holiday / Boogie wonderland / Saturday nite / Mighty mighty. *(UK-iss.May91 on 'Columbia' cd/c; 463200-2/-4)*

— added **RALPH JOHNSON** – percussion / **SONNY EMORY** – drums / + **session people**

Feb 90. (7"/c-s) *(EWF/+M 3) <73205>* **HERITAGE. / GOTTA FIND OUT** [ ] [ ]
(12"+=) *(EWFT 3)* – ('A'acappella) / Let's groove (extended).
(cd-s+=) *(CDEWF 3)* – Fantasy / September / ('A'extended).
(12"+=) *(EWFQT 3)* – Brazillian rhyme (interlude) / Got to get you into my life / I've had enough.
Mar 90. (cd/c/lp) *(466242-2/-4/-1) <45268>* **HERITAGE** [ ] Feb90 [70]
– Soweto / Takin' chances / Heritage / Good time / Body wrap / Anything you want / Bird / Wanna be the man / Close to home / Daydreamin' / King of the groove / I'm in love / For the love of you / Gotta find out / Motor / Faith / Welcome / Soweto (reprise).
Apr 90. (c-s) *<73344>* **FOR THE LOVE OF YOU / MOTOR** [–] [ ]
Sep 90. (7"/c-s) *<73436>* **WANNA BE THE MAN. / WELCOME** [ ] [ ]
(ext.12"+=/cd-s+=) *<73396>* – ('A'dub version).

Reprise Reprise
Sep 93. (cd/c) *<(9362 45274-2/-4)>* **MILLENNIUM** [ ] [39]
– Even if you wonder / Sunday morning / Blood brothers / Kalimba interlude / Spend the night / Divine / Two hearts / Honor the magic / Love is the greatest story / The L word / Just another lonely night / Super hero / Wouldn't change a thing about you / Love across the wire / Chicago (Chitown) blues / Kalimba blues.
Oct 93. (7"/c-s) *(W 0205/+C) <18461>* **SUNDAY MORNING. / THE L WORD** [ ] Aug93 [53]
(cd-s+=) *(W 0205CD)* – Just another lonely heart.

Avex not iss.
Nov 95. (cd/c) *(AVEX CD/MC 20)* **PLUGGED IN AND LIVE (live)** [ ] [–]
– In the stone / September / Let your feelings show / Let's groove / Sun goddess / Can't hide love / Boogie wonderland / Fantasy / Reason / That's the way of the world / Africano / I'll write a song for you / Be ever wonderful / After the love is gone / Shining star / System of survival / Sing a song / Devotion.

Eagle Rhino
Jul 97. (cd/c) *(EAG CD/MC 002) <R2/R4 72864>* **IN THE NAME OF LOVE** [ ] [ ]
– Revolution / Rock it / In the name of love / Revolution / When loves goes wrong / Fill you up / The right time / Round and round / Keep it real / Cruising / Love is life / Avatar (interlude).

Snapper Kalimba
Mar 04. (cd) *(SNAZ608CDX) <97300-2>* **THE PROMISE** [ ] May03 [89]
– All in the way / Betcha' / Wiggle / Why? / Wonderland / Where do we go from here? / Freedom / Hold me / Never / Prelude / All about love / Suppose you like me / The promise / She waits / The promise (continued) / Let me love you / Dirty.
Apr 04. (cd-s) *(SNAZ 605CD)* **ALL IN THE WAY / (mixes; Real people / Dogsun / Blacq & Wright)** [ ] [–]

— added guest **RAPHAEL SAADIQ** – vocals (ex-TONY! TONI! TONE!)

Sanctuary Sanctuary
Sep 05. (cd) *(SANCD 312) <87513>* **ILLUMINATION** [ ] [32]
– Lovely people / Pure gold / A talking voice (interlude) / Love's dance / Show me the way / This is how I feel / Work it out / Pass you by / The one / Elevated / Liberation / To you / The way you move.

– compilations, others, etc. –

on 'C.B.S.' UK / 'Columbia' US unless mentioned otherwise

Sep 74. (d-lp) *Warners; <2798>* **ANOTHER TIME** (first 2 albums) [–] [97]
1975. (7") *(13-33247)* **KEEP YOUR HEAD TO THE SKY. / EVIL** [ ] [–]
Apr 77. (7") *(CBS 5198)* **SING A SONG. / BIYO** [ ] [–]
Oct 79. (t-lp-box) *(CBS 66350)* **EARTH, WIND & FIRE** – (3 early albums) [ ] [–]
Aug 80. (7") *(CBS 8848)* **AFTER THE LOVE HAS GONE. / THAT'S THE WAY OF THE WORLD** [ ] [–]
Aug 80. (7") *(CBS 8876)* **FANTASY. / BOOGIE WONDERLAND** [ ] [–]
Oct 80. (lp) *Pickwick; (SSP 3078)* **EARTH, WIND & FIRE** [ ] [–]
1982. (c-ep) **SING A SONG / BIYO / SHINING STAR / THAT'S THE END OF THE WORLD** [ ] [–]
Sep 85. (7") *Old Gold; (OG 9556)* **FANTASY. / SEPTEMBER** [ ] [–]
Sep 85. (7") *Old Gold; (OG 9558)* **BOOGIE WONDERLAND. / LET'S GROOVE** [ ] [–]
Feb 86. (12"ep) *Old Gold; (OG 4008)* **STAR / SATURDAY NITE. / AFTER THE LOVE HAS GONE / I'VE HAD ENOUGH** [ ] [–]
May 86. (lp)(c)(cd) *K-Tel; (NE1/CD2/NCD3 322)* **THE COLLECTION** [ ] [–]
Jun 86. (7"/12") *(A/TA 7253)* **BOOGIE WONDERLAND. / LET'S GROOVE** [ ] [–]
May 88. (cd) *Arcade; (ADEHCD 821-0)* **THE VERY BEST OF . . . VOL.1** [ ] [–]
May 88. (cd) *Arcade; (ADEHCD 821-1)* **THE VERY BEST OF . . . VOL.2** [ ] [–]
Dec 90. (3xcd-box) *Columbia; (467388-2)* **I AM / ALL 'N' ALL / RAISE** [ ] [–]
Jan 93. (3xcd-box/3xc-box) *Columbia; (472614-2/-4)* **THE ETERNAL DANCE** [ ] [ ]
Jul 94. (3xcd-box) *Columbia; (468804-2)* **POWERLIGHT / ELECTRIC UNIVERSE / SPIRIT** [ ] [ ]
Dec 95. (cd/c) *Columbia; (467768-2/-4)* **THE LOVE SONGS** [ ] [ ]
Sep 96. (cd/c) *Telstar; (TCD/STAC 2879)* **BOOGIE WONDERLAND – THE BEST OF . . .** [35] [–]
Mar 97. (cd/lp) *Stax; (CDSXE/SXD 103)* **SWEET SWEETBACK'S BAADASSS SONG** (original soundtrack) [ ] [ ]
Jul 99. (12"/c-s/cd-s) *Incredible; (INCR 24/+MC/CD)* **SEPTEMBER 99 (mixes)** [25] [–]
Jul 99. (cd/c) *Sony TV; (SONYTV 66 CD/MC)* **THE ULTIMATE COLLECTION** [34] [–]
– Boogie wonderland / Shining star / That's the way of the world / September / Can't hide love / After the love has gone / Got to get you into my life / Sing a song / Gratitude / Serpentine fire / Fantasy / In the stone / Reasons / Saturday nite / Let's groove / Getaway / September '99 (Phats & Small remix) / Let's groove (Merchant Of Menace remix) / Boogie wonderland (Stretch & Vern remix).

☐ tha EASTSIDAZ (see under ⇒ SNOOP DOGG)

☐ EAZY-E (see under ⇒ N.W.A.)

ECHO & THE BUNNYMEN

Formed: Liverpool, England ... autumn 1978 by IAN McCULLOCH, WILL SERGEANT and LES PATTINSON. McCULLOCH had once been in The CRUCIAL THREE alongside future stars, JULIAN COPE and PETE WYLIE, the former two starting up another low key act, A SHALLOW MADNESS, together writing 'READ IT IN BOOKS' (the b-side of E&TB's debut single, 'PICTURES ON MY WALL'). The BUNNYMEN, complete with drum machine ECHO, released the aforementioned 45 as a one-off for the local 'Zoo' label, before signing to 'WEA/Warners' subsidiary, 'Korova', late in '79. By the following year, they'd had a Top 20 album, 'CROCODILES', and were soon breaking into the singles chart with 'RESCUE'. Overtly melancholy and DOORS-influenced, their material contained a fresher up-tempo feel which combined powerful melodrama and McCULLOCH's ego-fuelled attitude. From 1981-84, their albums 'HEAVEN UP HERE', 'PORCUPINE' and 'OCEAN RAIN', solidified a Merseyside revival that even crossed successfully over the Atlantic. They split after their last gig on the 26th April '88, and it surprised everyone, not least the solo bound McCULLOCH (he had issued a single in '84, Kurt Weill's 'SEPTEMBER SONG'), when The BUNNYMEN decided to carry on without him. However, in June '89, PETE DE FREITAS was tragically killed in a motorcycle accident. In the early 90's, The BUNNYMEN (SERGEANT, PATTINSON, plus NOEL BURKE – vocals, JACK BROCKMAN – keyboards and DAMON REECE – drums) struggled without their moody frontman. A disappointing album, 'REVERBERATION' (1990), did little to excite the public, the group forming their own 'Euphoric' label after 'Korova/WEA' dropped them. McCULLOCH meanwhile, had been continuing his search for glory, releasing two albums, the Top 20 'CANDLELAND' (1989) and the Top 50, 'MYSTERIO' (1992), the last of which was poorly received. Late in '94, McCULLOCH and SERGEANT were back with a new rock-driven tour de force, ELECTRAFIXION, their sole album, 'BURNED' (1995), was well received by the music press, went Top 40 and enjoyed moderate sales. There was considerably more media interest over the reformation of the original ECHO & THE BUNNYMEN line-up in 1997. A strong comeback single, 'NOTHING LASTS FOREVER', and album, 'EVERGREEN', both made the UK Top 10, while the band proved they could still cut it live with a tour and a series of summer festival appearances. McCULLOCH and SERGEANT returned in 1999 with the eagerly awaited 'WHAT ARE YOU GOING TO DO WITH YOUR LIFE?', a short but very, very sweet album (its running time is around thirty eight minutes). The set was very similar to other ECHO releases, but less jaded and cynical than the previous 'EVERGREEN', with songs 'HISTORY CHIMES' and 'GET IN THE CAR' all displaying McCULLOCH's tenderness towards songwriting. Meanwhile SERGEANT, who had been dabbling in psychedelic electronica since the late seventies (anyone remember the soundtrack album 'THEMES FOR GRIND' from 1983) had been completing a musical manifesto all on his ownsome. Named GLIDE, SERGEANT issued both live albums 'SPACE AGE FREAK OUT' ('97) and 'PERFORMANCE' along with a lost classic from 1978 called 'WEIRD AS FISH', both in 2000. All albums sounded similar to the Krautrock movement or BRIAN ENO in his better experimental stages. Lashings of psychedelia and weirdness was born from somebody who used to be a post-punk rocker, but that didn't diminish the originality of the albums. ECHO AND THE BUNNYMEN returned in 2001 with another accomplished set, 'FLOWERS'. Although considerably mellower than previous ECHO works, the album acted as a Part 2 to the fantastic 'WHAT ARE YOU GOING TO DO ...?'. Mixing pop rock with classy melancholy, songs such as 'EVERYBODY KNOWS' and 'HIDE AND SEEK' had set the standards for future records by a band who were quite happy spending a third decade together. Now well into middle age, it was a more sure-footed and centered McCULLOCH that re-emerged in 2003 with 'SLIDELING', his first solo album in over a decade. Relying on acoustic-based arrangements with sympathetic string accompaniment, the singer put aside any residual attitude and artifice for a more candid and resolute portrayal of his artistic position in the post-millennial rock arena. For many fans, 'SIBERIA' (2005), was the classicist record they'd been waiting for since the band's much trumpeted reformation in '97, particularly minor hit, 'STORMY WEATHER' and 'SCISSORS IN THE SAND'.

• **Songwriters:** Mainly group compositions, except covers PEOPLE ARE STRANGE (Doors) / PAINT IT BLACK (Rolling Stones) / ALL YOU NEED IS LOVE + TICKET TO RIDE (Beatles) / FRICTION (Television) / RUN RUN RUN (Velvet Underground) / SHIP OF FOOLS (John Cale). McCULLOCH covered: RETURN TO SENDER (hit; Elvis Presley) / LOVER, LOVER, LOVER (Leonard Cohen) / THE PRETTIEST STAR (David Bowie) / JEALOUS GUY (John Lennon). • **Trivia:** DAVE BALFE (of DALEK I LOVE YOU) played keyboards on their first JOHN PEEL session in August 1979.

Album rating: CROCODILES (*9) / HEAVEN UP HERE (*9) / PORCUPINE (*7) / OCEAN RAIN (*8) / SONGS TO LEARN AND SING compilation (*9) / ECHO & THE BUNNYMEN (*5) / REVERBERATION (*3) / BALLYHOO: THE BEST OF ECHO & THE BUNNYMEN compilation (*8) / EVERGREEN (*7) / WHAT ARE YOU GOING TO DO WITH YOUR LIFE? (*8) / FLOWERS (*6) / LIVE IN LIVERPOOL (*5) / SIBERIA (*6) / Ian McCulloch: CANDLELAND (*6) / MYSTERIO (*5) / SLIDELING (*6) / Electrafixion: BURNED (*6) / Will Sergeant: THEMES FOR GRIND (*3)

IAN McCULLOCH (b. 5 May'59) – vocals, guitar (ex-CRUCIAL THREE) **WILL SERGEANT** (b.12 Apr'58) – lead guitar / **LES PATTINSON** (b.18 Apr'58) – bass (& 'ECHO' a drum machine)

		Zoo	not iss.
Mar 79.	(7") *(CAGE 004)* **PICTURES ON MY WALL. / READ IT IN BOOKS**		–
	(re-iss. Mar91 on 'Document' 12"/cd-s; DC 3/+CD)		

— **PETE DE FREITAS** (b. 2 Aug'61, Port Of Spain, Trinidad) – drums repl. 'ECHO'

		Korova	Sire
Apr 80.	(7") *(KOW 1)* **RESCUE. / SIMPLE STUFF**	62	–
	(12"+=) *(KOW 1T)* – Pride.		
Jul 80.	(lp/c) *(KODE/CODE 1) <6096>* **CROCODILES**	17	
	– Going up / Stars are stars / Pride / Monkeys / Crocodiles / Rescue / Villier's terrace / Pictures on my wall / All that jazz / Happy death men. *(re-iss. Nov80 w/ free 7"; SAM 128)* DO IT CLEAN. / READ IT IN BOOKS *(re-iss. 1989 on 'WEA' lp/c/cd; same/same/2423162)*		
Sep 80.	(7") *(KOW 11)* **THE PUPPET. / DO IT CLEAN**		
Apr 81.	(12"ep)(c-ep) *(ECHOZ 1)(ECHO 1M)* **SHINE SO HARD (live)**	37	–
	– Crocodiles / Zimbo / Over the wall / All that jazz.		
May 81.	(lp/c) *(KODE/CODE 3) <3569>* **HEAVEN UP HERE**	10	
	– Show of strength / With a hip / Over the wall / It was a pleasure / A promise / Heaven up here / The disease / All my colours / No dark things / Turquoise days / All I want. *(cd-iss. Jul88 on 'WEA'; 2432173)*		
Jul 81.	(7"/12") *(KOW 15/+T)* **A PROMISE. / BROKE MY NECK**	49	–
May 82.	(7") *(KOW 24)* **THE BACK OF LOVE. / THE SUBJECT**	19	–
	(12"+=) *(KOW 24T)* – Fuel.		
Jan 83.	(7") *(KOW 26)* **THE CUTTER. / WAY OUT AND UP WE GO**	8	–
	(w/ free c-ep+=) *(KOW 26C)* – The cutter / Villier's terrace / Ashes to ashes (stars are stars) / Monkeys / Read it in books.		
	(12"+=) *(KOW 26T)* – Zimbo (live).		
Jan 83.	(lp/c) *(KODE/CODE 6) <23770>* **PORCUPINE**	2	
	– The cutter / The back of love / My white devil / Clay / Porcupine / Heads will roll / Ripeness / Higher hell / Gods will be gods / In bluer skies. *(free ltd.c-ep w/ above lp)* – 'JOHN PEEL SESSIONS' *(re-iss. Jul88 on 'WEA lp/c/cd; same/same/K 400 272)*		
Feb 83.	(7") **THE CUTTER. / GODS WILL BE GODS**	–	

Jul 83. (7") *(KOW 28)* **NEVER STOP. / HEADS WILL ROLL** 15 –
(12"+=) *(KOW 28T)* – ('A'-Discotheque) / ('B'-Summer version) / The original cutter (A drop in the ocean).

Jan 84. (7") *(KOW 32)* **THE KILLING MOON. / DO IT CLEAN** 9 –
(12"+=) *(KOW 32T)* – ('A'-All night version).

Jan 84. (m-lp) *<23987>* **ECHO AND THE BUNNYMEN** – ☐
– Back of love / Never stop / Rescue / The cutter / Do it clean.

Apr 84. (lp/c)(cd) *(KODE/CODE 8)(K 240388-2) <25084>* **OCEAN RAIN** 4 Jun84 87
– Silver / Nocturnal me / Crystal days / The yo yo man / Thorn of crowns / The killing moon / Seven seas / My kingdom / Ocean rain.

Apr 84. (7") *(KOW 34)* **SILVER. / ANGELS AND DEVILS** 30 –
(12"+=) *(KOW 34T)* – Silver (Tidal wave).

Jun 84. (7") *(KOW 35)* **SEVEN SEAS. / ALL YOU NEED IS LOVE** 16 –
(12"+=/d7"+=) *(KOW 35 T/F)* – The killing Moon / Stars are stars (acoustic) / Villier's terrace (acoustic).

Oct 85. (7"/7"pic-d) *(KOW 43/+P)* **BRING ON THE DANCING HORSES. / OVER MY SHOULDER** 21 –
(ext.12"+=) *(KOW 43T)* – Beds, bugs and ballyhoo.
(d7"+=) *(KOW 43F)* – Villier's terrace / Monkeys.

Nov 85. (lp/c)(pic-lp)(cd) *(KODE/CODE 13)(KODE 13P)(240 767-2) <25360>* **SONGS TO LEARN AND SING** (compilation) 6 ☐
– Rescue / The puppet / Do it clean / The promise / The back of love / The cutter / Never stop / The killing moon / Silver / Seven seas / Bring on the dancing horses. *(c+=/cd+=)* – Pride / Simple stuff / Read it in books / Angels and devils. *(free ltd.c-s w/ same extra tracks)*

— (Feb86) temp. **MARK FOX** – drums (ex-HAIRCUT 100) repl. DE FREITAS until return Sep'86.

WEA Sire

Jun 87. (7") *(YZ 134)* **THE GAME. / SHIP OF FOOLS** 28 –
(12"+=/12"w poster+=) *(YZ 134T/+W)* – Lost and found.

Jul 87. (lp/c)(cd) *(WX 108/+C)(242 137-2) <25597>* **ECHO AND THE BUNNYMEN** 4 51
– The game / Over you / Bedbugs and ballyhoo / All in your mind / Bombers bay / Lips like sugar / Lost and found / New direction / Blue blue ocean / Satellite / All my life. *(re-iss. cd Nov94)*

Jul 87. (7"/7"gf/7"box) *(YZ 144/+V/B)* **LIPS LIKE SUGAR. / ROLLERCOASTER** 36 –
(12"+=) *(YZ 144T/+X)* – People are strange.

Feb 88. (7"/c-s) *(YZ 175/+C)* **PEOPLE ARE STRANGE. / RUN RUN RUN (live)** 29 –
(12"+=) *(YZ 175T)* – Paint it black / Friction. *(re-iss. Feb91 7"/c-s; YZ 567/+C /12"/cd-s; YZ 567 T/CD)* – hit UK No.34)

— They split some unofficial time in '88. Re-formed after McCULLOCH went solo. PETE DE FREITAS joined SEX GODS. He died in motorcycle accident 14 Jun '89.

— **SERGEANT** and **PATTINSON** reformed group early 1990, with newcomers **NOEL BURKE** (b.Belfast, N.Ireland) – vocals (ex-St.VITAS DANCE) / **JACK BROCKMAN** – keyboards / **DAMON REECE** – drums

Korova Sire

Oct 90. (7"/c-s) *(9031 72796-7/-4)* **ENLIGHTEN ME. / LADY, DON'T FALL BACKWARDS** ☐ ☐
(12"+=/cd-s+=) *(9031 72796-1/-2)* – ('A'extended).

Nov 90. (cd)(c/lp) *(9031 72553-2)(CODE/KODE 14) <26388>* **REVERBERATION** ☐ Dec90 ☐
– Freaks dwell / Cut and dried / Revilement / Flaming red / Salvatore / Fine thing / Gone, gone, gone / Enlighten me / King of your castle / Senseless / Thick skinned world. *(cd+=)* – False goodbyes.

Euphoric not iss.

Oct 91. (12"ep/cd-ep) *(E 001 T/CDS)* **PROVE ME WRONG. / FINE THING / REVERBERATION (live)** ☐ –

Mar 92. (12"/cd-s) *(K 002 T/CD)* **INSIDE ME, INSIDE YOU. / WIGGED OUT WORLD** ☐ –

— The BUNNYMEN disbanded soon after the above and LES joined TERRY HALL'S backing group.

WILL SERGEANT

WEA not iss.

Jul 82. (7") *(K 19238)* **FAVOURITE BRANCHES. / (b-side by Ravi Shankar & Bill Lovelady)** ☐ –

92 Happy C. not iss.

Mar 83. (lp) *(HAPLP 1)* **THEMES FOR "GRIND"** ☐ –
– Grind starts the generator / The wheel turns / The small screen flickers. *(cd-iss. Jan98 +=; HAPSCD 1)* – Theme / Favourite branches / Aquarius dub.

Ochre not iss.

1995. (7"orange) *(OCH 003)* **COSMOS. / VENUS IN FLARES** ☐ –

— WILL went on to form project, GLIDE – (see Alt & Indie II book-only)

IAN McCULLOCH

IAN McCULLOCH – vocals while still a member of The BUNNYMEN

Korova not iss.

Nov 84. (7"/10") *(KOW 40/+L)* **SEPTEMBER SONG. / COCKLES & MUSSELS** 51 –
(12"+=) *(KOW 40T)* – ('A'extended).

— Now solo his back-up came from **RAY SHULMAN** – keyboards, programmer, bass, producer / plus guests **MICHAEL JOBSON** – bass / **BORIS WILLIAMS** – drums / **OLLE REMO** – drum programmer / **LIZ FRASER** – vox (of COCTEAU TWINS)

WEA Sire

Aug 89. (7"/7"box/c-s) *(YZ 417/+B/C)* **PROUD TO FALL. / POTS OF GOLD** 51 –
(12") *(YZ 417T)* – ('A'extended) / ('A'side) / The dead end.
(cd-s) *(YZ 417CD)* – (above 3 tracks) / ('A'version).
(12") *(YZ 417TX)* – ('A'side / Everything is real / The circle game.

Sep 89. (lp/c)(cd) *(WX 303/+C)(2292 46225-2) <26012>* **CANDLELAND** 18 ☐
– The flickering wall / The white hotel / Proud to fall / The cape / Candleland / Horse's head / Faith and healing / I know you well / In bloom / Start again.

Nov 89. (7"/c-s) *(YZ 436/+C)* **FAITH AND HEALING (remix). / TOAD** ☐ –
('A'mix-12"+=) *(YZ 436T)* – Fear of the known.
(cd-s++=) *(YZ 436CD)* – Rocket ship.
(12") *(YZ 436TX)* – ('A'side) / Fear of the known / Rocket ship.

Apr 90. (7"/c-s) *(YZ 436/+C)* **CANDLELAND (THE SECOND COMING). / THE WORLD IS FLAT** 75 –
(12"+=/12"gf+=/cd-s+=) *(YZ 452 T/TG/CD)* – Big days / Wassailing in the night.

— His backing band from late '89, were The PRODIGAL SONS; **MIKE MOONEY** – guitar / **JOHN McEVOY** – guitar, keyboards / **EDGAR SUMMERTIME** – bass / **STEVE HUMPHRIES** – drums

East West Warners

Feb 92. (7"/c-s) *(YZ 643/+C)* **LOVER, LOVER, LOVER. / WHITE HOTEL (acoustic) / THE GROUND BELOW** 47 –
('A'-Indian Dawn remix-12"+=/cd-s+=) *(YZ 643T)* – Vibor blue (acoustic).

Apr 92. (lp/c)(cd) *(WX 453/+C)(<9031 76264-2>)* **MYSTERIO** 46 ☐
– Mayreal world / Close your eyes / Dug for love / Honeydrip / Damnation / Lover, lover, lover / Webbed / Pomegranate / Vibor blue / Heaven's gate / In my head.

Apr 92. (7"/c-s) *(YZ 660/+C)* **DUG FOR LOVE. / POMMEGRANITE (live)** ☐ –
(12"+=)(cd-s+=) *(YZ 660 T/CD)* – Do it clean (live) / In my head (live).

ELECTRAFIXION

— **IAN McCULLOCH** – vocals, guitar / **WILL SERGEANT** – guitar / **LEON DE SYLVA** – bass / **TONY McGUIGAN** – drums

WEA Warners

Nov 94. (c-ep/12"ep/cd-ep) *(YZ 865 C/T/CD)* **THE ZEPHYR EP** 47 –
– Zephyr / Burned / Mirrorball / Rain on me.

Sep 95. (7"red/c-s) *(YZ 977 X/C)* **LOWDOWN. / HOLY GRAIL** 54 –
(cd-s+=) *(YZ 977CD)* – Land of the dying sun / Razors edge.

Sep 95. (cd/c) *(0630 11248-2/-4) <61793>* **BURNED** 38 Oct95 ☐
– Feel my pulse / Sister pain / Lowdown / Timebomb / Zephyr / Never / Too far gone / Mirrorball / Who's been sleeping in my head? / Hit by something / Bed of nails.

Oct 95. (c-s) *(WEA 022C)* **NEVER / NOT OF THIS WORLD** 58 –
(cd-s+=) *(WEA 022CD)* – Subway train / Lowdown (rest of the trash mix).
(cd-s) *(WEA 022CDX)* – ('A'side) / Lowdown / Work it on out / Never (Utah Saints blizzard on mix) / Sister pain.

Mar 96. (cd-ep) *(WEA 037CD1)* **SISTER PAIN / FEEL MY PULSE / ZEPHYR / LOWDOWN (live)** 27 –

(cd-ep) *(WEA 037CD2)* – ('A'side) / Burned / Loose (live) / Who's been sleeping in my head (acoustic).
(cd-ep) *(WEA 037CD3)* – ('A'live) / Holy grail (live) / Never (live) / Too far gone (live).

— the last set-up issued a very limited gold-7" in Sep'97, 'BASEBALL BILL' released on 'Phree' (PHREE 1)

ECHO & THE BUNNYMEN

— the original trio (**McCULLOCH, SEARGEANT + PATTINSON**) re-formed

London London

Jun 97. (7") *(LO 396)* **NOTHING LASTS FOREVER. / WATCHTOWER** [8] [–]
(cd-s+=) *(LONCD 396)* – Polly.
(cd-s) *(LONCDP 396)* – ('A'side) / Colour me in / Antelope.

Jul 97. (cd/c/lp) *(828905-2/-4/-1)* **EVERGREEN** [8] [–]
– Don't let it get you down / In my time / I want to be there (when you come) / Evergreen / I'll fly tonight / Nothing lasts forever / Baseball Bill / Altamont / Just a touch away / Empire state halo / Too young to kneel / Forgiven. *(d-cd-iss. Nov97; 828980-2) (cd re-iss. Sep99; 3984 29642-2)*

Aug 97. (cd-s) *(LOCD 399)* **I WANT TO BE THERE (WHEN YOU COME) / THE KILLING MOON (session) / NOTHING LASTS FOREVER (session)** [30] [–]
(cd-s) *(LOCDP 399)* – ('A'side) / Lips like sugar (live acoustic) / ('A'-live acoustic).

Oct 97. (cd-s) *(LOCD 406)* **DON'T LET IT GET YOU DOWN / BACK OF LOVE (live) / OVER THE WALL (live)** [50] [–]
(cd-s) *(LOCDP 406)* – ('A'side) / Rescue / Altamont.

— In Jun'98, McCULLOCH provided ENGLAND UNITED with their World Cup song, '(HOW DOES IT FEEL TO BE) ON TOP OF THE WORLD' which hit Top 10.

— a few months later, a joint single, 'GET IN THE CAR' with The FUN LOVIN' CRIMINALS, was withdrawn from release

Mar 99. (7") *(LO 424)* **RUST. / THE FISH HOOK GIRL** [22] [–]
(cd-s+=) *(LOCD 424)* – See the horizon.
(cd-s) *(LOCDP 424)* – ('A'side) / Sense of life / Beyond the green.

Apr 99. (cd/c) *(<556080-2/-4>)* **WHAT ARE YOU GOING TO DO WITH YOUR LIFE?** [21] Jun99 [ ]
– What are you going to do with your life? / Rust / Get in the car / Baby rain / History chimes / Lost on you / Morning sun / When it all blows over / Fools like us.

— **McCULLOCH + SERGEANT** brought in **CERI JAMES** – keyboards, synths

Cooking Vinyl Cooking Vinyl

Apr 01. (7") *(FRY 104)* **IT'S ALRIGHT. / SUPERMELLOW MAN (instrumental)** [41] [–]
(cd-s) *(FRYCD 104)* – ('A') / Marble towers / Rescue (Mindwinders remix).
(cd-s) *(FRYCD 104X)* – ('A') / Scratch the past / A promise (lo-fi lullaby #1) / ('A'-video).

May 01. (lp/cd) *(COOK/+CD 208)* *<608>* **FLOWERS** [56] [ ]
– King of kings / Supermellow man / Hide and seek / Make me shine / It's alright / Buried alive / Flowers / Everybody knows / Life goes on / An eternity turns / Burn for me.

Aug 01. (cd-s) *(FRYCD 112)* **MAKE ME SHINE / TICKET TO RIDE / NOTHING LASTS FOREVER (live)** [ ] [–]

— added **STEVE FLETT** – bass / **VINNY JAMIESON** – drums

Feb 02. (cd) *(COOKCD 223)* *<623>* **LIVE IN LIVERPOOL** (live August 2001) [ ] [ ]
– Rescue / Lips like sugar / King of kings / Never stop / Seven seas / Buried alive / Supermellow man / My kingdom / Zimbo / All the jazz / An eternity turns / The back of love / The killing moon / The cutter / Over the wall / Nothing lasts forever / Ocean rain.

Sep 05. (7") *(FRY 246)* **STORMY WEATHER. / MAKE ME SHINE (acoustic Brazilian radio session)** [55] [–]
(cd-s) *(FRYCD 246)* – ('A') / What if we are? (vocal & string version) / ('A'-instrumental).

Sep 05. (cd) *(COOKCD 297)* *<4697>* **SIBERIA** [ ] [ ]
– Stormy weather / All because of you days / Parthenon Drive / In the margins / Of a life / Make us blind / Everything kills you / Siberia / Sideways eight / Scissors in the sand / What if we are? *(d-lp iss.Apr06 on 'Let Them Eat Vinyl'; LETV 007LP)*

Oct 05. (cd-s) *(FRYCD 249)* **IN THE MARGINS / NOTHING LASTS FOREVER (acoustic) / IN THE MARGINS (instrumental)** [ ] [–]

– compilations, others, etc. –

Nov 88. (12"ep/cd-ep) *Strange Fruit; (SFPS/+CD 060)* **THE PEEL SESSIONS** (15.8.79) [ ] [–]
– Read it in books / Stars are stars / I bagsy yours / Villier's terrace. *(re-iss. cd-ep Dec94; same)*

Jul 90. (7") *Old Gold; (OG 9939)* **THE KILLING MOON. / SEVEN SEAS** [ ] [–]

Jul 90. (7") *Old Gold; (OG 9941)* **THE CUTTER. / THE BACK OF LOVE** [ ] [–]

Nov 91. (cd/lp) *Windsong; (WIN CD/LP 006)* **BBC RADIO 1 LIVE IN CONCERT (live)** [ ] [–]

Mar 93. (cd/c) *Pickwick-WEA; (4509-91886-2/-4)* **THE CUTTER** [ ] [–]
(re-iss. Sep95 on 'Warners'; same)

Jun 97. (cd/c) *W.E.A.; (0630 19103-2/-4)* **BALLYHOO – THE BEST OF ECHO & THE BUNNYMEN** [59] [–]
– Rescue / Do it clean / Villier's terrace / All that jazz / Over the wall / A promise / The disease / The back of love / The cutter / Never stop / The killing moon / Silver / Seven seas / Bring on the dancing horses / People are strange / The game / Lips like sugar / Bedbugs & ballyhoo.

Aug 01. (4xcd-box) *Rhino; (<8122 74263-2>)* **CRYSTAL DAYS 1979-1999** [ ] [ ]

IAN McCULLOCH

with session band, etc.

Cooking Vinyl SpinArt

Apr 03. (cd-s) *(FRYCD 146)* **SLIDING / CRACKERJACK / BLUE SKIES UP AHEAD** [61] [–]
(cd-s) *(FRYCD 146X)* – ('A'-acoustic) / Planet song / Jealous guy.

Apr 03. (cd) *(COOKCD 253)* *<SPIN 123>* **SLIDELING** [ ] May03 [ ]
– Love in veins / Playgrounds and city parks / Sliding / Baby hold on / Arthur / Seasons / Another train / High wires / She sings (all my life) / Kansas / Stake your claim.

Jul 03. (cd-s) *(FRYCD 158)* **LOVE IN VEINS / THE PRETTIEST STAR / ARTHUR (Prague)** [ ] [–]

EDITORS

Formed: Birmingham, England . . . 2003 initially as the PRIDE and then SNOWFIELD by Stafford University graduates TOM SMITH, CHRIS URBANOWICZ, RUSSELL LEETCH and ED LAY. Another bunch of funsters with a well-thumbed stack of 80s vinyl, EDITORS arrived well versed in the ways of ECHO & THE BUNNYMEN, KITCHENS OF DISTINCTION and ASSOCIATES. They even surfaced on the reactivated 'Kitchenware' imprint, a label last sighted as a rest home for PREFAB SPROUT. 2005 proved a good year for the band's miserabilist copy as their first three 45's, 'BULLETS', 'MUNICH' and 'BLOOD', circulated in ever greater numbers, the latter splashed across the UK Top 20. Debut album, 'THE BACK ROOM' (2005), drew predictable comparisons to Anglo-American IAN CURTIS acolytes, INTERPOL, although TOM SMITH has the impressive ability to subtly vary the effect of his fathoms-deep, CHAMELEON-ic vocal. A No.13 placing proved not so unlucky, as higher charting re-issues of 'BULLETS' and 'MUNICH' (plus final single from the album, 'ALL SPARKS'), eventually propelled the set into the Top 3.

• **Covers:** FRENCH DISKO (Stereolab) / ROAD TO NOWHERE (Talking Heads) / ORANGE CRUSH (R.E.M.).

Album rating: THE BACK ROOM (*8)

TOM SMITH – vocals, guitar / **CHRIS URBANOWICZ** – lead guitar / **RUSSELL LEETCH** – bass / **ED LAY** – drums

Kitchenware Fader

Jan 05. (7") *(SKX 77)* **BULLETS. / YOU ARE FADING** [54] [–]
(cd-s+=) *(SKCD 77)* – Dust in the sunlight.

Apr 05. (7") *(SKX 78)* **MUNICH. / DISAPPEAR** [22] [–]
(cd-s) *(SKCD 78)* – ('A') / Colours / Crawl down the wall.
(cd-s) *(SKCD 78-2)* – ('A') / Release.

ul 05. (7") *(SKX 79)* **BLOOD. / FOREST FIRE** 18 –
(cd-s) *(SKCD 79)* – ('A') / Let your good heart lead you home.
(cd-s) *(SKCD 79-2)* – ('A') / Heads in bags / ('A'-Freelance Hellraiser editorial).

ul 05. (cd/lp) *(KW CD/X 34)* **THE BACK ROOM** 13 –
– Lights / Munich / Blood / Fall / All sparks / Camera / Fingers in the factories / Bullets / Someone says / Open your arms / Distance. *(ltd d-cd+=; KWCD 34-2)* – Let your good heart lead you home / You are fading / Crawl down the wall / Colours / Release / Forest fire.

'ep 05. (7") *(SKX 80)* **BULLETS. / TIME TO SLOW DOWN** 27 –
(cd-s) *(SKCD 80)* – ('A') / Come share the view.
(cd-s) *(SKCD 80-2)* – ('A') / I buried the Devil / Blood (alt.) / ('A'-video).

an 06. (7") *(SKX 83)* **MUNICH. / CAMERA (demo)** 10 –
(cd-s) *(SKCD 83)* – ('A') / French disko.
(cd-s) *(SKCD 83-2)* – ('A') / Find yourself a safe place / ('A'-Cicada remix) / ('A'-video).

'eb 06. (cd; re-) *(as prev)* <905> **THE BACK ROOM** 2 Mar06

Iar 06. (7") *(SKX 84)* **ALL SPARKS. / SOMEONE SAYS (acoustic)** 21 –
(cd-s) *(SKCD 84)* – ('A') / The diplomat.
(cd-s) *(KWCD 84-2)* – ('A') / From the outside / ('A'-Cicada remix) / ('A'-video).

un 06. (10") *(SKX 87)* **BLOOD. / ROAD TO NOWHERE (Napster session) / CAMERA (obscured by J Spaceman)** 39 –
(cd-s) *(SKCD 87)* – ('A') / Orange crush / Camera (Oakenfold remix) / ('A'-video).

EELS

'ormed: Los Angeles, California, USA ... 1995 by E (MARK :VERETT), who had previously released two solo albums under his rather minimalist moniker (only in America). Hooking up vith fellow slippery characters TOMMY WALTER and BUTCH NORTON, they set free their electric debut album, 'BEAUTIFUL 'REAK'. Lyrically grim, EELS packaged their tales of dysfunctional Americana in deceptively effervescent indie melodies, the UK 'op 10 singles 'NOVOCAINE FOR THE SOUL' and 'SUSAN'S HOUSE' being prime examples of post-NIRVANA lo-fi rock. 1998's ELECTRO-SHOCK BLUES' was a more private and personal xploration of life's darker side, E exorcising the demons of his ister's suicide and his mother's death from cancer (his father had ied when MARK was 19). After the very morbid musings heard in ELECTRO . . .', EELS frontman and mainman E decided to record n album that harked back to the softer, more upbeat version of he band – the kind of styles presented as an introduction on the BEAUTIFUL FREAK' LP. Entitled 'DAISIES OF THE GALAXY' 2000), it was a fantastic journey into the heart of EVERETT's, m, heart. Standout single 'BEAUTIFUL DAY' saw the man inging about something more positive, although however bleak is songs were the message still stood the same: life is a beautiful hing . . . enjoy it! 'THE SOUND OF FEAR' displayed his brilliant acking band's use of instrumentation, with a creeping bass that ounded similar to NIRVANA's 'Lithium', before the jazzy snare icked in. 'IT'S A MOTHERFUCKER' made an example of his ongwriting talents in the way he could turn such a sour subject natter into such a sweet song. The amusing live set 'OH WHAT BEAUTIFUL DAY' (2000), saw a collection of live recordings aken from everywhere including Glasgow, L.A., New York and ondon (by this point bassist TOMMY WALTER had fled, to be eplaced by LISA GERMANO). The band threw in a few odd-ball overs along the way; EVERETT's staggering solo performances vere awesome. The strange and disjointed 'SOULJACKER' album ppeared in 2001 to tepid critical response. E, dressed as the otorious American terrorist the Unabomber, and taking the name om an equally notorious serial killer (who believed he stole his ictim's souls when he killed them), the album was patchy at best. 'ull of strange, unfinished ideas, the set had an uneven quality reflecting the 'ELECTRO SHOCK . . .' album almost to a tee. However, after the enigmatic and more mainstream 'DAISIES . . .' album, it was nice to see a little diversity in the group's music. Mr EVERETT was back with more twisted humour and self-consciously bleak lyrical portraits on 'SHOOTENANNY!' (2003), sounding more and more like the contrary, wilfully wayward troubadour he's always threatened to become. There's a beguiling charm about E's determinedly downbeat outlook, a strength which he continued to play to with this release. 'BLINKING LIGHTS AND OTHER REVELATIONS' (2005) was his first album for 'Vagrant' records ('Polydor' in Britain), an even more self-reflective double-set. The blinking lights of the title shone across E's tattered back pages, resulting in some of his most revealing, intimate songwriting to date, fleshed out with the help of JOHN SEBASTIAN and PETER BUCK; surprisingly, the record returned him to the UK Top 20 and finally broke him through in his homeland. Like many a hallowed great before him, the lone EEL subsequently recorded a 'LIVE AT TOWN HALL' set (as in New York) – "WITH STRINGS"! and rootin' tootin' accompaniment courtesy of BIG AL and CHET ATKINS III (alias LYSTER). Covers on the night included 'PRETTY BALLERINA' (Left Banke), 'GIRL FROM THE NORTH COUNTRY' (Bob Dylan) and 'POOR SIDE OF TOWN' (Johnny Rivers).

• **Songwriters:** Most songs by E, some with JIM JACOBSEN, JIM WEATHERLY, MARK GOLDENBERG, JON BRION or JILL SOBULE.

Album rating: E: A MAN CALLED E (*7) / BROKEN TOY SHOP (*5) / Eels: BEAUTIFUL FREAK (*7) / ELECTRO-SHOCK BLUES (*6) / DAISIES OF THE GALAXY (*6) / OH WHAT A BEAUTIFUL MORNING (*5) / SOULJACKER (*6) / SHOOTENANNY! (*7) / BLINKING LIGHTS AND OTHER REVELATIONS (*7) / WITH STRINGS: LIVE AT TOWN HALL (*6)

(E)

E (b. MARK OLIVER EVERETT, 9 Apr'63, Virginia, USA) – vocals, piano, multi

not iss. Polydor

Dec 91. (cd-s) *<CDP 654>* **HELLO CRUEL WORLD** –

Feb 92. (cd/c) *<511570-2/-4>* **A MAN CALLED (E)** –
– Hello cruel world / Fitting in with the misfits / Are you and me gonna happen / Looking out the window with a blue / Nowheresville / Symphony for toy piano in G minor / Mockingbird Franklin / I've been kicked around / Pray / E's tune / You'll be the scarecrow.

Mar 92. (cd-s) **NOWHERESVILLE / STRAWBERRY BLONDE** –

— now with various personnel incl. **PARTHENON HUXLEY + SEAB COLEMAN**

Dec 93. (cd/c) *<519976-2/-4>* **BROKEN TOY SHOP** –
– Shine it all on / Standing at the gate / The only thing I care about / Manchester girl / L.A. river / Most unpleasant man / Mass / Tomorrow I'll be nine / The day I wrote you off / Someone to break the spell / She loves a puppet / My old raincoat / Permanent broken heart / Eight lives left.

Dec 93. (cd-ep) *<SACD 772>* **NOT FOR AIRPLAY** –
– Shine it all on / L.A. river / Tomorrow I'll be nine / Everything's gonna be cool this summer.

EELS

— E with **TOMMY WALTER** – bass, vocals / **BUTCH NORTON** (b. JONATHAN) – drums, vocals

Dreamworks Dreamworks

Aug 96. (cd-s; promo) **RAGS TO RICHES / ANIMAL** –

Feb 97. (cd/c) *<(DRD/DRC 50001)>* **BEAUTIFUL FREAK** 5 Aug96
– Novocaine for the soul / Susan's house / Rags to rags / Beautiful freak / Not ready yet / My beloved monster / Flower / Guest list / Mental / Spunky / Your lucky day in Hell / Manchild. *(UK+=)* – BBC tracks:- Novocaine for the soul (live from Hell) / Manchester girl / My beloved mad monster party / Flower. *(re-iss. Feb00; same)*

Feb 97. (7"/c-s) *(DRM S/C 22174)* **NOVOCAINE FOR THE SOUL. / FUCKER** 10 –
(cd-s+=) *(DRMCD 22174)* – Guest list / My beloved monster (live).

May 97. (7"/c-s) *(DRM S/C 22238)* **SUSAN'S HOUSE. / STEPMOTHER** [9] [–]
(cd-s+=) *(DRMCD 22238)* – Manchester girl (BBC session).

Sep 97. (7"/c-s) *(DRM S/C 22277)* **YOUR LUCKY DAY IN HELL. / SUSAN'S APARTMENT** [35] [–]
(cd-s+=) *(DRMCD 22277)* – Altar boy.

Sep 98. (7"/c-s) *(DRM S/C 22346)* <5112> **LAST STOP: THIS TOWN. / FUNERAL PARLOUR** [23] [–]
(cd-s+=) *(DRMCD 22346)* – Novocaine for the soul (Moog Cookbook version).

Sep 98. (cd/c) <*(DRD/DRC 50052)*> **ELECTRO-SHOCK BLUES** [12] [ ]
– Elizabeth on the bathroom floor / Going to your funeral part 1 / Cancer for the cure / My descent into madness / 3 speed / Hospital food / Electro-shock blues / Efils' god / Going to your funeral part II / Last stop: this town / Baby genius / Climbing to the moon / Ant farm / Dead of winter / The medication is wearing off / P.S. you rock my world. *(re-iss. Feb00; same)*

Nov 98. (7"/c-s) *(DRM S/C 22373)* **CANCER FOR THE CURE. / EVERYTHING'S GONNA BE COOL THIS CHRISTMAS** [60] [–]
(cd-s+=) *(DRMCD 22373)* – Exodus part III.

—— **ADAM SIEGAL** – bass; repl. TOMMY WALTER

Feb 00. (7"pic-d) *(450978-7)* **MR. E'S BEAUTIFUL BLUES. / BIRDGIRL ON A CELL PHONE** [15] [–]
(cd-s+=) *(450976-2)* – ('A'-CD-Rom).
(cd-s) *(450977-2)* – ('A'side) / Hospital food (live) / Cancer for the cure (video).

Feb 00. (cd) <*(450218-2)*> **DAISIES OF THE GALAXY** [8] Mar00 [ ]
– Grace Kelly blues / Packing blankets / The sound of fear / I like birds / Daisies of the galaxy / Flyswatter / It's a motherfucker / Estate sales / Tiger in my tank / A daisy through concrete / Jeannie's diary / Wooden nickels / Something is sacred / Selective memory / Mr. E's beautiful blues. *(lp-iss.Apr00 on 'Bongload'; BL 47)*

Jun 00. (7"pic-d/cd-s) *(45094 5-7/6-2)* **FLYSWATTER. / OPEN THE DOOR (BBC live) / FLYSWATTER (polka dot remix)** [55] [–]
(cd-s) *(450947-2)* – ('A'side) / Something is sacred / Vice President Fruitley.

—— **LISA GERMANO** – bass (solo artist) repl. SIEGAL

Dec 00. (cd) *<net>* **OH WHAT A BEAUTIFUL MORNING** (live) [–] [–]
– Feeling good / Overture:- (a) Last stop: this town (b) Beautiful freak (c) Rags to riches (d) Your lucky day in Hell (e) My descent into madness (f) Novocaine for the soul (g) Flower / Oh what a beautiful morning / Abortion in the sky / It's a motherfucker / Fucker / Ant farm / Climbing to the Moon / Grace Kelly blues / Daisies of the galaxy / Flyswatter / Vice President Fruitley / Hot and cold / Mr. E's beautiful blues / Not ready yet / Susan's house / Something is sacred.

—— **E + BUTCH** recruited **JOHN PARISH** – guitars, keyboards, co-writer, etc + **KOOOL G** – synthesizers / **ADAM** (still here!)

Sep 01. (7") *(450893-7)* **SOULJACKER (part 1). / I WRITE THE B-SIDES** [30] [–]
(cd-s+=) *(450893-2)* – Can't help falling in love / ('A'video).
(cd-s) *(450893-5)* – ('A'side) / Jennifer Eccles / My beloved monstrosity / Flyswatter (video).

Sep 01. (cd/lp) *(450335-2/-1)* <*450346*> **SOULJACKER** [12] [ ]
– Dog faced boy / That's not really funny / Fresh feeling / Woman driving, man sleeping / Souljacker, pt.I / Friendly ghost / Teenage witch / Bus stop boxer / Jungle telegraph / World of shit / Souljacker, pt.II / What is this note? *(d-cd+=; 450346-2)* – I write the B-sides / (hidden track) / Jehovah's witness / Rotten world blues.

Jun 03. (cd) *(4504588)* <*03902*> **SHOOTENANNY!** [35] [ ]
– All in a day's work / Saturday morning / The good old days / Love of the loveless / Dirty girl / Agony / Rock hard times / Restraining order blues / Lone wolf / Wrong about Bobby / Numbered days / Fashion awards / Somebody loves you.

Polydor Vagrant

Apr 05. (d-cd) *(9881785)* <*VR 406*> **BLINKING LIGHTS AND OTHER REVELATIONS** [16] [93]
– Theme from Blinking Lights / From which I came – A magic world / Son of a bitch / Blinking lights (for me) / Trouble with dreams / Marie floating over the backyard / Suicide life / In the yard, behind the church / Railroad man / The other shoe / Last time we spoke / Mother Mary / Going fetal / Understanding salesmen / Theme for a pretty girl that makes you believe God exists / Checkout blues / Blinking lights (for you) / Dust of ages / Old shit – New shit / Bride of theme from Blinking Lights / Hey man (no[w] you're really living) / I'm going to stop pretending that I didn't break you[r] heart / To lick your boots / If you see Natalie / Sweet li'l thing / Dusk: peach in the orchard / Whatever happened to Soy bomb / Ugly love / God silence / LOsing streak / Last days of my bitter heart / The stars shine i[n] the sky tonight / Things that grandchildren should know.

May 05. (cd-s) *(9881879)* **HEY MAN (NOW YOU'RE REALLY LIVING) / AFTER THE OPERATION / THE BRIGHT SIDE / LOVE OF THE LOVELESS (live)** [45] [–]

—— E with **ALAN "BIG AL" HUNTER** – piano, upright bass / **CHET LYSTE[R]** (aka CHET ATKINS III) – guitar, mandolin, etc. / + other strings

Feb 06. (cd) *(910423-2)* <*VR 423*> **WITH STRINGS: LIVE AT TOWN HALL** (live) [ ] [ ]
– Blinking lights (for me) / Bride of theme from Blinking Lights / Bus sto[p] boxer / Dirty girl / Trouble with dreams / The only thing I care about / My beloved monster / Pretty ballerina / It's a motherfucker / Flyswatter / Novocaine for the soul / Girl from north country / Railroad man / I lik[e] birds / If you see Natalie / Poor side of town / Spunky / I'm going to sto[p] pretending that I didn't break your heart / Suicide life / Losing streak / He[y] man (now you're really living) / Things the grandchildren should know

ELBOW

Formed: Bury, Manchester, England . . . 1994 by GUY GARVEY, RICHARD JUPP, CRAIG POTTER, his brother MARK POTTER and PETE TURNER. Shortlisted for the Mercury Music Prize, thi[s] bittersweet collective were living proof that the Manchester music scene didn't just comprise of arrogant guitar bands kissing the feet of major labels. That said, ELBOW have mostly been kicke[d] in the face by the majors: 'Island' dropped them as did 'E.M.I.' But thankfully, they came bounding back to astound us with their melancholic blend of (in their own words) "prog rock, withou[t] the solos". It began when all five members met at college an[d] frequented local haunts before they attracted the watchful eye o[f] 'Island'. This in turn led to their debut EP, 'THE NOISEBOX' its title track 'POWDER BLUE' gaining a spot in John Peel's Festive 50 late '98. Independent record label 'Uglyman' raised th[e] money to fund the EP's 'THE NEWBORN' and 'ANY DAY NOW' two breezy, rousing tracks heir to TURIN BRAKES, KINGS OF CONVENIENCE and the spiralling New Acoustic Movement. Th[e] acclaim for the tracks was phenomenal, with music journos citin[g] ELBOW as the millennium's answer to RADIOHEAD (if there wa[s] such a thing!). This led to the release of their debut set 'ASLEE[P] IN THE BACK' (2001), an album of inspired beauty and eleganc[e]. Tracks such as 'POWDER BLUE' and 'CAN'T STOP' made yo[u] wonder what the major labels were thinking when they gave the[m] the proverbial elbow. The album, unsurprisingly, was nominate[d] for a Mercury music prize while it also managed a few weeks i[n] the Top 20. ELBOW would return in summer 2003 to issue th[e] downbeat, but excellent 'CAST OF THOUSANDS', a record whic[h] saw the lads unrestrained and reaching new creative peaks via the[ir] complex melodies and lyrics of torn relationships. The poignanc[e] of SPIRITUALIZED resonated somewhere in the backgroun[d], especially when the large, full-on gospel choirs kicked in, but [it] never sounded cheesy or over-orchestrated. Predictably, the albu[m] was critically acclaimed on its release, also striking a chord wit[h] the introspective COLDPLAY crowd, as 'CAST OF THOUSANDS' deservedly entered the British Top 10. Like PETER GABRIE[L] fronting the corpse of the BETA BAND, the anthemic 'FORGE[T] MYSELF' was the lead single for third Top 20 album, 'LEADERS OF THE FREE WORLD' (2005). Now a producer in his own right [(I] AM KLOOT, etc.), GUY GARVEY's man-of-the-people touch sa[w] his band leading the way on the Manchester scene.

• **Covers:** INDEPENDENT WOMAN (Destiny's Child).

Album rating: ASLEEP IN THE BACK (*8) / CAST OF THOUSANDS (*7) / LEADERS OF THE FREE WORLD (*7)

GUY GARVEY – vocals / CRAIG POTTER – organ / MARK POTTER – guitar / PETE TURNER – bass / RICHARD JUPP – drums

Soft | not iss.

an 98. (ltd;cd-ep) **THE NOISEBOX EP** [ ] [–]
– Powder blue / Red / George lassoes the Moon / Theme from Munroe Kelly / Can't stop.

Uglyman | not iss.

Aug 00. (cd-ep) *(UGLY 20)* **THE NEWBORN EP** [ ] [–]
– Newborn / Kisses / Bitten by the tailfly / None one.

an 01. (cd-ep/10"ep) *(UGLY 25/+V)* **ANY DAY NOW EP** [ ] [–]
– Any day now / Wurzel / George lassoes the moon / Don't mix your drinks.
(cd-s) *(UGLY 25VID)* – ('A'-video).

V2 | V2

Apr 01. (7") *(VVR 501615-7)* **RED. / VUM GARDA** [36] [–]
(cd-s+=) *(VVR 501615-3)* – About time.
(cd-s) *(VVR 501615-8)* – ('A'side) / Crow (acoustic) / Newborn (acoustic).

May 01. (cd/d-lp) *(<VVR 101588-2/-1>)* **ASLEEP IN THE BACK** [14] Jun01 [ ]
– Any day now / Red / Little beast / Powder blue / Bitten by the tailfly / Newborn / Don't mix your drinks / Presuming Ed (rest easy) / Coming second / Can't stop / Scattered black and whites. *(cd re-iss. Feb02; VVR 101901-2)*

ul 01. (cd-s) *(VVR 501616-3)* **POWDER BLUE / SUFFER / ABOUT TIME (acoustic)** [41] [–]
(cd-s) *(VVR 501616-8)* – ('A'side) / Red (session) / Powder blue (Andy Votel mix).

Oct 01. (12"/cd-s) *(VVR 501617-6/-3)* **NEWBORN. / LUCKY WITH DISEASE / PRESS YOUR LIPS (NEWBORN) – El Presidente remix** [42] [–]
(cd-s) *(VVR 501617-8)* – ('A'side) / One thing that was bothering me / None one.

Feb 02. (cd-s) *(VVR 501870-3)* **ASLEEP IN THE BACK / COMING SECOND / STUMBLE** [19] [–]
(cd-s) *(VVR 501870-8)* – ('A'side) / Coming second (Misery Lab mix) / Stumble.

Aug 03. (cd-s) *(VVR 502180-3)* **FALLEN ANGEL / LOSS / WHISPER GRASS** [19] [–]
(cd-s) *(VVR 502180-8)* – ('A'side) / Brave new shave / ('A'-remix).

Aug 03. (cd/lp) *(VVR 102181-2/-1) <27161>* **CAST OF THOUSANDS** [7] Jan04 [ ]
– Ribcage / Fallen angel / Fugitive motel / Snooks (progress report) / Switching off / Not a job / I've got a number / Buttons and zips / Crawling with idiot / Grace under pressure / Flying dream 143. *(cd re-iss. Nov03 +dvd; VVR 102181-0)*

Oct 03. (cd-s) *(VVR 502182-3)* **FUGITIVE MOTEL / SWITCHING OFF (acoustic) / RIBCAGE (Andy Cato mix)** [44] [–]
(cd-s) *(VVR 502182-8)* – ('A'-RJD2 mix) / Love blown down / Ribcage (Kinobe mix).

Feb 04. (cd-s) *(VVR 502467-8)* **NOT A JOB / TEARDROP** [26] [–]
(cd-s) *(VVR 5022467-3)* – ('A') / Lay down your cross / Live on my mind / ('A'-Soup Collective alt. video).
(dvd-s) *(VVR 8022467-8)* – ('A'-video) / Fugitive motel (video) / Theme from Munroe Kelly (2004 version).

ul 04. (cd-s) *(VVR 502670-3)* **GRACE UNDER PRESSURE / SWITCHING OFF / WAVING FROM WINDOWS / FUGITIVE HOTEL (acoustic) / GRACE UNDER PRESSURE (live from Glastonbury)** [ ] [–]

Sep 05. (7") *(VVR 503254-7)* **FORGET MYSELF. / McGREGOR** [22] [–]
(cd-s) *(VVR 503254-8)* – ('A') / The good day.
(cd-s) *(VVR 503254-3)* – ('A') / Strangeways to Holcombe Hill in 4 minutes and 20 seconds / My finger / ('A'-video).

Sep 05. (cd/lp) *(VVR 103255-2/-1) <27275>* **LEADERS OF THE FREE WORLD** [12] [ ]
– Station approach / Picky bugger / Forget myself / The stops / Leaders of the free world / An imagined affair / Mexican standoff / The everthere / My very best / Great expectations / Puncture repair. *(ltd-cd w/dvd; VVR 103255-8)* – (DVD footage).

Nov 05. (7") *(VVR 503562-7)* **LEADERS OF THE FREE WORLD. / GENTLE AS** [53] [–]
(cd-s) *(VVR 503562-8)* – ('A') / The long war shuffle.
(cd-s) *(VVR 503562-3)* – ('A') / Mexican standoff (Spanish version) / The drunken engineer.

☐ ELECTRAFIXION
(see under ⇒ ECHO & THE BUNNYMEN)

ELECTRIC LIGHT ORCHESTRA

Formed: Birmingham, England . . . 1968 by ROY WOOD, as an alternative to his other group The MOVE who were drifting into cabaret circuit decline. In 1969, he offered close friend JEFF LYNNE a place in The MOVE, although the singer he resisted and waited until ROY came up with ELO in 1971. Gathering in an array of outlandish but highly talented musicians (namely BEV BEVAN, RICHARD TANDY, BILL HUNT, WILF GIBSON, HUGH McDOWELL and ANDY CRAIG), the two outfits co-existed at this period, the eponymous ELECTRIC LIGHT ORCHESTRA debut, finally hitting the shops later that year. Much lawded by the critics, it didn't hit the UK Top 40 until the single, '10538 OVERTURE', made the Top 10 in August 1972. WOOD subsequently departed both ELO and The MOVE to form glam/flash rockers, WIZZARD, which left JEFF LYNNE as the group's main man. A creative BEATLES influenced rock/pop outfit who relied heavily on string-laden themes and a romanticised lyrical future, the new line-up (without WIZZARD bound HUNT and McDOWELL) rejuvenated a past Chuck Berry classic 'ROLL OVER BEETHOVEN' to the heights of the Top 10. The accompanying follow-up album, 'II' (1973), again made the British Top 40 and ELO enjoyed a further major chart hit with the infectious 'SHOWDOWN' single later that year. The track's more pop-friendly approach indicated the direction LYNNE would steer the band over the coming decade; both 'ON THE THIRD DAY' (1973) and 'EL DORADO . . .' (1974) saw him hone his songwriting skills, something which paid off when 'CAN'T GET IT OUT OF MY HEAD' became a surprise US Top 10 hit, boosting Statside sales of the latter album and taking it into the American Top 20. Subsequent album, 'FACE THE MUSIC' (1975), established the band as a major concert attraction across the Atlantic, where they spent much of their time touring. Though that album's 'EVIL WOMAN' had made the UK Top 10, they finally re-established themselves in their home country with 'A NEW WORLD RECORD' (1976). ELO reached a commercial peak towards the end of the decade when their finely crafted, harmony-laden songs represented everything the thriving punk scene set out to destroy; both 'OUT OF THE BLUE' (1977) and 'DISCOVERY' (1979) were massive transatlantic successes, while the band scored a formidable run of chart hits including 'MR. BLUE SKY', 'SWEET TALKIN' WOMAN', 'SHINE A LITTLE LOVE' and the classic 'DON'T BRING ME DOWN'. In summer 1980, a collaboration with OLIVIA NEWTON JOHN on the dreamy 'XANADU' provided the band with their only No.1 hit, the track taken from the soundtrack to the film of the same name. The hits continued to roll in with the inimitable cheesiness of 'TICKET TO THE MOON', 'HOLD ON TIGHT' and 'ROCK'N'ROLL IS KING', the latter track being their last Top 40 hit. As their chart success dried up in the mid-80's, LYNNE helped form The TRAVELING WILBURYS alongside BOB DYLAN, GEORGE HARRISON, ROY ORBISON and TOM PETTY. BEVAN eventually emerged in the early 90's with an ELO Mk.II, although their material inevitably lacked LYNNE's songwriting spark. The bearded one had produced DAVE EDMUNDS (1981-84), BRIAN WILSON (1988) and TOM PETTY (1989), to name just a few and released a solo album, 'ARMCHAIR THEATER' in 1990 which hit the UK Top 30. More than a decade later, LYNNE chose to resurrect the ELO moniker for 'ZOOM' (2001), a solo set in all but name but as close to the band's classic 70's sound as anything since, well, the 70's. Featuring JEFF's girlfriend (and former solo artiste), ROSIE VELA, the album touched all the bases that made ELO great way back when: a pristine pop sensibility, larger than life BEATLES-esque harmonies, retro bubblegum tendencies, lavish arrangements and flawless but sympathetic production. Unsurprisingly it failed to make much of a mark commercially, despite the fact that LYNNE knows more about so called "pop" music than most of the two-bit acts pimping their vacuous wares in the Top 20.

Album rating: ELECTRIC LIGHT ORCHESTRA (aka 'NO ANSWER' US) (*5) / ELECTRIC LIGHT ORCHESTRA II (*4) / ON THE THIRD DAY (*6) / THE NIGHT THE LIGHTS WENT ON IN LONG BEACH (*4) / ELDORADO (*7) / FACE THE MUSIC (*6) / OLE ELO compilation (*6) / A NEW WORLD RECORD (*6) / OUT OF THE BLUE (*8) / DISCOVERY (*5) / ELO'S GREATEST HITS compilation (*8) / XANADU soundtrack with Olivia Newton-John (*4) / TIME (*4) / SECRET MESSAGES (*4) / BALANCE OF POWER (*4) / PART II (*2; as Electric Light Orchestra Part II) / MOMENT OF TRUTH (*3; as Electric Light Orchestra Part II) / STRANGE MUSIC: THE BEST OF ELECTRIC LIGHT ORCHESTRA compilation (*7) / ZOOM (*6)

ROY WOOD (b. 8 Nov'46) – cello, vocals, multi (ex-MOVE) / **JEFF LYNNE** (b.30 Dec'47) – vocals, guitar (ex-MOVE, ex-IDLE RACE) / **BEV BEVAN** (b. BEVERLEY, 24 Nov'46) – drums, vocals (ex-MOVE) / **RICHARD TANDY** (b.26 Nov'48) – bass, keyboards, vocals (ex-BALLS, ex-UGLYS) / **BILL HUNT** – keyboards, French horn / **WILF GIBSON** – violin / **HUGH McDOWELL** (b.31 Jul'53, London, England) – cello / **ANDY CRAIG** – cello

Harvest U.A.

Dec 71. (lp) *(SHVL 797)* *<5573>* **THE ELECTRIC LIGHT ORCHESTRA** <US-title 'NO ANSWER'> [32] [ ]
– 10538 overture / Look at me now / Nellie takes her bow / The battle of Marston Moor (July 2nd, 1644) / First movement (jumpin' biz) / Mr. Radio / Manhattan rumble (49th Street massacre) / Queen of the hours / Whisper in the night. *(re-iss. Nov83 on 'Fame' lp/c; FA/TCFA 4130841)*

Jul 72. (7") *(HAR 5053)* **10538 OVERTURE. / FIRST MOVEMENT (JUMPIN' BIZ)** [9] [–]

Sep 72. (7") *<50914>* **10538 OVERTURE. / THE BATTLE OF MARSTON MOOR (JULY 2ND, 1644)** [–] [ ]

— **MIKE EDWARDS** – cello repl. ROY WOOD who formed WIZZARD (also went solo) **JEFF LYNNE** – (now lead vocals)

MICHAEL DE ALBUQUERQUE – bass repl. HUNT and McDOWELL who joined WIZZARD / **COLIN WALKER** – cello repl. ANDY CRAIG

Jan 73. (7") *(HAR 5063)* *<173>* **ROLL OVER BEETHOVEN. / QUEEN OF THE HOURS** [6] Apr73 [42]

Feb 73. (lp) *(SHVL 806)* *<040>* **ELECTRIC LIGHT ORCHESTRA II** [35] [62]
– In old England town (boogie #2) / Momma / Roll over Beethoven / From the sun to the world (boogie #1) / Kuiama. *(re-iss. May82 on 'Fame' lp/c; FA/TCFA 3003)*

Sep 73. (7") *(HAR 5077)* *<337>* **SHOWDOWN. / IN OLD ENGLAND TOWN** [12] Nov73 [53]

— **MIK KAMINSKI** (b. 2 Sep'51, Harrogate, England) – violin repl. GIBSON / **HUGH McDOWELL** – cello returned to repl. WALKER (above 2 in septet with **LYNNE, BEVAN, TANDY, WALKER ALBUQUERQUE** and **EDWARDS.**

Warners U.A.

Dec 73. (lp/c) *(K/K4 56021)* *<188>* **ON THE THIRD DAY** [ ] [52]
– Ocean breakup – King of the universe / Daybreaker / Bluebird is dead / Oh no, not Susan / New world rising / Ocean breakup (reprise) / Showdown / Daybreaker / Ma-Ma-Ma belle / Dreaming of 4000 / In the hall of the Mountain King. *(re-iss. 1977 on 'United Artists' lp/c; UAG/UAC 30091) (re-iss. Jun77 on 'Jet' clear-lp/c; JET LP/CA 202)*

Mar 74. (7") *(K 16349)* **MA-MA-MA BELLE. / CAN'T FIND THE TITLE** [22] [–]

Mar 74. (lp) *<UALA 318>* **THE NIGHT THE LIGHT WENT OUT IN LONG BEACH (live)** [–] [ ]
– Daybreaker / Showdown / Daytripper / 10538 overture / Mik's solo / Orange blossom special / Medley: In the hall of the mountain king – Great balls of fire / Roll over Beethoven. *(UK-iss.Nov85 on 'Epic' lp/c; EPC/40 32700)*

Apr 74. (7") *<405>* **DAYBREAKER (live). / MA-MA-MA BELLE (live)** [–] [87]

Jun 74. (7") *(K 16510)* *<573>* **CAN'T GET IT OUT OF MY HEAD. / ILLUSIONS IN G MAJOR** [ ] Dec74 [9]

Oct 74. (lp/c) *(K/K4 56090)* *<UALA 339>* **ELDORADO – A SYMPHONY BY THE ELECTRIC LIGHT ORCHESTRA** [ ] [16]
– Eldorado – overture / Can't get it out of my head / Boy blue / Larend tornado / Poor boy (the greenwood) / Mister Kingdom / Nobody's child Illusions in G major / Eldorado – finale. *(re-iss. 1977 on 'United Artists' lp/c UAG/UAC 30092) (re-iss. Jun77 on 'Jet' yellow-lp/c; JET LP/CA 203) (re-iss 1986; JETLP 32397)*

Nov 74. (7") **ELDORADO. / BOY BLUE** [–] [ ]

— **KELLY GROUCUTT** (b. 8 Sep'45, Coseley, England) – bass, vocals rep ALBUQUERQUE / **MELVYN GALE** (b.15 Jan'52, London) – cello rep EDWARDS

Jet Jet

Oct 75. (lp/c) *(JET LP/TC 11)* *<546>* **FACE THE MUSIC** [ ] [8]
– Fire on high / Waterfall / Evil woman / Night rider / Poker / Strang magic / Down home town / One summer dream. *(re-iss. Oct76 o 'Jet-United Artists' lp/c; UAG/UAC 30034) (re-iss. Mar77 green-lp/c; JE LP/CA 201) (re-iss. Jun85 on 'Epic'; lp/c; (EPC/40 32544) (cd-iss. Nov91 o 'Pickwick'; 9825962) (re-iss. cd Mar94 on 'Sony Collectors')*

Dec 75. (7") *(JET 764)* *<JET 729>* **EVIL WOMAN. / 10538 OVERTURE (live)** [10] Oct75 [10]

Mar 76. (7") *(JET 769)* **NIGHT RIDER. / DAYBREAKER** [ ] [–]

Mar 76. (7") *<JET 770>* **STRANGE MAGIC. / NEW WORLD RECORD** [–] [14]

Jun 76. (7") *(JET 779)* **STRANGE MAGIC. / SHOWDOWN (live)** [38] [–]

Jul 76. (7") *<JET 842>* **SHOWDOWN. / DAYBREAKER (live)** [–] [59]

U.A. Jet

Oct 76. (7",7"blue) *(UP 36184)* **LIVIN' THING. / FIRE ON HIGH** [4] [–]

Oct 76. (7") *<JET 888>* **LIVIN' THING. / MA-MA-MA BELLE** [–] [13]

Nov 76. (lp/c) *(UAG/UAC 30017)* *<679>* **A NEW WORLD RECORD** [6] Oct76 [5]
– Tightrope / Telephone line / Rockaria! / Mission (a new world record) So fine / Livin' thing / Above the clouds / Do ya / Shangri-la. *(re-iss. Jun7 red-lp/c; JET LP/CA 200) (re-iss. 1985 on 'Epic' lp/c; JET LP/CA 32545) (cd iss. Mar87; CDJET 200) (re-iss. cd Apr89; JETCD 32545) (re-iss. Sep89 o 'Pickwick' lp/c/cd; 902198-1/-4/-2)*

Jan 77. (7") *<JET 939>* **DO YA. / NIGHTRIDER** [–] [24]

Feb 77. (7") *(UP 36209)* **ROCKARIA!. / POKER** [9] [ ]
(re-iss. May78; SJET 100)

May 77. (7"m) *(UP 36254)* **TELEPHONE LINE. / POORBOY (THE GREENWOOD) / KING OF THE UNIVERSE** [8] [–]
(re-iss. May78; SJET 101)

May 77. (7") *<JET 1000>* **TELEPHONE LINE. / POORBOY (THE GREENWOOD)** [–] [7]

Oct 77. (7") *(UP 36313)* *<1099>* **TURN TO STONE. / MISTER KINGDOM** [18] Nov77 [13]
(re-iss. May78; SJET 103)

Nov 77. (d-lp/d-c) *(UAR/UAC 100)* *<823>* **OUT OF THE BLUE** [4] [4]
– Turn to stone / It's over / Sweet talkin' woman / Across the border / Nig in the city / Starlight / Jungle / Believe me now / Steppin' out / Standin in the rain / Summer and lightning / Mr. Blue Sky / Sweet is the night The whale / Wild west hero / Birmingham Blues. *(re-iss. 1978 on doubl blue-lp; JETDP 400) (re-iss. May87 on 'Epic' d-lp/d-c/d-cd; 450885-1/-4/- (re-iss. cd Jun91 on 'Epic')*

Jan 78. (7") *(UP 36342)* *<5050>* **MR. BLUE SKY. / ONE SUMMER DREAM** [6] Jun78 [35]
(re-iss. May78 in 7"blue; SJET 104)

Jet Jet

Feb 78. (7") *<1145>* **SWEET TALKIN' WOMAN. / FIRE ON HIGH** [–] [17]

Jun 78. (7"/12"yellow) *(SJET/+12 109)* **WILD WEST HERO. / ELDORADO** [6] [–]

Oct 78. (7") *<5052>* **IT'S OVER. / THE WHALE** [–] [75]

Sep 78. (7",7"mauve/12"mauve) *(SJET/+12 121)* **SWEET TALKIN' WOMAN. / BLUEBIRD IS DEAD** [6] [–]

May 79. (7"/12",12"white) *(SJET/+12 144)* *<5057>* **SHINE A LITTLE LOVE. / JUNGLE** [6] [8]

Jun 79. (lp/c) *(JET LX/CX 500)* *<35769>* **DISCOVERY** [1] [5]
– Shine a little love / Confusion / Need her love / The diary Horace Wimp / Last train to London / Midnight blue / On t run / Wishing / Don't bring me down. *(re-iss. Nov86 on 'Epic' lp EPC/40 450083-1/-4) (cd-iss. Apr87; CDJET 500) (re-iss. cd Jun91 on 'Epi 450083-2)*

Jul 79. (7") *(JET 150)* **THE DIARY OF HORACE WIMP. / DOWN HOME TOWN** 6 –

Aug 79. (7"/12") *(JET/+12 153) <5060>* **DON'T BRING ME DOWN. / DREAMING OF 4000** 3 4

Oct 79. (7") *<5064>* **CONFUSION. / POKER** – 37

Nov 79. (7") *(JET 166)* **CONFUSION. / LAST TRAIN TO LONDON** 8 –

Nov 79. Jet; (lp/c) *(JET LX/CX 525) <36310>* **ELO'S GREATEST HITS** (compilation) 7 30
– Telephone line / Evil woman / Livin' thing / Can't get it out of my head / Showdown / Turn to stone / Rockarai / Sweet talkin' woman / Ma-ma-ma belle / Strange magic / Mr. Blue sky. *(re-iss. Jan87 on 'Epic' lp/c; 450357-1/-4) (cd-iss. Dec86 on 'Epic; CDJET 525)*

Jan 80. (7") *<5067>* **LAST TRAIN TO LONDON. / DOWN HOME TOWN** – 39

— Now trimmed basic quartet of **LYNNE, BEVAN, TANDY** and **GROUCUTT** (KAMINSKI formed VIOLINSKI) (McDOWELL and GALE also departed)

Jet M.C.A.

May 80. (7") *(JET 179) <41246>* **I'M ALIVE. / DRUM DREAMS** 2 16

Jun 80. (7"/10"pink; by OLIVIA NEWTON-JOHN and ELECTRIC LIGHT ORCHESTRA) *(JET/+10 185)* **XANADU. / (track by OLIVIA NEWTON-JOHN)** 1 –

Jul 80. (lp/c) *(JET LX/CX 526) <6100>* **XANADU** (soundtrack shared w/ Olivia Newton-John) 2 Jun80 4
– (OLIVIA NEWTON-JOHN tracks) / I'm alive / The fall / Don't walk away / All over the world / Xanadu (w/ OLIVIA NEWTON-JOHN). *<(cd-iss. Dec03 on 'Epic'; 486620-2)>*

Jul 80. (7") *<41285>* **XANADU. / (other track by Gene Kelly & Olivia Newton-John)** – 8

Jul 80. (7"/10"blue) *(JET/+10 195)* **ALL OVER THE WORLD. / MIDNIGHT BLUE** 11 –

Jul 80. (7") *<41289>* **ALL OVER THE WORLD. / DRUM DREAMS** – 13

Nov 80. (7") *(JET 7004)* **DON'T WALK AWAY. / ACROSS THE BORDER** 21 –

Jul 81. (7") *(JET 7011) <02408>* **HOLD ON TIGHT. / WHEN TIME STOOD STILL** 4 10

Aug 81. (lp/c) *(JET LP/CA 236) <37371>* **TIME** 1 16
– Prologue / Twilight / Yours truly, 2095 / Ticket to the Moon / The way life's meant to be / Another heart breaks / Rain is falling / From the end of the world / The lights go down / Here is the news / 21st century man / Hold on tight / Epilogue. *(re-iss. Feb88 on 'Epic'; 460212) (cd-iss. May88 on 'Jet'; ZK 37371) (re-iss. cd Jun91; 460212-2)*

Oct 81. (7") *(JET 7015) <02559>* **TWILIGHT. / JULIE DON'T LIVE HERE** 30 33

Dec 81. (7"/12"pic-d) *(JET/+P12 7018)* **TICKET TO THE MOON. / HERE IS THE NEWS** 24 –

Jan 82. (7") *<02693>* **RAIN IS FALLING. / ANOTHER HEART BREAKS** – ☐

Mar 82. (7") *(JET 7021)* **THE WAY LIFE'S MEANT TO BE. / WISHING** ☐ –

Jet-Epic Jey-CBS

Jun 83. (7") *(JETA 3500) <03964>* **ROCK'N'ROLL IS KING. / AFTER ALL** 13 19
(12"+=) *(JETTA 3500)* – Time after time.

Jun 83. (lp/c) *(JET LX/CX 527) <38490>* **SECRET MESSAGES** 4 36
– Secret messages / Loser gone wild / Bluebird / Take me on and on / Four little diamonds / Stranger / Danger ahead / Letter from Spain / Train of gold / Rock'n'roll is king. *(cd-iss. May87; CDJET 527)* – Time after time. *(re-iss. Jun91 cd/c; 462487-2/-4) (re-iss. Mar93 cd/c)*

Aug 83. (7"/7"pic-d) *(JET A/WA 3720)* **SECRET MESSAGES. / BUILDINGS HAVE EYES** 48 –

Oct 83. (7") *(JETA 3869) <04130>* **FOUR LITTLE DIAMONDS. / LETTER FROM SPAIN** ☐ Sep83 86
(12"+=) *(JETTA 3869)* – The bouncer.

Jan 84. (7") *<04208>* **STRANGER. / TRAIN OF GOLD** – ☐

— after a brief spell in BLACK SABBATH, **BEVAN** rejoined ELO with others **JEFF LYNNE** and the returning **MICK KAMINSKI**

Epic C.B.S.

Feb 86. (7") *(A 6844) <05766>* **CALLING AMERICA. / CAUGHT IN A TRAP** 28 Jan86 18
(12"+=) *(QTA 6844)* – Destination unknown.

Mar 86. (lp/c) *(EPC/40 26467) <40048>* **BALANCE OF POWER** 9 Feb86 49
– Heaven only knows / So serious / Getting to the point / Secret lives / Is it alright? / Sorrow about to fall / Without someone / Calling America / Endless lies / Send it. *(cd-iss. May87; CD 26467) (re-iss. Jun91 cd/c; 468576-2/-4) (re-iss. Mar93 cd/c)*

Apr 86. (7") *(A 7090)* **SO SERIOUS. / A MATTER OF FACT** ☐ –
(12"+=) *(TA 7090)* – ('A'-alternative mix).

May 86. (7") *<05892>* **SO SERIOUS. / ENDLESS LIES** – ☐

Jul 86. (7") *(A 7317)* **GETTING TO THE POINT. / SECRET LIVES** ☐ –
(12"+=) *(TA 7317)* – Elo megamix.

— continued without LYNNE! who went solo and joined TRAVELING WILBURYS

— JEFF LYNNE had released two solo 45's while a ELO member. These were 'DOIN' THAT CRAZY THING'. / 'GOIN' DOWN TO RIO' in 1977. BEV BEVAN issued a single in 1976, 'LET THERE BE DRUMS'. / 'HEAVY HEAD'.

JEFF LYNNE

Virgin Virgin

Jul 84. (7"/12") *(VS 695/+12) <04570>* **VIDEO! / SOONER OR LATER** ☐ 85

Reprise Reprise

Jun 90. (7") *(W 9799) <19799>* **EVERY LITTLE THING. / I'M GONE** 59 ☐
(12"+=) *(W 9799T)* –

Jul 90. (cd)(lp/c) *(<7599 26134-2>)(WX 347/+C)* **ARMCHAIR THEATRE** 24 Jun90 83
– Every little thing / Don't let go / Lift me up / Nobody home / September song / Now you're gone / Don't say goodbye / What would it take / Stormy weather / Blown away / Save me now.

ELECTRIC LIGHT ORCHESTRA PART II

— now with **BEVAN, KAMINSKI, McDOWELL, GROUCUTT, LOUIS CLARK, PETE HAYCOCK** – vocals (ex-CLIMAX BLUES BAND) / session **NEIL LOCKWOOD, ERIC TROYER**

Telstar Scotti Bros

Apr 91. (7"/c-s) *(ELO 100/+C) <75248>* **HONEST MAN. / LOVE FOR SALE** 60 ☐
(12"+=/cd-s+=) *(ELO 100 T/CD)* – ('A'extended).

May 91. (cd/c/lp) *(TCD/STAC/STAR 2503) <75222>* **PART II** 34 ☐
– Hello / Honest man / Every night / Once upon a time / Heartbreaker / Thousand eyes / For the love of a woman / Kiss me red / Heart of hearts / Easy street.

Oct 91. (c-s) *<75292>* **FOR THE LOVE OF A WOMAN** – ☐

— **ERIC TROYER + PHIL BATES** – guitar, vocals repl. HAYCOCK (now solo again)

Ultrapop Curb

Aug 94. (c-s/cd-s) *(9612-4/-5 ULT)* **POWER OF A MILLION LIGHTS** ☐ –

Oct 94. (cd/c) *(9610-2/-4 ULT) <77692>* **MOMENT OF TRUTH** ☐ ☐
– Moment of truth (overture) / Breakin' down the walls / Power of a million lights / Interlude / One more tomorrow / Don't wanna / Voices / Interlude 2 / Vixen / The fox / Love or money / Blue violin / Whiskey girls / Interlude / Twist of the knife / So glad you said goodbye / Underture / The leaving.

Oct 94. (c-s/cd-s) **BREAKIN' DOWN THE WALLS / (album version) / DON'T WANNA** ☐ –

ELECTRIC LIGHT ORCHESTRA

— **JEFF LYNNE** + band **RICHARD TANDY** + guests ROSIE VELA, GEORGE HARRISON, RINGO STARR, etc

Epic Sony

Jun 01. (cd) *(502500-2) <85336>* **ZOOM** 34 94
– Alright / Moment in paradise / State of mind / Just for love / Stranger on a quiet street / In my own time / Easy money / It really doesn't matter / Ordinary dream / A long time gone / Melting in the sun / All she wanted / Lonesome lullaby.

Sep 01. (cd-s) *<671136>* **ALRIGHT** – ☐

– compilations, etc. –

on 'Harvest' unless mentioned otherwise

Oct 74. (lp/c) *(SHSP/TC-SHSP 4037)* **SHOWDOWN** ☐ –

Apr 77. (lp/c) *(SHSM/TC-SHSM 2015)* **THE LIGHT SHINES ON** [ ] [–]

Dec 77. (7"/12") *(HAR/+12 5121)* **SHOWDOWN. / ROLL OVER BEETHOVEN** [ ] [–]

Jun 76. (lp) *Jet; (JETLP 19 w/drawn) <35528>* **OLE ELO** [–] [32]

Dec 78. (7"ep) *Jet; (ELO 1)* **E.L.O. EP** [34] [–]
– Can't get it out of my head / Strange magic / Evil woman / Ma-ma-ma-belle.

Dec 78. Jet; (3xlp-box) *(JETBX 1)* **THREE LIGHT YEARS** [38] [–]
– (ON THE THIRD DAY / ELDORADO / FACE THE MUSIC)

Mar 79. (lp/c) *(SHSM/TC-SHSM 2027)* **THE LIGHT SHINES ON (VOL.2)** [ ] [–]

Nov 80. (4xlp-box) *Jet; (JETBX 2)* **FOUR LIGHT YEARS** [ ] [–]
– (A NEW WORLD RECORD / OUT OF THE BLUE / DISCOVERY)

May 84. (7") *EMI Gold; (G45 22)* **ROLL OVER BEETHOVEN. / 10538 OVERTURE** [ ] [–]

Apr 86. (lp/c) *(EMS/EMC 1128)* **FIRST MOVEMENT** [ ] [–]
(cd-iss. Oct87; CZ 14)

1988. (cd) *Jet; (JETCD 24043)* **A PERFECT WORLD OF MUSIC** [ ] [–]

May 88. (cd) *Arcade; (01024661)* **ALL OVER THE WORLD** [ ] [–]

Dec 89. (lp/c/cd) *Telstar; (STAR/+T/CD 2370)* **THE VERY BEST OF ELO** [23] [–]
– Evil woman / Livin' thing / Can't get it out of my head / Showdown / Turn to stone / Rockaria! / Sweet talkin' woman / Telephone line / Ma ma ma belle / Strange magic / Mr blue sky *(re-iss. Oct90 as 'THE VERY BEST OF THE ELECTRIC LIGHT ORCHESTRA'; same)* – hit UK No.28

Aug 91. (cd/c/d-lp) *E.M.I.; (CD/TC/LP EM 1419)* **EARLY ELO** [ ] [ ]
– (first 2 albums, plus bonus tracks)

Sep 92. (cd/c) *Collection; (R 450357-2/-4)* **GREATEST HITS VOL.2** [ ] [–]

Oct 92. Epic; (3xcd-box) *(EPC 472267 123)* **BOXED SET** [ ] [–]
– (OUT OF THE BLUE / ELDORADO / A NEW WORLD RECORD)

Dec 92. (3xcd-box) *Epic; (472267-2)* **ELDORADO / A NEW WORLD RECORD / OUT OF THE BLUE** [ ] [–]

Jun 94. Dino; (cd/c) *(DIN CD/C 30)* **THE VERY BEST OF THE ELECTRIC LIGHT ORCHESTRA** [4] [–]

Jul 94. (3xcd-box) *Legacy-Epic; (CD 46090)* **AFTERGLOW** [ ] [–]

Oct 94. (3xcd-box) *Epic; (477526-2)* **TIME / SECRET MESSAGES / DISCOVERY** [ ] [–]

May 96. (cd/c) *EMI Gold; (CD/TC GOLD 1002)* **THE GOLD COLLECTION** [ ] [–]

Oct 97. (cd/c) *Epic; (3013-2/-4)* **ONE NIGHT IN AUSTRALIA LIVE VOL.1 (live)** [ ] [–]

Oct 97. (cd/c) *Epic; (3014-2/-4)* **ONE NIGHT IN AUSTRALIA LIVE VOL.2 (live)** [ ] [–]

Nov 97. (cd/c) *Epic; (489039-2/-4)* **LIGHT YEARS – THE VERY BEST OF** [60] [–]

Nov 97. (3xcd-box) *Epic; (485340-2)* **DISCOVERY / OUT OF THE BLUE / TIME** [ ] [–]

Oct 01. (d-cd) *Sony TV; (STVCD 126)* **THE ULTIMATE COLLECTION** [18] [ ]

ELECTRIC SIX

Formed: Detroit, Michigan, USA . . . 1996 as the WILDBUNCH by JACKSON POUNDER and MARTIN M. The pair released the warped garage single, 'I LOST CONTROL (OF MY ROCK'N'ROLL)', on the tiny 'Uchu Cult' label before recruiting MOJO FREZZATO, DISCO, THE ROCK-N-ROLL INDIAN and the brilliantly named DR. BLACKLIPS HOFFMAN for 1997's 'Flying Bomb' release, 'THE BALLADE OF MC SUCKA DJ'. More pseudonymous japery followed as DICK VALENTINE (i.e. JACKSON, accompanied by one FRANK LLOYD BONNAVENTURE and SURGE JOEBOT amongst others) took the mic for the calculated, demented stooge-rock of 'DANGER! HIGH VOLTAGE'. It was electrifying enough to come within sniffing distance of the UK No.1 spot and, newly signed to Britain's 'X.L.' label, ELECTRIC SIX released the long awaited 'FIRE' (2003). Mutant disco, swaggering, sardonic stadium rock and good old underground subversiveness (just listen to 'GAY BAR' if you're short on laughs) were the key ingredients in the band's tongue-in-cheek armoury, proving that Detroit's font of alt-rock evangelism hasn't dried up quite yet. Turning irreverence into an art form, the Michigan maniacs returned to the charts late in 2004 with sophomore album taster, Queen's 'RADIO GA GA'. Released on 'Warners', 'SENOR SMOKE' (2005) featured some of the best disco-rock chops since the late 70s, showing peers the DARKNESS how it was done. And no one pronounces "Deviiillle" like DICK VALENTINE.

• **Covers:** ROCKSHOW (Peaches).

Album rating: FIRE (*7) / SENOR SMOKE (*6)

the WILDBUNCH

JACKSON POUNDER (b. JACKSON SPENCER) – vocals, guitar, bass, synthesizer / **MARTIN M.** (b. CORY MARTIN) – drums

not iss. / Uchu Cu

1996. (7"ep) *<SC 001>* **I LOST CONTROL (OF MY ROCK & ROLL) / TINY LITTLE MEN. / GAY BAR / I KNOW KARATE** [–] [ ]

1996. (ltd;m-lp) *<none>* **AN EVENING WITH THE MANY MOODS OF THE WILDBUNCH'S GREATEST HITS . . . TONIGHT! 8 TRACK** [–] [ ]

— added **THE ROCK-N-ROLL INDIAN** (b. ANTHONY SELPH) – guitar / **MOJO FREZZATO** – guitar / **DISCO** (b. STEVE NAWARA) – bass / plus **DR. BLACKLIPS HOFFMAN** – keyboards

not iss. / Flying Bomb

1997. (7"m) *<FLB 105>* **THE BALLADE OF MC SUCKA DJ. / TAKE OFF YOUR CLOTHES / NUCLEAR WAR (ON THE DANCE FLOOR)** [–] [ ]

not iss. / Off Woodwa

1998. (cd) *<none>* **DON'T BE AFRAID OF THE ROBOT: LIVE AT THE GOLD DOLLAR (live)** [–] [ ]

— **DICK VALENTINE** (was the new name for JACKSON)

— **SURGE JOEBOT** – guitar; repl. MOJO

not iss. / Flying Bomb

2001. (7"m) *<FLB 117>* **DANGER (HIGH VOLTAGE). / NEUROCAMERAMAN / SHE'S GUATEMALA** [–] [ ]

ELECTRIC SIX

VALENTINE, DISCO, SURGE + THE ROCK-N-ROLL INDIAN + M. with **TAIT NUCLEUS** – keyboards / **FRANK LLOYD BONNAVENTURE + DR. BLACKLIPS HOFFMAN + JEFF SIMMONS + TAIT NUCLEUS + JOHNNY VEGAS-HENTCH**

X.L. / Beggars X

Jan 03. (7") *(XLS 151) <BQTX 41157>* **DANGER! HIGH VOLTAGE. / I LOST CONTROL (OF MY ROCK'N'ROLL)** [2] Feb03 [ ]
(cd-s+=) *(XLS 151CD)* – Remote control (me).
('A'-Soulchild mix; 12"+=) *(XLT 151)* – ('A'-Thin White Duke remix).
(cd-s++=) *(XLS 151CD2)* – ('A'-kilogram mix).

— now with **THE COLONEL + JOHNNY NAS$HINAL** repl. TAIT

Jun 03. (7") *(XLS 158)* **GAY BAR. / THE LIVING END** [5] [–]
(cd-s) *(XLS 158CD)* – ('A') / Don't be afraid of the robot / Take off your clothes.

Jun 03. (ltd-7") *(XLS 159)* **ROCKSHOW. / Peaches: ROCKSHOW** [ ] [–]

Jun 03. (cd/lp) *(XLCD/XLLP 169) <40169>* **FIRE** [7] May03 [ ]
– Dance commander / Electric demons in love / Naked pictures (of your mother) / Danger! high voltage / She's white / I invented the night / Improper dancing / Gay bar / Nuclear war (on the dance floor) / Getting into the jam / Vengeance and fashion / I'm the bomb / Synthesizer. *(cd re-iss. Dec03 w/dvd+=; XLCD 169X)* – (videos).

Oct 03. (cd-s) *(XLS 170CD)* **DANCE COMMANDER / I AM DETROIT / ('A'-Soulchild extended remix)** [40] [–]
(cd-s) *(XLS 170CD2)* – ('A'-Benny Benassi satisfaction remix) / ('A'-Fatboy Slim dub mix) / ('A'-video).
(12") *(XLT 170)* – ('A'-Soulchild mix) / ('A'-Benny . . . mix).

Warners / Warner

Dec 04. (7"pic-d/cd-s) *(WEA 381/+CD1)* **RADIO GA GA. / GAY BAR (live at Manumission)** [21] [–]
(cd-s) *(WEA 381CD2)* – ('A') / Vibrator (download mix) / ('A'-Vertigo remix) / ('A'-video).

Feb 05. (cd) *(2564 62153-2)* **SENOR SMOKE** [ ] [ ]
– Rock and roll evacuation / Devil nights / Bite me / Jimmy Carter / Pleasant interlude I / Dance epidemic / Future boys / Dance-a-thon 2005 / Be my dark angel / Vibrator / Boy or girl? / Pleasant interlude II / Radio Ga Ga / Taxi to nowhere / The future is the future.

—— (Nov'04) drummer M departed; repl. by **PERCUSSION WORLD**

❑ ELECTRONIC (see under ⇒ NEW ORDER)

❑ Mama Cass ELLIOT
(see under ⇒ MAMAS AND THE PAPAS)

Missy ELLIOTT

Born: MELISSA ARNETTE ELLIOTT, 1 Jul'71, Portsmouth, Virginia, USA. Both a respected figure in the Hip-hop world and a self-proclaimed musical icon, MISSY ELLIOTT (along with DR DRE and super producer TIMBALAND) has contributed greatly to the rise of 'ghetto styl-ee' in modern music. MISSY began her musical legacy when DEVANTE SWING (of JODECI) signed her outfit SISTA to the 'Swing Mob' label. This is where she met TIMBALAND, a friend of SWING's and an inspiring Rap producer. JODECI's 'Diary Of A Mad Band' (1994) was to be the start of a long-term relationship with TIMBALAND, even if the Swing Mob' label eventually went bust. Abandoning SISTA, MISSY jumped at the chance to collaborate once again with her mentor on AALIYAH's 'One In A Million' album in '96, writing tracks Aaliyah' and the set's title track. After the astonishing success of the LP, MISSY was contracted to work with a number of rising stars by record execs, including writing, producing and rapping credits on songs from BOYZ II MEN, PAULA COLE and The RUFF RYDERS. She finally struck a solo deal with 'Elektra' in 1996 and issued the breakthrough album 'SUPA DUPA FLY' to critical and commercial acclaim, thanks to the stomping, adrenaline-fuelled single 'THE RAIN'. She continued producing tracks for WHITNEY HOUSTON, EVE and most notably DESTINY'S CHILD before the release of 1999's 'DA REAL WORLD' which spawned two massive singles 'SHE'S A BITCH' and 'HOT BOYZ' and boasted a collaboration with EMINEM. Between appearing in ads for Gap and Sprite, MISSY kept herself busy producing a rendition of 'LADY MARMALADE' featuring the girls from 'Moulin Rouge', aka PINK, CHRISTINA AGUILERA and LIL' KIM. The song was a Number One hit in both the States and the UK, paving the way for her third and best outing 'MISS E . . . SO ADDICTIVE' (2001), a record which featured the massive hit single 'GET UR FREAK ON', a tribal, operatic hip-hop track that sounded like no other. 'ONE MINUTE MAN' followed, and MISSY ELLIOTT was perhaps the most respected hip-hop artist/producer/rapper/songwriter in the industry. Southern rapper BUBBA SPARXXX asked to borrow elements from 'GET UR FREAK ON'. MISSY, of course obliged, but cheekily changed the lyrics to: "I'm Copywritten, so don't copy me . . .' However, many artists in the industry have, and with a talent this big, who could resist. The album 'UNDER CONSTRUCTION' was issued in 2002 to brilliant acclaim and featured possibly the most absurd and downright unusual single in the form of 'WORK IT'. Using spasmodic beats, industrial rhythms and elephant noises (!), it became a truly infectious bugged-out club hit. Elsewhere, MISSY ELLIOTT, brought in the cream of the R&B crop; from her right-hand man TIMBALAND (possibly the hardest working man in the Urban music game), JAY-Z and a duet with uber diva BEYONCE KNOWLES on 'NOTHING'S OUT THERE FOR ME'. It was a startling set of songs that put most R&B acts to shame with its use of warped time signatures, throbbing bass and colourful inventiveness. It would be hard to top the sheer size and scope of 'UNDER CONSTRUCTION', so it was no surprise that a year later and the release of 'THIS IS NOT A TEST!' failed to match up to the brilliance of its predecessor. However, the two albums were very similar, so much so, in fact, that they could have been issued as a double album. Single 'PASS THAT DUTCH', about dope-smoking among other things, was indeed 'WORK IT' only slightly watered down. The regulars were at the helm yet again, from TIMBALAND to JAY-Z, and a duet with Southern homeboy NELLY ('PUMP IT UP') being a particular highlight, although an R. KELLY collaboration 'IS THIS OUR LAST TIME' would have not been greatly missed. With 'THE COOKBOOK' (2005), ELLIOTT combined some of her spiciest ingredients to date, including recent American Pop Idol winner, FANTASIA (on '4 MY MAN'), SLICK RICK (on 'IRRESISTABLE'), MARY J. BLIGE & GRAND PUBA ('MY STRUGGLES') and, on transatlantic Top 10 single, 'LOSE CONTROL', a clutch of vintage KRAFTWERK-esque samples.

Album rating: SUPA DUPA FLY (*6) / DA REAL WORLD (*7) / MISS E . . . SO ADDICTIVE (*8) / UNDER CONSTRUCTION (*7) / THIS IS NOT A TEST! (*5) / THE COOKBOOK (*7)

MISSY 'MISDEMEANOR' ELLIOTT

- vocals / with session people, etc

Elektra Elektra

Jul 97. (cd/c) *<(7559 62062/-2/-4)>* **SUPA DUPA FLY** [ ] [3]
– Busta's intro / Hit 'em wit da hee / Sock it 2 me / The rain (supa dupa fly) / Beep me 911 / They don't wanna fuck wit me / Pass da blunt / Bite our style (interlude) / Friendly skies / Best friends / Don't be comin' (in my face) / Izzy izzy ahh / Why you hurt me / I'm talkin' (the biz) / Gettaway / Busta's outro / Missy's finale.

—— In Jul'97, MISSY ELLIOTT was featured on the collaborative hit single 'Not Tonight' by LIL' KIM, DA BRAT, LEFT EYE and ANGIE MARTINEZ

Aug 97. (c-s) *(E 3919C)* **THE RAIN (SUPA DUPA FLY) / (instrumental)** [16] [ ]
(cd-s+=) *(E 3919CD)* – (acappella).

Nov 97. (c-s/cd-s) *(E 3890 C/CD)* **SOCK IT 2 ME / (Da Brat instrumental & acappella) / RELEASE THE TENSION** [33] Oct97 [12]
(cd-s) *(E 3890CDX)* – ('A'side) / The rain (supa dupa fly) / Release the tension.

Apr 98. (c-s) *(E 3859C)* **BEEP ME 911 / (instrumental)** [14] [ ]
(cd-s+=) *(E 3859CD)* – ('A'mix).

—— in Jun'98, MISSY 'MISDEMEANOR' ELLIOTT (& MOCHA) featured on NICOLE's US Top 5 hit (UK No.22), 'Make It Hot' *(E 3821 C/T/CD)*
(below as MISSY 'MISDEMEANOR' ELLIOTT featuring LIL' KIM)

Aug 98. (12"/cd-s) *(E 3824 T/CD2)* **HIT 'EM WIT DA HEE. / BEEP ME 911** [25] [ ]
(12"/cd-s) *(E 3824 TX/CD1)* – ('A'mixes) / The rain.

—— in Sep'98, MISSY featured on MELANIE B's UK No.1, 'I Want You Back'

—— in Oct'98, she also guested for TOTAL on the US hit 'Trippin''

—— in Nov'98, MISSY featured on LIL' MO's single, '5 Minutes'

—— in Mar'99, a three-way collaboration with TIMBALAND and MAGOO heralded another minor hit, 'Here We Come'

Jun 99. (cd/c/lp) *(7559 62436-2/-4/-1) <62232>* **DA REAL WORLD** [40] [10]
– Mysterious / Beat biter / Funky white boy / All 'n my grill / Smooth chick / Hot boyz / Mr DJ / You don't know / We did it / She's a bitch / Dangerous mouths / Sticking chickens / Checkin' for you / U can't resist / Crazy feelings / Religious / All 'n my grill.

Jul 99. (c-s) *(E 3745C) <63751>* **SHE'S A BITCH / (clean)** [ ] May99 [90]
(12"+=/cd-s+=) *(E 3745 T/CD)* – ('A'mixes).

Sep 99. (c-s) *(E 3742C) <radio cut>* **ALL 'N MY GRILL / (version)** [20] Jul99 [64]
(12"+=/cd-s+=) *(E 3742 T/CD)* – ('A'mixes).
(above as MISSY 'MISDEMEANOR' ELLIOTT featuring MC SOLAAR)
(below as MISSY 'MISDEMEANOR' ELLIOTT featuring NAS, EVE & Q-TIP)

Elektra East West

Jan 00. (c-s) *(E 7002C) <64029>* **HOT BOYZ / (clean)** [18] Nov99 [5]
(12"+=/cd-s+=) *(E 7002 T/CD)* – (remix original).

—— in Jun'00, MISSY featured on TORREY CARTER's minior hit, 'Take That'

—— late 2000, she appeared on MEMPHIS BLEEK's hit, 'Is That Your Chick'

MISSY ELLIOTT

— a slight change of moniker

Apr 01. (c-s) *(E 7206C)* *<67190>* **GET UR FREAK ON / (clean)** [4] Mar01 [7]
(12"+=/cd-s+=) *(E 7206 T/CD)* – (instrumental)

May 01. (cd/c) *<(7559 62639-2/-4)>* **MISS E . . . SO ADDICTIVE** [10] [2]
– So addictive (with CHARLENE 'TWEET' KAYE) / Dog n heat (with REDMAN & METHOD MAN) / One minute man (with LUDACRIS) / Old school joint / Get Ur freak on / Lick shots / Take away (with GINUWINE) / 4 my people (with EVE) / Step off / Busta bus interlude (with BUSTA RHYMES) / Whatcha gon' do (with TIMBALAND) / Screen AKA itchin' / X tasy / Slap slap (with DA BRAT & JADE) / I've changed (with LIL' MO) / One minute man (with JAY-Z) / Higher ground. *<(clean version; 7559 62643-2/-4)> (new version cd-iss. Apr02 +=; 7559 62777-2)*

Aug 01. (c-s) *(E 7245C)* *<radio cut>* **ONE MINUTE MAN / (version)** [10] Jul01 [15]
(12"+=/cd-s+=) *(E 7245 T/CD)* – ('A'mixes).

Oct 01. (cd-s) *(7559 67255-0)* **SUPERFREAKON (mixes)** [72] [–]

— in Nov'01, MISSY featured on JANET JACKSON's hit, 'Son Of A Gun'

Dec 01. (c-s; by MISSY ELLIOTT featuring GINUWINE & TWEET) *(E 7263C)* **TAKE AWAY / (album version)** [ ] [50]
(cd-s+=) *(E 7263CD1)* – One minute man (original) / Get ur freak on (superchumba superfreakon remix + Cd-Rom).
(cd-s) *(E 7263CD2)* – ('A'mixes).

Jan 02. (cd-s) *<6727-2>* **TAKE AWAY** [–] [45]

Mar 02. (cd-s; by MISSY "MISDEMEANOR" ELLIOTT featuring EVE) *(E 7286CD1)* **4 MY PEOPLE / ('A'-Basement Jaxx mix) / TAKE AWAY** [5] [–]
(cd-s) *(E 7286CD2)* – ('A'side) / Get ur freak on (superchumbo's superfreakon remix) / Get ur freak on (video).

Nov 02. (c-s) *(E 7344C)* **WORK IT / (mix)** [6] Oct02 [2]
(12") *(E 7344T)* *<ELEK 67340>* – ('A'side) / P***ycat / My people.
(cd-s+=) *(E 7344CD)* – ('A'-video).

Nov 02. (cd/lp) *<(7559 62813-2/-4)>* **UNDER CONSTRUCTION** [23] [3]
– Intro – Go to the floor / Bring the pain (with METHOD MAN) / Gossip folks (with LUDACRIS) / Work it / Back in the day (with JAY-Z) / Funky fresh dressed (with MS. JADE) / P***ycat / Nothing out there for me (with BEYONCE KNOWLES) / Slide / Play that beat / Ain't that funny / Hot / Can you hear me (with TLC) / Work it (reprise with 50 CENT). *(cd re-iss. Mar03 +=; 7559 62875-2)* – Gossip folks (Fatboy Slim remix with LUDACRIS) / Gossip folks (Mousse T remix with LUDACRIS).

Mar 03. (12"/cd-s; by MISSY ELLIOTT & LUDACRIS) *(E 7380 T/CD)* *<67356>* **GOSSIP FOLKS (mixes by Fatboy Slim + video)** [9] [8]

— late in 2003, MISSY ELLIOTT duetted with WYCLEF JEAN on the hit single, 'Party To Damascus'

Nov 03. (12"/cd-s) *(E 7509 T/CD)* **PASS THAT DUTCH / (version) / HURT SUMTHIN** [10] [27]

Nov 03. (cd/lp) *<(7559 62905-2/-1)>* **THIS IS NOT A TEST!** [49] [13]
– Baby girl intro (with MARY J. BLIGE) / Pass that Dutch / Wake up (with JAY-Z) / Keep it movin' (with ELEPHANT MAN) / Is this our last time (with FABOLOUS) / I'm really hot / Dats what I'm talkin about (with R. KELLY) / Don't be cruel / Toyz / Let it bump / Pump it up (with NELLY) / It's real / Let me fix my weave / Spelling bee / I'm not perfect (with CLARK SISTERS) / Outro (with MARY J. BLIGE).
in Mar'04, MISSY feat. on TIMBALAND & MAGOO's hit, 'Cop That Shit'

Mar 04. (cd-s) *(E 7552CD)* **I'M REALLY HOT / PASS THAT DUTCH** [22] [–]
(dvd-s+=) *(E 7552DVD)* – ('A'-video) / ('B'-promo video).
in Jul'04, GHOSTFACE KILLAH feat. her on hit 'Push'
in Nov'04, the 'Car Wash' hit by CHRISTINA AGUILERA feat. MISSY
in Mar'05, MISSY feat. on TWEET's hit, 'Turn Da Lights Off'
in Apr'05, MISSY feat. on CIARA's hit, '1.2 Step'

Jul 05. (cd) *<(7567 83779-2)>* **THE COOKBOOK** [33] [2]
– Joy (feat. MIKE JONES) / Partytime / Irresistible delicious (feat. SLICK RICK) / Lose control (feat. CIARA & FAT MAN SCOOP) / My struggles (feat. MARY J. BLIGE & GRAND PUBA) / Meltdown / On & on / We run this / Remember when / 4 my man (feat. FANTASIA) / Can't stop / Teary eyed / Mommy / Click clack / Time and time again / Bad man (feat. VYBEZ CARTEL & M.I.A.).

Jul 05. (12") *(7567 93880-0)* *<93787>* **LOSE CONTROL (Jacques Lu Cont mix) /. / (dub)** [7] May05 [3]

Sep 05. (12"/cd-s) *(AT 0215 T/CD)* *<93943>* **TEARY EYED / (instrumental) / (a cappella) / (Jacques Lu Cont mix)** [47] Jan06 [ ]

Oct 05. (12") *<94030>* **WE RUN THIS** [–] [48]

EMBRACE

Formed: Huddersfield, England ... 1993 by Irish-rooted songwriting brothers, DANNY (lyrics) and RICHARD McNAMARA (the music), who enlisted the rhythm team of STEVE FIRTH and MIKE KEATON. After the stunning OASIS-esque grandeur of the early '97 debut, 'ALL YOU GOOD GOOD PEOPLE', for the 'Fierce Panda' set-up, they signed to Virgin offshoot, 'Hut'. The band made an immediate impact on the singles chart with the EP, 'FIREWORKS', increasing their chart exposure with the summer '97 follow-up, 'ONE BIG FAMILY'. However, the pop nation finally clutched them to their proverbial bosom with the re-issue of 'ALL YOU GOOD GOOD PEOPLE', which cracked the Top 10 in the Autumn. The following year, the much vaunted songwriting siblings scored a further two Top 10 hits, 'COME BACK TO WHAT YOU KNOW' and 'MY WEAKNESS IS NONE OF YOUR BUSINESS', both taken from their chart-topping debut album, 'THE GOOD WILL OUT'. Towards the end the decade and with part-timer MICKEY DALE now their official 5th member, EMBRACE previewed their forthcoming sophomore set via a Top 20 hit, 'HOOLIGAN'. When it finally arrived, 'DRAWN FROM MEMORY' (2000) revealed a more mature band, conscious of their more overblown tendencies and determined to pare their sound down somewhat. Thus the Britpop-inspired orchestration which characterised this album's predecessor wasn't quite so conspicuous, although the record's highlights were still centered around soul searching balladry such as the title track. In the event, 'DRAWN FROM MEMORY' (2000), in addition to making the UK Top 10 itself, spawned a further three hits in the shape of 'YOU'RE NOT ALONE', 'SAVE ME' and 'I WOULDN'T WANNA HAPPEN TO YOU'. Although the worst excesses of orchestration had been reined in, EMBRACE seemed to be working with the philosophy that if it ain't broke, don't fix it. If so, it was an ethos that ensured them a Top 10 placing for 'IF YOU'VE NEVER BEEN' (2001), along with two singles: the Top 20 'WONDER' and 'MAKE IT LAST'. Finding a natural home at 'Independiente' (alongside TRAVIS and PAUL WELLER), the Huddersfield lads proved with 'OUT OF NOTHING' (2004), they were the missing link between latter-period PINK FLOYD, OASIS and COLDPLAY, British and anthemic to the core. The presence of COLDPLAY's CHRIS MARTIN on second single 'GRAVITY' ('ASHES' had already hit the UK Top 10), suggested they kept their influences as close as their harmonies. The YOUTH-produced 'THIS NEW DAY' (2006) gave them two consecutive No.1 albums, with DANNY's vocal progess in evidence on classy, near chart-topper 'NATURE'S LAW'. Following in the grand tradition of the LIGHTNING SEEDS and NEW ORDER, EMBRACE were musically capped for England with the official World Cup (2006) song, 'WORLD AT YOUR FEET', a record that went Top 3.

Album rating: THE GOOD WILL OUT (*8) / DRAWN FROM MEMORY (*6) / IF YOU'VE NEVER BEEN (*6) / FIREWORKS: SINGLES 1997-2002 compilation (*7) / OUT OF NOTHING (*6) / DRY KIDS compilation (*6) / THIS NEW DAY (*8)

DANNY McNAMARA (b.31 Dec'70, Bailiff Bridge, nr. Bradford) – vocals / **RICHARD McNAMARA** (b.23 Oct'72, Bailiff Bridge) – guitar, vocals / **STEVE FIRTH** – bass / **MIKE KEATON** – drums, vocals

Fierce Panda — not iss.

Feb 97. (ltd-7") *(NING 29)* **ALL YOU GOOD GOOD PEOPLE. / MY WEAKNESS IS NONE OF YOUR BUSINESS** [ ] [–]

Hut Geffen

May 97. (c-ep/12"ep/cd-ep) *(HUT C/T/CD 84)* **FIREWORKS EP** 34 –
– The last gas / Now you're nobody / Blind / Fireworks. *(12"ep re-iss. Nov98; same)*

Jul 97. (c-ep/12"ep/cd-ep) *(HUT C/T/CD 86)* **ONE BIG FAMILY EP** 21 –
– One big family / Dry kids / You've only got to stop to get better / Butter wouldn't melt. *(12"ep re-iss. Nov98; same)*

Oct 97. (c-ep/12"ep/cd-ep) *(HUT C/T/DX 90)* **ALL YOU GOOD GOOD PEOPLE EP** 8 –
– All you good good people (extended) / You won't amount to anything – this time / The way I do / Free ride. *(12"ep re-iss. Nov98; same)*
(cd-ep) *(HUTCD 90)* – ('A') / One big family (Perfecto mix) / ('A'-Fierce Panda version) / ('A'-orchestral mix).

May 98. (c-s) *(HUTC 93)* *<95132>* **COME BACK TO WHAT YOU KNOW / LOVE IS BACK** 6 Jul98
(12"+=/cd-s+=) *(HUT T/DX 93)* – If you feel like a sinner / Perfect way.
(cd-s) *(HUTCDX 93)* – ('A') / Butter wouldn't melt (live) / Dry kids (live) / ('A'-orchestral).

Jun 98. (cd/c/d-lp) *(CDHUT/HUTMC/HUTDLP 46)* *<25165>* **THE GOOD WILL OUT** 1 Jul98
– Intro / All you good good people / My weakness is none of your business / Come back to what you know / One big family / Higher sights / Retread / I want the world / You've got to say yes / Fireworks / The last gas / That's all changed forever / Now you're nobody / The good will out.

Aug 98. (7") *(HUT 103)* **MY WEAKNESS IS NONE OF YOUR BUSINESS. / FEELINGS I THOUGHT YOU SHARED** 9 –
(c-s+=/cd-s+=) *(HUT C/CD 103)* – Don't turn your back on love.
(cd-s) *(HUTDX 103)* – ('A'-live) / Higher sights (live) / Retread (live). *(12"ep re-iss. Nov98; HUTT 103)*

Nov 98. (12"ep) *(HUTT 107)* **THE GOOD WILL OUT. / BUTTER WOULDN'T MELT (live) / DRY KIDS (live) / BLIND** –

—— added p/t (now f/t) 5th member **MICKEY DALE** (b.22 Mar'68) – keyboards (ex-CUD)

Hut E.M.I.

Nov 99. (c-s/cd-s) *(HUT C/CD 123)* **HOOLIGAN / I'VE BEEN RUNNING / I CAN'T FEEL BAD ANYMORE** 18 –
(cd-s) *(HUTDX 123)* – ('A') / Like a believer / With the one who got me here.

Mar 00. (cd-s) *(HUTCD 126)* **YOU'RE NOT ALONE / BROTHERS AND SISTERS / HAPPY AND LOST** 14 –
(cd-s/12"+=) *(HUT DX/T 126)* – ('A') / Come on and smile / Tap on your shoulder.

Mar 00. (cd/c/lp) *(CDHUT/HUTMC/HUTLP 60)* *<849014>* **DRAWN FROM MEMORY** 8
– The love it takes / You're not alone / Save me / Drawn from memory / Bunker song / New Adam new Eve / Hooligan / Yeah you / Liars tears / I wouldn't wanna happen to you / I had a time.

May 00. (c-s/12"/cd-s) *(HUT C/X/CD 133)* **SAVE ME / GET ON BOARD / STILL SO YOUNG** 29 –
(cd-s) *(HUTDX 133)* – ('A') / ('A'mixes).

Aug 00. (7") *(HUT 137)* **I WOULDN'T WANNA HAPPEN TO YOU. / 3 IS A MAGIC NUMBER** 23 –
(cd-s+=) *(HUTCDX 133)* – Top of the heap.
(12"++=) *(HUTT 133)* – First cut / I know what's going on.
(cd-s) *(HUTCD 133)* – ('A') / First cut / I know what's going on.

Aug 01. (c-s/cd-s) *(HUT C/CD 142)* **WONDER / ANYWHERE YOU GO / EVERYDAY** 14 –
(cd-s) *(HUTDX 142)* – ('A') / Today / Caught in a rush.

Sep 01. (cd/c/lp) *(CDHUT/HUTMC/HUTLP 68)* *<810973>* **IF YOU'VE NEVER BEEN** 9 Oct01
– Over / I hope you're happy now / Wonder / Many will learn / It's gonna take time / Hey, what you trying to say / If you've never been in love with anything / Make it last / Happiness will get you in the end / Satellites.

Nov 01. (cd-s) *(HUTCD 144)* **MAKE IT LAST / FIGHT YER CORNER / IT'S YOU I MAKE FOR** 35 –
(cd-s) *(HUTDX 144)* – ('A') / ('A'-orchestral) / Giving forgiving and giving in / What you've never had you'll never have.

Mar 02. (cd) *(CDHUT 74)* *<812083>* **FIREWORKS: SINGLES 1997-2002** (compilation) 36
– All you good good people / You're not alone / Come back to what you know / Make it last / 3 is a magic number / One big family / My weakness is none of your business / I wouldn't wanna happen to you / Save me / Hooligan / The good will out / Wonder / Fireworks.

Independiente Lava-Atlantic

Aug 04. (7"red) *(ISOM 87S)* **GRAVITY. / WASTED** 7 –
(cd-s) *(ISOM 87MS)* – ('A') / Too many times.
(cd-s) *(ISOM 87SMS)* – ('A') / The shot's still ringing / Waterfall / ('A'-video).

Sep 04. (cd/lp) *(ISOM 45 CD/LP)* *<93821>* **OUT OF NOTHING** 1 Jun05
– Ashes / Gravity / Someday / Looking as you are / Wish 'em all away / Keeping / Spell it out / A glorious day / Near life / Out of nothing. *(ltd-cd-iss. Nov04 +=; ISOM 45CDX)* – (bonus dvd).

Nov 04. (7"yellow) *(ISOM 89S)* **ASHES. / ENOUGH** 11 –
(cd-s) *(ISOM 89MS)* – ('A') / Maybe I wish.
(cd-s) *(ISOM 89SMS)* – ('A') / Flaming red hair / How come (live on Jo Whiley sessions) / ('A'-video).

Feb 05. (7"grey) *(ISOM 91S)* **LOOKING AS YOU ARE. / THE FINAL SAY** 11 –
(cd-s) *(ISOM 91MS)* – ('A') / Madelaine.
(cd-s) *(ISOM 91SMS)* – ('A') / I ache / Soldiers hours / ('A'-video).

May 05. (7"/cd-s) *(ISOM 94 S/MS)* **A GLORIOUS DAY. / MILK AND HONEY** 28 –
(cd-s) *(ISOM 94SMS)* – ('A') / Feels like glue / Red eye shot / ('A'-video).

Mar 06. (7") *(ISOM 103S)* **NATURE'S LAW. / SOULMATES** 2 –
(cd-s) *(ISOM 103MS)* – ('A') / Deliver me / Collide.

Mar 06. (cd/lp) *(ISOM 60 CD/LP)* **THIS NEW DAY** 1 –
– No use crying / Nature's law / Target / Sainted / I can't come down / Celebrate / Exploding machines / Even smaller stones / End is near / This new day. *(ltd-cd iss.Jun06 +=; ISOM 60CDX)* – World at your feet / World at your feet (documentary).

Jun 06. (7"pic-d) *(ISOM 107S)* **WORLD AT YOUR FEET. / WHAT LIES BEHIND US** 3 –
(cd-s) (ISOM 107MS) – ('A') / Celebrate.
(cd-s) *(ISOM 107SMS)* – ('A') / Love order / Whatever it takes / ('A'-video).

– compilations, etc. –

Oct 05. (cd) *Hut; (CDHUT 86)* **DRY KIDS (1997-2005)** –

EMERSON, LAKE & PALMER

Formed: London, England ... mid-1970 by KEITH EMERSON, GREG LAKE and CARL PALMER, who had all cut their teeth in late 60's acts/combos (see below). After an aborted collaboration with HENDRIX (just prior to his death) and an appearance at the Isle Of Wight festival on the 29th August '70, they signed to 'Island'. Later in the year, they unleashed their eponymous debut, which immediately established the band as one of the leading purveyors of 70's prog-rock. In fact, they focused more on the classical side of things, proving that rock could be adapted for more high-brow tastes (EMERSON had previously explored this field while with The NICE). Next-up was 'TARKUS' (1971), a misguided concept piece which was based around a battle between a Manticore (a mythical beast) and a mechanised armadillo (!). Riding on the coat-tails of their debut success, it nevertheless reached No.1 (Top 10 in the States). Their third album was a live adaptation of Mussorgsky's 'PICTURES AT AN EXHIBITION', a fine effort which was let down by the closing track, a pointless cover of B.BUMBLE & THE STINGERS' early 60's hit 'NUTROCKER'. In 1972, they fulfilled their early potential with 'TRILOGY', an album that also made the Top 3, showcasing their most accomplished work to date on tracks such as 'THE ENDLESS ENIGMA', 'LIVING SIN' and 'ABADDON'S BOLERO'. The following year, ELP created the label 'Manticore', its first release being the 'BRAIN SALAD SURGERY' album which consolidated their position as one of the 70's leading bands, at least in commercial terms. Once again, former part-time KING CRIMSON member PETE SINFIELD was drafted in to collaborate on the lyrics. Tracks like the romantic 'STILL ... YOU TURN ME ON' and the grandiose epic, 'KARN EVIL 9' were skillfully placed side by side with an arresting re-working of the hymn 'JERUSALEM'. While the band took a 2-year hiatus, they released a stop-gap triple live set entitled, 'WELCOME BACK MY FRIENDS' that was a little too overblown, pricey and pretentious for many. In 1975, the fans cringed when a solo GREG LAKE returned with the festive 'I BELIEVE IN FATHER CHRISTMAS' which hit No.2. The multi-talented keyboard maestro, KEITH EMERSON, also had a solo outing, a surprisingly basic rock'n'roll cover of Meade Lux Lewis' 'HONKY TONK TRAIN BLUES'. In 1977, ELP eventually returned with the double album, 'WORKS 1', a patchy affair which nevertheless spawned an inspired cover of Aaron Copeland's 'FANFARE FOR THE COMMON MAN'. In its edited form, the track gave the band a near No.1 in the UK. This however, was to be their last work of any relevance. All went solo in the 80's, and when PALMER formed PM, ELP conviently found a replacement (P) in the guise of Cozy POWELL. This set-up was short-lived although the original EMERSON, LAKE & PALMER re-formed once more in 1991. They were found floundering on past glories with the mediocre 'BLACK MOON' album the following year.

• **Trivia:** 'Manticore', the label they formed in 1973, also signed PETE SINFIELD, P.F.M. and LITTLE RICHARD!

Album rating: EMERSON, LAKE & PALMER (*6) / TARKUS (*5) / PICTURES AT AN EXHIBITION (*6) / TRILOGY (*8) / BRAIN SALAD SURGERY (*8) / WELCOME BACK MY FRIENDS TO THE SHOW THAT NEVER ENDS – LADIES AND GENTLEMEN . . . EMERSON, LAKE & PALMER (*5) / WORKS 1 (*5) / WORKS 2 (*3) / LOVE BEACH (*3) / IN CONCERT (*4) / THE BEST OF EMERSON, LAKE & PALMER compilation (*5) / EMERSON, LAKE & POWELL (*4) / TO THE POWER OF THREE (er . . . *3; by 3) / BLACK MOON (*4) / THE ATLANTIC YEARS compilation (*7) / LIVE AT THE ROYAL ALBERT HALL (*4) / IN THE HOT SEAT (*4)

KEITH EMERSON (b. 2 Nov'44, Todmorden, England) – keyboards (ex-NICE, ex-GARY FARR & THE T-BONES / **GREG LAKE** (b.10 Nov'48, Bournemouth, England) – vocals, guitar, bass (ex-KING CRIMSON) / **CARL PALMER** (b.20 Mar'47, Birmingham, England) – drums, percussion (ex-ATOMIC ROOSTER, ex-CRAZY WORLD OF ARTHUR BROWN)

Island Cotillion

Nov 70. (lp/c) *(ILPS/ILPC 9132)* <9040> **EMERSON, LAKE & PALMER** [4] [18]
– The barbarian / Take a pebble / Knife edge / The three fates:- Clotho – Lachesis – Acropus / Tank / Lucky man. *(re-iss. Dec73 on 'Manticore' lp/c; K/K4 43503) (cd-iss. 1988 on 'WEA'; 191202) (re-iss. cd Dec93 on 'Victory'; 828264-2) (cd re-iss. Mar96 on 'Essential'; ESMCD 340) (lp re-iss. Sep98 on 'Get Back'; GET 528) (cd re-iss. Mar01 on 'Castle'; CMRCD 165)*

Mar 71. (7") <44106> **LUCKY MAN. / KNIFE EDGE** [–] [48]
<US re-iss. Jan73 on 'Atlantic'; 13153> hit No.51>

Jun 71. (lp/c) *(ILPS/ILPC 9155)* <9900> **TARKUS** [1] [9]
– Tarkus:- Eruption – Stones of years – Iconoclast – The mass – Manticore – Battlefield – Aquatarkus – (conclusion) / Jeremy Bender / Bitches crystal / The only way / Infinite space / A time and a place / Are you ready Eddy?. *(re-iss. Dec73 on 'Manticore' lp/c; K/K4 43504) (cd-iss. Sep89 on 'WEA'; 781202) (re-iss. cd Dec93 on 'Victory'; 828465-2) (cd re-iss. Mar96 on 'Essential'; ESMCD 341)*

Sep 71. (7") <44131> **STONES OF YEARS. / A TIME AND A PLACE** [–] [ ]

Nov 71. (lp/c) *(HELP/HELC 1)* <66666> **PICTURES AT AN EXHIBITION** [3] Jan72 [10]
– Promenade: The gnome – Promenade – The sage – The old castle – Blues variation – Promenade / The hut of Baba Yaga – The curse of Baba Yaga – The hut of Baba Yaga – The great gates of Kiev – Nutrocker. *(re-iss. Dec73 on 'Manticore' lp/c; K/K4 33501) (cd-iss. 1988 on 'Cotillion'; 19122-2) (cd re-iss. Sep89 on 'WEA'; 781521-2) (re-iss. Dec93 on 'Victory'; 828466-2) (cd re-iss. Mar96 on 'Essential'; ESMCD 342) (cd re-iss. Mar01; CMRCD 167)*

Mar 72. (7") <44151> **NUTROCKER. / THE GREAT GATES OF KIEV** [–] [70]

Jul 72. (lp/c) *(ILPS/ILPC 9186)* <9903> **TRILOGY** [2] [5]
– The endless enigma (part 1) – Fugue – The endless enigma (part 2) / From the beginning / The sheriff / Hoedown / Trilogy / Living sin / Abaddon's bolero. *(re-iss. Dec73 on 'Manticore' lp/c; K/K4 43505) (cd-iss. Jun89 on 'Atlantic'; 781522-2) (re-iss. cd Dec93 on 'Victory'; 828467-2) (cd re-iss. Mar96 on 'Essential'; ESMCD 343)*

Aug 72. (7") *<44158>* **FROM THE BEGINNING. / LIVING SIN** [–] [39]

Manticore Manticore

Dec 73. (lp/c) *(K/K4 53501) <66669>* **BRAIN SALAD SURGERY** [2] [11]
– Jerusalem / Toccata / Still . . . you turn me on / Benny the bouncer / Karn evil 9. 1st impression – part 1 & 2 – 2nd impression – 3rd impression. *(cd-iss. Jun89 on 'WEA'; 781523-2) (re-iss. cd Dec93 on 'Victory'; 828468-2) (cd re-iss. Mar96 on 'Essential'; ESMCD 344) (<cd re-iss. May01 on 'Castle'+=; CMRCD 201)* – Brain salad surgery (single version) / When the apple blossoms bloom in the windmills of your mind / Excerpts from Brain Salad Surgery flexi.

Dec 73. (7") *(K 13503)* **JERUSALEM. / WHEN THE APPLE BLOSSOM BLOOMS IN THE WINDMILLS OF YOUR MIND, I'LL BE YOUR VALENTINE** [ ] [–]

Dec 73. (7") *<2003>* **BRAIN SALAD SURGERY. / STILL YOU TURN ME ON** [–] [ ]

Aug 74. (t-lp/d-c) *(K/K4 63500) <200>* **WELCOME BACK MY FRIENDS, TO THE SHOW THAT NEVER ENDS – LADIES AND GENTLEMEN . . . EMERSON, LAKE & PALMER (live)** [5] [4]
– Hoedown / Jerusalem / Toccata / Tarkus:- Eruption – Stones of years – Iconoclaust – The mass – Manticore – Battlefield – Epitaph – Aquatarkus – (conclusion) / Take a pebble – Piano improvisations – Take a pebble (conclusion) / Jeremy Bender / The sheriff / Karn evil 9. 1st impression – 2nd impression – 3rd impression. *(re-iss. d-cd Dec93 on 'Victory'; 828474-2) (d-cd re-iss. Mar96 on 'Essential'; ESDCD 359)*

Nov 75. (7"; by GREG LAKE) *(K 13511) <3305>* **I BELIEVE IN FATHER CHRISTMAS. / HUMBUG** [2] [95]
(re-iss. Nov82, hit No.72 – Dec83 hit No.65) (re-iss. Nov92 on 'Atlantic'; A 7393)

Apr 76. (7"; by KEITH EMERSON) *(K 13513)* **HONKY TONK TRAIN BLUES. / BARREL HOUSE SHAKE DOWN** [21] [–]

Atlantic Atlantic

Mar 77. (d-lp/d-c) *(K/K4 80009) <7000>* **WORKS 1** [9] [12]
– Piano concerto No.1 – 1st movement: Allegro giojoso / 2nd movement: Andante molto cantabile / 3rd movement: Toccata con fuoco / Lend your love to me tonight / C'est la vie / Hallowed by thy name / Nobody loves you like I do / Closer to believing / The enemy God dances with the black spirits / L.A. nights / New Orleans / Bach: Two part invention in D minor / Food for your soul / Tank / Fanfare for the common man / Pirates. *(cd-iss. Jun89; 781372-2) (re-iss. d-cd Dec93 on 'Victory'; 828470-2)*

Jun 77. (7"/12") *(K 10946/+T) <3398>* **FANFARE FOR THE COMMON MAN (edit). / BRAIN SALAD SURGERY** [2] [ ]

Aug 77. (7"; A-side by GREG LAKE) *(K 10990) <3405>* **C'EST LA VIE. / JEREMY BENDER** [ ] [91]

Nov 77. (lp/c) *(K/K4 50422) <19147>* **WORKS 2** (compilation of rare and demo work) [20] [37]
– Tiger in a spotlight / When the apple blossoms bloom in the windmills of your mind, I'll be your valentine / Bullfrog / Brain salad surgery / Barrel house shake down / Watching over you / So far to fall / Maple leaf rag / I believe in Father Christmas / Close but not touching / Honky tonk train blues / Show me the way to go home. *(cd-iss. Jun89; 781538-2) (re-iss. cd Dec93 on 'Victory'; 828473-2)*

Jan 78. (7"; A-side by GREG LAKE) **WATCHING OVER YOU. / HALLOWED BE THY NAME** [ ] [ ]

Nov 78. (lp/c) *(K/K4 50552) <19211>* **LOVE BEACH** [48] [55]
– All I want is you / Love beach / Taste of my love / The gambler / For you / Canario / Memoirs of an officer and a gentleman – Prologue – The education of a gentleman / Love at first sight / Letters from the front / Honourable company. *(cd-iss. Jun89; K2 50552) (re-iss. cd Dec93 on 'Victory'; 828469-2)*

Nov 78. (7") *(K 11225)* **ALL I WANT IS YOU. / TIGER IN A SPOTLIGHT** [ ] [ ]

—— disbanded December '78

Oct 79. (lp/c) *(K/K4 50652) <19255>* **EMERSON, LAKE & PALMER IN CONCERT (live 1978)** [ ] [73]
– (introductory fanfare) / Peter Gunn / Tiger in a spotlight / C'est la vie / The enemy god dances with the black spirits / Knife edge / Piano concerto No.1 / Pictures at an exhibition.

Dec 79. (7") *(K 11416)* **PETER GUNN (live). / KNIFE EDGE (live)** [ ] [ ]

KEITH EMERSON

Atlantic Cinevox

Sep 80. (7") *(K 11612)* **THE TAXI RIDE. / MATER TENEBRARUM** [ ] [–]

Dec 80. (lp) *(K 50753) <CIA 33138>* **INFERNO** (soundtrack) [ ] [ ]
– Inferno / Rose's descent into a cellar / The taxi ride / The library / Sarah in the library vaults / Bookbinder's delight / Rose leaves the apartment / Rose gets it / Elisa's story / A cat attic attack / Kazanian's tarantella / Mark's discovery / Matter tenebrarum / Inferno (finals) / Cigarettes, ices, etc. *(re-iss. Mar90 on 'Cinevox'; CIA 5022) (cd-iss. Feb98 on 'Cinevox'; CDMF 3060)*

— added **NEIL SYMONETTE** – drums / **TRISTAN FRY** – percussion / **GREG BOWEN** – trumpet / **JEROME RICHARDSON** – sax / **PAULETTE McWILLIAMS** – vocals

M.C.A. Backstreet

Apr 81. (7") *(MCA 697)* **I'M A MAN. / NIGHTHAWKS MAIN TITLE THEME** [ ] [ ]

Apr 81. (lp) *(MCF 3107) <BSR 5196>* **NIGHTHAWKS** (soundtrack) [ ] [ ]
– Nighthawks (main title) / Mean stalkin' / The bust / Nighthawking / The chase / I'm a man / The chopper / Tramway / I'm comin' in / Face to face / The flight of the hawk. *(re-iss. Jan89; MCA 1521) <US cd-iss. 2002 on 'Emersongs'; A 12802-2>*

Red Bus not iss.

Dec 83. (7") *(RBUS 85)* **UP THE ELEPHANT AND ROUND THE CASTLE. / ('A'instrumental)** [ ] [–]
(above featured comedian JIM DAVIDSON)

Chord not iss.

Apr 85. (lp) *(ESP 1)* **THE BEST OF KEITH EMERSON** (compilation) [ ] [–]

Apr 85. (lp) *(CHORD 001)* **BEST REVENGE** (1983 soundtrack) [ ] [–]
– Dream runner / The runner / Wha'dya mean / Straight between the eyes / Orchestral suite to "Best Revenge" / Playing for keeps (main title theme). *(cd-iss. Nov86 +=; CDCO 3)* – MURDEROCK tracks

— **MOTT** – guitar / **DICK MORRISSEY + ANDREW BRENNAN + PETE KING** – saxophone

Apr 85. (lp/cd) *(CHORD/+CD 002)* **HONKY** [ ] [–]
– Hello sailor / Bach before the mast / Salt cay / Green ice / Intro-juicing / Big horn breakdown / Yancey special / Rum-a-thing / Jesus loves me. *(re-iss. May86)*

Apr 85. (lp) *(CHORD 003)* **HARMAGEDON / CHINA FREE FALL** (soundtracks; B-side by DEREK AUSTIN) [ ] [–]
– Theme from Floi / Joe and Micheko / Children of the light / Funny's skate state / Zamedy stomp / Challenge of the psonic fighters / (other tracks by DEREK AUSTIN). *(re-iss. Feb87) (cd-iss. Feb99 on 'Volcano'; CPC8 3003)*

— next with **DOREEN CHANTER** – vocals / **MIKE SEBBAGE** – vocals / **TOM NICOL + DEREK WILSON** – drums / **MICHAEL SHEPPARD** – bass, guitar, co-producer

May 86. (lp/cd) *(CHORD/+CD 004)* **MURDEROCK – UCCIDE A PASSO DI DANZA** (soundtrack) [ ] [–]
– Murderock / Tonight is your night / Streets to blame / Not so innocent / Prelude to Candice / Don't go in the shower / Coffee time / Candice / New York dash / Tonight is not your night / The spill one. *(cd-iss. Oct01 Italy on 'Cinevox'+=; CD-MDF 345)* – Murderock (pt.1) / Murderock (pt.2) / Murderock (pt.3) / Murderock (pt.4).

— next with The National Philharmonic Orchestra, plus **BRAD DELP, LEVON HELM**

Dec 86. (cd) *(CDCOLL 1)* **THE EMERSON COLLECTION** (compilation) [ ] [–]

Priority not iss.

Nov 88. (lp/c/cd) *(KEITH LP/MC/CD 1)* **EMERSON – THE CHRISTMAS ALBUM** [ ] [–]
(cd-iss. Jun93 & Dec95 on 'Amp'; AMPCD 018)

Emerson not iss.

Dec 88. (7") *(KEITH 1)* **WE THREE KINGS OF ORIENT ARE. / CAPTAIN STARSHIP HOPKINS** [ ] [–]

Cinevox not iss.

Apr 89. (lp) *(MDF 33/192)* **LA CHIESA** (soundtrack w/ others) [–] Italy [–]
– The church (main theme) / La chiesa (GOBLIN) / Prelude 24 (from "Well Tempered Clavier") / Possessione (GOBLIN) / The possession / Lotte (GOBLIN) / Go to hell (ZOOMING ON THE ZOO) / The wire blaze / The church revisted. *(cd-iss. Oct01 +=; CD-MDF 329)* – The church (single mix) / La chiesa – suite (GOBLIN) / Suspence chiesa 1 (GOBLIN) / Suspence chiesa 2 (GOBLIN).

Amp not iss.

Apr 95. (cd) *(AMPCD 026)* **CHANGING STATES** [ ] [–]

Dec 95. (cd-s) **TROIKA (THE CHRISTMAS SINGLE). /** [ ] [–]

GREG LAKE BAND

GREG LAKE – vocals, guitar, bass with **TOMMY EYRE** – keyboards / **GARY MOORE** – guitar (ex-solo artist ex-THIN LIZZY ex-COLOSSEUM) / **TRISTRAM MARGETTS** – bass / **TED McKENNA** – drums (ex-SENSATIONAL ALEX HARVEY BAND)

Chrysalis Chrysalis

Sep 81. (7") *(CHS 2553)* **LOVE YOU TOO MUCH. / SOMEONE** [ ] [–]

Oct 81. (lp/c) *(<CHR/ZCHR 1357>)* **GREG LAKE** [62] [62]
– Nuclear attack / Love you too much / It hurts / One before you go / Loving goodbye / Retribution drive / Black and blue / Let me love you once / The lies / For those who dare.

Dec 81. (7") *<2571>* **LET ME LOVE YOU ONCE. / RETRIBUTION DRIVE** [–] [48]

Feb 82. (7") *(CHS 2567)* **IT HURTS. / RETRIBUTION DRIVE** [ ] [ ]

Jul 83. (lp/c) *(<CHR/ZCHR 1392>)* **MANOEUVRES** [ ] [ ]
– Manoeuvres / Too young to love / Paralysed / A woman like you / I don't want to lose your love tonight / It's you, you've got to believe / Famous last words / Slave to love / Haunted / I don't know why I still love you.

— LAKE joined ASIA with PALMER

PM

CARL PALMER with **TODD COCHRAN** – keyboards / **BARRY FINNERTY** – guitar, vocals / **JOHN NITZINGER** – guitar, vocals / **ERIK SCOTT** – bass, vocals

Ariola Ariola

May 80. (lp/c) *(ARL/ZCARL 5048)* **1 PM** [ ] [ ]
– Dynamite / You've got me rockin' / Green velvet splendour / Dreamers / Go on carry on / D'ya go all the way / Go for it / Madeleine / You're too much / Children of the air age.

Apr 80. (7") *(ARO 217)* **YOU GOT ME ROCKIN'. / GO FOR IT** [ ] [–]

Jul 80. (7") *(ARO 234)* **DYNAMITE. / D'YA GO ALL THE WAY** [ ] [–]

— (Jan81) PALMER joined ASIA

EMERSON, LAKE & POWELL

— are the new set up **COZY POWELL** (b.29 Dec'47, Cirencester, England) – drums, (ex-solo artist, ex-RAINBOW, etc.)

Polydor Polydor

Jul 86. (lp/c)(cd) *(POLD/+C 5191)(<829 297-2>)* **EMERSON, LAKE & POWELL** [35] Jun86 [23]
– Mars, the bringer of war / The score / Learning to fly / Touch and go / Miracle / Love blind / Step aside / Lay down your guns.

Jul 86. (7") *(POSP 804) <885101>* **TOUCH AND GO. / LEARNING TO FLY** [ ] Jun86 [60]
(12"+=) *(POSPX 804)* – The locomotion.

Sep 86. (7") **LAY DOWN YOUR GUNS. /** [–] [ ]

— (1987 originals reformed but disbanded Oct87)

3

was the unit formed by **EMERSON, PALMER** and American **ROBERT BERRY** – vocals (ex-HUSH)

Geffen Geffen

Feb 88. (lp/c/cd) *(924181-1/-4/-2) <24181>* **TO THE POWER OF THREE** [ ] [ ]
– Talkin' about / Lover to lover / Chains / Desde la vida / Eight miles high / Runaway / You do or you don't / On my way home.

Feb 88. (7") **TALKIN' ABOUT. / LA VISTA** [–] [ ]

EMERSON, LAKE & PALMER

— re-formed 1992

Victory-London Victory

Apr 92. (cd/c/lp) *(828 318-2/-4/-2) <480003>* **BLACK MOON** [ ] Jun92 [78]
– Black Moon / Paper blood / Affairs of the heart / Romeo and Juliet / Farewell to arms / Changing states / Burning bridges / Close to home / Better days / Footprints in the snow. *(cd re-iss. Apr97 on 'Essential'; ESMCD 506)*

London London

May 92. (7") *(LON 320)* **BLACK HOLE. / MILES IZ DEAD** –
(12"+=/cd-s+=) *(LON X/CD 320)* – A blade of grass.

Nov 92. (7"/c-s) *(LON/+C 327)* **AFFAIRS OF THE HEART. / BETTER DAYS** –
(cd-s+=) *(LONCD 327)* – A blade of grass / Black moon.
(cd-s) *(LOCDP 327)* – ('A'side) / Black moon (radio) / Fanfare for the common man / Jerusalem.

Feb 93. (cd/c) *(<828 933-2/-4>)* **LIVE AT THE ROYAL ALBERT HALL (live)**
– 1st impression part 2 / Tarkus: Eruption – Stones of years – Iconoclast / Knife edge / Paper blood / Romeo & Juliet / Creole dance / Still . . . you turn me on / Lucky man / Black moon / The pirates / Finale / Fanfare for the common man / America / Blue rondo A la Turk. *(cd re-iss. Apr97 on 'Essential'; ESMCD 504) (cd re-iss. Sep01; CMRCD 228)*

Nov 93. (4xcd-box) *(<828 459-2>)* **RETURN OF THE MANTICORE** (old & new material)
(re-iss. Nov96 on 'Essential'; ESFCD 421)

Dec 93. (cd) *(<828 477-2>)* **WORKS LIVE (live)**

Sep 94. (cd/c) *(<828 554-2/-4>)* **IN THE HOT SEAT**
– Hand of truth / Daddy / One by one / Heart on ice / Thin line / Man in the long black coat / Change / Give me a reason to stay / Gone too soon / Street war. *(cd+=)* – Pictures at an exhibition: a) Promenade – b) The gnome – c) Promenade – d) The sage – e) The hut of Baba Yaga – f) The great gates of Kiev.

Metal Minds Metal Minds

Sep 99. (cd) *(PROGCD 006)* <405613> **LIVE IN POLAND (live 1997)** May01
– Welcome back / Touch and go / From the beginning / Knife edge / Bitches crystal / Piano solo / Take a pebble / Lucky man / Medley: Tarkus – Pictures at an exhibition / Medley: Fanfare for the common man – Rondo. *(re-iss. Sep02 on 'Castle'; CMRCD 558)*

– compilations, others, etc. –

Nov 80. (lp/c) *Atlantic; (K/K4 50757)* <19283> **THE BEST OF EMERSON, LAKE & PALMER**
– Hoedown / Lucky man / Karn evil 9 / Trilogy / Fanfare for the common man / Still . . . you turn me on / Tiger in a spotlight / Jerusalem / Peter Gunn. *(cd-iss. 1983; K2 50757) (cd re-iss. Nov95 on 'Essential'; ESSCD 296)*

Jul 92. (cd/c/lp) *Atlantic; (<7567 82403-2/-4>)* **THE ATLANTIC YEARS**

Apr 97. (d-cd; GREG LAKE) *Essential; (ESDCD 522)* **FROM THE BEGINNING: THE GREG LAKE RETROSPECTIVE** –

Oct 98. (3xcd-box) *Essential; (ESMBX 303)* **EMERSON, LAKE & PALMER / TARKUS / PICTURES AT AN EXHIBITION**

Oct 98. (d-cd) *Eagle; (EDGCD 040)* **THEN & NOW (live 1974 & now)** –

Jan 01. (d-cd) *Castle; (CMEDD 110)* **FANFARE FOR THE COMMON MAN: THE ANTHOLOGY** –

Aug 01. (5xcd-box) *Castle; (<CMXBX 309>)* **THE ORIGINAL BOOTLEG SERIES FROM THE MANTICORE VAULTS VOL.1**

Aug 01. (8xcd-box) *Castle; (<CMXBX 330>)* **THE ORIGINAL BOOTLEG SERIES FROM THE MANTICORE VAULTS VOL.2**

Oct 01. (d-cd) *Snapper; (SMDCD 370)* **THE SHOW THAT NEVER ENDS** –

Feb 02. (cd) *Castle; (CMRCD 458)* **LIVE AT THE ISLE OF WIGHT FESTIVAL 1970 (live)** –

May 02. (d-cd) *Castle; (<CMDDD 442>)* **BEST OF THE BOOTLEGS**

Jul 02. (4xcd-box) *Castle; (<CMYBX 524>)* **THE ORIGINAL BOOTLEG SERIES FROM THE MANTICORE VAULTS VOL.3**

Oct 02. (cd) *Delta; (CD 47098)* **FANFARE (THE 1997 WORLD TOUR)** –

Oct 02. (3xcd-box) *Burning Airlines; (<PILOT 145>)* **RE-WORKS**
(lp-box-set-iss.Jul03 on 'Get Back'; GET 632)

Jan 03. (d-cd) *King Biscuit; (KBCCD 109)* **IN CONCERT (live)** –

May 03. (cd) *Music Club; (MCCD 520)* **FANFARE: THE BEST OF . . . LIVE** –

Aug 03. (cd) *Invisible Hands; (IHCD 23)* **RE-WORKS (BRAIN SALAD PERJURY)** –

EMINEM

Born: MARSHALL BRUCE MATHERS III, 17 Oct'72, St. Joseph, Missouri, USA. Spending his childhood roaming from one State to the next, the gifted rapper and one time SOUL INTENT member began freestyling in his friend's basement at the age of fifteen. Five years (and, apparently, a lot of mushrooms and NWA albums) later, the white MC decided to try his luck in the increasing world of hip hop. He debuted with the poorly distributed album 'INFINITE' (1996) and failed blindly at attracting attention from any major labels. Legend DR DRE apparently discovered EMINEM (a word play on his initials) when he found a demo tape on Interscope's Jimmy Iovines' garage floor. To be fully convinced by the rapper, DRE travelled to watch him perform in the 1997 Rap Olympics before rushing over and signing him on the spot. His major label debut, 'THE SLIM SHADY LP', appeared in the Spring of '99, sales boosted after the rather offensive massive hit single, 'MY NAME IS'. The aforementioned platter rocketed to the top spot in America and sent parents into a fit of rage over the filth and obscenities our white chump was slobbering about on tape. The American media, senseless rock stars and a few bad words about his dear old momma were all mentioned in the single, that had such an infectious chorus it made listeners fall under the spell of EMINEM's crazy, high-speed, nasal-pinching slur. The sophomore album did not do so bad either, selling nearly a million copies in its first week and a further million in the months after its release. But the waging battle between him and the general public continued, when songs that depicted rape, murder, violence, excessive drug taking, child molesting and, erm, his poor old mother were all raised in frequent "morality" debates. The second single (and to some, his finest), 'GUILTY CONSCIENCE', featured DRE as his alter ego, who pops up to discuss EMINEM's relationship problems when he finds his wife in bed with another man. Not surprising to see then, that EMINEM returned the favour by contributing to DRE's '2001' LP on the brilliant and humourous track 'IT'S ALL ABOUT DRE'. The crown king of confrontation returned in 2001 with 'THE MARSHALL MATHERS LP', an even darker journey through his tortured psychscape, shot through with as much humour as ever but pinned back with (un)healthy doses of stark realism. The pairing of MATHERS and cooing pop songbird DIDO on 'STAN' was a true stroke of genius, one that resulted in a huge UK No.1 single. This was preceded by 'THE REAL SLIM SHADY', a shuffling, propulsive groove taking it to the top; he was now taking the alter-ego of the Texas Chainsaw Massacre on stage – a tough life indeed! 2001 saw the emergence of D-12, a project from the preceding decade initiated by BIZARRE and PROOF (aka RUFUS JOHNSON and DeSHAUN HOLTON). Joined by KON ARTIS, KUNIVA plus BUGZ (the latter was shot dead in 1998 and replaced by SWIFTY McVAY), the alter-ego outfit that was the DIRTY DOZEN soon got together with childhood buddy EMINEM. The Slim Shady MATHERS and his five cohorts soon put together some tracks, the first of which being the extremely controversial, '$#!* ON YOU'. A hit in the UK early 2001, it was pursued by their OTT set that was 'DEVIL'S NIGHT'. No.1 in America (No.2 in the UK) it showed EMINEM and his juvenile rap partners (aged between 23 and 25 at the time) full of expletives, explicit lyrics and explosive violence incorporating the usual drugs-talk; 'PURPLE PILLS' was a single hit on both sides of the Atlantic. The enfant terrible of the rap scene returned in May 2002 with his ego firmly in place, delivering 'THE EMINEM SHOW'. The album consisted of the usual disgruntled outbursts at his critics and enemies, personal and international; if the 'MARSHAL MATHERS LP' was a concept album about his emotional strife, then this was centered upon the ever-looming

EMINEM

media circle that surrounded him. Bad and good in equal measures, 'WHITE AMERICA', with its guitar riffs and bludgeoning beats was a poisoned reaction against the American government that recalled the recently defunct RAGE AGAINST . . . Elsewhere, 'WITHOUT ME' was typical jestering EMINEM, all jokey lyrics and poppy hooks. 'SQUARE DANCE' was also a particular highlight, with DRE at the helm once again, whereas 'SUPERMAN' was a sleazy as they come, demonstrating some warped synthesiser and a porn star endorsed video to boot. The weaker moments, the AEROSMITH sampled 'DREAM ON' and 'CLEANING OUT MY CLOSET' (Lennon's 'Jealous Guy', anyone?) were simply dripping in melted cheese. Not surprising then that both were massive hits, but, like they say, kids will do anything for the taste of Dairylea. Having already made a guest appearance on the soundtrack to EMINEM's 2002 biopic '8 MILE' (which also generated one of his hardest hitting raps in the Oscar winning 'LOSE YOURSELF'), D-12 were back on top of both the US and UK charts with 'D12 WORLD' (2004). Trailed by the health-endangeringly catchy US Top 10 hit, 'MY BAND', and featuring production cameos for DR DRE and man-of-the-moment KANYE WEST, the record was criticised in many quarters for its calculatedly offensive rhymes; just another day at the office for MATHERS. 'ENCORE' (2004) saw him back at the helm of his own work, his third transatlantic No.1 album in succession. The singles flowed thick and fast – kicking off with the MICHAEL JACKSON-baiting 'JUST LOSE IT', a UK No.1/US Top 10 in late 2004, followed to the top of the British charts by the song 'LIKE TOY SOLDIERS' a few months later – but the multi-million sales didn't quite creep into double figures, with critics citing a lacklustre production and lyrics. Yet the hits continued to roll, with both 'MOCKINGBIRD' and 'ASS LIKE THAT' making the UK Top 5. Tragedy – both personal and professonial – was to hit the EMINEM camp in spring 2006, with the death (in a shooting at an 8 Mile Road nightclub) of D12 star and close friend, PROOF.

Album rating: INFINITE (*4) / THE SLIM SHADY LP (*9) / MARSHALL MATHERS LP (*9) / THE EMINEM SHOW (*7) / ENCORE (*6) / CURTAIN CALL: THE HITS compilation (*9) / D12: DEVIL'S NIGHT (*7) / D12 WORLD (*6)

EMINEM – vocals / with **MARKY** + **JEFF BASS**

not iss. Indep . . .

1996. (cd-s; as SOUL INTENT) *<none>* **FUCKING BACKSTABBER / BITERPHOBIA** [–] [ ]

1997. (d-lp) *<INF 01P>* **INFINITE** [–] [ ]
– Infinite / W.E.G.O. (interlude) / It's ok / 313 / Tonite / Maxine / Open mic / Never 2 far – Searchin' / Backstabber / Jealousy. *(UK-iss.Jan03; same as US)*

Interscope Interscope

Oct 98. (c-s,cd-s)(12") *<97044><95037>* **JUST DON'T GIVE A F***. / BRAIN DAMAGE** [–] [ ]

Mar 99. (c-s) *(INC 95638) <95040>* **MY NAME IS / (clean)** [2] Feb99 [36]
(cd-s) *(IND 95638)* – ('A'-instrumental).
(12") *(INT 95638)* – ('A'mixes).

Apr 99. (cd/c-d-lp)(clean;cd/c) *<(IND/INC/INT 90287)><(IND/INC 90321)>* **THE SLIM SHADY LP** [12] Feb99 [2]
– (Public service announcement) / My name is / Guilty conscience / Brain damage / Paul / If I had / 97' Bonnie & Clyde / Bitch / Role model / Lounge / My fault / Ken Kaniff / Cum on everybody / Rock bottom / Just don't give a fuck / Soap / As the world turns / I'm shady / Bad meets evil / Still don't give a fuck.

May 99. (12") *(RWK 193)* **ANY MAN. / ('A'mix)** [ ] [–]
(above issued on 'Rawkus')

Aug 99. (c-s; by EMINEM & DR.DRE) *(497129-4) <97097>* **GUILTY CONSCIENCE / ('A'mix with gunshots)** [5] Jun99 [25]
(cd-s) *(497128-2)* – ('A'side) / ('A'-acappella) / ('A'video).
(cd-s+=) *(497129-2)* – My name is (video).

May 00. (cd/c/d-lp) *<(490629-2/-4/-1)>* **THE MARSHALL MATHERS LP** [1] [1]
– (Public service announcement 2000) / Kill you / Stan / Paul (skit) / Who knew / Steve Berman / The way I am / The real Slim Shady / Remember me? / I'm back / Marshall Mathers / Kem Kaniff (skit) / Drug ballad / Amityville / Bitch please II / Kim / Under the influence / Criminal. *(censored version; 490632-2)*

— In Jun'00, EMINEM was also credited on DR DRE's UK Top single, 'Forget About Dre'

Jun 00. (c-s) *(497379-4) <497334>* **THE REAL SLIM SHADY / (instrumental)** [1] Apr00 [4]
(12"+=/cd-s+=) *(497379-1/-2)* – Bad influence / My fault (pizza mix).

Oct 00. (c-s) *(497425-4) <497399>* **THE WAY I AM / BAD INFLUENCE** [8] Aug00 [58]
(cd-s+=) *(497425-2)* – My fault (pizza mix) / ('A'-video).
(12") *(497425-1)* – ('A'side) / ('A'-instrumental).

Dec 00. (c-s; as EMINEM & DIDO) *(497470-4) <radio cut>* **STAN / MY NAME IS** [1] Nov00 [51]
(cd-s+=) *(497470-2)* – Get you mad / Stan (video).
(12") *(497470-1)* – ('A'side) / Get you mad / ('A'instrumental).

— in Aug'01, EMINEM featured on BAD MEETS EVIL's hit, 'Scary Movies'

May 02. (c-s) *(497728-4) <497731>* **WITHOUT ME / (instrumental)** [1] [2]
(12"+=) *(497728-1)* – The way I am (w/ MARILYN MANSON).
(cd-s+=) *(497728-2)* – ('A'-acappella).

May 02. (cd/c/d-lp) *<(493290-2/-4/-1)>* **THE EMINEM SHOW** [1] [1]
– Curtains up / White America / Business / Cleanin' out my closet / Square dance / The kiss / Soldier / Say goodbye Hollywood / Drips (with OBIE TRICE) / Without me / (Paul Rosenberg – skit) / Sing for the moment / Superman (with DINA RAE) / Hailie's song / (Steve Berman – skit) / When the music stops (with D-12) / Say what you say (with DR. DRE) / 'Till I collapse (with NATE DOGG) / My dad's gone crazy (with HAILIE JADE) / Curtains close.

Sep 02. (c-s) *(497394-4) <radio>* **CLEANIN' OUT MY CLOSET / RENEGADE** [4] [4]
(cd-s+=) *(497394-2)* – ('A'-instrumental) / ('A'-video).
(12") *(497394-1)* – ('A'side) / ('A'-instrumental) / ('A'-acappella) / Stimulate.

— EMINEM contributed acting & tracks to the movie, '8 Mile', which featured below song

Dec 02. (c-s) *(497828-4) <497815>* **LOSE YOURSELF / ('A'-instrumental)** [1] [ ]
(cd-s+=) *(497828-2)* – Renegade / ('A'-video).
(12") *(497828-1) <INTR 7815>* – ('A'side & mixes).

Dec 02. (cd-s) **SUPERMAN (mixes)** [–] [15]

Mar 03. (c-s/12") *(497871-4/-1)* **SING FOR THE MOMENT / SING FOR THE MOMENT (instrumental) / RABBIT RUN** [6] [14]
(cd-s+=) *(497871-2)* – ('A'video).

Jul 03. (12") *(980838-3)* **BUSINESS. / CONSPIRACY (freestyle – DJ Green Lantern version) / BUMP HEADS (DJ Green Lantern mix)** [6] [–]
(cd-s+=) *(980838-2)* – ('A'-live video).
(cd-s) *(980938-1)* – ('A'side) / Bump heads (DJ Green Lantern mix) / ('A'-live from Barcelona video).

Nov 04. (cd-s) *<(2103183)>* **JUST LOSE IT / LOSE YOURSELF** [1] [6]
(12") *(9864881)* – ('A') / (acapella) / (instrumental).
(cd-s++=) *(986881)* – (video).

Nov 04. (cd) *(9864884) <37717-2>* **ENCORE** [1] [1]
– Curtains up / Evil deeds / Never enough / Yellow brick road / Like toy soldiers / Mosh / Puke / My 1st single / Paul (skit) / Rain man / Big weenie / Em calls Paul (skit) / Just lose it / Ass like that / Spend some time / Mockingbird / Crazy in love / One shot 2 shot / Final thought (skit) / Encore. *(UK w/cd+=)* – We as Americans / Love you more / Ricky Ticky Toc. *<US d-lp; B0003771-01>*

Jan 05. (cd-s) *(2103963) <2103757>* **LIKE TOY SOLDIERS / RABBIT RUN (soundtrack explicit version)** [1] [34]
(cd-s+=) *(2103964)* – ('A'-instrumental) / ('A'-video).
(dvd-s) *(9880006)* – ('A'-video) / (behind the scenes).
(12") *<INTR 11313-1>* – ('A'-edit / explicit / instrumental / acapella).

Apr 05. (cd-s) *(9882074) <4833>* **MOCKINGBIRD / ENCORE** [4] [11]
(12"+=) *(9882075)* – Just lose it (DJ Green Lantern remix).
(cd-s) *(9882073)* – ('A') / ('A'-instrumental) / Just lose it (DJ Green Lantern remix) / ('A'-video).

Jul 05. (7"pic-d) *(9883871)* **ASS LIKE THAT. / (instrumental)** [4] [60]
(12"+=) *(9884117) <490111>* – Business (live).
(cd-s++=) *(9883904)* – ('A'-video; director's cut).

Dec 05. (cd) *(9887893) <588101>* **CURTAIN CALL: THE HITS** (compilation) [1] [1]
– (intro) / F.A.C.K. / The way I am / My name is / Stan / Lose yourself –

soundtrack version / Shake that / Sing for the moment / Without me / Like toy soldiers / The real Slim Shady / Mockingbird / Guilty conscience (w/ DR. DRE) / Cleanin' out my closet / Just lose it / When I'm gone / Stan (live w/ ELTON JOHN). *(ltd d-cd+=; 9889084)* – Dead wrong (feat. the NOTORIOUS B.I.G.) / Role model / Kill you / Shit on you (feat. D12) / Criminal / Renegade (feat. JAY-Z) / Just don't give a fuck.

Dec 05. (12") *(9879552)* **WHEN I'M GONE. / BUSINESS / WHEN I'M GONE (instrumental)** [4] [8]
(cd-s+=) *(9889581)* <8958> – ('A'-video).

D12

EMINEM + **PETER S. BIZARRE** (b. RUFUS JOHNSON) – vocals (of OUTSIDAZ) / **PROOF** (b. DeSHAUN HOLTON) – vocals / **KUNIVA** (aka VON CARLISLE or HANNZ G) – vocals / **SWIFTY McVAY** (aka O. MOORE) – vocals; repl. BUGZ (who died 1998) + **KON ARTIS** (b. DENINE PORTER) – producer

Interscope Interscope

Mar 01. (c-s) *(497496-4)* <497484> **$#!* ON YOU / (version)** [10] Dec00 [ ]
(12"+=) *(497496-1)* – Under the influence (explicit) / $#!* on you (instrumental).
(cd-s++=) *(497496-2)* – ('A'-CD-Rom).

Jun 01. (d-cd/c/d-lp) *(493079-2/-4/-1)* <490897> **DEVIL'S NIGHT** [2] [1]
– Another public announcement / Shit can happen / Pistol pistol / Bizarre (skit) / Nasty mind (with TRUTH HURTS) / Ain't nuthin' but music / American psycho / That's how (skit) / That's how . . . / Purple pills / Fight music / Instigator / Pimp like me (featuring DINA RAE) / Blow my buzz / Obie trice (skit by RONDELL BEENE & OBIE TRICE) / Devil's night / Steve Berman (by STEVE BERMAN & EMINEM) / Revelation / Girls / $#!* on you / Words are weapons / These drugs. *(clean version w/ less tracks Sep01; 490896-2)*

Jul 01. (c-s) *(497565-4)* <497569> **PURPLE PILLS / $#!* ON YOU (explicit)** [2] Jun01 [19]
(12"+=/cd-s+=) *(497587-1/-2)* – That's how . . . (explicit).
(cd-s) *(497569-2)* – ('A'-clean) / $#!* on you (clean) / That's how . . . (clean) / ('A'-CD-Rom).

Nov 01. (c-s/12") *(497652-4/-1)* <497645> **FIGHT MUSIC. / FREESTYLE / WORDS ARE WEAPONS** [11] [ ]
(cd-s+=) *(497652-2)* – ('A'-CD-Rom).

Apr 04. (cd-s) *(9862333)* **MY BAND / B N U** [2] [6]
(cd-s+=) *(9862352)* <11118> – ('A'-instrumental) / ('A'-video).
(12"+=) *(9862342)* – ('A'-instrumental) / ('A'- A cappella).

Apr 04. (cd) *(9862431)* **D12 WORLD** [1] [1]
– Git up / Loyalty (w/ OBIE TRICE) / Just like U / I'll be damned / Dude (skit) / My band / U R the one / 6 in the morning / How come / Leave dat boy alone / Get my gun / Bizarre (skit) / Bitch / Steve's coffee house (skit) / D12 world / 40 oz. / Commercial break (skit) / American psycho II / Bugz (skit) / Good die young / Keep talkin'.

Jul 04. (12") *(9863085)* <327011> **HOW COME / (instrumental). / 40 OZ. / (instrumental)** [4] [27]
(cd-s+=) *(9863083)* – ('A'-video).

— PROOF was shot dead in April '06

Brian ENO

Born: BRIAN PETER GEORGE ST. JOHN LE BAPTISTE DE LA SALLE ENO, 15 May'48, Suffolk, England. After leaving art school, where he fronted heavy group MAXWELL DEMON, he joined ROXY MUSIC in 1971. Contributing greatly to their image and sound on the albums, 'ROXY MUSIC' & 'FOR YOUR PLEASURE', he left due to a dispute over their increasingly pop-rock orientated direction. His first post-ROXY venture was (NO PUSSYFOOTING)' in 1973 with ROBERT FRIPP (of KING CRIMSON). This was nothing more than extreme experimentation of synth-electronics and treated guitar. However, it did provide art covers with a photo-shot of ENO & FRIPP in a multi-mirrored room. His first solo work in early 1974, 'HERE COME THE WARM JETS', disappointed the critics, who gave it the thumbs down, bar one gem, 'BABY'S ON FIRE'. He released two more greatly improved efforts for 'Island' before he formed his own label in 1975, appropriately titled 'Obscure'. Preceding this, in a fit of depression, he joined The WINKIES for a short tour during Feb-Mar'74, but departed after being diagnosed with a collapsed lung. He recovered to find himself on an 'Island records' concert bill on '1st JUNE, 1974', alongside stablemates KEVIN AYERS, NICO and JOHN CALE. The following year, he was hit by a car, which caused slight but not lasting brain damage. 1975's 'ANOTHER GREEN WORLD' represented the fruition of ENO's aural experimentation, sculpting instrumental, insidiously melodic soundscapes while the title track was subsequently used as the theme tune for the BBC TV arts series, 'Arena'. 'BEFORE AND AFTER SCIENCE' (1977) was an equally brilliant, if colder sounding, tapestry of sonic delights. Around this time, ENO began working with DAVID BOWIE on a trilogy of lp's that included 'LOW' (1977) and 'HEROES' (1977), while the following year he hooked up with TALKING HEADS, producing three of their albums during the period 1978-'80. He also collaborated with DAVID BYRNE on the ethnic-flavoured 'MY LIFE IN THE BUSH OF GHOSTS' (1981). With 'AMBIENT 1: MUSIC FOR AIRPORTS' (1978), ENO created an innovative classic while 'APOLLO: ATMOSPHERS AND SOUNDTRACKS' (1983) was a beguiling fusion of country and ambient, the gorgeous 'DEEP BLUE DAY' belatedly cropping up on the 'TRAINSPOTTTING' (1996) soundtrack. After initially collaborating with Canadian producer/engineer DANIEL LANOIS for production duties on such early 80's projects as 'THE PEARL' (a HAROLD BUDD/ENO album), the two worked wonders on U2's seminal 'UNFORGETTABLE FIRE' (1984). ENO clocked up further U2 production credits on 'THE JOSHUA TREE' (1987) and 'ACHTUNG BABY' (1991), scooping a joint Grammy (with LANOIS) in 1992 for the latter. The same year saw the release of a long awaited ENO solo album, 'NERVE NET', which took its cue from the burgeoning ambient techno scene. Throughout the 90's, this electronic auteur has continued to work on a dizzying array of music and other multi media projects, even publishing a volume of diaries in 1996, 'A YEAR WITH SWOLLEN APPENDICES'. The balding genius once described himself as a non-musician who just turned dials and switches. Maybe, but he happens to turn the right dials and switches, and this technically brilliant ambient experimentalist's obscure new musak is possibly a direct link to what listeners will appreciate in the 21st century. Following on from his collaboration with JAH WOBBLE on 1995's 'SPINNER', 'DRAWN FROM LIFE' (2001) once again proved that ENO is probably most effective when he has someone to bounce ideas off. This time around it was J. PETER SCHWALM, a German DJ with whom he'd previously worked on a Japanese-only release. LAURIE ANDERSON also contributed her inimitable vocals although the bulk of the tracks were instrumental. ENO subsequently turned to the inner workings of the humble bell, exploring the tonal complexity of various models across 75 meditative minutes: the project was released under the title 'JANUARY 07003: BELL STUDIES FOR THE CLOCK OF THE LONG NOW' (2003), with all proceeds going to the American foundation currently building the clock of the title. Released around the same time as another bit of "Pussyfootin'" by FRIPP & ENO, 'THE EQUATORIAL STARS', the man's almost as long awaited solo follow-up to his "conventional" mid-70s classics finally arrived in 2005: 'ANOTHER DAY ON EARTH' wasn't met with quite the same enthusiasm as back in his post-ROXY days, if satisfying long-time fans nevertheless. ENO even gave his vocals (amongst others) a rare outing on the likes of opening track, 'THIS'.

• **Songwriters:** All composed by ENO. • **Trivia:** His 1977 song 'KING'S LEAD HAT' was in fact an anagram of TALKING HEADS. ENO has also done session and production work for JOHN CALE (1974-75), ROBERT WYATT (1975), ROBERT CALVERT (1975), DAVID BOWIE (1977) / DEVO (1978) / TALKING HEADS (1978-80) / U2 (1985-91 with Daniel Lanois) / etc.

Album rating: HERE COME THE WARM JETS (*7) / TAKING TIGER MOUNTAIN (BY STRATEGY) (*7) / ANOTHER GREEN WORLD (*9) / DISCREET MUSIC (*6) / BEFORE AND AFTER SCIENCE (*8) / CLUSTER AND ENO with Cluster (*6) / AFTER THE HEAT with Moebius & Roedelius (*6) / MUSIC FOR FILMS soundtrack compilation (*6) / AMBIENT 1: MUSIC FOR AIRPORTS (*7) / AMBIENT 2: THE PLATEAUX OF MIRROR with Harold Budd (*5) / FOURTH WORLD VOL.1: POSSIBLE MUSICS with Jon Hassell (*6) / MY LIFE IN THE BUSH OF GHOSTS with David Byrne (*8) / AMBIENT 4: ON LAND (*7) / APOLLO, ATMOSPHERES & SOUNDTRACKS with Daniel Lanois & Roger Eno (*8) / THE PEARL with Harold Budd & Daniel Lanois (*5) / THURSDAY AFTERNOON (*6) / HYBRID with Michael Brook & Daniel Lanois (*5) / VOICES with Roger Eno (*5) / MORE BLANK THAN FRANK compilation (*7) / DESERT ISLAND SELECTION compilation (*7) / MUSIC FOR FILMS 2 (*6) / WRONG WAY UP with JOHN CALE (*7) / NERVE NET (*6) / THE SHUTOV ASSEMBLY (*6) / :NEROLI: (*5) / SPINNER with Jah Wobble (*6) / THE DROP (*5) / DRAWN FROM LIFE with J. Peter Schwalm (*5) / JANUARY 07003: BELL STUDIES FOR THE CLOCK OF THE LONG NOW (*6) / ANOTHER DAY ON EARTH (*6)

ENO had already released 'NO PUSSYFOOTIN' with FRIPP (King Crimson); he shared another 'EVENING STAR' in '75

— now solo with guest session people, including ROXY MUSIC musicians and ROBERT FRIPP, CHRIS SPEDDING, PAUL RUDOLPH and others.

Island Island

Jan 74. (lp/c) *(ILPS/ICT <9268>)* **HERE COME THE WARM JETS** [26] [ ]
– Needles in the camel's eye / The paw paw Negro blowtorch / Baby's on fire / Cindy tells me / Driving me backwards / On some faraway beach / Black rank / Dead finks don't talk / Some of them are old / Here come the warm jets. *(re-iss. Mar77 on 'Polydor'; 2302 063) (re-iss. Jan87 on 'E.G.' lp/c/cd; EG LP/MC/CD 11) (cd re-iss. Mar91; same)*

Mar 74. (7") *(WIP 6178)* **SEVEN DEADLY FINNS. / LATER ON** [ ] [ ]

— guests incl. PORTSMOUTH SINFONIA ORCHESTRA, PHIL COLLINS – drums / etc.

Nov 74. (lp/c) *(ILPS/ICT <9309>)* **TAKING TIGER MOUNTAIN (BY STRATEGY)** [ ] [ ]
– Burning airlines give you so much more / Back in Judy's jungle / The fat lady of Limbourg / Mother whale eyeless / The great pretender / Third uncle / Put a straw under baby / The truth wheel / China my China / Taking tiger mountain. *(re-iss. Mar77 on 'Polydor'; 2302 068) (re-iss. Jan87 on 'E.G.' lp/c/cd; EG LP/MC/CD 17) (cd re-iss. Mar91; same)*

Aug 75. (7") *(WIP 6233) <036>* **THE LION SLEEPS TONIGHT (WIMOWEH). / I'LL COME RUNNING** [ ] [ ]

— now with **FRIPP** (3) / **COLLINS** (3) / **JOHN CALE** – viola (2) / **PAUL RUDOPLH** (3) / **PERCY JONES** – bass (3) / **ROD MELVIN** – piano (3) / **BRIAN TURRINGTON** – bass, piano (1)

Sep 75. (lp/c) *(ILPS/ICT <9351>)* **ANOTHER GREEN WORLD** [ ] [ ]
– Sky saw / Over Fire Island / St. Elmo's fire / In dark trees / The big ship / I'll come running / Another green world / Sombre reptiles / Little fishes / Golden hours / Becalmed / Zawinul – Lava / Everything merges with the night. *(re-iss. Mar77 on 'Polydor'; 2302 069) (re-iss. Jan87 & Mar91 on 'E.G.' lp/c/cd; EG LP/MC/CD 21)*

Obscure Antilles

Nov 75. (lp) *(OBS 3) <7030>* **DISCREET MUSIC** [ ] [ ]
– Discreet music 1 & 2 / Three Variations on canon in D major; a) Fullness of wind – b) French catalogues – c) Brutal ardour. *(re-iss. Jan87 on 'EG-Editions' lp/c/cd; EGED/EGEDC/EEGCD 23)*

— For the next couple of years he worked with 801 (PHIL MANZANERA's band). He also produced his own 'Obscure' label, discovering people including PENGUIN CAFE ORCHESTRA, MICHAEL NYMAN, MAX EASTLEY & DAVID TOOP, HAROLD BUDD plus JAN STEELE / JOHN CAGE. More commercially he also played on and produced 1977 albums by DAVID BOWIE, TALKING HEADS, ULTRAVOX.

BRIAN ENO

Polydor Island

Dec 77. (lp) *(2302 071) <9478>* **BEFORE AND AFTER SCIENCE** [ ] May78 [ ]
– No one receiving / Backwater / Kurt's rejoiner / Energy fools the magician / King's lead hat / Here he comes / Julie with . . . / By this river / Through hollow lands / Spider and I. *(re-iss. Jan87 on 'E.G.' lp/c/cd; EG LP/MC/CD 32) (cd re-iss. Mar91; same)*

Jan 78. (7") *(2001 762)* **KING'S LEAD HAT. / R.A.F. (by "ENO & SNATCH")** [ ] [ ]

Ambient P.V.C.

Mar 79. (lp/c) *(AMB/+C 001) <7908>* **AMBIENT 1: MUSIC FOR AIRPORTS** [ ] [ ]
– 1'1 / 2'1 / 1'2 / 2'2. *(re-iss. Jan87 on 'E.G.' lp/c/cd; EGED/EGEDC/EEGCD 17)*

— Early in '79, ENO and MOEBIUS & ROEDILIUS (from CLUSTER) released album 'AFTER THE HEAT' *(Sky 021)*

— Late in 1979, ENO collaborated with trumpeter JON HASSELL on album 'FOURTH WORLD VOL.1: POSSIBLE MUSICS' on 'E.G.'; *EGED 007)*

— next with **HAROLD BUDD** – piano

E.G.-Ambient E.G.

Apr 80. (lp; ENO & BUDD) *(EGAMB 002) <EGS 107>* **AMBIENT 2: THE PLATEAUX OF MIRRORS** [ ] [ ]
– First light / Steal away / The plateau of mirror / Above Chiangmai / An arc of doves / Not yet remembered / The chill air / Among fields of crystal / Wind in lonely fences / Failing light. *(re-iss. Jan87 on 'EG')*

— next with DAVID BYRNE, vocalist and instrumentalist w/ TALKING HEADS

E.G. Sire

Feb 81. (lp/c; BRIAN ENO & DAVID BYRNE) *(EG LP/MC 48) <6093>* **MY LIFE IN THE BUSH OF GHOSTS** [29] [44]
– America is waiting / Mea culpa / Regiment / Help me somebody / The Jezebel spirit / Qu'ran / Moonlight in glory / The carrier / A secret life / Come with us / Mountain of needles. *(re-iss. Jan87 on 'E.G.' lp/c/cd; EG LP/MC/CD 48)*

May 81. (7"; BRIAN ENO & DAVID BYRNE) *(EGO 1)* **THE JEZEBEL SPIRIT. / REGIMENT** [ ] [ ]
(12"+=) *(EGOX 1)* – Very very hungry (Qu'ran).

Mar 82. (lp/c) *('EG-Editions'; EGED/+C 20)* **AMBIENT (4): ON LAND** [93] [–]
– Lizard point / The lost day / Tal coat / Shadow / Lantern marsh / Unfamiliar wind / A clearing / Dunwich Beach, Autumn 1960. *(cd-iss. Jan87 on 'E.G.'; EEGCD 20)*

Jul 83. (lp; BRIAN ENO with DANIEL LANOIS & ROGER ENO) *(EGLP 53)* **APOLLO: ATMOSPHERES & SOUNDTRACKS** [ ] [–]
– Under stars / The secret place / Matta / Signals / An ending (ascent) / Under stars II / Drift / Silver morning / Deep blue day / Weightless / Always returning / Stars. *(re-iss. Jan87 & Mar91 on 'E.G.' lp/c/cd; EG LP/MC/CD 53)*

EG-Editions not iss

Aug 84. (lp; HAROLD BUDD & BRIAN ENO with DANIEL LANOIS) *(EGED 37)* **THE PEARL** [ ] [–]
– Late October / A stream with bright fish / The silver ball / Against the sky / Lost in the humming air / Dark-eyed sister / Their memories / The pearl / Foreshadowed / An echo of night / Still return. *(re-iss. Jan87 on 'E.G.' lp/c/cd; EG LP/MC/CD 37)*

— In 1984, he released 2 albums 'BEGEGNUNGEN I & II' with MOEBIUS ROEDILUS & PLANK.

Aug 85. (lp/c; MICHAEL BROOK with BRIAN ENO & DANIEL LANOIS) *('EG-Editions'; EGED/+C 41)* **HYBRID** [ ] [–]
– Hybrid / Distant village / Mimosa / Pond life / Ocean motion / Midday / Earth floor / Vacant. *(re-iss. Nov86 on 'E.G.' lp/c/cd; EG LP/MC/CD 41)*

Aug 85. (lp; ROGER ENO with BRIAN ENO) *('EG-Editions'; EGED 42)* **VOICES** [ ] [–]
– A place in the wilderness / The day after / At the water's edge / Grey promenade / A paler sky / Through the blue / Evening tango / Recalling winter / Voices / The old dance / Reflections on I.K.B. *(re-iss. Jan87 on 'E.G.' lp/c/cd; EG LP/MC/CD 42)*

Jan 87. (lp/cd) *(EG LP/CD 64)* **THURSDAY AFTERNOON** [ ] [–]
– Thursday afternoon. *(1 track only) (re-iss. cd Mar91; same)*

ENO / CALE

(collaboration **JOHN CALE** – vocals, multi-)with **ROBERT AHWAI** – rhythm guitar / **DARYL JOHNSON** – bass / **NEIL CATCHPOLE** – violin / **RONALD JONES** – drums, tabla / **DAVE YOUNG** – guitars, bass

Land Opal-Warne

Oct 90. (lp/c/cd) *(AS/+C/CD 12) <7599 26421-1/-4/-2>* **WRONG WAY UP** [ ] [ ]
– Lay my love / One word / In the backroom / Empty frame / Cordoba / Spinning away / Footsteps / Been there done that / Crime in the desert / The river. *(re-iss. Jul92; same)*

Nov 90. (12"ep/cd-ep) *(LANDHO 4) <9 40001-1/-2>* **ONE WORD. / GRANDFATHER'S HOUSE / PALAQUIN** [ ] [–]

BRIAN ENO

Opal-WEA Opal-Warner

Jul 92. (7") *(48496-7) <9 40539-2>* **FRACTIAL ZOOM. / ('A'-Moby mix)**
(12"+=) *(48496-1)* – (4 mixes).
(cd-s++=) *(48496-2)* – (another mix) / The roil, the choke.

Sep 92. (cd/c) *(<9362 45033-2/-4>)* **NERVE NET** [70]
– Fractial zoom / Wire shock / What actually happened? / Pierre in mist / My squelchy life / Decentre / Juju space jazz / The roil, the choke / Ali click / Distributing being / Web.

Oct 92. (7") *(40618-7) <9 40650-2>* **ALI CLICK (Beirut mix). / ('A'-Rural mix)**
(12"+=) *(40618-1)* – ('A'-Markus Draws + Grid mixes).
(cd-s) *(40618-2)* – ('A'side) / ('A'-Markus Draws + Grid mixes) / ('A'-trance long darkly mad mix) / ('A'-trance instrumental).

Nov 92. (cd/c) *(<9362 45010-2/-4>)* **THE SHUTOV ASSEMBLY**
– Triennale / Alhondiga / Markgraph / Lanzarote / Francisco / Riverside / Innocenti / Stedelijk / Ikebukero / Cavallino.
(above music inspired by Moscow painter Sergei Shutov)

— Around the same time as above, he lectured at Sadler's Wells, and is the brunt of NME jokes as Professor Eno.

All Saints Caroline

Jun 93. (cd) *(ASCD 015) <6600-2>* **:NEROLI:**
– :Neroli:
above's long piece of music was used in hospitals for childbirth!

— Sep 94; ENO was credited on JAMES' ltd. album 'WAH WAH'.

All Saints Gyroscope

Oct 95. (lp/c/cd; by ENO / WOBBLE) *(AS/+C/CD 023) <8190 6614-2>* **SPINNER** (soundtrack to 'Glitterbug') [71]
– Where we lived / Like organza / Steam / Garden recalled / Marine radio / Unusual balance / Space diary 1 / Spinner / Transmitter and trumpet / Left where it fell.

All Saints Thirsty Ear

Jun 97. (cd) *(ASCD 032) <6603-2>* **THE DROP**
– Slip dip / But if / Belgiam drop / Cornered / Black drop / Out-out / Swanky / Coasters / Blissed / M.C. Organ / Boomcubist / Hazard / Rayonism / Dutch blur / Back clack / Dear world / Iced world. *(re-iss. Jun05 on 'Hannibal'; HNCD 1479)*

— In March 2000, ENO (alongside BONO, DANIEL LANOIS & The MDH BAND) contributed the bulk of tracks to 'THE MILLION DOLLAR HOTEL' OST

Venture Astralwerks

May 01. (cd; as BRIAN ENO & J. PETER SCHWALM) *(CDVE 954) <10148>* **DRAWN FROM LIFE**
– From this moment / Persis / Like pictures (part 1) / Like pictures (part 2) / Night traffic / Rising dust / Intenser / More dust / Bloom / Two voices / Bloom (instrumental).

Opal Opal

May 03. (cd) *(<02>)* **JANUARY 07003: BELL STUDIES FOR THE CLOCK OF THE LONG NOW**
– Fixed radio harmonic bells / Changes where bell number = repeat number / 2 harmonic studues / Deep glass bells (with harmonic clouds) / Dark cracked bells with bass / German-style ringing / Ephasizing enharmonic partials / Changes for January 07003, soft bells, hillis algorithm / Lithuanian bell study / Large bell change improvisation / Reverse harmonic bells / Bell improvisation 2 / Virtual dream bells, thick glass / Tsar kolokol III (and friends) / 1st-14th January 07003, hard bells, hillis algorithm.

— in April 2005, FRIPP & ENO released 'THE EQUATORIAL STARS'

Hannibal Hannibal

Jun 05. (cd) *<(HNCD 1475)>* **ANOTHER DAY ON EARTH** [75]
– This / And then so clear / A long way down / Going unconscious / Caught between / Passing over / How many worlds / Bottomliners / JUst another day / Under / Bone bomb.

– compilations, others, etc. –

on 'E.G.' unless mentioned otherwise

Sep 78. (lp) *Polydor; (2310 623) / E.G.; <EGS 105>* **MUSIC FOR FILMS** [55]
– Aragon / From the same hill / Inland sea / Two rapid formations / Slow water / Sparrowfall (1) / Sparrowfall (2) / Sparrowfall (3) / Alternative 3 / Quartz / Events in dense fog / 'There is nobody' / Patrolling wire borders / A measured room / Task force / M386 / Strange light / Final sunset. *(re-iss. Jan87 on 'E.G.' lp/c/cd; EGED/EGEDC/EEGCD 5)*

Apr 82. (d-c; FRIPP & ENO) *(EGDC 2)* **NO PUSSYFOOTIN' / EVENING STAR** –

Nov 83. (10xlp-box) *(EGBS 002)* **WORKING BACKWARDS 1983-1973** –
– (first 9 lp's, plus MUSIC FOR FILMS VOL.2 / + RARITIES m-lp:- Seven deadly finns / The lion sleeps tonight / Strong flashes of light / More volts / Mist rhythm)

Mar 86. (lp/c) *(EG LP/MC 65)* **MORE BLANK THAN FRANK** –
(cd-iss. Jun87 & Mar91; EGCD 65)

Jan 87. (cd) *(EGCD 65)* **DESERT ISLAND SELECTION** –
– Here he comes / Everything merges with the night / I'll come running (edit) / On some faraway beach (edit) / Spirits drifting / Back in Judy's jungle / St. Elmo's fire / No one receiving / Julie with . . . / Taking tiger mountain (edit) / 1'1.

Jan 87. (lp/c) *EG-Editions; (EGED/+C 35)* **MUSIC FOR FILMS 2** –
– The dove / Roman twilight / Matta / Dawn, marshland / Climate study / The secret place / An ending (ascent) / Always returning 1 / Signals / Under stars / Drift / Study / Approaching Taidu / Always returning 2.

Mar 89. (cd-s) *(CDT 41)* **ANOTHER GREEN WORLD / DOVER BEACH / DEEP BLUE DAY / 2'1** –

Dec 89. (3xc-box)(3xcd-box) *(EG BM/BC 7)* **ISLAND VARIOUS ARTISTS** –
– (ANOTHER GREEN WORLD / BEFORE AND AFTER SCIENCE / APOLLO)

Nov 93. (3xcd-box) *Virgin; (ENOBX 1)* **BRIAN ENO** (collaborations) –

Nov 93. (3xcd-box) *Virgin; (ENOBX 2)* **BRIAN ENO 2** (collaborations) –

Feb 94. (cd/c) *Venture; (CD/TC VE 920)* **THE ESSENTIAL FRIPP AND ENO** –

Oct 94. (3xcd-box) *Virgin; (TPAK 36)* **THE COMPACT COLLECTION** –

May 99. (cd) *Materiali Sonori; (129570110-2)* **SONORA PORTRAITS** –

— ENO contributed 2 tracks on live lp 'JUNE 1st, 1974' with KEVIN AYERS, NICO and JOHN CALE. He also with brother ROGER and DANIEL LANOIS provided one track to DUNE film (1984). For albums by CLUSTER & ENO; see CLUSTER.

EURYTHMICS

Formed: London, England . . . 1976, by Aberdonian, ANNIE LENNOX and Sunderland-born, DAVE STEWART. They formed the CATCH in 1977 with PETE COOMBES, which, by 1979, had evolved into the TOURISTS. Signing to 'Logo' records, they scored with some Top 10 pop hits, namely'I ONLY WANT TO BE WITH YOU' and 'SO GOOD TO BE BACK HOME', before they broke with COOMBES late in 1980. The duo, now EURYTHMICS, began recording their debut at Conny Plank's Cologne studio. Featuring contributions from the likes of CAN's HOLGER CZUKAY and JAKI LIEBEZEIT as well as MARCUS STOCHHAUSEN (son of KARLHEINZ), 'IN THE GARDEN' (1981) was a radical musical departure. Icy synth-pop with avant-garde tendencies, the band's closest musical compadres were the lipstick 'n' legwarmers 'New Romantic' crowd, although EURYTHMICS' vision was unique. So unique, in fact, that the record languished in relative obscurity, given scant support by 'R.C.A.'. Undeterred, the band recorded 'SWEET DREAMS (ARE MADE OF THIS)' (1983), the title track giving the band an international breakthrough. This time around, the sculpted synth soundscapes were fashioned with a studied pop nous, LENNOX's mournful vocals heavy with dark implications. Visually striking, the duo's image was also highly marketable and ANNIE became the chameleon queen of the new video generation, leading to overnight success in the States. 'TOUCH' (1983) consolidated the EURYTHMICS position as pop frontrunners, the single 'HERE COMES THE RAIN AGAIN' going Top 10 on both sides of the Atlantic. While their next project, the soundtrack for the film '1984 – For The Love Of Big Brother' was a relative success in Britain, it stiffed big time in the US amid recriminations from both parties; the director, MICHAEL RADFORD and EURYTHMICS themselves. 'BE YOURSELF TONIGHT' (1985) saw LENNOX in soul diva mode, belting out the likes of 'SISTERS ARE DOIN' IT FOR THEMSELVES' and putting in a breathtaking feat of vocal histrionics on the No.1 hit, 'THERE MUST BE AN ANGEL (PLAYING WITH MY HEART)'. Perhaps playing all those stadiums was beginning to affect the band, as 'REVENGE' saw the band veering towards big-rock, tracks like 'MISSIONARY MAN' sounding downright clumsy. By the release of 'WE TOO ARE ONE', (1989) the band were clearly on their last legs and it was obvious, on listening to the record, that the working relationship between LENNOX and STEWART had finally broken down. LENNOX went on to do charity work before releasing 'DIVA' in 1992, her multi-platinum selling solo debut. She also released a collection of covers, 'MEDUSA', in 1995. STEWART, meanwhile, recorded the soundtrack 'LILY WAS HERE' with sax-diva, CANDY DULFER, before going on to form his SPIRITUAL COWBOYS and generally receive a bit of a pasting from the critics. 1999 saw the return of EURYTHMICS via the hit single, 'I SAVED THE WORLD TODAY' and Top 5 album, 'PEACE'. LENNOX and STEWART were briefly reunited musically for what will probably be their final set of melodic pop songs. ANNIE LENNOX returned in 2003 with one of her intermittent solo releases, 'BARE'. As its title intimated, it was the most unflinchingly personal and self-excoriating song cycle she's yet recorded. Completely self-penned and unrelentingly melancholy, yet blessed with sympathetic arrangements and alluring use of electronica, the record's naked emotional force was as hypnotic as it was unprecedented. Her solo talent subsequently won her a Grammy (2004) for her contribution ('INTO THE WEST') to the final part in 'The Lord Of The Rings' trilogy. Whether the 1991 EURYTHMICS anthology actually needed updating was debateable; 'ULTIMATE COLLECTION' (2005) justified its existence with the inclusion of tracks from the 'PEACE' album and a new hit, 'I'VE GOT A LIFE'.

• **Songwriters:** COOMBES penned songs in the TOURISTS, except I ONLY WANT TO BE WITH YOU (Dusty Springfield). DAVE and ANNIE wrote together in The EURYTHMICS. Now a solo writer, ANNIE LENNOX covered KEEP YOUNG AND BEAUTIFUL (Al Dubin-Harry Warren) / FEEL THE NEED (Detroit Emeralds) / RIVER DEEP MOUNTAIN HIGH (Phil Spector) / DON'T LET ME DOWN (Beatles) / NO MORE "I LOVE YOU'S" (Lover Speaks) / TAKE ME TO THE RIVER (Al Green) / A WHITER SHADE OF PALE (Procol Harum) / DON'T LET IT BRING YOU DOWN (Neil Young) / TRAIN IN VAIN (Clash) / I CAN'T GET NEXT TO YOU (Strong-Whitfield) / DOWNTOWN LIGHTS (Blue Nile) / THE THIN BLUE LINE BETWEEN LOVE AND HATE (Pretenders; hit) / WAITING IN VAIN (Bob Marley) / SOMETHING SO RIGHT (Paul Simon) / LADIES OF THE CANYON (Joni Mitchell) / I'M ALWAYS TOUCHED BY YOUR PRESENCE DEAR (Blondie). DAVE STEWART's VEGAS covered SHE (Charles Aznavour). • **Trivia:** In March '84 ANNIE, now not involved intimately with DAVE, married German Hare Krishna RADHA RAMAR, although this only lasted six months. She married again in the early 90's and gave birth to her first child in the Spring pf '93. On the 1st of August '84, DAVE married SHAKESPEAR'S SISTER/ex-BANANARAMA singer, SIOBHAN FAHEY. The bearded one has also produced many artists including FEARGAL SHARKEY, MARIA McKEE, DARYL HALL, BOB GELDOF, BOB DYLAN, TOM PETTY, MICK JAGGER, BORIS GREBENSHIKOV (Russian rocker) and LONDONBEAT. Just a wee note to say, DAVE was not the DAVE STEWART that had a No.1 hit with BARBARA GASKIN.

Album rating: the Tourists: THE TOURISTS (*4) / REALITY EFFECT (*4) / LUMINOUS BASEMENT (*5) / Eurythmics: IN THE GARDEN (*5) / SWEET DREAMS (ARE MADE OF THIS) (*8) / TOUCH (*7) / TOUCH DANCE mini remix (*3) / 1984 (FOR THE LOVE OF BIG BROTHER) (*4) / BE YOURSELF TONIGHT (*7) / REVENGE (*6) / SAVAGE (*5) / WE TOO ARE ONE (*6) / EURYTHMICS' GREATEST HITS compilation (*8) / EURYTHMICS LIVE 1983-1989 collection (*4) / ULTIMATE COLLECTION compilation (*8) / Dave Stewart: LILY WAS HERE soundtrack (*5) / DAVE STEWART & THE SPIRITUAL COWBOYS (*6) / HONEST soundtrack (*5) / GREETINGS FROM THE GUTTER (*5) / Annie Lennox: ANNIE LENNOX – DIVA (*7) / MEDUSA (*5) / Eurythmics: PEACE (*5) / Annie Lennox: BARE (*6)

the CATCH

ANNIE LENNOX (b.25 Dec'54, Aberdeen, Scotland) – vocals, keyboards, flute / **DAVE STEWART** (b. 9 Sep'52, Sunderland, England) – guitar, keyboards (ex-LONGDANCER) / **PETE COOMBES** – guitar, vocals

Logo — not iss.

Nov 77. (7") *(GO 103)* **BORDERLINE. / BLACK BLOOD** [ ] [–]

the TOURISTS

added **EDDY CHIN** – bass / **JIM TOOMEY** – drums

Logo — Epic

May 79. (7") *(GO 350)* **BLIND AMONG THE FLOWERS. / HE WHO LAUGHS LAST LAUGHS LONGEST** [52] [ ]
(d7"+=) *(GOD 350)* – The golden lamp / Wrecked.

Jun 79. (lp) *(LOGO 1018)* **THE TOURISTS** [72] [ ]
– Blind among the flowers / Save me / Fool's paradise / Can't stop laughing / Don't get left behind / Another English day / Deadly kiss / Ain't no room / The loneliest man in the world / Useless duration of time / He who laughs last laughs longest / Just like you. *(re-iss. Jun81 on 'RCA Int.' lp/c; INT S/K 5096)*

Aug 79. (7"/7"pic-d) *(GO/+P 360)* **THE LONELIEST MAN IN THE WORLD. / DON'T GET LEFT BEHIND** [32] [ ]

Oct 79. (lp/c) *(LOGO/KLOGO 1019)* **REALITY EFFECT** [23] [ ]
– It doesn't have to be this way / I only want to be with you / In the morning / All life's tragedies / Everywhere you look / So good to be back home / Nothing to do / Circular fever / In my mind / Something in the air tonight / Summers night.

Oct 79. (7") *(GO 370)* *<50850>* **I ONLY WANT TO BE WITH YOU. / SUMMER NIGHT** [4] Apr80 [83]

Jan 80. (7") *(TOUR 1)* **SO GOOD TO BE BACK HOME. / CIRCULAR SAW** [6] [ ]

R.C.A. — R.C.A.

Sep 80. (7") *(TOUR 2)* **DON'T SAY I TOLD YOU SO. / STRANGE SKY** [40] [ ]

Oct 80. (lp/c) *(RCA LP/K 5001)* **LUMINOUS BASEMENT** [75] [ ]
– Walls and foundations / Don't say I told you so / Week days / So you want to go away now / One step nearer the edge / Angels and demons / Talk to me / Round round blues / Let's take a walk / Time drags so slow / I'm going to change my mind. *(free-7"yellow) (FREE 5001)* – FROM THE MIDDLE ROOM. / INTO THE FUTURE

— The TOURISTS split late '80.

EURYTHMICS

— were formed by **ANNIE LENNOX** + **DAVE STEWART** with guests **ROBERT GORL** and **GABI DELGADO** of D.A.F. / **JAKI LIEBEZEIT** – percussion and **HOLGER CZUKAY** – bass (both ex-CAN)

R.C.A. — R.C.A.

Jun 81. (7"/ext.12") *(RCA/+T 68)* **NEVER GONNA CRY AGAIN. / LE SINISTRE** [63] [ ]

Aug 81. (7") *(RCA 115)* **BELINDA. / HEARTBEAT, HEARTBEAT** [ ] [ ]

Oct 81. (lp/c) *(RCA LP/K 5061)* **IN THE GARDEN** [ ] [ ]
– English summer / Belinda / Take me to your heart / She's invisible now / Your time will come / Caveman head / Never gonna cry again / All the young (people of today) / Sing sing / Revenge. *(re-iss. Mar84 lp/c; PL/PK 70006) (cd-iss. Jan87; PD 70006) (re-iss. Sep91 cd/c/lp; ND/NK/NL 75036)*

— **ANNIE** and **DAVE** now augmented with synthesisers, also guests **CLEM BURKE** – drums (ex-BLONDIE, who later joined RAMONES in '87)

Mar 82. (7") *(RCA 199)* **THIS IS THE HOUSE. / HOME IS WHERE THE HEART IS** [ ] [ ]
(12") *(RCAT 199)* – ('A'side) / Your time will come (live) / 4-4 In leather (live) / Never gonna cry again (live) / Take me to your heart (live).

Jun 82. (7"m) *(RCA 230)* **THE WALK. / STEP ON THE BEAST / THE WALK (part 2)** [ ] [ ]
(12"+=) *(RCAT 230)* – Invisible hands / Dr. Trash.

Sep 82. (7"/7"pic-d) *(DA 1)* **LOVE IS A STRANGER. / MONKEY, MONKEY** [54] [ ]
(12"+=) *(DAT 1)* – Let's just close our eyes.
(re-iss. Apr83, hit No.6) <US re-iss. Sep83; 13618); hit No.23>

an 83. (7"/7"pic-d) *(DA/+P 2)* *<13533>* **SWEET DREAMS (ARE MADE OF THIS). / I COULD GIVE YOU (A MIRROR)** 2 Apr83 1
(12"+=) *(DAT 2)* – Baby's gone blue.

'eb 83. (lp/pic-lp/c) *(RCA LP/LPP/K 6063)* *<4681>* **SWEET DREAMS (ARE MADE OF THIS)** 3 May83 15
– Sweet dreams (are made of this) / Jennifer / This city never sleeps / This is the house / Somebody told me / The walk / I've got an angel / Love is a stranger / Wrap it up / I could give you (a mirror). *(re-iss. Aug84 lp/c; PL/PK 70014) (cd-iss. Jan84; RCD 25447) (re-iss. Oct87 lp/c/cd; NL/NK/ND 71471)*

ul 83. (7"/7"pic-d) *(DA/+P 3)* **WHO'S THAT GIRL?. / YOU TAKE SOME LENTILS . . . AND YOU TAKE SOME RICE** 3 –
(12"+=) *(DAT 3)* – ABC (freeform).

)ct 83. (7"/7"pic-d) *(DA/+P 4)* *<13695>* **RIGHT BY YOUR SIDE. / ('A'party mix)** 10 Jul84 29
(7"w/ free-c-s) *(DA 4-EUC 001)* – Intro speech / Step on the beast / Invisible hands / Angel (dub) / Satellite of love.
(12"+=) *(DAT 4)* – Plus something else.

— **ANNIE** and **DAVE** were augmented on album by **CLEM** – drums plus **DICK CUTHELL** – brass MARTIN DOBSON – horns / **DEAN GARCIA** – bass(above 3 also went on tour adding) **VIC MARTIN** – synthesizers / **PETE PHIPPS** – drums / and backing singers **GILL O'DONOVAN, SUZIE O'LISZT and MAGGIE RYDER**

Iov 83. (lp/pic-lp/c) *(PL/PLP/PK 70109)* *<4917>* **TOUCH** 1 Jan84 7
– Here comes the rain again / Regrets / Right by your side / Cool blue / Who's that girl? / The first cut / Aqua / No fear, no hurt, no pain (no broken hearts) / Paint a rumour. *(cd-iss. Sep84; PD 70109) (re-iss. Sep89 lp/c/cd; NL/NK/ND 90369)*

an 84. (7"/7"pic-d) *(DA/+P 5)* *<13725>* **HERE COMES THE RAIN AGAIN. / PAINT A RUMOUR** 8 4
(ext.12"+=) *(DAT 5)* – This city never sleeps (live).

.pr 84. (7") *<13800>* **WHO'S THAT GIRL?. / AQUA** – 21

.ın 84. (m-lp/c) *(PG/PH 70354)* *<5086>* **TOUCH DANCE** (remixes) 31
– The first cut (instrumental) / Cool blue (instrumental) / Paint a rumour (instrumental) / The first cut / Cool blue / Paint a rumour / Regrets. *(cd-iss. Dec91; ND 75151)*

)ct 84. (7") *(VS 728)* *<13956>* **SEXCRIME (NINETEEN EIGHTY-FOUR). / I DID IT JUST THE SAME** 4 81
(12"/12"pic-d) *(VS 728-12)* – ('A'extended).

Iov 84. (lp/c) *(V/TCV 1984)* *<ABL-1 5349>* **1984 – FOR THE LOVE OF BIG BROTHER (soundtrack)** 23 93
– I did it just the same / Sexcrime (Nineteen Eighty-Four) / For the love of Big Brother / Winston's diary / Greetings from a dead man / Julia / Doubleplusgood / Ministry of love / Room 101. *(re-iss. Jan88 lp/c; OVED/+C 207) (cd-iss. Apr89; CDV 1984) (cd re-iss. Dec95 on 'Virgin'VIP'; CDVIP 135)*

ın 85. (7"/7"pic-d) *(VS 734)* **JULIA. / MINISTRY OF LOVE** 44
(12"+=) *(VS 734-12)* – ('A'extended).
(above album & two singles were issued UK on 'Virgin')

.pr 85. (7",7"red,7"yellow,7"blue) *(PB 40101)* *<14078>* **WOULD I LIE TO YOU? / HERE COMES THAT SINKING FEELING** 11 5
(ext.remix; 12",12"red,12"yellow,12"blue;+=) *(PT 40102)* – ('A'-E.T.mix).

Iay 85. (lp/c/cd) *(PL/PK/PD 70711)* *<5429>* **BE YOURSELF TONIGHT** 3 9
– It's alright (baby's coming back) / Would I lie to you / There must be an angel (playing with my heart) / I love you like a ball and chain / Sisters are doin' it for themselves / Conditioned soul / Adrian / Here comes that sinking feeling / Better to have lost in love (than never to have loved at all). *(re-iss. May90 cd/c/lp; ND/NK/NL 74602)*

.ın 85. (7")(12"/dance mix-12") *(PB 40247)(PT 40248/+R)* *<14160>* **THERE MUST BE AN ANGEL (PLAYING WITH MY HEART). / GROWN UP GIRLS** 1 22

)ct 85. (7"; as EURYTHMICS & ARETHA FRANKLIN) *(PB 40339)* *<14214>* **SISTERS ARE DOIN' IT FOR THEMSELVES. / I LOVE YOU LIKE A BALL AND CHAIN** 9 18
(12"+=) *(PT 40340)* – ('A'-E.T. remix with ARETHA).

.ın 86. (7") *(PB 40375)* *<14284>* **IT'S ALRIGHT (BABY'S COMING BACK). / CONDITIONED SOUL** 12 78
(d7"+=/d12"+=) *(PB/PB 40375/40376; 2nd-free in yellow, blue or red)* – Would I lie to you? / Here comes that sinking feeling.
(12"+=) *(PT 40376)* – Tous les garcons et les filles.

Jun 86. (7") *(DA 7)* **WHEN TOMORROW COMES. / TAKE YOUR PAIN AWAY** 30
(ext.12"+=) *(DAT 7)* – ('A'-orchestral).

Jul 86. (lp/c/cd) *(PL/PK/PD 71050)* *<5847>* **REVENGE** 3 12
– Let's go / Take your pain away / A little of you / Thorn in my side / In this town / I remember you / Missionary man / The last time / When tomorrow comes / The miracle of love. *(cd re-iss. Sep93; 74321 12529-2)*

Jul 86. (7"/12") *<14414>* **MISSIONARY MAN. / TAKE YOUR PAIN AWAY** – 14

Aug 86. (7") *(DA 8)* *<5058>* **THORN IN MY SIDE. / IN THIS TOWN** 5 Oct86 68
(12"+=) *(DAT 8)* – ('A'extended or Houston mix).

Nov 86. (7"/7"sha-pic-d) *(DA/+P 9)* **THE MIRACLE OF LOVE. / WHEN TOMORROW COMES (live)** 23
(12"+=) *(DAT 9)* – Who's that girl? (live).

Feb 87. (7"/ext.12") *(DA/+T 10)* **MISSIONARY MAN. / THE LAST TIME (live)** 31 –

Oct 87. (7"/7"w-poster) *(DA 11/+P)* **BEETHOVEN (I LOVE TO LISTEN TO). / HEAVEN** 25
(ext.12"+=)(cd-s+=) *(DAT 11)(DA 11CD)* – ('A'dance mix).

Nov 87. (lp/c/cd) *(PL/PK/PD 71555)* *<6794>* **SAVAGE** 7 41
– Beethoven (I love to listen to) / I've got a lover (back in Japan) / Do you want to break up? / You have placed a chill in my heart / Shame / Savage / I need a man / Put the blame on me / Heaven / Wide eyed girl / I need you / Brand new day. *(re-iss. cd May93; 74321 13440-2)*

Dec 87. (7") *(DA 14)* **SHAME. / I'VE GOT A LOVER (BACK IN JAPAN)** 41
(12"+=/12"s+=) *(DAT 14/+P)* – ('A'dance mix).
('A'dance mix-cd-s+=) *(DA 14CD)* – There must be an angel (playing with my heart).

Dec 87. (7") *<5361>* **I NEED A MAN. / HEAVEN** – 46

Mar 88. (7") *(DA 15)* **I NEED A MAN. / I NEED YOU** 26 –
(12"+=) *(DAT 15)* – ('A'-macho mix).
(cd-s++=) *(DA 15CD)* – Missionary man (live).
(10"+=) *(DA 15X)* – There must be an angel (playing with my heart).
(7"m+=) *(DA 15R)* – I need a man (live).

May 88. (7") *(DA 16)* **YOU HAVE PLACED A CHILL IN MY HEART. / ('A'acoustic mix)** 16 64
(12"+=) *(DAT 16)* – ('A'dance).
(cd-s++=) *(DA 16CD)* – Do you want to break up / Here comes the rain again (live).

— In Oct'88, ANNIE was credited with AL GREEN on single 'PUT A LITTLE LOVE IN YOUR HEART' on 'A&M' 7"/12"; *(AM/+Y 484)*

R.C.A. Arista

Aug 89. (7"/c-s) *(DA/+K 17)* **REVIVAL. / PRECIOUS** 26
(12"+=/cd-s+=) *(DAT/DACD 17)* – ('A'dance mix).
(12"+=/12"s+=) *(DAT 18/+P)* – ('A'-extended E.T. dance mix).

Sep 89. (lp/c/cd) *(PL/PK/PD 74251)* *<8606>* **WE TOO ARE ONE** 1 34
– We two are one / The King and Queen of America / (My my) Baby's gonna cry / Don't ask me why / Angel / Revival / You hurt me (and I hate you) / Sylvia / How long? / When the day goes down. *(re-iss. cd Jun94; 74321 20898-2)*

Oct 89. (7"/c-s) *(DA/+K 19)* *<9880>* **DON'T ASK ME WHY. / RICH GIRL** 25 Sep89 40
(12"+=/12"pic-d+=/cd-s+=) *(DA T/P/CD 19)* – Sylvia.
(12"+=/cd-s+=) *(DA T/CD 20)* – ('A'acoustic) / When the day goes down.

Jan 90. (7"/c-s) *(DA/+K 23)* **KING AND QUEEN OF AMERICA (remix). / SEE NO EVIL** 29 –
(cd-s+=) *(DACD 23)* – There must be an angel (playin' with my heart) (live) / I love you like a ball and chain (live) / ('A'dub).
(12") *(DAT 23)* – ('A'dance mix) / ('B'side) / ('A'dub mix).
(12"+=/cd-s+=) *(DA T/CD 24)* – (as extra above except 'A'dub).

Apr 90. (7"/c-s) *(DA/+K 21)* **ANGEL. / ANGEL (choir version)** 23 –
(12"+=/cd-s+=) *(DA T/CD 21)* – Missionary man (acoustic).
(12") *(DAT 25)* – ('A'remix) / Sweet dreams (are made of this) (Nightmare mix).

Apr 90. (c-s) *<9917>* **ANGEL / PRECIOUS** –

Jun 90. (c-s) *<9939>* **(MY MY) BABY'S GONNA CRY / ('A'acoustic)** –

— split after the above release

ANNIE LENNOX

in 1992 with **STEPHEN LIPSON** – guitars, prog., keyboards / **PETER-JOHN VITTESE** – keyboards, recorder / **MARIUS DE VRIES** – programming, keyboards/ also **LOUIS JARDIM** – percussion / **ED SHEARMUR** – piano / **KEITH LeBLANC**

– drums / **DOUG WIMBUSH** – bass / **KENJI JAMMER** – guitar / **STEVE JANSON** – drum pro / **DAVE DeFRIES** – trumpet / **GAVON WRIGHT** – violin / **PAUL MOORE** – keyboards (co-writer on 1)

R.C.A. Arista

Mar 92. (7"/c-s) *(PB/PK 45317) <12419>* **WHY. / PRIMITIVE** [5] [34]
(12"+=) *(PT 45317)* – Keep young and beautiful.
(cd-s+=) *(PD 45317)* – ('A'instrumental).

Apr 92. (cd/c/lp) *(PL/PK/PD 75326) <18704>* **ANNIE LENNOX – DIVA** [1] [27]
– Why / Walking on broken glass / Precious / Legend in my living room / Cold / Money can't buy it / Little bird / Primitive / Stay by me / The gift. *(cd+=)* – Keep young and beautiful. *(re-iss. Feb96 cd/c; 74321 33102-2/-4)*

May 92. (7"/c-s) *(74321 10025-7/-4)* **PRECIOUS. / ('A'version)** [23] [ ]
(cd-s+=) *(74321 10025-2)* – Step by step / Why.

Aug 92. (7"/c-s/cd-s) *(74321 10722-7/-4/-2)* **WALKING ON BROKEN GLASS. / LEGEND IN MY OWN LIVING ROOM** [8] [–]
(12"+=/cd-s+=) *(74321 28483-1/-2)* – Don't let me down.

Aug 92. (c-s) *<12452>* **WALKING ON BROKEN GLASS / DON'T LET ME DOWN** [–] [14]

Oct 92. (7") *(74321 11688-7)* **COLD. / ('A'live)** [26] [ ]
(c-s) *(74321 11688-4)* – River deep mountain high / You have placed a chill in my heart / Why.
(cd-s) *(74321 11690-2)* – ('A'side) / River deep mountain high / Feel the need in me / Don't let me down.
(cd-s) *(74321 11689-2)* – ('A'side) / Why / The gift / Walking on broken glass.
(cd-s) *(74321 11688-2)* – ('A'side) / It's alright / Here comes the rain again / You have placed a chill in my heart.

Jan 93. (7"/c-s/12") *(74321 123383-7/-4/-1) <12508>* **LITTLE BIRD. / LOVE SONG FOR A VAMPIRE** [3] [49]
(cd-s+=) *(74321 12383-2)* – Feel the need (live).
(cd-s+=) *(74321 12383-5)* – River deep mountain high (live).
(cd-s+=) *(74321 12383-8)* – Don't let me down (live).

—— with **STEPHEN LIPSON** – programmer, guitar, keyboards, bass

Feb 95. (7"/c-s) *(74321 25716-7/-4) <12804>* **NO MORE "I LOVE YOU'S". / LADIES OF THE CANYON** [2] [23]
(cd-s+=) *(74321 25551-2)* – Love song for a vampire.
(cd-s) *(74321 25716-2)* – ('A'side) / Why (acoustic) / Cold (acoustic) / Walking on broken glass (acoustic).

Mar 95. (cd/c/lp) *(<74321 25717-2/-4/-1>)* **MEDUSA** [1] [11]
– No more "I love you's" / Take me to the river / A whiter shade of pale / Don't let it bring you down / Train in vain / I can't get next to you / Downtown lights / The thin line between love and hate / Waiting in vain / Something so right. *(re-iss. d-cd Dec95; 74321 33163-2)* – w/ free 'LIVE IN CENTRAL PARK')

May 95. (c-s) *(74321 28482-4)* **A WHITER SHADE OF PALE / HEAVEN** [16] [ ]
(cd-s+=) *(74321 26482-2)* – I'm always touched by your presence dear / Love song for a vampire.
(cd-s) *(74321 28483-2)* – ('A'side) / Don't let it bring you down / You have placed a chill in my heart / Here comes the rain again.

Sep 95. (c-s) *(74321 31612-4)* **WAITING IN VAIN. / NO MORE "I LOVE YOU'S"** [31] [ ]
(cd-s+=) *(74321 31613-2)* – (interview) / ('A'-Strong body mix).
(cd-s) *(74321 31612-2)* – ('A'side) / Train in vain (3 mixes).
(12") *(74321 31612-1)* – ('A'side) / ('A'-Strong body mix) / ('A'-Howie B mix).
(below featured PAUL SIMON)

Nov 95. (cd-s) *(74321 33238-2)* **SOMETHING SO RIGHT / SWEET DREAMS (ARE MADE OF THIS) (live)** [44] [ ]
(c-s+=) *(74321 33238-4)* – Who's that girl (live) / Waiting in vain (live).
(cd-s) *(74321 33239-2)* – ('A'side) / I love you like a ball and chain / Money can't buy it.

EURYTHMICS

—— re-formed in 1999 after a decade split

Arista Arista

Oct 99. (c-s/cd-s) *(74321 69563-4/-2)* **I SAVED THE WORLD TODAY / LIFTED** [11] [–]
(cd-s) *(74321 69564-2)* – ('A') / You have placed a chill in my heart / There must be an angel playing with my heart.

Oct 99. (cd/c) *(74321 69582-2/-4) <14617>* **PEACE** [4] [25]
– 17 again / I saved the world today / Power to the meek / Beautiful child / Anything but strong / Peace is just a word / I've tried everything / I want it all / My true love / Forever / Lifted.

Jan 00. (c-s/cd-s) *(74321 72626-4/-2)* **17 AGAIN / GOSPEL MEDLEY:- BALL AND CHAIN – WOULD I LIE TO YOU – SISTERS ARE DOIN' IT FOR THEMSELVES** [27] [–]
(cd-s) *(74321 72627-2)* – ('A') / Here comes the rain again / Why.

ANNIE LENNOX

R.C.A. J-Reco

Jun 03. (cd) *(82876 52405-2) <52072>* **BARE** [3] [4]
– A thousand beautiful things / Pavement cracks / The hurting time Honestly / Wonderful / Bitter pill / Loneliness / The saddest song I've got Erased / Twisted / Oh God (prayer). *(ltd-cd w/ dvd+=; 82876 52247-2)* – thousand beautiful things (live) / Wonderful (live) / (interview).

Oct 03. (12"/cd-s) *(82876 56920-1/-2)* **WONDERFUL / PAVEMENT CRACKS (Goldtrix full vocal mix) / A THOUSAND BEAUTIFUL THINGS (Gabriel & Dresden tech funk mix)** [ ] [–]
(cd-s) *(82876 56921-2)* – ('A'side) / Pavement cracks (Scumfrog mix) / thousand beautiful things (Bimbo Jones stealth mix).

– compilations, others, etc. –

on 'RCA' UK / 'Arista' US unless otherwise stated

Nov 88. (3"cd-ep/5"cd-ep) *Virgin; (CDT/CDF 22)* **SEXCRIME (1984 extended mix) / JULIA (extended) / I DID IT JUST THE SAME** [ ] [–]

Mar 89. (3"cd-ep) *(PD 42651)* **SWEET DREAMS (ARE MADE OF THIS) / I COULD GIVE YOU (A MIRROR) / HERE COMES THE RAIN AGAIN / PAINT A RUMOUR** [ ] [–]

Mar 91. (cd/c/lp) *(PD/PK/PL 74856) <8680>* **EURYTHMICS' GREATEST HITS** [1] [72]
– Love is a stranger / Sweet dreams (are made of this) / Who's that girl? Right by your side / Here comes the rain again / There must be an ang (playing with my heart) / Sisters are doin' it for themselves / It's alrigh (baby's coming back) / When tomorrow comes / You have placed a ch in my heart / Sexcrime (nineteen eighty-four) / Thorn in my side Don ask me why. *(cd+=/c+=)* – Miracle of love / Angel / Would I lie to you? Missionary man / I need a man.

Mar 91. (7"/c-s) *(PB/PK 44265)* **LOVE IS A STRANGER. / JULIA** [46] [–]
(12"+=/cd-s+=) *(PT/PD 44266)* – ('A'obsession mix) / There must be a angel (playin' with my heart).
(12") *(PT 44268)* – ('A'-JC meets the Obsessor mix) / ('A'instrumental) ('A'-Coldcut mix).

Nov 91. (7"/c-s) *(PB/PK 45031) <2243>* **SWEET DREAMS (ARE MADE OF THIS) '91. / KING AND QUEEN OF AMERICA** [48] [ ]
(12") *(PT 45032)* – ('A'side) / ('A'-house mix) / ('A'-nightmare mix) ('A'-hot remix).
(cd-s) *(PD 45032)* – ('A'side) / Beethoven (I love to listen to) / Shame This city never sleeps.

Nov 93. (d-cd/d-c) *(74321 17145-2/-4)* **EURYTHMICS LIVE 1983-1989** (live) [22] [–]
– Never gonna cry again / Love is a stranger / Sweet dreams (are made this) / This city never sleeps / Somebody told me / Who's that girl? / Rig by your side / Here comes the rain again / Sex crime / I love you like ball and chain / There must be an angel (playing with my heart) / Thor in my side / Let's go / Missionary man / The last time / Miracle of love / need a man / We two are one / (My my) Baby's gonna cry / Don't ask m why / Angel. *(cd includes free 7 track EP) (re-iss. Oct95; same)*

Apr 95. (d-cd) *(74321 26442-2)* **BE YOURSELF TONIGHT / REVENGE** [ ] [–]

Oct 05. (cd-s) *(82876 74834-2)* **I'VE GOT A LIFE / SWEET DREAMS (ARE MADE OF THIS) – Steve Angello remix** [14] [–]
(cd-s) *(82876 74835-2)* – ('A') / ('A'-Sander Kleinenberg's You're It remix) Sweet dreams (are made of this) / ('A'-video).

Nov 05. (cd) *(82876 74841-2) <73799-2>* **ULTIMATE COLLECTION** [5] [ ]
– I've got a life / Love is a stranger / Sweet dreams (are made of this) Who's that girl? / Right by your side / Here comes the rain again / Wou I lie to you? / There must be an angel (playing with my heart) / Siste are doin' it for themselves / It's alright (baby's coming back) / Whe tomorrow comes / Thorn in my side / The miracle of love / Missiona man / You have placed a chill in my heart / I need a man / I saved th world today / 17 again / Was it just another love affair?

EVANESCENCE

Formed: Little Rock, Arkansas, USA . . . 1998 by BEN MOODY and AMY LEE. Having first clocked the budding young singer/songwriter playing piano at a youth camp, MOODY quickly formed a musical partnership with her and the pair began crafting their gloomy, SARAH McLACHLAN goes nu-metal-lite, sub-goth, pro-Christian rock. A series of limited, self-financed EP's proved popular at live gigs and after expanding to a four piece – with the addition of ROCKY GRAY and JOHN LeCOMPT – they recorded the 'ORIGIN' demo. This in turn led to a major label deal with 'Sony' subsidiary 'Wind Up', who issued their debut album, 'FALLEN', in 2003. Spurred on by the chart success of the 'BRING ME TO LIFE' single (which had previously featured on the soundtrack to the movie, 'Daredevil'), the album made the US Top 3, showcasing LEE's admittedly powerful vocal chops against a piano-led backdrop swathed in the usual goth fallbacks of ominous keyboards, horror film strings and operatic choirs. While their chart profile remained high with UK Top 10 hits, 'GOING UNDER' and 'MY IMMORTAL', the band's stability remained volatile; no sooner had they found bassist WILLIAM BOYD than MOODY left abruptly citing creative differences – the latter would subsequently be replaced by TERRY BALSAMO. AMY LEE, meanwhile, occupied herself with a SEETHER collaboration on the US Top 20 hit, 'Broken'. Keeping product in the shops (and the US Top 40), EVANESCENCE released the obligatory stop-gap CD/DVD, 'ANYWHERE BUT HOME' (2004).

Covered: HEART-SHAPED BOX (Nirvana) / THOUGHTLESS (Korn).

Album rating: FALLEN (*7) / ANYWHERE BUT HOME (*6)

AMY LEE (b.13 Dec'81, Riverside, Calif.) – vocals, piano / **BEN MOODY** (b.22 Jan'81) – guitar / **DAVID HODGES** – keyboards (left Dec'02)

not iss. — own label

Dec 98. (cd-ep) *<none>* **EVANESCENCE** [–] [ ]

— added **JOHN LeCOMPT** (b.10 Mar'73) – guitar / **ROCKY GRAY** (b. WILLIAM, 2 Jul'74) – drums

Epic — Wind-Up

Apr 03. (cd) *(510879-2) <13063>* **FALLEN** [1] Mar03 [3]
– Going under / Bring me to life / Everybody's fool / My immortal / Haunted / Tourniquet / Imaginary / Taking over me / Hello / My last breath / Whisper.

May 03. (c-s; as EVANESCENCE feat. PAUL McCOY) *(673976-4) <radio>* **BRING ME TO LIFE / FARTHER AWAY / BRING ME TO LIFE (bliss mix)** [1] [5]
(cd-s+=) *(673976-2)* – ('A'-video).
(dvd-s) *(673976-9)* – ('A'-video) / ('A') / ('A'-live acoustic) / My immortal (live acoustic) / (interview footage).

— added **WILLIAM BOYD** (b.27 Apr'79) – bass

Sep 03. (cd-s) *(674352-2)* **GOING UNDER / GOING UNDER (live acoustic) / HEART-SHAPED BOX (live acoustic) / GOING UNDER (video)** [8] [–]

Dec 03. (cd-s) *(674542-2)* **MY IMMORTAL (band version, guitars down) / (version)** [7] [ ]
(cd-s) *(674542-5)* – ('A') / ('A'-live from Cologne) / Haunted (live from sessions @ AOL) / ('A'-video) / ('A'-behind the scenes).

Jun 04. (cd-s) *(674824-2)* **EVERYBODY'S FOOL / TAKING OVER ME (live in Cologne) / WHISPER (live in Cologne) / ('A'-instrumental)** [34] [–]

— (Oct'03) MOODY left; repl. by **TERRY BALSAMO** (b. 9 Oct'73) – guitar (ex-COLD)

— in Aug'04, AMY LEE feat. on SEETHER Top 20 US hit, 'Broken'

Nov 04. (cd+dvd) *(5192073) <13106>* **ANYWHERE BUT HOME** (live in Paris) [ ] [39]
– Haunted / Going under / Taking over me / Everybody's fool / Thoughtless / My last breath / Farther away / Missing / Breathe no more / My immortal / Bring me to life / Tourniquet / Imaginary / Whisper // (+dvd tracks).

☐ the EVENS (see under ⇒ FUGAZI)

EVERCLEAR

Formed: Portland, Oregon, USA . . . 1991 by former teenage junkie, ART ALEXAKIS (he gave up alcohol, drugs and nicotine in June '84). Coming from a broken home, he was also dogged by the drug deaths of his girlfriend and older brother, George. At the turn of the decade, ART was involved in two bands, The EASY HOES (lp released 'Tragic Songs Of Life' on 'Shindig') and COLORFINGER (cd issued 'Deep In The Heart Of The Beast In The Sun' – a demo cassette was also issued with future EVERCLEAR tracks!). Another founder member, CRAIG MONTOYA (other two, STEVEN BIRCH and SCOTT CUTHBERT) helped produce their debut indie album, 'WORLD OF NOISE', in 1994 and after rave reviews they were whisked away by 'Capitol' A&R man PERRY WATTS-RUSSELL. It was alleged that they were released from the indie, only when the gun-totting ALEXAKIS convinced the boss to let them go. By Spring '96 (and now with GREG EKLUND who had replaced CUTHBERT and BIRCH), their second album, 'SPARKLE AND FADE', had climbed into the US Top 30. A stylish anti-drug affair, it was described as ELVIS COSTELLO fused with LED ZEPPELIN, HUSKER DU or NIRVANA! ALEXAKIS and Co. returned in 1998 with a third set proper (the previous year's 'WHITE TRASH HELL' consisted of outtakes), 'SO MUCH FOR THE AFTERGLOW', the US Top 40 album almost spawning another UK Top 40 single, 'EVERYTHING TO EVERYONE'. While many of the tail-end grunge acts imploded before the 90's were through, EVERCLEAR entered the new millennium with their most ambitious project to date, a two-volume concept set exploring ALEXAKIS' divorce. 'SONGS FROM AN AMERICAN MOVIE, VOL.1: LEARNING HOW TO SMILE' (2000) covered the dating years with a peppy soundtrack inspired by the A.M. pop/rock of the frontman's youth (including a cover of Van Morrison's timeless 'BROWN EYED GIRL'). 'SONGS FROM AN AMERICAN MOVIE, VOL.2: GOOD TIME FOR A BAD ATTITUDE' (2000), meanwhile, hit the shelves a few months later and documented the dream turning sour. Unsurprisingly, the music was harder and the subject matter heavier as ALEXAKIS exorcised the pain of lost love and broken friendship. The Portland songwriter returned in 2003 with 'SLOW MOTION DAYDREAM', a respectable effort but one which made it difficult to shake off the impression that the whole concept of EVERCLEAR and their approach to rock was perhaps a little dated. ALEXAKIS proved he can still cut to the quick on the likes of opener 'HOW TO WIN FRIENDS AND INFLUENCE PEOPLE', although the cliche-ridden 'VOLVO DRIVING SOCCER MOM', hinted at desperation rather than inspiration.

• **Covered:** HOW SOON IS NOW (Smiths).

Album rating: WORLD OF NOISE (*6) / SPARKLE AND FADE (*9) / SO MUCH FOR THE AFTERGLOW (*7) / SONGS FROM AN AMERICAN MOVIE VOL.1: LEARNING HOW TO SMILE (*7) / SONGS FROM AN AMERICAN MOVIE VOL.2: GOOD TIME FOR A BAD ATTITUDE (*5) / SLOW MOTION DAYDREAM (*5)

ART ALEXAKIS (b.12 Apr'62) – vocals, guitar / **STEVEN BIRCH** – guitar / **CRAIG MONTOYA** (b.14 Sep'70) – bass, vocals / **SCOTT CUTHBERT** – drums, vocals

not iss. — Tim/Kerr

Oct 93. (7",7"colrd) *<TK 937055>* **NERVOUS & WEIRD. / ELECTRA MADE ME BLIND** [–] [ ]
(cd-ep+=) *<TK 93CD57>* – Drunk again / Lame / Connection / Slow motion genius (instrumental).

Nov 93. (cd/lp) *(FIRE CD/LP 46) <TK 59>* **WORLD OF NOISE** [–] [ ]
– Your genius hands / Sick & tired / The laughing world / Fire maple song / Pennsylvania is . . . / Nervous and weird / Malevolent / Sparkle / Trust fund / Loser makes good / Invisible / Evergleam. *<US re-iss. Nov94 on 'Capitol' cd/c; 30562-2/-4> (UK-iss.Feb95 on 'Fire' cd/lp; FIRE CD/LP 46) (cd re-iss. Oct02; SFIRE 021CD)*

Fire / Capitol

Nov 94. (cd-ep) *<58255>* **FIRE MAPLE SONG EP** [–] [ ]
– Fire maple song / Detroit / 1975 / Blondes / Pacific wonderland (instrumental) / Fire maple song (acoustic version).

Feb 95. (cd-ep) *(BLAZE 77CD)* **FIRE MAPLE SONG EP** [ ] [–]
– Fire maple song / Loser makes good / Lame / Connection.

—— **GREG EKLUND** (b.18 Apr'70) – drums, vocals; repl. CUTHBERT + BIRCH

Nov 95. (7") *<23261-7>* **HEROIN GIRL. / AMERICAN GIRL** [–] [ ]
(cd-s+=) *<23261-2>* – Annabella's song / Nahalem (alt. mix).

Capitol / Capitol

Mar 96. (cd/c/lp) *(CD/TC+/EST 2257) <30929>* **SPARKLE AND FADE** [ ] May95 [25]
– Electra made me blind / Heroin girl / You make me feel like a whore / Santa Monica / Summerland / Strawberry / Heartspark dollar / The twistinside / Her brand new skin / Nehalem / Queen of the air / Pale green stars / Chemical smile / My sexual life. *(d-cd re-iss. Jun98; CDESTX 2257)* – (extra tracks).

Apr 96. (cd-ep) *<58538>* **HEARTSPARK DOLLARSIGN / HEROIN GIRL (acoustic) / SIN CITY / HAPPY HOUR** [–] [85]

May 96. (7"clear) *(CL 773)* **HEARTSPARK DOLLARSIGN. / LOSER MAKES GOOD (live)** [48] [–]
(cd-s+=) *(CDCL 773)* – Sparkle (live).
(cd-s) *(CDCLS 773)* – ('A'side) / Pennsylvania is . . . (live) / Nervous & weird (live).

Aug 96. (7") *(CL 775)* **SANTA MONICA (WATCH THE WORLD DIE). / AMERICAN GIRL (KDGE version)** [40] [–]
(cd-s+=) *(CDCL 775)* – Strawberry (KDGE version) / Fire maple song (KDGE version).
(cd-s) *(CDCLS 775)* – ('A'side) / Heroin girl (KDGE version) / Summerland (KDGE version) / Sin city.

Sep 96. (cd-s) *<promo>* **YOU MAKE ME FEEL LIKE A WHORE / AMERICAN GIRL (live) / LIKE BRANDON DOES (by Klinger)** [–] [ ]

—— added **CHRIS BIRCH** – guitar

Mar 98. (cd/c) *<(36503-2/-4/-1)>* **SO MUCH FOR THE AFTERGLOW** [63] Oct97 [33]
– So much for the afterglow / Everything to everyone / Ataraxia / Normal like you / I will buy you a new life / Father of mine / One hit wonder / El distorto de melodica / Amphetamine / White men in black suits / Sunflower / Why don't I believe in God / Like a California king.

Apr 98. (7") *(CL 799)* **EVERYTHING TO EVERYONE. / OUR LIPS ARE SEALED** [41] [ ]
(cd-s+=) *(CDCL 799)* – What do I get / ('A'-CD-Rom video).
(cd-s) *(CDCLS 799)* – ('A'side) / Walk don't run / Search and destroy / Santa Monica heroin (CD-Rom video).

Jul 98. (cd-ep) *<85592>* **I WILL BUY YOU A NEW LIFE EP** [–] [ ]
– I will buy you a new life / So much for the afterglow (live) / Heroin girl (live) / Local god (live).

Nov 98. (cd-ep) *<86181>* **FATHER OF MINE EP** [–] [70]
– Father of mine / So much for the afterglow (live) / Heroin girl (live) / Local god (live).

Aug 00. (cd) *(527864-2) <97061>* **SONGS FROM AN AMERICAN MOVIE VOL.1 – LEARNING HOW TO SMILE** [51] Jul00 [9]
– Songs from an American movie (part 1) / Here we go again / AM radio / Brown eyed girl / Learning how to smile / The honeymoon song / Now that it's over / Thrift store chair / Otis Redding / Unemployed boyfriend / Wonderful / Annabella's song.

Oct 00. (c-s) *(TCCL 824) <58870>* **WONDERFUL / FATHER OF MINE (remix) / I'M ON YOUR TIME** [36] Aug00 [11]
(cd-s+=) *(CDCLS 824)* – ('A'-CD-ROM video)>

Mar 01. (cd-s) *(CDCL 827)* **AM RADIO / I'M ON YOUR TIME / SANTA MONICA (live from Woodstock)** [ ] [–]

Apr 01. (cd) *(530419-2) <95873>* **SONGS FROM AN AMERICAN MOVIE VOL.2 – GOOD TIME FOR A BAD ATTITUDE** [69] Nov00 [ ]
– When it all goes wrong again / Slide / Babytalk / Rock star / Short blonde hair / Misery whip / Out of my depth / The good witch of the north / Halloween Americana / All f**ked up / Overwhelming / Song from an American movie (part 2).

Mar 03. (cd) *<(5 38270-0)>* **SLOW MOTION DAYDREAM** [ ] [33]
– How to win friends and influence people / Blackjack / I want to die a beautiful death / Volvo driving soccer mom / Science fiction / New blue champion / TV show / Chrysanthemum / Sunshine (that acid summer) / A beautiful life / The New York Times. *<(bonus += untitled/dub)>*

—— (late 2003) **EKLUND + MONTOYA departed**

– compilations, etc. –

Aug 95. (cd) *Imprint; <97633>* **LIVE FROM TORONTO** (live) [–] [ ]

Apr 97. (m-cd) *Fire; (MCD 45)* **WHITE TRASH HELL** [ ] [–]
– Heroin girl (demo) / Detroit / 1975 / Blondes / Pacific wonderland (instrumental) / For Pete's sake / Fire maple song (acoustic). *(re-iss. May02; SFIRE 009CD)*

the EVERLY BROTHERS

Formed: Kentucky, USA . . . 1955 by brothers DON and PHIL EVERLY, the offspring of country singing parents, Ike and Margaret. No strangers to the music scene (the boys having appeared on numerous radio shows alongside their folks), they went to Nashville later that year hoping that hillbilly artists would buy their close harmony songs. The following year, they secured a deal with 'Columbia' records, the label releasing one country-style single, 'KEEP A LOVIN' ME', before opting out as the rock'n'roll era began to kick in. After a short struggle in an attempt to find another label, their father contacted old friend, star picker CHET ATKINS, who got them signed as writers for the legendary Roy Acuff/Wesley Rose songsmith team. ROSE subsequently became the siblings' manager, persuading Archie Bleyer of 'Cadence' records to take them on as recording artists in 1957. Adopting a new style combining their vocal harmonies with easy going pop'n'roll strumming, The EVERLY BROTHERS made an immediate impact with 'BYE BYE LOVE', a million selling single which peaked at No.2 that summer. Their profile heightened by a handful of TV appearances (i.e. the Ed Sullivan and Perry Como shows), the brothers' clean-cut apple-pie good looks and teen heartbreak appeal saw further singles, 'WAKE UP LITTLE SUSIE', 'ALL I HAVE TO DO IS DREAM' and 'BIRD DOG' fare equally well over the ensuing three years. In 1960, they signed to 'Warners', scoring a transatlantic chart topper with their label debut, 'CATHY'S CLOWN', a 45 that had to battle for chart supremacy against reissued 'Cadence' material. The lads were now also relying on their own material having left the Felice & Boudleaux Bryant songwriting duo behind when they switched stables. A further clutch of major hits, 'SO SAD (TO WATCH GOOD LOVE GO BAD)', 'WALK RIGHT BACK', 'TEMPTATION', 'CRYIN' IN THE RAIN' etc, saw them dominate the pre-BEATLES pop charts in both America and Britain, although it would be the UK who stood by the duo when the onslaught of 1963-64 British Invasion took hold. In 1965, as their American profile was on the wane, they scored considerable critical and commercial success as the classic, 'THE PRICE OF LOVE' hit No.2 in Britain (criminally ignored in their homeland). Their records continued to sell moderately throughout the latter half of the 60's although a dalliance with country rock in the early 70's brought little commercial reward; the increasingly estranged brothers finally parted company on less than amicable terms during a disastrous gig on the 14th of July '73. Over the next ten years, the brothers followed sporadically successful solo careers (PHIL, together with CLIFF RICHARD, had a 1983 UK Top 10 hit 'SHE MEANS NOTHING TO ME'), eventually coming together again for a reunion concert in '83; they were back on speaking terms after attending the funeral of their father. The resulting live album put The EVERLY BROTHERS back in the UK Top 50 as did the following year's eponymous (PAUL McCARTNEY-produced) comeback set, and although they maintained their working relationship they failed to keep up the momentum.

• **Covered:** CLAUDETTE (Roy Orbison) / LET IT BE ME (Gilbert Becaud)

BE-BOP-A-LULA (Gene Vincent) / LUCILLE (Little Richard) / WALK RIGHT BACK (Sonny Curtis; of Crickets) / EBONY EYES + IT'S MY TIME (John D. Loudermilk) / TEMPTATION (Bing Crosby) / CRYING IN THE RAIN (Carole King & Howard Greenfield) / BOWLING GREEN (Terry Slater) / ABANDONED LOVE (Bob Dylan) / THE GIRL SANG THE BLUES + LOVE HER (Mann-Weill) / YVES (Scott McKenzie). After an inter-label rift between Wesley Rose was rectified, The BRYANTS returned on late 1964's 'GONE GONE GONE'. The album 'ROCK'N'SOUL' featured many classic rock'n'roll oldies. • **Trivia:** Many famous musicians have passed through their ranks, including FLOYD CHANCE – bass (1957) / JOEY PAGE – guitar (1962) / JIM GORDON and BILLY PRESTON. Other 60's sessioners stemmed from The BYRDS, The HOLLIES and LED ZEPPELIN!

Best CD compilation: THE DEFINITIVE EVERLY BROTHERS (*8)

DON EVERLY (b.ISAAC DONALD EVERLY, 1 Feb'37, Brownie, Kentucky, USA) – vocals, guitar / **PHIL EVERLY** (b.19 Jan'39, Chicago, Illinois, USA) – vocals, guitar

not iss. | Columbia

Feb 56. (7") *<21496>* **KEEP A LOVIN' ME. / THE SUN KEEPS SHINING** [–] [ ]

London | Cadence

Jun 57. (7",78) *(HLA 8440)* *<1315>* **BYE BYE LOVE. / I WONDER IF I CARE AS MUCH** [6] May57 [2]
(re-iss. Jul82 on 'Old Gold'; OG 9060)

Oct 57. (7",78) *(HLA 8498)* *<1337>* **WAKE UP LITTLE SUSIE. / MAYBE TOMORROW** [2] Sep57 [1]
(re-iss. Jul82 on 'Old Gold'; OG 9061)

Feb 58. (7",78) *(HLA 8554)* *<1342>* **THIS LITTLE GIRL OF MINE. / SHOULD WE TELL HIM** [ ] [26]

Mar 58. (lp) *(HA-A 2081)* *<3003>* **THE EVERLY BROTHERS** [ ] Jan58 [16]
– This little girl of mine / Maybe tomorrow / Bye bye love / Brand new Heartache / Keep a knockin' / Be-bop-a-lula / Rip it up / I wonder if I care as much / Wake up little Susie / Leave my woman alone / Should we tell him / Hey doll baby.

May 58. (7",78) *(HLA 8554)* *<1348>* **ALL I HAVE TO DO IS DREAM. / CLAUDETTE** [1] [1] Apr58 [30]
<re-iss. Jul61, A-side hit No.96> (re-iss. Jul82 on 'Old Gold'; OG 9062)

Sep 58. (7",78) *(HLA 8685)* **BIRD DOG. / DEVOTED TO YOU** [2] [1] Jul58 [10]
(re-iss. Apr79 on 'Lightning; LIG 9018)

Nov 58. (lp) *(HA-A 2150)* *<3016>* **SONGS OUR DADDY TAUGHT US** [ ] Sep58 [ ]
– Roving gambler / Down in the willow garden / Longtime gone / Lightning express / That silver haired daddy of mine / Who's gonna shoe your pretty little feet / Barbara Allen / Oh so many years / I'm here to get my baby out of jail / Rockin' alone (in an old rocking chair) / Kentucky / Put my little shoes away. *(re-iss. Aug83 on 'Charly' CH 75)*

Jan 59. (7",78) *(HLA 8781)* *<1355>* **PROBLEMS. / LOVE OF MY LIFE** [6] [2] Nov58 [40]
(re-iss. Jul82 on 'Old Gold'; OG 9063)

May 59. (7",78) *(HLA 8863)* *<1364>* **POOR JENNY. / TAKE A MESSAGE TO MARY** [14] [22] Apr59 [16]
(re-iss. Jul82 on 'Old Gold'; OG 9064)

Sep 59. (7",78) *(HLA 8934)* *<1364>* **TILL I KISSED YOU. / OH WHAT A FEELING** [2] Aug59 [4]
(re-iss. Jul82 on 'Old Gold'; OG 9065)

Feb 60. (7",78) *(HLA 9039)* *<1376>* **LET IT BE ME. / SINCE YOU BROKE MY HEART** [13] Jan60 [7]
(re-iss. Jul82 on 'Old Gold'; OG 9066)

Warners | Warners

Apr 60. (7",78) *(WB 1)* *<5151>* **CATHY'S CLOWN. / ALWAYS IT'S YOU** [1] [1] [56]

Jun 60. (lp) *(WM 4012)* *<1381>* **IT'S EVERLY TIME!** [2] May60 [9]
– So sad / Just in case / Memories are made of this / That's what you do to me / Sleepless nights / What kind of girl are you / Oh true love / Carol Jane / Some sweet day / Nashville blues / You thrill me / I want you to know. *(re-iss. May85 on 'Rollercoaster'; ROLI 313)*

Sep 60. (7",78) *(WB 19)* *<5163>* **LUCILLE. / SO SAD (TO WATCH GOOD LOVE GO BAD)** [4] [21] Aug60 [7]

Jan 61. (7") *(WB 33)* *<5199>* **WALK RIGHT BACK. / EBONY EYES** [1] [7] [8]

Feb 61. (lp) *(WM 4028)* *<1395>* **A DATE WITH THE EVERLY BROTHERS** [3] Nov60 [9]
– Made to love / That's just too much / Stick with me baby / Baby what you want me to do / Sigh cry almost die / Always it's you / Love hurts / Lucille / So how come / Donna Donna / A change of heart / Cathy's clown. *(re-iss. May85 on 'Rollercoaster'; ROLI 314)*

Jun 61. (7") *(WB 42)* *<5199>* **TEMPTATION. / STICK WITH ME BABY** [1] [27] [41]

Sep 61. (7") *(WB 50)* *<5501>* **DON'T BLAME ME. / MUSKRAT** [20] [20] [82]

1961. (lp) *(WM 4052)* *<1418>* **BOTH SIDES OF AN EVENING** [ ] [ ]
– My mamma / Muskrat / My gal Sal / My grandfather's clock / Bully of the town / Chloe / Mention my name in Sheboygan / Hi Lili hi lo / Wayward wind / Don't blame me / Now is the hour / Little old lady / When I grow too old to dream / Love is where you find it.

Jan 62. (7") *(WB 56)* *<5250>* **CRYIN' IN THE RAIN. / I'M NOT ANGRY** [6] [6]

May 62. (7") *(WB 67)* *<5273>* **HOW CAN I MEET HER. / THAT'S OLD FASHIONED (THAT'S THE WAY LOVE SHOULD BE)** [12] [75] [9]

Jul 62. (lp) *(WM 4061)* *<1430>* **INSTANT PARTY** [20] [ ]
– Jezebel / Oh my papa / Step it up and go / True love / Bye bye blackbird / Trouble in mind / Love makes the world go round / Long lost John / Autumn leaves / Party's over / Ground hawg / When it's night time in Italy. *(re-iss. Oct86 on 'Rollercoaster'; ROLI 321)*

Sep 62. (lp; mono/stereo) *(WM/WS 8108)* *<1471>* **THE GOLDEN HITS OF THE EVERLY BROTHERS** (compilation) [ ] [35]
– That's old fashioned (that's the way love should be) / How can I meet her? / Crying in the rain / I'm not angry / Don't blame me / Ebony eyes / Cathy's clown / Walk right back / Lucille / So sad (to watch good love go bad) / Muskrat / Temptation. *(re-iss. Dec65 mono/stereo; W/WS 1471) (cd+c-iss 1991 on 'WEA')*

Oct 62. (7") *(WB 79)* *<5297>* **NO ONE CAN MAKE MY SUNSHINE SMILE. / DON'T ASK ME TO BE FRIENDS** [11] B-side [48]

Dec 62. (lp; mono/stereo) *(WM/WS 8116)* *<1483>* **CHRISTMAS WITH THE EVERLY BROTHERS AND THE BOYS TOWN CHOIR** (trad Xmas songs) [ ] [ ]

Mar 63. (7") *(WB 94)* *<5346>* **SO IT WILL ALWAYS BE. / NANCY'S MINUET** [23] [ ]

May 63. (lp; mono/stereo) *(WM/WS 8138)* *<1513>* **. . . SING GREAT COUNTRY HITS** [ ] [ ]
– Oh lonesome me / Born to lose / Just one time / Send me the pillow you dream on / Release me / Please help me I'm falling / I walk the line / Lonely street / Silver threads and golden needles / I'm so lonesome I could cry / Sweet dreams / This is the last song I'm ever going to sing. *(re-iss. Dec85 on 'Rollercoaster'; ROLI 329)*

Jun 63. (7") *(WB 99)* *<5362>* **IT'S BEEN NICE. / I'M AFRAID** [26] [ ]

Oct 63. (7") *(WB 109)* *<5389>* **THE GIRL SANG THE BLUES. / LOVE HER** [25] [ ]

Apr 64. (7") *(WB 129)* *<5422>* **AIN'T THAT LOVIN' YOU BABY. / HELLO AMY** [ ] [ ]

Jun 64. (7") *(WB 135)* *<5441>* **THE FERRIS WHEEL. / DON'T FORGET TO CRY** [22] [72]

Jan 65. (lp; mono/stereo) *(WM/WS 8163)* *<1554>* **THE VERY BEST OF THE EVERLY BROTHERS** (re-recorded hits) [ ] Jul64 [ ]
– Bye bye love / (Til) I kissed you / Wake up little Susie / Crying in the rain / Walk right back / Cathy's clown / Bird dog / All I have to do is dream / Devoted to you / Lucille / So sad (to watch good love go bad) / Ebony eyes. *(re-iss. May74 lp/c; K/K4 46008)* – hit UK No.43

1964. (7") *<5466>* **RING AROUND MY ROSIE. / YOU'RE THE ONE I LOVE** [–] [ ]

Nov 64. (7") *(WB 146)* *<5478>* **GONE GONE GONE. / TORTURE** [36] [31]

Dec 64. (lp; mono/stereo) *(WM/WS 8169)* *<1585>* **GONE GONE GONE** [ ] [ ]
– Donna, Donna / Lonely island / The facts of life / Ain't that lovin' you baby / Love is all I need / Torture / The drop out / Radio and TV / Honolulu / It's been a long dry spell / The ferris wheel / Gone gone gone. *(re-iss. 1970 on 'Valient'; VS 109) (re-iss. May85 on 'Rollercoaster'; ROLI 316)*

Feb 65. (7") *(WB 154)* <5600> **YOU'RE MY GIRL. / DON'T LET THE WHOLE WORLD KNOW** [ ] [ ]

Apr 65. (7") *(WB 158)* <5611> **THAT'LL BE THE DAY. / GIVE ME A SWEETHEART** [30] [ ]

May 65. (lp; mono/stereo) *(WM/WS 8171)* <1578> **ROCK'N'SOUL** [ ] [ ]
– That'll be the day / So fine / Maybelline / Dancing in the street / Kansas City / I got a woman / Love hurts / Slippin' and slidin' / Susie Q / Hound dog / I'm gonna move to the out-skirtsd of town / Lonely weekends. *(re-iss. May85 on 'Rollercoaster'; ROLI 317)*

May 65. (7") *(WB 161)* <5628> **THE PRICE OF LOVE. / IT ONLY COSTS A DIME** [2] [ ]

Aug 65. (7") *(WB 5539)* <5639> **I'LL NEVER GET OVER YOU. / FOLLOW ME** [35] [ ]

Sep 65. (lp) <*(WS 1605)*> **BEAT AND SOUL** [ ] [ ]
– Love is strange / Money / What am I living for / High heel sneakers / C.C. rider / Lonely avenue / Man with money / People get ready / My babe / Walking the dog / I almost lost my mind / The girl can't help it. *(re-iss. Dec85 on 'Rollercoaster'; ROLI 319)*

Oct 65. (7") <*(WB 5649)*> **LOVE IS STRANGE. / MAN WITH MONEY** [11] [ ]

Mar 66. (7") *(WB 5743)* <5808> **THE POWER OF LOVE. / LEAVE MY GIRL ALONE** [ ] [ ]

Mar 66. (lp) <*(WS 1620)*> **IN OUR IMAGE** [ ] [ ]
– Leave my girl alone / Chained to a memory / I'll never get over you / The doll house is empty / Glitter and gold / The power of love / The price of love / It's all over / I used to love you / Lonely Kravezit / June is as cold as December / It only cost a dime. *(re-iss. May85 on 'Rollercoaster'; ROLI 318)*

Mar 66. (7") <5682> **I USED TO LOVE YOU. / IT'S ALL OVER** [–] [ ]

1966. (7") <5698> **THE DOLL HOUSE IS EMPTY. / LONELY KRAVEZIT** [–] [ ]

Jul 66. (lp) <*(WS 1646)*> **TWO YANKS IN ENGLAND** [ ] [ ]
– Somebody help me / So lonely / Kiss your man goodbye / Signs that will never change / Like everytime before / Pretty flamingo / I've been wrong before / Have you ever loved somebody / The collector / Don't run and hide / Fifi the flea / Hard, hard year. *(re-iss. Feb89 on 'Edsel'; ED 297)*

Aug 66. (7") *(WB 5754)* **I'VE BEEN WRONG BEFORE. / HARD, HARD YEAR** [ ] [–]

Sep 66. (7") <5833> **SOMEBODY HELP ME. / HARD, HARD YEAR** [–] [ ]

Dec 66. (7") <5857> **FIFI THE FLEA (by "DON"). / LIKE EVERYTIME BEFORE (by "PHIL")** [–] [ ]

Feb 67. (lp) <*(WS 1676)*> **THE HIT SOUND OF THE EVERLY BROTHERS** [ ] [ ]
– Blueberry Hill / Movin' on / Devil's child / Trains and boats and planes / Sea of heartbreak / Oh boy / (I'd be a) Legend in my time / Let's go get stoned / Sticks and stones / The house of the rising Sun / She never smiles anymore / Good golly Miss Molly.

Mar 67. (7") <5901> **THE DEVIL'S CHILD. / SHE NEVER SMILES ANYMORE** [–] [ ]

Mar 67. (7") *(WB 6074)* **OH BOY. / GOOD GOLLY MISS MOLLY** [ ] [–]

Jun 67. (7") <*(WB 7020)*> **BOWLING GREEN. / I DON'T WANT TO LOVE YOU** [ ] [40]

Sep 67. (7") <*(WB 7062)*> **MARY JANE. / TALKING TO THE FLOWERS** [ ] [ ]

Nov 67. (7") <*(WB 7088)*> **LOVE OF THE COMMON PEOPLE. / A VOICE WITHIN** [ ] [ ]

Apr 68. (7") <*(WB 7192)*> **IT'S MY TIME. / EMPTY BOXES** [39] [ ]

Aug 68. (7") <*(WB 7226)*> **MILK TRAIN. / LORD OF THE MANOR** [ ] [ ]

Nov 68. (lp) <*(WS 1752)*> **ROOTS** (new & re-old material) [ ] [ ]
– Introduction: The Everly family / Mama tried / Less of me / T for Texas / I wonder if I care as much / Ventura boulevard / Shady grove / Illinois / Living too close to the ground / You done me wrong / Turn around / Sing me back home / Montage : The Everly family-Shady grove-Kentucky. *(re-iss. 1971; K 46128) (re-iss. Sep86 on 'Rollercoaster'; ROLI 322) (re-iss. 1987 on 'Edsel'; ED 203) (cd-iss. May95)*

Apr 69. (7") <7290> **I'M ON MY WAY HOME AGAIN. / THE CUCKOO BIRD** [–] [ ]

1969. (7") *(7262)* **T – FOR TEARS. / I WONDER IF I CARE AS MUCH** [–] [ ]

1969. (7") <7290> **CAROLINA ON MY MIND. / MY LITTLE YELLOW BIRD** [–] [ ]

Feb 70. (d-lp) <*(WS 1858)*> **THE EVERLY BROTHERS SHOW (live at The Grand Hotel)** [ ] [ ]
– Mama tried / Kentucky / Bowling green / Till I kissed you / Wake up little Susie / Cathy's clown / Bird dog / Maybelline / Lord of the manor / I wonder if I care as much / Love is strange / Let it be me / Give peace a chance / Rock and roll music / The end / Aquarius / If I were a carpenter / The price of love / The thrill is gone / Games people play / Baby what you want me to do / All I have to do is dream / Walk right back / Susie Q / Hey Jude.

Oct 70. (7") <*(WB 7425)*> **YVES. / HUMAN RACE** [ ] Feb70 [ ]

RCA Victor RCA Vict

1972. (7") *(RCA 2232)* <74-0717> **RIDIN' HIGH. / STORIES WE COULD TELL** [ ] [ ]

Jun 72. (lp) *(SF 8270)* <4620> **STORIES WE COULD TELL** [ ] [ ]
– All we really want to do / Breakdown / Green river / Mandolin wind / Up in Mabel's room / Del Rio Dan / Ridin' high / Brand new Tennessee waltz / Stories we can tell / Christmas eve can kill you / I'm tired of singing my songs in Las Vegas.

1972. (7") <74-0849> **PARADISE. / LAY IT DOWN** [–] [ ]

1973. (7") <74-0901> **NOT FADE AWAY. / LADIES LOVE OUTLAWS** [–] [ ]

1973. (7") *(RCA 2286)* **NOT FADE AWAY. / LAY IT DOWN** [ ] [–]

Feb 73. (lp) *(SF 8332)* <4781> **PASS THE CHICKEN AND LISTEN** [ ] [ ]
– Lay it down / Husbands and wives / Woman don't you try to tie me down / Sweet memories / Ladies love outlaws / Not fade away / Watchin' it go / Paradise / Somebody nobody knows / Good-hearted woman / A nickel for the fiddler / Rocky top. *(re-iss. +cd.Jul91 on 'Edsel')*

— Announced their break-up at a 14 Jul'73 concert. PHIL went solo later.

DON EVERLY

with one lp under his belt, also continued with solo career.

A&M Ode

1971. (7") <66009> **TUMBLIN' TUMBLEWEEDS. / ONLY ME** [–] [ ]

1971. (lp) *(AMLS 2007)* <77005> **DON EVERLY** [ ] [ ]
– Don't drink the water / Eyes of Asia / February 15th / My baby / My friend / Omaha / Safari / Sweet dreams of you / Tumbling tumbleweed / Thinking it over / When I stop dreaming.

— His next album featured group HEADS, HANDS & FEET

Ode Ode

Aug 74. (7") <*(ODS 66046)*> **WARMIN' UP THE BAND. / EVELYN SWING** [ ] [ ]

Oct 74. (lp) <*(ODE 77023)*> **SUNSET TOWERS** [ ] [ ]
– Melody train / Jack Daniels Old No.7 / Warmin' up the band / Helpless when you're gone / Did it rain / Brand new rock and roll band / Takin' shots / The way you remain / Evelyn swing / Southern California.

D.J.M. Hickory

Jul 76. (7") *(DJS 10692)* <368> **YESTERDAY JUST PASSED MY WAY AGAIN. / NEVER LIKE THIS** [ ] [ ]

Mar 77. (7") *(DJS 10760)* **SO SAD TO WATCH GOOD LOVE GO BAD. / LOVE AT LAST SIGHT** [ ] [–]

1976. (7") <54002> **OH, I'D LIKE TO GO AWAY. / LOVE AT LAST SIGHT** [–] [ ]

1976. (7") *(54005)* **DEEP WATER. / SINCE YOU BROKE MY HEART** [–] [ ]

Mar 77. (lp) *(20501)* <44003> **BROTHER JUKE BOX** [ ] [ ]
– Brother juke box / Love at last sight / So sad to watch good love go bad / Lettin' go / Since you broke my heart / Never like this / Deep water / Yesterday just passed my way again / Oh I'd like to go away / Oh what a feeling / Turn the memories back again. *(re-iss. May88 on 'Sundown' lp/c SDLP/SDC 002) (cd-iss. Aug94)*

Mar 78. (7") *(DJS 10842)* <54012> **BROTHER JUKE BOX. / OH, WHAT A FEELING** [ ] [ ]

Polydor Polydor

Aug 81. (7") *(POSP 315)* **LET'S PUT OUR HEARTS TOGETHER. / SO SAD TO WATCH GOOD LOVE GO BAD** [ ] [–]

Sundown Sundown

Nov 85. (7") *(SDS 1)* **BROTHER JUKE BOX. / NEVER LIKE THIS** [ ] [ ]

PHIL EVERLY

solo with **JAMES BURTON / WARREN ZEVON, JIM HORN and EARL PALMER**

R.C.A. R.C.A.

Sep 73. (7") *(RCA 2409)* **THE AIR THAT I BREATHE. / GOD BLESS OLD LADIES** [ ] [–]

;ep 73. (lp) *(SF 8370) <APL-1 0092>* **STAR SPANGLED SPRINGER** [ ] [ ]
– The air that I breathe / Sweet grass country / God bless older ladies (for they made rock and roll) / It pleases me to please you / Lady Anne / Red, white and blue / Our song / Poisonberry pie / La divorce / Snowflake bombadier.

Pye Pye

Mar 74. (7") *<71014>* **OLD KENTUCKY RIVER. / SUMMERSHINE** [–] [ ]
un 74. (7") *<71036>* **NEW OLD SONG. / BETTER THAN NOW** [–] [ ]
Aug 74. (7") *(7N 45398))* **INVISIBLE MAN. / IT'S TRUE** [ ] [–]
Nov 74. (7") *(7N 45415)* **SWEET MUSIC. / GOODBYE LINE** [ ] [–]
an 75. (lp) *(NSPL 18448) <12104>* **THERE'S NOTHING TOO GOOD FOR MY BABY** <US-title 'PHIL'S DINER'> [ ] [ ]
– Sweet music / Goodbye line / Feather bed / Summershine / Too blue / There's nothing too good for my baby / Invisible man / Caroline / We're running out / It's true / New old song. *(US title – 'PHIL'S DINER')*
)ct 75. (7") *(7N 45544)* **BETTER THAN NOW. / YOU AND I ARE A SONG** [ ] [ ]
Nov 75. (lp) *(NSPL 18473) <12121>* **MYSTIC LINE** [ ] [ ]
– Patiently / Lion and the lamb / Mystic line / Jammy butterfly / You and I are a song / Worlds in your eyes / Better than now / When will I be loved / Back when the bands played in ragtime / Friends.
976. (7") *<71055>* **WORLDS IN YOUR EYES. / BACK WHEN THE BAND PLAYED IN RAGTIME** [–] [ ]
976 (7") *(APBO 0064)* **GOD BLESS OLDER LADIES. / SWEET GRASS COUNTRY** [–] [ ]

not iss. Elektra

979. (lp) *<6E 213>* **LIVING ALONE** [–] [ ]
– It was too late for the party / Ich bin dein (I am yours) / You broke it / Living alone / Buy me a beer / California gold / Love will pull us through / I just don't feel like dancing / Charleston guitar / The fall of '59.

— guested on SANDRA LOCKE single 'Don't Say You Don't Love Me No More'

979 (7") *<46519>* **LIVING ALONE. / I JUST DON'T FEEL LIKE DANCING** [–] [ ]
979. (7") *<46556>* **YOU BROKE IT. / BUY ME A BEER** [–] [ ]

Epic Curb

1ar 81. (7") *(EPCA 9575) <5401>* **DARE TO DREAM AGAIN. / LONELY DAYS LONELY NIGHTS** [ ] [ ]
981. (7") *<ZS6 02116>* **SWEET SOUTHERN LOVE. / IN YOUR EYES** [–] [ ]

Capitol Capitol

)ct 82. (7") *(CL 266)* **LOUISE. / SWEET SUZANNE** [47] [–]
ın 83. (7"; PHIL EVERLY & CLIFF RICHARD) *(CL 276)* **SHE MEANS NOTHING TO ME. / A WOMAN AND A MAN** [9] [–]
983. (7") *<5197>* **WHO'S GONNA KEEP ME WARM. / ONE WAY LOVE ON A TWO WAY STREET)** [–] [ ]
.pr 83. (lp/c) *(EST/TC-EST 27670)* **PHIL EVERLY** [61] [ ]
– She means nothing to me / I'll mend your broken heart / God bless older ladies / Sweet pretender / Never gonna dream again / Better than now / A woman and a man / Louise / When I'm dead and gone / Sweet Suzanne / Oh baby oh (you're the star). *(re-iss. Aug87 as 'LOUISE' on 'Magnum Force' lp/c; MFLP/MFC 053) (cd-iss. Jan88; CDMF 053) (cd-iss. Oct93 & Feb95 on 'B.G.O.')*
.pr 83. (7") *(CL 285)* **SWEET PRETENDER. / BETTER THAN NOW** [ ] [–]
ın 83. (7") *(CL 294)* **OH BABY OH (YOU'RE THE STAR). / GOD BLESS OLDER LADIES** [ ] [–]

he EVERLY BROTHERS

:-united

Impression Passport

ov 83. (7"ep)(12"ep) *(IMS 1)* **DEVOTED TO YOU / EBONY EYES. / LOVE HURTS / THE PRICE OF LOVE (all live)** [ ] [–]
)ec 83. (lp/c) *(IMDP/IMDK 1) <11001>* **EVERLY BROTHERS' REUNION CONCERT** (Royal Albert Hall – Sep'83) [47] [ ]
– The price of love / Walk right back / Claudette / Crying in the rain / Love is strange / Live medley / Take a message to mary / Maybe tomorrow / I wonder if I care as much / When will I be loved / Bird dog / Live medley; Devoted to you – Ebony eyes – Love hurts / Barbara Allen / Lightning Express / Put my little shoes away / Long time gone / Down in the willow garden / Step it up and go / Cathy's clown / Gone, gone, gone / You send me / So sad (to watch good love go bad) / Blues (stay away from me) / Bye bye love / All I have to do is dream / Wake up little Susie / ('Til) I kissed you / Temptation / Be-bop-a-lula / Lucille / Let it be me / Good golly Miss Molly. *(cd-iss. May86 on 'Mercury') (re-iss. cd in 2 parts Jul95 on 'Charly'; CDCD 1226/7) (re-iss. cd/c Sep95 on 'Emporio'; EMPR CD/MC 587) (d-cd re-iss. May97 on 'Charly'; CPCD 8299-2) (d-cd re-iss. Nov99 on 'Snapper'; SMDCD 216) (d-cd re-iss. May00 on 'Castle Pie'; PIEDD 230) (d-cd re-iss. Jul01 on 'K-Box'; KBOX 226)*

Mercury Mercury

Aug 84. (7") *(MER 170) <880 213-7>* **ON THE WINGS OF A NIGHTINGALE. / ASLEEP** [41] [50]
Oct 84. (d-lp/c)(cd) *(MERH/+C 44)<(822431-2)>* **THE EVERLY BROTHERS** <US-title 'EB 84'> [36] [38]
– Danger, danger / The first in line / On the wings of a nightingale / The story of me / I'm taking my time / Lay lady lay / Following the Sun / You make it seem so easy / More than I can handle / Asleep. *(re-iss. Jun87 lp/c; REICE/PRIMC 110) <(cd-iss. Nov98 as 'EB84' on 'Razor & Tie'; RE 2040)>*
Nov 84. (7") *(MER 180)* **THE STORY OF ME. / FOLLOWING THE SUN** [ ] [ ]
Nov 84. (7") *<880 423-7>* **THE STORY OF ME. / THE FIRST IN LINE** [–] [ ]
Oct 85. (7") *(MER 206)* **AMANDA RUTH. / BORN YESTERDAY** [ ] [ ]
Oct 85. (7") *<884 428-7>* **BORN YESTERDAY. / DON'T SAY GOODNIGHT** [–] [ ]
Nov 85. (lp/c)(cd) *(MERH/+C 80)<(826142-2)>* **BORN YESTERDAY** [ ] [83]
– Amanda Ruth / I know love / Born yesterday / These shoes / Arms of Mary / That uncertain feeling / Thinkin' about you / Why worry / Abandoned love / Don't say goodnight / Always drive a Cadillac. (c-cd+=) – You send me.
Feb 86. (7') *<884 694-7>* **I KNOW LOVE. / THESE SHOES** [–] [ ]
Nov 88. (7"; EVERLY BROTHERS & The BEACH BOYS) *(MER 280)* **DON'T WORRY BABY. / BORN YESTERDAY** [ ] [–]
(cd-s+=) *(MERCD 280)* – On the wings of a nightingale.
Apr 89. (lp/c/cd) *<(832520-1/-4/-2)>* **SOME HEARTS** [ ] Nov88 [ ]
– Some hearts / Ride the wind / Can't get it over / Brown eyes / Julianne / Don't worry baby / Be my love again / Angel of the darkness / Three bands of steel / Any single – solitary heart.
Apr 89. (7") *<872 098-7>* **DON'T WORRY BABY. / RIDE THE WIND** [–] [ ]

– (selective) compilations, etc. –

Jul 60. (7") *(HLA 9157) <1380>* **WHEN WILL I BE LOVED. / BE-BOP-A-LULA** [4] [8] Jun60 [74]
(re-iss. Oct80 on 'Old Gold; OG 9067)
Oct 60. (lp) *London; (HA-A 2266) / <25040>* **THE FABULOUS STYLE OF THE EVERLY BROTHERS** [4] Aug60 [23]
<re-iss. Jan86 on 'Rhino'; RNLP 213> (cd-iss. Dec91 on 'Ace')
Nov 60. (7") *Cadence; <1388>* **LIKE STRANGERS. / BRAND NEW HEARTACHE** [–] [22]
Dec 60. (7") *London; (HLA 9250)* **LIKE STRANGERS. / LEAVE MY WOMAN ALONE** [11] [–]
Oct 62. (7") *Cadence; <1429>* **I'M HERE TO GET MY BABY OUT OF JAIL. / LIGHTNING EXPRESS** [–] [76]
Oct 75. (lp/c) *Warners; <(K/K4 56168)>* **WALK RIGHT BACK WITH THE EVERLYS** [10] [ ]
Mar 77. (lp) *Warwick; (WW 5027)* **LIVING LEGENDS** ('Cadence' hits) [12] [–]
Sep 77. (lp/c) *Warners; <(K/K4 56415)>* **THE NEW ALBUM** (from vaults) [ ] [ ]
Dec 82. (lp/c) *K-Tel; (NE1/CD2 197)* **LOVE HURTS** [31] [–]
(re-iss. Sep84; same)
May 93. (cd/c) *Warners; <(9548 31992-2/-4)>* **THE GOLDEN YEARS OF THE EVERLY BROTHERS – THEIR 24 GREATEST HITS** [26] [ ]
Jul 01. (cd) *WEA; <(9362 47869-2)>* **IT'S EVERLY TIME / A DATE WITH THE EVERLY BROTHERS** [ ] [ ]
Jul 01. (cd) *WEA; <(9362 47870-2)>* **BOTH SIDES OF AN EVENING / INSTANT PARTY** [ ] [ ]
May 02. (d-cd) *W.S.M.; (0927 47304-2) <73049>* **THE DEFINITIVE EVERLY BROTHERS** [10] Oct02 [ ]
– Bye bye love / I wonder if I care as much / Wake up little Susie / Maybe tomorrow / All I have to do is dream / Claudette / Bird dog / Devoted to

you / Problems / Poor Jenny / Take a message to Mary / Till I kissed you / Let it be me / Since you broke my heart / Cathy's clown / When will I be loved / Love hurts / Lucille / So sad / Like strangers / Sleepless nights / Walk right back / Ebony eyes / Temptation / Muskrat / Don't blame me / Crying in the rain / How can I meet her / No one can my sunshine smile / So it was so it is so it always will be / It's been nice (goodnight) / The girl sang the blues / Love her / Ferris wheel / Gone gone gone / That'll be the day / The price of love / I'll never get over you / Love is strange / It's all over / Bowling queen / It's my time / Empty boxes / Lord of the manor / Milk train / Yves / The stories we could tell / Green river / Lay it down / On the wings of a nightingale.

] the FACES (see under ⇒ SMALL FACES)

] Donald FAGEN (see under ⇒ STEELY DAN)

FAIRPORT CONVENTION

'ormed: Muswell Hill, London, England ... mid-1967 by ꝚICHARD THOMPSON, SIMON NICOL, ASHLEY ꞪUTCHINGS, JUDY DYBLE and original drummer SHAUN 'RATER. By the end of the year, FRATER was superseded by ɅARTIN LAMBLE, and after a debut 45 for 'Polydor', they added AIN MATTHEWS. This new sextet with Joe Boyd on production, ecorded their 1968 eponymous debut lp, although after its release, UDY left and was replaced by SANDY DENNY. They signed ɔ 'Island' around the same time and issued a second album, WHAT WE DID ON OUR HOLIDAYS' which was the last to eature MATTHEWS (a year later, he was at the UK No.1 spot vith his SOUTHERN COMFORT version of 'Woodstock'). After he completion of their third set, 'UNHALFBRICKING', and while n tour, tragedy struck on the 14th of May '69, when MARTIN AMBLE was killed as their van crashed. With the help of their 'op 30 French version of a Dylan song ('IF YOU GOTTA GO, GO ꞪOW'), 'SI TU DOIS PARTIR', the aforementioned album was ne first of four consecutive UK Top 20 entries. At this stage, the and were Britain's answer to US West Coast folk-rock, although ney increasingly adopted a more traditional folk sound in the 70's nd subsequently influenced many other acts. After the classic, LIEGE AND LIEF' (1969), HUTCHINGS left for STEELEYE SPAN nd DENNY formed FOTHERINGAY, both outfits enjoying their wn bit of fame. Recruiting DAVE PEGG on bass, the band ecorded another album, 'FULL HOUSE' (1970), before RICHARD HOMPSON departed for an acclaimed solo career which stretched quarter of a century (plus). While 'ANGEL DELIGHT' (1971), it the UK Top 10, the concept album 'BABBACOMBE LEE' 1971) stiffed and throughout the 70's, FAIRPORT underwent a izzying series of personnel changes (DENNY eventually rejoining ɔr 'LIVE CONVENTION' in '74). SANDY's stunning vocals made one of the band's best releases of the 70's and she stayed for one ırther studio album, 'RISING FOR THE MOON' (1975), before oing solo once more. Tragedy struck on the 21st of April 1978, hen SANDY died from a brain haemorrhage after falling down flight of stairs. Despite cutting a farewell live album in 1979, ıe band continued recording throughout the 80's and 90's amid ɔnstantly changing line-ups. In the early 80's, they limited their ve appearances to an annual bash at Cropredy in Oxfordshire, an vent which has now become something of a mini-festival attracting ıousands of folk/roots fans each year. Various line-ups continued record the occasional studio set through the 80's and 90's, with 996's largely acoustic 'OLD NEW BORROWED BLUE' and 1997's)th Anniversary set, 'WHO KNOWS WHERE THE TIME GOES', rawing favourable reviews. The latter featured a live version of SANDY DENNY's signature tune as well as an unlikely cover of Marvin Gaye's 'I HEARD IT THROUGH THE GRAPEVINE' and a reading of Jethro Tull's 'LIFE'S A LONG SONG'. 'TULL mainman ANDERSON, meanwhile, contributed his inimitable flute to 2002's 'XXXV', an album which took the veteran folk-rockers into the new millennium at the same time as it resurrected past classics. The appropriately-titled 'OVER THE NEXT HILL' (2004) saw SIMON NICOL and Co looking to new horizons if never really straying from their latter day path.

• **Songwriters:** Mainly group compositions, with numerous renditions of traditional English folk tunes. Other writers:- IF I HAD A RIBBON BOW (Maxine Sullivan) / NOTTAMUN TOWN + SHE MOVED THROUGH THE FAIR + loads more (trad.) / MILLION DOLLAR BASH (Bob Dylan) / GOLD (Peter Blegvad). The 1972 album as The BUNCH was full of covers. • **Trivia:** In 1970, their B-side, 'SIR B. McKENZIE'S DAUGHTER, ... ' entered The Guinness Book Of Records for having longest song title ever at the time.

Album rating: FAIRPORT CONVENTION (*6) / WHAT WE DID ON OUR HOLIDAYS (*8) / UNHALFBRICKING (*8) / LIEGE AND LIEF (*8) / FULL HOUSE (*7) / ANGEL DELIGHT (*6) / BABBACOMBE LEE (*6) / THE HISTORY OF FAIRPORT CONVENTION compilation (*8) / ROSIE (*5) / FAIRPORT NINE (*5) / LIVE CONVENTION (*5) / RISING FOR THE MOON (*5) / GOTTLE O' GEER (*3) / BONNY BUNCH OF ROSES (*4) / TIPPLER'S TALES (*4) / FAREWELL, FAREWELL (*6) / MOAT ON THE LEDGE (*5) / GLADYS' LEAP (*6) / EXPLETIVE DELIGHTED (*5) / IN REAL TIME: LIVE '87 (*4) / RED AND GOLD (*4) / FIVE SEASONS (*5) / JEWEL IN THE CROWN (*5) / OLD NEW BORROWED BLUE (*7) / WHO KNOWS WHERE THE TIME GOES? (*7) / CROPREDY BOX (*5) / XXXV (*5) / OVER THE NEXT HILL (*6)

RICHARD THOMPSON (b. 3 Apr'49) – guitar, vocals / **SIMON NICOL** (b.13 Oct'50) – guitar, banjo, dulcimer, bass, viola, vocals / **JUDY DYBLE** (b.1948) – vocals, autoharp / **ASHLEY HUTCHINGS** (b.Jan'45) – bass / **MARTIN LAMBLE** (b.Aug'49) – drums repl. SHAUN FRATER

Polydor Cotillion

Nov 67. (7") *(604 020)* **IF I HAD A RIBBON BOW. / IF (STOMP)** ☐ ☐

— added **IAIN MATTHEWS** (b.IAN MATTHEW MacDONALD, 16 Jun'46, Scunthorpe, England) – vocals, guitar, percussion (ex-PYRAMIDS)

Jun 68. (lp) *(583 035) <SD 9024>* **FAIRPORT CONVENTION** ☐ ☐
– Time will show the wiser / I don't know where I stand / If (stomp) / Decameron / Jack O'Diamonds / Portfolio / Chelsea morning / Sun shade / The lobster / It's alright ma, it's only witchcraft / One sure thing / M1 breakdown. *(re-iss. Jul75; 238 4047) (re-iss. Aug90 cd/c; 835 230-2/-4) (<cd re-mast.Mar03 +=; 068291-2>)* – Suzanne / If I had a ribbon bow / Morning glory / Reno, Nevada.

— **SANDY DENNY** (b.ALEXANDRA ELENE McLEAN DENNY, 6 Jan'47) – vocals (ex-STRAWBS, etc) repl. JUDY who joined GILES, GILES and FRIPP

Island A&M

Nov 68. (7") *(WIP 6047)* **MEET ON THE LEDGE. / THROWAWAY STREET PUZZLE** ☐ −

Jan 69. (lp) *(ILPS 9092)* **WHAT WE DID ON OUR HOLIDAYS** ☐ −
– Fotheringay / Mr. Lacey / Book song / The Lord is in his place / No man's land / I'll keep it with mine / Eastern rain / Nottamun town / Tale in hard time / She moves through the fair / Meet on the ledge / End of a holiday. *(re-iss. May89 on 'Carthage' lp/c; CG LP/C 4430) (cd-iss. Feb90; IMCD 97) (<cd re-mast.Mar03 +=; IMCD 294)<063597>* – Throwaway street puzzle / You're gonna need my help / Some sweet day.

1969. (7") *<1108>* **FOTHERINGAY. / I'LL KEEP IT WITH MINE** − ☐

FAIRPORT CONVENTION

— Trimmed to a quintet when IAIN formed MATTHEW'S SOUTHERN COMFORT

Jul 69. (7") *(WIP 6064)* <1155> **SI TU DOIS PARTIR. / GENESIS HALL** [21] [ ]

Jul 69. (lp) *(ILPS 9102)* <4206> **UNHALFBRICKING** [12] [ ]
– Genesis Hall / Si tu dois partir / Autopsy / A sailor's life / Cajun woman / Who knows where the time goes? / Percy's song / Million dollar bash. *(cd-iss. Feb87; CID 9102) (re-iss. May89 on 'Carthage' lp/c; CG LP/C 4418) (cd-iss. Nov89; IMCD 61) (lp re-iss. Jan00 on 'Simply Vinyl'; SVLP 164) (<cd re-mast.Mar03 +=; IMCD 293)<63596>* – Dear landlord / The ballad of easy rider.

— **DAVE MATTACKS** (b.Mar'48, London) – drums; repl. MARTIN LAMBLE who died 14 May'69 in tour bus crash / also added **DAVE SWARBRICK** (b. 5 Apr'41, New Malden, Surrey, England) – fiddle, vocals

Dec 69. (lp) *(ILPS 9115)* <4257> **LIEGE & LIEF** [17] [ ]
– Come all ye / Reynardine / Matty Groves / Farewell, farewell / The deserter / The lark in the morning – Rakish Paddy – Foxhunter's jig – Toss the feathers / Tam Lin / Crazy man Michael. *(re-iss. Sep86 lp/c/cd; ILPM/ICM/CID 9115) (cd re-iss. Oct89; IMCD 60) (<cd re-mast.May02 +=; IMCD 291)<586929>* – Sir Patrick Spens (alt.) / Quiet joys of brotherhood.

— **DAVE PEGG** (b. 2 Nov'47, Birmingham, England) – bass, vocals (ex-UGLYS) repl HUTCHINGS who joined STEELEYE SPAN (**PEGG** now in quintet with **THOMPSON, NICOL, MATTACKS** and **SWARBRICK** because SANDY DENNY also departed to form FOTHERINGAY)

Jul 70. (lp) *(ILPS 9130)* <4265> **FULL HOUSE** [13] [ ]
– Walk awhile / Doctor of physick / Dirty linen / Sloth / Sir Patrick Spens / Flatback caper / Poor Will and the jolly hangman / Flowers of the forest. *(re-iss. Jul87 on 'Hannibal'; HNBL 4417) (c-iss.May89; HNBC 4417) (re-iss. Jan92 cd/c; HNCD/HNBC 4417) (<cd re-mast.Sep01 +=; IMCD 285)<586375>* – Now be thankful (mono) / Sir B. McKenzie's daughter's lament . . . / Bonny bunch of roses / Now be thankful (stereo).

Oct 70. (7") *(WIP 6089)* **NOW BE THANKFUL. / SIR B. McKENZIE'S DAUGHTER'S LAMENT FOR THE 77th MOUNTED LANCERS' RETREAT FROM THE STRAITS OF LOCH KOMBE IN THE YEAR OF OUR LORD 1727, ON THE LAIRD OF KINLEAKIE** [ ] [–]

Nov 70. (7") <1195> **WALK AWHILE. / SIR PATRICK SPENS** [–] [ ]

— Now a quartet when RICHARD THOMPSON left to go solo

Jun 71. (7") <1333> **THE JOURNEYMAN'S GRACE. / THE WORLD HAS SURELY LOST IT'S HEAD** [–] [ ]

Jun 71. (lp) *(ILPS 9162)* <4319> **ANGEL DELIGHT** [8] [ ]
– Lord Marlborough / Sir William Gower / Bridge over the River Ash / Wizard of the worldly game / The journeyman's grace / Angel delight / Banks of the sweet primroses / Instrumental medley:- Cuckoo's nest – Hardiman the fiddler – Papa stoor / The bonny black hare / Sickness and diseases. *(cd-iss. Mar93; IMCD 166)*

Sep 71. (7") *(WIP 6128)* <1348> **JOHN LEE. / THE TIME IS NEAR** [ ] [ ]

Nov 71. (lp) *(ILPS 9176)* <4333> **BABBACOMBE LEE** [ ] [ ]
– John Babbacombe Lee: (John's reflection of his boyhood / His struggle with his family / Then the happiest period of his life, the Navy / Returning reluctantly to his job after being invalided out of the service / And the senseless murder of his mistress and the three attempts to hang him – Hanging song). *(cd-iss. Aug92; IMCD 153)*

— **ROGER HILL** – guitar, vocals repl. NICOL who joined ALBION COUNTRY BAND / **TOM FARNAL** – drums repl. MATTACKS who joined ALBION COUNTRY BAND

— In Jun72, **DAVID REA** – guitar repl. ROGER HILL until Aug72 when **MATTACKS** returned to repl. FARNALL / **TREVOR LUCAS** (b.25 Dec'43, Bungaree, Australia) – guitar, vocals (ex-FOTHERINGAY) repl. REA / **adding JERRY DONAHUE** (b.24 Sep'46, New York City, N.Y.) – guitar, vocals (ex-FOTHERINGAY)

Mar 73. (7") *(WIP 6155)* **ROSIE. / KNIGHTS OF THE ROAD** [ ] [–]

Mar 73. (lp) *(ILPS 9208)* <4386> **ROSIE** [ ] [ ]
– Rosie / Matthew, Mark, Luke and John / Knights of the road / Peggy's pub / The plainsman / Hungarian rhapsodie / My girl / Me with you / The hen's march through the midden & the four-poster bed / Furs and feathers. *(cd-iss. Aug92; IMCD 152)*

Oct 73. (lp) *(ILPS 9246)* <4407> **FAIRPORT NINE** [ ] [ ]
– The Hexamshire lass / Polly on the shore / The brilliancy medley and Cherokee shuffle / To Althea from prison / Tokyo / Bring 'em down / Big William / Pleasure and pain / Possibly Parsons Green. *(cd-iss. Aug92; IMCD 154)*

— added the returning **SANDY DENNY** – vocals (from solo career)

Oct 74. (lp) *(ILPS 9285)* **LIVE CONVENTION (live)** [ ] [–]
– Matty Groves / Rosie / Fiddlestix / John the gun / Something you got / Sloth / Dirty linen / Down in the flood / Sir B. MacKenzie . . . *(cd-iss. Feb90; IMCD 95)*

— **PAUL WARREN** – drums repl. MATTACKS who rejoined ALBION DANCE BAND

— **BRUCE ROWLANDS** – drums (ex-RONNIE LANE, ex-JOE COCKER) repl. WARREN

Island / Island

Jul 75. (7") *(WIP 6241)* **WHITE DRESS. / TEARS** [ ] [–]

Jul 75. (lp) *(ILPS <9313>)* **RISING FOR THE MOON** [52] [ ]
– Rising for the Moon / Restless / White dress / Let it go / Stranger to himself / What is true? / Iron lion / Dawn / After halloween / Night-time girl / One more chance. *(cd-iss. Aug92; IMCD 155)*

— FAIRPORT Basic trio **SWARBRICK, PEGG** and **ROWLANDS** recruited new folks **DAN AR BRAS** – guitar repl. SANDY DENNY who went solo again. (She later died of a brain haemorrage on 21 Apr78 after falling down her stairs) **BOB BRADY** – piano (ex-WIZZARD) repl. LUCAS who became producer. **ROGER BURRIDGE** – mandolin, fiddle repl. DONAHUE who became session man

Island / not iss.

May 76. (lp; as FAIRPORT) *(ILPS 9389)* **GOTTLE O'GEER** [ ] [–]
– When first into this country / Our band / Lay me down easy / Cropedy capers / The frog up the pump / Don't be late / Sandy's song / Come and get it / Limey's lament. *(cd-iss. Aug99; IMCD 262)*

— as **FAIRPORT CONVENTION** again because founder member **SIMON NICOL** – guitar returned to repl. BRADY, BRAS and BURRIDGE

Vertigo / not iss.

Feb 77. (lp) *(9102 015)* **BONNY BUNCH OF ROSES** [ ] [–]
– James O'Donnell's jig / The Eynsham poacher / Adieu adieu / The bonny bunch of roses / The poor ditching boy / General Taylor / Run Johnny run / The last waltz / Royal Selection No.13. *(re-iss. Oct88 on 'Woodworm' lp/c/cd; WR/+C/CD 011)*

May 78. (lp) *(9102 022)* **TIPPLER'S TALES** [ ] [–]
– Ye mariner's all / Three drunken maidens / Jack O'rion / Reynard the fox / Lady of pleasure / Bankruptured / The widow of Westmorland / The hair of the dogma / As bitme / John Barleycorn. *(re-iss. 1989 on 'Beat Goes On' lp/c/cd; BGO LP/MC/CD 72)*

Simons / not iss.

Oct 79. (7") *(PMW 1)* **RUBBER BAND. / BONNY BLACK HARE** [ ] [–]

Nov 79. (lp) *(GAMA 1)* **FAREWELL FAREWELL (live)** [ ] [–]
– Matty Groves / Orange blossom special / John Lee / Bridge over the River Ash / Sir Patrick Spens / Mr. Lacey / Walk awhile / Bonny black hare / Journeyman's grace / Meet on the ledge. *(re-iss. Apr80 on 'Woodworm'; BEAR 22) (cd-iss. May96 on 'Red Steel'; SIXCD 0002) (<cd re-mast.Sep97 as 'ENCORE ENCORE' on 'Folkprint'; FP 001CD)<4168> (cd re-iss. Jun99 as 'ENCORE ENCORE' on 'Eagle'; EMDCD 083)*

Woodworm / Varrick

1982. (lp) *(WR 001)* **MOAT ON THE LEDGE – LIVE 1981 (live)** [ ] [–]
– Walk awhile / Country pie / Rosie / Matty Groves / Both sides now / Poor Will and the hangman / The brilliancy medley – Cherokee shuffle / Woman or man / High school confidential. *(c-iss.1985 on 'Stoney Plain'; SP5 1052) (cd-iss. Apr03 on 'Talking Elephant'; TECD 052)*

— **DAVE MATTACKS and DAVE PEGG** returned to repl. SWARBRICK and ROWLANDS; **NICOL** also recruited sessioners **MARTIN ALLCOCK** (b. 5 Jan'57, Manchester, England) – strings / **RIC SAUNDERS** – violin (ex-SOFT MACHINE)

Aug 85. (lp/c/cd) *(WR/+C/CD 007)* *<V/VRC/CDVR 023>* **GLADYS' LEAP** [ ] 1988 [ ]
– How many times / Bird from the mountain / Honour and praise / The hiring fair / Instrumental medley '85: The riverhead – Glady's leap – The wise maid / My feet are set for dancing / Wat Tyler / Head in a sack. *(cd-iss. Aug94 on 'Terrapin Truckin'; TRUCKCD 015) (cd re-iss. May96 on 'Red Steel'; SIVCD 0003) (cd re-mast.Sep01 on 'Talking Elephant'+=; TECD 034)* – Angel delight / Polly on the shore / Lucky old sun.

1986. (lp/c/cd) *(WR/+C/CD 009)* *<CDVR 029>* **EXPLETIVE DELIGHTED!** [ ] 1988 [ ]
– Medley; The Rutland reel – Sack the juggler / Medley; The cat on the mixer – Three left feet / Bankruptured / Portmeirion / James O'Donnell's jig / Expletive delighted / Sigh beg sigh mor / Innstuck / The gas almost works / Hanks for the memory; Shazam – Pipeline – Apache – Peter Gunn. *(re-iss. Aug94 on 'Terrapin Truckin' cd/c; TRUCK CD/MC 016) (cd re-iss. Jun96 on 'Red Steel'; SIVCD 0004)*

Island / not iss.

Nov 87. (lp/c/cd) *(ILPS/ICT/CID 9883)* **IN REAL TIME: LIVE '87 (live)**
– Reynard the fox / The widow of Westmorland's daughter / The hiring fair / Crazy man Michael / Close to the wind / Big three medley – the swirling pit: Matty groves – The Rutland reel – Sack the juggler / Meet on the ledge. *(cd re-iss. 1989; IMCD 10) (c re-iss. Jul93; ICM 2026)*

— now 7-piece of **ALLCOCK, SAUNDERS, PEGG, MATTACKS, NICOL, DONAHUE** and **RICHARD THOMPSON**

New Routes / Rough Trade

Jan 89. (lp/c/cd) *(RUE/+MC/CD 002) <ROUGH-US 63/+C/CD>* **RED AND GOLD** 74
– Set me up / The noise club / Red and gold / The beggars song / The battle / Dark eyed Molly / The rose hip / Summer before the war / Open the door Richard. *(cd re-iss. Dec95 on 'H.T.D.'; HTDCD 47) (<cd re-iss. Jun01 on 'Talking Elephant'+=; TECD 014>)* – Close to the wind.

Dec 90. (lp/c/cd) *(RUE/+MC/CD 005)* **THE FIVE SEASONS** –
– Cloudy beats: medley – Cup of tea! – A loaf of bread – Miss Monahan's / All your beauty / Sock in it / Gold / Ginnie / Mock Morris '90:- The green man – The cropedy badger – Molly on the jetty / Medley:- The card song – Shuffle the pack – The wounded whale. *(cd re-iss. Jan96 on 'H.T.D.'; HTDCD 48) (cd re-iss. Aug01 on 'Talking Elephant'+=; TECD 019) <cd re-iss. 2002 on 'Sanctuary'+=; 81217>* – Caught in a whisper.

— **NICOL, ALLCOCK, PEGG, MATTACKS + SAUNDERS**

Woodworm / Green Linnet

Jan 95. (c/cd) *(WRC/+D 023) <3103>* **JEWEL IN THE CROWN** Jun95
– Jewel in the crown / Slip jigs and reels / A surfeit of lampreys / Kind of fortune / Diamonds and gold / The naked highwayman / The islands / The youngest daughter / London Danny / Summer in December / Travelling by steam / (Travel by steam) / She's like the swallow / Red tide / Home is where the heart is / Closing time.

— In Jun'96, they featured on DAVE SWARBRICK's '50th Birthday Concert' on 'Cooking Vinyl'; *MASHCD 001)*

Jun 96. (cd) *(WRCD 024) <3114>* **OLD NEW BORROWED BLUE**
– Woodworm swing / Men / Aunt Sally shuffle / There once was love – Innstuck / Frozen man / Mr. Sands is in the building / Lalla rookh / Foolish you / Crazy man Michael / Widow of Westmorland's daughter / Genesis hall / The deserter / The swimming song / Struck it right / The hiring fair / Matty Groves – Dirty linen.

— FAIRPORT CONVENTION reunion of nearly all past members

Woodworm / Mooncrest

May 98. (3xcd-box) *(WR3CD 026) <6804>* **THE CROPREDY BOX: THIRTIETH ANNIVERSARY 3 CD SET** (live August 1997) 1999
– Rory McLeod to Joe Byrd (introduction) / Wings / Jack o' diamonds / Time will show the wiser / Mr. Lacey / Suzanne / Genesis hall / Million dollar bash / Come all ye / Reynardine / Matty Groves / Danny boy / Ashley (introduction) / Walk awhile / Now be thankful / Poor Will and the jolly hangman / Angel delight / Rain / Cut across Shorty / Sloth / Rosie / Solo / John Barleycorn / Wat Tyler / Red and gold / Jewel in the crown / Woodworm swing / John Gaudie / Fiddlestix / Dirty linen / Si tu dois partir / Meet on the ledge / Seventeen come Sunday / The April fool tape. *(re-iss. Sep99 on 'Mooncrest'; CRESTBCD 042)*

— **PEGG, MATTACKS, NICOL + MARTIN ALLCOCK + CHRIS LESLIE**

Woodworm / Green Linnet

Aug 97. (cd/c) *(WRCD/WRC 025) <3122>* **WHO KNOWS WHERE THE TIME GOES?**
– John Gaudie / Sailing boat / Here's to Tom Paine / The bowman's retreat / Spanish main / The golden glove / Slipology / The wishfulness waltz / Life's a long song / Dangerous / Heard it through the grapevine (with RICHARD THOMPSON & ROY WOOD) / Who knows where the time goes? (live). *<US cd-iss. Mar00 as 'WISHFULNESS WALTZ' on 'Mooncrest'++; CRESTCD 48>* – Poor Will and the jolly hangman / Rosie / Jack o' diamonds / Come all ye.

Woodworm / Compass

Jan 02. (cd) *(WRCD 038) <4332>* **XXXV – 1967-2002: THE 35th ANNIVERSARY ALBUM** Feb02
– Madeleine / My love is in America / The happy man / Portmeiron / The crowd / Banks of the sweet primroses / The deserter / The light of day / I wandered by a brookside / Niel Gow's apprentice / Everything but the skirl / Talking about my love / Now be thankful / The crowd revosited.

Talking Elephant / not iss.

Jun 03. (d-cd) *(TECD 054)* **CROPREDY FESTIVAL 2002** (live) –
– Time will show the wiser / One sure thing / Jack o' Diamonds / It takes a lot to laugh / I'll keep it with mine / Nottamun town / Cajun woman / Million dollar bash / Tam Lin / Who knows where the time goes / Red and gold / Widow of Westmoreland / Neil's Morris / Journeyman's grace / Walk awhile / Doctor of Physick / You ain't goin' nowhere / Poor Will and the jolly hangman / Sloth / Rising for the Moon / John the gun / Rosie / Naked highwayman / Meet on the ledge. *(re-iss. Nov03 on 'Castle'; CMETD 815)*

Matty Grooves / Compas

Aug 04. (cd) *(MGCD 041) <4391>* **OVER THE NEXT HILL** Sep04
– Over the next hill / I'm already there / Wait for the tide to come in / Canny capers / Over the falls / The wassail song / The fossil hunter / Willow creek / Westward / Some special place / Si tu dois partir.

– compilations etc. –

on 'Island' unless mentioned otherwise

Jul 70. (7") *Polydor; (2058 014)* **IF (STOMP). / CHELSEA MORNING**

Nov 72. (d-lp) *(ICD 4)* **THE HISTORY OF FAIRPORT CONVENTION**
– Meet on the ledge / Fotheringay / Mr.Lacey / Book song / Sailor's life / Si tu dois partir / Who knows where the time goes / Matty Groves / Crazy man Michael / Now be thankful (medley) / Walk awhile / Sloth / The bonny black hare / Angel delight / Bridge over the river Ash / John Lee / Breakfast in Mayfair / Hanging song / The hen's march through the midden / The four-poster bed. *(cd-iss. Apr88; CIDD 4)* – (omits 2 tracks). *(re-iss. Jul91 cd)(c; IMCD 128)(ICM 2073)*

1976. (lp) *A&M; <3530>* **FAIRPORT CHRONICLES** –

Dec 76. (lp) *Help-Island; (HELP 28)* **LIVE AT THE L.A. TROUBADOUR 1970 (live)** –
(re-iss. Jan87 as 'HOUSE FULL' on 'Hannibal' lp/c; HN BL/BC 1319) (re-iss. Jan92 cd/c; HNCD/HNBC 1319) (cd re-mast.Oct01 on 'Island'+=; IMCD 289) – (bonus tracks).

1982. (c) *Woodworm; (none)* **THE AIRING CUPBOARD TAPES** –
(cd-iss. Nov02 on 'Talking Elephant'; TECD 046)

Sep 84. (c) *Woodworm; (WRC 1)* **AT 2 (THE AIRING CUPBOARD TAPES)** –

1985. (d-c) *Woodworm; (none)* **THE BOOT** –

1987. (d-c) *Woodworm; (none)* **THE OTHER BOOT** –

May 87. (7") *(IS 324)* **MEET ON THE LEDGE (re-recorded). / SIGH BHEG SIGH MHOR (live)** –
(12"+=) *(12IS 324)* – John Barleycorn (live).

Sep 87. (lp/c/cd) *Hannibal; (HN BL/BC/CD 1329)* **HEYDAY (BBC sessions '68-'69)** –
(<cd re-iss. Mar02 on 'Island'; IMCD 290>)

Apr 88. (cd) *(CIDD 4)* **THE BEST OF FAIRPORT CONVENTION** –

Aug 89. (d-c) *Woodworm; (none)* **THE THIRD LEG** –

Jan 92. (cd/c) *Woodworm; (WR CD/C 015)* **THE WOODWORM YEARS** –
(cd re-iss. Feb98 on 'Folkprint'; FP 003CD)

Aug 92. (4xcd-box) *(FCBX 1)* **25th ANNIVERSARY PACK** –
– (ROSIE / JOHN BABBACOMBE LEE / NINE / RISING FOR THE MOON)

Feb 98. (d-cd) *Folkprint; (FP 002CD)* **GLADYS' LEAP / EXPLETIVE DELIGHTED** –

Apr 98. (cd) *Mooncrest; (CRESTCD 035)* **CLOSE TO THE WIND** –

Nov 98. (cd) *Raven; (<RVCD 47>)* **FIDDLESTIX: THE BEST OF FAIRPORT CONVENTION 1972-1984**

Apr 99. (d-cd) *(<564687-2>)* **MEET ON THE LEDGE: THE CLASSIC YEARS** –

Sep 99. (cd) *Delta; (4700-2)* **RHYTHM OF THE TIME** –

Feb 00. (d-cd) *Snapper; (SMDCD 214)* **KING FORTUNE** –

Mar 01. (cd) *Rialto; (RMCD 2312)* **THE FAIRPORT CONVENTION ARCHIVE** –

Nov 01. (d-cd) *Castle; (CMDDD 367)* **ANTHOLOGY** –

Feb 02. (cd) *Metro; (METRCD 076)* **THEN AND NOW: 1982-1996 – THE BEST OF FAIRPORT CONVENTION**

May 02. (4xcd-box) *(FRQCD 35)* **FAIRPORT UNCONVENTIONAL**

May 02. (cd) *Talking Elephant; (TECD 042)* **FROM CROPREDY TO PORTMEIRON (live)** [ ] [–]

Jun 02. (d-cd) *Burning Airlines; (<PILOT 133>)* **BEFORE THE MOON (live in Denver, 1974)** [ ] [ ]

Mar 03. (cd) *Disky; (<SI 905323>)* **HERITAGE** [ ] [ ]

Aug 03. (3xcd-box) *Eureka; (<EURBX 1>)* **SHINES LIKE GOLD** [ ] [ ]

Oct 03. (d-cd) *Snapper; (SMDCD 484)* **ACROSS THE DECADES** [ ] [–]

FAITH NO MORE

Formed: Los Angeles & San Francisco, California, USA ... 1980 by BILL GOULD and MIKE BORDIN, although they only started gigging in 1982. With CHUCK MOSELEY and JIM MARTIN completing the line-up, the band began to carve out their innovative fusion of funk, rap, hardcore and metal. In 1985, they issued their eponymous debut album on local indie label, 'Mordam', the single, 'WE CARE A LOT' drawing the attention of 'Slash' records, who unleashed 'INTRODUCE YOURSELF' the same year. In 1988, due to musical differences and off-beat stage humour, MOSELEY was discharged from the band. His replacement was magnetic, Kyle Mclachlan-like, MIKE PATTON who immediately became a focal point, his impressive vocal theatrics and commanding stage presence transforming FAITH NO MORE into a formidable live act. PATTON also penned the bizarre, enigmatic lyrics for the band's breakthrough record, 'THE REAL THING' (1989). Arguably the best metal album of the decade, if you could call it metal, it veered from the stuttering rap-rock of 'EPIC' to the sublimely aquatic 'UNDERWATER LOVE' and on to a searing cover of BLACK SABBATH's 'WAR PIGS'. The record went on to sell over a million copies, gave a tired heavy metal scene a much needed boot up the arse and more importantly, gave FAITH NO MORE the convenience of a bigger budget for their next album. 'ANGEL DUST' (1992) wreaked aural havoc, a mish-mash of styles even more diverse than its predecessor. By turns defiantly inaccessible ('MALPRACTICE') and pop-friendly ('MIDLIFE CRISIS'), the record was characterised by a fractured, schizophrenic sound that seemed to tally with PATTON's increasingly outrageous antics. Following on from their live TECHNOTRONIC/NEW KIDS ON THE BLOCK (ironic? Americans? nah) medley, the band released their rather uninspired cover of The COMMODORES' 'I'M EASY'. It became their biggest selling UK single to date, while the album also sold by the truckload following a world tour with GUNS N' ROSES. By the release of 'KING FOR A DAY ... FOOL FOR A LIFETIME' (1995), MARTIN had been replaced with TREY SPRUANCE, who played alongside PATTON in his part-time side project, MR. BUNGLE. The record was as uncompromising as ever, venom-spewing hardcore rage sitting side by side with wilful weirdness. A blistering headlining set at that year's Phoenix festival (almost topping PUBLIC ENEMY's poignant farewell slot earlier that day) proved once more that live, FAITH NO MORE have few peers and even less scruples. While the group maintain they're simply a rock band and nothing more, they remain one of the genre's quintessential outsiders, image-unfriendly and maverick to the last, as evidenced on their last studio set, 'ALBUM OF THE YEAR' (1997). If not quite living up to the rather presumptious title, the record illustrated that FAITH NO MORE still have their collective finger in more than one pie, 'LAST CUP OF SORROW' being their most affecting single for years. Unfortunately, it would also be their epitaph as the band split up the following April.

• **Covered:** THE RIGHT STUFF (Edwin Starr) / MIDNIGHT COWBOY (John Barry) / MALPRACTICE (sampled: Kronos Quartet No.8) / LET'S LYNCH THE LANDLORD (Dead Kennedys) / I'M EASY (Commodores) / I STARTED A JOKE (Bee Gees) / GREENFIELDS (Gilykson-Dehr-Miller) / SPANISH EYES (hit; Al Martino) / THIS GUY'S IN LOVE WITH YOU (Burt Bacharach) / HIGHWAY STAR (Deep Purple). IMPERIAL TEEN covered SHAYLA (Blondie).

Album rating: FAITH NO MORE (*5) / INTRODUCE YOURSELF (*8) / THE REAL THING (*8) / LIVE AT BRIXTON ACADEMY (*6) / ANGEL DUST (*8) / KING FOR A DAY – FOOL FOR A LIFETIME (*7) / ALBUM OF THE YEAR (*6) / WHO CARES A LOT? compilation (*9) / THIS IS IT: THE BEST OF FAITH NO MORE compilation (*8)

CHUCK MOSELEY – vocals / **BILLY GOULD** (b.24 Apr'63, L.A.) – bass / **RODDY BOTTUM** (b. 1 Jul'63, L.A.) – keyboards / **JIM MARTIN** (b.JAMES, 21 Jul'61, Oakland, Calif.) – guitar / **MIKE BORDIN** (b.27 Nov'62) – drums

not iss. Mordan

1985. (lp) *<MDR 1>* **FAITH NO MORE** [–] [ ]
– We care a lot / The jungle / Mark Bowen / Jim / Why do you bother / Greed / Pills for breakfast / As the worm turns / Arabian disco / New beginnings. *(imported into UK.Feb88 as 'WE CARE A LOT'; same)*

Slash Slash

Oct 87. (lp/c)(cd) *(SLAP/SMAC 21)<(828051-2)>* **INTRODUCE YOURSELF** [ ] [ ]
– Faster disco / Anne's song / Introduce yourself / Chinese arithmetic / Death march / We care a lot / R'n'r / Crab song / Blood / Spirit.

Jan 88. (7") *(LASH 17) <28287>* **WE CARE A LOT. / SPIRIT** [53] [ ]
(12"+=) *(LASHX 17)* – Chinese Arithmetic (radio mix).

Apr 88. (7"/7"pic-d/12") *(LASH/+P/X 18)* **ANNE'S SONG (remix). / GREED** [ ] [ ]

—— **MIKE PATTON** (b.27 Jan'68, Eureka, Calif.) – vocals (of-MR. BUNGLE) repl. CHUCK who later (1991) joined BAD BRAINS

Jul 89. (lp/c/cd) *(828154-1/-4/-2) <25878>* **THE REAL THING** [30] [11]
– From out of nowhere / Epic / Falling to pieces / Surprise, you're dead / Zombie eaters / The real thing / Underwater love / The morning after / Woodpecker from Mars. *(cd+=)* – Edge of the world / War pigs. *(actually hit charts early 1990) (re-iss. Sep92 cd/c; same)*

Oct 89. (7") *(LASH 19)* **FROM OUT OF NOWHERE. / COWBOY SONG** [ ] [ ]
(12"+=) *(LASHX 19)* – The grave.

Jan 90. (7"/7"sha-pic-d) *(LASH/LASPD 21)* **EPIC. / WAR PIGS (live)** [37] [–]
(7"m+=) *(LASHG 21)* – Surprise you're dead (live).
(12"++=/cd-s++=) *(LASHX/LASCD 21)* – Chinese arithmetic.

Apr 90. (c-s) *(LASCS 24)* **FROM OUT OF NOWHERE. / WOODPECKER FROM MARS (live)** [23] [ ]
(7"m+=) *(LASHG 24)* – Epic (live).
(12"++=/12"pic-d++=/cd-s++=) *(LASHX/LASPX/LASCD 24)* – The real thing (live).

Jun 90. (c-s) *<19813>* **EPIC / EDGE OF THE WORLD** [–] [9]

Jul 90. (7") *(LASHP 25)* **FALLING TO PIECES. / WE CARE A LOT (live)** [41] [–]
(7"m+=)(c-s+=) *(LASHG/LASCS 25)* – Underwater love (live).
(12"++=/12"w-poster++=/cd-s++=) *(LASHX/LASPX/LASCD 25)* – From out of nowhere (live).

Sep 90. (7"sha-pic-d) *(LASPD 26)* **EPIC. / FALLING TO PIECES (live)** [25] [–]
(7"m+=/c-s+=) *(LASH/LASCS 26)* – Epic (live).
(12"++=/cd-s++=) *(LASHX/LASCD 26)* – As the worm turns.

Oct 90. (c-s) *<19563>* **FALLING TO PIECES / ZOMBIE EATERS** [–] [92]

Feb 91. (cd/c/lp) *(828238-2/-4/-1)* **LIVE AT BRIXTON ACADEMY (live)** [20] [–]
– Falling to pieces / The real thing / Pump up the jam / Epic / War pigs / From out of nowhere / We care a lot / The right stuff / Zombie eaters / Edge of the world. *(cd+=/c+=)* – The grade / Cowboy song.

May 92. (7"/7"colrd/c-s) *(LASH//LASCS 37)* **MIDLIFE CRISIS. / JIZZLOBER / CRACK HITLER** [10] [ ]
(12"pic-d+=/pic-cd-s+=) *(LASHX/LASCD 37)* – Midnight cowboy.

Jun 92. (cd/c/lp) *(828321-2/-4/-1) <26785>* **ANGEL DUST** [2] [10]
– Land of sunshine / Caffeine / Midlife crisis / RV / Smaller and smaller / Everything's ruined / Malpractise / Kindergarten / Be aggressive / A small victory / Crack Hitler / Jizzlober / Midnight cowboy. *(lp w/ free-12"ep)* – MIDLIFE CRISIS (remix) / (2). *(re-iss. Feb93) (+=)* – I'm easy.

Aug 92. (7"/c-s) *(LASH/LASCS 39)* **A SMALL VICTORY. / LET'S LYNCH THE LANDLORD** [29] [ ]
(12"+=)(12"pic-d+=) *(LASHX 39)* – Malpractise.
(cd-s++=) *(LASCD 39)* – ('A'extended).

Sep 92. (12"ep/cd-ep) *(LASHX/LASCD 40)* **A SMALL VICTORY (Youth remix) / R-EVOLUTION 23 (Full Moon mix) / SUNDOWN (mix) / SUNDOWN (instrumental)** [55] [–]

Nov 92. (7"/c-s) *(LASH/LASCS 43)* **EVERYTHING'S RUINED. / MIDLIFE CRISIS (live)** [28] [ ]
(cd-s+=) *(LASCD 43)* – Land of sunshine (live).
(cd-s) *(LASHCD 43)* – ('A'side) / Edge of the world (live) / RV (live).

Jan 93. (7"/c-s/12"/cd-s) *(LASH/LASCS/LASHX/LACDP 44)*
I'M EASY. / BE AGGRESSIVE [3] [–]

Mar 93. (c-s) *<18569>* **EASY / DAS SCHUTENFEST** [–] [58]

Oct 93. (12"ep/c-ep/cd-ep; by FAITH NO MORE & BOO-YAA T.R.I.B.E.) *(659794-6/-4/-2)* **ANOTHER BODY MURDERED. / Just Another Victim (by "HELMET / HOUSE OF PAIN")** [26] [–]
(above from the film 'Judgment Night', released on 'Epic')

— **DEAN MENTA** – guitar; repl. JIM MARTIN (TREY SPRUANCE played on below album) – JIM MARTIN released a solo album, 'MILK AND BLOOD' for 'S.P.V.' in 1997

Mar 95. (7"/c-s) *(LASH/LASCS 51)* **DIGGING THE GRAVE. / UGLY IN THE MORNING** [16] [ ]
(12"blue+=) *(LASHX 51)* – Absolute zero / Get out.
(cd-s+=) *(LASCD 51)* – Absolute zero / Cuckoo for Caca.
(cd-s) *(LASHCD 51)* – ('A'side) / I started a joke / Greenfields.

Mar 95. (cd/c/lp) *(828 560-2/-4/-1) <45723>* **KING FOR A DAY – FOOL FOR A LIFETIME** [5] [31]
– Get out / Ricochet / Evidence / The great art of making enemies / Star A.D. / Cuckoo for Caca / Caralho Voador / Ugly in the morning / Digging the grave / Take this bottle / King for a day / What a day / The last to know / Just a man. *(7"box-set)* – (interviews). *(re-iss. Sep97 cd/c; same)*

May 95. (c-s) *(LASCS 53)* **RICOCHET / SPANISH EYES** [27] [ ]
(cd-s+=) *(LASCD 53)* – I wanna f**k myself.
(cd-s) *(LACDP 53)* – ('A'side) / Midlife crisis (live) / Epic (live) / We care a lot (live).

Jul 95. (c-s) *(LASCS 54)* **EVIDENCE / EASY (live)** [32] [ ]
(cd-s+=) *(LASCD 54)* – Digging the grave (live) / From out of nowhere (live).
(cd-s) *(LACDP 54)* – ('A'side) / Das schutzenfest / (interview).

— **JON HUDSON** – guitar; repl. MENTA

May 97. (cd-ep) *(LASCD 61) <5915>* **ASHES TO ASHES / LIGHT UP AND LET GO / COLLISION / ASHES TO ASHES (DJ Icey & Mystero mix)** [15] [ ]
(cd-ep) *(LASCDP 61) <5909>* – ('A'side) / The big Kahuna / Mouth to mouth / ('A'-Hard Knox alternative mix).
(12"ep) *(LASX 61)* – ('A'side) / ('A'-Hard Knox alternative mix) / ('A'-DJ Icey & Mystero mix) / ('A';-DJ & Mystero dub mix).

Jun 97. (cd/c/lp) *(828 901-2/-4/-1) <46629>* **ALBUM OF THE YEAR** [7] [41]
– Collision / Strip search / Last cup of sorrow / Naked in front of the computer / Helpless / Mouth to mouth / Ashes to ashes / She loves me not / Got that feeling / Paths of glory / Home sick home / Pristina. *(cd with free cd Jan98; 828902-2)*

Jul 97. (cd-ep) *(LASCD 62)* **LAST CUP OF SORROW / LAST CUP OF SORROW (Bonehead mix) / SHE LOVES ME NOT (Spinna main mix) / SHE LOVES ME NOT (Spinna crazy dub)** [ ] [–]
(cd-ep) *(LASDP 62)* – ('A'side) / Pristina (Billy Gould mix) / Last cup of sorrow (Roli Mosimann mix) / Ashes to ashes (Dillinja remix).

— In Nov'97, they teamed up with 70's popsters SPARKS on a combined version of 'THIS TOWN AIN'T BIG ENOUGH FOR BOTH OF US'.

Jan 98. (cd-s) *(LASCD 63)* **ASHES TO ASHES / LAST CUP OF SORROW (Rammstein mix) / LAST CUP OF SORROW (Sharam Vs FNM club mix)** [29] [–]
(cd-s) *(LASCX 63)* – ('A'side) / ('A'-Dillinja remix) / The gentle art of making enemies / ('A'live).
(12") *(LASHX 63)* – ('A'-Dillinja mix) / ('A'-Hardknox mix).

— the band had already split in April '98

– compilations, etc. –

Oct 98. (cd-s) *London; (LONCD 65) / Slash; <570331>* **I STARTED A JOKE / THE WORLD IS YOURS / THEME FROM MIDNIGHT COWBOY** [49] Nov98 [ ]
(cd-s) *(LASCX 65) <570333>* – ('A'side) / This guy's in love with you / We care a lot (CD-rom).

Nov 98. (d-cd/d-c) *London; (556 057-2/-4) / Slash; <47149>* **WHO CARES A LOT? – THE GREATEST HITS** (compilation) [37] [ ]
– We care a lot (original) / Introduce yourself / From out of nowhere / Epic / Falling to pieces / Midlife crisis / A small victory / Easy / Digging the grave / The gentle art of making enemies / Evidence / I started a joke / Last cup of sorrow / Ashes to ashes / Stripsearch // The world is yours / Hippie jam song / Instrumental / I won't forget you / Introduce yourself (4-track demos) / Highway star / Theme from Midnight Cowboy / This guy's in love with you.

Feb 03. (cd) *Rhino; <(8122 76099-2)>* **THIS IS IT: THE BEST OF FAITH NO MORE** [ ] Jan03 [ ]
– Arabian disco / We care a lot / Anne's song / Introduce yourself / From out of nowhere / Epic / Falling to pieces / War pigs / The cowboy song / As the worm turns (live) / Midlife crisis / A small victory / Be aggressive / Easy / Digging the grave / Evidence / Last cup of sorrow / Ashes to ashes / The perfect crime.

Marianne FAITHFULL

Born: 29 Dec'46, Hampstead, London, England, daughter of a university lecturer and an Austrian baroness, who sent her to St. Joseph's convent school in Reading, Berkshire. At the age of 17, while attending a party with her artist boyfriend, JOHN DUNBAR, she was spotted by ANDREW LOOG OLDHAM (the ROLLING STONES' manager), who signed her to 'Decca' records. MARIANNE's debut 45, 'AS TEARS GO BY' (from the pen of JAGGER and RICHARDS), soon careered into the UK Top 10 and the US Top 30, however, her follow-up, Dylan's 'BLOWIN' IN THE WIND', flopped. Early in '65, 'COME AND STAY WITH ME' gave MARIANNE her biggest hit to date (and subsequently ever) and this was followed by two simultaneously issued folk/pop albums, 'COME MY WAY' and the eponymous, 'MARIANNE FAITHFULL' (both of which hit the Top 20). Later the same year, she gave birth to a son, Nicholas, although she was soon to separate from DUNBAR. The sultry blonde bombshell then began a much-publicised affair with MICK JAGGER after allegedly bedding the other three! (not WATTS). Busted for drugs with JAGGER and Co. on many occasions, the couple visiting the Maharishi Yogi in '68, although her career in the flower-power years had taken a sharp nosedive. Around the same time, she also began acting and starred in 'The Three Sisters' (a Chekhov play) and in the film, 'Girl On A Motorcycle', with Alain Delon. Later in '68, she miscarried with JAGGER's baby and six months later, both were arrested in their London home for possession of marijuana. A single, 'SISTER MORPHINE' (written with JAGGER and RICHARDS), was withdrawn and it looked like her music career was about to end. In the summer of '69, while on the set of the movie, 'Ned Kelly', alongside JAGGER, she was found in a coma after overdosing on barbituates (100+ Tuinal). MARIANNE was sadly dropped from the film and subsequently went into hospital to try and cure her heroin addiction and depression. A year later, after a season playing Ophelia in 'Hamlet' (alongside Nicol Williamson), much was made out of her suspected suicide bids which were reported by the press; her divorce from DUNBAR and split with JAGGER, also in the dailys. After five years in the proverbial wilderness, MARIANNE returned with a new contract on 'Nems', the single, 'DREAMING MY DREAMS' a pleasant if not brilliant comeback. Two albums appeared for the label, 'DREAMIN' MY DREAMS' (1977) and 'FAITHLESS' (1978), before she signed to 'Island', returning to the UK Top 50 in 1979 with her rendition of Shel Silverstein's, 'THE BALLAD OF LUCY JORDAN' (once a hit by DR. HOOK). On the 23rd of November '79, she married BEN BRIERLY (of punk rock band, The VIBRATORS), although her future seemed always to be dogged by her drug intake. Her last album's unfruitful attempt at C&W was soon forgotten when she unleashed what was to become her greatest achievement, the 'BROKEN ENGLISH' album. Released nearing the end of, what was for her, a torturous 70's, it marked a pinnacle in her up and down career and was helped in the writing department by her long-time guitarist, BARRY REYNOLDS. Highlighted by her xplicit, 'WHY D'YA DO IT' track, the leather-clad mistress was n full swing using sex as her vocal weapon backed by "the in-hing" electro/new wave; her cover of John Lennon's 'WORKING CLASS HERO' also a must-hear. Two albums followed in relatively quick succession, 'DANGEROUS ACQUAINTANCE' (1981) and A CHILD'S ADVENTURE' (1983), showing too desperately for ome, that she wanted to retain her new "rock" street cred. In 1987, till surprisingly contracted to 'Island' and now living in Cambridge, Aassachusetts with new husband and writer, Giorgio Della, she ssued a comeback album of sorts, 'STRANGE WEATHER'. It lelivered some powerful and poignant messages, showing her once roaky voice to shining effect; EDITH PIAF would have been proud of her. However, the following year, MARIANNE was deported rom the States, the singer subsequently choosing to settle in reland to finish off her autobiography, simply titled 'Faithfull'. In he mid-90's, she released a handful of albums (including 1995's A SECRET LIFE' and 1996's '20th CENTURY BLUES'), she even ook time out to appear with the likes of The CHIEFTAINS. A few ears onwards, MARIANNE chose to sing a full set of Kurt Weill ongs under the banner of 'THE SEVEN DEADLY SINS' (1998) – ery ambitious with a full orchestra as backing. Like a 'BROKEN NGLISH' part II, in the sense that it was just as lyrically intriguing, VAGABOND WAYS' (1999) delivered her back into the critical melight. Tracks such as 'ELECTRA' (accounting all the infamous vomen of history), 'INCARCERATION OF A FLOWER CHILD' a late 60's number written by ROGER WATERS about SYD ARRETT) and a cover of Leonard Cohen's 'TOWER OF SONG' vere excellent by today's high standards – FAITHFULL was indeed he saving grace amongst her contemporary divas. With 'KISSIN' IME' (2002), the seemingly indomitable singer surpassed herself et again, roping in a raft of cutting edge artists from the rock world create one of her most intriguing and challenging works to date. he presence of BECK, DAMON ALBARN, JARVIS COCKER and ILLY CORGAN might at best, have threatened to overshadow AITHFULL's singular talent, at worst, have become a muddled elebrity knees-up. In the event, she managed to meld the various nk-ups into a seamless whole without compromising either her wn artistic vision or that of her guests, each of whom succeeded in easing out different facets of FAITHFULL's musical character. On 004's critically acclaimed 'BEFORE THE POISON', FAITHFULL vas as sociable as ever, calling upon the songwriterly services of ICK CAVE, PJ HARVEY, DAMON ALBARN (again!) and JON RION, and sounding ever more like the grand dame of avant-pop.

Songwriters: Penned some herself, although she initially covered others; LL BE YOUR BABY TONIGHT (Bob Dylan) / GREENSLEEVES + HOUSE F THE RISING SUN + SCARBOROUGH FAIR (trad.) / COME AND TAY WITH ME (Jackie DeShannon) / GREEN ARE YOUR EYES (Bert nsch) / THE LAST THING ON MY MIND (Tom Paxton) / THE FIRST IME EVER I SAW YOUR FACE (Ewan MacColl) / SALLY FREE AND EASY ... Tannery) / COCKLESHELLS (... Taylor) / THIS LITTLE BIRD (John . Loudermilk) / SUNNY GOODGE STREET + THE MOST OF WHAT LEAST (Donovan) / YESTERDAY (Beatles) / SOMETHING BETTER Goffin-King) / IS THIS WHAT I GET FOR LOVING YOU (Ronettes) / REAMING MY DREAMS (Waylon Jennings) / STRANGE WEATHER Tom Waits) / MADAME GEORGE (Van Morrison) / GHOST DANCE Patti Smith), etc. • **Trivia:** In 1967, she appeared and supplied backing vocals r The BEATLES on their 'All You Need Is Love', single & TV video.

lbum rating: COME MY WAY (*4) / MARIANNE FAITHFULL (*6) / GO WAY FROM MY WORLD (*5) / NORTH COUNTRY MAID (*4) / FAITHFULL OREVER (*4) / LOVE IN A MIST (*4) / DREAMING MY DREAMS (*3) / AITHLESS (*4) / BROKEN ENGLISH (*8) / DANGEROUS ACQUAINTANCES 6) / A CHILD'S ADVENTURE (*5) / THE VERY BEST OF MARIANNE AITHFULL compilation (*7) / STRANGE WEATHER (*7) / BLAZING AWAY 6) / FAITHFULL: A COLLECTION OF HER BEST RECORDINGS compilation 5) / A SECRET LIFE (*5) / 20th CENTURY BLUES (*4) / THE SEVEN DEADLY NS (*6) / VAGABOND WAYS (*7) / KISSIN' TIME (*6) / BEFORE THE OISON (*7)

MARIANNE FAITHFULL – vocals (with session people)

Decca London

Jul 64. (7") *(F 11923) <9697>* **AS TEARS GO BY. / GREENSLEEVES** [9] Oct64 [22]

Oct 64. (7") *(F 12007)* **BLOWIN' IN THE WIND. / THE HOUSE OF THE RISING SUN** [ ] [ ]

Feb 65. (7") *(F 12075) <9731>* **COME AND STAY WITH ME. / WHAT HAVE I DONE WRONG** [4] [26]

Apr 65. (7") *(F 12162) <9759>* **THIS LITTLE BIRD. / MORNING SUN** [6] May65 [32]

May 65. (lp) *(LK 4688)* **COME MY WAY** [12] [–]
– Come my way / Jabberwock / Portland town / The house of the rising sun / Spanish is a loving tongue / Fare thee well / Lonesome traveller / Down in the Salley garden / Mary Ann / Full fathom five / Four strong winds / Black girl / Once I had a sweetheart / Bells of freedom. *(re-iss. Sep91 on 'Deram' lp/cd+=; 820 629-2)* – Blowin' in the wind / Et maintenant (what now my love) / That's right baby / Sister Morphine.

May 65. (lp) *(LK 4689) <3423>* **MARIANNE FAITHFULL** [15] [12]
– Come and stay with me / They will never leave you *(UK-only)* / / What have they done to the rain / In my time of sorrow / What have I done wrong / I'm a loser / As tears go by / If I never get to love you / Time takes time / He'll come back to me / Paris bells / Plasir d'amour. *(re-iss. Aug84; DOA 3) (cd-iss. Jun89 on 'London'+=; 820 630-2)* – Can't you hear my heartbeat? / Downtown.

Jul 65. (7") *(F 12193) <9780>* **SUMMER NIGHTS. / THE SHA LA LA SONG** [10] Aug65 [24]

Oct 65. (7") *(F 12268)* **YESTERDAY. / OH LOOK AROUND YOU** [36] [ ]

Nov 66. (7") *<9802>* **GO AWAY FROM MY WORLD. / OH, LOOK AROUND YOU** [–] [89]

Dec 65. (lp) *<3452>* **GO AWAY FROM MY WORLD** [–] [81]
– Go away from my world / Yesterday / Come my way / Last thing on my mind / How should true love / Wild mountain time / Summer nights / Mary Ann / Scarborough Fair / Lullabye / North country maid / Sally free and easy.

Apr 66. (lp) *(LK 4778)* **NORTH COUNTRY MAID** [ ] [–]
– Green are your eyes / Scarborough fair / Cockleshells / The last thing on my mind / The first time ever I saw your face / Sally free and easy / Sunny Goodge Street / How should your true love know / She moved through the fair / North country maid / Lullaby / Wild mountain thyme. *(cd-iss. Aug90+=; 820 631-2)* – The most of what is least / Come my way / Mary Ann.

May 66. (7") *(F 12408)* **TOMORROW'S CALLING. / THAT'S RIGHT BABY** [ ] [ ]

Jul 66. (7") *(F 12443)* **COUNTING. / I'D LIKE TO DIAL YOUR NUMBER** [ ] [ ]

Nov 66. (lp) *<3482>* **FAITHFULL FOREVER** [–] [ ]
– Counting / Tomorrow's calling / The first time / With you in mind / In the night time / Ne me quitte pas (love theme from Umbrellas of Cherbourg) / Monday Monday / Some other Spring / That's right baby / Lucky girl / I'm the sky / I have a love.

Feb 67. (7") *(F 22524)* **IS THIS WHAT I GET FOR LOVING YOU?. / TOMORROW'S CALLING** [43] [ ]

Feb 67. (lp; mono/stereo) *(LK/SKL 4854)* **LOVEINAMIST** [ ] [–]
– Yesterday / You can't go where the roses go / Our love has gone / Don't make promises / In the night time / This little bird / Ne me quite pas / Counting / Reason to believe / Conquillage / With you in mind / Young girl blues / Good guy / I love a love. *(cd-iss. Oct88+=; 820 632-2)* – Rosie, Rosie.

Feb 69. (7"; w-drawn) *(F 12889)* **SOMETHING BETTER. / SISTER MORPHINE** [ ] [ ]

—— She retired from music business for around half a decade

NEMS not iss.

Nov 75. (7") *(NES 004)* **DREAMIN' MY DREAMS. / LADY MADELAINE** [ ] [–]

Sep 76. (7") *(NES 013)* **ALL I WANNA DO IN LIFE. / WRONG ROAD AGAIN** [ ] [–]

Jan 77. (lp)(c) *(NEL 6007)* **DREAMIN' MY DREAMS** [ ] [–]
– Fairy tale hero / This time / I'm not Lisa / he way you want me to be / Wrong road again / All I wanna do in life / I'm looking for blue eyes / Somebody loves you / Vanilla O'lay / Dreamin' my dreams / Lady Madelaine / Sweet little sixteen.

Jan 77. (7") *(NES 014)* **WRONG ROAD AGAIN. / THE WAY YOU WANT ME TO BE** [ ] [–]

—— she was now backed by **The GREASE BAND**

Mar 78. (lp) *(NEL 6012)* **FAITHLESS** [ ] [–]
– Dreamin' my dreams / Vanilla O'Lay / Wait for me down by the river / I'll be your baby tonight / Lady Madelaine / All I wanna do in life / The way you want me to be / Wrong road again / This was the day (Nashville) / This time / I'm not Lisa / Honky tonk angels. *(re-iss. Apr89 on 'Castle' lp/c/cd; CLA LP/MC/CD 148) (cd re-iss. Apr99 on 'Essential'; ESSCD 713)*

Mar 78. (7") *(NES 117)* **THE WAY YOU WANT ME TO BE. / THAT WAS THE DAY (NASHVILLE)** [ ] [–]

—— now with **BARRY REYNOLDS** – guitar, co-producer / **STEVE YORK** – bass / **TERRY STANNARD** – drums / **JOE HAVETY** – keys / etc.

Island Island

Oct 79. (7") *(WIP 6491)* **THE BALLAD OF LUCY JORDAN. / BRAIN DRAIN** [48] [ ]

Oct 79. (lp) *(M 1) <ILPS 9570>* **BROKEN ENGLISH** [57] [82]
– Broken English / Witches song / Brain drain / Guilt / The ballad of Lucy Jordan / What's the hurry / Working class hero / Why d'ya do it? *(c-iss.May81; ICT 9570) (re-iss. Sep86 lp/c; ILPM/ICM 9570) (cd-iss. May89; IMCD 11) (re-iss. May94; ILPS 9570)*

Jan 80. (7") *<49121>* **BROKEN ENGLISH. / BRAIN DRAIN** [–] [ ]

Jan 80. (7") *(WIP 6542)* **BROKEN ENGLISH. / WHAT'S THE HURRY** [ ] [–]
(12") *(12WIP 6542)* – ('A'side) / Why d'ya do it?.

Oct 81. (7") *(WIP 6737)* **INTRIGUE. / FOR BEAUTY'S SAKE** [ ] [ ]

Oct 81. (lp/c) *(ILPS/ICT 9648)* **DANGEROUS ACQUAINTANCE** [45] [ ]
– Sweetheart / Intrigue / Easy in the city / Strange one / Tenderness / For beautie's sake / So sad / Eye communication / Truth bitter truth. *(cd-iss. May95; IMCD 205)*

Nov 81. (7") *(WIP 6752)* **SWEETHEART. / OVER HERE** [ ] [–]

Jan 82. (7") **SWEETHEART. / FOR BEAUTIE'S SAKE** [–] [ ]

May 82. (7") *(MF 100)* **BROKEN ENGLISH. / SISTER MORPHINE** [ ] [ ]

—— **BEN BRIERLEY + MIKEY CHUNG** – guitar repl. MAVETY **FERNANDO SAUNDERS** – bass + **WALLY BADAROU** – keyboards repl. YORK

Feb 83. (lp) *(ILPS 9734) <90066>* **A CHILD'S ADVENTURE** [99] [ ]
– Times Square / The blue millionaire / Falling from grace / Morning come / Ashes in my hand / Running for our lives / Ireland / She's got a problem. *(re-iss. Apr87 lp/c; ILPM/ICM 9734) (cd-iss. May95; IMCD 206)*

Mar 83. (7") *(IS 105)* **RUNNING FOR OUR LIVES. / SHE'S GOT A PROBLEM** [ ] [ ]

—— now w/ **many on session, incl. SAUNDERS**

Jun 87. (7") *(IS 323)* **AS TEARS GO BY. / TROUBLE IN MIND (THE RETURN)** [ ] [–]
(12"+=) *(12IS 323)* – This hawk el Galvion.

Jul 87. (lp/c/cd) *(ILPS/ICT/CID 9874) <842593>* **STRANGE WEATHER** [78] [ ]
– Stranger intro / Boulevard of broken dreams / I ain't goin' down to the well no more / Yesterdays / Sign of judgement / Strange weather / Love, life and money / I'll keep it with mine / Hello stranger / Penthouse serenade / As tears go by / A stranger on Earth. *(cd re-iss. May89; IMCD 12)*

—— now with **BARRY REYNOLDS** – guitar / **MARC RIBOT** / **LEW SOLOFF** / **GARTH HUDSON**

May 90. (cd/c/lp) *(CID/ICT/ILPS 9957) <842794>* **BLAZING AWAY** (live + 1 studio) [ ] [ ]
– Les prisons du roi / Guilt / Sister morphine / Why d'ya do it? / The ballad of Lucy Jordan / Blazing away / Broken English / Strange weather / Working class hero / As tears go by / When I find my life / Times Square / She moved through the fair. *(re-iss. cd May95; IMCD 207) (c re-iss. May95; same)*

Sep 94. (cd/c) *(DID/ICT 8023) <524004>* **FAITHFULL – A COLLECTION OF HER BEST RECORDINGS** (compilation) [ ] [ ]
– Broken English / Ballad of Lucy Jordan / Working class hero / Guilt / Why d'ya do it? / Ghost dance / Trouble in mind (the return) / Times Square (live) / Strange weather / She / As tears go by.
below from a VAN MORRISON tribute album on 'Exile-Polydor' / 'M.C.A.'

Sep 94. (c-s) **MADAME GEORGE. / ('b'side by Brian Kennedy)** [ ] [ ]
(cd-s+=) – (other by Brian Kennedy + Shana Morrison).
below with composer ANGELO BADALEMENTI

Apr 95. (cd/c) *(CID/ICT 8038) <524096>* **A SECRET LIFE** [ ] [ ]
– Prologue / Sleep / Love in the afternoon / Flaming September / She / Bored by dreams / Losing / The wedding / The stars line up / Epilogue. *(cd re-iss. Jul02 on 'Spectrum'; 524096-2)*

RCA Victor RCA Vi

Sep 96. (cd) *(<74321 38656-2>)* **20th CENTURY BLUES** [ ] Jan97 [ ]
– Alabama song / Want to buy some illusions / Pirate Jenny / Salomo song / Boulevard of broken dreams / Complainte de la Seine / The balla of the soldier's wife / Intro / Mon ami (my friend) / Falling in love again Mack the knife / 20th century blues / Don't forget me / Surabaya Johnny Outro: street singers farewell.

Aug 97. (cd-ep) *(CDDISC 10)* **HANG IT ON YOUR HEART / (TV theme version) / (instrumental)** [ ] [–]
(above issued on 'EMI Disc')

—— next with the Vienna Radio Orchestra conducted – Dennis Russell Davis

Sep 98. (cd) *(<74321 60119-2>)* **THE SEVEN DEADLY SINS** [ ] [ ]
– Prologue / Sloth / Pride / Anger / Gluttony / Lust / Covetousness / Envy Epilogue / Alabama song / The ballad of sexual dependency / Bilbao song Pirate Jenny.

I.T.R. I.T.F

Jun 99. (cd) *(ITRCD 1) <47759>* **VAGABOND WAYS** [ ] [ ]
– Vagabond ways / Incarceration of a flower child / File it under fun fro the past / Electra / Wilder shores of love / Marathon kiss / For wantir you / Great expectations / Tower of song / After the ceasefire.

Nov 99. (cd-s) *(896309)* **ELECTRA** [–] Europe [–]

Hut E.M.

Mar 02. (cd) *(CDHUT 71) <12009>* **KISSIN' TIME** [ ] [ ]
– Sex with strangers / The pleasure song / Like being born / I'm on fire Wherever I go / Song for Nico / Sliding through life on charm / Love an money / Nobody's fault / Kissin' time / Something good.

Naive Naiv

Oct 04. (cd) *(NV 800111) <86732>* **BEFORE THE POISON** [ ] Jan05 [ ]
– The mystery of love / My friends have / Crazy love / Last song / No chi' of mine / Before the poison / There is a ghost / In the factory / Desperanto City of Quartz.

– compilations, etc. –

on 'Decca' unless mentioned otherwise

May 65. (7"ep) *(DFE 8624)* **MARIANNE FAITHFULL** [ ] [–]
– Go away from my world / The most of what is least / El main tena (what now my love) / The sha la la song.

Feb 69. (lp) *(SPA 17)* **THE WORLD OF MARIANNE FAITHFULL** [ ] [–]

Apr 69. (lp) *London; <3547>* **MARIANNE FAITHFULL'S GREATEST HITS** (same tracks as above) [–] [ ]

Jul 80. (7"ep) *(F 13890)* **AS TEARS GO BY / COME AND STAY WITH ME. / THIS LITTLE BIRD / SUMMER NIGHTS** [ ] [–]

Feb 81. (lp) *(TAB 13)* **AS TEARS GO BY** [ ] [–]

Apr 83. (7") *Old Gold; (OG 9335)* **AS TEARS GO BY. / COME AND STAY WITH ME** [ ] [–]

Mar 84. (lp) *(TAB 78)* **SUMMER NIGHTS** [ ] [–]

Nov 85. (d-lp/c/cd) *Castle; (CCS LP/MC/CD 107)* **RICH KID BLUES** [ ] [–]
(cd re-iss. Jul98 on 'Diablo'; DIAB 861) (cd re-iss. Jun02 on 'Diablo'; DIA 8043)

Mar 87. (cd) *London; (820 482-2)* **THE VERY BEST OF MARIANNE FAITHFULL** [ ] [–]
– As tears go by / Come and stay with me / Scarborough Fair / Monda Monday / Yesterday / The last thing on my mind / What have they do to the rain / This little bird / Something better / In my time of sorrow / this what I get for loving you? / Tomorrow's calling / Reason to believe Sister Morphine / Go away from my world / Summer nights *(re-iss. Sep lp/c; 820 482-1/-4)*

Nov 92. (d-cd) *Island; (IRSCD 10)* **BROKEN ENGLISH / STRANGE WEATHER** [ ] [–]

Oct 93. (cd/c) *Spectrum; (550 097-2/-4)* **THIS LITTLE BIRD** [ ] [–]

Nov 98. (d-cd) *Island; (<524579-2>)* **PERFECT STRANGER: THE ISLAND ANTHOLOGY** [ ] [ ]

Nov 99. (cd) *Spectrum; (544 180-2)* **THE BEST OF MARIANNE FAITHFULL** [ ] [–]

Jan 00. (cd) *Repertoire; (REP 4799)* **IT'S ALL OVER NOW, BABY BLUE** [ ] [–]

Oct 00. (d-cd) *Universal; (E 542853-2)* **BROKEN ENGLISH / FAITHFULL** [ ] [–]

Sep 01. (cd) *Mercury; (585152-2)* **STRANGER ON EARTH: AN INTRODUCTION TO MARIANNE FAITHFULL** [ ] [–]

FAITHLESS

Formed: London, England . . . early '95 by veterans of the hip-hop dance scene MAXI JAZZ and ROLLO. The former had founded 'The Soul Food Cafe Sound System" in 1984, later spending time at the 'Acid Jazz' label before forming his own imprint in '92; 'Namu'. He released three solo outings under various guises and toured the world supporting SOUL II SOUL and JAMIROQUAI. The man also worked with JAH WOBBLE on his 'INVADERS OF THE HEART', ust prior to meeting ROLLO in the studio. ROLLO (a member of Mensa), worked on FELIX's massive seller 'DON'T YOU WANT ME', before remixing the likes of SIMPLY RED, GABRIELLE, LIVIN' JOY, M-PEOPLE and PET SHOP BOYS. One of the top producers/mixers in the world, he also worked on GLOWORM's 'Lift My Cup' among others on his own 'Cheeky' records. JAMIE CATTO was a singer/songwriter, who became frontman for BIG TRUTH BAND, while SISTER BLISS had outings as a solo singer. FAITHLESS revived 'Cheeky' records and had a Top 10 hit with the house dramatics of 'INSOMNIA' at the end of '96, pushing their album into the big league. ROLLO's ascendance from the narrow onfines of the dance scene to muso acceptance was confirmed with FAITHLESS' appearance on Jools Holland's 'Later With . . .' show. 1998's 'SUNDAY 8PM' was a well-anticipated follow-up, but although it contained a handful of major UK hits ('GOD IS A DJ', 'TAKE THE LONG WAY HOME' and 'BRING MY FAMILY BACK'), it failed to match its predecessor, at least with the critics. Three years in the making, 'OUTROSPECTIVE', hit the shops in 2001. A Top 5 hit only in Britain, it nevertheless yielded another massive smash for ROLLO and BLISS in the shape of 'WE COME 1'. Almost a decade into their career, the collective (now with oaster, LSK) kept the faith with chart-topping album 'NO ROOTS' (2004), launched by the TRICKY-esque attack of lead Top 10 single, 'MASS DESTRUCTION'. Both this and follow-up single, 'I WANT MORE', featured on No.1 anthology, 'FOREVER FAITHLESS' (2005), the size of its re-issue schedule showing just how popular the group was with the now thirty-something club generation.

Songwriters: Permutation of quartet, some with ROLLO's younger sister, DIDO. • **Trivia:** ROLLO had four hits:- 'Get Off Your High Horse' by ROLLO GOES CAMPING, which hit the UK Top 50 twice in 1994, while 'Love Love Love – Here I Come' by ROLLO GOES MYSTIC hit No.32 in the summer of '95. His final effort, 'Let This Be A Prayer' hit No.26 around a year later and was as ROLLO GOES SPIRITUAL WITH PAULINE TAYLOR.

Album rating: REVERENCE (*7) / SUNDAY 8PM (*6) / OUTROSPECTIVE (*7) / NO ROOTS (*6) / FOREVER FAITHLESS: THE GREATEST HITS compilation (*8)

MAXI JAZZ (b. MAXWELL FRASER) – vocals / **JAMIE CATTO** – vocals / **SISTER BLISS** (b. AYALAH BEN-TOVIM) – keyboards, vocals / **ROLLO** (b. ROLAND ARMSTRONG) – programming / with others **DIDO** ARMSTRONG) – vocals / **PAULINE TAYLOR** – vocals / + more musicians

Cheeky — Arista

Jul 95. (c-s) *(CHEKK 008)* **SALVA MEA (SAVE ME) / ('A'-Epic mix)** [30] [–]
(12"+=/cd-s+=) *(CHEK 12/CD 008)* – ('A'mixes; Tuff / Sister Bliss).

Nov 95. (c-s) *(CHEKK 010)* **INSOMNIA / ('A'-monster mix)** [27] [–]
(12"+=/cd-s+=) *(CHEK 12/CD 010)* – ('A'-moody mix).

Mar 96. (c-s) *(CHEKK 012)* **DON'T LEAVE / ('A'-deep mix)** [34] [–]
(12"+=/cd-s+=) *(CHEK 12/CD 012)* – ('A'mixes; Nellee Hooper / simple).

Apr 96. (cd/c/d-lp) *(CHEK CD/K/LP 500)* <18966> **REVERENCE** [63] Nov96 [ ]
– Reverence / Don't leave / Salva Mea / If lovin' you is wrong / Angeline / Insomnia / Dirty ol' man / Flowerstand man / Baseball cap / Drifting away. *(re-dist.Nov96 hit UK No.26; same)* (free cd w/cd) *(CHEKXCD 500)* **IRREVERENCE** – Flowerstand man (Matty's remix) / Angeline (The Innocents mix) / Reverence (Tamsin's re-fix) / Soundcheck jam / Salva Mea (Way Out West remix) / Don't leave (Floating remix) / Drifting away (Paradiso mix) / Insomnia (Moody mix) / Baseball dub (Cheeky All Stars remix). *(re-iss. Jun01 on 'Arista'; 74321 85859-1) <US-iss.May01 on 'Mushroom'; 54150>*

Jun 96. (12") *(VENMX 07ST)* **SALVA MEA (mixes)** [ ] [–]
(above issued on 'Vendetta')

Oct 96. (c-s) *(CHEKK 017)* <13333> **INSOMNIA / ('A'mix)** [3] Mar97 [62]
(12"+=/cd-s+=) *(CHEK 12/CD 017)* – ('A'mixes; CEC / monster).
(cd-s+=) *(CHEKXCD 017)* – ('A'mixes; moody / tuff).

Dec 96. (c-s) *(CHEKK 018)* **SALVA MEA / ('A'-C.E.C. mix) / ('A'-Epic mix)** [9] [ ]
(12"+=/cd-s+=) *(CHEK 12/CD 018)* – ('A'mixes; '96 / Way Out West / Tuff).
(cd-s+=) *(CHEKXCD 018)* – ('A'mixes; Sister Bliss / DJ Quicksilver).

Apr 97. (c-s) *(CHEKK 019)* **REVERENCE / INSOMNIA** [10] [ ]
(12"/cd-s) *(CHEK 12/CD 019)* – ('A'mixes; Matty's / monster).
(cd-s) *(CHEKXCD 019)* – ('A'mixes; Epic / Tamsin's drum & bass).

Nov 97. (c-s) *(CHEKK 024)* **DON'T LEAVE / ('A'-floating mix)** [21] [ ]
(cd-s+=) *(CHEKCD 024)* – ('A'-big mixes, etc).
(cd-s+=) *(CHEKXCD 024)* – ('A'-euphoric mixes, etc).

—— **DAVE RANDALL** – guitar; repl. ROLLO (still producer, etc)

Aug 98. (c-s) *(CHEKK 028)* **GOD IS A DJ / ('A'-monster mix)** [6] [ ]
(12"+=/cd-s+=) *(CHEK 12/CD 028)* – ('A'mixes; serious danger / sharp, etc).

Sep 98. (cd/c/d-lp) *(CHEK CD/K/LP 503)* <19029> **SUNDAY 8PM** [10] [ ]
– The garden / Bring my family back / Hour of need / Postcards / Take the long way home / Why go? / She's my baby / God is a DJ / Hem of his garment / Sunday 8 pm / Killer's lullaby.

Nov 98. (c-s) *(CHEKK 031)* <INT 886486-6> **TAKE THE LONG WAY HOME / ('A'-Rollin' mix)** [15] Dec98 [ ]
(cd-s+=) *(CHEKCD 031)* – ('A'-Epic mix) / ('A'-16c+ mix) / ('A'-Grant Nelson / Driver's powerpack / Timewriter's where the heart is.
(12") *(CHEK12 031)* – ('A'mixes).

Apr 99. (12") *(CHEK12 035)* **BRING MY FAMILY BACK (mixes; Boombastic / Robbie Rivera's Phat Funked up mix)** [14] [ ]
(cd-s) *(CHEKCD 035)* – ('A'side) / ('A'-Paul Van Dyk mix) / ('A'-Jan Driver boombastic mix) / ('A'-Rollo & Sister Bliss monster mix).
(cd-s) *(CHEKXCD 035)* – ('A'side) / God is a DJ (first ever mix) / Insomnia (Armand's unreleased mix).

Oct 99. (d-cd) *(CHEKXCD 503)* **SATURDAY 3AM** (remixes) [ ] [ ]

Nov 99. (12"/cd-s; by FAITHLESS & BOY GEORGE) *(CHEK 12/CD 038)* **WHY GO? (mixes; Ferry Corsten)** [ ] [ ]
(cd-s) *(CHEKXCD 038)* – ('A'mixes; Lange / Fused why).

Arista — Arista

Jun 01. (cd-s) *(74321 85084-2)* **WE COME 1 / WE COME 1 (Rollo & Sister Bliss remix) / WE COME 1 (Dave Clarke remix)** [3] [ ]
(cd-s) *(74321 85835-2)* – ('A'side) / ('A'-Wookie remix) / ('A'-Rocket vs Jeno remix).
(12") *(74321 85084-1)* – ('A'-Rollo & Sister Bliss remix) / ('A'-Elliott J remix).

Jun 01. (cd/d-lp) *(74321 85083-2/-1)* <14713> **OUTROSPECTIVE** [4] [ ]
– Donny X / Not enuff love / We come 1 / Crazy English summer / Muhammad Ali / Machines R us / One step too far / Tarantula / Giving myself away / Code / Evergreen / Lion tamer. *(cd+=)* – We come 1 (video).

Sep 01. (cd-s) *(74321 88544-2)* **MUHAMMAD ALI / (mixes: full intention club / Rollo & Sister Bliss sweet love)** [29] [ ]
(12") *(74321 88544-1)* – ('A'side & mixes, etc.)
(cd-s) *(74321 88645-2)* – ('A'side) / ('A'-Architech's remix) / ('A'-Inland Knight's alley mix).

Dec 01. (12"/cd-s) *(74321 90359-1/-2)* **TARANTULA (mixes; radio / Rollo & Sister Bliss funky as fuck / Tiesto)** [29] [–]
(cd-s) *(74321 90360-2)* – ('A'mixes; Rollo & Sister Bliss / Hiver & Hammer).

Apr 02. (12"/cd-s; by FAITHLESS & DIDO) *(74321 92641-1/-2)* **ONE STEP TOO FAR (mixes; radio / Rollo & Sister Bliss / Alex Neri club rah / Alex Neri club vocal)** [6] [ ]

Aug 02. (d-cd/d-lp) *(74321 95346-2/-1)* **REPERSPECTIVE** (remixes) [64] [–]

—— added **LSK** – vocals

Jun 04. (cd-s) *(82876 61491-2)* **MASS DESTRUCTION / WE COME 1** [7] [–]
(12") *(82876 61491-1)* – ('A'-mixes; Paul Jackson big weapon / Tom Middleton cosmos / P*nut & Sister Bliss).

(cd-s) *(82876 61492-2)* – ('A') / ('A'-mixes; Paul Jackson big weapon / Tom Middleton cosmos / Paul Jackson's destruction dub / Tom Middleton cosmos dub).

Jun 04. (cd/lp) *(82876 61870-2/-1) <63497>* **NO ROOTS** [1] [ ]
– Intro / Mass destruction / I want more (part 1) / I want more (part 2) / Love lives on my street / Bluegrass / Sweep / Miss U less, see U more / No roots / Swingers / Pastoral / Everything will be alright tomorrow / What above love / In the end / Mass destruction.

Aug 04. (cd-s) *(82876 64190-2)* **I WANT MORE / GOD IS A DJ** [22] [–]
(12") *(82876 64174-1)* – ('A'-main mix) / ('A'-Beginerz mix).
(cd-s+=) *(82876 64174-2)* – ('A') / ('A'-mixes; Filterheadz / video).

Nov 04. (cd-s) *(82876 66340-2)* **MISS U LESS, SEE U MORE / (mixes; Beginerz / Pete Heller's phela Detroit / Switch's chops)** [ ] [–]
(12") *(82876 66340-1)* – (Pete Heller mix) / Switch's chops).

Apr 05. (re-12") *(82876 69030-1)* **INSOMNIA (remix)** [49] [–]

May 05. (cd) *(82876 68155-2) <8398>* **FOREVER FAITHLESS: THE GREATEST HITS** (compilation) [1] [ ]
– Insomnia / Mass destruction / God is a DJ / Don't leave / Muhammad Ali / We come 1 / Reverence / Salva mea / One step too far / Bring my family back / Miss U less, see U more / Tarantula / Reasons (Saturday night) / Why go? / I want more.

Jun 05. (re; cd-s) *(82876 69929-2)* **WHY GO?** [49] [–]

Aug 05. (re-12") *(82876 71986-1)* **GOD IS A DJ** [66] [–]

Aug 05. (re-12") *(82876 71987-1)* **WE COME 1** [73] [–]

Sep 05. (cd-s) *(82876 72468-2)* **INSOMNIA (Blissy and Armand Van Helden 2005 re-work) / (monster mix)** [17] [–]
(cd-s+=) *(82876 72469-2)* – (Sasha B.A remix) / (Armand's European vacation remix).

– compilations, others, etc. –

on 'Arista' unless mentioned otherwise

Oct 00. (cd) *D.M.C.; (BACKCD 5) / Ultra; <1080>* **BACK TO MINE** (compiled and mixed by ROLLO & SISTER BLISS) [ ] FEb01 [ ]

Nov 00. (d-cd) *(74321 81165-2)* **SUNDAY 8PM / SATURDAY 3AM** [ ] [–]

Nov 00. (d-cd) *(74321 81169-2)* **REVERENCE / IRREVERENCE** [ ] [–]

the FALL

Formed: Salford, Manchester, England . . . late '76 by vocalist MARK E. SMITH, guitarist MARTIN BRAMAH and bassist TONY FRIEL. Completing the line-up with UNA BAINES (electric piano) and KARL BURNS (drums), the unusual punk band completed a 1977 session for Radio One's John Peel show, before signing to indie outlet, 'Step Forward'. In summer of the following year, The FALL released their debut, the 'BINGO-MASTERS BREAK-OUT! EP'. Sharp-witted right from the outset, the shrieking MARK E traversed the minefield of punk sterotypes, the last track, 'REPETITION' a slow teaser to the other quickfire numbers, 'PSYCHO MAFIA' and 'BINGO-MASTER'. The first of many personnel changes was to occur soon after, MARC RILEY and YVONNE PAWLETT coming in for the departing FRIEL (to The PASSAGE) and BAINES (to The BLUE ORCHIDS) respectively. A weird, disappointing follow-up, 'IT'S THE NEW THING' was thankfully not on their glorious Bob Sergeant-produced debut album, 'LIVE AT THE WITCH TRIALS'. Unleashed to an ever-changing alternative rock audience (who were probably now holding down office jobs while daydreaming of their pogoing dancefloor days of yore!?), the studio set (recorded in two days) packed a lyrical angst not heard since the days of The VELVET UNDERGROUND (one of MARK E's inspirators). Quirky punk tracks such as 'FUTURES AND PASTS' and 'REBELLIOUS JUKEBOX' fitted in nicely with longer excursions into experimentation, 'FRIGHTENED' and 'MUSIC SCENE', making this a classic debut worthy of more listeners. MARK E was now in full control after the remaining founding members, BRAMAH and BURNS bailed out (also joining BLUE ORCHIDS and The PASSAGE) to be subsequently replaced b STEVE HANLEY and MIKE LEIGH respectively. What came nex was a piece of punk rock genius, the single 'ROWCHE RUMBLE ditching conventional rhythms in mindblowing style. PAWLET left the band soon after and was replaced by guitarist, CRAI SCANLON, just in time for yet another masterful set that year 'DRAGNET' (1979). A darker, even more experimental affair MARK E's twisted tales of life's stranger characters were summed u best on tracks such as 'MUZOREWI'S DAUGHTER', 'A FIGUR WALKS', 'SPECTRE VS. RECTOR' and the "rockabilly" 'PSYKIC DANCEHALL'. The FALL kickstarted the 80's in fine fashion wit another punkabilly classic, 'FIERY JACK', an ever better versio appearing on 'THE FALL LIVE – TOTALE'S TURNS', their firs for 'Rough Trade' a couple of months later. With PAUL HANLE taking over the vacant drum stool, Mark and Co. delivered tw more classic 45's, 'HOW I WROTE ELASTIC MAN' and 'TOTALL WIRED', their third studio set, 'GROTESQUE (AFTER TH GRAMME)', being released later in 1980. An impressive if no brilliant album, it featured such acidic, "Manc-abilly" screechers 'THE CONTAINER DRIVERS', 'PAY YOUR RATES' and 'NEV FACE IN HELL', the kazoo backing provided by the group manager and MARK E's girlfriend, KAY CARROLL. Next up wa another unusual concept, the 10" mini-set that was 'SLATES (1981), a patchy affair that nevertheless contained another gem, 'A OLDER LOVER ETC'. With founder member KARL BURNS (th second drummer! and extra keyboard player) now back in tow, Th FALL signed to 'Kamera', releasing another diamond of a singl 'LIE DREAM OF A CASINO SOUL' (backed by 'FANTASTIC LIF on the B-side; like all 45's at this time, not from the accompanyin album). They finally found some degree of commercial succes when 1982's 'HEX ENDUCTION HOUR' broke silently into th Top 75. Recorded in Iceland, it was sixty minutes of lyrical abandor excellent songs, however confusing, came in the shape of 'TH CLASSICAL', 'WHO MAKES THE NAZIS?', 'HIP PRIEST' an their most commercial tune to date, 'JAW-BONE AND THE AIR RIFLE'. Later that year, the most prolific band on earth issue yet another long-player, 'ROOM TO LIVE', a more self-indulge delivery that disappointed their growing college/uni fanbase. I 1983, they lost the talents of MARC RILEY, who formed his ow outfit, the CREEPERS (another great band!), KAY also leaving afte she split (not for the first time!) with the grumpy one. Returnin to 'Rough Trade', The FALL excelled once more with two splendi singles, 'THE MAN WHOSE HEAD EXPANDED' and 'KICKE CONSPIRACY', before MARK E's new Californian girlfrien BRIX, came into the fold. She immediately made her mar augmenting on vocals, playing guitar and co-writing a few numbe on The FALL's late 1983 album, 'PERVERTED BY LANGUAGE This set was another to whet the appetite of the faithful (an another illustrious indie chart topper), MARK's mental executio of tracks like 'EAT Y'SELF FITTER' and 'TEMPO HOUSE' t pick of a bizarre bunch. Advancing to 'Beggars Banquet', MAR E, BRIX E and Co. delivered a couple of odd pop singles in th shape of 'OH BROTHER' and 'C.R.E.E.P.', the records not featurin on their forthcoming eighth set, 'THE WONDERFUL AN FRIGHTENING WORLD OF . . .' (1984). Their buoyant rockabil was back in full flow on two numbers, 'LAY OF THE LAND' an '2 x 4', while GAVIN FRIDAY of The VIRGIN PRUNES guest on a couple of tracks. A month later, a 12"ep, 'CALL FOR ESCAP ROUTE', saw the FALL experimenting once more, although th was their last with PAUL HANLEY, who was superseded by th numerous talents of SIMON ROGERS (he had been a member panpipes afficionados, INCANTATION!). With STEVE HANLE on summer vacation in 1985, the band released the disappointir 'COULDN'T GET AHEAD' single, its flipside containing their fir cover, Gene Vincent's 'ROLLIN DANY'. STEVE was back in tin

Mark E. Smith of The FALL

to record their most accessible recording to date, 'THIS NATION'S SAVING GRACE' (1985). Regarded as their best work since their debut, the UK Top 60 album housed the excellent 'PAINTWORK', 'MY NEW HOUSE' and 'I AM DAMO SUZUKI', the latter track MARK E's tribute (sort of!) to the CAN singer. BURNS jumped ship after the obligatory set of singles, SIMON WOOLSTENCROFT taking his place for the FALL's first hit (well, No.75), a cover version of The Other Half's 'MR. PHARMACIST'. This seemed to pay off commercially, especially when the accompanying (for once) 'BEND SINISTER' album reached the dizzy heights of the Top 40 in 1986. Another minor hit 45, 'HEY! LUCIANI' (Top 60 this time), preceded the following year's Top 30 embarrassment coming in the shape of R. Dean Taylor's 'THERE'S A GHOST IN MY HOUSE'. Some time later in 1987, BRIX brought in her old friend, MARSHA SCHOFIELD (both were in BANDA DRATSING together), the keyboard player and vocalist arriving in time for two more hits, 'HIT THE NORTH' and 'VICTORIA' (the latter from the pen of Ray Davies). Now without SIMON, who stayed on as their producer, MARK E and Co. hit the charts (Top 20!) with 'THE FRENZ EXPERIMENT' (1988), a confused set that nevertheless contained one standout song, 'CARRY BAG MAN'. Having also been a friend of ballet dancer, MICHAEL CLARK (who used FALL tapes as his backing soundtrack), MARK E and the FALL collaborated with the bare-arsed performer on the band's next ambitious concept, 'I AM KURIOUS ORANJ' (1988). It was indeed, curious, although the Top 60 album did have its moments, especially in 'CAB IT UP!' and a tongue-in-cheek rendition of William Blake's 'JERUSALEM' (segued with the 'DOG IS LIFE' poem). A concert set, 'SEMINAL LIVE' (1989) filled in time during which MARK and BRIX split up, the blonde (who had initiated her own band, ADULT NET, some time ago) eventually becoming the girlfriend of posh/cockney (you choose) classical violinist, NIGEL KENNEDY; he had previously guested on an earlier FALL album (she stunned many after appearing on 'This Is Your Life', which looked back over NIGEL's short career). BRAMAH was now back in the fold, enrolling in time for their umpteenth long-player, 'EXTRICATE' (1990), their first album jointly controlled by the group's new imprint, 'Cog Sinister' and major 'Fontana' label. Premiered by a hit version of Cold Cut's 'TELEPHONE THING', the cynical but accessible set featured other acidic attacks, 'SING! HARPY', 'THE LITTLEST REBEL' and two more obscure covers, 'POPCORN DOUBLE FEATURE' (Searchers) and 'BLACK MONK THEME' (Monks). MARK then trimmed the band down to a quartet, retaining only CRAIG, STEVE and JOHN to record an excellent SID VICIOUS-esque version of Big Bopper's 'WHITE LIGHTNING'. This minor hit was followed by an uncharacteristic flop, 'HIGH TENSION LINE', although both tracks appeared on the follow-up album, 'SHIFT-WORK' (1991), which added a fifth member, violinist KENNY BRADY. Split into two, titled sides, the UK Top 20 record was highlighted by two more excellent pieces of wordplay, 'EDINBURGH MAN' (still makes me sad) and their umpteenth rockabilly delivery, 'A LOT OF WIND' (as in, you talk . . .). BRADY was let go soon after, DAVID BUSH coming in as a more permanent fixture on their next set, 'CODE: SELFISH' (1992). The album disappointed many of the faithful, although some FALL diehards regard it as one of the best (I'm in the former I'm afraid), its re-working of Hank Williams' 'JUST WAITING' not the MARK E of old, although the hit single, 'FREE RANGE' gets back to grips. Moving to 'Permanent' records (not the most appropriate label title for them), MARK and the lads released their biggest seller to date, 'THE INFOTAINMENT SCAN', which went Top 10 in 1993. Short of a classic MARK E song, it collected together another bunch of covers, this time in the shape of Sister Sledge's 'LOST IN MUSIC', S. Bent's (who?!) 'I'M GOING TO SPAIN' and Lee Perry's 'WHY ARE PEOPLE GRUDGEFUL?' (a Top 50 hit). For many, The FALL "lost it" from then on, their formula of sticking several good (not brilliant) songs together with a few obscure covers saw their fanbase dwindle dramatically. Early in '94, a collaboration between MARK and The INSPIRAL CARPETS on the brilliant 'I WANT YOU' single gave him another hit, the mainman subsequently being invited to do similar things for other acts (notably, COLD CUT and DOSE). The return of KARL BURNS for the disappointing 'MIDDLE CLASS REVOLT' (Top 50, 1994) and BRIX for the bittersweet 'CEREBRAL CAUSTIC' (Top 75, 1995), did little to rectify this change in commercial climate. Now signed to 'Jet' records (once home to ELO!), they added JULIA NAGLE and a few guest members to the fold for their next effort, 'THE LIGHT USER SYNDROME' (1996), gaining some critical respect once again, as well as brief chart action. Returning early '98 on 'Artful' records with 'LEVITATE', MARK E and his crew seemed a tad "lost in music", the album being under par for once. Evidently, there had been friction between him and his "employees", three of them (STEVE HANLEY, KARL BURNS and guitarist TOMMY CROOKS) subsequently bailing out after the frontman became "impossible" to work with. Unperturbed, MARK E talked about a spoken-word album, 'THE POST NEARLY MAN', while the DOSE track, 'INCH' (a No.7 in John Peel's 1997 Festive 50), finally hit the shops early in '99. The FALL (Mk.1998/99) were back soon after, NAGLE standing by her man while newcomers NEVILLE WILDING, TOM HEAD and ADAM HALAL (the former two both session men on the last set – ADAM replaced KAREN LATHAM) were beginning to "fall" into place. That spring, album number thirty odd, 'THE MARSHALL SUITE', was dispatched to the shops and although it was a slight improvement the record found no new fans in the way of sales. Never far from the music biz tabloids, MARK E appeared (as a janitor!) in the low-budget movie, 'Glow Boys', while he collaborated with the CLINT BOON EXPERIENCE (ex-INSPIRAL CARPETS man) on the track, 'I Wanna Be Your Dog'. The millennium finally kicked off for The FALL in November 2000 via studio set, 'THE UNUTTERABLE'. Synth-riddled, sharp-lyrically and positively beaming with chaotic rhythms, the set shone out in all the right places, the obscure cover this time being 'HANDS UP BILLY'. A year on and returning to their own 'Cog Sinister' imprint (having escaped for the previous shot on elephant's graveyard label 'Eagle' – once home to STATUS QUO and GARY NUMAN), MARK E and his "classmates" drove out album #f--- knows, 'ARE YOU ARE MISSING WINNER' (2001). A winner it was certainly not, from the obscure nine and a half minutes of 'IBIS-AFRO MAN' trailing after a decent cover of R Dean Taylor's 'GOTTA SEE JANE', it failed to register among even the loyal fanbase. Get back to basics was the call. MARK E and his cohorts issued a rather disappointing album of studio outtakes and nine new live tracks (mostly culled from the band's 2001 US tour) in the form of '2G+2' (2002). Suffering from bad quality and even worse musicianship, the album didn't highlight the full live potential of the group, whilst the studio tracks seemed like the same regurgitated garage riffs over SMITH's stammering/strained vocals. A typical FALL release, nonetheless, but just not their best effort. Towards the end of 2003, the FALL (MARK E., JIM WATTS, BEN PRITCHARD, DAVE MILNER and ELINI POULOU) delivered their umpteenth studio set, 'THE REAL NEW FALL LP', a confusing title that was to have been called 'COUNTRY ON THE CLICK'. With producer Grant Showbiz at the controls, the band even managed a love song of sorts, 'GREEN EYED LOCO-MAN'. The appropriately-titled and muddily-recorded live/rehearsal set, 'INTERIM' (2004), Mark-E'd time before umpteenth studio set, 'FALL HEADS ROLL' (2005). Three tracks ('CLASP HANDS', 'BLINDNESS' and 'WHAT ABOUT US?') were carried over from 'INTERIM' albeit in more "polished" form side by side with another inimitable choice of cover, the Move's 'I CAN HEAR THE GRASS GROW', sung in slurred E. SMITH-ese.

• **Other covers:** A DAY IN THE LIFE (Beatles) / LEGEND OF XANADU (Dave Dee, Beaky, Mick and Tich) / SHUT UP! (Monks) / JUNK MAN (McFree) / WAR (Slapp Happy) / I'M NOT SATISFIED (Frank Zappa) / JUST WAITING (Hank Williams) / ROADHOUSE (John Barry) / STAY AWAY (OLD WHITE TRAIN) (Johnny Paycheck) / LAST CHANCE TO TURN AROUND (hit; Gene Pitney) / JUNGLE ROCK (Hank Mizell) / THIS PERFECT DAY (Saints) / F-'OLDIN' MONEY (Tommy Blake) / LOOP41 'HOUSTON (Lee Hazlewood). • **Trivia:** MARK E. featured on TACKHEAD b-side of 'Dangerous Sex' in mid 1990, alongside ADRIAN SHERWOOD and GARY CLAIL. Just previous to this, he had a solo track 'ERROR-ORROR I' for the Various Artists compilation 'HOME'.

Album rating: LIVE AT THE WITCH TRIALS (*9) / DRAGNET (*8) / THE FALL LIVE – TOTALE'S TURNS (IT'S NOW OR NEVER) (*6) / GROTESQUE (AFTER THE GRAMME) (*7) / SLATES (*6) / EARLY YEARS 77-79 compilation (*7) / HEX ENDUCTION HOUR (*7) / ROOM TO LIVE (*6) / PERVERTED BY LANGUAGE (*7) / THE WONDERFUL AND FRIGHTENING WORLD OF . . . (*7) / HIP PRIESTS & KAMERADS compilation (*6) / THIS NATION'S SAVING GRACE (*8) / BEND SINISTER (*7) / IN PALACE OF SWORDS REVERSED collection (*6) / THE FRENZ EXPERIMENT (*6) / I AM KURIOUS, ORANJ (*7) / SEMINAL LIVE (*4) / 458489 A-SIDES compilation (*8) / 458489 B-SIDES compilation (*7) / EXTRICATE (*8) / SHIFT-WORK (*8) / CODE: SELFISH (*7) / THE INFOTAINMENT SCAN (*7) / MIDDLE CLASS REVOLT (*6) / CELEBRAL CAUSTIC (*6) / THE TWENTY-SEVEN POINTS (*5) / THE LIGHT USER SYNDROME (*7) / LEVITATE (*6) / THE MARSHALL SUITE (*7) / THE UNUTTERABLE (*7) / ARE YOU ARE MISSING WINNER (*5) / 2G + 2 (*4) / THE REAL NEW FALL LP: FORMERLY 'COUNTRY ON THE CLICK' (*7) / INTERIM (*4) / FALL HEADS ROLL (*6)

MARK E. SMITH (b. MARK EDWARD SMITH, 5 Mar'57) – vocals / **TONY FRIEL** – bass / **MARTIN BRAMAH** – guitar / **UNA BAINES** – electric piano / **KARL BURNS** – drums

Step Forward | I.R.S.

Jun 78. (7"ep) *(SF 7)* **BINGO-MASTERS BREAK-OUT!** [ ] [–]
– Psycho Mafia / Bingo-Master / Repitition.

— **MARC RILEY** – bass; repl. ERIC and JOHNNIE BROWN who had repl. FRIEL (he formed The PASSAGE) / **YVONNE PAWLETT** – keyboards; repl. BAINES who formed BLUE ORCHIDS

Nov 78. (7") *(SF 9)* **IT'S THE NEW THING. / VARIOUS TIMES** [ ] [–]

Jan 79. (lp) *(SFLP 1) <SP 003>* **LIVE AT THE WITCH TRIALS** [ ] [ ]
– Frightened / Crap rap 2 – Like to blow / Rebellious jukebox / No Xmas for John Quays / Mother-sister! / Industrial estate / Underground medecin / Two steps back / Live at the witch trials / Futures and pasts / Music scene. *(cd-iss. Jun97 & Nov01 on 'Cog Sinister'; COGVP 103CD) <US cd-iss. 1997 on 'Resurgent'; 4107> (lp re-iss. Aug02 on 'Turning Point'; TPM 02208) (cd re-iss. Nov01 on 'Cog Sinister'; COGVP 103CD) <(US+cd re-iss. Nov02 on 'Cog Sinister'+=; COGVP 138CD>)* – Bingo master / Psycho mafia / Repetition. *(d-cd iss.Jan04 on 'Castle'+=; CMQCD 847)* – (bonus tracks).

— **MARK E.** (now sole founder), **RILEY** (now guitar) and **PAWLETT** recruited **STEVE HANLEY** (b.20 May'59, Dublin, Ireland) – bass repl. BRAMAH who also joined BLUE ORCHIDS / **MIKE LEIGH** – drums repl. BURNS who also joined The PASSAGE and P.I.L.

Jul 79. (7") *(SF 11)* **ROWCHE RUMBLE. / IN MY AREA** [ ] [–]

— **CRAIG SCANLON** (b. 7 Dec'60) – guitar (RILEY now guitar, keyboards) repl. PAWLETT

Oct 79. (lp) *(SFLP 4)* **DRAGNET** [ ] [–]
– Psykick dancehall / A figure walks / Printhead / Dice man / Before the Moon falls / Your heart out / Muzorewi's daughter / Flat of angles / Choc-stock / Spectre vs. rector / Put away. *(re-iss. Dec90 lp/cd; SFAL/SPLPCD 4) (cd re-iss. Nov01 on 'Cog Sinister'; COGVP 113CD) (lp re-iss. Aug02 on 'Turning Point'; TPM 02209) (<US+cd re-iss. Nov02 on 'Cog Sinister'+=; COGVP 140>)* – Rowche rumble / In my area / Fiery Jack / 2nd dark age / Psykick dancehall No.2. *(d-cd iss.Jan04 on 'Castle'+=; CMQDD 848)* – (bonus tracks).

Jan 80. (7") *(SF 13)* **FIERY JACK. / SECOND DARK AGE / PSYKICK DANCEHALL II** [ ] [–]

Rough Trade | not iss.

May 80. (lp) *(ROUGH 10)* **THE FALL LIVE – TOTALE'S TURNS (IT'S NOW OR NEVER)** (live) [ ] [–]
– (intro) – Fiery Jack / Rowche rumble / Muzorewi's daughter / In my area / Choc-stock / Spectre vs. rector 2 / Cary Grant's wedding / That man / New puritan / No Xmas for John Quays. *(cd-iss. Nov92 on 'Dojo'; DOJOCD 83) (cd re-iss. Mar04 on 'Castle'+=; CMRCD 882)*

— **PAUL HANLEY** – drums; repl. LEIGH

Jun 80. (7") *(RT 048)* **HOW I WROTE ELASTIC MAN. / CITY HOBGOBLINS** [ ] [–]

Sep 80. (7") *(RT 056)* **TOTALLY WIRED. / PUTTA BLOCK** [ ] [–]

— **KAY CARROLL** their manager augmented p/t on backing vocals, kazoo

Nov 80. (lp) *(ROUGH 18)* **GROTESQUE (AFTER THE GRAMME)** [ ] [ ]
– Pay your rates / English scheme / New face in Hell / C'n'c Smithering / The container drivers / Impression of J. Temperance / In the park / W.M.C. – Blob 59 / Gramme Friday / The N.W.R.A. *(<cd-iss. Sep93 on 'Castle'; CLACD 391>) (cd re-iss. Jun98 on 'Essential'; ESMCD 640) (lp re-iss. Oct02 on 'Turning Point'; TPM 02210) (cd re-iss. Mar04 on 'Castle'+=; CMRCD 883)*

Apr 81. (10"m-lp) *(RT 071)* **SLATES** [ ] [–]
– Middle mass / An older lover etc. / Prole art threat / Fit and working again / Slates, slags, etc. / Leave the capitol. *(cd-iss. Sep04 on 'Castle'+=; CMRCD 1006)* – (Peel sessions).

— **KARL BURNS** – drums returned now alongside **SMITH, RILEY, SCANLON, S and P HANLEY**

Kamera | not iss.

Nov 81. (7") *(ERA 001)* **LIE DREAM OF A CASINO SOUL. / FANTASTIC LIFE** [ ] [–]

Mar 82. (lp) *(KAM 005)* **HEX ENDUCTION HOUR** [71] [–]
– The classical / Jaw-bone and the air-rifle / Hip priest / Fortress – Deer park / Mere psued mag. ed / Winter / Winter 2 / Just step s'ways / Who makes the Nazis? / Iceland / And this day. *(re-iss. 1987 on 'Line'; LILP 400126) (<cd-iss. Sep89 & Mar98; LICD 900126>) <US cd-iss. 1999 on 'Resurgent'; 4486> (<cd re-iss. Nov02 on 'Cog Sinister'; COGVP 141CD>) (d-cd iss.Jan05 on 'Castle'+=; CMQDD 1059)* – I'm into CB / Session musician (live) / Jazzed up funk shit (live) / I'm into CB (live) / And this day (live) / Deer park (live) / And this day – revisited (live). *(d-lp iss.Sep05 on 'Narnack'+=; 40040)*

Apr 82. (7") *(ERA 004)* **LOOK KNOW. / I'M INTO C.B.** [ ] [–]

Nov 82. (lp) *(KAM 011)* **ROOM TO LIVE** [ ] [–]
– Joker hysterical face / Marquee cha-cha / Hard life in the country / Room to live / Detective instinct / Solicitor in studio / Papal visit. *(re-iss. Oct87 on 'Line'; LILP 400109) (cd-iss. Apr98 & Nov01 on 'Cog Sinister'; COGVP 105CD) <US cd-iss. 1998 on 'Resurgent'; 4257> (cd re-iss. Apr02 on 'Cog Sinister'; COGVP 119CD) (<US+cd-iss. Nov02 on 'Cog Sinister'; COGVP 139CD>) (cd re-iss. May05 on 'Castle'+=; CMRCD 1135) (d-lp iss.Sep05 on 'Narnack'+=; 40041)* – (bonus tracks).

— reverted to quintet when RILEY left to form MARC RILEY & THE CREEPERS (note that their manager and p/t member KAY CARROLL also departed)

Rough Trade | not iss.

Jun 83. (7") *(RT 133)* **THE MAN WHOSE HEAD EXPANDED. / LUDD GANG** [ ] [–]

Oct 83. (d7") *(RT 143)* **KICKER CONSPIRACY. // WINGS / CONTAINER DRIVERS (live) / NEW PURITANS (live)** [ ] [–]

— added **LAURA-ELISE** (now BRIX E. SMITH) (b. California, USA) – guitar, vocals (ex-BANDA DRATSING) P. HANLEY added keyboards and BURNS added lead bass to their repertoire

Dec 83. (lp/c) *(ROUGH/+C 62)* **PERVERTED BY LANGUAGE** [ ] [–]
– Eat y'self fitter / Neighbourhood of infinity / Garden / Hotel Bloedel / I feel voxish / Tempo house / Hexen definitive / Strife knot. *(re-iss. Oct87 on 'Line'; LILP 400116) (cd-iss. Sep89+=; LICD 900116)* – Oh! brother / God-box / C.R.E.E.P. / Pat-trip dispenser. *(<cd re-iss. Sep93 on 'Castle'; CLACD 392>) (cd re-iss. Feb98 on 'Cog Sinister – Voiceprint'; COGVP 104CD) (cd re-iss. Jun98 on 'Essential'; ESMCD 639) (d-cd iss.May05 on 'Castle'+=; CMQDD 1134)*

Beggars Banquet | Beggars Banquet

Jun 84. (7") *(BEG 110)* **OH BROTHER. / GOD-BOX** [ ] [–]
(12"+=) *(BEG 110T)* – ('A'instrumental).

Aug 84. (7") *(BEG 116)* **C.R.E.E.P. / PAT-TRIP DISPENSER** [ ] [–]
(12"green+=/12"s) *(BEG 116T/+P)* – ('A'extended).

— added **GAVIN FRIDAY** – some vocals (of VIRGIN PRUNES) (on next 2 releases)

Sep 84. (lp/c) *(<BEGA/+C 58>)* **THE WONDERFUL AND FRIGHTENING WORLD OF . . .** [62] [ ]
– Lay of the land / 2 x 4 / Copped it / Elves / Slang king / Bug day / Stephen song / Craigness / Disney's dream debased. *(re-iss. Jul88 on 'Beggars Banquet' lp/c)(cd+=; BBL/+C 58)(BBL 58CD)* – Oh! brother / Draygo's guilt / God-box / Clear off! / C.R.E.E.P. / Pat-trip dispenser / No bulbs.

Oct 84. (12"ep) *(BEG 120E)* **CALL FOR ESCAPE ROUTE** [ ] [–]
– Draygo's Guilt / No bulbs / Clear Off!.
(with free-7") **NO BULBS 3. / SLANG KING**

— **SIMON ROGERS** – bass, keyboards repl. P. HANLEY (he cont. with KISS THE BLADE) (GAVIN returned to VIRGIN PRUNES and S. HANLEY took a holiday)

Jul 85. (7") *(BEG 134)* **COULDN'T GET AHEAD. / ROLLIN' DANY** [ ] [ ]
(12"+=) *(BEG 134T)* – Petty (thief) lout.

— **STEVE HANLEY** returned to join **MARK E., BRIX, CRAIG, KARL and SIMON**

Sep 85. (lp/c)(cd) *(<BEGA/BEGC 47)(BEGA 67CD>)* **THIS NATION'S SAVING GRACE** [54] [ ]
– Mansion / Bombast / Barmy / What you need / Spoilt Victorian child / L.A. / Out of the quantifier / My new house / Paintwork / I am Damo Suzuki / To nkroachment: yarbles. *(re-iss. Feb90 lp/c)(cd+=; BBL/+C 67)(BBL 67CD)* – Vixen / Couldn't get ahead / Pretty (thief) lout / Rollin' Dany / Cruiser's creek.

Oct 85. (7") *(BEG 150)* **CRUISER'S CREEK. / L.A.** [ ] [-]
(12"+=) *(BEG 150T)* – Vixen.

Jul 86. (7") *(BEG 165)* **LIVING TOO LATE. / HOT AFTER-SHAVE BOP** [ ] [-]
(12"+=) *(BEG 165T)* – Living too long.

— **JOHN SIMON WOOLSTENCROFT** (b.19 Jan'63, Altringham, England) – drums (ex-WEEDS) repl. BURNS who formed THIRST

Sep 86. (7") *(BEG 168)* **MR. PHARMICIST. / LUCIFER OVER LANCASHIRE** [75] [ ]
(12"+=) *(BEG 168T)* – Auto-tech pilot.

Oct 86. (lp/c) *(BEGA/BEGC 75)* **BEND SINISTER** [36] [ ]
– R.O.D. / Dktr. Faustus / Shoulder pads #1 / Mr. Pharmicist / Gross chapel – British grenadiers / U.S. 80's-90's / Terry Waite sez / Bournemouth runner / Riddler / Shoulder pads #2. *(cd-iss. Jan88+=; BEGA 75CD)* – Living too late / Auto-tech pilot.

Nov 86. (7") *(BEGA 176)* **HEY! LUCIANI. / ENTITLED** [59] [ ]
(12"+=) *(BEG 176T)* – Shoulder pads.

Apr 87. (7") *(BEG 187)* **THERE'S A GHOST IN MY HOUSE. / HAF FOUND, BORMAN** [30] [ ]
(12"+=/c-s+=) *(BEG 187 T/C)* – Sleepdebt / Snatches / Mark'll sink us.

— added **MARSHA SCHOFIELD** (b.1963, Brooklyn, N.Y.) – keyboards, vocals of ADULT NET, (ex-BANDA DRATSING)

Oct 87. (7"/7"pic-d) *(BEG 200/+P)* **HIT THE NORTH. / (part 2)** [57] [ ]
(12"+=) *(BEG 200T)* – Australians in Europe.
(cd-s+=) *BEG 200C)* – Northerns in Europe / (Hit the north versions).

— reverted back to sextet of **MARK E., BRIX, CRAIG, JOHN S., STEVE** and **MARSHA** when **SIMON** became their producer & studio guitarist only

Jan 88. (7") *(BEG 206)* **VICTORIA. / TUFF LIFE BOOGIE** [35] [ ]
(12"+=) *(BEG 206T)* – Guest informant / Twister.

Mar 88. (lp/c)(cd) *(BEGA/BEGC 91)(BEGA 91CD) <6987>* **THE FRENZ EXPERIMENT** [19] [ ]
– Frenz / Carry bag man / Get a hotel / Victoria / Athlete cured / In these times / The steak place / Bremen nacht / Guest informant (excerpt) / Oswald defence lawyer. *(c/cd+=)* – Tuff life boogie / Guest informant / Twister / There's a ghost in my house / Hit the north (part 1).

Oct 88. (lp/c)(cd) *(BEGA/BEGC 96)(BEGA 96CD) <9582>* **I AM KURIOUS, ORANJ** [54] [ ]
– New big prinz / Overture from 'I Am Curious, Orange' / Dog is life – Jerusalem / Wrong place, right time / Guide me soft * / C.D. win fall 2088 ad / Yes, o yes / Van plague? / Bad news girl / Cab it up! / Last nacht * / Big new priest *. *(c+=/cd+= *)*

Nov 88. (d7"ep/d3"cd-ep) *(FALL 2 B/CD)* **JERUSALEM / ACID PRIEST 2088. / BIG NEW PRINZ / WRONG PLACE, RIGHT TIME** [59] [-]

Jun 89. (7") *(BEG 226)* **CAB IT UP. / DEAD BEAT DESCENDENT (out take from ballet** [ ] [-]
(12"+=) *(BEG 226T)* – Kurious oranj (live) / Hit the north (live).

Beggars Banquet – Lowdown | not iss.

Jun 89. (lp/c)(cd) *(BBL/+C 102)(BBL 102CD) <9807>* **SEMINAL LIVE** (some studio) [40] [-]
– Dead beat descendant / Pinball machine / H.O.W. / Squid law / Mollusc in Tyrol / 2 x 4 / Elf prefix – L.A. / Victoria / Pay your rates / Cruiser's creek. *(c+=/cd+=)* – Kurious oranj / Hit the north / In these times / Frenz.

— **MARTIN BRAMAH** – guitar returned to repl. BRIX E. who continued with ADULT NET.

Cog Sinister-Fontana | Fontana

Jan 90. (7"/c-s) *(SIN/+MC 4)* **TELEPHONE THING. / BRITISH PEOPLE IN HOT WEATHER** [58] [-]
(12"+=)(cd-s+=) *(SIN 4-12)(SINCD 4)* – Telephone (dub).

Feb 90. (cd/c/lp) *(<842204-2/-4/-1>)* **EXTRICATE** [31] [ ]
– Sing! Harpy / I'm Frank / Bill is dead / Black monk theme part 1 / Popcorn double feature / Telephone thing / Hilary / Chicago, now! / The littlest rebel / British people in hot weather / And therein. (c+cd+=) – Arms control poseur / Black monk theme part II / Extricate. *(cd re-iss. Nov01 on 'Cog Sinister'; COGVP 122CD)*

Mar 90. (7"/c-s) *(SIN/+MC 5)* **POPCORN DOUBLE FEATURE. / BUTTERFLIES 4 BRAINS** [ ] [-]
(12"+=) *(SIN 5-12)* – Arms control poseur.
(cd-s+=) *(SINCD 5)* – Zandra / Black monk theme part II.

— trimmed to basic quartet of **MARK E, CRAIG, STEVE and JOHN.**

Aug 90. (7") *(SIN 6)* **WHITE LIGHTNING. / BLOOD OUTTA STONE** [56] [-]
(12"+=) *(SINR 6-12)* – Zagreb.
(12"ep+=)(cd-ep+=) **THE DREDGER EP** *(SIN 6-12)(SINCD 6)* – Life just bounces.

Dec 90. (7") *(SIN 7)* **HIGH TENSION LINE. / XMAS WITH SIMON** [ ] [-]
(12"+=)(cd-s+=) *(SIN 7-12)(SINCD 7)* – Don't take the pizza.

— added guest **KENNY BRADY** – violin

Apr 91. (cd/c/lp) *(<848594-2/-4/-1>)* **SHIFT-WORK** [17] [ ]
– EARTH'S IMPOSSIBLE DAY :-So what about it? / Idiot joy showland / Edinburgh man / Pittsville direkt / The book of lies / High tension line / The war against intelligence/ / NOTEBOOKS OUT PLAGIARISTS :-Shift-work / You haven't found it yet / The mixer / White lightning / A lot of wind / Rose / Sinister waltz. *(<US+cd re-iss. Sep02 on 'Cog Sinister'+= COGVP 134CD>)* – Blood outta stone / Xmas with Simon.

— **DAVID BUSH** (b. 4 Jun'59, Taplow, England) – keyboards, machines repl BRADY

Mar 92. (7") *(SINS 8)* **FREE RANGE. / EVERYTHING HURTZ** [40] [-]
(12"+=)(pic-cd-s+=) *(SIN 8-12)(SINCD 8)* – Dangerous / Return.

Mar 92. (cd/c/lp) *(<512162-2/-4/-1>)* **CODE: SELFISH** [21] [ ]
– The Birmingham school of business school / Free range / Return / Time enough at last / Everything hurtz / Immorality / Two-face! / Just waiting / So-called dangerous / Gentlemen's agreement / Married, 2 kids / Crew filth. *(cd re-iss. Aug93; same) (<US+cd re-iss. Sep02 on 'Cog Sinister'+= COGVP 133CD>)* – Ed's babe / Free ranger.

Jun 92. (12"ep)(cd-ep) *(SIN 9-12)(SINCD 9)* **ED'S BABE / PUMPKIN HEAD XSCAPES / THE KNIGHT, THE DEVIL AND DEATH / ARID'S AL'S DREAM / FREE RANGER** [ ] [-]

Permanent | Matador

Apr 93. (7") *(SPERM 9) <OLE 053>* **WHY ARE PEOPLE GRUDGEFUL? / GLAM-RACKET** [43] [ ]
(12"+=/cd-s+=) *(12/CD SPERM 9) <OLE 054>* – The re-mixer / Lost in music.

Apr 93. (cd/c/lp) *(PERM CD/MC/LP 12) <OLE 055>* **THE INFOTAINMENT SCAN** [9] May93 [ ]
– Ladybird (green grass) / Lost in music / Glam-racket / I'm going to Spain / It's a curse / Paranoia man in cheap sh*t room / Service / The league of bald-headed men / A past gone mad / Light fireworks / League Moon monkey mix. *(cd+=)* – Why are people grudgeful? *(cd re-iss. Jul99 on 'Artful'; ARTFULCD 22) (d-cd iss.Jan06 on 'Castle'+=; CMQDD 1227)* – (extra sessions).

— added the returning **KARL BURNS** – percussion(now 6-piece yet again)

Dec 93. (d-cd-ep/d12"ep) *(CD/12 SPERM 13)* **BEHIND THE COUNTER EP** [75] [-]
– Behind the counter / War / M5 / Happy holiday / Cab driver / (1).

— Feb94; MARK guested for INSPIRAL CARPETS on their single 'I Want You

Apr 94. (10"clear-ep/12"ep/cd-ep) *(10/12/CD SPERM 14) <OLE 094>* **15 WAYS. / HEY! STUDENT / THE $500 BOTTLE OF WINE** [65] May94 [ ]

May 94. (cd/c/lp) *(PERM CD/MC/LP 18) <OLE 095>* **MIDDLE CLASS REVOLT (aka THE VAPOURISATION OF REALITY** [48] Jul94 [ ]
– 15 ways / The reckoning / Behind the counter / M5#1 / Surmount all obstacles / Middle class revolt! / You're not up to much / Symbol of Mordgan / Hey! student / Junk man / The $500 bottle of wine / City dweller / War / Shut up!. *(cd re-iss. Jul99 on 'Artful'; ARTFULCD 23) (d-cd iss.Jan06 on 'Castle'+=; CMQDD 1226)* – (extra tracks).

— added on tour the returning **BRIX SMITH**– guitar, vocals

Permanent Permanent

Feb 95. (cd/c/lp) *(<PERM CD/MC/LP 30>)* **CEREBRAL CAUSTIC** [67] May95 [ ]
– The joke / Don't call me darling / Rainmaster / Feeling numb / Pearl city / Life just bounces / I'm not satisfied / The aphid / Bonkers in Phoenix / One day / North west fashion show / Pine leaves. *(cd re-iss. Jul99 on 'Artful'; ARTFULCD 24) (cd re-iss. Mar06 on 'Castle'; CMRCD 1299)*

Aug 95. (d-cd/d-c/d-lp) *(<PERM CD/MC/LP 36>)* **THE TWENTY-SEVEN POINTS** (live) [ ] Sep95 [ ]
– Mollusc in Tyrol / Return / Lady bird (green grass) / Idiot – Walk-out / Ten points / Idiot – Walk-out / Big new prinz / Intro: Roadhouse / The joke / ME's jokes – The British people in hot weather / Free range / Hi-tension line / The league of the bald headed men / Glam racket: Star / Lost in music / Mr. Pharmacist / Cloud of black / Paranoia man in cheap shit room / Bounces / Outro / Passable / Glasgow advice / Middle class revolt: Simon, Dave and John / Bill is dead / Strychnine / War! / Noel's chemical effluence / Three points – Up too much. *(re-iss. May06 on 'Castle'; CMQCD 1351)*

— added **JULIA NAGLE** – keyboards, guitar / + 7th & 8th members **LUCY RIMMER** – vocals / **MIKE BENNETT** – vocals, co-producer (to MARK E., BRIX, SIMON, STEPHEN + KARL)

Jet Jet

Feb 96. (12"ep/c-ep/cd-ep) *(JET/+MC/SCD 500)* **THE CHISELERS / CHILINIST. / INTERLUDE / CHILINISM** [60] [–]

— MARK E. worked with DOSE on their single 'PLUG MYSELF IN', released on Pete Waterman's new label 'Coliseum'!

Jun 96. (cd/c/lp) *(<JET CD/MC/LP 1012>)* **THE LIGHT USER SYNDROME** [54] [ ]
– D.I.Y. meat / Das vulture ans ein nutter-wain / He Pep! / Hostile / Stay away (old white train) / Spinetrak / Interlude – Chilinism / Powder keg / Oleano / Cheetham Hill / The Coliseum / Last chance to turn around / The ballard of J. Drummer / Oxymoron / Secession man. *(cd re-iss. Feb99 on 'Receiver'; RRCD 264) (cd re-iss. Sep02 on 'Castle'; CMRCD 570)*

Artful Artful

Feb 98. (10"ep/cd-ep) *(10/CD ARTFUL 1)* **MASQUERADE / CALENDAR. / SCAREBALL / OL' GANG (live)** [69] [–]
(cd-ep) *(CXARTFUL 001)* – ('A'side) / Ivanhoes two pence / Spencer must die / Ten houses of Eve.

Feb 98. (cd/c/lp) *(<ARTFUL CD/MC/LP 9>)* **LEVITATE** [ ] [ ]
– Ten houses of Eve / Masquerade / Hurricane Edward / I'm a mummy / Quartet of Doc Shanley / Jap kid / 4 1/2 inch / Spencer must die / Jungle rock / Ol' gang / Tragic days / I come and stand at your door / Levitate / Everybody but myself. *(cd re-iss. May99; ARTFULCDX 9)*

— **SMITH** retained **NAGLE** and recruited **NEVILLE WILDING** – guitar + **TOM HEAD** – drums

— **ADAM HALAL** – bass; repl. temp. KAREN LATHAM

Mar 99. (12"/cd-s) *(12/CD ARTFUL 2)* **TOUCH SENSITIVE. / ANTIDOTE / TOUCH SENSITIVE (dance mix)** [ ] [–]

Apr 99. (cd/c/lp) *(<ARTFUL CD/MC/LP 17>)* **THE MARSHALL SUITE** [ ] Oct99 [ ]
– Touch sensitive / F-'oldin' money / Snake-off / Bound / This perfect day / (Jung Nev's) Antidotes / Inevitable / Anecdotes + anecdotes in B# / Early life of crying Marshal / Birthday song / Mad. men-eng, dog / On my own.

Aug 99. (cd-s) *(CDARTFUL 3)* **F-'OLDIN' MONEY / THIS PERFECT DAY (remix) / BIRTHDAY SONG (remix)** [ ] [–]
(cd-s) *(CDXARTFUL 3)* – ('A') / The early life of the crying marshall (remix) / Tom Raggazzi (remix).

Eagle Mister E

Nov 00. (cd) *(EAGCD 164)* <3> **THE UNUTTERABLE** [ ] [ ]
– Cyber insekt / Two Librans / W.B. / Sons of temperance / Dr. Buck's letter / Hot runes Way round / Octo realm – Ketamine sun / Serum / The unutterable / Pumpkin soup and mashed potatoes / Hands up Billy / Midwatch 1953 / Devolute / Das katerer.

— **SMITH + NAGLE** with **BERNARD FANNING** – guitar, vocals / **JIM WATTS** – bass, guitar

Cog Sinister Cog Sinister

Nov 01. (cd) *(<COGVP 131CD>)* **ARE YOU ARE MISSING WINNER** [ ] Dec01 [ ]
– Jim's the fall / Bourgeois town / Crop dust / My ex-classmate's kids / Kick the can / Gotta see Jane / Ibis afro man / Acute / Hollow mind / Reprise (Jane – Prof Mick – Ey bastardo). *(pic-lp iss.Feb02; COGVP 131LP) (re-iss. May06 on 'Castle'+=; CMRCD 1352)* – Rude all the time / Wake up in the city / New formation sermon / Distilled mug art / My ex-classmates' kids (live on Cologne) / Where's the fuckin' taxi cunt.

Action Telegraph

Jun 02. (cd) *(TAKE 18CD)* <1099-2> **2G + 2** (live) [ ] Aug02 [ ]
– The joke / New formation sermon / My ex-classmates' kids / Enigrammatic dream / I wake up in the city / Kick the can / F-'oldin' money / Bourgeois town / Distilled mug art / Ibis Afro-man / Mr. Pharmacist / I am Damo Suzuki.

Nov 02. (7"ep/cd-ep) *(TAKE 20/+CD)* **FALL VS. 2003** [64] [–]
– Susan vs. nightclub / Janet vs. Johnny.

— **SMITH + WATTS** plus **BEN PRITCHARD** – lead guitar / **DAVE MILNER** – drums, keyboards / **ELINI POULOU** – keyboards

Oct 03. (lp/cd) *(TAKE 21/+CD)* **THE REAL NEW FALL LP: FORMERLY 'COUNTRY ON THE CLICK'** [ ] [–]
– Green eyed loco-man / Mountain energei / Theme from Sparta F.C. / Contraflow / Last commands of xyralothep via M.E.S. / Open the boxoctosis #2 / Janet, Johnny + James / The past #2 / Loop41 'Houston / Mike's love xexagon / Proteinprotection / Recovery kit.

— **SPENCER BIRTWISTLE** – drums; repl. MILNER

Dec 03. (d7"ep/cd-ep) *(TAKE 22/+CD)* **(WE WISH YOU) A PROTEIN CHRISTMAS** [ ] [–]
– (We wish you) A protein Christmas / (We are) Mod mock goth / (Birtwistle's) Girl in shop / Recovery kit 2#.

Jun 04. (7") *(TAKE 23)* **THEME FROM: SPARTA F.C.#2. / MY EX CLASSMATE'S KIDS (live in Cologne 2001)** [66] [–]
(cd-s+=) *(TAKE 23CD)* – ('A'-original video).

Hip Priest Hip Priest

Nov 04. (cd) *(<HIPP 004CD>)* **INTERIM** (rehearsals + live) [ ] Jan05 [ ]
– All clasp hands / Blindness / What about us? / I'm Rodney the oney / Green-eyed snorkel / Mod mock goth / Wrong place / Sparta FC No.3 / Mere pseud mag ed / Spoilt Victorian childe / Boxoctosis alarum.

Feb 05. (cd-s) *(HIPP 005CD)* **RUDE (ALL THE TIME) / WAKE UP IN THE CITY / MY EX-CLASSMATES' KIDS / DISTILLED MUG ART** [ ] [–]

— **STEVE TRAFFORD** – bass; repl. WATTS

Slogan NarNack

Sep 05. (7") *(SLOSI 005)* **I CAN HEAR THE GRASS GROW. / CLASP HANDS** [ ] [–]
(cd-s) *NarNack; (NCK 7034)* – ('A') / (slow version) / Bo Doodak.

Oct 05. (cd/lp) *(SLO CD/LP 003)* *<NCK 7033-2/-1>* **FALL HEADS ROLL** [ ] [ ]
– Ride away / Pacifying joint / What about us? / Midnight aspen / Assume / Midnight aspen reprise / Blindness / I can hear the grass grow / Bo Demmick / Youwanner / Clasp hands / Early days of channel fuhrer / Breaking the rules / Trust in me. *(d-lp iss.Nov05 on 'NarNack'; NCK 7033-1)*

— (May '06) **SMITH + POULOU** recruited **TIM PRESSLEY** – guitar (of DARKER MY LOVE) / **ROB BARBATO** – bass (of DARKER MY LOVE) / **ORPHEO McCORD** – drums (of ON THE HILL)

– compilations, etc. –

Sep 81. (lp) *Step Forward; (ROUGH 18)* **77-EARLY YEARS-79** [ ] [–]
– Repetition / Bingo-masters breakout / Psycho mafia / Various times / It's the new thing / Rowche rumble / In my area / Dice man / Psykick dancehall / Second dark age / Fiery Jack / Stepping out / Last orders. *<US cd-iss. 2000 on 'Resurgent'; 4540> (cd-iss. Nov01 on 'Cog Sinister'; COGVP 123CD) (cd re-iss. Dec02 as 'THE EARLY SINGLES 1978-1982' on 'Cog Sinister'; COGVP 136CD)*

Mar 82. (c) *Chaos; (LIVE 006)* **LIVE AT ACKLAM HALL, LONDON 1980** [ ] [–]
(cd-iss. Jan96 as 'THE LEGENDARY CHAOS TAPES'; SAR 1005) (cd re-iss. Jul97 & Nov01 on 'Cog Sinister – Voiceprint'; COGVP 101CD) (cd re-iss. Sep04 as 'LIVE IN LONDON – CHAOS TAPES' on 'Castle'+=; CMRCD 1005) – (bonus tracks).

Nov 82. (lp) *Cottage; <none>* **A PART OF AMERICA THEREIN** [–] [ ]

Nov 83. (7") *Kamera; (KAM 014)* **MARQUEE CHA-CHA. / ROOM TO LIVE / / (PAPAL VISIT original b-side)** [ ] [–]

Mar 85. (lp/c) *Situation 2; (SIT U/C 13)* **HIP PRIESTS AND KAMERADS** (81-82 material) [ ] [–]
(c+=) – (has 4 extra tracks) *(cd-iss. Mar88+= same 4; SITU 13CD) (re-iss. 1988 on 'Situation 2-Lowdown' lp/c)(cd+=; SITL/+C 13)(SITU 13CD) (cd re-iss. Sep95 on 'Beggars Banquet')*

May 87. (12"ep/c-ep) *Strange Fruit; (<SFPF/SFPSC 028>)* **THE PEEL SESSIONS** (28.11.78) [ ] 1991 [ ]
– Put away / No Xmas for John Quay / Like to blow / Mess of my.

Nov 87. (cd/c/lp) *Cog Sinister; (CD/C+/COG 1)* **IN PALACE OF SWORDS REVERSED (80-83)** [ ] [–]
(cd re-iss. Nov01; COGVP 107CD)

Sep 90. (cd)(lp/c) *Beggars Banquet; (BEGA 111CD)(BEGA/+C 111)* <2430> **458489** ('A'sides; 1984-89) 47
– Oh! brother / C.R.E.E.P. / No bulbs 3 / Rollin' Dany / Couldn't get ahead / Cruiser's creek / L.A. / Living too late / Hit the north (part 1) / Mr. Pharmacist / Hey! Luciani / There's a ghost in my house / Victoria / Big new prinz / Wrong place, right time No.2 / Jerusalem / Dead beat descendant. // God-box / Pat-trip dispenser / Slang king 2 / Draygo's guilt / Clear off! / No bulbs / Petty thief lout / Vixen / Hot aftershave bop / Living too long / Lucifer over Lancashire / Auto tech pilot / Entitled / Shoulder pads #1 / Sleep debt snatches / Mark'll sink us / Haf found Bormann / Australians in Europe / Northerns in Europe / Hit the north (part 2) / Guest informant / Tuff life boogie / Twister / Acid priest 2088 / Cab it up. *<US cd re-iss. 1994 on 'Atlantic'; 92380>*

Dec 90. (cd)(d-lp/c) *Beggars Banquet; (BEGA 116CD)(BEGA/+C 116)* <2430> **458489** (B'sides; 1984-89)
– God-box / Pat-trip dispenser / Slang king 2 / Draygo's guilt / Clear off! / No bulbs / Petty thief lout / Vixen / Hot aftershave bop / Living too long / Lucifer over Lancashire / Auto tech pilot / Entitled / Shoulder pads £1 / Sleep debt snatches / Mark'll sink us / Haf found Bormann / Australians in Europe / Northerns in Europe / Hit the north (part 2) / Guest informant / Tuff life boogie / Twister / Acid priest 2088 / Cab it up. *(cd+=)* – Bremen nache run out / Mark'll sink us (live) / Kurious oranj. *<US cd re-iss. 1994 on 'Atlantic'; 92474>*

Mar 93. (7"ep/cd-ep) *Strange Fruit; (SFPS/SFPCD 087) / Dutch East India; <8355>* **KIMBLE**
– Kimble / C'n'c hassle schmuk / Spoilt Victorian child / Words of expectation.

Apr 93. (cd) *Castle; (CCSCD 365)* **THE COLLECTION** –

Aug 93. (m-cd) *Windsong; (WINCD 038) / Griffin; <404>* **BBC RADIO 1 LIVE IN CONCERT** –

Feb 94. (cd) *Loma; (LOMACD 10)* **SLATES / PART OF AMERICA IN THERIN 1981** –

Aug 94. (cd) *Matador; <OLE 62>* **THE LEAGUE OF BALD HEADED MEN** –

Feb 96. (cd) *Receiver; (<RRCD 209>)* **SINISTER WALTZ**

Apr 96. (cd) *Receiver; (<RRCD 211>)* **FIEND WITH A VIOLIN**

Apr 96. (cd/lp) *Receiver; (<RRCD/RRLP 213>)* **OSWALD DEFENCE LAWYER**

Oct 96. (3xcd-box) *Receiver; (<RRXCD 506>)* **THE OTHER SIDE OF THE FALL** (above 3 albums)

Apr 97. (d-cd) *Cog Sinister – Voiceprint; (COGVP 102CD)* **FALL IN A HOLE** –
(was originally a New Zealand release on 'Flying Nun') (re-iss. Nov97 on 'Resurgence'; RSG 4016) (re-iss. Nov01 on 'Cog Sinister'; COGVP 102CD) (re-iss. Dec02 on 'Cog Sinister'; COGVP 137CD) (re-iss. Jan06 on 'Castle'; CMQDD 1225)

Jun 97. (d-cd) *Snapper; (<SMDCD 132>)* **THE LESS YOU LOOK THE MORE YOU FIND**

Aug 97. (cd) *Receiver; (RRCD 239)* **15 WAYS TO LEAVE YOUR MAN (live)** –

Nov 97. (cd) *Receiver; (<RRCD 246>)* **OXYMORON**

Nov 97. (cd) *Rialto; (<RMCD 214>)* **THE FALL ARCHIVES**

Dec 97. (cd) *Receiver; (<RRCD 247>)* **CHEETHAM HILL**

Mar 98. (cd) *Strange Fruit; (SFRSCD 048)* **THE PEEL SESSIONS** –

Mar 98. (cd) *Castle; (CCSCD 823)* **SMILE . . . IT'S THE BEST OF THE FALL** –

Apr 98. (cd) *Cog Sinister – Voiceprint; (COGVP 108CD)* **LIVE ON AIR IN MELBOURNE 1982 (live)** –
(re-iss. Nov01; same)

Jun 98. (cd) *M.C.I.; (MCCD 350)* **NORTHERN ATTITUDE** –

Jun 98. (cd) *Artful; (ARTFULCD 3)* **IN THE CITY (live in Manchester 1995)**

Aug 98. (cd) *Cog Sinister – Voiceprint; (COGVP 111CD)* **LIVE VARIOUS YEARS (live)** –
(re-iss. Nov01; same)

Jan 99. (3xcd-box) *Receiver; (RRXCD 508)* **THE FALL BOX SET** –

Jan 99. (cd) *Strange Fruit; (SFRSCD 048)* **THE PEEL SESSIONS** –

Feb 00. (cd/d-lp) *Artful; (ARTFUL CD/LP 30)* **A PAST GONE MAD (THE BEST OF 1990-2000)** –

Aug 00. (3xcd-box) *Eagle; (EEECD 010)* **PSYKICK DANCEHALL – THE MASTERS** –

Feb 01. (d-cd) *Artful; (ARTFULCD 35)* **A WORLD BEWITCHED – THE BEST OF THE FALL 1990-2000** –

Feb 01. (cd) *Cog Sinister; (COGVP 115CD)* **LIVE IN CAMBRIDGE 1988 (live)** –

Jun 01. (cd) *Cog Sinister; (COGVP 109CD)* **LIVE IN ZAGREB (live)** –

Nov 01. (cd) *Cog Sinister; (COGVP 125CD)* **LIVE IN REYKJAVIK (May 6th 1983)** –

Nov 01. (cd) *Cog Sinister; (COGVP 127CD)* **BACKDROP** –

Nov 01. (cd) *Cog Sinister; (COGVP 110CD)* **LIVE IN NOTTINGHAM (live)** –

Dec 01. (cd) *Cog Sinister; (COGVP 115CD)* **LIVE IN CAMBRIDGE 1988 (live)** –

Dec 01. (cd) *Cog Sinister; (COGVP 118CD)* **LIVERPOOL '78 – LIVE AT MR. PICKWICK'S LIVERPOOL 1978** –

Apr 02. (cd) *Cog Sinister; (COGVP 114CD)* **LIVE 1977** –

Jun 02. (cd) *Cog Sinister; (COGVP 112CD)* **LIVE AT THE DERBY HALL, BURY 1982 (live)** –

Jul 02. (d-cd) *Castle; (CMDDD 461) / Sanctuary; <81205>* **TOTALLY WIRED: THE ROUGH TRADE ANTHOLOGY** Aug02

Jul 02. (4xcd-box) *Castle; (CMEBX 526)* **THE ROUGH TRADE SINGLES BOX** –

Sep 02. (d-cd) *Snapper; (SMDCD 443) / Recall; <443>* **HIGH TENSION LINE** Oct02

Nov 02. (cd) *Cog Sinister; (COGVP 132CD)* **LISTENING IN: LOST SINGLES TRACKS 1990-92** –

Feb 03. (cd) *Cog Sinister; (COGVP 143CD)* **LIVE IN AMERICA** (live) –

Mar 03. (cd) *Castle; (CMQCD 697) / Sanctuary; <81303>* **IT'S THE NEW THING! – THE STEP FORWARD YEARS** Jun03

Apr 03. (3xcd-box) *Castle; (CMETD 706) / Sanctuary; <81304>* **TIME ENOUGH AT LAST** (out-takes & live)
– OXYMORON / CHEETHAM HILL / 15 WAYS TO LEAVE YOUR MAN)

Jun 03. (d-cd) *Burning Airlines; (<PILOT 173>)* **THE IDIOT JOY SHOW** (rare live) Sep03

Jul 03. (5xcd-box) *Castle; (CMYBX 752) / Sanctuary; <81315>* **TOUCH SENSITIVE . . .BOOTLEG BOX SET (live)** Sep03

Aug 03. (cd) *Strange Fruit; (SFRSCD 120)* **LIVE AT THE PHOENIX FESTIVAL (live)** –

Sep 03. (d-cd) *Voiceprint; (VO 241 004CD)* **LIVE IN CAMBRIDGE / LIVE VARIOUS YEARS** –

Sep 03. (d-cd) *Voiceprint; (VP 241 019CD)* **IN A HOLE / LIVERPOOL 1978 (live)** –

Oct 03. (cd) *Fontana; (077000-2)* **THE WAR AGAINST INTELLIGENCE: THE FONTANA YEARS** –

May 04. (d-cd) *Sanctuary; (SMEDD 017)* **50,000 FALL FANS CAN'T BE WRONG (39 GOLDEN GREATS)**

Nov 04. (4xlp-box) *Get Back; (GET 123)* **THE IDIOT JOY SHOW** –

Nov 04. (lp) *Get Back; (GET 125)* **PEARL CITY** –

Apr 05. (6xcd-box) *Castle; (CMXBX 962)* **THE COMPLETE PEEL SESSIONS** –

Jul 05. (cd) *Hip Priest; (<HIPP 006CD>)* **LIVE FROM THE VAULTS VOL.1** (live Oldham '78)

Jul 05. (cd) *Hip Priest; (<HIPP 007CD>)* **LIVE FROM THE VAULTS VOL.2** (live Retford '79)

Jul 05. (cd) *Hip Priest; (<HIPP 008CD>)* **LIVE FROM THE VAULTS VOL.3** (live Los Angeles '79)

Aug 05. (d-cd+dvd) *Snapper; (SBOX 015)* **REBELLIOUS JUKEBOX** –

Nov 05. (cd) *Hip Priest; (<HIPP 009CD>)* **LIVE FROM THE VAULTS VOL.4** (live Glasgow '81)

Nov 05. (d-cd) *Hip Priest; (<HIPP 010CD>)* **LIVE FROM THE VAULTS VOL.5** (live Hoff Alter Banhoff '81)

May 06. (cd) *Artful; (ARTFULCD 53)* **THE PERMANENT YEARS: PARANOIA MAN IN CHEAP SHIT ROOM** –

FALL OUT BOY

Formed: Wilmette, Illinois, USA . . . 2001 by PATRICK STUMP, PETER WENTZ, ANDY HURLEY and JOE TROHMAN. Coalescing around the metropolitan centre of Chicago and its famous/infamous hardcore scene, FOB became radio-active in '02 via the release of a split EP (with PROJECT ROCKET). After 2003's convoluted 'FALL OUT BOY'S EVENING OUT WITH YOUR GIRLFRIEND', they signed to Gainesville, Florida imprint, 'Fueled By Ramen' (owned by LESS THAN JAKE's VINNIE BALZANO)

Despite the quartet's plea, 'TAKE THIS TO YOUR GRAVE' (2003), it's difficult to imagine anyone but GOOD CHARLOTTE or BUSTED fans requesting this sub-GREEN DAY whining to be played at their funeral. Love them or hate them, however, the album eventually achieved gold-status and attracted the attentions of 'Island' records. The regulation mental health problems dogged the band as bass player WENTZ survived an overdose of Ativan in early 2005. FOB bounced back with the Neal Avron-produced Top 10 sophomore set, 'FROM UNDER THE CORK TREE' (2005), an album for spiky happy people. Unlike the bulk of the album's ham-fisted titles (see below), singles 'DANCE, DANCE' and 'SUGAR, WE'RE GOIN' DOWN' were easier on the tongue, the ear and the charts.

• **Covers:** LOVE WILL TEAR US APART (Joy Division).

Album rating: FALL OUT BOY'S EVENING OUT WITH YOUR GIRLFRIEND mini (*6) / TAKE THIS TO YOUR GRAVE (*7) / FROM UNDER THE CORK TREE (*8)

PATRICK STUMP (b. PATRICK MARTIN STUMPH, 27 Apr'84, Glenview, Illinois) – vocals, guitar / **JOE TROHMAN** (b. 1 Sep'84, Hollywood, Florida) – lead guitar / **PETE WENTZ** (b. 5 Jun'79) – bass, vocals / **ANDY HURLEY** (b.31 May'80, Milwaukee, Wisconsin) – drums (of RACETRAITOR) / plus **CHRIS ENVY** – vocals, guitar (of SHOWOFF)

not iss. Uprising

May 02. (cd-ep) *<UPR 22CD>* **PROJECT ROCKET / FALL OUT BOY** (split) [–] [ ]
– (PROJECT ROCKET tracks) / Growing up / Switchblades and infidelity / Moving pictures. *(UK-iss.Apr06; same as US)*

Jan 03. (m-cd) *<UPR 24CD>* **FALL OUT BOY'S EVENING OUT WITH YOUR GIRLFRIEND** [–] [ ]
– Honorable mention / Calm before the storm / Switchblades and infidelity / Pretty in punk / Growing up / The world's not waiting (for five tired boys in a broken down van) / Short, fast and loud / Moving pictures / Parker Lewis can't lose (but I'm gonna give it my best shot).

— now without ENVY who rejoined SHOWOFF (aka the FOLD)

Sorepoint Fueled By Ramen

Mar 04. (cd) *(SORE 009CD) <FBR 061CD>* **TAKE THIS TO YOUR GRAVE** [ ] May03 [ ]
– Tell that Mick he just made my list of things to do today / Dead on arrival / Grand theft autumn – Where is your boy / Saturday / Homesick at space camp / Sending postcards from a plane crash (wish you were here) / Chicago is so two years ago / The pros and cons of breathing / Genade jumper / Calm before the storm / Reinventing the wheel to run myself over / The patron saint of liars and fakes.

Mar 04. (7") *(SORE 010S)* **DEAD ON ARRIVAL. /** [ ] [–]

May 04. (cd-ep) *<FBR 067CD>* **MY HEART WILL ALWAYS BE THE B-SIDE TO MY TONGUE** [–] [ ]
– My heart is the worst kind of weapon / "It's not a side effect of the cocaine, I am thinking it must be love" / Nobody puts baby in the corner / Love will tear us apart / Grand theft autumn – Where is your boy (acoustic).

Mercury Island

May 05. (cd) *(9880014) <B00041400-2>* **FROM UNDER THE CORK TREE** [ ] [9]
– Our lawyer made us change the name of this song so we wouldn't get sued / Of all the gin joints in all the world / Dance, dance / Sugar, we're goin' down / Nobody puts baby in the corner / I've got a dark alley and a bad idea that says you should shut your mouth / 7 minutes in Heaven (atavan Halen) / Sophomore slump or comeback of the year / Champagne for my real friends, real pain for my sham friends / I slept with someone in Fall Out Boy and all I got was this stupid song / A little less Sixteen Candles, a little more "touch me" / Get busy living or get busy dying (do you part to save the scene and St) / Xo.

Feb 06. (7") *(9850075)* **SUGAR, WE'RE GOIN' DOWN. / NOBODY PUTS BABY IN THE CORNER (acoustic)** [8] Jun05 [8]
(cd-s) *(9884652)* – ('A'-guitars down version) / Music or the misery.
(cd-s) *<(9850371)>* – ('A') / Dance, dance (Patrick Stump secret agent mix) / Snitches and talkers get stitches and walkers / ('A'-video).

Feb 06. (re-cd) *(as prev.)* **FROM UNDER THE CORK TREE** [12] [–]

Apr 06. (7") *(9877932)* **DANCE, DANCE. / SUGAR, WE'RE GOIN' DOWN (Zane Lowe session 2006)** [8] [9]
(cd-s) *<(9878031)>* – ('A') / It's not a side-effect of the cocaine, I think It must be love (acoustic).
(dvd-s) *(9856366)* – ('A'-videos) / A little less Sixteen Candles, a little more "touch me" (video).

☐ Jay FARRAR (see under ⇒ SON VOLT)

☐ Perry FARRELL (see under ⇒ JANE'S ADDICTION)

☐ FATBOY SLIM (see under ⇒ COOK, Norman)

FEEDER

Formed: London, England ... 1993 by Newport-born frontman GRANT NICHOLAS, fellow Welshman JON HENRY LEE on bass and through many auditions, Japanese bassist TAKA HIROSE, the group now set out to become the British answer to the SMASHING PUMPKINS. After slogging around the toilet circuit, the band signed to 'Echo' (home of JULIAN COPE and BABYBIRD), releasing their debut single 'TWO COLOURS' at the end of '95. The mini-album, 'SWIM' (mid '96), consolidated their pop-metal/grunge credentials, while an appearance at the CMJ music business conference in New York, led them to sign for 'Elektra'. Following on from the glistening dynamics and sonic confetti of their well-received debut album, 'POLYTHENE' (1997), they scored a number of minor UK chart successes culminating in the Top 30 single 'HIGH'. Never far from the pages of Kerrang! or the NME, FEEDER continued to scale the charts via two equally enterprising hard rock-meets-indie sets, 'YESTERDAY WENT TOO SOON' (1999) and 'ECHO PARK' (2001). The band were subsequently dealt the cruellest of blows with the suicide hanging of JON LEE on the 7th of January 2002. After deciding to carry on at the behest of LEE's family, they recruited former SKUNK ANANSIE drummer MARK RICHARDSON and set about recording 'COMFORT IN SOUND' (2002). As its title inferred, this was an attempt to both come to terms with, and find some kind of meaning in tragedy. Often uncomfortably intimate, the record nevertheless achieved its own natural catharsis over the course of its song cycle and reached the UK Top 10. While a new wave of Welsh acts stormed the pop barricades, veterans like NICHOLAS still had enough good tunes to count: January 2005 saw the release of Top 5 single, 'TUMBLE AND FALL', and near chart-topping fifth album, 'PUSHING THE SENSES', co-produced by Gil Norton. For the remainder of the year, FEEDER served up three major hits, 'FEELING A MOMENT', 'PUSHING THE SENSES' and the double-A side, 'SHATTER' / 'TENDER', all lining up – together with fresh recording 'LOST & FOUND' – on career retrospective 'THE SINGLES' (2006).

• **Covered:** CAN'T STAND LOSING YOU (Police) / THE POWER OF LOVE (Frankie Goes To Hollywood).

Album rating: POLYTHENE (*6) / YESTERDAY WENT TOO SOON (*6) / ECHO PARK (*6) / COMFORT IN SOUND (*7) / PUSHING THE SENSES (*6) / THE SINGLES compilation (*7)

GRANT NICHOLAS (b.12 Nov'67, Newport, Wales) – vocals, guitar / **TAKA HIROSE** (b.28 Jul'67, Nagoya, Japan) – bass / **JON HENRY LEE** (b.26 Mar'68, Newport, Wales)- drums

Echo Elektra

Oct 95. (7"/cd-s) *(ecs/+cd 13)* **TWO COLOURS** [ ] [–]
– Chicken on a bone / Pictures of pain.

May 96. (m-cd/m-c/m-lp) *(ech cd/mc/lp 9)* **SWIM** [ ] [–]
– Sweet 16 / Stereo world / W.I.T. / Descend / World asleep / Swim. *(m-cd re-iss. Oct98; same) (re-iss. Jul01 as 'SWIM (resurfaced)'+=; echcd 38)* – Shade / Elegy / Chicken on a bone / Spill / Forgiven / Crash (video) / Cement (video).

Oct 96. (7") *(ecs 27)* **STEREO WORLD. / MY PERFECT DAY** [ ] [–]
(cd-s+=) *(ecscd 27)* – World asleep / Change.

Feb 97. (7") *(ecs 32)* **TANGERINE. / RHUBARB** [60] [–]
(cd-s+=) *(ecscd 32)* – Rain.
(cd-s+=) *(ecscx 32)* – ('A'side) / TV me / Elegy.

Apr 97. (7") *(ecs 36)* **CEMENT. / PICTURES OF PAIN** 53 –
(cd-s+=) *(ecscd 36)* – Undivided.
(cd-s) *(ecscx 36)* – ('A'live) / Tangerine (live) / Shade (live) / Stereo world (live).

May 97. (cd/c/lp) *(ech cd/mc/lp 15)* <62085> **POLYTHENE** 65
– Polythene girl / My perfect day / Cement / Crash / Radiation / Suffocate / Descend / Stereo world / Tangerine / Waterfall / Forgive / Twentieth century trip. *(re-iss. Oct97 & Oct99 cd/c; ech cd/mc 19)*

Aug 97. (7") *(ecs 42)* **CRASH. / HERE IN THE BUBBLE** 48 –
(cd-s+=) *(ecscd 42)* – Forgive (acoustic) / Stereo world (video).
(cd-s) *(ecscx 42)* – ('A'side) / Undivided / Swim (version) / Tangerine (video).

Oct 97. (7"colrd) *(ecs 44)* **HIGH. / WHEN THE MORNING COMES** 24 –
(cd-s+=) *(ecscd 44)* – Women in towels / Cement (video cd-rom).
(cd-s) *(ecscx 44)* – ('A'side) / ('A'acoustic) / Sweet 16 / Crash (video cd-rom).

Feb 98. (7"purple) *(ecs 52)* **SUFFOCATE. / ECLIPSE** 37 –
(cd-s+=) *(ecscd 52)* – Cockroach / High (video – live).
(cd-s) *(ecscx 52)* – ('A'side) / Dry (acoustic) / Teddy bear / Descend (live).

Mar 99. (7") *(ecs 75)* **DAY IN DAY OUT. / CAN'T DANCE TO DISCO / HONEYFUZZ** 31 –
(cd-s) *(ecscd 75)* – ('A'side) / I need a buzz / Fly.
(cd-s) *(ecscx 75)* – ('A'side) / Can't dance to disco / Don't bring me down.

May 99. (c-s/cd-s) *(ecs mc/cd 77)* **INSOMNIA / SPACE AGE HERO / LIVING IN PARANOID** 22 –
(cd-s) *(ecscx 77)* – ('A'side) / Divebomb / Fly.

Aug 99. (c-s) *(ecsmc 79)* **YESTERDAY WENT TOO SOON / OXIDISE / TOMORROW SHINE** 20 –
(cd-s) *(ecscd 79)* – ('A'side) / Getting to know you well / Tomorrow shine.
(cd-s) *(ecscx 79)* – ('A'side) / Rubberband / Slide.

Aug 99. (cd/c/lp) *(ech cd/mc/lp 28)* <62400> **YESTERDAY WENT TOO SOON** 8 Oct99
– Anaesthetic / Insomnia / Picture of perfect youth / Yesterday went too soon / Waiting for changes / Radioman / Day in day out / Tinsel town / You're my evergreen / Dry / Hole in my head / So well / Paperfaces. *(d-cd; echcx 28)* – Bubble head.

Nov 99. (c-s) *(ecsmc 85)* **PAPERFACES / WHOOEY / WAITING FOR CHANGES (session)** 41 –
(cd-s) *(ecscd 85)* – (first two tracks) / Tinsel town (session).
(cd-s) *(ecscx 85)* – ('A'side) / Crash mat / You're my evergreen (session).

Echo Pony Canyon

Jan 01. (7"orange) *(ecs 106)* **BUCK ROGERS. / SEX TYPE DRUG** 5 –
(cd-s) *(ecscd106)* – ('A'side) / Purple / Heads.
(cd-s) *(ecscx 106)* – ('A'side) / We the electronic / 21st Century meltdown / ('A'-CD-Rom).

Apr 01. (7") *(ecs 107)* **SEVEN DAYS IN THE SUN. / JUST A DAY** 14 –
(c-s+=/cd-s+=) *(esc mc/cd 107)* – Home for the summer.
(cd-s) *(ecscx 107)* – ('A'side) / Reminders / Forever glow / ('A'-CD-Rom).

Apr 01. (cd/c/lp) *(ech cd/mc/lp 34)* **ECHO PARK** 5 –
– Standing on the edge / Buck Rogers / Piece by piece / Seven days in the sun / We can't rewind / Turn / Choka / Oxygen / Tell all your friends / Under the weather / Satellite news / Bug / Just a day.

Jul 01. (7"/cd-s) *(ech/+cd 116)* **TURN. / COMING BACK AROUND / BRING IT HOME** 27 –
(c-s) *(echcs 116)* – (first & third tracks) / San Diego.
(cd-s) *(echcx 116)* – ('A'side) / Bad hair day / ('A'-CD-Rom) / (the making of Echo Park).

Sep 01. (cd) <1521> **SEVEN DAYS IN THE SUN** –
– Seven days in the sun / Satellite news / Home for summer / Reminders / Forever glow / We the electronic / W.I.T. / High acoustic / Sry acoustic.

Dec 01. (7"orange) *(ecs/+mc 121)* **JUST A DAY. / EARLY** 12 –
(cd-s+=) *(ecscd 121)* – Slowburn.
(cd-s) *(ecscx 121)* – ('A'side) / Can't stand losing you / Piece by piece (video).

— JON LEE committed suicide on 7th January '02

— **MARK RICHARDSON** (b.28 May'70, Leeds, England) – drums (ex-SKUNK ANANSIE) joined other two

Echo Universal

Sep 02. (cd-s) *(ecscd 130)* **COME BACK AROUND / FEEL IT AGAIN / BULLET** 14 –
(cd-s) *(ecscx 130)* – ('A'side) / Opaque / ('A'-acoustic).

Oct 02. (cd/c/lp) *(ech cd/mc/lp 43)* <01180-2> **COMFORT IN SOUND** 6 May03
– Just the way I'm feeling / Come back around / Helium / Child in you / Comfort in sound / Forget about tomorrow / Summers gone / Godzilla / Quick fade / Find the colour / Love pollution / Moonshine. *(cd re-iss. Sep03 w/dvd+=; echdv 43)*

Jan 03. (cd-s) *(ecscd 133)* **JUST THE WAY I'M FEELING / BROKEN / THE POWER OF LOVE** 10 –
(cd-s) *(ecscx 133)* – ('A'-radio) / Redemption / Child in you (acoustic living room session) / ('A'-video).

May 03. (cd-s) *(ecscd 135)* **FORGET ABOUT TOMORROW / LOSE THE FEAR / TINSELTOWN (acoustic) / ('A'-video)** 12 –
(cd-s) *(ecscx 135)* – ('A'side) / Bring it together / Helium (acoustic) / ('A'-live video from Brixton Academy).

Sep 03. (7"white) *(ecs 145)* **FIND THE COLOUR. / REMEMBER THE SILENCE** 24 –
(cd-s+=) *(ecscd 145)* – Circles / ('A'-video).

Echo Liberation

Jan 05. (7"/cd-s) *(ecs/+cd 157)* **TUMBLE AND FALL. / VICTORIA** 5 –
(cd-s) *(ecscx 157)* – ('A') / Shatter / ('A'-acoustic) / ('A'-video).

Jan 05. (cd/lp) *(ech cd/lp 60)* <71562> **PUSHING THE SENSES** 2
– Feeling a moment / Bitter glass / Tumble and fall / Tender / Pushing the senses / Frequency / Morning life / Pilgrim soul / Pain on pain / Dove grey sands. *(ltd cd w/dvd+=; echdv 60)* – (DVD tracks).

Apr 05. (7"pic-d) *(ecs 163)* **FEELING A MOMENT. / MURMUR** 13 –
(cd-s+=) *(ecscx 163)* – Frequency (vox & piano version) / ('A'-U-MYX) / ('A'-video).
(cd-s) *(ecscd 163)* – ('A') / Bruised.

Jul 05. (7") *(ecs 173)* **PUSHING THE SENSES. / FEELING A MOMENT (Pete Lavelle's squeaky clean U-myx)** 30 –
(cd-s) *(ecscx 173)* – ('A') / I for you / Crowd of stars / ('A'-video).

Oct 05. (7"pic-d) *(ecs 180)* **SHATTER. / TENDER** 11 –
(cd-s+=) *(ecscx 180)* – Everybody hurts (full version) / ('B'-video).
(dvd-s) *(ecsdvd 180)* – ('A'-video) / Shattered (behind the scenes video) / (gallery) / Everybody hurts (Warchild video).
(above taken from the movie, 'Nightwatch')

May 06. (7"blue) *(esc 184)* **LOST & FOUND. / HIGH 5** 12 –
(cd-s+=) *(ecscx 184)* – ('A'-acoustic) / ('A'-video).
(7") *(ecx 184)* – ('A') / Uptight.

May 06. (cd/d-lp) *(ech cd/lp 69)* **THE SINGLES** (compilation) 2 –
– Come back around / Buck Rogers / Shatter / Just the way I'm feeling / Lost & found / Just a day / High / Comfort in sound / Feeling a moment / Burn the bridges / Tumble and fall / Forget about tomorrow / Tender / Pushing the senses / Save us / Seven days in the sun / Insomnia / Turn / Yesterday went too soon / Suffocate. *(ltd-cd w/dvd+=; echdv 69)* – (DVD tracks).

the FEELING

Formed: London, England ... 2005 by DAN GILLESPIE SELLS, CIARAN JEREMIAH, his brother KEVIN JEREMIAH, PAUL STEWART and RICHARD JONES, the latter the hubby of SOPHIE ELLIS-BEXTOR. Swimming against the tide of neo-New Wave noise and posturing, this MOR quintet clearly valued harmony over attitude, reincarnating the mid-70s, FM-friendly values of 10cc, ELO and WINGS, and occasionally bringing to mind a less tortured TRAVIS or a more Anglophone JELLYFISH. Not surprisingly this pop formula generated a major label deal off the bat, 'Island' releasing a limited-edition of the COCKNEY REBEL-ish 'FILL MY LITTLE WORLD', later to be a massive hit after the band had initially charmed the Top 10 in early 2006 with debut single proper, 'SEWN'. Moving along the corridor to 'M.C.A.', the FEELING subsequently embraced the lucrative album market with 'TWELVE STOPS AND HOME'.

Album rating: TWELVE STOPS AND HOME (*7)

DAN GILLESPIE SELLS – vocals, guitar / **CIARAN JEREMIAH** – keyboards, vocals / **KEVIN JEREMIAH** – guitar / **RICHARD JONES** – bass / **PAUL STEWART** – drums

Island | not iss.

Nov 05. (ltd-7") *(IS 912)* **FILL MY LITTLE WORLD. / ALL YOU NEED TO BE** [ ] [–]

Mar 06. (7") *(IS 920)* **SEWN. / FUNNY CIGARETTE** [7] [–]
(cd-s) *(CID 920)* – ('A') / Sun is shining / When I return / ('A'-video).

M.C.A. | not iss.

May 06. (7") *(MCS 40464)* **FILL MY LITTLE WORLD. / NOT BE TURNED** [10] [–]
(cd-s+=) *(MCSTD 40464)* – One thing that I want.

Jun 06. (cd/lp) *(MCD/MCA 60100)* **TWELVE STOPS AND HOME** [2] [–]
– I want you now / Never be lonely / Fill my little world / Kettle's on / Sewn / Anyone / Strange / Love it when you call / Rose / Same old stuff / Helicopter / Blue Piccadilly.

□ Bryan FERRY (see under ⇒ ROXY MUSIC)

50 CENT

Born: CURTIS JACKSON, 6 Jul'76, Queens, New York, USA. One of the most highly anticipated and hyped MCs in recent years, the much lauded 50 CENT, it seems, spent years on the street, and on the shelf, before breaking through to the mainstream with his DR.DRE/EMINEM-endorsed set, 'GET RICH OR DIE TRYIN'', in 2003. Raised by his drug-dealing mother (who died when he was eight), and then subsequently his grandmother in the impoverished area of Southside Jamaica, 50 CENT himself took to hustling crack-cocaine in his late teens, seeing a stint of prison sentences which eventually turned his attention towards hip-hop. Somehow, he managed to acquaint himself with the late JAM MASTER JAY (of RUN-D.M.C.), who signed him to his 'J.M.J.' imprint, although nothing much arose from the deal. However, through this young JACKSON made friends with the producing duo TRACKMASTERS (POKE and TONE, respectively) whose work with JAY-Z and NAS was notorious on the East Coast scene. They signed him to their 'Columbia' subsidiary, and recorded a batch of singles, the best of the bunch being 'THUG LOVE' (featuring, of all people, DESTINY'S CHILD) and the minor hit 'HOW TO ROB'. Tragedy would strike, when, after being stabbed three months earlier, 50 CENT was shot several times outside a studio in Queens as he was sitting in the passenger seat of a friend's car. 'Columbia' balked and his 'POWER OF THE DOLLAR' album was shelved indefinitely, turning a wounded and disappointed 50 CENT back on the streets, broke and disgruntled. Refusing to quit the music industry, he formed the underground trio G-UNIT with LLOYD BANKS and TONY YAYO and started touting himself on the underground "mix-tape" circuit, his bootlegged songs all appearing on 2002's 'GUESS WHO'S BACK?' outtakes compilation. After EMINEM openly cited 50 CENT as an inspiration on a live radio broadcast, the bidding wars for this notorious enigmatic MC began to escalate, with – guess who – EMINEM finally winning over, signing 50 CENT to his and DRE's 'Shady/Aftermath' imprint; EMINEM even included the underground hit 'WANKSTA' on his '8 Mile' movie soundtrack. Which would bring us to the crossover hit of 2003, and perhaps the most massive hip-hop single of the year, 'IN DA CLUB'. Beginning with the now famous lines "Hey Shorty, it's your birthday, we're gonna party like it's your birthday . . .", the single with its DRE produced beats and catchy hooks proved to be a massive hit in clubs and saw the once rebuked hip-hop artist win massive acclaim with sales and music awards et al. Around the same time, he issued his debut album proper 'GET RICH OR DIE TRYIN'', which was critically acclaimed during the hype. 2003 also saw him strike chart gold with a special DVD/CD, 'THE NEW BREED' and two further singles, '21 QUESTIONS' and 'P.I.M.P.'. Amid the obligatory hip-hop circus of controversy, back-biting and merchandising, 50 CENT released 'THE MASSACRE' (2005) on his own G-Unit imprint. Rap's seemingly endless marketability saw it crown charts in both America and Britain, breaking the 10 million sales barrier without breaking much new stylistic ground. Lead single, 'DISCO INFERNO', went US Top 3, while follow-up 'CANDY SHOP' made No.1, as well the UK Top 5. 'JUST A LIL BIT' made the UK Top 10 later that summer, while 'OUTTA CONTROL' did the same in America a few months later. With EMINEM having already kicked off the craze for biopics of artists still in the first flush of success, 50 CENT starred in his own (allegedly) semi-autobiographical film, 'Get Rich Or Die Tryin'' (2005). Bascially a showcase for G-Unit and its portfolio – MOBB DEEP, LLOYD BANKS, YOUNG BUCK etc. – as well as new material from the big man himself, the soundtrack went Top 3 US (Top 20 UK).

Album rating: GUESS WHO'S BACK? (*5) / GET RICH OR DIE TRYIN' (*7) / THE NEW BREED multimedia (*5) / THE MASSACRE (*6) / GET RICH OR DIE TRYIN' soundtrack w/ Various others (*5)

50 CENT – vocals

not iss. | Sony

Aug 99. (cd-s) <79252> **HOW TO ROB** [–] [ ]

Sep 99. (cd-s; as 50 CENT & DESTINY'S CHILD) *<79271>* **THUG LOVE (mixes; extra clean / instrumental / clean)** [–] [ ]

Oct 99. (12") *<79296>* **YOUR LIFE'S ON THE LINE** [–] [ ]

Feb 00. (12"; by 50 CENT & DESTINY'S CHILD) *<79297>* **THUG LOVE (mixes; explicit / clean / instrumental / explicit acappella)** [–] [ ]

Aug 00. (12"; with DESTINY'S CHILD, NOREAGA & The MADD RAPPER) *<79479>* **THUG LOVE. / I'M A HUSTLER** [–] [ ]

Full Clip | Full Clip

Aug 02. (cd) *<(FCR 2003)>* **GUESS WHO'S BACK?** [ ] Apr02 [28]
– Killa tape intro / Rotten apple / Drop (skit) / That's what's up (with G UNIT) / U not like me / 50 bars / Life's on the line / Get out the club / Be a gentleman / Fuck you / Too hot (with NAS & NATURE) / Who U rep with (with NAS & BRAVEHEARTS) / Corner bodega / Ghetto qua ran / As the world turns (with U.G.K.) / Whoo kid (freestyle) / Stretch Armstrong (freestyle) / Doo wop (freestyle). *<(d-lp-iss.Nov02; FCR 2003DLP)>*

Nov 02. (12") *<7816>* **WANKSTA** [–] [13]

Nov 02. (12") *<(FCR 4001)>* **ROTTEN APPLE** [ ] Jan03 [ ]

Polydor | Interscope

Feb 03. (cd) *(493564-2) <493544>* **GET RICH OR DIE TRYIN'** [2] [1]
– Intro / What up gangsta / Patiently waiting (with EMINEM) / Many men (wish death) / In da club / High all the time / Heat / If I can't / Blood hound (with YOUNG BUCK) / Back down / P.I.M.P. / Like my style (with TONY YAYO) / Poor lil rich / 21 questions (with NATE DOGG) / Don't push me (with LLOYD BANKS & EMINEM) / Gotta make it to Heaven / Wanksta / U not like me / Life's on the line. *(ltd-d-cd+=; 493564-2)* – In da club (acappella) / Wanksta (video).

Mar 03. (c-s) *(497874-4) <497856>* **IN DA CLUB / IN DA CLUB (explicit)** [4] [1]
(12"+=/cd-s+=) *(497874-1/-2)* – Wanksta.

May 03. (dvd+cd) *(493678-0) <10800DVD>* **THE NEW BREED** [ ] Apr03 [2]
– (the documentary) / (the interview) / Wanksta / Wanksta (video) / In da club / In da club (video) / Not like me (live) / Wanksta (live) / Patiently waiting (live) / Love me (live) / Rap game (live) / In da club (live) / The Detroit show: behind the scenes / Wanksta (AOL sessions) / In da club (AOL sessions) / Round here (AOL sessions) / 8 Mile (DVD trailer) / True loyalty / 8 Mile road / In da hood.

May 03. (12"; as 50 CENT & NATE DOGG) *<INT 063511>* **21 QUESTIONS / 21 QUESTIONS (instrumental). / MANY MEN (WISH DEATH) / MANY MEN (WISH DEATH) (instrumental)** [–] [1]

Jun 03. (c-s; as 50 CENT & NATE DOGG) *(980877-4)* **21 QUESTIONS / SOLDIER (with G UNIT)** [6] [–]
(12"+=) *(9808773)* – ('A'-live in NY) / ('A'-instrumental).
(cd-s++=) *(9807195)* – ('A'-video).

Oct 03. (c-s) *(9812336)* **P.I.M.P. / 8 MORE MILES (freestyle with G UNIT)** [5] Jul03 [3]
(12"+=) *(9812334) <INT 088811>* – ('A'-version).
(cd-s++=) *(9812333)* – ('A'-video).

Feb 04. (cd-s; 50 CENT & G UNIT) *(9815279)* <504761> **IF I CAN'T / POPPIN' THEM THANGS / IN DA CLUB (live in NYC) / If I can't (video) / Poppin' them thangs (video)** [10] Mar04 [ ]
Feb 04. (12") *<INT 414211>* **DISCO INFERNO (mixes)** [–] [3]
Mar 05. (cd)(d-lp) *(9880667)(2103890) <43170-2/-1>* **THE MASSACRE** [1] [1]
– Intro / In my hood / This is 50 / I'm supposed to die tonight / Piggy bank / Gatman and robbin' / Candy shop / Outta control / Get in my car / Ski mask way / A Baltimore love thing / Ryder music / Disco inferno / Just a lil bit / Gunz come out / My toy soldier / Position of power / Build you up / God gave me style / So amazing / I don't need 'em / Hate it or love it (G Unit remix). *(cd w/cd+=)* – P.I.M.P. (video) / Blood hound (video) / Back down (video). *(cd w/dvd+=; 9885127)* – (DVD tracks).
Mar 05. (cd-s)(12") *(9880547)(9880635) <9881084>* **CANDY SHOP (mixes) / DISCO INFERNO** [4] Jul05 [1]
Jun 05. (cd-s) *(9882949)* **JUST A LIL BIT / DISCO INFERNO (AOL live session)** [10] [–]
Sep 05. (cd-s; 50 CENT feat. MOBB DEEP) *(9885436)* **OUTTA CONTROL / (other explicit mix)** [7] [6]
(cd-s+=) *(9885269)* – ('A'-instrumental) / ('A'-video).
(12") *(9885302)* – ('A'-instrumental) / ('A'-a cappella).
Oct 05. (-) *<radio>* **PIGGY BANK** [–] [88]
Nov 05. (cd/lp) *(988799-2-1) <56060-2/-1>* **GET RICH OR DIE TRYIN'** (soundtrack w/ others) [18] [2]
– Hustler's ambition / What if / Things change (w/ SPIDER LOC feat. LLOYD BANKS) / You already know (w/ LLOYD BANKS feat. YOUNG BUCK) / When death becomes you (w/ MOP) / Have a party (w/ MOBB DEEP feat. NATE DOGG) / We both think alike (w/ OLIVIA) / (3 by other artists) / Window shopper / (other artist) / You a shooter (w/ MOBB DEEP) / I don't know officer (w/ LLOYD BANKS, PRODIGY, SPIDER LOC & MA$E) / Talk about me / When it rains it pours / (other artist) / Best friend / I'll whip ya head boy (w/ YOUNG BUCK).
Nov 05. (cd-s) *<(9888358)>* **WINDOW SHOPPER / I'LL WHIP YA HEAD BOY / WINDOW SHOPPER versions** [11] Dec05 [20]
Jan 06. (cd-s) *(9879772)* **HUSTLER'S AMBITION / IN DA CLUB (live in Glasgow) / (video)** [13] [65]
(12") *(9879773)* – ('A') / ('A'-P.I.M.P. (live in Glasgow).
Feb 06. (12") *<640411>* **BEST FRIEND** [–] [56]

□ Neil/Tim FINN (see under ⇒ CROWDED HOUSE)

□ the FIRM (see under ⇒ LED ZEPPELIN)

the FLAMING LIPS

Formed: Oklahoma City, Oklahoma, USA . . . 1983 by the COYNE brothers WAYNE and MARK, who reputedly stole instruments from a church hall to get their act off the ground. After a rare and weird EP in 1985, MARK left brother WAYNE to recruit new members for the 'Enigma' album, 'HEAR IT IS'. Their next, 'OH MY GAWD!!!', in '87, saw them strike with many poetic assaults, including the near 10-minute track 'ONE MILLION BILLIONTH OF A MILLISECOND ON A SUNDAY MORNING'. Their reputation grew, with wild, climactic live appearances, highlighting albums 'TELEPATHIC SURGERY' and 'IN A PRIEST-DRIVEN AMBULANCE (WITH SILVER SUNSHINE STARES)'. Phew!!!. Signed to 'Warners' in 1992, and between appearing at the Reading Festival, they released 'HIT TO DEATH IN THE MAJOR HEAD' and the US No.108 (!) album 'TRANSMISSIONS FROM THE SATELLITE HEART'. By the mid-90's, they had secured weirdo posterity, after giving birth to the drug-orientated, narrative track, 'WATERBUG'. Their avant-garde psychedelic (BARRETT / FLOYD) approach was now well behind them, their barrage of sound, once described as the JESUS & MARY CHAIN meeting BLACK FLAG or the DEAD KENNEDYS, took a sharp detour and ended up in DAVE FRIDMANN's (of MERCURY REV) up state New York studio, where the LIPS (now consisting of only three; WAYNE COYNE, STEVE DROZD and MICHAEL IVINS) recorded the spooky but highly commercial 'THE SOFT BULLETIN' (1999) for 'Warners'. The album spawned two hit singles, 'RACE FOR THE PRIZE' and the echo fronted 'WAITIN' FOR A SUPERMAN', which was their most pop orientated work since the 1995 release 'BAD DAYS'. 'THE SOFT BULLETIN' marked the work of a band who had matured in age and in sound. Adding the FRIDMANN formula, the album sounded similar to MERCURY REV's 'Deserter's Songs', although relying largely on its YES-type chord changes/structures and BEACH BOYS harmonies with COYNE attempting to sing in tune (possibly for the very first time). The group returned three years later with an album just as stunning and as beautiful as 'THE SOFT BULLETIN', influenced by Japanese counter-culture named 'YOSHIMI BATTLES THE PINK ROBOTS' (it's a concept album, kind of). From the lush title track, with its swirling analogue synth to the emotionally sweeping 'DO YOU REALIZE', 'YOSHIMI . . .' could be categorized easily alongside GRANDADDY's 'The Sophtware Slump' and RADIOHEAD's 'Kid A', although it seems that the FLAMING LIPS had a lot more fun. 'FIGHT TEST' was issued on the back of 'YOSHIMI . . .' in 2003, an EP of B-sides, remixes and obscure covers that extended the band's diversity even further. In amongst the oddities was the truly hilarious and rather downbeat cover of Kylie's monster hit 'CAN'T GET YOU OUT OF MY HEAD', beginning in a dramatic orchestral sweep, the listener couldn't help but think that the 'LIPS were extracting the urine a little, while making a notable improvement on the original. More obvious was their choices of covering Radiohead's 'KNIVES OUT' and touring partner Beck's 'GOLDEN AGE'. Both songs were given that added weirdness and would probably sit well with their original authors. As for the remix side, there was the overlong but joyous Scott Hardkiss redux of 'YOSHIMI . . .'s 'DO YOU REALIZE', clocking in at almost nine-and-a-half minutes it's always interesting to hear another musician's take on what was already a brilliant song. The 'LIPS were back in 2006 with the highest charting album of their career (UK Top 10/US Top 20), 'AT WAR WITH THE MYSTICS'. Released almost simultaneously with the sledgehammer protests of NEIL YOUNG's 'Living With War', the album was a less overt but no less scathing verdict on Bush and his cronies, as well as the terrorists they claim to be fighting. Groovy 'FLOYD-ian psychedelia was the vehicle for the message, road tested at assorted vintage checkpoints – dig the sample in 'IT OVERTAKES ME', a track used for a Beck's TV ad.

• **Songwriters:** Group except; SUMMERTIME BLUES (Eddie Cochran) / WHAT'S SO FUNNY 'BOUT PEACE, LOVE & UNDERSTANDING (Brinsley Schwarz) / PLASTIC JESUS (George Cromarty) / THANK YOU + COMMUNICATION BREAKDOWN (Led Zeppelin) / DEATH VALLEY '69 (Sonic Youth & Lydia Lunch) / STRYCHNINE (Sonics) / AFTER THE GOLD RUSH (Neil Young) / ALL THAT JAZZ + HAPPY DEATH MEN (Echo & The Bunnymen) / LIFE ON MARS (David Bowie) / WHAT A WONDERFUL WORLD (Nat King Cole) / ICE DRUMMER (Suicide) / CHOSEN ONE + LITTLE DRUMMER BOY (Smog).

Album rating: HEAR IT IS (*5) / OH MY GAWD!!! . . . THE FLAMING LIPS (*7) / TELEPATHIC SURGERY (*5) / IN A PRIEST-DRIVEN AMBULANCE (*6) / HIT TO DEATH IN THE FUTURE HEAD (*6) / TRANSMISSIONS FROM THE SATELLITE HEART (*8) / CLOUDS TASTE METALLIC (*7) / ZAIREEKA (*7) / THE SOFT BULLETIN (*9) / YOSHIMI BATTLES THE PINK ROBOTS (*8) / AT WAR WITH THE MYSTICS (*8)

MARK COYNE – vocals / **WAYNE COYNE** (b.13 Jan'61) – guitar, vocals / **MICHAEL IVINS** (b.17 Mar'63, Omaha, Nebraska) – bass / **RICHARD ENGLISH** – drums

not iss. Lovely Sc Of Dea

1985. (7"green-ep) *<L-19679>* **THE FLAMING LIPS E.P.** [ ] [ ]
– Bag full of thoughts / Out for a walk / Garden of eyes – Forever is a long time / Scratching the door / My own planet. *(re-iss. 1986 red-ep; same) (re-iss. 1987 on 'Pink Dust' 7"ep/c-ep; 731881-1/-4)*

The FLAMING LIPS

— **WAYNE** now on vox (MARK departed)

Enigma Restless

Nov 86. (white-lp,lp/c/cd) *<72173-1/-4/-2>* **HEAR IT IS** [–] [ ]
– With you / Unplugged / Trains, brains and rain / Jesus shootin' heroin / Just like before / She is death / Charles Manson blues / Man from Pakistan / Godzilla flick / Staring at sound – With you. *(cd+=)* – Bag full of thoughts / Out for a walk / Garden of eyes – Forever is a long time / Scratching the door / My own planet / Summertime blues. *(cd re-iss. Jul99; same)*

Nov 87. (clear-lp,lp/c/cd) *<72207-1/-4/-2>* **OH MY GAWD!!! . . . THE FLAMING LIPS** [–] [ ]
– Can't exist / Can't stop the spring / Ceiling is bending / Everything's explodin' / Love yer brain / Maximum dream for Evil Knievel / Ode to CC / One million billionth / Prescription: Overkill / Thank.

Feb 89. (lp/c/cd) *(ENVLP/TCENV/CDENV 523) <72350-1/-4/-2>* **TELEPATHIC SURGERY** [ ] [ ]
– Drug machine / Michael time to wake up / Miracle on 42nd Street / UFO story / Shaved gorilla / Begs and achin' / Right now / Hare Krishna stomp wagon / Chrome plated suicide / Redneck school of technology / Spontaneous combustion of John / The last drop of morning dew. *(cd re-iss. Jul99 on 'Restless'; same as US)*

— **JONATHAN PONEMANN** – guitar + **JOHN DONAHUE** – guitar

City Slang Sub Pop

Jun 89. (7"m) *(EFA 40153) <SP-28>* **DRUG MACHINE / STRYCHNINE. / (WHAT'S SO FUNNY ABOUT) PEACE, LOVE AND UNDERSTANDING** [ ] Jan89 [ ]

— **NATHAN ROBERTS** – drums repl. ENGLISH

City Slang Atavistic

Jan 91. (12"ep) *(EFA 04063-05)* **UNCONSCIOUSLY SCREAMIN' EP** [ ] [ ]
– Unconsciously screamin' / Lucifer rising / Ma, I didn't notice / Let me be it.

City Slang Restless

Feb 91. (pink-lp,lp/c/cd) *(SLANG 005/+C/CD) <72359>* **IN A PRIEST-DRIVEN AMBULANCE (WITH SILVER SUNSHINE STARES)** [ ] Sep90 [ ]
– Shine on sweet Jesus – Jesus song No.5 / Unconsciously screamin' / Rainin' babies / Take me ta Mars / Five stop Mother Superior rain / Stand in line / God walks among us now / Jesus song No.6 / There you are / Jesus song No.7 / Mountain song / What a wonderful world. *(cd re-iss. Sep96 on 'Restless'; 72359-2)*

Warners Warners

Jul 92. (cd-ep) *<40244>* **. . .WASTIN' PIGS IS STILL RADICAL** [–] [ ]
– Talkin' 'bout the smiling deathporn immorality blues (everyone wants to live forever) / All that jazz – Happy death men / Jets (Cupid's kiss vs. the psyche of death).

Aug 92. (cd/c/lp) *<(7599 26838-2/-4/-1)>* **HIT TO DEATH IN THE MAJOR HEAD** [ ] [ ]
– Talkin' about the smiling deathporn immorality blues (everyone wants to live forever) / Hit me like you did the first time / The Sun / Felt good to burn / Gingerale afternoon (the astrology of a Saturday) / Halloween on the Barbary Coast / The magician vs. the headache / You have to be joking (autopsy of the Devil's brain) / Frogs / Hold your head. *(re-iss. Apr95; same)*

— **RONALD JONES** – guitar; repl. JOHN who joined MERCURY REV

— **STEVEN DROZD** (b.11 Jun'69, Houston, Texas) – drums; repl. NATHAN

Jun 93. (cd/c/lp) *<(9362 45334-2/-4/-1)>* **TRANSMISSIONS FROM THE SATELLITE HEART** [ ] [ ]
– Turn it on / Pilot can at the queer of God / Oh my pregnant head (labia in the sunlight) / She don't use jelly / Chewin' the apple of your eye / Superhumans / Be my head / Moth in the incubator / Plastic Jesus / When yer twenty-two / Slow nerve action.

Aug 94. (7"/c-s) *(W 0246/+C) <9362 18131-2>* **SHE DON'T USE JELLY. / TURN IT ON (bluegrass version)** [ ] Nov94 [55]
(cd-s+=) *(WO 246CD)* – Translucent egg.
(cd-s) *(WO 246CDX)* – ('A'side) / The process / Moth in the incubator.

Apr 95. (cd-s) *<9362 43509-2>* **TURN IT ON / PUT THE WATERBUG IN THE POLICEMAN'S EAR / SHE DON'T USE JELLY (demo)** [–] [ ]

Jul 95. (m-cd) *<9362 45748-2>* **PROVIDING NEEDLES FOR YOUR BALLOONS** [–] [ ]
– Bad days / Jets part 2 (my two days as an ambulance driver) / Ice drummer / Put the waterbug in the policeman's ear / Chewin the apple of yer ear / Chosen one / Little drummerboy / Slow nerve action.

Sep 95. (cd/c) *<(9362 45911-2/-4)>* **CLOUDS TASTE METALLIC** [ ] [ ]
– The abandoned hospital ship / Psychiatric explorations of the fetus with needles / Placebo headwood / This here giraffe / Brainville / Guy who lost a headache and accidentally saves the world / When you smile / Kim's watermelon gun / They punctured my yolk / Lightning strikes the postman / Christmas at the zoo / Evil will prevail / Bad days (aurally excited version).

Dec 95. (c-s) *(W 0322C)* **BAD DAYS / GIRL WITH HAIR LIKE AN EXPLOSION** [ ] [–]
(cd-s+=) *(W 0322CD)* – She don't use jelly / Giraffe (demo).
(cd-s) *(W 0322CDX)* – ('A'side) / Ice drummer / When you smiled I lost my only idea / Put the water bug in the policeman's ear.

Mar 96. (cd-s) *(W 0335CD)* **THIS HERE GIRAFFE / JETS pt.2 (MY TWO DAYS AS AN AMBULANCE DRIVER) / LIFE ON MARS** [72] [–]
(c-s/cd-s) *(W 0335 C/CDX)* – ('A'side) / The sun / Hit me like you did the first time.
above was the first ever shaped cd single.

Aug 96. (3D-cd-s) *(W 0370CD)* **BRAINVILLE / EVIL WILL PREVAIL (live) / WATERBUG (live)** [ ] [–]
(c-s/cd-s) *(W 0370 C/CDX)* – ('A'side) / Brainville (live) / Raindrops keep falling on my head.

Oct 97. (4xcd-box) *<(9362 46804)>* **ZAIREEKA** [ ] [ ]
– Okay I'll admit that I really don't care / Riding to work in the year 2025 (your invisible now) / Thirty-five thousand feet of despair / Machine in India / The train runs over the camel but is . . . / How will we know? (futuristic crashendos) / March of the rotten vegetables / Big ol' bug is the new baby now.
(above was an unusual concept in that you needed 4 separate CD players to hear the simultaneous recordings at its full potential)

— now down to a trio of **WAYNE COYNE, STEVEN DROZD + MICHAEL IVINS**

May 99. (cd/c) *<(9362 47393-2/-4)>* **THE SOFT BULLETIN** [39] [ ]
– Race for the prize / A spoonful weighs a ton / The spark that bled / Slow motion / What is the light? / The observer / Waitin' for a superman / Suddenly everything has changed / The gash / Feeling yourself disintigrate / Sleeping on the roof / Race for the prize (remix) / Waitin' for a superman (remix) / Buggin' (remix). *<(lp-iss.Aug02 on 'PIAS USA'; PIASA 09LP)>*

Jun 99. (cd-s) *(W 494CD1)* **RACE FOR THE PRIZE / RIDING TO WORK IN THE YEAR 2025 (YOUR INVISIBLE NOW) (from 'Zaireeka' disc 1 / THIRTY THOUSAND FEET OF DESPAIR (from 'Zaireeka' disc 1)** [39] [–]
(cd-s) *(W 494CD2)* – ('A'side) / (same B's except from 'Zaireeka' disc 2).

Nov 99. (c-s/cd-s) *(W 505 C/CD2) <44793>* **WAITIN' FOR A SUPERMAN / RIDING TO WORK IN THE YEAR 2025 / YOU'RE INVISIBLE / 35,000 FEET OF DESPAIR** [ ] Feb00 [ ]
(cd-s) *(W 505CD1)* – ('A'mixes).

Jul 02. (cd) *<(9362 48141-2)>* **YOSHIMI BATTLES THE PINK ROBOTS** [13] [50]
– Fight test / One more robot – 3000-21 / Yoshimi battles the pink robots pt.1 / Yoshimi battles the pink robots pt.2 / In the morning of the magicians / Ego tripping at the gates of Hell / Are you a hypnotist? / It's summertime / Do you realize? / All we have is now / Approaching pavonis mons by balloon (utopia planitia). *<(lp-iss.Aug02 on 'PIAS USA'; PIASA 101LP)>*

Aug 02. (cd-s) *(W 586CD1)* **DO YOU REALIZE? / IF I GO MAD – FUNERAL IN MY HEAD / SYRTIS MAJOR** [32] [–]
(cd-s) *(W 586CD2)* – ('A'side) / Up above the daily hum / Zanthe terra.

Aug 02. (7"pic-d) *<RE-1>* **DO YOU REALIZE? / UP ABOVE THE DAILY HUM** [–] [ ]

Jan 03. (cd-s) *(W 597CD1)* **YOSHIMI BATTLES THE PINK ROBOTS PT.1 / CAN'T GET YOU OUT OF MY HEAD (KEXP version) / YOSHIMI BATTLES THE PINK ROBOTS PT.1 (AOL sessions version)** [18] [–]
(cd-s) *(W 597CD2)* – ('A'side) / Do you realize?? (Scott Hardkiss floating in space vocal mix) / ('A'-Japanese version).

Feb 03. (7"pic-d) *<FL 1>* **YOSHIMI BATTLES THE PINK ROBOTS PT.1 / YOSHIMI BATTLES THE PINK ROBOTS PT.1 (AOL sessions live in L.A.)** [–] [ ]

Apr 03. (m-cd) *<48433>* **FIGHT TEST** [–] [93]
– Fight test / Strange design of conscience / Thank you Jack White (for the fiber-optic Jesus that you gave me) / Do you realize (Scott Hardkiss mix) / Can't get you out of my head / The golden age / Knives out.

Jun 03. (cd-s) *(W 611CD1)* **FIGHT TEST / THANK YOU JACK WHITE (FOR THE FIBER-OPTIC JESUS THAT YOU GAVE ME) / DETEORATION OF THE FIGHT OR FLIGHT RESPONSE** 28 –
(cd-s) *(W 611CD2)* – ('A'side) / Strange design of conscience / ('A'-helium voice demo).

Jul 03. (7"pic-d) *<16659>* **FIGHT TEST. / THANK YOU JACK WHITE (FOR THE FIBER-OPTIC JESUS THAT YOU GAVE ME)** –

Nov 03. (m-cd) *<48514>* **EGO TRIPPING AT THE GATES OF HELL** –
– Assassination of the sun / I'm a fly in a sunbeam (following the funeral procession of a stranger) / Sunshine balloons / Do you realize?? / Ego tripping (ego in acceceration) / Ego tripping / A change at Christmas (say it isn't so).

Apr 06. (cd)<d-lp> *<(9362 49966-2)><44250-1>* **AT WAR WITH THE MYSTICS** 6 11
– The yeah yeah yeah song (with all your power) / Free radicals (a hallucination of the Christmas skeleton pleading with a suicide bomber) / The sound of failure – It's dark . . . is it always this dark?? / My cosmic autumn rebellion (the inner life as blazing shield of defiance and optimism as celestial spear of action) / Vein of stars / The wizard turns on . . . the giant silver flashlight and puts on his werewolf moccasins / It overtakes me – The stars are so big . . . I am so small . . . do I stand a chance? / Mr. Ambulance driver / Haven't got a clue / The W.A.N.D. (the will always negates defeat) / Pompeii am Gotterdammerung / Goin' on.

Apr 06. (7"pic-d) *(W 711)* **THE YEAH YEAH YEAH SONG. / WHY DOES IT END?** 16
(cd-s+=) *(W 711CD2)* – Time travel . . . yes!! / ('A'-video).
(cd-s) *(W 711CD1)* – ('A') / The gold in the mountain of our madness.

– compilations, etc. –

Oct 98. (cd) *Restless; <(RST 72963)>* **A COLLECTION OF SONGS REPRESENTING AN ENTHUSIASM FOR RECORDING . . . BY AMATEURS** (1984-1990) Sep98
– Bag full of thoughts / Jesus shootin' heroin / One million billionth / Chrome plated suicide / Michael time to wake up / Hell's angels cracker factory / Unconsciously screamin' / God walks among us now / Stychnini – Peace, love and understanding / Death valley '69 / Thank you / Ma, I didn't notice / After the gold rush / I want to kill my brother: The cymbal.

Sep 02. (3xcd-box) *Restless; <(REST 73764)>* **FINALLY, THE PUNK ROCKERS ARE TAKING ACID**
– (THE FLAMING LIPS ep / HEAR IT IS / OH MY GAWD!!! / TELEPATHIC SURGERY / others).

Sep 02. (2xcd-box) *Restless; <(REST 73765)>* **THE DAY WE SHOT A HOLE IN THE JESUS EGG**
– (IN A PRIEST DRIVEN AMBULANCE / DRUG MACHINE / UNCONSCIOUSLY SCREAMIN' / etc.)

FLEETWOOD MAC

Formed: London, England . . . July 1967, by MICK FLEETWOOD, PETER GREEN and BOB BRUNNING. They quickly inducted JEREMY SPENCER and made their live debut at the prestigious Windsor Jazz & Blues Festival on the 12th of August '67. Replacing BRUNNING with another ex-BLUESBREAKERS member, JOHN McVIE, they signed to 'Blue Horizon'. Initially billed as PETER GREEN'S FLEETWOOD MAC, the group made little impact in late '67 with their first 45, 'I BELIEVE MY TIME AIN'T LONG'. Around the same time, they became the in-house band for blues artists like OTIS SPANN and DUSTER BENNETT. Early in '68, the debut album, 'PETER GREEN'S FLEETWOOD MAC' hit the Top 5, a fairly derivative set of white-boy blues which nevertheless introduced GREEN's incredibly instinctive feeling for the music, both in his guitar playing and his bruised, soulful vocals. The promise was fully realised with 'BLACK MAGIC WOMAN', a classic slice of brooding voodoo blues with a lean, blistering GREEN solo. Another single, 'NEED YOUR LOVE SO BAD', followed into the lower regions of the chart soon after, while the follow-up album, 'MR. WONDERFUL', again made the Top 10 album charts. But the real breakthrough came with the billowy wistfulness of the GREEN instrumental, 'ALBATROSS', which made No.1 and saw the band melding their blues fixation into something more original. Listening to 'MAN OF THE WORLD', arguably GREEN's most affecting composition (presumably included for those who found the single too sensitive, was the charmingly titled B-side, 'SOMEBODY'S GONNA GET THEIR HEAD KICKED IN TONIGHT'!) , it was clear that all was not well with the band's frontman, and indeed he abruptly left the band the following year. Taking LSD had seriously affected GREEN and he began giving all his money away in line with his newly acquired religious beliefs, his last recording with the band, 'GREEN MANALISHI (WITH THE TWO PRONGED CROWN)', giving light to his demons in chilling style. Truly one of the most tragic cases in the history of rock, GREEN never really recovered from his mental problems and at one particularly low ebb in the 80's, was even sleeping rough around Richmond, Surrey. Despite his difficulties, GREEN did record a number of solo albums in the 70's and more recently, the man undertook a 1997 comeback tour under the moniker PETER GREEN & THE SPLINTER GROUP. Rarely has a white man played the blues with such feeling (legendary bluesman B.B. KING was one of his biggest fans) and it was inevitable that with his departure, FLEETWOOD MAC would be a radically different proposition. The remaining quartet of FLEETWOOD, McVIE, SPENCER and (DANNY) KIRWAN (who had joined a couple of years previous) cut a further album, 'KILN HOUSE' (1970), before recruiting CHRISTINE PERFECT (ex-CHICKEN SHACK) on keyboards/vocals. The next casualty to depart from FLEETWOOD MAC in bizarre circumstances was JEREMY SPENCER, who, in an infamous incident, went AWOL while the band were on tour in Los Angeles. When they eventually tracked him down, he was living with a religious cult, the Children Of God, and informed the band he was staying put. Surprisingly, GREEN returned briefly to fill in on the remainder of the tour although SPENCER was eventually replaced with session pro BOB WELCH. The addition of WELCH saw the band move ever further into the melodic rock vein in which PERFECT and KIRWAN had been steering the band since GREEN's departure. KIRWAN was next to leave, however, DAVE WALKER (ex-SAVOY BROWN) and BOB WESTON (ex-LONG JOHN BALDRY) briefly joining up. When the band cancelled a US tour, manager CLIFFORD DAVIS formed a 'new' FLEETWOOD MAC around WALKER and WESTON, the real FLEETWOOD MAC not unreasonably slapping an injunction on the imposters. Amid much legal wrangling, the band severed themselves from DAVIS and moved to California in 1974, only FLEETWOOD and JOHN and CHRISTINE McVIE (the pair had since been hitched) remaining. And so began the second chapter in the marathon MAC saga, as the band hooked up with studio maestro LINDSEY BUCKINGHAM and the sexiest woman to ever walk the planet, STEVIE NICKS. This girlfriend/boyfriend team had previously released an album on 'Polydor', 'BUCKINGHAM-NICKS', and FLEETWOOD was suitably impressed. For once, the band line-up gelled and by the following year, in an incredible reversal of fortunes, FLEETWOOD MAC were sitting pretty at the top of the US charts with the eponymous 'FLEETWOOD MAC' album. Highly melodic, airbrushed pop/rock was the order of the day while in NICKS, the band had a singer of a distinctiveness to match the likes of EMMYLOU HARRIS. The classic 'RHIANNON' found NICKS at her most alluring, fuelling the fantasies of clean cut American boys the country over with her breathy purr. While creatively the band were reaching for the stars, personally they were hitting the depths; JOHN and CHRISTINE divorced the following year, while BUCKINGHAM and NICKS had split acrimoniously. To top it all, FLEETWOOD was in the process of divorcing his wife, JENNY. Instead of imploding, the band channelled the emotional turmoil into writing songs, creating one of the most phenomenally successful records ever released. 'RUMOURS' (1977) remains the quintessential break-up record, every track, from 'GO YOUR OWN WAY' to 'GOLD DUST WOMAN' giving a different perspective on the situation. The songwriting was impeccable, not a duffer in sight, and in terms of AOR the record has yet to meet its match. 'TUSK' (1979), meanwhile, was a completely different kettle of fish; expensive, often experimental and bloody long. A double album, it was hard going in places yet there were moments of genius, notably NICKS' 'SARA', a beautifully melancholic ballad which arguably stands as the highlight of her career. Come 1980, various members began work on solo projects, FLEETWOOD recording 'THE VISITOR' (1981) with African musicians while NICKS started out on a successful solo career with 'BELLADONNA' (1981). The next MAC project was 'MIRAGE' (1982), a pleasant but ultimately unsatisfying attempt to recreate their winning 70's formula. It was relatively successful nevertheless, reaching No.1 in the States, although it would be the last band effort for five years. In the interim, BUCKINGHAM released his well-received 'GO INSANE' (1984) album (he'd made his solo debut three years earlier with 'LAW AND ORDER') while CHRISTINE McVIE released a self-titled album in 1984. Eventually regrouping in 1985, the band began working on what would become 'TANGO IN THE NIGHT' (1987). Basically the MAC sound translated into modern musical currency, the record surprisingly made more of an impact in Britain than the States. Like 'RUMOURS', the record was characterised by varying moods and textures, from BUCKINGHAM's clever, insistent 'BIG LOVE' to the cascading 'LITTLE LIES', and spawned a number of major chart hits. This marked the end of the classic line-up, however, as BUCKINGHAM departed the following summer after escalating tension with NICKS. RICK VITO and BILLY BURNETT were drafted in as replacements but on the showing of 'BEHIND THE MASK' (1990), BUCKINGHAM's midas touch was sorely missed. While the record made No.1 in the States, it failed to produce any singles, more calamity befalling the band later that year as NICKS bailed out following allegations in MICK FLEETWOOD's recently published autobiography. While BUCKINGHAM and NICKS played with the band at Bill Clinton's inauguration in 1993, there was no question of them rejoining, and ex-TRAFFIC man, DAVE MASON was hired along with BEKKA BRAMLETT (daughter of the legendary DELANEY & BONNIE). The resultant album, 'TIME' (1995), was released to general indifference although it was competent enough. Maybe the album should've been titled 'TIME, GENTLEMEN' as the band seemed something of an irrelevance in the 1990's. Then again, given their chequered history, anything is possible, an album of drum 'n' bass remixes, anyone? Anything is usually possible with the 'MAC and in 'SAY YOU WILL' (2003), they indeed pulled off the seemingly impossible: getting the original mid-70's band back together to record a fully fledged album – a double set no less – of new material. Admittedly, CHRISTINE McVIE was only a bit-part player but it was as close to a fully fledged reunion as longtime fans could have wished. The end result wasn't exactly spectacular, however, coming in at just under the hour and a half mark. With NICKS and BUCKINGHAM dominating the songwriting, there was an unevenness to proceedings, something only exacerbated by the wildly indulgent running time.

• **Songwriters:** GREEN compositions, except early covers; NEED YOUR LOVE SO BAD (Little Willie John) / NO PLACE TO GO (Howlin' Wolf) / DUST MY BROOM (Robert Johnson) / LOVE MINUS ZERO – NO LIMIT (Bob Dylan) / etc. • **Trivia:** Late 1973, their manager Clifford Davis, put together a bogus FLEETWOOD MAC, which resulted in a legal court battle, in which they won. The bogus group became STRETCH, and had a late '75 UK Top 20 hit with 'Why Did You Do It'.

Album rating: PETER GREEN'S FLEETWOOD MAC (*7) / MR. WONDERFUL (*6) / ENGLISH ROSE (*7) / PIOUS BIRD OF GOOD OMEN compilation (*7) / THEN PLAY ON (*7) / KILN HOUSE (*6) / FLEETWOOD MAC IN CHICAGO exploitation (*5) / FUTURE GAMES (*6) / GREATEST HITS compilation on 'CBS' (*9) / BARE TREES (*5) / PENGUIN (*4) / MYSTERY TO ME (*5) / HEROES ARE HARD TO FIND (*6) / FLEETWOOD MAC (*8) / RUMOURS (*10) / TUSK (*7) / FLEETWOOD MAC LIVE (*5) / MIRAGE (*6) / TANGO IN THE NIGHT (*6) / GREATEST HITS compilation on 'Warners' (*8) / BEHIND THE MASK (*5) / TIME (*3) / THE DANCE (*4) / THE VERY BEST OF FLEETWOOD MAC double compilation (*8) / SAY YOU WILL (*5)

JEREMY SPENCER (b. 4 Jul'48, Hartlepool, England) – guitar, vocals / **PETER GREEN** (b. PETER GREENBAUM, 29 Oct'49) – guitar, vocals (ex-JOHN MAYALL'S BLUESBREAKERS, ex-SHOTGUN EXPRESS) / **MICK FLEETWOOD** (b.24 Jun'42, Redruth, England) – drums (ex-JOHN MAYALL'S BLUESBREAKERS) / **JOHN McVIE** (b.26 Nov'45) – bass (ex-JOHN MAYALL'S BLUESBREAKERS) repl. BOB BRUNNING who formed SUNFLOWER BLUES BAND after recording B-side)

Blue Horizon — Epic

Nov 67. (7"; as PETER GREEN'S FLEETWOOD MAC) *(57-3051)* **I BELIEVE MY TIME AIN'T LONG. / RAMBLING PONY** [ ] [–]
(re-iss. 1969 on 'C.B.S.'; 3051)

Feb 68. (lp; stereo/mono) *(S+/7-63200)* <26402> **PETER GREEN'S FLEETWOOD MAC** <US-title 'FLEETWOOD MAC'> [4] Aug68 [ ]
– My heart beat like a hammer / Merry go round / Long grey mare / Shake your moneymaker / Looking for somebody / No place to go / My baby's good to me / I love another woman / Cold black night / The world keep on turning / Got to move. *(re-iss. Oct73 on 'CBS-Embasssy'; EMB 31036) (re-iss. Jul77 on 'CBS' lp/c; CBS/40 31494) (cd-iss. Aug94 as 'FLEETWOOD MAC' on 'Columbia Rewind'; 477 358-2)*

Mar 68. (7") *(57-3138)* **BLACK MAGIC WOMAN. / THE SUN IS SHINING** [37] [–]

Apr 68. (7") *<10351>* **BLACK MAGIC WOMAN. / LONG GREY MARE** [–] [ ]

Jul 68. (7") *(57-3139)* *<10386>* **NEED YOUR LOVE SO BAD. / STOP MESSIN' ROUND** [31] [ ]

Aug 68. (lp) *(7-63025)* **MR. WONDERFUL** [10] [–]
– Stop messin' round / Coming home / Rollin' man / Dust my broom / Love that burns / Doctor Brown / Need your love tonight / If you be my baby / Evenin' boogie / Lazy poker blues / I've lost my baby / Trying so hard to forget. *(re-iss. Nov89 on 'Essential' lp/c/cd; ESS LP/MC/CD 010) (re-iss. cd on 'Castle'; CCSCD 368)*

—— added **DANNY KIRWAN** (b.13 Mar'50) – guitar, vocals (ex-BOILERHOUSE)

Nov 68. (7") *(57-3145)* *<10436>* **ALBATROSS. / JIGSAW PUZZLE BLUES** [1] [ ]
(re-iss. Nov71 on 'C.B.S.'; CBS 3145)

Feb 69. (lp) *<BN 26446>* **ENGLISH ROSE** [–] [ ]
– Stop messin' round / Jigsaw puzzle blues / Doctor Brown / Something inside of me / Evenin' boogie / Love that burns / Black magic woman / I've lost my baby / One sunny day / Without you / Coming home / Albatross.

Immediate — not iss.

Apr 69. (7"; b-side by EARL VINCE & THE VALIENTS) *(IM 080)* **MAN OF THE WORLD. / SOMEBODY'S GONNA GET THEIR HEAD KICKED IN TONIGHT** [2] [–]
(re-iss. Feb83; same)

Reprise — Reprise

Sep 69. (7") *<0860>* **RATTLESNAKE SHAKE. / COMING YOUR WAY** [–] [ ]

Sep 69. (7") *(RS 27000)* *<0883>* **OH WELL (part 1). / OH WELL (part 2)** [2] Jan70 [55]

—— (note that SPENCER, for some reason did not play on the below album)

Sep 69. (lp) *(RSLP 9000)* *<6368>* **THEN PLAY ON** [6] [ ]
– Coming your way / Closing my eyes / Showbiz blues / Underway / Oh well / Although the sun is shining / Rattlesnake shake / Searching for Madge / Fighting for Madge / Closing my eyes / When you say / One sunny day / Although the sun is shining / Like crying / Before the beginning. *(re-iss. Jul71 lp/c; K/K4 44103) ;re-iss. Apr77) (cd-iss. Jun88 with extra tracks; 927 448-2)*

May 70. (7") *(RS 27007)* *<0925>* **THE GREEN MANALISHI (WITH THE TWO-PRONG CROWN). / WORLD IN HARMONY** [10] [ ]

—— Now a quartet of **FLEETWOOD, McVIE, SPENCER and KIRWAN** when GREEN went solo

Sep 70. (lp) *(RSLP 9004)* *<6408>* **KILN HOUSE** [39] [69]
– This is the rock / Station man / Blood on the floor / Hi ho silver / Jewel eyed Judy / Buddy's song / Earl Grey / One together / Tell me all the things you do / Mission bell. *(re-iss. Jul71 lp/c; K/K4 54001) (cd-iss. Feb93 on 'Warners'; 7599 27453-2)*

FLEETWOOD MAC

Jan 71. (7") *<0984>* **JEWEL EYED JUDY. / STATION MAN** –

— added **CHRISTINE** (PERFECT) **McVIE** (b.12 Jul'43, Birmingham, England) – keyboards, vocals (ex-CHICKEN SHACK) (she had already guested on 'MR. WONDERFUL' album)

Mar 71. (7") *(RS 27010)* **DRAGONFLY. / PURPLE DANCER** –

— **BOB WELCH** (b.31 Jul'46, Los Angeles, Calif.) – guitar, vocals (ex-HEAD WEST) repl. SPENCER who formed CHILDREN OF GOD

Sep 71. (lp/c) *(K/K4 44153) <6465>* **FUTURE GAMES** 91
– Women of 1000 years / Morning rain / What a shame / Future games / Sands of time / Sometimes / Lay it all down / Show me a smile. *(re-iss. Apr77; same) (cd-iss. Feb93 on 'Warners'; 7599 27458-2)*

Sep 71. (7") *<1057>* **SANDS OF TIME. / LAY IT ALL DOWN** –

Apr 72. (lp/c) *(K/K4 44181) <2080>* **BARE TREES** 70
– Child of mine / The ghost / Homeward bound / Sunny side of Heaven / Bare trees / Sentimental lady / Danny's chant / Spare me a little of your love / Dust / Thoughts on a grey day. *(re-iss. Apr77; same) (cd-iss. Feb93 on 'Warners'; 7599 27240-2)*

Aug 72. (7") *<1093>* **SENTIMENTAL LADY. / SUNNY SIDE OF HEAVEN** –

Aug 72. (7") *(K 14194)* **SPARE ME A LITTLE OF YOUR LOVE. / SUNNY SIDE OF HEAVEN** –

— **DAVE WALKER** – vocals (ex-SAVOY BROWN) repl. KIRWAN who went solo / added **BOB WESTON** – guitar, vocals (ex-LONG JOHN BALDRY) (above two now with FLEETWOOD, J. McVIE, C. McVIE and WELCH)

May 73. (7") *<1157>* **REMEMBER ME. / DISSATISFIED** –

May 73. (lp/c) *(K/K4 44235) <2138>* **PENGUIN** Apr73 49
– Remember me / Bright fire / Dissatisfied / (I'm a) Road runner / The derelict / Revelation / Did you ever love me / Night watch / Caught in the rain. *(re-iss. Apr77; same) (cd-iss. Feb93 on 'Warners'; 7599 26178-2)*

Jun 73. (7") *<1172>* **DID YOU EVER LOVE ME. / REVELATION** –

Jun 73. (7") *(K 14280)* **DID YOU EVER LOVE ME. / THE DERELICT** –

— Reverted to a quintet when WALKER departed forming HUNGRY FIGHTER

Jan 74. (lp/c) *(K/K4 44248) <2158>* **MYSTERY TO ME** Nov73 67
– Emerald eyes / Believe me / Just crazy love / Hypnotized / Forever / Keep on going / The city / Miles away / Somebody / The way I feel / Good things come to those who wait / Why / For your love. *(re-iss. Apr77; same) (cd-iss. Feb93 on 'Warners'; 7599 25982-2)*

Mar 74. (7") *(K 14315) <1188>* **FOR YOUR LOVE. / HYPNOTIZED**

— Trimmed to quartet when WESTON also left

Sep 74. (lp/c) *(K/K4 54026) <2196>* **HEROES ARE HARD TO FIND** 34
– Heroes are hard to find / Coming home / Angel / The Bermuda Triangle / Come a little bit closer / She's changing me / Bad loser / Silver heels / Prove your love / Born enchanter / Safe harbour. *(cd-iss. Feb93 on 'Warners'; 7599 27216-2)*

Feb 75. (7") *(K 14388) <1317>* **HEROES ARE HARD TO FIND. / BORN ENCHANTER**

— **LINDSEY BUCKINGHAM** (b. 3 Oct'47. Palo Alto, Calif.) – guitar, vocals (as below; ex-BUCKINGHAM-NICKS) repl. WELCH / added **STEVIE NICKS** (b. STEPHANIE NICKS, 26 May'48, Phoenix, Arizona) – vocals

Aug 75. (lp,white-lp/c) *(K/K4 54043) <2225>* **FLEETWOOD MAC** 1
– Monday morning / Warm ways / Blue letter / Rhiannon / Over my head / Crystal / Say you love me / Landslide / World turning / Sugar daddy / I'm so afraid. *(Nov76 hit UK No.23) (cd-iss. 1983; 2281-2) (cd-iss. Dec85 on 'Warners'; K2 54043) (re-iss. Feb93 cd/c/lp; 7599 27241-2/-4/-1)*

Oct 75. (7") *(K 14403)* **WARM WAYS. / BLUE LETTER** –

Feb 76. (7") *(K 14413) <1339>* **OVER MY HEAD. / I'M SO AFRAID** Nov75 20

Apr 76. (7") *(K 14430) <1345>* **RHIANNON. / SUGAR DADDY** Feb76 11
(re-iss. Feb78 reached UK-No.46)

Sep 76. (7") *(K 14447) <1356>* **SAY YOU LOVE ME. / MONDAY MORNING** 40 Jun76 11

Warners Warners

Jan 77. (7") *(K 16872) <8304>* **GO YOUR OWN WAY. / SILVER SPRINGS** 38 10

Feb 77. (lp,white-lp/c) *(K/K4 56344) <3010>* **RUMOURS** 1 1
– Second hand news / Dreams / Never going back again / Don't stop / Go your own way / Songbird / The chain / You make loving fun / I don't want to know / Oh daddy / Gold dust woman. *(cd-iss. Dec83; K2 56344) (re-iss. Jun88 lp/c; K/K4 56344) (re-iss. Feb93 cd/c/lp; 7599 27313-2/-4/-1) (re-hit No.18 UK in Sep'97)*

Apr 77. (7") *(K 16930) <8413>* **DON'T STOP. / GOLD DUST WOMAN** 32 Jul77 3

Jun 77. (7") *(K 16969) <8371>* **DREAMS. / SONGBIRD** 24 Apr77 1

Sep 77. (7") *(K 17013)* **YOU MAKE LOVING FUN. / NEVER GOING BACK AGAIN** 45 –

Oct 77. (7") *<8483>* **YOU MAKE LOVING FUN. / GOLD DUST WOMAN** – 9

Sep 79. (7") *(K 17468) <49077>* **TUSK. / NEVER MAKE ME CRY** 6 8

Oct 79. (d-lp/c) *(K/K4 66088) <3350>* **TUSK** 1 4
– Over & over / The ledge / Think about me / Save me a place / Sara / Wha makes you think you're the one / That's all for everyone / Not that funny / Sisters of the Moon / Angel / That's enough for me / Brown eyes / Neve make me cry / I know I'm not wrong / Honey hi / Beautiful child / Wal a thin line / Tusk / Never forget. *(cd-iss. Mar87; K2 66088) (re-iss. Feb9 cd/c/d-lp; 7599 27395-2/-4/-1)*

Dec 79. (7") *(K 17533) <49150>* **SARA. / THAT'S ENOUGH FOR ME** 37 7

Feb 80. (7") *(K 17577)* **NOT THAT FUNNY. / SAVE ME A PLACE** –

Mar 80. (7") *<49196>* **THINK ABOUT ME. / SAVE ME A PLACE** – 20

Mar 80. (7") *(K 17614)* **THINK ABOUT ME. / HONEY HI** –

Jun 80. (7") *<49500>* **SISTERS OF THE MOON. / WALK A THIN LINE** – 86

Nov 80. (d-lp/c) *(K/K4 66097) <3500>* **FLEETWOOD MAC LIVE (live)** 31 14
– Monday morning / Say you love me / Dreams / Oh well / Over & over Sara / Not that funny / Never going back again / Landslide / Fireflies Over my head / Rhiannon / Don't let me down again / One more night Go your own way / Don't stop / I'm so afraid / The farmer's daughter.

Jan 81. (7") *<49660>* **FIREFLIES. / OVER MY HEAD** – 60

Feb 81. (7") *(K 17746)* **THE FARMER'S DAUGHTER (live). / DREAMS (live)** –

Mar 81. (7") *<49700>* **THE FARMER'S DAUGHTER (live). / MONDAY MORNING (live)** –

Jul 82. (7") *(K 17965) <29966>* **HOLD ME. / EYES OF THE WORLD** Jun82 4

Jul 82. (lp/c) *(K/K4 56952) <23607>* **MIRAGE** 5 1
– Love in store / Can't go back / That's alright / Book of love / Gypsy Only over you / Empire state / Straight back / Hold me / Oh Diane / Ey of the world / Wish you were here. *(cd-iss. Dec83; K2 56952) (re-iss. Feb9 cd/c/lp; 7599 23607-2/-4/-1)*

Sep 82. (7") *(K 17997) <29918>* **GYPSY. / COOL WATER** 46 Aug82 12

Nov 82. (7") *<29848>* **LOVE IN STORE. / CAN'T GO BACK** – 22

Dec 82. (7"/7"pic-d) *(FLEET 1/+P)* **OH DIANE. / ONLY OVER YOU** 9 –
(12"+=) *(FLEET 1T)* – The chain.

Feb 83. (7") *<29698>* **OH DIANE. / THAT'S ALRIGHT** –

Apr 83. (7") *(W 9848)* **CAN'T GO BACK. / THAT'S ALRIGHT** –
(12") *(W 9848T)* – ('A'side) / Rhiannon / Tusk / Over and over.

Mar 87. (7"/ext.12"/ext.12"pic-d) *(W 8398/+T/TP) <28398>* **BIG LOVE. / YOU AND I, PART 1** 9 5
(d7"+=) *(W 8398F)* – The chain / Go your own way.

Apr 87. (lp/c)(cd) *(WX 65/+C)(925 471-2) <25471>* **TANGO IN THE NIGHT** 1 7
– Big love / Seven wonders / Everywhere / Caroline / Tango in the night Mystified / Little lies / Family man / Welcome to the room . . . Sara / Isn it midnight / When I see you again / You and I, part II.

Jun 87. (7") *(W 8317) <28317>* **SEVEN WONDERS. / BOOK OF MIRACLES (instrumental)** 56 19
(ext-remix.12"+=/ext-remix.12"pic-d+=) *(W 8317T/+P)* – ('A'dub).

Aug 87. (7") *(W 8291) <28291>* **LITTLE LIES. / RICKY** 5 4
(ext.c-s+=/ext.12"+=/ext.12"pic-d+=) *(W 8291/+C/T/TP)* – ('A'dub).

Nov 87. (7") *(W 8114) <28114>* **FAMILY MAN. / DOWN ENDLESS STREET** 54 Mar88 90
(7"box/12") *(W 8114 B/T)* – ('A'extended vocal remix) / Family party bonu beats / You and I, part II.

Feb 88. (7") *(W 8143) <28143>* **EVERYWHERE. / WHEN I SEE YOU AGAIN** 4 Nov 87 14
(12"+=) *(W 8143T)* – ('A'extended) / ('A'dub version).
(3"cd-s+=) *(W 8143CD)* – Rhiannon / Say you love me.

Jun 88. (7") *(W 7860)* **ISN'T IT MIDNIGHT. / MYSTIFIED** 60 –
(12"+=/3"cd-s+=) *(W 7860 T/CD)* – Say you love me / Gypsy.

Nov 88. (7") *(W 7644) <27644>* **AS LONG AS YOU FOLLOW. / OH WELL (live)** 66 43
(12"+=/3"cd-s+=) *(W 7644 T/CD)* – Gold dust woman.

Nov 88. (lp/c)(cd) *(WX 221/+C)(925 838-2) <25801>* **FLEETWOOD MAC'S GREATEST HITS** (compilation) [3] [14]
– As long as you follow / No questions asked / Rhiannon / Don't stop / Go your own way / Hold me / Everywhere / Gypsy / Say you love me / Dreams / Little lies / Sara / Tusk. *(c+=/cd+=)* – Oh Diane / Big love / You making loving fun / Seven wonders.

Feb 89. (7") *(W 7528)* **HOLD ME. / NO QUESTIONS ASKED** [ ] [–]
(12"+=/3"cd-s+=) *(W 7528 T/CD)* – I loved another woman (live).

— (Jul'88) when BUCKINGHAM departed, he was repl. by **RICK VITO** (b.13 Oct'49, Darby, Pennsylvania) – guitar / **BILLY BURNETT** (b. 8 May'53, Memphis, Tenn.) – guitar (ex-MICK FLEETWOOD'S ZOO)

Apr 90. (7"/c-s) *(W 9866/+C) <19866>* **SAVE ME. / ANOTHER WOMAN (live)** [53] [33]
(12"+=/cd-s+=/s-cd-s+=) *(W 9866 T/CD/CDX)* – Everywhere (live).

Apr 90. (cd)(lp/c) *(<7599 26111-2>)(WX 335/+C)* **BEHIND THE MASK** [1] [18]
– The skies the limit / In the back of my mind / Do you know / Save me / Affairs of the heart / When the Sun goes down / Behind the mask / Stand on the rock / Hard feelings / Freedom / When it comes to love / The second time. *(also cd-box; 7599 26206) (cd re-iss. Feb95; same)*

Aug 90. (7"/c-s) *(W 9739/+C)* **IN THE BACK OF MY MIND. / LIZARD PEOPLE** [58] [–]
(12"/cd-s) *(W 9739 T/CD)* – ('A'side) / Little lies (live) / The chain (live).
(s-cd-s+=) *(W 9739CDX)* – Lizard people.

Nov 90. (7"/c-s) *(W 9740/+C)* **THE SKIES THE LIMIT. / LIZARD PEOPLE** [ ] [–]
(12"/cd-s) *(W 9740 T/CD)* – ('A'side) / Little lies (live) / The chain (live).

Feb 91. (7") **SKIES THE LIMIT. / THE SECOND TIME** [–] [ ]

— (late 1990) STEVIE NICKS left to go solo, and CHRISTINE departed due to MICK's new book allegations.

Jan 93. (7"/c-s) *(W 0145/+C)* **LOVE SHINES. / THE CHAIN (alt.mix)** [ ] [ ]
(cd-s+=) *(W 0145CD)* – The chain (Not That Funny live version) / Isn't it midnight (alt.version).

— **MICK FLEETWOOD, JOHN McVIE, CHRISTINE McVIE** (latter departed in '94, but on below) + **BILLY BURNETTE** added **DAVE MASON** (b.10 May'46, Worcester, England) – vocals, guitars (ex-TRAFFIC, ex-solo artist)/ **BEKKA BRAMLETT** (b.19 Apr'68, Westwood, Calif.) – vocals (daughter of DELANEY & BONNIE)

Oct 95. (cd/c) *(<9362 45920-2/-4>)* **TIME** [47] [ ]
– Talkin' to my heart / Hollywood (some other kind of town) / Blow by blow / Winds of change / I do / Nothing without you / Dreamin' the dream / Sooner or later / I wonder why / Nights in Estoril / I got it in for you / All over again / These strange times.

— the famous mid-late 70's line-up reformed for one-off MTV performance below (complete with orchestra/band!)

Aug 97. (cd/c) *(<9362 46702/-2/-4>)* **THE DANCE** [15] [1]
– The chain / Dreams / Everywhere / Rhiannon / I'm so afraid / Temporary one / Bleed to love her / Big love / Landslide / Say you love me / My little demon / Silver springs / You make loving fun / Sweet girl / Go your own way / Tusk / Don't stop.

Jul 98. (12"ep/cd-ep) *<9362 44540-1/-2>* **LANDSLIDE (mixes; live album version / remix / string / analog)** [–] [51]

— line-up **MICK FLEETWOOD + JOHN McVIE** brought back **STEVIE NICKS + LINDSEY BUCKINGHAM** (CHRISTINE McVIE was a guest player)

Apr 03. (cd) *(9362 48479-2) <49467>* **SAY YOU WILL** [6] [3]
– What's the world coming to / Murrow turning over in his grave / Illume / Thrown down / Miranda / Red rover / Say you will / Peacekeeper / Come / Smile at you / Running through the garden / Silver girl / Steal your heart away / Bleed to love her / Everybody finds out / Destiny rules / Say goodbye / Goodbye baby. *(ltd d-cd+=; 9362 48467-2)* – Love minus zero – No limit / Not make believe / Peacekeeper (live) / Say you will (live).

Nov 03. (cd-s) *(W 632CD) <radio>* **PEACEKEEPER (Tin Tin Out radio edit) / PEACEKEEPER / SMILE AT YOU** [ ] [80]

– (with PETER GREEN) compilations, others, etc. –

Note all 'Blue Horizon' releases were on 'Epic' US.

Jul 69. (7") *Blue Horizon; (57-3157)* **NEED YOUR LOVE SO BAD. / NO PLACE TO GO** [32] [–]

Aug 69. (lp) *Blue Horizon; (7-63215)* **PIOUS BIRD OF GOOD OMEN** [18] [–]
– Need your love so bad / Coming home / Rambling pony / The big boat / I believe my time ain't long / The sun is shining / Albatross / Black magic woman / Just the blues / Jigsaw puzzle blues / Looking for somebody / Stop messin' around. *(re-iss. Jun81 on 'C.B.S.'; CBS 32050) (cd-iss. Jun95 on 'Columbia-Rewind'; 480 524-2)*
Note all CBS releases were on 'Epic' US.

May 71. (lp) *C.B.S.; (63875)* **THE ORIGINAL FLEETWOOD MAC BEFORE THE SPLIT** [ ] [ ]
(re-iss. +c/cd.Jun90 on 'Castle')

Jun 71. (d-lp) *Blue Horizon; <3801>* **FLEETWOOD MAC IN CHICAGO** [–] [ ]
<US-iss.Nov75 on 'Sire'; SASH 37152> <re-iss. 1977; 2XS 6009>

Oct 71. (d-lp) *Epic; <KE 30632>* **BLACK MAGIC WOMAN** [–] [ ]
– (US lp's; 'FLEETWOOD MAC' (1968) & 'ENGLISH ROSE')

Nov 71. (lp/c) *C.B.S.; (CBS/40 69011)* **GREATEST HITS** [36] [ ]
– The green Manalishi (with the two-pronged crown) / Oh well (part 1 & 2) / Shake your moneymaker / Need your love so bad / Rattlesnake shake / Dragonfly / Black magic woman / Albatross / Man of the world / Stop messin' around / Love that burns. *(re-iss. Feb88 lp/c; CBS 460 704-1/4) (cd-iss. Apr89; 460 704-2) (re-iss. cd Dec94 on 'Columbia-Rewind'; 477 512-2)*

May 72. (7") *Reprise; (K 14174)* **THE GREEN MANALISHI (WITH THE TWO-PRONG CROWN). / OH WELL (Pt.1)** [ ] [ ]
(re-iss. Mar73 & Nov76; same)

May 73. (7") *C.B.S.; (CBS 8306)* **ALBATROSS. / NEED YOUR LOVE SO BAD** [2] [ ]
(re-iss. Feb78; CBS 5957) (re-iss. Nov90 on 'Old Gold'; OG 9955)

Aug 73. (7") *C.B.S.; (CBS 1722)* **BLACK MAGIC WOMAN. / STOP MESSIN' ROUND** [ ] [ ]

Jun 75. (d-lp) *C.B.S.; (CBS 22025)* **THE ORIGINAL FLEETWOOD MAC / ENGLISH ROSE** [ ] [ ]
(re-iss. Jun76; 81308-9) (re-iss. Jun90 on 'Essential' cd/c/lp; ESS CD/MC/LP 026) (re-iss. cd May94 on 'Castle'; CLACD 344)

Oct 75. (7"; b-side by DANNY KIRWAN) *D.J.M.; (DJS 10620)* **MAN OF THE WORLD. / SECOND CHAPTER** [ ] [–]
(re-iss. Feb76 & Jun78 on 'Epic'; EPC 6466)

Mar 77. (d-lp/c) *C.B.S. / Sire; (CBS/40 88227) <3706>* **VINTAGE YEARS** [ ] [ ]
(re-iss. May82 as 'THE VINTAGE YEARS: HISTORY OF FLEETWOOD MAC'; CBS 22122)

Aug 77. (lp) *Embassy; (EMB 31569)* **ALBATROSS** (1 side by 'CHRISTINE PERFECT') [ ] [–]
(cd-iss. Feb91 on 'Columbia'; CD 31569)

Sep 78. (lp/c) *C.B.S.; (CBS/40 83110)* **MAN OF THE WORLD** [ ] [–]

Feb 80. (lp) *C.B.S.; (CBS 31798)* **BLACK MAGIC WOMAN** [ ] [–]

Aug 83. (c) *C.B.S.; (40-22163)* **FLEETWOOD MAC / THE PIOUS BIRD OF GOOD OMEN** [ ] [–]

Jul 84. (7") *C.B.S.; (A 4578)* **ALBATROSS. / MAN OF THE WORLD** [ ] [–]

Jan 85. (lp) *Shanghai; (HAI 107)* **LIVE IN BOSTON (live)** [ ] [–]
(re-iss. May88 on 'Line'; IMLP 400129) (cd-iss. Oct85 on 'Shanghai'; HAI 400) (cd-iss. Oct89 on 'Castle')

Aug 85. (d-lp/c) *Shanghai; (HAI/HAC 300)* **CERULEAN (LIVE IN BOSTON Part II)** [ ] [–]

Sep 85. (7") *Old Gold; (OG 9529)* **MAN OF THE WORLD. / ('Natural Born boogie' by Humble Pie)** [ ] [–]

Oct 85. (lp) *Platinum; (24076)* **RATTLESNAKE SHAKE** [ ] [–]

Oct 85. (lp) *Platinum;(24077)* **MADISON BLUES** [ ] [–]

Dec 85. (lp) *Platinum; (24082)* **OH WELL** [ ] [–]

Apr 86. (lp) *Commander; (LP 39006)* **RATTLESNAKE SHAKE LIVE** [ ] [–]

Apr 86. (lp) *Commander; (LP 39007)* **OH WELL LIVE** [ ] [–]

Apr 86. (lp) *Commander; (LP 39008)* **GREEN MANALISHI LIVE** [ ] [–]

Nov 86. (cd) *Commander; (CD 99011)* **FLEETWOOD MAC LIVE (live 1968)** [ ] [–]
(re-iss. May88; same) (re-iss. May94//Nov94 on 'Arc'; MEC 949020//MO 3016) (re-iss. Aug95 on 'Abracadabra'; AB 3017)

Nov 86. (lp/c/cd) *Thunderbolt; (THBL/THBC/CDTB 1.038)* **LONDON LIVE '68 (live)** [ ] [–]

Jul 87. (d-lp/c/cd) *Castle; (CCS LP/MC/CD 157)* **THE COLLECTION** [ ] [–]
(re-iss. cd Jan94)

Sep 87. (lp) *Commander; (224 821-7)* **GREATEST HITS LIVE** [ ] [–]
(re-iss. Dec89 lp/c/cd; 264 821-7/-4/-2) (re-iss. cd Apr93 on 'Zillion'; 261 0992)

1988. (lp) *Varrick; <VR 020>* **JUMPING AT SHADOWS** [–] [ ]
– (same as above)

Feb 89. (7") *C.B.S.; (654 613-7)* **ALBATROSS. / MAN OF THE WORLD** [ ] [–]
(12"+=/cd-s+=) *(654 613-6/-2)* – Black magic woman / Love that burns.

Apr 89. (lp/c/cd) *Castle; (CCS LP/MC/CD 216)* **THE BLUES COLLECTION** ☐ -
1989. (3"cd-ep) *C.B.S.; (655 171-3)* **ALBATROSS / BLACK MAGIC WOMAN / NEED YOUR LOVE SO BAD / I'D RATHER GO BLIND** ☐ -
Oct 89. (lp/c/cd) *Castle; (CLA LP/MC/CD 152)* **BOSTON LIVE** ☐ -
Nov 89. (lp/c/cd) *Mainline; (264 824-1/-4/-2)* **OH WELL** ☐ -
Nov 89. (lp/c) *Hallmark; (SHM/HSC 3268)* **LOOKING BACK ON FLEETWOOD MAC** ☐ -
(cd-iss. May90 on 'Pickwick'; PWKS 533)
Jul 90. (cd) *Marble Ach; (CMACD 125)* **FLEETWOOD MAC LIVE (live)** ☐ -
Feb 91. (3xcd/5xlp) *Essential; (ESB CD/LP 138)* **THE BLUES YEARS** ☐ ☐
Jun 91. (cd/c) *Elite; (ELITE 008 MC/CD)* **LIKE IT THIS WAY** ☐ -
(re-iss. Sep93; same)
Mar 92. (cd/lp; as PETER GREEN'S FLEETWOOD MAC) *Receiver; (RR CD/LP 157)* **LIVE AT THE MARQUEE (live)** ☐ -
(re-iss. cd Jun92 on 'Sunflower'; SF-CD 104)
Sep 92. (cd; as PETER GREEN'S FLEETWOOD MAC) *Dojo Early Years; (EARLD 5)* **THE EARLY YEARS** ☐ -
Feb 93. (cd) *Castle; (SSLCD 207)* **LIVE** ☐ -
Jun 93. (cd) *Point; (261 0202)* **21 GREATEST HITS LIVE** ☐ -
Mar 94. (cd) *Castle; (MACCD 187)* **MADISON BLUES LIVE** ☐ -
May 94. (cd) *Castle; (MATCD 266)* **THE BLUES YEARS** ☐ -
Jul 94. (cd/c) *Success;* **LIVE (live)** ☐ -
Jun 95. (cd) *Renaissance; (551 776-2)* **FLEETWOOD MAC** ☐ -
Sep 95. (d-cd/d-c; as PETER GREEN'S FLEETWOOD MAC) *Fleetwood; (EDF CD/MC 297)* **LIVE AT THE BBC** 48 -

– (GREEN on some) compilations, others, etc. –

on 'Warners' unless mentioned otherwise
1978. (lp/c) *Reprise; (K/K4 44138)* **THE BEST OF FLEETWOOD MAC** ☐ -
Oct 82. (c) *(K4 66103)* **RUMOURS / FLEETWOOD MAC** ☐ ☐
Nov 92. (4xcd-box/4xc-box) *(<9362 45129-2/-4>)* **25 YEARS – THE CHAIN** ☐ ☐
Feb 93. (d-cd) *(<9362 45188-2>)* **25 YEARS – SELECTIONS FROM THE CHAIN** ☐ -
Oct 02. (cd) *W.S.M.; (8122 73635-2)* **THE VERY BEST OF FLEETWOOD MAC** 7 -
– Go your own way / Don't stop / Dreams / Little lies / Everywhere / Albatross / You make loving fun / Rhiannon / Black magic woman / Tusk / Say you love me / Man of the world / Seven wonders / Family man / Sara / Monday morning / Gypsy / Over my head / Landslide / The chain / Big love (live 1997).
Oct 02. (d-cd) *Reprise; <73775>* **THE VERY BEST OF FLEETWOOD MAC** - 12
– Monday morning / Dreams / You make loving fun / Go your own way / Rhiannon / Say you love me / I'm so afraid / Silver springs / Over my head / Never going back again / Sara / Love in store / Tusk / Landslide / Songbird / Big love / Storms / The chain / Don't stop / What makes you think you're the one / Gypsy / Second hand news / Little lies / Think about me / Go insane / Gold dust woman / Hold me / Seven wonders / World turning / Everywhere / Sisters of the Moon / Family man / As long as you follow / No questions asked / Skies the limit / Paper doll.

☐ John FOGERTY
(see under ⇒ CREEDENCE CLEARWATER REVIVAL)

FOO FIGHTERS

Formed: Seattle, Washington, USA ... April/May '94, after the death of KURT COBAIN (Nirvana), by drummer turned singer/guitarist DAVE GROHL. He subsequently brought in COBAIN stand-in, PAT SMEAR, along with NATE MANDEL and WILLIAM GOLDSMITH, taking the group name from the mysterious lights reported by pilots during World War II. Continuing the UFO concept, the group founded their own 'Roswell' label, (funded by 'Capitol') and debuted in the summer of '95 with UK Top 5 single, 'THIS IS A CALL'. More harmonic and positively life-affirming than NIRVANA (comparisons were inevitable), The FOO FIGHTERS' offered up one of the most exciting debuts of the year; while the lyrics may have been somewhat cryptic, the obvious grunge influences were tempered with an infectious, pop-hardcore rush that was impossible to resist. The album sold well on both sides of the Atlantic, with GROHL & Co heading out on a successful series of festival dates. Work on the Gil Norton-produced follow-up, 'THE COLOUR AND THE SHAPE', got off to a difficult start with initial sessions in Seattle being scrapped. Further problems arose with the departure of sticksman GOLDSMITH halfway through recording, although GROHL subsequently completed the drum parts and the record was finally released in Spring '97 to rave reviews. Outpacing even the debut, The FOO FIGHTERS had come on leaps and bounds in the songwriting department, their rich post-grunge tapestry markedly more diverse. With good old romantic love as the driving theme of the record, the likes of the heart-rending (UK Top 20) 'EVERLONG' took starry-eyed, melodic distortion-pop to new (neck) hair-raising limits (complete with 'Evil Dead'-style video for that true-love atmosphere!), while more mellow musings like 'WALKING AFTER YOU' (used on the movie 'X-Files: Fight The Future') and 'DOLL' suggested GROHL was gaining enough confidence in his writing to chill out and reflect rather than continually going for the jugular. The group's growing self-belief was confirmed by some storming festival sets, while the album later came out top in rock 'bible', 'Kerrang!'s yearly critic's poll. After GROHL's brief expedition into film score work (with soundtrack 'TOUCH' being issued mid-'98), the band inked a deal with 'R.C.A. and were ready to unleash a third album. 'THERE IS NOTHING LEFT TO LOSE' (1999), which disappointed no one with its melodic, HUSKER DU/PIXIES-inspired rock tunes, especially the hit 'LEARN TO FLY' (although I hear RUSH's 'Finding My Way' every time). GROHL and the mighty FOO FIGHTERS went straight to No.1 in October 2002, courtesy of album, 'ONE BY ONE', a clean, polished-up rock album that seemed to be lacking any kind of sparkle or charisma or just plain damn rawness. Top 10 hit, 'ALL MY LIFE' was very reminiscent of the thrash-attack of QUEENS OF THE STONE AGE (well, GROHL had joined as drummer!), while elsewhere on the album, ballads were stuck clumsily alongside clean-cut out-and-out rock songs, and with no attempt made at rekindling the punk spirit. In short, papa GROHL's gonna have to get a brand new bag. As it turned out, he played with his heroes, just for one album: 'PROBOT' (2004) was the name of both record and project, approaching the 80s revival from a louder angle than most with a Fantasy League-style line-up of heavy/black/death-metallers including LEMMY, KING DIAMOND, MAX CAVALERA, LEE DORRIAN and CRONOS. Having got the Gwarrrgh factor out of his system, GROHL found the headspace to record a part acoustic, occasionally Nirvana-esque FOO FIGHTERS double-set 'IN YOUR HONOR' (2005), another transatlantic Top 3 unit shifter. The irrepressible DG must be the only man in showbiz who can shout at the Devil one minute and duet on a NORAH JONES' bossa nova the next. Fair do's to the man for his mind-boggling eclecticism but let's face it, most fans will have Disc 1 on repeat, specifically the UK Top 5 'BEST OF YOU'.

• **Covers:** OZONE (Kiss) / GAS CHAMBER (Angry Samoans) / DRIVE ME WILD (Vanity 6) / BAKER STREET (Gerry Rafferty) / DANNY SAYS (Ramones) / IRON & STONE (Obsessed) / REQUIEM (Killing Joke) / DOWN IN THE PARK (Tubeway Army) / SISTER EUROPE (Psychedelic Furs) / HAVE A CIGAR (Pink Floyd) / NEVER TALKING TO YOU AGAIN (Husker Du) / DARLING NIKKI (Prince) / I'M IN LOVE WITH A GERMAN FILMSTAR (Passions) / I FEEL FREE (Cream) / BORN ON THE BAYOU (Creedence Clearwater Revival). • **Trivia:** GREG DULLI (Afghan Whigs) played guitar on 'X-static'.

Album rating: FOO FIGHTERS (*8) / THE COLOUR AND THE SHAPE (*9) / TOUCH soundtrack by Dave Grohl (*6) / THERE IS NOTHING LEFT TO LOSE (*8) / ONE BY ONE (*6) / PROBOT by Probot (*7) / IN YOUR HONOR (*7)

DAVE GROHL (b.14 Jan'69, Warren, Ohio) – vocals, guitar (ex-NIRVANA) / **PAT SMEAR** – guitar (ex-GERMS) / **NATE MANDEL** – bass / **WILLIAM GOLDSMITH** – drums (both of SUNNY DAY REAL ESTATE)

Roswell Roswell

Jun 95. (7",7"red) *(CL 753)* **THIS IS A CALL. / WINNEBAGO** [5] [–]
(12"luminous+=/cd-s+=) *(12/CD CL 753)* – Podunk.

Jun 95. (cd/c/lp) *(CD/TC+/EST 2266) <34027>* **FOO FIGHTERS** [3] [23]
– This is a call / I'll stick around / Big me / Alone + easy target / Good grief / Floaty / Weenie beenie / Oh, George / For all the cows / X-static / Wattershed / Exhausted.

Sep 95. (c-s/7"red) *(TC+/CL 757)* **I'LL STICK AROUND. / HOW I MISS YOU** [18] [–]
(12"+=/cd-s+=) *(12/CD CL 757)* – Ozone.

Nov 95. (c-s/7"blue) *(TC+/CL 762)* **FOR ALL THE COWS. / WATTERSHED (live at Reading)** [28] [–]
(cd-s+=) *(CDCL 762)* – ('A'-live at Reading).

Mar 96. (c-s/7"white) *(TC+CL 768)* **BIG ME. / FLOATY (BBC session) / GAS CHAMBER (BBC session)** [19] [–]
(cd-s+=) *(CDCL 768)* – Alone + easy target (BBC session).

— **TAYLOR HAWKINS** – drums (of-ALANIS MORISSETTE) repl. GOLDSMITH

Apr 97. (7") *(CL 788)* **MONKEY WRENCH. / THE COLOUR AND THE SHAPE** [12] [–]
(cd-s+=) *(CDCLS 788)* – Up in arms (slow version).
(cd-s) *(CDCL 788)* – ('A'side) / Down in the park / See you (acoustic).

May 97. (cd/c/lp) *(CD/TC+/EST 2295) <58530>* **THE COLOUR AND THE SHAPE** [3] [10]
– Doll / Monkey wrench / Hey Johnny Park / My poor brain / Wind up / Up in arms / My hero / See you / Enough space / February stars / Everlong / Walking after you / New way home.

Aug 97. (7"blue) *(CL 792)* **EVERLONG. / DRIVE ME WILD** [18] [–]
(cd-s+=) *(CDCL 792)* – See you (live).
(cd-s) *(CDCLS 792)* – ('A'side) / Requiem / I'll stick around (live).

— now without SMEAR who was repl. by **FRANZ STAHL** (ex-SCREAM)

Jan 98. (7"red) *(CL 796)* **MY HERO. / DEAR LOVER** [21] [–]
(cd-s+=) *(CDCL 796)* – Baker Street (BBC session). *(with enhanced cd+=)* – Everlong (video) / Monkey wrench (video).

Aug 98. (7"/c-s/cd-s) *(E 4100/+C/CD)* **WALKING AFTER YOU (remix). / (Ween: Beacon Light)** [20] [–]
(above from the movie, 'X-Files: Fight The Future' on 'Elektra')

— now trio of **GROHL, MENDEL + HAWKINS**/ added on tour **CHRIS SHIFLETT** – guitar (ex-NO USE FOR A NAME)

R.C.A. R.C.A.

Oct 99. (c-s) *(74321 71308-4) <album cut>* **LEARN TO FLY / HAVE A CIGAR** [21] [19]
(cd-s+=) *(74321 71308-2)* – Iron & stone.
(cd-s+=) *(74321 71310-2)* – Make a bet.

Nov 99. (cd/c/lp) *<(07863 67892-2/-4/-1)>* **THERE IS NOTHING LEFT TO LOSE** [10] [10]
– Stacked actors / Breakout / Learn to fly / Gimme stitches / Generator / Aurora / Live-in skin / Next year / Headwires / Ain't it the life / M.I.A.

Mar 00. (cd-ep) *(74321 74958-2)* **GENERATOR EP** [ ] [–]
– Generator / Ain't it the life (two meter Dutch session) / Floaty (two meter Dutch session) / Fraternity / Breakout (live).
(cd-ep) *<74321 74617-2>* – ('A'side) / Learn to fly (live in Australia) / Stacked actors (live in Australia) / Breakout (live).

Sep 00. (7") *(74321 79012-7)* **BREAKOUT. / STACKED ACTORS (live)** [29] [–]
(cd-s+=) *(74321 79011-2)* – Monkey wrench.
(cd-s) *(74321 79010-2)* – ('A'side) / Iron and stone / Learn to fly (live).

Dec 00. (7"/c-s) *(74321 80926-7/-4)* **NEXT YEAR. / BIG ME (live/session)** [42] [–]
(cd-s+=) *(74321 80926-2)* – Next year (live/session).
(cd-s) *(74321 80927-2)* – ('A'side) / Baker street (live/session) / ('A'-CD-ROM).

Oct 02. (7") *(74321 97315-7)* **ALL MY LIFE. / SISTER EUROPE** [5] [–]
(cd-s+=) *(74321 97314-2)* – Win or lose / ('A'-video).
(cd-s) *(74321 97315-2)* – ('A'side) / Danny says / One.

Oct 02. (cd/lp) *(74321 97348-2/-1) <68008>* **ONE BY ONE** [1] [3]
– All my life / Low / Have it all / Times like these / Disenchanted lullaby / Tired of you / Halo / Lonely as you / Overdrive / Burn away / Come back.

Jan 03. (7") *(74321 98955-7)* **TIMES LIKE THESE. / LIFE OF ILLUSION** [12] [–]
(cd-s+=) *(74321 98955-2)* – Planet Claire / ('A'-video).
(cd-s) *(74321 98956-2)* – ('A'side) / Normal / Learn to fly (live) / (video footage).

Jun 03. (7") *(82876 52256-7)* **LOW. / NEVER TALKING TO YOU AGAIN (live)** [21] [–]
(cd-s+=) *(82876 52256-2)* – ('A'-video).
(cd-s) *(82876 52257-2)* – ('A'side) / Enough space (live) / ('A'video).

Sep 03. (7") *(82876 56370-7)* **HAVE IT ALL. / DARLING NIKKI** [37] [–]
(cd-s+=) *(82876 56370-2)* – Times like these (session).

Jun 05. (7") *(82876 70121-7)* **BEST OF YOU. / SPILL** [4] [18]
(cd-s) *(82876 70121-2)* – ('A') / I'm in love with a German filmstar.
(cd-s) *(82876 70101-2)* – ('A') / FFL / Kiss the bottle / What an honor (video interview).

Jun 05. (d-cd/q-lp) *(82876 70193-2)<(68038-2/-1)>* **IN YOUR HONOR** [2] [2]
– In your honor / No way back / Best of you / DOA / Hell / The last song / Free me / Resolve / The deepest blues are back / End over end // Still / What if I do? / Miracle / Another round / Friend of a friend / Over and out / On the mend / Virginia moon / Cold day in the sun / Razor. *(ltd d-cd w/dvd+=; 82876 70195-2)* – (DVD tracks).

Sep 05. (7"yellow) *(82876 72279-7)* **DOA. / RAZOR (acoustic)** [25] [68]
(cd-s) *(82876 72031-2)* – ('A') / I feel free.
(cd-s+=) *(82876 72032-2)* – Skin and bones / Best of you (video).

Oct 05. (cd-ep) *<BMK 96143>* **FIVE SONGS & A COVER** [–] [ ]
– Best of you (live) / DOA (demo) / Skin and bones / World (demo) / I feel free / FFL.

Nov 05. (7") *(82876 74965-7)* **RESOLVE. / WORLD (demo)** [32] [–]
(cd-s+=) *(82876 73890-2)* – Born on the bayou / ('A'-video).
(cd-s) *(82876 73891-2)* – ('A') / DOA (demo).

Mar 06. (cd-s) *(82876 80473-2)* **NO WAY BACK / COLD DAY IN THE SUN / BEST OF YOU (live in the winter 2005)** [64] [–]

DAVE GROHL

— featured guests LOUISE POST + JOHN DOE plus BARRETT JONES keyboards + ERIC RICHARDS slide guitar

Roswell – Capitol Roswell – Capitol

Mar 97. (cd) *<(7243 8 55632-25)>* **TOUCH** (soundtrack) [ ] Jun98 [ ]
– Bill Hill theme / August Murray theme / How do you do / Richie Baker's miracle / Making popcorn / Outrage / Saints in love / Spinning newspapers / Remission my ass / Scene 6 / This loving thing / Final miracle / Touch.

PROBOT

DAVE GROHL – vocals, multi / + guests (see album)

Southern Lord Southern Lord

Dec 03. (7") *<SUNN 30.5>* **CENTURIES OF SIN. / EMERALD LAW** [–] [ ]

Feb 04. (cd/lp) *<(SUNN 30 CD/LP)>* **PROBOT** [34] [68]
– (intro) / Centuries of sin (feat. CRONOS) / Red war (feat. MAX CAVALERA) / Shake your blood (feat. LEMMY) / Access Babylon (feat. MIKE DEAN) / Silent spring (feat. KURT BRECHT) / Ice cold man (feat. LEE DORRIAN) / Emerald law (feat. WINO) / Big sky (feat. TOM G. WARRIOR) / Dictatosaurus (feat. SNAKE) / My tortured soul (feat. ERIC WAGNER) / Sweet dreams (feat. KING DIAMOND).

□ the FOR CARNATION (see under ⇒ SLINT)

FOREIGNER

Formed: New York, USA . . . early 1976 by English expatriot MICK JONES, who was already the owner of a rather chequered music biz CV. After beginning his career in England with 60's outfit NERO & THE GLADIATORS, he later worked with French singer JOHNNY HALLIDAY as well as undergoing a stint in SPOOKY TOOTH before moving to New York and securing a job as an A&R man. Eventually hooking up with Englishmen, IAN McDONALD and DENNIS ELLIOTT alongside New Yorkers, LOU GRAMM, AL

GREENWOOD and ED GAGLIARI, JONES formed FOREIGNER. After a year in the studio, the group unleashed an eponymous debut album for 'Atlantic'. Although the record failed to chart in the UK, it hit Top 5 in the States, becoming a multi-million seller and staying in the chart for a year. Its success boosted by two hit singles, 'FEELS LIKE THE FIRST TIME' and 'COLD AS ICE', FOREIGNER rapidly became established as prime staples for American FM radio. Though their material was harder-edged than the likes of REO SPEEDWAGON etc., FOREIGNER captured the middle ground perfectly, their AOR/hard rock-straddling sound gaining them massive sales for subsequent releases such as 'DOUBLE VISION' (1978) and 'HEAD GAMES' (1979), the former's title track narrowly missing the US top spot. Despite the group headlining the 1978 Reading Festival, the latter album (which saw another seasoned player, RICK WILLS, replacing GREENWOOD) failed to chart in the UK. FOREIGNER would have to wait until the release of the huge, Mutt Lange-produced '4' (1981) album, before they enjoyed transatlantic success. This was secured on the back of the UK/US Top 10, 'WAITING FOR A GIRL LIKE YOU'. It would be another histrionic AOR ballad, 'I WANT TO KNOW WHAT LOVE IS' (featuring the gospel talents of the New Jersey Mass Choir), that would become the group's best known song, its success even furnishing the band with a UK No.1 album. Released after a lengthy sabbatical, 'AGENT PROVOCATEUR' (1984), gave FOREIGNER yet another multi-million selling set, the success of the single making the band a household name. While LOU GRAMM cut a successful solo set in 1987, 'READY OR NOT', MICK JONES flopped with an eponymous set in '89, GRAMM eventually leaving the band for a time at the beginning of the 90's. While FOREIGNER had enjoyed reasonable success with the 1987 set, 'INSIDE INFORMATION', their first GRAMM-less set (with JOHNNY EDWARDS on vocals) was a relative commercial failure. GRAMM finally returned in 1994 although it was clear FOREIGNER's glory days were over.

• **Songwriters:** JONES penned some with GRAMM, until his 1987 departure.

Album rating: FOREIGNER (*5) / DOUBLE VISION (*6) / HEAD GAMES (*6) / 4 (*7) / RECORDS compilation (*8) / AGENT PROVOCATEUR (*6) / INSIDE INFORMATION (*5) / UNUSUAL HEAT (*5) / THE VERY BEST OF FOREIGNER or THE VERY BEST . . . AND BEYOND compilations (*7) / MR. MOONLIGHT (*4) / JUKEBOX HEROES: THE FOREIGNER ANTHOLOGY compilation (*7) / THE DEFINITIVE compilation (*8)

LOU GRAMM (b. 2 May'50, Rochester, New York) – vocals (ex-BLACK SHEEP) / **MICK JONES** (b.27 Dec'47, London, England) – guitar (ex-SPOOKY TOOTH) / **IAN McDONALD** (b.25 Jun'46, London) – guitar, keyboards (ex-KING CRIMSON) / **AL GREENWOOD** (b. New York) – keyboards / **ED GAGLIARI** (b.13 Feb'52, New York) – bass (ex-STORM) / **DENNIS ELLIOTT** (b.18 Aug'50, London) – drums (ex-IAN HUNTER BAND)

Atlantic Atlantic

Apr 77. (7") *(K 10917) <3394>* **FEELS LIKE THE FIRST TIME. / WOMAN OH WOMAN** [ ] Mar77 [4]

Apr 77. (lp/c) *(K/K4 50356) <18215>* **FOREIGNER** [ ] Mar77 [4]
– Feels like the first time / Cold as ice / Starrider / Headknocker / The damage is done / Long, long way from home / Woman oh woman / At war with the world / Fool for you anyway / I need you. *(cd-iss. Apr85; 250356) (re-iss. cd Oct95; same) <(cd re-mast.May02 on 'Rhino'+=; 8122 74270-2)>* – Feels like the first time (demo) / Woman oh woman (demo) / At war with the world (demo) / Take me to your leader (demo).

Jul 77. (7",7"clear) *(K 10986) <3410>* **COLD AS ICE. / I NEED YOU** [ ] [6]
(hit UK No.24 in Jul'78)

Dec 77. (7") *<3439>* **LONG, LONG WAY FROM HOME. / THE DAMAGE IS DONE** [–] [20]

Apr 78. (7"m) *(K 11086)* **FEELS LIKE THE FIRST TIME. / LONG, LONG WAY FROM HOME / COLD AS ICE** [39] [–]

Aug 78. (lp/c) *(K/K4 50476) <19999>* **DOUBLE VISION** [32] Jul78 [3]
– Hot blooded / Blue morning, blue day / You're all I am / Back where you belong / Love has taken its toll / Double vision / Tramontaine / I have waited so long / Lonely children / Spellbinder. *(cd-iss. 1988 & Oct95; K2 50476) <(cd re-mast.Aug02 on 'Rhino'+=; 8122 78187-2)>* – Hot blooded (live) / Love maker (live).

Oct 78. (7",7"red) *(K 11167) <3488>* **HOT BLOODED. / TRAMONTANE** [42] Jun78 [3]

Dec 78. (7") *(K 11199) <3514>* **DOUBLE VISION. / LONELY CHILDREN** [ ] Sep78 [2]

Feb 79. (7",7"pic-d) *(K 11236) <3543>* **BLUE MORNING, BLUE DAY. / I HAVE WAITED SO LONG** [45] Dec78 [15]

—— **RICK WILLS** – bass (ex-ROXY MUSIC, ex-SMALL FACES) repl. AL (he joined The SPYS)

Sep 79. (7") *(K 11373) <3618>* **DIRTY WHITE BOY. / REV ON THE RED LINE** [ ] [12]

Sep 79. (lp/c) *(K/K4 50651) <29999>* **HEAD GAMES** [ ] [5]
– Dirty white boy / Love on the telephone / Women / I'll get even with you / Seventeen / Head games / The modern day / Blinded by science / Do what you like / Rev on the red line. *(cd-iss. Feb93 on 'Atco'; 7567 81598-2) (re-iss. cd Nov95; 250651) <(cd re-mast.Aug02 on 'Rhino'+=; 8122 78198-2)>* – Zalia.

Feb 80. (7") *(K 11417) <3633>* **HEAD GAMES. / DO WHAT YOU LIKE** [ ] Nov79 [14]

Apr 80. (7") *(K 11456) <3651>* **WOMEN. / THE MODERN DAY** [ ] Feb80 [41]

Sep 80. (7") *(K 11602)* **I'LL GET EVEN WITH YOU. / BLINDED BY SCIENCE** [ ] [–]

—— Trimmed to quartet, when GAGLIARI and McDONALD left

Jul 81. (7") *(K 11665) <3831>* **URGENT. / GIRL ON THE MOON** [54] Jun81 [4]

Jul 81. (lp/c) *(K/K4 50796) <16999>* **4** [5] [1]
– Night life / Juke box hero / Break it up / Waiting for a girl like you / Luanne / Urgent / I'm gonna win / Woman in black / Urgent / Girl on the Moon / Don't let go. *(cd-iss. Aug85; 250796) (re-iss. cd Feb91; 7567 82795-2) <(cd re-mast.May02 on 'Rhino'+=; 8122 78275-2)>* – Juke box hero (nearly unplugged) / Waiting for a girl like you (nearly unplugged).

Sep 81. (7") *(K 11678) <4017>* **JUKE BOX HERO. / I'M GONNA WIN** [48] Feb82 [26]

Oct 81. (7") *<3868>* **WAITING FOR A GIRL LIKE YOU. / I'M GONNA WIN** [–] [2]

Nov 81. (7"m) *(K 11696)* **WAITING FOR A GIRL LIKE YOU. / FEELS LIKE THE FIRST TIME / COLD AS ICE** [8] [–]

Mar 82. (7") *(K 11718)* **DON'T LET GO. / FOOL FOR YOU ANYWAY** [ ] [–]

Apr 82. (7") *<4044>* **BREAK IT UP. / LUANNE** [–] [26]

Apr 82. (7") *(K 11728)* **URGENT. / HEAD GAMES (live)** [45] [–]
(12") *(K 11728T)* – ('A'side) / Hot blooded (live).

Jul 82. (7") *<4072>* **LUANNE. / FOOL FOR YOU ANYWAY** [–] [75]

Dec 82. (lp/c)(cd) *(A 0999/+4)(780 999-2) <80999>* **RECORDS (THE BEST OF . . .)** (compilation) [58] [10]
– Cold as ice / Double vision / Head games / Waiting for a girl like you / Feels like the first time / Urgent / Dirty white boy / Jukebox hero / Long long way from home / Hot blooded. *<(re-iss. cd Oct95; 7567 82800-2)>*

Nov 84. (7",7"sha-pic-d) *(A 9596) <89596>* **I WANT TO KNOW WHAT LOVE IS. / STREET THUNDER** [1] [1]
(12"+=) *(A 9596T)* – Urgent.

Dec 84. (lp/c/cd) *(781999-1/-4/-2) <81999>* **AGENT PROVOCATEUR** [1] Nov84 [4]
– Tooth and nail / That was yesterday / I want to know what love is / Growing up the hard way / Reaction to action / Stranger in my own house / A love in vain / Down on love / Two different worlds / She's too tough *(re-iss. cd Oct95; same)*

Mar 85. (7") *(A 9571) <89571>* **THAT WAS YESTERDAY (remix). / TWO DIFFERENT WORLDS** [28] [12]
(12"+=) *(A 9571T)* – ('A'-orchestral version).

May 85. (7") *<89542>* **REACTION TO ACTION. / SHE'S TOO TOUGH** [–] [54]

Jun 85. (7") *(A 9539)* **COLD AS ICE (remix). / REACTION TO ACTION** [64] [–]
(12"+=) *(A 9539T)* – Head games (live).
(d7"++=) *(A 9539/SAM 247)* – Hot blooded (live).

Aug 85. (7") *<89493>* **DOWN ON LOVE. / GROWING UP THE HARD WAY** [–] [54]

—— LOU GRAMM left to go solo

Jul 87. (7") *(A 9169) <89169>* **SAY YOU WILL. / A NIGHT TO REMEMBER** [71] Nov87 [6]
(7"box+=/12"+=/cd-s+=) *(A 9169 B/T/CD)* – Hot blooded (live).

Dec 87. (lp/c)(cd) *(WX 143/+C)(781808-2) <81808>* **INSIDE INFORMATION** [64] [15]
– Heart turns to stone / Can't wait / Say you will / I don't want to live

without you / Counting every minute / Inside information / The beat of my heart / Face to face / Out of the blue / A night to remember.

May 88. (7") *(A 9101) <89101>* **I DON'T WANT TO LIVE WITHOUT YOU. / FACE TO FACE** [ ] Mar88 [5]
(12"+=/cd-s+=) *(A 9101 T/CD)* – Urgent.

Jul 88. (7") *<89046>* **HEART TURNS TO STONE. / COUNTING EVERY MINUTE** [–] [56]

— (1990) added **JOHNNY EDWARDS** – vocals to join **JONES + THOMAS**

Jun 91. (7"/c-s) *(A 7666/+C)* **LOWDOWN AND DIRTY. / FLESH WOUND** [ ] [ ]
(12"+=/cd-s+=) *(A 7666 T/CD)* – No hiding place.

Jul 91. (cd)(lp/c) *<(7567 82299-2)>(WX 424/+C)* **UNUSUAL HEAT** [56] [ ]
– Only Heaven knows / Lowdown and dirty / I'll fight for you / Moment of truth / Mountain of love / Ready for the rain / When the night comes down / Safe in my heart / No hiding place / Flesh wound / Unusual heat. *(cd-iss. Nov93; same)*

Aug 91. (7"/c-s) *(A 7608/+MC)* **I'LL FIGHT FOR YOU / MOMENT OF TRUTH** [ ] [ ]
(12"+=/cd-s+=) *(A 7608 T/CD)* – Dirty white boy (live).

Apr 92. (cd)(lp/c) *(7597 80511-2)(WX 469/+C) <89999>* **THE VERY BEST OF FOREIGNER** (compilation) [19] [ ]
– Feels like the first time / Cold as ice / Starrider / Hot blooded / Blue morning, blue day / Double vision / Dirty white boy / Women / Head games / Juke Box hero / Waiting for a girl like you / Urgent / That was yesterday / I want to know what love is / Say you will / I don't want to live without you. *(re-iss. Dec92 as 'THE VERY BEST . . . AND BEYOND' cd; 7567 89999-2)(+=)* – (3 extra tracks).

Apr 92. (7"/c-s) *(7567 85696-7/-4)* **WAITING FOR A GIRL LIKE YOU (live). / COLD AS ICE (live)** [ ] [–]
(cd-s+=) *(7567 85696-2)* – That was yesterday (live) / Feels like the first time (live).

Dec 93. (cd/c) *<(7567 82525-2/-4)>* **CLASSIC HITS LIVE (live)** [ ] [ ]
– Double vision / Cold as ice / Damage is done / Women / Dirty white boy / Fool for you anyway / Head games / Not fade away – Mona / Waiting for a girl like you / Juke box hero / Urgent / Love maker / I want to know what love is / Feels like the first time.

— **JONES + GRAMM** recruited **MARK SCHULMAN** – drums / **JEFF JACOBS** – keyboards / **BRUCE TURGON** – bass

B.M.G. Rhythm Safari

Oct 94. (7"/c-s) *(74321 23286-7/-4)* **WHITE LIE. / UNDER THE GUN** [58] [ ]
(cd-s+=) *(74321 23286-2)* – ('A'-alternate version).

Nov 94. (cd/c) *<(74321 23285-2/-4)>* **MR. MOONLIGHT** [59] [ ]
– Under the gun / Rain / Until the end of time / White lie / Big dog / Real world / All I need to know / Hole in my soul / I keep hoping / Running the risk / Hand on my heart.

Mar 95. (c-s) *<53183>* **UNTIL THE END OF TIME / UNDER THE GUN** [–] [42]

Mar 95. (c-s) *(74321 25457-4)* **UNTIL THE END OF TIME / HAND ON MY HEART** [ ] [–]
(cd-s+=) *(74321 25457-2)* – ('A'mix).

– compilations, etc. –

Oct 00. (d-cd) *Rhino; <(8122 79884-2)>* **JUKEBOX HEROES – THE FOREIGNER ANTHOLOGY** [ ] Aug00 [ ]
– Feels like the first time / Long, long way from home / Cold as ice / Headknocker / Starrider / At war with the world / Double vision / Blue morning, blue day / Hot blooded / I have waited so long / Dirty white boy / Head games / Women / Rev on the red line / Break it up / Juke box hero / Luanne / Urgent / Waiting for a girl like you / All sewn up (SPOOKY TOOTH) / The hoofer (SPOOKY TOOTH) / I want to know what love is / Down on love / Street thunder / Reaction to action / That was yesterday / Ready or not / Midnight blue / Heart turns to stone / I don't want to live without you / Say you will / Can't wait / Just wanna hold (MICK JONES) / Everything that comes around (MICK JONES) / Just between you and me (LOU GRAMM) / Lowdown and dirty / Soul doctor / Until the end of time / Under the gun.

Sep 02. (cd) *Rhino; <(8122 73596-2)>* **THE DEFINITIVE FOREIGNER** [ ] [ ]
– Cold as ice / Waiting for a girl like you / I want to know what love is / That was yesterday / Urgent / Say you will / Double vision / Blue morning, blue day / Heart turns to stone / Feels like the first time / Long, long way from home / I don't want to live without you / Starrider / White lie / Break it up / Hot blooded / Dirty white boy / Down on love / Juke box hero / Urgent (live).

☐ Robert FORSTER (see under ⇒ GO-BETWEENS)

☐ Roddy FRAME (see under ⇒ AZTEC CAMERA)

FRANKIE GOES TO HOLLYWOOD

Formed: Liverpool, England ... August '80 (initially as HOLLYCAUST) by HOLLY JOHNSON, who had issued two solo singles, 'YANKEE ROSE' and 'HOBO JOE', after once being part of punk experimentalists, BIG IN JAPAN. Taking their name from a news headline concerning singer, FRANKIE VAUGHAN going into the movies, FGTH enjoyed some on TV exposure in late 1982. After a session on David Jensen's Radio One show, they were invited onto Channel 4's 'The Tube', where they sang an embryonic, 'RELAX'. This led to 'Z.T.T.' (Zang Tumb Tumm) label, run by PAUL MORLEY and TREVOR HORN (ex-BUGGLES) signing them in Autumn 1983. With HORN's clever production, the song 'RELAX' soon climbed to the top in the UK, aided by another Radio One DJ, Mike Read, who helped it get banned from airplay due to its risqué lyrics. In June '84, with 'RELAX' still in the chart, the follow-up, 'TWO TRIBES', went straight in at No.1, and gave a new lease of life to the debut (it resurged back up to No.2, while 'TWO TRIBES' was at No.1!). This well-produced, power-disco/rock outfit were always at the front end of controversy (so to speak!), their gay/S&M sex themes (provided by leather clad HOLLY and boyfriend/dancer, PAUL RUTHERFORD) were the toast of the burgeoning mid-80's dance scene. Their debut (a double!) album in October '84, 'WELCOME TO THE PLEASURE DOME', also hit peak position, as did their third consecutive No.1 single, 'THE POWER OF LOVE' (a feat only previously achieved by another Mersey group, GERRY & THE PACEMAKERS). In March '85, their fourth single, the title track from the album, spoiled the run when it stalled at No.2. The group returned in late summer '86 after over a year off, their fifth single, 'RAGE HARD', only just scraping into the UK Top 5. Poor reviews of their follow-up album, 'LIVERPOOL', saw the group fading into a sharp commercial decline with each subsequent single release. HOLLY JOHNSON was back early in 1989. Having signed a contract with 'M.C.A.', the singer subsequently charted high with the singles, 'LOVE TRAIN' and 'AMERICANOS', which previewed his No.1 album, 'BLAST'. In mid-1990, HOLLY was asked by friend RICHARD O'BRIEN, to act as FRANK 'N' FURTER in the 'Rocky Horror Picture Show'. HOLLY's second solo album, 'DREAMS THAT MONEY CAN'T BUY' (1991), failed miserably, its sales so poor that the set didn't achieve a Top 75 placing. Sadly, HOLLY was subsequently diagnosed with the AIDS virus and was HIV postive as he wrote his autobiography, entitled 'A Bone In My Flute' (1994). Prior to delivering his third solo set, 'SOULSTREAM' (1999) – on his own 'Pleasuredome' imprint', JOHNSON exhibited his artwork at a London gallery.

• **Songwriters:** All group compositions except; FERRY ACROSS THE MERSEY (Gerry & The Pacemakers) / BORN TO RUN (Bruce Springsteen) / WAR (Edwin Starr) / SUFFRAGETTE CITY (David Bowie) / GET IT ON (T.Rex) / SAN JOSE (Bacharach-David). HOLLY solo covered; LOVE ME TENDER (Elvis Presley). The track 'ACROSS THE UNIVERSE' was not The BEATLES original. • **Trivia:** The 'TWO TRIBES' video (directed by GODLEY & CREME) featured Ronald Reagan & Chernenko lookalikes fighting in a wrestling ring.

Album rating: WELCOME TO THE PLEASURE DOME (*7) / LIVERPOOL (*5) / Holly Johnson: BLAST (*5) / DREAMS THAT MONEY CAN'T BUY (*3) / SOULSTREAM (*3)

HOLLY JOHNSON (b. WILLIAM JOHNSON, 9 Feb'60, Khartoum, Sudan) – vocals (ex-solo artist, ex-BIG IN JAPAN) / **PAUL RUTHERFORD**

(b. 8 Dec'59) – vocals (ex-SPITFIRE BOYS) / **BRIAN NASH** (b.20 Mar'63) – guitar repl. GED O'TOOLE / **MARK O'TOOLE** (b. 6 Jan'64) – bass / **PETER GILL** (b. 8 Mar'64) – drums

ZTT-Island Island

Oct 83. (7"pic-d/7") *(P+/ZTAS 1) <99805>* **RELAX. / ONE SEPTEMBER MORNING** [1] Mar84 [67]
(12"/12"pic-d) *(12/+P ZTAS 1)* – ('A'version) / Ferry across the Mersey.
(c-ep) *(CTIS 102)* – "Relax's Greatest Bits" – (various mixes).

Jun 84. (7"pic-d/7") *(P+/ZTAS 3) <99695>* **TWO TRIBES. / ONE FEBRUARY MORNING** [1] Oct84 [43]
(12"/12"pic-d) *(12/+P ZTAS 3)* – ('A'version) / War (hide yourself).
(12"pic-d) *(XZTAS 3)* – (all 3 tracks above)
(c-ep) *(CTIS 103)* – "Two Tribes (Keep The Peace)" – (various mixes).

Nov 84. (d-lp/c/cd) *(ZTTIQ/ZCIQ/CDIQ 1) <90232>* **WELCOME TO THE PLEASURE DOME** [1] [33]
– Well . . . / The world is my oyster / Snatch of fury / Welcome to the pleasure dome / Relax / War / Two tribes / Ferry / Born to run / San Jose / Wish the lads were here (inc. 'Ballad of 32') / Black night white light / The only star in Heaven / The power of love / Bang . . . *(also d-pic-lp; NEAT 1) (re-iss. May94 & Feb95 cd/c; same) (re-hit No.16 in Jun99) (cd re-iss. Jul00 on 'Repertoire'; RR 4896) (cd re-iss. Aug00 on 'ZTT'; ZTT 157CD)*

Nov 84. (7"pic-d/7") *(P+/ZTAS 5)* **THE POWER OF LOVE. / THE WORLD IS MY OYSTER** [1] [ ]
(12"+=) *(12XZTAS 5)* – ('A'-Pleasurefix mix) / ('A'-Starfix mix).
(12"pic-d)(c-s) *(12PZTAS 5)(CTIS 105)* – ('A'side) / Trapped and scrapped / Holier than thou.

Mar 85. (7"sha-pic-d/7") *(P+/ZTAS 7) <99653>* **WELCOME TO THE PLEASURE DOME. / HAPPY HI / GET IT ON** [2] [48]
(12"+=) *(XTAS 7)* – Born to run (live).
(c-s+=) *(CTIS 107)* – How to remake the world.

Aug 86. (7") *(ZTAX 22)* **RAGE HARD. / (DON'T LOSE WHAT'S LEFT) OF YOUR LITTLE MIND** [4] [ ]
(12"+=) *(12ZTAQ 22)* – Suffragette City.
(12"+=/12"box+=) *(12ZTAX/+B 22)* – Roadhouse blues.
(cd-s+=) *(ZCID 22)* – Suffragette city / Roadhouse blues.

Sep 86. (lp/c/cd) *(ZTT/ZC/ZCD IQ 8) <90546>* **LIVERPOOL** [5] [88]
– Warriors of the wasteland / Rage hard / Kill the pain / Maximum joy / Watching the wildlife / Lunar bay / For Heaven's sake / Is anybody out there?. *(re-iss. 1989 on 'Island'; IMCD 13) (re-iss. May94 & Nov98 cd/c; ZTT 107CD) (cd re-iss. Jul00 on 'Repertoire'; RR 4897)*

Nov 86. (7") *(ZTAS 25)* **WARRIORS OF THE WASTELAND. / WARRIORS (instrumental)** [19] [ ]
(12"+=/c-s+=/cd-s+=) *(12ZTAS/CTIS/ZCID 25)* – Warriors (lots of different mixes).

Feb 87. (7") *(ZTAS 26)* **WATCHING THE WILDLIFE. / THE WAVES** [28] [ ]
(12"+=) *(12ZTAX 26)* – Wildlife (Bit 3 & 4).
(c-s+=/cd-s+=) *(CTIS/ZCID 26)* – (various mixes, etc).

—— they split after legal contractual problems; RUTHERFORD went solo

—— In the spring of '93, HOLLY revealed he was HIV positive (AIDS)

– compilations, etc. –

releases on 'ZTT'

Sep 93. (7"/c-s) *(FGTH 1/+C)* **RELAX. / RELAX MCMXCIII** [5] [ ]
(12"+=/cd-s+=) *(FGTH 1 T/CD)* – ('A'mixes; Jam & Spoon, etc).

Oct 93. (cd/c/lp) *(4509 93912-2/-4/-1)* **BANG! . . . THE GREATEST HITS OF . . .** [4] [ ]
– Relax / Two tribes / War / Ferry / Warriors of the wasteland / For Heaven's sake / The world is my oyster / Welcome to the Pleasure dome / Watching the wildlife / Born to run / Rage hard / The power of love / Bang . . . *(re-iss. Jun94 cd/c; same) (cd re-iss. Jul00 on 'Repertoire'; RR 4898) (cd re-iss. Aug00; ZTT 159CD)*

Nov 93. (7"/c-s) *(FGTH 2/+C)* **WELCOME TO THE PLEASURE DOME. / ('A'-Elevatorman's non-stop top floor mix)** [18] [ ]
(12"+=/cd-s+=) *(FGTH 2 T/CD)* – ('A'mixes; Brothers In Rhythm, etc).

Dec 93. (7"/c-s) *(FGTH 3/+C)* **THE POWER OF LOVE. / ('A'mix)** [10] [ ]
(cd-s+=) *(FGTH 3CD)* – Rage hard (original DJ mix) / Holier than thou.

Feb 94. (7"/c-s) *(FGTH 4/+C)* **TWO TRIBES (Fluke's minimix). / ('A'mix)** [16] [ ]
(12"+=/cd-s+=) *(FGTH 4 T/CD)* – ('A'mixes).

May 94. (cd/c/lp) *(4509 95292-2/-4/-1)* **RELOAD – THE WHOLE 12 INCHES** [ ] [–]
(cd re-iss. Jul00 on 'Repertoire'; RR 4899) (cd re-iss. Aug00; ZTT 160CD)

Jun 00. (c-s/12"/cd-s) *(ZTT 150 C/T/CD)* **THE POWER OF LOVE (mixes)** [6] [–]

Jul 00. (cd-s) *Repertoire; (RR 8024)* **THE POWER OF LOVE (remix)** [ ] [–]

Aug 00. (c-s/12"/cd-s) *(ZTT 154 C/T/CD)* **TWO TRIBES (mixes)** [17] [–]

Sep 00. (cd/c) *(ZZT 160 CD/C)* **MAXIMUM JOY** [54] [–]

Nov 00. (c-s/12"/cd-s) *(ZTT 166 C/T/CD)* **WELCOME TO THE PLEASURE DOME** [45] [–]

HOLLY JOHNSON

had earlier returned to a solo career

M.C.A. Uni

Jan 89. (7") *(MCA 1306)* **LOVE TRAIN. / MURDER IN PARADISE** [4] [ ]
(12"+=/cd-s+=) *(MCAT/DMCA 1306)* – ('A'mix).

Mar 89. (7"/c-s) *(MCA/+C 1323)* **AMERICANOS. / ('A'dub version)** [4] [ ]
(cd-s+=/12"+=) *(D+/MCAT 1323)* – ('A'-Liberty mix).
(12") *(MCAX 1323)* – ('A'remixes).

Apr 89. (lp/c/cd) *(DMCG/MCGC/MCG 6042) <603>* **BLAST** [1] [ ]
– Atomic city / Heaven's here / Americanos / Deep in love / S.U.C.C.E.S.S. / Love train / Got it made / Love will come / Perfume / Fee good.

Jun 89. (12"/c-s) *(MCA T/C 1342)* **ATOMIC CITY. / BEAT THE SYSTEM** [18] [–]
(12"+=/cd-s+=) *(MCAX/DMCAT 1342)* – ('A'extended).

Sep 89. (7"/7"pic-d/c-s) *(MCA/+P/C 1365)* **HEAVEN'S HERE. / HALLELUJAH** [62] [–]
(cd-s+=/12"+=) *(D+/MCAT 1365)* – ('A'version).

Jul 90. (cd/c/lp) *(DMCL/MCLC/MCL 1902)* **HALLELUJAH, THE REMIX ALBUM** (BLAST remixed) [ ] [–]

Nov 90. (7"/c-s) *(MCA/+C 1460)* **WHERE HAS LOVE GONE. / PERFUME** [73] [–]
(cd-s+=/12"+=) *(D+/MCAT 1460)* – ('A'version).

Mar 91. (7"/c-s) **ACROSS THE UNIVERSE. / FUNKY PARADISE** [ ] [–]
(cd-s+=/12"+=) – ('A'-Space a-go-go mix).

May 91. (lp/c/cd) *(MCA/+C/D 10278)* **DREAMS THAT MONEY CAN'T BUY** [ ] [–]
– Across the universe / When the party's over / The people want to dance / I need your love / Boyfriend '65 / Where has love gone? / Penny arcade / Do it for love / You're a hit / The great love story.

Aug 91. (7"/c-s) **PEOPLE WANT TO DANCE. / ('A'-Apollo 440 mix)** [ ] [ ]
(12"+=/cd-s+=) – Love train (anxious big beat version).

Club Tool not is

Sep 94. (12"ep/cd-ep) **LEGENDARY CHILDREN (ALL OF THEM QUEER). / (4-'A'mixes)** [ ] [–]

Pleasuredome not is

Aug 99. (12"/cd-s) *(PLD/+CD1 004)* **DISCO HEAVEN (mixes; Sicario club radio / Daz & Andy's Heavenly / Sicario club)** [ ] [–]

Oct 99. (cd/c) *(PLD CD/MC 001)* **SOULSTREAM** [ ] [–]
– Lady luck / Soulstream / Disco heaven / Don't give up / Hope / The be invention / Hallelujah! / All U need is love / Legendary children (2000 The power of love / Urban jungle – In the house of the rising sun.

Dec 99. (c-s/cd-s) *(PLD MC/CD1 005)* **THE POWER OF LOVE (mix) / IN THE HOUSE OF THE RISING SUN (mixes; 12" & Doggs House)** [56] [–]
(cd-s) *(PLCD 2005)* – ('A'-Millennium mix) / In the house of the rising su (DNA instrumental) / All U need is love (demo).

– early solo as HOLLY –

Eric's not i

Dec 79. (7"m) *(ERIC'S 003)* **YANKEE ROSE. / TREASURE ISLAND / DESPERATE DAN** [ ] [–]

Jun 80. (7") *(ERIC'S 007)* **HOBO JOE. / STARS OF THE BARS** [ ] [–]

Aretha FRANKLIN

Born: 25 Mar'42, Memphis, Tennessee, USA. She was one of six children (future recording artists ERMA and CAROLYN among them) raised by her well-to-do preacher father, Rev. C.L. Franklin (a much revered figure, who himself had released a catalogue of recordings of his famous sermons) after they moved to Detroit, Michigan. In the early 50's, ARETHA was given singing lessons by family friends, MAHALIA JACKSON and CLARA WARD, who influenced her early career. ARETHA's initial recordings (included in the recently re-released 'Chess Masters' CD series) were primarily gospel releases, the celebratory, acappella black religious singing style that had developed from the old time spirituals and which went on to form a cornerstone of popular music. Inspired by the secular success of SAM COOKE, ARETHA subsequently moved to New York where she found manager, Joe King. There, she was spotted by music biz legend, JOHN HAMMOND, and in 1960 she signed to 'Columbia', releasing her debut single, 'TODAY I SING THE BLUES' In the autumn. After a minor hit, 'WON'T BE LONG', the gospel diva scored her first US Top 40 entry in 1961 with the standard, 'ROCK-A-BYE YOUR BABY WITH A DIXIE MELODY'. She continued to break the Hot 100 many times but FRANKLIN's wild creative spirit was essentially stifled by record company attempts to market her as a mainstream blues torch singer. Things really took off when she signed to 'Atlantic' in late '66, veteran producer Jerry Wexler relocating FRANKLIN to the legendary 'Muscle Shoals' studio in Alabama, the combination of WEXLER's experience and the "down home" style of the resident musicians, allowing FRANKLIN's formidable talents to flower in a manner that previous producer, Mitch Miller, hadn't touched on. With a team of WEXLER, engineer TOM DOWD and arranger ARIF MARDIN behind her, ARETHA was unstoppable and in the ensuing two years notched up a staggering run of hit singles, every one a timeless classic. 'I NEVER LOVED A MAN (THE WAY I LOVE YOU)' heralded her creative rebirth, FRANKLIN marking her territory with a seductive, primal femininity. The flip side was a sensitive cover of the DAN PENN/SPOONER OLDHAM classic, 'DO RIGHT WOMAN, DO RIGHT MAN', a potential hit in its own right. The same could be said of the follow-up, a blistering interpretation of Otis Redding's 'RESPECT', released with FRANKLIN's slow burning 'DR. FEELGOOD' in America and backed with the equally impressive 'SAVE ME' in Britain. The single was a US chart topper, the album 'I NEVER LOVED A MAN (THE WAY I LOVE YOU)' (1967) arguably her magnum opus and certainly a landmark soul release. More hits followed in the shape of the GOFFIN/KING-penned, '(YOU MAKE ME FEEL LIKE) A NATURAL WOMAN' (No.8 US), a cover of Don Covay's 'CHAIN OF FOOLS' (No.2 US) and 'SINCE YOU'VE BEEN GONE (SWEET SWEET BABY)'. All were included on 'LADY SOUL' (1968), another essential album which could've conceivably been titled 'FIRST LADY OF SOUL', ARETHA consolidating her position as the most talented female soul vocalist in the world as well as a highly accomplished piano player. 'THINK' was next up, a sexy soul juggernaut of a record and arguably the most uplifting call to feminist arms in the history of recorded music, while 'I SAY A LITTLE PRAYER', a beautifully sweet cover of the BACHARACH & DAVID number, was another million selling single, backed with the insidiously funky 'HOUSE THAT JACK BUILT' on the American release. As the decade drew to a close however, FRANKLIN began to lose her focus, splitting with her husband and sometime songwriting partner, TED WHITE. Nevertheless, 1970 saw a masterful gospel set, 'SPIRIT IN THE DARK', which contained the brilliant 'DON'T PLAY THAT SONG'. 'LIVE AT FILLMORE WEST' (1971) was a smoking concert set, while 'YOUNG GIFTED AND BLACK' (1972) featured the gritty funk of FRANKLIN's 'ROCK STEADY', proving that the 'Queen Of Soul' could compete with the Godfather, JAMES BROWN. 1972 also saw the release of 'AMAZING GRACE', Aretha's spellbinding double gospel set recorded with JAMES CLEVELAND & THE SOUTHERN CALIFORNIA COMMUNITY CHOIR. 'UNTIL YOU COME BACK TO ME (THAT'S WHAT I'M GONNA DO)', partly composed by STEVIE WONDER, was FRANKLIN's last major hit of the 70's and despite a reunion in 1974 with WEXLER and MARDIN, she couldn't match the depth and power of her late 60's heyday. Following a move to 'Arista' at the turn of the decade, FRANKLIN teamed up with LUTHER VANDROSS, releasing a string of slicker and poppier, if equally bland albums, the best of which, 'WHO'S ZOOMIN' WHO' (1985), providing her with her last Top 10 hit to date in the title track (excluding her smash hit duets with ANNIE LENNOX snd GEORGE MICHAEL). More interesting was the 1987 gospel album, 'ONE LORD, ONE FAITH, ONE BAPTISM', her voice still a revelation on a set which included contributions from the likes of MAVIS STAPLES and JESSE JACKSON. More's the pity then, that ARETHA seems to be lost without some kind of guiding hand, her wonderful voice wasted on uninspired projects. All her records from the golden period of '67-'72 are worth shelling out for, as is the Grammy Award-winning 4CD Box Set, covering the cream of the 'Atlantic' years. While the hip-hop smarts of 1998's 'A ROSE IS STILL A ROSE' had endeared her to a younger audience and regained her a place in the Top 40, FRANKLIN undertook a bonafide return to the roots with 2003's 'SO DAMN HAPPY'. If the hip-hop influence remained courtesy of two – admittedly rather wonderful – MARY J. BLIGE collaborations, ARETHA soared once more on the wholesome, retro soul likes of 'WONDERFUL'.

• **Songwriters:** Although ARETHA wrote many songs herself, her greatest success came with 'Atlantic' covers: SEE SAW (Don Covay) / YOU SEND ME (Sam Cooke) / SATISFACTION (Rolling Stones) / THE WEIGHT (Band) / TRACKS OF MY TEARS (Miracles) / GENTLE ON MY MIND (John Hartford) / ELEANOR RIGBY + LET IT BE (Beatles) / SON OF A PREACHER MAN (Dusty Springfield) / BRIDGE OVER TROUBLED WATER (Simon & Garfunkel) / DON'T PLAY THAT SONG + SPANISH HARLEM (Ben E. King) / WHOLY HOLY (Marvin Gaye) / YOU'RE ALL I NEED TO GET BY + AIN'T NOTHING LIKE THE REAL THING (Marvin Gaye & Tammi Terrell) / ANGEL (Jimi Hendrix) / WHEN YOU GET RIGHT DOWN TO IT (Ronnie Dyson) / WHAT A FOOL BELIEVES (Doobie Brothers) / EVERYDAY PEOPLE (Staple Singles) / etc. • **Trivia:** On her 1969 recordings, DUANE ALLMAN played slide guitar. She had been produced by many greats including QUINCY JONES (1973) / CURTIS MAYFIELD (1976) / LAMONT-DOZIER (1977) / ARIF MARDIN (1980) / LUTHER VANDROSS (1982-83) / NARADA MICHAEL WALDEN (1985-87). In 1980, she appeared as a waitress in the film, 'The Blues Brothers'.

Album rating: ARETHA (*4) / THE ELECTRIFYING ARETHA FRANKLIN (*4) / THE TENDER, THE MOVING, THE SWINGING (*5) / LAUGHING (ON THE OUTSIDE) (*4) / UNFORGETTABLE: A TRIBUTE TO DINAH WASHINGTON (*4) / SONGS OF FAITH gospel (*4) / RUNNIN' OUT OF FOOLS (*5) / YEAH!!! (*4) / SOUL SISTER (*4) / I NEVER LOVED A MAN (THE WAY I LOVE YOU) (*9) / ARETHA FRANKLIN'S GREATEST HITS exploitation compilation (*6) / ARETHA ARRIVES (*7) / ARETHA: LADY SOUL (*9) / ARETHA NOW (*8) / ARETHA IN PARIS (*6) / ARETHA FRANKLIN: SOUL '69 (*7) / ARETHA'S GOLD compilation (*8) / THIS GIRL'S IN LOVE WITH YOU (*6) / SPIRIT IN THE DARK (*6) / ARETHA LIVE AT FILLMORE WEST (*6) / ARETHA'S GREATEST HITS compilation (*7) / YOUNG, GIFTED & BLACK (*5) / AMAZING GRACE (*7) / HEY NOW HEY (THE OTHER SIDE OF THE SKY) (*6) / LET ME IN YOUR LIFE (*6) / WITH EVERYTHING I FEEL IN ME (*5) / YOU (*4) / SPARKLE soundtrack (*5) / SWEET PASSION (*4) / ALMIGHTY FIRE (*4) / LA DIVA (*3) / ARETHA (*5) / LOVE ALL THE HURT WAY (*4) / JUMP TO IT (*5) / GET IT RIGHT (*5) / WHO'S ZOOMIN' WHO (*6) / ARETHA [1986] (*5) / ONE LORD, ONE FAITH, ONE BAPTISM (*4) / THROUGH THE STORM (*5) / WHAT YOU SEE IS WHAT YOU SWEAT (*4) / QUEEN OF SOUL – THE VERY BEST OF ARETHA FRANKLIN compilation (*8) / RESPECT – THE VERY BEST OF ARETHA FRANKLIN compilation (*9) / SO DAMN HAPPY (*6)

ARETHA FRANKLIN

ARETHA FRANKLIN – vocals (with session people)

not iss. Checker

1960. (7") *<861>* **NEVER GROW OLD. / YOU GROW CLOSER** – [ ]

1960. (7") *<941>* **PRECIOUS LORD. / (part 2)** – [ ]

Fontana Columbia

Jan 61. (7") *(H 271) <41793>* **LOVE IS THE ONLY THING. / TODAY I SING THE BLUES** [ ] Oct60 [ ]
<re-iss. 1970>

Feb 61. (7") *<41923>* **WON'T BE LONG. / RIGHT NOW** – 76

Jul 61. (7") *<41985>* **MAYBE I'M A FOOL. / ARE YOU SURE** – [ ]

Oct 61. (7") *(H 343) <42157>* **ROCK-A-BYE YOUR BABY WITH A DIXIE MELODY. / OPERATION HEARTBREAK** [ ] 37

Jan 62. (lp) *(TFL 5173) <8412>* **ARETHA** [ ] Oct61 [ ]
– Won't be long / Over the rainbow / Love is the only thing / Sweet lover / All night long / Who needs you? / Right now / Are you sure / Maybe I'm a fool / It ain't necessarily so / Blue by myself / Today I sing the blues. *(re-iss. Jan84 on 'Cameo-CBS')*

C.B.S. Columbia

Jan 62. (7") *<42266>* **I SURRENDER, DEAR. / ROUGH RIDER** – 87 / 94

Apr 62. (lp) *<8561>* **THE ELECTRIFYING ARETHA FRANKLIN** – [ ]
– You made me love you / I told you so / Rockabye your baby with a Dixie melody / Nobody like you / Exactly like you / It's so heartbreakin' / Rough lover / Blue holiday / Just for you / That lucky old sun / I surrender, dear / Ac-cent-tchu-ate the positive.

Jun 62. (7") *<42456>* **DON'T CRY BABY. / WITHOUT THE ONE YOU LOVE** – 92

Sep 62. (7") *<42520>* **TRY A LITTLE TENDERNESS. / JUST FOR A THRILL** – 100

Nov 62. (lp) *<8676>* **THE TENDER, THE MOVING, THE SWINGING ARETHA FRANKLIN** – 69
– Don't cry baby / Try a little tenderness / I apologize / Without the one you love / Look for the silver lining / I'm sitting on top of the world / Just for a thrill / God bless the child / I'm wandering / How deep is the ocean / I don't know you anymore / Lover come back to me.

Dec 62. (7") *<42625>* **TROUBLE IN MIND. / GOD BLESS THE CHILD** – 86

Jan 63. (lp) *<8897>* **LAUGHING (ON THE OUTSIDE)** – [ ]
– Skylark / For all we know / Make someone happy / I wonder / Solitude / Laughing on the outside / Say it isn't so / Until the real thing comes along / If ever I would leave you / Where are you / Mr.Ugly / I wanna be around.

1963. (7") *<42796>* **SAY IT ISN'T SO. / HERE'S WHERE I CAME IN** – [ ]

1963. (7") *<42874>* **SKYLARK. / YOU'VE GOT HER** – [ ]

1963. (7") *<42933>* **JOHNNY. / KISSIN' BY THE MISTLETOE** – [ ]

1964. (7") *<43009>* **SOULVILLE. / EVIL GAL BLUES** – [ ]

Sep 64. (7") *<43113>* **RUNNIN' OUT OF FOOLS. / IT'S JUST A MATTER OF TIME** – 57

Oct 64. (lp) *<8963>* **UNFORGETTABLE: A TRIBUTE TO DINAH WASHINGTON** – [ ]
– Unforgettable / Cold cold heart / What a difference a day made / Drinking again / Evil gal blues / Nobody knows the way I feel this morning / Don't say you're sorry again / This bitter Earth / If I should lose you / Soulville. *(cd-iss. Jun95)*

Nov 64. (7") *<43177>* **WINTER WONDERLAND. / THE CHRISTMAS SONG** – [ ]

Dec 64. (lp) *<9081>* **RUNNIN' OUT OF FOOLS** – 84
– Mockingbird / How glad I am / Walk on by / My guy / Every little bit hurts / Shoop shoop song / You'll lose a good thing / I can't wait until I see my baby's face / It's just a matter of time / Runnin' out of fools / Two sides of love / One room Paradise.

Mar 65. (7") *<43203>* **CAN'T YOU JUST SEE ME. / LITTLE MISS RAGGEDY ANNE** [ ] Jan65 96

May 65. (7") *<43241>* **I CAN'T WAIT UNTIL I SEE MY BABY'S FACE. / ONE STEP AHEAD** – [ ]

Nov 65. (lp; stereo/mono) *(S+/BPG 62566) <9151>* **YEAH!!! – IN PERSON** [ ] Jul65 [ ]
– This could be the start of something / Once in a lifetime / Misty / More / There is no greater love / Muddy water / If I had a hammer / Impossible / Today I love everybody / Without the one you love / Trouble in mind / Love for sale.

Jul 66. (7") *<4333>* **SWEET BITTER LOVE. / I'M LOSING YOU** – [ ]

Aug 66. (lp; stereo/mono) *(S+/BPG 62744) <9321>* **SOUL SISTER** [ ] [ ]
– Until you were gone / You made me love you / Follow your heart / Ol' man river / Sweet bitter love / Mother's love / Swanee / I'm losing you / Take a look / Can't you just see me / Cry like a baby.

1966. (7") *<43442>* **THERE IS NO GREATER LOVE. / YOU MADE ME LOVE YOU** – [ ]

1966. (7") *<43515>* **HANDS OFF. / TIGHTEN UP YOUR TIE, BUTTON UP YOUR JACKET** – [ ]

1967. (7") *<43637>* **UNTIL YOU WERE GONE. / SWANEE** – [ ]

Atlantic Atlantic

Apr 67. (7") *(584 084) <2386>* **I NEVER LOVED A MAN (THE WAY I LOVE YOU). / DO RIGHT WOMAN, DO RIGHT MAN** [ ] Mar67 9

Apr 67. (7") *<2403>* **RESPECT. / DR. FEELGOOD** – 1

May 67. (7") *(584 115)* **RESPECT. / SAVE ME** 10 –

Jul 67. (lp; mono/stereo) *(587/588 066) <8139>* **I NEVER LOVED A MAN (THE WAY I LOVE YOU)** 36 Apr67 2
– Respect / Drown in my own tears / I never loved a man (the way I loved you) / Soul serenade / Don't let me lose this dream / Baby, baby, baby / Dr. Feelgood / Good times / Do right woman – do right man / Save me / A change is gonna come. *(re-iss. 1972) (cd-iss. Jun93)*

Aug 67. (7") *(584 127) <2427>* **BABY I LOVE YOU. / GOING DOWN SLOW** 39 Jul67 4

Sep 67. (7") *<2441>* **A NATURAL WOMAN (YOU MAKE ME FEEL LIKE). / BABY BABY BABY** – 8

Oct 67. (lp; mono/stereo) *(587/588 085) <8150>* **ARETHA ARRIVES** [ ] Aug67 5
– Satisfaction / You are my sunshine / Never let me go / 96 tears / Prove it / Night life / That's life / I wonder / Ain't nobody (gonna turn me around) / Going down slow / Baby, I love you. *(re-iss. 1972) (cd-iss. Aug93 on 'Rhino')*

Oct 67. (7") *(584 141)* **(YOU MAKE ME FEEL LIKE A) NATURAL WOMAN. / NEVER LET ME GO** [ ] –

Nov 67. (7") *<2464>* **CHAIN OF FOOLS. / PROVE IT** – 2

Dec 67. (7") *(584 157)* **CHAIN OF FOOLS. / SATISFACTION** 37 –

Mar 68. (7") *(584 172) <2486>* **(SWEET SWEET BABY) SINCE YOU'VE BEEN GONE. / AIN'T NO WAY** 47 5 / Feb68 16

Mar 68. (lp; mono/stereo) *(587/588 099) <8176>* **ARETHA: LADY SOUL** 25 Feb68 2
– Chain of fools / Money won't change You / People get ready / Niki Hoeky / (You make me feel like) A natural woman / Since you've been gone (sweet sweet baby) / Good to me as I am to you / Come back baby / Groovin' / Ain't no way. *(re-iss. Jun88, cd-iss. Sep89) (cd-iss. Jun93)*

May 68. (7") *(584 186) <2518>* **THINK. / YOU SEND ME** 26 7 / 56

Jul 68. (7") *(584 206)* **I SAY A LITTLE PRAYER. / SEE-SAW** 4 –

Aug 68. (7") *<2546>* **THE HOUSE THAT JACK BUILT. / I SAY A LITTLE PRAYER** – 6 / 10

Sep 68. (7") *(584 239)* **THE HOUSE THAT JACK BUILT. / DON'T LET ME LOSE THIS DREAM** [ ] –

Sep 68. (lp; mono/stereo) *(587/588 114) <8186>* **ARETHA NOW** 6 Jul68 3
– Think / I say a little prayer / See saw / Night time is the right time / You send me / You're a sweet sweet man / I take what I want / Hello sunshine / A change / I can't see myself leaving you *(cd-iss. Aug93 on 'Rhino')*

Nov 68. (7") *<2574>* **SEE SAW. / MY SONG** – 14 / 31

Dec 68. (lp; mono/stereo) *(587/588 149) <8207>* **ARETHA IN PARIS – LIVE AT THE OLYMPIA (live)** [ ] Nov68 13
– (I can't get no) Satisfaction / Don't let me lose this dream / Soul serenade / Night life / Baby I love you / Groovin' / Natural woman / Come back baby / Dr. Feelgood / Since you've been gone / I never loved a man (the way I love you) / Chain of fools / Respect. *(re-iss. cd Dec94 on 'Rhino-Atlantic')*

Mar 69. (7") *(584 252) <2603>* **THE WEIGHT. / THE TRACKS OF MY TEARS** [ ] 19 / Feb69 71

Mar 69. (lp) *(588 169) <8212>* **SOUL '69** [ ] Feb69 15
– Ramblin' / Today I sing the blues / River's invitation / Pitiful / Crazy he calls me / Bring it on home to me / Tracks of my tears / If you gotta make

a fool of somebody / Gentle on my mind / So long / I'll never be free / Elusive butterfly *(cd-iss. Feb94 on 'Rhino-Atlantic')*

Apr 69. (7") *<2619>* **I CAN'T SEE MYSELF LEAVING YOU. / GENTLE ON MY MIND** [–] [28] [76]

Aug 69. (7") *(584 285) <2650>* **SHARE YOUR LOVE WITH ME. / PLEDGING MY LOVE / THE CLOCK** [ ] Jul69 [13]

Nov 69. (7") *(584 306) <2683>* **ELEANOR RIGBY. / IT AIN'T FAIR** [ ] Oct69 [17]

Mar 70. (7") *(584 322) <2706>* **CALL ME. / SON OF A PREACHER MAN** [ ] Feb70 [13]

Apr 70. (lp) *(2400 004) <8248>* **THIS GIRL'S IN LOVE WITH YOU** [ ] Feb70 [17]
– Son of a preacher man / Share your love with me / The dark end of the street / Let it be / Eleanor Rigby / This girl's in love with you / It ain't fair / The weight / Call me / Sit down and cry *(cd-iss. Feb94 on 'Rhino-Atlantic')*

May 70. (7") *(2091 008)* **LET IT BE. / MY SONG** [ ] [–]

May 70. (7") *<2731>* **SPIRIT IN THE DARK. / THE THRILL IS GONE** [–] [23]

— Her new band comprised **KING CURTIS** – saxophone / **CORNELL DUPREE** – guitar / **RICHARD TEE** – piano / **JERRY JEMMOTT** – bass / **BERNARD PURDIE** – drums

Jul 70. (7") *<2751>* **DON'T PLAY THAT SONG. / LET IT BE** [–] [11]

Aug 70. (7") *(2091 027)* **DON'T PLAY THAT SONG. / THE THRILL IS GONE** [13] [–]

Sep 70. (lp) *(2400 021) <8265>* **DON'T PLAY THAT SONG** <US-title 'SPIRIT IN THE DARK'> [ ] [25]
– Don't play that song / The thrill is gone / Pullin' / You and me / Honest I do / Spirit in the dark / When the battle is over / One way ticket / Try Matty's / That's all I want from you / Oh no, not my baby / When I sing the blues. *(cd-iss. Feb94 on 'Rhino-Atlantic')*

Dec 70. (7") *(2091 044)* **OH NO NOT MY BABY. / YOU AND ME** [ ] [–]

Dec 70. (7") *<2772>* **BORDER SONG (HOLY MOSES). / YOU AND ME** [–] [37]

Feb 71. (7") *<2787>* **YOU'RE ALL I NEED TO GET BY. / PULLIN'** [–] [19]

Mar 71. (7") *(2091 063)* **YOU'RE ALL I NEED TO GET BY. / BORDER SONG** [ ] [–]

May 71. (7") *(2091 090) <2796>* **BRIDGE OVER TROUBLED WATER. / A BRAND NEW ME** [ ] Apr71 [6]

Jul 71. (lp) *(2400 136) <7205>* **LIVE AT FILLMORE WEST (live)** [ ] May71 [7]
– Respect / Love the one you're with / Bridge over troubled water / Eleanor Rigby / Make it with you / Don't play that song / Dr. Feelgood / Spirit in the dark / Spirit in the dark (reprise with RAY CHARLES) / Reach out and touch (somebody's hand). *(cd-iss. Feb94 on 'Rhino-Atlantic')*

Jul 71. (7"m) *(2091 111)* **I SAY A LITTLE PRAYER (live). / (I CAN'T GET NO) SATISFACTION (live)** [ ] [–]

Aug 71. (7") *(2091 127)* **A BRAND NEW ME. / SPIRIT IN THE DARK** [ ] [–]

— On the 13th August '71, her legendary sax player and soloist, KING CURTIS, was stabbed to death on the street. She and her father sang and gave sermon at funeral. She attended another funeral 6 months later of her friend/mentor Mahalia Jackson.

Sep 71. (7") *(2091 138) <2817>* **SPANISH HARLEM. / LEAN ON ME** [14] Jul71 [2]

Oct 71. (7") *<2838>* **ROCK STEADY. / OH ME OH MY (I'M A FOOL FOR YOU BABY)** [–] [9] [73]

Mar 72. (7") *(K 10154) <2866>* **DAYDREAMING. / I'VE BEEN LOVING TOU TOO LONG** [ ] [5]

Mar 72. (lp) *(K 40323) <7213>* **YOUNG, GIFTED AND BLACK** [ ] Feb72 [11]
– Oh me oh my (I'm a fool for you baby) / Daydreaming / Rock steady / Young, gifted and black / All the king's horses / A brand new me / April fools / I've been loving you too long / First snow in Kokomo / The long and winding road / Didn't I (blow your mind this time) / Border song. *(cd-iss. Feb94 on 'Rhino-Atlantic')*

May 72. (7") *<2883>* **ALL THE KING'S HORSES. / APRIL FOOLS** [–] [26]

Aug 72. (7") *<2901>* **WHOLY HOLY. / GIVE YOURSELF TO JESUS** [–] [81]

Sep 72. (7") *(K 10224)* **ALL THE KING'S HORSES. / ROCK STEADY** [ ] [–]

Sep 72. (d-lp) *(K 60023) <906>* **AMAZING GRACE (live)** [ ] Jun72 [7]
– Mary don't you weep / Medley / Precious Lord, Take my hand / You've got a friend / Old landmark / Give yourself to Jesus / How I got over / What a friend we have in Jesus / Amazing grace – Precious memories / Climbing higher mountains / Remarks by Reverend C L Franklin / God will take care of you / Wholy holy / You'll never walk alone / Never grow old. *(re-iss. Nov87)(cd-iss. Aug93)*

Mar 73. (7") *(K 10288) <2941>* **MASTER OF EYES (THE DEEPNESS OF YOUR EYES). / MOODY'S MOOD FOR LOVE** [ ] Feb73 [33]

Aug 73. (7") *(K 10346) <2969>* **ANGEL. / SISTER FROM TEXAS** [37] Jul73 [20]

Aug 73. (lp/c) *(K/K4 40504) <7265>* **HEY NOW HEY (THE OTHER SIDE OF THE SKY)** [ ] Jul73 [30]
– Hey now hey / Somewhere / So well when you're well / Angel / Sister from Texas / Mister Spain / That's the way I feel about cha / Moody's mood / Just right tonight. *(re-iss. cd Dec94 on 'Rhino-Atlantic')*

Jan 74. (7") *(K 10399) <2995>* **UNTIL YOU COME BACK TO ME (THAT'S WHAT I'M GONNA DO). / IF YOU DON'T THINK** [26] Nov73 [3]

Apr 74. (lp/c) *(K/K4 50031) <7292>* **LET ME IN YOUR LIFE** [ ] Mar74 [14]
– Let me in your life / Every natural thing / Ain't nothing like the real thing / I'm in love / Until you come back to me (that's what I'm gonna do) / The masquerade is over / With pen in hand / Oh baby / Eight days on the road / If you don't think / A song for you. *(re-iss. cd Dec94 on 'Rhino-Atlantic')*

Jun 74. (7") *(K 10447) <2999>* **I'M IN LOVE. / OH BABY** [ ] Apr74 [19]

Aug 74. (7") *<3200>* **AIN'T NOTHING LIKE THE REAL THING. / EIGHT DAYS A WEEK** [–] [47]

Jan 75. (7") *(K 10543) <3224>* **WITHOUT LOVE. / DON'T GO BREAKING MY HEART** [ ] Nov74 [45]

Feb 75. (lp/c) *(K/K4 50093) <18116>* **WITH EVERYTHING I FEEL IN ME** [ ] Jan75 [57]
– Without love / Don't go breaking my heart / When you get right down to it / You'll never get to Heaven / With everything I feel in me / I love every little thing about you / Sing it again – say it again / All of these things / You move me.

Mar 75. (7") *(K 10577)* **WHEN YOU GET RIGHT DOWN TO IT. / SING IT AGAIN – SAY IT AGAIN** [ ] [–]

Apr 75. (7") *<3249>* **SING IT AGAIN – SAY IT AGAIN. / WITH EVERYTHING I FEEL IN ME** [–] [ ]

Oct 75. (7") *(K 10669) <3289>* **MR. D.J. (5 FOR THE D.J.). / AS LONG AS YOU ARE THERE** [ ] Sep75 [53]

Dec 75. (7") *<3311>* **YOU. / WITHOUT LOVE** [–] [ ]

Dec 75. (lp/c) *(K/K4 50159) <18151>* **YOU** [ ] Nov75 [83]
– Mr D.J. / It only happens / I'm not strong enough to love you again / Walk softly / You make my life / Without you / The sha-la bandit / You got all the aces / As long as you are there.

Sep 76. (7") *(K 16765) <3326>* **SOMETHING HE CAN FEEL. / LOVING YOU BABY** [ ] Jun76 [28]

Sep 76. (7") *<3358>* **JUMP. / HOOKED ON YOUR LOVE** [–] [72]

Jan 77. (7") *<3373>* **LOOK INTO YOUR HEART. / ROCK WITH ME** [–] [82]

Apr 77. (lp/c) *(K/K4 56248) <18176>* **SPARKLE (Soundtrack)** [ ] Jun76 [18]
– Sparkle / Something he can feel / Hooked on your love / Look into your heart / I get high / Jump / Loving you baby / Rock with me. *<(cd-iss. Jun00 on 'Rhino'; 8122 71148-2)>*

May 77. (7") *(K 10938) <3393>* **BREAK IT TO ME GENTLY. / MEADOWS OF SPRINGTIME** [ ] [85]

Jun 77. (lp/c) *(K/K4 50368) <19102>* **SWEET PASSION** [ ] [49]
– Break it to me gently / When I think about you / What I did for love / No one could ever love you more / Tender touch / Touch me up / Sunshine will never be the same / Meadows of Springtime / Mumbles / I've got the music in me / Passion.

Sep 77. (7") *(K 11007) <3418>* **WHEN I THINK ABOUT YOU. / TOUCH ME** [ ] [ ]

Jun 78. (lp/c) *(K/K4 50445) <19161>* **ALMIGHTY FIRE** [ ] May78 [63]
– Almighty fire (woman of the future) / Lady day / More than just a joy / Keep on loving you / I needed you baby / Close to you / No matter who you love / This you can believe / I'm your speed.

Jun 78. (7") *<3468>* **ALMIGHTY FIRE. / I'M YOUR SPEED** [–] [ ]

Nov 78. (7") *<3495>* **THIS YOU CAN BELIEVE. / MORE THAN JUST A JOY** [–] [ ]

Oct 79. (7") *(K 11390) <3605>* **LADIES ONLY. / WHAT IF I SHOULD EVER NEED YOU** [ ] [ ]

Oct 79. (lp/c) *(K/K4 50637) <19248>* **LA DIVA** [ ] [ ]
– Ladies only / It's gonna get a bit better / What if I should ever need you / Honey I need your love / I was made for you / Only star / Reasons why / You brought me back to life / Half a love / The feeling.

Jan 80. (7") *<3632>* **HALF A LOVE. / ONLY STAR** [–] [ ]

Arista Arista

Oct 80. (7"/12") *(ARIST/+12 377)* **WHAT A FOOL BELIEVES. / SCHOOLDAYS** [46] [–]

Oct 80. (lp/c) *(SPART/TCART 1147) <9538>* **ARETHA** [ ] [47]
– Come to me / I can't turn you loose / United together / Take me with you / Whatever it is / What a fool believes / Together / Love me forever / Schooldays. *(re-iss. May88 lp/c/cd; 208/408/258 883)*

Mar 81. (7") *(ARIST 395) <0569>* **UNITED TOGETHER. / I CAN'T TURN YOU LOOSE** [ ] Dec80 [56]

May 81. (7") *<0600>* **COME TO ME. / SCHOOL DAYS** [–] [84]

Aug 81. (7"/12"; ARETHA FRANKLIN & GEORGE BENSON) *(ARIST/+12 428) <0624>* **LOVE ALL THE HURT AWAY. / HOLD ON I'M COMING** [49] [46]

Sep 81. (lp/c) *(SPART/TCART 1170) <9552>* **LOVE ALL THE HURT AWAY** [ ] [36]
– Hold on I'm coming / You can't always get what you want / It's my turn / Living in the streets / Love all the hurt away / There's a star for everyone / Truth and honesty / Search on / Whole lot of me / Kind of man *(cd-iss. 1988; 253 913)*

Jan 82. (7") *<0646>* **IT'S MY TURN. / KIND OF MAN** [–] [ ]

Feb 82. (7"/12") *(ARIST/+12 442)* **HOLD ON I'M COMING. / KIND OF MAN** [ ] [–]

Apr 82. (7") *<0665>* **LIVIN' IN THE STREETS. / THERE'S A STAR FOR EVERYONE** [–] [ ]

Aug 82. (7"/12") *(ARIST/+12 479) <0699>* **JUMP TO IT. / JUST MY DAYDREAM** [42] [24]

Aug 82. (lp/c) *(204/404 742) <9602>* **JUMP TO IT** [ ] [23]
– Love me right / 16 she don't want your love / This is for real / (It's just) Your love / I wanna make it up to you / It's your thing / Just my day dream. *(re-iss. May88 lp/c/cd; 209/409/259 060)*

Jan 83. (7"/12") *(ARIST/+12 500) <1023>* **LOVE ME RIGHT. / (IT'S JUST) YOUR LOVE** [ ] [ ]

Mar 83. (7") *<1043>* **THIS IS FOR REAL. / I WANT TO MAKE IT UP TO YOU** [–] [ ]

Jul 83. (7"/12") *(ARIST/+12 537)* **GET IT RIGHT. / JUMP TO IT** [74] [–]

Jul 83. (7") *<9034>* **GET IT RIGHT. / GIVING IN** [–] [61]

Jul 83. (lp/c) *(205/405 544) <8019>* **GET IT RIGHT** [ ] [36]
– Get it right / Pretender / Every girl (wants my guy) / When you love me like that / I wish it would rain / Better friends than lovers / I got your love / Giving in.

Oct 83. (7") *<9095>* **EVERY GIRL (WANTS MY GIRL). / I GOT YOUR LOVE** [–] [ ]

— In Jul'85, while attending a civil rights campaign, her father C.L. is shot and went into a coma. He never recovered fully and died in Jul'87.

Jul 85. (7") *(ARIST 624) <9354>* **FREEWAY OF LOVE. / UNTIL YOU SAY YOU LOVE ME** [68] Jun85 [3]
(12"+=) *(ARIST12 624)* – Jump to it.
(d7"++=) *(ARIST22 624)* – Zoomin' to the freeway.
(7"/12" – re-dist.Apr86, hit UK No.51)

— (Oct85) She duets with EURYTHMICS on her 'SISTERS ARE DOIN' IT FOR THEMSELVES'. It hit UK No.9 + US No.18.

Nov 85. (lp/c/cd) *(207/407 202) <8286>* **WHO'S ZOOMIN' WHO?** [49] Jul85 [13]
– Who's zoomin' who / Freeway of love / Another night / Sweet bitter love / Sisters are doin' it for themselves / Until you say love me / Push / Ain't nobody ever loved you / Integrity. *(re-iss. Jul88 lp/c/cd; 259/409/259 053)*

Nov 85. (7") *(ARIST 633) <9410>* **WHO'S ZOOMIN' WHO. / SWEET BITTER LOVE** [11] Sep85 [7]
(12"+=) *(ARIST12 633)* – ('A'dub version) / ('A'acappella mix).

Feb 86. (7")(12") *(ARIST 657) <9453>* **ANOTHER NIGHT. / KIND OF MAN** [54] [22]
(12"+=) *(ARIST12 657)* – School days / Together again.
(d7"++=) *(ARIST22 657)* – ('A'-Nightlife mix).

Aug 86. (7") *(ARIST 667) <9474>* **AIN'T NOBODY EVER LOVED YOU. / INTEGRITY** [ ] [ ]
(12"+=) *(ARIST12 667)* – ('A'dub mix) / ('A-Percappella mix).

Oct 86. (lp/c/cd) *(208/408/258 020) <8442>* **ARETHA** [51] [32]
– Jimmy Lee / I knew you were waiting (for me) / Do you still remember / Jumpin' Jack Flash / Rock-a-lott / An angel cries / He'll come along / If you need my love tonight / Look to the rainbow. *(cd re-iss. Nov93 on 'Entertainers')*

Oct 86. (7") *(ARIST 678) <9528>* **JUMPIN' JACK FLASH. / INTEGRITY** [58] Sep86 [21]
(12"+=) *(ARIST12 678)* – Who's zoomin' who / Sweet bitter love.

Nov 86. (7") *<9546>* **JIMMY LEE. / IF YOU NEED MY LOVE TONIGHT** [–] [28]

— She hit No.1 UK/US with GEORGE MICHAEL duet 'I KNEW YOU WERE WAITING (FOR ME)', This was released 'Epic' UK / 'Arista' US.

Feb 87. (7") *(RIS 6) <9557>* **JIMMY LEE. / AN ANGEL CRIES** [ ] Apr87 [ ]
(12"+=/cd-s+=) *(RIST/RICD 6)* – ('A'dub version) / Aretha megamix.

Jun 87. (7") *(RIS 20) <9574>* **ROCK-A-LOTT. / LOOK TO THE RAINBOW** [ ] [82]
(12") *(RIST 20)* – ('A'side) / ('A'dub) / ('A'cappella mix).

Oct 87. (7") *<9623>* **IF YOU NEED MY LOVE TONIGHT. / HE'LL COME ALONG** [–] [ ]

Nov 87. (lp/c/cd) *(208/408/258 715) <8497>* **ONE LORD, ONE FAITH, ONE BAPTISM** [ ] [ ]
– Walking in the light / Prayer invitation by Cecil Franklin / Introduction by Rev. Jesse Jackson / Jesus hears every prayer / Surely God is able / The Lord's prayer / Oh happy day / We need prayer / Speech by Rev. Jesse Jackson / Ave Maria / Introduction by Rev. Jasper Williams / Higher ground / Prayer by Rev. Donald Person / I've been in the storm too long / Waking up ready to go.

Feb 88. (7"/12") *(109780/610978) <9672>* **OH HAPPY DAY. / THE LORD'S PRAYER** [ ] [ ]
(above featured MAVIS STAPLES)

Apr 89. (7"/c-s/7"pic-d; ARETHA FRANKLIN & ELTON JOHN) *(112 185/409957/112377) <9809>* **THROUGH THE STORM. / COME TO ME** [41] [ ]
(12"+=/cd-s+=) *(612/162 185)* – Oh happy day.

May 89. (lp/c/cd) *(209/409/259 842) <8572>* **THROUGH THE STORM** [46] [55]
– Through the storm / Gimme your love / He's the boy / It ain't never gonna be / Think / Mercy / It isn't, it wasn't, it ain't never gonna be / If ever a love there was.

Jun 89, (7"; ARETHA FRANKLIN & WHITNEY HOUSTON) *<9850>* **IT ISN'T, IT WASN'T, IT AIN'T NEVER GONNA BE. / IF EVER A LOVE THERE WAS** [–] [41]

Sep 89. (7"/c-s; ARETHA FRANKLIN & WHITNEY HOUSTON) *(112545/410093)* **IT ISN'T, IT WASN'T, IT AIN'T NEVER GONNA BE. / THINK '89** [29] [–]
(12"+=) *(612545)* – ('A'extended remix).
(cd-s++=) *(662545)* – ('A'-Hip hop remix).

Nov 89. (7") *(112728) <9884>* **GIMME YOUR LOVE. / HE'S THE BOY** [ ] [ ]
(12"+=/cd-s+=) *(612/662 727)* – ('A'parts 1 & 2 versions).

Jul 91. (7") *(114420) <2239>* **EVERYDAY PEOPLE. / YOU CAN'T TAKE ME FOR GRANTED** [69] [ ]
(12") *(114420) <2340>* – ('A'side) / ('A'people remix) / ('A'people dub).
(cd-s+=) *(114420)* – ('A'remixed).

Aug 91. (cd/c/lp) *(261/411/211 724) <8628>* **WHAT YOU SEE IS WHAT YOU SWEAT** [ ] [ ]
– Everyday people / Everchanging times (with MICHAEL McDONALD / What you see is what you sweat / Mary goes round / I dreamed a dream / Someone' else's eyes / Doctor's orders / You can't take me for granted / What did you give / Everyday people (remix). *(cd re-iss. Feb94; same)*

Sep 91. (c-s) *<2350>* **SOMEONE ELSE'S EYES / WHAT DID YOU GIVE** [–] [ ]

Nov 91. (c-s) *<2380>* **WHAT YOU SEE IS WHAT YOU SWEAT /** [–] [ ]

Feb 92. (c-s) *<2394>* **YOU CAN'T TAKE ME FOR GRANTED / EVERCHANGING TIMES** [–] [ ]

Jan 94. (c-s) *(74321 18702-4) <12657>* **A DEEPER LOVE. / ('A'-Tribesman mix)** [5] [63]
(12"+=/cd-s+=) *(74321 18702-1/-2)* – (2 other mixes).

Mar 94. (cd/c) *(74321 16202-2/-4) <18722>* **GREATEST HITS 1980-1994** (compilation) [27] [85]
– Freeway of love / I knew you were waiting (for me) (w/ GEORGE MICHAEL) / Jump to it / Willing to forgive / Doctor's orders / United together / Who's zoomin' who / A deeper love / Honey / Get it right / Another night / Ever changing times / Jimmy Lee / (You make me fee like) A natural woman / I dreamed a dream / Jumpin' Jack Flash.

Jun 94. (c-s) *(74321 21334-4) <12680>* **WILLING TO FORGIVE / JUMP TO IT** [17] [26]
(12"+=/cd-s+=) *(74321 21334-1/-2)* – ('A'mix).

Apr 98. (c-s/cd-s) *(74321 56974-4/-2) <13465>* **A ROSE IS STILL A ROSE / ('A'mix)** [22] Mar98 [26]
(cd-s) *(74321 58035-2)* – ('A'mixes).

May 98. (cd/c) *<(0782 2 18987-2/-4)>* **A ROSE IS STILL A ROSE** [ ] Apr98 [30]
– A rose is still a rose / Never leave you again / In case you forgot / Here we go again / Every little bit hurts / In the morning / I'll dip / How many times / Watch my back / Love pang / Woman.

Sep 98. (c-s/cd-s) *(74321 61274-4/-2)* <13502> **HERE WE GO AGAIN / IN THE MORNING / NESSUN DORMA (live)** 68 Jul98 76
(cd-s) *(74321 61275-2)* – ('A'side) / Who's zoomin' who / Everyday people.
Sep 03. (12") *<56474>* **THE ONLY THING MISSIN. / (mix)** –
Sep 03. (cd) *(82876 55279-2) <50174>* **SO DAMN HAPPY** 33
– The only thing missin' / Wonderful / Holdin' on / No matter what / Everybody's somebody's fool / So damn happy / You are my joy / Falling out of love / Ain't no way / Good news / You are my joy (reprise).

– (selective) compilations, etc. –

on 'CBS' / 'Columbia' unless mentioned otherwise
Jun 67. (lp) *(CBS 64536) <9473>* **GREATEST HITS: ARETHA FRANKLIN 1960-65** 94
(re-iss. Apr87 lp/c;)
Aug 67. (7") *<44270>* **TAKE A LOOK. / FOLLOW YOUR HEART** – 56
Dec 67. (7") *<44381>* **MOCKINGBIRD. / A MOTHER'S LOVE** – 94
Jan 68. (lp) *(CBS 63269) <9554>* **TAKE A LOOK** Oct67
Feb 68. (7") *<44441>* **SOULVILLE. / EVIL GAL BLUES** – 83
on 'Atlantic' unless mentioned otherwise
Jul 69. (lp) *(588 182) <8227>* **ARETHA'S GOLD** 18
(re-iss. 1972) (cd-iss. Aug93)
1970. (lp) *(2464 007)* **I SAY A LITTLE PRAYER** –
Sep 71. (lp) *(K 40279) <8295>* **ARETHA'S GREATEST HITS** 19
(re-iss. 1982) (cd-iss. Aug93)
May 86. (d-lp/d-c) *Stylus; (SMR/SMC 8506)* **THE FIRST LADY OF SOUL** 89 –
Mar 90. (7") *East West; (A 7951)* **THINK. / (b-side by Blues Brothers)** 31 –
(12"+=/cd-s+=) (TA/CDA 7951) – ('A'mixes).
May 93. (cd) *<(7567 81230)>* **ARETHA'S JAZZ**
Jun 93. (d-cd) *<(7567 81668-2)>* **30 GREATEST HITS**
Oct 94. (cd/c) *<(7567 80606-2/-4)>* **QUEEN OF SOUL – THE VERY BEST OF . . .** 23
Apr 97. (cd) *Chess-MCA; <(MCD 91521)>* **ARETHA GOSPEL**
May 97. (cd) *Rhino; <(8122 72576-2)>* **LOVE SONGS**
May 98. (cd) *Sony Jazz; (CK 65050)* **THIS IS JAZZ**
May 98. (cd) *Rhino; <(8122 72942-2)>* **DELTA MEETS DETROIT: ARETHA'S BLUES**
Aug 98. (cd) *C.B.S.; (491454-2)* **SOUL SISTER (THE BEST OF ARETHA FRANKLIN)**
Nov 98. (d-cd/d-c) *Global TV; (RAD CD/MC 110)* **GREATEST HITS** 38
Jul 99. (d-cd) *<(8122 75627-2)>* **AMAZING GRACE: THE COMPLETE GOSPEL RECORDINGS**
Sep 00. (cd) *Universal; (AAMCAD 11850)* **YOU GROW CLOSER: THE PEACOCK GOSPEL CLASSICS**
Feb 01. (cd) *Columbia; (501495-2)* **LOVE SONGS** –
Apr 01. (cd) *Camden; (74321 84088-2)* **LOVE SONGS** –
Jun 02. (d-cd) *Warners; (0927 47054-2)* **RESPECT – THE VERY BEST OF ARETHA FRANKLIN** 15 –
– Respect / Think / Spanish Harlem / You make me feel like a natural woman / I say a little prayer / Son of a preacher man / I never loved a man / Chain of fools / Don't play that song / Angel / Border song (holy Moses) / Rock steady / See saw / The house that Jack built / Oh no not my baby / Until you come back to me / Good times / Since you've been gone / You're all I need to get by / Ain't nothing like the real thing / Do right woman do right man / Share your love with me / Something he can feel / Ain't no way / Sisters are doin' it for themselves (with ANNIE LENNOX) / I knew you were waiting (for me) (with GEORGE MICHAEL) / Through the storm (with ELTON JOHN) / Love all the hurt away / Willing to forgive / Let it be / Never let me go / The night time is the right time / Call me / Drown in my tears / People get ready / My song / The dark end of the street / Today I sing the blues / A rose is still a rose / Who's zoomin' who / Freeway of love / Daydreaming / Bridge over troubled water.

FRANZ FERDINAND

Formed: Glasgow, Scotland . . . late 2001 by singer/guitarist ALEX KAPRANOS, BOB HARDY and NICK McCARTHY; ex-YUMMY FUR sticksman PAUL THOMSON was added before they ventured into the studio. Half-Greek, half-English, with an encyclopedic CV, KAPRANOS had been a prime mover on the Glasgow indie scene in the decade prior to forming FRANZ (when he still called himself ALEX HUNTLEY), playing with the AMPHETAMEANIES, QUINN, URUSEI YATSURA and the BLISTERS, who evolved into the all-but-forgotten the KARELIA. Named after the Austro-Hungarian archduke whose assassination led to the first World War, his new band began cultivating their art school cool in an abandoned Gorbals warehouse they dubbed the Chateau. As the brains behind FRANZ FERDINAND's distinctive, post-New Wave/Punk aesthetic, KAPRANOS timed the band's entrance perfectly, incubating their sound (think the FIRE ENGINES, GANG OF FOUR, TALKING HEADS and JOSEF K) through the summer of 2002 to their zeitgeist-coasting appearance at T In The Park 2003. Even hotter than July was their demo track 'TELL HER TONIGHT', touted by the STROKES and inspiration for 'Domino' records to offer them a deal. The now highly collectable 'DARTS OF PLEASURE' single reached a modest No.44 in the UK charts, consolidated with support slots to HOT HOT HEAT and INTERPOL. It might have been released in January, but 'TAKE ME OUT' was already being touted as Single Of The Year (2004) after reaching UK Top 3. Their eponymous debut album more than lived up to the hype, likewise topping most critics' end of year rundowns as well as the British charts. A major label US deal was probably inevitable but what wasn't so predictable was the fact that, for the first time since fellow Glaswegians SIMPLE MINDS two decades earlier, a Scottish band cracked the notoriously resistant American mainstream. Back home, the band's drainpipe-skinny chic was everywhere, as follow-up 45, 'MATINEE', racked them up another Top 10 hit, and successive singles, 'MICHAEL' and 'THIS FFFIRE' went Top 20. Before the winner had even been announced, they looked to pretty much have the Mercury Music Prize in the bag, a fact confirmed in early 2005, along with two Brit awards. Given the unrelenting media attention, the self-consciously retro 'DO YOU WANT TO' was a comeback single in name only, its Top 5, playlist saturation making it seem as if FRANZ F had never been away. Chart-topping sophomore set, 'YOU COULD HAVE IT SO MUCH BETTER' (2005), couldn't quite match the dark glamour of their debut, but as both Top 20 singles, 'WALK AWAY' and 'THE FALLEN', and spastic-funk album tracks like 'OUTSIDERS' proved, their suave chemistry looks likely to burn for a few years yet.

Album rating: FRANZ FERDINAND (*9) / YOU COULD HAVE IT SO MUCH BETTER (*8)

ALEX KAPRANOS (b.20 Mar'72, Almondsbury, England) – vocals, guitar (ex-KARELIA) / **NICK McCARTHY** – guitar, keyboards, vocals / **BOB HARDY** – bass / **PAUL THOMSON** – drums (ex-YUMMY FUR)

Domino Domino

Sep 03. (7") *(RUG 164)* **DARTS OF PLEASURE. / SHOPPING FOR BLOOD** 44 –
(12"+=/cd-s+=) (RUG 164 T/CD) – Van tango.
Jan 04. (7") *(RUG 172)* **TAKE ME OUT. / TRUCK STOP** 3 May04 66
(12") *(RUG 172T)* – ('A') / ('A'-Morgan Geist re-version).
(cd-s) *(RUG 172CD) <Sony; 76774>* – ('A') / All for you, Sophia / Words so leisured.
(dvd-s) *(RUG 172DVD)* – ('A') / ('A'-video & extras).
Feb 04. (cd/lp) *(WIG CD/LP 27) <DN 027 CD/LP>* **FRANZ FERDINAND** 1 Mar04
– Jacqueline / Tell her tonight / Take me out / The dark of the matinee / Auf achse /Cheating on you / This fire / Darts of pleasure / Michael / Come on home / 40'.

Domino Epic/Sony

Apr 04. (cd/lp; re-) *<EK 92441-2/-1>* **FRANZ FERDINAND** – 32
<d-cd-iss. Nov04 +=; EK 93630> – This Ffire / Van tango / Shopping for blood / All for you, Sophia / Words so leisured.
Apr 04. (7") *(RUG 176)* **MATINEE. / MICHAEL (live at KCRW)** 8 –
(12"/cd-s) *(RUG 176 T/CD)* – ('A') / Better in Hoboken / Forty feet.
(dvd-s) *(RUG 176CD)* – ('A'-video & extras).
Aug 04. (7") *(RUG 184)* **MICHAEL. / MICHAEL (Simon Bookish version)** 17 –
(12"/cd-s) *(RUG 184 T/CD1)* – ('A') / Love and destroy / Missing you.

FRANZ FERDINAND

(cd-s) *(RUG 184CD2)* – ('A') / Don't start / Tell her tonight (Paul sings).
(cd-s) *(RUG 184CD3)* – ('A') / Don't start.
Nov 04. (dl-s) *(RUG 192DL)* **THIS FFFIRE (Rich Costey re-record) / THIS FIRE (Playgroup remix)** 8 –
Sep 05. (dl-s) *(RUG 211DL)* *<radio>* **DO YOU WANT TO** 4 76
(cd-s+=) *(RUG 211CD)* – Your diary.
(cd-s+=) *(RUG 211CDX)* – Fabulously lazy / What you meant (acoustic).
Oct 05. (cd/lp) *(WIG CD/LP 161)* *<1EK/1E 94800>* **YOU COULD HAVE IT SO MUCH BETTER** 1 8
– The fallen / Do you want to / This boy / Walk away / Evil and a heathen / You're the reason I'm leaving / Eleanor put your boots on / Well that was easy / What you meant / I'm your villain / You could have it so much better / Fade together / Outsiders. *(ltd-cd w/dvd+=; WIGCD 161X)* – (extras & videos).
Dec 05. (cd-s) *(RUG 215CD)* **WALK AWAY / SEXY BOY** 13 –
(7") *(RUG 215)* ('A') / The fallen (acoustic).
(cd-s) *(RUG 215dvd)* – ('A') / ('A'-video) / This boy (live) / (extras).
Apr 06. (7") *(RUG 219)* **THE FALLEN. / LINDSEY WELLS** 14 –
(7"m+=) *(RUG 219X)* – Brown onions.
(cd-s++=) *(RUG 219CD)* – Jeremy Fraser / ('A'-video).
(12") *(RUG 219T2)* – ('A'-Ruined by justice) / ('A') / Do you want to (Max Tundra remix) / Do you want to (Max Tundra instrumental).

□ FREAK POWER (see under ⇒ COOK, Norman)

FREE

Formed: London, England . . . Spring 1968 by PAUL RODGERS (vocals), PAUL KOSSOFF (guitar) and SIMON KIRKE (drums). The latter two had been members of blues combo BLACK CAT BONES before poaching RODGERS from another blues outfit, BROWN SUGAR. With the addition of young ex-BLUESBREAKER, ANDY FRASER, on bass, this precocious line-up was complete, adopting the name FREE at the suggestion of blues grandaddy ALEXIS KORNER. KORNER also tipped off 'Island' supremo CHRIS BLACKWELL, and after resisting an extremely misguided BLACKWELL attempt to rename them The HEAVY METAL KIDS, FREE duly signed to his label and began work on their debut album, TONS OF SOBS (1968). Emerging from the shadow of CREAM, the album was an impressive set of heavy, organic blues, KOSSOFF stealing the show with his emotionally charged, liquid gold guitar style, in full effect on BOOKER T's 'THE HUNTER'. By the release of 'FREE' (1969), RODGERS soulful voice was developing into one of the best in rock, while FRASER had taken on joint songwriting duties with RODGERS. The band also had a blistering live reputation and had already built up a sizeable following by the time 'ALL RIGHT NOW' was a massive worldwide hit. It's gritty R&B stomp paved the way for FREE's magnum opus, 'FIRE AND WATER' (1970), a No.3 UK album that boasted such enduring fare as the introspective ballads, 'OH I WEPT' and 'HEAVY LOAD' while RODGERS' wonderfully evocative vocals lent 'REMEMBER' a mellow resonance. That summer, cresting the wave of their popularity, the band played to over half a million people at the Isle Of Wight festival. With pressure to come up with a successful follow-up to 'ALL RIGHT NOW', FREE were confident that the 'THE STEALER' would do the business. When it stiffed completely things started to go seriously awry, the 'HIGHWAY' (1970) album receiving a similarly lukewarm reception. This relative commercial failure increased tensions in what was already a perilously fraught intra-band relationship, the group deciding to call it a day after fulfilling touring commitments in Japan and Australia. The split eventually came in May '71, ironically almost coinciding with their biggest hit since 'ALL RIGHT NOW', a FACES-style romp entitled 'MY BROTHER JAKE'. Solo projects by RODGERS (PEACE) and FRASER (TOBY) came to little, although KOSSOFF and KIRKE's eponymous collaboration with Texan keyboard player, JOHN 'RABBIT' BUNDRICK, and Japanese bassist TETSU YAMAUCHI, was released to relative critical an commercial success, KOSSOFF relishing the opportunity to realis his ideas outwith the confines of FREE. The band subsequentl regrouped in early 1972 and recorded the 'FREE AT LAST' album a reasonable effort which spawned a Top 20 hit with the 'LITTLI BIT OF LOVE' single, a highly melodic slice of rock, the sort o thing RODGERS would go on to perfect with BAD COMPANY While the album made the Top 10, KOSSOFF was spiralling int serious drug dependence, and following a disastrous America tour, the band's stability received a further blow when FRASEI departed for the group SHARKS (he subsequently released a fe melodic rock albums in the mid 70's). With TETSU and RABBI filling in, FREE undertook a Japanese tour prior to recording a fina album, 'HEARTBREAKER' (1973). Although KOSSOFF was too i to make much of a contribution, the album stands among FREE' best, boasting RODGER's desperate plea to KOSSOFF, 'WISHIN WELL', and the superb, BEATLES-esque 'COME TOGETHER II THE MORNING'. Following a final tour of America with TRAFFIC FREE finally split in summer '73, RODGERS and KIRKE goin on to form BAD COMPANY. KOSSOFF, meanwhile, had alread begun his ill-fated solo career, forming BACK STREET CRAWLER After a handful of relatively well-received albums, KOSSOFF finall succumbed to heroin addiction, dying in his sleep on the 19t March '76. It was a tragic end for a guitarist who was onc destined to be remembered in the same breath as the likes of ERI CLAPTON and JIMI HENDRIX.

Album rating: TONS OF SOBS (*7) / FREE (*6) / FIRE AND WATER (*8) HIGHWAY (*5) / FREE LIVE (*6) / FREE AT LAST (*5) / HEARTBREAKER (*6) THE FREE STORY compilation (*8) / COMPLETELY FREE compilation (*7) THE BEST OF FREE – ALL RIGHT NOW compilation (*8) / MOLTEN GOL THE ANTHOLOGY compilation (*8) / KOSSOFF, KIRKE, TETSU & RABBI (*4) / Back Street Crawler: BACK STREET CRAWLER (*6) / AND THE BAN PLAYS ON (*5) / posthumous:- KOSS (*6) / THE COLLECTION (*6) / STON FREE (*6)

PAUL RODGERS (b.12 Dec'49, Middlesbrough, England) – vocals (e BROWN SUGAR) / **PAUL KOSSOFF** (b.14 Sep'50, Hampstead, Londo England) – guitar (ex-BLACK CAT BONES) / **SIMON KIRKE** (b.2 Jul'49, Shrewsbury, England) – drums (ex-BLACK CAT BONES) / **AND FRASER** (b. 7 Aug'52, Shropshire, England) – bass (ex-JOHN MAYALL BLUESBREAKERS)

Island A&
Nov 68. (lp) *(ILPS 9089)* *<4198>* **TONS OF SOBS** Aug69
– Over the green hills (part 1) / Worry / Walk in my shadow / Wild Indi woman / Goin' down slow / I'm a mover / The hunter / Moonshine Sweet tooth / Over the green hills (part 2). *(cd-iss. Jun88; CID 908 (cd re-iss. 1989; IMCD 62) (<cd re-mast.Oct01 on 'Island-Universal'+ IMCD 289><586149>* – I'm a mover (BBC session) / Waitin' on you (BB session) / Guy Stevens blues (blues jam) / Moonshine (alt.) / Sweet too (alt.) / Visions of Hell (mix) / Woman by the sea (alt.) / Over the gre hills (BBC session).
Mar 69. (7") *<1099>* **I'M A MOVER. / WORRY** –
Mar 69. (7") *(WIP 6054)* **BROAD DAYLIGHT. / THE WORM** –
Jul 69. (7") *(WIP 6062)* **I'LL BE CREEPIN'. / SUGAR FOR MR. MORRISON** –
Aug 69. (7") *<1172>* **I'LL BE CREEPIN'. / MOUTHFUL OF GRASS** –
Oct 69. (lp) *(ILPS 9104)* *<4204>* **FREE** 22
– I'll be creepin' / Songs of yesterday / Lying in the sunshine / Trouble double time / Mouthful of grass / Woman / Free me / Broad dayligh Mourning sad morning. *(cd-iss. Jun88; CID 9104) (lp re-iss. Jan00 'Simply Vinyl'; SVLP 165) (cd re-mast.Oct01 on 'Island-Universal'+=; IM 282)* – Broad daylight (mono) / Worm (mono) / I'll be creepin' (mono Sugar for me Mr. Morrison (mono) / Broad daylight (BBC session) / Son of yesterday (BBC session) / Mouthful of grass (solo acoustic) / Wom (alt.) / Trouble on double time (Songs of yesterday version) / Mourni sad morning (alt.).
May 70. (7") *(WIP 6082)* *<1206>* **ALL RIGHT NOW. / MOUTHFUL OF GRASS** 2 Jul70 4
(re-iss. Jul73 hit UK No.15)
Jun 70. (lp) *(ILPS 9120)* *<4268>* **FIRE AND WATER** 2 Aug70 17
– Fire and water / Oh I wept / Remember / Heavy load / Mr. Big / Don't s

you love me / All right now. *(re-iss. Sep86 lp/c/cd; ILPM/ICM/CID 9120) (cd-iss. Apr90; IMCD 80) (re-iss. lp Jan94 + May94; ILPS 9120) (lp re-iss. Jul99 on 'Simply Vinyl'; SVLP 97) (<cd re-mast.Oct01 on 'Island-Universal'+=; IMCD 284)<586227>* – Oh I wept (alt.) / Fire and water (new stereo) / Fire and water (BBC session) / All right now (BBC session) / All right now (single version) / All right now (Songs of yesterday version).

Nov 70. (7") *(WIP 6093)* **THE STEALER. / LYING IN THE SUNSHINE** [ ] [–]

Nov 70. (7") *<1230>* **THE STEALER. / BROAD DAYLIGHT** [–] [49]

Dec 70. (lp) *(ILPS 9138) <4287>* **HIGHWAY** [41] Feb71 [ ]
– The highway song / The stealer / On my way / Be my friend / Sunny day / Ride on pony / Love you so / Bodie / Soon I will be gone. *(cd-iss. Jun88; CID 9138) (cd re-iss. 1989; (IMCD 63) (<cd re-mast.Feb02 on 'Island-Universal'+=; IMCD 283)<586226>* – My brother Jake / Only my soul / Ride on a pony (BBC session) / Be my friend (BBC session) / Rain (alt.) / The stealer (single version).

Jan 71. (7") *<1248>* **THE HIGHWAY SONG. / LOVE YOU SO** [–] [ ]

Mar 71. (7") *<1266>* **I'LL BE CREEPIN'. / MR. BIG** [–] [ ]

Apr 71. (7") *(WIP 6100) <1276>* **MY BROTHER JAKE. / ONLY MY SOUL** [4] [ ]

Jun 71. (lp) *(ILPS 9160) <4306>* **FREE LIVE! (live)** [4] Aug71 [89]
– All right now / I'm a mover / Be my friend / Fire and water / Ride on pony / Mr. Big / The hunter / Get where I belong (studio). *(cd-iss. Jun88; CID 9160) (cd re-iss. 1989; IMCD 73) (<cd re-mast.Feb02 on 'Island-Universal'+=; IMCD 286)<586228>* – Woman / Walk in my shadow / Moonshine / Trouble on double time / Mr. Big / All right now / Get where I belong (alt.).

— they had already split May'71. FRASER formed TOBY, while RODGERS formed the short-lived PEACE.

KOSSOFF, KIRKE, TETSU & RABBIT

were formed by the other two plus **TETSU YAMAUCHI** (b.21 Oct'47, Fukuoka, Japan) – bass / **JOHN 'RABBIT' BUNDRICK** – keyboards, vocals / and guest **B.J. COLE** – steel guitar

Nov 71. (lp) *(<ILPS 9188>)* **KOSSOFF, KIRKE, TETSU & RABBIT** [ ] [ ]
– Blue grass / Sammy's alright / Just for the box / Colours / Hold on / Yellow house / Dying fire / Fool's life / Anna / I'm on the run. *(re-iss. Aug91 cd)(c; IMCD 139)(ICM 9188)*

FREE

— re-formed originals Feb'72 (**RODGERS, KOSSOFF, FRASER + KIRKE**)

May 72. (7") *(WIP 6129) <1352>* **LITTLE BIT OF LOVE. / SAIL ON** [13] [ ]

Jun 72. (lp/c) *(ILPS/ICT 9192) <4349>* **FREE AT LAST** [9] [69]
– Catch a train / Soldier boy / Magic ship / Sail on / Travelling man / Little bit of love / Guardian of the universe / Child / Goodbye. *(cd-iss. Jun88; CID 9192) (cd re-iss. Feb90; IMCD 82) (<cd re-mast.Feb02 on 'Island-Universal'+=; IMCD 287)<586229>* – Burnin' (molten gold) (alt.) / Honky tonk women / Magic ship / Little bit of love / Guardian of the universe (Paul Rodgers solo) / Child (early version).

— **TETSU YAMAUCHI** – bass (see above); repl. FRASER who joined SHARKS / added **JOHN 'RABBIT' BUNDRICK** – keyboards (see above) / **RODGERS** – also added guitar

Dec 72. (7") *(WIP 6146)* **WISHING WELL. / LET ME SHOW YOU** [7] [–]

Jan 73. (lp/c) *(ILPS 9217) <9324>* **HEARTBREAKER** [9] [47]
– Wishing well / Come together in the morning / Travellin' in style / Heartbreaker / Muddy water / Common mortal man / Easy on my soul / Seven angels. *(cd-iss. Jun88; CID 9217) (cd re-iss. Feb90; IMCD 81) (<cd re-mast.Feb02 on 'Island-Universal'+=; IMCD 288)<586230>* – Wishing well (US mix) / Let me show you / Muddy water (alt.) / Hand me down – Turn me around / Heartbreaker (rehearsal) / Easy on my soul (rehearsal).

Mar 73. (7") *(WIP 6160)* **TRAVELLIN' IN STYLE. / EASY ON MY SOUL** [ ] [–]
(re-iss. Mar74; WIP 6223)

— **WENDELL RICHARDSON** – guitar of OSIBISA, on UK & US tour early '73) repl. KOSSOFF who formed BACK STREET CRAWLER. He died in his sleep 19 Mar'76 after years of drug abuse. FREE split early '73. RABBIT went solo before joining (KOSSOFF's) CRAWLER. TETSU joined The FACES. RODGERS and KIRKE formed BAD COMPANY.

– compilations, etc. –

on 'Island' UK / 'A&M' US unless mentioned otherwise

Mar 74. (d-lp) *(ISL D4)* **THE FREE STORY** [2] [ ]
– I'm a mover / I'll be creepin' / Mourning sad morning / All right now / Heavy load / Fire and water / Be my friend / The stealer / Soon I will be gone / Mr. Big / The hunter / Get where I belong / Travelling man / Just for the box / Lady / My brother Jake / Little bit of love / Sail on / Come together in the morning. *(re-iss. Oct89 lp/c/cd; ILPS/ICT/CID 9945) (cd re-iss. Sep96; IMCD 226)*

1974. (7") *<1629>* **LITTLE BIT OF LOVE. / THE STEALER** [–] [ ]

1974. (7") *<1720>* **ALL RIGHT NOW. / THE STEALER** [–] [ ]

Apr 75. (lp) *<3663>* **THE BEST OF FREE** [–] [ ]

Nov 76. (lp) *(ILPS 9453)* **FREE AND EASY, ROUGH AND READY** [ ] [–]

Nov 76. (7") *(WIP 6351)* **THE HUNTER. / WORRY** [ ] [–]

Feb 78. (7"ep) *(IEP 6)* **THE FREE EP** [11] [–]
– All right now / My brother Jake / Wishing well. *(re-iss. Oct82 as 12"pic-d; PIEP 6)* – hit UK No.57.

Oct 82. (lp/c) *(ILPS/ICT 9719)* **COMPLETELY FREE** [ ] [–]

May 85. (7") *(IS 221)* **WISHING WELL. / WOMAN** [ ] [–]
(12"+=) *(12IS 221)* – Walk in my shadow.

Feb 91. (c-s/7") *(C+/IS 486)* **ALL RIGHT NOW. / I'M A MOVER** [8] [ ]
(12"+=/cd-s+=) *(12IS/CID 486)* – Get where I belong.

Feb 91. (cd/c/lp) *(CID/IC/ILP TV 2)* **ALL RIGHT NOW – THE BEST OF FREE** [9] [ ]
– Wishing well / All right now / Little bit of love / Come together in the morning / The stealer / Sail on / Mr. Big / My brother Jake / The hunter / Be my friend / Travellin' in style / Fire and water / Travelling man / Don't say you love me.

Apr 91. (c-s/7") *(C+/IS 495)* **MY BROTHER JAKE (remix). / WISHING WELL (remix)** [ ] [ ]
(12"+=/cd-s+=) *(12IS/CID 495)* – The stealer (extended) / Only my soul (extended).

Nov 92. (d-cd) *(ITSCD 3)* **FIRE AND WATER / HEARTBREAKER** [ ] [–]

May 94. (d-cd) *(CRNCD 2) <518456>* **MOLTEN GOLD: THE ANTHOLOGY** [ ] [–]

Nov 98. (cd) *(IMCD 255)* **WALK IN MY SHADOW – AN INTRODUCTION TO FREE** [ ] [–]

Oct 99. (cd) *Spectrum; (544167-2)* **ALL RIGHT NOW** [ ] [–]

May 00. (5xcd-box) *(IBXCD 3)* **SONGS OF YESTERDAY** [ ] [–]

Oct 01. (cd) *Universal; (<E 586315>)* **THE UNIVERSAL MASTERS COLLECTION** [ ] [ ]

☐ FREEHEAT (see under ⇒ JESUS & MARY CHAIN)

☐ Ace FREHLEY (see under ⇒ KISS)

☐ FREUR (see under ⇒ UNDERWORLD)

☐ Glenn FREY (see under ⇒ EAGLES)

☐ Robert FRIPP (see under ⇒ KING CRIMSON)

☐ Edgar FROESE (see under ⇒ TANGERINE DREAM)

FUGAZI

Formed: Washington DC, USA ... 1987 by IAN MacKAYE), who had the previous year featured on an album by EMBRACE (not the more recent outfit!). MacKAYE and drummer JEFF NELSON subsequently founded the 'Dischord' label, a bedrock of the Washington DC hardcore scene and an outlet for the pair's new band, MINOR THREAT. Completing the line-up with LYLE PRESLAR and BRIAN BAKER, this highly influential outfit released two singles in 1981, before they added STEVE HANSEN to boost their minimalist sound on the album, 'OUT OF STEP' (1983). A further album, the eponymous 'MINOR THREAT', contained the track 'STRAIGHT EDGE', a term which would be adopted by a generation of fans who followed MacKAYE and Co.'s example of abstinence and individual responsibility. Following their split, mainman MacKAYE formed FUGAZI, sharing vocal and songwriting duties with GUY PICCIOTTO (ex-leader of RITES OF SPRING and INSURRECTION – the latter outfit having released a self-titled effort for 'Peaceville'). With the FUGAZI line-up crystallising around BRENDAN CANTY and JOE LALLY, they released two HENRY ROLLINS-produced mini-sets, the eponymous 'FUGAZI' and 'MARGIN WALKER' (1989), before fully realising their aggressively economical sound on the acclaimed 'REPEATER' (1990) album. Bringing to mind the once wilfully obscure vocals of DAVID THOMAS (PERE UBU) backed by the hardcore of NO MEANS NO, FUGAZI delivered a fourth set, 'STEADY DIET OF NOTHING' (1991), their perseverance paying off with a minor placing in the UK charts. Two years later, 'IN ON THE KILLTAKER' scored a deserved UK Top 30 and dominated the indie charts for months; despite persistent major label interest, FUGAZI have admirably refused to play the corporate game (how many bands can you say that about?). The mid 90's saw the release of 'RED MEDICINE', the album taking the staunchly independent hardcore crusaders into previously uncharted territory, i.e. the UK Top 20 (appropriately enough, the commercial behemoth that is the American music industry has so far prohibited the band's domestic success). MacKAYE, PICCIOTTO and crew were back in '98, although 'END HITS' (not a compilation) suffered a little commercially due to their long absence. Unperturbed, FUGAZI worked on a soundtrack album. Jem Cohen's docu-film, 'INSTRUMENT', was delivered the following spring, the music (with sparse vocals!) a return of sorts to their abrasive best. Now with the addition of second sticksman, JERRY BUSHER, FUGAZI returned via the 2001 set, 'THE ARGUMENT', a record that even boasted a minor UK hit single, 'FURNITURE' and the classic 'CASHOUT'. Finally tiring of the FUGAZI format, MacKAYE went out on a limb with girlfriend AMY FARINA (ex-WARMERS) as the EVENS. Although formed in 2001, the duo's release sheet remained blank until March 2005 when 'Dischord' finally delivered a stark, eponymous album, a lo-fi harmony punk departure from the DC hardcore sound of old.

• **Covered:** 12XU (Wire). • **Trivia:** MacKAYE produced the early '89 BEEFEATER single, 'House Burning Down'.

Album rating: 13 SONGS compilation (*8) / REPEATER (*8) / STEADY DIET OF NOTHING (*7) / IN ON THE KILLTAKER (*7) / RED MEDICINE (*6) / END HITS (*6) / INSTRUMENT soundtrack (*7) / THE ARGUMENT (*7) / Minor Threat: COMPLETE DISCOGRAPHY compilation (*8) / the Evens: THE EVENS (*7)

MINOR THREAT

IAN MacKAYE (b.16 Apr'62) – vocals, guitar / **LYLE PRESLAR** – guitar / **BRIAN BAKER** – bass (ex-GOVERNMENT ISSUE) / **JEFF NELSON** – drums

Dischord Dischord

Jun 81. (7"ep) *<Dischord 3>* **MINOR THREAT EP** [-]
– Out of step (with the world) / Guilty of being white / Steppin' stone.

Dec 81. (7",7"red) *<Dischord 5-Limp 41>* **IN MY EYES. / STAND UP / 12XU** [-]

—— added **STEVE HANSEN** – bass (BAKER now on second guitar)

1983. (lp/c) *<(DISCHORD 10/+C)>* **OUT OF STEP**
– Betray / It follows / Think again / Look back and laugh / Sob story / No reason / Little friend / Out of step.

Jun 84. (lp/c) *<(DISCHORD 12/+C)>* **MINOR THREAT**
– Filler / I don't wanna hear it / Seeing red / Straight edge / Small man, big mouth / Screaming at a wall / Bottled violence / Minor threat.

Aug 85. (7"ep) *<(DISCHORD 15)>* **SALAD DAYS / GOOD GUYS (DON'T WEAR WHITE). / STUMPED / CASHING IN**

Mar 90. (cd) *<(DISCHORD 40)>* **COMPLETE DISCOGRAPHY** (compilation)

FUGAZI

IAN MacKAYE – vocals, guitar (ex-MINOR THREAT, ex-TEEN IDES, ex-EMBRACE) / **GUY PICCIOTTO** (b. 1966) – guitar (ex-INSURRECTION, ex-RITES OF SPRING, ex-ONE LAST WISH) / **JOE LALLY** (b. 3 Dec'63, Silver Spring, Maryland) – bass / **BRENDAN CANTY** (b. 9 Mar'66, Teaneck, New Jersey) – drums

Dischord Dischor

Dec 88. (m-lp/m-c) *<(DISCHORD 30/+C)>* **FUGAZI**
– Waiting room / Bulldog front / Bad mouth / Burning / Give me the cure / Suggestion / Glue man. *(re-iss. Apr98; same)*

Jul 89. (m-lp/m-c) *<(DISCHORD 35/+C)>* **MARGIN WALKER**
– Margin walker / And the same / Burning too / Provisional / Lockdown / Promises. *(cd-iss. Oct89 as '13 SONGS'+=; DIS 36)* – FUGAZI *(re-iss Apr98; same)*

Feb 90. (7",7"green) *<(DISCHORD 43)>* **JOE #1. / BREAK IN / SONG #1**

Mar 90. (lp/c/cd) *<(DISCHORD 44/+C/CD)>* **REPEATER**
– Turnover / Repeater / Brendan /1 / Merchandise / Blueprint / Sieve-fisted grind / Greed / Two beats off / Styrofoam / Reprovisional / Shut the door *(cd+=)* – Song #1 / Joe /1 / Break in. *(re-iss. Apr98; same)*

Aug 91. (lp/c/cd) *<(DISCHORD 60/+C/CD)>* **STEADY DIET OF NOTHING** [63]
– Exit only / Reclamation / Nice new outfits / Stacks / Latin roots / Steady diet / Long division / Runaway return / Polish / Dear justice letter K.Y.E.O. *(re-iss. Apr98; same)*

Jun 93. (m-lp/m-c/m-cd) *<(DIS 70/+C/D)>* **IN ON THE KILLTAKER** [24]
– Facet squared / Public witness program / Returning the screw / Smallpox champion / Rend it / 23 beats off / Sweet and low / Cassavetes / Great cop Walken's syndrome / Instrument / Last chance for a slow dance. *(re-iss. Apr98; same)*

May 95. (lp/cd) *(DIS 90/+CD) <EFA 17990-2>* **RED MEDICINE** [18]
– Do you like me / Bed for the scraping / Latest disgrace / Birthday pony Forensic scene / Combination lock / Fell, destroyed / By you / Version Target / Back to base / Downed city / Long distance runner. *(re-iss. Apr98; same)*

—— FUGAZI were put in backburner until their return below

Apr 98. (cd/c/lp) *<(DIS 110 CD/C/V)>* **END HITS** [47]
– Break / Place position / Recap modotti / No surprise / Five corporations Caustic acrostic / Closed captioned / Floating boy / Foreman's dog Arpeggiation / Guilford fall / Pink frosty / F/D.

Apr 99. (cd/c/lp) *<(DIS 120 CD/C/V)>* **INSTRUMENT** (soundtrack compilation)
– Pink frosty (demo) / Lusty scripps / Arpeggiator (demo) / Afterthought Trio's / Turkish disco / Me and Thumbelina / Floating boy (demo) / Lin track / Little Debbie / H.B. / I'm so tired / Rend it (demo) / Closed captio (demo) / Guildford fall (demo) / Swingset / Shaken all over / Slow crostic

—— now with second drummer **JERRY BUSHER**

Oct 01. (7"/cd-s) *<(DIS 129/+CD)>* **FURNITURE. / NUMBER / HELLO MORNING** [61]

Oct 01. (cd/lp) *<(DIS 130 CD/V)>* **THE ARGUMENT** [63]
– Untitled / Cashout / Full disclosure / Epic problem / Life and limb / Th kill / Strangelight / Oh / Ex-spectator / Nightshop / Argument.

the EVENS

IAN MacKAYE + AMY FARINA

Dischord Disch

Mar 05. (cd) *<(DIS 150CD)>* **THE EVENS**
– Shelter two / Around the corner / All these governors / Crude bomb Sara Lee / Mt. Pleasant isn't / Blessed not lucky / If it's water / Un they're clear / On the face of it / Minding ones business / You won't fe a thing.

FUNERAL FOR A FRIEND

Formed: Bridgend, South Wales . . . 2001 by singer MATT 'TH RAT' DAVIES, KRIS ROBERTS, DARREN SMITH, drumme RANDY RICHARDS and bassist GARETH DAVIES. Issuing plethora of singles and EP's during 2002 and receiving considerab interest from the UK music press, FUNERAL FOR A FRIEN took their emo-infused prog-metal to 'Warners' and began wor on their 2003 debut 'CASUALLY DRESSED AND IN DEEP CONVERSATION'; a set which was later to reach the Top 20. Melding AT THE DRIVE-IN's synthetic funk with TOOL's dark metal offerings, FFAF out-sold their subsequent tour and were regularly featured during music slots on MTV2. They had recently delivered a compilation of the best material from their earlier EPs, acting as an introduction for US distribution only, entitled 'SEVEN WAYS TO SCREAM YOUR NAME' (2003). Employing virtually the same formula, the Welsh rawkers gave their all on Terry Date-produced sophomore set, 'HOURS' (2005), scoring a series of UK Top 40 hits, 'STREETCAR', 'MONSTERS', 'HISTORY' and 'ROSES FOR THE DEAD'. Later that year, Kerrang! stayed true to type by voting them "Best British Band".

• **Covers:** BABYLON'S BURNING (Ruts) / SUNDAY BLOODY SUNDAY (U2) / BOYZ ARE BACK IN TOWN (Thin Lizzy).

Album rating: CASUALLY DRESSED & DEEP IN CONVERSATION (*6) / HOURS (*7)

MATT "THE RAT" DAVIES – vocals / **KRIS ROBERTS** – guitar / **DARREN SMITH** – guitar / **GARETH DAVIES** – bass / **RANDY RICHARDS** – drums

Mighty Atom not iss.

Sep 02. (cd-ep) *(MTY 338CD)* **BETWEEN ORDER AND MODEL** [ ] [–]
– 10:45 Amsterdam conversations / Juno / Red is the new black / The art of American football. *(re-iss. Nov03; same)*

Infectious not iss.

Apr 03. (7"ep/cd-ep) *(INFEC 126 S/CDS)* **FOUR WAYS TO SCREAM YOUR NAME** [ ] [–]
– This year's most open heartbreak / She drove me to daytime television / Kiss and makeup (all bets are off) / Escapes artists never die.

East West Ferret

Jul 03. (7"white) *(EW 269)* **JUNEAU. / THE GETAWAY PLAN** [19] [–]
(cd-s+=) *(EW 269CD1)* – Kiss and makeup.
(cd-s) *(EW 269CD2)* – ('A'side) / The art of American football (BBC Wales session) / This year's most open heartbreak (Radio 1 session) / ('A'-video).

Oct 03. (m-cd) <*41*> **SEVEN WAYS TO SCREAM YOUR NAME** [–] [ ]
– 10:45 Amsterdam conversations / Red is the new black / The art of American football / The getaway plan / This year's most open heartbreak / Kiss and makeup / Escape artists never die.

Oct 03. (7") *(EW 274)* **SHE DROVE ME TO DAYTIME TELEVISION. / BULLET THEORY** [20] [–]
(cd-s+=) *(EW 274CD1)* – The system (session).
(cd-s+=) *(EW 274CD2)* – Juno (session).

Oct 03. (cd/lp) *(82564 60947-2/-1)* <*48*> **CASUALLY DRESSED AND DEEP IN CONVERSATION** [12] Feb04 [ ]
– Rookie of the year / Bullet theory / Juneau / Bend your arms to look like wings / Escape artists never die / Storytelling / Moments forever faded / She drove me to daytime television / Red is the new black / Your revolution is a joke / Waking up / Novella.

Feb 04. (7"clear) *(EW 283)* **ESCAPE ARTISTS NEVER DIE. / YOU WANT ROMANCE?** [19] [–]
(cd-s+=) *(EW 283CD)* – 10 scene points to the winner / ('A'-video) / ('B'-video).
(dvd-s) *(EW 283DVD)* – ('A') / ('A'-video) / Moments forever faded (live video) / Rookie of the year (2 minute live clip).

Atlantic Atlantic

Jun 05. (7"blue) *(ATUK 009)* **STREETCAR. / THE LETTER** [15] [–]
(cd-s) *(ATUK 009CD)* – ('A') / Lazarus (in the wilderness).
(cd-s) *(ATUK 009CDX)* – ('A') / I am the arsonist / ('A'-video) / ('A'-making of video).

Jun 05. (cd) *(5046 78438-2)* <*62386*> **HOURS** [12] [ ]
– All the rage / Streetcar / Roses for the dead / Hospitality / Drive / Monsters / History / Recovery / The end of nothing / Alvarez / Sonny.

Aug 05. (7"red) *(ATUK 012)* **MONSTERS. / BABYLON'S BURNING** [36] [–]
(cd-s) *(ATUK 012CD)* – ('A') / Sunday bloody Sunday.
(cd-s) *(ATUK 012CDX)* – ('A') / Boyz are back in town / ('A'-Jagz Kooner mix) / ('A'-video).

Nov 05. (7"blue) *(ATUK 017)* **HISTORY (Jeremy Wheatley mix). / DRIVE (Tiscali session)** [21] [–]
(7"violet) *(ATUK 017X)* – ('A') / The art of American football (Tiscali session).
(cd-s) *(ATUK 017CD)* – ('A') / Pirate song.

Feb 06. (7"pink) *(ATUK 022)* **ROSES FOR THE DEAD. / KISS & MAKE UP (ALL BETS ARE OFF) (live at the Garage 2003)** [39] [–]
(7"green) *(ATUK 022X)* – ('A') / This year's most open heartbreak (live Xfm Rock Show 2003).
(7"white) *(ATUK 022XX)* – ('A') / 10.45 Amsterdam conversations (live at the Astoria 2003).

☐ FUNKADELIC (see under ⇒ CLINTON, George)

the FUTUREHEADS

Formed: Sunderland, Tyne And Wear, England . . . 2000 by BARRY HYDE, PETE BREWIS and JAFF, subsequently expanding into a quartet with the addition of ROSS MILLARD. With a day job as workers at an inner city youth project, BREWIS and HYDE were no art school poseurs, even if their sound was as WIRE-d and emaciated as any of the noughties neo-New Wavers and even if BREWIS was later replaced by BARRY's brother DAVE. Feted by critics for their uniquely awkward, quasi-rhythmic updates of classic GANG OF FOUR, XTC and the JAM, the Northerners nevertheless took their moniker from a FLAMING LIPS album. Selecting the time-honoured media of EP's to create their snazz – 'NUL BOOK STANDARD', '1-2-3-NUL!' and 'FIRST DAY' – the FUTUREHEADS subsequently inked a deal with '679 Recordings' and entered the studio with none other than ANDY GILL (of GANG OF FOUR). The result of their labours was an eponymous debut set, hailed by most of the music press as representing the vanguard of the fertile North-East scene. The last of a trio of singles ('DECENT DAYS AND NIGHTS', 'MEANTIME' among them), their crash and splinter cover of Kate Bush's 'HOUNDS OF LOVE' (think Devo's deconstruction of the Stones' '..Satisfaction') landed in the UK Top 10 and re-booted sales of their album as well as a re-issue of 'DECENT DAYS AND NIGHTS'. Towards the end of the year, 'AREA' also cracked the Top 20, satiating demand until the release of second set, 'NEWS AND TRIBUTES' (2006).

• **Covers:** A PICTURE OF DORIAN GRAY (Ebb / Kander).

Album rating: THE FUTUREHEADS (*8) / NEWS AND TRIBUTES (*8)

BARRY HYDE – vocals, guitar / **ROSS MILLARD** – vocals, guitar / **JAFF** (b. DAVID CRAIG) – bass / **DAVE HYDE** – drums; repl. PETE BREWIS

Project Cosmonaut not iss.

Jul 02. (ltd;7"ep) *(PCOS 001)* **NUL BOOK STANDARD** [ ] [–]
– Park Inn / Robot / My rules / Stupid and shallow.

Fantastic Plastic not iss.

Mar 03. (ltd;7"ep) *(FP7 035)* **1-2-3-NUL!** [ ] [–]
– Carnival kids / Ticket / Cabaret / A picture of Dorian Gray.

Jul 03. (7"red-or-clear/cd-s) *(FP7/FPS 036)* **FIRST DAY. / BALSCH / PIECE OF CRAP** [58] [–]

679 Recordings Sire

Jul 04. (cd/d-lp) *(5046 73848-2/-1)* <*48908*> **THE FUTUREHEADS** [ ] Sep04 [ ]
– Le garage / Robot / A to B / Decent days and nights / Meantime / Alms / Danger of the water / Carnival kids / The city is here for you to use / First day / He knows / Stupid and shallow / Trying not to think about time / Hounds of love / Man Ray.

Jul 04. (7") *(679L 080)* **DECENT DAYS AND NIGHTS. / (Phone's bad acid remix)** [26] [–]
(7") *(679L 080X)* – ('A'-student broadcast network session) / The city is here for you to use (live at Astoria) / Piece of crap (live at Astoria).
(cd-s) *(679L 080CD)* – ('A') / Remote control.

Oct 04. (7") *(679L 088)* **MEANTIME. / SPOILT FOR CHOICE** [49] [–]
(cd-s) *(679L 088CD1)* – ('A') / Alms (acappella version).
(cd-s) *(679L 088CD2)* – ('A') / Le garage (live at The Garage) / He knows (live at The Garage) / ('A'-Echo Channel polite mix) / ('A'-video).

Feb 05. (7") *(679L 099)* **HOUNDS OF LOVE. / MAN MADE (A MISTAKE)** [8] [–]
(cd-s+=) *(679L 099CD2)* – Decent days and nights (acoustic) / ('A'-Mystery

Jets' pirate invasion mix) / ('A'-video).
(cd-s) *(679L 099CD1)* – ('A') / ('A'-Phone's wolf at the door remix).

Mar 05. (cd+=; re-) *(5046 77946-2)* **THE FUTUREHEADS** 11 –
– Decent days and nights (radio mix) / Hounds of love (radio mix). *(re-iss. Mar05 w/dvd+=; 5046 77640-2)* – (video tracks).

May 05. (cd-s) *(679L 104CD1)* **DECENT DAYS AND NIGHTS / BANQUO** 26 –
(cd-s) *(679L 104CD2)* – ('A') / ('A'-Max Tundra remix) / Boring the children / Hounds of love (U-MYX version) / ('A'-video).

679 Recordings | Vagrant

Nov 05. (7") *(679L 117)* **AREA. / WE CANNOT LOSE** 18 –
(cd-s+=) *(679L 117CD2)* – Help us out / ('A'-video).
(cd-s) *(679L 117CD1)* – ('A') / Decent days and nights (shy child mix).

May 06. (7"pic-d) *(679L 128)* **SKIP TO THE END. / HISTORY ITSELF** 24 –
(7") *(679L 128X)* – ('A') / Last time ever.
(cd-s) *(679L 128CD)* – ('A') / Easy for us.

May 06. (cd) *(2564 63352-2)* <VR 436> **NEWS AND TRIBUTES** 12 Jun06
– Yes, no / Cope / Fallout / Skip to the end / Burnt / News and tributes / Return of the beserker / Back to the sea / Worry about it later / Favours for favours / Thursday / Face / Area / Help us out / We cannot lose / Decent days & nights.

G

Peter GABRIEL

Born: PETER BRIAN GABRIEL, 13 May'50, Cobham, Surrey, England. After 8 years as leader of GENESIS, he left in May '75 to pursue a solo career, releasing the first of his four self-titled studio albums in 1977. Produced by BOB EZRIN (more often found working with heavy-rock acts), the album's overwrought feel found GABRIEL struggling for a musical identity despite including such enduring songs as the classic 'SOLISBURY HILL', a Top 20 hit single, and its creepy flipside, 'MORIBUND THE BURGERMEISTER'. 1978's follow-up boasted ROBERT FRIPP at the production helm, and a somewhat pared-down sound, GABRIEL illustrating his admiration for the punk ethos on 'D.I.Y.' and rocking out on the raging 'ON THE AIR'. His third, in 1980, moved towards a radically different style of songwriting, based around rhythm rather than chord sequences. With the use of a pioneering sampler, the Fairlight CMI, GABRIEL was able to construct tracks around the rhythm, adding instrumentation to enhance the sound. With STEVE LILLYWHITE producing and a cast of collaborators including FRIPP, KATE BUSH and PHIL COLLINS, he created a compelling set of minimalistic songs, the hypnotic anti-war single 'GAMES WITHOUT FRONTIERS', taking GABRIEL into the Top 5. The album also included his inspired tribute to murdered black South African activist (STEVE) 'BIKO'. This introduced GABRIEL's growing interest in world music, an area he would explore further on his fourth album (released in the States as 'SECURITY'). Incorporating ethnic sounds and rhythms into his distinctive songwriting technique, GABRIEL discovered a new found artistic freedom, creating one of his most accomplished and inventive albums in the process. Highlights included the single, 'SHOCK THE MONKEY', the African tribal drumming of 'RHYTHM OF THE HEAT', and the exotic 'THE FAMILY AND THE FISHING NET'. His increasing immersion in all things ethnic saw him become involved with the newly conceived WOMAD festival in 1982, highlighting music from the furthest flung corners of the globe. After a shaky start, the festival has now become an annual event with an affiliated world music label, 'Real World'. The 80's also saw GABRIEL record two soundtrack albums, Alan Parker's 'BIRDY' (1985) and Martin Scorsese's 'THE LAST TEMPTATION OF CHRIST' (1989). The former was made-up largely of revamped tracks from his earlier work, the original songs transformed into atmospheric mood pieces to impressive effect, while the latter was an eerily affecting collage of folksy, world music stylings. Sandwiched between these two, was the album which finally marked his arrival as a major league rock star. 'SO', released in 1986, saw GABRIEL incorporating his ethnic experimentation into the pop format with remarkable dexterity. The track, 'SLEDGEHAMMER', with its polished funk and famous, award winning video, shot into the upper regions of the charts, propelling the album to No.1 in the UK (No.2 in America). The record was a free ranging world trip, showcasing strong melodies ('DON'T GIVE UP' with KATE BUSH) against exotic backdrops, the culmination of his work to date. The long awaited "proper" follow-up, 'US' was eventually released in 1992, just held off the top spot on both sides of the Atlantic. The album was a markedly more downbeat, introspective affair, the single 'DIGGING IN THE DIRT', highlighting GABRIEL's return to more personal songwriting. It was also inspired by his mid-80's divorce from childhood sweetheart JILL MOORE and the split with his girlfriend, actress Rosanna Arquette. GABRIEL continued to devote much of his time to the 'Real World' label, although he did find some time for a tour and a live album, 'SECRET WORLD' in 1994. Not strictly a solo album as such, 'OVO: MILLENNIUM SHOW' (2000) was the ambitious soundtrack to an installation commissioned for London's Millennium Dome. A healthy list of collaborators as varied as the BLACK DYKE MILLS BAND, NENEH CHERRY and the AFRO-CELT SOUND SYSTEM ensured that the record encompassed everything from hip hop to folk and ethnic percussion. Released a full decade since his last album (not forgetting a soundtrack set 'RABBIT-PROOF FENCE' the same year), 'UP' (2002) was even more hermetic and insular, an often impenetrably personal work destined to appeal to dedicated fans with the patience and perseverence to coax out its secrets.

• **Covered;** STRAWBERRY FIELDS FOREVER (Beatles) / SUZANNE (Leonard Cohen). • **Trivia:** In 1982, he co-wrote & produced 'Animals Have More Fun' for JIMMY PURSEY (ex-SHAM 69). He has also guested for ROBBIE ROBERTSON (his 1987 album) & JONI MITCHELL (her 1991 album).

Album rating: PETER GABRIEL [1] (*7) / PETER GABRIEL [2] (*6) / PETER GABRIEL [3] (*7) / PETER GABRIEL (SECURITY) (*6) / PETER GABRIEL – PLAYS LIVE (*5) / BIRDY soundtrack (*6) / SO (*8) / PASSION: MUSIC FOR THE LAST TEMPTATION OF CHRIST (*6) soundtrack / SHAKIN' THE TREE: SIXTEEN GOLDEN GREATS compilation (*8) / US (*6) / SECRET WORLD LIVE (*5) / OVO (*4) / LONG WALK HOME – 'Rabbit-Proof Fence' soundtrack (*7) / UP (*5) / HIT – THE DEFINITIVE COLLECTION compilation (*8)

PETER GABRIEL – vocals, keyboards (ex-GENESIS, ex-GARDEN WALL) with **TONY LEVIN** – bass / **STEVE HUNTER** – guitar / **LARRY FAST** – keyboards / **JIMMY MAELEN** – percussion / **ALAN SCHWARTZBERG** – drums / **ROBERT FRIPP** – guitar

		Charisma	Atco
Feb 77.	(lp/c) *(CDS/+MC 4006)* *<36-147>* **PETER GABRIEL**	7	38
	– Moribund the burgermeister / Solisbury Hill / Modern love / Excuse me / Humdrum / Slowburn / Waiting for the big one / Down the Dolce Vita / Here comes the flood. *(cd-iss. May83; CDSCD 4006) (re-iss. Aug88 lp/c; CHC/+MC 38) (cd re-iss. May87; PGCD 1)*		
Mar 77.	(7") *(CB 301)* *<7079>* **SOLISBURY HILL. / MORIBUND THE BURGERMEISTER**	13	68
Jun 77.	(7") *(CB 302)* **MODERN LOVE. / SLOWBURN**		–

— now with **FRIPP**, plus **JERRY MAROTTA** – drums / **ROY BITTAN** – piano / **SID McGINNIS** – guitar / **BAYETE** – keyboards

		Charisma	Atlantic
May 78.	(7") *(CB 311)* **D.I.Y. / PERSPECTIVE (long)**		–
Jun 78.	(lp/c) *(CAS/+MC 4013)* *<19181>* **PETER GABRIEL**	10	45
	– On the air / D.I.Y. / Mother of violence / A wonderful day in a one-way world / White shadow / Indigo / Animal magic / Exposure / Flotsam and jetsam / Perspective / Home sweet home. *(re-iss. Mar84 lp/c; CHC/+MC 24) (cd-iss. May87; PGCD 2)*		

PETER GABRIEL

Jun 78. (7") *(CB 319)* **D.I.Y. (remix). / MOTHER OF VIOLENCE / TEDDY BEAR** [ ] [–]

Charisma Mercury

Feb 80. (7"m) *(CB 354)* **GAMES WITHOUT FRONTIERS. / THE START / I DON'T REMEMBER** [4] [–]

May 80. (7") *(CB 360)* **NO SELF CONTROL. / LEAD A NORMAL LIFE** [33] [–]

Jul 80. (7") *<76086>* **GAMES WITHOUT FRONTIERS. / LEAD A NORMAL LIFE** [–] [48]

Sep 80. (7") *<76086>* **I DON'T REMEMBER. /** [–] [ ]

— now with **FRIPP, LEVIN + MAROTTA** plus guests **PHIL COLLINS** – drums / **KATE BUSH** – vocals + **PAUL WELLER** – guitar

May 80. (lp/c) *(CAS/+Mc 4019) <3848>* **PETER GABRIEL** [1] [22]
– Intruder / No self control / Start / I don't remember / Family snapshot / And through the wire / Not one of us / Lead a normal life / Biko. *(re-iss. Sep83 lp/c; CDS/+MC 4019) (cd-iss. May87; PGCD 3) (cd's re-iss. Jul02; PGCDX/PGCDR 1)*

Aug 80. (7"/12") *(CB 370/+12)* **BIKO. / SHOSHOLOZA / JETZT KOMMT DIE FLUT** [38] [ ]

— guests on next incl. **DAVID LORD** – synthesizers, co-producer / **JOHN ELLIS** – guitar / + some of last line-up

Charisma Geffen

Sep 82. (lp/c) *(PG/+MC 4) <2011>* **PETER GABRIEL** <US-title 'SECURITY'> [6] [28]
– The rhythm of the heat / San Jacinto / I have the touch / The family and the fishing net / Shock the monkey / Lay your hands on me / Wallflower / Kiss of life. *(re-iss. Sep83 lp/c; same) (cd-iss. 1986; PGCD 4)*

Sep 82. (7"/7"pic-d/12") *(SHOCK 1/+22/12) <29883>* **SHOCK THE MONKEY. / SOFT DOG (instrumental)** [58] [29]
(7"/12") *(SHOCK 1/350)* – ('A'side) / ('B'-instrumental).

Dec 82. (7") *(CB 405)* **I HAVE THE TOUCH. / ACROSS THE RIVER** [ ] [–]

Jun 83. (d-lp/c) *(PGD L/MC 1) <4012>* **PETER GABRIEL PLAYS LIVE (live)** [8] [44]
– The rhythm of the heat / I have the touch / Not one of us / Family snapshot / D.I.Y. / The family and the fishing net / Intruder / I go swimming / San Jacinto / Solisbury Hill / No self control / I don't remember / Shock the monkey / Humdrum / On the air / Biko. *(cd-iss. Jun85; PGDLD 1) (cd re-iss. 1988; CDPGD 100)* – (omits 4 tracks).

Jun 83. (7") *(GAB 1)* **I DON'T REMEMBER (live). / SOLISBURY HILL (live)** [62] [–]
(12"+=) *(GAB 12)* – Kiss of life (live).
(free-12"w- 12") *(GAB 122)* – GAMES WITHOUT FRONTIERS (live). / SCHNAPPSCHUSS (EIN FAMILIENFOTO)

Virgin Geffen

Nov 83. (7") *<29542>* **SOLISBURY HILL (live). / I GO SWIMMING (live)** [–] [84]

May 84. (7") *<89668>* **WALK THROUGH THE FIRE. / (other by Mike Rutherford)** [–] [ ]

May 84. (7") *(VS 689)* **WALK THROUGH THE FIRE. / (other artist)** [69] [–]
(12"+=) *(VS 689-12)* – I have the touch (remix).
(above single from the movie OST, 'Against All Odds')

Mar 85. (lp/c/cd) *(CAS/+MC/CD 1167) <GEF/+C/D 24070>* **BIRDY** (music from the film soundtrack) [51] [ ]
– At night / Floating dogs / Quiet and alone / Close up / Slow water / Dressing the wound / Birdy's flight / Slow marimbas / The heat / Sketchpad with trumpet and voice / Under lock and key / Powerhouse at the foot of the mountain. *(re-iss. Apr90 on 'Virgin' lp/c; OVED/+C 283)*

— with **MAROTTA, LEVIN** plus **DANIEL LANOIS** – guitar, co-producer / **MANU KATCHE** – percussion / **YOUSSOU N'DOUR + KATE BUSH** – guest vocals / **STEWART COPELAND** – drums / etc.

Apr 86. (7") *(PGS 1) <28718>* **SLEDGEHAMMER. / DON'T BREAK THIS RHYTHM** [4] May86 [1]
(12"+=) *(PGS 112)* – ('A'dance mix).
('A'dance-12"+=) *(PGS 113)* – Biko (extended) / I have the touch ('85 remix).

May 86. (lp/c/cd) *(PG/+MC/CD 5) <24088>* **SO** [1] [2]
– Red rain / Sledgehammer / Don't give up / That voice again / In your eyes / Mercy street / Big time / We do what we're told. *(pic-cd.Dec88+=; PGCDP 5)* – This is the picture (excellent birds). *(re-iss. Feb97 on 'E.M.I.'; LPCENT 16)*

Sep 86. (7") *<28622>* **IN YOUR EYES. / ('A'-Special mix)** [–] [26]

Oct 86. (7"; PETER GABRIEL & KATE BUSH) *(PGS/+P 2)* **DON'T GIVE UP. / IN YOUR EYES (special mix)** [9] [–]
(12"+=) *(PGS 2-12)* – This is the picture (excellent birds).

Jan 87. (7") *<28503>* **BIG TIME. / WE DO WHAT WE'RE TOLD** [–] [8]

Mar 87. (7") *(PGS 3)* **BIG TIME. / CURTAINS** [13] [–]
(12"+=) *(PGS 312)* – ('A'extended).
('A'ext-c-s) *(PGT 312)* – Across the river / No self control (live). *(re-iss. 3"cd-s.1989; GAIL 312)*

Mar 87. (7"; PETER GABRIEL & KATE BUSH) *<28463>* **DON'T GIVE UP / CURTAINS** [–] [72]

Jun 87. (7") *(PGS 4)* **RED RAIN. / GA GA (I GO SWIMMING instrumental)** [46] [–]
(12"+=/c-s+=) *(PGS/+C 412)* – Walk through the fire.

Jan 88. (7"/c-s) *(PGS/+C 6)* **BIKO (live). / NO MORE APARTEID** [49] [–]
(12"+=/cd-s+=) *(PGS/CDPGS 6-12)* – I have the touch ('85 remix).

— In May 89, PETER ws credited with YOUSSOU N'DOUR on minor hit single 'SHAKING THE TREE' *(VS/+T/CD 1167)*

Real World Geffen

Jun 89. (d-lp/c/cd) *(RW LP/MC/CD 1) <24206>* **PASSION** (music for The Last Temptation Of Christ) [29] [60]
– The feeling begins / Gethsemane / Of these, hope / Lazarus raised / Of these, hope – reprise / In doubt / A different drum / Zaar / Troubled / Open* / Before night falls / With this love / Sandstorm / Stigmata** / Passion / With this love – choir / Wall of breath / The promise of shadows / Disturbed / It is accomplished / Bread and wine. *(*= with SHANKAR) (**= with MAHMOUD TABRIZI ZADEH)*

Nov 90. (lp/c/cd) *(PGTV/+C/D 6) <24326>* **SHAKING THE TREE – SIXTEEN GOLDEN GREATS** (compilation) [11] [48]
– Solisbury Hill / I don't remember / Sledgehammer / Family snapshot / Mercy Street / Shaking the tree / Don't give up / Here comes the flood / Games without frontiers / Shock the monkey / Big time / Biko. *(cd+=/c+=)* – San Juanito / Red rain / I have the touch / Zaar. *(cd re-iss. Feb02; PGTVDR 6)* – (hit No.61)

Dec 90. (7"/c-s) *(VS/+C 1322)* **SOLISBURY HILL. / SHAKING THE TREE** (w/ YOUSSOU N'DOUR) [57] [–]
(12"+=/cd-s+=) *(VS T/CD 1322)* – Games without frontiers.

Sep 92. (7"/c-s) *(PGS/+C 7) <19136>* **DIGGING IN THE DIRT. / QUIET STEAM** [24] [52]
(cd-s+=) *(PGSDG 7)* – ('A'instrumental).
(cd-s++=) *(PGSCD 7)* – Bashi-bazouk.

Oct 92. (lp/c/cd) *(PG/+MC/CD 7) <24473>* **US** [2] [2]
– Come talk to me / Love to be loved / Blood of Eden / Steam / Digging in the dirt / Fourteen black paintings / Kiss that frog / Secret world.

Dec 92. (c-s) *<19145>* **STEAM / GAMES WITHOUT FRONTIERS (live)** [–] [32]

Jan 93. (7"/c-s) *(PGS/+C 8)* **STEAM. / ('A'-Carter mix)** [10] [–]
(cd-s) *(PGSDG 8 / PGSDX 8)* – ('A' mix) / Games without frontiers (mix) / (2 'A' extended + dub mix or Games (other mix)

Mar 93. (7"/c-s) *(PGS/+C 9)* **BLOOD OF EDEN. / MERCY STREET** [43] [ ]
(cd-s+=) *(PGSDG 9)* – ('A'-special mix)
(cd-s+=) *(PGCDX 9)* – Sledgehammer.

Sep 93. (7"/c-s) *(PGS/+C 10)* **KISS THAT FROG. / ('A'-mindblender mix)** [46] [ ]
(cd-s+=) *(PGSDG 10)* – Digging in the dirt.
(cd-s+=) *(PGSDX 10)* – Across the river / Shaking the tree (Bottrill remix).

— Below single, another from 'Philadelphia' film on 'Epic' records.

Jun 94. (7"/c-s) *(660480-7/-4)* **LOVE TOWN. / LOVE TO BE LOVED** [49] [ ]
(cd-s+=) *(660480-2)* – Different drum.

— live with **TONY LEVIN** – bass, vocals / **DAVID RHODES** – guitar, vocals / **MANU KATCHE** – drums / **PAULA COLE** – vocals / **JEAN CLAUDE NAIMRO** – keyboards, vocals / **RAVI SHANKAR** – violin, vocals / **LEVON MINASSIAN** – doudouk

Aug 94. (c-s) *(PGSC 11)* **SECRET WORLD (live). / COME TALK TO ME** [39] [ ]
(cd-ep) *(PGSCD 11)* – ('A'live) / Red rain (live) / San Jacinto (live) / Mercy Street (live).

Sep 94. (d-cd/d-c) *(PG DCD/MC 8) <24722>* **SECRET WORLD LIVE (live)** [10] [23]
– Come talk to me / Steam / Across the river / Slow marimbas / Shaking the tree / Red rain / Blood of Eden / Kiss that frog / Washing of the water / Solisbury Hill / Digging in the dirt / Sledgehammer / Secret world / Don't give up / In your eyes.

Real World E.M.I.

Jun 00. (cd) *(PGCD 9) <849540>* **OVO (live millennium show)** [24] Aug00 [ ]
– The story of Ovo / Low light / The time of the turning / The man who

loved the earth – The hand that sold shadows / The time of the turning (reprise) / Father, son / The tower that ate people / Revenge / White ashes / Downside up / The nest that sailed the sky / Make tomorrow.

Jun 02. (cd) *(PGCD 10) <887131>* **LONG WALK HOME** (music from the film RABBIT-PROOF FENCE) ☐ Apr02 ☐
– Jigalong / Stealing the children / Unlocking the door / The tracker / Running to the rain / On the map / A sense of home / Go away Mr. Evans / Moodoo's secret / Gracie's recapture / Crossing the salt pan / The return (pts.1-3) / Ngankarrparni (sky blue) / The rabbit-proof fence / Cloudless.

Sep 02. (cd-s) *(PGSCD 13)* **THE BARRY WILLIAMS SHOW / (unadulterated) / MY HEAD SOUNDS LIKE THAT (Royksopp remix) / CLOUDLESS (radio edit)** ☐ –

Sep 02. (cd/c/d-lp) *(PG CD/MC/DLP 11) <493536>* **UP** 11 9
– Darkness / Growing up / Sky blue / No way out / I grieve / The Barry Williams show / My head sounds like that / More than this / Signal to noise / The drop.

Dec 02. (cd-s) *(PGSCD 14)* **MORE THAN THIS / MORE THAN THIS (Polyphonic Spree remix) / MORE THAN THIS (Elbow mix)** 47 –
(12") *(PGST 14)* – ('A'side) / My head sounds like this (Royksopp mix).

Nov 03. (d-cd) *(595237-2) <14860-2>* **HIT – THE DEFINITIVE COLLECTION** (compilation) 29 100
– Solisbury hill / Shock the monkey / Sledgehammer / Don't give up (with KATE BUSH) / Games without frontiers / Big time / Burn you up, burn you down / Growing up (Tom Lord – Alge mix) / Digging in the dirt / Blood of Eden / More than this / Biko / Steam / Red rain / Here comes the flood / San Jacinto / No self control *[UK-only]* / I don't remember *[US-only]* / Cloudless / The rhythm of the heat / I have the touch *[UK-only]* / Loved to be loved *[US-only]* / I grieve / D.I.Y. *[UK-only]* / Family snapshot *[US-only]* / Different drum *[UK-only]* / In your eyes *[US-only]* / The drop / The tower that ate people (Steve Osborne mix) / Lovetown / Father, son / Signal to noise / Downside up (live) / Washing of the water *[UK-only]*.

Nov 03. (cd-s) *(GABRIEL 003)* **BURN YOU UP, BURN YOU DOWN / DARKNESS (Engelspost remix)** ☐ –

– compilations, others, etc. –

on 'Virgin' UK / 'Geffen' US, unless mentioned otherwise

Jan 83. (7") *Old Gold; (OG 9265)* **SOLISBURY HILL. / GAMES WITHOUT FRONTIERS** ☐ –

Mar 83. (d-c) *Charisma; (CASMC 102)* **PETER GABRIEL 1 / PETER GABRIEL 2** ☐ –

1988. (3"cd-ep) *(CDT 33)* **SOLISBURY HILL / MORIBUND THE BURGERMEISTER / SOLISBURY HILL (live)** ☐ –
(re-iss. Apr90; VVCS 8)

Jun 88. (cd) *XCDSD 4018)* **PETER GABRIEL 3 (German version)** ☐ –

May 89. (7") *W.T.G.; <68936>* **IN YOUR EYES. / (track by Fishbone)** – 41
(above from the movie, 'Say Anything')

Oct 90. (3xcd-box) *(TPAK 9)* **PETER GABRIEL 1 / 2 / 3** ☐ ☐

☐ GADGETS (see under ⇒ the THE)

☐ Dave GAHAN (see under ⇒ DEPECHE MODE)

Rory GALLAGHER

Born: 2 Mar'49, Ballyshannon, Donegal, Ireland. After playing in various school bands in Cork, RORY formed The FONTANA SHOWBAND, who subsequently became The IMPACT. By 1965, they'd secured residencies in Hamburg, mostly playing CHUCK BERRY songs to post-BEATLES audiences. A year later, just as the British blues revival was gathering steam, he formed TASTE with NORMAN DAMERY and ERIC KITTERINGHAM, although the latter two were eventually replaced by CHARLIE McCRACKEN and JOHN WILSON. After an eponymous debut album failed to break through, TASTE hit the UK Top 20 in 1970 with the follow-up set, 'ON THE BOARDS'. The album established GALLAGHER as Ireland's ambassador of the blues guitar, setting the stage for his forthcoming solo career. A self-titled debut appeared in 1971, the record selling enough initial copies to give it a Top 40 placing. Worshipping at the altar of blues KING-s; B.B., FREDDIE and ALBERT that is, GALLAGHER was revered by loyal fans for his musical integrity and down-to-earth approach (described as the working man's guitarist, due to his unconformist attire – i.e. lumberjack shirt, jeans and ruffled hair – GALLAGHER could also drink many a rock star under the table, eventually into the grave). After another blistering studio set in 1971, 'DEUCE', he scored a massive UK Top 10 with the concert album, 'LIVE IN EUROPE' (1972). Recorded at the peak of GALLAGHER's powers, 'BLUEPRINT' (1972) and 'TATTOO' (1973) stand among the Irishman's most overlooked albums, although the former nearly hit the UK Top 10. To coincide with the projected release of an in-concert rockumentary, GALLAGHER released yet another live set, the electrifying double set, 'IRISH TOUR '74'. Moving to 'Chrysalis' records soon after, GALLAGHER's form slumped slightly just as the new, leaner breed of guitar acts were up and coming, his commercial appeal subsiding under this pressure with each successive release. Nevertheless he continued to record some worthwhile material and perform live for a hardcore following, persevering with the rock industry well into the 90's. Death was the only thing that could prise GALLAGHER away from his guitar, the Irishman passing away on the 14th June '95 after suffering complications with a liver transplant.

• **Covers:** SUGAR MAMA + DON'T START ME TALKING (Sonny Boy Williamson) / I'M MOVING ON (Hank Snow) / I TAKE WHAT I WANT (Hayes-Porter-Hedges) / ALL AROUND MAN (Davenport) / OUT ON THE WESTERN PLAINS (Leadbelly) / RIDE ON RED, RIDE ON (Levy-Glover-Reid) / I WONDER WHO (. . . Boyle) / AS THE CROW FLIES (Josh White) / JUST A LITTLE BIT (Dexter Gordon) / MESSING WITH THE KID (Julie London) / PISTOL SLAPPER BLUES (. . . Allen) / etc. • **Trivia:** VINCENT CRANE of ATOMIC ROOSTER guested on RORY's debut lp in '71. GALLAGHER also sessioned on albums by MUDDY WATERS (London Sessions) / JERRY LEE LEWIS (London Sessions) / LONNIE DONEGAN (Putting On The Style) / etc.

Album rating: Taste: TASTE (*6) / ON THE BOARDS (*7) / LIVE TASTE (*4) / LIVE AT THE ISLE OF WIGHT exploitation (*4) / Rory Gallagher: RORY GALLAGHER (*6) / DEUCE (*5) / LIVE IN EUROPE (*6) / BLUEPRINT (*7) / TATTOO (*7) / IRISH TOUR '74 (*8) / SINNER . . . AND SAINT early stuff (*5) / AGAINST THE GRAIN (*5) / THE STORY SO FAR compilation (*6) / CALLING CARD (*7) / PHOTO FINISH (*5) / TOP PRIORITY (*5) / STAGE STRUCK (*5) / JINX (*5) / DEFENDER (*4) / THE BEST OF RORY GALLAGHER & TASTE compilation (*6) / EDGED IN BLUE (*7) / BIG GUNS: THE VERY BEST OF RORY GALLAGHER compilation (*8)

TASTE

RORY GALLAGHER – vocals, guitar / **CHARLIE McCRACKEN** (b.26 Jun'48) – bass repl. ERIC KITTERINGHAM / **JOHN WILSON** (b. 3 Dec'47) – drums (ex-THEM) repl. NORMAN DAMERY

Major Minor not iss.

Apr 68. (7") *(MM 560)* **BLISTER ON THE MOON. / BORN ON THE WRONG SIDE OF TIME** ☐ –
(re-iss. Jul70; MM 718)

Polydor Atco

Mar 69. (7") *(56313)* **BORN ON THE WRONG SIDE OF TIME. / SAME OLD STORY** ☐ –

Apr 69. (lp) *(583 042)* **TASTE** ☐ ☐
– Blister on the moon / Leaving blues / Sugar mama / Hail / Born on the wrong side of time / Dual carriageway pain / Same old story / Catfish / I'm moving on. *(re-iss. 1977; 2384 076) (cd-iss. Aug92; 841 600-2)*

Jan 70. (lp) *(583 083)* **ON THE BOARDS** 18 ☐
– What's going on / Railway and gun / It's happened before, it'll happen again / If the day was any longer / Morning sun / Eat my words / On the boards / If I don't sing I'll cry / See here / I'll remember. *(cd-iss. Apr94; 841 599-2)*

Feb 71. (lp) *(2310 082)* **LIVE TASTE (live)** ☐ –
– Sugar mama / Gamblin' blues / Feel so good (part 1) / Feel so good (part 2) / Catfish / Same old story.

—— GALLAGHER went solo. The other two formed STUD. McCRACKEN also joined SPENCER DAVIS GROUP

RORY GALLAGHER

solo – vocals, guitar with **GERRY MacAVOY** – bass (ex-DEEP JOY) / **WILGAR CAMPBELL** – drums (ex-METHOD)

Polydor Atlantic

May 71. (lp) *(2383 044)* <33368> **RORY GALLAGHER** [32] [ ]
– Laundromat / Just the smile / I fall apart / Wave myself goodbye / Hands up / Sinner boy / For the last time / It's you / I'm not surprised / Can't believe it's true. *(re-iss. 1979 on 'Chrysalis' lp/c; CHR/ZCHR 1258) (cd-iss. Sep98 on 'Capo'; CAPO 101)*

Jun 71. (7"m) *(2814 004)* **IT'S YOU. / JUST THE SMILE / SINNER BOY** [ ] [ ]

Nov 71. (lp) *(2383 076)* <7004> **DEUCE** [39] [ ]
– Used to be / I'm not awake yet / Don't know where I'm going / Maybe I will / Whole lot of people / In your town / Should've learn't my lesson / There's a light / Out of my mind / Crest of a wave. *(re-iss. 1979 on 'Chrysalis' lp/c; CHR/ZCHR 1254) (cd-iss. Sep98 on 'Capo'; CAPO 102)*

Polydor Polydor

May 72. (lp) *(2383 112)* <5513> **LIVE! IN EUROPE (live)** [9] [ ]
– Messin' with the kid / Laundromat / I could've had religion / Pistol slapper blues / Going to my home town / In your town / Bullfrog blues. *(re-iss. 1979 on 'Chrysalis' lp/c; CHR/ZCHR 1257) (cd-iss. Mar95 on 'Castle'; CLACD 406) (cd re-iss. Feb99 on 'Capo'; CAPO 103)*

— **ROD DE'ATH** – drums (ex-KILLING FLOOR) repl. CAMPBELL / added **LOU MARTIN** – keyboards, mandolin (ex-KILLING FLOOR)

Feb 73. (lp) *(2383 189)* <5522> **BLUEPRINT** [12] [ ]
– Walk on hot coals / Daughter of the Everglades / Banker's blues / Hands off / Race the breeze / The seventh son of a seventh son / Unmilitary two-step / If I had a reason. *(re-iss. 1979 on 'Chrysalis' lp/c; CHR/ZCHR 1253) (cd-iss. Feb94 on 'Castle; CLACD 316) (cd re-iss. Feb00 on 'Capo'; CAPO 104)*

Aug 73. (lp) *(2383 230)* <5539> **TATTOO** [32] [ ]
– Tattoo'd lady / Cradle rock / 20:20 vision / They don't make them like you anymore / Livin' like a trucker / Sleep on a clothes-line / Who's that coming / A million miles away / Admit it. *(re-iss. 1979 on 'Chrysalis' lp/c; CHR/ZCHR 1259) (cd-iss. Jan94 on 'Castle'; CLACD 315) (cd re-iss. Feb00 on 'Capo'; CAPO 105)*

Jul 74. (d-lp) *(2659 031)* <9501> **IRISH TOUR '74 (live)** [36] [ ]
– Cradle rock / I wonder who (who's gonna be your sweet man) / Tattoo'd lady / Too much alcohol / As the crow flies / A million miles away / Walk on hot coals / Who's that coming / Back on my (stompin' ground) / Just a little bit. *(re-iss. 1979 on 'Chrysalis' lp/c; CTY/ZCTY 1256) (re-iss. May88 on 'Demon' d-lp)(d-c/d-cd; DFIEND 120)(FIEND CASS/CD 120) (cd re-iss. Sep98 on 'Capo'; CAPO 106)*

Chrysalis Chrysalis

Oct 75. (lp/c) *(<CHR/ZCHR 1098>)* **AGAINST THE GRAIN** [ ] [ ]
– Let me in / Cross me off your list / Ain't too good / Souped-up Ford / Bought and sold / I take what I want / Lost at sea / All around man / Out on the western plain / At the bottom. *(re-iss. May91 on 'Castle' cd/c/lp; CLA CD/MC/LP 223) (cd re-iss. Feb99 on 'Capo'; CAPO 107)*

Nov 75. (7") *(CDV 102)* **SOUPED-UP FORD. / I TAKE WHAT I WANT** [ ] [–]

Oct 76. (lp/c) *(<CHR/ZCHR 1124>)* **CALLING CARD** [32] [ ]
– Do you read me / Country mile / Moonchild / Calling card / I'll admit you're gone / Secret agent / Jack-knife beat / Edged in blue / Barley and grape rag. *(re-iss. Apr91 on 'Essential' cd/c/lp; ESS CD/MC/LP 143) (re-iss. cd Mar94 on 'Castle'; CLACD 352) (cd re-iss. Sep98 on 'Capo'; CAPO 108)*

— **TED McKENNA** – drums (ex-SENSATIONAL ALEX HARVEY BAND) repl.DE'ATH and MARTIN (to RAMROD)

Oct 76. (lp/c) *(<CHR/ZCHR 1170>)* **PHOTO FINISH** [ ] [ ]
– Shin kicker / Brute force and ignorance / Cruise on out / Cloak and dagger / Overnight bag / Shadow play / The Mississippi sheiks / The last of the indepenents / Fuel to the fire. *(cd-iss. Sep98 on 'Capo'; CAPO 109)*

Jan 79. (7"m) *(CHS 2281)* **SHADOW PLAY. / SOUPED UP FORD / BRUTE FORCE AND IGNORANCE** [ ] [–]
(10"+=) *(CXP 2281)* – Moonchild

Aug 79. (7",7"colrd) *(CHS 2364)* **PHILBY. / HELLCAT / COUNTRY MILE** [ ] [ ]

Sep 79. (lp/c) *(<CHR/ZCHR 1235>)* **TOP PRIORITY** [56] [ ]
– Follow me / Philby / Wayward child / Keychain / At the depot / Bad penny / Just hit town / Off the handle / Public enemy No.1. *(re-iss. May88 on 'Demon' lp/c/cd; FIEND/+CASS/CD 123) (cd re-iss. Feb99 on 'Capo'; CAPO 110)*

Aug 80. (7",7"colrd) *(CHS 2453)* **WAYWARD CHILD (live). / KEYCHAIN** [ ] [–]

Sep 80. (lp/c) *(<CHR/ZCHR 1280>)* **STAGE STRUCK (live)** [40] [ ]
– Shin kicker / Wayward child / Brute force and ignorance / Moonchild / Follow me / Bought and sold / The last of the independents / Shadow play. *(cd-iss. Mar95 on 'Castle'; CLACD 407) (cd re-iss. Feb00 on 'Capo'; CAPO 111)*

Dec 80. (7") *(CHS 2466)* **HELLCAT. / NOTHIN' BUT THE DEVIL** [ ] [ ]

— (May'81) **GALLAGHER** with **McAVOY** brought in **BRENDAN O'NEILL** – drums; repl. McKENNA who joined GREG LAKE BAND then MSG

Chrysalis Mercury

Apr 82. (lp/c) *(CHR/ZCHR 1359)* *<SRMI 4051>* **JINX** [68] [ ]
– Signals / The Devil made me do it / Double vision / Easy come, easy go / Big guns / Jinxed / Bourbon / Ride on Red, ride on / Loose talk. *(re-iss. May88 on 'Demon' lp/c/cd; FIEND/+CASS/CD 126) (cd re-iss. Feb00 on 'Capo'; CAPO 112)*

Jun 82. (7") *(CHS 2612)* **BIG GUNS. / THE DEVIL MADE ME DO IT** [ ] [ ]

1983. (10"ep) *(CXP 2281)* **SHADOW PLAY / BRUTE FORCE AND IGNORANCE. / MOONCHILD / SOUPED UP FORD** [ ] [–]

Capo-Demon Intercord

Jul 87. (lp)(c/cd) *(XFIEND 98)(FIEND CASS/CD 98)* **DEFENDER** [ ] [–]
– Kickback city / Loanshark blues / Continental op / I ain't no saint / Failsafe day / Road to Hell / Doing time / Smear campaign / Don't start me talkin' / Seven days. *(c+=/cd+=) (free-7")* – SEEMS TO ME. / NO PEACE FOR THE WICKED *(cd-iss. Feb99 on 'Capo'+=; CAPO 113)* – Seems to me / No peace for the wicked.

— guests **MARK FELTHAM** – harmonica / **LOU MARTIN** – piano / **JOHN EARL** – saxophones / **GERAINT WATKINS** – accordion / **JOHN COOKE** – keyboards / **RAY BEAVIS** – tenor sax / **DICK HANSON** – trumpet

Capo Intercord

Jun 90. (cd/c/lp) *(CAPO CD/MC/LP 14)* **FRESH EVIDENCE** [ ] [ ]
– 'Kid' gloves / The king of Zydeco (to: Clifton Chenier) / Middle name / Alexis / Empire state express / Ghost blues / Heaven's gate / The loop / Walkin' wounded / Slumming angel. *(re-iss. cd Oct92 on 'Essential'; ESSCD 155) (cd re-iss. Sep98 on 'Capo'; CAPO 114)*

— on the 14th June 1995, RORY died after complications from a liver transplant operation

– compilations etc. –

1974. (c) *Emerald-Gem; (GES 1110) / Springboard; <SPB 4056>* **IN THE BEGINNING (VOCAL AND GUITAR)** (rec.'67) <US-title 'TAKE IT EASY BABY'> [ ] 1976 [ ]

Aug 72. (lp; by TASTE) *Polydor; (2383 120)* **TASTE – LIVE AT THE ISLE OF WIGHT (live)** [41] [–]
(cd-iss. Apr94; 841 601-2)

Feb 75. (lp) *Polydor; (2383 315)* <6510> **SINNER . . . AND SAINT** (1971 material) [ ] [ ]

Oct 82. (7"ep/12"ep) *Polydor; (POSP/+X 609)* **BLISTER ON THE MOON / SUGAR MAMA. / CATFISH / ON THE BOARDS** [ ] [–]

Feb 76. (lp) *Polydor; (2383 376)* <6519> **THE STORY SO FAR** [ ] [ ]

1977. (lp) *Polydor: (2384 079)* **LIVE** [ ] [–]

May 80. (lp) *Hallmark; (HSC 3041)* **RORY GALLAGHER** [ ] [–]

Feb 88. (cd) *Razor; (MACH 10D)* **THE BEST OF RORY GALLAGHER & TASTE** [ ] [–]
– Blister on the moon / Hail / Born on the wrong side of time / Dual carriageway pain / Same old story / On the boards / See here / I'll remember / Sugar mama (live) / Sinner boy (live) / I feel so good (live) / Catfish / I'm movin' on / What's going on / Ralway and gun / Morning Sun / Eat my words.

May 89. (d-lp/d-c/d-cd) *That's Original; (TFO LP/MC/CD 20)* **LIVE! IN EUROPE / STAGE STRUCK** [ ] [–]

Jul 89. (d-lp/d-c/d-cd) *That's Original; (TFO LP/MC/CD 21)* **TATTOO / BLUEPRINT** [ ] [–]

May 91. (4xcd-box) *Demon; (RORY G1)* **RORY GALLAGHER** [ ] [–]
– (IRISH TOUR '74 / DEFENDER / TOP PRIORITY / JINX)

Jun 92. (lp/c/cd) *Demon; (FIEND/+C/CD 719)* **EDGED IN BLUE** [ ] [–]

Nov 92. (3xcd-box) *Essential; (ESBCD 187)* **G-MEN: BOOTLEG SERIES VOLUME ONE** [ ] [–]

Nov 98. (cd) *I.R.S.; (35783)* **A BLUE DAY FOR THE BLUES** [ ] [ ]

Nov 98. (cd) *Camden; (74321 62797-2)* **ETCHED IN BLUE** [ ] [–]

Aug 99. (d-cd) *Capo; (CAPO 701)* **THE BBC SESSIONS** [ ] [ ]

Oct 01. (4xcd-box) *Capo; (CAPO 702)* **LET'S GO TO WORK** [ ] [–]

Mar 03. (cd) *Capo; (82876 50387-2) / Buddha; <99787>* **WHEELS WITHIN WHEELS** [ ] [ ]

Jun 05. (d-cd) *Capo; (<CAPO 705>)* **BIG GUNS: THE VERY BEST OF RORY GALLAGHER** [31] [ ]
– Big guns / What's going on / Tattoo'd lady / Bad penny / Shadow play / Kickback city / Bourbon / Sinnerboy / Used to be (live) / Goin' to my hometown / Bullfrog blues (live) / Messin' with the kid (live) / The loop / Born on the wrong side of time / A million miles away / Calling card / Out on the western plains / Lonesome highway / Just the smile / I'm not awake yet / Daughter of the Everglades / I'll admit you're gone / The king of Zydeco / They don't make them like you anymore. *(ltd d-cd w/dvd; CAPOX 705)*

the GAME

Born: JAYCEON TERELL TAYLOR, 27 Nov'79, Compton, California, USA. Raised by parents who were allegedly affiliated gang members, and an alleged member of L.A. gang the Bloods himself, the GAME flaunted the kind of CV that a gangsta rapper would die for, no pun intended. As boasted on album opener, 'WESTSIDE STORY' (and elaborated on the defiant 'DON'T NEED YOUR LOVE'), he "took five" back in the day, as in five bullet wounds, suffered during a 2001 drug-deal-gone-wrong. After recovering from a three day coma, his brush with death inspired a career change and – namechecking his West Coast forebears (NWA, TUPAC, SNOOP etc.) as he went – he signed to 'Aftermath' at the behest of DR DRE. With DRE and 50 CENT at the helm alongside an all-star cast including TIMBALAND and KANYE WEST, 'THE DOCUMENTARY' finally appeared in 2005, a US No.1 (UK Top 10) introduced by a 30 second resume of latter day hip-hop's guiding philosophy: play the system, make the money, look after number one. The GAME's freestyling talent was undeniable even if the subject matter – "West Side" shout-outs, hard-knock flashbacks and unrelenting sex'n'violence – was nothing new: on US Top 10 'DREAMS', he envisaged a new breed of rap stars rising from near-death experience, while fondly recalling his pre-fame, R&B diva fantasies and somehow fitting in MARVIN GAYE and STEVIE WONDER. Earlier in the year, both the x-rated 'HOW WE DO' and 'HATE IT OR LIVE IT' had been 50 CENT-featuring singles, UK/US Top 5 successes both. Among his various feuds (including 'Roc-A-Fella' and 'Death Row'), the recent spat with 50 CENT/G-UNIT has been the most well publicised, the subject of his infamous diss, '300 BARS AND RUNNIN'.

Album rating: THE DOCUMENTARY (*8)

JAYCEON – rapper, etc. / with guests/producers

Aftermath – Interscope / Aftermath – Interscope

Nov 04. (12"; feat. 50 CENT) **WESTSIDE STORY** [–] [93]

Jan 05. (cd/lp) *(9864143) <B00035620-2/-1>* **THE DOCUMENTARY** [7] [1]
– Intro / Westside story (feat. 50 CENT) / Dreams / Hate it or love it (feat. 50 CENT) / Higher / How we do (feat. 50 CENT) / Don't need your love (feat. FAITH EVANS) / Church for thugs / Put you on the game / Start from scratch (feat. MARSHA of FLOETRY) / The documentary / Runnin' (feat. TONY YAYO) / No more fun and games / We ain't (feat. EMINEM) / Where I'm from (feat. NATE DOGG) / Special (feat. NATE DOGG) / Don't worry (feat. MARY J. BLIGE) / Like father, like son (feat. BUSTA RHYMES). *(ltd-cd w/dvd+=; 9880631)* – (DVD tracks).

Feb 05. (12"; feat. 50 CENT) *(9880368)* **HOW WE DO. / WESTSIDE STORY / HOW WE DO (instrumental)** [5] [4]
(cd-s+=) *(9880361)* – ('A'-video).

May 05. (cd-s; feat. 50 CENT) *(9882208)* **HATE IT OR LOVE IT / HIGHER** [4] [2]
(12"+=/cd-s+=) *(988220-6/-5)* – ('A'-mixes).

Aug 05. (12"/cd-s) *(9883904)* **DREAMS (mixes)** [8] [32]
in Sep'05, the GAME feat. on R. KELLY's hit, 'Playa's Only'

Nov 05. (12") *(9887826)* **PUT YOU ON THE GAME** [46] [–]
(cd-s+=) *(9887827)* – ('A'-video).

GANG OF FOUR

Formed: Leeds, England . . . 1977 by journalist ANDY GILL, JON KING, DAVE ALLEN and HUGO BURNHAM. After releasing a debut EP, 'DAMAGED GOODS' for Bob Last's 'Fast' label, they signed to 'E.M.I.' in late '78. Their debut 45 for the label, 'AT HOME HE'S A TOURIST', hit the Top 60 and should have reached a lot higher but for a BBC ban due to the use of the word 'Rubbers' (i.e. contraceptives) in the lyrics. In Autumn '79, their debut album 'ENTERTAINMENT' hit the Top 50, a startling showcase for the band's adrenaline fuelled post-punk sound, GILL's rifling staccato guitar slicing through the twisted funk rhythms. Lyrically, they were also pretty incendiary, although their radical political agenda rarely descended into heavy handed preaching or took precedence over the music. It would be another couple of years before they released a follow-up, 'SOLID GOLD' (1981) mixing down GILL's patented feedback assault and coming in for some critical stick. Although he played on the landmark 'TO HELL WITH POVERTY' single (released in summer '81), ALLEN subsequently left the band to form his own outfit, SHRIEKBACK, his replacement being SARA LEE. Thereafter, the band favoured a more conventional approach, 'SONGS OF THE FREE' (1982) notable for its barbed comments on the Falklands war, 'CALL ME UP' and 'I LOVE A MAN IN UNIFORM (another single blacklisted by Radio 1). Following the departure of BURNHAM, they moved further towards a slick funk/Philly sound with 'HARD' (1983), employing a cast of studio professionals and female backing singers. With diminishing artistic and commercial returns, the band finally split in mid-'84 following the release of live set, 'AT THE PALACE' (1984). While GILL subsequently relocated to America and concentrated on production work, renewed interest in the band towards the end of the decade saw a GANG OF FOUR reformation, although GILL and KING were the only original members involved in the project. The result was a one-off album for 'Polydor', 'MALL' (1991), the label soon losing interest after it failed to sell; there was more grief for them the following year when, despite their best efforts in supplying the soundtrack for the Labour Party's 1992 campaign, the Tories romped home yet again. The duo initiated yet another reincarnation of the band in 1995 for the 'SHRINKWRAPPED' set, although sales were again disappointing. With everybody and their adolescent dog citing GANG OF FOUR as inspiration, it wasn't surprising the originals took it on themselves to definitively reform, and straight to a major label no less. 'RETURN THE GIFT' (2005) was an understandable attempt to perfect the cream of their back catalogue which so many bands were apparantly listening to.

• **Songwriters:** Penned by KING / ALLEN / GILL, until ALLEN departed. Covered SOUL REBEL (Bob Marley).

Album rating: ENTERTAINMENT (*7) / SOLID GOLD (*6) / SONGS OF THE FREE (*6) / HARD (*5) / AT THE PALACE (*3) / A BRIEF HISTORY OF THE 20TH CENTURY compilation (*8) / MALL (*4) / SHRINKWRAPPED (*5) / RETURN THE GIFT (*6)

JON KING (b. 8 Jun'55, London) – vocals, melodica / **ANDY GILL** (b. 1 Jan'56, Manchester) – guitar / **DAVE ALLEN** (b.23 Dec'55, Cumbria) – bass / **HUGO BURNHAM** (b.25 Mar'56, London) – drums

Fast / not iss.

Oct 78. (7"m) *(FAST 5)* **DAMAGED GOODS. / LOVE LIKE ANTHRAX / ARMALITE RIFLE** [ ] [–]

E.M.I. / Warner

Mar 79. (7") *(EMI 2956)* **AT HOME HE'S A TOURIST. / IT'S HER FACTORY** [58] [–]

Sep 79. (lp/c) *(EMC/TC-EMC 3313) <BSK 3446>* **ENTERTAINMENT** [45] [ ]
– Ether / Natural's not in it / Not great men / Damaged goods / Return the gift / Guns before butter / I found that essence rare / Glass / Contract / At home he's a tourist / 5-45 / Anthrax. *(re-iss. 1985 lp/c; ATAK/TC-ATAK 41) (cd-iss. Feb95; CZ 541) <cd-iss. 1995 on 'Infinite Zero'+=; 14502-2>* – YELLOW EP

GANG OF FOUR

Regal Zonophone — not iss.

Apr 80. (7") *(Z 1)* **OUTSIDE THE TRAINS DON'T RUN ON TIME. / HE'D SEND IN THE ARMY** [ ] [-]

Regal Zonophone — Warners

Oct 80. (12"ep) *<MINI 3494>* **OUTSIDE THE TRAINS DON'T RUN ON TIME / HE'D SEND IN THE ARMY. / IT'S HER FACTORY / ARMALITE RIFLE** [-] [ ]

Mar 81. (7"/12") *(EMI/12EMI 5146)* **WHAT WE ALL WANT. / HISTORY'S BUNK** [ ] [-]

Mar 81. (lp/c) *(EMC/TC-EMC 3364) <BSK 3565>* **SOLID GOLD** [52] [ ]
– Paralysed / What we all want / If I could keep it for myself / Outside the trains don't run on time / Why theory? / Cheeseburger / The republic / In the ditch / A hole in the wallet / He'd send in the army.

May 81. (7") *(EMI 5177)* **CHEESEBURGER. / PARALYSED** [ ] [-]

— (tour) **BUSTA CHERRY JONES** – bass (ex-SHARKS) repl. ALLEN (to SHRIEKBACK)

Jul 81. (7"/12") *(EMI/12EMI 5193)* **TO HELL WITH POVERTY. / CAPITAL (IT FAILS US NOW)** [ ] [-]

Feb 82. (m-lp) *<MINI 3646>* **ANOTHER DAY / ANOTHER DOLLAR** [-] [ ]
– To hell with poverty / What we all want / Cheeseburger / Capital (it fails us now) / History's bunk!

— **SARA LEE** – bass, vocals (ex-JANE AIRE, ex-ROBERT FRIPP) repl. BUSTA

Apr 82. (7"/12") *(EMI/12EMI 5299)* **I LOVE A MAN IN A UNIFORM. / WORLD AT FAULT** [65] [-]

May 82. (lp/c) *(EMC/TCEMC 3412) <23683>* **SONGS OF THE FREE** [61] [ ]
– Call me up / I love a man in a uniform / Muscle for brains / It is not enough / Life, it's a shame / I will be a good boy / History of the world / We live as we dream, alone / Of the instant.

Jun 82. (7") *<29921>* **I LOVE A MAN IN A UNIFORM. / I WILL A GOOD BOY** [-] [ ]
(12"+=) *<29907>* – ('A'extended).

Jul 82. (7") *(EMI 5320)* **CALL ME UP. / I WILL BE A GOOD BOY** [ ] [-]

— (KING, GILL + BURNHAM were joined by) **JON ASTROP / CHUCK KIRKPATRICK + JOHN SOMBATERO** – bass repl. SARA / added backing singers **ALFA ANDERSON** and **BRENDA WHITE**

Aug 83. (7"/12") *(EMI/12EMI 5418)* **IS IT LOVE. / MAN WITH A GOOD CAR** [ ] [-]

Sep 83. (lp/c) *(EMC 165219-1/-4) <23936>* **HARD** [ ] [ ]
– Is it love / I fled / Silver lining / Woman town / A man with a good car / It don't matter / Arabic / A piece of my heart / Independence.

Sep 83. (7") *<29449>* **IS IT LOVE. / ARABIC** [-] [ ]

Nov 83. (7") *(EMI 5440)* **SILVER LINING. / INDEPENDENCE** [ ] [-]

— **STEVE GOULDING** – drums (ex-RUMOUR) repl. BURNHAM who joined ILLUSTRATED MAN

Mercury — not iss.

Oct 84. (12"m) *(GANG 12)* **I WILL BE A GOOD BOY (live). / IS IT LOVE (live) / CALL ME UP (live)** [ ] [-]

Nov 84. (lp/c) *(MERL/+C 51)* **AT THE PALACE (live)** [ ] [-]
– We live as we dream, alone / History is not made by great men / Silver lining / The history of the world / I love a man in uniform / Paralysed / Is it love / Damaged goods / At home he's a tourist / To hell with poverty. *(c+=)* – I will be a good boy / Call me up.

— (split mid-84) **JON** later formed KING BUTCHER

— they re-formed 1990 w/ **JON KING + ALAN GILL** adding **HIROMI + STAN LOUBIERES**

Scarlett — not iss.

Jun 90. (7") *(SCART 4)* **MONEY TALKS (The Money mix). / USE THE COLOUR FROM THE TUBE** [ ] [-]
(12") *(SCART 4T)* – ('A'side) / ('A'dub version).
(cd-s) *(SCART 4CD)* – ('A'extended) / (above 3 tracks).

Polydor — Polydor

May 91. (cd/c/lp) *<849 124-2/-4/-1>* **MALL** [-] [ ]
– Cadillac / Motel / Satellite / F.M.U.S.A. / Don't fix what ain't broke / Impossible / Money talks / Soul rebel / Hiromi & Stan talk / Colour from the tube / Hey yeah / Everybody wants to come / World falls apart.

Aug 91. (12") *(P2 152DJ)* **CADILLAC. / MOTEL / FAVOURITES** [ ] [-]

— disbanded again when their record label dropped them. GILL then supplied the soundtrack in 1992 for the Labour Party's unsuccessful general election campaign. Re-formed again in 1994.

— **GILL + KING + STEVE MONTI** (ex-CURVE) + **PHIL BUTCHER** (ex-IGGY POP)

When! — not iss.

Aug 95. (7"/c-s) *(WEN 7/M 1002)* **TATTOO. / BANNED WORDS / COP GOES HOME** [ ] [-]
(cd-s+=) *(WENX 1002)* – ('A'-Quiet guy mix).

Sep 95. (cd/c) *(WEN CD/MC 003)* **SHRINKWRAPPED** [ ] [-]
– Tattoo / Sleepwalker / I parade myself / Unburden / Better him than me / Something 99 / Showtime, valentine / Unburden, unbound / The dark side / I absolve you / Shrinkwrapped. *(cd re-iss. Apr01 on 'Castle'; CMRCD 197)*

— original members re-united for re-recordings

V2 — V2

Oct 05. (cd) *(VVR 103443-2) <27270>* **RETURN THE GIFT** [ ] [ ]
– To hell with poverty / Damaged goods / Natural's not in it / Not great men / Why theory? / Anthrax / Paralysed / What we all want / Ether / He'd send the army / Capital / I love a man in uniform / At home he's a tourist / We live as we dream, alone. *(UK cd w/cd+=)* – (remixes of above tracks).

– compilations etc. –

Oct 86. (12"ep) *Strange Fruit; (SFPS 008)* **THE PEEL SESSIONS (16.1.89)** [ ] [-]
– I found that essence rare / Return the gift / 5-45 / At home he's a tourist *(c-ep.iss.Jun87; SFPSC 008)*

May 90. (lp/c/cd) *Strange Fruit; (SFR LP/C/CD 107) / Dutch East India; <8101>* **THE PEEL SESSIONS (COMPLETE SESSIONS 1979-81)** [ ] [ ]

Mar 90. (cd)(c/lp) *Greenlight – Capitol; (CDP 795051-2)(TC+/GO 2028)* **YOU CATCH UP WITH HISTORY (1978-1983)** [ ] [-]

Nov 90. (cd/c/lp) *E.M.I.; (CD/TC+/EMC 3583) / Warners: <26448>* **A BRIEF HISTORY OF THE 20th CENTURY** [ ] Dec90 [ ]
– At home he's a tourist / Damaged goods / Natural's not in it / Not great men / Anthrax / Return the gift / It's her factory / What we all want (live) / Paralysed / A hole in the wallet / Cheeseburger / To hell with poverty / Capital (it fails us now) / Call me up / I will be a good boy / History of the world / I love a man in a uniform / Is it love / Woman town / We live as we dream, alone. *(c+=/cd+=)* – (4 tracks). *(cd re-iss. Jan04; 596541-2)*

Jan 91. (7"ep/c-ep/12"ep/cd-ep) *E.M.I.; (EMS/TCEM/12EM/CDEM 172)* **TO HELL WITH POVERTY (the loaded edit) / ('A'-original version). / CHEESEBURGER (live) / CALL ME UP** [ ] [-]

Oct 95. (cd) *Warners; <43035>* **SOLID GOLD / ANOTHER DAY – ANOTHER DOLLAR** [-] [ ]

Nov 98. (d-cd) *Rhino; <RCD 75479>* **100 FLOWERS BLOOM** (rare tracks) [-] [ ]

Jan 03. (cd) *Wounded Bird; (WOU 3936)* **HARD / SOLID GOLD** [ ] [-]

Apr 04. (cd) *E.M.I.; (CZ 561)* **SOLID GOLD / ANOTHER DAY ANOTHER DOLLAR** [ ] [ ]

GARBAGE

Formed: Madison, Wisconsin, USA ... 1994 by BUTCH VIG DUKE ERIKSON and STEVE MARKER, out of the ashes of FIRE TOWN and SPOONER. BUTCH's latter ham-pop/rock act, had been on the go since early 1978 and released their debut ep 'CRUEL SCHOOL' a year later <Boat; SP 4001>. Another soon followed, 'WHERE YOU GONNA RUN?' <Boat; SP 3001>, before an album, 'EVERY CORNER DANCE' surfaced in '82; <Mountain Railroad; HR 8005>. BUTCH then set up his own studio and produced KILLDOZER, before giving SPOONER another outing with the album 'WILDEST DREAMS' <Boat; SP 1004>. In 1986 their final flop 45, 'MEAN OLD WORLD' <Boat; SP 1018>, made BUTCH form FIRE TOWN, with old buddy STEVE MARKER and co-songwriter DOUG ERIKSON. A few singles, 'CARRY THE TORCH' <7-89242> and 'RAIN ON YOU' <7-89204>, appeared from the 'Atlantic' stable alongside albums 'IN THE HEART OF THE HEART COUNTRY' <Boat; 1013 / re-iss. Atlantic; 81754> & 'THE GOOD LIFE' cd/lp; <781945-2/-1>. In 1989/90, BUTCH re formed with the original line-up of SPOONER, DUKE ERIKSON, DAVE BENTON, JEFF WALKER and JOEL TAPPERO, to release one-off comeback cd 'THE FUGITIVE DANCE' <Dali-Chameleon; 89026>. He was then to find fame in production work for greats like NIRVANA, SONIC YOUTH, SMASHING PUMPKINS, NINE INCH NAILS and U2, before coming across Edinburgh-born vixen SHIRLEY MANSON fronting the band ANGELFISH on MTV. The new-look GARBAGE contributed the electro-goth of 'VOW' to a 'Volume' various artists compilation and this ended up as their limited edition debut 45 in 1995. By that year's summer, they had signed to Geffen's 'Almo Sounds' (UK 'Mushroom') records, which helped them break into the UK Top 50 with 'SUBHUMAN'. Success finally came with the 'ONLY HAPPY WHEN IT RAINS' single, a grungey, more tuneful affair that retained the goth overtones, MANSON weaving her deep throat vocals around the melody like a spider's web. She was an obvious focal point for the group; on their Top Of The Pops debut the singer made like a brooding, 90's incarnation of CHRISSIE HYNDE while the rest of the band remained comfortably anonymous in uniform black. The eponymous debut album, released later that year, was a mixed bag of styles that worked fairly effectively. Subsequent single, 'QUEER', kind of summed up the GARBAGE ethos, a deceptively poppy number featuring a MANSON vocal positively dripping with loathing, self or otherwise. GARBAGE continued their rise to the top of the pile with a UK chart-topping second set, 'VERSION 2.0', masterfully treading the finest of lines between alternative credibility and outright mainstream success; the hits kept on coming with 'PUSH IT', 'I THINK I'M PARANOID' and 'SPECIAL' all making the UK Top 20. After the phenomenal success of their previous albums, the group re-united in the studio to record their third album proper, the strange and often confused 'BEAUTIFUL GARBAGE' (2001). A slice of every popular genre imaginable, the set offered the listener a wide range of uncommercial tracks, shot through with MANSON's sexual imagery and VIG's scorching production techniques. The sassy 'SILENCE IS GOLDEN' saw MANSON taking some hints from feminine hero PJ HARVEY, while 'SHUT YOUR MOUTH' and hit single 'ANDROGYNY' were classic GARBAGE and would have fitted anywhere on the group's debut album. 'CHERRY LIPS (GO BABY GO!)' was the surprise track out of them all; a funky, sexy take-on of new wave, which just proved that GARBAGE still had a few tricks up their sleeves. Usurped by the younger generation of garage whipper-snappers, SHIRLEY and Co returned in 2005 to fight their increasingly predictable case with Top 10 ultimatum, 'WHY DO YOU LOVE ME'. Referencing the same influences and production as ever, right down to the PJ HARVEY-esque title, 'BLEED LIKE ME' (2005) found MANSON brooding over typically introspective subject matter against typically heavyweight choruses.

Covered: KISS MY ASS (Vic Chesnutt) / WILD HORSES (Rolling Stones) / sampled the CLASH's 'Train In Vain' on 'STUPID GIRL'.

Album rating: GARBAGE (*8) / VERSION 2.0 (*7) / BEAUTIFUL GARBAGE (*6) / BLEED LIKE ME (*5)

SHIRLEY MANSON (b. 3 Aug'66, Edinburgh, Scotland) – vocals, guitar (ex-GOODBYE MR MACKENZIE) / **STEVE MARKER** – guitar, samples, loops / **DUKE ERIKSON** (b. DOUG) – guitar, keyboards, bass / **BUTCH VIG** (b. BRYAN VIG, Viroqua, Wisconsin) – drums, loops, efx

Discordant AlmoSounds

Mar 95. (7") *(CORD 001)* <89000> **VOW. / VOW (Torn Apart version)** [ ] Jul95 [97]

Mushroom AlmoSounds

Aug 95. (s7"/7") *(SX/S 1138)* <89001> **SUBHUMAN. / £1 CRUSH** [50] [ ]
(cd-s+=) *(D 1138)* – Vow.

Sep 95. (7"/c-s/cd-s) *(SX/C/D 1199)* <89002> **ONLY HAPPY WHEN IT RAINS. / GIRL DON'T COME / SLEEP** [29] Feb96 [55]

Oct 95. (cd/c/2x45rpm-lp/6x7"box) *(D/C/L/LX 31450)* <80004> **GARBAGE** [6] Aug95 [20]
– Supervixen / Queer / Only happy when it rains / As Heaven is wide / Not my idea / A stroke of luck / Vow / Stupid girl / Dog new tricks / My lover's box / Fix me now / Milk. *(d-lp re-iss. Sep99 on 'Simply Vinyl'+=; SVLP 123)* – Dumb (live) / Stupid girl (live) / Temptation waits (live) / Vow (live). *(cd re-iss. JUl04; 5046 68875-2)*

—— on above **MIKE KASHAN** – bass / **PAULI RYAN** – percussion

Nov 95. (7") *(SX 1237)* <89003> **QUEER. / QUEER (Adrian Sherwood remix)** [13] Mar96 [ ]
(silver-cd-s) *(D 1237)* – ('A'side) / Trip my wire / ('A'-The very queer dub-bin mix) / ('A'-The most beautiful girl in town mix).
(gold-cd-s) *(DX 1237)* – ('A'side) / Butterfly collector / ('A'-Rabbit in the Moon remix) / ('A'-Danny Saber remix).

Mar 96. (7") *(SX 1271)* **STUPID GIRL. / DOG NEW TRICKS (pal mix)** [4] [–]
(red-cd-s+=) *(D 1271)* – Driving lesson / ('A'-Red Snapper mix).
(blue-cd-s) *(DX 1271)* – ('A'side) / Alien sex fiend / ('A'-Dreadzone dub) / ('A'-Dreadzone vox).

Jul 96. (c-s) <89004> **STUPID GIRL / DRIVING LESSON** [–] [24]

Nov 96. (7") *(SX 1494)* <89007> **MILK (The wicked mix). / MILK (the Tricky remix)** [10] [ ]
(cd-s) *(D 1494)* – Milk (the wicked mix featuring TRICKY) / ('A'-Goldie's completely trashed remix) / ('A'-original version) / Stupid girl (Tees radio mix by TODD TERRY).
(cd-s) *(DX 1494)* – Milk (the wicked mix featuring TRICKY) / ('A'-Massive Attack classic remix) / ('A'-Rabbit in the moon udder remix) / Stupid girl (the Danny Saber remix).

May 98. (c-s) *(MUSH 28MCS)* <89014> **PUSH IT / LICK THE PAVEMENT** [9] [52]
(cd-s+=) *(MUSH 28CDS)* – ('A'-Boom Boom Satellites remix).
(3"cd-s) *(MUSH 28CDSX)* – ('A'side) / Thirteen.

May 98. (cd/c/lp) *(74321 55410-2/-4/-1)* <80018> **VERSION 2.0** [1] [13]
– Temptation waits / I think I'm paranoid / When I grow up / Medication / Special / Hammering in my head / Push it / The trick is to keep breathing / Dumb / Sleep together / Wicked ways / You look so fine. *(d-cd-iss. Jun99; MUSH 29CDX) (cd re-iss. Mar05; 5046 68876-2)*

Jul 98. (c-s) *(MUSH 35MCS)* <40035> **I THINK I'M PARANOID / DEADWOOD** [9] [ ]
(cd-s+=) *(MUSH 35CDS)* – Afterglow.
(cd-s) *(MUSH 35CDX)* – ('A'side) / ('A'extended) / ('A'-Purity mix).
(3"cd-ep+=) *(MUSH 35CDXXX)* – (all of the above).

Oct 98. (c-s) *(MUSH 39MCS)* <827> **SPECIAL / THIRTEEN X FOREVER** [15] Nov98 [52]
(cd-s+=) *(MUSH 39CDS)* – ('A'-Brothers In Rhythm mix).
(cd-s) *(MUSH 39CDSX)* – ('A'side) / Medication (acoustic) / Push it (Victor Calderone remix).
(3"cd-s) *(MUSH 39CDSXXX)* – (all 5 above).

Jan 99. (c-s) *(MUSH 43MCS)* **WHEN I GROW UP / CAN'T SEEM TO MAKE YOU MINE** [9] [ ]
(cd-s+=) *(MUSH 43CDS)* – ('A'-Danny Tenaglia club mix).
(cd-s+=) *(MUSH 43CDSXXX)* – Tornado / ('A'-Danny Tenaglia club).
(cd-s) *(MUSH 43CDSX)* – ('A'side) / Tornado / Special (Rickidy raw mix).

May 99. (c-s) *(MUSH 49MCS)* **YOU LOOK SO FINE / SOLDIER THROUGH THIS** [19] [ ]
(cd-s+=) *(MUSH 49CDS)* – ('A'-Fine Young Cannibals remix).
(cd-s) *(MUSH 49CDSX)* – ('A'side) / Get busy with the fizzy / ('A'-Eric Kupper mix).
(3"cd-s) *(MUSH 49CDSXXX)* – ('A'side) / ('A'-Fine Young Cannibals mix) / ('A'-Eric Kupper mix) / ('A'-Plaid mix).

Nov 99. (c-s/cd-s) *(RAX C/TD 40)* **THE WORLD IS NOT ENOUGH (mixes; original / UNKLE / Ice Bandits)** [11] [ ]
(above from Bond movie of the same name – issued on 'Radioactive')

Sep 01. (cd-s) *(MUSH 94CDS)* **ANDROGYNY / BEGGING BONE / ANDROGYNY (Felix Da Housecat 'thee glitz remix')** [24] [–]
(cd-s) *(MUSH 94CDX)* – ('A'side) / ('A'-Neptunes remix) / ('A'-Architechs remix).

Oct 01. (cd/c/lp) *(MUSH 95 CD/MC/LP)* <493115> **BEAUTIFUL GARBAGE** [6] [13]
– Shut your mouth / Androgyny / Can't cry these tears / Till the day I die / Cup of coffee / Silence is golden / Cherry lips (go baby go!) / Breaking up the girl / Drive you home / Parade / Nobody loves you / Untouchable / So like a rose. *(cd re-iss. Nov04; 5046 68884-2)*

Jan 02. (cd-s) *(MUSH 98CDSE)* **CHERRY LIPS / CHERRY LIPS (Roger Sanchez tha S man's release mix)** [22] [–]
(cd-s+=) *(MUSH 98CDSX)* – Enough is never enough.

(cd-s) *(MUSH 98CDS)* – ('A'side) / Use me / ('A'-Howie B remix) / ('A'-video).
(12") *(MUSH 98T)* – ('A'-Roger Sanchez tha S man's release mix) / ('A'-mauve dark vocal mix with accapella mix).

Apr 02. (cd-s) *(MUSH 101CDS)* **BREAKING UP THE GIRL / CANDY SAYS / BREAKING UP THE GIRL (Brothers In Rhythm remix) / BREAKING UP THE GIRL (video)** 27 –
(cd-s) *(MUSH 101CDSX)* – ('A'version) / Happiness (p.2) / ('A'-Tino Maas remix).
(cd-s) *(MUSH 101CDSXXX)* – ('A'-acoustic version) / Confidence / Cherry lips (go go jam; Eli Janey remix).

Sep 02. (cd-s) *(MUSH 106CDS)* **SHUT YOUR MOUTH / SEX NEVER GOES OUT OF FASHION / SHUT YOUR MOUTH (jolly scary music mix) / SHUT YOUR MOUTH (video)** 20 –
(cd-s) *(MUSH 106CDSX)* – ('A'side) / April tenth / ('A'-Jags Kooner full vocal mix).
(cd-s) *(MUSH 106CDSXXX)* – ('A'side) / I'm really into techno / Wild horses (live).

Mar 05. (7") *(WEA 385)* **WHY DO YOU LOVE ME. / SPACE COME CAN THROUGH ANYTHING** 7 94
(cd-s) *(WEA 385CD) <8002>* – ('A') / Nobody can win.
(dvd-s) *(WEA 385DVD)* – ('A') / Cherry lips (Le Royale remix) / ('A'-video) / (interview footage).

Apr 05. (cd) *(5046 77681-2) <00041951-2>* **BLEED LIKE ME** 4 4
– Bad boyfriend / Run baby run / Right between the eyes / Why do you love me / Bleed like me / Metal heart / Sex is not the enemy / It's all over but the crying / Boys wanna fight / Why don't you come over / Happy home.

Jul 05. (7") *(WEA 391)* **SEX IS NOT THE ENEMY. / NEVER BE FREE** 24 –
(cd-s) *(WEA 391CD)* – ('A') / Honey bee.
(dvd-s) *(WEA 391DVD)* – ('A') / ('A'-video) / (documentary).

□ Jerry GARCIA (see under ⇒ GRATEFUL DEAD)

□ Art GARFUNKEL (see under ⇒ SIMON & GARFUNKEL)

Marvin GAYE

Born: MARVIN PENTZ GAY JR., 2 Apr'39, Washington, D.C., USA, son of an apostolic minister. In 1957, after being discharged from the army, MARVIN joined doo-wop outfit The MARQUEES, releasing two singles (HEY LITTLE SCHOOL GIRL; produced by Bo Diddley, + BABY YOU'RE THE ONLY ONE) for the 'Okeh' label. The following year, HARVEY FUQUA invited them to become his new MOONGLOWS, and after moving to 'Chess' land, Chicago, they recorded the 'ALMOST GROWN' and 'MAMA LOOCIE' singles. In 1960, FUQUA, who accompanied GAY to the motor city of Detroit with the intention of becoming a solo artist, helped arrange for GAY to play session drums on 45's by The MIRACLES. In 1961, after more session work for 'Motown' artists such as The MARVELETTES, he signed as a solo artist to 'Tamla Motown' as well as marrying boss BERRY GORDY's younger sister, ANNA. Suffixing his surname with an E, MARVIN initially had his heart set on becoming a jazz balladeer, although an album, 'THE SOULFUL MOODS OF MARVIN GAYE' (1961), flopped and he was eventually cajoled into recording R&B/soul. The result was the rawer, 'STUBBORN KIND OF FELLOW' single, an immediate success which provided MARVIN with his first R&B Top 10 hit in 1962. 'HITCH HIKE', 'PRIDE AND JOY' and CAN I GET A WITNESS followed in quick succession, all charting in the US Top 50 and establishing GAYE as one of Motown's foremost talents. Like most artists on the label, GAYE was assigned material by various writers (mainly the in-house team of HOLLAND-DOZIER-HOLLAND) although even in those early days, many of his songs were self-penned, including the classic 'WHEREVER I LAY MY HAT (THAT'S MY HOME)' (later made famous again by PAUL YOUNG). In 1964, although still mainly a credible solo artist, Berry Gordy teamed him up with MARY WELLS, and later KIM WESTON with whom he recorded the Top 20 soul-pop brilliance of 'IT TAKES TWO' as well as recording a whole album of duets under a similar title. The mid-60's also saw him developing the super smooth vocal prowess that would become his trademark on such hits as 'HOW SWEET IT IS (TO BE LOVED BY YOU)' and 'ONE MORE HEARTACHE'. The WESTON alliance was dissolved in mid-67 when GAYE found Philadelphia born singer, TAMMI TERRELL, their charmed partnership yielding a three-year run of hits on both sides of the Atlantic and producing some of the most sublime duets in the history of soul ('AIN'T NO MOUNTAIN HIGH ENOUGH', 'YOU'RE ALL I NEED TO GET BY', 'AIN'T NOTHING LIKE THE REAL THING' etc.). Tragically, to the obvious dismay of MARVIN, TAMMI died of a brain tumour in March 1970, aged only 24. The previous year, MARVIN had scored his biggest hit to date when 'I HEARD IT THROUGH THE GRAPEVINE' hit No.1 in America and Britain, a brooding, experimental epic that became Motown's biggest selling record in the label's history. But TERRELL's death hit MARVIN hard and his subsequent work was to take on a considerably more introspective bent. Although MARVIN didn't write it, the melancholy 'ABRAHAM, MARTIN AND JOHN' single (released in Spring '70) was an indicator of the direction GAYE was headed. Taking his cue from STEVIE WONDER, MARVIN decided to take complete control of his career, from the writing to the recording, making his first major artistic statement with 'WHAT'S GOING ON' (1971). A radical departure, the album (along with WONDER's early 70's material) changed the way soul music was made and challenged people's perceptions of the genre. Like a black 'Astral Weeks' (in feeling if not lyrically), the album was a lush, orchestral stream of consciousness collage, GAYE gazing into the ether and pleading for some kind of redemption for mankind. Addressing such pertinent issues as war, environmental disaster and God, 'Motown' were extremely reluctant to release the album, only relenting when GAYE threatened to leave the label. The singer was vindicated when the record became his biggest seller to date, as well as being recognised as one of the greatest albums in recording history. GAYE solved the problem of following up such a milestone by recording the soundtrack to blaxploitation flick, 'TROUBLE MAN'. Largely instrumental, the album was an enjoyable collection of jazz-funk grooves, a stop gap rather than a step forward. A bona fide successor came with 1973's steamy 'LET'S GET IT ON', the title track providing GAYE with the second No.1 of his career. The album itself reached No.2, becoming the most commercially successful release of his career. Like all truly transcendent artists, GAYE embraced both the profane and the sacred, his best work both overtly sexual and deeply spiritual; for GAYE, spiritual healing was sexual healing. Yet, ironically, GAYE's marriage to ANNA GORDY foundered in 1975, MARVIN detailing the break-up in his underrated double album, 'HERE MY DEAR' (1979), its title a sarcastic reference to the fact that GORDY was to receive all royalties from the disc as part of the divorce settlement. Despite having scored a third No.1 single two years previously with the disco epic, 'GOT TO GIVE IT UP', GAYE's personal life was a mess. As well as a second failed marriage, GAYE was constantly hounded by the taxman and fell into heavy cocaine use. Escaping to Europe GAYE worked on another concept album, 'IN OUR LIFETIME'. Following its release in 1981, GAYE accused Motown of tampering with both the sound of the album and the artwork prior to release. This marked the bitter end to his long standing relationship with the label, and he subsequently signed with 'Columbia'. 'MIDNIGHT LOVE' (1982) was a resounding return to form, the seminal 'SEXUAL HEALING' going Top 5 in Britain and America. Lyrically the album explored familiar GAYE themes on the nature of God

MARVIN GAYE

and love, but while the singer was still actively following some kind of spiritual path, he was also sinking deeper into drug dependence and depression. Retreating to his parents' home in L.A., MARVIN's depression and mood swings brought him into continual conflict with his father and after one particularly violent argument on the 1st of April 1984, MARVIN GAYE SNR. shot his son dead. It was a tragic end to the life of one of the most pivotal figures soul music has produced.

• **Covered:** ... GRAPEVINE (Whitfield-Strong) / ABRAHAM, MARTIN AND JOHN (c.Dick Holler). MARVIN's songs have been recorded by many international stars including ROBERT PALMER (Mercy Mercy Me) / CYNDI LAUPER (What's Going On).

Album rating: THE SOULFUL MOODS OF MARVIN GAYE (*5) / THAT STUBBORN KINDA FELLA (*6) / RECORDED LIVE ON STAGE (*4) / WHEN I'M ALONE I CRY (*4) / TOGETHER with Mary Wells (*6) / MARVIN GAYE GREATEST HITS compilation (*7) / HOW SWEET IT IS TO BE LOVED BY YOU (*5) / HELLO BROADWAY THIS IS MARVIN (*5) / A TRIBUTE TO THE GREAT NAT KING COLE (*4) / MOODS OF MARVIN GAYE (*5) / TAKE TWO with Kim Weston (*5) / MARVIN GAYE GREATEST HITS, VOL.2 compilation (*6) / UNITED with Tammi Terrell (*6) / YOU'RE ALL I NEED (*6) / IN THE GROOVE (*6) / M.P.G. (*6) / MARVIN GAYE AND HIS GIRLS collection (*6) / EASY with Tammi Terrell (*6) / THAT'S THE WAY LOVE IS (*5) / MARVIN GAYE & TAMMI TERRELL GREATEST HITS compilation (*6) / MARVIN GAYE SUPER HITS exploitation (*6) / WHAT'S GOING ON (*10) / TROUBLE MAN soundtrack (*8) / LET'S GET IT ON (*9) / ANTHOLOGY compilation (*8) / MARVIN GAYE LIVE! (*4) / I WANT YOU (*6) / MARVIN GAYE'S GREATEST HITS compilation (*7) / MARVIN GAYE LIVE AT THE LONDON PALLADIUM (*5) / HERE, MY DEAR (*7) / IN OUR LIFETIME (*6) / MIDNIGHT LOVE (*7) / DREAM OF A LIFETIME posthumous (*5)

MARVIN GAYE – vocals, drums, etc. (ex-MOONGLOWS, etc.) with Motown session people

not iss. — Tamla Motown

May 61. (lp) <221> **THE SOULFUL MOODS OF MARVIN GAYE** [–] [ ]
– The masquerade is over / Love for sale / My funny valentine / Let your conscience be your guide / etc.

May 61. (7") <54041> **LET YOUR CONSCIENCE BE YOUR GUIDE. / NEVER LET YOU GO (SHA LA BOP)** [–] [ ]

1962. (7") <54055> **I'M YOURS, YOU'RE MINE. / SANDMAN** [–] [ ]

1962. (7") <54063> **TAKING MY TIME. / SOLDIER'S PLEA** [–] [ ]

Nov 62. (lp) <239> **THAT STUBBORN KINDA FELLA** [–] [ ]
– That stubborn kinda fella / Pride and joy / Hitch hike / Get my hands on some lovin' / Soldier's plea / I'm yours, you're mine / Wherever I lay my hat (that's my home) / Taking my time / It hurt me too / Hello there angel.

Dec 62. (7") <54075> **HITCH HIKE. / HELLO THERE ANGEL** [–] [30]

Oriole — Tamla

Feb 63. (7") *(CBA 1803)* <54068> **STUBBORN KIND OF FELLOW. / IT HURT ME TOO** [ ] Jul62 [46]

Jul 63. (7") *(CBA 1846)* <54079> **PRIDE AND JOY. / ONE OF THESE DAYS** [ ] Apr63 [10]

Jul 63. (lp) <242> **RECORDED LIVE ON STAGE (live)** [–] [ ]
– That stubborn kinda fella / Hitch hike / One of these days / Days of wine and roses / You are my sunshine / etc.

Stateside — Tamla

Nov 63. (7") *(SS 243)* <54087> **CAN I GET A WITNESS. / I'M CRAZY 'BOUT MY BABY** [ ] [22] Oct63 [77]

1964. (lp) <251> **WHEN I'M ALONE I CRY** [–] [ ]
– You've changed / I was telling her about you / I wonder / I'll be around / Because of you / I don't know why / I've grown accustomed to her face / When your lover has gone / When I'm alone I cry / If my heart could sing.

Apr 64. (7") *(SS 284)* <54093> **YOU'RE A WONDERFUL ONE. / WHEN I'M ALONE I CRY** [ ] Feb64 [15]

—— Apr64, saw MARVIN duet with MARY WELLS on hit single ONCE UPON A TIME and album TOGETHER. (See further below and for collaborations/duets with **KIM WESTON and TAMMI TERRELL**)

Aug 64. (7") *(SS 326)* <54095> **TRY IT BABY. / IF MY HEART COULD SING** [ ] May64 [15]

Sep 64. (7") <54101> **BABY DON'T YOU DO IT. / WALK ON THE WILD SIDE** [–] [27]

Nov 64. (lp) *(SL 10100)* **MARVIN GAYE** (compilation from '63 & '64 lp's) [ ] [–]
– You're a wonderful one / Get my hands on some lovin' / Taking my time / Soldier's plea / Hello there, angel / I'm crazy 'bout my baby / Try it, baby / I'm yours, you're mine / Sandman / Hitch hike / Wherever I lay my hat / Can I get a witness.

Nov 64. (7") *(SS 360)* <54107> **HOW SWEET IT IS TO BE LOVED BY YOU. / FOREVER** [49] [6]

Tamla Motown — Tamla

Apr 65. (lp) *(STML 11004)* <258> **HOW SWEET IT IS TO BE LOVED BY YOU** [ ] Feb65 [ ]
– How sweet it is to be loved by you / Try it baby / Baby don't you do it / You're a wonderful one / Now that you've won me / Me and my lonely room / Stepping closer to your heart / No good without you / One of these days / Need your lovin' (want you back) / Forever. *<US-tracks slightly different> (cd-iss. Mar91; WD 72732)*

Apr 65. (7") *(TMG 510)* <54112> **I'LL BE DOGGONE. / YOU'VE BEEN A LONG TIME COMING** [ ] Feb65 [8]

Aug 65. (7") *(TMG 524)* <54117> **PRETTY LITTLE BABY. / NOW THAT YOU'VE WON ME** [ ] Jun65 [25]

Sep 65. (lp) *(STML 11015)* <259> **HELLO BROADWAY THIS IS MARVIN** [ ] [ ]
– Walk on the wild side / What kind of fool am I / Party's over / Days of wine and roses / People / My way / On the street where you live / Hello Dolly / Hello Broadway / My kind of town / This is the life.

Nov 65. (7") *(TMG 539)* <54122> **AIN'T THAT PECULIAR. / SHE'S GOT TO BE REAL** [ ] Sep65 [8]

Feb 66. (lp) *(STML 11022)* <261> **A TRIBUTE TO GREAT NAT KING COLE** [ ] [ ]
– Nature boy / Ramblin' Rose / Too young / Pretend / Straighten up and fly right / Mona Lisa / Unforgettable / To the ends of the Earth / Sweet Lorraine / It's only a paper Moon / Send for me / Calypso blues. *(re-iss. Jul82 lp/c; WL/WK 72210) (cd-iss. Jul92; 530054-2)*

Mar 66. (7") *(TMG 552)* <54129> **ONE MORE HEARTACHE. / WHEN I HAD YOUR LOVE** [ ] Feb66 [29]

Jun 66. (7") *(TMG 563)* <54132> **TAKE THIS HEART OF MINE. / NEED YOUR LOVIN' (WANT YOU BACK)** [ ] May66 [44]

Sep 66. (7") *(TMG 574)* <54138> **LITTLE DARLING (I NEED YOU). / HEY DIDDLE DIDDLE** [50] Aug66 [47]

Aug 67. (7") *(TMG 618)* <54153> **YOUR UNCHANGING LOVE. / I'LL TAKE CARE OF YOU** [ ] Jul67 [33]

Jan 68. (7") *(TMG 640)* <54160> **YOU. / CHANGE WHAT YOU CAN** [ ] [34]

Nov 68. (7") *(TMG 676)* <54170> **CHAINED. / AT LAST (I FOUND A LOVE)** [ ] [32]

Nov 68. (7") <54176> **I HEARD IT THROUGH THE GRAPEVINE. / YOU'RE WHAT'S HAPPENING (IN THE WORLD TODAY)** [–] [1]

Jan 69. (lp) *(STML 11091)* <285> **IN THE GROOVE** [ ] Oct68 [63]
– You / Tear it on down / Chained / I heard it through the grapevine / At last (I found a love) / Some kind of wonderful / Loving you is sweeter than ever / Change what you can / It's love I need / Every now and then / You're what's happening (in the world today) / There goes my baby. *(re-iss. Apr85 as 'I HEARD IT THROUGH THE GRAPEVINE' lp/c; WL/WK 72374) (cd-iss. Jun89; WD 72374)*

Feb 69. (7") *(TMG 686)* **I HEARD IT THROUGH THE GRAPEVINE. / NEED SOMEBODY** [1] [–]

Jul 69. (7") *(TMG 705)* <54181> **TOO BUSY THINKING ABOUT MY BABY. / WHEREVER I LAY MY HAT** [5] Apr69 [4]
(re-iss. Oct81 on 'Motown'; same)

Nov 69. (lp) *(STML 11119)* <292> **M.P.G.** [ ] Jun69 [33]
– Too busy thinking about my baby / This magic moment / I got to get to California / That's the way love is / The end of our road / Seek and you shall find / It's a bitter pill to swallow / Only a lonely man would know / Try my true love / Memories / More than a heart can stand / It don't take too much to keep me. *(re-iss. Jul82 lp/c; STMS/CSTMS 5064) (cd-iss. Aug93; 530210-2)*

Nov 69. (7") *(TMG 718)* <54185> **THAT'S THE WAY LOVE IS. / GONNA KEEP TRYIN' TILL I WIN YOUR LOVE** [ ] Aug 69 [7]

Jan 70. (7") <54190> **HOW CAN I FORGET. / GONNA GIVE HER ALL THE LOVE I'VE GOT** [–] [41] [67]

Apr 70. (lp) *(STML 11136)* <299> **THAT'S THE WAY LOVE IS** [ ] Oct69 [ ]
– Gonna give her all the love i've got / Yesterday / Groovin' / I wish it would rain / That's the way love is / How can I forget / Abraham, Martin and John / Gonna keep on tryin' till I win your love / No time for tears /

Cloud nine / Don't you miss me a little bit baby / So long. *(cd-iss. Apr91; WD 72736) (cd re-iss. Aug93; 530214-2)*

Apr 70. (7") *(TMG 734)* **ABRAHAM, MARTIN AND JOHN. / HOW CAN I FORGET** [9] [–]

Jun 70. (7") *<54195>* **THE END OF OUR ROAD. / ME AND MY LONELY ROOM** [–] [40]

Jun 71. (7") *(TMG 775) <54201>* **WHAT'S GOING ON. / GOD IS LOVE** [ ] Feb71 [2]
(re-iss. Mar83 on 'Motown')

Oct 71. (lp) *(STML 11190) <310>* **WHAT'S GOING ON** [ ] Jun71 [6]
– What's going on / What's happening brother / Flyin' high (in the friendly sky) / Save the children / God is love / Mercy mercy me (the ecology) / Right on / Wholy holy / Inner city blues (make me wanna holler). *(re-iss. Apr88 lp/c/cd; WL/WK/WD 72611) (re-iss. Jul94; 530022-2/-4) (deluxe d-cd-iss. Mar01 +=; 013404-2)* – (alt. mixes). *<(cd re-mast.Jan03 +=; 064022-2)>* – God is love (version) / Sad tomorrows (aka Flyin' high – in the friendly sky).

Nov 71. (7") *(TMG 796)* **SAVE THE CHILDREN. / LITTLE DARLING** [41] [ ]

Feb 72. (7") *(TMG 802)* **MERCY MERCY ME. / SAD TOMORROWS** [ ] Jul71 [4]

May 72. (7") *(TMG 817) <54209>* **INNER CITY BLUES (MAKE ME WANNA HOLLER). / WHOLY HOLY** [ ] Oct71 [9]

May 72. (7") *<54221>* **YOU'RE THE MAN. / (part 2)** [–] [50]

Feb 73. (lp) *(STML 11225) <T322L>* **TROUBLE MAN** [ ] Dec72 [14]
– Main theme from "Trouble Man" / "T" plays it cool / Poor Abbey Walsh / The break in (police shoot Big) / Cleo's apartment / Trouble man / Theme from "Trouble Man" / "T" stands for trouble / Main theme from "Trouble Man" / Life is a gamble / Deep-in-it / Don't mess with Mister "T" / There goes Mister "T". *(re-iss. Jul82 lp/c; STMS/CSTMS 5065) (re-iss. 1986 lp/c; WL/WK 72215) (cd-iss. Sep91; WD 72215) (cd re-iss. Apr93; 530 097-2)*

Mar 73. (7") *(TMG 846) <54228>* **TROUBLE MAN. / DON'T MESS WITH MISTER "T"** [ ] Dec72 [7]

Aug 73. (7") *(TMG 868) <54234>* **LET'S GET IT ON. / I WISH IT WOULD RAIN** [31] Jul73 [1]

Nov 73. (lp) *(STMA 8013) <329>* **LET'S GET IT ON** [39] Sep73 [2]
– Let's get it on / Please don't stay (once you go away) / If I should die tonight / Keep gettin' it on / Come get to this / Distant lover / You sure love to ball / Just to keep you satisfied. *(re-iss. Mar82 lp/c; STMS/XSTMS 5034) (re-iss. Apr84 on 'Motown' lp/c; WL/WK 72085) (cd-iss. Apr88; WD 72085) (cd-iss. Jul92; 530055-2) (deluxe d-cd-iss. Oct01 +=; 014757-2)* – (alt. versions). *(cd re-mast.Jan03 +=; 064021-2)* – Let's get it on (single version) / You sure love to ball (version).

— Around this time MARVIN teams up with DIANA ROSS, on album DIANA AND MARVIN. Many hits were lifted from it including YOU ARE EVERYTHING.

Jan 74. (7") *(TMG 882) <54241>* **COME GET TO THIS. / DISTANT LOVER** [ ] Nov73 [21]

Jan 74. (7") *<54244>* **YOU SURE LOVE TO BALL. / JUST TO KEEP YOU SATISFIED** [–] [50]

Sep 74. (lp) *(STMA 8018) <333>* **MARVIN GAYE LIVE! (live)** [ ] Jul74 [8]
– (the beginning: introduction & overture) / Trouble man – Inner city blues – Distant lover / Jan / Fossil medley: I'll be doggone – Try it baby – Can I get a witness – Subborn kind of fellow – How sweet it is to be loved by you / Now: Let's get it on – What's going on. *(re-iss. Mar82; same) (cd-iss. Feb88) (cd-iss. Sep93 on 'Stardust'; STAMCD 536)*

Sep 74. (7") *<54253>* **DISTANT LOVER. / TROUBLE MAN** [–] [28]

Apr 76. (7") *(TMG 1026) <54264>* **I WANT YOU. / I WANT YOU (instrumental)** [ ] [15]

May 76. (lp) *(STML 12025) <342>* **I WANT YOU** [22] Mar76 [4]
– I want you / Come live with me angel / After the dance (instrumental) / Feel all my love inside / I wanna be where you are / I want you / All the way around / Since I had you / Soon I'll be loving you again / I want you (intro jam) / After the dance. *(re-iss. Oct81; same) (re-iss. 1986 on 'Motown'; WL 72027) (cd-iss. Mar90; WD 72027) (cd re-iss. Jul94 & Sep98; 530887-2) (deluxe d-cd-iss. Aug03 +=; 038656-2)* – (alt. versions).

Aug 76. (7") *(TMG 1035) <54273>* **AFTER THE DANCE. / FEEL ALL MY LOVE INSIDE** [ ] [74]

Motown Motown

Apr 77. (7") *(TMG 1069) <54280>* **GOT TO GIVE IT UP (part 1). / GOT TO GIVE IT UP (part 2)** [7] [1]

— next d-lp, * – duets with FLORENCE LYLES

May 77. (d-lp) *(TMSP 6006) <352>* **LIVE AT THE LONDON PALLADIUM (live)** [ ] Mar77 [3]
– (intro theme) / All the way around / Since I had you / Come get to this / Let's get it on / Trouble man / Ain't peculiar / You're a wonderful one / Stubborn kind of fellow / Pride and joy / Little darling (I need you) / I heard it through the grapevine / Hitch hike / You / Too busy thinking about my baby / How sweet it is to be loved by you / Inner city blues (make me wanna holler) / God is love / What's going on / Save the children / You're all I need to get by * / Ain't nothing like the real thing * / Your precious love * / It takes two * / Ain't no mountain high enough * / Distant lover / (closing theme) / Got to give it up. *(re-iss. Aug86 lp/c; WL/WK 72213) (cd-iss. Mar87; ZD 72213) (cd re-iss. May89; WD 72213) (cd re-iss. Sep98; 530886-2)*

Jan 79. (d-lp) *(TMSP 6008) <364>* **HERE, MY DEAR** [ ] [26]
– Here, my dear / I met a little girl / When did you stop loving me, when did I stop loving you / Anger / Is that enough / Everybody needs love / Time to get it together / Sparrow / Anna's song / When did you stop loving me, when did I stop loving you (instrumental) / A funky space reincarnation / You can leave, but it's going to cost you / Falling in love again / When did you stop loving me, when did I stop loving you (reprise). *(re-iss. Oct81 lp/c; TMSP/CTMSP 6008) (cd-iss. Nov93; 530253-2)*

Feb 79. (7") *(TMG 1138) <54298>* **A FUNKY SPACE REINCARNATION (part 1). / (part 2)** [ ] [ ]
(12"+=) *(TMGT 1138)* – ('A'disco).

— Around this a collaboration with SMOKEY ROBINSON, DIANA ROSS and STEVE WONDER gave them a minor hit single 'POPS WE LOVE YOU'.

Nov 79. (7") *(TMG 1168) <54305>* **EGO TRIPPING OUT. / ('A' instrumental)** [ ] [ ]
(12") *(TMGT 1168)* – ('A'side) / What's going on / What's happening brother.

Feb 81. (lp) *(STML 12149) <374>* **IN OUR LIFETIME** [48] [ ]
– Praise / Life is for learning / Love party / Funk me / Far cry / Love me now or love me later / Heavy love affair / In our lifetime. *(cd-iss. Oct94; 530274-2)*

Feb 81. (7") *(TMG 1225) <54322>* **PRAISE. / FUNK ME** [ ] [ ]

Oct 81. (7") *(TMG 1232) <54326>* **HEAVY LOVE AFFAIR. / FAR CRY** [ ] [ ]

— MARVIN now played all instruments (or most of anyway)

C.B.S. Columbia

Oct 82. (lp/c) *(CBS/40 85977) <38197>* **MIDNIGHT LOVE** [10] [7]
– Midnight lady / Sexual healing / Rockin' after midnight / 'Til tomorrow / Turn on some music / Third world girl / Joy / My love is waiting. *(re-iss. Apr86 lp/c; CBS/40 32776) (cd-iss. Jul94; CD 85977) (cd re-iss. Aug00; 498169-2)*

Oct 82. (7"/12") *(A/TA 2855) <03302>* **SEXUAL HEALING. / ('A'instrumental)** [4] [3]

Nov 82. (7") *<03589>* **ROCKIN' AFTER MIDNIGHT. / 'TIL TOMORROW** [–] [ ]

Jan 83. (7"/12") *(A/TA 3048)* **MY LOVE IS WAITING. / ROCKIN' AFTER MIDNIGHT** [34] [–]

Jan 83. (7") *<03860>* **JOY. / ('A' instrumental)** [–] [ ]

Feb 83. (7") *<03870>* **STAR SPANGLED BANNER. / TURN ON SOME MUSIC** [–] [ ]

Mar 83. (7") *(A 3242) <03935>* **JOY. / TURN ON SOME MUSIC** [ ] [ ]

— On the 1st April 1984, MARVIN was shot dead by his father.

May 85. (7"/12") *(A/TA 4894) (04861>* **SANCTIFIED LADY. / ('A'instrumental)** [51] [ ]
(d7"+=) *(DA 4894)* – Sexual healing / Rockin' after midnight.

Jun 85. (lp/c) *(CBS/40 26239) <39916>* **DREAM OF A LIFETIME** (2 new & recordings from the 70's) [46] [41]
– Sanctified lady / Savage in the sack / Masochistic beauty / It's madness / Ain't it funny (how things turn around) / Symphony / Life's opera / Dream of a lifetime. *(cd-iss. Jun91 on 'Pickwick'; 982591-2)*

Jul 85. (7") *(A 6462) <05542>* **IT'S MADNESS. / AIN'T IT FUNNY (HOW THINGS TURN AROUND)** [ ] [ ]
(12"+=) *(TA 6462)* – Joy.

Dec 85. (lp/c) *(CBS/40 26744) <40208>* **ROMANTICALLY YOURS** [ ] [ ]
– More / Why did I choose you? / Maria / The shadow of your smile / Fly me to the Moon (in other words) / I won't cry anymore / Just like / Walkin' in the rain / I live for you / Stranger in my life / Happy go lucky. *(cd-iss. Jul89 on 'Pickwick' 902121-2) (re-iss. Jun94 on 'Sony Collectors' cd/c; 463158-2/-4)*

Jan 86. (7") *<05791>* **JUST LIKE. / MORE** [–] [ ]

Jun 86. (7") *(ZB 40758)* **THE WORLD IS RATED X. / LONELY LOVER** [ ] [–]
(12"+=) *(ZT 40758)* – ('A'instrumental).
Jun 86. (7") *<1836>* **THE WORLD IS RATED X. / NO GREATER LOVE** [–] [ ]

– (selective) compilations, etc. –

note all below on 'Tamla Motown' unless mentioned otherwise
Mar 64. (lp) *<252>* **GREATEST HITS** [–] [72]
Feb 68. (lp) *(STML 11065)* **MARVIN GAYE'S GREATEST HITS** [40] [–]
Jun 74. (d-lp) *(TMSP 1128)* **ANTHOLOGY** [ ] [61]
(d-cd-iss. Oct86) (d-cd re-iss. Apr93)
Nov 76. (lp) *(STML 12042) <348>* **THE BEST OF MARVIN GAYE** [56] [ ]
(re-iss. Oct81)
Oct 83. (lp) *<6058>* **EVERY GREAT MOTOWN HIT OF MARVIN GAYE** [–] [80]
(cd-iss. Jul00; AA314 549517-2)
Nov 83. (lp/c) *Telstar; (STAR/STAC 2234)* **GREATEST HITS** [13] [–]
– I heard it through the grapevine / Let's get it on / Too busy thinking about my baby / How sweet it is to be loved by you / You're all I need to get by / Got to give it up / You are everything / Midnight lady / Sexual healing / What's going on / Abraham, Martin & John / It takes two / Stop, look, listen (to your heart) / My love is waiting / The onion song / Wherever I lay my hat.
Apr 85. (lp/c) *(WK/WL 72374)* **I HEARD IT THROUGH THE GRAPEVINE** [ ] [–]
(cd-iss. Nov86; ZD 72457) (cd re-iss. Jun89; WD 72374) (cd re-iss. Aug99 on 'Spectrum'; 530793-2)
Mar 86. (cd) *(ZD 72422)* **COMPACT COMMAND PERFORMANCES VOL.1** [ ] [–]
Apr 86. (7") *(ZB 40701)* **I HEARD IT THROUGH THE GRAPEVINE. / CAN I GET A WITNESS** [8] [–]
(ext; 12"/c-s) *(ZT/ZV 40702)* – ('A'side) / That's the way love is / You're a wonderful one.
Jun 86. (lp/c) *(ZL/ZK 72463) <6172>* **MOTOWN REMEMBERS MARVIN GAYE** [ ] Apr86 [ ]
Jul 86. (cd) *(TCD 2234)* **THE VERY BEST OF MARVIN GAYE** [ ] [–]
Nov 86. (d-cd) *(ZD 72456)* **WHAT'S GOING ON / LET'S GET IT ON** [ ] [ ]
Feb 87. (d-cd) *(ZD 72500)* **TROUBLE MAN / M.P.G.** [ ] [–]
Mar 87. (cd) *(ZD 72508)* **COMPACT COMMAND PERFORMANCES – VOL.2** [ ] [–]
Jul 87. (d-cd) *(ZD 72562)* **THAT STUBBORN KINDA FELLA / HOW SWEET IT IS** [ ] [–]
Nov 88. (lp/c/cd; shared with SMOKEY ROBINSON) *Telstar; (STAR/STAC/TCD 2331)* **LOVE SONGS** [69] [–]
Oct 90. (cd/c/lp) *Telstar; (TCD/STAC/STAR 2427)* **LOVE SONGS** [39] [–]
Oct 92. (cd) *Columbia; (461017-2)* **MIDNIGHT LOVE / DREAM OF A LIFETIME** [ ] [–]
Mar 94. (cd/c) *(530292-2/-4)* **THE VERY BEST OF MARVIN GAYE** [3] [–]
May 94. (7"/c-s) *(TMG/+C 1426)* **LUCKY LUCKY ME. / ('A'extended)** [67] [ ]
(12"+=/cd-s+=) *(TMG T/CD 1426)* – ('A'instrumental mix) / ('A'jazz mix) / ('A'ragga vibe mix).
Oct 94. (3xcd-box) *Columbia; (477525-2)* **DREAM OF A LIFETIME / ROMANTICALLY YOURS / MIDNIGHT LOVE** [ ] [–]
Nov 95. (3xcd-box) **HOW SWEET IT IS / TRIBUTE TO NAT KING COLE / M.P.G.** [ ] [–]
Jul 96. (cd) *Spectrum; (552118-2)* **MOTOWN EARLY CLASSICS** [ ] [ ]
Nov 96. (cd) *Summit; (SUMCD 4043)* **THE MIDNIGHT LOVER: LIVE IN CONCERT (live)** [ ] [–]
May 97. (cd) *A-Play; (10030-2)* **IN CONCERT (live)** [ ] [–]
Sep 97. (d-cd) *Alpha; (ALPCD 102)* **THE LEGENDARY MARVIN GAYE** [ ] [ ]
Nov 98. (cd) *Creole; (CP 1008)* **THE LEGEND** [ ] [ ]
Nov 98. (cd) *Columbia; (491572-2)* **MIDNIGHT LOVE / THE SEXUAL HEALING SESSIONS** [ ] [ ]
Dec 99. (cd) *Castle Pie; (PIESD 180)* **LIVE** [ ] [–]
Feb 00. (cd/c) *Universal TV; (545470-2/-4)* **THE LOVE SONGS** [8] [–]
May 00. (4xcd-box) *(530492-2)* **THE MASTER 1961-1984** [ ] [ ]
Jul 00. (cd) *(153868-2)* **MOTOWN LOST AND FOUND: LOVE STARVED HEART** [ ] [ ]
Jul 00. (cd) *157609-2)* **AIN'T NOTHING LIKE THE REAL THING: AN INTRODUCTION TO MARVIN GAYE** [ ] [ ]
Oct 00. (d-cd) *(E 530831-2)* **WHAT'S GOING ON / IN OUR LIFETIME** [ ] [ ]
Oct 00. (cd) *(153426-2)* **I HEARD IT THROUGH THE GRAPEVINE / WHAT'S GOING ON** [ ] [ ]
Oct 00. (3xcd-box) *(E 530910-2)* **WHAT'S GOING ON / LET'S GET IT ON / TROUBLE MAN** [ ] [ ]
Oct 00. (d-cd) *(E 530832-2)* **LET'S GET IT ON / HERE, MY DEAR** [ ] [ ]
Feb 01. (cd) *(013184-2)* **THAT STUBBORN KINDA FELLOW / HOW SWEET IT IS TO BE LOVED BY YOU** [ ] [ ]
Feb 01. (cd) *(013185-2)* **MOODS OF MARVIN GAYE / IN THE GROOVE** [ ] [ ]
Feb 01. (cd) *(013187-2)* **M.P.G. / THAT'S THE WAY LOVE IS** [ ] [ ]
Feb 01. (cd) *(013216-2)* **HERE, MY DEAR / IN OUR LIFETIME** [ ] [ ]
Feb 01. (cd) *Burning Airlings; (PILOT 005)* **THE REAL THING** [ ] [ ]
(re-iss. Aug03 on 'Snapper'; SNAP 157CD)
Aug 01. (d-cd) *Universal TV; (014367-2)* **THE VERY BEST OF MARVIN GAYE** [15] [ ]
Feb 02. (cd) *016815-2)* **LOVE SONGS: BEDROOM BALLADS** [ ] [ ]
Aug 02. (d-cd) *Proper Pairs; (PVCD 110)* **MARVIN GAYE LIVE** [ ] [ ]
Sep 02. (cd) *Cleopatra; (CLP 1204CD)* **PERFORMANCE** [ ] [ ]
Oct 02. (cd) *Armoury; (ARMCD 069)* **BEST OF LIVE** [ ] [–]
Oct 02. (d-cd) *Delta Blues; (63060)* **GOT TO GIVE IT UP (live)** [ ] [–]
Nov 02. (cd) *Planet Media; (PML 1090)* **FINAL CONCERT (live)** [ ] [ ]
Jan 03. (cd) *Universe; (UV 061)* **NORTH AMERICAN TOUR** [ ] [ ]
Mar 03. (cd) *Universal; (AA121 53363-2)* **20th CENTURY MASTERS VOL.1** [ ] [ ]
Mar 03. (cd) *Universal; (AA121 53732-2)* **20th CENTURY MASTERS VOL.2** [ ] [ ]
May 03. (d-cd) *Eagle; (EDGCD 234)* **LIVE IN MONTREUX 1980 (live)** [ ] [–]
Aug 03. (3xcd-box) *Spectrum; (9808968)* **I HEARD IT THROUGH THE GRAPEVINE / MARVIN GAYE AND FRIENDS / EARLY CLASSICS** [ ] [ ]

☐ Bob GELDOF (see under ⇒ BOOMTOWN RATS)

☐ GENERATION X (see under ⇒ IDOL, Billy)

GENESIS

Formed: Godalming, Surrey, England ... early 1967 b Charterhouse public school boys PETER GABRIEL and TON BANKS (both ex-The GARDEN WALL). They teamed up wit former members of The ANON; MICHAEL RUTHERFORD ANTHONY PHILLIPS and CHRIS STEWART. Still at schoo they signed to 'Decca', having sent demos to solo artist an producer JONATHAN KING. Their first 2 singles flopped, as di their 1969 MOODY BLUES-styled album, 'FROM GENESIS T REVELATION', which only sold around 500 copies. Early in 197 they were seen live by TONY STRATTON-SMITH, who becam their manager after signing them to his 'Charisma' label. The second album, 'TRESPASS', failed to break through, although contained the live favourite and edited 45, 'THE KNIFE'. Afte its release, they found new members PHIL COLLINS and STEV HACKETT, who replaced recent additions JOHN MAYHEW an ANTHONY PHILLIPS. Late in '71, they issued their set, 'NURSER CRYME', which featured another two gems, 'THE MUSICA BOX' and 'THE RETURN OF THE GIANT HOGWEED'. By th point the band transformed into one of the leading purveyors o progressive rock, bizarre extrovert GABRIEL proving a compellin theatrical focus for the critically-lauded group. It was also th brief debut on lead vox for COLLINS, who sang on the trac

'FOR ABSENT FRIENDS'. A year later, with many gigs behind them, they had their first taste of chart success when 'FOXTROT' hit the UK Top 20. This contained the excellent concept piece, 'SUPPER'S READY', which lasted all of 23 minutes. In 1973, a live album of their best work so far, hit the Top 10, as did their studio follow-up, 'SELLING ENGLAND BY THE POUND'. This boasted another epic track, 'THE BATTLE OF EPPING FOREST', plus another COLLINS lead vocal in 'MORE FOOL ME'. Lifted from it, was a near Top 20 single, 'I KNOW WHAT I LIKE (IN YOUR WARDROBE)'. Late in 1974, they again made Top 10, with the concept double album, 'THE LAMB LIES DOWN ON BROADWAY', which was their first US Top 50 placing, the band performing the album in its entirety as part of a worldwide live show. Shortly after a last concert in May '75, GABRIEL left for a solo career, COLLINS taking over the vocal duties. Surprisingly, this did not harm the commercial appeal of the group when they returned in 1976 with the Top 3 album, 'A TRICK OF THE TAIL'. His drum-stool was filled for live gigs by the seasoned BILL BRUFORD, then CHESTER THOMPSON, who appeared on the 1977 live double album, 'SECONDS OUT'. This was also the last album to feature STEVE HACKETT, who also left for a lucrative solo career. In 1978, their next album, appropriately titled '. . . AND THEN THERE WERE THREE' (COLLINS, BANKS & RUTHERFORD), hit No.3 and also climbed into the US Top 20. The 80's were even more fruitful for the band, as they hit the top spot in the UK with each successive album (from 'DUKE' to 'WE CAN'T DANCE'), also amassing a number of hit singles over the same period. During this era, PHIL COLLINS (who had moonlighted in his own BRAND X) scored a number of easier-listening hit singles and albums. Although they remain one of the stadium rock circuit's largest grossing bands, the band have lost all trace of their pioneering 70's sound. With PHIL COLLINS now out of the picture, BANKS and RUTHERFORD took on the relatively younger Scotsman, RAY WILSON, who had previously fronted chart-toppers, STILTSKIN. TONY BANKS also released some solo work, as did MIKE RUTHERFORD, who made coffee-table pop/rock with his outfit, MIKE + THE MECHANICS. In 2004, GENESIS finally released a career-spanning anthology, 'PLATINUM COLLECTION', compiled in reverse chronology with the third disc covering the cream of the GABRIEL period.

Songwriters: GABRIEL lyrics and group compositions. From 1978, the trio collaborated on all work.

Album rating: FROM GENESIS TO REVELATION (*5) / TRESPASS (*6) / NURSERY CRYME (*8) / FOXTROT (*9) / GENESIS LIVE (*7) / SELLING ENGLAND BY THE POUND (*10) / THE LAMB LIES DOWN ON BROADWAY (*9) / A TRICK OF THE TAIL (*7) / WIND & WUTHERING (*6) / . . . AND THEN THERE WERE THREE (*6) / DUKE (*6) / ABACAB (*6) / THREE SIDES LIVE (*6) / GENESIS (*5) / INVISIBLE TOUCH (*6) / WE CAN'T DANCE (*5) / THE WAY WE WALK VOLUME 1: THE SHORTS (*5) / LIVE – THE WAY WE WALK VOLUME 2: THE LONGS (*6) / CALLING ALL STATIONS (*4) / TURN IT ON AGAIN – THE HITS compilation (*8) / PLATINUM COLLECTION compilation (*8)

PETER GABRIEL (b.13 May'50, London, England) – vocals / **TONY BANKS** (b.27 Mar'51, East Heathly, Sussex, England) – keyboards, vocals / **ANTHONY PHILLIPS** (b.Dec'51, Putney, England) – guitar, vocals / **MICHAEL RUTHERFORD** (b. 2 Oct'50, Guildford, Surrey, England) – bass, guitar / **CHRIS STEWART** – drums

Decca / Parrot

Feb 68. (7") *(F 12735) <3018>* **THE SILENT SUN. / THAT'S ME** [ ] [ ]

May 68. (7") *(F 12775)* **A WINTER'S TALE. / ONE-EYED HOUND** [ ] [–]

— **JOHN SILVER** – drums; repl. CHRIS

Mar 69. (lp; mono/stereo) *(LK/SKL 4990)* **FROM GENESIS TO REVELATION** [ ] [ ]
– Where the sour turns to sweet / In the beginning / Fireside song / The serpent / Am I very wrong? / In the wilderness / The conqueror / In hiding / One day / Window / In limbo / The silent sun / A place to call my own. *(re-iss. 1974 as 'IN THE BEGINNING'; same) (re-iss. Oct93 on 'Music Club' cd/c;)*

Jun 69. (7") *(F 12949)* **WHERE THE SOUR TURNS TO SWEET. / IN HIDING** [ ] [–]

— (Jul'69) **JOHN MAYHEW** – drums; repl. JOHN SILVER

Charisma / Impulse

Oct 70. (7"w-drawn) *(GS 1)* **LOOKING FOR SOMEONE. / VISIONS OF ANGELS** [–] [–]

Oct 70. (lp) *(CAS 1020) <9295>* **TRESPASS** [ ] [ ]
– Looking for someone / White mountain / Visions of angels / Stagnation / Dusk / The knife. *<US re-iss. 1974 on 'ABC'; 816> (re-iss. Mar83; CHC/+MC 12)(hit 98; Apr84) (cd-iss. Jun88; CASCD 1020) (cd re-iss. Aug94; CASCDX 1020)*

Jun 71. (7") *(CB 152)* **THE KNIFE (part 1). / THE KNIFE (part 2)** [ ] [–]

— (Dec70) **GABRIEL, BANKS + RUTHERFORD** recruited new members **PHIL COLLINS** (b.31 Jan'51, Chiswick, London, England) – drums, vocals (ex-FLAMING YOUTH) repl. MAYHEW / **STEVE HACKETT** (b.12 Feb'50, London) – guitar (ex-QUIET WORLD) repl. ANTHONY PHILLIPS who went solo

Charisma / Charisma

Nov 71. (lp)(c) *(<CAS 1052>)(7208 552)* **NURSERY CRYME** [ ] [ ]
– The musical box / For absent friends / The fountain of Salmacis / Seven stones / Harold the barrel / Harlequin / The return of the giant hogweed. *(hit UK No.39 May74) (re-iss. Feb84 lp/c; CHC/+MC 22); hit 68) (cd-iss. Sep85; CASCD 1052) (cd re-iss. Aug94; CASCDX 1052)*

May 72. (7") *(CB 181)* **HAPPY THE MAN. / SEVEN STONES** [ ] [ ]

Oct 72. (lp)(c) *(<CAS 1058>)(7208 553)* **FOXTROT** [12] [ ]
– Get 'em out by Friday / Time-table / Watcher of the skies / Can-utility and the coastliners / Horizon / Supper's ready; (i) Lover's leap, (ii) The guaranteed eternal sanctuary man, (iii) Ikhaton and Itsacon and their band of merry men, (iv) How dare I be so beautiful, (v) Willow farm, (vi) Apocalypse in 9/8 co-starring the delicious talents of Gabble Ratchet, (vii) As sure as eggs is eggs (aching men's feets). *(re-iss. Sep83 lp/c; CHC/+MC 38) (cd-iss. Jul86; CASCD 1058) (cd re-iss. Aug94; CASCDX 1058)*

Feb 73. (7") *<103>* **WATCHER OF THE SKIES. / WILLOW FARM** [–] [ ]

Jul 73. (lp)(c) *(CLASS 1)(7299 288) <1066>* **GENESIS LIVE (live)** [9] May74 [ ]
– Watcher of the skies / Get 'em out by Friday / The return of the giant hogweed / The musical box / The knife. *(re-iss. Feb86 lp/c; CHC/+MC 23) (cd-iss. Jul87; CLACD 1) (cd re-iss. Aug94; CLACDX 1)*

Oct 73. (lp)(c) *(CAS 1074)(7208 554) <6060>* **SELLING ENGLAND BY THE POUND** [3] [70]
– Dancing with the moonlit knight / I know what I like (in your wardrobe) / Firth of fifth / More fool me / The battle of Epping Forest / After the ordeal / The cinema show / Aisle of plenty. *(re-iss. Oct86 lp/c; CHC/+MC 46) (cd-iss. Feb86; CASCD 1074) (cd re-iss. Aug94; CLACDX 1074) (re-iss. Feb97 on 'E.M.I.'; LPCENT 17)*

Mar 74. (7") *(CB 224) <26002>* **I KNOW WHAT I LIKE (IN YOUR WARDROBE). / TWILIGHT ALEHOUSE** [21] [ ]

Charisma / Atco

Nov 74. (d-lp)(d-c) *(CGS 101)(7599 121) <401>* **THE LAMB LIES DOWN ON BROADWAY** [10] [41]
– The lamb lies down on Broadway / Fly on a windshield / Broadway melody of 1974 / Cuckoo cocoon / In the cage / The grand parade of lifeless packaging / Back in N.Y.C. / Hairless heart / Counting out time / Carpet crawlers / The chamber of 32 doors // Lilywhite Lilith / The waiting room / Anyway / Here comes the supernatural anaesthetist / The lamia / Silent sorrow in empty boats / The colony of Slippermen (The arrival – A visit to the doktor – Raven) / Ravine / The light dies down on Broadway / Riding the scree / *it. (re-iss. Sep83 d-lp/c; CGS/+MC 101) (d-cd-iss. Feb86; CGSCD 1) (cd re-iss. Aug94; CGSCDX 1)*

Nov 74. (7") *(CB 238)* **COUNTING OUT TIME. / RIDING THE SCREE** [ ] [–]

Dec 74. (7") *<7013>* **COUNTING OUT TIME. / THE LAMB LIES DOWN ON BROADWAY** [–] [ ]

Apr 75. (7") *(CB 251)* **CARPET CRAWLERS. / THE WAITING ROOM (evil jam) (live)** [ ] [–]

— Now just a quartet when PETER GABRIEL left to go solo.

Feb 76. (lp)(c) *(CDS 4001) <129>* **A TRICK OF THE TAIL** [3] [31]
– Dance on a volcano / Entangled / Squonk / Mad mad Moon / Robbery, assault and battery / Ripples / A trick of the tail / Los endos. *(re-iss. Sep83 lp/c; CDS/+MC 4001) (cd-iss. Apr86; CDSCD 4001) (re-iss. Apr90 on 'Virgin' lp/c; OVED/+C 306) (cd re-iss. Oct94; CDSCDX 4001)*

Mar 76. (7") *(CB 277)* **A TRICK OF THE TAIL. / RIPPLES** [ ] [-]
Mar 76. (7") *<7050>* **RIPPLES. / ENTANGLED** [-] [ ]
Jan 77. (lp)(c) *(CDS 4005)(7208 611) <144>* **WIND AND WUTHERING** [7] [26]
– Eleventh Earl of Mar / One for the vine / Your own special way / Wot gorilla? / All in a mouse's night / Blood on the rooftops / Unquiet slumbers for the sleepers . . .In that quiet Earth / Afterglow. *(re-iss. Sep83 lp/c; CDS/+MC 4005) (cd-iss. Apr86; CDSCD 4005) (re-iss. Apr90 on 'Virgin' lp/c; OVED/+C 332) (cd re-iss. Oct94; CDSCDX 4005)*
Feb 77. (7") *(CB 300)* **YOUR OWN SPECIAL WAY. / IT'S YOURSELF** [43] [-]
Feb 77. (7") *<7076>* **YOUR OWN SPECIAL WAY. / . . .IN THAT QUIET EARTH** [-] [62]
May 77. (7"ep) *(GEN 001)* **SPOT THE PIGEON** [14] [-]
– Match of the day / Inside and out / Pigeons. *(cd-ep-iss.1988 on 'Virgin'; CDT 40)*

— added **BILL BRUFORD** – drums (ex-YES, ex-KING CRIMSON) **CHESTER THOMPSON** – drums (ex-FRANK ZAPPA) they were both used on live album below, with CHESTER augmenting on tours.

Oct 77. (d-lp)(d-c) *(GE 2001)(7649 067) <9002>* **SECONDS OUT (live)** [4] [47]
– Sqounk / Carpet crawlers / Robbery, assault and battery / Afterglow / Firth of fifth / I know what I like (in your wardrobe) / The lamb lies down on Broadway / The musical box / Supper's ready / The cinema show / Dance on a volcano / Los endos. *(re-iss. Sep83 d-lp/d-c; GE/+MC 2001) (d-cd-iss. Nov85; GECD 2001) (d-cd re-iss. Oct94; GECDX 2001)*

— (Jun77) Now a trio of **COLLINS, BANKS & RUTHERFORD** when STEVE HACKETT continued solo career.

Charisma Atlantic

Mar 78. (7") *(CB 309)* **FOLLOW YOU FOLLOW ME. / BALLAD OF BIG** [7] [-]
Mar 78. (7") *<3474>* **FOLLOW YOU FOLLOW ME. / INSIDE AND OUT** [-] [23]
Apr 78. (lp)(c) *(CDS 4010)(7208 619) <19173>* **. . .AND THEN THERE WERE THREE** [3] [14]
– Down and out / Undertow / Ballad of big / Snowbound / Burning rope / Deep in the motherlode / Many too many / Scene from a night's dream / Say it's alright Joe / The lady lies / Follow you follow me. *(re-iss. Sep83 lp/c; CDS/+MC 4010) (cd-iss. May83; 800 059-2) (re-iss. Aug91 on 'Virgin' lp/c; OVED/+C 368) (cd re-iss. Oct94; CDSCDX 4010)*
Jun 78. (7") *(CB 315)* **MANY TOO MANY. / THE DAY THE LIGHT WENT OUT IN VANCOUVER** [43] [-]
Jul 78. (7") *<3511>* **SCENE FROM A NIGHT'S DREAM. / DEEP IN THE MOTHERLODE** [-] [ ]
Mar 80. (7") *(CB 356)* **TURN IT ON AGAIN. / BEHIND THE LINES (part 2)** [8] [-]
Mar 80. (lp/c) *(CBR/+C 101) <16014>* **DUKE** [1] [11]
– Behind the lines / Duchess / Guide vocal / Man of our time / Misunderstanding / Heathaze / Turn it on again / Alone tonight / Cul-de-sac / Please don't ask / Duke's end / Duke's travels. *(re-iss. Sep83 lp/c; CBR/+C 101) (cd-iss. Apr85; CBRCD 101) (re-iss. Mar91 on 'Virgin' lp/c; OVED/+C 345) (cd re-iss. Oct94; CBRCDX 101)*
May 80. (7") *(CB 363)* **DUCHESS. / OPEN DOOR** [46] [-]
May 80. (7") *<3662>* **MISUNDERSTANDING. / BEHIND THE LINES** [-] [14]
Sep 80. (7") *(CB 369)* **MISUNDERSTANDING. / EVIDENCE OF AUTUMN** [42] [-]
Sep 80. (7") *<3751>* **TURN IT ON AGAIN. / EVIDENCE OF AUTUMN** [-] [58]
Aug 81. (7") *(CB 388)* **ABACAB. / ANOTHER RECORD** [9] [-]
Sep 81. (lp/c) *(CBR/+C 102) <19313>* **ABACAB** [1] [7]
– Abacab / No reply at all / Me and Sarah Jane / Keep it dark / Dodo / Lurker / Who dunnit? / Man on the corner / Like it or not / Another record. *(cd-iss. May83; 800 044-2) (re-iss. Mar91 on 'Virgin' lp/c; OVED/+C 344) (cd re-iss. Oct94; CBRCDX 102) (lp re-iss. Jan01 on 'Simply Vinyl'; SVLP 278)*
Oct 81. (7") *(CB 391)* **KEEP IT DARK. / NAMINANU** [33] [-]
(12"+=) *(CB 391-12)* – Abacab (long version).
Oct 81. (7") *<3858>* **NO REPLY AT ALL. / HEAVEN LOVE MY LIFE** [-] [29]
Jan 82. (7") *<3891>* **ABACAB. / WHO DUNNIT?** [-] [26]
Feb 82. (7") *(CB 393) <4025>* **MAN IN THE CORNER. / SUBMARINE** [41] Mar82 [40]
May 82. (7") *<4053>* **PAPERLATE. / YOU MIGHT RECALL** [-] [32]
May 82. (7"ep) *(GEN 1)* **3 X 3 E.P.** [10] [-]
– Paperlate / You might recall / Me and Virgil.
Jun 82. (d-lp/d-c) *(GE/+MC 2002) <2000>* **THREE SIDES LIVE (live except ***)** [2] [10]
– Turn it on again / Dodo / Abacab / Behind the lines / Duchess / Me and Sarah Jane / Follow you follow me / Misunderstanding / In the cage / Afterglow / One for the vine * / Fountain of Salmacis * / Watcher of the skies * / It * / Paperlate *** / You might recall *** / Me and Virgil *** / Evidence of Autumn *** / Open door *** / You might recall II ***. *(cd-iss. Apr85; GECD 2002) <US-cd.repl.* w/ The cinema show + The colony of Slippermen> (re-iss. Apr92 d-lp/c; DOVD/+C 2) (cd re-iss. Oct94; GECDX 2002)*

Virgin Atco

Aug 83. (7"/ext.12") *(MAMA 1/+12) <89770>* **MAMA. / IT'S GONNA GET BETTER** [4] [73]
(cd-ep.iss.Jun88; CDT 5)
Oct 83. (lp/c/cd) *(GEN LP/MC/CD 1) <80116>* **GENESIS** [1] [9]
– Mama / That's all / Home by the sea / Second home by the sea / Illegal alien / Taking it all too hard / Just a job to do / Silver rainbow / It's gonna get better. *(re-iss. Jul87; same)*
Nov 83. (7") *(TATA 1)* **THAT'S ALL. / TAKING IT ALL TOO HARD** [16] [-]
(12"+=) *(TATAY 1)* – Firth of fifth (live).
Nov 83. (7") *<89724>* **THAT'S ALL. / SECOND HOME BY THE SEA** [-] [6]
Feb 84. (7"/7"sha-pic-d) *(AL/+S 1) <89698>* **ILLEGAL ALIEN. / TURN IT ON AGAIN (live)** [46] [44]
(12"+=) *(AL 1-12)* – ('A'extended).
Jun 84. (7") *<89656>* **TAKING IT ALL TOO HARD. / SILVER RAINBOW** [-] [50]
May 86. (7",7"clear) *(GENS 1)* **INVISIBLE TOUCH. / THE LAST DOMINO** [15] [1]
(12"+=) *(GENS 1-12)* – ('A'extended).
Jun 86. (lp/c/cd) *(GEN LP/MC/CD 2) <81641>* **INVISIBLE TOUCH** [1] [3]
– Invisible touch / Tonight, tonight, tonight / Land of confusion / In too deep / Anything she does / Domino:- In the glow of the night – The last domino / Throwing it all away / The Brazilian. *(pic-cd.Dec88; GENCDP 2*
Aug 86. (7"/12") *(GENS 2/+12)* **IN TOO DEEP. / DO THE NEUROTIC** [19] [-]
Aug 86. (7") *<89372>* **THROWING IT ALL AWAY. / DO THE NEUROTIC** [-] [4]
Nov 86. (7") *(GENS 3) <89336>* **LAND OF CONFUSION. / FEEDING THE FIRE** [14] Oct86 [4]
(12"+=) *(GENS 3-12)* – Dance the neurotic.
(cd-s++=) *(SNEG 3-12)* – ('A'extended).
Mar 87. (7"/12") *(GENS 4/+12)* **TONIGHT, TONIGHT, TONIGHT. / IN THE GLOW OF THE NIGHT (part 1)** [18] Feb87 [3]
(12"+=/cd-s+=) *(GENS/DRAW 4-12)* – Paperlate / ('A'ext.remix).
(cd-s+=) *(CDEP 1)* – Invisible touch (extended) / ('A'-John Potoker remix).
Apr 87. (7") *<89316>* **IN TOO DEEP. / I'D RATHER BE WITH YOU** [-] [3]
Jun 87. (7") *(GENS 5)* **THROWING IT ALL AWAY. / I'D RATHER BE WITH YOU** [22] [-]
(12"+=/c-s+=) *(GENS/+C 5-12)* – Invisible touch (live).
Oct 91. (7"/c-s) *(GENS/+C 6) <87571>* **NO SON OF MINE. / LIVING FOREVER** [6] [13]
(12"+=/cd-s+=) *(GENS/GENCD 6)* – Invisible touch (live).
Nov 91. (cd/c/d-lp) *(GEN CD/MC/LP 3) <82344>* **WE CAN'T DANCE** [1] [4]
– No son of mine / Jesus he knows me / Driving the last spike / I can't dance / Never a time / Dreaming while you sleep / Tell me why / Living forever / Hold on my heart / Way of the world / Since I lost you / Fading lights.
Jan 92. (7"/c-s) *(GENS/+C 7) <87532>* **I CAN'T DANCE. / ON THE SHORELINE** [7] [7]
(cd-s+=) *(GENDG 7)* – In too deep (live) / That's all (live).
(cd-s+=) *(GENDX 7)* – ('A'-sex mix).
Apr 92. (7"/c-s) *(GENS/+C 8) <87481>* **HOLD ON MY HEART. / WAY OF THE WORLD** [16] [12]
(cd-s+=) *(GENDG 8)* – Your own special way (live).
(cd-s+=) *(GENDX 8)* – Home by the sea.
Jul 92. (7"/c-s) *(GENS/+C 9) <87454>* **JESUS HE KNOWS ME. / HEARTS OF FIRE** [20] [23]
(cd-s+=) *(GENDG 9)* – I can't dance (mix).
(cd-s+=) *(GENDX 9)* – Land of confusion (rehearsal version).
Nov 92. (cd/c/d-lp) *(GEN CD/MC/LP 4) <82452>* **THE WAY WE WALK VOLUME 1: THE SHORTS (live)** [3] [35]
– Land of confusion / No son of mine / Jesus he knows me / Throwing it all away / I can't dance / Mama / Hold on my heart / That's all / In too

deep / Tonight, tonight, tonight / Invisible touch.

Nov 92. (7"/c-s) *(GENS/+C 10)* **INVISIBLE TOUCH (live). / ABACAB (live)** [7] [–]
(cd-s+=) *(GENDG 10)* – The Brazilian.

Nov 92. (c-s) *<87411>* **NEVER A TIME / TONIGHT, TONIGHT, TONIGHT (live) / INVISIBLE TOUCH (live)** [–] [21]

Jan 93. (cd/c/lp) *(GEN CD/MC/LP 5) <82461>* **LIVE / THE WAY WE WALK VOLUME 2: THE LONGS** (live) [1] Feb93 [20]
– Old medley: Dance on a volcano – Lamb lies down on Broadway – The musical box – Firth of fifth – I know what I like . . . / Driving the fast spike / Domino: part I – In the glow of the night, part II – The last domino / Home by the sea – Second home by the sea / Drum duet.

Feb 93. (7"/c-s) *(GENS/+C 11)* **TELL ME WHY. / DREAMING WHILE YOU SLEEP** [40] [–]
(cd-s+=) *(GENDG 11)* – Tonight, tonight, tonight.

— **RAY WILSON** – vocals (ex-STILTSKIN) repl. COLLINS who continued his solo career (see own entry ⇒)

Sep 97. (cd/c/lp) *(GEN CD/MC/LP 6) <83037>* **CALLING ALL STATIONS** [2] [54]
– Calling all stations / Congo / Shipwrecked / Alien afternoon / Not about us / If that's what you need / The dividing line / Uncertain weather / Small talk / There must be some other way / One man's fool.

Sep 97. (c-s/cd-s) *(GENS C/D 12)* **CONGO / PAPA HE SAID / BANJO MAN** [29] [–]

Nov 97. (c-s/cd-s) *<84063>* **NOT ABOUT US / TURN IT ON AGAIN (live acoustic)** [–] [ ]
(cd-s+=) *(GENSDX 12)* – Second by the sea.

Dec 97. (c-s/cd-s) *(GENS C/D 14)* **SHIPWRECKED / NO SON OF MINE / LOVERS LEAP / TURN IT ON AGAIN** [54] [–]
(cd-s) *(GENSDX 14)* – ('A'side) / Phret / 7-8.

Feb 98. (c-s/cd-s) *(GENS C/D 15)* **NOT ABOUT US / (extended)** [66] [–]
(cd-s+=) *(GENSDX 15)* – Dancing with the moonlit knight / Follow you, follow me.

– compilations etc. –

on 'Charisma' unless mentioned otherwise

May 74. (d-lp-box) *(CGS 102)* **GENESIS COLLECTION VOLUME ONE** [ ] [–]
– (TRESPASS / NURSERY CRYME)

May 74. (d-lp-box) *(CGS 103)* **GENESIS COLLECTION VOLUME TWO** [ ] [–]
– (FOXTROT / SELLING ENGLAND BY THE POUND)

May 76. (lp/c) *Decca; (ROOTS/KRTC 1)* **ROCK ROOTS: GENESIS** [ ] [–]
– (debut lp + early 45's)

Mar 83. (d-c) *(CASMC 112)* **FOXTROT / SELLING ENGLAND BY THE POUND** [ ] [–]

Apr 86. (lp/pic-lp) *Metal Masters; (MACHM/+P 4)* **WHEN THE SOUR TURNS TO SWEET** [ ] [–]
(cd-iss. Oct87; MACD 4) (re-iss. Jul91;)

Mar 87. (cd) *London; (820496-2)* **AND THE WORLD WAS** (early) [ ] [–]

Jun 88. (7") *Old Gold; (OG 9263)* **I KNOW WHAT I LIKE (IN YOUR WARDROBE). / COUNTING OUT TIME** [ ] [–]

Jun 88. (7") *Old Gold; (OG 9264)* **FOLLOW YOU FOLLOW ME. / A TRICK OF THE TAIL** [ ] [–]

Nov 90. (pic-cd-box) *Virgin; (TPAK 1)* **GENESIS CD COLLECTORS EDITION** [ ] [ ]
– (TRESPASS / NURSERY CRYME / FOXTROT)

Jun 98. (4xcd-box) *(CDBOX 6)* **ARCHIVE 1967-1975** [35] [ ]

Nov 00. (d-cd) *(MILBOX 41)* **GENESIS / ABACAB** [ ] [–]

Nov 00. (3xcd-box) *(CDBOX 7)* **ARCHIVE VOL.2 1976-1992** [ ] [ ]

Oct 99. (cd) *(GENMD 8) <83244>* **TURN IT ON AGAIN – THE HITS** [4] [65]
– Turn it on again / Invisible touch / Mama / Land of confusion / I can't dance / Follow you, follow me / Hold on my heart / Abacab / I know what I like (in your wardrobe) / No son of mine / Tonight, tonight, tonight / In too deep / Congo / Jesus he knows me / That's all / Misunderstanding / Throwing it all away / The carpet crawlers (1999).

Nov 04. (3xcd-box) *(GENCDX 9) <863730-2>* **PLATINUM COLLECTION** [21] [100]
– No son of mine / I can't dance / Jesus he knows me / Hold on my heart / Invisible touch / Throwing it all away / Tonight, tonight, tonight (edit) / Land of confusion / In too deep / Mama / That's all / Home by the sea / Second home by the sea / Illegal alien (2004 remix) / Paperlate (2004 remix) / Calling all stations // Abacab / Keep it dark / Turn it on again / Behind the lines / Duchess / Misunderstanding / Many too many / Follow you, follow me / Undertow / In that quiet earth / Afterglow / Your own special way / A trick of the tail / Ripples / Los endos // The lamb lies down on Broadway / Counting out time / The carpet crawlers / Firth of fifth / The cinema show / I know what I like (in your wardrobe) / Supper's ready / The musical box / The knife.

☐ GENIUS/GZA (see under ⇒ WU-TANG CLAN)

☐ Lowell GEORGE (see under ⇒ LITTLE FEAT)

☐ GHOSTFACE KILLAH (see under ⇒ WU-TANG CLAN)

☐ Beth GIBBONS & RUSTIN MAN (see under ⇒ PORTISHEAD)

☐ GILES, GILES & FRIPP (see under ⇒ KING CRIMSON)

☐ David GILMOUR (see under ⇒ PINK FLOYD)

☐ GLASS ONION (see under ⇒ TRAVIS)

☐ the GLOVE (see under ⇒ SIOUXSIE & THE BANSHEES)

GNARLS BARKLEY

Formed: Atlanta, Georgia, USA . . . 2003 by producer DANGER MOUSE (aka BRIAN BURTON) and frontman CEE-LO GREEN (aka THOMAS CALLOWAY). Contender for moniker of the decade, the name GNARLS BARKLEY seemingly materialised from nowhere in spring 2006, when the warped, modern day spiritual, 'CRAZY', became Britain's first ever No.1 calculated solely on download sales (a result of new chart rules allowing for internet sales in lieu of a subsequent physical release). Of course, the GNARLS boys hadn't come from nowhere; they already had bulging CV's: BURTON was a New Yorker transplanted to Georgia, where he'd issued his first recordings under the alias PELICAN CITY. Pensive, heavily cinematic trip-tronica tinkering with the work of NEUTRAL MILK HOTEL amongst others, debut album 'THE CHILLING EFFECT' (1999) was issued as a soundtrack to a shelved movie. As DANGER MOUSE, BURTON went on to record various remix and collaborative projects with the likes of JEMINI (on whose 'GHETTO POP LIFE' set he first worked with CEE-LO) and SAGE FRANCIS, finally hitting the headlines with 2004's 'THE GREY ALBUM'. An ingenious mash-up of 'THE WHITE ALBUM' (as in the BEATLES) and 'THE BLACK ALBUM' (as in JAY-Z), the record was never intended as an official release, becoming an internet/word-of-mouth phenomenon which ended up in many critics' end of year polls. As well as the attention of DAMON ALBARN, it also earned its creator a cease-and-desist order from 'E.M.I.'. ALBARN was nevertheless impressed enough to enlist BURTON as producer on his GORILLAZ follow-up, 'Demon Days' (2005). BURTON's work earned him a Grammy nomination, while a link-up with rapper MF DOOM (as DANGER DOOM) resulted in another acclaimed avant-hip hop opus, 'THE MOUSE AND THE MASK' (2005). Ostensibly inspired by cult US cartoon series, 'Adult Swim', the record was a savvy, hugely charming collage of BURTON's spot-that-70s-soundbite production and DOOM's balmy flow. With a guest appearance from CEE-LO GREEN amongst others, it also set the scene nicely for the poppier GNARLS BARKLEY. An Atlanta native born – on the 30th of May 1974 – to Baptist parents, the church-trained CEE-LO started out in the music biz as a prominent member of Dirty South hip-hop collective the GOODIE MOB. Pioneers of the Southern style alongside OUTKAST (with whom CEE-LO is also connected via the DUNGEON FAMILY clan), the group recorded three albums for 'Arista' – 'SOUL FOOD' (1995), 'STILL STANDING' (1998) and 'WORLD PARTY' (1999) – before being dropped. Leaving the 'MOB but sticking with 'Arista', GREEN went on to release a freethinking solo debut, 'CEE-LO GREEN AND HIS PERFECT IMPERFECTIONS' (2002). When GREEN wasn't making like a hyperactive LAST POET on mushrooms (check the psychedelic, church organ sleeve and Funkadelicised freak-grooves), he showcased a croon too ecstatically soulful to be confined to hip-hop. It was a voice developed over a more streamlined sophomore set, 'CEE-LO GREEN . . . IS THE SOUL MACHINE' (2004), with support from the likes of PHARRELL WILLIAMS and TIMBALAND. With both GREEN and BURTON really getting into their respective strides mid-decade, 'ST. ELSEWHERE' (2006) would've been a highly anticipated collaboration even without the success of 'CRAZY'. And if anything, it was with GREEN's solo output that the cracked, post-millennial psyche-pop of 'ST. ELSEWHERE' shared a pew, wilfully disregarding stylistic fault lines and poking its nose into cobwebbed corners of the mind.

Album rating: ST. ELSEWHERE (*8) / Pelican City: THE CHILLING EFFECT (*7) / RHODE ISLAND (*6) / Danger Mouse: GHETTO POP LIFE (*6) / THE GREY ALBUM internet (*9) / THE MOUSE AND THE MASK as Danger Doom (*8) / Cee-Lo: CEE-LO GREEN AND HIS PERFECT IMPERFECTIONS (*6) / CEE-LO GREEN . . . IS THE SOUL MACHINE (*7)

DANGER MOUSE (b. BRIAN BURTON, White Plains, New York, USA) – producer, electronics / **CEE-LO (GREEN)** (b. THOMAS DeCARLO CALLAWAY, 30 May'74, Atlanta, Georgia, USA) – vocals (ex-GOODIE MOB, Solo artist)

Warners Downtown

Mar 06. (dl-s)<cd-s> (-) <11374-2> **CRAZY** [1] [5]
(Apr06; 7"pic-d+=/cd-s+=) *(WEA 401/+CD)* – Just a thought.
(Apr06; 12"+=) *(WEA 401T)* – ('A'-instrumental).

Apr 06. (cd) *(2564 63267-2) <70003>* **ST. ELSEWHERE** [1] May06 [8]
– Go-go gadget gospel / Crazy / St. Elsewhere / Gone daddy gone / Smiley faces / The boogie monster / Feng shui / Just a thought / Transformer / Who cares? / Online / Necromancer / Storm coming / The last time.

PELICAN CITY

BRIAN BURTON – multi-electronics/instruments, producer / with **TODD MONFALCONE** + **SCOTT PATTON** – guitars / **JOSH PERRY** – horns

December First / December First

Dec 99. (cd) *<DF 001CD>* **THE CHILLING EFFECT** [-] [ ]
– Over from the start (intro/outro) / The city / The bleeding fader / Still alone / The search / The fool (Neutral Milk Hotel) – a Pelican City experiment / Danger's theme part I / Danger's theme part II / Calling the birds / The chase / Come on air (Wunderkind) – a Pelican City experiment / The bedroom / The rainstorm / The end of life / An exodus. *(UK-iss.May04; same as US)*

Oct 00. (cd) *<DF 002CD>* **RHODE ISLAND** [-] [ ]
– The icefields (Alan Parker) – a Pelican City experiment / Sesame Street / The northside / Chestnut park / The bordello / Jake's tavern / The beach / The movie theater / El Dorado diner / The pier. *(UK-iss.May04; same as US)*

2002. (cd-ep; w/ SCANNER) **PELICAN CITY vs SCANNER** [-] [ ]

DANGER MOUSE & JEMINI

BRIAN BURTON – multi, etc. / **JEMINI** – rapper

Lex Lex

Jul 03. (cd) *<(LEX 010CD)>* **GHETTO POP LIFE** [ ] Apr04 [ ]
– Born-A-MC / Ghetto pop life intro / Ghetto pop life / Omega supreme / What U sittin' on? (feat. LIKS) / The only one / Take care of business (feat. J-ZONE) / That Brooklyn shit / Yoo-hoo! / Copy cats (feat. PRINCE PO) / Don't do drugs / Medieval (feat. PHARCYDE) / Bush boys / Here we go again / I'm a DooMee / Knuckle sandwich.

Nov 03. (12"ep) *(LEX 022EP) <5220>* **TWENTY SIX INCH EP** [ ] Apr04 [ ]
– What U sittin' on? (26" remix feat. CEE-LO & the LIKS) / What we have here / Ghetto pop life (part 1 feat. SADAT) / Ghetto pop life (part 2).
(cd-ep+=) *(LEX 022CD) <5220>* – Omega supreme / Live on both sides.

DANGER MOUSE

internet

Feb 04. (internet) *(-)* **THE GREY ALBUM** [-] [-]
– Public service announcement / What more can I say / Encore / December 4th / 99 problem / Dirt off your shoulder / Moment of clarity / Change of clothes / Allure / Justify my thug / Lucifer 9 / My first song.

DANGER DOOM

BRIAN BURTON + rapper **MF DOOM** (b. DUMILE)

Lex Epitaph

Oct 05. (cd/d-lp) *(LEX 036 CD/LP) <86775>* **THE MOUSE AND THE MASK** [ ] [41]
– El chupa nibre / Sofa king / The mask / Perfect hair / Benzie box / Old school / A.T.H.F. / Basket case / No names / Crosshairs / Mince meat / Vats of urine / Space ho's / Bada bing.

CEE-LO

— ex-GOODIE MOB (three albums & still going strong) & DUNGEON FAMILY

Arista Arista

May 02. (cd) *<(07822 14682-2)>* **CEE-LO AND HIS PERFECT IMPERFECTIONS** [ ] Apr02 [11]
– Bad mutha / Close encounter (break) / Big ole words (damn) / Closet freak / Live (right now) / El Dorado sunrise (sper chicken) / A thug's concern (break) / One for the road (break) / Let him sing if he wants to / Spend the night in your mind / Suga baby (feat. BIG GIPP & BACKBONE) / Gettin' grown / Bass head jazz / MicroHard (feat. JAHALLA & KIRKLAND UNDERWATER) / Under the influence (follow me) / Medieval times (great pretender) / Country love (feat. JOHN POPPER) / Awful thing / Maintenance man (break) / Young man (Sierra's song) / Well damn, Lo (break).

May 02. (-) *<radio>* **CLOSET FREAK** [-] [99]

Mar 04. (cd) *(82876 58233-2) <52111>* **CEE-LO GREEN . . . IS THE SOUL MACHINE** [ ] [13]
– Intro / Soul machine / The art of noise (with PHARRELL) / iving again / I'll be around / The one / My kind of people / Childz play (with LUDACRIS) / I am selling soul / All day love affair / Evening news (with CHAZZIE) / Scrap metal (with BIG RUBE) / Glockapella / When we were friends / Sometimes / Let's stay together (with PHARRELL) / Die trying / What don't you do? (outro).

the GO-BETWEENS

Formed: Brisbane, Australia . . . 1978 by ROBERT FORSTER (guitar, vocals) and GRANT McLENNAN (vocals, lead guitar, bass) with DENNIS CANTWELL on drums. After a debut Australian-only 7" single, 'LEE REMICK', CANTWELL was replaced with TIM MUSTAFA while organist MALCOLM KELLY was brought in briefly for the early classic, 'PEOPLE SAY', the band's second and final domestic release (were also on the books of 'Beserkley' UK for a few months). Finally settling with LINDY MORRISON on drums, the GO-BETWEENS recorded two singles for seminal Scottish indie label, 'Postcard', before settling in London and signing with 'Rough Trade'. Their debut, 'SEND ME A LULLABY' (1982), drew comparisons with TALKING HEADS although their root influences remained the classic songwriting of BOB DYLAN and The VELVET UNDERGROUND. Following the addition of ROBERT VICKERS on bass, allowing McLENNAN to switch to guitar, 'BEFORE HOLLYWOOD' (1983) was a marked improvement. The twin songwriting and singing strength of McLENNAN and FORSTER was developing apace, the former's

'CATTLE AND CANE' a yearning, melancholy highlight. Rave reviews abounded and the band were soon signed to the Warner Brothers-affiliated 'Sire' label. 'SPRING HILL FAIR' (1984) marked the GO-BETWEENS major label debut, their swooning melodies enhanced by a superior production on classics like 'BACHELOR KISSES'. Again the band were heralded by the press and adored by a cult following yet a commercial breakthrough proved elusive. The group switched labels yet again (moving to 'Beggar's Banquet') for 'LIBERTY BELLE AND THE BLACK DIAMOND EXPRESS' (1986), the band's most accessible, and probably finest effort of their career; it remains a mystery why the lush guitar-pop of 'SPRING RAIN' failed to breach the charts. With the addition of AMANDA BROWN (guitar, violin, oboe, keyboards), the band cut the more ambitious 'TALLULAH' (1987) and despite a couple of strong singles, were still confined to the indie margins. Understandably, the group were miffed at their lack of any real success and '16 LOVERS LANE' (1988), another sterling set of consummate, painstakingly crafted songs, proved to be their final effort. The record reached a lowly No.81 on the UK chart, the GO-BETWEENS finally going their own way with McLENNAN and FORSTER both embarking on solo careers. FORSTER's 1991 debut, 'DANGER IN THE PAST' was a fine effort, its sound not much of a departure from the later GO-BETWEENS albums. 'CALLING FROM A COUNTRY PHONE' (1993) was rootsier, employing such traditional instrumentation as banjo and mandolin. McLENNAN initially worked on the more avant-garde project, JACK FROST, with STEVE KILBEY of the CHURCH, before releasing 'WATERSHED' in 1991 as G.W. McLENNAN. Another two fine albums followed with 'FIREBOY' (1993) and 'HORSEBREAKER STAR' (1994), FORSTER releasing an album of covers the same year, 'I HAD A NEW YORK GIRLFRIEND'. 'BELLAVISTA TERRACE: THE BEST OF THE GO-BETWEENS' was issued as a sort of updated version of the lost and very rare '1978-1990', containing some of the group's best tracks that never made it into the charts (FORSTER's bitter liner notes are a tad tiresome). Yes, they were all there in their full glory: 'PART COMPANY', 'HEAD FULL OF STEAM' and the truly fantastic 'BYE BYE PRIDE' were some of the best singles that nobody heard for a long time. In a strange twist to the band's legacy, FORSTER and McLENNAN re-joined to split the songwriting credits on a brand new GO-BETWEENS album entitled 'FRIENDS OF RACHEL WORTH' (2000). Enlisting the help of SLEATER-KINNEY (the other members of the GO-B's refused to take part), the album sounded like it was recorded by LOU REED's mountain dwelling brother, with tracks such as 'GOING BLIND' and 'GERMAN FARMHOUSE' both returing back to the folksy, rock/pop sound that made the band so attractive in the beginning. 'BRIGHT YELLOW BRIGHT ORANGE' (2003) basically picked up where that album left off with FORSTER and McLENNAN cementing their renewed partnership. Bolstered this time around by the rhythm section of ADELE PICKVANCE and GLENN THOMPSON, the pair eased into their performances with the kind of confident intimacy and almost telepathic anticipation that only comes with such long-term collaboration. Largely acoustic, satisfyingly literate and unadorned, with harmony vocals from PICKVANCE, the songs basked in the rosy glow of bittersweet, middle-aged contentment. 'OCEANS APART' (2005) followed in the same Antipodean, DYLAN-esque slipstream, although who was to know it would turn out to be McLENNAN's swansong; he died in his sleep on 6th of May 2006, aged only 48.

Songwriters: All compositions by FORSTER and McLENNAN, with LINDY MORRISON contributing some. McLENNAN covered BALLAD OF EASY RIDER (Byrds). FORSTER covered; NATURE'S WAY (Spirit) / BROKEN HEARTED PEOPLE (Guy Clark) / ECHO BEACH (Martha & The Muffins) / TELL ME THAT IT ISN'T TRUE (Bob Dylan) / 2541 (Bob Mould) / ANYTIME (. . . Nelson) / LOCKED AWAY (Richards-Jordan) / LOOK OUT HERE COMES TOMORROW (Neil Diamond) / ALONE (I-Ten) / BIRD (. . .Hansoms) / FRISCO DEPOT (Mickey Newbury) / 3 A.M. (Anderson-Todd) / TOWER OF SONG (Leonard Cohen). • **Trivia:** In 1991, FORSTER and McLENNAN did support slot to LLOYD COLE on a Toronto gig, which prompted GO-BETWEENS reformation rumours.

Album rating: SEND ME A LULLABY (*7) / BEFORE HOLLYWOOD (*8) / SPRING HILL FAIR (*7) / LIBERTY BELLE AND THE BLACK DIAMOND EXPRESS (*7) / TALULAH (*7) / 16 LOVERS LANE (*8) / THE GO-BETWEENS 1979-1990 compilation (*9) / Robert Forster: DANGER IN THE PAST (*6) / CALLING FROM A COUNTRY PHONE (*6) / I HAD A NEW YORK GIRLFRIEND (*5) / WARM NIGHTS (*5) / G.W. McLennan: WATERSHED (*7) / FIREBOY (*6) / HORSEBREAKER STAR (*7) / IN YOUR BRIGHT RAY (*6) / the Go-Betweens: BELLAVISTA TERRACE compilation (*8) / THE FRIENDS OF RACHEL WORTH (*7) / BRIGHT YELLOW BRIGHT ORANGE (*7) / OCEANS APART (*7)

GRANT McLENNAN (b.12 Feb'58, Rockhampton, Queensland) – vocals, lead guitar, bass / **ROB FORSTER** (b.29 Jun'57) – guitar, vocals / **DENNIS CANTWELL** – drums

Abel / not iss.

Oct 78. (7") *(AB 001)* **LEE REMICK. / KAREN** [–] Austra [–]

— added **TIM MUSTAFA** – drums + **MALCOLM KELLY** – organ to repl. CANTWELL

Oct 79. (7") *(AB 004)* **PEOPLE SAY. / DON'T LET HIM COME BACK** [–] Austra [–]
(above released UK Nov86 as 12"ep on 'Situation 2'; *SIT 44T)*

— **LINDY MORRISON** (b. 2 Nov'51) – drums (ex-ZERO) repl. TIM + MALCOLM

Postcard / not iss.

Nov 80. (7") *(80-4)* **I NEED TWO HEADS. / STOP BEFORE YOU SAY IT** [ ] [–]

Jul 81. (7") *(81-9)* **YOUR TURN, MY TURN. / WORLD WEARY** [ ] [–]
(possibly not issued in UK, released on their Australian label, 'Missing Link'; MISS 29)

Rough Trade / not iss.

Jun 82. (lp) *(ROUGH 45)* **SEND ME A LULLABY** [ ] [–]
– Your turn, my turn / One thing can hold us / People know / The girls have moved / Midnight to neon / Eight pictures / Careless / All about strength / Ride / Hold your horses / Arrow in a bow / It could be anyone. *<US cd-iss. 1990 on 'Beggars Banquet'; 92702> (cd re-mast.Jun02 on 'Circus'+=; FYL 009)* – Sunday night / One word / I need two heads / Clowns are in town / Serenade sound / Hope / Stop before you say it / World weary / Distant hands / Undo what you did / Cracked wheat / After the fireworks / Your turn my turn (video).

Jul 82. (7") *(RT 108)* **HAMMER THE HAMMER. / BY CHANCE** [ ] [–]

— added **ROBERT VICKERS** (b.25 Nov'59) – bass

Feb 83. (7") *(RT 124)* **CATTLE AND CANE. / HEAVEN SAYS** [ ] [–]

Sep 83. (lp) *(ROUGH 54)* **BEFORE HOLLYWOOD** [ ] [–]
– A bad debt follows you / Two steps step out / Before Hollywood / Dusty in here / Ask / Cattle and cane / By chance / As long as that / On my block / That way. *(cd-iss. Jun90; LCD 54) <US cd-iss. 1990 on 'Beggars Banquet'; 92703> (cd re-mast.Jun02 on 'Circus'+=; FYL 010)* – Hammer the hammer / Heaven says / Just a king in mirrors / Peaceful wreck / Man o' sand to girl o' sea / Near the chimney / This girl black girl / Exception of deception / Cattle and cane (video).

Oct 83. (7") *(RT 114)* **MAN O' SAND TO GIRL O' SEA. / THIS GIRL BLACK GIRL** [ ] [–]

Sire / not iss.

Jul 84. (7") *(W 9211)* **PART COMPANY. / JUST A KING IN MIRRORS** [ ] [–]
(12"+=) *(W 9211T)* – Newton told me.

Sep 84. (lp) *(925 179-1)* **SPRING HILL FAIR** [ ] [–]
– Bachelor kisses / Five words / The old way out / You've never lived / Part company / Slow slow music / Draining the pool for you / River of money / Unkind and unwise / Man o' sand girl o' sea. *<US cd-iss. 1990 on 'Beggars Banquet'; 82003> (cd re-mast.Jun02 on 'Circus'+=; FYL 011)* – Emperor's courtesan / Rare breed / Newton told me / Just right for him / Attraction / The power that I now have / Second hand furniture / Marco Polo Jr. / Sweet tasting hours / Unkind and unwise (instrumental) / Bachelor kisses (video).

Sep 84. (7") *(W 9156)* **BACHELOR KISSES. / RARE BREED** [ ] [–]
(12"+=) *(W 9156T)* – Unkind and unwise (instrumental).

Beggars Banquet | Big Time

Feb 86. (7") *(BEG 155)* **SPRING RAIN. / LIFE AT HAND** ☐ –
(12"+=) *(BEG 155T)* – Little Joe.

Mar 86. (lp/c) *(BEGA/BEGC 72)* *<6010>* **LIBERTY BELLE AND THE BLACK DIAMOND EXPRESS** ☐ ☐
– Spring rain / The ghost and the black hat / The wrong road / To reach me / Twin layers of lightning / In the core of the flame / Head full of steam / Palm Sunday (on board the S.S.Within) / Apology accepted. *(re-iss. Feb89 on 'Beggars Banquet-Lowdown' lp/c)(cd; BBL/+C 72)(BBL 72CD)*

May 86. (7") *(BEG 159)* **HEAD FULL OF STEAM. / DON'T LET HIM COME BACK** ☐ –
(12"+=) *(BEG 159T)* – The wrong road.

—— added **AMANDA BROWN** (b.17 Nov'65) – keyboards, violin, guitar, oboe

Feb 87. (7") *(BEG 183)* **RIGHT HERE. / WHEN PEOPLE ARE DEAD** ☐ –
(12"+=) *(BEG 183T)* – Don't call me gone.
(d7"++=) *(BEG 183D)* – A little romance (live).

May 87. (7") *(BEG 190)* **CUT IT OUT. / TIME IN DESERT** ☐ –
(12"+=) *(BEG 190T)* – Doo wop in "A".

Jun 87. (lp/c)(cd) *(BEGA/BEGC 81)(BEGA 81CD)* *<6042>* **TALLULAH** 91 ☐
– Right here / You tell me / Someone else's wife / I just get caught out / Cut it out / The house that Jack Kerouac built / Bye bye pride / Spirit of a vampyre / The Clarke sisters / Hope then strife. *(re-iss. Feb90 on 'Beggars Banquet-Lowdown' cd)(c/lp; BEGA 81CD)(BEGC/BEGA 81)*

Aug 87. (7"/12") *(BEG 194/+T)* **BYE BYE PRIDE. / THE HOUSE THAT JACK KEROUAC BUILT** ☐ –

—— **JOHN WILSTEED** (b.13 Feb'57) – bass; repl. VICKERS

Beggars Banquet | Capitol

Jul 88. (7") *(BEG 218)* *<4BX 44262>* **STREETS OF YOUR TOWN. / WAIT UNTIL JUNE** ☐ ☐
(12"+=) *(BEG 218T)* – Casanova's last words.
(cd-s++=) *(BEG 218CD)* – Spring rain / Right here.

Aug 88. (lp/c)(cd) *(BEGA/BEGC 95)(BEGA 95CD)* *<91230>* **16 LOVERS LANE** 81 ☐
– Love goes on / Quiet heart / Love is a sign / You can't say no forever / The Devil's eye / Streets of your town / Clouds / Was there anything I could do? / I'm alright / Dive for your memory.

Oct 88. (7") *(BEG 219)* **WAS THERE ANYTHING I COULD DO. / ROCK'N'ROLL FRIEND** ☐ –
(12"+=) *(BEG 219T)* – Mexican postcard.
(cd-s++=) *(BEG 219CD)* – Bye bye pride.

—— split on the day we moved into the 90's. FORSTER and McLENNAN went solo. The latter also being part of JACK FROST with STEVE KILBEY of The CHURCH. AMANDA formed CLEOPATRA WONG.

ROBERT FORSTER

—— (solo, with MICK HARVEY – producer)

Beggars Banquet | Beggars Banquet

Sep 90. (7") *(BEG 245)* **BABY STONES. / THE LAND THAT TIME FORGOT** ☐ –

Oct 90. (cd)(c/lp) *(BEGA 113CD)(BEGA/BEGC 113)* *<3028>* **DANGER IN THE PAST** ☐ ☐
– Baby stones / The river people / Leave here satisfied / Heart out to tender / Is this what you call change / Dear black dream / Danger in the past / I've been looking for somebody / Justice.

Apr 93. (cd/c) *(BBQ CD/MC 127)* **CALLING FROM A COUNTRY PHONE** ☐ –
– Atlanta lie low / 121 / The circle / Falling star / I want to be quiet / Cats life / Girl to a world / Drop / Beyond theit law / Forever & time. *(cd re-iss. Sep95 on 'Beggars Banquet-Lowdown'; BBL 127CD)*

—— with **JOHN KEANE** – guitars, banjos, keyboards, bass, etc / **JOEL MORRIS** – drums / **STEVE VENZ** – bass / **ANDY CARLSON** – guitars, mandolin / **TIM WHITE & BILL HOLMES** – porga & piano / **DWIGHT MANNING** – oboe / **SYD STRAW** – backing vocals

Beggars Banquet | Atlantic

Jul 94. (cd-ep) *(BBQ 38CD)* **2541 / 3 a.m. / FREDDIE FENDER / DANGER IN THE PAST (live)** ☐ –

Aug 94. (cd/c) *(BBQ CD/MC 161)* *<92482>* **I HAD A NEW YORK GIRLFRIEND** ☐ ☐
– Nature's way / Broken hearted people / Echo beach / Tell me that it isn't true / 2541 / Anytime / Locked away / Look out loves comes tomorrow / Alone / Bird / Frisco depot / 3 a.m.

Beggars Banquet | Beggar Banqu

Jul 96. (cd-ep) *(BEG 300CD)* **CRYIN' LOVE / HALF THE WAY HOME / HYPNOTIZED** ☐ –

Aug 96. (cd)(lp) *(BEGL 185CD)(BEGA 185)* *<80185>* **WARM NIGHTS** ☐ Sep96 ☐
– I can do / Warn nights / Cryin' love / Snake skin lady / Loneliness / Ju of wine / Fortress / Rock-n-roll friend / On a street corner / I'll jump.

G.W. McLENNAN

Beggars Banquet | Beggar Banqu

Mar 91. (12"ep/cd-ep) *(BEG 247 T/CD)* **WHEN WORD GETS AROUND / BLACK MULE / SHE'S SO STRANGE / THE MAN WHO DIED IN RAPTURE** ☐ –

May 91. (12"ep/cd-ep) *(BEG 254 T/CD)* **EASY COME EASY GO. / MAKING IT RIGHT FOR HER / STONES FOR YOU (trumpet version)** ☐ –

Jun 91. (cd)(c/lp) *(BEGACD 118)(BEG/BEGC 118)* **WATERSHED** ☐ –
– When word gets around / Haven't I been a fool / Haunted house / Stone for you / Easy come easy go / Black mule / Rory the weeks back on / Yo can't have everything / Sally's revolution / Broadway bride / Just get tha straight / Dream about tomorrow.

Beggars Banquet | Atlant

Jan 93. (cd-ep) *(BBQ 2CD)* **FINGERS / WHOSE SIDE ARE YOU ON? / WHAT WENT WRONG (original)** ☐ –

Feb 93. (cd-ep) *(BBQ 11CD)* **LIGHTING FIRES / DARK SIDE OF TOWN / IF I SHOULD FALL BEHIND** ☐ –

Mar 93. (cd/c) *(BBQ CD/MC 127)* *<92387>* **FIREBOY** ☐ Jun94 ☐
– Lighting fires / Surround me / One million miles from here / The dar side of town / Things will change / The pawnbroker / Whose side are yo on? / Fingers / Signs of life / The day my eyes Came back / Bathe (in th water) / When I close my eyes / Riddle in the rain.

Nov 94. (d-cd/c) *(BBQ CD/MC 162)* **HORSEBREAKER STAR** ☐ –
– Simone & Perry / Ice in Heaven / What went wrong / Race day rag / Don you cry for me no more / Put you down / Late afternoon in early August Coming up for air / Ballad of Easy Rider / Open invitation / Open my eyes From my lips / / Dropping you / Hot water / Keep my word / Do your ow thing / That's that / If I was a girl / Head over heels / Girl in a beret / A her songs / No peace in the palace / I'll call you wild / Horsebreaker sta *(re-iss. d-cd Sep95 on 'Beggars Banquet-Lowdown'; BEGA 162CD)*

Jun 95. (cd-ep) *(BBQ 57CD)* **SIMONE & PERRY / DON'T YOU CRY FOR ME NO MORE / BALLAD OF EASY RIDER / WHAT WENT WRONG (original)** ☐ –

Jul 97. (cd) *(BBQCD 192)* **IN YOUR BRIGHT RAY** ☐ –
– In your bright ray / Cave in / One plus one / Sea breeze / Malibu '69 Who said love was dead / Room for skin / All them pretty angels / Com scar / Down here / Lamp by lamp / Do you see the lights / Parade shadows.

the GO-BETWEENS

—— re-formed with **FORSTER + McLENNAN** plus SLEATER-KINNEY **CORIN TUCKER, CARRIE BROWNSTEIN + JANET WEISS**

Circus | Jetse

Sep 00. (cd) *(CIRCUSCD 004)* *<TWA 31>* **THE FRIENDS OF RACHEL WORTH** ☐ ☐
– Magic in here / Spirit / The clock / German farmhouse / He liv my life / Heart and home / Surfing magazines / Orpheus beach / Goir blind / When she sang about angels. *(lp-iss.on 'Clear Spot'; 05425 (re-mast.Jun02; FYL 003)*

Oct 00. (cd-s) *(CIRCUSCDS 002)* *<TWA 32>* **GOING BLIND / WOMAN ACROSS THE WAY / THE LOCUST GIRLS** ☐ ☐

—— **FORSTER + McLENNAN** added **ADELE PICKVANCE** – vocals, bass **GLENN THOMPSON** – drums

Feb 03. (cd) *(CIRCUSCD 016)* *<TWA 58>* **BRIGHT YELLOW BRIGHT ORANGE** ☐ ☐
– Caroline and I / Poison in the walls / Mrs. Morgan / In her diary Too much of one thing / Crooked lines / Old Mexico / Make her day Something for myself / Unfinished business. *(lp-iss.Mar03 on 'Clearspo efa 60211-1)*

Lo-Max | Yep R

Apr 05. (cd) *(LOMAXCD 007)* *<2105>* **OCEANS APART** ☐ May05 ☐
– Here comes a city / Finding you / Born to a family / No reasons to cr Boundary rider / Darlinghurst nights / Lavender / The statue / This nigh

for you / The mountains near Dellray. *(ltd-cd w/cd+=; LOMAXCD 007X)* – live:- People say / He lives my life / The wrong road / Bye bye pride / When people are dead / Streets of your town.

Nov 05. (cd-ep) *(LOMAX 022V)* **WORLDS APART EP** [ ] [–]
– Finding you / Ashes on the lawn / City of lights / Crystal shacks.

– compilations, others, etc. –

1982. (lp) *Man Made;* **VERY QUICK ON THE EYE – BRISBANE 1981 (demo)** [ ] [–]

1985. (lp) *P.V.C.; <PVC 8942>* **METAL AND SHELLS** [–] [ ]

Oct 89. (12"ep/cd-ep) *Strange Fruit; (SFPS/+CD 074) / Dutch East India; <8339>* **THE PEEL SESSIONS** [ ] 1991 [ ]
– The power that I have now / Second hand furniture / Fire woods / Rare breed.

Mar 90. (cd)(c/d-lp) *Beggars Banquet; (BEGA 104CD)(BEGC/BEGA 104) / Capitol; <94681>* **THE GO-BETWEENS 1979-1990** [ ] [ ]
– Hammer the hammer / I need two heads / Cattle and cane / When people are dead / Man o' sand to girl o' sea / Bachelor kisses / People say / Draining the pool for you / World weary / Spring rain / Rock and roll friend / Dusty in here / The Clarke sisters / Right here / Second-hand furniture / Bye bye pride / This girl, black girl / The house that Jack Kerouac built / Don't call me gone / Streets of our own town / Love is a sign / You won't find it again. *(c+=/d-lp+=)* – Karen / 8 pictures / The sound of rain / The wrong road / Mexican postcard.

Apr 99. (cd) *Tag; (TAGCD 002) / Jetset; <TWA 019>* **THE LOST ALBUM 1978-1979** [ ] [ ]

May 99. (d-cd) *Beggars Banquet; (BBL2 020CD) <82020>* **BELLAVISTA TERRACE: THE BEST OF THE GO-BETWEENS** [ ] [ ]
– Was there anything I could do? / Head full of steam / That way / Part company / Cattle and cane / Draining the pool for you / The wrong road / Bye bye pride / Man o' sand to girl o' sea / The house that Jack Kerouac built / Bachelor kisses / Streets of your town / Spring rain / Dive for your memory.

GODSMACK

Formed: Boston, Massachusetts, USA ... 1996 by frontman SALLY ERNA and his musical mates, TONY ROMBOLO, ROBBIE MERRILL and TOMMY STEWART, who named themselves after an ALICE IN CHAINS track. If you were to put the aforementioned ALICE IN CHAINS, METALLICA and the rest of the Grunge crew together – and without getting too sarcy – you would probably come up with GODSMACK. This dour 4-piece got their break from noneother than PAUL GEARY (former sticksman with EXTREME), who sorted out a contract with 'Universal' in 1998. By the following year, their self-titled debut album was high in the US Top 30, with an invite to Woodstock and Ozzfest to boot. Heralded by young trendy Americans into "that sort of thing", the band also had a surprise alternative rock hit with probably their finest five minutes, 'WHATEVER'. By late 2000, the lads thought we'd enjoy a second set. 'AWAKE' was not an appropriate title. 'FACELESS' (2003) – with new drummer SHANNON LARKIN – was much more appropriate given their utterly derivative take on what rock music has descended into over the last five years or so. That GODSMACK and their ilk continued to make not the slightest impression on the UK Top 40 was less surprising than ever. The band's sound was just as listless unplugged, as US Top 5 mini-set 'THE OTHER SIDE' (2004) proved. The ERNA-produced, imaginatively titled 'IV' (2006) was another No.1, suggesting that grunge just ain't supposed to die a natural death.

Album rating: GODSMACK (*5) / AWAKE (*4) / FACELESS (*4) / THE OTHER SIDE mini (*5) / IV (*6)

SULLY ERNA (b. SALVATORE PAUL ERNA, 7 Feb'68, Lawrence, Mass.) – vocals / **TONY ROMBOLO** – guitar / **ROBBIE MERRILL** – bass / **TOMMY STEWART** – drums; repl. JOE D'ARCO (although he did return)

Universal Universal

Aug 99. (cd) *(UND 53190) <153190>* **GODSMACK** [ ] Aug98 [22]
– Moon baby / Whatever / Keep away / Time bomb / Bad religion / Immune / Someone in London / Get up, get out! / Now or never / Stress / Situation / Voodoo. *<clean version as 'ALL WOUND UP'; UND 53183>*

Oct 00. (cd) *<(159688-2)>* **AWAKE** [ ] [5]
– Sick of life / Awake / Greed / Bad magick / Goin' down / Mistakes / Trippin' / Forgive me / Vampires / The journey / Spiral. *(re-iss. Apr01; same)*

—— **SHANNON LARKIN** (b.24 Apr'67) – drums (ex-WRATHCHILD AMERICA, ex-UGLY KID JOE, ex-AMEN) repl. D'ARCO

Apr 03. (cd) *(19900-2) <067854>* **FACELESS** [ ] [1]
– Straight out of line / Faceless / Changes / Make me believe / I stand alone / Re-align / I fucking hate you / Releasing the demons / Dead and broken / I am / The awakening / Serenity. *(UK+=)* – Keep away (live) / Awake (live).

Nov 03. (cd-s) *<19866>* **STRAIGHT OUT OF LINE / KEEP AWAY (live)** [–] [73]
(above was actually a Canadian import!)

Mar 04. (m-cd) *<15390-2>* **THE OTHER SIDE** [–] [5]
– Running blind / Re-align / Touche / Voices / Keep away / Spiral / Asleep.

Feb 06. (-) *<radio>* **SPEAK** [–] [85]

Apr 06. (cd) *(9855036) <65480-2>* **IV** [ ] [1]
– Livin' in sin / Speak / The enemy / Shine down / Hollow / No rest for the wicked / Bleeding me / Voodoo too / Temptation / Mama / Our rainy day.

GOLDFRAPP

Formed: Bath, England . . . 1998 by vocalist/keyboardist ALISON GOLDFRAPP and composer WILL GREGORY. Before bringing GOLDFRAPP together, ALISON was a regular contributor to the independent music scene in Britain. She began experimenting with music as part of her fine-art degree studies at Middlesex University, and while still majoring, managed to appear on TRICKY's debut album 'Maxinquaye' in 1995. Throughout the decade she seemed rather busy, appearing on both ORBITAL's 'Snivilization' in '96 and ADD N TO (X)'s undisputed masterpiece 'Avant Garde' in '98. Cameo appearances on alternative records such as these helped ALISON establish a reputation in both the independent and mainstream circles. By 1999, ALISON had completed a tape of demo material that would ultimately find its way onto the startling debut album proper, 'FELT MOUNTAIN' (2000), a set which was co-written with composer and fellow group member, WILL GREGORY. It took the music press by surprise, with many critics placing the set high on their top Albums Of The Year list. 'FELT MOUNTAIN' displayed such beauty and inspiration that peers PORTISHEAD and BROADCAST paled in comparison. The lush strings on 'HORSE TEARS' or ALISON's wilting vocals on 'PILOTS' set the standards for anybody who dared to be as good as them. But 'LOVELY HEAD', with its strange creeping JOHN BARRY-meets-STREISAND esque orchestra, reminiscent of MERCURY REV's darker period, and nostalgic whistling (very MORRICONE, indeed!), was perhaps the stand-out track on the entire album. Unfortunately, it was spoiled by an appearance in an Altman-esque mobile phone ad starring a very creepy Gary Oldman in cameo role. That said, everybody went about the next day asking everybody else: "Who sings that tune in that Gary Oldman advert?" Of course, it was GOLDFRAPP, and by the following year, both the album and singles ('UTOPIA' and 'LOVELY HEAD') were hitting the lower rungs of the UK charts. 2003's 'BLACK CHERRY' (featuring hits 'TRAIN', 'STRICT MACHINE' and 'TWIST') served up more intoxicating, strangely familiar and deceptively futuristic pop, less traditionalist and more experimental than the debut but still operating broadly within that record's parameters. The clue to 'SUPERNATURE' (2005) was in the title, and even if GOLDFRAPP didn't cover the CERRONE nugget, the near chart-topping album played as a potted history of glam-rock/vintage-disco/electro-pop.

Boosted by exposure in a T-mobile TV ad, lead single 'OOH LA LA' went Top 5, its Norman Greenbaum-sampled subtext worshipping that "Spirit In The Sky" all over again; further singles 'NUMBER 1' and 'RIDE A WHITE HORSE' also reached the UK Top 20. You didn't need to be a paid-up trainspotter to pick out the references: HUMAN LEAGUE, GARY NUMAN and DONNA SUMMER were all on the duo's internal playlist.

Album rating: FELT MOUNTAIN (*8) / BLACK CHERRY (*7) / SUPERNATURE (*7)

ALISON GOLDFRAPP (b.13 May'68, Enfield, England) – vocals, keyboards, synthesizer / **WILL GREGORY** – keyboards, synthesizer / with session people + guests

Mute Mute

May 00. (12"/cd-s) *(12/CD MUTE 247)* **LOVELY HEAD. / ('A'-star mix) / ('A'-Miss World mix)** [ ] [–]

Sep 00. (cd/lp) *(CD+/STUMM 188)* <9135> **FELT MOUNTAIN** [ ] [ ]
– Lovely head / Paper bag / Human / Pilots / Deer stop / Felt mountain / Oompa radar / Utopia / Horse tears. *(d-cd iss.Oct01+=; LCDSTUMM 188)* – Pilots (on a star) / UK girls (physical) / Lovely head (Miss World mix) / Utopia (new ears mix) / Human (Calexico vocal) / Human (Massey's cro-magnon mix) / Utopia (Tom Middleton cosmos vocal). *(re-dist.Aug01)* – hit No.57

Oct 00. (12"/cd-s) *(12/CD MUTE 253)* **UTOPIA. / UTOPIA (new ears mix) / UTOPIA (sunroof mix)** [ ] [–]

Feb 01. (12") *(12MUTE 259)* **HUMAN. / HUMAN (Calexico vocal mix) / HUMAN (Calexico instrumental) / HUMAN (Massey's neanderthal mix)** [ ] [–]
(cd-s) *(CDMUTE 259)* – ('A'side) / ('A'-Massey's cro-magnon).

Jun 01. (cd-s) *(CDMUTE 264)* **UTOPIA / UK GIRLS (physical) / HUMAN (live)** [62] [–]
(12"/cd-s) *(12/CDS MUTE 264)* – ('A'side) / ('A'-Jori Hulkonnen mix) / ('A'-Tom Middleton cosmos vocal) / ('A'-Tim Wright mix).

Nov 01. (cd-s) *(CDMUTE 267)* **LOVELY HEAD / PILOTS (ON A STAR) / HORSE TEARS (live)** [68] [–]
(cd-s) *(LCDMUTE 267)* – ('A'side) / ('A'-stare mesto mix) / Utopia (Tom Middleton cosmos acid dub) / Pilots (on a star) (video).

Apr 03. (cd-s) *(CDMUTE 291)* <2907> **TRAIN / TRAIN (village hall mix) / BIG BLACK CLOUD LITTLE WHITE LIE / TRAIN (video)** [23] [ ]
(12") *(12MUTE 291)* – ('A'side) / El train (T Raumschmiere remix) / ('A'-Ewan Pearson 4/4 instrumental).
(cd-s) *(LCDMUTE 291)* – El train (T Raumschmiere remix) / ('A'-Ewan Pearson 6/8 vocal mix) / ('A'-Ewan Pearson 4/4 instrumental).

Apr 03. (cd/lp) *(CD+/STUMM 196)* <9206> **BLACK CHERRY** [19] May03 [ ]
– Crystalline green / Train / Black cherry / Tiptoe / Deep honey / Hairy trees / Twist / Strict machine / Forever / Slippage.

Jul 03. (cd-s) *(CDMUTE 295)* **STRICT MACHINE / WHITE SOFT ROPE (featuring the Midwich Children Choir) / HAIRY TREES (live)** [25] [–]
(cd-s) *(LCDMUTE 295)* – ('A'-Ewan Pearson instrumental remix) / ('A'-Rowan's remix) / Train (Ewan Pearson dub).
(dvd-s) *(DVDMUTE 295)* – ('A'-Ewan's strippedmachine remix) / Deep honey (live in London) / Lovely head (live in London video).

Nov 03. (cd-s) *(CDMUTE 311)* **TWIST / YES SIR / DEER STOP (live)** [31] [–]
(cd-s) *(LCDMUTE 311)* – ('A'-Jacques Le Cont's conversation perversion mix) / Forever (Mountaineers remix) / ('A'-Dimitri Tokovol remix).

Mar 04. (cd-s) *(CDMUTE 320)* **BLACK CHERRY / GONE TO EARTH** [28] [–]
(cd-s) *(LCDMUTE 320)* – ('A'-M83 remix) / Twist (Kurtis Mantronik's twist and vac mix) / ('A'-live in London video) / Twist (video).
(dvd-s) *(DVDMUTE 320)* – ('A'-Lawrence remix) / Strict machine (video) / Utopia (live in London video) / Utopia (Tom Middleton cosmos acid dub mix).

May 04. (cd-s) *(CDMUTE 335)* **STRICT MACHINE / (Benny Benassi Sfaction edit)** [20] [ ]
(cd-s) *(LCDMUTE 335)* – Paris loaded / We are glitter / ('A'-Benny Benassi Sfaction extended + dub).
(cd-ep) <9215-2> – ('A') / White soft rope / Hairy trees (live in London) / Strict machine (mixes; Rowan's / Caulderone & Suryanto / Peter Rauhofer NYC + UK / Benny Benassi Sfaction extended / Ewan's strippedmachine).

Jul 04. (cd-ep) <9253-2> **BLACK CHERRY** [–] [ ]
– Black cherry / Gone to earth / Forever (Mountaineers' remix) / Black cherry (M83 remix) / Black cherry (Lawrence remix) / Black cherry (live in London video) / Sartorius (live video) / Strict machine (video) / Twist (video).

Aug 05. (cd-s) *(CDMUTE 342)* **OOH LA LA / ALL NIGHT OPERATOR (part 1)** [4] [ ]
(12") *(12MUTE 342)* – ('A') / ('A'-Phonesz re-edit).
(cd-s) *(LCDMUTE 342)* – ('A'-Benny Benassi extended) / ('A'-Phonesz re-edit) / ('A'-Tiefschwarz dub).
(dvd-s) *(DVDMUTE 342)* – ('A'-video) / ('A'-little pictures) / ('A'-When Andy Bell met Manhattan Clique remix).

Aug 05. (cd/lp) *(CD+/STUMM 250)* <9296> **SUPERNATURE** [2] [ ]
– Ooh la la / Lovely 2 C U / Ride a white horse / U never know / Let it take U / Fly me away / Slide in / Koko / Satin chic / Time out from the world / Number 1. *(ltd-cd+=; LCDSTUMM 250)* – (making of) / (documentary).

Oct 05. (cd-s) *(CDMUTE 351)* **NUMBER 1 / BEAUTIFUL** [9] [ ]
(cd-s+=) <9304-2> – All night operator / ('A'-Alan Braxe & Fred Falke mix) / Ooh la la (Tieschwarz mix) / ('A'-postcards from the summer video).
(12") *(12MUTE 351)* – ('A'-Alan Braxe & Fred Falke club & instrumental remixes).
(cd-s) *(LCDMUTE 351)* – ('A'-Alan Braxe & Fred Falke main remix) / Ooh la la (live) / ('A'-video) / Ooh la la (video).
(dvd-s) *(DVDMUTE 351)* – ('A'-postcards from the video) / Satin chic (special performance film) / Lovely 2 C U (T.Raumschmiere remix).

Feb 06. (cd-s) *(CDMUTE 356)* **RIDE A WHITE HORSE / SLIDE IN (DFA remix)** [15] [–]
(12") *(12MUTE 356)* – ('A'-Serge Santiago re-edit) / ('A'-FK-EK vocal).
(cd-s+=) *(LCDMUTE 356)* – ('A'-FK disco whores dub) / ('A'-Ewan Pearson disco odyssey parts 1 & 2).
(dvd-s) *(DVDMUTE 356)* – ('A'-live in London) / (Supernature tour access all areas) / Number 1 (Mum rmx).

May 06. (cd-s) *(CDMUTE 361)* **FLY ME AWAY / SATIN CHIC (Bombay mix by the Shortwave Set)** [??] [–]
(cd-s) *(LCDMUTE 361)* – ('A'-C2 rmx 4) / ('A'-Ladytron remix) / You never know (Mum remix).
(dvd-s) *(DVDMUTE 361)* – ('A'-inflight movies – Paris – New York – London) / Ride a white horse (video) / Time out from the world (Field remix).

□ the GOLLIWOGS (see under ⇒ CREEDENCE CLEARWATER REVIVAL)

GOMEZ

Formed: Southport, England . . . 1997 originally as GOMEZ, KILL KILL THE VORTEX by college lads BEN OTTEWELL, TOM GRAY, IAN BALL, PAUL BLACKBURN and OLLY PEACOCK. A home-recorded tape of the band found its way into the hands of record shop worker and former COMSAT ANGELS member STEVE FELLOWS, who almost immediately became their manager. He in turn set up time in a Sheffield rehearsal studio in which he invited a plethora of A&R men to witness the unique talent of the band. After a fortnight, over thirty record labels were showing signs of interest, although FELLOWS and his protegees opted for Virgin offshoot, 'Hut'. Their early 70's to early 90's sound – like a hybrid of LOWELL GEORGE, GRATEFUL DEAD and BECK – was much in debt to the bluesy whisky-throated chords of lead singer BEN, whose boyish, bespectacled look stunned an unsuspecting but appreciative audience on their debut single, '78 STONE WOBBLE'. It was their first UK Top 50 entry and was pursued a month later – in April '98 – by their classic debut album, 'BRING IT ON'. A critical and soon-to-be commercial success, its highlights were the tracks, 'GET MILES' (gruffly reminiscent of The BEATLES' 'Come Together'), 'WHIPPIN' PICCADILLY' and 'GET MYSELF ARRESTED', all of which helped it win the much lauded Mercury prize early in '99. Later that year, two brand-new GOMEZ tracks 'BRING IT ON' (surprisingly not a part of the debut!) and 'RHYTHM & BLUES ALIBI' hovered around the Top 20, while parent follow-up set, 'LIQUID SKIN' (1999) smashed in at No. On reflection, the band might've been better to wait a little longer

Good on GOMEZ though, as it says a lot for a band who release a fresh set of songs every year – here's hoping America could be their next prize. Prior to that difficult third album, GOMEZ stopped the proverbial gap with 'ABANDONED SHOPPING TROLLEY HOTLINE' (2000). Ostensibly a collection of the usual B-sides, live material and outtakes, this record merely served to underline GOMEZ's talent by transcending the implied second division quality of such material. Indeed, this could almost have been a third album proper in its own right save for the fact there are no obvious singles. 'IN OUR GUN' (2002) was a welcome return from GOMEZ. Still not surpassing the initial brilliance of their debut, the boys had a good shot at recreating that timid, stoned and gruff sound. Even more stoned here, with a lot of dub influences thrown in for good measure, these romantic-orientated ballads didn't seem too out of place (i.e. the title track). However, the production was as smooth as a polished stone, and the songs could get a little too Americana for their own good. Despite these small gripes, GOMEZ delivered one of the most enjoyable and entertaining records of the year. 'SPLIT THE DIFFERENCE' (2004) fulfilled their contract with 'Hut' records, a rootsy UK Top 40 return to the sound of their debut, featuring minor hits 'CATCH ME UP' and 'SILENCE' alongside a cover of Junior Kimbrough's 'MEET ME IN THE CITY'. The Southport quintet fulfilled another one of their retro-rock fantasies by playing three nights at San Francisco's legendary concert hall, the Fillmore, collecting the highlights for their 'Independiente' debut, 'OUT WEST' (2005). From the sombrero-psych artwork to the covers of Tom Waits' 'WAY OUT WEST' and Nick Drake's 'BLACK DOG', the album effectively drew the dots between their Anglo-mariachi-Americana aesthetic. One which Gil Norton tampered with on 6th studio set, 'HOW WE OPERATE' (2006), smoothing out the vocals and filtering at least some of the band's rootsier influences, a formula that just missed out on their career-long quest to break the Stateside market.

Album rating: BRING IT ON (*9) / LIQUID SKIN (*7) / ABANDONED SHOPPING TROLLEY HOTLINE collection (*6) / IN OUR GUN (*6) / SPLIT THE DIFFERENCE (*7) / OUT WEST (*6) / HOW WE OPERATE (*5)

BEN OTTEWELL – vocals / **IAN BALL** – guitar, vocals, harmonica (ex-SEV) / **TOM GRAY** – keyboards, vocals, guitar, multi / **PAUL BLACKBURN** – bass / **OLLY PEACOCK** – percussion

Hut — Virgin

Mar 98. (cd-s) *(HUTCD 95)* **78 STONE WOBBLE / WHO'S GONNA GO TO THE BAR / STEVE McCROSKI** [44] [–]
(12"+=/c-s+=) *(HUT T/C 95)* – Wham bam.

Apr 98. (cd-c/d-lp) *(CDHUT/HUTMC/HUTDLP 49)* *<45592>* **BRING IT ON** [11] May98 [ ]
– Get miles / Whippin' Piccadilly / Make no sound / 78 stone wobble / Tijuana lady / Here comes the breeze / Love is better than a warm trombone / Get myself arrested / Free to run / Bubble gum years / Rie's wagon / The comeback.

Jun 98. (c-s) *(HUTC 97)* **GET MYSELF ARRESTED / THE COWBOY SONG** [45] [–]
(12"+=/cd-s+=) *(HUT T/CD 97)* – Flavours / Old school shirt.

Aug 98. (c-s) *(HUTC 105)* <95293> **WHIPPIN' PICCADILLY / PUSSYFOOTIN'** [35] Nov98 [ ]
(12"+=/cd-s+=) *(HUT T/CD 105)* – Pick up the pieces.

Jun 99. (c-s/cd-s) *(HUT C/CD 112)* **BRING IT ON / DIRE TRIBE / M57** [21] [–]
(cd-s) *(HUTDX 112)* – ('A') / Chicken bones / Step inside.
(12"+=) *(HUTT 112)* – (all 5 tracks above).

Aug 99. (c-s/cd-s) *(HUT C/CD 114)* **RHYTHM & BLUES ALIBI / THE BEST IN THE TOWN / SO** [18] [–]
(cd-s) *(HUTDX 114)* – ('A'-Pre-mellotron version) / ZYX / Tijuanalaska (Tijuana lady – live version).
(12"+=) *(HUUT 114)* – (all 6 tracks above).

Sep 99. (cd/c/d-lp) *(CDHUT/HUTMC/HUTDLP 54)* *<48218>* **LIQUID SKIN** [2] [ ]
– Hangover / Revolutionary kind / Bring it on / Blue moon rising / Las Vegas dealer / We haven't turned around / Fill my cup / Rhythm & blues alibi / Rosalita / California / Devil will ride.

Nov 99. (c-s/cd-s) *(HUT C/CD 117)* **WE HAVEN'T TURNED AROUND / FLIGHT / ROSEMARY** [38] [–]
(cd-s/12") *(HUT DX/T 117)* – ('A'-mix) / Gomez in a bucket (a seaside town made of ice cream slowly melting) / Emergency surgery.

Sep 00. (cd/c/lp) *(CDHUTX/HUTMCX/HUTLP 64)* *<50260>* **ABANDONED SHOPPING TROLLEY HOTLINE** (collection) [10] Oct00 [ ]
– Shitbag 9 / Bringin' your lovin' back here / Emergency surgery (remix) / Hit on the head / Flavors / 78 stone shuffle (BBC live session) / We haven't turned around (x-ray version) / Buena vista / Shitbag / Steve McCroski (BBC live session) / Wharf me / High on liquid skin / Rosemary (BBC live session) / Cowboy song / Getting better.

Mar 02. (7") *(HUT 149)* **SHOT SHOT. / SILHOUETTES** [28] [–]
(cd-s+=) *(HUTCD 149)* – Coltrane.
(cd-s) *(HUTDX 149)* – Shot shot (folk shot) / Air hostess song / Pop juice.

Mar 02. (cd/d-lp) *(CDHUT/HUTDLP 72)* *<811950>* **IN OUR GUN** [8] [ ]
– Shot shot / Rex Kramer / Detroit swing 66 / In our gun / Even song / Ruff stuff / Sound of sounds / Army dub / Miles end / Ping one down / 1000 times / Drench / Ballad of nice and easy.

Jun 02. (7") *(HUT 154)* **SOUND OF SOUNDS. / PING ONE DOWN** [48] [–]
(cd-s+=) *(HUTCD 154)* – Where are your friends / ('A'-video).
(cd-s) *(HUTDX 154)* – ('B') / ('A'-instrumental) / Click click / ('B'-video).

Mar 04. (7"/cd-s) *(HUT/+CD 175)* **CATCH ME UP. / BIG MAN** [36] [–]
(cd-s) *(HUTDX2)* – ('A') / Why bother / Mississippi boweevil blues / ('A'-video).

May 04. (7"/cd-s) *(HUT/+CD 178)* **SILENCE. / BLIND** [41] [–]
(cd-s) *(HUTDX 178)* – ('A') / Tanglin' / Butterfly / ('A'-video).

May 04. (cd) *(CDHUT 84)* *<98492>* **SPLIT THE DIFFERENCE** [35] [ ]
– Do one / These 3 sins / Silence / Me, you and everybody / We don't know where we're going / Sweet Virginia / Catch me up / Where ya going? / Meet me in the city / Chicken out / Extra special guy / Nothing is wrong / There it was.

Sep 04. (7") *(HUT 179)* **SWEET VIRGINIA. / ROYALTY** [42] [–]
(cd-s+=) *(HUTCD 179)* – Champagne for monkeys / Bed hairdo.

Independiente — A.T.O.

Jul 05. (d-cd) *(ISOM 50CD)* *<21538>* **OUT WEST** (live) [ ] [ ]
– Get miles / Shot shot / Hangover / Going out west / Here comes the breeze / We haven't turned around / Fill my cup / Do one / Revolutionary kind / Bring it on / Nothing is wrong / Love is better than a warm trombone / Do's and don'ts / Black eyed dog – Free to run / Ping one down / Blue moon rising / Get myself arrested / These 3 sins / Make no sound / Whippin' Piccadilly.

May 06. (7") *(ISOM 105S)* **GIRLSHAPEDLOVEDRUG. / HOW WE OPERATE (acoustic)** [66] [–]
(cd-s) *(ISOM 105MS)* – ('A') / Caravan / Troubleshooting.

Jun 06. (cd) *(ISOM 63CD)* *<21548>* **HOW WE OPERATE** [69] [ ]
– Notice / See the world / How we operate / Hamoa beach / Girlshapedlovedrug / Chasing ghosts with alcohol / Tear your love apart / Charley Patton songs / Woman! man! / All too much / Cry on demand / Don't make me laugh.

– compilations, etc. –

Oct 02. (d-cd) *Hut; (543175-2)* **IN OUR GUN / ABANDONED SHOPPING TROLLEY HOTLINE** [ ] [–]

Oct 02. (d-cd) *Hut; (543416-2)* **LIQUID SKIN / BRING IT ON** [ ] [–]
(re-iss. Sep04; VBX 14)

Jose GONZALEZ

Born: 1978, Gothenberg, Sweden. Raised by Argentinean parents, GONZALEZ grew up playing classical guitar and Brazilian bossa nova in the chilly environs of Scandinavia. Although influenced by punk/hardcore (he even released a 90s single with RENASCENCE for the label 'Destination'), the JOSE GONZALEZ that people raved over in the mid 00s was an entirely different proposition, laid-back to the point of being horizontal. Post-millennium, the swarthy Swede was still concentrating on the domestic market, initially recording as JUNIP (with TOBIAS WINTERKORN and ELIAS ARAYA) before striking out as a solo artist via a series of singles and low-key debut album, 'VENEER' (2003). With a voice so unobtrusive as to be beyond low-key, the focus was on GONZALEZ' close-mic'd, heavy fingered and engagingly ragged acoustic picking, a post-modern update of 70s avant-folkies NICK DRAKE, JOHN MARTYN and TIM BUCKLEY. The record finally saw a UK release in spring 2005 on prog-techno label 'Peacefrog', although it never really took off until JOSE's sublime cover of the Knives' 'HEARTBEATS' was used on a striking Sony/Bratvia TV ad (the one with the coloured balls bouncing around a San Francisco street). Both the single and the album went UK Top 10 in early 2006, making him into one of the most unlikely indie pop stars of his New Wave-centric generation.

• **Covers:** HAND ON YOUR HEART (Kylie Minogue) / LOVE WILL TEAR US APART (Joy Division) / TEARDROP (Massive Attack) / BORN IN THE U.S.A. + THE GHOST OF TOM JOAD (Bruce Springsteen).

Album rating: VENEER (*8)

JOSE GONZALEZ – vocals, classical guitar, percussion

Kakafoni | not iss.

2001. (7"; by JUNIP) *(KAKAFONI 1)* **STRAIGHT LINES** [–] Sweden [–]

— the same outfit issued 'BLACK REFUGEE' EP on mp3 in 2005

2003. (7") *(KAKAFONI 2)* **DEADWEIGHT ON VELVETEEN** [–] Sweden [–]

Imperial | not iss.

2003. (7") *(IMP 004S)* **CROSSES. / STORM** [–] Sweden [–]
(cd-s+=) *(IMP 005CDS)* – Hints / Deadweight on velveteen.

2003. (cd) *(IMP 007CD)* **VENEER** [–] Sweden [–]
– Slow moves / Remain / Lovestain / Heartbeats / Crosses / Deadweight on velveteen / All you deliver / Stay in the shade / Hints / Save your day / Broken arrows.

2003. (12") *(IMP 008T)* **CROSSES (remix)** [–] Sweden [–]

2004. (7") *(IMP 010)* **REMAIN. / SUGGESTIONS** [–] Sweden [–]
(cd-ep+=) *(IMP 009CDS)* – Lovestain / Love will tear us apart.

2004. (7") *(IMP 011S / SERV 012)* **HAND ON YOUR HEART. / (other by JENS LEKMAN)** [–] Sweden [–]

2004. (cd-ep) *(IMP 016CDS)* **STAY IN THE SHADE** [–] Sweden [–]

2004. (7") *(IMP 019S)* **DOWN THE HILLSIDE** [–] Sweden [–]

Peacefrog | Hidden Agenda

Mar 05. (7"/cd-s+=) *(PFG 065/+CD)* **CROSSES. / STORM** [ ] [–]

Apr 05. (lp/cd) *(PFG 066/+CD)* <74> **VENEER** [ ] Aug05 [ ]

Oct 05. (cd-ep) *(PFG 069CD)* <81> **STAY IN THE SHADE** [ ] Jan06 [ ]
– Stay in the shade / Down the hillside / Sensing owls / Hand on your heart / Instrumental.

Jan 06. (7"/cd-s) *(PFG 076/+CD)* **HEARTBEATS. / SUGGESTIONS** [9] [–]
(dvd-s) *(PFG 076DVD)* – ('A') / ('A'-live) / (live in London video documentary) / ('A'-Colour Like No Other video).

Jan 06. (lp/cd; re-) *(as prev)* **VENEER** [7] [–]

Apr 06. (7"/cd-s; re-) *(PFG 065/+CDX)* **CROSSES** [ ] [–]

the GOO GOO DOLLS

Formed: Buffalo, New York, USA . . . 1985 by ROBBY TAKAC (a former DJ), JOHNNY RZEZNIK and GEORGE TUTUSKA. Like a grunge-punk fusion of CHEAP TRICK, the LEMONHEADS and the DESCENDENTS, they debuted the following year with a low-rent eponymous debut album thankfully not given a release in Britain. A follow-up, 'JED' (1989), was also sprinkled with the odd cover version, a reading of Creedence Clearwater Revival's 'DOWN ON THE CORNER' presided over by guest crooner, LANCE DIAMOND. In the early 90's, 'Metal Blade' took over the reins, their powerful metal-punk winning new audiences after the release of their third set, 'HOLD ME UP' (1990). Three years on, the GOO GOO DOLLS returned with 'SUPERSTAR CARWASH', a transitional set preceding their break for the big time. GEORGE had now been replaced by MIKE MALININ, the sticksman coming in for the band's LOU GIORDANO-produced set, 'A BOY NAMED GOO' (1995), a US Top 30 success that featured Top 5 smash, 'NAME'. However, unlike many of their peers (GREEN DAY, OFFSPRING, etc), the 'DOLLS didn't really translate to the saturated British market despite having another two radio airplay hits in the States, both taken from 1998 album, 'DIZZY UP THE GIRL'. Now irrevocably part of the major league despite their unassuming aesthetic, the band recorded 'GUTTERFLOWER' (2002) as an unashamedly major league album with a suitably pristine production to match. That said, the spirit – if not the sound – of their more ragged earlier releases was still intact, indicating a potential longevity which has outlasted many of their formative influences. Boosted by a US Top 40 cover of Supertramp's 'GIVE A LITTLE BIT', the GOO GOOs got in on the CD/DVD-package action with 'LIVE IN BUFFALO' (July 4th 2004), shooting the breeze before the release of umpteenth studio set, 'LET LOVE IN' (2006). Flawlessly produced by Glen Ballard (ALANIS MORISSETTE, etc.), the record once again courted a mainstream audience and went Top 10 in America, while singles 'BETTER DAYS' and 'STAY WITH YOU' also fared quite well.

• **Covered:** I WANNA DESTROY YOU (Soft Boys) / DON'T FEAR THE REAPER (Blue Oyster Cult) / SUNSHINE OF YOUR LOVE (Cream) / I COULD NEVER TAKE THE PLACE OF YOUR MAN (Prince) / GIMME SHELTER (Rolling Stones) / I DON'T WANNA KNOW (Fleetwood Mac) / etc.

Album rating: GOO GOO DOLLS (*4) / JED (*4) / HOLD ME UP (*5) / SUPERSTAR CARWASH (*5) / A BOY NAMED GOO (*7) / DIZZY UP THE GIRL (*5) / EGO, OPINION, ART & COMMERCE compilation (*7) / GUTTERFLOWER (*6) / LIVE IN BUFFALO: JULY 4TH 2004 (*5) / LET LOVE IN (*5)

JOHNNY RZEZNIK (b. 5 Dec'65) – vocals, guitar / **ROBBY TAKAC** (b.30 Sep'64) – bass, vocals / **GEORGE TUTUSKA** – drums

GOO GOO DOLLS

Celluloid | Mercena

1987. (lp) *(2211)* *<97292-2>* **GOO GOO DOLLS** [–] French [ ]
– Torn apart / Messed up / Livin' in a hut / I'm addicted / Sunshine of your love / Hardsores / Hammering eggs (the metal song) / (Don't fear) The reaper / Beat me / Scream / Slaughterhouse / Different light / Come on / Don't beat my ass (with a baseball bat). *(re-iss. Nov95 on 'Metal Blade' 14079-2)*

Roadracer | Death-Enigma

Apr 89. (lp/cd) *(RO 9477-1/-2)* *<847859>* **JED** [ ] [ ]
– Out of sight / Up yours / No way out / 7th of last month / Love dolls Sex maggot / Down on the corner / Had enough / Road to Salinas / Em Elbmuh / Misfortune / Artie / Gimme shelter / James Dean. *(cd re-iss Feb94 on 'Metal Blade'; CDZORRO 70)*

Fun After All | Metal Bl

Nov 90. (lp/cd) *(AFTER 8/+CD)* *<26259-1/-2>* **HOLD ME UP** [ ] [ ]
– Laughing / Just the way you are / So outta line / There you are / You know what I man / Out of the red / I could never take the place of your man / Hey / On your side / 22 seconds / Kevin's song / Know my name Million miles away / Two days in February. *(cd re-iss. May96 on 'Meta Blade'; 3984 17018CD)*

Warners | Warne

1993. (cd/c) *<9362 45206-2/-4>* **SUPERSTAR CARWASH** [–] [ ]
– Fallin' down / Lucky star / Cuz you're gone / Don't worry / Girl righ next to me / Domino / We are the normal / String of lies / Another secon time around / Stop the world / Already there / On the lie / Close your eyes So far away. *(UK-iss.Aug99 on 'Edel'; 0102702HWR)*

— **MIKE MALININ** (b.10 Oct'67, Washington, DC) – drums, vocals; repl GEORGE

Apr 95. (cd/c) *<(9362 45750-2/-4)>* **A BOY NAMED GOO** [ ] [27]
– Long way down / Burnin' up / Naked / Flat top / Impersonality / Name Only one / Somethin' bad / Ain't that unusual / So long / Eyes wide open Disconnected / Slave girl. *(cd re-iss. Aug99 on 'Edel'; 0103122HWR)*

May 95. (c-s) *(W 0293C)* **ONLY ONE / IMPERSONALITY** [ ] [ ]
(cd-s+=) *(W 0293CD)* – Hit or miss.

Sep 95. (c-s) *<17758>* **NAME / BURNIN' UP / HIT OR MISS** [–] [5]

Feb 96. (c-s) *(W 0333C)* **NAME / NOTHING CAN CHANGE YOU** [ ] [–]
(cd-s+=) *(W 0333CD)* – I wanna destroy you.

Jul 96. (c-s) *(W 0362C)* **LONG WAY DOWN / NAME (live)** [ ] [–]
(cd-s+=) *(W 0362CD)* – Don't change (live).

Jul 98. (c-s) *(W 0449C)* <44525> **IRIS / LAZY EYE** 50 Sep98 9
(cd-s+=) *(W 0449CD)* – I don't want to know.

the GOO GOO DOLLS

Hollywood Imprint-Warners

Mar 99. (c-s) *(010239HWR)* <1763> **SLIDE / ACOUSTIC #3** 43 Nov98 8
(cd-s+=) *(010205HWR)* – Nothing can change you.
Jul 99. (c-s/cd-s) *(01024 89/42 HWR)* **IRIS / IRIS (acoustic)** 26 –
Jul 99. (cd/c) *(0102042HWR)* <47058-2/-4> **DIZZY UP THE GIRL** 47 Sep98 15
– Dizzy / Slide / Broadway / January friend / Black balloon / Bullet proof / Amigone / All eyes on me / Full forever / Acoustic #3 / Iris / Extra pale / Hate this place.
Nov 99. (c-s/cd-s) *(010535 9/5 HWR)* **DIZZY / SLIDE (acoustic)** –
Feb 00. (c-s/cd-s) *(010311 9/5 HWR)* <16946> **BLACK BALLOON / BLACK BALLOON (album version) / NAKED** Jul99 16
Apr 00. (cd-s) **BROADWAY / NAKED (live) / BLACK BALLOON (live)** – 24
Jul 01. (cd) *(0127112HWR)* <47945> **EGO, OPINION, ART & COMMERCE** (compilation) May01
– Bulletproof / All eyes on me / Amigone / Acoustic #3 / Naked / Ain't that unusual / Burning up / Flat top / Eyes wide open / Fallin' down / Another second time around / Cuz you're gone / We are the normal / Girl right next to me / Lucky star / On the lie / Just the way you are / Two days in February / Laughing / There you are / Up yours / I'm addicted.

Warners Warners

Apr 02. (cd) *(9362 48311-2)* <48206> **GUTTERFLOWER** 56 4
– Big machine / Think about me / Here is gone / You never know / What a scene / Up, up, up / It's over / Sympathy / What do you need? / Smash / Tucked away / Truth is a whisper.
Jul 02. (c-s) *(W 583C)* <radio> **HERE IS GONE / WE ARE THE NORMAL** 18
(cd-s+=) *(W 583CD1)* – Burnin' up / Two days in February.
(cd-s+=) *(W 583CD2)* – Burnin' up.
Sep 02. (cd-s) <42475> **BIG MACHINE / BLACK BALLOON / BROADWAY** – 64
Mar 03. (7") <16663> **SYMPATHY. / THINK ABOUT ME** –
Oct 04. (cd-s) <242804> **GIVE A LITTLE BIT / SYMPATHY / GIVE A LITTLE BIT (live)** – 37
Nov 04. (cd w/dvd) <9362 48867> **LIVE IN BUFFALO: JULY 4TH 2004** (live) –
– Give a little bit / Big machine / Naked / Slide / Think about me / Smash / Tucked away / Black balloon / Dizzy / Name / Cuz you're gone / Sympathy / January friend / Here is gone / What a scene / Acoustic #3 / Two days in February / Broadway / Iris / Give a little bit. // (DVD tracks).
Nov 05. (cd-s) <15870> **BETTER DAYS / BETTER DAYS (acoustic)** – 36
Apr 06. (-) <radio> **STAY WITH YOU** – 28
Apr 06. (cd) <(9362 49748-2)> **LET LOVE IN** 9
– Stay with you / Let love in / Feel the silence / Better days / Without you here / Listen / Give a little bit / Can't let it go / We'll be here (when you're gone) / Strange love / Become.

GOOD CHARLOTTE

Formed: Waldorf, Maryland, USA … 1996 by twins JOEL and BENJI MADDEN, together with schoolfriends PAUL and BILLY. Famously inspired to pick up a guitar by a show on the BEASTIE BOYS' 'Ill Communication' tour of the mid-90's, the lads unfortunately failed to absorb much of the BEASTIES' style, wit, charisma and originality, never mind their awkward, endearing funkiness or encyclopaedic knowledge of black music. Instead, they took the usual route of local gigging then demo straight to major label amid the continuing corporate rush to sign anything with a faint whiff of adolescent angst or spiky hair. The fact that the MADDEN twins were moonlighting as MTV presenters didn't exactly do the band much harm either. Settling for a deal with 'Epic/Sony', GOOD CHARLOTTE released their eponymous debut album in 2000, sounding as assembly line-manufactured as they looked. Which was great if you were a fan of BLINK-182, GREEN DAY and their ilk, but not so great if you'd heard those chugging guitar chords and whining lyrics just once too often. 'THE YOUNG AND THE HOPELESS' (2002) was as tired as its title suggested, with more heavy handed hormonal musings and join-the-dots "punk" – example major hits, 'LIFESTYLES OF THE RICH AND FAMOUS', 'GIRLS AND BOYS' and 'THE ANTHEM'. Third album, 'THE CHRONICLES OF LIFE AND DEATH' (2004), served up more of the same creatively and commercially (transatlantic Top 10); the UK Top 20 singles said it all, 'PREDICTABLE' and 'I JUST WANNA LIVE' – bring back SUICIDAL TENDENCIES.

Album rating: GOOD CHARLOTTE (*5) / THE YOUNG AND THE HOPELESS (*6) / THE CHRONICLES OF LIFE AND DEATH (*6)

JOEL MADDEN (b.11 Mar'79) – vocals / **BENJI MADDEN** (b.11 Mar'79) – guitar, vocals / **BILLY MARTIN** (b.15 Jun'81, Naptown, MD) – guitar / **PAUL THOMAS** (b. 5 Oct'80) – bass / **AARON** – drums

Epic Sony

Sep 00. (cd) <61452> **GOOD CHARLOTTE** –
– Little things / Waldorfworldwide / Motivation proclamation / East Coast anthem / Festival song / Complicated / Seasons / I don't wanna stop / I heard you / Walk by / Let me go / Screamer / Change. *(UK-iss.Feb03 on 'Epic'+=; 510974-2)* – Thank you mom.
Mar 01. (cd-s) <670738> **LITTLE THINGS / CLICK / THANK YOU MOM** –
Aug 01. (cd-s) <671309> **MOTIVATION PROCLAMATION / YEP / YEP (version)** –
Jan 03. (cd) *(509488-9)* <86486> **THE YOUNG AND THE HOPELESS** 15 Sep02 7
– A new beginning / The anthem / Lifestyles of the rich and famous / Wondering / The story of my old man / Girls and boys / My bloody valentine / Hold on / Riot girl / Say anything / The day that I die / The young and the hopeless / Emotionless / Movin' on.
Feb 03. (cd-s) *(673556-2)* **LIFESTYLES OF THE RICH AND FAMOUS / THE ANTHEM (demo) / LIFESTYLES OF THE RICH AND FAMOUS (live acoustic) / CEMETERY (live acoustic)** 8 20
(cd-s) *(673556-5)* – ('A') / Little things / ('A'-live acoustic).
May 03. (c-s) *(673877-4)* **GIRLS AND BOYS / LIFESTYLES OF THE RICH AND FAMOUS (instrumental)** 6 48
(cd-s) *(673877-2)* – ('A') / Riot girl (acoustic) / ('A'video).
(cd-s) *(673877-5)* – ('A') / Lifestyles of the rich and famous (live acoustic) / The young and the hopeless (live acoustic).
Aug 03. (c-s) *(674255-4)* <79932> **THE ANTHEM / THE ANTHEM (instrumental)** 10 Jul03 43
(cd-s) *(674255-2)* – ('A') / If you leave / Motivation proclamation (live acoustic) / ('A'-video).
(cd-s) *(674255-5)* – ('A') / Acquiesce (live on BBC3) / Complicated (version).
Dec 03. (7") *(674543-7)* **THE YOUNG AND THE HOPELESS. / LIFESTYLES OF THE RICH AND FAMOUS** 34 –
(cd-s) *(674543-5)* – ('A') / Girls and boys (Abbey Road session) / Hold on (video).
(cd-s) *(674543-2)* – Hold on / The story of my old man (Abbey Road session) / ('A'video).
Oct 04. (7"pic-d/cd-s) *(675388-7/-1)* **PREDICTABLE. / THE CHRONICLES OF LIFE AND DEATH (acoustic)** 12
(cd-s) *<(675388-2)>* – ('A') / The anthem (live from Abbey Road sessions) / Hold on (live from Abbey Road sessions) / ('A'-video).
Oct 04. (cd) *(517685-2)* <92425> **THE CHRONICLES OF LIFE AND DEATH** 8 3
– Once upon a time: The battle of life and death / The chronicles of life and death / Walk away (maybe) / S.O.S. / I just wanna live / Ghost of you / Predictable / Secrets / The truth / The world is black / Mountain / We believe / It wasn't enough / In this world (murder). *<(bonus+=)>* – Falling away. *(ltd-cd+=; 517685-9)* – Meet my maker / Wounded.
Jan 05. (7") *(675649-7)* **I JUST WANNA LIVE. / S.O.S. (live session)** 9 Mar05 51
(cd-s+=) *<(675649-2)>* – The world is black (live session).
(cd-s) *(675649-1)* – ('A') / Mountain (live session).
Jun 05. (7"orange/cd-s) *(675943-7/-1)* **THE CHRONICLES OF LIFE AND DEATH. / (live version)** 30 –
(cd-s+=) *(675943-5)* – Mountain (live) / I just wanna live (full Phatt remix) / ('A'-video).

— **CHRIS WILSON** (b. 5 May'81, Provo, Utah) – drums; repl. AARON

– compilations, others, etc. –

Sep 04. (d-cd) *Epic; (5175539)* **GOOD CHARLOTTE / THE YOUNG AND THE HOPELESS** ☐ [–]

☐ Martin L. GORE (see under ⇒ DEPECHE MODE)

☐ GORILLAZ (see under ⇒ BLUR)

☐ GRADUATE (see under ⇒ TEARS FOR FEARS)

GRANDADDY

Formed: Modesto, California, USA . . . 1992 by ex-skater, JASON LYTLE, who, with the help of HOWE GELB (of GIANT SAND), found a sympathetic ear at 'Big Cat' records. The line-up around this time also included JIM FAIRCHILD, TIM DRYDEN, KEVIN GARCIA and AARON BURTCH, although it took time aplenty to finally emerge with debut release, the mini-set, 'A PRETTY MESS BY THIS ONE BAND'. 'UNDER THE WESTERN FREEWAY' followed in '98, another based on classic West Coast Americana, their BRIAN WILSON/MERCURY REV-esque sound marked them out as the Sunday drivers of the alt-country brigade. JASON LYTLE and his band of beardy brothers returned one year after the release of the 'BROKEN DOWN COMFORTER COLLECTION' with perhaps the best album of the year, 'THE SOPHTWARE SLUMP' (2000). As prog and as concept as you can get, 'THE SOPHTWARE SLUMP' began with what could only be described as an American Lo-Fi version of 'Paranoid Android' entitled 'HE'S SIMPLE, HE'S DUMB, HE'S THE PILOT'. On it LYTLE sang "How's it going 2000 man, I heard all of your controls were jammed . . .", and continued the theme of man against machine through the entirety of the set. Backed by FAIRCHILD's psychedelic, effect-laden guitar and DRYDEN's electric piano, that doubled up as a space-age synth, LYTLE wandered like a lost child in a daunting sc-fi mountain landscape singing eleven sad songs about drunken robots, smashed up computers, lost love and ultimately, hope, all in his unsure NEIL YOUNG/DANIEL JOHNSTON-esque croon. Tracks 'HEWLETT'S DAUGHTER' and 'THE CRYSTAL LAKE' must've been two of the best psychedelic pop songs ever written, whereas on 'CHARSANDGRAFS', the band cranked up all of their instruments for what sounded like progressive grunge. In turn, a humble band who were thought to only make sad, sun-blasted Lo-Fi had created one of the strongest concept albums since 'Ok Computer'. Even if it was pitched somewhere between the aforementioned set, FLAMING LIPS' 'The Soft Bulletin' and MERCURY REV's 'Deserter's Songs', the biggest compliment the listener could've paid GRANDADDY was by saying that it sounded mostly like them. After all of the acclaim, GRANDADDY issued the somewhat disappointing third set proper, 'SUMDAY', in 2003. Not that the album was bad, it was just many fans had expected something a bit more extravagant or even adventurous. What they got instead seemed like a watered-down version of their first two albums, with LYTLE's production moving towards a more polished, mainstream direction. Single 'NOW IT'S ON' was far too simple for a band that had given us the mindbending prog of 'HE'S DUMB . . .', and their slamming synth sounds, fuzzy guitars and looped beats were becoming a tad tiresome. But, it still seemed like an average album by GRANDADDY was still twice as good as other bands' outputs. 2005's across the board mini-set 'EXCERPTS FROM THE DIARY OF TODD ZILLA', preceded what was to be LYTLE and Co's last musical will and testament, the oddly titled 'JUST LIKE THE FAMBLY CAT' (2006). Like all their best work, it was an album with a scope and ambition to rival the FLAMING LIPS and their ilk; but despite positivist pop symphonies like 'ELEVATE MYSELF', 'REAR VIEW MIRROR' and 'THE ANIMAL WORLD', it looked as if a lack of mainstream appreciation had consigned GRANDADDY to pipe and slippers all too soon.

• **Covers:** REVOLUTION (Beatles).

Album rating: A PRETTY MESS BY THIS ONE BAND mini (*6) / UNDER THE WESTERN FREEWAY (*8) / THE BROKEN DOWN COMFORTER COLLECTION compilation (*8) / THE SOPHTWARE SLUMP (*9) / CONCRETE DUNES collection (*5) / SUMDAY (*6) / EXCERPTS FROM THE DIARY OF TODD ZILLA mini (*5) / JUST LIKE THE FAMBLY CAT (*7)

JASON LYTLE – vocals / **JIM FAIRCHILD** – guitar / **TIM DRYDEN** – keyboards / **KEVIN GARCIA** – bass / **AARON BURTCH** – drums

not iss. Big Jesus

Apr 94. (c) *<none>* **COMPLEX PARTY COME-ALONG THEORIES** [–] ☐

1994. (7") *<none>* **COULD THIS BE LOVE. / KIM, YOU BORE ME TO DEATH** [–] ☐

1994. (7") *<none>* **TASTER. / NEBRASKA** [–] ☐

1995. (c) *<w-drawn>* **DON'T SOCK THIS TRYER** [–] [–]

Big Cat Will

Apr 96. (m-cd) *<WIL 041>* **A PRETTY MESS BY THIS ONE BAND** [–] ☐
– Away birdies with special sounds / Taster / Peeano / Kim you bore me to death / Pre Merced / Gentle spike resort / Egg hit and Jack too.

1997. (7"ep) *<none>* **MACHINES ARE NOT SHE E.P.** [–] mail-o ☐
– Levitz / For the dishwasher / Lava kiss / Wretched songs / Sikh in a Baja VW bug / Fentry. *<re-iss. 1998 on 'Big Cat'; ABB 128P>*

Feb 98. (7") *(ABB 157S)* **EVERYTHING BEAUTIFUL IS FAR AWAY. / FOR THE DISHWASHER** ☐ [–]
(cd-s+=) *(ABB 157SCD)* – Glass dusty.

Mar 98. (7"/cd-s) *(ABB 161S/+CD)* **LAUGHING STOCK. / G.P.C. / 12-PAK 599** ☐ [–]

Apr 98. (lp/cd) *(ABB 152/+CD) <33646>* **UNDER THE WESTERN FREEWAY** ☐ Oct97 ☐
– Nonphenomenal lineage / A.M. 180 / Collective dreamwish of upper class / Summer here kids / Laughing stock / Under the western freeway / Everything beautiful is far away / Poisoned at Hartsy Thai food / Go progress chrome / Why took your advice / Lawn and so on. *(cd re-iss. Aug00; ABB 100248-2)*

May 98. (7"/cd-s) *(ABB 162S/+CD)* **SUMMER HERE KIDS. / LEVITZ (BIRDLESS) / MY SMALL LOVE** ☐ [–]

Oct 98. (7") *(ABB 500 350-7)* **A.M. 180. / HERE** ☐ [–]
(cd-s) *(ABB 164SCD)* – ('A'side) / For the dishwasher.

V2 V2

Sep 99. (7"ep) *<27612>* **SIGNAL TO SNOW** [–] ☐
– Hand crank transmitter / Jeddy's 3's poem / MGM grand / Protected from the rain.

May 00. (cd) *(VVR 101225-2) <27068>* **THE SOPHTWARE SLUMP** [36] ☐
– He's simple, he's dumb, he's the pilot / Hewlett's daughter / Jed the humanoid / The crystal lake / Chartsengrafs / Underneath the weeping willow / Broken household appliance national forest / Jed's other poem (beautiful ground) / E. Knievel interlude (the perils of keeping it real) / Miner at the dial-a-view / So you'll aim toward the sky. *(re-iss. Aug00 +=; VVR 101225-8)* – THE CRYSTAL LAKE tracks *(d-cd iss.Nov00 +=; VVR 101389-8)* – OUR DYING BRAIN tracks *(d-cd iss.Feb01 +=; VVR 101613-2)* – SIGNAL TO SNOW tracks

May 00. (7") *(VVR 501301-7)* **THE CRYSTAL LAKE. / OUR DYING BRAIN** ☐ [–]
(cd-s+=) *(VVR 501301-3)* – First movement / Message send: ID#5646766.

Aug 00. (7") *(VVR 501433-7)* **HEWLETT'S DAUGHTER. / LFO** [71] [–]
(cd-s) *(VVR 501433-3)* – ('A'side) / XD-data-II / Street bunny.
(cd-s++=) *(VVR 501465-3)* – Wonder why in L.A. / ('A'mix).
(cd-s) *(VVR 501433-8)* – ('A'side) / Wonder why in L.A. / Chartsengrafs.

Nov 00. (12"/cd-s) *(VVR 501493-6/-3)* **HE'S SIMPLE, HE'S DUMB, HE'S THE PILOT. / WIVES OF FARMERS / N. BLENDER** ☐ [–]

Jan 01. (7") *(VVR 501515-7)* **THE CRYSTAL LAKE. / RODE MY BIKE TO MY STEPSISTER'S WEDDING** [38] [–]
(cd-s) *(VVR 501515-3)* – ('A'side) / Moe Bandy mountaineers / She-deleter.
(cd-s) *(VVR 501515-8)* – ('A'-chilly mix) / What can't be erased / I don' want to record anymore.

Jun 03. (7") *(VVR 502224-7)* **NOW IT'S ON. / TROUBLE WITH A CAPITAL T** [23] [–]
(cd-s+=) *(VVR 502224-3)* – Hey cowboy, the phone's for you.
(cd-s) *(VVR 502224-8)* – ('A'side) / Getting jipped.

ın 03. (cd/lp) *(VVR 102223-2/-1)* <27155> **SUMDAY** [22] May03 [84]
– Now it's on / I'm on standby / The go in the go-for-it / The group who couldn't say / Lost on yer merry way / El caminos in the west / "Yeah" is what we had / Saddest vacant lot in all the world / Stray dog and the chocolate shake / O.K. with my decay / The warming sun / The final push to the sum. *(ltd-d-cd-iss. Nov03 +=; VVR 102223-0)* – Crystal lake (live) / For the dishwasher / "Yeah" is what we had / A.M. 180 / Our dying brains / Laughing stock / The go in go-for-it (Radio Frances Black session) / Saddest vacant lot in all the world / He's simple, he's dumb, he's the pilot.

ug 03. (cd-s) *(VVR 502366-3)* **EL CAMINOS IN THE WEST / BEAUTIFUL GROUND (live XM satellite radio) / MY LITTLE SKATEBOARDING PROBLEM** [48] [–]
(cd-s) *(VVR 502366-8)* – ('A'side) / Now it's on (Colin Murray Radio 1 session) / Derek Spears.

ın 04. (7") *(VVR 502460-7)* **I'M ON STANDBY. / STRAY DOG AND THE CHOCOLATE SHAKE** [ ] [–]
(cd-s+=) *(VVR 502460-3)* – The town where I'm livin' now / (hidden track).

ıl 05. (7") *(BMR 053-7)* **THE RUGGED AND SPLINTERED ENTERTAINMENT CENTER. / (flip by the Polyphonic Spree)** [ ] [–]
(above issued on 'Birdman')

ct 05. (m-lp/m-cd) *(VVR 103529-1/-2)* <27273> **EXCERPTS FROM THE DIARY OF TODD ZILLA** [ ] Sep05 [ ]
– Pull my curtains / At the post / A valley son (sparing) / Cinderland / F**k the valley fudge / Florida / Goodbye? *(bonus track+=)* – Hidden health announcement. *<US-lp on 'Devil In The Woods'; DIW 089>*

lay 06. (7") *(VVR 504008-7)* **ELEVATE MYSELF. / WINNERS** [ ] [–]

ay 06. (cd) *(VVR 102947-2)* <27277> **JUST LIKE THE FAMBLY CAT** [ ] [ ]
– What happened.. / Jeez Louise / Summer . . . it's gone / Oxygen – Aux send / Rear view mirror / The animal world / Skateboarding saves me twice / Where I'm anymore / 50% / Guide down denied / Elevate myself / Campershell dreams / Disconnecty / This is how it always starts.

– compilations, etc. –

996. (cd) *none; <none>* **THE WINDFALL VARIETAL** [–] [ ]

ın 99. (cd) *Big Cat; (ABB 100569-2)* **THE BROKEN DOWN COMFORTER COLLECTION** [ ] [–]
– (A PRETTY MESS BY THIS ONE BAND / MACHINES ARE NOT SHE).

ct 02. (cd) *Lakeshore; <(LAK 33690CD)>* **CONCRETE DUNES** [ ] Feb02 [ ]
– Why should I want to die / My small love / 12-pak-599 / Wretched songs / Levitz / For the dishwasher / Sikh in a baja VW bug / Lava kiss / Fentry / Gentle spike resort / Away birdies with spacial sounds / Kim you bore me to death / Pre merced / Taster / Egg hit and Jack too.

;RANDMASTER FLASH

orn: 1 Jan'58, Barbados, West Indies as JOSEPH SADDLER, :hough he moved to the Bronx district of New York at an ırly age. Taking his cue from pioneering DJ's like KOOL ERC, a teenage SADDLER began spinning records at local block ırties, eventually developing the complex technique of "cutting" :tween records on two separate turntables, creating a continuous ›w of beats punctuated by repetitive rhythmic "breaks". While ese tricks later proved to be one of the most revolutionary ıd money-spinning developments in the evolution of popular usic, for the time being SADDLER aka DJ GRANDMASTER .ASH (so called for his lightning speed turntable techniques) ıs content to demonstrate his considerable skills at local hip ›p events. Enlisting a cast of rappers to complement his inning, FLASH created The FURIOUS FIVE, originally consisting GRANDMASTER MELLE MEL (born MELVIN GLOVER), other KID CREOLE (born NATHANIEL GLOVER and no, ›t THAT KID CREOLE!), COWBOY (born KEITH WIGGINS), UKE BOOTEE (born EDWARD FLETCHER) and KURTIS .OW. The latter was subsequently replaced by RAHIEM (born GUY TODD WILLIAMS), the crew creating a buzz around New York and finally making their vinyl debut in 1979 for 'Enjoy' records with the track 'SUPERRAPPIN''. Like its follow-up, 'WE RAP MORE MELLOW', the track was a massive underground hit, although the band failed to grab the attention of the wider music community. It was only after signing to Sylvia and Joe Robinson's 'Sugar Hill' records that FLASH and his FURIOUS FIVE began to make major waves. With the addition of SCORPIO (born ED MORRIS), the group released the 'FREEDOM' single which hit the American R&B Top 20, closely followed by 'BIRTHDAY PARTY', but it was 'THE ADVENTURES OF GRANDMASTER FLASH ON THE WHEELS OF STEEL' (1981) that really set the hip hop world alight. A revolutionary cut'n'paste of sampling, scratching, breaks and boisterous rapping, the record used Chic's 'GOOD TIMES' and Queen's 'ANOTHER ONE BITES THE DUST' as its base material. Another precedent was set almost a year later with the SYLVIA ROBINSON/DUKE BOOTEE-penned 'THE MESSAGE', as powerful a record as has ever emerged from hip hop. With its hard hitting account of inner city life, the record pre-empted Gangsta-rap with half the bluster and twice the effectiveness, topping the charts on both sides of the Atlantic in 1982. Financial and personal squabbling led to a split in the ranks the following year during the recording of 'WHITE LINES (DON'T DO IT)', FLASH heading off with RAHEIM and KID CREOLE, eventually securing a contract with 'Elektra'. The latter track, released under the moniker GRANDMASTER FLASH & MELLE MEL was another revelatory piece of old skool electro-hip hop, all reverberating bass and apocalyptic vocals warning of the dangers of drug addiction. It was a warning that FLASH would've done well to heed, now a freebase cocaine addict himself, and although he eventually won a court battle with MELLE MEL over the use of the group name, his major label records made little impact, FLASH fading into obscurity as the 80's wore on, while young bucks like ERIC B and PUBLIC ENEMY took over. MELLE MEL, meanwhile, who had remained with COWBOY and SCORPIO, continued to record for 'Sugarhill' although he too, was afforded about as much interest with his later work as his estranged colleague. FLASH, MELLE MEL and THE FURIOUS FIVE eventually re-united in 1987 for a New York charity concert organised by PAUL SIMON. Tragically, it was the last time the original line-up would be on the same stage together as COWBOY died on the 8th of September '89 as a result of crack addiction. More recently, FLASH played at the 1997 Essential Music Festival in Brighton, England, while MELLE MEL released a solo album the same year.

• **Songwriters:** All written by FLASH and MELLE (VAUGHAN), except loads of sampling and covers, including WHO'S THAT LADY (Isley Brothers).

Album rating: THE MESSAGE (*7) / GREATEST MESSAGES compilation (*6) / THEY SAID IT COULDN'T BE DONE (*4) / THE SOURCE (*5) / BA-DOP-BOOM-BANG (*4) / ON THE STRENGTH (*3) / THE GREATEST HITS compilation (*7)

GRANDMASTER FLASH & THE FURIOUS FIVE

GRANDMASTER FLASH (b. JOSEPH SADDLER, 1 Jan '58, Barbados) – turntables / **MELLE MEL** (b. MELVIN GLOVER) – vocals / **COWBOY** (b. KEITH WIGGINS, 20 Sep'60) – vocals / **KID CREOLE** (b. NATHANIEL GLOVER) – vocals / added **MR. NESS** (b. EDDIE MORRIS) – rapper / and **RAHEIM** (b. GUY WILLIAMS) – vocals repl. KURTIS BLOW who went solo

not iss. Enjoy

1979. (7") **SUPERRAPPIN'. / ('A'instrumental)** [–] [ ]

not iss. Brass

1979. (7"; as The YOUNGER GENERATION) **WE RAP MORE MELLOW. / ('A' instrumental)** [–] [ ]

—— added **SCORPIO** – electronics

Sugar Hill — Sugar Hill

Apr 81. (7") *(SH 555) <759>* **BIRTHDAY PARTY. / ('A'instrumental)** [ ] [ ]
Jul 81. (7") **FREEDOM. / ('A'instrumental)** [–] [ ]
Dec 81. (12") *(SHL 557)* **THE ADVENTURES OF GRANDMASTER FLASH ON THE WHEELS OF STEEL. / THE BIRTHDAY PARTY** [ ] Oct81 [ ]
Dec 81. (7") **FLASH TO THE BEAT. / ('A'instrumental)** [–] [ ]
(originally issued 1979 on 'Bozo Meko')
Mar 82 (7"/12") *(SH/+L 111)* **IT'S NASTY (GENIUS OF LOVE). / BIRTHDAY PARTY** [ ] [–]
May 82. (7"/12") *(SH/+L 117) <584>* **THE MESSAGE. / THE MESSAGE (part 2)** [8] Sep82 [62]
Oct 82. (lp/c) *(SHLP/ZCSH 1007) <268>* **THE MESSAGE** [77] [53]
– She's fresh / It's nasty (genius of love) / Scorpio / It's a shame / Dreamin' / You are / The message / Adventures of Grandmaster Flash on the wheels of steel.
Dec 82. (7"/12") *(SH/+L 118) <790>* **SCORPIO. / IT'S A SHAME** [ ] [ ]
Jan 83. (7"/12"; by MELLE MEL & DUKE BOOTEE) *(SH/+L 119) <792>* **MESSAGE II (SURVIVAL). / ('A'instrumental)** [74] [ ]
May 83. (7"/12"; by The FURIOUS FIVE) *(SH/+L 125)* **NEW YORK, NEW YORK. / ('A'instrumental)** [ ] [–]

GRANDMASTER FLASH & MELLE MEL

Sugarhill — Sugarhill

Nov 83. (7"/12") *(SH/+L 130) <465>* **WHITE LINES (DON'T DO IT). / ('A'version)** [7] [ ]
(Jul84; 12"pic-d+=) *(SHLX 130)* – White lines (New York remix) / ('A'original) / ('A'-US mix). *(re-iss. Oct84 as 'CONTINUOUS WHITE LINES'; SHLM 130) (re-iss. Jun87 on 'Blatant' 7"/12"; BLAT 7/12 1)*

—— GRANDMASTER FLASH, MELLE MEL & THE FURIOUS FIVE split Nov83. FLASH and MEL split two ways, and went to court to use full group name. MEL adopted

GRANDMASTER MELLE MEL & THE FURIOUS FIVE

—— taking with him **SCORPIO** and **COWBOY**. He recruited new members **LEWIS GLOVER** (MEL's brother) / **TOMMY GUN CHEV / LES DE LA CRUZ**

Sugar Hill — Sugar Hill

1984. (7"/12") *(SH/+L 133)* **JESSE. / ('A' instrumental)** [ ] [–]
—— (below from the film 'Beat Street' on 'Atlantic')
Jun 84. (7") *(A 9659) <89659>* **BEAT STREET BREAKDOWN. / (part II)** [42] [86]
(12"+=) *(TA 9659)* – Internationally known.
Jun 84. (lp/c) *(SHLP/ZCSH 5552)* **GREATEST MESSAGES** (compilation) [41] [–]
– The message / Survival (The message II) / Freedom / Flash to the beat / Jesse / White lines (don't do it) / New York New York / Internationally known / Birthday party / Adventures on the wheels of steel / Scorpio / It's nasty (genius of love).
Sep 84. (7"/12") *(SH/+L 136) <92011>* **WE DON'T WORK FOR FREE. / ('A'instrumental)** [45] [ ]
Oct 84. (lp/c) *(SHLP/ZCSH 5553)* **WORK PARTY** [45] [ ]
– Rustler's convention / Yesterday / At the party / The truth / White lines (new UK master mix) / We don't work for free / World war III / Can't keep running away / The new adventures of Grandmaster.
Nov 84. (7") *(SH 139)* **STEP OFF (part 1). / STEP OFF (part 2)** [8] [ ]
(12"+=) *(SHL 139)* – The message.
(12"+=) *(SHLX 139)* – Continuous white lines.
Mar 85. (7") *(SH 141)* **PUMP ME UP. / ('A' instrumental)** [45] [–]
(12"+=/12"pic-d+=) *(SHL/+X 141)* – ('A'version).
May 85. (lp/c) *(SHLP/ZCSH 5555)* **STEPPING OFF** (compilation) [ ] [–]
– Pump me up / Step off / The message / We don't work for free / White lines (don't do it) / Jesse / Survival (the message II) / The megaMelle mix.
Jul 85. (7") *(SH 143)* **WORLD WAR III. / THE TRUTH** [ ] [–]
(12"+=) *(SHL 143)* – Step off / The message (version).
Nov 85. (7") *(SH 146) <92015>* **VICE (from 'Miami Vice' TV). / KING OF THE STREET** [ ] [ ]

GRANDMASTER FLASH

—— went solo, taking **RAHEIM** and **KID CREOLE** plus new people **LEVON BROADWAY** and **LARRY LOVE**

Elektra — Elektr

Feb 85. (7") *(E 9677) <69677>* **SIGN OF THE TIMES. / LARRY'S DANCE THEME** [72] [ ]
(12"+=) *(E 9677T)* – ('A'instrumental).
Feb 85. (lp/c) *(960389-1/-4) <60389>* **THEY SAID IT COULDN'T BE DONE** [95] [ ]
– Girls love the way he spins / The joint is jumpin' / Rock the house Jailbait / Sign of the times / Larry's dance theme / Who's that lady Alternative groove / Paradise.
May 85. (7") *<69643>* **GIRLS LOVE THE WAY HE SPINS. / LARRY'S DANCE THEME** [–] [ ]
Jul 85. (7") *<69617>* **WHO'S THAT LADY. / ALTERNATIVE GROOVE** [–] [ ]
Apr 86. (lp/c) *(960476-1/-4) <60476>* **THE SOURCE** [ ] [ ]
– Street scene / Style (Peter Gunn theme) / Ms. Thang / P.L.U. (Peac Love and Unity) / Throwin' down / Behind closed doors / Larry's danc theme (part 2) / Lies / Fastest man alive / Freelance.
May 86. (7") *(EKR 39) <69552>* **STYLE (PETER GUNN THEME). / ('A'instrumental)** [ ] [ ]
(12"+=) *(EKR 39T)* – ('A'remix).
Jul 86. (7") *<69530>* **LIES. / BEHIND CLOSED DOORS** [–] [ ]
Mar 87. (7"/12") *(EKR 54/+T) <69490>* **U KNOW WHAT TIME IT IS? / BUS DIS (WOO)** [ ] [ ]
Mar 87. (lp/c/cd) *(960723-1/-4/-2) <60723>* **BA-DOP-BOOM-BANG** [ ] [ ]
– Ain't we funkin' now / U know what time it is? / Underarms / Ki named Flash / Get yours / Then jeans / We will rock you / All wrappe up / Tear the roof off / Big black caddy / House that rocked / Bus dis / am somebody / Ain't we funkin' now (reprise).
May 87. (7") *<69459>* **ALL WRAPPED UP. / KID NAMED FLASH** [–] [ ]

GRANDMASTER FLASH & THE FURIOUS FIVE

(originals re-formed for 'Elektra')
Feb 88. (7") *(EKR 70) <69416>* **GOLD. / BACK IN THE OLD DAYS OF HIP HOP** [ ] [ ]
(12"+=) *(EKR 70T)* – ('A'acappella) / ('A'acappella dub).
Mar 88. (lp/c/cd) *(960769-1/-4/-2) <60769>* **ON THE STRENGTH** [ ] [ ]
– Gold / Cold in effect / Yo baby / On the strength / The king / Fly gir Magic carpet ride / Leave here / This is where you got it from / The b is dope. *(cd+=)* – Back in the old days of hip-hop. *(cd re-iss. Jan97; 75 60769-2)*
May 88. (7") *<69400>* **COLD IN EFFECT. / FLY GIRL** [–] [ ]
Jul 88. (7") *<69380>* **ON THE STRENGTH. / MAGIC CARPET RIDE** [–] [ ]

GRANDMASTER MELLE MEL

Edel — unkn

Jul 97. (12") *(0098470 RAP)* **MR. BIG STUFF. / CHINA WHITE** [ ] [–]

– compilations, etc. –

1988. (3"cd-ep) *Special Edition; (CD3-1)* **WHITE LINES (DON'T DO IT). / JESSE / THE MESSAGE II** [ ] [–]
1988. (3"cd-ep) *Special Edition; (CD3-2)* **THE ADVENTURES OF GRANDMASTER FLASH ON THE WHEELS OF STEEL. / THE MESSAGE / IT'S NASTY (GENIUS OF LOVE)** [ ] [–]
Mar 89. (d-c) *Sugar Hill; (IED 33)* **THE BEST OF GRANDMASTER FLASH & THE FURIOUS FIVE** [ ] [–]
Nov 89. (12") *Old Gold; (OG 4152)* **THE MESSAGE. / THE ADVENTURES ON THE WHEELS OF STEEL** [ ] [–]
Jul 90. (7") *Castle;* **WHITE LINES (DON'T DON'T DO IT) (freestyle Ben Legrand mix). / (Part 2)** [ ] [–]
Jul 91. (cd/c) *Kwest; (KWEST 5/4 193)* **WHITE LINES & OTHER MESSAGES – THE SILVER COLLECTION** [ ] [–]
May 92. (cd) *Sequel; (NEMCD 622)* **THE GREATEST HITS** [ ] [–]
– White lines (don't do it) / Step off / Pump me up / Jesse / Beat Stre

	Vice / Freedom / Birthday party / Flash to the beat / It's nasty (genius of love) / The message / Scorpio / Survival (Message II) / New York, New York.		
Dec 93.	(12"/cd-s) *W.G.A.F.; (WGAF/+CD 103)* **WHITE LINES (DON'T DO IT) (D&S 7" Remix) / HEY HEY (D&S 7" Remix)**	59	–
Mar 94.	(12"/cd-s) *W.G.A.F.; (WGAF/+CD 104)* **THE MESSAGE. / ('A'remixes)**		–
Aug 95.	(cd-s) *Old Gold; (OG 6314)* **WHITE LINES (DON'T DO IT) / PUMP ME UP**		–
Sep 95.	(cd-s) *Old Gold; (12623 6300-2)* **THE MESSAGE / SURVIVAL (MESSAGE II)**		–
Nov 96.	(cd/lp) *Deep Beats; (DEEP M/X 004)* **MORE HITS**		–
Jul 97.	(12"/cd-s) *Deep Cuts; (DEEP 12/CD 001)* **THE MESSAGE (mixes)**		–
Jul 97.	(d-cd; shared with SUGARHILL GANG) *Snapper; (SMDCD 164)* **GRANDMASTER FLASH VS THE SUGARHILL GANG**		–
Mar 99.	(12") *Sugarhill-Sequel; (NEET 1003)* **THE MESSAGE. / THE ADVENTURES OF GRANDMASTER FLASH ON THE WHEELS OF STEEL**		–
Mar 99.	(12") *Sugarhill-Sequel; (NEET 1007)* **WHITE LINES (DON'T DO IT). / SCORPIO**		–
Mar 99.	(3xcd-box) *Sequel; (NXTCD 305)* **BACK TO THE OLD SCHOOL**		–
Oct 99.	(12") *Hot Classics; (HCL 2261)* **THE MESSAGE. / IT'S NASTY**		–
Oct 99.	(12") *Hot Classics; (HCL 2262)* **WHITE LINES. / THE MESSAGE II**		–
May 02.	(cd; & MELLE MEL) *Sequel; (NEMCD 622)* **GREATEST HITS**		–
Sep 02.	(cd) *Camden; (74321 96051-2)* **GRANDMASTER FLASH & THE SUGARHILL GANG**		

☐ GRANDPABOY (see under ⇒ REPLACEMENTS)

☐ GRASSHOPPER & THE GOLDEN CRICKETS (see under ⇒ MERCURY REV)

GRATEFUL DEAD

Formed: San Francisco, California, USA ... 1965 by JERRY GARCIA, who had spent nine months of 1959 in the army before finding lyricist extrordinaire ROBERT HUNTER and forming folk outfit The THUNDER MOUNTAIN TUB THUMPERS. Along the way, this loose collective of musicians included soon-to-be GRATEFUL DEAD members BOB WEIR and RON McKERNAN (aka PIGPEN), JERRY going on to make demos in 1963 as duo JERRY & SARAH GARCIA. It wasn't until 1965 that the earliest incarnation of The GRATEFUL DEAD, The WARLOCKS, set out on their "golden road to unlimited gigging", when they took centre stage as house band for KEN KESEY's (author of 'One Flew Over The Cuckoo's Nest') legendary acid tests. Created by KESEY and his band of merry pranksters, the main objective of these psychedelic shindigs was to bombard the tripping hordes with as much sensory overload as posible; flashing lights, pre-recorded chants, hidden speakers hissing subversive messages and of course, the ear splitting racket of The WARLOCKS. With crowd and band liberally dosed with LSD courtesy of acidmeister AUGUSTUS STANLEY III, the events were clearly a formative part of their career. By this time, the band had gone electric, inspired by the raucous rock'n'roll of The BEATLES, bolstering the sound with drummer BILL KREUTZMANN and bassist PHIL LESH. Changing their name to the equally hoary sounding GRATEFUL DEAD (picked at random from a dictionary), the band toured California alongside JEFFERSON AIRPLANE. In 1966, they issued a one-off 45, 'DON'T EASE ME IN' for 'Fantasy' off-shoot label 'Scorpio', which led to 'Warners' signing them up in 1967. Recorded in three amphetamine-fuelled days, 'THE GRATEFUL DEAD' was released to the expectant hippy faithful in December of the same year, an admirable but untimately doomed attempt to recreate their fabled live sound in the studio. After an impromptu guest spot at one of their early shows, drummer MICKEY HART augmented the band's rhythm section, creating a more subtly complex rather than powerful sound. The group also recruited keyboardist TOM CONSTANTEN, whose avant-garde influences included JOHN CAGE and STOCKHAUSEN. Adding to the DEAD's psychedelic stew, these two further inspired the band's live improvisation, partly captured on 'ANTHEM OF THE SUN' in 1968. An ambitious collage of live and studio pieces, the album was another flawed attempt to seize the essence of the elusive beast that was the band's live show. It did however, contain bizarrely experimental sections with wonderful cod-hippy titles like, 'CRYPTICAL ENVELOPMENT' and 'THE FASTER WE GO, THE ROUNDER WE GET', these worth the admission price alone. The experimentation continued with 'AOXOMOXOA' in 1969, GARCIA's old mate ROBERT HUNTER marking his first collaboration with the band and helping to contain the explorations inside defined song structures. Highlights included 'MOUNTAINS OF THE MOON', with its celestial harpsicord and 'ST STEPHEN', a song that would go on to become a staple of the band's live set. With the release of 'LIVE DEAD' in 1970, The GRATEFUL DEAD finally did itself justice on vinyl, silencing the critics of their previous output who couldn't understand why the band were held in such high esteem by their fiercely loyal San Franciscan fanbase. On the track 'DARK STAR', the band crystallised their free-flowing improvisation in breathtaking style, while the celebratory 'TURN ON YOUR LOVE LIGHT', was also a standard of the band's now legendary live shows. Attracting multitudes of tye-dyed freaks, affectionately nicknamed "Deadheads", the band's gigs became communal gatherings, where both the crowd and band could lose themselves in the spaced-out jams which would often stretch songs over an hour or more. Forget 15 minutes of fame (as ANDY WARHOL once gave us all), the DEAD needed 15 minutes just for the intro! Ironically the band's next two studio albums marked a radical new direction with pared-down sets of harmony laden country-folk. With CONSTANTEN out of the picture by early 1970 and mounting debts, the group went for a simpler sound, clearly influenced by CROSBY, STILLS and NASH and GARCIA's part-time dabblings with The NEW RIDERS OF THE PURPLE SAGE. 'WORKINGMAN'S DEAD' was symptomatic of the times as bands began to move away from the psychedelic claustrophobia of the late 60's (note 'NEW SPEEDWAY BOOGIE' about the end of the hippy dream; the Altamont Festival at which a ROLLING STONES fan was killed by a drug-crazed Hell's Angel). 'AMERICAN BEAUTY' carried on where the previous album left off, 'SUGAR MAGNOLIA' and 'RIPPLE' being the highlights of this highly regarded piece of roots rock. By 1971, HART had departed and the band were reduced to five core members. Two live albums followed, the double 'GRATEFUL DEAD' and 'EUROPE 72', the latter stretching to three slabs of vinyl. 1972 also saw the release of WEIR's solo album, 'ACE', actually a GRATEFUL DEAD album in all but name. It included the glorious tongue-in-cheek romp, 'MEXICALI BLUES' and also saw WEIR begin writing with JOHN PERRY BARLOW, a partnership that would see HUNTER's input diminish over the following years. Years of alcohol abuse led to PIGPEN dying on 8th May '73 and he was replaced by KEITH GODCHAUX, who had toured with them the previous year. His wife DONNA also joined, taking up vocal duties. Around this time the band set up their own label, imaginatively titled 'Grateful Dead Records', releasing 'WAKE OF THE FLOOD' in July '73. The album was their most successful to date, containing the melancholy 'STELLA BLUE', although ironically, profits were lost to bootleggers. 'BLUES FOR ALLAH', from 1975, signalled a jazzier, fuller sound, though by this juncture the band were in financial deep water and signed with 'United Artists'. The source of much of their money problems was a concert movie which ate up most of their resources. 'STEAL YOUR FACE' was next in line and was intended for the movie, although it remained in the can due to the album's relative critical failure. Signing to 'Arista' and drafting in KEITH OLSEN on production duties they released 'TERRAPIN STATION' in 1977, an album which showcased a lusher, fuller sound. For '78's 'SHAKEDOWN STREET', the band collaborated with LOWELL GEORGE, and what could have been an interesting pairing, came out sounding limp and uninspiring; a pale reflection of what the DEAD were capable of. Despite the inconsistent quality of their studio work, the DEAD were always a safe live bet and they played the gig to surely top all gigs with their series of dates at the Pyramids in Egypt. Still carrying a hippy torch (even through the punk days), they filled large venues wherever they played and became a multi-million dollar industry in their own right. However, as they concentrated on live work, their studio outings suffered, their 1980 album 'GO TO HEAVEN' being particularly disappointing although it spawned their first success in the US singles chart with 'ALABAMA GETAWAY'. Another two live sets followed in 1981, 'DEAD SET' and 'RECKONING'. The latter was an acoustic album featuring classics like 'RIPPLE' and 'CASSIDY'. Soon after their release, GARCIA became a full blown heroin addict, narrowly escaping death when he fell into a diabetic coma in in 1986. Once he rehabilitated, the DEAD came back to life with 'IN THE DARK', a spirited set that reached the Top 10 in the US chart, even resulting in top selling 45, 'TOUCH OF GREY'. Their tribute to growing old with pride, it was a first when the band agreed to make a video for MTV. The awful 'DYLAN & THE DEAD' (yes with Mr. Zimmerman) was muted and dull, as was the studio 1989 offering, 'BUILT TO LAST'. Tragedy hit the band yet again, when keyboardist BRENT MYDLAND (who himself had replaced KEITH GODCHAUX in '79) was killed by a hard drugs cocktail. BRUCE HORNSBY (yes that solo geezer) was drafted in temporarily for touring commitments, while VINCE WELNICK joined full-time. The band released yet another live album the same year, the hardly dangerous 'WITHOUT A NET' and also started issuing the DICK'S PICKS series of archive recordings from great days of yore. On 9th August, 1995, the ailing JERRY GARCIA died of heart failure in a rehab unit after his arteries clogged up. It seemed inevitable that the long strange trip of the GRATEFUL DEAD had come to an end, GARCIA's guiding light relocating to find his "Dark Star" once again. The DEAD left behind a rich musical legacy, including numerous solo outings and off-shoot projects, but will always be remembered, by the Deadheads at least, for their transcendental live performances. WEIR, HART and LESH formed a new 'Dead' outfit, The OTHER ONES (along with BRUCE HORNSBY, DAVE ELLIS, MARK KARAN, JOHN MOLO and STEVE KIMOCK, etc), delivering a surprise oddity set, 'ONLY THE STRANGE REMAIN' (1999).

• **Songwriters:** Most by HUNTER-GARCIA or WEIR, LESH and some by others, including JOHN BARLOW. Covered; GOOD MORNING LITTLE SCHOOLGIRL (Don & Bob) / NEW MINGLEWOOD BLUES + SAMSON AND DELILAH (trad.) / JOHNNY B. GOODE (Chuck Berry) / NOT FADE AWAY (Buddy Holly) / ME AND BOBBY McGEE (Kris Kristofferson) / BIG BOSS MAN (Bo Diddley) / DANCING IN THE STREET (hit; Martha & The Vandellas) / STAGGER LEE (Lloyd Price) / LITTLE RED ROOSTER (Willie Dixon) / DEAR MR. FANTASY (Traffic) / WALKIN' BLUES (Robert Johnson) / NEXT TIME YOU SEE ME (Junior Parker) / etc. GARCIA covered; IT TAKES A LOT TO LAUGH + POSITIVELY 4TH STREET + KNOCKIN' ON HEAVEN'S DOOR (Bob Dylan) / LET'S SPEND THE NIGHT TOGETHER + WILD HORSES (Rolling Stones) / HE AIN'T GIVE YOU NONE (Van Morrison) / THAT'S ALL RIGHT MAMA (Arthur Crudup) / MY FUNNY VALENTINE / WHEN THE HUNTER GETS CAPTURED BY THE GAME (Smokey Robinson) / LET IT ROCK (Chuck Berry) / RUSSIAN LULLABY (Irving Berlin) / MIDNIGHT TOWN (Kahn-Hunter) / I SAW HER STANDING THERE (Beatles) / etc. • **Trivia:** An editec 'DARK STAR', was used as theme in the US 70's series of 'Twilight Zone'.

Album rating: THE GRATEFUL DEAD (*5) / ANTHEM OF THE SUN (*7) AOXOMOXOA (*8) / LIVE/DEAD (*7) / WORKINGMAN'S DEAD (*8) AMERICAN BEAUTY (*10) / GRATEFUL DEAD live double (*6) / EUROPE '7 (*6) / HISTORY OF THE GRATEFUL DEAD, VOL.1 (BEAR'S CHOICE) (*5) WAKE OF THE FLOOD (*5) / SKELETON'S FROM THE CLOSET: THE BES OF . . . compilation (*5) / GRATEFUL DEAD FROM THE MARS HOTEL (*5) BLUES FOR ALLAH (*5) / STEAL YOUR FACE (*4) / TERRAPIN STATION (*6) WHAT A LONG STRANGE TRIP IT'S BEEN compilation (*8) / SHAKEDOWN STREET (*4) / GO TO HEAVEN (*1) / RECKONING (*5) / DEAD SET (*5) / IN THE DARK (*7) / BUILT TO LAST (*4) / WITHOUT A NET (*4) / ONE FROM THE VAULT early concert (*5) / INFRARED ROSES concert (*4) / TWO FROM THE VAULT early concert (*5) / DICK'S PICK, VOL.1 early concert (*5) / DICK'S PICK, VOL.2 early concert (*5) / HUNDRED YEAR HALL early concert (*5) DICK'S PICK, VOL.3 early concert (*6) / DICK'S PICK, VOL.4 early concert (*8) THE VERY BEST OF THE GRATEFUL DEAD compilation (*8) / Jerry Garcia HOOTEROLL (*5) / GARCIA (*7) / LIVE AT THE KEYSTONE (*4) / GARCIA or 'Round' (*6) / OLD & IN THE WAY (*4) / REFLECTIONS (*5) / CATS UNDE THE STARS (*6) / RUN FOR THE ROSES (*6) / ALMOST ACOUSTIC (*6) JERRY GARCIA BAND (*6) / JERRY GARCIA & DAVID GRISMAN (*6) / NO FOR KIDS ONLY with David Grisman (*5) / HOW SWEET IT IS early gig (*5) GRATEFUL DAWG soundtrack w/ David Grisman (*7) / the Other Ones: ONL THE STRANGE REMAIN (*5)

JERRY GARCIA (b. JEROME JOHN GARCIA, 1 Aug'42) – vocals, lea guitar / **BOB WEIR** (b. ROBERT HALL, 6 Oct'47) – rhythm guitar / **RO 'PIGPEN' McKERNAN** (b. 8 Sep'45, San Bruno, Calif.) – keyboards, vocal mouth harp / **PHIL LESH** (b. PHILIP CHAPMAN, 15 Mar'40, Berkele Calif.) – bass / **BILL KREUTZMANN** (b. 7 Apr'46, Palo Alto, Calif.) – drum (DAN MORGAN left before recording)

not iss. Scorp

Jun 66. (7") *<003-201>* **DON'T EASE ME IN. / STEALIN'** [–] [ ]

Warners Warn

Feb 67. (7") *<7016>* **THE GOLDEN ROAD (TO UNLIMITED DEVOTION). / CREAM PUFF WAR** [–] [ ]

Dec 67. (lp; mono/stereo) *(<W/+S 1689>)* **THE GRATEFUL DEAD** [ ] Feb67 **73**

– The golden road (to unlimited devotion) / Cold rain and snow / Goo morning little schoolgirl / Beat it on down / Sitting on top of the world Cream puff war / Morning dew / New, new Minglewood blues / Viola Le blues. *(re-iss. Mar87 on 'Edsel'; ED 221) <US cd-iss. 1987; 2-1689> (cd-is Jul88 on 'Atlantic'; K 259302) <(cd-iss. Feb94; 7599 27167-2)> <(cd r mast.Mar03 on 'Rhino'+=; 8122 74398-2)>* – Alice D. millionaire / Oversea stomp (the Lindy) / Tastebud / Death don't have no mercy / Viola Le blues (edit) / Viola Lee blues (live).

— added **TOM CONSTANTEN** – keyboards / **MICKEY HART** (b.1950, Lon Island, N.Y.) – percussion and returning lyricist **ROBERT HUNTER**

Oct 68. (7") *(WB <7186>)* **BORN CROSS-EYED. / DARK STAR** [ ] [ ]

Nov 68. (lp) *(<WS 1749>)* **ANTHEM OF THE SUN** [ ] Aug 68 **87**

– That's it for other one:- Cryptical envelopment – Quadlibet for tend feet – The faster we go, the rounder we get – We leave the castle New potato caboose / Born cross-eyed / Alligator / Caution (do n stop on the tracks). *(re-iss. Jul71; K 46021) <US cd-iss. 1987; 2-174 (re-iss. Jul88 on 'WEA' lp/cd; K2 4602-1/2) <(re-iss. cd Feb94; 75 27173-2)> <(cd re-mast.Mar03 on 'Rhino'+=; 8122 74393-2)>* – Alligat (live) / Caution (do not stop on the tracks) (live) / Feedback (live) (untitled).

Oct 69. (lp) *(<WS 1790>)* **AOXOMOXOA** [ ] Jun 69 **73**

– St. Stephen / Dupree's diamond blues / Rosemary / Doin' the rag Mountains of the Moon / China cat sunflower / What's become of t baby / Cosmic Charlie. *(re-iss. Jul71; K 46027) ;re-iss. Jan77) <US cd-i 1987; 2-1790> (re-iss. Jun89 on 'WEA' c/cd; K4 46027/ K927128-2) <(cd re-i Feb94; 7599 27178-2)> <(cd re-mast.Mar03 on 'Rhino'+=; 8122 74394-2* – Clementine jam / Nobody's spoonful jam / The eleven jam / Cosm Charlie (live).

Oct 69. (7") *<7324>* **DUPREE'S DIAMOND BLUES. / COSMIC CHARLIE** [–] [ ]

Feb 70. (d-lp) *<2(WS 1830)>* **LIVE/DEAD (live in the studio)** [ ] Dec 69 **64**

– Dark star / St. Stephen / The eleven / Turn on your love light / Dea don't have no mercy / Feedback / And we bid you goodnight. *(re-iss. Jul7 K 66002) <US cd-iss. 1987; 2-1830> (cd-iss. Jun89 on 'WEA'; K927 181- <(cd re-mast.Mar03 on 'Rhino'; 8122 74395-2)>*

— **DAVID NELSON** – acoustic guitar; repl. CONSTANTEN / added gu **JOHN DAWSON** – guitar, vocals (on some)

above pairing also formed off-shoot band The NEW RIDERS OF THE PURPLE SAGE, who initially toured as support to DEAD, with GARCIA in their ranks.

Sep 70. (lp) *(<WS 1869>)* **WORKINGMAN'S DEAD** Jun 70 27
– Uncle John's band / High time / Dire wolf / New speedway boogie / Cumberland blues / Black Peter / Easy wind / Casey Jones. *(re-iss. Jul71; K 46049) <US cd-iss. 1987; 2-1889> (re-iss. 1988 lp/c) (cd-iss. Jun89 on 'WEA'; K2 46049) <(cd re-mast.Mar03 on 'Rhino'+=; 8122 74396-2)>* – New speedway boogie (alt.) / Dire wolf (live) / Black Peter (live) / Easy wind (live) / Cumberland blues (live) / Mason's children (live) / Uncle John's band (live).

Aug 70. (7") *(WB <7410>)* **UNCLE JOHN'S BAND. / NEW SPEEDWAY BOOGIE** 69

— added guest **DAVID TORBERT** – bass (1)

Dec 70. (lp) *(<WS 1893>)* **AMERICAN BEAUTY** 30
– Box of rain / Friend of the Devil / Sugar magnolia / Operator / Candyman / Ripple / Brokedown palace / Till the morning comes / Attics of my life / Truckin'. *(re-iss. Jul71; K 46074) ;re-iss. Jan77) <US cd-iss. 1987; 2-1893> (re-iss. Jun89 on 'WEA' c/cd; K2/K4 46074) <(cd re-mast.Mar03 on 'Rhino'+=; 8122 74397-2)>* – Truckin' (single version) / Friend of the DEvil (live) / Candyman (live) / Till the morning comes (live) / Attics of my life (live) / Truckin' (live).

Jan 71. (7") *<7464>* **TRUCKIN. / RIPPLE** – 64

— Now **GARCIA, WEIR, LESH, KREUTZMANN** and **'PIGPEN'** with new members **MERL SAUNDERS** – keyboards (repl. PIGPEN for a while when he was ill) all guests had departed, incl. HART and NELSON.

Oct 71. (d-lp) *(K 66009) <2WS 1935>* **GRATEFUL DEAD** (SKULL & ROSES) (live) 25
– Bertha / Mama tried / Big railroad blues / Playing in the band / The other one / Me & my uncle / Big boss man / Me & Bobby McGhee / Johnny B. Goode / Wharf rat / Not fade away / Goin' down road feeling bad. *<US cd-iss. 1987; 2-1935> (cd-iss. 1988; 927 192-2) <(cd re-iss. Feb03; 7599 27192-2)> <(cd re-mast.Mar03 on 'Rhino'+=; 8122 74392-2)>* – Oh, boy! / I'm a hog for you.

Jan 72. (7") **JOHNNY B. GOODE. / SO FINE (by 'Elvin Bishop')** –

— added on tour **KEITH GODCHAUX** (b.14 Jul'48) – keyboards (ex-DAVE MASON band) and **DONNA GODCHAUX** (b.22 Aug'47) – vocals (They both repl. SAUNDERS)

Dec 72. (t-lp) *(K 66019) <3WS 2668>* **EUROPE '72 (live)** Nov 72 24
– Cumberland blues / He's gone / One more Saturday night / Jack Straw / You win again / China cat sunflower / I know you rider / Brown-eyed woman / Hurts me too / Ramble on Rose / Sugar magnolia / Mr. Charlie / Tennessee Jed / The stranger (two souls in communion) *[re-mast.only]* / Truckin' / Epilogue / Prelude / Morning dew. *<(cd-iss. Nov94; 7599 27265-2)> <(cd re-mast.Mar03 on 'Rhino'+=; 8122 74399-2)>* – Looks like rain / Good lovin' / Caution (do not stop on the tracks) / Who do you love? / Caution (do not stop on the tracks) (alt.) / Good lovin' (alt.).

Dec 72. (7") *<7667>* **SUGAR MAGNOLIA (live). / MR. CHARLIE (live)** – 91

— Now just basic 4 of **GARCIA, WEIR, LESH, KREUTZMANN** and both **GODCHAUX'S.** ('PIGPEN' sadly died 8 May'73 after a long and threatening bout of illness) note that ROBERT HUNTER was still writing their lyrics, next 2 albums also included ten or more session people.

Warners / Grateful Dead

Jul 73. (lp/c) *(K/K4 49301) <GD 01>* **WAKE OF THE FLOOD** Oct 73 18
– Mississippi half-step uptown toodeloo / Let me sing your blues away / Row Jimmy / Stella blue / Here comes sunshine / Eyes of the world / Weather Report suite (part 1; Prelude – part 2; Let it grow). *(re-iss. Jan76 on 'United Artists'; UAS 29903) (<re-iss. Apr89 on 'Grateful Dead' lp/c/cd; GDV/GDTCGDCD 4002>) (pic-cd Feb90; GDPD 4002) <(cd re-iss. Oct03 on 'Falcon'; UN 3862)>*

Nov 73. (7") *(K 19301) <01>* **LET ME SING YOUR BLUES AWAY. / HERE COMES SUNSHINE**

Jan 74. (7") *<02>* **EYES OF THE WORLD. / WEATHER REPORT SUITE (part 1; PRELUDE)** –

Jul 74. (lp/c) *(K/K4 59302) <GD 102>* **FROM THE MARS HOTEL** 47 16
– Scarlet begonias / Ship of fools / Pride of Cucamonga / Loose Lucy / U.S. blues / Unbroken chain / China doll / Money money. *(re-iss. Jan76 on 'United Artists'; UAS 29904) <US cd-iss. Dec85 on 'Mobile Fidelity'; MFCD 830> (re-iss. Mar89 on 'Grateful Dead' lp/c/cd; GDV/GDTCGDCD 4007) (pic-cd Feb90; GDPD 4007)*

Aug 74. (7") *(UP 36030) <03>* **U.S. BLUES. / LOOSE LUCY**

— added the returning **MICKEY HART** – percussion

U.A. / Grateful Dead

Oct 75. (lp) *(UAS 29895) <LA 494>* **BLUES FOR ALLAH** 45 Sep75 12
– Help on the way / Slipknot / Franklin's tower / King Solomon's marbles / Stronger than dirt or milkin' the turkey / The music never stopped / Crazy fingers / Sage & spirit / Blues for Allah / Sand castles & glass camels / Unusual occurances in the desert. *(<re-iss. Mar89 on 'Grateful Dead' lp/c/cd; GDV/GDTCGDCD 4001>) (pic-cd Feb90; GDPD 4001)*

Oct 75. (7") *<718>* **THE MUSIC NEVER STOPPED. / HELP IS ON THE WAY** – 81

Jun 76. (d-lp) *(UAD 60131-2) <LA 620>* **STEAL YOUR FACE (live)** 42 56
– The promised land / Cold rain and snow / Around and around / Stella blue / Mississippi half-step uptown toodeloo / Ship of fools / Beat it down the line / Big river / Black-throated wind / U.S. blues / El Paso / Sugaree / It must have been the roses / Casey Jones. *(re-iss. Mar89 on 'Grateful Dead' lp/c/cd; GDV2/GDTCGDCD2 4006) (pic-cd Feb90; GDPD2 4006)*

1976. (7") *<762>* **FRANKLIN'S TOWER. / HELP IS ON THE WAY** –

Arista / Arista

Aug 77. (lp/c) *(SPART/TC-ARTY 1016) <AL 7001>* **TERRAPIN STATION** 28
– Estimated prophet / Samson and Delilah / Passenger / Dancing in the street / Sunrise / Terrapin station. *(re-iss. 1983; SPARTY 1016) (re-iss. Jan87 lp/c; 201/401 190) <US cd-iss. 1986; ARCD 8065> (cd-iss. Nov90; 260175)*

Oct 77. (12")<7"> *(DEAD 1) <0276>* **DANCING IN THE STREETS. / TERRAPIN STATION**

Feb 78. (7") *<0291>* **PASSENGER. / TERRAPIN STATION** –

Dec 78. (lp/c) *(ARTY/TC-ART 159) <AB 4198>* **SHAKEDOWN STREET** 41
– Good lovin' / France / Shakedown street / Serangetti / Fire on the mountain / I need a miracle / From the heart of me / Stagger Lee / New, new Minglewood blues / If I had the world to give. *<US cd-iss. 1986; ARCD 4198> (cd-iss. Jun91; 251 133)*

Dec 78. (7") *(ARIST 236) <0383>* **GOOD LOVIN'. / STAGGER LEE**

Mar 79. (7") *<0410>* **SHAKEDOWN STREET. / FRANCE** –

— **BRENT MYDLAND** (b.1953, Munich, Germany) – keyboards repl. both GODCHAUX'S (KEITH was killed in car crash 23 Jul'80)

May 80. (lp/c) *(SPART/TCART 1115) <AL 9508>* **GO TO HEAVEN** 23
– Far from home / Althea / Feel like a stranger / Alabama getaway / Don't ease me in / Easy to love you / Lost sailor / Saint of circumstance. *<US cd-iss. 1986; ARCD 9508>*

Jun 80. (7") *<0519>* **ALABAMA GETAWAY. / FAR FROM ME** – 68

Jan 81. (7") *<0546>* **DON'T EASE ME IN. / FAR FROM ME** –

Apr 81. (d-lp) *(DARTY 9) <A2L 8604>* **RECKONING (live)** (all line-ups) 43
– Dire wolf / The race is on / Oh babe it ain't no lie / It must have been the roses / Dark hollow / China doll / Been all around the world / Monkey and the engineer / Jack-a-roe / Deep Elam blues / Cassidy / To lay me down / Rosalie McFall / On the road again / Bird song / Ripple.

1981. (7") *<116>* **ALABAMA GETAWAY. / SHAKEDOWN STREET** –

Sep 81. (d-lp) *(DARTY 11) <A2L 8606>* **DEAD SET (live)** 29
– Samson and Delilah / Friend of the Devil / New, new Minglewood blues / Deal / Candyman / Little red rooster / Loser / Passenger / Feel like a stranger / Franklin's tower / Fire on the mountain / Rhythm devils / Greatest story ever told / Brokedown palace. *<US cd-iss. 1986; ARCD 8112>*

Sep 87. (7"/12") <cd-s/7",7"grey> *(RIS/+T 35) <ASCD+/9606>* **TOUCH OF GREY. / MY BROTHER ESAU** Jul87 9

Oct 87. (lp/c/cd) *(208/408/258 564) <AL/AC/ARCD 8452>* **IN THE DARK** 57 Jul87 6
– Touch of grey / Hell in a bucket / When push comes to shove / West L.A. fadeaway / Tons of steel / Throwing stones / Black muddy river. *(re-iss. Nov90 cd/lp; 261/211 145)*

Nov 87. (cd-s/7") *<ASCD+/9643>* **THROWING STONES. / WHEN PUSH COMES TO SHOVE** –

— Late '87, they recorded live album 'DYLAN AND THE DEAD' with BOB DYLAN, which was released early 1989, and hit US No.37.

Nov 89. (lp/c/cd) *(210/410/260 326)* *<AL/AC/ARCD 875>* **BUILT TO LAST** [ ] [27]
– Foolish heart / Just a little light / Built to last / Blow away / Standing on the Moon / Victim or the crime / We can run / Picasso moon / I will take you home.

Nov 89. (cd-s/7") *<ASCD+/9899>* **FOOLISH HEART. / WE CAN RUN** [–] [ ]

Oct 90. (d-cd/t-lp) *(303/353 935)* *<ACD2 8634>* **WITHOUT A NET (live)** [ ] [43]
– Feel like a stranger / Mississippi half-step uptown toodeloo / Walkin' blues / Althea / Cassidy / Let it grow / China cat sunflower – I know you rider / Looks like rain / Eyes of the world / Victim or the crime / Help on the way – Slipknot! – Franklin's tower / Bird song / One more Saturday night / Dear Mr. Fantasy.

—— BRETT MYDLAND died 26 Jul'90 of a drug overdose. Replaced by **VINCE WELNICK** (b.22 Feb'52, Phoenix, Arizona) – keyboards (ex-TUBES, ex-TODD RUNDGREN)

– compilations etc. –

on 'Grateful Dead' records unless mentioned otherwise

Apr 72. (lp) *Polydor; (2310 171) / Sunflower; <SNF 5004>* **HISTORIC DEAD** (rare '66) [ ] Jun71 [ ]

Apr 72. (lp) *Polydor; (2310 172) / Sunflower; <SUN 5001>* **VINTAGE DEAD (live '66)** [ ] Oct70 [ ]

1972. (lp) *Pride; <PRD 0016>* **THE HISTORY OF GRATEFUL DEAD** [–] [ ]

Sep 73. (lp) *Warners; (K 46246) <BS 2721>* **HISTORY OF THE DEAD – BEAR'S CHOICE (live rarities)** [ ] Jul73 [60]
– Katie Mae / Dark hollow / I've been all around the world / Wake up little Susie / Black Peter / Smokestack lightnin' / Hard to handle. *<US cd-iss. 1988; 2721-2> <(cd re-iss. Jun00; 7599 27274-2)> <(cd re-mast.Mar03 on 'Rhino'+=; 8122 74400-2)>* – Good lovin' / Big boss man / Smokestack lightnin' (version 2) / Sitting on top of the world.

Mar 74. (lp) *Warners; (K 56024) <BS 2674>* **SKELETONS FROM THE CLOSET** [ ] [75]
(re-iss. Oct86 on 'Thunderbolt' lp/c/cd; THBL/THBCCDTB 018) <US cd-iss. 1988; 2764-2>

Apr 74. (7") *Warners; <WB 21988>* **SUGAR MAGNOLIA. / MR. CHARLIE** [–] [ ]

—— All below on 'Grateful Dead' US records, unless otherwise mentioned.

Feb 77. (d-lp) *United Artists; (UDM 103-4)* **WAKE OF THE FLOOD / FROM MARS HOTEL** [ ] [ ]

Feb 78. (d-lp) *Warners; (K 66073)* **WHAT A LONG STRANGE TRIP IT'S BEEN: THE BEST OF GRATEFUL DEAD** [ ] Nov 77 [ ]
– New, new Minglewood blues / Cosmic Charlie / Truckin' / Black Peter / Born cross-eyed / Ripple / Doin' that rag / Dark star / High time / New speedway boogie / St. Stephen / Jack Straw / Me & my uncle / Tennessee Jed / Cumberland blues / Playing in the band / Brown-eyed woman / Ramble on Rose. *<US cd-iss. 1989; 3091-2>*

1987. (6xcd-box) *Arista; <ACD6 8530>* **DEAD ZONE: THE GRATEFUL DEAD CD COLLECTION 1977-1987** [–] [ ]
– (Arista albums from 77-87)

1987. (cd) *Pair; <ARP2 1053>* **FOR THE FAITHFUL** [–] [ ]

Jun 91. (d-cd/d-c/t-lp) *<(GDCD2/GDTC2/GDV2 4015)>* **ONE FROM THE VAULT** (live 13 Aug'75, Great American Music Hall, San Francisco) [ ] May91 [ ]
– (introduction) / Help on the way / Franklin's tower / Music never stopped / It must have been the roses / Eyes of the world – drums / King Solomon's marbles / Around and around / Sugaree / Big river / Crazy fingers – drums / The other one / Sage and spirit / Goin' down the road feeling bad / U.S. blues / Blues for Allah.

Jan 92. (cd) *<(GDCD 4016)>* **INFRARED ROSES (live)** [ ] [ ]
– Crowd sculpture / Parallelogram / Little Nemo in Lightland / Riverside rhapsody / Post-modern highrise table top stomp / Infrared roses / Silver apples of the Moon / Speaking in swords / Magnesium night light / Sparrow hawk row / River of nine sorrows / Apollo at the Ritz.

Aug 92. (d-cd/d-lp) *<(GDCD2/GDV2 4018)>* **TWO FROM THE VAULT** (live 23/24 Aug'68, Shrine Auditorium, L.A.) [ ] May92 [ ]
– Good morning little schoolgirl / Dark star / St. Stephen / The eleven / Death don't have no mercy / The other one / New potato caboose / Turn on your lovelight / Morning dew.

Dec 93. (d-cd) *<(GDCD 4019)>* **DICK'S PICK: VOLUME ONE (live Tampa, Florida 12/19/73)** [ ] [ ]
– Here comes sunshine / Big river / Mississippi half-step uptown toodeloo / Weather report suite (Prelude – part 1, Let it grow – part 2) / Big railroad blues / Playing in the band / He's gone / Truckin' / Nobody's fault but mine / Jam / The other one / Jam / Stella blue / Around and around.

Jan 94. (cd/c) *Dare International; (DIL CD/C 1001)* **RISEN FROM THE VAULTS** [ ] [ ]

Jun 95. (cd) *<(GDCD 4020)>* **DICK'S PICKS: VOLUME TWO** (live Columbus, Ohio 10/3/71) [ ] [ ]
– Dark star / Jam / Sugar magnolia / St. Stephen / Not fade away / Going down the road feeling bad / Not fade away.

Oct 95. (d-cd/d-c) *<(GD CD/MC 4021)>* **HUNDRED YEAR HALL** (live 26th April 1972, Jahrhundert Halle, Frankfurt) [ ] [26]
– Bertha / Me & my uncle / The next time you see me / China cat sunflower / I know you rider / Jack Straw / Big railroad blues / Playing in the band / Turn on your love light / Going down the road feeling bad / One more Saturday night / Truckin' / Cryptical envelopment / Comes a time / Sugar magnolia.

Nov 95. (d-cd) *<(GDCD2 4022)>* **DICK'S PICKS: VOLUME THREE** (live Pembroke Pines, Florida, 5/22/77) [ ] [ ]

Oct 96. (d-cd/d-c) *Arista; <(07822 18934-2/-4)>* **THE ARISTA YEARS 1977-95** [ ] [95]

Dec 96. (t-cd) *<(GRCD3 4023)>* **DICK'S PICK: VOLUME FOUR** (live February 13-14 1970) [ ] [ ]

Jan 97. (t-cd) *<(GDCD3 4024)>* **DOZIN' AT THE KNICK** [ ] Nov96 [74]

Dec 96. (t-cd) *<(GDCD3 4025)>* **DICK'S PICKS: VOLUME FIVE** (live Oakland Auditorium Arena 12/26/79) [ ] [ ]

Jan 97. (t-cd) *<(GDCD3 4026)>* **DICK'S PICKS: VOLUME SIX** (live Hartford Civic Center 10/04/83) [ ] [ ]

Apr 97. (t-cd) *<(GDCD3 4027)>* **DICK'S PICKS: VOLUME SEVEN** (live Alexandra Palace 9-11 Sep'74) [ ] [ ]

May 97. (cd) *Metro; (OTR 1100024)* **NIGHT OF THE GRATEFUL DEAD** [ ] [–]

Jun 97. (d-cd) *<(GDCD2 4052)>* **FALLOUT FROM THE PHIL ZONE** [ ] [83]

Jun 97. (d-cd; with JOHN OSWALD) *Swell Artifact; (SA 1969)* **GRAYFOLDED** [ ] [ ]
(re-iss. Aug99 on 'Snapper'; SMDCD 215)

Jun 97. (cd; MICKEY & THE HEARTBEATS) *Anthology; (ANT 2912)* **HARTBITS VOL.2** [ ] [ ]

Jul 97. (t-cd) *<GDCD3 4028>* **DICK'S PICK: VOLUME EIGHT** (live Harpur College 5/02/70) [–] [ ]

Oct 97. (t-cd) *<GDCD3 4029>* **DICK'S PICKS: VOLUME NINE** (live Madison Square Garden September 16, 1990) [ ] [ ]

Nov 97. (d-cd) *<GDCD2 4054>* **FILLMORE EAST 2-11-69 (live)** [–] [77]

Jun 98. (t-cd) *<ARI1 4031>* **DICK'S PICKS: VOLUME ELEVEN** (live August 27, 1972 Oregon & Jersey City) [–] [ ]

Mar 99. (t-cd) *<ARI1 4033>* **DICK'S PICKS: VOLUME THIRTEEN** (live 6/5/81 Nassau Coliseum, Long Island, NY) [–] [ ]
(UK-iss.May02; same as US)

Jun 99. (q-cd) *<ARI1 4034>* **DICK'S PICKS: VOLUME FOURTEEN** (live Boston Music Hall 11/30/73 & 12/2/73) [–] [ ]
(UK-iss.May02; same as US)

Aug 99. (t-cd) *<ARI1 4035>* **DICK'S PICKS: VOLUME FIFTEEN** (live English Town New Jersey 9/3/77) [–] [ ]
(UK-iss.May02; same as US)

Nov 99. (5xcd-box) *<14066>* **SO MANY ROADS (1965-1995) (live)** [–] [ ]

Dec 99. (pic-lp) *Ugo; (UGO 2)* **THE DEAD LIVE IN CONCERT (live)** [ ] [–]

Mar 00. (t-cd) *<ARI1 4036>* **DICK'S PICKS: VOLUME SIXTEEN** (live Fillmore Auditorium 11/8/69) [–] [ ]
(UK-iss.May02; same as US)

May 00. (t-cd) *<ARI1 4037>* **DICK'S PICKS: VOLUME SEVENTEEN** (live Boston Garden 9/25/91) [–] [ ]
(UK-iss.May02; same as US)

Jun 00. (t-cd) *<ARI1 4038>* **DICK'S PICKS: VOLUME EIGHTEEN** (live Dane County Coliseum 3/2/78 + University of North Iowa 5/2/78) [–] [ ]
(UK-iss.May02; same as US)

Jul 00. (t-cd) *<ARI1 4030>* **DICK'S PICKS: VOLUME TEN** (live 1977 San Francisco) [–] [ ]

Jul 00. (t-cd) *<ARI1 4032>* **DICK'S PICKS: VOLUME TWELVE** (live 1974 Providence & Boston) [–] [ ]

Oct 00. (t-cd) *<ARI1 4039>* **DICK'S PICKS: VOLUME NINETEEN** (live Fairgrounds Arena, Oklahoma City 10/19/73) [–] [ ]

Oct 00. (4xcd-box) *<14075>* **LADIES AND GENTLEMEN . . . FILLMORE EAST: NEW YORK CITY: APRIL 1971** [–] [ ]

Jan 01. (4xcd) *<ARI1 4040>* **DICK'S PICKS: VOLUME TWENTY** (live September 1976) [–] [ ]

Feb 01. (t-cd) *<ARI1 4041>* **DICK'S PICKS: VOLUME TWENTY-ONE** (live Richmond Coliseum 11/1/85 & 9/2/80 Community War Memorial, Rochester, NY) [–] [ ]

Jul 01. (d-cd) *<ARI1 4042>* **DICK'S PICKS: VOLUME TWENTY-TWO** (live 23/24 February 1968, Kings Beach, Lake Tahoe) [–] [ ]

Sep 01. (d-cd) *ARI1 4081>* **NIGHTFALL OF DIAMONDS** (live October 10, 1989) [–] [ ]

Oct 01. (t-cd) *<ARI1 4043>* **DICK'S PICKS: VOLUME TWENTY-THREE** (live September 17, 1972, Baltimore Civic Center) [–] [ ]

Oct 01. (12xcd-box) *Rhino; <(8122 74401-2)>* **THE GOLDEN ROAD (1965-1973)** [ ] [ ]

Feb 02. (d-cd) *<ARI1 4044>* **DICK'S PICKS: VOLUME TWENTY-FOUR** (live Bay Area 1974) [–] [ ]

Mar 02. (cd) *<ARI1 4069>* **POSTCARDS OF THE HANGING: . . .PERFORM THE SONGS OF BOB DYLAN** [–] [ ]

ul 02. (t-cd) *<ARI1 4045>* **DICK'S PICKS 25** (live 1978 New Haven, CT, May 10 – Springfield, MA, May 11) [–] [ ]

ul 02. (4xcd-box) *<(ARI1 4084)>* **STEPPIN' OUT WITH THE GRATEFUL DEAD** (live) [ ] [ ]

Oct 02. (t-cd) *<ARI1 4046>* **DICK'S PICKS: TWENTY-SIX** (live Electric Theater, Chicago, IL, April 26, 1969 & Labor Temple, Minneapolis, MN, April 27, 1969) [–] [ ]

Nov 02. (d-cd) *<(ARI1 4085)>* **GO TO NASSAU (live May 15-16, 1980)** [ ] Oct02 [ ]

an 03. (t-cd) *<ARI1 4047>* **DICK'S PICKS: VOLUME TWENTY-SEVEN** (live December 16, 1992, Oakland Coliseum Arena) [–] [ ]

Mar 03. (d-cd) *Rhino; <(8122 74391-2)>* **BIRTH OF THE DEAD** [ ] [ ]

Apr 03. (t-cd) *<ARI1 4048>* **DICK'S PICKS 28** (live Salt Palace, Salt Lake City, UT, February 28, 1973 & Lincoln, NE, February 28, 1973) [–] [ ]

ul 03. (6xcd-box) *<ARI1 4049>* **DICK'S PICKS 29** (live spring & summer 1977) [–] [ ]

ep 03. (cd) *Rhino; <(8122 73899-2)>* **THE VERY BEST OF THE GRATEFUL DEAD** [ ] [69]
– Truckin' / Touch of grey / Sugar magnolia / Casey Jones / Uncle John's band / Friend of the Devil / Franklin's tower / Estimated prophet / Eyes of the world / Box of rain / U.S. blues / The golden road (to unlimited devotion) / One more Saturday night (live) / Fire on the mountain / The music never stopped / Hell in a bucket / Ripple.

Oct 03. (t-cd) *<ARI1 4050>* **DICK'S PICKS 30** (live Academy Of Music, New York City, March 25 & 26, 1972) [–] [ ]

May 04. (3xcd-box) *Rhino; <(8122 78921-2)>* **ROCKIN' THE RHEIN WITH THE GRATESFUL DEAD** (live) [ ] [75]

ul 05. (d-cd) *Rhino; <(8122 73192-2)>* **TRUCKIN' UP TO BUFFALO, JULY 4th 1989** (live) [ ] [ ]

JERRY GARCIA

solo – used session men from the DEAD plus others

C.B.S. Douglas

ul 71. (lp; by HOWARD WALES & JERRY GARCIA) *(69013)* *<KZ 30859>* **HOOTEROLL?** [ ] [ ]
– South side strut / A trip to what next / Up from the desert / DC-502 / One a.m. approach / Uncle Martin's / Da bird song. *(cd-iss. Oct87 & Jul92 on 'Rykodisc'; <RCD 10052>) <US cd+=>* – Morning in Marin / Evening in Marin.

an 72. (7"; by HOWARD WALES & JERRY GARCIA) *<7-6501>* **SOUTH SIDE STRUT. / UNCLE MARTIN'S** [–] [ ]

Warners Warners

an 72. (lp) *(K 46139) <BS 2582>* **GARCIA** (aka 'The Wheel') [ ] [35]
– Deal / Bird song / Sugaree / Loser / Late for supper / Spiderdawg / Eep hour / To lay me down / An odd little place / The wheel. *(<re-iss. Feb89 as 'THE WHEEL' on 'Grateful Dead' lp/c/cd; GDV/GDTC/<GDCD 4003>)*

973. (7") *<7551>* **THE WHEEL. / DEAL** [–] [ ]

973. (7") *<7569>* **SUGAREE. / EEP HOUR** [–] [ ]

not iss. Fantasy

Dec 73. (d-lp) *<F 79002>* **LIVE AT THE KEYSTONE (live with MERLE SAUNDERS)** [–] [ ]
– Let's spend the night together / It takes a lot to laugh, it takes a train to cry / The harder they come / That's all right mama / He ain't give you none / Positively 4th street / My funny valentine / etc.

Round Round

Jun 74. (lp) *(RX 59301) <RX 102>* **GARCIA** (aka 'Compliments Of Garcia') [ ] [49]
– Let it rock / When the hunter gets captured by the game / That's what love will make us do / Russian lullabye / Turn on the bright lights / He ain't give you none / What goes around / Let's spend the night together / Mississippi moon / Midnight town. *(<re-iss. Apr89 as 'COMPLIMENTS OF GARCIA' on 'Grateful Dead' lp/c/cd; GDV/GDC/<GDCD 4011>)*

Jul 74. (7") *<4504>* **LET IT ROCK. / MIDNIGHT TOWN** [–] [ ]

— **GARCIA, DAVID GRISMAN, PETER ROWAN, JOHN KAHN, VASSAR CLEMENTS**

Mar 75. (lp; by OLD & IN THE WAY) *<RX 103>* **OLD AND IN THE WAY** [–] [ ]
– Pig in a pen / Midnight moonlight / Old and in the way / Knockin' on your door / The hobo song / Panama red / Wild horses / Kissimmee kid / White dove / Land of the Navajo. *(UK-iss.Feb85 on 'Sugarhill' lp/cd; SH/+CD 3746) <US cd-iss. 1987 on 'Rykodisc'; RCD 1009> (re-iss. cd 1990 on 'Grateful Dead'; GDCD 4014)*

U.A. Round

Feb 76. (lp) *(UAG 29921) <RX 107>* **REFLECTIONS** [ ] [42]
– Might as well / Mission in the rain / They love each other / I'll take a melody / It must have been the roses / Tore up over you / Catfish John / Comes a time. *(re-iss. Feb89 on 'Grateful Dead' lp/cd; GDV/GDTC/GDCD 4008)*

Arista Arista

Apr 78. (lp; by JERRY GARCIA BAND) *(SPART 1053) <AB 4160>* **CATS UNDER THE STARS** [ ] [ ]
– Rubin and Cherise / Love in the afternoon / Palm Sunday / Cats under the stars / Rhapsody in red / Rain / Down home / Gomorrah. *<US cd-iss. 1988; ARCD 8535>*

Nov 82. (lp) *(1204973) <AL 9603>* **RUN FOR THE ROSES** [ ] [ ]
– Run for the roses / I saw her standing there / Without love / Midnight getaway / Leave the little girl alone / Valerie / Knockin' on Heaven's door. *<US cd-iss. 1986; ARCD 8557>*

not iss. Fantasy

1988. (lp) *<MPF 4533>* **KEYSTONE ENCORES VOLUME 1** [–] [ ]

1988. (cd) *<FCD 7701-2>* **LIVE AT KEYSTONE VOLUME 1** [–] [ ]

1988. (lp) *<MPF 4534>* **KEYSTONE ENCORES VOLUME 2** [–] [ ]

1988. (cd) *<FCD 7702-2>* **LIVE AT KEYSTONE VOLUME 2** [–] [ ]

1988. (cd) *<FCD 7703-2>* **KEYSTONE ENCORES** (compilation of above) [–] [ ]
(above credited with MERLE SAUNDERS; lp/cd's with diff.titles)

Grateful Dead Grateful Dead

Mar 89. (lp/c/cd; as JERRY GARCIA ACOUSTIC BAND) *(GDV/GDC/GDCD 4005)* **ALMOST ACOUSTIC** [ ] [ ]
– Swing low, sweet chariot / Deep Elam blues / Blue yodel £9 (standing on the corner) / Spike driver blues / I've been all around this world / I'm here to get my baby out of jail / I'm troubled / Oh, the wind and the rain / The girl at the Crossroads bar / Oh babe it ain't no lie / Casey Jones / Diamond Joe / Gone home / Ripple.

— with **JOHN KAHN** – bass / **DAVID KEMPER** – drums / **MARVIN SEALS** – keyboards / and backing vocalists **JACKIE LA BRANCH** and **GLORIA JONES**

Arista Arista

Sep 91. (d-cd) *(354284) <18690-2>* **JERRY GARCIA BAND (live)** [ ] [97]
– The way you do the things you do / Waiting for a miracle / Simple twist of fate / Get out of my life / My sister and brothers / I shall be released / Dear Prudence / Deal / Stop that train / Senor (tales of Yankee power) / Evangeline / The night they drove old Dixie down / Don't let go / That lucky old Sun / Tangled up in blue.

not iss. Acoustic Disc

1993. (cd; by DAVID GRISMAN / JERRY GARCIA) *<ACD-9>* **NOT FOR KIDS ONLY** [–] [ ]

Apr 97. (cd; JERRY GARCIA & DAVID GRISMAN) *<(ACD-21)>* **SHADY GROVE** [ ] [ ]

Grateful Dead | Grateful Dead

May 97. (cd; JERRY GARCIA BAND) <*(GDCD 4051)*> **HOW SWEET IT IS** — Apr97 81

Acoustic Disc | Acoustic Disc

Sep 01. (cd; by JERRY GARCIA & DAVID GRISMAN) <*(ACD 46)*> **GRATEFUL DAWG** (soundtrack with Various others)
– Intro / Grateful dawg (live) / Wayfaring stranger (BILL MONROE) / Sweet sunny south / Old & In The Way intro (PETER ROWAN) / Pig in a pen (OLD & IN THE WAY) / Dawg's waltz / Sitting here in limbo / Off to sea once more (EWAN MacCOLL) / Off to sea once more / Jenny Jenkins / Arabia / The thrill is gone / Friend of the Devil / Grateful dawg (studio).

David GRAY

Born: 13 Jun'68, Sale, Manchester, England. As a young boy of nine, GRAY moved to Solva (in Wales) with his family where he found the joys of guitar playing while taking in the local punk and folk scene. In 1992 (through manager/A&R man Rob Holden), he signed to Virgin offshoot, 'Hut' and issued his debut set 'A CENTURY ENDS' (1993), which brilliantly displayed his tender and sparse songwriting skills. 'FLESH' (1994) appeared one year later, by now, GRAY had made a promising name for himself, attracting a huge cult following around Britain and Europe. The aforementioned album was not bad for somebody who was still learning his trade, comparisons to DYLAN, EDDIE VEDDER and MIKE SCOTT were bandied about like confetti at a wedding. The acoustic guitars, bouncing pedal steel and occasional piano made stand out tracks 'WHAT ARE YOU NOW', 'FALLING FREE' and 'NEW HORIZONS' levitate above some recent attempts at melancholic music, proving GRAY to be one of Britain's best kept secrets and filing him along with assets THOM YORKE and RICHARD ASHCROFT. 'SELL, SELL, SELL' (1996) was perhaps too proverbial for its own good and thus it didn't gain enough exposure to hit the shops in the UK. Nevertheless, it still received some airplay from Radio One's Steve Lamaque and went on to sustain GRAY's reputation in the alt-music world. It was 1999's 'WHITE LADDER' (on new imprint 'iht' through 'eastwest') which caught the attention of music critics and audiences alike. A fine album in every sense, GRAY took us into the underworld of his soul . . . and deeper, with tracks 'SAIL AWAY' and Soft Cell's 'SAY HELLO WAVE GOODBYE' bringing something delicate and strangely human to the work. Easily the highlight from the set was 'BABYLON', a chart flop first time around although album opener 'PLEASE FORGIVE ME' slightly compensated for this, clocking in at No.72. Aaah! what a difference a year can make. Now signed to 'east west', the single 'BABYLON' was re-issued to a wider audience and after massive playlisting it finally peaked at No.5. A resurrected 'WHITE LADDER' also climbed the charts post-millennium, rising to No.1 a whole year later. A newcomer of sorts (tell that to the struggling 30-something troubadour!), GRAY proceeded to have three further hits during 2001, 'PLEASE FORGIVE ME', 'THIS YEARS LOVE' and 'SAIL AWAY'. The tender singer/songwriter returned in 2002 to issue 'A NEW DAY AT MIDNIGHT', an altogether more thoughtful and intimate set than 'WHITE LADDER'. It included the soaring piano lament 'SEE YOU ON THE OTHER SIDE', a deep but nevertheless uplifting feel through GRAY's psyche. Another surefire hit with fans was the song 'BE MINE', a slight hark back to GRAY's earlier days. But it was the bitterly bitter-sweet sound of his piano on the frosty ballad 'DECEMBER' which set him apart from many copyists. UK chart-topper 'LIFE IN SLOW MOTION' (2005) – featuring the hits 'THE ONE I LOVE' and talismanic 'HOSPITAL FOOD' – didn't bring much extra colour to GRAY's signature sound, a sound which had already spawned the equally pedestrian Daniel Blunt and James Powter (? or is it vice versa, and who really cares?).

Album rating: A CENTURY ENDS (*6) / FLESH (*6) / SELL, SELL, SELL (*6) / WHITE LADDER (*9) / LOST SONGS 95-98 collection (*6) / THE EP'S 1992-1994 ALBUM collection (*5) / A NEW DAY AT MIDNIGHT (*7) / LIFE IN SLOW MOTION (*6)

DAVID GRAY – vocals, guitar, keyboards / with **NEILL MacCOLL** – guitar, mandolin, vocals / **ROBIN MILLAR** – guitar / **"FAMOUS DAVE" ANDERSON** – keyboards / **STEVE SIDELNYK** – programming

Hut | Caroline

Nov 92. (12"/cd-s) *(HUT/+CD 23)* **BIRDS WITHOUT WINGS. / L'S SONG / THE LIGHT** — –

Mar 93. (12"/cd-s) *(HUT/+CD 27)* **SHINE. / BRICK WALLS / THE RICE** — –

Apr 93. (cd/c/lp) *(CDHUT/HUTMC/HUTLP 9)* <*CAROL 1739*> **A CENTURY ENDS** — Nov93
– Shine / A century ends / Debauchery / Let the truth sting / Gathering dust / Wisdom / Lead me upstairs / Living room / Birds without wings / It's all over. *(cd re-iss. Jul01; CDHUTX 9)*

Jul 93. (12"/cd-s) *(HUT/+CD 32)* **WISDOM. / LOVERS / 4AM** — –

— with **MacCOLL** plus **ANDY METCALFE** – hammond organ / **SIMON EDWARDS + DAVID NOLTE** – bass / **ROY DODS** – drums / **CLUNE** – drums, vocals, keyboards, bass, co-writer

Hut | not iss.

Sep 94. (cd/c) *(CDHUT/HUTMC 17)* **FLESH** — –
– What are you? / The light / Coming down / Falling free / Mystery of love / Lullaby / New horizons / Loves old song / Flesh. <*US cd-iss. Jul0? on 'Vernon Yard'; 39770*> *(cd re-iss. Jul01; CDHUTX 17)*

— now with different session people incl. **CLUNE + TIM BRADSHAW**

E.M.I. | not iss.

Apr 96. (cd) *(7243 8 37357)* **SELL, SELL, SELL** — – Europe –
– Faster, sooner, now / Late night radio / Sell, sell, sell / Hold on to nothing / Everytime / Magdalena / Smile / Only the lonely / What am I doing wrong? / Gutters full of rain / Forever is tomorrow is today / Folk song. *(UK-iss.Jul00; CDEMC 3755)* <*US-iss.Sep00 on 'Nettwerk'*>

— GRAY with **(Mc)CLUNE** + 3rd p/t co-writer/producer, **POLSON**

Iht | A.T.O.

Mar 99. (cd) *(ihtcd 001)* **WHITE LADDER** — –
– Please forgive me / Babylon / My oh my / We're not right / Nightblindness / Silver lining / White ladder / This years love / Sail away / Say hello wave goodbye.

Mar 99. (cd-s) *(ihtcds 001)* **THIS YEARS LOVE / NIGHTBLINDNESS / OVER MY HEAD** — –

Jul 99. (cd-s) *(ihtcds 002)* **BABYLON / LEAD ME UPSTAIRS (live) / NEW HORIZONS (live)** — –

Nov 99. (12")(cd-s) *(ihtv 001)(ihtcds 003)* **PLEASE FORGIVE ME. / PLEASE FORGIVE ME (Paul Hartnoll remix)** 72 –

Apr 00. (re-cd) *(8573 82983-2)* <*21539*> **WHITE LADDER** 1 Jan00

Jun 00. (c-s/cd-s) *(EW 215 C/CD1)* <*radio cut*> **BABYLON / TELL ME MORE LIES / OVER MY HEAD** 5 Nov00 57
(cd-s+=) *(EW 215CD2)* – ('A'-video).

eastwest | R.C.A.

Aug 00. (re-cd) <*69351*> **WHITE LADDER** – 35

Oct 00. (c-s) *(EW 219C)* **PLEASE FORGIVE ME / (Paul Hartnoll remix)** 18 –
(cd-s+=) *(EW 219CD)* – Babylon (live at the Point) (video).

Mar 01. (c-s/cd-s) *(EW 228 C/CD1)* **THIS YEARS LOVE (strings remix) / FLAME TURNS BLUE / THE LIGHTS OF LONDON** 20 –
(cd-s) *(EW 228CD2)* – ('A'-live) / Roots of love / Tired of me.

Jul 01. (c-s) *(EW 234C)* **SAIL AWAY / (club mix)** 26 –
(cd-s+=) *(EW 234CD)* – ('A'-Rae & Christian remix).

Dec 01. (cd-s) *(EW 244CD)* **SAY HELLO WAVE GOODBYE (edit)** 26 –

Oct 02. (cd) *(5046 61658-2)* <*68154*> **A NEW DAY AT MIDNIGHT** 1 Nov02 17
– Dead in the water / Caroline / Long distance call / Freedom / Kangaroo / Last boat to America / Real love / Knowhere / December / Be mine / Easy way to cry / The other side.

Dec 02. (cd-s) *(EW 259CD)* **THE OTHER SIDE / LORELEI / DECIPHER** 35 –

Apr 03. (cd-s) *(EW 264CD)* **BE MINE / LOVERBOY / FALLING DOWN FROM THE MOUNTAINSIDE (live 2002)** 23 –

Atlantic A.T.O.

Sep 05. (7"/cd-s) *(ATUK 013/+CD)* **THE ONE I LOVE. / GOING IN BLIND (piano & strings version)** 8 –
(cd-s) *(ATUK 013CDX)* – ('A'-acoustic) / With open arms / Everybody's leaving town.

Sep 05. (cd) *(5046 79766-2) <71068>* **LIFE IN SLOW MOTION** 1 16
– Alibi / The one I love / Lately / Nos da cariad / Slow motion / From here you can almost see the sea / Ain't no love / Hospital food / Now and always / Disappearing world.

Nov 05. (7"/cd-s) *(ATUK 018/+CD)* **HOSPITAL FOOD. / SMILE LIKE YOU MEAN IT (BBC Radio 1 live version)** 34 –
(cd-s) *(ATUK 018CDX)* – ('A') / Baltimore (live at V2003) / Crimson lightning / ('A'-live at the Church studios 26.07.05).

Mar 06. (7") *(ATUK 027)* **ALIBI. / GOLDEN RAY** 71 –
(cd-s) *(ATUK 027CD)* – ('A') / Tracer.
(cd-s) *(ATUK 027CDX)* – ('A'-live) / Long gone now / SAcred ground / ('A'-video).

– compilations, etc. –

Jul 00. (cd) *iht; (IHTCD 002) / A.T.O.; <69375>* **LOST SONGS 95-98** Apr01
– Flame turns blue / Twilight / Hold on / As I'm leaving / If your love is real / Tidal wave / Falling down the mountainside / January rain / Red moon / A clean pair of eyes / Wurlitzer. *(re-iss. Feb01 on 'eastwest' cd/c; 8573 86953-2/-4)* – hit No.7

Jul 01. (cd) *Hut; (CDHUT 67)* **THE EP'S 1992-1994 ALBUM** 68

Oct 02. (d-cd) *Hut; (543413-0)* **FLESH / A CENTURY ENDS** –

Oct 02. (d-cd) *Hut; (543414-0)* **SELL, SELL, SELL / THE EP'S 1992-1994 ALBUM** –

Al GREEN

Born: AL GREENE, 13 Apr'46, Forrest City, Arkansas, USA. AL got off to an early start when, at the age of nine, he formed his first group, The GREEN BROTHERS, a gospel outfit which included siblings ROBERT, WALTER and WILLIAM. After touring throughout the South, AL was dropped from the group after his Dad caught him listening to the sweet sounds of JACKIE WILSON, and in doing so instilled an instant love for soul music. By the time AL was sixteen, he had formed his own outfit, AL GREEN & THE CREATIONS, who performed R&B tracks before drifting more into soul. Two members of the group, meanwhile, had formed their own label, 'Hot Line Music Journal', recording the newly-renamed AL GREENE & THE SOUL MATES. Their one and only hit, 'BACK UP TRAIN', was the sole measure of success until 1969 when AL met WILLIE MITCHELL, then bandleader and vice-president of 'Hi' Records. After hearing GREEN sing, MITCHELL immediately signed him to the label, where the soul brother recorded his most soulful and funky tracks. The debut album, 'GREEN IS BLUES', released in early '70, proved MITCHELL had made the right move. GREEN's incredible falsetto voice blended with the MITCHELL-arranged horn and strings punctuated a sexy groove that led to the trademark "love man" persona in the early 70's. Although no hits were forthcoming, his second set, 'AL GREEN GETS NEXT TO YOU', proved more accessible, spawning the classic 'TIRED OF BEING ALONE'; this benchmark was to precede four further hits in the next two years. Lifted from his next album, 'LET'S STAY TOGETHER', the title track became the first No.1 of GREEN's glorious career, his alluring voice subsequently gracing the heart-stopping 'I'M STILL IN LOVE WITH YOU' and the spicy 'HERE I AM (COME AND TAKE ME)'. By this point in his career, GREEN was widely recognised as a commercial and critical success, an artist at the pinnacle of his singing career who scored with six consecutive Top 10 singles between '72-'73. His life and career took a dramatic change of course when, on the 25th of October '74, his former girlfriend inflicted second degree burns on his back by pouring boiling grits over him before killing herself with the singer's gun. This led GREEN to follow a life in the Church, believing that the assault was a sign from God; by 1976 he had become pastor of the Full Gospel Tabernacle in Memphis. Though still making albums with MITCHELL, his sound had become too formulaic and he began to record solely self-produced religious music through his own studio ('American Music') to mixed critical acclaim and significantly smaller sales. The '80s saw GREEN releasing Gospel sets on the 'Myrrh' label, as well as the curious duet with ANNIE LENNOX, 'PUT A LITTLE LOVE IN YOUR HEART'. Now primarily a Gospel artist, the 90's have seen GREEN recording the occasional R&B number, the best of the bunch being 1995's 'YOUR HEART IN GOOD HANDS'. Over the years, his songs have been interpreted by many top artists; TAKE ME TO THE RIVER (Talking Heads), L.O.V.E. (Orange Juice), LET'S STAY TOGETHER (Tina Turner), HERE I AM (UB 40), to name but a few. All the more reason for celebration among classic soul fans then, when news leaked out that GREEN was back in the Hi studio with WILLIE MITCHELL at the controls and original sessioneers backing him up. The end result was 'I CAN'T STOP' (2003), an album which allayed fears of a limp retread with the soul don sounding like he'd never hung up his funk chops in the first place. Highlights included the joyous title track, as revelatory a slice of retro-soul as has been aired this decade. The good Reverend returned in 2005 to assure his soul flock: 'EVERYTHING'S OK', and it was, at least in terms of GREEN's ongoing resurgence. With MITCHELL back at the helm, capturing an even more authentic vibe than last time around, critics hailed it as his best since the 70s, mining the kind of spiritual/physical motherlode which an ageing MARVIN GAYE might've tapped had he still been around.

• **Covered:** I WANT TO HOLD YOUR HAND + GET BACK (Beatles) / MEMPHIS, TENNESSEE (Chuck Berry) / CAN'T GET NEXT TO YOU (Temptations) / YOU ARE SO BEAUTIFUL (Billy Preston) / etc. • **Trivia:** On the 13th of February '78, L.A. declared this the 'Al Green Day'.

Album rating: BACK UP TRAIN (*5) / GREEN IS BLUES (*6) / AL GREEN GETS NEXT TO YOU (*7) / LET'S STAY TOGETHER (*8) / I'M STILL IN LOVE WITH YOU (*8) / CALL ME (*8) / LIVIN' FOR YOU (*8) / AL GREEN EXPLORES YOUR MIND (*7) / AL GREEN'S GREATEST HITS compilation (*9) / AL GREEN IS LOVE (*6) / FULL OF FIRE (*5) / HAVE A GOOD TIME (*5) / AL GREEN'S GREATEST HITS, VOLUME II compilation (*7) / THE BELLE ALBUM (*7) / TRUTH 'N' TIME (*6) / THE LORD WILL MAKE A WAY (*6) / HIGHER PLANE (86) / TOKYO LIVE (*7) / TRUST IN GOD (*5) / HE IS THE LIGHT (*6) / GOING AWAY (*5) / SOUL SURVIVOR (*5) / I GET JOY (*6) / LOVE IS REALITY (*5) / THE SUPREME AL GREEN: THE GREATEST HITS compilation (*8) / YOUR HEART'S IN GOOD HANDS (*4) / HI AND MIGHTY: THE STORY OF AL GREEN 1969-78 compilation (*8) / TESTIFY: THE BEST OF THE A&M YEARS compilation (*7) / I CAN'T STOP (*7) / LOVE – THE ESSENTIAL AL GREEN compilation (*8) / EVERYTHING'S OK (*7)

AL GREEN – vocals with **CURTIS ROGERS** + **PALMER JONES**

Stateside Bell

Jan 68. (7"; by AL GREEN & The SOUL MATES) *(SS 2079)* *<1188>* **BACK UP TRAIN. / DON'T LEAVE ME** Oct67 41

Action Hot Line

Feb 69. (7"; as AL GREENE) *(ACT 4540)* **DON'T HURT ME NO MORE. / GET YOURSELF TOGETHER** –

Mar 69. (lp) *(ACLP 6008) <1500>* **BACK UP TRAIN**
– Back up train / Hot wire / Stop and check myself / Let me help you / I'm reaching out / Don't hurt me no more / Lovers hideaway / Don't leave me / What's it all about / I'll be good to you / Guilty / That's all it takes (lady) / Get yourself together. *<(cd-iss. Mar02 on 'Camden'; 74321 92482-2)>*

— now using 'Hi' records house band **THE MEMPHIS HORNS** who were **WAYNE JACKSON** – trumpet / **JAMES MITCHELL** – baritone sax. / **ANDREW LOVE** – tenor sax. / **JACK HALE** – trombone / **ED LOGAN** – tenor sax. / plus **LEROY HODGES** – bass / **MABON HODGES** – guitar. / **CHARLES HUGHES** – organ and **HOWARD GRIMES** – drums who repl. AL JACKSON who joined BOOKER T.

London / Hi

1969. (7") <2159> **I WANT TO HOLD YOUR HAND. / WHAT AM I TO DO WITH MYSELF** [–] [ ]

1969. (7") <2164> **ONE WOMAN. / TOMORROW'S DREAM** [–] [ ]

1969. (lp) <32055> **GREEN IS BLUES** [–] [ ]
– One woman / Talk to me / My girl / I stand accused / Gotta find a new world / What am I gonna do with myself / Tomorrow's dream / What am I gonna do with myself / Get back baby / Get back / Summertime. *<re-iss. Jan73, hit No.19> (UK-iss.Apr86 on 'Hi'; HIUKLP 401) <(cd-iss. Jan99; HILO 150)> <cd re-mast.Feb03 on 'Capitol'+=; CAP 42474>* – I want to hold your hand / Nothing impossible with love / Baby, what's wrong with you? / Memphis, Tennessee.

Feb 70. (7") *(HLU 10300)* <2172> **YOU SAY IT. / GOTTA FIND A NEW WORLD** [ ] [ ]

Apr 70. (7") <2177> **RIGHT NOW RIGHT NOW. / ALL BECAUSE I'M A FOOLISH ONE** [–] [ ]

Jan 71. (7") *(HLU 10324)* <2182> **I CAN'T GET NEXT TO YOU. / RIDE SALLY RIDE** [ ] Nov70 [60]

Apr 71. (7") <2188> **DRIVIN' WHEEL. / TRUE LOVE** [–] [ ]

Jul 71. (7") <2194> **TIRED OF BEING ALONE. / GET BACK BABY** [–] [11]

Aug 71. (7") *(HLU 10337)* **TIRED OF BEING ALONE. / RIGHT NOW RIGHT NOW** [4] [–]

Nov 71. (lp) *(SHU 8424)* <32062> **AL GREEN GETS NEXT TO YOU** [ ] Aug71 [58]
– I can't get next to you / Are you lonely for me baby / God is standing by / Tired of being alone / I'm a ram / Drivin' wheel / Light my fire / You say it / Right now right now / All because. *(re-iss. Apr86 on 'Hi' lp/cd; HIUK LP/CD 403) <(cd-iss. Jan99; HILO 151)> <cd re-mast.Feb03 on 'Capitol'+=; CAP 42679>* – Ride Sally ride / True love / I'll be standing by.

Dec 71. (7") *(HLU 10348)* <2202> **LET'S STAY TOGETHER. / TOMORROW'S DREAM** [7] Nov71 [1]

Mar 72. (lp) *(SHU 8430)* <32070> **LET'S STAY TOGETHER** [ ] Feb72 [8]
– Let's stay together / La-la for you / So you're leaving / What is this feeling / Old time lovin' / I've never found a girl / How can you mend a broken heart / Judy / It ain't no fun to me. *(re-iss. Jul86 on 'Hi' lp/cd; HIUK LP/CD 405) <(cd-iss. Nov98; HILO 152)> <cd re-mast.Feb03 on 'Capitol'+=; CAP 42678>* – Eli's game / Listen.

Mar 72. (7") <2211> **LOOK WHAT YOU DONE FOR ME. / LA-LA FOR YOU** [–] [4]

May 72. (7") *(HLU 10369)* **LOOK WHAT YOU DONE FOR ME. / I'VE NEVER FOUND A GIRL** [44] [–]

Jul 72. (7") *(HLU 10382)* <2216> **I'M STILL IN LOVE WITH YOU. / OLD TIME LOVIN'** [35] Jun72 [3]

Oct 72. (7") *(HLU 10393)* <2227> **YOU OUGHT TO BE WITH ME. / WHAT IS THIS FEELING** [ ] [3]

Dec 72. (lp) *(SHU 8443)* <32074> **I'M STILL IN LOVE WITH YOU** [ ] Oct72 [4]
– I'm still in love with you / I'm glad you're mine / Love and happiness / What a wonderful thing love is / Simply beautiful / Oh, pretty woman / For the good times / Look what you done for me / One of these good old days. *(re-iss. Jul86 on 'Hi'; HIUKLP 407) <(cd-iss. Nov98; HILO 153)> <cd re-mast.Feb03 on 'Capitol'+=; CAP 42677>* – I think it's for the feeling / Up above my head.

Feb 73. (7") *(HLU 10406)* <2235> **CALL ME (COME BACK HOME). / WHAT A WONDERFUL THING LOVE IS** [ ] [10]

Apr 73. (7") *(HLU 10419)* **LOVE AND HAPPINESS. / SO YOU'RE LEAVING** [ ] [–]

Jul 73. (7") *(HLU 10426)* <2247> **HERE I AM (COME AND TAKE ME). / I'M GLAD YOU'RE MINE** [ ] Jun73 [10]

Nov 73. (lp) *(SHU 8457)* <32077> **CALL ME** [ ] May73 [10]
– Call me (come back home) / Have you been making out o.k. / Stand up / I'm so lonesome I could cry / Your love is like the morning sun / Here I am (come and take me) / You ought to be with me / Jesus is waiting. *(re-iss. Jul86 on 'Hi'; HIUKLP 409) <(cd-iss. Nov98; HILO 154)>*

Jan 74. (7") *(HLU 10443)* <2257> **LIVIN' FOR YOU. / IT AIN'T NO FUN TO ME** [ ] Dec73 [19]

Apr 74. (lp) *(SHU 8464)* <32082> **LIVIN' FOR YOU** [ ] Dec73 [24]
– Livin' for you / Home again / Free at last / Let's get married / So good to be here / My sweet sixteen / Unchained melody / My God is real / Beware. *(re-iss. Jul86 on 'Hi'; HIUKLP 411) <(cd-iss. Mar99; HILO 155)>*

Apr 74. (7") *(HLU 10452)* <2262> **LET'S GET MARRIED. / SO GOOD TO BE HERE** [ ] Mar74 [32]

Oct 74. (7") *(HLU 10470)* <2274> **SHA-LA-LA (MAKE ME HAPPY). / SCHOOL DAYS** [20] Sep74 [7]

Dec 74. (lp) *(SHU 8479)* <32087> **AL GREEN EXPLORES YOUR MIND** [ ] Nov74 [15]
– Sha-la-la (make me happy) / Take me to the river / God blessed our love / The city / One nite stand / Stay with me forever / Hangin' on / School days. *(re-iss. Sep86 on 'Hi' lp/cd; HIUK LP/CD 413) <(cd-iss. Mar99; HILO 156)>*

Feb 75. (7") *(HLU 10482)* <2282> **L-O-V-E. (LOVE). / I WISH YOU WERE HERE WITH ME** [24] [13]

Jul 75. (7") *(HLU 10493)* <2288> **OH ME, OH MY (DREAMS IN MY ARMS). / STRONG AS DEATH (SWEET AS LIFE)** [ ] [48]

Oct 75. (lp) *(SHU 8488)* <32092> **AL GREEN IS LOVE** [ ] Sep75 [28]
– L.O.V.E. (love) / Rhymes / The love sermon / There is love / Could I be the one / Love ritual / I didn't know / Oh me, oh my (dreams in my heart) / I wish you were here. *(re-iss. Jul86 on Hi'; HIUKLP 415) <(cd-iss. Jun99; HILO 157)>*

Nov 75. (7") *(HLU 10511)* <2300> **FULL OF FIRE. / COULD I BE THE ONE** [ ] [28]

Mar 76. (lp) *(SHU 8493)* <32097> **FULL OF FIRE** [ ] [59]
– Glory glory / That's the way it is / Always / There's no way / I'd fly away / Full of fire / Together again / Soon as I get home / Let it shine. *(re-iss. Sep86 on 'Hi'; HIUKLP 417) <(cd-iss. Jun99; HILO 158)>*

May 76. (7") *(HLU 10527)* <2306> **LET IT SHINE. / THERE'S NO WAY** [ ] [ ]

Oct 76. (7") *(HLU 10542)* <2319> **KEEP ME CRYIN'. / THERE IS LOVE** [ ] [37]

Dec 76. (lp) *(SHU 8505)* <32103> **HAVE A GOOD TIME** [ ] Nov76 [93]
– Keep on cryin' / Smile a little bit more / I tried to tell myself / Something / The truth marches on / Have a good time / Nothing takes the place of you / Happy / Hold on forever. *(re-iss. Jul86 on 'Hi'; HIUKLP 419)*

Apr 77. (7") <2322> **I TRIED TO TELL MYSELF. / SOMETHING** [–] [ ]

May 77. (7"ep) **I TRIED TO TELL MYSELF / SOMETHING. / WHAT AM I GONNA DO WITH MYSELF / SUMMERTIME** [ ] [–]

Nov 77. (7") <2324> **LOVE AND HAPPINESS. / GLORY GLORY** [–] [ ]

Jan 78. (lp) <6009> **TRUTH 'N' TIME** [–] [ ]
– Blow me down / Lo and behold / Wait here / To sir with love / Truth 'n' time / King of all / Say a little prayer / Happy days. *<(cd-iss. Nov99; HILO 161)>*

—— AL GREEN completely changed his backing musicians recruiting **JAMES BASS** – guitar / **RUEBEN FAIRFAX** – bass / **JOHNNY TONEY** – drums / **FRED JORDAN** – trumpet / **BUDDY JARRETT** – alto sax. / **RON ECHOLS** – baritone sax

Hi-Cream / Hi

Jan 78. (7") <77505> **BELLE. / CHARIOTS OF FIRE** [–] [83]

Aug 78. (7") <78511> **FEELS LIKE SUMMER. / I FEEL GOOD** [–] [ ]

Nov 78. (7") <78522> **TO SIR WITH LOVE. / WAIT HERE** [–] [ ]

Aug 79. (7") *(HCS 101)* **BELLE. / TO SIR WITH LOVE** [ ] [–]

Sep 79. (lp) <(6004)> **THE BELLE ALBUM** [ ] Dec77 [ ]
– Belle / Loving you / Feels like summer / Georgia boy / I feel good / Chariots of fire / All in all / Dream. *(re-iss. Nov86 on 'Hi'; HIUKLP 421) <(cd-iss. Nov99; HILO 160)>*

Jul 81. (d-lp/d-c) *(HCD/ZHCD 5001)* <6005> **TOKYO LIVE (live)** [ ] [ ]
– L.O.V.E. (love) / Tired of being alone / Let's stay together / How can you mend a broken heart / All n all / Belle / Sha-la-la (make me happy) / Let's get married / God blessed our love / You ought to be with me / For the good times / Dream / I feel good / Love and happiness. *(re-iss. Aug87; 8302 ML2) (cd-iss. Mar90; HIUKCD 104) <(cd re-iss. Nov99; HILO 162)>*

—— The Rev. now used mainly session people and gospel backing singers.

Hi / Hi

Feb 82. (lp/c) <(HLP/ZCHLP 6006)> **HIGHER PLANE** [ ] [ ]
– Where love rules / Amazing Grace / His name is Jesus / Battle hymn of the republic / Higher plane / People get ready / By my side / Amazing grace / The spirit might come – on and on. *(re-iss. Nov86; HIUKLP 431)*

Nov 82. (lp) <(HLP 6007)> **PRECIOUS LORD** [ ] [ ]
– Glory to his name / Rock of ages / In the garden / Hallelujah (I just want to praise the Lord) / Precious Lord / What a friend we have in Jesus / The old rugged cross / Morningstar / How great thou art. *(re-iss. Nov86; HIUKLP 429)*

Feb 85. (lp) *(HIUKLP 423)* **TRUST IN GOD** [ ] [ ]
– Don't it make you wanna go home / Trust in God / Holy Spirit / Up the ladder to the roof / Ain't no mountain high enough / No not one / Lean on me / Never met anybody like you / Trust in God (reprise) / All we need is a little more love. *(cd-iss. Jul86; HIUKCD 423)*

Feb 85. (7") *(UK45 7003)* **NEVER MET NOBODY LIKE YOU. / HIGHER PLANE** [ ] [–]

A&M A&M

Nov 85. (7") *<2786>* **GOING AWAY. / BUILDING UP** [–] [ ]

Nov 85. (lp/c) *<(AMA/AMC 5120)>* **GOING AWAY** [ ] [ ]
– Going away / True love / He is the light / I feel like going on / Be with me Jesus / You brought the sunshine / Power / Building up / Nearer my God to thee.

Jan 86. (7") *(AM 302)* **TRUE LOVE. / YOU BROUGHT THE SUNSHINE** [ ] [–]
(12"+=) *(AMY 302)* – Going away.

Jan 86. (7") *<2807>* **TRUE LOVE. / HE IS THE LIGHT** [–] [ ]

Feb 87. (7") *<2919>* **EVERYTHING'S GONNA BE ALRIGHT. / SO REAL TO ME** [–] [ ]

Apr 87. (lp/c) *<(AMA/AMC 5150)>* **SOUL SURVIVOR** [ ] [ ]
– Everything's gonna be alright / Jesus will fix it / You know and I know / Yield not to temptation / So real to me / Soul survivor / You've got a friend / He ain't heavy / 23rd psalm.

Jun 87. (7") *<2952>* **YOU KNOW AND I KNOW. / TRUE LOVE** [–] [ ]

Sep 87. (7") *<2962>* **SOUL SURVIVOR. / JESUS WILL FIX IT** [–] [ ]

Nov 88. (7"; ANNIE LENNOX & AL GREEN) *(AM 484) <1255>* **PUT A LITTLE LOVE IN YOUR HEART. / Spheres Of Celestial Influence: A GREAT BIG PIECE OF LOVE** [28] [9]
(12"+=/cd-s+=) *(AMY/CDEE 484)* – (2-'A'versions).

Breakout-A&M Brreakout-A&M

Jun 89. (7") *(USA 654)* **AS LONG AS WE'RE TOGETHER. / BLESSED** [ ] [ ]
(12"+=) *(USAT 654)* – ('A'other mix).

Jun 89. (lp/c/cd) *(395228-1/-4/-2)* **I GET JOY** [ ] [ ]
– You're everything to me / All my praise / The end is near / Mighty clouds of joy / I get joy / As long as we're together / Praise him / Blessed / Tryin' to do the best I can / Tryin' to get over you.

— He provided the vocals on ARTHUR BAKER + BACKSTREET DISCIPLES Oct89 single THE MESSAGE IS LOVE.

— Co-writes w / **DAVID STEELE** (ex-BEAT). **ANDY COX** also appears and is co-producer. The song 'DON'T LOOK BACK' was written by SMOKEY ROBINSON, and featured CURTIS STIGERS. JOE ROBERTS + A.GLASS wrote 'Fountain of Love'. LOVE IN MOTION was a cover, as was his single below, which was penned by S.SWIRSKY.

Word Word

Apr 92. (cd/c) *(7019271 60X/502)* **LOVE IS REALITY** [ ] [ ]
– Just can't let you go / I can feel it / Love is reality / Positive attitude / Again / Sure feels good / I like it / You don't know me / A long time / A lone time / Why (with DON BYAS).

Arista R.C.A.

Sep 93. (7"/c-s) *(74321 16269-7/-4)* **LOVE IS A BEAUTIFUL THING. / ('A'mix)** [56] [ ]
(12"+=/cd-s+=) *(74321 16269-6/-2)* – ('A'mixes).

Sep 93. (cd/c/lp) *(74321 16310-2/-4/-1)* **DON'T LOOK BACK** [ ] [ ]
– Best love / Love is a beautiful thing / Waiting on you / What does it take / Keep on pushing love / You are my everything / One love / People in the world (keep on lovin' you) / Give it everything / Your love (is more than I ever hoped for) / Fountain of love / Don't look back / Love in motion. *(cd re-iss. Feb97; same)*

Mar 94. (7"/c-s) *(74321 19694-7/-4)* **KEEP ON PUSHING LOVE. / ('A'mix)** [ ] [ ]
(12"+=/cd-s+=) *(74321 19694-1/-2)* – ('A'mix).

— In May 94, AL did duet 'Funny How Time Slips Away' with LYLE LOVETT on 'Geffen' c-s/cd-s; (MCS C/TD 1974). Originally a 1962 hit for JIMMY ELLEDGE.

Jul 94. (c-s) *(74321 19349-4)* **WAITING ON YOU. / ('A'mix)** [ ] [ ]
(12"+=/cd-s+=) *(74321 19349-1/-2)* – (2-'A'mixes).

not iss. M.C.A.

Nov 95. (cd) *<AAMCAD 11350>* **YOUR HEART'S IN GOOD HANDS** [–] [ ]
– Your heart's in good hands / Keep on pushing love / Could this be love / Love is a beautiful thing / On love / Don't look back / The best love / Your love (is more than I ever hoped for) / What does it take / People in the world (keep on lovin' you). *(UK-iss.Mar03; same as US)*

Blue Note Blue Note

Nov 03. (cd/d-lp) *<(5 93556-2/-1)>* **I CAN'T STOP** [ ] [53]
– I can't stop / Play to win / Rainin' in my heart / I've been waitin' on you / You / Not tonight / Million to one / My problem is you / I'd still choose you / I've been thinkin' 'bout you / I'd write a letter / Too many.

Nov 04. (cd-s) *<19026>* **PERFECT TO ME (mixes)** [–] [ ]

Mar 05. (cd) *<(8 74584-2)>* **EVERYTHING'S OK** [ ] [50]
– Everything's OK / You are so beautiful / Build me up / Perfect to me / Nobody but you / Real love / I can make music / Be my baby / Magic road / I wanna hold you / Another day / All the time.

– compilations, etc. –

on 'Hi' unless mentioned otherwise

Sep 72. (lp) *Bell; <6076>* **AL GREEN** (early recordings) [–] [ ]

Sep 72. (7") *Bell; <45258>* **GUILTY. / LET ME HELP YOU** [–] [69]

Jan 73. (7") *Bell; <45305>* **HOT WIRE. / DON'T LEAVE ME** [–] [71]

Mar 75. (lp) *London; (SHU 8481) / Hi; <32089>* **AL GREEN'S GREATEST HITS** [18] Mar75 [17]
– Let's stay together / I can't get next to you / You ought to be with me / Look what you done to me / Let's get married / Tired of being alone / Call me / I'm still in love with you / Here I am (come and take me) / How can you mend a broken heart. *(re-iss. Jul86 on 'Hi' lp/c/cd; HIUK LP/CASS/CD 425)*

Jul 77. (lp) *<32105>* **GREATEST HITS VOL.2** [–] [ ]
(UK-iss.Oct87 as 'TAKE ME TO THE RIVER – GREATEST HITS VOL.2' on 'Hi' lp/c/cd; HIUK LP/CASS/CD 438)

Jan 80. (lp/c) *Cream; (HLPC/ZCHLP 101)* **THE CREAM OF AL GREEN** [ ] [–]

Jan 80. (7"/12") *Cream; (HCS/12HCS 102)* **TIRED OF BEING ALONE. / HOW CAN YOU MEND A BROKEN HEART** [ ] [–]

May 81. (lp) *Myrrh; (MYR 1109)* **THE LORD WILL MAKE A WAY** [ ] [ ]
– Highway to heaven / Pass me not / The Lord will make a way / Too close / None but the righteous / I have a friend above all others / Saved / In the holy name of Jesus. *(re-iss. Jul86 on 'Hi'; HIUKLP 433)*

Oct 81. (d-lp/d-c) *P.R.T.; (SPOT/ZCSPT 1016)* **SPOTLIGHT ON AL GREEN** [ ] [–]

1984. (7") *Cream; (HCS 107)* **TIRED OF BEING ALONE. / LET'S STAY TOGETHER** [ ] [ ]
(12"+=) *(12HCS 107)* – How can you mend a broken heart.

Sep 85. (7") *(HIUK45 7001)* **LET'S STAY TOGETHER. / I'M STILL IN LOVE WITH YOU** [ ] [–]
(12"+=) *(HIUK45T 7001)* – You ought to be with me.

Jul 86. (lp) *(HIUKLP 425)* **THE BEST OF AL GREEN** [ ] [ ]

Jul 86. (lp) *(XHIUKLP 437)* **WHITE CHRISTMAS** [ ] [ ]
(cd-iss. Nov95 +=; HILOCD 21) – (extra tracks).

Sep 88. (lp/c/cd) *K-Tel; (NE1/CD2/NCD3 420)* **HI LIFE – THE BEST OF AL GREEN** [34] [–]

Mar 89. (lp/c/cd) *(HIUK LP/CASS/CD 443)* **LOVE RITUAL – RARE AND PREVIOUSLY UNRELEASED (1968-76)** [ ] [ ]

Jun 90. (lp) *(HIUK 444)* **YOU SAY IT!** [ ] [–]

1990. (cd) *Word;* **ONE IN A MILLION** [–] [ ]

Apr 91. (cd/c) *(HIUK CD/CASS 107* **COVER ME GREEN** [ ] [–]

May 91. (cd) *(HIUKCD 113)* **LIVIN' FOR YOU / AL GREEN EXPLORES YOUR MIND** [ ] [–]

May 91. (cd) *(HIUKCD 114)* **AL GREEN IS LOVE / FULL OF FIRE** [ ] [–]

Sep 91. (cd) *(HIUKCD 119)* **HAVE A GOOD TIME / THE BELLE ALBUM** [ ] [–]

Apr 92. (cd/c) *(HIUK CD/CASS 130)* **THE SUPREME AL GREEN: THE GREATEST HITS** [ ] [–]
– Tired of being alone / I can't get next to you / Let's stay together / How can you mend a broken heart / Love & happiness / I'm still in love with you / Simply beautiful / What a wonderful thing love is / Call me (come back home) / My God is real / Let's get married / Sha-la-la (make me happy) / Take me to the river / Love ritual / L-O-V-E / I didn't know / Full of fire / Belle.

Oct 92. (cd; AL GREEN & ACE CANNON) *(HIUKCD 126)* **CHRISTMAS CHEERS** [ ] [ ]

Nov 92. (cd/c/lp) *Beechwood; (AGREE CD/MC/LP 1)* **AL** [41] [–]

Jul 93. (cd) *(HIUKCD 141)* **THE FLIP SIDE OF AL GREEN** [ ] [ ]

May 95. (cd) *Universal; (E 540255-2)* **. . .AND THE MESSAGE IS LOVE** [ ] [–]

Feb 97. (3xcd-box) *(HIBOOK 12)* **A DEEP SHADE OF GREEN** [ ] [ ]

Aug 98. (cd) *<(HEX 35)>* **THE HI MASTERS** [ ] [ ]

Sep 98. (cd/lp) *D.C.C.; (CDZ/LPZ 2058)* **GREATEST HITS** [ ] [–]

Oct 98. (d-cd) *<(HEXD 41)>* **HI AND MIGHTY – THE STORY OF AL GREEN (1969-78)** [ ] [ ]

Mar 99. (cd) *Music Club; (MCCD 378)* **TRUE LOVE (A COLLECTION)** [ ] [–]

Jul 00. (d-cd) <*(HEXD 52)*> **THE HI SINGLES A'S AND B'S** [ ] [ ]
Sep 00. (cd) *(HIUKCD 251)* **LISTEN – THE RARITIES** [ ] [–]
Apr 01. (cd) *Spectrum; (544294-2)* **THE GOSPEL COLLECTION** [ ] [–]
Aug 01. (3xcd-box+book) *(FBOOK 26)* **LOVE AND HAPPINESS** [ ] [–]
Aug 01. (cd) *Capitol; <33603>* **FEELS LIKE CHRISTMAS** [–] [ ]
Sep 01. (cd) *A&M; <(493122-2)>* **TESTIFY: THE BEST OF THE A&M YEARS** [ ] [ ]
– Put a little love in your heart (with ANNIE LENNOX) / Going away / True love / I feel like going on / You brought the sunshine / Power / Building up / Everything's gonna be alright / You know and I know / You've got a friend / He ain't heavy (he's my brother) / Soul survivor / You're everything to me / Mighty clouds of joy / As long as we're together / Tryin' to do the best I can / I get joy / So real to me.
Oct 01. (cd) *Music Club; (MCCD 476)* **THE VERY BEST OF AL GREEN** [ ] [–]
Jun 02. (cd) <*(HILO 189)*> **THE LORD WILL MAKE A WAY / HIGHER PLANE** [ ] [ ]
Aug 02. (cd) <*(HILO 190)*> **PRECIOUS LORD / I'LL RISE AGAIN** [ ] [ ]
Sep 02. (cd) *(HIUKCD 252)* **UNCHAINED MELODIES** [ ] [–]
Oct 02. (cd) <*(HILO 191)*> **TRUST IN GOD / WHITE CHRISTMAS** [ ] [ ]
Feb 02. (d-cd) <*(ALTV 2002)*> **LOVE: THE ESSENTIAL AL GREEN** [18] Feb04 [ ]
– I can't get next to you / Tired of being alone / Look what you done for me / Let's stay together / What am I gonna do with myself / Light my fire / I've never found a girl / I'm still in love with you / How can you mend a broken heart / What a wonderful thing love is / You ought to be with me / Call me (come back home) / Judy / Here I am (come and take me) / I wish you were here / Lean on me / I'm hooked on you / Simply beautiful / L.O.V.E. / Livin' for you / Love and happiness / My girl / Take me to the river / Sha la la (makes me happy) / Let's get married / Oh me oh my (dreams in my arms) / Full of fire / Have a good time / Let it shine / Could I be the one / Keep me cryin' / I tried to tell myself / Belle / Love is a beautiful thing / The message is love (with ARTHUR BAKER).

GREEN DAY

Formed: Rodeo, nr. Berkeley, California, USA . . . early 90's out of The SWEET CHILDREN by BILLY JOE ARMSTRONG and MIKE DIRNT. When TRE COOL replaced BILLY JOE's sister ANA on drums, they became GREEN DAY, this line-up releasing their debut LP, '39 / SMOOTH', which was recorded in under 24 hours. Their third album, 'DOOKIE' (their first for 'Reprise'), was a surprise US smash in 1994 due to its college/MTV favourite, 'BASKET CASE'. Retro punk-rock for young Americans (and now older Brits) who missed out on BUZZCOCKS, DICKIES, RAMONES (and even earlier 60's pop outfit, the MONKEES), GREEN DAY became a phenomenon in the States; like the SEX PISTOLS' revolution all over again, without the danger, unpredictability and raw excitement. Instead we got formulaic, annoyingly and yes, inanely catchy punk retreads that took you way back to '77. Still, the multi-millions who bought the record ensured that GREEN DAY were indeed radio-friendly unit shifters. A follow-up set, 'INSOMNIAC' (1995), was another massive seller, although it had to compete with the hordes of equally faceless acts clogging up the charts with similar material. A fifth set, 'NIMROD' (1997), made sure they were still in touch with their fanbase, the tried and tested formula again getting them into the Top 10. The album also spawned a surprise hit single in the shape of a rare ballad, 'TIME OF YOUR LIFE (GOOD RIDDANCE)', geeing the band on to er, express their more feminine side, or at least their less frantic side. With 'WARNING' (2000), GREEN DAY went ahead and exorcised those pop demons which had clearly been haunting them since way back when. By investing their punk-pop formula with a measure of melodic sparkle and a hint of vintage 60's flavour, the 3-chord thumpers had come up with their most consistently listenable album to date. The release of compilations, 'INTERNATIONAL SUPERHITS' (2001) and 'SHENANIGANS' (2002), might've made it seem that the band were marking time; in actual fact they were at work on their piece de resistance, 'AMERICAN IDIOT' (2004). Possibly the most celebrated work to come out of rock's post 9/11 ferment, the album was nothing less than a politicised post-millennial rock opera, and a transatlantic chart-topper into the bargain. The Bush-blasting title track served as a lead single, setting the tone for the high charting series of singles to follow: 'BOULEVARD OF BROKEN DREAMS', 'HOLIDAY' and 'WAKE ME UP WHEN SEPTEMBER ENDS'. ARMSTRONG's political commitment filtered through to the accompanying, award-winning videos, while the album itself scooped a Grammy. After being voted Best Show On Earth in a Kerrang! poll, the trio's semi-legendary Milton Keynes Bowl summer 2005 double-header was officially released later that year as a CD/DVD package, 'BULLET IN A BIBLE'.

• **Songwriters:** Lyrics; BILLIE JOE, group songs except TIRED OF WAITING FOR YOU (Kinks). • **Trivia:** DIRNT guested on the SCREECHING WEASEL album, 'How to Make Enemies And Irritate People'. BILLIE JOE was also a member of PINHEAD GUNPOWDER, who released an album, 'Jump Salty', plus a few EP's (also for 'Lookout').

Album rating: 39/SMOOTHED OUT SLAPPY HOURS compilation (*5) / KERPLUNK! (*5) / DOOKIE (*7) / INSOMNIAC (*6) / NIMROD (*6) / WARNING (*6) / INTERNATIONAL SUPERHITS compilation (*7) / SHENANIGANS compilation (*6) / AMERICAN IDIOT (*9) / BULLET IN A BIBLE (*6)

BILLIE JOE ARMSTRONG (b.17 Feb'72, San Pablo, Calif.) – vocals, guitar / **MIKE DIRNT** (b. PRITCHARD, 4 May'72) – bass, vocals / **TRE COOL** (b. FRANK EDWIN WRIGHT III, 9 Dec'72, Germany) – drums (ex-LOOKOUTS) repl. JOHN KIFTMEYER who had repl. AL SOBRANTE

not iss. Lookout

Apr 89. (7"ep) <*LK 17*> **1000 HOURS EP** [–] [ ]
– 1000 hours / Dry ice / Only of you / The one I want. *(UK-iss.Dec94; as above)*
Apr 90. (lp/c/cd) <*LO 22/+CS/CD*> **39 / SMOOTH** [–] [ ]
– At the library / Don't leave me / I was there / Disappearing boy / Green day / Going to Pasalacgua / 16 / Road to exceptance / Rest / The judge's daughter / Paper lanterns / Why do you want him? / 409 in your coffeemaker / Knowledge / 1000 hours / Dry ice / Only of you / The one I want / I want to be alone. *<re-iss. Nov91 lp/cd; LOOKOUT 22/+CD> (UK-iss.Sep94 as '1,039 / SMOOTHED OUT SLAPPY HOURS'; as above) (cd re-iss. Aug97 on 'Epitaph'; 6522-2)*
Mar 90. (7"ep) <*LK 35*> **SLAPPY EP** [–] [ ]
– Paper lanterns / Why do you want him? / 409 in your coffeemaker / Knowledge. *(UK-iss.Sep94; as above)*
Dec 91. (lp) <*LOOKOUT 46*> **KERPLUNK!** [–] [ ]
– 2000 light years away / One for the razorbacks / Welcome to Paradise / Christie Road / Private ale / Dominated love slave / One of my lies / 80 / Android / No one knows / Who wrote Holden Caulfield? / Words I might have ate. *(UK-iss.Sep94 on 'Lookout' lp/cd+=; LOOKOUT 46/+CD)* – Sweet children / Best thing in town / Strangeland / My generation. *(by SWEET CHILDREN and released US 1990 on 'Skene') (cd re-iss. Aug97 on 'Epitaph'; 6517-2)*

Reprise Reprise

Feb 94. (cd/c) <*(9362 45529-2/-4)*> **DOOKIE** [ ] [2]
– Burnout / Having a blast / Chump / Longview / Welcome to Paradise / Pulling teeth / Basket case / She / Sassafras roots / When I come around / Coming clean / Emenius sleepus / In the end / F.O.D. *(cd+=)* – (hidden track). *(re-dist.Oct94 on green-lp soon hit UK No.13; 9362 45795-2/-4)*
Jun 94. (7") *(W 0247)* **LONGVIEW. / ON THE WAGON** [ ] [–]
(10"/cd-s) *(W 0247 T/CD)* – ('A'side) / Going to Pasalacqua (infatuation) / F.O.D. (live) / Christy Road (live).
Aug 94. (7"green/c-s) *(W 0257/+C)* **BASKET CASE. / TIRED OF WAITING FOR YOU** [55] [–]
(cd-s+=) *(W 0257CD2)* – On the wagon / 409 in your coffeemaker.
(cd-s) *(W 0257CD)* – ('A'side) / Longview (live) / Burnout (live) / 2000 light years away (live).
Oct 94. (c-s) *(W 0269C)* **WELCOME TO PARADISE. / CHUMP (live)** [20] [–]
(12"green+=/cd-s+=/cd-s+=) *(W 0269 T/CD/CDX)* – Emenius sleepus.

Billie Joe Armstrong of GREEN DAY

Jan 95. (7"green/c-s) *(W 0279/+C)* **BASKET CASE. / 2,000 LIGHT YEARS AWAY (live)** [7] [–]
(cd-s+=) *(W 0279CD)* – Burnout (live) / Longview (live).

Mar 95. (7"/c-s) *(W 0278/+C)* **LONGVIEW. / WELCOME TO PARADISE (live)** [30] [–]
(cd-s+=) *(W 0278CD)* – One of my lies (live).

May 95. (7"pic-d/c-s) *(W 0294/+C)* **WHEN I COME AROUND. / SHE (live)** [27] [–]
(cd-s+=) *(W 0294CD)* – Coming clean (live).

Sep 95. (7"red/c-s) *(W 0320/+C)* **GEEK STINK BREATH. / I WANT TO BE ON T.V.** [16] [–]
(cd-s+=) *(W 0320CD)* – Don't want to fall in love.

Oct 95. (cd/c/lp) *<(9362 46046-2/-4/-1)>* **INSOMNIAC** [8] [2]
– Armatage Shanks / Brat / Stuck with me / Geek stink breath / No pride / Bab's Uvula who? / 86 / Panic song / Stuart and the Ave. / Brain stew / Jaded / Westbound sign / Tight wad hill / Walking contradiction.

Dec 95. (7") *(W 0327X)* **STUCK WITH ME. / WHEN I COME AROUND (live)** [24] [–]
(c-s+=) *(W 0327C)* – Jaded (live).
(cd-s) *(W 0327CD)* – ('A'side) / Dominated love slave (live) / Chump (live).

Jun 96. (c-s) *(W 0339C)* **BRAIN STEW / JADED / TIME OF YOUR LIFE (GOOD RIDDANCE)** [28] [–]
(cd-s+=) *(W 0339CD)* – Do da da.
(brain-shaped cd-s++=) *(W 0339CDX)* – Brain stew (radio).

Sep 97. (c-s) *(W 0424C)* *<43945>* **HITCHIN' A RIDE / SICK** [25] Jun98 [ ]
(cd-s+=) *(W 0424CD)* – Espionage.

Oct 97. (cd/c) *<(9362 46794-2/-4)>* **NIMROD** [11] [10]
– Nice guys finish last / Hitchin' a ride / The grouch / Reduntant / Scattered / Worry rock / Desensitized / All the time / Platypus (I hate you) / Last ride in / Jinx / Haushinka / Walking alone / Suffocate / Uptight / Take back / King for a day / Good riddance / Prosthetic head.

Jan 98. (c-s) *(W 0430C)* *<43974>* **TIME OF YOUR LIFE (GOOD RIDDANCE) / DESENSITIZED** [11] Jun98 [ ]
(cd-s+=) *(W 0430CD1)* – Rotting.
(cd-s) *(W 0430CD2)* – ('A'side) / Suffocate / You lied.

Apr 98. (7") *(W 0438)* **REDUNDANT. / THE GROUCH (live)** [27] [–]
(cd-s+=) *(W 0438CD1)* – Paper lanterns (live).
(cd-s) *(W 0438CD2)* – ('A'side) / Reject all American (live) / She (live).

Sep 00. (c-s) *(W 532C)* **MINORITY / BRAT (live)** [18] [–]
(cd-s+=) *(W 532CD)* – 86 (live).
(7"ep iss.Nov00 on 'Adeline'+=; ADELINE 013) – Jackass.

Oct 00. (cd/c) *<(9362 48030-2/-4)>* **WARNING** [4] [4]
– Warning / Blood, sex and booze / Church on Sunday / Fashion victim / Castaway / Misery / Deadbeat holiday / Hold on / Jackass / Waiting / Minority / Macy's day parade. *<US version+=; 47857>* – Brat (live) / 86 (live). *<(lp; 9362 47613-1)>* *<US lp-iss.Oct00 on 'Adeline'; ADELINE 012>*

Dec 00. (7"orange) *(W 548)* **WARNING. / SUFFOCATE** [27] [–]
(c-s+=/cd-s+=) *(W 548 C/CD2)* – Outsider. *(7"iss.Feb01 on 'Adeline'; ADELINE 014)*
(cd-s) *(W 548CD1)* – ('A'side) / Scumbag / I don't want to know if you are lonely.

Oct 01. (cd-s) *(W 570CD)* **WAITING / MACY'S DAY PARADE / BASKET CASE** [34] [–]
(cd-s) *(W 570CDX)* – ('A'side) / She / F.O.D.

Nov 01. (cd/c) *<(9362 48145-2/-4)>* **INTERNATIONAL SUPERHITS** (compilation) [15] [40]
– Maria / Poprocks and coke / Longview / Welcome to paradise / Basket case / When I come around / She / J.A.R. (Jason Andrew Relva) / Geek stink breath / Brain stew / Jaded / Walking contradiction / Stuck with me / Hitchin' a ride / Good riddance (time of your life) / Reduntant / Nice guys finish last / Macy's day parade.

Jul 02. (cd/c) *<(9362 48208-2/-4)>* **SHENANIGANS** (B-sides, etc, compilation) [32] [27]
– Suffocate / Desensitized / You lied / Outsider / Don't wanna fall in love / Espionage / I want to be on T.V. / Scumbag / Tired of waiting for you / Sick of me / Rotting / Do da da / On the wagon / Ha ha you're dead.

Sep 04. (7"pic-d/cd-s) *(W 652/+CD1)* *<16375-2>* **AMERICAN IDIOT. / TOO MUCH TOO SOON** [3] [61]
(cd-s) *(W 652CD2)* – ('A') / Shoplifter governator / Governator.

Sep 04. (cd/d-lp) *<(9362 48877-2/-1)>* **AMERICAN IDIOT** [1] [1]
– American idiot / Jesus of suburbia: i) Jesus of suburbia, ii) City of the damned, iii) I don't care, iv) Dearly beloved, v) Tales of another broken home / Holiday / Boulevard of broken dreams / Are we the waiting / St. Jimmy / Give me novacaine / She's a rebel / Extraordinary girl / Letterbomb / Wake me up when September ends / Homecoming: i) The death of St. Jimmy, ii) East 12th St., iii) Nobody like you, iv) Rock and roll girlfriend, v) We're coming home again / Whatsername.

Nov 04. (7"pic-d/cd-s) *(W 659/+CD1)* *<916147>* **BOULEVARD OF BROKEN DREAMS. / LETTERBOX (live)** [5] Jan05 [2]
(cd-s) *(W 659CD2)* – ('A') / American idiot (live) / She's a rebel (live).

Mar 05. (7"pic-d/cd-s) *(W 664/+CD1)* **HOLIDAY. / MINORITY (live)** [11] Apr05 [19]
(cd-s) *(W 664CD2)* *<radio>* – ('A') / ('A'-live) / Boulevard of broken dreams (live).

Jun 05. (7"pic-d/c-s) *(W 674/+CD1)* **WAKE ME UP WHEN SEPTEMBER ENDS. / GIVE ME NOVACAINE (live from Storytellers)** [8] Aug05 [6]
(cd-s) *(W 674CD2)* *<radio>* – ('A') / Homecoming (live from Storytellers) / Hitchin' a ride.

Nov 05. (10"/cd-s) *(W 691 TE/CD)* **JESUS OF SUBURBIA. / ST. JIMMY (live from Storytellers)** [17] [–]
(dvd-s) *(W 691DVD)* – ('A') / ('A'-live at the Irving PLate video) / Bullet In A Bible (1 min. trailer).

Nov 05. (cd w/dvd) *<(9362 49466-2)>* **BULLET IN A BIBLE** (live) [6] [8]
– American idiot / Jesus of suburbia: Jesus of suburbia – City of the damned – I don't care – Dearly beloved – Tales of another broken home / Holiday / Are we the waiting / St. Jimmy / Longview / Hitchin' a ride / Brain stew / Basket case / King for a day – Shout / Wake me up when September ends / Minority / Boulevard of broken dreams / Good riddance (time of your life). *(dvd+=)* – (visual tracks + bonus features).

☐ GREEN RIVER (see under ⇒ PEARL JAM)

☐ Jonny GREENWOOD (see under ⇒ RADIOHEAD)

☐ Dave GROHL (see under ⇒ FOO FIGHTERS)

GUNS N' ROSES

Formed: Los Angeles, California, USA ... early 1985 by AXL ROSE, IZZY STRADLIN and moonlighting L.A. GUNS member TRACII GUNS, who was soon to return to said outfit. With the addition of SLASH, DUFF McKAGAN and STEVEN ADLER, the seminal G N' R line-up was complete, the ramshackle collection of fun loving musical vagabonds subsequently embarking on the 'hell' tour of the US. Although this outing was a disaster, the band created a major buzz with their residency at L.A.'s Troubadour club and in the summer of '86 unleashed their debut recording, a 7"ep entitled 'LIVE ?!*' LIKE A SUICIDE'. A short, sharp shock of visceral rock'n'raunch, the record struck a major chord with critics and fans alike, quickly selling out of its limited 10,000 pressing. Snapped up by 'Geffen', the band released their debut album, 'APPETITE FOR DESTRUCTION', the following year. A head-on collision of AC/DC, AEROSMITH and the SEX PISTOLS, what the record lacked in originality, it made up for with sheer impact. The opening unholy trinity ('WELCOME TO THE JUNGLE', 'IT'S SO EASY', 'NIGHTRAIN') alone laid the rest of the L.A. hairspray pack to waste, while with 'PARADISE CITY' and 'SWEET CHILD O' MINE', the band staked their claim to chart domination and stadium stardom. In spite of its controversial cover art featuring a robot raping a woman (later withdrawn), the record went on to sell a staggering 20 million copies worldwide and remains one of metal's defining moments. It also remains one of the most vivid portrayals of the claustrophobic seediness of the L.A. metal scene in much the same way as N.W.A. captured the fuck-you nihilism of the city's black ghetto with 'Straight Outta Compton'. Live, GUNS N' ROSES were caustic and volatile, as likely to produce tabloid headlines as blistering performances. Image wise, they had SLASH as an unmistakable focal point; his trademark top hat perched on a nest of thick curls that all but obscured his face, fag constantly hanging from his lips a la KEITH RICHARDS. Controversy turned into tragedy the following summer, however, when two fans were crushed to death during a G N' R set at the 1988 Castle Donington

GUNS N' ROSES

Monsters Of Rock festival. Later that year, the band released 'G N' R LIES', a half live/ half studio affair that combined their earlier EP with four new acoustic numbers. On the lovely 'PATIENCE', ROSE was transformed from sneering vocal acrobat to mellow songsmith, although by 'ONE IN A MILLION', he was back to his old ways with a vengeance. While the song was performed with undeniable passion, it was all the more worrying given the subjects he was railing against. The track was basically an unforgivable tirade of abuse aimed at 'niggers', 'faggots' and 'immigrants', hmmm.. ironic? Yeah, right. Still, the good citizens of America snapped up the record and it peaked at No.2. in the US, No.22 in Britain. Come 1990, the band were supporting the ROLLING STONES on a world tour, their star status rapidly assuming the same magnitude as their drug habits. ADLER's heroin problems eventually saw him kicked out later that summer, CULT drummer MATT SORUM taking his place on the drum stool. The band also recruited a keyboard player, DIZZY REED, a sure sign they were beginning to lose the plot. A terminally dull cover of DYLAN's 'KNOCKIN' ON HEAVEN'S DOOR' (included on the 'Days Of Thunder' soundtrack) seemed to confirm this although 'CIVIL WAR', their contribution to Romanian orphan project, 'Nobody's Child', was more encouraging. When it eventually surfaced, the band's next studio project, 'USE YOUR ILLUSION' (1991), was a resounding disappointment. The very fact they released the disc in 2 volumes showed a severe lack of objectivity and needless to say, the quality control was non-existent. A sprawling, unfocused jumble, the collection nevertheless included a few inspired moments (notably the classic 'NOVEMBER RAIN') and both albums reached No.1 and 2 respectively in both Britain and America. During the subsequent world tour, STRADLIN walked out, finally leaving the band soon after for a solo career (his replacement was GILBY CLARKE). Among the dates on the record-breaking 28 month world tour was a performance at AIDS benefit concert, The Freddie Mercury Tribute, rather ironic in light of ROSE's lyrical homophobic tendencies. The bandana'ed one courted further outrage when the group included a CHARLES MANSON song on their 1993 covers album, 'THE SPAGHETTI INCIDENT', a record that also saw the band rework their faves from NAZARETH to the UK SUBS. They also massacred 'SYMPATHY FOR THE DEVIL' for the 'Interview With The Vampire' soundtrack, their last outing to date. CLARKE has subsequently left the band following a solo release, 'PAWNSHOP GUITARS', while SLASH also released a side project, 'IT'S FIVE O'CLOCK SOMEWHERE', in 1995 under the moniker SLASH'S SNAKEPIT. The cat in the top hat finally quit GN'R in '96, although it hardly mattered as the band were seemingly in terminal creative limbo; he eventually resurfaced in 2001 with a solo album, 'AIN'T LIFE GRAND', although rumours continued to circulate about a SLASH-less new GN'R album with a working title of 'Chinese Democracy'. By 2004, the release sheet was still blank and fans had to make do with another 'GREATEST HITS' collection, albeit without the consent of AXL ROSE (and ex-GN'R members) who unsuccessfully attempted to block its release with a court injunction. In the midst of this will-they-won't-they soap opera, SLASH, McKAGAN and MATT SORUM regrouped under the VELVET REVOLVER banner, and while they found a second guitarist in the shape of DAVE KUSHNER, it would take several high-profile auditions before they settled on erratic frontman, SCOTT WEILAND (formerly of STONE TEMPLE PILOTS). Surprise surprise, more grief followed as the band attempted to record a debut album around WEILAND's court appearances and drug rehabiliation. 'CONTRABAND' finally appeared in June 2004, sating the patience-strained appetite of long-time GN'R fans for some swaggering R'n'R destruction, scaling the charts and generating a couple of minor hits, 'SLITHER' and 'FALL TO PIECES'. Yet the reclusive ROSE continued to hog the headlines, previewing new material at sporadic live appearances and talking up his creative progress. While some of the tracks were inevitably leaked onto the internet, a concrete release date seems assured for the second half of 2006 – or is it?

• **Songwriters:** All written by AXL except; MAMA KIN (Aerosmith) / NICE BOYS DON'T PLAY ROCK'N'ROLL (Rose Tattoo) / WHOLE LOTTA ROSIE (Ac-Dc) / LIVE AND LET DIE (Paul McCartney & Wings). Punk covers album; SINCE I DON'T HAVE YOU (Skyliners) / NEW ROSE (Damned) / DOWN ON THE FARM (UK Subs) / HUMAN BEING (New York Dolls) / RAW POWER (Iggy & The Stooges) / AIN'T IT FUN (Dead Boys) / BUICK MAKANE (T.Rex) / HAIR OF THE DOG (Nazareth) / ATTITUDE (Misfits) / BLACK LEATHER (Sex Pistols) / YOU CAN'T PUT YOUR ARMS AROUND A MEMORY (Johnny Thunders) / I DON'T CARE ABOUT YOU (Fear) / WHAT'S YOUR GAME! (Charles Manson). McKAGAN covered CRACKED ACTOR (David Bowie) / VELVET REVOLVER covered: NEGATIVE CREEP (Nirvana) / BODIES (Sex Pistols).
• **Trivia:** On 28 Apr'90, AXL was married to ERIN, daughter of DON EVERLY (Brothers), but a couple of months later, they counterfiled for divorce. BAILEY was AXL's step-father's surname, and he found out real surname ROSE in the 80's.

Album rating: APPETITE FOR DESTRUCTION (*10) / G N' R LIES (*8) / USE YOUR ILLUSION I (*7) / USE YOUR ILLUSION II (*6) / THE SPAGHETTI INCIDENT (*5) / LIVE ERA '87-'93 exploitation (*6) / GREATEST HITS compilation (*7) / Duff McKagan: BELIEVE IN ME (*5) / Slash's Snakepit: IT'S FIVE O'CLOCK SOMEWHERE (*^0 / AIN'T LIFE GRAND (*5) / Velvet Revolver: CONTRABAND (*6)

W. AXL ROSE (b. WILLIAM BAILEY, 6 Feb'62, Lafayette, Indiana, USA) – vocals / **SLASH** (b. SAUL HUDSON, 23 Jul'65, Stoke-On-Trent, England) – lead guitar / **IZZY STRADLIN** (b.JEFFREY ISBELL, 8 Apr'62, Lafayette) – guitar / **DUFF McKAGAN** (b. MICHAEL, 5 Feb'64, Seattle, Wash.) – bass (ex-10 MINUTE WARNING, ex-FASTBACKS) / **STEVE ADLER** (b.22 Jan'65, Ohio) – drums repl. ROB to L.A. GUNS again.

not iss. Uzi Suicide

Aug 86. (7"ep) *<USR 001>* **LIVE ?!*' LIKE A SUICIDE** [–] [ ]
– Mama kin / Reckless life / Move to the city / Nice boys (don't play rock'n'roll). *<re-iss. Jan87 on 'Geffen'; >*

Geffen Geffen

Jun 87. (7") *(GEF 22)* **IT'S SO EASY. / MR. BROWNSTONE** [ ] [ ]
(12"+=/12"pic-d+=) *(GEF 22T/+P)* – Shadow of your love / Move to the city.

Aug 87. (lp/c)(cd) *(WX 125/+C)(924148-2) <24148>* **APPETITE FOR DESTRUCTION** [5] [1]
– Welcome to the jungle / It's so easy / Nightrain / Out ta get me / Mr. Brownstone / Paradise city / My Michelle / Think about you / Sweet child o' mine / You're crazy / Anything goes / Rocket queen. *(peaked UK-No.5 in 1989) (re-iss. Nov90 lp/c/cd; GEF/+C/D 24148) (re-iss. Oct95 cd/c;)*

Sep 87. (7") *(GEF 30)* **WELCOME TO THE JUNGLE. / WHOLE LOTTA ROSIE (live)** [67] [ ]
(12"+=/12"w-poster/12"pic-d+=) *(GEF 30 T/TW/P)* – It's so easy (live) / Knockin' on Heaven's door (live).

Aug 88. (7") *(GEF 43) <27963>* **SWEET CHILD O' MINE. / OUT TA GET ME** [24] Jun88 [1]
(12"+=/12"s+=/10"+=) *(GEF 43T/+V/E)* – Rocket queen.

Oct 88. (7") *(GEF 47) <27759>* **WELCOME TO THE JUNGLE. / NIGHTRAIN** [24] [7]
(12"+=/12"w-poster+=/12"w-patch+=/12"pic-d+=/cd-s+=) *(GEF 47 T/TW/TV/TP/CD)* – You're crazy.

Dec 88. (lp/c)(cd) *(WX 218/+C)(924198-2) <24198>* **G N' R LIES (live)** [22] [2]
– Reckless life / Nice boys (don't play rock'n'roll) / Move to the city / Mama kin / Patience / I used to love her / You're crazy / One in a million. *(re-iss. Nov90 lp/c/cd; GEF/+C/D 24198) (re-iss. Oct95 cd/c;)*

Mar 89. (7"/7"sha-clear/7"white-pic-d) *(GEF 50/+P/X) <27570>* **PARADISE CITY. / I USED TO LOVE HER** [6] Jan89 [5]
(c-s+=)(12"+=) *(9275 704)(GEF 50T)* – Anything goes.
(cd-s++=) *(GEF 50CD)* – Sweet child o' mine.

May 89. (7"/7"s/c-s) *(GEF 55/+W/C)* **SWEET CHILD O' MINE (remix). / OUT TA GET ME** [6] [–]
(7"sha-pic-d+=) *(GEF 55P)* – Rocket queen.
(12"/3"cd-s) *(GEF 55 T/CD)* – ('A'side) / Move to the city / Whole lotta Rosie (live) / It's so easy (live).

Jun 89. (7"/c-s) *(GEF 56/+C) <22996>* **PATIENCE. / ROCKET QUEEN** [10] Apr89 [4]
(12"+=/3"cd-s+=) *(GEF 56 T/CD)* – (W. Axl Rose interview).

Aug 89. (7"/7"sha-pic-d/c-s) *(GEF 60/+P/C)* *<22869>*
NIGHTRAIN. / RECKLESS LIFE [17] Jul89 [93]
(12"+=/3"cd-s+=) *(GEF 60 T/CD)* – Knockin' on Heaven's door (live '87).

— (Aug'90) **MATT SORUM** (b.19 Nov'60, Long Beach, Calif.) – drums (ex-CULT) repl. ADAM MARPLES (ex-SEA HAGS) who repl. ADLER due to bouts of drunkenness / added **DIZZY REED** (b. DARREN REED, 18 Jun'63, Hinsdale, Illinois) – keyboards

Jul 91. (7"/c-s/12"clear-pic-d/cd-s) *(GFS/+C/TP/TD 6)*
<19039> **YOU COULD BE MINE. / CIVIL WAR** [3] [29]

Sep 91. (d-lp/c/cd) *<(GEF/+C/D 24415)>* **USE YOUR ILLUSION I** [2] [2]
– Right next door to Hell / Dust n' bones / Live and let die / Don't cry (original) / Perfect crime / You ain't the first / Bad obsession / Back off bitch / Double talkin' jive / November rain / The garden / Garden of Eden / Don't damn me / Bad apples / Dead horse / Coma.

Sep 91. (d-lp/c/cd) *<(GEF/+C/D 24420)>* **USE YOUR ILLUSION II** [1] [1]
– Civil war / 14 years / Yesterdays / Knockin' on Heaven's door / Get in the ring / Shotgun blues / Breakdown / Pretty tied up / Locomotive / So fine / Estranged / You could be mine / Don't cry (alt.lyrics) / My world.

Sep 91. (7"/c-s) *(GFS/+C 9)* *<19027>* **DON'T CRY (original). / DON'T CRY (alternate lyrics)** [8] [10]
(12"+=/cd-s+=) *(GFST/+D 9)* – ('A'demo).

Dec 91. (7"/c-s/12") *(GFS/+C/X 17)* *<19114>* **LIVE AND LET DIE. / ('A'live)** [5] [33]
(cd-s+=) *(GFSTD 17)* – Shadow of your love.

— (Sep'91) **DAVID NAVARRO** – guitar (of JANE'S ADDICTION) repl. IZZY who walked out on tour. **GILBY CLARKE** (b.17 Aug'62, Cleveland, Ohio) – guitar finally repl. IZZY who formed IZZY STRADLIN & THE JU JU HOUNDS

Feb 92. (7"/c-s) *(GFS/+C 18)* *<19067>* **NOVEMBER RAIN. / SWEET CHILD O' MINE (live)** [4] Jun92 [3]
(12"+=/pic-cd-s+=) *(GFST/+D 18)* – Patience.

May 92. (7"/c-s/12"/cd-s) *(GFS/+C/T/TD 21)* **KNOCKIN' ON HEAVEN'S DOOR (live '92 at Freddie Mercury tribute). / ('A'studio)** [2] [–]

Oct 92. (7"/c-s) *(GFS/+C 27)* **YESTERDAYS. / NOVEMBER RAIN** [8] [–]
(12"pic-d+=/cd-s+=) *(GFST/+D 27)* – ('A'live) / Knockin' on Heaven's door (live '87).

Nov 92. (c-s) *<19142>* **YESTERDAYS / ('A'live)** [–] [72]

May 93. (cd-ep) *(GFSTD 43)* **CIVIL WAR EP** [11] [–]
– Civil war / Garden of Eden / Dead horse / (interview with Slash).

Nov 93. (c-s) *(GFSC 62)* **AIN'T IT FUN. / DOWN ON THE FARM** [9] [–]
(cd-s+=) *(GFSTD 62)* – Attitude.

Nov 93. (cd/c/lp) *<(GED/GEC/GEF 24617)>* **THE SPAGHETTI INCIDENT** [2] [4]
– Since I don't have you / New rose / Down on the farm / Human being / Raw power / Ain't it fun / Buick Makane / Hair of the dog / Attitude / Black leather / You can't put your arms around a memory / I don't care about you / What's your game!.

May 94. (7"colrd/c-s) *(GFS/+C 70)* *<19266>* **SINCE I DON'T HAVE YOU. / YOU CAN'T PUT YOUR ARMS AROUND A MEMORY** [10] Feb94 [69]
(cd-s+=) *(GFSTD 70)* – Human being.
(cd-s) *(GFSXD 70)* – ('A'side) / Sweet child o' mine / Estranged.

— **PAUL HUGE** – guitar; repl. the sacked and solo bound GILBY (below from the movie 'Interview With A Vampire')

Jan 95. (c-s) *(GFSC 86)* **SYMPATHY FOR THE DEVIL / LIVE AND LET DIE** [9] Dec94 [55]
(cd-s) *(GFSTD 86)* *<19381>* – ('A') / (track by Elliot Goldenthal).

— DUFF and MATT teamed up with STEVE JONES (Sex Pistols) and JOHN TAYLOR (Duran Duran) to form mid '96 supergroup, The NEUROTIC OUTSIDERS; released an eponymous album and single, 'JERK', for 'Maverick' records. In early November, SLASH quit, citing ill feeling between him and AXL.

– compilations, others, etc. –

on 'Geffen' unless mentioned otherwise

Nov 99. (d-cd/d-c) *<(490514-2/-4)>* **LIVE ERA '87-'93** (live) [45] [45]
– Nightrain / Mr. Brownstone / It's so easy / Welcome to the jungle / Dust n' bones / My Michelle / You're crazy / Used to love her / Patience / It's alright / November rain / Out to get me / Pretty tied up (the perils of rock'n'roll) / Yesterdays / Move to the city / You could be mine / Rocket queen / Sweet child o' mine / Knockin' on Heaven's door / Don't cry / Estranged / Paradise city.

Mar 04. (cd) *(9862108)* *<17140-2>* **GREATEST HITS** [1] [3]
– Welcome to the jungle / Sweet child o' mine / Patience / Paradise city / Knockin' on Heaven's door / Civil war / You could be mine / Don't cry / November rain / Live and let die / Yesterdays / Ain't in fun / Since I don't have you / Sympathy for the Devil.

DUFF McKAGAN

with **TED ANDREADIS** + **DIZZY REED** – keyboards / **WEST ARKEEN** – lead guitar (co-wrote 'Man In The Meadow') / plus other guests **SLASH** – lead guitar / **MATT SORUM** – drums (co-wrote 'F@*ked Up Beyond Belief'), **GILBY CLARKE** – guitars (co-wrote '10 Years'), **JOIE MASTROKALOS** – b.vocals (co-wrote 'Just Not There'), **DOC NEWMAN** – vocals (+ co-wrote 'F@*k You'), **SNAKE, SEBASTIAN BACH, LENNY KRAVITZ + JEFF BECK**

Geffen Geffen

Oct 93. (cd/c/lp) *<(GED/GEC/GEF 24605)>* **BELIEVE IN ME** [27] [ ]
– Believe in me / I love you / Man in the meadow / (F@*ked up) Beyond belief / Could it be U / Just not there / Punk rock song / The majority / 10 years / Swamp song / Trouble / F@*k you / Lonely tonite.

Nov 93. (cd-s) *(GED 21865)* **BELIEVE IN ME / BAMBI / CRACKED ACTOR** [ ] [ ]

— In 1997, DUFF couldn't wait for GN'R to regroup; he re-formed 10 MINUTE WARNING – a solo set, 'BEAUIFUL DISEASE' was shelved

SLASH'S SNAKEPIT

SLASH – guitar with **MATT SORUM + GILBY CLARKE / + ERIC DOVER** – vocals (ex-JELLYFISH)/ **MIKE INEZ** – bass (of ALICE IN CHAINS)

Geffen Geffen

Feb 95. (cd/c/lp) *<(GED/GEC/GEF 24730)>* **IT'S FIVE O'CLOCK SOMEWHERE** [15] [70]
– Neither can I / Dime store rock / Beggars and hangers-on / Good to be alive / What do you want to be / Monkey chow / Soma city ward / Jizz da pit / Lower / Take it away / Doin' fine / Be the ball / I hate everybody (but you) / Back and forth again.

— now with **MATT LAUG** – drums / **RYAN ROXIE** – guitar, vocals / **JACK DOUGLAS** – sitar, vocals / **ROD JACKSON** – vocals

Koch Koch

Oct 00. (cd/c) *<(KOC CD/MC 8198)>* **AIN'T LIFE GRAND** [ ] [ ]
– Been there lately / Just like anything / Shine / Mean bone / Back to the moment / Life's sweet drug / Serial killer / The truth / Landslide / Ain't life grand / Speed parade / Alien.

VELVET REVOLVER

SLASH, McKAGAN + SORUM recruited **SCOTT WEILAND** – vocals (ex-STONE TEMPLE PILOTS) + **DAVE KUSHNER** – guitar (ex-WASTED YOUTH, ELECTRIC LOVE HOGS)

R.C.A. R.C.A.

Jun 04. (cd/d-lp) *(82876 62835-2/-1)* *<82876 59794-2/-1>* **CONTRABAND** [11] [1]
– Sucker train blues / Do it for the kids / Big machine / Illegal I song / Spectacle / Fall to pieces / Headspace / Superhuman / Set me free / You got no right / Slither / Dirty little thing / Loving the alien. *(UK cd+=)* – Bodies (live). *(cd re-iss. Jun05 'Tour Edition' w/cd+=; 82876 70197-2)* – Surrender / No more no more / Fall to pieces (acoustic) / Slither (video) / Fall to pieces (video) / Dirty little thing (video).

Jul 04. (12"pic-d) *(82876 63331-1)* **SLITHER. / SET ME FREE** [35] [56]
(cd-s) *<(82876 63331-2)>* – ('A') / Negative creep / Bodies (live).
(cd-s) *(82876 63331-9)* – ('A') / Money / Set me free (video).

Oct 04. (7"/cd-s) *(82876 64797-7/64769-2)* *<63786>* **FALL TO PIECES. / SURRENDER** [32] Nov04 [67]
(dvd-s) *(82876 64769-9)* – ('A'-video) / Slither (video) / (making of Slither video).

☐ Robin GUTHRIE (see under ⇒ COCTEAU TWINS)

Bill HALEY

Born: WILLIAM HALEY, 6 Jul'25, Highland Park, Detroit, USA. After leaving school in Pennsylvania, BILL became a travelling musician and yodeller for country bands, The DOWN HOMERS and The RANGE DRIFTERS. In 1948, he was hired as a DJ for the local W-PWA station in Chester, taking up the opportunity to air recordings of his new outfit, The FOUR ACES. He subsequently abandoned them in the early 50's, recruiting new backers, The SADDLEMEN, whose reputation was beginning to spread around the hillbilly community. In 1952, HALEY signed to 'Essex' and issued the 78, 'ICY HEART' / 'ROCK THE JOINT', although this was only a minor seller. Renaming the outfit BILL HALEY & HIS COMETS, they hit upon a winning combination of rockabilly fused with their own interpretation of black R&B, scoring their first US Top 20 hit with 'CRAZY MAN CRAZY'. In 1954, the group shifted stables to 'Decca', where they cut 'THIRTEEN WOMEN' as a single, although this was to initially flop. The record's flip side, 'ROCK AROUND THE CLOCK', began to garner airplay from some of the more non-conformist radio stations and their next single, 'SHAKE, RATTLE AND ROLL' became a Top 20 hit (on both! sides of the Atlantic). Due to unprecedented public demand, 'ROCK AROUND THE CLOCK' was reissued, this landmark track eventually becoming a transatlantic chart topper. It was undeniably the birth of popular rock'n'roll, the youth culture transforming virtually overnight (parents hated its rebellious overtones, their offspring bopping uninhibitedly around the nation's dancehalls). HALEY was now giving legendary performances up and down the States, although his clean-cut and well-dressed appearance disappointed his newfound British following who were looking for a thinner, unmarried figurehead to portray this hip new sound. The formula was repeated on subsequent 45's/78's throughout the mid-late 50's, songs such as 'ROCK-A-BEATIN' BOOGIE', 'SEE YOU LATER, ALLIGATOR', 'THE SAINTS ROCK'N'ROLL' and 'ROCKIN' THROUGH THE RYE' dominating the charts prior to the advent of rock'n'roll as an image industry for fresh faced youngsters (i.e. ELVIS, EDDIE, and even CLIFF). The 60's were virtually a non-starter for HALEY, although his revival concerts of the following decade saw obligatory reissues of 'ROCK AROUND THE CLOCK' hit the UK Top 20. Sadly, after a year spent in and out of hospital with a brain tumor, he died of a heart attack at his home in Harlingen, Texas on the 9th of February, 1981.

• **Songwriters:** HALEY adapted songs from obscure originals, writing many himself. Covered ROCK THE JOINT (Jimmy Preston) / ROCKET 88 (hit. Jackie Brenston) / RIP IT UP (Little Richard) / WHEN THE SAINTS GO MARCHING IN (trad.) / ROCKIN' THROUGH THE RYE (Scot. trad) / etc.

Best CD compilation: THE VERY BEST OF BILL HALEY & HIS COMETS (*7)

BILL HALEY and the 4 ACES OF WESTERN SWING

BILL HALEY – vocals, guitar; and unknown backers

not iss. Cowboy

1948. (78) *<1201>* **TOO MANY PARTIES, TOO MANY PALS. / FOUR LEAF CLOVER BLUES** [–] [ ]

1948. (78) *<1202>* **CANDY KISSES. / TENNESSEE BORDER** [–] [ ]

JOHNNY CLIFTON & HIS STRING BAND

not iss. Center

1949. (78) *<102>* **STAND UP AND BE COUNTED. / LOVELESS BLUES** [–] [ ]

— In 1950, BILL HALEY's vocals were credited on RENO BROWNE and her BUCKAROOS single, 'MY SWEET LITTLE GIRL FROM NEVADA' <1701>

BILL HALEY and his SADDLEMEN

— with **JOHNNY GRANDE** – piano / **BILLY WILLIAMSON** – steel guitar

not iss. Keystone

1950. (78) *<5101>* **DEAL ME A HAND (I PLAY THE GAME ANYWAY). / TEN GALLON STETSON (WITH A HOLE IN THE CROWN)** [–] [ ]

1950. (78) *<5102>* **SUSAN VAN DUREN. / I'M NOT TO BLAME** [–] [ ]

(below was backing for **LOU GRAHAM**

not iss. Atlantic

1950. (78) *<727>* **WHY DO I CRY OVER YOU. / I'M GONNA DRY EVERY TEAR WITH A KISS** [–] [ ]

not iss. Holiday

1951. (78) *<105> (TU 103)* **ROCKET 88. / TEARSTAINS ON MY HEART** [–] [ ]

(UK-iss.Feb81 on 'Thumbs Up')

1951. (78) *<108>* **GREEN TREE BOOGIE. / DOWN DEEP IN MY HEART** [–] [ ]

1951. (78) *<110>* **I'M CRYING. / PRETTY BABY** [–] [ ]

1951. (78) *<111>* **A YEAR AGO THIS CHRISTMAS. / I DON'T WANT TO ALONE THIS CHRISTMAS** [–] [ ]

1952. (78) *<113>* **JUKEBOX CANNONBALL. / SUNDOWN BOOGIE** [–] [ ]

not iss. Essex

1952. (78) *<303>* **ICY HEART. / ROCK THE JOINT** [–] [ ]

1952. (78) *<305>* **ROCKING CHAIR ON THE MOON. / DANCE WITH THE DOLLY (WITH A HOLE IN HER STOCKING)** [–] [ ]

BILL HALEY and his COMETS

— with **GRANDE + WILLIAMSON** plus **DANNY SEDRONE** – lead guitar / **MARSHALL PINGATORE** – up.bass / **DICK RICHARDS** – drums / **JOEY D'AMBROSIA** – tenor sax.

London Essex

1952. (78) *<310>* **STOP BEATIN' ROUND THE MULBURRY BUSH. / REAL ROCK DRIVE** [–] [ ]

Aug 53. (78) *(L 1190) <321>* **CRAZY MAN, CRAZY. / WHATCHA GONNA DO** [ ] Feb53 [ ]

Nov 53. (78) *(L 1216) <327>* **PAT-A-CAKE. / FRACTURED** [ ] Apr53 [ ]

1953. (78) *<332>* **LIVE IT UP. / FAREWELL, SO LONG, GOODBYE** [–] [ ]

1953. (78) <340> **I'LL BE TRUE. / TEN LITTLE INDIANS** [–] [ ]
1953. (78) <348> **STRAIGHT JACKET. / CHATTANOOGA CHOO-CHOO** [–] [ ]
1954. (78) <374> **SUNDOWN BOOGIE. / JUKEBOX CANNONBALL** [–] [ ]
1954. (78) <381> **ROCKET 88. / GREEN TREE BOOGIE** [–] [ ]
1954. (lp) *<LP 202>* **ROCK WITH BILL HALEY & THE COMETS** [–] [ ]
(re-iss. 1954 on 'Trans World'; same)

— **BILLY GUSACK** – session drums (only 1)

Brunswick Decca

Sep 54. (7",78) *(05317) <29124>* **ROCK AROUND THE CLOCK. / THIRTEEN WOMEN** [ ] May54 [ ]
(re-dist.UK Dec54 hit No.17, Oct55 hit No.1, Sep56 hit No.5, stayed Top 30 until early next year) (re-dist.US Apr55, after 'Blackboard Jungle' film appearance, hit No.1, stayed in Top 50 for 1/2 a year)

— **FRANNY BEECHER** – lead guitar repl. CEDRONE who died of heart attack / **RUDY POMPILLI** – saxophone / **AL POMPILLI** – bass / **RALPH JONES** – drums repl. others

Nov 54. (7",78) *(05338) <29204>* **SHAKE, RATTLE AND ROLL. / ABC BOOGIE** [4] Jul54 [12]
Jan 55. (7",78) *(05373) <29317>* **DIM, DIM THE LIGHTS (I WANT SOME ATMOSPHERE). / HAPPY BABY** [ ] Nov54 [11]
Mar 55. (7",78) *(05405) <29418>* **MAMBO ROCK. / BIRTH OF THE BOOGIE** [14] [18] Feb55 [17]
Jul 55. (7",78) *(05405) <29552>* **RAZZLE-DAZZLE. / TWO HOUND DOGS** [ ] [15]
(UK re-dist.Sep56; hit No.13)
Sep 55. (10"lp) *<DL 5560>* **SHAKE RATTLE AND ROLL** [–] [ ]
Nov 55. (7",78) *(05509) <29713>* **ROCK-A-BEATIN' BOOGIE. / BURN THAT CANDLE** [4] [9] [23]
Feb 56. (7",78) *(05530) <29791>* **SEE YOU LATER, ALLIGATOR. / THE PAPER BOY** [7] Jan56 [6]
(re-dist.UK Sep56; hit No.12)
May 56. (7",78) *(05565) <29870>* **THE SAINTS ROCK'N'ROLL. / R-O-C-K** [5] Mar56 [18] [16]
Jun 56. (lp) *(LAT 8117) <DL 8225>* **ROCK AROUND THE CLOCK** [ ] Jan56 [12]
– (virtually a compilation, didn't make it in UK due to no lp chart until Nov'58)
– Rock around the clock / Shake rattle and roll / ABC boogie / (You hit the wrong note) Billy goat / Thirteen women (and only one man in town) / Tonight's the night / Razzle dazzle / Two hound dogs / Dim dim the lights / Happy baby / Birth of the boogie / Rockin' rollin' Rover / Mambo rock / Hide and seek / Burn that candle / Rock-a-beatin' boogie. *(re-iss. 1961 on 'Ace Of Hearts', re-iss. May68, hit UK No.34) (re-iss. Jan71 on 'Coral') (re-iss. Sep81 on 'M.C.A.')*
Aug 56. (7",78) *(05582) <29948>* **ROCKIN' THROUGH THE RYE. / HOT DOG BUDDY BUDDY** [3] [78] [60]
Nov 56. (7",78) *(05615) <30028>* **RIP IT UP. / TEENAGER'S MOTHER (ARE YOU RIGHT?)** [4] [25] Aug56 [68]
Nov 56. (lp) *(LAT 8139) <DL 8345>* **ROCK'N'ROLL STAGE SHOW** (hit singles chart=) [30] Sep56 [18]
– Calling all comets / Rockin' through the rye / A rocking little tune / Hide and seek / Hey then there now / Goofin' around / Hook line and sinker / Rudy's rock / Choo choo ch'boogie / Blue comet blues / Hot dog buddy buddy / Tonight's the night. *(re-iss. Aug83 on 'Charly')*
Nov 56. (7",78) *(05615) <30085>* **RUDY'S ROCK. / BLUE COMET BLUES** [26] [34]
Dec 56. (7") *<30148>* **DON'T KNOCK THE ROCK. / CHOO CHOO CH'BOOGIE** [–] [45]
Feb 57. (7",78) *(05640)* **DON'T KNOCK THE ROCK. / CALLING ALL COMETS** [7] [–]
Feb 57. (7",78) *(05641)* **HOOK, LINE AND SINKER. / GOOFIN' AROUND** [ ] [–]
Mar 57. (7") *<30214>* **FORTY CUPS OF COFFEE. / HOOK, LINE AND SINKER** [–] [70]
Apr 57. (7",78) *(05658)* **FORTY CUPS OF COFFEE. / CHOO CHOO CH'BOOGIE** [ ] [–]

— **FRANKIE SCOTT** – saxophone repl. RUDY (He was to die 5 Feb'76)

Jul 57. (7",78) *(05688) <30314>* **(YOU HIT THE WRONG NOTE) BILLY GOAT. / ROCKIN' ROLLIN' ROVER** [ ] [ ]
Oct 57. (7",78) *(05719) <30394>* **MISS YOU. / THE DIPSY DOODLE** [ ] [ ]
Dec 57. (lp) *(LAT 8219) <DL 8569>* **ROCKIN' THE OLDIES** [ ] [ ]
– The dipsy doodle / You can't stop me from dreamin' / (I'll be with you) In apple blossom time / Moon over Miami / Is it true what they say about Dixie / Carolina in the morning / Miss you / Please don't talk about me when I'm gone / Ain't misbehavin' (I'm savin' my love for you) / One sweet letter from you / I'm gonna sit right down and write myself a letter / Somebody else is taking my place. *(re-iss. Oct62 on 'Ace Of Hearts')*
Feb 58. (7",78) *(05735) <30530>* **MARY, MARY LOU. / IT'S A SIN** [ ] [ ]
Apr 58. (7",78) *(05742) <30592>* **SKINNY MINNIE. / HOW MANY** [ ] [22]
Aug 58. (7",78) *(05753) <30681>* **LEAN JEAN. / DON'T NOBODY MOVE** [ ] [67]
Nov 58. (lp) *(LAT 8268) <DL 8775>* **ROCKIN' THE JOINT** [ ] [ ]
– Rock the joint / Rockin' chair on the Moon / Farewell – So long – Goodbye / Real rock drive / Fractured / Stop beatin' around the mulberry bush / Crazy man, crazy / Pat-a-cake / Live it up / Watcha gonna do / I'll be true to you / Dance with a dolly (with a hole in her stockin').
Nov 58. (7",78) *(05766) <30741>* **WHOA MABEL! / CHIQUITA LINDA** [ ] [ ]
Jan 59. (7",78) *<30781>* **CORRINE, CORRINA. / B-B-BETTY** [–] [ ]
Mar 59. (7",78) *(05788) <30844>* **I GOT A WOMAN. / CHARMAINE** [ ] [ ]
Jun 59. (lp) *(LAT 8295) <DL 8821>* **BILL HALEY'S CHICKS** [ ] [ ]
– Whoa Mabel! / Ida, sweet as apple cider / Eloise / Dinah / Skinny Minnie / Mary, Mary Lou / Sweet Sue – Just you / B-B-Betty / Charmaine / Corrine Corrina / Marie / Lean Jean. *(re-iss. 1960 stereo; STA 3011) (re-iss. Jan64 on 'Ace Of Hearts'; AH 66)*
Jun 59. (7") *<30873>* **WHERE DID YOU GO LAST NIGHT? / (NOW AND THEN THERE'S) A FOOL SUCH AS I** [–] [ ]
Aug 59. (7",78) *(05805) <30926>* **SHAKY. / CALEDONIA** [ ] [ ]
Jan 60. (7",78) *(05810) <30956>* **JOEY'S SONG. / LOOK-A-THERE, AIN'T SHE PRETTY** [ ] Sep59 [46]
Feb 60. (7") *(05818) <31030>* **SKOKIAAN. / PUERTO RICAN JUGGLER** [ ] Dec59 [70]
Apr 60. (7") *<31080>* **MUSIC! MUSIC! MUSIC!. / STRICTLY INSTRUMENTAL** [–] [ ]
Apr 60. (lp) *(LAT 8326) <DL 8964>* **STRICTLY INSTRUMENTAL** [ ] [ ]
– Joey's song / (Put another nickel in) Music, music, music / Mack the knife / In a little Spanish town ('twas on a night like this) / Two shadows / Shaky / Strictly instrumental / Skokiaan (South African song) / Puerto Rican peddlar / Drowsy waters / Chiquita Linda (un poquito de tu amor) / The catwalk.

Warners Warners

May 60. (7") *(WB 6)* **CANDY KISSES. / TAMIAMI** [ ] [–]
1960. (7") *<5154>* **CHUCK SAFARI. / HAWK** [–] [ ]
1960. (7") *<5171>* **SO RIGHT TONIGHT. / LET THE GOOD TIMES ROLL, CREOLE** [–] [ ]
Nov 60. (lp) *(W 1391)* **HALEY'S JUKE BOX** [ ] [ ]
– Sing the blues / Candy kisses / No letter today / This is the thanks I get / Bouquet of roses / There's a new Moon over my shoulder / Cold, cold heart / Wild side of life / Any time / Afraid / I don't hurt anymore.
1960. (7") *<5228>* **FLIP, FLOP AND FLY. / HONKY TONK** [–] [ ]

London Gone

Dec 61. (7") *(HLU 9471) <5111>* **SPANISH TWIST. / MY KIND OF WOMAN** [ ] [ ]
1962. (7") *<5116>* **RIVIERA. / WAR PAINT** [–] [ ]

not iss. Orfeon

1962. (7") **FLORIDA TWIST. / NEGRA CONSENTIDA** [–] Mexico [–]
1962. (7") **PURE DE PAPAS. / ANOCHE** [–] Mexico [–]

not iss. Logo

1962. (7") *<7005>* **YAKETY SAX. / BOOTS RANDOLPH – BOOTS BLUES** [–] [ ]

Columbia Columbia

Oct 62. (lp) *(33SX 1460)* **TWISTIN' KNIGHTS AT THE ROUNDTABLE (LIVE!)** [ ] [ ]
– Lullaby of Birdland twist / Twist Marie / One two three twist / Down by the riverside twist / Queen of the twisters / Caravan twist / I want a little girl / Whistlin' and walkin' twist / Florida twist / Eight more miles to Louisville. *(re-iss. May81 on 'P.R.T.')*

Stateside Newtown

Jun 63. (7") *(SS 196) <5013>* **TENOR MAN. / UP GOES MY LOVE** [ ] [ ]
1963. (7") *<5014>* **MIDNIGHT IN WASHINGTON. / WHITE PARAKEET** [–] [ ]

1963. (7") *<5024>* **DANCE AROUND THE CLOCK. / WHAT CAN I SAY AFTER I SAY I'M SORRY** [–] [ ]

1963. (7") *<5025>* **TANDY. / YOU CALL EVERYBODY DARLING** [–] [ ]

Brunswick Decca

Aug 64. (7") *(05910)* **HAPPY BABY. / BIRTH OF THE BOOGIE** [ ] [–]

Oct 64. (7") *(05917) <31650>* **GREEN DOOR. / (YEAH!) SHE'S EVIL** [ ] [ ]

not iss. Apt

1965. (7") *<25051>* **BIG DADDY. / ST. LOUIS** [–] [ ]

1965. (7") *<25081>* **BURN THAT CANDLE. / STOP, LOOK AND LISTEN** [–] [ ]

1965. (7") *<25087>* **HALEY A GO-GO. / TONGUE TIED TONY** [–] [ ]

not iss. U.A.

1969. (7") *<50483>* **THAT'S HOW I GOT TO MEMPHIS. / AIN'T LOVE FUNNY, HA! HA! HA!** [–] [ ]

not iss. Kama Sutra

1970. (7") *<508>* **ROCK AROUND THE CLOCK. / FRAMED** [–] [ ]

Sonet GNP Cres

1971. (lp) *(SNTF 623) <2097>* **ROCK AROUND THE COUNTRY** [ ] [–]
– Dance around the clock / Games people play / A little piece at a time / I wouldn't have missed it for the world / Bony Moronie / There's a new Moon over my shoulder / Me and Bobby McGee / How many / Who'll stop the rain / Pink eyed pussycat / Travelin' band / No letter today. *(re-iss. Jun74 on 'Hallmark')*

1972. (7") *<162>* **A LITTLE PIECE AT A TIME. / TRAVELIN' BAND** [–] [ ]

May 73. (7") *(SON 2016)* **ME AND BOBBY McGEE. / I WOULDN'T HAVE MISSED IT FOR THE WORLD** [ ] [–]

1973. (lp) *(SNTF 645)* **JUST ROCK AND ROLL MUSIC** [ ] [ ]
– I'm walkin' / High-heel sneakers / Blue suede shoes / Tossin' and turnin' / Flip, flop and fly / Whole lotta shakin' goin' on / CC rider / Lawdy Miss Clawdy / Bring it on home to me / Personality / Crazy man crazy / Rock'n'roll music.

1974. (lp) **LIVE IN SWEDEN (live)** [–] [ ]

Jun 74. (7") *(SON 2043)* **CRAZY MAN CRAZY (live). / LAWDY MISS CLAWDY (live)** [ ] [–]

Atlantic Atlantic

Jun 74. (lp) *(K 51501)* **LIVE IN LONDON '74 (live)** [ ] [ ]
– Shake, rattle & roll / Rudy's rock / Rip it up / Spanish eyes / Razzle dazzle / Rock-a-beatin' boogie / Caravan / See you later alligator / Saints rock and roll / Rock around the clock / Rock the joint.

—— HALEY became ill, leading him into retirement. Although in England, he had given final appearance at Royal Variety Show, Nov79. In 1980, now at age 55, he was diagnosed with brain tumor. On 9 Feb'81 he died of a heart attack.

– (selective) compilations, etc. –

Feb 57. (7") *London; (HLF 8371)* **ROCK THE JOINT. / YES INDEED** [20] [–]

Mar 68. (7") *M.C.A.; (MU 1013)* **ROCK AROUND THE CLOCK. / SHAKE RATTLE AND ROLL** [20] [ ]

May 68. (lp) *M.C.A.; (MUP 318)* **RIP IT UP** [ ] [ ]

Mar 74. (7") *M.C.A.; (MCA 128)* **ROCK AROUND THE CLOCK. / RIP IT UP** [12] [–]

Mar 74. (7") *M.C.A.; <60025>* **(WE'RE GONNA) ROCK AROUND THE CLOCK. / THIRTEEN WOMEN (AND ONLY ONE MAN IN TOWN)** [–] [39]

Apr 81. (7") *M.C.A.; (MCA 694)* **HALEY'S GOLDEN MEDLEY. / ABC BOOGIE** [50] [ ]

Sep 82. (5xlp-box) *Bear Family; <BFX 15068-5>* **ROCKIN' ROLLIN' HALEY** [–] [ ]
(UK-iss.Sep84 on 'Rollercoaster'; same) <(5xcd-box iss.Oct90; BCD 15506)>

Dec 89. (cd/c) *Accord; (30137-2/-4)* **SEE YOU LATER ALLIGATOR** [ ] [–]

Jul 92. (cd/c) *Music Club; (MC CD/TC 068)* **THE VERY BEST OF BILL HALEY & HIS COMETS** [ ] [–]
– Rock around the clock / Shake, rattle and roll / See you later alligator / The saints rock and roll / Rock-a beatin' boogie / Rockin' thru the rye / Rip it up / Don't knock the rock / Mambo rock / Rudy's rock / Razzle dazzle / Skinny Minnie / R.O.C.K. / Thirteen women / ABC boogie / Birth of the boogie / Forty cups of coffee / Two hound dogs / Burn that candle / Calling all Comets.

Oct 94. (cd) *Timeless Treasures; (CD 114)* **BILL HALEY & THE COMETS** [ ] [–]

Feb 95. (cd/c) *More Music; (MOCD/MOMC 3015)* **ROCK AROUND THE CLOCK** [ ] [–]

Aug 96. (cd) *Marble Arch; (MACCD 231)* **BEST OF BILL HALEY** [ ] [–]

May 97. (cd) *A-Play; (10059-2)* **THE HITS COLLECTION** [ ] [ ]

Jan 98. (cd) *Members Edition; (UAE 3001-2)* **BILL HALEY** [ ] [–]

Mar 98. (cd) *Eagle; (EABCD 083)* **THE MASTERS** [ ] [–]

May 99. (6xcd-box) *Bear Family; <(BCD 16157)>* **THE WARNER BROTHERS YEARS AND MORE** [ ] [ ]

Jun 99. (cd) *Half Moon; (HMNCD 043)* **THE VERY BEST OF BILL HALEY & THE COMETS** [ ] [ ]

Aug 99. (cd) *Ultimate; (ULT 4019-2)* **ULTIMATE LEGENDS** [ ] [ ]

Oct 99. (cd) *Nervous; (RSRCD 013)* **THE HOUSE IS ROCKIN'** [ ] [ ]

Jan 00. (cd) *Members Edition; (UAE 30886-2)* **BILL HALEY & HIS COMETS** [ ] [–]

Jan 00. (cd) *Universal; (E 112174-2)* **THE UNIVERSAL MASTERS COLLECTION** [ ] [ ]

Jan 00. (cd) *Hydra; (BCK 27100)* **WE'RE GONNA PARTY** [ ] [–]

Jan 00. (cd) *Hydra; (BCL 27103)* **YOU'RE NEVER TOO OLD TO ROCK** [ ] [–]

Jul 00. (d-cd) *Duoline; (99011)* **ROCK AROUND THE CLOCK** [ ] [–]

Jan 01. (d-cd) *Ember; (EMCDCD 004)* **MR. ROCK 'N' ROLL / FRIENDS FROM THE BEGINNING (Little Richard & Jimi Hendrix)** [ ] [–]

Jul 01. (cd) *Platinum; (PLATCD 664)* **ROCK'N'ROLL LEGEND** [ ] [–]

Jul 01. (cd) *Hydra; (BCK 2711-2)* **ON THE AIR** [ ] [ ]

Sep 01. (cd) *Ember; (EMBCD 3401)* **MR. ROCK 'N' ROLL** [ ] [ ]

Feb 02. (cd/c) *Castle Pulse; (PLS CD/MC 566)* **THE BEST OF BILL HALEY** [ ] [ ]

Nov 02. (cd) *Planet Media; (PML 1051)* **ROCK AROUND THE CLOCK** [ ] [ ]

Dec 02. (cd) *Jerden; (JRCD 7023)* **THE BILL HALEY TAPES** [ ] [–]

Mar 03. (cd) *Universal; (AAMCAD 11957)* **20th CENTURY MASTERS** [ ] [ ]

Mar 03. (cd) *Universal; (E 320161-2)* **GREATEST HITS** [ ] [ ]

Jul 03. (cd) *Rock'n'roll Heroes; (RR 005)* **ROCK'N'ROLL HERO** [ ] [–]

Daryl HALL & John OATES

Formed: Philadelphia, Pennsylvania, USA . . . 1972 by the duo, wh signed to 'Atlantic', following their work with the band, GULLIVER They had originally met in 1967, while attending local Templ University; HALL had undergone classical training as a boy, an progressed to doo-wop groups while also featuring on a singl recorded by future producer KENNY GAMBLE & THE ROMEOS He then sessioned for many including THE TEMPTONES an SMOKEY ROBINSON, before forming GULLIVER with TI MOORE, TOM SELLERS and JIM HELMER. They released on self-titled lp in 1969 for 'Elektra', before being joined by OATES although they broke up before OATES could cut any songs wit them. The duo's debut album, 'WHOLE OATS', was produce by Arif Mardin, and was followed in 1974 by 'ABANDONE LUNCHEONETTE', the latter set containing the first of HAL & OATES' chartbound torch ballads in 'SHE'S GONE'. Thoug not a hit upon its original release, the single made the US To 10 two years later. The latter track featured on 'WAR BABIES (1974), a heavier, more experimental set (produced by TOD RUNDGREN) whose commercial failure marked the end of the ill-fated tenure with 'Atlantic'. Moving to 'R.C.A.', the grou concentrated on developing their white soul-rock/R&B, scorin almost immediately when their eponymous 1975 set climbed int the US Top 20 following the massive success of the infectio 'SARA SMILE' (co-written by HALL's sometime collaborator an girlfriend, Sara Allen). A follow-up set, 'BIGGER THAN BOTH O US' (1976) was even more successful, spawning the duo's first No. hit, 'RICH GIRL'. Though their profile took a bit of a batterin towards the end of the decade, HALL & OATES emerged with a gleaming new synth/pop-soul sound on 'VOICES' (1980), making the Top 20 with a cover of The Righteous Brothers' 'YOU'VE LOST THAT LOVIN' FEELIN' and scoring a belated second No.1 with 'KISS ON MY LIST' (it also included the original version of EVERY TIME YOU GO AWAY', later a hit for PAUL YOUNG). Vaguely akin to a two-headed American version of PHIL COLLINS (granted, a disturbing thought), HALL & OATES cleaned up in both the singles and albums market with a string of MOR hits including 'PRIVATE EYES', 'I CAN'T GO FOR THAT' (NO CAN DO)', 'MANEATER' and 'SAY IT ISN'T SO'; 'PRIVATE EYES' (1981) and 'H2O' (1982) remain among their best selling albums. The mid-80's concert set, 'LIVE AT THE APOLLO', saw them hooking up with TEMPTATIONS heroes, DAVID RUFFIN and EDDIE KENDRICKS, after which they took time out to work on side projects. Returning in 1988, they scored with the Top 5 hit, EVERYTHING YOUR HEART DESIRES', although subsequent albums, 'OOH YEAH!' (1988) and 'CHANGE OF SEASON' (1990) failed to scale the commercial heights of yesteryear. While 1997's MARIGOLD SKY' garnered few column inches, 2003's 'DO IT FOR LOVE' (2003) enjoyed a more hospitable reception from both the press and longtime fans. While hardly breaking any new ground, the record was a more than passable attempt at resurrecting the slick, blue-eyed soul vibe of their best work while both DARYL and OHN were in fine voice throughout, if a little burnished by the ntervening years.

Songwriters: HALL-OATES except; THE WAY YOU DO THE THINGS YOU DO – MY GIRL (Temptations) / CAN'T HELP FALLING IN LOVE Elvis Presley) / LOVE TRAIN (O'Jays) / etc. HALL covered; WRITTEN IN STONE (J.Allen-S.Dubin-K.Savigar) / ME AND MRS. JONES (Billy Paul). **Trivia:** ROBERT FRIPP (of KING CRIMSON) produced HALL's solo outing 'SACRED SONGS'.

Album rating: WHOLE OATS (*5) / ABANDONED LUNCHEONETTE (*7) / WAR BABIES (*4) / DARYL HALL & JOHN OATES (*6) / BIGGER THAN BOTH OF US (*5) / NO GOODBYES compilation (*4) / BEAUTY ON A BACK STREET (*6) / LIVETIME (*4) / ALONG THE RED LEDGE (*6) / X-STATIC (*4) / SACRED SONGS (*4; by Daryl Hall) / VOICES (*6) / PRIVATE EYES (*7) / H20 (*7) / ROCK'N'SOUL PART 1 compilation (*8) / BIG BAM BOOM (*6) / LIVE AT THE APOLLO with David Ruffin & Eddie Kendrick (*5) / THREE HEARTS IN A HAPPY ENDING MACHINE (*4; by Daryl Hall) / OOH YEAH! (*4) / CHANGE OF SEASON (*4) / THE BEST OF HALL & OATES – LOOKING BACK compilation (*8) / SOUL ALONE (*4; by Daryl Hall) / MARIGOLD SKY (*3)

DARYL HALL (b.DARYL HOHL, 11 Oct'48, Pottstown, Philadelphia) – vocals, keyboards (ex-TEMPTONES, ex-solo artist, ex-CELLAR DOOR, ex-EXECUTIVE SUITE, ex-GULLIVER) / **JOHN OATES** (b. 7 Apr'49, New York, USA) – vocals, guitar (ex-MASTERS) with various personnel session players.

Atlantic Atlantic

ep 72. (7"; as WHOLE OATS) *<2922>* **GOODNIGHT AND GOOD MORNING. / ALL OUR LOVE** [–] [ ]

lov 72. (lp) *<7242>* **WHOLE OATS** [–] [ ]
– I'm sorry / All our love / Georgie / Fall in Philadelphia / Water wheel / Lazy man / Good night & good morning / They needed each other / Southeast city window / Thank you for . . . / Lily (are you happy). *(UK-iss.Sep76; K 50306) (cd-iss. Feb93; 7567 81423)*

lov 72. (7") *<2939>* **I'M SORRY. / LILY (ARE YOU HAPPY)** [–] [ ]

an 74. (lp) *(K 40534) <7269>* **ABANDONED LUNCHEONETTE** [ ] [ ]
– I'm just a kid (don't make me feel like a man) / Laughing boy / She's gone / Las Vegas turnaround / Had I known you better then / Lady rain / When the morning comes / Abandoned luncheonette / Everytime I look at you. *<US re-iss. Oct76 hit No.33> (cd-iss. Jun93; 7567 81537-2)*

an 74. (7") *(K 19422)* **LAS VEGAS TURNAROUND. / I'M JUST A KID** [ ] [–]

eb 74. (7") *<2993>* **SHE'S GONE. / I'M JUST A KID (DON'T MAKE ME FEEL LIKE A MAN)** [–] [60]

il 74. (7") *(K 10459) <3026>* **WHEN THE MORNING COMES. / LADY RAIN** [ ] [ ]

ep 74. (7") *(K 10502)* **SHE'S GONE. / ABANDONED LUNCHEONETTE** [ ] [–]

Nov 74. (lp) *(K 50086) <18109>* **WAR BABIES** [ ] Oct74 [86]
– Can't stop the music (he played it much too long) / Is it a star / Beanie G and the rose tattoo / You're much too soon / 70's scenario / War baby son of Zorro / I'm watching you (a mutant romance) / Better watch your back / Screaming through December / Johnny Gone and the "C" eaters. *(cd-iss. Jul96; 7567 81489-2)*

Nov 74. (7") *<3239>* **CAN'T STOP THE MUSIC (HE PLAYED IT MUCH TOO LONG). / 70'S SCENARIO** [–] [ ]

R.C.A. R.C.A.

Sep 75. (lp) *<(APL-1 1144)>* **DARYL HALL & JOHN OATES** [56] [17]
– Camelia / Sara smile / Alone too long / Out of me, out of you / Nothing at all / Gino (the manager) / (You know) It doesn't matter anymore / Ennui on the mountain / Grounds for separation / Soldering. *(re-iss. Apr80; INTS 5010)*

Sep 75. (7") *(2614) <10373>* **CAMELIA. / ENNUI ON THE MOUNTAIN** [ ] [ ]

Nov 75. (7") *<10436>* **ALONE TOO LONG. / NOTHING AT ALL** [–] [ ]

Jan 76. (7") *(2656) <10530>* **SARA SMILE. / SOLDERING** [ ] [4]

May 76. (7") *(2684)* **GINO (THE MANAGER). / SOLDERING** [ ] [–]

Sep 76. (lp) *<(APL-1 1467)>* **BIGGER THAN BOTH OF US** [25] Aug76 [13]
– Back together again / Rich girl / Crazy eyes / Do what you want, be what you are / Kerry / London luck and love / Room to breathe / You'll never learn / Falling.

Oct 76. (7") *<10808>* **DO WHAT YOU WANT, BE WHAT YOU ARE. / YOU'LL NEVER LEARN** [–] [39]

— late in '76 DARYL duetted with RUTH COPELAND on single 'Heaven'.

Jan 77. (7") *<10860>* **RICH GIRL. / LONDON LUCK & LOVE** [–] [1]

Jan 77. (7") *(2757)* **RICH GIRL. / YOU'LL NEVER LEARN** [ ] [–]

May 77. (7") *<10970>* **BACK TOGETHER AGAIN. / ROOM TO BREATHE** [–] [28]

May 77. (7") *(PB 9053)* **BACK TOGETHER AGAIN. / ENNUI ON THE MOUNTAIN** [ ] [–]

Oct 77. (lp/c) *(PL/PK 12300) <2300>* **BEAUTY ON A BACK STREET** [40] Sep77 [30]
– Don't change / Why do lovers (break each other's heart?) / You must be good for something / The emptyness / Love hurts (love heals) / Bigger than both of us / Bad habits and infections / Winged bull / The girl who used to be. *(re-iss. Jul84; NL 82300)*

Oct 77. (7") *(PB 1132) <11132>* **WHY DO LOVERS (BREAK EACH OTHER'S HEART?). / THE GIRL WHO USED TO BE** [ ] [73]

Jan 78. (7") *<11181>* **DON'T CHANGE. / THE EMPTYNESS** [–] [ ]

— **CHARLES DE CHANT** – saxophone, keyboards, perc. repl. TOM SCOTT / **KENNY PASSARELLI** – bass repl. LEE SKLAR & SCOTT EDWARDS / **ROGER POPE** – drums repl. JEFF PORCARO / **CALEB QUAYE** – lead guitar / **DAVID KENT** – keyboards repl. other sessioners.

Jun 78. (lp/c) *(PL/PK 12802) <2802>* **LIVE TIME (live)** [ ] May78 [42]
– Rich girl / The emptyness / Do what you want, be what you are / I'm just a kid / Sara smile / Abandoned luncheonette / Room to breathe. *(re-iss. Jun83; INTS 5252)*

Aug 78. (7") *<111371>* **IT'S A LAUGH. / SERIOUS MATTER** [–] [20]

Sep 78. (7") *(PB 9324)* **THE LAST TIME. / SERIOUS MATTER** [ ] [–]

Sep 78. (lp/c) *(PL/PK 12804) <2894>* **ALONG THE RED LEDGE** [ ] [27]
– It's a laugh / Melody for a memory / The last time / I don't wanna lose you / Have I been away too long / Alley katz / Don't blame it on love / Serious matter / Pleasure beach / August day. *(re-iss. Jun83; INTS 5258) (re-iss. 1987 lp/c; NL/NK 84231)*

Jan 79. (7") *(PB 1424) <11424>* **I DON'T WANNA LOSE YOU. / AUGUST DAY** [ ] Dec78 [42]

— They retained **DECHANT, PASSARELLI** (on next only), and brought in **TOM 'T-Bone' WOLK** – bass, synthe / **G.E. SMITH** – guitar / **MICKEY CURRY** – drums

Nov 79. (7") *(PB 9466)* **PORTABLE RADIO. / NUMBER ONE** [ ] [–]

Nov 79. (lp/c) *<(AFL-1 3494)>* **X-STATIC** [ ] Oct79 [33]
– The woman comes and goes / Wait for me / Portable radio / All you want is Heaven / Who said the world was fair / Running from Paradise / Number one / Bebop – Drop / Hallofon / Intravino.

May 80. (7") *(PB 1747) <11747>* **WAIT FOR ME. / NO BRAIN NO PAIN** [ ] Oct79 [18]

May 80. (7") *<11920>* **WHO SAID THE WORLD WAS FAIR. / ALL YOU WANT IS HEAVEN** [–] [ ]

Jun 80. (7") *(RUN 1)* **RUNNING FROM PARADISE. / BEBOP – DROP** [41] [–]

Jul 80. (7") *<12048>* **HOW DOES IT FEEL TO BE BACK. / UNITED STATE** [–] [30]

Aug 80. (lp/c) *(PL/PK 13646) <AQL-1 3646>* **VOICES** [ ] [17]
– How does it feel to be back / Big kids / United state / Hard to be in love with you / Kiss on my list / Gotta lotta nerve (perfect perfect) / You've lost that lovin' feelin' / You make my dreams / Everytime you go away / Africa / Diddy doo wop (I hear the voices). *(re-iss. Sep81; RCALP 3044) (re-iss. Oct87 lp/c/cd; NL/NK/ND 90078)*

Sep 80. (7") *<12103>* **YOU'VE LOST THAT LOVIN' FEELIN' / DIDDY DOO WOP (I HEAR THE VOICES)** [–] [12]

Sep 80. (7") *(RCA 1)* **YOU'VE LOST THAT LOVIN' FEELIN'. / UNITED STATE** [55] [–]

Nov 80. (7") *(RCA 15) <12142>* **KISS ON MY LIST. / AFRICA** [33] Jan81 [1]

Jun 81. (7") *(RCA 86) <12217>* **YOU MAKE MY DREAMS. / GOTTA LOTTA NERVE (PERFECT PERFECT)** [ ] Apr81 [5]

Sep 81. (7"/12") *(RCA/+T 134) <12296>* **PRIVATE EYES. / TELL ME WHAT YOU WANT** [ ] Aug81 [1]
(re-promoted.Mar82; hit UK No.32)

Sep 81. (lp/c) *(RCA LP/K 6001) <AFL-1 4028>* **PRIVATE EYES** [8] [5]
– Private eyes / Loking for a good gun / I can't go for that (no can do) / Mama a mano / Did it in a minute / Head above water / Tell me what you want / Friday let me down / Ungaurded minute / Your imagination / Some men. *(cd-iss. Dec84; PD 84028) (re-iss. Oct87 lp/c/cd; NL/NK/ND 90079)*

Jan 82. (7"/12") *(RCA/+T 172) <12361>* **I CAN'T GO FOR THAT (NO CAN DO). / UNGUARDED MINUTE** [8] Nov81 [1]

Mar 82. (7") *<13065>* **DID IT IN A MINUTE. / HEAD ABOVE WATER** [–] [9]

Jun 82. (7"/12") *(RCA/+T 239) <13252>* **YOUR IMAGINATION. / SARA SMILE** [ ] [33]

Oct 82. (7"/12") *(RCA/+T 290) <13354>* **MANEATER. / DELAYED REACTION** [6] [1]

Oct 82. (lp/c) *(RCA LP/K 6056) <4383>* **H2O** [24] [3]
– Maneater / Crime pays / One on one / Art of heartbreak / Open all night / Family man / Italian girls / Guessing games / Delayed reaction / At tension / Go solo. *(cd-iss. 1985; PD 84383)*

Jan 83. (7"/12") *(RCA/+T 305) <13421>* **ONE ON ONE. / ART OF HEARTBREAK** [63] [7]
(US 12") *<13421>* – ('A'club) / I can't go for that (no can do) (extended).

Apr 83. (7") *<13507>* **FAMILY MAN. / OPEN ALL NIGHT** [–] [6]

Apr 83. (7") *(RCA 323)* **FAMILY MAN. / CRIME PAYS** [15] [–]
(12") *(RCAT 323)* – Open All Night.

Sep 83. (7") *<13654>* **SAY IT ISN'T SO. / KISS ON MY LIST** [–] [2]

Oct 83. (7"/12") *(RCA/+T 375)* **SAY IT ISN'T SO. / DID IT IN A MINUTE** [69] [–]

Oct 83. (lp/c) *(PL/PK 84858) <4858>* **ROCK'N SOUL, PART 1** (compilation) [16] [7]
– Sara smile / She's gone / Rich girl / Kiss on my list / You make my dreams / Private eyes / I can't go for that (no can do) / Maneater / One on one / Wait for me (live) / Adult education / Say it isn't so. *(cd-iss. Oct84; PD 84858)*

Feb 84. (7") *<13714>* **ADULT EDUCATION. / MANEATER** [–] [8]

Feb 84. (7") *(RCA 396)* **ADULT EDUCATION. / SAY IT ISN'T SO** [63] [–]
(12"+=) *(RCAT 396)* – I can't go for that (no can do).

Oct 84. (7"/12") *(RCA/+T 449) <13916>* **OUT OF TOUCH. / COLD DARK AND YESTERDAY** [48] Sep84 [1]

Oct 84. (lp/c/cd) *(PL/PK/PD 85309) <5309>* **BIG BAM BOOM** [28] [5]
– Going thru the motions / Cold dark and yesterday / All American girl / Possession obsession / Dance on your knees / Out of touch / Method of modern love / Bank on your love / Some things are better left unsaid.

Jan 85. (7"/12") *(RCA/+T 472) <13960>* **METHOD OF MODERN LOVE. / BANK ON YOUR LOVE** [21] Dec84 [5]
(d7"+=) *(RCAD 472)* – I can't go for that (live) / Maneater (live).

Mar 85. (7") *<14035>* **SOME THINGS ARE BETTER LEFT UNSAID. / ALL AMERICAN GIRL** [–] [18]

May 85. (7") *(PB 49967)* **OUT OF TOUCH (remix). / DANCE ON YOUR KNEES** [62] [–]
(12"+=) *(PT 49968)* – Every time you go away.

May 85. (7") *<14098>* **POSSESSION OBSESSION. / DANCE ON YOUR KNEES** [–] [30]

Aug 85. (7") *<14178>* **A NITE AT THE APOLLO! (live medley:- THE WAY YOU DO THE THINGS YOU DO – MY GIRL). / EVERY TIME YOU GO AWAY** [–] [20]

Sep 85. (7")(12") *(PB 49935)(PT 49936)* **A NITE AT THE APOLLO LIVE! (live medley: – THE WAY YOU DO THE THINGS YOU DO – MY GIRL). / ADULT EDUCATION** [58] [–]
(above & below credited eith DAVID RUFFIN & EDDIE KENDRICKS; ex-Temptations)

Sep 85. (lp/c/cd) *(PL/PK/PD 87035) <7035>* **LIVE AT THE APOLLO (WITH DAVID RUFFIN & EDDIE KENDRICKS)** [32] [21]
– Get ready – Ain't too proud to beg – The way you do the things you do – My girl / When something is wrong with my baby / Everytime you go away / I can't go for that (no can do) / One by one / Possession obsession / Adult education. *(cd-iss. Sep93; 74321 16003-2)*

— In 1986, they split for a while, HALL made solo album

Arista Arista

Apr 88. (7"/12") *(109/609 869) <9684>* **EVERYTHING YOUR HEART DESIRES. / REALOVE** [ ] [3]

Jun 88. (lp/c/cd) *(208/408/258 895) <8539>* **OOH YEAH!** [52] May88 [24]
– Downtown life / Everything your heart desires / I'm in pieces / Missed opportunity / Talking all night / Rockability / Rocket to God / Soul love / ReaLove / Keep on pushin' love.

Jul 88. (7") *<9727>* **MISSED OPPORTUNITY. / SOUL LOVE** [–] [29]

Sep 88. (7") *<9753>* **DOWNTOWN LIFE. / ('A'-Urban mix)** [–] [31]

Sep 90. (7") *<2085>* **SO CLOSE. / SO CLOSE (unplugged version)** [–] [11]

Sep 90. (7")(c-s) *(113600)(411050)* **SO CLOSE. / CAN'T HELP FALLING IN LOVE** [69] [–]
(12"+=)(cd-s+=) *(613600)(663600)* – She's gone (live).

Nov 90. (cd/c/lp) *(210/410/260 548) <8614>* **CHANGE OF SEASON** [44] Oct90 [61]
– So close / Starting all over again / Sometimes a mind changes / Change of season / I ain't gonna take it this time / Everywhere I look / Give it up (old habits) / Don't hold back your love / Halfway there / Only love / Heavy rain / So close – unplugged.

Dec 90. (c-s) *<2157>* **DON'T HOLD BACK YOUR LOVE / CHANGE OF SEASON** [–] [41]

Jan 91. (7")(c-s) *(113980)411329)* **EVERYWHERE I LOOK. / SOMETIMES A MIND CHANGES** [74] [–]
(12"+=)(cd-s+=) *(613980)(663980)* – I can't go for that (Ben Liebrand mix).

Oct 91. (cd/c) *(PD/PK 90388)* **LOOKING BACK – THE BEST OF DARYL HALL & JOHN OATES** (compilation) [9] [ ]
– She's gone / Sara smile / Rich girl / You've lost that lovin' feelin' / Kiss on my list / Every time you go away / Private eyes / I can't go for that (no can do) / Maneater / One on one / Family man / Adult education / Out of touch / Method of modern love / Starting all over again. *(cd+/c+=)* Back together again / So close / Everything your heart desires.

DARYL HALL

not iss. Parallax

1968. (7") *<404>* **A LONELY GIRL / VICKY, VICKY** [–] [ ]

not iss. Amy

1968. (7") *<11049>* **THE PRINCESS & THE SOLDIER. / (part 2)** [–] [ ]

R.C.A. R.C.A.

Apr 80. (lp/c) *(PL/PK 13573) <3573>* **SACRED SONGS** (rec.1977) [ ] [58]
– Sacred songs / Something in 4/4 time / Babs and Babs / Urban landscape / NYNCY / The farther away (I am) / Why was it so easy / Don't leave me alone with her / Survive / Without tears. *(re-iss. Jul84; NL 83573)*

Apr 80. (7") *<12001>* **SACRED SONGS. / SOMETHING IN 4-4 TIME** [–] [ ]

Jul 86. (7"/12") *(HALL/+T 1) <14387>* **DREAMTIME. / LET IT OUT** [28] [5]

Aug 86. (lp/c/cd) *(PL/PK/PD 87196) <7196>* **THREE HEARTS IN THE HAPPY ENDING MACHINE** [26] [29]
– Dreamtime / Only a vision / I wasn't born yesterday / Someone like you / Next stop / For you / Foolish pride / Right as rain / Let it out / What's going to happen to us. *(re-iss. May88)*

Oct 86. (7") *<5038-7>* **FOOLISH PRIDE. / WHAT'S GOING TO HAPPEN TO US** [–] [33]

Nov 86. (7") *(HALL 2)* **I WASN'T BORN YESTERDAY. / WHAT'S GONNA HAPPEN TO US** [ ] [–]
(12"+=) *(HALLT 2)* – Dreamtime.

Jan 87. (7") *<5105-7>* **SOMEONE LIKE YOU. / ('A'sax solo version)** [–] [57]

— writes with **PETER LORD MORELAND** – keyboards / **V. JEFFREY SMITH** – synth.bass / **ALAN GORRIE** – bass / other musicians **TOMMY EYRE** – keyboards / **MEL WESSON** – programming / **TREVOR MURRELL** – drums / **BOB BITSAND** – bass / **MYLES BOULD** – percussion

Epic Epic

Sep 93. (7"/c-s) *(659 555-7/-4)* *<77139>* **I'M IN A PHILLY MOOD (Edit) / MONEY CHANGES EVERYTHING** [59] [82]
(cd-s+=) *(659 555-2)* – I've finally seen the light.
(cd-s) *(659 555-5)* – ('A'side) / Love T.K.O. (live) / Me and Mrs. Jones (live).
(re-iss. Mar94, hit UK 52)

Oct 93. (cd/c/lp) *(473921-2/-4/-1)* *<53937>* **SOUL ALONE** [57] [ ]
– Power of seduction / This time / Love revelation / I'm in a Philly mood / Borderline / Stop loving me, stop loving you / Help me find a way to your heart / Send me / Wildfire / Money changes everything / Written in stone.
(re-dist.Jan94)

Jan 94. (c-s) *(659 998-4)* **STOP LOVING ME, STOP LOVING YOU. / MONEY CHANGES EVERYTHING** [30] [ ]
(12"+=/cd-s+=) *(659 998-6/-2)* – (4 more 'A'mixes).

May 94. (7"/c-s) *(660 410-7/-4)* **HELP ME FIND A WAY TO YOUR HEART. / POWER OF SEDUCTION** [70] [ ]
(cd-s+=) *(660 410-2)* – Stop loving me, stop loving you (live) / I'm in a Philly mood (live).

— Below on 'Mercury' & the theme from USA soccer World Cup Finals.

Jun 94. (7"pic-d/c-s/cd-s; DARYL HALL & SOUNDS OF BLACKNESS) *(662 059-7/-4/-2)* **GLORYLAND. / ('A'mixes)** [36] [ ]

Aug 94. (c-s) *(660 719-4)* **WILDFIRE / THIS TIME** [ ] [-]
(cd-s+=) *(660 719-2)* – ('A'extended).

— DARYL surfaced again when credited in May95 on DUSTY SPRINGFIELD's UK Top 50 hit single 'WHEREVER WOULD I BE'.

C.N.R. Liquid 8

Jul 03. (cd) *(2299957-2)* *<12109>* **CAN'T STOP DREAMING** (issued Japan 1999) [ ] [ ]
– Cab driver / Let me be the one / Can't stop dreaming / Never let me go / Holding out for love / Justify / What's in your world / Hold on to me / She's gone / All by myself / Fools rush in.

DARYL HALL & JOHN OATES

— reformed in 1997

Eagle Push

Nov 97. (cd/c) *(EAG CD/MC 011)* *<90200>* **MARIGOLD SKY** [ ] Oct97 [95]
– Romeo is bleeding / Marigold sky / The sky is falling / Out of the blue / Want to / Love out loud / Throw the roses away / I don't think so / Promise ain't enough / Time won't pass me by / Hold on to yourself / War of words / Hold on to yourself (remix).

Feb 98. (c-s) *(EAGCS 011)* **THE SKY IS FALLING / SHE'S GONE (live)** [ ] [ ]
(cd-s+=) *(EAGXA 011)* – Sara smile (live) / Out of touch (live).

Sanctuary U-Watch

Mar 03. (cd) *(SANCD 166)* *<480100>* **DO IT FOR LOVE** [37] Feb03 [ ]
– Man on a mission / Do it for love / Someday we'll know / Forever for you / Life's too short / Getaway car / Make you stay / Miss DJ / "She" got me bad / Breath of your life / Intuition / Heartbreak time / Something about you / Love in a dangerous time.

'un 03. (cd-s) *(SANXD 199)* **MAN ON A MISSION / KISS ON MY LIST (live) / OUT OF TOUCH (live)** [ ] [-]

– compilations, etc. –

›n 'Atlantic' unless mentioned otherwise

ul 76. (7") *<3332>* **SHE'S GONE. / I'M JUST A KID (DON'T MAKE ME FEEL LIKE A MAN)** [-] [ ]

›ep 76. (7"ep) *(K 10828)* **SHE'S GONE / WAR BABY SON OF ZORRO / LAZY MAN** [42] [-]

an 77. (7") *(K 10887)* **LAS VEGAS TURNAROUND. / HAD I KNOWN YOU BETTER THEN** [ ] [-]

Mar 77. (lp) *(K 50347)* *<18213>* **NO GOODBYES** [ ] [92]
(cd-iss. Jul96; 7567 80430-2)

Apr 77. (7") *(K 10915)* **IT'S UNCANNY. / BEANIE G. & THE ROSE TATTOO** [ ] [-]

Apr 77. (lp) *Chelsea; (CHL 547)* **PAST TIMES BEHIND** (71-72) [ ] [ ]

Iay 77. (7") *Chelsea; <3063>* **THE REASON WHY (Daryl Hall & GULLIVER). / IF THAT'S WHAT MAKES YOU HAPPY (Hall & Oates)** [ ] [-]

un 77. (7") *<3397>* **IT'S UNCANNY. / LILY (ARE YOU HAPPY)** [-] [80]

ul 81. (7") *(K 11597)* **SHE'S GONE. / WHEN THE MORNING COMES** [ ] [-]

May 82. (7") *RCA Gold; (GOLD 547)* **KISS ON MY LIST. / RUNNING FROM PARADISE** [ ] [-]

May 83. (c-ep) *R.C.A.; (RCXK 007)* **CASSETTE EP** [ ] [-]
– I can't go for that (no can do) / Maneater / Private eyes / Kiss on my list.

Jun 84. (lp) *Magnum Force; (THBM 003)* **THE PROVIDER** [ ] [-]

Oct 85. (lp) *Thunderbolt; (THBL 035)* **REALLY SMOKIN'** [ ] [-]
(cd-iss. Jul93; CDTB 122)

Apr 86. (lp/c) *Showcase; (SHLP/SHTC 134)* **THE EARLY YEARS** [ ] [-]

Nov 86. (7") *Old Gold; (OG9658)* **MANEATER. / I CAN'T GO FOR THAT (NO CAN DO)** [ ] [-]

Nov 86. (lp/c/cd) *Meteor; (SMT/SMTC/CDSM 006)* **20 CLASSIC TRACKS** [ ] [-]

Nov 88. (lp/c/cd) *Big Time; (221/211/241 5012)* **FIRST SESSIONS** [ ] [-]

Oct 92. (cd-ep) *Old Gold; (OG 6184)* **I CAN'T GO FOR THAT (NO CAN DO) / PRIVATE EYES / KISS IS ON MY LIST** [ ] [-]

Oct 92. (cd-ep) *Old Gold; (OG 6188)* **MANEATER / FAMILY MAN / METHOD OF MODERN LOVE** [ ] [-]

Feb 94. (cd/c) *Javelin; (HAD CD/MC 107)* **SPOTLIGHT ON HALL & OATES** [ ] [-]

Sep 94. (cd) *Wisepack; (LECD 084)* **LEGENDS IN MUSIC** [ ] [-]

Sep 94. (cd) *Prestige; (CDSGP 0128)* **A LOT OF CHANGES COMIN'** [ ] [-]

Feb 95. (cd) *B.A.M.;* **PEARLS OF THE PAST** [ ] [-]

Oct 95. (cd) *R.C.A.; (74321 28983-2)* **ROCK'N'SOUL PART 2 (GREATEST HITS)** [ ] [-]

Jul 96. (cd) *(812272205-2)* **ATLANTIC COLLECTION – THE BEST OF HALL & OATES** [ ] [-]

Feb 98. (cd) *R.C.A.; (74321 43662-2)* **WITH LOVE FROM HALL & OATES (THE BEST OF THE BALLADS)** [ ] [ ]

Sep 01. (cd/c) *(74321 88697-2/-4)* **THE ESSENTIAL COLLECTION** [26] [ ]
– Sara smile / She's gone / Rich girl / Wait for me / Kiss on my list / I can't go for that (no can do) / Private eyes / Maneater / One on one / Family man / Say it isn't so / Adult education / Out of touch / Method of modern love / Everything your heart desires / So close / Starting it all over again / I can't go for that (no can do) (Hoax remix).

Oct 01. (c-s) *(74321 89092-4)* **I CAN'T GO FOR THAT (NO CAN DO) (remix) / ('A'mix)** [ ] [-]
(12"+=/cd-s+=) *(74321 89092-1/-2)* – ('A'mixes).

☐ Pete HAM (see under ⇒ BADFINGER)

☐ Peter HAMMILL
(see under ⇒ VAN DER GRAAF GENERATOR)

HAPPY MONDAYS

Formed: Salford, Manchester, England ... 1984 by brothers SHAUN and PAUL RYDER. In 1985, with the help of A&R man and producer Mike Pickering, they signed a contract with Tony Wilson's 'Factory' records, issuing a debut 12", 'FORTY-FIVE'. With the addition of MARK BERRY aka BEZ on 'percussion', the band released the 'FREAKY DANCIN' single, as good a description as any for BEZ's onstage contortions. A JOHN CALE-produced debut album followed in 1987, the acclaimed mutant indie funk of 'SQUIRREL AND G-MAN . . .' winning the band many converts in the music press and the beginnings of a cult following. The early live shoes have been elevated to almost mythical status, SHAUN and co allegedly giving away drugs on the door to their own fans in true scally style. Despite sounding like it'd been recorded in a shed, the Martin Hannett-produced 'BUMMED' (1988) was a classic, a freewheeling groovy noise, punctuated intermittently by RYDER's stoned Mancunian slur. 'MAD CYRIL', 'LAZYITIS' and 'WROTE FOR LUCK' were all brilliant singles, the latter given a dance remix treatment by VINCE CLARKE (Erasure). 'Factory' supremo WILSON decided to take this a step further and set the band to work with the DJ/production team of PAUL OAKENFOLD and STEVE OSBORNE. The result was the pivotal 'MADCHESTER

RAVE ON EP', a druggy mash-up of dance, indie, pop and funk that acted as a catylyst for the "Baggy" scene alongside the STONE ROSES' 'FOOL'S GOLD' single (spookily released exactly the same month), inspiring a whole string of bands in Manchester and beyond, some good, some not so good (just don't mention the FARM). Early the following year, the 'MONDAYS hit the Top 5 with their anthemic remake of JOHN KONGOS' 'He's Gonna Step On You Again', retitled 'STEP ON' and injected with typically laissez faire funk. 'KINKY AFRO' also made the Top 5, preceding the band's biggest success of their career, the 'PILLS 'N' THRILLS AND BELLYACHES' (1990) album. This time around there was a cleaner production and a melodic accessibility coating the trademark melange of dirty 'STONES'-style guitar, raggedy-assed funk and cheesy disco. In addition to the singles, the album's highlights included a tribute to 60's folk-popster DONOVAN, a leering piece of porn-funk, 'BOB'S YER UNCLE' and the classic 'GOD'S COP' (featuring the timeless RYDER line "God laid his E's all on me"). While much of the band's music sounded continuously on the point of collapse and live, HAPPY MONDAYS often seemed as if they'd arrived onstage purely by accident, RYDER was no space cadet, his inimitable lyrical couplets sussed, sharp and dryly witty. Almost inevitably though, the backlash began in earnest with an NME interview painting RYDER and BEZ as dim witted homophobes. Whatever RYDER actually said, it's likely that his tongue was planted firmly in cheek, and besides, to expect the HAPPY MONDAYS to stand up as right-on, PC role models for student NME readers displays a naivety that beggars belief. Retreating to the Bahamas with Talking Heads' CHRIS FRANTZ and TINA WEYMOUTH at the production helm, the band struggled through sessions for the '. . .YES PLEASE!' album, amid tales of general strife, severe drug abuse and obligatory debauchery. The album, an expensive disaster (critically and commercially) that reputedly bankrupted 'Factory', eventually emerged in late '92. Generally ignored and panned by the press, the album nevertheless contained some stellar 'MONDAYS moments, not least the low-key brilliance of 'STINKIN' THINKIN' and the darkly hypnotic 'ANGEL', both tracks using female backing vocals to impressive effect. After a washout of a tour, HAPPY MONDAYS drifted apart, a messy end for a band that were capable of true musical genius against all the odds. The loose limbed spirit of the 'MONDAYS lived on, though, in BLACK GRAPE, the band RYDER formed along with rapper KERMIT and JED from the RUTHLESS RAP ASSASSINS and a host of extras. SHAUN's brilliant return from oblivion was complete by summer 1995 when the storming 'REVEREND BLACK GRAPE' launched him back into the Top 10. The mouthiest, grooviest low-slung Manc rave-up to grace the charts since the 'MONDAYS peak, the record pointed squarely in the direction where the party was really happening, bypassing completely the tedious Brit-pop posturing. As ever, RYDER and entourage were never far from controversy, both the song and video subsequently banned from TV as the Catholic church alleged the lyrics condoned Venezuelan terrorist, Carlos The Jackal (which also angered the New York based ADL – Anti-Defamation League). Another classic single, 'IN THE NAME OF THE FATHER', followed into the Top 10, funk rhythms and a sitar tinged intro previewing the eclecticism of the accompanying No.1 album, 'IT'S GREAT WHEN YOU'RE STRAIGHT . . . YEAH!'. Its title a reference to RYDER's clean living new ways (his inimitable cut 'n' paste lyrics apparently fuelled solely by Guinness!?), the record was compared favourably against The HAPPY MONDAYS' best work, and the second coming-style fuss over RYDER's critical rebirth seemed at least partly justified. Loping through a dayglo musical smarty pack of hip-hop, rock, indie-dance, soul and indeed, anything close to hand, RYDER proved his subversive genius was well intact, while KERMIT's hyperactive rapping assaults were a perfect foil for his stoned immaculate drawl. During this time, they were one of the successes at Hamilton Park's 'T In The Park' 2-day festival (near Glasgow), even though KERMIT broke his leg and had to sit out most of the gig on a speaker! During an eventful 1996 of regular touring and high profile press coverage, BEZ and RYDER finally parted ways, while KERMIT embarked on a side project, MAN MADE, the following year. A follow-up album, 'STUPID, STUPID, STUPID' finally emerged at the end of '97 amid furious interband disputes, claims and counter claims. The feuding saw the band cancel their New Year's Eve show at London's Alexandra Palace. SHAUN resurrected HAPPY MONDAYS and in the meantime, BEZ was up to all sorts, including a TV spot on the Lee & Herring Sunday brunch show (dedicated to strange scientific happenings, mad for it, man). He also began writing an autobiography, no really man! The HAPPY MONDAYS (i.e. SHAUN, his brother PAUL, GAZ, 'WAGS', 'NUTS', ROWETTA and of course a reluctant BEZ!) were "smokin" once again when a new single, 'THE BOYS ARE BACK IN TOWN' (described as only inspired by the THIN LIZZY number!) hit the Top 30. However, after all the hype, the promise and the fuss, only an accompanying 'GREATEST HITS' package was supplied as a stop-gap to feed their fans; PAUL RYDER left on the 11th of August after the Eclipse '99 festival in Cornwall. By which time, SHAUN had paid off the taxman (and child maintenance) from his royalties, but really what did the 'MONDAYS give us during this spell apart from another chance to see the bleary-eyed singer trying to read a cue card on a stage monitor; you're answers please on the back of a postage stamp. In the month of July 2000, the most embarrassing sham on TV since the days of Oliver Reed and George Best when a sober-looking SHAUN was a guest on the Jim Davidson Friday show, er . . . singing 'BARCELONA' (yes, that one!) side by side with opera singer RUSSELL WATSON. With ongoing legal wrangles stalling RYDER from recording under his old banners, the man took off to his cousin Pete's house in Perth, Australia. There, SHAUN talked about retiring and, with the help of 'MONDAY's sleeve designer Pete, he set about putting his memoirs to music. In the summer of 2003, his fun tales of drugs, fights, prison and er . . . drugs, were duly delivered as 'CLOWNS AND PET SOUNDS' under the AMATEUR NIGHT IN THE BIG TOP banner. Opener 'THE STORY' and the single 'SCOOTER GIRL' (the latter produced by CABARET VOLTAIRE man STEPHEN MALLINDER), were both experimental and techno showcasing his dark wit and cheeky Mancunian humour to the fore. HAPPY MONDAYS were back in 2005 via a minor hit, 'PLAYGROUND SUPERSTAR', from the feature film, 'Goal!'.

• **Songwriters:** Group compositions except; DESMOND (Ob-la-di Ob-la-da; Beatles) / LAZYITIS (Ticket To Ride; Beatles) / TOKOLOSHE MAN (John Kongos). For BLACK GRAPE, SHAUN & KERMIT wrote alongside DANNY SABER, although in October '95, INTASTELLA members MARTIN WRIGHT and MARTIN MITTLER served a writ, claiming they co-wrote with SHAUN on early demos before they departed.

Album rating: SQUIRREL AND G-MAN TWENTY FOUR HOUR PARTY . . (*8) / BUMMED (*8) / PILLS N' THRILLS AND BELLYACHES (*9) / LIVE (BABY BIG HEAD Bootleg album) (*4) / . . .YES PLEASE (*6) / LOADS – THE BEST OF . . . compilation (*8) / Black Grape: IT'S GREAT WHEN YOU'RE STRAIGHT . . . YEAH! (*9) / STUPID, STUPID, STUPID (*7) / Happy Mondays: THE GREATEST HITS compilation (*8) / STEP ON (*5) / Amateur Night In The Big Top: CLOWNS AND PET SOUNDS (*7)

SHAUN RYDER (b.23 Aug'62) – vocals / **PAUL RYDER** (b.24 Apr'64) – bass / **MARK DAY** (b.29 Dec'61) – guitar / **PAUL DAVIS** (b. 7 Mar'66) – keyboards / **GARY 'GAZ' WHELAN** (b.12 Feb'66) – drums

		Factory	Rough Trade
Sep 85.	(12"ep) *(FAC 129)* **FORTY-FIVE EP** – Delightful / This feeling / Oasis.		–
——	added **BEZ** (b. MARK BERRY, 18 Apr'64) – percussion, dancer		
Jun 86.	(7") *(FAC 142)* **FREAKY DANCIN'. / THE EGG** (ext.12"+=) *(FAC 142)* – ('A'live).		–
Mar 87.	(12") *(FAC 176)* **TART TART. / LITTLE MATCHSTICK OWEN'S RAP**		–

Apr 87. (lp) *(FACT 170)* **SQUIRREL & G-MAN TWENTY-FOUR HOUR PARTY PEOPLE PLASTIC FACE CARNT SMILE (WHITE OUT)** [ ] [–]
– Kuff dam / Tart tart / 'Enery / Russell / Olive oil / Weekends / Little matchstick Owen / Oasis / Desmond * / Cob 20. *(re-iss. Nov88; same)(track * repl. by)* – Twenty four hour party people. *(cd-iss. Mar90 +=; FACD 170)* – Little matchstick Owen's rap. *(cd re-iss. May99 on 'London'; 520012-2) (cd re-iss. Jan00 on 'Factory Too'; 3984 28252-2)*

Oct 87. (12") *(FAC 192)* **TWENTY FOUR HOUR PARTY PEOPLE. / YAHOO / WAH WAH (THINK TANK)** [ ] [–]

Nov 88. (7") *(FAC 212-7)* **WROTE FOR LUCK. / BOOM** [ ] [–]
(12"+=/cd-s+=) *(FAC/+D 212)* – ('A'dance mix) / ('A'club mix).

Nov 88. (lp/cd)(d/dat) *(FACT/FACD 220)(FACT 220 C/D)* **BUMMED** [ ] [–]
– Country song / Moving in with / Mad Cyril / Fat lady wrestlers / Performance / Brain dead / Wrote for luck / Bring a friend / Do it better / Lazyitis. *(hit UK 59 UK Jan90) (cd re-iss. May99 on 'London'; 520013-2) (cd re-iss. Jan00 on 'Factory Too'; 3984 28250-2)*

May 89. (12"/7"/c-s; as HAPPY MONDAYS & KARL DENVER) *(FAC 222/+7/C)* **LAZYITIS – ONE ARMED BOXER. / MAD CYRIL – HELLO GIRLS** [85] [–]
(re-iss. May90; same); hit No.46)

Sep 89. (12"/7") *(FAC 232/+7)* **WFL (Vince Clarke mix). / WFL – THINK ABOUT THE FUTURE (the Paul Oakenfold mix)** [68] [–]
(cd-s+=) *(FACD 232)* – Lazyitis – one armed boxer.

Nov 89. (7"clear/12"clear) **MAD CYRIL – HELLO GIRLS. / DO IT BETTER** [–] [ ]

Nov 89. (12"ep/cd-ep)(7"ep/c-ep) *(FAC/+D 242)(FAC 242-7/-C)* **MADCHESTER RAVE ON EP** [19] [–]
– Hallelujah / Holy ghost / Clap your hands / Rave on.
(7") *(FAC 242R-7)* – Hallelujah (the MacColl mix). / Hallelujah (in out mix).
(c-s)(12"/cd-s) *(FAC 242RC)(FAC/+D 242R)* – ('A'club mix) / Rave on (club mix).

— added guest **ROWETA** – backing vocals to repl. other guest KIRSTY MacCOLL

Factory Elektra

Mar 90. (12"/7") *(FAC 272/+7)* *<64899>* **STEP ON (stuff it in mix). / ('A'-One louder mix)** [5] Feb91 [57]
(c-s+=)(cd-s+=) *(FAC 272C)(FACD 272)* – ('A'-Twistin' my melons mix).

Oct 90. (12"/7"/c-s) *(FAC 302/+7/C)* **KINKY AFRO. / KINKY AFRO (live)** [5] [–]
(cd-s+=) *(FACD 302)* – ('A'radio edit).

Nov 90. (cd/lp)(c) *(FACD/FACT 320)(FAC 320C)* *<60986>* **PILLS 'N THRILLS AND BELLYACHES** [4] [89]
– Kinky Afro / God's cop / Donovan / Grandbag's funeral / Loose fit / Dennis & Lois / Bob's your uncle / Step on / Holiday / Harmony. *(cd re-iss. May99 on 'London'; 828223-2) (re-hit.Jul02 at No.47) (cd re-iss. Sep99 on 'Factory Too'; 3984 28251-2)*

Feb 91. (12"/7"/c-s) *(FAC 312/+7/C)* **LOOSE FIT. / BOB'S YOUR UNCLE** [17] [–]
(cd-s+=) *(FACD 312)* – Kinky Afro (Euro mix).

Sep 91. (cd/d-lp)(c) *(FACD/FACT 322)(FAC 322C)* **LIVE** (live BABY BIG HEAD Bootleg album) [21] [–]
– Hallelujah / Donovan / Kinky Afro / Clap your hands / Loose fit / Holiday / Rave on / E / Tokoloshe man / Dennis and Lois / God's cop / Step on / W.F.L. *(d-lp+=)(c+=)* – Bob's your uncle.

Nov 91. (12"/7"/c-s) *(FAC 332/+7/C)* **JUDGE FUDGE. / TOKOLOSHE MAN** [24] [–]
(cd-s+=) *(FACD 332)* – ('A'version).

Sep 92. (7"/c-s) *(FAC 362 7/C)* **STINKIN' THINKIN'. / ('A'-Boys Own mix)** [31] [–]
(12"+=/cd-s+=) *(FAC/+D 362)* – ('A'-Terry Farley mix) / Baby bighead.

Oct 92. (cd/lp)(c) *(FACD/FACT 420)(FAC 420C)* *<61391>* **. . . YES PLEASE!** [14] [ ]
– Stinkin' thinkin' / Monkey in the family / Sunshine & love / Dustman / Angel / Cut 'em loose Bruce / Theme from Netto / Love child / Total Ringo / Cowboy Dave. *(cd re-iss. May99 on 'London'; 520026-2) (cd re-iss. Jan00 on 'Factory Too'; 3984 28253-2)*

Nov 92. (7"/c-s) *(FAC 372 7/C)* **SUNSHINE & LOVE. / STAYING ALIVE (mix) / TWENTY FOUR HOUR PARTY PEOPLE (remix)** [62] [–]
(12"+=/cd-s+=) *(FAC/+D 372)* – ('A'dance mix).

— they disbanded early '93, with SHAUN and other two briefly forming The MONDAYS which evolved into BLACK GRAPE

BLACK GRAPE

SHAUN RYDER + BEZ with **KERMIT** (b.PAUL LEVEREDGE) – rapper (ex-RUTHLESS RAP ASSASINS) / **JED BIRTWHISTLE** – rapper (ex-RUTHLESS RAP ASSASSINS) / **WAGS** – guitar (ex-PARIS ANGELS) / **CRAIG GANNON** – guitar (ex-SMITHS) who replaced INTASTELLA guitarists **MARTIN WRIGHT + MARTIN MITTLER**

Radioactive Radioactive

May 95. (c-s) *(RAXC 16)* **REVEREND BLACK GRAPE / STRAIGHT OUT OF TRUMPTON (BASEMENT TAPES)** [9] [ ]
(cd-s+=) *(RAXTD 16)* – ('A'-dark side mix).
(12") *(RAXT 16)* – ('A'side) / ('A'-dub collar mix) / ('A'-dark side mix).

Jul 95. (c-s) *(RAXC 19)* **IN THE NAME OF THE FATHER / LAND OF A THOUSAND KAMA SUTRA BABIES** [8] [ ]
(cd-s+=) *(RAXTD 19)* – ('A'-chopper's mix) / ('A'-chopper's instrumental).
(12") *(RAXT 19)* – ('A'side) / (above 2).

Aug 95. (cd/c/lp) *(<RAD/RAC/RAR 11224>)* **IT'S GREAT WHEN YOU'RE STRAIGHT . . . YEAH** [1] [ ]
– Reverend Black Grape / In the name of the father / Tramazi party / Kelly's heroes / Yeah yeah brother / Big day in the north / Shake well before opening / Shake your money / Little Bob.

Nov 95. (c-s) *(RAXC 22)* **KELLY'S HEROES / ('A'-The Milky Bar Kid mix)** [17] [ ]
(cd-s+=) *(RAXTD 22)* – ('A'-The Archibald mix) / Little Bob (live).
(cd-s) *(RAXXD 22)* – ('A'live) / In the name of the father (live) / Fat neck.

— BEZ quit due to argument with SHAUN over his role in the group.

— On Channel 4's TFI Friday, SHAUN caused more controversy by adding loads of live f words on their version on SEX PISTOLS 'Pretty Vacant'.

May 96. (c-s) *(RAXC 24)* **FAT NECK / PRETTY VACANT (live)** [10] [ ]
(cd-s+=) *(RAXTD 24)* – Yeah yeah brother (Outlaw Josey Wales mix).
(12") *(RAXT 24)* – ('A'-GOLDIE Beat the f*** down mix) / Yeah yeah brother (Clockwork Orange mix) / Yeah yeah brother (Dog day afternoon mix).

Jun 96. (c-s) *(RAXC 25)* **ENGLAND'S IRIE / (Pass the Durazac mix)** [6] [ ]
(12"+=/cd-s+=) *(RAXT/+D 25)* – ('A'-Suedehead dub) / ('A'-Mel's L.A. Irie mix).
above featured JOE STRUMMER and KEITH ALLEN

— In Oct'96, SHAUN moonlighted with The HEADS (ex-TALKING HEADS) on minor hit single 'Don't Take My Kindness For Weakness'.

Oct 97. (c-s/cd-s) *(RAX C/TD 32)* **GET HIGHER / ('A'mixes)** [24] [–]
(cd-s) *(RAXXD 32)* – ('A'mixes).

Nov 97. (lp/c/cd) *(RAR/+C/D 11716)* **STUPID STUPID STUPID** [11] [–]
– Get higher / Squeaky / Marbles / Dadi was a badi / Rubber band / Spotlight / Tell me something / Money back guarenteed / Lonely / Words.

Feb 98. (cd-s) *(RAXTD 33)* **MARBLES (remixes by R.I.P. and FABIO PARAS) / MARBLES (demo)** [46] [–]
(12"+=) *(RAXT 33)* – ('A'-Tricky remix).
(cd-s) *(RAXXD 33)* – ('A'-Tricky remix) / Harry the dog / Get higher (uncensored video on CD-ROM).

HAPPY MONDAYS

— re-formed **SHAUN + PAUL RYDER, GAZ WHELAN, PAUL 'WAGS' WAGSTAFF, 'NUTS', BEZ + ROWETTA**

London not iss.

May 99. (12") *(LONX 432)* **THE BOYS ARE BACK IN TOWN. / ('A'-Dirty mix)** [24] [–]
(cd-s) *(LONCD 432)* – ('A'side) / Kinky Afro / ('A'extended).
(cd-s) *(LOCDP 432)* – ('A'-Dirty mix) / Loose fit (Perfecto mix) / Bob's yer uncle (Perfecto mix).

May 99. (cd/c) *(556105-2/-4)* **GREATEST HITS** (compilation) [11] [–]
– Step on / WFL (Vince Clarke mix) / The boys are back in town / Kinky Afro (Perfecto mix) / Hallelujah (club mix) / Mad Cyril / Lazyitis (One Armed Boxer mix) / Loose fit (Perfecto mix) / Bob's yer uncle / Judge fudge / Stinkin' thinkin' / 24 hour party people / WFL (Think About The Future mix) / Stayin' alive / Step on (Twisting My Melon mix). *(cd re-iss. Apr05; same)*

— in Jul'00, SHAUN RYDER er, collaborated on a version of 'BARCELONA' with opera singer RUSSELL WATSON (it hit UK No.68)

AMATEUR NIGHT IN THE BIG TOP

SHAUN RYDER – vocals / + cohorts on electronics, etc.

Offworld not iss.

Jun 03. (12"/cd-s) *(LOWS/COWS 1)* **SCOOTER GIRL. / CLOWNS (Gripper remix) / SCOOTER GIRL (Soundlab remix)** ☐ ☐-
Jul 03. (cd) *(POWS 1)* **CLOWNS AND PET SOUNDS** ☐ ☐-
– The story / Long legs (parts 1-3) / Scooter girl / Clowns / Murder / Northern soul brother (shapeshifter) / Monster / In 1987.

HAPPY MONDAYS

re-formed (originals)

Snapper not iss.

Aug 05. (cd) *(SMACD 902)* **STEP ON** (recorded live in Barcelona 2004) ☐ ☐-
– Kinky afro / Loose fit / Reverend Black Grape / Bob's yer uncle / Step on / Donovan / Hallelujah / Mad Cyril / WFL (Wrote For Luck) / Stinkin' thinkin' / 24 hour party people.

Big Brother not iss.

Oct 05. (7") *(RKID 34)* **PLAYGROUND SUPERSTAR. / (Graeme Revell track)** 51 ☐-
(cd-s) *(RKIDSSCD 34)* – ('A') / ('A'-Redanka's 4-4-2 vocal mix).
(above from the film, 'Goal!'

– compilations, etc. –

May 90. (12"ep/c-ep/cd-ep) *Strange Fruit; (SFPS/+C/CD 077) / Dutch East India; <8306>* **THE PEEL SESSION** ☐ ☐
– Tart tart / Mad Cyril / Do it better. *(cd-ep re-iss. Feb92; same)*
Nov 91. (cd-ep) *Strange Fruit;* **THE PEEL SESSION (1986)** ☐ ☐-
– Freaky dancin' / Kuff dam / Olive Oil / Cob 20.
Sep 93. (cd,c) *Elektra; <61543>* **DOUBLE EASY: THE US SINGLES** ☐- ☐
Oct 95. (cd/c) *London; (520036-2/-4)* **LOADS** 41 ☐-
– Step on / W.F.L. / Kinky Afro / Hallelujah – MacColl mix / Mad Cyril / Lazyitis / Tokoloshe man / Loose fit / Bob's yer uncle / Judge fudge / Stinkin' thinkin' / Sunshine & love / Angel / Tart tart / Kuff dam / Twenty four hour party people. *(some cd's w/ free cd+=)* **LOADS MORE** – Lazyitis – one armed boxer mix / W.F.L. (Perfecto mix) / Bob's yer uncle (Perfecto mix) / Loose fit (Perfecto mix) / Hallelujah (Deadstock mix) / Freaky dancing / Delightful.
May 02. (12") *London; (LONX 466)* **24 HOUR PARTY PEOPLE (mixes)** ☐ ☐-

HARD-FI

Formed: Staines, Middlesex, England ... 2002 by RICHARD ARCHER, ROSS PHILLIPS, KAI STEPHENS and STEVE KEMP. They might be from the homeboy territory of Ali G (alias Sacha Baron Cohen), but HARD-FI are more FRANZ FERDINAND meets the MERTON PARKAS than suburban freestyle. Dominated by ARCHER's adolescent wail, their claustrophobically titled mini-set, 'STARS OF CCTV' (2004), sold out of its limited pressing and got them signed to indie imprint, 'Necessary'. Debut single, 'CASH MACHINE', failed to pay out first time around, although follow-ups 'TIED UP TOO TIGHT', 'HARD TO BEAT' and 'SOMETHING FOR THE WEEKEND', paved the Top 20 way for a successful re-release in late 2005. That summer a re-vamped 'STARS OF CCTV' had generated overwhelmingly positive reviews and a UK Top 10 entry. It would finally top the charts early the following year, attracting both a Mercury Music Prize nomination and two Brit Award nominations.

• **Covered:** SEVEN NATION ARMY (White Stripes) / PEACHES (Stranglers).

Album rating: STARS OF CCTV (*7)

RICHARD ARCHER – vocals / **ROSS PHILIPS** – guitar / **KAI STEPHENS** – bass / **STEVE KEMP** – drums

Necessary not iss.

Oct 04. (ltd;m-cd) *(NR 2)* **STARS OF CCTV** ☐ ☐-
– Cash machine / Hard to beat / Middle Eastern holiday / Stronger / Hard to beatmix / Gotta reason / Feltham is singing out / Move on now *(originally iss.Jun04 on 'Genepool')*

Necessary – Atlantic Necessary – Atlantic

Jan 05. (7") *(HARDFI 01)* **CASH MACHINE. / DUB MACHINE** ☐ ☐-
(cd-s) *(HARDFI 01CD)* – ('A') / Sick of it all / ('A'-video).
Apr 05. (7"yellow) *(HARDFI 02)* **TIED UP TOO TIGHT. / SEVEN NATIONS ARMY** 15 ☐-
(cd-s) *(HARDFI 02CD)* – ('A') / Middle Eastern holiday.
(10") *(HARDFI 02TE)* – ('A') / Middle Eastern holiday (chicken lips vocal mix) / Middle Eastern holiday (chicken lips dub).
Apr 05. (cd-s) *<62413-2>* **CASH MACHINE EP** ☐- ☐
– Cash machine / Tied up too tight / Sick of it all / Seven nations army.
Jun 05. (7"yellow) *(HARD 03)* **HARD TO BEAT. / BETTER DUB BETTER** 9 ☐-
(12") *(HARD 03T)* – ('A') / ('A'-Axwell remix).
(cd-s) *(HARD 03CD)* – ('A') / Tied up too tight (BBC Radio 1 live lounge session).
(cd-s) *(HARD 03CDX)* – ('A') / Stronger / ('A'-video) / Tied up too tight (video) / (caught on CCTV.. making of video).
Jul 05. (cd/lp) *(5046 78691-2/-1)* **STARS OF CCTV** 6 ☐-
– Cash machine / Middle Eastern holiday / Tied up too tight / Gotta reason / Hard to beat / Unnecessary trouble / Move on now / Better do better / Feltham is singing out / Living for the weekend / Stars of CCTV
Sep 05. (7") *(HARD 04)* **LIVING FOR THE WEEKEND. / (dub)** 15 ☐-
(cd-s) *(HARD 04CD)* – ('A') / Unnecessary trouble (live).
(cd-s) *(HARD 04CDX)* – ('A') / Peaches (Radio 1 live session) / ('A'-video) / (caught on CCTV.. making of pt.2).
Dec 05. (7"yellow) *(HARD 05)* **CASH MACHINE. / (Roots Manuva mix)** 14 ☐-
(cd-s+=) *(HARD 05CDX)* – ('A'-new video) / ('A'-old video) / (making of the new video).
(cd-s) *(HARD 05CD)* – ('A') / ('A'-acoustic).
Dec 05. (re-cd) *(as prev) <as UK>* **STARS OF CCTV** 1 Mar06 ☐
Apr 06. (7"yellow) *(HARD 06)* **BETTER DO BETTER. / (WrongTom Wild inna 81 version)** 14 ☐-
(7"pic-d) *(HARD 06X)* – ('A') / Polish love song.
(cd-s+=) *(HARD 06CD)* – ('A'-video) / Hard to beat (U-Myx software).

☐ HARMONY ROCKETS (see under ⇒ MERCURY REV)

Ben HARPER

Born: 28 Oct'69, Claremont, California, USA. Born to music loving parents, HARPER was hooked by the blues as a child, subsequently taking up the guitar and graduating from a hands-on apprenticeship that found him playing on the same stage as such respected veterans as TAJ MAHAL. It was MAHAL who "discovered" HARPER drawing attention to the distinctive sound the young musician would ring from his vintage Weissenborn lap steel guitar and before long, the lad was added to the roster of 'Virgin America'. Prior to this, the man had made his recording debut, 'PLEASURE AND PAIN' (1992), with fellow troubadour TOM FREUND. Steeped in the essence of the blues but written in a thoroughly modern context, HARPER's songs addressed current events while reflecting age old themes. Racism for one; released as his debut single, 'LIKE A KING' was a barbed comment on the Rodney King affair. Cloaked in the sparsest of arrangements, HARPER's more personal material on 'WELCOME TO THE CRUEL WORLD' (1994) was equally forthright, succinct and resonant. While many cited him as the new HENDRIX (how many times have we heard that?), more sympathetic comparisons would be GIL SCOTT-HERON (who he subsequently played and toured with) and, if only for the purity and soulfulness of his slide playing, the late LOWELL GEORGE (of LITTLE FEAT). Yet while his influences were manifold, HARPER was singing the blues in his own style, accumulating gushing critical praise for his cathartic live performances. 1995's follow-up set, 'FIGHT FOR YOUR MIND', saw the addition of a drummer, OLIVER CHARLES, and a bassist, JUAN NELSON, although the songs were as sparingly radical as ever, if even more intense and imbued with a sense of human truth. Incredibly, perhaps, HARPER maintains that he has only written a handful of "blues" songs in his life, with only one ('HOMELESS CHILD') making it into the recording studio. What can't be disputed is that HARPER's music is about as far from the conception of blues as crusty old pub-rock as it is possible to get, a fact borne out by the continuing support of a wide cross-section of the music press, from the dance and style mags to the inkies. While major chart success continues to elude him, HARPER's third full-length release, 'THE WILL TO LIVE' (1997), suggested that, like his mate TAJ MAHAL, the best is yet to come. Now credited as BEN HARPER AND THE INNOCENT CRIMINALS, the man and his 3-piece backing combo had a well-deserved US Top 75 entry with fourth set, 'BURN TO SHINE' (1999). 2001's concert double set, 'LIVE FROM MARS', was an enjoyable, occasionally visceral insight into HARPER's hard-touring ethos. It only takes a couple of spins to realise that the guitarist lives and breathes this music, never more so than when he's onstage and inspired by the live dynamic. Two whole discs in one sitting may be a bit much for the average listener but even the covers (Marvin Gaye's 'SEXUAL HEALING' and Led Zep's 'WHOLE LOTTA LOVE') are soaked in HARPER's 100% proof soul power. The cleverly titled 'DIAMONDS ON THE INSIDE' (2003), his first new studio material in four years, was almost certainly worth the wait. As the likes of 'TOUCH FROM YOUR LUST', 'TEMPORARY REMEDY' and 'BRING THE FUNK' demonstrated, HARPER was perhaps more in tune with the spirit of raw funk than he's ever been, while guest vocals by LADYSMITH BLACK MAMBAZO lent the record an even deeper, African-rooted appeal. Having guested on the BLIND BOYS OF ALABAMA's 'Higher Ground', HARPER welcomed the acclaimed gospel troupe for a return favour on collaborative set, 'THERE WILL BE A LIGHT' (2004). The most mellow and traditional album of the guitarist's career, it saw BEN's hectoring slide take a back seat behind testifying southern soul; only on a very 'O Brother, Where Art Thou?' cover of Bob Dylan/Danny O'Keefe's 'WELL, WELL, WELL' did his guitar really wail. With everyone and his surfboard releasing a double-set in the mid-00s, HARPER followed suit with 'BOTH SIDES OF THE GUN' (2006), a sprawling personal/political odyssey split into two discs: one meditational acoustic, the other very BLACK CROWES-esque roots rock, both part of the same US Top 10 package.

Covers: STRAWBERRY FIELDS FOREVER (Beatles).

Album rating: WELCOME TO THE CRUEL WORLD (*6) / FIGHT FOR YOUR MIND (*7) / THE WILL TO LIVE (*6) / BURN TO SHINE (*6) / LIVE FROM MARS (*6) / DIAMONDS ON THE INSIDE (*7) / THERE WILL BE A LIGHT (*7) / LIVE AT THE APOLLO (*5) / BOTH SIDES OF THE GUN (*6)

BEN HARPER – vocals, acoustic guitar / **TOM FREUND** – guitar

not iss. Cardas

Mar 92. (lp; as BEN HARPER & TOM FREUND) *<none>* **PLEASURE AND PAIN** [–] ltd [–]
– Whipping boy / Jesus on the main line / Pay the man / Quarter of a man / Mama's got a girlfriend now / Angel from Montgomery / Click'yo heels / You should have come to me / Dust my broom / Sweet home Chicago / Pleasure and pain.
(above album was half covers w/ BEN + TOM writing 2 each separately)

— now with **JOHN McKNIGHT** – bass + **ROCK DEADRICK** – drums

Virgin Virgin

Jul 94. (cd/c) *(CDVUS/VUSMC 69) <V2/V4 39320>* **WELCOME TO THE CRUEL WORLD** [ ] Feb94 [ ]
– The three of us / Whipping boy / Breakin' down / Don't take that attitude to your grave / Waiting on an angel / Mama's got a girlfriend now / Forever / Like a king / Pleasure and pain / Walk away / How many miles must we march / Welcome to the cruel world / I'll rise.

Nov 94. (12"/cd-s) *(VUS T/DG 86)* **LIKE A KING / (remix). / WHIPPING BOY / (remix)** [ ] [–]

— now with **JUAN NELSON** – bass / **OLIVER CHARLES** – drums

Jul 95. (cd/c/d-lp) *(CDVUS/VUSMC/VUSDLP 93) <40620>* **FIGHT FOR YOUR MIND** [ ] [ ]
– Oppression / Ground on down / Another lonely day / Please me like you want to / Gold to me / Burn one down / Excuse me Mr. / People lead / Fight for your mind / Give a man a home / By my side / Power of the gospel / God fearing man / One road to freedom.

Mar 96. (c-ep/cd-ep) *(VUS C/CD 99)* **GROUND ON DOWN EP** [ ] [–]
– Ground on down / Not fire not ice / Wicked man / If I could only hear my mother pray again.

May 97. (cd/c/lp) *(CDVUS/VUSMC/VUSLP 128) <44178>* **THE WILL TO LIVE** [ ] [89]
– Faded / Homeless child / Number three / Roses from my friends / Jah work / I want to be ready / The will to live / Ashes / Widow of a living man / Glory and consequence / Mama's trippin' / I shall not walk alone.
(cd re-iss. Apr98; CDVUSX 128)

Oct 97. (c-s) *(VUSC 120)* **FADED / VOODOO CHILE** [ ] [–]
(cd-s+=) *(VUSCD 120)* – Gold to me (live) / Fight for your mind.

Mar 98. (cd-s) *(VUSCD 134)* **FADED / REMEMBER – SUPERSTITION (live) / LIKE A KING (remix)** [54] [–]
(cd-s) *(VUSCDX 134)* – ('A'side) / Fight for your mind (live) / Faded:-Heroes Dollis Hill groove (instrumental).

Jul 98. (cd-s) *<95139>* **MAMA'S TRIPPIN' / MAMA'S TRIPPIN' (the Freedom mix) / EXCUSE ME MUSTER – BURNIN' & LOOTIN' (live)** [–] [ ]

Feb 99. (cd-s) *<893726>* **EXCUSE ME MISTER / NOBODY'S FAULT BUT MINE / SEXUAL HEALING (live)** [–] [ ]

BEN HARPER & THE INNOCENT CRIMINALS

Sep 99. (cd/d-lp) *(CDVUS/VUSLP 160) <48151>* **BURN TO SHINE** [ ] [67]
– Alone / The woman in you / Less / Two hands of a prayer / Please bleed / Suzie blue / Steal my kisses / Burn to shine / Show me a little shame / Forgiven / Beloved one / In the Lord's arms.

Nov 99. (cd-s) **JAH WORK / MAMA'S TRIPPIN' (live) / POWER OF THE GOSPEL (live) / EXCUSE ME MR – BURNIN' & LOOTIN' (live)** [–] [ ]

Jan 00. (cd-s) *<896471>* **PLEASE BLEED** [–] [ ]

2000. (cd-s) **STEAL MY KISSES / NUMBER THREE (live) / BY MY SIDE (live) / STEAL MY KISSES (Neptune beat box)** [–] [ ]

May 01. (d-cd) *(CDVUSDX 187) <10079>* **LIVE FROM MARS (live)** [ ] Mar01 [70]
– Glory & consequence / Excuse me Mr. / Alone / Sexual healing / Woman in you / Ground on down / Steal my kisses / Burn one down / Mama's got a girlfriend / Welcome to the cruel world / Forgiven / Faded – Whole lotta love / Waiting on an angel / Roses from my friends / Power of the gospel / Pleasure and pain / Please bleed / The drugs don't work / In the Lord's arms / Not fire not ice / Beloved one / Number three / Walk away / Another lonely day / Like a king – I'll rise.

Mar 03. (cd; as BEN HARPER) *(CDVUS 234) <83003>* **DIAMONDS ON THE INSIDE** [ ] [19]
– With my own two hands / When it's good / Diamonds on the inside / Touch from your lust / When she believes / Brown eyed blues / Bring the funk / Everything / Amen omen / Temporary remedy / So high so low / Blessed to be a witness / Picture of Jesus / She's only happy in the sun.

Jun 03. (cd-s) *(VUSCD 266)* **DIAMONDS ON THE INSIDE / AMEN OMEN (solo acoustic version) / STRAWBERRY FIELDS FOREVER** [ ] [–]

BEN HARPER & THE BLIND BOYS OF ALABAMA

Sep 04. (cd) *(CDVUS 254) <71206>* **THERE WILL BE A LIGHT** [ ] [81]
– Take my hand / Wicked man / Where could I go / Church house steps / 11th commandment / Well, well, well / Picture of Jesus / Satisfied mind / Mother pray / There will be a light / Church on time.

Mar 05. (cd) *(CDVUS 262)* **LIVE AT THE APOLLO** (live) [ ] [–]
– 11th commandment / Well, well, well / I want to be ready / Take my hand / Picture of Jesus / Church house steps / Give a man a home / Wicked man / Mother pray / I shall not walk alone / Church on time / Where could I go / There will be a light / Satisfied mind.

BEN HARPER

Mar 06. (d-cd) *(CDVUSD 279) <57446>* **BOTH SIDES OF THE GUN** [ ] [7]
– Morning yearning / Waiting for you / Picture in a frame / Never leave lonely alone / Sweet nothing serenade / Reason to mourn / More than sorry / Cryin' won't help you now / Happy everafter in your eyes / Better way / Both sides of the gun / Engraved invitation / Black rain / Gather 'round the stone / Please don't talk about murder while I'm eating / Get it while you like it / The way you found me / Serve your soul. *(ltd-t-cd+=; CDVUSXX 279)* – Gather 'round the stone (alt.) / Reason to mourn (alt.) / Get it like you like it (live acoustic Nashville) / Waiting for you (alt.) / Morning yearning (alt.) / Beloved one (live in Atlanta).

– compilations, etc. –

Oct 02. (3xcd-box) *Virgin; (812906-2)* **BURN TO SHINE / WELCOME TO THE CRUEL WORLD / FIGHT FOR YOUR MIND** [ ] [ ]

Roy HARPER

Born: 12 Jun'41, Rusholme, Manchester, England. He was raised by his father, following his mother's death during childbirth. His step-mother was a Jehovah's Witness, leading to him becoming anti-religious. As a young teenager, he played in a skiffle group with his brother DAVID, but at 15, after leaving school, he joined the R.A.F. Not finding it to his liking, he feigned madness to escape further service. Roy then underwent ECT treatment at a mental hospital, later being institutionalised in Lancaster Moor. He then spent a year in jail at Walton Prison, Liverpool. In 1964, after busking around Europe, he moved to London and gained a solo residency at LES COUSINS' folk club in Soho. In 1966, he was signed to Peter Richards's 'Strike' records, who issued his debut lp, 'THE SOPHISTICATED BEGGAR'. The record encompassed his best pieces of poetry, only using a simple revox machine as backing. The following year, he signed to 'C.B.S.', issuing a second flop 45, which preceded the album, 'COME OUT FIGHTING, GENGHIS SMITH'. This featured an 11-minute track, 'CIRCLE' another of his highly personal folk/blues confessionals. In the summer of '68, he played free concerts at London's Hyde Park, which brought him a new underground audience. In 1969, he released the album, 'FOLKJOKEOPUS', which also featured a similarily lengthy track, the 15-minute 'McGOOGHAN'S BLUES'. Signing to 'Harvest' early in 1970, he released his fourth album in as many years, 'FLAT BAROQUE AND BERSERK' (it featured an uncredited guest spot from The NICE on the track, 'HELL'S ANGEL'). ROY then embarked on a US tour, but after arriving there drunk and jet-lagged he was arrested for abusive behaviour. He slept on West Coast beaches, while playing many gigs. In 1971, he released the highly regarded 'STORMCOCK' set, which hosted DAVID BEDFORD on orchestration and friend JIMMY PAGE (of LED ZEPPELIN) on the first of many guitar sessions for him. PAGE had already written an ode, 'Hats Off To Harper' for their LED ZEPPELIN III album. In 1972, he made his acting debut in the low-budget British film, 'Made', alongside Carol White. Most of the music from the film appeared in his next project, 'LIFEMASK', which was written as his last will and testament, following a near fatal, recurring blood disorder. On the 14th of February '74, he released the appropriately titled, 'VALENTINE', which gave him his first entry into the UK album chart. It was premiered at a concert on Valentine's Day at London's Rainbow theatre, with backing from PAGE, BEDFORD, KEITH MOON and JOHN BONHAM. Later in 1974, he formed the band TRIGGER (with BILL BRUFORD – drums / CHRIS SPEDDING – guitar & DAVE COCHRAN – bass), and supported PINK FLOYD at Knebworth. In 1975, he sang lead vox on PINK FLOYD's 'Have A Cigar', featured on the album, 'Wish You Were Here'. FLOYD had already guested on his next album, 'HQ', which like its 1977 follow-up, 'BULLINAMINGVASE', hit the UK Top 40. In between the aforementioned projects, he had briefly resided in the States. In 1982 with MARK THOMPSON, he set up his own 'Public' records, who issued ROY's return to form with the 'WORK OF HEART' album. Early in 1985, he scored his last UK Top 50 album, the JIMMY PAGE collaboration, 'WHATEVER HAPPENED TO JUGULA'. He continued to take an active part in the music scene, the album, 'DEATH OR GLORY' being his last effort for some time in 1992. HARPER's son NICK proved he was a chip off the old block when he contributed some fine acoustic guitar to the opening track ('SONGS OF LOVE') on ROY's 1998 album 'The DREAM SOCIETY'. Other guests included former JETHRO TULL man, IAN ANDERSON, who obliged with his trademark flute on the ambitious 'THESE FIFTY YEARS'. 'THE GREEN MAN' (2000), on the other hand, was a back to basics acoustic set recorded by HARPER alone with lyrics which were as reliably oblique as ever. Concert set, 'ROYAL FESTIVAL HALL LIVE 2001' featured both NICK and PENTANGLE plucker JOHN RENBOURN, running the gamut of his career.

• **Trivia:** PAUL and LINDA McCARTNEY guested on his 'ONE OF THOSE DAYS IN ENGLAND' album. Meanwhile, KATE BUSH guested on ROY's 'THE UNKNOWN SOLDIER' album, returning the compliment by appearing on her hit 45, 'Breathing'.

Album rating: THE SOPHISTICATED BEGGAR (*8) / COME OUT FIGHTING GENGHIS SMITH (*6) / FOLKJOKEOPUS (*5) / FLAT BAROQUE AND BERSERK (*6) / STORMCOCK (*8) / LIFEMASK (*7) / VALENTINE (*6) / FLASHES FROM THE ARCHIVES OF OBLIVION (*6) / HQ (*7) / BULLINAMINGVASE (*7) / ROY HARPER 1970-75 compilation (*6) / THE UNKNOWN SOLDIER (*4) / WORK OF HEART (*6) / BORN IN CAPTIVY (*5) / WHATEVER HAPPENED TO JUGULA with Jimmy Page (*5) / IN BETWEEN EVERY LINE (*4) / DESCENDENTS OF SMITH (*6) / LOONY ON THE BUS early/rare (*4) / ONCE (*5) / BURN THE WORLD (*5) / DEATH OR GLORY (*6) / AN INTRODUCTION TO ROY HARPER collection (*6) / THE DREAM SOCIETY (*6) / THE GREEN MAN (*5) / ROYAL FESTIVAL HALL LIVE 2001 (*5)

ROY HARPER – vocals, guitar (with session people)

Strike — not is[sued]

Mar 66. (7") *(JH 304)* **TAKE ME IN YOUR EYES. / PRETTY BABY** [ ] [–]

Dec 66. (lp) *(JHL 105)* **THE SOPHISTICATED BEGGAR** [ ] [–]
– China girl / Goldfish / Sophisticated beggar / My friend / Big fat silve[r] aeroplane / Blackpool / Legend / Girlie / October the twelfth / Blac[k] clouds / Mr. Station master / Forever / Committed. *(re-iss. Aug70 & 197[?] as 'RETURN OF THE SOPHISTICATED BEGGAR' on 'Youngblood' an[d] 'Birth' respectively; SSYB 7 & RAB 3) (re-iss. 1977 on 'Big Ben'; BBX 502) (re-iss. Jan89 on 'Sundown' lp/cd; SDLP/CDSM 051) (cd re-iss. Oct94 on 'J.H.D.'; JHDCD 064) (cd re-iss. Oct96 on 'Science Friction'; HUCD 007)*

C.B.S. — not is[sued]

Oct 67. (7") *(CBS 203001)* **MIDSPRING DITHERING. / ZENGEM** [ ] [–]

Jan 68. (lp) *(CBS 63184)* **COME OUT FIGHTING GHENGIS SMITH** [ ] [–]
– Freak street / You don't need money / Ageing raver / In a beautif[ul] rambling mess / All you need is / What you have / Circle / Highga[te] Cemetary / Come out fighting Ghengis Smith / Zaney Janey / Ballad [of a] songwriter / Midspring dithering / Zenjem / It's tomorrow and today [is] yesterday / Francesca / She's the one / Nobody's got any money in th[e] summer. *(re-iss. Jun77 as 'THE EARLY YEARS' on 'CBS-Embassy'; EM[B] 31544) (re-iss. Sep91 on 'Awareness' lp/cd;) (cd re-iss. Nov94 & Oct96 o[n] 'Science Friction'; HUCD 006)*

Apr 68. (7") *(CBS 3371)* **LIFE GOES BY. / NOBODY'S GOT ANY MONEY IN THE SUMMER** [ ] [–]

Liberty — Wor[ld] Paci[fic]

Apr 69. (lp; mono/stereo) *(LBL/LBS 83231) <21888>* **FOLKJOKEOPUS** [ ] [ ]
– Sergeant Sunshine / She's the one / In the time of water / Composer [of] life / One for all / Exercising some control / McGoohan's blues / Manan[a] *(re-iss. Sep77 on 'Sunset'; SLS 50373) <US re-iss. 1978 on 'Chrysalis'; 116[?]> (re-iss. Aug86 & Nov88 on 'Awareness' lp/c; AWL/AWT 1003) (cd-iss. Oct8[?]; AWCD 1003) (cd re-iss. Oct94 & Oct96 on 'Science Friction'; HUCD 009)*

Harvest Harvest

Jun 70. (lp) *(SHVL 766) <418>* **FLAT BAROQUE AND BERSERK** [ ] [ ]
– Don't you grieve / I hate the white man / Feeling all the Saturday / How does it feel / Goodbye / Another day / Davey / East of the sun / Tom Tiddler's ground / Francesca / Song of the ages / Hell's angels. *(re-iss. Jul85 lp/c; 260585-1/-4) (cd-iss. 1992 & Jun94 on 'Hard Up' respectively; HUCD 003 & HUP 3LTDCD)*

May 71. (lp) *(SHVL 789)* **STORMCOCK** [ ] [–]
– Hors d'oeuvres / The same old rock / One man rock and roll band / Me and my woman. *<US-iss.1978 on 'Chrysalis'; 1161> (re-iss. Apr87 on 'Awareness' lp/c; AWL/AWT 2001) (cd re-iss. Oct94 & Oct96 on 'Science Friction'; HUCD 004)*

Oct 72. (7") *(HAR 5059)* **BANK OF THE DEAD (VALERIE'S SONG). / LITTLE LADY** [ ] [–]

Feb 73. (lp) *(SHVL 808)* **LIFEMASK** (music from film soundtrack 'MADE') [ ] [–]
– Highway blues / All Ireland / Little lady / Bank of the dead (Valerie's song) / South Africa / The Lord's prayer: Poem – Modal song (part 1-4) – Front song – Middle song – End song – Front song (reprise). *<US-iss.1978 on 'Chrysalis'; 1162> (re-iss. Apr87 on 'Awareness' lp/c; AWL/AWT 1007) (cd-iss. Sep94 & Oct96 & Sep02 on 'Science Friction'+=; HUCD 005)* – Ballad of songwriter / Zaney Janey / Midspring dithering / Zenjam.

Feb 74. (7") *(HAR 5080)* **(DON'T YOU THINK WE'RE) FOREVER. / MALE CHAUVINIST PIG BLUES** [ ] [–]

Feb 74. (lp) *(SHSP 4027)* **VALENTINE** [27] [–]
– Forbidden fruit / Male chauvinist pig blues / I'll see you again / Twelve hours of sunset / Acapulco gold / Commune / Magic woman / Che / North country / (Don't you think we're) Forever. *<US-iss.1978 on 'Chrysalis'; 1163> (re-iss. Apr89 on 'Awareness' lp/c/cd; AWL/AWT/AWCD 1015)* – Home (studio) / Too many movies / Home (live). *(cd re-iss. Nov94 & Oct96 & Sep02 on 'Science Friction'+=; HUCD 015)*

Oct 74. (7") *(HAR 5089)* **HOME (live). / HOME (studio)** [ ] [–]

Nov 74. (d-lp) *(SHDW 405)* **FLASHES FROM THE ARCHIVES OF OBLIVION (live)** [ ] [–]
– Home / Commune / Don't you grieve / Twelve hours of sunset / Kangaroo blues / All Ireland / Me and my woman / South Africa / Interference / Highway blues / One man rock and roll band / Another day / M.C.P. blues / Too many movies / Home (studio version) *<US-iss.1978 on 'Chrysalis'; 1164> (re-iss. Apr89 on 'Awareness' d-lp/c/cd; AW CD/TD/LD 1012) (cd re-iss. Sep94 & Oct96 on 'Science Friction'; HUCD 010)*

Harvest Chrysalis

May 75. (lp) *(SHSP 4046) <1105>* **HQ** <US-title 'WHEN AN OLD CRICKETER LEAVES THE CREASE'> [31] Feb 76 [ ]
– The game (part I-V) / The spirit lives / Grown-ups are just silly children / Referendum / Forget-me-not / Hallucinating light / When an old cricketer leaves the crease / Referendum. *(re-iss. Mar86 on 'E.M.I.' lp/c; ATAK/TCATAK 68) (cd-iss. Aug95 & Oct96 on 'Science Friction'; HUCD 019)*

May 75. (7") *(HAR 5096)* **WHEN AN OLD CRICKETER LEAVES THE CREASE. / HALLUCINATING LIGHT (acoustic)** [ ] [ ]

Oct 75. (7") *(HAR 5102)* **GROWN-UPS ARE JUST SILLY CHILDREN. / REFERENDUM (LEGEND)** [ ] [–]

Feb 77. (lp) *(SHSP 4060)* **BULLINAMINGVASE** [25] [–]
– One of those days in England / These last days / Cherishing the lonesome / Naked flame / Watford Gap * / One of those days in England (parts 2-10). *(free 7"w/a) (PSR 407)* REFERENDUM / ANOTHER DAY (live). / TOM TIDDLER'S GROUND (live) *(lp re-iss. Mar77, track * repl. by;* – Breakfast in bed. *(re-iss. Apr87 on 'E.M.I.' lp/c; EMS/TCEMS 1259)*

Mar 77. (7") *(HAR 5120)* **ONE OF THOSE DAYS IN ENGLAND. / WATFORD GAP** [ ] [–]

Nov 77. (7"; as ROY HARPER'S BLACK SHEEP) *(HAR 5140)* **SAIL AWAY. / CHERISHING THE LONESOME** [ ] [–]

Mar 80. (7") *(HAR 5203)* **PLAYING GAMES. / FIRST THING IN THE MORNING** [ ] [–]

Jun 80. (lp) *(SHVL 820)* **THE UNKNOWN SOLDIER** [ ] [–]
– Playing games / I'm in love with you / The flycatcher / You / Old faces / Short and sweet / First thing in the morning / The unknown soldier / Ten years ago / True story.

Jun 80. (7"m) *(HAR 5207)* **SHORT AND SWEET. / WATER SPORTS (live) / UNKNOWN SOLDIER (live)** [ ] [–]

Public not iss.

Oct 82. (7") *(PUBS 1001)* **NO ONE EVER GETS OUT ALIVE. / CASUALITY (live)** [ ] [–]

Nov 82. (lp/c) *(PUBLP/TCPUBLP 5001)* **WORK OF HEART** [ ] [–]
– Drawn to the flames / Jack of hearts / I am a child / Woman / I still care / Work of heart; (i) No one ever gets out alive – (ii) Two lovers in the Moon – (iii) We are the people – (iv) All us children (so sadly far apart) – (v) We are the people (reprise) – (vi) No one ever gets out alive (finale). *(re-iss. Nov86 on 'Awareness' lp,c; AWL 1002) (lp w/free 7"x2; PUBS 1001/1002; 2nd very ltd) (cd-iss. Oct89; AWCD 1002)*

Mar 83. (7") *(PUBS 1002)* **I STILL CARE. / GOODBYE LADYBIRD** [ ] [–]

Hardup not iss.

1984. (lp; ltd) *(PUB 5002)* **BORN IN CAPTIVITY** (demos) [ ] [–]
– Stan / Drawn to the flames / Come to bed eyes / No woman is safe / I am a child / Elizabeth / Work of heart; (i) No one ever gets out alive – (ii) Two lovers on the Moon – (iii) We are the people – (iv) All us children (so sadly far apart) – (v) We are the people (reprise) – (vi) No one ever gets out alive (finale). *(re-iss. Jul85 & Nov88 on 'Awareness' lp/c; AWL/AWT 1001) (cd-iss. Apr89; AWCD 1001) (cd re-iss. Oct96 on 'Blueprint'; HUCD 008)*

ROY HARPER and JIMMY PAGE

with **JIMMY PAGE** – guitar (ex-LED ZEPPELIN)

Beggars Banquet P.V.C.

Feb 85. (lp/c) *(BEGA/BEGC 60) <8937>* **WHATEVER HAPPENED TO JUGULA** [44] [ ]
– Nineteen forty-eightish / Hangman / Elizabeth / Advertisement / Bad speech / Hope / Twentieth century man. *(re-iss. Aug88 & Jul91 on 'Lowdown – Beggars Banquet' lp/c/cd; BBL/+C 60/+CD)*

Mar 85. (7") *(BEG 131)* **ELIZABETH. / ADVERTISEMENT** [ ] [–]
(12"+=) *(BEG 131T)* – (I hate the) White man (live).

ROY HARPER

E.M.I. not iss.

Jun 86. (d-lp/c) *(EM/TCEM 5004)* **IN BETWEEN EVERY LINE (live)** [ ] [–]
– One of those days in England / Short and sweet / True story / Referendum / Highway blues / One man rock and roll band / The game / Hangman. *(cd-iss. Nov94 & Oct96 on 'Science Friction'; HUCD 018)*

Mar 88. (7") *(EM 46)* **LAUGHING INSIDE. / LAUGHING INSIDE (acoustic)** [ ] [–]
(above single was also released as 3 promos in the disguise of palindromes; RORY PHARE / HARRY ROPE / PER YARROH; *(Regal Zonophone; RP 1 / HP 1 / PY 1)*

Mar 88. (cd/c/lp) *(CD/TC+/EMC 3524)* **DESCENDANTS OF SMITH** [ ] [–]
– Laughing inside / Garden of uranium / Still life / Pinches of salt / Desert island / Government surplus / Surplus liquorice / Liquorice alltime / Maile lei / Same shoes / Descendants of Smith. *(cd+=)* – Laughing inside (rough and ready version). *(cd-iss. Sep94 & Oct96 as 'GARDEN OF URANIUM' on 'Science Friction' respectively; HUCD 014)*
below featured DAVE GILMOUR, KATE BUSH & STEVE BROUGHTON

Awareness I.R.S.

May 90. (cd/c/lp) *(AW CD/T/L 1018) <13078>* **ONCE** [ ] [ ]
– Once / Once in the middle of nowhere / Nowhere to run to / Black cloud of Islam / If / Winds of change / Berliners / Sleeping at the wheel / For longer than it takes / Ghost dance. *(cd re-iss. Oct94 on 'Line'; LICD 900892) (cd re-iss. Oct96 on 'Science Friction'; HUCD 011)*

Nov 90. (cd/c/lp) *(AW CD/T/L 1019)* **BURN THE WORLD** [ ] [–]
– Burn the world (studio) / Burn the world (live). *(cd re-iss. Oct94 & Oct96 on 'Science Friction'; HUCD 013)*

Nov 92. (cd/c/lp) *(AW CD/T/L 1037)* **DEATH OR GLORY** [ ] [–]
– Death or glory / War came home / Tonight duty / Waiting for Godot / Part zed next to me / Man kind / Tallest tree / Miles remains / Fourth world / Why / Cardboard city / One more tomorrow / Plough / On summer day / If I can. *(cd re-iss. Dec94 & Oct96 & Sep99 on 'Science Friction'; HUCD 012)*

Resurgent not iss.

Jun 98. (cd) *(4305)* **THE DREAM SOCIETY** [ ] [–]
– Songs of love / Songs of love (part 2) / Dancing all the night / Psychopath / I want to be in love / Drugs for everybody / Come the revolution / Angel of the night / The dream society / Broken wing / These fifty years. *(re-iss. Sep99 on 'Science Friction'; HUCD 030)*

Science Friction Science Friction

Apr 01. (cd) *(<HUCD 033>)* **THE GREEN MAN** [ ] May01 [ ]
– The green man / Wishing well / Sexy woman / The apology / Midnight sun / Glasto / The monster / New England / Solar wind sculptures / Rushing Camelot / All in all.

Dec 01. (cd) *(HUCD 035)* **ROYAL FESTIVAL HALL LIVE 2001** (live) [ ] [–]

– Commune / I'll see you again / Rushing Camelot / Another day / North country / Hallucinating light / The same old rock / Sexy woman / Key to the highway / Sophisticated beggar / Highway blues / Twelve hours of sunset / Me and my woman / The flycatcher / The green man.

– compilations, others, etc. –

May 78. (7") *Harvest; (HAR 5160)* **WHEN AN OLD CRICKETER LEAVES THE CREASE. / HOME (studio)**

May 78. (lp) *Harvest; (SHSM 2025)* **ROY HARPER 1970-75**
– Don't you grieve / (I hate the) White man / Tom Tiddler's ground / Me and my woman / Little lady / South Africa / Forbidden fruit / I'll see you again / Commune / Another day / When an old cricketer leaves the crease / Home.

Dec 88. (lp/c/cd) *Awareness; (AWL/AWT/AWCD 1011)* **LOONY ON THE BUS** (rare)
– No change (ten years ago) / Sail away / / Playing prison / I wanna be part of the news / Burn the world / Casuality / Cora / Loony on the bus / Come up and see me / The flycatcher / Square boxes.

1992. (c) *Hard Up; (HU 2)* **BORN IN CAPTIVITY II (live)**

Nov 94. (cd) *Awareness;* **BORN IN CAPTIVITY / WORK OF HEART**
(re-iss. cd Nov94 on 'Science Friction'; HUCD 008)

Dec 94. (cd) *Awareness;* **COMMERCIAL BREAKS** (unreleased from 1977 on 'Harvest'; *SHSP 4077)*
– My little girl / I'm in love with you / Ten years ago / Sail away / I wanna be part of the news / Cora / Come up and see me / The flycatcher / Too many movies / Square boxes / Burn the world (part 1) / Playing prisons.
(re-iss. Feb95 & Oct96 on 'Science Friction'; HUCD 016)

Dec 94. (cd) *Awareness; (234)* **AN INTRODUCTION TO ROY HARPER**
– Legend / She's the one / Tom Tiddler's ground / Highway blues / Che / Hallucinating light / One of those days in England / You / Nineteen forty-eightish / Pinches of salt / Ghost dance / The tallest tree / Miles remains.
(re-iss. Feb95 & Oct96 on 'Science Friction'; HUCD 017)

Aug 95. (cd) *Griffin; (132-2)* **UNHINGED**
– Descendants of Smith / Legend / North country / When an old cricketer leaves the crease / Three hundred words / Hope / Naked flame / Commune / South Africa / Back to the stones / Frozen moment / Highway blues / The same old rock. *(re-iss. Oct96 on 'Blueprint'; HUCD 020)*

May 96. (cd) *Blueprint; (BP 220CD)* **LIVE AT LES COUSINS (live)**

Apr 97. (cd) *Science Friction; (HUCD 022)* **LIVE AT THE BBC VOL.1**

Apr 97. (cd) *Science Friction; (HUCD 023)* **LIVE AT THE BBC VOL.2**

Jun 97. (cd) *Science Friction; (HUCD 024)* **LIVE AT THE BBC VOL.3**

Jun 97. (cd) *Science Friction; (HUCD 025)* **LIVE AT THE BBC VOL.4**

Jun 97. (cd) *Science Friction; (HUCD 026)* **LIVE AT THE BBC VOL.5**

Jun 97. (cd) *Science Friction; (HUCD 027)* **LIVE AT THE BBC VOL.6**

Jun 01. (cd) *Capitol; <27640>* **HATS OFF**

Emmylou HARRIS

Born: 2 Apr'47, Birmingham, Alabama, USA. She later moved to Washington, playing sax in a high school band before going to the University of North Carolina where she made her first forays into the world of folk music, playing as part of a duo. From here it was but a short step to the folk clubs of Greenwich Village in New York where she released her debut 1969 album, 'GLIDING BIRD' for the 'Jubilee' label. The record was hardly a resounding success and after a spell in Nashville in the early 70's, she drifted back with baby Hallie to Washington following the failure of her first marriage. By a twist of fate, this apparent setback proved to be the beginning of her career proper after she was spotted in a local club by the The FLYING BURRITO BROTHERS. The band informed ex-member and founding father of Cosmic American Music (country-rock, basically), GRAM PARSONS, who was after a partner for his forthcoming solo project. The two hit it off immediately, GRAM schooling her in the ways of classic country. Over the course of two albums, 'G.P.' (1972) and 'GRIEVOUS ANGEL' (1973), the pair recorded some of the most sublime duets in the history of recorded music ('WE'LL SWEEP OUT THE ASHES IN THE MORNING', 'LOVE HURTS' etc.), HARRIS' mournful soprano combining with PARSON's cracked chords to create music of a fragile beauty. PARSONS was on a crash course in self-destruction, however, and after he O.D.'d in 1973, HARRIS's career was once again in limbo. Down but not out, she eventually formed a new backing outfit from the ashes of GRAM's FALLEN ANGELS, retaining JAMES BURTON (guitar, previously of ELVIS PRESLEY's band) and GLENN D.HARDIN (piano), bringing in EMORY GORDY (bass), RODNEY CROWELL (rhythm guitar, vocals), HANK DE VITO (pedal steel) and JOHN WARE (drums). Remaining with PARSON's label, 'Reprise', HARRIS released 'PIECES OF THE SKY' in 1975, a masterful set which included one of her finest compositions, 'BOULDER TO BIRMINGHAM', a lilting eulogy to GRAM, alongside the beautiful 'SLEEPLESS NIGHTS' and a rousing cover of the LOUVIN BROTHERS 'IF I COULD ONLY WIN YOUR LOVE' which became an American country No.1. HARRIS possessed one of the most haunting and alongside STEVIE NICKS, one of the most distinctive, white female voices in the business. Over a string of excellent albums and consummate choice of cover material, she built up a reputation as one of country's leading ladies as well as winning over rock and pop fans. Her tonsils much in demand, she even appeared in The BAND's 'Last Waltz', performing ROBBIE ROBERTSON's 'EVANGELINE', and during the 70's provided backing vocals on a number of classic albums, including LITTLE FEAT's 'Dixie Chicken' and BOB DYLAN's 'Desire'. Following her marriage to producer BRIAN AHERN, HARRIS released her second Top 30 album, 'LUXURY LINER' (1977), arguably her strongest set of the decade wherein she performed a spine-tingling run through of the late, great Townes Van Zandt's 'PANCHO AND LEFTY' while covering The Carter Family's 'HELLO STRANGER' in fine style. With 'QUARTER MOON IN A TEN CENT TOWN' (1978), the singer moved towards straight country, scoring a Top 3 country hit with her touching cover of Dolly Parton's 'TO DADDY'. 'BLUE KENTUCKY GIRL' (1979) and 'ROSES IN THE SNOW' (1980) were rootsier, the latter stripped down to bare acoustic guitar. 'EVANGELINE' (1981) once more saw HARRIS at her best covering classic material, GRAM's 'HOT BURRITO No.2' and CREEDENCE CLEARWATER REVIVAL's 'BAD MOON RISING' both given a thorough going over. Heading back to Nashville in the mid-80's, HARRIS even recorded a country concept album (!), 'THE BALLAD OF SALLY ROSE' (1985). As the decade wore on, HARRIS and her HOT BAND were met with an increasingly cold reception, commercially at least, and she eventually replaced said backing crew with The NASH RAMBLERS, a rootsier acoustic group. The 90's saw HARRIS re-appraising her sound, hip producer DANIEL LANOIS working on her acclaimed 1995 album, 'WRECKING BALL', a set that also saw the likes of a similarly revamped STEVE EARLE guesting. If anyone can keep the spirit of roots country alive and relevant in an increasingly hi-tech musical world, then it's EMMYLOU, whose dedication to the genre through the ever changing dictats of fashion is admirable. Three whole decades and nearly thirty albums under her belt, HARRIS finally tapped her latent songwriting talent on the acclaimed 'RED DIRT GIRL' (2000). She may still dress like a cowgirl but you'd be hard pushed to find anything to tempt the Nashville mainstream on this record. Instead, EMMYLOU – with the help of producer Malcolm Burn and an extensive cast of friends that included BRUCE SPRINGSTEEN, GUY CLARK, KATE McGARRIGLE and DAVE MATTHEWS – put in some of the best performances of her career against a backdrop that encompassed elements of starry-eyed pop, atmospheric rock, ethnic textures and driving percussion. 2003's 'STUMBLE INTO GRACE', meanwhile, found the singer growing – if not exactly stumbling – older with as much elegance as the title suggested. Although she's arguably been working towards a state of musical grace since the earliest days of her career, in recent years she seems to have intensified that quest and the mistitled 'STUMBLE..' was another step in the right direction. Again laying its arrangements open to elements outwith her previous remit, the record found HARRIS flirting with haunting fragments of folk, pop and world music to often mesmerising effect. Featuring such career touchstones as 'LOVE HURTS', 'PANCHO AND LEFTY' and 'ORPHAN GIRL', 'THE VERY BEST OF EMMYLOU HARRIS: HEARTACHE & HIGHWAYS' (2005) was a long overdue summary, updating the two 'PROFILE' sets from way back, and spanning the GRAM PARSONS era, the country-rock chic 70's, the refined 80's and the bold alt-country experiments of her latter years. In April 2006, her collaboration ('ALL THE ROADRUNNING') with former DIRE STRAITS mainman, MARK KNOPFLER, returned her to the Top 20.

• **Songwriters:** Writes some herself, collaborates with others, except covers I'LL BE YOUR BABY TONIGHT (Bob Dylan) / THE PRICE YOU PAY + MY FATHER'S HOUSE + BORN TO RUN + TOUGHER THAN THE REST (Bruce Springsteen) / YOU NEVER CAN TELL (Chuck Berry) / THE BOXER (Simon & Garfunkel) / MISTER SANDMAN (Chordettes) / TO DADDY (Dolly Parton) / BURN THAT CANDLE (Bill Haley) / TWO MORE BOTTLES OF WINE (Delbert McClinton) / PLEDGING MY LOVE (Johnny Ace) / DIAMONDS ARE A GIRL'S BEST FRIEND (Jule Styne) / WILD MONTANA SKIES (duet w / JOHN DENVER) / HERE, THERE AND EVERYWHERE + FOR NO ONE (Beatles) / NO REGRETS (Tom Rush) / ICY BLUE HEART (John Hiatt) / LOVE IS (Kate McGarrigle) / WHEELS OF LOVE (Marjy Plant) / SAVE THE LAST DANCE FOR ME (Drifters) / JAMBALAYA (Hank Williams) / BAD MOON RISING + LODI (Creedence Clearwater Revival) / ROSE OF CIMARRON (Poco) / HOT BURRITO + SLEEPLESS NIGHTS (Gram Parsons) / BRAND NEW DANCE (Paul Kennerley) / SWEET DREAMS OF YOU (Kennerley-David) / BETTER OFF WITHOUT YOU (Chapman-Walker-Brown) / NEVER BE ANYONE ELSE BUT YOU (Baker Knight) / RED RED ROSE (David Mallett) / GUITAR TOWN (Steve Earle) / ROLLIN' AND RAMBLIN' (Williams-Williams-Clark) / EASY FOR YOU TO SAY (Routh-Sharp) / IN HIS WORLD (Kostas-Reynolds) / ABRAHAM, MARTIN & JOHN (hit; Marvin Gaye) / SCOTLAND (... Monroe) / CATTLE CALL (Buck Owens) / THANKS TO YOU (Jesse Winchester) / BALLAD OF A RUNNING HORSE (Leonard Cohen) / etc. • **Trivia:** In 1980, she won a Grammy for her country lp 'BLUE KENTUCKY GIRL'.

Album rating: GLIDING BIRD (*4) / PIECES OF THE SKY (*7) / ELITE HOTEL (*8) / LUXURY LINER (*8) / QUARTER MOON IN A TEN CENT TOWN (*7) / PROFILE – BEST OF . . . compilation (*7) / BLUE KENTUCKY GIRL (*6) / ROSES IN THE SNOW (*7) / LIGHT OF THE STABLE (*6) / EVANGELINE (*7) / CIMARRON (*6) / LAST DATE (*6) / WHITE SHOES (*6) / PROFILE II – BEST OF . . . compilation (*6) / THE BALLAD OF SALLY ROSE (*5) / THIRTEEN (*5) / TRIO with Dolly Parton & Linda Ronstadt (*5) / ANGEL BAND (*5) / BLUEBIRD (*5) / DUETS (*5) / BRAND NEW DANCE (*5) / AT THE RYMAN (*7) / NASHVILLE COUNTRY DUETS with Carl Jackson (*5) / COWGIRL'S PRAYER (*6) / SONGS OF THE WEST (*6) / WRECKING BALL (*8) / NASHVILLE (*5) / RED DIRT GIRL (*8) / STUMBLE INTO GRACE (*7) / HEARTACHES & HIGHWAYS: THE VERY BEST OF EMMYLOU HARRIS compilation (*8)

EMMYLOU HARRIS – vocals, acoustic guitar; with session people

not iss. | Jubilee

1969. (lp) *<JGS 0031>* **GLIDING BIRD** [-] [ ]
– I'll be your baby tonight / Fugue for the fox / I saw the light / Clocks / Black gypsy / Gliding bird / Everybody's talkin' / Bobbie's gone / I'll never fall in love again / Waltz of the magic man. *(UK-iss.Apr79 as 'THE LEGENDARY GLIDING BIRD ALBUM' on 'Pye Special'; PKL 5577)*

1969. (7") *<5679>* **I'LL BE YOUR BABY TONIGHT. / I'LL NEVER FALL IN LOVE AGAIN** [-] [ ]

1969. (7") *<5697>* **FUGUE FOR THE FOX. / PADDY** [-] [ ]

— he then went solo, augmented soon by The HOT BAND:- **JAMES BURTON** – guitar / **GLEN D.HARDIN** – piano / **EMORY GORDY** – bass / **RODNEY CROMWELL** – rhythm guitar, vocals / **HANK DE VITO** – pedal steel guitar / **JOHN WARE** – drums

Reprise | Reprise

Apr 75. (lp/c) *(L/K4 54037) <2213>* **PIECES OF THE SKY** [ ] Mar75 [45]
– Bluebird wine / Too far gone / If I could only win your love / Boulder to Birmingham / Before believing / Bottle let me down / Sleepless nights / Coat of many colours / For no one / Queen of the silver dollar. *(cd-iss. Feb89; 7599 27244-2)*

May 75. (7") *<1326>* **BOULDER TO BIRMINGHAM. / TOO FAR GONE** [-] [ ]

Jun 75. (7") *(K 14396)* **BOULDER TO BIRMINGHAM. / QUEEN OF THE SILVER DOLLAR** [ ] [-]

Nov 75. (7") *(K 14404) <1332>* **IF I COULD ONLY WIN YOUR LOVE. / QUEEN OF THE SILVER DOLLAR** [ ] Aug75 [58]

Jan 76. (7") *(K 14410) <1341>* **LIGHT OF THE STABLE. / BLUEBIRD WINE** [ ] [ ]

Jan 76. (lp/c) *(K/K4 54060) <2213>* **ELITE HOTEL** [17] [25]
– Amarillo / Together again / Feelin' single – seeing double / Sin city / One of these days / Till I gain control again / Here, there and everywhere / Ooh Las Vegas / Sweet dreams / Jambalaya / Satan's jewel crown / Wheels. *(re-iss. May89 on 'Edsel'; ED 306)*

Feb 76. (7") *(K 14415)* **HERE, THERE AND EVERYWHERE. / AMARILLO** [30] [-]

Mar 76. (7") *<1346>* **HERE, THERE AND EVERYWHERE. / TOGETHER AGAIN** [-] [65]

May 76. (7") *(K 14439)* **TOGETHER AGAIN. / WHEELS** [ ] [-]

Jul 76. (7") *<1353>* **ONE OF THESE DAYS. / TILL I GAIN CONTROL AGAIN** [-] [ ]

Sep 76. (7") *<1371>* **AMARILLO. / SWEET DREAMS** [-] [ ]

Nov 76. (7") *<1379>* **LIGHT OF THE STABLE. / BOULDER TO BIRMINGHAM** [-] [ ]

— **ALBERT LEE** – guitar (ex-Solo artist) repl. BURTON (returned to ELVIS)

Warners | Warners

Jan 77. (lp/c) *(K/K4 56334) <3115>* **LUXURY LINER** [17] [21]
– Luxury liner / Pancho & Lefty / Making believe / You're supposed to be feeling good / I'll be your San Antone rose / (You never can tell) C'est la vie / When I stop dreaming / Hello stranger / She / Tulsa queen. *(cd-iss. Jun89; 927338-2)*

Feb 77. (7") *(K 16888)* **(YOU NEVER CAN TELL) C'EST LA VIE. / HELLO STRANGER** [ ] [-]

Feb 77. (7") *<8329>* **(YOU NEVER CAN TELL) C'EST LA VIE. / YOU'RE SUPPOSED TO BE FEELING GOOD** [-] [ ]

May 77. (7") *<8388>* **MAKING BELIEVE. / I'LL BE YOUR SAN ANTONE ROSE** [-] [ ]

Jan 78. (lp/c) *(K/K4 56443) <3141>* **QUARTER MOON IN A TEN CENT TOWN** [40] [29]
– Easy from now on / Two more bottles of wine / To daddy / My songbird / Leavin' Louisiana in the broad daylight / Defying gravity / I ain't livin' long like this / One paper kid / Green rolling hills / Burn that candle. *(cd-iss. 1989; 927345-2)*

Feb 78. (7") *(K 17095) <8498>* **TO DADDY. / TULSA QUEEN** [ ] [ ]

Apr 78. (7") *<8553>* **I AIN'T LIVIN' LONG LIKE THIS. / TWO MORE BOTTLES OF WINE** [-] [ ]

Apr 78. (7") *(K 17133)* **I AIN'T LIVIN' LONG LIKE THIS. / ONE PAPER KID** [ ] [-]

Jun 78. (7") *<8623>* **EVEN FROM NOW ON. / YOU'RE SUPPOSED TO BE FEELING GOOD** [-] [ ]

May 79. (7") *<8815>* **SAVE THE LAST DANCE FOR ME. / EVEN COWGIRLS GET THE BLUES** [-] [ ]

Jun 79. (lp/c) *(K/K4 56627) <3318>* **BLUE KENTUCKY GIRL** [ ] May79 [43]
– Sister's coming home / Beneath still waters / Rough and rocky / Hickory wind / Save the last dance for me / Sorrow in the wind / They'll never take his love from me / Everytime you leave / Blue Kentucky girl / Even cowgirls get the blues. *<(cd-iss. Jan93; 7599 29392-2)>*

Jul 79. (7") *<49056>* **BLUE KENTUCKY GIRL. / LEAVIN' LOUISIANA IN THE BROAD DAYLIGHT** [-] [ ]

Oct 79. (7") *<49164>* **BENEATH STILL WATERS. / TILL I GAIN CONTROL AGAIN** [-] [ ]

Nov 79. (lp/c) *(K/K4 56757) <3484>* **LIGHT OF THE STABLE (THE CHRISTMAS ALBUM)** (festive) [ ] Nov80 [ ]

Nov 79. (7") *(K 17528)* **THE FIRST NOEL. / SILENT NIGHT** [ ] [-]

May 80. (7") *<49239>* **GREEN PASTURES. / WAYFARING STRANGERS** [-] [ ]

May 80. (lp/c) *(K/K4 56796) <3422>* **ROSES IN THE SNOW** [ ] [26]
– Roses in the snow / Wayfaring stranger / Green pastures / The boxer / Darkest hour just before dawn / I'll go stepping too / You're learning / Jordan / Miss the Mississippi / Gold watch and chain. *<(cd-iss. Feb90; 7599 23422-2)> <(cd re-mast.Jul02 on 'W.S.M.'+=; 8122 78140-2)>* – You're gonna change / Root like a rose.

Jul 80. (7") *(K 17649)* *<49262>* **THAT LOVIN' YOU FEELIN' AGAIN. / (b-side by Craig Hindley)** Jun80 55
(above from the film 'Roadie' and credited with ROY ORBISON)

Jul 80. (7") *<49551>* **THE BOXER. / PRECIOUS LOVE** –

Nov 80. (7") *<49633>* **BEAUTIFUL STAR OF BETHLEHEM. / LITTLE DRUMMER BOY** –

Dec 80. (7") *<49645>* **LIGHT OF THE STABLE. / LITTLE DRUMMER BOY** –

Feb 81. (7") *<49684>* **MISTER SANDMAN. / FOOLS THIN AIR** – 37

Feb 81. (7") *(K 17758)* **MISTER SANDMAN. / ASHES BY NOW** –

Feb 81. (lp/c) *(K/K4 56880)* *<3508>* **EVANGELINE** 53 22
– I don't have to crawl / How high the Moon / Spanish Johnny / Bad Moon rising / Evangeline / Hot burrito £2 / Millworker / Oh Atlanta / Mister Sandman / Ashes by now.

May 81. (7") *<49739>* **COLORS OF YOUR HEART. / I DON'T HAVE TO CRAWL** –

May 81. (7") *(K 17804)* **BAD MOON RISING. / I DON'T HAVE TO CRAWL** –

Nov 81. (7") *<49892>* **MAMA HELP. / TENNESSEE ROSE** –

Nov 81. (lp/c) *(K/K4 56955)* *<3603>* **CIMARRON** 46
– Rose of cimarron / Spanish is a loving tongue / If I needed you / Another lonesome morning / The last cheater's waltz / Born to run / The price you pay / Son of a rotten gambler / Tennessee waltz / Tennessee rose.

Feb 82. (7") *<29993>* **BORN TO RUN. / COLORS OF YOUR HEART** –

Feb 82. (7") *(K 17896)* **BORN TO RUN. / ASHES BY NOW** –

Nov 82. (lp/c) *(923740-1/-4)* *<23740>* **LAST DATE (live)** 65
– I'm moving on / It's not love (but it's not bad) / So sad (to watch good love so bad) / Grevious angel / Restless / Racing in the streets / Long may you run / Well sweep out the ashes (in the morning) / Juanita / Devil in disguise / (Lost his love) On our last date / Buckaroo / Love's gonna live here.

Nov 82. (7") *<29898>* **(LOST HIS LOVE) ON OUR LAST DATE. / ANOTHER POT O' TEA** –

Feb 83. (7") *<29729>* **I'M MOVIN' ON (live). / MAYBE TONIGHT** –

Apr 83. (7") *<29583>* **SO SAD (TO WATCH GOOD LOVE GO BAD) (live). / AMARILLO (live)** –

Oct 83. (7") *<29443>* **DRIVIN' WHEEL. / GOOD NEWS** –

Oct 83. (lp/c) *(923961-1/-4)* *<23961>* **WHITE SHOES**
– Drivin' wheel / Pledging my love / In my dreams / White shoes / On the radio / It's only rock'n'roll / Diamonds are a girl's best friend / Good news / Baby, better start turnin' 'em down / Like an old fashoined waltz. *(cd-iss. Jan84; 923961-2) (cd re-iss. Jan96; 7599 23961-2)*

Jan 84. (7") *<29329>* **LIKE AN OLD FASHIONED WALTZ. / IN MY DREAMS** –

May 84. (7") *<29218>* **PLEDGING MY LOVE. / BABY, BETTER START TURNIN' 'EM DOWN** –

May 84. (7") *(W 9364)* **ON THE RADIO. / GOOD NEWS** –

Nov 84. (7") *<29138>* **SOMEONE LIKE YOU. / LIGHT OF THE STABLE** –

Feb 85. (7") *<29041>* **WHITE LINE. / LONG TALL SALLY ROSE** –

Feb 85. (lp/c/cd) *(925205-1/-4/-2)* *<25205>* **THE BALLAD OF SALLY ROSE**
– The ballad of Sally Rose / Rhythm guitar / I think I love him – (instrumental; You are my flower) – Heart to heart / Woman walk the line / Bad news / Timberline / Long tall Sally Rose / White line / Diamond in my crown / The sweetheart of the rodeo / K-S-O-S (instrumental medley; Ring of fire – Wildwood flower – Six days on the road) – Sweet chariot. *(cd re-iss. Jan96; 7599 25205-2)*

May 85. (7") *<28952>* **DIAMOND IN MY CROWN. / RHYTHM GUITAR** –

Aug 85. (7") *<28852>* **TIMBERLINE. / SWEET CHARIOT** –

—— in Mar'87, EMMYLOU, DOLLY PARTON & LINDA RONSTADT released 'TRIO'

Mar 87. (7") *<28770>* **I HAD MY HEART SET ON YOU. / YOUR LONG JOURNEY** –

Apr 87. (lp/c/cd) *(925352-1/-4/-2)* *<25352>* **THIRTEEN** Mar87
– Mystery train / You're free to go / Sweetheart of the pines / Just someone in the know / My father's house / Lacassine special / Today I started loving you again / When I was yours / I had my heart set on you / Your long journey.

Jun 87. (7") *<28770>* **TODAY I STARTED LOVING YOU AGAIN. / WHEN I WAS YOURS** –

Jul 87. (lp/c/cd) *<25585-1/-4/-2>* **ANGEL BAND** –
– Where could I go to the Lord / Angel band / If I be lifted up / Precious memories / Bright morning stars / When he calls / We shall rise / Drifting too far / Who will sing for me / Someday my ship will sail / The other side of your life / When they ring those golden bells.

Aug 87. (7") *<28302>* **SOMEDAY MY SHIP WILL SAIL. / WHEN HE CALLS** –

Feb 89. (7") *<27635>* **HEARTBREAK HILL. / ICY BLUE HEART** –

Feb 89. (lp/c/cd) *(925776-1/-4/-2)* *<25776>* **BLUEBIRD**
– Heaven only knows / You've been on my mind / Icy blue heart / Love is / No regrets / Lonely street / Heartbreak hill / I still miss someone / A river for him / If you were a bluebird.

Reprise Reprise

May 89. (7") *<22999>* **HEAVEN ONLY KNOWS. / A RIVER FOR HIM** –

Aug 89. (7") *<22850>* **I STILL MISS SOMEONE. / NO REGRETS** –

Jul 90. (cd/c/lp) *Reprise; <(7599 25791-2/-4/-1)>* **DUETS**

Nov 90. (lp/c/cd) *(WX 396/+C/CD)* **BRAND NEW DANCE**
– Wheels of love / Tougher than the rest / In his world / Sweet dreams of you / Easy for you to say / Rollin' and ramblin' (the death of Hank Williams) / Better off without you / Never be anyone else but you / Brand new dance / Red red rose. *(cd re-iss. Feb95; same)*

Jan 91. (7") *<19870>* **GULF COAST HIGHWAY (w/ WILLIE NELSON). / EVANGELINE** –

Apr 91. (7") *<19707>* **RED RED ROSE. / NEVER BE ANYONE ELSE BUT YOU** –

Jan 92. (cd/c/d-lp; EMMYLOU HARRIS & The NASH RAMBLERS) *<(7599 26664-2/-4/-1)>* **AT THE RYMAN (live)**
– Guitar town / Halk as much / Cattle call / Guess things happen that way / Hard times / Mansion on the hill / Scotland / Montana cowboy / Like strangers / Lodi / Calling my children home / If I could be there / Walls of time / Get up John / Medley:- It's a hard life wherever you go / Smoke along the track. *(cd re-iss. Feb95; same)*

Grapevine Asylum

Apr 94. (cd-s) *(CDGPS 101)* **HIGH POWERED LOVE. / BALLAD OF A RUNAWAY HORSE** –

May 94. (cd/c/lp) *(GRA 101 CD/C)* *<61541>* **COWGIRL'S PRAYER**
– A ways to go / The night / High powered love / You don't know me / Prayer in open D / Cresent city / Lovin' you again / Jerusalem tomorrow / Thanks to you / I hear a call / Ballad of a runaway horse.

Sep 94. (c-s/cd-s) *(CS/CD GPS 102)* **YOU DON'T KNOW ME. / A WAYS TO GO** –

Oct 95. (cd/c/lp) *(GRA CD/MC/LP 102)* *<61854>* **WRECKING BALL** 46 94
– Where will I be / Goodbye / All my tears / Wrecking ball / Goin' back to Harlan / A deeper well / Every grain of sand / Sweet old world / May this be love / Orphan girl / Blackhawk / Waltz across Texas tonight.

Aug 98. (cd/c) *(GRA CD/MC 241)* *<25001>* **SPYBOY (live)** 57
– My songbird / Where will I be / I ain't living long like this / Love hurts / Green pastures / A deeper well / Prayer in open D / Calling my children home / Tulsa queen / Wheels / Born to run / Boulder to Birmingham / All my tears / Maker.

—— In Sep'99, she and LINDA RONSTADT released the 'WESTERN WALL – THE TUCSON SESSIONS' set, which scraped into the US Top 75

Grapevine Nonesuch

Sep 00. (cd) *(GRACD 103)* *<79616>* **RED DIRT GIRL** 45 54
– The pearl / Michelangelo / I don't wanna talk about it now / Tragedy / Red dirt girl / My baby needs a shepherd / Bang the drum slowly / J'ai fait tout / One big love / Hour of gold / My Antonia / Boy from Tupelo.

Sep 03. (cd) *<(7559 79805-2)>* **STUMBLE INTO GRACE** 52 58
– Here I am / I will dream / Little bird / Time in Babylon / Can you hear me now / Strong hand (just one miracle) / Jupiter rising / O Evangeline / Plaisir d'Amour / Lost unto this world / Cup of kindness.

– compilations, etc. –

on 'Warners' unless mentioned otherwise

Nov 78. (lp/c) *(K/K4 56570)* **PROFILE – THE BEST OF EMMYLOU HARRIS** 81
– One of these days / Sweet dreams / To daddy / You never can tell (C'est la vie) / Making believe / Easy from now on / Together again / If I could only win your love / Too far gone / Two more bottles of wine / From Boulder to Birmingham / Hello stranger. *(cd-iss. Jul84; 256570)*

Nov 78. (7") *<8732>* **TOO FAR GONE. / TULSA QUEEN** [–] [ ]

Mar 80. (7") *(K 17580)* **(YOU NEVER CAN TELL) C'EST LA VIE. / BOULDER TO BIRMIMGHAM** [ ] [–]

Mar 80. (lp) *K-Tel; (NE 1058)* **HER BEST SONGS** [36] [–]

Oct 82. (d-c) **ELITE HOTEL / LUXURY LINER** [ ] [–]

— In Nov '83, 'Magnum Force' released lp 'LIVE' with GRAM PARSONS

Oct 84. (lp/c) *<25161>* **PROFILE II – THE BEST OF EMMYLOU HARRIS** [–] [ ]
(UK-iss.Feb94; 7599 25161-2)

— In July '93, 'Magnum Force' released a cd 'NASHVILLE COUNTRY DUETS' with CARL JACKSON

Nov 94. (cd/c) *<(9362 45725-2/-4)>* **SONGS OF THE WEST** [ ] [ ]

Dec 96. (3xcd-box) *<(9362 45308-2)>* **PORTRAIT** [ ] [ ]

Jul 02. (cd) *Catfish; (KATCD 226)* **NOBODY'S DARLING BUT MINE** [ ] [–]

Jul 05. (cd) *Rhino; <(8122 73123-2)>* **HEARTACHES & HIGHWAYS: THE VERY BEST OF EMMYLOU HARRIS** [ ] [ ]
– Love hurts / Boulder to Birmingham / Making believe / Pancho and Lefty / One of these days / (Lost his love) On our last date (live) / Born to run / Beneath still waters / If I could only win your love / Together again / That lovin' you feelin' again / To know him is to love him / Two more bottles of wine / Wayfaring stranger / Calling my children home / Green pastures / Orphan girl / Michaelangelo / Here I am / The connection.

George HARRISON

Born: 25 Feb'43, Wavertree, Liverpool, England. Released in late 1968, HARRISON's 'WONDERWALL' was the first solo release by a BEATLE, although it flopped in the UK. He followed it up with a classic piece of late 60's self-indulgence, the awful 'ELECTRONIC SOUNDS' (released on his own 'Zapple' label). While HARRISON's pioneering sitar work was praise-worthy, the same experimental spirit applied to a Moog synthesizer, (strung out over a whole album), was downright dull. Despite being overshadowed by the writing partnership of LENNON and McCARTNEY, HARRISON's songs rank among the BEATLES' best, not least 'SOMETHING' and 'HERE COMES THE SUN'. When the BEATLES officially split in 1969, it was perhaps an opportunity for GEORGE to really go for it and prove his writing skills over a whole album. Not content with two sides of vinyl, he went for six, releasing the triple-set 'ALL THINGS MUST PASS' in 1970. The Herculean task of keeping a consistently high standard over three albums was beyond even the mercurial talent of HARRISON, although the peaks definitely outweigh the troughs. PHIL SPECTOR's legendary production skills enhance the gorgeous melodies of 'MY SWEET LORD' and DYLAN's 'IF NOT FOR YOU', while HARRISON's well-documented spirituality is given a voice in the title track and 'THE ART OF DYING'. The aforementioned 'MY SWEET LORD' was released as a single in early '71 topping the charts on both sides of the Atlantic. Success was bittersweet though, as BRIGHT TUNES (owners of songwriter RONNIE MACK's estate) claimed the song plagiarised their CHIFFONS song, 'HE'S SO FINE'. Five years later, the court gave 6-figure royalties to the plaintiff. HARRISON helped to organise a huge famine relief benefit gig in New York, playing alongside a cast of musicians that included his old mucker RINGO STARR as well as BOB DYLAN. The gig was released on another triple-set in 1972 as 'CONCERT FOR BANGLADESH'. May '73 saw yet another No.1 US single, 'GIVE ME LOVE (GIVE ME PEACE ON EARTH)' taken from the similarly successful album, 'LIVING IN THE MATERIAL WORLD'. If HARRISON was riding the crest of a wave, then he was soon to be dallying listlessly in a stagnant creative pond. In 1974, he set up his own 'Dark Horse' label, releasing the clueless album of the same name as well as signing up artists like RAVI SHANKAR and SPLINTER. He and his wife PATTI were divorced in June '77, after her much publicised affair with ERIC CLAPTON. In 1979, he founded his own 'Homemade' film productions, which released the 80's movies: 'Life Of Brian', 'The Long Good Friday', 'Time Bandits', 'The Missionary', 'Mona Lisa', 'A Private Function', 'Water', and 'Shanghai Surprise'. Mediocre albums were his forte at the turn of the decade, and even the tribute to LENNON, 'ALL THOSE YEARS AGO', (from 1981's 'SOMEWHERE IN ENGLAND'), seemed uninspired. HARRISON teamed up with ELO's JEFF LYNNE for 1987's 'CLOUD NINE'; his production, along with the hit, 'GOT MY MIND SET ON YOU', helping to make the record HARRISON's most successful of the 80's (and 90's for that matter). In the decade since, HARRISON has been involved in the relatively brief TRAVELING WILBURYS project (with LYNNE, DYLAN, PETTY & ROY ORBISON under various brotherly guises) as well as releasing 'LIVE IN JAPAN' in 1992, culled from a series of Japanese concerts with CLAPTON. In the mid-90's, he was involved in the archive project which saw the release of a BEATLES documentary, rarities/outtakes albums and even a "new" single, 'FREE AS A BIRD'. As ever though, the man remained an enigma, the quintessential rock star hermit content to do his own thing with a minimum of fuss. In December 1999, just when things looked settled and peaceful for the quiet man of rock, HARRISON and his wife Olivia were subjected to a break-in from a so-called fan at their mansion home in Henley-on-Thames. Both received injuries and, for a time, HARRISON's stab wounds looked serious enough for the media to speculate on his survival. It was also around this time that GEORGE found out he had cancer of the throat (later spreading to lung and brain cancer). By the 29th of November, 2001, tributes were overwhelming when GEORGE finally lost his battle for life. At the subsequent tribute concert at London's Royal Albert Hall, JEFF LYNNE featured prominently, as did HARRISON's son Dhani. In fact, the pair were to finish off GEORGE's final work, 'BRAINWASHED' (2002), roundly hailed as among the best of the former Beatle's career. Surprisingly light of touch in view of the pain of his final years, the album was the sound of a man content in himself and in his music.

• **Covered:** I'D HAVE YOU ANYTIME + I DON'T WANT TO DO IT (Bob Dylan) / BYE BYE LOVE (Everly Brothers) / GOT MY MIND SET ON YOU (James Ray) / ROLL OVER BEETHOVEN (Chuck Berry).

Album rating: WONDERWALL MUSIC (*4) / ELECTRONIC SOUND (*3) / ALL THINGS MUST PASS (*9) / THE CONCERT FOR BANGLA DESH with Various Artists (*6) / LIVING IN THE MATERIAL WORLD (*6) / DARK HORSE (*3) / EXTRA TEXTURE (READ ALL ABOUT IT) (*4) / THE BEST OF GEORGE HARRISON compilation (*6) / THIRTY-THREE & 1/3 (*6) / GEORGE HARRISON (*5) / SOMEWHERE IN ENGLAND (*4) / GONE TROPPO (*3) / CLOUD NINE (*7) / THE BEST OF DARK HORSE 1976-89 compilation (*7) / LIVE IN JAPAN (*4) / BRAINWASHED (*7)

GEORGE HARRISON – instruments (no vocals)

Apple Zapple

Nov 68. (lp; stereo/mono) *(S+/APCOR 1) <ST 3350>* **WONDERWALL MUSIC (Soundtrack)** [ ] Jan69 [49]
– Microbes / Red lady too / Tabla and Pavajak / In the park / Drilling a hole / Guru Vandana / Greasy legs / Ski-ing / Gat Kirwani / Dream scene / Party Seacombe / Love scene / Crying / Cowboy music / Fantasy sequins / On the bed / Glass box / Wonderwall to be here / Singing om. *(cd-iss. Jun92; CDSAPCOR 1) <US cd-iss. Jun92 on 'Capitol'; C2 98706>*

— **GEORGE** – moog synthesizer (no vocals)

Zapple Zapple

May 69. (lp) *(02) <ST 3358>* **ELECTRONIC SOUND** [ ] [ ]
– Under the Mersey wall / No time or space.

— He became in-house 'Apple' producer, before gigging with DELANEY & BONNIE late 1969. The BEATLES broke-up and he went solo again. Now with vocals, etc + augmented by **DEREK & THE DOMINOES** (Eric Clapton and his band) / **BADFINGER / BILLY PRESTON** – keyboards / **RINGO STARR, GINGER BAKER** – drums / etc.

Apple Apple

Nov 70. (t-box-lp) *(<STCH 639>)* **ALL THINGS MUST PASS** [4] [1]
– I'd have you anytime / My sweet Lord / Wah-wah / Isn't it a pity / What is life / If not for you / Behind that locked door / Let it down / Run of the mill / Beware of darkness / Apple scruffs / Ballad of Frankie Crisp (let it

roll) / Awaiting on you all / All things must pass / I dig love / Art of dying / Isn't it a pity / Hear me Lord / Out of the blue / It's Johnny's birthday / Plug me in / I remember Jeep / Thanks for the pepperoni. *(d-cd.iss.May87 on 'E.M.I.'; CDS 746688-2) (d-cd/t-lp re-iss. Jan01; 530474-2/-1)* – hit No.68

Nov 70. (7") *<2995>* **MY SWEET LORD. / ISN'T IT A PITY** [–] [1]

Jan 71. (7") *(R 5884)* **MY SWEET LORD. / WHAT IS LIFE** [1] [–]
(re-iss. Nov76; same)

Feb 71. (7") *<1828>* **WHAT IS LIFE. / APPLE SCRUFFS** [–] [10]

Jul 71. (7") *(R 5912) <1836>* **BANGLA-DESH. / DEEP BLUE** [10] [23]

Jan 72. (t-lp) *<(STCX 3385)>* **THE CONCERT FOR BANGLA DESH** (with Various Artists) [1] [2]
– introduction (* & RAVI SHANKAR) / Bangla dhun (RAVI SHANKAR) / Wah wah (*) / My sweet Lord (*) / Awaiting on you all (*) / That's the way God planned it (BILLY PRESTON) / It don't come easy (RINGO STARR) / Beware of darkness (*) / While my guitar gently weeps (*) / Jumping Jack Flash – Youngblood (LEON RUSSELL) / Here comes the sun (*) / A hard rain's gonna fall (BOB DYLAN) / It takes a lot to laugh, it takes a train to cry (BOB DYLAN) / Blowin' in the wind (BOB DYLAN) / Mr. Tambourine man (BOB DYLAN) / Just like a woman (BOB DYLAN) / Something (*) / Bangla Desh (*). *<(d-cd/d-c iss.Aug91 & Jan02; 468835-2/-4)>*

—— **GEORGE** now with various session people

May 73. (7") *(R 5988) <1862>* **GIVE ME LOVE (GIVE ME PEACE ON EARTH). / MISS O'DELL** [8] [1]

Jun 73. (lp/c) *(PAS 10006) <3410>* **LIVING IN THE MATERIAL WORLD** [2] [1]
– Give me love (give me peace on earth) / Sue me, sue you blues / The light that has lighted the world / Don't let me wait too long / Who can see it / Living in the material world / The Lord loves the one (that loves the Lord) / Be here now / Try some buy some / The day the world gets 'round / That is all. *(cd-iss. Jan92 on 'E.M.I.'; CDPAS 10006)*

Dec 74. (7") *(R 6002) <1879>* **DING DONG; DING DONG. / I DON'T CARE ANYMORE** [38] Jan75 [36]

Dec 74. (lp/c) *(PAS 10008) <3418>* **DARK HORSE** [ ] [4]
– Hari's on tour (express) / Simply shady / So sad / Bye bye love / Maya love / Ding dong; ding dong / Dark horse / Far East man / Is it he (Jai Sri Krishna). *(re-iss. Dec80 on 'Music For Pleasure'; MFP 50510) (cd-iss. Jan92 on 'E.M.I.'; CDPAS 10008)*

Feb 75. (7") *(R 6001) <1877>* **DARK HORSE. / HARI'S ON TOUR (EXPRESS)** [ ] Nov74 [15]

Sep 75. (7") *(R 6007) <1884>* **YOU. / WORLD OF STONE** [38] [20]

Oct 75. (lp/c) *(PAS 10009) <3420>* **EXTRA TEXTURE (READ ALL ABOUT IT)** [16] [8]
– The answer's at the end / This guitar (can't keep from crying) / You / Ooh baby (you know that I love you) / World of stone / A bit more of you / Can't stop thinking about you / Tired of midnight blue / Grey cloudy lies / His name is legs (ladies & gentlemen). *(cd-iss. Jan92 on 'E.M.I.'; CDPAS 10009)*

Feb 76. (7") *(R 6012) <1885>* **THIS GUITAR (CAN'T KEEP FROM CRYING). / MAYA LOVE** [ ] [ ]

Apple Capitol

Oct 76. (lp/c) *(PAS 10011) <11578>* **THE BEST OF GEORGE HARRISON** (compilation) [ ] [31]
– Something (BEATLES) / If I needed someone (BEATLES) / Here comes the sun (BEATLES) / Taxman (BEATLES) / Think for yourself (BEATLES) / While my guitar gently weeps (BEATLES) / For you blue (BEATLES) / My sweet Lord / Give me love (give me peace on Earth) / You / Bangla-Desh / Dark horse / What is life. *(re-iss. Oct81 on 'Music For Pleasure' lp/c; MFP 50523) (cd-iss. May87 on 'Parlophone'; CDP 746682-2)*

Dark Horse Dark Horse

Nov 76. (7") *(K 16856) <8294>* **THIS SONG. / LEARNING HOW TO LOVE YOU** [ ] [25]

Nov 76. (lp/c) *(K/K4 56319) <3005>* **THIRTY-THREE AND A THIRD** [35] [11]
– Woman don't you cry for me / Dear one / Beautiful girl / This song / See yourself / It's what you value / True love / Pure Smokey / Crackerbox palace / Learning how to love you.

Jan 77. (7") *<8313>* **CRACKERBOX PALACE. / LEARNING HOW TO LOVE YOU** [–] [19]

Feb 77. (7") *(K 16896)* **TRUE LOVE. / PURE SMOKEY** [ ] [–]

Jun 77. (7") *(K 16967)* **IT'S WHAT YOU VALUE. / WOMAN DON'T YOU CRY FOR ME** [ ] [–]

Feb 79. (7") *<8763>* **BLOW AWAY. / SOFT-HEARTED HANA** [–] [16]

Feb 79. (7") *(K 17327)* **BLOW AWAY. / SOFT TOUCH** [51] [–]

Feb 79. (lp/c) *(K/K4 56562) <3255>* **GEORGE HARRISON** [39] [14]
– Love comes to everyone / Not guilty / Here comes the moon / Soft-hearted Hana / Blow away / Faster / Your love is forever / Dark sweet lady / Soft touch / If you believe.

Apr 79. (7") *(K 17284)* **LOVE COMES TO EVERYONE. / SOFT-HEARTED HANA** [ ] [–]

Apr 79. (7") *<8844>* **LOVE COMES TO EVERYONE. / SOFT TOUCH** [–] [ ]

Jul 79. (7"/7"pic-d) *(K 17423/+P)* **FASTER. / YOUR LOVE IS FOREVER** [ ] [–]

May 81. (7") *(K 17807) <49725>* **ALL THOSE YEARS AGO. / WRITING'S ON THE WALL** [13] [2]

Jun 81. (lp/c) *(K/K4 56870) <3492>* **SOMEWHERE IN ENGLAND** [13] [11]
– Blood from a clone / Unconsciousness rules / Life itself / All those year ago / Baltimore oriole / Teardrops / That which I have lost / Writing's o the wall / Hong Kong blues / Save the world.

Jul 81. (7") *(K 17837) <49785>* **TEARDROPS. / SAVE THE WORLD** [ ] [ ]

Oct 82. (7") *(929864-2) <29864>* **WAKE UP MY LOVE. / GREECE** [ ] [53]

Nov 82. (lp/c) *(K 923734-1/-4) <23734>* **GONE TROPPO** [ ] [ ]
– Wake up my love / That's the way it goes / I really love you / Greece Gone troppo / Mystical one / Unknown delight / Baby don't run away Dream away / Circles.

Jan 83. (7") *<29744>* **I REALLY LOVE YOU. / CIRCLES** [–] [ ]

—— Took long time off from solo career to establish his film production wor Returned after nearly five years with new session people.

Sep 87. (lp/c)(cd) *(WX 123/+C)(925643-2) <25643>* **CLOUD NINE** [10] Nov87 [8]
– Cloud 9 / That's what it takes / Fish on the sand / Just for today / Th is love / When we was fab / Devil's radio / Someplace else / Wreck of th Hesperus / Breath away from Heaven / Got my mind set on you.

Oct 87. (7") *(W 8178) <28178>* **GOT MY MIND SET ON YOU. / LAY HIS HEAD** [2] [1]
(12"+=/12"pic-d+=) *(W 8178T/+P)* – ('A'extended).

Feb 88. (7") *(W 8131) <28131>* **WHEN WE WAS FAB. / ZIGZAG** [25] [23]
(12"+=/12"pic-d+=/3"cd-s+=) *(W 8131 T/TX/CD)* – That's the way it go (remix) / ('A'mix).

Jun 88. (7") *(W 7913) <27913>* **THIS IS LOVE. / BREATH AWAY FROM HEAVEN** [55] [ ]
(12"+=) *(W 7913T)* – All those wasted years ago.
(3"cd-s++=) *(W 7913CD)* – Hong Kong blues.

—— Later in 1988, HARRISON teamed up with BOB DYLAN, ROY ORBISO JEFF LYNNE and TOM PETTY in The TRAVELLING WILBURYS. He al continued solo work below.

Oct 89. (lp/c)(cd) *(WX 312/+C)(K 925643-2) <25726>* **THE BEST OF DARK HORSE (1976-1989)** (compilation) [ ] [ ]
– Poor little girl / Blow away / That's the way it goes / Cockamam business / Wake up my love / Life itself / Got my mind set on you / He comes the Moon / Gone troppo / When we was fab / Love comes everyone / All those years ago / Cheer down. *(c+=/cd+=)* – Crackerb Palace.

Nov 89. (7") *(W 2696)* **CHEER DOWN. / POOR LITTLE GIRL** [ ] [–]
(12"+=/cd-s+=) *(W 2696 T/CD)* – Crackerbox palace.

Jul 92. (cd/c) *(<7599 26964-2/-4>)* **LIVE IN JAPAN (with ERIC CLAPTON AND BAND)** [ ] [ ]
– I want to tell you / Old brown shoe / Taxman / Give me love (give m peace on Earth) / If I needed someone / Something / What is life / Da horse / Piggies / Got my mind set on you / Cloud nine / Here comes t Sun / My sweet Lord / All those years ago / Cheer down / Devil's radi Isn't it a pity / While my guitar gently weeps / Roll over Beethoven.

—— GEORGE died of cancer on the 29th November, 2001

Parlophone Capi

Jan 02. (cd-s) *(CDR 6571) <50438>* **MY SWEET LORD / LET IT DOWN / MY SWEET LORD (2000)** [1] [94]

E.M.I. Capi

Nov 02. (cd)(lp/c) *(543246-2)(541969-1/-4) <41969>* **BRAINWASHED** [52] [18]
– Any road / P2 Vatican blues (last Saturday night) / Pisces fish / Looki for my life / Rising sun / Marwa blues / Stuck inside a cloud / Run far / Never get over you / Between the Devil and the deep blue se Rocking chair in Hawaii / Brainwashed. *(cd-iss. w/ dvd+=; 580345-0)* (extra tracks).

May 03. (7") *(R 6601)* **ANY ROAD. / MARWA BLUES** [37] [ ]
(cd-s+=) *(CDRS 6601)* – ('A'-video).

– compilations etc. –

Oct 82. (d-cd) *Dark Horse; (K 466101)* **THIRTY-THREE AND A THIRD / GEORGE HARRISON** – –

❑ Jerry HARRISON (see under ⇒ TALKING HEADS)

❑ Deborah / Debbie HARRY (see under ⇒ BLONDIE)

Alex HARVEY

Born: 5 Feb'35, "the Gorbals" area, Glasgow, Scotland. ALEX grew up in a politically aware, well-read family, taking his stance as a conscientious objector from his father. Following loads of jobs (36 to be exact, including a stint lion-taming!) he played in various skiffle groups and after winning a local talent contest in 1956, he was dubbed "The TOMMY STEELE Of Scotland". In 1959, his BIG SOUL BAND backed touring American stars, EDDIE COCHRAN and GENE VINCENT, the former subsequently being killed in a car crash a few months later. By 1964, ALEX HARVEY AND HIS SOUL BAND were taking the well-trodden path to Hamburg, Germany, while back home LULU was capitalising on a hit version of 'Shout!', an ISLEY BROTHERS track which featured prominently in HARVEY's repertoire. During this heady mid-60's period, HARVEY himself released two LP's, the second of which 'THE BLUES' (1965) featured the precocious guitar playing of his younger brother LES. Travelling between London and Glasgow, ALEX subsequently struggled on with his ever evolving musical vision, psychedelic GIANT MOTH backing him up during the flower-power era of '67. After a run of flop singles, HARVEY joined the crew of the 'Hair' musical in London's West End, earning his crust by night (mainly as the guitarist but also contributing the occasional vocal) and continuing to write his own material by day. Towards the end of the decade, HARVEY released his first bonafide solo album, 'ROMAN WALL BLUES' (1969), backed up by his brother LES and some of the crew from the ROCK WORKSHOP ensemble in which ALEX was briefly involved. Through a third party, ALEX was introduced to Glasgow band TEAR GAS (ZAL CLEMINSON, HUGH McKENNA, CHRIS GLEN and TED McKENNA), with whom he was so impressed he moved back to Scotland and secured them as his backing outfit. Early in 1972 they became The SENSATIONAL ALEX HARVEY BAND, and, after nationwide tours and a signature for 'Vertigo', released their debut album 'FRAMED'. 1972 was set to be an eventful, often traumatic year for ALEX, what with the tragic death of his brother LES (electrocuted while on stage with STONE THE CROWS) and a challenging support slot to Brummie chart-toppers SLADE. ALEX had his own way of approaching such a challenge, frequently goading audiences (especially if they happened to be from south of the border!) into a reaction, negative or otherwise – JOHNNY ROTTEN obviously took note. Visually, HARVEY was a larger than life JOHNNY KIDD-esque pirate figure with more than a hint of hidden menace. With his buccaneer attitude and dishevelled look, he was nothing less than a musical visionary, only matched by his clown-faced guitarist, ZAL CLEMINSON. Late in '73, SAHB issued the excellent 'NEXT . . .', promoting the album with an extensive tour which included of all places, Falkirk Town Hall. The unadulterated combination of European style seediness, OTT theatrics and futuristic comic book imagery came together in such classics as 'THE FAITH HEALER' (a 7 minute+ masterpiece), the self-explanatory 'GANG BANG' and Jacques Brel's 'NEXT'. HARVEY was also a rather unlikely advocate of cleaning up the nation's streets, inventing the "Vambo" comic book character to push home his anti-vandal message. The track 'VAMBO MARBLE EYE', was the first and also the most memorable in a series of "Vambo" songs, urging fans "don't pish in your own water supply". A year later, SAHB secured their first UK Top 20 album spot with 'THE IMPOSSIBLE DREAM' (1974), a more accessible effort which sacrificed some of its predecessor's grubby intensity although 'THE TOMAHAWK KID' and 'ANTHEM' kept the fans on HARVEY's alternative yellow brick road. The pinnacle of HARVEY and SAHB's colourful career came in 1975, a year that saw both a UK Top 10 album 'TOMORROW BELONGS TO ME' and a Top 10 rendition of Tom Jones' 'DELILAH' (from the 'LIVE' set), culminating in a series of three sold out Xmas shows at Glasgow's Apollo theatre. Gallus as ever, HARVEY entered the stage to the strains of Irving Berlin's 'CHEEK TO CHEEK', joined by a troupe of dancing girls who eventually turned their backs to the crowd and revealed their cheeky bare-ass attire; ALEX was so impressed he kissed each bum in turn before blessing each one with a rose . . . The aforementioned 'CHEEK . . .' featured on SAHB's next offering 'THE PENTHOUSE TAPES' (1976), a slightly disappointing covers set that led to the band signing a fresh deal with 'Mountain' records (also home to NAZARETH). Shortly afterwards, ALEX and the boys scored their second major UK hit, 'BOSTON TEA PARTY', although again the accompanying album 'SAHB STORIES' (1976), left most fans let down. While ALEX took off to Northern Scotland for a bizarre documentary album, ' . . .PRESENTS THE LOCH NESS MONSTER', SAHB WITHOUT ALEX (as they were briefly billed!) released their own set, 'FOURPLAY' (1977). Even though ALEX had in some respects anticipated the advent of Punk Rock, SAHB were ill-equipped to compete in the brave new (wave) world. The 'ROCK DRILL' (1978) album was a final disappointing nail in the coffin while the death of HARVEY's mentor/manager BILL dealt him an emotional hammer blow. The band effectively came to an end when ALEX refused to board a plane for Stockholm, claiming that he'd seen a purple light and therefore couldn't cross water. Although his drinking and eccentric behaviour became more pronounced, he did subsequently form the not so sensational ALEX HARVEY BAND, returning to the recording studio with a new line-up for 1979's cult fave 'THE MAFIA STOLE MY GUITAR'. Years of hard living finally took its toll on ALEX as he succumbed to a heart attack on the 4th of February 1982, bizarrely enough just prior to boarding a return ferry from Belgium; he left behind wife Trudy and two sons.

• **Songwriters:** Most by himself and HUGH McKENNA, with additions from either ZAL or producer DAVE BATCHELOR. Covered; FRAMED (Leiber-Stoller) / I JUST WANT TO MAKE LOVE TO YOU (Willie Dixon) / GIDDY-UP-A-DING-DONG (Freddie Bell & The Bellboys) / THE IMPOSSIBLE DREAM (Leigh-Darion) / MONEY HONEY (. . . Stone) / RIVER OF LOVE / TOMORROW BELONGS TO ME (Ebb-Kander) / DELILAH (hit; Tom Jones) / GAMBLIN' BAR ROOM BLUES (Alley-Rodgers) / CHEEK TO CHEEK (Irving Berlin) / LOVE STORY (Jethro Tull) / CRAZY HORSES (Osmonds) / SCHOOL'S OUT (Alice Cooper) / RUNAWAY (Del Shannon) / GOODNIGHT IRENE (Leadbelly) / SHAKIN' ALL OVER (Johnny Kidd) / SNOWSHOES THOMPSON (Buddy Ebson).
• **Trivia:** HARVEY's 'LOCH NESS' lp, released unusually on 'K-Tel', featured only interviews from sightings of the monster.

Album rating: ALEX HARVEY & HIS SOUL BAND (*5) / THE BLUES (*5) / ROMAN WALL BLUES (*4) / Sensational Alex Harvey Band: FRAMED (*6) / NEXT . . . (*9) / THE IMPOSSIBLE DREAM (*7) / TOMORROW BELONGS TO ME (*7) / THE SENSATIONAL ALEX HARVEY BAND "LIVE" (*7) / PENTHOUSE TAPES (*5) / SAHB STORIES (*5) / FOURPLAY without Alex (*4) / ROCK DRILL (*5) / THE MAFIA STOLE MY GUITAR (*5) / THE SOLDIER ON THE WALL (*5) / THE BEST OF THE SENSATIONAL ALEX HARVEY BAND compilation (*8)

ALEX HARVEY & HIS SOUL BAND

ALEX HARVEY – vocals / **RICKY BARNES** – saxophone, vocals / **ISOBEL BOND** – vocals / **GIBSON KEMP** – drums / **IAN HINDS** – organ / **BILL PATRICK** – guitar

Polydor — not iss.

Jan 64. (7"; as ALEX HARVEY) *(NH 52264)* **I JUST WANNA MAKE LOVE TO YOU. / LET THE GOOD TIMES ROLL** [ ] [–]

Mar 64. (lp) *(LPHM 46424)* **ALEX HARVEY AND HIS SOUL BAND (live)** [ ] [–]
– Framed / I ain't worrying baby / Backwater blues / Let the good times roll / Going home / I've got my mojo working / Teensville U.S.A. / New Orleans / Bo Diddley is a gunslinger / When I grow too old to rock / Evil hearted man / I just wanna make love to you / The blind man / Reeling and rocking. *(Germany re-iss. Oct87 lp/c; 831887-1/-4)*

Jun 64. (7") *(NH 52907)* **GOT MY MOJO WORKING. / I AIN'T WORRIED BABY** [ ] [–]

— ALEX HARVEY brought in new soul band, (his brother **LES HARVEY** – guitar / **BOBBY THOMPSON** – bass / **GILSON KEMP** – drums)

Jul 65. (7") *(BM 56017)* **AIN'T THAT JUST TOO BAD. / MY KIND OF LOVE** [ ] [–]

Nov 65. (lp) *(LPHM 46441)* **THE BLUES** [ ] [–]
– Trouble in mind / Honey bee / I learned about woman / Danger zone / The riddle song / Waltzing Matilda / The blues / The big rock candy mountain / The Michegan massacre / No peace / Nobody knows you when you're down and out / St. James infirmary / Strange fruit / Kisses sweeter than wine / Good God almighty.

ALEX HARVEY

solo with session musicians.

Fontana — not iss.

Sep 65. (7") *(TF 610)* **AGENT OO SOUL. / GO AWAY BABY** [ ] [–]

Nov 66. (7") *(TF 764)* **WORK SONG. / I CAN'T DO WITHOUT YOUR LOVE** [ ] [–]

— HARVEY now backed by **GIANT MOTH:- JIM CONDRON** – guitar, bass / **MOX** – flute / **GEORGE BUTLER** – drums

Decca — not iss.

Jul 67. (7") *(F 12640)* **THE SUNDAY SONG. / HORIZON'S** [ ] [–]

Sep 67. (7") *(F 12660)* **MAYBE SOME DAY. / CURTAINS FOR MY BABY** [ ] [–]

— next with backing from ROCK WORKSHOP which incl. brother LES and loads of others. In 1970/71 for 'CBS', they released two lp's 'ROCK WORKSHOP' *(64075) & not with ALEX, a double 'THE VERY LAST TIME' (64394)*. Taken from first lp was 45; 'YOU TO LOSE'.

Fontana — not iss.

Oct 69. (lp; stereo/mono) *(S+/TL 5534)* **ROMAN WALL BLUES** [ ] [–]
– Midnight Moses / Hello L.A., bye bye Birmingham / Broken hearted fairytale / Donna / Roman wall blues / Jumping Jack Flash / Hammer song / Let my bluebird sing / Maxine / Down at Bart's place / Candy. *(cd-iss. May02 on 'Red Bus'; RF 609)*

Nov 69. (7") *(TF 1063)* **MIDNIGHT MOSES. / ROMAN WALL BLUES** [ ] [–]

— ALEX then formed his trio (**IAN ELLIS** – bass, ex-CLOUDS, **DAVE DUFORT** – drums) This was broken up after the death, by stage electrocution, of his brother LES, who had been part of STONE THE CROWS since '69 (Aug72) **ALEX** recruited a whole band

— **TEAR GAS** who had already made two albums – Nov70 'PIGGY GO BETTER' on 'Famous', without the McKENNA brothers. Aug71. 'TEAR GAS' on 'Regal Zonophone', with all the members of below . . .

the SENSATIONAL ALEX HARVEY BAND

ALEX – vocals, guitar / **ZAL CLEMINSON** (b. 4 May'49) – guitar, vocals / **CHRIS GLEN** (b. 6 Nov'50) – bass / **HUGH McKENNA** (b.28 Nov'49) – keyboards / **TED McKENNA** (b.10 Mar'50) – drums

Vertigo — Vertigo

Dec 72. (7") *(6059 070)* **THERE'S NO LIGHTS ON THE CHRISTMAS TREE, MOTHER, THEY'RE BURNING BIG LOUIE TONIGHT. / HARP** [ ] [–]

Jan 73. (lp) *(6360 081)* **FRAMED** [ ] [–]
– Framed / Hammer song / Midnight Moses / Isobel Goudie (part 1 – My lady of the night, part 2 – Coitus interruptus, part 3 – The virgin and the hunter) / Buff's bar blues / I just want to make love to you / Hole in her stocking / There's no lights on the Christmas tree, mother, they're burning big Louie tonight / St. Anthony. *(re-iss. Mar79 on 'Mountain';) (re-iss. Jul86 on 'Sahara' lp/c; (SAH 119/+TC) (cd-iss. 1986 on 'Samurai'+=; SAMRCD 00119)* – Smouldering / Chase it into the night.

Mar 73. (7") *(6059 075)* **JUNGLE JENNY. / BUFF'S BAR BLUES** [ ] [–]

Nov 73. (lp) *(6360 103) <1017>* **NEXT . . .** [ ] [ ]
– Swampsnake / Gang bang / The faith healer / Giddy up a ding dong / Next / Vambo marble eye / The last of the teenage idols (part I-III). *(re-iss. Mar79 on 'Mountain';) (re-iss. Nov84 on 'Sahara'; SAH 114) (pic-lp May86; SAH 114CD) (cd-iss. 1986 on 'Samurai'; SAMRCD 00114) (re-iss. Mar87 on 'Fame' lp/c; FA/TC-FA 3169)*

Feb 74. (7") *(6059 098)* **THE FAITH HEALER (edit). / ST. ANTHONY** [ ] [–]

Feb 74. (7") *<113>* **SWAMPSNAKE. / GANG BANG** [–] [ ]

Aug 74. (7") *(6059 106)* **SERGEANT FURY. / GANG BANG** [ ] [–]

Sep 74. (7") *<200>* **SERGEANT FURY. / TOMAHAWK KID** [–] [ ]

Sep 74. (lp)(c) *(6360 112) <2000>* **THE IMPOSSIBLE DREAM** [16] [ ]
– The hot city symphony; (part 1 – Vambo, part 2 – Man in the Jar) / River of love / Long hair music / Sergeant Fury / Weights made of lead / Money honey – The impossible dream / Tomahawk kid / Anthem. *(re-iss. Mar79 on 'Mountain';) (re-iss. Jul86 on 'Samurai' lp/c; SAH 116/+TC)*

Nov 74. (7") *(6059 112)* **ANTHEM. / ANTHEM (version)** [ ] [–]

Apr 75. (lp)(c) *(6360 120) <2004>* **TOMORROW BELONGS TO ME** [9] [ ]
– Action strasse / Snake bite / Soul in chains / The tale of the giant stoneater / Ribs and balls / Give my compliments to the chef / Shark teeth / Ribs and balls / Shake that thing / Tomorrow belongs to me / To be continued . . . *(re-iss. Nov84 on 'Sahara'; SAH 111) (cd-iss. Jul86 on 'Samurai'+=; SAMRCD 00111)* – Big boy / Pick it up and kick it.

Vertigo — Atlantic

Jul 75. (7") *(ALEX 001) <3293>* **DELILAH (live). / SOUL IN CHAINS (live)** [7] [ ]

Sep 75. (lp)(c) *(9102 007) <18184>* **THE SENSATIONAL ALEX HARVEY BAND "LIVE" (live)** [14] [100]
– Fanfare (justly, skillfully, magnanimously) / The faith healer / Tomahawk kid / Vambo / Give my compliments to the chef / Delilah / Framed. *(re-iss. Jul86 on 'Sahara' c/lp/pic-lp; TC+/SAH 117/+PD) (re-iss. Oct86 on 'Fame' lp/c; FA/TC-FA 3161) (cd-iss. 1986 on 'Samurai'; SAMRCD 00117)* – I wanna have you back / Jungle Jenny / Runaway / Love story / School's Out.

Nov 75. (7") *(ALEX 002)* **GAMBLIN' BAR ROOM BLUES. / SHAKE THAT THING** [38] [–]

Mar 76. (7") *(ALEX 003)* **RUNAWAY. / SNAKE BITE** [ ] [–]

Mar 76. (lp)(c) *(9102 007)* **PENTHOUSE TAPES** (old covers) [14] [–]
– I wanna have you back / Jungle Jenny / Runaway / Love story / School's out / Goodnight Irene / Say you're mine / Gamblin' bar room blues / Crazy horses / Cheek to cheek. *(re-iss. Mar79 on 'Mountain';) (re-iss. Nov84 on 'Sahara'; SAH 112) (cd-iss. Jul86 on 'Samurai'; SAMRCD 00112)*

Mountain — not iss.

May 76. (7") *(TOP 12)* **BOSTON TEA PARTY. / SULTAN'S CHOICE** [13] [–]

Jul 76. (lp)(c) *(TOPS 112)* **SAHB STORIES** [11] [–]
– Boston Tea Party / Sultan's choice / $25 for a massage / Dogs of war / Dance to your daddy / Amos Moses / Jungle rub out / Sirocco. *(re-iss. Nov84 on 'Sahara'; SAH 115)*

Aug 76. (7") *(TOP 19)* **AMOS MOSES. / SATCHEL AND THE SCALP HUNTER** [ ] [–]

— now all 4 members without ALEX HARVEY. (HUGH on vocals)

Jan 77. (lp; SAHB WITHOUT ALEX) *(TOPC 5006)* **FOURPLAY** [ ] [–]
– Smouldering / Chase it into the night / Shake your way to Heaven / Outer boogie / Big boy / Pick it up and kick it / Love you for a lifetime / Too much American pie. *(re-iss. Nov84 on 'Sahara'; SAH 113)*

Jan 77. (7"; SAHB WITHOUT ALEX) **PICK IT UP AND KICK IT. / SMOULDERING** [ ] [–]

— In Apr'77, **ALEX HARVEY** released but withdrew, solo narrative lp 'PRESENTS THE LOCH NESS MONSTER' on 'K-Tel'; *NE 984)*

— re-formed **HARVEY, CLEMINSON, TED McKENNA and GLEN** recruited **TOMMY EYRE** – keyboards who repl. HUGH McKENNA

Aug 77. (7") *(TOP 32)* **MRS. BLACKHOUSE. / ENGINE ROOM BOOGIE** [ ] [–]

Mar 78. (lp)(c) *(TOPS 114)* **ROCK DRILL** [ ] [–]
– The rock drill suite: Rock drill – The dolphins – Rock and roll – King Kong / Booids / Who murdered sex / Nightmare city / Water beastie / Mrs Blackhouse. *(re-iss. Nov84 on 'Sahara'; SAH 118)*

— (had already split late '77) CHRIS and TED joined ZAL in his own named band. ZAL later joined NAZARETH. TED later joined RORY GALLAGHER and then GREG LAKE BAND. TED and CHRIS later moved on to the MICHAEL SCHENKER GROUP.

the ALEX HARVEY BAND

with **TOMMY EYRE** – keyboards / **MATTHEW CANG** – guitar / **GORDON SELLAR** – bass (ex-BEGGARS OPERA) / **SIMON CHATTERTON** – drums

R.C.A. not iss.

Oct 79. (7") *(PB 5199)* **SHAKIN' ALL OVER. / WAKE UP DAVIS** [ ] [–]
Nov 79. (lp/c) *(PL/PK 25257)* **THE MAFIA STOLE MY GUITAR** [ ] [–]
– Don's delight / Back in the depot / Wait for me mama / The Mafia stole my guitar / Shakin' all over / The whalers (thar she blows) / Oh Sparticus / Just a gigolo / I ain't got nobody. *(cd-iss. Sep91 on 'Mau Mau'; MAUCD 608) (cd re-iss. May98 on 'Edsel'; EDCD 562)*
May 80. (7") *(PB 5252)* **BIG TREE SMALL AXE. / THE WHALERS (THAR SHE BLOWS)** [ ] [–]

— ALEX HARVEY died of a heart attack on the 4th of February 1982 while on a ferry from Belgium; he recorded last set late in 1981

Power Supply not iss.

Nov 83. (7") *(OHM 3)* **THE POET AND I. /** [ ] [–]
Nov 83. (c/lp) *(C+/AMP 2)* **SOLDIER ON THE WALL** (rec.late 1981) [ ] [–]
– Mitzi / Billy Bolero / Snowshoes Thompson / Roman wall blues / The poet and I / Nervous / Carry the water / Flowers Mr. Florist / The poet and I (reprise). *(<cd-iss. Aug03 on 'Diablo'; DIAB 8047>)*

the SENSATIONAL ALEX HARVEY BAND

— actually re-formed for live gigs (as Harvey tribute)

Meantime not iss.

Apr 94. (cd/c) *(JIMBO/JIMMC 001)* **LIVE IN GLASGOW 1993 (live)** [ ] [–]
– The faith healer / St. Anthony / Framed / Gang bang / Amos Moses / Boston tea party / Midnight Moses / Vambo / Armed and dangerous / Delilah.

– (SAHB) compilations, etc. –

May 77. (lp) *Vertigo; (6360 147)* **BIG HITS AND CLOSE SHAVES** [ ] [–]
(re-iss. Apr79 on 'Mountain')
Jun 77. (7") *Vertigo; (6059 173)* **CHEEK TO CHEEK. / JUNGLE JENNY** [ ] [–]
Jul 80. (c/lp) *Mountain; (T+/TOPS 129)* **COLLECTOR'S ITEMS** [ ] [–]
Jul 80. (7"m) *Mountain; (HOT 2)* **DELILAH (live). / BOSTON TEA PARTY / THE FAITH HEALER** [ ] [–]
Aug 82. (d-lp/d-c) *R.C.A.; (RCA LP/K 9003)* **THE BEST OF THE SENSATIONAL ALEX HARVEY BAND** [ ] [–]
– Next / Framed / The faith healer / Tomahawk kid / The hot city symphony; part 1 – Vambo, part 2 – Man in the jar / Sergeant Fury / The tale of the giant stoneater / Action strasse / Delilah / Weights made of lead / Boston Tea Party / Anthem / Runaway / Crazy horses / Big tree small axe / The Mafia stole my guitar / Gang bang / Tomorrow belongs to me. *(re-iss. May84 d-lp/d-c; PL/PK 70276)*
Nov 85. (lp/c) *Sahara; (SAH/+TC 041)* **LEGEND** [ ] [–]
(cd-iss. 1986 on 'Samurai'; SAMR 041CD)
Jan 86. (c) *Sahara; (SAH 041TC)* **ANTHOLOGY** [ ] [–]
Apr 86. (c) *Aura;* **DOCUMENT** [ ] [–]
Sep 86. (d-lp/c/cd) *Castle; (CCS LP/MC/CD 149)* **THE COLLECTION** [ ] [–]
– $25 for a massage / The tale of the giant stoneater / Action strasse / Gang bang / Next / Give my compliments to the chef / Framed / Tomorrow belongs to me / Dance to your daddy / Sgt.Fury / Sultan's choice / Delilah (live) / Soul in chains / The faith healer / Boston tea party / Vambo (part 1) / Dogs of war / There's no lights on the Christmas tree mother, they're burning big Louie tonight / Giddy up a ding dong.
Jul 87. (lp/c)(cd) *K-Tel; (NE1/CE2 368)(NCD 5139)* **THE BEST OF THE SENSATIONAL ALEX HARVEY BAND** [ ] [–]
– Delilah / The faith healer / Framed / Sergeant Fury / Jungle rub out / Love story / School's out / Boston Tea Party / Gamblin' bar room blues / Next / The man in the jar / Snake bite / Give my compliments to the chef / Cheek to cheek.
Sep 87. (lp/c/cd) *Start; (STF L/C/CD 1)* **PORTRAIT** [ ] [–]
(re-iss. Jan91 lp/c/cd; same)
Feb 91. (cd/c) *Music Club; (MC CD/TC 001)* **THE BEST OF THE SENSATIONAL ALEX HARVEY BAND** [ ] [–]
(re-iss. Jul94 on 'Success';)
Oct 91. (lp) *Windsong; (WINCD 002)* **BBC RADIO 1 LIVE IN CONCERT (live)** [ ] [–]
Jun 92. (cd/c) *Vertigo; (512 201-2/-4)* **ALL SENSATIONS** [ ] [–]
Nov 94. (cd) *Windsong; (WHISCD 004)* **LIVE ON THE TEST** [ ] [–]
Sep 94. (cd/c) *Spectrum; (550 663-2/-4)* **DELILAH** [ ] [–]
Feb 99. (lp) *Get Back; (GET 536)* **THE RISE AND FALL OF THE SENSATIONAL ALEX HARVEY BAND** [ ] [–]
May 99. (cd) *Bear Family; (<BCD 1630-2>)* **ALEX HARVEY AND HIS SOUL BAND** (not original LP) [ ] [ ]
Feb 02. (cd) *Mercury; (<586392-2>)* **FAITH HEALER – AN INTRODUCTION TO THE SENSATIONAL ALEX HARVEY BAND** [ ] [ ]
Apr 02. (d-cd) *Mercury; (<586696-2>)* **FRAMED / NEXT . . .** [ ] May02 [ ]
Apr 02. (d-cd) *Mercury; (<586697-2>)* **THE IMPOSSIBLE DREAM / TOMORROW BELONGS TO ME** [ ] May02 [ ]
Apr 02. (d-cd) *Mercury; (<586698-2>)* **THE PENTHOUSE TAPES / LIVE** [ ] May02 [ ]
Apr 02. (d-cd) *Mercury; (<586699-2>)* **ROCK DRILL / SAHB STORIES** [ ] May02 [ ]
Mar 03. (d-cd) *Mercury; (<065005-2>)* **CONSIDERING THE SITUATION: THE ANTHOLOGY** [ ] [ ]
May 03. (cd) *Neon; (NE 34559)* **ICE COLD** [ ] [–]
Jun 03. (cd) *Burning Airlines; (<PILOT 159>)* **TEENAGE A GO GO** [ ] [ ]

PJ HARVEY

Born: POLLY JEAN HARVEY, 9 Oct'69, Corscombe, nr.Yeovil, England. Born to music-loving hippie parents, HARVEY was acquainted with music and musicians from an early age. Her first songwriting experience was with rootsy outfit the POLEKATS, HARVEY later joining Somerset-based group AUTOMATIC DLAMINI, who had been around for some five years. Numbered in their ranks were ROBERT ELLIS on drums, JOHN PARISH (ex-THIEVES LIKE US) on guitar and vocals (both ex-HEADLESS HORSEMEN; alongside bassist DAVE DALLIMORE). With bassist JAMIE ANDERSON, they finally released a well-received debut EP, 'THE CRAZY SUPPER', in June '86; PARISH also went into production work for the CHESTERFIELDS and BRILLIANT CORNERS. Early members of AUTOMATIC DLAMINI included ex-CLEANERS FROM VENUS keyboard man and future rock critic GILES SMITH, and IAN OLLIVER. 1987 was their busiest year, releasing singles, 'I DON'T KNOW YOU BUT . . .' and 'ME AND MY CONSCIENCE', and album, 'THE D IS FOR DRUM'. ELLIS departed soon after and POLLY finally convinced PARISH to let her play guitar, sax and contribute backing vocals. Unfortunately, recordings (i.e. 12" 'WATER', an album, 'HERE CATCH SHOUTED HIS FATHER') didn't quite reach the retail stage. In August 1992, the group released 'FROM A DIVA TO A DIVER', after which PARISH took time out to produce WALL OF VOODOO and play with ENSENADA JOYRIDE, whose 'Hey Lady' POLLY had always wanted to cover. She then turned up on GRAPE's single 'BABY IN A PLASTIC BAG' and two tracks by the FAMILY CAT; 'COLOUR ME GREY' and 'RIVER OF DIAMONDS'. With ELLIS and OLLIVER, she had already formed PJ HARVEY in 1991, and they signed for 'Too Pure'. With POLLY on vocals, their first release, 'DRESS', immediately caught the attention of John Peel and achieved the dubious honour of a Melody Maker single of the week. A driving, primal howl of a record, it introduced HARVEY's lyrical preoccupation with the darker corners of female sexuality, a theme continued with 'SHEELA-NA-GIG' (without OLLIVER who was subsequently replaced by STEPHEN VAUGHAN) in early '92. The single hit the UK Top 75 and and there was enough of a buzz around the band for the debut album, 'DRY', to reach the fringes of the Top 10. HARVEY's impact had been immediate, her raw, defiantly individual interpretation of feminism sparking much debate in the music press, especially after an NME cover shot in which she appeared topless, back to the camera. Signing to 'Island', PJ HARVEY began work on the Steve Albini (ex-BIG BLACK)-produced follow-up, 'RID OF ME', which went Top 3 upon its release in the spring of '93. As one might expect from the man who gave us 'Songs About Fucking', Albini's production didn't exactly make for an easy listen, HARVEY turning in her most ferocious performance to date. With the likes of 'LEGS', 'MAN SIZE' and 'RUB TILL IT BLEEDS', the singer continued to explore the contradictory and unsavoury aspects of sexuality/relationships with unparallelled feminine fury. Following the departure of ROB ELLIS, HARVEY assembled a backing band that includuded JOHN PARRISH (guitar, ex-AUTOMATIC DLAMINI), NICK BAGNALL (keyboards/bass), JOE GORE (guitar) and ERIC FELDMAN (keyboards) and JEAN-MARC BUTTY (drums). In 1995, with FLOOD and BAD SEED, MICK HARVEY on production duties, she/they unleashed HARVEY's finest work to date, 'TO BRING YOU MY LOVE', which also hit the US Top 40 and was nominated for a UK "Mercury" award. A more balanced affair, HARVEY's dark rage chose to simmer below the surface this time around, creating the feeling of creeping unease that runs through much of NICK CAVE's work (her new acquaintance!?). In 1996, she gave JOHN PARISH a full credit on their dual album 'DANCE HALL AT LOUSE POINT', which sold relatively poorly. As well as featuring on TRICKY's 'Broken Homes' single, 1998 saw the release of 'IS THIS DESIRE', the singer's most introspective, inscrutable work to date. Recorded amid a period of retreat from the vagaries and distractions of the rock world, the album's relatively restrained textures suggested an artist in transition. This was confirmed with the release of the widely acclaimed 'STORIES FROM THE CITY, STORIES FROM THE SEA' (2000), an album – a Mercury prize contender – with the energy of New York (where it was partly written) and the visceral thrill of self discovery coursing through its glamorous veins. Many commentators mentioned PATTI SMITH, a reference that HARVEY would be unlikely to dispute given the cathartic power she wielded throughout. Given her track record of collaborations (everyone from JOHN PARISH to NICK CAVE to SPARKLEHORSE), it wasn't too surprising when the West Country troubadour made her mark on Volumes 9 & 10 of JOSH HOMME's "Desert Sessions" series; a single 'CRAWL HOME' almost grazed the UK Top 40 in late 2003. Remarkably, perhaps, for such a fiercely independent artist, 'UH HUH HER' (2004), was the singer's first self-produced, self-contained album for well over a decade. HARVEY played all the instruments herself (save for the drums), lending the record a stripped-down, off-kilter feel while retaining her experimental edge. Her partisan fanbase ensured at least a few weeks' residence in both the UK and US Top 30, while HARVEY lent some of her creative fire to MARIANNE FAITHFULL's 'Before The Poison' (2004).

• **Songwriters:** POLLY, and covers; HIGHWAY 61 (Bob Dylan) / DADDY (Willie Dixon) / BALLAD OF THE SOLDIER'S WIFE (Kurt Weill).

Album rating: DRY (*9) / RID OF ME (*8) / TO BRING YOU MY LOVE (*9) / DANCE HALL AT LOUSE POINT with John Parish (*5) / IS THIS DESIRE (*6) / STORIES FROM THE CITY, STORIES FROM THE SEA (*9) / UH HUH HER (*7)

POLLY HARVEY – vocals, guitar, cello, violin, organ / **IAN OLLIVER** – bass / **ROBERT ELLIS** (b.13 Feb'62, Bristol, England) – drums, vocals

Too Pure | Indigo

Oct 91. (12"ep) *(PURE 5)* **DRESS. / WATER (demo) / DRY (demo)** [ ] [–]
(cd-iss. Mar92; PURECD 5)

— **STEPHEN VAUGHAN** (b.22 Jun'62, Wolverhampton, England) – bass repl. OLLIVER who returned to brief reformation of AUTOMATIC DLAMINI

Feb 92. (7"ltd.) *(PURE S8)* **SHEELA-NA-GIG. / JOE (demo)** [69] [–]
(12"+=/cd-s+=) *(PURE 8/+CD)* – Hair (demo).

Mar 92. (lp/cd/s-lp) *(PURE 10/+CD/D)* <ING 5001> **DRY** [11] Jun92 [ ]
– Oh my lover / O Stella / Dress / Victory / Happy and bleeding / Sheela-na-gig / Hair / Joe / Plants and rags / Fountain water. *(s-lp w/ free 'Demonstration' lp; PURED 10)*

Island | Island

Apr 93. (7"/c-s) *(IS/CIS 538)* **50FT QUEENIE. / REELING / MAN-SIZE (demo)** [27] [–]
(12"+=/cd-s+=) *(12IS/CID 538)* – Hook (demo).

Apr 93. (cd/c/lp) *(CID/ICT/ILPS 8002)* <514696> **RID OF ME** [3] May93 [ ]
– Rid of me / Missed / Legs / Rub 'til it bleeds / Hook / Man-size sextet / Highway '61 revisited / 50ft Queenie / Yuri-G / Man-size / Dry / Me-Jane / Snake / Ecstasy.

Jul 93. (12"ep/cd-ep) *(12IS/CID 569)* **MAN-SIZE. / WANG DANG DOODLE / DADDY** [42] [–]

— drummer ELLIS departed after above.

Oct 93. (cd/c/lp) *(IMCD/ICT/ILPM 2079)* <518450> **4-TRACK DEMOS** (demos) [19] Nov93 [ ]
– Rid of me / Legs / Reeling / Snake / Hook / 50ft Queenie / Driving / Ecstasy / Hardly wait / Rub 'til it bleeds / Easy / M-bike / Yuri-G / Goodnight.

— POLLY now with **JOHN PARISH** – drums, guitar / **JOE GORE** (b. San Francisco) – guitar (ex-TOM WAITS) / **NICK BAGNALL** – keyboards, bass / **ERIC FELDMAN** (b. San Francisco) – keyboards (ex-CAPTAIN BEEFEART) / **JEAN-MARC BUTTY** (b. France) – drums

Feb 95. (7"ep/12"ep/cd-ep) *(IS/12IS/CID 607)* **DOWN BY THE WATER. / LYING IN THE SUN / SOMEBODY'S DOWN, SOMEBODY'S NAME** [38] [–]

Feb 95. (cd/c/lp) *(CID/ICT/ILPS 8035)* <524085> **TO BRING YOU MY LOVE** [12] [40]
– To bring you my love / Meet ze monsta / Working for the man / C'mon Billy / Teclo / Long snake moan / Down by the water / I think I'm a mother / Send his love to me / The dancer. *(re-iss. d-cd Dec95 w/ extra B-sides; CIDZ 8035)*

Jul 95. (12"/cd-s) *(12IS/CID 614)* **C'MON BILLY. / DARLING BE THERE / MANIAC** [29] [–]
(cd-s+=) *(CIDX 614)* – One time too many.

Oct 95. (7"pic-d) *(IS 610)* **SEND HIS LOVE TO ME. / LONG TIME COMING (session)** [34] [–]
(cd-s+=) *(CID 610)* – Harder.
(cd-s) *(CIDX 610)* – ('A'side) / Hook (live) / Water (live).

— enjoyed more chart success on duet with NICK CAVE; 'Henry Lee' single released early '96.

JOHN PARISH & POLLY JEAN HARVEY

— with **JEREMY HOGG** – guitar / **ERIC DREW FELDMAN** – bass, keyboards (ex-CAPTAIN BEEFHEART) / **ROB ELLIS** – drums

Island | Island

Sep 96. (cd/c/lp) *(CID/ICT/ILPS 8051)* <524278> **DANCE HALL AT LOUSE POINT** [46] [ ]
– Girl / Rope bridge crossing / City of no sun / That was my veil / Urn with dead flowers in a drained pool / Civil war correspondent / Taut / Un cercle autour du soleil / Heela / Is that all there is / Dance hall at Louse Point / Lost fun zone.

Nov 96. (7") *(IS 648)* **THAT WAS MY VEIL. / LOSING GROUND** [75] [–]
(12"+=/cd-s+=) *(12IS/CID 648)* – Who will love me now? / Civil war correspondent (Global Communications mix).

— ELLIS joined 'Too Pure' outfit, LAIKA

PJ HARVEY

— In 1998, she featured with TRICKY on his 'Broken Homes' single.

Island | Polygram

Sep 98. (7") *(IS 718)* <572408> **A PERFECT DAY ELISE. / SWEETER THAN ANYTHING / INSTRUMENTAL #3** [25] Oct98 [ ]
(cd-s) *(CID 718)* – (first & third tracks) / The Northwood.
(cd-s) *(CIDX 718)* – (first two tracks) / The bay.

Sep 98. (cd/c/lp) *(CID/ICT/ILPS 8076)* <524563> **IS THIS DESIRE?** [17] [54]
– Angelene / Sky lit up / Wind / My beautiful Leah / A perfect day Elise / Catherine / Electric light / Garden / Joy / River / No girl so sweet / Is this desire?

Jan 99. (7") *(IS 730)* **THE WIND. / NINA IN ECSTASY 2** [29] [ ]
(cd-s+=) *(CID 730)* – The faster I breathe, the further I go.
(cd-s) *(CIDX 730)* – ('A'side) / Rebecca / Instrumental No.2.

Oct 00. (cd/c/lp) *(CID/ICT/ILPS 8099)* <548144> **STORIES FROM THE CITY, STORIES FROM THE SEA** [23] Nov00 [42]
– Big exit / Good fortune / A place called home / One line / Beautiful

PJ HARVEY

feeling / The whores hustle and the hustlers whore / This mess we're in / You said something / Kamikaze / This is love / Horses in my dreams / We float. *(cd+=)* – This wicked tongue.

Nov 00. (7") *(IS 769)* **GOOD FORTUNE. / 66 PROMISES** [41] [–]
(cd-s+=) *(CID 769)* – Memphis.
(cd-s) *(CIDX 769)* – ('A'side) / Memphis / 30.

Feb 01. (7") *(IS 771)* **A PLACE CALLED HOME. / KICK TO THE GROUND (demo)** [43] [–]
(cd-s) *(CID 771)* – ('A'side) / As close as this / My own private revolution.

Oct 01. (7") *(IS 785)* **THIS IS LOVE. / ANGELINE (live)** [41] [–]
(cd-s) *(CID 785)* – ('A'side) / You said something / Place called home (live).

May 04. (7") *(IS 861)* **THE LETTER. / BOWS & ARROWS** [28] [–]
(cd-s+=) *(CIDX 861)* – The phone song.
(cd-s) *(CID 861)* – ('A') / The falling.

May 04. (cd/lp) *(CID/ILPS 8143)* <27510-2> **UH HUH HER** [12] Jun04 [29]
– The life and death of Mr. Badmouth / Shame / Who the fuck? / Pocket knife / The letter / The slow drug / No child of mine / Cat on the wall / You come through / It's you / The end / The desperate kingdom of love / Seagulls / The darker days of me & him. *(bonus +=)* – Who the fuck (video).

Jul 04. (7") *(IS 869)* **YOU COME THROUGH. / STONE** [41] [–]
(cd-s+=) *(CIDX 869)* – Who the fuck? (4-track demo).
(cd-s) *(CID 869)* – ('A') / Angel.

Sep 04. (7") *(IS 873)* **SHAME. / DANCE** [45] [–]
(cd-s) *(CID 873)* – ('A') / 97.
(dvd-s) *(DV 873)* – ('A') / The letter (video) / You come through (video).

HAWKWIND

Formed: London, England ... mid-'69 as GROUP X, by ex-FAMOUS CURE members DAVE BROCK and MICK SLATTERY, who were joined by NIK TURNER, TERRY OLLIS, DIK MIK and JOHN HARRISON. They subsequently became HAWKWIND ZOO, although SLATTERY opted out for a gypsy lifestyle in Ireland after they signed to 'United Artists' in late '69. Now as HAWKWIND and many free concerts later (mostly at open-air festivals), they released their eponymous debut in late summer 1970. While this album was a melange of bluesy, heavy psychedelic rock, the band added more personnel for the follow-up, 'IN SEARCH OF SPACE' (1971), including synth player DEL DETTMAR and vocalist/poet ROBERT CALVERT. His sci-fi musings featured heavily on the album, while the scattered electronic stabs and saxophone honking merged with the driving rhythm section to create their own tripped-out take on space rock. The record saw HAWKWIND break into the Top 20, while the following summer they smashed into the Top 3 with the classic 'SILVER MACHINE' (1972) single, LEMMY KILMISTER's pile driving bass fuelling the beast with a turbo-charged power. The track previously featured on the live various artists 'GREASY TRUCKERS' PARTY' album, as well as appearing on the similar 'GLASTONBURY FAYRE' compilation. The success of the single secured the band Top 20 placings on all four of their future albums for 'United Artists', although come 1975, after the semi-classic 'WARRIOR ON THE EDGE OF TIME' album, LEMMY had departed to form MOTORHEAD, while CALVERT had been replaced by sci-fi writer, MICHAEL MOORCOCK. HAWKWIND signed to 'Charisma' and despite continuing moderate success, were dogged by legal battles over their moniker (HAWKLORDS was used for one album, 1978's '25 YEARS ON'). With a substantially altered line-up, HAWKWIND continued to release albums on their own 'Flicknife' label throughout the 80's. Tragedy struck when CALVERT died from a heart attack on the 14 of August '88, although yet another line-up saw HAWKWIND into the 90's with the 'SPACE BANDITS' (1990) album. The band consistently attracted a loyal following of die-hard hippies and the emergence of the psychedelic/crusty techno scene had done them no harm, many young stoners citing HAWKWIND as a prominent influence, even if BROCK was the only remaining original member. As he did on early 90s albums, 'ELECTRIC TEPEE' (1992) and 'ALIEN 4' (1995), the man (and his HAWKs, RON TREE, RICHARD CHADWICK and JERRY RICHARDS) continued to vary the space-rock sound with elements of that scene across records like 'DISTANT HORIZONS' (1997), the half-live/half-studio 'IN YOUR AREA' (1999), the ostensibly solo 'SPACEBROCK' (2000), the Xmas-cracking double concert set, 'YULE RITUAL' (2001) and reunion of sorts 'CANTERBURY FAYRE 2001' (2003), the latter featuring a cameo from flame-helmeted guru, ARTHUR BROWN.

• **Songwriters:** Mostly by BROCK or CALVERT until the latter's departure, ALAN DAVEY eventually replacing him. Other various personnel over the years also took part in writing.

Album rating: HAWKWIND (*6) / IN SEARCH OF SPACE (*8) / DOREMI FASOL LATIDO (*5) / SPACE RITUAL ALIVE (*8) / HALL OF THE MOUNTAIN KING (*6) / WARRIOR ON THE EDGE OF TIME (*7) / ROADHAWKS live collection (*6) / ASTOUNDING SOUNDS AND AMAZING MUSIC (*5) / QUARK, STRANGENESS AND CHARM (*4) / 25 YEARS ON (*4) / PRX 5 (*5) / LIVE 1979 (*4) / LEVITATION (*5) / SONIC ATTACK (*6) / CHURCH OF HAWKWIND (*6) / CHOOSE YOUR MASQUES (*6) / ZONES (*5) / THIS IS HAWKWIND, DO NOT PANIC (*4) / CHRONICLE OF THE BLACK SWORD (*6) / THE XENON CODEX (*6) / STASIS – THE U.A. YEARS 1971-1975 compilation (*8) / SPACE BANDITS (*6) / ELECTRIC TEEPEE (*6) / IT'S THE BUSINESS OF THE FUTURE TO BE DANGEROUS (*6) / THE BUSINESS TRIP (*4) / ALIEN 4 (*5) / LOVE IN SPACE (*5) / DISTANT HORIZONS (*5) / IN YOUR AREA (*6) / SPACEBROCK (*4) / YULE RITUAL: LONDON ASTORIA 29.12.00 (*5) / CANTERBURY FAYRE 2001 (*6)

DAVE BROCK (b. 20 Aug'41, Isleworth, England) – vocals, guitar / **NIK TURNER** (b. 26 Aug'40, Oxford, England) – vocals, saxophone / **HUW-LLOYD LANGTON** – guitar repl. MICK SLATTERY (Oct69, when as HAWKWIND ZOO) **JOHN HARRISON** – bass / **TERRY OLLIS** – drums / **DIK MIK** (b. S. McMANUS, Richmond, England) – electronics engineer synthesizers

Liberty U.A.

Jul 70. (7") *(LBF 15382)* **HURRY ON SUNDOWN. / MIRROR OF ILLUSION** [ ] [ ]

Aug 70. (lp) *(LBS 83348)* <5519> **HAWKWIND** [ ] [ ]
– Hurry on sundown / The reason is? / Be yourself / Paranoia (part 1) / Paranoia (part 2) / Seeing it as you really are / Mirror of illusion. *(re-iss. Sep75 on 'Sunset'; SLS 50374) (re-iss. Feb80 as 'ROCKFILE' on 'United Artists'; LBR 1012) (re-iss. Feb84 on 'E.M.I.' lp/pic-lp; SLS/+P 1972921) (hit UK 75) (cd-iss. Feb94 & Nov02 on 'Repertoire'; REP 4403) (cd re-mast.Aug0 on 'E.M.I.'+=; 530028-2)* – Bring it on home / Hurry on sundown (alt.) / Kiss of the velvet whip / Cymbaline.

— (Sep'70) **THOMAS CRIMBLE** – bass repl. JOHN HARRISON / **DEL DETTMAR** – synthesizer repl. LANGTON (partway through next album)

— (May'71) **DAVE ANDERSON** – bass (ex-AMON DUUL II) repl. CRIMBLE On stage they also added on vocals **ROBERT CALVERT** (b. 9 Mar'45 Pretoria, South Africa) – poet, vocals, **MICHAEL MOORCOCK** – sci-fi writer and **STACIA** – exotic dancer

U.A. U.A.

Oct 71. (lp) *(UAG 29202)* <5567> **IN SEARCH OF SPACE** [18] [ ]
– You shouldn't do that / You know you're only dreaming / Master of the universe / We took the wrong step years ago / Adjust me / Children of the sun. *(re-iss. Jan81 on 'Liberty'; LBG 29202) (re-iss. Jun85 on 'Liberty-EMI' lp/c; ATAK/TCATAK 9) (re-iss. Oct87 on 'Fame' lp/c; FA/TCFA 3192) (cd-iss. May89 & Dec95 on 'Fame'; CDFA 3192) (cd re-mast.Aug01 on 'E.M.I.'+=; 530030-2)* – Silver machine / Seven by seven / Born to go (live).

— (Sep'71) **LEMMY** (b. IAN KILMISTER, 24 Dec'45, Stoke-On-Trent England) – bass, vocals repl. ANDERSON

— (Jan'72) **SIMON KING** – drums (ex-OPAL BUTTERFLY) repl. OLLIS (group now **KING, LEMMY, BROCK, TURNER, DIK MIK, DETTMAR CALVERT, STACIA** and p/t **MOORCOCK**)

Jun 72. (7") *(UP 35381)* <50949> **SILVER MACHINE. / SEVEN BY SEVEN** [3] [ ]
(re-iss. '76) (re-iss. Oct78, hit UK 34) (re-hit 67 when re-iss. Dec82 7"/7"pic d/12"; UP/UPP/12UP 35381)

Nov 72. (lp) *(UAG 29364)* <LA 001> **DOREMI FASOL LATIDO** [14] [ ]
– Brainstorm / Space is deep / One change / Lord of light / Down through the night / Time we left this world today / The watcher. *(re-iss. 1979) (re-iss. Jun85 on 'Liberty-EMI') (US cd-iss. Jul91 on 'One Way') (cd re-iss. Mar96 on 'E.M.I.'+=; HAWKS 3)* – Urban guerilla / Brainbox pullution / Lord of light / Ejection. *(cd re-mast.Aug01 on 'E.M.I.'+=; 530031-2)*

May 73. (d-lp) *(UAD 60037-8) <LA 120>* **SPACE RITUAL – RECORDED LIVE IN LIVERPOOL AND LONDON (live)** [9] [ ]
– Earth calling / Born to go / Down through the night / The awakening / Lord of light / The black corridor / Space is deep / Electronic No.1 / Orgone accumulator / Upside down / 10 seconds of forever / Brainstorm / 7 by 7 / Sonic attack / Time we left this world today / Master of the universe / Welcome to the future. *(re-iss. 1979;) (cd re-mast.Aug01 on 'E.M.I.'+=; 530032-2)* – You shouldn't do that / Masters of the universe / Born to go.

Aug 73. (7") *(UP 25566) <314>* **URBAN GUERILLA. / BRAINBOX POLLUTION** [39] [ ]

— Now a trim sex/septet when DIK MIK and CALVERT departed. The latter going solo. (Apr74) **SIMON HOUSE** – keyboards, synthesizers, violin (ex-THIRD EAR BAND, ex-HIGH TIDE) repl. DETTMAR who emigrated to Canada

Aug 74. (7") *(UP 35715)* **PSYCHEDELIC WARLORDS (DISAPPEAR IN SMOKE). / IT'S SO EASY** [ ] [ ]

Sep 74. (lp/c) *(UAG/UAC 29672) <LA 328>* **HALL OF THE MOUNTAIN GRILL** [16] [ ]
– The psychedelic warlords (disappear in smoke) / Wind of change / D-rider / Web weaver / You'd better believe it / Hall of the Mountain Grill / Lost Johnnie / Goat willow / Paradox. *(re-iss. Jan81 on 'Liberty'; LBG 29672) (re-iss. Jun85 on 'Liberty-EMI';) (re-iss. Sep85 on 'Fame'; FA41 3133-1) (cd-iss. May89 & Dec95; CD-FA 3133) (cd re-mast.Aug01 on 'E.M.I.'+=; 530030-2)* – You'd better believe it (single version) / Psychedelic warlords (disappear in smoke) (single version) / Paradox / It's so easy.

— added **ALAN POWELL** – 2nd drums (ex-STACKRIDGE, ex-CHICKEN SHACK, etc)

Charisma Atco

Mar 75. (7") *(UP 35808)* **KINGS OF SPEED. / MOTORHEAD** [ ] [ ]

May 75. (lp/c) *(UAG/UAC 29766) <35115>* **WARRIOR ON THE EDGE OF TIME** [13] [ ]
– Assault and battery – part one / The golden void – part two / The wizard blew his horn / Opa-Loka / The demented man / Magnu / Standing at the edge / Spiral galaxy 28948 / Warriors / Dying seas / Kings of speed. *(re-iss. 1979; same) (re-iss. Jan81 + Jun85 on 'Liberty-EMI'; TCK 29766) (re-iss. Feb94 on 'Dojo'; DOJOCD 84) (cd re-iss. Aug03 on 'Hawkwind'; HAWKVP 6CD)*

— **PAUL RUDOLPH** – bass (ex-PINK FAIRIES) repl. LEMMY who formed MOTORHEAD **BOB CALVERT** – vocals returned, STACIA the dancer left to get married. **CALVERT** and **RUDOLPH** now with **BROCK, TURNER, KING, HOUSE** and **POWELL**. note also that MOORCOCK left to form his DEEP FIX

Charisma Sire

Jul 76. (7") *(CB 289)* **KERB CRAWLER. / HONKY DORKY** [ ] [–]

Aug 76. (lp/c) *(CDS 4004)* **ASTOUNDING SOUNDS, AMAZING MUSIC EMPORIUM** [33] [–]
– Reefer madness / Steppenwolf / City of lagoons / The aubergine that ate Rangoon / Kerb crawler / Kadu flyer / Chronoglide skyway. *(re-iss. Mar83; CHC 14) (cd-iss. Apr89 on 'Virgin'; CDSCD 4004) (cd re-iss. Aug03 on 'Hawkwind'; HAWKVP 28CD)*

Jan 77. (7") *(CB 299)* **BACK ON THE STREETS. / THE DREAM OF ISIS** [ ] [ ]

— **ADRIAN SHAW** – bass TURNER who formed SPHINX then INNER CITY BLUES

Jun 77. (lp/c) *(CDS/CDC 4008) <6047>* **QUARK, STRANGENESS AND CHARM** [30] [ ]
– Spirit of the age / Damnation alley / Fable of a failed race / Quark, strangeness and charm / Hassan I Sahba / The forge of Vulcan / Days of the underground / Iron dream. *(re-iss. Oct86 lp/c; CHC/MC 50) (cd-iss. Apr89 on 'Virgin'; CDSCD 4008) (cd re-iss. Aug03 on 'Hawkwind'; HAWKVP 26CD)*

Jul 77. (7") *(CB 305)* **QUARK, STRANGENESS AND CHARM. / THE FORGE OF VULCAN** [ ] [–]

— **PAUL HAYLES** – keyboards repl. HOUSE who joined DAVID BOWIE on tour

HAWKLORDS

BROCK and **CALVERT** recruiting new members **STEVE SWINDELLS** – keyboards (ex-STRING DRIVEN THING, ex-PILOT) / **HARVEY BAINBRIDGE** – bass / **MARTIN GRIFFIN** – drums

Charisma Charisma

Oct 78. (lp/c) *(CDS/CDC 4014) <2203>* **25 YEARS ON** [48] [ ]
– PSI power / Free fall / Automoton / 25 years / Flying doctor / The only ones / (only) The dead dreams of the cold war kid / The age of the micro man. *(re-iss. Aug82; CHC 10) (cd-iss. Apr89 on 'Virgin'; CDS4014)*

Oct 78. (7") *(CB 323)* **PSI POWER. / DEATH TRAP** [ ] [–]

Dec 78. (7") *<CAS 701>* **PSI POWER. / ('A'extended)** [–] [ ]

Mar 79. (7") *(CB 332)* **25 YEARS. / (ONLY) THE DEAD DREAMS OF THE COLD WAR KID** [ ] [ ]
(12"grey+=) *(CB 332-12)* – P.X.R. 5.

HAWKWIND

recorded '78 by **BROCK, TURNER, SHAW, KING / + HAYLES**

May 79. (lp/c) *(CDS 4016)* **P.X.R. 5** [59] [–]
– Death trap / Jack of shadows / Uncle Sam's on Mars / Infinity / Life form / Robot / High rise / P.X.R. 5. *(re-iss. Mar84; CHC 25) (cd-iss. Apr89 on 'Virgin'; CDSCD 4016)*

— **HAWKWIND** in 1979 were **SIMON KING** – drums returned from QUASAR, to repl. GRIFFITHS in Dec78 (CALVERT left to go solo). **TIM BLAKE** – keyboards (ex-GONG) repl. SWINDELLS who went solo

— added **HUW-LLOYD LANGTON** – guitar who returned from QUASAR

— now:- **BROCK, LANGTON, BAINBRIDGE, KING + BLAKE**

Bronze not iss.

Jul 80. (lp/c) *(BRON/TCBRON 527)* **LIVE 1979 (live)** [15] [–]
– Shot down in the night / Motorway city / Spirit of the age / Brainstorm / Lighthouse / Master of the universe / Silver machine (requiem). *(cd-iss. Feb92 on 'Castle'; CLACD 243) (cd re-iss. Jul99 on 'Essential'; ESMCD 735)*

Jul 80. (7") *(BRO 98)* **SHOT DOWN IN THE NIGHT (live). / URBAN GUERILLA (live)** [59] [–]

— **GINGER BAKER** – drums (ex-CREAM, ex-BLIND FAITH, ex-AIRFORCE etc) repl. KING who teamed up with SWINDELLS

Nov 80. (7") *(BRO 109)* **WHO'S GONNA WIN THE WAR. / NUCLEAR TOYS** [ ] [ ]

Nov 80. (blue-lp/c) *(BRON/TCBRON 530)* **LEVITATION** [21] [–]
– Levitation / Motorway city / Psychosis / World of tiers / Prelude / Who's gonna win the war / Space chase / The 5th second forever / Dust of time. *(re-iss. Jul87 on 'Castle' lp/cd; CLA/+CD 129) (cd-iss. Jul99 on 'Essential'; ESMCD 736)*

— **MARTIN GRIFFIN** – drums returned to repl. BAKER / **KEITH HALE** – keyboards repl. BLAKE

RCA Active not iss.

Oct 81. (7") *(RCA 137)* **ANGELS OF DEATH. / TRANS-DIMENSIONAL** [ ] [–]

Oct 81. (lp/c) *(RCA LP/K 6004)* **SONIC ATTACK** [19] [–]
– Sonic attack / Rocky paths / Psychosonia / Virgin of the world / Angels of death / Living on a knife edge / Coded languages / Disintigration / Streets of fear / Lost chances. *(cd-iss. Nov97 on 'Emergency Broadcast'; EBSCD 123)*

May 82. (lp/c) *(RCA LP/K 9004)* **CHURCH OF HAWKWIND** [26] [–]
– Angel voices / Nuclear drive / Star cannibal / The phenomena of luminosity / Fall of Earth city / The church / The joker at the gate / Some people never die / Light specific data / Experiment with destiny / The last Messiah / Looking in the future. *(cd-iss. Jun94 on 'Dojo')*

— **NIK TURNER** – vocals, saxophone returned to repl. HALE

Aug 82. (7"/7"pic-d) *(RCA/+P 267)* **SILVER MACHINE (remix). / PSYCHEDELIC WARLORDS (remix)** [ ] [–]

Oct 82. (lp/c) *(RCA LP/K 6055)* **CHOOSE YOUR MASQUES** [29] [–]
– Choose your masques / Dream worker / Arrival in Utopia / Utopia / Silver machine / Void city / Solitary mind games / Fahrenheit 451 / The scan / Waiting for tomorrow. *(cd-iss. Nov97 on 'Emergency Broadcast'; EBSCD 124)*

Flicknife not iss.

Oct 83. (lp) *(SHARP 014)* **ZONES** (live, with other 80's line-ups) [57] [–]
– Zones / Dangerous vision / Running through the back brain / The island / Motorway city / Utopia 84 / Society alliance / Sonic attack / Dream worker / Brainstorm. *(re-iss. Mar84 on pic-lp; PSHARP 014)*

Oct 83. (7") *(FLS 025)* **MOTORWAY CITY (live). / MASTER OF THE UNIVERSE (live)** [ ] [–]

Jan 84. (7") *(7FLEP 104)* **NIGHT OF THE HAWKS. / GREEN FINNED DEMON** [ ] [–]
(12"ep+=) *(FLEP 104)* - **THE EARTH RITUAL PREVIEW** – Dream dancers / Dragons + fables.

Nov 84. (lp) *(SHARP 022)* **STONEHENGE: THIS IS HAWKWIND, DO NOT PANIC** [ ] [–]
– Psy power / Levitation / Circles / Space chase / Death trap / Angels of death / Shot down in the night / Stonehenge decoded / Watching the grass grow. *(cd-iss. May92 on 'Anagram'; CDM GRAM 54)*

— **ALAN DAVEY** – bass, vocals repl. BAINBRIDGE and TURNER / **CLIVE**

DEAMER – drums repl. GRIFFIN

Nov 85. (lp/c/cd) *(SHARP 033/+C/CD)* **CHRONICLE OF THE BLACK SWORD** [65] [–]
– Song of the swords / Shade gate / The sea king / The pulsing cavern / Elric the enchanter / Needle gun / Zarozinia / The demise / Sleep of a thousand tears / Chaos army / Horn of destiny. *(cd-iss. w / 3 extra tracks) (re-iss. cd Aug92 on 'Dojo'; DPJPCD 72)*

Nov 85. (7") *(FLS 032)* **NEEDLE GUN. / ARIOCH** [ ] [–]
(12"+=) *(FLST 032)* – Song of the swords.

Mar 86. (7") *(FLS 033)* **ZAROZINIA. / ASSAULT AND BATTERY** [ ] [–]
(12"+=) *(FLST 033)* – Sleep of a 1000 tears.

— **HAWKWIND** are now **BROCK**, as DR. HASBEEN – vocals, guitar, keyboards, synthesizers, **LANGTON, DAVEY, BAINBRIDGE** now vocals, keyboards, synthesizer and **DANNY THOMPSON** – drums, percussion, vocals

G.W.R. Roadrunner

May 88. (lp/c/cd) *(GW/+C/CD 26)* **THE XENON CODEX** [79] 1989 [ ]
– The war I survived / Wastelands of sleep / Neon skyline / Lost chronicles / Tides / Heads / Mutation zone / E.M.C. / Sword of the east / Good evening. *<US-iss. on pic-d> (cd re-iss. Jul99 on 'Essential'; ESMCD 737)*

— **BROCK, BAINBRIDGE, DAVEY** plus **SIMON HOUSE, RICHARD CHADWICK & BRIDGETT WISHART**

Oct 90. (lp/c/cd) *(GW/+C/CD 103)* **SPACE BANDITS** [70] [–]
– Images / Black elk speaks / Wings / Out of the shadows / Realms / Ship of dreams / TV suicide. *(re-iss. cd Feb92 on 'Castle'; CLACD 282) (cd re-iss. Jul99 on 'Essential'; ESMCD 738)*

Essential not iss.

May 92. (cd/c/d-lp) *(ESSCD/ESSMC/ESSD 181)* **ELECTRIC TEPEE** [53] [–]
– LSD / Blue shift / Death of war / The secret agent / Garden pests / Space dust / Snake dance / Mask of the morning / Rites of Netherworld / Don't understand / Sadness runs deep / Right to decide / Going to Hawaii / Electric teepee. *(re-iss. Jul95 on 'Dojo'; DOJOCD 244) (cd re-iss. May00; ESMCD 885)*

Oct 93. (cd/c/lp) *(ESD CD/MC/LP 196)* **IT IS THE BUSINESS OF THE FUTURE TO BE DANGEROUS** [75] [ ]
– It's the business of the future to be dangerous / Space is their (Palestine) / Tibet is not China (pt.1 & 2) / Let barking dogs lie / Wave upon wave / Letting in the past / The camera that could lie / 3 or 4 erections during the course of the night / Technotropic zone exists / Give me shelter / Avante. *(cd re-iss. Jul99; ESMCD 740)*

4 Real not iss.

Jun 93. (12"ep/c-ep/cd-ep) *(4R 1 T/CS/D)* **SPIRIT OF THE AGE (The Solstice remixes)** [ ] [–]
– (Full Vocal / Hard Trance / Cyber Trance / Flesh To Phantasy)

Nov 93. (12"ep/cd-ep) *(4R 2 T/D)* **DECIDE YOUR FUTURE EP** [ ] [–]
– Right to decide / The camera that could lie / Right to decide (radio edit mix) / Assassin (Magick Carpet mix).

Emergency Broadcast not iss.

Sep 94. (12"ep/cd-ep) *(EBT/+D 110)* **QUARK, STRANGENESS AND CHARM** [ ] [–]
– Uncle Sam's on Mars (Red Planet radio mix) / Quark, strangeness and charm / Black sun / Uncle Sam's on Mars (Martian Conquest mix).

Sep 94. (cd/c/d-lp) *(EBS CD/MC/LP 111)* **THE BUSINESS TRIP (live)** [ ] [–]
– Altair / Quark, strangeness and charm / LSD / The camera that would lie / Green finned demon / Do that / The day a wall came down / Berlin axis / Void of golden light / Right stuff / Wastelands / The dream goes on / Right to decide / The dream has ended / The future / Terra mystica.

Sep 95. (12"ep/cd-ep) *(EB T/CD 107)* **AREA S.4.** [ ] [–]
– Alien / Sputnik Stan / Medley: Death trap – Wastelands of sleep – Dream has . . ..

Oct 95. (cd/lp) *(EB SCD/LP 118)* **ALIEN 4** [ ] [–]
– Abducted / Alien (I am) / Reject your human touch / Blue skin / Beam me up / Vega / Xenomorph / Journey / Sputnik Stan / Kapal / Festivals / Deah trap / Wastelands / Are you losing your mind? / Space sex.

May 96. (cd/lp) *(EBS CD/LP 120)* **LOVE IN SPACE** (live October 1995) [ ] [–]
– Abducted / Death trap / Wastelands / Are you losing your mind? / Photo encounter / Blue skin / Robot / Alien I am / Sputnik Stan / Xenomorph / Vega / Love in space / Kapal / Elfin / Silver machine / Welcome.

— line-up: **BROCK, RON TREE, RICHARD CHADWICK + JERRY RICHARDS**

Nov 97. (cd) *(EBSCD 139)* **DISTANT HORIZONS** [ ] [–]
– Distant horizons / Phetamine Street / Waimea Canyon drive / Alchemy / Clouded vision / Reptoid vision / Population overload / Wheels / Kauai / Taxi for Max.

Hawkwind Griffin

Apr 00. (cd) *(HAWKVP 17CD)* <740> **IN YOUR AREA** (live + new) [ ] Jan99 [ ]
– Brainstorm – Hawkwind in your area – Alchemy / Love in space / Rat race / Aerospace inferno / First landing on Medusa / I am the reptoid / The Nazca / Hippy / Prairie / Your fantasy / Luxotica / Diana Park.

— **BROCK** with **DR. TECHNICAL + HAWKMAN**

Hawkwind Blueprint

Feb 01. (cd) *(HAWKVP 18CD)* <4739> **SPACEBROCK** [ ] Sep01 [ ]
– Life form / Some people never die / Dreamers / Earth breath / You burn me up / The right way / Sex dreams / To be or not / Kauai / Earth calling / The starkness of the capsule / Behind the face / SpaceBrock / Space pilots / 1st landing / The journey / Do you want this body.

— added **TIM BLAKE, ALAN DAVEY, MIKE MOORCOCK + SIMON HOUSE**

Oct 01. (d-cd) *(HAWKVP 19CD)* **YULE RITUAL: LONDON ASTORIA 29.12.00** (live) [ ] [–]
– Electronic intro / Leviation / Money tree / Space is deep / Flying doctor / Warrior at the edge of time / Angels of death / High rise / Damage of life / Lighthouse / Sonic attack / Freefall / Motorway city / Hurry on sundown / Spirit of the age / Assassins of Allah.

— added **KEITH KNIVETON** (on above)

Feb 03. (d-cd) *(HAWKVP 22CD)* **CANTERBURY FAYRE 2001** (live) [ ] [–]
– 5th second of forever / Levitation / Spiral galaxy / Solitary mind games / Angels of death / Spirit of the age / Magnu / Dust of time (excerpt) / Motorway city / Hurry on sundown / Assassins of Allah / Silver machine / Arthur's poem / Assault and battery / Void of golden light / Ejection.

– compilations, etc. –

1973. (d7") *United Artists;* **HURRY ON SUNDOWN. / MASTER OF THE UNIVERSE/ / SILVER MACHINE. / ORGONE ACCUMULATOR** [–] [ ]

Apr 76. (lp) *United Artists; (UAK 29919)* **ROADHAWKS** [34] [ ]
– Hurry on sundown / Paranoia (excerpt) / You shouldn't do that (live) / Silver machine (live) / Urban guerilla / Space is deep / Wind of change / The golden void. *(re-iss. Apr84 on 'Fame' lp/c; FA 413096-1/-4)*

Feb 77. (lp) *United Artists; (UAG 30025)* **MASTERS OF THE UNIVERSE** [ ] [–]
– Master of the universe / Brainstorm / Sonic attack / Orgone accumulator / It's so easy / Lost Johnnie. *(re-iss. May82 on 'Fame' lp/c; FA/C 3008) (re-iss. Jun87 & Dec95 on 'Liberty' lp/c; EMS/TCEMS 1258) (re-iss. May89 on 'Fame' lp/c/cd; FA/TCFA/CDFA 3220) (re-iss. Jul90 on 'Marble Arch' c/cd; CMA/+CD 129) (re-iss. Jul94 on 'Success' cd/c;) (cd-iss. Apr97 on 'Spalax'; 14972)*

Sep 80. (lp/c) *Charisma; (BG/+C 2)* **REPEAT PERFORMANCE** [ ] [–]
– Kerb crawler / Back on the streets / Quark strangeness and charm / Spirit of the age / Steppenwolf / 25 years / PSI power / The only ones / High rise / Uncle Sam's on Mars.

May 81. (12"ep; as HAWKWIND ZOO) *Flicknife; (FLEP 100)* **HURRY ON SUNDOWN. / SWEET MISTRESS OF PAIN / KINGS OF SPEED (live)** [ ] [–]
(re-iss. Dec83)

Jul 81. (7"/12") *Flicknife; (FLS/+EP 205)* **MOTORHEAD. / VALIUM TEN** [ ] [–]
(re-iss. 12" Oct82)

Nov 81. (12"ep; as SONIC ASSASSINS) *Flicknife; (FLEP 101)* **OVER THE TOP. / FREEFALL / DEATH TRAP** [ ] [–]

Mar 82. (lp) *Flicknife; (SHARP 001)* **FRIENDS & RELATIONS** (1/2 live '77-78, 1/2 studio '82) [ ] [–]
(re-iss. Nov83) (re-iss. Nov94 on 'Emporio' cd/c)

Jun 82. (7"; as HAWKLORDS) *Flicknife; (FLS 209)* **WHO'S GONNA WIN THE WAR. / TIME OFF** [ ] [–]

Feb 83. (7") *Flicknife; (FLS 14)* **HURRY ON SUNDOWN. / LORD OF THE HORNETS / DODGEM DUKE** [ ] [–]

Mar 83. (d-c) *Charisma; (CASMC 110)* **QUARK, STRANGENESS & CHARM / PXR 5** [ ] [–]
(re-iss. '88)

1983. (lp) *Flicknife; (SHARP 107)* **TWICE UPON A TIME: HAWKWIND FRIENDS AND RELATIONS VOL.2** [ ] [–]

Jul 83. (d-lp) *Illuminated; (JAMS 29)* **TEXT OF FESTIVAL (live '70-72)** [ ] [–]
(1-lp re-iss. Jul85 as 'IN THE BEGINNING' on 'Demi Monde'; DM 005) (re-iss. cd Mar94 on 'Charly') (re-iss. Dec88 on 'Thunderbolt'; THBL 2.068) (cd-iss. first 3 sides) (cd re-iss. Mar97; CDTB 068)

Jun 84. (10"m-lp) *Flicknife; (SHARP 109)* **INDEPENDENTS DAY** ☐ –
Nov 84. (d-lp/d-c) *A.P.K.; (APK/+C 8)* **SPACE RITUAL 2 (live)** ☐ –
(cd-iss. 1987 on 'The CD Label'; CDTL 003)
Feb 85. (lp) *Demi-Monde; (DM 002)* **BRING ME THE HEAD OF YURI GAGARIN** (live '73 Empire Pool) ☐ –
(cd-iss. Nov86 on 'Charly'; CDCHARLY 40) (cd-iss. Nov92 on 'Thunderbolt'; CDTB 101) (cd re-iss. Apr97 on 'Spalax'; 14846)
Feb 85. (lp) *Flicknife; (SHARP 024)* **HAWKWIND, FRIENDS AND RELATIONS VOL.3** ☐ –
(c-iss.Apr84 with VOL.1 on reverse; *SHARP C1024) (other c-iss.Apr84 with VOL.2 on reverse; SHARP C2024)*
Jul 85. (lp) *Dojo; (DOJOLP 11)* **LIVE 70-73 (live)** ☐ –
May 85. (lp) *Mausoleum; (SKULL 8333369)* **UTOPIA 1984** ☐ –
Nov 85. (lp) *Mausoleum; (SKULL 83103)* **WELCOME TO THE FUTURE** ☐ –
Nov 85. (lp) *Obsession; (OBLP 1)* **RIDICULE** ☐ –
(re-iss. of disc 2 of 'SPACE RITUAL') (re-iss. 1990 cd/lp; OBSESS CD/LP 1)
Nov 85. (lp/pic-lp)(cd) *Samurai; (SAMR 038/+PD)(SAMRCD 038)* **ANTHOLOGY – HAWKWIND VOL.1** ☐ –
(cd+=) – Silver machine. *(re-iss. pic-lp.Nov86 as 'APPROVED HISTORY OF HAWKWIND'; SAMR 046) (re-iss. Apr90 as 'ACID DAZE 1' on 'Receiver'; RR 125)*
Mar 86. (lp/cd)(c) *Samurai; (SAMR/+CD 039)(TCSAMR 039)* **ANTHOLOGY – HAWKWIND VOL. 2** ☐ –
(cd-iss. 1986 extra 4 tracks) (re-iss. Apr90 as 'ACID DAZE 2' on 'Receiver'; RR 126)
May 86. (7"/7"sha-pic-d) *Samurai; (HW 7001/001)* **SILVER MACHINE. / MAGNU** ☐ –
(12"+=) *(HW12-001)* – Angels of death.
Jul 86. (7") *Flicknife; (FLS 034-A)* **MOTORHEAD. / HURRY ON SUNDOWN** ☐ –
Jul 86. (lp/c) *Samurai; (SAMR 040/+TC)* **ANTHOLOGY – HAWKWIND VOL.3** ☐ –
(re-iss. Apr90 as 'ACID DAZE 3' on 'Receiver'; RR 127)
Jul 86. (lp) *Hawkfan; (HWFB 2)* **HAWKFAN 12** ☐ –
Sep 86. (d-lp/d-c/cd) *Castle; (CCS LP/MC/CD 148)* **THE HAWKWIND COLLECTION (Pts. 1 & 2)** ☐ –
(cd-iss. Dec86 omits some tracks)
Nov 86. (lp/c) *Flicknife; (SHARP 036/+C)* **INDEPENDENTS DAY VOL.2** ☐ –
Jan 87. (lp/c) *R.C.A.; (NL/NK 71150)* **ANGELS OF DEATH** ☐ –
Apr 87. (lp/c/cd) *Flicknife; (SHARP 040/+C/CD)* **OUT AND INTAKE** ☐ –
(cd+=) – (2 extra tracks).
Sep 87. (lp/c/cd) *Start; (STF L/C/CD 2)* **BRITISH TRIBAL MUSIC** ☐ –
Oct 87. (3xbox-pic-lp) *Flicknife; (HWBOX 1)* **OFFICIAL PICTURE LOGBOOK** ☐ –
– ('STONEHENGE' / 'BLACK SWORD' / 'OUT & INTAKE' / '(interview)' lp *(cd-iss. Nov94 on 'Dojo';)*
Dec 87. (lp/c) *Thunderbolt; (THBL/THBC 044)* **EARLY DAZE (THE BEST OF HAWKWIND)** ☐ –
(cd-iss. Jun88; CDTB CDTB 044)
Sep 88. (cd) *Virgin; (COMCD 8)* **SPIRIT OF THE AGE** ☐ –
(re-iss. Oct91 on 'Elite'; ELITE 021CD) (re-iss. Sep 93)
Nov 88. (cd) *Flicknife; (SHARP 1422CD)* **ZONES / STONEHENGE** ☐ –
Nov 88. (cd) *Flicknife; (SHARP 1724CD)* **BEST OF HAWKWIND, FRIENDS & RELATIONS** ☐ –
Dec 88. (d-lp/cd) *Flicknife; (SHARP 2045/+CD)* **THE TRAVELLERS AID TRUST** ☐ –
Dec 88. (d-lp/d-cd) *That's Original; (TFO 17/+CD)* **LEVITATION / HAWKWIND LIVE** ☐ –
Mar 89. (cd) *Avanti; (ISTCD 004)* **IRONSTRIKE** ☐ –
May 89. (lp) *Legacy; (GWSP 1)* **LIVE CHRONICLES** ☐ –
(re-iss. Feb92 cd/c on 'Castle; CCS CD/MC 123) (cd re-iss. Sep00 on 'Essential'; CMDDD 013)
May 89. (lp/c/cd) *Powerhouse; (POW/+C/CD 5502)* **NIGHT OF THE HAWK** ☐ –
(cd-iss. has 3 extra tracks)
1990. (cd/c) *Action Replay; (ARLC/CDAR 1018)* **BEST AND THE REST OF HAWKWIND** ☐ –
Mar 90. (2xcd-box)(3xlp-box) *Receiver; (RRDCD 1X)(RRBX 1)* **ACID DAZE (re-issue)** ☐ –
(3 VOLUMES re-iss. cd Jul93)
May 90. (cd)(c/lp) *E.M.I.; (CDP 746694-2)(TC+/NTS 300)* **STASIS, THE U.A. YEARS 1971-1975** ☐ –
– Urban guerilla / Psychedelic warlords (disappear in smoke) / Brainbox pollution / 7 by 7 / Paradox / Silver machine / You'd better believe it / Lord of light / The black corridor (live) / Space is deep (live) / You shouldn't do that (live). *(re-iss. cd Dec95 on 'Fame')*
Dec 90. (12"blue-ep) *Receiver; (REPLAY 3014)* **THE EARLY YEARS LIVE** ☐ –
– Silver machine / Spirit of the age / Urban guerilla / Born to go.
1990. (c) *Capitol; <4XLL 57286>* **METAL CLASSICS 2: BEST OF HAWKWIND** – ☐
1990. (cd/c) *Knight; (KN CD/MC 10017)* **NIGHT RIDING** ☐ –
Jun 91. (lp/c/cd) *G.W.R.; (GW/+MC/CD 104)* **PALACE SPRINGS** ☐ –
– (remixed tracks from 'WARRIORS ... ' & 'XENON ...) *(re-iss. cd Jul92 on 'Castle'; CLACD 303) (cd re-iss. Jul99 on 'Essential'; ESMCD 739)*
Oct 91. (cd/c) *Windsong; (WIN CD/MC 007)* **BBC RADIO 1 LIVE IN CONCERT (live)** ☐ –
Feb 92. (3xcd-box) *Castle; (CLABX 911)* **3 ORIGINALS** ☐ –
Feb 92. (cd) *Raw Fruit; (FRSCD 005)* **THE FRIDAY ROCK SHOW SESSIONS (live '86)** ☐ –
Jun 92. (cd) *Anagram; (GRAM 53)* **MIGHTY HAWKWIND CLASSICS 1980-1985** ☐ –
Aug 92. (cd) *Dojo; (DOJOCD 71)* **HAWKLORDS LIVE** ☐ –
Apr 94. (cd) *Cleopatra; (CLEO 57732)* **LORD OF LIGHT** ☐ –
Apr 94. (cd) *Cleopatra; (CLEO 57412)* **PSYCHEDELIC WARLORDS** ☐ –
Dec 94. (cd) *Cyclops; (CYCL 021)* **CALIFORNIA BRAINSTORM** ☐ –
Feb 95. (cd) *Emergency Broadcast; (EMBSCD 114)* **UNDISCLOSED FILES – ADDENDUM** ☐ –
Mar 95. (cd) *Anagram; (CDMGRAM 91)* **THE RARITIES . . .** ☐ –
May 95. (cd) *Spectrum; (550764-2)* **SILVER MACHINE** ☐ –
Oct 95. (cd) *Anagram; (CDGRAM 94)* **INDEPENDENTS DAY VOLUMES 1 & 2** ☐ –
Mar 97. (cd) *Emporio; (EMPRCD 710)* **ONWARD FLIES THE BIRD – LIVE AND RARE** ☐ –
Jul 97. (cd-ep) *E.B.S.; (EBCD 106)* **LOVE IN SPACE / LORD OF LIGHT / SONIC ATTACK** ☐ –
Sep 97. (d-cd) *Snapper; (SMDCD 121)* **AMBIENT ANARCHISTS** ☐ –
Nov 97. (cd/lp) *Emergency Broadcast; (EBS CD/LP 117)* **RITUAL OF THE SOLSTICE** ☐ –
Nov 97. (d-cd) *E.M.I.; (HAWKS 6)* **1999 PARTY** ☐ –
Mar 98. (cd) *Eagle; (EABCD 084)* **THE MASTERS** ☐ –
Apr 98. (cd) *Cleopatra; <(CLEO 2202)>* **WELCOME TO THE FUTURE** ☐ –
Sep 98. (cd) *Repertoire; (REP 4676)* **SONIC BOOM KILLERS** ☐ –
Sep 98. (d-cd) *Essential; (<ESDCD 664>)* **ANTHOLOGY** ☐ ☐
Feb 99. (cd) *Cleopatra; <(CLP 0471-2)>* **GOLDEN VOID 1969-1979** ☐ ☐
Mar 99. (lp) *Black Widow; (BWR/+CD 026)* **THE ELF AND THE HAWK** ☐ –
Apr 99. (cd) *Blueprint; (BP 309CD)* **THE DAWN OF HAWKWIND** ☐ –
May 99. (cd) *Anagram; (CDMGRAM 61)* **THE BEST OF FRIENDS AND RELATIONS** ☐ –
May 99. (4xcd-box) *Dressed To Kill; (REDTK 98)* **ENTIRE AND INFINITE** ☐ –
– (MASTERS OF THE UNIVERSE / BRING ME THE HEAD OF URI GAGARIN / SPACE RITUAL / TEXT OF FESTIVAL)
Jun 99. (cd) *Thunderbolt; (CDTB 099)* **SPACE RITUAL VOL.2** ☐ –
Aug 99. (cd) *EMI; (521747-2)* **EPOCH – ECLIPSE (THE ULTIMATE BEST OF HAWKWIND)** ☐ –
Aug 99. (3xcd-box) *EMI; (521751-2)* **EPOCH – ECLIPSE 30 YEAR ANTHOLOGY** ☐ –
Nov 99. (cd) *Hawkwind; (HAWKVP 1CD)* **LIVE AT THE GLASTONBURY FESTIVAL 1990** ☐ –
Nov 99. (cd) *Hawkwind; (HAWKVP 2CD)* **GREASY TRUCKERS (live at the Roundhouse 1972)** ☐ –
Nov 99. (d-cd) *Hawkwind; (HAWKVP 3CD)* **COLLECTORS SERIES VOL.1** ☐ –
Dec 99. (d-cd) *Hawkwind; (HAWKCD 4CD)* **COLLECTORS SERIES VOL.2** ☐ –
Apr 00. (cd) *Hawkwind; (HAWKVP 5CD)* **ATOM HENGE** ☐ –
Apr 00. (d-cd) *Hawkwind; (HAWKVP 13CD)* **LIVE IN NOTTINGHAM 1990** ☐ –

Jul 00. (d-cd) *Burning Airlines; (PILOT 033)* **YEAR 2000 – CODENAME HAWKWIND VOL.1 (live)** [ ] [–]
Jul 00. (cd) *Burning Airlines; (PILOT 064)* **LIVE FROM THE DARKSIDE** [ ] [–]
Jul 00. (d-cd) *Cleopatra; <(CLP 850)>* **THE STONEHENGE COLLECTION** [ ] [ ]

HAWTHORNE HEIGHTS

Formed: Dayton, Ohio, USA . . . June 2001 as A DAY IN THE LIFE by vocalist J.T. WOODRUFF, guitarist MICAH CARLI, bassist MATT RIDENOUR, drummer ERON BUCCIARELLI and guitarist/unholy growler CASEY CALVERT. After one self-financed mini-set, 'NINE REASONS TO SAY GOODBYE' (2001), the heavy-duty power-poppers re-christened themselves HAWTHORNE HEIGHTS, a name partly inspired by 19th Century American novelist Nathaniel Hawthorne. Sounding for all the world like an Americanized, metallicized CURE/ROBERT SMITH session being gatecrashed by LEE DORRIAN, debut long-player, 'THE SILENCE IN BLACK AND WHITE' (2004), made for 21st Century schizoid listening, and that's without even mentioning the un-SKYNYRD-like triple guitar assault. Chicago emo HQ, 'Victory', were also behind their US Top 3 sophomore set, 'IF ONLY YOU WERE LONELY' (2006), sporting a cleaner, shinier, happier hardcore sound once again spiked with CALVERT's absurd asides. Hardly as political as forebears GREEN DAY, the Christian 'HEIGHTS confirmed that growling is the new gospel according to MTV.

Album rating: NINE REASONS TO SAY GOODBYE mini as A Day In The Life (*5) / THE SILENCE IN BLACK AND WHITE (*5) / IF ONLY YOU WERE LONELY (*6)

J.T. WOODRUFF – vocals, guitar / **CASEY CALVERT** – guitar, vocals / **MICAH CARLI** – guitar / **MATT RIDENOUR** – bass, vocals / **ERON BUCCIARELLI** – drums

not iss. own label

2001. (m-cd; as A DAY IN THE LIFE) **NINE REASONS TO SAY GOODBYE** [–] [ ]
– The death of a dream / Control alt delete / Do you have a map, because I'm lost in your eyes / The girl that destroyed me / Candycanes and cola / Audrey in Sacramento / Photograph / Until her heart stops / I'm not crying, my eyeballs are sweating. *<re-iss. Apr05 on 'Confined'; 5164-2>*

Victory Victory

Aug 04. (cd) *<(VR 220CD)>* **THE SILENCE IN BLACK AND WHITE** [ ] Jun04 [56]
– Life on standby / Dissolve and decay / Niki FM / The transition / Blue burns orange / Silver bullet / Screenwriting an apology / Ohio is for lovers / Wake up call / Sandpaper and silk / Speeding up the octaves.

Feb 06. (cd) *<(VR 265CD)>* **IF ONLY YOU WERE LONELY** [ ] [3]
– This is who we are / We are so last year / Language lessons (five words or less) / Pens and needles / Saying sorry / Dead in the water / I am on your side / Breathing in sequence / Light sleeper / Cross me off your list / When can I stab myself in the ears / Decembers. *<(ltd-cd w/dvd+=; VR 266CD)>* – (VicTorV episode hosted by JT).

☐ the HEADS (see under ⇒ TALKING HEADS)

☐ HEATMISER (see under ⇒ SMITH, Elliott)

Jimi HENDRIX

Born: JOHNNY ALLEN HENDRIX, 27 Nov'42, Seattle, Washington, USA. He was raised by a part Cherokee Indian mother and black father, who, at age 3, changed his forenames to JAMES MARSHALL and bought him his first guitar. Being left-handed, he turned it upside down and reversed the strings, teaching himself by listening to blues and rock'n'roll artists such as ROBERT JOHNSON, MUDDY WATERS, B.B. KING and CHUCK BERRY. In the early 60's, he enlisted in the paratroopers, thus avoiding the draft into the US army. He was subsequently discharged for medical reasons in 1962, after injuring himself during a jump. Two years later, the young HENDRIX moved to New York and backed acts LITTLE RICHARD, The ISLEY BROTHERS and IKE & TINA TURNER. He soon struck up a partnership with soul singer CURTIS KNIGHT, also obtaining a contract with Ed Chalpin (KNIGHT is said to have written 'The Ballad Of Jimi' in 1965, after JIMI prophesied his own death circa 1970!). Early the following year, HENDRIX's first real band, JIMMY JAMES & THE BLUE FLAMES, were born. With JIMI's reputation now spreading, he was seen by ex-ANIMALS bassman CHAS CHANDLER, who invited him to London. After auditions, they found a rhythm section of NOEL REDDING and MITCH MITCHELL, smashing their way into the UK Top 10 in early '67 with the 'Polydor' one-off 45, 'HEY JOE'. CHANDLER then set up a deal with Kit Lambert's new 'Track' label, and The JIMI HENDRIX EXPERIENCE exploded onto the scene. Their first Hendrix-penned 45, the thundering acid-fever of 'PURPLE HAZE', made the UK Top 3, as did the scintillating debut album, 'ARE YOU EXPERIENCED?'. This was released hot on the heels of their third Top 10 single, 'THE WIND CRIES MARY'. Hendrix was a revelation, a black super-freak whose mastery of the guitar was above and beyond anything previously heard. In fact, he virtually re-invented the instrument, duly illustrating various methods of on-stage abuse (i.e. biting it, playing it with his teeth, shagging it and even setting fire to it!). He was duly booked on the Monterey International Pop Festival bill, where he proceeded to play an orgasmic version of 'WILD THING'. From the sublime to the ridiculous, the following month saw a wholly inappropriate US support tour with The MONKEES, leaving both him and teenybop audiences baffled, but no doubt entertained for seven nights. After another classic UK hit, 'THE BURNING OF THE MIDNIGHT LAMP', he released his second LP, 'AXIS: BOLD AS LOVE', which made the Top 5 early in '68, and was the first to chart and hit the Top 3 in his native America. In the Autumn of '68, JIMI revived and transformed BOB DYLAN's 'ALL ALONG THE WATCHTOWER', a song that broke into the US Top 20 and UK Top 5. It was trailed by a superb British Top 10 (US No.1) double-LP, 'ELECTRIC LADYLAND', the record featuring the now infamous naked women sleeve (much to JIMI's displeasure), which some shops sold in a brown cover! The beginning of the end came in 1969, when he was busted for drugs, leading to his band disintegrating; the trio played together for the last time on the 29th June at the Denver Pop Festival. REDDING had already formed FAT MATTRESS, MITCHELL returning with other musicians BILLY COX and LARRY LEE to make the group a quartet. The new "Experience" played the Woodstock Festival on the 17-18 August '69, performing an excellent version of 'STAR SPANGLED BANNER' that went down in the folklore of rock music. To end the year, JIMI was found not guilty of an earlier charge of heroin and marijuana possession and at the same time, he formed all-black outfit, BAND OF GYPSYS, along with COX and drummer BUDDY MILES. They released the self-titled live set in May '70 (recorded at FILLMORE EAST, New Year's Eve/Day 1969/70). This hit the Top 5 in the States, and, following a court order, he paid ex-manager Ed Chalpin $1m in compensation and a percentage of royalties. Tragically, after a few more open-air festival concerts and some bad drugs trips, he died in London on the 18th of September '70. He was said to have left a phoned message to Chandler saying "I need help bad, man". The official cause of death was an inhalation of vomit, due to barbiturate intoxication, leading to a coroner's decision of an open verdict. To many rock music buffs, he remains the greatest axegrinder of all-time and who knows what he might have become had he survived the heady sixties.

JIMI HENDRIX

• **Songwriters:** HENDRIX except other covers; HEY JOE (William Roberts) / JOHNNY B.GOODE (Chuck Berry) / GLORIA (Them) / SGT. PEPPER (Beatles) / HANG ON SLOOPY (McCoys) / TUTTI FRUTTI + LUCILLE (Little Richard) / BO DIDDLEY (Bo Diddley) / PETER GUNN (Henry Mancini) / HOOCHIE COOCHIE MAN (Muddy Waters) / BLUE SUEDE SHOES (Carl Perkins) / etc. • **Trivia:** In Jan'69, he and band play live tribute of CREAM's 'Sunshine Of Your Love' on The LULU Show, much to annoyance of TV controllers.

Album rating (selective): ARE YOU EXPERIENCED? (*10) / AXIS: BOLD AS LOVE (*9) / SMASH HITS compilation (*8) / ELECTRIC LADYLAND (*10) / BAND OF GYPSYS (*8) / posthumous:- THE CRY OF LOVE (*7) / EXPERIENCE (*3) / AT THE ISLE OF WIGHT (*4) / RAINBOW BRIDGE (*4) / HENDRIX IN THE WEST (*5) / WAR HEROES (*4) / SOUNDTRACK RECORDINGS FROM THE FILM 'JIMI HENDRIX' (*5) / CRASH LANDING (*4) / MIDNIGHT LIGHTNING (*4) / THE JIMI HENDRIX CONCERTS (*5) / THE SINGLES ALBUM (*7) / LIVE AT WINTERLAND (*7) / RADIO ONE (*7) / CORNERSTONES 1967-1970 (*8) / EXPERIENCE soundtrack (*5) / THE ULTIMATE EXPERIENCE (*10) / BLUES (*6) / JIMI HENDRIX: WOODSTOCK (*6) / VOODOO SOUP (*5) / FIRST RAYS OF THE NEW RISING SUN (*6) / VOODOO CHILD – THE JIMI HENDRIX COLLECTION (*8)

JIMI HENDRIX EXPERIENCE

JIMI HENDRIX – vocals, lead guitar (ex-CURTIS KNIGHT) with **NOEL REDDING** (b.DAVID REDDING, 25 Dec'45, Folkstone, Kent, England) – bass / **MITCH MITCHELL** (b.JOHN MITCHELL, 9 Jun'47, Ealing, London, England) – drums

Polydor | Reprise

Dec 66. (7"; as JIMI HENDRIX) *(56139)* **HEY JOE. / STONE FREE** [6] [–]
(re-iss. Jul84 on 'Old Gold')

Track | Reprise

Mar 67. (7") *(604 001)* **PURPLE HAZE. / 51ST ANNIVERSARY** [3] [–]
Mar 67. (7") *<0572>* **HEY JOE. / 51st ANNIVERSARY** [–] [ ]
May 67. (7") *(604 004)* **THE WIND CRIES MARY. / HIGHWAY CHILE** [6] [–]
May 67. (lp; mono/stereo) *(612/613 001) <6261>* **ARE YOU EXPERIENCED?** [2] Aug67 [5]
– Foxy lady / Manic depression / Red house / Can you see me / Love or confusion / I don't live today / May this be love / Fire / Third stone from the sun / Remember / Are you experienced? *(re-iss. Nov70; 2407 010) (re-iss. Nov81; 612 001) (re-iss. Sep85 on 'Polydor' lp/c; SPE LP/MC 97) (cd-iss. Jun91 & Oct93 cd/c; 521036-2/-4) (re-iss. Apr97 on 'MCA' cd/c; MCD/MCC 11608)*
Aug 67. (7") *<0597>* **PURPLE HAZE. / THE WIND CRIES MARY** [–] [65]
Aug 67. (7") *(604 007)* **THE BURNING OF THE MIDNIGHT LAMP. / THE STARS THAT PLAY WITH LAUGHING SAM'S DICE** [18] [–]
Dec 67. (7"; by JIMI HENDRIX) *<0641>* **FOXY LADY. / HEY JOE** [–] [67]
Dec 67. (lp; mono/stereo) *(612/613 003) <6281>* **AXIS: BOLD AS LOVE** [5] Feb68 [3]
– Experience / Up from the skies / Spanish castle magic / Wait until tomorrow / Ain't no telling / Little wing / If six was nine / You've got me floating / Castles made of sand / She's so fine / One rainy wish / Little Miss Lover / Bold as love. *(re-iss. Nov70;) (re-iss. Aug83 on 'Polydor' lp/c; (SPE LP/MC 71) (cd-iss. 1987 on 'Polydor'; 813 572-2) (re-iss. Jul91 & Oct93 on 'Polydor' lp/c/cd; 847243-1/-4/-2) (re-iss. Apr97 on 'MCA' cd/c; MCD/MCC 11601)*
Feb 68. (7") *<0665>* **UP FROM THE SKIES. / ONE RAINY WISH** [–] [82]
Apr 68. (lp; mono/stereo) *(612/613 004) <2025>* **SMASH HITS** (compilation) [4] Jul69 [6]
– Purple haze / Fire / The wind cries Mary / Can you see me / 51st anniversary / Hey Joe / Stone free / The stars that play with laughing Sam's dice / Manic depression / Highway chile / The burning of the midnight lamp / Foxy lady. *(re-iss. Jun73 on 'Polydor'; 2310 268) (re-iss. Aug83 on 'Polydor' lp/c; SPE LP/MC 3) (cd-iss. Feb85; 813 572-2)*
May 68. (7") *<0728>* **FOXY LADY. / PURPLE HAZE** [–] [ ]
Jul 68. (7") *<0742>* **ALL ALONG THE WATCHTOWER. / CROSSTOWN TRAFFIC** [–] [ ]

—— JIMI now brought in old session campaigners **AL KOOPER** and **STEVE WINWOOD** – keyboards plus **JACK CASADY** – bass / **BUDDY MILES** – drums / (to repl. MITCHELL and REDDING)

Sep 68. (7") *<0767>* **ALL ALONG THE WATCHTOWER. / BURNING OF THE MIDNIGHT LAMP** [–] [20]
Oct 68. (7") *(604 025)* **ALL ALONG THE WATCHTOWER. / LONG HOT SUMMER NIGHT** [5] [–]
Nov 68. (d-lp) *(613 008-9) <6307>* **ELECTRIC LADYLAND** [6] Oct68 [1]
– And the gods made love / (Have you ever been to) Electric Ladyland / Crosstown traffic / Voodoo chile / Rainy day, dream away / 1983 (a merman I should turn to be) / Moon, turn the tide . . . gently gently away / Little Miss Strange / Long hot summer night / Come on / Gypsy eyes / The burning of the midnight lamp / Still raining still dreaming / House burning down / All along the watchtower / Voodoo chile (slight return). *(also iss.lp/lp; 613 010/017) (re-iss. Jun73 on 'Polydor'; 2657 012) (re-iss. Jan84 on 'Polydor'; 350011-2) (re-iss. Jul91 & Oct93 on 'Polydor' lp/c/cd; 847233-1/-4/-2) (re-iss. Apr97 on 'MCA' cd/c; MCD/MCC 11600) (hit UK No.47 in Aug97)*
Apr 69. (7") *(604 029) <0798>* **CROSSTOWN TRAFFIC. / GYPSY EYES** [37] Nov68 [52]
Oct 69. (7") *(604 033)* **(LET ME LIGHT YOUR) FIRE. / THE BURNING OF THE MIDNIGHT LAMP** [ ] [ ]
Feb 70. (7") *<0853>* **STONE FREE. / IF 6 WAS 9** [–] [ ]
Apr 70. (7") *<0905>* **STEPPING STONE. / IZABELLA** [–] [ ]

JIMI HENDRIX

retained **BUDDY MILES** + recruited **BILLY COX** – bass

Track | Capitol

Jun 70. (lp) *(2406 002) <472>* **BAND OF GYPSYS (live)** [6] Apr70 [5]
– Who knows / Machine gun / Changes / Power of soul / Message to love / We gotta live together. *(re-iss. Aug83 on 'Polydor'; SPELP 16) (cd-iss. May88; 821 933-2) (re-iss. Dec89 & Jul91 on 'Polydor' lp/c/cd; 847 237-1/-4/-2) (re-iss. Apr97 on 'MCA' cd/c; MCD/MCC 11607)*

—— on the 18th September 1970 HENDRIX died of a drug overdose

– (selective) compilations, etc. –

on 'Polydor' unless mentioned otherwise / 'Reprise' US

Feb 68. (lp; with CURTIS KNIGHT) *London; (HA 8349) / Capitol; <2856>* **GET THAT FEELING (live 1964)** [39] [75]
Oct 70. (7"; JIMI HENDRIX with CURTIS KNIGHT) *London; (HLZ 10321)* **BALLAD OF JIMI. / GLOOMY MONDAY** [ ] [ ]
Sep 70. (lp; shared w/ OTIS REDDING) *Reprise; <MS 2029>* **MONTEREY INTERNATIONAL POP FESTIVAL (live soundtrack)** [–] [16]
Oct 70. (7"m) *Track; (2095 001)* **VOODOO CHILE (SLIGHT RETURN). / HEY JOE / ALL ALONG THE WATCHTOWER** [1] [–]
Mar 71. (lp) *Track; (2408 101) <2034>* **THE CRY OF LOVE** [2] [3]
– Freedom / Drifting / Ezy rider / Night bird flying / My friend / Straight ahead / Astro man / Angel / In from the storm / Belly button window. *(re-iss. Jun73 on 'Polydor' lp)(c; 2302 023)(3194 025) (re-iss. Sep85 on 'Polydor lp/c; SPE LP/MC 98) (cd-iss. Mar89; 829 926-2) (re-iss. Jul91 & Mar93 on 'Polydor' cd/c/lp; 847242-2/-4/-1)*
Mar 71. (7") *Reprise; <1000>* **FREEDOM. / ANGEL** [–] [59]
Aug 71. (lp) *Ember; (NR 5057)* **EXPERIENCE (live)** [9] [–]
– The sunshine of your love / Room full of mirrors / Bleeding heart / Smashing of amps. *(re-iss. Sep79 on 'Bulldog'; BDL 4002) (cd-iss. Jan87 & Nov91; BDCD 40023) (cd-iss. Mar95 on 'Nectar';)*
Oct 71. (7") *Reprise; <1044>* **DOLLY DAGGER (live). / THE STAR SPANGLED BANNER (live)** [–] [74]
Oct 71. (7"ep) *Track; (2094 010)* **GYPSY EYES. / REMEMBER / PURPLE HAZE / STONE FREE** [35] [ ]
Nov 71. (lp) *Reprise; (K 44159) <2040>* **RAINBOW BRIDGE (live soundtrack)** [16] Oct71 [15]
– Dolly dagger / Earth blues / Pali gap / Room full of mirrors / The star spangled banner / Look over yonder / Hear my train a comin' / Hey baby (new rising sun). *(cd-iss. Mar87; K2 44159) (cd re-iss. Apr89 +=; 831 312-2)* – Izabella / (I'm not your) Steppin' stone.
Nov 71. (lp) *(2302 016)* **JIMI HENDRIX AT THE ISLE OF WIGHT (live)** [17] [–]
– Midnight lightning / Foxy lady / Lover man / Freedom / All along the watchtower / In from the storm. *(re-iss. Apr84 lp/c; SPE LP/MC 71) (cd-iss Mar89; 831 813-2) (re-iss. Jul91 & Mar93 cd/c/lp; 847 236-2/-4/-1)*
Jan 72. (lp) *(2302 018) <2049>* **HENDRIX IN THE WEST (live)** [7] [12]
– Johnny B. Goode / Lover man / Blue suede shoes / Voodoo chile (slight return) / The queen / Sergeant Pepper's lonely hearts club band / Little wing / Red house.

Feb 72. (7") *(2001 277)* **JOHNNY B. GOODE. / LITTLE WING** 35 –

Nov 72. (lp) *(2302 020)* <2103> **WAR HEROES** 23 48
– Bleeding heart / Highway chile / Tax free / Peter Gunn / Catastrophe / Stepping stone / Midnight / 3 little bears / Beginning / Izabella. *(re-iss. Aug83 on 'Polydor' lp/c; SPE LP/MC 4) (cd-iss. Mar89; 813 573-2) (re-iss. Jul91 cd/c/lp;) (re-iss. cd+c Mar93)*

Jul 73. (d-lp) *Reprise; (K 64017)* <6481> **SOUNDTRACK RECORDINGS FROM THE FILM 'JIMI HENDRIX'** 37 89
– Hey Joe / Red house / Purple haze / Johnny B. Goode / Like a rolling stone / The star spangled banner / Rock me / Wild thing / Machine gun / In from the storm / Hear my train a comin'.

Mar 75. (lp) *(2343 080)* **JIMI HENDRIX** 35 –

Sep 75. (lp) *(2310 398)* <2204> **CRASH LANDING** 35 Mar75 5
– Message to love / Somewhere over the rainbow / Crash landing / Coming down hard on me / Peace in Mississippi / With the power / Stone free again / Captain Coconut. *(re-iss. Mar83 lp/c; SPE LP/MC 94) (cd-iss. Mar89;) (cd-iss. Jun91 & Mar93 cd/c/lp; 847263-2/-4/-1)*

Nov 75. (lp) *(2310 415)* <2229> **MIDNIGHT LIGHTNING** 46 43
– Trashman / Midnight lightning / Hear my train a coming / Hey baby (new rising sun) / Blue suede shoes / Machine gun / Once I had a woman / Beginnings. *(re-iss. Mar89 lp/c/cd; 825 166-1/-4/-2)*

Aug 82. (d-lp) *C.B.S.; (88592) / Reprise;* <22306> **THE JIMI HENDRIX CONCERTS (live)** 16 79
– Fire / I don't live today / Red house / Stone free / Are you experienced? / Little wing / Voodoo chile (slight return) / Bleeding heart / Hey Joe / Wild thing / Hear my train a-comin'. *(re-iss. Aug89 on 'Media Motion' lp/c/cd; MEDIA/+C/CD 1) (re-iss. Feb90 on 'Castle' lp+=/c+=/cd+=; CCS LP/MC/CD 235)* – Foxy lady.

Feb 83. (lp/c) *(PODV/+C 6)* **SINGLES ALBUM** 77 –

Nov 88. (12"ep/cd-ep) *Strange Fruit; (SFPS/+CD 065)* **THE PEEL SESSIONS** –
– Radio One theme / Day tripper / Wait until tomorrow / Hear my train a'comin' / Spanish castle magic. *(cd re-iss. Apr96; same)*

Feb 89. (d-lp/c/cd) *Castle; (CCS LP/MC/CD 212) / Rykodisc;* <RALP 00782> **THE RADIO ONE SESSIONS** 30
– Stone free / Radio one theme / Day tripper / Killing floor / Love or confusion / Catfish blues / Drivin' south / Wait until tomorrow / Hear my train a-comin' / Hound dog / Fire / Hoochie coochie man / Purple haze / Spanish castle magic / Hey Joe / Foxy lady / The burning of the midnight lamp.

Nov 89. (5xlp/3xc/3xcd-box) *Castle; (HB LP/MC/CD 100)* **LIVE AND UNRELEASED – THE RADIO SHOWS (live)**

Mar 90. (7"/c-s) *(PO/+CS 71)* **CROSSTOWN TRAFFIC. / PURPLE HAZE** 61
(12"+=) *(PZ 71)* – All along the watchtower.
(cd-s++=) *(PZCD 71)* – Have you ever been (to Electric Ladyland).

Oct 90. (cd/c/lp) *(847 231-2/-4/-1)* **CORNERSTONES (1967-1970, FOUR YEARS THAT CHANGED THE MUSIC) (live)** 5
– Hey Joe / Foxy lady / Purple haze / The wind cries Mary / Have you ever been to (Electric Ladyland) / Crosstown traffic / All along the watchtower / Voodoo chile (slight return) / Star spangled banner / Stepping stone / Room full of mirrors / Ezy rider / Freedom / Drifting / In from the storm / Angel. *(cd+=/c+=)* – Fire (live) / Stone free (live).

Oct 90. (7"ep) *(PO 100)* **ALL ALONG THE WATCHTOWER. / VOODOO CHILE / HEY JOE** 52
(12"+=/c-s+=) *(POCS/PZCD 100)* – Crosstown traffic.

Nov 90. (4xcd-box) <9-26435-2> **LIFELINES: THE JIMI HENDRIX STORY (live)** –

Feb 91. (4xcd-box) *(847232-2)* **SESSIONS BOX – ARE YOU EXPERIENCED? / AXIS: BOLD AS LOVE / ELECTRIC LADYLAND / CRY OF LOVE**

Mar 91. (4xcd-box) *(847 235-2)* **FOOTLIGHTS (live)**
– JIMI PLAYS MONTEREY / ISLE OF WIGHT / BAND OF GYPSIES / LIVE AT WINTERLAND

Feb 92. (4xcd-box) *(511 763-2)* **STAGES (live)**
– (Stockholm 5 Sep'67 / Paris 29 Jan'68 / San Diego 24 May'69 / Atlanta 4 Jul'70)

Nov 92. (cd/c) *Polygram TV; (517235-2/-4) / M.C.A.;* <10829> **THE ULTIMATE EXPERIENCE** 25 Jul93 72
– All along the watchtower / Purple haze / Hey Joe / The wind cries Mary / Angel / Voodoo chile (slight return) / Foxy lady / Burning of the midnight lamp / Highway chile / Crosstown traffic / Castles made of sand / Long hot summer night / Red house / Manic depression / Gypsy eyes / Little wing / Fire / Wait until tomorrow / Star spangled banner (live) / Wild thing (live). *(re-iss. Sep95; same)*

Feb 94. (cd) *I.T.M.; (ITM 960004)* **PURPLE HAZE IN WOODSTOCK (live)**

Apr 94. (3xcd-box) *Pulsar; (PULSE 301)* **GREATEST HITS** –
'Polydor' (the ones not mentioned), were issued on 'M.C.A.' in US.

Apr 94. (cd/c) *(521037-2/-4)* <11060> **BLUES** 10 45

Aug 94. (cd/c) *(523384-2/-4)* <11063> **AT WOODSTOCK (live)** 32 37
– (introduction) / Fire / Izabella / Hear my train a comin' / Red house / Jam back at the house (beginnings) / Voodoo child (slight return) – Stepping stone / The star spangled banner / Purple haze / Woodstock improvisation / Villanova junction / Farewell.

Apr 95. (cd/c) *(527 520-2/-4)* <11236> **VOODOO SOUP** 66
– The new rising sun / Belly button window / Stepping stone / Freedom / Angel / Room full of mirrors / Midnight / Night bird flying / Drifting / Ezy rider / Pali gap / Message to love / Peace in Mississippi / In from the storm.

May 97. (cd/c/d-lp) *M.C.A.; (MCD/MCC/MCA2 11599)* **FIRST RAYS OF THE NEW RISING SUN** 37 49

Sep 97. (cd/c) *Telstar; (TTV CD/MC 2930)* **EXPERIENCE HENDRIX – THE BEST OF** 21
– Purple haze / Fire / The wind cries Mary / Hey Joe / All along the watchtower / Stone free / Crosstown traffic / Manic depression / Little wing / If six was nine / Foxy lady / Bold as love / Castles made of sand / Red house / Voodoo chile (slight return) / Freedom / Night bird flying / Angel / Dolly dagger / Star spangled banner.

Oct 97. (cd/c/d-lp) *M.C.A.; (MCD/MCC/MCA 11684)* **SOUTH SATURN DELTA** 51

Jun 98. (d-cd/d-c/t-lp) *M.C.A.;* <*(MCD/MCC/MCA 11742)*> **THE BBC SESSIONS** 42 50

Jun 98. (cd) *Charly; (CDGR 246)* **EXPERIENCE** (soundtrack) –
– Sunshine of your love / Bleeding heart / Fire / Little wing / Voodoo child (slight return) / Room full of mirrors / Purple haze / Wild thing / Smashing of the amps. *(re-iss. Feb00 on 'Brilliant'; BT 33045) (<re+US-iss.Feb01/Jul01 on 'Snapper'; SNAP 004>)*

Feb 99. (d-cd/d-c/t-lp) *M.C.A.;* <*(MCD/MCC/MCA 11931)*> **LIVE AT FILLMORE EAST** 65

Jul 99. (d-cd/d-c) *M.C.A.;* <*(MCD 11987)*> **JIMI HENDRIX LIVE AT WOODSTOCK (live)** 90
– (introduction) / Message to love / Hear my train a comin' / Spanish castle magic / Red house / Lover man / Foxy lady / Jam back at the house / Izabella / Fire / Voodoo child (slight return) / The star spangled banner / Purple haze / Woodstock improvisation / Villanova junction / Hey Joe.

Jul 99. (10x7"box) *M.C.A.; (MCA 55578)* **THE CLASSIC SINGLES COLLECTION**

Apr 00. (cd) *Stony Plain; (7253 20068-2)* **WOKE UP THIS MORNING AND FOUND MYSELF DEAD**

Sep 00. (4xcd-box/8xlp-box) *Universal TV;* <*(112316-2/-1)*> **EXPERIENCE HENDRIX: THE BEST OF JIMI HENDRIX** 10 78

May 01. (3xcd-box) *K-Box; (KBOX 3270)* **THE BEST OF JIMI HENDRIX** –

Jul 02. (d-cd) *M.C.A.; (170322-2) / Universal;* <*112603-2*> **VOODOO CHILD – THE JIMI HENDRIX COLLECTION** 10 May01
– Purple haze / Hey Joe / The wind cries Mary / Fire / Highway chile / Are you experienced? / Burning of the midnight lamp / Little wing / All along the watchtower / Crosstown traffic / Voodoo child (slight return) / Spanish castle magic / Stone free / Izabella / Band of gypsys / Stepping stone / Angel / Dolly dagger / Hey baby (new rising sun) / Fire (live) / Hey Joe (live) / I don't live today (live) / Hear my train a comin' (live) / Foxy lady (live) / Machine gun (live) / Johnny B. Goode (live) / Red house (live) / Freedom (live) / Purple haze (live) / Star spangled banner (live) / Wild thing (live).

Nov 03. (cd) *Universal;* <*(006980-2)*> **MARTIN SCORSESE PRESENTS THE BLUES**

Apr 04. (d-cd) *Purple Haze; (HAZE 002CD)* **AXIS OUTTAKES**

Sep 04. (d-cd) *Snapper; (SNAD 539CD)* **THE ALBERT HALL EXPERIENCE**

Nov 04. (d-cd) *Purple Haze; (HAZE 006CD)* **AM I BLUE**

□ Don HENLEY (see under ⇒ EAGLES)

H.I.M.

Formed: Helsinki, Finland . . . 1991 as the brainchild of VILLE HERMANNI VALO, together with LILY LAZER and MIGE AMOUR. By the mid 90s, an expanded line-up (including JUHANA TUOMAS "PATKA" RANTALA and ANTTO EINARI MELASNIEMI), signed to 'B.M.G.' and delivered their first release, the EP '666 WAYS TO LOVE: PROLOGUE', in 1996. The hopefully titled debut LP, 'GREATEST LOVESONGS, VOL.666' (1997), carried on the satanic theme and occult trimmings; despite the fact that H.I.M. was reputed to stand for His Infernal Majesty, the Finnish quintet's sound was more 80s hair-metal than hellish. While a cover of Blue Oyster Cult's '(DON'T FEAR) THE REAPER' was credible enough, the choice of Chris Isaak's 'WICKED GAME' as a single wasn't exactly demonic. Towards the end of the millennium, two pseudonymous new members (ZOLTAN PLUTO and GAS LIPSTICK) were in place for a follow-up set, 'RAZORBLADE ROMANCE', in early 2000. Both the Germans and the Finns themselves were sold on its Euro-goth agenda, with the track 'JOIN ME IN DEATH' going on to become the biggest selling single in Finnish rock history. In America, meanwhile, the record was released under the H.E.R. moniker (due to a legal battle over their name) by JIMMY POP of the BLOODHOUND GANG. 2001 saw yet another personnel change with EMERSON BURTON superseding PLUTO for third LP, 'DEEP SHADOWS AND BRILLIANT HIGHLIGHTS' (2002), more noteworthy for VALO's transformation into a sub-Johnny Depp teen heart-throb. 'LOVE METAL' (2003) finally broke the Scandinavian sorcerers in Britain, with a trio of singles, 'BURIED ALIVE BY LOVE', 'THE SACRAMENT' and 'THE FUNERAL OF HEARTS', all hitting the Top 30. H.I.M. subsequently became the latest act to stylize a Neil Diamond song, going Top 10 with 'SOLITARY MAN' (a track included on compilation 'AND LOVE SAID NO . . . 1997-2004'). The band's self-styled "Love Metal" was actually camouflage for an unashamedly revisionist trawl through the 80s, as overseen by U2/ROBERT PLANT producer Tim Palmer on 2005's 'DARK LIGHT', a transatlantic Top 20 success. It had to happen sometime: the mouldy corpses of MIDGE URE's ULTRAVOX and the MISSION were re-animated on UK Top 30 singles such as 'WINGS OF A BUTTERFLY' and 'KILLING LONELINESS'.

• **Covers:** REBEL YELL (Billy Idol) / POISON HEART (Ramones).

Album rating: GREATEST LOVESONGS, VOL.666 (*7) / RAZORBLADE ROMANCE (*5) / DEEP SHADOWS AND BRILLIANT HIGHLIGHTS (*4) / LOVE METAL (*7) / AND LOVE SAID NO . . . 1997-2004 compilation (*7) / DARK LIGHT (*6)

VILLE VALO (b.22 Nov'76) – vocals / **LILY LAZER** (aka MIKKO VILJAMI "LINDE" LINDSTROM, b.12 Aug'76) – guitar / **ANTTO EINARI MELASNIEMI** – keyboards / **MIGE AMOUR** (b. MIKKO HENRIK JULIUS PAANANEN) – bass / **JUHANA TUOMAS "PATKA" RANTALA** – drums

B.M.G. B.M.G.

Oct 96. (cd-ep) **666 WAYS TO LOVE: PROLOGUE** [–] Fin [–]
– Stigmata diaboli / Wicked game / Dark sekret love / The heartless.

1997. (cd-s) **WHEN LOVE AND DEATH EMBRACE / (mix)** [–] Fin [–]

Nov 97. (cd) *(74321 62348-2)* <58914> **GREATEST LOVESONGS, VOL.666** [–] 1998 [ ]
– Your sweet six six six / Wicked game / The heartless / Our diabolical rapture / It's all tears (drown in this love) / When love and death embrace / The beginning of the end / (Don't fear) The reaper / For you. *(UK-iss.Jun00; same)*

1998. (cd-s) **YOUR SWEET SIX SIX SIX / BEGINNING OF THE END (Tandeberg B74 mix) / BEGINNING OF THE END (Satanik love mix)** [–] Fin [–]

Sep 98. (cd-ep) **WICKED GAME / FOR YOU / OUR DIABOLIKAL RAPTURE / WICKED GAME (video)** [–] Fin [–]

1999. (cd-s) **IT'S ALL TEARS (DROWN IN THIS LOVE) / THE HEARTLESS (club remix)** [–] Fin [–]

—— (1998) **ZOLTAN PLUTO** (aka JUSSI-MIKKO "JUSKA" SALMINIERI) – keyboards; repl. ANTTO

—— (1999) **GAS LIPSTICK** (b. MIKA KARPPINEN) – drums; repl. JUHANA

R.C.A. R.C.A.

1999. (cd-ep) *(74321 70454-2)* **JOIN ME / IT'S ALL TEARS (unplugged) / REBEL YELL (live) / DARK SEKRET LOVE** [–] Fin [–]

—— next released as H.E.R. in the USA

May 00. (cd) *(74321 79060-2)* *<73221>* **RAZORBLADE ROMANCE** [ ] [ ]
– Your sweet 666 (2000 re-recording) / Poison girl / Join me in death / Right here in my arms / Bury me deep inside your heart / Wicked game (2000 re-recording) / I love you (prelude to tragedy) / Gone with the sin / Razorblade kiss / Resurrection / Death is in love with us / Heaven tonight. *<US+=>* – Sigillum diaboli / One last time / The 9th circle (HER version).

2000. (cd-s) **RIGHT HERE IN MY ARMS / I'VE CROSSED OCEANS OF WINE TO FIND YOU / SIGILLUM DIABOLI** [–] Fin [–]

2000. (cd-s) **POISON GIRL / RIGHT HERE IN MY ARMS (live) / IT'S ALL TEARS (live)** [–] Fin [–]

2000. (cd-s) **GONE WITH THE SIN / GONE WITH THE SIN (O.D. version) / FOR YOU (acoustic) / GONE WITH THE SIN (version)** [–] Fin [–]

—— in 2001, LINDSTROM (aka DANIEL LIONEYE) released an album

—— (2001) **JANNE PUURTINEN** (b. EMERSON BURTON) – keyboards; repl. ZOLTAN

2001. (cd-ep) *(74321 86512-2)* **PRETENDING / PRETENDING (alt.) / PRETENDING (the cosmic Pope jam version) / PLEASE DON'T LET IT GO (acoustic) / LOOSE YOU TONIGHT (caravan version)** [–] Euro [–]

Feb 02. (cd) *(74321 87749-2)* *<87933-2>* **DEEP SHADOWS AND BRILLIANT HIGHLIGHTS** [ ] Mar02 [ ]
– Salt in our wounds / Heartache every moment / Lose you tonight / In joy and sorrow / Pretending / Close to the flame / Please don't let it go / Beautiful / Don't close your heart / Love you like I do.

2002. (cd-ep) *(74321 91249-2)* **HEARTACHE EVERY MOMENT** [–] Sweden [–]
– Heartache every moment / Close to the flame / acoustic:- Salt in our wounds / In joy and sorrow / Pretending / Heartache every moment / Close to the flame / videos:- Heartache every moment / Close to the flame.

Apr 03. (cd) *(82876 50501-2)* **LOVE METAL** [55] 2005 [ ]
– Buried alive by love / The funeral of hearts / Beyond redemption / Sweet pandemonium / Soul on fire / The sacrament / This fortress of tears / Circle of fear / Endless dark / The path.

May 03. (cd-s) *(82876 52316-2)* **BURIED ALIVE BY LOVE / BURIED ALIVE BY LOVE (live in Finland)** [30] [–]
(82876 52316-5) – ('A') / Join me (Razorblade mix) / Rebel yell (live).

Sep 03. (cd-s) *(82876 55880-2)* **THE SACRAMENT / SIGILLIUM DIABOLI / ONE LAST TIME / THE SACRAMENT (video)** [23] [–]
(cd-s) *(82876 55889-2)* – ('A') / Again / In joy & sorrow (string version) / In joy & sorrow (video).
(10") *(82876 59692-4)* – ('A') / Please don't let it go / The 9th circle.

Jan 04. (7") *(82876 58579-7)* **THE FUNERAL OF HEARTS. / BURIED ALIVE BY LOVE (Deliverance version)** [15] [–]
(cd-s) *(82876 58579-2)* – ('A') / Hand of doom (live in Turku).
(dvd-s) *(82876 58579-5)* – ('A'-video) / Join me (ice version – video) / (video; making of..) / Lonely road (live) / ('A'-acoustic) / ('A'-Dr. Dagon's dub).

Mar 04. (cd) *(82876 60606-2)* **AND LOVE SAID NO . . . 1997-2004** (compilation) [30] [ ]
– And love said no / Join me / Buried alive by love / Heartache every moment / Solitary man / Right here in my arms / The funeral of hearts / In joy and sorrow / Your sweet 666 / Gone with the sin / Wicked game / The sacrament / Close to the flame / It's all tears *[UK-only]* / Poison girl / Pretending / When love and death embrace. *(ltd-cd w/dvd+=; 82876 60610-2)* – (DVD tracks).

Apr 04. (etched-7") *(82876 61065-7)* **SOLITARY MAN** [9] [–]
(cd-s+=) *(82876 61065-2)* – Please don't let it go (punk rock version – live).
(dvd-s+=) *(82876 61065-9)* – ('A'-video) / Right here in my arms (video) / (Bam Marguera's making of Buried Alive By Love video) / (slideshow) / Your sweet 666 (live October 15, 2003).

		Warners	Warners
Sep 05.	(7"pic-d/cd-s) *(W 686/+CD1)* **WINGS OF A BUTTERFLY. / POISON HEART**	10	97
	(cd-s) *(W 686CD2)* – ('A') / And love said no (616 version) / Vampire heart (live) / ('A'-video).		
Sep 05.	(cd) *(<9362 49284-2>)* **DARK LIGHT**	18	18
	– Vampire heart / Rip out the wings of a butterfly / Under the rose / Killing loneliness / Dark light / Behind the crimson door / Face of God / Drunk on shadows / Play ahead / In the nightside of Eden. *(re-iss. Dec05 +=; 9362 48436-2)* – The cage. *(d-lp iss.May06 ++=; 9362 49284-1)* – Venus (in our blood) / Poison heart.		
Nov 05.	(etched-7") *(W 697)* **VAMPIRE HEART**		–
Apr 06.	(7"blue/cd-s) *(W 699/+CD1)* **KILLING LONELINESS. / UNDER THE ROSE (live at the Electric Factory, Philadelphia)**	26	–
	(cd-s) *(W 699CD2)* – ('A') / Rip the wings of a butterfly (live) / Play dead (live) / ('A'-video).		

– compilations, etc. –

Nov 02.	(10xcd-s; box) *B.M.G.; (74321 96173-2)* **THE SINGLES SET**		–
Sep 04.	(3xcd-box) *R.C.A.; (82876 64985-2)* **BOX SET**		
	– (RAZORBLADE ROMANCE / DEEP SHADOWS & BRILLIANT HIGHLIGHTS / LOVESONGS, VOL.666)		

□ HINDU LOVE GODS (see under ⇒ R.E.M.)

the HIVES

Formed: Fagersta, Sweden . . . 1993 by NICHOLAUS ARSON, his brother HOWLIN' PELLE ALMQVIST – later, CHRIS DANGEROUS, DR. MATT DESTRUCTION AND VIGILANTE CARLSTROEM were added to the line-up. Owing as much style and zeitgeist to the STOOGES, the KINKS and the ROLLING STONES as the STROKES did, this punky, mod-looking collective were banging out quasi-garage rock tunes before the STROKES had even left private school. In hindsight, possibly the only reason the HIVES became so popular after four years of industry/consumer ignorance was because of the Garage rock explosion during the summer of 2001, but, unlike the dull-ish LOU REED drone of the STROKES, the HIVES partied like it was 1969 . . . and boy did they rock some! Clad in Al Capone gangster uniform (black suit, white tie, naturally), the HIVES originally began playing rock'n'roll to annoy the commercial punk pundits who sifted around their hometown of Fagersta. After an inaugural EP in '96 ('OH LORD! WHEN? HOW?'), the quintet issued their debut album 'BARELY LEGAL' in September 1997 and practically became local heroes, selling-out clubs and venues and rocking up a storm with the Swedish music press. Soon the word spread like wildfire around Scandinavia and the HIVES issued 'aka I-D-I-O-T' as a mini-set at the beginning of '98. A thrash blend of rawk'n'roll and punk, the release was to be the band's last for almost two years as they began to experience management problems. However, this break turned out to be a blessing in disguise as they re-emerged in 2000 with a killer album and a re-invented, semi-fictional history involving a mysterious MONKEES-esque manufacturing. 'VENI VIDI VICIOUS' smacked the European music press in the face with its screeeeching guitars, fuzz-bass and hollering, but nobody seemed to be paying any attention – for now. The British music buying public missed the soaring KINKS driven anthems that were 'HATE TO SAY I TOLD YOU SO' and 'MAIN OFFENDER' the first time around when they were issued as singles in 2000 and 2001, but thanks to a Garage-rock revival, a few TV promos and ALAN McGEE (now boss at the newly-formed 'Poptones' imprint), the HIVES legacy was finally realised with the premiere of their "Best Of . . ." compilation 'YOUR NEW FAVOURITE BAND' (2001, and a title taking a subtle dig at the histrionic coverage that the STROKES received in the NME). The two aforementioned singles were re-released the following year to – hurrah! – critical acclaim, which just shows that sometimes you can't just lead a horse to the water, you have to make it drink the damn thing as well. Inking a honeypot deal with 'Polydor' ('Interscope' in the US), ALMQVIST and his killer buzz returned with the short, sharp sting of 'TYRANNOSAURUS HIVES' (2004), more spastic garage than MARC BOLAN. A UK Top 10 (US Top 40!), the record spawned a couple of hits, 'WALK IDIOT WALK, 'TWO-TIMING TOUCH AND BROKEN BONES' – the BOOMTOWN RATS revival starts here.

• **Trivia:** Their mysterious 6th member/writer, FITZSIMMONS was actually mainman PELLE who seemingly took the name of his old school teacher.

Album rating: BARELY LEGAL (*7) / a.k.a. I-D-I-O-T mini (*5) / VENI VIDI VICIOUS (*8) / YOUR NEW FAVOURITE BAND compilation (*8) / TYRANNOSAURUS HIVES (*7)

HOWLIN' PELLE ALMQVIST (b.29 May'79) – vocals / **NICHOLAUS ARSON** (b. ALMQVIST) – guitar / **VIGILANTE CARLSTROEM** – guitar / **DR MATT DESTRUCTION** – bass / **CHRIS DANGEROUS** – drums

		Burning Heart	Gearhead
Jun 96.	(cd-ep) *(JABSCD 001)* **OH LORD! WHEN? HOW?**		–
	– You think you're so darn special / Cellblock / Some people / How will I cope with that? / Bearded lady / Let me go.		
Sep 97.	(cd) *(BHR 068CD)* **BARELY LEGAL**		–
	– Well, well, well / a.k.a. I-D-I-O-T / Here we go again / I'm a wicked one / Automatic schmuck / King of asskissing / Hail hail spit n' drool / Black Jack / What's that spell? . . . go to hell! / Theme from . . . / Uptempo venomous poison / Oh Lord! when? how? / The stomp / Closed for the season. *<(US+re-iss. cd/lp-iss.Mar01/Jan02 on 'Gearhead'; RPM 030 CD/LP)>*		
Mar 98.	(m-cd,m-lp) *(BHR 072)* *<RPM 023>* **a.k.a. I-D-I-O-T**		
	– a.k.a. I-D-I-O-T / Outsmarted / Untutored youth / Fever / Mad man / Numbers. *(re-iss. Mar01 on 'Gearhead' m-lp/m-cd; same as US)*		
Apr 00.	(cd/lp) *(BHR 107-2/-1)* *<82005-2>* **VENI VIDI VICIOUS**		Sep00
	– The Hives – declare guerre nucleaire / Die, all right! / A get together to tear it apart / Main offender / Outsmarted / Hate to say I told you so / The Hives – introduce the metric system in time / Find another girl / Statecontrol / Inspection wise 1999 / Knock knock / Supply and demand. *(lp re-iss. Jul02 on 'Gearhead'; RPM 040LP)(hit US No.63)*		
Dec 00.	(7"/cd-s) *(BHR 122-2)* *<RPM 024/+CD>* **HATE TO SAY I TOLD YOU SO. / DIE, ALL RIGHT! / THE HIVES ARE LAW, YOU ARE CRIME**		
	(re-iss. Jan02 on 'Gearhead'; same as US)		
Sep 01.	(cd-s) *(BHR 134-2)* **MAIN OFFENDER / LOST AND FOUND / HOWLIN' PELLE TALKS TO THE KIDS**		–
		Poptones	Poptones
Sep 01.	(7") *(MC 50555)* **SUPPLY AND DEMAND. / THE STOMP**		–
Oct 01.	(cd) *(<MC 5055CD>)* **YOUR NEW FAVOURITE BAND** (compilation)	7	Apr02
	– Hate to say I told you so / Main offender / Supply and demand / Die, all right! / Untutored youth / Outsmarted / Mad man / Here we go again / a.k.a. I-D-I-O-T / Automatic schmuck / Hail hail spit n' drool / Hives are law you are crime. *(cd bonus+=)* – Main offender (video) / Hate to say I told you so (video) / a.k.a. I-D-I-O-T (video) / Die, all right! (video). *(lp-iss.Mar02; MC 5055LP)*		
Nov 01.	(7") *(7SN 006)* **MAIN OFFENDER. / LOST AND FOUND / HOWLIN' PELLE TALKS TO THE KIDS**		–
	(above issued on 'Sweet Nothing') (re-iss. Dec01 on 'Big Wheel' 7"/cd-s; BWR 0248/+CD)		
Feb 02.	(7") *(BHR 1058-7)* **HATE TO SAY I TOLD YOU SO. / UPTEMPO VENOMOUS POISON**	23	86
	(cd-s+=) *(BHR 1057-2)* – Gninrom ytic kcorknup.		
	(cd-s) *(BHR 1059-2)* – ('A'side) / Fever / Barely homosapien.		
	(above issued on 'Burning Heart') (below on 'Hard On' records)		
Mar 02.	(7"ep; split w/ PRICKS) *(HARDON 2)* **3:30 PUNK ROCK CITY MORNING / GNINROM YTIC KCOR KNUP 3:30 / NUMBERS. / (other side by the Pricks)**		–
May 02.	(7") *(MC 5076S)* **MAIN OFFENDER. / LOST AND FOUND**	24	–
	(cd-s+=) *(MC 5076SCD)* – Hate to say I told you so (live on Top Of The Pops + video).		
Oct 02.	(cd-s) *(MC 5078SCD)* **DIE, ALL RIGHT! / SUPPLY AND DEMAND**		–

		Polydor	Interscope
Jul 04.	(7"white) *(9867039)* **WALK IDIOT WALK. / GENE POOL CONVULSIONS**	13	–
	(cd-s+=) *(9867038)* – Keel hauling class of '89 / ('A'-video).		
Jul 04.	(cd/lp) *(98669 91/88)* *<27560-2>* **TYRANNOSAURUS HIVES**	7	33
	– Abra cadaver / Two-timing touch and broken bones / Walk idiot walk / No pun intended / A little more for little you / B is for Brutus / See through head / Diabolic scheme / Missing link / Love in plaster / Dead quote Olympics / Antidote. *(UK cd+=)* – Up tight / The Hives meet the Norm.		
Oct 04.	(7") *(9868352)* **TWO-TIMING TOUCH AND BROKEN BONES. / BORN TO CRY**	44	–
	(cd-s+=) *(9868351)* – Little Lil / ('A'-video).		

HOLE

Formed: Los Angeles, California, USA . . . late 1989 by COURTNEY LOVE (bizarrely enough, a two-piece indie band of the same moniker – see under LOIS – surfaced with a few 45's a year later!) and six foot plus guitarist and Capitol records employee, ERIC ERLANDSON. LOVE, who had previously worked as an exotic dancer and an actress (she appeared in the 1986 punk movie, 'Sid & Nancy') and played alongside JENNIFER FINCH (L7) and KAT BJELLAND (Babes In Toyland) in a band called SUGAR BABY DOLL, was also involved in an early incarnation of FAITH NO MORE. Taking the name HOLE from a line in Euripides' Medea, they placed an ad in a local paper, 'Flipside', finding a bassist and drummer, namely JILL EMERY and CAROLINE RUE. In the Spring of 1990, HOLE released the 'RAT BASTARD' EP, subsequently relocating to the burgeoning Seattle area. Early the following year, 'Sub Pop' issued the 'DICKNAIL' EP, the band duly signing to 'Caroline' records for their debut album, 'PRETTY ON THE INSIDE'. Produced by KIM GORDON and DON FLEMING, it hit the lower regions of the US charts, the record being voted album of the year by New York's Village Voice magazine. A harrowing primal howl of a record, LOVE's demons were confronted mercilessly on such psyche-trawling dirges as 'TEENAGE WHORE' and 'GARBAGE MAN'. Around the same time, LOVE's relationship with NIRVANA's KURT COBAIN, was the talk of the alternative rock world, the singer subsequently marrying him in February '92, giving birth to his daughter, Frances Bean, later that summer. The following year, with newcomers PATTY SCHEMEL (drums) and KRISTEN PFAFF (bass), the group secured a deal with the David Geffen Company ('D.G.C.'), much to the dismay of MADONNA who wanted HOLE for her newly formed 'Maverick' label. In Spring 1994, LOVE finally celebrated a UK Top 20 album, 'LIVE THROUGH THIS', although its success was overshadowed by the shocking suicide of KURT on the 8th of April. She subsequently held a memorial two days later, hailing everyone there to call him an asshole. More press coverage followed later that summer, when PFAFF was found dead in her bath on the 16th June (it was believed to be another tragic drug related death). Despite the press circus surrounding LOVE, the band played a rather disappointing Reading Festival stint in August that year, her at times lethargic vox letting some of the more discerning fans down (EVAN DANDO of The LEMONHEADS was rumoured to be her new boyfriend, although a number of lucky people – including DANDO – were privy to her womanly charms – both of them – when she "flashed" at the side of the stage). With a new bassist, MELISSA AUF DER MAUR, the group released two UK hits, 'DOLL PARTS' and 'VIOLET', LOVE certainly back on top form with her incendiary Top Of The Pops performances (LYDIA LUNCH eat your heart out!?). Back in the news again, she was fined for assaulting BIKINI KILL's KATHLEEN HANNA, LOVE and SCHEMEL conversely taking three security guards to court following an alleged assault incident while signing autographs stagefront at a GREEN DAY concert in Lakefront Arena (yet more column inches were devoted to the controversial singer in August '96, when LOVE was acquitted of a stage assault nine months previous on two teenage fans in Florida). More recently, LOVE has played down her wild child character, exchanging the Seattle grunge mantle for a more respectable Hollywood career. This was largely down to her acclaimed roles in the movies, 'Feeling Minnesota' and more so with the controversial, 'The People Vs. Larry Flint'. On the recording front, only a lone version of FLEETWOOD MAC's 'GOLD DUST WOMAN' has surfaced (this was included on the film soundtrack from 'The Crow II: City Of Angels'). In '98, COURTNEY (and HOLE) was once again writing new material, this time with BILLY CORGAN of the SMASHING PUMPKINS, although a dispute over who actually wrote what the public thought were collaborations was subsequent tabloid news. The album in question, 'CELEBRITY SKIN' (1998), was worthy of its Top 10 placing although a little commercialised for some. The following year (in November), MELISSA bailed out of the band and more shocking still was that she joined COURTNEY's old pal CORGAN in the SMASHING PUMPKINS. After a Golden Globe performance in the movie 'The People Vs. Larry Flynt' in '99, LOVE subsequently entered a legal wrangle over her dead husband's legacy once again. She tried to halt CHRIS NOVOSELIC and DAVE GROHL as they prepared to mix two new NIRVANA tracks and issue a 'Best Of . . .' compendium. Opening the situation up to the press as well as the television media, LOVE sought even more attention by publicly warring with the ex-NIRVANA casualties. However, it was all in vain as a settlement was agreed by both camps, leaving our favourite female rock'n'roll attention-seeker to direct her anger towards her own record company (whom she sued), before getting arrested over drug-related offences during 2002-03. On the songwriting front, ex-4 NON BLONDES dame, LINDA PERRY, was recruited to shore up her long vaunted solo debut, the narcissistically titled (and illustrated) 'AMERICA'S SWEETHEART' (2004). Various court appearances and er.. court non-appearances didn't exactly make for a smooth promotional schedule while underwhelming reviews helped relegate the album to the fringes of both the US and UK Top 50. She was never far away from the tabloid spotlight, though, an alleged, short-lived romance with Radio Norwich's star presenter Alan "a-ha" Partridge (alias comedian Steve Coogan) plastered all over Britain's newspapers in August 2005 – rumours which were subsequently refuted by both parties.

• **Covers:** STAR BELLY sampled DREAMS (Fleetwood Mac) + INTO THE BLACK (Neil Young) / DO IT CLEAN (Echo & The Bunnymen) / CREDIT IN THE STRAIGHT WORLD (Young Marble Giants) / HUNGRY LIKE THE WOLF (Duran Duran) / SEASON OF THE WITCH (Donovan) / HE HIT ME (IT FELT LIKE A KISS) (Goffin-King) / IT'S ALL OVER NOW, BABY BLUE (Bob Dylan). 'I THINK THAT I WOULD DIE' was co-written w / KAT BJELLAND (Babes In Toyland). • **Note:** Not to be confused with band who released in the late 80's; OTHER TONGUES, OTHER FLESH (LP) and DYSKINSIA (12") both on 'Eyes Media'.

Album rating: PRETTY ON THE INSIDE (*7) / LIVE THROUGH THIS (*9) / MY BODY, THE HAND GRENADE collection (*6) / CELEBRITY SKIN (*7) / Courtney Love: AMERICA'S SWEETHEART (*4)

COURTNEY LOVE (b. MICHELLE HARRISON, 9 Jul'64, San Francisco, Calif.) – vocals, guitars / **ERIC ERLANDSON** (b. 9 Jan'63) – guitars / **JILL EMERY** – bass, vocals / **CAROLINE RUE** – drums

		not iss.	Sympathy
Jul 90.	(7"white-ep) *<SFTRI 53>* **RETARD GIRL. / PHONEBILL SONG / JOHNNIES IN THE BATHROOM**	–	
	(UK-iss.cd-ep Sep97 +=; SFTRI 53CD) – Turpentine.		
		not iss.	Sub Pop
Apr 91.	(7"colrd-various) *(SP 93)* **DICKNAIL. / BURNBLACK**	–	
		City Slang	Caroline
Aug 91.	(7"colrd-various) *(EFA 04070-45)* **TEENAGE WHORE. / DROWN SODA**		

(12"+=/cd-s+=) *(EFA 04070-02/-03)* – Burnblack.

Oct 91. (cd/c/lp-some red) *(EFA 0407-2/-C/-1)* <SLANG 012>
PRETTY ON THE INSIDE 59 Jul91 [ ]
– Teenage whore / Babydoll / Garbage man / Sassy / Goodsister – bad sister / Mrs. Jones / Berry / Loaded / Star belly / Pretty on the inside / Clouds. *(re-iss. Sep95; same)*

— **LESLEY** – bass repl. JILL / **PATTY SCHEMEL** (b.24 Apr'67, Seattle Washington) – drums repl. CAROLINE

City Slang D.G.C.

Apr 93. (7") *(EFA 04916-45)* **BEAUTIFUL SON. / OLD AGE** 54 –
(12"+=/cd-s+=) *(EFA 04916-02/-03)* – 20 years in the Dakota.

— **KRISTEN PFAFF** – bass, piano, vocals repl. LESLEY

Mar 94. (7"some pink) *(EFA 04936-7)* **MISS WORLD. / ROCK STAR (alternate mix)** 64 [ ]
(cd-s+=) *(EFA 04936-2)* – Do it clean (live).

Apr 94. (cd/c/lp;some white) *(EFA 04935-2/-4/-1)* <24631>
LIVE THROUGH THIS 13 52
– Violet / Miss World / Plump / Asking for it / Jennifer's body / Doll parts / Credit in the straight world / Softer, softest / She walks on me / I think that I would die / Gutless / Rock star. *(re-iss. cd/lp Mar95 on 'Geffen'; GED/GEF 24631)*

— KRISTEN was found dead in her bath 16th June 1994. COURTNEY, ERIC + PATTI continued and later recruited **MELISSA AUF DER MAUR** (b.17 Mar'72, Montreal, Canada) – bass. As HOLEZ (HOLE + PAT SMEAR of GERMS) they released tribute GERMS cover 'CIRCLE 1' on 'Dutch East India' Mar95.

Geffen D.G.C.

Nov 94. (c-s) *<19379>* **DOLL PARTS / PLUMP (live)** – 58

Apr 95. (7") *(GFS 91)* **DOLL PARTS. / THE VOID** 16 –
(cd-s+=) *(GFSTD 91)* – Hungry like the wolf (live).
(cd-s) *(GFSXD 91)* – ('A'side) / Plump (live) / I think that I would die (live) / Credit in the straight world (live).

Jul 95. (7") *(GFS 94)* **VIOLET. / OLD AGE** 17 [ ]
(7"colrd) *(GFSP 94)* – ('A'side) / He hit me (it felt like a kiss).
(cd-s++=) *(GFSCD 94)* – Who's porno you burn (black).

Nov 96. (etched-d7") *(573164-7)* **GOLD DUST WOMAN. / (NY LOOSE: Spit)** [ ] [ ]
(above 45 was a limited edition on 'Polydor' UK, 'Hollywood' US)

Sep 98. (7"/c-s) *(GFS/+C 22345)* *<radio play>* **CELEBRITY SKIN. / BEST SUNDAY DRESS** 19 85
(cd-s+=) *(GFSTD 22345)* – Dying (original demo).

Sep 98. (cd/c/lp) *<(GED/GEC/GEF 25164)>* **CELEBRITY SKIN** 11 9
– Celebrity skin / Awful / Hit so hard / Malibu / Reasons to be beautiful / Dying / Use once & destroy / Northern star / Boys on the radio / Heaven tonight / Playing your song / Petals. *(special cd w/tour cd Jun99 +=; IND 90385)* – Pretty on the inside / Heaven tonight / Northern star / Awful / Paradise city / Celebrity skin.

Jan 99. (7") *(GFS 22369)* *<radio cut>* **MALIBU. / DRAG** 22 81
(cd-s+=) *(GFSTD 22369)* – It's all over now, baby blue.
(cd-s) *(GFSCX 22369)* – ('A') / Celebrity skin (live) / Reasons to be beautiful (live).

Interscope Interscope

Jun 99. (7") *(INTS7 97098)* **AWFUL. / VIOLET (live)** 42 [ ]
(cd-s) *(INTDE 97099)* – ('A') / Miss World (live) / Celebrity skin (video).
(cd-s) *(INTDE 97098)* – ('A') / She walks on me (live) / Malibu (video).

– compilations, etc. –

Oct 95. (m-cd) *Caroline; <1470>* **ASK FOR IT** (radio session) – [ ]

Sep 97. (cd/c/lp) *City Slang; <(EFA 04995-2/-4/-1)>* **MY BODY, THE HAND GRENADE** [ ] Oct97 [ ]
– Turpentine / Phonebill song / Retard girl / Burn black / Dicknail / Beautiful son / 20 years in Dakota / Miss World / Old age / Softer softest / He hit me (it felt like a kiss) / Season of the witch / Drown soda / Asking for it.

COURTNEY LOVE

Virgin Virgin

Feb 04. (cd) *(CDVUS 249)* *<91459>* **AMERICA'S SWEETHEART** 56 53
– Mono / But Julian, I'm a little bit older than you / Hold on to me / Sunset Strip / All the drugs / Almost golden / I'll do anything / Uncool / Life despite God / Hello / Zeplin song / Never gonna be the same.

Mar 04. (7"pink)<cd-s> *(VUS 283)* *<548290>* **MONO / FLY** 41 [ ]
(cd-s+=) *(VUSDX 283)* – ('A'-alt) / ('A'-video).

the HOLLIES

Formed: Manchester, England . . . 1961 by ALLAN CLARKE and GRAHAM NASH, who quickly found DON RATHBONE and ERIC HAYCOCK. In 1963, they signed to EMI's 'Parlophone' label, adding a 5th member, TONY HICKS. Their debut 45, '(AIN'T THAT) JUST LIKE ME', made the UK Top 30, being followed by 'SEARCHIN'', their first of 21 consecutive Top 20 hits until 1971's 'HEY WILLY' (later a hit for the SWEET as 'Little Willy') failed to register. During the early part of their career, The HOLLIES were basically a pop industry beat group, jumping on the psychedelic bandwagon in 1968 with the mythical pretentiousness of 'KING MIDAS IN REVERSE'. However, following the departure of NASH, they increasingly moved into the cabaret scene. They regained a bit of credibility in late 1969, however, with the much-loved ballad, 'HE AIN'T HEAVY'. In December '71, CLARKE left for the first time, returning in mid-73 after his Swedish replacement MICHAEL RICKFORS failed to impress the buying public. They immediately reinstated themselves when a Top 30 hit was followed by near No.1 smash, 'THE AIR THAT I BREATHE'. Although future hits were few and far between, they ploughed on throughout the 70's and 80's, even returning to the top of the UK charts in 1988 with the ad-friendly 'HE AIN'T HEAVY'. Not really an album kind of band (1983's 'WHAT GOES AROUND' put the lid on their earlier career), it was all the more surprising when they re-emerged in 2006 with the more rock-centric 'STAYING POWER'.

• **Songwriters:** CLARKE-HICKS-NASH, until latter's departure to CROSBY, STILLS & NASH. HOLLIES covered; (AIN'T THAT) JUST LIKE ME + SEARCHIN' (Coasters) / STAY (Maurice Williams & The Zodiacs) / JUST ONE LOOK (Doris Troy) / YES I WILL (Goffin-Titelman) / I'M ALIVE (Clint Ballard Jr.) / LOOK THROUGH ANY WINDOW + BUS STOP (Graham Gouldman) / IF I NEEDED SOMEONE (George Harrison; Beatles) / I CAN'T LET GO + THE BABY (Chip Taylor) / SORRY SUZANNE (T.MacAuley & G.Stephens) / GASOLINE ALLEY BRED (T.MacAuley-R.Cook-R.Greenaway) / WHEN THE SHIP COMES IN (Bob Dylan) / JESUS WAS A CROSSMAKER (Judee Sill) / SANDY (Bruce Springsteen) / STOP IN THE NAME OF LOVE (Supremes) / SOLDIER'S SONG (Mike Batt) / CARRIE (John Miles) / STAND BY ME (Ben E.King) / SHINE SILENTLY (Nils Lofgren) / etc. Also cover albums 'HOLLIES SING (Bob) DYLAN' and 'BUDDY HOLLY'. KENNY LYNCH collaborated on several with HICKS on 1971's 'DISTANT LIGHT'. • **Trivia:** In 1988 after exposure on Miller lite UK TV ad, the 1969 hit 'HE AIN'T HEAVY, HE'S MY BROTHER' re-charted, hitting No.1.

Best CD compilation: GREATEST HITS (*8)

ALLAN CLARKE (b. 5 Apr'42, Salford, Manchester, England) – vocals / **TONY HICKS** (b.16 Dec'43, Nelson, Lancashire, England) – lead guitar / **GRAHAM NASH** (b. 2 Feb'42, Blackpool, England) – guitar / **ERIC HAYDOCK** (b. 3 Feb'43) – bass / **DON RATHBONE** – drums

Parlophone Liberty

May 63. (7") *(R 5030)* **(AIN'T THAT) JUST LIKE ME. / HEY WHAT'S WRONG WITH ME** 25 –

Aug 63. (7") *(R 5052)* **SEARCHIN'. / WHOLE WORLD OVER** 12 –

— **BOBBY ELLIOTT** (b. 8 Dec'42, Burnley, England) – drums (ex-SHANE FENTON & THE FENTONES) repl. RATHBONE (still on next single b-side and album track – *)

Nov 63. (7") *(R 5077)* *<55674>* **STAY. / NOW'S THE TIME** 8 Mar64 [ ]

Jan 64. (lp) *(PMC 1220)* **STAY WITH THE HOLLIES** 2 –
– I'm talkin' 'bout you / Mr. Moonlight / You better move on / Lucille / Baby don't cry / Memphis / Stay / Rockin' Robin / What'cha gonna do about it? / Do you love me / It's only make believe / What kind of girl are you / Little lover / Candy man. *(re-iss. Oct87 on 'Beat Goes On'; BGOLP 4) (cd-iss. Oct88; BGOCD 4) (cd re-iss. Dec99 on 'Magic'; 524412-2)*

Parlophone Imperial

Feb 64. (7") *(R 5104)* *<66026>* **JUST ONE LOOK. / KEEP OFF THAT FRIEND OF MINE** 2 Apr64 98

May 64. (7") *(R 5137)* **HERE I GO AGAIN. / BABY THAT'S ALL** 4 –

Jul 64. (7") *<66044>* **HERE I GO AGAIN. / LUCILLE** [–] [ ]

Sep 64. (7") *(R 5178) <66070>* **WE'RE THROUGH. / COME ON BACK** [7] Oct64 [ ]

Nov 64. (lp) *(PMC 1235)* **IN THE HOLLIES STYLE** [ ] [–]
– Nitty gritty – Something's got a hold on me / Don't you know / To you my love / It's in her kiss / Time for love / What kind of boy / Too much monkey business / I thought of you last night / Please don't feel too bad / Come on home / Set me free. *(re-iss. Mar88 & Apr97 on 'Beat Goes On' lp/cd; BGO LP/CD 8) (cd re-iss. Oct00 on 'Magic'; 525127-2)*

Jan 65. (7") *(R 5232)* **YES I WILL. / NOBODY** [9] [–]

May 65. (7") *(R 5287)* **I'M ALIVE. / YOU KNOW HE DID** [1] [–]

Aug 65. (7") *(R 5322) <66134>* **LOOK THROUGH ANY WINDOW. / SO LONELY** [4] Nov65 [32]

Sep 65. (lp) *(PMC 1261) <12312>* **THE HOLLIES** [8] Jun66 [ ]
– Put yourself in my place / When I come home to you / That's my desire / Mickey's monkey / Very last day / Down the line / Lawdy Miss Clawdy / You must believe me / Too many people / Fortune teller / I've been wrong. *(re-iss. Nov69 as 'REFLECTION' on 'Regal Starline'; SRS 5008) (re-iss. Jul88 on 'Beat Goes On'; BGOLP 25) (cd-iss. Apr91; BGOCD 25)*

Dec 65. (7") *(R 5392)* **IF I NEEDED SOMEONE. / I'VE GOT A WAY OF MY OWN** [20] [–]

Jan 66. (lp) *<12299>* **HEAR! HERE!** [–] [ ]
– I'm alive / Very last day / You must believe me / Put yourself in my place / Down the line / That's my desire / Look through any window / Lawdy Miss Clawdy / When I come home to you / Lonely / I've been wrong / Too many people.

Feb 66. (7") *(R 5409) <66158>* **I CAN'T LET GO. / I'VE GOT A WAY OF MY OWN** [2] Mar66 [42]

Jun 66. (lp; mono/stereo) *(PMC/PCS 7008) <12330>* **WOULD YOU BELIEVE?** <US-title 'BUS STOP'> [16] Oct66 [75]
– I take what I want / Hard hard year / That's how strong my love is / Sweet little sixteen / Oriental sadness (I'll never trust in anybody no more) / I am a rock / Take your time / Don't you even care (what's gonna happen) / Fifi the flea / Stewball / I've got a way of my own / I can't let go. *(re-iss. Oct88 on 'Beat Goes On'; BGOLP 24) (cd-iss. Apr91; BGOCD 24)*

—— **BERNIE CALVERT** (b.16 Sep'43, Burnley) – bass repl. HAYDOCK who formed HAYDOCK'S ROADHOUSE **JOHN PAUL JONES** – bass sessioned on the next b-side. (Later to LED ZEPPELIN)

Jun 66. (7") *(R 5469) <66186>* **BUS STOP. / DON'T RUN AND HIDE** [5] Jul66 [5]

—— in Aug'66, they teamed up with actor/comedian PETER SELLERS on single 'AFTER THE FOX', from the film on 'United Artists'

Oct 66. (7") *(R 5508) <66214>* **STOP! STOP! STOP!. / IT'S YOU** [2] [7]

Oct 66. (lp; mono/stereo) *(PMC/PCS 7011) <12339>* **FOR CERTAIN BECAUSE . . .** <US-title 'STOP! STOP! STOP!'> [23] Feb67 [91]
– What's wrong with the way I live / Pay you back with interest / Tell me to my face / Clown / Suspicious look in your eyes / It's you / High classed / Peculiar situation / What went wrong / Crusader / Don't even think about changing / Stop! stop! stop! *(re-iss. Dec71 as 'STOP! STOP! STOP!' on 'Regal Starline'; SRS 5088) (re-iss. Apr88 on 'Beat Goes On' lp/c; BGO MC/CD 9) (cd-iss. Dec89; BGOCD 9) (cd re-iss. Jan99 on 'E.M.I.'; 528241-2)*

Feb 67. (7") *(R 5562) <66231>* **ON A CAROUSEL. / ALL THE WORLD IS LOVE** [4] Mar67 [11]

May 67. (7") *<66240>* **PAY YOU BACK WITH INTEREST. / WHAT'CHA GONNA DO ABOUT IT** [–] [28]

—— between Feb'67 and Mar'67 they used session drummer **DOUGIE WRIGHT** to repl. ill ELLIOTT (CLEM CATTINI + MITCH MITCHELL also guested)

Parlophone Epic

May 67. (7") *(R 5602) <10180>* **CARRIE-ANNE. / SIGNS THAT WILL NEVER CHANGE** [3] Jun67 [9]

Jun 67. (lp; mono/stereo) *(PMC/PCS 7022) <26315>* **EVOLUTION** [13] Jul67 [43]
– Then the heartaches begin / Stop right there / Water on the brain / Lullaby to Tim / Have you ever loved somebody / You need love / Rain on the window / Heading for a fall / Ye olde toffee shoppe *[UK-only]* / When your lights turned on / Leave me *[UK-only]* / The games we play. *<US+=>* – Carrie-Anne / Jennifer Eccles / Signs that will never change / Open up your eyes. *(re-iss. Feb72 as 'HOLLIES' on 'Music For Pleasure'; MFP 5252) (re-iss. 1989 on 'Beat Goes On'; BGOLP 80) (cd-iss. Jun93; BGOCD 80) (cd re-iss. Feb99 on 'E.M.I.'; 528247-2) <(cd re-iss. Jun99 on 'Sundazed'++=; SC 6122)> (cd re-iss. Oct00 on 'Magic'; 497579-2)*

Sep 67. (7") *(R 5637)* **KING MIDAS IN REVERSE. / EVERYTHING IS SUNSHINE** [18] [–]

Sep 67. (7") *<10234>* **KING MIDAS IN REVERSE. / WATER ON THE BRAIN** [–] [51]

Oct 67. (lp; mono/stereo) *(PMC/PCS 7039) <26344>* **BUTTERFLY** <US-title 'DEAR ELOISE / KING MIDAS IN REVERSE'> [ ] Jan68 [ ]
– Dear Eloise / Away away away / Maker / Pegasus the flying horse / Would you believe / Wish you a wish / Postcard / Charlie and Fred / Try it / Elevated observations / Step inside / Butterfly. *<US+=>* – King Midas in reverse / Leave me / Do the best you can. *(re-iss. 1989 on 'Beat Goes On' lp/cd; BGO LP/CD 79) <(cd re-iss. Dec97 as US title on 'Sundazed'+=; SC 6123)> (cd re-iss. Mar99 on 'E.M.I.'; 528243-2)*

Nov 67. (7") *<10251>* **DEAR ELOISE. / WHEN YOUR LIGHTS TURNED ON** [–] [50]

Mar 68. (7") *(R 5680)* **JENNIFER ECCLES. / OPEN UP YOUR EYES** [11] [–]

Mar 68. (7") *<10298>* **JENNIFER ECCLES. / TRY IT** [–] [40]

Jun 68. (7") *<10361>* **DO THE BEST YOU CAN. / ELEVATED OBSERVATIONS** [–] [93]

Sep 68. (7") *(R 5733)* **LISTEN TO ME. / DO THE BEST YOU CAN** [11] [–]

Sep 68. (7") *<10400>* **LISTEN TO ME. / EVERYTHING IS SUNSHINE** [–] [ ]

—— **TERRY SYLVESTER** (b. 8 Jan'45, Liverpool, England) – vocals, guitar (ex-SWINGING BLUE JEANS) repl. NASH who joined CROSBY, STILLS & NASH. (**ELLIOT** also returned)

Feb 69. (7") *(R 5765) <10454>* **SORRY SUZANNE. / NOT THAT WAY AT ALL** [3] [56]

May 69. (lp; mono/stereo) *(PMC/PCS 7078) <26447>* **HOLLIES SING DYLAN** [3] [ ]
– When the ship comes in / I'll be your baby tonight / I want you / This wheel's on fire / I shall be released/ / Blowin' in the wind / Quit your low down ways / Just like a woman / The times they are a-changin' / All I really want to do / My back pages / The mighty Quinn (Quinn, the eskimo). *(re-iss. Oct87 on 'Music For Pleasure' lp/c; MFP/TC-MFP 5811) (cd-iss. Jun93 on 'E.M.I.'; CZ 520) (cd re-iss. Apr99 on 'E.M.I.'; 528246-2)*

Sep 69. (7") *(R 5806) <10532>* **HE AIN'T HEAVY, HE'S MY BROTHER. / 'COS YOU LIKE TO LOVE ME** [3] Dec69 [7]

Nov 69. (lp) *(PCS 7092) <26538>* **HOLLIES SING HOLLIES** <US-title 'HE AIN'T HEAVY, HE'S MY BROTHER'> [ ] [32]
– Do you believe in love / Please sign your letters / Please let me please / Goodbye tomorrow / My life is over with you / Soldier's dilemma / Marigold; Gloria swansong / You love 'cos you like it / Why didn't you believe / Look at life / Don't give up easily / Reflections of a time gone past. *<US version replaced; 'Marigold – Gloria Swansong' with>* – He ain't heavy, he's my brother. *(cd-iss. Apr99 on 'Magic'; 497757-2)*

Apr 70. (7") *(R 5837) <10613>* **I CAN'T TELL THE BOTTOM FROM THE TOP. / MAD PROFESSOR BLYTH** [7] May70 [82]

Sep 70. (7") *(R 5862) <10677>* **GASOLINE ALLEY BRED. / DANDELION WINE** [14] [ ]

Nov 70. (lp) *(PCS 7116) <30255>* **CONFESSIONS OF THE MIND** <US-title 'MOVING FINGER'> [30] [ ]
– Survival of the fittest / Man without a heart / Little girl / Isn't it nice? / Perfect lady housewife / Confessions of a mind / Lady please / Frightened lady / Too young to be married / Separated / I wanna shout. *<US+=>* – Marigold – Gloria Swansong / Gasoline alley bred / Dandelion wine / Mad Professor Blyth. *(re-iss. 1989 on 'Beat Goes On'; BGOLP 96) (cd-iss. Apr91; BGOCD 96) <(cd re-iss. Nov97 as US title on 'Sundazed'+=; SC 6126)> (cd re-iss. May99 on 'E.M.I.'; 528243-2)*

Jan 71. (7") *<10716>* **SURVIVAL OF THE FITTEST. / MAN WITHOUT A HEART** [–] [ ]

May 71. (7") *(R 5905)* **HEY WILLY. / ROW THE BOAT TOGETHER** [ ] [ ]

Jun 71. (lp) *(PAS 10005) <30958>* **DISTANT LIGHT** [ ] Jul71 [21]
– What a life I've led / Look what we've got / Hold on / Pull down the blind / To do with love / Promised land / Long cool woman (in a black dress) / You know the score / Cable car / A little thing like love / Long dark road. *(re-iss. Jul91 on 'Beat Goes On'; BGO LP/CD 97) (cd re-iss. May99 on 'E.M.I.'; 528242-2)*

Jun 72. (7") *<10871>* **LONG COOL WOMAN (IN A BLACK DRESS). / LOOK WHAT WE'VE GOT** [–] [2]

Aug 72. (7") *(R 5939)* **LONG COOL WOMAN (IN A BLACK DRESS). / CABLE CAR** [32] [–]

Nov 72. (7") *<10920>* **LONG DARK ROAD. / INDIAN GIRL** [–] [26]

—— (Aug71) **MICHAEL RICKFORS** – vocals (ex-BAMBOO) repl. CLARK who went solo

Polydor Epic

Feb 72. (7") *(2058 199) <10842>* **THE BABY. / OH! GRANNY** [26] [ ]

Nov 72. (7") *(2058 289)* **MAGIC WOMAN TOUCH. / INDIAN GIRL** [ ] [–]

Nov 72. (lp) *(2383 144)* *<31992>* **ROMANY** — 84
– Won't we feel good that morning / Touch / Words don't come easy / Magic woman touch / Lizzy and the rainman / Down river / Slow down – Go down / Delaware Taggett and the outlaw boys / Jesus was a crossmaker / Romany / Blue in the morning / Courage of your convictions. *(cd-iss. Oct00 on 'Magic'+=; 497578-2)* – The baby / Oh! granny / Indian girl / I had a dream / Don't leave the child alone / If it wasn't for the reason / A better place / The last wind.

Jan 73. (7") *<10951>* **MAGIC WOMAN TOUCH. / BLUE IN THE MORNING** – 60

Mar 73. (7") *<10989>* **JESUS WAS A CROSSMAKER. / I HAD A DREAM** –

May 73. (7") *<11025>* **SLOW DOWN. / WON'T WE FEEL GOOD** –

not iss. Polydor

May 73. (lp) **OUT ON THE ROAD (studio)** – German –
– Out on the road / A better place / They don't realize I'm down / The last wind / Mr. Heartbreaker / I was born a man / Slow down – Go down / Don't leave the child alone / Nearer to you / Pick up the pieces again / Transatlantic west bound jet.

— (Jul73) **ALLAN CLARKE** – vocals returned to repl. RICKFORS (CLARKE now joining others HICKS, SYLVESTER, CALVERT and ELLIOTT)

Oct 73. (7") *(2058 403)* *<11051>* **THE DAY THAT CURLY BILLY SHOT CRAZY SAM McGEE. / BORN A MAN** 24

Jan 74. (7") *(2058 435)* *<11100>* **THE AIR THAT I BREATHE. / NO MORE RIDERS** 2 Apr74 6

Mar 74. (lp) *(2383 262)* *<32574>* **THE HOLLIES** 38 May74 28
– Falling calling / It's a shame, it's a game / Don't let me down / Out on the road / The air that I breathe / Rubber Lucy / Transatlantic west bound jet / Pick up the pieces again / Down on the run / Love makes the world go round / The day that Curly Billy shot down crazy Sam McGee. *(cd-iss. Dec99 on 'Magic'; 497577-2)*

May 74. (7") *(2058 476)* **SON OF A ROTTEN GAMBLER. / LAYIN' TO THE MUSIC** –

May 74. (7") *<50029>* **DON'T LET ME DOWN. / LAY INTO THE MUSIC** –

Nov 74. (7") *(2058 533)* **I'M DOWN. / HELLO LADY GOODBYE** –

Feb 75. (lp) *(2441 128)* *<33387>* **ANOTHER NIGHT**
– Another night / 4th of July, Asbury Park (Sandy) / Lonely hobo lullaby / Secondhand hang-ups / Time machine jive / I'm down / Look out Johnny (there's a monkey on your back) / Give me time / You gave me life (with that look in your eyes) / Lucy. *(cd-iss. Dec99 on 'Magic'; 524408-2)*

May 75. (7") *(2058 595)* *<50086>* **4TH OF JULY, ASBURY PARK (SANDY). / SECONDHAND HANG-UPS** Mar75 85
<US re-iss. Apr76; 50359>

Jun 75. (7") *<50110>* **ANOTHER NIGHT. / TIME MACHINE JIVE** – 71

Aug 75. (7") *<50144>* **I'M DOWN. / LOOK OUT JOHNNY (THERE'S A MONKEY ON YOUR BACK)** –

— **ROD ARGENT** – moog, piano (on next opening track)

Jan 76. (lp) *(2442 141)* **WRITE ON** –
– Star / Write on / Sweet country calling / Love is the thing / I won't move over / Narida / Stranger / Crocodile woman (she bites) / My island / There's always goodbye. *(cd-iss. Dec99 on 'Magic'+=; 524414-2)* – Boulder to Birmingham / Samuel / Star (live) / My island (live) / Born to run.

Feb 76. (7") *<50204>* **WRITE ON. / CROCODILE WOMAN (SHE BITES)** –

Feb 76. (7") *(2058 694)* **BOULDER TO BIRMINGHAM. / CROCODILE WOMAN (SHE BITES)** –

Apr 76. (7") *(2058 719)* **STAR. / LOVE IS THE THING** –

Aug 76. (7") *(2058 779)* **DADDY DON'T MIND. / C'MON** –

Oct 76. (7") *(2058 799)* **WIGGLE THAT WOTSIT. / CORRINE** –

Dec 76. (lp) *(2382 421)* **RUSSIAN ROULETTE** –
– Wiggle that wotsit / Forty-eight hour patrol / Thanks for the memories / My love / Lady of the night / Russian roulette / Draggin' my heels / Louise / Be with you / Daddy don't mind.

Dec 76. (7") *<50422>* **DRAGGIN' MY HEELS. / I WON'T MOVE OVER** –

Mar 77. (lp) *(2383 428)* **HOLLIES LIVE HITS** (live in New Zealand) 4 –
– I can't let go / Just one look / I can't tell the bottom from the top / Another night / Bus stop / 4th of July, Asbury Park (Sandy) / Star / My island / I'm down / Stop, stop, stop / Long cool woman (in a black dress) / Carrie-Anne / The air that I breathe / Too young to be married / He ain't heavy, he's my brother.

May 77. (7") *(2058 880)* **HELLO TO ROMANCE. / 48 HOUR PAROLE** –

Jul 77. (7") *(2058 906)* **AMNESTY. / CROSSFIRE** –

Mar 78. (lp) *(2383 474)* *<3534>* **A CRAZY STEAL**
– Writing on the wall / What am I gonna do? / Let it pour / Burn out / Hello to romance / Amnesty / Caracas / Boulder to Birmingham / Clown service / Feet on the ground.

Apr 78. (7") *<50522>* **BURN OUT. / WRITING ON THE WALL** –

Mar 79. (7") *(POSP 35)* **SOMETHING TO LIVE FOR. / SONG OF THE SUN** –
(12"+=) *(POSPX 35)* – The air that I breathe.

Mar 79. (lp) *(2442 160)* **FIVE THREE ONE – DOUBLE SEVEN O FOUR** –
– Say it ain't so, Joe / Maybe it's dawn / Song of the sun / Harlequin / When I'm yours / Something to live for / Stormy waters / Boys in the band / Satellite three / It's in every one of us.

Mar 80. (7") *(2059 246)* **SOLDIER'S SONG. / DRAGGIN' MY HEELS** 58 –

Sep 80. (7") *(POSP 175)* **HEARTBEAT. / TAKE YOUR TIME** –

Oct 80. (lp/c) *(POLTV/+M 12)* **BUDDY HOLLY** –
– Take your time / Wishing / Peggy Sue / Heartbeat / Love's made a fool of you / That'll be the day / Think it over / Tell me how / Maybe baby / I'm gonna love you too / What to do / It doesn't matter / Peggy Sue got married / Midnight shift / Everyday.

— trimmed to a trio of CLARKE, HICKS and ELLIOTT when CALVERT and SYLVESTER left. Latter teamed with JAMES GRIFFIN (ex-BREAD) (next single b-side with **ALAN JONES** – bass)

Nov 81. (7") *(POSP 379)* **TAKE MY LOVE AND RUN. / DRIVER** –

— added returning **GRAHAM NASH** – vocals, guitar

WEA Atlantic

Jul 83. (7") *(U 9888)* *<89819>* **STOP! IN THE NAME OF LOVE. / MUSICAL PICTURES** May83 29

Jul 83. (lp/c) *(250139-1/-4)* *<80076>* **WHAT GOES AROUND** 90
– Casualty / Take my love and run / Say you'll be mine / Something ain't right / If the lights go out / Stop! In the name of love / I got what you want / Just one look / Someone else's eyes / Having a good time. *<(cd-iss. Jan02 on 'Wounded Bird'+=; WOU 8076)>* – Musical pictures.

Aug 83. (7") *<89784>* **SOMEONE ELSE'S EYES. / IF THE LIGHTS GO OUT** –

Oct 83. (7") *<89768>* **CASUALTY. / IF THE LIGHTS GO OUT** –

— basic trio of **CLARKE, HICKS** and **ELLIOTT** plus **ALAN COATES** – harmonies / **STEVE STROUD** – bass / **DENNIS HAYNES** – keyboards

Columbia not iss.

May 85. (7") *(DB 9110)* **TOO MANY HEARTS GET BROKEN. / YOU'RE ALL WOMAN** –
(12"+=) *(12DB 9110)* – Laughter turns to tears.

Jan 87. (7") *(DB 9146)* **THIS IS IT. / YOU GAVE ME STRENGTH** –
(12"+=) *(12DB 9146)* – You're all woman.

Mar 87. (7") *(DB 9151)* **REUNION OF THE HEART. / TOO MANY HEARTS GET BROKEN** –
(12"+=) *(12DB 9151)* – Hollidaze (medley).

— **RAY STILES** – bass (ex-MUD) repl. STROUD

Coconut not iss.

Jan 88. (7") **STAND BY ME. / FOR WHAT IT'S WORTH** – German –

Jun 88. (7") **SHINE SILENTLY. / YOUR EYES** – German –

E.M.I. E.M.I.

Feb 89. (7") *(EM 86)* **FIND ME A FAMILY. / NO RULES** –

Mar 93. (c-s/7") *(TC+/EM 264)* **THE WOMAN I LOVE. / PURPLE RAIN (live)** 42 –
(cd-s+=) *(CDEM 264)* – The air that I breathe / (Ain't) That just like me.

Mar 93. (cd/c/lp) *(CD/TC+/EMTV 74)* **THE AIR THAT I BREATHE (THE BEST OF THE HOLLIES)** (compilation) 15 –
– The air that I breathe / Bus stop / Just one look / Yes I will / Look through any window / He ain't heavy, he's my brother / I can't let go / We're through / Searchin' / Stay / I'm alive / If I needed someone / Here I go again / Stop stop stop / On a carousel / Carrie Ann / King Midas in reverse / Jennifer Eccles / Listen to me / Sorry Suzanne / I can't tell the bottom from the top / Gasoline alley bred / Hey Willy / The day that curly Billy shot down crazy Sam McGee / The woman I love.

— re-formed in 2005 as 6-piece: newcomers **PETER HOWARTH** – vocals + **STEVE LAURI** – guitar; joined **TONY HICKS, BOBBY ELLIOTT, RAY STILES + IAN PARKER**

Sep 05. (cd-s) *(340623-2)* **HOPE / SHINE ON ME** [ ] [ ]
Feb 06. (cd-s) *(354064-2)* **SO DAMN BEAUTIFUL / TOO MUCH TOO SOON** [ ] [–]
Feb 06. (cd) *(355983-2)* *<50505>* **STAYING POWER** [ ] [ ]
– Hope / So damn beautiful / Prove me wrong / Break me / Shine on me / Suspended animation / Touch me / Emotions / Weakness / Live it up / Yesterday's gone / Let love pass.

– (selective) compilations, etc. –

on 'Parlophone' unless mentiond otherwise

Sep 67. (7") *Imperial; <66258>* **JUST ONE LOOK. / RUNNING THROUGH THE NIGHT** [–] [44]
Aug 68. (lp) *(7057) <12350>* **HOLLIES' GREATEST HITS** [1] [11]
(US version different)
Jul 78. (lp/c) *E.M.I.; (EMTV/TC-EMTV 11)* **20 GOLDEN GREATS** [2] [–]
– The air that I breathe / Carrie Anne / Bus stop / Listen to me / Look through any window / I can't let go / Long cool woman in a black dress / Here I go again / I can't tell the bottom from the top / I'm alive / Yes I will / Stay / Sorry Suzanne / Gasoline alley bred / We're through / Jennifer Eccles / Stop! stop! stop! / On a carousel / Just one look / He ain't heavy, he's my brother. *(cd-iss. Mar87 & Jan89; CDP 238-2)*
Aug 81. (7") *E.M.I.; (EMI 5229)* **HOLLIEDAZE (MEDLEY). / HOLLIEPOPS** [28] [–]
Aug 88. (7") *E.M.I.; (EM 74)* **HE AIN'T HEAVY, HE'S MY BROTHER. / CARRIE** [1] [ ]
(12"+=/cd-s+=) *(12/CD EM 74)* – The air that I breathe.
Sep 88. (d-lp/d-c)(d-cd) *E.M.I.; (EM/TCEM 1301)(CDS 790 850-2)* **ALL THE HITS AND MORE – THE DEFINITIVE COLLECTION** [51] [–]
Nov 88. (7") *E.M.I.; (EM 80)* **THE AIR THAT I BREATHE. / WE'RE THROUGH** [60] [ ]
(12"+=) *(12EM 80)* – King Midas in reverse / Just one look.
(cd-s+=) *(CDEM 80)* – He ain't heavy, he's my brother.
Feb 95. (4xcd-box) *E.M.I.; (HOLLIES 1)* **FOUR HOLLIES ORIGINALS** [ ] [–]
– (ANOTHER NIGHT / RUSSIAN ROULETTE / 5317704 / BUDDY HOLLY)
Mar 95. (cd) *See For Miles; (SEECD 94)* **THE EP COLLECTION** [ ] [ ]
Feb 96. (4xcd-box) *Premier-EMI; (CDHOLLIES 2)* **FOUR MORE HOLLIES ORIGINALS** [ ] [–]
– (ROMANY / WRITE ON / THE HOLLIES / A CRAZY STEAL)
Feb 97. (cd) *E.M.I.; (CTMCD 311)* **THE BEST OF THE HOLLIES: CENTENARY COLLECTION** [ ] [ ]
Sep 97. (cd) *Connoisseur; (NSPCD 518)* **ARCHIVE ALIVE: LIVE AT KING'S ISLAND, CINCINNATI, OHIO)** [ ] [ ]
Oct 97. (cd) *E.M.I.; (CDABBEY 103)* **AT ABBEY ROAD 1963-1966** [ ] [ ]
Feb 98. (cd) *E.M.I.; (493450-2)* **AT ABBEY ROAD 1966-1970** [ ] [ ]
Mar 03. (d-cd) *E.M.I.; (<5 82012-2>)* **GREATEST HITS** [21] [ ]
– I'm alive / Sorry Suzanne / Here I go again / On a carousel / King Midas in reverse / Look through any window / Blowin' in the wind / The air that I breathe / Pay you back with interest / I've got a way of my own / Stay / The very last day / We're through / Carrie Anne / Magic woman touch / I'm down / Gasoline alley bred / I can't let go / 4th of July, Asbury Park (Sandy) / Long cool woman (in a black dress) / Stop, stop, stop / If I needed someone / Dear Eloise / Long dark road / I can't tell the bottom from the top / He ain't heavy, he's my brother / Bus stop / Jennifer Eccles / The day that Curly Billy shot down Crazy Sam McGee / Too young to be married / Listen to me / Just one look / Searchin' / Ain't that just like me / Yes I will (I'll be true to you) / What's wrong with the way I live / Lonely hobo lullaby / Daddy don't mind / The baby / Hey Willy / Son of a rotten gambler / Write on / Star / Boulder to Birmingham / Soldier's song / The woman I love / How do I survive.

Buddy HOLLY

Born: CHARLES HARDIN HOLLEY, 7 Sep'36, Lubbock, Texas, USA. In the late 40's, the young HOLLY formed a C&W duo with schoolmate, BOB MONTGOMERY. As BUDDY & BOB, they became regulars on a Saturday afternoon TV show (around 1953/54), the pair subsequently putting together a number of demos, later issued as 'HOLLY IN THE HILLS'. With the addition of bassman, LARRY WELBORN and drummer JERRY ALLISON in 1955, the revamped unit began to make a name for themselves locally. After a gig supporting BILL HALEY & HIS COMETS, and through agent Eddie Crandall, BUDDY HOLLY was signed up by 'Decca' early the following year. Rejecting MONTGOMERY (who went on to become a successful producer, etc), the bespectacled HOLLY formed backing band, The THREE TUNES, retaining JERRY and recruiting SONNY CURTIS on guitar, DON GUESS on bass. Following two flop singles, BUDDY and JERRY left the label, travelling to New Mexico in search of producer, NORMAN PETTY, who was soon to become their manager. Early in 1957, the pair were joined by NIKI SULLIVAN (rhythm guitar) and JOE B. MAUDLIN (bass), becoming The CRICKETS. Their debut single, 'THAT'LL BE THE DAY', hit the top of the charts on both sides of the Atlantic, selling a million in the process. As a solo artist (with CRICKETS backing), BUDDY set up a deal with 'Coral', who released 'PEGGY SUE', another transatlantic Top 10 smash. The single also introduced HOLLY's idiosyncratic vocal mannerisms, his exaggerated hiccuping framed by simple but effective arrangements and infectious hooks which influenced many of the biggest 60's rock/pop stars, including DYLAN, The BEATLES and The 'STONES. Over the course of the following year, he balanced a series of CRICKETS hits ('OH BOY', 'MAYBE BABY' and 'THINK IT OVER') with his own solo classics ('LISTEN TO ME', 'RAVE ON' and 'EARLY IN THE MORNING'). His partnership with The CRICKETS was eventually severed in August '58, BUDDY marrying Maria Elena Santiago and moving to New York. His first CRICKETS-less single, 'HEARTBEAT', was surprisingly disappointing in terms of native chart success (i.e. No.82), although it managed to scrape into the UK Top 30. This was certainly a transitional period, things looking promising early the following year when the singer set out as headliner on a winter-long package tour of the States. Tragically, on the morning of the 3rd of February 1959, HOLLY, along with fellow pop stars, RICHIE VALENS and the BIG BOPPER were killed when their chartered plane crashed just after take-off from Mason City airport in Iowa. A posthumous release (written by PAUL ANKA), 'IT DOESN'T MATTER ANYMORE' – backed by 'RAINING IN MY HEART' – became one of his biggest UK hits, while climbing the US Top 20. With a bulging vault of HOLLY material at his disposal, NORMAN PETTY proceeded to keep the legend's name alive via a series of his releases during the early 60's. Although fans might have disagreed on what direction HOLLY's career might have taken, there was no disputing the fact that the 22 year-old surely still had a wealth of music inside of him.

• **Songwriters:** HOLLY wrote most himself, except EARLY IN THE MORNING + NOW WE'RE ONE (Bobby Darin) / BABY I DON'T CARE (Elvis Presley) / etc. His songs were later covered by Rolling Stones (NOT FADE AWAY) / Mud (OH BOY) / Showaddywaddy (HEARTBEAT) / Leo Sayer (RAINING IN MY HEART). • **Trivia:** In Sep'58, HOLLY produces his new bass player's (WAYLON JENNINGS) debut single 'JOLE BLON'.

Best CD compilation: THE BUDDY HOLLY COLLECTION (*9)

BUDDY HOLLY – vocals, guitar (backed by The **CRICKETS**)

Brunswick Decca

Jul 56. (7",78) *(05581) <29854>* **BLUE DAYS BLACK NIGHTS. / LOVE ME** [ ] Apr56 [ ]
Dec 56. (7",78) *<30166>* **MODERN DON JUAN. / YOU ARE MY ONE DESIRE** [–] [ ]
(with The CRICKETS ⇒ , he hit No.1 (May57-US / Sep57-UK) with the single **THAT'LL BE THE DAY. / I'M LOOKING FOR SOMEONE TO LOVE**

Coral Coral

Jun 57. (7",78) *<61852>* **WORDS OF LOVE. / MAILMAN BRING ME NO MORE BLUES** [–] [ ]
Nov 57. (7",78) *(Q 72293) <61885>* **PEGGY SUE. / EVERYDAY** [6] Sep57 [3]
(re-iss. Jul82 on 'Old Gold')
—— (with The CRICKETS ⇒ again, he hit US No.10 (Nov57) / UK No.3 (Dec57) with single **OH BOY. / NOT FADE AWAY.**

— An album **THE CHIRPING CRICKETS** was issued Nov57-US / Mar58-UK. Another single **MAYBE BABY. / TELL ME HOW** hit US No.17 (Feb58) / UK No.4 (Mar58).

Mar 58. (7",78) *(Q 72288) <61947>* **LISTEN TO ME. / I'M GONNA LOVE YOU TOO** 16 □

Jun 58. (7",78) *(Q 72325) <61985>* **RAVE ON. / TAKE YOUR TIME** 5 Apr58 37

Jul 58. (lp) *(LVA 9085) <57210>* **BUDDY HOLLY** □ Mar58 □
– I'm gonna love you too / Peggy Sue / Look at me / Listen to me / Valley of tears / Ready Teddy / Everyday / Mailman, bring me no more blues / Words of love / Baby I don't care / Rave on / Little baby. *(re-iss. Jul75) (re-iss. Mar83 + Nov86 on 'M.C.A.', cd-iss. Nov92 on 'Sequel') (re-iss. Jul68 as 'LISTEN TO ME' on 'MCA', re-iss. Feb74; all UK)*
(with The CRICKETS ⇒ again, he hit US No.27 (Jun58) / UK No.11 (Jul58) with single **THINK IT OVER. / FOOL'S PARADISE**

Aug 58. (7",78) *(Q 72333) <62006>* **EARLY IN THE MORNING. / NOW WE'RE ONE** □ Jul58 32

— (with The CRICKETS ⇒ again, he was heard on their last single collaboration **IT'S SO EASY. / LONESOME TEARS** (which didn't chart US-Sep58 / UK-Oct58)

He had now left The CRICKETS to hop away on their own Oct'58.

Nov 58. (7",78) *(Q 72346) <62051>* **HEARTBEAT. / WELL ALL RIGHT** 30 82

Feb 59. (7",78) *(Q 72360) <62074>* **IT DOESN'T MATTER ANYMORE. / RAINING IN MY HEART** 1 13
Jan59 88
(re-iss. Apr83 on 'Old Gold')

— On the 3rd of Feb'59, BUDDY was killed in a plane crash alongside other pop stars RICHIE VALENS and BIG BOPPER.

– (selective) compilations, etc. –

Jul 59. (7",78) *Brunswick; (05800)* **MIDNIGHT SHIFT. / ROCK AROUND WITH OLLIE VEE** 26 –
(some below featured CRICKETS' songs)

Apr 59. (lp) *Coral; (LVA 9105)* **THE BUDDY HOLLY STORY** 2 Mar 59 11
(UK re-iss. Jul68 as 'RAVE ON' on 'M.C.A.', re-iss. Feb74, also iss.Aug75 on 'M.F.P.') (cd-iss. Oct01 on 'Spectrum'; 544670-2)

Aug 59. (7",78) *Coral; (Q 72376) <62134>* **PEGGY SUE GOT MARRIED. / CRYING, WAITING, HOPING** 13 Jul59 □

Mar 60. (7",78) *Coral; (Q 72392)* **HEARTBEAT. / EVERYDAY** 30 –

May 60. (7") *Coral; (Q 72397)* **TRUE LOVE WAYS. / MOONDREAMS** 25 –

Jun 60. (7") *Coral; <62210>* **TRUE LOVE WAYS. / THAT MAKES IT TOUGH** – □

Oct 60. (7") *Coral; (Q 72411)* **LEARNING THE GAME. / THAT MAKES IT TOUGH** 36 –

Oct 60. (lp) *Coral; (LVA 9127)* **THE BUDDY HOLLY STORY VOL.2** 7 Mar60 □
(UK re-iss. Jul68 as 'TRUE LOVE WAYS' on 'M.C.A.', re-iss. Feb74)

Jan 61. (7") *Coral; (Q 72419)* **WHAT TO DO. / THAT'S WHAT THEY SAY** 34 –

Jun 61. (7") *Coral; (Q 72432) <62283>* **BABY I DON'T CARE. / VALLEY OF TEARS** 12 □

Feb 62. (7") *Coral; (Q 724490)* **LISTEN TO ME. / WORDS OF LOVE** 48 –

Sep 62. (7") *Coral; (Q 72455) <62329>* **REMINISCING. / WAIT TILL THE SUN SHINES NELLIE** 17 Aug62 □

Mar 63. (7") *Coral; (Q 72459)* **BROWN-EYED HANDSOME MAN. / SLIPPIN' & SLIDIN'** 3 –
(below album was dubbed in 1962 with musicians The FIREBALLS)

Apr 63. (lp) *Coral; (LVA 9212) <57246>* **REMINISCING** 2 Feb63 40
– Reminiscing / Slippin' and slidin' / Bo Diddley / Wait till the Sun shines, Nellie / Baby, won't you come out tonight / Brown-eyed handsome man / Because I love you / It's not my fault / I'm gonna set my foot down / Changing all those changes / Rock-a-bye-rock. *(UK re-iss. Nov86 on 'M.C.A.') (UK re-iss. Jul68 as 'BROWN-EYED HANDSOME MAN' on 'M.C.A.', re-iss. Feb74) (re-iss. Feb89; MCL/+C/CD 1826) (cd-iss. Nov92 on 'Castle'; CLACD 308) (cd re-iss. Feb03 on 'Spectrum'; 112099-2)*

May 63. (7") *Coral; (Q 72463)* **BO DIDDLEY. / IT'S NOT MY FAULT** 4 –

Aug 63. (7") *Coral; (Q 72466)* **WISHING. / BECAUSE I LOVE YOU** 10 –

Dec 63. (7") *Coral; (Q 72469)* **WHAT TO DO. / UMM OH YEAH (DEAREST)** 27 –

Apr 64. (7"; BUDDY HOLLY & THE CRICKETS) *Coral; (Q 72472)* **YOU'VE GOT LOVE. / AN EMPTY CUP** 40 –

Jun 64. (lp) *Coral; (LVA 9222) <57450>* **SHOWCASE** 3 May64 □
(UK re-iss. Nov86 & Feb89 on 'M.C.A.') (UK re-iss. Jul68 as 'HE'S THE ONE' on 'M.C.A.') (cd-iss Apr 93 on 'Castle')

Sep 64. (7") *Coral; (Q 724750)* **LOVE'S MADE A FOOL OF YOU. / YOU'RE THE ONE** 39 –

Jun 65. (lp) *Coral; (LVA 9227) <57463>* **HOLLY IN THE HILLS** (1954 demos) 13 Jan65 □
(some lp's have track 'Reminiscing' instead of 'Wishing') (UK re-iss. Jul86 as 'WISHING' on 'M.C.A.')

Jun 67. (lp) *Ace Of Hearts; (AH 148)* **BUDDY HOLLY'S GREATEST HITS** 9 –
(UK re-iss. Nov69, re-iss. Aug71; hit No.32, on 'Coral')

Mar 68. (7") *M.C.A.; (MU 1012)* **PEGGY SUE. / RAVE ON** 32 –

Mar 69. (lp) *M.C.A.; (MUPS 371)* **GIANT** 13 Jan69 □
(re-iss. Feb74 + Nov86)

Mar 78. (lp/c) *M.C.A.; (MCTV/+C 1)* **20 GOLDEN GREATS** 1 55
– That'll be the day / Peggy Sue / Words of love / Everyday / Not fade away / Oh! boy / Maybe baby / Listen to me / Heartbeat / Think it over / It doesn't matter anymore / It's so easy / Well all right / Rave on / Raining in my heart / True love ways / Peggy Sue got married / Bo Diddley / Brown-eyed handsome man / Wishing. *(re-iss. Jun79; same) (cd-iss. Feb89 & Aug93; DMCTV 1)*

Feb 89. (lp/c/cd) *Telstar; (STAR/STAC/TCD 2339)* **TRUE LOVE WAYS** 8 –

May 94. (cd/c) *M.C.A.; (MCLD 19242)* **THAT'LL BE THE DAY / BUDDY HOLLY** □ □

Nov 96. (cd/c) *Dino; (DIN CD/MC 133)* **THE VERY BEST OF BUDDY HOLLY** 24 –

Aug 99. (cd/c) *Universal TV; (112048-2/-4)* **THE VERY BEST OF BUDDY HOLLY** 25 –

Mar 03. (cd) *Universal; (AAMCAD 11956)* **20th CENTURY MASTERS** □ □

□ HOLY BARBARIANS (see under ⇒ CULT)

□ the HONEYDRIPPERS (see under ⇒ LED ZEPPELIN)

HOOBASTANK

Formed: Agoura Hills, California, USA ... 1994 by DOUGLAS ROBB and DAN ESTRIN, together with MARKKU LAPPALAINEN and CHRIS HESSE. The self-financed, self-consciously titled 'THEY SURE DON'T MAKE BASKETBALL SHORTS LIKE THEY USED TO' marked their long-playing debut in 1998, while a millennial deal with 'Island' saw them secure tour spots with the likes of ALIEN ANT FARM. The heavily rotated likes of 'CRAWLING IN THE DARK' pushed up sales of the band's 2001-released eponymous major label debut, itself a fairly rote collection high on energy and low on inspiration. It nevertheless went platinum, while 2003's 'THE REASON' offered yet more meat and potatoes angst-rock lovingly sculpted for the restrictive confines of MTV rotation. The replacement of bassist MARKKU with JOSH MOREAU had little effect on the band's journeyman sound; 'EVERY MAN FOR HIMSELF' (2006) could've been released a decade earlier but stuck-in-the PUDDLE OF MUDD American audiences put it in the Top 20.

Album rating: HOOBASTANK (*4) / THE REASON (*6) / EVERY MAN FOR HIMSELF (*6)

DOUGLAS ROBB (b. 2 Jan'75) – vocals / **DAN ESTRIN** (b. 9 Jul'76) – guitar / **MARKKU LAPPALAINEN** – bass / **CHRIS HESSE** – drums

not iss. own label

1997. (c) *<none>* **MUFFINS** – –
– Educated fool / Invisible / Naked jock man / Pee wee / Prank call to Cobalt Cafe / Show me your titz.

1998. (cd) *<none>* **THEY SURE DON'T MAKE BASKETBALL SHORTS LIKE THEY USED TO** – □
– Earthsick / Foot in your mouth / Karma patrol / Stuck without a voice / Can I buy you a drink? / Naked jock man / Our song / The mirror / Educated fool / The dance that broke my jaw.

Mercury Island

Jan 02. (cd) *<(586435-2)>* **HOOBASTANK** [ ] Nov01 [25]
– Crawling in the dark / Remember me / Running away / Pieces / Let you know / Better / Ready for you / Up and gone / Too little too late / Hello again / To be with you / Give it back. *(ltd cd-iss. Jul02 +=; 586873-2)* – Critic.

Apr 02. (c-s) *(582862-4) <radio>* **CRAWLING IN THE DARK / PIECES** [47] [68]
(cd-s+=) *(582862-2)* – Losing my grip / ('A'-video).

Jul 02. (c-s) *(582969-4) <radio>* **RUNNING AWAY / CRAWLING IN THE DARK (acoustic)** [ ] [44]
(cd-s+=) *(582969-2)* – Up and gone (acoustic) / ('A'-video).

Apr 04. (cd) *(9862261) <14880-2>* **THE REASON** [41] Dec03 [45]
– Same direction / Out of control / What happened to us? / Escape / Just one / Lucky / From the heart / The reason / Let it out / Unaffected / Never there / Disappear. *(UK+=)* – Never saw it coming / Out of control (video).

May 04. (7") *(9862603)* **THE REASON. / OUT OF CONTROL (live)** [12] [2]
(cd-s+=) *(9862567)* – Running away (acoustic) / ('A'-video).
(cd-s) *(9862566)* – ('A') / Crawling in the dark (acoustic).

Oct 04. (cd-s) *(9862567)* **THE REASON** (as above) [ ] [–]
(dvd-s) *(9864425)* – ('A'-video) / Same direction (video).

— **JOSH MOREAU** – bass; repl. MARKKU

May 06. (cd) *(987988-2) <B00061620-2>* **EVERY MAN FOR HIMSELF** [ ] [12]
– The rules / Born to lead / Moving forward / Inside of you / The first of me / Good enough / If I were you / Without a fight / Don't tell me / Look where we are / Say the same / If only / More than a memory. *(bonus+=)* – If I were you (video) / Born to lead (video).

John Lee HOOKER

Born: 22 Aug'20, Clarksdale, Mississippi, USA. The last of the original bluesmen who travelled north from the Delta, VAN MORRISON once said that HOOKER was "a window into another age". Doubts remain about his actual birth date although HOOKER recently admitted that he lied about his age as a teenager to get into the army. Taught to play guitar by his stepfather (his birth father disapproved of the blues), a popular local blues guitarist by the name of WILL MOORE, HOOKER drifted north during his teens to Memphis, Cincinatti and finally, to Detroit, where he settled in 1943. The budding bluesman was given his first guitar by the legendary T-BONE WALKER in 1947, sitting in on early sessions with Robert Nighthawk. He worked as a janitor in a car factory by day and performed in clubs around Hastings Street (a notorious area known as 'Black Bottom' from which the dance was named) at night, slowly gaining a reputation which paralleled such Chicago masters as MUDDY WATERS, SONNY BOY WILLIAMSON and HOWLIN' WOLF. HOOKER always maintained that he didn't like Chicago because there were too many other blues guitarists there, his relocation to Detroit paying off when he was introduced to local distributor, record store owner and kingpin of the 'Sensation' record label, Bernie Bessman, in 1948. In November that year he undertook his debut recording session (just himself and his guitar, with his distinctive tapping sounds coming from Coca-Cola bottle tops attached to the soles of his shoes), his first single from the set, 'BOOGIE CHILLUN' topping the "race" chart, as it was then known. After Bessman leased the master to 'Modern', it eventually sold more than a million copies (when it broke, HOOKER was still working as a janitor in the Chrysler car factory). As well as a demon guitarist, he was also a wicked womaniser, almost copping it in 1950 when an aggrieved husband poisoned his whisky (12 years after ROBERT JOHNSON had fatally suffered in a similar manner). HOOKER subsequently signed to 'Modern' in 1951, staying with the label for five years; as with other blues artists of the time, he recorded for anyone who was willing to pay him and got round his contractual obligations by recording 70 singles on 21 different labels under 10 pseudonyms, TEXAS SLIM ('BLACK MAN BLUES' for 'KING' Records), BIRMINGHAM SAM ('Savoy' Records), JOHN LEE BOOKER ('Chess' Records), JOHN LEE COOKER ('King' Records), DELTA JOHN ('Regent' Records), JOHNNY LEE ('Deluxe' Records), JOHNNY WILLIAMS ('Gotham' Records), LITTLE PORK CHOPS, THE BOOGIE MAN ('Acorn' Records) and JOHN L'HOOKER. During this period, 'I'M IN THE MOOD' became his second major R&B hit and matched the one million sales of 'BOOGIE CHILLUN', while the following year he made his debut as a DJ on a local radio station. Although B.B. KING outshone him in the 50's, HOOKER signed to 'Vee-Jay', who recognised his wider appeal and crafted him into a tighter performer, backing him with seasoned session players including guitarist, EDDIE TAYLOR and drummer, TOM WHITEHEAD. During a subsequent 1959 session, HOOKER cut new versions of his most successful songs including 'I'M IN THE MOOD', 'BOOGIE CHILLUN', 'HOBO BLUES' and 'CRAWLIN' KINGSNAKE' (all with his distinctive guttural singing). The following year, he was one of only a few (traditional) blues artists to perform at the 2nd Newport Folk Festival (his set was recorded and later released as 'CONCERT AT NEWPORT'), while the following year, BOB DYLAN made his New York debut opening for HOOKER at Gerde's Folk City venue. 1964 saw the British R&B explosion in full flow with 'BOOM BOOM' becoming a US hit for The ANIMALS (they also covered three HOOKER compositions on their debut album) and HOOKER himself entering the UK chart at 23 with 'DIMPLES'. This success led to numerous UK tours backed by the likes of The SPENCER DAVIS GROUP and The GROUNDHOGS (who took their name from HOOKER's, 'GROUNDHOG BLUES'); many other British bands of the time including The YARDBIRDS, The WHO, The SMALL FACES and, in particular, The ROLLING STONES, were inspired by, and recorded many of HOOKER's songs. In America, meanwhile, he influenced many bands from ZZ TOP (whose 'LA GRANGE' is pure HOOKER) to BRUCE SPRINGSTEEN, the latter including 'BOOM BOOM' as part of his set on the 'Tunnel Of Love' tour in 1988. In 1966, the veteran bluesman signed to 'ABC' Records and, over the next eight years, recorded albums for their subsidiaries, 'Impulse' and 'Bluesway', as well as 'ABC' themselves. HOOKER left Detroit in 1970 after a nasty divorce, settling in San Francisco where he met CANNED HEAT; together they recorded the double album, 'HOOKER 'N' HEAT' (1971), which became the guitarists first US chart success, reaching the Top 75. Unfortunately, CANNED HEAT's ALAN 'Blind Owl' WILSON died before the album was mixed, the sleeve depicting everyone in sombre mood with a black framed picture of WILSON hanging in the background. HOOKER's ABC contract ended in 1974 and, on the verge of quitting to open a motel, he signed a deal with 'Atlantic' Records. He recorded two albums for the major, 'DETROIT SPECIAL' and 'DON'T TURN ME FROM YOUR DOOR', although by 1978's, 'THE CREAM', he had downshifted to 'Tomato' Records. In 1980, he had a cameo role in 'The Blues Brothers' alongside RAY CHARLES, JAMES BROWN and ARETHA FRANKLIN, while his music also featured in another movie, 'The Color Purple'. Later in the 80's, HOOKER starred in the title role of PETE TOWNSHEND's musical, 'THE IRON MAN' (singing 'I EAT HEAVY METAL' – far removed from his normal style but performed with typical HOOKER panache nonetheless) and at the turn of the decade he paired up with MILES DAVIS for the soundtrack to the Dennis Hopper movie, 'The Hot Spot' (which featured HOOKER's, 'I'M IN THE MOOD'). He's become more popular with age, 'THE HEALER' (1989) attracting a whole new army of fans and breaking him into the mainstream rock world. The project came about because the contributing artists were all fans of "THE HOOK" (they all lived locally), including CARLOS SANTANA on the title track, BONNIE RAITT on 'I'M IN THE

MOOD' (a Grammy winner), ROBERT CRAY on 'CUTTIN' OUT' and LOS LOBOS on 'THINK TWICE BEFORE YOU GO', while most of the songs were completed in one or two takes (a hallmark of HOOKER's career). His next album was the stunning 'Charisma' debut, 'MR. LUCKY', which, in reaching number 3 in Britain (only made number 101 in the US!), became the highest charting "real" blues album ever, and at the age of 71, it made HOOKER the oldest artist to reach the UK Top 5. This album was another collection of duets, including the collaborations 'CRAWLIN KINGSNAKE' with KEITH RICHARDS, 'MR. LUCKY' with the ROBERT CRAY BAND, 'SUZIE' with JOHNNY WINTER and 'I COVER THE WATERFRONT' with his No.1 fan, VAN MORRISON, although the stand-outs were 'THIS IS HIP' with RY COODER, 'STRIPPED ME NAKED' (on which HOOKER sounds like a man possessed and CARLOS SANTANA is at his wailing best) and the top of the lot, 'I WANT TO HUG YOU' with CHUCK BERRY's former pianist, JOHNNIE JOHNSON. 1992 saw a rare appearance on Top Of The Pops as 'BOOM BOOM' reached the UK Top 20, further singles, 'BOOGIE AT RUSSIAN HILL' and 'GLORIA' (recorded with VAN MORRISON) also reaching the charts. Although clocking in at a remarkable three quarters of a century, HOOKER retained his humour, ability and style, as witnessed on the 1995 and 1997 releases, 'CHILL OUT' and 'DON'T LOOK BACK'. Sadly, HOOKER was to die of natural causes on the 21st June, 2001, aged 80.

Album rating (selective): THE FOLK BLUES OF JOHN LEE HOOKER (*8) / I'M JOHN LEE HOOKER (*8) / TRAVELLIN' (*7) / SINGS THE BLUES (*7) / THAT'S MY STORY (*8) / THE FOLKLORE OF JOHN LEE HOOKER (*8) / THE BEST OF JOHN LEE HOOKER compilation (*7) / JOHN LEE HOOKER AT NEWPORT (*7) / REAL FOLK BLUES (*7) / THE HEALER (*10) / MR. LUCKY (*7) / BOOM BOOM (*6) / CHILL OUT (*7) / DON'T LOOK BACK (*6) / THE BEST OF FRIENDS (*5) / THE ULTIMATE COLLECTION compilation (*8)

JOHN LEE HOOKER – vocals, guitars

not iss. / Modern

Jan 49. (78) *<20-627>* **BOOGIE CHILLEN (BOOGIE CHILDREN). / SALLY MAE (THERE'S A DAY COMIN' BABY)** – [ ]

— now with **JAMES WATKINS** – piano / **CURTIS FOSTER** – drums

not iss. / King

Mar 49. (78; as TEXAS SLIM) *<4283>* **BLACK MAN BLUES. / STOMP BOOGIE (FLUB)** – [ ]

— now w/ **ANDREW DUNHAM** – guitar / **EDDIE BURNS** – harmonica

— released many US 78's over the next several years (some with pseudonyms)

not iss. / Regent

1949. (78; as DELTA JOHN) *<1001>* **HELPLESS BLUES. / GOIN' MAD BLUES** – [ ]

not iss. / Savoy

1949. (78; as BIRMINGHAM SAM & HIS MAGIC GUITAR) *<5558>* **LOW DOWN MIDNITE BOOGIE. / LANDING BLUES** – [ ]

not iss. / Modern

1949. (78) *<20-663>* **HOBO BLUES. / HOOGIE BOOGIE** – [ ]
1949. (78) *<20-688>* **WEEPING WILLOW (BOOGIE). / WHISTLIN' AND MOANIN' BLUES (HUMMIN' THE BLUES)** – [ ]
1949. (78) *<20-714>* **CRAWLING KING SNAKE. / DRIFTING FROM DOOR TO DOOR** – [ ]

not iss. / Prize

1949. (78; as JOHNNY WILLIAMS) *<704>* **MISS ROSIE MAE. / HIGHWAY BLUES** – [ ]

not iss. / Sensation

Mar 50. (78) *<21>* **MISS SADIE MAE. / BURNIN' HELL** – [ ]
Apr 50. (78) *<26>* **CANAL STREET BLUES. / HUCKLE UP BABY** – [ ]
May 50. (78) *<30>* **GOIN' ON HIGHWAY 51 (GOIN' DOWN HIGHWAY 51). / LET YOUR DADDY RIDE (SLOW DOWN YOUR CHATTER BABY)** – [ ]
Jun 50. (78) *<33>* **MY BABY'S GOT SOMETHIN'. / DECORATION DAY BLUES (LORD TAKETH MY BABY AWAY)** – [ ]
Jul 50. (78) *<34>* **BOOGIE CHILLEN 2 (I GOTTA BE COMIN' BACK). / MISS ELOISE (MISS ELOISE, MISS ELOISE)** – [ ]
Aug 50. (78; as JOHN LEE COOKER) *<4504>* **MOANING BLUES. / STOMP BOOGIE (FLUB)** – [ ]

not iss. / Acorn

1949. (78; as THE BOOGIE MAN) *<308>* **DO THE BOOGIE. / MORNING BLUES** – [ ]

not iss. / Chance

1949. (78; as JOHN LEE BOOKER) *<1108>* **MISS LORRAINE. / TALKIN' BOOGIE** – [ ]
1949. (78; as JOHN LEE BOOKER) *<1110>* **GRAVEYARD BLUES. / I LOVE TO BOOGIE** – [ ]
1949. (78; as JOHN L. BOOKER) *<1122>* **609 BOOGIE. / ROAD TROUBLE** – [ ]

not iss. / King

1950. (78; as TEXAS SLIM) *<4315>* **THE NUMBERS. / DEVIL'S JUMP** – [ ]
1950. (78; as TEXAS SLIM) *<4323>* **I'M GONNA KILL THAT WOMAN. / NIGHTMARE BLUES** – [ ]
1950. (78; as TEXAS SLIM) *<4329>* **HEART TROUBLE BLUES. / SLIM'S STOMP (instrumental)** – [ ]
1950. (78; as TEXAS SLIM) *<4334>* **DON'T GO BABY. / WANDERING BLUES** – [ ]
Oct 50. (78; as TEXAS SLIM) *<4366>* **LATE LAST NIGHT. / DON'T YOU REMEMBER ME** – [ ]
Nov 50. (78; as TEXAS SLIM) *<4377>* **MOANING BLUES. / THINKING BLUES** – [ ]

not iss. / Modern

Apr 50. (78) *<20-730>* **PLAYIN' THE RACES (DREAM A NUMBER). / WELL I GOT TO LEAVE** – [ ]
May 50. (78) *<20-746>* **NO FRIEND AROUND (T.B.'S KILLIN' ME). / WEDNESDAY EVENING (SHE LEFT ME – ON MY BENDED KNEE)** – [ ]
Jun 50. (78) *<20-767>* **GIMME YOUR PHONE NUMBER (IT'S A CRIME AND A SHAME). / ROCK'N'ROLL (I CRIED THE WHOLE NIGHT LONG)** – [ ]
Jul 50. (78) *<20-790>* **ONE MORE TIME (LET'S TALK IT OVER). / LET YOUR DADDY RIDE** – [ ]

not iss. / Regal

1950. (78) *<3304>* **NEVER SATISFIED (JUST LIKE A WOMAN). / NOTORIETY WOMAN (NO PLACE TO STAY)** – [ ]

not iss. / Gone

1950. (78; as JOHN LEE BOOKER) **MAD MAN BLUES. / BOOGIE NOW (HEY BOOGIE)** – [ ]

not iss. / Modern

1950. (78) *<814>* **QUEEN BEE. / JOHN L'S HOUSE RENT BOOGIE (OUT THE DOOR I WENT)** – [ ]

not iss. / Staff

1950. (78; as JOHNNY WILLIAMS) *<710>* **HOUSE RENT BOOGIE. / WANDERING BLUES** – [ ]
1950. (78; as JOHNNY WILLIAMS) *<718>* **PRISON BOUND. / BUMBLE BEE BLUES** – [ ]

not iss. / Gotham

1951. (78; as JOHNNY WILLIAMS) *<509>* **REAL GONE GAL. / QUESTIONNAIRE BLUES** – [ ]
1951. (78; as JOHNNY WILLIAMS) *<513>* **LITTLE BOY BLUE. / MY DADDY WAS A JOCKEY** – [ ]
1951. (78' as JOHN LEE) *<515>* **CATFISH. / MEAN OLD TRAIN** – [ ]

not iss. / Chess

Jun 51. (78; as JOHN LEE BOOKER) *<1467>* **LEAVE MY WIFE ALONE. / RAMBLIN' BY MYSELF** – [ ]
Jul 51. (78; as JOHN LEE BOOKER) *<1482>* **GROUND HOG BLUES. / LOUISE** – [ ]

<above also iss.Jan52 as JOHN L. HOOKER on 'Modern'; 852>

Aug 51. (78) *<1505>* **HIGH PRICED WOMAN. / UNION STATION BLUES** – [ ]
Jul 52. (78) *<1513>* **WALKIN' THE BOOGIE. / SUGAR MAMA** – [ ]

not iss. Modern

Sep 51. (78) *<829>* **(FOUR) WOMEN IN MY LIFE. / TEASE ME BABY (TEASE YOUR DADDY)** [–] [ ]

Nov 51. (78) *<835>* **I'M IN THE MOOD. / HOW CAN YOU DO IT** [–] [ ]

Dec 51. (78; as JOHN L. HOOKER) *<847>* **TURN OVER A NEW LEAF. / ANYBODY SEEN MY BABY (JOHNNY SAYS COME BACK)** [–] [ ]

Feb 52. (78) *<862>* **ROCK ME MAMA (GOOD ROCKIN' MAMA). / COLD CHILLS (ALL OVER ME)** [–] [ ]

Vogue Modern

1952. (78) *(V 2102)* **HOOGIE BOOGIE. / WHISTLIN' AND MOANIN' BLUES** [ ] [–]

Sep 52. (78; as JOHN LEE HOOKER & "LITTLE" EDDIE KIRKLAND) *<876>* **IT HURTS ME SO. / I GOT EYES FOR YOU** [–] [ ]

Nov 52. (78) *<886>* **KEY TO THE HIGHWAY. / BLUEBIRD BLUES** [–] [ ]

Feb 53. (78) *<897>* **IT'S BEEN A LONG TIME BABY. / ROCK HOUSE BOOGIE** [–] [ ]

Apr 53. (78) *<901>* **RIDE 'TIL I DIE. / IT'S STORMIN' AND RAININ'** [–] [ ]

Jun 53. (78) *<1562>* **IT'S MY OWN FAULT (BABY, I PROVE MY LOVE TO YOU). / WOMEN AND MONEY** [–] [ ]

1953. (78; as JOHNNY LEE HOOKER) *<30>* **BOOGIE RAMBLER. / NO MORE DOGGIN'** [–] [ ]
<above issued on 'J.V.B.'>

Jul 53. (78; as JOHNNY LEE HOOKER) *<908>* **PLEASE TAKE ME BACK. / LOVE MONEY CAN'T BUY** [–] [ ]

Aug 53. (78; as JOHNNY LEE HOOKER) *<916>* **NEED SOMEBODY. / TOO MUCH BOOGIE** [–] [ ]
(UK-iss.1954 on 'London'; HL 8037)

Sep 53. (78; as JOHNNY LEE HOOKER) *<931>* **I WONDER (LITTLE DARLING). / JUMP ME (ONE MORE TIME)** [–] [ ]

not iss. DeLuxe

Sep 53. (78; as JOHN LEE BOOKER) *<6004>* **BLUE MONDAY (I AIN'T GOT NOBODY). / LOVIN' GUITAR MAN** [–] [ ]

Oct 53. (78; as JOHNNY LEE) *<6009>* **I'M A BOOGIE MAN. / I CAME TO SEE MY BABY** [–] [ ]

Dec 53. (78; as JOHN LEE BOOKER) *<6046>* **MY BABY DON'T LOVE ME. / REAL REAL GONE** [–] [ ]

not iss. Rockin'

Oct 53. (78; as JOHN LEE BOOKER) *<524>* **BLUE MONDAY (I AIN'T GOT NOBODY). / LOVIN' GUITAR MAN** [–] [ ]

Nov 53. (78; as JOHN LEE BOOKER) *<525>* **STUTTERIN' BLUES. / POURING DOWN RAIN (WOBBLIN' BABY)** [–] [ ]

not iss. Chart

1954. (78) *<609>* **GOIN' SOUTH. / WOBBLIN' BABY** [–] [ ]

1954. (78) *<614>* **BLUE MONDAY (I AIN'T GOT NOBODY). / MISBELIEVING BABY (MY BABY PUT YOU DOWN)** [–] [ ]

not iss. Modern

1954. (78) *<923>* **DOWN CHILD. / GOTTA BOOGIE (GONNA BOOGIE)** [–] [ ]

1954. (78) *<935>* **LET'S TALK IT OVER. / I TRIED HARD** [–] [ ]

1954. (78) *<942>* **BAD BOY. / COOL LITTLE CAR** [–] [ ]

1954. (78) *<948>* **SHAKE, HOLLER AND RUN. / HALF A STRANGER** [–] [ ]

1955. (78) *<958>* **TAXI DRIVER. / YOU RECEIVE ME** [–] [ ]

1955. (78) *<966>* **HUG AND SQUEEZE (YOU). / THE SYNDICATOR (SYNDICATE)** [–] [ ]

1955. (78) *<978>* **LOOKIN' FOR A WOMAN. / I'M READY** [–] [ ]

not iss. Vee Jay

Dec 55. (7") *<164>* **MAMBO CHILLUN. / TIME IS MARCHING** [–] [ ]

Apr 56. (7") *<188>* **TROUBLE BLUES. / EVERY NIGHT** [–] [ ]

Jun 56. (7") *<205>* **DIMPLES. / BABY LEE** [–] [ ]

Sep 56. (7") *<233>* **I'M SO WORRIED BABY. / THE ROAD IS SO ROUGH** [–] [ ]

Apr 57. (7") *<245>* **I'M SO EXCITED. / I SEE YOU WHEN YOU'RE WEAK** [–] [ ]

Aug 57. (7") *<255>* **LITTLE WHEEL. / ROSIE MAE** [–] [ ]

Sep 57. (7") *<265>* **YOU CAN LEAD ME BABY. / UNFRIENDLY WOMAN** [–] [ ]

Jul 58. (7") *<293>* **I LOVE YOU HONEY. / YOU'VE TAKEN MY WOMAN** [–] [ ]

Feb 59. (7") *<308>* **I'M IN THE MOOD. / MAUDIE** [–] [ ]

Apr 59. (7") *<319>* **BOOGIE CHILLUN. / TENNESSEE BLUES** [–] [ ]

Jun 59. (7") *<331>* **CRAWLIN' KINGSNAKE. / HOBO BLUES** [–] [ ]

Riverside Riversic

1960. (lp) *<321>* **THAT'S MY STORY** [–] [ ]
– I need some money / I'm wanderin' / Democrat man / I want to talk about you / Gonna use my rod / Wednesday evening blues / No more doggin' / One of these days, I'll believe I'll go back home / You're leavin' me baby / That's my story / Black snake / How long blues / Wobblin' baby / She's long, she's tall, she weeps like . . . / Peavine special / Tupelo blues / I rowed a little boat / Water boy / Church bell tone / Bundle up and go *(UK-iss.Nov88 on 'Ace')*

1962. (lp) *(RLP 12-838)* *<838>* **THE FOLK BLUES OF JOHN LEE HOOKER** [ ] 1959 [ ]
– Black snake / How long blues / Wobblin' baby / She's long, she's tall she weeps like a willow tree / Pea-vine special / Tupelo blues / I'm prison bound / I rowed a little boat / Water boy / Church bell tone / Bundle up and go / Good mornin' lil' school girl / Behind the plow.
- singles on other labels at the time

not iss. Elmor

1959. (7") *<303>* **609 BOOGIE. / (MISS SADIE MAE) CURL MY BABY'S HAIR** [–] [ ]

not iss. Fortur

1960. (7") *<853>* **CRY BABY. / LOVE YOU BABY** [–] [ ]

1960. (7") *<855>* **CRAZY ABOUT THAT WALK. / WE'RE ALL GOD'S CHILLUN** [–] [ ]

not iss. Hi-Q

1959. (7") *<5018>* **BIG FINE WOMAN. / BLUES FOR CHRISTMAS** [–] [ ]

not iss. Laure

1960. (7") *<361>* **BALLAD TO ABRAHAM LINCOLN (HE GOT ASSASSINATED). / MOJO HAND (RISIN' SUN)** [–] [ ]

1960. (7") *<362>* **I LOST MY JOB (TELL YOU A STORY). / DEEP DOWN IN MY HEART (HOW LONG CAN THIS GO ON)** [–] [ ]

not iss. Galax

1960. (7") *<716>* **SHAKE IT UP (JOHNNY LEE & THE THING). / (I) LOST MY JOB (TELL YOU A STORY)** [–] [ ]

Stateside Vee Ja

Apr 60. (7") *<349>* **SOLID SENDER. / NO SHOES** [–] [ ]

Jul 60. (7") *<366>* **TUPELO (BACKWATER BLUES). / DUSTY ROAD** [–] [ ]

Feb 61. (7") *<379>* **I'M MAD AGAIN. / I'M GOING UPSTAIRS** [–] [ ]

Apr 61. (7") *<397>* **WANT AD BLUES. / TAKE ME AS I AM** [–] [ ]

Feb 62. (7") *<438>* **BOOM BOOM. / DRUG STORE WOMAN** [–] [60]

Apr 62. (7") *<453>* **SHE'S MINE (KEEP YOUR HANDS TO YOURSELF). / A NEW LEAF** [–] [ ]

1962. (lp) *(SL 10014)* **THE FOLK LORE OF JOHN LEE HOOKER** [ ] [–]
– Tupelo / I'm mad again / I'm going upstairs / Wanted blues / Five year long / I like to see you walk / The hobo / Hard headed woman / Wednesda evening blues / Take me as I am / My first wife left me / You're lookin good tonight. *(re-iss. 1974 on 'Joy')*

Nov 62. (7") *<493>* **FRISCO BLUES. / TAKE A LOOK AT YOURSELF** [–] [ ]

1963. (7") *<538>* **I'M LEAVING. / BIRMINGHAM BLUES** [–] [ ]

1963. (7") *<575>* **DON'T LOOK BACK. / SEND ME YOUR PILLOW** [–] [ ]

1964. (lp) *(SL 10053)* **THE BIG SOUL OF JOHN LEE HOOKER** [ ] [–]
– Frisco blues / Take a look at yourself / Send me your pillow / She sho me down / I love her / Old time shimmy / You know I love you / Big soul Good rocking mama / Onions / No one told me. *(re-iss. 1969 + 1974 o 'Joy')*

Jul 63. (7") *(SS 203)* **BOOM BOOM. / FRISCO BLUES** [ ] [–]

May 64. (7") *(SS 297)* **DIMPLES. / I'M LEAVING** [23] [–]

Sep 64. (7") *(SS 341)* **I LOVE YOU HONEY. / SEND ME YOUR PILLOW** [ ] [–]

1964. (lp) *(SL 10074)* **I WANT TO SHOUT THE BLUES** [ ] [–]
– I'm leaving / Love is a burning thing / Birmingham blues / I want t shout / Don't look back / I want to hug you / Poor me / I want to ramble Half a stranger / My grinding mill / Bottle up and go / One way ticket.

1964. (7") *<670>* **YOUR BABE AIN'T SWEET LIKE MINE. / BIG LEGS, TIGHT SHIRT**

1964. (7") *<708>* **IT SERVES ME RIGHT (TO SUFFER). / FLOWERS ON THE HOUR**

Polydor not iss.

1964. (7") *(NH 52930)* **SHAKE IT BABY. / LET'S MAKE IT BABY**

Pye Int. Chess

Aug 64. (7") *(7N 25255)* **HIGH PRICED WOMAN. / SUGAR MAMA**

Nov 64. (7"ep) *(NEP 44034)* **LOVE BLUES**

Sue not iss.

Jun 65. (7") *(WI 361)* **I'M IN THE MOOD. / BOOGIE CHILLUN'**

Fontana not iss.

Nov 65. (lp) *(FJL 119)* **BLUE** (rec.1960)

not iss. Impulse

Jan 66. (7") *<242>* **BOTTLE UP AND GO. / MONEY**

Planet Planet

Feb 66. (7"; as JOHN LEE'S GROUNDHOGS) **I'LL NEVER FALL IN LOVE AGAIN. / OVER YOU BABY**

May 66. (7") *<(PLF 114)>* **MAI LEE. / DON'T BE MESSING WITH MY BREAD**

Chess Chess

Aug 66. (7") *(CRS 8039) <1965>* **LET'S GO OUT TONIGHT. / I'M IN THE MOOD**

Jan 67. (7") *(CRL 4527)* **REAL FOLK BLUES**
– Let's go out tonight / Please lovin' man / Stella Mae / I put my trust in you / I'm in the mood / You know, I know / I'll never trust your love again / One bourbon, one Scotch, one beer / The waterfront. *(cd-iss. Feb90 on 'M.C.A.';)*

H.M.V. Impulse

1968. (lp) *(CLP 5032) <9103>* **IT SERVES YOU RIGHT TO SUFFER** Feb66
– Sugar mama / Declaration day / Money (that's what I want) / It serves you right to suffer / Shake it baby / Country boy / Bottle up and go / You're wrong. *(re-iss. 1977 on 'Impulse') (re-iss,Feb84 on 'Jasmine')*

H.M.V. Bluesway

1968. (lp) *(CLP 3612) <BLS 6002>* **LIVE AT THE CAFE AU GO-GO (live)** Jul66
– I'm bad like Jesse James / She's long, she's tall / When my first wife left me / Heartaches and misery / One bourbon, on scotch and one beer / I don't want no trouble / I'll never get out of these blues alive / Seven days. *(re-iss. 1973 on 'Bluesway') (re-iss. +c+cd.Oct88 on 'B.G.O.')*

Jan 68. (7") *<61010>* **WANT AD BLUES. / THE MOTOR CITY IS BURNING**

Mar 68. (7") *<61014>* **CRY BEFORE I GO. / MR. LUCKY**

Stateside Bluesway

1968. (lp) *(SSL 10246) <BLS 6012>* **URBAN BLUES**
– Cry before I go / Boom boom / Backbiters & syndicaters / Mr.Lucky / I can't stand to leave you / My own blues / Think twice before you go / I'm standing in line / Hot water springs (pt.1 & 2) / Wand ad blues *(re-iss. Oct91 on 'B.G.O.')*

Jun 68. (7") *<61017>* **THINK TWICE BEFORE YOU GO. / BACKBITERS AND SYNDICATER**

1969. (lp) *(SSL 10208)* **SIMPLY THE TRUTH**
– I don't wanna go to Vietnam / I wanna boogaloo / Tantalizing with the blues / I'm just a drifter / Mini skirts / Mean mean woman / One room country shack. *(re-iss. +cd.Feb89 on 'B.G.O.')*

Probe Bluesway

1969. (lp) *(SPB 1016) <BLS 6038>* **IF YOU MISS 'IM . . . I GET 'IM**
– Hookers (if you miss 'im . . .I got 'im) / Baby I love you / Lonesome mood / Bang bang bang / If you take care of me, I'll take care of you / Baby, be strong / I wanna be your puppy / I don't care when you go / Have mercy on my soul.

— next with **PRETTY PURDIE** – drums / **ERNIE HAYES** – mouth harp

Feb 69. (7") *<61023>* **MEAN MEAN WOMAN. / I DON'T WANNA GO TO VIETNAM**

– below set are exploitation releases

1968. (lp) *(RLP 008)* **BURNIN'**
– Boom boom / Process / Lost a good girl / A new leaf / Blues before sunrise / Let's make it / I got a letter / Thelma / Drug store woman / Keep you hands to yourself / What do you say. *(re-iss. 1974 on 'Joy'; JOYS 124) (re-iss. +c.May87 on 'Topline')*

Joy Vee-Jay

1968. (lp) *(JOYS 101)* **I'M JOHN LEE HOOKER**

1969. (lp) *(JOYS 129)* **TRAVELIN'**
– No shoes / I wanna walk / Canal Street blues / Keep on / I'm a stranger / Whiskey and wimmen / Solid sender / Sunny land / Goin' to California / I can't believe / I'll know tonight / Dusty road. *(re-iss. 1974)*

1969. (lp) *(JOYS 142) <VJS 1078>* **CONCERT AT NEWPORT (live 24 Jun'60)**
– I can't quit you now blues / Stop baby don't hold me that way / Tupelo / Bus station blues / Freight train be my friend / Boom boom boom Talk that talk baby / Sometime baby you make me feel so bad / You've got to walk by yourself / Let's make it / The mighty fire.

1969. (lp) *(JOYS 152)* **IN PERSON**
– I'm leaving Love is a burning thing / Birmingham blues / I want to shout / Don't look back / I want to hug youu / Poor me / I want to ramble / Half a stranger / My grinding mill / Bottle up and go / One way ticket.

— In 1970, he recorded dual live album 'HOOKER'N'HEAT' with CANNED HEAT

Probe A.B.C.

May 71. (7") **KICK HIT 4 HIT KIX U. / DOIN' THE SHOUT**

May 71. (d-lp) *(SPB 1034) <ABCX 720>* **ENDLESS BOOGIE** Mar71
– (I got) A good 'un / Pots on, gas on high / Kick hit 4 hit kix u / I don't need no stream heart / We might as well call it through . . . / Sittin' in my dark room / Endless boogie parts 27 & 28.

— next with **ROBERT HOOKER** – organ / **LUTHER TUCKER** – guitar / **ELVIN BISHOP** + **DON 'Sugarcane' HARRIS** – piano / **CHARLIE MUSSELWHITE** – harmonica / **VAN MORRISON**

Apr 72. (lp) *(SPB 1057) <ABCX 736>* **NEVER GET OUT OF THESE BLUES ALIVE** Mar72
– Bumblebee bumblebee / Hit the road / Country boy / Boogee with the Hook / If you take care of me (I'll take care of you) / I've got a go / T.B. sheets / Letter to my baby / Never get out of these blues alive / Baby I love you / Lonesome road. *(cd-iss. Feb90 & Jan91 on 'See For Miles', 4 extra tracks)*

Apr 72. (7") **BOOGIE WITH THE HOOK. / NEVER GET OUT OF THESE BLUES ALIVE**

Dec 72. (lp) *<ABCX 761>* **LIVE AT SOLEDAD PRISON (live)**
– Super lover / I'm your crosscut saw / What's the matter baby Lucille / Boogie everywhere I go / Serve me right to suffer / Bang bang bang bang.

1973. (lp) *<ABCX 768>* **BORN IN MISSISSIPPI, RAISED UP IN TENNESSEE**
– Born in Mississippi, raised up in Tennessee / How many more years you gonna dog me 'round / Going down ./ Younger stud / King of the world / Tell me you love me.

A.B.C. A.B.C.

Nov 74. (lp) *(ABCL 5059)* **FREE BEER & CHICKEN**
– Make it funky / Five long years / 713 blues / 714 blues / One bourbon one Scotch one beer / Homework / Bluebird / Sittin' on top of the world / (You'l never amount to anything if you don't go to) College (a fortuitous concatenation of events (a) I know how to rock, (b) Nothin' but the best, (c) The scratch. *(re-iss. +cd.Oct91 on 'B.G.O.')*

not iss. Tomato

1977. (d-lp) *<2-7009>* **THE CREAM (live)**
– Hey hey / Rock steady / Tupelo / You know it ain't right / She's gone / T.B. sheets / Sugar mama / One room country shack / Drug store woman / I want you to roll me / Bar room drinking / Little girl / Louise / When my first wife left me* / Boogie on*. *(UK-iss.+c+cd.Jan88 on 'Charly', cd-omits*)(re-iss. cd Jun93)*

— In 1980, he cameos with loads of other stars in the film, 'BLUES BROTHERS'.

Silvertone Chameleon

Oct 89. (lp/c/cd) *(ORE LP/C/CD 508) <74808>* **THE HEALER** 63 62
– The healer / I'm in the mood / Baby Lee / Cuttin' out / Think twice before you go / Sally Mae / That's alright / Rockin' chair / My dream / No substitute.

Dec 89. (7"/12"; JOHN LEE HOOKER & CARLOS SANTANA) *(ORE/+T 10)* **THE HEALER. / ROCKIN' CHAIR**
(cd-s+=) *(ORECD 10)* – ('A'mix) / No substitute.

May 90. (7"; JOHN LEE HOOKER & BONNIE RAITT) *(ORE 18)* **I'M IN THE MOOD. / MY DREAM**
(cd-s+=) *(ORECD 18)* – ('A'version) / That's alright.

Oct 90. (7"/c-s; JOHN LEE HOOKER & ROBERT CRAY) **BABY LEE. / CUTTIN' OUT**
(cd-s+=) – ('A'mix).
(re-iss. Apr96; ORECD 81) – hit UK No.65

— with **STEVE EHERMAN** – bass / **SCOTT MATTHEWS** – drums + loads on sessions **CARLOS SANTANA / ALBERT COLLINS / VAN MORRISON / KEITH RICHARDS / BOOKER T. / RY COODER / etc.**

Silvertone Charisma

Aug 91. (cd/c/lp) *(ORE CD/C/LP 519) <91724>* **MR. LUCKY** [3] [ ]
– I want to hug you / Mr. Lucky / Backstabbers / This is hip / I cover the waterfront / Highway 13 / Stripped me naked / Susie / Crawlin' Kingsnake / Father was a jockey.

Aug 91. (7") *(ORE 29)* **MR. LUCKY. / THIS IS HIP** [ ] [–]
(12"+=/cd-s+=) *(ORE T/CD 29)* – ('A'-mix).

Pointblank Pointblank

Oct 92. (7"/c-s) *(POB/+C 3)* **BOOM BOOM. / HOMEWORK** [16] [ ]
(cd-s+=) *(POBCD 3)* – The blues will never die / Thought I heard.
(cd-s) *(POBDX 3)* – ('A'version) / Thought I heard.

Nov 92. (cd/c/lp) *(VPB CD/TC/LP 12)* **BOOM BOOM** (new rec.old tunes) [15] [–]
– Boom boom / I'm bad like Jesse James / Same old blues again / Sugar mama / Trick bag (shoppin' for my tombstone) / Boogie at Russian Hill / Hittin' the bottle again / Bottle up and go / Thought I heard / I ain't gonna suffer no more. *(re-iss. Oct93)*

Jan 93. (7"/c-s) *(POB/+C 4)* **BOOGIE AT RUSSIAN HILL. / THE BLUES WILL NEVER DIE** [53] [ ]
(cd-s+=) *(POBDX 4)* – I'm bad like Jesse James / Driftin' blues (w/ JOHN HAMMOND).

— In May'93, he teamed up with VAN MORRISON on UK No.31 hit 'GLORIA'.

— with **ROY ROGERS** – slide guitar / **CHARLES BROWN** – piano / **DANNY CARON** – guitar / **RUTH DAVIS + JIM GYETT** – bass / **GAYLORD BIRCH + BOWEN BROWN** – drums / guests **CARLOS SANTANA + CHESTER THOMPSON** (track 1) / **VAN MORRISON + BOOKER T** (track 4)

Feb 95. (7"/c-s) *(POB/+C 10)* **CHILL OUT (THINGS GONNA CHANGE). / TUPELO** [45] [ ]
(cd-s+=) *(POBDG 10)* – Boom boom.
(cd-s+=) *(POBD 10)* – Up and down / Thought I heard.

Feb 95. (cd/c/lp) *(VPB CD/TC/LP 22) <40107>* **CHILL OUT** [23] [ ]
– Chill out (things gonna change) / Deep blue sea / Kiddio / Medley: Serves me right to suffer – Syndicator / One bourbon, one scotch, one beer / Tupelo / Woman on my mind / Annie Mae / Too young / Talkin' the blues / If you've never been in love / We'll meet again.

Mar 97. (cd/c) *(VPB CD/TC 39) <42771>* **DON'T LOOK BACK** [63] [ ]
– Dimples / Healing game / Ain't no gig thing / Don't look back / Blues before sunrise / Spellbound / Travellin' blues / I love you honey / Frisco blues / Red house / Rainy day.

— next feat. duets with VAN MORRISON, ERIC CLAPTON, ROBERT CRAY, BONNIE RAITT, CARLOS SANTANA, RY COODER, etc.

Oct 98. (cd) *(VPBCD 49) <46424>* **THE BEST OF FRIENDS** [ ] [ ]
– Boogie chillen / This is hip / The healer / I cover the waterfront / Boom boom / I'm in the mood / Burning hell / Tupelo / Baby Lee / Dimples / Chill out (things gonna change) / Big legs, tight skirt / Don't look back.

— JOHN LEE HOOKER died in Los Altos, Ca., on the 21st of June 2001

– (selective) compilations, etc. –

Jul 64. (lp) *Pye Int./ US= Chess; (NPL 28042)* **HOUSE OF THE BLUES** (50's recordings) [ ] 1960 [ ]
(UK re-iss. Jan67 on 'Marble Arch'; MAL 663) – hit No.34 *(re-iss. Oct87 on 'Chess') (cd-iss. Dec86 on 'Vogue')*

1971. (lp) *United Artists; (UAS 29235)* **COAST TO COAST** [ ] [–]
(cd-iss. Sep97 on 'Beat Goes On'; BGOCD 363)

Feb 77. (d-lp) *D.J.M.; (DJD 28026)* **DIMPLES** [ ] [–]

Apr 82. (lp) *Chess; (CXMD 4005)* **CHESS MASTERS** [–] [ ]

Feb 87. (cd) *Charly; (CDCHARLY 62)* **HOUSE RENT BOOGIE** [ ] [–]
(re-iss. Mar01 on 'Ace'; CDCHD 799)

May 91. (cd) *Music Club; (MCCD 020)* **THE BEST OF JOHN LEE HOOKER** [ ] [–]
– Boom boom / Shake it baby (original) / The right time / Dimples / Boogie chillun / Mambo chillun / Wheel and deal / I'm so excited / Trouble blues / Everybody's rockin' / Unfriendly woman / Time is marchin' / I see you when you're weak / I'm in the mood / Will the circle be unbroken / This is hip / Hobo blues / Solid sender.

Sep 92. (cd) *Ace; (CDCHD 421)* **GRAVEYARD BLUES** [ ] [–]

May 93. (cd) *Ace; (CDCHD 315)* **THE LEGENDARY MODERN RECORDINGS 1948-1954** [ ] [–]

Jul 93. (cd) *Ace; (CDCHD 474)* **EVERYBODY'S BLUES** [ ] [–]

Nov 93. (cd) *Ace; (CDCHD 405)* **BLUES BROTHER** [ ] [ ]

Mar 94. (cd) *Ace; (CDCHM 530)* **ORIGINAL FOLK BLUES OF JOHN LEE HOOKER** [ ] [–]

Jul 94. (cd) *See For Miles; (SEECD 402)* **THE EP COLLECTION** [ ] [–]

Feb 95. (cd) *Castle; (CCSCD 410)* **THE COLLECTION: 20 BLUES GREATS** [ ] [–]

Apr 95. (4xcd-box+book) *Charly; (CDDIG 5)* **THE BOOGIE MAN** [ ] [–]

Jul 95. (3xcd-box) *Charly; (VBCD 301)* **THE VERY BEST OF JOHN LEE HOOKER** [ ] [–]

Aug 95. (cd) *Imp; (IMP 301)* **WHISKEY & WIMMEN** [ ] [–]

Oct 96. (d-cd) *Charly; (CPCD 8242-2)* **THE VERY BEST OF JOHN LEE HOOKER** [ ] [ ]

Jun 99. (d-cd) *Snapper; (SMDCD 187)* **THIS IS HIP: THE BEST OF JOHN LEE HOOKER** [ ] [ ]

Sep 99. (cd/c) *Platinum; (PLATCD 535)* **THE BEST OF JOHN LEE HOOKER** [ ] [–]

Oct 99. (cd) *Castle Pie; (PIESD 148)* **BOOM BOOM** [ ] [ ]

Mar 00. (cd) *Krazy Kat; (KKCD 05)* **BOOGIE AWHILE 1948-1953** [ ] [ ]

Feb 01. (cd) *M.C.A.; (MCBD 19507)* **THE BEST OF JOHN LEE HOOKER** [ ] [ ]

Jun 01. (cd) *Indigo; (IGOCD 2122)* **BOOGIE CHILLEN: THE ESSENTIAL RECORDINGS OF JOHN LEE HOOKER 1948-1949** [ ] [ ]

Sep 01. (cd) *R.P.M.; (RPMSH 208)* **THE COMPLETE 1964 RECORDINGS** [ ] [ ]

Sep 01. (3xcd-box) *Snapper; (SNAJ 705CD)* **TESTAMENT** [ ] [ ]

Sep 01. (3xcd-box) *E.M.I.; (833912-2)* **ALTERNATIVE BOOGIE: EARLY STUDIO RECORDINGS 1948-1952** [ ] [ ]

Oct 01. (d-cd) *Pointblank; (810908-2)* **BOOM BOOM / THE HEALER** [ ] [ ]

Jun 02. (cd) *Delta Blue; (63049)* **BLUES IS MY MIDDLE NAME** [ ] [ ]

Mar 03. (d-cd) *E.M.I.; (581727-2)* **BOOM BOOM / CHILL OUT** [ ] [ ]

Mar 03. (cd) *Corazong; (255018)* **ALONE – THE 1ST CONCERT (live)** [ ] [ ]

Mar 03. (cd) *Corazong; (255028)* **ALONE – THE 2ND CONCERT (live)** [ ] [ ]

HOPE OF THE STATES

Formed: Chichester, West Sussex, England ... late 2000 b[y] SAM HERLIHY, ANTHONY THEAKER and JIMMI LAWRENCE expanding to a six-piece when they added PAUL WILSON SIMON JONES and MIKE SIDDELL. After a self-financed part-demo release, 'BLACK DOLLAR BILLS' in 2003, they finally got [a] foot on the major label ladder, signing to 'Sony'. However, JIMM[I] was to only see the release of one hit single for the company 'ENEMIES/FRIENDS'; the band discovered him hanging from th[e] rafters of 'Real World' studios – where work was in progress o[n] a debut album – on the 15th of January 2004. After much sou[l] searching, recording was eventually picked up with new guitaris[t] MIKE HIBBERT. The new line-up's first single, 'THE RED TH[E] WHITE THE BLACK THE BLUE', hit the UK Top 20, whetting th[e] appetite for the much anticipated long-player, 'THE LOST RIOTS (2004). Opening with string-shredding instrumental, 'THE BLAC[K] AMNESIAS', a MOGWAI-meets-CALEXICO epic, the record wa[s] nevertheless comprised largely of snare-rattling, HERLIHY-led alt pop spiritually akin to Canadians ARCADE FIRE. Two year[s] on, HOTS snubbed the charts with the non-eligible 'BLOO[D] MERIDIAN' EP, a precursor to sophomore set, 'LEFT' (2006), no[t] quite as revolutionary although – along with accompanying 45 'SING IT OUT' – it did squeeze into the UK Top 50.

Album rating: THE LOST RIOTS (*9) / LEFT (*6)

SAM HERLIHY – vocals, guitar, keyboards / **ANTHONY THEAKER** – guitar keyboards / **JIMMI LAWRENCE** (b.25 Jan'77) – guitar / **PAUL WILSON** – bass / **MIKE SIDDELL** – violin / **SIMON JONES** – drums

Seeker / not iss.

Mar 03. (ltd;cd-s) *(SEEK 001)* **BLACK DOLLAR BILLS / EVERYTHING FOR EVERYONE (demo) / STS'IKEL (demo)** [ ] [–]

Sony / Epic

Sep 03. (7") *(674257-7)* **ENEMIES/FRIENDS. / WHY'D I LET MY HEART COME LAST** [25] [–]
(cd-s) *(674257-2)* – ('A') / 101st lament / Static in the cities (demo) / ('A'-video).

— tragically, LAWRENCE committed suicide on 15th January 2004

— the band decided to continue with new guitarist, **MIKE HIBBERT**

May 04. (7") *(674992-7)* **THE RED THE WHITE THE BLACK THE BLUE. / THE WORKMISER HARMONIES** [15] [–]
(cd-s) *(674992-1)* – ('A') / The last picture show.
(cd-s+=) *(674992-2)* – Angels over Kilburn / ('A'-video).

Jun 04. (cd/d-lp) *(517264-2/-1)* *<92886>* **THE LOST RIOTS** [21] Oct04 [ ]
– The black amnesias / Enemies/friends / 66 sleepers to summer / Don't go to pieces / The red the white the black the blue / Black dollar bills / George Washington / Me ves y sufres / Sadness on my back / Nehemiah / Goodhorsehymn / 1776. *(ltd-cd; 517264-9)*

Aug 04. (7") *(675247-7)* **NEHEMIAH. / THIS HOUSE WAS ONCE A HOME** [30] [–]
(cd-s) *(675247-2)* – ('A') / Thee seventies song / A heart can stop a bullet / ('A'-video).

Columbia / Sony

Apr 06. (10"ep) *(LEFT 02)* **BLOOD MERIDIAN EP** [–] non-ch [–]
– Blood meridian / Under the wires / A horse / Drinkers on the dry.

Jun 06. (7") *(LEFT7 03)* **SING IT OUT. / A REK** [39] [–]
(cd-s) *(LEFTCD 03)* – ('A') / Morning ghosts / My son the crow.
(7") *(LEFT72 037)* – ('A') / Hum.

Jun 06. (cd/d10"lp) *(LEFT CD/10 04)* *<682286-2>* **LEFT** [50] [ ]
– Seconds / Blood meridian / Sing it out / Bonfires / The good fight / Left / Industry / This is a question / Little silver birds (feat. JO APPS) / Four / January / Forwardirection / The church choir.

HOT HOT HEAT

Formed: Victoria, British Columbia, Canada . . . 1999 STEVE BAYS, MATT MARNIK, PAUL HAWLEY and DUSTIN HAWTHORNE. The band began as guitar-less new wave/punk revival rock outfit, using disturbing synthesizer sound and pounding bass to create a lively and vital piece of alt rock while carving their space out amongst their more garage rock obsessed peers. This early sound was probably best witnessed on subsequent compilation, 'SCENES ONE THROUGH TO THIRTEEN' (2002), which collected material from the period from about 2000 through to 2001. The following year saw the departure of frontman MARNIK, who was replaced by guitarist DANTE DeCARO. This led the band's sound down a punkier road as evidenced on the EP, 'KNOCK KNOCK KNOCK', released on the influential 'Sub Pop' indie imprint. A packed year of touring ensued to support this record and their subsequent debut album, 'MAKE UP THE BREAKDOWN' (2002) which, with its non-stop synth-punk attack, led to a major deal with 'Warners' by the year end. An album laden with catchy hooks and screaming keyboards, HOT HOT HEAT were certainly disproving their critics who had written them off as bandwagon jumping retroists hitching a ride on the STROKES' cart. Nevertheless, they joined the growing number of no-wave bands popping out of the underground scene; from YEAH YEAH YEAHS to the RAPTURE, something seemed different about HHH's spasmo-techno punk/funk assault. First of all they were great songwriters, as evident on 'NO, NOT NOW' and the infectious 'BANDAGES'. Second, they were just great young musicians, very tight, focused and well-oiled both in the studio and live. 'MAKE UP THE BREAKDOWN' sold a truck-load of albums and sent the band on a whirlwind tour in 2003. The STROKES influences weren't any less in-yer-face on 2005's Top 40 album 'ELEVATOR' (there was a little bit of horn-rimmed ELVIS COSTELLO in there as well; check out the phrasing on 'GOODNIGHT GOODNIGHT'), and like the hip-hyped New Yorkers, the 'HEAT didn't always blast at full furnace.

Album rating: SCENES ONE THROUGH THIRTEEN compilation (*6) / MAKE UP THE BREAKDOWN (*7) / ELEVATOR (*6)

STEVE BAYS (b. 2 May'78) – vocals, keyboards / **MATT MARNICK** – vocals, guitar / **DUSTIN HAWTHORNE** (b.21 Jul'76) – bass, vocals / **PATRICK HAWLEY** (b.24 Oct'80) – drums

Apr 00. (7"red-ep) *<ACHE 001>* **HOT HOT HEAT** [–] [ ]
– Fashion fight pause / Tourist in your town / Matador at the door / Spelling live backwards. *(UK-iss.Sep02; same)*

Nov 00. (lp) *<ACHE 002>* **HOT HOT HEAT / THE RED LIGHT STING** [–] [ ]
– Case that they gave me / Haircut economics / Circus maximus / Tokyo vogue / I blew a fuse in my personality / (others by RED LIGHT STING). *(UK cd-iss. Aug03 & May04; ACHE 002CD)*

not iss. / Monoton Studios

Jun 01. (7"ep) **HOT HOT HEAT** [–] [ ]
– Keep my name out of your mouth / Word to water / Paco Pena.

Ohev / Ohev

Feb 02. (cd) *<(OHEV 009CD)>* **SCENES ONE THROUGH THIRTEEN** (compilation) [ ] [ ]
– Keep my name out of your mouth / Word to water / Haircut economics / The case that they gave me / Paco Pena / Circus maximus / I blew a fuse in my personality / Tokyo vogue / Fashion fight pause / Spelling live backwards / Matador at the door / Tourist in your own town / You're ruining it for everyone.

— **DANTE DeCARO** – guitar, vocals; repl. MATT

Sub Pop / Sub Pop

Jul 02. (cd-ep) *<(SPCD 594)>* **KNOCK KNOCK KNOCK** [ ] Apr02 [ ]
– Le le low / 5 times out of 100 / Have a good sleep / Touch you touch you / More for show. *<(neon pink-12"ep iss.Oct02; SP 594)> (re-iss. Sep03; same)*

B-Unique / Sub Pop

Mar 03. (7") *(BUN 045-7)* **BANDAGES. / APT. 101** [25] [–]
(cd-s+=) *(BUN 045CDS)* – Move on.

WEA / Sub Pop

Mar 03. (lp/cd) *(5046 64225-2)* *<SP/+CD 599>* **MAKE UP THE BREAKDOWN** [35] Oct02 [ ]
– Naked in the city again / No not now / Get in or get out / Bandages / Oh, godamnit / Aveda / This town / Talk to me, dance with me / Save us S.O.S. / In Cairo.

Jul 03. (7") *(W 615)* **NO NOT NOW. / 5 TIMES OUT OF A 100 (thoughts out of a 100 remix)** [38] [–]
(cd-s+=) *(W 615CD)* – This town (live).

Nov 03. (cd-s) *(W 626CD)* **TALK TO ME, DANCE WITH ME / OH, GODDAMMIT** [ ] [–]

Dec 03. (cd-s) *<70637>* **TALK TO ME, DANCE WITH ME / OH, GODDAMMIT / LE LE LOW (live)** [–] [ ]

— (Oct'04) DeCARO left after recording new set (formed WOLF PARADE)

Sire / Sire

Apr 05. (7"pic-d/cd-s) *(W 670/+CD1)* **GOODNIGHT GOODNIGHT. / WHEN WE WERE KIDS (demo)** [36] [–]
(cd-s) *(W 670CD2)* – ('A') / Wait a second (demo) / Eyes ear mouth (demo) / ('A'-video).

Apr 05. (cd) *<(9362 48988-2)>* **ELEVATOR** [34] [34]
– Introduction / Running out of time / Goodnight goodnight / Ladies and gentleman / You owe me an IOU / No jokes – fact / Jingle jangle / Pickin' it up / Island of the honest man / Middle of nowhere / Dirty mouth / Soldier in a box / Untitled / Shame on you / Elevator.

Jul 05. (7"pic-d/cd-s) *(W 677/+CD1)* **MIDDLE OF NOWHERE. / GOODNIGHT GOODNIGHT (EL-P remix)** [47] [–]
(cd-s) *(W 677CD2)* – ('A') / 48th hour (demo) / Jingle jangle (acoustic).

— (Apr'05) added **LUKE PAQUIN** – guitar, vocals

☐ HOURGLASS
(see under ⇒ ALLMAN BROTHERS BAND)

☐ Steve HOWE (see under ⇒ YES)

the HUMAN LEAGUE

Formed: Sheffield, England ... autumn 1977 by computer operators MARTYN WARE and IAN CRAIG-MARSH. As The FUTURE, with vocalist ADI NEWTON, they recruited former hospital porter PHIL OAKEY, who soon replaced ADI (later to CLOCKDVA). Now as HUMAN LEAGUE, the trio recorded demo, which was accepted by Edinburgh-based indie 'Fast', run by Bob Last. Their debut 45 'BEING BOILED', became NME single of the week in mid-78. They added ADRIAN WRIGHT on visuals and synths, and after a dire instrumental EP 'THE DIGNITY OF LABOUR', they signed to 'Virgin' in Apr'79. Their first 45 for the label, 'I DON'T DEPEND ON YOU', was credited to The MEN, but their credibility was restored later that year when 'EMPIRE STATE HUMAN', nearly gave them a hit. This was duly followed by a debut album, 'REPRODUCTION', which failed to build on their early promise. In Spring 1980, they went into UK Top 60 with double-7" EP, 'HOLIDAY '80', and Top 20 with album, 'TRAVELOGUE'. In October '80, OAKEY and WRIGHT brought in teenage girls JOANNE and SUZANNE to replace WARE and CRAIG-MARSH who left to form HEAVEN 17. Twelve months later, with new additions IAN BURDEN and JO CALLIS, they were at No.1 with both the 'DARE' album, and 'DON'T YOU WANT ME' single, which also peaked at the top in the States. By now, the experimental industrial leanings of their early work had given way to a chart dominating new romantic/pop synth sound which made 'DARE' one of the definitive albums of the era. They were also responsible, or at least OAKEY was, for perhaps the worst 80's haircut of them all (yes, even worse than the mullet), the accident-with-a-pair-of-garden-shears number that featured one side long and erm ... one side short! Barnet's aside, the hits were consistent ('KEEP FEELING FASCINATION', 'MIRROR MAN', 'THE LEBANON'), if not exactly prolific and, like many similar 80's acts, by the time they got around to releasing a follow-up set, the fuss had died down. Nevertheless, 'HYSTERIA' (1984) made the UK Top 3, while OAKEY teamed up with disco veteran, GIORGIO MORODER, for the soppy but brilliant 'TOGETHER IN ELECTRIC DREAMS', another massive Top 5 hit in Autumn '84 (the pair subsequently recorded a full length album together, 'CHROME'). Produced by the soul/R&B team of Jimmy Jam and Terry Lewis, 'CRASH' (1986) didn't do the band any favours, although it did spawn the melancholy 'HUMAN', a surprise US No.1 and their biggest hit single since the early 80's heyday. Though a 1988 greatest hits album kept the band's profile high, poor sales of 'ROMANTIC' (1990) saw the end of their tenure with 'Virgin', and it looked like permanent relegation was imminent. A new deal with 'East West' and a 1994 Top 10 album, 'OCTOPUS', suggested otherwise, things coming full circle when a remixed version of 'DON'T YOU WANT ME' made the Top 20 in late '95. Conspicuous only by his absence, PHIL OAKEY has since provided some vocals (alongside 60's crooner, TONY CHRISTIE) on the ALL SEEING I album in '99. With 'SECRETS' (2001), the HUMAN LEAGUE entered their fourth decade of recording although you wouldn't have guessed it by OAKEY's ever youthful looks. A fair attempt at reconciling current trends in electronic music with their classic sound, this largely instrumental effort scraped into the UK Top 50. The occasionally ragged 'LIVE AT THE DOME' (2005), had in fact been recorded in Brighton two years previously, proof that OAKEY and Co were at heart a studio band.

• **Songwriters:** WARE and CRAIG-MARSH before their departure, and OAKEY and WRIGHT on all since early 80's. The 90's, featured OAKEY composing alongside new member NEIL SUTTON. Covered:- YOU'VE LOST THAT LOVIN' FEELIN' (Righteous Brothers) / ROCK'N'ROLL (Gary Glitter) / NIGHTCLUBBIN' (Iggy Pop) / ONLY AFTER DARK (Mick Ronson).

Album rating: REPRODUCTION (*5) / TRAVELOGUE (*5) / DARE (*8) / LOVE AND DANCING mixes set (*4) / HYSTERIA (*5) / CRASH (*5) / GREATEST HITS compilation (*8) / ROMANTIC? (*4) / OCTOPUS (*6) / SECRETS (*4) / THE VERY BEST OF ... compilation (*7) / LIVE AT THE DOME (*3) / Phil Oakey & Giorgio Moroder: CHROME (*4)

PHIL OAKEY (b. 2 Oct'55) – vocals / **IAN CRAIG-MARSH** (b.19 Nov'56) – synthesizers / **MARTYN WARE** (b.19 May'56) – synthesizers

Fast | not iss.

Jun 78. (7") *(FAST 4)* **BEING BOILED. / CIRCUS OF DEATH** [ ] [-]
(re-iss. Jan82 reached No.6 UK; same)

— added **ADRIAN WRIGHT** (b.30 Dec'56) – synthesizers, visuals

Apr 79. (12"ep) *(FAST 10)* **THE DIGNITY OF LABOUR** [ ] [-]
– (part 1 / part 2 / part 3 / part 4) *(contains free spoken word flexi; VF 1)*

Virgin | A&M

Jul 79. (7"/12"; as The MEN) *(VS 269/+12)* **I DON'T DEPEND ON YOU. / CRUEL (instrumental)** [ ] [-]

Sep 79. (7") *(VS 294)* **EMPIRE STATE HUMAN. / INTRODUCING** [ ] [-]

Oct 79. (lp/c) *(V/TCV 2133)* **REPRODUCTION** [ ] [-]
– Almost medieval / Circus of death / The path of least resistance / Blind youth / The word before last / Empire state human / Morale / You've lost that lovin' feelin' / Austerity / Girl one / Zero as a limit. *(re-pro.Aug81, hit UK No.49) (re-iss. Jun88 lp/c; OVED/+C 114) (cd-iss. Dec88; CDV 2133)*

Apr 80. (d7"ep) *(SV 105)* **HOLIDAY '80** [56] [-]
– Rock'n'roll / Being boiled / Nightclubbing / Dancevision. *(re-iss. Nov81 as 12"ep+=)* – Marianne. *(hit UK No.46)*

May 80. (lp/c) *(T/TCV 2160)* **TRAVELOGUE** [16] [-]
– The black hit of space / Only after dark / Life kills / Dreams of leaving / Toyota city / Crow and a baby / The touchables / Gordon's Gin / Being boiled / WXJL tonight. *(re-iss. Jun88 lp/c; OVED/+C 115)*

Jun 80. (7") *(VS 351)* **ONLY AFTER DARK. / TOYOTA CITY** [62] [-]
(free 7" w/) – EMPIRE STATE HUMAN. / INTRODUCING

— **JO CATHERALL** (b.18 Sep'62) **& SUSANNE SULLEY** (b.22 Mar'63) – b.vocals repl. WARE and MARSH who formed HEAVEN 17. also added **IAN BURDEN** (b.24 Dec'57) – bass, synthesizers

Feb 81. (7") *(VS 395)* **BOYS AND GIRLS. / TOM BAKER** [48] [-]

Apr 81. (7"/ext.12"; as HUMAN LEAGUE RED) *(VS 416/+12)* **THE SOUND OF THE CROWD. / ('A'instrumental)** [12] [-]

— added **JO CALLIS** (b. 2 May'55, Glasgow, Scotland) – guitar (ex-REZILLOS, ex-BOOTS FOR DANCING, ex-SHAKE)

Jul 81. (7"; as HUMAN LEAGUE RED) *(VS 435)* **LOVE ACTION (I BELIEVE IN LOVE). / HARD TIMES** [3] Apr82 [ ]
(12"+=) *(VS 435-12)* – ('A'&'B'instrumental).
(cd-ep.iss.Jun88; – the four 12"tracks)

Oct 81. (7"; as HUMAN LEAGUE BLUE) *(VS 453)* **OPEN YOUR HEART. / NON-STOP** [6] [-]
(12"+=) *(VS 453-12)* – ('A'instrumental) / ('B'instrumental).

Oct 81. (lp/pic-lp/c) *(T/TP/TCV 2192)* <4892> **DARE** [1] Feb82 [3]
– Things that dreams are made of / Open your heart / The sound of the crowd / Darkness / Do or die / Get Carter / I am the law / Seconds / Love action (I believe in love) / Don't you want me. *(cd-iss. 1983; OVED 177) (re-iss. Sep90 lp/c; OVED/+C 333) (cd-iss. Nov01; SACDV 2192)*

Nov 81. (7"; as HUMAN LEAGUE 100) *(VS 466)* <2397> **DON'T YOU WANT ME. / SECONDS** [1] Feb82 [1]
(2"+=) *(VS 466-12)* – ('A'extended).

Jul 82. (lp/c; as LEAGUE UNLIMITED ORCHESTRA) *(OVED/OVEC 6)* <3209> **LOVE AND DANCING** [6] Sep92 [ ]
– (instrumental versions of "DARE" except;) / Get Carter / Darkness *(cd-iss. Jan86; CDOVED 6)*

Aug 82. (7") **THINGS THAT DREAMS ARE MADE OF. / ('A' instrumental)** [-] [ ]

Oct 82. (7"; as LEAGUE UNLIMITED ORCHESTRA) **DON'T YOU WANT ME. / (part 2)** [-] [ ]

Nov 82. (7"/7"pic-d) *(VS/+Y 522)* **MIRROR MAN. / (YOU REMIND ME OF) GOLD** [2] [-]
(ext.12"+=) *(VS 522-12)* – Gold (instrumental).

Apr 83. (7"; as HUMAN LEAGUE RED) *(VS 569)* <2547> **(KEEP FEELING) FASCINATION. / TOTAL PANIC** [2] May83 [8]
(ext.12"+=) *(VS 569-12)* – ('A'improvisation).

Jul 83. (m-lp) <12501> **FASCINATION** (import, recent hits) [-] [22]

Sep 83. (7") <2587> **MIRROR MAN. / NON-STOP** [-] [30]

Apr 84. (7") *(VS 672)* <2641> **THE LEBANON. / THIRTEEN** [11] Jul84 [64]
(ext.12"+=) *(VS 672-12)* – ('A'instrumental).

The HUMAN LEAGUE

May 84. (lp/c/cd) *(T/TCV/CDV 2315)* <4923> **HYSTERIA** [3] [62]
– I'm coming back / I love you too much / Rock me again and again and again and again and again and again / Louise / The Lebanon / Betrayed / The sign / So hurt / Life on your own / Don't you know I want you. *(re-iss. Feb88 lp/c; OVED/+C 177)*

Jun 84. (7") *(VS 688)* **LIFE ON YOUR OWN. / THE WORLD TONIGHT** [16] [–]
(12"+=) *(VS 688-12)* – ('A'extended).

Aug 84. (7") **DON'T YOU KNOW I WANT TO. / THIRTEEN** [–] [ ]

Oct 84. (7"/7"pic-d)(12") *(VS/+Y 723)(VS 723-12)* **LOUISE. / THE SIGN** [13] [–]

Oct 84. (7") **LOUISE. / THE WORLD TONIGHT** [–] [ ]

—— Trimmed down to main trio of **PHIL, SUSANNE, JOANNE** plus **ADRIAN / JIM RUSSELL** – synthesizer repl. BURDEN and CALLIS

Aug 86. (7") *(VS 880)* <2861> **HUMAN. / ('A'instrumental)** [8] [1]
(ext.12"+=) *(VS 880-12)* – ('A'acappella).

Sep 86. (lp/c/cd) *(V/TCV/CDV 2391)* <5129> **CRASH** [7] [24]
– Money / Swang / Human / Jam / Are you ever coming back? / I need your loving / Party / Love on the run / The real thing / Love is all that matters.

Nov 86. (7") *(VS 900)* **I NEED YOUR LOVING. / ('A'instrumental)** [72] [–]
(ext.12"+=) *(VS 900-12)* – ('A'dub).

Nov 86. (7") <2893> **I NEED YOUR LOVING. / ARE YOU EVER COMING BACK** [–] [44]

Jan 87. (7") **LOVE IS ALL THAT MATTERS. / ('A'instrumental)** [–] [ ]

Apr 87. (7") **ARE YOU EVER COMING BACK. / JAM** [–] [ ]

Oct 88. (7") *(VS 1025)* **LOVE IS ALL THAT MATTERS. / I LOVE YOU TOO MUCH** [41] [ ]
('B'dub.12"+=/'B'dub.cd-s+=) *(VS T/CD 1025)* – ('A'extended).

Nov 88. (lp/c/cd/pic-cd) *(HL TV/MC/CD/CDP 1)* <75021 5227-1/-4/-2> **GREATEST HITS** (compilation) [3] [ ]
– Mirror man / (Keep feeling) Fascination / The sound of the crowd / The Lebanon / Human / Together in electric dreams (PHIL OAKEY & GIORGIO MORODER) / Don't you want me? / Being boiled (re-boiled) / Love action (I believe in love) / Louise / Open your heart / Love is all that matters / Life on your own. *(re-iss. Nov95 cd/c;)*

—— The basic trio, added **RUSSELL BENNETT** – guitar / **NEIL SUTTON** – keyboards

Aug 90. (7"/c-s) *(VS/+C 1262)* <1520> **HEART LIKE A WHEEL. / REBOUND** [29] Sep90 [32]
(12"+=) *(VST 1262)* – ('A'extended).
(cd-s++=) *(VSCDT 1262)* – ('A'remix).
(cd-s++=) *(VSCDX 1262)* – A doorway (dub mix).

Sep 90. (cd/c/lp) *(V/TCV/CDV 2624)* <75021 5316-2/-4/-1> **ROMANTIC?** [24] [ ]
– Kiss the future / A doorway / Heart like a wheel / Men are dreamers / Mister Moon and Mister Sun / Soundtrack to a generation / Rebound / The stars are going out / Let's get together again / Get it right this time.

Nov 90. (7"/c-s) *(VS/+C 1303)* **SOUNDTRACK TO A GENERATION. / ('A'instrumental)** [ ] [–]
(12"+=) *(VST 1303)* – ('A'-Orbit mix).
(cd-s++=) *(VSCDT 1303)* – ('A'-Pan Belgian mix).
(cd-s) *(VSCDX 1303)* – ('A'-Pan Belgian dub) / ('A'-808 instrumental mix) / ('A'-Dave Dodd's mix) / ('A'-acappella).

East West / East West

Dec 94. (c-s) *(YZ 882C)* <64443> **TELL ME WHEN. / ('A'mix 1)** [6] Mar95 [31]
(cd-s+=) *(YZ 882CD1)* – Kimi ni mune kyun / The bus to Crookes.
(12"/cd-s) *(YZ 882 T/CD2)* – ('A'side) / ('A'-Overworld mix) / ('A'-Red Jerry mix) / ('A'-Strictly blind dub mix).

Jan 95. (cd/c/lp) *(4509 98750-2/-4/-1)* <61788> **OCTOPUS** [6] [ ]
– Tell me when / These are the days / One man in my heart / Words / Filling up with Heaven / House full of nothing / John Cleese; is he funny? / Never again / Cruel young lover.

Mar 95. (c-s/cd-s) *(YZ 904 C/CD1)* **ONE MAN IN MY HEART / THESE ARE THE DAYS (Ba ba mix)** [13] [–]
(cd-s+=) *(YZ 904CD2)* – These are the days (sonic radiation) / ('A'version).
(12") *(YZ 904T)* – ('B'side) / ('B'-Symphone Ba Ba mix) / ('B'instrumental) / ('A'-T.O.E.C. unplugged).

Jun 95. (c-s/cd-s) *(YZ 944 C/CD1)* **FILLING UP WITH HEAVEN / JOHN CLEESE, IS HE FUNNY?** [36] [–]
(cd-s) *(YZ 944CD2)* – ('A'side) / ('A'-Hardfloor mix) / ('A'-Neil McLellen mix).

Jan 96. (c-s) *(EW 020C)* **STAY WITH ME TONIGHT / ('A'mix)** [40] [–]
(cd-s) *(EW 020CD)* – ('A'mixes).

Papillion / Ark 21

Jul 01. (cd-s) *(BTFLYS 0012)* <1220> **ALL I EVER WANTED / TRANQUILITY / ALL I EVER WANTED (vanity case mix)** [47] [ ]
(cd-s) *(BTFLYX 0012)* – ('A'-original) / ('A'-Oliver Lieb mix).

Aug 01. (cd) *(BTFLYCD 0019)* <810075> **SECRETS** [44] [ ]
– All I ever wanted / Nervous / Love me madly? / Shameless / 122.3 bpm / Never give your heart / Ran / The snake / Ringinglow / Liar / Lament / Reflections / Brute / Sin city / Release / You'll be sorry.

—— in Apr'03, PHILIP OAKEY featured on ALEX GOLD's single, 'LA Today'

Snapper / Secret

Jul 05. (cd) *(SMACD 904)* <2170858> **LIVE AT THE DOME** (live 2003 Brighton) [ ] Aug05 [ ]
– Hard times – Love action / Mirror man / Louise / The snake / Darkness / All I ever wanted / Open your heart / The Lebanon / Human / Things that dreams are made of / (Keep feeling) Fascination / Don't you want me / (Together in) Electric dreams / (+ DVD tracks).

– compilations, etc. –

Oct 90. (3xcd-box) *Virgin; (TPAK 3)* **DARE / HYSTERIA / CRASH** [ ] [–]

Oct 95. (c-s) *Virgin; (VSC 1557)* **DON'T YOU WANT ME (remix) / ('A'-Snap remix) / (2-'A'-Red Jerry mix)** [16] [ ]
(12") *(VST 1557)* – ('A'-Snap remix extended) / ('A'-Red Jerry remix extended).
(cd-s) *(VSCDT 1557)* – (all 6-'A'versions).

Oct 96. (cd) *Disky; (VI 87530-2)* **SOUNDTRACK TO A GENERATION** [ ] [ ]

Apr 02. (12") *Klang; (KLANG 62)* **ALL I EVER WANTED (mixes)** [ ] [–]

Sep 03. (d-cd) *Virgin; (HLCDX 2) / E.M.I.; <592391>* **THE VERY BEST OF THE HUMAN LEAGUE** [24] [ ]
– Don't you want me / Love action (I believe in love) / Open your heart / The sound of the crowd / Mirror man / (Keep feeling) Fascination / The Lebanon / Life on your own / Together in electric dreams / Louise / Human / Heart like a wheel / Tell me when / One man in my heart / All I ever wanted / Being boiled (Fast version) / Empire State human // Don't you want me (Majik J original booty vocal mix) / Open your heart (Laid remix) / The sound of the crowd (Trisco's popclash mix) / Love action (Brooks red line vocal mix) / (Keep feeling) Fascination ((groove collision TMC mix) / Empire State human (Chamber's reproduced mix) / The things that dreams are made of (Jimmy 19 the A509 PWC remix) / The sound of the crowd (Freaksblamredo) / Open your heart (Strand remix) / The sound of the crowd (Rilton re-dub) / Love action (Fluke's dub action remix).

PHIL OAKEY & GIORGIO MORODER

– synthesizers

Virgin / A&M

Sep 84. (7"/7"pic-d/ext.12") *(VS/+Y 713/+12)* **TOGETHER IN ELECTRIC DREAMS. / ('A'instrumental)** [3] [ ]

Jun 85. (7") *(VS 772)* **GOODBYE BAD TIMES. / ('A'instrumental)** [44] [ ]

Jul 85. (lp/c/cd) *(V/TCV/CDV 2351)* **CHROME** [52] [ ]
– Goodbye bad times / Together in electric dreams / Valerie / Why must the show go on / Be me lover now / Shake it up / Brand new lover / In transit / Now. *(re-iss. Oct87; OVED 187)*

Aug 85. (7"/12") *(VS 800/+12)* **BE MY LOVER NOW. / ('A' instrumental)** [ ] [ ]

Nov 88. (7") *Old Gold; (OG 9825)* **TOGETHER IN ELECTRIC DREAMS. / GOODBYE BAD TIMES** [ ] [–]

HUMBLE PIE

Formed: Essex, England . . . spring 1969 as a mini-supergroup by STEVE MARRIOT (ex-SMALL FACES, vocals, guitar) and PETER FRAMPTON (ex-HERD, vocals, guitar). Recruiting GREG RIDLEY (bass, ex-SPOOKY TOOTH) and JERRY SHIRLEY (drums, ex-LITTLE WOMEN), the band signed to Andrew Loog Oldham's 'Immediate' label and released their debut album, 'AS SAFE AS YESTERDAY', in the summer of '69. A solid collection of rootsy

·ock, the record spawned a Top 5 UK single with 'NATURAL BORN BUGIE', MARRIOT ditching the chirpy cockney popster persona ıe'd developed with the SMALL FACES in favour of an 'authentic' R&B rasp. The more acoustic-based follow-up, 'TOWN AND COUNTRY' (1969) flopped, and HUMBLE PIE returned from an American tour in late '69 to discover that their record label had gone under. Severe financial problems ensued until help came in he form of US lawyer, Dee Anthony, who helped secure the band a ıew deal with A&M. The eponymous 'HUMBLE PIE' (1970) failed o resurrect their fortunes, as did the harder-edged 'ROCK ON' 1971), Anthony subsequently packing the band off to America on nother tour from whence came the US gold-selling live album, PERFORMANCE-ROCKIN' THE FILLMORE' (1971). Despite his liminutive size, MARRIOT had a towering stage presence, the inger blazing his way through a fiery set of boogie-based blues-·ock, both HUMBLE PIE originals and frenetic covers including Muddy Waters' 'ROLLIN' STONE' and Dr. John's 'I WALK ON GILDED SPLINTERS'. FRAMPTON departed for a solo career ater that year, ex-COLOSSEUM man, DAVE CLEMPSON taking iis place. While FRAMPTON had proved a melodic acoustic-·ock foil to MARRIOT's hard rockin' excess, the new-look 'PIE ontinued to move in a heavier direction with 'SMOKIN'' (1972), he highest charting album in the band's career, reaching No.6 in he States. Augmented by all-girl backing trio, The BLACKBERRIES CLYDIE KING, BILLIE BARNUM & VANETTA FIELDS), the and attempted a hard rock/soul fusion with the half live/half studio louble set, 'EAT IT' (1973). The album was another American Top 20 hit but HUMBLE PIE's popularity was on the wane, a urther two efforts, 'THUNDERBOX' (1974) and 'STREET RATS' 1975) barely making the charts and receiving a scathing critical eaction. The group finally split shortly after the release of the latter lbum, SHIRLEY forming NATURAL GAS with ex-BADFINGER uitarist JOEY MOLLAND while MARRIOT put together the short ved STEVE MARRIOTT ALL-STARS with MICKEY FINN (guitar, x-T.REX), IAN WALLACE (drums, ex-KING CRIMSON) and DAMON BUTCHER (keyboards). CLEMPSON, meanwhile, joined GREENSLADE. After a brief SMALL FACES reunion in the late 0's, MARIOTT reformed HUMBLE PIE along with SHIRLEY and ıew members BOBBY TENCH (guitar, ex-STREETWALKERS, ex-EFF BECK GROUP) and ANTHONY JONES (bass). Signed to Atco', the band released two generally ignored albums, 'ON TO VICTORY' (1980) and 'GO FOR THE THROAT' (1981) before isbanding finally in 1981. MARRIOT continued to tour, releasing low key solo album, 'PACKET OF THREE', in 1986. Hopes of a ıusical reunion between MARIOTT and FRAMPTON were finally ashed on 20th April '91 when MARIOTT was tragically killed in a re at his Essex cottage.

Songwriters: All took a shot at writing, with MARRIOTT the main ontributor. Covers:- C'MON EVERYBODY + HALLELUJAH I LOVE HER O (Eddie Cochran) / ROADRUNNER (Junior Walker) / HONKY TONK VOMAN (Rolling Stones) / ROCK'N'ROLL MUSIC (Chuck Berry) / ALL HOOK UP (Elvis Presley) / etc.

lbum rating: AS SAFE AS YESTERDAY (*6) / TOWN AND COUNTRY (*5) / UMBLE PIE (*5) / ROCK ON (*6) / PERFORMANCE – ROCKIN' THE ILLMORE (*7) / SMOKIN' (*5) / EAT IT (*5) / THUNDERBOX (*4) / STREET ATS (*3) / ON TO VICTORY (*3) / GO FOR THE THROAT (*2) / HOT N' ASTY – THE ANTHOLOGY compilation (*7) / Steve Marriott: MARRIOTT 4) / PACKET OF THREE (what else ... *3) / 30 SECONDS TO MIDNIGHT xploitation (*4)

TEVE MARRIOTT (b.30 Jan'47, London, England) – vocals, guitar, eyboards (ex-SMALL FACES) / **PETER FRAMPTON** (b.22 Apr'50, eckenham, England) – vocals, guitar (ex-HERD) / **GREG RIDLEY** (b.23 ct'47, Carlisle, England) – bass (ex-SPOOKY TOOTH) / **JERRY SHIRLEY** ›. 4 Feb'52) – drums (ex-LITTLE WOMEN)

Immediate Immediate

Jul 69. (lp) *(IMSP 025)* <101> **AS SAFE AS YESTERDAY** [32] [ ]
– Desperation / Stick shift / Buttermilk boy / Growing closer / As safe as yesterday / Bang? / Alabama '69 / I'll go alone / A nifty little number like you / What you will. *(cd-iss. Nov89 on 'Line'; LICD 900296) (cd re-iss. Dec92 on 'Repertoire'+=;)* – Natural born bugie / Wrist job. *(lp re-iss. Dec99 on 'Get Back'; GET 549)*

Sep 69. (7") *(IM 082)* **NATURAL BORN BUGIE. / WRIST JOB** [4] [ ]
(re-iss. Feb83; same)

Oct 69. (7") <101> **NATURAL BORN BUGIE. / I'LL GO ALONE** [–] [ ]

Dec 69. (lp) *(IMSP 027)* **TOWN AND COUNTRY** [ ] [–]
– Take me back / The sad bag of shaky Jake / The light of love / Cold lady / Down home again / Ollie Ollie / Every mother's son / Heartbeat / Only you can say / Silver tongue / Home and away. *(re-iss. 1978 on 'Charly'; CR 300016) (cd-iss. Nov93; CDIMM 020) (cd-iss. Dec92 on 'Repertoire'+=;)* – Greg's song / 79th Street blues. *(cd re-iss. Feb95 on 'Charly'; CDIMM 020)*

A&M A&M

Jul 70. (lp) *(AMLS 986)* <4270> **HUMBLE PIE** [ ] [ ]
– Live with me / Only a roach / One eyed trouser-snake rumba / Earth and water song / I'm ready / Theme from Skint (see you later liquidator) / Red light mamma / Red hot / Sucking on the sweet vine.

Mar 71. (lp) *(AMLS 203)* <4301> **ROCK ON** [ ] [ ]
– Shine on / Sour grain / 79th and sunset / Stone cold fever / Rollin' stone / A song for Jenny / The light / Big George / Strange days / Red neck jump. *(cd-iss. 1988 on 'Mobile Fidelity'; MFCD 847)*

Sep 71. (7") <1282> **I DON'T NEED NO DOCTOR (live). / SONG FOR JENNY** [–] [73]

Nov 71. (d-lp/d-c) *(AMLH/CDM 63506)* <3506> **PERFORMANCE – ROCKIN' THE FILLMORE (live)** [32] [21]
– Four day creep / I'm ready / Stone cold fever / I walk on guilded splinters / Rollin' stone / Hallelujah (I love her so) / I don't need no doctor. *(re-iss. 1974;)*

— **DAVE CLEMPSON** (b. 5 Sep'45) – guitar (ex-COLOSSEUM) repl. FRAMPTON who went solo

Mar 72. (lp) *(AMLS 64342)* <4342> **SMOKIN'** [28] [6]
– Hot 'n' nasty / The fixer / You're so good to me / C'mon everybody / Old time feelin' / 30 days in the hole / (I'm a) Road runner / Roadrunner "G" jam / I wonder who / Sweet peace and time.

Apr 72. (7") <1349> **HOT 'N' NASTY. / YOU"RE SO GOOD FOR ME** [–] [52]

Sep 72. (7") <1366> **30 DAYS IN THE HOLE. / SWEET PEACE AND TIME** [–] [ ]

— now augmented by all-girl backing trio The BLACKBERRIES (**CLYDIE KING / BILLIE BARNUM + VANETTA FIELDS**)

Jan 73. (7") *(AMS 7052)* <1406> **BLACK COFFEE. / SAY NO MORE** [ ] [ ]

Apr 73. (d-lp) *(AMLD 6004)* <3701> **EAT IT** (1-side live) [34] Mar73 [13]
– Get down to it / Good booze and bad women / Is it for love / Drugstore cowboy / Black coffee / I believe to my soul / Shut up and don't interrupt me / That's how strong my love is / Say no more / Oh, Bella (all that's hers) / Summer song / Beckton dumps / Up our sleeve / Honky tonk woman / (I'm a) Road runner.

Jun 73. (7") *(AMS 7070)* <1440> **GET DOWN TO IT. / HONKY TONK WOMAN (live)** [ ] [ ]

Oct 73. (7") *(AMS 7090)* **OH LA DE DA. / THE OUTCROWD** [ ] [–]

Feb 74. (lp) *(AMLH 63611)* <3611> **THUNDERBOX** [ ] [52]
– Thunderbox / Groovin' with Jesus / I can't stand the rain / Anna / No way / Rally with Ali / Don't worry, be happy / Ninety-nine pounds / Every single day / No money down / Drift away / Oh la de da.

May 74. (7") <1530> **NINETY-NINE POUNDS. / RALLY WITH ALI** [–] [ ]

Feb 75. (lp) *(AMLS 68282)* <4514> **STREET RATS** [ ] [100]
– Street rat / Rock'n'roll music / We can work it out / Scored out / Road hog / Rain / Funky to the bone / Let me be your lovemaker / Countryman / Stomp / Drive my car / Queens and nuns.

Mar 75. (7") *(AMS 7185)* **ROCK'N'ROLL MUSIC. / SCORED OUT** [ ] [–]

Jul 75. (7") <1711> **ROCK'N'ROLL MUSIC. / ROAD HOG** [–] [ ]

— Disbanded Spring 1975. JERRY SHIRLEY formed NATURAL GAS, and the others joined

STEVE MARRIOTT ALL-STARS

also included **DAMON BUTCHER** – keyboards / **IAN WALLACE** – drums (ex-KING CRIMSON) / **MICKEY FINN** – guitar (ex-T.REX)

A&M A&M

May 76. (lp) *(AMLH 64572)* <4572> **MARRIOTT**
– Star in my life / Are you lonely for me baby / You don't know me / Late night lady / Early evening light / East side struttin' / Lookin' for love / Help me through the day / Midnight rock'n'rollin' / Wam bam thank you ma'am.

Jun 76. (7") *(AMS 7230)* **STAR IN MY LIFE. / MIDNIGHT ROCK'N'ROLLIN'** – –

Jun 76. (7") *<1825>* **STAR IN MY LIFE. / EAST SIDE STRUTTIN'** –

—— CLEMPSON and BUTCHER joined ROUGH DIAMOND. WALLACE toured with BOB DYLAN. MICKEY FINN joined PHIL MAY'S FALLEN ANGELS. MARRIOTT re-formed The SMALL FACES

HUMBLE PIE

also re-formed in 1979, with **STEVE MARRIOTT** – vocals, guitar / **JERRY SHIRLEY** – drums / **BOBBY TENCH** – guitar (ex-STREETWALKERS, ex-JEFF BECK) / **ANTHONY JONES** – bass

Jet Atco

Apr 80. (7") *(JET 180)* <7216> **FOOL FOR A PRETTY FACE. / YOU SOPPY PRATT** 52

Apr 80. (lp) *(JET LP/CA 231)* <38122> **ON TO VICTORY** 60
– Fool for a pretty face / You soppy pratt / Get it in the end / Infatuation / Further down the road / My lover's prayer / Take it from here / Baby don't do it.

Jun 81. (lp) *(38131)* <131> **GO FOR THE THROAT** May81
– All shook up / Chip away / Driver / Go for the throat / Keep it on the island / Lottie and the charcoal queen / Restless blood / Teenage anxiety / Tin soldier.

—— Finally called it a day in '81

– compilations, others –

Sep 72. (d-lp) *A&M; <3513>* **LOST AND FOUND** (1st-2 lp's) – 37

Jul 76. (lp) *Immediate; (IML 1005)* **BACK HOME AGAIN** –

Jan 78. (lp) *Immediate; (IML 2005)* **HUMBLE PIE'S GREATEST HITS** –

Sep 85. (7") *Old Gold; (OG 9529)* **NATURAL BORN BUGIE. / (other artist)** –

Nov 85. (d-lp/c/cd) *Castle; (CCS LP/MC/CD 104)* **THE COLLECTION** –
– Bang? / Natural born bugie / I'll go alone / Buttermilk boy / Desperation / Nifty little number like you / Wrist job / Stick shift / Growing closer / As safe as yesterday / Heartbeat / Down home again / Take me back / Only you can see / Silver tongue / Every mother's son / The sad bag of Shaky Jake / Cold lady / Home and away / Light of love. *(cd-iss. Apr94;)*

1988. (cd) *A&M; (393 208-2)* **THE BEST OF HUMBLE PIE**

Nov 92. (cd) *Dojo; (EARLD 4)* **THE EARLY YEARS** –

Feb 95. (cd) *Band Of Joy; (BOJCD 101)* **NATURAL BORN BOOGIE** –

May 95. (cd) *A&M; (540 179-2)* **A PIECE OF THE PIE**

Nov 95. (d-cd) *Charly; (CDIMMBOX 3)* **THE IMMEDIATE YEARS** –

Jul 98. (cd) *Strange Fruit; (SFRSCD 066)* **NATURAL BORN BOOGIE** –

Aug 98. (cd) *King Biscuit; (<KBFHCD 017>)* **KING BISCUIT PRESENTS . . .**

Nov 99. (cd) *Eagle; (EAGCD 114)* **THE SCRUBBERS SESSIONS** –

Jul 00. (cd) *Burning Airlines; (<PILOT 048>)* **RUNNING WITH THE PACK**

STEVE MARRIOTT

solo again

Aura not iss.

Jan 85 (7") *(AUS 145)* **WHAT'CHA GONNA DO ABOUT IT. / ALL SHOOK UP** –

Aura not iss.

Apr 86. (lp/c; STEVE MARRIOTT'S PACKET OF THREE) *(AUL/AUC 729)* **PACKET OF THREE** –
– What'cha gonna do about it / Bad moon rising / All shook up / The fixer / All or nothing / Five long years / I don't need no doctor.

—— STEVE MARRIOT died 20 Apr'91, after accidentally setting his Essex cottage on fire with a lighted cigarette.

– his compilations, others –

Sep 89. (lp/c/cd) *Trax; (MOD EM/EMC/CD 1037)* **30 SECONDS TO MIDNIGHT** –
(re-iss. Apr93 on 'Castle' cd/c; CLA CD/MC 386)

Nov 91. (cd) *Mau Mau; (MAUCD 609)* **DINGWALLS 6.7.84 (live)** –

Feb 92. (cd) *Maste – Elastic Cat;* **SCRUBBERS** (rec.1974, **STEVE MARRIOTT / TIM HINKLEY / GREG RIDLEY)** –

May 97. (cd) *Metro; (OTR 1100020)* **LIVE AT THE PALACE (with A PACKET OF THREE)** –

May 97. (d-cd) *Metro; (OTR 1100021)* **THE MARRIOTT ANTHOLOGY** –

May 97. (cd) *Metro; (OTR 1100023)* **INTEREPRETATIONS** –

HUSKER DU

Formed: St. Paul, Minnesota, USA . . . 1978 by BOB MOULD, GRANT HART and GREG NORTON. In 1980-82, they issued a few 45's and a live LP, 'LAND SPEED RECORD', on their own label, 'New Alliance'. The record typified the band's early uncompromising hardcore which was often tediously workmanlike in its adherence to the steadfast confines of the genre. 'EVERYTHING FALLS APART' (1983) was also unflinching in its intensity and it was all the more surprising when the band showed glimmers of noise-pop greatness on their 1983 debut for 'SST', 'METAL CIRCUS'. They consolidated this by cross-fertilising the previously polarised worlds of psychedelia and hardcore punk on an electrifying cover of The BYRDS' 'EIGHT MILES HIGH' (1984). The follow-up double set, 'ZEN ARCADE' (1984) was a further giant step for hardcore-kind. A concept album no less, the twin songwriting attack of MOULD and HART was becoming sharper and even the sprawling, unfocused feel of the whole affair wasn't enough to blunt the edges of songs like 'WHATEVER' and 'TURN ON THE NEWS'. The songwriting on 'NEW DAY RISING' (1985) was even more trenchant, the band's adrenaline fuelled pop-core hybrid developing at breakneck speed. 'FLIP YOUR WIG' (1985), the band's last indie release, marked a stepping stone to their major label debut for 'Warners', 'CANDY APPLE GREY' (1986). While HART perfected HUSKER DU's melodic dischord on tracks like 'DEAD SET ON DESTRUCTION', MOULD showcased darkly introspective, acoustic elegies 'TOO FAR DOWN' and 'HARDLY GETTING OVER IT'. The more musically-challenged among HUSKER DU's following were none too taken with this new fangled unplugged business although the album was released to unanimous critical acclaim. The band's swansong, 'WAREHOUSE: SONGS AND STORIES' (1987) was the culmination of a decade's experimentation and possessed an unprecedented depth, clarity and consistency. By the time of its release, though, tension in the band was reaching breaking point and HUSKER DU was disbanded in 1987. While GRANT HART and BOB MOULD went on to solo careers, as well as respectively forming NOVA MOB and SUGAR, they were always better together and the magic of HUSKER DU is inestimable in its influence on a generation of alternative guitar bands. Upon the demise of HUSKER DU in 1987, MOULD signed to 'Virgin America' and subsequently entered PRINCE's 'Paisley Park' studios to lay down his first solo set, 'WORKBOOK' (1989). Augmented by the former PERE UBU rhythm section of ANTON FIER and TONY MAIMONE and employing cellists JANE SCARPANTONI and STEVE HAIGLER, MOULD confounded expectations with a largely acoustic affair trading in melodic distortion for fragments of contemplative melancholy; only the closing 'WHICHEVER WAY THE WIND BLOWS' acknowledged the sonic assault of prime HUSKER DU. Despite the guaranteed critical plaudits and the more accessible nature of the material, 'WORKBOOK's sales were modest. Perhaps as a reaction, the following year's 'BLACK SHEETS OF RAIN' – again recorded with FIER and MAIMONE – was a searing return to bleaker, noisier pastures; 'HANGING TREE' remains among the most tormented work of MOULD's career, while the likes of 'HEAR ME CALLING' and 'IT'S TOO LATE' combined keening melody with blistering soloing/discordant riffing in patented MOULD fashion. When this album also failed to take off, the singer parted company from 'Virgin' and undertook a low-key acoustic tour. His wilderness period was brief, however, the emerging grunge vanguard citing HUSKER DU as a massive influence and inspiring MOULD to form another melodic power trio. Comprising fellow songwriter/bassist, DAVE BARBE and drummer MALCOLM TRAVIS, SUGAR signed to 'Creation' and proceeded to cut one of the most feted albums of the era in 'COPPER BLUE' (1992). Leaner, tighter and cleaner, the record's bittersweet pop-hardcore crunch finally provided MOULD with a springboard for commercial success; a UK Top 10 hit, the album even spawned a Top 30 hit single in the sublime 'IF I CAN'T CHANGE YOUR MIND'. 'BEASTER', 1993's mini-album follow-up, took tracks from the 'COPPER BLUE' sessions and buried them in a multi-tiered blanket of howling distortion. Unsurprisingly it failed to spawn a hit, although its Top 3 success was no doubt sweet for the ever contrary MOULD, his follow-up proper, 'FILE UNDER EASY LISTENING (F.U.E.L.)' (1994), suggesting that he'd become bored with the whole concept. MOULD eventually disbanded the project in spring '96, releasing a third solo album the same year, simply titled 'BOB MOULD'. Bowing out of the music industry treadmill with 'THE LAST DOG AND PONY SHOW' (1998), MOULD eventually resurfaced in 2002 with 'MODULATE', an ambitious if ultimately flawed attempt at re-examining his muse through the lens of post-millennial electronica. His most commercial LP to date, 'BODY OF SONG' (2005), was an occasionally uncomfortable compromise between his clubbier impulses (including DAFT PUNK-style vocoder-singing) and 80s/90s alt-rock.

Songwriters: MOULD-HART compositions except; SUNSHINE SUPERMAN (Donovan) / TICKET TO RIDE + SHE'S A WOMAN + HELTER SKELTER (Beatles) / EIGHT MILES HIGH (Byrds). NOVA MOB covered I JUST WANT TO MAKE LOVE TO YOU (Willie Dixon) / SHEENA IS A PUNK ROCKER (Ramones). Solo GRANT HART covered SIGNED D.C. (Love). MOULD covered; SHOOT OUT THE LIGHTS (Richard Thompson). • **Trivia:** HUSKER DU means DO YOU REMEMBER in Swedish.

Album rating: LAND SPEED RECORD mini (*6) / EVERYTHING FALLS APART (*5) / ZEN ARCADE (*9) / NEW DAY RISING (*9) / FLIP YOUR WIG (*9) / CANDY APPLE GREY (*7) / WAREHOUSE: SONGS & STORIES (*9) / THE LIVING END live compilation (*6) / Bob Mould: WORKBOOK (*7) / BLACK SHEETS OF RAIN (*6) / Sugar: COPPER BLUE (*9) / BEASTER mini (*7) / FILE UNDER: EASY LISTENING (*7) / BESIDES collection (*6) / Bob Mould: BOB MOULD (*8) / THE LAST DOG AND PONY SHOW (*7) / MODULATE (*4) / BODY OF SONG (*6)

BOB MOULD (b.12 Oct'61, Malone, New York) – vocals, guitar, keyboards, percussion / **GRANT HART** (b. GRANTZBERG VERNON HART, 18 Mar'61) – drums, keyboards, percussion, vocals / **GREG NORTON** (b.13 Mar'59, Rock Island, Illinois) – bass

not iss. Reflex

Jan 81. (7") *<38285>* **STATUES. / AMUSEMENT (live)** -

Alternative Tentacles New Alliance

Jan 82. (m-lp) *(VIRUS 25) <NAR 007>* **LAND SPEED RECORD (live)**
– All tensed up / Don't try to call / I'm not interested / Big sky / Guns at my school / Push the button / Gilligan's Island / MTC / Don't have a life / Bricklayer / Tired of doing things / You're naive / Strange week / Do the bee / Ultracore / Let's go die / Data control. *(re-iss. Nov88 on 'S.S.T.'; SST 195) (re-iss. cd/c/lp Oct95)*

May 82. (7"m) *<NAR 010>* **IN A FREE LAND. / WHAT DO I WANT? / M.I.C.** -

not iss. Reflex

Jan 83. (lp; @45rpm) *<D>* **EVERYTHING FALLS APART** -
– From the gut / Blah, blah, blah / Punch drunk / Bricklayer / Afraid of being wrong / Sunshine Superman / Signals from above / Everything falls apart / Wheels / Obnoxious / Gravity. *(cd-iss. May93 on 'WEA'+=; 8122 71163-2)* – In a free land / What do I want / M.I.C. / Statues / Let's go die / Amusement (live) / Do you remember?

S.S.T. S.S.T.

Dec 83. (m-lp) *<(SST 020)>* **METAL CIRCUS** Oct83
– Real world / Deadly skies / It's not funny anymore / Diane / First of the last calls / Lifeline / Out on a limb.

Apr 84. (7"colrd) *<(SST 025)>* **EIGHT MILES HIGH. / MASOCHISM WORLD**
(3"cd-s iss.Dec88; SST 025CD)

Sep 84. (d-lp) *<(SST 027)>* **ZEN ARCADE** Jul84
– Something I learned today / Broken home, broken heart / Never talking to you again / Chartered trips / Dreams reoccurring / Indecision time / Hare Krishna / Beyond the threshold / Pride / I'll never forget you / The biggest lie / What's going on / Masochism world / Standing by the sea / Somewhere / One step at a time / Pink turns to blue / Newest industry / Monday will never be the same / Whatever / The tooth fairy and the princess / Turn on the news / Reoccurring dreams. *(cd-iss. Oct87; SST 027CD) (re-iss. cd/c/d-lp Oct95 & Jun97; same)*

Feb 85. (lp) *<(SST 031)>* **NEW DAY RISING** Jan85
– New day rising / Girl who lives on Heaven Hill / I apologize / Folklore / If I told you / Celebrated summer / Perfect example / Terms of psychic warfare / 59 times the pain / Powerline / Books about UFO's / I don't know what you're talking about / How to skin a cat / Watcha drinkin' / Plans I make. *(cd-iss. Oct87; SST 031CD) (re-iss. cd/c/lp Oct95; same)*

Aug 85. (7") *<(SST 051)>* **MAKE NO SENSE AT ALL. / LOVE IS ALL AROUND (MARY'S THEME)**

Oct 85. (lp) *<(SST 055)>* **FLIP YOUR WIG** Sep85
– Flip your wig / Every everything / Makes no sense at all / Hate paper doll / Green eyes / Divide and conquer / Games / Find me / The baby song / Flexible flyer / Private plane / Keep hanging on / The wit and the wisdom / Don't know yet. *(cd-iss. Oct87; SST 055CD) (re-iss. cd/c/lp Oct95; same)*

Warners Warners

Feb 86. (7") *(W 8746)* **DON'T WANT TO KNOW IF YOU ARE LONELY. / ALL WORK NO PLAY**
(12"+=) *(W 8746T) <20446-0>* – Helter skelter (live).

Mar 86. (lp/c) *(WX 40/+C) <25385>* **CANDY APPLE GREY**
– Crystal / Don't want to know if you are lonely / I don't know for sure / Sorry somehow / Too far down / Hardly getting over it / Dead set on destruction / Eiffel Tower high / No promises have I made / All this I've done for you. *(cd-iss. Nov92; 7599 25385-2)*

Sep 86. (7") *(W 8612)* **SORRY SOMEHOW. / ALL THIS I'VE DONE FOR YOU** -
(d7+=/12"+=) *(W 8612 F/T)* – Flexible flyer / Celebrated summer.

Jan 87. (7") *(W 8456)* **COULD YOU BE THE ONE. / EVERYTIME** -
(12"+=) *(W 8456T)* – Charity, chastity, prudence, hope.

Jan 87. (d-lp/d-c) *(925544-1/-4) <25544>* **WAREHOUSE: SONGS & STORIES** 72
– These important years / Charity, chastity, prudence and hope / Standing in the rain / Back from somewhere / Ice cold ice / You're a soldier / Could you be the one? / Too much spice / Friend, you've got to fall / Visionary / She floated away / Bed of nails / Tell you why tomorrow / It's not peculiar / Actual condition / No reservations / Turn it around / She's a woman (and now he is a man) / Up in the air / You can live at home. *(cd-iss. Oct92; 7599 25544-2)*

Jun 87. (7") *(W 8276)* **ICE COLD ICE. / GOTTA LETTA** -
(12"+=) *(W 8276T)* – Medley.

—— disbanded in '87 after manager DAVID SAVOY Jr. committed suicide. GRANT HART went solo as did BOB MOULD; in 1992 the latter formed SUGAR

– compilations, etc. –

May 94. (cd/c) *Warners; <(9362 45582-2/-4)>* **THE LIVING END (live)** Apr94
– New day rising / Heaven Hill / Standing in the rain / Back from somewhere / Ice cold ice / Everytime / Friend you're gonna fall / She floated away / From the gut / Target / It's not funny anymore / Hardly

getting over it / Terms of psychic warfare / Powertime / Books about UFO's / Divide and conquer / Keep hangin' on / Celebrated summer / Now that you know me / Ain't no water in the well / What's goin' on / Data control / In a free land / Sheena is a punk rocker.

BOB MOULD

BOB MOULD (b.12 Oct'61, Malone, New York) – vocals, guitar, etc (ex-HUSKER DU) / with **ANTON FIER** – drums / **TONY MAIMONE** – bass, (both ex-PERE UBU) / **JANE SCARPANTONI** – cello (of TINY LIGHTS) / **STEVE HAIGLER** – cello

Virgin Virgin

Jun 89. (7") *(VUS 2)* **SEE A LITTLE LIGHT. / ALL THOSE PEOPLE KNOW** [ ] [–]
(12"+=/cd-s+=) *(VUS 2T/CD2)* – Shoot out the lights / Composition for the young and the old (live).

Jul 89. (lp/cd) *(VUS LP/CD 2)* <91240> **WORKBOOK** [ ] Apr89 [ ]
– Sunspots / Wishing well / Heartbreak a stranger / See a little light / Poison years / Sinners and their repentances / Lonely afternoon / Brasilia crossed the Tranton / Compositions for the young and old / Dreaming, I amd / Whichever way the wind blows. *(re-iss. Sep90; OVED 340)*

Aug 90. (cd/c/lp) *(VUS CD/MC/LP 21)* <91395> **BLACK SHEETS OF RAIN** [ ] May90 [ ]
– Black sheets of rain / Stand guard / It's too late / One good reason / Stop your crying / Hanging tree / The last night / Hear me calling / Out of your life / Disappointed / Sacrifice – let there be peace.

Virgin Virgin

May 94. (cd) *(CDVM 9030)* <39587> **THE POISON YEARS** (compilation from first two sets) [ ] Jul94 [ ]

SUGAR

BOB MOULD – vox, guitar, keyboards, percussion / **DAVE BARBE** – bass (ex-MERCYLAND) / **MALCOLM TRAVIS** – drums, percussion (ex-ZULUS)

Creation Rykodisc

Jul 92. (cd-ep) <1024> **HELPLESS / NEEDLE HITS E / IF I CAN'T CHANGE YOUR MIND / TRY AGAIN** [–] [ ]

Aug 92. (12"ep)(cd-ep) *(CRE 126T)(CRESCD 126)* **CHANGES / NEEDLE HITS E. / IF I CAN'T CHANGE YOUR MIND / TRY AGAIN** [ ] [–]

Sep 92. (cd/lp)(c) *(CRE CD/LP 129)(C-CRE 129) <RCD/RACS 10239>* **COPPER BLUE** [10] [ ]
– The act we act / A good idea / Changes / Helpless / Hoover dam / The slim / If I can't change your mind / Fortune teller / Slick / Man on the Moon.

Oct 92. (7"ep/c-ep) *(CRE/+CS 143)* <1030> **A GOOD IDEA. / WHERE DIAMONDS ARE HALOS / SLICK** [65] [ ]
(12"ep+=)(cd-ep+=) *(CRE 143T)(CRESCD 143)* – Armenia city in the sky.

Jan 93. (7"/c-s) *(CRE/+CS 149)* **IF I CAN'T CHANGE YOUR MIND. / CLOWN MASTER** [30] [ ]
(12"+=) *(CRE 149T)* *<1031>* – Anyone (live) / Hoover dam (live).
(cd-s) *(CRESCD 149)* *<1032>* – ('A'side) / The slim / Where diamonds are halos.

Apr 93. (m-cd/m-lp)(m-c) *(CRE CD/LP 153)(C-CRE 153)* *<50260>* **BEASTER** [3] [ ]
– Come around / Tilted / Judas cradle / JC auto / Feeling better / Walking away.

Aug 93. (7") *(CRE 156)* **TILTED. / JC AUTO (live)** [48] [–]

Aug 94. (7"/c-s) *(CRE/+CS 186)* **YOUR FAVORITE THING. / MIND IS AN ISLAND** [40] [ ]
(12"+=)(cd-s+=) *(CRE 186T)(CRESCD 186)* *<1038>* – Frustration / And you tell me (T.V. mix).

Sep 94. (cd/lp)(c) *(CRE CD/LP 172)(C-CRE 172)* <10300> **FILE UNDER EASY LISTENING (F.U.E.L.)** [7] [50]
– Gift / Company book / Your favorite thing / What you want it to be / Gee angel / Panama city hotel / Can't help it anymore / Granny cool / Believe what you're saying / Explode and make up.

Oct 94. (7"/c-s) *(CRE/+CS 193)* **BELIEVE WHAT YOU'RE SAYING. / GOING HOME** [73] [ ]
(cd-s+=) *(CRESCD 193)* *<1039>* – In the eyes of my friends / And you tell me.

Dec 94. (cd-ep) *<RCD5 1040>* **GEE ANGEL / EXPLODE AND MAKE UP / SLIM / AFTER ALL THE ROADS HAVE LED TO . . .** [–] [ ]

Jul 95. (d-cd) *<10321>* **BESIDES** (compilation of b-sides, live, etc) [–] [ ]

— disbanded and BARBE formed BUZZHUNGRY / TRAVIS went to CUSTOMIZED

BOB MOULD

— solo again with various back-up

Creation Rykodisc

Dec 95. (cd-s) *<51050>* **EGOVERRIDE** [–] [ ]

Apr 96. (cd/lp) *(CRE CD/LP 188)* <10342> **BOB MOULD** [52] [ ]
– Anymore time between / I hate alternative rock / Fort Knox, King Solomon / Next time that you leave / Egoverride / Thumbtack / Hair stew / Hair stew / Deep karma canyon / Art crisis / Roll over and die.

— now with **MATT HAMMON** – drums / **ALISON CHESLEY** – cello

Aug 98. (7") *(CRE 206)* **CLASSIFIEDS. / MOVING TRUCKS** [ ] [–]

Aug 98. (cd/lp) *(CRE CD/LP 215)* <10443> **THE LAST DOG AND PONY SHOW** [58] [ ]
– New #1 / Moving trucks / Taking everything / First drag of the day / Classifieds / Who was around? / Skintrade / Vaporub / Sweet serene / Megamaniac / Reflecting pool / Along the way / (interview).

Cooking Vinyl Granary

Apr 02. (cd) *(COOKCD 237)* <2021> **MODULATE** [ ] Mar02 [ ]
– 180 rain / Sunset safety glass / Semper fi / Homecoming parade / Lost zoloft / Without? / Slay – Sway / The receipt / Quasar / Soundonsound / Hornery / Comeonstrong / Trade / Author's lament.

— added **BRENDAN CANTY** – drums (of FUGAZI)

Cooking Vinyl Yep Roc

Jul 05. (cd) *(COOKCD 337)* <2091> **BODY OF SONG** [ ] [ ]
– Circles / (Shine your) Light love hope / Paralyzed / I am vision, I am sound / Underneath days / Always tomorrow / Days of rain / Best thing / High fidelity / Missing you / Gauze of friendship / Beating heart the prize.

□ Michael HUTCHENCE (see under ⇒ INXS)

ICE CUBE

Born: O'SHEA JACKSON, 15 Jun'69, Crenshaw, Los Angeles, California, USA. After starting out as a founding member of seminal rap terrorists N.W.A., CUBE took a sabbatical from the band following the release of the first album, going to study architecture at the Phoenix Institute of Technology. Returning in 1988, he worked on the pivotal 'STRAIGHT OUTTA COMPTON' (1989). After touring the record, the rapper had a dispute with manager JERRY HELLER over royalties, eventually settling in court in 1990. Following the incident, CUBE went solo with his backing crew DA LENCH MOB, releasing his debut, 'AMERIKKKA'S MOST WANTED' the same year. Produced by PUBLIC ENEMY's BOMB SQUAD, the album was as uncompromising, both lyrically and musically, as his best work for N.W.A., following the same gangsta rap blueprint and never budging from his old adage that "Life ain't nothing but bitches and money". Consistently controversial and contradictory, ICE CUBE puts down women at every opportunity yet offers female rapper YO YO a chance to have her say on 'IT'S A MAN'S WORLD', and say it she does, in fine style. 'DEATH CERTIFICATE' (1991) was an even more vicious verbal attack, CUBE railing against the usual targets like the police and the media, although the track's 'NO VASELINE' and 'BLACK KOREA' brought the most criticism. The former was an anti-Semitic outburst against his former boss, the jewish JERRY HELLER, while the latter advocated setting fire to Korean-owned grocery stores. He didn't stop there though, going on to include white "devils", middle class blacks and gay men in his litany of hate. Inevitably, the album brought widespread condemnation, the only thanks the rapper received for his troubles was from the Ku Klux Klan. On 'THE PREDATOR' (1992) CUBE's anger was more focused, the record debuting at No.1 in America and becoming a million seller within a month. It also spawned CUBE's biggest UK hit to date in the deceptively mellow 'IT WAS A GOOD DAY'. The rapper's P-Funk preoccupation continued with 'LETHAL INJECTION' (1993), wherein he spars with GEORGE CLINTON on the 'One Nation Under A Groove'-sampling 'BOP GUN (ONE NATION)', a single that almost made the Top 20 in both Britain and America. The remainder of the 90's was characterised by the rapper's absence from the scene save for a couple of compilations (1994's 'BOOTLEGS & B-SIDES' and '97's 'FEATURING . . .'), a one-off flop single ('THE WORLD IS MINE' from the movie 'Dangerous Ground') and a collaborative effort with KRS-ONE, B-REAL and SHAQUE O'NEILL ('Men Of Steel'). He finally emerged with a new album's worth of material in 1998's 'WAR & PEACE VOL.1 (THE WAR DISC)', the first instalment in a double whammy partnered by 'VOL.2 THE PEACE DISC' (2000). Through the late 90s and into the new millennium, the rapper – having already appeared in the iconic 'Boyz 'N The Hood' (1991) – morphed into a Hollywood/TV standby, appearing in countless action and comedy flicks. He only returned to recording in 2006 with 'LAUGH NOW, CRY LATER', welcomed back with open arms by fans and a US Top 5 placing in the charts.

• **Songwriters:** Co-writes with SADLER or JINX. Sample the ISLEYS, JAMES BROWN, STEELY DAN and MICHAEL JACKSON, OHIO PLAYERS, PUBLIC ENEMY, DAS EFX, MOMENTS + GRANDMASTER FLASH.
• **Trivia:** ICE-T starred and contributed to soundtracks for the films 'Boyz 'n' The Hood' and 'Trespass' (circa early 90's). In 1991, he co-wrote with JAMES BROWN and produced female hardcore rapper YO-YO on their 'East-West' debut US hit single 'You can't Play With My World'.

Album rating: AMERIKKKA'S MOST WANTED (*8) / DEATH CERTIFICATE (*8) / THE PREDATOR (*6) / LETHAL INJECTION (*5) / BOOTLEGS & B-SIDES collection (*5) / WAR & PEACE VOL.1 (THE WAR DISC) (*5) / WAR & PEACE VOL.2 (THE PEACE DISC) (*5) / GREATEST HITS compilation (*8) / LAUGH NOW, CRY LATER (*6)

ICE CUBE – vocals (with backing from DA LENCH MOB)

Ruthless — Priority

May 90. (12") *(VL 7220)* **AMERIKKKA'S MOST WANTED. / ONCE UPON A TIME IN THE PROJECTS**

4th & Broad — Priority

Jun 90. (cd/c/lp) *(CR CD/CA/LP 551)* *<57120>* **AMERIKKKA'S MOST WANTED** — 48 May90 19
– Better off dead / The nigga ya love to hate / Amerikkka's most wanted / What they hittin' foe? / You can't fade me / JD's gaffilin' / Once upon a time in the projects / Turn off the radio / Endangered species (tales from the darkside) / A gangsta's fairytale / I'm only out for one thing / Get off my Dick and tell yo bitch to come here / The drive-by / Rollin' with the Lench Mob / Who's the Mack? / It's a man's world / The bomb. *(cd re-iss. Sep96 on 'Island'; IMCD 230) <(cd re-mast.Mar03 on 'Priority'+=; 5 37601)>* – KILL AT WILL

Mar 91. (m-cd/m-c/m-lp) *(BRECD/BRCM/BRLM 572)* *<7230>* **KILL AT WILL** (above remixes) — 66 Dec90 34
– Endangered species (tales from the darkside) / Jackin' for beats / Get off my Dick and tell yo bitch to come here / The product / Dead Homiez / JD's gaffilin (part 2) / I gotta say what up!!!.

Nov 91. (cd/c/lp) *(BR CD/CA/LP 581)* *<57155>* **DEATH CERTIFICATE** — 2
– The funeral / The wrong nigga to fuck wit / My summer vacation / Steady mobbin' / Robin Lench / Givin' up the nappy dug out / Look who's burnin' / A bird in the hand / Man's best friend / Alive on arrival / Death / The birth / I wanna kill Sam / Horny lil' devil / True to the game / Color blind / Doing dumb shit / Us. *(cd+=)* – No Vaseline / Black Korea. *(cd re-iss. Sep96 on 'Island'; IMCD 232) <(cd re-mast.Mar03 on 'Priority'+=; 5 543341-2)>*– How to survive in South Central.

Dec 91. (7") *<7247>* **STEADY MOBBIN' / US**
(12"+=/cd-s+=) – Dead Homrez / Endangered species (tales from the dark side) (remix).

Nov 92. (cd-s) *<53813>* **WICKED (2 versions) / U AIN'T GONNA TAKE MY LIFE (2 versions)** — - 55

Nov 92. (7"/c-s) *(BRW/BRCA 282)* **WICKED. / WE HAD TO TEAR THIS MOTHAFUCKA UP** — -
(12"+=/cd-s+=) *(12BRW/BRCD 282)* – ('A'instrumental) / The wrong nigga to fuck wit. *(re-iss. Aug93, hit UK 62; same)*

Nov 92. (cd/c/lp) *(BR CD/CA/LP 592)* *<57185>* **THE PREDATOR** — 73 1
– (the first day of school intro) / When will they shoot? / (I'm scared) / Wicked / Now I gotta wet 'cha / The predator / It was a good day / We had to tear this mothafucka up / **** 'em / Dirty Mack / Don't trust 'em / Gangsta's fairytale 2 / Check yo self / Who's got the camera? / Integration / Say hi to the bad guy. *(cd re-iss. Sep96 on 'Island'; IMCD 328) <(cd re-mast.Mar03 on 'Priority'+=; 5 43339-2)>* – Check yo self (the message remix) / It was a good day (remix) / 24 with an L / U ain't gonna take my life.

Feb 93. (c-s) *<53813>* **IT WAS A GOOD DAY / ('A'instrumental)** [–] [15]

Mar 93. (c-s) *(BRCA 270) <53817>* **IT WAS A GOOD DAY. / AIN'T GONNA TAKE MY LIFE** [27] [–]
(12"+=/cd-s+=) *(12BRW/BRCD 270)* – ('A'&'B'instrumentals).

Jul 93. (c-s; as ICE CUBE featuring DAS EFX) *(BRCA 283) <53830>* **CHECK YO SELF / IT WAS A GOOD DAY (radio mix)** [36] [20]
(12"+=/cd-s+=) *(12BRW/BRCD 283)* – 24 with an L / ('A'version).
(cd-s+=) *(BRCDX 283)* – It was a good day (instrumental) / Who got the camera.

Dec 93. (cd/c/lp) *(BR CD/CA/LP 609) <53876>* **LETHAL INJECTION** [52] [5]
– The shot / Really doe / Ghetto bird / You know how we do it / Cave bitch / Bop gun (one nation) / What can I do? / Lil ass gee / Make it ruff, make it smooth / Down for whatever / Enemy / When I get to Heaven. *(cd re-iss. Sep96 on 'Island'; IMCD 229) <(cd re-mast.Mar03 on 'Priority'+=; 5 37602-2)>* – What can I do? (westside remix) / What can I do? (eastside remix) / You know how we do it (part 2) / Lil ass gee (eerie gumbo remix).

Dec 93. (12") *(12BRW 302) <53843>* **REALLY DOE. / MY SKIN IS MY SKIN** [66] [54]
(cd-s+=) *(BRCD 302)* – ('A'&'B'mixes).

Mar 94. (7"/c-s) *(BRW/BRCA 303) <53847>* **YOU KNOW HOW WE DO IT. / 2 N THE MORNING** [41] [30]
(12"+=/cd-s+=) *(12BRW/BRCD 303)* – ('A'instrumental).
(re-entered UK No.46 Dec94)
(cd-s+=) *(BRCDX 303)* – D-voidofpopniggafiedmegamix.

Aug 94. (7"/c-s; by ICE CUBE featuring GEORGE CLINTON) *(BR W/CA 308) <53155>* **BOP GUN (ONE NATION). / DOWN FOR WHATEVER** [22] Jul94 [23]
(12"+=) *(12BRW 308)* – ('A'-MYR mix) / Ghetto jam.
(cd-s+=) *(BRCD 308)* – Ghetto bird (Dr. Jam's mix).

—— snippets from the FUNKADELIC song 'One Nation Under A Groove'.

Dec 94. (cd/c/d-lp) *(BR CD/CA/LP 616) <53921>* **BOOTLEGS AND B-SIDES** (compilation) [ ] [19]
– Robin Hood (cause it ain't all good) / What can I do (remix) / 24 with an L / You know how we do it (remix) / 2 n the morning / Check yo self (remix) / You don't want to fuck with these (unreleased '93 shit) / Lil piss gee (eerie gumbo mix) / My skin is my sin / It was a good day (remix) / D'voidofpopniggafied – megamix. *(cd re-iss. Sep96 on 'Island'; IMCD 231)*

—— In 1995, ICE CUBE featured on minor hits by SCARFACE ('People Don't Believe') and WC AND THE MAAD CIRCLE 'West Up!'.

Priority Priority

Mar 97. (cd-s) *(894176-2)* **THE WORLD IS MINE / ('A'mixes)** [60] [ ]

—— In Aug'97, ICE CUBE collaborated with KRS-ONE, B-REAL and SHAQUE O'NEILL on minor US hit single, 'Men Of Steel'.

Dec 97. (cd) *<51037>* **FEATURING . . . ICE CUBE** (compilation) [–] [ ]
– Bend a corner with me / Natural born killaz / Bow down / Bop gun (one nation) / Check yo self / Endangered species (tales from the . . . .) / Trespass / It's a man's world / West up! / Game over / Wicked ways / Two to the head.

Oct 98. (c-s,12",cd-s; ICE CUBE featuring MR. SHORT KHOP) *<5345>* **PUSHIN' WEIGHT / (mixes)** [–] [26]

Nov 98. (cd/lp) *(CDPTY/PTYLP 1616) <50700>* **WAR & PEACE VOL.1 (THE WAR DISC)** [ ] [7]
– Ask about me / Pushin weight / Dr. Frankenstein / Fuck dying / War & peace / Ghetto vet / Greed / MP / Cash over ass / Curse of money / Peckin' order / Limos, demos & bimbos / Once upon a time in the projects 2 / If I was fuckin you / X-bitches / Extradition / 3 strikes you in / Penitentiary.

Nov 99. (12"/cd-s; ICE CUBE feat. MACK 10) *<53577>* **YOU CAN DO IT. / (other artist)** [–] [35]
(above from the film, 'Next Friday' starring ICE CUBE)

Mar 00. (cd/d-lp) *(CDPTY/PTYLP 183) <50015>* **WAR & PEACE VOL.2 (THE PEACE DISC)** [56] Feb00 [3]
– Hello / (pimp homeo) / You ain't gonna lie (ta kick it) / The guitar shit / Supreme hustle / (mental warfare) / 24 mo' hours / Until we rich / You can do it / (mackin' and drivin') / Gotta be insanity / Roll all day / Can you bounce? / (dinner with the CEO) *[d-lp-only]* / Record company pimpin' *[d-lp-only]* / Waitin' ta hate / Nigga of the century / You can do it (instrumental).

May 00. (12"/cd-s; as ICE CUBE featuring MACK 10 & MS. TOI) *(PTY ST/CD 125)* **YOU CAN DO IT. / UNTIL WE RICH** [ ] [–]

Dec 01. (cd) *(CDPTY 221) <29091>* **GREATEST HITS** (compilation) [ ] [54]
– Pushin' weight / Check yo' self / We be clubbin' / $100 bill y'all / Once upon a time in the projects / Bow down (WESTSIDE CONNECTION) / Hello / You can do it / You know how we do it / It was a good day / Bop gun (one nation) / What can I do? (remix) / My summer vacation / Steady mobbin' / Jackin' for beats / The nigga ya love to hate / Late night hour.

Lench Mob Lench Mob

Jun 06. (cd) *<6 5939-2>* **LAUGH NOW, CRY LATER** [–] [4]
– Definition of a West Coast G – intro / Why we thugs / Smoke some weed / Dimes & nicks (a call from Mike Epps) / Child support / 2 decades ago (insert) / Doin what it 'pose 2do / Laugh now, cry later / Stop snitchin' / Go to church (feat. SNOOP DOGG & LIL JON) / The nigga trapp / A history of violence / Growin' up / Click, clack – get back! / The game lord / Chrome & paint (feat. WC) / Steal the show / You gotta lotta that (feat. SNOOP DOGG) / Spittin' pollaseeds (feat. WC & KOKANE) / Holla @ cha' boy.

ICE-T

Born: TRACY MORROW, 16 Feb'58, Newark, New Jersey, USA. With a ghetto background that reportedly involved copious amounts of unlawful activity, a name derived from superpimp, ICEBERG SLIM, and a mean line in caustic wit, ICE-T set himself up as the original 'gangsta' rapper. The fact of the matter is he wasn't actually the first gangsta rapper, although he did invent the particularly potent West Coast strain. With backing from AFRIKA ISLAM and DJ ALADDIN, his debut for 'Warners', 'RHYME PAYS' (1987), set out the ICE-T agenda of unashamed criminal glorification over tough, made-to-measure beats. 'POWER' (1988) thankfully laid off the "I'm mental, me" sentiments to a certain degree, allowing room for more objectively intelligent lyrics, although that obviously couldn't be applied to 'GIRLS L.G.B.N.A.F.' (LET'S GET BUTT NAKED AND FUCK, dummy). Hardly the most offensive or potentially damaging lyrics in the ICE-T canon, the song nevertheless upset those nice people at the PMRC (an American institutionalised neighbourhood watch scheme for bad pop stars), not the first time he'd upset the powers that be (or would be). This storm in a teacup informed much of 1989's 'THE ICEBERG: FREEDOM OF SPEECH . . . JUST WATCH WHAT YOU SAY', a more rock-based, anti-censorship rant that laid the ground-work for his subsequent BODY COUNT project. The record that really took ICE-T's dubious message to the masses was the landmark 'O.G. ORIGINAL GANGSTER' (1991), a UK Top 5 album that saw ICE powering his way through a hardcore rap set of unrelenting intensity. As ever, the lyrics were sharp, witty and artfully articulate but ultimately offensive. While ICE-T argues that he tells it like it is, his lame attempts to justify his continual objectification of women are rarely satisfactory. It's one of hip hop's great tragedies that a rapper as charismatic, intelligent and creative as ICE-T continues to reinforce prejudice and stereotyping; for every inch that CHUCK D advances the black cause, ICE-T drags it back two. The next logical step for ICE was a foray into the world of heavy metal, another genre not exactly noted for its tolerance. Recruiting ERNIE-C (guitar), D-ROC (guitar), MOOSEMAN (bass) and BEATMASTER V (drums), ICE-T debuted his hardcore/speed metal band, BODY COUNT, on the 1991 Lollapalooza tour prior to the release of their eponymous debut the following year. While the record addressed racism on the likes of 'MOMMA'S GOTTA DIE TONIGHT', the rapper's trademark misogyny was ever present, notably on 'KKK BITCH'. However, the track that really hit the fan squarely with the shit was 'COP KILLER', a nasty little ditty about "taking out" some lawmen. While the LAPD were hardly in a postion to come over all moral, they perhaps understandibly took offence to such sentiments. As did President George Bush and good ol' Ollie North

ICE-T subsequently being given the honour of the biggest threat to American security since McCARTHY flushed out "those damn commies" in the 50's. The final straw for 'Warners' was when record company personnel started receiving death threats, the label finally giving in and removing the offending song from subsequent pressings. While it's arguably one of the functions of art to question the "norm", to go about it in such a club-footed manner ultimately benefits no-one. ICE-T was as defiant as ever, though, moving to 'Virgin' for 'BORN DEAD' (1994), another accomplished collection that wasn't quite so inflammatory. The rapper's solo career continued, meanwhile, with 'HOME INVASION' (1993) upon which, gasp!, the rapper actually admitted to feelings for his fellow man in 'GOTTA LOTTA LOVE' while remaining as unrepentant about his lifestyle as ever, ('THAT'S HOW I'M LIVIN'). It was to be another three years before the next album and in the interim, ICE-T used his not inconsiderable talent to host a Channel 4 documentary on Blaxploitation movies as well as presenting 'Baadaasss TV', a semi-successful attempt at catering for black culture. He also published a book of his forthright opinions which only served to furnish his opponents with yet more ammunition. ICE-T resumed his recording career in typically bigoted fashion with, 'VI: RETURN OF THE REAL' (1996), a cliched gangsta affair that added anti-semitic sentiment to his litany of hate. After a third BODY COUNT effort, 'VIOLENT DEMISE (THE LAST DAYS)' in '97, ICE-T was out on his own once more courtesy of the David Fincher 'Seven'-inspired 'THE SEVENTH DEADLY SIN' (1999). Featuring the 2PAC and BIGGIE tribute track, 'VALUABLE GAME', the album failed to generate much media or chart interest. Had ICE-T finally lost out to his younger rivals.

Album rating: RHYME PAYS (*5) / POWER (*5) / THE ICEBERG: FREEDOM OF SPEECH . . . JUST WATCH WHAT YOU SAY (*7) / O.G. ORIGINAL GANGSTER (*8) / BODY COUNT (*8; with Body Count) / HOME INVASION (*6) / BORN DEAD (*5; with Body Count) / IV: RETURN OF THE REAL (*5) / VIOLENT DEMISE (THE LAST DAYS (*4; with Body Count) / THE SEVENTH DEADLY SIN (*5) / GREATEST HITS: THE EVIDENCE compilation (*7)

ICE-T – vocals / w/**AFRIKA ISLAM** – synthesizers

Sire Sire

ul 87. (12") *(YZ 145)* **MAKE IT FUNKY. / SEX** [ ] [ ]

ul 87. (lp/c/cd) *(925602-1/-4/-2) <25602>* **RHYME PAYS** [ ] [93]
– (intro) / Rhyme pays / 6 'n the mornin' / Make it funky / Somebody gotta do it (pimpin' ain't easy) / 409 / I love ladies / Sex / Pain / Squeeze the trigger. *(cd-iss. Jan93 on 'Warners'; 7599 25602-2)*

Nov 87. (12") *<020805>* **SOMEBODY GOT DO IT (PIMPIN' AIN'T EASY). / OUR MOST REQUESTED RECORD** [ ] [ ]

un 88. (12") *<27902>* **COLORS. / SQUEEZE THE TRIGGER** [–] [10]

Sep 88. (lp/c/cd) *(925765-1/-4/-2)* **POWER** [ ] [35]
– (intro) / Power / Drama / Heartbeat / The syndicate / Radio suckers / I'm your pusher / Personal / High rollers / Girls L.G.B.N.A.F. / Grand larceny / Soul on ice / (outro).

Nov 88. (7") *<27768>* **I'M YOUR PUSHER. / GIRLS L.G.B.N.A.F.** [–] [ ]
(12"+=) – ('A'instrumental) / ('A'acappella) / ('B'instrumental) / ('B'acappella).

Warners Sire

Mar 89. (7") *(W 7574) <27574>* **HIGH ROLLERS. / THE HUNTED CHILD** [63] [ ]
(12"+=/12"s+=) *(W 7574T/+W)* – Power.

Sep 89. (7") *(W 2802) <11810>* **LETHAL WEAPON. / HEARTBEAT (remix)** [ ] [ ]
(12"+=/cd-s+=) *(W 2802 T/CD)* – ('A'instrumental).

Oct 89. (lp/c)(cd) *(WX 316/+C)<(926028-2)>* **THE ICEBERG: FREEDOM OF SPEECH . . . JUST WATCH WHAT YOU SAY** [42] [37]
– (intro) / Shut up, be happy / The iceberg / Lethal weapon / You played yourself / Peel their caps back / The girl tried to kill me / Black'n'decker / Hit the deck / This one's for me / The hunted child / What ya wanna do? / Freedom of speech / My word is bond. *(cd re-iss. Feb95)*

— guested on CURTIS MAYFIELD's re-make of classic 'Superfly'.

Feb 90. (c-s) *<19994>* **YOU PLAYED TOURSELF / FREEDOM OF SPEECH** [–] [ ]

Feb 90. (7") *(W 9994)* **YOU PLAYED YOURSELF. / MY WORD IS BOND** [64] [–]
(12"+=) *(W 9994T)* – Freedom of speech (with HENDRIX sample)

Apr 90. (c-s) **WHAT DO YOU WANNA DO? / THE GIRL TRIED TO KILL ME** [–] [ ]

Apr 91. (c-s) *<19442>* **NEW JACK HUSTLER (NINO'S THEME) / ('A'instrumental)** [ ] [67]

— <above from the film of the same name on US label 'Giant-Sire'>

May 91. (7") **O.G. ORIGINAL GANGSTER. / BITCHES 2** [ ] [ ]
(12"+=/cd-s+=) – Mind over matter / Midnight.

May 91. (cd)(lp/c) *<(7599 26492-2)>(WX 412/+C)* **O.G. ORIGINAL GANGSTER** [38] [5]
– Home of the bodybag / First impression / Ziplock / Mic contract / Mind over matter / New Jack hustler / Ed / Bitches 2 (incl. sample:- Dr. Funkenstein) / Straight up nigga / O.G. Original Gangster / The house / Evil E – what about sex? / Fly by / Midnight / Fried chicken / M.V.P.'s / Lifestyles of the rich and infamous / Body count / Prepared to die / Escape from the killing fields / Street killer / Pulse of the rhyme / The tower / Ya should killed me last year. *(cd re-iss. Feb95; same)*

Rhyme Syndicate Rhyme Syndicate

Mar 93. (d-lp/d-c/d-cd) *(RSYN/+C/D 1) <53858>* **HOME INVASION** [15] [14]
– Warning / It's on / Ice MFT / Home invasion / G style / Addicted to danger / Question and answer / Watch the ice break / Race war / That's how I'm livin' / I ain't new ta this / Pimp behind the wheels (DJ Evil E the great) / Gotta lotta love / Hit the fan / Depths of Hell (featuring DADDY NITRO) / 99 problems (featuring BROTHER MARQUIS) / Funky gripsta / Message to the soldier / Ain't a damn thing changed.

Apr 93. (12"ep/c-ep/cd-ep) *(SYND D/C/R 1)* **I AIN'T NEW TA THIS. / MIXED UP / MIXED UP (instrumental)** [62] [ ]

Dec 93. (12"ep/c-ep/cd-ep) *(SYND T/C/D 2)* **THAT'S HOW I'M LIVIN'. / COLOURS – RICOCHET – NEW JACK HUSTLER (film excerpts)** [21] [ ]

Mar 94. (c-s/12"/cd-s) *(SYND C/T/D 3)* **GOTTA LOTTA LOVE. / (2-'A'mixes) / excerpt from book 'The Ice Opinion (who gives a f***)'** [24] [ ]
(cd-s) *(SYNDD 3)* – ('A'mix) / Addicted to danger / G style / Racewar (remixes).

— In Dec 94, ICE-T was credited with WHITFIELD CRANE (Ugly Kid Joe) on MOTORHEAD single 'Born To Raise Hell', hit UK No.47

May 96. (12"/cd-s) *(SYND T/D 5)* **I MUST STAND. / ('A'mixes)** [41] [ ]

May 96. (d-lp/c/cd) *(RSYN/+C/D 3) <53933>* **VI – THE RETURN OF THE REAL** [26] [89]
– Pimp anthem / Where the shit goes down / Bouncin' down the strezeet / Return of the real / I must stand / (Alotta niggas) / Rap games hijacked / How does it feel / The lane / (Rap is fake) / Make the loot loop / Syndicate 4 ever / The 5th / (It's goin' down) / They want me back in / Inside of a gangsta / Forced to do dirt / (Haters) / Cramp your style / (Real).

Nov 96. (12"ep/cd-ep) *(SYND T/D 6)* **THE LANE / ('A'mixes). / BOUNCIN' DOWN THE STREZEET / GET MY CASH ON** [18] [ ]

Roadrunner Coroner

Oct 99. (cd/d-lp) *(RR 8614-2/-1) <3>* **THE SEVENTH DEADLY SIN** [ ] [ ]
– (intro) / Don't hate the playa / Check your game / Get your moneyman / 7th / NY NY / Valuable game / Eye of the storm / Always wanted to be a ho / Brother Marguis (interlude) / Fuck it / CJ Mac (interlude) / Retaliation / Threat / Check your heart / Sondoobiest (interlude) / Hardcore / In common sense / Numbskull (interlude) / God forgive me / Exodus.

Nov 99. (cd-s) *(RR 2137-3)* **VALUABLE GAME / VALUABLE GAME (instrumental) / ICE'S EXODUS (clean version)** [ ] [ ]

– compilations, etc. –

May 93. (cd/c) *Warners; (8122 71170-2/-4)* **THE CLASSIC COLLECTION** [ ] [ ]

Oct 00. (cd/c/lp) *Street Knowledge; (9362 46500-2/-4/-1) / Atomic Pop; <11>* **GREATEST HITS: THE EVIDENCE** [ ] Aug00 [ ]
– 6 'n the mornin' / I'm your pusher / High rollers / You played yourself / Peel their caps back / O.G. Original Gangster / Colors / New

jack hustler / Power / I ain't new ta this / That's how I'm livin' / I must stand / Squeeze the trigger / The tower / The lane / Money, power, women.

BODY COUNT

ICE-T with **ERNIE C** – lead guitar / **D-ROC** – rhythm guitar / **MOOSEMAN** – bass / **BEATMASTER 'V'** – drums

Sire | Sire

Jan 92. (12"/cd-s; w-drawn) **COP KILLER. / (withdrawn)** [–] [ ]

Mar 92. (cd/c) *(9362 45139-2/-4) <26876>* **BODY COUNT** [ ] [26]
– Smoked pork / Body Count's in the house / New sports / Body count / A statistic / Bowels of the Devil / The real problem / KKK bitch / C note / Voodoo / The winner loses / There goes the neighborhood / Oprah / Evil Dick / Body Count anthem / Momma's gotta die tonight / Freedom of speech.

Jun 92. (12") **THERE GOES THE NEIGHBORHOOD. / KKK BITCH** [ ] [ ]

Rhyme Syndicate | Virgin

Sep 94. (red-lp/c/cd) *(RSYN/+C/D 2) <39802>* **BORN DEAD** [15] [74]
– Body M-F Count / Masters of revenge / Killin' floor / Necessary evil / Drive by / Last breath / Hey Joe / Shallow graves / Surviving the game / Who are you / Sweet lobotomy / Born dead.

Sep 94. (c-s) *(SYNDC 4)* **BORN DEAD / BODY COUNT'S IN THE HOUSE (live)** [28] [ ]
(12"pic-d+=) *(SYNDTP 4)* – ('A'live).
(cd-s+=) *(SYNDD 4)* – Body M-F Count (live) / On with the Body Count (live).

Virgin | Virgin

Dec 94. (etched-10"pic-d) *(VSA 1529)* **NECESSARY EVIL / NECESSARY EVIL (live) / BOWELS OF THE DEVIL (live)** [45] [ ]
(cd-s) *(VSCDX 1529)* – ('A'side) / Body Count anthem (live) / Drive by (live) / There goes the neighborhood (live).

—— **GRIZ** – bass + **O.T.** – drums; repl. MOOSEMAN + BEATMASTER V

Mar 97. (cd/c/lp) *(CD/TC+/V 2813) <41915>* **VIOLENT DEMISE (THE LAST DAYS)** [ ] [ ]
– (interview) / My way (BODY COUNT & RAW BREED) / Strippers intro / Strippers / Truth or death / Violent demise / Bring it to pain / Music business / I used to love her / Root of all evil / Dead man walking / (interview end) / You're fuckin' with BC / Ernie's intro / Dr. K / Last days.

IDLEWILD

Formed: Edinburgh, Scotland . . . late '95 by RODDY WOOMBLE, ROD JONES and COLIN NEWTON, each having a penchant for noise veterans, SONIC YOUTH and FUGAZI. Having met at a party, the erstwhile students whittled away their revision time with ramshackle rehearsals, eventually channelling their frustrations into a debut single, 'QUEEN OF THE TROUBLED TEENS'. Famously financed by a student loan (and issued on their own 'Human Condition' imprint), the track was championed by Radio One DJ Steve Lamacq, duly rescuing the band from eternal toilet gig hell and setting in motion the mechanics of A&R overload. A follow-up single, 'CHANDELIER', appeared on 'Fierce Panda' while an acclaimed mini-album on 'Deceptive', 'CAPTAIN', kickstarted '98 and became their final fully fledged indie release prior to a deal with 'Food'. Somewhere along the way the band also picked up bassist BOB FAIRFOULL and began to coax some melancholic tunefulness from the blizzard of sound and fury that characterised their youthful approach. 'A FILM FOR THE FUTURE' announced their major label arrival in fittingly convulsive style, the first of many minor hits which have cemented the band's reputation as one of Scotland's most talked about and possibly most dedicated sonic abusers. Their highly anticipated first album proper, 'HOPE IS IMPORTANT' (late '98), made the UK Top 60 and the band's steady rise proves that noisy guitars never go out of fashion. '100 BROKEN WINDOWS' (2000) might've been the casualties of noise, perhaps. But surprisingly enough, the four-piece turned the screeching guitars down for this commercially-orientated release. The single, 'THESE WOODEN IDEAS' unveiled another side to the band that used to literally knee-cap themselves on stage. Still, with its edge intact 'LITTLE DISCOURAGE' found IDLEWILD adopting an R.E.M.-esque style (circa 1995), and 'THERE'S A GLORY IN YOUR STORY' saw them unplugging their guitars altogether. Still, this set could make ears bleed if played at the correct volume. They toned it down, however, for their next release, the bleakly entitled 'THE REMOTE PART' (2002), an album which flirted with a lot of influences; from the Top 20, AZTEC CAMERA-inspired single 'YOU HELD THE WORLD IN YOUR ARMS' to the punky R.E.M. 'Murmur'-era led 'AMERICAN ENGLISH'. The same formula (seen on the latter LP) remained with 'I NEVER WANTED', a soft, heartfelt acoustic numbe[r] and even a bit of spoken-word on 'THE REMOTE PART'. The album also crashed into the UK charts at No.3, providing one o[f] Scotland's premier rock bands with the recognition they've bee[n] striving for since their musical birth. Holing up in the Highlands IDLEWILD (now without FAIRFOULL who was replaced b[y] GAVIN FOX and guitarist ALLAN STEWART) spent much o[f] 2004 crafting 4th set, 'WARNINGS/PROMISES' (2005), a rootsie[r] record which went Top 10 and spawned three hits, 'LOV[E] STEALS US FROM LONELINESS', 'I UNDERSTAND IT' and 'E[L] CAPITAN'. On an even folkier note, WOOMBLE busied himsel[f] with a solo project following an amicable parting of the ways wit[h] 'Parlophone'.

Album rating: HOPE IS IMPORTANT (*7) / 100 BROKEN WINDOWS (*7) THE REMOTE PART (*8) / WARNINGS – PROMISES (*6)

RODDY WOOMBLE (b.13 Aug'76) – vocals / **ROD JONES** (b. 3 Dec'76) – guitar / **COLIN NEWTON** (b.18 Apr'77) – drums / **PAUL TIPLER** (helpe[d] out on) bass

Human Condition | not iss.

Mar 97. (7") *(HC 0017)* **QUEEN OF THE TROUBLED TEENS. / FASTER / SELF HEALER** [ ] [–]
(re-iss. Jan98; same)

—— **BOB FAIRFOULL** (b. 6 Aug'76) – bass; repl. PAUL

Fierce Panda | not iss.

Dec 97. (ltd-7") *(NING 42)* **CHANDELIER. / I WANT TO BE A WRITER** [ ] [–]

Deceptive | not iss.

Jan 98. (m-cd) *(BLUFF 058CD)* **CAPTAIN** [ ] [–]
– Self healer / Annihilate now / Captain / Last night I misse[d] all the fireworks / Satan polaroid / You just have to be who you are.

Feb 98. (7") *(BLUFF 057)* **SATAN POLAROID. / HOUSE ALONE** [ ] [–]

Food | Odeon-[EMI]

Apr 98. (7") *(FOOD 111)* **A FILM FOR THE FUTURE. / MINCE SHOWERCAP (part I)** [53] [–]
(cd-s+=) *(CDFOOD 111)* – What am I going to do?

Jul 98. (7") *(FOOD 113)* **EVERYONE SAYS YOU'RE SO FRAGILE. / MINCE SHOWERCAP (part II)** [47] [–]
(cd-s+=) *(CDFOOD 113)* – Theory of achievement.

Oct 98. (7") *(FOOD 114)* **I'M A MESSAGE. / MINCE SHOWERCAP (part III)** [41] [–]
(cd-s+=) *(CDFOOD 114)* – This is worse.
(cd-s) **THE SESSIONS EP** *(CDFOODS 114)* – ('A'live) / Satan polaroi[d] (live) / You've lost your way (live).

Oct 98. (cd/c/lp) *(497132-2/-4/-1) <9504>* **HOPE IS IMPORTANT** [53] [ ]
– You've lost your way / A film for the future / Paint nothing When I argue I see shapes / 4 people do good / I'm happy t[o] be here tonight / Everyone says you're so fragile / I'm a message You don't have the heart / Close the door / Safe and sound / Lo[w] light.

Feb 99. (7") *(FOOD 116)* **WHEN I ARGUE I SEE SHAPES. / (1903-70) / CHANDELIER (10.15 version)** [19] [–]
(cd-s) *(CDFOOD 116)* – (first 2 tracks) / Last night I missed all the firewor[ks] (live).
(cd-s) *(CDFOODS 116)* – (first & third tracks) / Palace flophouse.

Sep 99. (7") *(FOOD 124)* **LITTLE DISCOURAGE. / BROKEN WINDOWS** [24] [–]
(cd-s+=) *(CDFOOD 124)* – A-Tone.
(cd-s) *(CDFOODS 124)* – ('A') / You don't have the heart (live) / 1990 – night-time.

Mar 00. (7") *(FOOD 127)* **ACTUALLY IT'S DARKNESS. / MEET ME AT THE HARBOUR** [23] [–]
(cd-s+=) *(CDFOODS 127)* – West Haven.
(cd-s) *(CDFOOD 127)* – ('A') / Forgot to follow / It'll take a long time.

Apr 00. (cd/c/lp) *(FOOD CD/TC/LP 32)* *<65397>* **100 BROKEN WINDOWS** [15] May00 [ ]
– Little discourage / I don't have the map / These wooden ideas / Roseability / Idea track / Let me sleep (next to the mirror) / Listen to what you've got / Actually it's darkness / Rusty / Mistake pageant / Quiet crown / The bronze medal.

Jun 00. (7") *(FOOD 132)* **THESE WOODEN IDEAS. / THERE'S GLORY IN YOUR STORY** [32] [–]
(c-s) *(TCFOOD 132)* – ('A') / When the ship comes in.
(cd-s+=) *(CDFOODS 132)* – (three tracks above).
(cd-s) *(CDFOOD 132)* – ('A') / Actually it's darkness (acoustic) / Rescue.

Oct 00. (7") *(FOOD 134)* **ROSEABILITY. / RUSTY (the poop soldier mix)** [38] [–]
(cd-s+=) *(CDFOOD 134)* – A thousand.
(cd-s) *(CDFOODS 134)* – ('A') / I've only just begun / Self healer (live acoustic version) / ('A'-video).

Parlophone E.M.I.

Apr 02. (7") *(R 6575)* *<55078-2>* **YOU HELD THE WORLD IN YOUR ARMS. / A DISTANT HISTORY** [9] May02 [ ]
(cd-s+=) *(CDR 6575)* – I was made to think it.
(cd-s) *(CDRS 6575)* – ('A') / All this information / No generation.

Jul 02. (7") *(R 6582)* **AMERICAN ENGLISH. / POOR THING** [15] [–]
(cd-s+=) *(CDRS 6582)* – These are just years / ('A'-CD-video).
(cd-s) *(CDR 6582)* – ('A') / The nothing I know / We always have to impress.

Jul 02. (cd/lp) *(540243-2/-1)* **THE REMOTE PART** [3] [–]
– You held the world in your arms / A modern way of letting go / American English / I never wanted / (I am) What I am not / Live in a hiding place / Out of routine / Century after century / Tell me ten words / Stay the same / In remote part – Scottish fiction.

Oct 02. (7") *(R 6587)* **LIVE IN A HIDING PLACE. / GREAT TIMES WASTED** [26] [–]
(cd-s+=) *(CDR 6587)* – Everything flows / ('A'-video).
(cd-s) *(CDRS 6587)* – ('A') / Found that essence rare / I'm happy to be here tonight (live).

— FAIRFOULL had already departed September 2002 (joined DEGRASSI)

Feb 03. (7") *(R 6598)* **A MODERN WAY OF LETTING GO. / IN REMOTE PART** [28] [–]
(cd-s+=) *(CDR 6598)* – Scottish fiction (live) / ('A'-live).

— **GAVIN FOX** – bass; repl. FAIRFOULL

— added **ALLAN STEWART** – guitar

Feb 05. (cd-s/7") *(CD+/R 6658)* **LOVE STEALS US FROM LONELINESS. / HOLD ON TO YOUR BREATH** [16] [–]
(cd-s) *(CDRS 6658)* – ('A') / Gone too long / Don't let me change / ('A'-video) / (making of video).

Mar 05. (cd) *(560775-2)* **WARNINGS/PROMISES** [9] [–]
– Love steals us from loneliness / Welcome home / I want a warning / I understand it / As if I hadn't slept / Too long awake / Not just sometimes but always / The space between all things / El capitan / Blame it on obvious ways / Disconnected / Goodnight.

May 05. (cd-s/7") *(CD+/R 6662)* **I UNDERSTAND IT. / THE WORK WE NEVER DO** [32] [–]
(cd-s) *(CDRS 6662)* – ('A') / Pleasure and pain / Love steals us from loneliness (acoustic) / ('A'-video) / (making of video).

Jul 05. (7") *(R 6667)* **EL CAPITAN. / BRONZE MEDAL (acoustic)** [39] [–]
(7"red) *(R 6667X)* – ('A') / Winter is blue.
(cd-s+=) *(CDRS 6667)* – ('A'-acoustic).

— (Dec'05) **GARETH RUSSELL** – bass (ex-ASTRID) repl. GAVIN

– compilations, etc. –

Oct 02. (d-cd) *Parlophone; (543148-2)* **100 BROKEN WINDOWS / HOPE IS IMPORTANT** [ ] [–]

Billy IDOL

Born: WILLIAM BROAD, 30 Nov'55, Stanmore, Middlesex, England. In 1976, this aspring punk formed GENERATION X alongside BOB ANDREWS and ex-CHELSEA members, TONY JAMES and JOHN TOWE (the latter was soon replaced by former SUBWAY SECT man, MARK LAFF). Though they attracted a loyal fanbase, GENERATION X were never considered a dyed-in-the-wool punk band per se, their more commercial, hooky power pop at odds with the genre's inherent nihilism. Signed to 'Chrysalis', the band hit the Top 40 with their first single, 'YOUR GENERATION', following it up with 'WILD YOUTH' and 'READY STEADY GO', the latter track a decidedly un-punk 60's tribute. An eponymous debut album hit the Top 30 in Spring '78, while the band's sound grew increasingly commercial on successive albums, 'VALLEY OF THE DOLLS' (1979; produced by IAN HUNTER) and 'KISS ME DEADLY' (1981; released under the slightly clipped moniker of GEN X). Following their split in '81, JAMES later formed SIGUE SIGUE SPUTNIK, while the bleached-blond IDOL was free to pursue his barely concealed desire for pop stardom. Relocating to New York, he met manager, Bill Aucoin and producer, Keith Forsey, recruiting guitarist STEVE STEVENS and cutting a cover of Tommy James & The Shondells' 'MONY MONY' (along with a few other tracks – including the GENERATION X song, 'DANCING WITH MYSELF' – it formed part of a US-only mini-set, 'DON'T STOP'). A full length eponymous debut album followed in summer '82, the record including many songs which wouldn't hit the UK charts for another five years. The loping 'HOT IN THE CITY', for example, which became IDOL's first major US success; with the not inconsiderable, IDOL transformed himself into a leather-clad, lip-sneering hard rocker, his anthemic, dancefloor-friendly tunes lapped up by American teeny boppers and older fans alike. 'REBEL YELL' (1984) and the attendant 'EYES WITHOUT A FACE' single gave him further Stateside success, while a re-released 'WHITE WEDDING' gave IDOL a belated UK Top 10 hit in summer '85. A remix compilation, 'VITAL IDOL', was rush released the following month to build on the breakthrough, precipitating a rash of re-issued singles; while sales of his 'WHIPLASH SMILE' (1986) opus certainly benefitted, these re-issues were all bigger hits than his new material, not exactly a good sign. Just prior to the release of 'CHARMED LIFE' (1990), IDOL, ironically enough, suffered a near fatal motorbike crash, the climax to a troubled late 80's period which had seen the singer living out the rock'n'roll lifestyle to the full in sunny Los Angeles. Bluesy and confessional, the album's only hit was 'CRADLE OF LOVE', while the less said about IDOL's cover of the Doors' 'L.A. WOMAN', the better. An ill-advised concept album, 'CYBERPUNK' (1993), was even less well received, although it did feature UK Top 30 hit, 'SHOCK TO THE SYSTEM'. When IDOL re-emerged in the 00s, classicist cable channel, 'VH1', provided a perfect platform for a live comeback as part of their 'STORYTELLERS' series (IDOL also popped up in the movie, 'The Wedding Singer' for a musical cameo alongside Adam Sandler). 'Sanctuary' was another redoubt for ageing rockers, and they signed him on for a set of bonafide new material, 'DEVIL'S PLAYGROUND' (2005). Critics weren't too keen but it did scrape into the US Top 50, while one of the tracks, 'PLASTIC JESUS' (written by George Cromarty) was used in the Oscar-nominated film, 'Crash'.

• **Songwriters:** GENERATION X:- IDOL – JAMES, except GIMME SOME TRUTH (John Lennon) / SHAKIN' ALL OVER (hit; Johnny Kidd & The Pirates). Solo, IDOL & STEVENS collaborated until 1990 when IDOL wrote with WERNER. Solo Covers; HEROIN (Lou Reed) / MOTHER DAWN (McBrook – Youth).

Album rating: Generation X: GENERATION X (*6) / VALLEY OF THE DOLLS (*5) / KISS ME DEADLY (*5) / PERFECT HITS compilation (*7) / Billy Idol: BILLY IDOL (*6) / REBEL YELL (*7) / WHIPLASH SMILE (*5) / VITAL IDOL remixes (*5) / CHARMED LIFE (*6) / CYBERPUNK (*3) / IDOL SONGS – 11 OF THE BEST compilation (*7) / GREATEST HITS compilation (*7) / VH-1 STORYTELLERS (*5) / DEVIL'S PLAYGROUND (*4)

GENERATION X

BILLY IDOL – vocals (ex-CHELSEA, ex-INFANTS) / **BOB 'Derwood' ANDREWS** – guitar / **TONY JAMES** – bass, vocals (ex-CHELSEA, ex-INFANTS) / **MARK LAFF** – drums (ex-SUBWAY SECT) repl. JOHN TOWE (ex-CHELSEA, ex-INFANTS) who joined ALTERNATIVE TV then ADVERTS, etc

Chrysalis Chrysalis

Sep 77. (7") *(CHS 2165)* **YOUR GENERATION. / DAY BY DAY** 36

Dec 77. (7") *(CHS 2189)* **WILD YOUTH. / WILD DUB**
(some copies were mispressed with b-side 'NO NO NO')

Mar 78. (7") *(CHS 2207)* **READY STEADY GO. / NO NO NO** 47

Mar 78. (lp/c) *(CHR/ZCHR 1169)* **GENERATION X** 29
– From the heart / One hundred punks / Listen / Ready steady go / Kleenex / Promises promises / Day by day / The invisible man / Kiss me deadly / Too personal / Youth, youth, youth. *(cd-iss. Jan86; CCD 1169) (re-iss. cd Mar94; CD25CR 14) (cd re-iss. Jul96 on 'EMI Gold'; CDGOLD 1039)*

Jan 79. (7",7"red,7"pink,7"orange,7"yellow) *(CHS 2261)* **KING ROCKER. / GIMME SOME TRUTH** 11

Jan 79. (lp/c) *(CHR/ZCHR 1193)* **VALLEY OF THE DOLLS** 51
– Running with the boss sound / Night of the Cadillacs / Paradise west / Friday's angels / King rocker / Valley of the dolls / English dream / Love like fire / Paradise west / The prime of Kenny Silvers. *(cd-iss. Jan86; CCD 1193)*

Mar 79. (7",7"brown) *(CHS 2310)* **VALLEY OF THE DOLLS. / SHAKIN' ALL OVER** 23

Jun 79. (7",7"pink) *(CHS 2330)* **FRIDAY'S ANGELS. / TRYING FOR KICKS / THIS HEAT** 62

— **TERRY CHIMES** – drums (ex-CLASH, ex-COWBOYS INTERNATIONAL) repl. LAFF / **JAMES STEPHENSON** – guitar (ex-CHELSEA) repl. 'DERWOOD' (later to WESTWORLD)

GEN X

Sep 80. (7") *(CHS 2444)* **DANCING WITH MYSELF. / UGLY RASH** 62
(12"+=) *(CHS12 2444)* – Loopy dub / What do you want

Jan 81. (lp/c) *(CHR/ZCHR 1327)* **KISS ME DEADLY**
– Dancing with myself / Untouchables / Happy people / Heaven's inside / Triumph / Revenge / Stars look down / What do you want / Oh mother. *(cd-iss. Jan86; CCD 1327)*

Jan 81. (7"ep,7"clear-ep/12"ep) *(CHS/+12 2488)* **DANCING WITH MYSELF / UNTOUCHABLES. / KING ROCKER / ROCK ON** 60

— split early '81, when BILLY went solo. CHIMES rejoined The CLASH, TONY JAMES later formed SIGUE SIGUE SPUTNIK. STEPHENSON later joined GENE LOVES JEZEBEL, then The CULT.

– compilations, etc. –

on 'Chrysalis' unless otherwise mentioned

Nov 85. (lp/c) *(CHM/ZCHM 1521)* **THE BEST OF GENERATION X**

Feb 87. (7") *Old Gold; (OG 9693)* **KING ROCKER. / VALLEY OF THE DOLLS** –

Jun 87. (lp) *M.B.C.; (JOCKLP 9)* **THE ORIGINAL GENERATION X** –

Jun 88. (lp) *M.B.C.; (JOCKLP 11)* **GENERATION X LIVE (live)** –

Oct 91. (cd/c/lp) *(CCD/ZCHR/CHR 1854)* **PERFECT HITS (1975-81)**
– Dancing with myself / Your generation / Ready steady go / The untouchables / Day by day / Wild youth / Wild dub / One hundred punks / King rocker / Kiss me deadly / Gimme some truth / New order / English dream / Triumph / Youth, youth, youth.

BILLY IDOL

— with **STEVE STEVENS** – guitar / **PHIL FEIT** – bass / **STEVE MISSAL** – drums (same label)

Sep 81. (7") *(CHS 2543)* **MONY MONY. / BABY TALK**
(12"+=) *(CHS12 2543)* – Untouchables / Dancing with myself (extended). *<US-title 'DON'T STOP' m-lp; 4000>; hit No.71.*

Jul 82. (lp/c) *(CHR/ZCHR 1377) <41377>* **BILLY IDOL** 45
– Come on, come on / White wedding (part 1 & 2) / Hot in the city / Dead on arrival / Nobody's business / Love calling / Hole in the wall / Shooting stars / It's so cruel / Congo man. *(cd-iss. Jan86; CCD 1377) (re-iss. Jul94 cd/c;) (cd re-iss. Jan02 ++; 532860-2)* – Dancing with myself.

Aug 82. (7"/7"pic-d/ext.12") *(CHS/+P/12 2625) <2605>* **HOT IN THE CITY. / DEAD ON ARRIVAL** 58 Jun82 23

Oct 82. (7"/ext.12") *(CHS/+12 2656) <42697>* **WHITE WEDDING. / HOLE IN THE WALL** 36

Sep 83. (7",7"clear) *(IDOL 1)* **WHITE WEDDING. / HOT IN THE CITY** –
(12"+=) *(IDOLX 1)* – Love calling / Dancing with myself.

Jan 84. (lp/c) *(CHR/ZCHR 1450) <41450>* **REBEL YELL** Nov83 6
– Rebel yell / Daytime drama / Eyes without a face / Blue highway / Flesh for fantasy / Catch my fall / Crank call / (Do not) Stand in the shadows / The dead next door. *(hit UK No.36 Sep85) (cd-iss. Jan86; CCD 1450) (re-iss. cd Mar94;)*

Feb 84. (7"/7"square-pic-d) *(IDOL/+P 2) <42762>* **REBEL YELL. / CRANK CALL** 62 Jan84 46
(12"+=) *(IDOLX 2)* – White wedding.
(d7"++=) *(IDOLD 2)* – Hot in the city.

Jun 84. (7") *(IDOL 3) <42786>* **EYES WITHOUT A FACE. / THE DEAD NEXT DOOR** 18 Apr84 4
(d7"+=/12"+=/12"pic-d+=) *(IDOL D/X/P 3)* – Dancing with myself / Rebel yell.

Sep 84. (7") *(IDOL 4) <42809>* **FLESH FOR FANTASY. / BLUE HIGHWAY** 54 Aug84 29
(12"+=/12"pic-d+=) *(IDOL X/P 4)* – ('A'extended).

Oct 84. (7") *<42840>* **CATCH MY FALL. / DAYTIME DRAMA** – 50

Jun 85. (7",7"white) *(IDOL 5)* **WHITE WEDDING. / FLESH FOR FANTASY** 6 –
(7"clear/12",12"white/12"pic-d) *(IDOL/+X/P 5)* – ('A'-Shotgun mix pts.1 & 2) / Mega-Idol-mix.

Jul 85. (lp/c) *(CUX/ZCUX 1502) <41620>* **VITAL IDOL** (remix compilation) 7 Oct87 10
– White wedding (part 1 & 2) / Mony mony (downtown mix) / Hopt in the city / Dancing with myself (uptown mix) / Flesh for fantasy (below the belt mix) / To be a lover (mother of mercy mix) / Love calling (rub a dub dub mix) / Catch my fall (remix). *(cd-iss. Jan86; CCD 1502) (cd re-iss. Jan02; 532859-2)*

Sep 85. (7"/7"pic-d) *(IDOL/+P 6)* **REBEL YELL. / (DO NOT) STAND IN THE SHADOWS (live)** 6
(12"+=/12"pic-d+=) *(IDOL X/P 6)* – Blue highway.

Sep 86. (7",7"colrd) *(IDOL 8) <43024>* **TO BE A LOVER. / ALL SUMMER SINGLE** 22 6
(12"+=/12"pic-d+=) *(IDOL X/P 8)* – ('A'-Mercy mix).
(d12"++=) *(IDOLD 8)* – White wedding.

Oct 86. (lp/c/cd) *(CDL/ZCDL/CCD 1514) <41514>* **WHIPLASH SMILE** 8 6
– Worlds forgotten boy / To be a lover / Soul standing by / Sweet sixteen / Man for all seasons / Don't need a gun / Beyond belief / Fatal charm / All summer single / One night, one chance. *(re-iss. Mar93 cd/c;)*

Feb 87. (7",7"colrd) *(IDOL 9) <43087>* **DON'T NEED A GUN. / FATAL CHARM** 26 Jan87 37
(12"+=/12"pic-d+=) *(IDOL X/P 9)* – ('A'version).
(d7"+=) *(IDOLD 9)* – (free single).

May 87. (7") *(IDOL 10) <43114>* **SWEET 16. / BEYOND BELIEF** 17 Apr87 20
(12"+=/12"pic-d+=) *(IDOL X/P 10)* – Rebel yell.

Sep 87. (7") *(IDOL 11) <43161>* **MONY MONY (live). / SHAKIN' ALL OVER (live)** 7 Aug87 1
(12"+=) *(IDOLX 11)* – ('A'-Hung like a pony mix).

Jan 88. (7") *(IDOL 12) <43203>* **HOT IN THE CITY (remix). / CATCH MY FALL (remix)** 13 Dec87 48
(12"+=) *(IDOLX 12)* – Soul standing by.
('A'-Exterminator mix-cd-s++=) *(IDOLCD 12)* – Mony Mony (live).

Jun 88. (lp/c/cd) *(BILTV/ZBILTV/BILCD 1)* **IDOL SONGS – 11 OF THE BEST** (compilation) 2 –
– Rebel yell / Hot in the city / White wedding / Eyes without a face / Catch my fall / Mony mony / To be a lover / Sweet sixteen / Flesh for fantasy / Don't need a gun / Dancing with myself.

Aug 88. (7"/12"/cd-s) *(IDOL/+X/CD 13)* **CATCH MY FALL (the remix fix). / ALL SUMMER SINGLE (remix)** 63 –

— now with **MARK YOUNGER-SMITH** – guitar, bass / **KEITH FORSEY** – drums, producer **VITO** and **PHIL SOUSSAN** – bass / **ARTHUR BARROW** – keyboards / **MIKE BAIRD** – drums

Apr 90. (7"/c-s) *(IDOL/+C 14) <23509>* **CRADLE OF LOVE. / 311 MAN** 34 2
(12") *(IDOLX 14)* – ('A'extended) / Rob the cradle of love.
(cd-s) *(IDOLCD 14)* – (all 3 tracks above).

Apr 90. (cd/c/lp) *(CD/Z+/CHR 1735) <21735>* **CHARMED LIFE** 15 11
– The loveless / Pumping on steel / Prodigal blues / L.A. woman / Trouble with the sweet stuff / Cradle of love / Mark of Caine / Endless sleep / Love unchained / The right way / License to thrill.

Jul 90. (7"/c-s) *(IDOL/+C 15) <23571>* **L.A. WOMAN. / LICENSE TO THRILL** 70 52
(12"+=/cd-s+=) *(IDOL X/CD 15)* – Love child.

Dec 90. (7"/c-s) *(IDOL/+C 16)* **PRODIGAL BLUES. / MARK OF CAINE** 47
(12"+=/cd-s+=) *(IDOL X/CD 16)* – Flesh for fantasy.

— retained co-writer **YOUNGER-SMITH** + recruited **ROBIN HANCOCK** – keyboards, producer / **DOUG WIMBUSH** – bass / **JAMIE MAMOBERAC** – organ / **TAL BERGHAN** – drums

Jun 93. (7"/12") *(CHS/+12 3994)* **SHOCK TO THE SYSTEM. / HEROIN (overloads mix) / HEROIN (durge trance dub)** 30
(cd-s) *(CHSCD1 3994)* – ('A'side) / Heroin (original) / Rebel yell.
(cd-s) *(CHSCD2 3994)* – ('A'side) / Heroin (smack attack) / White wedding.

Jun 93. (cd/c/lp) *(CD/Z+/CHR 6000) <26000>* **CYBERPUNK** 20 48
– Wasteland / Shock to the system / Tomorrow people / Adam in chains / Neuromancer / Power junkie / Love labours on / Heroin / Shangrila / Concrete kingdom / Venus / Then the night comes / Mother Dawn.

Sep 93. (c-s/7") *(TC+/CHS 5002)* **ADAM IN CHAINS. / SHOCK TO THE SYSTEM / VENUS** –
(cd-s) *(CSCHSS 5002)* – (first 2) / Eyes without a face.
(cd-s) *(CDCHS 5002)* – ('A'side) / Tomorrow people / Mony Mony.

Fox-Arista Fox-Arista

Sep 94. (7"/c-s/cd-s) *(74321 22347-7/-4/-2)* **SPEED. / REBEL YELL (acoustic)** 47 –
(above from the film of the same name)

Chrysalis Capitol

Feb 02. (cd) *(<5 36919-2>)* **VH-1 STORYTELLERS** (live)
– Cradle of love / Don't need a gun / Flesh for fantasy / White wedding / Sweet sixteen / To be a lover / Rebel yell / Kiss me deadly / Eyes without a face / Dancing with myself / Ready steady go / Blue highway / Mony Mony / L.A. woman.

Sanctuary Sanctuary

Mar 05. (cd-s) *(SANXS 355)* **SCREAM / SCREAM (album version) / BLEEDING ME INSANE / SCREAM (Call Out Hook)** –

Mar 05. (cd) *(SANCD 339) <84735>* **DEVIL'S PLAYGROUND** 46
– Super overdrive / World comin' down / Rat race / Sherri / Plastic Jesus / Scream / Yellin' at the Xmas tree / Romeo's waiting / Body snatcher / Evil eye / Lady do or die / Cherie / Summer running.

– compilations, others, etc. –

on 'Chrysalis' unless mentioned otherwise

Mar 01. (cd) *(<5 28812-2>)* **GREATEST HITS** 74
– Dancing with myself / Mony Mony (studio) / Hot in the city / White wedding / Rebel yell / Eyes without a face / Flesh for fantasy / Catch my fall / To be a lover / Don't need a gun / Sweet sixteen / Cradle of love / L.A. woman / Shock to the system / Rebel yell (live acoustic) / Don't you forget about me.

Mar 03. (cd) *E.M.I.; (58221-2)* **THE ESSENTIAL BILLY IDOL** –

Mar 03. (d-cd) *(581768-2)* **VITAL IDOL / CHARMED LIFE** –

❑ James IHA (see under ⇒ SMASHING PUMPKINS)

❑ the IN-BE-TWEENS (see under ⇒ SLADE)

the INCREDIBLE STRING BAND

Formed: Glasgow, Scotland ... early 1966 by ROBIN WILLIAMSON, London-born CLIVE PALMER and MIKE HERON. From the early 60's, WILLIAMSON had played London gigs alongside BERT JANSCH (future PENTANGLE), before he returned to Glasgow. In April 1961, he formed a duo with Englishman PALMER, although they found it difficult to establish themselves, that is, until 1965 when PALMER set up the 'Incredible' folk club in Sauchiehall Street. That same year, the pair performed at the Edinburgh Folk Festival, catching the eye of Nathan Joseph of 'Transatlantic' records who recorded them for the concert's Various Artists compilation. After their folk club was shut down by the police, they became a trio, adding MIKE HERON to become The INCREDIBLE STRING BAND. After months tracking them down, American producer JOE BOYD finally found them and duly signed them to 'Elektra'. He subsequently took them to London, where they recorded their eponymous debut album (summer '66). With this well-received record under their belt, PALMER departed for Afghanistan. When he returned he declined to re-join the act, who were now broke but under the management of BOYD. Upon ROBIN's return from Morocco, the duo (augmented by some friends), played an 'Elektra' records package alongside TOM PAXTON and JUDY COLLINS, at The Royal Albert Hall. It helped promote their second album, 'THE 5000 SPIRITS OR THE LAYERS OF THE ONION', which made the UK Top 30 in 1967. Their underground blend of psychedelic folk was crystallised on such charming tracks as, 'CHINESE WHITE', 'FIRST GIRL I LOVED' and 'PAINTING BOX'. In Spring '68, they surprisingly crashed into the UK Top 5 with their third set, 'THE HANGMAN'S BEAUTIFUL DAUGHTER'. The album's witty lyrics (alternately penned by HERON or WILLIAMSON) and ethnic multi-instrumentation was embellished with the vocals of the duo's girlfriends, LICORICE and ROSE. The highlights of this album, arguably the group's finest hour, were 'A VERY CELLULAR SONG', 'THE MINOTAUR'S SONG' and 'KOEEOADDI THERE'. Late that year, they issued 2 single lp's as a double-set, 'WEE TAM' & 'THE BIG HUGE'. However, this brilliant but confused package failed to sell. Over the next two years, they released three UK Top 40 albums ('I LOOKED UP', a collection of baroque eclecticism – 'U' verging on pantomine), but after a move to 'Island' in 1971, they soon faded from the commercial limelight. Nevertheless, the second 'Island' album, 'LIQUID ACROBAT AS REGARDS THE AIR', hit the Top 50, boasting the spine-tingling melancholy of the 11-minute 'DARLING BELLE'. HERON and WILLIAMSON went their separate ways in the mid-70's, the former writing 'DON'T KILL IT CAROL' (later a hit for MANFRED MANN'S EARTH BAND), the latter becoming something of a self-styled cosmic folk storyteller (complete with harp). WILLIAMSON recorded a plethora of albums and poetry between 1977 to the present day and even established his own imprint, 'Pig's Whisker'. Although HERON hasn't been quite as visible since the ISB's split, he has surfaced with the occasional solo set, harking back to an ISB-style sound on 1996's 'WHERE THE MYSTICS SWIM'. Another old ISB face cropped up in 1999 as ROBIN recorded 'AT THE PURE FOUNTAIN' with CLIVE PALMER, the pair completing a second set, 'JUST LIKE THE IVY', the following year. The big news, however, was a full INCREDIBLE STRING BAND reunion at the 2001 Celtic Connections Festival in Glasgow, messrs WILLIAMSON, HERON, PALMER plus newcomers LAWSON DANDO and BINA WILLIAMSON (ROBIN's wife) putting in an acclaimed performance which more than justified the hype and boded well for the future. No sooner had the critics begun to rave however, than ROBIN resumed his solo career, leaving HERON, PALMER and DANDO at the helm of the good ship ISB for an intimate live set, 'NEBULOUS NEARNESSES' (2004).

Album rating: THE INCREDIBLE STRING BAND (*6) / THE 5000 SPIRITS OR THE LAYERS OF THE ONION (*9) / THE HANGMAN'S BEAUTIFUL DAUGHTER (*9) / WEE TAM (*8) / THE BIG HUGE (*7) / CHANGING HORSES (*5) / I LOOKED UP (*4) / "U" (*4) / RELICS OF . . . compilation (*7) / BE GLAD FOR THE SONG HAS NO ENDING (*4) / LIQUID ACROBAT AS REGARDS THE AIR (*5) / EARTHSPAN (*4) / NO RUINOUS FEUD (*5) / HARD ROPE AND SILKEN TWINE (*4) / SEASONS THEY CHANGE – THE BEST OF THE INCREDIBLE STRING BAND compilation (*8) / BLOOMSBURY 2000 (*6) / NEBULOUS NEARNESSES (*5)

ROBIN WILLIAMSON (b.24 Nov'43, Edinburgh, Scotland) – vocals, guitars, etc. / **CLIVE PALMER** (b. 1943, Edmonton, London, England) – guitar, banjo, vocals / **MIKE HERON** (b.12 Dec'42, Glasgow, Scotland) – vocals, rhythm guitar, sitar, etc.

Elektra Elektra

Jun 66. (lp) *(EUK 254) <EKS 7322>* **THE INCREDIBLE STRING BAND** ☐ ☐
– Maybe someday / October song / When the music starts to play / Schaeffer's jig / Womankind / The tree / Whistle tune / Dandelion blues / How happy am I / Empty pocket blues / Smoke shovelling song / Can't keep me here / Good as gone / Footsteps of the heron / Niggertown / Everything's fine right now. *(re-iss. Jul68; EKL 254); hit No.34) (cd-iss. Jul93; 7559 61547-2) (cd re-iss. Jun94 on 'Hannibal'; HNCD 4437)*

— now a duo when PALMER went to abroad; he later formed FAMOUS JUG BAND — added **CHRISTINA 'LICORICE' McKECHNIE** – some vocals, organ (a guest on below) plus guests **DANNY THOMPSON** – double bass (of PENTANGLE) / **JOHN HOPKINS** – piano

Jul 67. (lp; mono/stereo) *(EUK/+S7 257) <EKS 74010>* **THE 5000 SPIRITS OR THE LAYERS OF THE ONION** [26] ☐
– Chinese white / No sleep blues / Painting box / The Mad Hatter's song / Little cloud / The eyes of fate / Blues for the muse / The hedgehog's song / First girl I loved / You know that you could be / My name is death / Gently tender / Way back in the 1960s. *(re-iss. 1968; EKS 7257) (re-iss. Jan73 + 1976; K 42001) (cd-iss. Mar92; 7559 60913-2) (cd re-iss. Jun94 on 'Hannibal'; HNCD 4438)*

Mar 68. (7") *(EKSN 45028)* **PAINTING BOX. / NO SLEEP BLUES** ☐ [-]

Mar 68. (lp; mono/stereo) *(EUK/+S7 258) <EKS 74021>* **THE HANGMAN'S BEAUTIFUL DAUGHTER** [5] Jun68 ☐
– Koeeoaddi there / The minotaur's song / Witches hat / A very cellular song / Mercy I cry city / Waltz of the new Moon / The water song / Three is a green crown / Swift as the wind / Nightfall. *(re-iss. Jan73 + 1976; K 42002) (cd-iss. Mar92; 7559 60835-2) (cd re-iss. Jun94 on 'Hannibal'; HNCD 4437)*

— **MIKE, ROBIN** and his girlfriend **LICORICE** introduced MIKE'S girlfriend **ROSE SIMPSON** – some vocals, bass, percussion, violin

Oct 68. (d-lp; mono/stereo) *(EKL/EKS7 4036-7)* **WEE TAM / THE BIG HUGE** ☐ [-]
(d-cd-iss. Nov94 on 'Hannibal'; HNCD 4802) (d-cd re-iss. Jul02 on 'Collector's Choice'; CCM 0290-2)

Oct 68. (lp; mono/stereo) *(EKL/<EKS7 4036>)* **WEE TAM** ☐ Mar69 ☐
– Job's tears / Puppies / Beyond the see / The yellow snake / Log cabin home in the sky / You get brighter / The half-remarkable question / Air / Ducks on a pond. *(re-iss. Jan73 + 1976; K 42021) (cd-iss. Feb92 & Sep99; 7559 60914-2) (<cd re-iss. Nov94 on 'Hannibal'; HNCD 4802>)*

Oct 68. (lp; mono/stereo) *(EKL/<EKS7 4037>)* **THE BIG HUGE** ☐ Mar69 ☐
– Maya / Greatest friend / The son of Noah's brother / Lordly nightshade / The mountain of God / Cousin caterpillar / The iron stone / Douglas Traherne Harding / The circle is unbroken. *(re-iss. Jan73 + 1976; K 42022) (cd-iss. Jul93; 7559 61548-2)*

— LICORICE was now a full-time member

Oct 69. (7") *(EKSN 45074)* **BIG TED. / ALL WRIT DOWN** ☐ [-]

Nov 69. (lp) *(<EKS 74057>)* **CHANGING HORSES** [30] ☐
– Big Ted / White bird / Dust be diamonds / Sleepers, awake! / Mr. & Mrs. / Creation. *(cd-iss. Jul93 & May01; 7559 61549-2) (cd-iss. Dec94 on 'Hannibal'; HNCD 4439)*

— added guest **DAVE MATTACKS** – drums of FAIRPORT CONVENTION

Apr 70. (lp) *(<EKS 7401>)* **I LOOKED UP** [30] Jul70 ☐
– Black Jack Davey / Letter / Pictures in a mirror / This moment / When you find out who you are / Fair as you. *(re-prom.1970; 2469 002) (cd-iss. Dec94 on 'Hannibal'; HNCD 4440) (cd re-iss. Jul02; 7559 62760-2)*

Apr 70. (7") *(2101 003)* **THIS MOMENT. / BLACK JACK DAVEY** ☐ [-]

May 70. (7") *<45696>* **THIS MOMENT. / BIG TED** [-] ☐

— augmented by **JANET SHANKMAN** – b.vocals (ROBIN married her Dec70) **PETE GRANT** – banjo / **GREG HART** – sitar (of STONE MONKEY) plus guest **MALCOLM LE MAISTRE** – keyboards, bass (of EXPLODING GALAXY)

Oct 70. (d-lp) *(2665 001) <7E 2002>* **"U"** [34] Jan71 ☐
– El wool suite / The juggler's song / Time / Bad Sadie Lee / Queen of love / Partial belated overture / Light in the time of darkness – Glad to see you / Walking along with you / Hirem pawnitof – Fairies' hornpipe // Bridge theme / Bridge song / Astral plane theme / Invocation / Robot blues / Puppet song / Cutting the strings / I know you / Rainbow. *(re-iss. Jan73; K 62002) (d-cd iss.Jul02 on 'Collector's Choice'; CCM 0288-2) (d-cd re-iss. Aug02; 7559 62761-2)*

— Back to basic duo of **ROBIN + MIKE** plus **LICORICE + ROSE**

Island Elektra

Apr 71. (lp) *(ILPS 9140)* **BE GLAD FOR THE SONG HAS NO ENDING** ☐ [-]
– Come with me / All writ down / Vishangro / See all the people / Waiting for you / (Be glad for) The song has no ending. *(cd-iss. Jun98 on 'Edsel'; EDCD 564)*

— **MALCOLM LE MAISTRE** – keyboards, bass, vocals returned to repl. ROSE

Oct 71. (lp) *(ILPS 9172) <74112>* **LIQUID ACROBAT AS REGARDS THE AIR** [46] Feb72 ☐
– Talking of the end / Dear old battlefield / Cosmic boy / Worlds they rise and fall / Evloution rag / Painted chariot / Adam and Eve / Red hair / Here till here is there / Tree / Jigs: Eyes like leaves – Sunday is my wedding day – Drops of whiskey – Grumbling old men / Darling Belle. *(re-iss. Aug91 cd)(c; IMCD 130)(ICM 9172)*

— added **GERARD DOTT** – clarinet, saxophone (he played on HERON's 1972 solo album) and guest on one **STUART GORDON** – viola

Oct 72. (lp) *(ILPS 9211)* **EARTH SPAN** ☐ [-]
– My father was a lighthouse keeper / Antoine / Restless night / Sunday song / Black Jack David / Banks of sweet Italy / The actor / Moon hang low / The sailor and the dancer / Seagull. *(cd-iss. Dec92 on 'Edsel'; EDCD 360)*

Nov 72. (7") *(WIP 6145)* **BLACK JACK DAVID. / MOON HANG LOW** ☐ [-]

— **STAN LEE** – bass repl. LICORICE who joined WOODY WOODMANSEY Band **JACK INGRAM** – drums (added to ROBIN, MIKE, MALCOLM, GERARD and STAN)

Island Reprise

Feb 73. (7") *(WIP 6158)* **AT THE LIGHTHOUSE DANCE. / JIGS** ☐ [-]

Feb 73. (lp) *(ILPS 9229) <2139>* **NO RUINOUS FEUD** ☐ ☐
– Explorer / Down before Cathy / Saturday maybe / Jigs / Old Buccaneer / At the lighthouse dance / Second fiddle / Circus girl / Turquoise blue / My blue tears / Weather the storm / Little girl. *(cd-iss. Nov92 on 'Edsel'; EDCD 367)*

— **GRAHAM FORBES** – electric guitar (ex-POWERHOUSE) repl. GERARD / **JOHN GILSTON** – drums repl. INGRAM

Mar 74. (lp) *(ILPS 9270) <2198>* **HARD ROPE & SILKEN TWINE** ☐ ☐
– Maker of islands / Cold February / Glancing love / Dreams of no return / Dumb Kate / Ithkos. *(cd-iss. Feb93 on 'Edsel'; EDCD 368)*

— WILLIAMSON + HERON went onto solo careers; the pair re-formed late 1999 with PALMER, LAWSON DANDO + BINA WILLIAMSON

Pig's Whisker Pig's Whisker

Aug 01. (cd) *(<PWMD 5024>)* **BLOOMSBURY 2000 (live)** ☐ Nov01 ☐
– Maker of islands / Ducks on a pond / Air / The storm is on the ocean / Big city blues / Waltz of the new moon / Goodbye / You know what you could be / October song.

— when the WILLIAMSON's departed, **HERON, PALMER + DANDO** brought in **FLUFF** – vocals, multi / **GAVIN DRAKE** – bass / **STEINI GUDMUNDSSON** – percussion

Amoeba Amoeba

Jan 04. (cd) *(<AR 002CD>)* **NEBULOUS NEARNESSES** (live) ☐ Apr04 ☐
– You know what you could be / Cousin caterpillar / Everything's fine right now / Chinese white / Ducks on a pond / How happy I am / The water song / Banjo tune / Log cabin home in the sky / Painting box / Empty pocket blues / The hedgehog's song / A very cellular song.

– compilations etc. –

Mar 71. (lp) *Elektra; (EKS 74065) / Reprise; <7E 2004>* **RELICS OF THE INCREDIBLE STRING BAND** □ □

Nov 76. (d-lp) *Island; (ISLD 9)* **SEASONS THEY CHANGE – BEST OF THE INCREDIBLE STRING BAND** □ -
– Black Jack Davey / Blues for the muse / Nightfall / Puppies / Cold days of February / Worlds they rise and fall / Chinese white / Empty pocket blues / When the music starts to play / Saturday maybe / Red hair / The circle is unbroken / First girl I loved / Cosmic boy / Darling Belle / My father was a lighthouse keeper / Queen Juanita and her fisherman lover.

Oct 91. (cd/lp) *Band Of Joy; (BOJ CD/LP 004)* **ON AIR** (live) □ -

Nov 92. (cd) *Windsong; (WINCD 029)* **BBC RADIO 1 LIVE IN CONCERT** (live) □ -

Jun 97. (cd) *Blueprint; (PWMD 5003)* **THE CHELSEA SESSIONS 1967** □ -
(<re-iss. Mar98 on 'Pig's Whisker'; PWCD 5003)> (re-iss. Jul00; PWCD 5023)

Aug 98. (cd) *Mooncrest; (<CRESTCD 002>)* **FIRST GIRL I LOVED** (live) □ □
– Cousin caterpillar / I know that man / The circle is unbroken / Wild cat blues / The first girl I loved / Everything's fine right now / Old buccaneer / Catwalk rag / Giles crocodile / Turquoise blue / My father was a lighthouse keeper / Black Jack Davey / Ithkos.

May 01. (cd) *Island; (IMCD 280)* **HERE TILL THERE IS HERE (AN INTRODUCTION TO THE INCREDIBLE STRING BAND)** □ -

Jul 01. (cd) *Warner ESP; (9548 39803-2)* **THE BEST OF THE INCREDIBLE STRING BAND 1966-1970** □ -

Jul 02. (d-cd) *Collector's Choice; (CCM 0289-2)* **5000 SPIRITS OR THE LAYERS OF THE ONION / THE HANGMAN'S BEAUTIFUL DAUGHTER** □ -

Jul 02. (d-cd) *Collector's Choice; (CCM 0291-2)* **CHANGING HORSES / I LOOKED UP** □ -

Mar 03. (cd) *Disky; (<SI 90532-2>)* **HERITAGE** □ □

Jun 04. (cd) *Beat Goes On; (BGOCD 627)* **BE GLAD FOR THE SONG HAS NO ENDING / LIQUID ACROBAT AS REGARDS THE AIR** □ □

Jul 04. (cd) *Beat Goes On; (BGOCD 628)* **EARTHSPAN / NO RUINOUS FEUD** □ □

Aug 04. (d-cd) *Elektra; (8122 76504-2)* **THE INCREDIBLE STRING BAND / THE 5000 SPIRITS** □ □

— HERON and WILLIAMSON also released solo albums before their split. HERON = 'SMILING MEN WITH BAD REPUTATIONS' and WILLIAMSON = 'MYRRH'. Plus they went onto solo careers in 1975.

INCUBUS

Formed: Calabasas, California, USA ... summer 1990 by BRANDON BOYD, MIKE EINZIGER, ALEX KATUNICH, GAVIN POPPEL and JOSE ANTONIO PASILLAS II. Taking their moniker from an evil spirit purported to indulge in sexual activities with sleeping women, the band were nevertheless an uptempo funk/metal combo rather than a ghoulish death-metal act. One of the better acts to stay faithful to the spirit of classic RED HOT CHILI PEPPERS and FAITH NO MORE, updating the jack-in-the-box slap bass of the former and the resounding vocal depth of the latter, the group signed to Epic subsidiary 'Immortal' for their debut album, 'ENJOY INCUBUS' (1996) – actually they had self-financed a "real" debut album in '94. Well received in the metal press, 'ENJOY ...' transcended the barriers of the genre to successfully embrace everything from reggae to laid-back jazz, and still sounded funkin' great! Equally challenging and inventive, their next set, 'S.C.I.E.N.C.E.', was another mish-mash of styles even incorporating BOYD's didgeridoo, although don't let that put you off! In 1999, INCUBUS were back with new DJ, CHRIS GILMORE and a second full-set, 'MAKE YOURSELF', an album that finally gave them a US Top 50 success. More willing than many of their peers to mellow out, the band surprised many observers with the intelligence and relative soulfulness of 'MORNING VIEW' (2001), a near US chart topper (and UK Top 20) that generated major hits, 'DRIVE' and 'WISH YOU WERE HERE'. With newcomer BEN KENNEY filling the shoes of departed bassman ALEX, INCUBUS advanced their sound even further on the Brendan O'Brien-produced set, 'A CROW LEFT OF THE MURDER' (2004). More technically flashy and lyrically conscious, the record became the band's second successive album to hit No.2 boosted by lead track/hit, 'MEGALOMANIAC'. The quintet were subsequently commissioned to write part of the soundtrack for feature film, 'Stealth', contributing three new tracks and the previously released, 'AQUEOUS TRANSMISSION'.

• **Note:** Not the same group who released records on 'Nuclear Blast'.

Album rating: ENJOY INCUBUS mini (*6) / S.C.I.E.N.C.E. (*6) / MAKE YOURSELF (*7) / WHEN INCUBUS ATTACKS VOL.1 mini (*5) / FUNGUS AMONGUS collection (*5) / MORNING VIEW (*7) / A CROW LEFT OF THE MURDER (*7)

BRANDON BOYD (b.15 Feb'76, Van Nuys, Calif.) – vocals, percussion / **MIKE EINZIGER** (b.21 Jun'76, Los Angeles, Calif.) – guitar / **DIRK LANCE** (b. ALEX KATUNICH, 18 Aug'76) – bass / **KID LYFE** (b. GAVIN POPPEL) – scratches / **JOSE ANTONIO PASILLAS II** (b.26 Apr'76) – drums

Immortal – Epic / Immortal – Epic

Feb 97. (m-cd/m-c) *<(487102-2/-4)>* **ENJOY INCUBUS** □ Nov96 □
– You will be a hot dancer / Shaft / Trouble in 421 / Take me to your leader / Medium / Speak free / The answer / Psychopsilocybin / Sink beneath the line / Hilikus. *<US re-iss. Nov00 as 'FUNGUS AMONGUS'; 61497>*

Oct 97. (cd) *<(4882616)>* **S.C.I.E.N.C.E.** □ □
– Redefine / New skin / Idiot box / Glass / Magic medicine / Certain shade of green / Favourite things / Anti-gravity love song / Nebula / Deep inside / Calgon. *(re-iss. Jan01 & Jan02; same)*

— **CHRIS KILMORE** (b.21 Jan'73) – turntables; repl. GAVIN

Oct 99. (cd/c) *(495040-2/-4) <63652>* **MAKE YOURSELF** □ 47
– Privilege / Nowhere fast / Consequence / Warmth / When it comes / Stellar / Make yourself / Drive / Clean / Battle star / I miss you / Pardon me / Out from under. *(cd re-iss. May01 w/ extra cd; 495040-9)* – Pardon me (acoustic) / Stellar (acoustic) / Make yourself (acoustic) / Drive (live orchestral).

May 00. (7"red) *(669346-7)* **PARDON ME. / PARDON ME (acoustic)** 61 -
(cd-s) *(669346-2)* – ('A') / I miss you / Crowded elevator / ('A'-video).

Aug 00. (m-cd) *<61395>* **WHEN INCUBUS ATTACKS VOL.1** - 41
– Pardon me (acoustic) / Stellar (acoustic) / Make yourself (acoustic) / Crowded elevator / Favorite things (live) / Pardon me (live).

Jun 01. (cd-s) *(671378-2) <radio play>* **DRIVE / DRIVE (acoustic) / CLEAN (live)** 40 Feb01 9
(7"m) *(671378-7)* – ('A'live) / Favourite things (live) / Pardon me (live).

Oct 01. (cd) *(504061-2) <85272>* **MORNING VIEW** 15 2
– Nice to know you / Circles / Wish you were here / Just a phase / 11 a.m. / Blood on the ground / Mexico / Warning / Echo / Have you ever / Are you in? / Under my umbrella / Aqueous transmission. *(special cd+=; 504061-9)*– (the making of Morning View). *(re-iss. Apr06; 504061-5)*

Jan 02. (cd-s) *(672255-2) <671976>* **WISH YOU WERE HERE / NEW SKIN / DRIVE (orchestra) / ('A'video)** 27 Sep01 60
(cd-s) *(672255-5)* – ('A') / ('A'live) / Warmth (live) / Mexico (live).

Sep 02. (cd-s) *(672848-2) <67283-2>* **ARE YOU IN? / ARE YOU IN? (Paul Oakenfold remix) / STELLAR (acoustic) / ARE YOU IN? (video)** 34 Jun02 □
(cd-s) *(672848-5)* – ('A') / Wish you were here (live) / Pardon me (live video).

— **BEN KENNEY** – bass (of TIME-LAPSE CONSORTIUM) repl. ALEX

Jan 04. (7"red/cd-s) *(674646-7/-2)* **MEGALOMANIAC. / MONUMENTS AND MELODIES** 23 Dec03 55
(cd-s) *(674646-5)* – ('A') / Pistola (live at Lollapalooza 2003) / Nowhere fast (live at Lollapalooza 2003) / ('A'-video).

Feb 04. (cd) *(515047-2) <90890>* **A CROW LEFT OF THE MURDER** 6 2
– Megalomaniac / A crow left of the murder / Agoraphobia / Talk shows on mute / Beware! criminal / Sick sad little world / Pistola / Southern girl / Priceless / Zee Deveel / Made for TV movie / Suite lines / Here in my room / Leech. *(ltd-cd w/dvd+=; 515047-3)* – (DVD chapters). *<(re-iss. Sep05 w/dvd+=; <EN 92076>(515047-7)>* – (extended extras).

Jun 04. (7"yellow) *(674902-7)* **TALK SHOWS ON MUTE. / HERE IN MY ROOM (BBC Radio 1 session) / VITAMIN (live "bootleg" version) / HELLO (live "bootleg" version)** 43 -

(cd-s) *(674902-2)* – ('A') / Wish you were here (live "bootleg" version) / ('A'-live "bootleg" version) / Hello (BBC Radio 1 version) / ('A'-video).

– compilations, others, etc. –

Sep 05. (d-cd) *Epic; (520529-2)* **MAKE YOURSELF / MORNING VIEW** ☐ ☐

Apr 06. (d-cd) *(82876 82103-2)* **SCIENCE / FUNGUS AMONGUS** ☐ ☐

☐ INSPECTAH DECK (see under ⇒ WU-TANG CLAN)

☐ INSTITUTE (see under ⇒ BUSH)

☐ INTERNATIONAL SUBMARINE BAND (see under ⇒ PARSONS, Gram)

INTERPOL

Formed: New York City, New York, USA . . . 1998 by students DANIEL KESSLER, CARLOS D, and an old acquaintance PAUL BANKS. After some early gigging in the millennium the band settled on the inclusion of drummer SAMUEL FOGARINO, delivering a self-financed EP on the Scottish imprint 'Chemikal Underground' (as part of the 'fukd i.d.' series) in 2001; the group could also be found on several compilations, not least the British indie label Fierce Panda's 'Clooney Tunes'. INTERPOL were garnering interest in the music press both in their stateside homeland and in the UK; they toured Britain in April, and took the well-trodden track of alternative acts by appearing on the – need it be said – legendary John Peel slot on Radio One. Comparisons were being bandied about by the music hacks, not least of which was their likeness to celebrated Mancunian icons JOY DIVISION and less celebrated post-New Wavers the CHAMELEONS. The darker tones of the band's material did echo back to MARK BURGESS' et al's melancholy output, but it would have been wrong to have taken this analogy too far, as INTERPOL also ran in the tradition of many of the great American East Coast alternative acts. The New Yorkers were brought to the attention of 'Matador', who signed them up in 2002, and released a triple-track single in the early summer of that year. Hot on its heels came the release of their debut album 'TURN ON THE BRIGHT LIGHTS' (2002), widely hailed as one of the most enduring works to come out of the 00's neo-New Wave period. One of its most vocal supporters was the NME, who had INTERPOL perform in their annual awards show at the beginning of 2003, while the band strengthened their chart status with a re-issue of the classy 'OBSTACLE 1' single. If that difficult second album was guaranteed to be more difficult than most for INTERPOL, 'ANTICS' (2004) fulfilled expectations by never really straying from their glowering blueprint. It also more than fulfilled commercial expectations by reaching the US Top 20 (UK No.21); hit singles such as 'SLOW HANDS', 'EVIL' and 'C'MERE', all contributed to the INTERPOL myth, even if singer PAUL BANKS seemed to be in communion with the spectre of pre-Warners period MICHAEL STIPE.

Album rating: TURN ON THE BRIGHT LIGHTS (*9) / ANTICS (*8)

DANIEL KESSLER (b.25 Sep'74, London, England) – vocals, guitar / **PAUL BANKS** (b. 3 May'78, Clacton-on-Sea, Essex, England) – guitar, vocals / **CARLOS D** (b. DENGLER, 23 Apr'74) – bass, keyboards / **SAMUEL FOGARINO** (b. 9 Aug'68, Philadelphia, Pennsylvania, USA) – drums; repl. GREG

Chemikal Underground / Chemikal Underground

Dec 00. (12"ep/cd-ep) *(<CHEM 047/+CD>)* **fukd i.d. #3: PDA** ☐ ☐
– PDA / Precipitate / Roland / 5.

Matador / Matador

Jul 02. (7"ep/cd-ep) *<(OLE 546-7/-2)>* **THE INTERPOL EP** ☐ Jun02 ☐
– PDA / NYC / Specialist.

Aug 02. (cd/lp) *<(OLE 545-2/-1)>* **TURN ON THE BRIGHT LIGHTS** ☐ ☐
– Untitled / Obstacle 1 / NYC / PDA / Say hello to the angels / Hands away / Obstacle 2 / Stella was a diver and she was always down / Roland / The new / Leif Erikson.

Nov 02. (7") *(OLE 570-7)* **OBSTACLE 1. / OBSTACLE 2 (Peel session)** 72 –
(cd-s) *(OLE 570-2)* – ('A'side) / PDA (KCRW session) / Hands away (Peel session).

Apr 03. (7") *(OLE 582-7)* **SAY HELLO TO THE ANGELS. / N.Y.C. (demo)** 65 –
(cd-s+=) *(OLE 582-2)* – N.Y.C.

Aug 03. (cd-ep) *<592157-2>* **THE BLACK EP** – ☐
– Say hello to the angels / NYC (demo) / Obstacle 1 / Specialist / Leif Erikson / PDA. *(UK-iss.Mar05; same as US)*

Sep 03. (7") *(OLE 594-7)* **OBSTACLE 1 (remix). / OBSTACLE 1 (live black session)** 41 –
(cd-s) *(OLE 594-2)* – ('A'-Arthur Baker remixes).
(dvd-s) *(OLE 594-9)* – ('A'-video) / Specialist (live Black session) / Leif Erikson (live Black session).

Sep 04. (7") *(OLE 636-7)* **SLOW HANDS. / (Britt Daniel of Spoon remix)** 36 –
(cd-s) *(OLE 636-2)* – ('A') / (Dan The Automator remix).

Sep 04. (cd/lp) *<(OLE 616-2/-1)>* **ANTICS** 21 15
– Next exit / Evil / Narc / Take you on a cruise / Slow hands / Not even jail / Public pervert / C'mere / Length of love / A time to be so small.

Jan 05. (7") *(OLE 637-7)* **EVIL. / LEIF ERIKSON (Zane LOwe BBC session)** 18 –
(cd-s+=) *(OLE 637-6)* – Narc (Zane Lowe BBC session) / Slow hands (video).
(cd-s) *(OLE 637-2)* – ('A') / Song seven.

Apr 05. (7") *(OLE 664-7)* **C'MERE. / NOT EVEN JAIL (remix)** 19 –
(7") *(OLE 665-7)* – ('A') / Narc (Paul Banks remix).
(cd-s) *(OLE 664-2)* – ('A') / Public pervert (Carlos D remix) / Length of love (Fog vs. Mould remix).

Oct 05. (7") *(OLE 669-7)* **SLOW HANDS. / NEXT EXIT (Eden session)** 44 –
(cd-s) *(OLE 669-2)* – ('A') / C'mere (Eden session).
(7") *(OLE 670-7)* – ('A') / ('A'-Eden session).

Nov 05. (cd-ep) *<OLE 675-2>* **REMIX** – ☐
– Narc (Paul Banks remix) / Not even jail (Daniel Kessler remix) / (Fog vs. Mould for) The length of love / Public pervert (Carlos D remix).

INXS

Formed: Sydney, Australia . . . 1977 as The FARRISS BROTHERS by TIM, ANDREW and JON, plus MICHAEL HUTCHENCE, KIRK PENGILLY and GARRY BEERS. After briefly moving to Perth in 1978, they returned the following year as INXS, gigging extensively and eventually landing a deal with 'Deluxe' through 'RCA'. Their second single, 'JUST KEEP WALKING' was a domestic hit in 1980 and after a couple of straightahead rock efforts, 'INXS' (1980) and 'UNDERNEATH THE COLOURS' (1981), the band were eventually picked up by the American-based, 'Atlantic'-affiliated 'Atco' label. Their major label debut, 'SHABOOH SHOOBAH' (1982) eventually reached the lower fringes of the US Top 40 on the strength of single, 'THE ONE THING', which MTV had latched onto, the band's new groove-rock sound and HUTCHENCE's classic rock-god looks making them hot property in the emerging video generation. They caught the eye of top producer and ex-CHIC maestro NILE RODGERS who worked on the 'ORIGINAL SIN' single, a propulsive slice of funk rock that was the highlight of 'THE SWING', the band's 1984 album that once again almost breached the US Top 40. The break eventually came with the 'LISTEN LIKE THIEVES' opus, a Top 20 album in Britain with the single 'WHAT YOU NEED' reaching the UK Top 5. The band also gained valuable exposure by playing the Australian

Live Aid that year, rather ironic bearing in mind HUTCHENCE's future relationship with BOB GELDOF. With 'KICK' (1987), the band moved into the mega stardom league, the album a multi-million worldwide success, spawning four international hit singles. 'NEW SENSATION' and 'NEED YOU TONIGHT' (UK No.1) typified the INXS sound; glossy, supple, danceable rock with chunky basslines and HUTCHENCE's breathy vocals magnifying the raunch factor. 'NEVER TEAR US APART', meanwhile, was a rare ballad, uncharacteristically poignant with atmospheric strings. 1987 also saw the frontman's acting debut in Richard Lowenstein's cult movie, 'Dogs In Space'. The following year, after a gruelling world tour, HUTCHENCE recorded an album with IAN OLSEN under the title of MAX Q (named after his dog!), before re-emerging in 1990 with a new INXS album, 'X'. The record trod the same territory as 'KICK' without achieving quite the same effect, only 'SUICIDE BLONDE' and 'DISAPPEAR' making any impact on the singles charts. After packing out London's Wembley Stadium in 1991, an admirable feat for any band, INXS attempted to cast off the stadium rock tag by recording a more ambitious and experimental record, 'WELCOME TO WHEREVER YOU ARE' (1992). As well as a couple of US hits, the album contained the lovely 'BEAUTIFUL GIRL' single, as good as anything the band have recorded to date. With 'FULL MOON, DIRTY HEARTS' (1993), INXS aimed for a rocking return to their earliest recordings, featuring contributions from RAY CHARLES and CHRISSIE HYNDE. The result was only partly successful, the record stiffing completely in the UK. HUTCHENCE had always played the part of the decadent rock star to the max (Q), dating supermodels and allegedly indulging in copious drug use. Although HUTCHENCE had apparently found some sort of stability through a very public romance with Paula Yates (the final nail in the coffin of her doomed marriage to BOB GELDOF), friends and colleagues were apparently worried about his increasing drug use in recent years. However, no one could have predicted that HUTCHENCE would take his own life, the apparent cause of death after the singer was tragically found hanging from his hotel room door in Sydney, Australia on November 22, 1997. With tabloids speculating that HUTCHENCE was a casualty of a bizarre sex act gone wrong, and Paula Yates (also now deceased) laying the blame firmly at GELDOF's feet (hysterically calling him "the devil"). Whatever the outcome, the sad fact is that the music world has lost a talented and well loved star, the future of INXS looking decidedly shakey. 'V2' delivered MICHAEL's final solo recordings as his eponymous debut album in October '99, although what critics might have said – had he been still alive – about this basic self-written set (featuring guests BONO and JOE STRUMMER), we'll never know. Meanwhile, attempts to rekindle the embers of INXS were intially fanned with former 80s soul-rock star TERENCE TRENT D'ARBY and the less high profile JON STEPHENS; neither proved the right man for the job and in the end, it came down to a "reality" TV dogfight won by Canadian Elvis impersonator, J.D. FORTUNE. Judging by comeback album, 'SWITCH' (2005), FORTUNE had been a keen student of the HUTCHENCE mannerisms, fronting an 80s big-rock sound tailor-made for the American market, where it went Top 20.

• **Songwriters:** Most by ANDREW FARRISS and HUTCHENCE, except some B-sides by TIM. Covered; THE LOVED ONE (The Loved One).

Album rating: INXS (*4) / UNDERNEATH THE COLOURS (*5) / SHABOOH SHOOBAH (*5) / THE SWING (*6) / LISTEN LIKE THIEVES (*7) / KICK (*7) / X (*5) / LIVE BABY LIVE (*3) / WELCOME TO WHEREVER YOU ARE (*6) / FULL MOON, DIRTY HEARTS (*5) / INXS – THE GREATEST HITS compilation (*8) / ELEGANTLY WASTED (*5) / DEFINITIVE INXS compilation (*8) / SWITCH (*5) / Max Q: MAX Q (*5) / Michael Hutchence: MICHAEL HUTCHENCE (*4)

MICHAEL HUTCHENCE (b.12 Jan'60, Lain Cove, Sydney, Australia) – vocals / **ANDREW FARRISS** (b.27 Mar'59, Perth, Australia) – keyboards, guitar / **TIM FARRISS** (b.16 Aug'57, Perth) – guitar / **KIRK PENGILLY** (b. 4 Jul'58) – saxophone, guitar, vocals / **GARRY GARY BEERS** (b.22 Jun'57) – bass, vocals / **JON FARRISS** (b.18 Aug'61, Perth) – drums

Deluxe | not iss.

May 80. (7") *(103586)* **SIMPLE SIMON. / WE ARE ALL VEGETABLES** [–] Austra [–]

Oct 80. (lp) *(790184-1)* **INXS** [–] Austra [–]
– On a bus / Doctor / Just keep walking / Learn to smile / Jumping in vain / Roller skating / Body language / Newsreel babies / Wishy washy. *<US-iss.Aug84 on 'Atco' lp/c; 7.90184-1/-4> (UK-iss.Jul89 on 'Vertigo' lp/c/cd; 838776-1/-4/-2) (re-iss. May90 on 'Vertigo' cd/c/lp; 838925-2/-4/-1)*

Feb 81. (7") *(103741)* **THE LOVED ONE. / THE UNLOVED ONE** [–] Austra [–]

Sep 81. (7") *(103884)* **STAY YOUNG. / LACA VOCAL** [–] Austra [–]

Jan 82. (7") *(103734)* **NIGHT OF REBELLION. / PREHISTORIA** [–] Austra [–]

R.C.A. | not iss.

Sep 81. (7") *(RCA 89)* **JUST KEEP WALKING. / SCRATCH** [ ] [–]

Mar 82. (lp) *(RCALP 3058)* **UNDERNEATH THE COLOURS** [ ] [–]
– Stay young / Horizons / Big go-go / Underneath the colours / Fair weather ahead / Night of rebellion / What would you do / Follow / Barbarian / Just to learn again. *(re-iss. Jul89 on 'Vertigo' lp/c/cd; 838777-1/-4/-2)*

Mercury | Atco

Oct 82. (lp) *<90072>* **SHABOOH SHOOBAH** [–] [46]
– The one thing / To look at you / Spy of love / Soul mistake / Here comes / Black and white / Golden playpen / Jan's song / Old world new world / Don't change. *(UK-iss.Jun87 lp/c; PRICE/PRIMC 94) (cd-iss. May90; 812084-2)*

Oct 82. (7") *(100232)* **DON'T CHANGE. / GO WEST** [–] Austra [–]

Mar 83. (7") *<99905>* **THE ONE THING. / PHANTOM OF THE OPERA** [–] [30]

Jun 83. (7") *<99874>* **DON'T CHANGE. / LONG IN TOOTH** [–] [80]

Jun 83. (7") *(INXS 1)* **DON'T CHANGE. / YOU NEVER USED TO CRY** [ ] [–]
(12"+=) *(INXS 12-1)* – Golden playpen.

Sep 83. (7") *(INXS 2)* **THE ONE THING. / THE SAX THING** [ ] [–]
(12") *(INXS 2-12)* – ('A'extended) / Black and white.
(12") *(INXS 2-22)* – ('A'side) / Black and white / Here comes II.

Sep 83. (m-lp) *<7.90115>* **DEKADANCE** (remixes) [–] [ ]
– Black and white / Here comes / The one thing / To look at you.

Feb 84. (7") *(INXS 3)* **ORIGINAL SIN. / JAN'S SONG (live) / TO LOOK AT YOU (live)** [ ] [–]
(12"+=) *(INXS 3-12)* – ('A'extended).

Apr 84. (7") *<99766>* **ORIGINAL SIN. / STAY YOUNG** [–] [58]

May 84. (lp/c) *(MERL/+C 39) <90160>* **THE SWING** [ ] [52]
– Original sin / Melting in the sun / I send a message / Dancing on the jetty / The swing / Johnson's aeroplane / Love is (what I say) / Face the change / Burn for you / All the voices. *(cd-iss. Jul86; 818 553-2)*

Philips | Atco

May 84. (7") *(PH 2) <99731>* **I SEND A MESSAGE. / MECHANICAL** [ ] Jul84 [77]
(12"+=) *(PH 2-12)* – ('A'-long distance version).

Oct 84. (7") *<99703>* **BURN FOR YOU. / JOHNSON'S AEROPLANE** [–] [ ]

Mercury | Atlantic

Oct 85. (lp/c)(cd) *(MERH/+C 82)(824 957-2) <81277>* **LISTEN LIKE THIEVES** [48] [11]
– What you need / Listen like thieves / Kiss the dirt (falling down the mountain) / Shine like it does / Good and bad times / Biting bullets / This time / Three sisters / Same direction / One x one / Red red sun. *(initial copies cont. 'THE SWING') (re-iss. Apr95 cd/c;)*

Feb 86. (7") *(INXS 4) <89497>* **THIS TIME. / ORIGINAL SIN (long)** [ ] Nov85 [81]
(12"+=/d7"+=) *(INXS 4-12/D4)* – Burn for you / Dancing on the jetty.

Apr 86. (7") *(INXS 5) <89460>* **WHAT YOU NEED. / SWEET AS SIN** [51] Jan86 [5]
(w/ free c-s+=) *(INXSC 5)* – This time / What you need (live) / I'm over you / (lp excerpts).
(remix-12"+=) *(INXS 5-12)* – ('A'live) / The one thing.
(remix-d12"++=) *(INXSD 5-12)* – Don't change / Johnsons aeroplane.

Jun 86. (7"/7"sha-pic-d) *(INXS/+P 6) <89429>* **LISTEN LIKE THIEVES. / BEGOTTEN** [46] May86 [54]
(ext.12"+=) *(INXS 6-12)* – ('A'instrumental remix) / ('A'live).
(d7"+=) *(INXSSD 6)* – One x one / Xs verbiage (band interview).

Aug 86. (7") *(INXS 7)* **KISS THE DIRT. / 6 KNOTS / THE ONE THING (live)** [54] [–]
(12"+=) *(INXS 7-12)* – Spy of love.
(d7"+=) *(INXSD 7)* – This time / Original sin.

— In Jun'87, INXS were credited with JIMMY BARNES (ex-COLD CHISEL singer), on US single 'GOOD TIMES' <Atlantic; *89237*>, which hit No.47 and was lifted from the film 'The Lost Boys'. Early in 1991, it was finally a UK No.18 hit (Atlantic; *A 7751*).

Oct 87. (7") *(INXS 8) <89188>* **NEED YOU TONIGHT. / I'M COMING (HOME)** 58 1
(12"+=/cd-s+=) *(INXS 8-12/CD8)* – Mediate.

Nov 87. (lp/c)(cd) *(MERH/+C 114)(832 721-2) <81796>* **KICK** 9 3
– Guns in the sky / New sensation / Devil inside / Need you tonight / Mediate / The loved one / Wild life / Never tear us apart / Mystify / Kick / Calling all nations / Tiny daggers. *(pic-lp.Nov88; MERHP 114)*

Dec 87. (7"/7"pic-d) *(INXS/+R 9)* **NEW SENSATION. / DO WOT YOU DO** 25 –
(ext.12"+=) *(INXSR 9-12)* – Love is (what I say).
(12"++=/12"w-poster++=)(c-s++=/cd-s++=) *(INXS/+P 9-12)(INSM/INXSCD 9)* – Same direction.

Feb 88. (7"/7"s) *(INXS/+P 10) <89144>* **DEVIL INSIDE. / ON THE ROCKS** 47 2
(12"+=) *(INXS 10-12)* – ('A'extended).
(cd-s++=) *(INXSCD 10)* – What you need.
(10"+=) *(INXS 10-10)* – Dancing on the jetty / Shine like it does (live).

May 88. (7") *<89080>* **NEW SENSATION. / GUNS IN THE SKY (kookaburra mix)** – 3

Jun 88. (7"/7"w-poster)(7"pic-d/ext.12") *(INXS/+P 11)(INXS 11/+12/00)* **NEVER TEAR US APART. / GUNS IN THE SKY (Kickass remix)** 24 –
(12"+=) *(INXSG 11-12)* – Burn for you / One world new world.
(ext.cd-s+=) *(INXSCD 11)* – Different world / This time.
(10"white+=) *(INXS 11-10)* – Need you tonight / Listen like thieves.

Aug 88. (7") *<89038>* **NEVER TEAR US APART. / DIFFERENT WORLD** – 7

Oct 88. (7"/7"s) *(INXS/+G 12)* **NEED YOU TONIGHT. / MOVE ON** 2 –
('A'-Mendolsohn mix-cd-s+=) *(INXSCD 12)* – Original sin / Don't change.
(12"+=) *(INXS 12-12)* – Kiss the dirt / ('A'-Mendelsohn mix).
('A'-Ben Liebrand mix-12"+=) *(INXSR 12-12)* – New sensation.

Mar 89. (7"/7"g-f) *(INXS/+G 13)* **MYSTIFY. / DEVIL INSIDE (extended)** 14 –
(cd-s+=) *(INXSCD 13)* – What you need (extended) / Listen like thieves.
(12"+=) *(INXS 13-12)* – Never tear us apart (live) / Shine like it does (live).
(12") *(INXS 13-22)* – ('A'side) / Biting bullets / Shine like it does (live) / Never tear us apart (live).

Sep 90. (7") *(INXS 14) <87860>* **SUICIDE BLONDE. / EVERYBODY WANTS U TONIGHT** 11 9
(12"+=)(cd-s+=) *(INXS 14-12)(INXSCD 14)* – ('A'-milk mix).

Sep 90. (cd/c/lp) *(846668-2/-4/-1) <82140>* **X** 2 5
– Suicide blonde / Disappear / The stairs / Faith in each other / By my side / Lately / Who pays the price / Know the difference / Bitter tears / On my way / Hear that sound. *(re-iss. cd/c Apr95)*

Nov 90. (7") *(INXS 15) <87784>* **DISAPPEAR. / MIDDLE BEAST** 21 8
(12"+=)(cd-s+=) *(INXS 15-12)(INXSCD 15)* – What you need (Cold Cut force mix).
(12") *(INXS 15-22)* – ('A'side) / Need you tonight (mix) / New sensation.

Mar 91. (7"/c-s) *(INX S/MC 16)* **BY MY SIDE. / THE OTHER SIDE** 42 –
(12"+=) *(INXS 16-12)* – Faith in each other (live).
(cd-s++=) *(INXSCD 16)* – Disappear (mix).

Mar 91. (c-s) *<87760>* **BITTER TEARS / THE OTHER SIDE** – 46

Jul 91. (7") *(INXS 17)* **BITTER TEARS. / SOOTHE ME** 30 –
(12"+=) *(INXS 17-12)* – Disappear (mix) / ('A'tears are bitter mix) / ('A'other mix).
(cd-s+=) *(INXSCD 17)* – Original sin / Listen like thieves (extended remix).

Oct 91. (7"ep/12"ep/cd-ep) *(INXS/+12/CD 18)* **SHINING STAR** 27
– Shining star / Send a message (live) / Faith in each other (live) / Bitter tears (live).

Nov 91. (cd/c/lp) *(510580-2/-4/-1) <82294>* **LIVE BABY LIVE (live)** 8 72
– New sensation / Mystify / Never tear us apart / Need you tonight / Suicide blonde / By my side / Mediate / Hear that sound / The stairs / What you need / Shining star (studio).

Jul 92. (7"/7"pic-d/c-s/12"/cd-s) *(INX S/P/T/D 19)* **HEAVEN SENT. / IT AIN'T EASY** 31 –

Aug 92. (c-s) *<87437>* **NOT ENOUGH TIME / DEEPEST RED** – 28

Aug 92. (cd/c/lp) *(512507-2/-4/-1) <82394>* **WELCOME TO WHEREVER YOU ARE** 1 16
– Questions / Heaven sent / Communication / Taste it / Not enough time / All around / Baby don't cry / Beautiful girl / Wishing well / Back on line / Strange desire / Men and women. *(re-iss. cd/c Apr95)*

Sep 92. (7"/c-s) *(INX S/MC 20)* **BABY DON'T CRY. / (part 2)** 20
(cd-s+=) *(INXSCD 20)* – Ptar speaks / Question 8 (instrumental) / ('A'acappella mix).

Nov 92. (7"/c-s) *(INX S/MC 23)* **TASTE IT. / LIGHT THE PLANET** 21
(cd-s+=) *(INXCD 23)* – Youth / Not enough time (mix).

Feb 93. (7"/c-s) *(INX S/MC 24)* **BEAUTIFUL GIRL. / IN MY LIVING ROOM / ASHTAR SPEAKS** 23 –
(cd-s) *(INXCD 24)* – ('A'side) / Strange desire.
(cd-s) *(INXCT 24)* – ('A'side) / Underneath my colours / Wishing well.

Feb 93. (c-s) *<87383>* **BEAUTIFUL GIRL / STRANGE DESIRE** – 46

Oct 93. (7"/c-s) *(INX S/MC 25)* **THE GIFT. / ('A'mix)** 11
(cd-s+=) *(INXCD 25)* – Born to be wild.
(cd-s+=) *(INXCT 25)* – Heaven sent (live).

Nov 93. (cd/c/lp) *(518637-2/-4/-1) <82541>* **FULL MOON, DIRTY HEARTS** 3 53
– Days of rust / The gift / Make your peace / Time / I'm only looking / Please (you got that . . .) / Full moon, dirty hearts / Freedom deep / Kill the pain / Cut your roses down / The messenger / Viking juice.
(below single featured RAY CHARLES)

Dec 93. (12"/c-s) *(INX S/MC 26)* **PLEASE (YOU GOT THAT . . .). / TASTE IT (live)** 50
(cd-s) *(INXCD 26)* – ('A'side) / ('A'edit) / Freedom deep (extended 12"mix) / Communication (live).

Oct 94. (7"red/c-s) *(INX S/MC 27)* **THE STRANGEST PARTY (THESE ARE THE TIMES). / WISHING WELL** 15
(cd-s+=) *(INXCD 27)* – ('A'mix) / Sing something.
(cd-s) *(INXCT 27)* – ('A'side) / Need you tonight (remix) / I'm only looking (remix).

Nov 94. (cd/c/lp) *(526230-2/-4/-1) <82622>* **INXS – THE GREATEST HITS** (compilation) 3
– Mystify / Suicide blonde / Taste it / The strangest party (these are the times) / Need you tonight / Original sin / Heaven sent / Disappear / Never tear us apart / The gift / Devil inside / Beautiful girl / Deliver me / New sensation / What you need / Listen like thieves / Bitter tears / Baby don't cry.

Mar 97. (c-s/cd-s) *(INX MC/CD 28)* **ELEGANTLY WASTED / I'M ONLY LOOKING** 20
(cd-s+=) *(INXDD 28)* – Need you tonight / Original sin (mix).

Apr 97. (cd/c) *(<534 613-2/-4>)* **ELEGANTLY WASTED** 16 41
– Show me (cherry baby) / Elegantly wasted / Everything / Don't lose your head / Searching / I'm just a man / Girl on fire / We are thrown together / Shake the tree / She is rising / Building bridges / Shine.

May 97. (c-s) *(INXMC 29)* **EVERYTHING / BELIEVE** 71 –
(cd-s+=) *(INXCD 29)* – Suicide blonde.
(cd-s) *(INXDD 29)* – ('A'side) / Never tear you apart / What you need.

Sep 97. (promo;cd-s) *(INXCD 30)* **SEARCHING (mixes; leadstation / album / Alex Reece drum n' bass / Linslee Campbell R'n'B)** –

— On the 22nd November '97, HUTCHENCE committed suicide after a party in his hotel room.

— **JON STEVENS** took over on vocals (TERENCE TRENT D'ARBY temp)

— **J.D. FORTUNE** – vocals; repl. STEVENS

Sony Sony

Nov 05. (cd) *<SNY 97727-2>* **SWITCH** – 17
– Devil's party / Pretty Vegas / Afterglow / Hot girls / Perfect strangers / Remember, who's your man / Hungry / Never let you go / Like it or not / Us / God's top ten.

Jan 06. (cd-s) *<75609>* **PRETTY VEGAS / (version)** – 37

– compilations, etc. –

on 'Mercury' unless mentioned otherwise

Oct 02. (d-cd) *Raven; (RVCD 145)* **STAY YOUNG 1979-1982: THE COMPLETE DELUXE YEARS**

Oct 02. (cd-s) *(63885-2)* **TIGHT (mixes; Randy Nicklaus / Thick Dick vocal / Dino Lenny)** –
(cd-s) *(63884-2)* – ('A'side) / ('A'-Automator mix).

Oct 02. (cd/c) *(<63356-2/-4>)* **DEFINITIVE INXS** 15 Dec02
– Need you tonight / What you need / Disappear / Baby don't cry / Elegantly wasted / Mystify / Just keep walking / Suicide blonde / Never tea

us apart / Shining star / Beautiful girl / Listen like thieves / New sensation / Bitter tears / Original sin / The Devil inside / Gift / By my side / Born to be wild / Salvation Jane / Tight (Randy Nicklaus mix). *(<ltd d-cd+=; 63355-2>)* – Mystify (live) / Suicide blonde (live) / New sensation (live) / Tight (automator mix) / Precious heart / I'm so crazy / Suicide blonde / Need you tonight / Mystify.

MAX Q

(HUTCHENCE with **IAN 'OLLIE' OLSEN** duo named after his dog!)

		Mercury	Atlantic
Sep 89.	(7") *(MXQ 1) <88844>* **WAY OF THE WORLD. / ZERO 2-0**		
	(c-s+=/cd-s+=)(12"+=) *(MXQ MC/CD 1)(MXQ 1-12)* – Ghost of the year (Todd Terry mix).		
Oct 89.	(lp/c/cd) *(838942-1/-4/-2) <82014>* **MAX Q**	69	
	– Sometimes / Way of the world / Ghost of the year / Everything / Zero 2-0 / Soul engine / Buckethead / Monday night by satellite / Tight / Ot-ven-rot.		
Feb 90.	(7"/7"w-poster/c-s) *(MXQ/+P/MC 2)* **SOMETIMES. / LOVE MAN**	53	–
	(12"+=) *(MXQ 22-12)* – ('A'instrumental).		
	(12"+=/cd-s+=) *(MXQ 2-12/CD2)* – ('A'-land of Oz mix) / ('A'-rock house mix).		
Feb 90.	(7") *<88754>* **SOMETIMES. / GHOST OF THE YEAR**	–	

MICHAEL HUTCHENCE

		V2	Sony
Oct 99.	(c-s/cd-s) *(VVR 501079-5/-3)* **A STRAIGHT LINE / STANDING ON THE ROOFTOP / THE PASSENGER**		–
Oct 99.	(cd) *(VVR 100788-2) <707888>* **MICHAEL HUTCHENCE**		Dec99
	– Let me show you / Possibilties / Get on the inside / Fear / All I'm saying / A straight line / Baby it's alright / Don't save me from myself / She flirts for England / Flesh and blood / Put the pieces back together / Breathe / Slide away.		

☐ Tony IOMMI (see under ⇒ BLACK SABBATH)

IRON MAIDEN

Formed: Leytonstone, East London, England ... mid 1976 by STEVE HARRIS, DAVE MURRAY, PAUL DiANNO and DOUG SAMPSON, who played their earliest gigs around mid '77 – an embryonic late '75 IRON MAIDEN included HARRIS, PAUL DAY (vocals), DAVE SULLIVAN (guitar), TERRY RANCE (guitar) and RON MATTHEWS (drums). The band's amphetamine-fuelled trad-metal soon procured them a rabid following around the capital and the following year they released a self-financed debut EP, 'THE SOUNDHOUSE TAPES'. The cassette came to the attention of Rock DJ, Neal Kay, who sent them on a 'Heavy Metal Crusade' tour at London's Music Machine, the resultant publicity and increasing interest in the band leading to a deal with 'E.M.I.' in 1979 (this coincided with personnel changes, CLIVE BURR replacing SAMPSON, while DENNIS STRATTON replaced brief member TONY PARSONS. Their debut single, the 100 horsepower outlaw fantasy, 'RUNNING FREE', hit the shops and UK Top 40 early in 1980, soon followed by a self-titled debut album which made the Top 5. IRON MAIDEN were the leading lights of the New Wave Of British Heavy Metal; carrying on where BLACK SABBATH and URIAH HEEP left off, they helped to create and embody the cartoon caricature that the genre would become. Despite production problems, the debut album remains one the most enduring of their career, the material raw and hungry where later efforts have tended towards flabbiness. Masters of the power chord, tracks like 'IRON MAIDEN' and 'CHARLOTTE THE HARLOT' (Politically Correct this band were not, although the phrase could be interpreted in a different way with regards to the 'KILLERS' album sleeve, a depiction of Thatcher meeting an untimely end) were prime headbanging material, DI'ANNO's vocals more guttural punk than metal warbling. Yet the band were no musical novices, the stop-start exhilaration of 'PHANTOM OF THE OPERA' sounding considered and spontaneous at the same time. A hasty follow-up, the aforementioned 'KILLERS' (1981), lacked the focus of the debut, something which didn't deter metal fans from buying it in droves. By the release of 'THE NUMBER OF THE BEAST' (1982), DI'ANNO had been replaced by BRUCE DICKINSON, more of a vocal acrobat in the traditional metal sense. More accessible and melodic, if not as exciting, the record was a massive success (No.1 in Britain), packed with songs that would go on to form the backbone of the 'MAIDEN live set. 'RUN TO THE HILLS' was a particular favourite, giving the band their first Top 10 placing in the pop singles chart. 'PIECE OF MIND' (1983) and 'POWERSLAVE' (1984) carried on in much the same anthemic vein, the band capitalising on their staggering worldwide popularity with a mammoth touring schedule. With their trademark ghoulish mascot, 'EDDIE', horror fantasy artwork and readily identifiable sound, the band were arguably the very essence of 'Heavy Metal', a phenomenon which traversed all language boundaries in much the same way as dance music in the 90's. 'SOMEWHERE IN TIME' (1986) marked something of a departure, a more ambitious and musically diverse collection both in terms of songwriting and playing. This avenue was further explored on 'SEVENTH SON OF A SEVENTH SON' (1988), a concept affair that piled on the synth and sharpened the harmonies, resulting in four consecutive Top 10 singles. The steadfast reliability of the band's fanbase was amply illustrated when a series of EP's repackaging the band's singles went Top 10 almost without exception. But there was tension in the ranks with HARRIS favouring a return to their chest beating roots while guitarist ADRIAN SMITH was less than pleased with the prospect. In the event, SMITH was replaced with JANICK GERS and the band released the no-frills 'NO PRAYER FOR THE DYING' (1990), a back to basics effort which spawned IRON MAIDEN's first No.1 single, the side-splittingly titled 'BRING YOUR DAUGHTER ... TO THE SLAUGHTER'. 'FEAR OF THE DARK' (1992) gave the band yet another No.1 album, the last to feature the tonsils of DICKINSON, who soon departed for a solo career. DICKINSON's eventual replacement was BLAZE BAILEY (ex-WOLFSBANE) who made his debut on 'THE X-FACTOR' (1995), a record that achieved their lowest chart placing since 'KILLERS'. 1998's 'VIRTUAL XI' was another relative disappointment although the MAIDEN hordes took heart when BRUCE DICKINSON returned to the fray in early '99. The resulting tour was a blockbuster and paved the way for a new studio album featuring the classic line-up of DICKINSON, HARRIS, MURRAY, McBRAIN and SMITH alongside JANICK GERS who was retained as a third guitarist. 'BRAVE NEW WORLD' was released in spring 2000 amid much fanfare and expectation, the album's return to MAIDEN's halcyon mid-80's period – in terms of both gothic fantasy songwriting and crunching powerchord assault – pleasing longtime fans no end and seemingly securing the band's place in the post-metal wilderness. If the rather pointless 'ROCK IN RIO' (2002) live set perhaps showed up – however unintentionally – the gap in ambition between classic 'MAIDEN and their stodgier latter day fare, the back to basics 'DANCE OF DEATH' (2003) succeeded in harnessing at least some of that kinetic energy of old as they fast approached their 30th year in business. A belated souvenir from the accompanying tour, 'DEATH ON THE ROAD', was released in 2005, generating a spin-off hit in IRON nugget, 'THE TROOPER'.

• **Songwriters:** All mostly HARRIS and group. In the 90's, HARRIS or DICKINSON + GERS. Covered; COMMUNICATION BREAKDOWN (Led

IRON MAIDEN

Zeppelin) / KILL ME, CE SOIR (Golden Earring) / SPACE STATION No.5 (Montrose). DICKINSON solo re-hashed; ALL THE YOUNG DUDES (hit; Mott The Hoople). • **Trivia:** Derek Riggs became the group's artistic designer and created 'EDDIE', an evil skeleton comic-strip character, who appeared on album sleeves, poster bills & theatrical stage shows. Banned in Chile for being interpreted as 'devils and satanists'. First band to play "live" on Top Of The Pops since the Who.

Album rating: IRON MAIDEN (*9) / KILLERS (*6) / THE NUMBER OF THE BEAST (*7) / PIECE OF MIND (*6) / POWERSLAVE (*6) / LIVE AFTER DEATH (*8) / SOMEWHERE IN TIME (*6) / SEVENTH SON OF A SEVENTH SON (*7) / NO PRAYER FOR THE DYING (*7) / FEAR OF THE DARK (*7) / A REAL LIVE ONE (*5) / A REAL DEAD ONE (*5) / LIVE AT DONINGTON 1992 (*5) / THE X FACTOR (*6) / THE BEST OF THE BEAST compilation (*9) / VIRTUAL XI (*5) / BRAVE NEW WORLD (*7) / BACK IN RIO (*4) / EDWARD THE GREAT: THE GREATEST HITS compilation (*8) / DANCE OF DEATH (*6) / DEATH ON THE ROAD (*5)

PAUL DI'ANNO (b.17 May'59, Chingford, Essex, England) – vocals / **DAVE MURRAY** (b.23 Dec'58) – guitar / **STEVE HARRIS** (b.12 Mar'57) – bass, vocals / **DOUG SAMPSON** – drums

Rock Hard — not iss.

an 79. (7"ep) *(ROK 1)* **THE SOUNDHOUSE TAPES** [ ] [–]
– Invasion / Iron Maiden / Prowler.

— (Nov79) **CLIVE BURR** (b. 8 Mar'57) – drums repl. SAMPSON / **DENNIS STRATTON** (b. 9 Nov'54) – guitar repl. TONY PARSONS (brief stay)

E.M.I. — Harvest

eb 80. (7") *(EMI 5032)* **RUNNING FREE. / BURNING AMBITION** [34] [–]

pr 80. (lp/c) *(EMC/TCEMC 3330)* **IRON MAIDEN** [4] [ ]
– Prowler / Remember tomorrow / Running free / Phantom of the opera / Transylvania / Strange world / Charlotte the harlot / Iron maiden. *(re-iss. May85 on 'Fame' lp/c; FA/TCFA 41-3121-1) –* hit 71 *(cd-iss. Oct87 on 'Fame'; CDFA 3121) (re-iss. cd Jul94; CDEMS 1538) (re-iss. cd Dec95; CDEM 1570) (cd re-iss. Sep98; 496916-0)*

ay 80. (7"m) *(EMI 5065)* **SANCTUARY. / DRIFTER / I'VE GOT THE FIRE (live)** [29] [–]

ct 80. (7") *(EMI 5105)* **WOMEN IN UNIFORM. / INVASION** [35] [–]
(12"+=) *(12EMI 5105)* – Phantom of the opera (live).

— **ADRIAN SMITH** (b.27 Feb'57) – guitar (ex-URCHIN) repl. STRATTON who formed LIONHEART

eb 81. (lp/c) *(EMC/TCEMC 3357)* <12141> **KILLERS** [12] [78]
– The ides of march / Wrathchild / Murders in the Rue Morgue / Another life / Ghenghis Khan / Innocent exile / KIllers / Prodigal son / Purgatory / Drifter. *(re-iss. May85 on 'Fame' lp/c; FA/TCFA 41-3122-1) (cd-iss. Oct87 on 'Fame'; CDFA 3122) (re-iss. cd Jul94; CDEMS 1539) (re-iss. cd Dec95; CDEM 1571) (cd re-iss. Sep98; 496917-0)*

ar 81. (7",7"clear,7"red,c-s) *(EMI 5145)* **TWILIGHT ZONE. / WRATH CHILD** [31] [–]

un 81. (7") *(EMI 5184)* **PURGATORY. / GHENGIS KHAN** [52] [–]

ep 81. (12"ep)<m-lp> *(12EMI 5219)* <15000> **MAIDEN JAPAN** [43] [89]
– Remember tomorrow / Killers / Running free / Innocent exile.

— **BRUCE DICKINSON** (b. PAUL BRUCE DICKINSON, 7 Aug'58, Sheffield, England) – vocals (ex-SAMSON) repl. DI'ANNO who formed LONE WOLF

eb 82. (7"/7"pic-d) *(EMI/+P 5263)* **RUN TO THE HILLS. / TOTAL ECLIPSE** [7] [–]

ar 82. (lp/pic-lp)(c) *(EMC/EMCP/TCEMC 3400)* <12202> **THE NUMBER OF THE BEAST** [1] [33]
– Invaders / Children of the damned / The prisoner / 22, Acacia Avenue / The number of the beast / Run to the hills / Gangland / Hallowed be thy name. *(re-iss. May87 on 'Fame'; FA/TCFA 3178) (cd-iss. Apr88 on 'Fame'; CDFA 3178) (re-iss. cd Jul94; CDEMS 1533) (re-iss. Dec95 on d-cd w/bonus tracks; CDEM 1572) (cd re-iss. Sep98; 496918-0)*

pr 82. (7"/7"red) *(EMI 5287)* **THE NUMBER OF THE BEAST. / REMEMBER TOMORROW** [18] [–]

— now **HARRIS, MURRAY, DICKINSON** and **SMITH** were joined by **NICKO McBRAIN** (b. MICHAEL, 5 Jun'54) – drums (ex-PAT TRAVERS, ex-TRUST, ex-STREETWALKERS) repl. BURR who joined STRATUS

E.M.I. — Capitol

pr 83. (7"/12"pic-d)(c-s) *(EMI/12EMIP 5378)(TC IM4)* <5248> **FLIGHT OF ICARUS. / I'VE GOT THE FIRE** [11] [ ]

ay 83. (lp/c) *(EMA/TCEMA 800)* <12274> **PIECE OF MIND** [3] [14]
– Where eagles dare / Revelations / Flight of Icarus / Die with your boots on / The trooper / Still life / Quest for fire / Sun and steel / To tame a land. *(cd-iss. Dec86; CZ 82) (re-iss. 1989 lp/c; ATAK/CDATAK 139) (re-iss. cd Jun91 on 'Fame'; CDFA 3245) (re-iss. cd Jul94; CDEMS 1540) (re-iss. Dec95 on d-cd w/bonus tracks; CDEM 1573) (cd re-iss. Sep98; 496919-0)*

Jun 83. (7",7"sha-pic-d) *(EMI 5397)* **THE TROOPER. / CROSS-EYED MARY** [12] [–]

Aug 84. (7") *(EMI 5489)* **2 MINUTES TO MIDNIGHT. / RAINBOW'S GOLD** [11] [–]
(12"pic-d+=) *(12EMI 5489)* – Mission from 'Arry.

Sep 84. (lp/pic-lp)(c)(cd) *(POWER/+P 1)(TCPOWER 1)(746045-2)* <12321> **POWERSLAVE** [2] [21]
– Aces high / 2 minutes to midnight / Losfer words (big 'orra) / Flash of the blade / The duellists / Back in the village / Powerslave / Rime of the ancient mariner. *(re-iss. 1989 lp/c; ATAK/TCATAK 140) (re-iss. Jun91 on 'Fame'; FA 3244) (re-iss. cd Jul94; CDEMS 1539) (re-iss. Dec95 d-cd w/bonus tracks; CDEM 1574) (cd re-iss. Sep98; 496920-0)*

Oct 84. (7") *(EMI 5502)* **ACES HIGH. / KING OF TWILIGHT** [20] [–]
(12"+=/12"pic-d+=) *(12EMI/+P 5502)* – The number of the beast (live).

Sep 85. (7") *(EMI 5532)* **RUNNING FREE (live). / SANCTUARY (live)** [19] [–]
(12"+=/12"pic-d+=) *(12EMI/+P 5532)* – Murders in the Rue Morgue (live).

Oct 85. (d-lp/c)(cd) *(RIP/TCRIP 1)(746186-2)* <12441> **LIVE AFTER DEATH (live)** [2] [19]
– Aces high / 2 minutes to midnight / The trooper / Revelations / Flight of Icarus / The rime of the ancient mariner / Powerslave / The number of the beast / Hallowed be thy name / Iron maiden / Run to the hills / Running free. *(d-lp+=/c+=)* – Wrathchild / 22 Acacia Avenue / Children of the damned / Die with your boots on / Phantom of the opera. *(re-iss. 1989 lp/c; ATAK/TCATAK 141) (re-iss. Jun91 on 'Fame' w/ less tracks; CDFA 3248) (re-iss. cd Jul94 w/ fewer tracks; CDEMS 1535) (re-iss. Dec95 d-cd w/ bonus tracks; CDEM 1575) (d-cd re-iss. Sep98; 496921-0)*

Nov 85. (7") *(EMI 5542)* **RUN TO THE HILLS (live). / PHANTOM OF THE OPERA (live)** [26] [–]
(12"+=/12"pic-d+=) *(12EMI/+P 5542)* – Losfer words (The big 'orra) (live).

Aug 86. (7"/7"sha-pic-d) *(EMI/+P 5583)* **WASTED YEARS. / REACH OUT** [18] [–]
(12"+=) *(12EMI 5583)* – The sheriff of Huddersfield.

Sep 86. (lp/c)(cd) *(EMC/TCEMC 3512)(746341-2)* <12524> **SOMEWHERE IN TIME** [3] [11]
– Caught somewhere in time / Wasted years / Sea of madness / Heaven can wait / The loneliness of the long distance runner / Stranger in a strange land / Deja-vu / Alexander the Great. *(re-iss. 1989 lp/c; ATAK/TCATAK 142) (re-iss. Jun91 on 'Fame'; CDFA 3246) (re-iss. cd Jul94; CDEMS 1537) (re-iss. Dec95 d-cd w/bonus tracks; CDEM 1576) (cd re-iss. Sep98; 496924-0)*

Nov 86. (7") *(EMI 5589)* **STRANGER IN A STRANGE LAND. / THAT GIRL** [22] [–]
(12"+=/12"pic-d+=) *(12EMI/+P 5589)* – Juanita.

Mar 88. (7"/7"w sticker & transfer/7"sha-pic-d) *(EM/+S/P 49)* <44154> **CAN I PLAY WITH MADNESS. / BLACK BART BLUES** [3] [ ]
(12"+=/cd-s+=) *(12EM/CDEM 49)* – Massacre.

Apr 88. (cd/c/lp)(pic-lp) *(TC/CD+/EMD 1006)(EMDP 1006)* <90258> **SEVENTH SON OF A SEVENTH SON** [1] [12]
– Moonchild / Infinite dreams / Can I play with madness / The evil that men do / Seventh son of a seventh son / The prophecy / The clairvoyant / Only the good die young. *(re-iss. 1989 lp/c; ATAK/TCATAK 143) (re-iss. Jun91 on 'Fame'; CDFA 3247) (re-iss. cd Jul94; CDEMS 1534) (re-iss. Dec95 d-cd w/bonus tracks; CDEM 1577) (cd re-iss. Sep98; 496864-0)*

Aug 88. (7"/7"g-f/7"sha-pic-d) *(EM/+G/P 64)* **THE EVIL THAT MEN DO. / PROWLER '88** [5] [ ]
(12"+=/12"poster)(cd-s+=) *(12EM/+S 64)(CDEM 64)* – Charlotte the harlot '88.

Nov 88. (7"/7"clear/7"sha-pic-d) *(EM/+S/P 79)* **THE CLAIRVOYANT (live). / THE PRISONER (live)** [6] [ ]
(12"+=/12"pic-d+=)(cd-s+=) *(12EM/+P 79)(CDEM 79)* – Heaven can wait (live).

Nov 89. (7"/7"sha-pic-d)(c-s) *(EM/+PD 117)(TCEM 117)* **INFINITE DREAMS (live). / KILLERS (live)** [6] [ ]
(12"+=/cd-s+=)(12"etched+=) *(12/CD EM 117)* – Still life (live).

— (Feb'90) **JANICK GERS** – guitar (ex-GILLAN, ex-WHITE SPIRIT, etc.) repl. SMITH who formed A.S.A.P.

E.M.I. — Epic

Sep 90. (7"/c-s) *(EM/TCEM 158)* **HOLY SMOKE. / ALL IN YOUR MIND** [3] [ ]
(12"+=/12"pic-d+=)(cd-s+=) *(12EM/+P 158)(CDEM 158)* – Kill me ce soir.

Oct 90. (cd/c/lp)(pic-lp)<red-lp> *(CD/TC+/EMD 1017)(EMPD 1017)* <E 46905> **NO PRAYER FOR THE DYING** [2] [17]

– Tailgunner / Holy smoke / No prayer for the dying / Public enema number one / Fates warning / The assassin / Run silent run deep / Hooks in you / Bring your daughter . . . to the slaughter / Mother Russia. *(re-iss. cd Jul94; CDEMS 1541) (re-iss. Dec95 d-cd w/bonus tracks; CDEM 1578) (cd re-iss. Sep98; 496865-4)*

Dec 90. (7"/7"pic-d)(c-s) *(EM/+PD 171)(TCEM 171)* **BRING YOUR DAUGHTER . . . TO THE SLAUGHTER. / I'M A MOVER** [1] [ ]
(12"+=/12"pic-d+=)(cd-s+=) *(12EM/+P 171)(CDEM 171)* – Communication breakdown.

—— In Summer 1991, HARRIS and McBAIN back up tennis stars McENROE & CASH on their version of LED ZEPPELIN'S 'Rock And Roll'. In Mar'92, BRUCE DICKINSON was to feature on single with Rowan Atkinson's comic character 'MR.BEAN & SMEAR CAMPAIGN' on a version of an Alice Cooper song '(I Want To Be) Elected'.

Apr 92. (7") *(EM 229)* **BE QUICK OR BE DEAD. / NODDING DONKEY BLUES** [2] [ ]
(12"+=/12"pic-d+=)(cd-s+=) *(12EM/+P 229)(CDEM 229)* – Space station No.5.

May 92. (cd/c/d-lp) *(CD/TC+/EMD 1032) <48993>* **FEAR OF THE DARK** [1] [12]
– Be quick or be dead / From here to eternity / Afraid to shoot strangers / Fear is the key / Childhood's end / Wasting love / The fugitive / Chains of misery / The apparition / Judas be my guide / Weekend warrior / Fear of the dark. *(re-iss. cd Jul94; CDEM 1542) (re-iss. Dec95 d-cd w/bonus tracks +=; CDEM 1579)* – Nodding donkey blues / Space station No.5 / I can't see my feeling / No prayer for the dying (live) / Public enema No.1 (live) / Hook in you (live). *(cd re-iss. Sep98; 496925-0)*

Jul 92. (7"etched) *(EM 240)* **FROM HERE TO ETERNITY. / ROLL OVER VIC VELLA** [21] [ ]
(12"+=/cd-s+=) *(12/CD EM 240)* – Public enema number one / No prayer for the dying.
(7"sha-pic-d) *(EMPD 240)* – ('A'side) / I can't see my feeling.

E.M.I. Capitol

Mar 93. (7"/7"sha-pic-d) *(EMP/+D 263)* **FEAR OF THE DARK (live). / TAILGUNNER (live)** [8] [ ]
(cd-s+=) *(CDEM 263)* – Hooks in you (live) *(on some 7"sha-pic-d)* / Bring your daughter . . .to the slaughter (live).

Mar 93. (cd/c/lp) *(CD/TC+/EMD 1042) <81456>* **A REAL LIVE ONE (live)** [3] [ ]
– Be quick or be dead / From here to eternity / Can I play with madness / Wasting love / Tailgunner / The evil that men do / Afraid to shoot strangers / Bring your daughter . . .to the slaughter / Heaven can wait / The clairvoyant / Fear of the dark.

—— DICKINSON had already announced he had departed to go solo in '94

Oct 93. (7"red) *(EM 288)* **HALLOWED BE THY NAME (live). / WRATHCHILD (live)** [9] [ ]
(12"pic-d+=/cd-s+=) *(12EMP/CDEM 288)* – The trooper (live) / Wasted years (live).

Oct 93. (cd/c/lp) *(CD/TC+/EMD 1048) <89248>* **A REAL DEAD ONE (live)** [12] [ ]
– The number of the beast / The trooper / Prowler / Transylvania / Remember tomorrow / Where eagles dare / Sanctuary / Running free / Run to the hills / 2 minutes to midnight / Iron Maiden / Hallowed be thy name. *(this & last "live" set, re-iss. Sep98; 496926-0)*

Nov 93. (d-cd/d-c/t-lp) *(CD/MC+/DON 1)* **LIVE AT DONINGTON 1992 (live)** [23] [–]
– Be quick or be dead / The number of the beast / Wrathchild / From here to eternity / Can I play with madness / Wasting love / Tailgunner / The evil that men do / Afraid to shoot strangers / Fear of the dark / Bring your daughter . . . to the slaughter / The clairvoyant / Heaven can wait / Run to the hills / 2 minutes to midnight / Iron maiden / Hallowed be thy name / The trooper / Sanctuary / Running free. *(re-iss. Sep98; 496929-0)*

—— **BLAZE BAILEY** – vocals (ex-WOLFSBANE) now his replacement

E.M.I. CMC Int.

Sep 95. (c-s) *(TCEM 398)* **MAN ON THE EDGE / THE EDGE OF DARKNESS** [10] [ ]
(12"pic-d+=) *(12EM 398)* – I live my way.
(cd-s+=) *(CDEMS 398)* – Judgement day / (Blaze Bailey interview part 1).
(cd-s+=) *(CDEM 398)* – Justice of the peace / (Blaze Bailey interview part 2).

Oct 95. (cd/c/clear-d-lp) *(+CD/TC EMD 1087) <8003>* **THE X FACTOR** [9] [ ]
– Sign of the cross / Lord of the flies / Man on the edge / Fortunes of war / Look for the truth / The aftermath / Judgement of Heaven / Blood on the world's hands / The edge of darkness / 2 a.m. / The unbeliever.

Sep 96. (12") *(12EM 443)* **VIRUS. / PROWLER (the Soundhouse tapes) / INVASION (the Soundhouse tapes)** [16] [ ]
(cd-s) *(CDEM 443)* – ('A'side) / My generation / Doctor, doctor.
(cd-s) *(CDEMS 443)* – ('A'side) / Sanctuary (metal for muthas) / Wrathchild (metal for muthas).

Sep 96. (d-cd/q-lp) *(CDEMDS 1097)* **BEST OF THE BEAST** (compilation with all line-ups) [16] [ ]
– Virus / Sign of the cross / Afraid to shoot strangers (live) / Man on the edge / Be quick or be dead / Fear of the dark (live) / Holy smoke / Bring your daughter . . . to the slaughter / Seventh son of a seventh son / Can I play with madness / The evil that men do / The clairvoyant / Heaven can wait / Wasted years / / 2 minutes to midnight / Running free (live) / Rime of the ancient mariner (live) / Aces high / Where eagles dare / The trooper * / The number of the beast / Revelations * / The prisoner * / Run to the hills / Hallowed be thy name / Wrathchild / Killers * / Remember tomorrow * / Phantom of the opera / Sanctuary / Prowler * / Invasion * / Strange world / Iron maiden. *(q-lp+= *)*

Mar 98. (7"pic-d) *(EM 507)* **THE ANGEL AND THE GAMBLER. / BLOOD ON THE WORLD'S HANDS (live) / THE AFTERMATH (live)** [18] [ ]
(cd-s) *(CDEMS 507)* – (first 2 tracks) / Afraid to shoot strangers (CD-Rom video).
(cd-s) *(CDEM 507)* – (first & third tracks) / The aftermath (live) / Man on the edge (CD-Rom video).

Mar 98. (cd/c/d-lp) *(493915-2/-4/-1) <86240>* **VIRTUAL XI** [16] [ ]
– Futureal / The angel and the gambler / Lightning strikes twice / Clansman / When two worlds collide / Educated fool / Don't look to the eyes of a stranger / Como estais amigos.

Sep 98. (7"pic-d) *(EM 525)* **FUTUREAL. / THE EVIL THAT MEN DO (live) / MAN ON THE EDGE (live)** [–] [–]
(cd-s) *(CDEM 525)* – (first 2) / Futureal (CD-rom).
(cd-s) *(CDEMS 525)* – (first & third) / The angel and the gambler (CD-rom).
(above only available through the internet shopping channel)

—— early in '99, **BRUCE DICKINSON** was now back at the helm (as wa **ADRIAN SMITH** – guitar (now a six-piece)

May 00. (12"pic-d) *(12EM 568)* **THE WICKER MAN. / POWERSLAVE (live) / Killers (live)** [9] [–]
(cd-s) *(CDEMS 568)* – (first two tracks) / Man on the edge (live) ('A'-CD-Rom).
(cd-s) *(CDEM 568)* – (first & third tracks) / Futureal (live) / Futurea (CD-Rom).

May 00. (cd/c/d-lp) *(526605-2/-4/-1) <62208>* **BRAVE NEW WORLD** [7] [39]
– The wicker man / Ghost of the navigator / Brave new world / Bloo brothers / The mercenary / Dream of mirrors / The fallen angel / Th nomad / Out of the silent planet / The thin line between love and hate.

Oct 00. (7"red) *(EM 576)* **OUT OF THE SILENT PLANET. / ACES HIGH (live)** [20] [–]
(12"pic-d+=) *(12EM 576)* – Wasted years (live).
(cd-s+=) *(CDEM 576)* – ('A'-video).

Mar 02. (7"red) *(EM 612)* **RUN TO THE HILLS (live in Rio 2001). / RUN TO THE HILLS (original) / TOTAL ECLIPSE (live 1982)** [9] [–]
(cd-s+=) *(CDEM 612)* – Children of the damned (live 1982) / ('A'-vide live in Rio 2001).
(cd-s) *(CDEMS 612)* – ('A'side) / 22 Acacia Avenue (live 1982) / Prisone (live 1982) / ('A'-video Camp Chaos version of 1982 promo).

Mar 02. (d-cd/d-c/t-lp) *(538643-0/-4/-1) <54269>* **ROCK IN RIO** (live) [15] [ ]
– Intro / The wicker man / Ghost of the navigator / Brave new world Wrathchild / 2 minutes to midnight / Blood brothers / Sign of the cross The mercenary / The trooper / Brave new world (enhanced video) / Dream of mirrors / The clansman / The evil that men do / Fear of th dark / Iron maiden / The number of the beast / Hallowed be thy name Sanctuary / Run to the hills / A day in the life (enhanced video).

E.M.I. Colum

Sep 03. (7"green) *(EM 627)* **WILDEST DREAMS. / PASS THE JAM** [6] [–]
(cd-s+=) *(CDEM 627)* – Blood brothers (orchestral mix).

Sep 03. (cd/d-lp) *(592340-2/-1) <89061>* **DANCE OF DEATH** [2] [18]
– Wildest dreams / Rainmaker / No more lies / Montsegur / Dance o death / Gates of tomorrow / New frontier / Paschendale / Face in the sand Age of innocence / Journeyman.

Nov 03. (7"blue) *(EM 633)* **RAINMAKER. / DANCE OF DEATH (orchestral version 2)** [13] [–]
(cd-s+=) *(CDEM 633)* – More tea vicar.

Aug 05. (7"blue) *(EM 662)* **THE TROOPER (live 2003). / ANOTHER LIFE (live 2005)** 5 –
(12"pic-d) *(12EM 662)* – ('A') / ('A'-original version) / Murders in the Rue Morgue (live 2005).
(cd-s) *(CDEM 662)* – ('A') / ('A'-original) / Prowler (live 2005) / ('A'-video) / ('A'-original video).
(cd-s+=) *(CDEMS 666)* – Hallowed be thy name (live at Brixton 2002) / ('A'-original promo – Camp Chaos video) / ('A'-live at Brixton '02 video).

Aug 05. (d-cd) *(336437-2) <96429>* **DEATH ON THE ROAD (live)** 22
– Wildest dreams / Wrathchild / Can I play with madness / The trooper / Dance of death / Rainmaker / Brave new world / Paschendale / Lord of the flies / No more lies / Hallowed by thy name / Fear of the dark / Iron maiden / Journeyman / The number of the beast / Run to the hills.

– compilations, etc. –

on 'E.M.I.' unless otherwise stated

Feb 90. (cd-ep/d12") *(CD+/IRN 1)* **RUNNING FREE / BURNING AMBITION / SANCTUARY / DRIFTER (live) / I'VE GOT THE FIRE (live) / Listen with Nicko (part 1)** 10

Feb 90. (cd-ep/d12") *(CD+/IRN 2)* **WOMEN IN UNIFORM / INVASION / PHANTOM OF THE OPERA / TWILIGHT ZONE / WRATHCHILD / Listen with Nicko (part 2)** 10

Feb 90. (cd-ep/d12") *(CD+/IRN 3)* **PURGATORY / GENGHIS KHAN / RUNNING FREE / REMEMBER TOMORROW / KILLERS / INNOCENT EXILE / Listen with Nicko (part 3)** 5

Mar 90. (cd-ep/d12") *(CD+/IRN 4)* **RUN TO THE HILLS / TOTAL ECLIPSE / THE NUMBER OF THE BEAST / REMEMBER TOMORROW (live) / Listen with Nicko (part 4)** 3

Mar 90. (cd-ep/d12") *(CD+/IRN 5)* **FLIGHT OF ICARUS / I'VE GOT THE FIRE / THE TROOPER / CROSS-EYED MARY / Listen with Nicko (part 5)** 7

Mar 90. (cd-ep/d12") *(CD+/IRN 6)* **2 MINUTES TO MIDNIGHT / RAINBOW'S GOLD / MISSION FROM 'ARRY / ACES HIGH / KING OF TWILIGHT / THE NUMBER OF THE BEAST (live) / Listen with Nicko (part 6)** 11

Apr 90. (cd-ep/d12") *(CD+/IRN 7)* **RUNNING FREE / SANCTUARY / MURDERS IN THE RUE MORGUE / RUN TO THE HILLS / PHANTOM OF THE OPERA / LOSFER WORDS (THE BIG 'ORRA) / Listen with Nicko (part 7)** 9

Apr 90. (cd-ep/d12") *(CD+/IRN 8)* **WASTED YEARS / REACH OUT / THE SHERIFF OF HUDDERSFIELD / STRANGER IN A STRANGE LAND / THAT GIRL / JUANITA / Listen with Nicko (part 8)** 9

Apr 90. (cd-ep/d12") *(CD+/IRN 9)* **CAN I PLAY WITH MADNESS / BLACK BART BLUES / MASSACRE / THE EVIL THAT MEN DO / PROWLER '88 / CHARLOTTE THE HARLOT '88 / Listen with Nicko (part 9)** 10

Apr 90. (cd-ep/d12") *(CD+/IRN 10)* **THE CLAIRVOYANT (live) / THE PRISONER (live) / HEAVEN CAN WAIT (live) / INFINITE DREAMS (live) / KILLERS (live) / STILL LIFE (live) / Listen with Nicko (part 10)** 11

— (all 10 singles above, basically hit peak number before crashing out)

Aug 94. (cd,cd-vid) *(SAV 4913103)* **MAIDEN ENGLAND (live)** –
– Moonchild / The evil that men do / Prisoner / Still life / Die with your boots on / Infinite dreams / Killers / Heaven can wait / Wasted years / The clairvoyant / Seventh son of a seventh son / The number of the best / Iron maiden.

Dec 98. (16xcd-box) *(4979990)* **EDDIE'S HEAD**

May 99. (3xcd-ROM) *(5205200)* **ED HUNTER** –

Nov 02. (cd/c/d-lp) *(543103-2/-4/-1)* / *Sony; <86969>* **EDWARD THE GREAT: THE GREATEST HITS** 57
– Run to the hills / The number of the beast / Flight of Icarus / The trooper / 2 minutes to midnight / Wasted years / Can I play with madness / The evil that men do / The clairvoyant / Infinite dreams / Holy smoke / Bring your daughter . . . to the slaughter / Man on the edge / Futureal / The wicker man / Fear of the dark.

Nov 02. (6xcd-box) *(541277-2)* **EDDIE'S ARCHIVE**

Jan 05. (7"red) *(EM 666)* **THE NUMBER OF THE BEAST. / THE NUMBER OF THE BEAST (live at Brixton '02)** 3 –
(12"pic-d+=) *(12EM 666)* – Remember tomorrow (live original).

☐ Yusuf ISLAM (see under ⇒ STEVENS, Cat)

the ISLEY BROTHERS

Formed: Cincinatti, Ohio, USA . . . early 50's by RONALD, RUDOLPH, O'KELLY and VERNON ISLEY, all experienced gospel singers. The subsequent death of VERNON led to the remaining brothers moving from Cincinnati to New York in '56, where they began their recording career. After achieving some early success with 'SHOUT' in '59, the siblings recorded the enduring 'TWIST AND SHOUT' a couple of years later, a song The BEATLES would later cover to significantly greater commercial success. Eager for more creative control, the ISLEY BROTHERS took the unprecedented step of setting up their own label, 'T-Neck' (named after their new location, Teaneck in New Jersey). Their first homegrown recording, 'TESTIFY', was largely ignored although the featured lead guitarist would go on to influence the playing of generations, the axe-man in question one JIMI HENDRIX. In an effort to achieve a higher profile, the group signed to 'Motown' in '65. Unfortunately, the label insisted on moulding the band to their formulaic 'hit-factory' approach, stifling their creative input and producing only one hit, 1966's 'THIS OLD HEART OF MINE'. The brothers' finest recordings came after they split with Berry Gordy and Co. in '68, relaunching 'T-Neck' the following year. With creative control firmly back in the hands of the outfit, they let rip with funky grooves and even funkier outfits, their evolution complete with the addition of three more members of the ISLEY clan, brothers ERNIE and MARVIN and cousin CHRIS JASPER. The latter contributed the classic single, 'IT'S YOUR THING', a record which became an instant hit and earned the band a Grammy. Touring frequently in the late 60's and early 70's, a distribution deal with 'C.B.S.' in '73 led to the release of '3 + 3', an album which showcased the roots of the "Isley Sound"; ERNIE's Hendrix-influenced guitar work was a vital component in the trademark blend of dance rhythms and funk laden grooves best sampled on the sexy 'THAT LADY'. Through '73 to '83, the band scored nine consecutive gold or platinum albums, their sound switching back and forth between RONALD's soulfully smooth ballads and the hard and funky stuff. The two styles combined especially well on the 1975 offering, 'THE HEAT IS ON', alternating the furious vocals of 'FIGHT THE POWER' with a song addressing the need for social awareness and global peace in 'HARVEST FOR THE WORLD'. Towards the early 80's the family released a series of songs with a highly erotic content, a sure-fire winner in terms of sales, which produced the hits 'BETWEEN THE SHEETS' and 'CHOOSY LOVER'. There was a certain amount of compromise to their output, however, and in '84, the band split; the original members signed to 'Warner Bros.' while the "youngsters" went on to form the short-lived ISLEY-JASPER-ISLEY unit. The latter outfit penned the hymnal 'CARAVAN OF LOVE' in '85, later a UK No.1 hit for the HOUSEMARTINS. ERNIE ISLEY subsequently recorded a blistering solo album on 'Elektra', while RONALD, together with his future wife ANGELA WINBUSH, topped the R&B charts with 'SPEND THE NIGHT'. Influencing legions of recording artists throughout their four decades, the ISLEY BROTHERS were inducted into the Rock & Roll Hall Of Fame in '92. While a mid-90's effort on 'Island', 'MISSION TO PLEASE' (1996) made the US Top 40, the ISLEY BROTHERS became one of the few old skool soul acts to roll with the punches on the new R&B block come the new millennium. Deservedly, the acclaimed 'ETERNAL' (2001) made the US Top 3 alongside the Top 20 hit, 'CONTAGIOUS'. While the record featured a roll call of R&B scenesters such as R KELLY and JILL SCOTT, the real star of the show was RONALD's falsetto vocal, still as fresh as that 70's summer breeze after all these years. KELLY was to play a much bigger role in 2003's huge 'BODY KISS', producing and writing the bulk of the album. A No.1 hit in the States, the record fulfilled the potential hinted at in its predecessor, freeing up the full, stratospheric power of RONALD's vocals with a collection of contemporary R&B love songs. The ISLEYs were truly hip(-hop) once more with the release of a full-blown remix set, 'TAKEN TO THE NEXT PHASE' (2004), a record featuring MOS DEF amongst others. Back to bread-and-butter soul for the 00s, the siblings carried on their platinum resurgence with the US Top 5, 'BABY MAKIN' MUSIC' (2005), remarkably half a century in the music biz and still going strong.

• **Songwriters:** Producers LEIBER & STOLLER provided them with their 'Atlantic' material in '61, while the following year, producer BERT BERNS wrote 'RIGHT NOW' and produced their hit Medley-Russell-penned 'TWIST AND SHOUT'. In 1966, with 'Tamla Motown', HOLLAND-DOZIER-HOLLAND provided them with some hits. In 1969, their formation of 'T-Neck' saw them writing their own material. During this time they also covered LOVE THE ONE YOU'RE WITH (Stephen Stills) / LAY LADY LAY (Bob Dylan) / SPILL THE WINE (War) / COLD BOLOGNA (Bill Withers) / FIRE AND RAIN (James Taylor) / MACHINE GUN (Jimi Hendrix) / OHIO (Neil Young) / SUMMER BREEZE (Seals & Croft) / IT'S TOO LATE + BROTHER, BROTHER, BROTHER (Carole King) / etc.

Album rating: SHOUT! (*5) / TWIST & SHOUT! (*6) / THE FABULOUS ISLEY BROTHERS TWISTING AND SHOUTING (*4) / THIS OLD HEART OF MINE (*5) / SOUL ON THE ROCKS (*4) / IT'S OUR THING (*7) / THE BROTHERS: ISLEY (*4) / GIVIN' IT BACK (*5) / BROTHER, BROTHER, BROTHER (*6) / THE ISLEYS LIVE (*5) / 3 + 3 (*8) / LIVE IT UP (*6) / THE HEAT IS ON (*7) / HARVEST FOR THE WORLD (*6) / GO FOR YOUR GUNS (*6) / FOREVER GOLD compilation (*7) / SHOWDOWN (*6) / WINNER TAKES ALL (*6) / GO ALL THE WAY (*6) / GRAND SLAM (*6) / INSIDE YOU (*5) / THE REAL DEAL (*5) / BETWEEN THE SHEETS (*6) / MASTERPIECE (*5) / SMOOTH SAILIN' (*5) / Isley Brothers featuring Ronald Isley: SPEND THE NIGHT (*4) / TRACKS OF LIFE (*4) / MISSION TO PLEASE (*6) / ISLEY BROTHERS STORY VOL.1 (THE ROCK'N'ROLL YEARS 1959-68) compilation (*8) / ISLEY BROTHERS STORY VOL.2 (THE T-NECK YEARS 1969-1985) compilation (*8) / ETERNAL (*5) / BODY KISS (*6) / TAKEN TO THE NEXT PHASE (*7) / BABY MAKIN' MUSIC (*6) / SUMMER BREEZE – GREATEST HITS compilation (*8)

RONALD ISLEY (b.21 May'41) – lead vocals / **RUDOLPH ISLEY** (b. 1 Apr'39) – vocal / **O'KELLY ISLEY** (b.25 Dec'37) – vocals

not iss. / Teenage

1957. (7") *<1004>* **THE COW JUMPED OVER THE MOON. / ANGELS CRIED** [-] [ ]

not iss. / Mark-X

1957. (7") *<7003>* **ROCKIN' McDONALD. / DON'T BE JEALOUS** [-] [ ]

not iss. / Gone

1958. (7") *<5022>* **EVERYBODY'S GONNA ROCK'N'ROLL. / I WANNA KNOW** [-] [ ]

1958. (7") *<5048>* **THE DRAG. / THE LOVE** [-] [ ]

not iss. / Cindy

1958. (7") *<3009>* **THIS IS THE END. / DON'T BE JEALOUS** [-] [ ]

R.C.A. / R.C.A.

1959. (7") *<7537>* **TURN TO ME. / I'M GONNA KNOCK ON YOUR DOOR** [-] [ ]

Oct 59. (7") *(RCA 1149) <7588>* **SHOUT. / SHOUT (Pt.2)** [ ] Sep59 [47]
(re-iss. US Mar 62, hit No.94)

Jun 60. (lp) *(RD 27165) <LSP 2156>* **SHOUT!** [ ] Oct59 [ ]
– Shout! (part 1 & 2) / Tell me who / How deep is the ocean (part 1 & 2) / Respectable (parts 1 & 2) / Say you love me / Open up your heart / He's got the whole world in his hands / Without a song / Yes indeed / Ring a ling a ling / That lucky old sun / When the saints go marching in / Gypsy love song / St. Louis blues / Rock around the clock / Turn to me / Not one minute more / I'm gonna knock on your door. *(re-iss. Nov70; INTS 1098) (cd-iss. DEc88 on 'Bear Family'; BCD 15425)* – (extra tracks).

Feb 60. (7") *<7657>* **RESPECTABLE. / WITHOUT A SONG** [-] [ ]

Feb 60. (7") *(RCA 1172)* **RESPECTABLE. / I'M GONNA KNOCK ON YOUR DOOR** [ ] [-]

May 60. (7") *(RCA 1190) <7718>* **HE'S GOT THE WHOLE WORLD IN HIS HANDS. / HOW DEEP IS THE OCEAN** [ ] [ ]

Aug 60. (7") *<7746>* **GYPSY LOVE SONG. / OPEN UP YOUR HEART** [-] [ ]

Nov 60. (7") *(RCA 1213) <7787>* **TELL ME WHO. / SAY YOU LOVE ME TOO** [ ] [ ]

not iss. / Atlantic

1961. (7") *<2092>* **TELL ME HOW TO SHIMMY. / JEEPERS CREEPERS** [-] [ ]

1961. (7") *<2100>* **SHINE ON HARVEST MOON. / STANDING ON THE DANCE FLOOR** [-] [ ]

1961. (7") *<2110>* **WRITE TO ME. / YOUR OLD LADY** [-] [ ]

1961. (7") *<2122>* **A FOOL FOR YOU. / JUST ONE MORE TIME** [-] [ ]

Stateside / Wand

Feb 62. (7") *<118>* **RIGHT NOW. / THE SNAKE** [-] [ ]

Jun 62. (7") *(SS 112) <124>* **TWIST AND SHOUT. / I.B. Special: SPANISH TWIST** [ ] May62 [17]
(re-act.Jul63 reached UK No.42)

Oct 62. (7") *(SS 132) <127>* **TWISTING WITH LINDA. / YOU BETTER COME HOME** [ ] Sep62 [54]

Oct 62. (lp) *<653>* **TWIST AND SHOUT** [-] [61]
– Twist and shout / Don't you feel / Hold on baby / Time after time / Twisting with Linda / I say love / Right now / Spanish twist / The drag / Don't be jealous / This is the end / Rockin' McDonald. *(UK-iss.Feb76 on 'D.J.M.'; 2628) (c-iss.Oct82 on 'Orchid'; ORC 009) (cd-iss. 1988 on 'K-Tel'; NCD 5162)*

Aug 63. (7") *(SS 128) <127>* **NOBODY BUT ME. / I'M LAUGHING TO KEEP FROM CRYING** [ ] [ ]

Oct 63. (7") *<137>* **HOLD ON BABY. / I SAY LOVE** [-] [ ]

U.A. / U.A.

Oct 63. (7") *(UP 1034) <605>* **TANGO. / SHE'S GONE** [ ] [ ]

Dec 63. (7") *<638>* **SURF AND SHOUT. / WHAT'CHA GONNA DO** [-] [ ]

Feb 64. (7") *<659>* **YOU'LL NEVER LEAVE HIM. / PLEASE, PLEASE, PLEASE** [-] [ ]

Apr 64. (7") *<714>* **WHO'S THAT LADY. / MY LITTLE GIRL** [-] [ ]

Apr 64. (7") *(UP 1050)* **SHAKE IT WITH ME BABY. / STAGGER LEE** [ ] [-]

May 64. (lp) *(ULP 1064) <6313>* **THE FABULOUS ISLEY BROTHERS – TWISTING AND SHOUTING** [ ] [ ]
– Surf and shout / Please please please / Do the twist / She's the one / Tango / What'cha gonna do / Stagger Lee / You'll never leave him / Let's go, let's go, let's go / Shake it with me baby / She's gone / Long tall Sally.

Atlantic / T-Neck

May 64. (7") *<501>***TESTIFY. / (part 2)** [-] [ ]

Atlantic / Atlantic

Oct 64. (7") *(AT 4010) <2263>* **THE LAST GIRL. / LOOKING FOR A LOVE** [ ] [ ]

1965. (7") *<2277>* **SIMON SAYS. / WILD AS A TIGER** [-] [ ]

1965. (7") *<2303>* **MOVE OVER AND LET ME DANCE. / HAVE YOU EVER BEEN DISAPPOINTED** [-] [ ]

Tamla Motown / Tamla

Mar 66. (7") *(TMG 555) <54128>* **THIS OLD HEART OF MINE (IS WEAK FOR YOU). / THERE'S NO LOVE LEFT** [47] Jan66 [12]
(re-act.Oct68 reached UK No.3)

Oct 66. (lp) *(TML 11034) <269>* **THIS OLD HEART OF MINE (IS WEAK FOR YOU)** [ ] Jun66 [ ]
– Nowhere to run / Stop in the name of love / This old heart of mine (is weak for you) / Take some time out for love / I guess I'll always love you / Baby don't you do it / Who could ever doubt my love / Put yourself in my place / Just ain't enough love / I hear a symphony / There's no love left / Seek and you shall find. *(re-act.Dec68 hit UK No.23) (re-iss. Jul81 lp/c; STMS/CSTMS 5026)*

Jun 66. (7") *(TMG 556) <54133>* **TAKE SOME TIME OUT FOR LOVE. / WHO COULD EVER DOUBT MY LOVE** [ ] May66 [66]
(re-iss. Nov69; TMG 719)

Aug 66. (7") *(TMG 572) <54135>* **I GUESS I'LL ALWAYS LOVE YOU. / I HEAR A SYMPHONY** [45] Jul66 [61]

1967. (lp) *<37080>* **TAMLA MOTOWN PRESENTS . . . THE ISLEY BROTHERS** [-] [ ]
(UK-iss.Mar73 on 'Music For Pleasure';)

May 67. (7") *(TMG 606) <54146>* **GOT TO HAVE YOU BACK. / JUST AIN'T ENOUGH LOVE** [ ] [93]

Jan 68. (7") <54154> **ONE TOO MANY HEARTACHES. / THAT'S THE WAY LOVE IS** [–] [ ]
Feb 68. (lp) *(STML 11066)* <275> **SOUL ON THE ROCKS** [ ] [ ]
– Got to have you back / That's the way love is / Whispers (gettin' louder) / Tell it's just a rumour baby / One too many heartaches / It's out of the question / Why when love is gone / Save me from the misery / Little Miss Sweetness / Good things / Catching up on time / Behind a painted smile.
Apr 68. (7") *(TMG 652)* <54164> **TAKE ME IN YOUR ARMS (ROCK ME A LITTLE WHILE). / WHY WHEN LOVE IS GONE** [ ] [ ]
1968. (7") <54175> **BEHIND A PAINTED SMILE. / ALL BECAUSE I LOVE YOU** [–] [ ]
1968. (7") <54182> **TAKE SOME TIME OUT FOR LOVE. / JUST AIN'T ENOUGH LOVE** [–] [ ]

Major Minor T-Neck

Jun 69. (7") *(MM 621)* <901> **IT'S YOUR THING. / DON'T GIVE IT AWAY** [ ] Feb69 [2]
Jul 69. (lp) *(SMLP 59)* <3001> **IT'S OUR THING** [ ] Apr69 [22]
– This old heart of mine (is weak for you) / Who could ever doubt my love / I guess I'll always love you / That's the way love is / One too many heartaches / Why when love is gone / Just ain't enough love / Got to have you back / There's no love left / I hear a symphony / Take me in your arms (rock me for a while) / Take some time out for love.
Jul 69. (7") <903> **TURN ON, TUNE IN, DROP OUT. / (part 2)** [–] [ ]
Aug 69. (7") <906> **BLACK BERRIES. / (part 2)** [–] [79]
Sep 69. (7") *(MM 631)* <902> **I TURNED YOU ON. / I KNOW WHO YOU BEEN SOCKING IT TO** [ ] May69 [23]

— RONNIE, RUDOLPH and O'KELLY (who was now just KELLY) with brass section added **ERNIE ISLEY** (b. 7 Mar'52) – guitar, percussion, guitar (later EVERETT COLLINS – drums) / **MARVIN ISLEY** (b.18 Aug'53) – bass, percussion / **CHRIS JASPER** – keyboards

Stateside T-Neck

Dec 69. (7") <912> **BLESS YOUR HEART. / GIVE THE WOMEN WHAT THEY WANT** [–] [ ]
Feb 70. (7") *(SS 2162)* <908> **WAS IT GOOD TO YOU. / I GOT TO GET MYSELF TOGETHER** [ ] Sep69 [83]
Feb 70. (7") <914> **KEEP ON DOIN'. / SAVE ME** [–] [75]
Apr 70. (7") <919> **IF HE CAN, YOU CAN. / HOLDIN' ON** [–] [ ]
Jun 70. (lp) *(SSL 10300)* **THE BROTHERS: ISLEY** [ ] Oct69 [ ]
– Black berries / Vacuum cleaner / I turned you on / Was it good to you / She's my girl / Get down off the train / Gotta get myself together / Feel like the world / Holdin' on.
Jul 70. (7") <921> **GIRLS WILL BE GIRLS, BOYS WILL BE BOYS. / GET DOWN OFF THE TRAIN** [–] [75]
Sep 70. (7") <924> **GET INTO SOMETHING. / (part 2)** [–] [89]
Sep 70. (lp) <3004> **LIVE AT THE YANKEE STADIUM (live)** [–] Oct69 [ ]
– (shared with The Edwin Hawkins Singers + Brooklyn Bridge)
Dec 70. (7") <927> **FREEDOM. / I NEED YOU SO** [–] [72]
May 71. (7") *(SS 2188)* <929> **WARPATH. / I GOT TO FIND ME ONE** [ ] [ ]
Sep 71. (7") <932> **SPILL THE WINE. / TAKE INVENTORY** [–] [49]
Sep 71. (lp) **GIVIN' IT BACK** (all covers) [–] [71]
– Fire and rain / Ohio machine gun / Lay lady lay / etc
Oct 71. (7") *(SS 2193)* <930> **LOVE THE ONE YOU'RE WITH. / HE'S GOT YOUR LOVE** [ ] Jun71 [18]
Dec 71. (7") <933> **LAY LADY LAY. / VACUUM CLEANER** [–] [71]
Mar 72. (7") <934> **LAY AWAY. / FEEL LIKE THE WORLD** [–] [54]
Jun 72. (lp) <3009> **BROTHER, BROTHER, BROTHER** [–] [29]
– Brother, brother / Put a little love in your heart / Sweet seasons / Keep on walkin' / Work to do / Pop that thang / Lay away / It's too late / Love put me on the corner.
Jun 72. (7") <935> **POP THAT THANG. / I GOT TO FIND ME ONE** [–] [24]
Oct 72. (7") <936> **WORK TO DO. / BEAUTIFUL** [–] [51]
Mar 73. (lp) <3010> **ISLEY BROTHERS LIVE (live)** [–] [ ]
– Work to do / It's too late / It's your thing / Pop that thang / Love the one you're with / Lay lady lay / Lay away / Ohio / Machine gun.
May 73. (7") <937> **IT'S TOO LATE. / NOTHING TO DO BUT TODAY** [–] [ ]

Epic T-Neck

Aug 73. (7") *(EPC 1704)* <2251> **THAT LADY. / THAT LADY (part 2)** [14] Jul73 [6]
Nov 73. (lp) *(EPC 65740)* <32453> **3 + 3** [ ] Sep73 [ ]
– That lady / Don't let me be lonely tonight / If you were there / You walk your way / Listen to the music / What it comes down to / Sunshine (go away today) / Summer breeze / The highways of my life. *(re-iss. Mar81 lp/c; EPC/40 32039) (cd-iss. Apr94 on 'Sony'; 962615-2) (cd re-iss. Jul97; 487937-2)*

Nov 73. (7") <2252> **WHAT IT COMES DOWN TO. / HIGHWAYS OF MY LIFE** [–] [55]
Dec 73. (7") *(EPC 1980)* **THE HIGHWAYS OF MY LIFE. / DON'T LET ME BE LONELY TONIGHT** [25] [–]
Apr 74. (7") *(EPC 2244)* <2253> **SUMMER BREEZE. / SUMMER BREEZE (part 2)** [16] Mar74 [60]
Aug 74. (7") *(EPC 2578)* <2254> **LIVE IT UP. / (part 2)** [ ] Jul74 [52]
Sep 74. (lp/c) *(EPC/40 80317)* <33070> **LIVE IT UP** [ ] [14]
– Live it up / Brown eyed girl / Need a little taste of love / Lover's eye / Midnight sky / Hello it's me / Ain't I been good to you.
Nov 74. (7") *(EPC 2803)* **NEED A LITTLE TASTE OF LOVE. / IF YOU WERE THERE** [ ] [–]
Feb 75. (7") *(EPC 3034)* <2255> **MIDNIGHT SKY. / (part 2)** [ ] Nov74 [73]
Jul 75. (7") *(EPC 3434)* <2256> **FIGHT THE POWER. / (part 2)** [ ] Jun75 [4]
Jul 75. (lp/c) *(EPC/40 69139)* <33536> **THE HEAT IS ON** [ ] Jun75 [1]
– Fight the power / The heat is on (pts.1 & 2) / Hope you feel better love (pts.1 & 2) / For the love of you (pts.1 & 2) / Sensuality (pts.1 &2) / Make me say it again girl (pts.1 & 2). *(cd re-mast.Sep01 +=; 504041-2)* – Fight the power.
Jan 76. (7") *(EPC 3865)* <2259> **FOR THE LOVE OF YOU. / YOU WALK YOUR WAY** [ ] Nov75 [22]
Jun 76. (7") *(EPC 4369)* **HARVEST FOR THE WORLD. / LET ME DOWN EASY** [10] [–]
Jun 76. (lp/c) *(EPC/40 81268)* <33809> **HARVEST FOR THE WORLD** [50] May76 [9]
– Harvest for the world (prelude) / Harvest for the world / People of today / Who loves you better / Let me down easy / (At your best) You are love / So you wanna stay down / You still feel the need. *(re-iss. Jun85 lp/c; EPC/40 32652) (cd re-mast.Sep01 +=; 50404-2)* – Summer breeze.
Aug 76. (7") <2260> **HARVEST FOR THE WORLD. / (part 2)** [–] [63]
Sep 76. (7") *(EPC 4373)* <2260> **WHO LOVES YOU BETTER. / WHO LOVES YOU BETTER (part 2)** [ ] May76 [47]
Apr 77. (lp/c) *(EPC/40 86027)* <34432> **GO FOR YOU GUNS** [46] [6]
– Livin' in the life / Go for your guns / Voyage to Atlantis / Footsteps in the dark (part 1 & 2) / Tell me when you need it again (part1 & 2) / The pride (part 1 & 2). *(re-iss. May93 on 'Sony Collectors')*
May 77. (7") <2262> **THE PRIDE. / (part 2)** [–] [63]
Jul 77. (7") *(EPC 5443)* **VOYAGE TO ATLANTIS. / TELL ME WHEN YOU NEED IT AGAIN** [ ] [–]
Apr 78. (7") *(EPC 6292)* **TAKE ME TO THE NEXT PHASE. / LIVIN' IN THE LIFE** [ ] [–]
Apr 78. (7") <2264> **LIVIN' IN MY LIFE. / GO FOR YOUR GUNS** [–] [40]
Apr 78. (lp/c) *(EPC/40 86039)* <34930> **SHOWDOWN** [46] [4]
– Showdown (part 1 & 2) / Groovin' with you / Ain't givin' up no love / Rockin' with fire (part 1 & 2) / Take me to the next phase (part 1 & 2) / Coolin' me out (part 1 & 2) / Fun and games / Love fever (part 1 & 2).
May 78. (7") <2270> **SO YOU WANNA STAY DOWN. / VOYAGE TO ATLANTIS** [–] [ ]
Jun 78. (7") <2276> **TAKE ME TO THE NEXT PHASE. / TELL ME WHEN YOU NEED IT AGAIN** [–] [ ]
Jul 78. (7") *(EPC 6481)* <2277> **GROOVE WITH YOU. / FOOTSTEPS IN THE DARK** [ ] [ ]
Jul 79. (d-lp/c) *(EPC/40 88460)* <36077> **WINNER TAKES ALL** [ ] [14]
– I wanna be with you / Liquid love / Winner takes all / Life in the city / It's a disco night (rock don't stop) / Let's fall in love / (Can't you see) What you do to me / How lucky I am / You're the key to my heart / You're beside me / Love comes and goes / Let me into your life / Go for what you know / Mind over matter.
Aug 79. (7") *(EPC 7757)* **LIFE IN THE CITY. / (part 2)** [ ] [–]
Oct 79. (7") *(EPC 7911)* <2287> **IT'S A DISCO NIGHT (ROCK DON'T STOP). / AIN'T GIVIN' UP ON LOVE** [14] [90]
Jan 80. (7") *(EPC 7795)* <2284> **WINNER TAKES ALL. / FUN AND GAMES** [ ] Aug79 [ ]
Apr 80. (lp/c) *(EPC/40 65740)* <36035> **GO ALL THE WAY** [ ] [8]
– Go all the way / Say you will / Pass it on / The belly dancer / Here we go again / Don't say goodnight (it's time for love).
Jun 80. (7") *(EPC 8664)* <2290> **DON'T SAY GOODNIGHT (IT'S TIME FOR LOVE). / (part 2)** [ ] Apr80 [39]
Apr 81. (7") *(EPCA 1122)* **TONIGHT IS THE NIGHT (IF I HAD YOU). / WHO SAID** [ ] [–]
Apr 81. (lp/c) *(EPC/40 84914)* <37080> **GRAND SLAM** [ ] Mar81 [28]
– Tonight is the night (if I had you) / Hurry up and wait / I once had your love (and I can't let go) / Young girls / Party night / Don't let go / Who said.
Apr 81. (7") <02033> **HURRY UP AND WAIT. / ('A' instrumental)** [–] [58]

Jul 81. (7") *<02179>* **I ONCE HAD YOUR LOVE (AND CAN'T LET GO). / ('A'instrumental)** [–] [ ]

Nov 81. (7") *<02531>* **INSIDE YOU. / (part 2)** [–] [ ]

Nov 81. (7") *(EPCA 1741)* **INSIDE YOU. / LOVE ZONE** [ ] [–]

Nov 81. (lp/c) *(EPC/40 85252) <37533>* **INSIDE YOU** [ ] Oct81 [45]
– Inside you (part 1 & 2) / Baby hold on / First love / Welcome into my heart / Don't hold back your love (part 1 & 2) / Love merry-go-round / Love zone.

Jan 82. (7") *<02705>* **WELCOME INTO MY HEART. / PARTY NIGHT** [–] [ ]

Sep 82. (7") *<02985>* **THE REAL DEAL. / ('A'instrumental)** [–] [ ]

Sep 82. (lp/c) *(EPC/40 85790) <38047>* **THE REAL DEAL** [ ] Aug82 [87]
– The real deal (part 1 & 2) / Are you with me / I'll do it all for you / Stone cold lover / It's alright with me / All in my lover's eyes / Under the influence.

Nov 82. (7") *<03281>* **IT'S ALRIGHT WITH ME. / ('A'instrumental)** [–] [ ]

Feb 83. (7") *<03420>* **ALL IN MY LOVER'S EYES. / I'LL DO IT ALL FOR YOU** [–] [ ]

Jun 83. (lp/c) *(EPC/40 25419) <38674>* **BETWEEN THE SHEETS** [ ] May83 [19]
– Choosey lover / Touch me / I need your body / Let's make love tonight / Between the sheets / Ballad for the fallen soldier / Slow down children / Way out love / Gettin' over you / Rock you.

Jun 83. (7") *<03797>* **BETWEEN THE SHEETS. / (part 2)** [–] [ ]

Jun 83. (7"/12") *(A/TA 3513)* **BETWEEN THE SHEETS. / THAT LADY** [52] [–]

Aug 83. (7"/12") *(A/TA 3690) <03994>* **CHOOSEY LOVER. / CHOOSEY LOVER (part 2)** [ ] [ ]

Nov 83. (7") *<04320>* **LETS MAKE LOVE TONIGHT. / ('A'instrumental)** [–] [ ]

—— Reverted to original trio when others formed ISLEY, JASPER, ISLEY

Warners Warners

Nov 85. (7") *<28860>* **COLDER ARE MY NIGHTS. / BREAK THIS CHAIN** [–] [ ]

Dec 85. (7"/12") *(WB 8860/+T)* **COLDER ARE MY NIGHTS. / ('A'instrumental)** [ ] [–]

Dec 85. (lp/c) *(925347-1/-4/-2) <25347>* **MASTERPIECE** [ ] [ ]
– May I / My best was good enough / If leaving me is easy / You never know when you're gonna fall in love / Stay gold / Colder are my nights / Come to me / Release your love / The most beautiful girl.

Mar 86. (7") *<28764>* **MAY I. / ('A'instrumental)** [–] [ ]

—— Now a duo of RONNIE and RUDOLF, when O'KELLY died of a heart attack on the 31st of March '86

Jun 87. (7") *<28385>* **SMOOTH SAILIN' TONIGHT. / (part 2)** [–] [ ]

Jul 87. (lp/c/cd) *(925586-1/-4/-2) <25586>* **SMOOTH SAILIN'** [ ] Jun87 [64]
– Everything is alright / Pick it out / It takes a good woman / Send a message / Smooth sailin' tonight / Somebody I used to know / Come my way / I wish.

Sep 87. (7") *<28241>* **COME MY WAY. / (part 2)** [–] [ ]

Nov 87. (7") *<28129>* **I WISH. / ('A'instrumental)** [–] [ ]

Feb 88. (7") *<27954>* **IT TAKES A GOOD WOMAN. / (part 2)** [–] [ ]

ISLEY BROTHERS featuring RONALD ISLEY

—— **RONALD, ERNIE + MARVIN**

Jun 89. (7") *<22990>* **SPEND THE NIGHT (CE SOIR). / ('A'instrumental)** [–] [ ]

Jul 89. (lp/c/cd) *(925940-1/-4/-2) <25940>* **SPEND THE NIGHT** [ ] [89]
– Spend the night (ce soir) / You'll never walk alone / One of a kind / Real woman / Come together / If you ever need somebody / Baby come back home / One of a kind (reprise).

Oct 89. (7") *<22748>* **YOU'LL NEVER WALK ALONE. / ONE OF A KIND** [–] [ ]

Feb 90. (7") *<19910>* **IF YOU EVER NEED SOMEBODY. / ONE OF A KIND** [–] [ ]

May 90. (c-s) *<19814>* **COME TOGETHER /** [–] [ ]

—— In Mar 90, RONALD ISLEY backed ROD STEWART on a US Top 10 version of THIS OLD HEART OF MINE. ROD, of course, had earlier made UK No.4 with the song. ERNIE released his solo album, 'HIGH WIRE' early in 1990.

Jun 92. (cd/c) *<(7559 26620-2/-4)>* **TRACKS OF LIFE** [ ] [ ]
– Turn on the demon / Bedroom eyes / Morning love / Sensitive lover / Searching for a miracle / No axe to grind / Brazilian wedding song (setembro) / Dedicate this song / Got my licks in / I'll be there 4 u / Koolin' out / Lost in your love / Red hot.

4th & Broad Island

May 96. (c-s,cd-s) *<854586>* **LET'S LAY TOGETHER / ('A'instrumental)** [–] [93]

May 96. (cd/c) *<(524214-2/-4)>* **MISSION TO PLEASE** [ ] [31]
– Floatin' on your love / Whenever you're ready / Let's lay together / Can I have a kiss (for old time's sake)? / Mission to please you / Make your body sing / Let's het intimate / Show us the way / Tears . . . Ron crying alone.

Oct 96. (c-s) *(BRAC 338) <854738>* **FLOATIN' ON YOUR LOVE / ('A'remix)** [ ] Sep96 [47]
(12"+=/cd-s+=) *(12BRW/BRCD 338)* – ('A'remixes by LIL' KIM and 112).

Jan 97. (cd-s) *<854862>* **TEARS / TEARS (album) / MAKE YOUR BODY SING** [–] [55]

the ISLEY BROTHERS featuring RONALD ISLEY AND MR. BIGGS

Dreamworks Dreamwor

Jul 01. (-) *<radio cut>* **CONTAGIOUS** [–] [19]

Aug 01. (cd) *<(450291-2)>* **ETERNAL** [ ] [3]
– Move your body / Contagious / Warm summer night / You deserve better / Just like this / Secret lover / You're all I need / Settle down / Eternal / If you leave me now / Said enough / You didn't see me / Ernie's jam / Think.

May 03. (-) *<radio cut>* **WHAT WOULD YOU DO?** [–] [49]

May 03. (cd) *<(450409-2)>* **BODY KISS** [ ] [1]
– Superstar / Lucky charm / What would you do? / Body kiss / Busted / Showdown Vol.1 / Keep it flowin' / Prize posession / Take a ride / I want that / I like / What would you do? (part 2 remix).

the ISLEY BROTHERS

Def Soul Def Soul

Jun 06. (cd) *<48010-2>* **BABY MAKIN' MUSIC** [ ] May06 [5]
– You're my star / Blast off / Just came here to chill / Gotta be with you / Pretty woman / Forever mackin' / Show me / Give it to you / Beautiful / Heaven hooked us up / You help me write this song.

– (selective) compilations, etc. –

on 'Tamla Motown' until otherwise mentioned

Jan 69. (7") *(TMG 683)* **I GUESS I'LL ALWAYS LOVE YOU. / IT'S OUT OF THE QUESTION** [11] [ ]

Apr 69. (7") *(TMG 693)* **BEHIND A PAINTED SMILE. / ONE TOO MANY HEARTACHES** [5] [ ]

Aug 69. (7") *(TMG 708)* **PUT YOURSELF IN MY PLACE. / LITTLE MISS SWEETNESS** [13] [ ]

Oct 77. (lp) *Epic; (EPC 86040) <34452>* **FOREVER GOLD** [ ] [58]
(re-iss. Aug84 lp/c; EPC/40 32238) (cd-iss. Jan98; CD 32238)

Mar 88. (lp/c/cd) *Telstar; (STAR/STAC/SCD 2306)* **GREATEST HITS** [41] [–]

Sep 69. (lp) *(STML 1112)* **BEHIND A PAINTED SMILE** [ ] [ ]
– Behind a painted smile / Got to have you back / Take me in your arms (rock me a little while) / Catching up on a time / Save me from this misery / Little Miss Sweetness / Good things / All because I love you / That's the way love is / Tell me it's just a rumour baby / It's out of the question / Why when love is gone / One too many heartaches / Whispers (gettin' louder).

Nov 02. (cd) *(017190-2)* **THIS OLD HEART OF MINE / SOUL ON THE ROCKS** [ ] [ ]

Dec 02. (d-cd) *(509456-2)* **HARVEST FOR THE WORLD / THE HEAT IS ON** [ ] [ ]

Aug 04. (cd) *Epic; (512909-2) <86669-2>* **TAKEN TO THE NEXT PHASE** (remixes) [ ] [ ]

Jul 05. (cd) *Epic; (520461-2)* **SUMMER BREEZE – GREATEST HITS** [69] [–]

☐ the IVEYS (see under ⇒ BADFINGER)

JA RULE

Born: JEFFREY ATKINS, 29 Feb'76, Queens, New York, USA. JA RULE got his first break in the late 90's when 'Def Jam' producer IRV GOTTI took the young man under his 'Murder Inc.' associated wing. Hardcore gangsta rap with a leaning to DMX and The RUFF RYDERS crew, JA found his particular branding of his genre a hit with the East Coast public via debut single, 'HOLLA HOLLA' and JS Top 3 album, 'VENNI VETTI VECCI' (1999). Featuring the ikes of ERICK SERMON, JAY-Z, CASE, RONALD ISLEY and the aforementioned DMX, the long-player set the tone for a future post-millennium supergroup project, The MURDERERS. Together with AY-Z and DMX on initial recordings, JA and IRV also introduced new rappers such as BLACK CHILD, TAH MURDAH and VITA for their collaborative one-off 'IRV GOTTI PRESENTS . . .' (2000). To end what was to be a very busy year for JA, the man also despatched a follow-up chart-topping solo set, 'RULE 3:36' (2000), featuring no less than three further hits, 'PUT IT ON ME' (with VITA), BETWEEN ME AND YOU' (with CHRISTINA MILIAN) and 'I CRY' (with LIL' MO). However, it wasn't until 2001's 'PAIN IS LOVE' album that JA became the critically acclaimed superstar and household name (well, at least in the US). Another to peak at No.1, his collaborative R&B divas this time around included ASHANTI on the chart-topping 'ALWAYS ON TIME'), JENNIFER LOPEZ and MISSY ELLIOTT. With this hit formula JA RULE continued to expand his risky musical horizons on his fourth solo set, 'THE LAST TEMPTATION' (2002), although this only reached the Top 5 (Top 0 in Britain). Whether his choice of pop-friendly collaborations with the likes of BOBBY BROWN (on 'THUG LOVIN') and the aforementioned ASHANTI again (on major smash 'MESMERIZE') was a little diverse to say the least, JA RULE and his GOTTI-produced mates made their mark once more. However, fall-outs with DMX and newcomer 50 CENT (the latter saw him as a 2PAC impersonator), saw JA RULE subsequently crack under the strain. This was evident on the poor showing both critically and chartwise or 2003's 'BLOOD IN MY EYE', an album that took a swipe at most of his rivals including 50 CENT and EMINEM – it was time to get real! If the title of 'R.U.L.E.' (2004) was an attempt to restate his mission, the album failed to recapture his millennial salad days. Still, he chalked up his first UK No.1 with lead single, 'WONDERFUL', aided and abetted by R. KELLY and ASHANTI. Come 2005, a JA RULE compilation was in the stores: 'EXODUS' (2005) may have referenced BOB MARLEY but the sentiments weren't quite so spiritual.

lbum rating: VENNI VETTI VECCI (*5) / IRV GOTTI PRESENTS . . . THE MURDERERS (by the Murderers; *5) / RULE 3:36 (*5) / PAIN IS LOVE (*7) / THE LAST TEMPTATION (*6) / BLOOD IN MY EYE (*4) / R.U.L.E. (*4) / EXODUS compilation (*5)

A RULE – vocals / with various session people

Def Jam — Def Jam

ar 99. (c-s/12"/cd-s; by JA RULE, DMX & JAY-Z) *<566959>* **HOLLA HOLLA (mixes)** [–] [35]

May 99. (cd) *<(538920-2)>* **VENNI VETTI VECCI** [ ] [3]
– The March prelude / We here now / World's most dangerous (with NEMESIS) / Let's ride / Holla holla / Kill 'em all (with JAY-Z) / I hate nigguz (skit) / Nigguz theme / Suicide freestyle (with CASE) / Story to tell / Chris Black (skit) / Count on your nigga / It's murda (with DMX & JAY-Z) / E-dub & Ja (with ERICK SERMON) / 187 murda baptiss church (skit) / Murda 4 life (with MEMPHIS BLEEK) / Daddy's little baby (with RONALD ISLEY) / Race against time / Only begotten son / The murderers (with BLACK CHILD & TAH MURDAH).

—— The MURDERERS: **JA RULE + VITA + BLACK CHILD + TAH MURDAH + 0-1 + RONNIE BUMPS**

Feb 00. (12"; as The MURDERERS) *<56266-1>* **VITA, VITA, VITA (mixes)** [–] [ ]

Mar 00. (cd; as The MURDERERS) *<(542258-2)>* **IRV GOTTI PRESENTS . . . THE MURDERERS** [ ] [15]
– Intro / Murderers / Dem niggaz / We don't give a fuck / Clowns (skit) / Shit gets ugly / We Murderers baby / Interview with Vita (skit) / Vita, Vita, Vita / How many wanna die / Fuck parole (skit) / We getting high tonight / Tales from the darkside / I love the Yankees (skit) / Get it right / We different / Remo (skit) / Rebels symphony / Black or white / The 187 murda baptist church picknicing / If you were my bitch / 96R-0709 / Crime scene / Somebody's gonna die tonight / Holla holla (remix).

Oct 00. (cd) *<(542934-2)>* **RULE 3:36** [ ] [1]
– Intro / Watching me / Between me and you (with CHRISTINA MILIAN) / Put it on me (with VITA) / 6 feet underground / Love me, hate me / Die (with TAH MURDAH, BLACK CHILD & DAVE BING) / Fuck you (with 01 & VITA) / I'll fuck you girl (skit) / Grey box (skit with TAH MURDAH & BLACK CHILD) / Extasy (with TAH MURDAH & BLACK CHILD) / It's your life (with SHADE SHEIST) / I cry (with LIL' MO) / One of us / Chris Black (skit) / The rule won't die.

Nov 00. (12") *<572701>* **6 FEET UNDERGROUND (mixes)** [–] [ ]

Dec 00. (12"; with LIL' MO & VITA) *<572751>* **PUT IT ON ME** [–] [8]

Feb 01. (12"/cd-s; by JA RULE & CHRISTINA MILIAN) *<(572740-2)>* **BETWEEN ME AND YOU (mixes)** [26] Jan01 [11]

Apr 01. (12"; with LIL' MO) *<572856>* **I CRY (mixes)** [–] [40]

Oct 01. (cd/d-lp) *<(586437-2/-1)>* **PAIN IS LOVE** [17] Sep01 [1]
– Pain is love (skit) / Dial M for murder / Livin' it up (with CASE) / The Inc. (with CADDILLAC TAH & BLACK CHILD) / Always on time (with ASHANTI) / Down ass bitch (with CHUCK) / Never again / Worldwide gangsta (with CADDILLAC TAH & BLACK CHILD) / Leo (skit) / I'm real (with JENNIFER LOPEZ) / Smokin' and ridin' (with JODIE MACK & 0-1) / X (with MISSY ELLIOTT & TWEET) / Big Remo (skit) / Lost little girl / So much pain (with2PAC) / Pain is love. *(re-iss. Oct02; same)* – hit UK No.3

Oct 01. (c-s/12"/cd-s; JA RULE featuring CASE) *(588814-4/-1/-2)* *<588741>* **LIVIN' IT UP (mixes)** [27] Aug01 [6]

Jan 02. (c-s; JA RULE & ASHANTI) *(588946-4)* *<588795>* **ALWAYS ON TIME / I CRY (with Lil' Mo)** [6] Oct01 [1]
(12"+=) *(588946-1)* – ('A'-radio version).
(cd-s++=) *(588946-2)* – ('A'-video).

Feb 02. (12"/cd-s) *<588941-1/-2>* **DOWN ASS CHICK. / SMOKIN' & RIDIN'** [–] [21]

—— in Mar'02, JA RULE & CADDILLAC TAH featured on J.LO's Top 5 hit 'Ain't It Funny'

Jul 02. (c-s; JA RULE featuring CASE) *(063978-4)* **LIVIN' IT UP / LIVIN' IT UP (live at the London Astoria)** [5] [–]
(12"+=) *(063978-1)* – Always on time (Agent X mix) / Always on time (delight camp dub).
(cd-s+=) *(063978-2)* – Always on time (Agent X mix) / ('A'-video).

Nov 02. (cd/d-lp) *<(063487-2/-1)>* **THE LAST TEMPTATION** [14] [4]
– Intro / Thug lovin' (with BOBBY BROWN) / Mesmerize (with ASHANTI) / Pop niggas / The pledge (remix with ASHANTI, NAS &

2PAC) / Murder reigns / Last temptation (with CHARLI BALTIMORE) / Murder me (with CADDILLAC TAH & ALEXI) / The warning / Connected (with EASTWOOD & CROOKED I) / Emerica (with YOUNG LIFE & CHINK SANTANA) / Rock star / Destiny (outro).

Dec 02. (c-s; by JA RULE & BOBBY BROWN) *(63787-4)* *<63770>* **THUG LOVIN' / THE PLEDGE** — 15 Nov02 — 42
(12"+=) *(63787-4)* – ('A'-remix) / The pledge (remix).
(cd-s++=) *(63787-2)* – ('A'-video).

Mar 03. (c-s; by JA RULE & ASHANTI) *(077958-4) <063773>* **MESMERIZE / (instrumental)** — 12 Jan03 — 2
(12"+=) *(077958-1)* – Between you and me (explicit) / Pop niggaz (explicit).
(cd-s++=) *(077958-2)* – ('A'-video).

Nov 03. (cd) *(9861329) <015770-2>* **BLOOD IN MY EYE** — 51 — 6
– Murder intro / The life (with HUSSEIN FATAL & CADDILLAC TAH) / Clap back / The crown (with SIZZLA) / Kay slay / Things gon' change – 2 punk ass quarter (by I. GOTTI) / Race against time II / Bobby creep / Niggas & bitches / The INC is back (with SHADOW, SEKOU 720 & BLACK CHILD) / Remo / Blood in my eye (with HUSSEIN FATAL). *(bonus +=)* – It's murda (with HUSSEIN FATAL) / The wrap (with HUSSEIN FATAL).

Nov 03. (12") *(9814619) <981461>* **REIGNS. / MURDER REIGNS (by Jay-Z) / CLAP BACK (instrumental)** — 9 — 44
(cd-s+=) *(9814618)* – ('A'-video) / Murder reigns (video).

Oct 04. (cd-s; JA RULE feat. R KELLY & ASHANTI) *(986460-6) <348211>* **WONDERFUL (mixes) / CAUGHT UP** — 1 Sep04 — 5
(12"+=) *(986460-4)* – ('A'-radio) / ('A'-instrumental).
(cd-s) *(986460-5)* – ('A') / Livin' it up / Always on time.

Nov 04. (cd/d-lp) *(9862918)(2995501) <295550-2/-1>* **R.U.L.E.** — 33 — 7
– The Inc intro / Last of the Mohicans / Wonderful / What's my name / New York / Stripping game (skit) / The manual / Get it started / R.U.L.E. / True story (skit) / Caught up / Gun talk / Never thought / Life goes on / Weed (skit) / Where I'm from / Bout my business / Passion.

Feb 05. (-) *<radio>* **NEW YORK** — – — 27

Apr 05. (cd-s; JA RULE feat. LLOYD) *(988123-5)* **CAUGHT UP / (instrumental)** — 20 — –
(12")(cd-s) *(988125-6)(988123-2)* – ('A') / New York / Better days.

Dec 05. (cd/d-lp) *(98873-28/-31) <581301>* **EXODUS** (compilation) — 50 —
– Exodus (intro) / Me / Holla holla / It's murda / Put it on me / I cry / Livin' it up / Always on time / Ain't it funny / Thug lovin' / Mesmerize / Clap back / New York / Wonderful / Never again / Daddy's little baby / Love me or hate me / Exodus (outro).

Joe JACKSON

Born: 11 Aug'54, Burton-On-Trent, Staffordshire, England, although raised from a very early age in Gosport, near Portsmouth. He left school with top grade music honour and enrolled at the Royal College Of Music in 1973. After a spell in JOHNNY DANKWORTH's NATIONAL YOUTH JAZZ ORCHESTRA, he joined pub rock outfit, ARMS & LEGS; they released three flop singles for 'M.A.M.' between 1976-1977, before he quit. In 1977, he became a musical director for 'Opportunity Knocks' (TV talent show, hosted by Hughie Green) winners, COFFEE AND CREAM (yuk!). The following year, he moved away from the cabaret scene to London, where he recorded demo tape, which A&M's David Kershenbaum approved, producing first solo attempt, 'IS SHE REALLY GOING OUT WITH HIM?' (it took a re-issue of this single in Summer 1979 to break him into UK and US charts). The debut album, 'LOOK SHARP!' (1979), subsequently hit the US Top 20, its jazzy new-wave power-pop and acerbic lyrics inevitably drawing comparisons with ELVIS COSTELLO. 'I'M THE MAN' (1979), and its accompanying UK Top 5 hit single, the sly 'IT'S DIFFERENT FOR GIRLS', carried on in a similar vein although JACKSON veered off into more unsettling, eclectic musical textures with 1980's self-produced 'BEAT CRAZY'. Although credited to the JOE JACKSON BAND, the line-up remained identical to that which had played on the first two releases, namely GRAHAM MABY, GARY SANFORD and DAVE HOUGHTON. For 'JOE JACKSON'S JUMPIN' JIVE' (1981), only the former remained from the original formation, an array of jazz musicians employed in a fairly successful attempt to update the 40's swing style of LOUIS JORDAN and CAB CALLOWAY. The exotic musical landscape of New York was JACKSON's next stop; having relocated to the Big Apple following the breakdown of his marriage, he proceeded to soak up the spicy latin jazz/salsa influences for his 'NIGHT AND DAY' (1982) album. A transatlantic Top 5 hit, it spawned JACKSON's biggest hit single to date in the dancefloor friendly 'STEPPIN' OUT' and eventually went gold. JACKSON recruited another new group of musicians for 'BODY AND SOUL' (1984), while 'BIG WORLD' was an ambitious live double set featuring all-new material recorded over three successive nights. The vocal-free 'WILL POWER' (1987) set saw JACKSON dabbling in classical orchestration and accordingly failed to chart, while the autobiographical 'BLAZE OF GLORY' (1989) covered all JACKSON's stylistic bases to date. A change of label to 'Virgin', saw the man pen his most direct, accessible material in years with 'LAUGHTER AND LUST' (1991), a welcome diversion from his constant experimentation. 'HEAVEN & HELL' (1997) was another classically influenced work comprised of seven pieces relating to the biblical seven deadly sins, the likes of SUZANNE VEGA and JANE SIBERRY guesting. Even more straightforward in its classical intentions, 'SYMPHONY No.1' (1999) was conceived as a symphonic piece although with the likes of STEVE VAI on board it never completely abandoned the realm of rock and jazz idioms. On a completely different note, 'SUMMER IN THE CITY: LIVE IN NEW YORK' (2000) documented a summer '99 gig wherein the breadth of JACKSON's musical reach was demonstrated in a choice of covers which ranged from Lovin' Spoonful and the Beatles ('ELEANOR RIGBY') to Duke Ellington's 'MOOD INDIGO'. Later the same year, JACKSON, always full of surprises, released 'NIGHT AND DAY II', a belated sequel to his early 80's classic. 2003's confusingly titled 'VOLUME 4', meanwhile, found JACKSON and BAND reunited for the first time in over twenty years. While any fan expecting a re-run of those late 70's glory years could only ever be in for a let-down, this was the most authentic and committed JACKSON had sounded for many a year, eclipsing most of his work since the early 80's. Live set, 'AFTERLIFE' (2004) continued the band theme, finally revisiting the new wave nuggets he first made his name with.

• **Covered:** OH WELL (Fleetwood Mac) / MAKING PLANS FOR NIGE[L] (Xtc). • **Trivia:** He also produced The KEYS in '81, and reggae outfits RASSE[L] and The TOASTERS.

Album rating: LOOK SHARP! (*8) / I'M THE MAN (*7) / BEAT CRAZY (*7) / JUMPIN' JIVE (*7) / NIGHT AND DAY (*7) / BODY AND SOUL (*5) / MIKE MURDER part soundtrack (*6) / BIG WORLD (*5) / WILL POWER (*4) / LIVE . . . 1980-1986 (*6) / TUCKER: THE MAN AND HIS DREAM soundtra[ck] (*7) / BLAZE OF GLORY (*5) / STEPPIN' OUT – THE VERY BEST OF JO[E] JACKSON compilation (*8) / LAUGHTER AND LUST (*5) / NIGHT MUSIC (*3) / GREATEST HITS compilation (*8) / THIS IS IT! THE A&M YEARS compilati[on] (*8) / HEAVEN & HELL (*3) / SYMPHONY NO.1 (*4) / SUMMER IN TH[E] CITY – LIVE IN NEW YORK (*5) / NIGHT AND DAY II (*4) / VOLUME 4 (*6) / AFTERLIFE (*6)

ARMS AND LEGS

JOE JACKSON – piano, violin, vocals, harmonica / **MARK ANDREWS** – vocals / **GRAHAM MABY** – bass

M.A.M. — not i[ssued]

Apr 76. (7") *(MAM 140)* **JANICE. / SHE'LL SURPRISE YOU** — — –

Aug 76. (7") *(MAM 147)* **HEAT OF THE NIGHT. / GOOD TIMES** — — –

Feb 77. (7") *(MAM 156)* **IS THERE ANY MORE WINE. / SHE'LL SURPRISE YOU** — — –

JOE JACKSON

solo – lead vocals, piano with backing band **GRAHAM MABY** – bass / **GA[RY] SANFORD** – guitar / **DAVE HOUGHTON** – drums

A&M A&M

Sep 78. (7") *(AMS 7392)* <2132> **IS SHE REALLY GOING OUT WITH HIM? / (DO THE) INSTANT MASH** [ ] May79 [21]

Jan 79. (lp/c) *(AMLH/CAM 64743)* <4743> **LOOK SHARP!** [40] [20]
– One more time / Sunday papers / Is she really going out with him? / Happy loving couples / Throw it away / Baby stick around / Look sharp! / Fools in love / (Do the) Instant mash / Pretty girls / Got the time. *(re-iss. Aug79 on white-lp; same) (re-iss. Mar82; AMID 120) (re-iss. Sep84 on 'Hallmark' lp/c; SHM/HSC 3154) (cd-iss. Nov84; CDA 64743) (re-iss. 1988 lp/c; AMA/AMC 3187) (cd re-iss. Oct92; CDMID 115)*

Feb 79. (7") *(AMS 7413)* **SUNDAY PAPERS. / LOOK SHARP!** [ ] [–]

May 79. (7"/10"white) *(AMS/+P 7433)* **ONE MORE TIME. / DON'T ASK ME** [ ] [–]

Jul 79. (7") *(AMS 7459)* **IS SHE REALLY GOING OUT WITH HIM?. / YOU GOT THE FEVER** [13] [–]

Aug 79. (7") *<2186>* **IT'S DIFFERENT FOR GIRLS. / COME ON** [–] [ ]

Oct 79. (7") *(AMS 7479)* *<2209>* **I'M THE MAN. / COME ON (live)** [ ] [ ]

Oct 79. (lp/c)(5x7"box) *(AMLH/CAM 64794)(none)* <4794> **I'M THE MAN** [12] [22]
– On your radio / Geraldine and John / Kinda kute / It's different for girls / I'm the man / The band wore blue shirts / Don't wanna be like that / Amateur hour / Get that girl / Friday. *(cd-iss. 1988; CDA 3221) (cd re-iss. Oct92; CDMID 117)*

Dec 79. (7") *(AMS 7493)* **IT'S DIFFERENT FOR GIRLS. / FRIDAY** [5] [–]

Mar 80. (7") *(AMS 7513)* **KINDA KUTE. / GERALDINE AND JOHN** [ ] [–]

JOE JACKSON BAND

un 80. (7"/7"w-poster) *(AMS/+P 7536)* **THE HARDER THEY COME. / OUT OF STYLE / TILT** [ ] [–]

Oct 80. (7") *(AMS 7563)* **MAD AT YOU. / ENOUGH IS NOT ENOUGH** [ ] [–]

Oct 80. (lp/c) *(AMLH/CAM 64837)* <4837> **BEAT CRAZY** [42] [41]
– Beat crazy / One to one / In every dream home (a nightmare) / The evil eye / Mad at you / Crime don't pay / Someone up there / Battleground / Biology / Pretty boys / Fit. *(cd-iss. 1988; CDA 3241)*

Nov 80. (7") *<2276>* **ONE TO ONE. / ENOUGH IS NOT ENOUGH** [–] [ ]

an 81. (7") *(AMS 8100)* **BEAT CRAZY. / IS SHE REALLY GOING OUT WITH HIM?** [ ] [–]

Mar 81. (7") *(AMS 8116)* **ONE TO ONE. / SOMEONE UP THERE** [ ] [–]

JOE JACKSON'S JUMPIN' JIVE

OE retained **GRAHAM MABY** plus **PETE THOMAS** – sax / **RAUOL OLIVERA** – trumpet / **DAVE BITELI** – wind instr. NICK WELDON – piano / **LARRY TOLFREE** – drums / **NICK WELDON** – piano

un 81. (7") *(AMS 8145)* *<2365>* **JUMPIN' JIVE. / KNOCK ME A KISS** [43] [ ]

un 81. (lp/c) *(AMLH/CAM 68530)* <4871> **JOE JACKSON'S JUMPIN' JIVE** [14] [42]
– Jumpin' with symphony Sid / Jack, you're dead / Is you or is you ain't my baby / We the cats will help ya / San Francisco fan / Five guys named Moe / Jumpin' jive / You run your mouth (and I'll run my business) / What's the use of getting sober (when you're gonna get drunk again) / You're my meat / Tuxedo junction / How long must I wait for you. *(cd-iss. 1988; CDA 3271) (re-iss. May93 on 'Spectrum' cd/c; 550062-2/-4)*

ug 81. (7") *(AMS 8161)* **JACK, YOU'RE DEAD. / FIVE GUYS NAMED MOE** [ ] [–]

JOE JACKSON

— **SUE HADJOPOULOS** – percussion, flute; repl. WELDON + horns

un 82. (7"pic-d) *(AMS 8231)* **REAL MEN. / CHINATOWN** [ ] [–]

un 82. (lp/c) *(AMLH/CAM 64906)* <4906> **NIGHT AND DAY** [3] [4]
– Another world / Chinatown / T.V. age / Target / Steppin' out / Breaking us in two / Cancer / Real men / A slow song. *(cd-iss. 1983; CDA 64906) (re-iss. Oct92 cd/c; CD/C MID 158)*

ug 82. (7") *(AMS 8247)* **BREAKING US IN TWO. / EL BLANCO** [ ] [–]

ug 82. (7") *<2428>* **STEPPIN' OUT. / CHINATOWN** [–] [6]

Oct 82. (7") *(AMS 8262)* **STEPPIN' OUT. / ANOTHER WORLD** [6] [–]

Jan 83. (7") *<2510>* **BREAKING US IN TWO. / TARGET** [–] [18]

Feb 83. (7") *(AM 101)* **BREAKING US IN TWO. / EL BLANCO** [59] [–]
(12"+=) *(AMX 101)* – T.V. age.

May 83. (7") *(AM 114)* **A SLOW SONG. / REAL MEN** [ ] [–]

Jul 83. (7") *<2548>* **ANOTHER WORLD. / ORTO MUNDO** [–] [ ]

— added **JOY ASKEW** – synthesizers

Aug 83. (7") *(AM 134)* **COSMOPOLITAN. / BREAKDOWN** [ ] [–]

Sep 83. (lp/c) *(AMLH/CAM 64931)* *<SP/CS 4931>* **MIKE'S MURDER (soundtrack)** [ ] [64]
– Cosmopolitan / 1-2-3- go (this town's a fairground) / Laundromat Monday / Memphis / Moonlight / Zemeo / Breakdown / Moonlight theme.

Nov 83. (7") *<2601>* **MEMPHIS. / BREAKDOWN** [–] [85]

— retained only **MABY** and brought in **GARY BURKE** – drums / **VINNIE ZUMMO** – guitar / **ED ROYNESDAL** – keyboards, violin / **TONY AIELLO** – sax, flute / **MICHAEL MORREALE** – wind

Mar 84. (lp/c) *(AMLX/CXM 65000)* <5000> **BODY AND SOUL** [14] [20]
– The verdict / Cha cha loco / Not here, not now / You can't get what you want ('till you know what you want) / Go for it / Loisaida / Be my number two / Heart of ice. *(cd-iss. Oct84; CXM 65000) (cd re-iss. Oct92; CDMID 118)*

Apr 84. (7"/12") *(AM/+X 186)* *<2635>* **HAPPY ENDING. / LOISAIDA** [58] Jul84 [57]

Jun 84. (7") *(AM 200)* **BE MY NUMBER TWO. / IS SHE REALLY GOING OUT WITH HIM?** [70] [–]
(7") *(AMX 200)* – ('A'side) / Heart of ice.

Sep 84. (7") *(AM 212)* *<2628>* **YOU CAN'T GET WHAT YOU WANT ('TILL YOU KNOW WHAT YOU WANT). / CHA CHA LOCO** [ ] Apr84 [15]
(12"+=) *(AMX 212)* – ('A' dub version).

— **RICK FORD** – bass, guitar, vox repl. MABY, AIELLO, ROYNESDAL + MORREALE

Mar 86. (3.sided.d-lp/c/cd) *(JWA/JWC/JWD 3)* *<6021>* **BIG WORLD (live)** [41] [34]
– Wild west / Right and wrong / (It's a) Big world / Precious time / Tonight and forever / Shanghai sky / Fifty dollar love affair / We can't live together / Forty years / Survival / Soul kiss / The jet-set / Tango Atlantico / Hometown / Man in the street.

Apr 86. (7") *(AM 312)* *<2829>* **RIGHT OR WRONG. / BREAKING US IN TWO (live)** [ ] [ ]
(12"+=) *(AMY 312)* – I'm the man (live).

Jun 86. (7"/12") *(AM/+Y 324)* **HOME TOWN. / TANGO ATLANTICO** [ ] [–]

Jun 86. (7") *<2847>* **HOME TOWN. / I'M THE MAN (live)** [–] [ ]

Apr 87. (lp/c/cd) *(<AMA/AMC/CDA 3908>)* **WILL POWER** [ ] [ ]
– No Pasaran / Solitude / Will power / Nocturne / Symphony in one movement. *(cd re-iss. Apr89 on 'Mobile Fidelity'; UDCD 503)*

May 87. (7") *<2944>* **WILL POWER. / NOCTURNE** [–] [ ]

Apr 88. (7") *(AM 441)* **JUMPIN' JIVE (live). / MEMPHIS (live)** [ ] [ ]
(12"+=) *(AMY 441)* – You can't get what you want (till you know what you want).

May 88. (d-lp/c/cd) *(<AMA/AMC/CDA 6706>)* **LIVE 1980/86 (live)** [66] [91]
– One to one / I'm the man / Beat crazy / Is she really going out with him? / Cancer / Don't wanna be like that / On your radio / Fools in love / Cancer / Is she really going out with him? (acappella version) / Look sharp! / Sunday papers / Real men / Is she really going out with him? (acoustic) / Memphis / A slow song / Be my number two / Breaking us in two / It's different for girls / You can't get what you want ('till you know what you want) / Jumpin' jive / Steppin' out.

Jun 88. (7") *<1207>* **LOOK SHARP (live). / MEMPHIS (live)** [–] [ ]

Aug 88. (7") *(AM 481)* *<1228>* **(HE'S A) SHAPE IN A DRAPE. / SPEEDWAY** [ ] [ ]
(12"+=) *(AMY 481)* – Sometime in Chicago.

Nov 88. (lp/c/cd) *(<AMA/AMC/CDA 3917>)* **TUCKER: THE MAN AND HIS DREAM** (soundtrack) [ ] [ ]
– Captain of industry (overture) / Car of tomorrow . . . today! / No chance blues / (He's a) Shape in a drape / Factory / Vera / It pays to advertise / Tiger rag / Showtime in Chicago / Lone bank loan blues / Speedway / Marilee / Hangin' in Howard Hughes' hangar / The toast of the town / Abe's blues / The trial / Freedom swing – Tucker jingle / Rhythm delivery.

— Now with 10-piece line-up, **MABY, ZUMMO, BURKE, ASKEW, AIELLO, FORD, ROYNESDAL, HADJOPOULOS + TOM TEELEY** – guitar / **ANTHONY COX** – bass

Apr 89. (lp/c/cd) *(<AMA/AMC/CDA 5249>)* **BLAZE OF GLORY** [36] [61]
– Tomorrow's child / Me and you (against the world) / Down to London / Sentimental thing / Acropolis now / Blaze of glory / Rant and rave / Nineteen forever / The best I can do / Evil empire / Discipline / The uman touch.

May 89. (7") *(AM 506) <1404>* **NINETEEN FOREVER. / ACROPOLIS NOW (instrumental)** [ ] [ ]
(cd-s+=) *(CDEE 506)* – ('A'extended).

Oct 89. (7") *(AM 512)* **DOWN TO LONDON. / YOU CAN'T GET WHAT YOU WANT (TIL YOU KNOW WHAT YOU WANT)** [ ] [–]
(cd-s+=) *(CDEE 512)* – Sunday papers.

Aug 90. (7"/c-s) *(AM/+MC 583)* **STEPPIN' OUT (re-mix). / SENTIMENTAL THING** [ ] [–]
(cd-s+=) *(AMCD 583)* – It's a big worth.

Sep 90. (cd/c/lp) *(397052-2/-4/-1)* **STEPPIN' OUT – THE VERY BEST OF JOE JACKSON** (compilation) [7] [–]
– Is she really going out with him? / Fools in love / I'm the man / It's different for girls / Beat crazy / Jumpin' jive / Breaking us in two / Steppin' out / Slow song (live) / You can't get what you want ('till you know what you want) / Be my number two / Right and wrong / Home town / Down to London / Nineteen forever.

Virgin America | Virgin America

Apr 91. (c-s) *(VUSC 40)* **STRANGER THAN FICTION. / DROWNING** [ ] [–]
(cd-s+=) *(VUSCD 40)* – It's different for girls (acoustic).

Apr 91. (cd/c/lp) *(CDVUS/VUSMC/VUSLP 34) <91628>* **LAUGHTER & LUST** [41] [ ]
– Obvious song / Goin' downtown / Stranger than fiction / Oh well / Jamie G / Hit single / It's all too much / When you're not around / The other me / Trying to cry / My house / The old songs / Drowning.

Oct 94. (cd/c) *(CDVUS/VUSMS 78) <39880>* **NIGHT MUSIC** [ ] [ ]
– Nocturne No.1 / Flying nocturne No.2 / Ever after / The man who wrote Danny Boy / Nocturne No.3 / Lullaby / Only the future / Nocturne No.4 / Sea of secrets.

Sony Classical | Sony Classical

Sep 97. (cd) *<60273>* **HEAVEN & HELL** [–] [ ]
– Prelude / Fugue 1 – More is more (gluttony) / Angel (lust) / Tuzla (avarice) / Passacaglia – A bud and a slice (sloth) / Right (anger) / The bridge (envy) / Fugue 2 – Song of Daedalus (pride).

Oct 99. (cd) *(<SK 64435>)* **SYMPHONY NO.1** [ ] [ ]
– First movement / Fast movement / Slow movement / Last movement.

Jun 00. (cd) *(<SK 89237>)* **SUMMER IN THE CITY: LIVE IN NEW YORK (live)** [ ] May00 [ ]
– Summer in the city / Obvious song / Another world / Fools in love – For your love / Mood indigo / The crowd – Down to London / Eleanor Rigby / Be my number two / Home town / It's different for girls / King of the world / You can't get what you want / One more time.
(above also credited **GRAHAM MABY + GARY BURKE**

Sony Jazz | Sony Jazz

Oct 00. (cd) *(<SK 89261>)* **NIGHT AND DAY II** [ ] [ ]
– Prelude / Hall of a town / Stranger than you / Why / Glamour and pain / Dear mom / Love got lost / Just because / Happyland / Stay.

JOE JACKSON BAND

JOE with **GARY SANFORD** – guitar / **GRAHAM MABY** – bass / **DAVE HOUGHTON** – drums

Rykodisc | Rykodisc

Mar 03. (cd) *(<RCD 10639>)* **VOLUME 4** [ ] [ ]
– Take it like a man / Still alive / Awkward age / Chrome / Love at first light / Fairy dust / Little bit stupid / Blue flame / Dirty martini / Thugz 'R' us / Bright grey. *(<ltd-d-cd iss.+=; RCD 10638>)* – live:- One more time / Is she really going out with him? / On your radio / Got the time / It's different for girls / I'm the man.

Jul 03. (cd-s) *(RCD 51074)* **CHROME / IS SHE REALLY GOING OUT WITH HIM? (live) / COULDN'T I JUST TELL YOU** [ ] [–]

Mar 04. (cd) *(<RCD 10665>)* **AFTERLIFE** [ ] [ ]
– Steppin' out / One more time / Take it like a man / Awkward age / Look sharp! / Down to London / Beat crazy / Fools in love / Love at first light / Fairy dust / Sunday papers / Don't wanna be like that / Got the time.

– compilations, etc. –

Oct 93. (d-cd) *A&M; (CDA 24121)* **NIGHT AND DAY / LOOK SHARP!** [ ] [–]

Mar 96. (cd-s) *A&M; (581396)* **STEPPIN' OUT** [ ] [–]

May 96. (cd) *A&M; <540524>* **GREATEST HITS** [–] [ ]

Feb 97. (d-cd) *A&M; (540402-2)* **THIS IS IT! THE A&M YEARS** [ ] [ ]

Jul 00. (cd) *Universal; (E 497277-2)* **UNIVERSAL MASTERS COLLECTION** [ ] [–]

Feb 01. (cd) *Spectrum; (<544513-2>)* **THE COLLECTION** [ ] Apr01 [ ]

Michael JACKSON (& the JACKSONS)

Born: 29 Aug'58, Gary, Indiana, USA. Brought up in a family of child prodigies guided by musician father, JOE (no, not that one!), MICHAEL was groomed for a lead vocal spot from an early age, soon taking pole position alongside his brothers (JACKIE, TITO, JERMAINE and MARLON) in the all singing, all dancing JACKSON 5. Musically inspired by legendary 'Godfather' of soul, JAMES BROWN, along with the choreographed moves of Motown's best acts, this youthful posse initially recorded a couple of tracks for small local label, 'Steeltown', having proved themselves in the prestigious talent contests of The Apollo Theater in New York. Inevitably, the group were subsequently signed up by 'Motown' in 1968, the label quick to spot the potential of a group who were perfect for moulding and developing in their established style. Label guru Berry Gordy moved the family en masse to Hollywood, got the crack in-house team of writers on the job (it's rumoured 'Motown initially refused to use the group's own material) and sharpened up their moves before eventually releasing a debut single in late '69 'I WANT YOU BACK'. The label had struck gold yet again and the single became the first of four consecutive US No.1 hits, its pre-pubescent naivety and sugary charm a winning formula (and a treasure trove for hip hop samplers) which saw the classic 'ABC' 'THE LOVE YOU SAVE' and 'I'LL BE THERE' all topping the charts in quick succession. Like many soul outfits, The JACKSON 5 were primarily a singles venture and while albums such as 'DIANA ROSS PRESENTS THE JACKSON 5' (1970), 'ABC' (1970) and 'THE THIRD ALBUM' (1971) had more than their fair share of filler, the emotional charge of the early hits can still get a dancefloo grinning ear to ear. After another clutch of Top 20 single in '71 (including the timeless 'NEVER CAN SAY GOODBYE') MICHAEL was singled out for a solo career, debuting with th ballad, 'GOT TO BE THERE' early the following year. The singl was a transatlantic Top 5 smash, MICHAEL JACKSON the pop sta had arrived; the album of the same name hit the American To 20, while a sassy cover of Bobby Day's 'ROCKIN' ROBIN' repeate the success of the debut. His most famous hit of the era, howeve arrived in the shape of the syrupy 'BEN', an unlikely ode to a pet ra Although the track gave MICHAEL the first No.1 of his illustriou career, the ensuing few years would see commercial fortunes take bit of a back seat, both for him and his brothers (with whom he wa maintaining a parallel career in The JACKSON 5). From the head heights of starring in their very own cartoon series, the JACKSON began to struggle as they made the transistion from using 'Motown' penned material to writing their own stuff, the proto-disco of the 'DANCING MACHINE' (1974) album rejuvenating the somewhat despite it being their penultimate set for the label. The (all but JERMAINE who stayed with 'Motown' and was replace by younger brother RANDY) finally jumped ship for 'Epic' in 197 (presumably procuring a better royalty rate than the whoppin 2.7% they'd been getting at 'Motown'), although GORDY sue them for alleged breach of contract the following year and they we obliged to change their name to the JACKSONS; the case was finally settled at the turn of the decade with the siblings paying GORDY a tidy sum and giving up the rights to the JACKSON 5 name. Ensconced at 'Epic', the brothers enjoyed almost instant succes in 1976 with Top 10 hit, 'ENJOY YOURSELF', while the second single lifted from the eponymous major label debut album, 'SHOW YOU THE WAY TO GO', became the family's first UK No.1. In line with the burgeoning disco craze, the JACKSON's adopted a tougher, more mature sound as the decade wore on, the 'DESTINY' (1979) album spawning such enduring glitterball favourites as 'BLAME IT ON THE BOOGIE' and 'SHAKE YOUR BODY (DOWN TO THE GROUND)'. MICHAEL was also developing his stunning vocal prowess, his seminal solo set, 'OFF THE WALL' (released the same year) seeing the singer reinvented as a boogie-down pop powerhouse, sophisticated yet gloriously loose limbed. Seasoned producer/arranger QUINCY JONES was JACKSON's creative foil for the project, the pair having met while working on 'The Wiz', a commercially disastrous attempt at revamping the 'Wizard Of Oz' musical in an Afro-American stylee. JONES' expertise seemingly freed MICHAEL up to put in a career best performance on such electric material as 'DON'T STOP 'TIL YOU GET ENOUGH' (a massive transatlantic hit and a US No.1), 'ROCK WITH YOU' (another to top the American charts) and tear-jerker 'SHE'S OUT OF MY LIFE'. The album itself – a milestone in pop/soul – went on to become a multi-million worldwide seller and secure a place in history as the first record by a solo artist to spawn four consecutive Top 10 hits. Its success also had a knock-on effect for the subsequent JACKSONS album, 'TRIUMPH' (1980), which sold in bucketloads and prompted a huge US tour, wherein MICHAEL took the opportunity to develop his solo material and work on the moves which would eventually flower into his celebrated stage show. The next phase in the singer's solo career came as he and JONES reunited in 1982 to work on an obscure spoken word set based on the 'E.T.' movie (the record was subsequently withdrawn due to legal problems) before beginning work on a follow-up proper, the legendary 'THRILLER'. Quite literally the biggest selling album in the world . . . ever (40-odd million and counting), JACKSON's second masterpiece was released in late '82, and despite its predecessor's plaudits, few could've predicted the stratospheric commercial heights it would scale. Previewed by the PAUL McCARTNEY duet, 'THE GIRL IS MINE' (which almost reached the US Top spot), the 'THRILLER' phenomenon only really kicked into gear with the release of 'BILLIE JEAN' early the following year, a huge UK/US No.1 which set an ice-cool, tightrope disco-pop groove to a blinding visual backdrop of fleet-footed, snake-hipped choreography and revolutionary effects. Next up was the compulsive 'BEAT IT', a throbbing dancefloor killer utilising the guitar wizardry of EDDIE VAN HALEN and, incredibly, the first video by a black artist to be aired on MTV. JACKSON was now at the cutting edge of the all-important video medium (still in relative infancy) as it mushroomed with the all-pervasive influence of the aforementioned MTV; not content with merely recording the greatest selling album in history, JACKSON went ahead and filmed the most popular, the most talked about, and possibly the most hyped video in history. The near quarter of an hour long promo for 'THRILLER' (the single) came with the added kudos of JOHN LANDIS (director) and VINCENT PRICE (spook voice-over), featuring JACKSON strutting his funky stuff (he'd already debuted his legendary 'moonwalk' on American TV) amid a cast of moonlit grotesqueries. The film's mildly controversial content also marked his first, but by no means his last, major encounter with critical pressure (this time around a fairly mild fracas with his fellow Jehovah's Witnesses). Nevertheless, the hits kept on coming, JACKSON scoring with a further three hits from the album, the jittering 'WANNA BE STARTIN' SOMETHING', 'HUMAN NATURE' and 'P.Y.T. (PRETTY YOUNG THING)'. At the tail end of '83, he also enjoyed a further extended run at the top of the charts with another PAUL McCARTNEY duet, 'SAY SAY SAY' (from the latter's 'Pipes Of Peace' album), the singer's newfound superstar status netting him a record breaking sponsorship deal with Pepsi. While recording a commercial for the company, an accident led to JACKSON suffering second-degree burns requiring scalp and facial treatment. Much has since been made of JACKSON's alleged cosmetic surgery, and while the singer has constantly denied it, the evidence that he's become progressively "whiter" is in-your-face as it were, or indeed his face. While a whole book could probably be devoted to JACKSON's more colourful behaviour, surely any sentient being would struggle to cope with the pressure of following up such a colossal artistic and commercial feat. In the immediate aftermath of 'THRILLER's success, JACKSON recorded a further album with his brothers, 'VICTORY' (1984), and reluctantly undertook an ecstatically received, yet turbulent tour, the last time he'd perform/record with The JACKSONS as a group. Although the singer subsequently helped pen the huge USA For Africa famine-relief single, 'WE ARE THE WORLD', more controversy followed as he snapped up the rights to the catalogue of music publishers, ATV. This included the bulk of BEATLES material penned by LENNON/McCARTNEY, and, surprisingly enough, no further JACKSON/McCARTNEY collaborations ensued. Instead, JACKSON once again hooked up with QUINCY JONES to record a belated follow-up album, 'BAD' (1987). Previewed by a duet with SIEDAH GARRETT, 'I JUST CAN'T STOP LOVING YOU' (another transatlantic No.1), the album once again topped the charts in too many countries to mention and spawned a further four US No.1's, 'THE WAY YOU MAKE ME FEEL', 'MAN IN THE MIRROR', 'DIRTY DIANA' and the title track. Inevitably, the record paled in comparison to what had gone before, both commercially and artistically, even though its sales figures would've counted as blockbusting had they been enjoyed by almost any other artist. He did manage to break one record though, with the accompanying world tour, a gargantuan feat of logistical mastery which was touted as the biggest operation of its kind so far. The late 80's also saw the publication of JACKSON's autobiography, 'Moonwalker', though if fans were hoping for any juicy insights into what made the man tick, they were sorely disappointed. More newsworthy was his record breaking new contract with 'Sony', a multi-media billion dollar deal in which the singer negotiated, amongst other things, a sizable royalty rate, humungous advances and his own label (MJJ) to play around with. The first release under the new agreement was 1991's 'DANGEROUS' opus, JACKSON partially opting for a more street smart sound on tracks such as 'WHY YOU WANNA TRIP ON ME' and 'IN THE CLOSET', the pared-back style courtesy of New Jack Swing maestro, Teddy Riley. The biggest hits, however, 'BLACK OR WHITE' (a transatlantic No.1 addressing the controversy over his skin colour), 'HEAL THE WORLD' etc., were in the patented JACKSON style. The resulting world tour was plagued with misfortune and bad press; JACKSON attracted flak for his alleged arrogance during the African leg of the jaunt, while persistent poor health forced the singer to cancel a number of European shows after collapsing onstage at Wembley Stadium in London. The following year proved even worse, the tabloid machine going into overkill following allegations of sexual impropriety with a 13-year old boy. JACKSON strenuously denied the charge, although, bearing in mind the singer's family appeal, the controversy looked set to wreak havoc on his career. His love of children was already well publicised; the singer regularly invited underprivileged kids to his Neverland theme home, while he'd also set up the 'Heal The World Foundation' to tackle child-based issues. Opinion was understandably split although the press had a field day with the reclusive star, endlessly speculating on the reality behind the accusations. The pressure became too much and the exhausted JACKSON subsequently sought help for an addiction to painkillers before returning to the US to face the music; in the event, he reputedly paid off a sum of between 13 and 30 million dollars to the boy and his family, the LAPD also finally dropping a rumoured criminal case. Though some saw the settlement as a tacit admission of guilt, JACKSON emerged relatively unscathed (commercially at least) from the scandal; while he lost his Pepsi sponsorship, sales of 'DANGEROUS' didn't suffer too badly and he signed a new multi-million dollar deal with 'E.M.I' to handle his ATV catalogue. More surprises were in store as JACKSON announced his marriage to Lisa Marie Presley (ELVIS' daughter) in late '94, doubters proved correct when the relationship hit the rocks less than two years later. On the recording front, he was back in the news again by summer '95, an astronomically expensive video for the 'SCREAM' single (a duet with sister JANET) and a semi-retrospective double set, 'HIStory – PAST, PRESENT AND FUTURE, BOOK 1' ensuring media hyperbole. The latter set predictably topped the charts everywhere, while two new tracks, 'YOU ARE NOT ALONE' and 'EARTH SONG' (his best song ever!?) both topped the UK charts, another unprecedented feat for the veteran pop star. While JACKSON, in all his egocentric, asexual eccentricity, continues to be adored by fanatical fans the world over, some remain less impressed; just ask PULP's JARVIS COCKER, who took such a dislike to JACKSON's Christ-like appearance (rather unadvisedly with 'beggar' children in tow) during his 1997 Brit Awards performance that he invaded the stage and caused another press beano, this time with JACKSON as the victim rather than the villain. Despite everything, MICHAEL JACKSON remains a mythic figure, his increasingly rare recorded output unlikely to yield any clues and even more unlikely to match the towering standards of his early 80's heyday. The optimistically titled 'INVINCIBLE' (2001) opened yet another decade in the MICHAEL JACKSON saga although this time around, in a surprising lack of bad press, the music was forced to do the talking. Another US and UK No.1, the record benefitted from a raft of outside writing talent although apart from sounding convincingly modern, it was hardly the great comeback effort his career needed. In fact, JACKSON's career took a massive nosedive (so to speak) when, from a surgical mask, he revealed what was left of his nose due to cosmetic surgery. Days later, the phantom JACKO horrified even his most ardent fans and certainly the press by dangling his 11-month baby son over the balcony on the 7th floor of a German hotel – who's bad indeed. A subsequent Martin Bashir special TV report also didn't show the King Of Pop at his best and, with MICHAEL stating some children slept with him in his room at his Neverland ranch, police were called into action. In November 2003, with a compilation of his best work (entitled 'NUMBER ONES') at No.1 in the charts, the California police raided Neverland and in turn charged him with child molestation. Over the course of a near two-year media circus, JACKSON's case polarised public opinion, his hardcore fans coming to his defence while the TV audiences were left to make up their own mind on the daily turn of events. From spring '05 until his acquital of the ten charges that June (13th), the jury, the commentators and the rest of the world were in "Neverland" about the truth behind the accusations. While EMINEM made his own comment on the case with his controversial video for 'Just Lose It', JACKSON's own backlog of 20 video-singles hit the UK charts from February 2006. JACKSON, himself, meanwhile, has retreated to the shores of Bahrain, from where it's still possible he may yet have a comeback.

• **Songwriters:** JACKSON 5 singles covered NEVER CAN SAY GOODBYE (Clifton Davis) / LITTLE BITTY PRETTY ONE (Thurston Harris) / DOCTOR MY EYES (Jackson Browne) / FOREVER CAME TODAY (Supremes) / etc. The JACKSONS:- BLAME IT ON THE BOOGIE (Mick Jackson; no relation). MICHAEL covered ROCKIN' ROBIN (Bobby Day) / AIN'T NO SUNSHINE (Bill Withers) / GIRLFRIEND (Paul McCartney; who he also had two Top 3 duets with) / COME TOGETHER (Beatles). • **Miscellaneous:** In the late 80's, the Jackson family was at the centre of a controversial allegation by daughter/singer LaTOYA, who stated in a book and on US TV, that she was beaten as a child by her/their father. This divided the family into either defending their father or saying nothing. LaTOYA, of course had recently shocked them all by baring herself in the centre spread of Playboy magazine.

Album rating: GOT TO BE THERE (*5) / BEN (*6) / MUSIC AND ME (*4) / FOREVER MICHAEL (*4) / THE BEST OF MICHAEL JACKSON compilation (*6) / OFF THE WALL (*8) / THRILLER (*10) / BAD (*7) / DANGEROUS (*6) / HIStory: PAST, PRESENT AND FUTURE – BOOK 1 part compilation (*8) / BLOOD ON THE DANCE FLOOR: HIStory In The Mix (*5) / INVINCIBLE (*5) / NUMBER ONES compilation (*8) / THE ULTIMATE COLLECTION the best Jackson 5/Jacksons compilation (*8) / THE ESSENTIAL MICHAEL JACKSON compilation (*8)

the JACKSON 5

MICHAEL JACKSON – lead vocals / **JACKIE JACKSON** (b.SIGMUND, 4 May'51) – vocals / **TITO JACKSON** (b.TORIANO, 15 Oct'53) – vocals / **JERMAINE JACKSON** (b.11 Dec'54) – vocals / **MARLON JACKSON** (b.12 Mar'57) – vocals

		not iss.		Steeltown
1968.	(7") *<681>* **BIG BOY. / YOU'VE CHANGED**	–		
1969.	(7") *<684>* **SOME GIRLS WANT ME FOR THEIR LOVE. / YOU DON'T HAVE TO BE 21 TO FALL IN LOVE** *<re-iss. 1980s on 'Dynamo'; 146>*	–		
		Tamla Motown		Motown
Jan 70.	(7") *(TMG 724) <1157>* **I WANT YOU BACK. / WHO'S LOVING YOU** *(re-iss. Oct81)*	2	Nov69	1
Mar 70.	(7") *<1163>* **ABC. / IT'S ALL IN THE GAME**	–		1
Apr 70.	(lp) *(STML 11142) <700>* **DIANA ROSS PRESENTS THE JACKSON 5** – Zip-a dee doo-dah / Nobody / I want you back / Can you remember / Standing in the shadows of love / You've changed / My Cherie amour / Who's loving you / Chained / I'm losing you / Stand / Born to save you. *(re-iss. Aug81)*	16	Jan70	5
May 70.	(7") *(TMG 738)* **ABC. / THE YOUNG FOLKS**	8		–
Jul 70.	(7") *(TMG 746) <1166>* **THE LOVE YOU SAVE. / I FOUND THAT GIRL**	7	May70	1
Aug 70.	(lp) *(STML 11156) <709>* **ABC** – The love you save / One more chance / ABC / Come round here (I'm the one you need) / Don't know why I love you / Never had a dream come true / True love can be beautiful / La la means I love you / I'll bet you / I found that girl / The young folks. *(re-iss. Jun82)*	22	May70	4
Nov 70.	(7") *(TMG 758) <1171>* **I'LL BE THERE. / ONE MORE CHANCE**	4	Sep70	1
Dec 70.	(7") *<1174>* **SANTA CLAUS IS COMING TO TOWN. / CHRISTMAS WON'T BE THE SAME THIS YEAR**	–		
Dec 70.	(lp) *(STML 11168) <713>* **THE JACKSON 5 CHRISTMAS ALBUM** (festive – hit No.1 US Xmas chart) *(cd-iss. Nov94 on 'Spectrum')*			
Feb 71.	(lp) *(STML 11174) <718>* **THE THIRD ALBUM** – I'll be there / Ready or not here I come / Oh how happy / Bridge over troubled water / Can I see you in the morning / Goin' back to Indiana / How funky is your chicken / Mama's pearl / Reach in / The love I saw in you was just a mirage / Darling dear. *(re-iss. Mar82) (cd-iss. Sep93)*		Sep70	4
Apr 71.	(7") *(TMG 769) <1177>* **MAMA'S PEARL. / DARLING DEAR**	25	Jan71	2
Jun 71.	(7") *(TMG 778) <1179>* **NEVER CAN SAY GOODBYE. / SHE'S GOOD**	33	Mar71	2
Jul 71.	(7") *<1186>* **MAYBE TOMORROW. / I WILL FIND A WAY**	–		20
Oct 71.	(lp) *(STML 11188) <735>* **MAYBE TOMORROW** – Maybe tomorrow / She's good / Never can say goodbye / The wall / Petals / 16 Candles / (We've got) blue skies / My little baby / It's great to be here / Honey chile / I will find a way. *(cd-iss. Aug93)*		Apr71	11
Oct 71.	(lp) *<742>* **GOIN' BACK TO INDIANA (TV Soundtrack)** – (contained live hits from TV show)	–		16

Mar 72. (7") *(TMG 809)* <1194> **SUGAR DADDY. / I'M SO HAPPY** [ ] Dec71 [10]

Sep 72. (lp) *(STML 11212)* <741> **THE JACKSON 5 GREATEST HITS** (compilation) [26] Jan72 [12]
(re-iss. Mar 82, re-iss. +cd.Feb88)

MICHAEL JACKSON

started solo career as well on same label.

Jan 72. (7") *(TMG 797)* <1191> **GOT TO BE THERE. / MARIA (YOU WERE THE ONLY ONE)** [5] Oct71 [4]

May 72. (7") *(TMG 816)* <1197> **ROCKIN' ROBIN. / LOVE IS HERE AND NOW YOU'RE GONE** [3] Mar72 [2]

May 72. (lp) *(STML STML 11205)* <747> **GOT TO BE THERE** [37] Feb72 [14]
– Ain't no sunshine / I wanna be where you are / Girl don't take your love from me / In our small way / Got to be there / Rockin' robin / Wings of my love / Maria (you were the only one) / Love is here and now / You're gone / You've got a friend. *(re-iss. Aug81 & May84) (cd-iss. Jun89) (re-iss. cd Aug93)*

May 72. (7") <1202> **I WANNA BE WHERE YOU ARE. / WE GOT A GOOD THING GOIN'** [–] [16]

Jul 72. (7") *(TMG 826)* **AIN'T NO SUNSHINE. / I WANNA BE WHERE YOU ARE** [8] [–]
(re-iss. Oct81)

Nov 72. (7") *(TMG 834)* <1207> **BEN. / YOU CAN CRY ON MY SHOULDER** [7] Aug72 [1]
(re-iss. Oct81)

Dec 72. (lp) *(STML 11220)* <755> **BEN** [17] Sep72 [5]
– Ben / Greatest show on Earth / People make the world go round / We've got a good thing going / Everybody's fool / My girl / What goes around comes around / In our small way / Shoo-be-doo-be-doo-da-day / You can cry on my shoulder. *(re-iss. Oct81 + May84) (cd-iss. Feb90) (cd re-iss. Sep93)*

May 73. (7") <1218> **WITH A CHILD'S HEART. / MORNING GLOW** [–] [50]

Jul 73. (lp) *(STML 11235)* <767> **MUSIC AND ME** [ ] Apr73 [92]
– With a child's heart / Up again / All the things you are / Happy / Too young / Doggin' around / Johnny Raven / Euphoria / Morning glow / Music and me. *(re-iss. Nov84) (re-iss. cd/c May93 on 'Spectrum')*

Jul 73. (7") *(TMG 863)* **MORNING GLOW. / MY GIRL** [ ] [–]

May 74. (7") *(TMG 900)* **MUSIC AND ME. / JOHNNY RAVEN** [ ] [–]

Feb 75. (7") <1341> **WE'RE ALMOST THERE. / TAKE ME BACK** [–] [54]

Mar 75. (lp) *(STMA 8022)* <825> **FOREVER MICHAEL** [ ] [ ]
– We're almost there / Take me back / One day in your life / Cinderella stay awhile / We've got forever / Just a little bit of you / You are there / Dapper Dan / Dear Michael / I'll come home to you. *(re-iss. Jun83 + Jun88) (cd-iss. Mar90)*

Apr 75. (7") *(TMG 946)* **ONE DAY IN YOUR LIFE. / WITH A CHILD'S HEART** [ ] [–]

Oct 75. (7") *(TMG 1006)* <1349> **JUST A LITTLE BIT OF YOU. / DEAR MICHAEL** [ ] Jun75 [23]

Oct 75. (lp) *(STML 12005)* <851> **THE BEST OF MICHAEL JACKSON** (compilation) [ ] [ ]
(re-iss. Mar80 + May84) (Jul81 saw it hit UK No.11)

the JACKSON 5

MICHAEL had continued as the group's main singer

Apr 72. (7") <1199> **LITTLE BIT PRETTY ONE. / IF I HAVE TO MOVE A MOUNTAIN** [–] [13]

Sep 72. (7") *(TMG 825)* **LITTLE BITTY PRETTY ONE. / MAYBE TOMORROW** [ ] [–]

Oct 72. (lp) *(STML 11214)* <750> **LOOKIN' THROUGH THE WINDOWS** [16] Jun72 [7]
– Ain't nothing like the real thing / Lookin' through the windows / Don't let your baby catch you / To know / Doctor my eyes / Little bitty pretty one / E-ne-me-ne-mi-ne-moe / I'll have to move a mountain / Don't want to see you tomorrow / Children of the light / I can only give you love. *(re-iss. Feb83)*

Oct 72. (7") *(TMG 833)* <1205> **LOOKIN' THROUGH THE WINDOWS. / LOVE SONG** [9] Jul72 [16]

Nov 72. (7") <1214> **CORNER OF THE SKY. / TO KNOW** [–] [18]

Dec 72. (7"m) *(TMG 837)* **SANTA CLAUS IS COMING TO TOWN. / SOMEDAY AT CHRISTMAS / CHRISTMAS WON'T BE THE SAME THIS YEAR** [43] [–]

Feb 73. (7") *(TMG 842)* **DOCTOR MY EYES. / MY LITTLE BABY** [9] [–]

Mar 73. (7") <1224> **HALLELUJAH DAY. / YOU MAKE ME WHAT I AM** [–] [16]

May 73. (7") *(TMG 856)* **HALLELUJAH DAY. / TO KNOW** [20] [–]

Jul 73. (lp) *(STML 11231)* <761> **SKYWRITER** [ ] Apr73 [44]
– Skywriter / Hallelujah day / Boogie man / Touch / Corner of the sky / I can't quit your love / Uppermost / World of sunshine / Ooh, I'd love to be with you / You made me what I am. *(re-iss. Nov84) (cd-iss. Aug93)*

Aug 73. (7") *(TMG 865)* **SKYWRITER. / AIN'T NOTHING LIKE THE REAL THING** [25] [–]

Nov 73. (7") *(TMG 878)* <1277> **GET IT TOGETHER. / TOUCH** [ ] Sep73 [28]

Nov 73. (lp) *(STML 11243)* <783> **GET IT TOGETHER** [ ] [100]
– Dancing machine / Get it together / Don't say goodbye again / Reflections / Hum along and dance / Mama I gotta brand new thing (don't say no) / It's too late to change the time / You need love like I do (don't you).

Apr 74. (7") *(TMG 895)* **THE BOOGIE MAN. / DON'T LET YOUR BABY CATCH YOU** [ ] [–]

Jun 74. (7") *(TMG 904)* <1286> **DANCING MACHINE. / IT'S TOO LATE TO CHANGE THE TIME** [ ] Mar74 [2]

Nov 74. (lp) *(STML 11275)* <780> **DANCING MACHINE** [ ] Oct74 [16]
– Dancing machine / I am love / Whatever you got, I want / She's a rhythm child / The life of the party / What you don't know / If I don't love you this way / It all begins and ends with love / The mirrors of my mind.

Nov 74. (7") <1308> **WHATEVER YOU GOT, I WANT. / I CAN'T QUIT YOUR LOVE** [–] [38]

Nov 74. (7") *(TMG 927)* **WHATEVER YOU GOT, I WANT. / THE LIFE OF THE PARTY** [ ] [–]

Mar 75. (7") *(TMG 942)* <1310> **I AM LOVE. / (Part 2)** [ ] Feb75 [15]

Jun 75. (7") <1356> **FOREVER CAME TODAY. / ALL I DO IS THINK OF YOU** [–] [60]

Jul 75. (lp) *(STML 11290)* <829> **MOVING VIOLATION** [ ] [36]
– Forever came today / Moving violation / (You were made) Especially for me / Honey love / Body language (do the love dance) / All I do is think of you / Breezy / Call of the wild / Time explosion.

Sep 75. (7") *(TMG 1001)* **FOREVER CAME TODAY. / I CAN'T QUIT YOUR LOVE** [ ] [–]

the JACKSONS

RANDY JACKSON (b.29 Oct'62) – vocals; repl. JERMAINE who is having own solo career. Temporarily added sisters **LaTOYA** (b.29 May'56) – vocals / **REBBIE** (b. MAUREEN, 29 May'50) – vocals. In 1976, another sister **JANET** also appeared on tours.

Epic Epic

Feb 77. (7") *(EPC 4708)* <50289> **ENJOY YOURSELF. / STYLE OF LIFE** [42] Oct76 [6]

Feb 77. (lp/c) *(EPC/40 86009)* <34229> **THE JACKSONS** [54] Nov76 [36]
– Enjoy yourself / Think happy / Good times / Keep on dancing / Blues away / Show you the way to go / Living together / Strength of one man / Dreamer / Style of life. *(also on pic-lp US) (re-iss. cd Jun94 on 'Sony')*

May 77. (7") *(EPC 5266)* <50350> **SHOW YOU THE WAY TO GO. / BLUES AWAY** [1] Apr77 [28]

Jul 77. (7") *(EPC 5458)* **DREAMER. / GOOD TIMES** [22] [–]

Oct 77. (7") *(EPC 5732)* <50454> **GOIN' PLACES. / DO WHAT YOU WANNA** [26] [52]

Oct 77. (lp/c) *(EPC/40 86035)* <34835> **GOIN' PLACES** [45] [63]
– Music's takin' over / Goin' places / Different kind of lady / Even though you're gone / Jump for joy / Heaven knows I love you girl / Man of war / Do you wanna / Find me a girl. *(also iss.pic-lp US) (re-iss. cd Jun94 on 'Sony')*

Jan 78. (7") <50496> **FIND ME A GIRL. / DIFFERENT KIND OF LADY** [–] [ ]

Jan 78. (7") *(EPC 5919)* **EVEN THOUGH YOU'RE GONE. / DIFFERENT KIND OF LADY** [31] [–]

Apr 78. (7") *(EPC 6263)* **MUSIC'S TAKING OVER. / MAN OF WAR** [ ] [–]

Sep 78. (7") *(EPC 6683)* **BLAME IT ON THE BOOGIE. / DO WHAT YOU WANNA** [8] [–]

Oct 78. (7") <50595> **BLAME IT ON THE BOOGIE. / EASE ON DOWN THE ROAD** [–] [54]

Dec 78. (7") *(EPC 6983)* **DESTINY. / THAT'S WHAT YOU GET** [39] [–]
(12"+=) *(EPC13 6983)* – Blame it on the boogie.

Apr 79. (lp/c) *(EPC/40 83200)* <35552> **DESTINY** [33] Dec78 [11]
– Blame it on the boogie / Push me away / Things I do for you / Shake your body (down to the ground) / Destiny / Bless his soul / All night dancin' / That's what you get. *(re-iss. 1984)*

Mar 79. (7"/12") *(EPC/+13 7181)* **SHAKE YOUR BODY (DOWN TO THE GROUND). / ALL NIGHT DANCIN'** [4] [–]

Mar 79. (7") *<50656>* **SHAKE YOUR BODY (DOWN TO THE GROUND). / THAT'S WHAT YOU GET (FOR BEING POLITE)** [–] [7]

MICHAEL JACKSON

solo again. In Oct78, he duetted with DIANA ROSS ⇒ on 'MCA' Top 50 US/UK single 'EASE ON DOWN THE ROAD'. (re-iss. May84)

Epic Epic

May 79. (7"pic-d/12") *(EPC/+13 7135)* *<50654>* **YOU CAN'T WIN. / (Part 2)** [ ] Feb79 [81]

Aug 79. (7") *(EPC 7763)* *<50742>* **DON'T STOP 'TIL YOU GET ENOUGH. / I CAN'T HELP IT** [3] [1]

Aug 79. (lp/c) *(EPC/40 83458)* *<35745>* **OFF THE WALL** [5] [3]
– Don't stop 'til you get enough / Rock with you / Working day and night / Get on the floor / Off the wall / Girlfriend / She's out of my life / I can't help it / It's the falling in love / Burn this disco out. *(re-dist.1980 w / free 7" YOU CAN'T WIN) (re-iss. Nov86) (cd-iss. 1983 & Dec95) (re-iss. Aug92, hit UK No.48)*

Oct 79. (7") *<50797>* **ROCK WITH YOU. / WORKING DAY AND NIGHT** [–] [1]

Nov 79. (7") *(EPC 8045)* **OFF THE WALL. / WORKING DAY AND NIGHT** [7] [–]

Feb 80. (7") *<50838>* **OFF THE WALL. / GET ON THE FLOOR** [–] [10]
(re-iss. Apr82)

Feb 80. (7")(12") *(EPC 8206)* **ROCK WITH YOU. / GET ON THE FLOOR** [7] [–]
(re-iss. Apr82)

Apr 80. (7") *(EPC 8384)* **SHE'S OUT OF MY LIFE. / Jacksons: PUSH ME AWAY** [3] [–]

Apr 80. (7") *<50871>* **SHE'S OUT OF MY LIFE. / GET ON THE FLOOR** [–] [10]

Jul 80. (7") *(EPC 8782)* **GIRLFRIEND. / Jacksons: BLESS HIS SOUL** [41] [–]

the JACKSONS

— returned to the fold

Oct 80. (7") *<50938>* **LOVELY ONE. / BLESS HIS SOUL** [–] [12]

Oct 80. (7") *(EPC 9302)* **LOVELY ONE. / THINGS I DO FOR YOU** [29] [–]

Oct 80. (lp/c) *(EPC/40 86112)* *<36424>* **TRIUMPH** [13] [10]
– Can you feel it / Lovely one / Your ways / Everybody / Heartbreak hotel / Time waits for no one / Walk right now / Give it up / Wondering who.

Dec 80. (7") *<50959>* **HEARTBREAK HOTEL. / THINGS I DO FOR YOU** [–] [22]

Dec 80. (7") *(EPC 9391)* **HEARTBREAK HOTEL. / DIFFERENT KIND OF LADY** [44] [–]

Feb 81. (7") *(EPC 9554)* **CAN YOU FEEL IT. / WONDERING WHO** [6] [–]

Apr 81. (7") *<01032>* **CAN YOU FEEL IT. / EVERYBODY** [–] [77]

Jun 81. (7") *(EPC 1294)* *<02132>* **WALK RIGHT NOW. / YOUR WAYS** [7] [73]

Sep 81. (7") *(EPC 1579)* **TIME WAITS FOR NO ONE. / GIVE IT UP** [ ] [–]

Nov 81. (7") *<02720>* **THE THINGS I DO FOR YOU (live). / WORKING DAY AND NIGHT (live)** [–] [ ]

Nov 81. (d-lp/d-c) *(EPC/40 88562)* *<37545>* **THE JACKSONS – LIVE! (live)** [53] [30]
– Opening: Can you feel it? Things I do for you / Off the wall / Ben / Heartbreak hotel / She's out of my life / Movie and rap medley (a) I want you back, (b) Never can say goodbye, (c) Got to be there / The love you save / I'll be there / Rock with you / Lovely one / Working day and night / Don't stop 'til you get enough / Shake your body (down to the ground).

Nov 81. (7") *(EPC 1902)* **THINGS I DO FOR YOU (live). / DON'T STOP 'TIL YOU GET ENOUGH (live)** [ ] [–]

MICHAEL JACKSON

returned to solo work again

Epic Epic

Nov 82. (7"/7"pic-d; by MICHAEL JACKSON & PAUL McCARTNEY) *(EPCA/+11 2729)* *<03288>* **THE GIRL IS MINE. / CAN'T GET OUT OF THE RAIN** [10] [2]

— (Nearly a year later they had another hit, 'SAY SAY SAY' a No.2 UK / No.1 US)

Dec 82. (lp/c/cd) *(EPC/40/CD 85930)* *<38112>* **THRILLER** [1] [1]
– Wanna be startin' something / Baby be mine / The girl is mine / Thriller / Beat it / Billie Jean / Human nature / P.Y.T. (Pretty Young Thing) / The lady in my life. *(pic-lp.Jul83; EPC11 85930) (re-iss. Aug92 hit UK No.17)*

Jan 83. (7") *<03509>* **BILLIE JEAN. / CAN'T GET OUT OF THE RAIN** [–] [1]

Jan 83. (7") *(EPC 3084)* **BILLIE JEAN. / IT'S FALLING IN LOVE** [1] [–]
(12"+=) *(EPC/+13 3084)* – ('A'extended).

Mar 83. (7") *<03759>* **BEAT IT. / GET ON THE FLOOR** [–] [1]

Mar 83. (7"/12") *(EPC/+13 3258)* **BEAT IT. / BURN THIS DISCO OUT** [3] [–]

May 83. (7") *<03914>* **WANNA BE STARTIN' SOMETHING. / (part 2)** [–] [5]

May 83. (7") *(A 3427)* **WANNA BE STARTIN' SOMETHING. / Jacksons: ROCK WITH YOU** [8] [–]
(12"+=) *(TA 3427)* – ('A'instrumental).

Jul 83. (7") *<03914>* **HUMAN NATURE. / BABY BE MINE** [–] [7]

Oct 83. (7") *<04165>* **P.Y.T. (PRETTY YOUNG THING). / WORKING DAY AND NIGHT** [–] [10]

Nov 83. (7"/12") *(EPCA/TA 3643)* **THRILLER. / THE THINGS I DO FOR YOU** [10] [–]

Jan 84. (7") *<04364>* **THRILLER. / CAN'T GET OUTTA THE RAIN** [–] [4]

Mar 84. (7") *(A 4136)* **P.Y.T. (PRETTY YOUNG THING). / HEARTBREAK HOTEL** [11] [–]
(12"+=) *(TA 4136)* – Thriller (instrumental).

the JACKSONS

— now 6-piece when **JERMAINE** returned to join the 5 brothers.

Jun 84. (7"pic-d/12") *(A/TA 4431)* **STATE OF SHOCK. / YOUR WAYS** [14] [3]
(above featured MICK JAGGER on dual vocals with MICHAEL)

Jul 84. (pic-lp/c) *(EPC/40 86303)* *<38946>* **VICTORY** [3] [4]
– Torture / Wait / One more chance / Be not always / State of shock / We can change the world / The hurt / Body. *(cd-iss. May87) (cd-iss. Dec94)*

Aug 84. (7") *(A 4675)* *<04575>* **TORTURE. / ('A'instrumental)** [26] [17]
(12"+=) *(TA 4675)* – Show you the way to go / Blame it on the boogie.

Nov 84. (7"/12") *(A/TA 4883)* *<04673>* **BODY. / ('A'instrumental)** [ ] [47]

Feb 85. (7"/12") *(A/TA 6105)* **WAIT. / SHE'S OUT OF MY LIFE** [ ] [–]

MICHAEL JACKSON

Jul 87. (7"/7"s/12") *(650 202-7/-0/-6)* *<07253>* **I JUST CAN'T STOP LOVING YOU. / BABY BE MINE** [1] [1]
(above featured duet with SIEDAH GARRETT)

Sep 87. (7") *<07418>* **BAD. / I CAN'T HELP IT** [–] [1]

Sep 87. (7") *(651 155-7)* **BAD. / ('A'instrumental)** [3] [–]
(12"+=) *(651 155-6)* – ('A'acappella mix) / ('A'dub version).
(c-s+=) *(651 155-4)* – ('A'extended).

Sep 87. (lp/c/cd) *(450 290-1/-4/-2)* *<40600>* **BAD** [1] [1]
– Bad / The way you make me feel / Speed demon / Liberian girl / Just good friends / Another part of me / Man in the mirror / I just can't stop loving you / Dirty Diana / Smooth criminal. *(pic-lp Nov87; 450 290-0) (re-iss. Jul88 as 5x7"box; 450 290-9) (re-iss. Aug92, hit UK No.14)*

Nov 87. (7") *(651 275-7)* *<07645>* **THE WAY YOU MAKE ME FEEL. / ('A'instrumental)** [3] [1]
(12"+=) *(651 275-0)* – ('A'dance mix) / ('A'dub mix).
(cd-s+=) *(651 275-2)* – ('A'acappella mix).

Feb 88. (7"/7"sha-pic-d) *(651 388-7/-9)* *<07668>* **MAN IN THE MIRROR. / ('A'instrumental)** [21] [1]
(12"+=/cd-s+=) *(651 388-6/-2)* – ('A'mix).

— (In Apr'88, he did a duet single, 'GET IT', with STEVIE WONDER which hit UK Top40 & US No.80)

Jul 88. (7") *(651 546-7)* *<07739>* **DIRTY DIANA. / ('A'instrumental)** [4] [1]
(12"+=/cd-s+=) *(651 546-6/-9)* – Bad (extended dance).
(3"cd-s+=) *(651 546-2)* – ('A'-album version).

Sep 88. (7"/7"s) *(652 844-7/-9)* *<07962>* **ANOTHER PART OF ME. / ('A'instrumental)** [15] [11]
(12"+=/cd-s+=) *(652 844-6/-2)* – ('A'acappella) / ('A'radio).
(3"cd-s+=) *(653 004-2)* – ('A'drum mix) / ('A'acappella).

Nov 88. (7"/7"s) *(653 026-7/-0)* <08044> **SMOOTH CRIMINAL. / ('A'instrumental)** [8] [7]
(12"+=/cd-s+=) *(653 026-1/-2)* – ('A'extended) / ('A'acappella) / ('A'dance dub).
(cd-s++=) *(653 026-2)* – ('A'Annie mix).

eb 89. (7"/7"s) *(654 672-7/-0)* **LEAVE ME ALONE. / HUMAN NATURE** [2] [–]
(c-s+=/3"cd-s+=) *(654 672-4/-3)* – Don't stop 'til you get enough.
(cd-s++=) *(654 672-2)* – Wanna be startin' something (extended).

ul 89. (7"/7"s/c-s) *(654 947-7/-0/-4)* **LIBERIAN GIRL. / GIRLFRIEND** [13] [–]
(3"cd-s+=) *(654 947-3)* – Get on the floor.
(cd-s++=) *(654 947-2)* – The lady in my life.

he JACKSONS

pr 89. (7"/c-s) *(654 808-7/-4)* <68688> **NOTHIN' (THAT COMPARES 2 U). / HEARTBREAK HOTEL / ALRIGHT WITH ME** [ ] [77]
(12"+=/cd-s+=) *(654 808-6/-2)* – ('A'choice dub extended).

un 89. (lp/c/cd) *(463 352-1/-4/-2)* <40911> **2300 JACKSON STREET** [ ] [59]
– Art of madness / Nothin' (that compares 2 U) / Maria / Private affair / 2300 Jackson Street / Harley / She / Alright with me / Play it up / Midnight rendezvous / If you'd only believe.

ug 89. (7"/c-s) *(655 206-7/-4)* <69022> **2300 JACKSON STREET. / WHEN I LOOK AT YOU** [ ] [ ]
(12"+=) *(655 206-6)* – Please come back to me.
(cd-s++=) *(655 206-2)* – ('A'lp version) / Keep her.

MICHAEL JACKSON

Nov 91. (7"/c-s) *(657 598-7/-4)* <74100> **BLACK OR WHITE. / ('A'instrumental)** [1] [1]
(12"+=) *(657 598-6)* – Bad / Thriller.
(cd-s+=) *(657 598-2)* – Smooth criminal.
(12"+=/cd-s+=) – (other mixes by and 1 by C&C MUSIC FACTORY)

ec 91. (cd/c/lp) *(465 802-2/-4/-1)* <45400> **DANGEROUS** [1] [1]
– Jam / Why you wanna trip on me / In the closet / She drives me wild / Remember the time / Can't let her get away / Heal the world / Black or white / Who is it / Give in to me / Will you be there / Keep the faith / Gone too soon / Dangerous.

n 92. (c-s) <74200> **REMEMBER THE TIME / BLACK OR WHITE (Clivilies & Cole mix)** [–] [3]

eb 92. (7"/c-s/12"/cd-s) *(657 774-7/-4/-6/-2)* **REMEMBER THE TIME. / COME TOGETHER** [3] [–]

pr 92. (7"/c-s) *(658 018-7/-4)* <74266> **IN THE CLOSET. / ('A'remix)** [8] [6]
(12"+=/cd-s+=) *(658 018-6/-2)* – (other 'A'mixes).

l 92. (7"/c-s) *(658 179-7/-4)* **WHO IS IT. / ROCK WITH YOU (mix)** [10] [–]
(12"+=/cd-s+=) *(658 179-6/-2)* – Don't stop 'til you get enough (remix).

l 92. (c-s) <74333> **JAM / ROCK WITH YOU (remix)** [–] [26]

p 92. (7"/c-s) *(658 360-7/-4)* **JAM. / BEAT IT (Moby mix)** [13] [–]
(12"+=) *(658 360-6)* – Wanna be starting something (Brothers In Rhythm house mix).
(cd-s) *(658 360-2)* – ('A'side) / ('A'-Roger's Jeep mix) / ('A'-Atlanta techno mix) / Wanna be startin' something (Brothers In Rhythm house mix).

ov 92. (7"/c-s) *(658 488-7/-4)* <74708> **HEAL THE WORLD. / SHE DRIVES ME WILD** [2] Dec92 [27]
(12"+=) *(658 488-6)* – Man in the mirror.
(cd-s) *(658 488-2)* – ('A'side) / Wanna be starting something / Don't stop till you get enough / Rock with you.

b 93. (7"/c-s) *(659 069-7/-4)* **GIVE IN TO ME. / DIRTY DIANA** [2] [–]
(cd-s+=) *(659 069-2)* – Beat it.

pr 93. (c-s) <74406> **WHO IS IT / (Oprah Winfrey intro)** [–] [14]

n 93. (7"/c-s) *(659 222-7/-4)* <77060> **WILL YOU BE THERE. / GIRLFRIEND** [9] [7]
(cd-s+=) *(659 222-2)* – Keep the faith.

ec 93. (7"/c-s) *(659 976-7/-4)* **GONE TOO SOON. / ('A'instrumental)** [33] [–]
(12"/cd-s) *(659 976-6/-2)* – ('A'side) / Human nature / She's out of my life / Thriller.

n 95. (7"/c-s/cd-s; MICHAEL JACKSON & JANET JACKSON) *(662 022-7/-4/-2)* <78000> **SCREAM / CHILDHOOD** [3] [5]
(cd-s/12"/12") *(662 022-2/-6/-8)* – ('A'album version) / ('A'-Pressurized dub pt.1 & 2) / ('A'-Naughty By Nature pretty-pella mix) / ('A'-N.B.N. acappella).
(12") – ('A'-classic club mix) / ('A'-David Morales R&B extended mix) / ('A'-Def radio mix). / ('A'-Naughty By Nature main mix) / ('A'-Naughty By Nature main mix no rap) / ('A'-Dave "Jam" Hall's extended urban remix). *(note the above 4th & 5th formats hit UK No.43)*

Jun 95. (d-cd/d-c/t-lp) *(474 709-2/-4/-1)* <59000> **HIStory: PAST, PRESENT AND FUTURE – BOOK 1** [1] [1]
– Billie Jean / The way you make me feel / Black or white / Rock with you / She's out of my life / Bad / I just can't stop loving you / Man in the mirror / Thriller / Beat it / The girl is mine / Remember the time / Don't stop 'til you get enough / Wanna be startin' somethin' / Heal the world. // Scream / They don't care about us / Stranger in Moscow / This time around / Earth song / DS / Money / Come together / You are not alone / Childhood / Tabloid junkie / 2 bad / History / Little Susie / Smile.

Aug 95. (c-s) *(662 310-4)* <78002> **YOU ARE NOT ALONE / SCREAM LOUDER (Flyte Tyme mix with JANET JACKSON)** [1] [1]
(cd-s/12") *(662 310-2/-8)* – ('A'-Frankie Knuckles remix) / ('A'-Jon B remix).
(cd-s) *(662 310-5)* – ('A'-R Kelly remix) / Rock with you (Masters At work remix) / Rock with you (Frankie Knuckles remix).

Nov 95. (c-s) *(662 695-4)* **EARTH SONG / ('A'-Hani's extended radio experience)** [1] [–]
(cd-s) *(662 695-2)* – ('A'side) / ('A'-Hani's club experience) / Michael Jackson DMC megamix.
(cd-s) *(662 695-5)* – ('A'side) / Wanna be startin' somethin' / ('A'-Brothers In Rhythm mix) / ('A'-Tommy D's main mix).

Apr 96. (c-s/cd-s) *(662 950-4/-2)* <78060> **THEY DON'T CARE ABOUT US / ROCK WITH YOU / EARTH SONG** [4] Jun96 [30]
(cd-s) *(662 950-2)* – ('A'mixes) / Beat it.

— In Aug'96, MICHAEL featured on nephews 3T (offspring of TITO) Top 3 hit 'Why'.

Nov 96. (c-s) *(663 787-4)* **STRANGER IN MOSCOW / ('A'-Tee's radio mix)** [4] Aug97 [91]
(cd-s) *(663 787-2)* – ('A'-side) / ('A'-Todd Terry mix) / ('A'-Charles 'The Mixologist' Roane mix).
(cd-s) *(663 787-5)* – ('A'side) / ('A'-Hani mix) / ('A'-Basement Boys mix).

Apr 97. (c-s/12"/cd-s) *(664 462-4/-0/-2)* **BLOOD ON THE DANCEFLOOR / (mixes)** [1] [42]
(12"/12"/cd-s) *(664 462-6/-8/-5)* – ('A'remixes).

May 97. (cd/c) *(487 500-2/-4)* <68000> **BLOOD ON THE DANCEFLOOR** (remixes) [1] [24]
– Blood on the dancefloor / Morphine / Superfly sister / Ghosts / Is it scary / Scream louder / Money / 2 bad / Stranger in Moscow / This time around / Earth song / You are not alone / History.

Jul 97. (c-s/cd-s) *(664 796-4/-2)* **HISTORY / GHOSTS** [5] [–]
(cd-s) *(664 796-5)* – ('A'mixes).

Oct 01. (c-s) *(672029-4)* <*radio cut*> **YOU ROCK MY WORLD / (mix)** [2] Sep01 [10]
(12"+=) *(672029-6)* – ('A'-instrumental) / ('A'-acappella).
(cd-s++=) *(672029-2)* – ('A'-video).

Oct 01. (cd/c/d-lp) *(495174-2/-4/-1)* <69400> **INVINCIBLE** [1] [1]
– Unbreakable / Heartbreaker / Invincible / Break of dawn / Heaven can wait / You rock my world / Butterflies / Speechless / 2000 watts / You are my life / Privacy / Don't walk away / Cry / The lost children / Whatever happens / Threatened.

Nov 01. (-) <*radio cut*> **BUTTERFLIES** [–] [19]

Dec 01. (12"/c-s) *(672182-4/-6)* **CRY. / SHOUT / STREETWALKER** [25] [–]
(cd-s+=) *(672182-2)* – ('A'-video).

Nov 03. (cd/d-lp) *(513800-2/-1)* <88998> **NUMBER ONES** (compilation) [1] [13]
– Don't stop 'til you get enough / Rock with you / Billie Jean / Beat it / Thriller / I just can't stop loving you (with SIEDAH GARRETT) / Bad / Smooth criminal / The way you make me feel / Man in the mirror / Dirty Diana / Black or white / You are not alone / Earth song / You rock my world / Break of dawn / One more chance / Ben (live).

Nov 03. (12"/cd-s) *(674480-6/-2)* <*radio*> **ONE MORE CHANCE (mixes; incl. Paul Oakenfold)** [5] [83]
(cd-s) *(674480-5)* – ('A'mixes; Oakenfold / Metro / Ron G club).

– (MICHAEL JACKSON) compilations, others –

Note; All below on 'Motown' unless stated

Apr 80. (7") **BEN. / ('B'by MARVIN GAYE)** [ ] [ ]
(re-iss. Oct81)

Oct 80. (7") *(TMG 973)* **GOT TO BE THERE. / ('B'by MARV JACKSON)** ☐ ☐
(re-iss. Oct81)

Apr 81. (7") *(TMG 976)* **ONE DAY IN YOUR LIFE. / TAKE ME BACK** 1 55
(re-iss. Oct81)

Jul 81. (lp/c) *(STML 12158/CSTML 12158)* **ONE DAY IN YOUR LIFE** 29 ☐
– One day in your life / We're almost there / You're my best friend, my love / Don't say goodbye again / Take me back / It's too late to change the time / We've got a good thing going / You are there / Doggin' around / Dear Michael / Girl, don't take your love from me / I'll come home to you. *(re-iss. Mar85)*

Jul 81. (7"/12") *(TMG/+T 977)* **WE'RE ALMOST THERE. / WE GOT A GOOD THING GOING** 46 ☐

Jul 83. (7"pic-d/12"/7") *(TMG P/T 986/TMG 986)* **HAPPY (LOVE THEME FROM 'LADY SINGS THE BLUES'). / WE'RE ALMOST THERE** 52 ☐

Jul 83. (c-ep) *(CTME 2035)* **FLIPHITS** ☐ –
– One day in your life / Got to be there / Ben / Ain't no sunshine.

May 84. (7"/12") *TMG/+T 1342)* **FAREWELL MY SUMMER LOVE. / CALL ME** 7 38

Aug 84. (lp/c) *(Z L/K 72227)* **FAREWELL MY SUMMER LOVE** 9 46
– Don't let it get you down / You've really got a hold on me / Melodie / Touch the one you love / Girl you're so together / Farewell my summer love / Call on me / Here I am / To make my father proud.
(re-iss. Jun88, cd-iss. Oct89)

Aug 84. (7") *(TMG 1355)* **GIRL YOU'RE SO TOGETHER. / TOUCH THE ONE YOU LOVE** ☐ ☐
(12"+=) – Ben / Ain't no sunshine.

Nov 84. (lp/c) *(W L/K 72289)* **THE GREAT LOVE SONGS OF MICHAEL JACKSON** ☐ ☐

May 86. (lp/c) *(W L/K 72424)* **LOOKING BACK TO YESTERDAY** ☐ ☐

Apr 87. (d-cd) *(ZD 72530)* **MICHAEL JACKSON ANTHOLOGY** ☐ ☐
– Got to be there / Rockin' Robin / Ain't no sunshine / Maria (you were the only one) / I wanna be where you are / Girl don't take your love from me / Love is here and now you're gone / Ben / People make the world go 'round / Shoo-be-doo-be-doo-da-day / With a child's heart / Everybody's somebody's fool / In our small way / All the things you are / You can cry on my shoulder / Maybe tomorrow / I'll be there / Never can say goodbye / It's too late to change the time / Dancing machine / When I come of age / Dear Michael / Music and me / You are there / One day in your life / Love's gone bad / That's what love is made of / Who's looking for a lover / Lonely teardrops / We're almost there / Take me back / Just a little bit of you / Melodie / I'll come home to you / If'n I was God / Happy / Don't let it get you down / Call on me / To make my father proud / Farewell my summer love. – (w / JACKSON 5 tracks) *(re-iss. d-cd Apr93)*

1987. (7") **25 MILES. / UP ON THE HOUSETOP** – ☐

Feb 92. (cd/c/lp) *(530014 – 2/-4/-1)* **MOTOWN'S GREATEST HITS** ☐ ☐

Apr 82. (7") *Epic; (EPC 8046)* **OFF THE WALL. / DON'T STOP 'TIL YOU GET ENOUGH** ☐ ☐

Dec 82. (c-ep) *Epic; (EPC 2906)* **GREATEST ORIGINAL HITS** ☐ –
(re-iss. Mar83 as 7"ep)

Nov 83. (9x7"red-pack) *Epic; (MJ 1)* **SINGLES PACK** 66 ☐
(re-iss. Jul88)

Sep 86. (c-ep) *Epic; (4501274)* **THE 12" TAPE** ☐ ☐
– Billie Jean / Beat it / Wanna be startin' something / Thriller.

Jul 88. (singles pack) *Epic; (MJ 5)* **SOUVENIR SINGLES PACK** 91 –

Jul 92. (4xpic-cd-ep's) *Epic; (MJ 4)* **TOUR SOUVENIR PACK** 32 ☐
– (3 tracks on each disc)

Jul 82. (lp/c) *Pickwick; (2/4 0038)* **AIN'T NO SUNSHINE** ☐ –
(re-iss. Nov84 on 'Astan')

Jul 83. (lp/c/cd) *Telstar; (STA R/C 2232/TCD 2232)* **18 GREATEST HITS (by MICHAEL JACKSON / JACKSON 5)** 1 ☐
(re-iss. Jun88)

May 84. (cd) *Motown; (MCD 06070MD)* **COMPACT COMMAND PERFORMANCES: 18 GREATEST HITS** ☐ ☐
(re-iss. Oct87)

Nov 86. (d-cd) *Motown; (ZD 72468)* **GOT TO BE THERE / BEN** ☐ ☐

Oct 87. (lp/c/cd) *Telstar;* **LOVE SONGS (w / DIANA ROSS)** 15 ☐

Nov 87. (lp/c/cd) *Stylus; (SM R/C/D 745)* **THE MICHAEL JACKSON MIX** 27 ☐

Nov 95. (3xcd-box) *Motown;* **FOREVER MICHAEL / MUSIC & ME / BEN** ☐ –

Jun 97. (cd/c) *Polygram TV; (530804-2/-4)* **THE BEST OF MICHAEL JACKSON & THE JACKSON 5** 5 –
– I want you back / ABC / Love you save / I'll be there / Mama's pearl / Never can say goodbye / Got to be there / Rockin' robin / Ain't no sunshine / Looking through the windows / Ben / Doctor my eyes / We're almost there / Farewell my summer love / Girl you're so together.

Nov 01. (cd) *MJJ Music; (501869-2) <85250>* **GREATEST HITS: HISTORY VOL.1** 68 85

Jun 04. (cd; as the JACKSONS) *Sony TV; (5163669)* **THE VERY BEST OF THE JACKSONS** 7 –

—— all below on 'Epic' (+ w/ 'A'/ 'A'-version + 'A'-video)

Nov 04. (cd) *(5177433) <92600>* **THE ULTIMATE COLLECTION** 75 ☐

Jul 05. (d-cd) *(520422-2) <94287-2>* **THE ESSENTIAL** 2 96
– I want you back / ABC / The love you save / Got to be there / Rockin' robin / Ben / Blame it on the boogie / Shake your body (down to the ground) / Don't stop 'til you get enough / Off the wall / Rock with you / She's out of my life / Can you feel it / The girl is mine / Billie Jean / Beat it / Wanna be startin' somethin' / Human nature / P.Y.T. (Pretty Young Thing) / I just can't stop loving you / Thriller / Bad / The way you make me feel / The man in the mirror / Dirty Diana / Another part of me / Smooth criminal / Leave me alone / Black or white / Remember the time / In the closet / Who is it / Heal the world / Will you be there / You are not alone / Earth song / They don't care about us / You rock my world.

Feb 06. (dvd-s) *(82876 72511-2)* **DON'T STOP 'TIL YOU GET ENOUGH** 17 –
Feb 06. (dvd-s) *(82876 72513-2)* **ROCK WITH YOU** 15 –
Mar 06. (dvd-s) *(82876 72517-2)* **BILLIE JEAN** 11 –
Mar 06. (dvd-s) *(82876 72518-2)* **BEAT IT** 15 –
Mar 06. (dvd-s) *(82876 72524-2)* **BAD** 16 –
Mar 06. (dvd-s) *(82876 72525-2)* **THE WAY YOU MAKE ME FEEL** 17 –
Apr 06. (dvd-s) *(82876 72527-2)* **DIRTY DIANA** 17 –
Apr 06. (dvd-s) *(82876 72529-2)* **SMOOTH CRIMINAL** 19 –
Apr 06. (dvd-s) *(82876 72530-2)* **LEAVE ME ALONE** 15 –
Apr 06. (dvd-s) *(82876 77330-2)* **BLACK OR WHITE** 18 –
May 06. (dvd-s) *(82876 77332-2)* **REMEMBER THE TIME** 22 –
May 06. (dvd-s) *(82876 77334-2)* **IN THE CLOSET** 20 –
May 06. (dvd-s) *(82876 77336-2)* **JAM** 22 –
May 06. (dvd-s) *(82876 77338-2)* **HEAL THE WORLD** 27 –
May 06. (dvd-s) *(82876 77340-2)* **YOU ARE NOT ALONE** 30 –
Jun 06. (dvd-s) *(82876 77342-2)* **EARTH SONG** 34 –
Jun 06. (dvd-s) *(82876 77344-2)* **THEY DON'T CARE ABOUT US** 26 –
Jun 06. (dvd-s) *(82876 77346-2)* **STRANGER IN MOSCOW** 22 –
Jun 06. (dvd-s) *(82876 77348-2)* **BLOOD ON THE DANCEFLOOR** 19 –

☐ Mick JAGGER (see under ⇒ ROLLING STONES)

the JAM

Formed: Woking, Surrey, England . . . late '73 by PAUL WELLER, BRUCE FOXTON, RICK BUCKLER and 4th member STEVE BROOKS – guitar. This quartet first gigged mid-74, progressing to the likes of London's Marquee, 101 Club & Red Cow in late '76, by which time BROOKS had departed. Peddling amphetamine charged retro R&B, the band rode in on the first wave of punk's brave new musical world. Incendiary live performances had generated a loyal following and considerable record company interest, the band signing with 'Polydor' early the following year via A&R man Chris Parry. In Spring '77, their debut, 'IN THE CITY', cracked the UK Top 40, an album of the same name following a month later. Image-wise, the band were kitted out in unashamed allegiance to the mod masterplan of yore; sharp suits, parkas, scooters etc., another factor that set the band apart from the anti-fashion of punk. Something WELLER did share with his glue-sniffing peers was anger; yes, before WELLER the 'red-wedge' soul smoothie and WELLER the

Paul Weller of The JAM

patron of 'Dad Rock' came WELLER the angry young man, so angry in fact, that he professed to voting conservative. Politics aside, 'IN THE CITY' was a cut above the average three chord punk thrash, bristling with adolescent fury yet possessed of an irresistible melodic verve. 'THIS IS THE MODERN WORLD' (1977) was a hastily recorded follow-up, and it showed. Only the pounding title track (the single backed with a cover of Arthur Conley's 'SWEET SOUL MUSIC') really hit the target, the rest of the album pointlessly recycling WHO riffs ad nauseam. With 'ALL MOD CONS' (1978), however, The JAM were onto something big, WELLER's cutting social reportage and songwriting genius translating into such gems as 'DOWN IN THE TUBE-STATION AT MIDNIGHT', a cover of The Kinks' 'DAVID WATTS' indicating the heights he was aiming for. Come 'SETTING SONS' (1979), and with the bile-spewing 'ETON RIFLES', in particular, WELLER came pretty damn close to updating RAY DAVIES' class-conscious agenda for a harsh new age. The single gave the band their first Top 5 success and the album achieved a similar feat upon its release a month later. In February of the following year, the band went straight in at No.1 with 'GOING UNDERGROUND', a snarling critique of the establishment. The band followed this up with 'START!', a virtual remake (well, intro definitely) of George Harrison/Beatles' 'TAXMAN', quite why there's never been a court case over the matter remains a mystery. Still, the single marked a move into more ambitious musical territory, WELLER penning his most accomplished tune to date in the lilting, understated ennui of 'THAT'S ENTERTAINMENT'. The album, 'SOUND AFFECTS' (1980), confirmed the shift away from powerchord aggression with the use of horns and more obviously black music-derived rhythms. By this point, the JAM were one of, if not the, biggest band in Britain although, despite repeated attempts, the American market was apparently impossible for the band to crack. Then again, it's not hard to see that their defiantly British sound just didn't translate in the States, in much the same way as, more recently, BLUR's idiosyncratic Englishness has precluded US recognition. Back home though, the band were No.1 again in early 1982 with the heavily Motown-influenced 'TOWN CALLED MALICE', 'THE GIFT' album being released the following month. It was to be the band's swansong as WELLER, at the peak of the band's fame later that summer, announced he was to break the group up to explore his soul fixation with the STYLE COUNCIL. After a final kiss-off with 'THE BITTEREST PILL' and the brilliant 'BEAT SURRENDER', the band were no more. While WELLER went on to a undergo many musical rebirths, there was no such joy for FOXTON, who later joined aging punks STIFF LITTLE FINGERS. BUCKLER, meanwhile, forsook the evils of the music business for furniture restoration. Thankfully, with no reunion so far, and the possibility of one rather slim, the legend of the JAM remains intact.

• **Songwriters:** WELLER penned except; BACK IN MY ARMS AGAIN (Holland-Dozier-Holland) / DAVID WATTS (Kinks) / MOVE ON UP (Curtis Mayfield). • **Trivia:** In Oct'81, WELLER started own record company 'Respond', and signed acts The QUESTIONS and TRACIE.

Album rating: IN THE CITY (*6) / THIS IS THE MODERN WORLD (*5) / ALL MOD CONS (*8) / SETTING SONS (*8) / SOUND EFFECTS (*8) / THE GIFT (*6) / DIG THE NEW BREED live collection (*6) / compilations: SNAP! (*10) / GREATEST HITS (*8) / DIRECTION REACTION CREATION boxed (*9) / THE VERY BEST OF THE JAM (*8) / THE SOUND OF THE JAM (*8) / THE JAM AT THE BBC (*7) / COMPACT SNAP! (*10)

PAUL WELLER (b. JOHN WELLER, 25 May'58) – vocals, guitar / **BRUCE FOXTON** (b. 1 Sep'55) – bass, vocals / **RICK BUCKLER** (b. PAUL RICHARD BUCKLER, 6 Dec'55) – drums

Polydor Polydor

Apr 77. (7") *(2058 866)* **IN THE CITY. / TAKIN' MY LOVE** [40] [–]
(re-iss. Apr80) – hit No.40 *(re-iss. Jan83)* – hit No.47 *(re-iss. Apr02; 587611-7)* – hit No.36

May 77. (lp) *(2383 447) <6110>* **IN THE CITY** [20] [ ]
– Art school I've changed my address / Slow down / I got by in time / Away from the numbers / Batman / In the city / Sounds from the street / Non stop dancing / Time for truth / Takin' my love / Bricks and mortar. *(re-iss. Aug83 lp/c; SPE LP/MC 27) (re-iss. Jul90 cd/c/lp; 817124-2/-4/-1) (cd re-iss. Jul97; 537417-2)*

Jul 77. (7") *(2058 903)* **ALL AROUND THE WORLD. / CARNABY STREET** [13] [–]
(re-iss. Apr80) – hit No.43 *(re-iss. Jan83)* – hit No.38

Oct 77. (7"m) *(2058 945)* **THE MODERN WORLD. / SWEET SOUL MUSIC (live) / BACK IN MY ARMS AGAIN (live) / BRICKS AND MORTAR (live)** [36] [–]
(re-iss. Apr80) – hit No.52 *(re-iss. Jan83)* – hit No.51

Nov 77. (lp) *(2383 475) <6129>* **THIS IS THE MODERN WORLD** [22] [ ]
– The modern world / London traffic / Standards / Life from the window / The combine / Don't tell them you're sane / In the street today / London girl / I need you / Here comes the weekend / Tonight at noon / In the midnight hour. *(re-iss. Aug83 lp/c; SPE LP/MC 66) (re-iss. Jul90 cd/c/lp; 823281-2/-4/-1) (cd re-iss. Jul97; 537418-2)*

Feb 78. (7") *<14462>* **I NEED YOU. / IN THE CITY** [–] [ ]

Mar 78. (7"m) *(2058 995)* **NEWS OF THE WORLD. / AUNTIES AND UNCLES / INNOCENT MAN** [27] [–]
(re-iss. Apr80) – hit No.53 *(re-iss. Jan83)* – hit No.39

Aug 78. (7") *(2059 054)* **DAVID WATTS. / 'A' BOMB IN WARDOUR STREET** [25] [–]
(re-iss. Apr80) – hit No.54 *(re-iss. Jan83)* – hit No.50

Oct 78. (7"m) *(POSP 8)* **DOWN IN THE TUBE STATION AT MIDNIGHT. / SO BAD ABOUT US / THE NIGHT** [15] [–]
(re-iss. Apr80) (re-iss. Jan83) – hit No.30

Nov 78. (lp/c) *(POLD/+C 5008) <6218>* **ALL MOD CONS** [6] [ ]
– All mod cons / To be someone (didn't we have a nice time) / Mr. Clean / David Watts / English rose / In the crowd / Billy Hunt / It's too bad / Fly 3.18 / The place I love / 'A' bomb in Wardour Street / Down in the tube station at midnight. *(cd-iss. 1989; 823282-2) (cd re-iss. Jul97; 537419-2) (lp re-iss. Aug99 on 'Simply Vinyl'; SVLP 108)*

Mar 79. (7") *(POSP 34) <14553>* **STRANGE TOWN. / THE BUTTERFLY COLLECTOR** [15] [ ]
(re-iss. Apr80) – hit No.44 *(re-iss. Jan83)* – hit No.42

Jun 79. (7") *<14566>* **DOWN IN THE TUBE STATION AT MIDNIGHT. / MR. CLEAN** [–] [ ]

Aug 79. (7") *(POSP 69)* **WHEN YOU'RE YOUNG. / SMITHERS-JONES** [17] [–]
(re-iss. Jan83) – hit No.53

Oct 79. (7") *(POSP 83)* **THE ETON RIFLES. / SEE-SAW** [3] [–]
(re-iss. Jan83) – hit No.54

Nov 79. (lp/c) *(POLD/+C 5028) <6249>* **SETTING SONS** [4] [ ]
– Girl on the phone / Thick as thieves / Private hell / Little boy soldiers / Waste land / Burning sky / Smithers-Jones / Saturday's kids / The Eton rifles / Heat wave. *(cd-iss. May88; 831314-2) (cd re-iss. Jul97; 537420-2) (lp re-iss. May00 on 'Simply Vinyl'; SVLP 209) (cd re-iss. Nov01 on 'Collector Choice'+=; CCM 0247-2)* – Strange town / When you're young / Smithers-Jones / See saw / Going underground / Dreams of children / So sad about us / Hey mister / Start.

Dec 79. (7") *<2051>* **THE ETON RIFLES. / SMITHERS-JONES** [–] [ ]

Feb 80. (7") *(POSP 113)* **GOING UNDERGROUND. / DREAMS OF CHILDREN** [1] [–]
(d7"+=) *(POSPJ 113 – 2616 024)* – The modern world (live) / Away from the numbers (live) / Down in the tube station at midnight (live). *(re-iss Jan83)* – hit No.21

Apr 80. (7") *<2074>* **SATURDAY'S KIDS. / (LOVE IS LIKE A) HEATWAVE** [–] [ ]

Aug 80. (7") *(2059 266)* **START! / LIZA RADLEY** [1] [–]
(re-iss. Jan83) – hit No.60

Sep 80. (7") *<2155>* **START! / WHEN YOU'RE YOUNG** [–] [ ]

Nov 80. (lp/c) *(POLD/+C 5035) <6315>* **SOUND AFFECTS** [2] [72]
– Pretty green / Monday / But I'm different now / Set the house ablaze / Start! / That's entertainment / Dreamtime / Man in the cornershop / Musi for the last couple / Boy about town / Scrape away. *(re-iss. Apr90 cd/c/lp 823284-2/-4/-1) (cd re-iss. Jul97; 537421-2)*

Jan 81. (7") *(0030 364)* **THAT'S ENTERTAINMENT. / DOWN IN THE TUBE STATION AT MIDNIGHT (live)** [21] [–]
(above 45, was actually imported into Britain by German 'Metrognome' *(re-iss. Jan83 on 'Polydor'; 2059 482)* – hit No.60

May 81. (7") *(POSP 257)* **FUNERAL PYRE. / DISGUISES** [4] [ ]
(re-iss. Jan83)

Oct 81. (7") *(POSP 350)* **ABSOLUTE BEGINNERS. / TALES FROM THE RIVERBANK** [4] [ ]
(re-iss. Jan83)

Dec 81. (m-lp) *<503>* **THE JAM** –
– Absolute beginners / Funeral pyre / Liza Radley / Tales from the riverbank / Disguises.

Feb 82. (7"/12") *(POSP/+X 400)* **TOWN CALLED MALICE. / PRECIOUS** 1
(re-iss. Jan83) – hit No.73

Mar 82. (lp/c) *(POLD/+C 5055) <6349>* **THE GIFT** 1 82
– Happy together / Ghosts / Precious / Just who is the 5 o'clock hero? / Trans-global express / Running on the spot / Circus / The planner's dream goes wrong / Carnation / Town called Malice / The gift. *(re-iss. Apr90 cd/c/lp; 823285-2/-4/-1) (cd re-iss. Jul97; 537422-2)*

Jun 82. (7") *(2059 504)* **JUST WHO IS THE 5 O'CLOCK HERO?. / THE GREAT DEPRESSION** 6
(12"+=) *(2141 558)* – War.

Sep 82. (7") *(POSP 505)* **THE BITTEREST PILL (I EVER HAD TO SWALLOW). / PITY POOR ALFIE / FEVER – PITY POOR ALFIE** 2
<US-iss.Nov82 as 12"m-lp> – Great depression.

Nov 82. (7") *(POSP 540)* **BEAT SURRENDER. / SHOPPING** 1 Mar83
(d7"+=)<m-lp> *(POSPJ 540 – JAM 1) <810751>* – Move on up / War / Stoned out of my mind.

Dec 82. (lp/c) *(POLD/+C 5075) <6365>* **DIG THE NEW BREED (live 77-82)** 2
– In the city / All mod cons / To be someone / It's too bad / Start! / Big bird / Set the house ablaze / Ghosts / Standards / In the crowd / Going underground / Dreams of children / That's entertainment / Private hell. *(re-iss. Jun87 lp/c; SPE LP/MC 107) (re-iss. Jun90 cd/c/lp; 810041-2/-4/-1) (cd re-iss. Sep95)*

—— They split late '82. WELLER formed The STYLE COUNCIL, before making it huge as a solo star. FOXTON, meanwhile, went solo, delivering a solitary solo album, 'TOUCH SENSITIVE' (May 1984) for 'Arista'; the Top 75 breaker contained his only Top 30 hit, 'FREAK', released a year earlier. BUCKLER formed TIME UK who had one minor hit, 'THE CABARET' (Sep'83), before he and FOXTON teamed up with TIME UK singer, JIMMY EDWARDS, to become mid-late 80's outfit, SHARP.

– compilations, etc. –

on 'Polydor' unless mentioned otherwise

Sep 80. (d-lp) *(2683 074)* **IN THE CITY / THIS IS THE MODERN WORLD** –
(re-iss. Jan91 cd/c; 847730-2/-4)

Jan 83. (d-c) *(TWOMC 1)* **SOUND AFFECTS / THE GIFT** –

Feb 83. (d-c) *(1574 098)* **ALL MOD CONS / SETTING SONS** –

Oct 83. (d-lp/d-c) *(SNAP/+C 1)* **SNAP!** 2 –
– In the city / Away from the numbers / All around the world / The modern world / News of the world / Billy Hunt / English Rose / Mr. Clean / David Watts / 'A' bomb in Wardour Street / Down in the tube station at midnight / Strange town / The butterfly collector / When you're young / Smithers-Jones / Thick as thieves / The Eton rifles / Going underground / Dreams of children / That's entertainment / Start! / Man in the cornershop / Funeral pyre / Absolute beginners / Tales from the riverbank / Town called Malice / Precious / The bitterest pill (I ever had to swallow) / Beat surrender. *(d-lp.with free 7"ep)* **LIVE AT WEMBLEY (live)** – The great depression / But I'm different now / Move on up / Get yourself together. *(cd-iss. Sep84 as 'COMPACT SNAP'; 821712-2)* – (omits 8 tracks). *(re-iss. Jun90 cd/c/lp; 815537-2/-4/-1)*

Mar 90. (7") *Old Gold; (OG 9894)* **TOWN CALLED MALICE. / ABSOLUTE BEGINNERS** –

Mar 90. (7") *Old Gold; (OG 9895)* **BEAT SURRENDER. / THE BITTEREST PILL (I EVER HAD TO SWALLOW)** –

Mar 90. (7") *Old Gold; (OG 9896)* **THE ETON RIFLES. / DOWN IN THE TUBE STATION AT MIDNIGHT** –

Mar 90. (7") *Old Gold; (OG 9897)* **GOING UNDERGROUND. / START!** –

Sep 90. (12"ep/cd-ep) *Strange Fruit; (SFPS/+CD 080)* **THE PEEL SESSIONS** (26.4.77) –
– In the city / Art school / I've changed my address / The modern world. *(cd-ep re-iss. Sep96; same)*

Jun 91. (7"/c-s) *(PO/+CS 155)* **THAT'S ENTERTAINMENT. / DOWN IN THE TUBE-STATION AT MIDNIGHT (live)** 57 –
(12"+=/cd-s+=) *(PZ/+CD 155)* – Town called Malice (live).

Jul 91. (cd/c/lp) *(849554-2/-4/-1)* **GREATEST HITS** 2 –
– In the city / All around the world / Modern world / News of the world / David Watts / A bomb in Wardour Street / Down in the tube-station at midnight / Strange town / When you're young / Eton rifles / Going underground / Dreams of children / Start / That's entertainment / Funeral pyre / Absolute beginners / A town called Malice / Precious / Just who is the 5 o'clock hero / The bitterest pill (I ever had to swallow) / Beat surrender.

Mar 92. (7"/c-s) *(PO/+CS 199)* **THE DREAMS OF CHILDREN. / AWAY FROM THE NUMBERS (live)** –
(12"+=/cd-s+=) *(PZ/+CD 199)* – This is the modern world (live).

Apr 92. (cd/c/lp) *(513177-2/-4/-1)* **EXTRAS: A COLLECTION OF RARITIES** –

Oct 92. (cd/c) *Pickwick; (PWK S/MC 4129P)* **WASTELAND** –

Oct 93. (cd/c/d-lp) *(519667-2/-4/-1)* **LIVE JAM** (live) 28
– The modern world / Billy Hunt / Thick as thieves / Burning sky / Mr. Clean / Smithers-Jones / Little boy soldiers / The Eton Rifles / Away from the numbers / Down in the tube station at midnight / Strange town / When you're young / 'A' Bomb In Wardour Street / Pretty green / Boy about town / Man in the cornershop / David Watts / Funeral pyre / Move on up / Carnation / The butterfly collector / Precious / Town called Malice / Heatwave. *(cd re-iss. Apr02; same)*

Jul 96. (d-cd/d-c/d-lp) *(531493-2/-4/-1)* **THE JAM COLLECTION** 58 –

May 97. (5xcd-box) *(537143-2)* **DIRECTION REACTION CREATION** 8 –

Sep 97. (7"/c-s) *(571598-7/-4)* **THE BITTEREST PILL (I EVER HAD TO SWALLOW). / THE BUTTERFLY COLLECTOR** 30 –
(cd-s+=) *(571598-2)* – That's entertainment / ('A'version).

Oct 97. (cd/c) *(537423-2/-4)* **THE VERY BEST OF THE JAM** (all the singles 1977-1982) 9 –
– (see 'GREATEST HITS' for track details).

Nov 98. (cd/c) *Spectrum; (550006-2/-4)* **BEAT SURRENDER** –

Apr 01. (9xcd-s-box) *(587610-2)* **THE SINGLES 1977-1979** –

Apr 01. (9xcd-s-box) *(587620-2)* **THE SINGLES 1980-1982** –

May 02. (cd/d-lp) *(589781-2/-1) <065635>* **THE SOUND OF THE JAM** 3 Feb03
– In the city / Away from the numbers / The modern world / David Watts / Down in the tube-station at midnight / To be someone (didn't we have a nice time) / Mr. Clean / English rose / The butterfly collector / The Eton rifles / Thick as thieves / Going underground / Start! / Lisa Radley / Pretty green / That's entertainment / Tales from the riverbank / Town called Malice / Ghosts / Beat surrender.

Jun 02. (3xcd-box) *(<589690-2>)* **THE JAM AT THE BBC** 33

Jun 05. (d-cd; re-) *(821712-2) <9877181>* **COMPACT SNAP** 39 Mar06

JAMES

Formed: Manchester, England ... 1982 by JIM GLENNIE, songwriter TIM BOOTH, LARRY GOTT and GAVAN WHELAN. In 1983 they signed to Tony Wilson's 'Factory' label, issuing a debut 3-track, the 'JIMONE EP'. Their folksy idiosyncracy and wilful weirdness was beloved of the music press almost from the off and their cult standing increased considerably after their 2nd classic 45, 'HYMN FROM A VILLAGE', topped the indie chart early in '85. They were soon snapped up by Seymour Stein's 'Sire', legendary underground mover and shaker Lenny Kaye producing the debut album, 'STUTTER'. BOOTH's overtly accented vocals were the primary focus of the band's often erratic and unorthodox, cerebral, improvisation-driven indie rock/folk and this bizarre combination made the band a compelling live act. However, financial difficulties led to the band moving label to WEA subsidiary 'Blanco Y Negro', where they released 'STRIP MINE' (1988). In 1990, after a change of personnel and a spell on 'Rough Trade', JAMES had their first Top 40 hit on 'Fontana' with 'HOW WAS IT FOR YOU?'. It was soon followed by a Top 20 album, 'GOLD MOTHER', that when re-promoted early 1991 with No.2 hit, the outrageously anthemic and subsequently tediously annoying 'SIT DOWN', also hit No.2. Suddenly the band were riding on the frayed, flared coat-tails of the baggy scene alongside fellow Manchester bands like the HAPPY MONDAYS and the STONE ROSES. Their obstinately obscure sound of old had now been bolstered by chant-along choruses of almost terrace proportions and the ubiquitous JAMES t-shirt was de rigeur for fresher students up and down the country. The band were now playing to stadium-sized audiences and they made their follow-up, 'SEVEN' (1992), to match, all big production and bombast that went down like a lead balloon with critics. With 'LAID' (1993), the band roped in BRIAN ENO, and went for a more opaque, stripped-down sound that recalled their experimental, earlier work. Lyrically, the album was as complex and as vivid as ever while the gorgeous 'SOMETIMES' gave the band their first Top 20 hit since early '92. The ENO sessions also provided the material for the 'WAH WAH' (1994) album, a collection of ambient improvisations with the aging electronic wizard. Of late, TIM BOOTH teamed up with ANGELO BADALAMENTI (he of 'Twin Peaks' fame') and ex-SUEDE guitarist, BERNARD BUTLER to release one-off set, 'BOOTH AND THE BAD ANGEL' (1996). Last year (1997), JAMES were again in the UK Top 10, the single 'SHE'S A STAR' and its parent album, 'WHIPLASH', both achieving the feat. Of late, a stop-gap 'best of' package was treated well by the fans (who made it UK No.1) but 'MILLIONAIRES' (1999) fell short of requirements. Although the near chart-topping record featured hit singles, 'I KNOW WHAT I'M HERE FOR' and 'JUST LIKE FRED ASTAIRE', it had none of the zip and lyrical sparkle of old. Ten albums in and JAMES were showing little sign of middle age spread although 'PLEASED TO MEET YOU' (2001) imparted the wisdom of maturity rather than the arrogance of youth. Although the album didn't quite make the Top 10 and 'GETTING AWAY WITH IT' should've been a bigger hit, the veteran Mancunians proved that mid-life musical crisis is all in the mind. Yet it was to be the band's parting shot as TIM BOOTH returned to his first love, theatre/dance, while keeping his music career on the boil with 'BONE' (2004), a sunny solo sojourn aided and abetted by co-producer/multi-instrumentalist, LEE "MUDDY" BAKER. 2005 saw him playing the role of Mr Zsasz in the movie, 'Batman Begins'.

• **Covers:** SUNDAY MORNING (Velvet Underground) / CHINA GIRL (Iggy Pop & David Bowie).

Album rating: STUTTER (*6) / STRIP MINE (*6) / ONE MAN CLAPPING (*6) / GOLD MOTHER (*8) / SEVEN (*8) / LAID (*7) / WAH WAH (*6) / WHIPLASH (*6) / THE BEST OF JAMES compilation (*8) / MILLIONAIRES (*5) / PLEASED TO MEET YOU (*6) / ULTRA: B-SIDES collection (*5) / GETTING AWAY WITH IT . . . LIVE (*5) / Booth & The Bad Angel: BOOTH & THE BAD ANGEL (*5) / Tim Booth: BONE (*5)

TIM BOOTH (b. 4 Feb'60, Bradford, England) – vocals / **LARRY GOTT** (b. JAMES GOTT) – guitar / **JIM GLENNIE** (b.10 Oct'63) – bass / **GAVAN WHELAN** – drums

Factory | not iss.

Sep 83. (7") *(FAC 78)* **JIMONE** [ ] [–]
– What's the world / Fire so close / Folklore.

Feb 85. (7") *(FAC 119)* **JAMES II** [ ] [–]
– Hymn from a village / If things were perfect.

Jun 85. (12"ep) *(FAC 138)* **VILLAGE FIRE** [ ] [–]
– What's the world / Fire so close / Folklore / Hymn from a village / If things were perfect.

Sire | Warners

Feb 86. (7") *(JIM 3)* **CHAIN MAIL. / HUP STRINGS** [ ] [–]
(12"+=) *(JIM 3T)* **SIT DOWN EP** – Uprising.

Jul 86. (7") *(JIM 4)* **SO MANY WAYS. / WITHDRAWN** [ ] [–]
(12"+=) *(JIM 4T)* – Just hipper.

Jul 86. (lp/c) *(JIM LP/C 1)* **STUTTER** [68] [–]
– Skullduggery / Scarecrow / So many ways / Just hip / Johnny Yen / Summer song / Really hard / Billy's shirts / Why so close / Withdrawn / Black hole. *(cd-iss. Nov91; 7599 25437-2)*

Blanco Y Negro | Sire

Sep 87. (7") *(NEG 26)* **YAHO. / MOSQUITO** [ ] [–]
(12"+=) *(NEG 26T)* – Left out of her will / New nature.

Mar 88. (7") *(NEG 31)* **WHAT FOR. / ISLAND SWING** [ ] [–]
(c-s+=/12"+=) *(NEG 31 C/T)* – Not there.

Sep 88. (lp/c)(cd) *(JIM LP/C 2)(925657-2)* **STRIP MINE** [90] [ ]
– What for / Charlie Dance / Fairground / Are you ready / Yaho / Medieval / Not there / Riders / Vulture / Strip mining / Refrain. *(re-iss. Jul91; same) (cd re-iss. Feb95; 925657-2)*

Rough Trade | not iss.

Mar 89. (lp/c/cd) *(ONEMAN 001/+C/CD)* **ONE MAN CLAPPING (live in Bath)** [ ] [–]
– Chain mail / Sandman (hup strings) / Whoops / Riders / Why so close / Leaking / Johnny Yen / Scarecrow / Are you ready / Really hard / Burned / Stutter. *(cd+=)* – Yaho.

—— **DAVE BAYNTON-POWER** – drums repl. WHELAN / added **SAUL DAVIS** – violin, percussion, guitar / **MARK HUNTER** – keyboards

Jun 89. (7") *(RT 225)* **SIT DOWN. / SKY IS FALLING** [ ] [–]
(12"+=/3"cd-s+=) *(RTT 225/+CD)* – Goin' away / Sound investment.

—— added **ANDY DIAGRAM** – trumpet (ex-PALE FOUNTAINS, ex-DIAGRAM BROS)

Nov 89. (7") *(RT 245)* **COME HOME. / PROMISED LAND** [ ] [–]
(12"+=/cd-s+=) *(RTT 245/+CD)* – ('A'extended) / Slow right down (demo).

Fontana | Mercury

May 90. (7") *(JIM 5)* **HOW WAS IT FOR YOU? / WHOOPS (live)** [32] [–]
(12") *(JIM 5-12)* – ('A') / Hymn from a village (live) / Lazy.
(cd-s) *(JIMCD 5)* – ('A') / Hymn from a village (live) / Undertaker.
(12") *(JIMM 5-12)* – ('A') / ('A'different mix) / Lazy / Undertaker.

Jun 90. (cd/c/lp) *(<846189-2/-4/-1>)* **GOLD MOTHER** [16] Aug90 [ ]
– Come home / Government walls / God only knows / You can tell how much suffering (on a face that's always smiling) / How was it for you? / Crescendo / Hang on / Walking the ghost / Gold mother / Top of the world. *(re-iss. Apr91 cd/c/lp; 848595-2/-4/-1); hit No.2) (cd+=)* – Sit down / Lose control. *(cd re-iss. Dec01 ++; 548785-2)* – Come home (skunk weed skank mix) / Lose control (live) / Sit down (live) / Gold mother (remix).

Jul 90. (7"/c-s) *(JIM/+C 6)* **COME HOME (Flood mix). / DREAMING UP TOMORROW** [32] [–]
(12") *(JIM 6-12)* – ('A'extended) / Stutter (live) / Fire away.
(cd-s) *(JIMCD 6)* – ('A'side) / ('A'extended) / Gold mother (remix) / Fire away.
(12") *(JIMM 6-12)* – ('A'live) / Gold mother (Warp remix) / ('A'-Andy Weatherall Boys own remix).

Nov 90. (7"/c-s) *(JIM/+C 7)* **LOSE CONTROL. / SUNDAY MORNING** [38] [–]
(ext.12"+=/ext.cd-s+=) *(JIM 7-12/CD7)* – Out to get you.

Mar 91. (7"/c-s) *(JIM/+C 8)* **SIT DOWN. / ('A'live)** [2] [ ]
(12"+=/cd-s+=) *(JIM 8-12/CD8)* – Tonight.

Nov 91. (7"/c-s) *(JIM/+C 9)* **SOUND. / ALL MY SONS** [9] [ ]
(12"+=/cd-s+=) *(JIM 9-12/CD9)* – ('A'extended) / Come home (Youth mix).

Jan 92. (7"/c-s) *(JIM/+C 10)* **BORN OF FRUSTRATION. / BE MY PRAYER** [13] [ ]
(12"+=/cd-s+=) *(JIM 10-12/CD10)* – Sound (mix).

Feb 92. (cd/c/lp) *(<510932-2/-4/-1>)* **SEVEN** [2] Mar92 [ ]
– Born of frustration / Ring the bells / Sound / Bring a gun / Mother / Don't wait that long / Live a life of love / Heavens / Protect me / Seven. *(cd+=/c+=)* – Next lover. *(re-iss. Aug98; same) (cd re-iss. Dec01 +=; 548786-2)* – live:- Protect me (acoustic) / Sound / Heavens / Don't wait that long.

Mar 92. (7"/c-s) *(JIM/+C 11)* **RING THE BELLS. / FIGHT** [37] [ ]
(12"+=/cd-s+=) *(JIM 11-12/CD11)* – The skunk weed skank / Come home (live dub version).
(12"++=) *(JIM 11-122)* – Once a friend.

Jul 92. (7"ep/c-ep/cd-ep) *(JIM/+C/CD 12)* **SEVEN (remix) / GOALIES BALL. / WILLIAM BURROUGHS / STILL ALIVE** [46] [–]

Sep 93. (7"/c-s) *(JIM/+C 13)* **SOMETIMES. / AMERICA** [18] [ ]
(12"+=/cd-s+=) *(JIM 13-12/CD13)* – Building a charge.

Sep 93. (cd/c/lp) *(<514943-2/-4/-1>)* **LAID** [3] Oct93 [72]
– Out to get you / Sometimes (Lester Piggott) / Dream thrum / One of the three / Say something / Five-o / P.S. / Everybody knows / Knuckle too far / Low, low / Laid / Lullaby / Skindiving. *(re-iss. Aug98; same) (cd re-iss. Dec01 +=; 548787-2)* – live at the BBC:- Laid / Sometimes / Five-O / Say something (live).

Nov 93. (7"/c-s) *(JIM/+C 14) <858217>* **LAID. / WAH WAH KITS** [25] Jan94 [61]
(cd-s+=) *(JIMCD 14)* – The lake / Seconds away.
(cd-s) *(JIMDD 14)* – ('A'live) / Five-O / Say something / Sometimes.

Mar 94. (c-s) *(JIMMC 15)* **JAM J / SAY SOMETHING** [24] [ ]
(12"+=)(cd-s+=) *(JIMX 15)(JMCD 15)* – Assassin / ('B'-version).
(cd-s) *(JIMCD 15)* – JAM J – James vs The Sabres Of Paradise (i) Arena dub (ii) Amphetamine pulsate / JAM J – James vs The Sabres Of Paradise (i) Sabresonic tremelo dub (ii) Spaghetti steamhammer.

Sep 94. (cd/c/d-lp;ltd) *(<314 526 408-2/-4/-1>)* **WAH WAH (w / BRIAN ENO)** [11] Oct94 [ ]

– Hammer strings / Pressure's on / Jam J / Frequency dip / Lay the law down / Burn the cat / Maria / Low clouds (1) / Building a fire / Gospel oak / DVV / Say say something / Rhythmic dreams / Dead man / Rain whistling / Low clouds (2) / Bottom of the well / Honest Joe / Arabic agony / Tomorrow / Laughter / Sayonara.

— **ADRIAN OXAAL** – repl. DIAGRAM

Feb 97. (cd-s) *(JIMED 16)* **SHE'S A STAR / STUTTER (live) / JOHNNY YEN (live)** 9 –
(cd-s) *(JIMDD 16)* – ('A'side) / Chunney chops / Fishknives / Van Gogh's dog.
(cd-s) *(JIMCD 16)* – ('A'-Dave Angel mix) / ('A'-Biosphere mix) / Come home (Weatherall mix).

Mar 97. (cd/c/lp) *(<534354-2/-4/-1>)* **WHIPLASH** 9
– Tomorrow / Lost a friend / Waltzing along / She's a star / Greenpeace / Go to the bank / Play dead / Avalanche / Homeboy / Watering hole / Blue pastures. *(cd re-iss. Dec01 +=; 548788-2)* – LOst a friend (live) / Greenpeace (live) / Homeboy (live) / Waltzing along (Flytronic mix).

Apr 97. (cd-ep) *(JIMCD 17)* **TOMORROW / GONE TOO FAR / HONEST PLEASURE / ALL ONE TO ME** 12 –
(cd-s) *(JIMDD 17)* – ('A'side) / Lost a friend (session) / Come home (session) / Greenpeace (session).
(cd-s) *(JIMED 17)* – ('A'mixes; Fila Brazilia / Archive / Dirty Beatnik).

Jun 97. (cd-s) *(JIMCD 18)* **WALTZING ALONG / ('A'mix)** 23 –
(cd-s) *(JIMED 18)* – ('A'side) / ('A'live) / (live).
(cd-s) *(JIMDD 18)* – ('A'remixes by; Midfield General & Flytronix).

Mar 98. (cd-ep) *(JIMCD 19)* **DESTINY CALLING / GOALIE'S BALL / ASSASSIN / THE LAKE** 17 –
(cd-ep) *(JIMDD 19)* – ('A'side) / Jam J (live) / Honest Joe (live) / Sound (live).
(cd-s) *(JIMED 19)* – ('A'side) / She's a star (CD-Rom video).

Mar 98. (cd/c) *(<536898-2/-4>)* **THE BEST OF** (compilation) 1
– Come home / Sit down / She's a star / Laid / Waltzing along / Say something / Tomorrow / Born of frustration / Destiny calling / Out to get you / Runaground / Lose control / How was it for you? / Seven / Sound / Ring the bells / Sometimes / Hymn from a village.
(also d-cd-iss. ; 558173-2)

May 98. (cd-ep) *(JIMCD 20)* **RUNAGROUND / CRESCENDO / HANG ON / BE MY POWER** 29 –
(cd-ep) *(JIMDD 20)* – ('A'side) / Say something (live) / Laid (live) / Lose control (live).
(cd-ep) *(JIMED 20)* – ('A'side) / ('A'remix) / Egoiste / Lost a friend (Aloof remix).

Nov 98. (c-s/cd-s) *(JIM MC/CD 21)* **SIT DOWN (1998 remix) / ('A'-Apollo 440 remix)** 7 –
(cd-s) *(JIMDD 21)* – China girl (radio 1 Iggy Pop tribute).

Jul 99. (c-s) *(JIMC 22)* **I KNOW WHAT I'M HERE FOR / ALL GOOD BOYS** 22
(cd-s+=) *(JIMCD 22)* – Imagine ourselves.
(cd-s) *(JIMDD 22)* – ('A'side) / Downstairs / Stolen horses.

Oct 99. (c-s) *(JIMC 23)* **JUST LIKE FRED ASTAIRE / I DEFEAT** 17
(cd-s+=) *(JIMCD 23)* – Long to see.
(cd-s) *(JIMDD 23)* – ('A'side) / Mary / Goal, goal, goal.

Oct 99. (cd/c) *(<546386-2/-4>)* **MILLIONAIRES** 2
– Crash / Just like Fred Astaire / I know what I'm here for / Shooting my mouth off / We're going to miss you / Strangers / Hello / Afro lover / Surprise / Dumb jam / Someone's got it in for me / Vervaceous. *(also d-cd+=; 546789-2)* – (live):- I know what I'm here for / Crash / Destiny calling / Someone's got it in for me / Just like Fred Astaire / I know what I'm here for (video) / Just like Fred Astaire (video).

Dec 99. (c-s) *(JIMMC 24)* **WE'RE GOING TO MISS YOU / WISDOM OF THE THROAT** 48
(cd-s+=) *(JIMCD 24)* – Top of the world (live).
(cd-s) *(JIMDD 24)* – ('A'side) / Pocketful of lemons ('A'-Eno's version).

— now without OXAAL

Jun 01. (cd-s) *(JIMCD 25)* **GETTING AWAY WITH IT (ALL MESSED UP) / MAKE IT ALRIGHT / SO SWELL (ambient mix)** 22 –
(cd-s) *(JIMDD 25)* – ('A'side) / Stand / Shining (live).

Jul 01. (cd) *(<586146-2>)* **PLEASED TO MEET YOU** 11
– Space / Falling down / English beefcake / Junkie / Pleased to meet you / The shining / Senorita / Give it away / Fine / Getting away with it (all messed up) / Alaskan pipeline.

— JAMES disbanded in December 2001

– compilations, etc. –

Dec 01. (cd) *Fontana; (<548440-2>)* **ULTRA: B-SIDES** Jan02
– Gone too far / Honest pleasure / Sunday morning / China girl / Still alive / The lake / I defeat / Goalie's ball / Chunny pops / Tonight / Dream up tomorrow / William Burroughs / Assassin / Stolen horse / Undertaker / Egoiste / Van Gogh's dog / Where you gonna run?

Jun 02. (d-cd) *Sanctuary; (SANDD 119) <84557>* **GETTING AWAY WITH IT . . . LIVE (live)**
– Say something / Waltzing along / Sometimes / Laid / I know what I'm here for / God only knows / Someone's got it in for me / Vervaceous / Protect me / Out to get you / Hymn from a village / Johnny Yen / Getting away with it / Tomorrow / Born of frustration / Ring the bells / Top of the world / Sound / Space / She's a star / Come home / Sit down.

BOOTH AND THE BAD ANGEL

TIM BOOTH / ANGELO BADALAMENTI / + BERNARD BUTLER (ex-Suede)

Fontana Mercury

Jun 96. (c-s) *(BBMC 1)* **I BELIEVE (edit) / I BELIEVE (long version)** 25 –
(cd-s+=) *(BBCD 1)* – When you smiled.
(cd-s+=) *(BBDD 1)* – Melting away.

Jul 96. (cd/c) *(<526 852-2/-4>)* **BOOTH AND THE BAD ANGEL** 35
– I believe / Dance of the bad angels / Hit parade / Fall in love with me / Old ways / Life gets better / Heart / Rising / Butterfly's dream / Stranger / Hands in the rain.
(below lifted from the film 'Martha Meet Franky, Daniel & Laurence'.

Jun 98. (c-s) *(MERMC 503)* **FALL IN LOVE WITH ME (live) / I BELIEVE (live)** 57 –
(cd-s+=) *(MERCD 503)* – Hit parade (live).
(cd-s) *(MERDD 503)* – ('A') / Butterfly's dream (live) ('A'-live).

TIM BOOTH

BOOTH – vocals / with **LEE "MUDDY" BAKER** – multi, producer + **KEVIN "KK" KERRIGAN** – bass

Sanctuary Koch Int.

Jun 04. (cd) *(SANCD 268) <KOCD 9626>* **BONE**
– Wave hello / Bone / Monkey god / Redneck / Love hard / Discover / Fall in love / Falling down / Down to the Jen / In the darkness / Eh mamma / Careful what you say.

Jun 04. (7") *(SANSE 279)* **DOWN TO THE SEA. / BRING IT ON** 68 –
(cd-s) *(SANXS 279)* – ('A') / Remember me.

Aug 04. (cd-s) *(SANXS 287)* **WAVE HELLO / SI TU VEUX** –

JAMIROQUAI

Formed: /based Ealing, London . . . early 1991, by the youthful, JASON KAY (aka JAY K). After scoring a minor hit on Eddie Pillar's 'Acid Jazz' label, with his debut single, 'WHEN YOU GONNA LEARN?', JAMIROQUAI switched labels to 'Sony Soho Square', the label no doubt hoping to cash in on the super-hip Acid Jazz scene which had already seen The BRAND NEW HEAVIES reap financial rewards for 'London' records, especially in the lucrative American market. And cash in on it they did; where Acid Jazz had once been the preserve of a London clique, JAY K sold the concept nationwide. The image was calculated but perfect; Adidas Gazelles, 70's cords, ethnic hats and funky soul-boy footwork. Vocally, the comparisons with STEVIE WONDER were unavoidable, all 'doo-doo-da-doo-doo' flourishes which seemed irreconcilable with a skinny white kid from London. 'TOO YOUNG TO DIE', his first effort for 'Sony', went Top 10, the debut album, 'EMERGENCY ON PLANET EARTH' (1993) reaching No.1 later that summer. Spontaneous, irresistibly funky and musically accomplished, what the record lacked in originality, it made up for with brazen charm. The only thing that indicated the album had been recorded in the 90's was the lavish use of digeridoo, although this added novelty value rather then any real innovation. Lyrically, the record was a platform for JAY's unceasingly positive guide to life and his often naive, if well meaning, political and ecological diatribes. In interviews and on stage, JAY's charisma was undeniable, rebuffing charges of being contrived with a cocksure cheekiness. By 'THE RETURN OF THE SPACE COWBOY' (1994) the image was still intact, it was just a case of different album, different hat. As well as cornering the money-spinning pop/teen market, the DAVID MORALES mix of the title track was a massive European club hit, further boosting sales of the album. Musically, the record more or less stuck to the same formula although there were signs of a growing maturity in JK's songwriting and lyrics. 'TRAVELLING WITHOUT MOVING' (1996) saw JAMIROQUAI consolidate their position as purveyors of reliable, chart-friendly pop-funk while JK has become as much of a 90's icon as OASIS, if a bit more stylish. Now "lord of the manor" in a Buckinghamshire country estate (he also owns a number of sports cars, etc.) and the beau of Big Breakfast starlet, Denise Van Outen, JASON KAY was back to what he knows best, writing songs; a new song from the 'Godzilla' movie, 'DEEPER UNDERGROUND' was his return to No.1. 'SYNKRONIZED' (1999) was JAMIROQUAI's fourth album in six years, although the slickness of JAY K's retro persona was wearing a little thin. Nevertheless, the album shot to the top of the UK charts (his first since his debut!) and produced three further hits, 'CANNED HEAT', 'SUPERSONIC' and 'KING FOR A DAY'. The man in the silly hat returned in 2001 with 'A FUNK ODYSSEY', sounding more and more like STEVIE WONDER with each album. The set, mostly based on the group's strained attempts at disco/funk, entered the UK charts at No.1 and the US Billboard's Top 50. It also reaped in the cash for JK and Co via the singles 'LITTLE L' and the estranged, break-up track 'YOU GIVE ME SOMETHING' both reaching the UK Top 10 and being shoved down the public's throats by repeated plays on MTV, etc. JAY and his funkateers returned to the UK Top 3 in 2005 with sixth set, 'DYNAMITE', effecting a fashionably 80s gloss here and there but otherwise fusing the tried and tested 70s funk and disco influences on hits like 'FEELS JUST LIKE IT SHOULD', 'SEVEN DAYS IN SUNNY JUNE' and '(DON'T) GIVE HATE A CHANCE'.

• **Songwriters:** JAY and TOBY are main writers, although ZENDER, McKENZIE and others contribute. • **Trivia:** Pronounced JAM-EAR-OH-KWAI, they took name from a tribe of Native Americans.

Album rating: EMERGENCY ON PLANET EARTH (*9) / RETURN OF THE SPACE COWBOY (*7) / TRAVELLING WITHOUT MOVING (*7) / SYNKRONIZED (*6) / A FUNK ODYSSEY (*5) / DYNAMITE (*6)

JAY K (b. JASON KAY, 30 Sep'69, Stretford, Lancashire, England) – vocals / **TOBY SMITH** (b. TOBY GRAFFETY-SMITH, 29 Oct'70) – keyboards / **NICK VAN GELDER** – drums / **STUART ZENDER** (b.18 Mar'74, Philadelphia, Pennsylvania, USA) – bass / **WALLIS BUCHANAN** (b.29 Nov'65) – didgeridoo / plus **KOFI KARIKARI** – percussion / **MAURIZIO RAVALIO** – percussion / **GLENN NIGHTINGALE + SIMON BARTHOLOMEW** – guitars / **D-ZIRE** – DJ / **GARY BARNACLE** – sax, flute / **JOHN THIRKELL** – trumpet, flugel horn / **RICHARD EDWARDS** – trombone

Acid Jazz | not iss.

Oct 92. (12") *(JAZID 46T)* **WHEN YOU GONNA LEARN (JK mix & instrumental). / WHEN YOU GONNA LEARN (mixes; Cante Hondo / original demo / Digeridoo instrumental)** [52] [–]
(re-iss. Feb93 hit No.69)
(cd-s+=) *(JAZID 46CD)* – ('A'-digeridon't mix).

Sony S2 | Epic

Mar 93. (12") *(659011-6)* **TOO YOUNG TO DIE (mixes; extended / original / instrumental)** [12] [–]
(cd-s+=) *(659011-2)* – ('A'edit).

May 93. (c-s) *(659297-4)* **BLOW YOUR MIND (part 1) / HOOKED UP** [10] [–]
(12"+=) *(659297-6)* – Blow your mind (part 2).
(cd-s++=) *(659297-2)* – When you gonna learn (JK mix).

Jun 93. (cd/c/lp) *(474069-2/-4/-2)* **EMERGENCY ON PLANET EARTH** [1] [ ]
– When you gonna learn (digeridoo) / Too young to die / Hooked up / If I like it, I do it / Music of the mind / Emergency on Planet Earth / Whatever it is, I just can't stop / Blow your mind / Revolution 1993 / Didgin' out.

Aug 93. (12"/c-s/cd-s) *(659578-6/-4/-2)* **EMERGENCY ON PLANET EARTH. / IF I LIKE IT, I DO IT (MTV acoustic) / REVOLUTION 1993 (demo)** [32] [ ]

Sep 93. (c-s) *(659695-6)* **WHEN YOU GONNA LEARN (Digeridoo). / DIDGIN' OUT (live at the Milky Way, Amsterdam)** [28] [ ]
(cd-s+=) *(659695-2)* – Too young to die (live) / ('A'-Cante Hondo mix).
(12") *(659695-6) <74925>* – ('A'mixes from 'Acid Jazz').

— **DERRICK McKENZIE** (b.27 Mar'62, Islington, London) – drums; repl. VAN GELDER

Sep 94. (12") *(660851-6)* **SPACE COWBOY. / JOURNEY TO ARNHEMLAND / SPACE COWBOY – STONED AGAIN** [17] [ ]
(cd-s) *(660851-2)* – (first two tracks) / Kids / ('A'demo).
(cd-s/12") *<77827+1>* – (6-'A'versions).

Oct 94. (cd/c/d-lp) *(477813-2/-4/-1)* **THE RETURN OF THE SPACE COWBOY** [2] [ ]
– Just another story / Stillness in time / Half the man / Light years / Manifest destiny / The kids / Mr. Moon / Scam / Journey to Arnhemland / Morning glory / Space cowboy. *(cd re-iss. Dec01; same)*

Nov 94. (c-s) *(661003-4)* **HALF THE MAN / SPACE CLAV** [15] [–]
(12"+=/cd-s+=) *(661003-6/-2)* – Emergency on Planet Earth.
(cd-s) *(661003-5)* – ('A'side) / Jamiroquai's Greatest Hits: When you gonna learn? / Too young to die / Blow your mind.

Feb 95. (c-s) *(661256-4)* **LIGHT YEARS / JOURNEY TO ARNHEMLAND (live)** [ ] [–]
(ext-12"+=) *(661256-6)* – Light years (live).
(cd-s+=) *(661256-2)* – Scam / We gettin' down.

Jun 95. (12"/cd-s) *(662025-6/-2)* **STILLNESS IN TIME. / SPACE COWBOY (mix)** [9] [ ]
(cd-s+=) *(662025-5)* – Emergency on Planet Earth / Light years.

— In Jun'96, JAMIROQUAI featured on M-BEAT's No.12 hit version of 'DO U KNOW WHERE YOU'RE COMING FROM'.

Aug 96. (7") *(663613-7)* **VIRTUAL INSANITY. / ('A'-Unreality mix)** [3] [–]
(c-s+=) *(663613-4)* – ('A'-album mix).
(12"/cd-s) *(663613-6/-2)* – ('A'side) / Do you know where you're coming from / Bullet / ('A'-album version).
(cd-s) *(663613-5)* – ('A'side) / Space cowboy (classic radio) / Emergency on Planet Earth (London-Rican mix) / Do you know where you're coming from.

Sep 96. (cd/c/lp) *(483999-2/-4/-1) <67903>* **TRAVELLING WITHOUT MOVING** [2] [24]
– Virtual insanity / Cosmic girl / Use the force / Everyday / Alright / High times / Drifting along / Didjerama / Didjital vibrations / Travelling without moving / You are my love / Spend a lifetime. *(cd+=)* – (bonus track).

Nov 96. (7"/c-s) *(663829-7/-4)* **COSMIC GIRL / SLIPIN 'N' SLIDIN'** [6] [ ]
(cd-s+=) *(663829-2)* – Didjital vibrations / ('A'-classic radio).
(12"/cd-s) *(663829-6/-5) <78501-2>* – ('A'mixes; radio / classic / Quasar / dub).

May 97. (cd-s) *(664235-2) <78703>* **ALRIGHT (mixes; radio / vocal version / dub vocal / DJ version excursion)** [6] Sep97 [78]
(cd-s) *(664235-5)* – ('A'mixes; extended / Tee's In House / Tee's Digital club / Tee's radio Jay).
(12") *(664235-6)* – ('A'-version vocal & Tee's In House mix) / Space cowboy (classic club) / Cosmic girl (classic mix).
(d12") *<786591>* – (7 version incl. above stuff).

Dec 97. (12"/cd-s) *(665370-6/-2)* **HIGH TIMES (mixes; original / Bionic Supachronic / Doobie dub / album or Jamiroquai dub)** [20] [ ]
(cd-s+=) *(665370-5)* – ('A'mixes; incl. Sanchez radio edit).

Jul 98. (c-s) *(666218-4)* **DEEPER UNDERGROUND / DEEPER UNDERGROUND (the metro mix)** [1] [ ]
(cd-s+=) *(666218-2)* – ('A'-instrumental).
(cd-s) *(666218-5)* – ('A'side & mixes; Ummah & S-Man Meets Da Northface Killa dub).
(cd-s+=) *<79032>* – (all above) / High times (album & Doobie dub).

May 99. (c-s) *(667302-4) <79189-4/-7>* **CANNED HEAT / WOLF IN SHEEP'S CLOTHING** [4] [ ]

(cd-s+=) *(667302-2)* – ('A'radio edit).
(cd-s) *(667302-5)* – ('A'versions) / Deeper underground (Chillington mix).
(cd-s) *<79162>* – (all above tracks).

Jun 99. (cd/c/lp) *(494517-2/-4/-1) <69973>* **SYNKRONIZED** 1 28
– Canned heat / Planet home / Black Capricorn day / Soul education / Falling / Destitute illusions / Supersonic / Butterfly / Where do we go from here? / King for a day. *(cd+=)* – Deeper underground. *(cd re-iss. Sep01; same)*

Sep 99. (c-s) *(667839-4)* **SUPERSONIC / SUPERSONIC (album version)** 22 ☐
(cd-s) *(667839-32) <79320><12"= 79307>* – ('A'side) / ('A'-Pete Heller – the love mix) / ('A'-Harvey's Fuel altered mix).
(cd-s) *(667839-5)* – ('A'side) / ('A'-Restless Soul main vocal) / ('A'-Sharp Razor remix).

Nov 99. (c-s) *(667973-4)* **KING FOR A DAY / PLANET HOME (Trabant Brothers Inc. remix)** 20 –
(cd-s+=) *(667973-2)* – Supersonic (Dirty Rotten Scoundrels mix).
(cd-s) *(667973-5)* – ('A'side) / Canned heat (Shanks & Bigfoot – extended master mix) / Supersonic (edit) / Supersonic (CD-Rom version).

— in Feb'01, JAMIROQUAI featured on JOOLS HOLLAND's UK hit, 'I'm In The Mood For Love'

Aug 01. (c-s) *(671718-4)* **LITTLE L / LITTLE L (wounded buffalo mix)** 5 –
(12"+=) *(671718-6)* – ('A'-Bob Sinclair mix) / ('A'-Boris Dlugosch mix).
(cd-s++=) *(671718-2)* – ('A'-video).

Sep 01. (cd/c/lp) *(504069-2/-4/-1) <85954>* **A FUNK ODYSSEY** 1 44
– Feel so good / Little L / You give me something / Corner of the earth / Love foolosophy / Stop don't panic / Black crow / Main vein / Twenty zero one / Picture of my life. *(UK+=)* – So good to feel real.

Nov 01. (c-s) *(672007-4)* **YOU GIVE ME SOMETHING / DO IT LIKE WE USED TO** 16 –
(cd-s) *(672007-2)* – ('A'side) / ('A'-mixes; Blacksmith R&B / Full intention / Cosmos / King Unique).

Feb 02. (cd-s) *(672325-2)* **LOVE FOOLOSOPHY / (Knee Deep remix) / (Bini & Martini's ocean remix) / (original video)** 14 –
(cd-s) *(672325-2)* – ('A'side) / (twin club remix) / (Blaze remix) / (alternate video).

Jul 02. (cd-s) *(672788-2)* **CORNER OF THE EARTH / MAIN VEIN (knee deep remix) / MAIN VEIN (deep swing jazzy thumper mix)** 31 –
(12"+=) *(672821-6)* – Main vein (knee deep vocal dub).
(cd-s) *(672788-5)* – ('A'side) / Bad girls (with ANASTACIA live at the Brits) / Little L (the making of the video).

Sony Sony

Jun 05. (cd-s) *(675968-1)* **FEELS JUST LIKE IT SHOULD / (Knee Deep remix)** 8 –
(12"/cd-s) *(675968-6/-2)* – ('A') / (Mark Ronson remix) / (Timo Maas remix).

Jun 05. (cd/d-lp) *(<520111-2/-1>)* **DYNAMITE** 3 ☐
– Feels just like it should / Dynamite / Seven days in sunny June / Electric mistress / Starchild / Loveblind / Talullah / (Don't) Give hate a chance / World that he wants / Black devil car / Hot tequila brown / Time won't wait.

Sep 05. (cd-s) *(676064-1)* **SEVEN DAYS IN SUNNY JUNE / (Steve Mac edit)** 14 –
(cd-s) *(676064-2)* – ('A') / ('A'-remixes; Steve Mac classic / Oliver Lang / Blackbeard).
(12") *(676064-6)* – ('A'-Steve Mac classic) / ('A'-Ashley Beedle heavy disco vocal mix).

Nov 05. (cd-s) *(82876 75064-2)* **(DON'T) GIVE HATE A CHANCE / (Steve Mac radio edit)** 27 –
(12") *(82876 75064-1)* – (Steve Mac radio edit) / (Freemasons mix).
(cd-s+=) *(82876 75064-5)* – (all 3 versions above).

JANE'S ADDICTION

Formed: Los Angeles, California, USA ... 1984 by Miami-raised PERRY FARRELL. The band's debut effort was a self-financed eponymous live album on 'Triple XXX', the record's naked intensity going some way towards capturing FARRELL's skewed musical vision. More successful was the band's debut for 'Warner Brothers', 'NOTHING'S SHOCKING' (1988), a wilfully perverse and eclectic blend of thrash, folk and funk that, musically and lyrically, made L.A.'s cock-rock brigade look like school boys. FARRELL's creepy shrill was something of an acquired taste, although it complemented the abrasive, mantra-like music perfectly, from the juddering 'PIGS IN ZEN' to the bleakly beautiful 'JANE SAYS'. The record courted controversy almost immediately, with its cover art depicting naked siamese twins strapped to an electric chair. Live, the band were just as confrontational, FARRELL stalking the stage like some transexual high priest. 'RITUAL DE LO HABITUAL' (1990) was JANE'S' masterstroke, combining the compelling musical dynamics of the debut with more rhythm and melody. The result was a UK Top 40 hit for 'BEEN CAUGHT STEALING', a funky paeon to the delights of shoplifting. Inevitably, JANE'S ADDICTION incurred, yet again, the wrath of America's moral guardians and the record was banned from several US retail chains. The band replied by re-releasing it in a plain white sleeve with only the First Amendment printed on it. The following year, FARRELL organised the first Lollapalooza tour, a travelling festival of indie, rap and alternative acts. It was while headlining this jaunt that the band reached its messy conclusion, FARRELL eventually coming to blows with guitarist NAVARRO and splitting soon after. While NAVARRO subsequently joined the RED HOT CHILI PEPPERS, FARRELL formed PORNO FOR PYROS with PERKINS and a cast of likeminded musicians. The 1993 eponymous debut was like a more aggressive, less mysterious JANE'S ADDICTION, reaching the Top 5. Following personal problems and a drug bust, the band eventually released a follow-up three years later, 'GOOD GOD'S URGE', a more heavy-lidded, narcotic-centric affair which even featured NAVARRO on one track, 'FREEWAY'. JANE'S ADDICTION have since reformed (with the 'CHILI's FLEA on bass), initially for some live work in 1997, although a handful of new tracks surfaced on the odds'n'sods collection, 'KETTLE WHISTLE'. Towards the end of the millennium, PERRY was back in a solo capacity, the album 'REV' receiving some tender reviews for his er, carnival of sound. The zen-like figure of FARRELL was back in 2001 with the second instalment of his solo career, 'SONG YET TO BE SUNG', a diversion into electronica which almost succeeds in capturing the spirit of global musical enlightenment FARRELL was so obviously after. While fans expecting a return to the serrated alchemy of yore would have been disappointed by 'STRAYS' (2003), JANE'S' first full length studio album in more than a decade, the warped genius of FARRELL was still evident in fits and starts. Hazy and unfocused, the album seemed unable to shake off the sense that it was a continuation of FARRELL's intermittent solo career, especially bearing in mind that AVERY was missing.

• **Songwriters:** Group penned, except SYMPATHY FOR THE DEVIL (Rolling Stones). Perry solo covered WHOLE LOTTA LOVE (Led Zeppelin) / TONIGHT (from 'West Side Story') / SATELLITE OF LOVE (Lou Reed) / RIPPLE (Grateful Dead).

Album rating: JANE'S ADDICTION (*7) / NOTHING'S SHOCKING (*8) / RITUAL DE LO HABITUAL (*9) / KETTLE WHISTLE part compilation (*6) / Porno For Pyros: PORNO FOR PYROS (*6) / GOOD GOD'S URGE (*8) / Perry Farrell: REV (*7) / SONG YET TO BE SUNG (*5) / Dave Navarro: TRUST NO ONE (*6) / Jane's Addiction: STRAYS (*6)

PERRY FARRELL (b. PERRY BERNSTEIN, 29 Mar'59, Queens, N.Y.) – vocals / **DAVE NAVARRO** (b. 6 Jun'67, Santa Monica, Calif.) – guitar / **ERIC AVERY** (b.25 Apr'65) – bass / **STEPHEN PERKINS** (b.13 Sep'67) – drums

not iss. Triple X

Aug 87. (lp) *<XXX 51004>* **JANE'S ADDICTION (live)** – ☐
– Trip away / Whores / Pigs in Zen / 1% / I would for you / My time / Jane says / Rock'n'roll / Sympathy / Chip away. *<re-iss. Dec88 lp/c/cd; TX 510041 LP/MC/CD> (UK-iss.Dec90 on 'WEA' cd/c/lp; 7599 26599-2/-4/-1)*

Warners Warners

Sep 88. (lp/c)(cd) *(WX 216/+C)(925727-2) <25727>* **NOTHING'S SHOCKING** ☐ ☐
– Up the beach / Ocean size / Had a dad / Ted, just admit it . . . / Standing in the shower . . . thinking / Summertime rolls / Mountain song / Idiots rule / Jane says / Thank you boys. *(cd+=)* – Pigs in Zen.

Mar 89. (7") *<27520>* **MOUNTAIN SONG. / STANDING IN THE SHOWER . . . THINKING** [–] [ ]

May 89. (7") *(W 7520)* **MOUNTAIN SONG. / JANE SAYS** [ ] [–]
(12"ep+=) **THE SHOCKING EP** *(W 7520T)* – Had a dad (live).

—— added guest **MORGAN** (a female) – violin

Aug 90. (cd)(lp/c) *(7599 25993-2)(WX 306/+C) <25993>* **RITUAL DE LO HABITUAL** [37] [19]
– Stop / No one's leaving / Ain't no right / Obvious / Been caught stealing / Three days / Then she did . . . / Of course / Classic girl.

Aug 90. (7"/c-s) *(W 9584/+C)* **THREE DAYS. / (part 2)** [ ] [ ]
(12"/cd-s) *(W 9584 T/CD)* – ('A'side) / I would for you (demo) / Jane says (demo).

Mar 91. (7"/c-s) *(W 0011/+C) <19574>* **BEEN CAUGHT STEALING. / HAD A DAD (demo)** [34] [ ]
(12"+=/12"box+=/cd-s+=) *(W 0011 T/TB/CD)* – ('A'remix) / L.A. medley:- L.A. woman / Nausea / Lexicon devil.

May 91. (7"/c-s) *(W 0031/+C)* **CLASSIC GIRL. / NO ONE'S LEAVING** [60] [ ]
(12"pic-d+=/cd-s+=) *(W 0031 TP/CD)* – Ain't no right.

—— Had already disbanded when FARRELL looked liked heading into film acting. NAVARRO had briefly filled in for IZZY STRADLIN in GUNS N' ROSES, before joining RED HOT CHILI PEPPERS.

PORNO FOR PYROS

—— **FARRELL + PERKINS** with **PETER DISTEFANO** (b.10 Jul'65) – guitar, samples, vocals / **MARTYN LE NOBLE** (b.14 Apr'69, Vlaardingen, Netherlands) – bass (ex-THELONIUS MONSTER) / and guest **DJ SKATEMASTER TATE** – keyboards, samples

Warners Warners

Apr 93. (cd/c/lp) *<(9362 45228-2/-4/-1)>* **PORNO FOR PYROS** [13] [3]
– Sadness / Porno for pyros / Meija / Cursed female – cursed male / Pets / Badshit / Packin' / • 25 / Black girlfriend / Blood rag / Orgasm.

Jun 93. (7"/c-s) *(W 0177/+C) <18480>* **PETS. / TONIGHT (from 'West Side Story')** [53] [67]
(12"pic-d+=/cd-s+=) *(W 0177 T/CD)* – Cursed female – cursed male (medley).

1994. (cd-s) *<41449>* **SADNESS / A LITTLE SADNESS / COOK THE RICE (live) / PETS (live) / PETE'S DAD (live)** [–] [ ]

—— **MIKE WATT** – bass (ex-fIREHOSE, ex-MINUTEMEN, ex-CICCONE YOUTH) repl. MARTYN (on most)

—— added **THOMAS JOHNSON** – samples, engineer and co-producer

May 96. (cd/c/lp) *<(9362 46126-2/-4/-1)>* **GOOD GOD'S URGE** [40] [20]
– Porpoise head / 100 ways / Tahitian moon / Kimberly Austin / Thick of it all / Good God's:// Urge! / Wishing well / Dogs rule the night / Freeway / Bali eyes.

JANE'S ADDICTION

—— re-formed **PERRY FARRELL / DAVE NAVARRO / STEPHEN PERKINS + FLEA**

Dec 97. (cd/c) *<(9362 46752-2/-4)>* **KETTLE WHISTLE** (4 new + live, demos & out-takes) [ ] Nov97 [21]
– Kettle whistle / Ocean size / Maceo / Hadadad / So what! / Jane says / Mountain song / Slow divers / Three days / Ain't no right / Up the beach / Stop / Been caught stealing / Whores / City.

Sep 99. (cd-s) *<44709-2>* **SO WHAT! (The Deep Red remixes)** [–] [ ]

PERRY FARRELL

with **STEPHEN PERKINS, KARL LEIKER + BRENDAN HAWKINS**

Warners Warners

Nov 99. (cd/c) *<(9362 47544-2/-4)>* **REV** (part comp) [ ] [ ]
– Rev / Whole lotta love / Been caught stealing / Jane says / Stop / Mountain song / Summertime rolls / Kimberley Austin / Tonight / Tahitian moon / Pets / Cursed male / 100 ways / Hard charger / Ripple / Satellite of love.

Virgin Virgin

Jul 01. (cd) *(CDVUS 197) <50030>* **SONG YET TO BE SUNG** [ ] [ ]
– Happy birthday jubilee / Song yet to be sung / Did you forget / Shekina / Our song / Say something / Seeds / King Z / To me / Nua nua / Admit I / Happy birthday jubilee (reprise).

DAVE NAVARRO

Chrysalis Capitol

Jul 01. (cd) *<(5 33280-2)>* **TRUST NO ONE** [ ] Jun01 [61]
– Rexall / Hungry / Sunny day / Mourning sun / Everything / Not for nothing / Avoiding the angel / Very little daylight / Venus in furs / Slow motion sickness.

JANE'S ADDICTION

FARRELL, NAVARRO, PERKINS plus **ERIC AVERY** – bass

Capitol Capitol

Jul 03. (7"/cd-s) *(CL/CDCL 847) <552637>* **JUST BECAUSE. / SUFFER SOME (live)** [14] [72]

Jul 03. (cd)(lp) *(592197-2)(590186-1) <90186>* **STRAYS** [14] [4]
– True nature / Strays / Just because / Price I pay / The riches / Superhero / Wrong girl / Everybody's fool / Suffer some / Hypersonic / To match the sun.

Oct 03. (7"/cd-s) *(CL/CDCL 850)* **TRUE NATURE. / BEEN CAUGHT STEALING (live)** [41] [ ]
(cd-s) *(CDCLS 850)* – ('A'side) / Just because (live) / Stop (Westwood One session) / ('A'-video).

JAPAN

Formed: Catford / Lewisham, London, England . . . mid-70's by DAVID SYLVIAN, his brother STEVE JANSEN, MICK KARN and RICHARD BARBIERI. In 1977, they added a second guitarist, ROB DEAN, subsequently signing to 'Ariola-Hansa' after winning a talent competition run by the label. They released a debut album, 'ADOLESCENT SEX', in the Spring of '78, followed six months later by 'OBSCURE ALTERNATIVES'. Basically pop music at the more accessible end of the avant-garde spectrum, JAPAN's proto-New Romantic image contrasted with SYLVIAN's (FERRY-esque) monotone croon. The following year, JAPAN scored a major hit in (of all places) Japan, with the GIORGIO MORODER-produced single, 'LIFE IN TOKYO'; a year on they finally gained a UK chart placing with 'QUIET LIFE'. By the turn of the decade, they'd secured a deal with 'Virgin', releasing the John Porter-produced Top 50 album, 'GENTLEMEN TAKE POLAROIDS'. The next year, after three minor hits in Britain, they went overground with a top selling classic album, 'TIN DRUM'. The record subsequently spawned the spectral 'GHOSTS' single in early '82, which hit the UK Top 5 after their former label had initiated a string of re-issues with 'EUROPEAN SON'; these exploitation releases graced the charts over the course of the next eighteen months while JAPAN officially folded. All band members went on to other projects, DAVID SYLVIAN enjoying most success. After a 1982 collaboration with RYUICHI SAKAMOTO ('BAMBOO HOUSES' and 'FORBIDDEN COLOURS' from the movie, 'Merry Xmas Mr. Lawrence'), the immaculately fringed frontman released his debut solo album, 'BRILLIANT TREES' (1984). The Top 5 album utilised the talents of world trumpeter, JON HASSELL, while JAPAN cohorts JANSEN and BARBIERI also helped to sculpt its sophisticated ambience. On future albums such as 'GONE TO EARTH' (1986), 'SECRETS OF THE BEEHIVE' (1987), 'PLIGHT AND PREMONITION' (1988) and 'FLUX AND MUTATION' (1989) – the latter two were collaborations with HOLGER CZUKAY (ex-CAN) – he worked with left-field luminaries like BILL NELSON and ROBERT FRIPP. In 1991, JAPAN re-formed as RAIN TREE CROW, although it became clear this set-up was only temporary, as all members (especially SYLVIAN), continued to pursue solo careers. SYLVIAN briefly returned to the charts in 1993 with the ROBERT FRIPP collaboration, 'THE FIRST DAY', a more accessible yet still inventive set. Although MICK KARN began a solo career at the same time as SYLVIAN (the bassist's work reminiscent of ENO or BILL NELSON), he went on to work as a sculptor; his track, 'TRIBAL

DAWN' (from the album, 'TITLES' – 1982), was used on Channel 4's arty TV programme, 'Altered States'. SYLVIAN was still gaining respect in some quarters of the music world when he turned up courtesy of a fresh set of scrumptious solo songs entitled 'DEAD BEES ON A CAKE' (1999), his aura and presence still on show when this returned him to the Top 40 (as did single, 'I SURRENDER').

• **Songwriters:** SYLVIAN lyrics / group compositions except; DON'T RAIN ON MY PARADE (Rogers-Hammerstein) / AIN'T THAT PECULIAR (Marvin Gaye) / I SECOND THAT EMOTION (Smokey Robinson) / ALL TOMORROW'S PARTIES (Velvet Underground).

Album rating: ADOLESCENT SEX (*6) / OBSCURE ALTERNATIVES (*6) / QUIET LIFE (*6) / GENTLEMEN TAKE POLAROIDS (*7) / TIN DRUM (*9) / ASSEMBLAGE compilation (*7) / OIL ON CANVAS live (*6) / EXORCISING GHOSTS compilation (*9) / Rain Tree Crow: RAIN TREE CROW (*4) / David Sylvian: BRILLIANT TREES (*8) / GONE TO EARTH (*6) / SECRETS OF THE BEEHIVE (*7) / PLIGHT AND PREMONITION with Holger Czukay (*7) / FLUX AND MUTABILITY with Holger Czukay (*6) / THE FIRST DAY with Robert Fripp (*6) / DEAD BEES ON A CAKE (*8) / APPROACHING SILENCE (*5) / EVERYTHING AND NOTHING compilation (*8) / CAMPHOR collection (*4) / BLEMISH (*7)

DAVID SYLVIAN (b. DAVID BATT, 23 Feb'58) – vocals, guitar, keyboards / **RICHARD BARBIERI** (b.30 Nov'57) – keyboards, synthesizers / **ROB DEAN** – guitar, mandolin / **MICK KARN** (b. ANTHONY MICHAELIDES, 24 Jul'58) – bass, saxophone / **STEVE JANSEN** (b. STEVE BATT, 1 Dec'59) – drums, percussion

Ariola Hansa — Ariola

Mar 78. (7") *(AHA 510)* **DON'T RAIN ON MY PARADE. / STATELINE** — –

Apr 78. (lp) *(AHAL 8004) <50037>* **ADOLESCENT SEX**
– Transmission / The unconventional / State line / Wish you were black / Performance / Lovers on Main Street / Don't rain on my parade / Suburban love / Adolescent sex / Communist China / Television. *(re-iss. Sep82; same) (re-iss. Sep84 on 'Fame' lp/c; FA41 3108-1/-4) (cd-iss. 1989 on 'Hansa Germany'; VDP 1153)*

Aug 78. (7") *(AHA 525)* **THE UNCONVENTIONAL. / ADOLESCENT SEX** — –

Nov 78. (lp) *(AHAL 8007) <50047>* **OBSCURE ALTERNATIVES**
– Automatic gun / Rhodesia / Love is infectious / Sometimes I feel so low / Obscure alternatives / Deviation / Suburban Berlin / The tenant. *(re-iss. Sep82; same) (re-iss. Apr84 on 'Fame' lp/c; FA41 3098-1/-4) (cd-iss. 1989 on 'Hansa Germany'; CDP 1154)*

Nov 78. (7",7"blue) *(AHA 529) <7727>* **SOMETIMES I FEEL SO LOW. / LOVE IS INFECTIOUS**

May 79. (7"red/ext.12"red) *(AHA/+D 540)* **LIFE IN TOKYO. / LIFE IN TOKYO (part 2)** — –

Jul 79. (12") *<7756>* **LIFE IN TOKYO. / LOVE IS INFECTIOUS** – —

Jan 80. (lp) *(AHAL 8011)* **QUIET LIFE** 53 –
– Quiet life / Fall in love with me / Despair / In-vogue / Halloween / All tomorrow's parties / Alien / The other side of life. *(re-iss. Sep82 on 'Fame' lp/c; FA/TCFA 3037) (cd-iss. 1989 on 'Hansa Germany'; VDP 1155)*

Feb 80. (7",7"maroon) *(AHA 559)* **I SECOND THAT EMOTION. / QUIET LIFE** — –

Virgin — not iss.

Oct 80. (7") *(VS 379)* **GENTLEMEN TAKE POLAROIDS. / THE EXPERIENCE OF SWIMMING** 60 –
(d7"+=) *(VS 379)* – The width of a room / Burning bridges.

Oct 80. (lp/c) *(V/TCV 2180)* **GENTLEMEN TAKE POLAROIDS** 45 –
– Gentlemen take polaroids / Swing / Some kind of fool / My new career / Methods of dance / Ain't that peculiar / Night porter / Taking islands in Africa. *(re-iss. Aug88 lp/c; OVED/+C 138) (cd-iss. Jun88; CDV 2180) <US cd-iss. 1991 on 'Caroline'; CAROL 1829-2>*

—— Trimmed to quartet when ROB DEAN left, to later form ILLUSTRATED MAN

Apr 81. (7"/12") *(VS 409/+12)* **THE ART OF PARTIES. / LIFE WITHOUT BUILDINGS** 48 –

Oct 81. (7") *(VS 436)* **VISIONS OF CHINA. / TAKING ISLANDS IN AFRICA** 32 –
(12"+=) *(VS 436-12)* – Swing. *(re-iss. Dec84; same)*

Nov 81. (lp/c) *(V/TCV 2209)* **TIN DRUM** 12 –
– The art of parties / Talking drum / Ghosts / Canton / Still life in mobile homes / Visions of China / Sons of pioneers / Cantonese boy. *(re-iss. Apr86 lp/c; OVED/+C 158) (cd-iss. Jun88; CDV 2209) <US cd-iss. 1991 on 'Caroline'; CAROL 1830-2>*

Jan 82. (7"/7"pic-d/12") *(VS/+Y 472)(VS 472-12)* **GHOSTS. / THE ART OF PARTIES (version)** 5 –

Feb 82. (7") **VISIONS OF CHINA. / CANTON** –

May 82. (d7") *(VS 502)* **CANTONESE BOY. / BURNING BRIDGES // GENTLEMEN TAKE POLAROIDS / THE EXPERIENCE OF SWIMMING** 24 –

—— They had earlier in the year quietly branched out into new projects. DAVID SYLVIAN went solo after a brief collaboration with RYUICHI SAKAMOTO. MICK KARN went solo, had one-off single with MIDGE URE, then went into sessions before forming DALI'S CAR with PETE MURPHY in '84. BARBERI and JANSEN produced Swedes LUSTAN LAKEJER. The pair formed their own duo (The DOLPHIN BROTHERS) before joining DAVID SYLVIAN again.

– compilations, exploitation releases etc. –

—— on 'Hansa-Ariola' unless otherwise mentioned

Apr 81. (7"/12") *(HANSA/+12 4)* **LIFE IN TOKYO. / EUROPEAN SON** — –

Aug 81. (7"/12") *(HANSA/+12 6)* **QUIET LIFE. / A FOREIGN PLACE / FALL IN LOVE WITH ME** 19 –

Sep 81. (lp)(c) *(HANLP 1)(ZCHAN 003)* **ASSEMBLAGE** 26 –
– Adolescent sex / State line / Communist China / Rhodesia / Suburban Berlin / Life in Tokyo / European son / All tomorrow's parties / Quiet life / I second that emotion. *(c+=)* – (12"extended versions). *(re-iss. Sep85 on 'Fame' lp/c; FA41 3136-1/-4)*

Jan 82. (7"/12") *(HANSA/+12 10)* **EUROPEAN SON. / ALIEN** 31 –

Jun 82. (7"/12") *(HANSA/+12 12)* **I SECOND THAT EMOTION. / HALLOWEEN** 9 –

Sep 82. (7"/12") *(HANSA/+12 17)* **LIFE IN TOKYO. / THEME** 28 –

—— now on 'Virgin' unless mentioned otherwise

Nov 82. (7") *(VS 554)* **NIGHT PORTER. / AIN'T THAT PECULIAR** 29 –
(12"+=) *(VS 554-12)* – Methods of dance.

Feb 83. (7"/12") *Hansa; (HANSA/+12 18)* **ALL TOMORROW'S PARTIES. / IN VOGUE** 38 –

May 83. (7") *(VS 581)* **CANTON (live). / VISIONS OF CHINA (live)** 42 –

Jun 83. (d-lp/c) *(VD/TCVD 2513)* **OIL ON CANVAS (live)** 5 —
– Oil on canvas / Sons of pioneers / Gentlemen take polaroids / Swing / Cantonese boy / Visions of china / Ghosts / Voices raised in welcome, hands held in prayer / Night porter / Still life in mobile homes / Methods of dance / Quiet life / The art of parties / Canton / Temple of dawn. *(cd-iss. Apr85; CDVD 2513)*

Aug 83. (d-c) *(XTWO 24)* **ADOLESCENT SEX / OBSCURE ALTERNATIVES** — –

Nov 84. (d-lp/c/cd) *(VGD/+C/CD 3510)* **EXORCISING GHOSTS** 45 —
– Methods of dance / Swing / Gentlemen take polaroids / Quiet life / A foreign place * / Night porter / My new career / The other side of life / Visions of China / Sons of pioneers * / Talking drum / The art of parties / Taking islands in Africa / Voices raised in welcome, hands held in prayer / Life without buildings / Ghosts. *(cd-omits *)*

Jun 88. (3"cd-ep) *(CDT 11)* **GHOSTS / THE ART OF PARTIES / VISIONS OF CHINA**

Nov 88. (3"cd-ep) *(CDT 32)* **GENTLEMEN TAKE POLAROIDS / CANTONESE BOY / METHODS OF DANCE**

Sep 87. (7") *Old Gold; (OG 9666)* **I SECOND THAT EMOTION. / ALL TOMORROW'S PARTIES** — –
(12"+=) *(OG 4020)* – Life in Tokyo.

Nov 87. (7") *Old Gold; (OG 4031)* **QUIET LIFE. / LIFE IN TOKYO** — –

Nov 88. (7") *Old Gold; (OG 9817)* **GHOSTS. / CANTONESE BOY** — –

Dec 89. (c/cd) *R.C.A.; (410/260 360)* **A SOUVENIR FROM JAPAN** — –

Nov 90. (3xcd-box) *(TPAK 6)* **COLLECTOR'S EDITION**
– (GENTLEMEN TAKE POLAROIDS / TIN DRUM / OIL ON CANVAS)

Nov 92. (cd-ep) *Old Gold; (OG 6187)* **I SECOND THAT EMOTION / QUIET LIFE / LIFE IN TOKYO** — –

Oct 91. (cd/c) *Receiver; (RR CD/MC 150)* **THE OTHER SIDE OF JAPAN** — –

Aug 96. (cd) *B.M.G.; (74321 39338-2)* **IN VOGUE**

DAVID SYLVIAN

- vocals, instruments (ex-JAPAN) / **RYUICHI SAKAMOTO** – synthesizers (ex-YELLOW MAGIC ORCHESTRA)

Virgin Caroline

Jul 82. (7"/ext.12"; by SYLVIAN / SAKAMOTO) *(VS 510)* **BAMBOO HOUSES. / BAMBOO MUSIC** [30] [–]
(below from the the film soundtrack 'Merry Christmas Mr. Lawrence')

Jun 83. (7"; by DAVID SYLVIAN & RYUICHI SAKAMOTO) *(VS 601)* **FORBIDDEN COLOURS. / THE SEED AND THE SOWER (by RYUICHI SAKAMOTO)** [16] [ ]
(12"+=) *(VS 601-12)* – Last regrets.
(3"/5"cd-ep of SYLVIAN tracks was iss.Aug88; CDT 18)

— now solo – vocals, keyboards, guitar, percussion, with **RICHARD BARBIERI** and **STEVE JANSEN** (ex-JAPAN) / **RYUICHI SAKAMOTO** – synthesizers / **HOLGER CZUKAY** – tapes / **DANNY THOMPSON** – upright bass / **KENNY WHEELER** – horns

May 84. (7"/7"pic-d)(12") *(VS/+Y 633)(VS 633-12)* **RED GUITAR. / FORBIDDEN COLOURS (version)** [17] [–]

Jun 84. (lp/c/cd) *(V/TCV/CDV 2290)* *<CAROL 1812>* **BRILLIANT TREES** [4] [ ]
– Pulling punches / The ink in the well / Nostalgia / Red guitar / Weathered wall / Backwaters / Brilliant trees. *(re-iss. Apr90 lp/c; OVED/+C 239)*

Aug 84. (7"/12") *(VS 700/+12)* **THE INK IN THE WELL (remix). / WEATHERED WALL (instrumental)** [36] [–]

Oct 84. (7"/ext.12") *(VS 717/+12)* **PULLING PUNCHES. / BACKWATERS (remix)** [56] [–]

— now with **JOHN HASSELL** and **ROBERT FRIPP** – guitar / **HOLGER CZUKAY** – tapes / **KENNY WHEELER** – horns

Nov 85. (12"ep) *(VS 835-12)* **WORDS WITH THE SHAMEN** [72] [–]
– Part 1:- Ancient evening / Part 2:- Incantation / Part 3:- Awakening.

Dec 85. (c) *(SLY 1)* **ALCHEMY (AN INDEX OF POSSIBILITIES)** [ ] [–]
– WORDS WITH THE SHAMEN / Preparations for a journey / Steel cathedrals.

— now with **ROBERT FRIPP** and **BILL NELSON** – guitar / **PHIL PALMER** – accoustic guitar / **MEL COLLINS** – soprano sax. / **KENNY WHEELER** – flugel horn

Virgin Virgin

Jul 86. (7"/7"sha-pic-d) *(VS/+Y 815)* **TAKING THE VEIL. / ANSWERED PRAYERS** [53] [–]
(remix-12"+=) *(VS 815-12)* – Bird of prey vanishes into a bright blue sky.

Aug 86. (d-lp)(c)(cd) *(VDL/TCVDL/CDVDL 1)* *<96003>* **GONE TO EARTH** [24] [ ]
– Taking the veil / Laughter and forgetting / Before the bullfight / Gone to earth / Wave / River man / Silver moon / The healing place / Answered prayers * / Where the railroad meets the sea / The wooden cross * / Silver moon over sleeping steeples * / Campfire: Coyote country * / A bird of prey vanishes into a blue cloudless sky * / Sunlight seen through the towering trees * / Upon this Earth. *(cd-omits tracks *)*

Sep 86. (7"/s7") *(VS/+P 895)* **SILVER MOON. / GONE TO EARTH** [ ] [–]
(12"+=) *(VS 895-12)* – Silver moon over sleeping steeples.

— DAVID was also credited on VIRGINIA ASTLEY's Feb87 'Some Small Hope'.

— now with **SAKAMOTO, PALMER, JANSEN** plus **DANNY CUMMINGS** – percussion / **DAVID TORN** – guitar / **DANNY THOMPSON** – d. bass / **MARK ISHAM** – trumpet

Oct 87. (lp)(c)(cd) *(V/TCV/CDV 2471)* *<86028>* **SECRETS OF THE BEEHIVE** [37] [ ]
– September / The boy with the gun / Maria / Orpheus / The Devil's own / When poets dreamed of angels / Mother and child / Let the happiness in / Waterfront.

Oct 87. (7") *(VS 1001)* **LET THE HAPPINESS IN. / BLUE OF MOON** [66] [ ]
(12"+=) *(VS 1001-12)* – Buoy (remix).

Apr 88. (7") *(VS 1043)* **ORPHEUS. / THE DEVIL'S OWN** [ ] [ ]
(12"+=) *(VS 1043-12)* – Mother and child.

— His touring band **JANSEN, BARBIERI, TORN, ISHAM** plus **IAN MAIDMAN** – bass, percussion / **ROBBY ALEDO** – guitar

DAVID SYLVIAN & HOLGER CZUKAY

with **JAKI LIEBEZEIT** – drums (ex-CAN)

Venture Virgin

Mar 88. (lp/c/cd) *(VE/TCVE/CDVE 11)* *<86053>* **PLIGHT AND PREMONITION** [71] [ ]
– Plight (the spiralling of winter ghosts) / Premonition (giant empty iron vessel).

— with **LIEBEZEIT, MICHAEL KAROLI** – guitar / **MARKUS STOCKHAUSEN** – flugel horn / **MICHI** – vocals

Venture Caroline

Sep 89. (lp/c/cd) *(VE/TCVE/CDVE 43)* *<CAROLCD 1602>* **FLUX AND MUTABILITY** [ ] [ ]
– Flux (a big, bright, colourful world) / Mutability ("a new beginning is in the offing").

DAVID SYLVIAN

Virgin not iss.

Nov 89. (7") *(VS 1221)* **POP SONG. / A BRIEF CONVERSATION ENDING IN DIVORCE** [ ] [–]
(12"+=/cd-s+=) *(VST/VSCDX 1221)* – ('A'remix).
(cd-s+=) *(VSCD 1221)* – Stigmas of childhood.

Nov 89. (5-cd-box) *(DXCD 1)* **WEATHERBOX** [ ] [–]
– (BRILLIANT TREES / GONE TO EARTH / GONE TO EARTH (instrumental) / SECRETS OF THE BEEHIVE / ALCHEMY – AN INDEX OF POSSIBILITIES)

Nov 91. (cd) *(DSRM 1)* **EMBRE GLANCE (THE PERMANENCE OF MEMORY)** [ ] [–]
– The beekeeper's apprentice / Epiphany.

— JAPAN had reformed quartet in 1990, but as . . .

RAIN TREE CROW

Virgin Virgin

Mar 91. (7"/c-s) *(VS/+C 1340)* **BLACK WATER. / RAIN TREE CROW / I DRINK TO FORGET** [62] [–]
(12") *(VST 1340)* – (1st + 3rd track) / Red Earth (as summertime ends).
(cd-s) *(VSCD 1340)* – (all above 4).

Apr 91. (cd/c/lp) *(CD/TC+/V 2659)* *<91774>* **RAIN TREE CROW** [24] [ ]
– Big wheels in Shanty town / Every colour you are / Rain tree crow / Red Earth (as summertime ends) / Rocket full of charge / Boat's for burning / New Moon Red Deer wallow / Black water / A reassuringly dull Sunday / Blackcrow hats shoe shine city.

SYLVIAN – SAKAMOTO

— next with **INGRID CHAVEZ**

Virgin America Virgin Am

Jun 92. (7"/c-s) *(VUS/+C 57)* **HEARTBEAT (TAINAI KAIKI II) RETURNING TO THE WOMB. / NUAGES** [58] [–]
(cd-s+=) *(VUSCD 57)* – The lost emperor.
(cd-s) *(VUSCDG 57)* – ('A'side) / Forbidden colours / Heartbeat.

DAVID SYLVIAN & ROBERT FRIPP

with **FRIPP** – guitar (of-KING CRIMSON & solo artist) / **TREY GUNN** – synthesizers, vocals, co-writer plus band **DAVID BOTTRILL** – synthesizers / **JERRY MAROTTA** – drums, percussion / **MARC ANDERSON** – percussion / **INGRID CHAVEZ** – backing vocals

Virgin Virgin

Jul 93. (cd/c/lp) *(CD/TC+/V 2712)* *<88208>* **THE FIRST DAY** [21] [ ]
– God's monkey / Jean the birdman / Firepower / Brightness falls / 20th century dreaming (a shaman's song) / Darshan (the road to Graceland).

Aug 93. (c-ep/cd-ep) *(VSC/DG 1462)* **JEAN THE BIRDMAN / EARTHBOUND – STARBLIND / ENDGAME** [68] [–]
(cd-ep) *(VSCDT 1462)* – ('A'side) / Tallow moon / Dark water / Gone to Earth.

Dec 93. (cd/c/lp) *(SYL CD/MC/LP 1)* **DARSHAN** (mixes) [ ] [–]
– Darshan (the road to Graceland) (remixed by The GRID & others).

Sep 94. (cd) *(DAMAGE 1)* *<39905>* **DAMAGE (live)** [ ] [ ]
– Damage / God's monkey / Brightness falls / Every colour you are / Firepower / Gone to Earth / 20th century dreaming (a shaman's song) / Wave / Riverman / Darshan (the road to Graceland) / Blinding light of Heaven / The first day. *(re-iss. Nov01 on 'Venture'; CDVE 958)*

— In 1996, SYLVIAN was credited on soundtrack of 'Marco Polo' film alongside NICOLA ALESINI & PIER LUIGI ANDREONI. It was released on 'Materiali Sonori'; *MASOCD 90069)*

DAVID SYLVIAN

Mar 99. (cd-s) *(VSCDT 1722)* **I SURRENDER / LES FLEURS DU MAL / STARRED AND DREAMING** 40 –
(cd-s) *(VSCDX 1722)* – ('A'side) / Whose trip is this / Remembering Julia.

Mar 99. (cd/c) *(CDV/TCV 2876)* *<47071>* **DEAD BEES ON A CAKE** 31
– I surrender / Dobro #1 / Midnight sun / Thalhelm / Godman / Alphabet angel / Krishna blue / Shining of things / Cafe Europe / Pollen path / All of my mother's name / Wanderlust / Praise / Darkest dreaming.

Venture Virgin

Sep 99. (cd-s) *(VEND 8)* **GODMAN (mixes) / SHADOWLAND (mixes)** –

Sep 99. (m-cd) *(CDVE 943)* *<848177>* **APPROACHING SILENCE** Oct99
– The beekeeper's apprentice / Epiphany / Approaching silence.

– compilations, etc. –

Oct 00. (d-cd/d-c) *Virgin; (CDVD/TCVD 2897)* *<50017>* **EVERYTHING AND NOTHING** 57
– The scent of magnolia / Heartbeat (Tainai kaiki II) / Blackwater / Albuquerque (dobro No.6) / Ride / The golden way / Ghosts / Pop song / Every colour you are / Wanderlust / God's monkey / Let the happiness in / I surrender / Thoroughly lost to logic / Jean the birdman / Cover me with flowers / The boy with the gun / Riverman / Aparna and Nimisha (dobro No.5) / Midnight sun / Orpheus / Some kind of fool / Cries and whispers / Godman / Laughter and forgetting / Buoy / Weathered wall / Bamboo houses / Come morning. *(3xcd-box+=; CDVDX 2897)* – Scent of magnolia (edit) / Blinding light of Heaven / Scent of magnolia (Portobello mix) / Brilliant trees (version 2000).

May 02. (cd/d-cd) *Venture; (CDVE/+X 962) / E.M.I.;* *<812201>* **CAMPHOR** (out-takes)

JAY-Z

Born: SHAWN CARTER, 4 Dec'70, Brooklyn, New York, USA. Despite being one of the most lauded yet egotistical rappers in the game, JAY-Z, who worked his way up from the slums of Brooklyn, had become one of the richest young entrepreneurs in the music industry thanks to his booming 'Roc-a-Fella' imprint. Raised in the Marcy projects of Brooklyn, the young JAY-Z (then known as 'Jazzy') began hustling on the streets in his teens until he met the aspiring rapper BIG JAZ, who was signed to a small label. Influenced by JAZ, JAY-Z decided to launch his own record label with just a few well-known rap artists around Brooklyn instead of trying to break into the already expanding rap industry. He enlisted DAMON DASH and KAREEM BURKE, and together they established 'Roc-a-Fella' records in 1995, just one year before JAY-Z issued his fantastic debut set 'REASONABLE DOUBT'. Critically acclaimed and pretty successful for an independent release, the set charted in the Billboard charts at number 23 but became a cult record amongst the fledgling rapsters on the East Coast scene. The album also boasted a fine line-up of guests (soon to become a common thing on JAY-Z records) such as MARY J BLIGE and the tragic NOTORIOUS B.I.G. The following year JAY-Z ditched his gangsta efforts and went for a more pop orientated direction for his subsequent release 'IN MY LIFE: VOL 1'. The usual guest stars appeared (PUFF DADDY, TEDD RILEY) but with an entourage of singles such as 'SUNSHINE' and 'THE CITY IS MINE', JAY-Z proved to a mainstream audience that he was no ghetto thug – but a sound producer with a lot to offer to the overground. Not surprisingly, the set entered the Billboard charts at Number 3, a huge climb from the self-produced debut. 'VOL 2: HARD KNOCK LIFE' (1998) surfaced the following year boasting the huge single 'HARD KNOCK LIFE (GHETTO ANTHEM)' which cleverly and bizarrely enough sampled the 'Annie' song, with piano and a chorus of orphaned children respectively. Other singles 'JIGGA WHAT?' and 'MONEY AIN'T A THING' climbed the charts but didn't possess the strangeness and quirkiness of the album's title track. By this point JAY-Z had turned his record company into a "dynasty", by producing his own clothing line and representing a huge host of New York's finest talents. Like usual, he unfettered another two albums over the next two years; vanity project 'VOL 3: LIFE AND TIMES OF S. CARTER' (1999) truly for only the most avid collector, and a sort of label sampler (but not quite) 'DYNASTY ROC LA FAMILIA' (2000), which included a whole host of in-house artists like MEMPHIS BLEEK and AMIL. These two albums were literally nothing compared to the excellent 'THE BLUEPRINT' album, issued in 2001 and heavily compared by critics to Z's breakthrough 'REASONABLE DOUBT'. It featured the track 'TAKEOVER', a vicious attack on East Coasters NAS and MOBB DEEP. Although the feud continued for many months after the release of the set – nobody is very clear why JAY-Z launched such a tirade on two very respected members of the hip-hop scene. The album spawned two other hit singles 'GIRLS, GIRLS, GIRLS' and 'JIGGA THAT NIGGA' and went on to rank high on many album-of-the-year polls. After sharing an album with R. KELLY, 'THE BEST OF BOTH WORLDS' (2002), New York's shrewdest cut double set, 'THE BLUEPRINT: THE GIFT & THE CURSE' (2002). A sprawling, near 2-hour trawl through contemporary hip hop featuring everyone from the NEPTUNES and DR. DRE to LENNY KRAVITZ and BEYONCe, the album represented an opportunity for JAY-Z to pander to his artistic whims without the editorial discipline required of a conventional set. While he's certainly not the first artist to do a 'BLACK ALBUM' (2003), JAY-Z is perhaps the first to instill the title with such meaning. And while his lyrics cut to the quick on the travails of the black experience, more often than not it was, as usual, from a strictly personal viewpoint. Which, of course, is what made the likes of 'DECEMBER 4' and the Russell Crowe-sampling 'WHAT MORE CAN I SAY', so compelling. Towards the end of the following year, JAY-Z continued his chart domination via two collaborations, the first with R&B crooner R KELLY ('2004 UNFINISHED BUSINESS'), the second with nu-metal rappers LINKIN PARK ('COLLISION COURSE'). The latter was an official "mash-up"/"mosh-up" cutting and pasting the best bits of the respective artists' catalogues, and spawning a one-off hit, 'NUMB / ENCORE'.

Album rating: REASONABLE DOUBT (*6) / IN MY LIFETIME, VOL.1 (*7) / VOL.2 ... HARD KNOCK LIFE (*8) / VOL.3 ... LIFE AND TIMES OF S. CARTER (*7) / THE DYNASTY ROC DA FAMILIA (2000) (*6) / THE BLUEPRINT (*8) / MTV UNPLUGGED (*5) / CHAPTER ONE compilation (*7) / THE BLUEPRINT 2: THE GIFT & THE CURSE (*6) / THE BLACK ALBUM (*7)

JAY-Z – vocals / with various guests

not iss. ffrr

Jul 95. (12"/cd-s) *<120072>* **IN MY LIFETIME (mixes; original ski / original ski street / skitrumental / big jazz radio / big jazzmental) / CAN'T GET WITH THAT (DJ Clark Kent version)** –

Feb 96. (12"/cd-s) *<53233>* **DEAD PRESIDENTS (mixes; clean / album instrumental) / AIN'T NO NIGGA (album / instrumental)** –

Northwest – Arista Roc-a-fella

Feb 97. (c-s; by JAY-Z featuring MARY J. BLIGE) *(74321 44719-4)* *<53242>* **CAN'T KNOCK THE HUSTLE (mixes; clean / dirty)** 30 73
(cd-s+=) *(74321 44719-2)* – (instrumental / acappella).

Mar 97. (cd/c/d-lp) *(74321 44720-2/-4/-1)* *<50592>* **REASONABLE DOUBT** Jul96 23
– Can't knock the hustle (with MARY J. BLIGE) / Politics as usual / Brooklyn's finest (with NOTORIOUS B.I.G.) / Dead presidents II Feelin' it (with MECCA) / D'Evils / 22 two's / Can I live / Ain't no nigga (with FOXY BROWN) / Friend or foe / Coming of age (with MEMPHIS BLEEK) / Cashmere thoughts / Bring it on (with BIG JAZ) / Regrets / Can I live II. *(re-iss. May99 cd/c; same)*

Apr 97. (12"/cd-s; by JAY-Z with FOXY BROWN) *(74321 47484-1/-2)* **AIN'T NO PLAYA/NIGGA (mixes; clean / original radio / Ganjo Kru / Fresh to Def / New York street / original)** 31 50

—— JAY-Z returned the favor to FOXY by featuring on her hit, 'I'll Be'

Aug 97. (12"/cd-s) *(W 0411 T/CD)* <43883> **WHO YOU WIT (mixes; clean / album / instrumental / acappella)** 65 84
(above issued on 'Qwest-Warners')

Oct 97. (c-s; by JAY-Z featuring BABYFACE & FOXY BROWN) *(74321 52870-4)* <574923> **(ALWAYS BE MY) SUNSHINE / DEAD PRESIDENTS II** 25 95
(12"+=/cd-s+=) *(74321 52870-1/-2)* – ('A'-mixes; radio / album / clean / TV acappella).

Feb 98. (c-s; by JAY-Z featuring GWEN DICKEY) *(74321 55463-4)* **WISHING ON A STAR (mixes; radio / masters / D Influence)** 13 –
(12"+=/cd-s+=) *(74321 55463-1/-2)* – Brooklyn's finest (featuring NOTORIOUS B.I.G.).

Feb 98. (cd/c)(t-lp) *(74321 55989-2/-4)(52869-1)* <536392> **IN MY LIFETIME, VOL.1** [ ] Nov97 3
– intro / A million and one questions / Rhyme no more / The city is mine (with BLACKstreet) / I know what girls like (with PUFF DADDY & LIL' KIM) / Imaginary player / Streets is watching / Friend or foe '98 / Lucky me / (Always be my) Sunshine (with BABYFACE & FOXY BROWN) / Who you wit – Face off / Real niggaz (with TOO SHORT) / Rap game – Crack game / Where I'm from / You must love me.

Jun 98. (c-s; by JAY-Z featuring BLACKstreet) *(74321 58801-4)* **THE CITY IS MINE / (version)** 38 Jan98 52
(12"+=/cd-s+=) *(74321 58801-1/-2)* – A million and one questions.

—— mid'98, JAY-Z had a US hit (w/ MEMPHIS BLEEK), 'It's Alright'

Nov 98. (c-s) *(74321 63533-4)* <566977> **HARD KNOCK LIFE (GHETTO ANTHEM) / CAN'T KNOCK THE HUSTLE** 2 15
(12"+=/cd-s+=) *(74321 63533-1/-2)* – ('A'mixes).

Jan 99. (cd/c/lp) *(74321 62555-2/-4/-1)* <558902> **VOL.2 . . . HARD KNOCK LIFE** [ ] Oct98 1
– intro / Hand it down (w/ MEMPHIS BLEEK) / Hard knock life (ghetto anthem) / If I should die / Ride or die / Nigga what, nigga who (originator 99) (with BIG JAZ) / Money cash hoes (with DMX) / A week ago (with TOO SHORT) / Coming of age (da sequel) (with MEMPHIS BLEEK) / Can I get a . . . (with AMIL & JA RULE) / Paper chase (with FOXY BROWN) / Reservoir dogs / It's like that (with KID CAPRI) / It's alright (with MEMPHIS BLEEK) / Money ain't a thing (with JERMAINE DUPRI).

Feb 99. (12") <566893> **MONEY CASH HOES (mixes)** – [ ]
Mercury Roc-A-Fella

Mar 99. (12"/cd-s; by JAY-Z featuring AMIL & JA RULE) *(566847-1/-2)* <567688> **CAN I GET A . . . (mixes)** 24 Oct98 19

Mar 99. (-; by JAY-Z featuring BIG JAZ) *<radio>* **JIGGA WHAT, JIGGA WHO / AIN'T NO NIGGA / BRING IT ON** – 84

—— in Apr'99, JAY-Z featured ANOTHER LEVEL's hit, 'Be Alone No More'

—— in Jun'99, he also featured on TIMBALAND's hit, 'Lobster & Scrimp'

Jun 99. (cd-s) <562201> **JIGGA MY NIGGA / MEMPHIS BLEEK IS / WHEN WILL U SEE / WHAT A THUG ABOUT** – 28

Aug 99. (cd-s) <668138> **GIRLS' BEST FRIEND** – 52

—— in Nov'99, the rapper appeared on MARIAH CAREY's Top 5 'Heartbreaker'

—— a month later, JAY-Z featured on yet another collaboration single (with MEMPHIS BLEEK), 'What You Think Of That'

Roc-A-Fella Roc-A-Fella

Dec 99. (cd-s; by JAY-Z featuring BEANIE SIGEL & AMIL) <562575> **DO IT AGAIN (PUT YA HANDS UP) (mixes) / SO GHETTO / JIGGA MY NIGGA** – 65

Feb 00. (c-s) *(562650-4)* <562670> **ANYTHING / GO GHETTO** 18 55
(cd-s+=) *(562650-2)* – There's been a murder.

Jun 00. (c-s/12"; JAY-Z featuring UGK) *(562833-4/-1)* <562774> **BIG PIMPIN'. / ANYTHING** 29 Apr00 18
(cd-s+=) *(562774-2)* – ('A'mixes).

Jun 00. (cd/c/lp) *(546815-2/-4/-1)* <546822> **VOL.3 . . . LIFE AND TIMES OF S. CARTER** [ ] Jan00 1
– Hova song (intro) / So ghetto / Do it again (put ya hands up) (with BEANIE SIGEL & AMIL) / Dope man (with SERENA ALTSHUL) / Things that U do (with MARIAH CAREY) / It's hot (some like it hot) / Snoopy track (with JUVENILE) / S. Carter / Pop 4 roc (with BEANIE SIGEL, MEMPHIS BLEEK & AMIL) / Hove interlude / Big pimpin' (with UGK) / Is that yo bitch (with TWISTA & MISSY) / Come and get me (with TWISTA & MISSY) / N.Y.M.P. (with TWISTA & MISSY) / Hova song (outro). *(UK+=)* – Anything. *(clean cd version; 546814-2)*

Aug 00. (cd-s; by JAY-Z feat. MEMPHIS BLEEK & AMIL) <562862> **HEY PAPI (mixes)** – 76

Nov 00. (cd/lp) <(548203-2/-1)> **ROC LA FAMILIA – THE DYNASTY** [ ] 1
– (intro) / Change the game / I just wanna love U (give it 2 me) / Streets is talking / This can't be life (with SCARFACE) / Get your mind right mami (with SNOOP DOGG) / Stick 2 the script / You, me, him and her / Guilty until proven innocent (with R. KELLY) / Parking lot pimpin' / Holla / 1-900 hustler / The R.O.C. / Soon you'll understand / Squeeze 1st / Where have you been.

Dec 00. (c-s) *(572746-4)* <572666> **I JUST WANNA LOVE U (GIVE IT 2 ME) / PARKING LOT PIMPIN' (radio)** 17 Oct00 11
(12"+=) *(572746-1)* – Hey papi.
(cd-s++=) *(572746-2)* – ('A'video).

Jan 01. (cd-s; by JAY-Z featuring BEANIE SIGEL & MEMPHIS BLEEK) <572761> **CHANGE THE GAME (mixes; radio / instrumental / research hook)** – 86

—— in Mar'01. JAY-Z featured on R KELLY's hit, 'Fiesta'

Apr 01. (cd-s; by JAY-Z & R KELLY) <572809> **GUILTY UNTIL PROVEN INNOCENT (radio / album) / CHANGE THE GAME** – 82

Sep 01. (cd/d-lp) <(586396-2/-1)> **THE BLUEPRINT** 30 1
– The ruler's back / Takeover / Izzo (H.O.V.A.) / Girls, girls, girls / Jigga that n**** / U don't know / Hola' hovita / Heart of the city (ain't no love) / Never change / Song cry / All I need / Renegade / Blueprint (momma loves me).

Oct 01. (c-s) *(588815-4)* <588701> **IZZO (H.O.V.A.) / (album)** 21 Jul01 8
(12"+=/cd-s+=) *(588815-1/-2)* – (instrumental).

Jan 02. (c-s) *(588906-4)* <588793> **GIRLS, GIRLS, GIRLS / (part 2)** 11 Oct01 17
(12"+=) *(588906-1)* – Big pimpin' (with UGK).
(cd-s++=) *(588906-2)* – ('A'video).

Mar 02. (cd) <(586614-2)> **MTV UNPLUGGED** (live) [ ] Dec01 34
– Izzo (H.O.V.A.) / Takeover / Girls, girls, girls / Jigga what, jigga who / Big pimpin' / Heart of the city (ain't no love) / Can I get a . . . / Hard knock life (ghetto anthem) / Ain't no / Can't knock the hustle – Family affair / Song cry / I just wanna love U (give it 2 me) / Jigga that nigga.

—— in Mar'02, JAY-Z collaborated with R. KELLY on the album, 'THE BEST OF BOTH WORLDS' and the single, 'HONEY'; both hits.

Nov 02. (d-cd/q-lp) <(63381-2/-1)> **THE BLUEPRINT 2: THE GIFT & THE CURSE** 23 1
– A dream (with FAITH EVANS & The NOTORIOUS B.I.G.) / Hovi baby / The watcher 2 (with DR. DRE & TRUTH HURTS) / '03 Bonnie & Clyde (with BEYONCE KNOWLES) / Excuse me miss / What they gonna do (with SEAN PAUL) / All around the world (with LaTOIYA WILLIAMS) / Poppin' tags (with BIG BOI, KILLER MIKE & TWISTA) / Fuck all nite / The bounce / I did it my way / Diamond is forever / Guns & roses (with LENNY KRAVITZ) / U don't know (remix) (with M.O.P.) / Meet the parents / Some how some way (with BEANIE SIGEL & SCARFACE) / Some people hate / Blueprint2 / Nigga please (with YOUNG CHRIS) / 2 many hoes / As one (with MEMPHIS BLEEK, FREEWAY & YOUNG GUNS) / A ballad for the fallen soldier / Show you how / Bitches & sisters / What they gonna do, pt.II. <*(re-iss. Apr03 as 'BLUEPRINT 2.1'; 077344-2)*> – <hit US No.17>

Jan 03. (c-s; by JAY-Z & BEYONCE KNOWLES) *(077010-4)* <063843> **'03 BONNIE & CLYDE / (explicit album version)** 2 Nov02 4
(12") *(077010-1)* – ('A'side) / U don't know (explicit remix) / ('A'-instrumental).
(cd-s++=) *(077010-2)* – ('A'-video).

Apr 03. (12"/cd-s) *(077912-1/-2)* <63717> **EXCUSE ME MISS. / ('A'-instrumental) / Heart of the city (ain't no love) (live)** 17 Feb03 8

—— in Jul'03, JAY-Z featured on PANJABI MC's hit 'Jogi' + also PHARRELL WILLIAMS' Top 10 smash, 'Frontin'

Nov 03. (cd/d-lp) *(9861121)* <15280-2/-1> **THE BLACK ALBUM** 40 1
– Interlude / December 4th / What more can I say / Encore / Change clothes / Dirt off your shoulder / Threat / Moment of clarity / 99 problems / Public service announcement (interlude) / Justify my thug / Lucifer / Allure / My 1st song.

Dec 03. (cd-s) *(981522-5)* <165111> **CHANGE CLOTHES / WHAT MORE CAN I SAY** 32 Nov03 10

(12"/cd-s) *(981522-7/-6)* – ('A'side) / Excuse me miss / I just wanna love U (give it 2 me) / Excuse me miss again.

May 04. (cd-s) *(9862391)* *<248411>* **99 PROBLEMS / DIRT OFF YOUR SHOULDER** [12] [30] [5]

— in Oct'04, R KELLY & JAY-Z released US No.1 set, '2004 UNFINISHED BUSINESS'

— late in 2004, JAY-Z collaborated on US No.1 album, 'COLLISION COURSE' with LINKIN PARK; featured 'NUMB' / 'ENCORE' Top 20 UK

– compilations, others, etc. –

Mar 02. (cd/lp) *B.M.G.; (74321 92046-2/-1)* *<86098>* **CHAPTER ONE** [65] [ ]
– Hard knock life (the ghetto anthem) / Wishing on a star / Sunshine (with FOXY BROWN & BABYFACE) / The city is mine / Can't knock the hustle / Ain't no nigga / Imaginary prayer / Money ain't a thang (with JERMAINE DUPRI) / Can I get a . . . (with AMIL & JA RULE) / Streets is watching / Money, cash, hoes (with DMX) / I know what girls like / Feelin' it / Dead presidents II / Wishing on a star / Can't knock the hustle (with MELISSA MORGAN) / Ain't no nigga (with FOXY BROWN).

Oct 03. (cd) *Camden-BMG; (82876 56697-2)* **BRING IT ON: THE BEST OF JAY-Z** [ ] [–]

JEFFERSON AIRPLANE

Formed: San Francisco, California, USA . . . early 1965 by MARTY BALIN and PAUL KANTNER. They recruited others and signed to 'RCA' in late '65, releasing a flop debut single, 'IT'S NO SECRET'. In September '66, their first album, ' . . . TAKES OFF', was finally issued, a competent hybrid of folk-rock and blues notable for the powerful singing of second vocalist SIGNE ANDERSON. By the time of the album's release, however, ANDERSON had left to have a baby and was replaced by GRACE SLICK (formerly of The GREAT SOCIETY). SKIP SPENCE also left and the drum stool was filled by SPENCER DRYDEN. The potential of this all-playing, all-writing group was fulfilled on the follow-up lp, 'SURREALISTIC PILLOW' (1967). A psychedelic classic, the record spawned two top 10 singles in the U.S., 'SOMEBODY TO LOVE' (1967) and 'WHITE RABBIT' (967), SLICK having brought both songs with her from her previous band. Her vocals were even stronger than ANDERSON's and her commanding clarity stamped itself indelibly on every song, particularly 'WHITE RABBIT', a neo classical, lysergic nursery rhyme (inspired by the Lewis Carroll book 'Alice In Wonderland') that managed to sound at once sinister and insidiously catchy. Even KAUKONEN's blistering guitar work and newcomer JACK CASADY's relentlessly inventive bass playing sounded more assured, the album going on to sell half a million copies. The band then took psychedelic experimentation ever further with 'AFTER BATHING AT BAXTER'S' (1968). Comprising a number of free-form song 'suites', the album was hard going; the melodies were still in there, they were just harder to find among the wilful weirdness and extended instrumental jams. 'R.C.A.' must have breathed a sigh of relief when the band came up with the relatively more accessible 'CROWN OF CREATION' (1968). A more conventional set of songs, it featured the scary 'THE HOUSE AT POOH CORNER', SLICK's haunting 'LATHER' and a cover of DAVID CROSBY's menage-a-trois elegy, 'TRIAD'. After a thundering live set, 'BLESS ITS POINTED LITTLE HEAD' (1969), the band recorded the last album to feature the classic JEFFERSON line-up, 'VOLUNTEERS' (1970). It featured the unflinching politicism of 'WE CAN BE TOGETHER' and though the title track was used in the 'Woodstock' movie, the band's own performance wasn't filmed. Soon after the album's release, DRYDEN left to join The NEW RIDERS OF THE PURPLE SAGE and was replaced by JOEY COVINGTON. BALIN also departed around this time after a prolonged period of tension with SLICK, violinist PAPA JOHN CREACH (was this the man behind MADONNA's 'Papa Don't Preach' we ask ourselves?) taking up the slack. The subsequent 'BARK' (1971) and 'LONG JOHN SILVER' (1972) albums (released on the band's newly formed 'Grunt' label) bore none of the intensity of The 'AIRPLANE's earlier work and the band's final effort, the live 'THIRTY SECONDS OVER WINTERLAND' (1973) was similarly underwhelming. By this point, JOHN BARBATA had replaced sticksman COVINGTON while DAVID FRIEBERG (ex-QUICKSILVER MESSENGER SERVICE) had been recruited on vocals. While CASSADY and KAUKONEN went full-time with their side project, HOT TUNA, SLICK and KANTNER formed JEFFERSON STARSHIP with the remaining 'AIRPLANE members. The name was taken from an earlier, KANTNER sci-fi inspired project that released one album, 1971's '(IT'S A FRESH WIND THAT) BLOWS AGAINST THE NORTH'. The debut JEFFERSON STARSHIP album, 'DRAGONFLY' (1974), was well written and skillfully executed but it was clear the band were headed towards the mainstream and with 'RED OCTOPUS' (1975), the band's sleek sound was crystallised, the album shifting a cool four million copies. MARTY BALIN was also back in the fold by this point and his song, 'MIRACLES', went Top 3 later the same year. Disillusioned with the new direction, SLICK soon left for a low key solo career while JEFFERSON STARSHIP continued to notch up hit albums. She later rejoined, although by 1984 even KANTNER had become tired of the group's commercial sound, leaving and taking the JEFFERSON part of the name with him. As STARSHIP, the SLICK fronted band went on to even bigger success, reeling off hits like 'WE BUILT THIS CITY ON ROCK 'N' ROLL' (1985) and the nauseous pop slush of 'NOTHING'S GONNA STOP US NOW' (1987). Incredibly/inevitably there was a full reunion of the classic JEFFERSON AIRPLANE line-up in 1989 which produced an eponymous album. A pointless exercise in crusty nostalgia, it was almost as dull as the dishwater STARSHIP were peddling. JEFFERSON STARSHIP might as well have called themselves JEFFERSON STARTREK given their "next generation" tenacity, releasing mid-90s set, 'DEEP SPACE – VIRGIN SKY'. BALIN, CASADY and KANTNER subsequently dropped the subtitle for three further GRACE-less albums, 'WINDOWS OF HEAVEN' (1998), 'GREATEST HITS: LIVE AT THE FILLMORE' (1999) and 'ACROSS THE SEA OF SUNS' (2001), vocals courtesy of DIANA MANGANO.

Album rating: JEFFERSON AIRPLANE TAKES OFF (*5) / SURREALISTIC PILLOW (*8) / AFTER BATHING AT BAXTER'S (*7) / CROWN OF CREATION (*7) / VOLUNTEERS (*6) / THE WORST OF JEFFERSON AIRPLANE compilation (*6) / BLOWS AGAINST THE EMPIRE (*5; as PAUL KANTNER & JEFFERSON STARSHIP) / SUNFIGHTER (*5; by Paul Kantner & Grace Slick) / BARK (*6) / LONG JOHN SILVER (*5) / THIRTY SECONDS OVER WINTERLAND (*5) / BARON VON TOLBOOTH & THE CHROME NUN (*4; by Paul Kantner, Grace Slick & David Freiberg) / EARLY FLIGHT early stuff (*4) / Grace Slick: MANHOLE (*4) / DREAMS (*4) / WELCOME TO THE WRECKING BALL (*5) / Jefferson Starship: DRAGON FLY (*6) / RED OCTOPUS (*7) / SPITFIRE (*6) / FLIGHT LOG 1966-1976 compilation (*6; Jefferson Airplane & Starship) / EARTH (*4) / GOLD compilation (*7) / FREEDOM AT POINT ZERO (*5) / MODERN TIMES (*5) / WINDS OF CHANGE (*4) / NUCLEAR FURNITURE (*4) / Starship: KNEE DEEP IN THE HOOPLA (*4) / 2400 FULTON STREET – AN ANTHOLOGY remastered early collection (*7) / NO PROTECTION (*4) / LOVE AMONG THE CANNIBALS (*4) / JEFFERSON AIRPLANE (*3; as Jefferson Airplane) / DEEP SPACE – VIRGIN SKY (*3) / GREATEST HITS (TEN YEARS AND CHANGE 1979-1991) compilation (*6; by Starship) / Jefferson Starship: WINDOWS OF HEAVEN (*6) / ACROSS THE SEA OF SUNS (*5)

MARTY BALIN (b. MARTYN JEREL BUCHWALD, 30 Jan'43, Cincinnati, Ohio, USA) – vocals, guitar (ex-solo) / **PAUL KANTNER** (b.12 Mar'42, San Francisco) – guitar, vocals / **JORMA KAUKONEN** (b.23 Dec'40, Washington, D.C.) – lead guitar / **SIGNE TOLY ANDERSON** (b.15 Sep'41, Seattle, Wash.) – vocals / **JACK CASADY** (b.13 Apr'44, Washington, D.C.) – bass repl. BOB HARVEY / **SKIP SPENCE** (b.18 Apr'46, Ontario, Canada) – drums (ex-QUICKSILVER MESSENGER SERVICE) repl. JERRY PELOQUIN

R.C.A. R.C.A.

Feb 66. (7") <8679> **IT'S NO SECRET. / RUNNIN' ROUND THIS TABLE** [–] [ ]

May 66. (7") <8848> **COME UP THE YEARS. / BLUES FROM AN AEROPLANE** [–] [ ]

Sep 66. (lp) <*LSP 3584*> **JEFFERSON AIRPLANE TAKES OFF** [–] [ ]
– Blues from an airplane / Let me in / It's no secret / Bringing me down / Tobacco road / Coming up the years / Run around / Let's get together / Don't slip away / Chauffeur blues / And I like it. *(UK-iss.Oct71; SF 8195) (re-iss. Jun74;)* <*(cd re-mast.Aug03 +=; 82876 50352-2)*> – Runnin' 'round this world / High flyin' bird / It's alright / Go to her / Let me in (alt.) / Run around (alt.) / Chauffeur blues (alt.) / And I like it (alt.).

Sep 66. (7") <8967> **BRINGING ME DOWN. / LET ME IN** [–] [ ]

— **GRACE SLICK** (b. GRACE BARNETT WING, 30 Oct'39, Chicago, Illinois) – vocals (ex-GREAT SOCIETY) repl. SIGNE who left to look after her baby / **SPENCER DRYDEN** (b. 7 Apr'38, New York City) – drums (ex-PEANUT BUTTER CONSPIRACY, ex-ASHES) repl. SKIP who formed MOBY GRAPE

Dec 66. (7") <9063> **MY BEST FRIEND. / HOW DO YOU FEEL** [–] [ ]

Sep 67. (lp; mono/stereo) *(RD/SF 7889)* <*LSP 3766*> **SURREALISTIC PILLOW** [ ] Feb67 [3]
– She has funny cars / Somebody to love / My best friend / Today / Comin' back to me / How do you feel / 3/5 mile in 10 seconds / D.C.B.A. – 25 / Embryonic journey / White rabbit / Plastic fantastic lover. *(UK-rel.had different tracks) (cd-iss. Sep84; PD 83766) (cd re-iss. Oct87; ND 83738)* <*(cd re-mast.Aug03 +=; 82876 50351-2)*> – In the morning / J.P.P. McStep B. blues / Go to her / Come back baby / Somebody to love / White rabbit.

May 67. (7") *(RCA 1594)* <9140> **SOMEBODY TO LOVE. / SHE HAS FUNNY CARS** [ ] Feb67 [5]

Sep 67. (7") *(RCA 1631)* <9248> **WHITE RABBIT. / PLASTIC FANTASTIC LOVER** [ ] Jun67 [8]

Nov 67. (7") *(RCA 1647)* <9297> **BALLAD OF YOU AND ME AND POONEIL. / TWO HEADS** [ ] Sep67 [42]

Jun 68. (lp; mono/stereo) *(RD/SF 7926)* <*LSP 1511*> **AFTER BATHING AT BAXTER'S** [ ] Dec67 [17]
– (Streetmasse): / Ballad of you and me and Pooneil – A small package of value will come to you, shortly – Young girl Sunday blues / (The war is over): / Martha – Wild thyme / (Hymn to an older generation): / The last wall of the castle – Rejoyce / How sweet it is:- Watch her ride – Spare chaynge / Shizoforest love suite: Two heads – Won't you try – Saturday afternoon. *(re-iss. Dec88 lp/c; NL/NK 84718) (cd-iss. May98; ND 84718)* <*(cd re-mast.Aug03 +=; 82876 53225-2)*> – The ballad of you and me and Pooneil (live) / Martha (version) / Two heads (alt.) / Things are better in the east (demo).

Jan 68. (7") <9389> **WATCH HER RIDE. / MARTHA** [–] Dec67 [61]

Jun 68. (7") *(RCA 1711)* <9496> **GREASY HEART. / SHARE A LITTLE JOKE** [ ] Mar68 [98]

Sep 68. (7") *(RCA 1736)* **IF YOU FEEL LIKE CHINA BREAKING. TRIAD** [ ] [–]

Oct 68. (7") <9644> **CROWN OF CREATION. / TRIAD** [–] [64]

Dec 68. (lp; mono/stereo) *(RD/SF 7976)* <*LSP 4058*> **CROWN OF CREATION** [ ] Sep68 [6]
– Lather / In time / Triad / Star track / Share a little joke / Chushingura / If you feel / Crown of creation / Ice cream Phoenix / Greasy heart / The house at Pooh Corner. *(re-iss. Oct85 lp/c; NL/NK 83797) (cd-iss. Jun88 & Jan98; ND 83660)* <*(cd re-mast.Aug03 ++; 82876 53226-2)*> – Ribump ba bap dum dum / Would you like a snack? / Share a little joke / The saga of Sydney Spacepig.

Jun 69. (lp; mono/stereo) *(RD/SF 8019)* <*LSP 4133*> **BLESS ITS POINTED LITTLE HEAD (live)** [38] Feb69 [17]
– Clergy / 3/5 of a mile in 10 seconds / Somebody to love / Fat angel / Rock me baby / The other side of this life / It's no secret / Plastic fantastic lover / Turn out the lights / Bear melt.

Jul 69. (7") <*0150*> **PLASTIC FANTASTIC LOVER (live). / THE OTHER SIDE OF THIS LIFE (live)** [–] [ ]

Feb 70. (lp) *(SF 8164)* <*LSP 4238*> **VOLUNTEERS** [34] Nov69 [13]
– We can be together / Good shepherd / The farm / Hey Frederick / Turn my life down / Wooden ships / Eskimo blue day / A song for all seasons / Meadowlands / Volunteers. *(re-iss. Oct85)*

Mar 70. (7") *(RCA 1933)* <*0245*> **VOLUNTEERS. / WE CAN BE TOGETHER** [ ] Nov69 [65]

— **JOEY COVINGTON** – drums repl. DRYDEN who joined NEW RIDERS OF THE PURPLE SAGE (above new with **SLICK, CASADY, BALIN** and **KAUKONEN**) (note also DRYDEN played on below 'A' side)

Aug 70. (7") *(RCA 1989)* <*0343*> **MEXICO. / HAVE YOU SEEN THE SAUCERS?** [ ] [ ]

— At this time various members, mainly KAUKONEN and CASADY side-lined HOT TUNA. PAUL KANTNER then recorded album with what was then p/t JEFFERSON STARSHIP (see further below and his late '71 co-credit with GRACE SLICK)

— **PAPA JOHN CREACH** (b.28 May 1917, Beaver Falls, Pennsylvania) – violin (of HOT TUNA) finally repl. BALIN who left earlier.

Grunt Grunt

Oct 71. (lp) <*(FTR 1001)*> **BARK** [42] Sep71 [11]
– When the Earth moves again / Feel so good / Crazy Miranda / Pretty as you feel / Wild turkey / Law man / Rock and roll island / Third week in Chelsea / Never argue with a German if you're tired or European song / Thunk / War movie. *(re-iss. Jul84; NL 84386)*

Oct 71. (7") <*(65-0500)*> **PRETTY AS YOU FEEL. / WILD TURKEY** [ ] [60]

— **JOHN BARBATA** – drums (ex-CROSBY & NASH, ex-TURTLES) repl. JOEY

Jun 72. (lp) <*(FTR 1007)*> **LONG JOHN SILVER** [30] [20]
– Long John Silver / Aerie (gang of eagles) / Twilight double leader / Milk train / Son of Jesus / Easter? / Trial by fire / Alexander the medium / Eat starch mom.

Sep 72. (7") <*(65-0506)*> **LONG JOHN SILVER. / MILK TRAIN** [ ] [ ]

1972. (7") <*(65-0511)*> **TWILIGHT DOUBLE DEALER. / TRIAL BY FIRE** [ ] [ ]

— **DAVID FREIBERG** (b.24 Aug'38, Boston, Mass.) – vocals (ex-QUICKSILVER MESSENGER SERVICE) (They made last album recorded between 71-72)

Apr 73. (lp) <*(FTR 0147)*> **30 SECONDS OVER WINTERLAND (live)** [ ] [52]
– Have you seen the saucers / Feel so good / Crown of creation / When the Earth moves again / Milk train / Trial by fire / Twilight double leader. *(re-iss. Oct85 lp/c; NL/NK 83867)*

— Now non-recording quintet of SLICK, KANTNER, FREIBERG, BARBATA and CREACH. CASADY and KAUKONEN made HOT TUNA their full-time band.

PAUL KANTNER & JEFFERSON STARSHIP

with JERRY GARCIA, DAVID CROSBY, GRAHAM NASH, MICKEY HART

R.C.A. R.C.A.

Jan 71. (7") <*0426*> **A CHILD IS COMING. / LET'S GO TOGETHER** [–] [ ]

Apr 71. (lp) *(SF 8163)* <*LSP 4448*> **(IT'S A FRESH WIND THAT) BLOWS AGAINST THE NORTH** [ ] Nov70 [20]
– Mau mau (Amerikon) / The baby tree / Let's go together / A child is coming / Sunrise / Hijack / Home / Have you seen the stars tonite / X-M / Starship.

PAUL KANTNER & GRACE SLICK

Grunt Grunt

Dec 71. (lp) <*(FTR 1002)*> **SUNFIGHTER** [ ] [89]
– Silver spoon / Diana (part 1) / Sunfighter / Titanic / Look at the wood / When I was a boy I watched the wolves / Million / China / Earth mother / Diana (part 2) / Universal Copernican mumbles / Holding together. *(re-iss. Apr89 on 'Essential' lp/cd; ESS LP/CD 001)*

Jan 72. (7") <*0503*> **SUNFIGHTER. / CHINA** [–] [ ]

— KANTNER later released a US only album 'THE PLANET EARTH ROCK AND ROLL ORCHESTRA iss.Aug83. After leaving JEFFERSON STARSHIP he formed KBC with BALIN and CASADY (ex-AIRPLANE members). They released a single and album early '83.

PAUL KANTNER, GRACE SLICK, DAVID FREIBERG

with guests **JORMA KAUKONEN** – guitar / **JACK CASADY** – bass / **CHAQUICO** – guitar / **JERRY GARCIA** ('Grateful Dead') / **DAVID CROSBY** ('Crosby, Stills & Nash')

Grunt Grunt

Jun 73. (lp) <*(BFL 1-0148)*> **BARON VON TOLBOOTH & THE CHROME NUN** [ ] [ ]
– Ballad of the chrome nun / Fat / Flowers of the night / Walkin' / You

mind has left your body / Across the board / Harp tree lament / White boy (transcaucasian airmachine blues) / Fishman / Sketches of China.

Jun 73. (7") <0094> **BALLAD OF THE CHROME NUN. / SKETCHES OF CHINA** [–] [ ]

JEFFERSON STARSHIP

(new name re-formed) **SLICK, KANTNER, FREIBERG, CREACH + BARBATA** recruited **CRAIG CHAQUICO** (b.26 Sep'54, Sacramento, Calif.) – guitar (ex-STEELWIND) repl. JORMA / **PETE SEARS** (b. England) – bass, keyboards, vocals repl. PETER KAUKONEN, who had repl. JACK

Grunt Grunt

Nov 74. (7") *<FB 10080>* **RIDE THE TIGER. / DEVIL'S DEN** [–] [84]

Dec 74. (lp) *<(BFL 1-0717)>* **DRAGONFLY** [ ] Oct74 [11]
– Ride the tiger / That's for sure / Be young you / Caroline / Devil's den / Come to life / All fly away / Hyperdrive.

1975. (7") *<FB 10206>* **BE YOUNG YOU. / CAROLINE** [–] [ ]

—— added the returning **MARTY BALIN** – vocals, guitar

Jul 75. (lp) *(FTR 2002) <BFL 1-0999>* **RED OCTOPUS** [ ] [1]
– Fast buck Freddie / Miracles / Git fiddler / Al Garimasu (there is love) / Sweeter than honey / Play on love / Tumblin' / I want to see another world / Sandalphon / There will be love. *(re-iss. Feb81 on 'RCA International' lp/c; INT S/K 5069) (re-iss. Oct84 on 'RCA' lp/c/cd; PL/PK/PD 80999) (re-iss. Jun86 on 'Fame' lp/c; FA/TC-FA 3156) (cd-iss. Oct87 & Jun88; ND 83464 & ND 83660)*

Sep 75. (7") *<(FB 10367)>* **MIRACLES. / AL GARIMASU (THERE IS LOVE)** [ ] Aug75 [3]

Nov 75. (7") *<FB 10456>* **PLAY ON LOVE. / I WANT TO SEE ANOTHER WORLD** [–] [49]

—— Trimmed to sextet when PAPA JOHN CREACH then GRACE SLICK went solo

Jul 76. (lp) *<(BFL 1-1557)>* **SPITFIRE** [30] [3]
– Hot water / Big city / Switchblade / Cruisin' / Love lovely love / St. Charles / Dance with the dragon / St. Charles / With your love / Song to the sun / Ozymandias / Don't let it rain. *(cd-iss. Jun97 on 'R.C.A.'; 0786366876-2)*

Aug 76. (7") *<(FB 10746)>* **WITH YOUR LOVE. / SWITCHBLADE** [ ] Jul76 [12]

Nov 76. (7") *<FB 10791>* **ST. CHARLES. / LOVE LOVELY LOVE** [–] [64]

Feb 78. (7") *<(FB 11196)>* **COUNT ON ME. / SHOW YOURSELF** [ ] [8]

Mar 78. (lp/c) *(FL/FK 12515) <2515>* **EARTH** [ ] [5]
– Love too good / Count on me / Take your time / Crazy feelin' / Skateboard / Fire / Show yourself / All nite long. *(cd-iss. Jun97 on 'R.C.A.'; 0786366878-2)*

Jun 78. (7") *<(FB 11274)>* **RUNAWAY. / HOT WATER** [ ] May 78 [12]

Aug 78. (7") *<FB 11374>* **CRAZY FEELIN' / LOVE TOO GOOD** [–] [54]

Nov 78. (7"/12") *<FB 11426/11469>* **LIGHT THE SKY ON FIRE. / HYPERDRIVE** [–] [66]

—— **MICKEY THOMAS** (b. Cairo, Georgia) – vocals (ex-ELVIN BISHOP) repl. BALIN who went solo / **AYNSLEY DUNBAR** (b.10 Jan'46, Liverpool, England) – drums (ex-JOURNEY ex-KGB) repl. BARBATA (above 2 joining **KANTNER, FREIBERG, CHAQUICO** and **SEARS**) / **GRACE SLICK** also guested uncredited on the next album (she joined full-time Feb81.)

Jan 80. (7") *<(FB 11750)>* **JANE. / FREEDOM AT POINT ZERO** [21] Nov79 [14]

Jan 80. (lp) *(FL 13452) <3452>* **FREEDOM AT ZERO POINT** [22] Nov79 [10]
– Girl with hungry eyes / Freedom at Zero Point / Fadiing lady night / Lightning Rose / Things to come / Just the same / Rock music / Awakening / Jane. *(re-iss. Sep81 lp/c; RCA LP/K 3038) (re-iss. Jun89; NL 89912) (cd-iss. Feb90; ND 89912)*

Apr 80. (7") *<(FB 11921)>* **GIRL WITH THE HUNGRY EYES. / JUST THE SAME** [ ] [55]

Jun 80. (7") *<FB 11961>* **ROCK MUSIC. / LIGHTNING ROSE** [–] [ ]

R.C.A. Grunt

May 81. (7"/12") *(RCA 66) <FB 1221-1/-3>* **FIND YOUR WAY BACK. / MODERN TIMES** [ ] Apr81 [29]

Jun 81. (lp) *(3050) <BZL 1-3848>* **MODERN TIMES** [ ] Apr81 [26]
– Find your way back / Stranger / Wild eyes / Save your love / Modern times / Mary / Free / Alien / Stairway to Cleveland. *(re-iss. Sep81 lp/c; RCA LP/K 3050)*

Jul 81. (7") *<12275>* **STRANGER. / FREE** [–] [48]

Oct 81. (7"/12") *<1233-2/-3>* **SAVE YOUR LOVE. / WILD EYES** [–] [ ]

Oct 82. (7") *<13350>* **BE MY LADY. / OUT OF CONTROL** [–] [28]

Feb 83. (lp/c) *(RCA LP/K 6060) <BXL 1-4372>* **WINDS OF CHANGE** [ ] Oct82 [26]
– Winds of change / Keep on dreamin' / Be my lady / I will stay / Out of control / Can't find love / Black widow / I came back from the jaws of the dragon / Quit wasting time. *(re-iss. Oct84 lp/c/cd; FL/FK/FD 84372)*

Jan 83. (7") *<13439>* **WINDS OF CHANGE. / BLACK WIDOW** [–] [38]

Apr 83. (7") *<13531>* **CAN'T FIND LOVE. / I WILL STAY** [–] [ ]

—— **DON BALDWIN** – drums (ex-ELVIN BISHOP BAND) repl. DUNBAR

Jun 84. (7") *(RCA 424) <13811>* **NO WAY OUT. / ROSE GOES TO YALE** [ ] May84 [ ]
(12"+=) *(RCA 424T) <13812>* – Be my lady.

Jun 84. (lp/c/cd) *(FL/FK/FD 84921) <4921>* **NUCLEAR FURNITURE** [ ] [28]
– Layin' it on the line / No way out / Sorry me, sorry you / Live and let live / Connection / Nuclear furniture / Rose goes to Vale / Magician / Assassin / Shining in the moonlight / Showdown / Champion.

Sep 84 (7") *<13872>* **LAYIN' IT ON THE LINE. / SHOWDOWN** [–] [66]

STARSHIP

was the name they were allowed to use after KANTNER left. Now **GRACE SLICK, MICKEY THOMAS, CRAIG CHAQUICO, PETE SEARS** and **DON BALDWIN**

Oct 85. (7") *(FB 49929) <14170>* **WE BUILT THIS CITY. / PRIVATE ROOM** [12] Sep85 [1]
(12"+=) *(FT 49930)* – ('A'extended).

Nov 85. (lp/c/cd) *(FL/FK/FD 85488) <5488>* **KNEE DEEP IN THE HOOPLA** [ ] Oct85 [7]
– We built this city / Sara / Tomorrow doesn't matter tonight / Rock myself to sleep / Desperate heart / Private room / Before I go / Hearts of the world (will understand) / Love rusts. *(re-iss. Sep89 lp/c/cd; NL/NK/ND 90367)*

Jan 86. (7") *(FB 49893) <14253>* **SARA. / HEARTS OF THE WORLD (WILL UNDERSTAND)** [ ] Dec85 [1]
(12"+=) *(FT 49894)* – Jane.

May 86. (7") *(FB 49855) <14332>* **TOMORROW DOESN'T MATTER TONIGHT. / LOVE RUSTS** [ ] Apr86 [26]
(12"+=) *(FT 49856)* – No way out / Layin' it on the line.

Jun 86. (7",12") *<14393>* **BEFORE I GO. / CUT YOU DOWN** [–] [68]

—— now w/out SEARS

R.C.A. RCA-Grunt

Mar 87. (7") *(FB 49757) <5109>* **NOTHING'S GONNA STOP US NOW. / LAYING IT ON THE LINE** [1] Jan87 [1]
(12"+=) *(FT 49757)* – We built this city / Tomorrow doesn't matter tonight.

Jul 87. (lp/c/cd) *(FL/FK/FD 86413) <6413>* **NO PROTECTION** [26] [12]
– Beat patrol / Nothing's gonna stop us now / It's not over ('til it's over) / Girls like you / Wings of a lie / The children / I don't know why / Transatlantic / Babylon / Set the night to music.

Aug 87. (7") *(RCA 5001) <5225>* **IT'S NOT OVER ('TIL IT'S OVER). / BABYLON** [ ] Jun87 [9]
(12"+=)<US-cd-s> *(RCAT 5000)* – Jane / Sara.

Nov 87. (7") *(RCA 5002) <5308>* **BEAT PATROL. / GIRLS LIKE YOU** [ ] Sep87 [46]
(12"+=) *(RCAT 5002)* – ('A'extended).

Feb 88. (7") *<6964>* **SET THE NIGHT TO MUSIC. / I DON'T KNOW WHY** [–] [ ]
(12"+=) *<6964>* – ('A'dub version) / ('A'instrumental).

—— STARSHIP in the 90's were: – **MICKEY THOMAS, DONNY BALDWIN, CRAIG CHAQUICO** plus **MARK MORGAN** – keyboards / **BRETT BLOOMFIELD** – bass

Feb 89. (7") *(EKR 88) <69349>* **WILD AGAIN. / LAYIN' IT ON THE LINE** [ ] Dec88 [73]
(12"+=) *(EKR 88T)* – Tutti Frutti.
(above was from the film 'Cocktail' on label 'Elektra')

R.C.A. R.C.A.

Sep 89. (7"/c-s) *(PB/PK 49357) <9032>* **IT'S NOT ENOUGH. / LOVE AMONG THE CANNIBALS** [ ] Jul89 [12]
(12"+=) *(PT 49358)* – Wild again.
(cd-s++=) *(PD 49356)* – Nothing's gonna stop us now.

Sep 89. (lp/c/cd) *(PL/PK/PD 90387) <9693>* **LOVE AMONG THE CANNIBALS** [ ] Aug89 [64]
– The burn / It's not enough / Trouble in mind / I didn't mean to stay all night / Send a message / Love among the cannibals / We dream in colour / Healing waters / Blaze of love / I'll be there. *(cd+=)* – Wild again.

Nov 89. (c-s) *(9109>* **I DIDN'T MEAN TO STAY ALL NIGHT / WE DREAM IN COLOR** [–] [75]
Apr 91. (c-s) *<2796>* **GOOD HEART / (3 album excerpts)** [–] [81]
Aug 91. (cd/c/lp) *(PD/PK/PL 82423)* **GREATEST HITS (TEN YEARS AND CHANGE 1979-1991)** (compilation) [ ] [–]
– Jane / Find your way back / Stranger / No way out / Layin' it on the line / Don't lose any sleep / We built this city / Sara / Nothing's gonna stop us now / It's not over ('til it's over) / It's not enough / Good heart. *(re-iss. cd Oct95)*

JEFFERSON AIRPLANE

were reformed with **SLICK, KANTNER, KAUKONEN, CASADY and BALIN.** Augmented by **KENNY ARONOFF** – drums / **PETER KAUKONEN and RANDY JACKSON** – guitar (ex-ZEBRA)

Epic Epic

Oct 89. (lp/c/cd) *(465 659-1/-4/-2) <45271>* **JEFFERSON AIRPLANE** [ ] [85]
– Planes / Solidarity / Summer of love / The wheel / True love / Now is the time / Panda / Freedom / Ice age / Madeleine Street / Common market madrigal / Upfront blues / Too many years.
Oct 89. (7") *<73044>* **SUMMER OF LOVE. / PANDA** [–] [ ]
Jan 90. (c-s) *<73080>* **TRUE LOVE /** [–] [ ]

—— JEFFERSON STARSHIP ("the next generation") were formed after above.

JEFFERSON STARSHIP ("the next generation")

KANTNER / CASADY / BALIN + SLICK (repl. CREACH) / **TIM GORMAN** – keyboards, vocals (ex-KBC BAND) / **PRAIRIE PRINCE** (b. 7 May'50, Charlotte, New Connecticut) / **MARK AUGUILAR** – guitar, vocals (ex-KBC BAND) / **DARBY GOULD** – vocals

Essential Intersound

Jul 95. (cd/c) *(ESM CD/MC 493) <9151>* **DEEP SPACE – VIRGIN SKY** [ ] [ ]
– Shadowlands / Ganja of love / Dark ages / I'm on fire / Papa John / Women who fly / Gold / The light / Crown of creation / Count on me / Miracles / Intro to lawman / Lawman / Wooden ships / Somebody to love / White rabbit.

JEFFERSON STARSHIP

—— **DIANA MANGANO** – vocals; repl. GRACE SLICK + GOULD

not iss. S.P.V.

Jul 98. (cd) *<SPV-085 2910-2>* **WINDOWS OF HEAVEN** [–] [ ]
– The light (ginger & metaphysics) / See the light / Borderland / Maybe for you / Let it live / Let me fly / Goddess / Blessings / Shadowlands / Which side are you on / Ways of love / Later on / The windows of Heaven / Out of the rain / Millennium beyond. *<re-iss. Feb99 on 'C.M.C.'; 86265> (UK-iss.Feb02 on 'S.P.V.'; SPV 230-2910-2) (UK re-iss. May03 on 'Neon'; NE 34558)*

not iss. C.M.C.

Sep 99. (cd) *<86276>* **GREATEST HITS: LIVE AT THE FILLMORE** (live) [–] [ ]
– 3/5 mile in 10 seconds / Plastic fantastic lover / Somebody to love / Crown of creation / It's no secret / The light (ginger & metaphysics) / White rabbit / Caroline / Miracles / Count on me / Volunteers / Wooden ships / Let me fly / Ride the tiger.

not iss. Zebra

Nov 01. (d-cd) *<44024>* **ACROSS THE SEA OF SUNS** (live) [–] [ ]
– Caroline / She has funny cars / When the earth moves again / Good shepard / Today / Dcba-25 / Eskimo blue day / How do you feel / Miracles / Have you seen the stars tonight? / Embryonic journey – Starship / There will be love / Hearts / Hey Frederick / When I was a boy I watched the wolves / Hyperdrive / You're bringing me down / The ballad of you and me and Pooneil / Mexico – Wooden ships / Somebody to love – Volunteers / You're my best friend / JPP McStep blues.

– (AIRPLANE) compilations, etc. –

on 'R.C.A.' unless mentioned otherwise
Jun 70. (7") *(RCA 1964)* **WHITE RABBIT. / SOMEBODY TO LOVE** [ ] [ ]
Nov 70. (lp) *(SF 8164) <4459>* **THE WORST OF JEFFERSON AIRPLANE** [ ] [12]
(re-iss. Sep86 on 'Fame' lp/c; FA/TC-FA 3167)
Apr 74. (lp) *Grunt; <(APL 1-0437)>* **EARLY FLIGHT** [ ] [ ]
Apr 76. (7"m) *(RCA 2676)* **WHITE RABBIT. / SOMEBODY TO LOVE / CROWN OF CREATION** [ ] [ ]
Dec 76. (d-lp) *(SF 7889) <1255>* **FLIGHT LOG** (1966-76 work) [ ] [37]
Apr 79. (12") *RCA Gold; (GOLD 4)* **WHITE RABBIT. / SOMEBODY TO LOVE** [ ] [–]
Jul 80. (lp/c) *(INT S/K 5030) <42727>* **THE BEST OF JEFFERSON AIRPLANE** [ ] [ ]
(re-iss. 1984 lp/c; NL/NK 89186)
Nov 86. (7") *Old Gold; (OG 9631)* **WHITE RABBIT. / SOMEBODY TO LOVE** [ ] [–]
1987. (7") *<5156>* **WHITE RABBIT. / PLASTIC FANTASTIC LOVER** [ ] [–]
May 87. (7") *Ariola; (JEFF 1)* **WHITE RABBIT. / SOMEBODY TO LOVE** [ ] [ ]
(12"+=) *(JEFFT 1)* – She has funny cars / Third week in Chelsea.
Jul 87 (d-lp/c/d-cd) *(NL/NK/ND 90036) <5724>* **2400 FULTON STREET – AN ANTHOLOGY** [ ] [ ]
– It's no secret / Come up the years / My best friend / Somebody to love / Comin' back to me / Embryonic journey / She has funny cars / Plastic fantastic lover / Wild tyme / The ballad of you & me & Pooneil – A small package of value will come to you, shortly / White rabbit / Won't you try Saturday afternoon / Lather / We can be together / Crown of creation / Mexico / Wooden ships / Rejoyce / Volunteers / Pretty as you feel / Martha / Today / Third week in Chelsea. *(d-cd+=)* – Let's get together / Blues from an airplane / J.P.P. McStep B. Blues / Fat angel / Greasy heart / We can be together / Have you seen the saucers / Eat starch mom / Good shepherd / Eskimo blue day / The Levi commercials. *(re-iss. d-cd.1992;)*
Oct 88. (d-lp/c/cd) *Castle; (CCS LP/MC/CD 200)* **THE COLLECTION** [ ] [–]
<US cd-iss. Oct92; >
1989. (3"cd-ep) *(PD 49463)* **WHITE RABBIT / PLASTIC FANTASTIC LOVER / SOMEBODY TO LOVE / SHE HAS FUNNY CARS** [ ] [–]
May 90. (cd/lp) *Thunderbolt; (CDTB/THBL 074)* **LIVE AT THE MONTEREY FESTIVAL (live)** [ ] [–]
Nov 92. (3xcd-box) **JEFFERSON AIRPLANE LOVES YOU** [ ] [ ]
Apr 93. (cd) *Pulsar;* **WOODSTOCK REVIVAL** [ ] [–]
Sep 93. (cd/c) *Remember; (RMB 7/4 5065)* **WHITE RABBIT (featuring GRACE SLICK)** [ ] [–]
Aug 96. (cd) *B.M.G. Special; <74321 40057-2>* **JOURNEY (THE BEST OF JEFFERSON AIRPLANE)** [ ] [–]
Sep 96. (cd; w-free pic-cd) *Experience; (EXP 021)* **JEFFERSON AIRPLANE LIVE** [ ] [–]
Jan 97. (cd) *Stampa Alternativa; (SB 03)* **WE ARE ALL ONE** [ ] [ ]

– (STARSHIP) compilations etc. –

Mar 79. (lp/c) *Grunt-RCA; (FL/FK 13247) <3247>* **GOLD** [ ] Feb79 [20]
(with free 7") – LIGHT THE SKY ON FIRE. / HYPERDRIVE
1979. (7") *Grunt-RCA;* **MIRACLES. / WITH YOUR LOVE** [–] [ ]
Nov 92. (cd-ep) *Old Gold;* **NOTHING'S GONNA STOP US NOW / WE BUILT THIS CITY / SARA** [ ] [–]

GRACE SLICK

solo, all featuring JEFFERSON's and session people

Grunt Grunt

Jan 74. (7") *<0183>* **THEME FROM MANHOLE. / COME AGAIN? TOUCAN** [–] [ ]
Jan 74. (lp) *<(BFL 1-0347)>* **MANHOLE** [ ] [ ]
– Jay / Theme from 'Manhole' / Come again? Toucan / It's only music / Better lying down / Epic (#38).

R.C.A. R.C.A.

May 80. (7") *<11939>* **SEASONS. / ANGEL OF NIGHT** [–] [ ]
May 80. (7") *(PB 9534)* **DREAMS. / ANGEL OF NIGHT** [50] [–]
May 80. (lp/c) *<(PL/PK 1-3544)>* **DREAMS** [28] [32]
– Dreams / El Diablo / Face to the wind / Angel of night / Seasons / Do it the hard way / Full Moon man / Let it go / Garden of man. *(re-iss. Sep81 lp/c; RCA LP/K 3040) (re-iss. Sep91 on 'Great Expectations' cd/c/lp; PIP CD/MC/LP 030)*
Jul 80. (7",12") *<1204-1/-2>* **DREAMS. / DO IT THE HARD WAY** [–] [ ]
Feb 81. (7") *(RCA 33)* **MISTREATER. / FULL MOON MAN** [ ] [ ]
Feb 81. (lp/c) *(RCA LP/K 5007) <3851>* **WELCOME TO THE WRECKING BALL** [ ] [48]
– Wrecking ball / Mistreater / Shot in the dark / Round & round / Shooting

star / Just a little love / Sea of love / Lines / Right kind / No more heroes. *(re-iss. Sep91 on 'Great Expectations' cd/c/lp; PIP CD/MC/LP 029)*

May 81. (7") *<12171>* **SEA OF LOVE. / FULL MOON MAN** [–] [ ]

Mar 84. (lp/c) *(PL/PK 84791)* **SOFTWARE** [ ] [–]
– Call it right call it wrong / Me and me / All the machines / Fox face / Through the window / It just won't stop / Habits / Rearrange my face / Bikini Atoll.

Mar 84. (12") *<13708>* **ALL THE MACHINES. / ('A'long version)** [–] [ ]

May 84. (7") *<13764>* **THROUGH THE WINDOWS. / HABITS** [–] [ ]

the JESUS & MARY CHAIN

Formed: East Kilbride, Scotland . . . 1983 by brothers WILLIAM and JIM REID, who took their name from a line in a Bing Crosby film. After local Glasgow gigs, they moved to Fulham in London, having signed for Alan McGhee's independent 'Creation' label in May'84. Their debut SLAUGHTER JOE-produced 45, 'UPSIDE DOWN', soon topped the indie charts, leading to WEA subsidiary label, 'Blanco Y Negro', snapping them up in early 1985. They hit the UK Top 50 with their next single, 'NEVER UNDERSTAND', and they were soon antagonising new audiences, crashing gear after 20 minutes on set. Riots ensued at nearly every major gig, and more controversy arrived when the next 45's B-side 'JESUS SUCKS', was boycotted by the pressing plant. With a new B-side, the single 'YOU TRIP ME UP', hit only No.55, but was soon followed by another Top 50 hit in October, 'JUST LIKE HONEY'. A month later they unleashed their debut album, 'PSYCHOCANDY', and although this just failed to breach the UK Top 30, it was regarded by many (NME critics especially) as the album of the year. Early in '86, BOBBY GILLESPIE left to concentrate on his PRIMAL SCREAM project and soon after, JAMC hit the Top 20 with the softer single, 'SOME CANDY TALKING'. In 1987 with new drummer JOHN MOORE, the single 'APRIL SKIES' and album 'DARKLANDS' both went Top 10. Later that year, they remixed The SUGARCUBES' classic 'Birthday' single.'BARBED WIRE KISSES' (1988) was a hotch-potch of B-sides and unreleased material, essential if only for the anarchic trashing of The Beach Boys' 'SURFIN' U.S.A.'. By the release of the 'AUTOMATIC' album in 1989, the Reid brothers had become the core of the band, enlisting additional musicians as needed. The record sounded strangely muted and uninspired although the 'ROLLERCOASTER' EP and subsequent tour (alongside MY BLOODY VALENTINE and a pre-'PARKLIFE' BLUR) were an improvement. True to controversial style, the band returned to the singles chart in 1992 with the radio un-friendly, post-industrial mantra, 'REVERENCE'. Perhaps the last great piece of venom-spewing noise the 'MARY CHAIN produced, the follow-up album, 'HONEY'S DEAD', was tame in comparison. No surprise then, that it received mixed reviews although there were a few low key highlights, notably the melodic bubblegum grunge of 'FAR GONE AND OUT'. After 1993's 'SOUND OF SPEED' EP, the band hooked up with MAZZY STAR'S Hope Sandoval for 'STONED AND DETHRONED', a mellow set of feedback free strumming. While still echoing the brooding portent of the THE VELVETS, the style of the record was more 'PALE BLUE EYES' than 'SISTER RAY'. Predictably, the band were seen as having 'sold out' by Indie-Rock dullards and a 1995 single, 'I HATE ROCK'N'ROLL', didn't even scrape the Top 50. 1998's comeback set, 'MUNKI', peaked at only No.47 in the charts; tension had been reported from other band members as WILLIAM and JIM fought out their differences. With the latter working on something solo (and Alan McGee's label coming to a close) it was inevitable that the brothers would split the 'CHAIN late in '99. WILLIAM had already delivered his first solo outing a year earlier, 'TIRED OF FUCKING' very low key. LAZYCAME's 'SATURDAY THE FOURTEENTH' finally featured his rejected penis sleeve (from creation days) and FREEHEAT (JIM's project) comprised of BEN LURIE (guitar), ROMI MORI (bass & ex-GUN CLUB) and NICK SANDERSON (drums of EARL BRUTUS)

• **Songwriters:** All written by JIM and WILLIAM except; VEGETABLE MAN (Syd Barrett) / SURFIN' USA (Beach Boys) / WHO DO YOU LOVE (Bo Diddley) / MY GIRL (Temptations) / MUSHROOM (Can) / GUITAR MAN (Jerry Lee Hubbard) / TOWER OF SONG (Leonard Cohen) / LITTLE RED ROOSTER (Willie Dixon) / (I CAN'T GET NO) SATISFACTION (Rolling Stones) / REVERBERATION (13th Floor Elevators) / GHOST OF A SMILE (Pogues) / ALPHABET CITY (Prince) / NEW KIND OF KICK (Cramps).
• **Trivia:** Their 1986 single 'SOME CANDY TALKING' was banned by Radio 1 DJ Mike Smith, due to its drug references. The following year in the States, they were banned from a chart show due to their blasphemous name.

Album rating: PSYCHOCANDY (*9) / DARKLANDS (*8) / BARBED WIRE KISSES collection (*7) / AUTOMATIC (*7) / HONEY'S DEAD (*8) / THE SOUND OF SPEED compilation (*7) / STONED AND DETHRONED collection (*6) / I HATE ROCK N ROLL (*5) / MUNKI (*5) / 21 SINGLES compilation (*9) / Lazycame: FINBEGIN (*8)

JIM REID (b.29 Dec'61) – vocals, guitar / **WILLIAM REID** (b.28 Oct'58) – guitar, vocals / **MURRAY DALGLISH** – drums (bass tom & snare) / **DOUGLAS HART** – bass

Creation / not iss.

Nov 84. (7") *(CRE 012)* **UPSIDE DOWN. / VEGETABLE MAN** [ ] [–]
(12"+=) *(CRE 012T)* – ('A' demo).

—— **BOBBY GILLESPIE** – drums (ex-WAKE, of PRIMAL SCREAM) repl. DALGLISH who formed BABY'S GOT A GUN

Blanco Y Negro / Reprise

Feb 85. (7") *(NEG 8)* **NEVER UNDERSTAND. / SUCK** [47] [–]
(12"+=) *(NEGT 8)* – Ambition.

Jun 85. (7") *(NEG 13)* **YOU TRIP ME UP. / JUST OUT OF REACH** [55] [–]
(12"+=) *(NEGT 13)* – Boyfriend's dead.

Oct 85. (7") *(NEG 017)* **JUST LIKE HONEY. / HEAD** [45] [–]
(12"+=) *(NEGT 17)* – Just like honey (demo) / Cracked.
(d7"+=) *(NEGF 17)* – ('A'demo) / Inside me.

Nov 85. (lp/c) *(BYN/+C 11) <25383>* **PSYCHOCANDY** [31] [ ]
– Just like honey / The living end / Taste the floor / Hardest walk / Cut dead / In a hole / Taste of Cindy / Never understand / It's so hard / Inside me / Sowing seeds / My little underground / You trip me up / Something's wrong. *(cd-iss. Aug86 & Jan97 +=; K 242 000-2)* – Some candy talking.

—— **JOHN LODER** – drums (on stage when BOBBY was unavailable)

Jul 86. (7") *(NEG 19)* **SOME CANDY TALKING. / PSYCHO CANDY / HIT** [13] [–]
(12"+=) *(NEGT 19)* – Taste of Cindy.
(d7"+=) *(NEGF 19)(SAM 291)* – Cut dead (acoustic) / You trip me up (acoustic) / Some candy talking (acoustic) / Psycho candy (acoustic).

—— now basic trio of **JIM, WILLIAM** and **DOUGLAS** brought in **JOHN MOORE** (b.23 Dec'64, England) – drums repl. GILLESPIE (who was busy with PRIMAL SCREAM) / **JAMES PINKER** – drums (ex-DEAD CAN DANCE) repl. MOORE now on guitar

Apr 87. (7") *(NEG 24)* **APRIL SKIES. / KILL SURF CITY** [8] [–]
(12"+=) *(NEGT 24)* – Who do you love.
(d7"+=) *(NEGF 24)* – Mushroom / Bo Diddley is Jesus.

Aug 87. (7") *(NEG 25)* **HAPPY WHEN IT RAINS. / EVERYTHING IS ALRIGHT WHEN YOU'RE DOWN** [25] [–]
(ext.12"+=) *(NEGT 25)* – Happy place / F-Hole.
(ext.10"+=) *(NEGTE 25)* – ('A'demo) / Shake.

—— trimmed to basic duo of REID brothers.

Sep 87. (lp/c)(cd) *(BYN/+C 25)(K 242 180-2) <25656>* **DARKLANDS** [5] [ ]
– Darklands / Deep one perfect morning / Happy when it rains / Down on me / Nine million rainy days / April skies / Fall / Cherry came too / On the wall / About you. *(cd re-iss. Nov94; K 242 180-2)*

Oct 87. (7"/7"g-f) *(NEG/+F 29)* **DARKLANDS. / RIDER / ON THE WALL (demo)** [33] [–]
(12"+=/12"g-f+=) *(NEGTF 29)* – Surfin' U.S.A.
(10"+=/cd-s+=) *(NEG TE/CD 29)* – Here it comes again.

—— **DAVE EVANS** – rhythm guitar repl. MOORE who formed EXPRESSWAY

The JESUS & MARY CHAIN

Mar 88. (7") *(NEG 32)* **SIDEWALKING. / TASTE OF CINDY (live)** [30] [–]
(12"+=) *(NEGT 32)* – ('A'extended) / April skies (live).
(cd-s++=) *(NEGCD 32)* – Chilled to the bone.

Apr 88. (lp/c)(cd) *(BYN/+C 29)(K 242 331-2)* <25729> **BARBED WIRE KISSES** (part compilation) [9] [ ]
– Kill Surf City / Head / Rider / Hit / Don't ever change / Just out of reach / Happy place / Psychocandy / Sidewalking / Who do you love / Surfin' USA / Everything's alright when you're down / Upside down / Taste of Cindy / Swing / On the wall. *(c+=/cd+=)* – Cracked / Here it comes again / Mushroom / Bo Diddley is Jesus. *(cd re-iss. Jan97; same)*

— In Nov'88, DOUGLAS HART moonlighted in The ACID ANGELS, who released 7"promo 'SPEED SPEED ECSTASY' on 'Product Inc.'; *FUEL 1)*

Nov 88. (7") <27754> **KILL SURF CITY. / SURFIN' USA (summer mix)** [–] [ ]

— Basically REID brothers, HART and EVANS. (added **RICHARD THOMAS** – drums) / **BEN LURIE** – rhythm guitar repl. EVANS

Sep 89. (7") *(NEG 41)* **BLUES FROM A GUN. / SHIMMER** [32] [–]
(10"+=) *(NEG 41TE)* – Break me down / Penetration.
(12"+=/c-s+=) *(NEG 41 T/C)* – Penetration / Subway.
(3"cd-s+=) *(NEG 41CD)* – Penetration / My girl.

Oct 89. (lp/c)(cd) *(BYN/+C 20)(K 246 221-2)* <26015> **AUTOMATIC** [11] [ ]
– Here comes Alice / Coast to coast / Blues from a gun / Between planets / UV ray / Her way of praying / Head on / Take it / Halfway to crazy / Gimme hell. *(cd re-iss. Jan97; same)*

Nov 89. (7") *(NEG 42)* **HEAD ON. / IN THE BLACK** [57] [–]
(12"+=) *(NEG 42T)* – Terminal beach.
(3"cd-s++=) *(NEG 42CD)* – Drop (acoustic re-mix).
(7") *(NEG 42XB)* – ('A'side). / DEVIANT SLICE
(7") *(NEG 42Y)* – ('A'side). / I'M GLAD I NEVER
(7") *(NEG 42Z)* – ('A'side). / TERMINAL BEACH

Mar 90. (7") <19891> **HEAD ON. / PENETRATION** [–] [ ]

Aug 90. (7") *(NEG 45)* **ROLLERCOASTER. / SILVER BLADE** [46] [–]
(12"+=) *(NEG 45T)* – Tower of song.
(7"ep++=/cd-ep++=) *(NEG 45 D/CD)* – Low-life.

— Trimmed again, when THOMAS joined RENEGADE SOUNDWAVE on U.S.tour. HART became video director. The **REID** brothers and **BEN** recruited **MATTHEW PARKIN** – bass + **BARRY BLACKER** – drums (ex-STARLINGS)

Blanco Y Negro / American

Feb 92. (7") *(NEG 55)* **REVERENCE. / HEAT** [10] [–]
(12"+=/cd-s+=) *(NEG 55 T/CD)* – ('A'radio remix) / Guitar man.

Mar 92. (cd/c/lp) *(9031 76554-2/-4/-1)* <26830> **HONEY'S DEAD** [14] [ ]
– Reverence / Teenage lust / Far gone and out / Almost gold / Sugar Ray / Tumbledown / Catchfire / Good for my soul / Rollercoaster / I can't get enough / Sundown / Frequency. *(cd re-iss. Jan97; same)*

Apr 92. (7") *(NEG 56)* **FAR GONE AND OUT. / WHY'D DO YOU WANT ME** [23] [–]
(12"+=/cd-s+=) *(NEG 56 T/CD)* – Sometimes you just can't get enough.

Jun 92. (7") *(NEG 57)* **ALMOST GOLD. / TEENAGE LUST (acoustic)** [41] [–]
(12"+=) *(NEG 57T)* – Honey's dead.
(gold-cd-s+=) *(NEG 57CD)* – Reverberation (doubt) / Don't come down.

Jun 93. (7"ep/c-ep/10"ep/cd-ep) *(NEG 66/+C/TE/CD)* **SOUND OF SPEED EP** [30] [–]
– Snakedriver / Something I can't have / White record release blues / Little red rooster.

Jul 93. (cd/c/lp) *(4509 93105-2/-4/-1)* **THE SOUND OF SPEED** (part comp '88-'93) [15] [–]
– Snakedriver / Reverence (radio mix) / Heat / Teenage lust (acoustic version) / Why'd you want me / Don't come down / Guitar man / Something I can't have / Sometimes / White record release blues / Shimmer / Penetration / My girl / Tower of song / Little red rooster / Break me down / Lowlife / Deviant slice / Reverberation / Sidewalking (extended version). *(cd re-iss. Jan97; same)*

— next album feat. guest vox HOPE SANDOVAL (Mazzy Star) + SHANE MacGOWAN / **STEVE MONTI** – drums repl. BLACKER

Jul 94. (7"/c-s) *(NEG 70/+C)* **SOMETIMES ALWAYS. / PERFECT CRIME** [22] [–]
(10"+=/cd-s+=) *(NEG 70 TE/CD)* – Little stars / Drop.

Aug 94. (cd/c/lp) *(4509 93104-2/-4/-1)* <45573> **STONED AND DETRONED** [13] [98]
– Dirty water / Bullet lovers / Sometimes always / Come on / Between us / Hole / Never saw it coming / She / Wish I could / Save me / Till it shines / God help me / Girlfriend / Everybody I know / You've been a friend / These days / Feeling lucky. *(cd re-iss. Jan97; same)*

Oct 94. (c-s) <18078> **SOMETIMES ALWAYS / DROP** [–] [96]

Oct 94. (7"/c-s) *(NEG 73/+C)* **COME ON. / I'M IN WITH THE OUT-CROWD** [52] [–]
(cd-s+=) *(NEG 73CD)* – New York City / Taking it away.
(cd-s) *(NEG 73CD)* – ('A'side) / Ghost of a smile / Alphabet city / New kind of kick.

Jun 95. (c-ep/12"ep/cd-ep) *(NEG 81 C/TEX/CD)* **I HATE ROCK N ROLL / BLEED ME. / 33 1-3 / LOST STAR** [61] [–]

Sep 95. (cd,c) <43043> **HATE ROCK N ROLL** (compilation of B-sides & rarities) [–] [ ]
– I hate rock'n'roll / Snakedriver / Something I can't have / Bleed me / Thirty three and a third / Lost star / Penetration / New York City / Taking it away / I'm in with the out crowd / Little stars / Teenage lust / Perfect crime.

— **JIM, WILLIAM + BEN** were joined by **NICK SANDERSON** – drums / **TERRY EDWARDS** – horns / + guests vocalists **HOPE SANDOVAL** + **SISTER VANILLA** (PAUL KING was also a member late '97)

Creation / Sub Pop

Apr 98. (7") *(CRE 292)* **CRACKING UP. / ROCKET** [35] [–]
(cd-s+=) *(CRESCD 292)* – Hide myself / Commercial.

May 98. (7"/c-s) *(CRE/+CS 296)* **I LOVE ROCK N ROLL. / EASYLIFE, EASYLOVE** [38] [–]
(cd-s+=) *(CRESCD 296)* – 40,000k / Nineteen 666.

Jun 98. (cd/c/d-lp) *(CRECD/CCRE/CRELP 232)* <SP 426> **MUNKI** [47] [ ]
– I love rock n roll / Birthday / Stardust remedy / Fizzy / Moe Tucker / Perfume / Virtually unreal / Degenerate / Cracking up / Commercial / Supertramp / Never understood / I can't find the time for times / Man on the moon / Black / Dream lover / I hate rock n roll. *(cd re-iss. Jan01; same)*

— they disbanded in October '99

– compilations, etc. –

Sep 91. (m-lp/m-c/m-cd) *Strange Fruit; (SFP MA/MC/CD 210)* **THE PEEL SESSIONS (1985-86)** [ ] [–]
– Inside me / The living end / Just like honey / all / Hapy place / In the rain.

Jun 94. (cd+book) *Audioglobe;* **LIVE (live)** [ ] [–]

Jul 01. (lp) *Strange Fruit; (SFRSLP 092)* **THE COMPLETE JOHN PEEL SESSIONS** [ ] [–]

May 02. (cd) *Blanco Y Negro; (0927 46141-2) / Rhino; <78256>* **21 SINGLES** [ ] Jul02 [ ]

LAZYCAME

WILLIAM REID – solo

Creation / not iss.

Apr 98. (cd-ep; as WILLIAM) *(CRESCD 295)* **TIRED OF FUCKING EP** [ ] [–]
– Tired of fucking / Lucibelle / Kissaround / Hard on.

Hot Tam / not iss.

Oct 99. (7"ep) *(HTAM 001)* **TASTER EP** [ ] [–]
– Muswileclouds / Stevinik / Dement / Engine8.
(cd-ep+=) *(HTAM 001CD)* – God / Complicated.

Dec 99. (cd) *(HOTTAMCD 002)* **FINBEGIN** [ ] [–]
– God / Complicated / Five one zero lovers / Rokit / Go get find / Fornicate / Unfinished business / Blue June / Naturallow / McIntosh lost.

May 00. (cd) *(HOTTAMCD 003)* **SATURDAY THE FOURTEENTH** [ ] [–]
– Drizzle / Last days of Creation / Lo Fi Li / Fuck you genius / You don't belong / Kill kool kid / Kissaround / Muswil clouds / Tired of fucking / Mayhem / Everyone knows / Dement / Unamerican.

Guided Missile / not iss.

Apr 00. (7"ep) *(GUIDE 41)* **YAWN! EP** [ ] [–]
– Drizzle / K to be lost.
(cd-ep+=) *(GUIDE 41CD)* – Who killed Manchester? / Male wife / Commercial.

FREEHEAT

JIM REID – vocals, guitar / **BEN LURIE** – guitar / **ROMI MORI** – bass (ex-GUN CLUB) / **NICK SANDERSON** – drums (ex-EARL BRUTUS)

Outafocus Hall Of Records

Nov 00. (cd-ep) <1104> **DON'T WORRY, BE HAPPY** [–] [ ]
– Two of us / Facing up to the facts / Shine on little star / Nobody's gonna trip my wire.

Feb 02. (cd-ep) *(OUTA 4CD)* **RETOX** [ ] [–]
– DON'T WORRY, BE HAPPY + / Long goodbye.

JET

Formed: Melbourne, Australia ... mid-90's as MOJO FILTER by NICK CESTER and CAMERON MUNCEY. NICK's younger brother CHRIS completed the core of a band hailed as Australia's great white hopes. Never tiring in their defence of "real" rock (which apparently means The ROLLING STONES, The BEATLES, LED ZEPPELIN etc etc etc ad nauseam) over almost anything else but particularly dance music, they even resurrected that essential piece of late 70's fashion, the 'Disco Sucks' t-shirt which, let's face it, wasn't even funny first time round. Aside from spouting tired, tedious musical fascism they made half decent attempts at approximating their beloved "real" music after being picked up by 'Elektra' amidst an A&R scramble in late 2002. With bass player MARK WILSON now completing the line-up, they released the limited edition 'DIRTY SWEET' EP in their home territory (then the UK) before 2003's 'GET BORN' album had critics namechecking about every classic rock influence in the book. The stand-out track on the Top 20 set was easily the classy hit single, 'ARE YOU GONNA BE MY GIRL'.

• **Covered:** THAT'S ALRIGHT MAMMA (Elvis Presley).

Album rating: GET BORN (*7)

NIC CESTER (b. 6 Jul'79, Dingley, Melbourne) – vocals, guitar / **CAMERON MUNCEY** (b. 8 Feb'80) – guitar / **MARK WILSON** (b. 6 Aug'79) – bass / **CHRIS CESTER** – drums

Elektra Elektra

May 03. (12"ep/cd-ep) *(<7559 62886-1/-2>)* **DIRTY SWEET EP** [ ] [–]
– Take it or leave it / Cold hard bitch / Move on / Rollover D.J.

Aug 03. (12") *(E 7456T)* **ARE YOU GONNA BE MY GIRL. / HEY KIDS / THAT'S ALRIGHT MAMMA** [23] [–]
(cd-s) *(E 7456CD1)* – ('A') / Hey kids / You were right (demo) / ('A'video).
(cd-s) *(E 7456CD2)* – ('A'-alt version) / That's alright mamma (live) / Take it or leave it (video).

Sep 03. (cd/lp) *(<7559 62892-2/-1>)* **GET BORN** [14] Oct03 [26]
– Last chance / Are you gonna be my girl / Rollover D.J. / Look what you've done / Get what you need / Move on / Radio song / Get me outta here / Cold hard bitch / Come around again / Take it or leave it / Lazy gun / Timothy.

Nov 03. (12") *(E 7486T)* **ROLLOVER D.J. / SGT. MAJOR / YOU DON'T LOOK THE SAME** [34] [–]
(cd-s) *(E 7486CD1)* – (first 2 tracks) / Are you gonna be my girl (live).
(cd-s) *(E 7486CD2)* – (first & third tracks) / Cold hard bitch (live) / ('A'-video).

Mar 04. (cd-s) *(E 7525CD)* <67527> **LOOK WHAT YOU'VE DONE / BRUISES** [28] Apr04 [37]
(12"+=) *(E 7525CD)* – Are you gonna be my girl (acoustic).
(dvd-s) *(E 7527DVD)* – ('A') / Backdoor Santa / ('A'-video) / Get what you need (live at the Astoria, London) / (behind the videos).

May 04. (12") *(E 7599T)* **ARE YOU GONNA BE MY GIRL. / AIN'T THAT A LOTTA LOVE / SWEET YOUNG THING** [16] [29]
(cd-s) *(E 7599CD)* – ('A') / Cigarettes & cola.
(dvd-s) *(E 7599DVD)* – ('A'-video) / Rollover DJ (video) / ('A') / Ain't that a lotta love.

Sep 04. (7") *(E 7607)* <549976> **COLD HARD BITCH. / MOVE ON (featuring the Stands live at Brixton Academy)** [34] [55]
(cd-s) *(E 7607CD)* – ('A') / Everlovin' man.
(dvd-s) *(E 7607DVD)* – ('A'-video) / Rollover DJ (video – international version) / ('A') / Sweet young thing (live at Brixton..)

Dec 04. (etched-7") *(E 7625)* **GET ME OUTTA HERE** [37] [–]

JETHRO TULL

Formed: London, England ... late 1967 by Scots-born IAN ANDERSON and GLENN CORNICK, who had both been in Blackpool band, JOHN EVANS' SMASH for four years alongside school friends EVANS and JEFFREY HAMMOND-HAMMOND. IAN and GLENN brought in former McGREGORY'S ENGINE members MICK ABRAHAMS plus CLIVE BUNKER, adopting the 18th century name of an English agriculturist/inventor, JETHRO TULL. It was often mistaken by the uninitiated as the name of the lead singer, IAN ANDERSON. Early in 1968, through agents Terry Ellis & Chris Wright, 'M.G.M.' issued their debut single, 'SUNSHINE DAY', mistakenly credited as JETHRO TOE at the pressing plant (it has since changed hands for over £100 at record fairs). On the 29th of June '68, after a residency at the Marquee Club, they supported PINK FLOYD at a free rock concert in Hyde Park, London. Following another enthusiastically received concert at Sunbury's Jazz & Blues Festival in August, they signed to 'Island'. By the end of the year, their debut album, 'THIS WAS' had cracked the UK Top 10, even managing to break into the American Top 75. Early in '69, they hired TONY IOMMI (future BLACK SABBATH) and DAVID O'LIST (of The NICE), for a few gigs following the departure of ABRAHAMS. In May '69, with the addition of MARTIN BARRE, they secured a UK Top 3 placing with the classic 'LIVING IN THE PAST' single. This was quickly followed by the UK No.1 album, 'STAND UP', which also made the Top 20 in the States. They then signed to associate label, 'Chrysalis', scoring two more UK Top 10 singles in 'SWEET DREAM' and 'THE WITCH'S PROMISE'. By this juncture, the band were moving away from their early blues-orientated sound into the murky waters of progressive rock, ANDERSON's songwriting voice becoming more vocal with each successive release. With his fevered, one-legged flute playing and laughably outlandish vagrant garb, ANDERSON gave the group its visual trademark, for many people he was *JETHRO TULL*. After a series of line-up changes and continued success in America, the band released 'AQUALUNG' (1971), a million selling concept album through which ANDERSON expressed his contempt for organised religion. This was nothing, however compared to the contempt which ANDERSON himself would be subject to from a volatile music press whose patience was wearing thin. If the ambitious 'THICK AS A BRICK' (1972) received a less than enthusiastic response from the press, then 'PASSION PLAY's whimsical self-indulgence was met with a critical mauling. As is often the case, the public ignored the reviews and queued up in droves for a copy, especially in America. 'WAR CHILD' and 'MINSTREL IN THE GALLERY' heralded a return to more traditional song structures but by this time, the critics had it in for the band. 'TULL did little to improve the situation by releasing the execrable 'TOO OLD TO ROCK'N'ROLL, TOO YOUNG TO DIE' (1976). Cast into the ghetto of eternal unhipness with the onslaught of punk, JETHRO TULL carried on unhindered, their live shows attracting hordes of die-hard fans. While their recorded output took on a more folky bent with 'SONGS FROM THE WOOD' and 'HEAVY HORSES', the beast that was the 'TULL live phenomenon was beamed around the world by satellite from a show at New York's Madison Square Garden in 1978. ANDERSON began working on a solo album in 1980 with ex-members of ROXY MUSIC and FAIRPORT CONVENTION, the finished article, "A", eventually being released as an official JETHRO TULL album. While the record was greeted with enthusiasm from fans the follow-up ANDERSON solo LP, 'WALK INTO THE LIGHT' (1983) and subsequent group project 'UNDER WRAPS' (1984) tested even the most ardent 'TULL devotees with their co electronica. After a few years break, the band released 'CREST OF A KNAVE' (1987), a harder rocking affair and a return to form of sorts. 'ROCK ISLAND' (1989) and 'CATFISH RISING' (1991) were disappointing in comparison while the live 1992 album, 'A LITTLE LIGHT MUSIC', saw the band in refreshing semi-acoustic mode. 1995 marked a fair solo effort by ANDERSON and a well received 'TULL album, 'ROOTS TO BRANCHES'. While the band's studio output continued to be inconsistent at best, the prospect of a JETHRO TULL live show still has old prog die-hards parting with their hard-earned cash. 'J-TULL.COM' (1999) found the band dragging themselves kicking and screaming into the Net era, in theory if not in actual musical practice. While song titles like 'HOT MANGO FLUSH' and 'BLACK MAMBA' might have suggested a deepening of the world music ties which characterised this album's predecessor, it was a remarkably pedestrian effort from ANDERSON and Co. Even the entirely predictable and highly polished live splurge, 'LIVING WITH THE PAST' (2002), was more engrossing. Drawing yet more mileage out of the back catalogue, JETHRO TULL revisited the classic 'AQUALUNG' album in full, in concert, recorded as part of XM Radio's 'Then Again' series and released in 2005.

• **Songwriters:** ANDERSON lyrics / group compositions, except BOUREE (J.S. Bach) / JOHN BARLEYCORN (trad.) / CAT'S SQUIRREL (Cream).
• **Trivia:** ANDERSON still controls his trout-farming business in Northern Scotland. In 1974, he produced STEELEYE SPAN's 'Now We Are Six' album.

Album rating: THIS WAS (*6) / STAND UP (*7) / BENEFIT (*6) / AQUALUNG (*8) / THICK AS A BRICK (*6) / LIVING IN THE PAST part compilation/live (*7) / A PASSION PLAY (*7) / WAR CHILD (*6) / MINSTREL IN THE GALLERY (*6) / M.U. – THE BEST OF JETHRO TULL compilation (*8) / TOO OLD TO ROCK'N'ROLL, TOO YOUNG TO DIE (*4) / SONGS FROM THE WOOD (*7) / REPEAT – THE BEST OF JETHRO TULL, VOL.II compilation (*6) / HEAVY HORSES (*6) / JETHRO TULL LIVE – BURSTING OUT (*5) / STORMWATCH (*4) / "A" (*4) / THE BROADSWORD AND THE BEAST (*4) / UNDER WRAPS (*3) / CREST OF A KNAVE (*6) / 20 YEARS OF JETHRO TULL boxed-set compilation (*8) / ROCK ISLAND (*4) / CATFISH RISING (*5) / A LITTLE LIGHT MUSIC (*3) / THE BEST OF JETHRO TULL: THE ANNIVERSARY COLLECTION compilation (*7) / NIGHTCAP rare material (*4) / ROOTS TO BRANCHES (*4) / J-TULL DOT COM (*3) / LIVING WITH THE PAST (*5) / AQUALUNG LIVE (*6) / Ian Anderson: WALK INTO LIGHT (*3)

IAN ANDERSON (b.10 Aug'47, Edinburgh, Scotland) – vocals, flute / **GLENN CORNICK** (b.24 Apr'47, Barrow-in-Furness, England) – bass / **MICK ABRAHAMS** (b. 7 Apr'43, Luton, England) – guitar, vocals (ex-McGREGORY'S ENGINE) / **CLIVE BUNKER** (b.12 Dec'46) – drums (ex-McGREGORY'S ENGINE)

M.G.M. — not iss.

Mar 68. (7"; as JETHRO TOE) *(MGM 1384)* **SUNSHINE DAY. / AEROPLANE** [ ] [–]

Island — Reprise

Aug 68. (7") *(WIP 6043)* **A SONG FOR JEFFREY. / ONE FOR JOHN GEE** [ ] [–]

Oct 68. (lp; mono/stereo) *(ILP/+S 9805)* <6336> **THIS WAS** [10] Feb69 [62]
– My Sunday feeling / Some day the sun won't shine for you / Beggar's farm / Move on alone / Serenade to a cuckoo / Dharma for one / It's breaking me up / Cat's squirrel / A song for Jeffrey / Round. *(re-iss. Jan74 lp/c; CHR/ZCHR 1041) (cd-iss. 1986; CCD 1041) (lp re-iss. Apr99; 499468-1) (<cd re-mast.Sep01 on 'EMI-Capitol'+=; 5 35459-2>)* – One for John Gee / Love story / Christmas song.

Dec 68. (7") *(WIP 6048)* **LOVE STORY. / A CHRISTMAS SONG** [29] [–]

Mar 69. (7") <0815> **LOVE STORY. / A SONG FOR JEFFREY** [–] [ ]

— **MARTIN BARRIE** (b.17 Nov'46) – guitar; repl. MICK ABRAHAMS who formed BLODWYN PIG

May 69. (7") *(WIP 6056)* **LIVING IN THE PAST. / DRIVING SONG** [3] [–]

Jul 69. (lp) *(ILPS 9103)* <6360> **STAND UP** [1] Oct69 [20]
– A new day yesterday / Jeffrey goes to Leicester Square / Bouree / Back to the family / Look into the sun / Nothing is easy / Fat man / We used to know / Reasons for waiting / For a thousand mothers. *(re-iss. Nov83 on 'Fame' lp/c; FA/TCFA 413086-1/-4) (cd-iss. Jan89; CCD 1042) (re-iss. Feb97 on 'E.M.I.'; LPCENT 8) (<cd re-mast.Sep01 on 'EMI-Capitol'+=; 5 35458-2>)* – Living in the past / Driving song / Sweet dream / 17.

Chrysalis — Reprise

Oct 69. (7") *(WIP 6070)* **SWEET DREAM. / 17** [9] [–]

Oct 69. (7") <0886> **SWEET DREAM. / REASONS FOR WAITING** [–] [ ]

Jan 70. (7") *(WIP 6077)* <0899> **THE WITCH'S PROMISE. / TEACHER** [4] [ ]

— augmented by **JOHN EVAN** (b.28 Mar'48) – keyboards (he later joined full-time)

Apr 70. (lp) *(ILPS 9123)* <6400> **BENEFIT** [3] [11]
– With you there to help me / Nothing to say / Alive and well and living in / Son / For Michael Collins, Jeffrey and me / To cry you a song / A time for everything / Inside / Play in time / Sossity; you're a woman. *(re-iss. Jan74 lp/c; CHR/ZCHR 1043) (cd-iss. Jun87; CPCD 1043) (<cd re-mast.Oct01 on 'EMI-Capitol'+=; 5 35457-2>)* – Singing all day / Witch's promise / Just trying to be / Teacher.

May 70. (7") *(WIP 6081)* **INSIDE. / ALIVE AND WELL AND LIVING IN** [ ] [–]

Jul 70. (7") <0927> **INSIDE. / A TIME FOR EVERYTHING** [–] [ ]

— **JEFFREY HAMMOND-HAMMOND** (b.30 Jul'46) – bass repl. CORNICK who formed WILD TURKEY

Mar 71. (lp) *(ILPS 9145)* <2035> **AQUALUNG** [4] Apr71 [7]
– Aqualung / Cross-eyed mary / Cheap day return / Mother goose / Wond'ring aloud / Up to me / My God / Hymn #43 / Slipstream / Locomotive breath / Wind up. *(re-iss. Jan74 lp/c; CHR/ZCHR 1044) (cd-iss. 1988; CCD 933-2) (re-iss. cd Mar94; CD25CR 08) (cd re-iss. Jun96 +=; CD25CR 08)* – (sessions):- Lick your fingers clean / Wind up (quad version) / (Ian Anderson interview) / Song for Jeffrey / Fat man / Bouree. *(<cd re-mast.Jun98 +=; 495401-2>)* – Lick your fingers clean / Wind up (quad) / (excerpts from the Ian Anderson interview) / A song for Jeffrey / Fat man / Bouree. *(lp re-iss. Aug00 on 'D.C.C.'; LPZ 2030)*

Jul 71. (7") <1024> **HYMN #43. / MOTHER GOOSE** [–] [91]

— **ANDERSON, BARRE, HAMMOND-HAMMOND** and **EVAN** were joined by **BARRIEMORE BARLOW** (b.10 Sep'49) – drums (ex-JOHN EVAN'S SMASH) who repl. BUNKER who joined BLODWYN PIG

Sep 71. (7"ep) *(WIP 6106)* **LIFE IS A LONG SONG / UP THE POOL. / DR. BOGENBROOM / FOR LATER / NURSIE** [11] [–]

Oct 71. (7") <1054> **LOCOMOTIVE BREATH. / WIND** [–] [ ]

Chrysalis — Reprise

Mar 72. (lp) *(CHR 1003)* <2071> **THICK AS A BRICK** [5] May72 [1]
– Thick as a brick (side 1) / Thick as a brick (side 2). *(re-iss. Jan74 lp/c; CHR/ZCHR 1003) (cd-iss. 1986; ACCD 1003) (cd-re-iss. Apr89 on 'Mobile Fidelity'; UDCD 510) (cd re-iss. Jun98 as part of 25th Anniversary on 'E.M.I.'+=; CDCNTAV 5)* – Thick as a brick (live at Madison Square Gardens 1978) / (interview).

Apr 72. (7") <1153> **THICK AS A BRICK (edit #1). / HYMN #43** [–] [ ]

Chrysalis — Chrysalis

Jul 72. (d-lp) *(CJT 1)* <2106> **LIVING IN THE PAST** (live / studio compilation) [8] Nov72 [3]
– A song for Jeffrey / Love story / Christmas song / Teacher / Living in the past / Driving song / Bouree / Sweet dream / Singing all day / Witches promise / Teacher / Inside / Just trying to be / By kind permission of / Dharma for one / Wond'ring again / Locomotive breath / Life is a long song / Up the pool / Dr. Bogenbroom / For later / Nursie. *(cd-iss. Oct87; CCD 1035) (re-iss. Mar94 cd/c; ZCJTD 1)*

Oct 72. (7") <2006> **LIVING IN THE PAST. / CHRISTMAS SONG** [–] [11]

May 73. (7") <2012> **A PASSION PLAY (edit #8). / A PASSION PLAY (edit #9)** [–] [80]

Jul 73. (lp) *(<CHR/ZCHR 1040>)* **A PASSION PLAY** [13] [1]
– A passion play (part 1; including 'The story of the hare who lost his spectacles' part 1)- /- (part 2) / A passion play (part 2). *(cd-iss. Jan89; CCD 1040) (<cd re-mast.Apr03 on 'EMI-Capitol'+=; 5 815690>)* – (enhanced video track).

Aug 73. (7") <2017> **A PASSION PLAY (edit #6). / A PASSION PLAY (edit #10)** [–] [ ]

Oct 74. (7") *(CHS 2054)* <2101> **BUNGLE IN THE JUNGLE. / BACK-DOOR ANGELS** [ ] [12]

Oct 74. (lp/c) *(<CHR/ZCHR 1067>)* **WAR CHILD** [14] [2]
– Warchild / Queen and country / Ladies / Back-door angels / Sealion / Skating away on the thin ice of a new day / Bungle in the jungle / Only solitaire / The third hooray / Two fingers. *(cd-iss. Apr99 on 'Mobile Fidelity'; UDCD 745) (cd re-iss. Aug00; CCD 1067) (<cd re-mast.Oct02 on 'EMI-Capitol'+=; 5 41571-2>)* – Warchild waltz / Quartet / Paradise steakhouse / Sealion (part 2) / Rainbow blues / Glory row / Saturation.

Jan 74. (7") *<2103>* **SKATING AWAY ON THE THIN ICE OF A NEW DAY. / SEALION** [–] [ ]

Sep 75. (lp/c) *(<CHR/ZCHR 1082>)* **MINSTREL IN THE GALLERY** [20] [7]
– Minstrel in the gallery / Cold wind to Valhalla / Black satin dancer / Requiem / One white duck / 0x10 = Nothing at all – Baker St. Muse (including Pig-me and the whore – Nice little tune – Crash barrier waltzer – Mother England reverie) / Grace. *(cd-iss. 1986; CCD 1082) (<cd re-mast.Oct02 on 'EMI-Capitol'+=; 5 41572-2>)* – Summerday sands / March the mad scientist / Pan dance / Minstrel in the gallery (live) / Cold wind to Valhalla (live).

Oct 75. (7") *(CHS 2075) <2106>* **MINSTREL IN THE GALLERY. / SUMMER DAY SANDS** [ ] [79]

—— **JOHN GLASCOCK** (b.1953) – bass (ex-CHICKEN SHACK, ex-TOE FAT) repl. HAMMOND-HAMMOND

Mar 76. (7") *(CHS 2086)* **TOO OLD TO ROCK'N'ROLL, TOO YOUNG TO DIE. / RAINBOW BLUES** [ ] [–]

Apr 76. (7") *<2114>* **TOO OLD TO ROCK'N'ROLL, TOO YOUNG TO DIE. / BAD-EYED AND LOVELESS** [–] [ ]

May 76. (lp/c) *(<CHR/ZCHR 1111>)* **TOO OLD TO ROCK'N'ROLL: TOO YOUNG TO DIE** [25] [14]
– Quizz kid / Crazed institution / Salamander / Taxi grab / From a dead beat to an old greaser / Bad-eyed and loveless / Big dipper / Too old to rock'n'roll: too young to die / Pied piper / The chequered flag (dead or alive). *(cd-iss. Nov86 & Aug00; CCD 1111) (<cd re-mast.Oct02 on 'EMI-Capitol'+=; 541573-2>)* – A small cigar / Strip cartoon.

—— added **DAVID PALMER** – keyboards (He had been their past orchestrator)

Nov 76. (7"ep) *(CXP 2)* **RING OUT, SOLSTICE BELLS / MARCH THE MAD SCIENTIST. / A CHRISTMAS SONG / PAN DANCE** [28] [–]

Jan 77. (7") *(CHS <2135>)* **THE WHISTLER. / STRIP CARTOON** [ ] Apr77 [59]

Feb 77. (lp/c) *(<CHR/ZCHR 1132>)* **SONGS FROM THE WOOD** [13] [8]
– Songs from the wood / Jack-in-the-green / Cup of wonder / Hunting girl / Ring out, solstice bells / Velvet green / The whistler / Pibroch (cap in hand) / Fire at midnight. *(cd-iss. 1986; ACCD 1132) (<cd re-mast.Apr03 on 'EMI-Capitol'+=; 581570-2>)* – Beltane / Velvet green (live).

Apr 78. (7") *(CHS 2214)* **MOTHS. / LIFE IS A LONG SONG** [ ] [–]

Apr 78. (lp/c) *(<CHR/ZCHR 1175>)* **HEAVY HORSES** [20] [19]
– . . .And the mouse police never sleeps / Acres wild / No lullaby / Moths / Journeyman / Rover / One brown mouse / Heavy horses / Weathercock. *(cd-iss. 1986; CCD 1175) (<cd re-mast.Apr03 on 'EMI-Capitol'+=; 581571-2>)* – Living in these hard times / Broadford bazaar.

Oct 78. (d-lp/c) *(CJT/ZCJT 4) <1201>* **LIVE – BURSTING OUT (live)** [17] [21]
– No lullaby / Sweet dream / Skating away on the thin ice of a new day / Jack in the green / One brown mouse / A new day yesterday / Flute solo improvisation – God rest ye merry gentlemen – Bouree / Songs from the wood / Thick as a brick / Hunting girl / Too old to rock'n'roll: too young to die / Conundrum / Cross-eyed Mary / Quatrain / Aqualung / Locomotive breath / The dambusters march.

Nov 78. (7",7"white) *(CHS 2260)* **A STITCH IN TIME. / SWEET DREAM (live)** [ ] [–]

Sep 79. (7") *(CHS 2378)* **NORTH SEA OIL. / ELEGY** [ ] [ ]

Sep 79. (lp/c) *(<CDL/ZCDL 1238>)* **STORMWATCH** [27] [22]
– North Sea oil / Orion / Home / Dark ages / Warm sporran / Something's on the move / Old ghosts / Dun Ringill / Flying Dutchman / Elegy. *(cd-iss. Jan89; CCD 1238)*

Nov 79. (7") *<2387>* **HOME. / WARM SPORRAN** [–] [ ]

Nov 79. (7"ep) *(CHS 2394)* **HOME / KING HENRY'S MADRIGAL (THEME FROM MAINSTREAM). / WARM SPORRAN / RING OUT SOLSTICE BELLS** [ ] [–]

—— ANDERSON for what was supposed to be a solo album retained **BARRE** / plus new **DAVE PEGG** (b. 2 Nov'47, Birmingham, England) – bass (ex-FAIRPORT CONVENTION) repl. GLASCOCK who died. / **EDDIE JOBSON** (b.28 Apr'55, England) – keyboards (ex-ROXY MUSIC, ex-CURVED AIR, etc) repl. EVANS and PALMER who took up session work / **MARK CRANEY** (b. Los Angeles, Calif.) – drums repl. BARLOW who went solo.

Aug 80. (lp/c) *(<CDL/CDC 1301>)* **"A"** [25] Sep 80 [30]
– Crossfire / Fylingdale flyer / Working John, working Joe / Black Sunday / Protect and survive / Batteries not included / 4.W.D. (low ratio) / The Pine Marten's jig / And further on. *(<cd re-mast.Oct02 on 'EMI-Capitol'; 321301-2>)*

Oct 80. (7") *(CHS 2468)* **WORKING JOHN, WORKING JOE. / FYLINGDALE FLYER** [ ] [–]

—— **PETER JOHN VITESSE** – keyboards repl. JOBSON who went solo / **GERRY CONWAY** – drums (ex-STEELEYE SPAN) repl. CRANEY

Apr 82. (lp/c) *(<CDL/CDC 1380>)* **THE BROADSWORD AND THE BEAST** [27] May82 [19]
– Beastie / Clasp / Fallen on hard times / Flying colours / Slow marching band / Broadsword / Pussy willow / Watching me watching you / Seal driver / Cheerio. *(cd-iss. Apr83; CCD 1380)*

May 82. (7") *<2613>* **PUSSY WILLOW. / FALLEN ON HARD TIMES** [–] [ ]

May 82. (7"/7"pic-d) *(CHS/+P 2616)* **BROADSWORD. / FALLEN ON HARD TIMES** [ ] [–]

—— **DOANNE PERRY** – drums repl. CONWAY

Sep 84. (lp/pic-lp/c/cd) *(CDL/CDLP/ZCDL/CCD 1461) <1-/0-/4-/2-1461>* **UNDER WRAPS** [18] [76]
– Lap of luxury / Under wraps #1 / European legacy / Later that same evening / Saboteur / Radio free Moscow / Nobody's car / Heat / Under wraps #2 / Paparazzi / Apogee. *(c+=/cd+=)* – Automatic engineering / Astronomy / Tundra / General crossing. *(<cd re-mast.Oct02; same>)*

Sep 84. (7") *(TULL 1)* **LAP OF LUXURY. / ASTRONOMY** [70] [ ]
(d7"+=/12"+=) *(TULL D/X 1)* – Tundra / Automatic engineering.

Jun 86. (7") *(TULL 2)* **CORONIACH. / JACK FROST AND THE HOODED CROW** [ ] [ ]
(12"+=) *(TULLX 2)* – Living in the past / Elegy.

—— **ANDERSON, BARRE, PEGG** and **PERRY** recruited new member **MARTIN ALLCOCK** – keyboards (ex-FAIRPORT CONVENTION) repl. VITESSE

Sep 87. (lp/c/cd) *(CDL/ZCDL/CCD 1590) <1-/4-/2-1590>* **CREST OF A KNAVE** [19] [32]
– Steel monkey / Farm on the freeway / Jump start / Said she was a dancer / Dogs in midwinter * / Budapest / Mountain men / The waking edge * / Raising steam. *(cd+= *) (cd re-iss. Aug00; same)*

Oct 87. (7"/7"pic-d) *(TULL/+P 3)* **STEEL MONKEY. / DOWN AT THE END OF YOUR ROAD** [ ] [ ]
(12"+=)(c-s+=) *(TULLX/ZTULL 3)* – Too many too / I'm your gun.

Dec 87. (7"/7"pic-d) *(TULL/+P 4)* **SAID SHE WAS A DANCER. / DOGS IN MIDWINTER** [55] [ ]
(12"+=) *(TULLX 4)* – The waking edge.
(cd-s+=) *(TULLCD 4)* – Down at the end of your road / Too many too.

Aug 89. (lp/pic-lp/c/cd) *(CHR/CHRP/ZCHR/CCD 1708) <1-/0-/4-/2-21708>* **ROCK ISLAND** [18] [56]
– Kissing Willie / The rattlesnake trail / Ears of tin / Undressed to kill / Rock Island / Heavy water / Another Christmas song / The whalers dues / Big Riff and Mando / Strange avenues.

Aug 89. (c-s) **KISSING WILLIE. / EARS OF TIN** [–] [ ]

Nov 89. (7") *(TULL 5)* **ANOTHER CHRISTMAS SONG. / SOLSTICE BELLS** [ ] [ ]
(12"+=) *(TULLX 5)* – Jack Frost.
(12"+=/cd-s) *(TULL EX/CD 5)* – ('A'side) / Intro – A Christmas song (live) / Cheap day return – Mother goose / Outro – Locomotive breath (live).

—— **ANDY GIDDINGS** – keyboards (3) / **MATT PEGG** – bass (3) / etc. repl. ALLCOCK

Aug 91. (7"/c-s) *(TULL/+XMC 6)* **THIS IS NOT LOVE. / NIGHT IN THE WILDERNESS** [ ] [ ]
(12"+=/cd-s+=) *(TULL X/CD 6)* – Jump start (live).

Sep 91. (cd/c/lp) *(CCD/ZCHR/DCHR 1886) <2-/4-/1-1863>* **CATFISH RISING** [27] [88]
– This is not love / Occasional demons / Rocks on the road / Thinking round corners / Still loving you tonight / Doctor to my disease / Like a tal thin girl / Sparrow on the schoolyard wall / Roll yer own / Gold-tipped boots, black jacket and tie. *(free 12"ep)* – WHEN JESUS CAME TO PLAY. / SLEEPING WITH THE DOG / WHITE INNOCENCE

—— **DAVID MATTACKS** – drums, percussion, keyboards repl. PERRY and guests

Mar 92. (12"pic-d) *(TULLX 7)* **ROCKS ON THE ROAD. / JACK-A-LYNN (demo) / AQUALUNG – LOCOMOTIVE BREATH (live)** [47] [ ]
(c-s) *(TULLMC 7)* – ('A'side) / Bouree (live) / Mother goose – Jack-a-Lyr (live).
(2xbox-cd-s++=) *(TULLCD 7)* – Tall thin girl (live) / Fat man (live).

Sep 92. (cd/c/d-lp) *(CCD/ZCHR/CHR 1954) <2-/4/-1-1954>* **A LITTLE LIGHT MUSIC (live in Europe '92)** [34] [ ]
– Someday the sun won't shine for you / Living in the past / Life is a long song / Rocks on the road / Under wraps / Nursie / Too old to rocl and roll, too young to die / One white duck / A new day yesterday / Johr Barleycorn / Look into the sun / A Christmas song / From a dead bea to an old greaser / This is not love / Bouree / Pussy willow / Locomotive breath.

— **PERRY** returned to repl. MATTACKS; bass playing was provided by **DAVE PEGG / STEVE BAILEY**

Sep 95. (cd/c/d-lp) *(CCD/ZCHR/CHR 6109) <2-/4-/1-6109>* **ROOTS TO BRANCHES** [20] [ ]
– Roots to branches / Rare and precious chain / Out of the noise / This free will / Valley / Dangerous veils / Beside myself / Wounded old and treacherous / At last, forever / Stuck in the August rain / Another Harry's bar.

— **ANDERSON, BARRE, GIDDINGS + PERRY** were joined by **JONATHAN NOYCE** – bass

Papillon Varese

Aug 99. (cd) *(BTFLYCD 0001) <1043>* **J-TULL DOT COM** [44] [ ]
– Spiral / Dot com / Awol / Nothing @ all / Wicked windows / Hunt by numbers / Hot mango flush / El Nino / Black mamba / Mango surprise / Bends like a willow / Far Alaska / The dog-ear years / A gift of roses.

Nov 99. (cd-s) *(BTFLYS 0001)* **BENDS LIKE A WILLOW / BENDS LIKE A WILLOW (version) / IT ALL TRICKLES DOWN** [ ] [–]

Eagle Fuel 2000

May 02. (cd) *(EAGCD 231) <061199>* **LIVING WITH THE PAST (live 2001)** [ ] [ ]
– (intro) / My Sunday feeling / Roots to branches / Jack in the green / The Habanero reel / Sweet dream / In the grip of stronger stuff / Aqualung / Locomotive breath / Living in the past / Protect and survive / Nothing is easy / Wond'ring aloud / Life is a long song / A Christmas song / Cheap day return / Mother goose / Dot com / Fat man / Dome day the sun won't shine for you / Cheerio.

— **ANDERSON, BARRE**, etc.

Random House not iss.

Sep 05. (cd) *(RANCD 0015)* **AQUALUNG LIVE** (live) [ ] [–]
– Aqualung / Crosseyed Mary / Cheap day return / Mother goose / Wond'ring aloud / Up to me / My god / Hymn 43 / Slipstream / Locomotive breath / Wind-up / narratives:- Riffs – Another monkey / Recording the original / Choosing my words with care / Hummmmmmmm 43 / A different kettle of very different fish / But is it any good?

– compilations, others, etc. –

on 'Chrysalis' unless mentioned otherwise

Jan 76. (7") *(CHS 2081)* **LIVING IN THE PAST. / REQUIEM** [ ] [ ]

Jan 76. (lp/c) *(<CHR/ZCHR 1078>)* **M.U. – THE BEST OF JETHRO TULL** [44] [13]
– Teacher / Aqualung / Thick as a brick (edit #1) / Bungle in the jungle / Locomotive breath / Fat man / Living in the past / A passion play (#8) / Skating away on the thin ice of a new day / Rainbow blues / Nothing is easy. *(cd-iss. Dec85; ACCD 1078)*

Feb 76. (7") *<2110>* **LOCOMOTIVE BREATH. / FAT MAN** [–] [62]

Nov 77. (lp/c) *(<CHR/ZCHR 1135>)* **REPEAT – THE BEST OF JETHRO TULL VOL.2** [ ] [94]
– Minstrel in the gallery / Cross-eyed Mary / A new day yesterday / Bouree / Thick as a brick (edit #1) / War child / A passion play (edit #9) / To cry you a song / Too old to rock'n'roll, too young to die / Glory row. *(cd-iss. Apr86; CCD 1135)*

Dec 82. (d-c) *(ZCDP 105)* **M.U. / REPEAT** [ ] [–]

Oct 85. (lp/c/cd) *(JTTV/ZJTTV/CCD 1515)* **ORIGINAL MASTERS** [63] [ ]

Aug 87. (7") *Old Gold; (OG 9637)* **LIVING IN THE PAST. / THE WITCHES' PROMISE** [ ] [–]

Jun 88. (5xlp-box/3xc-box/3xcd-box) *(T/MC/CD BOX 1) <41653>* **20 YEARS OF JETHRO TULL** [78] [97]
– THE RADIO ARCHIVES:- A song for Jeffrey / Love story * / Fat man / Bouree / Stormy Monday blues * / A new day yesterday * / Cold wind to Valhalla / Minstrel in the gallery / Velvet green / Grace * / The clasp / / Pibroch (pee-break) – Black satin dancer (instrumental) * / Fallen on hard times // THE RARE TRACKS:- Jack Frost and the hooded crow / I'm your gun / Down at the end of your road / Coronach * / Summerday sands * / Too many too / March the mad scientist * / Pan dance / Strip cartoon / King Henry's madrigal / A stitch in time / 17 / One for John Gee / Aeroplane / Sunshine day // FLAWED GEMS:- Lick your fingers clean * / The Chateau Disaster Tapes: Scenario – Audition – No reheasal / Beltane / Crossword * / Saturation * / Jack-A-Lynn * / Motoreyes * / Blues instrumental (untitled) / Rhythm in gold // THE OTHER SIDES OF TULL:- Part of the machine * / Mayhem, maybe * / Overhang * / Kelpie * / Living in these hard times / Under wraps II * / Only solitaire / Cheap day return / Wond'ring aloud * / Dun Ringill * / Salamander / Moths / Nursie * / Life is a long song * / One white duck – 0x10 = Nothing at all // THE ESSENTIAL TULL:- Songs from the wood / Living in the past * / Teacher * / Aqualung * / Locomotive breath * / The witches promise * / Bungle in the jungle / Farm on the freeway / Thick as a brick / Sweet dream. *(re-iss. Aug88 as d-lp/d-c/d-cd; tracks *; CHR/ZCHR/CCD 1655)*

Jun 88. (pic-cd) *(TULLPCD 1)* **PART OF THE MACHINE / STORMY MONDAY BLUES (live) / LICK YOUR FINGERS CLEAN (live) / MINSTREL IN THE GALLERY (live) / FARM ON THE FREEWAY (live)** [ ] [–]

Jan 91. (cd/c/lp) *Raw Fruit; (FRS CD/MC/LP 004)* **LIVE AT HAMMERSMITH 1984 (live)** [ ] [–]

Apr 93. (4xcd-box) *(CDCHR 60044)* **25th ANNIVERSARY BOXED SET** [ ] [ ]
– REMIXED (CLASSIC SONGS) / CARNEGIE HALL N.Y. (RECORDED LIVE NEW YORK CITY 1970) / THE BEACON'S BOTTOM (TAPES) / POT POURRI (LIVE ACROSS THE WORLD AND THROUGH THE YEARS)

May 93. (7") *(CHS 3970)* **LIVING IN THE PAST. / HARD LINER** [32] [ ]
(12") *(12CHS 3970)* – ('A'side) / ('A'club)/ ('A'dub ravey master) / ('A'dub N.Y. mix).
(d-cd-s) *(23970-1)* – Living in the (slightly more recent) past (live) / Silver river turning / Rosa on the factory floor / I don't want to be me / ('A'side) / Truck stop runner / Piece of cake / Man of principle.

May 93. (d-cd/d-c) *(CDCHR/ZCHR 6001)* **THE VERY BEST OF JETHRO TULL – THE ANNIVERSARY COLLECTION** [ ] [ ]
– A song for Jeffrey / Beggar's farm / A Christmas song / A new day yesterday / Bouree / Nothing is easy / Living in the past / To cry you a song / Teacher / Sweet dream / Cross-eyed Mary / Mother goose / Aqualung / Locomotive breath / Life is a long song / Thick as a brick (extract) / Skating away on the thin ice of a new day / Bungle in the jungle/ / Minstrel in the gallery / Too old to rock'n'roll / Songs from the wood / Jack in the green / The whistler / Heavy horses / Dun Ringill / Fylingdale flyer / Jack-a-Lynn / Pussy willow / Broadsword / Under wraps II / Steel monkey / Farm on the freeway / Jump start / Kissing Willie / This is not love.

Nov 93. (d-cd) *(CDCHR 6057)* **NIGHTCAP – THE UNRELEASED MASTERS 1973-1991** [ ] [ ]
– CHATEAU D'ISASTER – First post / Animelee / Tiger Moon / Look at the animals / Law of the bungle / Law of the bungle part II / Left right / Solitaire / Critique oblique / Post last / Scenario / Audition / No rehearsal/ / UNRELEASED & RARE TRACKS – Paradise steakhouse / Sealion II / Piece of cake / Quartet / Silver river turning / Crew nights / The curse / Rosa on the factory floor / A small cigar / Man of principle / Commons brawl / No step / Drive on the young side of life / I don't want to be me / Broadford bazaar / Lights out / Truck stop runner / Hard liner.

Apr 95. (cd) *Windsong; (WINCD 070)* **IN CONCERT (live)** [ ] [–]

Feb 97. (cd) *EMI Gold; (CDGOLD 1079)* **THROUGH THE YEARS** [ ] [–]
(re-iss. Apr00 on 'Disky'; SI 99195-2)

Mar 97. (cd) *Disky; (DC 87861-2)* **THE JETHRO TULL COLLECTION** [ ] [–]

Apr 97. (3xcd-box) *(CDOMB 021)* **THE ORIGINALS** [ ] [–]
– (THIS WAS / STAND UP / BENEFIT) *(re-iss. Sep00 on 'EMI'; 528364-2)*

Feb 98. (cd) *Strange Fruit; (SFRSCD 051)* **BBC LIVE IN CONCERT** [ ] [ ]

Mar 03. (d-cd) *(5 82353-2)* **STAND UP / THIS WAS** [ ] [–]

Mar 03. (cd) *EMI-Capitol; (582145-2)* **THE ESSENTIAL** [ ] [–]

Oct 03. (cd) *R&M; (RAMCD 004) / Fuel 2000; <061340>* **THE JETHRO TULL CHRISTMAS ALBUM** (festive recordings) [ ] [ ]

IAN ANDERSON

solo album augmented by **PETER JOHN VITESSE** – synth, keyboards

Chrysalis Chrysalis

Nov 83. (7") *(CHS 2746)* **FLY BY NIGHT. / END GAME** [ ] [–]

Nov 83. (lp/c) *<(CDL/ZCDL 1443)>* **WALK INTO LIGHT** [78] [ ]
– Fly by night / Made in England / Walk into light / Trains / End game / Black and white television / Toad in the hole / Looking for Eden / User-friendly / Different Germany. *(cd-iss. 1988; CCD 1443) (cd re-iss. Jun97 on 'Beat Goes On'; BGOCD 350)*

E.M.I. E.M.I.

Sep 98. (cd) *(<CDC 555262-2>)* **DIVINITIES (12 DANCES WITH GOD)** [ ] May95 [ ]
– In a stone circle / In sight of a minaret / In a black box / In the grip of stronger stuff / In material grace / In the moneylender's temple / At their

father's knee / En Afrique / In the olive garden / In the pay of Spain / In times of India (Bombay valentine).

Papillion Varese

Mar 00. (cd) *(BTFLYCD 2000)* <061053> **THE SECRET LANGUAGE OF BIRDS** [ ] [ ]
– The secret language of birds / Little flower girl / Montserrat / Postcard day / Water carrier / Set-aside / Better Moon / Sanctuary / Jasmine corridor / Habanero reel / Panama freighter / The secret language of birds, pt.2 / Boris dancing / Circular breathing / Stormont shuffle.

JIMMY EAT WORLD

Formed: Mesa, Arizona, USA … 1993 by JIM ADKINS, TOM LINTON, MITCH PORTER and ZACH LIND. Having begun life as a METALLICA covers band, the quartet soon developed a more lugubrious, melodic post-grunge sound as evidenced on their independently released debut 7". An eponymous album quickly followed as did a slew of split singles with the likes of CHRISTIE FRONT DRIVE and BLUEPRINT. Subsequently signed to 'Capitol', the group released 'STATIC PREVAILS' as their major label debut in 1996. Their contract nevertheless allowed for indie releases and they issued an eponymous five track EP in 1998 as a taster for the acclaimed 'CLARITY' (1999), a blinding, infused album of pure rock energy. Hailed by music journos as "the official Emo boys", the group settled on playing their abrasive, no bullshit, straight up rock'n'roll. But this wasn't three-chord idiot rock, oh no! JIMMY EAT WORLD incorporated intelligent lyrics and swirling, prolonged instrumentals, akin to the good ol' days of FUGAZI and straight-edged punk. After a split mini-album with Australian rockers JEBEDIAH, the group were dropped by majors 'Capitol'. They headed back into the studio and self-financed their sophomore set 'BLEED AMERICAN', later to be re-titled 'JIMMY EAT WORLD' (2001), after the 9/11 terrorists attacks. With runaway single 'THE MIDDLE' blasted all over MTV, and the growing popularity of emo-core, the 'EAT WORLD found themselves a distribution deal with Geffen/Spielberg label 'Dreamworks'. The album subsequently catapulted them into the mainstream while further single 'SWEETNESS' rocked the chart. With Gil Norton taking up the baton from Mark Trombino (ex-DRIVE LIKE JEHU), the band streamlined their sound on fifth album, 'FUTURES' (2004), a Top 10'er that also produced a couple of hits, 'PAIN' and 'WORK'.

• **Covered:** NEW RELIGION (Duran Duran) / SPANGLE (Wedding Present) / LAST CHRISTMAS (Wham) / FIRSTARTER (Prodigy).

Album rating: JIMMY EAT WORLD (*4) / STATIC PREVAILS (*5) / CLARITY (*6) / SINGLES compilation (*6) / BLEED AMERICAN (*7) / FUTURES (*7)

JIM ADKINS (b.10 Nov'75) – vocals, guitar / **TOM LINTON** (b. 8 Aug'75) – vocals, guitar / **MITCH PORTER** – bass / **ZACH LIND** (b.19 Mar'76) – drums

not iss. Wooden Blue

1994. (7"ep) **ONE, TWO, THREE, FOUR** [–] [ ]
– What would I say to you now / Speed read.

1994. (cd) **JIMMY EAT WORLD** [–] [ ]
– Chachi / Patches / Amphibious / Splat out of luck / House arrest / Usery / Wednesday / Crooked / Reason 346 / Scientific / Cars.

1995. (7") **OPENER. / 77 SATELLITES** [–] [ ]
<re-iss. 1995 on 'Jimmy Eat World'; >

1995. (7") **DIGITS. / (other by CHRISTIE FRONT DRIVE)** [–] [ ]

not iss. Ordinary

Nov 95. (7") **BETTER THAN OH. / (other by EMERY)** [–] [ ]

not iss. Abridged

Dec 95. (7"ep) **CHRISTMAS CARD / UNTITLED. / (other 2 by BLUEPRINT)** [–] [ ]

—— **RICK BURCH** (b. 4 Feb'75) – bass; repl. PORTER

not iss. Capitol

Jul 96. (cd/c) <32404> **STATIC PREVAILS** [–] [ ]
– Thinking, that's all / Rockstar / Claire / Call it in the air / Seventeen / Episode IV / Digits / Caveman / World is static / In the same room / Robot factory / Anderson Mesa. *(UK cd-iss. Jul02 on 'E.M.I.'+=; 539615-2)* – Rockstar (video).

1996. (7"ep) **LESS THAN JAKE / JIMMY EAT WORLD split** [–] [ ]
– Rockstar / Call it in the air / Seventeen / (other 3 by LESS THAN JAKE)

—— in 1997, the track 'CRUSH' featured on a 7" split alongside SENSEFIELD + MINERAL

1998. (7"ep) **JIMMY EAT WORLD / JEJUNE split** [–] [ ]
– What I would say to you now / Speed read / (other 2 by JEJUNE).
(above issued on 'Big Wheel Recreation') (below on 'Fueled By Ramen')

Oct 98. (cd-ep) *<FBR 020CD>* **JIMMY EAT WORLD** [–] [ ]
– Lucky Denver mint / For me this is heaven / Your new aesthetic (demo) / Softer / Roller queen. *(UK-iss.Apr99; same as US)*

Feb 99. (cd) <55950> **CLARITY** [–] [ ]
– Table for glasses / Lucky Denver mint / Your new aesthetic / Believe in what you want / Sunday / Crush / 12.23.95 / Ten / Just watch the fireworks / For me this is Heaven / Blister / Clarity / Goodbye sky harbor *(UK-iss.Jul02 on 'E.M.I.'+=; 539616-2)* – Lucky Denver mint (video).

Big Wheel Big Whe

Oct 00. (3x7"/cd-ep) *<(BWR 0232/+CD)>* **JEBEDIAH & JIMMY EAT WORLD** [ ] [ ]
– The most beautiful things / No sensitivity / Cautioners / (other 3 by JEBEDIAH).

Universal Dreamw

Aug 01. (cd) *(450348-2)* <450334> **BLEED AMERICAN** [ ] Jul01 [54]
– Bleed American / A praise chorus / The middle / Your house / Sweetness Hear you me / If you don't, don't / Get it faster / Cautioners / The authorit song / My sundown / Splash, turn, twist *[UK+lp-only]*. *<lp-iss.on 'Gran Royal'; GR 99> (lp-iss.Mar03 on 'I.M.S.'; E 450334-1) (lp re-iss. Jun03 o 'Western Tread'; WT 002)*

Oct 01. (cd-s) *(450897-2)* **BLEED AMERICAN / SPLASH, TURN, TWIST / YOUR HOUSE (demo) / THE AUTHORITY SONG (demo) / BLEED AMERICAN (video)** [ ] [–]

Nov 01. (7") *(450878-7)* **SALT SWEAT SUGAR. / YOUR HOUSE (demo)** [60] [–]
(c-s) *(450878-4)* – ('A') / Splash, turn, twist.
(cd-s+=) *(450878-2)* – ('A'-video).

Jan 02. (7"/c-s) *(450848-7/-4)* **THE MIDDLE. / A PRAISE CHORUS** [26] [5]
(cd-s) *(450848-2) <450794>* – ('A') / If you don't, don't / Game of pricks ('A'-video).

Jan 02. (cd) *(as prev.)* **JIMMY EAT WORLD** (aka 'BLEED AMERICAN') [62] [31]

Jun 02. (7") *(450832-7)* **SWEETNESS. / CLARITY (live)** [38] May02 [75]
(cd-s) *<(450833-2)>* – ('A') / Blister (live) / Your new acoustic (live).
(cd-s) *(450834-2)* – ('A') / A praise chorus (live) / Lucky Denver mint (live)

Dec 02. (7") *<BLR 16>* **LAST CHRISTMAS. / FIRESTARTER** [–] [ ]
(above issued on 'Better Looking' records)

Polydor Intersc

Oct 04. (7") *(9864181)* **PAIN. / YOU (demo) / WHEN I WANT (demo)** [37] [93]
(cd-s) *(9864179)* – ('A') / Shame (demo) / Yer feet (live) / ('A'-video).

Oct 04. (cd) *(9864241) <B000335810-2>* **FUTURES** [22] [6]
– Futures / Just tonight. . . / Work / Kill / The world you love / Pain / Drug or me / Polaris / Nothingwrong / Night drive / 23. *(UK+=)* – Shame When I want. *<(d-lp on 'Western Tread'; WT 004)> (ltd d-cd++=; 988018* – (demos of all tracks).

Mar 05. (cd-s) *(9880673)* **WORK / DRUGS OR ME (Styrofoam remix) / WORK (acoustic) / WORK (video)** [49] [–]

Oct 05. (cd-ep) *<B0005448-02>* **STAY ON MY SIDE TONIGHT** [–] [ ]
– Disintigration / Over / Closer / Half right / Drugs or me (Styrofoa remix).

– compilations, etc. –

Aug 01. (cd) *Big Wheel; <(BWR 0230CD)>* **SINGLES** [ ] [ ]
– Opener / 77 satellites / What would I say to you now / Speed read Spangle / H Ramina / Christmas card / Untitled / Carbon scoring / Digi *(cd re-iss. Oct01 on 'Golf'+=; CDGOLF 049)* – If model / Most beautif things / Cautioners.

Billy JOEL

Born: WILLIAM MARTIN JOEL, 9 May'49, Hicksville, Long Island, New York, USA. In 1965, the classically trained JOEL played piano in his first group, The ECHOES, having been a welterweight boxing champ for local Long Island boys' club. In 1967, he joined The HASSLES who signed to 'United Artists' and released a couple of albums, after an initial SAM & DAVE cover version 45, 'YOU GOT ME HUMMIN'. In 1969, JOEL became a rock critic for 'Changes' art-magazine and formed his own hard-rock duo, ATTILA, with JON SMALL. They issued one 1970 album for 'Epic', before disbanding. JOEL then suffered a bout of depression and entered Meadowbrook mental hospital, with psychiatric problems. In 1971 he was back in circulation to sign a solo contract with Family Productions' Artie Ripp (allegedly known as 'Ripp-off' to his employees, due to his large percentage of artist royalties). JOEL's debut solo effort, 'COLD SPRING HARBOR' was soon issued but, due to a mixing fault, was pressed at the wrong speed!! Embarrassingly for JOEL, who had been well-received by live audiences, this version hit the shops without being corrected, and it made him sound slightly Chipmunk-ish (an 80's re-release rectified matters). Nevertheless, JOEL's piano playing was faultless and with the ballad, 'SHE'S GOT A WAY', he proved his songwriting calibre. He subsequently moved to Los Angeles, soon marrying the ex-wife of JON SMALL, Elizabeth Weber. Culled from JOEL's experiences of playing incognito in piano bars, the 'PIANO MAN' (1973) opus gave him a deserved break with 'Columbia', after his 'CAPTAIN JACK' track was played on FM radio. The following year, the album made the US Top 30, as did its title track. 'STREETLIFE SERENADE' (1974) carried on in much the same vein, JOEL at his strongest on ballad material like 'ROBERTA'. 'TURNSTILES' (1976) sounded more assured, 'NEW YORK STATE OF MIND' JOEL's most accomplished track of his career up to that point. This promise was realised with 'THE STRANGER' (1977), which reached No.2 in the US chart and spawned such enduring candlelight smoochers as 'JUST THE WAY YOU ARE' (written for Elizabeth) and 'SHE'S ALWAYS A WOMAN'. The hits were coming thick and fast, '52nd STREET' (1978) giving JOEL another No.1 album, while the rollicking piano pop/rock of 'MY LIFE' hit NO.3 in the American singles chart and furnished the singer with his biggest UK hit single to date. 'GLASS HOUSES' (1980) kept up the momentum, the retro pastiche of 'IT'S STILL ROCK'N'ROLL TO ME' giving JOEL his first No.1 single (US) while proving he could still be relied upon for cringe-inducing lyrics. With 'THE NYLON CURTAIN' (1982), however, JOEL turned his attention to more pressing concerns, addressing, SPRINGSTEEN style, such issues as Vietnam veterans ('GOODNIGHT SAIGON') and unemployment ('ALLENTOWN'). 'AN INNOCENT MAN' (1984), on the other hand, saw JOEL revisiting his musical roots. By far the biggest success of his career, the record was a highly listenable blend of doo-wop, soul and early rock'n'roll. It was also packed with hits; 'UPTOWN GIRL' (his first UK No.1), 'TELL HER ABOUT IT' and the title track all went Top 10 on both sides of the Atlantic, JOEL enjoying his greatest UK success to date. 'THE BRIDGE' (1986) carried on in a vaguely similar, if not so successful vein, while 'STORM FRONT' (1989) rose to the top of the US charts on the back of the 'WE DIDN'T START THE FIRE' single, an uncharacteristically ballsy rocker which set the tone for the rest of the album, a partially successful attempt at stadium bombast. Employing a new cast of seasoned musicians, JOEL recorded 'RIVER OF DREAMS' (1993), another big selling opus. While the doo-wop influenced title track went Top 5, the other singles failed to make any headway. Nevertheless, over almost three decades, JOEL has proved himself a consistent writer and performer, an elder statesman of pop/rock who pays little heed to constant press barbs. '2000 YEARS: THE MILLENNIUM CONCERT' (2000) only partly lived up to its grandiose, overblown title, the record a document of JOEL's New Year's Eve '99 bash at New York's Madison Square Garden. Although the veteran pianist had ostensibly retired from the music biz, he hammed it up one more time with a crowd pleasing run through his back catalogue, even wheeling out the obligatory 'AULD LANG SYNE' at the bells. The pianist subsequently invested his creative energies in composing classical music, or rather classical music with populist flourishes. 'FANTASIES & DELUSIONS' (2001) was a collection of solo piano works written by JOEL but performed by RICHARD JOOS. While it might be argued that the record was not, strictly speaking, a BILLY JOEL album, the man's trademark, strident melodicism was neatly stamped over most of the material, making it a pleasurable listen even for pop fans not normally taken to buying classical pieces. With no new pop material forthcoming, JOEL fans had to dig in their pockets while their hero delved into his past on three consecutive stocktakers: the anthology 'PIANO MAN – THE VERY BEST OF..' (2004), the exhaustive boxed-set, 'MY LIVES' (2005) and the Madison-revisiting live set, '12 GARDENS' (2006).

• **Covered:** BACK IN THE USSR + I'LL CRY INSTEAD (Beatles) / THE TIMES THEY ARE A CHANGIN' + TO MAKE YOU FEEL MY LOVE (Bob Dylan) / LIGHT AS THE BREEZE (Leonard Cohen) / and a few more. • **Trivia:** Divorced from his wife (Elizabeth) in July '82, he soon married supermodel and star of his 'UPTOWN GIRL' promo video; Christine Brinkley. In 1989, he fired his manager ex-brother-in-law Frank Weber, after an audit of the accounts showed nearly $100 million missing. The following year, JOEL was awarded $2 million by the courts, and a countersuit by Weber for $30 million was thrown out.

Album rating: COLD SPRING HARBOR (*4) / PIANO MAN (*5) / STREETLIFE SERENADE (*5) / TURNSTILES (*6) / THE STRANGER (*8) / 52ND STREET (*7) / GLASS HOUSES (*6) / SONGS IN THE ATTIC (*6) / THE NYLON CURTAIN (*7) / AN INNOCENT MAN (*6) / GREATEST HITS, VOLUME 1 & 2 compilation (*8) / THE BRIDGE (*5) / KOHU,EPT (LIVE IN LENINGRAD) (*4) / STORM FRONT (*5) / RIVER OF DREAMS (*6) / GREATEST HITS, VOLUME III compilation (*6) / 2000 YEARS – THE MILLENNIUM CONCERT (*4) / THE ULTIMATE COLLECTION compilation (*8) / FANTASIES & DELUSIONS (*5) / PIANO MAN – THE VERY BEST OF.. (*8) / MY LIFE boxed (*8) / 12 GARDENS LIVE (*6)

Philips — Family

May 72. (7") *(6078 001) (0900>* **SHE'S GOT A WAY. / EVERYBODY LOVE YOU NOW** [ ] [ ]

Jun 72. (lp) *(6269 150) <2700>* **COLD SPRING HARBOUR** [ ] Nov71 [ ]
– She's got a way / You can make me free / Everybody loves you now / Why Judy why / Falling of the rain / Turn around / You look so good to me / Tomorrow is today / Nocturne / Got to begin again. *(re-iss. re-mixed Jan84 on 'C.B.S.' lp/c; CBS/40 32400)* – hit UK No.95 *(cd-iss. Jan84; CD 26108) (re-iss. Sep91 on 'Pickwick' cd/c; 982637-2/-4)*

Jan 73. (7") *<0906>* **TOMORROW IS TODAY. / EVERYBODY LOVES YOU NOW** [–] [ ]

Apr 74. (7") *(6078 018)* **THE BALLAD OF BILLY THE KID. / IF I ONLY HAD THE WORDS (TO TELL YOU)** [ ] [–]

—— Stage band around this time were **DON EVANS** – guitar / **PAT McDONALD** – bass / **TOM WHITEHORSE** – steel guitar, banjo / **RHYS CLARK** – drums

C.B.S. — Columbia

Jun 74. (7") *<46055>* **WORSE COMES TO THE WORST. / SOMEWHERE ALONG THE LINE** [–] [80]

Aug 74. (7") *<10015>* **TRAVELIN' PRAYER. / AIN'T NO CRIME** [–] [77]

Apr 75. (lp/c) *(CBS/40 80719) <32544>* **PIANO MAN** [ ] Nov73 [27]
– Travelin' prayer / Piano man / Ain't no crime / You're my home / The ballad of Billy The Kid / Worse comes to the worst / Stop in Nevada / If I only had the words (to tell you) / Somewhere along the line / Captain Jack. *(re-iss. Mar81 lp/c; CBS/40 32002)* – hit UK No.98 in Jun84 *(cd-iss. Sep85; CD 80719) (cd re-iss. Apr89; CD 32002) (cd re-iss. Jul97 on 'Columbia'; 487938-2)*
(above should have been released May74 by 'Philips' – withdrawn)

Nov 74. (7") *<10064>* **THE ENTERTAINER. / THE MEXICAN CONNECTION** [–] [34]

Apr 75. (7") *(CBS 3183) <45963>* **PIANO MAN. / YOU'RE MY HOME** [ ] Feb74 [25]

Sep 75. (7") *(CBS 3469)* **IF I ONLY HAD THE WORDS (TO TELL YOU). / STOP IN NEVADA** [ ] [–]

Jul 75. (lp/c) *(CBS/40 80766) <33146>* **STREETLIFE SERENADE** [ ] Nov74 [35]
– Streetlife serenader / Los Angelenos / The great suburban showdown / Root beer rag / Roberta / Last of the big time spenders / Weekend song / Souvenir / The Mexican connection. *(re-iss. Mar81 lp/c; CBS/40 32035) (cd-iss. Mar87; CD 80766) (cd re-iss. Feb97 on 'Columbia'; 484461-2)*

—— band now incl. **NIGEL OLSSON + DEE MURRAY** (both ex-ELTON JOHN)

Jul 76. (lp/c) *(CBS/40 81195) <33848>* **TURNSTILES** [ ] Jun76 [ ]
– Say goodbye to Hollywood / Summer, Highland falls / All you wanna do is dance / New York state of mind / James / Prelude / Angry young man / I've loved these days / Miami 2017 (seen the lights go on Broadway). *(re-iss. Nov81 lp/c; CBS/40 32057) (cd-iss. Mar87; Cd 81195) (re-iss. Nov89 on 'Pickwick' lp/c/cd; 902197-1/-4/-2) (cd re-iss. Feb97 on 'Columbia'; 474681-2)*

Jul 76. (7") *<10412>* **SUMMER, HIGHLAND FALLS. / JAMES** [–] [ ]

Oct 76. (7") *<10562>* **I'VE LOVED THESE DAYS. / SAY GOODBYE TO HOLLYWOOD** [–] [ ]

Nov 76. (7") *(CBS 4686)* **SAY GOODBYE TO HOLLYWOOD. / STOP IN NEVADA** [ ] [ ]

Sep 77. (7") *<10624>* **MOVIN' OUT (ANTHONY'S SONG). / SHE'S ALWAYS A WOMAN** [–] [ ]

Dec 77. (lp/c) *(CBS/40 82311) <34987>* **THE STRANGER** [25] Oct77 [2]
– Movin' out (Anthony's song) / The stranger / Just the way you are / Scenes from an Italian restaurant / Vienna / Only the good die young / She's always a woman / Get it right the first time / Everybody has a dream. *(re-iss. May87 lp/c; 450914-1/-4) (cd-iss. Dec85; CD 82311) (cd re-iss. Jun89; 450914-2)*

Jan 78. (7") *(CBS 5872) <10646>* **JUST THE WAY YOU ARE. / GET IT RIGHT THE FIRST TIME** [19] Nov77 [3]

Mar 78. (7") *<10708>* **MOVIN' OUT (ANTHONY'S SONG). / EVERYBODY HAS A DREAM** [–] [17]

Apr 78. (7") *(CBS 6266)* **SHE'S ALWAYS A WOMAN. / EVERYBODY HAS A DREAM** [ ] [–]

May 78. (7") *<10750)* **ONLY THE GOOD DIE YOUNG. / GET IT RIGHT THE FIRST TIME** [–] [24]

Jun 78. (7") *(CBS 6412)* **MOVIN' OUT (ANTHONY'S SONG). / VIENNA** [35] [–]

Aug 78. (7") *<10788>* **SHE'S ALWAYS A WOMAN. / VIENNA** [–] [17]

Nov 78. (lp/c) *(CBS/40 83181) 35609>* **52nd STREET** [10] Oct78 [1]
– Big shot / Honesty / My life / Zanzibar / Stiletto / Rosalind's eyes / Half a mile away / Until the night / 52nd Street. *(re-iss. Nov85 lp/c; CBS/40 32693) (cd-iss. Nov87; CD 83181) (cd re-iss. Feb95 on 'Columbia'; CK 64412)*

Nov 78. (7") *(CBS 6821) <10853>* **MY LIFE. / 52nd STREET** [12] [3]

Feb 79. (7") *<10913>* **BIG SHOT. / ROOT BEER BAG** [–] [14]

Mar 79. (7") *(CBS 7242)* **UNTIL THE NIGHT. / ROOT BEER RAG** [50] [–]

Jun 79. (7") *(CBS 7422) <10959>* **HONESTY. / THE MEXICAN CONNECTION** [ ] Apr79 [24]

Feb 80. (7") *<11229>* **SOUVENIR. / ALL FOR LENYA** [–] [ ]

Mar 80. (lp/c) *(CBS/40 86108) <36384>* **GLASS HOUSES** [9] [1]
– You may be right / Sometimes a fantasy / Don't ask me why / It's still rock'n'roll to me / All for Lenya / I don't want to be alone / Sleeping with the television on / C'Etait toi (you were the one) / Close to the borderline / Through the long night. *(cd-iss. Dec85; CD 86108) (re-iss. Nov86 lp/c; 450087-1/-4) (cd-iss. Mar91; 450087-2) (re-iss. May94 on 'Columbia' cd/c; 450067-2/-4)*

Mar 80. (7") *(CBS 8325)* **ALL FOR LEYNA. / CLOSE TO THE BORDERLINE** [40] [–]

Mar 80. (7") *<11231>* **YOU MAY BE RIGHT. / CLOSE TO THE BORDERLINE** [–] [7]

May 80. (7") *(CBS 8643)* **YOU MAY BE RIGHT. / THROUGH THE LONG NIGHT** [ ] [–]

Jul 80. (7") *(CBS 8753) <11276>* **IT'S STILL ROCK'N'ROLL TO ME. / THROUGH THE LONG NIGHT** [14] May80 [1]

Oct 80. (7") *(CBS 9031) <11331>* **DON'T ASK ME WHY. / C'ETAIT TOI (YOU WERE THE ONE)** [ ] Aug80 [19]

Oct 80. (7") *<11379>* **SOMETIMES A FANTASY. / ALL FOR LEYNA** [–] [36]

Jan 81. (7") *(CBS 9419)* **SOMETIMES A FANTASY. / SLEEPING WITH THE TELEVISION ON** [ ] [–]

Sep 81. (7") *(CBS 1642) <02518>* **SAY GOODBYE TO HOLLYWOOD (live). / SUMMER, HIGHLAND FALLS (live)** [ ] [17]

Sep 81. (lp/c) *(CBS/40 85273) <37461>* **SONGS IN THE ATTIC (live)** [57] [8]
– Miami 2017 (seen the lights go out on Broadway) / Summer, Highland Falls / Streetlife serenader / Los Angelenos / She's got a way / Everybody loves you now / Say goodbye to Hollywood / Captain Jack / You're my home / The ballad of Billy The Kid / I've loved these days. *(re-iss. Nov83 lp/c; CBS/40 32364) (cd-iss. May87; CD 85273) (cd re-iss. Jun89; CD 32364)*

Nov 81. (7") *(A 1808)* **YOU'RE MY HOME (live). / THE BALLAD OF BILLY THE KID (live)** [ ] [–]

Jan 82. (7") *(A 2002) <02628>* **SHE'S GOT A WAY (live). / THE BALLAD OF BILLY THE KID (live)** [ ] Nov81 [23]

Sep 82. (7") *(A 2730) <03244>* **PRESSURE. / LAURA** [ ] [20]

Sep 82. (lp/c) *(CBS/40 85959) <38200>* **THE NYLON CURTAIN** [27] [7]
– Allentown / Laura / Pressure / Goodnight Saigon / She's right on time / A room on your own / Surprises / Scandinavian skies / Pressure / Where's the orchestra. *(cd-iss. Jan83; CD 85959) (re-iss. Mar88 lp/c; 460186-1/-4)*

Nov 82. (7") *(A 2981) <03413>* **ALLENTOWN. / ELVIS PRESLEY BOULEVARD** [ ] [17]

Feb 83. (7") *(A 3029)* **GOODNIGHT SAIGON. / WHERE'S THE ORCHESTRA** [ ] [–]

Feb 83. (7") *<03780>* **GOODNIGHT SAIGON. / A ROOM OF OUR OWN** [–] [56]

Aug 83. (7") *(A 3655) <04012>* **TELL HER ABOUT IT. / EASY MONEY** [ ] Jul83 [1]

Sep 83. (lp/c) *(CBS/40 25554) <38837>* **AN INNOCENT MAN** [2] Aug83 [4]
– Easy money / An innocent man / The longest time / This night / Tell her about it / Uptown girl / Careless talk / Christie Lee / Leave a tender moment alone / Keeping the faith. *(cd-iss. Aug84; CD 25554)*

Oct 83. (7") *(A 3775) <04149>* **UPTOWN GIRL. / CARELESS TALK** [1] Sep83 [3]
(12"+=) *(TA 3775)* – Just the way you are / It's still rock'n'roll to me.

Dec 83. (7") *(A 3655)* **TELL HER ABOUT IT. / EASY MONEY** [4] [–]
(12"+=) *(TA 3655)* – You got me hummin' (live).

Dec 83. (7") *<04259>* **AN INNOCENT MAN. / I'LL CRY INSTEAD** [–] [10]

Feb 84. (7") *(A 4142)* **AN INNOCENT MAN. / YOU'RE MY HOME (live)** [8] [–]
(12"+=) *(TA 4142)* – She's always a woman / Until the night.

Apr 84. (7") *(A 4280) <0440>* **THE LONGEST TIME. / CHRISTIE LEE** [25] Mar84 [14]
(12"+=) *(TA 4280)* – Captain Jack (live) / The ballad of Billy the kid (live)

Jun 84. (7") *(A 4521)* **LEAVE A TENDER MOMENT ALONE. / GOODNIGHT SAIGON** [29] [–]
(12"+=) *(TA 4521)* – Movin' out (Anthony's song) / Big shot / You may be right.

Jul 84. (7") *<04514>* **LEAVE A TENDER MOMENT ALONE. / THIS NIGHT** [–] [27]

Nov 84. (7") *(A 4884)* **THIS NIGHT. / I'LL CRY INSTEAD (live)** [ ] [–]

Jan 85. (7") *<04681>* **KEEPING THE FAITH. / SHE'S RIGHT ON TIME** [–] [18]

—— featured on the 'USA FOR AFRICA' single, 'WE ARE THE WORLD'.

Jun 85. (7") *(A 6378) <05417>* **YOU'RE ONLY HUMAN. / SURPRISES** [ ] [9]
(12"+=) *(TA 6378)* – Keeping the faith / Scenes from an Italian restaurant

Oct 85. (7") *(A 6622) <05657>* **THE NIGHT IS STILL YOUNG. / SUMMER, HIGHLAND FALLS** [ ] [34]

Jul 86. (7") *(A 7247) <06118)* **MODERN WOMAN. / SLEEPING WITH THE TELEVISION ON** [ ] Jun86 [10]
(d7"+=) *(DA 7247)* – Uptown girl / All for love.
(12"+=) *(TA 7247)* – The night is still young / You're only human.

Aug 86. (lp/c/cd) *(CBS/40/CD 86323) <40402>* **THE BRIDGE** [38] [7]
– Running on ice / This is the time / A matter of trust / Modern woman / Baby grand (w/ RAY CHARLES) / Big man on Mulberry Street Temptation / Code of silence (w/ CYNDI LAUPER) / Getting closer *(re-iss. Oct89 lp/c; 465 561-1/-4) (re-iss. Feb94 on 'Columbia' cd/c; 465561-2*

Sep 86. (7") *(650057-7) <06108>* **A MATTER OF TRUST. / GETTING CLOSER** [52] Aug86 [10]
(12"+=) *(650057-6)* – An innocent man / Tell her about it.

Nov 86. (7") *<06526>* **THIS IS THE TIME. / CODE OF SILENCE (with CYNDI LAUPER)** [–] [18]

Mar 87. (7"; BILLY JOEL featuring RAY CHARLES) *<06994>* **BABY GRAND. / BIG MAN ON MULBERRY STREET** [–] [75]

Nov 87. (d-lp/c/cd) *(460407-1/-4/-2) <40996>* **KOHU.EPT – LIVE IN LENINGRAD (live)** [92] [38]

– Odoya / Angry young man / Honesty / Goodnight Saigon / Stiletto / Big man on Mulberry Street / Baby grand / An innocent man / Allentown / A matter of trust / Only the good die young / Sometimes a fantasy / Uptown girl / Big shot / Back in the U.S.S.R. / The times they are a-changin'. *(cd re-iss. Oct90 on 'Columbia'; 467448-2)*

Nov 87. (7") *(651206-7) <07626>* **BACK IN THE U.S.S.R. (live). / BIG SHOT (live)**
(12"+=)(cd-s+=) *(651206-6)(CDEWF 1)* – A matter of trust (live) / The times they are a-changin' (live).

Feb 88. (7") *<07664>* **THE TIMES THEY ARE A-CHANGIN' (live). / BACK IN THE U.S.S.R. (live)** –

— new band **MINDY JOSTIN** – rhythm guitar, violin, harp / **DAVID BROWN** – guitar / **MARK RIVIERA** – sax / **LIBERTY DeVITO** – drums / **SCHUYLER DEALE** – bass / **JEFF JACOBS** – synthesizers / **CRYSTAL TALIEFERO** – vocals, percussion

Sep 89. (7"/c-s) *(JOEL/+M 1) <73021>* **WE DIDN'T START THE FIRE. / HOUSE OF BLUE LIGHT** 7 Oct89 1
(12"+=/cd-s+=) *(JOEL T/C 1)* – Just the way you are.

Oct 89. (lp/c/cd) *(465658-1/-4/-2) <44366>* **STORM FRONT** 5 1
– That's not her style / We didn't start the fire / The downeaster "Alexa" / I go to extremes / Shameless / Storm front / Leningrad / State of Grace / When in Rome / And so it goes. *(cd re-iss. Mar96 on 'Columbia'; 4656583)*

Dec 89. (7"/c-s) *(JOEL/+M 3)* **LENINGRAD. / THE TIMES THEY ARE A-CHANGIN' (live)** 53 –
(cd-s+=) *(CDJOEL 3)* – Uptown girl (live) / Back in the USSR (live).
(3"cd-s+=) *(JOELC 3)* – Goodnight Saigon / Vienna / Scandinavian skies.

Mar 90. (7"/c-s) *(JOEL/+M 2) <73091>* **I GO TO EXTREMES. / WHEN IN ROME** 70 Jan90 6
(12"+=/cd-s+=) *(JOEL T/C 2)* – Uptown girl / All for Leyna.
(7"ep+=) *(JOELEP 2)* – Prelude / Angry young man / Tell her about it / Leave a tender moment alone.

Apr 90. (c-s) *<73333>* **THE DOWNEASTER "ALEXA" / AND SO IT GOES** – 57

May 90. (7"/c-s) *(JOEL/+M 4)* **THE DOWNEASTER "ALEXA". / AND SO IT GOES / STREETLIFE SERENADE** –
(12"+=/cd-s+=) *(JOELT/CDJOEL 4)* – I've loved these days / An innocent man.
(pic-cd-s+=) *(JOELC 4)* – Say goodbye to Hollywood / Allentown / Only the good die young.

Jul 90. (c-s) *<73602>* **THAT'S NOT HER STYLE / AND SO IT GOES** – 77

Oct 90. (7"ep/cd-ep) **THAT'S NOT HER STYLE / WE DIDN'T START THE FIRE / UNTIL THE NIGHT / JUST THE WAY YOU ARE** –

Oct 90. (c-s) *<73602>* **AND SO IT GOES / THE DOWNEASTER ALEXA / SHAMELESS / STATES OF GRACE** – 37

Jan 92. (c-s) *<74188>* **SHAMELESS / STORM FRONT (live)** –
(below from film 'Honeymoon In Vegas' on 'Epic records')

Aug 92. (7"/c-s/cd-s) *(658343-7/-4/-2) <74422>* **ALL SHOOK UP. / (b-side by Ricky Van Shelton)** 27 Jul92 92

— other musicians; **DAN KORTCHMAR, TOMMY BYRNES, LESLIE WEST** – guitar / **T.H. STEVENS, LONNIE HILLER** – bass / **STEVE JORDAN, ZACHARY ALFORD, LIBERTY DeVITTO** – drums

Jul 93. (7"/c-s) *(659543-7/-4) <77086>* **THE RIVER OF DREAMS. / NO MAN'S LAND** 3 3
(cd-s+=) *(659543-2)* – The great wall of China.

Aug 93. (cd/c/lp) *(473872-2/-4/-1) <53003>* **RIVER OF DREAMS** 3 1
– No man's land / The great wall of China / Blonde over blue / A minor variation / Shades of grey / All about soul / Lullabye (goodnight, my angel) / The river of dreams / Two thousand years / Famous last words.

Oct 93. (7"/c-s) *(659736-7/-4) <77254>* **ALL ABOUT SOUL. / YOU PICKED A REAL BAD TIME** 32 29
(cd-s+=) *(659736-2)* – (2-'A'mixes).

Feb 94. (7"/c-s) *(659920-7/-4)* **NO MAN'S ISLAND. / SHADES OF GREY (live)** 50 –
(cd-s+=) *(659920-2)* – ('A'mix).

Mar 94. (c-s) *<77363>* **LULLABYE (GOODNIGHT MY ANGEL) / TWO THOUSAND YEARS** – 77

Aug 97. (cd-s) *<78641>* **TO MAKE YOU FEEL MY LOVE / (bare bones version) / GOODBYE YELLOW BRICK ROAD / A HARD DAY'S NIGHT** – 50
(cd-s) *<78660>* – (first 2 tracks) / House of blue lights / Intro – Summer, Highland falls (live) / Goodbye yellow brick road (live).

Oct 97. (cd/c) *(488236-2/-4) <67347>* **GREATEST HITS – VOLUME III** (compilation) 23 Aug97 9
– Keeping the faith / An innocent man / A matter of trust / Baby grand / This is the time / Leningrad / We didn't start the fire / I go to extremes / And so it goes / Downeaster Alexa / Shameless / All about soul / Lullabye / River of dreams / To make you feel my love / Hey girl / Light as a breeze.

May 00. (d-cd/d-c) *(497981-2/-4) <63792-2>* **2000 YEARS – THE MILLENNIUM CONCERT** (live 31st December, 1999) 68 40
– Beethoven's ninth symphony / Big shot / Movin' out (Anthony's song) / Summer, Highland falls / The ballad of Billy The Kid / Don't ask me why / New York state of mind / I've loved these days / My life / Allentown / Prelude – Angry young man / Only the good die young / I go to extremes / Goodnight Saigon / We didn't start the fire / Big man on Mulberry street / 2000 years / Auld lang syne / River of dreams / Scenes from an Italian restaurant / Dance to the music / Honky tonk woman / It's still rock'n'roll to me / You may be right / This night / This is the time.

Nov 01. (cd) *<(SK 85397)>* **FANTASIES & DELUSIONS (MUSIC FOR SOLO PIANO)** Sep01 83
– Opus 3: Reverie (villa d'este) / Opus 2: Waltz #1 (Nunley's carousel) / Opus 7: Aria (grand canal) / Opus 6: Invention in C minor / Opus 1: Soliloquy (on a separation) / Opus 8: Suite for piano (star-crossed) I/II/III / Opus 5: Waltz #2 (Steinway hall) / Opus 9: Waltz #3 (for Lola) / Opus 4: Fantasy (film noir) / Opus 10: Air (Dublinesque).
(above on 'Sony Classical')

Jun 06. (d-cd) *<85176>* **12 GARDENS LIVE** (live) – 14
– Angry young man / My life / Everybody loves you now / The ballad of Billy The Kid / The entertainer / Vienna / New York state of mind / The night is still young / Zanzibar / Miami 2017 (I've seen the lights go out on Broadway) / The Great Wall of China / Allentown / She's right on time / Don't ask me why / Laura / A room of our own / Goodnight Saigon / Movin' out (Anthony's song) / An innocent man / The Downeaster "Alexa" / She's always a woman / Keeping the faith / The river of dreams / A matter of trust / We didn't start the fire / Big shot / You may be right / Only the good die young / Scenes from an Italian restaurant / Piano man / And so it goes / It's still rock & roll to me.

– compilations, etc. –

on 'CBS' UK / 'Columbia' US unless mentioned otherwise

Oct 79. (3-lp-box) *(CBS 66352)* **3-LP BOX SET** –
– 'TURNSTILES' / 'THE STRANGER' / '52nd STREET'

1980. (7") *Columbia;* **DOWN IN THE BOONDOCKS. / 21ST CENTURY MAN** –

Feb 83. (7"ep) *Epic; (EPCA 2619)* **GREATEST ORIGINAL HITS** –
– Just the way you are / Movin' out (Anthony's song) / My life / She's a woman. *(c-iss.Aug82)*

Jul 84. (7") *(A 4591)* **JUST THE WAY YOU ARE. / MY LIFE** –

Jul 85. (d-lp/c/cd) *(CBS/40/CD 88666)* **GREATEST HITS VOL.1 & VOL.2** 7 6
– Piano man / Say goodbye to Hollywood / New York state of mind / The stranger / Just the way you are / Movin' out (Anthony's song) / Only the good die young / She's always a woman / My life / Big shot / Honesty / You may be right / It's still rock and roll to me / Pressure / Allentown / Goodnight Saigon / Tell her about it / Uptown girl / The longest time / You're only human (second wind) / The night is still young. *(d-cd-iss. Sep92 on 'Columbia'; CD 88666)*

Feb 86. (7") *(A 6862)* **SHE'S ALWAYS A WOMAN. / JUST THE WAY YOU ARE** 53 –

Apr 86. (lp/c) *Showcase; (SHLP/SHTC 114)* **CALIFORNIA FLASH** –

Jul 87. (d-lp) *(BJ 241)* **THE STRANGER / AN INNOCENT MAN** –

1988. (d-c) *(4022143)* **PIANO MAN / STREETLIFE SERENADE** –

Aug 88. (3"cd-ep) *<38K 07950>* **IT'S STILL ROCK'N'ROLL TO ME. / JUST THE WAY YOU ARE** –

Nov 91. (4xcd-box/4xc-box) *Columbia; (469174-2/-4)* **THE BILLY JOEL SOUVENIR – THE ULTIMATE COLLECTION INTERVIEW WITH BILLY JOEL** –
– (GREATEST HITS VOL.1 & 2 / STORM FRONT / LIVE AT THE YANKEE STADIUM plus 50 minute interview)

Jun 92. (c/cd) *Tring; (MC+/JHD 004)* **FURTHER THAN HEAVEN** –

Sep 92. (d-cd) *Columbia;* **THE BRIDGE / GLASS HOUSES**

Mar 93. (d-cd) *(471604-2)* **AN INNOCENT MAN / THE STRANGER**
(re-iss. Feb95; 478478-2)

Oct 96. (3xcd-box) *(485320-2)* **AN INNOCENT MAN / STORM FRONT / THE STRANGER** [ ] [–]

Jun 98. (3xcd-box) *(491274-2)* **THE GREATEST HITS COLLECTION VOLUMES I, II & III** [33] [ ]

Mar 01. (d-cd/d-c) *Sony TV; (SONYTV 98 CD/MC)* **THE ULTIMATE COLLECTION** [4] [–]
– Just the way you are / My life / It's still rock & roll to me / An innocent man / Piano man / You're my home / Everybody loves you now / The entertainer / Streetlife serenader / New York state of mind / Say goodbye to Hollywood / She's got a way / Movin' out (Anthony's song) / She's always a woman / Honesty / You may be right / Don't ask me why / Miami 2017 / Uptown girl / Tell her about it / The river of dreams / The longest time / We didn't start the fire / Goodnight SAigon / Allentown / All for Leyna / This is the time / Leave a tender moment alone / A matter of trust / Modern woman / Baby grand / I go to extremes / Leningrad / The downeaster "Alexa" / You're only human (second wind) / All about soul (remix).

Oct 01. (4xcd-box) *(504502-2)* **THE COMPLETE HITS COLLECTION (BILLY JOEL'S GREATEST HITS 1973-1997)** [ ] [–]

Oct 01. (d-cd) *<86005>* **THE ESSENTIAL BILLY JOEL** [–] [29]

Nov 04. (cd) *(519018-2)* **PIANO MAN – THE VERY BEST OF BILLY JOEL** [40] [–]
– Tell her about it / Uptown girl / Don't ask me why / Piano man / New York state of mind / The river of dreams / It's still rock & roll to me / We didn't start the fire / Goodnight Saigon / My life / She's always a woman / She's got a way / Scandinavian skies / An innocent man / Movin' out (Anthony's song) / Only the good die young / All about soul / Honesty / Just the way you are.

Dec 05. (4xcd-box) *(82876 75474-2) <93520-2>* **MY LIVES** [ ] Nov05 [ ]

Elton JOHN

Born: REGINALD KENNETH DWIGHT, 25 Mar'47, Pinner, Middlesex, England. After learning piano at an early age, he attained a scholarship from Royal Academy Of Music. In the early 60's, he joined BLUESOLOGY, and by 1965 had written his first 45, 'COME BACK BABY' for 'Fontana', the band subsequently touring in the UK as back-up to American acts (i.e. MAJOR LANCE, The BLUE BELLES with PATTI LaBELLE, etc). Late in 1966, the group were joined by five others including singer LONG JOHN BALDRY, who virtually took over show, much to the dislike of the young REG DWIGHT. In 1967, he left BLUESOLOGY and auditioned for 'Liberty', but after failure found other writer BERNIE TAUPIN (b.22 May'50, Lincolnshire). They wrote LONG JOHN BALDRY's b-side, 'Lord You Made The Night Too Long', for his UK No.1 'Let The Heartaches Begin'. DWIGHT of course became ELTON JOHN, taking names from BLUESOLOGY members ELTON DEAN and LONG JOHN BALDRY. In 1968, ELTON and BERNIE joined the Dick James Music Publishing (later D.J.M.) stable, and earned around £10 a week each. With CALEB QUAYE (ex-BLUESOLOGY) on production, ELTON released debut solo single 'I'VE BEEN LOVING YOU TOO LONG' for 'Philips'. Early in '69, he gained needed airplay for 'LADY SAMANTHA', but when this failed, he tried to join KING CRIMSON, to no avail. The pair then wrote a number for the Eurovision Song Contest, 'I CAN'T GO ON LIVING WITHOUT YOU', which was heard but rejected by LULU for eventual winner, 'Boom Bang A Bang'. Early in 1969, ELTON signed to 'DJM', and flopped with both 45 'IT'S ME THAT YOU NEED' & lp 'EMPTY SKY'. To make ends meet, ELTON played on HOLLIES 'He Ain't Heavy . . . ' session, and worked for budget labels 'Pickwick' & 'MFP', on some pop covers. In 1970 after more HOLLIES sessions, he released 'BORDER SONG', which, when picked up by 'Uni', broke into US Top 100. The accompanying eponymous album (the first of many to be produced by Gus Dudgeon) made the American Top 5 and the UK Top 20, ELTON finally setting out on the road to superstardom that would see him become one of the most unlikely pop icons of the 70's. With the liltingly effective 'YOUR SONG', the JOHN/TAUPIN writing partnership also stepped up a gear, the chemistry obvious from the beginning despite TAUPIN's often impenetrable lyrics. Later that year, ELTON made his US stage debut (along with guitarist CALEB QUAYE – yes, part of the same clan as FINLAY – and the rhythm section of NIGEL OLSSON and DEE MURRAY) at the Troubadour in L.A., giving the Americans a taste of the flamboyant showmanship which would become ever more OTT as the decade wore on and which subsequently resulted in the LIBERACE comparisons. A relatively successful attempt at retro Americana, 'TUMBLEWEED CONNECTION' (1970) was another big seller and included the rustic beauty of 'COUNTRY COMFORT', later covered in memorable style by ROD STEWART, although 'MADMAN ACROSS THE WATER' (1971) saw Paul Buckmaster's overbearing string arrangements come in for some critical flak. With DAVY JOHNSTONE replacing QUAYE, 'HONKY CHATEAU' (1972) was the first album to be credited to the ELTON JOHN GROUP; a more robust affair and his first No.1 (US), it saw ELTON begin to adopt the musical maverick approach which would characterise most of his 70's albums, spawning a massive hit in the soaring 'ROCKET MAN'. 'DON'T SHOOT ME I'M ONLY THE PIANO PLAYER' (1973) consolidated his commercial appeal, a transatlantic No.1 which saw him flirting gamely with bubblegum pop on 'CROCODILE ROCK' (his first No.1 single) and adult balladry on 'DANIEL'. The pinnacle of JOHN's early career, however, came with 'GOODBYE YELLOW BRICK ROAD' (1973) a massive selling double set which saw ELTON's chameleon-like talent embrace a dazzling, occasionally over ambitious, array of styles, from the musclebound piano assault of 'SATURDAY'S ALRIGHT FOR FIGHTING' and the cloying bombast of 'BENNIE AND THE JETS' to his poignant Marilyn Monroe tribute, 'CANDLE IN THE WIND'. The same year, ELTON did the obligatory rock star thing and formed his own label, 'Rocket', KIKI DEE and NEIL SEDAKA being two of his more prominent signings, JOHN also working with JOHN LENNON the following year on his comeback single, 'Whatever Gets You Thru The Night'. 'CAPTAIN FANTASTIC AND THE BROWN DIRT COWBOY' (1975) was a concept affair documenting the development of the JOHN/TAUPIN partnership through the years, the soul baring 'SOMEONE SAVED MY LIFE TONIGHT' ranking among the pair's best. As well as making a cameo appearance in Ken Russell's screen version of The WHO's 'Tommy' (sporting one of the rather more erm, exotic models from his famed sunglasses collection), JOHN let go longstanding sidemen, MURRAY and OLSON, revamping his band prior to recording 'ROCK OF THE WESTIES' (1975), his last No.1 album for almost fifteen years. The latter half of the decade saw JOHN retire from performing, and, to a large extent, from recording; 1976's lengthy double-set, 'BLUE MOVES', marked the end of his partnership with TAUPIN, and JOHN subsequently busied himself with chairing his beloved Watford F.C. Though it spawned the Top 5 'SONG FOR GUY', 'A SINGLE MAN' (1978) was hardly a convincing return and the early 80's marked a creative nadir as ELTON fumbled his way through a series of confused albums and ill-advised musical experiments. Only a reunion with TAUPIN halted the slide on 1983's 'TOO LOW FOR ZERO' and its defiant hit single, 'I'M STILL STANDING'. 'BREAKING HEARTS' (1984) continued the renaissance with insidiously catchy 'PASSENGERS' and the cheesy but gorgeous 'SAD SONGS (SAY SO MUCH)', Top 10 hits both. Nevertheless, like many of his contemporaries, JOHN was now a card carrying member of the glossy, MOR brigade whose airbrushed, MTV sterility partly defined the 80's. But as his music became smoother, his personal life was in turmoil; an ill-fated marriage to Renate Blauer, well documented drug/alcohol problems and throat surgery all gave the gutter press hours of speculative fun. JOHN had the last laugh, however, when he successfully sued The Sun newspaper in October '88. Openly gay, JOHN increasingly devoted his time and money into AIDS care and research, founding the Elton John AIDS Foundation in 1992 and announcing that, from 'THE ONE' onwards, he'd donate all future royalties from singles sales. 1993 saw the release of the 'DUETS' album, featuring JOHN in tandem with everyone from TAMMY WYNETTE to LEONARD COHEN, while a suitably camp run through of 'DON'T GO BREAKING MY HEART' with RuPAUL hit the UK Top 10. The bland 'MADE IN ENGLAND' (1995) has been only the singer's second set of new material in the 90's, its embarrassingly awful title track incredibly/unsurprisingly hitting the UK Top 20. However, by far the most high profile of ELTON's more recent activities was his rendition of 'CANDLE IN THE WIND' at the funeral of Diana, Princess Of Wales, the single subsequently re-issued and a hysterical public pushing it to the top of the charts. Coincidentally, JOHN released his latest solo set, 'THE BIG PICTURE' (1997) the following month, a transatlantic Top 10 which spawned a couple of minor hits. More successful was another high profile duet (with LeANN RIMES), 'WRITTEN IN THE STARS', a prelude to a whole album's worth of coffee table bonhomie, 'ELTON JOHN AND TIME RICE'S AIDA' (1999). Credited to ELTON JOHN & FRIENDS, the record boasted a "galaxy" of stars in the mould of STING, SHANIA TWAIN, JANET JACKSON etzzzz . . . Come the new millennium and after two diverse soundtrack works ('THE MUSE' and 'THE ROAD TO EL DORADO'), the ubiquitous star decided to resurrect a raft of his old classics for 'ONE NIGHT ONLY' (2000), treating paying guests in New York's Madison Square Garden to a final, definitive rendering of the hits that made ELTON the man he is today. All this nostalgia seemed to rub off on him, inspiring a belated return to the rollicking, expansive musical sweep of his best 70's era recordings with 'SONGS FROM THE WEST COAST' (2001). Having already performed a duet of 'Stan' with controversial rapper EMINEM (making up after a previous tete-a-tete) at 2001's Grammy awards, ELTON continued his track record of collaborative hits in the varied company of ALESSANDRO SAFINA ('YOUR SONG') and BLUE ('SORRY SEEMS TO BE THE HARDEST WORD'), while a DJ-fied update of JOHN's Philly-soul era track 'ARE YOU READY FOR LOVE', topped the UK charts in 2003. The evergreen songsmith had clearly been keeping his best stuff for another back-to-basics critical fave, 'PEACHTREE ROAD' (2004), writing in collaboration with TAUPIN on a set which once again attracted comparisons with his piano-pounding early 70s works. At the same time as the man was on a revisionist trip, younger acts like SCISSOR SISTERS were exulting in their own unashamedly ELTON-influenced retro-camp. His next three collaborations were among his most newsworthy: an ill-advised Live8 duet with a regulation worse-for-wear PETE DOHERTY, a seriously incongruous chart-topping link-up with long-deceased gangsta rap legend 2PAC on 'Ghetto Gospel' and tying the knot with his longtime partner, David Furnish on the 21st of December, 2005.

• **Covered:** GET BACK + LUCY IN THE SKY WITH DIAMONDS + I SAW HER STANDING THERE (Beatles; on which ELTON did duet with JOHN LENNON) / PINBALL WIZARD (Who; from the film 'Tommy', in which he featured) / JOHNNY B. GOODE (Chuck Berry) / WHERE HAVE ALL THE GOOD TIMES GONE (Kinks) / I HEARD IT THROUGH THE GRAPEVINE (hit; Marvin Gaye) / I'M YOUR MAN (Leonard Cohen) / etc.

Album rating: EMPTY SKY (*4) / ELTON JOHN (*7) / TUMBLEWEED CONNECTION (*8) / "FRIENDS" soundtrack (*5) / 11-17-70 (*4) / MADMAN ACROSS THE WATER (*7) / HONKY CHATEAU (*8) / DON'T SHOOT ME I'M ONLY THE PIANO PLAYER (*8) / GOODBYE YELLOW BRICK ROAD (*9) / CARIBOU (*4) / GREATEST HITS compilation (*9) / CAPTAIN FANTASTIC AND THE BROWN DIRT COWBOY (*7) / ROCK OF THE WESTIES (*5) / HERE AND THERE (*4) / BLUE MOVES (*6) / GREATEST HITS, VOL.II compilation (*8) / A SINGLE MAN (*6) / VICTIM OF LOVE (*3) / 21 AT 33 (*5) / THE FOX (*4) / JUMP UP! (*5) / TOO LOW FOR ZERO (*6) / BREAKING HEARTS (*5) / ICE ON FIRE (*5) / LEATHER JACKETS (*5) / LIVE IN AUSTRALIA (*4) / GREATEST HITS, VOL.III, 1979-1987 compilation (*6) / REG STRIKES BACK (*5) / SLEEPING WITH THE PAST (*5) / THE VERY BEST OF ELTON JOHN compilation (*8) / THE ONE (*5) / DUETS (*4) / MADE IN ENGLAND (*6) / LOVE SONGS compilation (*6) / BIG PICTURE (5) / ELTON JOHN AND TIM RICE'S AIDA (*3) / THE MUSE soundtrack (*5) / THE ROAD TO EL DORADO soundtrack (*5) / ONE NIGHT ONLY – THE GREATEST HITS compilation (*6) / SONGS FROM THE WEST COAST (*7) / GREATEST HITS 1970-2002 compilation (*9) / PEACHTREE ROAD (*7)

BLUESOLOGY

REG DWIGHT – vocals, piano / **STUART BROWN** – guitar, vocals / **REX BISHOP** – bass / **MICK INKPEN** – drums

		Fontana	not iss.
Jul 65.	(7") *(TF 594)* **COME BACK BABY. / TIME'S GETTING TOUGHER THAN TOUGH**		–
Feb 66.	(7") *(TF 668)* **MISTER FRANTIC. / EVERYDAY (I HAVE THE BLUES)**		–

—— added **LONG JOHN BALDRY** – vocals / **CALEB QUAYE** – guitar / **ELTON DEAN** – sax / **PETE GAVIN, NEIL HUBBARD + MARK CHARIG** – wind

		Polydor	not iss.
Oct 67.	(7"; as STU BROWN & BLUESOLOGY) *(56195)* **SINCE I FOUND YOU BABY. / JUST A LITTLE BIT**		–

ELTON JOHN

(solo) – vocals, piano with session people, incl.**NIGEL OLSSON** (note most of BLUESOLOGY later joined SOFT MACHINE)

		Philips	Congress
Mar 68.	(7") *(BF 1643)* **I'VE BEEN LOVING YOU TOO LONG. / HERE'S TO THE NEXT TIME**		–
Jan 69.	(7") *(BF 1739)* **LADY SAMANTHA. / ALL ACROSS THE HEAVENS**		–
1969.	(7") *<6017>* **LADY SAMANTHA. / IT'S ME THAT YOU NEED**	–	
1969.	(7") *<6022>* **BORDER SONG. / BAD SIDE OF THE MOON**	–	

—— In 1969, ELTON was part of BREAD & BEER BAND, who issued 1 'Decca' single 'THE DICK BARTON THEME. / BREAKDOWN BLUES. (re-iss. 1972)

		D.J.M.	Uni
May 69.	(7") *(DJS 205)* **IT'S ME THAT YOU NEED. / JUST LIKE STRANGE RAIN**		–
Jun 69.	(lp; mono/stereo) *(DJMLP/DJLPS 403) <2130>* **EMPTY SKY**		
	– Empty sky / Valhalla / Western Ford gateway / Hymn 2000 / Lady what's tomorrow / Sails / The scaffold / Skyline pigeon / Gulliver – Hay chewed – Reprise. *<US re-iss. Jan75 on 'M.C.A.'; 2130>* – reached No.6 *(re-iss. May81 lp/c; DJM 2/-4 2086) (cd-iss. Oct86; DJMCD 13) (re-iss. May87 lp/c; PRICE/PRIMC 97) (cd re-iss. Jun87; 823017-2) <US cd-iss. Jun88; 31000> (cd re-iss. May95 on 'Rocket';)*		

—— now with band **NIGEL OLSSON** (b.10 Feb'49, Merseyside) – drums / **DEE MURRAY** (b.DAVID MURRAY OATES, 3 Apr'46, Southgate, London) – bass / **CALEB QUAYE** – guitar (ex-BLUESOLOGY)

Mar 70.	(7") *(DJS 217) <55246>* **BORDER SONG. / BAD SIDE OF THE MOON**		Jul70 92
Apr 70.	(lp/c) *(DJLPS 2/4 0406) <73090>* **ELTON JOHN**	11	Sep70 4
	– Your song / I need you to turn to / Take me to the pilot / No shoestrings on Louise / First episode at Heinton / Sixty years on / Border song / Greatest discovery / The cage / The king must die. *(re-iss. May81 lp/c; DJM 2/4 2087) (re-iss. Apr87 lp/c; PRICE/PRIMC 98) (cd-iss. Jun87; 827689-2) (cd re-iss. May95 on 'Rocket';)*		
Jun 70.	(7") *(DJS 222)* **ROCK AND ROLL MADONNA. / GREY SEAL**		–
Oct 70.	(lp/c) *(DJLPS 2/4 0410) <73096>* **TUMBLEWEED CONNECTION**	6	Jan71 5
	– Ballad of well-known gun / Come down in time / Country comfort / Son of your father / My father's gun / Where to now St. Peter / Love song / Amoreena / Talking old soldiers / Burn down the mission. *(re-iss. May81 lp/c; DJM 2/4 2088) (re-iss. Apr87 lp/c; PRICE/PRIMC 99) (cd-iss. Jun87; 829248-2) (cd re-iss. May95 on 'Rocket')*		
Nov 70.	(7") *<55265>* **YOUR SONG. / TAKE ME TO THE PILOT**	–	8
Jan 71.	(7") *(DJS 233)* **YOUR SONG. / INTO THE OLD MAN'S SHOES**	7	–

Apr 71. (7") *(DJS 244) <55277>* **FRIENDS. / HONEY ROLL** [ ] Mar71 34

Apr 71. (lp) *(SPFL 269) <PAS 6004>* **FRIENDS** (soundtrack) [ ] Mar71 36
– Friends / Michelle's song / Seasons / Variation on Michelle's song (a day in the country) / Can I put you on / Variation on Friends / I meant to do my work today (a day in the country) / Four moods / Seasons reprise. *(<cd-iss. Oct92 on 'RARE MASTERS' see below>)*
(above issued for 'Paramount')

Apr 71. (lp/c) *(DJLPS 2/4 0414) <93105>* **17.11.70 (live)** 20 May71 11
– Take me to the pilot / Honky tonk women / Sixty years on / Can I put you on / Bad side of the Moon / Burn down the mission: My baby left me – Get back. *(re-iss. Mar78 on 'Hallmark' lp/c; SHM 942/HSC 314) (cd-iss. Sep95 on 'Rocket')*

Nov 71. (lp/c) *(DJH 2/4 0420) <93120>* **MADMAN ACROSS THE WATER** 41 8
– Tiny dancer / Levon / Razor face / Madman across the water / Indian sunset / Holiday inn / Rotten Peaches / All the nasties / Goodbye. *(re-iss. May81 lp/c; DJM 2/4 2089) (re-iss. Apr87 lp/c; PRICE/PRIMC 100) (cd-iss. Jun87; 825487-2) (cd re-iss. Aug95 on 'Rocket')*

Dec 71. (7") *<55314>* **LEVON. / GOODBYE** – 24

Feb 72. (7") *<55318>* **TINY DANCER. / RAZOR FACE** – 41

— **DAVEY JOHNSTONE** (b. 6 May'51, Edinburgh, Scotland) – guitar (ex-MAGNA CARTA) repl. QUAYE. Added **RAY COOPER** – percussion

Apr 72. (7"m) *(DJX 501)* **ROCKET MAN. / HOLIDAY INN / GOODBYE** 2 –

May 72. (7") *<55328>* **ROCKET MAN. / SUZIE (DREAMS)** – 6

May 72. (lp/c) *(DJLPH 2/4 0423) <93135>* **HONKY CHATEAU** 2 Jun72 1
– Honky cat / Mellow / I think I'm going to kill myself / Susie (dramas) / Rocket man / Salvation / Slave / Amy / Mona Lisas and mad hatters / Hercules. *(re-iss. May81 lp/c; DJM 2/4 2090) (re-iss. Apr87 lp/c; PRICE/PRIMC 101) (cd-iss. Jun87; 829249-2) (cd re-iss. Aug95 on 'Rocket')*

Aug 72. (7"m) *(DJS 269)* **HONKY CAT. / LADY SAMANTHA / IT'S ME THAT YOU NEED** 31 –

Aug 72. (7") *<55343>* **HONKY CAT. / SLAVE** – 8

D.J.M. M.C.A.

Oct 72. (7") *(DJS 271) <40000>* **CROCODILE ROCK. / ELDERBERRY WINE** 5 Dec72 1

Jan 73. (7") *(DJS 275) <40046>* **DANIEL. / SKYLINE PIGEON** 4 Apr73 2

Feb 73. (lp/c) *(DJLPH 2/4 0427) <2100>* **DON'T SHOOT ME I'M ONLY THE PIANO PLAYER** 1 1
– Daniel / Teacher I need you / Elderberry wine / Blues for my baby and me / Midnight creeper / Have mercy on the criminal / I'm going to be a teenage idol / Texan love song / Crocodile rock / High flying bird. *(re-iss. May81 lp/c; DJM 2/4 2091) (re-iss. Apr87 lp/c; PRICE/PRIMC 105) (cd-iss. Jun87; 827690-2) (cd re-iss. May95 on 'Rocket')*

Jun 73. (7"m) *(DJX 502) <40105>* **SATURDAY NIGHT'S ALRIGHT FOR FIGHTING. / JACK RABBIT / WHEN YOU'RE READY (WE'LL GO STEADY AGAIN)** 7 Jul73 12

Sep 73. (7") *(DJS 285) <40148>* **GOODBYE YELLOW BRICK ROAD. / SCREW YOU** 6 –

Oct 73. (7") *<40148>* **GOODBYE YELLOW BRICK ROAD. / YOUNG MAN'S BLUES** – 2

Oct 73. (d-lp/d-c) *(DJE 2/4 9001) <10003>* **GOODBYE YELLOW BRICK ROAD** 1 1
– Funeral for a friend / Love lies bleeding / Bennie and the jets / Candle in the wind / Goodbye yellow brick road / This song has no title / Grey seal / Jamaica jerk off / I've seen that movie too / Sweet painted lady / The ballad of Danny Bailey (1909-34) / Dirty little girl / All the girls love Alice / Your sister can't twist (but she can rock'n'roll) / Saturday night's alright for fighting / Roy Rogers / Social disease / Harmony. *(re-iss. Nov87 lp/c; PRICE/PRIMC 13) (cd-iss. Nov87; DJMCD 2) (cd re-iss. May95 on 'Rocket')*

Nov 73. (7") *(DJS 290) <65018>* **STEP INTO CHRISTMAS. / HO! HO! HO! WHO'D BE A TURKEY AT CHRISTMAS** 24 [ ]

Feb 74. (7") *<40198>* **BENNY AND THE JETS. / HARMONY** – 1

Feb 74. (7") *(DJS 297)* **CANDLE IN THE WIND. / BENNIE AND THE JETS** 11 –

May 74. (7") *(DJS 302) <40259>* **DON'T LET THE SUN GO DOWN ON ME. / SICK CITY** 16 Jun74 2

Jun 74. (lp/c) *(DJLH 2/4 0439) <2116>* **CARIBOU** 1 1
– The bitch is back / Pinky / Grimsby / Dixie Lily / Solar prestige a gammon / You're so static / I've seen the saucers / Stinker / Don't let the sun go down on me / Ticking. *(re-iss. May81 lp/c; DJM 2/4 2092) (re-iss. Nov87 lp/c; PRICE/PRIMC 106) (cd-iss. Nov87; DJMCD 6) (cd re-iss. May95 on 'Rocket')*

Sep 74. (7") *(DJS 322) <40297>* **THE BITCH IS BACK. / COLD HIGHWAY** 15 4

Nov 74. (7") *(DJS 340) <40344>* **LUCY IN THE SKY WITH DIAMONDS. / ONE DAY AT A TIME** 10 1

Feb 75. (7"; ELTON JOHN BAND) *(DJS 354) <40364>* **PHILADELPHIA FREEDOM. / I SAW HER STANDING THERE (with JOHN LENNON)** 12 1

May 75. (lp/c) *(DJX 1) <2142>* **CAPTAIN FANTASTIC AND THE BROWN DIRT COWBOY** 2 1
– Captain Fantastic and the brown dirt cowboy / Tower of Babel / Bitter fingers / Tell me when the whistle blows / Someone saved my life tonight / (Gotta get a) Meal ticket / Better off dead / Writing / We fall in love sometimes / Curtains. *(re-iss. pic-disc '78; DJLPX 1) (re-iss. May81 lp/c; DJM 2/4 2094) (re-iss. Nov87 lp/c; PRICE/PRIMC 108) (cd-iss. Nov87; 821746-2) (cd re-iss. Aug95 on 'Rocket')*

Jun 75. (7") *(DJS 385) <40421>* **SOMEONE SAVED MY LIFE TONIGHT. / HOUSE OF CARDS** 22 4

— ELTON now w/ others, after firing MURRAY and OLSSON (to BILLY JOEL)

Sep 75. (7") *(DJS 610) <40461>* **ISLAND GIRL. / SUGAR ON THE FLOOR** 14 1

Nov 75. (lp/c) *(DJH 2/4 0464) <2163>* **ROCK OF THE WESTIES** 5 1
– Medley: Yell help – Wednesday night – Ugly / Dan Dare (pilot of the future) / Island girl / Grow some funk of your own / I feel like a bullet (in the gun of Robert Ford) / Street kids / Hard luck story / Billy Bones and the white bird. *(re-iss. May81 lp/c; DJM 2/4 2093) (re-iss. Nov87 lp/c; PRICE/PRIMC 107) (cd-iss. Nov87; DJMCD 9) (cd re-iss. Aug95 on 'Rocket')*

Jan 76. (7") *(DJS 629) <40505>* **GROW SOME FUNK OF YOUR OWN. / I FEEL LIKE A BULLET (IN THE GUN OF ROBERT FORD)** [ ] 14

Mar 76. (7") *(DJS 652)* **PINBALL WIZARD. / HARMONY** 7 –

May 76. (lp/c) *(DJH 2/4 0473) <2197>* **HERE AND THERE (live)** 6 4
– Skyline pigeon / Border song / Honky cat / Love song / Crocodile rock / Funeral for a friend / Love lies bleeding / Rocket man / Bennie and the jets / Take me to the pilot. *(re-iss. Sep78 as 'LONDON AND NEW YORK' on 'Hallmark' lp/c; SHM 942/HSC 333) (cd-iss. Sep95 on 'Rocket')*

Rocket M.C.A.

Jun 76. (7"; ELTON JOHN & KIKI DEE) *(ROKN 512) <40585>* **DON'T GO BREAKING MY HEART. / SNOW QUEEN** 1 1

Oct 76. (d-lp/d-c) *(ROLL/TC2ROLL 12) <11004>* **BLUE MOVES** 3 3
– Your starter for . . . / Tonight / One horse town / Chameleon / Boogie pilgrim / Cage the songbird / Crazy water / Shoulder holster / Sorry seems to be the hardest word / Out of the blue / Between seventeen and twenty / The wide-eyed and laughing / Someone's final song / Where's the shoorah / If there's a God in Heaven (what's he waiting for) / Idol / Theme from a non-existant TV series / Bite your lip (get up and dance!). *(re-iss. Sep84 d-lp/d-c; PRID/+C 2) (cd-iss. Jun89; 822818-2)*

Oct 76. (7") *(ROKN 517) <40645>* **SORRY SEEMS TO BE THE HARDEST WORD. / SHOULDER HOLSTER** 11 6

Feb 77. (7") *<40677>* **BITE YOUR LIP (GET UP AND DANCE!). / CHAMELEON** – 28

Feb 77. (7") *(ROKN 521)* **CRAZY WATER. / CHAMELEON** 27 –

May 77. (7")(12") *(RU 1)* **BITE YOUR LIP (GET UP AND DANCE!). / CHICAGO** 28 –

Apr 78. (7") *(ROKN 538) <40892>* **EGO. / FLINTSTONE BOY** 34 34

Oct 78. (7") *(XPRES 1) <40973>* **PART-TIME LOVE. / I CRY AT NIGHT** 15 22

Oct 78. (lp/c) *(TRAIN/SHUNT 1) <3027>* **A SINGLE MAN** 8 15
– Shine on through / Return to Paradise / I don't care / Big dipper / Georgia / It ain't gonna be easy / Part-time love / Georgia / Shooting star / Madness / Reverie / Song for Guy. *(re-iss. Jun83 lp/c; PRICE/PRIMC 24) (cd-iss. Jun83; 826805-2)*

Dec 78. (7") *(XPRES 5) <40993>* **SONG FOR GUY. / LOVESICK** 4 [ ]

May 79. (7") *(XPRES 13)* **ARE YOU READY FOR LOVE (part 1). / (part 2)** 42 –
(12"+=) *(XPRES 13-12)* – Three way love affair / Mama can't buy you love

Jun 79. (12"m) *<13921>* **THE THOM BELL SESSIONS** (recorded 1977) – 51
– Are you ready for love / Three way love affair / Mama can't buy you love

Jun 79. (7") *<41042>* **MAMA CAN'T BUY YOU LOVE. / THREE WAY LOVE AFFAIR** – 9

Sep 79. (7") *(XPRES 21) <41126>* **VICTIM OF LOVE. / STRANGERS** [ ] 31

Oct 79. (lp/c) *(HISPD/REWND 125) M5104>* **VICTIM OF LOVE** 41 35
– Johnny B. Goode / Warm love in a cold climate / Born bad / Thunde

in the night / Spotlight / Street boogie / Born Bad / Victim of love. *(re-iss. Jul84 lp/c; PRICE/PRIMC 70)*

Dec 79. (7") *<41159>* **JOHNNY B. GOODE. / GEORGIA** [–] [ ]

Dec 79. (7"/12") *(XPRES 24/+12)* **JOHNNY B. GOODE. / THUNDER IN THE NIGHT** [ ] [–]

May 80. (7") *(XPRES 32) <41236>* **LITTLE JEANNIE. / CONQUER THE SUN** [33] [3]

May 80. (lp/c) *(HISPD/REWND 126) <5121>* **21 AT 33** [12] [13]
– Chasing the crown / Little Jeannie / Sartorial eloquence / Two rooms at the end of the world / White lady, white powder / Dear God / Never gonna fall in love again / Take me back / Give me the love. *(re-iss. Jul84 lp/c; PRICE/PRIMC 71) (cd-iss. Jun89; 800055-2)*

Aug 80. (7") *(XPRES 41) <41293>* **SARTORIAL ELOQUENCE. / WHITE MAN DANCER; CARTIER** [44] [39]

Nov 80. (7") *(XPRESS 45)* **DEAR GOD. / TACTICS** [ ] [–]
(d7") *(XPRESS 45 – ELTON 1)* – Steal away child / Love so cold.

Rocket Geffen

May 81. (7") *(XPRES 54) <49722>* **NOBODY WINS. / FOOLS IN FASHION** [42] [21]

May 81. (lp/c) *(TRAIN/SHUNT 016) <2002>* **THE FOX** [12] [21]
– Breaking down barriers / Heart in the right place / Just like Belgium / Nobody wins / Fascist faces / Carla etude / Fanfare / Chloe / Heels of the wind / Elton's song / The fox. *(re-iss. Jul84 lp/c; PRICE/PRIMC 72) (cd-iss. Jun89; 800063-2)*

Jul 81. (7") *(XPRESS 59)* **JUST LIKE BELGIUM. / CAN'T GET OVER LOSING YOU** [ ] [–]

Jul 81. (7") *<49788>* **CHLOE. / TORTURED** [–] [34]

Mar 82. (7") *(XPRES 71) <29954>* **BLUE EYES. / HEY PAPA LEGBA** [8] Jul82 [12]

Apr 82. (lp/c) *(HISPD/REWND 127) <2013>* **JUMP UP!** [13] [17]
– Dear John / Spiteful child / Ball and chain / Legal boys / I am your robot / Blue eyes / Empty garden /Princess / Where have all the good times gone? / All quiet on the western front. *(cd-iss. 1983; 800037-2)*

May 82. (7"/7"pic-d) *(XPRES/XPPIC 77) <50049>* **EMPTY GARDEN. / TAKE ME DOWN TO THE OCEAN** [51] Mar82 [13]

Sep 82. (7") *(XPRES 85)* **PRINCESS. / THE RETREAT** [ ] [–]

Nov 82. (7") *(XPRES 88)* **ALL QUIET ON THE WESTERN FRONT. / WHERE HAVE ALL THE GOOD TIMES GONE?** [ ] [–]

Nov 82. (7") *<29846>* **BALL AND CHAIN. / WHERE HAVE ALL THE GOOD TIMES GONE?** [–] [ ]

Apr 83. (7") *(XPRES 91)* **I GUESS THAT'S WHY THEY CALL IT THE BLUES. / LORD CHOC ICE GOES MENTAL** [5] [–]

May 83. (7") *<29639>* **I'M STILL STANDING. / LOVE SO COLD** [–] [12]

Jun 83. (lp/c)(cd) *(HISPD/REWND 24)(811052-2) <4006>* **TOO LOW FOR ZERO** [7] [25]
– Cold at Christmas / I'm still standing / Too low for zero / Religion / I guess that's why they call it the blues / Crystal / Kiss the bride / Whipping boy / Saint / One more arrow. *(cd re-mast.Jun98; 558475-2)*

Jul 83. (7"/7"sha-pic-d)(12") *(EJ S/PIC 1)(EJS 1-12)* **I'M STILL STANDING. / EARN WHILE YOU LEARN** [4] [–]

Aug 83. (7") *<29568>* **KISS THE BRIDE. / LORD CHOC ICE GOES MENTAL** [–] [25]

Oct 83. (7"/12") *(EJS 2/+12)* **KISS THE BRIDE. / DREAMBOAT** [20] [–]
(d7"+=) *(EJS 2 – FREEJ 2)* – Ego / Song for Guy.

Oct 83. (7") *<29460>* **I GUESS THAT'S WHY THEY CALL IT HTE BLUES. / THE RETREAT** [–] [4]

Dec 83. (7") *(EJS 3)* **COLD AT CHRISTMAS. / CRYSTAL** [33] [–]
(12"+=) *(EJS 3-12)* – J'veux de la tendresse.
(d7"+=) *(EJS 3-2)* – Don't go breaking my heart / Snow queen.

May 84. (7"/7"sha-pic-d)(12") *(PH/+PIC 7)(PH 7-12) <29292>* **SAD SONGS (SAY SO MUCH). / SIMPLE MAN** [7] [5]

Jun 84. (lp/c)(cd) *(HISPD/REWND 25)(882088-2) <24031>* **BREAKING HEARTS** [2] [20]
– Restless / Slow down Georgie (she's poison) / Who wears these shoes? / Breaking hearts (ain't what it used to be) / Li'l fridgerator / Passengers / In neon / Burning bridges / Did he shoot her? / Sad songs (say so much).

Aug 84. (7"/12") *(EJS 5/+12)* **PASSENGERS (remix). / LONELY BOY** [5] [–]

Sep 84. (7") *<29189>* **WHO WEARS THESE SHOES? / LONELY EYES** [–] [16]

Oct 84. (7") *(EJS 6)* **WHO WEARS THESE SHOES? / TORTURED** [50] [–]
(12"+=) *(EJS 6-12)* – I heard it through the grapevine.

Nov 84. (7") *<29111>* **IN NEON. / TACTICS** [–] [38]

Feb 85. (7") *(EJS 7)* **BREAKING HEARTS (AIN'T WHAT IT USED TO BE). / IN NEON** [59] [–]

Jun 85. (7"; ELTON JOHN & MILLIE JACKSON) *(EJS 8) <28956>* **ACT OF WAR (part 1). / (part 2)** [32] [ ]
(12"+=) *(EJS 8-12)* – (part 3) / (part 4).

Sep 85. (7") *(EJS 9)* **NIKITA. / THE MAN WHO NEVER DIED** [3] [–]
(12"+=)(d7"+=) *(EJS 9-12)(EJSD 9)* – Sorry seems to be the hardest word (live) / I'm still standing (live).

Oct 85. (7") *<28873>* **WRAP HER UP. / THE MAN WHO NEVER DIED** [–] [ ]

Nov 85. (lp/c)(cd) *(HISPD/REWND 26)(826213-2) <24077>* **ICE ON FIRE** [3] [48]
– Wrap her up / Satellite / Tell me what the papers say / Candy by the pound / Shoot down the Moon / This town / Cry to heaven / Soul glove / Nikita / Too young. *(c+=/cd+=)* – Act of war (with MILLIE JACKSON). *(cd re-mast.Jun98; 558476-2)*

Nov 85. (7"/7"sha-pic-d) *(EJ SC/PIC 10)* **WRAP HER UP. / RESTLESS (live with GEORGE MICHAEL)** [12] [–]
(ext.d12"+=) *(EJS 10-12 – EJS 9-12)* – Nikita / The man who never died / Sorry seems to be the hardest word (live) / I'm still standing (live).

Jan 86. (7") *<28800>* **NIKITA. / RESTLESS** [–] [7]

Feb 86. (7") *(EJS 11)* **CRY TO HEAVEN. / CANDY BY THE POUND** [47] [–]
(12"+=) *(EJS 11-12)* – Rock'n'roll medley.
(d7"++=) *(EJSD 11)* – Your song.

Sep 86. (7") *(EJS 12) <28578>* **HEARTACHES ALL OVER THE WORLD. / HIGHLANDER** [45] [55]
(12"+=) *(EJS 12-12)* – ('A'version).
(d7"+=) *(EJSD 12)* – Passengers / I'm still standing.

Nov 86. (lp/c)(cd) *(EJLP/EJMC 1)(830487-2) <24114>* **LEATHER JACKETS** [24] [91]
– Leather jackets / Hoop of fire / Go it alone / Don't trust that woman / Gypsy heart / Slow rivers / Heartache all over the world / Angeline / Memory of love / Paris / I fall apart.

Nov 86. (7"pic-d/c-s; ELTON JOHN & CLIFF RICHARD) *(EJS P/C 13)* **SLOW RIVERS. / BILLY AND THE KIDS** [44] [–]
(12"+=) *(EJS 13-12)* – Lord of the flies.

Rocket M.C.A.

Jun 87. (7") *(EJS 14)* **YOUR SONG (live). / DON'T LET THE SUN GO DOWN ON ME (live)** [ ] [–]
(12"+=) *(EJS 14-12)* – I need you to turn to / The greatest discovery.

Sep 87. (d-lp/d-c/cd) *(EJBX L/C/D 1) <8022>* **LIVE IN AUSTRALIA (live)** [43] Jul87 [24]
– Sixty years on / I need you to turn to / The greatest discovery / Tonight / Sorry seems to be the hardest word / The king must die / Take me to the pilot / Tiny dancer / Have mercy on the criminal / Madman across the water / Candle in the wind / Burn down the mission / Your song / Don't let the Sun go down on me. *(cd re-mast.Jun98; 558477-2)*

Dec 87. (7"/7"pic-d) *(EJS/+P 15) <53196>* **CANDLE IN THE WIND (live). / SORRY SEEMS TO BE THE HARDEST WORD (live)** [5] Nov87 [6]
(12"+=)(cd-s+=) *(EJS 15-12)(EJSCD 15)* – Your song (live) / Don't let the sun go down on me (live).

Mar 88. (7") **TONIGHT. / TAKE ME TO THE PILOT** [–] [ ]

May 88. (7"/7"pic-d) *(EJS/+IP 16) <53345>* **I DON'T WANT TO GO ON WITH YOU LIKE THAT. / ROPE AROUND A FOOL / (interview)** [30] Jun88 [2]
(12"+=)(cd-s+=) *(EJS 16-12)(EJSCD 16)* – ('A'-Shep Pettibone mix).

Jun 88. (lp/c)(cd) *(EJLP/EJMC 3)(834701-2) <6240>* **REG STRIKES BACK** [18] [16]
– Town of plenty / A word in Spanish / Mona Lisas and mad hatters (part 2) / I don't want to go on with you like that / Japanese hands / Goodbye Marlon Brando / The camera never lies / Heavy traffic / Poor cow / Since God invented girls. *(cd re-mast.Jun98; 558478-2)*

Sep 88. (7") *(EJSLB 17)* **TOWN OF PLENTY. / WHIPPING BOY** [74] [–]
(12"+=) *(EJS 17-12)* – My baby's a saint.
(cd-s++=) *(EJSCD 17)* – I guess that's why they call it the blues.

Nov 88. (7") *(EJS 18) <53408>* **A WORD IN SPANISH. / HEAVY TRAFFIC** [ ] Sep88 [19]
(12"+=) *(EJS 18-12)* – Live in Australia medley: Song for Guy – I guess that's why they call it the blues – Blue eyes.
(cd-s++=) *(EJSCD 18)* – Daniel.

— In Apr'89, he was credited on 'THROUGH THE STORM' UK No.41 / No.16 single with ARETHA FRANKLIN.

Aug 89. (7"/c-s) *(EJS/+MC 19)* <53692> **HEALING HANDS. / DANCING IN THE END ZONE** | 45 | | 13
(12"+=)(cd-s+=) *(EJS 19-12)(EJCD 19)* – ('A'version).

Sep 89. (lp/c/cd) *(838839-1/-4/-2)* <6321> **SLEEPING WITH THE PAST** | 1 | | 23
– Durban deep / Healing hands / Whispers / Club at the end of the street / Sleeping with the past / Stone's throw from hurtin' / Sacrifice / I never knew her name / Amazes me / Blue avenue. *(cd re-mast.Jun98; 558479-2)*

Oct 89. (7"/c-s) *(EJS/+MC 20)* <53750> **SACRIFICE. / LOVE IS A CANNIBAL** | 55 | Jan90 | 18
(12"+=)(cd-s+=) *(EJS 20-12)(EJSCD 20)* – Durban deep.

Apr 90. (7") <53818> **CLUB AT THEN END OF THE STREET. / SACRIFICE** | – | | 28

Jun 90. (7"/c-s) *(EJS/+MC 22)* **SACRIFICE. / HEALING HANDS** | 1 | | –
(12"+=)(cd-s+=) *(EJS 22-12)(EJSCD 22)* – Durban deep.

Aug 90. (7"/c-s) *(EJS/+MC 23)* **CLUB AT THE END OF THE STREET. / WHISPERS** | 47 | | –
(12"+=) *(EJS 23012)* – I don't wanna go on with you like that.
(cd-s+=) *(EJSCD 23)* – Give peace a chance.

Oct 90. (7"/c-s) *(EJS/+MC 24)* <53953> **YOU GOTTA LOVE SOMEONE. / MEDICINE MAN** [UK-only] | 33 | Nov90 | 43
(12"+=)(cd-s+=) *(EJS 24-12)(EJSCD 24)* – ('B'-Adamski version).

Nov 90. (7"/c-s) *(EJS/+MC 25)* **EASIER TO WALK AWAY. / SWEAR I HEARD THE NIGHT TALKING** | 63 | | –
(12"+=)(cd-s+=) *(EJS 25-12)(EJSCD 25)* – Made for me.

—— DEE MURRAY died of a heart attack, after suffering from cancer

May 92. (7"/c-s) *(EJS/+MC 28)* <54423> **THE ONE. / SUIT OF WOLVES** | 10 | Jun92 | 9
(cd-s+=) *(EJSCD 28)* – Fat boys and ugly girls.

Jun 92. (cd/c/lp) *(512360-2/-4/-1)* <10614> **THE ONE** | 2 | | 8
– Simple life / The one / Sweat it out / Runaway train / Whitewash county / The North / When a woman doesn't want you / Emily / On dark street / Understanding women / The last song. *(cd re-mast.Jun98; 558477-2)*

Jul 92. (7"/c-s; ELTON JOHN & ERIC CLAPTON) *(EJS/+MC 29)* **RUNAWAY TRAIN. / UNDERSTANDING WOMEN** | 31 | | –
(cd-s+=) *(EJSCD 29)* – Made for me.
(cd-s) *(EJSCDX 29)* – ('A'side) / Through the storm (with ARETHA FRANKLIN) / Don't let the sun go down on me (with GEORGE MICHAEL) / Slow rivers (with CLIFF).

Oct 92. (7"/c-s) *(EJS/+MC 30)* <54510> **THE LAST SONG. / THE MAN WHO NEVER DIED / SONG FOR GUY** | 21 | | 23
(cd-s) *(EJSCD 30)* – ('A'side) / Are you ready / Three way love affair / Mama can't buy you love.

Feb 93. (c-s) <54581> **SIMPLE LIFE / THE NORTH** | – | | 30

May 93. (7"/c-s) *(EJS/+MC 31)* **SIMPLE LIFE. / THE LAST SONG** | 44 | | –
(cd-s+=) *(EJSCD 31)* – The north.

Nov 93. (7"/c-s; ELTON JOHN & KIKI DEE) *(EJS/+MC 32)* **TRUE LOVE. / THE SHOW MUST GO ON** | 2 | | –
(cd-s+=) *(EJSCD 32)* – Runaway train.
(cd-s) *(EJSCDX 32)* – ('A'side) / Wrap her up / That's what friends are for / Act of war.

Nov 93. (c-s; ELTON JOHN & KIKI DEE) <54762> **TRUE LOVE / RUNAWAY TRAIN (with ERIC CLAPTON)** | – | | 56

Nov 93. (cd/c/d-lp) *(516478-2/-4/-1)* <10926> **DUETS** (with other artists) | 5 | | 25
– Teardrops (k.d.LANG) / When I think about love (I think about you) (P.M.DAWN) / The power (LITTLE RICHARD) / Shakey ground (DON HENLEY) / True love (KIKI DEE) / If you were me (CHRIS REA) / A woman's needs (TAMMY WYNETTE) / Don't let the Sun go down on me (GEORGE MICHAEL) / Old friend (NIK KERSHAW) / Go on and on (GLADYS KNIGHT) / Don't go breaking my heart (RuPAUL) / Ain't nothing like the real thing (MARCELLA DETROIT) / I'm your puppet (PAUL YOUNG) / Love letters (BONNIE RAITT) / Born to lose (LEONARD COHEN) / Duets for one (ELTON JOHN solo).

Feb 94. (7"/c-s; ELTON JOHN & RuPAUL) *(EJS/+MC 33)* <54813> **DON'T GO BREAKING MY HEART. / DONNER POUR DONNER** | 7 | | 92
(cd-s+=) *(EJCD 33)* – A woman's needs.
(cd-s) *(ERJMX 33)* – ('A'side) / (5-'A'mixes).

—— In May 94, he & MARCELLA DETROIT (ex-SHAKESPEAR'S SISTER) hit UK No.24 with 'AIN'T NOTHIN' LIKE THE REAL THING'.

Jun 94. (7"/c-s) *(EJS/+MC 34)* <64543> **CAN YOU FEEL THE LOVE TONIGHT? / ('A'mix)** | 14 | May94 | 4
(cd-s+=) *(EJCD 34)* – (other artists).
(above & below from the animated 'Hollywood' movie 'The Lion King')

Sep 94. (c-s) *(EJSMC 35)* <64516> **THE CIRCLE OF LIFE / ('A'-other artist)** | 11 | Aug94 | 18
(cd-s+=/pic-cd-s+=) *(EJS CD/CX 35)* – I just can't wait to be king / (other artist).

—— with **GUY BABYLON** – keyboards/ **BOB BIRCH** – bass/ **DAVEY JOHNSTONE** – guitar, mandolin, banjo/ **CHARLIE MORGAN** – drums/ **RAY COOPER** – percusion

Feb 95. (c-s) *(EJSMC 36)* **BELIEVE / SORRY SEEMS TO BE THE HARDEST WORD (live)** | 15 | | –
(cd-s+=) *(EJCD 36)* – Believe (live).
(cd-s) *(EJCDX 36)* – ('A'side) / The one / The last song.

Rocket | | Rocket

Mar 95. (c-s) <856014> **BELIEVE / THE ONE (live)** | – | |
Mar 95. (cd/c/lp) *(<526185-2/-4/-1>)* **MADE IN ENGLAND** | 3 | | 13
– Believe / Made in England / House / Cold / Pain / Belfast / Latitude / Please / Man / Lies / Blessed.

May 95. (c-s) *(EJSMC 37)* <852092> **MADE IN ENGLAND / DANIEL (live) / CAN YOU FEEL THE LOVE TONIGHT** | 18 | | 52
(cd-s+=) *(EJSCD 37)* – Your song / Don't let the sun go down on me.
(cd-s) *(EJCDX 37)* – ('A'side) / Whatever gets you thru the night / Lucy in the sky with diamonds / I saw her standing there.

Oct 95. (c-s) *(EJSMC 38)* <852394> **BLESSED / LATITUDE** | | | 34
(cd-s) *(EJSCD 38)* – ('A'side) / Made in England (mixes).
(cd-s) *(EJSDD 38)* – ('A'side) / Honky cat (live) / Take me to the pilot (live) / The bitch is back (live).

Nov 95. (cd/c) *(528788-2/-4)* <11481> **LOVE SONGS** (compilation) | 7 | Sep96 | 24
– Sacrifice / Candle in the wind / I guess that's why they call it the blues / Don't let the sun go down on me (with GEORGE MICHAEL) / Sorry seems to be the hardest word / Blue eyes / Daniel / Nikita / Your song / The one / Someone saved my life tonight / True love (with KIKI DEE) / Can you feel the love tonight / Circle of life / Blessed / Please / Song for Guy.

Jan 96. (c-s) *(EJSMC 40)* **PLEASE / LATITUDE** | 33 | | –
(cd-s+=) *(EJSCD 40)* – Made in England (mixes).
(cd-s) *(EJSCDX 40)* – ('A'side) / Honky cat (live) / Take me to the pilot (live) / The bitch is back (live).

Oct 96. (c-s) <55222> **YOU CAN MAKE HISTORY (YOUNG AGAIN) / SONG FOR GUY** | – | | 70

Rocket | | Mercury

Dec 96. (c-s; by ELTON JOHN & LUCIANO PAVAROTTI) *(LLHMC 1)* **LIVE LIKE HORSES / ('A'live finale)** | 9 | |
(cd-s+=) *(LLHCD 1)* – ('A'solo studio) / I guess that's why they call it the blues.
(cd-s) *(LLHDD 1)* – ('A'side) / Step into Christmas / Blessed.

Sep 97. (c-s) *(EJSMC 41)* **SOMETHING ABOUT THE WAY YOU LOOK TONIGHT / I KNOW I'M IN LOVE** | | |
(cd-s+=) *(EJSCD 41)* – No valentines ('A'extended).
(cd-s+=) *(EJSCX 41)* – You can make history (young again) ('A'extended).
(above was withdrawn after the events below)

Sep 97. (c-s/cd-s) *(PT MC/CD 1)* **CANDLE IN THE WIND 1997 / SOMETHING ABOUT THE WAY YOU LOOK TONIGHT** | 1 | | 1
(cd-s+=) *(568108-2)* – You can make history (young again).
(above double 'A'side was a tribute to Princess Diana who recently died in a car crash)

Oct 97. (cd/c) <*(536266-2/-4>)* **THE BIG PICTURE** | 3 | | 9
– Long way from happiness / Live like horses / The end will come / I can't bend / Love's got a lot to answer for / Something about the way you look tonight / If the river can bend / The big picture / Recover your soul / January / I can't steer my heart / Wicked dreams.

Feb 98. (c-s) *(EJSMC 42)* <568762> **RECOVER YOUR SOUL / I KNOW WHY I'M IN LOVE** | 16 | Apr98 | 55
(cd-s+=) *(EJSCD 42)* – Big man in a little suit / ('A'mix).
(cd-s+=) *(EJSCX 42)* – No valentines.

Jun 98. (c-s) *(EJSMC 43)* **IF THE RIVER CAN BEND / BENNIE AND THE JETS** | 32 | |
(cd-s+=) *(EJSCD 43)* – Saturday night's alright for fighting / ('A'original).
(cd-s) *(EJSDD 43)* – ('A'side) / Don't let the sun go down on me (live) / I guess that's why they call it the blues (live) / Sorry seems to be the hardest word (live).

Feb 99. (c-s; ELTON JOHN & LeANN RIMES) *(EJSMC 45)* *<566918>* **WRITTEN IN THE STARS / (alternative version)** [10] [29]
(cd-s+=) *(EJSCD 45)* – Recover your soul.

— next with "friends" **STING, LENNY KRAVITZ, TINA TURNER, SHANIA TWAIN, the SPICE GIRLS, JAMES TAYLOR, JANET JACKSON, LeANN RIMES + HEATHER HEADLEY**

Mar 99. (cd/c; ELTON JOHN & FRIENDS) *<(524628-2/-4)>* **ELTON JOHN AND TIM RICE'S AIDA** [29] [41]
– Another pyramid / Written in the stars / Easy as life / My strongest suit / I know the truth / Not me / Amneris' letter / A step too far / Like father like son / Elaborate lives / How I know you / The messenger / Gods love Nubia / Enchantment passing through / Orchestral finale.

Aug 99. (cd) *<546517-2>* **THE MUSE** (soundtrack) [–] [ ]
– Driving home / Driving to Universal / Driving to Jack's / Walk of shame / Better have a gift / The wrong gift / The aquarium / Are we laughing / Take a walk with me / What should I do / Back to the aquarium / Steven redecorates / To the guesthouse / The cookie factory / Multiple personality / Sarah escapes / Back to Paramount / Meet Christine / The muse / The muse (Jermaine Dupri remix).

Rocket DreamWorks

Apr 00. (cd-s) *<459039>* **SOMEDAY OUT OF THE BLUE / CHELDORADO** [–] [49]

Jun 00. (cd) *(<4 50219-2>)* **THE ROAD TO EL DORADO** (soundtrack) [ ] Mar00 [63]
– El Dorado / Someday out of the blue (theme from 'El Dorado') / Without question / Friends never say goodbye / The trail we blaze / 16th Century man / The panic in me / It's tough to be a god (w/ RANDY NEWMAN) / Trust me / My heart dances / Queen of cities / Cheldorado / The brig / Wonders of the new world.

Rocket Universal

Nov 00. (cd/c) *(548334-2/-4)* *<013050>* **ONE NIGHT ONLY – THE GREATEST HITS (live)** [7] [65]
– Goodbye yellow brick road / Philadelphia freedom / Don't go breaking my heart (with KIKI DEE) / Rocket man / Daniel / Crocodile rock / Sacrifice / Can you feel the love tonight / Bennie and the jets / Your song (with RONAN KEATING) / Sad songs (say so much) (with BRYAN ADAMS) / Candle in the wind / The bitch is back / Saturday night's alright for fighting (with ANASTACIA) / I'm still standing / Don't let the sun go down on me / I guess that's why they call it the blues (with MARY J. BLIGE).

Sep 01. (c-s) *(588706-4)* **I WANT LOVE / NORTH STAR** [9] [ ]
(cd-s+=) *(588706-2)* – Tiny dancer (live) / ('A'video).
(cd-s) *(588706-5)* – ('A'side) / God never came there / One (live).

Oct 01. (cd) *(<586330-2>)* **SONGS FROM THE WEST COAST** [2] [15]
– The emperor's new clothes / Dark diamond / Look ma, no hands / American triangle / Original sin / Birds / I want love / The wasteland / Ballad of the boy in the red shoes / Love her like me / Mansfield / This train don't stop there anymore. *(special cd+=; 063194-2)* – Your song (with ALESSANDRO SAFINA) / Teardrops (with LULU) / Northstar (with LULU) / Original sin (Junior Earth's mix) / I want love (video) / This train don't stop there anymore (video) / Your song (video with ALESSANDRO SAFINA).

Jan 02. (c-s) *(588896-4)* **THIS TRAIN DON'T STOP THERE ANYMORE / DID ANYONE SLEEP WITH JOAN OF ARC** [24] [ ]
(cd-s+=) *(588896-2)* – I want love (live).
(cd-s) *(588897-2)* – ('A') / American triangle (live) / Philadelphia freedom (live).

Apr 02. (c-s) *(588999-4)* **ORIGINAL SIN / I'M STILL STANDING (live)** [39] [ ]
(cd-s+=) *(588999-2)* – This train don't stop there anymore (live) / This train don't stop there anymore (video).
(cd-s) *(582850-2)* – ('A') / ('A'-live) / All the girls love Alice (live) / ('A'-video).

Jul 02. (c-s; by ELTON JOHN & ALESSANDRO SAFINA) *(063997-4)* **YOUR SONG / (instrumental)** [4] [ ]
(cd-s+=) *(063997-2)* – ('A'-video).

Nov 02. (d-cd/d-c) *(63499-2/-4)* *<865570>* **GREATEST HITS 1970-2002** (compilation) [3] [12]
– Your song / Tiny dancer / Honky cat / Rocket man (I think it's going to be a long long time) / Crocodile rock / Daniel / Saturday night's alright for fighting / Goodbye yellow brick road / Candle in the wind / Bennie and the jets / Don't let the sun go down on me / The bitch is back / Philadelphia freedom / Someone saved my life tonight / Island girl / Don't go breaking my heart (with KIKI DEE) / Sorry seems to be the hardest word / Blue eyes / I'm still standing / I guess that's why they call it the blues / Sad songs (say so much) / Nikita / Sacrifice / The one / Kiss the bride / Can you feel the love tonight? / Circle of life / Believe / Made in England / Something about the way you look tonight / Written in the stars (with LeANN RIMES) / I want love / This train don't stop there anymore / Song for Guy / Levon / Border song / Lucy in the sky with diamonds / Pinball wizard / True love (with KIKI DEE) / Live like horses (with LUCIANO PAVAROTTI) / I don't wanna go on with you like that / Don't let the sun go down on me (with GEORGE MICHAEL) / Your song (with ALESSANDRO SAFINA) / Sorry seems to be the hardest word (with BLUE) / Are you ready for love.

— late in 2002, ELTON and BLUE hit No.1 with 'SORRY SEEMS TO BE THE HARDEST WORD'

Aug 03. (c-s/cd-s) *(ECB 50 MCS/CDS)* / *Ultra; <1177>* **ARE YOU READY FOR LOVE (1979 radio edit) / (full length version) / THREE WAY LOVE AFFAIR** [1] [ ]
(12") *(ECB 50)* – ('A') / ('A'-Freeform Five reform mix).
(above issued on 'Southern Fried')

Mercury Universal

Nov 04. (7") *(9868689)* **ALL THAT I'M ALLOWED (I'M THANKFUL). / NICE AND SLOW (Thom Bell session in Philadelphia 1977** [20] [–]
(cd-s) *(9868258)* – ('A') / Keep it a mystery.
(cd-s) *(9868257)* – ('A') / So sad the renegade / A little peace.

Nov 04. (cd) *(986876-2)* *<35670-2>* **PEACHTREE ROAD** [21] [17]
– Weight of the world / Porch swing in Tupelo / Answer in the sky / Turn the lights out when you leave / My elusive drug / They call her the cat / Freaks in love / All that I'm allowed (I'm thankful) / I stop and I breathe / Too many tears / It's getting dark in here / I can't keep this from you. *(re-iss. Jul05 cd+=/d-lp+=; 9871101/9872301)* – The letter / Merry Christmas Maggie Thatcher / Electricity. *(re-iss. Jul05 += w/ dvd+=; 9872303)* – (DVD tracks).

Apr 05. (cd-s) *(9870664)* **TURN THE LIGHTS OUT WHEN YOU LEAVE / THINGS ONLY GET BETTER WITH LOVE** [32] [–]
(cd-s) *(9870663)* – ('A') / How's tomorrow / Peter's song.
in Jul'05, ELTON feat. on 2PAC's posthumous No.1, 'Ghetto Gospel'

Jul 05. (7"blue) *(9872343)* **ELECTRICITY. / BITE YOUR LIP (GET UP AND DANCE) – live 2004** [4] [ ]
(cd-s) *(9872184)* – ('A') / Indian sunset.
(cd-s) *(9872183)* – ('A') / ('A'-orchestral version) / Your song (live 2004) / Your song (live 2004 video).

– compilations, others, etc. –

on 'DJM' UK / 'MCA' in the US unless mentioned otherwise

Nov 74. (lp/c) *(DJH 2/4 0442)* *<2128>* **ELTON JOHN'S GREATEST HITS** (compilation) [1] [1]
– Your song / Daniel / Honky cat / Goodbye yellow brick road / Saturday night's alright for fighting / Rocket man / Candle in the wind / Don't let the Sun go down on me / Border song / Crocodile rock / The bitch is back / Lucy in the sky with diamonds / Sorry seems to be the hardest word / Don't go breaking my heart / Someone saved my life tonight / Philadelphia freedom / Island girl / Grow some funk of your own / Benny & the jets / Pinball wizard. *(cd-iss. Oct84; DJMCD 3)*

Sep 76. (7") *(DJS 10705)* **BENNIE AND THE JETS. / ROCK AND ROLL MADONNA** [37] [–]

May 77. (7"ep) *(DJR 18001)* **FOUR FROM FOUR EYES** [ ] [–]
– Your song / Rocket man / Saturday night's alright for fighting / Whenever you're ready (we'll go steady again).

Sep 77. (lp/c) *(DJH 2/4 0520)* *<3027>* **GREATEST HITS VOL.2** [6] [21]

Sep 78. (12"ep) *(DJT 15000)* **FUNERAL FOR A FRIEND; LOVE LIES BLEEDING / CURTAINS / WE ALL FALL IN LOVE SOMETIMES** [ ] [–]

Sep 78. (12x7"box) *(EJ 12)* **THE ELTON JOHN SINGLES COLLECTION** [ ] [ ]
(also available separately as below)

Sep 78. (7") *(DJS 10901)* **LADY SAMANTHA. / SKYLINE PIGEON** [ ] [ ]

Sep 78. (7") *(DJS 10902)* **YOUR SONG. / BORDER SONG** [ ] [ ]

Sep 78. (7") *(DJS 10903)* **HONKY CAT. / SIXTY YEARS ON** [ ] [ ]

Sep 78. (7") *(DJS 10904)* **CROCODILE ROCK. / COUNTRY COMFORT** [ ] [ ]

Sep 78. (7") *(DJS 10905)* **ROCKET MAN. / DANIEL** [ ] [ ]

Sep 78. (7") *(DJS 10906)* **GOODBYE YELLOW BRICK ROAD. / SWEET PAINTED LADY** [ ] [ ]

Sep 78. (7") *(DJS 10907)* **DON'T LET THE SUN GO DOWN ON ME. / SOMEONE SAVED MY LIFE** [ ] [ ]

Sep 78. (7") *(DJS 10908)* **CANDLE IN THE WIND. / I FEEL LIKE A BULLET (. . .** [ ] [ ]

Sep 78. (7") *(DJS 10909)* **THE BITCH IS BACK. / GROW SOME FUNK OF YOUR OWN** [ ] [ ]

Sep 78. (7") *(DJS 10910)* **ISLAND GIRL. / SATURDAY NIGHT'S ALRIGHT FOR FIGHTING** [ ] [ ]

Sep 78. (7") *(DJS 10911)* **PHILADELPHIA FREEDOM. / BENNIE AND THE JETS** [ ] [ ]

Sep 78. (7") *(DJS 10912)* **PINBALL WIZARD. / BENNIE AND THE JETS** [ ] [ ]

Feb 79. (d-lp/d-c) *Pickwick; (PDA/PDC 047)* **THE ELTON JOHN LIVE COLLECTION** [ ] [–]
– (live albums of Apr71 + May76) *(re-iss. Nov88 as 'THE COLLECTION'; PWKS 551)*

Aug 79. (5xlp-box) *(DJV 2300)* **ELTON JOHN** [ ] [ ]
(originally released in US contains 'EARLY YEARS', 'ELTON ROCKS', 'MOODS', 'SINGLES' & 'CLASSICS')

Oct 80. (lp/c) *(DJM 2/4 2085)* **LADY SAMANTHA** (rare 'B's) [56] [ ]

Nov 80. (7") *(DJS 10961)* **HARMONY. / MONA LISA AND THE MAD HATTERS** [ ] [–]

Mar 81. (7") *(DJS 10965)* **I SAW HER STANDING THERE. / WHATEVER GETS YOU THROUGH THE NIGHT / LUCY IN THE SKY WITH DIAMONDS (with JOHN LENNON)** [30] [–]

1988. (d-c) **ROCK OF THE WESTIES / ELTON JOHN'S GREATEST HITS** [ ] [ ]

1988. (d-c) **EMPTY SKY / GREATEST HITS VOL.2** [ ] [ ]

1988. (d-c) **CAPTAIN FANTASTIC AND THE BROWN DIRT COWBOY / ELTON JOHN** [ ] [ ]

1988. (d-c) **DON'T SHOOT ME I'M ONLY THE PIANO PLAYER / TUMBLEWEED CONNECTION** [ ] [ ]

1988. (d-c) **GREATEST HITS / ROCK OF THE WESTIES** [ ] [ ]
Note; All 'Rocket' releases were issued on 'MCA' in the US.

Apr 77. (7"mail-order) *Rocket; (GOALD 1)* **THE GOALDIGGER SONG. / (spoken)** [ ] [–]

Mar 81. (7") *Rocket; (XPRESS 49)* **DON'T GO BREAKING MY HEART. / SNOW QUEEN** [ ] [–]

Sep 87. (cd,c,lp) *<24153>* **ELTON JOHN'S GREATEST HITS, VOLUME III, 1979-1987** [–] [84]

Oct 90. (cd/c/d-lp) *Rocket; (846947-2/-4/-1)* **THE VERY BEST OF ELTON JOHN** [1] [–]
– Your song / Rocket man / Crocodile rock / Daniel / Goodbye yellow brick road / Saturday night's alright for fighting / Candle in the wind / Don't let the Sun go down on me / Lucy in the sky with diamonds / Philadelphia freedom / Someone saved my life tonight / Don't go breaking my heart / Bennie and the jets / Sorry seems to be the hardest word / Song for Guy / Part time love / Blue eyes / I guess that's why they call it the blues / I'm still standing / Kiss the bride / Sad songs / Passengers / Nikita / Sacrifice / You gotta love someone. *(cd+=/c+=)* – Pinball wizard / The bitch is back / I don't wanna go on with you like that / Easier to walk away. *(re-iss. Nov91 hit UK No.29)*

Feb 91. (7"/c-s) **DON'T LET THE SUN GO DOWN ON ME. / SONG FOR GUY** [ ] [–]
(12"+=/cd-s+=) – Sorry seems to be the hardest word.

Nov 91. (cd-box/c-box) *<10110>* **TO BE CONTINUED . . .** [–] [82]

Oct 92. (d-cd/d-c) *Rocket; (<514305-2/-4>)* **RARE MASTERS** [ ] [ ]
– (includes the "FRIENDS" soundtrack)

Jan 78. (lp) *St.Michael; (2094 0102)* **CANDLE IN THE WIND** [ ] [–]

Oct 80. (lp) *K-Tel; (NE 1094)* **THE VERY BEST OF ELTON JOHN** [24] [–]

Sep 81. (lp/c) *Hallmark; (SHM/HSC 3088)* **THE ALBUM** [ ] [–]

Nov 82. (lp/c) *T.V.; (TVA/TVC 3)* **LOVE SONGS** [ ] [–]
(re-iss. Feb84 on 'Rocket' lp/c/cd; 814 085-2)

Jun 83. (lp/c) *Premier; (CBR/KCBR 1027)* **THE NEW COLLECTION** [ ] [–]

1984. (lp/c) *Premier; (CBR/KCBR 1036)* **THE NEW COLLECTION VOL.2** [ ] [–]

1983. (d-c) *Cambra; (CRT 003)* **ELTON JOHN (hits)** [ ] [–]

May 84. (d-c) *Cambra; (CRT 130)* **SEASONS . . . THE EARLY LOVE SONGS** [ ] [–]

Oct 84. (cd) *(DJMCD 4)* **THE SUPERIOR SOUND OF . . .** [ ] [–]

Feb 88. (7") *Old Gold; (OG 9776)* **NIKITA. / I'M STILL STANDING** [ ] [–]

Jun 88. (7") *Old Gold; (OG 9789)* **DON'T GO BREAKING MY HEART. / I GOT THE MUSIC IN ME (Kiki Dee)** [ ] [–]

Jun 88. (7") *Old Gold; (OG 9791)* **SONG FOR GUY. / BLUE EYES** [ ] [–]

1988. (cd) *Starr; (825 173-2)* **BIGGEST** [ ] [–]

below, a guest spot w/**KIKI DEE.**

Apr 81. (7") *Ariola; (ARO 269)* **LOVING YOU IS SWEETER THAN EVER. / 24 HOURS** [ ] [–]

May 87. (7") *CBS; (650865-7/-6) / Epic; <07119>* **FLAMES OF PARADISE. / CALL ON ME** [ ] [36]
above JENNIFER RUSH & ELTON JOHN single

Mar 94. (cd/c) *Spectrum; (550213-2/-4)* **ROCK & ROLL MADONNA** [ ] [–]

Feb 95. (cd-s) *D.J.;* **UNITED WE STAND / NEANDERTHAL MAN** [ ] [–]
(above credited to REG DWIGHT) (early recordings)

Apr 95. (cd) *RPM; (RPM 142)* **CHARTBUSTERS GOES POP** [ ] [–]

☐ JOHNNY & THE SELF-ABUSERS

(see under ⇒ SIMPLE MINDS)

☐ Holly JOHNSON

(see under ⇒ FRANKIE GOES TO HOLLYWOOD)

Jack JOHNSON

Born: 18 May'75, Hawaii, USA. A one-time pro-surfer equally handy with a film camera and a guitar, JACK JOHNSON's positivist slacker-blues and ethical ways have increasingly warmed the cockles of both American students and melodically inclined Brits. The man's initial move from riding waves to soundwaves came via a guest spot ('RODEO CLOWNS') on a G. LOVE & SPECIAL SAUCE album, 'Philadelphonic' (1999). Prior to this, he'd graduated from the University Of California with a film degree, putting it to good use by working on music videos before co-producing surf film, 'Thicker Than Water'. Like its follow-up, 'The September Sessions', the movie drew critical acclaim and awards in its field, as well as the attention of JP Plenier, BEN HARPER's manager/producer. It wasn't long before JOHNSON was recording an album, 'BRUSHFIRE FAIRYTALES' (2001), with Plenier at the helm and HARPER on lap steel. With a turn of phrase not dissimilar to ANTHONY KEIDIS and a frayed, funk-scratchy way with an acoustic guitar, JOHNSON succeeded in distilling the bronzed aura of white-rasta surfer-chic into both his singing and playing. Tours with HARPER increased his profile, with the release of a Mario Caldato Jr.-produced follow-up set, 'ON AND ON' (2003), just as his debut was going platinum. JOHNSON didn't exactly ape HARPER's brimstone resolve, but that hardly precluded politics from his songwriting on the likes of lead single, 'THE HORIZON HAS BEEN DEFEATED'. He finally broke into the British market with third set, 'IN BETWEEN DREAMS' (2004), another Caldato Jr.-helmed set which – without the help of a hit single – eventually climbed to the top of the album chart in mid-summer 2005 and at the time of writing, is still refusing to bow out of the Top 10. His street cred invested with guest spots for the likes of the underrated Handsome Boy Modelling School (and more famously the BLACK EYED PEAS), JOHNSON finally scored a major UK hit with 'BETTER TOGETHER'. The breakthrough came in early 2006 on the back of a Brit Award for Best International Newcomer coinciding with the release of his highest profile soundtrack to date. Having already co-ordinated some of the music for his surf movies – and played alongside the likes of MONEY MARK in 'Sprout' (2004) – JOHNSON made his mainstream celluloid debut with a suitably cross-generational soundtrack for kids' animation 'CURIOUS GEORGE' (2006).

Album rating: BUSHFIRE FAIRYTALES (*7) / ON AND ON (*6) / IN BETWEEN DREAMS (*7) / CURIOUS GEORGE soundtrack w/ friends (*7)

JACK JOHNSON – vocals, guitars, piano / with **MERLO** – bass / **ADAM TOPOL** – drums, percussion not iss. Enjoy

Feb 01. (lp/cd) <440075015> **BRUSHFIRE FAIRYTALES** [–] [ ]
– Inaudible melodies / Middle man / Posters / Sexy plexi / Flake / Bubble toes / Fortunate fool / The news / Drink the water / Mudfootball (for Moe Lerner) / F-stop blues / Losing hope / It's all understood.

Universal Universal

May 02. (-) <radio> **FLAKE** [–] [34]
Jun 02. (re-cd) <(AA422 860994-2)> **BRUSHFIRE FAIRYTALES** [ ] [34]
(UK re-iss. Oct02; 64956-2) – Flake (live) / Inaudible melodies (live).

— late 2002, JOHNSON featured in & contributed a few songs to the soundtrack of his feature documentary, 'The September Sessions'

Island Universal

Jun 03. (cd/lp) *(9807097)* <440007501-2/-1> **ON AND ON** [ ] May03 [3]
– Times like these / The horizon has been defeated / Traffic in the sky / Taylor / Gone / Cupid / Wasting time / Holes to Heaven / Dreams be dreams / Tomorrow morning / Fall line / Cookie jar / Rodeo clowns / Cocoon / Mediocre bad guys / Symbol in my driveway. *(UK+=)* – The horizon has been defeated (acoustic).

— late in 2003, his second documentary soundtrack was released, 'Thicker Than Water'; featured Various Artists again

Apr 05. (cd/lp) *(9881565)* <B0004149-02/-01> **IN BETWEEN DREAMS** [1] Mar05 [2]
– Better together / Never know / Banana pancakes / Good people / No other way / Sitting, waiting, wishing / Staple it together / Situations / Crying shame / If I could / Breakdown / Belle / Do you remember / Constellations.

Brushfire – M.C.A. Brushfire – Universal

May 05. (cd-s) *(MCSTD 40417)* **GOOD PEOPLE / NO OTHER WAY (acoustic) / BUTTERNUT** [ ] [ ]
Sep 05. (cd-s) *(MCSTD 40430)* **BREAKDOWN / CONSTELLATIONS / GIRL I WANNA LAY YOU DOWN / BREAKDOWN (video)** [73] [ ]
Nov 05. (cd-s) *(MCSXD 40407)* **SITTING, WAITING, WISHING / CONSTELLATIONS (live feat Dan Lebowitz) / GIVE IT TO YOU (feat. G. Love) / ('A'-video)** [65] [66]
Feb 06. (cd-s) *(9879916)* **BETTER TOGETHER / BETTER TOGETHER (version) / STAPLE IT TOGETHER / (video)** [24] [–]

— next as JACK JOHNSON and Friends

Feb 06. (cd) *(9850967)* <87969> **Sing-A-Longs and Lullabies for the Film: CURIOUS GEORGE** (soundtrack) [15] [1]
– Upside down / Broken / People watching / Wrong turn / Talk of the town / Jungle gym / We're going to be friends / The sharing song / The 3 R's / Lullaby / With my own two hands / Questions / Supposed to be.

Mar 06. (re-cd) *(as prev.)* **ON AND ON** [30] [–]
May 06. (re-cd) *(as prev.)* **BRUSHFIRE FAIRYTALES** [25] [–]
May 06. (cd-s) *(9853873)* **UPSIDE DOWN / TALK OF THE TOWN (AOL session) / LULLABY (feat. Matt Costa) / ('A'-video)** [30] [38]

❑ John Paul JONES (see under ⇒ LED ZEPPELIN)

Janis JOPLIN

Born: 19 Jan'43, Port Arthur, Texas, USA. In the early 60's, she hitched to California and San Francisco, where she sang in the WALLER CREEK BOYS trio alongside future 13th FLOOR ELEVATORS member R.POWELL ST.JOHN. In 1963, she subsequently appeared opposite JORMA KAUKONEN (later JEFFERSON AIRPLANE) at local night spots. In 1966, after nearly giving up singing and her hippy drug-taking ways for a life of domesticity, she returned to Texas where she briefly rehearsed with The 13th FLOOR ELEVATORS. That same year, she again ventured to San Francisco, this time joining BIG BROTHER & THE HOLDING COMPANY. They released two albums, the second of which, 'CHEAP THRILLS', stayed at the top of the US charts for 8 weeks. When they temporarily folded late in '68, she went solo, although her alcohol and drug abuse was becoming increasingly pronounced. After three major concerts; London's Royal Albert Hall, Newport Festival and New Orleans Pop Festival, she unleashed her 1969 solo debut, 'I GOT DEM OL' KOSMIC BLUES AGAIN', which made the US Top 5. In May '70, she formed her new backing group, the FULL-TILT BOOGIE BAND, beginning work on an album in the autumn of 1970. Before it was completed, however, on the 4th of October 1970, JANIS was found dead in her Hollywood hotel room. The coroner's verdict reported that her death was due to an accidental drug overdose. Early in 1971, her last recording, 'PEARL' was issued, topping the US charts for 9 weeks, also giving her a first taste of UK chart action. She again hit pole position in the States with a great version of Kris Kristofferson's 'ME AND BOBBY McGEE'. But for her death, she would probably have become the greatest female singer of all-time, her powerful 3-octave vocals having the capacity to transform the most run-of-the-mill tune into a tour de force.

• **Songwriters:** She used many outside writers, including JERRY RAGAVOY, and covered; PIECE OF MY HEART (hit; Erma Franklin) / MAYBE (Chantells) / TO LOVE SOMEBODY (Bee Gees) / etc. • **Trivia:** In 1979, a film, 'The Rose', was released based on her life, featuring BETTE MIDLER in her role.

Album rating: Big Brother & The Holding Co.: BIG BROTHER & THE HOLDING CO. (*5) / CHEAP THRILLS (*8) / Janis Joplin: I GOT DEM OL' KOSMIC BLUES AGAIN MAMA (*6) / PEARL (*7) / JOPLIN IN CONCERT posthumous (*5) / compilations: JANIS JOPLIN'S GREATEST HITS (*8) / JANIS soundtrack (*4) / FAREWELL SONG (*4) / 18 ESSENTIAL SONGS (*8)

BIG BROTHER & THE HOLDING CO.

SAM ANDREW (b.18 Dec'41, Taft, California) – guitar, vocals / **PETE ALBIN** (b. 6 Jun'44) – bass, vocals / **JAMES GURLEY** (b.22 Dec'39, Detroit, Mich.) – guitar repl. DAVE ESKERSON (left Nov65) / **DAVID GETZ** (b.24 Jan'40, Brooklyn, N.Y.) – drums repl. CHUCK JONES (left Feb'66) also on occasion / **ED BOGAS** – violin (left before summer'66, to NEW RIDERS OF THE PURPLE SAGE)

— (Jun'66) added **JANIS JOPLIN** – vocals

Fontana Mainstream

Jul 67. (7") <657> **BLIND MAN. / ALL IS LONELINESS** [–] [ ]
Sep 67. (7") <662> **DOWN ON ME. / CALL ON ME** [–] [ ]
<hit US No.43 in Aug'68> (UK-iss.Sep68 on 'London'; HLT 10226)
Nov 67. (lp; stereo/mono) *(S+/TL 5457)* <6099> **BIG BROTHER & THE HOLDING COMPANY** [ ] Aug67 [60]
– Bye bye baby / Easy rider / Intruder / Light is faster than sound / Call on me / Women is losers / Blind man / Down on me / Caterpillar / All is loneliness. *(re-iss. 1969 on 'London' mono/stereo; HA-T/SH-T 8377) <US re-iss. May71 on 'Columbia'; 30631>* – Coo Coo / The last mile. *(cd-iss. Apr93 as 'FIRST ALBUM' on 'Sony Europe';)*
Nov 67. (7") <666> **BYE BYE BABY. / INTRUDER** [–] [ ]
Dec 67. (7") *(TF 881)* **BYE BYE BABY. / ALL IS LONELINESS** [ ] [–]
Feb 68. (7") <675> **WOMEN IS LOSERS. / LIGHT IS FASTER THAN SOUND** [–] [ ]

C.B.S. Columbia

Aug 68. (7") *(CBS 3683)* <44626> **PIECE OF MY HEART. / TURTLE BLUES** [ ] [12]
Sep 68. (lp) *(CBS 63392)* <PC 9700> **CHEAP THRILLS** [ ] Aug68 [1]
– Combination of the two / I need a man to love / Summertime / Piece of my heart / Turtle blues / O sweet Mary / Ball and chain. *<US re-iss. Mar81; > (cd-iss. Jan91 & Jun92 on 'Columbia'; CD 32004)*

— folded late 1968; JANIS JOPLIN went solo, taking SAM ANDREW

JANIS JOPLIN

JANIS JOPLIN – vocals / **SAM ANDREW** – guitar / others in her KOZMIC BLUES BAND were **BRAD CAMPBELL** (aka KEITH CHERRY) – bass / **TERRY CLEMENTS** – saxophone / **RICHARD KERMODE** – organ repl. BILL KING (Feb69) / **LONNIE CASTILLE** – drums repl. ROY MARKOWITZ (Apr69) / **TERRY HENSLEY** – trumpet repl. MARCUS DOUBLEDAY (Apr69) / added **SNOOKY FLOWERS** – saxophone (Feb'69)

— (Jul'69) **JOHN TILL** – guitar, vocals; repl. SAM ANDREW / **MAURY BAKER** – drums; repl. CASTILLE / **DAVE WOODWARD** – trumpet; repl. GASCA who repl. HENSLEY

C.B.S. Columbia

Oct 69. (lp) *(CBS 63546)* <9913> **I GOT DEM OL' KOZMIC BLUES AGAIN MAMA!** [ ] [5]
– Try (just a little bit harder) / Maybe / One good man / As good as you've been to this world / To love somebody / Kozmic blues / Little girl blue / Work me, Lord. *(re-iss. 1983 lp/c; CBS/40 32063) (cd-iss. 1988; CD 63546) (cd re-iss. Jan91;)*

Nov 69. (7") *<45023>* **KOZMIC BLUES. / LITTLE GIRL BLUE** [–] [41]

Dec 69. (7"w-drawn) *(CBS 3683)* **TURTLE BLUES. / PIECE OF MY HEART** [–] [–]

Jan 70. (7") *<45080>* **TRY (JUST A LITTLE BIT HARDER). / ONE GOOD MAN** [–] [ ]

Apr 70. (7") *<45128>* **MAYBE. / WORK ME, LORD** [–] [ ]

— JANIS JOPLIN & THE FULL TILT BOOGIE BAND retained **CAMPBELL** and **TILL** / added **RICHARD BELL** – piano / **KEN PEARSON** – organ / **CLARK PIERSON** – drums/ On the 4th Oct70, JANIS died of a drug overdose. She had just recorded below album

Jan 71. (lp) *(CBS 64188)* <30322> **PEARL** [50] [1]
– Move over / Cry baby / A woman left lonely / Half Moon / Buried alive in the blues / My baby / Me and Bobby McGee / Mercedes Benz / Trust me / Get it while you can. *(re-iss. Jan84 lp/c; CBS/40 32064) (cd-iss. 1988; CD 64188) (cd re-iss. Jan91 & Jul95 on 'Columbia'; 480415-2)*

Jan 71. (7") *(CBS 7019)* *<45314>* **ME AND BOBBY McGEE. / HALF MOON** [ ] [1]

May 71. (7") *(CBS 7217)* *<45379>* **CRY BABY. / MERCEDES BENZ** [ ] [42]

Sep 71. (7") *<45433>* **GET IT WHILE YOU CAN. / MOVE OVER** [–] [78]

– other posthumous JANIS JOPLIN releases –

on 'CBS' UK / 'Columbia' US unless mentioned otherwise

Oct 71. (7"ep) *(CBS 9136)* **MOVE OVER / CRY BABY. / TRY (JUST A LITTLE BIT HARDER) / PIECE OF MY HEART** [ ] [ ]

Jul 72. (d-lp) *(CBS 67241)* <31160> **JANIS JOPLIN IN CONCERT (live half with BIG BROTHER & THE HOLDING COMPANY / half with FULL TILT BOOGIE BAND)** [30] May72 [4]
– Down on me / Bye, bye baby / All is loneliness / Piece of my heart / Road block / Flower in the sun / Summertime / Ego rock / Half moon / Kozmic blues / Move over / Try (just a little bit harder) / Get it while you can / Ball and chain. *(re-iss. Sep87; 460128-1/4) (cd-iss. Aug93; 466838-2)*

Jul 72. (7") *(CBS 8241)* *<45630>* **DOWN ON ME (live). / BYE, BYE BABY (live)** [ ] [91]

Jul 73. (lp) *(CBS 65470)* *<32168>* **JANIS JOPLIN'S GREATEST HITS** [ ] [37]
– Piece of my heart / Summertime / Try (just a little bit harder) / Cry baby / Me and Bobby McGee / Down on me / Get it while you can / Bye, bye baby / Move over / Ball and chain. *(re-iss. Sep82 & May90 lp/c; CBS/40 32190) (cd-iss. 1988; 831 726-2) (cd re-iss. Oct94 on 'Sony'; 476555-2)*

May 75. (d-lp) *(CBS 88115)* *<33345>* **JANIS** (soundtrack // early performances) [ ] [54]
– Mercedes Benz / Ball and chain / Try (just a little bit) / Summertime / Albert Hall / Cry baby / Move over / (Dick Cavett TV interview) / Piece of my heart / Port Arthur high school reunion / Maybe / Me and Bobby McGee // Trouble in mind / What good can drinkin' do / Silver threads and golden needles / Mississippi river / Stealin' stealin' / No reason for livin' / Black mountain blues / Walk right in / River Jordan / Mary Jane / Kansas City blues / Daddy, daddy, daddy / See see rider / San Francisco Bay blues / Winin' boy / Careless love / I'll drown in my own tears.

Jun 75. (7") *(13-33205)* **ME AND BOBBY McGEE. / GET IT WHILE YOU CAN** [ ] [–]

Mar 76. (7") *(CBS 3960)* **PIECE OF MY HEART. / KOZMIC BLUES** [ ] [–]

Jul 80. (d-lp) *<(CBS 88492)>* **ANTHOLOGY** [ ] [ ]
(d-cd-iss. Jun97 on 'Columbia'; 467 405-2)

Feb 82. (lp) *(CBS 85354)* **FAREWELL SONG** [ ] [ ]

Nov 84. (d-c) **PEARL / CHEAP THRILLS** [ ] [ ]

Jun 86. (lp/c) *(CBS/40 54731)* **GOLDEN HIGHLIGHTS OF JANIS JOPLIN** [ ] [–]

Dec 90. (3xcd-box) *(467387-2)* **CHEAP THRILLS / PEARL / I GOT DEM OL' KOZMIC BLUES AGAIN** [ ] [–]

Sep 92. (d-cd) *Sony; (4610202)* **PEARL / I GOT DEM OL' KOZMIC BLUES AGAIN!** [ ] [ ]

Nov 92. (cd) *I.T.M.; (ITM 960001)* **MAGIC OF LOVE** [ ] [–]

Sep 93. (cd) *I.T.M.; (ITM 960007)* **LIVE AT WOODSTOCK, 1969 (live)** [ ] [ ]

Jan 94. (3xcd-box) *Legacy; (CD 48845-2) <65409>* **JANIS** (not the soundtrack) [ ] Nov93 [ ]

Dec 94. (cd) *Columbia;* **THE BEST** [ ] [ ]

Apr 95. (cd) *Legacy; (478515-2)* **18 ESSENTIAL SONGS** [ ] [–]

Aug 98. (cd) *Sony; (491683)* **THE ULTIMATE COLLECTION** [26] [ ]

JOURNEY

Formed: San Francisco, California, USA . . . early 1973, originally as The GOLDEN GATE BRIDGE by NEAL SCHON, GEORGE TICKNER, ROSS VALORY and PRAIRIE PRINCE. Due to manager Walter Herbert auditioning through a radio station for the group name, they settled with JOURNEY. They made their live debut on the 31st of December 1973 in front of over 10,000 people at San Francisco's 'Wonderland' venue. Prior to the recording of their eponymous first album in 1975, (the group had secured a deal with 'Columbia'), another SANTANA veteran, GREGG ROLIE, was added, while English-born AYNSLEY DUNBAR replaced the TUBES-bound PRINCE. The debut, and subsequent releases, 'LOOK INTO THE FUTURE' (1976) and 'NEXT' (1977), focused on jazzy art-rock, although major changes were afoot by 1978's 'INFINITY'. With the addition of ex-ALIEN PROJECT vocalist, STEVE PERRY, the group were transformed from noodling jam-merchants into sleek AOR-pomp exponents set for American FM radio domination. Produced by Roy Thomas Baker (QUEEN), the album saw PERRY's strident, impressively dynamic vocals given free rein over a new improved pop-friendly format, gleaming synths and irresistible hooks now the order of the day. The record also gave JOURNEY a near brush with the Top 20, a feat they'd achieve with 'EVOLUTION' (1979). By this juncture, DUNBAR had departed for JEFFERSON STARSHIP, his replacement being STEVE SMITH on a set which provided JOURNEY with their biggest hit single to date (Top 20) in 'LOVIN', TOUCHIN', SQUEEZIN'. The following year's 'DEPARTURE' album performed even better, JOURNEY finally nearing their ultimate destination, i.e. the top of the US charts. Enhanced by the polished pop instincts of ex-BABYS' frontman JONATHAN CAIN (a replacement for ROLIE, who went solo, later forming The STORM with VALORY and SMITH), JOURNEY scored their first (and only) No.1 album with the massively successful 'ESCAPE' (1981). The record spawned an unprecedented three US Top 10 hits, namely 'WHO'S CRYING NOW', 'OPEN ARMS' and the swooning 'DON'T STOP BELIEVIN'. Despite almost universal critical derision from the more elitist factions of the music press, JOURNEY continued to capture the lucrative middle ground between pop and tasteful metal, even breaking into the previously impenetrable UK Top 10 with 'FRONTIERS' (1983). The same month, SCHON released his second solo collaboration with keyboard wizard, JAN HAMMER, 'HERE TO STAY', while PERRY subsequently launched his solo career to huge success with the melodramatic 'OH SHERRIE' single and 'STREET TALK' (1984) album. JOURNEY eventually regrouped in the mid-80's, the band now comprising the core trio of PERRY, SCHON and CAIN, augmented by RANDY JACKSON and LARRIE LONDIN. The resulting album, 'RAISED ON RADIO' (1986) proved to be JOURNEY's end, the group bowing out on a high point. Following an official split in early '87, CAIN (along with VALORY) joined MICHAEL BOLTON, while SCHON eventually hooked up with JOHN WAITE in BAD ENGLISH, before forming HARDLINE in '92 with ROLIE and SMITH. With reunion fever all the rage in the 90's, JOURNEY finally got back together in 1996 for the successful 'TRIAL BY FIRE' album. Fans were disappointed however, with the subsequent departure of PERRY and his replacement with STEVE AUGERI. Although a relative soundalike, AUGERI couldn't quite match PERRY's charisma on 'ARRIVAL'

(2001), a blatant attempt to capture the spirit of the band's early 80's golden period.

• **Trivia:** A couple of JOURNEY tracks, featured on the 1980 & 1981 film soundtracks of 'Caddyshack' & 'Heavy Metal'.

Album rating: JOURNEY (*3) / LOOK INTO THE FUTURE (*4) / NEXT (*3) / IN THE BEGINNING compilation (*4) / INFINITY (*6) / EVOLUTION (*5) / DEPARTURE (*4) / CAPTURED (*7) / ESCAPE (*8) / FRONTIERS (*6) / RAISED ON RADIO (*7) / THE BEST OF JOURNEY compilation (*8) / TIME 3 compilation (*7) / TRIAL BY FIRE (*4) / ARRIVAL (*5) / THE ESSENTIAL JOURNEY compilation (*8)

NEAL SCHON (b.27 Feb'54, San Mateo, Calif.) – lead guitar, vocals (ex-SANTANA) / **GREGG ROLIE** (b.17 Jun'47) – vocals, keyboards (ex-SANTANA) / **GEORGE TICKNER** – guitar, vocals / **ROSS VALORY** (b. 2 Feb'49) – bass, vocals (ex-STEVE MILLER BAND) / **AYNSLEY DUNBAR** (b.1946, Liverpool, England) – drums (ex-FRANK ZAPPA, ex-JOHN MAYALL, ex-JEFF BECK) repl. PRAIRIE PRINCE who joined The TUBES

C.B.S. | Columbia

Apr 75. (lp/c) *(CBS/40 80724)* *<33388>* **JOURNEY** [ ] [ ]
– Of a lifetime / In the morning day / Kohoutek / To play some music / Topaz / In my lonely feeling – Conversations / Mystery mountain. *(cd-iss. Oct93 on 'Sony Collectors'; 983313-2) (cd re-iss. Oct94 on 'Columbia'; 477854-2)*

Jun 75. (7") *<10137>* **TO PLAY SOME MUSIC. / TOPAZ** [–] [ ]

— (Apr'75) reverted to a quartet when TICKNER departed

Jan 76. (lp/c) *(CBS/40 69203)* *<33904>* **LOOK INTO THE FUTURE** [ ] [100]
– On a Saturday nite / It's all too much / Anyway / She makes me (feel alright) / You're on your own / Look into the future / Midnight dreamer / I'm gonna leave you. *(re-iss. Mar82; CBS 32102)*

Mar 76. (7") *<10324>* **ON A SATURDAY NIGHT. / TO PLAY SOME MUSIC** [–] [ ]

Jul 76. (7") *<10370>* **SHE MAKES ME (FEEL ALRIGHT). / IT'S ALL TOO MUCH** [–] [ ]

Feb 77. (7") *<10522>* **SPACEMAN. / NICKEL AND DIME** [–] [ ]

Feb 77. (lp/c) *(CBS/40 81554)* *<34311>* **NEXT** [ ] [85]
– Spaceman / People / I would find you / Here we are / Hustler / Next / Nickel & dime / Karma.

— (Jun'77) added **ROBERT FLEISCHMAN** – lead vocals

— (Oct77) **STEVE PERRY** (b.22 Jan'53, Hanford, Calif.) – lead vocals; repl. FLEISCHMAN

Mar 78. (7") *(CBS 6238)* *<10700>* **WHEEL IN THE SKY. / CAN DO** [ ] [57]

May 78. (lp/c) *(CBS/40 82244)* *<34912>* **INFINITY** [ ] Feb78 [21]
– Lights / Feeling that way / Anytime / La do da / Patiently / Wheel in the sky / Somethin' to hide / Winds of March / Can do / Opened the door. *(cd-iss. 1988; CD 82244) (cd re-iss. Nov96 on 'Columbia'; 486665-2)*

Jun 78. (7") *<10757>* **ANYTIME. / CAN DO** [–] [83]

Aug 78. (7") *(CBS 6392)* **LIGHTS. / OPEN THE DOOR** [ ] [–]

Aug 78. (7") *<10800>* **LIGHTS. / SOMETHIN' TO HIDE** [–] [68]

— (Nov'78) **STEVE SMITH** – drums repl. DUNBAR who joined JEFFERSON STARSHIP (above now alongside SCHON, ROLIE, PERRY and VALORY)

Apr 79. (lp/c) *(CBS/40 83566)* *<35797>* **EVOLUTION** [100] [20]
– Sweet and simple / Just the same way / Do you recall / City of angels / Lovin', touchin', squeezin' / Daydream / When you're alone (it ain't easy) / Lady luck / Too late / Lovin' you is easy / Majestic. *(re-iss. Jul83 lp/c; CBS/40 32342) (cd-iss. Oct93 on 'Sony Collectors'; 982737-2) (cd re-iss. Nov96 on 'Columbia'; 486666-2)*

Apr 79. (7") *<10928>* **JUST THE SAME WAY. / SOMETHIN' TO HIDE** [–] [58]

Sep 79. (7") *(CBS 7890)* *<11036>* **LOVIN', TOUCHIN', SQUEEZIN'. / DAYDREAM** [ ] Jul79 [16]

Dec 79. (7") *<11143>* **TOO LATE. / DO YOU RECALL** [–] [70]

Feb 80. (7") *<11213>* **ANY WAY YOU WANT IT. / WHEN YOU'RE ALONE (IT AIN'T EASY)** [–] [23]

Mar 80. (lp/c) *(CBS/40 84101)* *<36339>* **DEPARTURE** [ ] [8]
– Any way you want it / Walks like a lady / Someday soon / People and places / Precious time / Where were you / I'm cryin' / Line of fire / Departure / Good morning girl / Stay awhile / Homemade love. *(re-iss. Feb86 lp/c; CBS/40 32714) (cd-iss. 1987; CD 84101) (cd re-iss. Nov96 on 'Columbia'; 486667-2)*

May 80. (7"/12") *(CBS/12 8558)* **ANY WAY YOU WANT IT. / DO YOU RECALL** [ ] [–]

May 80. (7") *<11275>* **WALKS LIKE A LADY. / PEOPLE AND PLACES** [–] [ ]

Aug 80. (7") *<11339>* **GOOD MORNING GIRL. / STAY AWHILE** [–] [55]

Feb 81. (d-lp) *(CBS 88525)* *<37016>* **CAPTURED (live)** [ ] [9]
– Majestic / Where were you / Just the same way / Line of fire / Lights / Stay awhile / Too late / Dixie highway / Feeling that way / Anytime / Do you recall / Walks like a lady / La do da / Lovin', touchin', squeezin' / Wheel in the sky / Any way you want it / The party's over (hopelessly in love). *(re-iss. Sep87 d-lp/d-c/cd; 451132-1/-4/-2) (cd re-iss. Jun89; CD 88525) (cd re-iss. Nov96 on 'Columbia'; 486661-2)*

Mar 81. (7") *(CBS 9578)* *<60505>* **THE PARTY'S OVER (HOPELESSLY IN LOVE) (live). / WHEEL IN THE SKY (live)** [ ] Feb81 [34]

— (Apr'81) **JONATHAN CAIN** (b.26 Feb'50, Chicago, Illinois) – keyboards, guitar, vocals (ex-BABYS) repl. ROLIE who went solo, and later formed The STORM with VALORY and SMITH

Aug 81. (lp/c) *(CBS/40 85138)* *<37408>* **ESCAPE** [32] [1]
– Don't stop believin' / Stone in love / Who's crying now / Keep on runnin' / Still they ride / Escape / Lay it down / Dead or alive / Mother, father / Open arms. *(cd-iss. May87; CD 85138) (re-iss. Feb88 lp/c; 460185-1/-4) (cd re-iss. Apr89; 460285-2) (cd re-iss. Nov96 on 'Columbia'; 486662-2)*

Jul 81. (7") *<02241>* **WHO'S CRYING NOW. / MOTHER, FATHER** [–] [4]

Aug 81. (7"/12") *(A/TA 1467)* **WHO'S CRYING NOW. / ESCAPE** [ ] [–]

Dec 81. (7"/12"/12"pic-d) *(A/+13/11 1728)* *<02567>* **DON'T STOP BELIEVIN'. / NATURAL THING** [62] Oct81 [9]

Apr 82. (7") *(A 2057)* *<02687>* **OPEN ARMS. / LITTLE GIRL** [ ] Jan82 [2]

May 82. (7") *<02883>* **STILL THEY RIDE. / RAZA DEL SOL** [–] [19]

Aug 82. (7") *(A 2725)* **WHO'S CRYING NOW. / DON'T STOP BELIEVIN'** [46] [–]
(12") *(TA 2725)* – ('A'side) / The Journey story (14 best snips).

Oct 82. (7") *(A 2890)* **STONE IN LOVE. / ONLY SOLUTIONS** [ ] [–]

Feb 83. (lp/c) *(CBS/40 25261)* *<38504>* **FRONTIERS** [6] [2]
– Separate ways (worlds apart) / Send her my love / Chain reaction / After the fall / Faithfully / Edge of the blade / Troubled child / Back talk / Frontiers / Rubicon. *(cd-iss. 1988; CD 25261) (cd re-iss. Nov96 on 'Columbia'; 486663-2)*

Feb 83. (7"/12") *(A/+13 3077)* *<03513>* **SEPARATE WAYS (WORLDS APART). / FRONTIERS** [ ] [8]

Apr 83. (7") *<03840>* **FAITHFULLY. / FRONTIERS** [–] [12]

Apr 83. (7") *(A 3358)* **FAITHFULLY. / EDGE OF THE BLADE** [ ] [–]

Jul 83. (7") *<04004>* **AFTER THE FALL. / OTHER SOLUTIONS** [–] [23]

Jul 83. (7") *(A 3692)* **AFTER THE FALL. / RUBICON** [ ] [–]
(12"+=) *(TA 3692)* – Any way you want me / Don't stop believin'.

Sep 83. (7") *<04151>* **SEND HER MY LOVE. / CHAIN REACTION** [–] [ ]

— (the band take on some solo projects, see further below)

Feb 85. (7") *(A 6058)* *<29090>* **ONLY THE YOUNG. / (B-side by Sammy Hagar)** [ ] Jan85 [9]
(above songs from the film 'Vision Quest' on 'Geffen' records)

— **PERRY, SCHON and CAIN** regrouped and added **RANDY JACKSON** – bass (ex-ZEBRA) / **LARRIE LONDIN** – drums

Apr 86. (7") *(A 7095)* *<05869>* **BE GOOD TO YOURSELF. / ONLY THE YOUNG** [ ] [9]
(12"+=) *(TA 7095)* – Any way you want it / Stone in love.
(d7"+=) *(DA 7095)* – After the fall / Rubicon.

May 86. (lp/c/cd) *(CBS/40/CD 26902)* *<39936>* **RAISED ON RADIO** [22] [4]
– Girl can't help it / Positive touch / Suzanne / Be good to yourself / Once you love somebody / Happy to give / Raised on radio / I'll be alright without you / It could have been you / The eyes of a woman / Why can't this night go on forever. *(re-iss. Apr91 on 'Columbia' cd/c; 467992-2/-4) (cd re-iss. Nov96 on 'Columbia'; 486664-2)*

Jul 86. (7") *(A 7265)* *<06134>* **SUZANNE. / ASK THE LONELY** [ ] Jun86 [17]
(12"+=) *(TA 7265)* – Raised on radio.

— (Aug'86) **MIKE BAIRD** – drums repl. LONDIN

Oct 86. (7") *(650116-7)* *<06302>* **GIRL CAN'T HELP IT. / IT COULD HAVE BEEN YOU** [ ] Aug86 [17]

Dec 86. (7") *<06301>* **I'LL BE ALRIGHT WITHOUT YOU. / THE EYES OF A WOMAN** [–] [14]

Apr 87. (7") *<07043>* **WHY CAN'T THIS NIGHT GO ON FOREVER. / POSITIVE TOUCH** [–] [60]

— split early '87. CAIN and VALORY joined MICHAEL BOLTON. SCHON joined BAD ENGLISH in '89, then HARDLINE in '92 with ROLIE and SMITH

— re-formed the quintet in 1996:- **PERRY, SCHON, CAIN, VALORY + SMITH**

Columbia Columbia

Oct 96. (cd/c) *(485264-2/-4) <67514>* **TRIAL BY FIRE** [ ] [3]
– Message of love / One more / When you love a woman / If he should break your heart / Forever in blue / Castles burning / Don't be down on me baby / Still she cries / Colours of the spirit / When I think of you / Easy to fall / Can't tame the lion / It's just the rain / Trial by fire / Baby I'm leaving you. *(cd re-iss. Jan00; same)*

Oct 96. (c-s) *<78428>* **WHEN YOU LOVE A WOMAN / MESSAGE OF LOVE / OPEN ARMS** [–] [12]

— **DEAN CASTRONOVO** – drums (ex-BAD ENGLISH) repl. SMITH

Apr 01. (cd) *(498479-2) <69864>* **ARRIVAL** [ ] [56]
– Higher piece / All the way / Signs of life / All the things / Loved by you / Livin' to do / I got a reason / With your love / Lifetime of dreams / Live and breathe / Nothin' comes close / To be alive again / Kiss me softly / I'm not that way / We will meet again.

– compilations, others, etc. –

on 'CBS' UK / 'Columbia' US, unless mentioned otherwise

Sep 80. (d-lp) *(CBS 22073) <36324>* **IN THE BEGINNING** (from first 3 albums) [ ] Jan80 [ ]

Dec 82. (c-ep) *(40 2908)* **CASSETTE EP** [ ] [–]
– Don't stop believin' / Who's crying now / Open arms / Lovin' touchin' squeezin'.

Aug 82. (7") *<03133>* **OPEN ARMS. / THE PARTY'S OVER** [–] [ ]

Aug 82. (7") *<03134>* **DON'T STOP BELIEVIN'. / WHO'S CRYING NOW** [–] [ ]

Feb 83. (d-c) *(EPC-40 22150)* **INFINITY / NEXT** [ ] [–]

Aug 87. (d-lp) *(CBSJ 241)* **FRONTIERS / ESCAPE** [ ] [–]

Nov 88. (lp/c/cd) *(463149-1/-4/-2) <44493>* **GREATEST HITS** [ ] [10]
– Only the young / Don't stop believin' / Wheel in the sky / Faithfully / I'll be alright with you / Any way you want it / Ask the lonely / Who's crying now / Separate ways (worlds apart) / Lights / Lovin', touchin', squeezin' / Open arms / Girl can't help it / Send her my love / Be good to yourself. *(cd re-iss. Apr96 & Apr00 on 'Columbia'; 463149-2)*

Jan 89. (7") *(654541-7)* **WHO'S CRYING NOW. / OPEN ARMS** [ ] [–]
(12"+=/cd-s+=) *(654541-6/-2)* – Suzanne / Don't stop believing.

— (now on 'Columbia' unless mentioned otherwise)

Dec 92. (t-cd/t-c) *(472810-2/-4) <48937>* **TIME 3** [ ] [90]
(re-iss. Apr98; C3K 65159)

Jan 93. (c-s) *<74842>* **LIGHTS (live) / (6 album excerpts)** [–] [74]

Apr 98. (cd/c) *(489703-2/-4) <69139>* **GREATEST HITS LIVE (live)** [ ] [ ]

Nov 00. (3xcd-box) *(492658-2)* **INFINITY / ESCAPE / FRONTIERS** [ ] [ ]

Mar 01. (cd) *Sony; <2416>* **THE JOURNEY CONTINUES . . .** [–] [ ]

Nov 01. (cd) *<86080>* **THE ESSENTIAL JOURNEY** [–] [47]

JOY DIVISION

Formed: Salford, Manchester, England . . . mid '77 initially as The STIFF KITTENS by IAN CURTIS, BERNARD ALBRECHT, PETER HOOK and STEPHEN MORRIS. By the time they were ready to take the stage for the first time, the group were going under the WARSAW moniker, finally settling on JOY DIVISION later that year. A term used by the Nazis for Jewish prostitutes, the band had taken the name from the book, 'House Of Dolls'; unsurprisingly, they ran into a little media trouble, the press subsequently speculating about their supposedly fascistic tendencies and unfairly branding them little Adolfs. Particularly controversial was the track, 'AT A LATER DATE', included on the 'Virgin' various artists punk sampler, 'Short Circuit: Live At The Electric Circus'. A vinyl debut proper came with the limited EP, 'AN IDEAL FOR LIVING', although it was through manager Rob Gretton and a subsequent deal with the emerging 'Factory' records that JOY DIVISION's career really got off the ground. Their first recordings for the label were a couple of tracks, 'GLASS' and 'DIGITAL', featured on a 'Factory' sampler (in mid-'79, a further two tracks, 'AUTO-SUGGESTION' and 'FROM SAFETY TO WHERE', surfaced on the 'Fast' records compilation EP, 'Earcom 2'), while their legendary Martin Hannett-produced debut album, 'UNKNOWN PLEASURES' was finally released later that summer. Groundbreaking in its bass-heavy, skeletal sound and evocation of urban alienation, isolation and despair, the record ensured CURTIS's position as a latter day messiah of existential angst; while his lyrics trawled the underbelly of the human psyche with disturbing clarity, his sub-JIM MORRISON ruminations were a blueprint for every pasty-faced goth pretender of the next decade. Tony Wilson's faith in the band was such that he contributed his life savings of over £8,000 towards the album's cost, the 'Factory' supremo's investment rewarded as the record topped the indie charts and JOY DIVISION became the foremost post-punk cult act. Yet even as the hypnotic rhythms of sublime new single, 'TRANSMISSION', hinted at an equally compelling new direction, CURTIS's robotic contortions and trance-like stage presence were giving way to epileptic fits as the singer struggled to cope with the increasing demands of live work. Tragically, on the 18th May, 1980, depressed with the break-up of his marriage and his worsening illness, CURTIS hanged himself. Ironically, JOY DIVISION scored their first chart hit a month later with the seminal 'LOVE WILL TEAR US APART'; the loss of such a fiercely individual talent was underlined as the track suggested a singer (and indeed, band) at the very apex of their creative potential. CURTIS had actually recorded a full album's worth of material before his death, released that summer as 'CLOSER'; even more lyrically unsettling, the record's bleak vision nevertheless pre-empted rock's dancefloor embrace on the synth-laced likes of 'ISOLATION', as well as forming the basis for NEW ORDER's experiments in cross-genre innovation. The latter act were formed later that year from JOY DIVISION's ashes, while further CURTIS-era material was posthumously released in late '81 as 'STILL'. The band remain one of the most revered and certainly one of the most influential outfits to emerge from the punk 'revolution', the best of NEW ORDER's work an indication as to what musical heights JOY DIVISION might have scaled had CURTIS prolonged the battle with his personal demons.

Album rating: UNKNOWN PLEASURES (*10) / CLOSER (*10) / STILL part compilation/live (*8) / SUBSTANCE compilation (*9) / PERMANENT: JOY DIVISION 1995 remixes (*6)

IAN CURTIS (b.15 Jul'56, Macclesfield, England) – vocals / **BERNARD ALBRECHT** (b. BERNARD DICKEN, 4 Jan'56) – guitar, vocals / **PETER HOOK** (b.13 Feb'56, Salford, Manchester) – bass / **STEPHEN MORRIS** (b.28 Oct'57, Macclesfield) – drums

Enigma not iss

Jun 78. (7"ep) *(PSS 139)* **AN IDEAL FOR LIVING** [ ] [–]
– An ideal for living / Warsaw / Leaders of men / No love lost / Failures *(re-iss. Jul78 on 'Anonymous' 12"ep; ANON 1)*

Factory not iss

Aug 79. (lp) *(FACT 10)* **UNKNOWN PLEASURES** [ ] [–]
– Disorder / Day of the lords / Candidate / Insight / New dawn fades / She's lost control / Shadowplay / Wilderness / Interzone / I remember nothing. *(re-dist.Jul80, hit No.71) (re-iss. Jul82; same) (c-iss.Nov84; FACT 10C) (cd-iss. Apr86; FACD 10) (re-iss. Jul93 on 'Centredate-London' cd/c 520016-2) <US-iss.1989 on 'Qwest' lp/c/cd; 1-/4-/2-25840> (cd re-iss. Jan00 3984 28223-2)*

Oct 79. (7") *(FAC 13)* **TRANSMISSION. / NOVELTY** [ ] [–]
(re-iss. Oct80 as 12"; FAC 13-12)

Mar 80. (7") *(SS 33-002)* **ATMOSPHERE. / DEAD SOULS** [–] France [–]
(above single released on 'Sordide Sentimentale' & now worth lots)

Jun 80. (7") *(FAC 23)* **LOVE WILL TEAR US APART. / THESE DAYS** [13] [–]
(re-iss. Oct80 as 12"+=; FAC 23-12) – ('A'version). *(re-iss. Oct83; same); h UK No.19)*

Jul 80. (lp) *(FACT 25)* **CLOSER** [6] [–]
– Heart and soul / 24 hours / The eternal / Decades / Atrocity exhibition Isolation / Passover / Colony / Means to an end. *(c-iss.Jul82; FACT 25C (cd-iss. Apr86; FACD 25) (re-iss. Jul93 on 'Centredate-London' cd/c; 520015

2) <US-iss.1989 on 'Qwest' lp/c/cd; 1-/4/-2-25841> (cd re-iss. Sep99 on 'Factory Too'; 3984 28219-2)

— After another fit of depression, IAN CURTIS hanged himself 18th May 1980. The others became NEW ORDER

– compilations, others, etc. –

Sep 80. (12") *Factory Benelux; (FACTUS 2)* **ATMOSPHERE. / SHE'S LOST CONTROL** [ ] [–]

Apr 81. (free 7"flexi) *Factory; (FAC 28)* **KOMAKINO. / INCUBATION** [–] [–]

May 81. (7"ep/12"ep; as WARSAW) *Enigma; (PSS 138)* **THE IDEAL BEGINNING** [ ] [–]
– Inside the line / Gutz / At a later date.

Oct 81. (d-lp) *Factory; (FACT 40)* **STILL (live & rare)** [5] [–]
– Exercise one / Ice age / The sound of music / Glass / The only mistake / Walked in line / The kill / Something must break / Dead souls / Sister Ray / Ceremony / Shadowplay / Means to an end / Passover / New dawn fades / Transmission / Disorder / Isolation / Decades / Digital. *(c-iss.Dec86; FACT 40C) (cd-iss. Mar90; FACD 40) (re-iss. Jul93 on 'Centredate-London' cd/c; 520014-2/-4) <US-iss.1989 on 'Qwest' lp/c/cd; 26495> (cd re-iss. Jan00 on 'Factory Too'; 3984 28222-2)*

Nov 86. (12"ep) *Strange Fruit; (SFPS 013)* **THE PEEL SESSIONS (31.1.79)** [ ] [–]
– Exercise one / Insight / She's lost control / Transmission. *(re-iss. Jul88 cd-ep; SFPSCD 013)*

Sep 87. (12"ep) *Strange Fruit; (SFPS 033)* **THE PEEL SESSIONS 2 (26.11.79)** [ ] [–]
– Love will tear us apart / 24 hours / Colony / The sound of music. *(re-iss. Jul88 cd-ep; SFPSCD 033)*

1987. (7"ep+book) *Stampa; (SCONIC 001)* **YOU'RE NO GOOD FOR ME / KOMAKINO / INCUBATION / INCUBATION (version)** [–] Italy [–]

Jun 88. (7") *Factory; (FAC 213-7)* **ATMOSPHERE. / THE ONLY MISTAKE** [34] [–]
(12"+=) *(FAC 213)* – The sound of music.
(cd-s) *(FACD 213)* – ('A'side) / Love will tear us apart / Transmission.

Jul 88. (lp/c/dat)(cd) *Factory; (FACT 250/+C/D)(FACD 250) / Qwest; <1-/4-/2-25747>* **SUBSTANCE** (The best of..) [7] [ ]
– She's lost control / Dead souls / Atmosphere / Love will tear us apart / Warsaw / Leaders of men / Digital / Transmission / Auto-suggestion. *(cd+=)* – (7 extra tracks). *(re-iss. Jul93 on 'Centredate-London' cd/c; 520 014-2/-4) (cd re-iss. Sep99 on 'Factory Too'; 3984 28224-2)*

Sep 90. (cd/c) *Strange Fruit; (SFR CD/MC 111)* **COMPLETE PEEL SESSIONS** [ ] [–]

Jun 95. (c-s) *London; (YOJC 1)* **LOVE WILL TEAR US APART (radio version) / ('A'-original version)** [19] [ ]
(12"+=/cd-s+=) *(YOJ T/CD 1)* – These days / Transmission.

Jun 95. (cd/c/d-lp) *London; (828 624-2/-4/-1) / Warners; <45979>*
PERMANENT: JOY DIVISION 1995 (remixes) [16] Aug95 [ ]
– Love will tear us apart / Transmission / She's lost control / Shadow play / Day of the lords / Isolation / Passover / Heart and soul / 24 hours / These days / Novelty / Dead souls / The only mistake / Something must break / Atmosphere / Love will tear us apart (Permanent mix). *(cd re-iss. Sep99; 3984 28221-2)*

Jan 98. (4xcd-box) *London; (<828 968-2>)* **HEART AND SOUL** (all material) [70] [ ]
(re-iss. Sep99; 3984 29040-2)

Feb 98. (cd+book) *Sonic Book; (SB 10)* **ALL THE LYRICS** [ ] [–]

Jul 00. (cd) *Fractured; (FACD 260)* **PRESTON – THE WAREHOUSE 28/2/80 (live)** [ ] [ ]
(lp-iss.Oct00 on 'Get Back'; GET 69)

Aug 00. (cd) *Strange Fruit; (SFRSCD 094)* **THE COMPLETE RADIO ONE RECORDINGS** [ ] [ ]
(lp-iss.Apr01; SFRSCD 084)

Apr 01. (cd) *Fractured; (FACD 261)* **LES BAINS DOUCHES** [ ] [–]
(d-lp-iss.Jun01 on 'Get Back'; GET 79)

JUDAS PRIEST

Formed: Birmingham, England . . . 1969 by KK DOWNING and IAN HILL. In 1971, they completed the line-up with vocalist AL ATKINS – who named the band after a BOB DYLAN track, 'The Ballad Of Frankie Lee And Judas Priest' – and drummer JOHN ELLIS; the latter was replaced by ALAN MOORE then CHRIS CAMPBELL. In 1973, both CAMPBELL and ATKINS bailed out (the latter went solo in the 90's releasing 'Victim Of Changes') as the 'PRIEST recruited singer ROB HALFORD and drummer JOHN HINCH. Three years later, with a few hundred gigs behind them, they brought in second guitarist GLENN TIPTON. Signed to 'Decca' off-shoot label 'Gull', they unleashed a debut album, 'ROCKA ROLLA', the same year. The record made little impact and after replacing HINCH with the returning ALAN MOORE, the band surfaced again in '76 with the excellent 'SAD WINGS OF DESTINY'. Following a resoundingly triumphant appearance at that year's Reading Festival, they signed to 'C.B.S.' in early '77. They soon had a UK Top 30 album with the ROGER GLOVER (Deep Purple)-produced 'SIN AFTER SIN', another metal masterpiece which included an unlikely, but effective cover of Joan Baez's 'DIAMONDS AND RUST'. While the leather clad JUDAS PRIEST weren't exactly original in their steadfast adherence to the leaden riffing and helium overdose of heavy metal, they helped to shape the genre's increasing preoccupation with all things grim 'n' nasty. 'STAINED CLASS' (1978), another Top 30 UK album, proferred such lyrical delights as 'SAINTS IN HELL', 'SAVAGE' and 'BEYOND THE REALMS OF DEATH', plus a cover of SPOOKY TOOTH's 'BETTER BY YOU, BETTER THAN ME', the record later having serious repercussions for the band (see below). Coming at the height of the NWOBHM explosion, 'BRITISH STEEL' (1980) was the band's biggest critical and commercial success to date, the Top 20 success of the 'LIVING AFTER MIDNIGHT' and 'BREAKING THE LAW' singles showing the more accessible, hook-driven face of the band. This was to be one of the most fertile periods of the 'PRIEST's career with a trio of consistent Top 20 albums; 'POINT OF ENTRY' (1981), 'SCREAMING FOR VENGEANCE' (1982) and 'DEFENDERS OF THE FAITH' (1984) were all testosterone-saturated howlers, the kind of British metal that just doesn't exist anymore. The latter housed the PMRC-baiting 'EAT ME ALIVE', securing the band's position as perceived deviant enemy of the nation's lank-haired youth alongside the equally wholesome W.A.S.P. Late in 1985, two of their fans shot themselves while listening to a track off the 'STAINED CLASS' album, prompting the boys' parents to sue both JUDAS PRIEST and their label, 'Columbia'. They alleged the record contained subliminal satanic messages hidden in the lyrics, thus forcing the boys to commit suicide. This fiasco finally got to court in July '90, the judge ruling against the dead boys' parents, although he did fine the label a 5-figure sum for withholding the master tapes!!? Despite the controversy, fans were less enamoured with 'TURBO' (1986), PRIEST's attempts at guitar synthesized innovation cutting no ice with the band's metal diehards. 'RAM IT DOWN' (1988) was a return to harder fare while the band underwent a critical rebirth of sorts with the thrash-y 'PAINKILLER' (1990), their status acknowledged as grandaddies of heavy metal and a glaring influence on the likes of METALLICA and SLAYER. ROB HALFORD subsequently left the band after forming side-project, FIGHT, his new outfit turning into a full-time affair after releasing a debut album. 'PRIEST returned in 1997 with a new frontman, the cornily-monikered TIM "RIPPER" OWENS lending his eardrum rupturing shriek over the tuneless assault of the poorly-received comeback set, 'JUGULATOR'. OWENS' tenure in the pulpit was short-lived, 'LIVE IN LONDON' (2003) proving to be the frontman's swansong. The inimitable ROB HALFORD – who'd finally "come out" in '98 – was back at his screaming best on 'ANGEL OF RETRIBUTION' (2005), a US Top 20 entry mystifyingly touted as the completion of a concept begun with 'SAD WINGS..'. Quite where Nessie fitted into all this is anyone's guess, but ROB and the lads were the first rockers to sing about the 'LOCH NESS' Monster since Scots icon ALEX HARVEY.

• **Songwriters:** TIPTON, HALFORD & DOWNING on most, except extra covers; THE GREEN MANALISHI (Fleetwood Mac) / JOHNNY B. GOODE (Chuck Berry).

Album rating: ROCKA ROLLA (*2) / SAD WINGS OF DESTINY (*8) / SIN AFTER SIN (*7) / STAINED CLASS (*6; recommended only to those without access to a gun, a bazooka, a tank or any tactical nuclear weapon) / KILLING MACHINE (*6) / UNLEASHED IN THE EAST (*7) / BRITISH STEEL (*8) / POINT OF ENTRY (*4) / SCREAMING FOR VENGEANCE (*8) / DEFENDERS OF THE FAITH (*6) / TURBO (*5) / PRIEST . . . LIVE! (*6) / RAM IT DOWN (*6) / PAINKILLER (*8) / METAL WORKS compilation (*8) / JUGULATOR (*3) / MELTDOWN LIVE '98 (*4) / DEMOLITION (*4) / LIVE IN LONDON (*4) / ANGEL OF RETRIBUTION (*5)

ROB HALFORD (b.25 Aug'51, Walsall) – vocals; repl. ALAN ATKINS / **KK DOWNING** (b. KENNETH, 27 Oct'51, West Midlands) – guitars / **GLENN TIPTON** (b.25 Oct'48, West Midlands) – guitar, vocals (ex-FLYING HAT BAND) / **IAN HILL** (b.20 Jan'52, West Midlands) – bass / **JOHN HINCH** – drums; repl. CHRIS CAMPBELL who'd repl. ALAN MOORE who'd repl. JOHN ELLIS

Gull Janus

Aug 74. (7") *(GULS 6)* **ROCKA ROLLA. / NEVER SATISFIED** –

Sep 74. (lp) *(GULP 1005)* **ROCKA ROLLA** –
– One for the road / Rocka rolla / Winter / Deep freeze / Winter retreat / Cheater / Never satisfied / Run of the mill / Dying to meet you / Caviar and meths. *(re-iss. Sep77; same) <US-iss.Oct82 on 'Visa'; 7001> (re-iss. Nov85 on 'Fame' lp/c; FA41 3137-2/-4) (cd-iss. Nov87 on 'Line'; LICD 900101) (cd-iss. Mar93 on 'Repertoire'; RR 4305) (cd re-iss. Aug98 on 'Snapper'; SMMCD 562)*

— **ALAN MOORE** – drums (who had been 1971 member) returned to repl. HINCH

Mar 76. (7") *(GULS 31)* **THE RIPPER. / ISLAND OF DOMINATION** –

Apr 76. (lp) *(GULP 1015) <7019>* **SAD WINGS OF DESTINY**
– Prelude / Tyrant / Genocide / Epitaph / Island of domination / Victim of changes / The ripper / Epitaph / Dreamer deceiver. *(pic-lp.Sep77; PGULP 1015) (re-iss. 1984 on 'Line' white-lp; LILP 4.00112) (cd-iss. Nov87; LICD 9.00112) (re-iss. cd May95 on 'Repertoire';) (cd re-iss. Aug98 on 'Snapper'; SMMCD 562)*

— **SIMON PHILLIPS** – drums repl. MOORE

C.B.S. Columbia

Apr 77. (7") *(CBS 5222)* **DIAMONDS AND RUST. / DISSIDENT AGGRESSOR** –

Apr 77. (lp/c) *(CBS/40 82008) <34587>* **SIN AFTER SIN** 23
– Sinner / Diamonds and rust / Starbreaker / Last rose of summer / Let us prey / Call for the priest – Raw deal / Here come the tears / Dissident aggressor. *(re-iss. Mar81; CBS 32005) (re-iss. cd.Nov93 on 'Sony Collectors'; 983286-2) (cd re-iss. Feb97 on 'Epic'; 474684-2)*

— **LES BINKS** – drums repl. PHILLIPS

Jan 78. (7") *(CBS 6077)* **BETTER BY YOU, BETTER BY ME. / INVADER** –

Feb 78. (lp/c) *(CBS/40 82430) <35296>* **STAINED CLASS** 27
– Exciter / White heat, red hot / Better by you, better by me / Stained class / Invader / Saints in Hell / Savage / Beyond the realms of death / Heroes end. *(re-iss. Nov81; CBS 32075) (re-iss. May91 on 'Columbia' cd/c; CD/40 32075)*

Sep 78. (7") *(CBS 6719)* **EVENING STAR. / STARBREAKER** –

Nov 78. (red-lp/c) *(CBS/40 83135) <36179>* **KILLING MACHINE** <US-title 'HELL BENT FOR LEATHER'> 32
– Delivering the goods / Rock forever / Evening star / Hell bent for leather / Take on the world / Burnin' up / Killing machine / Running wild / Before the dawn / Evil fantasies. *(re-iss. red-lp.Sep82; CBS 32218)*

Oct 78. (7") *(CBS 6794)* **BEFORE THE DAWN. / ROCK FOREVER**

Jan 79. (7") *(CBS 6915)* **TAKE ON THE WORLD. / STARBREAKER (live)** 14
(12"+=) *(CBS12 6915)* – White heat red hot (live).

Apr 79. (7") *(CBS 7312)* **EVENING STAR. / BEYOND THE REALMS OF DEATH** 53
(12"clear+=) *(CBS12 7312)* – The green Manalishi.

May 78. (7") *<11000>* **ROCK FOREVER. / THE GREEN MANALISHI (WITH THE TWO-PRONGED CROWN)** –

Sep 79. (lp/c) *(CBS/40 83852) <36179>* **UNLEASHED IN THE EAST (live)** 10 70
– Exciter / Running wild / Sinner / The ripper / The green manalishi (with the two-pronged crown) / Diamonds and rust / Victim of changes / Genocide / Tyrant. *(free 7"w.a.)* **ROCK FOREVER / HELL BENT FOR LEATHER. / BEYOND THE REALMS OF DEATH** *(cd-iss. 1988; CD 83852) (re-iss. May94 on 'Columbia' cd/c; 468604-2/-4)*

Dec 79. (7") *<11135>* **DIAMONDS AND RUST (live). / STARBREAKER (live)** –

— **DAVE HOLLAND** – drums repl. BINKS

Mar 80. (7") *(CBS 8379)* **LIVING AFTER MIDNIGHT. / DELIVERING THE GOODS (live)** 12 –
(12"+=) *(CBS12 8379)* – Evil fantasies (live).

Apr 80. (lp/c) *(CBS/40 84160) <36443>* **BRITISH STEEL** 4 34
– Rapid fire / Metal gods / Breaking the law / Grinder / United / You don't have to be old to be wise / Living after midnight / The rage / Steeler. *(re-iss. Jan84 lp/c; CBS/40 32412) (cd-iss. 1988; CD 32412) (cd re-iss. Jun94 on 'Sony'; 982725-2)*

May 80. (7") *<11308>* **LIVING AFTER MIDNIGHT. / METAL GODS** –

May 80. (7") *(CBS 8644)* **BREAKING THE LAW. / METAL GODS** 12

Aug 80. (7") *(CBS 8897) <11396>* **UNITED. / GRINDER** 26

Feb 81. (7") *(CBS 9520)* **DON'T GO. / SOLAR ANGELS** 51 –

Feb 81. (lp/c) *(CBS/40 84834) <37052>* **POINT OF ENTRY** 14 39
– Heading out to the highway / Don't go / Hot rockin' / Turning circles / Desert plains / Solar angels / You say yes / All the way / Troubleshooter / On the run. *(cd-iss. Apr01 on 'Columbia'; 502132-2)*

Apr 81. (7") *(A 1153)* **HOT ROCKIN' / BREAKING THE LAW (live)** 60 –
(12") *(A12 1153)* – ('A'side) / Steeler / You don't have to be old to be wise.

Apr 81. (7") *<02083>* **HEADING OUT TO THE HIGHWAY. / ROCK FOREVER** –

Jul 82. (lp/c) *(CBS/40 85941) <38160>* **SCREAMING FOR VENGEANCE** 11 17
– The hellion / Electric eye / Riding on the wind / Bloodstone / (Take these) Chains / Pain and pleasure / Screaming for vengeance / You've got another thing comin' / Fever / Devil's child. *(re-iss. Feb86 lp/c; CBS/40 32712)*

Aug 82. (7"/7"pic-d) *(A/+11 2611)* **YOU'VE GOT ANOTHER THING COMIN'. / EXCITER (live)** 66 –

Oct 82. (7") *<03168>* **YOU'VE GOT ANOTHER THING COMIN'. / DIAMONDS AND RUST** – 67

Oct 82. (7") *(A 2822)* **(TAKE THESE) CHAINS. / JUDAS PRIEST AUDIO FILE**

Jan 84. (7") *(A 4054)* **FREEWHEEL BURNING. / BREAKING THE LAW** 42 –
(12"+=) *(TA 4054)* – You've got another thing comin'.

Jan 84. (lp/c) *(CBS/40 25713) <39219>* **DEFENDERS OF THE FAITH** 19 18
– Freewheel burning / Jawbreaker / Rock hard ride free / The sentinel / Love bites / Eat me alive / Some heads are gonna roll / Night comes down / Heavy duty / Defenders of the faith. *(cd-iss. Jul84; CD 25713)*

Feb 84. (7") *<04371>* **SOME HEADS ARE GONNA ROLL. / BREAKING THE LAW (live)** –

Mar 84. (7") *(A 4298)* **SOME HEADS ARE GONNA ROLL. / THE GREEN MANALISHI (WITH THE TWO-PRONGED CROWN)** –
(12"+=) *(TA 4298)* – Jawbreaker.

Apr 84. (7") *<04436>* **JAWBREAKER. / LOVE BITES** –

Apr 86. (lp/c/cd) *(CBS/40/CD 26641) <40158>* **TURBO** 33 17
– Turbo lover / Locked in / Private property / Parental guidance / Rock you all around the world / Out in the cold / Wild night, hot and crazy days / Hot for love / Reckless. *(re-iss. Feb89 lp/c/cd; 463365-1/-4/-2)*

Apr 86. (7") *(A 7048)* **TURBO LOVER. / HOT FOR LOVE** –

May 86. (7") *(A 7144)* **LOCKED IN. / RECKLESS** –
(ext.12"+=) *(QTA 7144)* – Desert plains (live) / Free wheel burning (live).

May 86. (7") *<05856>* **LOCKED IN. / HOT FOR LOVE** –

Aug 86. (7") *<06142>* **TURBO LOVER. / RESTLESS** –

Nov 86. (7") *<06281>* **PARENTAL GUIDANCE. / ROCK YOU AROUND THE WORLD** –

Jun 87. (d-lp/c/cd) *(450639-1/-4/-2) <40794>* **PRIEST . . . LIVE! (live)** 47 38
– Out in the cold / Heading out to the highway / Metal gods / Breaking the law / Love bites / Some heads are gonna roll / The sentinel / Private property / Rock you all around the world / Electric eye / Turbo lover / Free wheel burning / Parental guidance / Living after midnight / You've got another thing comin'. *(cd+=)* – Shout – Oh yeah!

Atlantic Columb

Apr 88. (7") *(A 9114) <89114>* **JOHNNY B. GOODE. / ROCK YOU ALL AROUND THE WORLD (live)** 64
(12"+=) *(AT 9114)* – Turbo lover (live).
(3"cd-s++=) *(A 9114CD)* – Living after midnight (live).

May 88. (lp/c/cd) *(461108-1/-4/-2)* **RAM IT DOWN** [24] [31]
– Ram it down / Heavy metal / Love zone / Come and get it / Hard as iron / Blood red skies / I'm a rocker / Johnny B. Goode / Love you to death / Monsters of rock.

— **SCOTT TRAVIS** – drums (ex-RACER-X) repl. HOLLAND

C.B.S. Columbia

Sep 90. (7"/c-s) *(656273-7/-4)* **PAINKILLER. / UNITED** [74] [ ]
(12"+=/cd-s+=) *(656273-6/-2)* – Better by you, better than me.

Sep 90. (cd/c/lp) *(467290-2/-4/-1)* *<46891>* **PAINKILLER** [24] [26]
– Painkiller / Hell patrol / All guns blazing / Leather rebel / Metal meltdown / Night crawler / Between the hammer and the anvil / A touch of evil / Battle hymn (instrumental) / One shot at glory.

Columbia Columbia

Mar 91. (7"/7"sha-pic-d/c-s) *(656589-7/-0/-4)* **A TOUCH OF EVIL. / BETWEEN THE HAMMER AND THE ANVIL** [58] [ ]
(12"+=/cd-s+=) *(656589-6/-2)* – You've got another thing comin' (live).

— In Oct'92, HALFORD left after already forming FIGHT in 1991, taking with him SCOTT TRAVIS.

Apr 93. (7"/c-s) *(659097-7/-4)* **NIGHT CRAWLER (Edit) / BREAKING THE LAW** [63] [ ]
(cd-s+=) *(659097-2)* – Living after midnight.

Apr 93. (d-cd/d-c/t-lp) *(473050-2/-4/-1)* *<53932>* **METAL WORKS '73-'93** (compilation) [37] [ ]
– The hellion / Electric eye / Victim of changes / Painkiller / Eat me alive / Devil's child / Dissident aggressor / Delivering the goods / Exciter / Breaking the law / Hell bent for leather / Blood red skies / Metal gods / Before the dawn / Turbo lover / Ram it down / Metal meltdown/ / Screaming for vengeance / You've got another thing comin' / Beyond the realms of death / Solar angels / Bloodstone / Desert plains / Wild nights, hot & crazy days / Heading out to the highway / Living after midnight / A touch of evil / The rage / Night comes down / Sinner / Freewheel burning / Night crawler.

— **TIM "RIPPER" OWENS** – vocals; completed the line-up

S.P.V. C.M.C.

Nov 97. (cd/c/lp) *(SPV 085 1878-2/-4/-1)* *<86224>* **JUGULATOR** [ ] [82]
– Jugulator / Blood stained / Dead meat / Death row / Decapitate / Burn in hell / Brain dead / Abductors / Bullet train / Cathedral spires.

Oct 98. (d-cd) *(SPV 0891954-2)* *<86261>* **MELTDOWN (live '98)** [ ] [ ]
– The hellion / Electric eye / Metal gods / Grinder / Rapid fire / Blood stained / The sentinnel / Touch of evil / Burn in hell / The ripper / Bullet train / Beyond the realms of death / Death row / Metal meltdown / Night crawler / Abductors / Victim of changes / Diamonds and rust / Breaking the law / The green manalishi (with the two-pronged crown) / Painkiller / You've got another thing comin' / Hell bent for leather / Living after midnight.

S.P.V. Atlantic

Jun 01. (cd-s) *(SPV 056-7245-2)* **MACHINE MAN / SUBTERFUGE / BURN IN HELL (video)** [ ] [-]

Jul 01. (cd/lp) *(SPV 085-7242-2/-1)* *<83480>* **DEMOLITION** [ ] [ ]
– Machine man / One on one / Hell is home / Jekyll and Hyde / Close to you / Devil digger / Bloodsuckers / In between / Feed on me / Subterfuge / Lost and found / Cyberface / Mental messiah.

S.P.V. S.P.V.

Jan 03. (d-cd) *(<SPV 092-7426-2>)* **LIVE IN LONDON** (live) [ ] Apr03 [ ]
– Metal gods / Heading out to the highway / Grinder / Touch of evil / Blood stained / Victim of changes / The sentinel / One on one / Running wild / The ripper / Diamonds & rust / Feed on me / The green manalishi (with the two-pronged crown) / Beyond the realms of death / Burn in Hell / Hell is home / Breaking the law / Desert plains / You've got another thing comin' / Turbo lover / Painkiller / Hellion – Electric eye / United / Living after midnight / Hell bent for leather.

— **ROB HALFORD** – vocals; returned to repl. OWENS

Sony Epic

Feb 05. (cd) *(519300-2)* *<92933>* **ANGEL OF RETRIBUTION** [39] Mar05 [13]
– Judas rising / Deal with the Devil / Revolution / Worth fighting for / Demonizer / Wheels of fire / Angel / Hellrider / Eulogy / Loch Ness. *(ltd-cd w/dvd+=; 519300-3)* – (live documentary from 'Reunited' Tour 2004).

– compilations, etc. –

Feb 78. (pic-lp/lp) *Gull; (P+/GULP 1026)* **THE BEST OF JUDAS PRIEST** (early work) [ ] [-]
(cd-iss. May87 +=; GUCD 1026) – (2 extra tracks).

Aug 80. (7") *Gull; (GULS 71)* **THE RIPPER. / VICTIMS OF CHANGE** [ ] [-]
(12"+=) *(GUL 71-12)* – Never satisfied.

Jun 83. (12"white) *Gull; (GULS 76-12)* **TYRANT. / ROCKA ROLLA / GENOCIDE** [ ] [-]

Jan 83. (c-ep) *C.B.S.; (A40 3067)* **CASSETTE EP** [ ] [-]
– Breaking the law / Living after midnight / Take on the world / United.

Aug 83. (d-c) *C.B.S.; (22161)* **SIN AFTER SIN / STAINED GLASS** [ ] [-]

Sep 83. (7"ep/c-ep) *(7SR/ 5018)* **6 TRACK HITS** [ ] [-]
– Sinner / Exciter / Hell bent for leather / The ripper / Hot rockin' / The green manalishi.

Aug 86. (pic-lp) *Shanghai; (PGLP 1026)* **JUDAS PRIEST** [ ] [-]

Nov 87. (cd) *Line; (LICD 900414)* **HERO HERO** [-] German [-]
(re-iss. 1988 on 'Gull' c/lp; ZC+/GUD 2005-6) (cd re-iss. Jul95 on 'Connoisseur'; CSAPCD 119)

Feb 89. (7") *Old Gold; (OG 9864)* **LIVING AFTER MIDNIGHT. / BREAKING THE LAW** [ ] [-]

May 89. (lp/c/cd) *Castle; (CCS LP/MC/CD 213)* **THE COLLECTION** [ ] [-]
– (first two albums)

Mar 93. (3xcd-box) *Columbia; (468328-2)* **BRITISH STEEL / SCREAMING FOR VENGEANCE / STAINED GLASS** [ ] [-]

Apr 97. (cd) *Columbia; (487242-2)* **LIVING AFTER MIDNIGHT** [ ] [-]

Jun 98. (cd) *Ranch Life; (CRANCH 3)* **CONCERT CLASSICS (live)** [ ] [-]

Nov 98. (3xcd-box) *Columbia; (492657-2)* **BRITISH STEEL / POINT OF ENTRY / SCREAMING FOR VENGEANCE** [ ] [-]

Jan 99. (cd) *Columbia; (493008-2) / Sony; <7713>* **LIVE AND RARE** [ ] Sep99 [ ]

Jul 99. (cd) *Eureka; (EURCD 401)* **TYRANT (THE ORIGINAL MASTERS)** [ ] [-]

Feb 00. (d-cd) *Snapper; (<SMDCD 273>)* **GENOCIDE** [ ] [ ]

Feb 01. (cd) *Koch; <8071>* **THE BEST OF JUDAS PRIEST** [-] [ ]

KAISER CHIEFS

Formed: Leeds, England . . . 2003 out of (RUNSTON) PARVA by RICKY WILSON, ANDREW WHITE, NICK BAINES, SIMON RIX and NICK HODGSON; named after a South African football team. A pulverising punk mantra, debut single 'OH MY GOD', sold out of its initial pressing (on 'Drowned In Sound') in a matter of days, scraping enough sales for a minor chart placing. The Yorkshire tribe were subsequently headhunted by the major labels, eventually opting for Universal subsidiary, 'B-Unique'. A post-millennium tale of the natives getting restless, 'I PREDICT A RIOT', was a festival anthem in the making, hyperkinetically marshalled by big Chief RICKY. The song initially went Top 30, re-energising a Top 10 'OH MY GOD' immediately prior to their hotly anticipated, Stephen Street-produced debut album, 'EMPLOYMENT' (2005). Although the record entered the UK chart at No.3, the band's ever-growing legions of subjects as well as further hits, 'EVERYDAY I LOVE YOU LESS AND LESS', 'I PREDICT A RIOT' (again!) and 'MODERN WAY', ensured its deserved place on top of the charts. Their infectious amphetamine-fuelled amalgam of good-time Brit-pop/rock/mod, together with kitchen-sink lyrics and WILSON's defiantly Northern phrasing was enough to see them clean up at the Brit awards, although they just missed out on a Mercury Music Prize 2006.

Album rating: EMPLOYMENT (*9)

RICKY WILSON (b. CHARLES RICHARD WILSON, 19 Jan'78, Keighley, West Yorkshire) – vocals, tambourine / **ANDREW 'Whitey' WHITE** – guitar / **NICK 'Peanut' BAINES** – keyboards / **SIMON RIX** (b. JAMES SIMON RIX, 1977) – bass / **NICK HODGSON** – drums, vocals

Drowned In Sound — not iss.

May 04. (cd-s) *(DIS 03)* **OH MY GOD / BORN TO BE A DANCER / CAROLINE, YES** — 66 — –

B-Unique — Universal

Nov 04. (7"m/cd-s) *(BUN 088 7/CD)* **I PREDICT A RIOT. / WRECKING BALL / TAKE MY TEMPERATURE** — 22 — –

Feb 05. (cd-s) *(BUN 092CD)* **OH MY GOD / THINK ABOUT YOU (AND I LIKE IT)** — 6 — –
(cd-s) *(BUN 092CDX)* – ('A') / Hard times send me / Born to be a dancer (demo).
(7"ep++=) *(BUN 0927)* – Brightest star.

Mar 05. (cd/d-lp) *(BUN 093 CD/DLP)* *<42150-2>* **EMPLOYMENT** — 1 — 86
– Everyday I love you less and less / I predict a riot / Modern way / Na na na na naa / You can have it all / Oh my god / Born to be a dancer / Saturday night / What did I ever give you? / Time honoured tradition / Caroline, yes! / Team mate. *(d-cd-iss. May05 +=; BUN 093CDX)* – Hard times send me / Modern way / I predict a riot / Time honoured tradition / Na na na na naa / Oh my god.

May 05. (cd-s) *(BUN 094CD)* **EVERYDAY I LOVE YOU LESS AND LESS / ANOTHER NUMBER** — 10 — –
(cd-s) *(BUN 094CDX)* – ('A'-Spike Stent mix) / Seventeen cups / Not surprised / ('A'-video).
(7"ep++=) *(BUN 0947)* – Letter song.

Aug 05. (cd-s) *(BUN 096CD)* **I PREDICT A RIOT / SINK THAT SHIP** — 9 — –
(cd-s/7"ep+=) *(BUN 096 CDX/7)* – ('A') / Less is more / Everyday I love you less and less (Boys Noize mix) / ('A'-video; new version).

Nov 05. (cd-s) *(BUN 100CD)* **MODERN WAY / PEOPLE NEED LIGHT** — 11 — Dec05 —
(cd-s) *(BUN 100CDX)* *<987517>* – ('A') / Moon / It ain't easy (demo) / ('A'-video).
(7"ep++=) *(BUN 1007)* – ('A'-version) / Run again.

☐ Paul KANTNER & Grace SLICK (see under ⇒ JEFFERSON AIRPLANE)

☐ KARA'S FLOWERS (see under ⇒ MAROON 5)

KASABIAN

Formed: Leicester, England ... 1999 by school friends TOM MEIGHAN, SERGE PIZZORNO, CHRIS KARLOFF and CHRISTOPHER EDWARDS. Steeping themselves in darkside rock'n'roll iconography from the start, the band named themselves after Manson "family" member, Linda Kasabian, going on to forge their swaggering sound in the time-honoured fashion (a la the BAND and CAPTAIN BEEFHEART/MAGIC BAND, etc.) of communal seclusion. The quartet finally came out of their shell in 2003/04 with a couple of collectable one-sided 10" singles, 'PROCESSED BEATS' and 'REASON IS TREASON', yet it was the jackhammer groove of third single, 'CLUB FOOT', that really booted the New Wave-influenced competition into touch: this was exactly the kind of post-modern ZEPPELIN-esque behemoth that JOHN SQUIRE never wrote. Follow-up Top 10 single, 'L.S.F. [LOST SOULS FOREVER]', showcased the kind of baggy beat and aggro-slurring vocals that suggested KASABIAN – for all their classic rock action – were a 90s band adrift in the 00s, the real "second coming". 'KASABIAN' the album (2004) was certainly received as such, with critics falling over themselves to hail the belated heirs to PRIMAL SCREAM/OASIS/STONE ROSES. To their growing catalogue of anthemic narco-classics they added 'CUTT OFF', along with subsequent re-issues of 'PROCESSED BEATS' and 'CLUB FOOT', massive chart hits all.

• **Covered:** HEROES (David Bowie).

Album rating: KASABIAN (*8)

TOM MEIGHAN – vocals / **SERGE PIZZORNO** – guitar, synths, vocals / **CHRIS KARLOFF** – lead guitar, bass, synths, omni chord / **CHRISTOPHER EDWARDS** – bass

B.M.G. — not iss.

2003. (10";1-sided) *(82876 569172)* **PROCESSED BEATS** — — –

R.C.A. — R.C.A.

Feb 04. (10";1-sided) *(PARADISE 04)* **REASON IS TREASON** — — –

May 04. (10") *(PARADISE 09)* **CLUB FOOT / CLUB FOOT (Jagz Kooner vocal mix) / (Paradise mix)** — 19 — –
(cd-s+=) *(PARADISE 08)* – Trash can / Sand clit (video).

Aug 04. (cd-s) *(PARADISE 13)* **L.S.F. [LOST SOULS FOREVER] / (Jagz Kooner mix edit)** — 10 — –
(cd-s+=) *(PARADISE 14)* – Lab twat / Pier song / ('A'-video).

(10"ep+=) *(PARADISE 15)* – ('A') / Club foot / ('A'-versions) / Lab twat / Pier song.

Sep 04. (cd/c/d10"lp) *(PARADISE 16/17/18)* <664317-2> **KASABIAN** [4] Nov04 [94]
– Club foot / Processed beats / Reason is treason / I.D. / (orange) / L.S.F. [Lost Souls Forever] / Running battle / Test transmission / (pinch roller) / Cutt off / Butcher blues / Ovary stripe / U boat.

Oct 04. (cd-s) *(PARADISE 20)* **PROCESSED BEATS / THE NIGHTWORKER'S** [17] [–]
(cd-s+=) *(PARADISE 21)* – L.S.F. [Lost Souls Forever] (live) / ('A'-Afrika Bambaataa remix) / ('A'-video).
(10") *(PARADISE 22)* – ('A') / Ovary stripe (remix) / ('A'-Afrika Bambaataa remix).

Dec 04. (cd-s) *(PARADISE 25)* **CUTT OFF / BENEFICIAL HERBS (demo)** [8] [–]
(10"+=) *(82876 67151-1)* – Pan Am slit scan / ('A'-versions) / Processed beats / Out of space.

Mar 05. (cd-s) *(82876 68247-2)* **CLUB FOOT / 55 (live)** [21] [–]
(10"+=) *(82876 68247-1)* – (below tracks).
(cd-s) *(82876 68248-2)* – ('A') / The duke / Bang / ('A'-Jimmy Douglass remix) / ('A'-video) / ('A'-live video).

KEANE

Formed: Battle, East Sussex, England ... 1997 by TIM RICE-OXLEY, DOMINIC SCOTT, TOM CHAPLIN and RICHARD HUGHES. With CHAPLIN studying at Edinburgh Uni, what began as a covers outfit only coalesced into a serious songwriting unit at the turn of the decade. Serving as pianist RICE-OXLEY's "write"-hand man until his departure in 2001, SCOTT picked up credits on a couple of self-distributed singles, 'CALL ME WHAT YOU LIKE' and 'WOLF AT THE DOOR'. Minus the man's guitar, KEANE's sound wasn't so dissimilar to COLDPLAY, drawing the attention of scribe turned 'Fierce Panda' boss Simon Williams, who'd already helped launched CHRIS MARTIN and Co's career. Williams of course wasn't wrong, as the chiming, post-millennial melancholia of 'EVERYBODY'S CHANGING' and 'THIS IS THE LAST TIME' had the major labels mad-KEANE on their signature. By early 2004, 'Island' had secured their services and begun conquering the UK Top 10 with the very COLDPLAY-esque, celestial prophecy of 'SOMEWHERE ONLY WE KNOW'. Looking and sounding like the kind of guy who'd find it hard to get served in a pub, the cherub-faced CHAPLIN was central to KEANE's appeal, with a voice pitched mournfully somewhere between MARTIN, THOM YORKE and MORTEN HARKET (of a-ha fame). The inevitable re-issue of 'EVERYBODY'S CHANGING' laid out the red carpet for chart-topping debut set, 'HOPES AND FEARS' (2004), the kind of music for depressed choirboys that so well defined the contemporary music scene. Subsequent singles, 'BEDSHAPED' and a re-vamped 'THIS IS THE LAST TIME' only underlined the songwriting strength which saw the trio pick up an Ivor Novello award the following year. Gloomier and more electro-fied than its predecessor, sophomore set, 'UNDER THE IRON SEA' (2006) – and its UK Top 3 lead single 'IS IT ANY WONDER?' – consolidated KEANE's position as heirs to the COLDPLAY throne.

• **Covers:** GOODBYE YELLOW BRICK ROAD (Elton John) / THE SUN AIN'T GONNA SHINE ANYMORE (Walker Brothers).

Album rating: HOPES AND FEARS (*8) / UNDER THE IRON SEA (*6)

TOM CHAPLIN (b. 8 Mar'79) – vocals / **TIM RICE-OXLEY** (b. 2 Jun'76) – piano, bass, keyboards / **RICHARD HUGHES** (b. 8 Sep'75, Gravesend, Kent, England) – drums / **DOMINIC SCOTT** – guitar, keyboards

Zoomorphic | not iss.

Feb 00. (ltd;cd-s) *(none)* **CALL ME WHAT YOU LIKE / RUBBERNECKING / CLOSER NOW** [ ] [–]

Jun 01. (ltd;cd-s) *(ZOO/2/01)* **WOLF AT THE DOOR / CALL ME WHAT YOU LIKE / SHE HAS NO TIME** [ ] [–]

— now without DOMINIC

Fierce Panda | not iss.

May 03. (cd-s) *(NING 133CD)* **EVERYBODY'S CHANGING / BEDSHAPED / THE WAY YOU WANT IT** [ ] [–]

Oct 03. (cd-s) *(NING 147CD)* **THIS IS THE LAST TIME / CAN'T STOP NOW / ALLEMANDE** [ ] [–]

Island | Universal

Feb 04. (7") *(IS 849)* **SOMEWHERE ONLY WE KNOW. / SNOWED UNDER** [3] [50]
(cd-s+=) *(CID 849)* <9816418> – Walnut tree / ('A'-video).

May 04. (7") *(IS 855)* **EVERYBODY'S CHANGING. / FLY TO ME** [4] [–]
(cd-s+=) *(CID 855)* – To the end of the earth / ('A'-video).

May 04. (cd/c/lp) *(CIS 8145)* <9866685> **HOPES AND FEARS** [1] [45]
– Somewhere only we know / Bend and break / We might as well be strangers / Everybody's changing / Your eyes open / She has no time / Can't stop now / Sunshine / This is the last time / On a day like today / Untitled 1 / Bedshaped.

Aug 04. (7") *(IS 870)* **BEDSHAPED. / SOMETHING IN ME WAS DYING** [10] Oct04 [ ]
(cd-s+=) *(CID 870)* <9867669> – Untitled 2 / ('A'-video).

Nov 04. (7") *(IS 880)* **THIS IS THE LAST TIME. / SHE OPENS HER EYES** [18] [–]
(cd-s+=) *(CID 880)* – ('A'-demo) / ('A'-video).

May 06. (7") *(IS 934)* **IS IT ANY WONDER? / LET IT SLIDE** [3] [–]
(cd-s) *(CID 934)* – ('A') / He used to be a lovely boy.

Jun 06. (cd/lp) *(CID/ILPS 8167)* <6855-02> **UNDER THE IRON SEA** [1] [4]
– Atlantic / Is it any wonder? / Nothing in my way / Leaving so soon / A bad dream / Hamburg song / Put it behind you / The iron sea / Crystal ball / Try again / Broken toy / The frog prince. *(ltd-cd w/dvd+=; CIDX 8167)* – (DVD tracks).

□ KILBURN & THE HIGH ROADS (see under ⇒ DURY, Ian)

the KILLERS

Formed: Las Vegas, Nevada, USA ... 2002 by ex-BLUSH RESPONSE singer BRANDON FLOWERS, alongside DAVID KEUNING plus anonymous bassist and drummer; MARK STOERMER and RONNIE VANNUCCI would be drafted in after a few gigs. The following year, the KILLERS released their first single for 'Lizard King', voyeurism meditation 'MR BRIGHTSIDE'. From the band's impressive digestion of various 80s gloom/glamour merchants and 'Born Slippy'-style megaphone vocals, you'd never guess they hailed from the neon lights of Nevada (Vegas!). Arguably the most engagingly sleazy and seductive proponents of Yankee New Romanticism, the KILLERS floored the UK Top 20 with gender-bending single 'SOMEBODY TOLD ME'. A re-released 'MR BRIGHTSIDE' cornered the same market, its setting off a chain reaction which propelled their debut album, 'HOT FUSS' (2004), into both the UK and US Top 10. Even DURAN DURAN themselves (inspired to recreate their classic sound on their 'Astronaut' set) couldn't nail that heady 'Rio' echo as well as FLOWERS and Co. Unlike the fairly clean-cut "Wild Boys", the KILLERS courted controversy on a regular basis, trading insults with US rivals the BRAVERY, and causing offence as far afield as Lothian, Scotland where a high profile murder case was allegedly the subject matter for one of FLOWERS' lyrics.

Album rating: HOT FUSS (*7)

BRANDON FLOWERS (b.21 Jun'81, Henderson, Nevada) – vocals, keyboards (ex-BLUSH RESPONSE) / **DAVID KEUNING** (b. Pella, Iowa) – guitar / **MARK AUGUST STOERMER** – bass / **RONNIE VANNUCCI JR.** (b.15 Feb'76) – drums, vocals (ex-ROMANCE FANTASY)

Lizard King | Island

Sep 03. (ltd;7"white) *(LIZARD 007X)* **MR BRIGHTSIDE. / SMILE LIKE YOU MEAN IT** [ ] [–]
(ltd-cd-s+=) *(LIZARD 007)* – On top / Who let you go.

Mar 04. (ltd;7"pink) *(LIZARD 009X)* **SOMEBODY TOLD ME. / THE BALLAD OF MICHAEL VALENTINE** [20] [–]
(ltd-cd-s+=) *(LIZARD 009)* – Under the gun.

May 04. (ltd;7"red) *(LIZARD 010CDX)* **MR BRIGHTSIDE. / SMILE LIKE YOU MEAN IT** 10 –
(cd-s) *(LIZARD 010CD1)* – ('A') / Change your mind.
(cd-s) *(LIZARD 010CD2)* – ('A') / Somebody told me (Insider remix) / Midnight show (SBN live session) / ('A'-video).

Jun 04. (cd/lp) *(LIZARD 011 CD/LP)* *<246802>* **HOT FUSS** 6 7
– Jenny was a friend of mine / Mr Brightside / Smile like you mean it / Somebody told me / All these things that I've done / Andy, you're a star / On top / Change your mind / Believe me Natalie / Midnight show / Everything will be alright. *<cd re-iss. Aug05 +=; 524102>* – Glamorous indie rock & roll / The ballad of Michael Valentine / Under the gun.

Aug 04. (12") *<B000 3253-11>* **SOMEBODY TOLD ME (mixes; Josh Harris x 2 + King Unique x2)** – 51
(cd-s) *<9863514>* – (see UK original).

Aug 04. (ltd;7"yellow) *(LIZARD 012X)* **ALL THESE THINGS THAT I'VE DONE. / ANDY, YOU'RE A STAR** 18 Nov04 74
(cd-s) *(LIZARD 012)* *<9883644>* – ('A') / Why don't you find out for yourself (Radio 1 session) / ('A'-radio) / ('A'-video).

Jan 05. (12") *(LIZARD 014X)* **SOMEBODY TOLD ME (Mylo mix). / SOMEBODY TOLD ME (the Glimmers GypoRock mix)** 3 –

Feb 05. (12") *<B000 4170-11>* **MR BRIGHTSIDE (mixes; Jacques Lu Cont x 2 + the Lindbergh Palace x3)** – 10
(cd-s) *<9880418/9>* – (see UK originals)

May 05. (ltd;7"cherry) *(LIZARD 015X)* **SMILE LIKE YOU MEAN IT. / RUBY, DON'T TAKE YOUR LOVE TO TOWN (session)** 11 –
(cd-s) *(LIZARD 015)* – ('A') / Get trashed.
(12") *(LIZARD 015Y)* – ('A') / Mr Brightside (Thin White Duke remix).

KILLING JOKE

Formed: Notting Hill, London, England ... 1979 by JAZ COLEMAN and PAUL FERGUSON, who subsequently added GEORDIE (K. WALKER) and YOUTH (MARTIN GLOVER). After borrowing money to finance a debut EP (contained three tracks including 'TURN TO RED'), the band were the subject of some interest to DJ John Peel who championed their alternative rock sound. This immediately led to KILLING JOKE signing a deal with 'Island', who virtually re-issued the aforementioned single/EP in abbreviated 7" form (A-side, 'NERVOUS SYSTEM'), adding a fourth track on the 12". While supporting the likes of JOY DIVISION and The RUTS, they released a follow-up double A-sided single, 'WARDANCE' / 'PSYCHE', resurrecting their own 'Malicious Damage' label in the process. The left-field 'E.G.' operation were quick to spot the group's potential, taking on both KILLING JOKE and their label. The first results of this partnership came in the form of 'REQUIEM', the single taken from their pioneering eponymous UK Top 40 album. Replacing the anger of punk with apocalyptic doom mongering, KILLING JOKE were akin to a sonically disturbing, industrialised BLACK SABBATH. Now regarded as a catalystic classic in metal circles, the album also inspired many US hardcore acts, as well as such big guns as METALLICA, MINISTRY, SOUNDGARDEN and NIRVANA. By the release of follow-up set, 'WHAT'S THIS FOR' (1981), KILLING JOKE had taken their occult punk-like chants/anthems to extreme new dimensions. Nevertheless, they retained a strange accessibility which saw the single, 'FOLLOW THE LEADERS' attaining a minor UK chart placing and incredibly, a hit on the American dancefloors! A third set, 'REVELATIONS' (1982), eased up a little on the intensity factor, although it peaked at No.12 having already spawned another hit single, 'EMPIRE SONG'. Convinced of imminent world destruction, the occult-fixated COLEMAN remained in Iceland after a tour, YOUTH initially returning home but later following his lead to the frozen north. He subsequently flew back to England, teaming up with FERGUSON and newfound friend, PAUL RAVEN to form BRILLIANT. However, both FERGUSON and RAVEN soon departed from YOUTH's group, taking off for Iceland in search of the missing COLEMAN. Eventually locating their frontman, all three returned to UK shores and re-entered the studio (GEORDIE also in tow) with a view to recording new KILLING JOKE material. The resulting album, 'FIRE DANCES' (1983), only managed to scrape into the Top 30, its lack of bite and experimentation possibly a hangover from their northern treks. The following year, KILLING JOKE released only two 45's, although one of them, 'EIGHTIES' (a minor hit), was showcased in all its eccentric glory on Channel 4's new pop show, 'The Tube'. Having overcome the mental obstacle of 1984 (and all of its apocalyptic implications), COLEMAN and Co. unleashed their most focused work to date in 'NIGHT TIME' (a near Top 10 album), the 'LOVE LIKE BLOOD' single preceding the set and breaking into the Top 20 in early '85. The latter half of the eighties weren't so kind, both critically and commercially, the albums, 'BRIGHTER THAN A THOUSAND SUNS' (1986) and 'OUTSIDE THE GATE' (1988), taking a more self-indulgent keyboard-orientated approach. Following major personnel upheavals, KILLING JOKE decided to take a brief sabbatical, COLEMAN finding time to release a collaborative album with ANNE DUDLEY (ex-ART OF NOISE), 'SONGS FROM THE VICTORIOUS CITY' (1990). The same year, COLEMAN, GEORDIE, RAVEN and newcomer MARTIN ATKINS, returned with the acclaimed 'EXTREMITIES, DIRT AND VARIOUS REPRESSED EMOTIONS' album. Having spent most of the early 90's globetrotting in various exotic locations, KILLING JOKE (now COLEMAN, GEORDIE and the returning YOUTH), were back with a vengeance on 1994's 'PANDEMONIUM'. Their biggest selling album to date, the record and the 'PANDEMONIUM' single from it both made the Top 30 (the previous 'MILLENNIUM' made Top 40), while also seeing an American release on the 'Zoo' label. Another, increasingly metallic/industrial set, 'DEMOCRACY' followed in 1996, although COLEMAN now spends the bulk of his time in New Zealand, where he is composer in residence for the country's Symphony Orchestra. After almost a decade, COLEMAN, GEORDIE, YOUTH (and DAVE GROHL on drums!) were back with the eponymous 'KILLING JOKE' (2003). If the stark title harked back to their classic 1980 debut, the uncompromising likes of 'TOTAL INVASION' and 'ASTEROID' – sharpened by an Andy Gill production – indeed seemed to suggest they'd come full circle, updating the steamrolling sound which initially made their name. The celebratory 'XXV GATHERING!' – recorded January 2005 at London's Shepherd's Bush Empire – was better experienced on DVD than CD, although 2006's studio comeback, 'HOSANNAS FROM THE BASEMENTS OF HELL', was a kind of "back-to-basements" set recorded on vintage equipment for that unmistakeable, ungodly grind of yore.

Album rating: KILLING JOKE (*9) / WHAT'S THIS FOR ...! (*7) / REVELATIONS (*5) / HA! KILLING JOKE LIVE (*5) / FIRE DANCES (*7) / NIGHT TIME (*7) / BRIGHTER THAN A THOUSAND SUNS (*6) / OUTSIDE THE GATE (*6) / EXTREMITIES, DIRT AND VARIOUS REPRESSED EMOTIONS (*7) / LAUGH? I NEARLY BOUGHT ONE! compilation (*8) / PANDEMONIUM (*8) / DEMOCRACY (*6) / KILLING JOKE (*7) / XXV GATHERING! (*5) / HOSANNAS FROM THE BASEMENTS OF HELL (*7)

JAZ COLEMAN (b. JEREMY, 26 Feb'60, Cheltenham, England; raised Egypt) – vocals, keyboards / **GEORDIE** (b. KEVIN WALKER, 18 Dec'58, Newcastle-upon-Tyne, England) – guitar, synthesizers / **YOUTH** (b. MARTIN GLOVER, 27 Dec'60, Africa) – bass, vocals (ex-RAGE) / **PAUL FERGUSON** (b.31 Mar'58, High Wycombe, England) – drums

Malicious Damage — not iss.

Oct 79. (10"ep) *(MD 410)* **ARE YOU RECEIVING ME. / TURN TO RED / NERVOUS SYSTEM** –

Island — not iss

Nov 79. (7") *(WIP 6550)* **NERVOUS SYSTEM. / TURN TO RED** –
(12"+=) *(12WIP 6550)* – Almost red / Are you receiving me.

Malicious Damage — not iss.

Mar 80. (7") *(MD 540)* **WARDANCE. / PSYCHE** [ ] [–]

E.G. – Malicious Damage — Editions

Sep 80. (7") *(EGMD 1.00)* **REQUIEM. / CHANGE** [ ] [–]
(12"+=) *(EGMX 1.00)* – Requiem 434 / Change (version).

Oct 80. (lp/c) *(EGMD/+C 545)* **KILLING JOKE** [39] [–]
– Requiem / Wardance / Tomorrow's world / Bloodsport / The wait / Complications / S.O. 36 / Primitive. *(re-iss. Jan87 lp/c/cd; EG LP/MC/CD 57) <US cd-iss. 1987 on 'Caroline'; 1538>*

May 81. (7") *(EGMDS 1.01)* **FOLLOW THE LEADERS. / TENSION** [55] [–]
(10"+=) *(EGMDX 1.010)* – Follow the leaders – dub.

Jun 81. (lp/c) *(EGMD/+C 550) <111>* **WHAT'S THIS FOR . . .!** [42] [ ]
– The fall of Because / Tension / Unspeakable / Butcher / Follow the leaders / Madness / Who told you how? / Exit. *(re-iss. Jan87 lp/c/cd; EG LP/MC/CD 58) <US cd-iss. 1987 on 'Caroline'; 1539>*

E.G. — Caroline

Mar 82. (7") *(EGO 4)* **EMPIRE SONG. / BRILLIANT** [43] [–]

— **GUY PRATT** – bass; repl. YOUTH who formed BRILLIANT

Apr 82. (lp/c) *(EGMD/+C 3)* **REVELATIONS** [12] [–]
– The hum / Empire song / We have joy / Chop chop / The Pandys are coming / Chapter III / Have a nice day / Land of milk and honey / Good samaritan / Dregs. *(re-iss. Jan87 lp/c/cd; EG LP/MC/CD 59) <US cd-iss. 1987 on 'Caroline'; 1540>*

Jun 82. (7") *(EGO 7)* **CHOP CHOP. / GOOD SAMARITAN** [ ] [–]

Oct 82. (7") *(EGO 10)* **BIRDS OF A FEATHER. / FLOCK THE B-SIDE** [64] [–]
(12"+=) *(EGOX 10)* – Sun goes down.

Nov 82. (10"m-lp/m-c) *(EGMD T/C 4)* **HA – KILLING JOKE LIVE (live)** [66] [–]
– Psyche / Sun goes down / The Pandys are coming / Take take take / Unspeakable / Wardance.

— **PAUL RAVEN** – bass (ex-NEON HEARTS) repl. PRATT who joined ICEHOUSE

Jun 83. (7") *(EGO 11)* **LET'S ALL GO (TO THE FIRE DANCES). / DOMINATOR (version)** [51] [–]
(12"+=) *(EGOX 11)* – The fall of Because (live).

Jul 83. (lp/c) *(EGMD/+C 5)* **FIRE DANCES** [29] [–]
– The gathering / Fun and games / Rejuvenation / Frenzy / Harlequin / Feast of blaze / Song and dance / Dominator / Let's all go (to the fire dances) / Lust almighty. *(re-iss. Jan87 lp/c/cd; EG LP/MC/CD 60) <US cd-iss. 1987 on 'Caroline'; 1541>*

Oct 83. (7") *(EGOD 14)* **ME OR YOU?. / WILFUL DAYS** [57] [–]
(with free 7") *(KILL 1-2)* – ('A'side) / Feast of blaze.
(d12"++=) *(EGOXD 14)* – Let's all go (to the fire dances) / The fall of Because (live) / Dominator (version).

Mar 84. (7") *(EGO 16)* **EIGHTIES. / EIGHTIES (Coming mix)** [60] [–]
(12"+=) *(EGOX 16)* – ('A'-Serious dance mix).

Jun 84. (7") *(EGO 17)* **A NEW DAY. / DANCE DAY** [56] [–]
(12"+=) *(EGOX 17)* – ('A'dub).

Jan 85. (7") *(EGO 20)* **LOVE LIKE BLOOD. / BLUE FEATHER** [16] [–]
(12"+=) *(EGOY 20)* – ('A'-Gestalt mix).
(12"++=) *(EGOX 20)* – ('A'instrumental).

Feb 85. (lp/c) *(EGMD/+C 6) <1531>* **NIGHT TIME** [11] [ ]
– Night time / Darkness before dawn / Love like blood / Kings and queens / Tabazan / Multitudes / Europe / Eighties. *(re-iss. Jan87 lp/c/cd; EG LP/MC/CD 61)*

Mar 85. (7") *(EGO 21)* **KINGS AND QUEENS. / THE MADDING CROWD** [58] [–]
(12"+=) *(EGOX 21)* – ('A'-Right Royal mix).
(12"+=) *(EGOY 21)* – ('A'-Knave mix).

Aug 86. (7") *(EGO 27)* **ADORATIONS. / EXILE** [42] [–]
(d7"+=) *(EGOD 27)* – Ecstacy / ('A'instrumental).

E.G. — Virgin

Oct 86. (7") *(EGO 30)* **SANITY. / GOODBYE TO THE VILLAGE** [70] [–]
(free c-s with-7") *(above tracks)* – Wardance (remix).
(12"+=) *(EGOX 30)* – Victory.

Nov 86. (lp/c/cd) *(EG LP/MC/CD 66) <90568-1/-4/-2>* **BRIGHTER THAN A THOUSAND SUNS** [54] [ ]
– Adorations / Sanity / Chessboards / Twilight of the mortal / Love of the masses / A southern sky / Wintergardens / Rubicon. *(c+=/cd+=)* – Goodbye to the village / Victory.

E.G. — Caroline

Apr 88. (7") *(EGO 40)* **AMERICA. / JIHAD (Beyrouth edit)** [ ] [–]
(12"+=) *(EGOX 40)* – ('A'extended).
(cd-s++=) *(EGOCD 40)* – Change (original 1980 mix).

Jun 88. (lp/c/cd) *(EG LP/MC/CD 73) <1378>* **OUTSIDE THE GATE** [92] [ ]
– America / My love of this land / Stay one jump ahead / Unto the ends of the Earth / The calling / Obsession / Tiahuanaco / Outside the gate. *(cd+=)* – America (extended) / Stay one jump ahead (extended).

Jul 88. (7") *(EGO 43)* **MY LOVE OF THIS LAND. / DARKNESS BEFORE DAWN** [ ] [–]
(12"+=) *(EGOX 43)* – Follow the leaders (dub) / Psyche.
(10"+=) *(EGOT 43)* – Follow the leaders (dub) / Sun goes down.

— **JAZ + GEORDIE** brought in new members **MARTIN ATKINS** (b. 3 Aug'59, Coventry, England) – drums (ex-PUBLIC IMAGE LTD.) repl. FERGUSON / **TAFF** – bass repl. ANDY ROURKE (ex-SMITHS) who had repl. RAVEN. Early 1990, **JAZ COLEMAN** teamed up with ANNE DUDLEY (see; ART OF NOISE)

— **KILLING JOKE** reformed (**COLEMAN, GEORDIE, ATKINS + RAVEN**)

Noise Int. — R.C.A.

Nov 90. (cd/c/lp) *(AGR 054-2/-4/-1) <4828-2/-4>* **EXTREMITIES, DIRT AND VARIOUS REPRESSED EMOTIONS** [ ] [ ]
– Money is not our god / Age of greed / Beautiful dead / Extremities / Inside the termite mound / Intravenus / Solitude / North of the border / Slipstream / Kalijuga struggle. *(cd re-iss. Sep98 on 'F.A.D.'; FAD 5054)*

Jan 91. (12"/cd-s) *(AG 054-6/-3)* **MONEY IS NOT OUR GOD. / NORTH OF THE BORDER** [ ] [–]

Invisible — Invisible

Jul 93. (d-lp) *(<INV 004>)* **THE COURTHOLD TALKS** [ ] [ ]
– (spoken word with JAZ, GEORDIE & JEFF SCANTLEBURY on percussion)

— **YOUTH** returned to repl. RAVEN

— **GEOFF DUGMORE** – drums (ex-ART OF NOISE) repl. ATKINS (to PIGFACE, etc)

Butterfly — Volcano-Zoo

Mar 94. (10"ep/cd-ep) *(BFL T/D 11)* **EXORCISM. / ('A'live) / ('A'-German mix) / WHITEOUT (Ugly mix) / ANOTHER CULT GOES DOWN (mix) / ('A'-Bictonic revenge mix)** [ ] [–]

Apr 94. (7"clear/c-s) *(BFL/+C 12)* **MILLENNIUM. / ('A'-Cybersank remix)** [34] [–]
(12"+=/cd-s+=) *(BFL T/D 12)* – ('A'-Drum Club remix) / ('A'Juno Reactor remix).

Jul 94. (12"/c-s/cd-s) *(BFL T/C/D 17) <14178>* **PANDEMONIUM. / ('A'mix)** [28] Oct94 [ ]
(cd-s) *(BFLD 17)* – ('A'side) / Requiem (Kris Weston & Greg Hunter remix).

Jul 94. (cd/c/d-lp) *(BFL CD/MC/LP 9) <31085>* **PANDEMONIUM** [16] Aug94 [ ]
– Pandemonium / Exorcism / Millenium / Communion / Black Moon / Labyrinth / Jana / Whiteout / Pleasures of the flesh / Mathematics of chaos.

— re-united originals **JAZ COLEMAN / GEORDIE + YOUTH**

Jan 95. (cd-ep) *(BFLDA 21)* **JANA (Youth remix) / JANA (Dragonfly mix) / LOVE LIKE BLOOD (live) / WHITEOUT** [54] [–]
(12"ep/cd-ep+=) *(BFL T/DB 21)* – Jana (live) / Wardance (live) / Exorcism (live) / Kings and queens (live).

Mar 96. (cd-s) *(BFLDA 33) <34262>* **DEMOCRACY / DEMOCRACY (Rooster mix by Carcass) / MASS** [39] [ ]
(cd-s) *(BFLDB 33)* – ('A'-United Nations mix) / ('A'-Russian tundra mix) / ('A'-Hallucinogen mix).

Apr 96. (cd/c) *(BFL CD/MC 17) <31127>* **DEMOCRACY** [71] [ ]
– Savage freedom / Democracy / Prozac people / Lanterns / Aeon / Pilgrimage / Intellect / Medicine wheel / Absent friends / Another bloody election. *(cd re-iss. Aug99; same)*

— added guest **DAVE GROHL** – drums (of FOO FIGHTERS) + **YOUTH**

Zuma — Zuma

Jul 03. (12"/cd-s) *(ZUMA/+D 004)* **LOOSE CANNON. / LOOSE CANNON (full version) / WARDANCE (the ultimate version)** [25] [–]

Jul 03. (cd) *(ZUMACD 002) <6365>* **KILLING JOKE** [43] Aug03 [ ]
– The death & resurrection show / Total invasion / Asteroid / Implant / Blood on your hands / Loose cannon / You'll never get to me / Seeing red / Dark forces / The house that pain built. *(bonus track+=)* – Wardance.

Oct 03. (cd-s) *(ZUMAD 005)* **SEEING RED (mixes; radio / full version / Jagz Kooner / Jagz Kooner instrumental)** -

—— **JAZ, GEORDIE + PAUL**

Cooking Vinyl Cooking Vinyl

Oct 05. (cd) *(<COOKCD 358>)* **XXV GATHERING!** (live)
– Communion / War dance / Song and dance / Primitive / Total invasion / Bloodsport / Requiem / Asteroid / The wait / Psyche / The Pandys are coming / Sun goes down / Are you receiving? / Love like blood / Pandemonium.

Mar 06. (cd-s) *(FRYCD 251)* **HOSANNAS FROM THE BASEMENTS OF HELL / UNIVERSE B. / AFTERBURNER** -

Apr 06. (cd) *(COOKCD 346) <4746>* **HOSANNAS FROM THE BASEMENTS OF HELL**
– This tribal antidote / Hosannas from the basements of Hell / Invocation / Implosion / Majestic / WAlking with the gods / The lightbringer / Judas goat / Gratitude. *(d-lp iss. on 'Let Them Eat Vinyl'; LETV 005LP)*

– compilations, etc. –

on 'Virgin' unless mentioned otherwise

Sep 92. (12"/c-s) *(VST/VSC 1432)* **CHANGE. / REQUIEM** -
(cd-s) *(VSCDT 1432)* – ('A'spiral tribe mix). / ('B'trash Greg Hunter mix).
(cd-s) *(VSCDX 1432)* – ('A'-Youth mix). / ('B'-Youth mix).

Oct 92. (cd/c) *(CDV/TCV 2693) / Caroline; <1596>* **LAUGH? I NEARLY BOUGHT ONE!**
– Turn to red / Psyche / Requiem / Wardance / Follow the leaders / Unspeakable / Butcher / Exit / The hum / Empire song / Chop-chop / The Sun goes down / Eighties / Darkness before dawn / Love like blood / Wintergardens / Age of greed.

May 95. (cd) *(CDOVD 440) / Caroline; (1884>* **WILFUL DAYS** (remixes)

Oct 95. (cd) *Windsong; (WINCD 068)* **BBC LIVE IN CONCERT (live)** -

Apr 98. (12") *Dragonfly; <48>* **LOVE LIKE BLOOD. / INTELLECT** -

Aug 99. (cd) *Butterfly; (BFLCD 9) <114151>* **WAR DANCE** (remix album) - Aug98

Apr 01. (d-cd) *Burning Airlines; <(PILOT 085)>* **NO WAY OUT BUT FORWARD GO (live 1985)** May01

Nov 02. (cd) *Brilliant; (BT 33087)* **LOVE LIKE BLOOD** -

B.B. KING

Born: RILEY B. KING, 16 Sep'25, Indianola, Mississippi, USA, the cousin of respected country bluesman, BUKKA WHITE. A self-taught guitarist (earliest influences being jazz players CHARLIE CHRISTIAN and DJANGO REINHARDT, although T-BONE WALKER would become his future idol), KING initiated a blues style that became a cornerstone of rock music. The son of a sharecropper, as a young man he picked cotton (through the depression) for around 20 dollars a week; the chances of buying a $200-$300 guitar were remote, not to mention the fact that his town didn't have any electricity! KING performed with The ELKHORN SINGERS in his teens and moved to Memphis in 1946 to look for work as a musician, linking up with SONNY BOY WILLIAMSON and initially playing a residency at the 16th Avenue Grill. Subsequently talent-spotted, he won his own, regular 10-minute spot (The Sepia Swing Show) on a black music radio station, WDIA, and word of his prowess spread; the station's PR man dubbed him 'The BEALE STREET BLUES BOY' which was shortened to 'BLUES BOY' and eventually 'BB'. Towards the end of 1949, KING signed to the 'Bullett' label and debuted with 'MISS MARTHA KING', while the following year, he inked a deal with the 'Kent/Modern/RPM' group of labels through their talent scout, IKE TURNER, remaining there until 1962 (he also formed his own, short-lived 'Blue Boy' label during the 50's). BB developed his own sound on his Gibson guitar, LUCILLE (so named because of an incident after a gig in Twist, Arkansas during which a fight – caused by a woman named Lucille – ended up in the venue being evacuated). In February 1952, KING hit US number 1 for fifteen weeks in the R&B charts with 'THREE O'CLOCK BLUES' (written by LOWELL FULSON), while in November, 'YOU DIDN'T WANT ME', repeated the feat. KING was to enjoy regular R&B chart success over the next five years, including two more chart toppers, 'PLEASE LOVE ME' (1953) and 'YOU UPSET ME BABY' (1954). The big man achieved his first national chart success in 1957 via 'BE CAREFUL WITH A FOOL' and followed it with 'I NEED YOU SO BAD' which also broke into the US Top 100. KING subsequently left 'Kent' in 1962 for the larger 'A.B.C.' label, with whom he was to record until their absorption into 'M.C.A.' in 1979. His first ABC release was a version of Louis Jordan's 'HOW BLUE CAN YOU GET', while in May '62, 'ROCK ME BABY' (written by ARTHUR 'BIG BOY' CRUDUP and recorded for 'Kent' before his move) was his first recognised pop hit, entering the US Top 40 and becoming the subject of countless cover versions by UK R&B bands. 'LIVE AT THE REGAL' recorded at the Regal Theatre, Chicago in 1960 and released in 1965, captured him at his best playing songs that were to be mainstays of his set for years to come – Memphis Slim's 'EVERYDAY I HAVE THE BLUES', 'HOW BLUE CAN YOU GET' and 'IT'S MY OWN FAULT' (written by JOHN LEE HOOKER). 'LIVE IN COOK COUNTY JAIL' (1971) was in the same vein featuring 'WORRY WORRY', 'THREE O'CLOCK BLUES' and the unmistakeable 'THE THRILL IS GONE' (his only US Top 20 single). At the end of the decade (after achieving his second US Top 40 hit with 'PAYING THE COST TO BE THE BOSS'), he left his long term manager, Lou Zito, after an argument over money, his accountant, Sidney Siedenberg, took over. On the 4th of April 1968 (the night that MARTIN LUTHER KING was assassinated) KING, BUDDY GUY and JIMI HENDRIX played an all-night blues session, passing the hat round to collect money for the Southern Leadership fund. The following year, after the release of albums, 'LUCILLE' and 'BLUES ON TOP OF BLUES', he made his first trip to Europe, appeared at numerous festivals including the Newport Jazz Festival and opened for The ROLLING STONES on their sixth US tour. KING's manager subsequently encouraged him to widen his fan base and steered him away from his traditional (although declining) black audience towards the middle class white kids involved in the R&B/blues revival. In December that year, his version of Roy Hawkins' 'THE THRILL IS GONE' gave him his biggest hit single so far, reaching the US Top 20, with the accompanying album, 'COMPLETELY WELL' achieving similar results. His next album, 'HUMMINGBIRD' and the jazzy Top 30 set, 'INDIANOLA MISSISSIPPI SEEDS' were both released at the turn of the decade, while 1971 brought him a Grammy for 'THE THRILL IS GONE'; a string of minor hits followed, both singles and albums. In August 1979, 'TAKE IT HOME', gave him his first UK album chart success (reaching No.60), although it struggled to achieve a similar position in the States. 'THERE MUST BE A BETTER WORLD SOMEWHERE' (1981), with music and lyrics by DR. JOHN and DOC POMUS, was one of his finest studio albums, cuts such as 'THE VICTIM' and the ironic 'LIFE AIN'T NOTHING BUT A PARTY' enduring highlights. In 1982, KING demonstrated what a thoroughly generous guy he was when he donated his entire record collection (20,000 discs including 7,000 rare blues 78's) to the Mississippi University Centre For The Study Of Southern Culture. His second Grammy came in February for 'THERE MUST BE A BETTER WORLD SOMEWHERE' and on September the 16th (his 57th birthday), he recorded 'BLUES N JAZZ' which won him another Grammy in 1984. He added yet another one to the trophy cabinet in 1986 with 'MY GUITAR SINGS THE BLUES', a track taken from his 50th album, 'SIX SILVER STRINGS'. In 1988, he surprisingly recorded a one-off track with U2, 'WHEN LOVE COMES TO TOWN' making the UK Top 10 for the first and only time in his chequered history

Meanwhile, KING continued with his charity work, performing at a concert for the National Coalition For The Homeless and a Dallas based group for the homeless, Common Ground (later performing at the Roy Orbison All Star Benefit Tribute and helping to raise $500,000 for homeless charities). In December 1989, he featured on the album, 'HAPPY ANNIVERSARY CHARLIE BROWN' which commemorated the 40th year of the Peanuts cartoon strip (he later continued his association with cartoon characters by playing guitar on 'BORN UNDER A BAD SIGN' for the 'SIMPSONS SINGS THE BLUES' album in 1990 and 'MONDAY MORNING BLUES' for 'AM I COOL, OR WHAT?', a homage to Garfield the cat in 1991). KING went into hospital in April 1990 because of problems relating to his diabetes, resulting in the cancellation of some concerts although he soon got back to his intensive recording and touring schedule (he averages 300 one-nighters a year – mainly to pay for his compulsive gambling habit). February 1991 brought him another Grammy, this time for 'LIVE AT SAN QUENTIN' (recorded 20 years earlier!) and in May that year he opened his own restaurant and night club (BB KING's MEMPHIS BLUES CLUB) on Beale Street, Memphis. This busy year continued in October with the release of his best studio album in a decade, 'THERE IS ALWAYS ONE MORE TIME', highlights being 'I'M MOVIN' ON' and 'THE BLUES COME OVER ME'. In 1992, he received a Grammy for 'LIVE AT THE APOLLO', reached UK Top 60 with GARY MOORE on 'SINCE I MET YOU BABY' and in December performed at the Gainsville Drug Treatment Centre in Florida before 300 prison inmates including his daughter, PATTY, who was serving a 3-year term for trafficking. March 1993 saw him headline a benefit concert in Chattanooga, raising $90,000 for the Bessie Smith Hall (opened later in the year) and in September, 'BLUES SUMMIT' (recorded with ROBERT CRAY, ALBERT COLLINS, ETTA JAMES, JOHN LEE HOOKER, BUDDY GUY and IRMA THOMAS) breached the US Top 200. The legend of US urban blues subsequently teamed up with the legend of white boy English blues, ERIC CLAPTON, for 'RIDING WITH THE KING' (2000). The two guitarists amicably trading licks on a bevvy of KING nuggets – 'TEN LONG YEARS', 'THREE O'CLOCK BLUES', 'WHEN MY HEART BEATS LIKE A HAMMER' etc.- and other assorted blues favourites such as 'KEY TO THE HIGHWAY'. Well into his 70's come the new millennium, KING kept on trucking with 'MAKIN' LOVE IS GOOD FOR YOU' (2000), perhaps a hint as to this blues colossus' longevity. Whatever it is, he still has that musical virility missing in many players half his age and on the likes of the title track and the cover of Barbara George's 'I KNOW', he proved he can still cut it a soul-man as well. 'REFLECTIONS' (2003), as its title suggests, was more of a taking stock affair, winding casually and unashamedly nostalgically back through the decades with readings of 'ALWAYS ON MY MIND', 'WHAT A WONDERFUL WORLD' and '(I LOVE YOU) FOR SENTIMENTAL REASONS' alongside straight-up blues cuts. KING returns to his old neighbourhood each year and puts on a weekend of free concerts; a tireless ambassador for the blues, he succeeded in bringing the form into the mainstream and remains one of the most well-known artists in the genre's near hundred year history. He'll be approaching the big ton himself soon: as it is, he recently turned eighty, celebrating a landmark that most musicians will likely never see in the company of premier division pop/rock acts including old buddies ERIC CLAPTON, BOBBY BLAND and VAN MORRISON, as well as less likely partners BILLY GIBBONS, ELTON JOHN and GLORIA ESTEFAN. The results were issued under the self-explanatory title '80' (2005), a record that met with critical ambivalence and a US Top 50 entry.

• **Covered:** LOVE ME TENDER (hit; Elvis Presley) / ONE OF THOSE NIGHTS (Conway Twitty) / DON'T CHANGE ON ME (James Holiday & Edward Reeves) / LEGEND IN MY TIME (Don Gibson) / YOU'VE ALWAYS GOT THE BLUES + TIME IS A THIEF (Mickey Newbury) / NIGHTLIFE (Willie Nelson) / PLEASE SEND ME SOMEONE TO LOVE (Percy Mayfield) / YOU AND ME, ME AND YOU (Will Jennings) / YOU SHOOK ME (Willie Dixon) / PLAYIN' WITH MY FRIENDS (Robert Cray & T-Bone Walker) / YOU'RE THE BOSS (Lieber-Stoller) / etc. • **Trivia:** He gave his "Lucille" guitar a cameo role in the 1985 movie, 'Into The Night' and two years later appeared in 'Amazon Women On The Moon'.

Album rating (selective): ROCK ME BABY (*7) / LIVE AT THE REGAL (*8) / BLUES IS KING (*7) / LUCILLE (*7) / LIVE AND WELL (*7) / COMPLETELY WELL (*6) / INDIANOLA MISSISSIPPI SEEDS (*7) / LIVE IN COOK COUNTY JAIL (*7) / B.B. KING IN LONDON (*6) / L.A. MIDNIGHT (*6) / GUESS WHO (*6) / THE BEST OF B.B. KING compilation (*7) / TO KNOW YOU IS TO LOVE YOU (*6) / FRIENDS (*6) / TOGETHER FOR THE FIRST TIME . . . LIVE with Bobby Bland (*7) / LUCILLE TALK BACK (*6) / TOGETHER AGAIN . . . LIVE with Bobby Bland (*6) / KING SIZE (*6) / MIDNIGHT BELIEVER (*6) / TAKE IT HOME (*6) / NOW APPEARING AT OLE MISS (*6) / THERE MUST BE A BETTER WORLD SOMEWHERE (*7) / BLUES 'N' JAZZ (*6) / BLUES SUMMIT (*7) / HEART & SOUL: A COLLECTION OF BLUES BALLADS compilation (*6) / RIDING WITH THE KING with Eric Clapton (*6) / MAKIN' LOVE IS GOOD FOR YOU (*5) / REFLECTIONS (*6) / 80 (*4)

B.B. KING – vocals, guitar

		not iss.	Bullet
1949.	(78) *<309>* **MISS MARTHA KING. / WHEN YOUR BABY PACKS UP AND GOES**	–	

Note: All release dates in the 50's & 60's are approximate guesses, through working out dates / years of session recordings relating to catalogue numbers.

		not iss.	Bullet
1949.	(78) *<315>* **GOT THE BLUES. / TAKE A SWING WITH ME**	–	

		not iss.	R.P.M.
Oct 50.	(78) *<304>* **MISTREATED WOMAN. / B.B.'S BOOGIE**	–	
Jan 51.	(78) *<311>* **THE OTHER NIGHT BLUES. / WALKIN' AND CRYIN'**	–	

B.B. KING & HIS ORCHESTRA

Mar 51.	(78) *<318>* **MY BABY'S GONE. / DON'T YOU WANT A MAN LIKE ME**	–	
Jun 51.	(78) *<323>* **SHE'S DYNAMITE. / B.B.'S BLUES**	–	
Sep 51.	(78) *<330>* **SHE'S A MEAN WOMAN. / HARD WORKING WOMAN**	–	
Dec 51.	(78) *<339>* **3 O'CLOCK BLUES. / THAT AIN'T THE WAY TO DO IT**	–	
Mar 52.	(78) *<348>* **SHE DON'T MOVE ME NO MORE. / FINE LOOKING WOMAN**	–	
May 52.	(78) *<355>* **MY OWN FAULT DARLIN'. / SHAKE IT UP AND GO**	–	
Jul 52.	(78) *<360>* **SOME DAY SOME WHERE. / GOTTA FIND MY BABY**	–	
Sep 52.	(78) *<363>* **YOU KNOW I LOVE YOU. / YOU DIDN'T WANT ME**	–	
Nov 52.	(78) *<374>* **STORY FROM MY HEART AND SOUL. / BOOGIE WOOGIE WOMAN**	–	
Jan 53.	(78) *<380>* **DON'T HAVE TO CRY (PAST DAY). / WOKE UP THIS MORNING (MY BABY WAS GONE)**	–	
Mar 53.	(78) *<386>* **PLEASE LOVE ME. / HIGHWAY BOUND**	–	
May 53.	(78) *<391>* **NEIGHBORHOOD AFFAIR. / PLEASE HURRY HOME**	–	
Jul 53.	(78) *<395>* **WHY DID YOU LEAVE ME. / BLIND LOVE (WHO CAN YOUR GOOD MAN BE)**	–	
Sep 53.	(78) *<403>* **PRAYING TO THE LORD. / PLEASE HELP ME**	–	

B.B. "BLUES BOY" KING & HIS ORCHESTRA

(same label)

Nov 53.	(78) *<408>* **I LOVE YOU BABY. / THE WOMAN I LOVE**	–	
Jan 54.	(78) *<411>* **EVERYTHING I DO IS WRONG. / DON'T YOU WANT A MAN LIKE ME**	–	
Feb 54.	(78) *<412>* **WHEN MY HEART BEATS LIKE A HAMMER. / BYE! BYE! BABY**	–	
1954.	(78) *<416>* **YOU UPSET ME BABY. / WHOLE LOT OF LOVIN'**	–	
1955.	(78) *<421>* **EVERYDAY I HAVE THE BLUES. / SNEAKIN' AROUND**	–	

1955. (78) *<425>* **JUMP WITH YOU BABY. / LONELY AND BLUE** –
1955. (78) *<430>* **SHUT YOUR MOUTH. / I'M IN LOVE** –
1955. (78) *<435>* **WHAT CAN I DO (JUST SING THE BLUES). / TEN LONG YEARS (I HAD A WOMAN)** –
Feb 56. (78) *<450>* **I'M CRACKING UP OVER YOU. / RUBY LEE** –
Mar 56. (78) *<451>* **SIXTEEN TONS. / CRYING WON'T HELP YOU** –
May 56. (78) *<457>* **DID YOU EVER LOVE A WOMAN. / LET'S DO THE BOOGIE** –
Jun 56. (78) *<459>* **DARK IS THE NIGHT. / (part 2)** –
Sep 56. (78) *<468>* **SWEET LITTLE ANGEL. / BAD LUCK** –
Feb 57. (78) *<479>* **ON MY WORD OF HONOUR. / BIM BAM** –
Apr 57. (78) *<486>* **EARLY IN THE MORNING. / YOU DON'T KNOW** –
May 57. (78) *<490>* **HOW DO I LOVE YOU. / YOU CAN'T FOOL MY HEART** –
Jun 57. (78) *<492>* **I WANT TO GET MARRIED. / TROUBLES TROUBLES (TROUBLES)** –
Jul 57. (78) *<494>* **BE CAREFUL WITH A FOOL. / (I'M GONNA) QUIT MY BABY** – 95
Oct 57. (78) *<498>* **I NEED YOU SO BAD. / I WONDER** – 85
Dec 57. (78) *<501>* **THE KEY TO MY KINGDOM. / MY HEART BELONGS TO YOU** –

not iss. Kent/Crown

1958. (lp) *<5020>* **SINGING THE BLUES** (compilation) –
– 3 o'clock blues / You know I love you / Woke up this morning / Please love me / You upset me baby / Everyday I have the blues / Ten years long (I had a woman) / Did you ever love a woman / Crying won't help you / Sweet little angel / Bad luck.

1958. (lp) *<5063>* **THE BLUES** (compilation) –
– Boogie woogie woman / Don't have to cry (past day) / Don't you want a man like me / When my heart beats like a hammer / What can I do (just sing the blues) / Ruby Lee / Early in the morning / I want to get married / Troubles troubles / Why does everything happen to me.

Sep 58. (7") *<301>* **WHY DOES EVERYTHING HAPPEN TO ME. / YOU KNOW I GO FOR IT** –
Nov 58. (7") *<307>* **DON'T LOOK NOW, BUT I'VE GOT THE BLUES. / DAYS OF OLD** –
Feb 59. (7"; by B.B.KING & THE VOCAL CHORDS) *<315>* **PLEASE ACCEPT MY LOVE. / YOU'VE BEEN AN ANGEL** –
1959. (lp) *<5115>* **WAILS** –
– Tomorrow is another day / We can't make it / I've got papers on you baby (do what I say) / Sweet thing / Treat me right (oh baby) / Time to say goodbye / I love you so / The woman I love / The fool (a fool too long) / Come by here.

B.B. KING

(same label)

Aug 59. (7") *<317>* **I AM. / WHY WORRY** –
Sep 59. (7") *<319>* **COME BY HERE. / THE FOOL (A FOOL TOO LONG)** –
Oct 59. (7") *<325>* **A LONELY LOVER'S PLEA. / THE WOMAN I LOVE** –
Nov 59. (7") *<327>* **EVERYDAY I HAVE THE BLUES. / TIME TO SAY GOODBYE** –
(above 'A'side featured members of The COUNT BASIE BAND)
Dec 59. (7") *<329>* **MEAN OLE FRISCO. / SUGAR MAMA** –
Jan 60. (7") *<5>* **SWEET SIXTEEN. / (part 2)** –
(above on 'Modern' records)
Feb 60. (lp) *<568>* **SWEET SIXTEEN** (compilation) –
– Sweet sixteen (parts 1 & 2) / Days old old / Be careful with a fool / (I'm gonna) Quit my baby / What can I do (just sing the blues) / Ten long years (I had a woman) / I was blind / Whole lotta lovin' / Someday baby.

Feb 60. (7") *<333>* **(I'VE) GOT A RIGHT TO LOVE MY BABY. / MY OWN FAULT** –
Mar 60. (7") *<336>* **CRYING WON'T HELP YOU. / PLEASE LOVE ME** –
Apr 60. (7") *<337>* **BLIND LOVE (WHO CAN YOUR GOOD MAN BE). / YOU UPSET ME BABY** –
May 60. (7") *<338>* **TEN LONG YEARS (I HAD A WOMAN). / EVERYDAY I HAVE THE BLUES** –
May 60. (7") *<339>* **THREE O'CLOCK BLUES. / DID YOU EVER LOVE A WOMAN** –
Jun 60. (7") *<340>* **YOU DONE LOST YOUR GOOD THING NOW. / SWEET LITTLE ANGEL** –
(above 4 singles were recorded between 1953-56)
Jul 60. (7") *<346>* **GOOD MAN GONE BAD. / PARTIN' TIME** –
Aug 60. (lp) *<5167>* **KING OF THE BLUES** –
– (I've) Got a right to love my baby / Good man gone bad / Partin' time / Long nights (the feeling they call the blues) / I'll survive / What a way to go / Feel like a million / If I lost you / You're on top / I'm king. *(UK-iss.1976 on 'Music For Pleasure'; 50259)*

Sep 60. (7") *<350>* **YOU DONE LOST YOUR GOOD THING NOW. / WALKING DR.BILL** –
Oct 60. (7") *<351>* **THINGS ARE NOT THE SAME. / FISHIN' AFTER ME (CATFISH BLUES)** –
Nov 60. (7") *<353>* **GET OUT OF HERE. / BAD LUCK SOUL** –
Jan 61. (lp) *<5188>* **MY KIND OF BLUES** –
– You done lost your good thing now / Walking Dr. Bill / Fishin' after me (catfish blues) / Hold that train / Understand / Someday baby / Mr. Pawnbroker / Driving wheel / My own fault (baby) / Please set a date.

Feb 61. (7") *<358>* **HOLD THAT TRAIN. / UNDERSTAND** –
Jun 61. (7") *<360>* **PEACE OF MIND. / SOMEDAY BABY** –
Jul 61. (lp) *<5230>* **MORE B.B.KING** –
– My reward / Don't cry anymore / You're breaking my heart / Blues for me (groovin' twist) / Just like a woman (rockin' twist) / Bad case of love / Bad luck soul / Get out of here / Shut your mouth.

Oct 61. (7") *<362>* **BAD CASE OF LOVE. / YOU'RE BREAKING MY HEART** –
Nov 61. (lp) *<5248>* **TWIST WITH B.B.KING** (compilation recent & old) –
Feb 62. (lp) *<5286>* **EASY LISTENING BLUES** –
– Hully gully (twist) / Easy listening (blues) / Blues for me / Slow walk (slow burn) / Shoutin' the blues / Night long / Confessin' / Don't touch / Rambler / Walkin'.

Mar 62. (7") *<372>* **HULLY GULLY (TWIST). / GONNA MISS YOU AROUND HERE** –
1962. (lp) *<7708>* **BLUES FOR ME** –
– Got 'em bad / I can't explain / You're gonna miss me / Troubles don't last / Strange things / Down hearted / So many days / I need you baby / The wrong road / The letter / You never know / Sundown / You won't listen. *<above issued on 'United'>*

H.M.V. ABC Paramount

Apr 62. (7") *<10316>* **YOU ASK ME. / I'M GONNA SIT IN TILL YOU GIVE IN** –
Jun 62. (7") *<10334>* **BLUES AT MIDNIGHT. / MY BABY'S COMIN' HOME** –
Sep 62. (7") *<10361>* **SNEAKIN' AROUND. / CHAINS OF LOVE** –
Nov 62. (7") *<10367>* **TOMORROW NIGHT. / A MOTHER'S LOVE** –
1963. (lp) *<456>* **MR. BLUES** –
– Young dreamers / By myself / Chains of love / A mother's love / Blues at midnight / Sneakin' around / On my word of honor / Tomorrow night / My baby's comin' home / Guess who / You ask me / I'm gonna sit in 'til you give in.

Mar 63. (7") *<10390>* **GUESS WHO. / BY MYSELF** –
Jun 63. (7") *<10455>* **YOUNG DREAMERS. / ON MY WORD OF HONOR** –
Oct 63. (7") *<10486>* **HOW DO I LOVE YOU. / SLOWLY LOSING MY MIND** –
Feb 64. (7") *<10527>* **HOW BLUE CAN YOU GET. / PLEASE ACCEPT MY LOVE** – 97
May 64. (7") *<10552>* **HELP THE POOR. / I WOULDN'T HAVE IT ANY OTHER WAY** – 98
Jul 64. (7") *<10576>* **THE HURT. / WHOLE LOTTA LOVIN'** –
Oct 64. (7") *<10599>* **NEVER TRUST A WOMAN. / WORRYIN' BLUES** – 90
Dec 64. (7") *<10616>* **WORST THING IN MY LIFE. / PLEASE SEND ME SOMEONE TO LOVE** –
Feb 65. (7") *<10634>* **IT'S MY OWN FAULT. / EVERYDAY I HAVE THE BLUES** –
Apr 65. (7") *<10675>* **TIRED OF YOUR JIVE. / NIGHT OWL** –
Jun 65. (7") *<10724>* **ALL OVER AGAIN. / THE THINGS YOU PUT ME THROUGH** –
Jul 65. (lp) *(CLP 1870)* *<ABCD 509>* **LIVE AT THE REGAL (live in Chicago 1964)**

– Everyday (I have the blues) / Sweet little angel / It's my own fault / How blue can you get / Please love me / You upset me baby / Worry, worry / Woke up this mornin' / You done lost you good thing / Help the poor. *<re-iss. Sep71; ABCS 724> (re-iss. Oct83 on 'Charly'; CH 86) (cd-iss. Dec94 on 'Beat Goes On'; BGOCD 235)*

Aug 65. (7") *<10754>* **I'D RATHER DRINK MUDDY WATER. / GOIN' TO CHICAGO BLUES** [–] [ ]

Mar 66. (lp) *(CLP 3514) <528>* **CONFESSIN' THE BLUES** [ ] [ ]
– See see rider / Do you call that a buddy / Wee baby blues / I'd rather drink muddy water / In the dark / Confessin' the blues / Goin' to Chicago blues / I'm gonna move to the outskirts of town / World of trouble / How long blues / Cherry red / Please send me someone to love.

Jun 66. (7") *<10766>* **TORMENTED. / YOU'RE STILL A SQUARE** [–] [ ]

Dec 66. (7") *<10856>* **DON'T ANSWER THE DOOR. / (part 2)** [ ] Oct66 [72]

Jan 67. (lp) *(CLP 3608) <704>* **BLUES IS KING** [ ] [–]
– Waitin' on you / Gambler's blues / Tired of your jive / Night life / Buzz me / Don't answer the door / Blind love / I know what you're puttin' down / Baby get lost / Gonna keep on loving you. *(re-iss. Nov87 on 'See For Miles'; SEE 216) (cd-iss. Jul92; SEECD 216)*

1967. (7") *(POP 1580) <10889>* **NIGHT LIFE. / WAITIN' ON YOU** [ ] [ ]

Stateside Bluesway

Jul 67. (lp) *(SSL 10238) <BLS 6011>* **BLUES ON TOP OF BLUES** [ ] [ ]
– Heartbreaker / Losing faith in you / Dance with me / That's wrong little mama / Having my say / I'm not wanted anymore / Worried dream / Paying the cost to be the boss / Until I found you / I'm gonna do what they do to me / Raining in my heart / Now that you've lost me. *(re-iss. 1989 on 'B.G.O.' lp/cd; BGO/+CD 69)*

1967. (7") *<61004>* **THINK IT OVER. / MEET MY HAPPINESS** [–] [ ]

1967. (7") *(POP 1594)* **I DON'T WANT YOU CUTTIN' YOUR HAIR. / THINK IT OVER** [ ] [–]

1967. (7") *<61007>* **WORRIED DREAM. / THAT'S WRONG LITTLE MAMA** [–] [ ]

1967. (7") *<61011>* **HEARTBREAKER. / RAINING IN MY HEART** [–] [ ]

1968. (7") *<61012>* **SWEET SIXTEEN. / (part 2)** [–] [ ]

May 68. (7") *(SS 2112) <61015>* **PAYING THE COST TO BE THE BOSS. / HAVING MY SAY** [ ] Feb68 [39]

Jun 68. (7") *<61018>* **I'M GONNA DO WHAT THEY DO TO ME. / LOSING FAITH IN YOU** [–] [74]

Sep 68. (7") *<61019>* **THE B.B. JONES. / YOU PUT IT ON ME** [ ] [98] [82]

Dec 68. (7") *<61021>* **DANCE WITH ME. / PLEASE SEND ME SOMEONE TO LOVE** [–] [ ]

— (below feat. musicians **The MAXWELL DAVIS BAND**

Jan 69. (lp) *(SSL 10272) <6016>* **LUCILLE** [ ] Oct68 [ ]
– Lucille / You move me so / Country girl / No money no luck / I need your love / Rainin' all the time / I'm with you / Stop putting the hurt on me / Watch yourself *(re-iss. 1977 on 'A.B.C.'; 712) (cd-iss. Feb89 on 'Beat Goes On' lp/cd; BGO/+CD 36)*

Feb 69. (7") *(SS 2141) <61022>* **DON'T WASTE MY TIME. / GET MYSELF SOMEBODY** [ ] [ ]

Mar 69. (lp) *(SSL 10284) <6022>* **THE ELECTRIC B.B.KING** (compilation) [ ] [ ]
– Tired of your jive / Don't answer the door / B.B.Jones / All over again / Paying the cost to the boss / Think it over / I done got wise / Meet my happiness / Sweet sixteen / You put it on me / I don't want you cuttin' off your hair. *(re-iss. Jan89 on 'Beat Goes On' lp/cd; BGO/+CD 37)*

Apr 69. (7") *<61024>* **WHY I SING THE BLUES. / FRIENDS** [–] [61]

Jun 69. (7") *<61026>* **GET OFF MY BACK WOMAN. / I WANT YOU SO BAD** [–] [74]

Jun 69. (lp) *(SSL 10297) <6031>* **LIVE AND WELL (half live)** [ ] [56]
– Don't answer the door / Just a little love / My mood / Sweet little angel / Please accept my love / I want you so bad / Friends / Get off my back woman / Let's get down to business / Why I sing the blues. *<cd-iss. Jun88 on 'M.C.A.'; 31191> (cd-iss. Jul94 on 'Beat Goes On'; BGOCD 233)*

Sep 69. (7") *(573161) <57-3161)* **EVERYDAY I HAVE THE BLUES. / FIVE LONG YEARS** [ ] [–]

— (above iss.UK on 'Blue Horizon')

Oct 69. (7") *<61029>* **JUST A LITTLE LOVE. / MY MOOD** [–] [76]

Feb 70. (7") *(SS 2161) <61032>* **THE THRILL IS GONE. / YOU'RE MEAN** [ ] Jan70 [15]

Feb 70. (lp) *(SSL 10299) <6037>* **COMPLETELY WELL** [ ] Dec69 [38]
– The thrill is gone / So excited / No good / You're losing me / What happened / Confessin' the blues / Key to my kingdom / Crying won't help you now / You're mean. *(cd-iss. Jul87 on 'M.C.A.'; CMCAD 31039)*

May 70. (7") *(SS 2169) <61035>* **SO EXCITED. / CONFESSIN' THE BLUES** [ ] Mar70 [54]

Probe A.B.C.

Aug 70. (7") *(SS 2176) <11268>* **HUMMINGBIRD. / ASK ME NO QUESTIONS** [ ] Jun 70 [48]

Oct 70. (7") *(PRO 516) <11280>* **CHAINS AND THINGS. / KING'S SPECIAL** [–] [45]

Nov 70. (lp) *(SPBA 6255) <713>* **INDIANOLA MISSISSIPPI SEEDS** [ ] Oct70 [26]
– Nobody loves me but my mother / You're still my woman / Ask me no questions / Until I'm dead and cold / King's special / Ain't gonna worry my life anymore / Chains and things / Go underground / Hummingbird. *(re-iss. May88 on 'Castle' lp/c/cd; CLA LP/MC/CD 141) (cd re-iss. Apr95 on 'Beat Goes On'; BGOCD 237)*

Feb 71. (7") *<11268>* **ASK ME NO QUESTIONS. / NOBODY LOVES ME BUT MY MOTHER** [–] [40]

Mar 71. (7") *(PRO 528)* **ASK ME NO QUESTIONS. / HELP THE POOR / HUMMING BIRD** [ ] [–]

Mar 71. (lp) *(SPB 1032) <723>* **LIVE IN COOK COUNTY JAIL (live)** [ ] Feb71 [25]
– Every day I have the blues / How blues can you get / Worry, worry, worry / 3 o'clock blues / Darlin' you know I love you / Sweet sixteen / The thrill is gone / Please accept my love. *(re-iss. Oct87 on 'M.C.A.'; IMCA 27005) <US cd-iss. Jun88 on 'M.C.A.'; 31080> (d-cd-iss. Jul96 on 'M.C.A.'; MCD 33007)*

Jun 71. (7") *<11302>* **HELP THE POOR. / LUCILLE'S GRANNY** [–] [90]

Aug 71. (7") *<11310>* **GHETTO WOMAN. / SEVEN MINUTES** [–] [68]

below feat. **RINGO STARR, DR.JOHN, ALEXIS KORNER + STEVE MARRIOTT**

Oct 71. (lp) *(SPB 1041) <730>* **B.B. KING IN LONDON** [ ] [57]
– Introduction / Every day I have the blues / Night life / Love the life I'm living / When it all comes down (I'll still be around) / I've got a right to give up livin' / Encore. *(re-iss. 1977 on 'A.B.C.'; ABC 5015) (re-iss. Oct88 on 'Beat Goes On' lp/cd; BGO/+CD 42)*

Oct 71. (7") *<11316>* **AIN'T NOBODY HOME. / ALEXI'S BOOGIE** [–] [46]

Feb 72. (7") *<11319>* **SWEET SIXTEEN. / I'VE BEEN BLUE TOO LONG** [–] [93]

Feb 72. (lp) *(SPB 1051) <743>* **L.A. MIDNIGHT** [ ] [53]
– I got some help I don't need help / The poor / Can't you hear me talking to you / Midnight / Sweet sixteen / I believe (I've been blue too long) / Lucille's granny.

May 72. (7") *<11321>* **I GOT SOME HELP I DON'T NEED IT. / LUCILLE'S GRANNY** [–] [92]

Aug 72. (7") *<11330>* **GUESS WHO. / BETTER LOVIN' MAN** [–] [62]

Aug 72. (lp) *(SPB 1063) <759>* **GUESS WHO** [ ] [65]
– Summer in the city / Just can't please you / Any other way / You don't know nothin' about love / Found what I need / Neighborhood affair / It takes a young girl / Better lovin' man / Guess who / Shouldn't have left me / Five long years *<re-iss. 1974 on 'A.B.C.'; 5021> (re-iss. May89 on 'Beat Goes On' lp/cd; BGO LP/CD 71)*

Oct 72. (7") *<11339>* **FIVE LONG YEARS. / SUMMER IN THE CITY** [–] [ ]

Nov 72. (7") *(PRO 573)* **SUMMER IN THE CITY. / FOUND WHAT I NEED** [ ] [–]

Jul 73. (7") *(PRO 603) <11373>* **TO KNOW YOU IS TO LOVE YOU. / I CAN'T LEAVE** [ ] [38]

Aug 73. (lp) *(SPB 1083) <794>* **TO KNOW YOU IS TO LOVE YOU** [ ] [71]
– I like to live the love / Respect yourself / Who are you / Love / I can't leave / To know you is to love you / Thank you for loving the blues / Oh to me. *(re-iss. Oct74 on 'A.B.C.'; 5083> (cd-iss. Feb02 on 'M.C.A.'; MCD 10414)*

Jan 74. (7") *(PRO 613) <11406>* **I LIKE TO LIVE THE LOVE. / LOVE** [ ] [28]

A.B.C. A.B.C.

Aug 74. (7") *(ABC 4005) <11433>* **WHO ARE YOU. / OH TO ME** [ ] Jun 74 [78]

Aug 74. (lp) *(ABCL 5051) <825>* **FRIENDS** [ ] [ ]
– Friends / I got them blues / Baby I'm yours / Up at 5 a.m. / Philadelphia / When everything else is gone / My song. *(cd-iss. Sep91 on 'Beat Goes On'; BGOCD 125)*

Oct 74. (7") *(ABC 4017) <12029>* **PHILADELPHIA. / UP AT 5 P.M.** □ [64]

Nov 74. (d-lp; B.B. KING & BOBBY BLAND) *Anchor; (ABCD 605) / Dunhill; <751096>* **TOGETHER FOR THE FIRST TIME . . . LIVE (live)** □ [43]
– Introduction / 3 o'clock in the morning / It's my own fault baby / Driftin' blues / That's the way love is / I'm sorry / I'll take care of you / Don't cry no more / Don't want a soul hangin' around / Medley / Everybody wants to know why I sing the blues / Goin' down slow / I like to live the love. *(cd-iss. Jun94 on 'Beat Goes On'; BGOCD 161)*

Jan 75. (7") *<12053>* **FRIENDS. / MY SONG** [–] □

Sep 75. (7") *<12158>* **HAVE FAITH. / WHEN I'M WRONG** [–] □

Oct 75. (lp) *(5149) <898>* **LUCILLE TALKS BACK** □ □
– Lucille talks back (copulation) / Breaking up somebody's home / Reconsider baby / Don't make me pay for his mistakes / When I'm wrong / I know the price / Have faith / Everybody lies a little.

Jul 76. (lp; BOBBY BLAND & B.B. KING) *Impulse; (IMPL 8027) <9317>* **TOGETHER AGAIN . . . LIVE (live)** □ [73]
– Let the good times roll / Strange things happen / Feel so bad / Mother-in-law blues / Mean old world / Everyday (I have the blues) / The thrill is gone / I ain't gonna be the first to cry. *(re-iss. Jan90 on 'M.C.A.' lp/cd; MCA/+D 4160) (cd re-iss. Feb93 on 'Beat Goes On'; BGOCD 162)*

1976. (7") *Impulse; <31006>* **LET THE GOOD TIMES ROLL. / STRANGE HINGS HAPPEN** [–] □

1976. (7") *Impulse; <31009>* **EVERYDAY (I HAVE THE BLUES). / THE THRILL IS GONE** [–] □

Feb 77. (lp) *(95148) <977>* **KINGSIZE** □ □
– Confessin' the blues / Paying the cost to be the boss / Think it over / You move me so / Heartbreaker / I'm gonna do what they do to me / What happened / By myself / That's wrong little mama / How long, how long blues / I'm not wanted anymore / My baby's comin' home.

1977. (7") *<12247>* **I WONDER WHY. / SLOW AND EASY** [–] □

1977. (7") *<12380>* **LET ME MAKE YOU CRY A LITTLE LONGER. / NEVER MADE A MOVE TOO SOON** [–] □

Mar 78. (7") *<12412>* **I JUST CAN'T LEAVE YOUR LOVE ALONE. / ?** □ □

Apr 78. (lp) *(ABCL 5246) <1061>* **MIDNIGHT BELIEVER** □ □
– When it all comes down / Midnight believer / I just can't leave your love alone / Hold on (I feel our love is changing) / Never make a move too soon / A world full of strangers / Let me make you cry a little longer. *(re-iss. Jun84 on 'M.C.A.' lp/c; MCL/+C 1802) (cd-iss. May90; DMCL 1802) (re-iss. Jan93 cd/c; MCL D/C 19170)*

Jun 78. (7") *(ABC 4236)* **HOLD ON (I FEEL OUR LOVE IS CHANGING). / MIDNIGHT BELIEVER** □ [–]

M.C.A. M.C.A.

Aug 79. (7") *(MCA 515) <41062>* **BETTER NOT LOOK DOWN. / HAPPY BIRTHDAY BLUES** □ □

Aug 79. (lp) *(MCF 3010) <3151>* **TAKE IT HOME** [60] □
– Better not look down / Same old story / Happy birthday blues / I've always been lonely / Second hand woman / Tonight I'm gonna make you a star / The beginning of the end / A story everybody knows / Take it home. *(re-iss. Feb84 lp/c; MCL/+C 1784)*

Oct 79. (7") *(MCA 535)* **TAKE IT HOME. / SAME OLD STORY** □ □

Apr 80. (d-lp) *<2-8016>* **NOW APPEARING AT OLE MISS (live)** □ □
– B.B. King theme / Caledonia / Don't answer the door / You done lost your good thing now / I need love so bad / Nobody loves me but my mother / Hold on (I feel our love is changing) / I got some outside help (I don't really need) / Darlin' you know I love you / When I'm wrong / The thrill is gone / Never made a move too soon / Three o'clock in the morning / Rock me baby / Guess who / I just can't leave your love alone. *(UK-iss.Feb86 d-lp/d-c; MCDL/+C 601)*

May 80. (7") *(MCA 588)* **CALEDONIA (live). / ROCK ME BABY (live)** □ [–]

Feb 81. (7") *<51101>* **THERE MUST BE A BETTER WORLD SOMEWHERE. / YOU'RE GOING WITH ME** [–] □

Feb 81. (lp) *(MCF 3095) <5162>* **THERE MUST BE A BETTER WORLD SOMEWHERE** □ □
– Life ain't nothing but a party / Born again human / There must be a better world somewhere / The victim / More, more, more / You're going with me. *(cd-iss. Sep91 on 'Beat Goes On'; BGOCD 124)*

Apr 82. (7") *(MCA 772)* **LEGEND IN MY TIME. / LOVE ME TENDER** □ □

Apr 82. (lp) *(MCF 3139) <5307>* **LOVE ME TENDER** □ □
– One of these nights / Love me tender / Don't change on me / (I'd be) A legend in my time / You've always got the blues / Please send me someone to love / You and me, me and you / Since I met you baby / Time is a thief / A world I never made.

Jun 82. (7") *(MCA 788) <52057>* **ONE OF THESE NIGHTS. / SINCE I MET YOU BABY** □ □

— augmented The CRUSADERS and The Royal Philharmonic Orchestra on the 'Street Life' single.

Sep 82. (7") *<52125>* **LOVE ME TENDER. / THE WORD I NEVER MADE** [–] □

Jul 83. (7") *<52218>* **INFLATION BLUES. / SELL MY MONKEY** [–] □

Jul 83. (lp) *(MCF 3170) <5413>* **BLUES 'N' JAZZ** □ Jun83 □
– Inflation blues / Broken hearted / Sell my monkey / Heed my warning / Teardrops from my eyes / Rainbow riot / Darlin' you know I love you / I can't let you go. *(re-iss. Oct87 lp/c; MCL/+C 1836)*

Jul 85. (7") *(MCA 947) <52530>* **INTO THE NIGHT. / CENTURY CITY CHASE** □ □
(12"+=) *(MCAT 947)* – Midnight believer.

Sep 85. (lp/c) *(MCF/+C 3281) <5616>* **SIX SILVER STRINGS** □ □
– Strings / Big boss man / In the midnight hour / Into the night / My Lucille / Memory lane / My guitar sings the blues / Double trouble.

Sep 85. (7") *<52574>* **MY LUCILLE. / Keep It Light (by Thelma Houston)** [–] □

Nov 85. (7") *<53675>* **BIG BOSS MAN. / MY GUITAR SINGS THE BLUES** [–] □

Feb 86. (7") *<52751>* **SIX SILVER STRINGS. / MEMORY LANE** [–] □

Mar 87. (7") *(MCA 1124)* **STANDING ON THE EDGE OF LOVE. / DON'T TELL ME NOTHNG** □ [–]
(12"+=) *(MCAT 1124)* – Let yourself in for it.

Sep 87. (7") *(MCA 1196)* **IN THE MIDNIGHT HOUR. / HEED MY WARNING** □ [–]

Jan 89. (7") *<53872>* **GO ON. / LAY ANOTHER LOG ON THE FIRE** [–] □

Feb 89. (lp/c/cd) *(MCG/MCGC/DMCG 6038) <42183>* **KING OF THE BLUES 1989** □ □
– (You've become a) Habit to me / Drowning in the sea of love / Can't get enough / Standing on the edge / Go on / Let's straighten it out / Change in your lovin' / Undercover man / Lay another log on the fire / Business with my baby tonight.

— Apr'89, BB was credited on U2's Top 10 hit 'WHEN LOVE COMES TO TOWN'

Aug 89. (7") *(MCA 1354)* **AIN'T NOBODY HOME. / LAY ANOTHER LOG ON THE FIRE** □ [–]
(cd-s+=/12"+=) *(D+/MCAT 1354)* – Standing on the edge.

Oct 91. (lp/c/cd) *<(MCA/+C/D 10295)>* **THERE IS ALWAYS ONE MORE TIME** □ □
– I'm moving on / Back in L.A. / The blues come over me / Fool me once / The lowdown / Mean and evil / Something up my sleeve / Roll, roll, roll / There is always one more time.

Feb 92. (c-s) *<54339>* **THE BLUES COME OVER ME (wild & bluesy club mix) / ('A'-integrity mix)** [–] □

Jul 93. (cd/c) *<(MCD/MCC 10710)>* **BLUES SUMMIT** □ □
– Playin' with my friends / Since I met you baby / I pity the fool / You shook me / Something you got / There's something on your mind / Call it stormy Monday / You're the boss / We're gonna make it / Medley: I gotta move out of this neighborhood – Nobody loves me but my mother / Little by little / Everybody had the blues.

Nov 93. (cd-s; by B.B.KING / PHILIP BENT & TONY REMY / DIANE SCHUUR) **MERRY CHRISTMAS BABY. /** □ □
(above on 'G.R.P.')

Nov 97. (cd) *<(MCD 1172-2)>* **DEUCES WILD** □ [73]
– If you love me / The thrill is gone / Rock me baby / Please send me someone to love / Baby I love you / Ain't nobody home / There must be a better world somewhere / Confessin' the blues / Paying the cost to be the boss / Dangerous mood / Keep it coming / Crying won't help you / Night life.

May 00. (cd) *<(112299-2)>* **MAKIN' LOVE IS GOOD FOR YOU** □ Apr00 □
– I got to leave this woman / Since I fell for you / I know / Peace of mind / Monday woman / Ain't nobody like my baby / Makin' love is good for you / Don't go no farther / Actions speak louder than words / What you bet / You're on top / Too good to you baby / I'm in the wrong business / She's my baby.

Reprise Reprise

Jun 00. (cd/c/lp; by B.B. KING & ERIC CLAPTON) *<(9362 47612-2/-4/-1)>* **RIDING WITH THE KING** [15] [3]
– Riding with the king / Ten long years / Key to the highway / Marry you

3 o'clock blues / Help the poor / I wanna be / Worried life blues / Days of old / When my heart beats like a hammer / Hold on! I'm coming / Come rain or shine.

		not iss.	M.C.A.
Nov 01.	(cd) *<112756>* **A CHRISTMAS CELEBRATION OF HOPE** (festive)	–	
un 03.	(cd) *<53202>* **REFLECTIONS**	–	

– Exactly like you / On my word of honor / I want a little girl / I'll string along with you / I need you / A mother's love / (I love you) For sentimental reasons / Neighborhood affair / Tomorrow night / There I've said it again / Always on my mind / Cross my heart / What a wonderful world.

		Island	Geffen
Oct 05.	(cd) *(9885355) <5263>* **80**	Sep05	45

– Early in the morning / Tired of your jive / The thrill is gone / Need your love so bad / Ain't nobody home / Hummingbird / All over again / Drivin' wheel / There must be a better world somewhere / Never make your move too soon / Funny how time slips away / Rock this house (live).

– (selective) compilations, etc. –

May 64.	(7") *Kent; <393>* **ROCK ME BABY. / I CAN'T LOSE** *(also iss.US on 'Modern')*		34
Apr 64.	(7") *<421>* **PLEASE LOVE ME. / BABY LOOK AT YOU**	–	
	note all below released on 'Kent'		
Oct 64.	(7") *<403>* **BEAUTICIAN BLUES. / I CAN HEAR MY NAME**	–	82
un 65.	(7") *<426>* **BLUE SHADOWS. / AND LIKE THAT**	–	97
Mar 67.	(7") *<462>* **THE JUNGLE. / LONG GONE BABY**	–	94
ep 68.	(7") *Blue Horizon; (57-3144) <492>* **THE WOMAN I LOVE. / YOU PUT IT ON ME**		94
Apr 71.	(7") *<4542>* **THAT EVIL CHILD. / HELP THE POOR**	–	97
ep 71.	(lp) *A.B.C.; (ABCD 509)* **LIVE AT THE REGAL live 1964)**		78
an 87.	(lp/c/cd) *Ace; (C H/HC/DCH 199)* **THE BEST OF B.B.KING VOLUME 2**		–
Apr 87.	(lp) *Ace; (CHD 201)* **ONE NIGHTER BLUES**		–
Aug 89.	(lp/cd) *Ace; (CHD 271)* **LUCILLE HAD A BABY**		–
ep 90.	(cd/c/lp) *M.C.A.; (DMCG/MCGC/MCG 6103)* **LIVE AT SAN QUENTIN (live 1970)** *(re-iss. cd+c Sep94)*		
Aug 91.	(cd/c) *Ace; (CDFAB/FABC 004)* **THE FABULOUS B.B.KING**		–
ul 92.	(cd) *Ace; (CDCHD 300)* **MY SWEET LITTLE ANGEL**		–
Nov 92.	(4xcd-box/4xc-box) *M.C.A.; (E 112418-2)* **KING OF THE BLUES**		
Aug 93.	(cd/c) *MCA; (MCL D/C 19214)* **KING OF THE BLUES 1989**		
eb 95.	(cd) *Castle; (CCSCD 412)* **THE COLLECTION**		–
ul 95.	(cd) *M.C.A.; (MCD 33008)* **LUCILLE / FRIENDS**		–
May 97.	(cd) *A-Play; (10033-2)* **THE BLUES COLLECTION**		
ul 98.	(cd) *Ace; (CDCHK 691)* **HE'S DYNAMITE**		
Oct 98.	(cd) *M.C.A.; (MCD 11879)* **BLUES ON THE BAYOU**		
Nov 98.	(cd/c) *Castle Pulse; (PLS CD/MC 298)* **THE GREAT B.B. KING**		
Dec 98.	(cd) *GP Records; (GP 2035)* **THE BEST**		
Mar 99.	(cd) *Ace; (CHCHD 712)* **THE RPM HITS 1951-1957**		
pr 99.	(cd/c) *Universal TV; (547340-2/-4)* **HIS DEFINITIVE GREATEST HITS**	24	
Aug 99.	(cd) *Castle Pie; (PIESD 051)* **ROCK ME BABY**		
Oct 99.	(cd) *M.C.A.; (112042-2)* **LET THE GOOD TIMES ROLL: THE MUSIC OF LOUIS JORDAN**		
an 00.	(cd) *Ace; (CDCHD 760)* **THE BEST OF THE KENT SINGLES 1958-1971**		
ul 00.	(cd) *M.C.A.; (MCBD 1905)* **THE VERY BEST OF B.B. KING**		
an 01.	(cd) *Castle Select; (SELCD 581)* **BB'S BLUES**		
pr 02.	(d-cd) *Ace; (CDCHM2 835)* **THE MODERN RECORDINGS 1950-1951**		
an 02.	(4xcd-box) *Ace; (ABOXCD 8)* **THE VINTAGE YEARS**		
Mar 03.	(cd) *King Biscuit; (KBCCD 114)* **IN CONCERT**		
Mar 03.	(cd) *Universal; (AAMCAD 11939)* **20TH CENTURY MASTERS**		
May 03.	(cd) *Ace; (CDCHM 881)* **MY KIND OF BLUES**		

Carole KING

Born: CAROLE KLEIN, 9 Feb'40, Brooklyn, New York, USA. Taught to play piano and sing by her mother from an early age, CAROLE's first serious forays into songwriting were with PAUL SIMON in 1958. She then met lyricist (and future husband) GERRY GOFFIN at college, the pair subsequently forming one of the most prolific and successful writing partnerships the music business has ever seen. Setting up shop in New York's famed 'Brill Building' (working for AL NEVINS and DON KIRSHNER's 'Aldon Music'), the duo scored their first success in 1961 when 'WILL YOU STILL LOVE ME TOMORROW' (by the SHIRELLES) and 'TAKE GOOD CARE OF MY BABY' (by BOBBY VEE), both hit the US top spot. The following year, 'THE LOCOMOTION' (by LITTLE EVA), gave them their third No.1, a track they also arranged, conducted and produced for the young singer. The hits kept on coming and meanwhile, KIRSHNER had persuaded CAROLE to release her solo version of 'IT MIGHT AS WELL RAIN UNTIL SEPTEMBER', which subsequently went UK Top 3 and US Top 30. The hit was a one-off though, and KING wasn't to resume her recording career until the late 60's. A relatively lean spell ensued (during which CAROLE and GERRY were divorced, although they kept the writing partnership going) before STEVE LAWRENCE took a GOFFIN-KING number back to the top of the US charts, 'GO AWAY LITTLE GIRL' (also a hit for DONNY OSMOND). Nor were the duo fazed by the onset of psychedelia, scoring hits for the ANIMALS ('DON'T BRING ME DOWN), THE MONKEES ('PLEASANT VALLEY SUNDAY', they also recorded 'TAKE A GIANT STEP') and The BYRDS (a brilliant version of 'GOIN' BACK', they also transformed 'WASN'T BORN TO FOLLOW' into a psych-country classic). At the height of the hippy scene in 1967, GOFFIN, KING and columnist, AL ARONOWITZ, founded their own label, 'Tommorrow', signing up flower power outfit, the MYDDLE CLASS. The project flopped, although the band's bass player, CHARLES LARKEY (ex-FUGS) would soon become KING's second husband. He and KING subsequently formed their own band, The CITY, with DANNY 'KOOTCH' KORTCHMAR (guitar, ex-FUGS) and JIM GORDON (drums). The outfit released one poor selling album, 'NOW THAT EVERYTHING'S BEEN SAID' (1969) on LOU ADLER's 'Ode' label, KING soon striking out on her own for a solo career. Encouraged to pen her own lyrics by fellow Laurel Canyon singer/songwriter JAMES TAYLOR (for whom CAROLE had played piano on his debut 'Apple' album, 'Sweet Baby James'), the first hesitant results came in the form of the 'WRITER' album in 1970, KING remaining with 'Ode' records. A breakthrough came with 'TAPESTRY' in 1971, a multi-million seller that became the biggest album in recording history up to that point. From the opening shimmy of 'I FEEL THE EARTH MOVE', to the melancholy reflection of 'SO FAR WAY' and 'HOME AGAIN', KING sounded more confident and self-possessed, her unpretentious vocal style and straight talking, confessional lyrics proving a winning combination. The record also benefitted from the midas touch of Lou Adler's production and the backing of 'The Section', the semi-legendary session team of KORTCHMAR, LELAND SKLAR (bass), RUSS KUNKEL (drums) and CRAIG DOERGE (keyboards), creating a highly commercial pop/rock/white soul fusion making up in melody what it lacked in earthiness. The album not only set the tone for the MOR dominated American music of the 70's, but initiated a slew of similar releases by songwriters desperate to get out from behind a desk. Sales of 'TAPESTRY' were further boosted when JAMES TAYLOR had a US No.1 in the summer of '71 with a cover of 'YOU'VE GOT A FRIEND'. KING's follow-up albums, 'MUSIC' (1971),

'RHYMES AND REASONS' (1972), 'FANTASY' (1973) and 'WRAP AROUND JOY (1974) all carried on in much the same vein, going gold and spawning such reliable AOR fare as 'SWEET SEASONS' (Top 10 in 1971) and 'JAZZMAN' (No.2 in 1974). The latter album employed the lyric-writing services of DAVID PALMER, later of STEELY DAN. None of the records, however, achieved the consistency of 'TAPESTRY', although they did cement KING's position as a fully paid-up superstar member of the L.A. elite. She eventually reunited with GOFFIN in 1976 for 'THOROUGHBRED' , her last album for 'Ode', subsequently signing for 'Capitol'. Her first release for the company, 'SIMPLE THINGS' (1977) saw her hooking up with backing band NAVARRO who numbered KING's future husband, RICK EVERS among their ranks. Tragedy struck the following year, however, when EVERS died of a drug overdose. It marked the beginning of a relatively barren period for KING, only her 'PEARLS – SONGS OF GOFFIN AND KING' (1980) album making any impact on the charts, and even that consisted of rehashed past glories. A brief move to 'Atlantic' and the return of KORTCHMAR and KUNKEL failed to resurrect her career and KING hasn't had a hit album or single since. She remains a respected figure within the business, however, and continues to tour and record, releasing material on her own 'King's X' label, finally receiving the dubious honour of being inducted into the Rock'n'roll Hall Of Fame in 1990. KING returned with a millennial comeback of sorts in the shape of 'LOVE MAKES THE WORLD' (2001), a partly successful attempt at recapturing the singer/songwriter grace of yore. Pared-down ballad fare such as 'YOU WILL FIND ME THERE' and 'THIS TIME' came closest to realising that early 70's magic, while guest spots from the likes of k.d. LANG and WYNTON MARSALIS kept things interesting. 'THE LIVING ROOM TOUR' (2005), interestingly enough, didn't do what it said on the tin, but it was an intimate double-set, with a 60-something KING in surprisingly spry vocal form against a sparse backdrop of piano and acoustic guitar. Taking stock of her expansive legacy and reaching right back to the early 60s, the record was emblematic of KING's multi-generational appeal, strong enough to lift her into the US Top 20 for the first time since 1977.

Album rating: WRITER: CAROLE KING (*6) / TAPESTRY (*8) / MUSIC (*7) / RHYMES & REASONS (*6) / FANTASY (*7) / WRAP AROUND JOY (*7) / REALLY ROSIE (*6) / THOROUGHBRED (*6) / SIMPLE THINGS (*4) / HER GREATEST HITS compilation (*7) / WELCOME HOME (*4) / TOUCH THE SKY (*4) / PEARLS – SONGS OF GOFFIN AND KING (*5) / ONE TO ONE (*4) / SPEEDING TIME (*3) / CITY STREETS (*4) / IN CONCERT (*3) / COLOR OF YOUR DREAMS (*3) / NATURAL WOMAN – THE VERY BEST OF ... compilation (*8) / LOVE MAKES THE WORLD (*5) / THE LIVING ROOM TOUR (*6)

CAROLE KING – vocals, piano (with session people)

not iss. / ABC-Paramount

Jan 59. (7") <9921> **GOIN' WILD. / THE RIGHT GIRL** –
Mar 59. (7") <9986> **BABY SITTIN'. / UNDER THE STARS** –

not iss. / RCA Victor

May 59. (7") <7560> **QUEEN OF THE BEACH. / SHORT MORT** –

not iss. / Alpine

Nov 59. (7") <57> **OH NEIL!. / A VERY SPECIAL BOY** –

—— She kept on writing for others alongside husband GERRY GOFFIN. After two and a half years she returned to solo work for ...

London / Dimension

Aug 62. (7") *(HLU 9591)* <2000> **IT MIGHT AS WELL RAIN UNTIL SEPTEMBER. / NOBODY'S PERFECT** 3 22
<first issued in US on 'Companion'; 2000> (re-iss. Sep72; HL 10391) (reached No.43 UK)

Nov 62. (7") <1004> **SCHOOL BELLS ARE RINGING. / I DIDN'T HAVE ANY** –

Apr 63. (7") <1009> **HE'S A BAD BOY. / WE GROW UP TOGETHER** – 94

—— Soon divorced her husband GERRY, although they still carried on writing.

London / Tomorr

Apr 66. (7") *(HL 10036)* <7502> **SOME OF YOUR LOVIN'. / ROAD TO NOWHERE**

the CITY

CAROLE KING with **CHARLES LARKEY** – bass (of FUGS) / **DANNY 'KOOTCH' KORTCHMAR** – guitar / **JIM GORDON** – drums

A & M / Ode

Jan 69. (lp) <244012> **NOW THAT EVERYTHING'S BEEN SAID** –
– Snow queen / I wasn't born to follow / Now that everything's been said / Paradise alley / Man without a dream / Victim of circumstance / Why are you leaving / Lady / My sweet home / I don't believe it / That old swee roll (hi-de-do) / All my time.

Feb 69. (7") <113> **PARADISE ALLEY. / SNOW QUEEN** –

May 69. (7") <119> **THAT OLD SWEET ROLL. / WHY ARE YOU LEAVING** –

CAROLE KING

solo, with session people

May 70. (lp) *(AMLS 996)* <77006> **WRITER: CAROLE KING**
– Spaceship races / No easy way down / Child of mine / Goin' back / T love / What have you got to lose / Eventually / Raspberry jam / Can't yo be real / I can't hear you no more / Sweet sweetheart / Up on the roo *<re-prom.Apr71 hit US No.84> (re-iss. Feb79 on 'Epic'; EPC 82318)*

Mar 70. (7") **EVENTUALLY. / UP ON THE ROOF** –

—— now again with regulars LARKEY and KORTCHMAR plus **RUSS KUNKE** – drums and guest **JAMES TAYLOR** – guitar, backing vocals (solo artist)

Nov 70. (lp/c) *(AMLS/CAM 2025)* <77009> **TAPESTRY** 4 1
– I feel the earth move / So far away / It's too late / Home again / Beautiful / Way over yonder / You've got a friend / Where you lead / Will you still lov me tomorrow / Smackwater Jack / Tapestry / (You make me feel like) natural woman. *(re-iss. 1977 on 'Epic'; EPC 82308) (re-iss. Aug84 on 'Epi lp/c; EPC/40 32110) (cd-iss. May84 on 'Polydor'; 821 194-1) (cd re-iss. 198 on 'C.B.S.'; CDCBS 82308) (cd re-iss. Jun89; CD 32110) (cd re-iss. Sep95 o 'Epic'; 480422-2)*

Apr 71. (7") *(AMS 849)* <66015> **IT'S TOO LATE. / I FEEL THE EARTH MOVE** 6 1

Jul 71. (7") *(AMS 867)* <66019> **SO FAR AWAY. / SMACKWATER JACK** 14

Dec 71. (lp/c) *(AMLH/CAM 67013)* <77013> **MUSIC** 18 1
– Brother, brother / Song of long ago / Brighter / Surely / Some kind c wonderful / It's going to take some time / Music / Sweet seasons / Car your load / Growing away from me / Too much rain / Back to Californi *(re-iss. Feb79 on 'Epic'; EPC 82319) (re-iss. 1983 on 'C.B.S.' lp/c; CBS/ 32066) (cd-iss. Jun91 on 'Pickwick'; 982595-2) (cd re-iss. Feb97 on 'Epic 484462-2)*

Jan 72. (7") *(AMS 887)* <66022> **SWEET SEASONS. / POCKET MONEY** 9

Mar 72. (7") **BROTHER, BROTHER. / IT'S GOING TO TAKE SOME TIME** –

Ode / Ode

Oct 72. (7") <(ODS 66031)> **BEEN TO CANAAN. / BITTER WITH THE SWEET** 24

Nov 72. (lp/c) <(77016)> **RHYMES AND REASONS** 40 Oct72 2
– Come down easy / My my she cries / Peace in the valley / Feeling sa tonight / The first day in August / Bitter with the sweet / Goodbye don mean I'm gone / Stand behind me / Gotta get through another day / I thin I can hear you / Ferguson Road / Been to Canaan.

Jun 73. (7") <(ODS 66035)> **YOU LIGHT UP MY LIFE. / BELIEVE IN HUMANITY** 28 67

Jul 73. (lp/c) <(77018)> **FANTASY** Jun73 6
– Fantasy beginning / You've been around too long / Being at w with each other / Directions / That's how things go down / Weekdays Haywood / A quiet place to live / Welfare symphony / You light up n life / Corazon / Believe in humanity / Fantasy end. *(cd-iss. Oct93 on 'So Collectors'; 983307-2) (cd re-iss. Jul97 on 'Epic'; 487939-2)*

Oct 73. (7") <ODS 66039> **CORAZON. / THAT'S HOW THINGS GO DOWN** – 37

—— added guest **TOM SCOTT** – saxophone

Jul 74. (7") <(ODS 66101)> **JAZZMAN. / YOU GO YOUR WAY, I'LL GO MINE** 2

Oct 74. (lp/c) <(77024)> **WRAP AROUND JOY** Sep74 1

– Nightingale / Change in mind, change of heart / Jazzman / You go your way, I'll go mine / You're something new / We are all in this together / Wrap around joy / You gentle me / My lovin' eyes / Sweet Adonis / A night this side of dying / The best is yet to come. *(cd-iss. May92 on 'Thunderbolt'; CDTB 137)*

Jan 75. (7") *<(ODS 66106)>* **NIGHTINGALE. / YOU'RE SOMETHING NEW** [ ] [9]

Mar 75. (lp) *<77027>* **REALLY ROSIE** (children's TV) [–] [20]
– Really Rosie / One was Johnny / Alligators all around / Pierre / Screaming and yelling / The ballad of chicken soup / Chicken soup and rice / Ave. P / My simple humble neighborhood / The awful truth / Such suffer / Really Rosie. *(cd-iss. Sep93 on 'Sony Collectors'; 983257-2)*

Jul 75. (7") <> **PIERRE. / CHICKEN SOUP WITH RICE** [–] [ ]

Jan 76. (7") *<ODS 66119>* **ONLY LOVE IS REAL. / STILL HERE THINKING OF YOU** [–] [37]

Jan 76. (lp/c) *<(77034)>* **THOROUGHBRED** [ ] [3]
– So many ways / Daughter of light / High out of time / Only love is real / There's a space between us / I'd like to know you better / We all have to be alone / Ambrosia / Still here thinking of you / It's gonna work out fine. *(re-iss. Jul84 on 'C.B.S.' lp/c; CBS/40 31841)*

Jul 76. (7") *<(ODS 66123)>* **HIGH OUT OF TIME. / I'D LIKE TO KNOW YOU BETTER** [ ] May76 [76]

— She now worked with backing band NAVARRO, which included new 3rd husband **RICK EVERS** – guitar

Capitol Capitol

Jul 77. (7") *(CL 15934) <4455>* **HARD ROCK CAFE. / TO KNOW THAT I LOVE YOU** [ ] [30]

Aug 77. (lp/c) *<(EA-ST 11667)>* **SIMPLE THINGS** [ ] [17]
– Simple things / Hold on / In the name of love / Labyrinth / You're the one who knows / Hard rock cafe / Time alone / God only knows / To know that I love you / One.

Oct 77. (7") *<4497>* **HOLD ON. / SIMPLE THINGS** [–] [ ]

Nov 77. (7") *(CL 15949)* **LABYRINTH. / SIMPLE THINGS** [ ] [–]

Apr 78. (lp/c) *<(EA-ST 11785)>* **WELCOME HOME** [ ] [ ]
– Main Street Saturday night / Sunbird / Venusian diamond / Changes / Morning sun / Disco tech / Ways of love / Ride the music / Everybody's got the spirit / Welcome home.

Apr 78. (7") *<4593>* **MAIN STREET SATURDAY NIGHT. / CHANGES** [–] [ ]

Aug 78. (7") *<4649>* **MORNING SUN. / SUNBIRD** [–] [ ]

Aug 78. (7") *(CL 16009)* **DISCO TECH. / VENUSIAN DIAMOND** [ ] [–]

— Her husband RICK died Mar78 of a drug overdose. She recorded next album with ex-JERRY JEFF WALKER's musicians.

Jul 79. (lp/c) *<(EA-ST 11953)>* **TOUCH THE SKY** [ ] Jun79 [ ]
– Time gone by / Move lightly / Dreamlike I wander / Walk with me / Good mountain people / You still want her / Passing of the days / Crazy / Eagle / Seeing red.

Aug 79. (7") *(CL 16093) <4718>* **MOVE LIGHTLY. / WHISKEY** [ ] [ ]

Oct 79. (7") *<4766>* **TIME GONE BY. / DREAMLIKE I WANDER** [–] [ ]

— ex-husband **LARKEY** returned on bass and **CHRISTOPHER CROSS** – guitar

Jun 80. (lp/c) *<(EA-ST 12073)>* **PEARLS – SONGS OF GOFFIN AND KING** (new versions old songs) [ ] [44]
– Dancin' with tears in my eyes / Locomotion / One fine day / Hey girl / Snow queen / Chains / Oh no not my baby / Hi de ho / Wasn't born to follow / Goin' back.

Jun 80. (7") *(CL 16152) <4864>* **ONE FINE DAY. / RULERS OF THE WORLD** [ ] May80 [12]

Aug 80. (7") *<4911>* **LOCOMOTION. / OH NO NOT MY BABY** [–] [ ]

Oct 80. (7") *<4941>* **CHAINS. / HEY GIRL** [–] [ ]

— Now with new session people

Atlantic Atlantic

Mar 82. (lp/c) *(K/K4 50880) <19344>* **ONE TO ONE** [ ] [ ]
– One to one / It's a war / Lookin' out for number one / Life without love / Golden man / Read between the lines / Love is like (a boomerang) / Goat Annie / Someone you never met before / Little prince.

Mar 82. (7") *<4026>* **ONE TO ONE. / GOAT ANNIE** [–] [45]

Apr 82. (7") *(K 11725)* **READ BETWEEN THE LINES. / GOLDEN MAN** [ ] [–]

May 82. (7") *<4062>* **READ BETWEEN THE LINES. / LIFE WITHOUT LOVE** [–] [ ]

Jun 82. (7") *(K 11738)* **LITTLE PRINCE. / SOMEONE YOU NEVER MET BEFORE** [ ] [–]

— **KUNKEL** and **KORTCHMAR** returned to line-up

Dec 83. (lp/c/cd) *<(780 118-1/-4)>* **SPEEDING TIME** [ ] [ ]
– Computer eyes / Small voice / Crying in the rain / Sacred heart of stone / Speeding time / Standin' on the border line / So ready for love / Chalis Borealis / Dancing / Alabaster lady.

Dec 83. (7") *<89756>* **CRYING IN THE RAIN. / A SACRED HEART OF STONE** [–] [ ]

Feb 84. (7") *<89694>* **SPEEDING TIME. /** [–] [ ]

In 1985, she and JOHN SEBASTIAN wrote songs for the "Care Bears" film

Capitol Capitol

Apr 89. (7") *<44336>* **CITY STREETS. / TIME HEALS ALL WOUNDS** [–] [ ]

Apr 89. (7") *(CL 527)* **CITY STREETS. / I CAN'T STOP THINKING ABOUT YOU** [ ] [–]
(12"+=/cd-s+=) *(12/CD CL 527)* – Time heals all wounds.

Apr 89. (cd/c/lp) *(CD/TC+/EST 2092) <90885>* **CITY STREETS** [ ] [ ]
– City streets / Sweet life / Down to the darkness / Lovelight / I can't stop thinking about you / Legacy / Ain't that the way / Midnight flyer / Homeless heart / Someone who believes in you.
(above featured ERIC CLAPTON – guitar / MAX WEINBERG – drums)

Jul 89. (7") *<44444>* **SOMEONE WHO BELIEVES IN YOU. / CITY STREETS** [–] [ ]

Quality Rhythm Safari

Mar 93. (cd) *<57197>* **COLOR OF YOUR DREAMS** [–] [ ]
– Lay down my life / Hold out for love / Standing in the rain / Now and forever / Wishful thinking / Color of your dreams / Tears falling down on me / Friday's tie-dye nightmare / Just one thing / Do you feel love / It's never too late.

Mar 94. (cd/c) *(CKING CD/MC 01) <53878>* **IN CONCERT – THE GREATEST HITS LIVE** (live) [ ] [ ]
– Hard Rock Cafe / Up on the roof / Smackwater Jack / So far away / Beautiful / A natural woman (you make me feel like) / Hold out for love / Will you love me tomorrow / Jazzman / It's too late / Chains / I feel the earth move / You've got a friend / The locomotion / You've got a friend.
above was recorded at LA's Amphitheater, with guest spots for CROSBY & NASH, plus SLASH of GUNS N' ROSES playing guitar on 'The Locomotion'.

not iss. Koch Int.

Sep 01. (cd) *<8346>* **LOVE MAKES THE WORLD** [–] [ ]
– Love makes the world / You can do anything / The reason / I wasn't gonna fall in love / I don't know / Oh no, not my baby / It could have been anyone / Monday without you / An uncommon love / You will find me there / Safe again / This time.

Rockingale Rockingale

Aug 05. (d-cd) *<(RCD2 6201-2)>* **THE LIVING ROOM TOUR** (live) [ ] Jul05 [17]
– Welcome to my living room / Peace in the valley / Love makes the world / Now and forever / Where you lead I will follow / Lay down my life / Jazzman / Smackwater Jack / Wishful thinking / Take good care of my baby – It might as well rain until September / Loving you forever / It's too late / So far away / Sweet seasons / Chains / Pleasant valley Sunday / Being at war with each other / I feel the earth move / (You make me feel like a) Natural woman / You've got a friend / Locomotion.

– compilations etc. –

Note; All below releases on 'Epic' were issued on 'Ode' US.

May 78. (lp/c) *Epic; (EPC 86043) / Ode; <34967>* **HER GREATEST HITS** [ ] Mar78 [47]
– Jazzman / So far away / Sweet seasons / I feel the Earth move / Brother, brother / Only love is real / It's too late / Nightingale / Smackwater Jack / Been to Canaan / Corazon / Believe in humility. *(re-iss. Jul83 lp/c; EPC/40 32345) (cd-iss. Mar87 on 'C.B.S.'; CD 86043) (cd re-iss. Mar91; CD 32345)*

Jun 79. (7") *Epic; (EPC 7067)* **IT'S TOO LATE. / YOU'VE GOT A FRIEND** [ ] [–]

Oct 83. (7") *Old Gold; (OG 9355)* **IT MIGHT AS WELL RAIN UNTIL SEPTEMBER. / THE ROAD TO NOWHERE** [ ] [–]

Jul 94. (cd) *Connoisseur; (VSOPCD 199)* **PEARLS / TIME GONE BY** [ ] [–]

Oct 94. (d-cd/d-c) *Legacy-Epic; (E2K/E2T 48833)* **A NATURAL WOMAN – THE ODE COLLECTION 1968-1976** [ ] [–]

Nov 96. (cd) *Epic; (485104-2)* **LIVE AT CARNEGIE HALL (live)** [ ] [–]

Jun 97. (cd) *Marginal; (MAR 010)* **HITS AND RARITIES** [ ] [–]

Sep 00. (cd/c) *Sony TV; (SONYTV 93 CD/MC)* **NATURAL WOMAN – THE VERY BEST OF . . .** 31 –

☐ KING BISCUIT TIME (see under ⇒ BETA BAND)

KING CRIMSON

Formed: Bournemouth, England . . . summer 1967 by ROBERT FRIPP, plus brothers MIKE and PETE GILES, who formed the soft-rock trio BRAIN, then GILES, GILES & FRIPP. After signing to 'Deram' early in '68 and adding couple, IAN McDONALD and JUDY DYBLE, they issued flop album, 'THE CHEERFUL INSANITY OF . . .', in September of that year. With IAN now replacing PETE, the trio soon became KING CRIMSON, adding new vocalist GREG LAKE, who debuted at The Speakeasy in London on the 9th of April 1969. Three months later, they supported The ROLLING STONES at Hyde Park's free concert, a performance which attracted the attention of the 'Island' label. Subsequently signed up, they unleashed 'IN THE COURT OF THE CRIMSON KING' in October '69, a masterful debut album which made UK Top 5 and US Top 30. At this stage, the group were basically a prog-rock neo-classical outfit, their initial MOODY BLUES' mellotron-sound soon swapped for experimental, occasionally self-indulgent guitar-mastery of FRIPP. KING CRIMSON found themselves in turmoil when a couple of group members departed, leaving FRIPP and lyricist/road manager, PETE SINFIELD, to work things out. Eventually, with augmentation from session men and ex-members, they recorded the 1970 follow-up album, 'IN THE WAKE OF POSEIDON'. An aggregation of KING CRIMSON members had earlier performed the weird 'CAT FOOD' single on 'Top Of The Pops'; this release signalled a move towards avant-jazz territory, a sound they'd develop over the course of early 70's albums, 'LIZARD', 'ISLANDS' and 'LARKS' TONGUES IN ASPIC'. Throughout this turbulent period, FRIPP and Co. went through even more upheavals, although they still scored with astounding album successes ('STARLESS AND BIBLE BLACK' and 'RED' – both 1974) until they disbanded for the first time late in '74. FRIPP had already been a prolific session man for the likes of VAN DER GRAAF GENERATOR and (BRIAN) ENO, and together with the latter was co-credited on two experimental budget lp's, 'NO PUSSYFOOTIN' (1973) and 'EVENING STAR' (1975). He then moved to New York in 1977 and worked with PETER GABRIEL on his first three albums, at the same time lending his expertise to BOWIE's 'Heroes'. In 1979, FRIPP released his debut solo album, 'EXPOSURE', which featured many of his close friends handling vocals (GABRIEL, HAMILL, etc). The following year, his instrumental set, 'GOD SAVE THE QUEEN / UNDER HEAVY MANNERS' developed his patented brand of electro-experimentation, dubbed "Frippertronics", the record trailed by a short-lived project/band, the LEAGUE OF GENTLEMEN. In 1981, he re-formed KING CRIMSON with BILL BRUFORD, ADRIAN BELEW and TONY LEVIN, recording a clutch of slightly more accessible albums, before FRIPP was again left contemplating a revived solo career. During the period, 1982-84, the guitarist collaborated on two albums, 'I ADVANCE MASKED' and 'BEWITCHED', with ANDY SUMMERS (POLICE guitarist). Like many of their contemporaries, KING CRIMSON reunited in 1994, issuing a series of studio and live sets. Come the new millennium, KING CRIMSON were still going strong, embracing the fad for treated vocals on 'HAPPY WITH WHAT YOU HAVE TO BE HAPPY WITH' (2002), a record which also featured some of the most aggressive material of the band's career. 'THE POWER TO BELIEVE' (2003) meanwhile, collected the cream of their more recent releases – including the startling 'EYES WIDE OPEN' – with new material. 2005 saw FRIPP deliver two Soundscape-style sets: a collaborative reunion set with ENO, 'THE EQUATORIAL STARS', and the solo 'LOVE CANNOT BEAR', pieced together from 22 years worth of "Frippertronics".

• **Trivia:** In the mid-80's, FRIPP married singer/actress, TOYAH WILLCOX, even collaborating on an album, 'THE LADY OR THE TIGER', in 1987.

Album rating: Giles, Giles & Fripp: THE CHEERFUL SANITY OF . . . (*5) / King Crimson: IN THE COURT OF THE CRIMSON KING (*9) / IN THE WAKE OF POSEIDON (*6) / LIZARD (*6) / ISLANDS (*7) / EARTHBOUND (*4) / LARKS' TONGUES IN ASPIC (*8) / STARLESS & BIBLE BLACK (*8) / RED (*8) / U.S.A. (*5) / A YOUNG PERSON'S GUIDE TO KING CRIMSON compilation (*8) / DISCIPLINE (*6) / BEAT (*6) / THREE OF A PERFECT PAIR (*5) / FRAME BY FRAME – THE ESSENTIAL KING CRIMSON compilation (*8) / VROOOM (*5) / THRAK (*5) / B'BOOM: OFFICIAL SOUNDTRACK – LIVE IN ARGENTINA (*5) / THRaKaTTaK (*4) / THE CONSTRUCkTION OF LIGHT (*6) / HAPPY WITH WHAT YOU HAVE TO BE HAPPY WITH mini (*6) / THE POWER TO BELIEVE (*6) / EleKtriK (*6) / Fripp & Eno: NO PUSSYFOOTIN' (*2 at the time – *6 now!?) / EVENING STAR (*2 at the time – *5 now!?) / THE EQUATORIAL STARS (*7) / Robert Fripp: EXPOSURE (*7) / GOD SAVE THE QUEEN – UNDER HEAVY MANNERS (*7) / LET THE POWER FALL (FRIPPERTRONICS) (6) / THE LEAGUE OF GENTLEMEN (*5) / NETWORK collection (*6) / GOD SAVE THE KING (*5) / ROBERT FRIPP AND THE LEAGUE OF CRAFTY GUITARISTS!: LIVE (*5) / THE BRIDGE BETWEEN (*5) / 1995 SOUNDTRACKS, VOLUME 2 – LIVE IN CALIFORNIA (*5) / RADIOPHONICS: 1995 SOUNDSCAPES VOLUME 1 (*5) / INTERGALACTIC BOOGIE EXPRESS – LIVE IN EUROPE 1991 (*5) / THAT WHICH PASSES (*5) / LOVE CANNOT BEAR live soundscapes collection (*6)

GILES, GILES & FRIPP

PETE GILES – bass / **MICHAEL GILES** (b.1942)– drums / **ROBERT FRIPP** (b.16 May'46, Wimbourne, Dorset, England)– guitar, mellotron

C.B.S. not iss.

May 67. (7"; as BRAIN) *(R 5595)* **NIGHTMARES IN RED. / KICK THE DONKEY** ☐ –

Deram not iss.

Jun 68. (7") *(DM 188)* **ONE IN A MILLION. / NEWLY-WEDS** ☐ –

— added **IAN McDONALD** (b.25 Jun'46, London) – keyboards / and guest **JUDY DYBLE** – vocals (ex-FAIRPORT CONVENTION) also featured as did KING CRIMSON lyricist **PETE SINFIELD**

Sep 68. (lp; mono/stereo) *(DML/SML 1022)* **THE CHEERFUL INSANITY OF GILES, GILES & FRIPP** ☐ –
– The Saga of Rodney Toady / One in a million / Just George / Thursday morning / North meadow / Call tomorrow / Newly-weds / Digging my lawn / Suite No.1 / Little children / The crukster / How do you know / The sun is shining / Brudite eyes / Elephant song. *(re-iss. 1970; SPA 423) (re-iss. Apr82 on 'Editions-EG'; EGED 16) (re-iss. Aug93 cd/c+=; 820 965-2/-4)* – (extra versions).

— IAN now on vocals (JUDY left to join TRADER HORNE)

Sep 68. (7") *(DM 210)* **THURSDAY MORNING. / ELEPHANT SONG** ☐ –

KING CRIMSON

ROBERT, IAN + MIKE recruited **GREG LAKE** (b.10 Nov'48) – vocals, bass (ex-GODS)

Island Atlantic

Oct 69. (7") *(WIP 6071) <2703>* **THE COURT OF THE CRIMSON KING (part 1). / (part 2)** ☐ Dec69 80

Oct 69. (lp) *(ILPS 9111) <8245>* **IN THE COURT OF THE CRIMSON KING** 5 Dec69 28
– 21st century schizoid man (including; Mirrors) / I talk to the wind / Epitaph (including; March for no reason – Tomorrow and tomorrow) / Moonchild (including; The dream – The illusion) / The court of the Crimson King (including: The return of the fire witch – The dance of the puppets). *<US re-iss. 1970; SD 19155> (re-iss. Mar77 on 'Polydor' lp)(c 2302 057)(3100 357) (cd-iss. May83 on 'Polydor'; 800 030-2) (re-iss. Jan87 & Nov91 on 'E.G.' lp/c/cd; EG LP/MC/CD 1)*

— **PETE GILES** – bass (ex-GILES, GILES & FRIPP) repl. IAN who with MIKE had formed McDONALD & GILES. IAN later formed FOREIGNER. MIKE appeared below. Added **KEITH TIPPET** – piano (other two were FRIPP & LAKE)

Mar 70. (7") *(WIP 6080)* **CAT FOOD. / GROON** ☐ –

— added **MEL COLLINS** – saxophone (ex-CIRCUS) / plus guest on 1 track **GORDON HASKELL** – vocals

May 70. (lp) *(ILPS 9127) <8266>* **IN THE WAKE OF POSEIDON** [4] Sep70 [31]
– Peace – a beginning / Pictures of a city (including; 42nd at Treadmill) / Cadence and cascade / In the wake of Poseidon (including; Libra's theme) / Peace – a theme / Cat food / The Devil's triangle: Merday morn – Hand of Sceiron – Garden of worm / Peace – an end. *(re-iss. Mar77 on 'Polydor' lp)(c; (2302 058)(3100 358) (re-iss. Jan87 & Nov91 on 'E.G.' lp/c/cd; EG LP/MC/CD 2)*

— **GORDON HASKELL** (now full-time) repl. GREG who formed EMERSON, LAKE & PALMER (earlier). FRIPP had also retained **MEL COLLINS / ANDY McCULLOCH** – drums repl. MIKE

Dec 70. (lp) *(ILPS 9141) <8278>* **LIZARD** [30] [ ]
– Cirkus (including; Entry of the chameleons) / Indoor games / Happy family / Lady of the dancing water / Lizard suite: Prince Rupert awakes – Bolero-The peacock's tale – The battle of glass tears; (a) Dawn song – (b) Last skirmish – (c) Prince Rupert's lament / Big top. *(re-iss. Apr77 on 'Polydor' lp)(c; 2302 059)(3100 359) (re-iss. Jan87 & Nov91 on 'E.G.' lp/c/cd; EG LP/MC/CD 4)*

— **BOZ BURRELL** (b. RAYMOND, 1946, Lincoln, England) – vocals, bass repl. HASKELL who went solo / **IAN WALLACE** (b.29 Sep'46, Bury, England) – drums repl. McCULLOCH who joined GREENSLADE

Dec 71. (lp) *(ILPS 9175) <7212>* **ISLANDS** [30] [76]
– Formentera lady / The sailor's tale / Letters / (prelude) / Song of the gulls – Islands / Ladies of the road. *(re-iss. Apr77 on 'Polydor' lp)(c; 2302 060)(3100 360) (re-iss. Jan87 on 'E.G.' lp/c/cd; EG LP/MC/CD 5)*

— FRIPP was sole survivor (lyricist PETE SINFIELD left early '72, to go into production for ROXY MUSIC's debut and be lyricist for Italians P.F.M.) / **JOHN WETTON** (b.12 Jul'49, Derby, England) – vocals, bass (ex-FAMILY) repl. BOZ who formed BAD COMPANY / **BILL BRUFORD** (b.17 May'48, London, England) – drums (ex-YES) repl. WALLACE who joined STREETWALKERS / **DAVID CROSS** (b.1948, Plymouth, England) – violin, flute repl. COLLINS who later joined CAMEL + sessions / added **JAMIE MUIR** – percussion and new lyricist **RICHARD PALMER-JAMES**

Mar 73. (lp) *(ILPS 9230) <7263>* **LARKS' TONGUES IN ASPIC** [20] [61]
– Larks' tongues in aspic (part one) / Book of Saturday / Exiles / Easy money / The talking drum / Larks' tongues in aspic (part two). *(re-iss. Apr77 on 'Polydor' lp)(c; 2302 061)(3100 361) (re-iss. Jan87 & Nov91 on 'E.G.' lp/c/cd; EG LP/MC/CD 7)*

— Reverted to a quartet when JAMIE became a Tibetan monk

Feb 74. (7") *(WIP 6189) <3016>* **THE NIGHT WATCH. / THE GREAT DECEIVER** [ ] [ ]

Feb 74. (lp) *(ILPS 9275) <7298>* **STARLESS AND BIBLE BLACK** [28] [64]
– The great deceiver / Lament / We'll let you know / The night watch / Trio / The mincer / Starless and bible black / Trio / Fracture. *(re-iss. Apr77 on 'Polydor' lp)(c; 2302 065)(3100 365) (re-iss. Jan87 & Nov91 on 'E.G.' lp/c/cd; EG LP/MC/CD 12)*

— now just basically a trio of FRIPP, WETTON and BRUFORD with old guests **MEL COLLINS, IAN McDONALD** and the departing **CROSS** augmenting on a track

Oct 74. (lp) *(ILPS 9308) <18110>* **RED** [45] [66]
– Red / Fallen angel / One more red nightmare / Providence / Starless. *(re-iss. Apr77 on 'Polydor' lp/c; 2302 066)(3100 366) (re-iss. Jan87 & Nov91 on 'E.G.' lp/c/cd; EG LP/MC/CD 15)*

— Split just before last album. Next live album was recorded with DAVID CROSS

Apr 75. (lp) *(ILPS 9316) <18136>* **U.S.A. (live)** [ ] [ ]
– Larks' tongues in aspic (part II) / Lament / Exiles / Asbury park / Easy money / 21st century schizoid man. *(re-iss. Dec79 on 'Polydor'; 2302 067) (re-iss. Jan87 on 'E.G.' lp/c/cd; EG LP/MC/CD 18)*

— JOHN WETTON joined BRIAN FERRY, then URIAH HEEP and later ASIA etc. As above BILL BRUFORD went solo and formed UK, after GONG stints.

FRIPP & ENO

ROBERT FRIPP – guitar of KING CRIMSON / **BRIAN ENO** – synthesizers, instruments

Island-Help Antilles

Nov 73. (lp) *(HELP 16) <7007>* **(NO PUSSYFOOTING)** [ ] [ ]
– The heavenly music corporation / Swastika girls. *(re-iss. Oct77 on 'Polydor'; 2343 095) (re-iss. Jan87 on 'E.G.' lp/cd; EGED/EEGCD 2)*

Dec 75. (lp) *(HELP 22) <7018>* **EVENING STAR** [ ] [ ]
– Wind on water / Evening star / Evensong / Wind on wind / An index of metals. *(re-iss. Oct77 on 'Polydor'; 2343 094) (re-iss. Jan87 on 'E.G.' lp/cd; EGED/EEGCD 3)*

ROBERT FRIPP

solo adding keyboards and a number of friends **PETER GABRIEL, PETER HAMILL & DARYL HALL** on vox, plus **PHIL COLLINS, BARRY ANDREWS, TONY LEVIN & MICHAEL NARADA WALDEN** – other instruments

E.G. E.G.-Polydor

Apr 79. (lp/c) *(EG LP/MC 101) <6201>* **EXPOSURE** [71] [79]
– (prelude) / You burn me up I'm a cigarette / Breathless / Disengage / North star / Chicago / NY3 / Mary / Exposure / Haaaden two / Urban landscape / I may not have had enough of me but I've had enough of you / (first inaugural address to the J.A.C.E. Sherborne House) / Water music I / Here comes the flood / Water music II / Postscript. *(cd-iss. Jan87 & Apr89; EGCD 41)*

Mar 80. (lp/c) *(EG LP 105) <PL 6266>* **GOD SAVE THE QUEEN / UNDER HEAVY MANNERS (instrumental)** [ ] [ ]
– Under heavy manners / The zero of the signified / Red two scorer / God save the Queen / 1983. *(re-iss. Jan87 lp/c/cd; EG LP/MC/CD 45)*

E.G.-Editions not iss.

Apr 81. (lp/c) *(EGED/+C 10)* **LET THE POWER FALL (FRIPPERTRONICS)** [ ] [–]
– 1984 / 1985 / 1986 / 1987 / 1988 / 1989. *(cd-iss. Jan87; EEGCD 10)*

the LEAGUE OF GENTLEMEN

FRIPP retained **BARRY ANDREWS** adding **SARA LEE** – bass (ex-JANE AIRE) / **JOHNNY TOOBAD** – drums

E.G.-Editions Polydor

Dec 80. (7") *(EGEND 1)* **HEPTAPARAPARSHINOKH. / MARRIAGEMUZIC** [ ] [–]

Mar 81. (lp) *(EGED 9) <16317>* **LEAGUE OF GENTLEMEN (instrumental)** [ ] [ ]
– Indiscreet / Inductive recurrance / Minor man / Heptaparaparshinokh / Dislocated / Pareto optimum 1 / Eye needles / Indiscreet II / Pareto optimum 2 / Cognitive dissonance / H.G. Wells / Trap / Ochre / Indiscreet III.

Mar 81. (7") *(EGEND 2)* **DISLOCATED. / 1984** [ ] [–]

KING CRIMSON

FRIPP along with past member BRUFORD recruits newcomers **ADRIAN BELEW** (b. ROBERT STEVEN BELEW, 23 Dec'49, Covington, Kentucky) – guitar, vocals (ex-TOM TOM CLUB) / **TONY LEVIN** (b. 6 Jun'46, Boston, Mass.) – bass (ex-session man including PETER GABRIEL)

E.G. Warners

Sep 81. (lp/c) *(EG LP/MC 49) <BSK 3629>* **DISCIPLINE** [41] [45]
– Elephant talk / Frame by frame / Matte Kudasai / Indiscipline / Thelahun ginjeet / The sheltering sky / Discipline. *(re-iss. Jan87 & Nov91 lp/c/cd; EG LP/MC/CD 49)*

Nov 81. (7") *(EGO 2)* **MATTE KUDASAI. / ELEPHANT TALK** [ ] [–]

Jun 82. (lp/c) *(EG LP/MC 51) <23692-1>* **BEAT** [39] [52]
– Neal and Jack and me / Heartbeat / Sartori in Tangier / Waiting man / Neurotica / Two hands / The howler / Requiem. *(cd-iss. Apr84 on 'Polydor'; 821 194-2) (re-iss. Jan87 & Nov91 lp/c/cd; EG LP/MC/CD 51)*

Jun 82. (7") *(EGO 6) <29964>* **HEARTBEAT. / REQUIEM (excerpt)** [ ] [ ]

Feb 84. (7") *(EGO 15) <29309>* **SLEEPLESS. / NUAGES** [ ] [ ]
(12") *(EGOX 15)* – ('A'side) / ('A'instrumental & dance mixes).

Mar 84. (lp/c/cd) *(EG LP/MC/CD 55) <25071>* **THREE OF A PERFECT PAIR** [30] [58]
– Three of a perfect pair / Model man / Sleepless / Man with an open heart / Nuages (that which passes, passes like clouds) / Industry / Dig me / No warning / Lark's tongues in aspic (part three). *(re-iss. Jan87 & Nov91; same)*

— FRIPP disbanded KING CRIMSON project for a decade

– compilations, others, etc. –

Jun 72. (lp) *Help-Island; (HELP 6)* **EARTHBOUND (live)** [ ] [–]
– 21st century schizoid man / Peoria / The sailor's tale / Earthbound / Groon. *(re-iss. Oct77 on 'Polydor' lp)(c; 2343 092)(3192 385) (re-iss. Apr82 on 'EG')*

Feb 76. (d-lp) *Island; (ISLP 7)* **A YOUNG PERSON'S GUIDE TO KING CRIMSON** [ ] [–]

– Epitaph (including; (a) March for no reason – (b) Tomorrow and tomorrow / Cadence and cascade / Ladies of the road / I talk to the wind / Red / Starless / The night watch / Book of Saturday / Peace – a beginning / Cat food / Groon / Coda from Larks' tongues in aspic part 2 / Moonchild; (a) Mirrors – (b) The illusion / Trio / The court of the crimson king (including; (a) The return of the fire witch – (b) Dance of the puppets / 21st century schizoid man. *(re-iss. Mar77 on 'Polydor' d-lp/c; 2612 035)(3500 123) (cd-iss. 1986 on 'E.G.'; EGCD 22)*

Feb 76. (7") *Island; (WIP 6274)* **21st CENTURY SCHIZOID MAN. / EPITAPH** ☐ ☐-

Dec 80. (d-lp) *Polydor;* **IN THE COURT OF THE CRIMSON KING / LARKS' TONGUES IN ASPIC** ☐ ☐-

Dec 86. (cd/d-lp/d-c) *E.G.; (EG CD/MC/LP 68)* **THE COMPACT KING CRIMSON** ☐ ☐

Apr 87. (7"; by BRAIN) *Bam Caruso; (OPRA 63)* **NIGHTMARES IN RED. / (other artist)** ☐ ☐-

Dec 89. (3xcd-box/3xc-box/3xlp-box) *E.G.; (EGBC/EGBM/EGBL 6)* **KING CRIMSON BOXED SET** ☐ ☐-
– (IN THE COURT OF THE CRIMSON KING / LARKS' TONGUES IN ASPIC / DISCIPLINE)
(above 3 albums were packaged with other 'Island' artists)

1991. (cd-ep) *Virgin;* **THE ABBREVIATED KING CRIMSON – HEARTBEAT (medley)** ☐ ☐-
– The King Crimson barber shop – 21st century schizoid man (abbreviated) – In the court of the crimson king (abbreviated) – Elephant talk (edit) – Matte Kudesai – Heartbeat (edit).

Dec 91. (4xcd-box) *Virgin; (KCBOX 1)* **FRAME BY FRAME: THE ESSENTIAL KING CRIMSON** ☐ ☐-

Nov 92. (4xcd-box) *Virgin; (KCDIS 1)* **THE GREAT DECEIVER** ☐ ☐-

Sep 93. (cd/c) *Virgin; (CDV/TCV 2721)* **SLEEPLESS: THE CONCISE KING CRIMSON** ☐ ☐
– 21st century schizoid man / Epitaph / In the court of the crimson king / Cat food / Ladies of the road / Starless (abridged) / Red / Fallen angel / Elephant talk / Frame by frame / Matte Kudasai / Heartbeat / Three of a perfect pair / Sleepless.

Dec 93. (3xcd-box) *Virgin;* **IN THE COURT OF THE CRIMSON KING / IN THE WAKE OF POSEIDON / LIZARD** ☐ ☐-

Apr 97. (d-cd) *Discipline; (DGM 9607)* **EPITAPH (live in 1969)** ☐ ☐-

ROBERT FRIPP / the LEAGUE OF GENTLEMEN

EG-Editions E.G.

Jun 85. (lp/c) *(EGED/+C 9)* **GOD SAVE THE KING** ☐ ☐
– God save the King / Under heavy manners / Heptaparparshinokh / Inductive resonance / Cognitive dissonance / Dislocated / HG Wells / Eye needles / Trap. *(cd-iss. Jan87; EEGCD 9)*

Nov 86. (lp/c/cd) *(EGED/+C 43)* **ROBERT FRIPP AND THE LEAGUE OF CRAFTY GUITARISTS: LIVE! (live)** ☐ ☐
– Guitar craft theme 1: Invocation / Tight muscle party at Love Beach / The chords that bind / Guitar craft theme 3: Eye of the needle / All or nothing II / Guitar craft theme 2: Aspiration / All or nothing I / Circulation / A fearful symmetry / The new world / Crafty march. *(cd-iss. Jan87; EEGCD 43)*

— Late 1988, FRIPP / FRIPP (TOYAH) toured augmented by **TREY GUNN** – stick bass / **PAUL BEAVIS** – percussion, drums

— In mid'93, ROBERT FRIPP collaborated with ex-JAPAN singer DAVID SYLVIAN on near UK Top 20 album 'THE FIRST DAY'.

— In Aug'94, FRIPP was part of FFWD alongside THOMAS FEHLYN, KRIS WESTON + Dr.ALEX PATTERSON of The ORB. In Sep'94, FRIPP again teamed up with DAVID SYLVIAN on album 'DAMAGE'.

KING CRIMSON

FRIPP / BRUFORD / BELEW / LEVIN / GUNN / PAT MASTELOTTO

Discipline Virgin

Dec 94. (cd) *(DGM 0004)* **VROOOM** ☐ ☐
– Vrooom / Sex, sleep, eat, drink, dream / Cage / Thrak / When I say stop, continue / One time.

Apr 95. (cd/cd/c) *(KC CDX/CDY/MC 1) <40313>* **THRAK** 58 83
– Vrooom / Coda: Marine 475 / Dinosaur / Walking on air / B'boom / Thrak / Inner garden I / People / Radio I / One time / Radio II / Inner garden II / Sex, sleep, eat, drink, dream / Vrooom vrooom / Vrooom vrooom coda.

Aug 95. (d-cd) *(<DGM 9503>)* **B'BOOM: OFFICIAL SOUNDTRACK – LIVE IN ARGENTINA** (live) ☐ ☐
– Vrooom / Frame by frame / Sex, sleep, eat, drink, dream / Red / One time / B'boom / Thrak / Improv – Two sticks / Elephant talk / Indiscipline // Vrooom vrooom / Matte Kudesai / The talking drum / Lark's tongues in aspic (part 2) / Heartbeat / Sleepless / People / B'boom / Thrak.

May 96. (cd) *(<DGM 9604>)* **THRaKaTTaK** (live 1995) ☐ Jun96 ☐
– Thrak / Fearless and highly thrakked / Mother hold the candle steady while I shave the chicken's lips / Thrakattak (pt.1) / The slaughter of the innocents / This night wounds time / Thrakattk (pt.2) / Thrak reprise.

Sep 96. (cd) *(DGMVC 1)* **LIVE IN JAPAN 1995** (live) ☐ ☐-
– Frame by frame / Dinosaur / One time / Red / B'room / Thrak / Matte kudasai / Three of a perfect pair / Vroom vroom / Sex, sleep, eat, drink, dream / Elephant talk / Indiscipline / Talking drum / Larks' tongues in aspic part II / People / Walking on air.

— **FRIPP, BELEW, GUNN + MASTELOTTO**

King Crimson Virgin

May 00. (cd) *(KCCDX2) <49261>* **THE CONSTRUCKTION OF LIGHT** ☐ ☐
– ProzaKc blues / The construcKtion of light (2 parts) / Into the frying pan / FraKctured / The world's my oyster soup kitchen floor wax museum / Larks' tongues in aspic – part IV / Coda: I have a dream / ProjeKct X: Heaven and Earth.

Sanctuary Sanctuary

Nov 02. (m-cd) *(SANEP 123) <84580>* **HAPPY WITH WHAT YOU HAVE TO BE HAPPY WITH** ☐ Oct02 ☐
– Bude / Happy with what you have to be happy with / Mie gakure / She shudders / Eyes wide open / Shoganai / I ran / Potato pie / Larks' tongues in aspic (pt.IV) / Clouds.

Feb 03. (cd) *(SANCD 155) <84585>* **THE POWER TO BELIEVE** ☐ Mar03 ☐
– The power to believe I: a cappella / Level five / Eyes wide open / Elektrik / Facts of life (intro) / Facts of life / The power to believe II / Dangerous curves / Happy with what you have to be happy with / The power to believe III / The power to believe IV: Coda (live).

ROBERT FRIPP

Discipline Virgin

Nov 94. (cd; ROBERT FRIPP STRING QUARTET) *(DGM 9303)* **THE BRIDGE BETWEEN** ☐ ☐

Feb 95. (cd) *(DGM 9402-2)* **1999 SOUNDSCAPES – LIVE IN ARGENTINA (live)** ☐ ☐-
– 1999 (part one) / 2000 / 2001 / Interlude / 2002.

Oct 95. (cd) *(DGM 9502)* **INTERGALACTIC BOOGIE EXPRESS – LIVE IN EUROPE 1991** (live with The LEAGUE OF CRAFTY GUITARISTS) ☐ ☐-
– A Connecticut Yankee in the court of King Arthur / Rhythm of the universe / Lark's hrak / Circulation 1 / Intergalactic boogie express / G force / Eye of the needle / Corrente / Driving force / Groove penetration / Flying home / Circulation II / Fireplace / Fragments of skylab / Asturias / Prelude circulation / Cheeseballs / Prelude in c minor / Wabash cannonball / Fractual Jazn / Ashesis. *(re-iss. Mar97; same)*

Mar 96. (cd) *(DGM 9505)* **RADIOPHONICS: 1995 SOUNDSCAPES VOL.1 (live in Argentina)** ☐ ☐-
– Radiophonic I / Radiophonic II / Buenos Aires suite: I- Atmosphere, II- Elegy (for mothers and children), III- Streets, IV- Sky.

Sep 96. (cd) *(DGM 9506)* **A BLESSING OF TEARS: 1995 SOUNDSCAPES – VOLUME TWO** (live in California) ☐ ☐-
– The cathedral of tears / First light / Midnight blue / Reflection 1 / Second light / A blessing of tears / Returning I / Returning II.

May 96. (cd; LEAGUE OF GENTLEMEN) *(DGM 9602)* **THRANG THRANG GOZINBULX** ☐ ☐

Sep 96. (cd) *(DGM 9507)* **THAT WHICH PASSES** ☐ ☐
– On acceptance / On the approach of doubt / Worm in Paradise / New worlds / On triumph / On awe / This too shall pass / Fear of light / Time to die.

Jun 97. (cd-ep) *(<DGM 9704>)* **PIE JESU EP** ☐ Sep97 ☐
– Pie Jesu / Midnight blue / Abandonment to divine providence / Sometimes God hides.

Apr 98. (cd) *(<DGM 9608>)* **GATES OF PARADISE** ☐ ☐
– Outer darkness: the outer darkness / Gates of Paradise: Abandonment to divine / Outer darkness: In fear of trembling / Gates of Paradise / Sometimes God hides.

– FRIPP compilations, etc. –

Jan 87. (10"m-lp/c) *E.G.; (EGM LP/MC 4)* **NETWORK** [ ] [ ]
– North star / (i) Water music 1 – (ii) Here comes the flood / God save the king / Under heavy manners.

May 91. (cd; ROBERT FRIPP & THE LEAGUE OF CRAFTY GUITARISTS) *E.G.; (EEG 21022)* **SHOW OF HANDS** [ ] [ ]

Oct 05. (cd) *(<DGM 0552>)* **LOVE CANNOT BEAR: SOUNDSCAPES – LIVE IN THE USA** (live) [ ] [ ]
– Acceptance – Affirming / Affirmation: Imac / On my mother's birthday / Affirmation: New York / Midnight blue / Easter Sunday / Love cannot bear / Requiem – Affirming.

FRIPP & ENO

Discipline Global — Discipline Global

Mar 05. (cd) *(<DGM 0550>)* **THE EQUATORIAL STARS** [ ] Apr05 [ ]
– Meissa / Lyra / Tarazed / Lupus / Ankaa / Altair / Terebellum.

KINGS OF LEON

Formed: Nashville, Tennessee, USA ... 2000 by brothers CALEB, JARED and NATHAN FOLLOWILL; cousin MATTHEW FOLLOWILL was recruited in a matter of months. Somewhat akin to the ALLMAN BROTHERS in their earliest incarnation, plaid shirts, drain-pipe jeans, et al, KINGS OF LEON were like preacher's sons gatecrashing a porn movie. After playing as a backing band in churches for their father and moving from one trailer park to the next when they were young 'uns, they decided the best route for their homegrown garage blues was to keep it strictly in the family (another cousin is their road manager). Swinging like the BAND meeting GRAM PARSONS' wandering ghost at a CREEDENCE CLEARWATER REVIVAL concert, KINGS OF LEON issued their southern fried debut EP 'HOLY ROLLER NOVOCAINE' (featuring superb lead track 'MOLLY'S CHAMBERS') early in 2003 and followed into the charts a few months later via 'WHAT I SAW', both lifted from their groundbreaking first set, 'YOUTH & YOUNG MANHOOD', Top 5 in Britain. Thanks to some hype from the NME, etc., their label ('Down') finally launched 'MOLLY'S CHAMBERS' into the UK charts in its own right and set up a possible challenge in their homelands. Elsewhere on the album, we heard songs of redemption, cross-dressing cowboys and tequila-stained bedsheets from a band of ex-religious nuts who had a penchant for the days of NEIL YOUNG and MC5. The KINGS continued to push back the wild frontiers of post-millennial Southern-rock on the cryptically named sophomore effort, 'AHA SHAKE HEARTBREAK' (2004), CALEB sounding even more like a horse-whipped RAY DAVIES than ever. Which is possibly why British fans continued to be more taken with their Muswell Hillboogie than the Americans; the album itself went Top 3 (Top 50 fringes in the US), while singles, 'THE BUCKET', 'FOUR KICKS' and 'KING OF THE RODEO', generated exponential chart returns.

Album rating: YOUTH & YOUNG MANHOOD (*8) / AHA SHAKE HEARTBREAK (*6)

CALEB FOLLOWILL (b. ANTHONY CALEB FOLLOWILL, 1982) – vocals, rhythm guitar / **MATTHEW FOLLOWILL** – lead guitar / **JARED FOLLOWILL** – bass / **NATHAN FOLLOWILL** – drums, percussion, vocals

Handmedown — R.C.A.

Feb 03. (cd-ep) *<7863 60614-2>* **HOLY ROLLER NOVOCAINE** [–] [ ]
– Molly's chambers / Wasted time / California waiting / Wicker chair / Holy roller novocaine.

Feb 03. (10"red-ep/cd-ep) *(HMD 20/21)* **HOLY ROLLER NOVOCAINE EP** [53] [–]
– Molly's chambers / California waiting / Holy roller novocaine.

Jun 03. (10"blue-ep) *(HMD 22)* **WHAT I SAW EP** [22] [–]
– Red morning light / Wicker chair.
(cd-ep+=) *(HMD 23)* – Talihina sky.
(dvd-ep) *(HMD 24)* – Red morning light (+ live video clips).

Jul 03. (cd)(d10"lp) *(HMD 27JC)(HMD 26) <52394>* **YOUTH & YOUNG MANHOOD** [5] Aug03 [ ]
– Red morning light / Happy alone / Wasted time / Joe's head / Trani / California waiting / Spiral staircase / Molly's chambers / Genius / Dusty / Holy roller novocaine. *(hidden track+=/d10"lp+=)* – Talihina sky.

Aug 03. (10") *(HMD 28)* **MOLLY'S CHAMBERS. / CALIFORNIA WAITING (live)** [23] [–]
(cd-s) *(HMD 29)* – ('A') / Wasted time (live) / Spiral staircase (live).
(cd-s) *(HMD 30)* – ('A'-live) / Red morning light (live).

Oct 03. (10") *(HMD 31)* **WASTED TIME. / MOLLY'S HANGOVER** [51] [–]
(cd-s) *(HMD 32)* – ('A') / Joe's head (live from LA) / ('A'-video).

Feb 04. (10"clear/cd-s) *(HMD 36/35)* **CALIFORNIA WAITING. / JOE'S HEAD (live from Brixton Academy 2003)** [61] [–]

Oct 04. (7") *(HMD 43)* **THE BUCKET. / TRANI (live)** [16] [–]
(10") *(HMD 42)* – ('A') / Slow nights so long / Wicker chair (live from Roskilde).
(cd-s) *(HMD 41)* – ('A') / Where nobody knows.

Nov 04. (cd/white;d-lp) *(HMD 39/40) <64544>* **AHA SHAKE HEARTBREAK** [3] Feb05 [55]
– Slow night, so long / King of the rodeo / Taper Jean girl / Pistol of fire / Milk / The bucket / Soft / Razz / Day old blues / Four kicks / Velvet snow / Rememo. *(bonus +=)* – Where nobody knows. *<US white-lp; CGO 026>*

Jan 05. (7"/cd-s) *(HMD 47/45)* **FOUR KICKS. / HEAD TO TOE** [24] [–]
(10") *(HMD 46)* – ('A') / ('A'-live in Belgium) / Razz (dub).

Apr 05. (7") *(HMD 50)* **KING OF THE RODEO. / SOFT (live in Belgium)** [41] [–]
(cd-s) *(HMD 49)* – ('A') / Taper Jean girl (live in Belgium) / Molly's chambers (live in Belgium) / ('A'-video).

the KINKS

Formed: Muswell Hill, London, England . . . 1963 by brothers RAY and DAVE DAVIES, who recruited PETER QUAIFE from The RAVENS. With help from managers Robert Wace and Grenville Collins, they met Larry Page who gave them the name KINKS late '63. He also arranged demos, which were soon heard by American SHEL TALMY, securing them a deal with 'Pye' early '64. Two singles flopped, but the third, 'YOU REALLY GOT ME', stormed the top spot in the UK, soon breaking into US Top 10. With its scuzzy, propulsive guitar riff, the song is oft cited as one of the first real "heavy rock" records, although it's debatable whether RAY DAVIES would admit to inspiring a multitude of poodle-maned Van Halen soundalikes. A top selling eponymous lp followed, as did a series of Top 10 sixties singles, including two more UK No.1's, 'TIRED OF WAITING FOR YOU' and 'SUNNY AFTERNOON'. As RAY's songwriting developed, the band moved to a quieter, more reflective sound, his camp, semi-detached vocals complementing the wry observations and quintessential Englishness of the lyrical themes. Come 1967, when every band worth their weight in spiked sugarcubes were looking towards the 'East', Davies looked no further than his proverbial back garden. 'SOMETHING ELSE', with its heartfelt eulogies to a mythical England past, still stands as the Kinks' greatest moment, the aching melancholy of 'WATERLOO SUNSET' its crowning glory. Davies' nostalgic bent continued on 1968's 'THE KINKS ARE THE VILLAGE GREEN PRESERVATION SOCIETY', an enchanting concept album that reached ever further into a faded history of rural simplicity. It also included the KINKS' sole dalliance with psychedelia, 'WICKED ANNABELLA', a Brothers Grimm-like fairytale come nightmare fantasy. DAVIES' lyrical obsessions were given centre stage once more on 'ARTHUR (OR THE DECLINE OF THE ROMAN EMPIRE)' (1969) wherein the rosy hue of the past was contrasted with the grey decline of modern day Britain. The mood lightened somewhat with 1970's surprise No.2 hit single, 'LOLA', a tongue in cheek tribute to a male cross-dresser and the standout track from the subsequent album,

The KINKS

'LOLA VERSUS POWERMAN AND THE MONEYGOROUND PART 1'. 1971's 'MUSWELL HILLBILLIES' echoed 'VILLAGE GREEN's collection of storybook vignettes although the band were beginning to lose their focus and the hits were about to dry up. 'SUPERSONIC ROCKETSHIP' went top 20 in 1972 but the follow-up, 'CELLULOID HEROES', failed to chart. Both songs were taken from the album, 'EVERYBODY'S IN SHOWBIZ', and were high points in an otherwise unremarkable affair. The remainder of the 70's saw the KINKS become bogged down in ill-advised concept albums and self-parody although while the band were virtually ignored in the UK, they still had a sizeable following in America, hitting the US Top 30 with the patchy 'SLEEPWALKER' album in 1977. With the release of the harder rocking 'LOW BUDGET' a couple of years later, the band were embraced fully by the US rock fraternity and hitched a lucrative ride on the stadium rock circuit as well as gaining a sizeable piece of chart action. While the early 80's albums, 'GIVE THE PEOPLE WHAT THEY WANT' and 'STATE OF CONFUSION' were competent albeit largely uninspired, the Americans lapped them up and the band even found themselves back in the UK Top 20 with the classic 'COME DANCING' single. Throughout the 80's the band once again descended into inconsistency and commercial wilderness, their live shows being the sole factor in keeping the KINKS' spirit intact. Fast forward to 1995 and BLUR were riding high on the 'Britpop' wave with their heavily KINKS-influenced 'Parklife' album. Overrated and trailing in the KINKS shadows, the album's success nevertheless gave Blur mainman DAMON ALBORN the opportunity to express his admiration for his hero RAY DAVIES and perform a poignant TV duet with the great man on 'WATERLOO SUNSET'. The renewed interest also resulted in a TV documentary on the KINKS and a solo tour by RAY, not to mention autobiographies by both RAY and DAVE. RAY's 1998 'THE STORYTELLER', meanwhile, was his first solo effort since 1985's low-key 'RETURN TO WATERLOO' soundtrack. Inspired by the the promotional tour he undertook after the release of his book, the album's appeal lay in its witty, intimate dialogue revealing the often amusing stories behind the songs – many of which were culled from the KINKS back catalogue. Save for a handful of early 80's solo albums, the plaintive tones of DAVE DAVIES went unheard for much of the 80's and 90's, which made the release of 'ROCK BOTTOM: LIVE AT THE BOTTOM LINE' (2000), all the more surprising. Recorded at the New York club in winter '97, the set was a robust summary of his KINKS heyday. Even more surprisingly, it was followed by an album of all-new material, 'BUG' (2002), his first for two decades and – save for the Moroder-pulsing soundclash of 'De-Bug' – unrepentantly in the 70's rockist/conspiracy theorist/lovelorn vein he signed off with twenty years earlier. 'TRANSFORMATION' (2005) was another live set, while 'KINKED' was a 'Koch'-issued best-of gathering material from the latter day albums as well as re-recorded KINKS tunes, tempting diehard fans with his GEORGE HARRISON tribute, 'GIVE ME LOVE, GIVE ME PEACE ON EARTH', as well as the newly recorded 'GOD IN MY BRAIN', frazzled boogie-rock conceived in the aftermath of a stroke. Brother RAY also turned up with new material in 2006, releasing 'OTHER PEOPLE'S LIVES' to general critical acclaim and Top 40 success. Documenting all the human folly and life-affirming minutiae he'd observed in the decade since 'PHOBIA', and still wrestling with his warring impulses of sympathy and contempt, the record confirmed DAVIES as Britain's most enduring social chronicler.

Songwriters: RAY DAVIES wrote all of work, except covers; LONG TALL SALLY (Ernie Johnson) / TOO MUCH MONKEY BUSINESS (Chuck Berry) / GOT LOVE IF YOU WANT IT (Slim Harpo) / MILK COW BLUES (Elvis Presley) / etc. • **Trivia:** RAY produced 1969 lp 'Turtle Soup' for The TURTLES. He was married on the 12th December '64 to Rasa Dicpetri, but later divorced her (see KINKS biography by Johnny Rogan). In 1981, he divorced his second wife Yvonne. (RAY had a relationship with CHRISSIE HYNDE of The PRETENDERS for three years). She gave him a daughter, Natalie, in February '83, although they separated when she started dating JIM KERR (of SIMPLE MINDS). In 1986, RAY appeared in the film musical, 'Absolute Beginners'.

Album rating: THE KINKS – YOU REALLY GOT ME (*6) / KINDA KINKS (*5) / KINKS-SIZE (*6) / THE KINK KONTROVERSY (*5) / KINKS KINKDOM (*5) / THE KINKS GREATEST HITS! compilation (*8) / FACE TO FACE (*8) / LIVE AT KELVIN HALL (*5) / SOMETHING ELSE BY THE KINKS (*7) / VILLAGE GREEN PRESERVATION SOCIETY (*8) / ARTHUR (OR THE DECLINE AND FALL OF THE BRITISH EMPIRE) (*8) / LOLA VERSUS POWERMAN AND THE MONEYGOROUND, PART ONE (*7) / PERCY soundtrack (*6) / MUSWELL HILLBILLIES (*7) / EVERYBODY'S IN SHOW-BIZ (*6) / THE GREAT LOST KINKS ALBUM early (*6) / PRESERVATION ACT I (*6) / PRESERVATION ACT II (*6) / SOAP OPERA (*4) / SCHOOLBOYS IN DISGRACE (*5) / SLEEPWALKER (*6) / MISFITS (*7) / LOW BUDGET (*6) / ONE FOR THE ROAD (*5) / GIVE THE PEOPLE WHAT THEY WANT (*6) / STATE OF CONFUSION (*6) / WORD OF MOUTH (*5) / THINK VISUAL (*4) / COME DANCING WITH THE KINKS – THE BEST OF . . . 1977-1986 compilation (*7) / THE ROAD (*4) / THE ULTIMATE COLLECTION compilation (*9) / UK JIVE (*4) / PHOBIA (*5) / TO THE BONE (*6) / THE ULTIMATE COLLECTION double compilation (*9) / Ray Davies: RETURN TO WATERLOO soundtrack (*5) / THE STORYTELLER (*6) / OTHER PEOPLE'S LIVES (*7) / Dave Davies: DAVE DAVIES – AFLI-3603 (*5) / GLAMOUR (*4) / CHOSEN PEOPLE (*5) / THE ALBUM THAT NEVER WAS exploitation (*7) / ROCK BOTTOM: LIVE AT THE BOTTOM LINE (*6) / BUG (*5) / TRANSFORMATION (*5) / KINKED compilation (*6)

RAY DAVIES (b.21 Jun'44) – vocals, guitar / **DAVE DAVIES** (b. 3 Feb'47) – guitar, vocals / **PETER QUAIFE** (b.31 Dec'43, Tavistock, Devon) – bass with session drummers

Pye | Cameo

Mar 64. (7") *(7N 15611)* <308> **LONG TALL SALLY. / I TOOK MY BABY HOME** [ ] Apr64 [ ]
<US re-iss. Nov64; 345>

May 64. (7") *(7N 15636)* **YOU STILL WANT ME. / YOU DO SOMETHING TO ME** [ ] [–]

Pye | Reprise

Aug 64. (7") *(7N 15673)* <0306> **YOU REALLY GOT ME. / IT'S ALRIGHT** [1] Sep64 [7]

—— **MICK AVORY** (b.15 Feb'44) – drums was now used although he joined 9 months previously

Oct 64. (lp) *(NPL 18096)* <6143> **THE KINKS** <US-title 'YOU REALLY GOT ME'> [3] Dec64 [29]
– Beautiful Delilah / So mystifying / Just can't go to sleep / Long tall Shorty / You really got me / Cadillac / Bald headed woman / Revenge / Too much monkey business / I've been driving on Bald mountain / Stop your sobbing / Got love if you want it. *(re-iss. Jan67 on 'Golden Guinea'; GGL 0357) (re-iss. May80 as 'YOU REALLY GOT ME'; NSPL 18615) (re-iss. Oct87 on 'P.R.T.' lp/c/cd; PYL/PYM/PYC 6002) (cd re-iss. Dec89 on 'Castle'; CLACD 155) (cd re-mast.Mar98 on 'Essential'+=; ESMCD 482)* – I took my baby home / I'm a lover not a fighter / You still want me / I don't need you any more.

Oct 64. (7") *(7N 15714)* <0334> **ALL DAY AND ALL OF THE NIGHT. / I GOTTA MOVE** [2] Dec64 [7]
(re-iss. Oct84 on 'P.R.T.'; KIS 003) (re-iss. Jan88 on 'P.R.T.'; PYS 4)

Jan 65. (7") *(7N 15759)* <0347> **TIRED OF WAITING FOR YOU. / COME ON NOW** [1] Mar65 [6]

Mar 65. (lp) <6158> **KINKS-SIZE** [–] [13]
– Tired of waiting for you / Louie Louie / I've got that feeling / Revenge / I gotta move / Things are getting better / I gotta go now / I'm a lover not a fighter / Come on now / All day and all of the night.

Mar 65. (lp) *(NPL 18112)* <6173> **KINDA KINKS** [3] Aug65 [60]
– Look for me baby / Got my feet on the ground / Nothin' in the world can stop me worryin' 'bout that girl / Naggin' woman / Wonder where my baby is tonight / Tired of waiting for you / Dancing in the street / Don't ever change / Come on now / So long / You shouldn't be sad / Something better beginning. *(re-iss. Oct87 on 'P.R.T.' lp/c/cd; PYL/PYM/PYC 6003) (cd re-iss. Dec89 on 'Castle'; CLACD 156) (cd re-mast.Mar98 on 'Essential'+=; ESMCD 483)* – I need you / See my friends / Never met a girl like you before / I go to sleep.

Mar 65. (7") *(7N 15813)* <0366> **EVERYBODY'S GONNA BE HAPPY. / WHO'LL BE THE NEXT IN LINE** [11] Apr65 [ ]
<above 45 flipped over in the States with B-side hitting No.34>

May 65. (7") *(7N 15854)* <0379> **SET ME FREE. / I NEED YOU** [9] Jun65 [23]

Jul 65. (7") *(7N 15919)* <0409> **SEE MY FRIENDS. / NEVER MET A GIRL LIKE YOU BEFORE** [10] [ ]

Nov 65. (7") *<0420>* **A WELL RESPECTED MAN. / MILK COW BLUES** [–] [13]

Nov 65. (7") *(7N 15981) <0454>* **TILL THE END OF THE DAY. / WHERE HAVE ALL THE GOOD TIMES GONE** [6] Mar66 [50]

Nov 65. (lp) *(NPL 18131) <6197>* **THE KINK KONTROVERSY** [9] Apr66 [95]
– Milk cow blues / Ring the bells / Gotta get the first plane home / When I see that girl of mine / Till the end of the day / The world keeps going round / I'm on the island / Where have all the good times gone / It's too late / What's in store for me / You can't win. *(re-iss. Oct87 on 'P.R.T.' lp/c/cd; PYL/PYM/PYC 6004) (cd re-iss. Dec89 on 'Castle'; CLACD 157) (cd re-mast.Mar98 on 'Essential'+=; ESMCD 507)* – Dedicated follower of fashion / Sittin' on my sofa.

Dec 65. (lp) *<6184>* **KINKS KINKDOM** [–] [47]
– A well respected man / Such a shame / Wait 'til the summer comes along / Naggin' woman / Who'll be the next in line / Don't you fret / I need you / It's all right / Louie Louie.

Feb 66. (7") *(7N 17064) <0471>* **DEDICATED FOLLOWER OF FASHION. / SITTING ON MY SOFA** [4] May66 [36]

—— **JOHN DALTON** – bass deputised on tour for QUAIFE while injured

Jun 66. (7") *(7N 17125) <0497>* **SUNNY AFTERNOON. / I'M NOT LIKE EVERYBODY ELSE** [1] Aug66 [14]

Aug 66. (lp) *<6217>* **THE KINKS GREATEST HITS** (compilation) [–] [9]
– Dedicated follower of fashion / Tired of waiting for you / All day and all of the night / You really got me / A well respected man / Who'll be the next in line / Everybody's gonna be happy / Till the end of the day / Set me free / Something better beginning.

—— **JOHN DALTON** sessioned between 66-69, QUAIFE's photo on covers

Oct 66. (lp; mono/stereo) *(NPL/NSPL 18145) <6228>* **FACE TO FACE** [12] Feb67 [ ]
– Party line / Rosy won't you please come home / Dandy / Too much on my mind / Session man / Rainy day in June / House in the country / Sunny afternoon / Holiday in Waikiki / Most exclusive residence for sale / Fancy / Little Miss Queen of Darkness / You're looking fine / I'll remember. *(re-iss. Oct87 on 'P.R.T.' lp/c/cd; PYL/PYM/PYC 6005) (cd re-iss. Dec89 on 'Castle'; CLACD 158) (cd re-mast.Mar98 on 'Essential'+=; ESMCD 479)* – I'm not like everybody else / Dead end street / Big black smoke / Mr. Pleasant / This I where I belong. *(cd re-iss. Aug01 on 'Castle'; CMTCD 302)*

Nov 66. (7") *(7N 17125) <0540>* **DEAD END STREET. / BIG BLACK SMOKE** [5] Jan67 [73]

May 67. (7") *(7N 17321)* **WATERLOO SUNSET. / ACT NICE AND GENTLE** [2] [–]

May 67. (lp; mono/stereo) *(NPL/NSPL 18191) <6260>* **LIVE AT KELVIN HALL (live in Glasgow)** <US-title 'THE LIVE KINKS'> [ ] Sep67 [ ]
– Till the end of the day / I'm on an island / You really got me / All day and all of the night / A well respected man / You're looking fine / Sunny afternoon / Dandy / Come on now / Milk cow blues – Batman theme – Tired of waiting for you. *(re-iss. Oct87 on 'P.R.T.' lp/c/cd; PYL/PYM/PYC 6007) (cd re-iss. Dec89 on 'Castle'; CLACD 160) (cd re-mast.May98 on 'Essential'; ESMCD 508) (cd re-iss. Sep01 on 'Castle'; CMTCD 323)*

Jun 67. (7") *<0587>* **MR. PLEASANT. / HARRY RAG** [–] [80]

Sep 67. (7") *<0612>* **WATERLOO SUNSET. / TWO SISTERS** [–] [ ]

Oct 67. (lp; mono/stereo) *(NPL/NSPL 18193) <6279>* **SOMETHING ELSE BY THE KINKS** [35] Feb68 [ ]
– David Watts / Death of a clown / Two sisters / No return / Harry Rag / Tin soldier man / Situation vacant / Love me till the sun shines / Lazy old sun / Afternoon tea / Funny face / End of the season / Waterloo sunset. *(re-iss. Oct87 on 'P.R.T.' lp/c/cd; PYL/PYM/PYC 6006) (cd re-iss. Dec89 on 'Castle'; CLACD 159) (cd re-mast.Mar98 on 'Essential'+=; ESMCD 480)* – Susannah's still alive / Autumn almanac / Act nice and gentle / Wonderboy / Pretty Polly / Lincoln County / There's no life without love. *(cd re-iss. Aug01 on 'Castle'; CMTCD 303)*

Oct 67. (7") *(7N 17400) <0647>* **AUTUMN ALMANAC. / MR. PLEASANT** [3] [ ]

Apr 68. (7") *(7N 17468) <0691>* **WONDERBOY. / POLLY** [37] [ ]

Jul 68. (7") *(7N 17573) <0762>* **DAYS. / SHE'S GOT EVERYTHING** [12] [ ]

Jul 68. (lp; mono/stereo) *(NPL/NSPL 18233) <6327>* **THE KINKS ARE THE VILLAGE GREEN PRESERVATION SOCIETY** [ ] [ ]
– Village green preservation society / Do you remember Walter / Picture book / Johnny Thunder / The last of the steam powered trains / Big sky / Sitting by the riverside / Animal farm / Village green / Starstruck / Phenomenal cat / All my friends were there / Wicked Annabella / Monica / People take pictures of each other. *(re-iss. Nov85 on 'Flashback-PRT'; FBLP 8091) (re-iss. Oct87 on 'P.R.T.' lp/c/cd; PYL/PYM/PYC 6008) (cd re-iss. Oct89 on 'Castle'; CLACD 161) (cd re-iss. Feb97 on 'Original Recordings'; ORRLP 005) (cd re-mast.Mar98 on 'Essential'; ESMCD 481) (cd re-iss. Sep01 on 'Castle'; CMTCD 319)*

Apr 69. (7") *(7N 17724) <0743>* **PLASTIC MAN. / KING KONG** [31] [ ]

Apr 69. (7") *<0806>* **STARSTRUCK. / PICTURE BOOK** [–] [ ]

—— **JOHN DALTON** (b.21 May'43) – bass officially repl. QUAIFE

Jun 69. (7") *<0847>* **WALTER. / VILLAGE GREEN PRESERVATION SOCIETY** [–] [ ]

Jun 69. (7"; b-side by KINKS featuring DAVE DAVIES) *<7N 17776>* **DRIVIN'. / MINDLESS CHILD OF MOTHERHOOD** [ ] [–]

Sep 69. (7") *(7N 17812)* **SHANGRI-LA. / THIS MAN HE WEEPS TONIGHT** [ ] [–]
(above initially had 'LAST OF THE STEAM-POWERED TRAINS' on B-side)

Oct 69. (lp) *(NSPL 18317) <6366>* **ARTHUR (OR THE DECLINE AND FALL OF THE BRITISH EMPIRE** [ ] [ ]
– Victoria / Yes sir, no sir / Some mother's son / Brainwashed / Australia / Shangri-la / Mr. Churchill says / She bought a hat like Princess Marina / Young and innocent days / Nothing to say / Arthur. *(re-iss. Oct87 on 'P.R.T.' lp/c/cd; PYL/PYM/PYC 6009) (cd re-iss. Oct89 on 'Castle'; CLACD 162) (cd re-mast.May98 on 'Essential'; ESMCD 511) (cd re-iss. Sep01 on 'Castle'; CMTCD 322)*

Dec 69. (7") *(7N 17865)* **VICTORIA. / MR. CHURCHILL SAYS** [33] [–]

Jan 70. (7") *<0863>* **VICTORIA. / BRAINWASHED** [–] [62]

Jun 70. (7") *(7N 17961)* **LOLA. / BERKELEY MEWS** [2] [–]

Aug 70. (7") *<0930>* **LOLA. / MINDLESS CHILD OF MOTHERHOOD** [–] [9]

Nov 70. (lp) *(NSPL 18359) <6423>* **LOLA VERSUS POWERMAN & THE MONEYGOROUND, PART ONE** [ ] [35]
– The contenders / Strangers / Denmark Street / Get back in line / Lola / Top of the pops / The moneygoround / This time tomorrow / A long way from home / Rats / Apeman / Powerman / Got to be free. *(re-iss. Oct87 on 'P.R.T.' lp/c/cd; PYL/PYM/PYC 6010) (cd re-iss. Oct89 on 'Castle'; CLACD 163) (cd re-mast.May98 on 'Essential'; ESMCD 509) (cd re-iss. Sep01 on 'Castle'; CMTCD 320)*

Nov 70. (7") *(7N 45016) <0979>* **APEMAN. / RATS** [5] Jan71 [45]

Mar 71. (lp) *(NSPL 18365)* **PERCY** (soundtrack) [ ] [–]
– God's children / Lola / The way love used to be / Completely / Running round town / Moments / Animals in the zoo / Just friends / Whip lady / Dreams / Helga / Willesden Green / God's children – end. *(re-iss. Oct87 on 'P.R.T.' lp/c/cd; PYL/PYM/PYC 6011) (cd re-iss. Oct89 on 'Castle'; CLACD 164) (cd re-mast.May98 on 'Essential'; ESMCD 510) (cd re-iss. Sep01 on 'Castle'; 321)*

Apr 71. (7") *(7N 8001)* **GOD'S CHILDREN. / MOMENTS** [ ] [–]
(7"m+=) *(7NX 8001)* – The way love used to be / Dreams.

Apr 71. (7") *<1017>* **GOD'S CHILDREN. / THE WAY LOVE USED TO BE** [–] [ ]

—— added **JOHN GOSLING** – keyboards (he guested on 'LOLA' album), plus **LAURIE BROWN** – trumpet / **JOHN BEECHAM** – trombone / **ALAN HOLMES** – saxophone recruited from The MIKE COTTON SOUND. The three became full-time members '73, adding to **R. DAVIES, D. DAVIES, AVORY and DALTON**

R.C.A. R.C.A.

Nov 71. (lp) *(SF 8243) <LSP 4644>* **MUSWELL HILLBILLIES** [ ] [100]
– 20th century man / Acute schizophrenia paranoia blues / Holiday / Skin and bone / Alcohol / Complicated life / Here come the people in the grey / Have a cuppa tea / Holloway jail / Oklahoma U.S.A. / Uncle son / Muswell hillbilly.

Feb 72. (7") *<74-0620>* **20th CENTURY MAN. / SKIN AND BONE** [–] [ ]

May 72. (7") *(RCA 2211) <74-0807>* **SUPERSONIC ROCKET SHIP. / YOU DON'T KNOW MY NAME** [16] [ ]

Aug 72. (d-lp) *(DPS 2035) <6065>* **EVERYBODY'S IN SHOWBIZ** [ ] [70]
– Here comes yet another day / Maximum consumption / Unreal reality / Hot potatoes / Sitting in my hotel / You don't know my name / Supersonic rocket ship / Look a little on the sunny side / Celluloid heroes / Motorway. / **EVERYBODY'S A STAR (live)** – Top of the pops / Brainwashed / Mr. Wonderful / Acute schizophrenia paranoia blues / Holiday / Muswell Hillbilly / Alcohol / Banana boat song / Skin and bone / Baby face / Lola.

Nov 72. (7") *(RCA 2299)* *<74-0852>* **CELLULOID HEROES. / HOT POTATOES** [ ] [ ]

Jun 73. (7") *<74-0940>* **ONE OF THE SURVIVORS. / SCRAPHEAP CITY** [–] [ ]

Jun 73. (7") *(RCA 2387)* **SITTING IN THE MIDDAY SUN. / ONE OF THE SURVIVORS** [ ] [–]

Sep 73. (7") *(RCA 2418)* **SWEET LADY GENEVIEVE. / SITTING IN MY HOTEL** [ ] [–]

Sep 73. (7") *<5001>* **SWEET LADY GENEVIEVE. / SITTING IN THE MIDDAY SUN** [–] [ ]

Dec 73. (d-lp) *(SF 8392)* *<LPL 5002>* **PRESERVATION ACT I** [ ] [ ]
– Morning song / Daylight / Sweet Lady Genevieve / There's a change in the weather / Where are they now / One of the survivors / Cricket / I am your man / Here comes Flash / Sitting in the midday Sun / Demolution.

—— next 45 only contained **RAY & DAVE DAVIES**, before full 5 + 3 again

Apr 74. (7") *(RCA 5015)* **MIRROR OF LOVE. / CRICKET** [ ] [–]

Jun 74. (7") *<0275>* **MONEY TALKS. / HERE COMES FLASH** [–] [ ]

Jun 74. (d-lp) *<(LPL2 5040)>* **PRESERVATION ACT II** [ ] [ ]
– (announcement) / Introduction to solution / When a solution comes / Money talks / (announcement) / Shepherds of the nation / Scum of the Earth / Secondhand car spiv / He's evil / Mirror of love / (announcement) / Nobody gives / Oh where oh where is love? / Flash's dream / Flash's confession / Nothing lasts forever / (announcement) / Artificial man / Scrapheap city / (announcement) / Salvation Road.

Jul 74. (7") *(RCA 5042)* *<APBO 10019>* **MIRROR OF LOVE. / HE'S EVIL** [ ] [ ]

Oct 74. (7") *(RCA 2478)* **HOLIDAY ROMANCE. / SHEPHERDS OF THE NATION** [ ] [–]

Oct 74. (7") *<APBO 10121>* **PRESERVATION. / SALVATION** [–] [ ]

Apr 75. (7") *<APBO 10251>* **ORDINARY PEOPLE. / STAR MAKER** [–] [ ]

Apr 75. (7") *(RCA 2546)* **DUCKS ON THE WALL. / RUSH HOUR BLUES** [ ] [–]

May 75. (lp) *(SF 8411)* *<LPI 5081>* **SOAP OPERA** [ ] [51]
– Everybody's a star (starmaker) / Ordinary people / Rush hour blues / Nine to five / When work is over / Have another drink / Underneath the neon sign / Holiday romance / You make it all worth while / Ducks on the wall / Face in the crowd / You can't stop the music. *(re-iss. Jul84)*

May 75. (7") *(RCA 2567)* **YOU CAN'T STOP THE MUSIC. / HAVE ANOTHER DRINK** [ ] [–]

Nov 75. (lp) *(RS 1028)* *<FLI 5102>* **SCHOOLBOYS IN DISGRACE** [ ] [45]
– Schooldays / Jack the idiot dunce / Education / The first time we fall in love / I'm in disgrace / Headmaster / The hard way / The last assembly / No more looking back / (finale).

Nov 75. (7") *<10551>* **THE HARD WAY. / I'M IN DISGRACE** [–] [ ]

Jan 76. (7"m) *(RCM 1)* **NO MORE LOOKING BACK. / JACK THE IDIOT DUNCE / THE HARD WAY** [ ] [–]

—— Now down to basic 5-piece after the 3 brass section members departed

Arista Arista

Feb 77. (lp/c) *(SP/TC ARTY 1002)* *<AL 4106>* **SLEEPWALKER** [ ] [21]
– Life on the road / Mr. Big man / Sleepwalker / Brother / Juke box music / Sleepless night / Stormy sky / Full moon / Life goes on.

Mar 77. (7") *(ARIST 97)* *<0240>* **SLEEPWALKER. / FULL MOON** [ ] [48]

Jun 77. (7") *(ARIST 114)* **JUKE BOX MUSIC. / SLEEPLESS NIGHT** [ ] [–]

Jun 77. (7") *<0247>* **JUKE BOX MUSIC. / LIFE GOES ON** [–] [ ]

—— **ANDY PYLE** – bass (ex-BLODWYN PIG, ex-SAVOY BROWN, etc) repl. DALTON

Dec 77. (7") *(ARIST 153)* *<0296>* **FATHER CHRISTMAS. / PRINCE OF THE PUNKS** [ ] [ ]

May 78. (lp/c) *(SP/TC ART 1055)* *<AL 4167>* **MISFITS** [ ] [40]
– Misfits / Hay fever / Live life / Rock'n'roll fantasy / In a foreign land / Permanent waves / Black Messiah / Out of the wardrobe / Trust your heart / Get up.

May 78. (7") *(ARIST 189)* *<0342>* **ROCK'N'ROLL FANTASY. / ARTIFICIAL LIGHT** [ ] Jul78 [30]

Jul 78. (7") *(ARIST 199)* **LIVE LIFE. / IN A FOREIGN LAND** [ ] [–]

Jul 78. (7") *<0372>* **LIVE LIFE. / BLACK MESSIAH** [–] [ ]

Sep 78. (7") *(ARIST 210)* **BLACK MESSIAH. / MISFITS** [ ] [–]

—— RAY DAVIES, DAVE DAVIES and MICK AVORY recruited new members **GORDON EDWARDS** – keyboards (ex-PRETTY THINGS) repl. GOSLING (to NETWORK) / **JIM RODFORD** (b. 7 Jul'45, St. Albans, England) – bass (ex-ARGENT, ex-PHOENIX) repl. PYLE (to NETWORK)

Jan 79. (7"/12") *(ARIST/+12 240)* **(WISH I COULD FLY LIKE) SUPERMAN. / LOW BUDGET** [ ] [–]

—— **IAN GIBBON** – keyboards repl. EDWARDS

Apr 79. (7") *<0409>* **(WISH I COULD FLY LIKE) SUPERMAN. / PARTY LINE** [–] [41]

Sep 79. (7") *(ARIST 300)* **MOVING PICTURES. / IN A SPACE** [ ] [–]

Sep 79. (lp/c) *(SP/TC ART 1099)* *<AB 4240>* **LOW BUDGET** [ ] Jul79 [11]
– Attitude / Catch me now I'm falling / Pressure / National health / (I wish I could fly like) Superman / Low budget / In a space / Little bit of emotion / Gallon of gas / Misery / Moving pictures. *(cd-iss. Apr88; 251 146)*

Sep 79. (7") *<0448>* **GALLON OF GAS. / LOW BUDGET** [–] [ ]

Nov 79. (7") *<0458>* **CATCH ME NOW I'M FALLING. / LOW BUDGET** [–] [ ]

Nov 79. (7") *(ARIST 321)* **PRESSURE. / NATIONAL HEALTH** [ ] [–]

Jul 80. (d-lp) *(DARTY 6)* *<8401>* **ONE FOR THE ROAD (live)** [ ] Jun80 [14]
– The hard way / Catch me now I'm falling / Where have all the good times gone / Lola / Pressure / All day and all of the night / 20th century man / Misfits / Prince of the punks / Stop your sobbing / Low budget / Attitude / (Wish I could fly like) Superman / National health / Till the end of the day / Celluloid heroes / You really got me / Victoria / David Watts.

Jul 80. (7"ep) *(ARIST 360)* **WHERE HAVE ALL THE GOOD TIMES GONE (live)** [ ] [–]
– Where have all the good times gone / Victoria / Attitude / David Watts.

Aug 80. (7") *<0541>* **LOLA (live). / CELLULOID HEROES (live)** [–] [81]

Oct 80. (7") *<0577>* **YOU REALLY GOT ME (live). / ATTITUDE (live)** [–] [ ]

Jun 81. (lp/c) *(SP/TC ART 1171)* *<9567>* **GIVE THE PEOPLE WHAT THEY WANT** [ ] [15]
– Around the dial / Give the people what they want / Killer's eyes / Predictable / Add it up / Destroyer / Yo-yo / Back to front / Art lover / A little bit of abuse / Better things.

Jun 81. (7") *(ARIST 415)* **BETTER THINGS. / MASSIVE REDUCTIONS** [46] [–]
(d7"+=) *(KINKS 1)* – Lola / David Watts.

Oct 81. (7",7"pic-d) *(ARIST 426)* **PREDICTABLE. / BACK TO FRONT** [ ] [–]

Oct 81. (7") *<0619>* **DESTROYER. / BACK TO FRONT** [–] [85]

Nov 81. (7") *<0649>* **BETTER THINGS. / YO-YO** [–] [92]

Jun 83. (lp/c) *(205/405 275)* *<8018>* **STATE OF CONFUSION** [ ] [12]
– State of confusion / Definite maybe / Labour of love / Come dancing / Property / Don't forget to dance / Young Conservatives / Heart of gold / Cliches of the world (B movie) / Bernadette. *(cd-iss. 1988 on 'Ariola')*

Jul 83. (7"/12") *(ARIST/+12 502)* *<1054/9016>* **COME DANCING. / NOISE** [12] May83 [6]

Aug 83. (7") *<9075>* **DON'T FORGET TO DANCE. / YOUNG CONSERVATIVES** [–] [29]

Sep 83. (7",12") *(ARIST 524)* **DON'T FORGET TO DANCE. / BERNADETTE** [58] [–]

Mar 84. (7") *(ARIST 560)* **STATE OF CONFUSION. / HEART OF GOLD** [ ] [–]
(12"+=) *(ARIST12 560)* – 20th century man (live) / Lola (live).

Jul 84. (7") *(ARIST 577)* **GOOD DAY. / TOO HOT** [ ] [ ]
(ext.12"+=) *(ARIST12 577)* – Don't forget to dance.

Nov 84. (lp/c) *(206/406 685)* *<8264>* **WORD OF MOUTH** [ ] [57]
– Do it again / Word of mouth / Good day / Living on a thin line / Sold me out / Massive reductions / Guilty / Too hot / Missing persons / Summer's gone / Going solo. *(cd-iss. Jun88; 259 047)*

Apr 85. (7") *(ARIST 617)* *<9309>* **DO IT AGAIN. / GUILTY** [ ] Dec84 [41]
(12"+=) *(ARIST12 617)* – Summer's gone.

Apr 85. (7") *<9334>* **SUMMER'S GONE. / GOING SOLO** [–] [ ]

Oct 86. (d-lp/c) *(302/502 778)* *<8428>* **COME DANCING WITH THE KINKS – THE BEST OF THE KINKS 1977-1986** (compilation) [ ] Jul86 [ ]

—— Returned to original line-up of **RAY, DAVE + MICK,** plus sessioners. (RODFORD and GIBBONS departed).

London M.C.A.

Nov 86. (7") *<52960>* **ROCK'N'ROLL CITIES. / WELCOME TO SLEAZY TOWN** [–] [ ]

Nov 86. (lp/c)(cd) *(LON LP/C 27)(828 030-2)* *<5822>* **THINK VISUAL** [ ] [81]
– Working at the factory / Lost and found / Repetition / Welcome to Sleazy Town / The video shop / Rock'n'roll cities / How are you / Think visual / Natural gift / Killing time / When you were a child.

Dec 86. (7") *(LON 119)* **HOW ARE YOU. / KILLING TIME** [ ] [–]
(12"+=) *(LONX 119)* – Welcome to Sleazy town.

Mar 87. (7") *(LON 132)* <53015> **LOST AND FOUND. / KILLING TIME**
(12"+=) *(LONX 132)* – (Ray Davies interview).

May 87. (7") *<53093>* **HOW ARE YOU. / WORKING AT THE FACTORY** –

Feb 88. (7") *(LON 165)* **THE ROAD. / ART LOVER**
(ext.12"+=) *(LONX 165)* – Come dancing.

May 88. (lp/c)(cd) *(LON LP/C 49)(828 078-2) <42107>* **THE ROAD (live / studio *)** Feb88
– The road * / Destroyer / Apeman / Come dancing / Art lover / Cliches of the world (B-movie) / Living on a thin line / Lost and found / It * / Around the dial / Give the people what they want.

—— **BOB HENRIT** (b. 2 May'45)- drums repl. AVORY / added **MARK HALEY** – keyboards, vocals

Sep 89. (7") *(LON 239)* **DOWN ALL THE DAYS (TILL 1992). / YOU REALLY GOT ME (live)** –
(12"+=/cd-s+=) *(LON X/CD 239)* – Entertainment.

Oct 89. (lp/c/cd) *(828 165-1/-4/-2) <6337>* **UK JIVE**
– Aggravation / How do I get close / UK jive / Now and then / What are we doing / Entertainment / War is over / Down all the days (till 1992) / Loony balloon / Dear Margaret. *(c+=/cd+=)* – Bright lights / Perfect strangers. *(re-iss. Apr91;)*

Feb 90. (7") *(LON 250)* **HOW DO I GET CLOSE. / DOWN ALL THE DAYS (TILL 1992)** –
(12"+=/cd-s+=) *(LON X/CD 250)* – War is over.

Mar 90. 7") *<53699>* **HOW DO I GET CLOSE. / WAR IS OVER** –

Columbia Columbia

Mar 93. (cd/c) *(472489-2/-4) <48724>* **PHOBIA**
– Opening / Wall of fire / Drift away / Still searching / Phobia / Only a dream / Don't / Babies / Over the edge / Surviving / It's alright (don't think about it) / The informer / Hatred (a duet) / Somebody stole my car / Close to the wire / Scattered. *(cd+=)* – Did ya.

Jul 93. (cd-s) **SCATTERED. / HATRED (A DUET) / DAYS** –

Nov 93. (7") *(659922-7)* **ONLY A DREAM (Radio Version) / SOMEBODY STOLE MY CAR**
(cd-s+=) *(659922-2)* – Babies.

Konk not iss.

Oct 94. (cd/c/lp) *(KNK CD/MC/LP 1)* **TO THE BONE (live)** –
– All day and all of the nigt / Apeman / Tired of waiting for you / See my friend / Death of a clown / Waterloo sunset / Muswell hillbillies / Better things / Don't forget to dance / Autumn almanac / Sunny afternoon / Dedicated follower of fashion / You really got me.

Oct 94. (cd-ep) *(KNKD 2)* **WATERLOO SUNSET E.P. (live)** –
– Waterloo sunset / You really got me / Elevator man / On the outside.

When! not iss.

Jan 97. (c-ep/cd-ep) *(WEN M/X 1016)* **DAYS EP** 35 –
– Days / You really got me / Dead end street / Lola.

– (selective) compilations, etc. –

on 'Pye' UK / 'Reprise' US, unless mentioned otherwise

Jun 66. (lp) *Marble Arch; (MAL 612)* **WELL RESPECTED KINKS** 5 –

Sep 67. (lp) *Marble Arch; (MAL 716)* **SUNNY AFTERNOON** 9 –

Oct 71. (lp) *Golden Hour; (GH 501)* **THE GOLDEN HOUR OF THE KINKS** 21 –
(cd-iss. Apr89 on 'Castle'; GHCD 1)

Apr 72. (lp) *<6454>* **THE KINK KRONICLES** – 94

Oct 78. (d-lp) *Ronco-Pye; (RPL 2031)* **THE KINKS 20 GOLDEN GREATS** 19 –

Oct 83. (d-lp) *P.R.T.; (KINK 1)* **KINKS' GREATEST HITS – DEAD END STREET** 96 –

Oct 83. (7"/7"pic-d) *P.R.T.; (KD/KPD 1)* **YOU REALLY GOT ME. / MISTY WATER** 47 –
(12"pic-d+=) *(DKL 1)* – All day and all of the night.

Sep 89. (lp/c/cd) *Castle; (CTV LP/MC/CD 001)* **THE ULTIMATE COLLECTION** 35 –
– You really got me / All day and all of the night / Tired of waiting for you / Everybody's gonna be happy / Set me free / Till the end of the day / Dedicated follower of fashion / Sunny afternoon / Dead end street / Waterloo sunset / Autumn almanac / Wonder boy / Days / Plastic man / Victoria / Lola / Apeman / David Watts / Where have all the good times gone / A well respected man / I'm not like everybody else / End of the season / Death of a clown (DAVE DAVIES) / Suzannah's still alive (DAVE DAVIES).

Jun 90. (lp/c/cd) *See For Miles; (SEE/+K/CD 295)* **THE EP COLLECTION** –

Feb 92. (cd/c) *See For MIles; (SEE CD/K 329)* **THE EP COLLECTION VOL.2** –

Sep 93. (cd/c) *Polygram TV; (516 465-2/-4)* **THE DEFINITIVE COLLECTION – THE KINKS' GREATEST HITS** 18 –
(re-iss. Mar97; same)

Apr 97. (cd/c) *Polygram TV; (537554-2/-4)* **THE VERY BEST OF THE KINKS** 42 –

Sep 97. (d-cd) *Essential; (ESSCD 592)* **THE SINGLES COLLECTION / WATERLOO SUNSET**

Nov 98. (10xcd-ep;box) *Essential; (ESFCD 667)* **THE KINKS EP COLLECTION VOL.1** –

Oct 99. (cd) *Castle Pie; (PIESD 134)* **IT'S THE KINKS**

Jan 00. (cd/c) *Castle Select; (SEL CD/MC 560)* **YOU REALLY GOT ME: THE BEST OF THE KINKS**

Jul 00. (10xcd-ep;box) *Essential; (ESFCD 904)* **THE KINKS EP COLLECTION VOL.2** –

Mar 01. (d-cd/3xlp) *Sanctuary; (SAN DD/TV 010)* **BBC SESSIONS 1964-1977**

Mar 01. (d-cd) *Essential; (CMEDD 018)* **LIVE AT THE BBC: SONGS WE SANG FOR AUNTIE 1964-1994**

Jun 01. (cd) *Castle; (CMRCD 212)* **THE SINGLES COLLECTION**

Jul 01. (3xcd-box) *Castle; (CMGBX 318)* **THE MARBLE ARCH YEARS**
– (WELL RESPECTED KINKS / SUNNY AFTERNOON / KINDA KINKS)

May 02. (d-cd) *Sanctuary; (SANDD 109)* **THE ULTIMATE COLLECTION** 32 –
– You really got me / All day and all of the night / Tired of waiting for you / Everybody's gonna be happy / Set me free / See my friend / Till the end of the day / Dedicated follower of fashion / Sunny afternoon / Dead end street / Waterloo sunset / Death of a clown (DAVE DAVIES) / Autumn almanac / Susannah's still alive (DAVE DAVIES) / Wonderboy / Days / Plastic man / Victoria / Lola / Apeman / Supersonic rocket ship / Better things / Come dancing / Don't forget to dance / David Watts / Stop your sobbing / Dandy / Mr. Pleasant / I gotta move / Who'll be the next in line / I need you / Where have all the good times gone / Sittin' on my sofa / A well respected man / I'm not like everybody else / Love me till the sun shines / She's got everything / Starstruck / Shangr-la / God's children / Celluloid heroes / Wish I could fly like Superman / Do it again / Living on a thin line.

Apr 04. (cd) *Sanctuary; (SMRCD 024)* **THE SINGLES COLLECTION** –

Sep 04. (cd-s) *Sanctuary; (SANXD 317)* **YOU REALLY GOT ME / IT'S ALL RIGHT / MISTY WATER** 42 –

DAVE DAVIES

Pye Reprise

Jul 67. (7") *(7N 17356) <0614>* **DEATH OF A CLOWN. / LOVE ME TILL THE SUN SHINES** 3 Aug67

Nov 67. (7") *(7N 17429) <0660>* **SUSANNAH'S STILL ALIVE. / FUNNY FACE** 21

Aug 68. (7") *(7N 17514)* **LINCOLN COUNTY. / THERE IS NO LOVE WITHOUT LIFE**

Jan 69. (7") *(7N 17678)* **HOLD MY HAND. / CREEPING JEAN**

R.C.A. R.C.A.

Sep 80. (7") *<PB 12089>* **IMAGINATION'S REAL. / WILD MAN** –

Sep 80. (lp/c) *(PL/PK 13603) <AFL-1-3603; the US title>* **DAVE DAVIES** Jul80 42
– Where do you come from / Doing the best for you / Move over / Visionary dreamer / Nothin' more to lose / Imagination real / In you I believe / See the beast / Run / The world is changing hands. *(<cd-iss. May05 on 'Kock'; KOCCD 9680>)*

Nov 80. (7") *<PB 12147>* **DOING THE BEST FOR YOU. / NOTHING MORE TO LOSE** –

Dec 80. (7") *(PB 9620)* **DOING THE BEST FOR YOU. / WILD MAN** –

Oct 81. (lp/c) *(RCA LP/K 6005) <AFL-1-4036>* **GLAMOUR** Jul81
– Is this the only way / Reveal yourself / World of our own / Two serious / Glamour / 7th channel / Body / Eastern eyes / Body. *(<cd-iss. May05 on 'Kock'; KOCCD 9681>)*

Warners Warners

ep 83. (lp/c) *(92-3917-1/-4)* *<23917-1/-4>* **CHOSEN PEOPLE** [ ] Aug 83 [ ]
– Mean disposition / Love gets you / Take one more / True story / Danger zone / Tapes / Freedom lies / Fire burning / Cold winter / Matter of decision / Is it any wonder / Charity / Chosen people.

ep 83. (7") *<7-29509>* **LOVE GETS YOU. / ONE NIGHT WITH YOU** [–] [ ]

Nov 83. (7") *<7-29425>* **MEAN DISPOSITION. / COLD WINTER** [–] [ ]

Sanctuary Koch

ep 01. (cd) *(SANCD 098)* *<KOCCD 8087>* **ROCK BOTTOM: LIVE AT THE BOTTOM LINE** (live 1997) [ ] Jun00 [ ]
– I need you / She's got everything / Beautiful Delilah / Creepin' Jean / Good to see yer / Look through any doorway / LOve me till the sun shines / Tired of waiting / The kiss / Milk cow blues / Imaginations real / Dave's got his reading glasses / Wicked Annabella / Picture book / Death of a clown / All the Kinks songs / Too much on my mind / Strangers / Psycho lounge / One night with you / Living on a thin line / All day and all of the night / Encore / Money (that's what I want) / David Watts / I'm not like everybody else / You really got me.

lay 02. (cd) *<KOCCD 8398>* **BUG** [–] [ ]
– Whose foolin' who / It ain't over, 'til it's done! . . . / The lie! . . . . / Displaced person / Rock you, rock me / Flowers in the rain / Fortis Green / Why?!! / True phenomenon / Bug . . ... / De-bug / Life after life (transformation). *(UK-iss.Jul04 on 'Angel Air'; SJPCD 179)*

Angel Air Angel Air

ep 05. (cd) *(<SJPCD 212>)* **TRANSFORMATION** (live May 2003) [ ] [ ]
– Transformation 1 / Who's foolin' who / Till the end of the day / I need you / The blues / See my friends / Dead end street / Rock you, rock me / Flowers in the rain / Death of a clown / Picture book / It ain't over (till it's done) / Bug / Transformation 2 / Livin' on a thin line / Father Christmas / You really got me / Outro.

– (DAVE DAVIES) compilations, etc. –

pr 68. (7"ep) *Pye; (NEP 24289)* **DAVE DAVIES HITS** [ ] [ ]

ug 82. (7") *Old Gold; (OG 9128)* **DEATH OF A CLOWN. / SUSANNAH'S STILL ALIVE** [ ] [–]

eb 88. (lp/c) *P.R.T.; (PYL/PYK 6012)* **DAVE DAVIES – THE ALBUM THAT NEVER WAS** [ ] [–]
– (1960's singles)

l 92. (cd) *Mau Mau; (MAUDCD 617)* **DAVE DAVIES / GLAMOUR** [ ] [–]
(<re-iss. Aug03 on 'Beat Goes On'; BGOCD 587>)

eb 06. (cd) *Koch; <KOCCD 9996>* **KINKED** [–] [ ]

RAY DAVIES

not iss. Arista

l 85. (lp) *<8380>* **RETURN TO WATERLOO** (soundtrack) [–] [ ]
– Intro / Return to Waterloo / Going solo / Missing persons / Sold me out / Lonely hearts / Not far away / Expectations / Voices in the dark – end title. *<cd-iss. Feb05 on 'Velvel'; VELV 79820>*

below was from the film 'Absolute Beginners'

Virgin not iss.

ay 86. (7"/12") *(VS 865/+12)* **QUIET LIFE. / VOICES IN THE DARK** [ ] [–]

E.M.I. Capitol

ar 98. (cd) *(<494168-2>)* **THE STORYTELLER** (live VH1) [ ] Apr98 [ ]
– Storyteller / Introduction / Victoria / My name (dialogue) / 20th century man / London song / My big sister (dialogue) / That old black magic / Tired of waiting / Set me free (instrumental) / Dad and the green amp (dialogue) / Set me free / The front room (dialogue) / See my friends / Autumn almanac / Hunchback (dialogue) / X-ray / Art school (dialogue) / Art school babe / Back in the front room / Writing the song (dialogue) / When big Bill speaks – The man who knew a man / It's alright (dialogue) / It's alright (dialogue) / It's alright (dialogue) / Julie Finkle (dialogue) / The ballad of Julie Finkle / The third single (dialogue) / You really got me / London song (studio).

V2 V2

b 06. (cd) *(VVR 103535-2)* *<27285>* **OTHER PEOPLE'S LIVES** [36] [ ]
– Things are gonna change (the morning after) / After the fall / Next door neighbour / All she wrote / Creatures of little faith / Run away from time / The tourist / Is there life after breakfast? / The gateway (lonesome train) / Other people's lives / Stand up comic / Over my head / Thanksgiving day.

KISS

Formed: New York City, New York, USA ... late '71 by ex-WICKED LESTER members GENE SIMMONS and PAUL STANLEY, who recruited guitarist ACE FREHLEY and drummer PETER CRISS. After a year of touring in '73, they were signed to the new 'Casablanca' label, hitting the US Top 100 with an eponymous debut album in early '74. This, together with subsequent follow-up albums, 'HOTTER THAN HELL' (1974) and 'DRESSED TO KILL' (1975) set the greasepainted scene for what was to follow; low-rent glitter-metal so tacky it almost stuck to the speakers. Though these early albums sound like they were recorded on a cheap walkman in a sawmill, they contained some of KISS' finest groin-straining moments; 'STRUTTER', 'DEUCE' and 'ROCK AND ROLL ALL NITE' were anthemic shout-alongs for white college kids who could pretend to be rebellious for three minutes. But KISS undoubtedly built their reputation on a garish image and the sensory overkill of their live show, ALICE COOPER-style make-up and onstage schlock the order of the day. Accordingly, it was the double live album, 'ALIVE' (1975) that finally powered the band into the US Top 10 and the stadium major league. With 'DESTROYER' (produced by COOPER mentor, BOB EZRIN), the band refined their sound slightly, even recording a ballad, the PETER CRISS-penned/crooned teen heartbreaker, 'BETH' which furnished the band with their biggest ever hit single. This mid-70's career peak also saw a further three releases achieve platinum status, 'ROCK AND ROLL OVER' (1976), 'LOVE GUN' (1977) and 'ALIVE II'. KISS had struck a resounding chord in some back alley of the American consciousness and now boasted a merchandise line almost as long as SIMMONS' grotesque tongue, a perverted, proto-SPICE GIRLS marketing job from the dark side. And you couldn't get a much better marketing coup than releasing four solo albums on the same day, which is exactly what KISS did (one by each member), probably because they knew they could get away with it. Unsurprisingly, most of the material was self-indulgent rubbish and, with the threat of punk never far away, the band began to falter. Although the 'DYNASTY' (1979) album went Top 10 and provided a massive hit with 'I WAS MADE FOR LOVIN' YOU', CRISS soon bowed out, the drum stool filled by session man ANTON FIG for the 'UNMASKED' (1980) album. A permanent replacement was found in ERIC CARR who made his debut on the ill-advised concept nonsense of 'THE ELDER' (1981), though the new musical direction was just too much for FREHLEY to take and he wisely departed the following year. His place was filled by VINNIE VINCENT, who played on the back to basics 'CREATURES OF THE NIGHT'. When this album failed to revive their commercial fortunes, the band did the unthinkable, removing their make-up for the 'LICK IT UP' album. Perhaps as a result of the public discovering they weren't blood sucking ghouls after all but (relatively) normal looking people, the album went Top 30. Ironically, the band had just started to re-establish themselves in Britain, where 'LICK IT UP' made the Top 10, no doubt giving them heart in their struggle back to world domination. KISS then went through more line-up changes, with VINCENT being replaced first by MARK ST. JOHN, then BOB KULICK. With the unashamedly commercial 'CRAZY CRAZY NIGHTS' single and 'CRAZY NIGHTS' (1987) album, the band enjoyed their biggest success since their 70's heyday, both releases reaching No.4 in the UK. After another reasonably successful album, 'HOT IN THE SHADE' (1989), tragedy struck the band in the early 90's when CARR died following heart problems and cancer. Shaken but unbowed the band carried on with ERIC SINGER on drums, going back to the hoary sound of old with the 'REVENGE' (1992) opus, an album that saw

KISS

them showing the young bucks who had patented the moves. It had to happen of course; 1996 marked a money-spinning, full-blown reunion tour with the original line-up and re-applied warpaint, the perfect KISS-off to those who had written them off for dead. Of course, this now meant that KULICK and SINGER were surplus to requirement; the pair were duly given their marching orders and the KISS album they'd just worked on, 'CARNIVAL OF SOULS: THE FINAL SESSIONS' was shelved. With bootleggers having a field day, the album was eventually given a belated release in 1997 although critics were generally agreed that its lacklustre contents should've been kept on the mastertape. Still, KISS were flying high after the runaway success of the reunion tour and even decided to record a full album together. The resulting 'PSYCHO CIRCUS' (1998) made the US Top 3 to incredibly become the highest charting album of their near three decade career! This despite the fact it offered nothing new or even compared to their glory days. Then again, when the mainstream modern alternatives are so bland is it any wonder people consistently cling to retro fantasies? The band proceeded to indulge in perhaps one of heavy metal's most annoying and consistently dull fantasies, that of classical orchestra meets rock band. 'KISS SYMPHONY: ALIVE IV' (2003) was as dire as anything they've done and that's saying something. A double set of preposterous, string-backed rehashes, minus FREHLEY (who'd wisely bailed out by this point, to be replaced by former BLACK 'N' BLUE man TOMMY THAYER) and plus a musical non-connection between KISS and the MELBOURNE SYMPHONY ORCHESTRA did not Grammy material make. SIMMONS radioactivated his solo career in 2004 with a couple of very different albums, the first of which, '***HOLE', was a bizarre mish-mash of covers ('FIRESTARTER' anyone?), writing collaborations – DYLAN(!) and ZAPPA no less, the latter made possible by the co-operation of FRANK's wife Gail – and out of character ballads. The other record was a stand-up (as in "comedy") effort, 'SPEAKING IN TONGUES', performed before an appreciative Australian audience. From 2005, British fans could tune in to his weekly patter on Reality TV show, 'Rock School', shaking up a staid, private school music department in much the same way as the 2003 movie, 'School Of Rock', starring Jack Black.

• **Songwriters:** Most by STANLEY or SIMMONS, with some ballads by CRISS. Covered; THEN (S)HE KISSED ME (Crystals) / GOD GAVE ROCK AND ROLL TO YOU (Argent). MICHAEL BOLTON co-wrote with STANLEY their minor hit ballad 'FOREVER'. GENE SIMMONS solo covered; WHEN YOU WISH UPON A STAR (Judy Garland). • **Trivia:** In 1977, Marvel Comics started a KISS feature series in their monthly mag. In 1984, SIMMONS starred as a villain in the film 'Runaway' alongside Tom Selleck. Two years later 'The Bat-Winged Vampire' featured in films 'Never Too Young To Die', 'Trick Or Treat' & 'Wanted Dead Or Alive'. In 1994, a tribute album 'KISS MY ASS' was released by 'Mercury'. It featured star cover versions by LENNY KRAVITZ, GARTH BROOKS, ANTHRAX, GIN BLOSSOMS, TOAD THE WET SPROCKET, SHANDI's ADDICTION, DINOSAUR JR., EXTREME, LEMONHEADS, etc.

Album rating: KISS (*7) / HOTTER THAN HELL (*7) / DRESSED TO KILL (*7) / ALIVE! (*8) / DESTROYER (*8) / ROCK AND ROLL OVER (*6) / LOVE GUN (*6) / ALIVE II (*7) / DOUBLE PLATINUM compilation (*8) / DYNASTY (*6) / UNMASKED (*5) / (MUSIC FROM) THE ELDER (*4) / KILLERS compilation (*5) / CREATURES OF THE NIGHT (*6) / LICK IT UP (*6) / ANIMALIZE (*5) / ASYLUM (*6) / CRAZY NIGHTS (*5) / SMASHES, THRASHES AND HITS compilation (*7) / HOT IN THE SHADE (*6) / REVENGE (*6) / ALIVE III (*7) / MTV UNPLUGGED (*5) / CARNIVAL OF SOULS (*5) / PSYCHO-CIRCUS (*4) / THE BOX SET collection (*6) / THE VERY BEST OF KISS compilation (*6) / KISS SYMPHONY: ALIVE IV (*3) / Gene Simmons: ***HOLE (*4) / SPEAKING IN TONGUES spoken (*4)

GENE SIMMONS (b. CHAIM KLEIN WITZ, 25 Aug'49, Haifa, Israel) – vocals, bass / **PAUL STANLEY** (b. STANLEY EISEN, 20 Jan'52, Queens, N.Y.) – guitar, vocals / **ACE FREHLEY** (b. PAUL FREHLEY, 22 Apr'51, Bronx, N.Y.) – lead guitar, vocals / **PETER CRISS** (b. PETER CRISSCOULA, 27 Dec'47, Brooklyn, N.Y.) – drums, vocals

		Casablanca	Casablanca
Feb 74.	(7") <0004> **NOTHIN' TO LOSE. / LOVE THEME FROM KISS**	–	
Feb 74.	(lp) <9001> **KISS**	–	87
	– Strutter / Nothin' to lose / Fire house / Cold gin / Let me know / Kissin' time / Deuce / Love theme from Kiss / 100,000 years / Black diamond. *(UK-iss.Feb75; CBC 4003) (re-iss. May77 red-lp; CAL 2006) (re-iss. Feb82 lp/c; 6399/7199 057) (re-iss. Jul84 lp/c; PRICE/PRIMC 68) (cd-iss. Aug88; 824146-2)*		
May 74.	(7") <0011> **KISSIN' TIME. / NOTHIN' TO LOSE**	–	83
Aug 74.	(7") <0015> **STRUTTER. / 100,000 YEARS**	–	
Nov 74.	(lp) <7006> **HOTTER THAN HELL**	–	100
	– Got to choose / Parasite / Goin' blind / Hotter than Hell / Let me go, rock'n roll / All the way / Watchin' you / Mainline / Comin' home / Strange ways. *(UK-iss.May77 red-lp; CAL 2007) (re-iss. Feb82 lp/c; 6399/7199 058) (cd-iss. Aug88; 824147-2)*		
Jan 75.	(7") *(CBX 503)* **NOTHIN' TO LOSE. / LOVE THEME FROM KISS**		–
Mar 75.	(7") <823> **LET ME GO ROCK'N'ROLL. / HOTTER THAN HELL**	–	
Aug 75.	(lp) *(CBC 4004)* <7016> **DRESSED TO KILL**		Mar75 32
	– Room service / Two timer / Ladies in waiting / Getaway / Rock bottom / C'mon and love me / Anything for my baby / She / Love her all I can / Rock and roll all nite. *(re-iss. May77 red-lp; CAL 2008) (re-iss. Feb82 lp/c; 6399/7199 059) (cd-iss. Aug88; 824148-2)*		
May 75.	(7") <829> **ROCK AND ROLL ALL NITE. / GETAWAY**	–	68
Jun 75.	(7") *(CBX 510)* **ROCK AND ROLL ALL NITE. / ANYTHING FOR MY BABY**		–
Oct 75.	(7") <841> **C'MON AND LOVE ME. / GETAWAY**	–	
Nov 75.	(7") <850> **ROCK AND ROLL ALL NITE (live). / ('A'studio mix)**	–	12
Apr 76.	(7") *(CBX 516)* <854> **SHOUT IT OUT LOUD. / SWEET PAIN**		Mar76 31
May 76.	(lp) *(CBC 4008)* <7025> **DESTROYER**	22	Mar76 11
	– Detroit rock city / King of the night time world / God of thunder / Great expectations / Flaming youth / Sweet pain / Shout it out loud / Beth / Do you love me. *(re-iss. May77 red-lp; CAL 2009) (re-iss. Feb82 lp/c; 6399/7199 064) (cd-iss. Apr87; 824149-2)*		
Jun 76.	(7") <858> **FLAMING YOUTH. / GOD OF THUNDER**	–	74
Jun 76.	(d-lp) *(CBC 4011+2)* <7020> **ALIVE! (live)**	49	Oct75 9
	– Deuce / Strutter / Got to choose / Hotter than Hell / Firehouse / Nothin' to lose / C'mon and love me / Parasite / She / Watchin' you / 100,000 years / Black diamond / Rock bottom / Cold gin / Rock and roll all nite / Let me go, rock'n'roll. *(re-iss. May77 red-lp; CALD 5001) (re-iss. Feb82; 6640 064) (re-iss. Sep84 d-lp/d-c; PRID/+C 3) (cd-iss. Apr87; 822780-2)*		
Aug 76.	(7") <863> **BETH. / DETROIT ROCK CITY**	–	7
Jul 76.	(7") *(CBX 519)* **BETH. / GOD OF THUNDER**		–
Feb 77.	(red-lp) *(CALH 2001)* <NBLP 7037> **ROCK AND ROLL OVER**		Nov76 11
	– I want you / Take me / Calling Dr. Love / Ladies room / Baby driver / Love 'em and leave 'em / Mr. Speed / See you in your dreams / Hard luck woman / Makin' love. *(re-iss. Feb82 lp/c; 6399/7199 060) (cd-iss. Aug88; 824150-2)*		
Dec 76.	(7") <873> **HARD LUCK WOMAN. / MR. SPEED**	–	15
Mar 77.	(7") <880> **CALLING DR. LOVE. / TAKE ME**	–	16
May 77.	(7"m) *(CAN 102)* **HARD LUCK WOMAN. / CALLING DR. LOVE / BETH**		–
Jun 77.	(lp) *(CALH 2017)* <7057> **LOVE GUN**		4
	– I stole your love / Christine sixteen / Got love for sale / Shock me / Tomorrow and tonight / Love gun / Hooligan / Almost human / Plaster caster / The she kised me. *(re-iss. Feb82 lp/c; 6399/7199 063) (re-iss. Jul84 lp/c; PRICE/PRIMC 69) (cd-iss. Aug88; 824151-2)*		
Jul 77.	(7") <889> **CHRISTINE SIXTEEN. / SHOCK ME**	–	25
Aug 77.	(7"m/12"m) *(CAN/L 110)* **THEN SHE KISSED ME. / HOOLIGAN / FLAMING YOUTH**		–
Sep 77.	(7") <895> **LOVE GUN. / HOOLIGAN**	–	61
Nov 77.	(d-lp/d-c) *(CALD/+C 5004)* <7076> **KISS ALIVE II**	60	7
	– Detroit rock city / King of the night time world / Ladies room / Makin' love / Love gun / Calling Dr. Love / Christine sixteen / Shock me / Hard luck woman / Tomorrow and tonight / I stole your love / Beth / God of thunder / I want you / Shout it out loud / All American man / Rockin' in the U.S.A. / Larger than life / Rocket ride / Anyway you want it. *(re-iss. Feb82 d-lp)(d-c; 6685 043)(7599 512) (cd-iss. May89; 822781-2)*		
Jan 78.	(7") <906> **SHOUT IT OUT LOUD (live). / NOTHIN' TO LOSE (live)**	–	54

Feb 78. (7") <915> **ROCKET RIDE. / TOMORROW AND TONIGHT** – 39

Mar 78. (7") *(CAN 117)* **ROCKET RIDE. / LOVE GUN (live)** – –

(12"+=) *(CANL 117)* – Detroit rock city (live).

Jun 78. (7") *(CAN 126)* **ROCK AND ROLL ALL NITE. / C'MON AND LOVE ME** –

—— Took time to do solo projects (all same label on below)

GENE SIMMONS

Sep 78. (lp/pic-lp) *<NBLP/NBPIX 7120>* **GENE SIMMONS** – 22

– Radioactive / Burning up with fever / See you tonite / Tunnel of love / True confessions / Living in sin / Always near you – Nowhere to hide / Man of 1000 faces / Mr. Make Believe / See you in your dreams / When you wish upon a star. *<re-iss. 1987 pic-lp; NBLPP 7120> <cd-iss. 1997 (UK Mar03) on 'Universal'; 532384-2>*

Oct 78. (7") *<NB 951>* **RADIOACTIVE. / SEE YOU IN YOUR DREAMS** –

Jan 79. (7",7"red) *(CAN 134)* **RADIOACTIVE. / WHEN YOU WISH UPON A STAR** 41 –

ACE FREHLEY

Sep 78. (lp/pic-lp) *<NBLP/NBPIX 7121>* **ACE FREHLEY** – 26

– Rip it out / Speedin' back to my baby / Snow blind / Ozone / What's on your mind / New York groove / I'm in need of love / Wiped-out / Fractured mirror. *<re-iss. 1987 pic-lp; NBLPP 7121> (cd-iss. May88; 826916-2) <cd re-iss. 1997 (UK Mar03) on 'Universal'; 532385-2>*

Nov 78. (7"blue) *(CAN 135) <NB 941>* **NEW YORK GROOVE. / SNOW BLIND** Sep78 13

PETER CRISS

Sep 78. (lp/pic-lp) *<NBLP/NBPIX 7122>* **PETER CRISS** – 43

– I'm gonna love you / You matter to me / Tossin' and turnin' / Don't you let me down / That's the kind of sugar papa likes / Easy thing / Rock me, baby / Kiss the girl goodbye / Hooked on rock'n'roll / I can't stop the rain. *<re-iss. 1987 pic-lp; NBLPP 7122> (cd-iss. Nov91; 826917-2) (re-iss. Aug94 cd+red-lp+book on 'Megarock') <cd re-iss. 1997 (UK Mar03) on 'Universal'; 532386-2>*

Dec 78. (7") *(NB 952)* **DON'T YOU LET ME DOWN. / HOOKED ON ROCK AND ROLL** –

Feb 79. (7"green) *(CAN 139)* **YOU MATTER TO ME. / HOOKED ON ROCK AND ROLL** –

PAUL STANLEY

Sep 78. (lp/pic-lp) *<NBLP/NBPIX 7123>* **PAUL STANLEY** – 40

– Tonight you belong to me / Move on / Ain't quite right / Wouldn't you like to know / Take me away (together as one) / It's alright / Hold me, touch me (think of me when we're apart) / Love in chains / Goodbye. *(re-iss. 1987 pic-lp; NBLPP 7123> (cd-iss. Nov91; 826918-2) <cd re-iss. 1997 (UK Mar03) on 'Universal'; 532387-2>*

Feb 79. (7",7"purple) *(CAN 140)* **HOLD ME TOUCH ME. / GOODBYE** –

KISS

—— returned to studio

Casablanca Casablanca

Jun 79. (7") *(CAN 152) <983>* **I WAS MADE FOR LOVIN' YOU. / HARD TIMES** 50 May79 11

(12") *(CANL 152)* – ('A'side) / Charisma.

Jun 79. (lp/c) *(CALH/+C 2051) <7152>* **DYNASTY** 50 9

– I was made for lovin' you / 2,000 man / Sure know something / Dirty livin' / Charisma / Magic touch / Hard times / X-ray eyes / Save your love. *(re-iss. Oct83 lp/c; PRICD/PRIMC 42) <cd-iss. 1988; > (cd-iss. Aug88; 812770-2)*

Aug 79. (7") *(CAN 163) <2205>* **SURE KNOW SOMETHING. / DIRTY LIVIN'** 47

Feb 80. (7"m/12"m) *(NB/+L 1001)* **2000 MAN. / I WAS MADE FOR LOVIN' YOU / SURE KNOW SOMETHING** –

Mercury Casablanca

Jun 80. (7") *<2282>* **SHANDI. / SHE'S SO EUROPEAN** – 47

Jun 80. (7") *(MER 19)* **TALK TO ME. / SHE'S SO EUROPEAN** –

Jun 80. (lp/c) *(6302 032) <7225>* **UNMASKED** 48 35

– Is that you / Shandi / Talk to me / Naked city / What makes the world go 'round / Tomorrow / Two sides of the coin / She's so European / Easy as it seems / Torpedo girl / You're all that I want. *(cd-iss. May83; 800041-2)*

Aug 80. (7") *(KISS 1)* **WHAT MAKES THE WORLD GO 'ROUND. / NAKED CITY** –

Aug 80. (7") *<2299>* **TOMORROW. / NAKED CITY** –

—— (May'80) **ERIC CARR** (b.12 Jul'50) – drums, producer repl. CRISS who went solo (early 80's pop albums; 'OUT OF CONTROL' / 'LET ME ROCK YOU')

Nov 81. (lp/c) *(6302/7144 163) <7261>* **MUSIC FROM 'THE ELDER'** 51 75

– The oath / Fanfare / Just a boy / Dark light / Only you / Under the rose / A world without heroes / Mr. Blackwell / Escape from the island / Odyssey / I. *(cd-iss. Jun89; 825153-2)*

Nov 81. (7") *<2343>* **A WORLD WITHOUT HEROES. / DARK LIGHT** – 56

Jan 82. (7"/7"pic-d) *(KISS/+P 2)* **A WORLD WITHOUT HEROES. / MR. BLACKWELL** 55 –

—— **VINNIE VINCENT** (b. VINCENT CUSANO) – guitar repl. BOB KULICK who had repl. FREHLEY (he formed FREHLEY'S COMET)

Casablanca Casablan

Oct 82. (7") *<2365>* **DANGER. / I LOVE IT LOUD** –

Oct 82. (7") *(KISS 3)* **KILLER. / I LOVE IT LOUD** –

(12"+=) *(KISS 3-12)* – I was made for lovin' you.

Oct 82. (lp/c) *(6302/7144 219) <7270>* **CREATURES OF THE NIGHT** 22 45

– Creatures of the night / Saint and sinner / Keep me comin' / Rock and roll Hell / Danger / I love it loud / I still love you / Killer / War machine. *(cd-iss. Aug88; 824154-2)*

Mar 83. (7") *(KISS 4)* **CREATURES OF THE NIGHT. / ROCK AND ROLL ALL NITE (live)** 34 –

(12"+=) *(KISS 4-12)* – War machine.

Vertigo Mercur

Oct 83. (7") *<814 671-7>* **LICK IT UP. / DANCE ALL OVER YOUR FACE** – 66

Oct 83. (7"/7"sha-pic-d) *(KISS 5/+P)* **LICK IT UP. / NOT FOR THE INNOCENT** 34 –

(12"+=) *(KISS 5-12)* – I still love you.

Oct 83. (lp/c) *(VERL/+C 9) <814 297>* **LICK IT UP** 7 24

– Exciter / Not for the innocent / Lick it up / Young and wasted / Gimme more / All Hell's breakin' loose / A million to one / Fits like a glove / Dance all over your face / And on the 8th day. *(cd-iss. Dec89 on 'Mercury'; 814297-2)*

Jan 84. (7") *<818 216-2>* **ALL HELL'S BREAKIN' LOOSE. / YOUNG AND WASTED** –

—— **MARK (NORTON) ST. JOHN** – guitar repl. VINCENT who formed VINNIE VINCENT'S INVASION

Sep 84. (7") *(VER 12) <880 205-7>* **HEAVEN'S ON FIRE. / LONELY IS THE HUNTER** 43 49

(12"+=) *(VERX 12)* – All hell's breakin' loose.

Sep 84. (lp/c) *(VERL/+C 18) <822 495>* **ANIMALIZE** 11 19

– I've had enough (into the fire) / Heaven's on fire / Burn bitch burn / Get all you can take / Lonely is the hunter / Under the gun / Thrills in the night / While the city sleeps / Murder in high-heels. *(cd-iss. Dec89 on 'Mercury'; 822 495-2)*

Nov 84. (7") *<880 535-2>* **THRILLS IN THE NIGHT. / BURN BITCH BURN** –

—— **BRUCE KULICK** – guitar repl. MARK who became ill

Oct 85. (lp/c) *(VERH/+C 32) <826 099>* **ASYLUM** 12 20

– King of the mountain / Any way you slice it / Who wants to be lonely / Trial by fire / I'm alive / Love's a deadly weapon / Tears are falling / Secretly cruel / Radar for love / Uh! All night. *(cd-iss. May89 on 'Mercury'; 82 303-2)*

Oct 85. (7") *<884 141-7>* **TEARS ARE FALLING. / ANY WAY YOU SLICE IT** – 51

Oct 85. (7") *(KISS 6)* **TEARS ARE FALLING. / HEAVEN'S ON FIRE (live)** 57 –

(12"+=) *(KISS 6-12)* – Any way you slice it.

Sep 87. (7"/7"s) *(KISS 7/+P) <888 796-7>* **CRAZY CRAZY NIGHTS. / NO, NO, NO** 4 65

(12"+=) *(KISS 7-12)* – Lick it up / Uh! All night.

(12"pic-d+=) *(KISSP 7-12)* – Heaven's on fire / Tears are falling.

Oct 87. (lp/c) *(VERH/+C 49) <832626>* **CRAZY NIGHTS** 4 18

– Crazy crazy nights / I'll fight Hell to hold you / Bang bang you / No, no, no / Hell or high water / My way / When your walls come down / Reason to live / Good girl gone bad / Turn on the night / Thief in the night. *(cd-iss. Feb91; 832 626-2)*

Dec 87. (7"/7"s) *(KISS/+P 8) <870 022-7>* **REASON TO LIVE. / THIEF IN THE NIGHT** [33] [64]
(c-s+=) *(KISSMC 8)* – Who wants to be lonely.
(12"++=) *(KISS 8-12)* – Thrills in the night.
(12"pic-d++=) *(KISSP 8-12)* – Secretly cruel.
(cd-s+=) *(KISCD 8)* – Tears are falling / Crazy crazy nights.

Feb 88. (7"/7"s) *(KISS/+P 9) <870 215-7>* **TURN ON THE NIGHT. / HELL OR HIGH WATER** [41] [ ]
(12"+=/12"pic-d+=) *(KISS/+P 9-12)* – King of the mountain / Any way you slice it.
(cd-s+=) *(KISCD 9)* – Heaven's on fire / I love it loud.

Oct 89. (7"/7"red/c-s) *(KIS S/R/MC 10) <876 146-7>* **HIDE YOUR HEART. / BETRAYED** [59] [66]
(12"+=/cd-s+=) *(KIS SX/CD 10)* – Boomerang.
(10"pic-d) *(KISP 10-10)* – ('A'side) / Lick it up / Heaven's on fire.

Oct 89. (lp/c/cd) *<(838 913-2/-4/-1)>* **HOT IN THE SHADE** [35] [29]
– Rise to it / Betrayed / Hide your heart / Prisoner of love / Read my body / Love's a slap in the face / Forever / Silver spoon / Cadillac dreams / King of hearts / The street giveth and the street taketh away / You love me to hate you / Somewhere between Heaven and Hell / Little Caesar / Boomerang.

Mar 90. (7"/7"s) *(KISS/+P 11) <876 716-7>* **FOREVER (remix). / THE STREET GIVETH AND THE STREET TAKETH AWAY** [65] Feb90 [8]
(12"white+=) *(KISS 12-12)* – Deuce (demo) / Strutter (demo).
(12"/12"g-f) *(KIS SX/XG 11)* – ('A'side) / All American man / Shandi / The Oath.
(cd-s) *(KISCD 11)* – ('A'side) / Creatures of the night / Lick it up / Heaven's on fire.

Jun 90. (c-s) *<875096>* **RISE TO IT. / SILVER SPOON** [–] [81]

— In May'91, ERIC CARR underwent open heart surgery. He was admitted to hospital again but they found malignant cancer growth. He died on the 24th Nov'91. In Jan'92, KISS hit UK No.4 with 'GOD GAVE ROCK AND ROLL TO YOU II' from the film 'Bill & Ted's Bogus Journey'. On the same single issued on 'Interscope' were tracks by KING'S X & SLAUGHTER.

— **ERIC SINGER** – drums (ex-BADLANDS, ex-BLACK SABBATH) repl. CARR

May 92. (7"/c-s) *(KISS/KISMC 12)* **UNHOLY. / GOD GAVE ROCK'N'ROLL TO YOU II** [26] [ ]
(12"+=/12"pic-d+=)(cd-s+=) *(KISS/+P 12-12)(KISCD 12)* – Partners in crime / Deva / Strutter (demos).

May 92. (cd/c/lp) *(848 037-2/-4/-1) <48037>* **REVENGE** [10] [6]
– Unholy / Take it off / Tough love / Spit / God gave rock'n'roll to you II / Domino / Heart of chrome / Thou shalt not / Every time I look at you / Paralyzed / I just wanna / Carr jam 1981.

May 93. (cd/c) *<(514 827-2/-4)>* **KISS ALIVE III (live)** [24] [9]
– Creatures of the night / Deuce / I just wanna / Unholy / Heaven's on fire / Watchin' you / Domino / I was made for lovin' you / I still love you / Rock'n'roll all nite / Lick it up (featuring BOBBY WOMACK) / Take it off / I love it loud / Detroit rock city / God gave rock'n'roll to you / Star spangled banner.

Mar 96. (cd/c/lp) *<(528 950-2/-4/-1)>* **MTV UNPLUGGED (live)** [74] [15]
– Comin' home / Plaster caster / Goin' blind / Do you love me / Domino / Sure know something / A world without heroes / Rock bottom / See you tonight / I still love you / Every time I look at you / 2,000 man / Beth / Nothin' to lose / Rock and roll all nite.

Oct 97. (cd/c) *<(536 323-2/-4)>* **CARNIVAL OF SOULS** [ ] [27]
– Hate / Rain / Master and slave / Childhood's end / I will be there / Jungle / In my head / It never goes away / Seduction of the innocent / I confess / In the mirror / I walk alone.

— originals were back again (**SIMMONS, STANLEY, FREHLEY + CRISS**)

Sep 98. (cd/c) *<(558 992-2/-4)>* **PSYCHO-CIRCUS** [47] [3]
– Psycho-circus / Within / I pledge allegience (to the state of rock & roll) / Into the void / We are one / You wanted the best / Raise your glasses / I finally found my way / Dreamin' / Journey of 1,000 years.

— **TOMMY THAYER** – guitar (ex-BLACK 'N' BLUE) repl. FREHLEY

— next with the MELBOURNE SYMPHONY ORCHESTRA

Sanctuary Sanctuary

Jul 03. (cd/t-lp) *(SAN DD/TV 195) <84617>* **KISS SYMPHONY: ALIVE IV (live)** [ ] [ ]
– Deuce / Strutter / Let me go rock & roll / Lick it up / Calling Dr. Love / Psycho circus / Beth / Forever / Goin' blind / Sure know something / Shandi / Detroit rock city / King of the night time world / Do you love me / Shout it out loud / God of thunder / Love gun / Black diamond / Great expectations / I was made for lovin' you / Rock and roll all nite.

– compilations etc. –

Aug 76. (t-lp) *Casablanca; <7032>* **THE ORIGINALS** (first 3 albums) [–] [ ]

May 78. (d-lp) *Casablanca; (CALD 5005) <7100 1-2>* **DOUBLE PLATINUM** [ ] [24]
(re-iss. Feb82; 6641 907) (re-iss. May85 d-lp/d-c; PRID/+C 8) cd-iss. Jun87; 824 148-2)

Jan 81. (lp) *Casablanca; (6302 060)* **THE BEST OF THE SOLO ALBUMS** [ ] [–]

Jun 82. (lp) *Casablanca; (CANL 1)* **KILLERS** [42] [–]

Nov 88. (7") *Mercury; <872 246-7>* **LET'S PUT THE 'X'. / CALLING DR. LOVE** [–] [97]

Nov 88. (lp/c/cd) *Vertigo / Mercury; <(836 759-1/-4/-2)>* **SMASHES, THRASHES AND HITS** [62] [21]
– Let's put the X in sex / Crazy, crazy nights / (You make me) Rock hard / Love gun / Detroit rock city / I love it loud / Reason to live / Lick it up / Heavens on fire / Strutter / Beth / Tears are falling / I was made for lovin' you / Rock and roll all nite / Shout it out loud.

Oct 88. (5"vid-cd) *Vertigo; (080 232-2)* **CRAZY, CRAZY NIGHTS. / NO, NO, NO / WHEN YOUR WALLS COME DOWN / THIEF IN THE NIGHT** [ ] [–]

1989. (7") *Mercury; <814 303-7>* **BETH. / HARD LUCK WOMAN** [–] [ ]

1989. (7") *Mercury; <814 304-7>* **ROCK AND ROLL ALL NITE. / I WAS MADE FOR LOVIN' YOU** [–] [ ]

Sep 89. (5"vid-cd) *Vertigo; (080 044-2)* **LICK IT UP. / DANCE ALL OVER YOUR FACE / GIMME MORE / FITS LIKE A GLOVE** [ ] [–]

Sep 89. (5"vid-cd) *Vertigo; (080 058-2)* **TEARS ARE FALLING. / ANY WAY YOU SLICE IT / WHO WANTS TO BE LONELY / SECRETLY CRUEL** [ ] [–]

— (all lp's were released as pic-lp's in Europe)

Jul 96. (cd/c) *Mercury; <(532 741-2/-4)>* **YOU WANTED THE BEST, YOU GOT THE BEST (live compilation)** [ ] [17]

Jul 97. (cd/c) *Polygram TV; <(536 159-2/-4)>* **GREATEST HITS** [58] Apr97 [77]

Dec 01. (5xcd-box) *<(586561-2)>* **THE BOX SET** [ ] Nov01 [ ]

Sep 02. (cd) *Universal; <(E 063122-2)>* **THE VERY BEST OF KISS** [ ] Aug02 [52]
– Strutter / Deuce / Got to choose / Hotter than hell / C'mon and love me / Rock and roll all nite / Detroit rock city / Shout it out loud / Beth / I want you / Calling Dr. Love / Hard luck woman / I stole your love / Christine sixteen / Love gun / New York groove / I was made for lovin' you / I love it loud / Lick it up / Forever / God gave rock & roll to you II.

GENE SIMMONS

Sanctuary Sanctuary

May 04. (cd) *(SANCD 245) <84670>* *****HOLE** [ ] Jun04 [ ]
– Sweet & dirty love / Firestarter / Weapons of mass destruction / Waiting for the morning light / Beautiful / ***hole / Now that you're gone / Whatever turns you on / Dog / Black tongue / Carnival of souls / If I had a gun / 1,000 dreams.

Sep 04. (cd) *(SANCD 298) <84707>* **SPEAKING IN TONGUES** (spoken word) [ ] [ ]

☐ Mark KNOPFLER (see under ⇒ DIRE STRAITS)

the KOOKS

Formed: Brighton, England ... 2004 by LUKE PRITCHARD (aka STEPHEN BEAN), HUGH HARRIS, MAX RAFFERTY and PAUL GARRED. Referencing Hunky Dory-era BOWIE in their moniker, the KOOKS stirred their Brit-Pop broth with a list of classic ingredients sourced as far back as the KINKS (witness PRITCHARD's elongated, DAVIES-esque diction) and as far forward as ARCTIC MONKEYS. Unlike the 'MONKEYS, LUKE had a formal grounding in showbiz at the Brits School, where he met his former girlfriend, KATIE MELUA, now a major pop artist in her own right. The experience must have come in handy as they signed to 'Virgin' in 2005 and released a string of increasingly buzz-worthy and higher charting singles: 'EDDIE'S GUN', 'SOFA SONG' and 'YOU DON'T LOVE ME'. Their semi-acoustic Anglo-centricity found full, fresh-faced expression on debut album, 'INSIDE IN / INSIDE OUT' (2006), a UK Top 3 entry whose secret weapon was the classy single, 'NAIVE', their biggest seller to date.

Album rating: INSIDE IN – INSIDE OUT (*7)

LUKE PRITCHARD (b. 1986) – vocals, guitar / **HUGH HARRIS** – lead guitar, vocals / **MAX RAFFERTY** – bass, vocals / **PAUL GARRED** – drums, percussion

		Virgin	not iss.
Jul 05.	(7") *(VS 2000)* **EDDIE'S GUN. / BUS SONG**	35	–
	(cd-s) *(VSCDT 2000)* – ('A') / California.		
Oct 05.	(7") *(VS 1904)* **SOFA SONG. / SOMETHING TO SAY**	28	–
	(cd-s) *(VSCDT 1904)* – ('A') / Be mine.		
	(dvd-s) *(VSDVD 1905)* – ('A'-video) / Eddie's gun (video) / Put your back to my face.		
Jan 06.	(7") *(VS 1910)* **YOU DON'T LOVE ME. / LONELY CAT (demo)**	12	–
	(cd-s) *(VSCDT 1910)* – ('A') / Slave to the game.		
	(cd-s) *(VSCDX 1910)* – ('A'-live @ The Garage) / See the world (acoustic live @ Abbey Road) / The window song / ('A'-video) / See the world (footage from Abbey Road).		
Jan 06.	(cd/lp) *(CD+/V 3016)* **INSIDE IN / INSIDE OUT** – Seaside / See the world / Sofa song / Eddie's gun / Oooh la / You don't love me / She moves in her own way / Matchbox / Naive / I want you back / If only / Jackie big tits / Time awaits / Got no love. *(lp w/free lp+=)* – LIVE & ACOUSTIC @ ABBEY ROAD	3	–
Mar 06.	(7"clear) *(VS 1911)* **NAIVE. / TEA AND BISCUITS**	5	–
	(cd-s) *(VSCDT 1911)* – ('A') / Hiding low.		
	(cd-s) *(VSCDX 1911)* – ('A') / I love that girl / ('A'-demo) / ('A'-video) / You don't love me (live from Fopp tour video).		
Jun 06.	(7") *(VS 1913)* **SHE MOVES IN HER OWN WAY. / I ALREADY MISS YOU**	7	–
	(cd-s) *(VSCDT 1913)* – ('A') / Do you love me still?		
	(cd-s) *(VSCDX 1913)* – ('A') / In my opinion / Give in / ('A'-video).		

KORN

Formed: Bakersfield / Huntington Beach, California, USA . . . 1993 out of CREEP, by JONATHAN DAVIS, J MUNKY SHAFFER, BRIAN 'HEAD' WELCH, FIELDY and DAVID SILVERIA. Signed to 'Epic' the following year, they unleashed to the public their eponymous US Top 75 debut. A barrage of aural psychosis, DAVIS' tortured performance more than lived up to the hype surrounding the record's release. Among its schizophrenic highs and lows were the disturbing but cathartic ten minute (+) emotional minefield, 'DADDY', which cried out from the core of DAVIS' very soul. Bizarrely, DAVIS turned his hand (and elbow) to the bagpipes on the nursery rhyme parody, 'SHOOTS AND LADDERS', a track that even GAVIN FRIDAY might have disowned in his VIRGIN PRUNES heyday! Consolidating this seminal meisterwork, KORN toured the world, resurfacing in 1996 with another primal scream of sinuous, bass-heavy angst-metal in the shape of 'LIFE IS PEACHY'. The album contained no less than three UK Top 30 hits, 'NO PLACE TO HIDE', 'A.D.I.D.A.S.' (which stands for "All Day I Dream About Sex"; nothing to do with the sports company) and 'GOOD GOD', the set also featuring covers of Oshea Jackson's 'WICKED' and War's 'LOWRIDER'. A US Top 3, the record also cracked the UK Top 40, due largely to the strong Kerrang! support only rivalled in 1997 by DAVIS's more attention-seeking contemporary, MARILYN MANSON. Two further chart-topping albums, 'FOLLOW THE LEADER' (1998) and the concept 'ISSUES' (1999), didn't sell quite so well in Britain, the grim storytelling of KORN's leader beginning to get short shrift from some of his gloomy disciples. While DAVIS' lyrical agenda continued in this brooding, navel-gazing vein for 'UNTOUCHABLES' (2002), KORN continued to forge a distinctively dense mesh of sound which further distanced them from the incestuous nu-metal scene, almost completely paring back the rap pretensions for an altogether more intimidating sound. 'TAKE A LOOK IN THE MIRROR' (2003), meanwhile, trimmed off any sonic excess they'd been accumulating over the years with an album which concentrated the essence of their root sound while still taking them forward. 'GREATEST HITS VOL.1' (2004), on the other hand, saw them take a retrospective step backwards, controversially leading in with two contrasting covers: a pointless run through Cameo's 'WORD UP!' and a spookier, personalised take on Pink Floyd's 'ANOTHER BRICK IN THE WALL, PTS.1-3'. Following a battle with crystal meth, WELCH subsequently announced his conversion to born-again Christianity. Not for the rest of the band though, whose seventh studio set, 'SEE YOU ON THE OTHER SIDE' (2005), dissed organised religion on the likes of 'HYPOCRITES'. Having signed to 'Virgin' and enlisted the skills of NiN producer Atticus Ross, KORN semi-industrialised their sound in anticipation of encroaching middle-age. Although the tribal grind of lead single, 'TWISTED TRANSISTOR', made the UK Top 30, the novelty had begun wearing thin on British album buyers; it was a different story in the US of course, where their not so nu-metal was still Top 3 bound.

• **Covered:** EARACHE MY EYE (Cheech & Chong) / SHOULD I STAY OR SHOULD I GO (Clash) / ONE (Metallica).

Album rating: KORN (*9) / LIFE IS PEACHY (*8) / FOLLOW THE LEADER (*5) / ISSUES (*6) / UNTOUCHABLES (*5) / TAKE A LOOK IN THE MIRROR (*4) / GREATEST HITS VOL.1 compilation (*7) / SEE YOU ON THE OTHER SIDE (*7) / LIVE & RARE (*5)

JONATHAN DAVIS (b.18 Jan'71) – vocals, bagpipes / **MUNKY** (b. JAMES SHAFFER, 6 Jun'70, Rosedale, Calif.) – guitar, vocals / **BRIAN 'HEAD' WELCH** (b.19 Jun'70, Torrance, Calif.) – guitar, vocals / **FIELDY** (b. REGINALD ARVIZU, 2 Nov'69) – bass, vocals / **DAVID SILVERIA** (b.21 Sep'72, San Leandro, Calif.) – drums, vocals

		Epic	Immortal
Jul 95.	(cd/c) *(478080-2/-4)* *<66633>* **KORN** – Blind / Ball tongue / Need to / Clown / Divine / Faget / Shoots and ladders / Predictable / Fake / Lies / Helmet in the bush / Daddy.		Nov94 72
Oct 95.	(10"ep) *(KORN 1)* **BLIND**		
Oct 96.	(7"white) *(663845-0)* **NO PLACE TO HIDE. / PROUD**	26	
	(cd-s+=) *(663845-2)* – Sean Olsen.		
	(cd-s) *(663845-5)* – ('A'side) / Shoots and ladders (Dust Brothers industrial mix) / Shoots and ladders (Dust Brothers hip-hop mix).		
Oct 96.	(cd/c/lp/cd-rom) *(485369-2/-4/-1/-6)* *<67554>* **LIFE IS PEACHY** – Twist / Chi / Lost / Swallow / Porno creep / Good God / Mr. Rogers / K"£0%! / No place to hide / Wicked / A.D.I.D.A.S. / Lowrider / Ass itch / Kill you.	32	3
Feb 97.	(10"white-ep) *(664204-0)* **A.D.I.D.A.S. / CHI (live). / LOWRIDER – SHOOTS AND LADDERS (live)**	22	
	(cd-ep+=) *(664204-2)* – Ball tongue (live).		
	(cd-ep) *(664204-5)* – ('A'side) / Faget / Porno creep / Blind.		
Jun 97.	(cd-ep) *(664658-2)* **GOOD GOD / GOOD GOD (Mekon mix) / GOOD GOD (Dub Pistols mix) / WICKED (Tear The Roof Off mix)**	25	
	(cd-ep) *(664658-5)* – ('A'side) / A.D.I.D.A.S. (Synchro dub) / A.D.I.D.A.S. (Under Pressure mix) / A.D.I.D.A.S. (The Wet Dream mix).		
	(12"ep) *(664658-6)* – ('A'-Mekon mix) / ('A'-Dub Pistols mix) / A.D.I.D.A.S. (Synchro dub) / A.D.I.D.A.S. (Under Pressure mix).		
Aug 98.	(ltd-cd-s) *(666391-2)* **GOT THE LIFE / (12"mixes by DeeJay Punk-Roc and D.O.S.E.)**	23	
	(cd-s) *(666391-5)* – ('A'side) / I can remember / Good god (oomph! vs such a surge mix).		
Aug 98.	(cd/c/lp) *(491221-2/-4/-1)* *<69001>* **FOLLOW THE LEADER** – It's on / Freak on a leash / Got the life / Dead bodies eveywhere / Children of the korn / B.B.K. / Pretty / All in the family / Reclaim my place / Justin / Seed / Cameltosis / My gift to you.	5	1
Apr 99.	(cd-s) *(667252-2)* **FREAK ON A LEASH / FREAK ON A LEASH (Dante Ross mix) / FREAK ON A LEASH (Josh A's beast on a leash mix)**	24	
	(cd-s) *(667252-5)* – ('A'-Freakin' bitch mix) / ('A'-Josh A's beast on a leash		

mix) / ('A'-Dante Ross mix).
(12") *(667252-6)* – ('A'mixes; above).

Nov 99. (cd/c/lp) *(496359-2/-4/-1)* *<63710>* **ISSUES** 37 1
– Dead / Falling away from me / Trash / 4U / Beg for me / Make me bad / It's gonna go away / Wake up / Am I going crazy / Hey daddy / Somebody someone / No way / Let's get this party started / Wish you could be me / Counting / Dirty. *(re-iss. Apr00 cd/cd/cd; 497850-2/-6/-9)*

Jan 00. (7"orange) *(668869-7)* **FALLING AWAY FROM ME. / JINGLE BALLS** 24
(cd-s+=) *(668869-2)* – ('A'-Krust remix) / ('A'-CD-Rom).
(cd-s) *(668869-5)* – ('A'side) / ('A'-Mantronik Beatdown formula) / Got the life (Josh Abraham remix).

May 00. (7") *(669433-7)* **MAKE ME BAD. / DIRTY (live)** 25
(cd-s+=) *(669433-2)* – ('A'-live).
(cd-s) *(669433-5)* – ('A'side) / ('A'mixes; Kornography / Sickness In Salvation / Sybil / Danny Saber).

— early 2002, JONATHAN DAVIS (alongside RICHARD GIBBS) contributed five songs to the Various Artists OST movie, 'Queen Of The Damned'

May 02. (cd-s) *(672742-2)* *<radio>* **HERE TO STAY / (T-Ray's mix) / (T-Ray's instrumental) / (video)** 12 Jun02 72
(cd-s) *(672742-5)* – ('A'side) / (T-Ray's mix) / (BT's managed anger mix).

Jun 02. (cd/d-lp) *(501770-2/-1)* *<61488>* **UNTOUCHABLES** 4 2
– Here to stay / Make believe / Blame / Hollow life / Bottled up inside / Thoughtless / Hating / One more time / Alone I break / Embrace / Beat it upright / Wake up hate / I'm hiding / No one's there. *(ltd-cd+=; 501770-2)* – Here to stay (T-Ray's mix) / Here to stay (video).

Sep 02. (cd-s) *(673157-2)* **THOUGHTLESS / (DJ Cooley remix) / (Dante Ross remix) / (video)** 37 –
(cd-s) *(673157-5)* – ('A'side) / Here to stay (mindless self indulgence mix) / Here to stay (Tone Toven & sleep remix).

Aug 03. (cd-s) *(674142-2)* **DID MY TIME / (greyedout mix) / ONE (live from MTV ICON: Metallica)** 15 –

Nov 03. (cd) *(513325-2)* *<90335>* **TAKE A LOOK IN THE MIRROR** 53 9
– Right now / Break some off / Counting on me / Here it comes again / Deep inside / Did my time / Everything I've known / Play me (with NAS) / Alive / Let's do this now / I'm done / Y'all want a single / When will this end. *(cd w/dvd+=; 513325-3)* – One (live) / Korn kut up / Right now (mirror mix video) / (Untouchables 2002 tour documentary).

Oct 04. (cd) *(518792-2)* *<92700-2>* **GREATEST HITS VOL.1** (compilation) 22 4
– Word up! / Another brick in the wall (pts.1-3) / Y'all want a single / Right now / Did my time / Alone I break / Here to stay / Trash / Somebody someone / Make me bad / Falling away from me / Got the life / Freak on a leash / Twist / A.D.I.D.A.S. / Clown / Shoots and ladders / Blind / Freak on a leash (Dante Ross mix). *<US cd w/dvd>*

— now without BRIAN WELCH

Virgin Virgin

Nov 05. (7"white/cd-s) *(VUS/+CD 316)* **TWISTED TRANSISTOR. / TOO LATE I'M DEAD** 27 64

Dec 05. (cd) *(CDVUS 274)* *<45889>* **SEE YOU ON THE OTHER SIDE** 71 3
– Twisted transistor / Politics / Hypocrites / Souvenir of sadness / 2-way / Throw me away / Love song / Open up / Coming undone / Getting off / Liar / For no one / Interlude #3 – I've seen it all / Tearjerker.

Jun 06. (7") *(VUS 323)* **COMING UNDONE. / TWISTED TRANSISTOR (live)** –
(cd-s) *(VUSCD 323)* – ('A') / Eaten up inside.

– compilations, others, etc. –

Sep 05. (d-cd) *Immortal; (520530-2)* **KORN / FOLLOW THE LEADER**

Apr 06. (d-cd) *Epic; (82876 82148-2)* **LIFE IS PEACHY / UNTOUCHABLES**

May 06. (cd) *Epic; <(82876 82247-2)>* **LIVE & RARE** (live 2003) 51
– live:- Did my time / Blind / Falling away from me / Right now / Got the life / Here to stay / Freak on a leash / Another brick in the wall pts.1, 2 & 3 / One / My gift to you / A.D.I.D.A.S. / rare:- Earache my eye / Proud.

KRAFTWERK

Formed: Dusseldorf, Germany . . . 1969 as ORGANISATION by RALF HUTTER, FLORIAN SCHNEIDER-ESLEBEN and three others, namely BUTCH HAUF, FRED MONICKS and BASIL HAMMOND. After one CONRAD PLANK-produced album, 'TONE FLOAT', for 'R.C.A.' in 1970, the pair broke away to form KRAFTWERK (German for POWERPLANT), with KLAUS DINGER and THOMAS HOMANN. After one album for 'Philips', RALF & FLORIAN became KRAFTWERK, releasing the 1973 album (titled after their Christian names) for 'Vertigo' in the process. In 1974, they added KLAUS ROEDER & WOLFGANG FLUR, issuing their magnus-opus 'AUTOBAHN'. This UK & US Top 5 album contained a 22-minute title track, which, edited into 3 minutes, also became a hit. The next album, 'RADIO ACTIVITY' (which was also issued on their own 'Kling Klang' label in Germany), disappointed most and failed to secure a Top 50 placing. In 1978, they were back in the UK Top 10 at least, with an excellent return to form, 'THE MAN MACHINE'. In the early 80's, they enjoyed another hit album, 'COMPUTER WORLD', and a run of UK hit singles, one of which, 'THE MODEL' (from 1978 lp) made the top spot. A projected album by the name of 'TECHNOPOP', was pencilled in for release in 1983 and allegedly 'E.M.I.' were even supplied with artwork. The record never appeared, and of course, given KRAFTWERK's reclusive reticence, no explanation was offered. The same year, however, the band did release a one-off 12" single, 'TOUR DE FRANCE', no doubt inspired by HUTTER's preoccupation with cycling. It was to be another three years before the band released a full album, the disappointing 'ELECTRIC CAFE'. By this point the band were starting to tread water, an assumption that seemed to be confirmed when fans had to wait another five years for 'new' material. 'THE MIX', released in 1991, was actually an album of reworkings of old tracks, a bit of a hit and miss affair which failed to deliver any original pieces per se. Both BARTOS and FLUR had left the band before the album's release, allegedly sick of the laboriously slow and detailed recording process and the band's reclusive inertia. Despite a reputation for a disciplined working ethos, the band remain defiantly distant from the music industry. Their studio apparently possesses neither fax nor phone, they've no management and they've turned down all offers of remix work and collaborations. Whether they can remain on the cutting edge in such a vacuum remains to be seen and for the moment, their Guru-like status is based on past glories, sounds that continue to permeate almost all strands of pop culture, now more than ever. It's testament to their towering influence that despite releasing no new material for more than a decade, they headlined the Tribal Gathering dance festival in the late 90's. This robotic electronic rock act with minimalist synth-tunes, being at times (on stage!) twiddled by dummies, were more inspirational than their contemporaries TANGERINE DREAM: KRAFTWERK became a major influence for ULTRAVOX!, GARY NUMAN, DAVID BOWIE ('77), JEAN-MICHEL JARRE, SIMPLE MINDS, AFRIKA BAMBAATAA (whose 'TRANS-EUROPE EXPRESS'-sampling 'Planet Rock' virtually invented electro), DAFT PUNK, etc. Back on the musical autobahn for the new millennium, KRAFTWERK released a single, 'EXPO 2000'. Their first album in two decades, incredible but true, followed in summer 2003. 'TOUR DE FRANCE SOUNDTRACKS', as its title might suggest, was inspired by the band's love of cycling. Preceded by an update of the track they originally released in 1983, the album was quintessential KRAFTWERK, as disciplined and precision-crafted as the race itself. The appropriately titled 'MINIMUM-MAXIMUM' (2005), was a live UK Top 30 double-disc set, the kind of record that would've been unthinkable from the studio boffins just a decade earlier; what next, a headlining spot at T In The Park 2010 to promote their "new" album?

Album rating: Organisation: TONE FLOAT (*4) / Kraftwerk: KRAFTWERK (HIGHRAIL) (*4) / KRAFTWERK 2 (VAR) (*4) / RALF AND FLORIAN (*5) / AUTOBAHN (*8) / RADIOACTIVITY (*4) / TRANS-EUROPE EXPRESS (*8) / THE MAN MACHINE (*8) / COMPUTER WORLD (*7) / ELECTRIC CAFE (*4) / THE MIX remixes (*5) / TOUR DE FRANCE SOUNDTRACKS (*6) / MINIMUM-MAXIMUM (*6)

ORGANISATION

RALF HUTTER (b.20 Aug'46, Krefeld, Germany) – electric organ, strings / **FLORIAN SCHNEIDER-ESLEBEN** (b. 7 Apr'47, Bodensee)– flute, echo unit, strings / **BUTCH HAUF** – bass, percussion / **FRED MONICKS** – drums / **BASIL HAMMOND** – percussion, vocals

R.C.A. — not iss.

Aug 70. (lp) *(SF 8111)* **TONE FLOAT** [ ] [-]
– Tone float / Milk float / Silver forest / Rhythm salad / Noitasinagro.

KRAFTWERK

HUTTER + SCHNEIDER with **KLAUS DINGER** – guitar, keyboards / **THOMAS HOMANN** – percussion

Philips — not iss.

1971. (lp) *(6305 058)* **KRAFTWERK** [-] German [-]
– Ruckzuck / Stratowargius / Megaherz / Vom Himmel hoch.

— **HUTTER + SCHNEIDER** trimmed to a duo. (DINGER and HOMANN formed NEU!)

1972. (lp) *(6305 117)* **KRAFTWERK 2** [-] German [-]
– Klingklang / Atem / Strom / Spule 4 / Wellenlange / Harmonika.

Vertigo — Vertigo

Nov 72. (d-lp) *(6641 077)* **KRAFTWERK** (2 German lp's combined) [ ] [-]

Nov 73. (lp) *(6360 616)* **RALF & FLORIAN** [ ] [-]
– Elektrisches roulette (Electric roulette) / Tongebirge (Mountain of sound) / Kristallo (Crystals) / Heimatklange (The bells of home) / Tanzmusik (Dance music) / Ananas symphonie (Pineapple symphony). *<US-iss.Sep75; 2006>*

— added **KLAUS ROEDER** – violin, guitar / **WOLFGANG FLUR** – percussion

Nov 74. (lp/c) *(6360/ 620)* *<2003>* **AUTOBAHN** [4] [5]
– Autobahn / Kometenmelodie 1 & 2 (Comet melody) / Mitternacht (Midnight) / Morgenspaziergang (Morning walk). *(re-iss. Mar82 on 'E.M.I.' lp/c; EMC/TC-EMC 3405); hit 61 UK) (re-iss. Jun85 on 'Parlophone' lp/c; AUTO/TCAUTO 1) (cd-iss. Jun87 & Aug95 on 'E.M.I.'; CDP 746153-2)*

Feb 75. (7") *(6147 012)* **AUTOBAHN. / KOMETENMELODIE** [11] [-]

Feb 75. (7") *<203>* **AUTOBAHN. / MORGENSPAZIERGANG** [-] [25]

Jul 75. (7") *(6147 015)* **KOMETENMELODIE 2. / KRISTALLO** [ ] [-]

Jul 75. (7") *<204>* **KOMETENMELODIE 2. / MITTERNACHT** [-] [ ]

— In Oct'75, **KARL BARTOS** – percussion repl. ROEDER

Capitol — Capitol

Nov 75. (lp/c) *(<EST/TC-EST 11457>)* **RADIO-ACTIVITY** [ ] [ ]
– Geiger counter / Radio-activity / Radioland / Airwaves / (intermission) / News / The voice of energy / Antenna / Radio stars / Uran / Transistor / Ohm sweet ohm. *(re-iss. Jun84 on 'Fame' lp/c; FA 413103-1/-4) (re-iss. 1985 on 'E.M.I.' lp/c; EMS/TC-EMS 1256) (cd-iss. May87 on 'E.M.I.'; CDP 746474-2) (re-iss. Aug87 on 'E.M.I.' lp/c; ATAK/TCATAK 104) (re-iss. cd Apr94 on 'Cleopatra';) (re-iss. cd Apr95 on 'E.M.I.';)*

Feb 76. (7") *(CL 15853)* *<4211>* **RADIO-ACTIVITY. / ANTENNA** [ ] [ ]

Apr 77. (lp/c) *(<EST/TC-EST 11603>)* **TRANS-EUROPE EXPRESS** [ ] [ ]
– Europe endless / The hall of mirrors / Showroom dummies / Trans-Europe express / Metal on metal / Franz Schubert / Endless endless. *(in Feb82, they hit UK No.49 Feb82) (re-iss. 1985 on 'E.M.I.' lp/c; ATAK/TCATAK 5) (re-iss. Jun86 on 'Fame' lp/c; FA 413151-1/-4) (cd-iss. May87 on 'E.M.I.'; CDP 746473-2) (re-iss. cd Apr94 on 'Cleopatra';)*

Apr 77. (7") *(CL 15917)* **TRANS-EUROPE EXPRESS. / EUROPE ENDLESS** [ ] [-]

Aug 77. (7") *(CLX 104)* **SHOWROOM DUMMIES. / EUROPE EXPRESS** [ ] [ ]

May 78. (7") *<4460>* **TRANS-EUROPE EXPRESS. / FRANZ SCHUBERT** [-] [67]

May 78. (lp/c) *(<EST/TC-EST 11728>)* **THE MAN MACHINE** [9] [ ]
– The robots / Spacelab / Metropolis / The model / Neon lights / The man machine. *(re-iss. Mar85 on 'Fame' lp/c; 413118-1/-4) (re-iss. Jul88 on 'Fame' cd/c/lp; CD/TC+/FA 3118) (re-iss. cd Apr94 on 'Cleopatra'; CLEO 5877CD) (re-iss. cd/c Apr95 on 'E.M.I.'; CD/TC EMS 1520) (cd re-iss. Jun97 on 'E.M.I.'; CDCNTAV 4)*

May 78. (7") *(CL 15981)* **THE ROBOTS (edit). / SPACELAB** [ ] [ ]

Jun 78. (7") *<4620>* **NEON LIGHTS. / THE ROBOTS** [-] [ ]

Sep 78. (7"/12"luminous) *(CL/12CL 15998)* **NEON LIGHTS. / TRANS-EUROPE EXPRESS / THE MODEL** [53] [ ]

Nov 78. (12"m) *(CL 16098)* **SHOWROOM DUMMIES. / EUROPE ENDLESS / SPACELAB** [ ] [-]

E.M.I. — Warners

Apr 81. (7") *(EMI 5175)* *<49723>* **POCKET CALCULATOR. / DENTAKU** [39] [ ]
(12"+=) *(12EMI 5175)* – Numbers.
(c-s) *(TCEMI 5175)* – ('A'extended) / ('A'side) / Numbers.

May 81. (lp/c) *(EMC/TC-EMC 3370)* *<3549>* **COMPUTER WORLD** [15] [72]
– Pocket calculator / Numbers / Computer-world / Computer love / Home computer / It's more fun to compute. *(re-iss. Apr95 cd/c; CD/TC EMS 1547)*

Jun 81. (7"/12") *(EMI/12EMI 5207)* **COMPUTER LOVE. / THE MODEL** [36] [-]
(Dec81; flipped over, hit UK No.1) (re-iss. May84; G45 16)

Jun 81. (7") *<49795>* **COMPUTER LOVE. / NUMBERS** [-] [ ]

Feb 82. (7") *(EMI 5272)* **SHOWROOM DUMMIES. / NUMBERS** [25] [-]
(12"+=) *(12EMI 5272)* – Pocket calculator.

— (In May'83, they had album 'TECHNO POP' cancelled)

Jul 83. (7") *(EMI 5413)* *<29342>* **TOUR DE FRANCE. / TOUR DE FRANCE (instrumental)** [22] [ ]
(c-s+=/12"+=) *(TC/12 EMI 5413)* – ('A'version).

Aug 84. (7") *(EMI 5413)* **TOUR DE FRANCE (remix). / TOUR DE FRANCE** [24] [-]
(12"+=) *(12EMI 5413)* – ('A'instrumental).

Oct 86. (7"/ext.12") *(EMI/12EMI 5588)* **MUSIQUE NON-STOP. / MUSIQUE NON STOP (version)** [ ] [ ]

Nov 86. (lp/c)(cd) *(EMD/TC-EMD 3370)(CDP 746416-2)* *<25525>* **ELECTRIC CAFE** [58] [ ]
– Boom boom tschak / Techno pop / Musique non stop / The telephone call / Sex object / Techno pop / Electric cafe. *(cd re-iss. Aug95; CDEMS 1546)*

Feb 87. (7") *(EMI 5602)* *<28441>* **THE TELEPHONE CALL. / DER TELEFON ANRUF** [ ] [ ]
(12"+=) *(12EMI 5602)* – House phone.

— **FRITZ HIJBERT** repl. WOLFGANG FLUR

May 91. (c-s/7") *(TC+/EM 192)* **THE ROBOTS (re-recorded). / ROBOTRONIK** [20] [ ]
(12"+=) *(12EM 192)* – ('A'album version).
(cd-s+=) *(CDEM 192)* – Robotnik.

Jun 91. (cd/c/d-lp) *(CD/TC+/EM 1408)* **THE MIX** ('91 remixes) [15] [ ]
– The robots / Computer love / Pocket calculator / Dentaku / Autobahn / Radioactivity / Trans-Europe express / Abzug / Metal on metal / Homecomputer / Musique non-stop. *(cd re-iss. Aug95; CDEM 1408)*

Oct 91. (c-s/7") *(TC+/EM 201)* **RADIOACTIVITY (Francois Kevorkian remix). / ('A'-William Orbit mix)** [43] [-]
(12"+=/cd-s+=) *(12/CD EM 201)* – ('A'extended).

— In Jul'91, BARTOS and FLUR formed their own project, ELEKTRIC

Oct 99. (12"/cd-s) *(887421-0/-6)* **TOUR DE FRANCE** (mixes) [61] [-]

Dec 99. (12"/cd-s) *(EXPO 1/+CD)* **EXPO 2000** (mixes) [ ] [-]
(above issued on German 'Kling Klang')

E.M.I. — Astralwe

Mar 00. (12"/cd-s) *(12EM/CDEM 562)* **EXPO 2000** (mixes) [27] [-]

Nov 00. (2x12"/m-cd) *(EMP/CDEM 583)* *<38768>* **EXPO REMIX** [ ] Oct01 [ ]
– (remixes: Orbital / Francois K & Rob Rives / DJ Rolando / Underground resistance / UR infiltrated / UR thought 3).

Jul 03. (2x12")(cd-s) *(552689-6)(CDEM 626)* *<52989>* **TOUR DE FRANCE 2003** [20] [ ]
– (version 1 / version 2 / version 3 / long distance version).

Aug 03. (cd)(d-lp) *(cd/d-lp)* *(CDEM 591710-2)(<5 91 708-1>)* **TOUR DE FRANCE SOUNDTRACKS** [21] [ ]

– Prologue / Tour de France etape 1 / Tour de France etape 2 (continued) / Tour de France etape 3 (continued) / Chrono / Vitamin / Aerodynamik / Titanium / Elektro kardiogramm / La forme / Regeneration / Tour de France.

Mar 04. (12") *(12EM 637)* <*ASW 48204*> **AERODYNAMIK (mixes; Kling Klang dynamix / Alex Gopher & Etienne De Crecy dynamix / Francois K. Aero)** [33] [ ]
(cd-s+=) *(CDEM 637)* – ('A'-radio edit).

Jun 05. (d-cd) *(<5 60611-2>)* **MINIMUM-MAXIMUM** (live) [29] [ ]
– The man-machine / Planet of visions / Tour de France etape 1 / Chrono / Tour de France etape 2 / Vitamin / Tour de France / Autobahn / The model / Neon lights / Radioactivity / Trans Europe express / Metal on metal / Numbers / Computer world / Home computer / Pocket calculator / Dentaku / The robots / Elektro kardiogramm / Aero dynamik / Music non stop.

– compilations, others, etc. –

on 'Vertigo' unless mentioned otherwise

Oct 75. (lp) *(6360 629)* **EXCELLER 8** [ ] [–]
Oct 80. (7") *(CUT 108)* **AUTOBAHN. / (b-side by BEGGAR'S OPERA)** [ ] [–]
Apr 81. (lp) *(6449 066)* **ELEKTRO KINETIC** [ ] [–]
May 81. (7") *(VER 3)* **KOMETENMELODIE 2. / VON HIMMEL HOCH** [ ] [–]
— <In the US compilation lp 'THE ROBOTS' on 'Capitol'; *9445*>
Apr 94. (cd) *Cleopatra; (CLEO 6843CD)* **SHOWROOM DUMMIES** [ ] [–]
(re-iss. May97; same)
Apr 94. (cd) *Cleopatra; (CLEO 5761-2)* **THE MODEL (The Best Of Kraftwerk 1975-1978)** [ ] [–]
Mar 97. (12") *Discopromo; (D 762)* **NUMBERS** [ ] [–]
Mar 97. (12") *Discopromo; (D 801)* **TOUR DE FRANCE** [ ] [–]
May 97. (d-cd) *Cleopatra; (CLEO 9416-2)* **THE CAPITOL YEARS** [ ] [–]

Lenny KRAVITZ

Born: 26 May'64, New York City, New York, USA, son of a Russian Jew and black Bahamas-born actress. As a teenager, he moved with his family to Los Angeles, where he joined the local boys' choir and taught himself to play guitar and piano. In 1987, KRAVITZ formed his own one-man band, ROMEO BLUE, marrying girlfriend of two years, 'Cosby Show' actress Lisa Bonet. Over the course of the ensuing two years, he recorded demos which were soon heard by Henry Hirsch, who recommended them to 'Virgin'. In October '89, after many arguments with the record company over production techniques, etc., KRAVITZ finally released a debut album and single, 'LET LOVE RULE'. A back to basics operation of luddite proportions, the record slavishly imitated KRAVITZ's paisley-shirted heroes of yesteryear (HENDRIX, CURTIS MAYFIELD, DYLAN) in much the same fashion as The BLACK CROWES paid homage to The FACES and The ALLMAN BROTHERS. Yet, despite charges of plagiarism from critics, much like The 'CROWES debut, 'LET LOVE RULE' was consistently listenable. Unsurprisingly then, the album subsequently notched up sales of half a million copies in the US, eventually reaching Top 60 in the UK. In 1990, the title track became KRAVITZ's first Top 40 success in Britain, tempting MADONNA into requesting his writing skills (along with INGRID CHAVEZ) for her controversial 'Justify My Love' single. Quite a celebrity in his own right, KRAVITZ played up the part of Hollywood socialite to the max, immaculately decked out in nouveau-retro clobber (a la PRINCE) and de rigueur dreadlocks. Later that year, he also appeared in Liverpool at YOKO ONO's tribute to her late husband JOHN LENNON. 'MAMA SAID' (1991) was a more accomplished, soulful affair which fleshed out the sound with brass and strings, songs alternating between introspective mood pieces (he'd recently split with his wife) and gritty funk-rock. Early in '92, LENNY settled out of court over royalties owing to INGRID CHAVEZ from the MADONNA collaboration, although the whole thing seemed a bit of a sham bearing in mind that the main thrust of the song was highly reminiscent of PUBLIC ENEMY's 'Security Of The First World'. Nevertheless, KRAVITZ could well afford to pay, 'MAMA SAID' notching up considerable American and British sales, while the single, 'IT AIN'T OVER 'TIL IT'S OVER' was a US No.2. After writing a passable album for sexy French goddess, VANESSA PARADIS, KRAVITZ re-emerged in thundering rock-God mode (replete with red leather trousers, no less) for 'ARE YOU GONNA GO MY WAY', a HENDRIX-esque song that made the UK Top 5. The album of the same name was KRAVITZ's biggest success to date, scaling the album charts in Britain, although it was clear the singer was running out of fresh ideas (or at least fresh ways of presenting old ideas). 'CIRCUS' (1995) carried on in much the same vein, successful but stale. The imaginatively titled '5' (1998) hardly broke the mould although, with the UK No.1 success of the 'FLY AWAY' single (aided at least in part by its use on a UK TV ad), the album was a resounding transatlantic success. A pointless cover of the Guess Who's 'AMERICAN WOMAN' (for the 'Austin Powers – The Spy Who Shagged Me' soundtrack and a 'GREATEST HITS' package) suggested that KRAVITZ was approaching creative meltdown. All the more surprising then, that 'LENNY' (2001), if being equally imaginatively titled, offered a return to his more varied, soulful palate of yesteryear. Never highly original, but certainly his most engaging work in almost a decade. More a critical death knell than a born-again comeback, 'BAPTISM' (2004) found KRAVITZ going through the usual HENDRIX/SLY STONE/PRINCE motions, and lamenting his rock'n'roll lifestyle into the bargain; the album nevertheless made the US Top 20, although only serving up one major hit, 'LADY'.

• **Covered;** COLD TURKEY + GIVE PEACE A CHANCE (John Lennon) / IF SIX WAS NINE (Jimi Hendrix) / DEUCE (Kiss). • **Trivia:** SLASH of GUNS N' ROSES played guitar on 2 tracks from 'MAMA SAID'.

Album rating: MAMA SAID (*8) / LET LOVE RULE (*7) / ARE YOU GONNA GO MY WAY (*7) / CIRCUS (*5) / 5 (*5) / GREATEST HITS compilation (*8) / LENNY (*5) / BAPTISM (*4)

LENNY KRAVITZ – vocals, guitar, piano, bass, drums with on session / **HENRY HIRSCH** – keyboards / **KARL DENSON** – sax / + guests

Virgin Virgin

Oct 89. (7"/7"w-poster) *(VUS/+P 10)* <*99166*> **LET LOVE RULE. / EMPTY HANDS** [ ] [89]
(12"+=/cd-s+=) *(VUS T/CD 10)* – Blues for Sister Someone / Flower child.

Nov 89. (lp/c/cd) *(VUSLP/VUSMC/CDVUS 10)* <*91290*> **LET LOVE RULE** [56] [61]
– Sitting on top of the world / Let love rule / Freedom train / My precious love / I build this garden for us / Fear / Does anybody out there even care / Mr. Cab driver / Rosemary / Be. *(c+=)* – Blues for Sister Someone / Flower child. *(cd++=)* – Empty hands.

Jan 90. (7"/c-s) *(VUS/+C 17)* **I BUILT THIS GARDEN FOR US. / FLOWER CHILD** [81] [–]
(12"+=/cd-s+=) *(VUS T/CD 17)* – Fear.

May 90. (7"/c-s) *(VUS/+C 20)* **MR. CAB DRIVER. / BLUES FOR SISTER SOMEONE (live) / DOES ANYBODY OUT THERE EVEN CARE (live)** [58] [ ]
(12"/cd-s) *(VUS T/CD 20)* – (first 2 tracks) / Rosemary (live).
(10") *(VUSA 20)* – ('A'side) / Rosemary (live) / Let love rule (live).

Jul 90. (7"/c-s) *(VUS/+C 26)* **LET LOVE RULE. / COLD TURKEY (live)** [39] [–]
(12"+=) *(VUSTG 26)* – Flower child (live).
(cd-s+=) *(VUSCD 26)* – My precious love (live).
(10") *(VUSA 26)* – ('A'side) / If six was nine (live) / My precious love (live).

Mar 91. (7"/c-s) *(VUS/+C 34)* **ALWAYS ON THE RUN. / ('A'instrumental)** [41] [–]
(12"+=/12"box+=) *(VUST/+X 34)* – Light skin girl from London.
(cd-s++=) *(VUSCD 34)* – Butterfly.

Apr 91. (cd)(c/lp) *(CDVUS 31)(VUS MC/LP 31)* <*91610*> **MAMA SAID** [8] [39]
– Fields of joy / Always on the run / Stand by my woman / It ain't over

'til it's over / More than anything in this world / What goes around comes around / The difference is why / Stop draggin' around / Flowers for Zoe / Fields of joy (reprise) / All I ever wanted / When the morning turns to night / What the . . .. are we saying? / Butterfly.

May 91. (7"/c-s) *(VUS/+C 43)* **IT AIN'T OVER 'TIL IT'S OVER. / THE DIFFERENCE IS WHY** 11 –
(12"+=/cd-s+=) *(VUST 43)* – I'll be around.
(12"pic-d) *(VUSTY 43)* – ('A'side) / (interview).

May 91. (c-s) *<98795>* **IT AIN'T OVER 'TIL IT'S OVER / I'LL BE AROUND** – 2

Sep 91. (7"/c-s) *(VUS/+C 45)* **STAND BY MY WOMAN. / FLOWERS FOR ZOE** 55 –
(12"+=) *(VUST 45)* – Stop dragging around (live).
(cd-s+=) *(VUSCD 45)* – What the . . .. are we saying? (live) / Always on the run (live).

Oct 91. (c-s) *<98736>* **STAND BY MY WOMAN / LIGHT SKIN GIRL FROM LONDON** – 76

— now with **CRAIG ROSS** – electric guitar (co-writes some music) / **TONY BRETT** – bass / **MICHAEL HUNTER** – flugel horn

Feb 93. (7"/c-s) *(VUS/+C 65)* **ARE YOU GONNA GO MY WAY. / MY LOVE** 4 –
(cd-s) *(VUSCD 65)* – ('A'side) / Always on the run / It ain't over 'til it's over / Let love rule.

Mar 93. (cd)(c/lp) *(CDVUS 60)(VUS MC/LP 60) <86984>* **ARE YOU GONNA GO MY WAY** 1 12
– Are you gonna go my way / Believe / Come on and love me / Heaven help / Just be a woman / Is there any love in your heart / Black girl / My love / Sugar / Sister / Eleutheria.

May 93. (7"/c-s) *(VUS/+C 72) <12662>* **BELIEVE. / FOR THE FIRST TIME** 30 60
(10"pic-d+=/cd-s+=) *(VUS T/CD 72)* – ('A'acoustic) / Sitar (acoustic).

Aug 93. (7"/c-s) *(VUS/+C 73)* **HEAVEN HELP. / ELEUTHERIA** 21 –
(cd-s+=) *(VUSDG 73)* – Ascension / Brother.

Nov 93. (7"pic-d/12") *(VUS P/T 76)* **IS THERE ANY LOVE IN YOUR HEART. / ALWAYS ON THE RUN (live)** 52
(cd-s+=) *(VUSDG 76)* – What goes around comes around (live) / Freedom train (live).

Mar 94. (c-s) *<38412>* **HEAVEN HELP. / SPINNING AROUND OVER YOU** – 80
(cd-s+=) *<38412>* – B-side blues / Are you gonna go my way / Freedom train – Always on the run (live).
(above b-side was from the movie, 'Reality Bites')

Aug 95. (c-s) *(VUSC 93)* **ROCK AND ROLL IS DEAD / ANOTHER LIFE** 22 –
(10"+=/cd-s+=) *(VUS AB/CD 93)* – Confused / Is it me or is it you.

Sep 95. (c-s) *<38514>* **ROCK AND ROLL IS DEAD / ANOTHER LIFE / ARE YOU GONNA GO MY WAY (live)** – 75

Sep 95. (cd/c/lp) *(CDVUS/VUSLP/MUSMC 86) <40696>* **CIRCUS** 5 10
– Rock and roll is dead / Circus / Beyond the 7th sky / Tunnel vision / Can't get you off my mind / Magdalene / God is love / Thin ice / Don't go and put a bullet in your head / In my life today / The resurrection.

Dec 95. (c-s) *(VUSC 96)* **CIRCUS / ('A'acoustic)** 54
(10"+=/cd-s+=) *(VUS A/CD 96)* – Tunnel vision (live) / Are you gonna go my way (live).

Feb 96. (7"/c-s) *(VUS A/C 100) <38535>* **CAN'T GET YOU OFF MY MIND. / EMPTY HANDS** 54 62
(cd-s+=) *(VUSCD 100)* – Stand by my woman.

Sep 96. (10"/cd-s) *(VUS A/CD 107)* **THE RESURRECTION (live). /** – w-drawn –

May 98. (c-s) *(VUSC 130)* **IF YOU CAN'T SAY NO / WITHOUT YOU** 48
(12"+=/cd-s+=) *(VUS T/CD 130)* – ('A'-Zero & BT . . . mixes).

May 98. (cd/c) *(CDVUS/VUSMC 140) <47758>* **5** 18 28
– Live / Supersoulfighter / I belong to you / Black velveteen / If you can't say no / Thinking of you / Take time / Fly away / It's your life / Straight cold player / Little girl's eyes / You're my flavor / Can we find a reason? *(cd re-iss. Jun99; CDVUSX 140)*

Sep 98. (c-s) *(VUSC 138)* **I BELONG TO YOU / IF YOU CAN'T SAY NO (Flunky in the attic mix)** 75
(cd-s+=) *(VUSCD 138)* – If you can't say no (BT twilo dub).

Feb 99. (c-s/cd-s) *(VUSC/+D 141) <radio cut>* **FLY AWAY / FLY AWAY (live acoustic) / BELIEVE (live acoustic)** 1 Nov98 12

Jun 99. (c-s) *(VUSC 146)* **BLACK VELVETEEN / LIVE / FLY AWAY** –
(cd-s) *(VUSCD 146)* – (first 2 tracks) / Supersoulfighter.
(cd-s) *(VUSCDX 146)* – (first & third tracks) / Straight cold player. *(re-iss. Dec99; same)*

Aug 99. (c-s) *(VUSC 153) <radio cut>* **AMERICAN WOMAN / THINKING OF YOU (Nick Hexam's dancehall mix)** Jul99 49
(cd-s+=) *(VUSCD 153)* – Straight cold player (live) / Fields of joy (live).

Mar 00. (-) *<album cut>* **I BELONG TO YOU** – 71

Oct 00. (cd/c) *(CDVUSX/VUSMCX 183) <50316>* **GREATEST HITS** (compilation) 12 2
– Are you gonna go my way / Fly away / Rock and roll is dead / Again / It ain't over 'til it's over / Can't get you off my mind / Mr. Cab driver / American woman / Stand by my woman / Always on the run / Heaven help / I belong to you / Believe / Let love rule / Velveteen.

Nov 00. (c-s) *(VUSC 187) <radio play>* **AGAIN / FLY AWAY (live) / ARE YOU GONNA GO MY WAY (live)** 4
(cd-s) *(VUSCD 187)* – (first two tracks) / Always on the run (live).
(cd-s) *(VUSCDG 187)* – (first & third tracks) / Let love rule (live).

Oct 01. (cd/lp) *(CDVUS/VUSLP 213) <11233>* **LENNY** 55 12
– Battlefield of love / If I could fall in love / Yesterday is gone (my dear Kay) / Stillness of heart / Believe in me / Pay to play / A million miles away / God save us all / Dig in / You were in my heart / Bank robber man / Let's get high.

Nov 01. (cd-s) *(VUSCD 229) <radio cut>* **DIG IN / ROSEMARY / CAN'T GET YOU OFF MY MIND** Sep01 31

Mar 02. (cd-s) *(VUSCD 236)* **STILLNESS OF HEART / STILLNESS OF HEART (acoustic) / FLOWERS FOR ZOE (acoustic)** 44 –

Jan 04. (12"/cd-s; LENNY KRAVITZ, P DIDDY, LOON & PHARRELL WILLIAMS) *(MCST/+D 40350)* **SHOW ME YOUR SOUL (mixes) / SHAKE A TAILFEATHER (corporate mix)** 35 –
(above on 'Puff Daddy – M.C.A.'; from the movie, 'Bad Boys II')

May 04. (cd-s) *<18510>* **WHERE ARE WE RUNNIN'? / UNCHARTED TERRAIN** – 69

May 04. (cd) *(CDVUS 252) <84145>* **BAPTISM** 74 14
– Minister of rock'n'roll / I don't want to be a star / Lady / Calling all angels / California / Sistamamalover / Where are we runnin'? / Baptized / Flash / What did I do with my life? / Storm / The other side / Destiny. *(d-cd iss.Nov04 +=; VBX 32)* – LENNY

Jul 04. (7") *(VUS 294)* **CALIFORNIA. / MR. CAB DRIVER (acoustic)** 62 –
(cd-s) *(VUSCD 294)* – ('A') / Where are we runnin' (live at WXRK, NYC).

Aug 04. (-) *<radio>* **STORM** – 98

Nov 04. (12") *(VUST 295)* **LADY. / STORM (a cappella)** 27
(cd-s) *(VUSCD 295)* – ('A') / Storm (Just Blaze remix).

– compilations, etc. –

Oct 01. (d-cd) *(810873-2)* **LET LOVE RULE / MAMA SAID** –

□ KYUSS (see under ⇒ QUEENS OF THE STONE AGE)

□ Greg LAKE (see under ⇒ EMERSON, LAKE & PALMER)

LAMBCHOP

Formed: Nashville, Tennessee, USA ... 1992 initially as POSTERCHILD by KURT WAGNER, the 90's country-lounge answer to 60's icons, CAT STEVENS and TIM HARDIN. His hesitant but heavy-lidded vocal monotone sat perfectly against the lethargic drowsiness of the country-jazz played by his large backing ensemble. Although they could hardly be termed rock, LAMBCHOP emerged from the flourishing alternative roots scene with an album on 'Merge' ('City Slang' UK) 'I HOPE YOU'RE SITTING DOWN' (1995). A post-modern cousin of CHET ATKINS (although at times at least twice removed!), the record revealed WAGNER's love of vintage string-laden production and his penchant for beer-soaked, meandering tales of ordinary madness. Early the following year, KURT and LAMBCHOP delivered another collection of near comatose country vignettes, 'HOW I QUIT SMOKING', this time around wrapped up in a classic 70's Nashville production sheen courtesy of arranger, John Mock. One of the record's highlights, 'THE MAN WHO LOVED BEER', was issued as the first LAMBCHOP single and has since been adopted as author, Martin C. Strong's theme tune. Joking aside, 1996 also saw the release of a third set, the critically acclaimed live/festival (1995) recorded 'HANK', relaxzzzed audiences no doubt giving WAGNER and Co the first ever horizontal standing ovation. A third studio album, meanwhile, sauntered onto the scene in 1997, the LAMBCHOP man surely being just a tad ironic in naming it 'THRILLER', although opening cuts, 'MY FACE YOUR ASS' and 'YOUR SUCKING FUNNY DAY', raised the pulse a little. Prolific as ever, WAGNER and his entourage (they had all worked on VIC CHESNUTT's 'The Salesman & Bernadette') returned in 1998 with possibly his/their best album to date, 'WHAT ANOTHER MAN SPILLS', featuring croonsome classic, 'THE SATURDAY OPTION', alongside a few covers by F.M. CORNOG (i.e. EAST RIVER PIPE) and one by Curtis Mayfield, 'GIVE ME YOUR LOVE'. The country-soul meets disco connection carried on to the acclaimed 'NIXON' (2000) wherein WAGNER's impenetrable songwriting was transformed into (relatively) more intelligible but no less fascinating observations on life's essential minutiae. As for the album title, it was apparently inspired by the infamous ex-American President, LAMBCHOP kindly supplying a reading list of related material on the sleeve. Take for instance minor hit, 'UP WITH PEOPLE' – complete with their hilarious and overlooked "Nixon" video – and opener 'THE OLD GOLD SHOE'; surely this was truly the album that set WAGNER and Co apart from anything remotely similar. LAMBCHOP returned with their most intimate and mature album to date, the breezy 'IS A WOMAN' in early 2002. If 'NIXON' was a Saturday night out on the town, then 'IS A WOMAN' was most certainly the sleepy Sunday morning afterwards. WAGNER muted the soul-thang to give us soft croaky songs, reminiscent of 70's RANDY NEWMAN. The tracks, all recorded bare-bones, like delicate little ornaments, also displayed WAGNER's impending talent which makes you wonder if this man was writing songs thirty years ago, he would be a living legend by now. MARK NEVER's production and spacey guitar was impeccable, with the last track even sliding into a reggae riff. Bloody marvellous. If NICK CAVE and TOM WAITS can do it, why not the 'CHOP?, a countrypolitan nation asked itself as WAGNER and crew released two puckishly titled albums on the same day (Feb 17th 2004, to be exact): 'AW C'MON' and 'NO, YOU C'MON'. Both were spruced up with the Nashville String Machine, their cellos and violas tracing the vagaries of WAGNER's five-and-dime operas. Even without the man's sage ramblings, their cinematic warmth rendered the likes of 'BEING TYLER' and 'THE LONE OFFICIAL' (both from 'AW..') as great lost 70's soundtrack music, or even some recently unearthed Jimmy Webb/Glen Campbell collaborations with the vocals erased. 'NO..' wasn't as dreamy if still a worthy companion piece. Worth picking up for the title alone, 'THE DECLINE OF COUNTRY & WESTERN CIVILIZATION, PT.2: THE WOODWIND YEARS' (2006), was a collection of rarities, alternate takes etc.

Album rating: I HOPE YOU'RE SITTING DOWN (*6) / HOW I QUIT SMOKING (*7) / HANK (*7) / THRILLER (*6) / WHAT ANOTHER MAN SPILLS (*7) / NIXON (*9) / TOOLS IN THE DRYER rarities compilation (*6) / IS A WOMAN (*8) / AW C'MON – NO, YOU C'MON (*7) / THE DECLINE OF THE COUNTRY & WESTERN CIVILIZATION (1993-1999) rarities compilation (*6) / THE DECLINE OF THE COUNTRY & WESTERN CIVILIZATION PART TWO: THE WOODWIND YEARS rarities compilation (*6)

KURT WAGNER – vocals, guitar / **BILL KILLEBREW** – guitar / **MARC TROVILLION** – bass / **STEVE GOODHUE** – drums / **ALLEN LOWREY** – percussion / **JONATHAN MARX** – clarinet, trumpet / **SCOTT CHASE** – washboard, maracas

		not iss.	Thump Audio
1992.	(7"ep; as POSTERCHILD) *<1>* **AN OPEN FRESCA / A MOIST TOWELETTE / (other two by Crop Circle Hoax)**	–	
		City Slang	Merge
1992.	(7") *<MRG 048>* **NINE. / MOODY FUCKER**	–	
1994.	(7") *<02>* **MY CLICHE. / LORETTA LUNG**	–	
	(re-iss. 1999 on Spanish label 'Elefant'; ER 15913-69>		
——	<above on 'Sunday Driver'>		
Aug 94.	(7") *<MRG 066>* **SOAKY IN THE POOPER. / TWO KITTENS DON'T MAKE A PUPPY**	–	
1994.	(7") **IT'S IMPOSSIBLE. / (other track by NONPAREILS AND BARTLEBEES)**	–	
	(above on 'Contrast International') <below on 'Bloodsucker'>		
1995.	(7"ep) *<19846>* **I CAN HARDLY SPELL MY NAME / THE SCARY CAROLER. / (other tracks by CYOD)**	–	

—— line-up **WAGNER, CHASE, MARX, TROVILLION, LOWREY, KILLEBREW + GOODHUE** added **PAUL NIEHAUS** – lap steel guitar, trombone, vocals / **JOHN DELWORTH** – organs / **DEANNA VARAGONA** – vocals, alto sax, banjo, cello / **MIKE DOSTER** – bass (on 1)

		City Slang	Merge
Mar 95.	(cd/d-lp) *(efa 04953-2/-1)* *<MRG 70>* **I HOPE YOU'RE SITTING DOWN / JACK'S TULIPS**		Sep94

– Begin / Betweemus / Soaky in the pooper / Because you are the very air he breathes / Under the same moon / I will drive slowly / Oh, what a disappointment / Hellmouth / Bon soir, bon soir / Hickey / Breathe deep / So I hear you're moving / Let's go bowling / What was he wearing? / Cowboy on the moon / The pack-up song. *(cd re-iss. May00; 8403530)*

1995. (7") *<7003-7>* **YOUR LIFE AS A SEQUEL. / SMUCKERS** [–] [ ]

— <above on 'Mute America'> <below issued for 'I-sore 5" club'>

1996. (5") *<#1>* **SCARED OUT OF MY SHOES. / (other track by Spent)** [–] [ ]

Jan 96. (cd/d-lp) *(efa 04969-2/-1) <MRG 97>* **HOW I QUIT SMOKING** [ ] [ ]
– For which we are truly thankful / The man who loved beer / The militant / We never argue / Life's little tragedy / Suzieju / All smiles and mariachi / The scary caroler / Smuckers / The militant / Garf / Your life as a sequel / Theone / Again.

Apr 96. (7"m)(cd-s) *(efa 04974-45)(efa 04977-03)* **THE MAN WHO LOVED BEER. / ALUMNI LAWN / BURLY & JOHNSON** [ ] [–]

— added guest **HANK TILBURY** – banjo

Jul 96. (m-cd/10"m-lp) *(efa 04979-2/-1) <MRG 108>* **HANK (live)** [ ] [ ]
– I'm a stranger here / Blame it on the brunettes / The tin chime / Randi / Doak's need / Poor bastard. *(cd+=)* – I sucked my boss's dick.
below by VIC CHESNUTT, DAVE LOWERY, KURT WAGNER + PAUL NIEHAUS

1996. (7") *<25075>* **A LOOSE CONFEDERATION OF SATURDAY CITY-STATES** [–] [ ]
– Plagarism / How can I face tomorrow.

— added **PAUL BIRCH JR., MARKY NEVERS, ALEX McMANUS + JOHN CATCHINGS**; to repl. STEVE + BILL

Jul 97. (7") *<(MRG 124)>* **CIGARETTIQUETTE. / MR. CRABBY** [ ] [ ]
(above & below 45's released on 'Merge' only)

Sep 97. (7") *<(MRG 126)>* **WHITEY. / PLAYBOY, THE SHIT** [ ] [ ]

Sep 97. (cd/lp) *(efa 04998-2/-1) <MRG 130>* **THRILLER** [ ] [ ]
– My face your ass / Your fucking sunny day / Hey, where's your girl / Crawl away / Gloria Leonard / Thriller / The old fat robin / Superstar in France.

Nov 97. (cd-ep) *(efa 0870-03)* **YOUR SUCKING FUNNY DAY / THE PETRIFIED FLORIST / THE THEME FROM THE NEAL MILLER SHOW** [ ] [–]

— added **DENNIS CRONIN, MIKE GRIFFITH, VIC CHESNUTT + TONY CROW**

Sep 98. (cd/lp) *(efa 08711-2/-1) <MRG 146>* **WHAT ANOTHER MAN SPILLS** [ ] [ ]
– Interrupted / The Saturday option / Shucks / Give me your love (love song) / Life #2 / Scamper / It's not alright / N.O. / I've been lonely for so long / Magnificent obsession / King of nothing never / The theme from the Neil Miller show.

Nov 98. (ltd-12") *<fu 003>* **GIVE ME YOUR LOVE (LOVE SONG) – Dopperganger remix. / ('A'-album & Doppelganger instrumental)** [–] [ ]

— <above on City Slang's 'For Us' records, below on own label>

Dec 98. (cd-s) *<none>* **CHRISTMAS TIME IS HERE / CHRISTMAS TIME IS HERE** [–] radio [–]

Apr 99. (ltd-7") *<(ER 198)>* **LA DISTANCIA DESCE ELLA HASTA ALLI (THE DISTANCE FROM HER TO THERE). / THE BOOK I HAVEN'T READ** [ ] [–]
(above issued on Spanish 'Elefant 6') (below on 'Third Gear')

— **MATT SWANSON** – bass + **DENNIS CRONIN** – trumpet, cornet; repl. KILLEBREW + CATCHINGS + CHESNUTT + GRIFFITH

Nov 99. (7") *(3G 23)* **UP WITH PEOPLE. / Dump: Die For The Memory** [ ] [–]

— Nov'99, KURT WAGNER was credited on an EP, 'Chester' with JOSH ROUSE

Feb 00. (cd/lp) *(20152-2/-1) <MRG 175>* **NIXON** [60] [ ]
– The good old shoe / Grumpus / You masculine you / Up with people / Nashville parent / What else could it be? / The distance from her to there / The book I haven't read / The petrified florist / The butcher boy.

May 00. (7") *(20165-7)* **UP WITH PEOPLE. / MISS PRISSY** [66] [–]
(cd-s+=) *(20159-2)* – ('A'-remix by Zero 7).
(12") *(20159-6)* – ('A'side) / ('A'-remix by Zero 7) / ('A'-reprise by Zero 7).

Feb 02. (cd/d-lp) *(20190-2/-1) <MRG 204>* **IS A WOMAN** [38] [ ]
– The daily growl / The new cobweb summer / My blue wave / I can hardly spell my name / Autumn's vicar / Flick / Caterpillar / D. Scott Parsley / Bugs / The old matchbook trick / Is a woman.

May 02. (cd-s) *(20196-0)* **IS A WOMAN / THE NEW COBWEB SUMMER (Schneider TM Lanzarote remix) / IS A WOMAN (Alpha remix) / IS A WOMAN (Maxwell implosion rework) / IS A WOMAN (video)** [ ] [–]

Feb 04. (d-cd/d-lp)<2xcd> *(595890-0/-1) <MRG 240/241>* **AW C'MON // NO, YOU C'MON** [45] [ ]
– Being Tyler / Four pounds in two days / Steve McQueen / The lone official / Something's going on / Nothing but a blur from a bullet train / Each time I bring it up it seems to bring you down / Timothy B. Schmidt / Women help to create the kind of men they despise / I hate candy / Haven't heard a word I said / Action figure. // Sunrise / Low ambition / There's still time / Nothing adventurous please / The problem / Shang a dang dang / About my lighter / Under a dream of a lie / Jan / The gusher / Listen / The producer.

Aug 04. (cd-s) *(549628-0)* **SOMETHING'S GOING ON (AND ON) / JANUARY 17B / THE PUPPY & THE LEAF** [ ] [–]
(12") *(549628-6)* – ('A') / Low ambition (Stratus remix) / I hate candy (Moabeat remix).

– compilations, others, etc. –

Feb 03. (cd) *Merge; <(MRG 200CD)>* **TOOLS IN THE DRYER** [ ] Sep01 [ ]
– Nine / Whitey / Cigaretiquette / Miss Prissy / Petrified florist / Each with a bag of fries / All over the world / Flowers of memory / Scared out of my shoes / Style monkeys / Militant / Up with people / Give me your love / Love T.K.O. / Or thousands of prizes / Moody fucker.

Apr 06. (cd) *City Slang; (SLANG 103834-2)* **THE DECLINE OF THE COUNTRY & WESTERN CIVILIZATION (1993-1999)** [ ] [–]
– Soaky in the pooper / Two kittens don't make a puppy / Nine / Moody fucker / Loretta Lung / Scared out of shoes / Your life as a sequel / Smuckers / Scary caroler / I can hardly spell my name / Alumni lawn / Playboy the shit / Whitey / Cigaretiquette / Mr. Crabby / Gettysburg address / Beyond belief.

Apr 06. (cd) *Merge; <MRG 274CD>* **THE DECLINE OF THE COUNTRY & WESTERN CIVILIZATION PART TWO: THE WOODWIND YEARS** [–] [ ]
– My cliche / Loretta Lung / Two kittens don't make a puppy / It's impossible / Ovary eyes / I can hardly spell my name / The scary caroler / Your life as a squel / Smuckers / Alumni lawn / Burly and Johnson / Mr. Crabby / Playboy, the shit / Gloria Leonard (alt.) / The old fat robin / The distance from her to there (alt.) / The book I haven't read (alt.) / Gettysburg address.

☐ Mark LANEGAN (see under ⇒ SCREAMING TREES)

the LA'S

Formed: Liverpool, England ... 1984 by songwriters MIKE BADGER (ex-KINDERGARTEN PAINTSET) and LEE MAVERS, along with drummer JOHN TIMSON; a limited V/A sampler 'A Secret Liverpool' exists of these times. When an inexperienced young bass player JOHN POWER joined the well-touted LA'S (alongside brief member PAUL HEMMINGS), things began to change, friction also set-in between BADGER and MAVERS, the former bailing out and disappearing into the world of sculpture and painting (he had been a great fan of CAPTAIN BEEFHEART!). Signing to 'Go! Discs' early in 1987, the new LA'S (with MAVERS at the helm) released the charming retro-pop debut single, 'WAY OUT'. The record was well received but failed to chart and replacing TIMSON with CHRIS SHARROCK, the band followed up the single with the seminal BYRDS-like pop genius of 'THERE SHE GOES', all soaring melodies and youthful vigour. Incredibly, the single failed to chart, although it later reached the Top 20 when it was re-released in 1990 at the same time as the eponymous debut. Over the two year period it took to record the album, MAVERS' friend BARRY SUTTON replaced SHARROCK on the drum stool while JAMES JOYCE was recruited for the departing POWER (who went on to form the highly successful CAST). CAMMY, another guitarist, was also added. Part of the problem was the notoriously perfectionist MAVERS who obsessed over every tiny detail of the recording process in his search for an 'authentic' sound. 'Go! Discs' became increasingly worried about the escalating cost of the project and decided to go ahead and release the album against MAVERS' wishes. He retaliated by criticising the company in press interviews and dismissed the debut as a collection of demos. In reality, the album was a seamless collection of post-baggy guitar pop, drawing comparisons with the STONE ROSES and garnering almost universal acclaim. After a tour of America and Japan in 1991, the band went to ground and little has been heard from them since, save a brief, disastrous appearance supporting PAUL WELLER in 1994. While rumours continue to abound, the band remain one of the greatest modern day musical enigmas. BADGER finally emerged as a solo artist (he had worked for SPACE on the cover of 'Tin Planet') at the beginning of 1999, an album 'VOLUME' (on his SPACE mate TOMMY SCOTT's new 'Viper' imprint and produced by now LIGHTNING SEEDS man PAUL HEMMINGS) was the missing piece in The LA's troubled rock'n'roll history. A subsequent tabloid grouch by the equally reclusive MAVERS on the worthiness of CAST frontman JOHN POWER was given short shrift – meanwhile SIXPENCE NONE THE RICHER (how well named) were high in the US charts with the LA'S classic, 'THERE SHE GOES'.

Album rating: THE LA'S (*8) / BREAKLOOSE (LOST LA'S 1983-86) (*6) / Mike Badger: VOLUME (*6)

LEE MAVERS (b. 2 Aug'62) – vocals, guitar / **JOHN TIMSON** – drums / added **JOHN POWER** (b.14 Sep'67) – bass

— (late '86) MIKE BADGER was repl. by **PAUL HEMMINGS** – guitar / **JOHN 'BOO' BYRNE** – guitar

		Go! Discs	London
Oct 87.	(7") *(GOLAS 1)* **WAY OUT. / ENDLESS** (12"+=) *(GOLAS 1-12)* – Knock me down. (12"++=) *(GOLAR 1-12)* – Liberty ship (demo) / Freedom song (demo).		

— **CHRIS SHARROCK** – drums (ex-ICICLE WORKS) repl. TIMSON

Nov 88.	(7") *(GOLAS 2)* **THERE SHE GOES. / COME IN, COME OUT** (12"+=)(cd-s+=) *(GOLAS 2-12)(LASCD 2)* – Who knows / Man I'm only human. (7"ep+=) *(LASEP 2)* – Who knows / Way out (new version).	59	
May 89.	(7";w-drawn) *(GOLAS 3)* **TIMELESS MELODY. / CLEAN PROPHET** (10"+=; w-drawn) *(LASEP 3)* – All by myself / There she goes. (cd-s+=; w-drawn) *(LASCD 3)* – All by myself / Ride yer camel.	–	–

— **NEIL MAVERS** (b. 8 Jul'71) – drums repl. SHARROCK / **JAMES JOYCE** (b.23 Sep'70) – bass repl. POWER who formed CAST / added **CAMMY** (b.PETER JAMES CAMELL, 30 Jun'67) – guitar (ex-MARSHMALLOW)

Sep 90.	(7"/c-s) *(GOLAS/LASMC 4)* **TIMELESS MELODY. / CLEAN PROPHET** (12"purple+=)(cd-s+=) *(GOLAS 4-12)(LASCD 4)* – Knock me down / Over.	57	
Oct 90.	(cd/c/lp) *(<828 202-2/-4/-1>)* **THE LA'S** – Son of a gun / I can't sleep / Timeless melody / Liberty ship / There she goes / Doledrum / Feelin' / Way out / I.O.U. / Freedom song / Failure / Looking glass. *(cd re-iss. Sep99 on 'Polydor'; same) (cd re-mast.Jan01 on 'Universal'+=; 549566-2)* – All by myself / Clean prophet / Knock me down / Over (live) / IOU (alt.take).	30	
Oct 90.	(7"/c-s) *(GOLAS/LASMC 5)* **THERE SHE GOES (new version). / FREEDOM SONG** (12"+=)(cd-s+=) *(GOLAS 5-12)(LASCD 5)* – All by myself.	13	–
Feb 91.	(7"/c-s) *(GOLAS/LASMC 6)* **FEELIN'. / DOLEDRUM** (12"+=)(cd-s+=)(7"ep+=) *(GOLAS 6-12)(LASCD 6)(GOLAB 6)* – I.O.U. (alt.version) / Liberty ship.	43	
Jun 91.	(c-s) *<869 370-4>* **THERE SHE GOES / ALL BY MYSELF**	–	49

— had already disbanded just prior to above. In Apr'97 a various artists EP (taken from the movie, 'Fever Pitch', featured 'THERE SHE GOES' (issued on 'Blanco Yo Negro'; *NEG 104 C/T/CD*)

– compilations, etc. –

Sep 99.	(cd-s) *Polydor; (561403-2)* **THERE SHE GOES / COME IN COME OUT / WHO KNOWS**	65	–
Oct 99.	(cd/lp) *Viper; (VIPER 2 CD/LP)* **BREAKLOOSE (LOST LA'S 1984-1986)** – Breakloose (live) / Open your heart / Sweet 35 / Trees and plants / Red deer stalk / Dovecot dub / Walk / Get down over / What do you do / I did the painting / My girl sits like reindeer / Money in your talk / You blue / Moonlight.		–
Jul 01.	(cd/lp) *Viper; (VIPER 8 CD/LP)* **CALLIN' ALL (LOST LA'S 1986-1987)**		–

☐ LAZYCAME (see under ⇒ JESUS & MARY CHAIN)

☐ the LEAGUE OF GENTLEMEN (see under ⇒ KING CRIMSON)

LED ZEPPELIN

Formed: London, England ... mid '68 out of The NEW YARDBIRDS, by guitar wizard JIMMY PAGE, session bassist JOHN PAUL JONES and frontman ROBERT PLANT. Another session musician, drummer JOHN BONHAM, completed the line-up, arriving in time for their live debut at Surrey University on the 15th October '68. Taking the group name from one of KEITH MOON's catchphrases, "going down like a lead zeppelin", the band came under the wing of PETER GRANT, one of the most notoriously shrewd managers in the history of rock and an integral part of the 'ZEPPELIN legend. Following some early dates in Scandinavia and the UK, GRANT secured a lucrative worldwide deal with 'Atlantic', the group subsequently touring America with fellow proto-metallers, VANILLA FUDGE. Universally saddled with the dubious honour of inventing heavy metal, the group nevertheless started out as a power-blues outfit, as evidenced on their blistering 1969 debut set, the eponymous 'LED ZEPPELIN'. From the beginning it was obvious 'ZEPPELIN had a musical chemistry more electric than any rock'n'roll band that had gone before; in spite of, or perhaps as a result of, the fact that BONHAM and JONES came from a soul background while PLANT and PAGE were coming from the heavy blues/R&B angle, the group had an almost superhuman grasp of dynamics. Whether negotiating the climactic blues of 'BABE I'M GONNA LEAVE YOU' or ripping out the power drill rhythms of 'COMMUNICATION BREAKDOWN', each musician wielded their instrument like a weapon, deadly accurate and timed to perfection. PLANT, meanwhile, had one of the most distinctive, orgasmic blues wails in rock, bringing it down to a rustic canter on the folkier numbers. These would come later, though, the sole folk song on the blues-dominated debut being the trad-based instrumental, 'BLACK MOUNTAIN SIDE'. The album's centrepiece was the tortured 'DAZED AND CONFUSED', PAGE's guitar trawling the depths of black despair, while PLANT put in one of his career best performances over a track which would become a mainstay of the LED ZEPPELIN live extravaganza. These were marathon events, with solos and improvisation aplenty, albeit in a more focussed way than the likes of the GRATEFUL DEAD. The shows were also concentrated, initially at least, in America, where GRANT was intent upon breaking the band. While the debut was a transatlantic Top 10 success, the follow-up, 'LED ZEPPELIN II' (1969), scaled both the UK and US charts later that year. Cited by many as the birthdate of British heavy metal, the sledgehammer, divebombing riff of 'WHOLE LOTTA LOVE' ushered in a new era for rock, blasting the competition out of the water. Recorded on the road, the album was graced with more than a little of the improvisatory tension of the live show; the grungy groove of 'MOBY DICK' panned out to a marathon display of BONHAM's rhythmic alchemy, while the middle part of 'WHOLE LOTTA LOVE' lingered in a kind of suspended animation as PAGE

LED ZEPPELIN

engendered all manner of bizarre effects and PLANT got himself all hot and bothered. 'THANK YOU' and 'RAMBLE ON' indicated the direction 'ZEPPELIN would follow on subsequent releases while 'LIVING LOVING MAID (SHE'S JUST A WOMAN)' and 'BRING IT ON HOME', were itchy, funky blues/metal barnstormers, the latter boasting one of the most effective intros and majestic, f***-off riffs in the 'ZEP pantheon. Prepared at 'Bron-Y-Aur' cottage in rural Wales, 'LED ZEPPELIN III' (1970) was something of a departure, at least in its equal billing for the gentler acoustic folk numbers such as 'THAT'S THE WAY' and 'TANGERINE'. Nevertheless, proceedings opened with the lumbering battlecry of 'IMMIGRANT SONG', while PAGE performed one of his most endearingly rocking solos midway through 'CELEBRATION DAY'. Though the album again topped the British and US charts (without the aid of any UK singles; LED ZEPPELIN famously never released any British singles, all part of GRANT's masterplan), critics were sceptical of the change in emphasis. They soon changed their tune with the arrival of the group's fourth effort, an untitled affair with four mystical runes adorning the cover. This immersion in myth and mysticism (PAGE had even purchased the notoriously haunted 'Boleskine Lodge' on the shores of Loch Ness, previously home to occult figurehead, Aleister Crowley) was reflected in the material contained within; the epic 'STAIRWAY TO HEAVEN' remains the most (in)famous LED ZEPPELIN song, its pseudo-hippie musings and acoustic strumming leading into one of the most revered guitar solos of all time. Basically, if you want to spank your plank, this is where you're supposed to start. 'MISTY MOUNTAIN HOP' was another hippie fantasy, while 'THE BATTLE OF EVERMORE' was a folk-rock epic blessed by the golden tonsils of SANDY DENNY. 'BLACK DOG' and 'ROCK AND ROLL' were funky, chunky riffathons, the album's heaviest track surprisingly placed at the end of side two, the wailing, harmonica driven, rolling thunder of 'WHEN THE LEVEE BREAKS', arguably 'ZEPPELIN's most hauntingly effective update of the delta blues tradition. BONHAM's drumming didn't get get much better than this, his molten rhythms subsequently sampled by arch-rappers The BEASTIE BOYS on their massive selling debut album. At the other end of the spectrum, the sun-bleached warmth of 'GOING TO CALIFORNIA' was 'ZEPPELIN at their folky, laidback best, PLANT adopting a mellow, down-home drawl. And this was exactly what the group did, spending most of their time on the road and a fair portion of it in America. With British bands not exactly known for their good manners abroad, LED ZEPPELIN had the most infamous reputation by far. Chief suspects were BONHAM and road manager RICHARD COLE, their alleged appetite for groupies and general debauchery the stuff of rock'n'roll legend; any reader with an interest in such matters will no doubt find the gory details in any of the many books written on ZEPPELIN's antics. The embodiment of 70's excess, the band even leased their own jet, nicknamed 'The Starship', which reportedly turned into a 'flying brothel'. With LED ZEPPELIN having released their most successful album to date, one of the most successful albums ever, in fact, they were now riding high as probably the biggest group on the planet. They knew they could get away with anything they wanted and with 'HOUSES OF THE HOLY' (1973), they clearly fancied a bit of experimentation. The majority of critics remained unimpressed with their half-baked attempts at funk ('THE CRUNGE') and reggae ('D'YER MAKER'), 'ZEPPELIN sounding more at home on familiar ground, especially the evocative 'OVER THE HILLS AND FAR AWAY' and JONES' scathing 'NO QUARTER'. Regardless of what commentators might've thought, ZEPPELIN remained the crown kings of rock, the album predictably topping the charts and the group undertaking their biggest US tour to date. Subsequently activating their own record label, 'Swan Song', the group took artistic control into their own hands, releasing the ambitious double set, 'PHYSICAL GRAFFITI' in Spring '75. While the quality control was spread rather thin in places, there were some unforgettable moments, obviously the exultant 'KASHMIR', but also the affecting 'CUSTARD PIE', the booty-shaking 'TRAMPLED UNDERFOOT' and the obligatory blues odyssey, 'IN MY TIME OF DYING'. Although the group's popularity ensured massive sales, 'PRESENCE' (1976) saw major cracks appearing in the LED ZEPPELIN armoury; in a set which sounded merely slung together, only 'ACHILLES LAST STAND' put up a fight. The double live set, 'THE SONG REMAINS THE SAME' (1976), was also overblown, the album a soundtrack to a rockumentary/movie of the same name featuring live footage from '73 spliced with dodgy 'dream sequences'. Having recovered from a car crash in 1975, PLANT was dealt another blow when his young son, KARAC, died from a viral infection in the summer of '77. Amid much speculation that the group would finally call it a day, LED ZEPPELIN re-emerged in 1979 with 'IN THROUGH THE OUT DOOR', another patchy effort which nevertheless initiated a comeback tour. Following UK dates at Knebworth and a European jaunt, the group went into rehearsals for a full-scale US tour. It never happened. On the 25th of September 1980, BONHAM was found dead after another sizeable drinking session and the group officially split shortly before Christmas. A posthumous collection of outtakes, 'CODA', was issued in late '82, while more recently, the celebrated 'REMASTERS' (1990) set brought together the cream of 'ZEPPELIN's material on shiny, remastered compact disc. While PLANT went on to record solo material in the early 80's, the transatlantic Top 5, 'PICTURES AT ELEVEN' (1982) and the equally fine 'THE PRINCIPLE OF MOMENTS' (1983), PAGE recorded a sole soundtrack effort, 'DEATH WISH II' (1982). PAGE and PLANT finally got back together in 1984 via the mediocre HONEYDRIPPERS R&B/soul project along with JEFF BECK. Then came The FIRM, PLANT and PAGE hooking up with veteran BAD COMPANY frontman, PAUL RODGERS. Despite the expectation, both 'THE FIRM' (1985) and 'MEAN BUSINESS' (1986) were disappointing, suffering from turgid supergroup syndrome. Much more worthy of attention were PLANT's 'SHAKEN 'N' STIRRED' (1985), 'NOW AND ZEN' (1988), and 'MANIC NIRVANA' (1990), the singer maintaining his experimental spirit throughout, dabbling with everything from hip hop rhythms to metallic blues. Even better was 1993's 'FATE OF NATIONS', the likes of '29 PALMS' and a delicate cover of TIM HARDIN's 'IF I WERE A CARPENTER' seeing PLANT in wistfully reflective, folky mood. Save a one-off collaboration with his old mucker, ROY HARPER ('Whatever Happened To Jugula?' 1985), PAGE's only solo outing proper came with 1988's 'OUTRIDER', a competent, if hardly rivetting set of hard rocking blues (vocals courtesy of seasoned hands JOHN MILES and CHRIS FARLOWE). In 1993 however, PAGE teamed up with WHITESNAKE frontman DAVID COVERDALE to record the highly successful but rather derivative album, 'COVERDALE – PAGE'. While PLANT and PAGE teamed up once more in the mid-90's for a startling album of ethnically reworked 'ZEPPELIN classics (including four new tracks), 'NO QUARTER – UNLEDDED' (1994), the prospect of a LED ZEPPELIN reunion looks as improbable as ever and with the death of PETER GRANT (of a heart attack) on the 21st November 1995, another part of the 'ZEPPELIN legend was laid to rest. Still, fans could console themselves with the release of the acclaimed 'BBC SESSIONS' at Christmas '97, featuring a couple of electrifying performances from the earliest part of their career. Early the following year, PAGE & PLANT were back again with a complete set of new recordings, 'WALKING INTO CLARKSDALE' (1998), the material on the album being close to LED ZEPPELIN standard. JOHN PAUL JONES, meanwhile, was working on his solo project, although why the appropriately titled 'ZOOMA' (1999) was ever issued is beyond me; "What is and what should never have been" are words that spring to mind.

When PLANT finally returned with 'DREAMLAND' (2002), his first studio set in a decade, critics were fairly unanimous in piling on the plaudits. Never mind that there were only a couple of original tunes, the choice of covers was as peerless as the quality of the interpretations. In the same way that he brought out the pathos in Tim Hardin's 'IF I WERE A CARPENTER' (on 'FATE OF NATIONS'), his ability to tap into the root emotions and psychological strata of relatively unsung classics like Bob Dylan's 'ONE MORE CUP OF COFFEE' and The Youngbloods' brooding 'DARKNESS DARKNESS' again demonstrated why he's perhaps still the most accomplished interpreter in rock. Anthology 'SIXTY SIX TO TIMBUKTU' (2003), only added further weight to that theory, gathering together startling, long forgotten covers from his pre-ZEP days as well as a comprehensive overview of his solo career in all its freewheeling glory. PAGE, meanwhile, wasn't exactly twiddling his thumbs, rather he was compiling a belated live album culled from American concerts recorded during the band's early 70's peak. 'HOW THE WEST WAS WON' (2003) was as exalted and regal as its title suggested, lining up a clean sweep of the band's most dynamic compositions performed in all their thundering, hammer-of-the-gods glory. JOHN PAUL JONES made one of his intermittent solo sojourns with 'THE THUNDERTHIEF' (2002), attracting more or less encouraging reviews on a record which save for a few helping hands (including ROBERT FRIPP on chugging opener 'LEAFY MEADOWS', and some lyrics courtesy of avant-gardist/cartoonist/former SLAPP HAPPY member PETER BLEGVAD) showcased JONES' self-contained agility on a dazzling array of instruments, best exemplified in the exotic arrangements of 'SHIBUYA BOP' and oriental closer 'FREEDOM SONG', as well as the beautifully rendered traditional, 'DOWN TO THE RIVER TO PRAY'. ROBERT PLANT was next out of the blocks on the solo front, releasing 'MIGHTY REARRANGER' to universal acclaim and a UK Top 5 position (US Top 30). Over a set of twelve straight originals, the fifty-something lung-welder marshalled a band – the STRANGE SENSATION – which drew on LED ZEPPELIN's uber-dynamism without sounding cliched, rooting and shaping PLANT's polyglottal wanderings, and directing his lemon-dripping blooze back to their African source.

• **Songwriters:** PAGE + PLANT wrote nearly all with some help from JONES and/or BONHAM. They also covered; I CAN'T QUIT YOU BABY (Otis Rush) / YOU SHOOK ME (Willie Dixon) / BRING IT ON HOME (Sonny Boy Williamson) / GALLOW'S POLE + HATS OFF TO HARPER (trad.) / etc. JIMMY PAGE covered; HUMMINGBIRD (B.B. King). The HONEYDRIPPERS;- SEA OF LOVE (Phil Phillips with the Twilights). ROBERT PLANT: LET'S HAVE A PARTY (Elvis Presley). • **Trivia:** In the early 70's, C.C.S. (aka. ALEXIS KORNER) had a Top 10 hit with 'WHOLE LOTTA LOVE' (later adopted for the Top Of The Pops theme). In 1985, with PHIL COLLINS on drums, LED ZEPPELIN played LIVE AID. JOHN BONHAM's drumming son, JASON, formed his own band, BONHAM in the late 80's. Around the same time, a kitsch mickey-take outfit DREAD ZEPPELIN, hit the music scene, playing reggae adaptations of the group's classics. In 1992, Australian 60's hitmaker and TV personality ROLF HARRIS destroyed 'STAIRWAY TO HEAVEN', hitting the charts in the process. It was even worse than 1985's FAR CORPORATION version, which also hit the UK Top 10. **Early work:** As well as session work with many (THEM, etc.), JIMMY PAGE released a solo single in early '65 ('SHE JUST SATIFIES' / 'KEEP MOVIN'') for 'Fontana' (TF 533) – it's now worth 250 quid! He had earlier played on 45's by NEIL CHRISTIAN & THE CRUSADERS, plus CARTER-LEWIS & THE SOUTHERNERS. JOHN PAUL JONES played in The TONY MEEHAN COMBO, before issuing a solo 45 in April '64 ('A FOGGY DAY IN VIETNAM' / 'BAJA'), for 'Pye' label. ROBERT PLANT had been part of LISTEN, who released one 45 in November '66; ('YOU'D BETTER RUN' / 'EVERYBODY'S GOTTA SAY') (CBS; 202456). He stayed with the label for two solo releases in March '67; ('OUR SONG' / 'LAUGHING, CRYING, LAUGHING') (202656), and July '67 ('LONG TIME COMING' / 'I'VE GOT A SECRET') (2858). He subsequently teamed up that year with BONHAM, to form Birmingham-based group, BAND OF JOY. All these rare singles now fetch upwards of 100 quid.

Album rating: LED ZEPPELIN (*9) / LED ZEPPELIN II (*10) / LED ZEPPELIN III (*9) / UNTITLED (LED ZEPPELIN IV) (*10) / HOUSES OF THE HOLY (*8) / PHYSICAL GRAFFITI (*10) / PRESENCE (*6) / THE SONG REMAINS THE SAME (*6) / IN THROUGH THE OUT DOOR (*6) / CODA (*5) / REMASTERS double compilation (*10) / EARLY DAYS AND LATTER DAYS – THE VERY BEST OF . . . double compilation (*10) / HOW THE WEST WAS WON live compilation (*8) / Robert Plant: PICTURES AT ELEVEN (*6) / PRINCIPLE OF MOMENTS (*7) / MANIC NIRVANA (*7) / FATE OF NATIONS (*7) / Jimmy Page: DEATH WISH II soundtrack (*4) / OUTRIDER (*6) / Page & Plant: UNLEDDED (*7) / WALKING INTO CLARKSDALE (*7) / John Paul Jones: SCREAM FOR HELP soundtrack (*3) / ZOOMA (*3) / THE THUNDERTHIEF (*5) / Robert Plant: DREAMLAND (*6) / SIXTY SIX TO TIMBUKTU compilation (*7) / MIGHTY REARRANGER (*6)

ROBERT PLANT (b.20 Aug'48, West Bromwich, England) – vocals (ex-LISTEN) / **JIMMY PAGE** (b. JAMES PATRICK PAGE, 9 Jan'44, Heston, England) – lead guitars (ex-YARDBIRDS) / **JOHN PAUL JONES** (b. JOHN BALDWIN, 3 Jun'46, Sidcup, Kent, England) – bass / **JOHN BONHAM** (b.31 May'48, Redditch, England) – drums

Atlantic Atlantic

Mar 69. (lp) *(588 171)* <8216> **LED ZEPPELIN** 6 Feb69 10
– Good times bad times / Babe I'm gonna leave you / You shook me / Dazed and confused / Your time is gonna come / Black mountain side / Communication breakdown / I can't quit you baby / How many more times. *(re-iss. Mar72 lp/c; K/K4 40031) (cd-iss. Jan87 & 1989 special; 240031) (re-iss. Jul94 & Aug97 cd/c; 7567 82632-2) (lp re-iss. Oct99 on 'Classic'; SD 19126)*

Mar 69. (7") <2613> **GOOD TIMES BAD TIMES. / COMMUNICATION BREAKDOWN** – 80

Oct 69. (lp) *(588 198)* <8236> **LED ZEPPELIN II** 1 1
– Whole lotta love / What is and what should never be / The lemon song / Thank you / Heartbreaker / Livin' lovin' maid (she's just a woman) / Ramble on / Moby Dick / Bring it on home. *(re-iss. Mar72 lp/c; K/K4 40037) (cd-iss. Jan87 & 1989 special; 240037) (re-iss. Jul94 & Aug97 cd/c; 7567 82633-2)*

Nov 69. (7") <2690> **WHOLE LOTTA LOVE. / LIVING LOVING MAID (SHE'S JUST A WOMAN)** – 4 / 65

Oct 70. (lp) *(2401 002)* <7201> **LED ZEPPELIN III** 1 1
– Immigrant song / Friends / Celebration day / Since I've been loving you / Out on the tiles / Gallows pole / Tangerine / That's the way / Bron-y-aur stomp / Hats off to (Roy) Harper. *(re-iss. Mar72 lp/c; K/K4 50002) (cd-iss. Jan87 & 1989 special; 250002) (cd-iss. Aug97; 7567 82678-2)*

Nov 70. (7") <2777> **IMMIGRANT SONG. / HEY HEY WHAT CAN I DO** – 16

Nov 71. (lp) *(2401 012)* <7208> **(UNTITLED – 4 SYMBOLS)** 1 2
– Black dog / Rock and roll / The battle of Evermore / Stairway to Heaven / Misty mountain hop / Four sticks / Going to California / When the levee breaks. *(re-iss. Mar72 lp/c; K/K4 50008) (lilac-lp Nov78; K 50008) (cd-iss. Jul83; 250008) (cd-iss. Jan87 & 1989 special; 250008) (re-iss. Jul94 & Aug97 cd/c; 7567 82638-2/-4)*

Dec 71. (7") <2849> **BLACK DOG. / MISTY MOUNTAIN HOP** – 15

Mar 72. (7") <2865> **ROCK AND ROLL. / FOUR STICKS** – 47

Apr 73. (lp/c) *(K/K4 50014)* <7255> **HOUSES OF THE HOLY** 1 1
– The song remains the same / The rain song / Over the hills and far away / The crunge / Dancing days / D'yer mak'er / No quarter / The ocean. *(cd-iss Jan87; 250014) (re-iss. Jul94 & Aug97 cd/c; 7567 82639-2/-4)*

Jun 73. (7") <2970> **OVER THE HILLS AND FAR AWAY. / DANCING DAYS** – 51

Oct 73. (7") <2986> **D'YER MAK'ER. / THE CRUNGE** – 20

Swan Song Swan So

Mar 75. (d-lp/d-c) *(SSK/SK4 89400)* <200> **PHYSICAL GRAFFITI** 1 1
– Custard pie / The rover / In my time of dying / Houses of the holy / Trampled underfoot / Kashmir / In the light / Bron-y-aur / Down by the seaside / Ten years gone / Night flight / The wanton song / Boogie with Stu / Black country woman / Sick again. *(d-cd-iss. Jan87; 294800) (re-iss Oct94 & Aug97 on 'Atlantic' cd/c; 7567 92442-2)*

Mar 75. (7") <70102> **TRAMPLED UNDERFOOT. / BLACK COUNTRY WOMAN** – 38

Apr 76. (lp/c) *(SSK/SK4 59402)* <8416> **PRESENCE** 1 1
– Achilles last stand / For your life / Royal Orleans / Nobody's fault bu mine / Candy store rock / Hots on for nowhere / Tea for one. *(cd-iss. Jun87 259402) (re-iss. Oct94 Aug97 on 'Atlantic' cd/c; 7567 92439-2/-4)*

May 76. (7") <70110> **CANDY STORE ROCK. / ROYAL ORLEANS** – –

Oct 76. (d-lp/d-c) *(SSK/SK4 89402)* <201> **The soundtrack from the film 'THE SONG REMAINS THE SAME' (live)** [1] [2]
– Rock and roll / Celebration day / The song remains the same / Rain song / Dazed and confused / No quarter / Stairway to Heaven / Moby Dick / Whole lotta love. *(d-cd-iss. Feb87; 289402) (cd re-iss. Aug97 on 'Atlantic'; SK2 89402)*

— Above was also a film from concerts at Madison Square Gardens in 1973. It featured some dream sequences / fantasies of each member.

Aug 79. (lp/c) *(SSK/SK4 59410)* <16002> **IN THROUGH THE OUT DOOR** [1] [1]
– In the evening / South bound Saurez / Fool in the rain / Hot dog / Carouselambra / All my love / I'm gonna crawl. *(cd-iss. Jan87; 259410) (re-iss. Oct94 & Aug97 on 'Atlantic' cd/c: 7567 92443-2)*

Dec 79. (7") <71003> **FOOL IN THE RAIN. / HOT DOG** [–] [21]

— Disbanded when JOHN BONHAM died after a drinking session 25 Sep'80.

— JOHN PAUL JONES was already a top producer. In 1992, he contributed string arrangements to R.E.M.'s classic album 'Automatic For The People'. ROBERT PLANT went solo and teamed up with JIMMY PAGE in The HONEYDRIPPERS. PAGE also went solo and formed The FIRM.

— In Aug 94; JOHN PAUL JONES turned up on an unusual collaboration (single 'Do You Take This Man') between himself and loud punk-opera diva DIAMANDA GALAS.

– compilations, others, etc. –

on 'Atlantic' unless mentioned otherwise

Nov 82. (lp/c) *Swan Song; (A 0051/+4)* <90051> **CODA** (demos from 68-79) [4] Dec82 [6]
– We're gonna groove / Poor Tom / I can't quit you baby / Walter's walk / Ozone baby / Darlene / Bonzo's Montreaux / Walter's walk / Wearing and tearing. *(cd-iss. Jul87; 790051) (cd re-iss. Aug97 on 'Atlantic'; 7567 92444-2)*

Oct 90. (4xcd/4xc/5xlp) *(<7567 82144-2/-4/-1>)* **LED ZEPPELIN: THE REMASTERS BOX** [48] [18]

Nov 90. (d-cd/d-c/t-lp) *(ZEP/+C/CD 1)* <82371> **REMASTERS** [10] Mar92 [47]
– Communication breakdown / Babe I'm gonna leave you / Good times bad times / Dazed and confused / Whole lotta love / Heartbreaker / Ramble on / Immigrant song / Celebration day / Since I've been loving you / Black dog / Rock and roll / The battle of Evermore / Misty mountain hop / Stairway to Heaven / The song remains the same / The rain song / D'yer mak'er / No quarter / Houses of the holy / Kashmir / Trampled underfoot / Nobody's fault but mine / Achilles last stand / All my love / In the evening. *(re-iss. cd Sep92; 7567 80415-2) (cd re-iss. Aug97 hit UK No.27; as last)*

Sep 93. (2xcd-box/2xc-box) *(<7567 82477-2/-4>)* **BOXED SET II** [56] [87]

Oct 93. (10xcd-box) *(<7567 82526-2>)* **REMASTERS 2** [ ] [ ]

Nov 96. (cd) *Tring; (QED 107)* **WHOLE LOTTA LOVE (Bootleg Zep)** [ ] [–]

Sep 97. (cd-s) *(AT 0013CD)* **WHOLE LOTTA LOVE / BABY COME ON HOME / TRAVELLING RIVERSIDE BLUES** [21] [–]

Nov 97. (d-cd/d-c) *(<7567 83061-2/-4>)* **BBC SESSIONS** [23] [12]
– You shook me / I can't quit you baby / Communication breakdown / Dazed and confused / The girl I love / What is and what should never be / Communication breakdown / Travelling riverside blues / Whole lotta love / Something else / Communication breakdown / I can't quit you baby / You shook me / How many more times / Immigrant song / Heartbreaker / Since I've been loving you / Black dog / Dazed and confused / Stairway to Heaven / Going to California / That's the way / Whole lotta love / Thank you.

Nov 99. (cd/c) *(<7567 83268-2/-4>)* **EARLY DAYS: THE BEST OF LED ZEPPELIN VOLUME ONE** [55] [71]
(<d-lp iss.Feb03; 83268-1>)

Mar 00. (cd/c) *(<7567 83278-2/-4>)* **LATTER DAYS: THE BEST OF LED ZEPPELIN VOLUME TWO** [40] [81]
(<d-lp iss.Feb03; 83278-1>)

May 00. (cd) *Thunderbolt; (CDTB 210)* **ROCK AND ROLL HIGHWAY** [ ] [–]

Feb 03. (d-cd) *(<7567 83619-2>)* **EARLY DAYS AND LATTER DAYS: THE VERY BEST OF LED ZEPPELLIN** [11] Nov02 [ ]
– Good times bad times / Babe I'm gonna leave you / Dazed and confused / Communication breakdown / Whole lotta love / What is and what should never be / Immigrant song / Since I've been loving you / Black dog / Rock and roll / The battle of evermore / When the levee breaks / Stairway to Heaven // The song remains the same / No quarter / Houses of the holy / Trampled underfoot / Kashmir / Ten years gone / Achilles last stand / Nobody's fault but mine / All my love / In the evening.

May 03. (t-cd) *(<7567 83587-2>)* **HOW THE WEST WAS WON** (live at the L.A. Forum & Long Beach Arena, 25 & 27th June 1972) [5] [1]
– (L.A. drone) / Immigrant song / Heartbreaker / Black dog / Over the hills and far away / Since I've been loving you / Stairway to Heaven / Going to California / That's the way / Bron-y-aur stomp // Dazed and confused / What is and what should never be / Dancing days / Moby Dick // Whole lotta love / Rock and roll / The ocean / Bring it on home.

ROBERT PLANT

with **BOBBIE BLUNT** – guitar / **JEZZ WOODRUFFE** – keyboards / **PAUL MARTINEZ** – bass / **COZY POWELL** – drums / guest **PHIL COLLINS** – drums, percussion

Swan Song Swan Song

Jul 82. (lp/c) *(SSK/+4 59418)* <8512> **PICTURES AT ELEVEN** [2] [5]
– Burning down one side / Moonlight in Samosa / Pledge pin / Slow dancer / Worse that Detroit / Fat lip / Like I've never been gone / Mystery title. *(cd-iss. 1984; SSK2 59418)*

Sep 82. (7") *(SSK 19429)* <99979> **BURNING DOWN ONE SIDE. / MOONLIGHT IN SAMOSA** [73] [44]
(12"+=) *(SSK 19429T)* – Far post.

Nov 82. (7") <99952> **PLEDGE PIN. / FAT LIP** [–] [74]

— **RITCHIE HAYWARD** – drums (ex-LITTLE FEAT) repl. COZY

— added **BOB MAYO** – keyboards, guitar

Es Paranza Es Paranza

Jul 83. (lp/c) *(790101-1/-4)* <90101> **THE PRINCIPLE OF MOMENTS** [7] [8]
– Other arms / In the mood / Messin' with the Mekon / Wreckless love / Thru with the two-step / Horizontal departure / Stranger here. . .than over there / Big log. *(cd-iss. 1984; 790101-2)*

Jul 83. (7") *(B 9848)* **BIG LOG. / MESSIN' WITH THE MEKON** [11] [–]
(12"+=) *(B 9848T)* – Stranger here . . . than over there.

Sep 83. (7") <99844> **BIG LOG. / FAR POST** [–] [20]

Nov 83. (7") <99820> **IN THE MOOD. / HORIZONTAL DEPARTURE** [–] [39]

Jan 84. (7") *(B 6970)* **IN THE MOOD. / PLEDGE PIN (live)** [ ] [–]
(12"+=) *(B 6970T)* – Horizontal departure.

May 85. (7") *(B 9640)* **PINK AND BLACK. / TROUBLE YOUR MONEY** [ ] [–]

May 85. (7") <99644> **LITTLE BY LITTLE. / TROUBLE YOUR MONEY** [–] [36]

May 85. (lp/c/cd) *(790265-1/-4/-2)* <90265> **SHAKEN 'N' STIRRED** [19] [20]
– Hip to hoo / Kallalou Kallalou / Too loud / Trouble your money / Pink and black / Little by little / Doo doo a do do / Easily led / Sixes and sevens.

Jul 85. (7") <99622> **TOO LOUD. / KALLALOU KALLALOU** [–] [ ]

Aug 85. (7") *(B 9621)* **LITTLE BY LITTLE (remix). / DOO DOO A DO DO** [ ] [–]
(ext.12"+=) *(B 9621T)* – Easily led (live).
(d7"++=) *(B 9621F)* – Rockin' at midnight (live).

— now with **DOUG BOYLE** – guitars / **PHIL SCRAGG** – bass / **PHIL JOHNSTONE** – keyboards, co-writer / **JIMMY PAGE** – guitar / **CHRIS BLACKWELL** – drums, percussion / **MARIE PIERRE, TONI HALLIDAY** + **KIRSTY MacCOLL** – backing vocals

Jan 88. (7") *(A 9373)* <99373> **HEAVEN KNOWS. / WALKING TOWARDS PARADISE** [33] [ ]
(ext.12"+=/ext.3"cd-s+=) *(A 9373 T/CD)* – Big log.
(ext.12"box+=) *(A 9373TB)* – ('A'-Astral mix).

Feb 88. (lp/c)(cd) *(WX 149/+C)(790863-2)* <90863> **NOW AND ZEN** [10] [6]
– Heaven knows / Dance on my own / Tall cool one / The way I feel / Helen of Troy / Billy's revenge / Ship of fools / Why / White, clean and neat. *(cd+=)* – Walking towards Paradise.

Apr 88. (7") *(A 9348)* <99348> **TALL COOL ONE (remix). / WHITE, CLEAN AND NEAT** [ ] [25]
(12"+=) *(A 9348T)* – ('A'extended).
(3"cd-s++=) *(A 9348CD)* – Little by little.

Aug 88. (7") *(A 9281)* **SHIP OF FOOLS. / HELEN OF TROY** [ ] [–]
(12"+=/12"w-poster+=) *(A 9281 T/TF)* – Heaven Knows (live).
(3"cd-s+=/3"box-cd-s+=) *(A 9281 CD/+B)* – Dimples (live).

Aug 88. (7") <99333> **SHIP OF FOOLS. / BILLY'S REVENGE** [–] [84]

— **PAT THORPE** – drums repl. BLACKWELL who became ill

— now with **BLACKWELL, CHARLIE JONES, JOHNSTONE and BOYLE**

Mar 90. (lp/c/cd) *(WX 229/+C/CD) <91336>* **MANIC NIRVANA** [15] [13]
– Hurting kind (I've got my eyes on you) / Big love / S S S & Q / I cried / She said / Nirvana / The dye on the highway / Your ma said you cried in your sleep last night / Anniversary / Liars dance / Watching you.

Mar 90. (7") *<98985>* **HURTING KIND (I'VE GOT MY EYES ON YOU). / I CRIED** [–] [46]

Apr 90. (7") *(A 8985)* **HURTING KIND (I'VE GOT MY EYES ON YOU). / OOMPAH (WATERY BINT)** [45] [–]
(12"+=) *(A 8985T)* – I cried / One love.
(cd-s+=) *(A 8985CD)* – Don't look back / One love.

Jun 90. (7"/c-s) *(A 8945/+C)* **YOUR MA SAID YOU CRIED IN YOUR SLEEP LAST NIGHT. / SHE SAID** [ ] [ ]
(12"/cd-s) *(A 8945 T/CD)* – ('A'side) / ('A'version) / One love.

— with **KEVIN SCOTT MACMICHAEL** – guitar / **PHIL JOHNSTONE** – electric piano / **CHARLIE JONES** – bass / **MICHAEL LEE** – drums / **CHRIS HUGHES** – drums, co-producer / plus guests **FRANCIS DUNNERY, MAIRE BRENNAN, NIGEL KENNEDY + RICHARD THOMPSON**

Fontana Es Paranza

Apr 93. (7") *(FATE 1)* **29 PALMS. / 21 YEARS** [21] [ ]
(c-s+=) *(FATEM 1)* – Dark moon.
(cd-s++=) *(FATEX 1)* – Whole lotta love (you need love).

May 93. (cd/c/lp) *(<514 867-2/-4/-1>)* **FATE OF NATIONS** [6] [34]
– Calling to you / Down to the sea / Come into my life / I believe / 29 palms / Memory song (hello, hello) / If I were a carpenter / Colours of a shade / Promised land / The greatest gift / Great spirit / Network news.

Jun 93. (7"/c-s) *(FATE/+M 2)* **I BELIEVE. / GREAT SPIRIT (acoustic mix)** [64] [ ]
(cd-s+=) *(FATEX 2)* – Hey Jayne.
(12"pic-d++=) *(FATETP 2)* – Whole lotta love (you need love).

Aug 93. (c-s) *(FATEM 3)* **CALLING TO YOU. / NAKED IF I WANT TO** [ ] [ ]
(12"+=/cd-s+=) *(FATE/+X 3)* – 8.05.

Dec 93. (c-s) *(FATEM 2)* **IF I WERE A CARPENTER / I BELIEVE (live)** [63] [ ]
(cd-s+=) *(FATED 4)* – Going to California (live).
(cd-s) *(FATEX 4)* – ('A'side) / Ship of fools (live) / Tall cool one (live).

JIMMY PAGE

— solo with **CHRIS FARLOWE** – vocals / **DAVE LAWSON + DAVID SINCLAIR WHITTAKER + GORDON EDWARDS** – piano / **DAVE PATON** – bass / **DAVE MATTACKS** – drums

Swan Song Swan Song

Feb 82. (lp) *(SSK 59415) <SS 8511>* **DEATH WISH II** (soundtrack) [40] Mar82 [50]
– Who's to blame / The chase / City sirens / Jam sandwich / Carole's theme / The release / Hotel rats and photostats / A shadow in the city / Jill's theme / Prelude / Big band, sax and violence / Hypnotizing ways (oh mamma). *<cd-iss. Dec99 on 'WEA'; 2745>*

— In 1985, PAGE provided the unreleased score for 'Death Wish 3'

— In 1985, PAGE collaborated with friend ROY HARPER on dual album 'WHATEVER HAPPENED TO JUGULA', which hit UK Top 50.

— In 1987, he released soundtrack blue-lp 'LUCIFER RISING' for 'Boleskine House'; *<BHR 666>*

— now guest vocals – **JOHN MILES, ROBERT PLANT, CHRIS FARLOWE JASON BONHAM** – drums / **DURBAN LEVERDE** – bass / **FELIX KRISH, TONY FRANKLIN, BARRYMORE BARLOW** – drums

Geffen Geffen

Jun 88 (lp/c)(cd) *(WX 155/+C)(924188-2) <24188>* **OUTRIDER** [27] [26]
– Wasting my time / Wanna make love / Writes of winter / The only one / Liquid mercury / Hummingbird / Emerald eyes / Prison blues / Blues anthem (if I cannot have your love . . .). *(re-iss. Feb91 & Aug99 cd/c; GEFD/GEFC 24188)*

Jun 88. (7"w-drawn) *(GEF 41)* **WASTING MY TIME. / WRITES OF WINTER** [ ] [–]

T.V.T. T.V.T.

Jul 00. (d-cd; by JIMMY PAGE and BLACK CROWES) *(TVT 61214) <2140>* **LIVE AT THE GREEK (live)** [39] [64]
– Celebration day / Custard pie / Sick again / What is and what should never be / Woke up this morning / Shapes of things / Sloppy drunk / Ten years gone / In my time of dyin' / Your time is gonna come / The lemon song / Nobody's fault but mine / Heartbreaker / Hey hey what can I do / Mellow down easy / Oh well / Shake your money maker / You shook me / Out on the tiles / Whole lotta love. *(d-cd iss.Jul00 on 'S.P.V.'; SPV 0917202-2)*

– other recordings, etc –

Jan 82. (lp; JIMMY PAGE, SONNY BOY WILLIAMSON & BRIAN AUGER) *Charly; (CR 30193)* **JAM SESSION** (rec.1964) [ ] [–]
– Don't send me no flowers / I see a man downstairs / She was so dumb / The goat / Walking / Little girl, how old are you / It'a a bloody life / Getting out of town.
below featured on session; **JOHN PAUL JONES / ALBERT LEE / NICKY HOPKINS + CLEM CATTINI**

Sep 84. (lp/c/cd; by JIMMY PAGE & FRIENDS) *Thunderbolt; (THBL/THBC/CDTB 007)* **NO INTRODUCTION NECESSARY** [ ] [–]
– Lovin' up a storm / Everything I do is wrong / Think it over / Boll Weevil song / Livin' lovin' wreck / One long kiss / Dixie friend / Down the line / Fabulous / Breathless / Rave on / Lonely weekends / Burn up. *(re-iss. cd May93;)*
below from early 70's featuring; **JOHN BONHAM, JEFF BECK, NOEL REDDING + NICKY HOPKINS** + actually a re-issue of LORD SUTCH AND HEAVY FRIENDS album.

May 85. (lp/c) *Thunderbolt; (THB L/C 2002)* **SMOKE AND FIRE** [ ] [–]
– Wailing sounds / 'Cause I love you / Flashing lights / Gutty guitar / Would you believe / Smoke and fire / Thumping beat / Union Jack car / One for you baby / L-O-N-D-O-N / Brightest lights / Baby come back. *(cd-iss. Aug86; CDTB 2002)*
below featured him in session with:- JET HARRIS & TONY MEEHAN / MICKIE MOST / DAVE BERRY / The FIRST GEAR / MICKEY FINN / solo / etc.

Jan 90. (lp/cd) *Archive Int.; <AIP/+CD 10041>* **JAMES PATRICK PAGE SESSION MAN VOLUME 1** [–] [ ]

Jul 90. (lp/cd) *Archive Int.; <AIP/+CD 10053>* **JAMES PATRICK PAGE SESSION MAN VOLUME 2** [ ] [–]

Aug 92. (cd) *Sony; <AK 52420>* **JIMMY'S BACK PAGES: THE EARLY YEARS** [–] [ ]
In the US, 'EARLY WORKS ' was issued on 'Springboard' <SPB 4038>

the HONEYDRIPPERS

ROBERT PLANT – vocals / **JIMMY PAGE** – guitar / **JEFF BECK** – guitar (solo artist) / **NILE RODGERS** – producer, etc.

Es Paranza Es Paranz

Oct 84. (7") *<99701>* **SEA OF LOVE. / I GET A THRILL** [–] [3]

Nov 84. (10"m-lp/c) *(790220-2/-4) <90220>* **VOLUME 1** [56] Oct84 [4]
– I get a thrill / Sea of love / I got a woman / Young boy blues / Rockin' at midnight. *(cd-iss. Feb93; 7567 90220-2)*

Jan 85. (7") *(YZ 33)* **SEA OF LOVE. / ROCKIN' AT MIDNIGHT** [56] [–]

Mar 85. (7") *<99686>* **ROCKIN' AT MIDNIGHT. / YOUNG BOY BLUES** [–] [25]

JOHN PAUL JONES

w/ JIMMY PAGE, MADELINE BELL + JON ANDERSON

Atlantic Atlantic

Apr 85. (lp/c) *<(780 190-1/-4)>* **SCREAM FOR HELP** (soundtrack) [ ] [ ]
– Spaghetti Junction / Bad child / Silver train / Crackback / Chilli sauce / Take it or leave it / Christie / When you fall in love / Here I am. *<cd-iss. 2000 on 'WEA'; 2746>*

the FIRM

JIMMY PAGE – guitar / **PAUL RODGERS** – vocals (ex-FREE, ex-BAD COMPANY) / **TONY FRANKLIN** – bass, keys / **CHRIS SLADE** – drums (ex-MANFRED MANN'S EARTH BAND)

Atlantic Atlantic

Feb 85. (lp/c/cd) *(781 239-1/-4/-2) <81239>* **THE FIRM** [15] [17]
– Closer / Make or break / Someone to love / Together / Radioactive / You've lost that lovin' feeling / Money can't buy satisfaction / Satisfaction guarenteed / Midnight moonlight.

Feb 85. (7"/7"sha-pic-d) *(A 9586/+P) <89586>* **RADIOACTIVE. / TOGETHER** [ ] [28]
(12") *(A 9586T)* – ('A'-special mix) / City sirens (live) / Live in peace (live).
(12") *(A 9586TE)* – (all 4 above).

Apr 85. (7") *<89561>* **SATISFACTION GUARENTEED. / CLOSER** [–] [73]

Apr 86. (lp/c)(cd) *(WX 43/+C)(781628-2) <81628>* **MEAN BUSINESS** [46] Feb86 [22]
– Fortune hunter / Cadillac / All the King's horses / Live in peace / Tear down the walls / Dreaming / Free to live / Spirit of love.

Apr 86. (7") *(A 9458) <89458>* **ALL THE KING'S HORSES. / FORTUNE HUNTER** [ ] [61]

Jun 86. (7") *<89421>* **LIVE IN PEACE. / FREE TO LIVE** [–] [ ]

— In 1993, JIMMY collaborated with DAVID COVERDALE (of WHITESNAKE) to make one hit album 'COVERDALE • PAGE'.

JIMMY PAGE & ROBERT PLANT

— with **CHARLIE JONES** – bass, percussion / **PORL THOMPSON** – guitar, banjo / **MICHAEL LEE** – drums, percussion / **NAJMA AKHTAR** – vocals / **JOE SUTHERLAND** – mandolin, bodhran / **NIGEL EASTON** – hurdy gurdy / **ED SHEARMUR** – hammond organ & orchestral arrangements for (large) English + Egyptian Ensemble + London Metropolitan Orchestra

Fontana Atlantic

Nov 94. (cd/c/d-lp) *(526362-2/-4/-1) <82706-2/-4/-1>* **NO QUARTER – UNLEDDED** [7] [4]
– Nobody's fault but mine / Thank you / No quarter / Friends / Yallah / City don't cry / Since I've been loving you / The battle of Evermore / Wonderful one / Wah wah / That's the way / Gallows pole / Four sticks / Kashmir.

Dec 94. (7") *(PP 2)* **GALLOWS POLE. / CITY DON'T CRY** [35] [–]
(pic-cd-s+=) *(PPCD 2)* – The rain song.
(pic-cd-s) *(PPDD 2)* – ('A'side) / Four sticks / What is and what should never be.

Mar 95. (cd-ep) *<CD5 85591-2>* **WONDERFUL ONE (2 versions) / WHAT IS AND WHAT SHOULD NEVER BE / WHEN THE LEVEE BREAKS** [–] [ ]

— **PLANT & PAGE** were actually a 4-piece with other rhythm section & co-writers, **CHARLIE JONES** – bass / **MICHAEL LEE** – drums

Mercury Atlantic

Mar 98. (7") *(PP 3)* **MOST HIGH. / THE WINDOW** [26] [ ]
(cd-s+=) *(PPCD 3)* – Upon a golden horse.

Apr 98. (cd/c/lp) *(558025-2/-4/-1) <83092>* **WALKING INTO CLARKSDALE** [3] [8]
– Shining in the light / When the world was young / Upon a golden horse / Blue train / Please read the letter / Most high / Heart in your hand / Walking into Clarksdale / Burning up / When I was a child / House of love / Sons of freedom.

Jun 98. (7") *(MER 506)* **SHINING IN THE LIGHT. / MOST HIGH (guitar mix)** [ ] [ ]
(cd-s+=) *(MERDD 506)* – How many more times (live).
(cd-s) *(MERCD 506)* – ('A'side) / Walking into Clarksdale (live) / No quarter (live).

JOHN PAUL JONES

Discipline Discipline

Sep 99. (cd) *(<DGM 9909>)* **ZOOMA** [ ] [ ]
– Zooma / Grind / Smile of your shadow / Bass'n'drums / B fingers / Snake eyes / Nosumi blues / Tidal.

Feb 02. (cd) *(<DGM 0104>)* **THE THUNDERTHIEF** [ ] [ ]
– Leafy meadows / The thunderthief / Hoediddle / Ice fishing at night / Daphne / Angry angry / Down to the river to pray / Shibuya bop / Freedom song.

ROBERT PLANT

with **JUSTIN "SCARECROW" ADAMS** – guitar / **PORL THOMPSON** – guitar / **CHARLIE JONES** – bass / **CLIVE DEAMER** – drums / **JOHN BAGGOT** – drums, percussion, string arrangements

Mercury Universal

Jun 02. (cd-s) *(582958-2)* **MORNING DEW / A HOUSE IS NOT A MOTEL (live) / (interview video) / MORNING DEW (video)** [ ] [–]

Jun 02. (cd)(lp) *(<586963-2>)(63094-1)* **DREAMLAND** [20] [40]
– Funny in my mind (I believe I'm fixin' to die) / Morning dew / One more cup of coffee / Last time I saw her / Song to the siren / Win my train fare home (if I ever get lucky) / Darkness, darkness / Red dress / Hey Joe / Skip's song. *(d-cd-iss. Oct02 +=; 063465-2)* – Dirt in a hole / Song to the siren (alpha mix) / Morning dew (BBC Radio 2 session) / Funny in my mind (I believe I'm fixin' to die) / Darkness, darkness (video).

Mar 03. (cd-s) *(77933-2)* **THE LAST TIME I SAW HER / SONG TO THE SIREN** [ ] [–]

Nov 03. (d-cd) *(981319-9) <83626>* **SIXTY SIX TO TIMBUKTU** (compilation) [27] [ ]
– Tie dye on the highway / Upside down / Promised land / Tall cool one / Dirt in a hole / Calling to you / 29 palms / If I were a carpenter / Sea of love / Darkness, darkness / Big log / Ship of fools / I believe / Little by little / Heaven knows / Song to the siren / You'd better run / Our song / Hey Joe (demo with BAND OF JOY) / For what it's worth (demo with BAND OF JOY) / Operator / Road to the sun / Philadelphia baby (with CRAWLING KINGSNAKES) / Red is for danger / Let's have a party / Hey Jayne / Louie, Louie / Naked if I want to / 21 years / If it's really got to be this way / Rude world (PLANT & PAGE) / Little hands / Life begin again (with AFRO CELT SOUND SYSTEM) / Let the boogie woogie roll / Win my train fare home.

ROBERT PLANT & the STRANGE SENSATION

PLANT – vocals / with **JUSTIN ADAMS** + **SKIN TYSON** – guitars / **JOHN BAGGOT** – keyboards / **BILLY FULLER** – bass / **CLIVE DEAMER** – drums

Sanctuary Sanctuary

Apr 05. (7"/cd-s) *(SAN SE/XS 369)* **SHINE IT ALL AROUND. / ALL THE MONEY IN THE WORLD** [32] [–]
(cd-d) *(SANXD 369)* – ('A') / ('A'-the girls remix) / ('A'-video).

May 05. (cd) *(SANCD 356) <84747>* **MIGHTY REARRANGER** [4] [22]
– Another tribe / Shine it all around / Freedom fries / Tin pan alley / All the king's horses / The enchanter / Takamba / Dancing in Heaven / Somebody knocking / Let the four winds blow / Mighty rearranger / Brother Ray. *(ltd-cd; SANDP 356)*

☐ Arthur LEE (see under ⇒ LOVE)

☐ Geddy LEE (see under ⇒ RUSH)

LEFTFIELD

Formed: London, England . . . 1990 by ex-teacher of English NEIL BARNES and PAUL DALEY, formerly of Balearic housers A MAN CALLED ADAM. Barnes had previously released the 'Mississippi Burning'-sampling 'NOT FORGOTTEN' on dance indie Outer Rhythm and when the single became an underground club hit, contractual problems ensued. Undeterred, the duo kept a high profile with remix work (including David Bowie and Inner City) before setting up the Hard Hands label and cutting two singles in 1992, 'RELEASE THE PRESSURE' and 'SONG OF LIFE', the latter a slow building progressive house epic which further enhanced their dancefloor reputation and nudged into the lower regions of the pop charts. But the song that really branded LEFTFIELD into the musical consciousness of the nation was the pounding crossover hit, 'OPEN UP'. A collaboration with P.I.L.'s JOHN LYDON, his blood curdling wail of 'BURN HOLLYWOOD BURN' was scarier than Michael Bolton's mullet cut and was enough to have the video banned from ITV's Chart Show. Spookily enough, the song was released at the same time as a spate of Californian fires . . . The single was a corking tune into the bargain and climbed to No.13 in the charts. The debut album, 'LEFTISM' was greeted with critical plaudits galore upon its release in 1995, reaching No.3 in the U.K. and even being nominated for The Mercury Music Prize . An exhilarating cross-fertilisation of musical stylings, the album took pumping techno trance as its base ingredient, interspersing this with everything from cerebral sonic tapestries ('MELT') to dark, foreboding drum 'n' bass ('STORM 3000'). It contained all the aforementioned singles (save the earlier 'NOT FORGOTTEN') as well as a vocal-led collaboration with goth goddess Toni Halliday. LEFTFIELD enjoyed further chart success with tracks and remixes from the album and contributed material to both the 'Shallow Grave' and 'Trainspotting' film soundtracks. A nationwide tour and a series of legendary festival appearances in 1996 cemented their position as one of the key players in the new techno vanguard alongside UNDERWORLD, PRODIGY et al. 'PHAT PLANET' (from that Guinness ad with the white horses riding the waves) was LEFTFIELD's first musical/video venture for some time, the duo finally releasing (in September '99) the excellent bass-heavy track on the B-side of another CHRIS CUNNINGHAM-directed single/promo, 'AFRIKA SHOX' (with of course, the man BAMBAATAA). Around the same time, the duo finally unleashed their (chart-topping) second album proper, 'RHYTHM AND STEALTH', an enjoyable journey through four years of hard toil in the studio; had their contemporaries beaten them to the prizes though? LEFTFIELD went their separate ways in March 2002.

• **Songwriters:** BARNES / DALEY / guests and some samples. • **Trivia:** Their label 'Hard Hands' run by manager LISA HORRAN, also included acts VINYL BLAIR, DELTA LADY, DEE PATTEN and SCOTT HARRIS.

Album rating: BACKLOG compilation (*6) / LEFTISM (*9) / RHYTHM AND STEALTH (*7) / A FINAL HIT: GREATEST HITS compilation (*8)

NEIL BARNES – DJ, percussion, synthesizers / **PAUL DALEY** – samples (ex-A MAN CALLED ADAM)

Outer Rhythm — not iss.

Mar 90. (12") *(FOOT 003)* **NOT FORGOTTEN. / PATELL'S ON THE CASE / ('A'version)** [ ] [–]

Feb 91. (12") *(FOOT 009)* **NOT FORGOTTEN (Hard Hands mix). / MORE THAN I KNOW** [ ] [–]
(12") *(FOOT 009R)* – ('A'&'B'remixes).

Hard Hands — Medicine

Aug 92. (12"ltd.; featuring EARL SIXTEEN) *(HAND 001T)* **RELEASE THE PRESSURE (3 track vocal)** [ ] [–]
(12"ltd.) *(HAND 001R)* – Release the dubs (instrumental mixes). *(re-iss. Mar99; same)*

Nov 92. (12"ltd.) *(HAND 002T)* **SONG OF LIFE. / FANFARE OF LIFE / DUB OF LIFE** [59] [ ]
(12") *(HAND 002R)* – ('A'-3 Underworld mixes).
(cd-s) *(HAND 002CD)* – ('A'side) / Fanfare of life / Release the dub. *(re-iss. Mar99; same)*

Dec 92. (cd) *(OUTERCD 001)* **BACKLOG** (compilation of above material on 'Outer Rhythm') [ ] [–]

below single with JOHN LYDON (of PUBLIC IMAGE LTD) on vocals

Nov 93. (7"/c-s; as LEFTFIELD / LYDON) *(HAND 009/+MC)* *<42232>* **OPEN UP (radio edit). / ('A'instrumental)** [13] Feb94 [ ]
(12"+=)(cd-s+=) *(HAND 009 T/CD)* – ('A'vocal 12"mix) / ('A'-Dervish overdrive mix) / ('A'-Andrew Weatherall mix) / ('A'-Dust Brothers mix). *(re-iss. Mar99; same)*
(12") *(HAND 9R)* – ('A'remixes).

Hard Hands — Sony-Columbia

Jan 95. (cd/c/d-lp) *(HAND CD/MC/LP 002/+D) <67231-2/-4/-1>* **LEFTISM** [3] [ ]
– Release the pressure / Afro-left / Melt / Song of life / Original / Black flute / Space shanty / Inspection (check one) / Storm 3000 / Open up / 21st century poem. *(iss.Apr95, 3x12"+=) (HANDLP 2T)* – Half past dub. *(cd w/ bonus disc)* – Afro-left (Afro-ride) / Release the pressure (release one) / Original (live dub) / Filter fish / Afro-left (Afro-Central) / Release the pressure (release four).

below single as featured TONI HALLIDAY (ex-CURVE) on vocals

Mar 95. (c-ep/cd-ep; as LEFTFIELD & HALLIDAY) *(HAND 018 MC/CD)* **ORIGINAL / ('A'-live mix) / ('A'jam mix) / FILTER FISH** [18] [–]
(12"ep) *(HAND 018T)* – ('A'-Drift version) – repl. ('A'live)

Jul 95. (12"ep/c-ep/cd-ep; LEFTFIELD featuring DJUM DJUM) *(HAND 023 T/MC/CD) <78045>* **AFRO-LEFT EP** [22] [ ]
– Afro left / Afro ride / Afro sol / Afro central.

Jan 96. (c-s) *(HAND 029MC)* **RELEASE THE PRESSURE (remix 96 vocal): RELEASE ONE / RELEASE TWO** [13] [ ]
(12"+=) *(HAND 029T)* – Release four.
(cd-s++=) *(HAND 029CD)* – Release three.

Sep 99. (12"/cd-s; as LEFTFIELD. BAMBAATAA) *(HAND 057 T/CD1)* **AFRIKA SHOX. / PHAT PLANET (Dave Clarke mix) / AFRIKA SHOX (Jedis elastic bass mix)** [7] [ ]
(cd-s) *(HAND 057CD2)* – ('A'mixes; VX / etc).

Sep 99. (cd/c/d-lp) *(HAND CD/MC/LP 004) <68529>* **RHYTHM AND STEALTH** [1] [ ]
– Dusted / Phat planet / Chant of a poor man / Double flash / El Cid / Afrika shox / Dub gussett / Swords / 6-8 war / Rhino's prayer. *(cd re-mixed May00; HANDCD 4X)*

Nov 99. (12"/cd-s; as LEFTFIELD w/ ROOTS MANUVA) *(HAND 058 T/CD)* **DUSTED (mixes)** [28] [ ]
(cd-s) *(HAND 058CD2)* – ('A'mixes).

—— split March 2002

– compilations, etc. –

Sep 05. (cd) *Hard Hands; (82876 72607-2)* **A FINAL HIT: GREATEST HITS** [32] [–]
– Release the pressure / Afro-Left / Song of life / Original / Storm 3000 / Open up / Dusted / Phay planet / Afrika shox / Not forgotten / A final hit / Swords / Shallow grave / Snakeblood / More than I know. *(ltd-cd w/dvd+= 82876 72608-2)* – (DVD tracks).

the LEMONHEADS

Formed: Boston, Massachusetts, USA . . . 1983 by EVAN DANDO. Raised by middle-class parents (they were divorced when he was 12), the singer was originally the band's drummer and in March '86 he was joined by one-time school-friend, jazz-bassist JESSE PORETZ. With BEN DEILY completing the line-up, this early incarnation of The LEMONHEADS released their debut EP, the amateurish indie squall of 'LAUGHING ALL THE WAY TO THE CLEANERS' on the recently formed Boston label, 'Taang!'. The band stayed with the label for their first three releases, belting out spirited melodic punk (drawing comparisons with DINOSAUR JR, HUSKER DU, REPLACEMENTS etc,) on 'HATE YOUR FRIENDS' (1987), 'CREATOR' (1988) and 'LICK' (1989), the latter the pick of the bunch with a beguiling cover of Suzanne Vega's 'LUKA'. 'Atlantic' records were sufficiently confident in the band's pop grunge abilities to offer them a deal, the initial fruits of which, the well received 'LOVEY' (1990), saw DANDO take more of a leading role following the departure of DEILY. From this point on he steered the band in an increasingly mellow, country-flavoured direction (an area he'd already explored on his 1990 solo EP 'FAVOURITE SPANISH DISHES') with a brilliant cover of Mike Nesmith's 'DIFFERENT DRUM', while 'LOVEY' featured a fairly faithful rendition of his hero Gram Parson's 'BRASS BUTTONS'. Yet the ever unpredictable DANDO split the band up after the major label debut, eventually reforming with the help of girlfriend JULIANA HATFIELD and DAVE RYAN, the latter having played on 'LOVEY'. A spell in Australia seemed to have further mellowed the singer and the resultant album, 'IT'S A SHAME ABOUT RAY' was the most accessible LEMONHEADS release to date, heavy on harmonies and melody. Despite a favourable critical reception, the album lingered in the lower reaches of the album chart and it was only when 'Atlantic' issued the band's power pop cover of Simon & Garfunkel's 'MRS. ROBINSON', that The LEMONHEADS became a household name. Re-released to include the track, 'IT'S A SHAME ABOUT RAY' enjoyed a commercial comeback, eventually making it into the UK Top 40. Suddenly DANDO's long-haired slacker-extraordinaire visage was staring out from every magazine cover from NME to The FACE, although this sudden thrust into the limelight seemed to drive DANDO further into drug abuse; a follow-up album, 'COME ON FEEL THE LEMONHEADS' eventually surfacing in late 1993. The record was another mellow beauty, powering into the UK Top 5 on the back of a successful Love Positions' cover, 'INTO YOUR ARMS', and even featuring contributions from legendary pedal steel player, SNEAKY PETE KLEINOW. Predictably, the Yanks just didn't get it, preferring the bluster of PEARL JAM instead. Lack of success in his home country sent DANDO spiralling further into drug use, although he had apparently cleaned up by the end of the year, undertaking a solo acoustic tour of the US. However, after a much criticised appearance at the 1995 Glastonbury festival, DANDO went to ground, spending much of his time in Australia strung out on heroin and LSD. A shorn, torn and frayed DANDO eventually surfaced in October 1996 with 'CAR BUTTON CLOTH', the first LEMONHEADS album in four years, finding DANDO in reflective and world weary mood, the melancholy side of his songwriting more pronounced than ever. After a seemingly interminable wait, DANDO came in from the wilderness with 'LIVE AT THE BRATTLE THEATRE / GRIFFITH SUNSET' (2001), a half live/half studio covers affair which revisited old favourites like 'DOWN ABOUT IT' and 'MY DRUG BUDDY'. If it was hardly a high profile comeback, we shouldn't be too surprised; thankfully DANDO still sounds as if he's doing it all off the cuff with the kind of haphazard enthusiasm his druggy days might well have leached out of him. It was a wiser, cleaned-up DANDO which eventually resurfaced in early 2003 with 'BABY I'M BORED', his debut studio album and his first collection of new material in years. Although the wiry angst of old was gone completely, the singer had unsurprisingly honed the poignant, bittersweet essence of his more reflective work, resulting in the least immediate but perhaps most rewarding album of his career thus far. While his voice betrayed the trials of recent years it had lost none of its melancholy charm and while his songs remained as deceptively basic as ever, they were permeated with the wisdom of encroaching middle age.

• **Songwriters:** DANDO, although DELLY or MADDOX were contributors early on. Covered; I AM A RABBIT (Proud Scum) / HEY JOE + AMAZING GRACE (trad.) / MOD LANG (Big Star) / STRANGE (Patsy Cline) / YOUR HOME IS WHERE YOU ARE HAPPY (C. MANSON / PLASTER CASTER (Kiss) / SKULLS (Misfits) / GONNA GET ALONG WITHOUT YA NOW (Hoagy Carmichael) / STEP BY STEP (New Kids On The Block) / FRANK MILLS (from 'Hair' musical) / KITCHEN (Hummingbirds) / MISS OTIS REGRETS (Cole Porter) / FADE TO BLACK (Metallica) / LIVE FOREVER (Oasis) / KEEP ON LOVING YOU (Reo Speedwagon) / TENDERFOOT (Tom Morgan / Adam Young) / GALVESTON (Jimmy Webb) / PIN YR HEART (Jacobites). Between 1994-1996, he co-wrote 'PURPLE PARALLELOGRAM' with Noel Gallagher (Oasis) + 'IF I COULD TALK I'D TELL YOU' with Eugene Kelly (Eugenius). • **Trivia:** DANDO and JOHN STROHM appeared on BLAKE BABIES lp, 'Slow Learners'.

Album rating: HATE YOUR FRIENDS (*4) / CREATOR (*4) / LICK (*7) / LOVEY (*5) / IT'S A SHAME ABOUT RAY (*8) / COME ON FEEL THE LEMONHEADS (*7) / CAR BUTTON CLOTH (*6) / THE BEST OF THE LEMONHEADS compilation (*8) / Evan Dando: LIVE AT THE BRATTLE THEATRE . . . (*5) / BABY I'M BORED (*7)

EVAN DANDO (b. 4 Mar'67) – vocals, guitar + some drums / **JESSE PERETZ** – bass / **BEN DEILY** – guitar, + some drums

not iss. ArmoryArms

Jul 86. (7"ep) <1-2-Huh-Bag 1> **LAUGHING ALL THE WAY TO THE CLEANERS** [–] [ ]
– Glad I don't know / I like to / I am a rabbit / So I fucked up.

— added **DOUG TRACHTON** – drums

World Service Taang!

May 88. (lp)<US-lp some colrd> *(SERVM 001)* <T 15> **HATE YOUR FRIENDS** [ ] Jun87 [ ]
– I don't wanna / 394 / Nothing time / Second change / Sneakyville / Amazing Grace / Belt / Hate your friends / Don't tell yourself it's ok / Uhhh / Fed up / Rat velvet. *(US-cd 1989; same +=)* – Glad I don't know / I like to / I am a rabbit / So I fucked up / Ever / Sad girl / Buried alive / Gotta stop. *(re-iss. cd Mar93 with the extra tracks)*

— **EVAN,** on bass, also joined BLAKE BABIES in 1988, alongside girlfriend JULIANA HATFIELD. **JOHN STROHM** – drums (ex-BLAKE BABIES) repl. DOUG.

Sep 88. (lp)(c) *(SERV 001)* <T 23> **CREATOR** [ ] [ ]
– Burying ground / Sunday / Clang bang clang / Out / Your home is where you're happy / Falling / Die right now / Two weeks in another town / Plaster caster / Come to my window / Take her down / Postcard / Live without. *(US-cd 1989; same +=)* – Luka (live) / Interview / Mallo cup. *(re-iss. Sep92 on 'Taang!', with 6 extra live tracks included) (re-iss. cd Mar93 with all re-issued tracks + 2 acoustic)*

— **COREY LOOG BRENNAN**– guitar (ex-BULLET LAVOLTA) repl. JOHN STROHM

Apr 89. (7"colrd) <T 31> **LUKA. / STRANGE / MAD** [ ] [–]
(scheduled UK Nov89 unissued 12"/cd-s; SEVS 010/+CD)
(UK-iss. 7"/12"/cd-s Apr93)

May 89. (lp/cd) *(SERV/+CD 007)* <T 32> **LICK** [ ] [ ]
– Mallo cup / Glad I don't know / 7 powers / A circle of one / Cazzo di ferro / Anyway / Luka / Come back D.A. / I am a rabbit / Sad girl / Ever. *(US-cd+=)* – Strange / Mad. *(re-iss. cd Mar93)*

— **MARK "BUDOLA"** – drums, toured until he checked out mid '89. (COREY also left to concentrate on his PhD)

Roughneck not iss.

Jun 90. (7") *(HYPE 3)* **DIFFERENT DRUM. / PAINT** [ ] [–]
(12"+=)(cd-s+=) *(12 HYPE 3)(HYPE 3CD)* – Ride with me. *(re-iss. Feb93 12"ep/cd-ep; HYPE 3 T/CD)*

Atlantic Atlantic

Jun 90. (cd-ep) <786088-2> **FAVORITE SPANISH DISHES EP** [–] [ ]
– Different drum / Paint / Ride with me / Skulls / Step by step.

— **DAVID RYAN** (b.20 Oct'64, Fort Wayne, Indiana) – drums repl. DEILY

Oct 91. (cd/c/lp) <(7567 82137-2/-4/-2)> **LOVEY** [ ] Aug90 [ ]
– Ballarat / Half the time / Year of the cat / Ride with me / Li'l seed / Stove / Come downstairs / Left for dead / Brass buttons / (The) Door. *(re-iss. cd/c/lp Nov93)*

— In Sep'90, **DANDO** recruited **BEN DAUGHTY** – drums (ex-SQUIRREL BAIT) repl. RYAN / **BYRON HOAGLAND** – bass (ex-FANCY PANTS) repl. PERETZ.

Sep 91. (7") *(A 7709)* **GONNA GET ALONG WITHOUT YA NOW. / HALF THE TIME** [ ] [–]
(12"ep+=) *(TA 7709)* – PATIENCE AND PRUDENCE EP: Stove (remix) / Step by step.

— **DANDO, RYAN + JULIANA HATFIELD** (b. 2 Jul'67, Wiscasset) – bass, vocals (ex-BLAKE BABIES)

Jul 92. (cd/c/lp) <(7567 82137-2/-4/-1)> **IT'S A SHAME ABOUT RAY** [69] [68]
– Rockin' stroll / Confetti / Rudderless / My drug buddy / The turnpike down / Bit part / Alison's starting to happen / Hannah and Gaby / Kitchen / Ceiling fan in my spoon / Frank Mills. *(album hit UK No.33 Jan'93) (re-iss. Feb95)*

Oct 92. (7"/c-s) *(A 7423/+C)* **IT'S A SHAME ABOUT RAY. / SHAKEY GROUND** [70] [–]
(10"+=/cd-s+=) *(A 7423 TE/CD)* – Dawn can't decide / The turnpike down.

Nov 92. (7"/c-s) *(A 7401/+C)* **MRS. ROBINSON. / BEING AROUND** [19] [–]
(10"+=/cd-s+=) *(A 7401 TE/CD)* – Divan / Into your arms.

— 1993 line-up: **DANDO, RYAN, NIC DALTON** (b.14 Jun'64, Australia) although she did provide b.vox for 1993 releases. – bass HATFIELD formed own trio)

Jan 93. (7"/c-s) *(A 7430/+C)* **CONFETTI (remix). / MY DRUG BUDDY** [44] [–]
(10"+=/cd-s+=) *(A 7430 TE/CD)* – Ride with me (live) / Confetti (acoustic).

Mar 93. (c-s) *(A 5764C)* **IT'S A SHAME ABOUT RAY / ALISON'S STARTING TO HAPPEN** [31] [–]
(cd-s+=) *(A 5764CD)* – Different drum (Evan acoustic) / Stove (Evan acoustic).
(10"+=) *(A 5764TE)* – Different drum (acoustic) / Rockin' stroll (live).
(cd-s) *(A 5764CDX)* – ('A'live) / Confetti / Mallo cup / Rudderless (all 4 live).

Oct 93. (7"/c-s) *(A 7302/+C)* <87294> **INTO YOUR ARMS. / MISS OTIS REGRETS** [14] [67]
(10"+=/cd-s+=) *(A 7302 TE/CD)* – Little black egg / Learning the game.

Oct 93. (cd/c/lp) <(7567 82537-2/-4/-1)> **COME ON FEEL THE LEMONHEADS** [5] [56]
– The great big no / Into your arms / It's about time / Down about it / Paid to smile / Big gay heart / Style / Rest assured / Dawn can't decide / I'll do it anyway / Rick James style / Being around / Favourite T / You can take it with you / The jello fund. *(lp+=)* – Miss Otis regrets.

Nov 93. (7"/c-s) *(A 7296/+C)* **IT'S ABOUT TIME. / RICK JAMES ACOUSTIC STYLE** [57] [–]
(10"+=/cd-s+=) *(A 7296 TE/CD)* – Big gay heart (demo) / Down about it (acoustic).

(above 'A'side was written about JULIANA. I'LL DO IT ANYWAY for BELINDA CARLISLE)

May 94. (c-ep/10"ep/cd-ep) *(A 7259 C/TE/CD)* **BIG GAY HEART / DEEP BOTTOM COVE. / HE'S ON THE BEACH / FAVORITE T (session)** 55 –

— Offending lyrics to above 'A'side, were changed; with Stroke & Brick.

— DALTON departed Sep '94

— **PATRICK MURPHY** – drums (ex-DINOSAUR JR) repl. RYAN

— other members with DANDO; **BILL GIBSON** – bass, guitar / **DINA WAXMAN** – bass / **KENNY LYON** – guitar / **RICH GILBERT** – pedal steel / **BRYCE GOGGIN** – vocals, keyboards / etc.

Sep 96. (c-s) *(A 5495C)* **IF I COULD TALK I'D TELL YOU /** 39 –
(cd-s) *(A 5495CD)* – ('A'side) / How will I know (acoustic & electric version) / I don't want to go home / Seagulls aren't free.
(cd-s) *(A 5495CDX)* – ('A'side) / It's all true (acoustic – no drums) / Sexual bryceulidge.

Oct 96. (cd/c) *<(7567 92726-2/-4)>* **CAR BUTTON CLOTH** 28
– It's all true / If I could talk I'd tell you / Break me / Hospital / The outdoor type / Losing your mind / Something's missing / Knoxville girl / 6ix / C'mon daddy / One more time / Tenderfoot / Secular rockulidge.

Nov 96. (c-s) *(A 5635C)* **IT'S ALL TRUE / LIVE FOREVER** 61 –
(10"+=/cd-s+=) *(A 5635 TE/CD)* – Fade to black / Keep on loving you.

Mar 97. (c-s) *(A 5620C)* **THE OUTDOOR TYPE (remix) / PIN YR HEART** –
(cd-s+=) *(A 5620CD)* – Losing your mind (live acoustic).

Aug 97. (7") *(AT 0012)* **BALANCING ACTS. / GALVESTON** –

– compilations, etc. –

1990. (cd) *Taang!; <T 15/T23>* **CREATE YOUR FRIENDS** –
– (HATE YOUR FRIENDS / CREATOR / LAUGHING E.P.)

Aug 98. (cd/c) *Atlantic; <(7567 80851-2/-4)>* **THE BEST OF THE LEMONHEADS**
– Confetti / Into the arms / Mrs. Robinson / Rudderless / It's a shame about Ray / The great big no / Ride with me (acoustic) / My drug buddy / Big gay heart / It's about time / The outdoor type / It's all true / If I could talk I'd tell you / Hospital / Rudy with a flashlight / Into your arms (acoustic) / Down about it (acoustic) / Being around / Rick James acoustic style.

EVAN DANDO

Modular Modular

Dec 01. (d-cd) *<(MODCD 017)>* **LIVE AT THE BRATTLE THEATRE / GRIFFITH SUNSET (live)** Nov01
– Down about it / The turnpike down / The outdoor type / My drug buddy / The same thing you thought hard about is . . . . / Ride with me / Frying pan / Excuse me mister / Thirteen / Stove / Half the time / Ba-de-da / Fraulein / Sam Stone / Nothin / My baby's gone / Tribute to Hank Williams / (untitled).

— next with **JON BRION, BROKAW, JOEY BURNS, JOHN COVERTINO, HOWE GELB, ROYSTON LANGDON + SIM CAIN**

Setanta Bar/None

Mar 03. (cd/lp) *(SET CD/LP 114) <141>* **BABY I'M BORED** 30 Feb03
– Repeat / My idea / Rancho Santa Fe / Waking up / Hard drive / Shots is fired / It looks like you / The same thing you thought hard about is the same part I can live without / Why do you do this to yourself? / Stop my head / In the grass all wine colored.

May 03. (7"red) *(SET 127)* **STOP MY HEAD. / THRASHER** 38 –
(cd-s) *(SETCDA 127)* – ('A') / Shots is fired / Tongue tied.
(cd-s) *(SETCDB 127)* – ('A') / Things have gone to pieces / Au bord la Seine / ('A'-video).

Dec 03. (7") *(SET 130)* **IT LOOKS LIKE YOU. / WHOOPS / THE TODD KILLINGS** 68 –
(cd-s) *(SETCDA 130)* – ('A') / The same thing you thought hard about is the same part I can live without (live) / Hannah and Gabi (live).

John LENNON

Born: JOHN WINSTON LENNON, 9 Oct'40, Liverpool, England. While still a member of the BEATLES (late 1968), he teamed up with his new girlfriend at the time, YOKO ONO, to record the controversial, 'UNFINISHED MUSIC NO.1: TWO VIRGINS'. The cover-shot displayed a full-frontal nude photo of the couple and the album was subsequently sold in brown paper wrapping to apparently save embarrassment to both the customers and the retailers! During spring next year, its follow-up, 'UNFINISHED MUSIC NO.2: LIFE WITH THE LIONS', hit the shops and continued their anti-commercial, free-form direction, the songs mainly recorded on a small cassette player. Now divorced from his wife Cynthia, JOHN married YOKO on the 20th March '69, even changing by deed poll, his middle name from WINSTON to ONO. After the LENNON's completed an 8-day peace protest by publicly lying/sitting in a hotel bed, they released the PLASTIC ONO BAND's debut hippy anthem, 'GIVE PEACE A CHANCE'. This gave JOHN his first non-BEATLES hit, rising into the UK Top 3 and US Top 20. Later that year, 'COLD TURKEY' (a drug withdrawal song), also gave him a Top 30 smash on both sides of the Atlantic. Late 1969, he unveiled two albums, one, another avant-garde collaboration with YOKO, 'THE WEDDING ALBUM', and the other a more standard commercial product from the PLASTIC ONO BAND, 'LIVE IN TORONTO 1969', a record which breached the US Top 10. They also scored with another UK/US Top 5 hit, 'INSTANT KARMA', which was produced by PHIL SPECTOR early in 1970. In May that year, the BEATLES officially split prior to the release of another No.1 album, 'Let It Be'. JOHN then concentrated wholly on his solo career, returning with the album, 'JOHN LENNON: PLASTIC ONO BAND'. This was followed by another Top 20 anthem, 'POWER TO THE PEOPLE'. On the 3rd of September '71, he went to New York to live with YOKO and a month later, his classic album, 'IMAGINE', topped the charts in both the US and the UK (its US-only released title track, hitting No.3). In 1971, he failed in a bid to have a Christmas hit in the States with 'HAPPY XMAS (WAR IS OVER)', although this reached the UK Top 5 a year later. During the next three years, during which he released three albums, he fought to stay in America after being ordered by immigration authorities to leave. During this period, in which he temporarily split from YOKO, he went through drinking bouts with his buddy HARRY NILSSON, the pair recording an album, 'PUSSY CATS', together. On the 9th of October '75, YOKO gave birth to their first child, SEAN. LENNON then went into retirement to look after the boy in their Manhattan apartment, leaving behind a charting greatest hits, 'SHAVED FISH'. He was soon to receive his green card, allowing him to permanently reside in the States. However, in 1980 he returned to the studio once again, David Geffen offering to release an album on his self-titled label. In November that year, 'DOUBLE FANTASY' was released, soon topping both US and UK album charts. There was also a return to the singles chart, when the appropriately titled '(JUST LIKE) STARTING OVER' made the Top 10. Tragically on the 8th of December 1980, JOHN was shot four times by a deranged fan, Mark Chapman, outside the LENNON's apartment block. He died shortly afterwards at Roosevelt hospital. Not surprisingly, the aforementioned 'STARTING OVER' 45 climbed back up the charts and peaked at No.1, with a re-issue of 'IMAGINE' following it to the top early in 1981. His killer was sent to a mental institution for the rest of his life, and we can only ponder what the 40-year-old might have achieved in the 80's & 90's had he lived. He remains a much revered genius, an artist who attempted to alienate the pop industry with non-conventional music styles. He was also a peaceful man, whose outbursts and human faults seemed to be portrayed falsely by the media, especially in his BEATLES days. His love of YOKO was undoubtably a turning point, finding both himself and the world around him a happier place to live. Although some of his songs exploded into frenetic rock anthems of anti-war and anti-government sentiments, his music, in its many facets, showed a poetic beauty and untouched romance.

• **Songwriters:** LENNON, except covers album 'ROCK'N'ROLL' which contained;- BE-BOP-A-LULA (Gene Vincent) / STAND BY ME (Ben

E.King) / PEGGY SUE (Buddy Holly) / AIN'T THAT A SHAME (Fats Domino) / SWEET LITTLE SIXTEEN + YOU CAN'T CATCH ME (Chuck Berry) / BONY MORONIE (Larry Williams) / BRING IT HOME TO ME + SEND ME SOME LOVIN' (Sam Cooke) / JUST BECAUSE (Lloyd Price) / YA YA (Lee Dorsey) / RIP IT UP + SLIPPIN' AND SLIDIN' + READY TEDDY (Little Richard) / DO YOU WANT TO DANCE (Bobby Freeman). • **Trivia:** In 1967, JOHN acted in the movie, 'How I Won The War', also appearing in many zany films with The BEATLES. In 1975, he co-wrote 'Fame' with DAVID BOWIE, which topped the US charts. His son from his first marriage, JULIAN, has previously enjoyed chart action, while SEAN has also been more visible, appearing at benefits, etc.

Album rating: UNFINISHED MUSIC NO.1: TWO VIRGINS (*3) / UNFINISHED MUSIC NO.2: LIFE WITH THE LIONS (*3) / THE WEDDING ALBUM (*2) / THE PLASTIC ONO BAND – LIVE PEACE IN TORONTO 1969 (*5) / JOHN LENNON – PLASTIC ONO BAND (*8) / IMAGINE (*9) / SOMETIME IN NEW YORK CITY (*5) / MIND GAMES (*7) / WALLS AND BRIDGES (*6) / ROCK'N'ROLL (*5) / SHAVED FISH compilation (*8) / DOUBLE FANTASY (*7) / posthumous collections: THE JOHN LENNON COLLECTION (*10) / MILK & HONEY (*4) / LIVE IN NEW YORK CITY (*4) / MENLOVE AVE. (*4) / IMAGINE: JOHN LENNON soundtrack (*7) / LENNON LEGEND boxed-set (*9) / WORKING CLASS HERO – THE DEFINITIVE LENNON (*9)

JOHN LENNON & YOKO ONO

JOHN LENNON – vocals, guitar, etc. / **YOKO ONO** (b.18 Feb'33, Tokyo, Japan) – wind, vocals

Apple Apple

Nov 68. (lp; stereo/mono) *(S+/APCOR 2) <5001>* **UNFINISHED MUSIC NO.1: TWO VIRGINS** [ ] [ ]
– Section 1, 2, 3, 4, 5, 6 / Side 2. *(cd-iss. Jan93 on'Rock Classics';) (cd re-iss. Jun97 on 'Rykodisc'; RCD 10411)*

Zapple Zapple

May 69. (lp) *(ZAPPLE 01) <3357>* **UNFINISHED MUSIC NO.2: LIFE WITH THE LIONS (1/2 live)** [ ] [ ]
– Cambridge 1969 / No bed for Beatle John / Baby's heartbeat / Two minutes silence / Radio play. *(cd-iss. Jun97 on 'Rykodisc'; RCD 10412)*

the PLASTIC ONO BAND

Apple Apple

Jul 69. (7") *(APPLE 13) <1809>* **GIVE PEACE A CHANCE. / REMEMBER LOVE** [2] [14]
(re-iss. Jan81, reached UK No.33)

Oct 69. (7") *(APPLES 1001) <1813>* **COLD TURKEY. / DON'T WORRY KYOKO (MUMMY'S ONLY LOOKING FOR A HAND IN THE SNOW)** [14] Dec69 [30]

Dec 69. (lp; as JOHN ONO LENNON & YOKO ONO LENNON) *(SAPCOR 11) <3361>* **WEDDING ALBUM** [ ] [ ]
– John and Yoko / Amsterdam. *(cd-iss. Jun97 on 'Rykodisc'; RCD 10413)*

— JOHN and YOKO hired the following musicians **ERIC CLAPTON** – guitar (ex-YARDBIRDS, ex-CREAM, ex-BLUESBREAKERS) / **KLAUS VOORMAN** – bass (ex-MANFRED MANN) / **ALAN WHITE** – drums

Dec 69. (lp) *(CORE 2001) <3362>* **THE PLASTIC ONO BAND – LIVE PEACE IN TORONTO 1969 (live 13 Sep'69)** [ ] Jan70 [10]
– Blue Suede shoes / Money (that's what I want) / Dizzy Miss Lizzy / Yer blues / Cold turkey / Give peace a chance / Don't worry Kyoko / John John (let's hope for peace).

Feb 70. (7"; LENNON / ONO WITH PLASTIC ONO BAND) *(APPLES 1003) <1818>* **INSTANT KARMA!. / Yoko Ono: WHO HAS SEEN THE WIND?** [5] [3]

JOHN LENNON & THE PLASTIC ONO BAND

— The **LENNON's** retained only **KLAUS** / **RINGO STARR** – drums (ex-BEATLES) repl. WHITE who later joined YES

Dec 70. (lp) *(SAPCOR 17) <3372>* **JOHN LENNON: PLASTIC ONO BAND** [11] [6]
– Mother / Hold on / I found out / Working class hero / Isolation / Remember / Love / Well well well / Look at me / God / My mummy's dead. *(re-iss. Jul84 on 'Fame' lp/c; 41-3102-1/-4) (cd-iss. Apr88 on 'E.M.I.'; CDP 746770-2) (cd re-iss. Dec94 on 'Fame'; CDFA 3310) (cd re-iss. Oct00 on 'Parlophone'+=; 528740-2)* – Power to the people / Do the oz.

Dec 70. (7") *<1827>* **MOTHER. / WHY (Yoko Ono)** [–] [43]

— next single also credited with **YOKO ONO**

Mar 71. (7") *(R 5892)* **POWER TO THE PEOPLE. / OPEN YOUR BOX** [7] [–]

Mar 71. (7") *<1830>* **POWER TO THE PEOPLE. / Yoko Ono: TOUCH ME** [–] [11]

Oct 71. (lp) *(PAS 10004) <3379>* **IMAGINE** [1] Sep71 [1]
– Imagine / Crippled inside / Jealous guy / It's so hard / I don't want to be a soldier / Give me some truth / Oh my love / How do you sleep? / How? / Oh Yoko!. *(also on quad-lp Jun72; Q4PAS 10004) (cd-iss. May87 on 'Parlophone'; CDP 746641-2) (re-iss. Nov97; LPCENT 27) (re-mast.Feb00 cd/c/lp; 524858-2/-4/-1)* – hit UK No.51

Oct 71. (7") *<1840>* **IMAGINE. / IT'S SO HARD** [–] [3]

May 72. (7") *<1848>* **WOMAN IS THE NIGGER OF THE WORLD. / Yoko Ono: SISTERS, OH SISTERS** [–] [57]

— with ELEPHANT'S MEMORY & FLUX / INVISIBLE STRINGS and lots of guests including **FRANK ZAPPA, ERIC CLAPTON,** etc.

Sep 72. (d-lp; JOHN & YOKO / PLASTIC ONO BAND) *(PCSP 7161) <3392>* **SOMETIME IN NEW YORK CITY (live)** [11] [48]
– Woman is the nigger of the world / Sisters o sisters / Attica state / Born in a prison / New York City / Sunday bloody Sunday / The luck of the Irish / John Sinclair / Angela / We're all water / (w/ CAST OF THOUSANDS); Cold turkey / Don't worry Kyoko / (w/ The MOTHERS); Jamrag / Scumbag / Au. *(re-iss. Feb86 on 'Parlophone'; see LIVE IN NEW YORK CITY')*

— Next single credited as **JOHN & YOKO / PLASTIC ONO BAND** with **The HARLEM COMMUNITY CHOIR**

Nov 72. (7",7"green) *(R 5970)* **HAPPY XMAS (WAR IS OVER). / LISTEN THE SNOW IS FALLING** [4] Nov71 [ ]
(re-iss. Dec74; same); hit No.48) (re-iss. Dec80; same); No.2) (re-iss. Dec81; same); No.28) (re-iss. Dec82; ; hit 56)

JOHN LENNON

Nov 73. (7") *(R 5994) <1868>* **MIND GAMES. / MEAT CITY** [26] [18]

Nov 73. (lp/c; JOHN LENNON & PLASTIC U.F.ONO BAND) *(PCS/TC-PCS 7165) <3414>* **MIND GAMES** [13] [9]
– Mind games / Tight a $ / Aisumasen (I'm sorry) / One day (at a time) / Bring on the Lucie (freda people) / Nutopian international anthem / Intuition / Out of the blue / Only people / I know (I know) / You are here / Meat city. *(re-iss. Oct80 on 'Music For Pleasure' lp/c; MFP/TCMFP 50509) (cd-iss. Aug87 & Sep91 on 'Parlophone'; CDP 746769-2) (cd re-mast.Oct02 +=; 542425-2)* – home versions:- Aisumasen (I'm sorry) / Bring on the Lucie (freda people) / Meat city.

Oct 74. (7"; JOHN LENNON & THE PLASTIC ONO NUCLEAR BAND featuring ELTON JOHN) *(R 5998) <1874>* **WHATEVER GETS YOU THRU' THE NIGHT. / BEEF JERKY** [36] Sep74 [1]

Oct 74. (lp/c) *(PC/+TC 253) <3416>* **WALLS AND BRIDGES** [6] [1]
– Going down on love / Whatever gets you thru the night / Old dirt road / What you got / Bless you / #9 dream / Surprise surprise (sweet bird of Paradise) / Steel and glass / Beef jerky / Nobody loves you (when you're down and out) / Ya-ya / Scared. *(re-iss. Jan85 on 'Parlophone' lp/c; ATAK/TC-ATAK 43) (cd-iss. Jul87; CDP 746768-2)*

Jan 75. (7") *(R 6003) <1878>* **#9 DREAM. / WHAT YOU GOT** [23] [9]

Feb 75. (lp/c) *(PCS/TC-PCS 7169) <3419>* **ROCK'N'ROLL** [6] [6]
– Be-bop-a-lula / Stand by me / Medley: Rip it up – Ready Teddy / You can't catch me / Ain't that a shame / Do you want to dance / Sweet little sixteen / Slippin' and slidin' / Peggy Sue / Medley: Bring it on home to me – Send me some lovin' / Ya ya / Just because. *(re-iss. Nov81 on 'Music For Pleasure' lp/c; MFP/TCMFP 50522) (cd-iss. Jul87 on 'Parlophone'; CDP 746 707-2) (re-iss. Feb97 on 'E.M.I.'; LPCENT 9)*

Apr 75. (7") *(R 6005) <1881>* **STAND BY ME. / MOVE OVER MS. L** [30] Mar75 [20]
(re-iss. Apr81; same)

Oct 75. (7") *(R 6009)* **IMAGINE. / WORKING CLASS HERO** [6] [–]
(re-iss. Dec80; same); hit No.1)

Nov 75. (lp/c) *(PCS 7173) <3421>* **SHAVED FISH** (compilation) [8] [12]
– Give peace a chance / Cold turkey / Instant karma / Power to the people / Mother / Woman is the nigger of the world / Imagine / Whatever gets you thru the night / Mind games / #9 dream / Happy Xmas (war is over) / Give peace a chance (reprise). *(cd-iss. May87 on 'E.M.I.'; CDP 746642-2)*

— JOHN was also credited on a few singles by ELTON JOHN – Feb75 'I Saw Her Standing There' which was also realeased Mar81 with 2 other. In Jul71 a rare single 'GOD SAVE US'/'DO THE OZ' was released by him and Plastic Ono Band backing 'BILL ELLIOT AND THE ELASTIC OZ BAND'

JOHN LENNON & YOKO ONO

returned after a long break

Geffen Geffen

Oct 80. (7") *(K 79186)* <49604> **(JUST LIKE) STARTING OVER. / KISS KISS KISS (Yoko Ono)** [1] [1]

Nov 80. (lp/c) *(K/K4 99131)* <2001> **DOUBLE FANTASY** [1] [1]
– (Just like) Starting over / Every man has a woman who loves him (YOKO ONO) / Clean up time / Give me something (YOKO ONO) / I'm losing you / I'm moving on (YOKO ONO) / Beautiful boy (darling boy) / Watching the wheels / I'm your angel (YOKO ONO) / Dear Yoko / Beautiful boys (YOKO ONO) / Kiss kiss kiss (YOKO ONO) / Woman / Hard times are over (YOKO ONO). *(re-iss. Jan89 on 'Capitol' cd)(c/lp; CDP 791 425-2)(TC+/EST 2083) (cd re-iss. Oct00 on 'Parlophone'+=; 528739-2)* – Help me to help myself / Walking on thin ice / Central Park stroll (dialogue).

Jan 81. (7"/c-s) *(K/MK 79195)* <49644> **WOMAN. / Yoko Ono: BEAUTIFUL BOYS** [1] [2]

Mar 81. (7"/c-s) *(K/MK 79207)* <49695> **WATCHING THE WHEELS. / Yoko Ono: YES, I'M YOUR ANGEL** [30] [10]

— His last two singles were released after his tragic murder 8th Dec'80

JOHN & YOKO

had recorded one more album prior to his death.

Polydor Polydor

Jan 84. (lp) *(<817 238-1>)* **A HEART PLAY: UNFINISHED DIALOGUE** (interview with Playboy) [ ] [ ]

Jan 84. (7") *(POSP 700)* <817254> **NOBODY TOLD ME. / O SANITY** [6] [5]

Jan 84. (lp/pic-lp/c)(cd) *(POLH/+P/C 5)(<817160-2>)* **MILK AND HONEY** [3] [11]
– I'm stepping out / Sleepless night (YOKO ONO) / I don't wanna face it / Don't be scared (YOKO ONO) / Nobody told me / O'sanity (YOKO ONO) / Borrowed time / Your hands (YOKO ONO) / (Forgive me) My little flower princess / Let me count the ways (YOKO ONO) / Grow old with me / You're the one (YOKO ONO). *(cd re-mast.Oct01 on 'Parlophone'+=; 535959-2)* – Every man has a woman who loves him / I'm moving on (home demo) / I'm stepping out (home demo) / (interview).

Mar 84. (7") *(POSP 701)* **BORROWED TIME. / YOUR HANDS (Yoko Ono)** [32] [ ]
(12"+=) *(POSPX 701)* – Never say goodbye.

Jul 84. (7") *(POSP 702)* <821107> **I'M STEPPING OUT. / SLEEPLESS NIGHT (Yoko Ono)** [ ] [55]
(12"+=) *(POSPX 702)* – Loneliness.

Nov 84. (7") *(POSP 712)* **EVERY MAN HAS A WOMAN WHO LOVES HIM. / IT'S ALRIGHT** [ ] [ ]
(above from various compilation 'B'-side by his son SEAN ONO LENNON)

– posthumous releases, etc. –

on 'Parlophone' UK /'Capitol' US, unless mentioned otherwise

Jun 81. (8xlp-box) *Apple; (JLB 8)* **JOHN LENNON (BOXED)** [ ] [ ]
– (all lp's from LIVE PEACE – SHAVED FISH) *(4xcd-box-iss.Oct90; LENNON 1)*

Nov 82. (lp/c) *E.M.I.; (EMTV/TC-EMTV 37) / Geffen; <GHSP 2023>* **THE JOHN LENNON COLLECTION** [1] [33]
– (nearly as 'SHAVED FISH') *(re-iss. Jun85; same) (cd-iss. Oct89; CDEMTV 37)* – (2 extra tracks).

Nov 82. (7") *(R 6059)* **LOVE. / GIVE ME SOME TRUTH** [41] [ ]

Mar 84. (7") *EMI Gold; (G45 2)* **GIVE PEACE A CHANCE. / COLD TURKEY** [ ] [–]

Nov 85. (7") *(R 6117)* **JEALOUS GUY / GOING DOWN ON LOVE** [65] [ ]
(12"+=) *(12R 6117)* – Oh Yoko!

Feb 86. (lp/c)(cd) *(PCS/TC-PCS 7301)(CDP 746 196-2) <12451>* **LIVE IN NEW YORK CITY (live)** [55] [41]

Nov 86. (lp/c/cd) *(PCS/TCPCS/CDPCS 7308) <12533>* **MENLOVE AVE.** (sessions 74-75) [ ] [ ]
– Here we go again / Rock'n'roll people / Angel baby / Since my baby left me / To know her is to love her / Steel and glass / Scared / Old dirt road / Nobody loves you (when you're down and out).

May 87. (7") *Antar;* **TWO MINUTES SILENCE. / TWO MINUTES SILENCE (dub!)** [ ] [ ]

Aug 87. (cd) **LIVE JAM** (half of SOMETIME lp) [ ] [ ]

Oct 88. (cd/d-c/d-lp) *(CD/TC+/PCSP 722) <90803>* **IMAGINE: JOHN LENNON** (soundtrack / some by The BEATLES *) [64] [31]
– Real love / Twist and shout (*) / Help! (*) / In my life (*) / Strawberry fields forever (*) / A day in the life (*) / Revolution (*) / The ballad of John & Yoko (*) / Julia (*) / Don't let me down (*) / Give peace a chance / How? / Imagine (rehearsal) / God / Mother / Stand by me / Jealous guy / Woman / Beautiful boy (darling boy) / (Just like) Starting over / Imagine.

Oct 88. (cd-s) *<44230>* **JEALOUS GUY / GIVE PEACE A CHANCE** [–] [80]

Nov 88. (7"/7"pic-d) *(R/RP 6199)* **IMAGINE. / JEALOUS GUY** [45] [–]
(12"+=/12"pic-d+=) *(12R/+P 6199)* – Happy Xmas (war is over).
(cd-s+=) *(CDR 6199)* – Give peace a chance.

Oct 97. (cd/c/lp) *(<8 21954-2/-4/-1>)* **LENNON LEGEND – THE VERY BEST OF JOHN LENNON** [4] Mar98 [65]
– Imagine / Instant karma / Mother / Jealous guy / Power to the people / Cold turkey / Love / Mind games / Whatever gets you thru the night / No.9 dream / Stand by me / (Just like) Starting over / Woman / Beautiful boy / Watching the wheels / Nobody told me / Borrowed time / Working class hero / Happy Xmas (war is over) / Give peace a chance. *(cd re-iss. Oct03; 595067-2)*

Sep 98. (3xcd-box) *Dressed To Kill; (DTKBOX 92)* **IN MY LIFE** [ ] [–]

Nov 98. (4xcd-box+book) *(<8 30614-2)>* **JOHN LENNON ANTHOLOGY** (alt.takes, live rarities and home recordings) [62] [99]
– ASCOT / NEW YORK CITY / THE LOST WEEKEND / DAKOTA)

Nov 98. (cd/c) *(497639-2/-4)* **WONSAPONATIME** (above highlights) [ ] [ ]

Dec 99. (c-s/cd-s) *(TCR/CDR 6534)* **IMAGINE / HAPPY XMAS (WAR IS OVER) / GIVE PEACE A CHANCE** [3] [–]

Dec 03. (7") *(R 6627)* **HAPPY XMAS (WAR IS OVER). / IMAGINE** [33] [–]
(cd-s+=) *(CDR 6627)* – Instant karma (version) / Imagine (instrumental).

Oct 05. (d-cd) *(340080-2) <40391>* **WORKING CLASS HERO – THE DEFINITIVE LENNON** [11] [ ]
– (Just like) Starting over / Imagine / Watching the wheels / Jealous guy / Instant karma (we all shine on) / Stand by me / Working class hero / Power to the people / Oh my love / Oh Yoko! / Nobody loves you (when you're down and out) / Nobody told me / Bless you / Come together (live) / New York City / I'm stepping out / You are here / Borrowed time / Happy Xmas (war is over) // Woman / Mind games / Out the blue / Whatever gets you thru the night / Love / Mother / Beautiful boy / Woman is the nigger of the world / God / Scared / #9 dream / I'm losing you / Isolation / Cold turkey / Intuition / Gimme some truth / Real love / Grow old with me.

□ Annie LENNOX (see under ⇒ EURYTHMICS)

Jerry Lee LEWIS

Born: 29 Sep'35, Ferriday, Louisiana, USA. In 1949, his parents mortgaged their house to buy him a piano which the young JERRY mastered in two weeks! A few years later, after being expelled from a religious school that taught music, he married a preacher's daughter; he soon deserted her however, bigamously marrying another girl in true shotgun style. In 1956, LEWIS went to Memphis, Tennessee with his father and through perseverance, set up recording time in Sam Phillips' 'Sun' studios. The following year, after his debut, 'CRAZY ARMS', was banned from airplay, LEWIS secured a couple of appearances on the Steve Allen TV Show, the exposure leading to massive sales of his second single, 'WHOLE LOTTA SHAKIN' GOIN' ON'. Although LEWIS didn't actually write any of his material, his demented rock'n'roll performances (he even pummelled the piano with his feet!) earned him the rather unfortunate nickname, "The Killer". Later in '57, JERRY bigamously married again!, this time secretly to his 13 year-old second cousin, Myra Gale Brown. Perhaps inspired by his recent activities, LEWIS scored two enormous worldwide classics in the appropriately titled 'GREAT BALLS OF FIRE' and 'BREATHLESS'. Meanwhile, he divorced his second wife and brought the wrath of the religious establishment and moral majority when his questionable lifestyle was disclosed; LEWIS' UK arrival (in May '58) caused uproar and near tour cancellation after newspapers had a field day over his "minor" misdemeanours. Although JERRY LEE made a few more sporadic returns to the charts, his career had been severely dented by this late 50's hysteria. While Myra gave birth to his second son, Steve Allen, in February '59, LEWIS's intake of alcohol and pills was increasing every month. Tragedy struck in April '62, when his aforementioned son drowned in a swimming pool accident. Around a year and a half later, coinciding with LEWIS' signature for new imprint 'Smash', Myra produced another child, this time a daughter, Phoebe Allen. In the early 70's, Myra finally divorced him, claiming neglect, etc. It didn't stop him marrying a fourth time, although this time he did it legally in late '71. With his career enjoying something of a resurrection in 1973 (by which time he'd traded in his blue suede shoes for Stetson-styled country-pop), tragedy struck again when his son (his drummer on tour) JERRY LEE JR was killed in a motoring accident. In 1976, LEWIS was involved in two gun incidents, one when he accidently shot his bassman, NORMAN OWENS, the other occurring outside Gracelands (Elvis Presley's home) hours after being charged with drunk driving. He signed to 'Elektra' in 1978, although a few albums and a serious stomach ulcer operation later, he sued the label. In 1982, his estranged fourth wife, Jaren Gunn Lewis (ne Pate), drowned in a mysterious swimming pool incident just prior to their divorce settlement. The following year, coming up for his 50th birthday, the irrepressible LEWIS tied the knot yet again, this time to a 25 year-old, Shawn Michelle Stevens; just over two months later, she was to be found dead in their home. Although suspected of foul play, no case was brought and LEWIS, proving that he was a family man at heart, went on to marry his sixth wife, the 22 year-old, Kerrie McCarver, who, in early '87, gave birth to a son, Jerry Lee Lewis III. A few years later, his biopic film story appeared (Nick Tosches' celebrated biography, 'Hellfire', had previously hit the shelves in 1982) featuring re-recordings of his oldies, his part played by actor, Dennis Quaid.

• **Songwriters:** Wrote own material, except CRAZY ARMS (Ray Price) / WHOLE LOTTA SHAKIN' GOIN' ON (D.Williams & Sunny Dave) / YOU WIN AGAIN + SETTIN' THE WOODS ON FIRE (Hank Willliams) / WHAT'D I SAY + HIT THE ROAD JACK (Ray Charles) / BREAK UP + I'LL MAKE IT ALL UP TO YOU (Charlie Rich) / SWEET LITTLE SIXTEEN + LITTLE QUEENIE (Chuck Berry) / GOOD GOLLY MISS MOLLY + LONG TALL SALLY (Little Richard) / ME AND BOBBY McGEE (Kris Kristofferson) / GREEN GREEN GRASS OF HOME (Curly Putnam) / CHANTILLY LACE (Big Bopper) / JACK DANIELS (Heads, Hands & Feet) / DRINKIN' WINE SPO . . . (Stick McGhee) / RITA MAE (Bob Dylan) etc.
• **Trivia:** His sister, LINDA GAIL LEWIS, also issued solo recordings between 1965 and 74. Another unlikely cousin of JERRY LEE is the TV evangelist, Jimmy Swaggart!

Best CD compilation: THE VERY BEST OF JERRY LEE LEWIS (*8)

JERRY LEE LEWIS – vocals, piano + sessions

London | Sun

Dec 56. (7") *<259>* **CRAZY ARMS. / END OF THE ROAD** [–] [ ]
Jul 57. (7",78) *(HLS 8457) <267>* **WHOLE LOTTA SHAKIN' GOIN' ON. / IT'LL BE ME** [8] Jun57 [3]
Nov 57. (7") *<281>* **GREAT BALLS OF FIRE. / YOU WIN AGAIN** [–] [2] [95]
Dec 57. (7",78) *(HLS 8529)* **GREAT BALLS OF FIRE. / MEAN WOMAN BLUES** [1] [–]
Feb 58. (7",78) *(HLS 8559)* **YOU WIN AGAIN. / I'M FEELIN' SORRY** [ ] [–]
Apr 58. (7",78) *(HLS 8592) <288>* **BREATHLESS. / DOWN THE LINE** [8] Feb58 [7]
Jun 58. (7") *<301>* **THE RETURN OF JERRY LEE. / LEWIS BOOGIE** [–] [ ]
Sep 58. (7",78) *(HLS8700) <303>* **BREAK-UP. / I'LL MAKE IT ALL UP TO YOU** [ ] [52] Aug58 [85]
Jan 59. (lp) *(HAS 2138) <1230>* **JERRY LEE LEWIS** [ ] Dec57 [ ]
– Don't be cruel / Goodnight Irene / Put me down / It all depends / Ubangi stomp / Crazy arms / Jambalaya / Fools like me / High school confidential / Where the saints go marching in Matchbox / It'll be me. *(re-iss. May82 on 'Mercury' lp/c; 6463/7145 042) (cd-iss. Apr86 on 'Pickwick'; PCD 814)*
Jan 59. (7",78) *(HLS 8780) <296>* **HIGH SCHOOL CONFIDENTIAL. / FOOLS LIKE ME** [12] May58 [21]
Apr 59. (7",78) *(HLS 8940) <317>* **LOVIN' UP A STORM. / BIG BLON' BABY** [28] [ ]
Sep 59. (7",78) *(HLS 8941) <324>* **LET'S TALK ABOUT US. / THE BALLAD OF BILLY JOE** [ ] [ ]
Nov 59. (7",78) *(HLS 8993) <330>* **LITTLE QUEENIE. / I COULD NEVER BE ASHAMED OF YOU** [ ] [ ]
Mar 60. (7") *(HLS 9083) <312>* **I'LL SAIL MY SHIP ALONE. / IT HURT ME SO** [–] Dec 58 [93]
May 60. (7") *(HLS 9131) <337>* **BABY, BABY, BYE, BYE. / OLD BLACK JOE** [47] [ ]
Oct 60. (7") *(HLS 9202) <344>* **JOHN HENRY. / HANG UP MY ROCK'N'ROLL SHOES** [ ] [ ]
Dec 60. (7") *<352>* **WHEN I GET PAID. / LOVE MADE A FOOL OF ME** [–] [ ]
Apr 61. (7") *(HLS 9335) <356>* **WHAT'D I SAY. / LIVIN' LOVIN' WRECK** [10] [30]
1961. (lp) *<1265>* **JERRY LEE'S GREATEST** (part compilation) [–] [ ]
Sep 61. (7") *(HLS 9414) <364>* **IT WON'T HAPPEN WITH ME. / COLD COLD HEART** [ ] [ ]
Oct 61. (7") *(HLS 9446)* **AS LONG AS I LIVE. / WHEN I GET PAID** [ ] [–]
Oct 61. (7") *<367>* **SAVE THE LAST DANCE FOR ME. / AS LONG AS I LIVE** [–] [ ]
Dec 61. (7") *<371>* **MONEY. / BONNIE B** [–] [ ]
Mar 62. (7") *(HLS 9526) <374>* **I'VE BEEN TWISTIN'. / RAMBLING ROSE** [ ] [ ]
May 62. (lp) *(HAS 2440)* **JERRY LEE LEWIS VOL.2** [14] [ ]
– Money / As long as I live / Country music is here to stay / Frankie and Johnny / Home / Hello baby / Let's talk about us / What'd I say Breakup / Great balls of fire / Cold, cold heart / Hello Josephine *(cd-iss. Apr86 on 'Pickwick'; PCD 840)*
Aug 62. (7") *(HLS 9584) <379>* **SWEET LITTLE SIXTEEN. / HOW'S MY EX TREATING YOU** [38] [95]
Feb 63. (7") *(HLS 9688) <382>* **GOOD GOLLY MISS MOLLY. / I CAN'T TRUST ME (IN YOUR ARMS ANYMORE)** [31] Dec62 [ ]
May 63. (7") *(HLS 9722) <384>* **TEENAGE LETTER. ("& LINDA GAIL LEWIS") / SEASONS OF MY HEART** [ ] Feb63 [ ]

Philips | Smash

1963. (7") *(AMT 1216) <1857>* **HIT THE ROAD JACK. / PEN AND PAPER** [–] [ ]
Mar 64. (7") *(BF 1324) <1886>* **I'M ON FIRE. / BREAD AND BUTTER MAN** [ ] [98]
1964. (7") *<1906>* **SHE WAS MY BABY. / THE HOLE HE SAID HE'D DIG FOR ME** [–] [ ]
Oct 64. (7") *(BF 1371) <1930>* **HI HEAL SNEAKERS. / YOU WENT BACK ON YOUR WORD** [ ] [91]
Dec 64. (7") **WHOLE LOTTA SHAKIN' GOIN' ON (live). / BREATHLESS (live)** [–] [ ]
Feb 65. (7") **GREAT BALLS OF FIRE (live). / HIGH SCHOOL CONFIDENTIAL (live)** [–] [ ]
Apr 65. (7") *(BF 1407) <1969>* **BABY HOLD ME CLOSE. / I BELIEVE IN YOU** [ ] [ ]
May 65. (lp) *(SBL 7650) <67650>* **THE GREATEST LIVE SHOW ON EARTH (live)** [ ] Dec64 [71]
– Jenny Jenny / Who will the next fool be / Memphis Tennessee / Hound dog / Mean woman blues / Hi-heel sneakers / No particular place to go / Together again / Long tall Sally / Whole lotta shakin' goin' on / Little Queenie (intro) / How's my ex treating you / Johnny B. Goode / Green, green grass of home / What'd I say (part 2) / You win again / I'll sail my ship alone / Cryin' time / Money / Roll over Beethoven.
Jul 65. (7") *(BF 1425)* **ROCKIN' PNEUMONIA AND THE BOOGIE WOOGIE FLU. / THIS MUST BE THE PLACE** [ ] [ ]
Jul 65. (lp) *(SBL 7668) <67063>* **THE RETURN OF ROCK** [ ] May65 [ ]
– I believe in you / Maybeline / Flip, flop and fly / Roll over Beethoven / Baby, hold me close / Herman the hermit / Don't let go / You went back on your word / Corrine, Corrina / Sexy ways / Johhny B.Goode / Got you on my mind.

1965. (7") *<2006>* **GREEN GREEN GRASS OF HOME. ("& LINDA GAIL LEWIS") / BABY, YOU'VE GOT WHAT IT TAKES** [–] [ ]

Jan 66. (lp) *(SBL 7688) <67071>* **COUNTRY SONGS FOR CITY FOLKS** [ ] [ ]
– Green green grass of home / Wolverton mountain Funny how time slips away North to Alaska / The wild side of life / Ray of fire / Detroit city / Crazy arms King of the road / Seasons of my heart.

1966. (7") *<2027>* **STICKS AND STONES. / WHAT A HECK OF A MESS** [–] [ ]

May 66. (lp) *(SBL 7706) <67079>* **MEMPHIS BEAT** [ ] [ ]
– Memphis beat / Mathilda / Darlin' wine spo-dee-o-dee / Hallelujah, I love her so / She thinks I still care / Just because / Sticks and stones / Whenever you're ready / Lincoln limousine / Big boss man / Too young / The urge.

Oct 66. (7") *(BF 1521) <2053>* **MEMPHIS BEAT. / IF I HAD TO DO IT OVER** [ ] [ ]

Jan 67. (lp) *(SBL 7746) <67086>* **BY REQUEST – MORE GREATEST LIVE SHOW ON EARTH (live)** [ ] [ ]
– Introduction / Little Queenie / How's my ex treating you / Johnny B.Goode / Green green grass of home / What'd I say / You win again / I'll sail my ship alone / Crying time / Money / Roll over Beethoven.

Jul 67. (7") *(BF 1594) <2103>* **IT'S A HANG-UP BABY. / HOLDIN' ON** [ ] [ ]

Mercury Smash

Mar 68. (7") *(MF 1020) <2146>* **ANOTHER TIME ANOTHER PLACE. / WALKING THE FLOOR OVER YOU** [ ] [97]

Jul 68. (lp) *(MCL 20117) <67097>* **SOUL MY WAY** [ ] [ ]
– Turn on your love light / It's a hang-up baby / Dream baby (how long must I dream / Just dropped in Wedding bells / He took it like a man / Hey baby / Treat her right / Holdin' on Shotgun man I bet you're gonna like it.

Aug 68. (7") *(MF 1045) <2164>* **WHAT MADE MILWALKEE FAMOUS. / ALL THE GOOD IS GONE** [ ] [94]

1968. (7") *<2186>* **SHE STILL COMES AROUND. / SLIPPIN' AROUND** [–] [ ]

Jan 69. (lp) *(SMWL 21011) <67104>* **ANOTHER PLACE ANOTHER TIME** [ ] Jun68 [ ]
– What made Milwaukee famous Play me a song I can cry to / On the back row / Walking the floor over you All night long / I'm a lonesome fugitive Another place, another time / Break my mind / Before the next teardrop falls / All the good is gone / We live in two different worlds (w/ Linda)

Mar 69. (7") *(MF 1088) <2202>* **TO MAKE LOVE SWEETER FOR YOU. / LET'S TALK ABOUT US** [ ] Dec68 [ ]

May 69. (lp) *(SMCL 20147) <67112>* **SHE STILL COMES AROUND (TO LOVE WHAT'S LEFT OF ME)** [ ] Feb69 [ ]
– To make love sweeter for you / Let's talk about us / I can't get over you / Out of my mind / Today I started loving you again / She still comes around (to love what's lkeft of me) / Louisiana man / Release me / Listen, they're playing my song / There stands the glass / Echoes.

May 69. (7") *(MF 1105)* **LONG TALL SALLY. / JENNY JENNY** [ ] [–]

1969. (7") *<2220>* **DON'T LET ME CROSSOVER. / WE LIVE IN TWO DIFFERENT WORLDS** [–] [ ]

1969. (7"; JERRY LEE LEWIS & LINDA GAIL LEWIS) *<2224>* **ONE HAS MY NAME. / I CAN'T STOP LOVING YOU** [–] [ ]

Feb 70. (lp; JERRY LEE LEWIS & LINDA GAIL LEWIS) *(SMCL 20172) <67126>* **TOGETHER** [ ] Nov69 [ ]
– Milwaukee here I come / Jackson / Don't take it out on me / Cryin' time / Sweet thing / Secret places / Don't let me cross over / Gotta travel on / We live in two different worlds / Earth up above / Roll over Beethoven.

1970. (7") *<2224>* **SHE EVEN WOKE ME UP TO SAY GOODBYE. / ECHOES** [–] [ ]

Jun 70. (lp) *(6338 010) <67128>* **SHE EVEN WOKE ME UP TO SAY GOODBYE** [ ] Feb70 [ ]
– Once more with feeling / Working man blues / Waiting for a train / Brown eyed handsome man / My only claim to fame / Since I met you baby / She woke me up to say goodbye / Wine me up / When the grass grows over me / You went out of your way / Echoes.

Aug 70. (7") *<2257>* **ONCE MORE WITH FEELING. / YOU WENT OUT OF YOUR WAY** [–] [ ]

Nov 70. (7") *<73155>* **I CAN'T HAVE A MERRY CHRISTMAS MARY (WITHOUT YOU). / IN LOVING MEMORIES** [–] [ ]

1971. (7") *<73099>* **THERE MUST BE MORE TO LOVE THAN THIS. / HOME AWAY FROM HOME** [–] [ ]

Jun 71. (lp) *(6338 045) <61323>* **THERE MUST BE MORE TO LOVE THAN THIS** [ ] Jan71 [ ]
– There must be more to love than this / Bottles and barstools / Rueben James / I'd be talkin' / All the time / One more time / Sweet Georgia Brown / Woman, woman / I forget more than you'll ever know / Foolaid / Home away from home / Life's little ups and downs.

Jul 71. (7") *<73192>* **TOUCHING HOME. / WOMAN, WOMAN** [–] [ ]

Jul 71. (lp) *<61343>* **TOUCHING HOME** [–] [ ]

1971. (7") *<73227>* **WHEN HE WALKS ON YOU. / FOOLISH KIND OF MAN** [–] [ ]

Feb 72. (lp) *(6338 071) <61346>* **WOULD YOU TAKE ANOTHER CHANCE ON ME?** [ ] Nov71 [ ]

Jan 72. (7") *(6052 117) <73248>* **ME AND BOBBY McGEE. / WOULD YOU TAKE ANOTHER CHANCE ON ME** [ ] [40]

Apr 72. (7") *(6502 141) <73273>* **CHANTILLY LACE. / THINK ABOUT IT DARLIN'** [33] [43]

Jun 72. (7") *<73296>* **TURN ON YOUR LOVELIGHT. / LONELY WEEKENDS** [–] [95]

Jun 72. (7") *(6052 162)* **TURN ON YOUR LOVELIGHT. / I'M WALKIN'** [ ] [–]

1972. (7"; JERRY LEE LEWIS & LINDA GAIL LEWIS) *<73328>* **WHO'S GONNA PLAY THIS OLD PIANO. / NO HONKY TONKS IN HEAVEN** [–] [ ]

Mar 73. (7") *(6052 260) <73374>* **DRINKIN' WINE SPO-DEE O'DEE. / ROCK & ROLL MEDLEY** [ ] [41]

Apr 73. (d-lp) *(6672 008) <803>* **THE SESSION** [ ] Mar73 [37]
– Johnny B. Goode / Trouble in mind / Early morning rain / No headstone on my grave / Pledgin' my love / Memphis / Drinkin' wine spo-dee o'dee / Music to the man / Bad Moon rising / Sea cruise / Sixty minute man / Moving on down the line / What'd I say / Medley: Good golly Miss Molly – Long tall Sally – Jenny . . . – Tutti frutti – Whole lotta shakin' goin' on. *(cd-iss. May85; 822751-2)*
(above recorded with PETER FRAMPTON, ALBERT LEE, RORY GALLAGHER, ALVIN LEE)

1973. (7") *<73361>* **NO MORE HANGING ON. / THE MERCY OF A LETTER** [–] [ ]

1973. (7") *<73402>* **NO HEADSTONE ON MY GRAVE. / JACK DANIELS (OLD No.7)** [–] [ ]

Jul 73. (lp) *(6338 148) <61278>* **LIVE AT THE INTERNATIONAL, LAS VEGAS (live)** [ ] Oct70 [ ]
– Mean woman blues / High school confidential / Money / Matchbox / What'd I say / What'd I say (pt.2) / Great balls of fire / Good golly Miss Molly / Lewis boogie / Your cheating heart / Hound dog / Long tall Sally / Whole lotta shakin' goin' on.

Sep 73. (7") *(6052 378)* **TAKING MY MUSIC TO THE MAN. / JACK DANIELS** [ ] [–]

1973. (7") *<73423>* **SOMETIMES A MEMORY AIN'T ENOUGH. / I NEED TO PRAY** [–] [ ]

1974. (7") *<73462>* **JUST A LITTLE BIT. / MEAT MAN** [–] [ ]

Mar 74. (lp) *(6338 452) <SRM-1 690>* **SOUTHERN ROOTS** [ ] [ ]
– Meat man / When a man loves a woman / Hold on I'm coming / Just a little bit / Born to be a loser / The haunted house / Blueberry hill The revolutionary man / Big blue diamond / That Old Bourbon Street church.

1974. (7") *<73491>* **TELL TALE SIGNS. / COLD, COLD MORNING LIGHT** [–] [ ]

1974. (7") *<73518>* **HE CAN'T FILL MY SHOES. / TOMORROW'S TAKING BABY AWAY** [–] [ ]

1974. (7") *<73661>* **I CAN STILL HEAR THE MUSIC IN THE RESTROOM. / REMEMBER ME I'M THE ONE WHO LOVES YOU** [–] [ ]

1975. (7") *<73685>* **BOOGIE WOOGIE COUNTRY MAN. / I'M STILL JEALOUS OF YOU** [–] [ ]

1975. (7") *<73729>* **A DAMN GOOD COUNTRY SONG. / WHEN I TAKE MY VACATION IN HEAVEN** [–] [ ]

Nov 75. (lp) *(6338 602)* **I'M A ROCKER** [ ] [–]

1976. (7") *<73763>* **DON'T BOOGIE WOOGIE. / THAT KIND OF FOOL** [–] [ ]

1976. (7") *<73822>* **LET'S PUT IT BACK TOGETHER AGAIN. / JERRY LEE'S ROCK'N' ROLL REVIVAL SHOW** [–] [ ]

1976. (7") *<73872>* **THE CLOSEST THING TO YOU. / YOU BELONG TO ME** [–] [ ]

1977. (7") *<55011>* **MIDDLE-AGE CRAZY. / GEORGIA ON MY MIND** [–] [ ]

1978. (7") *<55021>* **COME ON IN. / WHO'S SORRY NOW** [–] [ ]

1978. (7") *<55028>* **I'LL FIND IT WHERE I CAN. / DON'T LET THE STARS GET IN YOUR EYES** [–] [ ]

Nov 78. (d-lp) *(6641 869)* **BACK TO BACK** [ ] [–]

1979. (7") *<76146>* **I'M SO LONESOME I COULD CRY. / PICK ME UP ON THE WAY DOWN** [–] [ ]

Elektra Elektra

May 79. (7") *<46030>* **ROCKIN' MY LIFE AWAY. / I WISH I WAS EIGHTEEN AGAIN** [–] [ ]

May 79. (7") *(K 12351)* **DON'T LET GO. / I WISH I WAS EIGHTEEN AGAIN** [ ] [–]

Apr 79. (lp/c) *(K/K4 52132) <184>* **JERRY LEE LEWIS** [ ] [ ]
– Don't let go / Rita May / Every day I have to cry / I like it like that / Number one lovin' man / Rockin' my life away / Who will the next fool be (you've got) / Personality / I wish I was eighteen again / Rockin' little angel. *(re-iss. Apr90 as 'ROCKIN' MY LIFE AWAY' on 'Tomato' lp/c/cd; 269661-1/-4/-2)*

Aug 79. (7") *(K 12374)* **ROCKIN' MY LIFE AWAY. / RITA MAE** [ ] [–]

1979. (7") *<46067>* **WHO WILL THE NEXT FOOL BE? / RITA MAE** [–] [ ]

Nov 79. (7") *(K 12399)* **EVERYDAY I HAVE TO CRY. / WHO WILL THE NEXT FOOL BE?** [ ] [–]

Feb 80. (7") *(K 12432) <46642>* **ROCKIN' JERRY LEE. / GOOD TIME CHARLIE'S GOT THE BLUES** [ ] [ ]

Apr 80. (7") *<46591>* **WHEN TWO WORLDS COLLIDE. / GOOD NEWS TRAVELS FAST** [–] [ ]

Apr 80. (lp) *(K 52113) <254>* **WHEN TWO WORLDS COLLIDE** [ ] [ ]
– Rockin' Jerry Lee / Who will buy the wine / Love game / Alabama jubilee / Goodtime Charlie's got the blues / When two worlds collide / Good news travels fast / I only want a buddy not a sweetheart / Honky tonk stuff / Toot toot Tootsie.

1980. (7") *<46642>* **HONKY TONK STUFF. / ROCKIN' JERRY LEE** [–] [ ]

Jan 81. (7") *<47026>* **FOLSAM PRISON BLUES. / OVER THE RAINBOW** [–] [ ]

May 81. (lp) *(K 52246) <291>* **KILLER COUNTRY** [ ] [ ]
– Folsam prison blues / I'll do it all over again / Jukebox junkie / Too weak to fight / Late night lovin' man / Change places with me / Let me on / Thirty-nine and holding / Mama, this one's for you / Over the rainbow. *(re-iss. Feb87; ED 250)*

May 81. (7") *<47095>* **THIRTY-NINE AND HOLDING. / CHANGE PLACES WITH ME** [–] [ ]

Aug 81. (7") *<69962>* **I'D DO IT ALL AGAIN. / WHO WILL BUY THE WINE** [–] [ ]

— On Apr'82, he was one of the stars alongside JOHNNY CASH & CARL PERKINS to feature on 'THE SURVIVORS' album, recorded in Germany 1981 for 'CBS-Columbia'.

M.C.A. M.C.A.

Jan 83. (7") *(MCA 808) <52151>* **MY FINGERS DO THE TALKIN'. / FOREVER FORGIVING** [ ] [ ]

May 83. (lp) *(MCF 3162)* **MY FINGERS DO THE TALKING** [ ] [ ]
– My fingers do the talkin' / She sure makes leaving look easy / Why you been gone so long / She sings Amazing Grace / Better not look down / Honky tonk rock and roll piano man / Come as you were / Circumstantial evidence / Forever forgiving / Honky tonk Heaven.

May 83. (7") *<52188>* **CIRCUMSTANTIAL EVIDENCE. / COME AS YOU WERE** [–] [ ]

Aug 83. (7") *<52233>* **SHE SINGS AMAZING GRACE. / WHY YOU BEEN GONE SO LONG** [–] [ ]

Jun 84. (7") *<52369>* **I AM WHAT I AM. / THAT WAS THE WAY IT WAS THEN** [–] [ ]

Jul 84. (lp) *(MCL 1810)* **I AM WHAT I AM** [ ] [ ]
– I am what I am / Only you (and you alone) / Get out your big roll daddy / Have I got a song for you / Careless hands / Candy kisses / I'm looking over a four leaf clover / Send me the pillow that you dream on / Honky tonk heart / That was the way it was then. *(re-iss. May85 lp/c; MCL/+C 1810) (re-iss. Aug89 on 'Instant' cd/c/lp; CD/TC+/INS 5008)*

not iss. Sire

Jun 90. (7") *<19809>* **IT WAS THE WHISKEY TALKIN' (NOT ME). / ('A'-Rock'n'roll version)** [–] [ ]

Warners Warners

Jun 95. (cd/c) *<(7559 61795-2/-4)>* **YOUNG BLOOD** [ ] [ ]
– House of blue lights / Young blood / Things / It was the whiskey talkin' (not me) / Goosebumps / Crown Victoria custom '51 / Restless heart / High school pressure / One of them old things / Poison love / Down the road apiece / Gotta travel on / Miss the Mississippi and you / I'll never get out of this world alive.

Fabulous Fabulous

Sep 03. (cd) *<(FABCD 189)>* **MIDDLE AGED CRAZY** [ ] [ ]
– Whole lotta shakin' goin' on / Middle aged crazy / Roll over Beethoven / Little Queenie / Crazy arms / She even woke me up to say goodbye / You win again / Sweet little sixteen / What'd I say / Great balls of fire / Hadacol boogie / High school confidential / Boogie woogie country man – Rockin' my life away / I'll find it where I can / Come on in / Who will the next fool be? / Would you take another chance on me / No headstones on my grave.

– (selective) compilations, others, etc. –

Nov 65. (lp) *London; (HA-S 8251)* **WHOLE LOTTA SHAKIN' GOIN' ON** [ ] [–]
(re-iss. +c.Oct74) (re-iss. 10"lp.Jul82 on 'Charly') (re-iss. Jul86 on 'Sun')

Jun 67. (lp) *London; (HAS 8323)* **BREATHLESS** [ ] [–]

Dec 87. (cd) *Bear Family; (BCD 15408)* **UP THROUGH THE YEARS 1956-1963** [ ] [ ]

May 89. (cd) *Magnum Force; (CDMF 071)* **LIVE IN ITALY (live)** [ ] [–]

Nov 89. (lp/c/cd) *Polydor; <(839516-1/-4/-2)>* **GREAT BALLS OF FIRE!** [ ] Jul89 [62]
– Great balls of fire / High school confidential / Big legged woman (BOOKER T. LAURY) / I'm on fire / Rocket 88 (JACKIE BRENSTON) / Whole lotta shakin' goin' on / Whole lotta shakin' goin' on (VALERIE WELLINGTON) / Breathless / Crazy arms / Real wild child (wild one) / That lucky old sun (just rolls around Heaven all day) / Great balls of fire (original).

Sep 89. (8xcd-box) *Sun; (CDSUNBOX 1)* **THE SUN YEARS** [ ] [ ]

Dec 90. (lp/cd) *See For Miles; (SEE/+CD 307)* **THE EP COLLECTION** [ ] [–]

Apr 91. (cd) *Ace; (CDCH 326)* **LIVE AT THE VAPORS CLUB (live)** [ ] [–]

Dec 91. (cd) *Ace; (CDCH 332)* **HONKY TONK ROCK'N'ROLL PIANO MAN** [ ] [–]

Apr 92. (cd) *Ace; (CDCH 348)* **PRETTY MUCH COUNTRY** [ ] [–]

May 92. (cd) *See For Miles; (SEECD 397)* **THE EP COLLECTION . . . PLUS: VOLUME 2** [ ] [–]

Sep 92. (cd) *Music Club; (MCCD 081)* **THE BEST OF JERRY LEE LEWIS** [ ] [–]
– Great balls of fire / Whole lotta shakin' goin' on / Drinkin' wine spo-dee-o-dee / Lewis boogie / Mean woan blues / You win again / Jailhouse rock / Lovin' up a storm / Pumpin' piano rock / High school confidential / Fools like me / Down the line / Breathless / Wild one / Milkshake mademoiselle / Pink pedal pushers / I could never be ashamed of you / In the mood / Let's talk about us / What'd I say.

Jun 93. (d-cd) *Tomato; (2696742)* **THE COMPLETE PALOMINO CLUB RECORDINGS** [ ] [ ]

Feb 94. (cd) *Javelin; (HADCD 124)* **SPOTLIGHT ON . . .** [ ] [ ]

Dec 94. (9xcd-box) *Bear Family; (BCD 15783)* **LOCUST YEARS & THE RETURN TO THE PROMISED LAND** [ ] [ ]

Aug 95. (cd) *Charly; (CPCD 8121)* **WHOLE LOTTA HITS** [ ] [–]

Oct 96. (d-cd) *Charly; (CPCD 8243-2)* **THE VERY BEST OF JERRY LEE LEWIS** [ ] [ ]

Feb 97. (cd) *Charly; (CPCD 8206)* **GREAT BALLS OF FIRE** [ ] [ ]

May 97. (cd/c) *A-Play; (10041-2/-4)* **IN CONCERT** [ ] [ ]

May 97. (cd) *Koch; (399538)* **JERRY LEE LEWIS** [ ] [ ]

Jan 98. (cd) *Summit; (SUMCD 4167)* **THE DEFINITIVE COLLECTION** [ ] [ ]

Aug 99. (cd) *Castle Pie; (PIESD 053)* **COUNTRY CONCERT** [ ] [ ]

Jan 00. (cd) *Platinum; (PLATCD 512)* **GREAT BALLS OF FIRE** [ ] [ ]

Jan 00. (cd) *Castle Pie; (PIESD 185)* **GREAT BALLS OF FIRE** [ ] [ ]

May 00. (cd) *Music; (CD 41001)* **THE SUN YEARS VOL.1** [ ] [ ]

Jun 00. (cd) *Warners; <(7599 26689-2)>* **ROCKIN' MY LIFE AWAY: THE JERRY LEE LEWIS COLLECTION** [ ] [ ]

Jul 00. (cd) *Spectrum; (554379-2)* **THE COUNTRY COLLECTION: THE VERY BEST OF JERRY LEE LEWIS** [ ] [ ]

Jul 00. (cd) *Music; (CD 41002)* **THE SUN YEARS VOL.2** [ ] [ ]

Jul 00. (cd) *Music; (CD 41003)* **THE SUN YEARS VOL.3** [ ] [ ]

Jul 00. (cd) *Spectrum; (554193-2)* **THE KILLER COLLECTION** [ ] [ ]

Jul 00. (cd) *Spectrum; (554765-2)* **THE KILLER VOL.3: 1973-1977** [ ] [ ]

Feb 01. (cd) *EMI Plus; (5760220)* **THE STORY** [ ] [ ]

Oct 01. (cd) *Disky; (GO 64017-2)* **GREAT BALLS OF FIRE** [ ] [ ]

Jul 02. (cd) *Stomper Time; (STCD 2)* **THAT BREATHLESS CAT** [ ] [ ]

Aug 02. (cd) *Beat Goes On; (BGOCD 561)* **SINGS THE COUNTRY MUSIC HALL OF FAME HITS VOL.1 & 2** [ ] [ ]

Sep 02. (4xcd-box) *Snapper; (SNAB 904CD)* **SUN ESSENTIALS**
Oct 02. (cd) *Raven; (RVCD 155)* **ANOTHER PLACE ANOTHER TIME / SHE EVEN WOKE ME UP TO SAY GOODBYE**
Jan 03. (cd) *King Biscuit; (KBCCD 106)* **IN CONCERT**
Mar 03. (d-cd) *Ember; (EMBCD 505)* **BY INVITATION ONLY** (live in Dalton, Ga., 31 December 1972)
Jun 03. (cd) *Charly; (SNAP 124CD)* **HEARTBREAK**
Jul 03. (d-cd) *Gemini; (22040130-2)* **ROCK RIGHT NOW WITH THE PIANO MAN**
Jul 03. (cd) *Rock'n'roll Heroes; (RR 001)* **ROCK'N'ROLL HERO**

the LIBERTINES

Formed: Bethnal Green, London, England ... 2001 by CARL BARAT, PETE DOHERTY, both of whom shared guitar and vocal duties, along with the rhythm section of JOHN HASSALL on bass guitar and GARY POWELL on drums. Having secured a deal with 'Rough Trade', the LIBERTINES arrived on the music scene in 2002 by way of their debut single 'WHAT A WASTER'. Instantly they were compared with other groups such as the STROKES, the WHITE STRIPES and the HIVES who were, jointly, seen as the frontrunners in an emerging garage rock scene. The group were quickly recognised as serious contenders with the release of another, assured, single 'I GET ALONG', almost immediately followed by the debut album 'UP THE BRACKET' (2002). A blend of aggressive, catchy, melodies that the JAM would be proud of and a scuzzy guitar sound not unlike the STOOGES, the band's first long player demanded that you pay attention. The entire album brims with confidence and attitude; however, 'BOYS IN THE BAND', 'TIME FOR HEROES', and, third single and title track, 'UP THE BRACKET' are particularly rousing. It is no coincidence that the album was produced by MICK JONES of the CLASH as like their punk classics 'London Calling' and 'Give 'Em Enough Rope' this was music for trouble makers. Summer 2003 saw some weird goings-on in the LIBERTINES camp as according to the tabloids PETE and CARL split the band into two factions. It was later revealed that PETE had actually been charged with burglary and that his victim was none other than bandmate CARL! Drug addict PETE plead guilty and was subsequently sentenced to six months in Wandsworth prison, although this was reduced to two after an appeal that led to him being released in October. Both CARL and PETE put the past behind them and reunited the band; the LIBERTINES had already chalked up another major UK hit via 'DON'T LOOK BACK INTO THE SUN'. Making up for lost time, DOHERTY directed his surplus creativity into a couple of spring 2004 side-projects: a Top 10 single, 'FOR LOVERS', with poet WOLFMAN, and a limited-edition eponymous 7" under the banner of BABYSHAMBLES, an outfit which was to become a future full-time concern. Later that summer, as PETE dropped in and out of court and rehab clinics (including a botched stint at Thailand's famous Thamkrabok monastery), the likely lads released what was to be the LIBERTINES' epitaph, and what an epitaph: an eponymous, iconic trawl through the crumbling DOHERTY-BARAT dynamic, buoyed by the huge success of the candid 'CAN'T STAND ME NOW'. While the strength of its generation-defining songwriting might've gotten it there anyway, the album's chart-topping achievements weren't exactly hindered by the tabloid feeding frenzy. BARAT had already tired of DOHERTY's unreliability however, recruiting ANTHONY ROSSOMANDO as a tour/festival fill-in; DOHERTY for his part, couldn't even regularly turn up for his BABYSHAMBLES engagements. The latter had become his principle day/night job, scoring their first Top 10 with the twisted post-millennial wordplay of 'KILLAMANGIRO'. Ex-CLASH man MICK JONES bravely took on production duties for an album as the wildly erratic frontman courted controversy by the day: seemingly endless drug-related brushes with the law and the media painted DOHERTY as the proverbial accident waiting to happen, an increasingly tragic figure with the needle and the damage already done. Nor did a shambolic duet (Marc Bolan's 'Children Of The Revolution') with Sir ELTON JOHN in the media glare of Live8 help his cause. While BABYSHAMBLES did eventually manage to get some product on the market, and the single 'FUCK FOREVER' made the Top 5, the delayed 'DOWN IN ALBION' finally surfaced towards the end of 2005. Bigger news than the album's disappointment was PETE's papparazzi-frenzied relationship with supermodel Kate Moss. Amid further class-A drug revelations, court appearances and general career threatening rumours, the couple split the following year. With DOHERTY in creative freefall, it was left to CARL BARAT to carry on the spirit of the LIBERTINES via his new ensemble DIRTY PRETTY THINGS, alongside DIDZ HAMMOND, GARY POWELL and the aforementioned ROSSOMANDO. Signed to the resurgent 'Vertigo' imprint, the quartet released a controversy-free single, 'BANG BANG, YOU'RE DEAD' and album 'WATERLOO TO ANYWHERE' in spring 2006.

Album rating: UP THE BRACKET (*7) / THE LIBERTINES (*8) / BabyShambles: DOWN IN ALBION (*5) / Dirty Pretty Things: WATERLOO TO ANYWHERE (*6)

CARL BARAT (b. 6 Jun'78) – vocals, lead guitar / **PETE DOHERTY** (b.12 Mar'79) – vocals, rhythm guitar / **JOHN HASSALL** (b.17 Feb'81) – bass / **GARY POWELL** – drums

Rough Trade Sanctuary

Jun 02. (7") *(RTRADES 054)* **WHAT A WASTER. / I GET ALONG** 37 –
(cd-s+=) *(RTRADESCD 054)* – Mayday.
Sep 02. (7") *(RTRADES 064)* **UP THE BRACKET. / BOYS IN THE BAND** 29 –
(cd-s+=) *(RTRADESCD 064)* – Skag & bone man.
(cd-s) *(RTRADESCD 064X)* – ('A') / The Delaney / Plan A.
Oct 02. (cd/lp) *(RTRADE CD/LP 065)* *<83213>* **UP THE BRACKET** 35
– Vertigo / Death on the stairs / Horror show / Time for heroes / Boys in the band / Radio America / Up the bracket / Tell the king / The boy looked at Johnny / Begging / The good old days / I get along. *<US cd+=>* – What a waster / Mayday. *(re-iss. cd Sep03 w/dvd+=; RETRADECD 065)* – Up the bracket (video) / Time for heroes (video) / I get along (video).
Jan 03. (7") *(RTRADES 074)* **TIME FOR HEROES. / 7 DEADLY SINS** 20 –
(cd-s+=) *(RTRADESCD 074)* – ('A') / General smuts / Bangkok.
(cd-s) *(RTRADESCD 074X)* – ('A') / Mr Finnegan / Sally Brown.
Aug 03. (7") *(RTRADES 119)* **DON'T LOOK BACK INTO THE SUN. / DEATH ON THE STAIRS** 11 –
(cd-s+=) *(RTRADESCD 119)* – Tell the king (original version).
(cd-s) *(RTRADESCDS 120)* – ('A') / Skint and minted / Mockingbird.

— in Apr'04, PETE DOHERTY was credited on WOLFMAN's (aka PETER WOLFE) UK No.7 hit single, 'For Lovers' on 'Rough Trade' *(RTRADS/+CD 177)*

Rough Trade Rough Trad

Aug 04. (7") *(RTRADS 163)* **CAN'T STAND ME NOW. / (I'VE GOT) SWEETS** 2
(cd-s) *(RTRADSCD 163)* – ('A') / Never never.
(cd-s) *(RTRADSCDX 163)* *<06076-83254-2>* – ('A') / Cyclops / Dilly boys / ('A'-video).
(cd-s) *<06076 83255-2>* – ('A') / Never never / All at sea.
Aug 04. (cd/lp) *(RTRAD CD/LPX 166)* *<83250-2>* **THE LIBERTINES** 1
– Can't stand me now / Last post on the bugle / Don't be shy / The man who would be king / Music when the lights go out / Narcissist / The ha ha wall / Arbeit macht frei / Campaign of hate / What Katie did / Tomblands / The saga / Road to ruin / What became of the likely lads.
Oct 04. (7") *(RTRADS 215)* **WHAT BECAME OF THE LIKELY LADS. / BOYS IN THE BAND (live in Brixton)** 9 Feb05
(cd-s) *(RTRADSCD 215)* – ('A') / The Delaney (live Brixton).
(cd-s) *(RTRADSCDX 215)* – ('A') / Skag & bone man (live Brixton) / Time for heroes (live Brixton).
(cd-ep++=) *<RTA 30051-2>* – Don't look back into the sun.

The LIBERTINES

— the LIBERTINES had already started touring without DOHERTY (festival fill-in:- **ANTHONY ROSSOMANDO**)

BABYSHAMBLES

PETE DOHERTY – vocals, guitar / **PATRICK WALDEN** (b. 5 Oct'78) – guitar / **DREW McCONNELL** (b.10 Nov'78, Dublin, Ireland) – bass / **GEMMA CLARKE** – drums (of SUFFRAJETS)

High Society | not iss.

Apr 04. (ltd-7") *(HS7IN 011)* **BABYSHAMBLES. / FLOPHOUSE** [ ] [–]

Rough Trade | not iss.

Nov 04. (7") *(RTRADS 201)* **KILLAMANGIRO. / THE MAN WHO CAME TO STAY** [8] [–]
(cd-s+=) *(RTRADSCD 201)* – ('A'-video).

— **ADAM FICEK** – drums; repl. GEMMA

Aug 05. (7") *(RTRADS 210)* **F*CK FOREVER. / BLACK BOY LANE** [4] [–]
(cd-s) *(RTRADSCD 210)* – ('A') / Monkey casino.
(cd-s) *(RTRADSCDX 210)* – ('A') / East of Eden / Babyshambles / ('A'-video).

— in Oct'05, PETER DOHERTY was credited on LITTL'ANS' UK No.22 hit single, 'Their Way', on 'Rough Trade' *(RTRADS/+CD 367)*

Nov 05. (cd/d-lp) *(RTRAD CD/LP 240)* **DOWN IN ALBION** [10] [–]
– La belle et la bete / Fuck forever / A'rebours / The 32 of December / Pipedown / Sticks & stones / Killamangiro / 8 dead boys / In love with a feeling / Pentonville / What Katy did next / Albion / Back from the dead / Loyalty song / Up the morning / Merry go round.

Nov 05. (cd-s) *(RTRADSCD 260)* **ALBION / DO YOU KNOW ME** [8] [–]
(cd-s) *(RTRADSCDX 260)* – ('A') / Clementine / Why did you break my heart / ('A'-video) / ('A'-acoustic video footage).

DIRTY PRETTY THINGS

CARL BARAT – vocals, lead guitar / **ANTHONY ROSSOMANDO** (b. Hamden, Connecticut, USA) – guitar, vocals (of DAMN PERSONALS) / **DIDZ HAMMOND** (b. DAVID JONATHAN HAMMOND, 19 Jul'81) – bass, vocals (ex-COOPER TEMPLE CLAUSE) / **GARY POWELL** – drums

Vertigo | Universal

Apr 06. (7") *(9854374)* **BANG BANG YOU'RE DEAD. / WONDERING (acoustic)** [5] [–]
(cd-s) *(9854376)* – ('A') / Gin and milk (acoustic) / If you were wondering (tavern version).
(dvd-s) *(9854378)* – ('A'-video) / ('A'-documentary) / ('A'-Paris clip).

May 06. (cd)(lp) *(9853266)(9856133)* *<87898>* **WATERLOO TO ANYWHERE** [3] [ ]
– Deadwood / Doctors and dealers / Bang bang you're dead / Blood thirsty bastards / Gentry cove / Gin and milk / Enemy / If you love a woman / You fucking love it / Wondering / Last of the small town playboys / B.U.R.M.A. *(lp w/free 7")* – BANG BANG YOU'RE DEAD (acoustic). / B.U.R.M.A. *(ltd-cd w/dvd+=; 9856134)* – (DVD tracks).

LIMP BIZKIT

Formed: Jacksonville, Florida, USA ... 1994 by FRED DURST, WES BORLAND, SAM RIVERS, JOHN OTTO and DJ LETHAL, the latter snatched from the recently defunct, HOUSE OF PAIN. Drawing inevitable comparisons to KORN and RAGE AGAINST THE MACHINE, the band thrust their bass-chunky metal funk/rap into the melting pot of 90's rock with favourable results. Of a generally more sprightly disposition than the aforementioned bands, this goatee-bearded fly-shaded posse released their 'Interscope' debut, 'THREE DOLLAR BILL, Y'ALL$' in the summer of '97. Not content with BIZKIT's minor breakthrough, DURST also guested for COLD, SOULFLY and KORN on their early 1998 sets. With METHOD MAN from WU-TANG CLAN (on the track, 'N 2 GETHER NOW') and a celebrity feast of stars courtesy of KORN, STONE TEMPLE PILOTS and PRIMUS all on show, how could their follow-up album, 'SIGNIFICANT OTHER', fail. In fact, its MTV-friendly hardcore rap was all the rage with trendy young teenagers who helped it get all the way to No.1 on its first week of release. However, the more discerning Brit was not quite convinced (it only reached No.26). The new millennium got off to a flyer via a $2 million deal with Napster which was soon followed by a breakthrough Top 3 single in the UK, 'TAKE A LOOK AROUND' (the theme to 'MI:2'). Better still was when their 3rd set, 'CHOCOLATE STARFISH AND THE HOT DOG FLAVORED WATER' smashed in at No.1 in the US charts that Autumn; it finally reached peak spot in Britain after the 'ROLLIN' single did the same. In the unlikely event that you hadn't had your fill of LIMP BIZKIT's one dimensional rap-metal, 'NEW OLD SONGS' (2001) offered up remixes from the likes of TIMBALAND and DJ PREMIER. Just prior to this (October 2001), WES BORLAND had opted to bail out from the band. His departure had a resounding effect on the band as the long awaited 'RESULTS MAY VARY' (2003) testified. Having recorded and scrapped sessions more than once, DURST and Co (with newcomer MIKE SMITH) finally released an unfocused, creatively bankrupt set of songs – only Top 3 in US – which actually varied very little in their sheer monotony, notable only for the frontman's incoherent, vitriolic lyrical outbursts. Then there was the self-pity, poured into a cover of the Who's 'BEHIND BLUE EYES', a UK Top 20 hit later in the year. With BORLAND back in the BIZKIT tin for the following summer, DURST and Co got political with mini-set, 'THE UNQUESTIONABLE TRUTH (PART 1)' (2005), although the hard truth was dismissive reviews and an ailing chart profile. The album's underwhelming performance was the cue for a hastily released 'GREATEST HITZ', just in time for Xmazzz, with hellfireside faves alongside stocking-filler covers of George Michael's 'FAITH' and a DURST-ing down of Motley Crue chestnut 'HOME SWEET HOME' and the Verve's 'BITTERSWEET SYMPHONY' – in the same song . . .

Album rating: THREE DOLLAR BILL, Y'ALL$ (*7) / SIGNIFICANT OTHER (*5) / CHOCOLATE STARFISH AND THE HOT DOG FLAVORED WATER (*7) / NEW OLD SONGS (*5) / RESULTS MAY VARY (*4) / THE UNQUESTIONABLE TRUTH (PART 1) mini (*5) / GREATEST HITZ compilation (*7)

FRED DURST (b. WILLIAM FREDERICK DURST, 20 Aug'70) – vocals / **WES BORLAND** (b. WESLEY LOUDEN BORLAND, 7 Feb'75, Richmond, Virginia, USA) – guitar / **SAM RIVERS** (b. 2 Sep'77) – bass / **JOHN OTTO** (b.22 Mar'77) – drums / **DJ LETHAL** (b. LEOR DiMANT, 18 Dec'72, Latvia) – turntables (ex-HOUSE OF PAIN)

not iss. | Flip

Jun 96. (c-s) *<24894>* **COUNTERFEIT / POLLUTION / STUCK** [–] [ ]

Interscope | Interscope

Jul 97. (cd) *<(IND 90124)>* **THREE DOLLAR BILL, Y'ALL$** [ ] [22]
– Intro / Pollution / Counterfeit / Stuck / Nobody loves me / Sour / Stalemate / Clunk / Faith / Stinkfinger / Indigo flow / Leech / Everything. *(hit UK No.68 in Aug00 & No.50 in Jun01)*

Jul 99. (cd/c/d-lp) *(IND/INC/INT2 90335)* *<490335>* **SIGNIFICANT OTHER** [26] [1]
– Intro / Jusy like this / Nookie / Break stuff / Re-arranged / I'm broke / Nobody like you / Don't go off wandering / 9 teen 90 nine / N 2 gether now / Trust? / No sex / Show me what you got / A lesson learned / Outro. *(cd re-iss. Sep00+=; 490788-2)* – Re-arranged (live) / Nookie (live) / N 2 gether now / Break stuff (video).

Jul 99. (cd-s) *<497139-2>* **NOOKIE / COUNTERFEIT / COUNTERFEIT (mix)** [–] [80]

Nov 99. (c-s/cd-s; as LIMP BIZKIT featuring METHOD MAN) *<497183>* **N 2 GETHER NOW** [–] [73]

Nov 99. (cd-s) *<497138-2>* **RE-ARRANGED / FAITH** [–] [88]

Apr 00. (cd-s) *<497309-2>* **BREAK STUFF / CRUSHED / N 2 GETHER** [–] [ ]

Jul 00. (cd-s) *(497368-2)* **TAKE A LOOK AROUND (THEME FROM M:I-2) / FAITH** [3] [–]
(cd-s) *(497369-2)* – ('A'side) / N 2 gether now (live) / Break stuff (CD-Rom video) / ('A'-CD-Rom video).

Oct 00. (cd/d-lp) *(490770-2)* *<490759>* **CHOCOLATE STARFISH AND THE HOT DOG FLAVORED WATER** [1] [1]
– Intro / Hot dog / My generation / Full nelson / My way / Rollin' (air raid vehicle) / Livin' it up / One / Getcha groove on / Take a look around / It'll

be ok / Boiler / Hold on / Rollin' (urban assault vehicle) / Outro. *(special d-cd+=; 490793-2)* – Crushed / Faith / Counterfeit (Lethal Dose mix) / Faith (video) / Nookie (video) / Re-arranged (video) / N2 gether now (video).

Oct 00. (7"pic-d) *(497447-7)* **MY GENERATION. / IT'S LIKE THAT Y'ALL** 15 –
(cd-s+=) *(497447-2)* – Snake in your face.
(cd-s) *(497448-2)* – ('A'side) / Back on da bus / My generation (US mix) / My generation (video).

Jan 01. (c-s) *(INC 97474)* *<radio play>* **ROLLIN' (AIR RAID VEHICLE) / ROLLIN' (URBAN ASSAULT VEHICLE)** 1 Oct00 65
(cd-s+=) *(IND 97474)* – Take a look around (live) / My generation (live) / ('A'-CD-ROM).

— also in early 2001, FRED DURST teamed up with AARON LEWIS of STAIND to have a US hit single, 'OUTSIDE'

Jun 01. (c-s) *(497574-4)* *<radio play>* **MY WAY / ROLLIN' (Air Raid Vehicle remix)** 6 75
(cd-s) *(497573-2)* – ('A'side) / ('A'-William Orbit mix) / ('A'-DJ Premier remix).
(cd-s) *(497574-2)* – ('A'side) / ('A'-Dub Pistols remix) / ('A'-Dancehall dub remix) / ('A'-Dub Pistols remix instrumental).

Oct 01. (cd-s) *(497636-2)* **BOILER / FAITH / MY WAY (P Diddy remix) / BOILER (video)** 18

— WES BORLAND was now no longer a member

Dec 01. (cd/d-lp) *<(493192-2/-1)>* **NEW OLD SONGS** (remixes) 26
– Nookie – for the nookie / Take a look around (Timbaland) / Break stuff (DJ Lethal mix) / My way (P Diddy mix) / Crushed (Bosko mix) / N2gether now (all in together now) / Rearranged (Timbaland mix) / Getcha groove on (DJ Premier dirt road mix) (with XZIBIT) / Faith – Fame (mix) / My way (DJ Lethal mix) / Nookie (Androids vs. Las Putas mix) / Counterfeit (Lethal Dose extreme guitar mix) / Rollin' (DJ Monk vs. The Track Mack mix). *(cd+=)* – My way (DJ Premier mix) / My way (William Orbit mix) / My way (Dub Pistols dancehall mix).

— added **MIKE SMITH** – guitar (ex-SNOT)

Sep 03. (7") *(9811758)* **EAT YOU ALIVE. / SHOT** 10
(cd-s+=) *(9811757)* *<11013>* – Just drop dead / ('A'-video).

Sep 03. (cd) *(9860971)* *<12350-2>* **RESULTS MAY VARY** 7 3
– Re entry / Eat you alive / Gimme the mic / Underneath the gun / Down another day / Almost over / Build a bridge / Red light – green light / The only one / Let me down / Lonely world / Phenomenon / Creamer (radio is dead) / Behind blue eyes / Drown. *(UK+=)* – Let it go.

Nov 03. (7") *(9814743)* *<radio>* **BEHIND BLUE EYES. / JUST DROP DEAD** 18 71
(cd-s+=) *(9814744)* – Rollin' (DJ Monk-vs-The track Mack remix) / ('A'-video).

— **WES BORLAND** returned to repl. SMITH

Geffen Geffen

May 05. (m-cd) *(9882180)* **THE UNQUESTIONABLE TRUTH (PART 1)** 71 24
– The propaganda / The truth / The priest / The key / The channel / The story / The surrender.

Nov 05. (cd) *(9887830)* *<5631>* **GREATEST HITZ** (compilation) 47
– Counterfeit / Faith / Nookie / Break stuff / Re-arranged / N 2 gether now / Take a look around / My generation / Rollin' (air raid vehicle) / My way / Boiler / Eat you alive / Behind blue eyes / Build a bridge / Why / Lean on me / Home sweet home – Bittersweet symphony.

LINKIN PARK

Formed: Los Angeles, California, USA ... 1999 as HYBRID THEORY by high school friends BRAD DELSON, MIKE SHINODA and ROB BOURDON together with JOSEPH HAHN and CHESTER BENNINGTON. Influenced by the likes of NINE INCH NAILS, APHEX TWIN and the ROOTS, LINKIN PARK are yet another act to muscle in on the heavily saturated rap-metal market. Offered a publishing deal after their very first gig at L.A.'s Whisky, the band subsequently signed with 'Warners' for their debut album, '[HYBRID THEORY]' (2000). While admittedly pretty fly for white guys, LINKIN PARK, like most bands of their ilk, possess neither the fluid funk of the 'CHILI PEPPERS nor the wiry conviction of RATM. Remix set, '[REANIMATION]' (2002), found a posse of rappers, producers and DJ's making brave attempts at sprucing up tracks from the band's debut. Makeovers from the likes of PHAROAH MONCH and ALCHEMIST certainly improved on the originals although that wasn't exactly difficult. In fact, the LINKIN lads could've done with similar treatment on 'METEORA' (2003), where it was back to lumpen nu-metal business for the masses. There was little discernible creative progress from the debut but it was admittedly slick and professional enough to rely on cruise control, something which couldn't be said for 'LIVE IN TEXAS' (2003) which perhaps showed up more of the LP's non-studio shortcomings than they might've liked. In an age of collaborative madness (officially sanctioned or otherwise), LINKIN PARK became the latest metal rappers to splice their songs with a hip-hop luminary, JAY-Z. 'COLLISION COURSE' (2004) mashed its way to the top of the US charts, with 'NUMB / ENCORE' hybridising a path into the Top 20.

Album rating: [HYBRID THEORY] (*6) / [REANIMATION] (*5) / METEORA (*5) / LIVE IN TEXAS (*4) / COLLISION COURSE w/ Jay-Z (*6)

CHESTER BENNINGTON (b.20 Mar'76) – vocals (ex-GREY DAZE) **/ MIKE SHINODA** (b.11 Feb'77) – vocals/MC, sampling, keyboards, rhythm guitar / **BRAD DELSON** (b. BRADFORD, 1 Dec'77) – guitar / **JOSEPH HAHN** (b.15 Mar'77, Glendale, Calif.) – DJ, vocals / **ROB BOURBON** (b.20 Jan'79, Calabasa, Calif.) – drums / with **SCOTT KOZIOL** – bass

Warners Warners

Oct 00. (cd) *<(9362 47755-2)>* **[HYBRID THEORY]** 4 Apr00 7
– Papercut / One step closer / With you / Points of authority / Crawling / Runaway / By myself / In the end / A place for my head / Forgotten / Cure for the itch / Pushing me away. *(lp-iss.Oct01; 9362 47755-1)*

— **PHOENIX** (b. DAVE FARRELL, 8 Feb'77, Plymouth, Mass.) – bass; repl. part-timer SCOTT

Jan 01. (10"/c-s) *(W 550 TE/MC)* *<radio play>* **ONE STEP CLOSER. / MY DECEMBER** 24 75
(cd-s+=) *(W 550CD)* – High voltage / ('A'-CD-ROM).

Apr 01. (c-s) *(W 556MC)* *<radio cut>* **CRAWLING / PAPERCUT (live)** 16 Aug01 79
(cd-s+=) *(W 556CD)* – (CD-Rom video footage).
(dvd-s) *(W 556DVD)* – ('A') / ('A'-live snippets).

Jun 01. (c-s) *(W 562C)* **PAPERCUT / POINTS OF AUTHORITY (live)** 14
(cd-s+=) *(W 562CD)* – Papercut (live).

Oct 01. (cd-s) *(W 569CD)* *<42411>* **IN THE END / A PLACE FOR MY HEAD (live) / STEP UP** 8 2
(cd-s) *(W 569CDX)* – ('A') / ('A'-live) / Points of authority (live).

Jul 02. (c-s; as LINKIN PARK & EVIDENCE featuring PHAROAHE MONCH & DJ BABU) *(W 588C)* *<24247>*
H! VLTG3 / PTS.OF.ATHRTY (with JAY GORDON) 9 Aug02
(cd-s+=) *(W 588CD)* – Buy myself (with MARILYN MANSON).

Jul 02. (cd/c) *<(9362 48326-2/-4)>* **[REANIMATION]** (remixes) 3 2
– (Opening) / Pts.of.athrty (with JAY GORDON) / Enth e nd (with KAMASTA KURT & MOTION MAN) / (Chali) / Frgt-10 (with CHALI 2NA & ALCHEMIST) / P5hng me a*wy (with STEPHEN RICHARDS) / Plc.4 mie haed (with AMP LIVE & ZION) / X-ecutioner style (with BLACK THOUGHT) / H! Vltg3 (with EVIDENCE featuring PHAROAHE MONCH & DJ BABU) / (Riff raff) / Wth you (with CHAIRMAN HAHN & ACEYALONE) / (Ntr-mssion) / Ppr: kut (with CHEAPSHOT & JUBACCA) / Rnw@y (with BACKYARD BANGERS & PHOENIX ORION) / My (with MICKEY P. & KELLI ALI) / (Stef) / By myslf (with JOSH ABRAHAM) / Kyur4 th ich (with CHAIRMAN HAHN) / 1 stp klosr (with HUMBLE BROTHERS & JONATHAN DAVIS) / Krwlng (with AARON LEWIS) / Untitled (dub).

Mar 03. (7") *(W 602)* *<radio>* **SOMEWHERE I BELONG. / STEP UP (live)** 10 32
(cd-s+=) *(W 602CD)* – My December (live).

Mar 03. (cd/lp) *<(9362 48443-2/48186-1)>* **METEORA** 1 1
– (Foreword) / Don't stay / Somewhere I belong / Lying from you / Hit the floor / Easier to run / Faint / Figure.09 / Breaking the habit / From the inside / Nobody's listening / Session / Numb. *<(cd w/dvd+=; 9362 48461-2)>* – (the making of Meteora).

Jun 03. (7"pic-d) *(W 610)* <16652> **FAINT. / LYING FROM YOU (live)** 15 Oct03 48
(cd-s+=) *(W 610CD1)* – Somewhere I belong (video).
(cd-s) *(W 610CD2)* – ('A') / One step closer (live) / ('A'-video).

Sep 03. (cd-s) *(W 622CD1)* **NUMB / FROM THE INSIDE (live) / NUMB (video)** 14 11
(cd-s) *(W 622CD2)* – ('A') / Easier to run (live) / Faint (video).

Nov 03. (cd) *<(9362 48638-2)>* **LIVE IN TEXAS** (live) 47 23
– Somewhere I belong / Lying from you / Papercut / Points of authority / Runaway / Faint / From the inside / Pushing me away / Numb / Crawling / In the end / One step closer.

Mar 04. (-) *<radio>* **LYING FROM YOU** – 58

Jun 04. (cd-s) *(W 645CD)* <42721> **BREAKING THE HABIT / CRAWLIN' (live) / ('A'-video)** 39 20

Nov 04. (cd-s; by JAY-Z – LINKIN PARK) *(W 660CD)* <916123> **NUMB – ENCORE / (instrumental)** 14 Mar05 20

Nov 04. (cd+dvd; by JAY-Z – LINKIN PARK) *<(9362 48966-2)>* **COLLISION COURSE** 15 1
– Dirt off your shoulder – Lying from you / Big pimpin' – Papercut / Jigga what – Faint / Numb – Encore / Izzo – In the end / Points of authority – 99 problems – One step closer. *(w/ DVD tracks).*

LITTLE FEAT

Formed: Los Angeles, California, USA ... late 1969 out of The FACTORY, by ex-ZAPPA cohorts LOWELL GEORGE and ROY ESTRADA, plus BILL PAYNE and RICHIE HAYWARD, both recent members of cult act The FRATERNITY OF MAN. Having all previously played together in the aforementioned outfits, the formation of LITTLE FEAT was more of a natural progression, GEORGE bailing out of ZAPPA's band after playing on 'Hot Rats' and 'Weasels Ripped My Flesh'. Signed to 'Warners' on the strength of three demo tracks ('WILLIN'', 'TRUCK STOP GIRL' and 'BRIDES OF JESUS'), the band began work on their eponymous debut with producer RUSS TITELMAN. Eventually surfacing in late 1970, 'LITTLE FEAT' announced the arrival of a major force in American music; the aforementioned 'WILLIN' was GEORGE's statement of intent, a much covered nugget that gave LITTLE FEAT more exposure than was ever afforded their overlooked debut. In its earliest incarnation, the song was a lean sliver of poor-boy country blues, GEORGE on resolutely unadorned vocal form with RY COODER carving out shards of wiry slide guitar. Just as raggedly affecting was 'TRUCK STOP GIRL'; closer in spirit to traditional country heartbreak than anything GEORGE would subsequently write, the song was given a wonderfully sympathetic reading by CLARENCE WHITE the same year on The BYRDS self-titled, half live/half studio opus. The 'FORTY FOUR BLUES/HOW MANY MORE YEARS' medley called to mind the mutant blues of CAPTAIN BEEFHEART while 'SNAKES ON EVERYTHING' and 'STRAWBERRY FLATS' were by turns, swaggering and shambling R&B. Though the record was met with ecstatic reviews, LITTLE FEAT didn't appear to be high on 'Warners' list of priorities, a bottom of the bill slot on a BEEFHEART/RY COODER double header more or less the only exposure the band were afforded. Returning to the studio, they cut 'SAILIN' SHOES' (1972), an album that more successfully melted LITTLE FEAT's eclectic Americana into a rich, gumbo stew. 'WILLIN' had been lovingly refashioned into a work of resonant, almost transcendent beauty, embellished by wisps of pedal steel (courtesy of 'SNEAKY' PETE KLEINOW) and PAYNE's graceful piano. 'EASY TO SLIP' was as commercial as LITTLE FEAT got, and that was part of the problem, at least in terms of widespread commercial acceptance. There was a brilliantly gritty surreallism and warped humour to GEORGE's lyrics at odds with the prevailing Californian decadence of The EAGLES/DOOBIE BROTHERS axis and the hippie utopianism of CROSBY, STILLS and NASH. This skewed vision of modern America's seedy underbelly also touched the music, the likes of 'TRIPE FACE BOOGIE' and 'TEENAGE NERVOUS BREAKDOWN' highly original, blistering slabs of rock'n'roll while the title track was a subversive slice of gospel blues. 'SAILIN' SHOES' was also the first record to feature the gaudy, surrealist artwork of NEON PARK, a regular fixture for the remainder of the band's career. Although the record again sold poorly and ROY ESTRADA left for CAPTAIN BEEFHEART's MAGIC BAND, LITTLE FEAT regrouped with extra members KENNEY GRADNEY, SAM CLAYTON (both from DELANEY & BONNIE) and PAUL BARRERE, entering the studio in late '72 to begin work on 'DIXIE CHICKEN' (1973). The pinnacle of LITTLE FEAT's career, this release represented the band's most consistent and complete body of work. Rooted in the swamp funk of New Orleans, the album was a swaggering, intoxicating masterpiece. LOWELL had developed into a frighteningly good slide player, his soaring, smoking runs interlocking with PAYNE's piano and CLAYTON's percussion to create a vibe that many have since tried and failed to imitate. The title track, 'TWO TRAINS' and 'FAT MAN IN THE BATHTUB' were anthemic stuff, BONNIE BRAMLETT and LOWELL's close friend BONNIE RAIT providing suitably soulful backing vocals. Elsewhere, LOWELL navigated a cover of ALLEN TOUSSAINT's 'ON YOUR WAY DOWN' with trenchant ease, his gilt-edged gravel/molasses vocals oozing class. The PAYNE/BARRERE-penned 'WALKIN' ALL NIGHT', meanwhile, strutted like a catwalk model. Sensual, sexy and insidiously funky, it remains a mystery why 'Warners' failed to make any commercial headway with 'DIXIE CHICKEN'. Subsequent low sales led to tension in the ranks and the band briefly split up. In the interim, GEORGE worked on ROBERT PALMER's 'Sneakin' Sally Through The Alley' and BONNIE RAITT's 'Takin' My Time' amongst other session work while PAYNE toured with labelmates, The DOOBIE BROTHERS. By May '74, the band were back together, ensconced in their Maryland studio and working on a fourth album, 'FEATS DON'T FAIL ME NOW' (1974). While the record gave them belated success, it marked a turning point in LITTLE FEAT's musical evolution. The opening salvo of 'ROCK AND ROLL DOCTOR' and 'OH ATLANTA' were skintight R&B numbers, entertaining but hardly possessed of the trademark LITTLE FEAT genius. The VAN DYKE PARKS-produced 'SPANISH MOON' was more like it, slinky and sexy with a louche, after-midnight feel. Elsewhere on the album, there was a worrying move towards jazz fusion noodling, PAYNE and BARRERE muscling in on the songwriting as GEORGE took a backseat. This was partly due to his belief in band deomcracy and increasingly due to his immersion in more hedonistic pleasures rendering the ever more girthsome GEORGE unable to exert full control over the band's direction. Ironically, just as LOWELL began to retreat, Warner Brothers began to show some support, sending the band on a European package tour with The DOOBIE BROTHERS, MONTROSE, TOWER OF POWER etc., early in 1975. The London show became the stuff of legend, GEORGE and Co. receiving a rapturous reception that lasted well into the DOOBIE's set. 'THE LAST RECORD ALBUM' (1975) confirmed the worst, however, PAYNE/BARRERE collaborations dominating proceedings. While the likes of 'ALL THAT YOU DREAM' was charming, its jazz-pop sound strayed far from the path of LITTLE FEAT's original vision. Of GEORGE's contributions, 'LONG DISTANCE LOVE' saw him at his bittersweet best while 'DOWN BELOW THE BORDERLINE' and 'MERCENARY TERRITORY' showed his songwriting had lost none of its bite. 'TIME LOVES A HERO' (1977) continued the descent into WEATHER REPORT territory while the double concert set, 'WAITING FOR COLUMBUS' (1978) was met with mixed reviews, revealing little of the fire and spark that marked the numerous live bootlegs on the market. GEORGE had already released his solo album, 'THANKS, I'LL EAT IT HERE' (1979) by the time the band embarked on recording sessions for 'DOWN ON THE FARM' (1979). By the time the latter had been completed, LOWELL had left the band completely although a number of his compositions featured, notably the lovely 'KOKOMO'. Bloated and tired, LOWELL's heart finally packed in on him that summer (29th June) while promoting his album. Tragically cut down in his prime (aged just 34), GEORGE may have suffered a typical rock'n'roll death, but he was no ordinary musician; revered by everyone from MICK JAGGER to JIMMY PAGE, the man was a one-off, a troubled genius whose music had the rare power to move hearts, minds and feet and whose ultimate potential will sadly never be realised. LITTLE FEAT was subsequently reformed in the mid-80's by ESTRADA, PAYNE and HAYWARD together with past collaborator FRED TACKET and CRAIG FULLER (ex-PURE PRAIRIE LEAGUE). The new-look 'FEAT released a string of listenable, if ultimately forgettable albums in 'LET IT ROLL' (1988), 'SHAKE ME UP' (1991) and 'AIN'T HAD ENOUGH FUN' (1995), succeeding in keeping the name alive if not exactly adding to the legacy. The addition of sandpaper-throated female vocalist SHAUN MURPHY lent 'UNDER THE RADAR' (1998) an extra dimension, with the likes of 'CALLING THE CHILDREN HOME' attempting to reprise the old New Orleans magic with at least some degree of success. 'CHINESE WORK SONGS' (2000) was another worthy if hardly essential chapter in the band's second coming, turning in a rootsy cover of Bob Dylan's 'IT TAKES A LOT TO LAUGH, IT TAKES A TRAIN TO CRY'. The latter was also performed in the raw on 2003's 'DOWN UPON THE SUWANNEE RIVER, an electric follow-up to the more intimate, acoustic-based 'LIVE AT THE RAMS HEAD' (2002), the latest archival release on their own 'Hot Tomato' label, and featuring the usual set list of 'FEAT classics and latter day material. 'KICKIN' IT AT THE BARN' (2003) was the first studio album to appear on the imprint, its title a reference to FRED TACKETT's home studio. Unusually, the veteran guitarist shared many of the songwriting credits on what was to be a blip among the slew of live releases, a schedule which continued with 'HIGHWIRE ACT LIVE IN ST. LOUIS 2003' (2004).

• **Covered:** HOW MANY MORE YEARS (Howlin' Wolf) / ON YOUR WAY DOWN (Allen Toussaint) / etc. LOWELL solo:- EASY MONEY (Rickie Lee Jones) / + a few more.

Album rating: LITTLE FEAT (*6) / SAILIN' SHOES (*8) / DIXIE CHICKEN (*9) / FEATS DON'T FAIL ME NOW (*8) / THE LAST RECORD ALBUM (*7) / TIME LOVES A HERO (*7) / WAITING FOR COLOMBUS (*6) / DOWN ON THE FARM (*5) / HOY-HOY collection (*7) / AS TIME GOES BY – THE BEST OF LITTLE FEAT compilation (*9) / LET IT ROLL (*5) / REPRESENTING THE MAMBO (*4) / SHAKE ME UP (*4) / AIN'T HAD ENOUGH FUN (*5) / LIVE FROM NEON PARK (*4) / UNDER THE RADAR (*5) / CHINESE WORK SONGS (*5) / LIVE AT THE RAMS HEAD (*5) / DOWN UPON THE SUWANNEE RIVER (*5) / KICKIN' IT AT THE BARN (*5) / HIGHWIRE ACT LIVE IN ST. LOUIS 2003 (*5) / Lowell George: THANKS, I'LL EAT IT HERE (*6)

LOWELL GEORGE (b.13 Apr'45) – vocals, guitar (ex-MOTHERS OF INVENTION/**ZAPPA) / ROY ESTRADA** (b. Santa Ana) – bass, vocals (ex-MOTHERS OF INVENTION/ZAPPA) / **BILL PAYNE** (b.12 Mar'49, Waco, Texas) – keyboards, vocals (ex-FRATERNITY OF MAN) / **RICHIE HAYWARD** – drums (ex-FRATERNITY OF MAN)

Warners Warners

May 70. (7") *<7431>* **STRAWBERRY FLATS. / HAMBURGER MIDNIGHT** [–] [ ]

Nov 70. (lp) *(K 46072) <1890>* **LITTLE FEAT** [ ] [ ]
– Snakes on everything / Strawberry flats / Truck stop girl / Brides of Jesus / Willin' / Hamburger midnight; (a) Forty four blues, (b) How many more years / Crack in your door / I've been the one / Takin' my time / Crazy Captain Gunboat Willie. *<(cd-iss. Dec93; 7599 27189-2)>*

May 72. (7") *<7553>* **EASY TO SLIP. / CAT FEVER** [–] [ ]

May 72. (lp) *(K 46156) <2600>* **SAILIN' SHOES** [ ] [ ]
– Easy to slip / Cold cold cold / Trouble / Tripe face boogie / Willin' / Apolitical blues / Sailin' shoes / Teenage nervous breakdown / Got no shadows / Cat fever / Texas rose cafe. *<(cd-iss. 1988; K2 46156)> <(cd re-iss. May95; 7599 27258-2)>*

— **KENNY GRADNEY** (b. New Orleans) – bass (ex-DELANEY AND BONNY) repl. ESTRADA who joined CAPTAIN BEEFHEART & HIS MAGIC BAND / added **PAUL BARRERE** (b. 3 Jul'48, Burbank, California) – guitar, vocals / **SAM CLAYTON** – congas / **BONNIE BRAMLETT** – guest vocals

Nov 72. (7") *<7689>* **DIXIE CHICKEN. / LAFAYETTE RAILROAD** [–] [ ]

Feb 73. (lp) *(K 46200) <2686>* **DIXIE CHICKEN** [ ] [ ]
– Dixie chicken / Two trains / Roll um easy / On your way down / Kiss it off / Fool yourself / Walkin' all night / Fat man in the bathtub / Juliette / Lafayette railroad. *(cd-iss. Jul88; K2 46200)*

— Band split for 6 months (Oct '73-May '74). BILL joined DOOBIE BROTHERS and others, mainly LOWELL went into sessions. The sextet re-formed May74

Jul 74. (7") *<8054>* **OH ATLANTA. / DOWN THE ROAD** [–] [ ]

Sep 74. (7") *<8091>* **SPANISH MOON. / DOWN THE ROAD** [–] [ ]

Sep 74. (lp) *(K 56030) <2784>* **FEATS DON'T FAIL ME NOW** [ ] [36]
– Rock and roll doctor / Cold cold cold / Tripe face boogie / The fan / Oh Atlanta / Skin it back / Down the road / Spanish moon / Down the road / Feats don't fail me now. *(cd-iss. Jan89; K2 56030)*

Feb 75. (7") *(K 16524)* **DIXIE CHICKEN. / OH ATLANTA** [ ] [–]

Nov 75. (lp/c) *(K/K4 56156) <3015>* **THE LAST RECORD ALBUM** [36] [36]
– Romance dance / All that you dream / Long distance love / Day or night / One love / Down below the borderline / Somebody's leavin' / Mercenary territory. *(cd-iss. Jul88; K2 56156)*

Feb 76. (7") *(K 16689)* **LONG DISTANCE LOVE. / ROMANCE DANCE** [ ] Oct75 [ ]

Feb 76. (7") *<8219>* **ALL THAT YOU DREAM. / ONE LOVE** [–] [ ]

May 77. (lp/c) *(K/K4 56349) <3140>* **TIME LOVES A HERO** [8] [34]
– Time loves a hero / Hi roller / New elhi freight train / Old folks boogie / Red streamliner / Keepin' up with the Joneses / Rocket in my pocket / Missin' you / Day at the dog races. *(cd-iss. Jul88; K2 56349)*

Jun 77. (7") *<8420>* **TIME LOVES A HERO. / SAILIN' SHOES** [–] [ ]

Jul 77. (7") *(K 16694)* **TIME LOVES A HERO. / ROCKET IN MY POCKET** [ ] [–]

Mar 78. (d-lp/d-c) *(K/K4 66075) <3140>* **WAITING FOR COLUMBUS (live)** [43] [18]
– Join the band / Fat man in the bathtub / All that you dream / Oh Atlanta / Old folks boogie / Time loves a hero / Day or night / Mercenary territory / Spanish moon / Dixie chicken / Tripe face boogie / Rocket in my pocket / Don't bogart that joint / Willin' / Apolitical blues / Sailin' shoes / Feats don't fail me now. *<(cd-iss. Dec93; 7599 2734-2)> <(d-cd-iss. Apr02 on 'Rhino'+=; 8122 78274-2)>* – One love stand / Rock & roll doctor / Skin it back / On your way down / Walkin' all night / Cold, cold, cold / Day at the dog races / Skin it back / Red streamliner / Teenage nervous breakdown.

Jul 78. (7") *<8566>* **WILLIN' (live). / OH ATLANTA (live)** [–] [ ]

Oct 79. (lp/c) *(K/K4 56667) <3345>* **DOWN ON THE FARM** [46] [29]
– Down on the farm / Six feet of snow / Perfect imperfection / Kokomo / Be one now / Straight from the heart / Front page news / Wake up dreaming / Feel the groove. *(cd-iss. Jul88; K2 56667)*

— They had by this time split (Apr'79). BARRERE and CLAYTON joined NICOLETTE LARSON. BARRERE went solo '83 and released 'ON MY OWN TWO FEET'. The others went into sessions.

LOWELL GEORGE

— - solo (vocals, guitar) with **FRED TACKETT** – guitar / **EDDIE ZIP** – keyboards,vocals / **PETER WASNER** – keyboards / **JERRY JUMONVILLE** – saxophone / **LEE THORNBERG** – trumpet / **MAXINE DIXON** – b. vocals / **ARMANDO COMPION** – bass / **DON HEFFINGTON** – drums

Warners Warners

Apr 79. (7") *<8847>* **WHAT DO YOU WANT THE GIRL TO DO. / 20 MILLION THINGS** [–] [ ]

Apr 79. (lp/c) *(K/K4 56487) <3194>* **THANKS, I'LL EAT IT HERE** [ ] [71]
– What do you want the girl to do / Honest man / Two trains / Can't stand the rain / Cheek to cheek / Easy money / 20 million things / Find a river / Himmler's ring. *(cd-iss. Dec93; 7599 26755-2)*

Jul 79. (7") *(K 17379)* **CHEEK TO CHEEK. / HONEST MAN** [ ] [–]

— Tragically LOWELL died 29th June '79 of a drug induced heart attack. He had gigged the night before. In 1983, PAUL BARRERE issued his debut album 'ON MY OWN TWO FEET' for 'Mirage'; *25-0093-1/-4)*

LITTLE FEAT

— re-formed 1988. (**BARRERE, PAYNE, HAYWARD & FRED TACKETT**) plus **CRAIG FULLER** – vocals (ex-PURE PRAIRIE LEAGUE) / **KENNY GRADNEY** – bass / **SAM CLAYTON** – percussion, vocals

Warners Warners

Jul 88. (lp/c)(cd) *(WX 192/+C)(925750-2)* <*25750*> **LET IT ROLL** 36
– Hate to lose your lovin' / One clear moment / Cajun girl / Hangin' on to the good times / Listen to your heart / Let it roll / Long time till I get over you / Business as usual / Changin' luck / Voices on the wind.

Jul 88. (7") <*27728*> **HATE TO LOSE YOUR LOVIN'. / CAJUN GIRL** –

Sep 88. (7") <*27684*> **ONE CLEAR MOMENT. / CHANGIN' LUCK** –

Apr 90. (cd/c/lp) <*(7599 26163-2/-4/-1)*> **REPRESENTING THE MAMBO** 45
– Texas twister / Daily grind / Representing the mambo / Woman in love / Rad gumbo / Teenage warrior / That's her, she's mine / Feelin's all gone / Those feet'll steer ya wrong sometimes / The ingenue / Silver screen.

Polydor Morgan Creek

Sep 91. (c-s) <*23005*> **SHAKE ME UP** –

Oct 91. (cd/c/lp) *(511310-2/-4/-1)* <*20005*> **SHAKE ME UP**
– Spider's blues (might need it sometime) / Shake me up / Things happen / Mojo haiku / Loved and lied to / Don't try so hard / Boom boy car / Fast & furious / Livin' on dreams / Clownin' / Down in flames.

Oct 91. (c-s) <*3007*> **THINGS HAPPEN** –

— **SHAUN MURPHY** – vocals; repl. FULLER

Zoo Zoo

Jun 95. (cd/c/lp) <*(72445 11097-2/-4/-1)*> **AIN'T HAD ENOUGH FUN**
– Drivin' blind / Blue jean blues / Cadillac hotel / Romance without finance / Big bang theory / Cajun rage / Heaven's where you find it / Borderline blues / All that you can stand / Rock & roll every night / Shakeytown / Ain't had enough fun / That's a pretty good love.

Jun 96. (d-cd) <*11129*> **LIVE FROM NEON PARK (live)** –
– (introductions) / Two trains / Spanish moon – Skin it back / Rock & roll every night / Down on the farm / Willin' / Hate to lose / Can't be satisfied – They're red hot / Cadillac hotel / Changin' luck / You're taking up another man's place / Oh, Atlanta / Texas twister / Fat man in the bathtub / Representing the mambo / Long distance love / Rad gumbo / Dixie chicken / Feats don't fail me now / Sailin' shoes / Let it roll – High roller.

S.P.V. C.M.C.

Aug 98. (cd) *(SPV 0852924-2)* <*86253*> **UNDER THE RADAR** Jun98
– Home ground / Eden's wall / A distant thunder / Hoy hoy / Under the radar / Vale of tears / Loco motives / Ferocious morning / Voiceless territory (intro to Falling through the worlds) / Falling through the worlds / The blues don't tell it all / I got happiness / Calling the children home.

Jun 00. (cd) *(SPV 0857100-2)* <*607686295-2*> **CHINESE WORK SONGS**
– Rag mama rag / Evla / Bed of roses / Sample in a jar / Just another Sunday / Gimme a stone / Rio Esperenza / Tattoo heart / Marginal creatures / Chinese work songs / It takes a lot to laugh, it takes a train to cry.

Hot Tomato Hot Tomato

Nov 02. (d-cd) <*(HTR 0205)*> **LIVE AT THE RAMS HEAD** (live)
– Hate to lose your lovin' / Rocket in my pocket / Honest man / Oh, Atlanta / Calling the children home / Rag mama rag / Shake me up / Easy to slip – I know you rider / Bed of roses / One clear moment / Willin' / Gringo / Cajun rage / Cadillac hotel / Spanish moon / Skin it back / Hoy hoy / Let it roll / On your way down / Cajun girl / Feats don't fail me now.

Jan 03. (12"/cd-s) *S.P.V.;* <*293-9/-0*> **A DISTANT THUNDER / HOME GROUND** –

Sep 03. (d-cd) <*(HTR 0206)*> **DOWN UPON THE SUWANNEE RIVER** Jul03
– (introduction) / All that you dream / Spanish moon / Skin it back / Big bang theory / Bed of roses / Cajun girl / Sailin' shoes / Rag mama rag / Let it roll / Lafayette railroad / Dixie chicken / Tripe face boogie / It takes a lot to laugh, it takes a train to cry / Oh, Atlanta / Willin' / Fat man in the bathtub.

Nov 03. (cd) <*(HTR 0208)*> **KICKIN' IT AT THE BARN**
– Night on the town / Heaven forsaken / I'd be lyin' / Corazones y sombras / Walking as two / In a town like this / Fighting the mosquito wars / Stomp / Why don't it look like the way that it talk / I do what the telephone tells me to do / Bill's river blues.

Aug 04. (d-cd) <*(HTR 0210)*> **HIGHWIRE ACT LIVE IN ST. LOUIS 2003** (live) Apr04
– Time loves a hero / Day or night / Cadillac hotel / Spanish moon / Skin it back / Cajun girl / Night on the town / I'd be lyin' / The blues don't tell it all / Old folks' boogie / Oh, Atlanta / Dixie chicken / Tripe face boogie / Fat man in the bathtub / Let it roll / Willin' / Feats don't fail me now.

– compilations, etc. –

on 'Warners' unless otherwise mentioned

Oct 75. (d-lp) *(K 66038)* **TWO ORIGINALS OF LITTLE FEAT** –
– (LITTLE FEAT / DIXIE CHICKEN).

Aug 81. (d-lp/d-c) *(K/K4 66100)* <*3538*> **HOY-HOY!** (remixes of rare material) 76 39
– Rocket in my pocket / Rock and roll doctor / Skin it back / Easy to slip / Red streamliner / Lonesome whistle / Front page news / The fan / Forty-four blues: How many more years / Teenage nervous breakdown (live) / Framed / Strawberry flats / Gringo / Over the edge / Two trains / China white / All that you dream / Feats don't fail me now. <*(cd-iss. Jul02; WB 3538)*>

Aug 81. (7") <*49801*> **EASY TO SLIP. / FRONT PAGE NEWS** –

Oct 81. (7") <*49841*> **GRINGO. / STRAWBERRY FLATS** –

Aug 86. (lp/c)(cd) *(WX 36/+C)(240 863-2)* **THE BEST OF LITTLE FEAT – AS TIME GOES BY** –
– Dixie chicken / Willin' / Rock and roll doctor / Two trains *[cd-only *]* / Truck stop girl *[cd-only *]* / Fat man in the bathtub *[cd-only *]* / Trouble / Sailin' shoes / Spanish moon / Feats don't fail me now / Oh, Atlanta *[cd-only *]* / All that you dream / Long distance love / Mercenary territory / Rocket in my pocket *[cd-only *]* / Texas twister *[cd-only*]* / Let it roll *[cd-only *]* / Hate to lose your lovin' *[cd-only *]* / Old folks boogie / Twenty million things. *(cd re-iss. Aug93 * <US Feb94 *>; 9548 32247-2)*

Oct 00. (4xcd-box) *Rhino;* <*(8122 79912-2)*> **HOTCAKES & OUTTAKES** Sep00

Aug 01. (d-cd) *Burning Airlines; (PILOT 110)* **LATE NIGHT TRUCK STOP (live from Denver 1973)** –
(d-lp-iss.Nov02 on 'Fruit Tree'; FT 823)

Nov 01. (d-cd) *S.P.V.;* <*(31071180)*> **UNDER THE RADAR / CHINESE WORK SONGS**

Jul 02. (d-cd) *Hot Tomato;* <*(HTR 0203)*> **RAW TOMATOS: VOLUME ONE (live and rare)** Jun02

Jul 02. (d-cd) *Hot Tomato;* <*(HTR 0204)*> **RIPE TOMATOS: VOLUME ONE** (live and rare) Jun02

LITTLE RICHARD

Born: RICHARD WAYNE PENNIMAN, 5 Dec'35, Macon, Georgia, USA, raised in a large family by preacher parents who schooled him in the ways of gospel singing. Aged 16, the petite RICHARD was given the opportunity (through singer, BILLY WRIGHT) to record for 'RCA-Victor'. After four flop singles for the imprint, LITTLE RICHARD subsequently moved on to Don Robey's 'Peacock' label in 1953, where he sessioned for doo-wop group, The TEMPO-TOPPERS. After fronting The JOHNNY OTIS ORCHESTRA in 1955, the man signed a solo deal with 'Specialty'. His first single for the label, 'TUTTI FRUTTI', gave him his maiden entry into the US Top 20. Outrageously attired in flamboyant pink body-suits, this eccentric, clowning pioneer of rock'n'roll, was like nothing the white music establishment had ever encountered; in both his image and his hollering, tongue-in-cheek assault, the effeminate RICHARD borrowed nothing from his contemporaries. Over the course of the next few years, he flounced his way through a series of classic hits which would subsequently become standards:- 'LONG TALL SALLY', 'RIP IT UP', 'THE GIRL CAN'T HELP IT' (exposure from the rock'n'roll movie of the same name gave him yet another UK hit), 'LUCILLE', 'JENNY, JENNY', 'KEEP A KNOCKIN' and 'GOOD GOLLY, MISS MOLLY'. At the height of his fame, RICHARD was to publicly renounce his "evil" rock'n'roll music/lifestyle, reverting back to gospel and pledging his life to Jeeesus. In 1960, the now Rev. LITTLE RICHARD spent a couple of years under the production of QUINCY JONES, returning to rock'n'roll in 1964. Although he had a few minor hits, including 'BAMA LAMA BAMA LOO', his new material was overshadowed by British acts covering his earlier work. In the 70's, RICHARD released a few albums, while collaborating with the likes of CANNED HEAT and DELANEY & BONNIE, swinging back and fourth between rock'n'roll and God, homosexuality and heterosexuality. By the mid 80's, the veteran showman was back in the limelight when he took up the offer to appear in the movie, 'Down And Out In Beverly Hills'. From then on in, LITTLE RICHARD has successfully kept his profile high via guest spots in TV series including 'Miami Vice', while also fraternising with top named celebrities such as ELTON JOHN, TANYA TUCKER and er, KERMIT THE FROG!

Best CD compilation: 20 CLASSIC CUTS (*8)

LITTLE RICHARD – vocals, piano + sessions

not iss. | RCA Victor

1952. (7") <4392> **EVERY HOUR. / TAXI BLUES** – |

1952. (7") <4582> **GET RICH QUICK. / THINKIN' 'BOUT MY MOTHER** – |

1952. (7") <4772> **WHY DID YOU LEAVE. / AIN'T NOTHIN' HAPPENIN'** – |

1953. (7") <5025> **I BROUGHT IT ALL ON MYSELF. / PLEASE HAVE MERCY ON ME** – |

the TEMPO-TOPPERS featuring LITTLE RICHARD

not iss. | Peacock

1953. (7") <1616> **AIN'T THAT GOOD NEWS. / FOOL AT THE WHEEL** – |

1954. (7") <1628> **ALWAYS. / RICE, RED BEANS & TURNIP GREENS**

—— On the same label, he joined The JOHNNY OTIS BAND in 1955. They released 2

1955. (7") <1658> **LITTLE RICHARD BOOGIE. / DIRECTLY FROM MY HEART TO YOU** – |

1955. (7") <1673> **MAYBE I'M RIGHT. / I LOVE MY BABY** – |

LITTLE RICHARD

went solo again, backed by **RED TYLER** – saxophone / **LEE ALLEN** – saxophone / **FRANK FIELDS** – bass / **ERNEST McLEAN & JUSTIN ADAMS** – guitar / **EARL PALMER** – drums / plus pianists **HUEY SMITH, EDWARD FRANK, LITTLE BOOKER & SALVADOR DOUCHETTE.**

London | Specialty

Dec 55. (7") <561> **TUTTI FRUTTI. / I'M JUST A LONELY GUY** – | 17

Mar 56. (7") <572> **LONG TALL SALLY. / SLIPPIN' AND SLIDIN' (PEEPIN' AND HIDIN')** – | 6 | 33

Jul 56. (7",78) *(HLO 8336)* <579> **RIP IT UP. / READY TEDDY** 30 | 17 | 44

1956. (7") <584> **SHE'S GOT IT. / HEEBIE JEEBIES** – |

Jan 57. (7",78) *(HLO 8366)* **LONG TALL SALLY. / TUTTI FRUTTI** 3 | – | 29

Jan 57. (7") <591> **THE GIRL CAN'T HELP IT. / ALL AROUND THE WORLD** – | 49

Feb 57. (7",78) *(HLO 8382)* **SHE'S GOT IT. / THE GIRL CAN'T HELP IT** 15 | 9 | –

Jun 57. (7",78) *(HLO 8446)* <598> **LUCILLE. / SEND ME SOME LOVIN'** 10 | 21 | Mar57 54

Jul 57. (lp) *(HA-O 2055)* <2100> **HERE'S LITTLE RICHARD** | 13
– Tutti frutti / True fine mama / Ready Teddy / Baby / Slippin' and slidin' (peepin' and hidin') / Long tall Sally / Miss Ann / Oh why / Rip it up / Jenny, Jenny / She's got it / Can't believe you wanna leave. *(re-iss. Feb85 on 'Ace'; CH 128) (cd-iss. Jun89; CDCHM 128)*

Aug 57. (7",78) *(HLO 8470)* <606> **JENNY, JENNY. / MISS ANN** 11 | 14 | Jun57 56

Nov 57. (7",78) *(HLO 8509)* <611> **KEEP A KNOCKIN'. / CAN'T BELIEVE YOU WANNA LEAVE** 21 | Sep57 8

Feb 58. (7",78) <*HLU 8560*> <624> **GOOD GOLLY MISS MOLLY. / HEY HEY HEY HEY** 8 | 10

Jun 58. (7",78) *(HLO 8647)* <633> **OOH! MY SOUL. / TRUE FINE MAMA** 22 | 31 | 68

Dec 58. (7",78) *(HLU 8770)* <645> **BABY FACE. / I'LL NEVER YOU GO** 2 | Sep58 41

Dec 58. (lp) *(HA-U 2126)* <2103> **LITTLE RICHARD 2** |
– Keep a knocking / Send me some lovin' / I'll never let you go / All around the world / By the light of the silvery Moon / Good golly Miss Molly / Baby face / Hey hey hey hey / Ooh my soul / Lucille / The girl can't help it. *(re-iss. Feb85 on 'Ace'; CH 131) (cd-iss. Jul89; CDCHM 131)*

Jan 59. (7") <652> **SHE KNOWS HOW TO ROCK. / EARLY ONE MORNING** | –

Mar 59. (7") <660> **BY THE LIGHT OF THE SILVERY MOON. / WONDERING** – |

Mar 59. (7",78) *(HLU 8831)* **BY THE LIGHT OF THE SILVERY MOON. / EARLY ONE MORNING** 17 | –

May 59. (7",78) *(HLU 8868)* <664> **KANSAS CITY. / LONESOME AND BLUE** 26 | 95

1959. (lp) *(HA-U 2193)* <2104> **THE FABULOUS LITTLE RICHARD** |
– Shake a hand / Chicken little baby / All night long / Most I can offer / Lonesome and blue / Wonderin' / Whole lotta shakin' goin' on / She knows how to rock / Kansas City / Directly from my heart / Maybe I'm right / Early one morning / I'm just a lonely girl. *(re-iss. Jul80 on 'Sonet'; SNTF 5027) (re-iss. Feb85 on 'Ace'; CH 133) (cd-iss. Aug89; CDCHM 133) (cd re-iss. Aug91 on 'Ace'; CDFAB 001)*

1959. (7") <670> **SHAKE A HAND. / ALL NIGHT LONG** – |

1959. (7") <680> **WHOLE LOTTA SHAKIN' GOIN' ON. / MAYBE I'M RIGHT** – |

Feb 60. (7",78) *(HLU 9065)* <681> **BABY. / I GOT IT** | Dec 59

1960. (7") <686> **DIRECTLY FROM MY HEART. / THE MOST I CAN OFFER** – |

not iss. | Coral

1960. (7") <62366> **NEED HIM. / MILKY WHITE WAY** – |

Mercury | Mercury

1961. (7") *(AMT 1165)* <71884> **HE'S NOT JUST A SOLDIER. / JOY JOY JOY** |

1962. (7") <71911> **DO YOU CARE. / RIDE ON KING JESUS** – |

Sep 62. (7") *(AMT 1189)* <71965> **HE GOT WHAT HE WANTED. / WHY DON'T YOU CHANGE YOUR WAYS** 38 |

London | Woodman

Apr 63. (7") *(HLK 9708)* <2181> **CRYING IN THE CHAPEL. / HOLE IN THE WALL** |
(re-dist.US 1963 on 'Atlantic')

London | Atlantic

Jul 63. (7") *(HLK 9756)* <2192> **TRAVELLIN' SHOES. / IT IS NO SECRET** |

1964. (lp) *(LVA 9220)* <757446> **COMING HOME** |
– ust a closer walk with thee / Coming home / Search me Lord / I want Jesus to walk with me / Milky white way / Need him / Every time I feel the spirit / Does Jesus care / God is real / I'm trampin' / Jesus walked this lonesome valley / Precious Lord.

London | Specialty

Apr 64. (7") <692> **BAMA LAMA BAMA LOO. / ANNIE'S BACK** – | 82

May 64. (7") *(HL 9896)* **BAMA LAMA BAMA LOO. / KEEP A KNOCKIN'** 20 | –

Stateside | Vee-Jay

Sep 64. (7") *(SS 340)* <612> **WHOLE LOTTA SHAKIN' GOIN' ON. / GOODNIGHT IRENE** |

1964. (7") *(SON 5001)* <699>**POOR BOY PAUL. / WONDERIN'** – |
(UK-iss.1976 on 'Specialty')

Stateside | 20th Century

1964. (lp) *(SL 10054)* **LITTLE RICHARD SINGS GOSPEL** | –
– Every time I feel the spirit / I'm trampin' / Milky white way / Does Jesus care / Coming home / I know the Lord / I've just come from the fountain / God is real / Troubles of the world / Certainly Lord / Tell God my troubles / Precious Lord. *(re-iss. Jul82 on 'Bulldog')*

Mercury Mercury

Jan 65. (7") *(MF 841)* **PEACE IN THE VALLEY. / JOY JOY JOY**

Jan 65. (lp) *(MCL 20036)* **IT'S REAL**
– It's real / Joy, joy, joy / Do you care / The captain calls for you / In times like these / Do Lord, remember me / Ride on King Jesus / (There'll be) Peace in the valley (for me) / He's not just a soldier / My desire / He's my star / It takes everything to serve the Lord.

Fontana Vee-Jay

Jan 65. (7") *(H 519)* <625> **BLUEBERRY HILL. / CHERRY RED**

Feb 65. (lp) *(TL 5235)* <1107> **LITTLE RICHARD IS BACK!**
– A whole lotta shakin' goin' on / Going home tomorrow / Money honey / Only you ./ Hound dog / Goodnight Irene / Lawdy Miss Clawdy / Groovy little Suzy / Short Fat Fanny / Cherry red / Memories are made of this / Blueberry hill. *<re-iss Jul68 on 'Joy'; 100>*

Oct 65. (7") *(H 652)* <698> **I DON'T KNOW WHAT YOU'VE GOT BUT IT'S GOT ME. / (Part 2)** 92

Sue Vee-Jay

Feb 66. (7") *(SR 4001)* <665> **WITHOUT LOVE. / DANCE WHAT YOU WANNA**

Jul 66. (7") *(WI 4015)* <652> **CROSS OVER. / IT AIN'T WHAT'CHA DO**

Stateside Modern

May 66. (7") *(SS 508)* <1018> **HOLY MACKERAL. / BABY DON'T YOU WANT A MAN LIKE ME**

1966. (7") *<1019>* **DO YOU FEEL IT. / (Part 2)** –

1966. (7") *<1022>* **DIRECTLY FROM THE HEART. / I'M BACK** –

1966. (7") *<1043>* **BABY WHAT YOU WANT ME TO DO. / (Part 2)** –
<re-iss. Feb69 on 'Action'>

not iss. Kent

1966. (7") *<4567>* **IN THE NAME. / DON'T YOU KNOW I** –

Columbia Okeh

1966. (7") *(DB 7974)* *<7251>* **POOR DOG (WHO CAN'T WAG HIS TAIL). / WELL**

1966. (7") *(DB 8058)* *<7262>* **I NEED LOVE. / THE COMMANDMENTS OF LOVE**

Jan 67. (7") *(DB 8116)* **GET DOWN WITH IT. / ROSEMARY** –

Apr 67. (7") *(DB 8263)* *<7271>* **HURRY SUNDOWN. / I DON'T WANT TO DISCUSS IT** –

May 67. (lp) *(6136)* *<14117>* **THE EXPLOSIVE LITTLE RICHARD**
– I don't want to discuss it / Land of a 1000 dances / Commandments of love / Money / Poor dog / I need love / Never gonna let you go / Don't deceive me / Function at the junction / Well. *(cd-iss. Nov97 on 'Beat Goes On'; BGOCD 368)*

1967. (7") *<7278>* **DON'T DECEIVE ME (PLEASE DON'T GO). / NEVER GONNA LET YOU GO** –

Jul 67. (7") *(DB 8240)* **LITTLE BIT OF SOMETHING. / MONEY**

Aug 67. (lp) *<14121>* **LITTLE RICHARD'S GREATEST HITS (live)** –
<re-iss. Jul68 on 'Joy'; 100>

1967. (7") *<7325>* **LUCILLE. / WHOLE LOTTA SHAKIN' GOIN' ON** –

M.C.A. Brunswick

Mar 68. (7") *(MU 1006)* *<55362>* **TRY SOME OF MINE. / SHE'S TOGETHER** –

1968. (7") *<55377>* **TEAR MY CLOTHES. / STINGY JENNY** –

1968. (7") *<55386>* **SOUL TRAIN. / CAN I COUNT ON YOU** –

Reprise Reprise

Jun 70. (7") *(RS 20907)* *<0907>* **FREEDOM BLUES. / DEW DROP INN** 47

Aug 70. (7") *<0942>* **GREENWOOD MISSISSIPPI. / I SAW HER STANDING THERE** – 85

1970. (lp) *<(RSLP 6406)>* **THE RILL THING**
– Freedom blues / Greenwood, Mississippi / Two-time loser / Dew Drop Inn / Somebody saw you / Spreadin' Natta, what's the matter / The rill thing / Lovesick blues / I saw her standing there.

1971. (7") *<1005>* **SHAKE A HAND. / SOMEBODY SAW YOU** –

Nov 71. (lp) *(K 44156)* *<6462>* **THE KING OF ROCK AND ROLL**
– King of rock'n'roll / Joy to the world / Brown sugar / In the name / Dancing in the street / Midnight special / The way you do the things you do / Green power / I'm so lonesome I could die / Settin' the woods on fire / Born on the bayou. *(re-iss. Jul88 on 'Entertainers' lp/c; ENT LP/MC 13044) (cd-iss. same; ENTCD 264)*

Dec 71. (7") **SHAKE A HAND. / SOMEBODY SAW YOU** –

Feb 72. (7") *(K 14150)* *<1062>* **MONEY RUNNER. / MONEY IS**

1972. (7") *(K 14915)* **MOCKINGBIRD SALLY. / ROCKIN' ROCKIN' BOOGIE**

1972. (lp) *(K 44024)* *<2107>* **THE SECOND COMING**
– Mockingbird Sally / It ain't what you do, it's the way that you do it / The saints / Nuki Suki / Rockin' rockin' boogie / Prophet of peace / Thomasine / Sanctified, satisfied toe-tapper.

—— (Around this time, he teamed up with CANNED HEAT on lp, 'ROCKIN' WITH THE KING')

not iss. Green Mountain

1973. (7") *<413>* **IN THE MIDDLE OF THE NIGHT. / WHERE WILL I FIND A PLACE TO SLEEP THIS EVENING** –

Reprise not iss.

1974. (7"ep) *(K 14343)* **ROCKIN' ROLLIN' BOOGIE / KING OF THE ROCK'N'ROLL / SAINTS / MOCKINGBIRD SALLY** –

not iss. Atlantic

1976. (7") *<7007>* **CALL MY NAME. / STEAL MISS LIZA**

not iss. Mainstream

1979. (lp) **GOD'S BEAUTIFUL CITY** –

1980. (7") *<5572>* **TRY TO HELP YOUR BROTHER. / (part 2)**

—— next from the film, 'Down And Out In Beverly Hills'

M.C.A. M.C.A.

May 86. (7") *(MCA 1049)* *<52780>* **GREAT GOSH A'MIGHTY (IT'S A MATTER OF TIME). / THE RIDE** 62 Feb86 42
(12"+=) *(MCAT 1049)* – (movie theme).

W.E.A. Warners

Oct 86. (7"/12") *(YZ 89/+T)* **OPERATOR. / BIG HOUSE REUNION** 67

Oct 86. (lp/c)(cd) *(WX 72/+C)(242018-2)* *<42018>* **LIFETIME FRIEND**
– Great gosh a'mighty (it's a matter of time) / Operator / Somebody's comin' / Destruction / I found my way / The world can't do me / One ray of sunshine / Someone cares / Big house reunion.

Jan 87. (7") *(YZ 98)* **SOMEBODY'S COMIN'. / ONE RAY OF SUNSHINE**

Atco Atco

Nov 87. (7"pic-d/12"pic-d; LITTLE RICHARD & The BEACH BOYS) *(B 9392/+TP)* *<99392>* **HAPPY ENDING. / CALIFORNIA GIRLS**

—— collaborated with PHILIP BAILEY (Earth, Wind & Fire) on the the single, 'TWINS', which was from the film of the same name

not iss. Disney

1992. (cd/c) *<60849-2/-4>* **SHAKE IT ALL ABOUT** (childrens) –

– (selective) compilations, etc. –

1974. (lp) *Ember; (EMB 3434)* **FRIENDS FROM THE BEGINNING (with JIMI HENDRIX)** –
(cd-iss. Mar98; EMBCD 3434)

Jun 77. (7"m) *Creole; (CR 140)* **GOOD GOLLY MISS MOLLY. / RIP IT UP / BY THE LIGHT OF THE SILVERY MOON** 37 –

Oct 77. (lp) *Creole; (CRLP 510)* **LITTLE RICHARD – NOW** –
(cd-iss. Jun93 & Aug01 on 'Rhino'; RNCD 1007)

1980. (lp) *Charly; (CR 30190)* **GEORGIA PEACH** –

Dec 86. (lp) *Ace; (CH 195)* **20 CLASSIC CUTS** –
– Long tall Sally / Ready Teddy / The girl can't help it / Rip it up / Miss Ann / She's got it / Lucille / Keep a knockin' / Good golly Miss Molly / Send me some lovin' / Hey-hey-hey-hey / Slippin' and slidin' / Tutti frutti / Heeby jeebies / Baby face / Jenny Jenny / By the light of the silvery Moon / Ooh! my soul / True fine mama / Bama lama bama loo. *(re-iss. Jul90 +=; CDCH/CCH 195)* – Can't believe you leave / I'll never let you go.

Oct 89. (8xlp-box/6xc-box/6xcd-box) *Ace; (ABOX LP/MC/CD 1)* **THE SPECIALITY SESSIONS** –
(3xcd-box re-iss. Aug02 on 'Speciality'; 3SPCD 8508)

Jul 90. (cd) *Ace; (CDCHD 109)* **HIS GREATEST RECORDINGS**

Oct 90. (3xcd-box) *Ace; (ABOXCD 2)* **HERE'S LITTLE RICHARD / VOLUME 2 / THE FABULOUS LITTLE RICHARD**

Feb 93. (cd) *Charly; (CDCD 1014)* **THE WILDEST** – -

Mar 93. (cd) *See For Miles; (SEECD 366)* **THE E.P. COLLECTION** – -

Jun 95. (cd) *Collection; (COL 006)* **LITTLE RICHARD COLLECTION**

Oct 96. (cd) *Summit; (SUMCD 4019)* **THE VERY BEST OF LITTLE RICHARD** – -

May 97. (cd/c) *A-Play; (10154-2/-4)* **HITS COLLECTION** – -

Aug 01. (cd) *Ace; (CDCHM 729)* **THE ORIGINAL BRITISH HIT SINGLES**

Feb 01. (cd) *R.P.M.; (RPMSH 217)* **TALKING 'BOUT SOUL**

Jul 02. (d-cd) *Snapper; (SMDCD 413)* **ROCKIN' WITH THE GEORGIA PEACH**

Nov 02. (cd) *Repertoire; (REP 4876)* **THE BEST OF LITTLE RICHARD: KEEP A KNOCKIN'**

Nov 02. (cd) *Planet Media; (PML 1125)* **GOOD GOLLY MISS MOLLY** – -

Aug 03. (cd) *Castle Pulse; (PLS CD/MC 625)* **ROCKIN' WITH LITTLE RICHARD**

LL COOL J

Born: JAMES TODD SMITH, 14 Jan'68, Westchester County, New York, USA. From the age of four, young JAMES was beset by family troubles, culminating in the near-fatal shooting of his mother (and grandfather) by his father. When his mother finally met someone else, this would also prove abusive as LL was beaten consistently by his step-father. At 13 years of age, he began rapping as a way of counteracting these situations and through his working-class mother's finances he released a few demos. In the need to be cocksure from the start, L.(ADIES) L.(OVE) COOL J(AMES) was picked up by a young RICK RUBIN for his new 'Def Jam' label. Released in 1984, 'I NEED A BEAT' kickstarted not only the career of young JAMES but the 'Def Jam' empire, selling 100,000 copies and leading to L.L. prematurely abandoning his school career. Following up with the seminal B-Boy holler of 'I CAN'T LIVE WITHOUT MY RADIO', the rapper established himself as one of the key players in the new hip hop mafia alongside RUN D.M.C. and subsequently The BEASTIE BOYS. With RUBIN revving up L.L.'s solid arrangements via his trademark metal grind, 'RADIO' (1986) was the first in a string of groundbreaking 'Def Jam' albums, boasting such heavyweight knockouts as 'ROCK THE BELLS' alongside the first two singles. Live, L.L. could go twenty rounds with just about any other act on the scene, sleek with sweat from his gold-chained, bare-chested torso and stalking the stage like a panther. It came as something of a surprise, then, when L.L. played the sensitive, doomed romantic card with the rather limp ballad, 'I NEED LOVE' and although it broke him into both the UK Top 10 and the US Top 20, the track wasn't exactly representative of his street tough style. The accompanying concept album, 'BIGGER AND DEFFER' (1987) was also a bit of a disappointment to many, lacking the headstrong focus of the debut while the US Top 10 'WALKING WITH A PANTHER' (1989) alienated him from the more grassroots element of his fanbase with its overtly commercial sound, typified by the likes of 'I'M THAT TYPE OF GUY'. Its saving grace was the bizarre minimalism of 'GOING BACK TO CALI', a track featured on the 'Def Jam' soundtrack to cult film 'Less Than Zero' alongside metal acts like SLAYER and AEROSMITH. L.L.'s passport back to some kind of credibility came with the aid of veteran producer MARLEY MARL, the pair working together on the Grammy-winning 'MAMA SAID KNOCK YOU OUT' (1990), L.L.'s biggest selling and most consistently rounded release to date. In the early to mid 90's, COOL J again lost his way somewhat, taking vague aim at gangsta rap with '14 SHOTS TO THE DOME' (1993) and descending into self-parody and cliche with 'MR. SMITH' (1995). Ironically, it was via heavy metal, or rather heavy metal goons Beavis And Butt-Head ('. . . Do America'), that COOL J stormed his way back into the charts, collaborating with the gruesome twosome on a cover of CHAKA KHAN's 'AIN'T NOBODY'. The single was a UK No.1 in early '97, paving the way for L.L.'s re-invention as red-leather clad funk grinder on the brilliant 'PHENOMENON' single, another UK Top 10 later that year. Along with the likes of BUSTA RHYMES' scorching 'Put Your Hands Where My Eyes Can See', the track saw rap pared down to raw, minimalist funk, a visceral departure from the snooze-core, weed-obsessed hip hop of recent years. 'PHENOMENON' (1997) the album saw L.L. back in the US Top 10, back on form and working with some of the most respected artists in the game, including the aforementioned RHYMES, REDMAN and the WU TANG's METHOD MAN. His third decade in the business and the ladies were still loving cool James, at least going by the rap-meister's ever self regarding lyrics on 'G.O.A.T. FEATURING JAMES T. SMITH: THE GREATEST OF ALL TIME' (2000). Long winded as the title was, the record was basically another helping of occasionally tough talking, occasionally witty, often overtly sexual and almost always smooth and slick rap. Now in his 30's, LL shows no signs of growing old gracefully which, really, is something we should probably be thankful for. No surprise then that '10' (2002) was, incredibly perhaps, the man's tenth album of his career. While all the top name producers of the day showed their face, the record's half-hearted bluster and sweet talk served only to underline the fact that those halcyon recordings of the mid-80's are unlikely to be matched. Whether this was the case in 2004 via 11th set, 'THE DEFinition', the jury/critics remained unconvinced, although with the help of producer TIMBALAND and extras such as 7 AURELIUS, it still went Top 5 as did album opener, 'HUSH' (but only in Britain). 'TODD SMITH' (2006) – featuring everyone from JENNIFER LOPEZ to JAMIE FOXX – became another album that would secure massive sales in the US, but hardly anything outside the Hip-Hop world.

Album rating: RADIO (*7) / BIGGER AND DEFFER (*6) / WALKING WITH A PANTHER (*7) / MAMA SAID KNOCK YOU OUT (*8) / 14 SHOTS TO THE DOME (*5) / MR. SMITH (*6) / ALL WORLD: GREATEST HITS compilation (*8) / PHENOMENON (*5) / G.O.A.T. FEATURING JAMES T. SMITH THE GREATEST OF ALL TIME (*5) / 10 (*5) / THE DEFinition (*6) / TODD SMITH (*5)

L.L. COOL J – vocals (with various back-up)

Def Jam-CBS Def Jam

Jan 86. (7") *(A 6684)* **I CAN'T LIVE WITHOUT MY RADIO. / I CAN'T GIVE YOU MORE**
(12"+=) *(TA 6684)* – ('A'instrumental).

Feb 86. (lp/c) *(DEF/40 26745)* *<40239>* **RADIO** 71 Jan86 46
– I can't live without my radio / You can't dance / Dear Yvette / I can give you more / Dangerous / Rock the bells / I need a beat / You'll rock / I want you. *(cd-iss. Jul95; 527352-2)*

Mar 86. (7") *(A 7003)* **ROCK THE BELLS. / EL SHABAZZ**
(12"+=) *(TA 7003)* – ('A'original mix).
(d7"+=) *(DA 7003)* – I can't live without my radio / I can give you more.

Sep 86. (7") *(650113-7)* **I CAN'T LIVE WITHOUT MY RADIO. / ROCK THE BELLS**
(12"+=) *(650113-6)* – You'll rock / El shabazz.

Jun 87. (7") *(650856-7)* *<07120>* **I'M BAD. / GET DOWN** 71 May87 84
(12"+=) *(650856-6)* – Dangerous.
(7"pic-d) *(650856-8)* – ('A'side) / Rock the bells / I can't live without my radio.

Jun 87. (lp/c) *(450515-1/-4)* *<40793>* **BIGGER AND DEFFER** 54 3
– I'm bad / Get down / The Bristol hotel / The rhyme ain't done / 357 – Break it on down / Go cut creator go / Breakthrough / I need love / Ahh, let's get ill / The doo-wop / On the ill tip. *(cd-iss. 1991; 450515-2) (cd re-iss. Jul95; 527353-2)*

Aug 87. (7") *(651101-7) <07350>* **I NEED LOVE. / MY RHYME AIN'T DONE** 8 Jul87 14
(12"+=) *(651101-6)* – ('A'mixes).

Nov 87. (7"/7"pic-d) *(LLCJ/+P 1)* **GO CUT CREATOR GO. / I NEED LOVE** 66 –
(10"+=/12"+=/cd-s+=) *(LL CJQ/CJT/CD 1)* – The Bristol hotel / Kandy.

Feb 88. (7") *(LLCJ 2) <07679>* **GOING BACK TO CALI. / JACK THE RIPPER** 37 31
(10"+=/12"+=) *(LLCJ Q/T 2)* – I can't live without my radio.

May 89. (7"/c-s) *(LLCJ/+M 3) <68902>* **I'M THAT TYPE OF GUY. / IT GETS NO ROUGHER** 43 15
(12"+=) *(LLCJT 3)* – Rock the bells.
(cd-s+=) *(CDLLCJ 3)* – ('A'mixes).

Jun 89. (lp/c/cd) *(465112-1/-4/-2) <45172>* **WALKING WITH A PANTHER** 43 6
– Droppin' em / Smokin' dopin' / Fast peg / Clap your hands / Nitro / You're my heart / I'm that type of guy / Why do you think they call it dope? / It gets no rougher / Big ole butt / One shot at love / 1-900 LL Cool J / Two different worlds / Jealous / Jingling baby / Def jam in the motherland. *(cd+=)* – Going back to Cali / Crime stories. *(c++=)* – Change your ways / Jack the ripper. *(cd re-iss. Jul95; 527355-2)*

Sep 90. (c-s) *<73457>* **THE BOOMIN' SYSTEM / ('A'-Underground mix)** – 48

Oct 90. (cd/c/lp) *(467315-2/-4/-1) <46888>* **MAMA SAID KNOCK YOU OUT** 49 Sep90 16
– Boomin' system / Around the way girl / Eat 'em up L. Chill / Mr. Good bar / Murdergram (live at Rapmania) / Cheesy rat blues / Farmers boulevard (our anthem) / Mama said knock you out / Milky cereal / Jingling baby / To da break of dawn / 6 minutes of pleasure / Illegal search / Power of God. *(cd re-iss. Jul95; 523477-2) (cd re-iss. May00; 542428-2)*

Nov 90. (c-s) *<73609>* **AROUND THE WAY GIRL / ('A'remix)** – 9

Nov 90. (7") *(6564470-7)* **AROUND THE WAY GIRL. / MAMA SAID KNOCK YOU OUT** 41 –
(12"+=/cd-s+=) *(6564470-6/-2)* – ('A'mixes).
(re-iss. Mar91; hit UK No.36)

Apr 91. (c-s) *<73706>* **MAMA SAID KNOCK YOU OUT / ('A'-Hot mix)** – 17

Sep 91. (c-s) *<73820>* **6 MINUTES OF PLEASURE / EAT EM UP L CHILL** – 95

Mar 93. (7") *(659169-7) <74811>* **HOW I'M COMIN'. / BUCKIN 'EM DOWN** 37 57
(12"+=/cd-s+=) *(659169-6/-2)* – ('A'mixes).

Apr 93. (cd/c/lp) *(473678-2/-4/-1) <53325>* **14 SHOTS TO THE DOME** 74 5
– How I'm comin' / Buckin' em down / Stand by your man / Little somethin' / Pink cookies in a plastic bag getting crushed by buildings / Straight from Queens / Funkadelic relic / All we got left is the beat / (NFA) No frontin' allowed / Back seat / Soul survivor / Ain't no stoppin' this / Diggy down / Crossroads. *(cd re-iss. Jan96; 523488-2)*

Jun 93. (c-s) *<74984>* **BACK SEAT (OF MY JEEP) / PINK COOKIES IN A PLASTIC BAG GETTING CRUSHED BY BUILDINGS** – 42 96

Nov 95. (cd/c) *(529724-2/-4) <529583>* **MR. SMITH** – 20
– Make it hot / Hip hop / Hey lover (featuring BOYZ II MEN) / Doin' it / Life as / I shot ya / Mr. Smith / No aerplay / Loungin' / Hollis to Hollywood / God bless / Get the drop on 'em.

Jan 96. (c-s; LL COOL J featuring BOYZ II MEN) *(DEFMC 14) <577494>* **HEY LOVER / ('A'instrumental)** 17 Nov95 3
(12"+=/cd-s+=) *(12DEF/DEFCD 14)* – ('A'mix).
below featured guest vocals by LeSHAUN

May 96. (c-s) *(DEFMC 15) <576120>* **DOIN' IT / HEY LOVER (street version)** 15 Feb96 9
(12"+=/cd-s+=) *(12DEF/DEFCD 15)* – ('A'-unarmed mix) / Hey lover (street instrumental).

Sep 96. (c-s) *(DEFMC 30) <575062>* **LOUNGIN' / SUMMER LUV** 7 Jun96 3
(12"+=/cd-s+=) *(12DEF/DEFCD 30)* – ('A'-who do ya luv featuring TOTAL mix).

Nov 96. (cd/c/d-lp) *<(534125-2/-4/-1)>* **ALL WORLD: GREATEST HITS** (compilation) 23 –
– I can't live without my radio / Rock the bells / I'm bad / I need love / Going back to Cali / Jack the ripper / Jingling baby / Big ole butt / Boomin' system / Around the way girl / Mama said knock you out / Back seat / I need a beat / Doin' it / Loungin' (who do ya luv) / Hey lover (with BOYZ II MEN).

Jan 97. (c-s) *(GFSC 22195) <19410>* **AIN'T NOBODY / (track by Madd Head)** 1 Dec96 46
(12"+=/cd-s+=) *(GFST/+D 22195)* – ('A'mix).
(above on 'Geffen' & from the movie 'Beavis & Butt-Head Do America')

— in Apr'97, LL COOL J was one of a bunch of rap stars who featured on the UK Top 10 single, 'HIT EM HIGH (THE MONSTARS' ANTHEM)'

Oct 97. (cd/c/lp) *<(539186-2/-4/-1)>* **PHENOMENON** 37 7
– Phenomenon / Candy (with RALPH TRESVANT & RICKY BELL) / Starsky and Hutch (with BUSTA RHYMES) / Another dollar / Nobody can freak with you (with KEITH SWEAT & LeSHAUN) / Hot hot hot / 4,3,2,1 (with METHOD MAN, REDMAN, DMX, CANIBUS & MASTER P) / Wanna get paid (with LOST BOYZ) / Father / Don't be late don't come too soon (with TAMIA).

Oct 97. (c-s) *(568116-4) <568081>* **PHENOMENON / ('A'mix)** 9 56
(12"/cd-s) *(568117-1/-2)* – ('A'mix) / Wanna get paid / Mama said knock you out.

Dec 97. (cd-s; LL COOL J featuring METHOD MAN, REDMAN, DMX, CANIBUS & MASTER P) *<568321>* **4,3,2,1 /** – 75

Mar 98. (c-s) *(568117-4) <568332>* **FATHER / (instrumental)** 10 Jan98 18
(cd-s+=) *(568117-2) <568333>* – 4,3,2,1 (E-dub remix 6) (radio).

— In Jul'98, COOL J was credited on DR DRE's hit, 'Zoom'

— In Nov'98, he also appeared on 'Incredible' hit with KEITH MURRAY

Nov 99. (c-s/cd-s) *(W 512 C/CD)* **DEEPEST BLUEST (SHARK'S FIN) (mixes; album / instrumental / acappella)** – –
(above from the movie, 'Deep Blue Sea' + issued on 'Warners')

Jun 00. (cd-s) *<562827>* **IMAGINE THAT (mixes; radio / explicit / instrumental)** – 98

Sep 00. (cd) *(542997-2) <546819>* **G.O.A.T. FEATURING JAMES T. SMITH THE GREATEST OF ALL TIME** 29 1
– (intro) / Imagine that / Back where I belong / LL Cool J / Take it off / (skit) / Fuhgidabowdit / Farmers / This is us / Can't think / Hello / You and me / Homicide / U can't fuck with me / Queen is / The G.O.A.T.

— In Nov'01, LL COOL J was credited on the LUDACRIS hit, 'Fatty Girl'

Oct 02. (c-s) *(63872-4) <063956>* **LUV U BETTER / FA-HA** 7 Aug02 4
(12") *(63872-1)* – ('A'-instrumental).
(cd-s+=) *(63872-2)* – ('A'-video).

Oct 02. (cd) *<(63219-2)>* **10** 26 2
– (intro) / Born to love you / Luv U better / Paradise (with AMERIE) / Fa ha / Niggy nuts / Amazin' (with KANDICE LOVE) / Clockin' G's / Lollipop / After school (with P. DIDDY) / Throw ya L's up / U should / 10 million stars / Mirror mirror / Big mama (unconditional love) (with DRU HILL).

Feb 03. (c-s; by LL COOL J featuring AMERIE) *(63703-4) <063820>* **PARADISE / PARADISE (James Yarde mix with TERRI WALKER)** 18 Nov02 36
(12"+=) *(63703-1)* – ('A'-instrumental).
(cd-s++=) *(63703-2)* – ('A'-video).

— in Mar'03, LL COOL J featured on JENNIFER LOPEZ's hit, 'All I Have'

Aug 04. (cd-s) *<(9863759)>* **HEADSPRUNG / FEEL THE BEAT** 25 16
(cd-s) *(9863755)>* – ('A'-mixes).

Aug 04. (cd/lp) *(9863650) <29390-2/-1>* **THE DEFinition** 66 4
– Headsprung / Rub my back / I'm about to get her (feat. R. KELLY) / Move somethin' / Hush (feat. 7 AURELIUS) / Every sip / Shake it baby / Can't explain it / Feel the beat / Apple cobbler / 1 in the morning.

Feb 05. (cd-s; LL COOL J feat. 7 AURELIUS) *<(2103773)>* **HUSH / LUV U BETTER / HEY LOVER (video)** 3 26

Apr 06. (-) *<radio>* **CONTROL MYSELF** – 89

Apr 06. (cd) *(9853569) <6158-2>* **TODD SMITH** – 6
– It's LL and Santana (feat. JUELZ SANTANA) / Control myself (feat. JENNIFER LOPEZ) / Favorite flavor (feat. MARY J. BLIGE) / Freeze (feat. LYFE JENNINGS) / Best dress (feat. JAMIE FOXX) / Preserve the sex (feat. TEAIRRA MARI) / What you want (feat. FREEWAY) / I've change (feat. RYAN TOBY) / Ooh wee (feat. GINUWINE) / #1 fan / Down th aisle (feat. 112) / We're gonna make it (feat. MARY MARY) / So sic (remix) (feat. NE-YO). *(UK+=)* – Control myself (Nevins funktek remix)

– compilations, etc. –

Mar 93. (cd/c) *Def Jam; (473043-2/-4)* **12" TAPE** (versions) – –
– Rock the bells / I need love / I can't live without my radio / Boomin system / Around the way girl.

LONG-VIEW

Formed: Manchester, England . . . 2002 by ROB McVEY, DOUG MORCH, AIDAN BANKS and MATT DABBS. Taking the longview that ruminatory Brit-indie bands such as COLDPLAY, DOVES and EMBRACE were the future of rock, or at least the heirs of shoegazing, these Mancunian miserabilists entered 2003 with a couple of minor hits under their belt, 'WHEN YOU SLEEP' and 'NOWHERE'. Inking a deal with '14th Floor', the band hovered on the fringes of the mainstream as third single, 'FURTHER', and debut album, 'MERCURY' (2003), scraped the lower rungs of the charts. Despite another three attempts ('CAN'T EXPLAIN', 'STILL' and 'IN A DREAM') at getting past the Top 30, the band's soporific sound seemed to be taking a career slowdive. However, it took a name tweak (newly hyphenated as LONG-VIEW due to a coincidental clash with, bizarrely enough, an American bluegrass outfit!) and the remixing skills of MOGWAI, ELBOW, ANDY VOTEL and er, ULRICH SCHNAUSS, to refresh the parts they couldn't reach themselves. Titled 'SUBVERSIONS', the remix set surfaced in early 2005 around the same time as double A-sided Top 40 single, 'COMING DOWN' / 'WHEN YOU SLEEP'. Despite being signed to 'Columbia' for the much anticipated US release of 'MERCURY' that March, it was to be a re-packaged UK version (and a re-release of 'FURTHER') which finally made them a Top 30 band.

Album rating: MERCURY (*8)

LONGVIEW

ROB McVEY – vocals / **DOUG MORCH** – guitar / **AIDAN BANKS** – bass / **MATT DABBS** – drums

4.45 Recordings — not iss.

Oct 02. (7") *(LVIEW 02)* **WHEN YOU SLEEP. / STILL** [74] [–]
(cd-s+=) *(LVIEW 02CD)* – Say it once.

Jan 03. (7") *(LVIEW 03)* **NOWHERE. / JUST CAME TOO LATE** [72] [–]
(cd-s+=) *(LVIEW 03CD)* – Feel the same.

14th Floor — not iss.

Jul 03. (7") *(14FLR 01)* **FURTHER. / ONE MORE TRY** [27] [–]
(cd-s+=) *(14FLR 01CD1)* – Fading.
(cd-s) *(14FLR 01CD2)* – ('A') / Longview vs. Elbow Further / ('A'-video).

Jul 03. (cd) *(5046 66886-2)* **MERCURY** [45] [–]
– Further / Can't explain / Electricity / When you sleep / If you asked / I would / Nowhere / Falling for you / Falling without you / Still / Will you wait here / This is.

Sep 03. (cd-s) *(14FLR 02CD1)* **CAN'T EXPLAIN / LUCY / CAN'T EXPLAIN (live at ULU 31.07.03)** [51] [–]
(cd-s) *(14FLR 02CD2)* – ('A') / ('A'-video).
(dvd-s) *(14FLR 02DVD)* – ('A'-video) / Just waiting here / I would (Votel's Angels glum rock remix) / ('A'-making ov..).
(ltd-d12"; LONGVIEW and ULRICH SCHNAUSS converged) *(14FLR 03T)* – ('A'-vocal) / ('A'-instrumental) / Will you wait here (vocal & instrumental).

Jan 04. (cd-s) *(14FLR 04CD1)* **STILL / HOLD ON / GOODBYE / WILL YOU WAIT HERE (w/ ULRICH SCHNAUSS) / ('A'-video)** [ ] [–]
(cd-s/dvd-s) *(14FLR 04 CD2/DVD)* – ('A'-video) / Falling without you (live from ULU 31/07.03 – video) / ('A'-demo) / Can't explain (w/ ULRICH SCHNAUSS).

Jun 04. (7"yellow) *(14FLR 06)* **IN A DREAM. / STILL (acoustic)** [38] [–]
(w/ free 7"white) *(14FLR 06V)* – ('A'-demo) / River.
(cd-s) *(14FLR 06CD)* – ('A') / ('A'-Mogwai remix).

LONG-VIEW

14th Floor — Columbia

Jan 05. (7"white) *(14FLR 09)* **COMING DOWN. / WHEN YOU SLEEP** [32] [–]
(cd-s) *(14FLR 09CD)* – ('A') / ('B'-U.S. radio mix).
(7"clear) *(14FLR 09V)* – ('A') / ('A'-Zip it up mix) / Gently sleeping.

Jan 05. (lp) *(5046 76202-1)* **SUBVERSIONS** (remixes) [ ] [–]
– Further (Jacknife Lee) / Can't explain (Ulrich Schnauss) / In a dream (Mogwai) / Further (Elbow) / Will you wait here (Ulrich Schnauss) / I would (Andy Votel) / Further (Jacknife Lee instrumental) / Can't explain (Ulrich Schnauss instrumental) / Will you wait here (Ulrich Schnauss instrumental).

Jan 05. (d-cd) *(5046 76203-2)* **MERCURY / SUBVERSIONS** [ ] [–]

Jul 05. (re-cd) *(2564 62518-2)* <93669-2> **MERCURY** [29] Mar05 [ ]
– Further / Can't explain / Falling for you / In a dream / Nowhere / I would / Electricity / Still / One more try / When you sleep / If you asked / Will you wait here. *(bonus+=)* – Further (radio mix) / Falling without you.

Aug 05. (7"sky-blue) *(14FLR 12V1)* **FURTHER. / JEALOUSY** [24] [–]
(cd-s) *(14FLR 12CD)* – ('A'-radio) / Jealousy – with choir.
(7"maroon) *(14FLR 12V)* – ('A') / I want a reaction (demo).

☐ LOOSE FUR (see under ⇒ WILCO)

LOSTPROPHETS

Formed: Pontypridd, nr. Cardiff, Wales . . . summer 1997 from the ashes of PUBLIC DISTURBANCE by MIKE LEWIS and IAN WATKINS, who duly recruited MIKE CHIPLIN and LEE GAZE. After paying their dues on the local gig circuit, the so called boy band of nu-metal bolstered their line-up and pin-up factor with the addition of bass player STUART RICHARDSON. A deal with indie label 'Visible Noise' and a slow-burning debut album, 'THE FAKE SOUND OF PROGRESS' (2001) ensued amid encouraging reviews and mounting sales. While they contributed little to the advancement of their chosen genre and stood little chance of stealing the MANICS', or even the SUPER FURRY's Welsh rock crown, their spirited racket made them the darlings of the metal press. In 2001/2, JAMIE OLIVER (that's DJ – not celeb chef) was introduced, although he'd have to wait until late 2003 and the 'BURN BURN' single to contribute. Early the following year, the lads delivered their sophomore effort, 'START SOMETHING', a surprise Top 5 entry and even more surprisingly a Top 40 breakthrough over the pond. It featured no less than three major hits, 'LAST TRAIN HOME', 'WAKE UP (MAKE A MOVE)' and 'LAST SUMMER', living out their 80s fantasies at just the right time. Prior to work on a new Bob Rock-produced album, CHIPLIN made way for drummer ILAN RUBIN. 'LIBERATION TRANSMISSION' eventually appeared in late June 2006 (and topped the album chart early July), trailed by promotional UK Top 10 hit 'ROOFTOPS (A LIBERATION BROADCAST)'.

• **Covered:** A VIEW TO A KILL (Duran Duran) / BOYS DON'T CRY (Cure) / REPTILIA (Strokes) / IN THE AIR TONIGHT (Phil Collins) / SWEET DREAMS MY L.A. EX (Rachel Stevens).

Album rating: THE FAKE SOUND OF PROGRESS (*6) / START SOMETHING (*6) / LIBERATION TRANSMISSION (*8)

IAN WATKINS – vocals / **MIKE LEWIS** – guitar / **LEE GAZE** – guitar / **STUART RICHARDSON** – bass / **MIKE CHIPLIN** – drums / **DJ STEPZAK** – turntable

demos — not iss.

Nov 97. (cd-s) *(none)* **HERE COMES THE PARTY** [–] [–]

1998. (cd-s) *(none)* **PARA TODAS LAS PUTAS CE LOSAS** [–] [–]

1999. (cd-ep) *(none)* **THE FAKE SOUND OF PROGRESS** [–] [–]

Visible Noise — Columbia

Oct 00. (cd) *(TORMENT 5CD)* **THE FAKE SOUND OF PROGRESS** [ ] [–]
– Shinobi vs. Dragon Ninja / The fake sound of progress / Five is a four letter word / . . .And she told me to leave / Kobrakai / The handsome life of swing / A thousand apologies / Still laughing / For sure / Awkward / Ode to summer.

Nov 01. (7") *(TORMENT 18)* **SHINOBI VS. DRAGON NINJA. / MILES AWAY FROM NOWHERE** [41] [–]
(cd-s+=) *(TORMENT 17CD)* – Still laughing (BBC Radio 1 session).
(cd-s) *(TORMENT 16CD)* – ('A') / Directions / The lesson part 1.

Feb 02. (re-cd) *(TORMENT 10CD)* <85955> **THE FAKE SOUND OF PROGRESS** [44] [ ]

Mar 02. (7") *(TORMENT 21)* **THE FAKE SOUND OF PROGRESS. / HAPPY NEW YEAR, HAVE A GOOD 1985** [21] [–]
(cd-s+=) *(TORMENT 19CD)* – A view to a kill.
(cd-s) *(TORMENT 20CD)* – ('A') / Shoulder to the wheel / Need you tonight.

— **JAMIE OLIVER** (b. RICHARD OLIVER) – keyboards, samples; repl. STEPZAK

Nov 03. (7") *(TORMENT 31)* **BURN BURN. / OUR BROKEN HEARTS (SCENE FROM TOP GUN 2)** [17] [–]
(cd-s+=) *(TORMENT 29CD)* – Like a fire.
(cd-s) *(TORMENT 30CD)* – ('A') / Lucky you / Push out the jive, bring in the love.

Jan 04. (7") *(TORMENT 38)* **LAST TRAIN HOME. / SHINOBI VS. DRAGON NINJA (acoustic)** [8] [75]
(cd-s) *(TORMENT 36CD)* – ('A') / Cry me a river.
(cd-s) *(TORMENT 37CD)* – ('A') / ('A'-demo) / The politics of emotion / ('A'-video & making of..).

Feb 04. (cd) *(TORMENT 32CD)* <86554> **START SOMETHING** [4] [33]
– We still kill the old way / To Hell we ride / Last train home / Make a move / Burn burn / I don't know / Hello again / Goodbye tonight / Start something / A million miles / Last summer / We are Godzilla – You are Japan *[UK-only]* / Sway.

May 04. (7") *(TORMENT 41)* **WAKE UP (MAKE A MOVE). / START SOMETHING (Radio One Astoria gig)** [18] [–]
(cd-s) *(TORMENT 39CD)* – ('A') / ('A'-Chicago Q101 live).
(cd-s) *(TORMENT 40CD)* – ('A') / Holding on (demo) / ('A'-video).

Aug 04. (7"red) *(TORMENT 44)* **LAST SUMMER. / BOYS DON'T CRY** [13] [–]
(cd-s) *(TORMENT 42CD)* – ('A') / Sweet dreams my L.A. ex.
(cd-s) *(TORMENT 43CD)* – ('A') / Reptilia / In the air tonight / ('A'-demo).

Nov 04. (etched-7") *(TORMENT 48)* **GOODBYE TONIGHT** [42] [–]
(cd-s+=) *(TORMENT 46CD)* – Burn burn (no truth remix).
(cd-s+=) *(TORMENT 47CD)* – Last train home (Xanex broken heart remix) / Wake up and move (Nebuchednezzar mix) / ('A'-video, etc.)

— (Jun'05) **ILAN RUBIN** – drums (ex-FENIX*TX) repl. CHIPLIN

Jun 06. (etched-7") *(TORMENT 74)* **ROOFTOPS (A LIBERATION BROADCAST)** [8] [–]
(cd-s+=) *(TORMENT 72CD)* – Ordinary life (demo).
(cd-s+=) *(TORMENT 73CD)* – Dead to me (demo) / No way out (demo).

Jun 06. (cd) *(TORMENT 68CD)* **LIBERATION TRANSMISSION** [1] [ ]
– Everyday combat / A town called Hypocrisy / The new transmission / Rooftops (a liberation broadcast) / Can't stop, gotta date with hate / Can't catch tomorrow (good shoes won't save you this time) / Everybody's screaming!!! / Broken hearts, torn up letters and the story of a lonely girl / 4 am forever / For all these times son, for all these times / Heaven for the weather, Hell for the company / Always all ways (apologies, glances and messed up chances).

LOVE

Formed: Los Angeles, California, USA . . . early '65 originally as The GRASS ROOTS, by ARTHUR LEE and former BYRDS roadie BRYAN MacLEAN. The contrasting songwriters recruited JOHN ECHOLS, KEN FORSSI and DON CONKA (the latter being replaced by SNOOPY PFISTERER). When another band of the same name made the US charts, they became LOVE, soon signing to Jac Holzman's 'Elektra' records. In 1966, they released a snarling cover of Burt Bacharach's 'MY LITTLE RED BOOK', nearly breaking it into the US Top 50. With The LEAVES beating them to the US Top 40 on a cover of 'HEY JOE', LOVE opted instead for a British release, although it failed to chart. Soon after, an eponymous album hit the shops, a fairly competent folk-rock set that nevertheless contained the classics, 'SIGNED D.C.', 'CAN'T EXPLAIN' and the two singles. Around the same time, the band scored their only Top 40 success with the galloping HENDRIX-like psych-out of '7 AND 7 IS'. Early in 1967, they followed up with the classic, 'DA CAPO' album, containing the ambitious 20-minute 'REVELATION' alongside such timeless jewels, 'ORANGE SKIES', 'SHE COMES IN COLORS', 'STEPHANIE KNOWS WHO', 'THE CASTLE' and the previous 45. Shacked-up in LEE's Hollywood mansion, the band eventually emerged with 'FOREVER CHANGES', often cited as one of the greatest albums of all-time. A psychedelic tour de force, it combined acoustic musings, Latin rhythms and the eerily surreal LEE-penned lyrics. Almost every track was flawless and it remains one of rock's great mysteries why the album's two singles, 'ALONE AGAIN OR' and 'ANDMOREAGAIN', failed to chart. Equally baffling was the fact that the album only made the highest position of No.154, while in Britain it hit the Top 30. The band recorded a further brilliant single, 'YOUR MIND AND WE BELONG TOGETHER', before LEE sacked the rest of the group "cause they couldn't cut it". He subsequently formed a "new" LOVE with JAY DONELLAN, JIM HOBSON, FRANK FAYAD, GEORGE SURANOVICH and some additional members. This line-up cut a fourth album, the disappointing 'FOUR SAIL', following it up with two others in the early 70's, 'OUT HERE' and 'FALSE START'. Eventually LEE was again left on his own, leading him to carve out a solo career, the album 'VINDICATOR' (1972) being released to a lukewarm reception. He re-created yet another LOVE in 1974, fans again bitterly disappointed with a commercial set that even unadvisedly touched on disco! After various other re-unions in the late 70's, LEE released a self-titled solo effort in 1981, before going AWOL again. In the early 90's, with renewed LOVE interest, LEE re-formed the group for a re-union album, 'ARTHUR LEE AND LOVE'. The 90's weren't exactly kind to this revered eccentric, LEE being diagnosed with Parkinson's Disease and, more recently, receiving a 12-year sentence for firearms offences. His former partner, born-again christian BRYAN MacLEAN (who had virtually retired in 1970, although he did pen songs for his half-sister MARIA McKEE and country-star PATTY LOVELESS) tragically died of a suspected heart attack on Christmas Day, 1998. ARTHUR LEE quietly re-formed LOVE for a series of live concerts in the late 90's, 'ELECTRICALLY SPEAKING' (2001), was a document of some of these. Following LEE's release from prison, he eventually got a serious band together and began touring again to increasing UK acclaim and often sold out shows. The reverence afforded the wayward genius was such that he was able to stage a performance of 'FOREVER CHANGES' in its entirety at London's Royal Festival Hall in January 2003. The resulting live document, titled simply 'THE FOREVER CHANGES CONCERT' (2003), was testament to both the album's timeless appeal and LEE's enduring genius.

• **Trivia:** In 1970, LEE was about to initiate a supergroup, BAND AID (not the charity) with STEVE WINWOOD and HENDRIX, but JIMI died on September '70. In 1973, he recorded an album, 'BLACK BEAUTY' for 'Buffalo' records. This was shelved, although illegal bootlegs did surface.

Album rating: LOVE (*6) / DA CAPO (*8) / FOREVER CHANGES (*10) / FOUR SAIL (*6) / OUT HERE (*4) / FALSE START (*4) / REEL TO REAL (*4) / LOVE LIVE (*4) / ARTHUR LEE AND LOVE (*4) / COMES IN COLOURS compilation (*8) / LOVE STORY 1966-1972 compilation (*8) / ELECTRICALLY SPEAKING: LIVE IN CONCERT (*5) / FIVE STRING SERENADE (*6) / THE FOREVER CHANGES CONCERT (*7) / Bryan MacLean: IFYOUBELIEVEIN (*6) / posthumous CANDY'S WALTZ (*5)

ARTHUR LEE (b. ARTHUR TAYLOR PORTER, 1945, Memphis, Tennessee) – vocals, guitar (ex-LAG'S, ex-AMERICAN FOUR) / **BRYAN MacLEAN** (b.1947) – guitar, vocals / **JOHN ECHOLS** (b.1945, Memphis) – lead guitar (ex-LAG'S) / **KEN FORSSI** (b.1943, Cleveland, Ohio) – bass (ex-SURFARIS) / **ALBAN 'SNOOPY' PFISTERER** (b.1947, Switzerland) – drums; repl. DON CONKA

London Elektra

Mar 66. (7") <45603> **MY LITTLE RED BOOK. / A MESSAGE TO PRETTY** [–] [52]

Jun 66. (7") *(HLZ 10053)* **HEY JOE. / MY LITTLE RED BOOK** [ ] [–]

Sep 66. (7") *(HLZ 10073)* <45605> **7 AND 7 IS. / NO. FOURTEEN** [ ] Aug66 [33]

LOVE

Elektra Elektra

Sep 66. (lp; mono/stereo) *<(EKL/EKS 7-4001)>* **LOVE** [ ] Jul66 [57]
– My little red book / A message to Pretty / Softly to me / Emotions / Gazing / Signed D.C. / Mushroom clouds / Can't explain / My flash on you / No matter what you do / You I'll be following / Hey Joe / Coloured bells falling / And more. *(re-iss. Jan72 lp/c; K/K4 42068) (re-iss. Feb87 on 'Edsel'; ED 218) (cd-iss. Feb93 & Dec93; 7559 74001-2) <(cd re-iss. Sep01 +=; 8122 73567-2)>* – LOVE (stereo). *<(lp re-iss. Jan02 on 'Sundazed'; SCLP 5100)>*

— added **MICHAEL STUART** – drums (ex-SONS OF ADAM) ('SNOOPY' now on keyboards) + **TJAY CANTRELLI** – saxophone

Dec 66. (7") *(EKSN 45010) <45608>* **SHE COMES IN COLOURS. / ORANGE SKIES** [ ] [ ]

Feb 67. (lp; mono/stereo) *<(EKL/EKS 7-4005)>* **DA CAPO** [ ] [80]
– Stephanie knows who / Orange skies / Que vida / 7 and 7 is / The castle / She comes in colors / Revelation. *(re-iss. Jan72 lp/c; K/K4 42011) (cd-iss. 1989 on 'WEA'; 974005-2) <(lp re-iss. Jan02 on 'Sundazed'; SCLP 5101)>*

Mar 67. (7") *<45613>* **QUE VIDA (edit). / HEY JOE** [–] [ ]

Sep 67. (7") *(EKSN 45016)* **THE CASTLE. / SOFTLY TO ME** [ ] [–]

— Reverted to a quintet when 'SNOOPY' and TJAY left. (latter to DOMINIC TROIANO)

Jan 68. (7") *<45629>* **ALONE AGAIN OR (edit). / A HOUSE IS NOT A MOTEL** [–] [ ]

Jan 68. (7") *(EKSN 45024)* **ALONE AGAIN OR. / BUMMER IN THE SUMMER** [ ] [–]
(re-iss. Oct70; 2101-019)

Feb 68. (lp; mono/stereo) *<(EKL/EKS 7-4013)>* **FOREVER CHANGES** [24] Jan68 [ ]
– Alone again or / A house is not a motel / Andmoreagain / The daily planet / Old man / The red telephone / Maybe the people would be the times or between Clark and Hilldale / Live and let live / Good honor man he sees everything like this / Bummer in the summer / You set the scene. *(re-iss. Jan72 lp/c; K/K4 42015) (cd-iss. Jul88 on 'WEA'; 7559 60656-2) <(cd re-mast.Feb01 +=; 8122 73537-2)>* – Hummingbirds (demo) / Wonder people (I do wonder) (alt.) / Alone again or (alt.) / You set the scene (alt.) / Your mind and we belong together (alt.) / Your mind and we belong together (single) / Laughing stock (single). *<(lp re-iss. Jan02 on 'Sundazed'; SCLP 5102)>*

Mar 68. (7") *(EKSN 45024)* **ANDMOREAGAIN. / THE DAILY PLANET** [ ] [–]

Sep 68. (7") *(EKSN 45038) <45633>* **YOUR MIND AND WE BELONG TOGETHER. / LAUGHING STOCK** [ ] [ ]

— ARTHUR LEE dismissed others and recruited new people below **JAY DONELLAN** (LEWIS) – guitar / **JIM HOBSON** – keyboards / **FRANK FAYAD** – bass / **GEORGE SURANOVICH** – drums

— augmented by **PAUL MARTIN** and **GARY ROWLES** – guitar plus **DRACKEN THEAKER** – keyboards (ex-CRAZY WORLD OF ARTHUR BROWN)

Nov 69. (lp) *<(EKS 74049)>* **FOUR SAIL** [ ] Sep69 [ ]
– August / Your friend and mine – Neil's song / I'm with you / Good times / Singing cowboy / Dream / Robert Montgomery / Nothing / Talking in my sleep / Always see your face. *(re-iss. Jan72 lp/c; K/K4 42030) (re-iss. Nov87 on 'Thunderbolt'; THBL 047) (cd-iss. Jun88; CDBT 047) <(cd re-mast.Nov02; 8122 73640-2)>*

Mar 70. (7") *(EKSN 45086)* **I'M WITH YOU. / ROBERT MONTGOMERY** [ ] [–]

Harvest Blue Thumb

May 70. (d-lp) *(SHDW 3-4) <BTS 9000>* **OUT HERE** [29] Dec69 [ ]
– I'll pray for you / Abalony / Signed D.C. / Listen to my song / I'm down / Stand out / Discharged / Doggone / I still wonder / Love is more than words or better late than never / Nice to be / Car lights on in the day time blues / Run to the top / Willow willow / Instra-mental / You are something / Gather round. *(re-iss. Jul88 on 'Big Beat' lp; WIKA 69) (cd-iss. Jul90; CDWIKA 69)*

May 70. (7") *<BLU-7 106>* **I'LL PRAY FOR YOU. / STAND OUT** [–] [ ]

Nov 70. (7") *(HAR 5030) <BLU-7 116>* **KEEP ON SHINING. / THE EVERLASTING FIRST** [ ] [ ]

— **GARY ROWLES** now full time; repl. JAY

Jan 71. (lp) *(SHVL 787) <BTS 8822>* **FALSE START** [ ] Dec 70 [ ]
– The everlasting first / Flying / Gimi a little break / Stand out / Keep on shining / Anytime / Slick Dick / Love is coming / Feel daddy feel good / Ride that vibration. *(cd-iss. Jul92 on 'Beat Goes On'; BGOCD 127) (cd re-iss. Apr94 on 'One Way'; MCAD 22029)*

Mar 71. (7") *(HAR 5014)* **STAND OUT. / DOGGONE** [ ] [–]

ARTHUR LEE

— a solo venture with BAND AID: **FAYAD** and new men **CHARLES KARP** – guitar / **CRAIG TARWATER** – guitar / **CLARENCE McDONALD** – keyboards / **DON PONCHA** – drums / + guest **DAVID HULL** – bass

A&M A&M

Aug 72. (lp) *(AMLS 64356) <SP 4356>* **VINDICATOR** [ ] [ ]
– Sad song / You can save up to 50% / Love jumped through my window / Find somebody / He said she said / Everytime I look up / Everybody's gotta live / He knows a lot of good women / You want change for your re-run / Hamburger breath stinkfinger / Ol' morgue mouth / Busted feet. *(cd-iss. Apr97; 540697-2)*

Aug 72. (7") *<1361>* **EVERYBODY'S GOT TO LIVE. / LOVE JUMPED THROUGH MY WINDOW** [–] [ ]

Nov 72. (7") *<1381>* **SAD SONG. / YOU WANT TO CHANGE FOR YOUR RE-RUN** [–] [ ]

LOVE

— **ARTHUR LEE** recruited **MELVIN WHITTINGTON + JOHN STERLING** – guitar / **SHERWOOD AKUNA + ROBERT ROZENO** – bass / **JOE BLOCKER** – drums

R.S.O. R.S.O.

Dec 74. (7") *<SO 502>* **TIME IS LIKE A RIVER. / WITH A LITTLE ENERGY** [–] [ ]

Jan 75. (7") *(2090 151)* **TIME IS LIKE A RIVER. / YOU SAID YOU WOULD** [ ] [–]

Jan 75. (lp) *(2394 145) <SO 4804>* **REEL TO REAL** [ ] [ ]
– Time is like a river / Stop the music / Who are you? / Good old fashioned love / Which witch is which / With a little energy / Singing cowboy / Be thankful for what you got / You said you would / Busted feet / Everybody's gotta live.

Mar 75. (7") *<SO 506>* **YOU SAID YOU WOULD. / GOOD OLD FASHIONED DREAM** [–] [ ]

ARTHUR LEE

— solo again, using loads of session people

Da Capo not iss.

1977. (7"ep) *(CAP 001)* **I DO WONDER / JUST US. / DO YOU KNOW THE SECRET? / HAPPY YOU** [ ] [–]

Beggars Banquet Rhino

Jul 81. (lp) *(BEGA 26) <RNLP 020>* **ARTHUR LEE** [ ] [ ]
– One / I do wonder / Just us / Happy you / Do you know the secret / One and one / Seven and seven is / Mr. Lee / Bend down / Stay away from evil / Many rivers to cross.

— LOVE re-formed in Autumn '91, with **ARTHUR LEE, DON CONKA, SHUGGIE OTIS** – guitar / **MELLAN WHITTINGTON** – guitar / **SHERWOOD AKUNA** – bass

New Rose not iss.

May 92. (cd/lp) *(ROSE CD/LP 288)* **ARTHUR LEE AND LOVE** [ ] [–]
– Five string serenade / Somebody's watching you / Twenty on my way / You're the prettiest song / I believe in you / Ninety miles away / Seventeen / Love saga / The watcher / Passing by. *(re-iss. May94; 422214)*

— ARTHUR was diagnosed with Parkinson's Disease in the early 90's (see biog above)

LOVE

ARTHUR LEE – vocals, guitar / **MELVAN WHITTINGTON** – guitar / **SHERWOOD AKUNA** – bass / **GARY STERN** – drums

Yeaah Yeaah

Jun 01. (cd) *<(YEAAH 49)>* **ELECTRICALLY SPEAKING: LIVE IN CONCERT (live)** [ ] Nov01 [ ]
– Alone again or / My little red book / 7 and 7 is / Orange skies / Signed DC / The everlasting first / Andmoreagain / Hey Joe / She comes in colors / Everybody's gotta live – Instant karma / That's the way it goes / Signed DC / Andmoreagain / Little wing.

Last Call Last Call

Oct 01. (cd; as ARTHUR LEE & LOVE) *<(306986-2)>* **FIVE STRING SERENADE** [ ] [ ]
– Five string serenade / Somebody's watching you / Twenty on my way / You're the prettiest song / I believe in you / Nonety miles away / Seventeen / Love saga / Watcher / Passing by.

Snapper Snapper

Jul 03. (d-cd) <*(SMACD 868/869)*> **THE FOREVER CHANGES CONCERT** (live at The Royal Festival Hall) ☐ Sep03 ☐
– Alone again or / A house is not a motel / Andmoreagain / The daily planet / Old man / The red telephone / Maybe the people would be the times (or between Clark and Hilldale) / Live and let live / The good humor man he sees everything like this / Bummer in the summer / You set the scene / Seven and seven is / Your mind and we belong together / Signed D.C. / My little red book / Alone again or.

– LOVE compilations etc. –

on 'Elektra' unless mentioned otherwise

Aug 70. (7") <*45700*> **ALONE AGAIN OR. / GOOD TIMES** – 99

Dec 70. (lp) *(2469 009)* <*EKS 74049*> **LOVE REVISITED** ☐ Aug70 ☐
(re-iss. Jan72 lp/c; K/K4 42091) <*(re-iss. Jan02 on 'Sundazed'; SCLP 5104)*>

Feb 73. (lp/c) *(K/K4 32002)* **LOVE MASTERS** ☐ –
– My little red book / Signed D.C. / Hey Joe / 7 and 7 is / Stephanie knows who / Orange skies / Que vida / The castle / She comes in colours / Laughing stock / Your mind / And we belong together / Old man / The Daily Planet / A house is not a motel / Andmoreagain / Alone again or.

Jul 73. (7") *(K 12113)* **ALONE AGAIN OR. / ANDMOREAGAIN** ☐ –
(re-iss. Apr84; E 9740)

Sep 76. (7") *(K 12231)* **ALONE AGAIN OR. / THE CASTLE** ☐ ☐

1980. (lp) *Rhino;* <*RNLP 800*> **THE BEST OF LOVE** – ☐

1981. (pic-lp) *Rhino;* <*RNDF 251*> **LOVE LIVE (live)** – ☐

1982. (lp) *M.C.A.;* <*27025*> **STUDIO / LIVE** – ☐
(UK cd-iss. Apr94 on 'One Way'; MCAD 22036)

1986. (lp) *Rhino;* <*RNLP 70175*> **GOLDEN ARCHIVE** – ☐

Jan 93. (cd) *Raven; (RVCD 29)* **COMES IN COLOURS** ☐ –
– My little red book / Can't explain / Message to pretty / Softly to me / Hey Joe / Signed D.C. / And more / 7 and 7 is / No.14 / Stephanie knows who / Orange skies / Que vida / The castle / She comes in colors / Alone again or / Andmoreagain / Old man / A house is not a motel / Daily planet / Live and let live / Laughing stock / Your mind and we belong together / August / (Arthur Lee interview). *(re-iss. Feb99; same)*

May 00. (cd/lp; by ARTHUR LEE & SHACK) *Viper;* <*(VIPER 3 CD/LP)*> **LIVE IN LIVERPOOL 1992 (live)** ☐ ☐

BRYAN MacLEAN

—— solo recordings between 1966-82 + 1970's respectively

Sundazed Sundazed

Nov 97. (cd) <*(SC 11051)*> **IFYOUBELIEVEIN** ☐ ☐
– Barber John / Fresh hope / Kathleen / Orange skies / Strong commitment / Alone again or / Tired of sitting / Blues singer / Friday's party / People / Claudia / If you believe in / Orange skies (2nd version) / Alone again or (2nd version) / She looks good / Old man.

Oct 00. (cd) <*SC 11076*> **CANDY'S WALTZ** – ☐
– I can't remember / Most of us / Special joy / Love will be here / Candy's waltz / Always I wanted / Castle waltz / Hip-hip hooray / Claudia / Husband and father / If this is love / Claudine's samba / Candy's waltz (live) / Kathleen (live) / You could be here / Soon / Darlin / Love in the end / We'll be together again / (Bryan MacLean interview).

☐ Courtney LOVE (see under ⇒ HOLE)

LOW

Formed: Duluth, Minnesota, USA ... late 1993 by Mormons ALAN SPARHAWK, his wife MIMI PARKER and third member, JOHN NICHOLS (replaced by ZAK SALLY after debut). Their early efforts, 'I COULD LIVE IN HOPE' (1994) and 'LONG DIVISION' (1995), were more or less ignored, although critics pricked up their ears for the low-key Lo-Fi/ambient classic, 'THE CURTAIN HITS THE CAST' (1996). LOW subsequently completed a few UK gigs to promote it during that summer and later cut a single for the legendary 'Sub Pop', 'VENUS'. The trio delivered a further two sets, namely 'SONGS FOR A DEAD PILOT' (1997) and 'ONE MORE REASON TO FORGET' (1998), described as "sad-core" in the music tabloids; it also featured 17-minute track, 'DO YOU KNOW HOW TO WALTZ?'). 1999 saw the return of the trio and the release of their 5th and best work to date, the bruised and ultra sensitive 'SECRET NAME' album. Recorded over a 7-day period with West Coast rock throwback and ex-BIG BLACK frontman STEVE ALBINI riding the faders, the band had hit a new creative peak with this warm and whispering alternative classic. Tracks such as 'SOON' and the harmonic 'MISSOURI' evoked blissful sensation and echoed tingling country heir to GRAM PARSONS. Others like 'TWO-STEP' and 'I REMEMBER' could easily be compared to a CARPENTERS ballad or something reminising GALAXIE 500. Meanwhile, ZAK SALLY moonlighted with another minimalist trio, ENEMYMINE (along with MIKE KUNKA of GODHEADSILO and DANNY SASAKI), recording an eponymous mini-set for Calvin Johnson's 'K' imprint. Towards the end of the millennium, LOW came up with 'THE CHRISTMAS EP', which featured four brand new tracks and cover of four traditional hymns that would peacefully send the children off to sleep by the fire come the festive season. Prolific as always, LOW returned in 2001 with their most accessible album to date, the haunting 'THINGS WE LOST IN THE FIRE'. The album, produced by Steve Albini once again, saw the group head towards a more uptempo, song-based direction, although tracks such as 'WHITETAIL', 'JULY' and 'CLOSER' still upheld the LOW watermark. But songs 'DINOSAUR ACT' (issued as a single) and 'WHORE' stepped towards a rockier area, with fuzz guitar being used in the latter, in amongst the soaring vocals of PARKER, SPARHAWK and the crashing drums. Not as poignant or as beautiful as 'SECRET NAME' (every track was a classic), 'THINGS WE LOST IN THE FIRE' demonstrated the group's abilities to write great compositions, while still maintaining the sad-core motif that had became so synonymous with the group. A split EP was issued in April the same year with underground artist K and although LOW were on top form (produced by WARN DeFEVER), it was really K's tremendous contribution that shone most on the set. In another bizarre but brilliant twist in LOW's direction, the band issued a cover single of the Smiths' 'LAST NIGHT I DREAMT THAT SOMEBODY LOVED ME', which could've almost been better than the original, with strings fusing into crashing crescendos and PARKER's and SPARHAWK's vocals sounding as strange and as powerful as always. It's also worth mentioning the B-side track 'BECAUSE YOU STOOD STILL'; how did something so incredible get omitted from an album? LOW returned in September of 2002 with the delicately crafted 'TRUST', a slightly unadorned set, from the usually consistently reliable group. The album, which saw LOW delve deeper into sparse and darker terrain, may have been saved from droning obscurity by PARKER's light vocals and the group's undeniable knack for writing beautiful songs, no matter how dark and eerie. With the ubiquitous DAVID FRIDMANN at the helm, 'THE GREAT DESTROYER' – LOW's first for label 'Sub Pop' – marked what may be a turning point in the band's career. While 'SILVER RIDER' malingered with as sorrowful an intent as ever, it was the likes of 'JUST STAND BACK' and lead single, 'CALIFORNIA', that fulfilled the pre-release prophecies of a bonafide "rock" record, invigorated tempos, bouyant hooks and all. Even death-watch closer 'WALK INTO THE SEA' sounded liberated rather than oppressed. After more than a decade in the band, SALLY was replaced by MATT LIVINGSTON later in 2005.

• **Songwriters:** Group except SUNSHINE (Mitchell – Davis) / JACK SMITH (Supreme Dicks) / Transmission (Joy Division) / LONG LONG LONG (George Harrison) / DOWN BY THE RIVER (Neil Young) / LAST NIGHT I DREAMT THAT SOMEBODY LOVED ME (Smiths) / LITTLE DRUMMER BOY + BLUE CHRISTMAS + SILENT NIGHT + TAKING DOWN THE TREE (trad).

Album rating: I COULD LIVE IN HOPE (*7) / LONG DIVISION (*8) / THE CURTAIN HITS THE CAST (*7) / SECRET NAME (*8) / THINGS WE LOST IN

THE FIRE (*8) / TRUST (*6) / A LIFETIME OF TEMPORARY RELIEF boxed collection (*5) / THE GREAT DESTROYER (*7)

ALAN SPARHAWK – vocals, guitar / **JOHN NICHOLS** – bass / **MIMI PARKER** – vocals, drums

Quigley Quigley

Aug 94. (cd) *<QUIGD 5>* **I COULD LIVE IN HOPE**
– Words / Fear / Cut / Slide / Lazy / Lullaby / Sea / Down / Drag / Rope / Sunshine.

not iss. Summershine

1994. (cd-ep) *<shine 48CD>* **LOW** –
– Below & above / Lazy / Words / Caroline / Tired.

—— **ZAK SALLY** – bass; repl. NICHOLS

Vernon Yard Vernon Yard

1995. (cd) *<YARDCD 014>* **LONG DIVISION** –
– Violence / Below and above / Shame / Throw out the line / Swingin' / See-through / Turn / Caroline / Alone / Streetlight / Stay / Take. *(UK-iss.Feb97; same)*

Feb 96. (cd-ep) *(FLATSCD 24)* **TRANSMISSION EP** –
– Transmission / Bright / Cardine / Hands / Jack Smith / Untitled.
(above issued on 'Vernon Yard' UK)

May 96. (cd-ep) *<(YARD 022CD)>* **FINALLY**
– Anon / Tomorrow one / Prisoner / Turning over.

Aug 96. (d-lp/cd) *(YARD/+CD 018)* **THE CURTAIN HITS THE CAST**
– Anon / The plan / Over the ocean / Mom says / Coat tails / Standby / Laugh / Lust / Stars gone out / Same / Do you know how to waltz / Dark. *(d-lp+=)* – Prisoner / Tomorrow one.

Nov 96. (7"/cd-s) *<(YARD 024/+CD)>* **OVER THE OCEAN. / CIOLENCE / BE THERE**

Sub Pop Sub Pop

Sep 97. (7") *<(SP 392)>* **VENUS. / BOYFRIEND**

Wurlitzer Jukebox not iss.

Oct 97. (7") *(WJ 44)* **IF YOU WERE BORN TODAY (A SONG FOR LITTLE BABY JESUS). / BLUE CHRISTMAS**

Kranky Kranky

Oct 97. (m-lp/m-cd) *<(KRANKY 021/+CD)>* **SONGS FOR A DEAD PILOT**
– Will the night / Condescend / Born by the wires / Be there / Landlord / Hey Chicago.

Tugboat Kranky

May 98. (7") *(TUG 001)* **JOAN OF ARC. / LONG LONG LONG** –
(re-iss. Aug99 on 'Tugboat'; same)

Jul 98. (cd) *(INR 1040CD)* **ONE MORE REASON TO FORGET**
– Be there / Venus / Condescend / Landlord / Over the ocean / Do you know how to waltz? / Shame / If you were born today (song for the little baby Jesus).
(above issued on 'Bluesanct Musak')

—— In 1998, LOW, PIANO MAGIC & TRANSIENT WAVES shared a 7", 'SLEEP AT THE BOTTOM' (flip by TRANSIENT WAVES) on 'Rocket Girl' *(RGIRL 4)*

Feb 99. (7") *(TUGS 006)* **IMMUNE. / I REMEMBER** –

Apr 99. (cd/d-lp) *(TUG CD/LP 007)* *<KRANKY 035>* **SECRET NAME**
– I remember / Starfire / 2-step / Weight for water / Missouri / Don't understand / Soon / Immune / Lion – Lamb / Days of . . . / Will the night / Home.

Nov 99. (m-cd) *<(TUGCD 014–LOWXMASD 1)>* **CHRISTMAS**
– Just like Christmas / Long way around the sea / Little drummer boy / If you were born today / Blue Christmas / Silent night / Taking down the tree / One special gift.

May 00. (12"/cd-s; with SPRINGHEEL JACK) *(TUGS/+CD 017)* **BOMBSCARE EP** –
– Bombscare / Hand so small / So easy (so far) / The way behind.

Oct 00. (7") *(TUGS 024)* **DINOSAUR ACT. / OVERHEAD** –
(cd-s+=) (TUGSCD 024) – Don't carry it all.

Feb 01. (cd/lp) *(TUG CD/LP 027)* *<KRANKY 046>* **THINGS WE LOST IN THE FIRE**
– Sunflower / Whitehall / Dinosaur act / Medicine magazines / Laser beam / July / Embrace / Whore / Kind of girl / Like a forest / Closer / Funny noise / In metal. *(lp+=)* – Overhead / Don't carry it all.

not iss. Tiger Style

Apr 01. (7"ep; shared w/ K) *<15>* **THOSE GIRLS** –
– (track by K) / Those girls / Venus / (track by K).

Rough Trade Chairkicker's Music

Oct 01. (7") *(RTRADES 033)* *<CKM 003>* **LAST NIGHT I DREAMT THAT SOMEBODY LOVE ME. / BECAUSE YOU STOOD STILL**
(cd-s+=) (RTRADESCD 033) – Dinosaur act (dub).

Mar 02. (7") *<(MM 01)>* **split w/ VIBRACATHEDRAL**
(above issued on 'Misplaced') *(re-iss. Sep02; same)*

Rough Trade Kranky

Sep 02. (cd/d-lp) *(RTRAD CD/LP 061)* *<KRANKY 52>* **TRUST**
– (That's how you sing) Amazing grace / Canada / Candy girl / Time is the diamond / Tonight / The lamb / In the drugs / Last snowstorm of the year / John Prine / Little argument with myself / La la la song / Point of disgust / Shots & ladders.

Oct 02. (7"/cd-s) *(RTRADES/+CD 058)* **CANADA. / FEARLESS** –

Rough Trade Sub Pop

Jan 05. (cd) *(RTRADCD 206)* *<SP 643CD>* **THE GREAT DESTROYER** 72
– Monkey / California / Everybody's song / Silver rider / Just stand back / On the edge of / Cue the strings / Step / When I go deaf / Broadway (so many people) / Pissing / Death of a salesman / Walk into the sea.

Feb 05. (7"colrd) *(RTRADS 221)* **CALIFORNIA** 57 –

—— **MATT LIVINGSTON** – bass; repl. ZAK SALLY

– compilations, etc. –

Jul 98. (cd) *Vernon Yard; <YARD 27>* **OWL** (LOW remixes by other artists) –
– Down / Annon (spore) / Over the ocean / Laugh / Anon (pollen) / Do you know how to waltz / Over the ocean / Words.

May 01. (cd/lp; shared with DIRTY THREE) *In The Fishtank; (FISH 7 CD/LP)* **IN THE FISHTANK** –
– I hear . . . goodnight / Down by the river / Invitation day / When I called upon your seed / Cody / Lordy. *(re-iss. Sep05; same)*

Jul 04. (4xcd w/dvd) *Rough Trade; (RTRADCDX 195)* **A LIFETIME OF TEMPORARY RELIEF: 10 YEARS OF B-SIDES & RARITIES** –

☐ LUCKY PIERRE (see under ⇒ ARAB STRAP)

LUDACRIS

Born: CHRIS BRIDGES, 11 Sep'77, Atlanta, Georgia, USA. Having already honed his patter and his industry chops as a popular Atlanta-based radio DJ, LUDACRIS made his debut in 2000 with the wittily titled, independently released 'INCOGNEGRO'. With the album increasing his local fame to fever pitch, 'Def Jam' talent scout SCARFACE subsequently snapped up LUDACRIS as the flagship act on the newly created 'Def Jam South' imprint (itself created to get a piece of the increasingly hot hip hop action in America's deep south). Shrewdly (but no doubt annoyingly for fans who'd already bought the debut), the label re-packaged the album later the same year, re-issuing it with four new big name tracks (and soon to be hits) including a revamped version of his TIMBALAND collabo 'FAT RABBIT' (which had originally appeared on the producer's 1998 album, 'Tim's Bio'), the NEPTUNES floor filler 'SOUTHERN HOSPITALITY' and a FOXY BROWN-enhanced version of the risqué 'WHAT'S YOUR FANTASY', the song which had gotten LUDACRIS noticed in the first place and which became his national breakthrough hit. Not quite as enticingly underground but studded with an array of name talent, 'WORD OF MOUF' (2001) made the US Top 3 on the strength of larger than life singles 'ROLLOUT (MY BUSINESS)' and 'SATURDAY (OOOH OOOH!)'. From its wonderfully tacky cover to its razor-witted raps, 'CHICKEN-N-BEER' (2003) was roundly hailed as LUDACRIS' crowning achievement, a raucous round-up of Dirty South attitude, humour and street smart philosophy. Following a Screen Actors Guild Award for his role in Hollywood blockbuster, 'Crash' (his acting career had begun in the early 00s alongside

SNOOP DOGG and DR DRE in hip-hop comedy, 'The Wash'), LUDACRIS was back on top of the American charts with 'THE RED LIGHT DISTRICT' (2004), its in-with-a-bullet success apparently a fait accompli if the Austin Powers-referencing, 'Soul Bossa Nova'-mangling 'NUMBER ONE SPOT' was anything to go by. Like heavyweight lead single, 'GET BACK', it made the US Top 20/UK Top 30, while the BOBBY VALENTINO-abetted 'PIMPIN' ALL OVER THE WORLD' (NOT a tongue-in-cheek update of the JOHN FOGERTY classic, sadly) went Top 10. VALENTINO was back on 'DISTURBING THA PEACE' (2005), a LUDACRIS PRESENTS . . . effort also featuring the ubiquitous JAMIE FOXX still on a RAY CHARLES tip with minor US Top 40 hit, 'GEORGIA'.

Album rating: BACK FOR THE FIRST TIME (*6) / WORD OF MOUF (*7) / CHICKEN-N-BEER (*7) / THE RED LIGHT DISTRICT (*6)

LUDACRIS – vocals / with session people

not iss. | Disturbing The Peace

May 00. (cd) *<911>* **INCOGNEGRO** [–] [ ]
– (intro) / U got a problem? / Game got switched / 1st and 10 (with INFAMOUS 2-D & F.A.T.E.) / It wasn't us / (Come on over – skit) / Hood stuck / Get off me / Mouthing off / Midnight train (with CHIMERE) / (Ho – skit) / Ho / (Tickets sold out – skit) / Catch up (with INFAMOUS 2-D & F.A.T.E.) / What's your fantasy (with SHAWNA) / Rock and a hard place.

Def Jam | Def Jam

Oct 00. (cd) *<(548138-2)>* **BACK FOR THE THE FIRST TIME** [ ] [4]
– U got a problem? / Game got switched (with INFAMOUS 2.0 & FATE WILSON) / 1st and 10 / What's your fantasy (with SHAWNA) / (Come on over – skit) / Hood stuck / Get off me (with PASTOR TROY) / Mouthing off (with 4-IZE) / Stick 'em up (with UGK) / (Ho – skit) / Ho / Tickets sold out – skit) / Catch up (with INFAMOUS 2.0 & FATE WILSON) / Southern hospitality (with PHARRELL) / What's your fantasy (remix with TRINA, SHAWNA & FOXY BROWN) / Phat rabbit.

May 01. (12"; as LUDACRIS featuring SHAWNA) *(572948-1) <562944>* **WHAT'S YOUR FANTASY / (mixes)** [19] Sep00 [21]
(cd-s+=) *(572948-2)* – ('A'video).

—— in Aug'01, he featured on MISSY ELLIOTT's single, 'One Minute Man'

Sep 01. (c-s; as LUDACRIS featuring NATE DOGG) *(588772-4) <588671>* **AREA CODES / SOUTHERN HOSPITALITY** [25] [24] [23]
(12"+=/cd-s+=) *(588772-1/-2)* – ('A'mixes).

Nov 01. (cd/d-lp) *<(586446-2/-1)>* **WORD OF MOUF** [ ] [3]
– Coming 2 America / Rollout (my business) / Go 2 sleep (with I-20, LIL' WILSON & THREE 6 MAFIA) / Cry babies (oh no) / She said (with FATE WILSON) / (Howhere – skit) / Area codes (with NATE DOGG) / Growing pains (with FATE WILSON & KEON BRYCE) / (Greatest hits – skit) / Move bitch (with MYSTIKAL & I-20) / (Stop lying – skit) / Saturday (oooh oooh!) (with SLEEPY BROWN) / Keep it on the hush (with JAZZE PHA) / Word of mouf (freestyle) (with 4-IZE) / Get the fuck back (with SHAWNA, I-20 & FATE WILSON) / Freaky thangs (with TWISTA & JAGGED EDGE) / Cold outside / Block lockdown (with I-20). *(re-iss. Jun02; same)* – hit No.57

Dec 01. (cd-s) *<15531>* **FATTY GIRL** [–] [87]

Jun 02. (c-s) *(582963-4) <588914>* **ROLLOUT (MY BUSINESS) / (album version)** [20] Jan02 [17]
(12"+=) *(582963-1)* – ('A'-Wiley Cat instrumental).
(cd-s++=) *(582963-2)* – What's your fantasy (explicit version with SHAWNA) / ('A'-video).

May 02. (12") *<582948>* **MOVE B***H. / KEEP IT ON THE HUSH (with Jazze Pha)** [–] [10]

Sep 02. (c-s; as LUDACRIS featuring SLEEPY BROWN) *<(063914-4)>* **SATURDAY (OOOH! OOOH!) / (Southern hospitality remix with MS. DYNAMITE)** [31] [22]
(12"+=) *(063914-1)* – Move b***h (with MYSTIKAL).
(cd-s++=) *(063914-2)* – ('A'-video).

May 03. (12") *<053911>* **ACT A FOOL. / BLOCK REINCARNATED** [–] [32]

Oct 03. (cd) *(9861137) <93002>* **CHICKEN-N-BEER** [44] [1]
– Southern fried intro / Blow it out / Stand up (with SHAWNA) / (Rob quarters skit) / Splash waterfalls / Hard times (with 8 BALL, MJG & CARL THOMAS) / Diamond in the back / Screwed up / (T baggin' skit) / P-poppin' (with SHAWNA & LIL' FATE) / Hip hop quotables / (Black man's struggles skit) / Hoes in my room (with SNOOP DOGG) / Teamwork / (Interactive skit) / We got (with CHINGY, I-20 & TITY BOI) / Eyesbrows down (with TITY BOI & DOLLA BOY).

Nov 03. (12"; LUDACRIS feat. SHAWNA) *(981400-1)* **STAND UP. / WHAT'S YOUR FANTASY (with TRINA, SHAWNA & FOXY BROWN)** [14] [–]
(cd-s+=) *(981400-2)* – ('A'-video).

—— in Feb'04, LUDACRIS feat. on CHINGY single, 'Holidae In' (alongside SNOOP DOGG) hit UK 35

—— in Mar'04, LIL' JON & LUDACRIS feat. on USHER chart-topper, 'Yeah!'

Dec 04. (cd) *(9863801) <B00034830-2>* **THE RED LIGHT DISTRICT** [ ] [1]
– Intro / Number one spot / Get back / Put your money (feat. DMX) / Blueberry yum yum (feat. SLEEPY BROWN) / Child of the night (feat. NATE DOGG) / The potion / Pass out / (skit) / Spur of the moment (feat. DJ QUIK & KIMMI) / Who not me (feat. SMALL WORLD & DOLLA BOY) / Large amounts / Pimpin' all over the world (feat. BOBBY VALENTINO) / Two miles an hour / Hopeless (feat. TRICK DADDY) / Virgo (feat. NAS & DOUG E. FRESH). *(re-iss. May05; 2103527)*

Apr 05. (cd-s) *(9881720)* **NUMBER ONE SPOT / GET BACK** [30] [19] [13]
(12"/cd-s) *(988166-6/-5)* – ('A') / The potion / Get back (Sum 41 rock remix).
in May'05, he was credited on single, 'Get Low', by LIL JON..
also in May, he feat. on 'Sugar (Gimme Some)' by TRICK DADDY
late in 2005, LUDACRIS brought together various rap artists on collaboratine 'DISTURBING THA PEACE'

☐ John LYDON (see under ⇒ PUBLIC IMAGE LTD.)

☐ Jeff LYNNE (see under ⇒ ELECTRIC LIGHT ORCHESTRA)

☐ Phil LYNOTT (see under ⇒ THIN LIZZY)

LYNYRD SKYNYRD

Formed: Jacksonville, Florida, USA ... 1966 initially as MY BACKYARD, by RONNIE VAN ZANT (vocals) who carefully hand picked a line-up of GARY ROSSINGTON (guitar), ALLEN COLLINS (guitar), BOB BURNS (drums) and LARRY JUNSTROM (bass) to realise his boyhood dream of creating an American equivalent to the ROLLING STONES. The band were blown away after witnessing an early incarnation of the ALLMAN BROTHERS, vowing to conquer the world with their own unique take on the roots music of the South. Continually brought to task for having long hair by gym teacher, Leonard Skinner, VAN ZANT and co. packed in school at the earliest opportunity, spending up to sixteen hours a day honing the sound of the band they'd eventually dub LYNYRD SKYNYRD after their schoolhouse nemesis (name slightly changed to protect themselves from enforced circuit training). At the time, the band's home town of Jacksonville boasted a thriving and eclectic music scene that saw the likes of future ALLMAN's DICKY BETTS and BERRY OAKLEY paying their dues, as well as a young TOM PETTY amongst a slew of others. SKYNYRD's first victory in their campaign to resurrect the glory of the South was winning a support slot to psychedelic one-hit wonders, STRAWBERRY ALARM CLOCK. By 1970, the band had almost notched up a mind boggling 1,000 gigs and the real touring hadn't even started. Record wise, they had a limited issue single, 'NEED ALL MY FRIENDS', (released in 1968 by the local 'Shadetree' label) under their belts and in 1971, they issued a second single, 'I'VE BEEN YOUR FOOL', the cut taken from sessions the band had recorded at the famed Muscle Shoals studio in Sheffield, Alabama. Over the course of the sessions, the septet laid down early versions of the tracks that would later become their acclaimed debut,

'PRONOUNCED LEH-NERD SKIN-NERD' (1974), bassist LEON WILKINSON joining the band midway through the sessions, while future BLACKFOOT man, RICKY MEDLOCKE, contributed some drum and vocal parts. Manager ALAN WALDEN touted the demos around various companies to no avail, opportunity eventually knocking in the form of industry mover and shaker extraordinaire, AL KOOPER (ex-BLUES PROJECT), who was in the process of setting up the Atlanta-based 'Sounds Of The South' label with the backing of 'M.C.A.'. The purpose of this venture was to capitalise on the booming Southern music scene and in SKYNYRD, KOOPER knew he'd found a band to take Southern Rock to a new plateau. As Intense and driven as the band themselves, KOOPER constantly clashed with them during the recording of the debut which he had taken upon himself to produce. Nevertheless, KOOPER functioned like an extra member of the group, playing and singing on many of the tracks, his input pivotal in creating one of rock's great debut albums. A simmering gumbo stew that drew influences from the likes of The 'STONES, FREE and CREAM yet was also haunted by the spectre of raw country blues, the album's flagbearer and breathtaking finale was 'FREE BIRD', the song most people think of at the mention of SKYNYRD's name. From BILLY POWELL's piano-led intro (which, after writing, resulted in the former roadie being taken up as a full time member of the band), the song led into a gorgeously melancholy DUANE ALLMAN-style (whom the band would dedicate the song to after he was killed in a motorcycle crash) slide guitar part, eventually building up to a blistering triple guitar climax. The band achieved the latter by overdubbing an extra guitar part by COLLINS, authentically replicating the song live as LEON WILKINSON (who'd left prior to recording the album) later returned, allowing ED KING (who'd filled in as a bass player on the debut) to become a permanent member, switching to guitar and cementing the three-pronged attack of the classic 'SKYNYRD line-up. Alongside 'FREE BIRD', the album contained some of the finest songs of the band's career in the mournful 'TUESDAY'S GONE', VAN ZANT's normally commanding voice sounding as forlorn as hero's MERLE HAGGARD and WAYLON JENNINGS. 'SIMPLE MAN' was another earthy ballad, RONNIE's lyrics as succinct and unpretentious as ever. 'THINGS GOIN' ON', meanwhile, was a biting criticism of underhand political dealings set to a rollicking honky tonk backing. KOOPER secured the band a support slot on The WHO's 1973 American tour, and immediately the band were thrown in at the deep end, playing to stadium sized audiences. Incredibly, at almost every show, the band had won the normally fiercely partisan WHO crowd over by the end of their set and when 'SWEET HOME ALABAMA' (a rousing, tongue-in-cheek rebuke to NEIL YOUNG's 'Southern Man') made the US Top 10 the following year, the band were well on the way to becoming major league stars. 'SECOND HELPING' (1974) almost matched the power of the debut, the vicious sting of 'WORKIN' FOR M.C.A.' contrasting with the strum and slide of 'THE BALLAD OF CURTIS LOWE', a tribute to a black bluesman. And thus lay the contradiction with LYNYRD SKYNYRD; denounced as reactionary rednecks, their music was haunted by the music of black immigrants. As many commentators have noted, SKYNYRD didn't have any defined politics; VAN ZANT was fiercely proud of his upbringing, attempting in his own blunt way to speak out for a part of America that had been discredited after the civil war; charges of racism, however, were way off the mark. Similarly, an anti-firearms song, 'SATURDAY NIGHT SPECIAL', didn't exactly fit with the archetype of the rifle-toting redneck. The song formed the centrepiece of the band's third effort, 'NUTHIN' FANCY' (1975), a harder rockin' affair that nevertheless failed to break any new ground or capture the excitement of the band's live show. The album also marked the first of LYNYRD SKYNYRD's many casualties as BOB BURNS was replaced with ARTIMUS PYLE after freaking out on tour. The band had been on the road almost constantly from their inception and things began coming to a head, the trek that followed the release of 'NUTHIN' FANCY' coming to be dubbed the 'Torture Tour'. The tales of sex, drugs, violence and madness are legendary, VAN ZANT's infamous violent outbreaks particularly nauseating. While ED KING departed, the rest of the band soldiered on under the auspices of the notoriously unpredictable VAN ZANT, his dedication winning unfaltering loyalty despite his temper. KING's replacement was STEVE GAINES, brother of backing singer CASSIE. Though he was only featured on a handful of the tracks on the live 'ONE MORE FROM THE ROAD' (1976), his visceral playing re-energised a flagging 'SKYNYRD, helping to make 'STREET SURVIVORS' (1977) their best release since 'SECOND HELPING'. Inspired by the 'Outlaw' movement that saw country stars like WILLIE NELSON and TOMPALL GLASER moving away from the polished Nashville sound, 'STREET SURVIVORS' was more countrified than any previous release, right down to a cover of MERLE HAGGARD's 'HONKY TONK NIGHT TIME MAN'. It also included VAN ZANT's heartfelt anti-heroin track, 'THAT SMELL'. The song's lyrics and the album's cover art (featuring the band surrounded by flames) were to take on a chilling new resonance when, on October 20, en route to Baton Rouge, the aircraft carrying band and crew plummeted from the sky after both its engines failed. VAN ZANT was killed on impact, as were STEVE and CASSIE GAINES, and assistant road manager DEAN KILPATRICK. The remaining passengers were all seriously injured and the details of the crash were horrific, the effects of the tragedy still resonating to this day. The remaining members decided to disband LYNYRD SKYNYRD, even although 'STREET SURVIVORS' had become their biggest selling album ever, the remnants of 'SKYNYRD forming the ROSSINGTON-COLLINS BAND, who released two forgettable albums at the turn of the decade, COLLINS later forming his own band after the death of his wife KATHY. This wasn't the end to his strife; COLLINS was involved in a serious car accident in 1986 which killed his girlfriend and left him paralysed from the waist down (he died of pneumonia four years later). COLLINS wasn't the only one to suffer in the aftermath of the band's tragedy; suicide, drug addiction and even alleged child abuse dogged the survivors of the plane crash for years to come. In the late 80's, the remaining members regrouped for a memorial tour and subsequent live album, 'SOUTHERN BY THE GRACE OF GOD' (1988), RONNIE's brother, JOHNNY, fronting the band. Another reformation in 1991 resulted in the eponymous 'LYNYRD SKYNYRD 1991', a credible comeback that saw the return of ED KING. The band released a further three albums during the 90's, 'THE LAST REBEL' (1993), the unplugged 'ENDANGERED SPECIES' (1994) and 1997's 'TWENTY', the latter featuring BLACKFOOT man RICKY MEDLOCKE, who'd played on sessions for the debut over a quarter of a century previously. Of late, LYNYRD SKYNYRD have delivered three more sets, 'LYVE FROM STEEL TOWN' (1998), 'EDGE OF FOREVER' (1999) and the ill-advised 'CHRISTMAS TIME AGAIN' (2000). None of these albums captured the intensity of the original line-up, however, and those looking for a comprehensive musical history lesson are pointed in the direction of the 1991 'M.C.A.' boxed set. Alongside all the essential album cuts, the collection includes a spectral demo version of 'FREE BIRD' as well as unreleased gems like the impassioned 'HE'S ALIVE' and the spine-tingling 'ALL I CAN DO IS WRITE ABOUT IT', as revealing a song as to what drove the late VAN ZANT as the man ever penned. The new millennium saw the death of yet another longtime member when LEON WILKESON passed away as a result of natural causes on 27th July 2001. With EAN EVANS coming in to replace him, the group bounced back with one of their better latter day releases, 'VICIOUS CYCLE' (2003), with KID ROCK even turning up for a raucous run through

'GIMME BACK MY BULLETS'. To complement these recordings and commemorate 30 odd years in the business, 'SKYNYRD issued the double concert set, 'LYVE: THE VICIOUS CYCLE TOUR' in June 2004.

• **Songwriters:** Bulk by VAN ZANT + COLLINS or VAN ZANT + GAINES after '75. When they re-formed in '87, ROSSINGTON, KING and the new VAN ZANDT contributed all. Covered; SAME OLD BLUES + CALL ME THE BREEZE (J.J. Cale) / CROSSROADS (Robert Johnson) / NONE OF US ARE FREE (Mann-Weil-Russell) / etc.

Album rating: PRONOUNCED LEH-NERD SKIN-NERD (*8) / SECOND HELPING (*8) / NUTHIN' FANCY (*6) / GIMME BACK MY BULLETS (*6) / ONE MORE FROM THE ROAD (*8) / STREET SURVIVORS (*7) / SKYNYRD'S FIRST AND.. LAST posthumous (*6) / GOLD AND PLATINUM compilation (*9) / LEGEND rare live (*6) / SOUTHERN BY THE GRACE OF GOD: LYNYRD SKYNYRD TRIBUTE TOUR – 1987 (*5) / LYNYRD SKYNYRD 1991 (*5) / THE LAST REBEL (*5) / LYNYRD SKYNYRD boxed set (*9) / FREEBIRD – THE VERY BEST OF . . . compilation (*8) / ENDANGERED SPECIES (*4) / TWENTY (*4) / LYVE FROM STEEL TOWN (*5) / EDGE OF FOREVER (*5) / CHRISTMAS TIME AGAIN (*2) / VICIOUS CYCLE (*6) / THYRTY: 30th ANNIVERSARY COLLECTION (*8) / LYVE: THE VICIOUS CYCLE TOUR (*6) / GREATEST HITS double compilation (*9)

RONNIE VAN ZANT (b.15 Jan'48) – vocals / **GARY ROSSINGTON** (b. 4 Dec'51) – guitar / **ALLEN COLLINS** (b.19 Jul'52) – guitar / **GREG WALKER** (or) **LEON WILKESON** (b. 5 Apr'52) – bass / **RICKY MEDLOCKE** (or) **BOB BURNS** – drums

not iss. — Shade Tree

1968. (7") *<101>* **NEED ALL MY FRIENDS. / MICHELLE** [–] [ ]

1971. (7") *<102>* **I'VE BEEN YOUR FOOL. / GOTTA GO** [–] [ ]
(UK-iss.Oct82 on 'M.C.A.'; 799)

— **ED KING** – bass (ex-STRAWBERRY ALARM CLOCK) repl. LEON & GREG / added **BILLY POWELL** (b. 3 Jun'52) – piano (RICKY MEDLOCKE had now formed BLACKFOOT, after contributing vox + drums on 2 tracks 'White Dove' & 'The Seasons')

M.C.A. — M.C.A.

Nov 73. (7") *<40158>* **GIMME THREE STEPS. / MR. BANKER** [–] [ ]

Jan 74. (lp/c) *(MCG/+C 3502) <363>* **PRONOUNCED LEH-NERD SKIN-NERD** [ ] Sep73 [27]
– I ain't the one / Tuesday's gone / Gimme three steps / Simple man / Things goin' on / Mississippi kid / Poison whiskey / Free bird. *(re-iss. Jun84 lp/c; MCL/+C 1798) (cd-iss. Jul88; DMCL 1798) (cd re-iss. Nov91; MCLD 19072) (lp re-iss. Nov98 on 'Simply Vinyl'; SVLP 52)*

— added returning **LEON WILKESON** – bass (ED KING now 3rd guitarist)

May 74. (7") *(MCA 136) <40231>* **DON'T ASK ME NO QUESTIONS. / TAKE YOUR TIME** [ ] Jan74 [ ]

Oct 74. (lp/c) *(MCF/+C 2547) <413>* **SECOND HELPING** [ ] Apr74 [12]
– Sweet home Alabama / I need you / Don't ask me no questions / Workin' for MCA / The ballad of Curtis Loew / Swamp music / The needle and the spoon / Call me the breeze. *(re-iss. 1983 lp/c; MCL/+C 1746) (re-iss. Oct87 on 'Fame' lp/c; FA/TC-FA 3194) (cd-iss. Aug89; DMCL 1746) (cd re-iss. Oct92; MCLD 19073)*

Oct 74. (7") *(MCA 160) <40258>* **SWEET HOME ALABAMA. / TAKE YOUR TIME** [ ] Jul74 [8]

Nov 74. (7") *<40328>* **FREE BIRD (edit). / DOWN SOUTH JUKIN'** [–] [19]

— (Dec74) **ARTIMUS PYLE** (b. 15 Jul'48, Spartanburg, South Carolina) – drums repl. BURNS

May 75. (lp/c) *(MCF/+C 2700) <2137>* **NUTHIN' FANCY** [43] Apr75 [9]
– Saturday night special / Cheatin' woman / Railroad song / I'm a country boy / On the hunt / Am I losin' / Made in the shade / Whiskey rock-a-roller. *(re-iss. 1983 lp/c; MCL/+C 1760) (cd-iss. Aug87; CMCAD 31003) (cd re-iss. Nov94; MCLD 19074) (cd re-iss. Nov99; MCD 12024)*

Jul 75. (7") *(MCA 199) <40416>* **SATURDAY NIGHT SPECIAL. / MADE IN THE SHADE** [ ] May75 [27]

— Reverted to six-piece, when ED KING departed / added backing vocalists **CASSIE GAINES, LESLIE HAWKINS + JO JO BILLINGSLEY**

Feb 76. (7") *(MCA 229) <40532>* **DOUBLE TROUBLE. / ROLL GYPSY ROLL** [ ] [80]

Mar 76. (lp/c) *(MCF/+C 2744) <2170>* **GIMME BACK MY BULLETS** [34] Feb76 [20]
– Gimme back my bullets / Every mother's son / Trust / (I got the) Same old blues / Double trouble / Roll gypsy roll / Searching / Cry for the bad man / All I can do is write about it. *(re-iss. Feb82 lp/c; MCL/+C 1653) (cd-iss. Nov99; MCD 12023) (cd re-iss. Mar06 deluxe += w/dvd+=; 9833400)* – (live versions). // (video versions).

Jun 76. (7") *<40565>* **GIMME BACK MY BULLETS. / ALL I CAN DO IS WRITE ABOUT IT** [–] [ ]

Aug 76. (7"ep) *(MCA 251)* **FREE BIRD. / SWEET HOME ALABAMA / DOUBLE TROUBLE** [31] [–]
(re-iss. Nov79, hit No.43) (re-iss. May82 hit No.21) (re-iss. Dec83 12" /12"pic-d; MCAT/+P 251)

— added **STEVE GAINES** (b.14 Sep'49, Seneca, Missouri) – 3rd guitar (ex-SMOKEHOUSE)

Oct 76. (7") *<40647>* **TRAVELIN' MAN (live). / GIMME THREE STEPS (live)** [–] [ ]

Oct 76. (d-lp/d-c) *(MCSP/+C 279) <6001>* **ONE MORE FROM THE ROAD** (live) [17] Sep76 [9]
– Workin' for MCA / I ain't the one / Searching / Tuesday's gone / Saturday night special / Travelin' man / Whiskey rock-a-roller / Sweet home Alabama / Gimme three steps / Call me the breeze / T for Texas / The needle and spoon / Crossroads / Free bird. *<US cd-iss. 1991 with edited applause> (d-cd-ss.Dec92; MCLDD 19139)*

Nov 76. (7") *<40665>* **FREE BIRD (live). / SEARCHING (live)** [–] [38]

Jan 77. (7") *(MCA 275)* **FREE BIRD (live edit). / GIMME THREE STEPS (live)** [ ] [–]

Oct 77. (lp/c) *(MCG/+C 3525) <3029>* **STREET SURVIVORS** [13] [5]
– What's your name / That smell / One more time / I know a little / You got that right / I never dreamed / Honky tonk night time man / Ain't no good life. *(re-iss. Jul82 lp/c; MCL/+C 1694) (cd-iss. Oct94; MCLD 19248)*

— On 20th Oct'77, a few days after release of above album, the band's tour plane crashed. RONNIE VAN ZANT, STEVE & CASSIE GAINES plus roadie DEAN KILPATRICK were all killed. The remainder all suffered other injuries, but would recover. ARTIMUS went solo, the rest became ROSSINGTON-COLLINS BAND

Jan 78. (7") *(MCA 342) <40819>* **WHAT'S YOUR NAME. / I KNOW A LITTLE** [ ] Nov77 [13]

Mar 78. (7") *<40888>* **YOU GOT THAT RIGHT. / AIN'T NO GOOD LIFE** [–] [69]

ROSSINGTON-COLLINS BAND

— formed 1979 by **GARY & ALLEN** with **BILLY POWELL** – keyboards / **LEON WILKESON** – bass / **DALE KRANTZ** – vocals / **BARRY HAREWOOD** – guitars, slide / **DEREK HASS** – drums, percussion

M.C.A. — M.C.A.

Jul 80. (lp/c) *(MCG/+C 4011) <5130>* **ANYTIME, ANYPLACE, ANYWHERE** [ ] [13]
– Prime time / Three times as bad / Don't misunderstand me / Misery loves company / One good man / Opportunity / Getaway / Winners and losers / Sometimes you can put it out. *(re-iss. Jun87 lp/c; MCL/+C 1748) <US cd-iss. Jun88; 31220>*

Aug 80. (7") *(MCA 636) <41284>* **DON'T MISUNDERSTAND ME. / WINNERS AND LOSERS** [ ] [55]

Oct 80. (7") *<51023>* **GETAWAY. / SOMETIMES YOU CAN PUT IT OUT** [–] [ ]

Oct 80. (7") *(MCA 648)* **ONE GOOD MAN. / MISERY LOVES COMPANY** [ ] [–]

Jun 81. (7") *<51218>* **GOTTA GET IT STRAIGHT. / DON'T STOP ME NOW** [–] [ ]

Oct 81. (lp/c) *(MCF/+C 4018) <5207>* **THIS IS THE WAY** [ ] [24]
– Gotta get it straight / Teshauna / Gonna miss it when it's gone / Pine box / Fancy ideas / Don't stop me now / Seems like every day / I'm free today / Next phone call / Means nothing to you.

Oct 81. (7") *(MCA 752)* **TESHAUNA. / GONNA MISS IT WHEN IT'S GONE** [ ] [–]
(12"+=) *(MCAT 572)* – Don't stop me now.

ROSSINGTON

— with **GARY** & his wife **DALE** with **HASS** – drums / **JAY JOHNSON** – guitar / **TIM LINDSAY** – bass

not iss. — Atlantic

Nov 86. (lp) *<81672>* **RETURNED TO THE SCENE OF THE CRIME** [–] [ ]
– Turn it up / Honest hearts / God luck to you / Wounded again / Waiting in the shadows / Dangerous love / Can you forget about my love / Returned to the scene of the crime / Are you leaving me / Path less chosen.

Nov 86. (7") *<89364>* **TURN IT UP. / PATH LESS CHOSEN** [–] [ ]

— now with **TIM LINDSEY** – bass / **TIM SHARPTON** – keyboards / **RONNIE EADES** – sax / **MITCH RIGER** – drums

M.C.A. M.C.A.

Jul 88. (lp/c/cd; as The ROSSINGTON BAND) <*(MCA/+C/D 42166)*> **LOVE YOUR MAN** [ ] [ ]
– Losin' control / Welcome me home / Call it love / Holdin' my own / Rock on / Love your man / Stay with me / Nowhere to run / Say it from the heart / I don't want to leave you.

ALLEN COLLINS BAND

— with **COLLINS, HAREWOOD, POWELL, WILKESON, HESS,** plus **JIMMY DOUGHERTY** – vocals / **RANDALL HALL** – guitar

not iss. M.C.A.

1983. (lp) <*39000*> **HERE THERE AND BACK** [–] [ ]
– Just trouble / One known soldier / Hangin' judge / Time after time / This ride's on me / Ready to move / Chapter one / Commitments / Everything you need. <*US cd-iss. 1990's; MCAD 31324*>

— After a spell in prison, POWELL joined Christian band VISION. Also in 1986, ALLEN COLLINS was involved in a car crash which killed his girlfriend, and paralized himself from the waist down. On the 23rd Jan'90 he died of pneumonia.

LYNYRD SKYNYRD

— re-formed Autumn 1987 with **ROSSINGTON, POWELL, PYLE, WILKESON, KING** plus **DALE KRANTZ ROSSINGTON, RANDALL HALL + JOHNNY VAN ZANT** – vocals (ex-• 38 SPECIAL)

M.C.A. M.C.A.

Apr 88. (d-lp/d-c/cd) *(DCMDMCMDC/DMCMD 7004)* <*8027*> **SOUTHERN BY THE GRACE OF GOD (live)** [ ] [68]
– Workin' for MCA / That smell / I know a little / Comin' home / You got that right / What's your name / Gimme back my bullets / Swamp music / Call me the breeze / Dixie – Sweet home Alabama / Free bird.

— **LYNYRD SKYNYRD** re-formed again in 1991 with **ROSSINGTON, KING** and **HALL** – guitars / **JOHNNY VAN ZANT** – vocals / **POWELL** – keyboards / **WILKESON** – bass / **PYLE** – percussion, drums / **CUSTER** – drums, percussion

Atlantic Atlantic

Jun 91. (cd/c/lp) <*(7567 82258-2/-4/-1)*> **LYNYRD SKYNYRD 1991** [ ] [64]
– Smokestack lightning / Keeping the faith / Southern women / Pure & simple / I've seen enough / Good thing / Money man / Backstreet crawler / It's a killer / Mama (afraid to say goodbye) / End of the road.

— extended members **JERRY JONES** – bass, guitar / **DALE KRANTZ-ROSSINGTON** – backing vocals repl. ARTIMUS PYLE

Mar 93. (cd/c) <*(7567 82447-2/-4)*> **THE LAST REBEL** [ ] [64]
– Good lovin's hard to find / One thing / Can't take that away / Best things in life / The last rebel / Outta Hell in my Dodge / Kiss your freedom goodbye / South of Heaven / Love don't always come easy / Born to run. *(re-iss. cd Feb95; same)*

not iss. Capricorn

Aug 94. (cd/c) <*42028-2*> **ENDANGERED SPECIES** [–] [ ]
– Down south jukin' / Heartbreak hotel / Devil in the bottle / Things goin' on / Saturday night special / Sweet home Alabama / I ain't the one / Am I losin' / All I have is a song / Poison whiskey / Good luck, bad luck / The last rebel / Hillbilly blues.

S.P.V. S.P.V.

Jul 96. (d-cd) *(SPV 0874419-2)* **SOUTHERN KNIGHTS (live)** [ ] [ ]
– Working for MCA / Ain't the one / Saturday night special / Down south jukin' / Double trouble / T for Texas / Devil in the bottle / That smell / Simple man / Whiskey rock and roller / What's your name / Gimme three steps / Sweet home Alabama / Free bird.

— line-up now **ROSSINGTON, VAN ZANT, WILKESON, POWELL** plus **RICKEY MEDLOCKE** – guitars, vocals (ex-BLACKFOOT) / **HUGHIE THOMASSON** – guitars, vocals (ex-OUTLAWS) / **OWEN HALE** – drums, percussion

May 97. (cd) *(SPV 0854439-2)* **TWENTY** [ ] [97]
– We ain't much different / Bring it on / Voodoo lake / Home is where the heart is / Travelin' man / Talked myself right into it / Never too late / O.R.R. / Blame it on a sad song / Berneice / None of us are free / How soon we forget.

— **MICHAEL CARTELLONE** – drums (ex-DAMN YANKEES) repl. HALE

S.P.V. CMC Int.

Jun 98. (d-cd) *(SPV 0852916-2)* <*607686147*> **LYVE FROM STEEL TOWN (live)** [ ] Apr98 [ ]
– We ain't much different / Saturday night special / What's your name? / On the hunt / You got that right / Voodoo lake / That smell / Bring it on / Simple man / I know a little / Berneice / Gimme three steps / Sweet home Alabama / Travelin' man / Free bird / (interview pt.1 & 2).

Aug 99. (cd) *(SPV 0852964-2)* <*86272*> **EDGE OF FOREVER** [ ] [96]
– Workin' / Full moon night / Preacher man / Mean streets / Tomorrow's goodbye / Edge of forever / Gone fishin' / Through it all / Money back guarentee / G.W.T.G.G. / Rough around the edges / Fla.

Oct 00. (cd) *(SPV 0857102-2)* <*86298*> **CHRISTMAS TIME AGAIN** (festive) [ ] Sep00 [ ]

— **EAN EVANS** – bass; repl. WILKESON who died 21st July 2001

Sanctuary Sanctuary

May 03. (cd) *(SANCD 180)* <*84607*> **VICIOUS CYCLE** [ ] [30]
– That's how I like it / Pick 'em up / Dead man walkin' / The way / Red white and blue / Sweet mama / All funked up / Hell or Heaven / Mad hatter / Rockin' little town / Crawl / Jake / Life's lessons / Lucky man / Gimme back my bullets (with KID ROCK).

Jun 04. (d-cd) *(SANDD 262)* <*84699*> **LYVE: THE VICIOUS CYCLE TOUR** (live) [ ] [ ]
– That's how I like it / What's your name? / I know a little / Pick 'em up / Simple man / That smell / Red white and blue / Down south jukin' / Gimme back my bullets / Double trouble / The ballad of Curtis Loew / Tuesday's gone / Mississippi kid / Workin' / Gimme three steps / Call me the breeze / Sweet home Alabama / The way / Free bird. *(re-iss. May06 on 'Castle' w/dvd+=; CMFVD 1348)*

– compilations, others, etc. –

All 'M.C.A.' unless otherwise stated.

Oct 78. (lp/c) *(MCG/+C 3529)* <*3047*> **SKYNYRD'S FIRST AND . . .LAST** (rec.1970-72) [50] Sep78 [15]
– Down south jukin' / Preacher's daughter / White dove / Was I right or wrong / Lend a helpin' hand / Wino / Comin' home / The seasons / Things goin' on. *(re-iss. Aug81 lp/c; MCL/+C 1627)*

Oct 78. (7") <*40957*> **DOWN SOUTH JUKIN'. / WINO** [–] [ ]

Oct 78. (7"ep) *(MCEP 101)* **DOWN SOUTH JUKIN' / THAT SMELL. / LEND A HELPIN' HAND / CALL ME THE BREEZE** [ ] [–]

Jan 80. (d-lp/d-c) *(MCSP/+C 308)* <*11008*> **GOLD & PLATINUM** [49] Dec79 [12]
– Down south jukin' / Saturday night special / Gimme three steps / What's your name / You got that right / Gimme back my bullets / Sweet home Alabama / Free bird / That smell / On the hunt / I ain't the one / Whiskey rock-a-roller / Simple man / I know a little / Tuesday's gone / Comin' home. *(re-iss. Jul82 lp/c; MCDW/+C 456)*

Apr 82. (d-c) *(MCA2 107)* **PRONOUNCED LEH-NERD SKIN-NERD / SECOND HELPING** [ ] [–]

Nov 82. (lp) <*5370*> **THE BEST OF THE REST** [–] [ ]

Jul 84. (7") *Old Gold; (OG 9421)* **FREE BIRD (edit). / SWEET HOME ALABAMA** [ ] [–]
(re-iss. Aug95 on cd-s;)

Sep 86. (d-c) *(MCA2 111)* **NUTHIN' FANCY / GIVE ME BACK MY BULLETS** [ ] [–]

Mar 87. (d-lp/c) *Raw Power; (RAW LP/TC 031)* **ANTHOLOGY** [ ] [–]

Nov 87. (7") <*53206*> **WHEN YOU GOT GOOD FRIENDS. / TRUCK DRIVIN' MAN** [–] [ ]

Nov 87. (lp/c) *(MCF/+C 3405)* <*42084*> **LEGEND** (rare live) [ ] Oct87 [41]
– Georgia peaches / When you got good friends / Sweet little Missy / Four walls of Raiford / Simple man / Truck drivin' man / One in the sun / Mr. Banker / Take your time.

Jan 89. (7"/12") *(MCA/+T 1315)* **FREE BIRD. / SWEET HOME ALABAMA** [ ] [–]

Apr 89. (lp/c/cd) *(MCG/MCGC/DMCG 6046)* <*42293*> **SKYNYRD'S INNYRDS** [ ] [ ]

1990. (c-s) <*54306*> **FREE BIRD. / SWEET HOME ALABAMA** [–] [ ]

Feb 92. (3xcd-box) *(MCA3 10390)* **THE DEFINITIVE LYNYRD SKYNYRD COLLECTION** [ ] [ ]

Mar 94. (cd/c) *Nectar; (NTR CD/C 015)* **FREEBIRD – THE VERY BEST** [ ] [–]
– Saturday night special / Whiskey rock & roller / Workin' for MCA / I ain't the one / Sweet home Alabama / Ballad of Curtis Loew / Tuesday's gone / Gimme 3 steps / The needle & the spoon / Free bird / Call me the breeze / What's your name / Swamp music / Gimme back my bullets / That smell / You got that right.

Sep 94. (cd) *(MCLD 19248)* **STREET SURVIVORS / SKYNYRD'S FIRST AND . . . LAST** [ ] [–]

Sep 96. (cd) <*(MCD 1147-2)*> **FREEBIRD – THE MOVIE** (soundtrack) [ ] Aug96 [ ]
– Workin' for M.C.A. / I ain't the one / Saturday night special / Whisky rock-a-roller / Travellin' man / Searching / What's your name / That

smell / Gimme three steps / Call the breeze / T for Texas (blue yodel No.1) / Sweet home Alabama / Freebird / Dixie.

Jun 97. (d-cd) *Repertoire; (RR 4637)* **OLD TIME GREATS** [ ] [–]
Nov 98. (cd) *B.M.G.; <44845>* **EXTENDED VERSIONS** [–] [ ]
Nov 98. (cd) *<MCD 11888>* **SKYNYRD'S FIRST** [–] [ ]
Jan 99. (d-cd) *<(MCD 11807)>* **THE ESSENTIAL LYNYRD SKYNYRD** [ ] Aug98 [ ]
Mar 99. (cd) *<MCD 11941>* **THE MILLENNIUM COLLECTION: THE BEST OF LYNYRD SKYNYRD** [–] [ ]
Oct 99. (cd) *<MCD 12041>* **SOLO FLYTES** [–] [ ]
Jan 00. (cd) *Universal; (E 112173-2)* **UNIVERSAL MASTERS COLLECTION** [ ] [ ]
Mar 00. (cd) *<112229>* **ALL TIME GREATEST HITS** [–] [ ]
Mar 00. (cd) *Calamari; <12606>* **THE COMPLETE LYNYRD SKYNYRD LIVE** [–] [ ]
Jul 00. (cd) *S.P.V.; (SPV 0762994-2) / C.M.C.; <86293>* **THEN AND NOW** [ ] Apr00 [ ]
Aug 00. (cd) *Universal; <112341>* **DOUBLE TROUBLE** [–] [ ]
Oct 00. (3xcd-box) *Universal; (E 132182-2)* **NUTHIN' FANCY / SECOND HELPING / STREET SURVIVORS** [ ] [–]
Dec 00. (cd) *Universal; (AA 88112429-2) / M.C.A.; <429>* **COLLECTYBLES** [ ] Nov00 [ ]
Apr 00. (cd) *B.M.G.; <45721>* **YESTERDAY AND TODAY** [–] [ ]
Apr 01. (cd) *Spectrum; (544451-2)* **THE ESSENTIAL COLLECTION** [ ] [–]
Aug 03. (d-cd) *Universal TV; <2840-2>* **THYRTY: 30TH ANNIVERSARY COLLECTION** [–] [16]
– Sweet home Alabama / Need all my friends / Blues medley: Sweet little angel – How blue can you get – I got a mind to go / Down south jukin' / Was I right or wrong / I ain't the one / Tuesday's gone / Gimme three steps / Workin' for MCA / Ballad of Curtis Loew / Call me the breeze / Saturday night special / All I can do is write about it (acoustic) / Free bird // Whiskey rock-a-roller (live) / Simple man (live) / What's your name? / That smell / I know a little / You got that right / Comin' home (live) / Swamp music (live) / Gimme back my bullets (live) / Smokestack lightning / Last rebel / Things goin' on (acoustic) / Talked myself right into it / We ain't much different (live) / Workin' / Mad hatter.
Jun 05. (d-cd) *Universal TV; (9830565)* **GREATEST HITS** [47] [–]
– Freebird / Tuesday's gone / Gimme three steps / Simple man / Poison whiskey / Don't ask me no questions / Swamp music / I've been a fool / Comin' home / Down south jukin' / I ain't the one / White dove / Workin' for MCA / The needle and the spoon / Sweet home Alabama // Call me the breeze / Saturday night special / Railroad song / I'm a country boy / On the hunt / Whiskey rock-a-roller / Gimme back my bullets / I got the same old blues / Double trouble / Searchin' / Cry for the bad man / What's your name? / That smell / I know a little / You got that right.
Sep 05. (cd) *Lilith; (LR 101CD)* **POISON WHISKEY** [ ] [–]
May 06. (d-cd) *Universal; (9833088)* **THE LYNYRD SKYNYRD STORY** [ ] [–]

☐ Shane MacGOWAN & the POPES
(see under ⇒ POGUES)

☐ Billy MACKENZIE (see under ⇒ ASSOCIATES)

MADNESS

Formed: Camden, London, England ... early '79, out of Kentish Town ska outfit, The INVADERS. In its earliest incarnation MADNESS comprised MIKE BARSON (keyboards), LEE THOMPSON (saxophone, vocals) CHRIS FOREMAN (guitar), CHAS SMASH (horns, vocals, 'nutty' dancing), GRAHAM 'SUGGS' McPHERSON (vocals, equally 'nutty' dancing), MARK BEDFORD (bass) and DAN WOODGATE (drums). MADNESS were one of the leading lights of the ska revivalist '2-Tone' movement, the most exciting musical phenomenon since the advent of punk a few years earlier. Becoming friends with The SPECIAL AKA, MADNESS signed a one-off singles deal with JERRY DAMMERS' (the SPECIALS mainman) '2-Tone' label, releasing 'THE PRINCE' in August '79. An irrepressible dancefloor shuffle embellished with loose-limbed piano courtesy of BARSON, the track was a tribute to blue beat legend PRINCE BUSTER, whose song 'MADNESS' inspired the group's name and which they covered in their own inimitable style on the B-side. The track powered into the Top 20 and after a '2-Tone' tour with The SPECIALS and The SELECTER, MADNESS signed to 'Stiff', embarking upon an impressive run of chart domination. The follow-up single was 'ONE STEP BEYOND', its famous 'Hey you, don't watch that, watch this . . .' intro leading into a largely instrumental, sax-driven epic. The album of the same name reached No.2, confirming MADNESS had arrived. The group's "nutty boy" postures, madcap humour, cockney patois and unerringly catchy hooks won them a wide cross section of fans, from primary school kids and grannys to style-conscious teenagers, a far cry from their early audience of hardcore NF skinheads, most of whom they thankfully managed to shake off. As the band progressed from the likes of 'BAGGY TROUSERS' to the mordant social commentary of the '7' (1981) album, they moved away slightly from their ska roots, developing a highly original pop sound. After nine Top 10 hits, the band scored their first No.1 in 1982 with 'HOUSE OF FUN', a colourful coming of age yarn that contrasted with the increasing sense of melancholy that would come to mark their later work. Even earlier tracks like the brilliant 'BED AND BREAKFAST MAN' (from ONE STEP BEYOND) possessed a kind of bittersweet poignancy, as did the band's final single as a 7-piece, 'THE SUN AND THE RAIN'. MADNESS were still capable of a good old rave up of course, as they illustrated with their previous effort, the celebratory calypso vibe of 'WINGS OF A DOVE', a No.2 hit in the summer of '83. With the departure of MIKE BARSON (one the band's main writers), the band began to lose their trademark sound. Songs likes 'MICHAEL CAINE' were interesting but not the MADNESS fans knew and loved, their declining popularity marked by increasingly lower chart positions. In 1984, the band formed their own label, 'Zarjazz', releasing work by FEARGAL SHARKEY as well as their own material which was, by this point, largely uninspired, coming to a juddering anti-climax with a cover of Scritti Politti's 'SWEETEST GIRL' and 'WELCOME TO THE GHOST TRAIN'. The band had already decided to split by the time of the latter's release in October '86, BEDFORD and WOODFORD subsequently joining VOICE OF THE BEEHIVE. In 1988, McPHERSON, THOMPSON, FOREMAN and SMASH re-fromed the band as THE MADNESS, an eponymous album not even breaching the Top 50. They had split for good by the end of the year, SUGGS going on to become a suitably "nutty" TV presenter as well as inflicting the FARM upon an unsuspecting music world at the turn of the decade. SMASH became an A&R man for 'Go! Discs', while THOMPSON and FOREMAN went back to ska basics with a new outfit, the NUTTY BOYS, releasing an album, 'CRUNCH!', in 1990. Back by popular demand, the original line-up reformed in 1992 for two sell-out shows in London's Finsbury Park where an army of 20-something's donned their pork pie hats and relived their days down the youth centre disco. The event was such a triumph that MADNESS repeated it in successive years. Not content with merely presenting Top Of The Pops now and again, SUGGS released a solo album, 'THE LONE RANGER', in 1995, subjecting innocent pop kids to an awful cod-reggae version of Simon & Garfunkel's 'CECILIA'. Maybe he's finally lost it. No, SUGGS was back to give us a second helping of his nutty pop songs, 'THE THREE PYRAMIDS CLUB' in 1998 was followed a year later by a re-formed MADNESS set, 'WONDERFUL' (1999) – well, if you like that sort of thing. In 2005 and with 25 years or so in the business, MADNESS showed they could still cut a good tune, albeit from the pen of someone else. 'THE DANGERMEN SESSIONS, VOLUME ONE' (2005) was shaped in a similar stylee to UB40's 'Labour Of Love' – from way back in 1983 – and it certainly paid off as songs by Desmond Dekker, Max Romeo and even the Kinks were given the Nutty Boy treatment.

• **Songwriters:** Either McPHERSON-THOMPSON or BARSON or BEDFORD-FOREMAN. Covered; ONE STEP BEYOND (Cornell Campbell) / SWAN LAKE (Tchaikovski) / IT MUST BE LOVE (Labi Siffre) / THE HARDER THEY COME (Jimmy Cliff). SUGGS covered; I'M ONLY SLEEPING (Beatles). • **Trivia:** Early in 1982, SUGGS married singer and fellow 'Stiff' artist, BETTE BRIGHT.

Album rating: ONE STEP BEYOND (*8) / ABSOLUTELY (*6) / 7 (*6) / THE RISE AND FALL (*7) / COMPLETE MADNESS compilation (*9) / KEEP MOVING (*5) / MAD NOT MAD (*4) / UTTER MADNESS compilation (*6) / THE MADNESS (*6) / DIVINE MADNESS compilation (*9) / MADSTOCK (*5) / WONDERFUL (*5) / THE DANGERMEN SESSIONS VOLUME ONE (*6) / Suggs: THE LONE RANGER (*5) / THREE PYRAMIDS CLUB (*4)

GRAHAM 'SUGGS' McPHERSON (b.13 Jan'61, Hastings, England) – vocals / **MIKE BARSON** (b.21 May'58) – keyboards / **CHRIS 'CHRISSIE BOY' FOREMAN** (b. 8 Aug'58) – guitar / **LEE 'KIX' THOMPSON** (b. 5 Oct'57) – saxophone, vocals / **MARK 'BEDDERS' BEDFORD** (b.24 Aug'61) – bass / **DAN 'WOODY' WOODGATE** (b.19 Oct'60) – drums repl. JOHN HASLER / **CHAS SMASH** (b. CATHAL SMYTH, 14 Jan'59) – horns, vocals, dancer

		2-Tone-Chrysalis	not iss.
Aug 79.	(7") *(CHS TT3)* **THE PRINCE. / MADNESS** *(re-iss. Feb87 on 'Old Gold'; OG 9685)*	16	–
		Stiff	Sire
Oct 79.	(lp/c) *(SEEZ/CSEEZ 17)* <6085> **ONE STEP BEYOND . . .**	2	

– One step beyond / My girl / Night boat to Cairo / Believe me / Land of hope & glory / The prince / Tarzan's nuts / In the middle of the night / Bed and breakfast man / Razor blade alley / Swan Lake / Rockin' in Ab / Mummy's boy / Chipmunks are go. *(re-iss. Aug88 on 'Virgin' lp/c; OVED/+C 133) (cd-iss. Apr90; CDOVED 133)*

Oct 79. (7") *(BUY 56)* **ONE STEP BEYOND. / MISTAKES** [7] [ ]
(12"+=) *(BUYIT 56)* – Nutty theme.
(re-iss. Jun85 on 'Virgin' 7"; VS 780)

Dec 79. (7") *(BUY 62)* **MY GIRL. / STEPPING INTO LINE** [3] [ ]
(12"+=) *(BUYIT 62)* – In the rain.
(re-iss. Jun85 on 'Virgin' 7"; VS 781)

Mar 80. (7"ep) *(BUY 71)* **WORK, REST & PLAY EP** [6] [ ]
– Night boat to Cairo / Deceives the eye / The young and the old / Don't quote me on that. *(re-iss. Jun85 on 'Virgin' 7"ep; VS 782)*

Sep 80. (7") *(BUY 84)* **BAGGY TROUSERS. / THE BUSINESS** [3] [ ]
(re-iss. Jun85 on 'Virgin' 7"; VS 783)

Sep 80. (lp/c) *(SEEZ/CSEEZ 29)* <6094> **ABSOLUTELY** [2] [ ]
– Baggy trousers / Embarrassment / E.R.N.I.E. / Close escape / Not home today / On the beat Pete / Solid gone / Take it or leave it / Shadow of fear / Disappear / Overdone / In the rain / You said / The return of the Los Palmas 7. *(re-iss. Aug88 on 'Virgin' lp/c; OVED/+C 134) (cd-iss. Nov89; CDOVED 134)*

Nov 80. (7") *(BUY 102)* **EMBARRASSMENT. / CRYING SHAME** [4] [ ]

Jan 81. (7") *(BUY 108)* **THE RETURN OF THE LOS PALMAS 7. / THAT'S THE WAY TO DO IT** [7] [ ]
(12"+=) *(BUYIT 108)* – My girl (demo) / Swan Lake (live).

Apr 81. (7"/c-s) *(BUY/ZBUY 112)* **GREY DAY. / MEMORIES** [4] [–]

Sep 81. (7") *(BUY 126)* **SHUT UP. / A TOWN WITH NO NAME** [7] [–]
(12"+=) *(BUYIT 126)* – Never ask twice.

Oct 81. (lp/c) *(SEEZ/CSEEZ 39)* **7** [5] [–]
– Cardiac arrest / Shut up / Sign of the times / Missing you / Mrs. Hutchinson / Tomorrow's dream / Opium eaters / Grey day / Pac-amac / Promises promises / Benny bullfrog / When dawn arrives / The opium eaters / Aeroplane. *(re-iss. Aug88 on 'Virgin' lp/c; SEEZ/CSEEZ 135) (cd-iss. Nov89; CDOVED 135)*

Stiff / Geffen

Nov 81. (7"/12") *(BUY/S'BUY 134)* **IT MUST BE LOVE. / SHADOW ON THE HOUSE** [4] [–]

Feb 82. (7"/ext.12") *(BUY/+IT 140)* **CARDIAC ARREST. / IN THE CITY** [14] [ ]

Apr 82. (lp/c) *(HITTV/ZHITV 1)* **COMPLETE MADNESS** (compilation) [1] [–]
– Embarrassment / Shut up / My girl / Baggy trousers / It must be love / The prince / Bed and breakfast man / Night boat to Cairo / One step beyond / House of fun / Cardiac arrest / Take it or leave it / Madness / The return of the Los Palmas 7 / In the city. *(cd-iss. Jul 86 on 'Virgin'; HITCD 1)*

May 82. (7"/7"pic-d) *(BUY/P-BUY 140)* **HOUSE OF FUN. / DON'T LOOK BACK** [1] [ ]
(re-iss. Jun85 on 'Virgin' 7"; VS 784)

Jul 82. (7"/7"pic-d) *(BUY/P-BUY 153)* **DRIVING IN MY CAR. / ANIMAL FARM** [4] [ ]
(12"+=) *(S'BUY 153)* – Riding on my bike.
(re-iss. Jun85 on 'Virgin' 7"; VS 785)

Oct 82. (7"/7"pic-d) *(BUY/P-BUY 163)* **OUR HOUSE. / WALKING WITH MR WHEEZE** [5] [–]
(12"+=) *(BUYIT 163)* – ('A'extended).
(re-iss. Jun85 on 'Virgin' 7"; VS 786)

Nov 82. (lp/c) *(SEEZ/CSEEZ 46)* **PRESENTS THE RISE AND FALL** [10] [ ]
– Rise and fall / Tomorrow's (just another day) / Blue skinned beast / Primrose hill / Mr. Speaker (gets the word) / Sunday morning / Our house / Tiptoes / New Delhi / That face / Calling cards / Are you coming (with me) / Madness (is all in the mind). *(re-iss. Aug88 on 'Virgin' lp/c; OVED/+C 190) (cd-iss. Nov89; CDOVED 190)*

Feb 83. (7"/7"pic-d) *(BUY/P-BUY 169)* **TOMORROW'S (JUST ANOTHER DAY). / MADNESS (IS ALL IN THE MIND)** [8] [ ]
(ext.12"+=) *(BUYIT 169)* – Blue beast / ('A'version with ELVIS COSTELLO).
(re-iss. Jun85 on 'Virgin' 7"; VS 787)

Mar 83. (lp) <4003> **MADNESS** [–] [41]
– It must be love / Shut up / Rise and fall / Tomorrow's just another day / Primrose Hill / Madness (is all in the mind) / Grey day / House of fun / Blue skinned beast / Cardiac arrest / Night boat to Cairo / Shadow of fear.

May 83. (7")(12") <29668> **OUR HOUSE. / CARDIAC ARREST** [–] [7]

Aug 83. (7") <29562> **IT MUST BE LOVE. / CALLING CARDS** [–] [33]

Aug 83. (7"/7"pic-d) *(BUY/P-BUY 181)* **WINGS OF A DOVE. / BEHIND THE 8 BALL** [2] [ ]
('A'-Blue train mix-12"+=) *(BUYIT 181)* – One's second thoughtlessness.
(re-iss. Jun85 on 'Virgin' 7"; VS 788)

Oct 83. (7"/7"pic-d) *(BUY/P-BUY 192)* **THE SUN AND THE RAIN. / FIREBALL XL5** [5] [–]
(ext.12"+=) *(BUYIT 192)* – My girl (live).
(re-iss. Jun85 on 'Virgin' 7"; VS 789)

Jan 84. (7") <29350> **THE SUN AND THE RAIN. / TIME FOR TEA** [–] [72]

— trimmed to a 6-piece, when BARSON went to stay in Holland with his Dutch wife.

Jan 84. (7"/7"pic-d) *(BUY/P-BUY 196)* **MICHAEL CAINE. / IF YOU THINK THERE'S SOMETHING** [11] [ ]
(12"+=) *(BUYIT 196)* – ('A'extended).
(re-iss. Jun85 on 'Virgin' 7"; VS 790)

Feb 84. (lp/pic-lp/c) <4022> *(SEEZ/PSEEZ/CSEEZ 53)* **KEEP MOVING** [6] [ ]
– Keep moving / Michael Caine / Turning blue / One better day / March of the gherkins / Waltz into mischief * / Brand new beat / Victoria Gardens. *<US repl. * w/)* – Wings of a dove (a celebratory song) / The sun and the rain / Prospects / Samantha. *(re-iss. Aug88 on 'Virgin' lp/c; OVED/+C 191) (cd-iss. Nov89; CDOVED 191)*

May 84. (7"/7"pic-d) *(BUY/P-BUY 201)* **ONE BETTER DAY. / GUNS** [17] [ ]
(12"+=) *(BUYIT 201)* – Victoria Gardens / Sarah.
(re-iss. Jun85 on 'Virgin' 7"; VS 791)

Zarjazz / Virgin

Aug 85. (7") *(JAZZ 5)* **YESTERDAY'S MEN. / ALL I KNEW** [18] [ ]
(ext.12") *(JAZZ 5-12)* – ('A'demo).
(7"square-pic-d/incl.free-7"+=) *(JAZZ D5)* – YESTERDAY'S MEN (harmonica mix) / IT MUST BE LOVE (live)

Oct 85. (lp/c) *(JZ LP/MC 1)* **MAD NOT MAD** [16] [ ]
– I'll compete / Yesterday's men / Uncle Sam / White heat / Mad not mad / Sweetest girl / Burning the boats / Tears you can't hide / Time / Coldest day. *(cd-iss. Jul87; JZCD 1)*

Oct 85. (7"/s7") *(JAZZ/+F 7)* **UNCLE SAM. / PLEASE DON'T GO** [21] [ ]
(7"pic-d+=) *(JAZZY 7)* – Inanity over Christmas.
(ext.12"+=) *(JAZZ 7-12)* – ('A'demo).

Jan 86. (7"/one-sided-7"pic-d) *(JAZZ/+Y 8)* **SWEETEST GIRL. / JENNIE (A PORTRAIT OF)** [35] [ ]
(ext.12"+=) *(JAZZ 8-12)* – ('A'dub).
(d7"+=) *(JAZZ D8)* – Tears you can't hide / Call me.

— **BARSON** returned for swan-song

Oct 86. (7"/7"square-pic-d) *(JAZZ/+S 9)* **(WAITING FOR) THE GHOST TRAIN. / MAYBE IN ANOTHER LIFE** [18] [ ]
(12"+=/12"w-booklet+=) *(JAZZ/+B 9-12)* – Seven year scratch.

Nov 86. (lp/c/cd) *(JZ LP/MC/CD 2)* **UTTER MADNESS** (compilation) [29] [ ]
– Our house / Driving in my car / Michael Caine / Wings of a dove / Yesterday's men / Tomorrow's (just another day) / I'll compete / (Waiting for) The ghost train / Uncle Sam / The sun and the rain / Sweetest girl / One better day / Victoria Gardens. *(cd+=)* – Seven year scratch (hit megamix). *(re-iss. Apr90 on 'Virgin' lp/c; OVED/+C 287)*

— Had already split Sep'86. BEDDERS and WOODY joined VOICE OF THE BEEHIVE. They had recently backed female duo STRAWBERRY SWITCHBLADE.

the MADNESS

— **McPHERSON, THOMPSON, FOREMAN + SMYTH**, re-formed Feb'88, with slight change of name (allowed to just prefix THE), bringing in some session people; **JERRY DAMMERS, STEVE NIEVE + BRUCE THOMAS**

Virgin / Virgin

Mar 88. (7") *(VS 1054)* **I PRONOUNCE YOU. / PATIENCE** [44] [ ]
(d7"+=/12"+=/cd-s+=) *(VS X/T/CD 1054)* – 4 BF / 11th hour.

May 88. (lp/c/cd) *(V/TCV/CDV 2507)* **THE MADNESS** [65] [ ]

– Nail down the days / What's that / I pronounce you / Oh / In wonder / Song in red / Nightmare nightmare / Thunder and lightning / Beat the bride / Gabriel's horn. *(cd+=)* – 11th Hour / 4BF / Be Good Boy / Flashings.

May 88. (7"/7"sha-pic-d) *(VS/+S 1078)* **WHAT'S THAT. / BE GOOD BOY.** [ ] [ ]
(7"sha-pic-d) *(VSJ 1078)* – WHAT'S THAT. / FLASHINGS
(12"+=) *(VST 1078)* – Be good boy.

— Disbanded again in 1988. SUGGS became a TV presenter and the manager of The FARM, who he produced in 1985, and CHAS became A&R man for 'Go! Discs'. They were encouraged to re-unite for a one-off gig on 8 Aug'92 at Finsbury Park, after old hits re-charted (see further below).

MADNESS

(original line-up, see above)

Go! Discs London

Oct 92. (cd/c/lp) *(828367-2/-4/-1)* **MADSTOCK (live)** [22] [ ]
– One step beyond / The Prince / Embarrassment / My girl / The Sun and the rain / Grey day / It must be love / Shut up / Driving in my car / Bed and breakfast man / Close escape / Wings of a dove / Our house / Night boat to Cairo / Madness / House of fun / Baggy trousers / The harder they come.

Nov 92. (7"/c-s) *(GOD/+C 93)* **THE HARDER THEY COME (live). / TOMORROW'S JUST ANOTHER DAY (live) / TAKE IT OR LEAVE IT (live)** [44] [ ]
(cd-s+=) *(GODCD 93)* – Land of hope & glory.

SUGGS

WEA not iss.

Aug 95. (c-s) *(YZ 975C)* **I'M ONLY SLEEPING / OFF ON HOLIDAY** [7] [–]
(cd-s+=) *(YZ 975CD)* – Off on holiday (instrumental).
(cd-s+=) *(YZ 975CDX)* – Animal / When you came.

Oct 95. (7"/c-s) *(WEA 019/+C)* **CAMDEN TOWN. / BEDAZZLED** [14] [–]
(cd-s+=) *(WEA 019CD)* – ('A'-Chili pepper dub) / ('A'-Ragga in London mix).

Oct 95. (cd/c) *(0630 12478-2/-4)* **THE LONE RANGER** [14] [–]
– I'm only sleeping / Camden Town / Alcohol / 4 am / The tune / Cecilia / Haunted / Off on holiday / Green eyes / Fortune fish / She's gone.

Dec 95. (7") *(WEA 031)* **THE TUNE. / ALRIGHT** [33] [–]
(c-s+=/cd-s+=) *(WEA 031 C/CD)* – Sleigh ride.

Apr 96. (c-s/cd-s) *(WEA 042 C/CD)* **CECILIA / I FEEL GOOD** [4] [–]
(cd-s+=) *(WEA 052CDX)* – The tune.
above featured LOUCHIE LOU and MICHIE ONE, as did below

Sep 96. (c-s/cd-s) *(WEA 065 C/CD1)* **NO MORE ALCOHOL / FORTUNE FISH** [24] [–]
(cd-s+=) *(WEA 065CD2)* – ('A'mix).

May 97. (c-s/cd-s; as SUGGS & CO. featuring CHELSEA TEAM) *(WEA 112 C/CD)* **BLUE DAY / ALRIGHT** [22] [–]
(cd-s+=) *(WEA 112CD2)* – ('A'versions).

Aug 98. (c-s) *(WEA 174C)* **I AM / SAME AGAIN** [38] [–]
(cd-s+=) *(WEA 174CD)* – It really would be nice.

Sep 98. (cd/c) *(3984 23815-2/-4)* **THE THREE PYRAMIDS CLUB** [ ] [–]
– I am / So tired / Straight banana / Invisible man / Sing / Girl / The greatest show on earth / Our man / On drifting sand / The three pyramids club.

MADNESS

re-formed yet again

Virgin E.M.I.

Jul 99. (c-s) *(VSC 1737)* **LOVESTRUCK. / WE ARE LOVE** [10] [–]
(cd-s+=) *(VSCDT 1737)* – ('A'-CD-Rom).
(12") *(VSLH 1737)* – ('A'side) / Round & round / Maddley (album medley).

Oct 99. (cd-s) *(VSCDT 1740)* **JOHNNY THE HORSE / YOU'RE WONDERFUL (remix)** [44] [–]
(c-s/cd-s) *(VSC/+DX 1740)* – ('A'side) / I was the one / Dreaming man.

Oct 99. (cd/c) *(CDV/TCV 2889)* <848406> **WONDERFUL** [17] Dec99 [ ]
– Lovestruck / Johnny the horse / Communicator / 4 a.m. / Wizard / Drip fed Fred / Going to the top / Elysium / Saturday night Sunday morning / If I didn't care / No money.

Feb 00. (c-s; by MADNESS featuring IAN DURY) *(VSC 1768)* **DRIP FED FRED / WE WANT FREDDIE** [55] [–]
(cd-s+=) *(VSCDT 1768)* – Elysium.
(cd-s) *(VSCDX 1768)* – ('A'side) / Light of the way.

V2 V2

Aug 05. (cd-s) *(VVR 503324-2)* **SHAME AND SCANDAL / SKYLARKING / DREADER THAN DREAD** [38] [–]

Aug 05. (cd) *(VVR 103323-2)* <27269> **THE DANGERMEN SESSIONS VOLUME ONE** [11] [ ]
– This is where / Girl why don't you? / Shame and scandal / I chase the devil (aka Ironshirt) / Taller than you are / You keep me hanging on / Dangermen (aka High Wire) / Israelites / John Jones / Lola / You'll lose a good thing / Rain / So much trouble in the world.

– compilations, etc. –

on 'Virgin' unless otherwise stated

Oct 86. (12"ep) *Strange Fruit; (SFPS 007)* **THE PEEL SESSIONS (27.8.79)** [ ] [–]
– The prince / Bed and breakfast man / Land of hope & glory / Stepping into line. *(c-ep.Jun87; SFPSC 007) (cd-ep.Jul88; SFPSCD 007)*

Nov 88. (7") *Old Gold; (OG 9821)* **BAGGY TROUSERS. / EMBARRASSMENT** [ ] [ ]

Nov 88. (7") *Old Gold; (OG 9826)* **IT MUST BE LOVE. / MY GIRL** [ ] [ ]

May 89. (7") *(VS 1197)* **IT MUST BE LOVE. / THE RETURN OF THE LOS PALMAS 7** [6] [–]

Sep 90. (lp/c/cd) *Pickwick;* **IT'S . . . MADNESS** [ ] [–]
(re-iss. May94 on 'Virgin-VIP' cd/c; VVIP D/C 107)

Oct 90. (3xcd-box) *(TPAKJ 8)* **ONE STEP BEYOND / ABSOLUTELY / THE RISE AND FALL** [ ] [–]

Jul 91. (cd) *Pickwick; (cd)* **IT'S MADNESS . . . TOO** [ ] [–]
(re-iss. Oct94 on 'Virgin-VIP' cd/c; VVIP D/C 115)

Jan 92. (7"/c-s) *(VS/+C 1405)* **IT MUST BE LOVE. / BED AND BREAKFAST MAN** [6] [–]
(cd-s+=/pic-cd-s+=) *(VSCD T/P 1405)* – Airplane / Don't quote me on that.

Feb 92. (cd/c/d-lp) *(CD/TC+/V 2692)* **DIVINE MADNESS** [1] [ ]
– The Prince / One step beyond / My girl / Night boat to Cairo / Baggy trousers / Embarrassment / The return of Los Palmas 7 / Grey day / Shut up / It must be love / Cardiac arrest / House of fun / Driving in my car / Our house / Tomorrow's just another day / Wings of a dove / The sun and the rain / Michael Caine / One better day / Yesterday's men / Uncle Sam / (Waiting for) The ghost train.

Apr 92. (7"/c-s) *(VS/+C 1413)* **HOUSE OF FUN. / UN PASO ADELAINTE (ONE STEP BEYOND – Spanish version)** [40] [ ]
(12"+=/cd-s+=) *(VS T/CD 1413)* – Yesterday's men / Gabriel's horn (demo).

Aug 92. (7"/c-s) *(VS/+C 1425)* **MY GIRL. / MADNESS** [27] [ ]
(cd-s) *(VSCD 1425)* – ('A'side) / E.R.N.I.E. / Embarrassment / Tomorrow's dream.
(cd-s) *(VSCDX 1425)* – ('A'side) / Precious one (live) / My girl (live) / Disappear (live).

Feb 93. (7"/c-s) *(VS/+C 1447)* **NIGHT BOAT TO CAIRO. / ('A'mix)** [56] [ ]
(12"+=/cd-s+=) *(VS T/CD 1447)* – ('A'mixes).

Nov 93. (3xcd-box) *(MADBOX 1)* **THE BUSINESS – THE DEFINITIVE SINGLES COLLECTION** [ ] [–]

— In Oct'93, 'THE PRINCE' alongside other ska-revival bands on '2-TONE EP' hit UK No.30.

Jun 98. (cd/c) *(CDV/TCV 2862) / E.M.I.; <846040>* **THE HEAVY HEAVY HITS** [19] Feb99 [ ]
– Grey day / The sweetest girl / Michael Caine / Embarrassment / Night boat to Cairo / House of fun / Yesterday's men / It must be love / Driving in my car / (Waiting for the) Ghost train / Uncle Sam / Shut up / Cardiac arrest / Our house / My girl / The sun and the rain / Baggy trousers / Wings of a dove / Tomorrow's just another day / One better day / Return of the Los Palmas 7 / The prince / One step beyond.

Mar 99. (cd) *Goldenvoice; (GVC 0440-2)* **UNIVERSAL MADNESS (live)** [ ] [–]

Nov 99. (6xcd-box) *(MADBOX 2)* **THE LOT** [ ] [–]

Oct 02. (cd) *(CDV 2965)* **OUR HOUSE – THE ORIGINAL SONGS** [45] [–]
– House of fun / Our house / Simple equation / My girl / Baggy trousers / Prospects / Embarrassment / Driving in my car / Grey day / Shut up / The return of Los Palmas 7 / The sun and the rain / Tomorrow's just another day / Night boat to Cairo / Wings of a dove / One better day / Rise and fall / Sarah's song / White heat / Michael Caine / It must be love (remix).

MADONNA

Born: MADONNA LOUISE VERONICA CICCONE, 16 Aug'59, Rochester, Michigan, USA. After winning a scholarship to her local university (where she also learned ballet), the budding singer subsequently dropped out in the late 70's and headed for New York where she supported herself with waitressing and part-time model work (nude photos were later published in 1985 by top shelf mags, 'Penthouse' and 'Playboy'). To make ends meet (as they say), she also acted in a budget soft-porn flick, 'A Certain Sacrifice', later (1988) released on video without her consent; on first name terms with controversy from the beginning, MADONNA would nevertheless prove herself to be one of the 80's most deft media manipulators and arguably one of the most driven women in the history of the music business. Her first real experience of professional performance was as a touring dancer/backing singer for Hi-NRG legend, PATRICK HERNANDEZ (when will 'Born To Be Alive' ever get a re-release?!!!), although she soon returned to the Big Apple and began writing with ex-boyfriend, STEVE BRAY. Local DJ Mark Kamins was sufficiently impressed with the resulting material to help secure MADONNA a deal with 'Sire', the label releasing her debut single, 'EVERYBODY', late in '82. The track became a dancefloor favourite, as did US-only 12", 'BURNING UP', the singer subsequently hooking up with DJ 'Jellybean' Benitez to work on a whole albums worth of material. 'MADONNA' the album, hit the shelves in Autumn '83, its pilot single, 'HOLIDAY', finally making the jump from clubland to the charts (Top 20) a few months later. The track's unpretentious dance-pop and naive appeal served MADONNA well throughout this early period; the song also hit the UK Top 20 and prompted the re-issue of second single, 'LUCKY STAR', while the teen-love poignancy of 'BORDERLINE' gave the singer her first US Top 10 early the following year. The album itself was well on its way to becoming a multi-million seller and, in late summer '84, MADONNA firmly imprinted herself on public consciousness with US No.1 (album and single), 'LIKE A VIRGIN' and its attendant video. Through a winning combination of coy sexuality, pouting girlishness, Nile Rodgers-enhanced rhythmic backing and pop savvy, MADONNA had invented herself as an icon for not only the 80's 'MATERIAL GIRL', but legions of gay men and hormonal adolescents. Accordingly, manager Freddie DeMann was quick to break the singer into a parallel acting career, helping her secure a minor part in the film 'Vision Quest' and a more high profile role alongside Rosanna Arquette in 'Desperately Seeking Susan'. While these didn't exactly present a case for Oscar nominations, their soundtracks did provide MADONNA with two further No.1 singles in 'CRAZY FOR YOU' and 'INTO THE GROOVE'. More transatlantic hits followed in 'DRESS YOU UP', 'ANGEL' and 'GAMBLER', although it was only with the 'TRUE BLUE' (1986) album and preceding No.1 singles, 'LIVE TO TELL' and 'PAPA DON'T PREACH', that MADDY began to win the grudging respect of the rock press and fully blossom as a powerful vocalist. The latter track, in particular, showed a quantum leap in songwriting ability, its controversial, teenage pregnancy subject matter seeing MADONNA finally spark debate for something other than her risqué videos/stage show. Successive singles 'OPEN YOUR HEART' and the sultry 'LA ISLA BONITA' saw her top the charts yet again, while the album became her biggest selling to date. Summer '87 saw more movie action, her title track from the 'Who's That Girl' (in which she starred alongside Griffin Dunne) soundtrack scaling the charts on both sides of the Atlantic. Though the ensuing couple of years were a bit quieter on the recording front (save for a dodgy remix compilation, 'U CAN DANCE'), MADONNA's massive international superstar status and stormy marriage to actor Sean Penn (with whom she starred in 1986's 'Shanghai Surprise') ensured she was never far from the tabloid gossip columns. The more self-appointedly moralistic elements of the press had a field day with the video for 1989's 'LIKE A PRAYER', the sight of MADONNA making lewd advances to a black priest not going down (oops!) too well with the Vatican either. In the resulting furore, the pointy-bra'd one saw her sponsorship deal with 'Pepsi' go flat, although the intense interest guaranteed humungous sales of the accompanying album (also called 'LIKE A PRAYER'). Incidentally, the record was her most mature and fully realised piece of work to date, candidly exploring her favourite themes of religion and sex in a more frankly personal fashion than ever. The turn of the decade saw another feverish burst of activity with the release of two albums, 'I'M BREATHLESS' (as the sleeve states, 'Music Inspired By The Film Dick Tracy') and an impressive greatest hits set, wittily entitled 'THE IMMACULATE COLLECTION'. By far the most controversial offering of the year, however, was the 'JUSTIFY MY LOVE' single, its X-rated video (banned just about everywhere, it nevertheless enjoyed an airing on Channel 4's infamous ambassador of tack, 'The Word') and pre-orgasmic panting taking up almost as much column inches as the ensuing row over the writing credits (LENNY KRAVITZ and INGRID CHAVEZ at loggerheads). MADONNA took the increasingly overt sexuality angle to its ultimate conclusion with the simultaneous release of the 'EROTICA' (1992) album and 'Sex' book. The latter was MADONNA's first venture into publishing and possibly her last; the explicit soft-porn poses and woefully weak thematic thread saw the expensive (25 quid a throw, and you weren't even allowed to peruse the damn thing before you bought it!) panned by critics. Still, 1992 wasn't all bad as the singer signed a multi-million dollar agreement with 'Warners', giving added commercial oomph to her developing 'Maverick' label. Over the next five years, MADONNA was more often featured in the music press in connection with her business acumen (amongst others, she's secured the signatures of ALANIS MORISSETTE) than her recorded output, 1994's 'BEDTIME STORIES' album offering up a limp R&B sound. Nevertheless, MADONNA's longtime blonde ambition was fulfilled in 1996 as she played the lead part of Eva Peron in the screen version of 'EVITA', the singer finally winning unreserved critical plaudits from all quarters and even acquiring a fair degree of respectability among her moralising detractors. If her 90's output had been spotty overall, 1998's 'RAY OF LIGHT' album opened up a whole new chapter of creative birth and rebirth for the ageing (but seemingly ageless) pop chameleon. The recruitment of electronica sculptor WILLIAM ORBIT was a shrewd move yet few could have predicted how well the pairing's flawless marriage of star glamour and contemporary club sounds would imprint itself on the transatlantic musical consciousness. MADONNA had sculpted her singing style to suit this brave new style while her newfound spirituality permeated the album's surging grooves. The ballad, 'FROZEN', topped the UK chart, as did the album itself, a feat almost repeated on her home territory. While not incuded on the album, 'BEAUTIFUL STRANGER' (from the movie, 'Austin Powers: The Spy Who Shagged Me') became one of the singer's biggest UK hits in years, providing a stop gap and a musical link for her next album. Come the new millennium, MADONNA had subtly reinvented herself yet again, an urban cowgirl image complementing the electro panorama of 'MUSIC' (2000). ORBIT again supplied the deftest of touches while co-writer Mirwais Ahmadzai made a significant contribution to the record's post-modern digi-pop. The insistent, sensual, stuttering throb of the title track secured MADONNA yet another massive transatlantic hit while the album itself topped both the US and UK charts. MADDY was once again at the forefront of pop culture while her celebrity knew no bounds, a massively publicised marriage to ('Lock, Stock & Two Smoking Barrels') director Guy Ritchie in a Scottish Castle giving the tabloids material to chew on for weeks. If compilation set, 'GHV2' (2001) didn't sound as consistent and cohesive as 'IMMACULATE COLLECTION', it was due to the glaring gap between her average early 90's pop and her millennial revisionism. Few then, would've predicted the critical and commercial backwards step of 'AMERICAN LIFE' (2003), an uncharacteristically muted and sterile affair seemingly hung up on style over substance despite the weighty lyrical matter. Subsequent musical attempts to repair the damage via a Gap commercial with MISSY ELLIOTT and an MTV Video Music Awards performance of 'LIKE A VIRGIN – HOLLYWOOD' (with BRITNEY SPEARS, AGUILERA and ELLIOTT) were compressed into the equally dispensible 'REMIXED AND REVISITED' EP. London life seemed to sit well with the ageing diva, and a surprisingly controversy free couple of years preceded her umpteenth studio set, 'CONFESSIONS ON A DANCE FLOOR' (2005). As both the title and its Abba-sampling lead single, 'HUNG UP', made clear, the album was an unashamed glance back to the disco scene that first inspired her. It was also a full-frontal return to commercial form, both single and album topping most charts around the world. Early the following year, after yet another UK chart-topper, 'SORRY', MADONNA announced her retiral from acting, citing a fear of her screen reputation preceding her. However, she was still taking to the stage with her music, issuing a rare CD/DVD concert set under the title of 'I'M GOING TO TELL YOU A SECRET' (2006).

• **Songwriters:** She collaborated on most material, the bulk with ex-boyfriend STEVE BRAY. Others & covers; PHYSICAL ATTRACTION (Reggie Lucas) / HOLIDAY (Jellybean Benitez) / LOVE DON'T LIVE HERE ANYMORE (Rose Royce; hit) / LIKE A VIRGIN (Tom Kelly & Billy Steinberg) / CRAZY FOR YOU (Jon Lind & John Bettis) / JUSTIFY MY LOVE (Lenny Kravitz & Ingrid Chavez) / FEVER (Peggy Lee) / LOVE SONG (co-w/ PRINCE) / BEDTIME STORY (Bjork) / GUILT BY ASSOCIATION with Joe Henry (Vic Chesnutt) / I WANT YOU (Marvin Gaye).

Album rating: MADONNA (*6) / LIKE A VIRGIN (*6) / TRUE BLUE (*7) / YOU CAN DANCE remixes (*5) / LIKE A PRAYER (*8) / THE IMMACULATE COLLECTION compilation (*9) / I'M BREATHLESS soundtrack (*4) / EROTICA (*6) / BEDTIME STORIES (*7) / SOMETHING TO REMEMBER compilation (*7) / EVITA soundtrack (*6) / RAY OF LIGHT (*8) / MUSIC (*8) / GHV2 compilation (*7) / AMERICAN LIFE (*5) / CONFESSIONS ON A DANCE FLOOR (*7) / I'M GOING TO TELL YOU A SECRET (*5)

MADONNA – vocals with session people, producers, etc.

Sire Sire

Dec 82. (7"/12") *(W 9899/+T)* <29841> **EVERYBODY. / EVERYBODY (dub version)** [ ] [ ]

May 83. (7") <29609> **BURNING UP. / PHYSICAL ATTRACTION** – [ ]

Oct 83. (7") <29478> **HOLIDAY. / I KNOW IT** – 16

Oct 83. (7"/ext.12") *(W 9522/+T)* <29177> **LUCKY STAR. / I KNOW IT** [ ] Aug84 4
(12") *(W 9522TV)* – ('A'-U.S.remix) / I know it.
(re-prom.Mar84 hit UK No.14)

Sep 83. (lp/c) *(923867-1/-4)* <23867> **MADONNA** 6 Aug83 8
– Lucky star / Borderline / Burning up / I know it / Holiday / Think of me / Physical attraction / Everybody. *(re-iss. Sep85 as 'THE FIRST ALBUM'; WX 22)*

Nov 83. (7"/ext.12") *(W 9405/+T)* **HOLIDAY. / THINK OF ME** 6 –
(re-prom.Jul85, hit UK-No.2; also 12"pic-d; W 9405P)

Mar 84. (7") <29354> **BORDERLINE. / THINK OF ME** – 10

May 84. (7") *(W 9260)* **BORDERLINE. / PHYSICAL ATTRACTION** 56 –
(d7"+=) *(W 9260F)* – Holiday / Think of me.
(12") *(W 9260T)* – ('A'-U.S.remix) / ('A'dub remix) / ('B'side).
(re-Prom.Jan86, hit UK No.2 – also 7"sha-pic-d; W 9260P)

Nov 84. (7") *(W 9210)* <29210> **LIKE A VIRGIN. / STAY** 3 1
(12") *(W 9210T)* <20239> – ('A' US dance remix) / ('B'side).

Nov 84. (lp/c)(cd)) *(WX 20/+C)(925157-2)* <25157> **LIKE A VIRGIN** 1 1
– Material girl / Angel / Like a virgin / Over and over / Love don't live here anymore / Dress you up / Shoo-be-doo / Stay / Pretender. *(re-iss. Aug85 pic-lp)(cd+=; WX 20P)(925181-2)* – Into the groove.

Feb 85. (7") *(W 9083)* <29083> **MATERIAL GIRL. / PRETENDER** 3 2
(12") *(W 9083T)* <20304> – ('A'-Jellybean dance mix) / ('B'side).
(below single issued on 'Geffen' from the film 'Vision Quest')

Feb 85. (7")(12") <29051><26325> **CRAZY FOR YOU. / (B-side by Berlin)** – 1

Apr 85. (7") <29008> **ANGEL. / (dance mix)** – 5
(12") <20335> – Angel (extended dance mix) / Into the groove.

May 85. (7"/7"sha-pic-d) *(A/WA 6323)* **CRAZY FOR YOU. / (B-side by Sammy Hagar)** 2 –
(below from the movie 'Desperately Seeking Susan'; not on soundtrack)

Jul 85. (7"/7"sha-pic-d) *(W 8934/+P)* **INTO THE GROOVE. / SHOO-BEE-DOO** 1 –
(12"+=) *(W 8934T)* – Everybody.

Aug 85. (7") <28919> **DRESS YOU UP. / SHOO-BEE-DOO** – 5
(12"+=) <20369> – ('A'-Casual instrumental mix).

Sep 85. (7"/7"sha-pic-d) *(W 8881/+P)* **ANGEL. / BURNING UP** 5 –
(12") *(W 8881T)* – ('A'-12"extended dance mix) / ('B'side).
(below single issued on 'Geffen' from the film 'Vision Quest')

Oct 85. (7"/7"+poster) *(A/QA 6585)* **GAMBLER. / (B-side by Black 'n' Blue)** 4 –
(12") *(TA 6585)* – ('A'extended dance mix) / ('A'instrumental) / ('B'side).

Nov 85. (7"/7"sha-pic-d) *(W 8848/+P)* **DRESS YOU UP. / I KNOW IT** 5 –
(12"/12"+poster) *(W 8848T/+F)* – ('A'-instrumental).

Apr 86. (7") *(W 8717)* <28717> **LIVE TO TELL. / ('A'instrumental)** 2 1
(12"+=/12"+poster) *(W 8717T/+W)* <20461> – ('A'version).

Jun 86. (7")(ext.12") <28660><20492> **PAPA DON'T PREACH. / PRETENDER** – 1

Jun 86. (7") *(W 8636)* **PAPA DON'T PREACH. / AIN'T NO BIG DEAL** 1 –
(12"+=/12"+poster+=/12"pic-d+=) *(W 8636T/+W/P)* – ('A'extended).

Jul 86. (lp/c)(cd) *(WX 54/+C)(925442-2)* <25442> **TRUE BLUE** 1 1
– Papa don't preach / Open your heart / White heat / Live to tell / Where's the party / rue blue / La Isla Bonita / Jimmy Jimmy / Love makes the world go round.

Sep 86. (7") *(W 8550)* **TRUE BLUE (remix). / HOLIDAY (lp version)** 1 –
(12"/12"pic-d) *(W 8550T/+P)* – ('A'extended version version) / Holiday (full length).

Sep 86. (7",7"blue) <28591> **TRUE BLUE. / AIN'T NO BIG DEAL** – 3
(12"+=) <20533> – ('A'Colour mix) / ('A'instrumental).

Dec 86. (7") <28508> **OPEN YOUR HEART. / WHITE HEAT** – 1
(ext.12"+=) <20597> – ('A'dub version).

Dec 86. (7") *(W 8480)* **OPEN YOUR HEART. / LUCKY STAR** 4 –
(ext.12"+=/ext.12"pic-d+=) *(W 8480T/+P)* – ('A'dub mix).

Mar 87. (7") *(W 8378)* <28425> **LA ISLA BONITA (remix). / ('A'instrumental)** 1 4
(12"/12"pic-d) *(W 8378T/+P)* <20633> – ('A'extended remix) / ('A'extended instrumental).

Jul 87. (7"/ext.12"/ext.12"pic-d) *(W 8341/+T/TP)* <28341> **WHO'S THAT GIRL. / WHITE HEAT** 1 1
(ext.12") *(W 8341TX)* <20692> – ('A'dub version).

Jul 87. (lp/c)(cd) *(WX 102/+C)(925611-2)* <1-/4-/2-25611> **WHO'S THAT GIRL** (soundtrack w/ Various Artists) 4 7
– Who's that girl / Causing a commotion / The look of love / Can't stop (other artists). *(cd re-iss. Feb95; same)*

Sep 87. (7") *(W 8224)* <28224> **CAUSING A COMMOTION (Silver Screen mix). / JIMMY JIMMY** 4 2
(12"+=/12"pic-d+=/c-s+=) *(W 8224 T/TP/C)* <20762> – ('A'-movie house mix).

Nov 87. (lp/c)(cd) *(WX 76/+C)(925535-2)* <25535> **U CAN DANCE** (remixes) 5 14
– Spotlight / Holiday / Everybody / Physical attraction / Over and over Into the groove / Where's the party / Spotlight (dub) / Holiday (dub) Into the groove (dub) / Over and over (dub). *(re-iss. cd/c Feb95)*

Dec 87. (7") *(W 8115)* **THE LOOK OF LOVE. / I KNOW IT** 9 –
(12"+=/12"pic-d+=) *(W 8115T/+P)* – Love don't live here anymore.

Mar 89. (7") *(W 7539)* <27539> **LIKE A PRAYER. / ACT OF CONTRITION** 1 1
(ext.12"+=/ext.12"pic-d+=/c-s+=) *(W 7539 T/TP/C)* – ('A'club mix).
(12") *(W 7539TX)* <21170> – ('A'dance mix) / ('A'-Churchapella mix) ('A'side).
(3"cd-s) *(W 7539CD)* – ('A'extended remix) / ('A'club mix).

Mar 89. (lp/c)(cd) *(WX 239/+C)(925844-2) <25844>* **LIKE A PRAYER** [1] [1]
– Like a prayer / Express yourself / Love song / Till death us do part / Promise to try / Cherish / Dear Jessie / Oh father / Keep it together / Spanish eyes / Act of contrition.

May 89. (7"s/7"s/c-s) *(W 2948 X/W/C) <22948>* **EXPRESS YOURSELF. / THE LOOK OF LOVE** [5] [2]
(c-s/cd-s/12"pic-d) *(W 2948 CX/CD/TP)* – ('A'side) / ('A'-Non-stop mix) / ('A'-Stop & go mix).

Aug 89. (7"/c-s) *(W 2883/+C) <22883>* **CHERISH. / SUPERNATURAL** [3] [2]
(12"pic-d+=/cd-s+=) *(W 2883 TP/CD)* – ('A'extended).

Nov 89. (7"/7"pic-d/c-s) *(W 2668/+P/C)* **DEAR JESSIE. / TILL DEATH US DO PART** [5] [–]
(12"+=/cd-s+=/pic-cd-s+=) *(W 2668 TW/CD/CDX)* – Holiday (12"mix).

Nov 89. (7"/c-s) *<22723-7/-4>* **OH FATHER. / PRAY FOR SPANISH EYES** [–] [20]

Jan 90. (7"/c-s) *<19986-7/-4>* **KEEP IT TOGETHER. / (instrumental)** [–] [8]

Mar 90. (7"/7"pic-d/c-s) *(W 9851/+P/C)* **VOGUE. / KEEP IT TOGETHER** [1] [–]
(12"+=/cd-s+=) *(W 9851 TX/CD)* – ('A'-Strike-a-pose dub mix).
(12"pic-d+=) *(W 9851TW)* – ('A'-Bette Davis dub).

Apr 90. (7"/c-s) *<19863-7/-4>* **VOGUE. / ('A'-Bette Davis dub)** [–] [1]
(12"+=/c-s+=/cd-s+=) *<21513-0/-4/-2>* – ('A'-Strike-a-pose dub).

May 90. (cd)(lp/c) *<(7599 26209-2)>(WX 351/+C)* **I'M BREATHLESS** (music inspired by the film 'Dick Tracy') [2] [2]
– He's a man / Sooner or later / Hanky panky / I'm going bananas / Cry baby / Something to remember / Back in business / More / What can you lose / Now I'm following you (pt.1) / Now I'm following you (pt.2) / Vogue.

Jul 90. (7"/c-s) *(W 9789/+C) <19789>* **HANKY PANKY. / MORE** [2] Jun90 [10]
('A'-Bare Bottom mix;12"+=/12"pic-d+=/cd-s+=) *(W 9789 T/TP/CD) <21577>* – ('A'-Bare Bones mix).

Nov 90. (7"/c-s) *(W 9000/+C) <19485-7/-4>* **JUSTIFY MY LOVE. / EXPRESS YOURSELF** [2] [1]
(12"pic-d+=/cd-s+=) *(W 9000 TP/CD)* – ('A'-William Orbit mix).

Nov 90. (cd)(lp/c) *<(7599 26440-2)>(WX 370/+C)* **THE IMMACULATE COLLECTION** (compilation) [1] [5]
– Spotlight / Holiday / Everybody / Physical attraction / Over and over / Into the groove / Where's the party / Spotlight (dub) / Holiday (dub) / Into the groove (dub) / Over and over (dub).

Feb 91. (7"/7"sha-pic-d) *(W 0008/+P)* **CRAZY FOR YOU (remix). / KEEP IT TOGETHER** [2] [–]
(12"pic-d+=/c-s+=/cd-s+=) *(W 0008 TP/C/CD)* – Into the groove.

Feb 91. (c-s) *<19490-4>* **RESCUE ME (remix) / RESCUE ME (alternate mix)** [–] [9]

Apr 91. (7"/c-s) *(W 0024/+C)* **RESCUE ME (remix). / SPOTLIGHT (version)** [3] [–]
(cd-s+=) *(W 0024CD)* – ('A'-Titanic mix).

May 91. (7"/7"pic-d) *(W 0037/+P)* **HOLIDAY. / TRUE BLUE** [5] [–]
(cd-s+=/c-s+=) *(W 0037 CD/CT)* – Causin' a commotion / Who's that girl.
(12") *(W 0037T)* – ('A'side) / Where's the party / Everybody (remix).

— Below from the film, 'A League Of Their Own'.

Jul 92. (7"/c-s) *(W 0122/+C) <18822>* **THIS USED TO BE MY PLAYGROUND. / (long version)** [3] [1]
(12"+=/cd-s+=) *(W 0122 T/CD)* – ('A'mixes).

Maverick – Sire Maverick – Sire

Oct 92. (7"/7"pic-d/c-s) *(W 0138/+P/C) <18782>* **EROTICA. / (instrumental)** [3] [3]
(12"+=/12"pic-d+=/cd-s+=) *(W 0138 T/TP/CD) <40585>* – ('A'mixes; William Orbit / Jeep beats / Underground club / Kenlou B-boy / etc).

Oct 92. (cd/c/lp) *<(9362 45031-2/-4/-1)>* **EROTICA** [2] [2]
– Erotica / Fever / Where life begins / Bye bye baby / Bad girl / Waiting / Deeper and deeper / Thief of hearts / Words / Rain / Why it's so hard / In this life / Did you do it / Secret garden.

Dec 92. (7"/c-s) *(W 0146/+C) <18639>* **DEEPER AND DEEPER. / ('A'instrumental)** [6] [13]
(12"pic-d+=/cd-s+=) *(W 0146 TP/CD) <40722>* – ('A'mixes; Shep's deep beats / David's deeper dub / David's klub mix / etc).

Feb 93. (c-s/cd-s) *<18650-4/-2>* **BAD GIRL / FEVER** [–] [36]
(c-s+=/cd-s+=) *<40793-4/-2>* – ('A'mixes; Murk Boys Deep South mix / Oscar G's dope mix / Shep's remedy mix / etc.)

Feb 93. (7"/c-s) *(W 0145/+C)* **BAD GIRL. / EROTICA (William Orbit mix)** [10] [–]
(12"pic-+=/cd-s+=) *(W 0145 TP/CD)* – ('A'mixes; (see US above).

Mar 93. (7"pic-d/c-s) *(W 0168 P/C)* **FEVER. / ('A'remix)** [6] [–]
(12"pic-d+=/cd-s+=) *(W 0168 TP/CD)* – ('A'mixes).

Jul 93. (c-s/cd-s) *<18505-4/-2>* **RAIN / WAITING** [–] [14]
(12"+=/c-s+=/cd-s+=) *<40988-0/-4/-2>* – Up down suite / ('A'album version).

Jul 93. (7"/c-s) *(W 0190/+C)* **RAIN. / OPEN YOUR HEART** [7] [–]
(12"pic-d+=/cd-s+=) *(W 0190 TP/CD)* – Up down suite (dub).

— her backing; **DALLAS AUSTIN** – drums, keyboards, co-writer / **TOMMY MARTIN** – guitar / **ME'SHELL NDEGEOCELLO + COLIN WOLFE** – bass / **MARCUS DeVRIES** – prog. / **BABYFACE** – synth, drum prog / etc.

Mar 94. (7"/c-s) *(W 0240/+C) <18247>* **I'LL REMEMBER. / SECRET GARDEN** [7] [2]
(12"pic-d/cd-s) *(W 0240 TP/CD) <41355>* – ('A'-Orbit + Guerilla Beach mixes) / Why is it so hard? (live).

Sep 94. (c-s/cd-s) *<18035-4/-2>* **SECRET / (instrumental)** [–] [3]
(12"+=/cd-s+=) *<41772-0/-2>* – ('A'mixes; Junior Luscious various).

Sep 94. (7"pic-d/c-s) *(W 0268 P/C)* **SECRET. / LET YOUR GUARD DOWN (rough mix edit)** [5] [–]
(12"pic-d+=) *(W 0268TP)* – ('A'instrumental) / ('A'other version).
(cd-s) *(W 0268CD)* – ('A'side) / ('A'-Junior mixes).

Oct 94. (cd/c/lp) *<(9362 45767-2/-4/-1)>* **BEDTIME STORIES** [2] [3]
– Survival / Secret / I'd rather be your lover / Don't stop / Inside of me / Human nature / Forbidden love / Love tried to welcome me / Sanctuary / Bedtime story / Take a bow.

Dec 94. (7"pic-d/c-s) *(W 0278 T/C) <18000>* **TAKE A BOW. / ('A'-InDaSoul mix)** [17] [1]
(cd-s+=) *(W 0278CD) <41887>* – ('A'mixes; instrumental / Silky Soul).

— Above single co-written w /BABYFACE as was 7th track. The singular title track was written by NELLEE HOOPER, BJORK & MARCUS DeVRIES. DAVE HALL co-wrote 5th, 6th & 8th track. Many samples included The ISLEYS (written) / AALIYAH / GAP BAND / GUTTERSNYPES / MAIN SOURCE / GRANT GREEN / HERBIE HANCOCK.

Feb 95. (c-s) *(W 0285C)* **BEDTIME STORY / ('A'-Junior's mix)** [4] Apr95 [42]
(12"pic-d/cd-s) *(W 0285 TP/CD)* – ('A'side) / ('A'-Junior's wet dream mix) / ('A'-Junior's Dreamy drum dub) / ('A'-Orbital mix) / ('A'-Junior's sound factory mix).
(cd-s) *(W 0285CDX)* – ('A'-Junior's mix) / Secret (Allstar mix) / Secret (Some Bizarre mixes).

Apr 95. (c-s/cd-s) *<17924-4/-2>* **BEDTIME STORY / SURVIVAL** [–] [42]
(12"+=/cd-s+=) *<41895-0/-2>* – (see Junior mixes above).

Jul 95. (c-s/cd-s) *<17882-4/-2>* **HUMAN NATURE / SANCTUARY** [–] [46]
(12"/cd-s) *<41880-0/-2>* – ('A'mixes; I'm Not Your Bitch / Bottom Heavy dub / Love Is The nature / Runway Club / etc)

Aug 95. (c-s) *(W 0300C)* **HUMAN NATURE / ('A'-Chorus door slam mix)** [8] [–]
(cd-s+=) *(W 0300CD)* – ('A'club mix) / ('A'-Runway club mix) / I'm not your bitch.
(12"pic-d) *(W 0300TP)* – (all above except 'A'side).

Oct 95. (c-s) *(W 0324C) <17719>* **YOU'LL SEE / (instrumental)** [5] [6]
(cd-s+=) *(W 0324CD)* – Rain.
(cd-s) *(W 0324CDX)* – ('A'side) / Secret (Junior Luscious club mix) / Sooner or later / Bad girl.

Nov 95. (cd/c/lp) *<(9362 46100-2/-4/-1)>* **SOMETHING TO REMEMBER** (compilation) [3] [6]
– I want you / I'll remember (theme from "With Honors") / Take a bow / You'll see / Crazy for you / This used to be my playground / Live to tell / Love don't live here anymore (remix) / Something to remember / Forbidden love / One more chance / Rain / Oh father / I want you (orchestral).

Dec 95. (c-s) *(W 0326C)* **OH FATHER / LIVE TO TELL (live)** [16] [–]
(cd-s+=) *(W 0326CD)* – Why it's so hard (live).

Mar 96. (c-s) *(W 0337C)* **ONE MORE CHANCE / ('A'-Spanglish version)** [11] [–]
(cd-s+=) *(W 0337CD)* – You'll see (Spanish version).

Apr 96. (c-s/cd-s) *<17714-4/-2>* **LOVE DON'T LIVE HERE ANYMORE / ('A'-album version)** [–] [79]

Oct 96. (c-s/cd-s) *(W 0378 C/CD) <17495-4/-2>* **YOU MUST LOVE ME / RAINBOW HIGH** [10] [18]

Nov 96. (d-cd/d-c) *<(9362 46346-2/-4)>* **EVITA** (soundtrack w/ Cast Members) [1] [2]
– (tracks by *) / Oh what a circus (w/ **) / (track by ***) / Eva and

Magaldi – Eva beware of the city (w/ ***, ** & *****) / Beunos Aires / Another suitcase in another hall / Goodnight and thank you (w/ **) / (track by **) / Charity concert – The art of the possible (w/ ***, **** & **) / I'd be surprisingly good for you (w/ ****) / Hello and goodbye (w/ **** & ******) / Peron's latest flame (w/ **) / A new Argentina (w/ ** & ****) // (track by ****) / Don't cry for me Argentina / On the balcony of the Casa Rosada 2 / High flying, adored (w/ **) / Rainbow high / Rainbow tour (w/ **, ******* & ****) / The actress hasn't learned the lines (you'd like to hear) (w/ **) / (track by **) / Partido feminista / (track by ****) / (track by *) / Waltz for Eva and Che (w/ **) / Your little body's slowly breaking down (w/ ****) / You must love me / Eva's final broadcast / (track by *) / Lament (w/ **). *<US 1-cd iss.Aug97; 46692-2>*

— Cast, etc.:- ANDREW LLOYD WEBBER (*) / ANTONIO BANDERAS (**) / JIMMY NAIL (***) / JONATHAN PRYCE (****) / JULIAN LITTMAN (*****) / ANDREA CORR (******) / GARY BROOKER, PETER POLYCARPOU & JOHN GOWER (*******)

Dec 96. (c-s/cd-s) *(W 0384 C/CD)* **DON'T CRY FOR ME ARGENTINA / SANTA EVITA** [3] [–]
(cd-s+=) *(W 0384CDX)* – Latin chant.

Feb 97. (c-s/cd-s) *<43809-4/-2>* **DON'T CRY FOR ME ARGENTINA / ('A'mixes; Spanlish / Miami dub & instrumental / etc).** [–] [8]

Mar 97. (c-s) *(W 0388C)* **ANOTHER SUITCASE IN ANOTHER HALL / DON'T CRY FOR ME ARGENTINA** [7] [–]
(cd-s+=) *(W 0388CDX)* – Waltz for Eva and Che.
(cd-s) *(W 0388CD)* – ('A'dance mix) / Hello and goodbye / You must love me.

Feb 98. (c-s/cd-s) *(W 0433C) <17244>* **FROZEN / SHANTI-ASHTANGI** [1] [2]
(12") *(W 0433T)* ('A'extended) / ('A'-Stereo Mc's mix) / ('A'-Meltdown mix).
(cd-s+=) *(W 0433T)* – ('A'-Widescreen mix).

Mar 98. (cd/c/lp) *<(9362 46847-2/-4/-1)>* **RAY OF LIGHT** [1] [2]
– Drowned world – Substitute for love / Swim / Ray of light / Candy perfume girl / Skin / Nothing really matters / Sky fits Heaven / Shanti – Ashtangi / Frozen / The power of good-bye / To have and not to hold / Little star / Mer girl.

Apr 98. (c-s) *(W 0444C) <17206>* **RAY OF LIGHT / HAS TO BE** [2] Jun98 [5]
(12"+=/cd-s+=) *(W 0444 T/CD)* – ('A'mixes).
(cd-s) *(W 0444CD2)* – ('A'side) / ('A'-Sasha mix) / ('A'-Victor Calderone mix) / ('A'-William Orbit mix).

Aug 98. (c-s/cd-s) *(W 0453 C/CD2)* **DROWNED WORLD – SUBSTITUTE FOR LOVE / SKY FITS HEAVEN (Victor Calderone & Sasha remix)** [10] [–]
(cd-s) *(W 0453CD1)* – ('A'mixes by BT & Sasha).

Nov 98. (c-s/cd-s) *(W 0459 C/CD) <17160>* **THE POWER OF GOOD-BYE / LITTLE STAR** [6] Oct98 [11]
(12") *(W 0459T)* – ('A'mixes) / Mer girl.

Mar 99. (c-s) *(W 471C) <17102>* **NOTHING REALLY MATTERS / TO HAVE AND NOT TO HOLD** [7] Apr99 [93]
(cd-s) *(W 471CD1)* – ('A'mixes; album / club 69 / club 69 vocal / Kruder & Dorfmeister).
(cd-s+=) *(W 471CD2)* – ('A'-Vikram mix).
(12") *(W 471T)* – ('A'mixes).

Jun 99. (c-s) *(W 495C) <radio cut>* **BEAUTIFUL STRANGER / ('A'-Calderone radio mix)** [2] [19]
(cd-s+=) *(W 495CD)* – ('A'mixes; Calderone club).
(12") *(W 495T)* – ('A'mixes).

Mar 00. (c-s) *(W 519C) <radio cut>* **AMERICAN PIE / (Calderone filter dub)** [1] Feb00 [29]
(cd-s+=) *(W 519CD1)* – ('A'-Richard 'Humpty' vission mix).
(cd-s) *(W 519CD2)* – ('A'-Victor Calderone & Richard 'Humpty' mixes).
(12") *(W 519T)* – ('A'mixes).

Aug 00. (c-s) *(W 537C) <16826>* **MUSIC / (Calderone mix)** [1] [1]
(cd-s+=) *(W 537CD1)* – ('A'-Deep dish / Groove Armada / HQ2 mixes).
(cd-s) *(W 537CD2)* – ('A'mixes).

Sep 00. (cd/c/lp) *(9362 47865-2/-4/-1) <47598>* **MUSIC** [1] [1]
– Music / Impressive instant / Runaway lover / I deserve it / Amazing / Nobody's perfect / Don't tell me / What it feels like for a girl / Paradise (not for me) / Gone / American pie.

Nov 00. (c-s) *(W 547C) <16825>* **DON'T TELL ME / (Thunderpuss' hands in the air radio mix)** [4] Dec00 [4]
(cd-s+=) *(W 547CD1)* – ('A'-Tracy Young club & Vission mixes).
(cd-s+=) *(W 547CD2)* – ('A'-Victor Calderone sensory mix).

Apr 01. (c-s) *(W 553C) <42372>* **WHAT IT FEELS LIKE FOR A GIRL / (Calderone & Quayle dark side mix)** [7] [23]
(cd-s+=/12") *(W 553 CD1/T1)* – ('A'mixes; above & beyond / Paul Oakenfold Perfecto / Richard Vission).
(cd-s/12") *(W 553 CD2/T2)* – ('A'mixes; above & beyond / Spanish / Richard Vission velvet / Tracy Young club) / Lo que siente la muyer.

Nov 01. (cd/c) *<(9362 48000-2/-4)>* **GHV2 (GREATEST HITS VOL.2)** (compilation) [2] [7]
– Deeper and deeper / Erotica / Human nature / Secret / Don't cry for me Argentina / Bedtime story / The power of good-bye / Beautiful stranger / Frozen / Take a bow / Ray of light / Don't tell me / What it feels like for a girl / Drowned world – Substitute for love / Music.

Oct 02. (c-s) *(W 595C)* **DIE ANOTHER DAY / (Dirty Vegas main mix)** [3] [8]
(cd-s+=) *(W 595CD2) <42492>* – (Deepsky remix).
(cd-s) *(W 595CD1)* – ('A'side) / (Thunderpuss mix) / (Felix Da Housecat thee retroelectro mix).
(d12"+=) *(W 595T)* – (Dirty Vegas dub).

Apr 03. (cd-s) *(W 603CD1) <16658>* **AMERICAN LIFE / (Missy Elliott remix) / (Peter Rauhofer's American anthem)** [2] [37]
(cd-s) *(W 603CD2)* – ('A'side) / (Oakenfold downtempo remix) / (Felix Da Housecat Devin dazzle club mix).
(12") *(W 603T)* – ('A'side) / Die another day (Calderone & Quayle afterlife mix).
(d12"/cd-s) *(W 603 T2/CDX)* – (all above).

Apr 03. (cd/d-lp) *(9362 48454-2) <48439>* **AMERICAN LIFE** [1] [1]
– American life / Hollywood / I'm so stupid / Love profusion / Nobody knows me / Nothing fails / Intervention / X-static process / Mother and father / Die another day / Easy ride. *(special cd; 9362 48440-2)*

Jul 03. (cd-s) *(W 614CD1) <42638>* **HOLLYWOOD / (Oakenfold full remix) / (Deepsky HSH vocal mix)** [2] [ ]
(cd-s) *(W 614CD2)* – ('A'side) / (Jacques Lu Cont's Thin White Duck mix) / (Micronauts remix).
(12") *(W 614T)* – ('A'side) / (Micronauts remix) / (Oakenfold full remix).
(d12"/cd-s) *(W 614 T2/CDX)* – (all above tracks).

— In Nov'03, MADONNA feat. on BRITNEY SPEARS' hit, 'Me Against The Music'

Nov 03. (m-cd) *(W 631CD) <48624>* **REMIXED AND REVISITED** [ ] [ ]
– Nothing fails / Love profusion / Nobody knows me / American life / Like a virgin – Hollywood (live medley with CHRISTINA AGUILERA & BRITNEY SPEARS) / Into the Hollywood groove (with MISSY ELLIOTT) / Your honesty.

Dec 03. (cd-s) *(W 634CD1)* **LOVE PROFUSION / NOTHING FAILS / LOVE PROFUSION (passengerz club mix)** [11] [–]
(cd-s) *(W 634CD2)* – ('A'side) / (Ralph Rosario house vocal mix) / Nobody knows me (above and beyond 12" mix).
(12") *(W 634T) <42682>* – ('A'-Passengerz club mix) / Nobody knows me (above & beyond 12" mix).

Nov 05. (cd-s) *(W 695CD1)* **HUNG UP / (Tracy Young's Get Up And Dance Groove mix)** [1] [7]
(cd-s+=) *(W 695CD2)* – (SDP extended vocal).
(12"+=) *(W 695T)* – (SDP extended dub).
(d12"++=/cd-s++=) *<9362 42845-0/-2>* – (Bill Hamel remix) / (Chus & Ceballos remix).

Nov 05. (cd/lp) *<(9362 49460-2)>* **CONFESSIONS ON A DANCE FLOOR** [1] [1]
– Hung up / Get together / Sorry / Future lovers / I love New York / Let it will be / Forbidden love / Jump / How high / Isaac / Push / Like it or not. *(UK pink-d-lp iss.Mar06; 9362 49460-1)*

Feb 06. (cd-s) *(W 703CD1)* **SORRY / LET IT WILL BE (Paper Faces vocal)** [1] [58]
(12") *(W 703T)* – (remixes: radio / PSB maxi-mix / Paul Oakenfold / Green velvet).
(cd-s++=) *(W 703CD2)* – (Man with guitar remix).
(d12"/cd-s) *<42892-0/-2>* – (all above).

Jun 06. (cd+dvd) *<(9362 49990-2)>* **I'M GOING TO TELL YOU A SECRET** (live) [18] [33]
– The beast within / Vogue / Nobody knows me / American life / Hollywood / Die another day / Lament (from 'Evita') / Like a prayer / Mother and father / Imagine / Susan MacLeod – Into the groove / Music / Holiday / I love New York // (DVD tracks).

– compilations, others, etc. –

on 'Replay' unless mentioned otherwise (many with OTTO WERNHERR)

Feb 87. (12") *(3006)* **WILD DANCING. / ('A'dance mix)** ☐ [–]
(re-iss. cd-s Sep93 & Apr95)

Apr 89. (12") *(3000)* **COSMIC CLUB (extended dance mix). / WE ARE THE GODS** ☐ [–]
(re-iss. cd-s Sep93)

May 89. (12") *(3007)* **TIME TO DANCE (extended). / (instrumental) / (radio mix)** ☐ [–]
(cd-s-iss.Oct95; RRSCD 3007)

Sep 89. (12") *(3008)* **ON THE STREET (edit). / (extended mix)** ☐ [–]
(cd-s-iss.Oct95; RRSCD 3008)

May 90. (12") *(3009)* **OH MY!!! (edit). / ('A'disco mix)** ☐ [–]

Aug 90. (cd/c) *Action Replay; (CDAR/ARLC 1005)* **THE BEST & THE REST OF MADONNA AND OTTO WERNKERR** ☐ [–]

Sep 90. (12") *(3010)* **SHAKE (extended). / ('A'mix) / ('A'instrumental)** ☐ [–]
(cd-iss. Oct95; RRSCD 3010)

now on 'Receiver' unless mentioned otherwise

1989. (cd/c/lp) *(CD/TC+/KNOB 1)* **IN THE BEGINNING** ☐ [–]
(cd re-iss. Oct98 on 'Gravity'; GTY 2001-2) (cd re-iss. Feb99; same as original)

Oct 89. (lp/c/cd) *(RR LP/LC/CD 118)* **THE EARLY YEARS** ☐ [–]

Jul 91. (cdlp) *(RR CD/LP 144)* **GIVE IT TO ME** ☐ [–]

Apr 92. (7"/12"pic-d/pic-cd-s) **SHINE A LIGHT. / ON THE GROUND / LITTLE BOY** ☐ [–]

Jul 93. (cd/c) *(CDAR/ARLC 1033)* **BEST OF THE REST VOLUME II** ☐ [–]

☐ MAD SEASON (see under ⇒ ALICE IN CHAINS)

the MAGIC NUMBERS

Formed: Ealing, London, England ... 2004 by bearded blokes ROMEO STODART and SEAN GANNON along with their respective sisters MICHELE and ANGELA. The STODARTs had originally hailed from Trinidad via New York, bringing the sunny, harmony-rich spirit of the LOVIN' SPOONFUL and the MAMAS & THE PAPAS with them. Amid the spiky sounds of contemporary musical fashion, the 'NUMBERS transmitted the original ethos of hirsute, horizontal festival going to the summer calendar, building on the success of their early 'Heavenly' singles: 'FOREVER LOST' and 'LOVE ME LIKE YOU'. The band's easy going family values, together with ROMEO's classicist songwriting made 'THE MAGIC NUMBERS' (2005) one of the wild card hits of that year, spinning off further Top 30 entries, 'LOVE'S A GAME' and 'I SEE YOU, YOU SEE ME'. At least one of their summer 2005 appearances wasn't so magic, in fact it never happened at all due to the insensitive words of Top Of The Pops presenter Richard Bacon, who allegedly introduced them as a "big, fat melting pot of talent". At least he got the talent part right.

• **Covers:** CRAZY IN LOVE (Beyonce) / THERE IS A LIGHT THAT NEVER GOES OUT (Smiths).

Album rating: THE MAGIC NUMBERS (*7)

ROMEO STODART (b. Trinidad) – vocals, guitar, banjo, piano / **ANGELA GANNON** – percussion, melodica, vocals / **MICHELE STODART** – bass, vocals, keyboards / **SEAN GANNON** – drums

Heavenly / Capitol

2004. (ltd;7") *(HVN 143P)* **HYMN FOR HER. / OH SISTER** ☐ [–]

2004. (ltd;7") *(HVN 147)* **ANIMA SOLA. / (flip by Hal)** [–] tour [–]

May 05. (7"pic-d) *(HVN 151)* **FOREVER LOST. / HOPE YOU DON'T MIND** [15] [–]
(cd-s) *(HVN 151CD)* – ('A') / Idea of a feeling.
(dvd-s+=) *(HVN 151DVD)* – ('A'-version) / ('A'-live).

Jun 05. (d-lp/cd) *(HVNLP 53/+CD) <CAP 094633920521>* **THE MAGIC NUMBERS** [7] Jul05 ☐
– Mornings eleven / Forever lost / The mule / Long legs / Love me like you / Which way to happy / I see you, you see me / Don't give up the fight / This love / Wheels on fire / Love's a game / Try. *(d-lp w/ 7" + cd hidden track +=)* – Hymn for her.

Aug 05. (7"pic-d) *(HVN 153)* **LOVE ME LIKE YOU. / DELPHINA'S SONG** [12] [–]
(cd-s+=) *(HVN 153CDS)* – Drunk on your words.
(cd-s) *(HVN 153CD)* – ('A') / Travelling souls.

Oct 05. (7") *(HVN 154)* **LOVE'S A GAME. / LAST NIGHT I FELL** [24] [–]
(cd-s) *(HVN 154CD)* – ('A') / Keep it in the pocket.
(dvd-s) *(HVN 154DVD)* – ('A'-video) / Love me like you (video) / ('A'-original Swedish recording).

Feb 06. (7"red) *(HVN 156X)* **I SEE YOU, YOU SEE ME. / CRAZY IN LOVE (Jo Whiley live lounge version)** [20] [–]
(cd-s) *(HVN 156CD)* – ('A') / Forever lost (Tmsbury School) (the MAGIC FRACTIONS) / Close your eyes (live Shepherds Bush) / ('A'-video).
(7") *(HVN 156)* – ('A'-live from Shepherds Bush) / There is a light that never goes out (Dermot O'Leary session).

☐ MAKAVELI (see under ⇒ 2PAC)

☐ Stephen MALKMUS (see under ⇒ PAVEMENT)

the MAMAS AND THE PAPAS

Formed: St. Thomas, Virgin Islands, USA ... 1964 as The NEW JOURNEYMAN by DENNY DOHERTY, and two JOURNEYMEN; JOHN PHILLIPS and MICHELLE GILLIAM. They soon brought in the larger-than-life CASS ELLIOT, relocating to California where they became The MAMAS & THE PAPAS (Mama being Hell's Angels slang for girlfriend). They were introduced to producer and owner of 'Dunhill' records Lou Adler, by 'Eve Of Destruction'-man, BARRY McGUIRE. He contracted them initially as backing singers for McGUIRE's 1965 album, 'Precious Time', which included PHILLIPS' 'CALIFORNIA DREAMIN'. The following year, this classic piece of harmony-orientated folk-pop became their debut 45, hitting the US Top 5. Their follow-up, 'MONDAY MONDAY', topped the charts (No.3 in the UK), succeeded by a string of hits, abruptly halted by the split of the group in '68. This was the result of the eventual marriage break-up of JOHN and MICHELLE, as well as drug busts and alleged record company rip-offs. All subsequently took off on solo ventures, often re-uniting for one-off concerts, etc. Tragically, on the 29th of July '74, CASS ELLIOT died of a heart attack while choking on food. In 1982, the three remaining members re-grouped with a new singer, SPANKY McFARLANE (ex-SPANKY & HER GANG). MICHELLE had already begun an acting career, that has since seen her in US TV dramas such as 'Knot's Landing'. Sadly, great songwriter extraordinaire, JOHN PHILLIPS, died of a heart attack in March 2001.

• **Covered:** DANCING IN THE STREET (Martha & The Vandellas) / DEDICATED TO THE ONE I LOVE (Shireles) / DO YOU WANNA DANCE (Bobby Freeman) / I CALL YOUR NAME (Beatles) / etc. In 1967, PHILLIPS wrote No.1 smash, 'SAN FRANCISCO', for late 80's PAPA-to-be SCOTT McKENZIE. Twenty years later, JOHN co-wrote US No.1, 'Kokomo', with The BEACH BOYS. • **Trivia:** On the 31st October 1970, MICHELLE, now divorced from JOHN, married cult actor DENNIS HOPPER (but only for a week!).

Album rating: IF YOU CAN BELIEVE YOUR EYES AND EARS (*7) / THE MAMAS & THE PAPAS (*7) / THE MAMAS AND THE PAPAS DELIVER (*6) / FAREWELL TO THE FIRST GOLDEN ERA compilation (*7) / THE PAPAS & THE THE MAMAS (*6) / GOLDEN ERA, VOL.2 compilation (*6) / 16 OF

THEIR GREATEST HITS compilation (*8) / PEOPLE LIKE US (*3) / CREEQUE ALLEY: HISTORY OF THE MAMAS & THE PAPAS compilation (*8) / Mama Cass: DREAM A LITTLE DREAM (*5) / BUBBLE GUM, LEMONADE & ... SOMETHING FOR MAMA (*5) / MAMA'S BIG ONES compilation (*6) / John Phillips: JOHN, THE WOLFKING OF L.A. (*8)

JOHN PHILLIPS (b.30 Aug'35, Parris Island, South Carolina) – vocals / **CASS ELLIOT** (b. ELLEN NAOMI COHEN, 19 Sep'41, Baltimore, Maryland) – vocals / **MICHELLE GILLIAM** (b. HOLLY MICHELLE GILLIAM, 4 Jun'45, Long Beach, Calif.) – vocals (ex-JOURNEYMEN, with PHILLIPS) (ELLIOT ex-MUGWUMPS with DOHERTY) / **DENNY DOHERTY** (b.29 Nov'41, Halifax, Nova Scotia, Canada) – vocals

R.C.A. Dunhill

Jan 66. (7") *(1503)* <4020> **CALIFORNIA DREAMIN'. / SOMEBODY GROOVY** 23 Dec65 4

May 66. (7") *(1516)* <4026> **MONDAY MONDAY. / GOT A FEELIN'** 3 Apr66 1

Jun 66. (lp; mono/stereo) *(RD 7803)* <D/DS 50001> **IF YOU CAN BELIEVE YOUR EYES AND EARS** 3 Feb66 1
– Do you wanna dance / Go where you wanna go / California dreamin' / Spanish harlem / Somebody groovy / Hey girl / You baby / In crowd / Monday, Monday / Straight shooter / Got a feelin' / I call your name. *(cd-iss. 1990 on 'MCA';)*

Jul 66. (7") *(1533)* <4031> **I SAW HER AGAIN. / EVEN IF I COULD** 11 Jun66 5

— **JILL GIBSON** – vocals repl. MICHELLE for a while

Oct 66. (7") *(1551)* <4050> **LOOK THRU MY WINDOW. / ONCE THERE WAS A TIME I THOUGHT** 24

— **MICHELLE** returned when she reconciled with husband JOHN

Jan 67. (lp; mono/stereo) *(RD/SF 7834)* <D/DS 50010> **CASS JOHN MICHELLE DENNY** 24 Sep66 4
– No salt on her tail / Trip, stumble and fall / Dancing bear / Words of love / My heart stood still / Dancing in the steet / I saw her again / Strange young girl / I can't wait / Even if I could / That kind of girl / Once was a time I thought.

Jan 67. (7") *(1564)* <4057> **WORDS OF LOVE. / DANCING IN THE STREET** 47 5 / Nov66 75

Mar 67. (7") *(1576)* <4077> **DEDICATED TO THE ONE I LOVE. / FREE ADVICE** 2 Feb67 2

Apr 67. (7") <4083> **CREEQUE ALLEY. / NO SALT IN HER TAIL** – 5

Jun 67. (lp; mono/stereo) *(RD/SF 7880)* <D/DS 50014> **DELIVER** 4 Mar67 2
– Dedicated to the one I love / My girl / Creeque Alley / Sing for your supper / Twist and shout / Free advice / Look through any window / Boys and girls together / String man / Frustration / Did you ever want to cry / John's music box.

Jul 67. (7") *(1613)* **CREEQUE ALLEY. / DID YOU EVER WANT TO CRY** 9 –

Sep 67. (7") *(1630)* <4099> **12:30 (YOUNG GIRLS ARE COMING TO THE CANYON). / STRAIGHT SHOOTER** Aug67 20

Dec 67. (7") *(1649)* <4107> **GLAD TO BE UNHAPPY. / HEY GIRL** Oct67 26

Dec 67. (lp; mono/stereo) <D/DS 50025> **FAREWELL TO THE FIRST GOLDEN ERA** (compilation) Oct67 5
– Dedicated to the one I love / Go where you wanna go / Words of love / Look through any window / Dancing in the street / Monday Monday / Creeque Alley / Got a feelin' / 12:30 (young girls are coming to the canyon) / I call your name / I saw her again last night / California dreamin'.

Dec 67. (7") <4113> **DANCING BEAR. / JOHN'S MUSIC BOX** – 51

Jun 68. (7") *(1710)* <4125> **SAFE IN MY GARDEN. / TOO LATE** May68 53

Sep 68. (lp; mono/stereo) *(RD/SF 7960)* <DS 50031> **...PRESENTING THE PAPAS AND THE MAMAS** May68 15
– Dream a little dream of me / Gemini child / Ivy / Mansions / Meditation mama (transcendental woman travels) / Midnight voyage / Nothing's too good for my little girl / Rooms / Safe in my garden / The right somebody to love / Too late / Twelve thirty.

Sep 68. (7") *(1744)* <4150> **FOR THE LOVE OF IVY. / STRANGE YOUNG GIRLS** 81

Nov 68. (7") <4171> **DO YOU WANNA DANCE. / MY GIRL** – 76

— (Jul68) Disbanded, when JOHN and MICHELLE broke up. JOHN PHILLIPS later went solo, as did DENNY and MICHELLE.

MAMA CASS

had already gone solo.

R.C.A. Dunhill

Aug 68. (7") *(1726)* <4145> **DREAM A LITTLE DREAM OF ME (live). / MIDNIGHT VOYAGE** 11 Jul68 12
(above also credited with The MAMAS AND THE PAPAS)

Stateside Dunhill

Nov 68. (7") *(SS 8002)* 4166> **CALIFORNIA EARTHQUAKE. / TALKIN' TO YOUR TOOTHBRUSH** Oct68 67

Dec 68. (lp; stereo/mono) *(S+/SL 5004)* <DS 50040> **DREAM A LITTLE DREAM** Oct68 87
– Dream a little dream of me / California earthquake / The room nobody lives in / Talkin' to your toothbrush / Blues for breakfast / You know who I am / Rubber band / Long time loving you / Jane, the insane dog lady / What was I thinking of / Burn your hatred / Sweet believer.

Feb 69. (7") <4184> **MOVE IN A LITTLE BIT CLOSER. / ALL FOR ME** – 58

Mar 69. (7") *(SS 8014)* **MOVE IN A LITTLE BIT CLOSER. / I CAN DREAM, CAN'T I** –

Jul 69. (7") *(SS 8021)* <4195> **IT'S GETTING BETTER. / WHO'S TO BLAME** 8 May69 30

Nov 69. (lp; stereo/mono) *(S+/SL 5014)* <DS 50055> **BUBBLEGUM, LEMONADE AND... SOMETHING FOR MAMA** Jun69 91
– Blow me a kiss / It's getting better / Easy come, easy go / I can dream, can't I / Welcome to the world / Lady Love / He's a runner / Move in a little closer, baby / When I just wear my smile / Who's to blame / Sour grapes. *<US re-iss. Nov69 as 'MAKE YOUR OWN KIND OF MUSIC'; DS 50071>* – Make your own kind of music.

MAMA CASS ELLIOT

Nov 69. (7") *(SS 8031)* <4114> **MAKE YOUR OWN KIND OF MUSIC. / LADY LOVE** Oct69 36

Mar 70. (7") *(SS 8039)* <4225> **NEW WORLD COMING. / BLOW ME A KISS** Jan70 42

Mar 70. (7") <4226> **SOMETHING TO MAKE YOU HAPPY. / NEXT TO YOU** –

Sep 70. (7") *(SS 8057)* <4244> **A SONG THAT NEVER COMES. / I CAN DREAM, CAN'T I?** Jul70 99

Nov 70. (7") *(D 4253>* **THE GOOD TIMES ARE COMIN'. / A SONG THAT NEVER COMES** –

Mar 71. (lp) *(SPB 1020)* <DS 50093> **MAMA'S BIG ONES** (compilation)
– Dream a little dream of me / Make your own kind of music / It's getting better / Easy come, easy go / Words of love / Move in a little closer, baby / Song that never comes / One way ticket / Ain't nobody else like you / Don't let the good life pass you by / The good times are comin' / New world coming. *(re-iss. Oct74 on 'A.B.C.'; ABCL 5011)*

— Late 1970-early 1971, MAMA CASS teamed up with DAVE MASON on some releases.

the MAMAS AND THE PAPAS

re-united

Probe Dunhill

Nov 71. (lp) *(SPB 1048)* <DS 50106> **PEOPLE LIKE US** Oct 71 84
– Dream a little dream of me / Make your own kind of music / It's getting better / Easy come, easy go / Words of love / Move in a little closer, baby / Song that never comes / One way ticket / Ain't nobody else like you / Don't let the good life pass you by / The good times are coming / New world coming. *(re-iss. Oct74 on 'A.B.C.'; ABCL 5017) (re-iss. Nov76 on 'Music For Pleasure'; 50299)*

Jan 72. (7") <4301> **STEP OUT. / SHOOTING STAR** – 81

Feb 72. (7") *(PRO 552)* **SHOOTING STAR. / NO DOUGH** –

— Break-up, once again for final time. All try-out solo careers.

CASS ELLIOT

went solo again.

R.C.A. R.C.A.

1972. (7") *(2179)* <74-0644> **BABY I'M YOURS. / CHERRIES JUBILEE**

Feb 72. (lp) <*(LSP 4619)*> **CASS ELLIOT**
– Introduction – Dream a little dream of me / Extraordinary / I think a lot about you / Don't call me Mama anymore / My love / I'm coming

to the best part of my life / The torchsong medley: I came here to sing a torchsong – I got a right to sing the blues – I've got it bad and that ain't good – Mean to me – Why was a born – I came here to sing a torchsong (reprise) / The night before / I like what I like / I'll be seeing you / Closing – I don't call me Mama anymore (reprise).

1972. (7") *<74-0693>* **THAT SONG. / WHEN IT DOESN'T WORK OUT** [–] [ ]

1972. (7") *<74-0764>* **DISNEY GIRLS (1957). / BREAK ANOTHER HEART** [–] [ ]

1973. (7") *<74-0830>* **DOES ANYBODY LOVE YOU. / THE ROAD IS NO PLACE FOR A LADY** [–] [ ]

1973. (lp) *(SF 8306) <LSP 4753>* **THE ROAD IS NO PLACE FOR A LADY** [ ] [ ]
– (If you're gonna) Break another heart / Saturday suit / Does anybody love you / Walk beside me / All my life – Say hello / Who in the world / Love was not a word / Oh babe, what would you say / The road is no place for a lady.

1973. (7") *<74-0957>* **LISTEN TO THE WORLD. / I THINK A LOT ABOUT YOU** [–] [ ]

Jul 74. (7") *(LPB 07521)* **IF YOU'RE GONNA BREAK ANOTHER HEART. / DON'T CALL ME MAMA ANYMORE** [ ] [–]

Jul 74. (lp) *<(APL1-0303)>* **DON'T CALL ME MAMA ANYMORE** [ ] [ ]
– Introduction – Dream a little dream of me / Extraordinary / I think a lot about you / Don't call me Mama anymore / My love / I'm coming to the best part of my life / The torchsong medley: I came here to sing a torchsong – I got a right to sing the blues – I've got it bad and that ain't good – Mean to me – Why was a born – I came here to sing a torchsong (reprise) / The night before / I like what I like / I'll be seeing you / Closing – I don't call me Mama anymore (reprise).

—— on July '74, CASS ELLIOT died of a heart attack

– (MAMAS & PAPAS) compilations, etc. –

below on 'Stateside' UK / 'Dunhill' US unless mentioned otherwise

Dec 68. (lp; stereo/mono) *(S+SL 5002) <DS 50038>* **GOLDEN ERA, VOL.2** [ ] Sep68 [53]

Apr 69. (lp; stereo/mono) *(S+/SL 5007)* **HITS OF GOLD** [7] [–]
(re-iss. Oct74 on 'A.B.C.'; ABCL 5003) (re-iss. Aug81 on 'M.C.A.'; MCL 1614)

Sep 69. (lp) *<DS 50064>* **16 OF THEIR GREATEST HITS** [–] [61]

May 77. (lp) *Arcade; (ADEP 30)* **THE BEST OF THE MAMAS AND THE PAPAS** [6] [–]

May 91. (d-cd) *M.C.A.; (MCAD2-10195)* **CREEQUE ALLEY: THE HISTORY OF THE MAMAS & PAPAS** [ ] [ ]
– Wild women / Winken', blinkin' and nod / I'll remember tonight / I don't wanna know / This precious time / (John Phillips dialogue) / California dreamin' / Go where you wanna go / Monday, Monday / You baby / Do you wanna dance / I call your name / Spanish harlem / Straight shooter / Got a feelin' / I saw her again last night / Look through my window / Words of love / Dancing in the street / (Mama Cass dialogue) / Once was a time I thought / No salt in her tail / Trip, stumble and fall / Dancing bear / Dedicated to the one I love / Creeque Alley / My girl / Twist and shout / I call your name / Twelve thirty (young girls are coming to the canyon) / Glad to be unhappy / For the love of Ivy / Safe in my garden / Midnight voyage / Dream a little dream of me / California earthquake / It's getting better / Mississippi / Watcha gonna do / (Mama Cass dialogue) / Step out / The achin' kind.

Jun 92. (cd/c) *See For Miles; (SEE CD/K 333)* **THE EP COLLECTION** [ ] [–]

Dec 94. (cd/c) *Polygram TV; (523 973-2/-4)* **CALIFORNIA DREAMING – THE VERY BEST OF THE MAMAS & THE PAPAS** [14] [–]
(re-dist.Aug97; hit No.30)

Jul 97. (c-s/cd-s) *M.C.A.; (MCS C/TD 48058)* **CALIFORNIA DREAMIN' / DREAM A LITTLE DREAM OF ME / MONDAY MONDAY / MAKE YOUR OWN KIND OF MUSIC** [9] [–]

Aug 99. (cd) *Beat Goes On; (BGOCD 462)* **DELIVER / THE PAPAS & THE MAMAS** [ ] [ ]

Jan 00. (cd) *Universal; (E 112175-2)* **UNIVERSAL MASTERS COLLECTION** [ ] [ ]

Oct 00. (cd/c) *M.C.A.; (MCBD/MCBC 19519)* **THE BEST OF THE MAMAS & THE PAPAS** [ ] [ ]

Aug 01. (d-cd) *Universal; (AA88 112653-2)* **ALL THE LEAVES ARE BROWN** [ ] [ ]

Feb 02. (d-cd) *BR Music; (BS 8125-2)* **THE SINGLES PLUS** [ ] [–]

Mar 03. (cd) *Universal; (AAMCAD 11739)* **IF YOU CAN BELIEVE YOUR EYES** [ ] [ ]

Mar 03. (cd) *Universal; (AAMCAD 11740)* **GREATEST HITS** [ ] [ ]

Mar 03. (cd) *Universal; (AAMCAD 11945)* **20TH CENTURY MASTERS** [ ] [ ]

MANIC STREET PREACHERS

Formed: Blackwood, Caerphilly, Wales . . . 1988 by JAMES DEAN BRADFIELD (vocals, guitar) and cousin SEAN MOORE (drums). With the addition of former school friends NICKY WIRE (bass) and RICHEY EDWARDS (rhythm guitar), the line-up was complete and the band set about recording their self-financed debut single, 'SUICIDE ALLEY'. The group began to attract attention with the release of the 'NEW ART RIOT' EP (1990), derivative but impassioned neo-punk which drew interest more for the band's defiant slurs on a range of targets (fellow musicians were shown no mercy) than its musical content. While the band looked the part (low rent glamour chic) and namechecked all the right people (RIMBAUD, The CLASH, etc.), their philosophy of kill your idols and then burn out, smacked of contrivance to say the least. When journalist STEVE LAMACQ said as much in an interview with EDWARDS in 1991, the guitarist proceeded to carve '4 REAL' into his arm with a razor, upping the ante in the band's already precarious relationship with the music press and causing furious debate between doubters and obsessive fans. The group proceeded to release a couple of raging singles on 'Heavenly', 'MOTOWN JUNK' and the stinging 'YOU LOVE US' (aimed at the press), before signing to 'Columbia' in 1991. After a couple of minor hits, 'STAY BEAUTIFUL' and 'LOVE'S SWEET EXILE', the MANICS cracked the Top 20 with a re-released 'YOU LOVE US', their much anticipated debut album, 'GENERATION TERRORISTS' following in February 1992. A sprawling double set, it kicked convincingly against the pricks, lashing out at such deserving targets as high street banks ('NAT WEST-BARCLAYS-MIDLAND-LLOYDS') and our beloved monarch ('REPEAT'). The band also proved they had a way with melody and songwriting in the soaring melancholy of 'MOTORCYCLE EMPTINESS'. Despite their original well intentioned claims to break up after the debut, the band rather predictably toured the album and began work on a new collection, 'GOLD AGAINST THE SOUL' (1993). Lacking the vicious kick of the debut, the record nevertheless contained some fine moments in the likes of 'LA TRISTESSE DURERA (SCREAM TO A SIGH)' and 'LIFE BECOMING A LANDSLIDE', reaching No.8 in the album charts. The MANIC STREET PREACHERS continued to court controversy with NICKY WIRE making his infamous comments about MICHAEL STIPE at the 1993 Reading Festival. The following year RICHEY EDWARDS' depression, self-mutilation and anorexia reached a head, the guitarist eventually admitted to a clinic for several weeks. His trauma was detailed in the harrowing '4st 7lb' from their third album, 'The HOLY BIBLE' (1994), a dark night of the soul which centred on such grim topics as Nazi genocide. Then, on 1st February '95, with EDWARDS apparently recovered, he went AWOL from his London hotel. A fortnight later, his abandoned car was found at the Severn Bridge, and rumours of suicide abounded. Even after a protracted police search, there was no trace of the guitarist and at the time of writing , he is still missing. Numerous sightings have since been reported, most notably in Goa, India although the Police have continued to draw a blank. The remaining members eventually decided to carry on, contributing a poignant 'RAIN DROPS KEEP FALLING ON MY

HEAD' to the 1995 Warchild charity album, 'HELP', and releasing their fourth album, 'EVERYTHING MUST GO' (1996). The group's most accomplished work to date, the record was preceded by their biggest hit single (No.2), the bitter 'A DESIGN FOR LIFE'. Embellished with soaring strings and lavish arrangements, the band scored with a succession of brilliant songs including 'AUSTRALIA' and the title track, compositions that were almost transcendant in their emotive power, the memory of EDWARDS never far away. It seemed that at last the MANIC STREET PREACHERS had lived up to their early boasts and in early 1997 their talent was recognised when 'EVERYTHING MUST GO' won the coveted Mercury Music Award. The top of the singles chart was the only place the MANICS hadn't been. This was remedied late summer '98 when 'IF YOU TOLERATE THIS YOUR CHILDREN WILL BE NEXT' made No.1, a taster from their massive selling parent album, 'THIS IS THE TRUTH TELL ME YOURS' (1998). Classic anthems such as 'THE EVERLASTING', 'YOU STOLE THE SUN FROM MY HEART', and 'TSUNAMI', also became top selling in the UK charts, although what was happening to their records in America? Not that the staunchly socialist MANICS gave a fig for their Stateside oblivion, content to become the first Western rock band to play in Communist Cuba, that longtime thorn in Uncle Sam's bloated side. No need to ask then, what 'BABY ELIAN' was all about given the Cuba vs USA tussle of summer 2000. The latter track was served up for 'KNOW YOUR ENEMY' (2001), the band's sixth album and one of their most accomplished to date. The almost STOOGES-style savagery of 'FOUND THAT SOUL' (a dual Top 10 single released simultaneously with 'SO WHY SO SAD') set the tone, a blistering punk/garage track that put many of the so called American nu-metal/punk groups to shame and served as a timely reminder of how good angry rock music can be when it comes from the gut and not the marketing strategy. 'OCEAN SPRAY', in contrast, was a poignant homage to JAMES' mum's battle with cancer, Ocean Spray being a brand of cranberry juice used to combat the disease. Yet this album was primarily a politicised affair, again railing against the evils of the USA in the likes of 'FREE SPEECH WON'T FEED MY CHILDREN' and 'LET ROBESON SING', a tribute to the forgotten entertainer/political activist. They may be guilty of naivety, bombast and even double standards but few bands of the modern era write, play and perform with the emotional and political intensity, the dignity and the humbleness of the MANIC STREET PREACHERS. In the absence of any new material, the inevitable greatest hits and B-sides collections were released in 2002 and 2003 respectively. While 'FOREVER DELAYED' made a fair stab at charting their fascinating career curve, the dearth of representative material from the traumatic 'HOLY BIBLE' era meant it didn't tell the whole story. 'LIPSTICK TRACES', meanwhile, told a slightly different story, its disc of covers giving an often intimate insight into the roots and influences that made them the singular artists they are. The Caerphilly trio returned in late 2004, but not to the Top 10, their comeback album, 'LIFEBLOOD', attracting mixed reviews for its toned down maturity, even if its lyrics and song titles were as uncompromising as ever: 'THE LOVE OF RICHARD NIXON' and 'EMPTY SOULS' nevertheless both went to No.2.

• **Covered:** IT'S SO EASY (Guns N' Roses) / UNDER MY WHEELS (Alice Cooper) / SUICIDE IS PAINLESS (Theme from 'M.A.S.H.') / WE ARE BOURGEOIS NOW + CHARLES WINDSOR (McCarthy) / THE DROWNERS (Suede) / STAY WITH ME (Faces) / WROTE FOR LUCK (Happy Mondays) / RAINDROPS KEEP FALLING ON MY HEAD (Bacharach-David) / VELOCITY GIRL (Primal Scream) / TAKE THE SKINHEADS BOWLING (Camper Van Beethoven) / BEEN A SON (Nirvana) / OUT OF TIME (Rolling Stones) / BRIGHT EYES (Mike Batt) / I CAN'T TAKE MY EYES OFF YOU (hit; Andy Williams) / TRAIN IN VAIN + WHAT'S MY NAME (Clash) / LAST CHRISTMAS (George Michael) / DIDN'T MY LORD DELIVER DANIEL (trad.) / ROCK AND ROLL MUSIC (Chuck Berry).

Album rating: GENERATION TERRORISTS (*8) / GOLD AGAINST THE SOUL (*9) / THE HOLY BIBLE (*9) / EVERYTHING MUST GO (*9) / THIS IS MY TRUTH TELL ME YOURS (*8) / KNOW YOUR ENEMY (*7) / FOREVER DELAYED – GREATEST HITS compilation (*8) / LIPSTICK TRACES: A SECRET HISTORY OF . . . double compilation (*5) / LIFEBLOOD (*6)

JAMES DEAN BRADFIELD (b.21 Feb'69, Newport) – vocals, guitar / **RICHEY JAMES EDWARDS** (b.27 Dec'69) – rhythm guitar / **NICKY WIRE** (b. NICHOLAS JONES, 20 Jan'69, Tredegar) – bass / **SEAN MOORE** (b.30 Jul'70, Pontypool) – drums

S.B.S. — not iss.

Aug 89. (7") *(SBS 002)* **SUICIDE ALLEY. / TENNESSEE (I FEEL SO LOW)** [ ] [–]

Damaged Goods — not iss.

Jun 90. (12"ep) *(YUBB 4)* **NEW ART RIOT** [ ] [–]
– New art riot / Stip it down / Last exit on yesterday / Teenage 20-20. *(re-iss. Dec91, Jul93 + Sep96, 12"pink-ep/cd-ep; YUBB 4 P/CD)*

Heavenly — not iss.

Jan 91. (12"ep/cd-ep) *(HVN8 12/CD)* **MOTOWN JUNK. / SORROW 16 / WE HER MAJESTY'S PRISONERS** [92] [–]

May 91. (7") *(HVN 10)* **YOU LOVE US. / SPECTATORS OF SUICIDE** [62] [–]
(12"+=/cd-s+=) *(HVN 10 12/CD)* – Starlover / Strip it down (live).

Caff — not iss.

Jul 91. (7") *(CAFF 15)* **FEMININE IS BEAUTIFUL: NEW ART RIOT. / REPEAT AFTER ME** [ ] [–]

Columbia — Columbia

Jul 91. (7") *(657337-7)* **STAY BEAUTIFUL. / R.P. McMURPHY** [40] [ ]
(12"+=/12"w-poster/cd-s+=) *(657337-6/-8/-2)* – Soul contamination.
(US-cd-ep+=) – Motown junk / Sorrow 16 / Star lover.
(cd-ep re-iss. Sep97 on 'Epic' hit No.52; MANIC 1CD)

Nov 91. (7") *(657582-7)* **LOVE'S SWEET EXILE. / REPEAT** [26] [–]
(12"+=/cd-s+=) *(657582-6/-2)* – Democracy coma.
(12"ltd.++=) *(657582-8)* – Stay beautiful (live).
(cd-ep re-iss. Sep97 on 'Epic' hit No.55; MANIC 2CD)

Jan 92. (7"/c-s) *(657724-7/-4)* **YOU LOVE US. / A VISION OF DEAD DESIRE** [16] [–]
(12"+=) *(657724-6)* – It's so easy (live).
(cd-s++=) *(657724-2)* – We her majesty's prisoners.
(cd-ep re-iss. Sep97 on 'Epic' hit No.49; MANIC 3CD)

Feb 92. (pic-cd/cd/d-c/d-lp/pic-d-lp) *(471060-0/-2/-4/-1/-9)* <52474> **GENERATION TERRORISTS** [13] [ ]
– Slash 'n' burn / Nat West-Barclays-Midland-Lloyds / Born to end / Motorcycle emptiness / You love us / Love's sweet exile / Little baby nothing / Repeat (stars and stripes) / Tennessee / Another invented disease / Stay beautiful / So dead / Repeat (UK) / Spectators of suicide / Damn dog / Crucifix kiss / Methadone pretty / Condemned to rock'n'roll. *(cd re-iss. Jan99; same)*

Mar 92. (7"/c-s) *(657873-7/-4)* **SLASH 'N' BURN. / AIN'T GOING DOWN** [20] [–]
(12"+=) *(657873-6)* – Motown junk.
(cd-s++=/gold-cd-s++=) *(657873-2/-0)* – ('A'version).
(cd-ep re-iss. Sep97 on 'Epic' hit No.54; MANIC 4CD)

Jun 92. (7"/c-s) *(658083-7/-4)* **MOTORCYCLE EMPTINESS. / BORED OUT OF MY MIND** [17] [–]
(12"pic-d+=) *(658083-8)* – Under my wheels.
(cd-s++=/s-cd-s++=) *(658083-2/-9)* – Crucifix kiss (live).
(cd-ep re-iss. Sep97 on 'Epic' hit No.41; MANIC 5CD)

Sep 92. (7"/cd-s) *(658382-7/-2)* **THEME FROM M.A.S.H. (SUICIDE IS PAINLESS). / ('b'side by 'Fatima Mansions' – Everything I Do (I Do It For You)** [7] [–]

Nov 92. (7") *(658796-7)* **LITTLE BABY NOTHING. / SUICIDE ALLEY** [29] [–]
(12"+=/cd-s+=) *(658796-6/-2)* – Yankee drawl / Never want again.
(cd-ep re-iss. Sep97 on 'Epic' hit No.50; MANIC 6CD)

Jun 93. (c-s) *(659337-4)* **FROM DESPAIR TO WHERE. / HIBERNATION** [25] [–]
(12"+=) *(659337-6)* – Spectators of suicide (Heavenly version).
(cd-s+=) *(659337-2)* – Star lover (Heavenly version).

Jun 93. (cd/c/lp/pic-lp) *(474064-2/-4/-1/-9)* <57386> **GOLD AGAINST THE SOUL** [8] [ ]
– Sleepflower / From despair to where / La tristesse durera (scream to a sigh) / Yourself / Life becoming a landslide / Drug drug druggy / Roses in the hospital / Nostalgic pushead / Symphony of tourette / Gold against the soul.

Jul 93. (7"/c-s) *(659477-7/-4)* **LA TRISTESSE DURERA (SCREAM TO A SIGH). / PATRICK BATEMAN** [22] [–]

(12"+=) *(659477-6)* – Repeat (live) / Tennessee.
(cd-s+=) *(659477-2)* – What's my name (live) / Slash'n'burn (live).

Sep 93. (7"/c-s) *(659727-7/-4)* **ROSES IN THE HOSPITAL. / US AGAINST YOU / DONKEY** 15 –
(cd-s+=) *(659727-2)* – Wrote for luck.
(12") *(659727-6)* – ('A'side) / (5-'A' mixes).

Epic Epic

Feb 94. (c-s) *(660070-4)* **LIFE BECOMING A LANDSLIDE / COMFORT COMES** 36 –
(12"+=) *(660070-6)* – Are mothers saints.
(cd-s++=) *(660070-2)* – Charles Windsor.

Jun 94. (7"/c-s) *(660447-7/-4)* **FASTER. / P.C.P.** 16 –
(10"+=) *(660447-0)* – Sculpture of man.
(cd-s++=) *(660447-2)* – New art riot (in E-minor).

Aug 94. (10"/c-s) *(660686-0/-4)* **REVOL. / TOO COLD HERE** 22 –
(cd-s+=) *(660686-2)* – You love us (original Heavenly version) / Love's sweet exile (live).
(cd-s) *(660686-5)* – ('A'side) / (3 live at Glastonbury tracks).

— RICHEY booked himself into a health clinic, after wasting himself down to 5 stone.

Aug 94. (cd/c/pic-lp) *(477421-2/-4/-0)* <66967> **THE HOLY BIBLE** 6
– Yes / Ifwhiteamericatoldthetruthforonedayit'sworldwouldfallapart / Of walking abortion / She is suffering / Archives of pain / Revol / 4st 7lb / Mausoleum / Faster / This is yesterday / Die in the summertime / The intense humming of evil / P.C.P.

Oct 94. (10"/c-s) *(660895-0/-4)* **SHE IS SUFFERING. / LOVE TORN US UNDER (acoustic)** 25 –
(cd-s+=) *(660895-2)* – The drowners / Stay with me (both live w/ BERNARD BUTLER).
(cd-s) *(660895-5)* – ('A'side) / La tristesse durera (scream to a sigh) / Faster (Dust Brothers remixes).

— RICHEY was now fully recuperated . . . but on 1st Feb '95, he went AWOL again after walking out of London's Embassy Hotel at 7 that morning. Two weeks later, his car was found abandoned and after police frogmen searched the Severn, it was believed he might be dead. By the end of 1995, with RICHEY still missing, the group carried on as a trio.

— Meanwhile, BRADFIELD produced the debut of NORTHERN UPROAR.

Apr 96. (c-s) *(663070-4)* **A DESIGN FOR LIFE / BRIGHT EYES (live)** 2 –
(cd-s) *(663070-2)* – ('A'side) / Mr Carbohydrate / Dead passive / Dead trees and traffic islands.
(cd-s) *(663070-5)* – ('A'side) / ('A'-Howard Grey remix) / ('A'-Apollo 440 remix) / Faster (Chemical Brothers remix).

May 96. (cd/c/lp) *(483930-2/-4/-1)* <67709> **EVERYTHING MUST GO** 2
– Elvis impersonator: Blackpoool pier / A design for life / Kevin Carter / Enola – alone / Everything must go / Small black flowers that grow in the sky / The girl who wanted to be God / Removables / Australia / Interiors (song for Willem De Kooning) / Further away / No surface at all.

Jul 96. (c-s) *(663468-4)* **EVERYTHING MUST GO / RAINDROPS KEEP FALLING ON MY HEAD (live)** 5 –
(cd-s) *(663468-2)* – ('A'side) / Hanging on / Black garden / No-one knows what it's like to be me.
(cd-s) *(663468-5)* – ('A'side) / ('A'-Stealth Sonic Orchestra remix) / ('A'-Chemical Brothers remix).

Sep 96. (c-s) *(663775-4)* **KEVIN CARTER / EVERYTHING MUST GO (acoustic)** 9 –
(cd-s) *(663775-2)* – ('A'side) / Horses under starlight / Sepia / First republic.
(cd-s) *(663775-5)* – Kevin Carter busts loose (Jon Carter remix) / ('A'-Stealth Sonic Orchestra mixes).

Dec 96. (c-s) *(664044-4)* **AUSTRALIA / A DESIGN FOR LIFE (live)** 7 –
(cd-s) *(664044-2)* – ('A'side) / Velocity girl / Take the skinheads bowling / I can't take my eyes off you (acoustic).
(cd-s) *(664044-5)* – ('A'side) / ('A'-Lionrock remix) / Motorcycle emptiness (Stealth Sonic Orchestra version).

Epic Virgin

Aug 98. (c-s) *(666345-4)* **IF YOU TOLERATE THIS YOUR CHILDREN WILL BE NEXT / KEVIN CARTER (live)** 1 –
(cd-s) *(666345-2)* – ('A'side) / Prologue to history / Montana Autumn '78.
(cd-s) *(666345-5)* – ('A'side) / ('A'-Massive Attack remix) / ('A'-The Class Reunion Of The Sunset Marquis mix; aka David Holmes).

Sep 98. (cd/c/lp) *(491703-2/-4/-1)* <47579> **THIS IS MY TRUTH TELL ME YOURS** 1
– The everlasting / If you tolerate this your children will be next / You stole the sun from my heart / Ready for drowning / Tsunami / My little empire / I'm not working / You're tender and you're tired / Born a girl / Be natural / Black dog on my shoulder / Nobody loved you / S.Y.M.M. *(cd re-iss. Nov02; 491703-6)*

Nov 98. (c-s) *(666686-4)* **THE EVERLASTING / SMALL BLACK FLOWERS THAT GROW IN THE SUN (live at Nunex)** 11 –
(cd-s) *(666686-2)* – ('A'side) / Blackholes for the young / Valley boy.
(cd-s) *(666686-5)* – ('A'extended) / ('A'-Deadly Avenger's Psalm 315) / ('A'-Stealth Sonic Orchestra mix).

Mar 99. (c-s) *(666953-4)* **YOU STOLE THE SUN FROM MY HEART / IF YOU TOLERATE THIS YOUR CHILDREN WILL BE NEXT (live)** 5 –
(cd-s) *(666953-2)* – ('A'side) / Socialist serenade / Train in vain (live).
(cd-s) *(666953-5)* – ('A'side) / ('A'mixes by David Holmes & Mogwai).

Jul 99. (c-s) *(667411-4)* **TSUNAMI / MOTOWN JUNK (live)** 11 –
(cd-s) *(667411-2)* – ('A'side) / Buildings for dead people / A design for life (video).
(cd-s) *(667411-5)* – ('A'mixes by Cornelius & Stereolab).

Jan 00. (c-s) *(668530-4)* **THE MASSES AGAINST THE CLASSES / CLOSE MY EYES** 1 –
(10"+=/cd-s+=) *(668530-6/-2)* – Rock and roll music.

Feb 01. (c-s) *(670832-4)* **SO WHY SO SAD / YOU STOLE THE SUN FROM MY HEART (live from Cardiff Millennium Stadium 31st December 1999)** 8 –
(cd-s) *(670832-2)* – ('A'side) / ('A'-Avalanche remix) / Pedestal.

Feb 01. (7") *(670833-7)* **FOUND THAT SOUL. / THE MASSES AGAINST THE CLASSES (live)** 9 –
(cd-s) *(670833-2)* – ('A'side) / Locust valley / Ballad of the Bangkok Novotel.

Mar 01. (cd/c/lp) *(501880-2/-4/-1)* <10113> **KNOW YOUR ENEMY** 2
– Found that soul / Ocean spray / Intravenus agnostic / So why so sad / Let Robeson sing / The year of purification / Wattsville blues / Miss Europa disco dancer / Dead martyrs / His last painting / My Guernica / The convalescent / Royal correspondent / Epicentre / Baby Elian / Freedom of speech won't feed my children. *(untitled hidden track+=) (cd re-iss. Nov01; same)*

Jun 01. (c-s) *(671253-4)* **OCEAN SPRAY / OCEAN SPRAY (Ellis Island mix)** 15 –
(cd-s) *(671253-2)* – ('A'side) / The groundhog days / Just a kid.
(cd-s) *(671253-5)* – ('A'side) / ('A'-Medicine mix) / ('A'-Kinobe mix).

Sep 01. (12") *(671773-6)* **LET ROBESON SING. / ('A'-Ian Brown mix) / ('A'-thee glitz mix by Felix Da Housecat)** 19 –
(cd-s+=) *(671773-5)* – ('A'video).
(cd-s) *(671773-2)* – ('A'-side) / Masking tape / Didn't my Lord deliver Daniel / ('A'-video).

Oct 02. (cd-s) *(673166-2)* **THERE BY THE GRACE OF GOD / AUTOMATIK TEKNICOLOUR / IT'S ALL GONE / ('A'video)** 6 –
(cd-s) *(673166-5)* – ('A'-side) / Unstoppable salvation / Happy ending.

Oct 02. (cd/lp) *(509551-2/-1)* <87029> **FOREVER DELAYED – GREATEST HITS** (compilation) 4
– A design for life / Motorcycle emptiness / If you tolerate this your children will be next / La tristesse durera (scream to a high) / There by the grace of God / You love us / Australia / You stole the sun from my heart / Kevin Carter / Tsunami / Masses against the classes / From despair to where / Door to the river / Everything must go / Faster / Little baby nothing / M.A.S.H. (suicide is painless) / So why so sad / Everlasting / Motown junk. *(d-cd+=; 509551-9)* – (remixes).

Jul 03. (d-cd/t-lp) *(512386-2/-1)* <862000> **LIPSTICK TRACES: A SECRET HISTORY OF . . .** (compilation) 11
– Prologue to history / 4 ever delayed / Sorrow 16 / Judge yr'self / Socialist serenade / Donkeys / Comfort comes / Mr. Carbohydrate / Dead trees and traffic islands / Horses under starlight / Sepia / Sculpture of man / Spectators of suicide / Democracy coma / Strip it down (live) / Bored out of my mind / Just a kid / Close my eyes / Valley boy / We her Majesty's prisoners / We are all bourgeoise now / Rock and roll music / It's so easy (live) / Take the skingheads bowling / Been a son / Out of time / Raindrops keep falling on my head / Bright eyes (live) / Train in vain (live) / Wrote for luck / What's my name (live) / Velocity girl / Can't take my eyes off you / Didn't my Lord deliver Daniel / Last Christmas (live).

Oct 04. (cd-s) *(675342-1)* **THE LOVE OF RICHARD NIXON / EVERYBODY KNOWS – NOBODY CARES** 2 –
(cd-s) *(675342-2)* – ('A') / Everything will be (Andy Cato remix) / Askew road / ('A'-video).
(dvd-s) *(675342-9)* – ('A') / Quarantine (in my place of) (short film) / Voodoo polaroids.

Nov 04. (cd/lp) *(518885-2/-1)* *<91944>* **LIFEBLOOD** 13 Dec04
– 1985 / The love of Richard Nixon / Empty souls / A song for departure / I live to fall asleep / To repel ghosts / Emily / Glasnost / Always – Never / Solitude sometimes is / Fragments / Cardiff afterlife.

Jan 05. (cd-s) *(675610-1)* **EMPTY SOULS / ALL ALONE HERE** 2 –
(cd-s) *(675610-2)* – ('A') / No jubilees / Litany / ('A'-video).
(dvd-s) *(675610-9)* – ('A'-video) / Dying breeds (short film directed by Patrick Jones) / Failure bound.

Manfred MANN

Formed: London, England ... late '62, initially as The MANN-HUGG BLUES BAND, subsequently naming themselves MANFRED MANN after the band's keyboard player. MANN and HUGG then recruited DAVE RICHMOND, PAUL JONES and MIKE VICKERS, playing local gigs which secured them a deal with the 'H.M.V.' label. Early in 1964, after two flop singles, they had their first chart success, hitting the Top 5 with the harmonica-fuelled R&B classic, '5-4-3-2-1'. They continued to storm the charts throughout the 60's, reaching pole position three times with 'DOO WAH DIDDY DIDDY' (1964), 'PRETTY FLAMINGO' (1966) and 'THE MIGHTY QUINN' (1968). The latter was fronted by MIKE D'ABO, who had replaced the solo bound PAUL JONES. In 1969, MANN and HUGG churned out commercial jingles for Michelen tyres and Ski yogurt before forming the heavier jazz-rock outfit, MANFRED MANN CHAPTER THREE. They delivered a couple of albums for 'Vertigo', soon reverting back to their original name in 1971. The following year, they re-emerged minus HUGG, with the more ambitious and progressive MANFRED MANN'S EARTH BAND. They struggled initially, although they created their own take on GUSTAV HOLST's "Jupiter suite" (from 'The Planets') in the form of 'JOYBRINGER' (a top 10 hit in 1973). A dry period of three years ensued, during which time they released three accessible rock albums, 'SOLAR FIRE', 'THE GOOD EARTH' and 'NIGHTINGALES AND BOMBERS'. The band saw a return to chart action with a cover of BRUCE SPRINGSTEEN's, 'BLINDED BY THE LIGHT', which also hit No.1 in America. Their albums fared a lot better from this point on, another SPRINGSTEEN re-hash, 'SPIRIT IN THE NIGHT', denting the US Top 40 in 1977. In the 80's (and 90's!), his EARTH BAND continued to tread the same ground, releasing a plethora of mediocre cover versions for the coffee-table set. One particular song, 'THE RUNNER', saw them sprinting back into the US Top 30 early in 1984. Over the course of the decade or so, MANFRED MANN delivered the odd pop-rock album, although it was in 1999, that he would return to some kind of press coverage, albeit over the sample/use of his song 'TRIBUTE' on MASSIVE ATTACK's 'Black Mark'; the Bristol posse settled out of court.

• **Songwriters:** MANN-HUGG until latter's departure in '71. Covered; DOO WAH DIDDY DIDDY (Exciters) / SHA LA LA (Shirelles) / OH NO NOT MY BABY (Goffin-King) / SMOKESTACK LIGHTNING (Howlin' Wolf) / MY LITTLE RED BOOK (Bacharach-David) / WITH GOD ON OUR SIDE + IF YOU GOTTA GO, GO NOW + JUST LIKE A WOMAN + THE MIGHTY QUINN + PLEASE, MRS.HENRY + others (Bob Dylan) / SWEET PEA (Tommy Roe) / SO LONG DAD + LIVING WITHOUT YOU (Randy Newman) / MY NAME IS JACK (John Simon) / etc. His EARTH BAND covered FATHER OF DAY, FATHER OF NIGHT + YOU, ANGEL YOU + SHELTER FROM THE STORM (Bob Dylan) / SPIRIT IN THE NIGHT + BLINDED BY THE LIGHT + FOR YOU (Bruce Springsteen) / DON'T KILL IT CAROL (Mike Heron) / REDEMPTION SONG (Bob Marley) / DO ANYTHING YOU WANNA DO (Eddie & The Hot Rods) / GOING UNDERGROUND (Jam) / BANQUET (Joni Mitchell) / PLAY WITH FIRE (Rolling Stones) / NOTHING EVER HAPPENS (Del Amitri) / PLEASURE + PAIN (Chapman-Knight) / TUMBLING BALL (M. Spiro) / THE PRICE I PAY (Robert Cray) / LOSE THE TOUCH (C. Schumann) / THE COMPLETE HISTORY OF SEXUAL JEALOUSY (Momus) / 99 LBS (D Bryant) / etc. • **Trivia:** MIKE HUGG wrote 'SHAPES OF THINGS' in 1966 for fellow R&B hitmakers, The YARDBIRDS. MANFRED played Moog synthesizer on URIAH HEEP's 1971 album, 'Look At Yourself'. The 'GLORIFIED MAGNIFIED' track was used for the theme to Radio 1's 'Sound Of The 70's'.

Best CD compilation: WORLD OF MANN – THE VERY BEST OF MANFRED MANN & MANFRED MANN'S EARTH BAND (*8)

MANFRED MANN (b. MANFRED LUBOWITZ, 21 Oct'40, Johannesburg, South Africa) – keyboards / **PAUL JONES** (b.PAUL POND, 24 Feb'42, Portsmouth, England) – vocals, harmonica / **MIKE VICKERS** (b.18 Apr'41, Southampton, England) – guitar / **DAVE RICHMOND** – bass / **MIKE HUGG** (b.11 Aug'42, Andover, England) – drums

H.M.V. Prestige

Jul 63. (7") *(POP 1189)* **WHY SHOULD WE NOT. / BROTHER JACK** –

Oct 63. (7") *(POP 1225)* **COCK-A-HOOP. / NOW YOU'RE NEEDING ME** –

—— **TOM McGUINESS** (b. 2 Dec'41, Wimbledon, London, England) – bass (ex-ROOSTERS) repl. RICHMOND

Jan 64. (7") *(POP 1252)* **5-4-3-2-1. / WITHOUT YOU** 5 Mar64

H.M.V. Ascot

Apr 64. (7") *(POP 1282)* *<2151>* **HUBBLE BUBBLE TOIL AND TROUBLE. / I'M YOUR KINGPIN** 11

Jul 64. (7") *(POP 1320)* *<2157>* **DOO WAH DIDDY DIDDY. / WHAT YOU GONNA DO** 1 Aug64 1
(re-iss. Oct82; PMS 1003)

Sep 64. (lp) *(CLP 1731)* **THE FIVE FACES OF MANFRED MANN** 3 –
– Smokestack lightning / Don't ask me what I say / It's gonna work out fine / Sack of wool / What you gonna do / I'm your kingpin / Hoochie coochie / Down the road apiece / I've got my mojo working / Mr. Analles / Untie me / Bring it to Jerome / Without you / You've got to take it. *(cd-iss. Jun97 on 'E.M.I.'; DORIG 121)*

Oct 64. (7") *(POP 1346)* *<2165>* **SHA LA LA. / JOHN HARDY** 3 Nov64 12

Nov 64. (lp) *<16015>* **THE MANFRED MANN ALBUM** – 35
– Do wah diddy diddy / Sack o' woe / Don't ask me what I say / What you gonna do / Got my mojo working / I'm your hoochie coochie man / Smokestack lightning / It's gonna work out fine / Down the road apiece / Untie me / Bring it to Jerome / Without you.

Jan 65. (7") *(POP 1381)* *<2170>* **COME TOMORROW. / WHAT DID I DO WRONG** 4 Feb65 50

Mar 65. (lp) *<ALS 16018>* **THE FIVE FACES OF MANFRED MANN** –
– Sha la la / Come tomorrow / She / Can't believe it / John Hardy / Did you have to do that / Watermelon man / I'm your kingpin / Hubble bubble (toil and trouble) / You've got to take it / Dashing away with the smoothing iron / Groovin'.

Apr 65. (7") *(POP 1413)* **OH NO NOT MY BABY. / WHAT AM I DOING WRONG** 11 –

Apr 65. (7") *<2181>* **POISON IVY. / I CAN'T BELIEVE WHAT YOU SAY** –

Jun 65. (7") *<2184>* **MY LITTLE RED BOOK. / WHAT AM I DOING WRONG** –
<re-iss. 1966; 2241>

Jul 65. (lp) *<ALS 16201>* **MY LITTLE RED BOOK OF WINNERS** –
– My little red book / Oh no, not my baby / What am I to do / One in the middle / You gave me somebody to love / You're for me / Poison Ivy / Without you / Brother Jack / Love like yours / I can't believe what you say / With God on your side.

Sep 65. (7") *(POP 1466)* **IF YOU GOTTA GO, GO NOW. / STAY AROUND** 2 –

Oct 65. (lp) *(CLP 1911)* *<ALS 16024>* **MANN MADE** 7
– Since I don't have you / You're for me / Look away / L.S.D. / The abominable snowman / Watch your step / The way you do the things you do / Stormy Monday blues / Hi lili hi lo / I really do believe / Bear Hugg / You don't know me / I'll make it up to you. *(re-iss. Nov69 on 'Regal Starline'; SRS 5007)*

Oct 65. (7") *<2194>* **IF YOU GOTTA GO, GO NOW. / THE ONE IN THE MIDDLE** –

Jan 66. (7") *<2210>* **HI LILI, HI LO. / SHE NEEDS COMPANY** [–] [ ]

—— (PETE BURFORD and DAVID HYDE deputised for VICKERS on tour until) / **JACK BRUCE** (b.14 May'43, Lanarkshire, Scotland) – bass (ex-JOHN MAYALL, ex-GRAHAM BOND) repl. VICKERS / added **LYN DOBSON** – saxophone / **HENRY LOWTHER** – trumpet (McGUINESS now guitar)

H.M.V. U.A.

Apr 66. (7") *(POP 1523) <50040>* **PRETTY FLAMINGO. / YOU'RE STANDING BY** [1] Jun66 [29]

—— **MANN, HUGG** and **McGUINESS** added new members **MIKE D'ABO** (b. 1 Mar'44, Bethworth, England) – vocals (ex-BAND OF ANGELS) repl. JONES who went solo, etc. / **KLAUS VOORMAN** (b.29 Apr'42, Berlin, Germany) – bass repl. JACK BRUCE who formed CREAM.

Jun 66. (7") *(POP 1541)* **YOU GAVE ME SOMEBODY TO LOVE. / POISON IVY** [36] [–]

Sep 66. *<50066>* **DO YOU HAVE TO DO THAT. / WHEN WILL I BE LOVED** [–] [ ]

Fontana Mercury

Jul 66. (7") *(TF 730) <72607>* **JUST LIKE A WOMAN. / I WANNA BE RIGHT** [10] [ ]

Oct 66. (7") *(TF 757) <72629>* **SEMI-DETACHED SUBURBAN MR. JAMES. / MORNING AFTER THE PARTY** [2] [ ]

Oct 66. (lp; stereo/mono) *(S+/TL 5377)* **AS IS** [22] [–]
– Trouble and tea / A now and then thing / Each other's company / Box office draw / Dealer dealer / Morning after the party / Another kind of music / As long as I have lovin' / Autumn leaves / Superstitious guy / You're my girl / Just like a woman.

Dec 66. (lp) *<6549>* **PRETTY FLAMINGO** [–] [ ]
– Pretty flamingo / Let's go get stoned / Tired of trying / Bored with living / Scared of dying / I put a spell on you / It's getting late / You're standing by / Machines / Stay around / Tennessee waltz / Drive man / Do you have to do that.

Mar 67. (7") *(TF 812) <72676>* **HA! HA! SAID THE CLOWN. / FEELING SO GOOD** [4] [ ]

May 67. (7") *(TF 828)* **SWEET PEA. / ONE WAY** [36] [–]

Sep 67. (7") *(TF 862)* **SO LONG DAD. / FUNNIEST GIG** [ ] [–]

Jan 68. (7") *(TF 897) <72770>* **MIGHTY QUINN. / BY REQUEST EDWIN GARVEY** [1] [10]
(re-iss. Jun82 on 'Old Gold'; OG 9252)

Feb 68. (lp; stereo/mono) *(S+/TL 5460) <SR 61159>* **UP THE JUNCTION** (soundtrack) [ ] [ ]
– Up the junction (vocal) / Sing songs of love / Walking around / Up the junction (instrumental) / Love theme (instrumental) / Up the junction (vocal & instrumental) / Just for me / Love theme (instrumental) / Sheila's dance / Belgravia / Wailing horn / I need your love / Up the junction (vocal). *(re-iss. 1970; 6852 005) (cd-iss. Nov99 on 'R.P.M.'+=; RPM 189)* – Sleepy hollow.

Mar 68. (lp) *(SFL 13003)* **WHAT A MANN** (compilation) [ ] [–]
– Funniest gig / Sunny / Get away / With a girl like you / Sweet pea / Wild thing / The morning after the party / Feeling so good / One way / So long dad.

Mar 68. (7") *(TF 908)* **THEME – UP THE JUNCTION. / SLEEPY HOLLOW** [ ] [–]

May 68. (lp) *<61168>* **MIGHTY QUINN** [–] [ ]
– Mighty Quinn / Ha! ha! said the clown / Every day another hair turns grey / It's so easy falling / Big Betty / Cubist town / Country dancing / Semi-detached suburban Mr. James / The vicar's daughter / Each and every day / No better, no worse.

Jun 68. (lp; stereo/mono) *(S+/TL 5470)* **MIGHTY GARVEY!** [ ] [–]
– Happy families / No better, no worse / Each and every day / Country dancing / It's so easy falling / Happy families / Mighty Quinn / Big Betty / The vicar's daughter / Every day another hair turns grey / Cubist town / Ha! ha! said the clown / Harry the one-man band / Happy families.

Jun 68. (7") *(TF 943) <72872>* **MY NAME IS JACK. / THERE IS A MAN** [8] [ ]

Dec 68. (7") *(TF 985) <72879>* **FOX ON THE RUN. / TOO MANY PEOPLE** [5] [97]

May 69. (7") *(TF 1013) <72921>* **RAGAMUFFIN MAN. / A 'B' SIDE** [8] [ ]

—— split mid 69. TOM formed McGUINESS FLINT. D'ABO went solo, and VOORMAN joined JOHN LENNON's PLASTIC ONO BAND

MANFRED MANN'S CHAPTER III

MANFRED retained **MIKE HUGG** – vocals, electric piano. —— Recruited **BRIAN HUGG** – guitar / **STEVE YORK** – bass plus session singers, drummers and wind section

Vertigo Polydor

Nov 69. (lp) *(VO 3) <4013>* **MANFRED MANN CHAPTER THREE** [ ] [ ]
– Travelling lady / Snakeskin garter / Konekuf / Sometimes / Devil woman / Time / One way glass / Mister you're a better man than I / Ain't it sad / A study in inaccuracy / Where am I going. *(cd-iss. Feb94 on 'Cohesion'; MFMCD 14)*

Mar 70. (7") *<14026>* **SNAKESKIN GARTER. / SOMETIMES** [–] [ ]

—— on session **CHRIS SLADE** – drums (alongside others)

Sep 70. (7") *(6059 012)* **HAPPY BEING ME. / DEVIL WOMAN** [ ] [–]

Oct 70. (lp) *(6360 012)* **MANFRED MANN CHAPTER III, VOL.2** [ ] [–]
– Lady Ace / I ain't laughing / Poor sad Sue / Jump before you think / It's good to be alive / Happy being me / Virginia. *(cd-iss. Feb94 on 'Cohesion'; MFMCD 15) (cd re-mast.Dec99 on 'Cohesion'; MANN 002)*

MANFRED MANN'S EARTH BAND

—— His new band now featured **CHRIS SLADE** – drums (now a full time member) / **MICK ROGERS** – vocals, guitar repl. MIKE HUGG / **COLIN PATTENDEN** – bass repl. STEVE YORK and BRIAN HUGG

Philips Polydor

Jun 71. (7"; as MANFRED MANN; w-drawn) *<14074>* **CALIFORNIA COASTLINE. / PART TIME** [–] [ ]

Jun 71. (7"; as MANFRED MANN) *(6006 122) <14113>* **LIVING WITHOUT YOU. / TRIBUTE** [ ] Jan72 [69]

Sep 71. (7"; as MANFRED MANN) *(6006 251)* **MRS HENRY. / PRAYER** [ ] [ ]

Feb 72. (lp) *(6308 086) <5015>* **MANFRED MANN'S EARTH BAND** [ ] [ ]
– California coastline / Captain Bobby Stout / Sloth / Living without you / Tribute / Mrs Henry / Jump sturdy / Prayer / Part time man / I'm up and leaving. *(re-iss. Apr77 & 1981 on 'Bronze'; BRON 252) (re-iss. Jan90 on 'Castle' lp/cd; CLA LP/CD 150) (re-iss. Jan91 on 'Cohesion' lp/c/cd; COMME/+T/CD 6) (cd re-mast.Aug99 on 'Cohesion'; MANN 003)*

Mar 72. (7") *<14130>* **PART TIME MAN. / I'M UP AND LEAVING** [–] [ ]

Sep 72. (lp) *(6308 125) <5031>* **GLORIFIED MAGNIFIED** [ ] [ ]
– Meat / Look around / One way glass / I'm gonna have you all / Down home / Our friend George / Ashes to the wind / It's all over now, baby blue / Glorified magnified. *(re-iss. Apr77 & 1981 on 'Bronze') (cd-iss. Dec93 on 'Cohesion'; MFMCD 11) (cd re-mast.Dec99 on 'Cohesion'; MANN 004)*

Nov 72. (7") *(6006 251)* **MEAT. / GLORIFIED MAGNIFIED** [ ] [–]

Feb 73. (7") *<14164>* **IT'S ALL OVER NOW, BABY BLUE. / ASHES TO THE WIND** [–] [ ]

Vertigo Polydor

Apr 73. (7"; as EARTH BAND) *(6059 078)* **GET YOUR ROCKS OFF. / SADJOY** [ ] [–]

Jun 73. (lp) *(6360 087) <5050>* **MESSIN'** <US-title 'GET YOUR ROCKS OFF'> [ ] [ ]
– Buddah / Messin' / Cloudy eyes / Get your rocks off / Sadjoy / Black and blue / Mardi Gras day. *(re-iss. Apr77 & 1981 on 'Bronze'; BRON 261) (re-iss. Jan90 on 'Castle' lp/cd; CLA LP/CD 151) (re-iss. Jan91 on 'Cohesion' lp/c/cd; COMME/+T/CD 7)*

Jun 73. (7") *<14173>* **MARDI GRAS DAY. / SADJOY** [–] [ ]

Aug 73. (7") *<14191>* **GET YOUR ROCKS OFF. / ASHES TO THE WIND** [–] [ ]

Aug 73. (7") *(6059 083)* **JOYBRINGER. / CAN'T EAT MEAT** [9] [–]

Sep 73. (7") *<14205>* **JOYBRINGER. / CLOUDY EYES** [–] [ ]

Bronze Polydor

Nov 73. (lp) *(ILPS 9265) <6019>* **SOLAR FIRE** [ ] [96]
– Father of night, in the beginning / Pluto the dog / Solar fire / Saturn (Mercury) / Earth the circle (pts.1 & 2). *(re-iss. Apr77 & 1981; BRON 265) (re-iss. Nov87 on 'Legacy' lp/c/cd; LLP/LLK/LLCD 121) (re-iss. Jan91 on 'Cohesion' lp/c/cd; COMME/+T/CD 1)*

Mar 74. (7") **FATHER OF DAY, FATHER OF NIGHT. / SOLAR FIRE 2** [ ] [–]

Bronze Warners

Oct 74. (7") *(BRO 13)* **BE NOT TOO HARD. / EARTH HYMN (part 2a)** [ ] [–]

Oct 74. (lp/c) *(ILPS/ICT 9306) <BS 2826>* **THE GOOD EARTH** [ ] [ ]
– Give me the good earth / Launching place / I'll be gone / Earth hymn

(pts.1 & 2) / Sky high / Be not too hard. *(re-iss. Apr77 + 1981; BRON 306) (cd-iss. Dec93 on 'Cohesion'; MFMCD 12) (cd re-mast.Mar99 on 'Cohesion'; MANN 007)*

Jul 75. (7") *(BRO 18) <8152>* **SPIRIT IN THE NIGHT. / AS ABOVE SO BELOW (part 2)** [ ] [ ]

Aug 75. (lp/c) *(ILPS/ICT 9337) <BS 2877>* **NIGHTINGALES AND BOMBERS** [ ] [ ]
– Spirit in the night / Countdown / Time is right / Crossfade / Visionary mountains / Nightingales and bombers / Fat Nelly / As above so below. *(re-iss. Apr77 + 1981; BRON 337) (re-iss. 1987 on 'Castle' lp/cd; CLA LP/CD 137) (re-iss. Jan91 on 'Cohesion' lp/c/cd; COMME/+T/CD 8)*

Feb 76. (7") *<8176>* **SPIRIT IN THE NIGHT. / AS ABOVE SO BELOW** [–] [97]

— **CHRIS THOMPSON** – vocals repl. ROGERS who later formed AVIATOR / added **DAVE FLETT** – guitar

Aug 76. (7") *(BRO 29) <8252>* **BLINDED BY THE LIGHT. / STARBIRD No.2** [6] [1]

Aug 76. (lp/c) *(ILPS/ICT 9357) <BS 3055>* **THE ROARING SILENCE** [10] [10]
– Blinded by the light / Singing the dolphin through / Waiter, there's a yawn in my ear / The road to Babylon / This side of Paradise / Starbird / Questions. *(re-iss. Apr77 + 1981; BRON 357) (re-iss. Nov87 on 'Legacy' lp/c/cd; LLP/LLK/LLCD 122) (re-iss. Jan91 on 'Cohesion' lp/c/cd; COMME/+T/CD 2)*

Nov 76. (7") *(BRO 34)* **QUESTIONS. / WAITER, THERE'S A YAWN IN MY EAR No.2** [ ] [–]

Dec 76. (7") *<8355>* **QUESTIONS. / SPIRIT IN THE NIGHT** [–] [ ]

— **PAT KING** – bass (ex-SHANGHAI, etc.) repl. PATTENDEN (to TERRA NOVA)

Jun 77. (7") *<8355>* **SPIRIT IN THE NIGHT (remix). / ROAD TO BABYLON** [–] [40]

Nov 77. (7") *(BRO 48)* **CALIFORNIA. / CHICAGO INSTITUTE** [ ] [–]

Feb 78. (lp/c) *(BRON/+C 507) <BS 3157>* **WATCH** [33] [83]
– Circles / Drowning on dry land / Fish soup / California / Chicago institute / Davy's on the road again / Martha's madman / The mighty Quinn. *(re-iss. 1981; same) (re-iss. Nov87 on 'Legacy'; LLCD 123) (re-iss. Jan91 on 'Cohesion' lp/c/cd; COOME/+T/CD 3)*

Mar 78. (7") *(BRO 51)* **THE MIGHTY QUINN. / TINY** [ ] [–]

Apr 78. (7") *(BRO 52) <8620>* **DAVY'S ON THE ROAD AGAIN. / BOUILLABAISE** [6] Sep78 [ ]

Jul 78. (7") *<8574>* **CALIFORNIA. / BOUILLABAISE** [–] [ ]

— After a short split, MANN reformed band retaining **THOMPSON + KING / STEVE WALLER** – guitar (ex-GONZALES) repl. FLETT / **GEOFF BRITTON** – drums (ex-EAST OF EDEN, ex-WINGS, ex-ROUGH DIAMOND, ex-CHAMPION) repl. CHRIS SLADE who joined URIAH HEEP. He later joined The FIRM (see; LED ZEPPELIN)

Feb 79. (7") *(BRO 68)* **YOU ANGEL YOU. / OUT IN THE DISTANCE** [54] [–]

Mar 79. (lp/c) *(BRON/+C 516) <3302>* **ANGEL STATION** [30] [ ]
– Don't kill it Carol / You angel you / Hollywood town / Belle of the Earth / Platform end / Angels at my gate / You are I am / Waiting for the rain / Resurrection. *(re-iss. Nov87 on 'Legacy' lp/c/cd; LLP/LLK/LLCD 124) (re-iss. Jan91 on 'Cohesion' lp/c/cd; COMME/+T/CD 4) (cd re-mast.Aug99 on 'Cohesion'; MANN 011)*

May 79. (7") *<8850>* **YOU ANGEL YOU. / BELLE OF THE EARTH** [–] [58]

Jun 79. (7"/7"pic-d) *(BRO/BPO 77)* **DON'T KILL IT CAROL. / BLINDED BY THE LIGHT** [45] [ ]

— **JOHN LINGWOOD** – drums repl. BRITTON who became ill. / guests included **PETER MARSH, WILLY FINLAYSON.** (vocals – **CHRIS THOMPSON**)

Oct 80. (lp/c) *(BRON/+C 529) <BSK 3498>* **CHANCE** [ ] [87]
– Lies (through the 80's) / On the run / For you / Adolescent dream / Fritz the blank / Stranded / This is your heart / No guarentee / Heart on the street. *(re-iss. 1987 on 'Castle' lp/cd; CLA LP/CD 133) (re-iss. Jan91 on 'Cohesion' lp/c/cd; COMME/+T/CD 9) (cd re-mast.Aug99 on 'Cohesion'; MANN 012)*

Nov 80. (7") *(BRO 103) <49762>* **LIES (THROUGH THE 80'S). / ADOLESCENT DREAM** [ ] Jun81 [ ]

Jan 81. (7") *(BRO 113) <49678>* **FOR YOU. / A FOOL I AM** [ ] [ ]

— **MATT IRVING** – bass (ex-DREAM POLICE, ex-BABYS, ex-LONGDANCER) repl. KING

Nov 81. (7") *(BRO 137)* **I (WHO HAVE NOTHING). / MAN IN JAM** [ ] [–]

Bronze Arista

Feb 82. (7") *(BRO 141)* **EYES OF NOSTRADAMUS. / HOLIDAY'S END** [ ] [–]
(12"+=) *(BROX 141)* – Man in jam.

Jun 82. (7") *(BRO 150)* **REDEMPTION SONG (NO KWAZULU). / WARDREAM** [ ] [–]

Nov 82. (7") *(BRO 157)* **TRIBAL STATISTICS. / WHERE DO THEY SEND THEM** [ ] [–]

Jan 83. (lp/c) *(BRON/C 543) <8194>* **SOMEWHERE IN AFRIKA** [87] Mar84 [40]
– Tribal statistics / Eyes of Nostradamus / Third world service / Demolition man / Brothers and sisters of Azania:- (a) Afrika suite – (b) Brothers and sisters of Afrika – (c) To ban Tustan – (d) Koze Kobenini (how long must we wait?) / Lalela / Redemption song (no Kwazulu) / Somewhere in Afrika. *(re-iss. Nov87 on 'Legacy' lp/c/cd; LLP/LLK/LLCD 125) (re-iss. Jan91 on 'Cohesion' lp/c/cd; COMME/+T/CD 1) (cd re-mast.Aug99 on 'Cohesion'; MANN 013)*

Jan 83. (7") *(BRO 161)* **DEMOLITION MAN. / IT'S STILL THE SAME** [ ] [–]

Feb 84. (7") *(BRO 177)* **DAVY'S ON THE ROAD AGAIN (live). / THE MIGHTY QUINN (live)** [ ] [–]
(12"+=) *(BROX 177)* – Don't kill it Carol (live).

Feb 84. (lp/c) *(BRON/+C 550)* **BUDAPEST (live)** [ ] [ ]
– Spirits in the night / Demolition man / For you / Davy's on the road again / Lies (through the 80's) / Blinded by the light / Redemption song (no Kwazulu) / The mighty Quinn. *(cd-iss. 1988 on 'Ariola'; ACD 610163) (re-iss. Jan91 on 'Cohesion' lp/c/cd; COMME/+T/CD 10) (cd re-mast.Dec99 on 'Cohesion'; MANN 014)*

— **MICK RODGERS** – vocals, guitar returned to repl. WALLER (MANN, THOMPSON, LINGWOOD) also still in band. (IRVING left to join LORDS OF THE NEW CHURCH. He later joined PAUL YOUNG band).

Jan 84. (7") *(BRO 180)* **(THE) RUNNER. / NO TRANSKEI** [ ] [–]
(12"+=) *(BROX 180)* – Lies (through the 80's).

Jan 84. (7") *<9143>* **(THE) RUNNER. / WHERE DO THEY SEND THEM** [–] [22]

Jun 84. (7") *<9203>* **REBEL. / FIGURES ON A PAGE** [–] [ ]

10-Virgin not iss.

Mar 86. (7"/12") *(TEN 115/+12)* **DO ANYTHING YOU WANNA DO. / CROSSFIRE** [ ] [–]

May 86. (7"/12") *(TEN/+T 121)* **GOING UNDERGROUND. / I SHALL BE RESCUED** [ ] [–]

Jun 86. (lp/c/cd) *(XID/CXID/DIXCD 17)* **CRIMINAL TANGO** [ ] [–]
– Going underground / Who are the mystery kids / Banquet / Killer on the loose / Do anything you wanna do / Rescue / You got me through the heart / Hey bulldog / Crossfire. *(cd re-iss. Aug99 on 'Cohesion'+=; MANN 015)* – Going underground (alt.) / Do anything you wanna do (alt.) / (The) Runner / Rebel.

— **MAGGIE RYDER** – vocals repl. CHRIS THOMPSON who went solo (guests incl.**FRANK MEAD** – saxophone / **DENNY NEWMAN** – bass, vocals on 1)

Oct 87. (7"/12") *(TEN/+T 196)* **GERONIMO'S CADILLAC. / TWO FRIENDS** [ ] [–]

Nov 87. (lp/c/cd) *(DIX/CDIX/DIXCD 69)* **MASQUE** [ ] [–]
– Joybringer (from 'Jupiter') / Billies orno bounce (including Billies bounce) / What you give is what you get (start) / Rivers run dry / Planets schmanets / Geronimo's Cadillac / Sister Billies bounce (including Sister Sadie & Billies bounce) / Telegram to Monica / A couple of mates (from 'Mars' & 'Saturn') / Neptune *Icebringer) / The hymn (from 'Jupiter') / We're going wrong. *(cd re-mast.Dec99 on 'Cohesion'; MANN 016)*

Kaz Priority

Aug 92. (cd) *(KAZCD 902) <57123>* **MANFRED MANN'S PLAIN MUSIC** [ ] [ ]
– Kiowa / Medicine song / Wounded Knee / Sikelele / Hunting bow / Salmon fishing / Laguna / Instrumedicine song / Sikelele II. *(cd re-mast.Mar99 on 'Cohesion'; MANN 017)*

— **MANFRED MANN** with **CHRIS THOMPSON + NOEL McCALLA** – vocals / **MICK ROGERS** – guitars / **STEVE KINCH** – bass / **CLIVE BUNKER + DAVID FARMER** – drums / + guests

Grapevine not iss.

Jun 96. (cd/c) *(GRA CD/MC 213)* **SOFT VENGEANCE** [ ] [–]
– SOFT: Pleasure and pain / Play with fire / Nothing ever happens / Shelter from the storm / Tumbling ball / The price I pay / Lose the touch / Adults only / Wherever love drops (part one) / (interval 10 seconds) / VENGEANCE: The complete history of sexual jealousy / 99 lbs / Miss you / Nature of the beast / Wherever love drops (part two).

– compilations, others, etc. –

Jul 77. (lp) *Vertigo; (9199 107)* **MANFRED MANN'S EARTH BAND 1971-73** ☐ -

Oct 90. (7") *Cohesion;* **DAVY'S ON THE ROAD AGAIN. / BLINDED BY THE LIGHT** ☐ -

Jan 91. (cd/c/lp) *Cohesion; (BOMME 1 CD/MC/LP)* **20 YEARS OF MANFRED MANN'S EARTH BAND 1971-1991** ☐ -
– Blinded by the light / California / Joybringer / Tribal statistics / Somewhere in Africa / Davy's on the road again / You angel you / The runner / Questions / The mighty Quinn / Angels at the gate / For you / Demolition man.

Nov 92. (10xlp-box/10xc-box/10xcd-box) *Cohesion; (COMME/+T/CD 6)* **MANFRED MANN'S EARTH BAND** ☐ -
– (albums from 1972-1986) *(free-12"+=)*

Oct 99. (cd) *Cohesion; (MANN 018)* **THE BEST OF MANFRED MANN'S EARTH BAND REMASTERED VOL.1** ☐ ☐

Mar 00. (cd) *Music Club; (MCCD 414)* **BLINDIN': A STUNNING COLLECTION OF POWERFUL MASTERPIECES 1973-1982** ☐ -

Apr 02. (cd) *Brilliant; (BT 33085)* **ON THE ROAD** ☐ -

– (early MANN selective) compilations, etc. –

on 'H.M.V.' unless otherwise mentioned

Jul 65. (7"ep) *(7EG 8908)* **ONE IN THE MIDDLE** 6 -
– With God on our side / Watermelon man / What am I to do / One in the middle.

Sep 66. (lp) *(CLP 3559)* **MANN MADE HITS** 11 -
– Pretty flamingo / The one in the middle / Oh no not my baby / John Hardy / Spirit feel / Come tomorrow / Do wah diddy diddy / With God on our side / There's no living without your loving / Groovin' / I'm your kingpin / Sha la la / 5-4-3-2-1 / If you gotta go, go now.

Jan 67. (lp; mono/stereo) *(CLP/CSD 3594)* **SOUL OF MANN** (instrumentals) 40 -
– I got you babe / Bare Hugg / Spirit feel / Why should we not / L.S.D. / (I can't get no) Satisfaction / God rest ye merry gentlemen / My generation / Mr. Anello / Still I'm sad / Tengo tango / Brother Jack / The abominable snowman / Sack o' woe. *(re-iss. Jul85 on 'See For Miles'; SEE 52) (cd-iss. Jan99 on 'E.M.I.'; 498935-2)*

Sep 79. (d-lp/c) *E.M.I.; (EMTV/TC-EMTV 19)* **SEMI-DETACHED SUBURBAN (20 GREAT HITS OF THE SIXTIES)** 9 -
– Do wah diddy diddy / 5-4-3-2-1 / Sha la la / Hubble bubble, toil and trouble / Hi lili hi lo / One in the middle / Got my mojo working / With God on our side / Come tomorrow / If you gotta go, go now / Pretty flamingo / Semi-detached suburban Mr. James / There's no living without your loving / Just like a woman / Oh no not my baby / Ha ha said the clown / My name is Jack / Fox on the run / Ragamuffin man / Mighty Quinn.

Jun 89. (lp/c/cd) *E.M.I.; (SEE/+K/CD 252)* **THE EP COLLECTION** ☐ -
(re-iss. cd Nov94; same)

Jul 90. (cd/c/d-lp) *Castle; (CCS CD/MC/LP 245)* **THE COLLECTION** ☐ -

Jan 93. (cd/c/lp) *Polygram TV; (514362-2/-4/-1)* **AGES OF MANN (22 CLASSICS OF THE 60's)** 23 -
(re-iss. Sep95 cd/c; same)

Aug 94. (cd/c) *Arcade; (ARC 31001-62/-74)* **THE VERY BEST OF MANFRED MANN'S EARTH BAND** 69 -

Jun 06. (d-cd) *Universal TV; (983916-2)* **WORLD OF MANN – THE VERY BEST OF MANFRED MANN & MANFRED MANN'S EARTH BAND** 24 ☐
– 5-4-3-2-1 / Hubble bubble (toil & trouble) / Do wah diddy diddy / Sha la la / Come tomorrow / Oh no, not my baby / The one in the middle / If you gotta go, go now / Pretty flamingo / Just like a woman / Semi-detached suburban Mr. James / Ha! ha! said the clown / Sweet pea / The mighty Quinn / My name is Jack / Fox on the run / Ragamuffin man / Handbags and gladrags (MIKE D'ABO) // Blinded by the light / Davy's on the road again / Demolition man / Joybringer / For you / Spirits in the night / Don't kill it Carol / The runner / Lies (through the 80's) / Father of day, father of night / Questions / California / Redemption song / Pleasure & pain / It's all over now, baby blue / Demons and dragons / Mighty Quinn (live).

Marilyn MANSON

Formed: Fort Lauderdale, South Florida, USA ... early 90's by the once pneumonia-crippled MANSON (real name BRIAN WARNER), an ordained minister in the Church Of Satan (run by Anton LeVey), provoking the wrath of conservative America. MANSON had begun his infamous career as a music journalist, simultaneously forming MARILYN MANSON & THE SPOOKY KIDS and taking inspiration from schlock-meisters like ALICE COOPER, KISS and surprisingly, veteran UK goth throwbacks, ALIEN SEX FIEND. After interviewing TRENT REZNOR, he/they secured a support slot with Reznor's NINE INCH NAILS, ultimately resulting in a record deal with TRENT's 'Nothing' records. Although the ghoulish Edward Scissorhands lookalike MANSON dated porn-star TRACII LORDS, he caused uproar at a hometown show when he allegedly mouthed ROBIN FINCK's (NIN) "pink oboe". The piercingly contact-lensed MANSON, whose onstage regalia usually included surgical corset and stockings, completed his OTT persona by routinely mutilating himself with knives, light-bulbs and indeed anything that came to hand. Like ALICE COOPER before him, he overshadowed the rest of his band (who comprised DAISY BERKOWITZ, MADONNA WAYNE GACY, SARA LEE LUCAS and smackhead GIDGET GEIN – the latter was deposed by TWIGGY RAMIREZ). Typically subtle as the proverbial sledgehammer, the band members' names were stitched together from glamorous icons and serial killers! As for the music, MANSON's vinyl/cd freakshow began with 1994's sub-goth posturing of 'PORTRAIT OF AN AMERICAN FAMILY'. GINGER took over drum duties for their second set, a collection of remixes entitled 'SMELLS LIKE CHILDREN', which included gruesome versions of SWEET DREAMS (Eurythmics), I PUT A SPELL ON YOU (Screamin' Jay Hawkins) and ROCK'N'ROLL NIGGER (Patti Smith) – he had previously covered Gary Numan's 'DOWN IN THE PARK'. Later that year, MANSON and Co. finally launched a full-scale assault on the moral majority/minority (delete as appropriate) with the inflammatory 'ANTICHRIST SUPERSTAR', which crucified the Billboard chart at No.3. They finally drove a stake through England's conservative heart in 1997, when MANSON (at that time the beau of MTV babe Julia Valet) wowed audiences at secret gigs around the country. By this point, they had also introduced new guitarist ZIM ZUM, who replaced DAISY for the UK Top 20 single, 'BEAUTIFUL PEOPLE', the unholy climax of MANSON's bizarre career to date. Whatever else he is, MANSON is a consummate showman, enticing ghoulish audiences with threats of onstage suicide, the ultimate in 90's entertainment, presumably ? (that's if the Christian extremists don't get 'im first). MANSON (BRIAN) re-invented himself and became a BOWIE-clone/freak "undressed" eunuchoid-fashion on the cover of the band's 1998 US chart-topping set, 'MECHANICAL ANIMALS', "Aladdin INsane" you could say! The Manson who fell to Earth indeed, it looked like we'd have to wait even longer before his "Rock'n'roll Suicide". Earlier in the year, his first book, the autobiographical, 'The Long Hard Road Out Of Hell', was published and contained insights into how WARNER/MANSON's deranged brain evolved. With controversy never a light year away, the man's "evil-metal" music was even brought into question when two MARILYN MANSON-obsessed kamikaze teenagers gunned down thirteen people (12 students and a teacher – another 28 were injured) inside Columbine High School, near Denver. MANSON immediately cancelled the rest of the band's tour and sent his sympathies to the bereaved while answering Right-wing politicians who were intent on blaming MANSON and the world of Heavy Metal – they should ask themselves how easy it was for "easily-led" youngsters (and anyone with that constitution) to obtain firearms and does any other music genre such as Country or Pop get the same media furore when one of its klan goes haywire. Down but not out, the beleaguered scapegoat attempted a resurrection of sorts with 'HOLY WOOD' (2000), summoning up the darker forces which informed 'ANTICHRIST . . .' while retaining the more accessible textures of 'MECHANICAL . . .'. The question is whether MANSON's carefully manicured goth-horror schtick actually has the power to shock anymore. With a career so reliant on image, can the music exist independently once that image has become a cliche? Answers on the back of an inverted cross to the usual address. Judging by the lofty ambitions and even loftier concept of 'THE GOLDEN AGE OF GROTESQUE' (2003), MANSON's not content to become a caricature just yet. A barbed, twisted synthesis of pre-war European theatrics and his continuing obsession with the darker side of Hollywood, the record mightn't have restored him to his public enemy number one status but it at least demonstrated his willingness to at least try for some originality. With MANSON's music career on hold, 'Interscope' marked time with a "BEST OF.." anthology entitled 'LEST WE FORGET..' (2004) – how could we? The record was trailed by a cover of Depeche Mode's messianic classic 'PERSONAL JESUS', which also took him into the Top 20. The dark one was busier with his personal life; having already bedded a bevvy of adult-industry babes, WARNER/MANSON finally tied the knot with nude model, Dita Von Teese, in late 2005. The world of motion pictures was proving increasingly attractive to MARILYN in lieu of rock, and with a roll call of cameos and soundtrack credits (notably 2002's 'Resident Evil') behind him, he expressed his intentions to move into celluloid full-time.

• **Covers:** TAINTED LOVE (Soft Cell) / BIZARRE LOVE TRIANGLE (New Order) / SUICIDE IS PAINLESS (from 'M.A.S.H.') / PLEASE, PLEASE, PLEASE, LET ME GET WHAT I WANT (Smiths).

Album rating: PORTRAIT OF AN AMERICAN FAMILY (*6) / SMELLS LIKE CHILDREN (*6) / ANTICHRIST SUPERSTAR (*8) / MECHANICAL ANIMALS (*7) / THE LAST TOUR ON EARTH (*5) / HOLY WOOD (*7) / THE GOLDEN AGE OF GROTESQUE (*7) / LEST WE FORGET: THE BEST OF compilation (*7)

REVEREND MARILYN MANSON (b. BRIAN WARNER, 5 Jan'69, Canton, Ohio) – vocals / **MADONNA WAYNE GACY** (b. STEPHEN) – keyboards, organ, theremin, saxophone, samples / **DAISY BERKOWITZ** (b. SCOTT MITCHELL PUTESKY) – guitars / **TWIGGY RAMIREZ** – bass; repl. GIDGET GEIN (b.BRAD STEWART) / **SARA LEE LUCAS** (b. FREDDY STREITHORST) – drums

Nothing-Interscope Nothing-Interscope

Jun 94. (cd-ep) *<INTDM 95902>* **GET YOUR GUNN / MISERY MACHINE / MOTHER INFERIOR GOT HER GUNN / REVELATION No.9** –

Dec 94. (cd/c/d-lp) *<(IND 92344)>* **PORTRAIT OF AN AMERICAN FAMILY**
– Prelude (the family trip) / Cake and sodomy / Lunchbox / Organ grinder / Cyclops / Dope hat / Get your gunn / Wrapped in plastic / Dogma / Sweet tooth / Snake eyes and sissies / My monkey / Misery machine. *(re-iss. cd Jul96 on 'Nothing-Interscope'; same) (lp re-iss. Sep99 on 'Simply Vinyl'; SVLP 121)*

Feb 95. (cd-ep) *<INTDM 95806>* **LUNCHBOX / NEXT MOTHERFUCKER (remix) / DOWN IN THE PARK / BROWN BAG (remix) / METAL (remix)** –

— **GINGER FISH** – drums; repl. SARA LEE

Aug 96. (cd-ep) *(IND 95504)* **SWEET DREAMS (ARE MADE OF THIS) / DANCE OF THE DOPE HATS (remix) / DOWN IN THE PARK / LUNCHBOX (NEXT MOTHERF****R)**

Aug 96. (cd) *<(IND 92641)>* **SMELLS LIKE CHILDREN** Oct95 31
– The hands of small children / Diary of a dope fiend / S****y chicken gang bang / Kiddie grinder (remix) / Sympathy for the parents / Sweet dreams (are made of this) / Everlasting c***sucker (remix) / F*** Frankie / I put a spell on you / May cause discoloration of the urine or feces / Scatos, guns and peanut butter / Dance of the dope hats (remix) / White trash (remixed by Tony F. Wiggins) / Dancing with the one-legged . . . / Rock'n'roll nigger. *(cd re-iss. Aug98; same) (lp-iss.May00 on 'Simply Vinyl'; SVLP 208)*

— **ZIM ZUM** – guitar; repl. DAISY after below recording (he subsequently turned up with JACK OFF JILL in '98)

Oct 96. (cd/c) *<(IND 90006-2/-4)>* **ANTICHRIST SUPERSTAR** 73 3
– Irresponsible hate anthem / The beautiful people / Dried up, tied up and dead to the world / Tourniquet / Little horn / Cryptorchid / Deformography / Wormboy / Mister Superstar / Angel with the scabbed wings / Kinderfeld / Antichrist superstar / 1996 / Minute of decay / The reflecting God / Man that you fear. *(lp-iss.Nov98 on 'Simply Vinyl'; SVLP 55)*

Jun 97. (cd-ep) *(IND 95541)* **THE BEAUTIFUL PEOPLE / THE HORRIBLE PEOPLE (Danny Sabre remix) / SWEET DREAMS (lp version) / CRYPTORCHID** 18
(cd-ep) *(INDX 95541)* – ('A'side) / The not so beautiful people (Jim Thirlwell remix) / Snake eyes and sissies / Deformography.
(10"pic-d) *(INVP 95541)* – The horrible people (Danny Sabre remix) / The not so beautiful people (Jim Thirlwell remix).

Sep 97. (10"pic-d) *(INVP 95552)* **TOURNIQUET. / TOURNIQUET (Prosthetic dance mix)** 28
(cd-s+=) *(IND 95552)* – ('A'-Prosthetic dance mix edit).
(cd-s) *(INDX 95552)* – ('A'side) / Lunchbox / Next MF (remix).

Apr 98. (m-cd) *<(IND 95017)>* **REMIX & REPENT** Dec97
– The horrible people (remixed by Danny Saber) / Tourniquet (prosthetic dance mix) / Dried up, tied and dead to the world (live in Utica, NY) / Antichrist superstar (live in Hartford, CT) / Man that you fear (acoustic requiem for Antichrist Superstar).

— **JOHNNIE 5** – guitar; repl. ZIM ZUM

Sep 98. (cd/c) *<(IND/INC 98273)>* **MECHANICAL ANIMALS** 8 1
– Great big white world / The dope show / Mechanical animals / Rock is dead / Disassociative / The speed of pain / Posthuman / I want to disappear / I don't like the drugs (but the drugs like me) / New model No.15 / User friendly / Fundamentally loathsome / The last day on earth / Coma white. *(ltd-cd-iss. Jun99; IND 90394) (lp-iss.Apr00 on 'Simply Vinyl'; SVLP 195)*

Nov 98. (one-sided-10"pic-d) *(INVP 95610)* **THE DOPE SHOW** 12
(cd-s+=) *(IND 95610)* – Sweet dreams (live) / Apple of Sodom (live).
(cd-s+=) *(INDX 95610)* – The beautiful people (live) / ('A'-CD-rom video).

— now without the sacked ZIM ZUM; **JOHN LOWERY** was his replacement

Jun 99. (10"pic-d) *(W 486TE)* **ROCK IS DEAD. / I DON'T LIKE DRUGS (BUT THE DRUGS LIKE ME) (every day mix)** 23 –
(cd-s) *(W 486CD)* – ('A'side) / Man that you fear (acoustic requiem for Antichrist Superstar) / Baxter (television radio edit).
(cd-s) *(W 486CDX)* – ('A'side) / I don't like the drugs (but the drugs like me) (absinthe makes the heart grow fonder mix) / Baxter (I can't see why album version) / ('A'-CD-ROM video).
(above from the movie 'The Matrix' on 'Warner Bros.' records)

Nov 99. (d-cd) *<(490524-2)>* **THE LAST TOUR ON EARTH (live)** 61
– Inauguration of the mechanical Christ / The reflecting God / Great big white world / Get your gunn / Sweet dreams (are made of this) / Hell outro / Rock is dead / The dope show / Lunchbox / I don't like the drugs (but the drugs like me) / Antichrist superstar / The beautiful people / The irresponsible hate anthem / The last day on Earth. *(UK d-cd+=)* – Coma white / Get off my rocks / Coma white / A rose and a baby Ruth.

Nov 00. (12"pic-d) *(497458-1)* **DISPOSABLE TEENS. / WORKING CLASS HERO / FIVE TO ONE** 12 –
(cd-s) *(497437-2)* – (first two tracks) / Diamonds & pollen.
(cd-s) *(497438-2)* – (first & third tracks) / Astonishing panorama of the endtimes.

Nov 00. (cd/d-lp) *(490829-2/-1) <490790>* **HOLY WOOD** 23 13
– Godeatgod / The love song / The fight song / Disposable teens / Target audience (Narcissus narcosis) / President dead / In the valley of the shadow of Earth / Cruci-fiction in space / A place in the dirt / The nobodies / The death song / Lamb of God / Born again / Burning flag / Coma black: Eden eye – The apple of discord / Valentine's day / The fall of Adam / King kill 33 / Count to six and die.

Feb 01. (12"pic-d) *(497491-1)* **THE FIGHT SONG. / THE FIGHT SONG (Slipknot remix) / LOVE SONG (remix)** 24 –
(cd-s) *(497490-2)* – (first two tracks) / Disposable teens (CD-Rom video).
(cd-s) *(497491-2)* – (first & third tracks) / Disposable teens (remix).

Sep 01. (cd-s) *(497604-2)* **THE NOBODIES / THE NOBODIES (live) / DEATH SONG (with bible speech live) / (video)** 34 –

Mar 02. (cd-s) *(W 579CD1)* **TAINTED LOVE / MEST – I MELT WITH YOU / STABBING WESTWOOD – BIZARRE LOVE TRIANGLE** [5] [–]
(cd-s) *(W 579CD2)* – ('A'side) / Suicide is painless / Muse – Please, please, please, let me get what I want.

— MM tracks featured on the s/t to 'Resident Evil' movie 2002

May 03. (cd)(d-lp) *(980008-2)(980108-9) <37002>* **THE GOLDEN AGE OF GROTESQUE** [4] [1]
– Thaeter / This is the new shit / mOBSCENE / Doll-dagga buzz-buzz ziggety-zag / Use your fist and not your mouth / The golden age of grotesque / (s)AINT / Ka-boom ka-boom / Slutgarden / Spade / Paranoir / The bright young things / Vodevil / Obsequey (the death of art). *(UK+=)* – Tainted love / Baboon rape party.

Jun 03. (7") *(9807728)* **mOBSCENE. / PARANOIAC** [13] [–]
(cd-s) *(9807726)* – ('A'side) / Tainted love (re-Tainted interpretation) / ('A'-Flint & Youth's overnight mix) / ('A'-video).

Sep 03. (10"pic-d) *(9810794)* **THIS IS THE NEW SHIT. / THIS IS THE NEW SHIT (Marilyn Manson vs. Goldfrapp)** [29] [–]
(cd-s+=) *(9810793)* – Mind of a lunatic / ('A'-video).
(above from the movie, 'The Matrix: Reloaded')

Sep 04. (cd)(d-lp) *(9863883)(9864285) <34780-2>* **LEST WE FORGET: THE BEST OF** (compilation) [4] [9]
– The love song / Personal Jesus / mOBSCENE / The fight song / Tainted love / The dope show / This is the new shit / Disposable teens / Sweet dreams (are made of this) / Lunchbox / Tourniquet / Rock is dead / Get your gunn / The nobodies / Long hard road out of Hell / The beautiful people / The reflecting god. *(UK+=)* – (s)AINT / Irresponsible hate anthem. *(ltd-cd w/dvd+=; 9863975)* – (DVD tracks).

Oct 04. (7") *(986416-7)* **PERSONAL JESUS. / (rude photo motor remix)** [13] [ ]
(cd-s) *(986416-6)* – ('A') / New shit invective (Obiter Dictum mix by Bitteren Ende) / mOBSCENE replet (mea culpa mix by Betteren Ende) / ('A'-video; clean blurred version).
(12"+=) *<INTR 0263-1>* – ('A'-rude photo dub/instrumental).

– others, etc. –

Dec 96. (cd-ep) *Interscope; <INTDM 95806>* **LUNCHBOX** [ ] [ ]

Dec 96. (cd-ep) *Interscope; <INTDM 95902>* **GET YOUR GUN** [ ] [ ]

Nov 97. (cd+book) *UFO; (UFOCD 15BX)* **SMELLS LIKE WHITE TRASH** [ ] [–]

Jun 99. (cd-book) *Hallmark; (8086)* **STAR PROFILE** [ ] [–]

Mar 01. (cd; as MARILYN MANSON & THE SPOOKY KIDS) *Nightingale; <(ILLUSIONCD 2001)>* **BIRTH OF THE ANTI-CHRIST** [ ] [ ]

Mar 01. (cd; as MARILYN MANSON & THE SPOOKY KIDS) *Illusion; <(ILLUSIONCD 2002)>* **LIVE** [ ] [ ]

Mar 01. (d-cd/CD-Rom; as MARILYN MANSON & THE SPOOKY KIDS) *Illusion; <(ILLUSIONCD 2003)>* **THE WORD ACCORDING TO MANSON** [ ] [ ]

Jul 01. (lp/cd) *Megarock; <(COTP 7/+CD)>* **GENESIS OF THE DEVIL** [ ] [ ]

Apr 02. (cd; as MARILYN MANSON & THE SPOOKY KIDS) *Eastworld; <(EWO 012CD)>* **DANCING WITH THE ANTICHRIST** [ ] [ ]

□ MARC & THE MAMBAS (see under ⇒ ALMOND, Marc)

MARILLION

Formed: Aylesbury, Buckinghamshire, England . . . late '78 initially as SILMARILLION, by MICK POINTER and DOUG IRVINE. Taking their name from a J.R.R. Tolkien novel, they soon shortened it to MARILLION the following year. By this point, the all-instrumental outfit had added STEVE ROTHERY and BRIAN JELLIMAN, subsequently recruiting Scots vocalist, FISH (and DIZ MINNITT), after IRVINE departed late in 1980. By March '82, FISH (aka DEREK WILLIAM DICK), POINTER and ROTHERY, finally completed the line-up with Irishman MARK KELLY and PETE TREWAVAS. The band had now been gigging for almost four years and had built up a sizeable following, something that 'E.M.I.' had noticed before securing them a major deal. Soon after, the company issued 'MARKET SQUARE HEROES', the single denting the UK Top 60. Surprisingly, given their prog-rock pretensions, they were voted the best newcomer in the rock-centric (now defunct) Sounds magazine early in 1983. A second single, 'HE KNOWS, YOU KNOW', hit the Top 40, preceding the release of a debut album, 'SCRIPT FOR A JESTER'S TEAR'. Featuring one of their best-loved tracks, 'GARDEN PARTY' (also a UK Top 20 hit), the record reached the Top 10. With GENESIS pursuing a more commercial direction, MARILLION were perfectly poised to fill the gap in the market; a giant of a man, the enigmatic FISH updated PETER GABRIEL's early 70's vocal mannerisms over a keyboard-dominated backing. Like punk never happened, FISH and the lads took us back a decade, sporting ornate lyrical concepts masterminded by the hulking frontman. A harder-edged affair, the follow-up album, 'FUGAZI' strengthened the band's reputation among British rock fans looking for a genuine alternative to AOR-brushed material churning out of America. In the summer of '85, after a rather unnecessary live mini-set, 'REAL TO REEL', they wooed the mainstream with the wistful love song, 'KAYLEIGH', a near chart topper and an integral part of the conceptual yet accessible 'MISPLACED CHILDHOOD' opus. A UK No.1, the album also featured another top selling ballad, 'LAVENDER' and transformed MARILLION into a stadium-filling live proposition (although America proved impenetrable, 'KAYLEIGH' only scraping into their Hot 100). By 1987's top selling 'CLUTCHING AT STRAWS', FISH was uncomfortable with his newfound pop star status, his drink/drug problems fuelling speculation of an imminent split. The rumours proved all too true, when, just prior to the release of a double live set, 'THE THIEVING MAGPIE', the big man bailed out. While he contemplated a solo career, MARILLION decided to carry on, having found a worthy replacement in STEVE HOGARTH. An unknown quantity to many (although he had fronted minor chart group the EUROPEANS), HOGARTH's fluid, unassuming style nevertheless won over the majority of MARILLION fans, taking the band into unknown territory with the album, 'SEASON'S END' (1989). A competent set, the album's sole weak point was the Top 30 single, 'HOOKS IN YOU'. In 1992, they tried in vain to carry off a cover of Rare Bird's 'SYMPATHY', although this still managed a Top 20 placing, as did a singles collection. MARILLION found it hard to recapture the momentum of their halycon days, that is, until 1994's brilliant return to their conceptual roots with the album, 'BRAVE'. This fusion of folky melodic-rock and quasi-ambient atmospherics was their first to hit the Top 10 for some time, although two albums ('AFRAID OF SUNLIGHT' and the live 'MADE AGAIN') down the line, they finally parted company with 'E.M.I.'. Now on 'Raw Power' (rock's retirement stable), MARILLION subsequently released their 1997 set, 'THIS STRANGE ENGINE', a more accessible outing than previously. Its acoustic musings stood in contrast to 'RADIATION' (1998), a return to meatier, more conceptual waters which nevertheless retained an oblique pop edge. To their credit, MARILLION seemed unwilling to sit on their laurels and churn out music specifically created for their cult fanbase, instead making a concerted effort to update their influences for the new millennium as witnessed on 'MARILLION.COM' (1999). The wittily titled 'ANORAKNOPHOBIA' followed in 2001. In a novel attempt to free themselves from the shackles of a record company advance, the band financed the recording of the album with funds from 12,000 fans (who dutifully pre-ordered their copy before it was recorded), ironically letting their creative impulses stray from the prog template which so long served them. Accompanied by an infamous press release pleading for economy in using the p**g tag, the album was an admirable shot at casting off for pastures contemporary. So successful was the strategy that MARILLION employed it again on 'MARBLES' (2004), crediting the names of their donors in the sleevenotes. Not only was the music more au fait with modern palettes but for the first time since the FISH-fronted 'INCOMMUNICADO', MARILLION made the Top 10: while the album itself didn't chart, lead single 'YOU'RE GONE', made No.7, and 'DON'T HURT YOURSELF', followed into the Top 20, again underscoring the latent potential in globally connected fandom. 'MARBLES LIVE' (2005) was another contemporary move, documenting a performance of the album in its entirety.

Album rating: SCRIPT FOR A JESTER'S TEAR (*8) / FUGAZI (*6) / REAL TO REEL (*5) / MISPLACED CHILDHOOD (*7) / CLUTCHING AT STRAWS (*6) / THE THIEVING MAGPIE (*5) / SEASON'S END (*5) / A SINGLES COLLECTION 1982-1992 compilation (*8) / HOLIDAYS IN EDEN (*6) / BRAVE (*7) / AFRAID OF SUNLIGHT (*5) / THIS STRANGE ENGINE (*6) / RADIATION (*5) / MARILLION.COM (*4) / ANORAKNOPHOBIA (*5) / MARBLES (*6)

FISH (b. DEREK WILLIAM DICK, 25 Apr'58, Dalkeith, Scotland) – vocals / **MARK KELLY** (b. 9 Apr'61, Dublin, Eire) – keyboards repl. BRIAN JELLIMAN / **MICK POINTER** (b.22 Jul'56) – drums / **STEVE ROTHERY** (b.25 Nov'59) – guitar / **PETER TREWAVAS** (b.15 Jan'59) – bass repl. DOUG IRVINE

E.M.I. | Capitol

Oct 82. (7") *(EMI 5351)* **MARKET SQUARE HEROES. / THREE BOATS DOWN FROM THE CANDY** [60] [–]
(12"+=/12"pic-d+=) *(12EMI 5351/+P)* – Grendel. *(re-entered.Apr83; hit No.53)*

Jan 83. (7") *(EMI 5362)* **HE KNOWS, YOU KNOW. / CHARTING THE SINGLE** [35] [–]
(12"+=) *(12EMI 5362)* – ('A'extended).

Mar 83. (lp/c) *(EMC/TC-EMC 3429)* <12269> **SCRIPT FOR A JESTER'S TEAR** [7] [ ]
– Script for a jester's tear / He knows, you know / The web / Garden party / Chelsea Monday / Forgotten sons. *(pic-lp.Jun84; EMCP 3429) (cd-iss. Feb87; CDP 746237-2) (re-iss. May90 on 'Fame' cd/c/lp; CD/TC+/FA 3235) (re-iss. Mar96 on 'EMI Gold' cd/c; CD/TC GOLD 1012) (cd re-mast.Sep97 +=cd; REMARIL 001)* – Market Square heroes (battle priest version) / Three boats down from the candy / Grendel (fair deal studios version) / Chelsea Monday (demo) / He knows you know (demo) / Charting the single / Market Square heroes (alt.). *(cd re-iss. Aug00; 527115-2)*

Jun 83. (7"/7"sha-pic-d) *(EMI/+P 5393)* **GARDEN PARTY. / MARGARET (live)** [16] [–]
(ext.12"+=/ext.12"w-poster+=) *(12EMI/+P 5393)* – Charting the single (live).

— **ANDY WARD** – drums (ex-CAMEL) replaced POINTER / **IAN MOSLEY** (b.16 Jun'53) – drums (ex-STEVE HACKETT, ex-CURVED AIR) repl. WARD

Jan 84. (7") *(MARIL 1)* **PUNCH AND JUDY. / MARKET SQUARE HEROES (new version)** [29] [–]
(12"+=/12"pic-d+=) *(12MARIL/+P 1)* – Three boats down from the candy (new version).

Mar 84. (lp/pic-lp)(c) *(MRL/+P 1)(TC-MRL 1)* <46027> **FUGAZI** [5] [ ]
– Assassing / Punch and Judy / Jigsaw / Emerald lies / She chameleon / Incubus / Fugazi. *(re-iss. May88 on 'Fame' cd/c/lp; CD/TC+FA 3196) (cd re-iss. May94; CDEMS 1516) (cd re-mast.Mar98 +=cd; 493369-2)* – Cinderella search (12" version) / Assassing (alt.) / Three boats down from the candy / Punch and JUdy (demo) / She chameleon (demo) / Emerald lies (demo) / Incubus (demo).

Apr 84. (7")(ext;12"+=/12"pic-d+=) *(MARIL 2)(12MARIL/+P 2)* **ASSASSING. / CINDERELLA SEARCH** [22] [–]

Nov 84. (m-lp/c) *(JEST/TC-JEST 1)* **REAL TO REEL (live)** [8] [ ]
– Assassing / Incubus / Cinderella search / Forgotten sons / Garden party / Market square heroes. *(pic-lp.Jan85; EG 2603036) (re-iss. Nov85 on 'Fame' lp/c/cd+=; FA/TC-FA/CD-FA 3142)* – Emerald lies. *(cd re-iss. Oct87; CDM 752 021-2)*

May 85. (7"/7"pic-d) *(MARIL/+P 3)* **KAYLEIGH. / LADY NINJA** [2] [–]
(ext.12"+=/ext.12"pic-d+=) *(12MARIL/+P 3)* – ('A'-alternative).

Jun 85. (lp/pic-lp)(c)(cd) *(MRL/+P 2)(TC-MRL 2)(CDP 746160-2)* <12431> **MISPLACED CHILDHOOD** [1] [47]
– The pseudo silk kimono / Kayleigh / Lavender / Bitter suite – Heart of Lothian / Waterhole (expresso bongo) / Lords of the backstage / Blind curve / Childhood's end? / White feather. *(cd re-iss. May94; CDEMS 1518) (cd re-mast.Oct98 +=cd; 497034-2)* – Lady Nina / Freaks / Kayleigh (alt.) / Lavender blue / Heart Of Lothian (extended) / Pseudo silk komono (demo) / Kayleigh (demo) / Lavender (demo) / Bitter suite – Brief encounter – Lost weekend (demo) / LOrds of the backstage (demo) / Blue angel (demo) / Misplaced rendezvous / Heart of LOthian – Wide boy – Curtain call (demo) / Waterhole (express bongo) (demo) / Passing strangers – Mylo – Perimeter walk threshold (demo) / Childhood's end? (demo) / White feather (demo). *(cd re-iss. Aug00; 527116-20*

Aug 85. (7") *(MARIL 4)* *<5539>* **LAVENDER. / FREAKS** [5] [ ]
(12"+=/12"pic-d+=) *(12MARIL/+P 4)* – ('A'remix).

Sep 85. (7") *<5493>* **KAYLEIGH. / HEART OF LOTHIAN** [–] [74]

Nov 85. (7") *(MARIL 5)* **HEART OF LOTHIAN. / CHELSEA MONDAY (live)** [29] [–]
(12"+=/12"pic-d+=) *(12MARIL/+P 5)* – ('A'extended).

— early 1986, FISH teamed up with TONY BANKS (GENESIS) on a single.

Dec 85. (7") *<5561>* **HEART OF LOTHIAN. / LADY NINJA** [–] [ ]

Mar 86. (m-lp) *<15023>* **BRIEF ENCOUNTER** (3 live early '86) [–] [67]
– Freaks / Fugazi / Kayleigh / Lady Ninja / Script for a jester's tear.

May 87. (7") *(MARIL 6)* *<44043>* **INCOMMUNICADO. / GOING UNDER** [6] [ ]
(12"pic-d+=)(cd-s+=) *(12MARILP 6)(CDMARIL 6)* – ('A'alternate).

Jun 87. (lp/pic-lp)(c/cd) *(EMD/+P 1002)(TC/CD EMD 1002)* *<12539>* **CLUTCHING AT STRAWS** [2] [ ]
– Hotel hobbies / Warm wet circles / That time of the night (the short straw) / Going under * / Just for the record / White Russian / Incommunicado / Torch song / Slainte Mhath / Sugar mice / The last straw: happy ending. *(cd+= *) (re-iss. 1989 cd)(c/lp; CZ 214)(TC+/ATAK 135) (cd re-mast.Mar99 +=cd; 498611-2)* – Incommunicado (alt.) / Tux on / Going under (extended) / Beaujolais day / Story from a thin wall / Shadows on the barley / Sunset hill / Tic-tac-toe / Voice in the crowd / Exile on Princes Street / White Russians (demo) / Sugar mice in the rain. *(cd re-iss. Aug00; 527117-2) (cd re-iss. Feb01; 527117-2)*

Jul 87. (7"/7"pic-d) *(MARIL/+P 7)* *<44060>* **SUGAR MICE. / TUX ON** [22] [ ]
(12"+=/12"pic-d+=) *(12MARIL/+P 7)* – ('A'extended).

Oct 87. (7") *(MARIL 8)* **WARM WET CIRCLES. / WHITE RUSSIAN (live)** [22] [–]
(12"+=/12"pic-d+=) *(12MARIL/+P 8)* – Incommunicado (live).
(cd-s++=) *(CDMARIL 8)* – Up on top of a rainbow.

Nov 88. (d-cd/c/d-lp) *(CD/TC+/MARL 1)* *<C 191463>* **THE THIEVING MAGPIE (live)** [25] [ ]
– (intro) / La gazza ladra / Slainte mhath / He knows, you know / Chelsea Monday / Freaks / Jigsaw / Punch and Judy / Sugar mice / Fugazi / Script for a jester's tear / Incommunicado / White Russian / Misplaced childhood part 1:- Pseudo silk kimono – Kayleigh – Lavender – Bitter suite – Heart of Lothian. *(d-cd+=)* – Misplaced childhood part 2:- Waterhole (expresso bongo) – Lords of the backstage – Blind curve – Childhood's end? – White feather.

Nov 88. (7"/7"sha-pic-d) *(MARIL/+P 9)* **FREAKS (live). / KAYLEIGH (live)** [24] [–]
(12"+=/cd-s+=) *(12/CD MARIL 9)* – Childhood's end (live) / White feather (live).

— **STEVE HOGARTH** – vocals (ex-HOW WE LIVE, ex-EUROPEANS, ex-LAST CALL) finally repl. FISH. (He had left to go solo Sep'88).

Aug 89. (c-s/7") *(TC+/MARIL 10)* **HOOKS IN YOU. / AFTER ME** [30] [–]
(12"+=/12"pic-d+=) *(12MARIL 10/+P)* – ('A'-meaty mix).
(cd-s+=) *(CDMARIL 10)* – ('A'-seven mix).

Sep 89. (cd/c/lp) *(CD/TC+/EMD 1011)* *<C 192877>* **SEASON'S END** [7] [ ]
– King of sunset town / Easter / The uninvited guest / Season's end / Holloway girl / Berlin / After me / Hooks in you / The space. *(c+=/cd+=)* – After me. *(pic-lp.Dec89; EMDPD 1011) (cd re-mast.Sep97 +=cd; REMARIL 005)* – The uninvited guest (12" version) / The bell in the sea / The release / The king of sunset town / Holloway girl / Season's end / The uninvited guest / Berlin / The bell in the sea. *(cd re-iss. Aug00; 527118-2)*

Nov 89. (7"/7"sha-pic-d)(c-s) *(MARIL/+PD 11)(TC-MARIL 11)* **THE UNINVITED GUEST. / THE BELL IN THE SEA** [53] [–]
(12"+=/12"pic-d+=)(cd-s+=) *(12MARIL/+P 11)(CDMARIL 11)* – ('A'extended).

Mar 90. (7"/7"pic-d)(c-s) *(MARIL/+P 12)(TC-MARIL 12)* **EASTER. / THE RELEASE** [34] [–]
(12"+=/12"g-f+=)(cd-s+=) *(12MARIL/+G 12)(CDMARIL 12)* – ('A'extended) / The uninvited guest (live).

Jun 91. (c-s/7") *(TC+/MARIL 13)* **COVER MY EYES (PAIN AND HEAVEN). / HOW CAN IT HURT** [34] [–]
(12"+=/cd-s+=) *(12/CD MARIL 13)* – The party.

Jul 91. (cd/c/lp) *(CD/TC+/EMD 1022)* *<13138>* **HOLIDAYS IN EDEN** [7] [ ]
– Splintered heart / Cover my eyes (pain and Heaven) / The party / No one can / Holidays in Eden / Dry land / Waiting to happen / This town / The rakes progress / 100 nights. *(cd re-mast.Mar98 +=cd; 493372-2)* – Sympathy / How can it hurt / A collection / Cover my eyes (acoustic) / Sympathy (acoustic) / I will walk on water (acoustic) / You don't need anyone / No one can / The party / This town / Waiting to happen / Eric / The epic (fairground).

Jul 91. (7"/7"box)(c-s) *(MARIL/+S 14)(TC-MARIL 14)* **NO ONE CAN. / A COLLECTION** [33] [–]
(cd-s+=) *(CDMARIL 14)* – Splintered heart (live).

Sep 91. (c-s/7") *(TC+/MARIL 15)* **DRY LAND. / HOLLOWAY GIRL / AFTER ME** [34] [–]
(12"+=) *(12MARIL 15)* – Substitute.
(10"clear+=) *(10MARIL 15)* – Waiting to happen.
(cd-s+=) *(CDMARIL 15)* – Easter / Sugar mice.
(12"pic-d+=) *(12MARILP 15)* – King of Sunset town.

May 92. (c-s/7") *(TC+/MARIL 16)* **SYMPATHY. / KAYLEIGH (live)** [17] [–]
(cd-s+=) *(MARILS 16)* – I will walk on water.
(12"pic-d+=)(cd-s+=) *(12MARILPD 16)(CDMARIL 16)* – Dry land (live).

Jun 92. (cd/c/d-lp) *(CD/TC+/EMD 1033)* **A SINGLES COLLECTION 1982-1992** (compilation) [27] [–]
– Cover my eyes (pain & Heaven) / Kayleigh / Easter / Warm wet circles / Uninvited guest / Assassing / Hooks in you / Garden party / No one can / Incommunicado / Dry land / Lavender / I will walk on water / Sympathy.

Jul 92. (c-s/7") *(TC+/MARIL 17)* **NO ONE CAN. / A COLLECTION** [26] [–]
(cd-s+=) *(CDMARIL 17)* – Splintered heart.

Feb 94. (cd/c/d-lp) *(CD/TC+/EMD 1054)* *<28032>* **BRAVE** [10] [ ]
– Bridge / Living with the big lie / Runaway / Goodbye to all that (i) Wave (ii) Mad (iii) The opium den (iv) The slide (v) Standing in the swing / Hard as love / The hollow man / Alone again in the lap of luxury (i) Now wash your hands / Paper lies / Brave / The great escape (i) The last of you (ii) Fallin' from the Moon / Made again. *(cd re-mast.Oct98 +=cd; 497038-2)* – The great escape (orchestral) / Marouatte jam / The hollow man (acoustic) / Winter trees / Alone again in the lap of luxury (acoustic) / Runaway (acoustic) / Hard as love (acoustic) / Living with the big lie (demo) / Alone again in the lap of luxury (demo) / Dream sequence / The great escape (remix).

Mar 94. (c-s/7") *(TC+/EM 307)* **THE HOLLOW MAN. / BRAVE** [30] [–]
(cd-s+=) *(CDEMS 307)* – Marouatte jam.
(cd-s) *(CDEM 307)* – ('A'side) / The last of you – Falling from the Moon (the great escape) / Winter trees.

Apr 94. (c-s) *(TCEM 318)* **ALONE AGAIN IN THE LAP OF LUXURY / LIVING WITH THE BIG LIE (live)** [53] [–]
(12"pic-d+=) *(12EMPD 318)* – The space (live).
(cd-s+=) *(CDEMS 318)* – River (live) / Bridge (live).
(cd-s) *(CDEM 318)* – ('A'side) / Cover my eyes / Slainte Mhath / Uninvited guest (all live).

Jun 95. (c-s/cd-s) *(TC/CD MARIL 18)* **BEAUTIFUL / AFRAID OF SUNRISE / ICON** [29] [–]
(cd-s) *(CDMARILS 18)* – ('A'side) / Live forever / Great escape (demo) / Hard as love (demo).

Jun 95. (cd/c/lp) *(CD/TC+/EMD 1079)* *<33874>* **AFRAID OF SUNLIGHT** [16] [ ]
– Gazpacho / Cannibal surf babe / Beautiful / Afraid of sunrise / Out of this world / Afraid of sunlight / Beyond you / King. *(cd re-mast.Mar99 +=cd; 498614-2)* – Icon / Live forever / Second chance (aka Beautiful) / Beyond you (demo) / Cannibal surf babe / Out of this world / Bass frenzy / Mirages (demo) / Afraid of sunlight (acoustic demo).

E.M.I. Castle

Mar 96. (d-cd/d-c) *(CD/TC EMD 1094)* *<117>* **MADE AGAIN (live)** [37] [ ]
– Splintered heart / Easter / No one can / Waiting to happen / Cover my eyes / The space / Hooks in you / Beautiful / Kayleigh / Lavender / Afraid of sunlight / King // Brave (live in Paris):- Bridge / Living with the big life / Runaway / Goodbye to all that / Wave / Mad / The opium den / Slide / Standing in the swing / Hard as love / Hollow man / Alone again in the lap of luxury / Now wash your hands / Paper lies / Brave / The great escape / The last of you / Falling from the Moon / Made again. *(d-cd re-iss. Feb01 on 'Castle'; CMDDD 123)*

Raw Power Velvel

May 97. (cd/c/pic-lp) *(RAW CD/MC/DP 121)* *<79791>* **THIS STRANGE ENGINE** [27] Jul97 [ ]
– Man of 100 faces / One fine day / Eighty days / Estonia / Memory of water / An accidental man / Hope for the future / This strange engine. *(cd re-iss. Feb01 on 'Castle'; CMRCD 071)*

May 97. (cd-s) *(RAWX 1044)* **MAN OF 1000 FACES / BEAUTIFUL / MADE AGAIN / ('A'mix)** [ ] [–]

Oct 97. (cd-s) *(RAWX 1049)* **EIGHTY DAYS / THIS STRANGE ENGINE (extended – live) / BELL IN THE SEA (live)** [ ] [–]

Sep 98. (cd-s) *(RAWX 1051)* **THESE CHAINS / FAKE PLASTIC TREES (live) / MEMORY OF WATER (Big Beat mix)** [ ] [–]

Sep 98. (cd) *(RAWCD 126)* *<79760>* **RADIATION** [35] Oct98 [ ]
– Costa del Slough / Under the sun / The answering machine / Three minute boy / Now she'll never know / These chains / Born to run / Cathedral wall / Few words for the dead. *<US+=>* – Estonia / Memory of water. *(re-iss. Feb01 on 'Castle'; CMRCD 113)*

Raw Power Never

Oct 99. (cd) *(RAWCD 144)* *<4505>* **MARILLION.COM** [53] Nov99 [ ]
– A legacy / Deserve / Go / Rich / Enlightened / Built-in bastard radar / Tumble down the years / Interior Lulu / House.

Liberty Sanctuary

May 01. (cd) *(532321-2)* *<84506>* **ANORAKNOPHOBIA** [ ] [ ]
– Between you and me / Quartz / Map of the world / When I grow old / Fruit of the wild rose / Separated out / This is the 21st century / If my heart were a ball it would roll uphill.

Capitol Capitol

Apr 02. (cd) *(<538727-2>)* **ANORAK IN THE UK** (live) [ ] [ ]
– Separated out / Quartz / Map of the world / Out of this world / Between you and me / The great escape / King / If my heart were a ball it would roll uphill / Waiting to happen / Easter.

Intact not iss.

Apr 04. (cd-s) *(CDINTACT 1)* **YOU'RE GONE / THE DAMAGE** [7] [–]
(cd-s) *(CXINTACT 1)* – ('A') / Faith (live) / When I meet God (spirited away mix).
(dvd-s) *(CDVDINTACT 1)* – ('A') / ('A'-version) / Quartz (dreamtime remix) / ('A'-video) / (interview video).

May 04. (cd) *(INTACTCD 1)* **MARBLES** [ ] [–]
– The invisible man / Marbles 1 / You're gone / Angelina / Marbles II / Don't hurt yourself / Fantastic place / Marbles III / Drilling holes / Marbles IV / Neverland. *(bonus+=)* – You're gone (single mix). *(ltd live-cd+=; INTACTCD 9)* – Estonia.

Jul 04. (cd-s) *(CDINTACT 2)* **DON'T HURT YOURSELF / ANGELINA (Steven Wilson mix)** [16] [–]
(cd-s) *(CXINTACT 2)* – ('A') / Fantastic place (live in Hamburg, May 7th 2004) / The damage (live in Hamburg, May 9th) / ('A'-video).

– compilations etc. –

on 'E.M.I.' unless mentioned otherwise

Jan 88. (cd)(lp) *(CZ 39)(EMS 1295)* **B SIDES THEMSELVES (rare flips)** [64] [–]

Nov 95. (3xcd-box) *(CDOMB 015)* **THE ORIGINALS** [ ] [–]
– (SCRIPT FOR A JESTER'S TEAR / FUGAZI / MISPLACED CHILDHOOD). *(re-iss. Apr97; same)*

Oct 96. (cd) *EMI Gold; (CDGOLD 1058)* **THE COLLECTION** [ ] [–]

Feb 97. (d-cd) *(CDEMC 3761)* **THE BEST OF BOTH WORLDS** [ ] [–]

Apr 97. (d-pic-lp) *(EMCF 3761)* **THE BEST OF BOTH WORLDS 1982-88** [ ] [–]

Apr 97. (d-pic-lp) *(EMCH 3761)* **THE BEST OF BOTH WORLDS 1989-PRESENT** [ ] [–]

Jun 97. (d-cd) *(CDEM 1603)* **REAL TO REEL / BRIEF ENCOUNTER** [ ] [–]

Mar 99. (cd) *Disky; (DC 86718-2)* **KAYLEIGH** [ ] [–]

Jan 00. (cd/c) *Eagle; (EAG CD/MC 033)* **TALES FROM THE ENGINE ROOM** [ ] [–]
– (THIS STRANGE ENGINE remixed + MARILLION & THE POSITIVE LIGHT)

Jul 00. (12xcd-s) *(<888667-2>)* **THE CD SINGLES VOL.1: 1982-1988** [ ] [ ]

Oct 02. (12xcd-s) *(<550821-2>)* **THE CD SINGLES VOL.2: 1989-1995** [ ] [ ]

Mar 03. (cd) *Disky; (SI 90523-2)* **WARM WET CIRCLES** [ ] [–]

Bob MARLEY

Born: ROBERT NESTA MARLEY, 2 Feb'45, Rhoden Hall, St. Ann's, Jamaica, the son of an English sailor/captain and a Jamaican woman. By the early 60's, in common with most other Jamaicans (save older Calypso fans), he became influenced by ska and bluebeat, cutting his debut single, 'JUDGE NOT (UNLESS YOU JUDGE YOURSELF)' with the help of producer LESLIE KING. Another 7", 'ONE CUP OF COFFEE', followed early in '63, MARLEY subsequently forming vocal quintet, The WAILIN' WAILERS (shortened to The WAILERS after the first single) the following year. The outfit consisted of MARLEY (vocals, later also guitar), PETER TOSH (vocals, later also guitar), BUNNY LIVINGSTONE (vocals, percussion), JUNIOR BRAITHWAITE (vocals) and BEVERLEY KELSO (vocals) with instrumental backing by The SOUL BROTHERS and subsequently The SKATELITES. Teaming up with legendary producer COXSONE DODD, their first single, 'SIMMER DOWN', was a massive hit in Jamaica, the outfit recording a further string of 45's for DODD's seminal 'Studio One' and 'Coxsone' labels. MARLEY's career was put on hold, however, when he married RITA and subsequently spent a year in America visiting his mother who had moved there in 1963. He returned to his homeland in 1967, setting up his own 'Wailin' Soul' label with JOHNNY NASH and duly re-uniting with The WAILERS. Although their releases during this period met with little success, the group immersed themselves in the Rastafari religion which would subsequently influence much of their later work. In 1969, the outfit began working with pivotal songwriter/producer, LEE 'SCRATCH' PERRY, and over the course of the ensuing three years, developed from a soul/ska/R&B vocal outfit to form one of the cornerstones of reggae. With the addition of ASTON BARRETT on bass and brother CARLTON on drums (the former rhythm section of PERRY's UPSETTERS), the newly expanded WAILERS cut a further series of 7" singles under the guiding hand of PERRY, including such enduring tracks as 'KAYA', 'TRENCHTOWN ROCK' and 'SMALL AXE', as well as a debut album, 'SOUL REBEL' (1970). By 1971, The WAILERS had formed their own label, 'Tuff Gong', and had begun producing their own material. The following year, after JOHNNY NASH had taken MARLEY's 'STIR IT UP' into the UK Top 20, The WAILERS signed to 'Island', CHRIS BLACKWELL having previously distributed their early releases in the UK. He provided financial muscle for the outfit to record their major label debut in Jamaica, their first release to be promoted and widely available outside their home country. 'CATCH A FIRE' (1973) was scorching, bass-heavy vibrations providing a platform for impassioned, challenging lyrics on the likes of 'CONCRETE JUNGLE' and '400 YEARS', while the superior WAILERS version of 'STIR IT UP' glowed with laid back positivity. 'BURNIN' (1973) followed soon after, an even fierier set of spiritually and politically motivated songs that featured 'GET UP, STAND UP', a call for individual liberty powered by a knotty, insistent rhythm, as well as the plea for justice, 'I SHOT THE SHERIFF', a US No.1 for ERIC CLAPTON in the summer of '74. By the end of the year, however, PETER TOSH and BUNNY LIVINGSTONE (later renaming himself BUNNY WAILER) had both departed for solo careers, MARLEY recruiting the The I-THREES (a female vocal trio consisting of JUDY MOWAT, MARCIA GRIFFITHS and his wife, RITA) as a replacement as well as bringing in extra backing musicians. Under the revised moniker, BOB MARLEY & THE WAILERS, the outfit toured extensively for the first time in Europe, America and Africa, subsequently releasing the exceptional 'NATTY DREAD' (1975). A landmark roots reggae album, the set featured a studio version of the subsequent live hit, 'NO WOMAN NO CRY', a sublime love song with the I-THREES providing celestial harmonies and MARLEY putting in one of the most moving vocal performances of his career. Elsewhere, 'THEM BELLY FULL (BUT WE HUNGRY)' and 'REVOLUTION' were as politically charged as ever while 'SO JAH SEH' and the title track were ardent professions of MARLEY's rastafarian beliefs. 'LIVE!' was issused later that year, documenting an electric WAILERS performance in London the previous year, while 'RASTAMAN VIBRATION' (1976) gave The WAILERS their biggest commercial success to date, reaching Top 20 in the UK and Top 10 in the US on the back of the 'ROOTS, ROCK, REGGAE' single's Stateside success. Though 'EXODUS' (1977) made the US Top 20, it was the last release to make any significant commercial impact in America, the group's most vociferous fans residing in the UK, Europe, Africa and of course, Jamaica, where MARLEY was revered as if he was royalty. In general a more relaxed set than its predecessor, other highlights from 'EXODUS' included the gentle 'WAITING IN VAIN' and the hooky pop-reggae of 'THREE LITTLE BIRDS'. 'KAYA' (1978) carried on in a similar vein with the spliffed-out 'EASY SKANKING', the mellow 'SATISFY MY SOUL' and the meditative 'TIME WILL TELL' (later covered by The BLACK CROWES). After another live release, 'BABYLON BY BUS' (1978), the group recorded 'SURVIVAL' (1979), probably the most overtly political release of their career with MARLEY addressing the plight of his African brethren on 'ZIMBABWE' and 'AFRICA UNITE'. 'UPRISING' (1980) was released the same year as MARLEY was diagnosed with cancer, lending a new poignancy to tracks like 'REDEMPTION SONG', a beautiful, stripped down piece of African folk and arguably the singer's most spiritually resonant work. It also proved to be his epitaph, the final WAILERS release before MARLEY's death on the 11th of May '81. Later that summer, a Sunsplash Reggae Festival was dedicated to MARLEY and was attended by over 20,000 fans as well as his children, The MELODY MAKERS. More tragedy was to follow in 1987 when Ex-Wailers, CARLTON BARRETT and PETER TOSH, were both murdered in separate incidents, reflecting the inherently violent nature of Jamaican culture (MARLEY himself had earlier survived an attempt on his life in 1976 when gunmen broke into his Kingston home, shooting and injuring him, his wife and manager Don Taylor). Further controversy followed when RITA was ousted by the remaining WAILERS amid calls for an investigation into the MARLEY estate. Nevertheless, the legend of BOB MARLEY remains untarnished, the singer still a hero to countless Rastafarians and ordinary music fans alike. The singer's massive popularity was further illustrated in 1992 when 'SONGS OF FREEDOM', a collection of newly discovered demos, made the UK Top 10, a single culled from the set, 'IRON ZION LION', reaching No.5; MARLEY's has been hitting the charts in one way or another ever since (i.e. with LAURYN HILL). Original WAILERS singer, JUNIOR BRAITHWAITE, was sadly gunned down (in his hometown of Kingston, Jamaica) by an unknown assailant on the 2nd of June 1999.

Album rating (selective): CATCH A FIRE (*8) / BURNIN' (*8) / NATTY DREAD (*9) / LIVE! (*6) / RASTAMAN VIBRATION (*7) / EXODUS (*8) / KAYA (*8) / BABYLON BY BUS (*6) / SURVIVAL (*8) / UPRISING (*8) / CONFRONTATION posthumous (*6) / compilations:- LEGEND (*10) / SONGS OF FREEDOM boxed (*6) / NATURAL MYSTIC (*6) / ONE LOVE: THE VERY BEST OF . . . (*8) / AFRICA UNITE: THE SINGLES COLLECTION (*7)

ROBERT MARLEY

		Island	not issued
Dec 62.	(7") *(WI 088)* **JUDGE NOT (UNLESS YOU JUDGE YOURSELF). / DO YOU STILL LOVE ME?**		–
1963.	(7") *(WI 128)* **ONE CUP OF COFFEE. / (B-side by Ernest Ranglin)**		–

BOB MARLEY

the WAILERS

were formed by **MARLEY** (-vocals, +later guitar) plus **PETER TOSH** (b.WINSTON HUBERT MacINTOSH, 19 Oct'44, Westmoreland, Jamaica) – vocals, +later guitar / **BUNNY LIVINGSTONE** (b.NEVILLE O'RILEY LIVINGSTONE, 10 Apr'47, Kingston, Jamaica) – vocals, percussion / **JUNIOR BRAITHWAITE** – vocals / **BEVERLEY KELSO** – vocals / plus occasionally **RITA MARLEY** (b. ALPHARITA CONSTANTIA ANDERSON) – backing vocals / Instruments by SOUL BROTHERS then SKATELITES

Ska Beat — not iss.

Jan 65. (7"; as WAILIN' WAILERS) *(JB 186)* **SIMMER DOWN. / I DON'T NEED YOUR LOVE**

— Released in Jamaica earlier, UK in batches

Island — not iss.

Mar 65. (7") *(WI 188)* **IT HURTS TO BE ALONE. / MR.TALKATIVE**

Apr 65. (7") *(WI 206)* **PLAY BOY. / YOUR LOVE**

— added **CHERRY SMITH** – backing vocals

May 65. (7") *(WI 211)* **HOOT NANNY ROLL. / DO YOU REMEMBER**

(above A-side was actually credited to PETER TOUCH, the B-side BOB MARLEY, although all featured MARLEY, TOSH and The WAILERS)

May 65. (7") *(WI 212)* **HOOLIGAN. / MAGA DOG**

Jun 65. (7"; as PETER TOSH & THE WAILERS) *(WI 215)* **SHAME AND SCANDAL. / THE JERK**

Jun 65. (7") *(WI 216)* **DON'T EVER LEAVE ME. / DONNA**

Dec 65. (7") *(WI 254)* **WHAT'S NEW PUSSYCAT. / WHERE WILL I FIND**

Mar 66. (7") *(WI 260)***JUMBIE JAMBOUREE. / (B-side by The Skatelites)**

Apr 66. (7") *(WI 268)* **PUT IT ON (FEEL THE SPIRIT). / LOVE WON'T BE MINE**

Ska Beat — not iss.

Aug 65. (7") *(JB 211)* **LONESOME FEELINGS. / THERE SHE GOES**

Oct 65. (7") *(JB 226)* **I MADE A MISTAKE. / (B-side by The SOUL BROTHERS)**

(above A-side was probably by The WAILIN' RUDEBOYS)

1966. (7") *(JB 228)* **LOVE AND AFFECTION. / TEENAGER IN LOVE**

1966. (7") *(JB 230)* **AND I LOVE HER. / DO IT RIGHT**

1966. (7") *(JB 249)* **LONESOME TRACK. / SINNER MAN**

(below might be without MARLEY)

Rio — not iss.

1966. (7") *(R 116)* **DANCING SHOES. / DON'T LOOK BACK**

— MARLEY left Feb'66, to marry RITA but soon returned. CHERRY also left. LIVINGSTONE was imprisoned in 1966.

Doctor Bird — not iss.

1966. (7") *(DB 1013)* **RUDE BOY. / (B-side by Roland Al & The Soul Brothers)**

1966. (7") *(DB 1021)* **GOOD GOOD RUDIE. / (B-side by City Slickers)**

Nov 66. (7") *(DB 1039)* **RASTA PUT IT ON. / (B-side by Roland Al & The Soul Brothers)**

(re-iss. Apr67 on 'Island')

— (below iss.Jamaica on 'Rocksteady')

1967. (7") *(DB 1091)* **NICE TIME. / HYPOCRITE**

— (below 2 without MARLEY)

Island — not iss.

Nov 66. (7") *(WI 3001)* **HE WHO FEELS IT KNOWS IT. / SUNDAY MORNING**

Dec 66. (7") *(WI 3009)* **LET HIM GO (RUDE BOY GOT BAIL). / SINNER MAN**

Apr 67. (7") *(WI 3035)* **BABY I NEED YOU. / (B-side by Ken Boothe)**

— Now a trio of **MARLEY, TOSH & BUNNY.** (KELSO and BRAITHWAITE departed)

Apr 67. (7") *(WI 3043)* **BEND DOWN LOW. / FREEDOM TOWN**

Apr 67. (7"; PETER TOSH & THE WAILERS) *(WI 3042)* **I AM THE TOUGHEST. / (B-side by Marcia Griffiths)**

Studio One — not iss.

1967. (7") *(SO 2010)* **I STAND PREDOMINANT. / (B-side by Norma Fraser)**

Trojan — not iss.

Oct 68. (7") *(TR 617)* **STIR IT UP. / THIS TRAIN**

Bamboo — not iss.

1970. (7") *(BAM 55)* **JAILHOUSE. / (B-side by John Holt)**

Escort — not iss.

1970. (7") *(ERT 842)* **RUN FOR COVER. / TO THE RESCUE**

BOB MARLEY & THE WAILERS

— added **ASTON BARRETT** (b.22 Nov'46, KIngston) – bass / **CARLTON BARRETT** (b.17 Dec'50, Kingston) – drums

Upsetter — Shelter

1970. (7") *(US 340)* **MY CUP. / SON OF THUNDER (by "LEE PERRY & THE WAILERS")**

1970. (7"; by The WAILERS) *(US 342)* **VERSION OF CUP. / (B-side by The Upsetters)**

Dec 70. (7") *(US 348)* **DUPPY CONQUEROR. / (B-side by The Upsetters)**

Jan 71. (7") *(US 354)* **MR. BROWN. / (B-side by The Upsetters)**

Feb 71. (7") *(US 356)* **KAYA. / (version by The Upsetters)**

Feb 71. (7") *(US 357)* **SMALL AXE. / ALL IN ONE**

1971. (7"; as The WAILERS) *(US 351)* **DREAMLAND. / (B-side by The Upsetters)**

1971. (7") *(US 372)* **MORE AXE. / (B-side by The Upsetters)**

1971. (7"; as RAS DAWKINS & THE WAILERS) *(US 368)* **PICTURE ON THE WALL. / (B-side by The Upsetters)**

Trojan — not iss.

Sep 70. (7") *(TR 7759)* **SOUL SHAKEDOWN PARTY. / (B-side by The Beverley All-Stars)**

Dec 70. (lp) *(TBL 126)* **SOUL REBEL**

– There she goes / Put it on / How many times / Mellow mood / Changes are / Hammer / Tell me / Touch me / Treat you right / Soul rebel. *(re-iss. Sep81 on 'New Cross'; NC 001) (c-iss.Jan82 on 'Sun'; CFK 1020) (re-iss. Jun84 on 'Blue Moon' lp/c; BMLP/BMC 1018) (re-iss. Oct86 on 'Receiver' lp/c; RRLP/RRLC 106) (cd-iss. Jan90; RRCD 106) (re-iss. Apr90 on 'Action Replay' cd/c; CDAR/ARLC 1013)*

Jackpot — not iss.

1971. (7") *(JP 730)* **MR. CHATTERBOX. / WALK THROUGH THE WORLD**

Punch — not iss.

1971. (7") *(PH 69)* **MORE AXE. / (B-side by Dave Berber)**

1971. (7"; as The WAILERS) *(PH 77)* **DOWN PRESSER. / (B-side by Junior Byles)**

1972. (7") *(PH 101)* **SCREW FACE. / FACE MAN**

Bullet — not iss.

1971. (7") *(BU 464)* **SOULTOWN. / LET THE SUN SHINE ON ME**

1971. (7") *(BU 493)* **LICK SAMBA. / SAMBA**

Summit — not iss.

1971. (7") *(SUM 8526)* **STOP THE TRAIN. / CAUTION**

1971. (7") *(SUM 8530)* **FREEDOM TRAIN. /**

Green Door — Tuff Gon

1971. (7") *(GD 4002)* **LIVELY UP YOURSELF. / (B-side by Tommy McCook)**

Nov 71. (7") *(GD 4005)* **TRENCHTOWN ROCK. / GROOVING KINGDOM**

1972. (7") *(GD 4025)* **GUAVA JELLY. / REDDER THAN RED**

(below was 1968 demo)

C.B.S. — not iss.

May 72. (7") *(CBS 4902)* **REGGAE ON BROADWAY. / OH LORD I GOT TO GET THERE**

Trojan — not iss.

Sep 72. (7") *(US 392)* **KEEP ON MOVING. / AFRICAN HERBSMAN**

1972. (lp) *(TRL 62)* **AFRICAN HERBSMAN**

– Lively up yourself / Small axe / Duppy conqueror / African herbsman / Trenchtown rock / Keep on moving / Fussing and fighting / Stand alone / All in one / Don't rock the boat / Put it on / Sun is shining / Kaya / Riding high / 400 years / Brain washing. *(re-iss. Jul84 lp/c; TRLS/ZCTRL 62) (cd-iss. Jun88; CDTRL 62) (re-iss. Nov83 on 'Fame' lp/c; FA/TCFA 41-3082-1/-4) (cd re-iss. Mar94 on 'Trojan'; same)*

the WAILERS

Blue Mountain — not iss.

Jan 73. (7") *(1021)* **BABY WE'VE GOT A DATE (ROCK IT BABY). / STOP THAT TRAIN** [ ] [–]

Island — Island

Apr 73. (7") *<1211>* **STOP THAT TRAIN. / ROCK IT BABY** [–] [ ]

Apr 73. (lp/c) *(<ILPS/ICT 9241>)* **CATCH A FIRE** [ ] [ ]
– Concrete jungle / Slave driver / 400 years / Stop that train / Baby we've got a date (rock it baby) / Stir it up / Kinky reggae / No more trouble / Midnight ravers. *(re-iss. Oct86 lp/c; ILPM/ICM 9241) (re-iss. Jun90 on 'Tuff Gong' cd/c; RRCD/RRCT 1) (cd re-iss. Jun01 +=; 548893-2)* – High tide or low tide / All day all night.

Jun 73. (7") *(WIP 6164)* **CONCRETE JUNGLE. / REINCARNATION SOUL** [ ] [–]

Jul 73. (7") *<1215>* **CONCRETE JUNGLE. / NO MORE TROUBLE** [–] [ ]

Sep 73. (7") *(WIP 6167) <1218>* **GET UP, STAND UP. / SLAVE DRIVER** [ ] [ ]

Nov 73. (lp/c) *(<ILPS/ICT 9256>)* **BURNIN'** [ ] [ ]
– Get up, stand up / Hallelujah time / I shot the sheriff / Burnin' and lootin' / Put it on / Small axe / Pass it on / Duppy conqueror / One foundation / Rastaman chant. *(re-iss. Mar87; ILPM 9256) (re-iss. Jun90 on 'Tuff Gong' cd/c; RRCD/RRCT 2) (cd re-iss. Jun01 +=; 548894-2)* – Reincranated soul / No sympathy / Oppressed song.

Feb 74. (7") *<005>* **I SHOT THE SHERIFF. / PUT IT ON** [–] [ ]

—— added **The I-THREES** (female backers **JUDY MOWAT, MARCIA GRIFFITHS**, and **RITA**). They replaced PETER TOSH and BUNNY WAILER who both went solo.

BOB MARLEY & THE WAILERS

—— **MARLEY, ASTON** and **BARRETT** added **EARL LINDO** – keyboards / **BERNARD HARVEY** – keyboards / **AL ANDERSON** – guitar.

May 75. (lp/c) *(<ILPS/ICT 9281))* **NATTY DREAD** [43] [92]
– Lively up yourself / No woman no cry / Them belly full (but we hungry) / Rebel music (3 o'clock road block) / So jah seh / Natty dread / Bend down low / Talkin' blues / Revolution. *(re-iss. May87 lp/c/cd; ILPM/ICM/CID 9281) (re-iss. Jun90 on 'Tuff Gong' cd/c; RRCD/RRCT 3) (cd re-iss. Jul01 +=; 548895-2)* – Am a do.

Jun 75. (7") *(WIP 6212)* **NATTY DREAD. / SO JAH SEH** [ ] [–]

Jun 75. (7") *<027>* **LIVELY UP YOURSELF. / SO JAH SEH** [–] [ ]

—— **TYRONE DOWNIE** – keyboards repl. HARVEY / **ALVIN 'SHECO' PATTERSON** – percussion repl. LINDO / added **JULIAN 'JUNIOR' MURVIN** – guitar

Aug 75. (7") *(WIP 6244) <037>* **NO WOMAN NO CRY (live). / KINKY REGGAE** [22] [ ]

Dec 75. (lp/c) *(<ILPS/ICT 9376>)* **LIVE! (live)** [38] [90]
– Trenchtown rock / Burnin' and lootin' / Them belly full (but we hungry) / Lively up yourself / No woman no cry / I shot the sheriff / Get up, stand up. *(re-iss. Jul81 + Sep86 as 'LIVE AT THE LYCEUM' lp/c; ILPM/ICM 9376) (cd-iss. Jan87; CID 9376) (re-iss. Nov90 on 'Tuff Gong' cd/c; RRCD/RRCT 4) (cd re-iss. Jul01 +=; 548896-2)* – Kinky reggae.

Jan 76. (7") *(WIP 6265)* **JAH LIVE. / CONCRETE JUNGLE (live)** [ ] [–]

Apr 76. (7") *(WIP 6296)* **JOHNNY WAS (WOMAN HANG HER HEAD AND CRY). / CRY TO ME** [ ] [–]

Apr 76. (lp/c) *(<ILPS/ICT 9383>)* **RASTAMAN VIBRATION** [15] [8]
– Positive vibration / Roots, rock, reggae / Johnny was / Cry to me / Want more / Crazy baldhead / Who the cap fit / Night shift / War / Rat race. *(re-iss. Apr87 lp/c/cd; ILPM/ICM/CID 9383) (re-iss. Nov90 on 'Tuff Gong' cd/c; RRCD/RRCT 5) (cd re-iss. Jul01 +=; 548897-2)* – Jah live.

Jun 76. (7") *(WIP 6309)* **ROOTS ROCK REGGAE. / STIR IT UP** [ ] [–]

Jun 76. (7") *<061>* **ROOTS ROCK REGGAE. / CRY TO ME** [–] [51]

Nov 76. (7") *<072>* **WHO THE CAP FIT. /** [–] [ ]

May 77. (lp/c) *(<ILPS/ICT 9498>)* **EXODUS** [8] Jun77 [20]
– Natural mystic / So much things to say / Guiltiness / The heathen / Exodus / Jamming / Waiting in vain / Turn your lights down low / Three little birds / One love – People get ready. *(re-iss. Mar87 lp/c/cd; ILPM/ICM/CID 9498) (re-iss. Nov90 on 'Tuff Gong' cd/c; RRCD/RRCT 6) (cd re-mast.Nov01 +=; 548898-2)* – Jammin' (long version) / Punky reggae party (long version).

Jun 77. (7") *(WIP 6390) <089>* **EXODUS. / EXODUS (dub)** [14] [ ]

Aug 77. (7") *(WIP 6402) <092>* **WAITING IN VAIN. / ROOTS** [27] [ ]

Dec 77. (7") *(WIP 6410)* **JAMMING. / PUNKY REGGAE PARTY** [9] [–]

—— added the returning **EARL 'WIRE' LINDO** – keyboards

Feb 78. (7") *(WIP 6420) <099>* **IS THIS LOVE. / CRISIS (version)** [9] [ ]
(12"-iss.Jun81;)

Mar 78. (lp/c) *(<ILPS/ICT 9517>)* **KAYA** [4] [50]
– Easy shanking / Kaya / The sun is shining / Is this love / Satisfy my soul / She's gone / Misty morning / Crisis / Running away / Time will tell. *(re-iss. Feb87 lp/c/cd; ILPM/ICM/CID 9517) (re-iss. Nov90 on 'Tuff Gong' cd/c; RRCD/RRCT 7) (cd re-mast.Aug01 +=; 548899-2)* – Smile (Jamaica version).

May 78. (7") *(WIP 6440)* **SATISFY MY SOUL. / SMILE JAMAICA** [21] [–]

Dec 78. (d-lp/c) *(<ISLD/ICT 9542>)* **BABYLON BY BUS (live)** [40] [ ]
– Positive vibration / Punky reggae party / Exodus / Stir it up / Rat race / Concrete jungle / Kinky reggae / Lively up yourself / Rebel music (3 o'clock road block) / War / No more trouble / Is this love / The heathen / Jammin'. *(cd-iss. Feb87; CIDD 11) (re-iss. Nov90 on 'Tuff Gong' cd/c; RRCD/RRCT 8) (cd re-mast.Aug01 +=; 548900-2)* –

Jan 79. (7"; w-drawn) *(WIP 6478)* **STIR IT UP (live). / RAT RACE (live)** [–] [–]
(12") (WIP12 6478) – ('A'side) / War (live) / No more trouble (live).

Jul 79. (7") *<49080>* **WAKE UP AND LIVE. / (part 2)** [–] [ ]

Sep 79. (7") *(WIP 6510)* **SO MUCH TROUBLE IN THE WORLD. / ('A'instrumental)** [56] [–]

Oct 79. (lp/c) *(<ILPS/ICT 9542>)* **SURVIVAL** [20] [70]
– So much trouble in the world / Zimbabwe / Top ranking / Babylon system / Survival / Africa unite / One drop / Ride Natty ride / Ambush in the night / Wake up and live. *(re-iss. Mar87 lp/c/cd; ILPM/ICM/CID 9542) (re-iss. Nov90 on 'Tuff Gong' cd/c; RRCD RRCT 9) (cd re-mast.Aug01 +=; 548901-2)* – Ride Natty ride (12" mix) / Wake up and live (pt.1 & 2 – single version).

Nov 79. (7") *<49156>* **ONE DROP. / KAYA** [–] [ ]

Nov 79. (7") *(WIP 6553)* **SURVIVAL. / WAKE UP AND LIVE** [ ] [–]

Mar 80. (7") *(WIP 6597)* **ZIMBABWE. / SURVIVAL** [ ] [–]
(12") (WIP12 6597) – ('A'side) / Africa unite / Wake up and live.

May 80. (7") *(WIP 6610)* **COULD YOU BE LOVED. / ONE DROP** [5] [–]
(12"+=) (12WIP 6610) – Ride natty ride.

May 80. (7") *<49547>* **COULD YOU BE LOVED. / RIDE NATTY RIDE** [–] [ ]

Jun 80. (lp/c) *(<ILPS/ICT 9596>)* **UPRISING** [6] [45]
– Coming in from the cold / Real situation / Bad card / We and them / Work / Zion train / Pimper's paradise / Could you be loved / Forever loving Jah / Redemption song. *(cd-iss. Feb87; CID 9596) (re-iss. Nov90 on 'Tuff Gong' cd/c; RRCD/RRCT 10) (cd re-mast.Aug01 +=; 548902-2)* – Redemption song (band version) / Could you be loved (12" mix).

Aug 80. (7") *(WIP 6641)* **THREE LITTLE BIRDS. / EVERY NEED GOT AN EGO FEED** [17] [–]

Oct 80. (7"/12") *(WIP/12WIP 6653)* **REDEMPTION SONG. / ('A'-Band version)** [ ] [–]

Nov 80. (7") *<49636>* **REDEMPTION SONG. / COMING IN FROM THE COLD** [–] [ ]

—— in Oct'80, BOB was diagnosed with lung cancer and died 11th May '81

– (selective) compilations, etc. –

on 'Island' unless mentioned otherwise

Jul 74. (lp) *Trojan; (TRLS 89)* **RASTA REVOLUTION** [ ] [–]
(re-iss. 1981 + Jul84 lp/c; TRLS/ZCTRL 89) (cd-iss. Jun88; CDTRL 89) (re-iss. Jul85 on 'Fame' lp/c; FA/TCFA 41 3127) (cd re-iss. Mar94)

Jun 81. (12") *(12WIP 6244) <49755>* **NO WOMAN NO CRY (live). / JAMMIN'** [8] [ ]

Sep 81. (lp/c) *Warners; (K/K4 99183) / Cotillion; <5228>* **CHANCES ARE** [ ] [ ]

1982. (9xlp-box) *(EMSP 100)* **BOB MARLEY – THE BOXED SET** [ ] [–]

1982. (lp/c) *(ISTDA 1)* **COUNTRYMAN** (soundtrack with 8 MARLEY songs) [ ] [–]

Apr 83. (7"/12") *(IS/12IS 108)* **BUFFALO SOLDIER. / BUFFALO (dub)** [4] [ ]

May 83. (lp/c) *(ILPS/ICT 9760) <90085>* **CONFRONTATION** [5] [55]
– Chant down Babylon / Buffalo soldier / Jump Nyabinghi / Mix up, mix up / Give thanks and praises / Blackman redemption / Trenchtown / Stiff neked fools / I know / Rastaman live up!. *(re-iss. Mar87) (cd-iss. 1988 on 'Mango') (re-iss. cd+c Jun90 on 'Tuff Gong')*

Apr 84. (7") *(IS 169)* **ONE LOVE. / PEOPLE GET READY** [5] [ ]
(12"+=/12"pic-d+=) *(12IS/+P 169)* – Keep on moving / So much trouble.

May 84. (lp/c) *(BMW/+C 1)* <90169> **LEGEND** [1] [54]
– Is this love / Jamming / No woman no cry / Stir it up / Get up, stand up / Satisfy my soul / I shot the sheriff / One love / People get ready / Buffalo soldier / Exodus / Redemption song / Could you be loved / Want more. *(cd-iss. Aug85; CID 103) (cd re-iss. May91 on 'Tuff Gong' hit UK No.11, Mar92 No.18 / Jul92 No.25)*

Jun 84. (7") *(IS 180)* **WAITING IN VAIN. / BLACK MAN REDEMPTION** [31] [ ]
(12"+=) *(12IS 180)* – Marley mix-up.

Nov 84. (7"/7"pic-d) *(IS/+P 210)* **COULD YOU BE LOVED. / NO WOMAN NO CRY** [71] [ ]
(12"+=) *(12IS 210)* – Jamming / Coming in from the cold.

Jun 86. (lp/c/cd) *(ILPS/ICT/CID 9843)* <90169> **REBEL MUSIC** [54] [ ]
(re-iss. cd+c.Jun90 on 'Tuff Gong')

on 'Tuff Gong' unless mentioned otherwise

Mar 91. (cd/c/lp) *(TGL CD/MC/LP 12)* <848243> **TALKIN' BLUES** [ ] [–]
– (radio sessions 1973 + interviews 1975)

May 91. (c-s/7") *(TC+/TGX 1)* **ONE LOVE – PEOPLE GET READY. / SO MUCH TROUBLE IN THE WORLD** [42] [–]
(12"+=/cd-s+=) *(12/CD TGX 1)* – ('A'extended) / Keep on moving.

Sep 92. (c-s/7") *(TC+/TGX 2)* **IRON ZION LION ('74 track). / COULD YOU BE LOVED** [5] [ ]
(12"/cd-s) *(12/CD TGX 2)* – ('A') / Smile Jamaica / Three little birds.

Sep 92. (4xcd-box/4xc-box) *(TGCBX/TGMBX 1)* <512280> **SONGS OF FREEDOM** (discovered demos) [10] [86]
(re-iss. May93 as 8xlp-box; TGLBX 1)

Nov 92. (c-s/7") *(TC+/TGX 3)* **WHY SHOULD I. / ('A'-Kindread Spirit mix)** [42] [ ]
(cd-s+=) *(CDTGX 3)* – Exodus (rebel the remix)

May 95. (c-s) *(TCTGX 4)* **KEEP ON MOVING / PIMPER'S PARADISE** [17] [ ]
(12+=/cd-s+=) *(12/CD TGX 4)* – ('A'-mixes).

May 95. (lp/c/cd) *(BMW/+C/CD 2)* <524103> **NATURAL MYSTIC** [5] [67]

Jun 96. (c-s) *(ANACA 002)* **WHAT GOES AROUND COMES AROUND** [42] [ ]
(12"+=/cd-s+=) *(ANA12/ANACD 002)* –

Sep 99. (c-s/12"/cd-s; as BOB MARLEY VS FUNKSTAR DE LUXE) *Club Tools; (0066895 9/0/5 CLU)* **THE SUN IS SHINING (mixes)** [3] [–]

Nov 99. (c-s/cd-s; by BOB MARLEY & LAURYN HILL) *Ruffhouse; (668436-4/-2)* **TURN YOUR LIGHTS DOWN LOW / (mixes)** [15] [ ]
(cd-s) *(668436-5)* – ('A'-mixes) / Superstar.

Nov 99. (cd/lp) *(<546404-2/-1>)* **CHANT DOWN BABYLON** (remixed with modern artists) [ ] [60]

Jan 00. (12"/cd-s; by BOB MARLEY Vs FUNKSTAR DE LUXE) *Club Tools; (006722 0/5 CLU)* **RAINBOW COUNTRY (mixes)** [11] [–]

Jun 00. (c-s/12"/cd-s; as BOB MARLEY featuring MC LYTE) *(12TGX/TGXCT/TGXCD 9)* **JAMMIN' (mixes)** [42] [–]

Nov 00. (cd) *Prestige; (CDSGP 056)* **LIVELY UP YOURSELF** [ ] [–]

May 01. (cd) *(BMWCD 3) / Universal TV;* <542855> **ONE LOVE: THE VERY BEST OF BOB MARLEY & THE WAILERS** [5] [60]
– Stir it up / Get up, stand up / I shot the sheriff / Lively up yourself / No woman, no cry (live) / Roots, rock, reggae / Exodus / Jamming / Waiting in vain / Three little birds / Turn your lights down low / One love – People get ready / Is this love / Sun is shining / So much trouble in the world / Could you be loved / Redemption song (band version) / Buffalo soldier / Iron lion Zion / I know a place.

Jun 01. (re-cd) *Music Collection; (12691)* **LIVELY UP YOURSELF** [75] [–]

Oct 01. (d-cd) *Universal TV; (586551-2)* **ONE LOVE – THE VERY BEST OF BOB MARLEY & THE WAILERS** [24] [–]
– (original CD tracks) // Concrete jungle / Burnin' and lootin' / Rebel music (3 o'clock roadblock) / Jah live / Positive vibration / Smile Jamaica / Natural mystic / Punky reggae party / Satisfy my soul / Africa unite / Coming in from the cold / Rastaman live up! / Who colt the game.

May 04. (cd) *Trojan; (TJODX 176)* **ROOTS OF A LEGEND** [51] [ ]

2004. (10"pic-d) *Erica;* <ER 2002-20> **LIVELY UP YOURSELF / TRENCH TOWN ROCK. / SOUL REBEL / SUN IS SHINING** [–] [ ]

Oct 05. (7"/cd-s) *(TGX/+CD 13)* **NO WOMAN, NO CRY. / DUPPY CONQUEROR (live at Leeds 23/11/73)** [58] [–]

Nov 05. (7"/cd-s) *(TGX/+CD 14)* **I SHOT THE SHERIFF. / TRENCHTOWN ROCK (live at the Roxy 26th May 1976)** [67] [–]

Nov 05. (cd) *(BMWCD 4)* **AFRICA UNITE: THE SINGLES COLLECTION** [26] [ ]
– Soul rebel / Lively up yourself / Trench town rock / Concrete jungle / I shot the sheriff / Get up, stand up / No woman, no cry / Roots, rock, reggae / Exodus / Waiting in vain / Jamming / Is this love / Sun is shining / Could you be loved / Three little birds / Buffalo soldier / One love – People get ready / Africa unite / Slogans / Stand up Jamrock (Ashley Beedle remix).

Nov 05. (7"/cd-s) *(TGX/+CD 15)* **SUN IS SHINING. / JAMMING (live at the Rainbow 4th June 1977)** [54] [–]

Nov 05. (7"/cd-s) *(TGX/+CD 16)* **AFRICA UNITE (will.i.am remix). / I SHOT THE SHERIFF (live at the Roxy 26th May 1976)** [49] [–]

Nov 05. (7") *(TGXS 11)* **SLOGANS. / THE HEATHEN (live at the Rainbow 4th June 1977)** [45] [–]
(cd-s+=) *(TGXSCD 11)* – ('A'-mix).

Dec 05. (7"/cd-s) *(TGX/+CD 17)* **STAND UP JAMROCK. / STIR IT UP (live at Leeds Polytechnic, 23rd November 1973)** [56] [–]

MAROON 5

Formed: Los Angeles, California, USA . . . 1999, although four/fifths of the band (ADAM LEVINE, JESSE CARMICHAEL, MICKEY MADDEN and RYAN DUSICK) began life in the mid-90s as alt-pop rockers KARA'S FLOWERS. The latter found minor success via their one and only long-player, 'THE FOURTH WORLD' (1997), adolescent grunge-lite which, under the mellow gaze of the Californian sun, ripened into the burnished, soul-goes-rock of MAROON 5. Upon their collective return from college sabbatical (and adding second guitarist JAMES VALENTINE), M5 finally found a sympathetic new sponsor in 'Octone' records. After a sluggish start, the Matt Wallace-produced 'SONGS ABOUT JANE' (2002), came into its own at the turn of the following year, hitting both the American and British album charts. Coming on like a choreographed 'CHILI PEPPERS, breakthrough Top 20 single, 'HARDER TO BREATHE', took their horizontal MOR to the twenty-something masses. Follow-up single, 'THIS LOVE' writhed into the Top 5 on the back of a soft-focus, soft-porn video (featuring the apple of Adam's eye, model Kelly McKee). More sauce was to come in the promo for repeat transatlantic Top 5, 'SHE WILL BE LOVED', a cumulative controversy which seduced the album into, er.. pole position. The following year saw the quintet tread ever deeper water with makeweight acoustic and live releases, the former worth hearing for a parodic excavation of Ac/Dc's 'HIGHWAY TO HELL'.

Album rating: Kara's Flowers: THE FOURTH WORLD (*6) / Maroon 5: SONGS ABOUT JANE (*7) / 1.22.03 ACOUSTIC mini (*3) / LIVE: FRIDAY THE 13TH live cd w/dvd (*5)

KARA'S FLOWERS

ADAM LEVINE – vocals, guitar / **JESSE CARMICHAEL** – keyboards / **MICKEY MADDEN** – bass / **RYAN DUSICK** – drums

Reprise Reprise

Sep 97. (cd/c) <(9362 46578-2/-4)> **THE FOURTH WORLD** [ ] Aug97 [ ]
– Soap disco / Future kid / Myself / Oliver / Never saga / Loving the small time / To her with love / Sleepy windbreaker / Pantry queen / My ocean blue / Captain Splendid. *<re-iss. 2004 on 'Rhino'; 78963-2>*

Nov 97. (c-s/cd-s) *(W 0415 C/CD)* <17333> **SOAP DISCO / CAPTAIN SPLENDID** [ ] [ ]

—— went, er . . . underground in '99

MAROON 5

— the quartet added **JAMES VALENTINE** – guitar

J – Octone J – Octone

May 03. (cd) *(82876 52353-2)* *<82376 50001-2>* **SONGS ABOUT JANE** [ ] Jun02 [ ]
– Harder to breathe / This love / Shiver / She will be loved / Tangled / The sun / Must get out / Sunday morning / Secret / Through with you / Not coming home / Sweetest goodbye.

Dec 03. (re-cd+=)(lp) *(82876 58430-2)(58260-1)* *<as prev.>* **SONGS ABOUT JANE** [30] [6]
– (+=) Harder to breathe (video) / This love (video).

Jan 04. (cd-s) *(82876 56692-2)* *<55427-2>* **HARDER TO BREATHE / RAGDOLL / SECRET / ('A'-video)** [13] Mar04 [18]

Apr 04. (re-cd+=) *(as prev.)* **SONGS ABOUT JANE** [1] [–]

Apr 04. (cd-s) *(82876 60845-2)* *<63388-2>* **THIS LOVE / HARDER TO BREATHE (acoustic) / THE SUN (acoustic) / ('A'-video)** [3] Jul04 [5]

Aug 04. (cd-s) *(82876 64362-2)* *<65248-2>* **SHE WILL BE LOVED / (live acoustic)** [4] Sep04 [5]
(cd-s) *(82876 64363-2)* – ('A') / This love (live acoustic) / This love (Kanye West remix) / ('A'-video).

Dec 04. (cd-s) *(82876 66804-2)* *<66634-2>* **SUNDAY MORNING / SHIVER (live from "Hard Rock") / THROUGH WITH YOU (live from "Hard Rock")** [27] Jan05 [31]

Feb 05. (m-cd) *(82876 63230-2)* *<62468-2>* **1.22.03 ACOUSTIC** [58] Jun04 [42]
– This love / Sunday morning / She will be loved / Harder to breathe / The sun / If I fell. *(bonus+=)* – Highway to Hell (live).

Apr 05. (cd-s) *(82876 68906-2)* **MUST GET OUT / THIS LOVE (acoustic)** [39] [–]

Oct 05. (cd w/dvd) *(82876 70649-2)* *<69952-2>* **LIVE: FRIDAY THE 13th** (live) [ ] Sep05 [61]
– Shiver / Through with you / Tangled / Harder to breathe / The sun / Wasted years / Secret – Ain't no sunshine / Not coming home / This love / Must get out / Sunday morning / Sweetest goodbye / Hello / She will be loved. // (+ DVD equivalents).

☐ Steve MARRIOTT (see under ⇒ HUMBLE PIE)

☐ the MARS VOLTA (see under ⇒ AT THE DRIVE-IN)

John MARTYN

Born: IAIN McGEACHY, 11 Sep'48, New Malden, Surrey (he was partly brought up on a houseboat by his English mother, the other six months of the year by his father in Glasgow after they separated just after he was born – his grandmother subsequently brought him up in Scotland). Having learned guitar techniques from folk singer HAMISH IMLACH, MARTYN moved to London in 1967 after being the first white solo artist to secure a deal with Chris Blackwell's 'Island' label. His early albums, 'LONDON CONVERSATION' (1968) and 'THE TUMBLER' (1968) were competent folk sets, the latter revealing the first glimmers of MARTYN's nascent jazz/blues leanings, employing the services of respected flautist HAROLD McNAIR. Following MARTYN's marriage to Coventry girl, BEVERLEY KUTNER, the pair began recording together in 1969, releasing two albums, 'STORMBRINGER' and 'THE ROAD TO RUIN' the following year. The latter set was the first of many MARTYN albums to feature the double bass work of friend (and then PENTANGLE member) DANNY THOMPSON, the only musical collaborator who would become a fairly permanent fixture in the singer's career. Following the birth of the MARTYN's second child in 1971, JOHN resumed his solo career with 'BLESS THE WEATHER'. His most heavily jazz-influenced set to date, the record was a blueprint for much of MARTYN's subsequent work; here were the first signs of the singer's trademark lounge lizard slur (a defiantly unique hybrid of ERIC CLAPTON, LOWELL GEROGE and TOM WAITS) with which he'd dextrously negotiate the grey area where jazz, blues, folk and rock meet. With RICHARD THOMPSON on additional guitar (he also played on 'BLESS..') and a rhythm section courtesy of FAIRPORT CONVENTION (bassist DAVE PEGG and drummer DAVE MATTACKS), 'SOLID AIR' (1973) was the pivotal early MARTYN album. Pioneering use of acoustic guitar echo lent the album a uniquely haunting quality, the set featuring some of MARTYN's most affecting material. The title track was a drifting, twilight tribute to NICK DRAKE while among the more conventional, folk-ish numbers, 'OVER THE HILL' and lovely 'MAY YOU NEVER' (later covered by ERIC CLAPTON on his 'Slowhand' album) were soul stirring highlights. The album considerably widened his large cult following which numbered musicians like STEVE WINWOOD, a collaborator on the follow-up, 'INSIDE OUT' (1973). The record traced the same nebulous path as its predecessor, as did 'SUNDAY'S CHILD' (1975), the latter employing the services of the late PAUL KOSSOFF (ex-FREE and latterly BACKSTREET CRAWLER). In the two year gap prior to his next studio project, MARTYN released a limited (10,000) mail-order only (from his Sussex home) live album, the acclaimed 'LIVE AT LEEDS' (1975). The speed at which the pressing sold out indicated the extent of MARTYN's fanbase. Nevertheless, the singer was yet to make an overt attempt to turn his standing into commercial success; 'ONE WORLD' (1977) was as esoteric as ever. Extending his range of influences to include dub and oblique ambience, the record was another key release in MARTYN's career featuring both the gorgeous 'COULDN'T LOVE YOU MORE' and the sly, insidious skank of 'BIG MUFF', a collaboration with Jamaican legend LEE PERRY. The ensuing three years saw MARTYN split with wife BEVERLEY, this harrowing period providing much of the impetus for 1980's 'GRACE AND DANGER'. While the album was a relatively sombre affair, the emergence of PHIL COLLINS (here contributing percussion, vocals and production) signalled a move towards a more mainstream sound. Inevitably, then, his 1981 album, 'GLORIOUS FOOL' (a political assault on newly elected US president Ronald Reagan) made the UK Top 30, the follow-up, 'WELL KEPT SECRET' (1982) reaching No.20. Since then, however, he's failed to consolidate this brief flurry of chart action, conceivably because MARTYN's albums rarely include any glaring hit singles. Though the 80's were a fairly fallow period for MARTYN, he returned in fine style at the turn of the decade with 'THE APPRENTICE' (1990) and the sophisti-jazz of 'COOLTIDE' (1991). The latter set surfaced on 'Permanent' for whom he'd revisit a batch of old material on two studio sets and a live album over the course of the early-mid 90's. A surprise move to 'Go Discs!', resulted in his first Top 40 entry of the decade with 'AND' (1996). Upon the label's demise, MARTYN joined the new 'Independiente' stable (alongside TRAVIS!) and cut a low-key covers set, 'THE CHURCH WITH ONE BELL' (1998); he subsequently used the profits generated to help him procure the church pictured on the album sleeve(!). The millennial 'GLASGOW WALKER' (2000) wasn't much of a departure from the kind of vapourous, jazz-inflected atmospherics with which he's constructed much of his latter day output although that wasn't such a bad thing, especially bearing in mind the oblique allure which MARTYN's vocal still holds, even on material like 'CRY ME A RIVER' and 'YOU DON'T KNOW WHAT LOVE IS'. The hard-living legend was to subsequently undergo a partial amputation (below the knee) of his right leg after a cyst burst and became infected. Laid up after the operation, financial necessity became the driving force behind some new recordings. 'ON THE COBBLES' (2004) was as enthusiastically received as anything he'd done in the last decade, conclusive evidence that his health problems hadn't adversely affected his art. At least two of the tracks were familiar – 'BABY COME HOME', from a FRANKIE MILLER tribute, and 'SOLID AIR' classic, 'GO DOWN EASY', here rendered as percolating ambience. Also familiar, bringing back wispish visions of 'SOLID

AIR', was DANNY THOMPSON's bass playing on the illuminatory 'MY CREATOR'. Paying their respects to a man who's still perhaps the most criminally unsung legend in the history of British popular music were longtime admirer PAUL WELLER, ex-VERVE man NICK McCABE and even MAVIS STAPLES, who took centre stage on a cover of the Leadbelly nugget, 'GOODNIGHT IRENE'. MARTYN's body of work remains unique, a rich seam of inspiration for the uninitiated; it's just a pity his talents aren't more widely acknowledged.

• **Covered:** COCAINE BLUES (trad.) / I'D RATHER BE THE DEVIL (Skip James) / JOHNNY TOO BAD (Slickers) / TIGHT CONNECTION TO MY HEART (Bob Dylan) / NEVER LET ME GO (Joe Scott) / HE'S GOT ALL THE WHISKEY (Bobby Charles) / GOD'S SONG (Randy Newman) / HOW FORTUNATE THE MAN WITH NONE (Dead Can Dance; words Bertholt Brecht) / SMALL TOWN TALK (Bobby Charles & Rick Danko) / EXCUSE ME MISTER (Ben Harper) / STRANGE FRUIT (Billie Holiday) / THE SKY IS CRYING (Elmore James) / GLORY BOX (Portishead) / FEEL SO BAD (S. Hopkins) / DEATH DON'T HAVE NO MERCY (Reverend Gary Davis).
• **Trivia:** He has also guested on albums by CLAIRE HAMMILL, BURNING SPEAR and BACK STREET CRAWLER, to mention but a few.

Album rating: LONDON CONVERSATION (*5) / THE TUMBLER (*5) / STORMBRINGER (*6) / THE ROAD TO RUIN (*6) / BLESS THE WEATHER (*7) / SOLID AIR (*8) / SUNDAY'S CHILD (*6) / LIVE AT LEEDS (*6) / INSIDE OUT (*6) / SO FAR SO GOOD compilation (*7) / ONE WORLD (*7) / GRACE & DANGER (*7) / GLORIOUS FOOL (*6) / THE ELECTRIC JOHN MARTYN compilation (*6) / WELL KEPT SECRET (*6) / PHILENTROPHY (*5) / SAPPHIRE (*5) / PIECE BY PIECE (*6) / FOUNDATIONS (*5) / THE APPRENTICE (*6) / COOLTIDE (*6) / NO LITTLE BOY (*5) / COULDN'T LOVE YOU MORE (*6) / SWEET LITTLE MYSTERIES compilation (*9) / AND. (*5) / THE CHURCH WITH ONE BELL (*6) / GLASGOW WALKER (*6) / ON THE COBBLES (*6)

JOHN MARTYN – vocals, acoustic guitar

Island Warners

Oct 67. (lp) *(ILP 952)* **LONDON CONVERSATION** [ ] [–]
– Fairy tale lullaby / Sandy grey / London conversation / Ballad of an elder woman / Cocaine blues / Run honey run / Back to stay / Rolling home / Who's grown up now / Golden girl / This time / Don't think twice. *(re-iss. Aug91 cd)(c; IMCD 134)(ICM 2074)*

— added **HAROLD McNAIR** – flute / **PAUL WHEELER** – guitar / **DAVE MOSES** – bass

Dec 68. (lp) *(ILPS 9091)* **THE TUMBLER** [ ] [–]
– Sing a song of summer / The river / Goin' down to Memphis / The gardeners / A day at the sea / Fishin' blues / Dusty / Hello train / Winding boy / Fly on home / Knuckledy crunch and slipp ledee slee song / Seven black roses. *(cd-iss. Apr94; IMCD 173)*

JOHN & BEVERLEY MARTYN

(as BEVERLEY, she recorded solo 45's) **BEVERLEY** nee KUTNER – vocals, with + **LEVON HELM** – drums (The BAND) / **PAUL HARRIS** – piano / **HARVEY BROOKS** – bass / **BIUX MUNDI** + **HERBIE LOVELL** – drums

Jan 70. (7") *(WIP 6076)* **JOHN THE BAPTIST. / THE OCEAN** [ ] [–]
Feb 70. (lp) *(ILPS 9113)* *<1854>* **STORMBRINGER** [ ] [ ]
– Go out and get it / Can't get the one I want / Stormbringer / Sweet honesty / Woodstock / John the baptist / The ocean / Traffic light lady / Tomorrow time / Would you believe me. *(re-iss. Aug91 cd)(c; IMCD 131)(ICM 9113)*
Apr 70. (7") **GO OUT AND GET IT. / CAN'T GET THE ONE I WANT** [–] [ ]

— with **DANNY THOMPSON** – bass (of PENTANGLE) / **WELLS KELLY** – drums, bass + **PAUL HARRIS**

Nov 70. (lp) *(ILPS 9133)* *<1882>* **THE ROAD TO RUIN** [ ] [ ]
– Primrose hill / Parcels / Auntie aviator / New day / Give us a ring / Sorry to be so long / Tree garden / Say what you can / The road to ruin. *(cd-iss. Mar93; IMCD 165)*

JOHN MARTYN

went solo again, with **DANNY THOMPSON** – double bass / **RICHARD THOMPSON** – guitar (solo artist) / **TONY REEVES** – (of COLOSSEUM) / **IAN WHITEMAN** and **ROGER POWELL** (of MIGHTY BABY)

Island Island

Nov 71. (lp) *(ILPS 9167)* *<9311>* **BLESS THE WEATHER** [ ] [ ]
– Go easy / Bless the weather / Sugar lump / Walk to the water / Just now / Head and heart / Let the good times come / Back down the river / Glistening Glyndebourne / Singing in the rain. *(re-iss. Aug91 cd)(c; IMCD 135)(ICM 9167)*

— retained **DANNY, RICHARD** and brought in **JOHN 'RABBIT' BUNDRICK** – keyboards / **DAVE PEGG** – bass / **DAVE MATTACKS** – drums / and **SPEEDY** (NEEMOI ACQUAYE) – congas / (all of FAIRPORT CONVENTION).

Nov 72. (7") *(WIP 6116)* **MAY YOU NEVER. / JUST NOW** [ ] [–]
Feb 73. (lp) *(ILPS 9226)* *<9325>* **SOLID AIR** [ ] [ ]
– Over the hill / Don't want to know / I'd rather be with the Devil / Go down easy / Dreams by the sea / May you never / The man in the station / Easy blues / Solid air. *(re-iss. Nov86 lp/c; ILPM/ICM 9226) (cd-iss. Feb87; CID 9226) (cd re-mast.Oct00; IMCD 274)*
Mar 73. (7") **MAY YOU NEVER. / DON'T WANT TO KNOW ABOUT EVIL** [–] [ ]

— retained **DANNY,** and brought in **BOBBY KEYES** and **REMI KABAKA** plus **STEVE WINWOOD** and **CHRIS WOOD** (both of TRAFFIC)

Oct 73. (lp) *(ILPS 9253)* *<9335>* **INSIDE OUT** [ ] [ ]
– Fine lines / Eibhli ghail ghiuin ni chearbhaill / Ain't no saint / Outside in / The glory of love / Look in / Beverley / Make no mistake / Ways to cry / So much in love with you. *(cd-iss. Apr94; IMCD 172)*

— with **DANNY THOMPSON / JOHN STEVENS** – drums / **PAUL KOSSOFF** – guitar (ex-FREE) and guests **BEVERLEY MARTYN** – vocals

Jan 75. (lp) *(ILPS 9296)* *<9396>* **SUNDAY'S CHILD** [ ] [ ]
– One day without you / Lay it all down / Root love / My baby girl / Sunday's child / Spencer the rover / Clutches / The message / Satisfied mind / You can discover / Call me crazy. *(cd-iss. Mar93; IMCD 163)*
Sep 75. (lp; ltd-mail order) *(ILPS 9343)* **LIVE AT LEEDS (live)** [–] [–]
– Outside in / Solid air / Make no mistake / Bless the weather / The man in the station / I'd rather be the Devil. *(re-iss. Jun87 on 'Cacophony'; SKELP 001) (cd-iss. May92 on 'Awareness'; AWCD 1036) (re-iss. cd Jul95 on 'Hypertension'; HYCD 200114) (cd re-iss. Aug98 on 'Blueprint'; OW 107CD)*
Feb 77. (7") *(WIP 6385)* **OVER THE HILL. / HEAD AND HEART** [ ] [–]
Mar 77. (lp) *(<ILPS 9484>)* **SO FAR SO GOOD** (compilation) [ ] [ ]
– May you never / Bless the weather / Head and heart / Over the hill / Spencer the rover / Glistening Glyndebourne / Solid air / One day without you / I'd rather be the Devil.

— with guests **STEVE WINWOOD** – keyboards / **MORRIS PERT** – percussion.

Nov 77. (lp/c) *(ILPS/ZCI 9492)* **ONE WORLD** [54] [–]
– Couldn't love you more / Certain surprise / Dancing / Small hours / Dealer / One world / Smiling stranger / Big Muff. *(re-iss. Sep86 lp/c/cd; ILPM/ICM/CID 9492)*
Jan 78. (7") *(WIP 6414)* **DANCING. / DEALER (version)** [ ] [–]

— with **PHIL COLLINS** – drums,vocals / **JOHN GIBLIN** – bass (both of BRAND X) / **TOMMY EYRE** – keyboards (GREASE BAND) / **DAVE LAWSON** – keyboards (ex-GREENSLADE).

Island not iss.

Oct 80. (lp/c) *(ILPS/ICT 9560)* **GRACE AND DANGER** [54] [–]
– Some people are crazy / Grace and danger / Lookin' on / Johnny too bad / Sweet little mystery/ Hurt in your heart / Baby please come home / Save some for me / Our love. *(cd-iss. May87; CID 9560)*
Oct 80. (7") *(WIP 6495)* **JOHNNY TOO BAD. / ('A'instrumental)** [ ] [–]
Mar 81. (7") *(WIP 6547)* **JOHNNY TOO BAD. / ('A'version)** [ ] [–]
(12") *(IPR 2046)* – ('A'ext. dub version) / Big Muff (ext.mix).
May 81. (7") *(WIP 6718)* **SWEET LITTLE MYSTERY. / JOHNNY TOO BAD** [ ] [–]

— with **PHIL COLLINS** – drums, vocals, producer / **ALAN THOMSON** – bass / **MAX MIDDLETON** – keyboards / **DANNY CUMMINGS** – percussion / **DICK CUTHELL** – horns 2.

WEA Duke

Aug 81. (7") *(K 79243)* **PLEASE FALL IN LOVE WITH ME. / DON'T YOU GO** [ ] [–]
Sep 81. (lp/c) *(K/K4 99178)* **GLORIOUS FOOL** [25] [–]
– Couldn't love you more / Amsterdam / Hold on my heart / Perfect hustler / Hearts and keys / Glorious fool / Never say never / Oascanel (get back home) / Didn't do that / Please fall in love with me / Don't you go.
Feb 82. (7") **COULDN'T LOVE YOU MORE. /** [–] [ ]

— with **DANNY** and **ALAN** plus **JEFFREY ALLEN** – drums / **JIM PRIME** – keyboards / **MEL COLLINS** – sax / **MARTIN DROVER** – trumpet / **LEE KOSMIN** and **STEVE LANGE** – harmony.

Aug 82. (lp/c) *(K/K4 99255)* **WELL KEPT SECRET** [20] [–]
– Could've been me / You might need a man / Hung up / Gun money /

Never let me go / Love up / Changes her mind / Hiss on the tape / Back with a vengeance / Livin' alone.

Sep 82. (7") *(K 79336)* **HISS ON THE TAPE. / LIVIN' ALONE** [ ] [–]

Nov 82. (7") *(259987-7)* **GUN MONEY (US remix). / HISS ON THE TAPE (live)** [ ] [ ]

— touring line-up **ALAN THOMSON** – bass / **JEFFREY ALLEN** – drums / **DANNY CUMMINGS** – percussion / **RONNIE LEAHY** – keyboards

Body Swerve — not iss.

Nov 83. (lp) *(JMLP 001)* **PHILENTHROPY (live)** [ ] [–]
– Sunday's child / Don't want to know / Johnny too bad / Make no mistake / Root love / Lookin' on / Hung up / Smiling stranger. *(re-iss. Mar86 on 'Dojo' lp/c/cd; DOJO LP/TC/CD 26)*

— **MARTYN** retained **JIM** and **ALAN** plus **BARRY REYNOLDS** add. guitar / **JACK WALDMAN** – keyboards / **ROBIN RANKIN** – keyboards / **JAMES HOOKER** – keyboards / **STEVEN STANLEY** – linn drums / **ANDY LYDEN** – linn drums / **UZZIAH 'STICKY' THOMPSON** – percussion / **COLIN TULLY** – saxophone / harmony by **MORWENNE LAIDLAW, TERRY NELSON** and **LORNA BROOKS**

Island — Island

Oct 84. (7") *(IS 209)* **OVER THE RAINBOW. / ROPE SOUL'D** [ ] [–]

Nov 84. (lp/c) *(ILPS/ICT 9779)* **SAPPHIRE** [57] [ ]
– Sapphire / Over the rainbow / You know / Watching her eyes / Fisherman's dream / Acid rain / Mad dog days / Climb the walls / Coming in on time / Rope soul'd. *(cd-iss. Mar93; IMCD 164)*

— with **ALAN THOMSON** – fretless bass / **DANNY CUMMINGS** – percussion / **COLIN TULLY and FOSTER PATTERSON** – keyboards, vocals.

Feb 86. (lp/c/cd) *(ILPS/ICT/CID 9807)* **PIECE BY PIECE** [28] [–]
– Nightline / Lonely love / Angeline / One step too far / Piece by piece / Serendipity / Who believes in angels / Love of mine / John Wayne. *(cd+=)* – Tight connection to my heart / Solid air / One world / May you never.

Feb 86. (7") *(IS 265)* **ANGELINE. / TIGHT CONNECTION TO MY HEART** [ ] [–]
(12"+=) *(12IS 265)* – May you never / Certain surprise / One day without you.
(cd-ep+=) *(CID 265)* – May you never / Solid air / Glistening Glyndebourne.

May 86. (7") *(IS 272)* **LONELY LOVE. / SWEET LITTLE MYSTERY (live)** [ ] [–]
(12"+=) *(12IS 272)* – Fisherman's dream (live).

— **DAVID BALL** – bass repl. THOMPSON / added **ARRAN ABMUN** – drums + **JEFF CASTLE** – keyboards

Oct 87. (lp/c/cd) *(ILPS/ICT/CID 9884)* **FOUNDATIONS (live)** [ ] [–]
– Mad dog days / Angeline / The apprentice / May you never / Deny this love / Send me one line / John Wayne / Johnny too bad / Over the rainbow. *(re-iss. cd Apr94; IMCD 180)*

Permanent — not iss.

Mar 90. (cd/c/lp) *(PERM CD/MC/LP 1)* **THE APPRENTICE** [ ] [–]
– Live on love / Look at that gun / Send me one line / Hold me / The apprentice / The river / Income town / Deny this love / UPO / Patterns in the rain. *(cd+=)* – The moment. *(cd re-iss. Apr98 on 'Indelible'; INDELCD 1)*

Aug 90. (7") *(PERM S12)* **DENY THIS LOVE (remix). / THE APPRENTICE (live)** [ ] [–]
(cd-s+=) *(CDPERM 1)* – ('A'-lp version).

Nov 91. (cd/c/lp) *(PERM CD/MC/LP 4)* **COOLTIDE** [ ] [–]
– Hole in the rain / Annie says / Jack the lad / Number nine / The cure / Same difference / Father Time / Call me / Cooltide.

Apr 92. (cd-s) *(CDPERM 3)* **JACK THE LAD / ?** [ ] [–]

Sep 92. (7") *(PERM 6)* **SWEET LITTLE MYSTERY. / HEAD AND HEART** [ ] [–]
(12"+=/cd-s+=) *(12/CD PERM 6)* – Never let me go.

Oct 92. (cd/c/lp) *(PERM CD/MC/LP 9)* **COULDN'T LOVE YOU MORE** [65] [–]
– Lonely love / Couldn't love you more / Sweet little mystery / Head & heart / Could've been me / One day without you / Over the hill / Fine lines / May you never / One world / Way's to cry / Angeline / Man in the station / Solid air / Never let me go.

Jan 93. (cd-s; w-drawn) **LONELY LOVE** [ ] [–]

— with on next album **SPENCER COZENS** or **CHRIS CAMERON** – keyboards / **GERRY CONWAY** or **WAYNE STEWART** – drums / **ALAN THOMPSON** or **JOHN GIBLIN** – bass / **MILES BOULD** or **MARK WALKER** – percussion / **DAVE GILMOUR** or **ALAN DARBY** or **BILL RUPERT** – guitar / **ANDY SHEPHERD** or **GERRY UNDERWOOD** – sax / **FRED NELSON** – piano / **LEVON HELM** – guest / and of course **PHIL COLLINS** – b.vocals, etc.

Jul 93. (cd/c) *(PERM CD/MC 14)* **NO LITTLE BOY** (old songs re-worked) [ ] [–]
– Solid air / Ways to cry / Could've been me / I don't wanna know / Just now / One day without you / Sweet little mystery / Pascanel / Sunday's child / Head and heart / Fine lines / Bless the weather / Man in the station / One world / Rock salt and nails / Hole in the rain.

— with **PHIL COLLINS, JOHN GIBLIN + ALAN THOMPSON, JERRY UNDERWOOD, SPENCER COZENS**, etc

Go! Discs — not iss.

Aug 96. (cd/c) *(828 798-2/-4)* **AND.** [32] [–]
– Sunshine's better / Suzanne / The downward pull of human nature / All in your favour / A little strange / Who are they? / Step it up / Carmine / She's a lover.

— now with **GIBLIN, COZENS** / + **ARRAN AHMUN** – drums, percussion

Blueprint — not iss.

Dec 97. (cd-ep) *(BP 276CD)* **SNOOO . . . / SHE'S A LOVER / ALL IN YOUR FAVOUR / STEP IT UP / A LITTLE STRANGE** [ ] [–]

Independiente — Thirsty Ear

Mar 98. (cd) *(ISOM 3CD)* <57053> **THE CHURCH WITH ONE BELL** [51] [ ]
– He's got all the whiskey / God's song / How fortunate the man with none / Small town talk / Excuse me mister / Strange fruit / The sky is crying / Glory box / Feel so sad / Death don't have no mercy.

Jun 98. (cd-s) *(ISOM 14MS)* **EXCUSE ME MISTER / GOD'S SONG (live) / ROCK, SALT AND NAILS (live) / JOHN WAYNE (live)** [ ] [–]

May 00. (cd) *(ISOM 15CD)* **GLASGOW WALKER** [66] [–]
– So sweet / Wildflower / The field of play / Cool in the life / Feel so good / Cry me a river / Mama T / Can't live without / The cat won't work tonight / You don't know what love is.

— in Mar'01, MARTYN was credited on the SISTER BLISS (of FAITHLESS) UK No.31 single, 'Deliver Me'

Independiente — Independiente

Apr 04. (cd) *(<ISOM 43CD>)* **ON THE COBBLES** [ ] Jun04 [ ]
– Baby come home / Under my wing / Ghosts / Back to Marseilles / Cobbles / My creator / One for the road / Go down easy / Walking home / Goodnight Irene.

– compilations, etc. –

on 'Island' unless otherwise mentioned

Oct 82. (lp/c) *(ILPS/ICT 9715)* **THE ELECTRIC JOHN MARTYN** [ ] [ ]
(cd-iss. Apr88; CID 9715)

May 92. (cd) *Windsong; (WINCD 012)* **BBC RADIO 1 LIVE IN CONCERT (live)** [ ] [–]

Nov 92. (d-cd) *(ITSCD 2)* **SOLID AIR / ONE WORLD** [ ] [–]

Jun 94. (d-cd) *(CRNCD 4)* **SWEET LITTLE MYSTERIES – THE ISLAND ANTHOLOGY** [ ] [ ]

Jul 95. (d-cd/d-c) *Permanent; (PERM CD/MC 33) / Resurgent;* <1122> **LIVE (live at the Shaw Theatre, London, 31st March, 1990)** <US-title 'DIRTY, DOWN & LIVE'> [ ] Nov99 [ ]
– Easy blues / May you never / Dealer / Outside in / Never let me go / Sapphire / Couldn't love you more / Deny this love / Fisherman's dream / Big Muff / Angeline / Sweet little mystery / The river / Income town / The apprentice / John Wayne / Look at the girl / Looking on / Johnny too bad / One world.

Mar 98. (cd) *Artful; (ARTFULCD 13)* **THE REST OF THE BEST** [ ] [–]

Mar 00. (d-cd) *Artful; (ARTFULCD 31)* **CLASSICS** [ ] [–]
(re-iss. Apr02; same)

Jul 00. (d-cd) *Eagle; (EDMCD 102)* **THE MASTERS (live '91)** [ ] [–]

Nov 00. (cd) *One World; (OW 113CD)* **THE NEW YORK SESSION** [ ] [–]

Apr 01. (cd) *Mooncrest; (<CRESTCD 065>)* **PATTERNS IN THE RAIN (some live)** [ ] [ ]

Jul 01. (cd; by JOHN MARTYN & DANNY THOMPSON) *One World; (OW 118CD)* **LIVE IN GERMANY 1986 (live)** [ ] [ ]

Aug 01. (cd; by JOHN MARTYN & DANNY THOMPSON) *One World; (OW 115CD)* **LIVE AT THE BREWERY ARTS CENTRE KENDAL 1986 (live)** [ ] [–]

Aug 01. (cd) *One World; (OW 109CD)* **LIVE AT THE TOWN & COUNTRY CLUB 1986 (live)** [ ] [–]

Nov 01. (cd) *One World; (OW 116CD)* **LIVE AT THE BOTTOM LINE, NEW YORK 1983 (live)** [ ] [–]

Nov 01. (cd) *One World; (OW 119CD)* **SWEET CERTAIN SURPRISE (live)** ☐ -
May 02. (cd) *One World; (OW 117CD)* **LIVE IN MILAN (live)** ☐ -

☐ J. MASCIS (see under ⇒ DINOSAUR JR.)

☐ Nick MASON (see under ⇒ PINK FLOYD)

MASSIVE ATTACK

Formed: Bristol, England ... 1987 by 3-D, MUSHROOM and DADDY G. Having founded their own label, 'Wild Bunch' (named after the loose Bristol collective of DJ's, producers and musicians of which MASSIVE ATTACK were an integral part) five years earlier, they were subsequently snapped up by Virgin subsidiary, 'Circa' in 1990 and with only their second single, 'UNFINISHED SYMPATHY' – released under the revised moniker of MASSIVE (to distance themselves from any affiliation with the UN Gulf War policy) – crashed into the Top 20. Featuring the velvet tones of SHARA NELSON and luxuriant string arrangements to die for, this hypnotically beautiful track is oft cited as one of the most perfect singles ever crafted. While not boasting anything quite as tantalising, the classic debut album, 'BLUE LINES', hit the the Top 20 in Spring '91, a darkly sensual, spliff-heavy cocktail of sampladelic dub, hip-hop, funk and soul that can quite possibly lay claim to be the Big Daddy of that much-maligned genre, trip-hop. Alongside the aforementioned NELSON, the record featured guest vocalists, TRICKY (soon to carve out his own career in paranoid beats) and dub reggae veteran, HORACE ANDY. NELSON subsequently departed for a solo career and all was quiet from the MASSIVE' camp until the Autumn of '94, when they re-surfaced with the NELLEE HOOPER (Soul II Soul)-produced 'PROTECTION' album. An even darker, slinkier creature, it featured an array of guest vocalists, most effectively employing TRACEY THORN on the aching 'BETTER THINGS' and the title track; TRICKY, meanwhile, sounded almost catatonic on the spellbinding voodoo bass-psyche of 'KARMACOMA' while the exotic tones of NICOLETTE graced a couple of tracks. More cohesive soundwise, the record was characterised by a haunting dub-reggae feel and while it was perhaps pushing it a bit to revamp a Doors track ('LIGHT MY FIRE'), the claustrophobic brilliance of 'SPYING GLASS' (featuring HORACE ANDY in peerless form) more than made up for it. London dub producer, The MAD PROFESSOR, later gave it a bowel quaking, full-on dub reworking early in '95, the results surfacing as the mind scrambling 'NO PROTECTION'. Stunningly original and defiantly self-sufficient, MASSIVE ATTACK continue to shrug off any labels hopeful journos may pin on them (and woe betide anyone who mentions tr*p h*p), and while their perfectionism means lengthy periods between new material, fans have learned to be patient. In the summer of '97, the trio returned with their darkest, scariest track to date, 'RISINGSON', a solitary taster for the following year's long-awaited UK chart-topper, 'MEZZANINE'. Yet again cleaning up across the critical board, MASSIVE ATTACK had created a work many regarded as the pinnacle of their career, an unflinchingly bleak, downbeat and introspective record mired in paranoia, despair and apocalytic pre-millennium tension. Nevertheless, 3-D, MUSHROOM and DADDY-G explored more musical possibilities than most bands of their ilk put together, even hooking up with LIZ FRASER (of the COCTEAU TWINS) on the track, 'TEARDROPS', subsequently a Top 10 hit. 1999 started a little painfully for the trio when MANFRED MANN threatened a lawsuit against them for the use of his song 'Tribute' on their track 'BLACK MARK'; an out of court settlement was soon agreed on. However, that was the least of their problems, MUSHROOM opting to bail out in July that year. With DADDY G also departing on domestic duty, it was left to 3D to complete '100th WINDOW' (2003), the band's fourth album and the only one not to develop significantly from its predecessor. That said, its brooding, stifling atmospherics were almost as compelling as 'MEZZANINE', with SINEAD O'CONNOR taking up the role that SHARA NELSON, TRACEY THORN and LIZ FRASER filled with such grace in the past. Unsurprisingly, the Irish singer brought a different dimension to that role, illuminating the album's darker corners with her burning vision, and nowhere more so than 'WHAT YOUR SOUL SINGS'. HORACE ANDY also reported for duty once again, airing his timeless, genderless vocal chords on 'NAME TAKEN' and 'EVERYWHEN'. The baying industrio-grunge and abstract sonics of 'DANNY THE DOG' (2004) represented MASSIVE's first soundtrack venture, a genre which they'd been gravitating towards – at least aesthetically – for years. Typically for a film project, the album failed to spawn any hit singles although it did graze the Top 75. As inevitable as the soundtrack, was a best-of, finally released as 'COLLECTED' in 2006. Another near-No.1, its tracklist was split pretty much evenly among their various landmark opuses with an unreleased track to tempt diehards: 'LIVE WITH ME' offered a rare opportunity to hear soul-folk veteran TERRY CALLIER beyond his usual acoustic guitar arrangements, shrouding his mahogany baritone in unquiet strings and smoothing a path into the Top 20 for what was the first major hit of CALLIER's long career.

• **Songwriters:** Group except; BE THANKFUL FOR WHAT YOU'VE GOT (William DeVaughn) / LIGHT MY FIRE (Doors) / MAN NEXT DOOR (John Holt) / EXCHANGE (Bob Hilliard & Mort Garson). Sampled JAMES BROWN, PIECES OF A DREAM, YOUNG HOLT TRIO. • **Trivia:** Remixed PETER GABRIEL, LES NEGRESSES VERTES.

Album rating: BLUE LINES (*9) / PROTECTION (*9) / NO PROTECTION (*8; Massive Attack Vs. The Mad Professor) / MEZZANINE (*9) / 100th WINDOW (*6) / DANNY THE DOG soundtrack (*5) / COLLECTED compilation (*8)

3-D (b. ROBERT DEL NAJA, 21 Jan'65, Brighton, England) – vocals / **MUSHROOM** (b. ANDREW VOWLES, 10 Nov'67) – keyboards / **DADDY-G** (b. GRANT MARSHALL, 18 Dec'59) – keyboards

Warners Warners

Jul 88. (12") *(MASS 001)* **ANY LOVE. / ('A'mix)** ☐ ☐

— w / **SHARA NELSON** – vocals / **NELLEE HOOPER** – programmer / arranger

Wild Bunch-Circa Virgin

Nov 90. (7"/c-s) *(WBR S/C 1)* **DAYDREAMING. / ('A'instrumental)** ☐ -
(12"+=/cd-s+=) *(WBR T/X 1)* – Any love (2).
(12") *(WBR TX 1)* – ('A'-luv it mix) / ('A'-Brixton bass mix) / ('A'-luv it dub).

Feb 91. (7"/c-s; as MASSIVE) *(WBR S/C 2)* **UNFINISHED SYMPATHY. / ('A'-Nellee Hooper mix)** 13 -
(12"/cd-s) *(WBR T/X 2)* – ('A'side) / ('A'-Paul Oakenfold mix) / ('A'-P.O. instrumental) / ('A'instrumental).

— Below also featured **HORACE ANDY** – vox

Apr 91. (cd/c/2x12"lp) *(WBR CD/MC/LP 1) <91685>* **BLUE LINES** 13 Aug91 ☐
– Safe from harm / One love / Blue lines / Be thankful for what you've got / Five man army / Unfinished sympathy / Daydreaming / Lately / Hymn of the big wheel. *(re-iss. Sep96; same); hit UK 21)*

May 91. (7"/c-s) *(WBR S/C 3) <96332>* **SAFE FROM HARM. / ('A'version)** 25 ☐
(cd-s+=) *(WBRX 3)* – ('A'-Perfecto mix).
(12") *(WBRT 3)* – ('A'-Perfecto mix) / ('A'dub mix) / ('A'instrumental).

Feb 92. (7"ep/c-ep/12"ep/cd-ep) *(WBR S/C/T/X 4)* **MASSIVE ATTACK** 27 -
– Hymn of the big wheel / Home of the whale / Be thankful / Any love.

— now w / **TRACEY THORN** (Everything But The Girl) **/ NICOLETTE / TRICKY + HORACE ANDY** – vocals. **CRAIG ARMSTRONG** – piano / **CHESTER KAMEN** – guitar / **ROB MERRIL** – drums

Sep 94. (cd/c/lp) *(WBR CD/MC/LP 2) <39883>* **PROTECTION** 4 ☐
– Protection / Karmacoma / Three / Weather storm / Spying glass / Better things / Eurochild / Sly / Heat miser / Light my fire (live).

Oct 94. (c-s/cd-s) *(WBR C/X 5) <38465>* **SLY / ('A'mix by UNDERDOG) / ('A'-Mad Professor mix) / ('A'-Tim Simenon mix)** 24 Nov94 □
(12"s+=/cd-s+=) *(WBR T/DX 5)* – (extra-'A'mix).

Jan 95. (cd-s; by MASSIVE ATTACK with TRACEY THORN) *(WBRDX 6) <38471>* **PROTECTION / ('A'-J.Sw!ft mix) / THREE (Don T's house mix)** 14 Feb95 □
(c-s/cd-s) *(WBR C/X 6)* – (1st 2 tracks) / ('A'-Radiation for the nation mix) / ('A'-Eno mix).
(12"+=) *(WBRT 6)* – ('A'-Mad Professor mix).

Feb 95. (cd/c/lp; as MASSIVE ATTACK VS MAD PROFESSOR) *(WBR CD/MC/LP 3)* **NO PROTECTION** 10 –
– Radiation ruling the nation (Protection) / Bumper ball dub (Karmacoma) / Trinity dub (Three) / Cool monsoon (Weather storm) / Eternal feedback (Sly) / Moving dub (Better things) / I spy (Spying glass) / Backward sucking (Heat miser).

Mar 95. (12"ep) *(WBRT 7)* **KARMACOMA. / ('A'-Napoli trip mix) / ('A'-Unkle mix) / BLACKSMITH – DAYDREAMING** 28 Jul95 □
(cd-ep+=) *(WBRX 7)* – ('A'-Portishead experience mix) / ('A'-Bumper ball mix).
(c-ep++=/cd-ep++=) *(WBR C/DX 7)* – ('A'-Portishead mix).

— next album/releases saw the addition of vocalists **HORACE ANDY, ELIZABETH FRASER, SARA JAY, ROBERT DEL NAJA + GRANT MARSHALL** / guitars – **ANGELO BRUSCHINI** / bass – **JOHN HARRIS, BOB LOCKE + WINSTON** / drums – **ANDY GANGADEEN**

Jul 97. (12"/cd-s) *(WBR T/X 8)* **RISINGSON. / SUPERPREDATORS** 11 □

Apr 98. (cd/c/lp) *(WBR CD/MC/LP 4) <45599>* **MEZZANINE** 1 May98 60
– Angel / Risingson / Teardrop / Inertia creeps / Exchange / Dissolved girl / Man next door / Black milk / Mezzanine / Group four / (Exchange).
(below single featured LIZ FRAZER on vocals)

Apr 98. (c-s) *(WBRC 9)* **TEARDROP / EURO ZERO HERO** 10 –
(12"+=/cd-s+=) *(WBR T/X 9)* – ('A'mixes).

Jul 98. (c-s) *(WBRC 10)* **ANGEL / GROUP 4** 30 –
(12"+=/cd-s+=) *(WBR T/X 10)* – ('A'mixes by Blur & the Mad Professor).

Oct 98. (d12"ep/cd-ep) *(WBR TD/DDX 11)* **INERTIA CREEPS** – non –
– (mixes:- Manic Street Preachers / State of Bengal / Alpha / Back she comes – Inertia mixed by Mad Professor / Reflection).

— now without MUSHROOM who left mid-'99

Virgin Astralwerks

Feb 03. (cd/t-lp) *(CD+/V 2967) <81239>* **100th WINDOW** 1 69
– Future proof / What your soul sings / Everywhen / Special cases / Butterfly caught / A prayer for England / Small time shot away / Name taken / Antistar.

Feb 03. (cd-s) *(VSCDT 1839)* **SPECIAL CASES / SPECIAL CASES (Akufen remix) / I AGAINST I (featuring MOS DEF) / SPECIAL CASES (version 2)** 15 –
(12") *(VST 1839)* – (Akufeb remix) / Luono's casing.

Jun 03. (cd-s) *(VSCDT 1853)* **BUTTERFLY CAUGHT (mixes; Paul Daley / Octave One / RJD2 / Jagz Kooner / Version Point / video)** – –
(d12") *(VST 1853)* – (some above mixes).

Oct 04. (cd) *<(874393-2)>* **DANNY THE DOG** (soundtrack) 70 Nov04 □
– Opening title / Atta boy / P is for piano / Simple rules / Polaroid girl / Sam / One thought at a time / Confused images / Red light means go / Collar stays on / You've never had a dream / Right way to hold a spoon / Everybody's got a family / Two rocks and a cup of water / Sweet is good / Montage / Everything about you is new / The dog obeys / Danny the dog / I am home / The academy.
(above issued on 'E.M.I.')

Mar 06. (cd-s) *(VSCDX 1912)* **LIVE WITH ME / (alt. version) / FALSE FLAGS / ('A'-video)** 17 –

Mar 06. (cd/t-lp) *(CD+/V 3017) <60068>* **COLLECTED** (compilation) 2 Apr06 □
– Safe from harm / Karmacoma / Angel / Teardrop / Teardrop / Inertia creeps / Protection / Butterfly caught / Unfinished symphony / Risingson / What your soul sings / Future proof / Five man army / Sly / Live with me. *(ltd cd w/dvd+=; CDVX 3017)* – (DVD tracks).

□ MATCHING MOLE (see under ⇒ WYATT, Robert)

MAXIMO PARK

Formed: Newcastle Upon Tyne, England ... 2003 by PAUL SMITH, DUNCAN LLOYD, LUKAS WOOLLER, ARCHIE TRU and TOM ENGLISH. Along with the FUTUREHEADS and FRANZ FERDINAND, Geordie art-rockers MAXIMO PARK cast a glamourous shade of post-punk on Northern skies, being one of the privileged few guitar bands to ink a deal with cult electronic imprint, 'Warp'. Late 2004, the quintet delivered a minor hit, 'THE COAST IS ALWAYS CHANGING' (having already issued their debut single, 'GRAFFITI', on an independent label), a more probing, multi-layered sequel to '77 than many of their peers. Successive UK Top 20 singles, 'APPLY SOME PRESSURE' and 'GRAFFITI', as well as their Paul Epworth-produced, Mercury-nominated debut set, 'A CERTAIN TRIGGER' (2005), conjured a sonic 'PARK-life haunted by the ghosts of New Wave icons the JAM, WIRE and XTC. Three further highly desirable, multi-coloured singles, 'GOING MISSING', 'APPLY SOME PRESSURE' (again!) and 'I WANT YOU TO STAY', kept Northern geek chic in vogue.

• **Covers:** ISOLATION (John Lennon).

Album rating: A CERTAIN TRIGGER (*8)

PAUL SMITH – vocals / **DUNCAN LLOYD** – guitar / **LUKAS WOOLLER** – keyboards / **ARCHIE TIKU** – bass / **TOM ENGLISH** – drums (of FIELD MUSIC)

Billingham not iss.

Apr 04. (ltd-7"red) *(none)* **GRAFFITI. / GOING MISSING** □ –

Warp Warp

Nov 04. (7") *(7WAP 183)* **THE COAST IS ALWAYS CHANGING. / THE NIGHT I LOST MY HEAD** 63 –

Feb 05. (7") *(7WAP 185)* **APPLY SOME PRESSURE. / I WANT YOU TO LEAVE** 20 –
(cd-s) *(WAP 185CD)* – ('A') / Fear of falling.
(10") *(10WAP 185X)* – (above 3) / The coast is always changing.

May 05. (7") *(7WAP 187)* **GRAFFITI. / HAMMER HORROR** 15 –
(cd-s) *(WAP 187CD)* – ('A') / Trial and error.
(cd-s) *(WAP 187CDR)* – ('A'-demo) / Stray talk / Apply some pressure (demo).

May 05. (cd/lp) *(<WARP CD/LP 130>)* **A CERTAIN TRIGGER** 15 □
– Signal and sign / Apply some pressure / Graffiti / Postcard of a painting / Going missing / I want you to stay / Limassol / The coast is always changing / The night I lost my head / Once, a glimpse / Now I'm all over the shop / Acrobat / Kiss you better. *(ltd d-cd+=; WARPCD 130X)* – (live in Japan):- Signal and sign / The coast is always changing / I want you to stay / Limassol / Once, a glimpse / Kiss you better.

Jul 05. (7"etched) *(7WAP 190)* **GOING MISSING / (acoustic)** 20 –
(cd-s) *(WAP 190CD)* – ('A') / A19.
(cd-s) *(WAP 190CDR)* – ('A') / A year of doubt / Kiss you better (acoustic).

Oct 05. (7"orange) *(7WAP 198)* **APPLY SOME PRESSURE. / MY LIFE IN REVERSE** 17 –
(cd-s+=) *(WAP 198CD)* – Once, a glimpse.
(7"clear) *(7WAP 198R)* – ('A'-live in Japan) / Isolation.

Feb 06. (cd-s) *(WAP 201CD)* **I WANT YOU TO STAY / LA QUINTA / I WANT YOU TO STAY (Field Music J Xaverre mix)** 21 –
(7"blue) *(7WAP 201)* – ('A'-original demo) / ('A'-Field Music..)
(7"white) *(7WAP 201R)* – ('A'-Cristian Vogel mix) / La quinta.

□ MAX Q (see under ⇒ INXS)

□ Brian MAY (see under ⇒ QUEEN)

□ Phil MAY & the FALLEN ANGELS (see under ⇒ PRETTY THINGS)

John MAYALL

Born: 29 Nov'33, Macclesfield, Cheshire, England. A National Service veteran from the Korean war in 1951-1955, he became a graphic artist (studying at Manchester Art College and working in an art studio attached to a local advertising agency) and picked up a taste for boogie from his trombone playing father. MAYALL started to master piano styles from boogie-woogie 78s by CRIPPLE CLARENCE LOFTON, PINETOP SMITH and others, before going on to learn the basics of harmonica and guitar. Although he initiated his first band, JOHN MAYALL's POWERHOUSE FOUR, in Manchester, he subsequently went to London at ALEXIS KORNER's request to form the BLUES SYNDICATE; this became the first of many BLUESBREAKERS featuring JOHN McVIE on bass, BERNIE WATSON on guitar and PETER WARD on drums (the latter was replaced by MARTIN HART when the band went full-time and gained a residency at the Scene, Great Windmill Street, London). Renowned for being a bit eccentric (he spent some time living in a self constructed tree-house), MAYALL was a strict bandleader and maintained an almost religious belief in blues purism. His songs were excellent pastiches of his heros' compositions, his voice being reminiscent of OTIS RUSH, BUDDY GUY and his ultimate idol, J.B. LENOIR. Signing a short term deal with 'Decca', he released his 1965 debut album, 'JOHN MAYALL PLAYS JOHN MAYALL', a badly recorded live set which nevertheless captured the initimate atmosphere of a sweaty R&B club. One of the record's tracks (which was duly released as a single), 'CRAWLING UP A HILL', showcased MAYALL's soft voice being over-run by a distorted harmonica and Hammond organ. The best BLUESBREAKERS line-ups were those that included ERIC CLAPTON, PETER GREEN and MICK TAYLOR, all of whom left the band with greatly enhanced reputations which enabled them to command vast amounts of money. CLAPTON joined in 1965, straight from The YARDBIRDS – bringing respectability to the band as fans flocked to see the guitar hero – and virtually dominated the classic UK Top 10 'BLUESBREAKERS' (1966) set. CLAPTON departed the following year to form CREAM and was replaced by PETER GREEN (he had earlier replaced him for a one-off 3-day period), who played on 'A HARD ROAD'. GREEN excelled on the instrumentals 'THE STUMBLE' (a Freddie King number) and his own 'THE SUPERNATURAL' as well as providing soulful vocals on the likes of 'YOU DON'T LOVE ME' and 'THE SAME WAY'. GREEN eventually left in 1967, his replacement being a shy but exceptionally talented young guitarist by the name of MICK TAYLOR. Remaining with MAYALL until 1969 – before taking BRIAN JONES' slot in The ROLLING STONES – TAYLOR's tenure lasted up to and including 'BLUES FROM LAUREL CANYON' (a transatlantic Top 60 success), a period which also produced the brassier sounding 'CRUSADE' in 1967. 'DIARY OF A BAND VOLUMES 1 & 2' both hit the UK Top 30 in 1968 and featured the band's live sound from the previous year, the excellent work of KEEF HARTLEY and MICK TAYLOR a must to hear. 1968 also produced 'BARE WIRES', a record leaning towards jazz and featuring JON HISEMAN on drums and an experienced brass section of HENRY LOWTHER, CHRIS MERCER and DICK HECKSTALL-SMITH. Understandably, MAYALL became tired of running his band as a finishing school for aspiring megastars and disbanded The BLUESBREAKERS, subsequently signing to 'Polydor' and forming an acoustic band including guitarist JON MARK and saxophonist JOHNNY ALMOND. This formation recorded the live album, 'TURNING POINT' (his biggest seller, his only gold disc and a near UK Top 10) in 1969 at the Fillmore East, featuring his best known song, 'ROOM TO MOVE' (his finest harp solo) and 'THOUGHTS ABOUT ROXANNE'. MARK and ALMOND soon moved on (after 'EMPTY ROOMS', another UK Top 10'er which included MAYALL's only US chart single, 'DON'T WASTE MY TIME') to form their own group, MARK-ALMOND, while MAYALL moved to Los Angeles and formed his own record label, 'Crusade'. 'USA UNION' with a backing band of Americans, notably, HARVEY MANDEL, DON 'SUGARCANE' HARRIS and LARRY TAYLOR was another Top 50 success, although critics rounded on the insipid lyrics. Following the double set, 'BACK TO THE ROOTS', MAYALL's work-rate declined, his output over the next few years of poor quality. The struggling bluesman signed to 'ABC/Blue Thumb' in 1975, releasing 'NEW YEAR, NEW BAND, NEW COMPANY'; for the first time, MAYALL had employed a female vocalist, DEE McKIMMIE along with future FLEETWOOD MAC guitarist RICK VITO. The album was to be his last US chart entry for 15 years; a number of albums followed although their success was limited by inadequate exposure and MAYALL stopped recording, only playing the odd local gig near his home in California. MAYALL toured Europe in 1988 to small but enthusiastic audiences, signing to 'Island' Records and releasing a belated comeback album, 'CHICAGO LINE'. The man never regained his success of the 60's, although he's now recognised as the Father Of British Blues and is still nurturing the occasional rising blues star from his now reformed and ever-changing BLUESBREAKERS (WALTER TROUT being one of the most recent). The 90's were kinder to MAYALL, 1990's 'A SENSE OF PLACE' on 'Island' (which marked his return to the US charts) and the brilliant 'WAKE UP CALL' (1993) on 'Silvertone' (UK Top 75) – with guest appearances by ALBERT COLLINS, BUDDY GUY, MICK TAYLOR and MAVIS STAPLES – being his best albums in years. After a further trio of mid-late 90's efforts, of which 1999's 'PADLOCK ON THE DOOR' was the most successful, MAYALL rounded up a posse of pals and set to work on 'ALONG FOR THE RIDE' (2001). The list of collaborators read like a who's who of the 60's Brit blues scene, with the likes of MICK TAYLOR, JOHN McVIE and MICK FLEETWOOD lending their talents. The father-like figure of MAYALL even managed to coax PETER GREEN into making a contribution. 'STORIES' (2002) found MAYALL as undiminished by age as ever, the soon to be septuagenarian casting a knowing eye back over the history of his beloved blues with tributes such as 'OH LEADBELLY'. There aren't many men still cutting it in their 70's but then MAYALL was merely following the traditions of his chosen genre, and if there weren't many old time blues players afforded a bash as big as '70th BIRTHDAY CONCERT' (2003), then MAYALL made up for them all with a gutsy, heady trip down memory lane with guest spots by old friends MICK TAYLOR and ERIC CLAPTON. MAYALL & THE BLUESBREAKERS (with the addition of TOM CANNING and HANK VAN SICKLE) surfaced from the studio once again in 2005, courtesy of umpteenth set, 'ROAD DOGS', a modern-day take on a blues revival now 40 years old.

• **Songwriters:** Self-penned alongside covers; MY BABY IS SWEETER (Willie Dixon) / DOUBLE TROUBLE + ALL YOUR LOVE (Otis Rush) / BERNARD JENKINS (Eric Clapton) / WHAT'D I SAY (Ray Charles) / DOUBLE CROSSIN' TIME (w/ Clapton) / DUST MY BLUES (Elmore James) / THE SUPERNATURAL (Peter Green) / SO MANY ROADS (Paul) / LOOKING BACK (Johnny Guitar Watson) / ALL MY LIFE (Robinson) / RIDIN' ON THE L & N (Barley Hampton) / IT HURTS ME TOO (London) / OH, PRETTY WOMAN (Big Joe Williams) / MAN OF STONE (Eddie Kirkland) / NIGHT TRAIN / LUCILLE (Little Richard) / PARCHMAN FARM (Mose Allison) / STEPPIN' OUT (Charles Brackeen) / etc.

Album rating: JOHN MAYALL PLAYS JOHN MAYALL (*7) / BLUESBREAKERS WITH ERIC CLAPTON (*8) / A HARD ROAD (*7) / CRUSADE (*6) / THE BLUES ALONE (*6) / THE DIARY OF A BAND VOL.1 (*5) / THE DIARY OF A BAND VOL.2 (*5) / BARE WIRES (*8) / BLUES FROM LAUREL CANYON (*6) / THE TURNING POINT (*7) / EMPTY ROOMS (*7) / LOOKING BACK compilation

(*7) / U.S.A. UNION (*5) / BACK TO THE ROOTS (*5) / MEMORIES (*5) / JAZZ BLUES FUSION (*5) / MOVING ON (*5) / TEN YEARS ARE GONE (*5) / THE LATEST EDITION (*4) / NEW YEAR, NEW BAND, NEW COMPANY (*4) / TIME EXPIRED, NOTICE TO APPEAR (*4) / A BANQUET OF BLUES (*4) / LOTS OF PEOPLE (*4) / A HARD CORE PACKAGE (*4) / BOTTOM LINE (*4) / NO MORE INTERVIEWS (*4) / ROAD SHOW BLUES (*4) / BEHIND THE IRON CURTAIN (*4) / CHICAGO LINE (*4) / A SENSE OF PLACE (*7) / LONDON BLUES compilation (*7) / ROOM TO MOVE compilation (*7) / WAKE UP CALL (*7) / SPINNING COIN (*4) / BLUES FOR THE LOST DAYS (*5) / PADLOCK ON THE BLUES (*6) / ALONG FOR THE RIDE (*5) / STORIES (*6) / 70th BIRTHDAY CONCERT (*7) / ROAD DOGS (*6)

BLUESBREAKERS

JOHN MAYALL – vocals, keyboards, harmonica, guitar(ex-BLUES SYNDICATE) / **BERNIE WATSON** – guitar repl. JOHN GILBEY who had repl. SAMMY PROSSER / **JOHN McVIE** (b.26 Nov'45) – bass repl. PETE BURFORD who had repl. RICKY BROWN / **MARTIN HART** – drums repl. PETER WARD who had repl. KEITH ROBERTSON (note previous drummers early 1963 =BRIAN MYALL after SAM STONE.)

JOHN MAYALL'S BLUESBREAKERS

Decca not iss.

Apr 64. (7"; as JOHN MAYALL & BLUES BREAKERS) *(F 11900)* **CRAWLING UP A HILL. / MR. JAMES** [ ] [–]

— MAYALL retained only McVIE, and recruited **ROGER DEAN** – guitar replaced WATSON **HUGHIE FLINT** – drums (ex-BLUES SYNDICATE) repl. HART

Feb 65. (7"; by JOHN MAYALL) *(F 12120)* **CROCODILE WALK. / BLUES CITY SHAKEDOWN** [ ] [–]

Mar 65. (lp; by JOHN MAYALL) *(LK 4680)* **JOHN MAYALL PLAYS JOHN MAYALL (live at Klook's Kleek)** [ ] [–]
– Crawling up a hill / I wanna teach you everything / When I'm gone / I need your love / The hoot owl / R&B time; Night train – Lucille / Crocodile walk / What's the matter with you / Doreen / Runaway / Heartache / Chicago line. *(cd-iss. Jun88 on 'London'; 820 536-2)*

— **ERIC CLAPTON** (b.30 Mar'45, Ripley, England) – guitar, vocals (ex-YARDBIRDS) repl. DEAN

Immediate Immediate

Oct 65. (7") *(IM 012)* *<502>* **I'M YOUR WITCHDOCTOR. / TELEPHONE BLUES** [ ] [ ]
(re-iss. Sep67 by JOHN MAYALL and the BLUESBREAKERS with ERIC CLAPTON; IM 051)

— (a month earlier CLAPTON departed to join The GONADS.) (he was repl. by ?) **JACK BRUCE** (b.14 May'43, Lanarkshire, Scotland) – bass (ex-GRAHAM BOND ORGANISATION) repl. McVIE

— MAYALL's band were now FLINT, McVIE and CLAPTON again. (BRUCE joined MANFRED MANN)

Decca London

Jul 66. (lp; mono/stereo; by JOHN MAYALL WITH ERIC CLAPTON) *(LK 4804)* *<LL3/PS 492>* **BLUES BREAKERS WITH ERIC CLAPTON** [6] [ ]
– All your love / Hideaway / Little girl / Another man / Double crossin' time / What'd I say / Key to love / Parchman farm / Have you heard / Ramblin' on my mind; (a) Steppin' out – (b) It ain't right. *(re-iss. 1969 mono/stereo; LK/SLK 4804) <US re-iss. 1985 on 'Mobile Fidelity'; MFSL 183> (cd-iss. Feb89; 800 086-2) (re-iss. Aug90 on 'Deram' cd/lp; 800 086-2/-1)*

Sep 66. (7"; A-side solo) *(F 12490)* *<20016>* **PARCHMAN FARM. / KEY TO LOVE** [ ] [ ]

Nov 66. (7") *<20024>* **ALL YOUR LOVE. / HIDEAWAY** [–] [ ]

— (Jul66) **PETER GREEN** (b. PETER GREENBAUM, 29 Oct'46) – guitar(on above b-side) repl. CLAPTON who formed CREAM

— (Sep66) **AYNSLEY DUNBAR** – drums (ex-MOJOS) repl. FLINT who later formed McGUINNESS FLINT

Oct 66. (7"; as JOHN MAYALL'S BLUESBREAKERS & PETER GREEN) *(F 12506)* **LOOKING BACK. / SO MANY ROADS** [ ] [–]

Oct 66. (7") *(F 12545)* **SITTING IN THE RAIN. / OUT OF REACH** [ ] [ ]

Feb 67. (lp; mono/stereo) *(LK/SKL 4853)* *<PS 502>* **A HARD ROAD** [10] [ ]
– A hard road / It's over / You don't love me / The stumble / Another kinda love / Hit the highway / Leaping Christine / Dust my blues / There's always work / The same way / The super natural / Top of the hill / Someday after a while (you'll be sorry) / Living alone.

Mar 67. (7"; as BLUESBREAKERS) *(F 12588)* **CURLY. / RUBBER DUCK** [ ] [ ]

Apr 67. (7"ep) *(DFE-R 8673)* **BLUESBREAKERS WITH PAUL BUTTERFIELD** [ ] [ ]

— **MICK FLEETWOOD** (b.24 Jun'47, Redruth, England) – drums repl. MICKEY WALLER who had repl. DUNBAR (to JEFF BECK GROUP) (others still in band MAYALL, GREEN and McVIE)

Apr 67. (7") *(F 12621)* **DOUBLE TROUBLE. / IT HURTS ME TOO** [ ] [ ]

— added **TERRY EDMONDS** – rhythm guitar, (for Jun67 only before he joined FERRIS WHEEL) / **MICK TAYLOR** (b.17 Jan'48, Welwyn Garden City, England) – guitar, vocals (ex-GODS) repl. PETER who formed FLEETWOOD MAC / **KEEF HARTLEY** (b. 8 Mar'44, Preston, England) – drums (ex-ARTWOODS) repl. MICK who formed FLEETWOOD MAC / added **CHRIS MERCER + RIP KANT** – saxophones

Sep 67. (lp; mono/stereo) *(LK/SKL 4890)* *<PS 529>* **CRUSADE** [8] [ ]
– Oh pretty woman / Stand back baby / My time after a while / Snowy wood / Man of stone / Tears in my eyes / Driving sideways / The death of J.B. Lenoir / I can't quit you baby / Streamline / Me and my woman / Checkin' up on my baby.

— **MAYALL** retained **TAYLOR, HARTLEY** and **MERCER,** bringing in **PAUL WILLIAMS** – bass (ex-ZOOT MONEY) repl. McVIE who also joined FLEETWOOD MAC / **DICK HECKSTALL-SMITH** (b.26 Sep'34, Ludlow, England) – saxophone (ex-GRAHAM BOND) repl. KANT / added **HENRY LOWTHER** – trumpet

Sep 67. (7") *(F 12684)* **SUSPICIONS (part 1). / SUSPICIONS (part 2)** [ ] [–]

Sep 67. (7") *<20035>* **SUSPICIONS. / OH PRETTY WOMAN** [–] [ ]

— **KEITH TILLMAN** – bass repl. WILLIAMS

Dec 67. (7"; solo) *(F 12732)* *<20037>* **JENNY. / PICTURES ON THE WALL** [ ] [ ]

Jan 68. (lp; mono/stereo) *(LK/SKL 4918)* *<PS 570>* **THE DIARY OF A BAND VOL.1** (live interviews & chat) [27] Feb70 [93]
– Blood on the night / (chat; Edmonton cooks Ferry Inn) / I can't quit you baby / (Keef Hartley interview x2) / Anzio Annie / (John Mayall interview x2) / Snowy wood / The lesson / My own fault / God save the queen.

Jan 68. (lp; mono/stereo) *(LK/SKL 4919)* *<PS 589>* **THE DIARY OF A BAND VOL.2** (live interviews & chat) <US-title 'JOHN MAYALL LIVE IN EUROPE'> [28] Apr71 [ ]
– (Gimme some lovin') / The train / Crying shame / (chat); local boy makes good / Help me / Blues in Bb / Soul of a short fat man.

Feb 68. (7") **BROKEN WINGS. / SONNY BOY BLUE** [–] [ ]

— **TONY REEVES** – bass repl. ANDY FRASER (to FREE) who had repl. TILLMAN / **JON HISEMAN** (b.21 Jun'44) – drums (ex-GRAHAM BOND, ex-GEORGIE FAME) repl. HARTLEY (to solo)

Jun 68. (lp; mono/stereo) *(LK/SKL 4945)* *<PS 537>* **BARE WIRES** [3] [59]
– Where did I belong / I start walking / Open up a new door / Fire / I know now / Look in the mirror / I'm a stranger / Hartley quits / No reply / Killing time / She's too young / Sandy. *(cd-iss. Jun88 on 'London'; 820 538-2)*

Jun 68. (7") *(F 12792)* **NO REPLY. / SHE'S TOO YOUNG** [ ] [ ]

— **MAYALL** only retained **MICK TAYLOR / COLIN ALLEN** – drums (ex-ZOOT MONEY) repl. HISEMAN who formed COLOSSEUM / **STEVE THOMPSON** – bass repl. REEVES. (he & HECKSTALL-SMITH also formed above) (also note MERCER left going into sessions and LOWTHER joined KEEF HARLEY BAND)

Nov 68. (7") *(F 12846)* **THE BEAR. / 2401** [ ] [ ]

Dec 68. (lp; mono/stereo) *(LK/SKL 4972)* *<PS 545>* **BLUES FROM LAUREL CANYON** [33] [68]
– Vacation / Walking on sunset / Laurel Canyon home / 2401 / Ready to ride / Medicine man / Somebody's acting like a child / The bear / Miss James / First time alone / Long gone midnight / Fly tomorrow. *(cd-iss. Jan88 on 'London'; 820 539-2)*

Dec 68. (7") **WALKING ON SUNSET. / LIVING ALONE** [–] [ ]

JOHN MAYALL

(his new band played without a drummer) **DUSTER BENNETT** – guitar, vocals repl. TAYLOR who joined ROLLING STONES / **JON MARK** (b. Cornwall, England) – guitar / **JOHNNY ALMOND** (b.20 Jul'46, Enfield, England) – saxophone repl. ALLEN who joined STONE THE CROWS / (after below lp **ALEX DMOCHOWSKI** – bass repl. THOMPSON who joined STONE THE CROWS)

Polydor Polydor

Oct 69. (lp; mono/stereo) *(582/583 571) <PD 4004>* **THE TURNING POINT (live 1969)** 11 Sep69 32
– The laws must change / Saw mill Gulch road / I'm gonna fight for you J.B. / So hard to share / California / Thoughts about Roxanne / California / Room to move. *(re-iss. May82 lp)(c; 2485 222)(3201 294) (cd-iss. Aug87; 823 305) (cd re-iss. Aug92 on 'Beat Goes On'; BGOCD 145)*

Oct 69. (7") *(56544) <14004>* **DON'T WASTE MY TIME. / DON'T PICK A FLOWER** 81

Jan 70. (7") **ROOM TO MOVE. / SAW MILL GULCH ROAD** -

— **LARRY TAYLOR** – bass deputised for the ill THOMPSON. (DMOCHOWSKI tour)

Mar 70. (lp) *(583 580) <PD 4010>* **EMPTY ROOMS** 9 33
– Don't waste my time / Plan your revolution / Don't pick a flower / Something new / People cling together / Waiting for the right time / Thinking of my woman / Counting the days / When I go / Many miles apart / To a princess / Lying in my bed.

May 70. (7") *(2066 021)* **THINKING OF MY WOMAN. / PLAN YOUR REVOLUTION** -

— MAYALL's completely new band of US musicians **HARVEY MANDEL** (b.11 Mar'45, Detroit, Michigan) – guitar (ex-CANNED HEAT) repl. MARK who formed MARK-ALMOND / **DON 'SUGURCANE' HARRIS** – vocals (ex-FRANK ZAPPA) repl. ALMOND (as above) / **LARRY TAYLOR** – bass finally repl. DMOCHOWSKI

Dec 70. (lp) *(2425 020) <PD 4022>* **U.S.A. UNION** 50 Oct70 22
– Nature's disappearing / You must be crazy / Night flyer / Off the road / Possessive emotions / Where did my legs go / Took the car / Crying / My pretty girl / Deep blue sea.

Jan 71. (7") **NATURE'S DISAPPEARING. / MY PRETTY GIRL** -

— Next reunified MAYALL with nearly all old BLUESBREAKERS + new US musicians

Jun 71. (d-lp) *(2657 005) <PD 3002>* **BACK TO THE ROOTS** 31 Apr71 52
– Prisons on the road / My children / Accidental suicide / Groupie girl / Blue fox / Home again / Television eye / Marriage madness / Looking at tomorrow / Dream with me / Full speed ahead / Mr. Censor man / Force of nature / Boogie Albert / Goodbye December / Unanswered questions / Devil's tricks / Travelling.

— MAYALL retained only LARRY TAYLOR and recruited **JERRY McGEE** – guitar (ex-VENTURES) to replace MANDEL (who formed own band) and HARRIS

Nov 71. (lp) *(2425 085) <PD 5012>* **MEMORIES**
– Memories / Wish I knew a woman / Back from Korea / Home in a tree / Separate ways / The fighting line / Grandad / The city / Nobody cares / Play the harp.

Feb 72. (7") **NOBODY CARES. / PLAY THE HARP** -

— **MAYALL** and **TAYLOR** brought in a drummer! – **RON SELICO / plus FREDDY ROBINSON** – guitar to repl. McGEE / added **BLUE MITCHELL** – trumpet / **CLIFFORD SOLOMON** – saxophone

May 72. (lp) *(2425 103) <PD 5027>* **JAZZ-BLUES FUSION (live)** 64
– Country road / Mess around / Good time boogie / Change your ways / Dry throat / Exercise in c-major for harmonica, bass and shufflers / Got to be this way.

— **VICTOR GASKIN** – bass repl. LARRY / **KEEF HARTLEY** – drums returned to repl. RON

— added on next **CHARLES OWEN** – flute / **FRED JACKSON** + **ERNIE WATTS** – saxophones

Jan 73. (lp) *(2391 047) <PD 5036>* **MOVING ON** Oct72
– (a brief introduction by Bill Cosby) / Worried mind / Keep our country green / Christmas 71 / Things go wrong / Do it / Moving on / Red sky / Reasons / High pressure living.

Jan 73. (7") **MOVING ON. / KEEP OUR COUNTRY GREEN** -

Nov 73. (d-lp) *(2683 036) <PD 3005>* **TEN YEARS ARE GONE** Sep73
– Ten years are gone / Driving till the break of day / Drifting / Better pass you by / California campground / Undecided / Good looking stranger / I still care / Don't hang me up / (introduction) / Sitting here thinking / Harmonica free form / Burning Sun / Dark of the night.

Nov 74. (7") **GASOLINE BLUES. / BRAND NEW BAND** -

Dec 74. (lp) *(2391 141) <PD 6030>* **THE LATEST EDITION**
– Gasoline blues / Perfect peace / Going to take my time / Deep down feelings / Troubled times / The pusher man / One of the few / Love song / Little kitchen / A crazy game.

Feb 75. (7") **LET ME GIVE. / PASSING THROUGH** -

— MAYALL brought back **LARRY TAYLOR** and **SUGERCANE HARRIS** plus new members **DEE McKINNIE** – vocals / **RICK VITO** – guitar / **JAY SPELL** – keyboards / **SOKO / RICHARDSON** – drums

A.B.C. A.B.C.

Mar 75. (lp) *(ABCL 5115) <6019>* **NEW YEAR, NEW BAND, NEW COMPANY**
– Sitting on the outside / Can't get home / Step in the sun / To match the wind / Sweet Scorpio / Driving on / Taxman blues / So much to do / My train time / Respectively yours.

Apr 75. (7") **STEP IN THE SUN. / AL GOLDSTEIN BLUES** -

— **MAYALL** now totally solo.

Nov 75. (lp) *(ABCL 5142) <ABCD 926>* **TIME EXPIRED, NOTICE TO APPEAR**
– Lil boogie in the afternoon / Mess of love / That love / The boy most likely to succeed / Who's next who's now / Hail to the man who lives alone / There will be a way / Just knowing you is a pleasure / A hard day's night / Oldtime blues. *(cd-iss. Apr94 on 'M.C.A.'; MCAD 22070)*

— His following albums feature session musicians.

Apr 76. (lp) *(ABCL 5187) <ABCD 958>* **A BANQUET OF BLUES**
– Sunshine / You can't put me down / I got somebody / Turn me loose / Seven days too long / Table top girl / Lady / Fantasyland. *(cd-iss. Apr94 on 'M.C.A.'; MCAD 22075)*

May 76. (7") *<12216>* **SUNSHINE. / TURN ME LOOSE** -

Apr 77. (lp) *(ABCL 5126) <ABCD 992>* **LOTS OF PEOPLE (live)**
– (spoken introduction by Red Holloway) / Changes in the wind / Burning down / Play the harp / A helping hand / I got to get down with you / He's a travelling man / Separate ways / Room to move. *(cd-iss. Apr94 on 'M.C.A.'; MCAD 22073)*

— now with **JAMES QUILL SMITH** – vocals, guitar / **STEVE THOMPSON** – bass / **SOKO RICHARDSON** – drums / and a brass section

Feb 78. (lp) *<ABCD 1039>* **A HARD CORE PACKAGE** -
– Rock and roll hobo / Do I please you / Disconnected line / An old sweet picture / The last time / Make up your mind / Arizona bound / Now and then / Goodnight dreams / Give me a chance. *(cd-iss. Apr94 on 'M.C.A.'; MCAD 22071)*

— now with loads of session people.

D.J.M. D.J.M.

May 79. (lp) *(DJF 20556) <23>* **BOTTOM LINE**
– Bottom line / Dreamboat / Desert flower / I'm gonna do it / Revival / Game of love / Celebration / Come with me.

Jul 79. (7") *(DJS 10918)* **BOTTOM LINE. / DREAMBOAT**

Dec 79. (lp) *(DJF 20564) <29>* **NO MORE INTERVIEWS**
– Hard going up / A bigger slice of pie / Falling / Take me home tonight / Sweet honey bee / Stars in the night / Consideration / Gypsy lady / Wild new lover.

— now with **SMITH, RICHARDSON** + **KEVIN McCORMICK** – bass / **MAGGIE PARKER** – vox

May 81. (lp) *(DJF2/DJH4 0570)* **ROAD SHOW BLUES**
– Why worry / Road show / Mama talk to your daughter / A big man / Lost and gone / Mexico City / John Lee boogie / Reaching for a mountain / Baby what you want me to do. *(re-iss. Jun88 on 'Thunderbolt' lp/cd; THBL/CDTB 060)*

Jun 81. (7") **JOHN LEE BOOGIE. / WHY WORRY. / MAMA TALK TO YOUR DAUGHTER**

— **MAYALL'S** new line-up featured **COCO MONTAYA** + **WALTER TROUT** – guitar / **BOBBY HAYNES** – bass / **JOE YUELE** – drums

P.R.T. GNP Crescend

May 86. (lp/c) *(NCP/ZCNCP 709) <GNP S/5 2184>* **BEHIND THE IRON CURTAIN** (rec.1984) 1985
– Somebody's acting like a child / Rolling with the blues / The laws must change / Parchman farm / Have you heard / Fly tomorrow / Steppin' out. *(cd-iss. Dec95 on 'GNP Crescendo';)*

— After couple of years out of the studio he returned Spring '87. with famous guests **MICK TAYLOR, JOHN McVIE**, etc.

Charly Entente

Dec 88. (cd) *(CDCHARLY 202)* **CHICAGO LINE**
– Chicago line / Gimme one more day / One life to live / The last time / Dream about the blues / Fascination lover / Cold blooded woman / The dirty dozen / Tears came rollin' down / Life in the jungle.

— **FREEBO** – bass repl.HAYNES + TROUT

Island Island

Apr 90. (cd) *(CID/ICT/ILPS 9958) <842795>* **A SENSE OF PLACE**
– I want to go / Congo square / Send me down to Vicksburg / Without her / Sensitive kind / Jacksboro highway / Let's work together / I can't complain / Black cat moon / Sugarcane / All my life. *(cd re-iss. Mar93; IMCD 167)*

— **RICK CORTES** – bass repl. FREEBO

— guests; **MICK TAYLOR / BUDDY GUY + ALBERT COLLINS**

Silvertone Jive

Apr 93. (cd/c/lp) *(ORE CD/C/LP 527) <41518>* **WAKE UP CALL** 61
– Mail order mystics / Maydell / I could cry / Wake up call / Loaded dice / Undercover agent for the blues / Light the fuse / Anything I can say / Nature's disappearing / I'm a sucker for love / Not at home / Ain't that lovin' you baby.

1993. (cd-s) **WAKE UP CALL /** –

— the BLUESBREAKERS were MAYALL, MICK TAYLOR, COCO MONTOYA + DON McMINN

Sep 93. (cd/c) *(AIM CD/C 1004)* **RETURN OF THE BLUESBREAKERS** –
– An eye for an eye / The same old blues / Rock & roll kitchen / Rock it in the pocket / Keep on rollin' / My time after awhile (live) / Ridin' on the Santa Fe (live) / Howlin' moon (live) / You never can be trusted (live) / Lookin' for Willie (live) / My babe / A long long way / Black cat moan.
(above on 'Aim' records)

— **BUDDY WHITTINGTON** – guitar; repl. MONTOYA

Feb 95. (cd/c/lp) *(ORE CD/C/LP 537) <41541>* **SPINNING COIN**
– When the Devil starts crying / Spinning coin / Ain't no brakeman / Double life feelings / Run / What passes for love / Fan the flames / Voodoo music / Long story short / No big hurry / Remember this. *(cd re-iss. Mar97; same)*

Apr 97. (cd) *(ORECD 547) <41605>* **BLUES FOR THE LOST DAYS**
– Dead city / Stone cold deal / All those heroes / Blues for the lost days / Trenches / One in a million / How can you live like that / Some other day / I don't mind / It ain't safe / Sen-say-shun / You are for real.

JOHN MAYALL & THE BLUESBREAKERS

— (see above BLUESBREAKERS line-up)

Eagle Red Ink

Apr 99. (cd) *(EAGCD 077) <597>* **PADLOCK ON THE BLUES**
– Don't turn your back / Padlock on the blues / Hard road / Somebody's watching / Always a brand new road / My country girl / The strip / I've got to talk to you / Dancing shoes / Bad dream catcher / When the blues are bad / Ain't no surrender / White line fever.

Eagle Eagle

Apr 01. (cd; as JOHN MAYALL & FRIENDS) *(EAGCD 150) <18474>* **ALONG FOR THE RIDE** May01
– A world of hurt / Along for the ride / Put it right back / That's why I love you so / Yo yo man / If I don't get home / Testify / Early in the morning / Something about my baby / So many roads / World war blues / California / She don't play by the rules.

Aug 02. (cd) *(EAGCD 223) <59669>* **STORIES**
– Southside story / Dirty water / Feels just like home / Kids got the blues / The witching hour / Oh, Leadbelly / Demons in the night / Pride and faith / Kokomo / Romance classified / I wished I had / Pieces and parts / I thought I heard the Devil / The mists of time.
below friends:- ERIC CLAPTON / CHRIS BARBER / MICK TAYLOR

Nov 03. (d-cd; w/ FRIENDS) *(EAGCD 246) <20017>* **70th BIRTHDAY CONCERT**
– Grits ain't groceries / Jacksboro highway / Southside story / Kids got the blues / Dirty water / Somebody acting like a child / Blues for the lost days / Walking on sunset / Oh, pretty woman / No big hurry / Please Mr. Lofton / Hide away / All your love / Have you heard / (I'm your) Hoochie coochie man / I'm tore down / It ain't right / California / Talk to your daughter.

— added **TOM CANNING** – keyboards / **HANK VAN SICKLE** – bass

Jun 05. (cd) *(EAGCD 296) <20069>* **ROAD DOGS**
– Road dogs / Short wave radio / So glad / Forty days / To heal the pain / Burned bridges / Snake eye / Kona village / Beyond control / Chaos in the neighborhood / You'll survive / Awesome and spellbound / With you / Brumwell's beat / Scrambling.

– (selective) compilations, etc. –

Aug 66. (7"ltd; by JOHN MAYALL and ERIC CLAPTON)
Purdah; (45-3502) **LONELY HEARTS. / BERNARD JENKINS** –

Nov 67. (lp) *Ace Of Clubs; (SCL 1245) / London; <PS 543>* **THE BLUES ALONE** (nearly all instruments himself) 24
– Brand new start / Please don't tell / Down the line / Sonny Boy blow / Marsha's mood / No more tears / Catch that train / Cancelling out / Harp man / Brown sugar / Broken wings / Don't kick me. *(cd-iss. Jun88 on 'London'; 820 535-2)*

Aug 69. (lp; mono/stereo) *Decca; (LK/SKL 5010) / London; <562>* **LOOKING BACK** 14 79
– Mr. James / Blues city shakedown / They call it stormy Monday / So many roads / Looking back / Sitting in the rain / It hurts me too / Double trouble / Suspicions (part 2) / Jenny / Picture on the wall. *(cd-iss. Jan89 on 'London'; 820 331-2)*

Apr 86. (d-lp/c/cd) *Castle; (CCS LP/MC/CD 137)* **THE COLLECTION** –
– Key to love / Hideaway / Ramblin' on my mind / All your love / They call it stormy Monday / Hoochie coochie man / Crocodile walk (1st version) / Crawling up a hill / Marsha's mood / Sonny Boy blow / Looking back / A hard road / The supernatural / You don't love me / Leaping Christine / Suspicions (part 2) / Picture on the wall / The death of J.B. Lenoir / Sandy / The bear / Walking the sunset / Fly tomorrow.

Apr 86. (lp) *Decal; (LIK 1)* **SOME OF MY BEST FRIENDS ARE BLUES** –

Mar 92. (cd/c) *Charly; (CD/TC BM 4)* **LIFE IN THE JUNGLE** (rec.'84)

Apr 94. (cd) *One Way; (OW 30008)* **THE 1982 REUNION CONCERT (live)** –
(re-iss. Nov02 on 'Repertoire'; REP 4393)

Apr 99. (d-cd) *Eagle; (EDMCD 071)* **THE MASTERS**

Apr 99. (cd) *Indigo; (IGOXCD 102)* **ROCK THE BLUES TONIGHT** (live in Canada 1971)

Apr 99. (cd) *Eagle; (EAMCD 70)* **LIVE AT THE MARQUEE 1969**

Nov 99. (cd) *Deram; (844785-2)* **AS IT ALL BEGAN: THE BEST OF JOHN MAYALL & THE BLUESBREAKERS 1964-69**

May 00. (cd) *Beat Goes On; (BGOCD 492)* **NEW YEAR NEW BAND NEW COMPANY / LOTS OF PEOPLE**

Jun 00. (cd) *Beat Goes On; (BGOCD 493)* **A HARDCORE PACKAGE / THE LAST OF THE BRITISH BLUES**

Jun 00. (cd) *Beat Goes On; (BGOCD 495)* **NOTICE TO APPEAR / A BANQUET IN BLUES**

Mar 01. (cd) *Rialto; (RMCD 2322)* **THE JOHN MAYALL ARCHIVE**

Apr 01. (d-cd) *Universal; (AA314 549424-2)* **BACK TO THE ROOTS: A VERY SPECIAL DOUBLE ALBUM . . .**

May 01. (cd) *Silvertone; (059122-2)* **THE BEST OF JOHN MAYALL**

May 01. (cd) *Silvertone; (ORECD 547)* **BLUES FOR THE LOST DAYS**

Sep 01. (cd) *Deram; (882922-2)* **AN INTRODUCTION TO JOHN MAYALL AND THE BLUESBREAKERS: STEPPIN' OUT**

Jan 03. (d-cd) *Castle; (CMDDD 639)* **ROCKIN' THE ROADSHOW**

Apr 03. (cd) *Movieplay Gold; (MPG 74070)* **LOST AND GONE**

Curtis MAYFIELD

Born: 3 Jun'42, Chicago, Illinois, USA. Immersed in music from an early age, MAYFIELD was a self-taught guitarist and lyricist, strongly influenced by the sounds of the Northern Jubilee Gospel Singers (a local group that included JERRY BUTLER). In 1957, BUTLER asked MAYFIELD to join a newly formed group, The ROOSTERS, who would soon evolve into The IMPRESSIONS under the management of Eddie Thomas. As a songwriter for the group, MAYFIELD had his first hit in '58 with 'FOR

YOUR PRECIOUS LOVE', prior to BUTLER's departure. The IMPRESSIONS scored their first Top 20 hit in '60 with 'GYPSY WOMAN', MAYFIELD's prolific writing career taking off via a new contract with 'A.B.C.' records. During the 60's, he penned a wealth of hits, including 'WE'RE A WINNER', the lyrical content highlighting MAYFIELD's awareness of the civil rights movement and the increasing confidence and self-determination of the African-American community. The decade also saw the soul man writing for record labels such as Okeh and Veejay as well as Chicago based artists including GENE CHANDLER and MAJOR LANCE. This work inspired CURTIS to set up his own label, 'Curtom' (distributed through 'Buddah'), releasing material by a number of successful acts, among them DONNY HATHAWAY. Leaving The IMPRESSIONS to go solo in 1970, his critically acclaimed self-titled debut set was characterised by his trademark funky organic sounds blended with socially aware lyrics. This album was followed by 'ROOTS', a record which included the groove-laden, 'KEEP ON KEEPING ON'. The turning point from acclaimed artist to international stardom arrived in 1972 when MAYFIELD was asked to score and perform the soundtrack for the blaxploitation film, 'SUPERFLY'. The movie was a massive hit, MAYFIELD's soundtrack complementing the film perfectly and producing hits in the form of the title track and 'FREDDIE'S DEAD'. Still regarded as one of contemporary black music's most momentous recordings, 'SUPERFLY' represented the pinnacle of MAYFIELD's solo career. Although the man released some above average albums in the 70's and continued to oversee the creative development of the 'Curtom' imprint (now distributed by 'Warners'), he didn't really come close to matching the soundtrack's power. Arguably his finest post-'Superfly' work, 'SHORT EYES' was another soundtrack, written for a movie in which MAYFIELD also had an acting role. The 80's saw MAYFIELD touring regularly and scoring intermittent hits, a reunion tour with The IMPRESSIONS seen the return of his old sparring partner, BUTLER. The beginning of the 90's saw tragedy strike when in August 1990, MAYFIELD was hit by a lighting rig that had been dislodged by high winds during an open air concert in Brooklyn; he was paralysed from the neck down. The next few years saw MAYFIELD elected into the Rock And Roll Hall Of Fame and various lifetime achievement awards bestowed on him, so it was all the more remarkable when his comeback album, 'NEW WORLD ORDER', was released in '96. The recording process involved was time consuming, although the result was worth the wait, MAYFIELD achieving his best solo work since the early 70's. Tragically, it would be CURTIS' swansong as the great man died of (a long suffering) cancer on Boxing Day, 1999.

Album rating: CURTIS (*7) / CURTIS/LIVE! (*6) / ROOTS (*7) / SUPERFLY (*9) / BACK TO THE WORLD (*7) / CURTIS IN CHICAGO (*6) / SWEET EXORCIST (*6) / GOT TO FIND A WAY (*5) / THERE'S NO PLACE LIKE AMERICA TODAY (*6) / GIVE, GET, TAKE AND HAVE (*5) / NEVER SAY YOU CAN'T SURVIVE (*4) / SHORT EYES soundtrack (*6) / DO IT ALL NIGHT (*5) / HEARTBEAT (*6) / THE RIGHT COMBINATION with Linda Clifford (*4) / SOMETHING TO BELIEVE IN (*4) / LOVE IS THE PLACE (*5) / HONESTY (*7) / WE COME IN PEACE WITH A MESSAGE OF LOVE (*4) / LIVE IN EUROPE (*5) / TAKE IT TO THE STREET (*4) / A MAN LIKE CURTIS – THE BEST OF compilation (*8) / THE RETURN OF SUPERFLY soundtrack w/ Various Artists (*5) / NEW WORLD ORDER (*6)

CURTIS MAYFIELD – vocals, guitar, keyboards + live band

Buddah Curtom

Nov 70. (7") *(2011 055) <1955>* **(DON'T WORRY) IF THERE'S A HELL BELOW WE'RE ALL GOING TO GO. / THE MAKINGS OF YOU** [ ] [29]

Feb 71. (lp) *(2318 015) <8005>* **CURTIS** [ ] Sep70 [19]
– (Don't worry) If there's a Hell below we're all going to go / The other side of town / The makings of you / We the people who are darker than blue / Move on up / Miss Black America / Wild and free / Give it up. *(re-iss. Oct74; BDLH 5005) (re-iss. Jun76 on 'Warners'; K 56252) (cd-iss. Nov93 on 'Movieplay Gold'; MPG 74026) (re-iss. Mar94 on 'Curtom' cd/c; CUR 2012 CD/MC)*

May 71. (7") *<1960>* **GIVE IT UP. / BEAUTIFUL BROTHER OF MINE** [–] [ ]

Jun 71. (7"m) *(2011 080)* **MOVE ON UP. / GIVE IT UP / BEAUTIFUL BROTHER OF MINE** [12] [–]

Aug 71. (d-lp) *(2659 004) <8008>* **CURTIS / LIVE! (live)** [ ] May71 [21]
– Mighty mighty (spade and Whitey) / I plan to stay a believer / We're a winner (rap) / We've only just begun / Check out your mind / People get ready / Stare and stare / Gypsy woman / The makings of you / We the people who are darker than blue / (Don't worry) If there's a Hell below we're all going to go / Stone junkie. *(re-iss. Oct74; BDLP 2001) (re-iss. Jun76 on 'Warners'; K 66047) (d-cd-iss. Mar94 on 'Movieplay Gold'; MPG 74176) (d-cd-iss. Jun94 on 'Curtom'; CPCD 8038)*

Sep 71. (7") *<1963>* **MIGHTY MIGHTY (SPADE AND WHITEY) (live). /** [–] [ ]

Nov 71. (7") *(2011 101)* **WE GOT TO HAVE PEACE. / PEOPLE GET READY** [ ] [–]

Dec 71. (7") *<1966>* **GET DOWN. / WE'RE A WINNER** [–] [69]

Jan 72. (lp) *(2318 065) <8009>* **ROOTS** [ ] Oct71 [40]
– Get down / Keep on keeping on / Underground / We got to have peace / Beautiful brother of mine / Now you're gone / Love to keep you in my mind. *(re-iss. Oct74; BDLH 5006) (re-iss. Jun76 on 'Warners'; K 56249) (cd-iss. Nov93 on 'Movieplay Gold'; MPG 74027) (cd re-iss. Jun94 on 'Charly'; CPCD 8037)*

Feb 72. (7") *<1968>* **WE GOT TO HAVE PEACE. / WE'RE A WINNER** [–] [ ]

Apr 72. (7") *<1972>* **BEAUTIFUL BROTHER OF MINE. / LOVE TO KEEP YOU IN MY MIND** [–] [ ]

May 72. (7") *(2011 119)* **KEEP ON KEEPING ON. / STONE JUNKIE** [ ] [–]

Jun 72. (7") *<1974>* **MOVE ON UP. / UNDERGROUND** [–] [ ]

Sep 72. (7") *(2011 141) <1975>* **FREDDIE'S DEAD (theme from "Superfly"). / UNDERGROUND** [ ] Aug72 [4]

Nov 72. (lp) *(2318 065) <CRS 8014ST>* **SUPERFLY (Soundtrack)** [26] Aug72 [1]
– Little child runnin' wild / Pusherman / Freddie's dead / Junkie chase / Give me your love (love song) / Eddie you should know better / No thing on me (cocaine song) / Think / Superfly / Superfly theme: Freddie's dead / Superfly (mix). *(re-iss. Nov74; BDLH 4018) (re-iss. Aug79 on 'R.S.O.'; RSS 5) (re-iss. Jun88 on 'Curtom' cd/c/lp; CD/ZC+/CUR 2002) (cd re-iss. Jun94 on 'Charly'; CPCD 8039) (d-cd iss.Jun98 on 'Charly'+=; CDNEW 1302)* – (bonus tracks, etc.) *(cd re-iss. Mar01 on 'Snapper'; SNAP 005CD) <(d-cd iss.May02 on 'Snapper'+=; SNAD 507CD)> (d-cd-iss. Feb03 on 'Black Box'; BB 257) <lp re-iss. Jun03; same as>*

Nov 72. (7") *<1978>* **SUPERFLY. / UNDERGROUND** [–] [8]

Feb 73. (7") *(2011 156)* **SUPERFLY. / GIVE ME YOUR LOVE (LOVE SONG)** [ ] [–]

Jul 73. (7") *<1987>* **FUTURE SHOCK. / THE OTHER SIDE OF TOWN** [–] [39]

Sep 73. (lp) *(2318 085) <8015>* **BACK TO THE WORLD** [ ] Jun73 [16]
– Back to the world / Future shock / Right on for the darkness / If I were only a child again / Can't say nothin' / Keep on trippin' / Future song (love of a good woman, love of a good man). *(re-iss. Oct74; BDLH 5008) (re-iss. Jun76 on 'Warners'; K 56251) (cd-iss. Nov93 on 'Movieplay Gold'; MPG 74029) (cd re-iss. Jun94 on 'Charly'; CPCD 8040)*

Oct 73. (7") *(2011 187)* **BACK TO THE WORLD. / THE OTHER SIDE OF TOWN** [ ] [–]

Oct 73. (7") *<1991>* **IF I WERE ONLY A CHILD AGAIN. / THINK** [–] [71]

Jan 74. (7") *<1993>* **CAN'T SAY NOTHIN'. / FUTURE SHOCK** [–] [88]

Mar 74. (lp) *(2318 091) <8018>* **CURTIS IN CHICAGO (TV Soundtrack)** [ ] Nov73 [ ]
– Superfly / For your precious love / I'm so proud / Once in my life (IMPRESSIONS) / Preacher man (IMPRESSIONS) / Duke of Earl (GENE CHANDLER) / Love oh love (LEROY HUTSON) / Amen. *(re-iss. Oct74; BDLH 5009) (re-iss. Jun76 on 'Curtom'; K 56250) (cd-iss. Oct94 on 'Charly'; CPCD 8046)*

Aug 74. (lp) *(2318 099) <8601>* **SWEET EXORCIST** [ ] May74 [39]
– Ain't got time / Sweet exorcist / To be invisible / Power to the people / Kung Fu / Suffer / Make me believe in you. *(re-iss. Oct74; BDLH 5001) (re-iss. Aug76 on 'Curtom'; K 56284) (cd-iss. Oct94 on 'Charly'; CPCD 8047)*

Aug 74. (7") *(BDS 402) <1999>* **KUNG FU. / RIGHT ON FOR THE DARKNESS** [ ] Jun74 [40]

Oct 74. (7") *<2005>* **SWEET EXORCIST. / SUFFER** [–] [ ]

Jan 75. (lp) *(BDLP 4029) <8604>* **GOT TO FIND A WAY** [ ] Nov74 [76]
– Love me (right in the pocket) / So you don't love me / A prayer / Mother's son / Cannot find a way / Ain't no love lost. *(cd-iss. Oct94 on 'Charly'; CPCD 8048)*

CURTIS MAYFIELD

Mar 75. (7") *(BDS 426)* <2006> **MOTHER'S SON. / LOVE ME RIGHT IN THE POCKET**

Jun 75. (7") **STASH THAT BUTT, SUCKER. / ZANZIBAR** –
(above single issued on 'Columbia')

— His band from this period onwards **GARY THOMPSON** – guitar / **RICH TUFO** – keyboards / **LUCKY SCOTT** – bass / **QUINTON JOSEPH** – drums

Aug 75. (lp) *(BDLP 4033)* <5001> **THERE'S NO PLACE LIKE AMERICA TODAY** Jun75
– Billy Jack / When seasons change / So in love / Jesus / Blue Monday people / Hard times / Love to the people. *(re-iss. Jan89 on 'Curtom' cd/c/lp; CD/ZC+/CUR 2003)*

Sep 75. (7") *<0105>* **SO IN LOVE. / HARD TIMES** – 67

Jul 76. (7") *<0118>* **ONLY YOU BABE. / LOVE TO THE PEOPLE** –

Jul 76. (lp) *(BDLP 4042)* *<5007>* **GIVE, GET, TAKE AND HAVE** Jun76
– In your arms again / This love is sweet / P.S. I love you / Party night / Get a little bit (give, get, take and have) / Soul music / Only you babe / Mr. Welfare you. *(re-iss. Mar94 on 'Curtom' cd/c; CUR 2011 CD/MC) (cd re-iss. Jun94 on 'Charly'; CPCD 8070)*

Sep 76. (7") *<0122>* **PARTY NIGHT. / P.S. I LOVE YOU** –

Curtom Curtom

Mar 77. (7") *<0125>* **SHOW ME LOVE. / JUST WANT TO BE WITH YOU** –

Mar 77. (lp) *(K 56352)* *<5013>* **NEVER SAY YOU CAN'T SURVIVE**
– Show me love / Just want to be with you / When we're alone / Never say you can't survive / I'm gonna win your love / All night long / When you used to be mine / Sparkle. *(re-iss. Mar94 on 'Curtom' cd/c; CUR 2010 CD/MC) (cd-iss. Oct94 on 'Charly'; CPCD 8049)*

Nov 77. (7") *<0131>* **DO DO WAP IS STRONG IN HERE. / NEED SOMEONE TO LOVE** –

Feb 78. (lp) *(K 56430)* *<5017>* **SHORT EYES (Soundtrack)** Nov77
– Do do wap is strong in here / Back against the wall / Need someone to love / A heavy dude / Short eyes / Freak, freak, free, free, free (*) / Break it down / Another fool in love / Father confessor. *(cd-iss. Jun96 on 'Charly'+= *; CPCD 8183)*

Jul 78. (7") *<0135>* **YOU ARE, YOU ARE. / GET A LITLE BIT (GIVE, GET, TAKE AND HAVE)** –

Sep 78. (7") *<0141>* **DO IT ALL NIGHT. / PARTY PARTY** –

Oct 78. (lp) *<5022>* **DO IT ALL NIGHT** –
– Do it all night / No goodbyes / Party party / Keeps me loving you / In love, in love, in love / You are, you are. *(cd-iss. Oct94 on 'Charly'; CPCD 8050)*

Nov 78. (7") *<0142>* **IN LOVE, IN LOVE, IN LOVE. / KEEPS ME LOVING YOU** –

Atlantic not iss.

Dec 78. (12") *(LV 1)* **NO GOODBYES. / PARTY PARTY** 65 –

— With various session people

R.S.O. R.S.O.

Mar 79. (7") *(RSO 28)* *<919>* **THIS YEAR. / ('A'instrumental)**

Sep 79. (lp) *(RSS 4)* *<3053>* **HEARTBEAT** Aug79 42
– Tell me, tell me (how ya like to be loved) / What is my woman for? / Between you baby and me / Victory / Over the hump / You better stop / You're so good to me / Heartbeat. *(cd-iss. Jun94 on 'Charly'; CPCD 8071)*

Aug 79. (7"; by LINDA CLIFFORD & CURTIS MAYFIELD) *<RSO 43)* *<941>* **BETWEEN YOU BABY AND ME. / YOU'RE SO GOOD TO ME**

Jun 80. (lp; by LINDA CLIFFORD & CURTIS MAYFIELD) *(2394 269)* *<3084>* **THE RIGHT COMBINATION**
– Rock to your socks / The right combination / I'm so proud / Ain't no love lost / It's lovin' time / Love's sweet sensation / Between you baby and me. *(cd-iss. Jun94 on 'Charly'; CPCD 8072)*

1980. (7"; by LINDA CLIFFORD & CURTIS MAYFIELD) *<1029>* **LOVE'S SWEET SENSATION. / ('A'instrumental)** –

1980. (7") *<1036>* **LOVE ME, LOVE ME NOW. / IT'S ALRIGHT** –

Sep 80. (lp) *(2394 271)* *<3077>* **SOMETHING TO BELIEVE IN** Jul80
– Something to believe in / Love me, love me now / Never let me go / Tripping out / People never give up / It's alright / Never stop loving me. *(re-iss. Oct89 on 'Curtom' lp/c/cd; CUR/+MC/CD 2005) (cd re-iss. Jun94 on 'Charly'; CPCD 8073) (cd re-iss. Oct94 on 'Curtom'; CUR 2005CD)*

Sep 80. (7") *<1046>* **TRIPPING OUT. / NEVER STOP LOVING** –

Oct 80. (7") *(RSO 68)* **IT'S ALRIGHT. / SUPERFLY** –

Epic Boardwal

1981. (lp) *<2601 6012>* **LOVE IS THE PLACE** – German –
– She don't let nobody (but me) / Toot an' toot an' toot / Baby doll / Love is the place / Just ease my mind / You mean everything to me / You get all my love / Come free your people,

1981. (7") *<122>* **SHE DON'T LET NOBODY (BUT ME). / YOU GET ALL MY LOVE** –

1981. (7") *<132>* **COME FREE YOUR PEOPLE. / TOOT AN' TOOT AN' TOOT** –

Oct 82. (7") *<155>* **HEY BABY (GIVE IT ALL TO ME). / SUMMER HOT** –

Mar 83. (lp/c) *(EPC/40 25317)* *<2601 6022>* **HONESTY** German
– Hey baby (give it all to me) / Still within your heart / Dirty laundry / Nobody but you / If you need me / What you gawn do? / Summer hot.

Mar 83. (7") *<169>* **DIRTY LAUNDRY. / NOBODY BUT YOU** –

not iss. C.R.C.

Sep 85. (lp) *<447>* **WE COME IN PEACE WITH A MESSAGE OF LOVE** –
(UK-iss.Feb91 on 'Curtom' lp/c/cd; CRC 2001/+MC/CD)

98.6 98.6

Nov 86. (7"/12") *(CURT 1/+T)* **BABY IT'S YOU. / BREAKIN' IN THE STREETS**

— In mid'87 he was credited on BLOW MONKEYS single 'Celebrate The Day'.

Capitol Capitol

1987. (lp; withdrawn) **LIVE IN LOS ANGELES (live)** – –

Ichiban Ichiban

Jun 88. (cd/c/lp) *(CD/ZC+/CUR 2901)* **LIVE IN EUROPE (live)**
– (intro) / Freddie's dead / We gotta have peace / People get ready / Move on up / Back to the world / Gypsy woman / Pusher man / We've only just begun / When seasons change / (Don't worry) If there's a Hell below we're all going to go.

Jul 88. (7"/12") *(CUR/12CUR 101)* **MOVE ON UP (live). / LITTLE CHILD RUNNIN' WILD (live)**

Curtom Arista

May 89. (7"; w/ FISHBONE) **HE'S A FLY GUY. / ('A'instrumental)** –

May 89. (7") *(7CUR 102)* **I MO GIT U SUCKA. / HE'S A FLY GUY** –
(12"+=/cd-s+=) *(12/CD CUR 102)* – ('A'extended).

Feb 90. (7"/12") *(7/12 CUR 106)* **HOMELESS. / PEOPLE NEVER GIVE UP**

Mar 90. (cd/c/lp) *(CD/ZC+/CUR 2008)* **TAKE IT TO THE STREET**
– Homeless / Got to be real / Do be down / Who was that lady / On and on / He's a fly guy / Don't push / I mo git u sucka. *(cd re-iss. Apr96 on 'Charly'; CPCD 8179)*

Jun 90. (7") *(7CUR 108)* **DO BE DOWN. / GOT TO BE REAL**
(12"+=) *(12CUR 108)* – ('A'extended) / ('A'-radio version).

— On the 13th August, 1990, while CURTIS prepared for a gig, a high wind brought down a lighting scaffold which struck him. This left him permanently paralysed from the neck downwards (his house subsequently burned down a month later!).

Capitol Capitol

Sep 90. (7"; as CURTIS MAYFIELD & ICE-T) *(CL 586)* **SUPERFLY 1990. / ('A'mix)** 48
(12"+=/cd-s+=) *(12/CD CL 586)* – ('A'mixes).

Nov 90. (cd/c/lp) *(CD/TC+/EST 2129)* *<C2/C4 94244>* **THE RETURN OF SUPERFLY** (soundtrack w/ Various Artists) Oct90
– Superfly 1990 (w/ ICE-T) / Showdown / Forbidden / Superfly 1990 (hip-hop instrumental) / For the love of you.

— CURTIS returned to the studio 1995/96 with session backing

Warners WEA I

Jan 97. (cd/c) *<(9362 46348-2/-4)>* **NEW WORLD ORDER** 44
– New world order / Ms. Martha / Back to living again / No one knows about a good thing (you don't have to cry) / Just a little bit of love / We people who are darker than blue / I believe in you / Here but I'm gone / It was love that we needed / The got dang song / The girl I find stays on my mind / Let's not forget / Oh so beautiful.

— on the 26th of December 1999, after suffering with cancer for a long time CURTIS died in an Atlanta hospital

— posthumously, CURTIS was credited on BRAN VAN 3000's mid-2001 UK hit, 'Astounded'

– compilations, others, etc. –

Nov 74. (lp) *Buddah; (BDLP 4015)* **MOVE ON UP – THE BEST OF CURTIS MAYFIELD** ☐ ☐
Nov 74. (7") *Buddah; (BDS 410)* **MOVE ON UP. / GIVE IT UP** ☐ –
Jan 83. (7") *Flashback; (FBS 23)* **MOVE ON UP. / (b-side by Melba Moore)** ☐ –
Feb 90. (cd/c) *Essential; (ESS CD/MC 003)* **PEOPLE GET READY (live At Ronnie Scott's)** ☐ –
(cd re-iss. 1993 on 'Castle'; CLACD 329)
Nov 90. (d-lp/c/cd) *Curtom; (CUR 22902/+MC/CD)* **OF ALL TIME – THE CLASSIC COLLECTION** ☐ –
Nov 92. (cd) *Music Collection; (MUSCD 007)* **A MAN LIKE CURTIS – THE BEST OF . . .** ☐ –
– Move on up / Superfly / (Don't worry) If there's a Hell below we're all gonna go / You are, you are / Give me your love / Never stop loving me / Tripping out / Soul music / This year / Ain't no love lost / Pusherman / Freddie's dead / Do do wop is strong in here / Hard times / In your arms again (shake it) / So in love.
Sep 93. (cd) *Traditional Line; (TL 001333)* **HARD TIMES** ☐ –
Jan 94. (cd) *Windsong; (WINDCD 052)* **BBC RADIO 1 LIVE IN CONCERT** ☐ –
May 94. (cd/c) *Laserlight; (1/7 2364)* **CURTIS MAYFIELD** ☐ –
Jun 94. (cd) *Charly; (CPCD 1211)* **POWER FOR THE PEOPLE** ☐ –
Aug 94. (cd) *Charly; (CPCD 8043)* **GROOVE ON UP** ☐ –
Nov 94. (cd) *Charly; (CPCD 8065)* **TRIPPING OUT** ☐ –
Feb 95. (d-cd) *Charly; (CPCD 8034)* **GET DOWN TO THE FUNKY GROOVE** ☐ –
Mar 96. (cd) *Sequel; (NEMCD 783)* **LOVE IS THE PLACE / HONESTY** ☐ –
Apr 96. (cd) *Audiophile; (APH 102802)* **MOVE ON UP** ☐ –
Apr 96. (cd) *Castle; (CCSCD 806)* **THE VERY BEST OF CURTIS MAYFIELD** ☐ –

— CURTIS also collaborated on other Film Soundtracks, 'CLAUDINE' in Aug74 with GLADYS KNIGHT & THE PIPS, 'LET'S DO IT AGAIN' in Sep76 with STAPLE SINGERS and 'SPARKLE' Oct76 with ARETHA FRANKLIN. There were also a few tribute cd's about the shops in the mid-90's.

Paul McCARTNEY

Born: JAMES PAUL McCARTNEY, 18 Jun'42, Liverpool, England. An integral part of The BEATLES throughout the 60's, he and JOHN LENNON were easily the greatest contemporary writing partnership of the 20th Century. The band officially split on the 11 April 1970, prior to issuing their final album, 'LET IT BE', (there was also a docu-film of the same name, detailing the last days of the fab four). Released three weeks previous was McCARTNEY's first solo outing, the eponymous 'McCARTNEY', which included backing from new wife, LINDA (who he married on the 12th of March '69). By virtue of its relative acoustic simplicity (PAUL played every instrument himself), the record remains one of the better releases from a time when self indulgence and wildly ambitious concepts were the order of the day. Though berated by critics at the time, the album contained one of PAUL's finer efforts in 'MAYBE I'M AMAZED', going on to top the American charts but being held off the UK No.1 by SIMON & GARFUNKEL's 'Bridge Over Troubled Water'. The following year, McCARTNEY scored a cross-Atlantic Top 5 with his debut solo single, 'ANOTHER DAY', and then took the unusual step of co-crediting his wife LINDA (though she did actually contribute keyboards, backing vocals and percussion) on the subsequent album, 'RAM' (1971). Sales wise, the album reversed the chart positions of its predecessor, spawning the whimsical US-only No.1 single, 'UNCLE ALBERT – ADMIRAL HALSEY'.'RAM' had also featured the drumming talents of DENNY SEIWELL who, together with ex-MOODY BLUES man, DENNY LAINE (guitar, vocals), would form one half of McCARTNEY's new group, WINGS, later that year. With the husband and wife duo of PAUL and LINDA completing the line-up, McCARTNEY hit an unprecedented critical low with WINGS's vaguely reggae-ish debut effort, 'WILDLIFE'. Unfazed, McCARTNEY took his band out on a low key colllege tour, beefing up the sound with the addition of HENRY McCULLOUGH (who had previously worked with JOE COCKER) on guitar and backing vocals. The next WINGS's release was the controversial (and surprisingly successful given its political sentiments) 'GIVE IRELAND BACK TO THE IRISH'. Annoyed at a radio ban, WINGS then put music to nursery rhyme with 'MARY HAD A LITTLE LAMB', a rather excessive anti-censorship statement that made the UK Top 10 but lost the band valuable credibility. The McCARTNEY's then underwent a series of drug busts and another pedantic BBC ban with their next hit, 'HI HI HI'. In Spring '73, PAUL McCARTNEY & WINGS topped the US charts with the single, 'MY LOVE', and another under par album, 'RED ROSE SPEEDWAY'. Following later that summer was the much more impressive 'LIVE AND LET DIE', a much covered McCARTNEY-penned theme song for the James Bond film of the same name. With the departure of SEIWELL and McCULLOUGH immediately prior to recording the fourth album, WINGS were reduced to a core of The McCARTNEY's and LAINE, one that endured for the remainder of the band's career. Going it alone, the trio surprisingly came up with the most successful album of their career, 'BAND ON THE RUN' (1973). Where before, McCARTNEY's compositions had been perfectly formed but lacking in substance, he silenced his critics with impassioned pop/rock of the highest calibre, notably on 'JET' and the title track. The album went on to sell over 6 million copies during its two year-plus stay in both the UK & US charts, PAUL finally proving his post-BEATLES mettle. The subsequent addition of JIMMY McCULLOCH and GEOFF BRITTON saw the band expanded to a 5-piece again, BRITTON only playing on one single, 'JUNIOR'S FARM'. His replacement was JOE ENGLISH, the new line-up recording the mediocre quasi-concept album, 'VENUS AND MARS' (1975). The album topped the American and British charts all the same, although the single 'LETTING GO' didn't even make the Top 40, a pattern that would continue into the late 70's and beyond. 'WINGS AT THE SPEED OF SOUND' (1976) gets points deducted for McCARTNEY's well intentioned but annoying insistence that each band member get a lead vocal although 'SILLY LOVE SONGS' and 'LET 'EM IN' were finely honed hit singles. The triple live set, 'WINGS OVER AMERICA' (1977), was impressive if overly long proof of the band's well deserved live reputation, showcasing McCARTNEY's vocal and multi-instrumentalist talents to often dazzling effect. In early 1977, the band were reduced to a trio once more following the departure of McCULLOCH and ENGLISH for The SMALL FACES and SEA LEVEL respectively. Incredibly, WINGS bounced back with their biggest single to date, the windswept sentimental indulgence that was 'MULL OF KINTYRE'. Blissfully oblivious to punk, McCARTNEY even employed a warts and all Scottish pipe band to give the song that 'authentic' Caledonian appeal. It obviously worked; the record stood proudly at the top of the UK charts for nine weeks, becoming the biggest selling UK single ever. Incredibly, given the yanks taste for anything remotely celtic, the single's B-side was promoted in the States, consequently stalling in the lower regions of the chart. WINGS had more US success via the single, 'WITH A LITTLE LUCK', a No.1 from the otherwise forgettable 'LONDON TOWN' (1978). The addition of LAURENCRE JUBER and STEVE HOLLY failed to prevent another critical pasting with 'BACK TO THE EGG' (1979). By the time WINGS had officially been laid to rest, PAUL had already released the Yuletide cutesiness of the 'WONDERFUL

CHRISTMASTIME' single as well as the 'McCARTNEY II' (1980) album, a stripped down affair that heralded a new phase in his career. From the international chart topping 'EBONY AND IVORY' (a duet with STEVIE WONDER) onwards, the first half of the new decade saw McCARTNEY collaborating with the cream of the MOR elite. The results were sometimes intriguing, often downright dull. 'TUG OF WAR' (1982) and 'PIPES OF PEACE' (1983) kept the singer's profile high, the latter featuring 'SAY SAY SAY', a duet with buddy, MICHAEL JACKSON. While fans voted with their feet, critics were not so generous, although they saved their most vicious scorn for 'GIVE MY REGARDS TO BROAD STREET' (1984), McCARTNEY's own feature film and accompanying soundtrack. While 'NO MORE LONELY NIGHTS' was an affecting, if slight, ballad, the bulk of the project consisted of pointless BEATLES rehashes. It was two years before McCARTNEY surfaced again, although 'PRESS TO PLAY' (1986) failed to rectify matters. After finding a writing partner in ELVIS COSTELLO, McCARTNEY recroded his most committed and consistent work for more than a decade with 'FLOWERS IN THE DIRT' (1989). Recruiting a fairly permanent backing band: PAUL WICKENS (keyboards), CHRIS WHITTEN (drums), ROBBIE McINTOSH (guitar) and HAMISH STUART (guitar, bass), McCARTNEY set off on another world tour, documented on the fine 'TRIPPING THE LIVE FANTASTIC' (1990). An obligatory MTV unplugged set was released the following year, while an ambitious foray into classical music, 'LIVERPOOL ORATARIO' (1991) saw McCARTNEY working with the likes of CARL DAVIS and DAME KIRI TEKANEWA. His next album proper, 'OFF THE GROUND' (1993), failed to get that far, his solo career subsequently put on ice as he hooked up with his old chums, GEORGE HARRISON and RINGO STARR, to make the 'ANTHOLOGY' series of albums and videos tracing the history of The BEATLES. With his profile at its highest since the WINGS days, PAUL released 'FLAMING PIE' (1997), a work that even surpassed 'FLOWERS IN THE DIRT' and finally saw him live up to his reputation as one of the greatest songwriters popular music has ever known. However, tragedy was to strike the McCARTNEY's, when wife LINDA lost her battle against breast cancer on the 17th of April 1998 (PAUL was beside her to the end); a tribute album for her work, 'Wild Prairie' was issued that November while PAUL was inducted as a solo artist into the Rock And Roll Hall Of Fame – "about fucking time!" was fashion designer daughter STELLA's T-shirted opinion of the matter. On the music front, MACCA was back with a bluesy rock'n'roll covers set, 'RUN DEVIL RUN' (1999), although underneath all the showbiz glitz of a comeback tour, PAUL was still hurting inside. A long overdue WINGS anthology, 'WINGSPAN' (2001) was as fitting a tribute as any to LINDA's often unsung talents while the man himself was back with another solo set in the shape of 'DRIVING RAIN' later the same year. More adventurous and fresh sounding than much of the material he recorded in the previous decade, the record wasn't exactly a creative rebirth but suggested that the pioneering spirit of the BEATLES hadn't completely deserted him just yet. Meanwhile, PAUL had found a new love, thirty-something former model Heather Mills, whom he married on 12th June 2002. The double live 'BACK IN THE WORLD' (2003) – titled 'BACK IN THE US' in the States – was McCARTNEY back doing what he perhaps does best, entertaining a crowd and indulging that crowd with the kind of material they want to hear. Thus there was plenty LENNON/McCARTNEY material alongside WINGS and solo material although it was hard to avoid the impression of a man going through the motions. In 2004, McCARTNEY became the latest rock legend to headline Glastonbury, subsequently pulling off another concert coup when he appeared alongside U2 on a rare rendition of BEATLES talisman, 'SGT. PEPPER'S LONELY HEARTS CLUB BAND', at Live8. Later in 2005, Sir PAUL took a leaf out of Sir ELTON's book by cutting a back-to-basics solo set, 'CHAOS AND CREATION IN THE BACKYARD', produced by man-in-demand Nigel Godrich and a transatlantic Top 10. Harking back to his classicist songwriting of yore, much of the material could've slipped on any post-'67 BEATLES album, while the acoustic 'JENNY WREN' (a hit alongside the overtly Fab Four-ish 'FINE LINE') was McCARTNEY's most unadorned single in decades. His love life wasn't so simple however; in May 2006, it was announced that he and Heather were to separate, while newspapers speculated over the possibly record-breaking divorce settlement.

• **Songwriters:** 99% by PAUL, except some with group. Covered; MONY MONY (Tommy James & The Shandells) / GO NOW (Moody Blues) / RUDOLPH THE RED-NOSED REINDEER (Christmas trad.) / KANSAS CITY (Wilbert Harrison) / MATCHBOX (Carl Perkins) / TWENTY FLIGHT ROCK (Eddie Cochran) / LAWDY MISS CLAWDY + IT'S NOW OR NEVER + BLUE MOON OF KENTUCKY (Elvis Presley) / BE-BOP-A-LULA (Gene Vincent) / BACK ON MY FEET (co-with Elvis Costello) / HI-HEEL SNEAKERS (Tommy Tucker) / GIVE PEACE A CHANCE (John Lennon) / AIN'T THAT A SHAME (Fats Domino) / etc., and many past BEATLES songs live. • **Trivia:** The 'BAND ON THE RUN' album sleeve featured the group being caught escaping alongside celebrities; Michael Parkinson, Kenny Lynch, James Coburn, Clement Freud, Christopher Lee & John Conteh.

Album rating: McCARTNEY (*6) / RAM (*6) / WILD LIFE (*4) / RED ROSE SPEEDWAY (*5) / BAND ON THE RUN (*9) / VENUS AND MARS (*6) / WINGS AT THE SPEED OF SOUND (*4) / WINGS OVER AMERICA (*6) / LONDON TOWN (*5) / WINGS GREATEST compilation (*7) / BACK TO THE EGG (*5) / McCARTNEY II (*5) / TUG OF WAR (*5) / PIPES OF PEACE (*4) / GIVE MY REGARDS TO BROAD STREET soundtrack (*3) / PRESS TO PLAY (*4) / ALL THE BEST! compilation (*8) / FLOWERS IN THE DIRT (*6) / TRIPPING THE LIVE FANTASTIC (*4) / UNPLUGGED (THE OFFICIAL BOOTLEG) (*6) / CHOBA B CCCP – THE RUSSIAN ALBUM (*4) / OFF THE GROUND (*4) / PAUL IS LIVE! (*4) / FLAMING PIE (*6) / RUN DEVIL RUN (*5) / WINGSPAN boxed compilation (*8) / DRIVING RAIN (*7) / BACK IN THE U.S./WORLD (*5) / CHAOS AND CREATION IN THE BACKYARD (*6)

PAUL McCARTNEY – vocals, bass, guitar, keyboards, drums (ex-BEATLES) with **LINDA McCARTNEY** (b. LINDA EASTMAN, 24 Sep'42, Scarsdale, New York, USA) – backing vocals

Apple Apple

Apr 70. (lp/c) *(PCS/TC-PCS 7102) <3363>* **McCARTNEY** [2] [1]
– The lovely Linda / That would be something / Valentine day / Every night / Hot as sun / Glasses / Junk / Man we was lonely / Momma miss America / Teddy boy / Singalong junk / Maybe I'm amazed / Kreen-Akrove. *(re-iss. May84 on 'Fame' lp/c; FA41 3100-1/-4) (cd-iss. Apr87; CDP 746 611-2) (re-iss. Apr90 lp/c; ATAK/TC-ATAK 152) (re-iss. Jun93 cd/c;)*

Feb 71. (7") *(R 5889) <1829>* **ANOTHER DAY. / OH WOMAN OH WHY** [2] [5]

— **PAUL** – vocals, guitar, bass / **LINDA** – keyboards, backing vocals, percussion / added **DENNY SEIWELL** – drums, vocals (plus various session people)

May 71. (lp/c; PAUL & LINDA McCARTNEY) *(PAS/TC-PAS 10003) <3375>* **RAM** [1] [2]
– Too many people / Three legs / Ram on / Dear boy / Uncle Albert – Admiral Halsey / Smile away / Heart of the country / Monkberry moon delight / Eat at home / Long-haired lady / Ram on / The back seat of my car. *(re-iss. Jan85 on 'Parlophone'; CDP 746 612-2) (re-iss. Jan88; ATAK/TC-ATAK 12) (re-iss. Jun93 cd/c;)*

Aug 71. (7"; PAUL & LINDA McCARTNEY) *(R 5914)* **THE BACK SEAT OF MY CAR. / HEART OF THE COUNTRY** [39] [–]

Aug 71. (7"; PAUL & LINDA McCARTNEY) *<1837>* **UNCLE ALBERT – ADMIRAL HALSEY. / TOO MANY PEOPLE** [–] [1]

WINGS

— was the group the above trio formed; adding **DENNY LAINE** – guitar, vocals (ex-MOODY BLUES, ex-UGLYS, ex-BALLS, etc.)

Dec 71. (lp/c) *(PCS/TC-PCS 7142) <3386>* **WILD LIFE** [8] [10]
– Mumbo / Bip bop / Love is strange / Wild life / Some people never know / I am your singer / Tomorrow / Dear friend. *(re-iss. Apr84 on 'Fame' lp/c; FA/TCFA 3101) (cd-iss. Oct87 +=; CDFA 3101)* – Mary had a little lamb / Little woman love / Oh woman, oh why. *(re-iss. Jun93 cd/c;)*

— added **HENRY McCULLOCH** – guitar, vocals (ex-JOE COCKER, etc.)

Feb 72. (7") *(R 5936)* *<1847>* **GIVE IRELAND BACK TO THE IRISH. / ('A'version)** [16] Mar72 [21]

May 72. (7") *(R 5949)* *<1851>* **MARY HAD A LITTLE LAMB. / LITTLE WOMAN LOVE** [9] Jun72 [28]

Dec 72. (7") *(R 5973)* *<1857>* **C MOON. / HI HI HI** [5] [10]
(above flipped over in the States)

PAUL McCARTNEY AND WINGS

Mar 73. (7") *(R 5985)* *<1861>* **MY LOVE. / THE MESS (live)** [9] Apr73 [1]

May 73. (lp/c) *(TC+/PCTC 251)* *<3409>* **RED ROSE SPEEDWAY** [5] [1]
– Big barn bed / My love / Get on the right thing / One more kiss / Little lamb dragonfly / Single pigeon / When the night / Hold me tight – Lazy dynamite – Hands of love – Power cut / Loup (1st Indian on the Moon). *(re-iss. Jan85 on 'Parlophone' lp/c; ATAK/TC-ATAK 16) (re-iss. Oct87 on 'Fame' lp/c/cd+=; FA/TCFA/CDFA 3193) (re-iss. Jun93)* – The mess (live) / I lie around / Country dreamer.

Jun 73. (7"; as WINGS) *(R 5987)* *<1863>* **LIVE AND LET DIE. / I LIE AROUND** [9] Jul73 [2]

— **PAUL, LINDA + DENNY LAINER. (McCULLOCH went solo, SEIWELL to sessions)**

Oct 73. (7") *(R 5993)* *<1869>* **HELEN WHEELS. / COUNTRY DREAMER** [12] Nov 73 [10]

Dec 73. (lp/c) *(PAS/TC-PAS 10007)* *<3415>* **BAND ON THE RUN** [1] [1]
– Band on the run / Jet / Bluebird / Mrs. Vanderbilt / Let me roll it / Mamunia / No words / Picasso's last words (drink to me) / Nineteen hundred and eighty-five. *<US pic-lp; > (re-iss. Jan85 on 'Parlophone' lp/c; ATAK/TC-ATAK 19) (cd-iss. Feb85 +=; CDP 746055-2)* – Helen wheels. *(re-iss. Jun93 cd/c;) (special 25th anniversary edition Mar99 d-cd/d-lp; 499176-2/-1)* – (extra versions). *(hit No.69)*

Feb 74. (7") *(R 5996)* *<1871>* **JET. / LET ME ROLL IT** [7] [7]

Apr 74. (7") *<1873>* **BAND ON THE RUN. / 1985** [–] [1]

Jun 74. (7") *(R 5997)* **BAND ON THE RUN. / ZOO GANG** [3] [–]

— added **JIMMY McCULLOCH** (b. 4 Jun'53) – guitar, vocals (ex-THUNDERCLAP NEWMAN, ex-STONE THE CROWS) + **GEOFF BRITTON** – drums (ex-EAST OF EDEN)

Nov 74. (7") *(R 5999)* *<1875>* **JUNIOR'S FARM. / SALLY G** [16] [3] [17]

WINGS

— **JOE ENGLISH** (b. Rochester, New York) – drums (ex-JAM FACTORY) repl. BRITTON who joined CHAMPION

Capitol Capitol

May 75. (7") *(R 6006)* *<4091>* **LISTEN TO WHAT THE MAN SAID. / LOVE IN SONG** [6] [1]

Jun 75. (lp/c) *(PCTC/TC-PCTC 254)* *<11419>* **VENUS AND MARS** [1] [1]
– Venus and Mars rock show / Love in song / You gave me the answer / Magneto and Titanium man / Letting go / Venus and Mars (reprise) / Spirits of ancient Egypt / Medicine jar / Call me back again / Listen to what the man said / Treat her gently – lonely old people / Crossroads theme. *(re-iss. Jan85 on 'Parlophone' lp/c; ATAK/TC-ATAK 14) (cd-iss. Nov88 cd+=/c/lp; CD/TC+/FA 3213)* – Zoogang / My carnival / Lunch box – odd socks. *(re-iss. Jun93 cd/c;)*

Sep 75. (7") *(R 6008)* *<4145>* **LETTING GO. / YOU GAVE ME THE ANSWER** [41] [39]

Nov 75. (7") *(R 6010)* *<4175>* **VENUS AND MARS ROCK SHOW. / MAGNETO AND TITANIUM MAN** [ ] [12]

E.M.I. Capitol

Apr 76. (lp/c) *(PAS/TC-PAS 10010)* *<11525>* **WINGS AT THE SPEED OF SOUND** [2] [1]
– Let 'em in / The note you never wrote / She's my baby / Beware my love / Wino junko / Silly love songs / Cook of the house / Time to hide / Must do something about it / San Ferry Anne / Warm and beautiful. *(re-iss. Jan85 lp/c; ATAK/TCATAC 13) (cd-iss. Jul89 on 'Parlophone'; CDPAS 10010) (re-iss. Oct89 on 'Fame' cd/c/lp; CD/TC+/FA 3229) (re-iss. Jun93 cd/c;)*

May 76. (7") *(R 6014)* *<4256>* **SILLY LOVE SONGS. / COOK OF THE HOUSE** [2] Apr76 [1]

Jul 76. (7") *(R 6015)* *<4293>* **LET 'EM IN. / BEWARE MY LOVE** [2] [3]

Jan 77. (t-lp/d-c) *(PCSP/TC-PCSP 720)* *<11593>* **WINGS OVER AMERICA (live)** [8] Dec76 [1]
– Venus and Mars rock show / Jet / Let me roll it / Spirits of ancient Egypt / Medicine jar / Maybe I'm amazed / Call me back again / Lady Madonna / The long and winding road / Live and let die / Picasso's last words (drink to me) / Richard Cory / Bluebird / I've just seen a face / Yesterday / You gave me the answer / Magnet and Titanium man / Go now / My love / Listen to what the man said / Let 'em in / Time to hide / Silly love songs / Beware my love / Letting go / Band on the run / Hi hi hi / Soily. *(d-cd-iss. May87; CDS 746715-2) (re-iss. 1989 d-lp/d-c; ATAK/TC-ATAK 17)*

Feb 77. (7") *(R 6017)* *<4385>* **MAYBE I'M AMAZED (live). / SOILY (live)** [28] [10]

— cut to trio of **PAUL, LINDA** and **DENNY** when JIMMY joined SMALL FACES, and JOE joined SEA LEVEL (ex-ALLMANS).

Capitol Capitol

Nov 77. (7",7"blue) *(R 6018)* *<4504>* **MULL OF KINTYRE. / GIRLS SCHOOL** [1] [33]
(above flipped over in the States)

— added **STEVE HOLLY** – drums (on session but joined f/t Jul'78)

Parlophone Capitol

Mar 78. (7") *(R 6019)* *<4559>* **WITH A LITTLE LUCK. / CUFF LINK: BACKWARDS TRAVELLER** [5] [1]

Apr 78. (lp/c) *(PAS/TC-PAS 10012)* *<11777>* **LONDON TOWN** [4] [2]
– London town / Cafe on the Left Bank / I'm carrying / Backwards traveller – Cuff link / Children children / Girlfriend / I've had enough / With a little luck / Famous groupies / Deliver your children / Name and address / Don't let it bring you down / Morse Moose and the Grey Goose. *(re-iss. Jan85 lp/c; ATAK/TCATAK 18) (re-iss. Aug89 on 'Fame' cd/c/lp; CD/TC+/FA 3223) (re-iss. Jun93 cd/c;)*

Jun 78. (7") *(R 6020)* *<4594>* **I'VE HAD ENOUGH. / DELIVER YOUR CHILDREN** [42] [25]

Aug 78. (7") *(R 6021)* *<4625>* **LONDON TOWN. / I'M CARRYING** [60] [39]

Nov 78. (lp/c) *(PCTC/TC-PCTC 256)* *<11905>* **WINGS GREATEST** (compilation) [5] [29]
– Another day / Silly love songs / Live and let die / Junior's farm / With a little luck / Band on the run / Uncle Albert – Admiral Halsey / Hi hi hi / Let 'em in / My love / Mull of Kintyre. *(re-iss. Jan85 lp/c; ATAK/TCATAK 15) (cd-iss. 1989; CDP 746056-2) (re-iss. Aug93 cd/c;)*

— added **LAURENCE JUBER** – guitar, vocals

Parlophone Columbia

Mar 79. (7"/ext.12") *(R/12R 6023)* *<10939>* **GOODNIGHT TONIGHT. / DAYTIME NIGHTIME SUFFERING** [5] [5]

Jun 79. (7") *(R 6026)* **OLD SIAM, SIR. / SPIN IT ON** [35] [–]

Jun 79. (7") *<11020>* **GETTING CLOSER. / SPIN IT ON** [–] [20]

Jun 79. (lp/c) *(PCTC/TC-PCTC 257)* *<36057>* **BACK TO THE EGG** [6] [8]
– Reception / Getting closer / We're open tonight / Spin it on / Again and again and again / Old Siam, sir / Arrow through me / Rockestra theme / To you / After the ball – Million miles / Winter rose – Love awake / The broadcast / So glad to see you here / Baby's request. *<US pic-lp promo, became worth $1,000; PCTCP 257) (cd-iss. Jul89; CDPCTC 257) (re-iss. Aug93 cd/c;)*

Aug 79. (7") *(R 6027)* **GETTING CLOSER. / BABY'S REQUEST** [60] [–]

Sep 79. (7") *<11070>* **ARROW THROUGH ME. / OLD SIAM, SIR** [–] [29]

PAUL McCARTNEY

— went solo, augmented by LINDA plus session people

Parlophone Columbia

Nov 79. (7") *(R 6029)* *<11162>* **WONDERFUL CHRISTMASTIME. / RUDOLPH THE RED-NOSED REINDEER** [6] [ ]
<US re-iss. Nov83; same>

Apr 80. (7") *(R 6035)* *<11263>* **COMING UP. / COMING UP (live) / LUNCH BOX – ODD SOX** [2] [1]

May 80. (lp/c) *(PCTC/TCPCTC 258)* *<36511>* **McCARTNEY II** [1] [3]
– Coming up / Temporary secretary / On the way / Waterfalls / Nobody knows / Front parlour / Summer's day song / Frozen Jap / Bogey music / Darkroom / One of these days. *(re-iss. Sep87 on 'Fame' cd+=/c/lp; CD/TC+/FA 3191)* – Secret friend / Check my machine. *(re-iss. Aug93 cd/c;)*

Jun 80. (7") *(R 6037)* *<11335>* **WATERFALLS. / CHECK MY MACHINE** [9] [ ]

Sep 80. (12") *(12R 6039)* **TEMPORARY SECRETARY. / SECRET FRIEND** [ ] [–]

Apr 82. (7"; PAUL McCARTNEY & STEVIE WONDER) *(R 6054)* *<02860>* **EBONY AND IVORY. / RAINCLOUDS** [1] [1]
(12"+=) *(12R 6054)* – ('A'solo version).

Apr 82. (lp/c) *(PCTC/TC-PCTC 259) <37462>* **TUG OF WAR** [1] [1]
– Tug of war / Take it away / Somebody who cares / What's that you're doing? / Here today / Ballroom dancing / The pound is sinking / Wanderlust / Get it / Be what you see / Dress me up as a robber / Ebony and ivory. *(cd-iss. Jan85; CDP 746 057-2) (re-iss. Nov88 on 'Fame' cd/c/lp; CD/TC+/FA 3210) (re-iss. Aug93 cd/c;)*

Jun 82. (12"m) *(R 6056) <03018>* **TAKE IT AWAY. / I'LL GIVE YOU A RING / DRESS ME UP AS A ROBBER** [15] [10]

Sep 82. (7") *(R 6057) <03235>* **TUG OF WAR. / GET IT** [53] [53]

— (In Oct'82, duetted w/ MICHAEL JACKSON on 'THE GIRL IS MINE' Top 10)

Oct 83. (7"; by PAUL McCARTNEY & MICHAEL JACKSON) *(R 6062) <04168>* **SAY SAY SAY. / ODE TO KOALA BEAR** [2] [1]
(12"+=) *(12R 6062)* – ('A'instrumental).

Nov 83. (lp/c) *(PCTC/TCPCTC 1) <39149>* **PIPES OF PEACE** [4] [15]
– Pipes of peace / Say say say / The other me / Keep under cover / So bad / The man / Sweetest little show / Average person / Hey hey / Tug of peace / Through our love. *(cd-iss. Jan84; CDP 746 018-2) (re-iss. Aug93 cd/c;)*

Dec 83. (7") *(R 6064) <04296>* **PIPES OF PEACE. / SO BAD** [1] B-side [23]

Sep 84. (7") *(R 6080) <04581>* **NO MORE LONELY NIGHTS. / ('A' extended)** [2] [6]
(12"+=/12"pic-d+=) *(12R/+P 6080)* – Silly love songs.

Oct 84. (d-lp/c)(cd) *(PCTC/TCPCTC 2)(CDP 746043-2) <39613>* **GIVE MY REGARDS TO BROAD STREET** (soundtrack) [1] [21]
– No more lonely nights (ballad) / Good day sunshine – Corridor music / Yesterday / Here, there and everywhere / Wanderlust / Ballroom dancing / Silly love songs / Not such a bad boy / No values – No more lonely nights (reprise) / For no one / Eleanor Rigby – Eleanor's dream / The long and winding road / No more lonely nights (play out version). *(re-iss. Mar91 lp/c; ATAK/TC-ATAK 165) (cd re-iss. Mar91; CZ 395) (re-iss. Aug93 cd+=/c+=; CD/TC PMCOL 14)* – Good night princess.

Nov 84. (7"/7"sha-pic-d; by PAUL McCARTNEY & THE FROG CHORUS) *(R/+P 6086)* **WE ALL STAND TOGETHER. / ('A'-Humming version)** [3] [–]
(re-iss. Dec85, reached No.34)

Parlophone Capitol

Nov 85. (7"/7"sha-pic-d) *(R/+P 6118) <5537>* **SPIES LIKE US. / MY CARNIVAL** [16] [7]
(12"+=/12"pic-d+=) *(12R/+P 6118)* – ('A'-party mix).

Jul 86. (7") *(R 6133) <5597>* **PRESS. / IT'S NOT TRUE** [25] [21]
(12"+=) *(12R 6133)* – Hanglide. / ('A' dub).
(10"++=) *(10R 6133)* – ('A'version).

Sep 86. (cd/c/lp) *(CD/TC+/PCSD 103) <12475>* **PRESS TO PLAY** [8] [30]
– Stranglehold / Good times coming – Feel the sun / Talk more talk / Footprints / Only love remains / Press / Pretty little head / Move over busker / Angry / However absurd. *(cd+=)* – Write away / It's not true / Tough on a tightrope. *(re-iss. Aug93 cd/c;)*

Oct 86. (7") *(R 6145)* **PRETTY LITTLE HEAD. / WRITE AWAY** [ ] [–]
(12"+=/c-s+=) *(12R/TCR 6145)* – Angry.

Nov 86. (7") *<5636>* **STRANGLEHOLD. / ANGRY (remix)** [–] [81]

Dec 86. (7"/12") *(R/12R 6148) <5672>* **ONLY LOVE REMAINS. / TOUGH ON A TIGHTROPE** [34] [ ]
(7" w-free 7') *(R 6018)* – Mull of Kintyre / Girls school.

Nov 87. (7") *(R 6170)* **ONCE UPON A LONG AGO. / BACK ON MY FEET** [10] [–]
(12"+=) *(12R 6170)* – Midnight special / Don't get around much anymore.
(12"+=) *(12RX 6170)* – Lawdy Miss Clawdy / Kansas City.
(cd-s+=) *(CDR 6170)* – Don't get around much anymore / Kansas City.

Nov 87. (cd/c/lp) *(CD/TC+/PMTV 1) <48287>* **ALL THE BEST!** (compilation) [2] [62]
– Coming up / Ebony and ivory (w/ STEVIE WONDER) / Listen to what the man said / No more lonely nights / Silly love songs / Let 'em in / C Moon / Pipes of peace / Live and let die / Another day / Maybe I'm amazed / Goodnight tonight / Once upon a long time ago / Say say say / With a little luck / My love / We all stand together / Mull of Kintyre / Jet / Band on the run. *<US slightly different tracks>*

— now with **LINDA** / **WIX** (PAUL WICKENS) – keyboards / **CHRIS WHITTEN** – drums / **ROBBIE McINTOSH** – guitar / **HAMISH STUART** – guitar, bass (ex-AVERAGE WHITE BAND)

May 89. (7") *(R 6213) <44367>* **MY BRAVE FACE. / FLYING TO MY HOME** [18] [25]
(12"+=/c-s+=/cd-s+=) *(12R/TCR/CDR 6213)* – I'm gonna be a wheel someday / Ain't that a shame.

Jun 89. (cd/c/lp) *(CD/TC+/PCSD 106) <91653>* **FLOWERS IN THE DIRT** [1] [21]
– My brave face / Rough ride / You want her too / Distractions / We got married / Put it there / Figure of eight / This one / Don't be careless love / That day is done / How many people / Motor of love. *(cd+=)* – Ou est le soleil. *(re-iss. Nov89 as 'FLOWERS . . . WORLD TOUR PACK' cd/lp; CD+/PCSDX 106) (w/free 7")* – PARTY PARTY *(free 3"cd-s.w/cd version) (re-iss. Aug93 cd/c;)*

Jul 89. (c-s/7") *(TC+/R 6223) <44438>* **THIS ONE. / THE FIRST STONE** [18] [94]
(12"+=/cd-s+=) *(12R/CDR 6223)* – I wanna cry / I'm in love again.

Nov 89. (c-s/7") *(TC+/R 6235) <44489>* **FIGURE OF EIGHT. / OU EST LE SOLEIL?** [42] [92]
(12"+=) *(12R 6235)* – ('B'dub mix).
(3"cd-s+=) *(CD3R 6235)* – Rough ride.
(12") *(12RX 6235)* – ('A'side) / This one (club mix).
(cd-s) *(CDR 6235)* – ('A'side) / Long and winding road / Loveliest thing.

Feb 90. (c-s/7") *(TC+/R 6246)* **PUT IT THERE. / MAMA'S LITTLE GIRL** [32] [–]
(12"+=/cd-s+=) *(12R/CDR 6246)* – Same time next year.

Oct 90. (c-s/7") *(TC+/R 6271)* **BIRTHDAY (live). / GOOD DAY SUNSHINE (live)** [29] [–]
(12"+=/cd-s+=) *(12R/CDR 6271)* – P.S. I love you (live) / Let 'em in (live).

Nov 90. (d-cd/d-c/t-lp) *(CD/TC+/PCST 7346) <94778>* **TRIPPING THE LIVE FANTASTIC (live)** [17] [26]
– Figure of eight / Jet / Rough ride / Got to get you into my life / Band on the run / Birthday / Ebony and ivory / we got married / Inner city madness / Maybe I'm amazed / The long and winding road / Cracking up / Fool on the hill / Sgt. Pepper's lonely hearts club band / Can't buy me love / Matchbox / Put it there / Together / Things we said today / Eleanor Rigby / This one / My brave face / I saw her standing there / Back in the USSR / Twenty flight rock / Coming up / Sally / Let it be / Ain't that a shame / Live and let die / If I were not upon the stage / Hey Jude / Yesterday / Get back / Golden slumbers – Carry that weight – The end / Don't let the Sun catch you crying.

Dec 90. (c-s/7") *(TC+/R 6278)* **ALL MY TRIALS (live). / C MOON (live)** [35] [–]
(12"+=) *(12R 6278)* – Mull of Kintyre / Put it there.
(cd-s+=) *(CDR 6278)* – Live medley:- Strawberry fields forever / Help / Give peace a chance.

— **BLAIR CUNNINGHAM** – drums (ex-LLOYD COLE) repl. WHITTEN

Jun 91. (cd/c/lp) *(CD/TC+/PCSD 116) <96413>* **UNPLUGGED – THE OFFICIAL BOOTLEG** [7] [14]
– Be-bop-a-lula / I lost my little girl / Here there and everywhere / Blue Moon of Kentucky / We can work it out / San Francisco Bay blues / I've just seen a face / Every night / She's a woman / Hi-heel sneakers / And I love her / That would be something / Blackbird / Ain't no sunshine / Good rockin' tonight / Singing the blues / Junk. *(re-iss. Aug91 as 'CHOBA B CCCP' cd/c/lp; CD/TC+/PCSD 117)* – hit UK No.63 *(re-iss. Sep94)*

Jan 93. (c-s/7") *(TC+/R 6330) <44904>* **HOPE OF DELIVERANCE. / LONG LEATHER COAT** [18] [83]
(12"/cd-s) *(12R/CDR 6330)* – ('A'side) / Big boys bickering / Deliverance (dub) / Kicked around no more.

Feb 93. (cd/c/lp) *(CD/TC+/PCSD 125) <80362>* **OFF THE GROUND** [5] [17]
– Off the ground / Looking for changes / Hope of deliverance / Mistress and maid / I owe it all to you / Biker like an icon / Peace in the neighbourhood / Golden Earth girl / The lovers that never were / Get out of my way / Winedark open sea / C'mon people.

Feb 93. (c-s/7") *(TC+/R 6338)* **C'MON PEOPLE. / I CAN'T IMAGINE** [41] [–]
(cd-s+=) *(CDR 6338)* – Down to the river / Keep coming back to love.
(cd-s) *(CDRS 6338)* – ('A'side) / Deliverance / Deliverance (dub).

Nov 93. (cd/c/lp) *(CD/TC+/PCSD 147) <27704>* **PAUL IS LIVE! (live)** [34] [78]
– Drive my car / Let me roll it / Looking for changes / Peace in the neighbourhood / All my loving / Robbie's bit / Good rocking tonight / We can work it out / Hope of deliverance / Michelle / Biker like an icon / Here there and everywhere / My love / Magical mystery tour / C'mon people / Lady Madonna / Paperback writer / Penny Lane / Live and let die / Kansas City / Welcome to Soundcheck / Hotel in Benidorm / I wanna be your man / A fine day.

— In 1995, PAUL had his biggest hit in a long time (No.19), when he was part of The SMOKIN' MOJO FILTERS ('Come Together') alongside PAUL WELLER and NOEL GALLAGHER (Oasis).

May 97. (7"pic-d) *(RP 6462)* **YOUNG BOY. / LOOKING FOR YOU** [19] [ ]

(cd-s+=) *(CDRS 6462)* – Oobu Joobu medley (part 1).
(cd-s) *(CDR 6462)* – ('A'side) / Broomstick / Oobu Joobu medley (part 2).

May 97. (cd/c/lp) *(CD/TC+/PCSD 171)* <56500> **FLAMING PIE** 2 2
– Song we were singing / The world tonight / If you wanna / Somedays / Young boy / Calico skies / Flaming pie / Heaven on a Sunday / Used to be bad / Souvenir / Little willow / Really love you / Beautiful night / Great day.

Jul 97. (7"pic-d) *(RP 6472)* **THE WORLD TONIGHT. / USED TO BE BAD** 23 May97 64
(cd-s+=) *(CDRS 6472)* – Oobu joobu (part 3).
(cd-s) *(CDR 6472)* – Oobu joobu (part 1).

Dec 97. (c-s/7") *(TC+/R 6489)* **BEAUTIFUL NIGHT. / LOVE COME TUMBLING DOWN** 25 □
(cd-s+=) *(CDRS 6489)* – Oobu joobu (part 6).
(cd-s) *(CDR 6489)* – ('A'side) / Oobu joobu (part 6) / Same love.

Oct 99. (cd/c/lp) *(<5 22351-2/-4/-1>)* **RUN DEVIL RUN** 12 27
– Blue jean bop / She said yeah / All shook up / Run Devil run / No other baby / Lonesome town / Try not to cry / Movie mag / Brown eyed handsome man / What it is / Coquette / I got stung / Honey hush / Shake a hand / Party. *(8x7"box-iss.Nov99; 523229-1)*

Oct 99. (7") *(R 6527)* **NO OTHER BABY. / BROWN EYED HANDSOME MAN** 42 □
(cd-s+=) *(CDRS 6527)* – Fabulous.
(cd-s) *(CDR 6527)* – (all three tracks in mono).

Oct 01. (7") *(R 6567)* **FROM A LOVER TO A FRIEND. / RIDING TO JALPUL** 45 □
(c-s+=) *(TCR 6567)* – ('A'-David Kahne remix 2).
(cd-s) *(CDR 6567)* – ('A'side) / ('A'-David Kahne remix 1).

Nov 01. (cd/c/lp) *(<5 35510-2/-4>)* **DRIVING RAIN** 46 26
– Lonely road / From a lover to a friend / She's given up talking / Driving rain / I do / Tiny bubble / Magic / Your way / Spinning on an axis / About you / Heather / Back in the sunshine again / Your loving flame / Riding to Jaipur / Rinse the raindrops.

Dec 01. (cd-s) *<50291>* **FREEDOM / FROM A LOVER TO A FRIEND / FROM A LOVER TO A FRIEND (David Kahne remix 2)** – 97

Mar 03. (d-cd) *(5 83005-2)* *<42318>* **BACK IN THE WORLD** (live) <US title 'BACK IN THE U.S.'> 5 Nov02 8
– Hello goodbye / Jet / All my loving / Getting better / Coming up / Let me roll it / Lonely road / Driving rain / Your loving flame / Blackbird / Every night / We can work it out / Mother nature's son / Carry that weight / Fool on the hill / Here today / Something / Eleanor Rigby / Here, there and everywhere / Calico skies / Michelle / Band on the run / Back in the USSR / Maybe I'm amazed / Let 'em in / My love / She's leaving home / Can't buy me love / Live and let die / Let it be / Hey Jude / The long and winding road / Lady Madonna / I saw her standing there / Yesterday / Sgt. Pepper's lonely hearts club band / The end.

Sep 05. (7") *(R 6673)* **FINE LINE. / GROWING UP FALLING DOWN** 20 –
(cd-s) *(CDR 6673)* – ('A') / Comfort of love.

Sep 05. (cd/lp) *(337958-2/-1)* *<38299>* **CHAOS AND CREATION IN THE BACKYARD** 10 6
– Fine line / How kind of you / Jenny Wren / At the mercy / Friends to go / English tea / Too much rain / A certain softness / Riding to Vanity Fair / Follow me / Promise to you girl / This never happened before / Anyway. *(ltd cd w/dvd+=; 337961-2)* – (DVD tracks).

Nov 05. (7"mulberry) *(R 6678)* **JENNY WREN. / SUMMER OF 59** 22 –
(cd-s) *(CDR 6678)* – ('A') / I want you to fly.
(cd-s+=) *(CDRS 6678)* – This loving game.

– compilations, etc. –

Feb 81. (lp) *E.M.I.; (CHAT 1) / Columbia; <36987>* **McCARTNEY INTERVIEW** 34 □

May 01. (d-cd/d-c/q-lp) *Parlophone; (532850-2/-4/-1) / M.P.L.; <32946>* **WINGSPAN: HITS AND HISTORY** 5 2
– Listen to what the man said / Band on the run / Another day / Live and let die / Jet / My love / Silly love songs / Pipes of peace / C moon / Hi hi hi / Let 'em in / Goodnight tonight / Junior's farm / Mull of Kintyre / Uncle Albert – Admiral Halsey / With a little luck / Coming up / No more lonely nights / Let me roll it / Lovely Linda / Daytime nighttime suffering / Maybe I'm amazed / Helen wheels / Bluebird / Heart of the country / Every night / Take it away / Junk / Man he was lonely / Venus and Mars / Rockshow / Backseat of my car / Rockestra theme / Tomorrow / Too many people / Call me back again / Tug of war / Bip bop / Hey diddle / No more lonely nights (playout version).

– under an alias (various connections) –

— PAUL's brother MIKE McGEAR with a sibling collaboration

Oct 74. (7"; COUNTRY HAMS) *E.M.I.; (EMI 2220)* **WALKING IN THE PARK WITH ELOISE. / BRIDGE OVER THE RIVER SUITE** □ □

— PAUL under a new moniker

Apr 77. (7"; as PERCY 'THRILLS' THRILLINGTON) *E.M.I.; (EMI 2594)* **UNCLE ALBERT, ADMIRAL HALSEY. / EAST AT HOME** □ □
(also album, 'THRILLINGTON' lp/c; EMC/TC-EMC 3175)

— next by LINDA McCARTNEY's band

Aug 79. (7"/7"yellow; by SUZY & THE RED STRIPES) *A&M; (AMS/+P 7461) / Epic; <50403>* **SEASIDE WOMAN. / B SIDE TO SEASIDE** □ Jun77 59
(re-iss. Jul80, 7"/7"pic-d; AMS/+P 7548) (re-iss. 1986 on 'E,M,I,' 7"12"; EMI/12EMI 5572)

— PAUL had also guested on numerous singles and albums. DENNY LAINE has also had solo career, although with no commercial success.

□ John McENTIRE (see under ⇒ TORTOISE)

□ Roger McGUINN (see under ⇒ BYRDS)

□ Duff McKAGAN (see under ⇒ GUNS N' ROSES)

□ G.W. McLENNAN (see under ⇒ GO-BETWEENS)

□ Declan McMANUS (see under ⇒ COSTELLO, Elvis)

□ MC REN (see under ⇒ N.W.A.)

MEAT LOAF

Born: MARVIN LEE ADAY, 27 Sep'48, Dallas, Texas, USA, his nickname given to him after he trod on the toes of his school master. In 1966 he moved to Los Angeles and formed psychedelic-rock outfit POPCORN BLIZZARD, who opened for The WHO, AMBOY DUKES and The STOOGES, before disbanding in early 1969. That year, MEAT LOAF successfully auditioned for the 'Hair' musical, where he met female soul singer STONEY. In 1970, they made a self-titled lp together for 'Rare Earth', although he soon rejoined the 'Hair' tour in Cleveland, the behemoth subsequently taking the role of Buddha in the musical 'Rainbow'. A year and a half later, he starred in JIM STEINMAN's Broadway musical 'More Than You Deserve', a partnership that was to flower, both creatively and commercially, as the decade wore on. The following year, MEAT LOAF acted/sang in Richard O'Brien's Broadway musical 'The ROCKY HORROR PICTURE SHOW', which was soon made into a film with MEAT LOAF taking the part of EDDIE. He and STEINMAN went on to tour with the comedy show 'National Lampoon', MEAT LOAF playing the part of a priest in the 'Rockabye Hamlet' sketch. Keeping his finger in the rock'n'roll pie, he contributed vocals to TED NUGENT's 1976 set, 'Free For All'. Early the following year, the big man got together again in New York with STEINMAN, starting work on the 'NEVERLAND' project. They signed to 'R.C.A.', although the partnership changed stables (to 'Epic' affiliated label 'Cleveland International') after it was clear the label didn't want to work with producer TODD RUNDGREN. Late in 1977, they finally unleashed the finished article as 'BAT OUT OF HELL', and with heavy tours, the record eventually made the US Top 20 (also hitting the UK Top 10). A bombastic rock opera, the album shook up the punk/new wave dominated music scene, its heavyweight, anthemic choruses and vein-bursting vocal histrionics reclaiming the territory that "rock" had lost in the past few years. It crossed over to such an extent that it became part of nearly everyone's record collection, selling millions in the process and residing in the charts for over eight years. Songs such as 'YOU TOOK THE WORDS RIGHT OUT OF MY MOUTH', 'TWO OUT OF THREE AIN'T BAD', 'PARADISE BY THE DASHBOARD LIGHT' and the epic title track, took rock'n'roll to melodramatic new heights, its crescendos gripping and lulling the listener into submission. Sweating like a builder's arse crack, MEAT LOAF strained and contorted his way through each song with a theatrical passion as yet unwitnessed in rock. However, it wasn't without a price, the hairy one subsequently suffering throat and alcohol problems over the course of the next few years as the pressures of fame took their toll. Nevertheless, he starred in the film 'Roadie' (1980), alongside DEBBIE HARRY and her group BLONDIE. Impatient with MEAT LOAF's problems, STEINMAN released the 'BAD FOR GOOD' (May '81) album under his own name, although this was intended for MEAT. The long-awaited MEAT LOAF follow-up, 'DEAD RINGER FOR LOVE' was finally issued four months later, and although it hit the top of the charts, it only managed to scrape into US Top 50. Having used ELLEN FOLEY as a vocal foil on his last meisterwork, MEAT LOAF employed the powerful tonsils of CHER on the title track (also a hit single). With STEINMAN out of the picture, MEAT LOAF concentrated his activities in Britain, where he soon became a widely known celebrity, losing a few stone in the process. While mid 80's albums like 'MIDNIGHT AT THE LOST AND FOUND' (1983), 'BAD ATTITUDE' (1984) and 'BLIND BEFORE I STOP' (1986) did little to improve his critical standing, fans still came out in their droves for live appearances. Inevitably perhaps, MEAT LOAF and STEINMAN eventually got back together, 'Virgin' (having just lost MIKE OLDFIELD's massive selling 'Tubular Bells II' to 'Warners') being the lucky backer of a million-selling 1993 sequel, funnily enough called 'BAT OUT OF HELL II – BACK INTO HELL'. This provided the once 20-stone rocker with a return to transatlantic chart domination, the accompanying single 'I'D DO ANYTHING FOR YOU (BUT I WON'T DO THAT)'. This rejuvenated the singer's flagging career, a British beef ban unable to prevent MEAT LOAF (and new writer DIANE WARREN) once again making the UK Top 3 with the 'WELCOME TO THE NEIGHBORHOOD' album in 1995; a best of package hit the UK Top 20 late in 1998. MEAT was back in 2003 with 'COULDN'T HAVE SAID IT BETTER', MOTLEY CRUE's NIKKI SIXX (together with writing partner JAMES MICHAEL) surprisingly claiming the lion's share of the writing credits. The SIXX material most closely followed the hell-for-leather grandiloquence of MEAT in full flight, while the inclusion of Bob Dylan's 'FOREVER YOUNG' certainly made for interesting listening. With today's past veterans looking to older recordings/albums to get them back in the spotlight, it was no surprise then, that 'BAT OUT OF HELL' was re-vamped – complete with the backing of the Melbourne Symphony Orchestra – and released (into the UK charts) in 2004. It has to stop.

• **Songwriters:** MEATLOAF co-wrote w/ PAUL CHRISTIE + others in 1983. P. JACOBS + S. DURKEE took the bulk of the load in 1984. Covered; MARTHA (Tom Waits) / OH WHAT A BEAUTIFUL MORNING (Rogers-Hammerstein) / WHERE ANGELS SING (Davis) / WHATEVER HAPPENED TO SATURDAY NIGHT (Richard O'Brien) / COME TOGETHER + LET IT BE (Beatles).

Album rating: BAT OUT OF HELL (*10) / DEAD RINGER (*6) / MIDNIGHT AT THE LOST AND FOUND (*5) / HITS OUT OF HELL compilation (*7) / BAD ATTITUDE (*6) / MEAT LOAF LIVE AT WEMBLEY (*5) / BLIND BEFORE I STOP (*5) / BAT OUT OF HELL II: BACK INTO HELL (*6) / WELCOME TO THE NEIGHBOURHOOD (*4) / THE VERY BEST OF MEAT LOAF compilation (*7) / COULDN'T HAVE SAID IT BETTER (*5) / BAT OUT OF HELL LIVE (*4)

STONEY AND MEATLOAF

STONEY – vocals (later joined BOB SEGER)

Rare Earth Rare Earth

Apr 71. (7") *<5027-F>* **WHAT YOU SEE IS WHAT YOU GET. / LADY OF MINE** [–] [71]

Jun 71. (7") *<5033-F>* **IT TAKES ALL KINDS OF PEOPLE. / THE WAY YOU DO THE THINGS YOU DO** [–] [ ]

Oct 71. (7") *(RES 103)* **WHAT YOU SEE IS WHAT YOU GET. / THE WAY YOU DO THE THINGS YOU DO** [ ] [–]
(re-iss. Mar79 on 'Prodigal'; PROD 10)

Oct 72. (lp) *(SRE 3005) <R 528-1>* **STONEY AND MEATLOAF** [ ] Oct71 [ ]
– Jimmy Bell / She waits by the window / It takes all kind of people / Stone heart / Who is the leader of the people / What you see is what you get / Kiss me again / Sunshine (where's Heaven) / Jessica White / Lady be mine / Everything under the sun. *<(re-iss. Oct78/Mar79 as 'MEATLOAF (FEATURING STONEY AND MEATLOAF)' on 'Prodigal'; P7 10029> (PDL 2010) (re-iss. Oct81 c; CPDL 2010) (re-iss. 1986 as 'MEAT LOAF' on 'Motown'; ZL 72217)*

—— Returned to feature in the musical 'Hair' (plus see above biography).

MEAT LOAF

not iss. R.S.O.

1974. (7") *<RS 407>* **MORE THAN YOU DESERVE. / PRESENCE OF THE LORD** [–] [ ]

Ode Ode

Oct 75. (7"w-drawn) *(ODS 66304)* **CLAP YOUR HANDS AND STAMP YOUR FEET. / STAND BY ME** [ ] [ ]
(above was recorded in 1973)

—— **MEAT LOAF** – vocals / **JIM STEINMAN** – composer, keyboards, percussion / **TODD RUNDGREN** – multi- / **ROY BITTAN** – piano, keyboards / **MAX WEINBERG** – drums / **KASIM SULTAN** – bass / **ROGER POWELL** – synth. / **ELLEN FOLEY** + **RORY DODD** – back.vox

Epic Epic

Jan 78. (lp/c)(pic-lp) *(EPC/40 82419)(EPC11 82419) <34974>* **BAT OUT OF HELL** [9] Oct77 [14]
– You took the words right out of my mouth (hot summer night) / Heaven can wait / All revved up with no place to go / Two out of three ain't bad / Bat out of hell / For crying out loud / Paradise by the dashboard light: (I)- Paradise, (II)- Let me sleep on it, (II)- Praying for the end of time. *(cd-iss. 1983; EPCCDEPC 82419) (re-iss. pic-cd Dec90; 467732-2) (re-iss. Jul91 lp/c+=; EPC/40 82419)* – Dread ringer for love. *(hit UK No.14, re-entered Jan92, peaked again at No.24-Jul92, returned to hit UK No.19 Autumn 1993) (cd re-iss. Jul95; 480411-2) (lp re-iss. Jun99 on 'Simply Vinyl'; SVLP 86)*

Mar 78. (7") *(SEPC 5980) <50467>* **YOU TOOK THE WORDS RIGHT OUT OF MY MOUTH. / FOR CRYING OUT LOUD** [33] Jan78 [ ]

Jul 78. (7") *(SEPC 6281) <50513>* **TWO OUT OF THREE AIN'T BAD. / FOR CRYING OUT LOUD** [32] Mar78 [11]

Aug 78. (7") *<50588>* **PARADISE BY THE DASHBOARD LIGHT. / "BAT" OVERTURE** [–] [39]

Sep 78. (7") *(SEPC 6797)* **PARADISE BY THE DASHBOARD LIGHT. / ALL REVVED UP WITH NO PLACE TO GO** [ ] [–]

Nov 78. (7") *<50634>* **YOU TOOK THE WORDS RIGHT OUT OF MY MOUTH. / PARADISE BY THE DASHBOARD LIGHT** [–] [39]

Jan 79. (7"/ext.12"red) *(SEPC/+12 7018)* **BAT OUT OF HELL. / HEAVEN CAN WAIT** [15] [–]
(re-iss. Apr81)

—— MEAT LOAF now brought in many session people, including **CHER** on title track.

Sep 81. (lp/c)(pic-lp) *(EPC/40 83645)(EPC11 83645) <36007>* **DEAD RINGER** [1] [45]
– Peel out / I'm gonna love her for both of us / More than you deserve / I'll kill you if you don't come back / Read 'em and weep / Nocturnal pleasure / Dead ringer for love / Everything is permitted. *(re-iss. Nov85 lp/c; EPC 32692) (cd-iss. Nov87; EPCCD 83645)*

Sep 81. (7") *(EPCA 1580) <02490>* **I'M GONNA LOVE HER FOR BOTH OF US. / EVERYTHING IS PERMITTED** [62] [84]

Nov 81. (7"/7"pic-d) *(EPCA/+11 1697)* **DEAD RINGER FOR LOVE. / MORE THAN YOU DESERVE** [5] [–]
(re-iss. Aug88)

Mar 82. (7") *(EPCA 2012)* **READ 'EM AND WEEP. / EVERYTHING IS PERMITTED** [ ] [–]
(12"+=) *(EPCA 12-2012)* – (interview with MEAT LOAF).

Apr 82. (7") *<02607>* **READ 'EM AND WEEP. / PEEL OUT** [–] [ ]

1982. (12"ep-clear) *(EPCA 12-2251)* **MEAT LOAF IN EUROPE '82 (live)** [ ] [–]
– Two out of three ain't bad / You took the words right out of my mouth / I'm gonna love her for both of us / Dead ringer for love.

May 83. (lp)(c) *(EPC 25243)(450360-4)* **MIDNIGHT AT THE LOST AND FOUND** [7] [ ]
– Razor's edge / Midnight at the lost and found / Wolf at your door / Keep driving / The promised land / You never can be too sure about the girl / Priscilla / Don't you look at me like that / If you really want to / Fallen angel. *(re-iss. Jan87 lp/c/cd; EPC 450360-1/-4/-2)*

May 83. (7") *(A 3357)* **IF YOU REALLY WANT TO. / KEEP DRIVING** [59] [–]
(12"+=/12"pic-d+=) *(TA/WA 3357)* – Lost love.

Jul 83. (7"/7"pic-d) *(A/WA 3511)* **RAZOR'S EDGE. / YOU NEVER CAN BE TOO SURE ABOUT THE GIRL** [ ] [–]
(12"+=) *(TA 3511)* – Don't look at me like that.

Sep 83. (7"/7"pic-d) *(A/WA 3748)* **MIDNIGHT AT THE LOST AND FOUND. / FALLEN ANGEL** [17] [–]
(d7"+=/12"+=) *(DA/TA 3748)* – Bat out of Hell (live) / Dead ringer for love (live).

Jan 84. (7") *(A 4080) <04028>* **RAZOR'S EDGE (remix). / PARADISE BY THE DASHBOARD LIGHT** [41] [ ]
(12"+=) *(TA 4080)* – Read 'em and weep.

Arista R.C.A.

Sep 84. (7"/7"sha-pic-d) *(ARIS T/DP 585)* **MODERN GIRL. / TAKE A NUMBER** [17] [–]
(d7"/12")(12"pic-d) *(ARIST12 585/+D)(ARIPD12 585)* – ('A'-Freeway mix) / ('B'extended).

Nov 84. (lp)(c)(cd) *(206619)(406610)(610187) <5451>* **BAD ATTITUDE** [8] May85 [74]
– Bad attitude / Modern girl / Nowhere fast / Surf's up / Piece of the action / Jumpin' the gun / Cheatin' in your dreams / Don't leave your mark on me / Sailor to a siren. *(re-iss. May86 on 'Fame' lp/c; FA41/TCFA 3150) (cd re-iss. Jun88 & Feb94; 259049)*

Nov 84. (7"/7"s/7"g-f/7"sha-pic-d) *(ARI ST/PU/SG/SD 600)* **NOWHERE FAST. / CLAP YOUR HANDS** [67] [–]
(ext.12"+=) *(ARIST12 600)* – Stand by me.

Mar 85. (12") *<14050>* **MODERN GIRL. / ('A'long version)** [–] [ ]

Mar 85. (7"/7"sha-pic-d) *(ARIS T/D 603)* **PIECE OF THE ACTION. / SAILOR TO A SIREN** [47] [ ]
(d7"+=) *(ARIST 603 + FS603)* – Bat out of Hell (live) / Modern Girl (US remix).
(ext.12"+=) *(ARIST12 603)* – Bad attitude.
(ext.d12"++=) *(ARIST12 603 + FS12 603)* – (see d7"above FS603).

May 85. (7") *<14101>* **(GIVE ME THE FUTURE WITH A) MODERN GIRL. / SAILOR TO A SIREN** [–] [ ]

Aug 85. (7") *<14149>* **SURF'S UP. / JUMPIN' THE GUN** [–] [ ]
(12") *<14141>* – ('A'extended) / ('A'side) / Bad attitude.

Aug 86. (7"/7"sha-pic-d/7"white-sha-pic-d/12"/12"pic-d; by MEAT LOAF and JOHN PARR) *(ARIST 666/+P/XP)* **ROCK'N'ROLL MERCENARIES. / REVOLUTIONS PER MINUTE** [31] [–]

Sep 86. (lp/c/cd) *(207/407/257 741)* **BLIND BEFORE I STOP** [28] [ ]
– Execution day / Rock'n'roll mercenaries / Getting away with murder / One more kiss / Night of the soft parade / Blind before I stop / Burning down / Standing on the outside / Masculine / Man and a woman / Special girl / Rock'n'roll hero. *(re-iss. cd Feb94; 259741)*

Nov 86. (7"/7"sha-pic-d)(10") *(ARIST 683/+P)(ARIST10 683) <89340>* **GETTING AWAY WITH MURDER. / ROCK'N'ROLL HERO** [ ] [ ]
(12") *(ARIST12 683)* – ('A'-Scot free mix)/ ('B'extended).

Feb 87. (7"/12") *(RIS/+T 3)* **BLIND BEFORE I STOP. / EXECUTION DAY** [ ] [–]
(12"+=) *(RIST 3R)* – Dead ringer for love (live) / Paradise by the dashboard light (live).

Mar 87. (7") *<89303>* **ROCK'N'ROLL MERCENARY. / EXECUTION DAY** [–] [ ]

Apr 87. (7") *(RIS 14)* **SPECIAL GIRL. / ONE MORE KISS** [ ] [–]
(12"+=/cd-s+=) *(RIS T/CD 14)* – Dead ringer for love (live) / Paradise by the dashboard light (live).

Oct 87. (7"/ext.12") *(RIS/+T 41)* **BAT OUT OF HELL (live). / MAN AND A WOMAN** [ ] [–]

Nov 87. (lp/c/cd) *(208/408/258 599)* **LIVE AT WEMBLEY (live)** [60] [–]
– Blind before I stop / Rock & roll mercenaries / Took the words / Midnight at the lost and found / Modern girl / Paradise by the dashboard light / Two out of three ain't bad / Bat out of Hell. *(free 12"ep/cd+=) –* Masculine / Rock'n'roll medley: Johnny B. Goode – Slow down – Jailhouse rock – Blue suede shoes.

— now with **MRS LOUD** – female vocal / **ROY BITTAN & BILL PAYNE** – piano / **TIM PIERCE & EDDIE MARTINEZ** – guitar / **KENNY ARONOFF & RICK MAROTTA & BRIAN MEAGHER & JIMMY BRALOWER** – drums / **STEVE BUSLOWE** – bass / **PAT THRALL** – guitar solo / **LENNY PICKETT** – sax / **JEFF BOVA** – synth. & prog. / **etc.**

Virgin M.C.A.

Sep 93. (cd/c/lp) *(CDV/TCV/V 2710) <10699>* **BAT OUT OF HELL II: BACK INTO HELL** [1] [1]
– I'd do anything for love (but I won't do that) / Life is a lemon and I want my money back / Rock and roll dreams come through / It just won't quit / Out of the frying pan (and into the fire) / Objects in the rear view mirror may appear closer than they are / Wasted youth / Everything louder than everything else / Good girls go to heaven (bad girls go everywhere) / Back into Hell / Lost boys and golden girls. *(ltd.pic-lp Dec93; VP 2710) (re-iss. Nov95; same)*

Sep 93. (c-s) *<54626>* **I'D DO ANYTHING FOR LOVE (BUT I WON'T DO THAT) / ('A'edit)** [–] [1]

Oct 93. (7"/c-s) *(VS/+C 1443) <54626>* **I'D DO ANYTHING FOR LOVE (BUT I WON'T DO THAT). / BACK INTO HELL** [1] [–]
(cd-s+=) *(VSCDT 1443)* – Everything louder than everything else (live NYC).
(cd-s) *(VSCDG 1443)* – ('A'side) / You took the words right out of my mouth (live NYC) / Bat out of hell (live NYC).

Jan 94. (c-s) *<54757>* **ROCK AND ROLL DREAMS COME THROUGH / I'D DO ANYTHING FOR LOVE (BUT I WON'T DO THAT) (live)** [–] [13]

Feb 94. (7"pic-d/c-s) *(VSP/VSC 1479)* **ROCK AND ROLL DREAMS COME THROUGH. / WASTED YOUTH** [11] [–]
(cd-s+=) *(VSCDT 1479)* – I'd do anything for love (but I won't do that) (live NYC).
(cd-s+=) *(VSCDG 1479)* – Heaven can wait (live) / Paradise by the dashboard light (live).

Apr 94. (7"/c-s) *(VS/+C 1492) <54848>* **OBJECTS IN THE REAR VIEW MIRROR MAY APPEAR CLOSER THAN THEY ARE. / TWO OUT OF THREE AIN'T BAD (live)** [26] [38]
(cd-s) *(VSCDT 1492)* – ('A'side) / Rock and roll dreams come through (live) / All revved up (live).

Oct 95. (c-s) *(VSC 1563) <55134>* **I'D LIE FOR YOU (AND THAT'S THE TRUTH). / I'D DO ANYTHING FOR LOVE (BUT I WON'T DO THAT)** [2] [13]
(cd-s+=) *(VSCDG 1563)* – Whatever happened to Saturday night.
(cd-s) *(VSCDT 1563)* – ('A'-Fountain Head mix) / Oh, what a beautiful mornin' / Runnin' for the red light (I gotta life).

Oct 95. (cd/c/d-lp) *(CD/TC+/V 2799) <11341>* **WELCOME TO THE NEIGHBOURHOOD** [3] Nov95 [17]
– When the rubber meets the road / I'd lie for you (and that's the truth) / Original sin / 45 seconds of ecstacy / Runnin' for the red light (I gotta life) / Fiesta de las Almas Perdidas / Left in the dark / Not a dry eye in the house / Amnesty is granted / If this is the last kiss (let's make it last all night) / Martha / Where angels sing.

Jan 96. (c-s) *(VSC 1567) <55174>* **NOT A DRY EYE IN THE HOUSE / I'D LIE TO YOU (AND THAT'S THE TRUTH) (live)** [7] [82]
(cd-s+=) *(VSCDT 1567)* – Where the rubber meats the road (live).
(cd-s) *(VSCDX 1567)* – ('A'side) / Come together / Let it be.

Apr 96. (c-s) *(VSC 1582)* **RUNNIN' FOR THE RED LIGHT (I GOTTA LIFE) / LIFE IS A LEMON AND I WANT MY MONEY BACK (live) / AMNESTY IS GRANTED** [21] [–]
(cd-s+=) *(VSCDX 1582)* – Dead ringer for love.
(12"pic-d) *(VSTP 1582)* – ('A'side) / Dead ringer for love (live) / All revved up (live) / Midnight at the lost and found (live).

Nov 98. (d-cd/d-c) *(CDV/TCV 2868) <69335>* **THE VERY BEST OF MEAT LOAF** (compilation) [14] [ ]
– Home by now – No matter what / Life is a lemon and I want my money back / You took the words right out of my mouth (hot summer night) / Two out of three ain't bad / Modern girl / Rock and roll dreams come through / Is nothing sacred / Paradise by the dashboard light / Heaven can wait / I'd do anything for love (but I won't do that) / A kiss is a terrible thing to waste / I'd lie for you (and that's the truth) / Not a dry eye in the house / Nocturnal pleasure / Dead ringer for love / Midnight at the lost and found / Objects in the rear view mirror may appear closer than they are / Bat out of Hell.

Apr 99. (c-s/cd-s; by MEAT LOAF featuring PATTI RUSSO) *(VSC/+DT 1734)* **IS NOTHING SACRED / NO MATTER WHAT / DEAD RINGER FOR LOVE (live)** 15 –
(cd-s) *(VSCDX 1734)* – ('A'side) / What you see is what you get (live) / Out of the frying pan (and into the fire) (live).

Mercury Sanctuary

Apr 03. (cd-s) *(065684-2)* **COULDN'T HAVE SAID IT BETTER / ('A'radio) / UNSAID / ('A'-video)** 31 –

Apr 03. (cd) *(076099-2)* <84653> **COULDN'T HAVE SAID IT BETTER** 4 Sep03 85
– Couldn't have said it better / Did I say that / Why isn't that enough / Love you out loud / Man of steel – Intermezzo / Testify / Tear me down / You're right, I was wrong / Because of you / Do it! / Forever young / Bat out of Hell (live). *<US+=>* – Couldn't have said it better (video) / Did I say that (video).

Nov 03. (cd-s) *(9815114)* **MAN OF STEEL / TEAR ME DOWN (live) / LOVE YOU OUT LOUD (live)** 21 –

Oct 04. (cd) *(9868074)* *<84721>* **BAT OUT OF HELL LIVE** (with the Melbourne Symphony Orchestra) 14 Sep04
– Bat out of Hell / You took the words right out of my mouth (hot summer night) / Heaven can wait / All revved up with no place to go / Two out of three ain't bad / Paradise by the dashboard light / For crying out loud.

– compilations, others, etc. –

on 'Epic' records (unless stated)

Aug 82. (c-ep) *(EPCA40 2621)* **GREATEST ORIGINAL HITS EP** –
– Bat out of Hell / Read 'em and weep / Dead ringer for love / I'm gonna love her for both of us. *(7"ep-iss.Mar83; EPCA 2621)*

Jan 85. (lp/c/cd) *(EPC/40/EPCCD 26156)* **HITS OUT OF HELL** 2
– Bat out of Hell / Read 'em and weep / Midnight at the lost and found / Two out of three ain't bad / Dead ringer for love / Modern girl / I'm gonna love her for both of us / You took the words right out of my mouth (hot summer night) / Razor's edge / Paradise by the dashboard light. *(re-iss. Mar88 lp/c; 450447-1/-4) (re-iss. cd Mar91 & Jul99; EPC 450447-2)*

Sep 86. (c-ep) *(450131-4)* **MEAT LOAF** –
– Bat out of Hell / Dead ringer for love / Read 'em and weep / If you really want to / Razor's edge.

Aug 87. (d-lp) *(EPCML 241)* **BAT OUT OF HELL / HITS OUT OF HELL** –

Jan 88. (7") *Old Gold; (OG 9751)* **BAT OUT OF HELL. / DEAD RINGER FOR LOVE** –

Feb 89. (7") *Old Gold; (OG 9865)* **YOU TOOK THE WORDS RIGHT OUT OF MY MOUTH. / MIDNIGHT AT THE LOST AND FOUND** –

Nov 89. (lp/c/cd) *Arista; (210/410/260 363)* **PRIME CUTS**

Nov 89. (lp/c/cd; with tracks by BONNIE TYLER) *Telstar; (STAR/STAC/TCD 2361)* **HEAVEN AND HELL** –
(re-iss. cd-c.May93 & Dec95 on 'Columbia')

Jun 91. (7"/c-s) *(656982-7/-4)* **DEAD RINGER FOR LOVE. / HEAVEN CAN WAIT** 53
(12"+=/cd-s+=) *(656982-6/-2)* – Bat out of Hell.

Jun 92. (7"/c-s) *(657491-7/-4)* **TWO OUT OF THREE AIN'T BAD. / MIDNIGHT AT THE LOST AND FOUND** 69
(12"+=/cd-s+=) *(657491-6/-2)* – I'm gonna love her for both of us.

Jul 92. (c-s) *M.C.A.; <54557>* **PARADISE BY THE DASHBOARD LIGHT. /** –
(above from the 'Leap Of Faith' soundtrack starring Steve Martin)

Oct 92. (cd/c) *Pickwick; (PWK CD/S 4121)* **ROCK'N'ROLL HERO** –
(re-iss. May94; same)

Feb 93. (cd) *(CDX 82419)* **BAT OUT OF HELL – REVAMPED** –

Feb 93. (d-cd) *(CDX 82419D)* **DEAD RINGER / BAT OUT OF HELL** –

Apr 93. (d-cd) *(474032-2)* **DEAD RINGER / MIDNIGHT AT THE LOST AND FOUND** –
(re-iss. Feb95; 478486-2)

Sep 93. (cd/c) *Ariola; (74321 1528-2/-4)* **THE COLLECTION** –

Dec 93. (12"pic-d-ep/c-ep/pic-cd-ep) *(660006-6/-4/-2)* **BAT OUT OF HELL / READ 'EM AND WEEP. / OUT OF THE FRYING PAN (AND INTO THE FIRE) / ROCK AND ROLL DREAMS COME THROUGH (Jim Steinman)** 8

Oct 94. (cd; with BONNIE TYLER) **THE BEST**

Oct 94. (cd/c/lp) *Pure Music; (PM CD/MC/LP 7002)* **ALIVE IN HELL (live)** 33 –
– (tracks on 'LIVE AT WEMBLEY' album) + (studio tracks;-) Piece of the action / Bad attitude / Surf's up.

Apr 95. (cd) *Arista; (74321 25957-2)* **BLIND BEFORE I STOP / BAD ATTITUDE** –

Jun 96. (cd/c) *Camden; (74321 39336-2/-4)* **ROCK'N'ROLL HERO** –

Jul 98. (cd) *(488674-2)* **THE DEFINITIVE COLLECTION** –

Sep 99. (cd) *Beyond; <78065>* **VH1 STORYTELLERS (live)** –

Nov 03. (d-cd) *Epic; (513743-2)* **THE VERY BEST OF MEAT LOAF**

MEGADETH

Formed: San Francisco, California, USA ... 1983 by ex-METALLICA guitarist/vocalist, DAVE MUSTAINE, alongside DAVE ELLEFSON (bass), CHRIS POLAND (guitar) and GAR SAMUELSON (drums). MUSTAINE soon secured the band a deal with the small 'Combat' label, who released MEGADETH's breakneck debut album, 'KILLING IS MY BUSINESS . . . AND BUSINESS IS GOOD' (1985). Taking the aural assault of METALLICA as a template, MUSTAINE and Co. had carved out an even more intense, speed-driven variation on heavy metal, but unlike many of their similarly speed-obsessed peers, MEGADETH had the instrumental prowess to pull it off. Signing to 'Capitol', the band followed up with 'PEACE SELLS . . . BUT WHO'S BUYING?' (1986), after which MUSTAINE sacked both POLAND and SAMUELSON. Replacing them with JEFF YOUNG and CHUCK BEHLER respectively, the band returned in February '88 with a fierce cover of the SEX PISTOLS' 'ANARCHY IN THE U.K.' , complete with original 'PISTOLS' guitarist, STEVE JONES. 'SO FAR . . . SO GOOD . . . SO WHAT!' followed in March, the pinnacle of their career thus far and one of the finest metal albums of that year. Lyrically, MUSTAINE was as reliably pessimistic as ever, 'IN MY DARKEST HOUR' seeing the frontman wracked with bitterness and frustrated rage. Which possibly accounts for his headlong descent into substance abuse following the album's success, MUSTAINE again firing his musicians and not surfacing again until the cover of ALICE COOPER's 'NO MORE MR. NICE GUY' in late '89, his first Top 20 hit. Going on MUSTAINE's track record, there had never been a MR. NICE GUY, although new recruits MARTY FRIEDMAN (guitar) and NICK MENZA (drums) have been with the band now for an unprecedented eight years and MUSTAINE obviously had it together enough to record the critically acclaimed 'RUST IN PEACE' (1990). 'HOLY WARS . . . THE PUNISHMENT DUE' was the first single from the album, an uncannily prescient piece of writing in light of the Gulf War, the record made even more eerie by dint of its wailing Arab-esque embellishments. The whole set was more mature, both musically and lyrically, FRIEDMAN ripping out solo's at furious speed, note for perfect note while MUSTAINE tackled subjects from alien cover-ups ('HANGER 18', another Top 30 hit) to the threat of nuclear weapons ('RUST IN PEACE . . .POLARIS'). COUNTDOWN TO EXTINCTION (1992) featured equally topical lyrical themes, mainly dealing with the danger to the earth's environment. Musically, the band had inevitably slowed the pace down somewhat; allowing more consideration for melody and structure, MEGADETH scored their biggest success to date, the album reaching No.2 in America, No.5 in Britain. 'SKIN O' MY TEETH' recounted MUSTAINE's brushes with death; rather than banging on about saving the planet, perhaps MUSTAINE should have dealt with his own affairs first as rumours began to surface about drug problems marring sessions for the 'YOUTHANASIA' (1994) album. Nevertheless, by the time of the album's release, MUSTAINE had apparently finally cleaned up and on the strength of the record, no one could really argue. It was another masterful effort, a transatlantic Top 10 that signalled

MUSTAINE was hot on the heels of his old muckers METALLICA. After an odds'n'sods collection in '95, the band returned a few years later with 'CRYPTIC WRITINGS', a disappointing affair that should've served as MEGADETH's epitaph. However, they stood their ground for another cocktail of pitbull metal in the shape of 9th set, 'RISK' (1999); another transatlantic Top 30 entry. Having signed off (late in 2000) from 'Capitol' via an obligatory 'best of' package, 'CAPITOL PUNISHMENT: THE MEGADETH YEARS', the group signed a deal with 'Sanctuary' ('Metal-Is' in the UK), releasing the disappointing 'THE WORLD NEEDS A HERO' (2001). Following an arm injury MUSTAINE put the band on ice – apparently permanently – and fans had to be content with the limited thrills of double live set, 'RUDE AWAKENING' (2002), a fairly pedestrian summation of their helter skelter career if a better primer than ' . . .PUNISHMENT'. While its title harked back to the 80's glory years, 'STILL, ALIVE . . .AND WELL?' (2002) was an unashamed cash-in released in the absence of new material and featuring both a batch of live cuts trimmed from 'RUDE AWAKENING' and another batch of previously released stuff from the disappointing ' . . .HERO'. With MUSTAINE officially disbanding MEGADETH in April 2002 – citing nerve damage to his left arm – it really looked like the end of the road. Gradually regaining his guitar playing ability through physiotherapy and hard practice, he began working with guitarist/founding MEGADETH member CHRIS POLAND, onetime FRANK ZAPPA drummer VINNIE COLAIUTA and session bassist JIMMY SLOAS. 'THE SYSTEM HAS FAILED' (2004) was the band's first album to go Top 20 in America since 'YOUTHANASIA' a decade earlier, buoyed by the MUSTAINE/POLAND reunion and hailed by critics as a long overdue return to form. Against a background of law suit and counter law suit (involving another founder member DAVE ELLEFSON), MEGADETH's mainman took a comletely different line-up – ex-KING DIAMOND man GLEN DROVER, his brother SHAWN and former ICED EARTH guitarist JAMES MacDONOUGH (subsequently replaced with JAMES LOMENZO) – out on tour with him, a jaunt which he initially claimed would be the band's final bow before announcing an even bigger jaunt for 2005. That year also saw the release of greatest hits set, 'BACK TO THE START', its title confirmation of a new era.

Album rating: KILLING IS MY BUSINESS . . . AND BUSINESS IS GOOD (*6) / PEACE SELLS . . . BUT WHO'S BUYING? (*8) / SO FAR . . . SO GOOD . . . SO WHAT? (*7) / RUST IN PEACE (*7) / COUNTDOWN TO EXTINCTION (*7) / YOUTHANASIA (*6) / HIDDEN TREASURES (*5) / CRYPTIC WRITINGS (*4) / RISK (*3) / CAPITOL PUNISHMENT compilation (*6) / THE WORLD NEEDS A HERO (*4) / RUDE AWAKENING (*5) / STILL ALIVE . . . AND WELL? (*4) / THE SYSTEM HAS FAILED (*6) / GREATEST HITS: BACK TO THE START compilation (*7)

DAVE MUSTAINE (b.13 Sep'61, La Mesa, Calif.) – vocals, lead guitar (ex-METALLICA) / **CHRIS POLAND** – guitar / **DAVE ELLEFSON** (b.12 Nov'64, Minnesota) – bass / **GAR SAMUELSON** – drums

Music For Nations — Combat

Jun 85. (lp) *(MFN 46) <970546>* **KILLING IS MY BUSINESS . . . AND BUSINESS IS GOOD** [ ] [ ]
– Last rites – Loved to death / Killing in my business . . .and business is good / The skull beneath the skin / These boots / Rattlehead / Chosen ones / Looking down the cross / Mechanix. *(cd-iss. Aug87; CDMFN 46) (pic-lp May88; MFN 46P) (cd re-iss. Nov99 on 'Century Media'; 66034-2)*

— POLAND was replaced by MIKE ALBERT (ex-KING CRIMSON) briefly until his return

Capitol — Capitol

Nov 86. (lp/pic-lp)(c) *(EST/+P 2022)(TCEST 2022) <12526>* **PEACE SELLS . . . BUT WHO'S BUYING?** [ ] [76]
– Wake up dead / The conjuring / Peace sells / Devils island / Good mourning – Black Friday / Bad omen / I ain't superstitious / My last words. *(cd-iss. Sep88; CDP 746148-2) (re-iss. Jul94 cd/c; CDEST 2022)*

Nov 87. (7"/7"pic-d) *(CL/+P 476)* **WAKE UP DEAD. / BLACK FRIDAY (live)** [65] [ ]
(12"+=,12"w/7"pic-d) *(12CL 476)* – Devil's island (live).

— **CHUCK BEHLER** – drums replaced SAMUELSON / **JEFF YOUNG**– guitar repl. JAY REYNOLDS who had briefly repl. POLAND

Feb 88. (7"/7"pic-d) *(CL/+P 480)* **ANARCHY IN THE U.K. / LIAR** [45] [ ]
(12"+=) *(12CL 480)* – 502.

Mar 88. (lp/pic-lp)(c/cd) *(EST/+P 2053)(CD/TC EST 2053) <48148>* **SO FAR . . . SO GOOD . . . SO WHAT!** [18] Jan88 [28]
– Into the lungs of Hell / Set the world afire / Anarchy in the U.K. / Mary Jane / 502 / In my darkest hour / Liar / Hook in mouth.

May 88. (7"/7"pic-d) *(CL/+P 489)* **MARY JANE. / HOOK IN MOUTH** [46] [ ]
(12"+=) *(12CL 489)* – My last words.

— Late '88, YOUNG joined BROKEN SILENCE and BEHLER joined BLACK & WHITE

Nov 89. (7"/7"pic-d)(c-s) *(SBK/+PD 4)(TCSBK 4)* **NO MORE MR. NICE GUY. / DEAD ON: Different Breed** [13] [ ]
(12"+=/cd-s+=) *(12/CD SBK 4)* – DANGEROUS TOYS: Demon bell (the ballad of Horace Pinker).
(above single released on 'S.B.K.')

— (Mar90) **MUSTAINE + ELLEFSON** bring in new members **MARTY FRIEDMAN** (b. 8 Dec'62, Washington, D.C.) – guitar (ex-CACOPHONY) / **NICK MENZA** (b.23 Jul'64, Germany) – drums

Sep 90. (c-s/7") *(TC+/CLP 588)* **HOLY WARS . . . THE PUNISHMENT DUE. / LUCRETIA** [24] [ ]
(12"+=/cd-s+=) *(12/CD CLP 588)* – Information.
(12"pic-d) *(12CLP 588)* – ('A'side) / (13-minute interview).

Oct 90. (cd/c)(lp/pic-lp) *(CD/TC EST 2132)(EST/+P 2132) <91935>* **RUST IN PEACE** [8] [23]
– Holy wars . . . the punishment due / Hangar 18 / Take no prisoners / Five magics / Poison was the cure / Lucretia / Tornado of souls / Dawn patrol / Rust in peace . . . Polaris. *(re-iss. Sep94 cd/c; same)*

Mar 91. (7"/7"sha-pic-d) *(CL/+PD 604)* **HANGAR 18. / THE CONJURING (live)** [26] [ ]
(cd-s+=) *(12/CD CLG 604)* – ('A'live) / Hook in mouth (live).

Jun 92. (7") *(CLS 662)* **SYMPHONY OF DESTRUCTION. / PEACE SELLS (live)** [15] [–]
(12"clear+=/cd-s+=) *(12CLS/CDCL 662)* – Go to Hell / Breakpoint.
(7"pic-d) *(CLPD 662) – ('A'side) / In my darkest hour (live).*

Jul 92. (cd/c/lp) *(CD/TC+/ESTU 2175) <98531>* **COUNTDOWN TO EXTINCTION** [5] [2]
– Skin o' my teeth / Symphony of destruction / Architecture of aggression / Foreclosure of a dream / Sweating bullets / This was my life / Countdown to extinction / High speed dirt / Psychotron / Captive honour / Ashes in your mouth.

Oct 92. (c-s) *<44886>* **SYMPHONY OF DESTRUCTION / SKIN O' MY TEETH** [–] [71]

Oct 92. (7"/7"pic-d)(c-s) *(CL/+P 669)(TCCL 669)* **SKIN O' MY TEETH. / HOLY WARS . . . THE PUNISHMENT DUE (General Norman Schwarzkopf)** [13] [ ]
(cd-s+=) *(CDCL 669)* – ('A'version) / Lucretia.
(10"+=) *(10CL 669)* – High speed drill / (Dave Mustaine interview).

May 93. (c-s/7") *(TC+/CL 692)* **SWEATING BULLETS. / ASHES IN YOUR MOUTH (live)** [26] [ ]
(12"/cd-s) *(12/CD CL 692)* – ('A'side) / Countdown to extinction (live '92) / Symphony of destruction (gristle mix) / Symphony of destruction (live).

Oct 94. (cd/c/blue-lp) *(CD/TC+/EST 2244) <29004>* **YOUTHANASIA** [6] [4]
– Reckoning day / Train of consequences / Addicted to chaos / A tout le monde / Elysian fields / The killing road / Blood of heroes / Family tree / Youthanasia / I thought I knew it all / Black curtains / Victory.

Dec 94. (7"clear) *(CL 730)* **TRAIN OF CONSEQUENCES. / CROWN OF WORMS** [22] [ ]
(cd-s+=) *(CDCL 730)* – Peace sells . . . but who's buying? (live) / Anarchy in the UK (live).
(laser-etched 12") *(12CL 730)* – ('A'side) / Holy wars . . . the punishment due (live) / Peace sells . . . but who's buying? (live) / Anarchy in the U.K. (live).

Aug 95. (d-cd) *(CDESTS 2244) <33670>* **HIDDEN TREASURES** [28] [90]
– No more Mr. Nice guy / Breakpoint / Go to Hell / Angry again / 99 ways to die / Paranoid / Diadems / Problems.

Jul 97. (cd/c/lp) *(CD/TC+/EST 2297) <38262>* **CRYPTIC WRITINGS** [38] [10]
– Trust / Almost honest / Use the man / Mastermind / The disintegrators / I'll get even / Sin / A secret place / Have cool, will travel / She-wolf / Vortex / FFF.

Sep 99. (cd) *(499130-2) <99134>* **RISK** [29] [16]
– Insomnia / Prince of darkness / Enter the arena / Crush 'em / Breadline /

The doctor is calling / I'll be there / Wanderlust / Ecstasy / Seven / Time: the beginning / Time: the end.

Nov 00. (cd) *(525916-2)* *<25916>* **CAPITOL PUNISHMENT: THE MEGADETH YEARS** (compilation) [ ] Oct00 [66]
– Kill the king / Dread and the fugitive mind / Crush 'em / Use the man / Almost honest / Trust / A tout le monde / Train of consequences / Sweating bullets / Symphony of destruction / Hangar 18 / Holy wars . . . the punishment due / In my darkest hour / Peace sells. *(hidden tracks+=)*

Metal-Is Sanctuary

May 01. (cd/lp) *(MIS CD/LP 006) <84503>* **THE WORLD NEEDS A HERO** [45] [16]
– Disconnect / The world needs a hero / Moto psycho / 1000 times goodbye / Burning bridges / Promises / Recipe for hate . . . warhorse / Losing my senses / Dread and the fugitive mind / Silent scorn / Return to Hangar / When.

Mar 02. (d-cd) *(MISDD 019) <84544>* **RUDE AWAKENING** (live) [ ] [ ]
– Dread and the fugitive mind / Kill the king / Wake up dead / In my darkest hour / Angry again / She wolf / Reckoning day / Devil's island / Train of consequences / A tout le monde / Burning bridges / Hangar 18 / Return to hangar / Hook in mouth / Almost honest / 1000 times goodbye / Mechanix / Tornado of souls / Ashes in your mouth / Sweating bullets / Trust / Symphony of destruction / Peace sells / Holy wars.

— split April 2002 – MUSTAINE being diagnosed with radial neuropathy

Sep 02. (cd) *(MISCD 024) <84566>* **STILL ALIVE . . . AND WELL? (live & studio)** [ ] [ ]
– Time – Use the man / Conjuring / In my darkest hour / Sweating bullets / Symphony of destruction / Holy wars / Moto psycho / Dread and the fugitive mind / Promises / The world needs a hero / Burning bridges / Return to hangar.

— **MUSTAINE** reunited MEGADETH + added **CHRIS POLAND** – guitar

Sanctuary Sanctuary

Sep 04. (cd) *(SANCD 297) <84708>* **THE SYSTEM HAS FAILED** [60] [18]
– Blackmail the universe / Die dead enough / Kick the chair / The scorpion / Tears in a vial / I know Jack / Back in the day / Something that I'm not / Truth be told / Of mice and men / Shadow of deth / My kingdom.

– compilations, etc. –

Mar 97. (3xcd-box) *E.M.I.; (CDOMB 019)* **THE ORIGINALS** [ ] [–]
– (PEACE SELLS . . . BUT WHO'S BUYING / SO FAR . . . SO GOOD . . . SO WHAT / RUST IN PEACE). *(re-iss. Sep00; 528368-2)*

Jun 05. (cd) *Capitol; <(8 73929-2)>* **GREATEST HITS: BACK TO THE START** [ ] [65]
– Holy wars . . . the punishment due / In my darkest hour / Peace sells / Sweating bullets / Angry again / A tout le monde / Trust / Kill the king / Symphony of destruction / Mechanix / Train of consequences / Wake up dead / Hangar 18 / Dread and the fugitive mind / Skin o' my teeth / She-wolf / Prince of darkness. *(ltd cd w/dvd+=; 330771-2)* – Kill the king (video) / (tour footage live at the Auditorium 1999).

John (Cougar) MELLENCAMP

Born: 7 Oct'51, Seymour, Indiana, USA. After graduating from high school, where he played in two bands, CREPE SOUL (!) and SNAKEPIT BANANA BARN, the young MELLENCAMP left home in 1970 and moved to Valonia where he married his pregnant girlfriend, Priscilla. Although he formed glam-rock outfit, TRASH (alongside LARRY CRANE) in the early 70's, it would be be another three years before MELLENCAMP made any serious inroads into the music business. By this point, he'd graduated from university, separated from his wife and child and secured a deal with 'M.C.A.' as well as management company 'Mainman' (home to DAVID BOWIE), after sending a demo to the latter's Tony DeFries. Released in 1976, his debut album, 'CHESTNUT STREET INCIDENT', was credited (reportedly unbeknownst to MELLENCAMP) to JOHN COUGAR, as DeFries had christened him. Not that many people noticed anyway, poor sales of both his debut and the follow-up, 'THE KID INSIDE' (1977) seeing him part company with the label and sign to 'Riva', an imprint run by ROD STEWART's manager, Billy Gaff, and indeed the recording home of the leopard-print trousered legend himself. At this stage, MELLENCAMP's recycled rock'n'roll struggled to even match the negligible quality of STEWART's airbrushed fodder and both the UK-only 'A BIOGRAPHY' (1978) and 'JOHN COUGAR' (1979) failed to come up with anything resembling originality although the latter set nevertheless spawned a minor US hit in 'I NEED A LOVER'. The apallingly titled, STEVE CROPPER-produced 'NOTHIN' MATTERS, & WHAT IF IT DID' (1981) continued in the same empty, rock-posturing vein although for the first time, saw MELLENCAMP in the (US) Top 40. Finally managing to combine hard-bitten authenticity with epic anthem-rock a la TOM PETTY, MELLENCAMP scored a surprise US No.1 with the MTV favourite, 'JACK & DIANE'. The accompanying album, 'AMERICAN FOOL' (1982) also topped the chart and almost spawned a further two No.1's in 'HURTS SO GOOD' and 'HAND TO HOLD ON TO'. Now commanding a bit of commercial leverage, the singer ensured that 'UH-HUH!' (1984) was issued under the JOHN COUGAR MELLENCAMP moniker, his newfound confidence evident on a set which consolidated the earlier success and convincingly announced the arrival of a major league contender. Placing MELLENCAMP's small-town ideology into the context of the American farming crisis, 'SCARECROW' (1985) was a work of seemingly heartfelt conviction with cast-iron rockouts to match; the record spawned five hit singles (including the Top 10 triple whammy of 'LONELY OL' NIGHT', 'SMALL TOWN' and 'R.O.C.K. IN THE U.S.A.'), its impact lent extra weight via MELLENCAMP's role in organising Farm Aid (alongside NEIL YOUNG and WILLIE NELSON). Expanding his troupe of backing musicians to include the likes of LISA GERMANO (here playing violin), the proletarian rocker embraced a more folky approach on 'THE LONESOME JUBILEE' (1987). Painting a bleak picture of contemporary life for the average down-at-heel American, the record included some of MELLENCAMP's most memorable songs, not least the bitter 'PAPER IN FIRE'. The latter track made the Top 10, as did the album itself and for the first time, MELLENCAMP began making an impact in Britain where the record almost went Top 30. Perversely enough, the singer's most introspective album to date, 'BIG DADDY' (1989) – he had recently become a grandad – was his most successful UK release; utilising a distinctively more subdued musical approach, the rootsy, melancholy backing echoed the more intensely personal lyrical fare. The late 80'/early 90's proved a difficult time for the artist as he re-evaluated his musical direction (meantime starring in the film, 'Falling From Grace'), suffered nervous exhaustion and saw his keyboard player, JOHN CASCELLA, meet an untimely death aged only 35. MELLENCAMP himself would come face to face with his own mortality in 1994 when his touring plans were abandoned following a heart attack. Ironically, that year's album, 'DANCE NAKED', was his finest of the decade so far, following on from the return to harder territory of 'WHATEVER WE WANTED' (1991) and 'HUMAN WHEELS' (1993). It also spawned the rather unlikely (US) Top 3 duet with ME'SHELL NDEGECELLO on a cover of Van Morrison's 'WILD NIGHT'. You'd be hard pushed to come up with a more bizarre choice of producer for a JOHN MELLENCAMP album than New York DJ Don, Junior Vasquez, yet that was exactly who took the helm for the Top 10 'MR. HAPPY GO LUCKY' (1996). While the likes of MADONNA can successfully change her spots at will, a man with such an honest rock'n'roll pedigree was never going to benefit to any great extent from such an ambitious pairing. Still, it did suggest a willingness to explore different avenues, something which didn't hamper the back to basics sound of 'JOHN MELLENCAMP' (1998), as straightforward an album as the title might suggest, perhaps too straightforward: it failed to reach the US Top 40, an affront he hadn't suffered since the late 70's. While the latter marked the beginning of the man's new deal with 'Columbia', 1999's 'ROUGH HARVEST' was an interesting hodge podge of covers and acoustic readings of old favourites, ostensibly released as a contractual obligation to 'Mercury'. MELLENCAMP found himself back in the chart fold (US Top 20) with 'CUTTIN' HEADS' (2001), an easy-going return to form with guest appearances as varied as CHUCK D and TRISHA YEARWOOD, proof if nothing else that the veteran troubadour is something of a minor American institution. Ostensibly inspired by a well received cover of Robert Johnson's 'STONES IN MY PASSWAY' at a tribute gig, 'TROUBLE NO MORE' (2003) was the man's first full-blown covers album. Unsurprisingly, the emphasis was squarely on great American songs, from blues (Willie Dixon's 'DOWN IN THE BOTTOM') to folk (Woody Guthrie's 'JOHNNY HART') to Tin Pan Alley standards (Hoagy Carmichael's 'BALTIMORE ORIOLE'), with the mood fairly downbeat and edgdy throughout. An interesting diverson from the man's usual fare, it made the US Top 40 and boaded well for further similar excursions. While he's never quite lived up to the "new SPRINGSTEEN" tag which greeted his 70's arrival, MELLENCAMP has earned his place as a pillar of trad US rock by dint of sheer hard graft, honesty and not a little talent.

• **Songwriters:** Penned most himself, with collaborations mainly stemming from CRANE. Covered; KICKS (Paul Revere & The Raiders) / JAILHOUSE ROCK (Elvis Presley) / OH PRETTY WOMAN (Roy Orbison) / DO YOU BELIEVE IN MAGIC (Lovin' Spoonful) / UNDER THE BOARDWALK (Drifters) / etc. • **Trivia:** Due to his height, he produced under the alias of the Little Bastard. His work in this field has included; MITCH RYDER (Never Kick A Sleeping Dog) / BLASTERS (Hard Line).

Album rating: CHESTNUT STREET INCIDENT (*3) / THE KID INSIDE (*3) / A BIOGRAPHY (*4) / JOHN COUGAR (*5) / NOTHIN' MATTERS AND WHAT IF IT DID (*5) / AMERICAN FOOL (*6) / UH-HUH (*6) / SCARECROW (*7) / THE LONESOME JUBILEE (*7) / BIG DADDY (*8) / WHENEVER WE WANTED (*6) / HUMAN WHEELS (*6) / DANCE NAKED (*6) / MR. HAPPY GO LUCKY (*5) / JOHN MELLENCAMP (*5) / THE BEST THAT I COULD DO compilation (*7) / ROUGH HARVEST compilation (*6) / CUTTIN' HEADS (*6) / TROUBLE NO MORE (*5) / WORDS & MUSIC: JOHN MELLENCAMP'S GREATEST HITS compilation (*8)

JOHNNY COUGAR

JOHN MELLENCAMP – vocals, guitar; with session people

not iss. M.C.A.

Dec 76. (lp) <2225> **CHESTNUT STREET INCIDENT** [–] [ ]
– American dream / Oh pretty woman / Jailhouse rock / Dream killin' town / Supergirl / Chestnut street revisited / Good girls / Do you believe in magic / Twentieth century fox / Sad lady. *(UK-rel.Oct84 on 'MainMan'; MML 602) (re-iss. Apr86 on 'Castle' lp/c/cd; CLA LP/MC/CD 113) (cd re-iss. Feb98 on 'Snapper'; SMMCD 513)*

— his band **TIGER FORCE** were **LARRY CRANE** – guitars / **TOM WINCE** – keyboards / **DAVID PARMAN** – bass, guitar, violin, percussion / **TERENCE SALSA** – drums, percussion / **WAYNE HALL** – saxophone, flute, percussion

1977. (lp) **THE KID INSIDE** [–] [ ]
– Kid inside / Take what you want / Cheap shot / Side-walks and street lights / R.Gang / American son / Gearhead / Young genocides / Too young to live / Survive. *(UK-iss.May86 on 'Castle'; CLALP 112) (cd-iss. Nov86; CLACD 112) (cd re-iss. Feb98 on 'Snapper'; SMMCD 510)*

not iss. Gulcher

1977. (7"ep) **U.S. MALE** [–] [ ]
– 2000 a.d. / Lou-ser / Hot man / Kicks.

Riva Riva

Mar 78. (7") *(RIVA 14)* **I NEED A LOVER. / BORN RECKLESS** [ ] [–]
(re-iss. Nov79 as JOHN COUGAR; same)

Mar 78. (lp/c) *(RV LP/4 6)* **A BIOGRAPHY** [ ] [–]
– Born reckless / Factory / Night slumming / Taxi dancer / I need a lover / Alley of the angels / High "C" Cherie / Where the side walk ends / Let them run your lives / Goodnight.

Jun 78. (7") *(RIVA 16)* **FACTORY. / ALLEY OF THE ANGELS** [ ] [–]

JOHN COUGAR

Riva Riva

Jun 79. (7",7"pic-d) *(RIVA 20)* **MIAMI. / DO YOU THINK THAT'S FAIR** [ ] [–]

Jul 79. (lp/c) *(RV LP/4 9)* <7401> **JOHN COUGAR** [ ] [64]
– A little night dancin' / Small Paradise / Great mid-west / Miami / Take home pay / Sugar Marie / Welcome to Chinatown / Pray for me / Do you think that's fair / Taxi dancer. *(re-iss. Jun88 on 'Mercury'; PRICE 119) (cd-iss. Jan86; 814 995-2)*

Sep 79. (7") <202> **I NEED A LOVER. / WELCOME TO CHINATOWN** [–] [28]

Oct 79. (7") *(RIVA 21)* **TAXI DANCER. / SMALL PARADISE** [ ] [–]

Feb 80. (7") <203> **SMALL PARADISE. / SUGAR MARIE** [–] [87]

Apr 80. (7") <204> **PRAY FOR ME. / A LITTLE NIGHT DANCIN'** [–] [ ]

Sep 80. (7") *(RIVA 25)* *<RIVA 205>* **THIS TIME. / DON'T UNDERSTAND ME** [ ] [27]

Jan 81. (7") <207> **AIN'T EVEN DONE WITH THE NIGHT. / MAKE ME FEEL** [–] [17]

Feb 81. (lp/c) *(RV LP/4 10)* <7403> **NOTHIN' MATTERS AND WHAT IF IT DID** [ ] Sep80 [37]
– Hot night in a cold town / Ain't even done with the night / Don't understand me / This time / Make me feel / To M.G. (wherever she may be) / Tonight / Wild angel / Cheap shot. *(cd-iss. Jan86; 814 994-2)*

Feb 81. (7") *(RIVA 30)* **HOT NIGHT IN A COLD TOWN. / TONIGHT** [ ] [–]

May 81. (7") *(RIVA 31)* **AIN'T EVEN DONE WITH THE NIGHT. / TO M.G. WHEREVER SHE MAY BE** [ ] [–]

— his live band consisted of **LARRY CRANE** – guitar, vocals / **MIKE WANCHIC** – guitar, vocals / **TOBY MYERS** – bass, vocals / **KENNY ARONOFF** – drums, vocals

May 82. (7") *(RIVA 36)* <207> **HURTS SO GOOD. / CLOSE ENOUGH** [ ] Apr 82 [2]

Jul 82. (7") <210> **JACK & DIANE. / CAN YOU TAKE IT** [–] [1]

Nov 82. (lp/c) *(RV LP/4 16)* <7501> **AMERICAN FOOL** [37] May82 [1]
– Hurts so good / Jack & Diane / Hand to hold on to / Danger list / Can you take it / Thundering hearts / China girl / Close enough / Weakest moments. *(re-iss. Sep85 on 'Mercury' lp/c; PRICE/PRIMC 85) (cd-iss. Jan85; RVCD 7501) (re-iss. cd 1988; 814 993-2)*

Sep 82. (7") *(RIVA 37)* **JACK & DIANE. / DANGER LIST** [25] [–]
(12"+=) *(RIVA 37T)* – Need a lover.

Nov 82. (7") <211> **HAND TO HOLD ON TO. / SMALL PARADISE** [–] [3]

Jan 83. (7",7"pic-d/12") *(RIVA 38/+T)* **HAND TO HOLD ON TO. / HURTS SO GOOD** [ ] [–]

JOHN COUGAR MELLENCAMP

Nov 83. (7"/12") *(JCM 1/+12)* <214> **CRUMBLIN' DOWN. / GOLDEN GATES** [ ] Oct 83 [9]

Dec 83. (7") <215> **PINK HOUSES. / SERIOUS BUSINESS** [–] [8]

Feb 84. (lp/c) *(RIVL/+C 1)* <7504> **UH-HUH** [92] Oct83 [9]
– Crumblin' down / Pink houses / Authority song / Warmer place to sleep / Jackie O / Play guitar / Serious business / Lovin' mother fo ya / Golden Gates. *(cd-iss. Oct84; 814 485-2)*

Feb 84. (7") *(JCM 2)* **AUTHORITY SONG. / HURTS SO GOOD** [ ] [–]
(12"+=) *(JCM 212)* – Thundering hearts.

Mar 84. (7") <216> **AUTHORITY SONG. / PINK HOUSES (acoustic)** [–] [15]

Jun 84. (7") *(JCM 3)* **PINK HOUSES. / WARMER PLACE TO SLEEP** [ ] [–]

— added **JOHN CASCELLA** – keyboards plus others on session

Oct 85. (7") *(JCM 4)* <880 984-7> **LONELY OL' NIGHT. / JACK & DIANE** [ ] Aug 85 [6]
(12"+=) *(JCMX 4)* – Rumbleseat.

Nov 85. (lp/c)(cd) *(RIVH/+C 2)*<(824865-2)> **SCARECROW** [ ] Sep85 [2]
– Rain on the scarecrow / Grandma's theme / Small town / Minutes to memories / Lonely ol' night / The face of the nation / Justice and independence / Between a laugh and a tear / Rumbleseat / You've got to stand for somethin' / R.O.C.K. in the U.S.A. *(c+=)(cd+=)* – The kind of fella I am.

Jan 86. (7"/12") *(JCM/+X 5)* <884 202-7> **SMALL TOWN. / SMALL TOWN (acoustic)** [53] Oct 85 [6]
(d7"+=) *(JCMDP 5)* – Hurts so good / The kind of fella I am.
(d12"+=) *(JCMXD 5)* – Pink houses / Small town (acoustic).

Apr 86. (7") *(JCM 6)* <*884 455-7*> **R.O.C.K. IN THE U.S.A. / UNDER THE BOARDWALK** 67 Jan 86 2

Apr 86. (7") <*884 635-7*> **RAIN ON THE SCARECROW. / PRETTY BALLERINA** – 21

Jun 86. (7") <*884 856-7*> **RUMBLESEAT. / COLD SWEAT** – 28

Nov 86. (7") *(JCM 7)* **(as "CONSPIRACY OF HOPE"): PINK HOUSES. / (Howard Jones: No One Is To Blame)** –
(12"+=) *(JCMX 7)* – Pink houses (acoustic).

—— added **LISA GERMANO** – violin / **PAT PETERSON** – backing vocals, percussion.

Mercury Mercury

Sep 87. (7") *(JCM 8)* <*888 763-7*> **PAPER IN FIRE. / NEVER TO OLD** Aug 87 9
(12"+=) *(JCMX 8)* – Cold sweat.

Sep 87. (lp/c)(cd) *(MERH/+C 109)*<*(832465-2)*> **THE LONESOME JUBILEE** 31 6
– Paper in fire / Down and out in paradise / Check it out / Real life / Cherry bomb / We are the people / Empty hands / Hard times for an honest man / Hot dogs and hamburgers / Rooty toot toot.

Nov 87. (7") *(JCM 9)* <*888 934-7*> **CHERRY BOMB. / SHAMA LAMA DING DONG** Oct87 8
(12"+=) *(JCMX 9)* – Under the boardwalk.
(cd-s++=) *(JCMCD 9)* – Pretty ballerina (live).

Feb 88. (7") *(JCM 10)* <*870 126-7*> **CHECK IT OUT. / WE ARE THE PEOPLE** 14
(12"+=) *(JCMX 10)* – Shama lama ding dong / Pretty ballerina.
(cd-s+=) *(JCMCD 10)* – Pink houses (acoustic) / Check it out (live).

Jul 88. (7") *(JCM 11)* <*870 327-7*> **ROOTY TOOT TOOT. / CHECK IT OUT (live)** May 88 61
(12"+=) *(JCMX 11)* – Pretty ballerina / Like home (acoustic).
(cd-s+=) *(JCMCD 11)* – Never too old / Cold sweat.

Apr 89. (7") *(EKR 90)* **RAVE ON. / (Beach Boys: Kokomo)**
(12") *(EKRT 90)* – ('A'side) / (Fabulous Thunderbirds: Powerful Stuff) / (Starship: Wild Again).
(above single from the film 'Cocktail' on 'Elektra' label)

—— added **CRYSTAL TALIEFERO** – backing vocals, percussion

May 89. (lp/c/cd) <*(838220-1/-4/-2)*> **BIG DADDY** 25 7
– Big daddy of them all / To live / Martha say / Theo and weird Henry / Jackie Brown / Pop singer / Void in my heart / Mansions in Heaven / Sometimes a great notion / Country gentlemen / J.M.'s question. *(cd+=)* – Let it all hang out.

Jun 89. (7") *(JCM 12)* <*874 012-7*> **POP SINGER. / J.M.'S QUESTION** Apr 89 15
(12"+=) *(JCM 1212)* – Like a rolling stone (live).
(cd-s++=) *(JCMCD 12)* – Check it out (live).

Jul 89. (7") <*874 644-7*> **JACKIE BROWN. / JACKIE BROWN (acoustic)** – 48

JOHN MELLENCAMP

Sep 91. (7") *(MER 354)* <*867890-7*> **GET A LEG UP. / WHENEVER WE WANTED** 14
(c-s+=/12"+=/cd-s+=) *(MER MC/X/CD 354)* – Seventh son.

Oct 91. (cd/c/lp) <*(510151-2/-4/-1)*> **WHENEVER WE WANTED** 39 17
– Love and happiness / Now more than ever / I ain't ever satisfied / Get a leg up / Crazy ones / Last chance / They're so tough / Melting pot / Whenever we wanted / Again tonight. *(re-iss. cd Apr95)*

Jan 92. (7"/c-s) *(MER/+MC 362)* **LOVE AND HAPPINESS. / ('A'-L.A. rock dance mix)** –
(12") *(MERX 362)* – ('B'mix) / ('A'-Jezzard mix) / ('A'-dub).
(cd-s+=) *(MERCD 362)* – (all mixes + 'A'side above).

Feb 92. (c-s) <*866414-7*> **AGAIN TONIGHT / GET A LEG UP (live)** – 36

Apr 92. (7") *(MER 368)* **NOW MORE THAN EVER. / JACK AND DIANE (live)**
(cd-s+=) *(MERCD 368)* – Check it out (live) / Martha say (live).
(c-s) *(MERMC 368)* – ('A'side) / Lonely ol' night.
(cd-s) *(MERCB 368)* – (above 2) / Small town / Pink houses.

—— mid'92, MELLENCAMP suffered nervous exhaustion and cancelled gigs when his bassist MYERS severed a big toe in a boating accident. The 14th of November '92, also saw his keyboard player JOHN CASCELLA die. He was only 35, but still played on half of next album. He was replaced by **MALCOLM BURN** – organ, guitar, harmonica, synth.

—— **DAVID GRISSOM** – guitars, mandolin, bass repl. CRANE

Sep 93. (cd/c) <*(518088-2/-4)*> **HUMAN WHEELS** 37 7
– When Jesus left Birmingham / Junior / Human Wheels / Beige to beige / Case 795 (the family) / Suzanne and the jewels / Sweet evening breeze / What if I came knocking / French shoes / To the river. *(cd re-iss. Sep97; same)*

Oct 93. (c-s) <*862702-7*> **HUMAN WHEELS / ('A'edit)** – 48

—— now w / **WANCHIC, MYERS, ARONOFF, ME'SHELL NDEGECELLO** (bass, vocals), **GERMANO, PETERSON + ANDY YORK** – guitar

Jun 94. (cd/c) <*(522428-2/-4)*> **DANCE NAKED** 13
– Dance naked / Brothers / When Margaret comes to town / Wild night / L.U.V. / Another sunny day 12 / 25 / Too much to think about / The big jack / The breakout. *(cd re-iss. Sep97; same)*

Jun 94. (c-s) <*858738*> **WILD NIGHT / BROTHERS (live)** – 3

Aug 94. (7"yellow/c-s) *(MER/+MC 409)* **WILD NIGHT. / HURTS SO GOOD** 34 –
(cd-s) *(MERCD 409)* – ('A'side) / Jack and Diane / Pink houses / R.O.C.K. in the U.S.A. (a salute to the 60's).
(cd-s) *(MERCX)* – ('A'side) / Dance naked (live) / When Jesus left Birmingham / Small town (acoustic).

Nov 94. (c-s) <*856346*> **DANCE NAKED / R.O.C.K. IN THE U.S.A.** – 41
<with free live c-s> – Human wheels / Pink houses.

Aug 96. (c-s) <*578398*> **KEY WEST INTERMEZZO (I SAW YOU FIRST) / LIKE A ROLLING STONE** – 14

Sep 96. (cd-ep) *(MERCD 474)* **KEY WEST INTERMEZZO (I SAW YOU FIRST) / WILD NIGHT (live) / WHAT IF I CAME KNOCKING (live) / SMALL TOWN (live acoustic)** –
(cd-ep) *(MERCX 474)* – ('A'side) / Cold sweat (live) / Check it out (live) / Like a rolling stone (live).

Oct 96. (cd/c) <*(532896-2/-4)*> **MR. HAPPY GO LUCKY** Sep96 9
– Overture / Jerry / Key west intermezzo (I saw you first) / Just another day / This may not be the end of the world / Emotional love / Mr. Bellows / The full catastrophe / Circling around the Moon / Large world turning / Jackamo road / Life is hard.

Feb 97. (cd-s) <*578816*> **JUST ANOTHER DAY / KEY WEST INTERMEZZO (I SAW YOU FIRST) / COLD SWEAT (live) / CRUMBLIN' DOWN (live)** – 46

Columbia Columbia

Feb 99. (cd/c) *(491652-2/-4)* <*69602*> **JOHN MELLENCAMP** Oct98 41
– Fruit trader / Your life is now / Positively crazy / I'm not running anymore / Where the world began / It all comes true / Eden is burning / Chance meeting at the Tarantula / Miss Missy / Break me off some / Summer of love / Days of farewell.

Jan 02. (cd) *(503293-2)* <*85098*> **CUTTIN' HEADS** Oct01 15
– Cuttin' heads / Peaceful world / Deep blue heart / Crazy island / Just like you / The same way I do / Women seem / Worn out nervous condition / Shy / In our lives.

Columbia Best Buy C

Aug 03. (cd) *(512264-2)* <*2007201*> **TROUBLE NO MORE** Jun03 31
– Stones in my passway / Death letter / Johnny Hart / Baltimore oriole / Teardrops will fall / Diamond Joe / The end of the world / Down in the bottom / Lafayette / Joliet bound / John the revelator / To Washington.

– compilations, etc. –

Mar 86. (lp/c/cd; JOHN COUGAR) *Castle; (CCS LP/MC/CD 124)* **THE COLLECTION** (early) –

Jan 98. (cd/c) *Mercury; (536738-2/-4)* **THE BEST THAT I COULD DO** (1978-1988) 25 33
– Jack and Diane / R.O.C.K. in the U.S.A. / Hurts so good / I need a lover / Ain't even done with the night / Crumblin' down / Pink houses / Authority song / Lonely ol' night / Small town / Paper in fire / Cherry bomb / Check it out / Without expression.

Aug 99. (cd) *Mercury;* <*(558355-2)*> **ROUGH HARVEST** 99
– Love and happiness / In my time of dying / Between a laugh and a tear / Human wheels / Rain on the scarecrow / Farewell Angelina / Key West intermezzo (I saw you first) / Jackie Brown / When Jesus left Birmingham / Full catastrophe of life / Minutes to memories / Under the boardwalk / Wild night.

Mar 00. (d-cd) *Snapper; (SMDCD 280)* **SKIN IT BACK** –

May 00. (3xcd-box) *Snapper; (SMXCD 108)* **THE BOX** –
– (CHESTNUT STREET INCIDENT / THE KID INSIDE / SKIN IT BACK).

Oct 04. (d-cd) *Island; (9864810)* <*35920-2*> **WORDS & MUSIC: JOHN MELLENCAMP'S GREATEST HITS** 13
– Walk tall / Pink houses / Lonely ol' night / Jackie Brown / Rain on the scarecrow / Love and happiness / Check it out / Peaceful world / Paper in fire / Your life is now / Human wheels / When Jesus left Birmingham / Authority song / What if I came looking / Crumblin' down / Small town /

R.O.C.K. in the U.S.A. / Cherry bomb / Pop singer // Thank you / Martha say / Key West intermezzo (I saw you first) / Hand to hold on to / I need a lover / Hurts so good / Get a leg up / Wild night / Dance naked / Teardrops will fall / Ain't even done with the night / Just another day / Jack & Diane / Rumble seat / I'm not running anymore / Again tonight / This time / Now more than ever. *<US w/dvd+=>* – Crumblin' down / R.O.C.K. in the U.S.A. / Rain on the scarecrow / Check it out / Key West intermezzo (I saw you first).

☐ Freddie MERCURY (see under ⇒ QUEEN)

MERCURY REV

Formed: Buffalo, New York, USA ... 1988 by JONATHAN DONAHUE, DAVID BAKER, GRASSHOPPER (aka SEAN MACKIOWIAK), DAVE FRIDMANN, JIMY CHAMBERS and SUZANNE THORPE, who claimed they had all met while attending a psychiatric hospital. Admittedly, their sound, which came about by playing their own soundtrack to nature TV programmes! ('VERY SLEEPY RIVERS' indeed) was certainly deliciously deranged enough for this explanation of their secret history. Just over two years of rehearsals passed (DONAHUE, co-producer FRIDMANN and GRASSHOPPER were part-time members of FLAMING LIPS and utilised some spare studio time), before they finally surfaced with the mini-lp, 'YERSELF IS STEAM' (1991). Perhaps the most immaculate marriage of searing noise and crystalline pop ever committed to vinyl, this freaky guitar-angst rock classic mixed up psychedelia, noise, film dialogue and exhilarating experimentation in a way only previously matched by the FLAMING LIPS; other indie influences were also apparent (i.e. the BIRTHDAY PARTY, STUMP, the VERY THINGS and MY BLOODY VALENTINE). The inspired opening salvo of 'CHASING A BEE', 'SYRINGE MOUTH' and 'CONEY ISLAND CYCLONE', alone was enough to give the album a resounding thumbs-up by the British press and record buying public alike. Later that year, the 'CAR WASH HAIR' EP/track (recorded with DEAN WAREHAM of GALAXIE 500), further convinced commentators of MERCURY REV's volatile genius although squabbling and widely publicised, wildly unpredictable live shows led to break-up rumours. These were subsequently quashed when the band were snapped up by 'Beggars Banquet', a follow-up album, 'BOCES' (1993), carrying on in the established schizophrenic mould but too often straying into wanton self-indulgence at the expense of conventional tunes. However, it did satisfy some punters by becoming their first record to hit the UK Top 50. The following year, the band's infamous in-fighting reach a head as the proverbial time-honoured musical differences led to the wayward BAKER pursuing a noisier career of his own as SHADY. Although a solitary MERCURY REV single, 'EVERLASTING ARM', appeared in summer '94 (featuring ALAN VEGA of SUICIDE), it would be another long year before the release of 'SEE YOU ON THE OTHER SIDE' (1995), although by this time the first chapter of MERCURY REV's maverick career had already drawn to a close. While critics marvelled over the album's more accessible but wonderfully eclectic pop-jazz experiments, DONAHUE and GRASSHOPPER were in the process of completing a debut album, 'PARALYZED MIND OF THE ARCANGEL VOID' (1995) for their revamped side-project, HARMONY ROCKETS. A few years later, the pair resurrected the MERCURY REV moniker with a complete new cast (namely ADAM SNYDER, JUSTIN RUSSO, JASON RUSSO and JEFF MERCEL), although the subsequent return of THORPE, FRIDMANN and CHAMBERS (SNYDER was retained) resulted in a more fully-fledged reformation. V.I.P. HARMONY ROCKETS guests, LEVON HELM and GARTH HUDSON of the BAND, were also brought on board for the album no one thought was possible, 'DESERTER'S SONGS' (1998). Issued on Richard Branson's new imprint, 'V2' ('Epic' in the States), the record was widely hailed as THE album of the year as MERCURY REV enjoyed one of the critical rebirths of the decade. Older and wiser, the band (or the BAND, take your pick!) had possibly stumbled upon what GRAM PARSONS really meant when he dreamt of his "cosmic American music", a wistful (in a far-out sort of way) melange of quixotic pop, spacey orchestration and lullaby romanticism quite possibly unlike anything you've ever heard. If long-time fans were hoping to hear the anarchic spark of old they were in for a drastic shock, tracks such as 'TONITE IT SHOWS', 'OPUS 40', 'DELTA SUN BOTTLENECK BLUES' and 'ENDLESSLY', meandering to a more mature muse, the latter even incorporating their own heavy-lidded interpretation of traditional carol, 'Silent Night'. A couple of months previous to the album's release, GRASSHOPPER & HIS GOLDEN CRICKETS (including flautist, SUZANNE THORPE) had taken their own, more off-beat journey into the psychedelic musical galaxy with the album, 'THE ORBIT OF ETERNAL GRACE'. After recovering from the trailblazing glory of 'DESERTER'S SONGS', many fans and critics were pondering over the group's next release: how were they going to match the previous album? How would they write songs now that their woe and grief had disappeared thanks to their new found glory? MERCURY REV, however, answered both of these questions on the eve of the release of their fifth album, the epic 'ALL IS DREAM' (2001). A kaleidoscope of drifting thoughts, strange orchestral lulls, and dark, uncertain things that creeped around in the shadows, the set displayed all of the usual REV decorations, only with a brooding overtone. Darker than their last set, the record opened with the soaring, heart-wrenchingly poignant 'DARK IS RISING' (the unofficial sequel to 'HOLES') – a piano led wander into DONAHUE's subconscious, with aching violins and unnormally high choir voices that sounded like a collaboration between a broken-down NEIL YOUNG and a drunken SCOTT WALKER. Elsewhere on the album, 'DROP IN TIME', 'TIDES OF THE MOON' and 'HERCULES' were all fine demonstrations by the group that they hadn't lost any of their musical ambition (especially FRIDMANN, who was surely becoming the PHIL SPECTOR of the independent movement). If 'DESERTER'S SONGS' was the soundtrack to a sad children's Christmas movie, then 'ALL IS DREAM' was pitched somewhere between a classic romantic period drama and a high-tension adventure set in a faraway land. Three years on, the Mercurial New Yorkers released one of their most intimate AOP (Adult Orientated Psychedelia/Prog) meditations to date in the shape of 'THE SECRET MIGRATION' (2005), once again drawing the ubiquitous FLAMING LIPS comparisons. Somehow, DONAHUE and Co haven't quite enjoyed the same Stateside success as their LIP-py counterparts, although they always seemed to generate enough chart interest in the UK.

• **Covered:** IF YOU WANT ME TO STAY (Sly Stone) / SHHH – PEACEFUL (Miles Davis) / DEADMAN (Alan Vega) / RAINDROPS KEEP FALLING ON MY HEAD (Bacharach & David) / HE WAS A FRIEND OF MINE (Bob Dylan) / SILVER STREET (Nikki Sudden) / MOTION PICTURES (Neil Young) / OBSERVATORY CREST (Captain Beefheart) / I KEEP A CLOSE WATCH (John Cale) / STREETS OF LAREDO (Marty Robbins) – The HARMONY ROCKETS covered I'VE GOT A GOLDEN TICKET (from 'Charlie & The Chocolate Factory') / L'APOCALYPSE DES ANIMAUX (Vangelis) / etc..

Album rating: YERSELF IS STEAM (*8) / BOCES (*6) / SEE YOU ON THE OTHER SIDE (*8) / DESERTER'S SONGS (*9) / ALL IS DREAM (*8) / THE SECRET MIGRATION (*6) / Harmony Rockets: PARALYZED MIND OF THE ARCANGEL VOID (*6) / Grasshopper & The Golden Crickets: THE ORBIT OF ETERNAL GRACE (*7)

DAVID BAKER – vocals / **JONATHAN DONAHUE** – vocals, guitar (ex-FLAMING LIPS) / **SEAN 'Grasshopper' MACKIOWIAK** – guitar / **DAVID FRIDMANN** – bass / **JIMY CHAMBERS** – drums / **SUZANNE THORPE** – woodwind

Mint Films Mint Films

Feb 91. (cd/c/blue-lp) <*(MINT CD/C/LP 4)*> **YERSELF IS STEAM**
– (Rocket): Chasing a bee / Syringe mouth / Coney Island cyclone / Blue and black / Sweet oddysee of a cancer cell t' th' center of yer heart / (Harmony): Frittering / Continuous trucks and thunder under a mother's smile / Very sleepy rivers. *(re-iss. Nov92 on 'Beggars Banquet' as d-cd+=/d-c+=/d-lp+=; BBQ CD/MC/LP 125)* **LEGO MY EGO** – If you want me to stay / Shhh – Peaceful – Very sleepy rivers / Frittering / Coney Island cyclone / Car wash hair / Syringe mouth / Blood on the moon / Chasing a girl (inside a car). *<US cd re-iss. Nov92 on 'Columbia'; 53030> (re-iss. Feb99 +=; same)* – Space patrol / Uh . . . it's out there / I better let my pants back on / My mom is coming over. *(d-cd-iss. Jul02; MINTCD 0045)*

Nov 91. (12"ep/cd-ep) <*(MINT 5 T/CD)*> **CAR WASH HAIR (The Bee's Chasing me) full pull / CHASING A BEE (demo) / CONEY ISLAND CYCLONE (demo)**

Rough Trade not iss.

Apr 92. (7") *(45REV 6)* **IF YOU WANT ME TO STAY. / THE LEFT-HANDED RAYGUN OF PAUL SHARITS (RETIREMENT JUST LIKE THAT)** –

Beggars Banquet Columbia

Nov 92. (12"/cd-s) *(BBQ 1/+CD)* <*74717*> **CHASING A BEE. / CONEY ISLAND CYCLONE**

Mar 93. (10"/cd-s) *(BBQ 5 T/CD)* <*74907*> **THE HUM IS COMING FROM HER. / SO THERE (with ROBERT CREELY)** Apr93

May 93. (7") *(BBQ 14)* **SOMETHING FOR JOEY. / THREE SPIDER'S EGGS (live)** –
(12"+=) *(BBQ 14/+T)* – Suzanne peels out.
(cd-s++=) *(BBQ 14CD)* – Noise. *(re-iss. Jul93)*

Jun 93. (cd/c/lp) *(BBQ CD/MC/LP 140)* <*53217*> **BOCES** 43
– Meth of a rockette's kick / Trickle down / Bronx cheer / Boys peel out / Downs are feminine balloons / Something for Joey / Snorry mouth / Hi-speed boats / Continuous drunks and blunders / Girlfren.

Jul 93. (cd-ep) <*CSK 5532*> **SOMETHING FOR JOEY / SO THERE / BOYS PEEL OUT / VERY SLEEPY RIVERS / (Ron Jeremy interview)** –

Feb 94. (cd-ep) <*77112*> **BRONX CHEER / THERE'S SPIDER EGGS IN BUBBLA YHUM / SUZANNE PEELS OUT** –

— now without BAKER who re-surfaced as SHADY, releasing towards the end of '94, a solo album, 'WORLD' (for 'Beggars Banquet' UK, 'Atlantic' US), which included members of SWERVEDRIVER, ROLLERSKATE SKINNY, Th' FAITH HEALERS, SHARKBOY and BOO RADLEYS. A single, 'NARCOTIC CANDY' was taken from it with a subsequent single, 'PEARLS', coming out a year later.

Jun 94. (12"white/cd-s) *(BBQ 37 T/CD)* **EVERLASTING ARM. / DEADMAN** –

May 95. (cd/c/lp)(pic-lp) *(BBQ CD/MC/LP 176)(BBQ 176P)* <*64362*> **SEE YOU ON THE OTHER SIDE** Sep95
– Empire state (Sun House in excelsis) / Young man's stride / Sudden ray of hope / Everlasting arm / Racing the tide / Close encounters of the 3rd grade / A kiss from an old flame (a trip to the Moon) / Peaceful night.

— split late '94, as DONAHUE and GRASSHOPPER were already moonlighting as the HARMONY ROCKETS. The former and MERCURY REV collaborated on The CHEMICAL BROTHERS 'Dig Your Own Hole' track, 'Private Psychedelic Reel'.

HARMONY ROCKETS

— **DONAHUE + GRASSHOPPER** plus **LEVON HELMS + GARTH HUDSON** (the BAND) (they also guested on MERCURY REV's comeback album) / **ZOOT ROLLO HORN** (ex-CAPTAIN BEEFHEART)

Rockville Rockville

Jun 93. (7") *(ROCK 6113-7)* **SKELETON MAN. /**

Big Cat Big Cat

Oct 95. (lp/cd) <*(ABB 90/+CD)*> **PARALYZED MIND OF THE ARCHANGEL VOID** Sep98
– Paralyzed mind of the archangel void.

Big Cat No.6

Oct 97. (cd-s) *(ABB 151SCD)* <*45*> **I'VE GOT A GOLDEN TICKET EP** Nov98
– I've got a golden ticket / L'apocalypse des animaux / Tale scendeva l'etternale adore / I've got a golden ticket (version) / I've got a golden ticket (extended).

MERCURY REV

— **JONATHAN + GRASSHOPPER** reformed the band in the summer of '97 with **ADAM SNYDER** – keyboards / **JUSTIN RUSSO** – keyboards / **JASON RUSSO** – bass / **JEFF MERCEL** – drums

— by 1998, **SNYDER** was the only person that **JONATHAN + GRASSHOPPER** retained, bringing back **DAVE FRIDMANN, SUZANNE THORPE + JIMY CHAMBERS**

V2 Epic

Oct 98. (cd/lp) *(VVR 100277-2/-1)* <*27027*> **DESERTER'S SONGS** 27 Sep98
– Holes / Tonite it shows / Endlessly / I collect coins / Opus 40 / Hudson line / The happy end (the drunk room) / Goddess on a hiway / The funny bird / Pick up if you're there / Delta sun bottleneck stomp. *(also on special cd; VVR 100379-2)*

Nov 98. (7") *(VVR 500332-7)* **GODDESS ON A HIWAY. / RAGTAG** 51 –
(cd-s+=) *(VVR 5000332-3)* – I only have eyes for you.

Jan 99. (12") *(VVR 500541-6)* **DELTA SUN BOTTLENECK STOMP. / ('A'-Chemical Brothers mix) / ENDLESSLY (instrumental)** 26
(cd-s) *(VVR 500541-3)* – (first two tracks) / Vampire blues (live).
(cd-s) *(VVR 500616-3)* – ('A') / Holes (live) / Isolation (live).

May 99. (7") *(VVR 500696-7)* **OPUS 40. / MOTION PICTURES (live)** 31 –
(cd-s) *(VVR 500697-3)* – ('A') / He was a friend of mine (live) / Raindrops keep falling on my head (live).
(cd-s) *(VVR 500696-3)* – ('A') / He was a friend of mine (live) / Tonite is shows (live).

Aug 99. (7") *(VVR 500849-7)* **GODDESS ON A HIWAY. / CAROLINE SAYS** 26 –
(cd-s) *(VVR 500849-3)* – ('A') / I don't wanna be a soldier / Car wash hair (live).
(cd-s) *(VVR 500849-8)* – ('A') / I dreamt / Very sleepy rivers (live).

Aug 01. (cd/lp) *(VVR 101752-2/-1)* <*27106*> **ALL IS DREAM** 11
– The dark is rising / Tides of the Moon / Chains / Lincoln's eyes / Nite and fog / Little rhymes / A drop in time / You're my queen / Spiders and flies / Hercules. *(cd re-iss. Apr02 & Jan05 w/free cd+=; VVR 101752-0)* – Saw song (live) / Hercules (live) / Little rhymes (live) / Nite and fog (video) / The dark is rising (video) / (interview documentary).

Sep 01. (7") *(VVR 501772-7)* **NITE AND FOG. / NITE AND FOG (demo)** 47 –
(cd-s) *(VVR 501772-3)* – ('A') / A drop in time (demo) / Serpentine.
(cd-s) *(VVR 501772-8)* – ('A') / Cool waves / Nite & fog (alt. version feat. boys choir).

Jan 02. (cd-s) *(VVR 501871-3)* **THE DARK IS RISING / NOCTURNE IN C# MINOR – OPUS 27 NO.1 / PLANET CARAVAN** 16 –
(cd-s) *(VVR 501871-8)* – ('A') / Spiders and flies (live) / Blues skies.

Jul 02. (cd-s) *(VVR 501978-3)* **LITTLE RHYMES / CHAINS (Peter Stillman mix) / I KEEP A CLOSE WATCH** 51 –
(cd-s) *(VVR 501978-8)* – ('A') / Observatory crest / Streets of Laredo.

Jan 05. (7"pic-d) *(VVR 502922-7)* **IN A FUNNY WAY. / ANDROGYNOUS** 28 –
(cd-s) *(VVR 502922-3)* – ('A') / Good times ahead / Black swan.
(dvd-s) *(VVR 502922-9)* – ('A') / Moving on (video) / Down poured the heavens (video).

Jan 05. (cd/lp) *(VVR 102923-2/-1)* <*27244*> **THE SECRET MIGRATION** 16 Mar05
– Secret for a song / Across yer ocean / Diamonds / Black forest (Lorelei) / Vermillion / In the wilderness / In a funny way / My love / Moving on / The climbing rose / Arise / First-time mother's joy (flying) / Down poured the heavens.

Mar 05. (7"pic-d) *(VVR 503103-7)* **ACROSS YER OCEAN. / TENNESSEE BLUES** 54 –
(cd-s) *(VVR 503103-3)* – ('A') / Mirror for a bell / Afraid.

– compilations, others, etc. –

Jun 04. (d-cd) *V2; (VVR 102774-2)* **DESERTER'S SONGS / ALL IS DREAM** –

GRASSHOPPER AND THE GOLDEN CRICKETS

with **SUZANNE THORPE** – flute, co-producer (of MERCURY REV) + others

		Beggars Banquet	Beggars Banquet
Jul 98.	(7") *(BBQ 325)* **SILVER BALLOONS. / SOLAR POWERED HORNET BEYOND THE SHADOWS OF OVERLOOK MOUNTAIN**	☐	-
	(cd-s+=) *(BBQ 325CD)* – ('A'mix).		
Aug 98.	(cd/lp) *(BBQ CD/LP 201) <80201>* **THE ORBIT OF ETERNAL GRACE**	☐	☐

– Silver balloons / The ballad of the one-eyed angelfish / O-ring (baby talk) / Nickel in a lemon / The orbit of eternal grace / September's fool / Univac bug track / Smpte for the Devil / N.Y. avenue playground / Sketches of Saturn (love in space) / Midnight express / N.Y. avenue playground (reprise).

METALLICA

Formed: Norvale, California, USA . . . 1981 by LARS ULRICH (this Danish-born drummer had previously filled the stool on a UK tour by DIAMOND HEAD, whose songs METALLICA would later cover) and JAMES HETFIELD (guitar vocals; ex-OBSESSION). Recruiting LLOYD GRAND on guitar, the band recorded their first demo, 'NO LIFE TILL LEATHER' and a one-off 7" single, 'LET IT LOOSE'. In early '82, LLOYD was replaced by future MEGADETH mainman DAVE MUSTAINE, while RON McGOVNEY was brought in on bass. After a brief period of relative stability, MUSTAINE was fired for drunkenness early the following year, being replaced by former EXODUS guitarist KIRK HAMMETT. By this point CLIFF BURTON (ex-TRAUMA) had already joined on bass following the departure of McGOVNEY. This was the classic early METALLICA line-up that played on the first three albums, redefining the boundaries of metal and touring constantly until the tragic death of BURTON in 1986. Moving to New Jersey in early '83, the band signed to John Zazula's 'Megaforce' label and unleashed their high octane debut, 'KILL 'EM ALL' (licensed to 'Music For Nations' for UK release). While it certainly wasn't without cliche, both lyrically and musically, there was a vibrancy in the speed and loudness of their sonic attack that drew on hardcore and punk, particularly in 'SEEK AND DESTROY', a track that would come to be a staple of the band's live set. The record also featured, horror of horrors, a track that consisted entirely of a bass solo! But METALLICA weren't trying to resurrect the indulgence of the 70's, their follow-up opus, 'RIDE THE LIGHTNING' (1984), confirming METALLICA's status as one of the most inventive, promising bands in the metal canon. The group had welded a keening sense of melody to their visceral thrash, alternating between grinding, bass heavy, mid-tempo uber-riffing (the title track and 'FOR WHOM THE BELL TOLLS') and all out pummelling ('FIGHT FIRE WITH FIRE' and 'TRAPPED UNDER ICE'). They even came close to ballad territory with the bleakly beautiful 'FADE TO BLACK', arguably one of the best tracks the band have ever penned. Then came 'MASTER OF PUPPETS' (1986), a masterful collection that rightfully saw METALLICA hailed as one of, if not the, foremost metal act in the world, at the heavier end of the spectrum at least. Opening with the relentless fury of 'BATTERY', followed by the epic, breathtaking dynamics of the title track, the album was almost flawless from start to finish, again using the combination of all-out thrashers alternated with bowel-quaking grinders ('THE THING THAT SHOULD NOT BE', 'WELCOME HOME (SANITARIUM)') to maximum effect. The album went Top 30 in the States without the help of a hit single or even radio play, eventually achieving platinum status. The band subsequently toured with metal godfather, OZZY OSBOURNE, playing to rapturous crowds wherever they went. Disaster struck, however, when the band's tour bus crashed on 27th September '86, BURTON losing his life in the accident. METALLICA decided to carry on, replacing BURTON with JASON NEWSTED (ex-FLOTSAM & JETSAM) and fulfilling their touring commitments. The following summer, the band released an EP of covers, '$5.98 EP – GARAGE DAYS REVISITED', a hotch potch of inspired reworkings from the likes of DIAMOND HEAD, BUDGIE and The MISFITS. The record made both the UK and US Top 30, the US edition containing an extra former KILLING JOKE track (see below). Their next album proper, ' . . .AND JUSTICE FOR ALL' (1988), was marred by overly ambitious structures and complex arrangements as well as a poor production, subduing the trademark gut intensity. Nevertheless, there were moments of brilliance, most notably with 'ONE', a distressing first person narrative of a soldier kept alive on a life support machine. The song almost made the UK Top 10, winning the band a Grammy the following year for Best Metal Performance. With the eponymous transatlantic No.1, 'METALLICA' (1991), the band entered the major league alongside the likes of U2 and R.E.M. as one of the biggest rock bands in the world. The aptly named Bob Rock had given the record a cleaner, 'big rock' sound that complemented the more melodic and accessible material contained within. Not that METALLICA had gone limp on the Beavis & Butthead element of their fanbase, 'ENTER SANDMAN' was as crunchingly heavy as ever, yet the single possessed a sufficiently strong melodic hook to see it go Top 5 in the UK. With 'NOTHING ELSE MATTERS', METALLICA really had penned a WISHBONE ASH-esque ballad, replete with strings (!) which saw the band notch up another Top 10 UK hit. After undertaking the biggest tour heavy rock has ever seen (obliterating co-headliners GUNS N' ROSES in the process), the band came back with another work of mature rock majesty, 'LOAD' (1996). From morbid metal to LYNYRD SKYNYRD-style rootsy acoustics, METALLICA once more developed and expanded their sonic palate, gaining widespread acclaim. The album went on to sell almost ten million copies, the band headlining the American Lollapolooza tour to promote it, again blowing most of the other acts away. Not exactly the most prolific of bands, METALLICA surpassed themselves by releasing a successor to 'LOAD' the following year, entitled, appropriately enough, 'RE-LOAD'. While other heavy rock acts flounder under the weight of 90's expectations, METALLICA continue to innovate and energise a tired genre, even, God forbid, cutting their hair(!) in line with their new standing as the post-modern kings of metal. In the spring of '99, HETFIELD, ULRICH and Co were planning an orchestrated performance with composer MICHAEL KAMEN at the helm of the San Francisco Symphony Orchestra, a 'best of' live album, 'S&M' hitting the bemused public later in the year. Three years into the new millennium and more than two decades into a genre-defining career, the trio of HETFIELD, ULRICH and HAMMETT (together with longtime producer ROBERT TRUJILLO on bass, as a replacement for the departed NEWSTED) returned with, 'ST. ANGER' (2003), the sonic brutality and unalloyed rage that had perhaps been missing in their recent work was on show here. Judging by the fear and loathing within these pulverising grooves, HETFIELD's recent stint in rehab seemed to have unlocked a fearsome closet of skeletons, the frontman raging at the world and, in the process, unleashing a momentum that had his band members caged-in from the opening bars. In 2004, the band released their warts'n'all documentary film/DVD/mini-CD, 'SOME KIND OF MONSTER' – bow to the master who is therapist, Phil Towle.

• **Songwriters:** ULRICH-HETFIELD, bar other covers on record; BLITZKRIEG (Blitzkrieg) / CRASH COURSE IN BRAIN SURGERY + BREADFAN (Budgie) / AM I EVIL? + THE PRINCE + HELPLESS + IT'S ELECTRIC (Diamond Head) / LAST CARESS – GREEN HELL + DIE DIE

MY DARLING (Misfits) / KILLING TIME (Sweet Savage) / THE SMALL HOURS (Holocaust) / THE WAIT (Killing Joke) / STONE COLD CRAZY (Queen) / SO WHAT (Anti-Nowhere League) / SABBRA CADABRA (Black Sabbath) / Medley: EVIL – CURSE OF THE PHARAOHS – SATAN'S FALL – A CORPSE WITHOUT SOUL – INTO THE COVEN (Mercyful Fate) / LOVERMAN (Nick Cave) / WHISKEY IN THE JAR (Thin Lizzy) / TURN THE PAGE (Bob Seger & The Silver Bullet Band) / TUESDAY'S GONE (Lynyrd Skynyrd) / OVERKILL + STONE DEAD FOREVER + DAMAGE CASE + TOO LATE, TOO LATE (Motorhead) / FREE SPEECH FOR THE DUMB + THE MORE I SEE (Discharge) / ASTRONOMY (Blue Oyster Cult) / NOW I WANNA SNIFF SOME GLUE + CRETIN HOP (Ramones).

Album rating: KILL 'EM ALL (*7) / RIDE THE LIGHTNING (*8) / MASTER OF PUPPETS (*9) / . . . AND JUSTICE FOR ALL (*7) / METALLICA (*10) / LOAD (*8) / RE-LOAD (*6) / GARAGE INC. (*5) / S&M (*5) / ST. ANGER (*7) / SOME KIND OF MONSTER mini soundtrack (*4)

JAMES HETFIELD (b. 3 Aug'63, Los Angeles) – vocals, rhythm guitar (ex-OBSESSION, etc) / **LARS ULRICH** (b.16 Dec'63, Gentoss, Copenhagen, Denmark) – drums / with **LLOYD GRAND** – guitar

not iss. — Bootleg

Dec 81. (7") **LET IT LOOSE. / KILLING TIME** [–] [ ]

— (Jan'82) **DAVE MUSTAINE** (b.13 Sep'63, La Mesa, Calif.) – lead guitar, co-writer / **RON McGOVNEY** – bass repl. GRAND (JEF WARNER also played guitar in 1982)

— (early '83) **KIRK HAMMETT** (b.18 Nov'62, San Francisco) – lead guitar (ex-EXODUS) repl. MUSTAINE who was fired due to drunkenness. He was soon to form rivals MEGADETH.

— **CLIFF BURTON** (b.10 Feb'62) – bass (ex-TRAUMA) replaced McGOVNEY

Music For Nations — Megaforce

Jul 83. (lp) *(MFN 7) <MRI-069>* **KILL 'EM ALL** [ ] [ ]
– Hit the lights / The four horsemen / Motorbreath / Jump in the fire / (Anesthesia) Pulling teeth / Whiplash / Phantom Lord / No remorse / Seek and destroy / Metal militia. *<US re-iss. Mar86; same> (pic-lp.Aug86; MFN 7P) (cd-iss. Apr87; CDMFN 7) <US re-iss. Feb88 on 'Elektra'+=; 60766>* – Am I evil? / Blitzkrieg. *(re-iss. Nov89 on 'Vertigo' lp/c/cd; 838 142-1/-4/-2)*

Jan 84. (12",12"red) *(12KUT 105) <MRS 04>* **JUMP IN THE FIRE** / *[us-only]* WHIPLASH (special neckbrace mix). / SEEK AND DESTROY (live) / PHANTOM LORD [ ] [ ]
(re-iss. Mar86, 7"sha-pic-d; PKUT 105)

Jul 84. (lp/c) *(MFN/TMFN 27) <769>* **RIDE THE LIGHTNING** [87] [100]
– Fight fire with fire / Ride the lightning / For whom the bell tolls / Fade to black / Trapped under ice / Escape / Creeping death / The call of Ktulu. *(re-iss. Sep86 cd/pic-lp; CDMFN 27/CDMFN 27P) <US re-iss. Oct84 on 'Elektra'; 60396> (re-iss. Nov89 on 'Vertigo' lp/c/cd; 838410-1/-4/-2) (cd re-iss. Apr00 on 'DCC'; GZS 1136)*

Music For Nations — Elektra

Nov 84. (12"pic-d/12") *(P+/12KUT 112)* **CREEPING DEATH. / AM I EVIL. / BLITZKRIEG** [ ] [ ]
(re-iss. Jan87 12"gold/12"blue; GV/CV 12KUT 112)

Mar 86. (lp/pic-d-lp)(c/cd) *(MFN 60/+P)(T/CD MFN 60) <9-60439-1>* **MASTER OF PUPPETS** [41] [29]
– Battery / Master of puppets / The thing that should not be / Welcome home (sanitarium) / Disposable heroes / Leper messiah / Orion / Damage, Inc. *(re-iss. Dec87 d-lp; MFN 60DM) (re-iss. May89 on 'Vertigo' lp/c/cd; 838 141-1/-4/-2)*

— **JASON NEWSTEAD** (b. 4 Mar'63, Battle Creek, Missouri) – bass (ex-FLOTSAM AND JETSAM) repl. CLIFF who was killed in tour bus crash 27 Sep'86 Sweden.

Vertigo — Elektra

Aug 87. (12"ep) *(METAL 1-12) <60757>* **$5.98 EP – GARAGE DAYS RE-REVISITED** [27] [28]
– Helpless / Crash course in brain surgery / The small hours / Last caress – Green hell. *<US+=>* – The Wait. *(re-iss. May90 lp/c/cd; 888 788-1/-4/-2)*

Sep 88. (7") *<69357>* **EYE OF THE BEHOLDER. / BREADFAN** [–] [ ]

Sep 88. (12"ep/cd-ep) *(METAL 2-12/CD2)* **HARVESTER OF SORROW. / BREADFAN. / THE PRINCE** [20] [ ]

Oct 88. (d-lp)(c)(cd) *(VERH/+C 61)(836 062-2) <60812>* **. . .AND JUSTICE FOR ALL** [4] Sep88 [6]
– Blackened / . . .And justice for all / Eye of the beholder / One / The shortest straw / Harvester of sorrow / The frayed ends of sanity / To live is to die / Dyers eve.

Feb 89. (7") *<69329>* **ONE. / THE PRINCE** [–] [35]
(3"cd-s+=) – Eye of the beholder.

Mar 89. (7")(10"pic-d) *(MET 5)(METPD 5-10)* **ONE. / SEEK AND DESTROY (live)** [13] [–]
(12")(cd-s) *(MET 5-12)(METCD 5)* – ('A'demo) / For whom the bell tolls (live) / Welcome home (sanitarium) (live).
(12"g-f+=) *(METG 5-12)* – Creeping death (live).

Jul 91. (7"pic-d) *(METAL 7) <64857>* **ENTER SANDMAN. / STONE COLD CRAZY** [5] [16]
(12"+=/12"box+=)(cd-s+=) *(MET AL/BX 7-12)(METCD 7)* – Holier than thou.

Aug 91. (cd/c/d-lp) *(510022-2/-4/-1) <61113>* **METALLICA** [1] [1]
– Enter sandman / Sad but true / Holier than thou / The unforgiven / Wherever I may roam / Don't tread on me / Through the never / Nothing else matters / Of wolf and man / The god that failed / My friend of misery / The struggle within.

Nov 91. (7"/7"pic-d) *(METAL/METAP 8) <64814>* **THE UNFORGIVEN. / KILLING TIME** [15] [35]
(12"+=)(cd-s+=) *(METAL 8-12)(METCD 8)* – ('A'demo) / So what.

Apr 92. (7"/7"pic-d) *(META L/P 10) <64770>* **NOTHING ELSE MATTERS. / ENTER SANDMAN (live)** [6] Mar92 [34]
(12"+=)(cd-s+=) *(METAL 10-12)(METCD 10)* – Harvester of sorrow (live) / ('A'demo).
(live-cd-s+=) *(METCL 10)* – Stone cold crazy (live) / Sad but true (live).

— On tour only **JOHN MARSHALL (of METAL CHURCH)** repl. injured (burnt) HETFIELD

Oct 92. (7"/7"pic-d) *(METAL/METAP 9) <64741>* **WHEREVER I MAY ROAM. / FADE TO BLACK (live)** [25] Jul92 [82]
(pic-cd-s+=) *(METCD 9)* – ('A'demo).
(cd-s) *(METCB 9)* – ('A'side) / Last caress – Am I evil? – Battery (live medley).
(12"+=) *(METAL 9-12)* – ('A'demo).

Oct 92. (c-s) *<64696>* **SAD BUT TRUE / SO WHAT?** [–] [98]

Feb 93. (7") *(METAL 11) <64696>* **SAD BUT TRUE. / NOTHING ELSE MATTERS** [20] [–]
(12"+=,12"pic-d+=)(cd-s+=) *(METAL 11-12)(METCD 11)* – Creeping death (live) / ('A'demo).
(pic-cd-s) *(METCH 11)* – ('A'side) / ('B'live) / ('A'live).

Dec 93. (d-cd/d-c) *(518 726-2/-4) <61594>* **LIVE SHIT: BINGE & PURGE (live)** [54] [26]
– Enter sandman / Creeping death / Harvester of sorrow / Welcome home (sanitarium) / Sad but true / Of wolf and man / Guitar doodle / The unforgiven / And justice for all / Solos (bass/guitar) / Through the never / From whom the bell tolls / Fade to black / Master of puppets / Seek & destroy / Whiplash / Nothing else matters / Wherever I may roam / Am I evil? / Last caress / One / Battery. *(d-c+=)* – The four horsemen / Motorbreath / Stone cold crazy. *(also issued 3 videos + book etc 'METALLICAN')*

May 96. (10"red-ep) *(METAL 12)* **UNTIL IT SLEEPS. / 2x4 (live) / UNTIL IT SLEEPS (Moby remix)** [18] [–]
(cd-s) *(METCD 12)* – ('A'-Herman Melville mix) / 2x4 (live) / F.O.B.D (aka; Until It Sleeps – demo).
(cd-s) *(METCX 12)* – (first & third tracks) / Kill – Ride (medley; Ride the lightning – No remorse – Hit the lights – The four horsemen – Phantom Lord – Fight fire with fire).

May 96. (c-s) *<64276>* **UNTIL IT SLEEPS / OVERKILL** [–] [10]

Jun 96. (cd/c/d-lp) *(532 618-2/-4/-1) <61923>* **LOAD** [1] [1]
– Ain't my bitch / 2 x 4 / The house Jack built / Until it sleeps / King Nothing / Hero of the day / Bleeding me / Cure / Poor twisted me / Wasting my hate / Mama said / Thorn within / Ronnie / The outlaw torn.

Sep 96. (12"ep) *(METAL 13)* **HERO OF THE DAY / MOULDY (aka HERO OF THE DAY – early demo version). / HERO OF THE DAY (outta b sides mix) / OVERKILL** [17] [–]
(cd-ep) *(METCD 13)* – ('A'side) / Overkill / Damage case / Hero of the day (outta b sides mix).
(cd-ep) *(METCX 13)* – ('A'side) / Stone dead forever / Too late too late / Mouldy (aka 'Hero Of The Day' – early demo version).
(cd-ep) *(METCY 13)* – ('A'side) / Overkill / Damage case / Stone dead forever / Too late too late.
(because of length of above, it also hit 47 in UK album charts)

Oct 96. (c-s) *<64248>* **HERO OF THE DAY / KILL – RIDE (medley)** [–] [60]

Nov 96. (7"pic-d) *(METAL 14)* **MAMA SAID. / AIN'T MY BITCH (live)** [19] [ ]
(cd-s) *(METCD 14)* – ('A'side) / King Nothing (live) / Whiplash (live) / ('A'edit).

(cd-s) *(METCX 14)* – ('A'side) / So what (live) / Creeping death (live) / ('A'-early demo).

Feb 97. (cd-s) *<64197>* **KING NOTHING / AIN'T MY BITCH (live)** [–] [90]

Nov 97. (7") *(METAL 15) <64126>* **THE MEMORY REMAINS. / FOR WHOM THE BELL TOLLS (Haven't Heard It Yet mix)** [13] [28]
(cd-s) *(METCD 15)* – ('A'side) / Fuel for fire / Memory (demo).
(cd-s) *(METDD 15)* – ('A'side) / The outlaw torn (Unencumbered By Manufacturing Restrictions version) / King Nothing (Tepid mix).

— MARIANNE FAITHFULL supplied backing vocals on above single

Nov 97. (cd/c/d-lp) *(536409-2/-4/-1) <62126>* **RELOAD** [4] [1]
– Fuel / The memory remains / The Devil's dance / Unforgiven II / Better than you / Carpe diem baby / Prince Charming / Bad seed / Where the wild things are / Slither / Low man's lyric / Attitude / Fixxer.

Feb 98. (cd-ep) *(METCD 17) <64114>* **THE UNFORGIVEN II / HELPLESS (live) / The four horsemen (live) / Of wolf and man (live)** [15] Mar98 [59]
(cd-ep) *(METDD 17)* – ('A'side) / The thing that should not be (live) / The memory remains (live) / King nothing (live).
(cd-ep) *(METCX 17)* – ('A'side) / No remorse (live) / Am I evil? (live) / The unforgiven II (demo).

Jun 98. (cd-ep) *(METCD 16)* **FUEL / SAD BUT TRUE (live) / NOTHING ELSE MATTERS (live)** [31] [ ]
(cd-ep) *(METDD 16)* – ('A'side) / Wherever I roam (live) / One (live).
(cd-ep) *(METED 16)* – ('A'side) / Until it sleeps (live) / ('A'live) / ('A'demo).

Nov 98. (d-cd/d-c/d-lp) *(538351-2/-4/-1) <62323>* **GARAGE INC.** (the covers) [29] [2]
– Free speech for the dumb / It's electric / Sabba cadabra / Turn the page / Die die my darling / Loverman / Mercyful Fate medley:- Evil – Curse of the pharaohs – Satan's fall – A corpse without soul – Into the coven / Astronomy / Whiskey in the jar / Tuesday's gone / The more I see / Helpless / The small hours / The wait / Crash course in brain surgery / Last caress – Green hell / Am I evil? / Blitzkrieg / Breadfan / The prince / Stone cold crazy / So what? / Killing time / Overkill / Damage case / Stone dead forever / Too late, too late.

Nov 98. (cd-ep) *(566591-2)* **TURN THE PAGE / STONE COLD CRAZY (live) / THE WAIT (live) / BLEEDING ME (live)** [ ] [ ]

Feb 99. (cd-s) *(566855-2)* **WHISKEY IN THE JAR / BLITZKREIG (live) / THE PRINCE (live)** [29] [ ]
(cd-s) *(566857-2)* – ('A'side) / The small hours (live) / Killing time (live).
(cd-s) *(566859-2)* – ('A'side) / Last caress – Green hell (live) / Whiskey in the jar (live).

Jun 99. (cd-ep) *(METCD 20)* **DIE DIE MY DARLING / SABBRA CADABRA (live) / MERCYFUL FATE MEDLEY (live)** [ ] [ ]

Nov 99. (d-cd/d-c) *(546797-2/-4) <62463>* **S&M** (live with the San Francisco Symphony Orchestra) [33] [2]
– The ecstasy of gold / The call of the Ktulu / Master of puppets / Of wolf and man / The thing that should not be / Fuel / The memory remains / No leaf clover / Hero of the day / Devil's dance / Bleeding me / Nothing else matters / Until it sleeps / For whom the bell tolls / Human / Wherever I may roam / Outlaw torn / Sad but true / One / Enter sandman / Battery. *(re-iss. Apr00; same)*

Mar 00. (cd-s) *(562696-2) <album cut>* **NO LEAF CLOVER / ('A'-enhanced CD-Rom) / "S&M" Documentary (enhanced first 15 minutes)** [ ] Feb00 [74]
(cd-s) *(562697-2)* – ('A') / (photo gallery and album lyrics CD-Rom) / "S&M" Documentary (enhanced second 15 minutes).
(cd-s) *(562698-2)* – ('A') / (Metallica screensaver) / "S&M" Documentary (enhanced third 15 minutes).

Jul 00. (cd-s) *(0113875HWR) <album cut>* **I DISAPPEAR / I DISAPPEAR (instrumental)** [35] Feb00 [76]
(above iss.on 'Edel-Hollywood')

— **ROBERT TRUJILLO** – bass; repl. NEWSTED (left in 2001)

Mercury Elektra

Jun 03. (cd/c/d-lp) *(986533-2/-4/-6) <62853>* **ST. ANGER** [3] [1]
– Frantic / St. Anger / Some kind of monster / Dirty window / Invisible kid / My world / Shoot me again / Sweet amber / The unnamed feeling / Purify / All within my hands.

Jun 03. (7") *(986541-1)* **ST. ANGER. / WE'RE A HAPPY FAMILY** [9] [–]
(cd-s) *(986541-2)* – ('A') / Commando / Today your love tomorrow the world.
(cd-s) *(986541-3)* – ('A') / Now I wanna sniff some glue / Cretin hop / ('A'-video).

Sep 03. (12") *(981151-5)* **FRANTIC. / FRANTIC (UNKLE remix)** [16] [–]
(cd-s) *(981151-3)* – ('A') / Blackened (live) / Harvester of sorrow (live) / ('A'-video).
(cd-s) *(981151-4)* – ('A') / No remorse (live) / Welcome home – Sanitarium (live).

Jan 04. (12"pic-d) *(9815661)* **THE UNNAMED FEELING. / LEPER MESSIAH (live)** [42] Dec03 [ ]
(cd-ep+=) *<(9815881)>* – live – Paris:- The four horsemen / Damage Inc. / Motorbreath / Ride the lightning (w/intro) / Hit the lights / ('A'-video).

Aug 04. (m-cd) *(9867810) <48838>* **SOME KIND OF MONSTER** (soundtrack) [ ] Jul04 [37]
– Some kind of monster / The four horsemen (live) / Damage, Inc. (live) / Leper messiah (live) / Motorbreath (live) / Ride the lightning (live) / Hit the lights (live) / Some kind of monster (edit & movie trailer).

– compilations, others, etc. –

Aug 87. (7"ep/7"pic-ep) *Megaforce; <MRS 04/+P>* **WHIPLASH EP** [–] [ ]

Feb 90. (cd/c) *Vertigo; (642 219-2/-4)* **METALLICA** [ ] [ ]
– (JUMP IN THE FIRE + CREEPING DEATH singles).

May 90. (6x12"box) *Vertigo; (875 487-1)* **THE GOOD, THE BAD & THE LIVE – THE 6 1/2 YEARS ANNIVERSARY COLLECTION** [56] [–]

Apr 98. (cd) *Ranch Life; (CRANCH 1)* **BAY AREA THRASHERS** [ ] [ ]
(also pic-lp on 'Collectors Picture Disc Series'; CPD 014)

□ METHOD MAN (see under ⇒ WU-TANG CLAN)

□ Malcolm MIDDLETON (see under ⇒ ARAB STRAP)

□ MINOR THREAT (see under ⇒ FUGAZI)

Joni MITCHELL

Born: ROBERTA JOAN ANDERSON, 7 Nov'43, Fort MacLeod, Alberta, Canada. In 1964, she performed at the Mariposa Folk Festival in Ontario, and married CHUCK MITCHELL in June '65, although after they relocated to Detroit the following year, they divorced. She retained the surname and moved to New York, where her songs were gradually recorded by others, mainly JUDY COLLINS ('BOTH SIDES NOW' & 'MICHAEL FROM MOUNTAINS') and TOM RUSH ('THE CIRCLE GAME'). Her self-titled DAVID CROSBY-produced debut lp came out in Summer of '68 and managed to only scrape into US Top 200. In August 1969 on the advice of David Geffen, she pulled out of WOODSTOCK free festival, and instead wrote the classic song of that name. It was later a US hit for CROSBY, STILLS, NASH & YOUNG, and also a UK No.1 for MATTHEWS' SOUTHERN COMFORT. Her second lp, 'CLOUDS', broke through into US Top 40 after her non-appearance, another classic album of the late 60's. Her third outing, 'LADIES OF THE CANYON' contained the aforementioned hippie mysticism of 'WOODSTOCK' as well as the surprise UK hit 'BIG YELLOW TAXI', making MITCHELL a household name in Britain when the album went to No.8. The romanticism had all but vanished by 'BLUE', one of the starkest, most soul searching records of the singer/songwriter era. The autobiographical intensity of the record is borne out by the fact that MITCHELL allegedly allowed no one but the engineer into the studio during recording. Not quite so intense but arguably more introspective was her 1972 album, 'FOR THE ROSES', a more experimental edge creeping into the arrangements and the first signs of MITCHELL's increasing preoccupation with jazz stylings. A combination of glittering melody and a light jazz sheen created one of her most listenable and commercially successful albums, 1974's 'COURT AND SPARK'. The assured sophistication of MITCHELL's blossoming talent was also evident in her live work, 'MILES OF AISLES', matching 'COURT AND SPARK's No.2 position on the US chart. Her next two albums, 'THE HISSING OF SUMMER LAWNS' and 'HEJIRA' marked a significant move away from the relative simplicity of her earlier work into more sophisticated sonic textures, underscored by jazz and world-inflected rhythms while her lyrical musings followed suit, away from personal confession towards pointed observation and cultural commentary. Alienated from the rock community which had nurtured her and amid scathing reviews, she moved ever further into obscure jazz fusion throughout the latter half of the 70's with the double album 'DON JUAN'S RECKLESS DAUGHTER' (1977) and ultimately, her collaboration with jazz legend Charles Mingus, released in 1979 and simply titled, 'MINGUS'. Come the 80's, MITCHELL seemed to lose her focus. 'WILD THINGS RUN FAST', saw her treading water although 1985's THOMAS DOLBY-produced 'DOG EAT DOG' was an impassioned attack on the rampant materialism and hypocrisy of the 80's, singling out such worthy targets as the TV evangelists of the religious right. The insipid banality of 'CHALK MARK IN A RAINSTORM' (1988) is best passed over while 1991's 'NIGHT RIDE HOME' saw a return to from of sorts, combining the jazz textures and lyrical expaniveness of her earlier work. Around this time, MITCHELL exhibited some of her paintings in London and Edinburgh to critical acclaim while her most recent album to date, 'TURBULENT INDIGO' was a mature, accomplished set taking on such controversial issues as domestic violence. 1998's 'TAMING THE TIGER' was no exception, wherein MITCHELL expanded her sound with the use of guitar synthesizer, the jazzy arrangements and uncompromising lyrics (supplied, on 'The CRAZY CRIES OF LOVE', by boyfriend Don Freed) suggesting that the singer/songwriter was still restless despite her approaching 50th birthday. If not exactly likely to win many new converts, her loyal fanbase ensured the record a Top 75 placing on both sides of the Atlantic, a feat replicated by 'BOTH SIDES NOW' (2000). Directed and co-produced by former husband Larry Klein, the latter was a concept set based around the theme of romance and musically fleshed out by a 71-piece orchestra. Once more demonstrating MITCHELL's desire to push herself, the album found her interpreting pre-war songwriting in sympathetic and original style. 'TRAVELOGUE' (2002), announced as the coda to her long and ever winding music biz road, was perhaps the most ambitious and far sighted project of her near four decades of recording. Backed by a sizeable orchestra and accompanied by jazz luminaries like WAYNE SHORTER and HERBIE HANCOCK, MITCHELL took a long, unsentimental look at her back catalogue, re-imagining a choice selection of her compositions with often intoxicating results. Like her old musical sparring partner NEIL YOUNG, MITCHELL remains one of the few survivors of the hippy era to avoid falling in terminal self-parody, admirably still challenging herself and her fans with each successive release.

• **Songwriters:** All self-penned except; TWISTED (Annie Ross) / WHY DO FOOLS FALL IN LOVE (Frankie Lymon) / BABY I DON'T CARE (hit; Elvis Presley) / SLOUCHING TOWARDS BETHLEHEM (poem; W.B.Yeats).

Album rating: JONI MITCHELL (*7) / CLOUDS (*7) / LADIES OF THE CANYON (*9) / BLUE (*9) / FOR THE ROSES (*7) / COURT AND SPARK (*9) / MILES OF AISLES (*6) / THE HISSING OF SUMMER LAWNS (*8) / HEJIRA (*9) / DON JUAN'S RECKLESS DAUGHTER (*5) / MINGUS (*6) / SHADOWS AND LIGHT (*6) / WILD THINGS RUN FAST (*6) / DOG EAT DOG (*5) / CHALK MARK IN A RAINSTORM (*7) / NIGHT RIDE HOME (*5) / TURBULENT INDIGO (*6) / JONI MITCHELL HITS compilation (*8) / TAMING THE TIGER (*5) / BOTH SIDES NOW (*5) / TRAVELOGUE (*6) / THE BEGINNING OF SURVIVAL compilation (*6) / DREAMLAND compilation (*7)

JONI MITCHELL – vocals, acoustic guitar, piano with **STEPHEN STILLS** – bass / etc (on first)

Reprise Reprise

Jun 68. (lp) *(RSLP 6293)* <6293> **JONI MITCHELL** [Mar68]
– I CAME TO THE CITY:- I had a king / Michael from the mountains / Night in the city / Marcie / Nathan la Freneer / OUT OF THE CITY AND DOWN TO THE SEASIDE:- Sisotowbell Lane / The dawntreader / The pirate of penance / Song to a seagull / Cactus tree. *(cd-iss. Jan88; K2 44051)*

Jul 68. (7") *(RS 20694)* **NIGHT IN THE CITY. / I HAD A KING** [–]

Aug 69. (7") *(23402)* **CHELSEA MORNING. / BOTH SIDES NOW** [–]
<US-iss.Jun72; 1154>

Oct 69. (lp) *(RSLP 6341)* <6341> **CLOUDS** [May69] [31]
– Tin angel / Chelsea morning / I don't know where I stand / That song about the Midway / Roses blue / The gallery / I think I understand / Songs to ageing children come / The fiddle and the drum / Both sides now. *(cd-iss. Jan88; K2 44070)*

—— next guests **MILT HOLLAND** – percussion / **TERESSA ADAMS** – cello / **JIM HORN** – baritone sax / **PAUL HORN** – clarinet, flute

May 70. (lp) *(RSLP 6376)* <6376> **LADIES OF THE CANYON** [8] [Apr70] [27]
– Morning Morgantown / For free / Conversation / Ladies of the canyon / Willy / The arrangement / Rainy night house / The priest / Blue boy / Big yellow taxi / Woodstock / The circle game. *(cd-iss. Jul88; K2 44085)*

Jun 70. (7") *(RS 20906)* <0906> **BIG YELLOW TAXI. / WOODSTOCK** [11] [67]

—— with **STILLS** + **JAMES TAYLOR** – guitar / **SNEAKY PETE KLEINOW** – steel guitar / **RUSS KUNKEL** – drums / etc.

Jul 71. (lp) *(K 44128)* <2038> **BLUE** [3] [Jun71] [15]
– All I want / My old man / Little green / Carey / Blue / California / This flight tonight / River / A case of you / The last time I saw Richard. *(cd-iss. Jan87; K2 44128)*

Aug 71. (7") <1029> **CAREY. / THIS FLIGHT TONIGHT** [–] [93]

Aug 71. (7") *(K 14099)* **CAREY. / MY OLD MAN** [–]

Apr 72. (7") *(K 14130)* <1049> **CALIFORNIA. / A CASE OF YOU** [Oct71]

Jul 72. (7") <1155> **CAREY. / BIG YELLOW TAXI** [–]

—— Her band now **STILLS** + **NASH** (her recent boyfriend) + **KUNKEL** / **WILTON FELDER** / **JAMES BURTON** – guitar / **TOM SCOTT** – wind

Asylum Asylum

Nov 72. (7") *(AYM 511)* <11010> **YOU TURN ME ON, I'M A RADIO. / URGE FOR GOING** [25]

Dec 72. (lp) *(SYLA 8753)* <5057> **FOR THE ROSES** [Nov72] [11]
– Banquet / Cold blue steel and sweet fire / Barangrill / Lesson in survival / Let the wind carry me / For the roses / See you sometime / Electricity / You turn me on, I'm a radio / Blonde in the bleachers / Woman of heart and mind / Judgement of the Moon and stars (Ludwig's tune). *(cd-iss. Dec87; K2 53007)*

Mar 73. (7") *(AYM 515)* **COLD BLUE STEEL AND SWEET FIRE. / BLONDE IN THE BLEACHERS** [–]

—— Retained **TOM SCOTT's L.A. EXPRESS** with new boyfriend **JOHN GUERIN** – drums / **WILTON FELDER** – bass / **LARRY CARLTON** – guitar / **CHUCK FINDLEY** – trumpet / **JOE SAMPLE** – keyboards / **ROBBIE ROBERTSON** – guitar

Jan 74. (7") *(AYM 524)* <11029> **RAISED ON ROBBERY. / COURT AND SPARK** [Dec73] [65]

Mar 74. (lp) *(SYLA 8756)* <7E 1001> **COURT AND SPARK** [14] [Feb74] [2]
– Court and spark / Help me / Free man in Paris / People's parties / The same situation / Car on a hill / Down to you / Just like this train / People's parties / Raised on robbery / Trouble child. *(re-iss. Jun76 lp/c; K/K4 53002) (cd-iss. May83; 253002-2)*

Mar 74. (7") <11034> **HELP ME. / JUST LIKE THIS TRAIN** [–] [7]

Jul 74. (7") <11041> **FREE MAN IN PARIS. / PEOPLE'S PARTIES** [–] [22]

Oct 74. (7") *(AYM 533)* **FREE MAN IN PARIS. / CAR ON A HILL** [–]

Jan 75. (7") *(AYM 537)* <45221> **BIG YELLOW TAXI (live). / RAINY NIGHT HOUSE (live)** [Dec74] [24]

Jan 75. (d-lp) *(SYSP 902)* <202> **MILES OF AISLES** [34] [Nov74] [2]
– You turn me on, I'm a radio / Big yellow taxi / Rainy night house / Woodstock / Cactus tree / Cold blue steel and sweet fire / Woman of heart and mind / A case of you / The circle game / People's parties / All I want / Real good for free / Both sides now / Carey / The last time I saw Richard / Jericho / Love or money. *(re-iss. Jun76 d-lp/d-c; K/K4 63001) (cd-iss. 1989; K2 63001)* – (omits some dialogue).
(above also with **TOM SCOTT & THE L.A. EXPRESS;- SCOTT / GUERIN** plus **ROBBEN FORD** – guitar / **LARRY NASH** – piano / **MAX BENNETT** – bass

Nov 75. (lp/c) *(K/K4 53018) <7E 1051>* **THE HISSING OF SUMMER LAWNS** [14] [4]
– In France they kiss on Main Street / The jungle line / Edith and the kingpin / Don't interrupt the sorrow / Shades of Scarlett conquering The hissing of summer lawns / The boho dance / Harry's house – Centerpiece / Sweet bird / Shadows and light. *(cd-iss. Nov87; K2 53018)*

Mar 76. (7") *(K 13035) <45296>* **IN FRANCE THEY KISS ON MAIN STREET. / BOHO DANCE** [ ] Feb76 [66]

Nov 76. (lp/c) *(K/K4 53053) <7E 1087>* **HEJIRA** [11] [13]
– Coyote / Amelia / Furry sings the blues / A strange boy / Hejira / Song for Sharon / Black crow / Blue motel room / Refuge of the roads. *(cd-iss. Oct87; 253053-2)*

Feb 77. (7") *(K 13072) <45377>* **COYOTE. / BLUE MOTEL ROOM** [ ] [ ]

— now with **JACO PASTORIUS** – bass / **GLENN FREY** – vocals / **WAYNE SHORTER** – sax / **J.D.SOUTHER + CHAKA KHAN** – both backing vocals

Dec 77. (d-lp/d-c) *(K/K4 63003) <101>* **DON JUAN'S RECKLESS DAUGHTER** [20] [25]
– Overture – Cotton Avenue / Talk to me / Jericho / Paprika plains / Otis and Marlena / The tenth world / Dreamland / Don Juan's reckless daughter / Off night backstreet / The silky veils of Ardor. *(cd-iss. 1988; K2 63003)*

Feb 78. (7") *(K 13110)* **OFF NIGHT BACKSTREET. / JERICHO** [ ] [–]

Feb 78. (7") *<45467>* **JERICHO. / DREAMLAND** [–] [ ]

— now with **JACO PASTORIUS** – bass / **WAYNE SHORTER** – sax / **HERBIE HANCOCK** – keyboards / **PETER ERSKINE** – drums / **DON ALIAS + EMIL RICHARDS** – percussion

Jun 79. (7") *(K 13154) <46506>* **THE DRY CLEANER FROM DES MOINES. / GOD MUST BE A BOOGIE MAN** [ ] [ ]

Jul 79. (lp/c) *(K/K4 53091) <505>* **MINGUS** [24] Jun79 [17]
– Happy birthday 1975 (rap) / God must be a boogie man / Funeral (rap) / A chair in the sky / The wolf that lives in Lindsey / I's a muggin' (rap) / Sweet sucker dance / Coin in the pocket (rap) / The dry cleaner from Des Moines / Lucky (rap) / Goodbye pork pie hat. *(cd-iss. 1988; K2 53091)*

— now with **PAT METHENY** – lead guitar / **JACO PASTORUS** – bass / **LYLE MAYS** – keyboards / **DON ALIAS** – drums / **MICHAEL BRECKER** – saxophone

Sep 80. (d-lp/d-c) *(K/K4 62030) <704>* **SHADOWS AND LIGHT (live)** [63] [38]
– (introduction) / In France they kiss on Main Street / Edith and the kingpin / Coyote / Goodbye pork pie hat / The dry cleaner from Des Moines / Amelia / Pat's solo / Hejira / Black crow / Don's solo / Dreamland / Free man in Paris / (band introduction) / Furry sings the blues / Why do fools fall in love? / Shadows and light / God must be a boogie man / Woodstock.

Oct 80. (7") *(K 12478) <47038>* **WHY DO FOOLS FALL IN LOVE? (live). / BLACK CROW (live)** [ ] [ ]

— **LARRY KLEIN** – bass (she married him Nov'82) / **LARRY WILLIAMS** – keyboards / **LARRY CARLTON / JOHN GUERIN / VICTOR FELDMAN** / etc.

Geffen Geffen

Nov 82. (7") *(GEF 2950) <29849>* **(YOU'RE SO SQUARE) BABY, I DON'T CARE. / LOVE** [ ] [47]

Nov 82. (lp/c) *(GEF/40 25102) <GHS 2019>* **WILD THINGS RUN FAST** [32] [25]
– Chinese cafe – Unchained melody / Wild things run fast / Ladies man / Moon at the window / Solid love / Be cool / (You're so square) Baby, I don't care / You dream flat tyres / Man to man / Underneath the streetlight / Love. *(cd-iss. Jul88; GEFD 02019) (re-iss. Jul92 cd/c; GFLD/GFLC 19129)*

Feb 83. (7") *<29757>* **BE COOL. / UNDERNEATH THE STREETLIGHT** [–] [ ]

Feb 83. (7") *(GEF 3122)* **CHINESE CAFE. / LADIES MAN** [ ] [–]
(d7"+=) *(DA 3122)* – (interview).

Nov 85. (7") *(A 6740) <28840>* **GOOD FRIENDS. / SMOKIN' (EMPTY TRY ANOTHER)** [ ] [85]

— Above feat. guest duet **MICHAEL McDONALD**

— now with co-producer **THOMAS DOLBY** – synthesizers / etc.

Nov 85. (lp/c) *(GEF/GEC 26455) <24074>* **DOG EAT DOG** [57] [63]
– Good friends / Fiction / Three great stimulants / Tax free / Smokin' (empty, try another) / Dog eat dog / Shiny toys / Ethiopia / Impossible dreamer / Lucky girl. *(cd-iss. May86; K 924074-2) (re-iss. Oct87 lp/c; K 924074-1/-4) (re-iss. Mar93 cd/c; GFLD/GFLC 19198)*

Apr 86. (7"/12") *(A/TA 7124)* **SHINY TOYS. / THREE GREAT STIMULANTS** [ ] [ ]

— guests **THOMAS DOLBY, TOM PETTY, WILLIE NELSON, DON HENLEY, WENDY & LISA, BILLY IDOL, PETER GABRIEL, etc. KLEIN** co-produced, as was next

Mar 88. (lp/c)(cd) *(WX 141/+C)(924172-2) <24172>* **CHALK MARK IN A RAIN STORM** [26] [45]
– My secret place / Number one / Lakota / The tea leaf prophecy / Dancing clown / The beat of black wings / Snakes and ladders / The recurring dream / The bird that whistles. *(re-iss. Jan91 lp/c/cd; GEF/+C/D 24172) (re-iss. Mar93 cd/c; GFLD/GFLC 19199)*

Apr 88. (7") *<27887>* **MY SECRET PLACE. / LAKOTA** [–] [ ]

May 88. (7") *(GEF 37)* **MY SECRET PLACE. / NUMBER ONE** [ ] [–]
(12"+=/3"cd-s+=) *(GEF 37 T/CD)* – Chinese eyes – Unchained melody / Good friends.

— ('A' featured **PETER GABRIEL**)

— retained **KLEIN** with band **VINNIE COLAIUTA** – drums / **ALEX ACUNA** – percussion / **WAYNE SHORTER** – saxophone / **BILL DILLON + MICHAEL LANDAU** – guitars

Mar 91. (lp/c/cd) *<(GEF/+C/D 24302)>* **NIGHT RIDE HOME** [25] [41]
– Night ride home / Passion play (when all the slaves are free) / Cherokee Louise / The windfall (everything for nothing) / Slouching towards Bethlehem / Come in from the cold / Nothing can be done / The only joy in town / Ray's dad's cadillac / Two grey rooms.

Jul 91. (7") *(GFS 4)* **COME IN FROM THE COLD. / RAY'S DAD'S CADILLAC** [ ] [–]
(cd-s+=/pic-cd-s+=) *(GFS 4CD/+P)* – ('A'extended).

Reprise Reprise

Oct 94. (cd/c) *<(9362 45786-2/-4)>* **TURBULENT INDIGO** [53] [47]
– Sunny Sunday / Sex kills / The Magdalene laundries / Turbulent indigo / How do you stop / Last chance lost / Not to blame / Borderline / Yvette in English / The sire of sorrow (Job's sad song).

Nov 94. (c-s/cd-s) *(W 0273 C/CD)* **HOW DO YOU STOP / THE SIRE OF SORROW / MOON AT THE WINDOW** [ ] [–]

Sep 98. (cd/c) *<(9362 46451-2/-4)>* **TAMING THE TIGER** [57] [75]
– Harlem in Havana / Man from Mars / Love puts on a new face / Lead balloon / No apologies / Taming the tiger / The crazy cries of love / Stay in touch / Face lift / My best to you / Tiger bones.

Feb 00. (cd/c) *<(9362 47620-2/-4)>* **BOTH SIDES NOW** [50] Mar00 [66]
– You're my thrill / At last / Comes love / You've changed / Answer me, my love / A case of you / Don't go to strangers / Sometimes I'm happy / Don't worry 'bout me / Stormy weather / I wish I were in love again / Both sides now (version).

Nonesuch Warners

Nov 02. (d-cd) *(7559 79817-2) <47965>* **TRAVELOGUE** [ ] [ ]
– Otis and Marlena / Amelia / You dream flat tires / Love / Woodstock / Slouching towards Bethlehem / Judgement of the Moon and stars (Ludwig's tune) / The sire of sorrow (Job's sad song) / For the roses / Trouble child / God must be a boogie man / Be cool / Just like this train / Sex kills / Refuge of the roads / Jejira / Chinese cafe – Unchained melody / Cherokee Louise / The dawntreader / The last time I saw Richard / Borderline / The circle game.

– compilations, others, etc. –

May 74. (7"ep) *Reprise; (K 14345)* **CAREY / BOTH SIDES NOW. / BIG YELLOW TAXI / WOODSTOCK** [ ] [–]

Oct 82. (d-c) *Reprise; (K4 64046)* **CLOUDS / BLUE** [ ] [–]

Jul 76. (7") *Asylum; (K 13048)* **YOU TURN ME ON, I'M A RADIO. / FREE MAN IN PARIS** [ ] [–]

Nov 83. (d-c) *Asylum;* **FOR THE ROSES / COURT AND SPARK** [ ] [–]

Oct 96. (cd/c) *Reprise; <(9362 46326-2/-4)>* **HITS** [ ] [ ]
– Urge for going / Chelsea morning / Big yellow taxi / Woodstock / The circle game / Carey / California / You turn me on I'm a radio / Raised on robbery / Help me / Free man in Paris / River / Chinese cafe / – Unchained melody / Come in from the cold / Both sides, now.

Oct 96. (cd/c) *Reprise; <(9362 46358-2/-4)>* **MISSES** [ ] [ ]

May 97. (cd) *Experience; (EXP 025)* **JONI MITCHELL** [ ] [–]

Jun 97. (cd) *Metro; (OTR 1100027)* **GHOSTS** [ ] [–]

Nov 03. (4xcd-box) *Geffen; <(81902)>* **THE COMPLETE GEFFEN RECORDINGS** [ ] Sep03 [ ]

Jul 04. (cd) *Geffen; <B00028360-2>* **THE BEGINNING OF SURVIVAL** [–] [ ]
– The reoccurring dream / The windfall (everything for nothing) / Slouching towards Bethlehem / Dog eat dog / Fiction / The beat of black wings / No apologies / Sex kills / The three great stimulants / Lakota / Ethiopia / Cool water / Tax free / The Magdalene laundries / Passion play

(the story of Jesus and Zachius . . . the little tax collector) / Impossible dreamer.

Sep 04. (cd) *Rhino; <(8122 76520-2)>* **DREAMLAND** [43] [ ]
– Free man in Paris / In France they kiss on Main Street / Dreamland / The jungle line / Furry sings the blues / You turn me on I'm a radio / Carey / Big yellow taxi / California / Help me / Nothing can be done / Dancin' clown / Come in from the cold / Amelia (version) / For the roses (version) / Both sides now (version) / The circle game.

MOBY

Born: RICHARD MELVILLE HALL, 11 Sep'65, New York City, New York, USA. After being raised by his middle-class mother in Darien, Connecticut, he joined hardcore outfit The VATICAN COMMANDOS, which led to him having a brief stint in the similar, FLIPPER. He didn't record anything with the band and moved back to New York to become a DJ, making hardcore techno/dance records under the guise of BRAINSTORM and UHF3, etc. He subsequently became a mixer for The PET SHOP BOYS, ERASURE and MICHAEL JACKSON, before and during his return into solo work in the early 90's. His UK debut, 'GO', hit the Top 10 in October '91, having just breached the charts 3 months earlier. Sampling the 'Twin Peaks' theme, the song was a compelling piece of techno-pop that remains a dancefloor favourite. Little was subsequently heard of him barring a few US imports, although this led to UK semi-indie, 'Mute', taking him on board in mid '93. First up was his near Top 20 single, 'I FEEL IT', beginning a series of hits, albeit sporadic. Early in 1995, his album 'EVERYTHING IS WRONG' had critics lavishing praise on the man for his combination of acid-dance and ambience. 'ANIMAL RIGHTS', the 1996 follow-up added a new dimension; heavy industrial punk-metal which gave him a new found Kerrang! audience. Towards the tail-end of '97, the shaven-headed Christian vegan released the James Bond Theme to 'TOMORROW NEVER DIES', and although it rocketed into the UK Top 10, the accompanying soundtracks album, 'I LIKE TO SCORE', failed to gain the same chart momentum. Eager to once more turn up his amps to number 11, MOBY this time took elements of Southern Blues (courtesy of BESSIE JONES' 'Sometimes') and threw it into his punk/dance melting pot for next single, 'HONEY'. Although it deserved a better chart placing than No.33, it did pave the way for a series of diverse releases kicking off with CANNED HEAT-esque 'RUN ON' (aka 'Run On For A Long Time' by BILL LANDFORD), a taster from his fourth 'Mute' album, 'PLAY' (1999). Opening with the aforementioned 'HONEY', the second track 'FIND MY BABY' took a similar trek back in time (via a sample of the BOY BLUE's 'Joe Lee's Rock') while further UK hit singles, 'BODYROCK' and 'WHY DOES MY HEART FEEL SO BAD', rattled and graced the dancefloors respectively. Following up the unprecedented success of 'PLAY' was always going to prove a difficult if not impossible task for MOBY, especially in light of his often radical musical departures. In the event, '18' (2002) was as warm and self-assured as its predecessor while pointedly not attempting to repeat that record's singular fusion. The spiritual residue of that record did remain, however, imbuing '18's more conventional electronica with an earthy worldliness lacking in his earlier work. Written and recorded without his famous samples, 'HOTEL' (2005) was never going to sound like the final third of a triptych. Instead, it found MOBY strapping on his guitar and stepping up to the mic for what played (no pun intended) as a regular, recorded-live-in-the-studio alt-rock record, interspersed with dancefloor excursions and graced with the soft-focus tones of LAURA DAWN (who shone on a slo-mo cover of New Order's 'TEMPTATION'). Those with a penchant for MOBY's ambient work could find more joy in the bonus disc, yet the album itself only made the US Top 30. As usual, the man was more successful in the UK, where the album made Top 10 and the single, 'LIFT ME UP' (a political broadside adding to what was beoming a litany of protest against the Bush administration) went Top 20.

• **Songwriters:** Himself, and a few with singer, MIMI GOESE:- 'Into The Blue' + 'When It's Cold I'd Like To Die'. Other singers on 1995 album; ROZZ MOREHEAD / MYIM ROSE / NICOLE ZARAY / KOOKIE BANTON / SAUNDRA WILLIAMS. Samples BADALAMENTI's 'Twin Peaks' on 'GO'. Covered NEW DAWN FADES (Joy Division) / THAT'S WHEN I REACH FOR MY REVOLVER (Mission Of Burma). • **Trivia:** In 1992, he remixed JAM & SPOON's club smash 'Stella', which had sampled his 'GO'. He also provided vox for RECOIL's 1992 album , 'Bloodline'. MOBY remixed The B-52's, ESKIMOS AND EGYPT, LFO, FORTRAN 5, ORBITAL, ENO, PET SHOP BOYS + The OTHER TWO.

Album rating: MOBY (*6) / EARLY UNDERGROUND compilation (*6) / THE STORY SO FAR compilation (*6) / AMBIENT (*5) / EVERYTHING IS WRONG (*9) / ANIMAL RIGHTS (*8) / I LIKE TO SCORE (*7) / PLAY (*9) / 18 (*7) / HOTEL (*4)

MOBY HALL – vocals, guitar, keyboards, etc

not iss. / Pregnant Nun

1983. (7"ep; by VATICAN COMMANDOS) *<#1>* **HIT SQUAD FOR GOD** [–] [ ]
– Why must I follow / It's so scary / Housewives on valium / Hit squad for God / Your way / Wonder bread.

— now with **PAUL JOHNSON** – bass + **ANDREW DeARUAJO** – drums

not iss. / Purity

1984. (12"ep; by AWOL) *<#1>* **AWOL** [–] [ ]
– Heart flag / Happy now / Holy mountain / One more dance / More than ever.

— now with **PAUL YATES** + **J. HARRELL**

1985. (lp; by SHOPWELL) *<HF-01>* **PEANUTS** [–] [ ]

— **TARQUIN KATIS** repl. HARRELL in a band called the PORK GUYS (MOBY still played drums with them in 1997!)

not iss. / Instinct

Sep 00. (12"; as the BROTHERHOOD) *<EX 224>* **TIME'S UP (mixes; deep / dope / bonus beats / radio / dust / acapella)** [–] [ ]

Nov 90. (12"ep) *<EX 226>* **MOBILITY / MOBILITY (aquamix). / GO / TIME SIGNATURE** [–] [ ]

Feb 91. (12"ep; as VOODOO CHILD) *<EX 227>* **VOODOO CHILD (contracted) / PERMANENT GREEN. / VOODOO CHILD (expanded) / M-FOUR** [–] [ ]

Mar 91. (12") *<EX 229>* **GO (mixes; Woodtick / Low spirit / Analog / Night time)** [–] [ ]

Low Spirit / Instinct

Apr 91. (12"; as BRAINSTORM) *(12YOBR 24) <EX 231>* **BRAINSTORM – ROCK THE HOUSE** [ ] [ ]
– Rock the house / Move the colors / Help me to believe.

May 91. (12"; as VOODOO CHILD) *<EX 232>* **VOODOO CHILD REMIXES (Brainstorm / original / Poor in N.Y.) / NO BUTTONS TO PUSH** [–] [ ]

C.T. / Instinct

May 91. (12"ep; as BARRACUDA) *<EX 233>* **DRUG FITS THE FACE / DRUG FITS THE FACE (drug free). / PARTY TIME / BARRACUDA** [–] [ ]

Jun 91. (12"ep; as BARRACUDA) *(CTT 31)* **DRUG FITS THE FACE. / DRUG FITS THE FACE (drug free) / MAD LOVE** [ ] [–]

Outer Rhythm / Instinct

Jul 91. (c-s) *(FOOT 15C)* **GO (low spirit) / GO (Woodtick)** [46] [–]
(cd-s+=) *(FOOT 15)* – GO (voodoo child mix).
(cd-s+=) *(FOOT 15CD)* – GO (analog mix).
(12") *(FOOT 15R)* – ('A'side) / ('A'-video aux w/ LYNCH & BADALAMENTI) / ('A'-Rain forest mix).
(re-iss. Oct91, hit No.10; same)

X.L. / Sonic

Nov 91. (12"ep/cd-ep; as UHF) *(XLT/XLS 25/+CD) <SNC 2002/+CD>* **UHF** [ ] [ ]
– UHF / Peacehead / Everything / Protect write.

Outer Rhythm / Instinct

Dec 91. (d-lp/cd; by various) *<EX 236/+CD>* **INSTINCT DANCE** [–] [ ]
– BARRACUDA: Party time / Drug fits the face / Besame / MOBY: Go / Mobility / BRAINSTORM: Rock the house / Move the colors / Drop a

beat / VOODOO CHILD: Voodoo child (remix) / Have you seen my baby? <cd+=> – Permanent green.

Jan 92. (12") *<EX 237>* **GO (mixes; radio / rainforest / subliminal / woodtick)** [–] [ ]
(cd-s+=) *<EX 237CDS>* – Go (mixes; soundtrack / original).

Mar 92. (12") *<EX 240-1>* **DROP A BEAT / ELECTRICITY. / DROP A BEAT (deep mix)** [–] [ ]
(cd-s+=) *(EX 240-2)* – UHF 2.

Jul 92. (cd/c/lp) *<EX 241-2/-4/-1>* **MOBY** [–] [ ]
– Drop a beat / Everything / Yeah / Electricity / Next is the E / Mercy. *<cd re-iss. 1995 on 'Elektra'+=; 61838>* – Go / Help me to believe / Have you seen my baby / Ah ah / Slight return / Stream.

Oct 92. (12") *<EX 247-1>* **NEXT IS THE E (mixes; I feel it / synthe / edit / victory) / THOUSAND** [–] [ ]
(cd-s+=) *<EX 247-2>* – Next is the E (cool world mix).

Mar 93. (cd/c) *<EX 250-2/-4>* **EARLY UNDERGROUND** [–] [ ]
– Besame / Rock the house / Move the colors / UHF3 / Party time / Protect write / Go (original) / Permanent green / Voodoo child / Drug fits the face / Time signature / Peace head / Barracuda / Mobility / M-four. *(UK cd-iss. Nov98 & Mar00 on 'Pinnacle'; PLRCD 016)*

Equator Instinct

Jun 93. (12") *(AXIST 001)* **I FEEL IT / I FEEL IT (synthe mix). / THOUSAND / I FEEL IT (victory mix)** [38] [–]
(12"/cd-s) *(AXIS TM/CD 001)* – I feel it (mixes; contentious / synthe / THK Tekk) / Thousand..
(12") *(AXISTX 001)* – (remixes; synthe / THK / I feel it) / Thousand.

Jul 93. (cd/c/lp) *(ATLAS CD/MC/LP 1)* **THE STORY SO FAR** (compilation) [ ] [–]
– Ah ah / I feel it (I feel it mix) / Everything / Help me to believe / Mercy *[cd-only]* / Go (woodtick mix) / Yeah / Drop a beat (the new version) / Thousand / Slight return / Go (subliminal mix unedited version) / Stream. *(cd re-iss. Nov98 & Mar00 on 'Pinnacle'; PLRCD 014)*

Oct 93. (cd/c) *(ATLAS CD/LP 2)* *<EX 253-2/4>* **AMBIENT** [ ] Aug93 [ ]
– My beautiful blue sky / Heaven / Tongues / J Breas / Myopia / House of blue leaves / Bad days / Piano & string / Sound / Dog / 80 / Lean on me. *(re-iss. Nov98 & Mar00 on 'Pinnacle'; PLRCD 015)*

Mute Elektra

Sep 93. (c-s) *(CMUTE 158)* *<61568>* **MOVE (YOU MAKE ME FEEL SO GOOD). / ('A'-disco threat mix)** [21] [ ]
(12"/cd-s) *(12/CD MUTE 158)* – ('A'side) / ('A'-Subversion) / ('A'-xtra mix) / ('A'-MK-Blades mix).
(cd-s) *(LCDMUTE 158)* – ('A'side) / All that I need is to be loved / Unloved symphony / Rainfalls and the sky shudders.
(12") *(L12MUTE 158)* – (last track repl. by)- Morning dove.

May 94. (c-s) *(CMUTE 161)* **HYMN – THIS IS MY DREAM (extended) / ALL THAT I NEED IS TO BE LOVED (H.O.S. mix)** [31] [ ]
(cd-s+=) *(CDMUTE 161)* – ('A'-European edit) / ('A'-Laurent Garnier mix).
(12") *(12MUTE 161)* – ('A'extended) / ('A'-Laurent Garnier mix) / ('A'-Upriver mix)/ ('A'-Dirty hypo mix).
(cd-s) *(LCDMUTE 161)* – Hymn (alternate quiet version 33 mins).

Oct 94. (c-s) *(CMUTE 173)* *<66180>* **FEELING SO REAL. / NEW DAWN FADES** [30] [ ]
(cd-s+=) *(CDMUTE 173)* – ('A'-Unashamed ecstatic piano mix) / ('A'-Old skool mix).
(cd-s) *(LCDMUTE 173)* – ('A'-Westbam remix) / ('A'-Ray Keith remix) / ('A'dub mix) / Everytime you touch me (remix parts).
(12") *(12MUTE 173)* – ('A'side) / (4-versions from cd's above).

Feb 95. (c-s/7"dinked) *(C+/MUTE 176/+D)* *<66154>* **EVERYTIME YOU TOUCH ME / THE BLUE LIGHT OF THE UNDERWATER SUN** [28] [ ]
(cd-s+=) *(CDMUTE 176)* – ('A'-Beatmasters mix) / ('A'-competition winner; Jude Sebastian mix) / ('A'Freestyle mix).
(cd-s++=) *(LCDMUTE 176)* – ('A'-Uplifting mix).
(12") *(12MUTE 176)* – ('A'-Sound Factory mix) / ('A'-SF dub) / ('A'-Follow me mix) / ('A'-Tribal mix).

Mar 95. (cd/c/d-lp) *(CD/C+/Stumm 130)* *<61701>* **EVERYTHING IS WRONG** [21] [ ]
– Hymn / Feeling so real / All that I need is to be loved / Let's go free / Everytime you touch me / Bring back my happiness / What love? / First cool hive / Into the blue / Anthem / Everything is wrong / God moving over the face of the waters / When it's cold I'd like to die. *(cd/c w/free cd/c) (XLCD/XLC+/Stumm 130)* – Underwater (parts 1-5).

Jun 95. (c-s) *(CMUTE 179)* **INTO THE BLUE / ('A'-Shining mix)** [34] [ ]
(cd-s+=) *(LCDMUTE 179)* – ('A'-Summer night mix) / ('A'-Beatmasters mix).
(12"/cd-s) *(12/CD MUTE 179)* – ('A'-Beastmasters mix) / ('A'-Jnr Vasquez mix) / ('A'-Phil Kelsey mix) / ('A'-Jon Spencer Blues mix).

Jan 96. (cd/c) *(XLStumm 130)* **EVERYTHING IS WRONG – MIXED AND REMIXED** [25] [ ]

— The track 'GOD MOVING OVER THE FACE OF THE WATERS' was used for the Rover 400 TV commercial. Toyota had earlier sampled his 'GO'.

Aug 96. (12") *(12MUTE 184)* **THAT'S WHEN I REACH FOR MY REVOLVER. / ('A'-Rollo & Si Star Bliss mix)** [50] [–]
(cd-s) *(CDMUTE 184)* – ('A'side) / Lovesick / Displaced / Sway.
(cd-s) *(LCDMUTE 184)* – ('A'side) / Every one of my problems / God moving over the face of the waters (dark mix).

Oct 96. (cd/c/d-lp) *(CD/C+/Stumm 150)* *<62031>* **ANIMAL RIGHTS** [38] [ ]
– Now I let it go / Come on baby / Someone to love / Heavy flow / You / My love will never die / Soft / Say it's all mine / That's when I reach for my revolver / Face it / Living / Love song for my mom. *(cd w/ free cd)* **LITTLE IDIOT** *(LCDStumm 150)* – Degenerate / Dead city / Walnut / Old / A season in Hell / Love song for my mom / The blue terror of lawns / Dead sun / Reject.

Nov 96. (12"ep) *(12MUTE 200)* **COME ON BABY / LOVE HOLE / WHIP IT / GO / ALL THAT I NEED TO BE IS LOVED / HYMN** [ ] [ ]
(cd-ep) *(CDMUTE 200)* – ('A'-Eskimos And Egypt mix) / ('A'-Crystal method mix) / ('A'-Eskimos And Egypt extended).

Jan 97. (7") *<SP 377>* **THAT'S WHEN I REACH FOR MY REVOLVER. / WHIP IT (death metal version)** [–] [ ]

— <above issued on 'Sub Pop'>

May 97. (12") *<0-63953>* **THAT'S WHEN I REACH FOR MY REVOLVER (mixes; Moby / Psychotic VE-gun / Moby's 2 / The Rollo & Sister Bliss vocal)** [–] [ ]

Jul 97. (cd) *<62092-2>* **THE END OF EVERYTHING** [–] [ ]
– Patient love / Great lake / Gentle love / Honest love / Slow motion suicide / Dog heaven / Reject.

Nov 97. (c-s/12"/cd-s) *(C/12/CD MUTE 210)* *<040>* **JAMES BOND THEME: TOMORROW NEVER DIES** [8] [ ]
– (mixes:- extended dance / Grooverider's Jeep remix / Da Bomb remix / CJ Bolland remix / Dub Pistols remix / CJ Bolland – Dubble-oh Heaven remix).
(12") *(XL12MUTE 210)* – ('A'mixes; re-version / Grooverider / Danny Tenaglia dub).

Nov 97. (cd/c/lp) *(CD/C+/Stumm 168)* *<62094>* **I LIKE TO SCORE** [ ] [ ]
– Novio / James Bond theme (Moby's re-version) / Go / Ah-ah / I like to score / Oil 1 / New dawn fades / God moving over the face of the waters / First cool hive / Nash / Love theme / Grace.

Aug 98. (cd-s) *(CDMUTE 218)* *<2186>* **HONEY / HONEY (Mario Caldato Jnr. mix) / MICRONESIA / MEMORY GOSPEL** [33] [ ]
(cd-s) *(LCDMUTE 218)* – ('A'-Rollo & Sister Bliss blunt edit) / ('A'-Moby's 118 mix) / ('A'-Westbam & Hardy mix) / ('A'-Aphrodite & Micky Finn mix).
(12") *(12MUTE 218)* – ('A'-Rollo & Sister Bliss mix) / ('A'-Sharam Jey's sweet honey mix) / ('A'-Moby's low side mix).

Mute V2

Apr 99. (cd-s) *(CDMUTE 221)* **RUN ON / SPIRIT / RUNNING** [33] [ ]
(cd-s) *(LCDMUTE 221)* – ('A'extended) / Sunday / Down slow.
(12") *(12MUTE 221)* – ('A'mixes; Moby young & funky / Dave Clarke / extended).

May 99. (cd/c/d-lp) *(CD/C+/STUMM 172)* *<27049>* **PLAY** [1] [38]
– Honey / Find my baby / Porcelain / Why does my heart feel so bad? / South side / Rushing / Bodyrock / Natural blues / Machete / 7 / Run on / Down slow / If things were perfect / Everloving / Inside / Guitar flute & string / The sky is broken / My weakness. *(d-cd+=; LCDSTUMM 172 / <27085>)* – THE B-SIDES (hit UK No.24)

Jul 99. (cd-s) *(CDMUTE 225)* **BODYROCK / SUNSPOT / ARP** [38] [ ]
(12"/cd-s) *(12/LCD MUTE 225)* – ('A'-Olav Basoski da hot funk mix) / ('A'-Da freak funk mix) / ('A'-B&H Bodyrock mix) / ('A'-Dani Konig mix).

Oct 99. (cd-s) *(LCDMUTE 230)* **WHY DOES MY HEART FEEL SO BAD / FLYING FOXES / PRINCESS** [16] [ ]
(12"/cd-s) *(12/CD MUTE 230)* – ('A'mixes by ATB, FERRY CORSTEN, SHARP BOYS + SUBSONIC LEGACY).

Mar 00. (12"/cd-s) *(12/CD MUTE 251)* **NATURAL BLUES / WHISPERING WIND / SICK IN THE SYSTEM** [11] [ ]
(12"/cd-s) *(L12/LCD MUTE 251)* – ('A'mixes).

Jun 00. (c-s) *(CMUTE 252)* **PORCELAIN / SUMMER** [5] [ ]
(cd-s+=) *(CDMUTE 252)* – Flying over the dateline.
(cd-s) *(LCDMUTE 252)* – ('A'mixes).

Oct 00. (c-s) *(CMUTE 255)* **WHY DOES MY HEART FEEL SO BAD / HONEY (remix)** [17] [ ]
(cd-s+=) *(CDMUTE 255)* – Flower (w/ KELIS).
(cd-s) *(LCDMUTE 255)* – ('A'side) / Honey (Fafu's 12"mix) / ('A'-Red Jerry's string and breaks mix) / The sun never stops setting.

Jan 01. (cd-s; by MOBY featuring GWEN STEFANI) <27665> **SOUTH SIDE / (original & mixes)** [–] [14]

Apr 02. (c-s) *(CMUTE 268)* **WE ARE ALL MADE OF STARS / WE ARE ALL MADE OF STARS (DJ Tiesto full vocal mix) / LANDING** [11] [ ]
(cd-s+=) *(CDMUTE 268)* – Soul to love.
(cd-s) *(LCDMUTE 268)* – ('A'-Downtempo mix) / ('A'-Timo Maas dub).

May 02. (cd/c/d-lp) *(CD/C+/STUMM 202)* <27172> **18** [1] [4]
– We are all made of stars / In this world / In my heart / Great escape / Signs of love / One of these mornings / Another woman / Fireworks / Extreme ways / Jam for the ladies (with ANGIE STONE & MC LYTE) / Sunday (the day before my birthday) / 18 / Sleep alone / At least we tried / Harbour (with SINEAD O'CONNOR) / Look back in / Rafters / I'm not worried at all.

Aug 02. (cd-s) *(CDMUTE 270)* **EXTREME WAYS / LOVE OF STRINGS / LIFE'S SO SWEET / EXTREME WAYS (video)** [39] [–]
(12"/cd-s) *(CD/12 MUTE 270)* – ('A'-DJ Tiesto mix) / ('A'-Junior Jack club mix).
(12"/cd-s) *(LCD/L12 MUTE 270)* – ('A'-Creamer & K mix) / ('A'-Lee Coombes remix).

Nov 02. (cd-s) *(CDMUTE 276)* **IN THIS WORLD / PIANO AND STRINGS / DOWNHILL** [35] [–]
(cd-s) *(LCDMUTE 276)* – ('A'-T&F remix) / ('A'-AFTC deep south vocal mix) / ('A'-Push vocal club mix).
(12") *(12MUTE 276)* – ('A'-ATFC deep south club mix) / ('A'-Slacker's rain before carnival mix).

Mar 03. (cd-s) *(CDMUTE 280)* **SUNDAY (THE DAY BEFORE MY BIRTHDAY) / AND I KNOW / I.S.S. / ('A'-video)** [ ] [–]
(cd-s/12") *(LCD/12 MUTE 280)* – ('A'-West London deep club mix) / ('A'-Boris Dlugosch & Michi Lange headbanger session) / In my heart (Ferry Corsten remix).

Jul 04. (12"/cd-s; as MOBY & PUBLIC ENEMY) *(12/CD MUTE 333)* **MAKE LOVE FUCK WAR / (instrumental) / (acappella)** [ ] [–]

Feb 05. (cd-s) *(CDMUTE 340)* **LIFT ME UP / MULHOLLAND** [18] [–]
(12") *(12MUTE 340)* – ('A'-mixes; Mylo / Superdiscount / Abe Duque).
(cd-s+=) *(LCDMUTE 340)* – ('A'-mixes; album / Superdiscount radio).

Mar 05. (cd/lp) *(CD+/STUMM 240)* <27243> **HOTEL** [8] [28]
– Hotel intro / Raining again / Beautiful / Lift me up / Where you end / Temptation / Spiders / Dream about me / Very / I like it / Love should / Slipping away / Forever / Homeward angel. *(ltd d-cd+=; LCDSTUMM 240)* – HOTEL.AMBIENT:- Swear / Snowball / Blue paper / Homeward angel (long version) / Chord sounds / Not sensitive / Lilly / The come down / Overland / Live forever / Aerial.

May 05. (7") *(MUTE 350)* **SPIDERS. / TEMPTATION** [50] [–]
(cd-s) *(CDMUTE 350)* – ('A') / It's OK.
(cd-s) *(LCDMUTE 350)* – ('A') / Put the headphones on / Raining again (Ewan Pearson vocal).

Aug 05. (7") *(MUTE 355)* **DREAM ABOUT ME. / (The Shortwave Set pick'n'mix)** [ ] [–]
(cd-s) *(CDMUTE 355)* – ('A') / Feeling so real (live).
(12") *(12MUTE 355)* – ('A'-mixes; Sebastian Ingrosso / MHC & Booka Shade).

Jan 06. (12") *(12MUTE 365)* **SLIPPING AWAY (Axwell vocal mix). / WHERE YOU END (Tiga's All You Need Is To Be Dubbed mix)** [53] [–]
(cd-s) *(LCDMUTE 365)* – ('A') / ('A'-mixes; Axwell instrumental) / MHC extended / Focus People That Slip remix by Mathew Jonson / Zloot).

– compilations, specials, etc. –

Nov 93. (12") *Mute; (12NEMY 2)* **ALL THAT I NEED IS TO BE LOVED. / (3 other 'A'mixes)** [ ] [–]

Sep 94. (c-s) *Mute; (CNOCAR 1)* **GO (woodtick mix). / ('A'-Low spirit mix)** [ ] [–]
(12"+=) *(12NOCAR 1)* – ('A'-Voodoo chile mix).
(12"+=) *(12LNOCAR 1)* – ('A'-Appathoski mix) / ('A'-Amphemetix mix).
(cd-s+=) *(CDNOCAR 1)* – ('A'-Delirium mix).

Mar 95. (10"ltd.) *Soapbar; (SBR 15)* **FEELING SO REAL (mixes)** [ ] [–]

Nov 98. (d-cd) *Pinnacle; (PLRCD 017)* **RARE** (collected B-sides) [ ] [–]
(re-iss. Mar00; same)

Jul 00. (cd) *Elektra; <62554>* **MOBYSONGS (1993-1998)** [–] [ ]

☐ the MODERN LOVERS
(see under ⇒ RICHMAN, Jonathan)

MODEST MOUSE

Formed: Issaquah, Washington, USA . . . 1993 by ISAAC BROCK, ERIC JUDY and JEREMIAH GREEN. After magnum practice sessions in a confined space called the "Shed" (a, erm, shed that was built by BROCK next to his mother's mobile home in their trailer park) the weirdo-trio entered the dark and mysterious circle of CALVIN JOHNSON (and his 'K' imprint'), cutting their first self-titled single in his 'Dub Narcotic' studio. A move to the 'Up' label was to follow, and the release of two further sets, 'THIS IS A LONG DRIVE FOR SOMEBODY WITH NOTHING TO THINK ABOUT' and 'INTERSTATE 8' in 1996. Never making their minds up, and shifting to 'K' once again, the 3-piece released 'THE FRUIT THAT ATE ITSELF' and the superior 'LONESOME CROWDED WEST' (1997), which contained the fabulous 'HEART COOKS BRAIN', a song for which the term "Slacker" could have been invented. The track had all the ingredients to become a generation-x anthem, with kooky scratching, lo-fi guitars, SLINT-like vocals, chicken noises and the lyrics: "I'm on my way to god knows, I don't care/in this place that I call home, the hours go fast and the days go so slow." The tracks on 'THE FRUIT THAT ATE ITSELF' rambled on in certain places and JOHNSON's deliberate messy production did the band no justice, certainly adding zero credibility to their name. BROCK and chums returned in 2000, issuing their major label ('Sony') debut 'THE MOON & ANTARCTICA', a wayward mix of downbeat, spacy lo-fi, jinxed-up no wave; the PIXIES show their looming influence as ever. Light rock/pop songs such as 'GRAVITY RIDES EVERYTHING' and the immensly enjoyable 'WILD PACK OF FAMILY DOGS' were immediate highlights. BROCK once again reminded us of how unique his voice was, because, like STIPE and CORGAN, there is no denying that he sounds like no-one else, with his trademark abrasive, broken-down lisp. The group also issued two previously unreleased sets; 2000's B-side and rarity collection 'BUILDING NOTHING OUT OF SOMETHING', and a brilliant "lost" album, 'SAD SAPPY SUCKER' (2001). The latter, supposedly recorded in 1994 (!) by 'K' record's CALVIN JOHNSON, was shelved and thought to have been destroyed. It played like JOHNSON's previous BECK effort 'One Foot In The Grave', all ramshackle recording and coughs and background noises. It also featured the ultra-rare 7" single 'WORMS VS. BIRDS", and a collection of BROCK's answerphone songs. But if his genius hadn't yet been fully realized then the delivery of 2002's 'SHARPEN YOUR TEETH' set, under the bizarre moniker UGLY CASANOVA (sounds more like a UK garage rap artist, than a fumbling indie hero), then all hope was lost. Issued to tremendous critical acclaim, BROCK insisted that the songs on the album were derived from a bunch of tapes left at 'Sub Pop's headquarters by a crazed MODEST MOUSE fan named Edgar Graham. A likely story indeed! It was, in fact, the work of BROCK, TIM RUTILI (of RED RED MEAT) and the recent CALIFONE, PALL JENKINS (from BLACK HEART PROCESSION) and post-rock producer BRIAN DECK (TORTOISE, SEA AND CAKE). A soft, gliding addition to the alt country hall of fame, the set shone with ballads from a nowhere place, where the roads were dusty and every day is like a Sunday. 'CAT FACES', 'PACIFICO' and 'SO LONG TO THE HOLIDAYS' displayed moments of brilliance, but its 'HOTCHA GIRLS', with its catchy acoustic guitar riff, building orchestral movement and psychedelic click-track beats made it one of the most uplifting and mournful songs of BROCK's career. A true gem of an album. After making the inevitable transition from 'Matador' to major label ('Epic'), MM's creative schedule was complicated with the mental health problems of drummer JEREMIAH GREEN, who quit the band in 2003. Replacements were found in BENJAMIN WEIKEL and DANN GALLUCCI, both of whom played on the long-awaited 'GOOD NEWS FOR PEOPLE WHO LOVE BAD NEWS' (2004). The real good news was its breakthrough into the US Top 20 (UK Top 40), even more surprising given its rambunctious, schizoid sprawl through recent and not so recent rock history: the awkward groove of TALKING HEADS, the sepulchral rasp of TOM WAITS and petulant outbursts of MALKMUS. With JEREMIAH GREEN back on the scene and JOHNNY MARR waiting in the wings, the 'MOUSE might have to leave their modesty behind.

Album rating: THIS IS A LONG DRIVE FOR SOMEONE WITH NOTHING TO THINK ABOUT (*6) / INTERSTATE 8 mini (*6) / THE FRUIT THAT ATE ITSELF mini (*7) / THE LONESOME CROWDED WEST (*8) / THE MOON & ANTARCTICA (*7) / SAD SAPPY SUCKER exploitation (*5) / GOOD NEWS FOR PEOPLE WHO LOVE BAD NEWS (*8) / Ugly Casanova: SHARPEN YOUR TEETH (*7)

ISAAC BROCK (b. 9 Jul'75) – vocals, guitar / **ERIC JUDY** – bass / **JEREMIAH GREEN** – drums

not iss. K

1994. (7"ep) *<IPU 58>* **BLUE CADET-3, DO YOU CONNECT?** –
– Blue cadet-3, do you connect? / Dukes up / Woodgrain / It always rains on a picnic / 5,4,3,2,1 . . . lisp off.

Sub Pop Sub Pop

Feb 96. (7"m) *<(SP 338)>* **BROKE. / WHENEVER I BREATHE OUT / POSITIVE NEGATIVE**
(re-iss. Aug99; same)

not iss. Up

Feb 96. (lp/cd) *<UP 27/+CD>* **THIS IS A LONG DRIVE FOR SOMEONE WITH NOTHING TO THINK ABOUT** –
– Dramamine / Breakthrough / Custom concern / Might / Lounge / Beach side property / Ionizes and atomizes / Head south / Dog paddle / Novocain stain / Tundra – Desert / Ohio / Exit does not exist / Talking shit about a pretty sunset / Make everyone happy – Mechanical birds / Space travel is boring. *(lp+=)* – Edit the sad parts / A manic depressive named laughing boy.

Nov 96. (m-lp/m-cd) *<UP 35/+CD>* **INTERSTATE 8** –
– Interstate 8 / All night diner / Sleepwalking (couples only dance prom) / Tundra – Desert / Edit the sad parts.

K K

Jun 97. (m-lp/m-cd) *<(KLP 63/+CD)>* **THE FRUIT THAT ATE ITSELF**
– Waydown / Dirty fingernails / Sunspots in the house of the late scapegoat / The fruit that ate itself / Summer / Karma's payment.

Suicide Square Suicide Square

Jan 98. (7") *<(SS 003)>* **LIFE OF ARCTIC SOUNDS. / MEDICATION** Nov97

Up Up

Feb 98. (lp/cd) *<(UP 44/+CD)>* **THE LONESOME CROWDED WEST** Oct97
– Teeth like God's shoeshine / Heart cooks brain / Convenient parking / Lounge (closing time) / Jesus Christ was an only child / Doin' the cockroach / Cowboy Dan / Trailer trash / Out of gas / Long distance drunk / Shit luck / Truckers atlas / Polar opposites / Bankrupt on selling / Styrofoam boots – It's all nice on ice, alright. *(lp+=)* – Baby blue sedan.

Feb 98. (7") *<(UP 47)>* **OTHER PEOPLE'S LIVES. / GREY ICE WATER**

Jul 98. (12"/cd-s) *<(UP 58/+CD)>* **WHENEVER YOU SEE FIT / ('A'-DJ Dynomite) / Omega (mixes by 764 HERO)**
(re-iss. 12" with 764 HERO on 'Suicide Squeeze'; SSQ 008)

not iss. Sub Pop

Oct 98. (7") **NEVERENDING MATH EQUATION. / WORKIN' ON LEAVIN' THE LIVIN'** –

Matador Sony

Jul 99. (7") *(OLE 382-7)* **HEART COOKS BRAIN. / SHIT LUCK** –

Jun 00. (12"ep) *<UP 90>* **NIGHT ON THE SUN** –
– Night on the sun / You're the good things (it's alright to die) / Wild pack of family dogs / Dark center of the universe / Your life.
(above issued on 'Up')

Jul 00. (cd/d-lp) *(OLE 450-2/-1)* *<EK 063871>* **THE MOON & ANTARCTICA** Jun00
– 3rd planet / Gravity rides everything / Dark center of the universe / Perfect disguise / Tiny cities made of ashes / A different city / The cold part / Alone down there / The stars are projectors / Wild packs of family dogs / Paper thin walls / I came as a rat / Lives / Life like weeds / What people are made of.

Nov 00. (12"ep) *(OLE 464-1)* **WILFUL SUSPENSION OF DISBELIEF / NIGHT ON THE SUN. / I CAME AS A RAT (LONG WALK OFF A SHORT DOCK) / YOU'RE THE GOOD THINGS** –

Epic Epic

Sep 01. (m-cd) *<62104>* **EVERYWHERE AND HIS NASTY PARLOR TRICKS** (collection) –
– Wilful suspension of disbelief / Night on the sun / 3 inch horses, two faced monsters / You're the good things / The air / So much beauty in dirt / Here it comes / I came as a rat (long walk off a short dock).

— (2003) **BENJAMIN WEIKEL** – drums; repl. JEREMIAH GREEN

— added **DANN GALLUCCI** – guitar

Jul 04. (7") *(675069-7)* **FLOAT ON. / BUKOWSKI (Congleton Godbey remix)** 46 May04 68
(cd-s) *(675069-2)* – ('A') / I've got it all (most) / Good times are killing me (alt.) / ('A'-video).
(cd-s) *<76685>* – (first 2 tracks).

Jul 04. (cd) *(516272-2)* *<87125>* **GOOD NEWS FOR PEOPLE WHO LOVE BAD NEWS** 40 Apr04 18
– Horn intro / The world at large / Float on / Ocean breathes salty / Dig your grave / Bury me with it / Dance hall / Bukowski / This devil's workday / The view / Satin in a coffin / Interlude (Milo) / Blame it on the Tetons / Black cadillacs / One chance / The good times are killing me.

— **JEREMIAH GREEN** returned to repl. DANN

– compilations, others, etc. –

Feb 00. (lp/cd) *<(UP 73/+CD)>* **BUILDING SOMETHING OUT OF NOTHING** Jan00
– Never ending math equation / Interstate 8 / Broke / Medication / Workin' on leavin' the livin' / All nite diner / Baby blue sedan A life of arctic sounds / Sleepwalkin' / Grey ice water / Whenever I breathe out / Other people's lives.

Apr 01. (cd) *K; <(KLP 131CD)>* **SAD SAPPY SUCKER** (rec.1994)
– Worm vs. birds / Four fingered fisherman / Wagon ride return / From point A to point B / Path of least resistance / It always rains on a picnic / Dukes up / Think long / Every penny fedcat / Mice eat cheese / Race car grin you ain't no landmark / Red hand case / Secret agent X-9 / Blue cadet-3, do you connect? / Call to dial a song / 5,4,3,2,1 lisp off / Woodgrain / BMX crash / Sucker betru / Black blood and old newagers / SWY / Australopithecus / Sin gun chaser.

UGLY CASANOVA

ISAAC BROCK – vocals / **BRIAN DECK** – multi / **TIM RUTILI** – fiddle, guitar, keyboards, vocals (of CALIFONE, of RED RED MEAT) / **PALL A. JENKINS** – guitar, keyboards, vocals (of BLACK HEART PROCESSION) / **JOHN ORTH** – drums (of HOLOPAW)

Sub Pop Sub Pop

Jun 02. (d-lp/cd) *<(SP 552/+CD)>* **SHARPEN YOUR TEETH** May02
– Barnacles / Spilled milk factory / Parasites / Hotcha girls / (no song) / Diamonds on the face of evil / Cat faces / Ice on the sheets / Beesting / Pacifico / Smoke like ribbons / Things I don't remember / So long to the holidays.

MOGWAI

Formed: Glasgow, Scotland . . . 1995 by STUART BRAITHWAITE (also of ESKA), DOMINIC AITCHISON and MARTIN BULLOCH. In the spring of '96, the band debuted with 'TUNER' / 'LOWER', a precursor to the band's double whammy NME Singles Of The Week, 'SUMMER' and 'NEW PATHS TO HELICON'. Early in 1997, they signed to the suffocatingly hip Glasgow-based 'Chemikal Underground' (home of BIS and friends, ARAB STRAP), the first outing being 'THE 4 SATIN EP'. A fine collection of their early singles was released a month later in June, although another label was responsible. That summer, the new 5-piece MOGWAI (complete with JOHN CUMMINGS and former TEENAGE FANCLUB member, BRENDON O'HARE) alternately bludgeoned/charmed the NME tent at Scotland's premier festival 'T In The Park' with their striking hybrid of SONIC YOUTH, METALLICA and pre-'Blue Monday' NEW ORDER! The feverishly anticipated "proper" debut album, 'MOGWAI YOUNG TEAM' was released late '97 to rave reviews, also scraping into the Top 75. Stunningly dynamic, the record shifted seamlessly from tranquil, bleakly beautiful soundscapes to brain scrambling white noise and sledgehammer riffing. Prime examples were 'LIKE HEROD', 'WITH PORTFOLIO' and 'MOGWAI FEAR SATAN', while 'TRACY' was a near 10-minute collage of drifting, childlike charm segueing into a taped phone conversation. Another track, 'R U STILL IN 2 IT', featured the mumbling vocal talents of ARAB STRAP's AIDAN MOFFAT. Prior to the album's release, O'HARE was summarily dismissed, apparently for yapping his way through an ARAB STRAP gig (tsk, tsk!). 1998 was indeed a busy year for the "young team", five releases hitting the shops between March and August and nearly all making the Top 75. The first of these, '. . ... DO THE ROCK BOOGALOO' was a split affair with fellow noisemongers MAGOO, the title not an EP but the "un"-covering of two classic BLACK SABBATH tracks, MOGWAI having a laugh with 'SWEET LEAF'. 'FEAR SATAN' was then chosen for the remix treatment (MY BLOODY VALENTINE's the highlight), while a full album, 'KICKING A DEAD PIG: MOGWAI SONGS REMIXED', was all their best tunes reworked by others including ARAB STRAP, KID LOCO and ALEC EMPIRE. 'Chemikal Underground' put their two-pennith in by issuing the 'NO EDUCATION = NO FUTURE (FUCK THE CURFEW)' ep, while 'TEN RAPID' was an early singles collection. The following March (with newcomer pianist BARRY BURNS now a fully-fledged member) 'COME ON DIE YOUNG' was the gangland war cry they chose as the title of their more sedate second album proper. A hard album indeed, in the sense that it took time to "get into" (probably due to the slight omission of their characteristic sonic crescendos), it unearthed a softer, more delicate style which was rewarded with a Top 30 entry. Opening with 'PUNK ROCK:' (complete with IGGY POP archive interview as voiceover), the Slo-Fi 'CODY' and the sludgedelic 'HELP BOTH WAYS, the album proved the young MOGWAI were top of the class; 'EX-COWBOY' and the emotional MORRICONE-inspired finale 'PUNK ROCK / PUFF DADDY / ANtICHRISt' were also noteworthy. Towards the end of '99, they delivered a self-titled EP, attributing 'STANLEY KUBRICK' as the lead track. 'BURN GIRL PROM QUEEN', an excellent diversion from the 'WAI featured the Cowdenbeath Brass Orchestra to eerie effect. Perhaps the best career move a band of their status could make, 'ROCK ACTION' (2001), saw MOGWAI reach new musical heights with their first release on their own 'Southpaw' label. The album, named after the band's other record label, focused its attention on the subtler side of life. It gladly took advice from the DAVID PAJO (who appears on the record) school of experimental rock, evoking his recent PAPA M meanderings. With its harmonic use of banjos, lap-steel and orchestra, the album harked back to the aforementioned 'STANLEY KUBRICK' EP. 'SINE WAVE' was briefly melodic, with hints of warped guitar static and BULLOCH's tom-toms adding an abrasive edge to the mix. '2 RIGHTS MAKE A WRONG' is quietly SLINT-ish, with the odd-kilter signature tune thrown in for good measure. But it's 'DIAL: REVENGE' with SUPER FURRY ANIMALS vocalist GRUFF RHYS which makes the album. His lingering Welsh vocals proved to be a catalyst for the overall structure, and the emotions that surface during the intensified verse-chorus-verse of the song. Preceding the album by a few weeks was an unusual and unique appearance at Rothesay in the Isle Of Bute for 500 fans lucky enough to get the "golden" tickets. The Glaswegians crowned 2001 with their most ambitious arrangement to date, a 20-minute long er, single inspired by a Jewish spiritual and produced by STEVE ALBINI; if that sounds an unlikely combination, be assured its skull-crushing crescendo is old time religion MOGWAI style. 'HAPPY SONGS FOR HAPPY PEOPLE' (2003) marked a slight departure for the band, downsizing on the "rock action" front. As MOGWAI albums went, this was certainly their weakest and most over-produced, but it was still bloody good! The solemn funereal pace of 'MOSES? I AMN'T' was something to make the late great JOY DIVISION proud; the riff at the end of epic 'RATTS OF THE CAPITAL' was pure grunge, and the chiming, symmetrical piano and programmed rhythmic structure of 'I KNOW YOU ARE BUT WHAT AM I?' was the band entering AERIAL-M territory. Elsewhere there was more fun to be had via the romantically-inclined 'GOLDEN PORSCHE' and the signature-like opening track 'HUNTED BY A FREAK' – even vocoder vocals! Happy songs for happy people? Happy MOGWAI fans in the knowledge that they had made another decent album, more like. The band's close relationship with the late John Peel was poignantly highlighted on 'GOVERNMENT COMMISSIONS: BBC SESSIONS 1996-2004' (2005), a timely round-up of live-in-session epics released only a matter of months after Peel's unexpected passing. Fifth album proper, 'MR BEAST' (2006), was once again hailed as a minor masterpiece, and touted as a return to the glacial simplicity of the early albums. They must have been doing something right, with 'FRIEND OF THE NIGHT' even cracking the charts, their first ever to hit the Top 40. Bookending it on the album was the cumulative, NYMAN-esque opening track, 'AUTO ROCK' and rib-splintering 'GLASGOW MEGA-SNAKE', paralleled by the penultimate 'I CHOSE HORSES' (a cinematic haiku featuring TETSUYA FUKAGAWA) and closing dirge, 'WE'RE NO HERE'.

• **Covered:** HONEY (Spacemen 3).

Album rating: MOGWAI YOUNG TEAM (*9) / KICKING A DEAD PIG: MOGWAI SONGS REMIXED (*7) / TEN RAPID compilation (*8) / COME ON DIE YOUNG (*10) / ROCK ACTION (*9) / HAPPY SONGS FOR HAPPY PEOPLE (*8) / GOVERNMENT COMMISSIONS: BBC Sessions 1996-2004 collection (*8) / MR. BEAST (*7)

STUART BRAITHWAITE (b.10 May'76) – guitar, vocals (also of ESKA, until autumn '96) / **DOMINIC AITCHISON** – bass / **MARTIN BULLOCH** – drums

		Rock Action	not iss.
Feb 96.	(ltd-7") *(RAR 001)* **TUNER. / LOWER**	☐	–
		Che	not iss.
May 96.	(ltd-7"green) *(che 61)* **ANGELS VERSUS ALIENS. / (other side by DWEEB)**	☐	–
		Love Train	not iss.
Sep 96.	(ltd-7"; "CAMDEN CRAWL II") *(PUBE 011)* **A PLACE FOR PARKS. / (other artists)**	☐	–
Oct 96.	(ltd-7"; "TEN DAY WEEKEND") *(PUBE 012)* **I AM NOT BATMAN. / (other artists)**	☐	–
Nov 96.	(ltd-7") *(PUBE 014)* **SUMMER. / ITHICA 27 o 9**	☐	–
		Wurlitzer Jukebox	not iss.
Jan 97.	(ltd-7") *(WJ 22)* **NEW PATHS TO HELICON** – Helicon 1 / Helicon 2.	☐	–

— added **JOHN CUMMINGS** – guitar

Chemikal Underground | Jetset

May 97. (12"ep/cd-ep) *(chem 015/+cd)* *<TWA 14CD>* **4 SATIN EP**
– Superheroes of BMX / Now you're taken / Stereo Dee. <US++> – Guardians of space. *(re-iss. Apr99; same)*

— added **BRENDAN O'HARE** – piano (of-MACROCOSMICA, ex-TEENAGE FANCLUB, ex-TELSTAR PONIES)

Oct 97. (cd/d-lp) *(chem 018 cd/lp)* *<7>* **MOGWAI YOUNG TEAM** | 75 |
– Yes! I am a long way from home / Like Herod / Radar maker / Tracy / Summer (Priority version) / With portfolio / R u still in 2 it / A cheery wave from stranded youngsters / Mogwai fear Satan. *(re-iss. Apr99; same)*

Feb 98. (7") *(SHaG 13.05)* **Club Beatroot Part Four** | | –
– Stereo Dee (live) / (other side by Ph FAMILY)
(above issued on 'Flotsam & Jetsam – 13th Note')

— now without O'HARE, who was sacked (see above)

Mar 98. (7"; split w/ MAGOO) *(NING 47CD)* **. . . .. DO THE ROCK BOOGALOO** | 60 | –
– Black Sabbath (by MAGOO) / Sweet leaf.
(above issued on 'Fierce Panda', below 2 for 'eye q' / US 'Jetset')

Apr 98. (cd-ep) *(eyeuk 032cd)* **FEAR SATAN remixes** | 57 | –
– Mogwai remix / U-ziq remix / Surgeon remix / My Bloody Valentine remix. *(re-iss. Apr99; same)*

May 98. (cd/d-lp) *(eyeuk cd/lp)* *<TWA 13 CD/LP>* **KICKING A DEAD PIG: MOGWAI SONGS REMIXED** | | Jun98
– Like Herod (Hood remix) / Helicon 2 (Max Tundra remix) / Summer (Klute's weird winter remix) / Gwai on 45 (Arab Strap remix) / A cheery wave from stranded youngsters (Third Eye Foundation tet offensive remix) / Like Herod (Alec Empire's face the future remix) / Mogwai fear Satan (Surgeon remix) / R U still in to it? (DJ Q remix) / Tracy (Kid Loco's playing with the young team remix) / Mogwai fear Satan (Mogwai remix). *(re-iss. Apr99; same) (cd re-iss. Sep01 on 'Chemikal Underground'; CHEM 057CD)*

Jun 98. (12"ep/cd-ep) *(chem 026/+cd)* *<111230>* **NO EDUCATION = NO FUTURE (FUCK THE CURFEW) e.p.** | 68 |
– Xmas steps / Rollerball / Small children in the background. *(re-iss. Apr99; same)*

— In Nov'98, their track 'I CAN'T REMEMBER' featured on the 'Glasgow' V/A EP along with EL HOMBRE TRAJEADO, the KARELIA and the YUMMY FUR

— added **BARRY BURNS** – piano, flute, guitar

Chemikal Underground | Matador

Mar 99. (d-lp/cd) *(chem 033/+cd)* *<OLE 365>* **COME ON DIE YOUNG** | 29 |
– Punk rock: / Cody / Helps both ways / Year 2000 non-compliant cardia / Kappa / Waltz for Aidan / May nothing but happiness come through your door / Oh! how the dogs stack up / Ex-cowboy / Chocky / Christmas steps / Punk rock – Puff Daddy – ANtICHRISt.

Oct 99. (12"ep/cd-ep) *(chem 036/+cd)* *<OLE 412>* **MOGWAI e.p.**
– Stanley Kubrick / Christmas song / Burn girl prom-queen / Rage: man. *(re-iss. Sep01 as 'MOGWAI+6'+=; CHEM 056CD)* – Xmas steps / Rollerball / Small children in the background / Superheroes of BMX / Now you're taken / Stereodee.

Southpaw | Matador

Apr 01. (cd/lp) *(PAW CD/LP 001)* *<OLE 490>* **ROCK ACTION** | 23 |
– Sine wave / Take me somewhere nice / O I sleep / Dial: revenge / You don't know Jesus / Robot chant / 2 rights make 1 wrong / Secret pint.

May 01. (12"ep) *<OLE 522-1>* **D TO E / DRUM MACHINE. / (other 2 by Bardo Pond)** | – | tour –

Rock Action | Matador

Oct 01. (cd-ep) *(ROCKACTCD 10)* *<OLE 538>* **MY FATHER MY KING**

Jun 03. (cd/lp) *(PIASX 035 CD/LP)* *<OLE 567>* **HAPPY SONGS FOR HAPPY PEOPLE** | 47 |
– Hunted by a freak / Moses? I amn't / Kids will be skeletons / Killing all the flies / Boring machines disturbs sleep / Ratts of the capital / Golden Porsche / I know you are but what am I? / Stop coming to my house.

Jan 06. (7") *(PIASX 064S)* **FRIEND OF THE NIGHT. / FRESH CROWN** | 38 | –
(cd-s+=) *(PIASX 064CD)* – 1% of monster / ('A'-video).

Mar 06. (cd/d-lp) *(PIASX 062 CD/LP)* *<OLE 681>* **MR. BEAST** | 31 |
– Auto rock / Glasgow mega-snake / Acid food / Travel is dangerous / Team handed / Friend of the night / Emergenct trap / Folk death 95 / I chose horses / We're no here. *(ltd-cd w/dvd+=; PIASX 062CDLTD)* – (the recording of..).

Jun 06. (12"ep/cd-ep) *(PIASX 066 T/CD)* **TRAVEL IS DANGEROUS EP** | | –
– Travel is dangerous / Auto rock (Errors remix) / Friend of the night (Acid Casuals remix) / Like Herod (live) / We're no here (live).

– compilations, etc. –

Aug 98. (cd) *Rock Action; (ROCKACTCD 5) / Jetset; <TWA 05LP>* **TEN RAPID (collected recordings 1996-1997)** | | Aug97
– Summer / Helicon 2 / Angels versus aliens / I am not Batman / Tuner / Ithica 27 o 9 / A place for parks / Helicon 1 / End.

Feb 05. (cd) *Rock Action; (PIASX 051CD) / Matador; <OLE 646>* **GOVERNMENT COMMISSIONS** (BBC Sessions 1996-2004)
– Hunted by a freak / R U still in 2 it / New paths TP helicon (part 2) / Kappa / Cody / Like Herod / Secret pint / Superheroes of BMX / New paths to helicon (part 1) / Stop coming to my house.

the MONKEES

Formed: Los Angeles, California, USA ... 1965, the brainchild of Hollywood TV producers, BOB RAFELSON and BERT SCHNEIDER. The pair had wanted to make a sit-com based around The BEATLES' film, 'A Hard Day's Night' and in September of that year, they ran a wanted ad for four boys aged between 17 and 21. Out of over four hundred applicants, they picked the lucky DAVY JONES, MICKEY DOLENZ, MIKE NESMITH & PETER TORK, signing them to the 'Colpix' label. All had fairly notable previous experience (see below), and were duly sent for acting/grooming lessons early in '66. Following difficulties on the songwriting front, BOB & BERT brought in pensmiths TOMMY BOYCE and BOBBY HART (on appointment from 'Screen Gems' top man, Don Kirshner), who also became the group's producers. Other writers were brought in, namely NEIL DIAMOND, GERRY GOFFIN & CAROLE KING, NEIL SEDAKA plus BARRY MANN & CYNTHIA WEIL. On the 12th of September 1966, "The MONKEES" TV show premiered on NBC, and although not an overnight success, became a teenage favourite. A month later, their debut 45, 'LAST TRAIN TO CLARKSVILLE', was released, showcasing their BEACH BOYS-style harmonies and soon climbing to US No.1. Their follow-up, 'I'M A BELIEVER' (penned by NEIL DIAMOND), also hit the top, and with their show now on BBC TV, it repeated the feat in Britain. Another DIAMOND composition, 'A LITTLE BIT ME, A LITTLE BIT YOU', made both Top 3's in March '67 (two of their albums also having amassed cross-Atlantic success). The aforementioned 45's virtually turned the group into an overnight pop phenomenon, their boyish good looks and "zany" antics endearing their bubblegum psychedelia to the nation's teenyboppers (although their music has surprisingly stood the test of time, giving them cult status). For the remainder of the 60's (with NESMITH increasingly dominating the songwriting), they carried on with further TV series' (one featuring ZAPPA, another with TIM BUCKLEY) and some major hits. Their show was axed towards the end of the decade, by which time they had gone into the movies, making the box-office disaster, 'HEAD', with writers BOB RAFELSON and JACK NICHOLSON (yes that one!).

• **Covered:** DAYDREAM BELIEVER (John Sebastian) / D.W. WASHBURN (Leiber-Stoller) / etc. • **Trivia:** In 1967, their 'RANDY SCOUSE GIT' (taken from the character Alf Garnett in British sit-com 'Til Death Us Do Part') was banned by the BBC, and later given the 'ALTERNATIVE TITLE' motif.

The MONKEES

Best CD compilation: HERE THEY COME – THE GREATEST HITS OF . . . (*8)

DAVY JONES (b.30 Dec'46, Manchester, England) – vocals, rhythm guitar (ex-apprentice jockey, actor UK TV 'Coronation Street' & 'Z Cars' / solo artist) / **MICKEY DOLENZ** (b. GEORGE MICHAEL DOLENZ JR., 8 Mar'45, Tarzana, Calif.) – drums, vocals (child actor 'Circus Boy' as Corky, 'Peyton Place', etc.) / **MIKE NESMITH** (b. ROBERT MICHAEL NESMITH, 30 Dec'42, Houston, Texas) – guitar, vocals (ex-folk solo act as MICHAEL BLESSING on 'Colpix' label) / **PETER TORK** (b. PETER THORKELSON, 13 Feb'44, Washington, D.C.) – bass, vocals (ex-AU GO GO SINGERS with RICHIE FURAY / recommended by STEPHEN STILLS)

Session men on discs were; JAMES BURTON, GLEN CAMPBELL, LEON RUSSELL, HAL BLAINE + DAVID GATES.

RCA Victor — Colgems

Oct 66. (7") *(RCA 1547)* *<1001>* **LAST TRAIN TO CLARKSVILLE. / TAKE A GIANT STEP** — [ ] Sep66 [1]
(late Jan'67; – debut single hit UK No.23)

Dec 66. (7") *(RCA 1560)* *<1002>* **I'M A BELIEVER. / I'M NOT YOUR STEPPING STONE** — [1] [1] [20]

Jan 67. (lp; mono/stereo) *(RD/SF 7844)* *<101>* **THE MONKEES** — [1] Oct66 [1]
– Theme from The Monkees / Saturday's child / I wanna be free / Tomorrow's gonna be another day / Papa Gene's blues / Take a giant step / Last train to Clarksville / This just doesn't seem to be my day / Let's dance on / I'll be true to you / Sweet young thing / Gonna buy me a dog. *<re-iss. Aug86 on 'Rhino' hit No.92; 70140> (cd-iss. Apr88 on 'Arista'; 258773) (cd-iss. Dec94 on 'Warners'; 4509 97655-2)*

Mar 67. (7") *(RCA 1580)* *<1004>* **A LITTLE BIT ME, A LITTLE BIT YOU. / THE GIRL I KNEW SOMEWHERE** — [3] [2] [39]

Apr 67. (lp; mono/stereo) *(RD/SF 7868)* *<102>* **MORE OF THE MONKEES** — [1] Feb67 [1]
– When love comes knockin' (at your door) / She / Mary, Mary / Hold on girl / Your Auntie Grizelda / (I'm not you) Steppin' stone / Look out (here comes tomorrow) / The kind of girl I could love / The day we fell in love / Sometime in the morning / Laugh / I'm a believer. *<re-iss. Aug86 on 'Rhino' hit No.96; 70142> (cd-iss. Jun88 on 'Arista'; 259052) (cd-iss. Dec94 on 'Warners'; 4509 97658-2)*

Jun 67. (7") *(RCA 1604)* **ALTERNATIVE TITLE. / FORGET THAT GIRL** — [2] [–]
(above was to have been called 'RANDY SCOUSE GIT')

Jul 67. (lp; mono/stereo) *(RD/SF 7868)* *<103>* **HEADQUARTERS** — [2] Jun67 [1]
– You told me / I'll spend my life with you / Forget that girl / Band 6 / You just may be the one / Shades of grey / I can't get her off my mind / For Pete's sake / Mr. Webster / Sunny girlfriend / Zilch / No time / Early morning blues and greens / Randy Scouse git. *<re-iss. Aug86 on 'Rhino'; 70143> (cd-iss. Feb95 on 'Warners'; 4509 97662-2)*

Jul 67. (7") *(RCA 1620)* *1007>* **PLEASANT VALLEY SUNDAY. / WORDS** — [11] [3] [11]

Nov 67. (7") *(RCA 1645)* *<1012>* **DAYDREAM BELIEVER. / GOING DOWN** — [5] [1]

Jan 68. (lp; mono/stereo) *(RD/SF 7912)* *<104>* **PISCES, AQUARIUS, CAPRICORN AND JONES LTD.** — [5] Nov67 [1]
– Salesman / She hangs out / The door into summer / Love is only sleeping / Cuddly toy / Words / Hard to believe / What am I doing hangin' round? / Peter Percival Patterson's pet pig Porky / Pleasant Valley Sunday / Daily nightly / Don't call on me / Star collector. *<re-iss. Aug86 on 'Rhino'; 70141> (cd-iss. Feb95 on 'Warners'; 4509 97663-2)*

Mar 68. (7") *(RCA 1673)* *<1019>* **VALLERI. / TAPIOCA TUNDRA** — [12] [3] [34]

May 68. (lp; mono/stereo) *(RD/SF 7948)* *<109>* **THE BIRDS, THE BEES & THE MONKEES** — [ ] [3]
– Dream world / Auntie's municipal court / We were made for each other / Tapioca tundra / Daydream believer / Writing wrongs / I'll be back on my feet / The poster / P.O. Box 9847 / Magnolia Simms / Valleri / Zor and Zam. *<re-iss. Aug86 on 'Rhino'; 70144> (cd-iss. Dec94 on 'Warners'; 4509 97665-2)*

Jun 68. (7") *(RCA 1706)* *<1023>* **D.W. WASHBURN. / IT'S NICE TO BE WITH YOU** — [17] [19] [51]

Sep 68. (7") *<1031>* **THE PORPOISE SONG. / AS WE GO ALONG** — [–] [62]

— now down to trio when TORK departed. (he still appeared on below s/track)

Mar 69. (7") *(RCA 1802)* *<5000>* **TEARDROP CITY. / A MAN WITHOUT A DREAM** — [46] Feb69 [56]

May 69. (lp; mono/stereo) *(RD/SF 8016)* *<113>* **INSTANT REPLAY** — [ ] Feb69 [32]
– Through the looking glass / Don't listen to Linda / I won't be the same without her / Me without you / Just a game / Don't wait for me / You and I / While I cry / Teardrop city / The girl I left behind me / Man without a dream / Shorty Blackwell. *<re-iss. Oct86 on 'Rhino'; 70147> (cd-iss. Feb95 on 'Warners'; 4509 97661-2)*

Jun 69. (7") *(RCA 1824)* *<5004>* **SOMEDAY MAN. / LISTEN TO THE BAND** — [47] [81] [63]

Aug 69. (7") *(RCA 1862)* **DADDY'S SONG. / THE PORPOISE SONG** — [ ] [ ]

Sep 69. (lp; mono/stereo) *(RD/SF 8051)* *<5008>* **HEAD (Soundtrack)** — [ ] Dec68 [45]
– Opening ceremony / The porpoise song (theme from 'Head') / Ditty Diego – War chant / Circle sky / (Supplicio) / Can you dig it / (Gravy) / Superstitious / As we go along / (Dandruff?) / Daddy's song / (Poll) / Long title: Do I have to do this all over again / Swami – Plus strings. *<re-iss. Oct86 on 'Rhino'; 70146> (cd-iss. Dec94 on 'Warners'+=; 4509 97659-2)* – Ditty Diego – War chant / Circle sky / Happy birthday to you / Can you dig it / Daddy's song / Head radio spot.

Sep 69. (7") *(RCA 1887)* *<5005>* **GOOD CLEAN FUN. / MOMMY AND DADDY** — [ ] [82]

Oct 69. (lp) *<117>* **THE MONKEES PRESENT . . .** — [–] [100]
– Little girl / Good clean fun / If I knew / Bye bye baby bye bye / Never tell a woman yes / Looking for the good times / Ladies Aid Society / Listen to the band / French song / Mommy and daddy / Oklahoma backroom dancer / Pillow time. *<re-iss. Nov86 on 'Rhino'; 70147> (cd-iss. Dec94 on 'Warners'; 4509 97660-2)*

— now down to **JONES + DOLENZ** duo when NESMITH left to go solo.

Jun 70. (7") *(RCA 1958)* *<5011>* **OH MY MY. / LOVE YOU BETTER** — [ ] [98]

1970. (lp) *<119>* **CHANGES** — [–] [ ]
– Oh my my / Ticket on a ferry ride / You're so good to me / It's got to be love / Acapulco sun / 99 pounds / Tell me love / Do you feel it too / I love you better / All alone in the dark / Midnight train / I never thought it peculiar. *<re-iss. Aug86 on 'Rhino'; 70148> (cd-iss. Dec94 on 'Warners'; 4509 97657-2)*

the MONKEES

— re-formed with **DOLENZ, JONES + TORK** and session people.

Arista — Arista

Oct 86. (7"pic-d-4/7") *(ARIST 1/2/3/4+/673)* *<9505>* **THAT WAS THEN, THIS IS NOW. / THEME FROM THE MONKEES** — [68] Jul86 [20]
(12"+=) *(ARIST 12-673)* – Pleasant valley Sunday / Last train to Clarksville.

Oct 86. (lp/c/cd) *(207/407/257 874)* *<8432>* **THEN & NOW . . . THE BEST OF THE MONKEES** (w/ 3 new) — [ ] Jul86 [21]
– Then and now / Tripwire / Theme from The Monkees / Last train to Clarksville / Take a giant step / I'm a believer / I'm not your stepping stone / A little bit me, a little you / Anytime, anyplace, anywhere / That was then, this is now / The girl I knew somewhere / Pleasant valley Sunday / What am I doing hangin' 'round / Daydream believer / Valeri / Kicks.

Oct 86. (7") *<9532>* **DAYDREAM BELIEVER. / RANDY SCOUSE GIT** — [–] [79]

Rhino — Rhino

Aug 87. (7") *<74408>* **HEART AND SOUL. / M.G.B.G.T.** — [–] [87]

Aug 87. (lp/c/cd) *<(RN IN/IC/CD 70706)>* **POOL IT!** — [ ] [72]
– Heart and soul / (I'd go the) Whole wide world / Long way home / Secret heart / Gettin' in / (I'll) Love you forever / Every step of the way / Don't bring me down / Midnight / She's movin' in with Rico / Since you went away / Counting on you. *(cd-iss. Nov95;)*

Nov 87. (7") **EVERY STEP OF THE WAY. / I LOVE YOU FOREVER** — [–] [ ]

— the original four re-formed in 1996

Artful — Artful

Jan 97. (cd/c) *(ARTFUL CD/MC 6)* *<72542>* **JUSTUS** — [ ] [ ]
– Circle sky / Never enough / Oh what a night / You and I / Unlucky stars / Admiral Mike / Dyin' of a broken heart / Regional girl / Run away from life / I believe you / It's my life / If't not too late.

– (selective) compilations, etc. –

Jun 69. (lp) *Colgems; <115>* **GREATEST HITS** [–] [89]
Aug 76. (lp) *Arista; <4089>* **THE MONKEES' GREATEST HITS** [–] [58]
Feb 80. (7"ep) *Arista; (ARIST 326)* **THE MONKEES** [33] [ ]
– Daydream believer / Last train to Clarksville / I'm a believer / A little bit me, a little bit you.
Jun 81. (7"ep) *Arista; (ARIST 402)* **THE MONKEES VOL.2** [ ] [ ]
– I'm not your stepping stone / Pleasant valley Sunday / Alternative title (Randy Scouse git) / What am I doing.
Jun 81. (d-lp/d-c) *Arista; (DARTY/TCDAR 12)* **THE MONKEES** [99] [ ]
Oct 87. (lp/c/cd) *Rhino; (RN LP/C/CD 70139)* **LIVE 1967 (live)** [–] [ ]
Oct 87. (lp/c) *Rhino; (RN LP/C 70150)* **MISSING LINKS** (rare) [–] [ ]
Mar 89. (7"ep/3"cd-ep) *Arista; (112/662 157)* **THE MONKEES** [62] [ ]
– Daydream believer / A little bit me, a little bit you / Theme from The Monkees.
Apr 89. (7"ep/3"cd-ep) *Arista; (112/662 158)* **THE MONKEES VOL.2** [ ] [ ]
– Last train to Clarksville / I'm a believer / Pleasant valley Sunday.
Apr 89. (lp/c/cd) *K-Tel; (NE1/CD2/NCD3 432)* **HEY HEY IT'S THE MONKEES – GREATEST HITS** [12] [–]
– Theme from The Monkees / Pleasant valley Sunday / The girl I knew somewhere / D.W. Washburn / Last train to Clarksville / A little bit me, a little bit you / teardrop city / Some day man / What am I doing hangin' 'round / Daydream believer / I'm not your stepping stone / Alternative title (randy scouse git) / Words / I'm a believer / Listen to the band / Valeri / Tapioca tundra / That was then, this is now.
Mar 97. (cd/c) *Telstar; (954835218-2/-4)* **HERE THEY COME: THE GREATEST HITS OF THE MONKEES** [15] [–]
Mar 00. (cd) *Audiophile; (APH 102811)* **20 GREATEST HITS** [ ] [–]
Feb 01. (d-cd/d-c) *Warners ESP; (8573 86691-2/-4)* **THE DEFINITIVE MONKEES** [15] [–]
Mar 01. (4xcd-box) *Rhino; <(8122 76706-2)>* **THE MONKEES MUSIC BOX** [ ] [ ]
Apr 03. (cd) *King Biscuit; (KBCCD 131)* **IN CONCERT** [ ] [ ]

the MOODY BLUES

Formed: Birmingham, England . . . May '64 by DENNY LAINE (who had just dissolved his DIPLOMATS band), MIKE PINDER, RAY THOMAS, CLINT WARWICK and GRAEME EDGE. They hooked up with manager, Tony Secunda, who subsequently secured them a deal with 'Decca' records. Their debut 45, 'LOSE YOUR MONEY', bombed, but by early '65 they were at the top spot with the Bessie Banks cover, 'GO NOW'. They tried desperately to emulate its success, and although they scored a few minor chart hits, they disbanded in October '66. The band quickly re-united a month later, after finding JUSTIN HAYWARD and JOHN LODGE to replace DENNY LAINE and recent member ROD CLARKE. Late in the summer of '67, they switched to the more adventurous 'Deram', immediately hitting with the concept album, 'DAYS OF FUTURE PASSED'. It broke from their mid-60's R&B/pop sound, to a more ambitious hybrid of rock and orchestral pop. A haunting piece from it, 'NIGHTS IN WHITE SATIN', became a massive seller and an all-time classic in the process. After a rare concert at London's Queen Elizabeth Hall, they issued a follow-up concept album, 'IN SEARCH OF THE LOST CHORD'. Another massive seller, it was succeeded by their first No.1 album, 'ON THE THRESHOLD OF A DREAM', in 1969. Later that year they founded their own label, 'Threshold', continuing the winning formula on a further clutch of early 70's albums, in addition to some finely crafted 45's, including 'QUESTION', 'ISN'T LIFE STRANGE' and 'I'M JUST A SINGER (IN A ROCK AND ROLL BAND)'. In the mid-70's, The MOODY BLUES was put on ice while they ventured into side projects. All had a relative degree of success, most notably the BLUE JAYS (aka HAYWARD & LODGE) who had a more mainstream sounding pop hit, 'BLUE GUITAR' (1975 & produced by 10cc). With new Swiss-born keyboard wizard PATRICK MORAZ on board (fresh from a spell with YES), they released the comeback album, 'OCTAVE', in 1978, the record subsequently returning them to platinum status. Although early 80's album, 'LONG DISTANCE VOYAGER', went Top 10 on both sides of the Atlantic (No.1 in the US), creatively, the band were becoming stale, subsequent studio sets such as 'THE PRESENT' (1983), 'THE OTHER SIDE OF LIFE' (1986), 'SUR LA MER' (1988), 'KEYS OF THE KINGDOM' (1991) and 'STRANGE TIMES' (1999) doing little to regain the credibility thay had in the 60s & 70s.

• **Songwriters:** LAINE wrote most of material, until LODGE or HAYWARD took over late '66. Also covered; I DON'T WANT TO GO ON WITHOUT YOU (Drifters) / IT AIN'T NECESSARILY SO (Gershwin) / TIME IS ON MY SIDE (Rolling Stones) / BYE BYE BIRD (Sonny Boy Williamson) / etc.

Album rating: THE MAGNIFICENT MOODIES (*5) / DAYS OF FUTURE PASSED (*8) / IN SEARCH OF THE LOST CHORD (*7) / ON THE THRESHOLD OF A DREAM (*8) / TO OUR CHILDREN'S CHILDREN'S CHILDREN (*6) / A QUESTION OF BALANCE (*6) / EVERY GOOD BOY DESERVES FAVOUR (*7) / SEVENTH SOJOURN (*6) / THIS IS THE MOODY BLUES compilation (*8) / CAUGHT LIVE + 5 (*5) / OCTAVE (*5) / LONG DISTANCE VOYAGER (*7) / THE PRESENT (*5) / VOICES IN THE SKY – THE BEST OF THE MOODY BLUES compilation (*8) / THE OTHER SIDE OF LIFE (*6) / SUR LA MER (*4) / GREATEST HITS compilation (*7) / KEYS OF THE KINGDOM (*4) / A NIGHT AT RED ROCKS WITH THE COLORADO SYMPHONY ORCHESTRA (*4) / TIME TRAVELLER boxed-set (*8) / STRANGE TIMES (*4) / HALL OF FAME (*4) / THE VERY BEST OF THE MOODY BLUES + STRANGE TIMES part compilation (*7) / DECEMBER (*5) / LOVELY TO SEE YOU (*6) / Justin Hayward & John Lodge: BLUE JAYS (*6)

DENNY LAINE (b. BRIAN HINES, 29 Oct'44, Jersey, England) – vocals, guitar (ex-DIPLOMATS) / **MIKE PINDER** (b.12 Dec'41) – keyboards, vocals (ex-CREWCATS) / **RAY THOMAS** (b.29 Dec'42, Stourport-on-Severn, England) – flute, vocals, harmonica / **CLINT WARWICK** (b. CLINTON ECCLES, 25 Jun'39) – bass, vocals / **GRAHAM EDGE** (b.30 Mar'42, Rochester, England) – drums (ex-GERRY LEVENE AND THE AVENGERS)

Decca London

Aug 64. (7"; as MOODYBLUES) *(F 11971)* **STEAL YOUR HEART AWAY. / LOSE YOUR MONEY (BUT DON'T LOSE YOUR MIND)** [ ] [–]
Nov 64. (7") *(F 12022)* **GO NOW! / IT'S EASY CHILD** [1] [–]
Feb 65. (7") *(F 12095)* **I DON'T WANT TO GO ON WITHOUT YOU. / TIME IS ON MY SIDE** [33] [ ]
Feb 65. (7") *<9726>* **GO NOW! / LOSE YOUR MONEY (BUT DON'T LOSE YOUR MIND)** [–] [10]
May 65. (7") *(F 12166) <9764>* **FROM THE BOTTOM OF MY HEART (I LOVE YOU). / AND MY BABY'S GONE** [22] [93]
Jul 65. (lp) *(LK 4711) <LP 428>* **THE MAGNIFICENT MOODIES** <US-title 'GO NOW! – THE MOODY BLUES'> [ ] [ ]
– I'll go crazy / Something you got / Go now! / Can't nobody love you / I don't mind / I've got a dream / Let me go / Stop! / Thank you baby / It ain't necessarily so / True story / Bye bye bird. *(cd-iss. Nov88 & Jan93; 820 758-2) (re-iss. Mar93 on 'Repertoire' +=;)*– Steal your heart away / Lose your money (but don't lose your mind) / It's easy child / I don't want to go on without you (come back) / Time is on my side / From the bottom of my heart (I love you) / And my baby's gone.
Oct 65. (7") *(F 12266)* **EVERYDAY. / YOU DON'T (ALL THE TIME)** [44] [ ]
Mar 66. (7") *<9810>* **STOP! / BYE BYE BIRD** [–] [98]

— (Jul66) **ROD CLARKE** – bass repl. WARWICK

Oct 66. (7") *(F 12498)* **BOULEVARD DE LA MADELAINE. / THIS IS MY HOUSE (BUT NOBODY CALLS)** [ ] [ ]

— (Nov'66) **JUSTIN HAYWARD** (b.14 Oct'46, Swindon, England) – vocals, guitar (ex-WILDE THREE, ex-solo artist) repl. DENNY who went solo (and later to WINGS) / **JOHN LODGE** (b.20 Jul'45) – bass, vocals (ex-EL RIOT & THE REBELS) repl. CLARKE

Jan 67. (7"; w-drawn after a day) *(F 12543)* **LIFE'S NOT LIFE. / HE CAN WIN** [–] [–]
May 67. (7") *(F 12607)* **FLY ME HIGH. / REALLY HAVEN'T GOT THE TIME** [ ] [ ]
Aug 67. (7") *(F 12670)* **LOVE AND BEAUTY. / LEAVE THIS MAN ALONE** [ ] [ ]

Deram Deram

Nov 67. (7") *(DM 161)* *<85023>* **NIGHTS IN WHITE SATIN. / CITIES** 19 [ ]

<re-iss. Jul72; same>; hit No.2> (re-iss. Nov72; same); hit No.9) (re-iss. Mar76; same) (re-iss. Oct79; same); hit No.14) (re-iss. Oct83 & Jun88 on 'Old Gold'; OG 9349)

Nov 67. (lp; mono/stereo) *(DML/SML 707)* *<18012>* **DAYS OF FUTURE PASSED** 27 Apr68 3

– The day begins / Dawn:- Dawn is a feeling / The morning:- Another morning / Lunch break:- Peak hour / The afternoon:- Forever afternoon (Tuesday) / Time to get away / Evening:- The sunset / Twilight time / The night:- Nights in white satin. *<US re-iss. Sep72 hit No.3> (cd-iss. 1983 on 'Threshold'; 800 082-2) (re-iss. Nov84 lp/c; DOA/KDOAC 6) (re-iss. Apr91 cd/c/lp; 820006-2/-4/-1) (cd re-iss. Apr00 on 'Polydor'; 844767-2)*

Jul 68. (7") *<85028>* **TUESDAY AFTERNOON (FOREVER AFTERNOON). / ANOTHER MORNING** – 24

Jul 68. (7") *(DM 196)* **VOICES IN THE SKY. / DR. LIVINGSTONE, I PRESUME** 23 –

Jul 68. (lp; mono/stereo) *(DML/SML 711)* *<18017>* **IN SEARCH OF THE LOST CHORD** 5 Sep68 23

– Departure / Ride my see-saw / Dr. Livingstone, I presume / House of four doors (part 1) / Legend of a mind / House of four doors (part 2) / Voices in the sky / The best way to travel / Visions of paradise / The actor / The word / Om. *(re-iss. Nov84 lp/c; DOA/KDOAC 7) (cd-iss. Aug86 & Apr91 on 'London'; 820 168-2) (cd re-iss. Apr00 on 'Polydor'; 844768-2)*

Oct 68. (7") *<85033>* **RIDE MY SEE-SAW. / VOICES IN THE SKY** – 61

Nov 68. (7") *(DM 213)* **RIDE MY SEE-SAW. / A SIMPLE GAME** 42 –

Apr 69. (7") *(DM 247)* *<85044>* **NEVER COMES THE DAY. / SO DEEP WITHIN YOU** [ ] 91

Apr 69. (lp; mono/stereo) *(DML/SML 1035)* *<18025>* **ON THE THRESHOLD OF A DREAM** 1 May69 20

– In the beginning / Lovely to see you / Dear diary / Send me no wine / To share our love / So deep within you / Never comes the day / Lazy day / Are you sitting comfortably / The dream / Have you heard (part 1) / The voyage / Have you heard (part 2). *(cd-iss. Aug86 on 'London'; 820 170-2) (cd re-iss. Apr00 on 'Polydor'; 844769-2)*

Threshold Threshold

Oct 69. (7") *(TH 1)* **WATCHING AND WAITING. / OUT AND IN** [ ] –

Nov 69. (lp; mono/stereo) *(<THM/THS 1>)* **TO OUR CHILDREN'S CHILDREN'S CHILDREN** 2 Jan70 14

– Higher and higher / Eyes of a child (part 1) / Floating / Eyes of a child (part 2) / I never thought I'd live to be a hundred / Beyond / Out and in / Gypsy / Eternity road / Candle of life / Sun is still shining / I never thought I'd live to be a million / Watching and waiting. *(cd-iss. Aug86 on 'London'; 820 364-2) (cd re-iss. Apr00 on 'Polydor'; 844770-2)*

Apr 70. (7") *(TH 4)* *<67004>* **QUESTION. / CANDLE OF LIFE** 2 21

(re-iss. Oct83 on 'Old Gold'; OG 9348)

Aug 70. (lp) *(<TH 3>)* **A QUESTION OF BALANCE** 1 Sep70 3

– Question / How is it (we are here) / And the tide rushes in / Don't you feel small / Tortoise and the hare / It's up to you / Minstrel's song / Dawning is the day / Melancholy man / The balance. *(cd-iss. Aug86 & Jul92 on 'London'; 820 211-2) (cd re-iss. Apr00 on 'Polydor'; 844771-2)*

Jul 71. (lp) *(<TH 5>)* **EVERY GOOD BOY DESERVES FAVOUR** 1 Aug71 2

– Procession / The story in your eyes / Our guessing game / Emily's song / After you came / One more time to live / Nice to be here / You can never go home / My song. *(cd-iss. Aug86 & Apr91 on 'London'; 820 160-2) (cd re-iss. Apr00 on 'Polydor'; 844772-2)*

Aug 71. (7") *<67006>* **THE STORY IN YOUR EYES. / MELANCHOLY MAN** – 23

Apr 72. (7") *(TH 9)* *<67009>* **ISN'T LIFE STRANGE. / AFTER YOU CAME** 13 29

Nov 72. (lp) *(<TH 7>)* **SEVENTH SOJOURN** 5 1

– Lost in a lost world / New horizons / For my lady / Isn't life strange / You and me / The land of make-believe / When you're a free man / I'm just a singer (in a rock'n'roll band). *(cd-iss. Sep86 on 'London'; 820 159-2) (cd re-iss. Apr00 on 'Polydor'; 844773-2)*

Jan 73. (7") *(TH 13)* *<67012>* **I'M JUST A SINGER (IN A ROCK'N'ROLL BAND). / FOR MY LADY** 36 12

— Split early '73 but only for a 5 year trial period, releasing own solos released (2) compilations while they split

Nov 74. (d-lp) *(MB 1-2)* *<2-12-13>* **THIS IS THE MOODY BLUES** 14 11

– Question / The actor / The word / Eyes of a child / Dear diary / Legend of a mind / In the beginning / Lovely to see you / Never comes the day / Isn't life strange / The dream / Have you heard / Voyage / Ride my see-saw / Tuesday afternoon / And the tide rushes in / New horizons / Simple game / Watching and waiting / I'm just a singer (in a rock'n'roll band) / For my lady / Story in your eyes / Melancholy man / Nights in white satin. *(d-cd-iss. Aug89; 820 007-2)*

Decca London

Apr 77. (d-lp) *(MB 3-4)* *<690-1>* **CAUGHT LIVE + 5** (live '69 +1 studio side) [ ] Jun77 26

– Gypsy / The sunset / Dr. Livingstone, I presume / Never comes the day / Peak hour / Tuesday afternoon / Are you sitting comfortably / Have you heard (part 1) / The voyage / Have you heard (part 2) / Nights in white satin / Legend of a mind / Ride my see-saw / Gimme a little somethin' / Please think about it / Long summer days / King and Queen / What am I doing here. *(cd-iss. Apr00; 820161-2)*

— re-formed mid 1978; **(HAYWARD, LODGE, EDGE, PINDER** and **THOMAS)**

Decca London

Jun 78. (lp/blue-lp/c) *(TX/+S/C 129)* *<PS 708>* **OCTAVE** 6 13

– Steppin' in a slide zone / Under moonshine / Had to fall in love / I'll be level with you / Driftwood / Top rank suite / I'm your man / Survival / One step into the light / The day we meet again. *(cd-iss. Oct86 & Jan93 & Apr00; 820 329-2)*

Jul 78. (7") *(F 13790)* *<270>* **STEPPIN' IN A SLIDE ZONE. / I'LL BE LEVEL WITH YOU** [ ] 39

Oct 78. (7") *(F 13809)* *<273>* **DRIFTWOOD. / I'M YOUR MAN** [ ] 59

— **PATRICK MORAZ** (b.24 Jun'48, Morges, Switzerland) – keyboards (ex-YES, solo artist, ex-REFUGEE) repl. PINDER

Threshold Threshold

May 81. (lp/c) *(TXS 139)* *<TRL-1 2901>* **LONG DISTANCE VOYAGER** 7 Jun81 1

– The voice / Talking out of turn / Gemini dream / In my world / Meanwhile / 22,000 days / Nervous / Painted smile / Reflective smile / Veteran cosmic rocker. *(cd-iss. Oct86 & Apr00; 820 105-2)*

Jun 81. (7") *(TH 27)* *<601>* **GEMINI DREAM. / PAINTED SMILE** [ ] 12

Jul 81. (7") *(TH 33)* *<602>* **THE VOICE. / 22,000 DAYS** [ ] 15

Nov 81. (7"/7"pic-d) *(TH/+PD 29)* *<603>* **TALKING OUT OF TURN. / VETERAN COSMIC ROCKER** [ ] 65

Aug 83. (7") *(TH 30)* **BLUE WORLD. / GOING NOWHERE** 35 –

Sep 83. (lp/c)(cd) *(TXS/+C 140)(810119-2)* *<2902>* **THE PRESENT** 15 26

– Blue world / Meet me halfway / Sitting at the wheel / Going nowhere / Hole in the world / Under my feet / It's cold outside of your heart / Running water / I am / Sorry. *(cd re-iss. Apr91 on 'London'; same)*

Sep 83. (7") *<604>* **SITTING AT THE WHEEL. / GOING NOWHERE** – 27

Oct 83. (7") *(TH 31)* **SITTING AT THE WHEEL. / SORRY** [ ] –

(12"+=) *(THX 31)* – Gemini dream.

Nov 83. (7") *<605>* **BLUE WORLD. / SORRY** – 62

Feb 84. (7") *<606>* **UNDER MY FEET. / RUNNING WATER** – [ ]

Polydor Polydor

Mar 86. (7"/12") *(POSP/+X 787)* *<883906>* **YOUR WILDEST DREAMS. / TALKIN' TALKIN'** [ ] Apr86 9

May 86. (lp/c)(cd) *(POLD/+C 5190)(829179-2)* *<829179>* **OTHER SIDE OF LIFE** 24 9

– Your wildest dreams / Talkin' talkin' / Rock'n'roll over you / I just don't care / Running out of love / The other side of life / The spirit / Slings and arrows / It may be a fire. *(cd re-iss. Feb97; same)*

Aug 86. (7") *(POSP 830)* *<885201>* **THE OTHER SIDE OF LIFE. / NIGHTS IN WHITE SATIN (live)** [ ] 58

(12"+=) *(POSPX 830)* – The spirit. *<US; b-side>*

May 88. (7") *(POSP 921)* *<887600>* **I KNOW YOU'RE OUT THERE SOMEWHERE. / MIRACLE** 52 30

(12"+=) *(POSPX 921)* – ('A'extended).

(cd-s+=) *(POCD 921)* – Rock'n'roll over you (live).

Jun 88. (lp/c)(cd) *(POLH/+C 43)(<835756-2>)* **SUR LA MER** 21 38

– I know you're out there somewhere / Want to be with you / River of endless love / No more lies / Here comes the weekend / Vintage wine / Breaking point / Miracle / Love is on the run / Deep. *(cd re-iss. Feb97; same)*

Dec 88. (7") *(PO 27)* **NO MORE LIES. / RIVER OF ENDLESS LOVE** [ ] [ ]

(12"+=) *(PZ 27)* – The other side of life.

Jun 91. (7"/c-s) **SAY IT WITH LOVE. / LEAN ON ME (TONIGHT)** [ ] [ ]

(12"+=/cd-s+=) – Highway.

Aug 91. (cd/c/lp) *(<849433-2/-4/-1>)* **KEYS OF THE KINGDOM** 54 94
– Say it with love / Bless the wings (that bring you back) / Is this Heaven? / Say what you mean (pt.1 & 2) / Lean on me (tonight) / Hope and pray / Shadows on the wall / Celtic sonant / Magic / Never blame the rainbows for the rain. *(cd+=/c+=)* – Once is enough. *(re-iss. Jan93; same)*

Mar 93. (cd/c) *(<517977-2/-4>)* **A NIGHT AT RED ROCKS** (with The Colorado Symphony Orchestra live)
– Overture / Late lament / Tuesday afternoon (forever afternoon) / For my lady / Lean on me (tonight) / Lovely to see you / I know you're out there somewhere / The voice / Your wildest dreams / Isn't life strange / The other side of life / I'm just a singer (in a rock and roll band) / Nights in white satin / Question / Ride my see-saw. *(cd re-iss. Feb97; 517977-2)* *(<deluxe d-cd-iss. Mar03; 065275-2>)*

Universal Universal

Sep 99. (cd) *(<1 53265-2>)* **STRANGE TIMES** 93
– English sunset / Haunted / Sooner or later (walkin' on air) / Wherever you are / Foolish love / Love don't come easy / All that is real is you / Strange times / Words you say / My little lovely / Forever now / One / Swallow / Nothing changes.

Apr 00. (d-cd)(c) *(541424-2)(535800-4)* **THE VERY BEST OF THE MOODY BLUES** (compilation; cd w/ 'STRANGE TIMES') 19 –
– Go now / Tuesday afternoon (forever autumn) / Nights in white satin / Ride my see-saw / Voices in the sky / Question / The story in your eyes / Isn't life strange / I'm just a singer (in a rock and roll band) / Blue guitar / Steppin' in a slide zone / Forever autumn / The voice / Gemini dream / Blue world / Your wildest dream / I know you're out there somewhere.

Sep 00. (cd) *(159537-2)* *<810059>* **HALL OF FAME** (live) Aug00
– Overture / Tuesday afternoon (forever afternoon) / English sunset / Words you say / The story in your eyes / I know you're out there somewhere / Haunted / Your wildest dreams / Isn't life strange / I'm just a singer (in a rock and roll band) / Nights in white satin / Legend of a mind / Question / Ride my see-saw.

— **HAYWARD, LODGE + EDGE** (RAY THOMAS left after 2003 tour)

Oct 03. (cd) *<15630-2>* **DECEMBER** (festive) –
– Don't need a reindeer / December snow / In the quiet of Christmas morning (Bach 147) / On this Christmas day / Happy Xmas (war is over) / A winter's tale / The spirit of Christmas / Yes I believe / When a child is born / White Christmas / In the bleak midwinter.

— added **PAUL BLISS** – keyboards / **BERNIE BARLOW** – keyboards, vocals / **GORDON MARSHALL** – percussion / **NORDA MULLEN** – flute

dvd-only Image

Nov 05. (d-cd) *<2851>* **LOVELY TO SEE YOU** (live) –
– Lovely to see you / Tuesday afternoon / Lean on me (tonight) / The actor / Steppin' in a slide zone / The voice / Talking out of turn / I know you're out there somewhere / The story in your eyes / Forever autumn / Your wildest dreams / Isn't life strange / The other side of life / December snow / Higher and higher / Are you sitting comfortably? / I'm just a singer (in a rock & roll band) / Nights in white satin / Question / Ride my see-saw.

– (selective) compilations, etc. –

Nov 84. (lp/c)(cd) *Threshold; (SKL/KSKC 5341) <820155>* **VOICES IN THE SKY – THE BEST OF THE MOODY BLUES** Mar85
– Ride my see-saw / Talking out of turn / Driftwood / Never comes the day / I'm just a singer (in a rock and roll band) / Gemini dream / The voice / After you came / Question / Veteran cosmic rocker / Isn't life strange / Nights in white satin. *(cd re-iss. Apr91)*

Oct 79. (lp/c) *K-Tel; (NE/+C 1051)* **OUT OF THIS WORLD** 15 –

Nov 89. (lp/c/cd) *Polydor; (<840 659-1/-4/-2>)* **GREATEST HITS** 71

Sep 94. (5xcd-box) *Polydor; (516436-2)* **TIME TRAVELLER** *(re-iss. Feb97; 535223-2)*

Sep 96. (cd/c) *Polygram TV; (535 800-2/-4)* **THE VERY BEST OF THE MOODY BLUES** 13 –
– Go now / Tuesday afternoon (forever afternoon) / Nights in white satin / Ride my see-saw / Voices in the sky / Questions / The story in your eyes / Isn't life strange / I'm just a singer (in a rock'n'roll band) / Blue guitar / Steppin' on a slide zone / Forever autumn / The voice / Gemini dream / Blue world / Your wildest dreams / I know you're out there somewhere.

Oct 98. (d-cd) *Universal; (AA314 565430-2)* **ANTHOLOGY**

Jan 00. (cd) *Universal; (E 541088-2)* **UNIVERSAL MASTERS COLLECTION**

Mar 01. (cd) *Ark 21; <810065>* **JOURNEY INTO AMAZING CAVES** (soundtrack with STEVE WOOD & DANIEL MAY) –
– To extremes / Search for daylight / Arizona / Water / Crystal chamber / Blue cathedral / Frozen in time / Home of the Mayan gods / Horizons turn inward / We can fly.

Jul 01. (d-cd) *Deram; (560241-2)* **THE COLLECTION**

Feb 02. (d-cd) *BR Music; (BS 8123-2)* **THE SINGLES PLUS**

Apr 02. (d-cd) *Universal TV; (583344-2)* **THE VERY BEST OF THE MOODY BLUES / HALL OF FAME LIVE AT THE ROYAL ALBERT HALL** 27 –
– (see THE VERY BEST OF . . .) / Overture / Tuesday afternoon / English sunset / Words you say / The story in your eyes / I know you're out there somewhere / Haunted / Your wildest dreams / Isn't life strange / I'm just a singer (in a rock'n'roll band) / Nights in white satin / Legend of a mind / Question / Ride my see-saw.

Alanis MORISSETTE

Born: 1 Jun'74, Ottawa, Ontario, Canada, to a French-Canadian father and Hungarian mother, both schoolteachers. She began writing songs at age ten and subsequently became a regular on the American cable show, 'You Can't Do That On Television'. Her debut, self-financed single 'FATE STAY WITH ME' (on 'Lamor'), was released around the same time and by the age of sixteen, the budding singer/songwriter had cut two disco/pop albums ('ALANIS' and 'NOW IS THE TIME'). MORISSETTE then left her native Canada for the lure of Los Angeles, subsequently hawking her demo unsuccessfully around almost every major record company. Salvation came in the form of MADONNA who recognised her talent, signing ALANIS to her own 'Maverick' label. 'JAGGED LITTLE PILL' (1995) was duly released to major critical acclaim, climbing to No.1 in America and scooping four Grammys and a Brit Award the following year. Confrontational and uncompromising as well as evocative and emotional, MORISSETTE's singing demanded attention, her pent-up adolescent angst finding an outlet in the likes of 'PERFECT', 'YOU OUGHTA KNOW' and 'ONE HAND IN MY POCKET', the latter two both fairly successful UK singles. Musically, the album was largely straightahead guitar rock, solid, if not exactly hard-edged, with ALANIS playing guitar while backed up by BENMONT TENCH (organ, ex-TOM PETTY), LANCE MORRISON (bass) and MATT LAUG (drums). Touting a decidedly more earthy strain of 'girl power' than the SPICE GIRLS, it remains to be seen whether MORISSETTE can keep the momentum going and achieve a similar career trajectory as comtemporaries like SHERYL CROW. A taster single from her new album, 'THANK U' became her biggest hit to date, reaching the US Top 5. Yet with its convoluted title and meandering feel, the album in question, 'SUPPOSED FORMER INFATUATION JUNKIE' (1998), was never likely to spawn any further hits or create the sensation of her debut despite its pole position on the American chart. Even in the stripped down 'ALANIS UNPLUGGED' (1999), where MORISSETTE attempted to reintroduce the material in a more palatable form, these songs retained an inscrutable edge. By 2002's 'UNDER RUG SWEPT', the singer had parted company with her longtime writing partner Glen Ballard, resulting in a more cohesive and accessible yet still relatively impenetrable set of songs. Heralded by the 'HANDS CLEAN' single, the album was, musically at least, a fair attempt at revising her mid-90's heyday, with all the restless tension which fuelled that era hardly having dissipated in the interim. 'SO-CALLED CHAOS' (2004) showcased a much-mellowed MORISSETTE, aglow with the thrill of romance (specifically, actor Ryan Reynolds) and reflecting on the realities of the big 3-0. ALANIS even carried this older and wiser attitude over to a wholesale acoustic re-recording of her 1995 debut, marking the 10th anniversary of its original release. It was a tactic that went down especially well with her Brit fanbase (almost Top 10), a water-treading episode compounded with 'THE COLLECTION' (2005), featuring her version of Seal's 'CRAZY'.

• **Trivia:** Guests on her debut included FLEA (Red Hot Chilis) and DAVE NAVARRO (ex-Jane's Addiction).

Album rating: JAGGED LITTLE PILL (*9) / SUPPOSED FORMER INFATUATION JUNKIE (*6) / MTV UNPLUGGED (*5) / UNDER RUG SWEPT (*6) / SO-CALLED CHAOS (*6) / JAGGED LITTLE PILL ACOUSTIC (*8) / THE COLLECTION compilation (*7)

ALANIS MORISSETTE – vocals / with **BENMONT TENCH** organ (ex-TOM PETTY) / **LANCE MORRISON** -bass / **MATT LAUG** -drums

Maverick Maverick

Jun 95. (cd/c/lp) *<(9362-45901-2/-4/-1)>* **JAGGED LITTLE PILL** [1] [1]
– All I really want / You oughta know / Perfect / Hand in my pocket / Right through you / Forgiven / You learn / Head over feet / Mary Jane / Ironic / Not the doctor / Wake up. *(cd+=)* – Your house.

Jul 95. (c-s) *(W 0307C)* **YOU OUGHTA KNOW (clean version) / PERFECT (version)** [22] [–]
(cd-s+=) *(W 0307CD)* – ('A'-Jimmy The Saint blend) / Wake up.

Oct 95. (c-s) *(W 0312C)* **HAND IN MY POCKET / HEAD OVER FEET (live acoustic)** [26] [–]
(cd-s+=) *(W 0312 CD1)* – Not the doctor (live acoustic).
(cd-s) *(W 0312 CD2)* – ('A'side) / Right through you (live acoustic) / Forgiven (live acoustic).

Feb 96. (c-s) *(W 0334C)* **YOU LEARN / YOUR HOUSE (live)** [24] [–]
(cd-s+=) *(W 0334CD)* – Wake up (modern rock live) / Hand in my pocket (version).

Mar 96. (c-s) *<17698>* **IRONIC / FORGIVEN (live) / NOT THE DOCTOR (live)** [–] [4]

Apr 96. (c-s) *(W 0343C)* **IRONIC / YOU OUGHTA KNOW (live acoustic)** [11] [–]
(cd-s+=) *(W 0343CD)* – Mary Jane (live) / All I really want (live).

Jul 96. (c-s) *<17644>* **YOU LEARN / YOU OUGHTA KNOW (live)** [–] [6]

Jul 96. (c-s) *(W 0355C)* **HEAD OVER FEET / HAND IN MY POCKET (live)** [7] [–]
(cd-s+=) *(W 0355CD)* – You learn (live) / Right through you (live).

Nov 96. (c-s) *(W 0382C)* **ALL I REALLY WANT / IRONIC (live from Sydney)** [59] [–]
(cd-s+=) *(W 0382CD)* – Hand in my pocket (live from Brisbane).

— now with **BENMONT** (again) + **NICK LASHLEY** + **JOEL SHEARER** – guitar / **CHRIS CHANEY** – bass / **GARY NOVAK** – drums

Oct 98. (c-s) *(W 0458C) <radio play>* **THANK U / UNINVITED (demo)** [5] [17]
(cd-s+=) *(W 0458CD)* – Pollyanna flower.

Nov 98. (cd/c/lp) *<(9362 47094-2/-4/-1)>* **SUPPOSED FORMER INFATUATION JUNKIE** [3] [1]
– Front row / Baba / Thank U / Are you still mad / Sympathetic character / That I would be good / The couch / Can't not / UR / I was hoping / One / Would not come / Unsent / So pure / Joining you / Heart of the house / Your congratulations.

Jan 99. (-) *<radio cut>* **UNSENT** [–] [58]

Mar 99. (c-s) *(W 472C)* **JOINING YOU / YOUR HOUSE (live)** [28] [–]
(cd-s+=) *(W 472CD2)* – London (live).
(cd-s+=) *(W 472CD1)* – These are the thoughts (live).

Jul 99. (c-s) *(W 492C)* **SO PURE / I WAS HOPING (acoustic modern rock live)** [38] [–]
(cd-s+=) *(W 492CD1)* – ('A'-Pure ecstasy mix).
(cd-s+=) *(W 492CD2)* – Would not come (live).

Nov 99. (cd/c) *<(9362 47589-2/-4)>* **MTV UNPLUGGED** (live) [59] [63]
– You learn / Joining you / No pressure over cappuccino / That I would be good / Head over feet / Princess familiar / I was hoping / Ironic / These R the thoughts / King of pain / You oughta know / Uninvited.

Dec 99. (c-s/cd-s) *(W 509 C/CD)* **THAT I WOULD BE GOOD (MTV unplugged live) / WOULD NOT COME (reverb live) / FORGIVE (reverb live) / I WAS HOPING (99X live)** [ ] [–]

Feb 02. (c-s) *(W 574C)* **HANDS CLEAN / UNPRODIGAL DAUGHTER** [12] [23]
(cd-s+=) *(W 574CD1) <42431>* – Symptoms.
(cd-s) *(W 574CD2)* – ('A') / Fear of bliss / Sister blister.

Mar 02. (cd/c) *<(9362 47988-2/-4)>* **UNDER RUG SWEPT** [2] Feb02 [1]
– 21 things I want in a lover / Narcissus / Hands clean / Flinch / So unsexy / Precious illusions / That particular time / A man / You owe me vnothing in return / Surrendering / Utopia.

Aug 02. (c-s) *(W 582C)* **PRECIOUS ILLUSIONS / HANDS CLEAN** [53] [–]
(cd-s+=) *(W 582CD1)* – Sorry 2 myself.
(cd-s) *(W 582CD2)* – ('A') / Offer / Bent 4 U.

May 04. (cd-s) *(W 641CD1)* **EVERYTHING / SO UNEASY (acoustic) / EVERYTHING (acoustic) / (video)** [22] [76]
(cd-s) *(W 641CD2)* – ('A') / Precious illusions (acoustic).

May 04. (cd) *<(9362 78773-2)>* **SO-CALLED CHAOS** [8] [5]
– Eight easy steps / Out is through / Excuses / Doth I protest too much / Knees of my bees / So-called chaos / Not all me / This grudge / Spineless / Everything. *(ltd cd w/cd+=; 9362 48555-2)* – Eight easy steps (live) / Excuses (live) / (the making of) / This grunge (acoustic).

Jul 04. (cd-s) *(W 647CD1)* **OUT IS THROUGH / SPINELESS (Vancouver sessions 2004)** [56] [–]
(cd-s) *(W 647CD2)* – ('A') / Eight easy steps (Vancouver sessions 2004) / This grudge (Vancouver sessions 2004).

Jul 05. (cd) *<(9362 49345-2)>* **JAGGED LITTLE PILL ACOUSTIC** [12] [50]
– All I really want / You oughta know / Perfect / Hand in my pocket / Right through you / Forgiven / You learn / Head over feet / Mary Jane / Ironic / Not the doctor / Wake up. *(hidden+=)* – Your house.

Oct 05. (cd-s) *(W 694CD)* **CRAZY / JOINING YOU (melancholy mix) / CRAZY (Claude de Gache club mix)** [65] [ ]
(cd-s/d12") *<42855-2/-1>* – ('A'-mixes; original / Claude de Gache club / Eddie Baez Coo Coo club / Monk's.. / Interstate).

Nov 05. (cd) *<(9362 49490-2)>* **THE COLLECTION** (compilation) [44] [51]
– Thank you / Head over feet / 8 easy steps / Everything / Crazy / Ironic / Princes Familiar (unplugged) / You learn / Simple together / You oughta know / That I would be good / Sister Blister / Hands clean / Mercy / Still (from 'Dogma') / Uninvited (from 'City Of Angels') / Let's do it (from 'De-Lovely') / Hand in my pocket. *<(ltd-cd w/dvd+=; 9362 49563-2)>* – (DVD tracks).

Van MORRISON

Born: GEORGE IVAN MORRISON, 31 Aug'45, Belfast, N.Ireland. Reared on such eclectic musical fare as HANK WILLIAMS, JIMMIE RODGERS, LEADBELLY and DUKE ELLINGTON, the young VAN began his professional musical apprenticeship on the Irish showband circuit, mastering guitar, piano and saxophone and laying the fertile seed bed of vocal improvisation and innovation that would come to distinguish his career. A rough and tumble tour of Germany with The MONARCHS was followed by spells in the The MANHATTAN SHOWBAND, The GOLDEN EAGLES and finally, The GAMBLERS, who, in turn, evolved into THEM, the brooding R&B bovver boys with whom MORRISON first stamped his gutteral howl on a nations's musical consciousness. Along with The ANIMALS, The PRETTY THINGS and The ROLLING STONES, THEM formed an integral part of the mid-60's British R&B boom from whence came rock music as we now know and love (or loathe, as the case may be) it today. Though the band only released two official albums, 'THEM' (1965) and 'THEM AGAIN' (1966), their place in legend was assured as the garage leer of 'GLORIA' came to be one of the most covered songs in rock history. One of the few constants in their ramshackle approach and ever changing line-up was MORRISON; his dour, threatening demeanour and erratically electric live performances coupled with a precocious gift for songwriting indicated a star in the ascendant. When THEM finally disintegrated, VAN took up an invitation from BERT BERNS (composer of THEM's hit, 'HERE COMES THE NIGHT' – he had also produced the band) to lay down some tracks in New York for his fledgling 'Bang' label. The resulting sessions produced eight finished songs, among them the youthful exuberance of 'BROWN EYED GIRL' and the harrowing, churning claustrophobia of 'T.B. SHEETS', polar opposites between which

Van MORRISON

MORRISON began to develop his songcraft. The former song edged its way into the US Top 10 during the summer of love in 1967, the label subsequently releasing all the tracks as an album, 'BLOWIN' YOUR MIND', in September (without the consent, and much to the annoyance, of MORRISON himself). Nevertheless, the singer entered the studio once again later that year to record another series of tracks, including early versions of 'BESIDE YOU' and 'MADAME GEORGE' (later appearing in their full glory on 'ASTRAL WEEKS'), some surfacing on the hopefully titled 1970 cash-in, 'THE BEST OF VAN MORRISON', while the remainder were eventually unearthed on 1974's 'T.B. SHEETS'. Following the sudden death of BERNS in December '67, VAN moved north to Cambridge, Massachusetts, where he was eventually spotted and signed to a management deal with New York's 'Inherit Productions'. A contract was subsequently secured with 'Warners' and the cream of the Big Apple's jazz musicians were rounded up to back VAN on his solo debut proper, 'ASTRAL WEEKS'. As hotly debated, analysed, shrouded in myth and generally deified as any recording in the history of music, the enigmatic, ethereal allure of the album remains ultimately impenetrable. Recorded, quintessentially MORRISON-style, in two spontaneous four-hour sessions, the record transcended any notion of "rock" per se, nor could it be bracketed under jazz. A darkly intoxicating stream of inspired musical consciousness, 'ASTRAL WEEKS' traded in conventional verse/chorus song structures for freefrom exporations and fragments, languidly vivid imagery floating in and out of focus. From the yearning warmth and acoustic strum of the title track and 'SWEET THING' to the harpsichord tapestry of 'CYPRUS AVENUE' and the epic, dizzying 'MADAME GEORGE', MORRISON set out the blueprint for much of his later work, an eternal quest for spiritual enlightenment that both embraced and transcended hope and despair, contentment and restlessness. Fittingly, then, this music is timeless, the only indication of its 1968 birthdate the supple potency of VAN's young voice. An instrument in its own right, MORRISON's vocal faculty is arguably among the most powerful, seductive and ultimately healing to have emerged in the last thirty or so years, capable of everything from a primal grunt a la JAMES BROWN, to a child-like, awestruck breathlessness. An album that has grown in stature with each passing year, 'ASTRAL WEEKS' was met with mixed reviews upon its original release, and it initially sold relatively poorly. Undeterred, VAN moved to Woodstock with his new wife, Janet Planet (yep, she was a fully paid up hippy), where he penned most of the material for a follow-up album, 'MOONDANCE'. Released in early 1970, the record was a more solidly constructed affair, MORRISON reigning in his more abstract tendencies into tighter, shorter, brassy bursts. Much of the album reflected VAN's love of soul and R&B, punchy horn flourishes replacing the meandering acoustics of 'ASTRAL WEEKS'. The soporific 'AND IT STONED ME' and the classic 'INTO THE MYSTIC' were closest in spirit to the debut, the latter track condensing the albums theme of the redemptive power of love. By this point, the critics were catching on to the stocky Irishman's genius, lauding the album and heralding MORRISON as one of the rock worlds most talented visionaries. He was also arguably one of the few white musicians to interpret black music forms in such a way as to retain the spontaneity and richness while creating something completely original. In saying that, it could be argued that 'VAN MORRISON, HIS BAND AND THE STREET CHOIR' (1970) relied too heavily on a straight soul/R&B formula, lacking any real depth as a result. 'DOMINO' was the standout track, a driving, hedonistic slice of white R&B that gave VAN his biggest (US) hit to date. The album's inside cover showed a scene of communal domesticity, an apparent contentedness (only rarely glimpsed since) that continued with 'TUPELO HONEY' (1971), a country-tinged collection celebrating love and romance. The lush balladeering of the title track saw VAN putting in one of the sweetest vocal performances of his career thus far, most of the songs finding the singer in laid-back, family man mode. Entertaining as the album was, 'ST. DOMINIC'S PREVIEW' (1972) was far more compelling. Tellingly, by the time VAN came to record the album, his relationship with Janet was on the rocks. While the disc opened with the life-affirming soul shout of 'JACKIE WILSON SAID', the epic 'LISTEN TO THE LION' formed the album's centrepiece, a musical and spiritual marathon that set out VAN's agenda of personal quest more explicitly than ever before. The title track was equally inspiring while the almost gospel-like 'REDWOOD TREE' was manna for the soul, healing harmonies of hope and forgiveness. The billowing, hypnotic ambience of 'INDEPENDENCE DAY' closed the album in suitably enigmatic style, and bizarrely enough, recalled the PINK FLOYD of 'Wish You Were Here' (though don't let that put you off!). 'ST. DOMINIC'S PREVIEW' came at a time when VAN was regaining his confidence on stage after a period of relative withdrawal from live performance. To catalogue the ever shifting personnel of MORRISON's various bands would probably warrant a book in its own right although the general concensus is that the man reached a zenith of sorts with his CALEDONIA SOUL ORCHESTRA. Recorded for posterity on the double live album, 'IT'S TOO LATE TO STOP NOW' (1974), MORRISON's summer '73 shows are the stuff of legend. One of the classic live albums, MORRISON takes his songs to places they were probably never designed for, stretching, remoulding and re-inventing them in his inimitable R&B preacher/spiritual warrior fashion. The result is rarely less than breathtaking. Ironically enough, 'HARD NOSE THE HIGHWAY' (1973), MORRISON's studio effort of the time, lacked the intensity of the live work although 'THE GREAT DECEPTION' is probably VAN's angriest song, berating the showbusiness falsity that he's always made a point of distancing himself from. The remainder of the 70's were MORRISON's wilderness years as he seemingly struggled to focus on any kind of musical direction, taking time out to explore his spiritual journey on a personal level. 'VEEDON FLEECE' (1974), apparently inspired by a return to his native Ireland after years in exile, presaged this more intense period of searching. Arguably closest in spirit to VAN's cosmic debut than anything else he's since released, the record shared 'ASTRAL WEEKS' otherworldly sense of drifting in and out of consciousness, set against a backdrop of Ireland's rich heritage. The Celtic folk influence was most prominent on 'STREETS OF ARKLOW', haunting Irish pipes conjuring up images of brooding, silent faces peering from rain lashed doorways. The album remains a pivotal release, signalling the more overtly Celtic and spiritual direction MORRISON's music would take in the 80's and after completing this milestone, the Irishman didn't surface again until 1977 with the poorly received 'PERIOD OF TRANSITION'. 'WAVELENGTH' (1978) saw VAN back on track, although 'INTO THE MUSIC' (1979) was really the beginning of a new phase in his career. Joyously religious but never dogmatic, the album found MORRISON flirting with Christianity; 'FULL FORCE GALE' was a revelation, a rock of strength and deep seated conviction. A rich seam of hope and inspiration runs through the whole album, culminating in 'AND THE HEALING HAS BEGUN'. From here on in, MORRISON's albums were increasingly concerned with religious redemption, Celtic mysteries and ultimately the healing power of music (or navel-gazing nonsense, if you erred towards cynicism) . 'COMMON ONE' (1980) divided the critics with its esoteric New Age slant, while other early 80's efforts like 'BEAUTIFUL VISION' (1982) and 'INARTICULATE SPEECH OF THE HEART' (1983) introduced a kind of airbrushed, synthesizer sound that didn't sit particularly well with MORRISON's organic voice and approach. 'NO GURU, NO METHOD, NO TEACHER' (1986) was a convincing return to form, 'ONE IRISH ROVER' a taster for his other great work of the decade, 'IRISH HEARTBEAT'

(1988), the triumphant collaboration with Irish traditionalists, The CHIEFTAINS. The record found MORRISON in boisterous form, the resulting tour inspiring some of the most positive reactions since his seminal live shows of the 70's. The devotional 'POETIC CHAMPIONS COMPOSE' (1987) was sandwiched between these two, another work of nomadic spiritual searching, MORRISON's singing his pain on the haunting 'SOMETIMES I FEEL LIKE A MOTHERLESS CHILD'. Incredibly, VAN's first Top 20 UK solo hit came with 'WHENEVER GOD SHINES HIS LIGHT', a duet with CLIFF RICHARD the following year. The success of the single helped to boost VAN's commercial clout, the mellow 'AVALON SUNSET' (1989) opus reaching No.13 while subsequent albums, 'ENLIGHTENMENT' (1990) and the heavily gospel-orientated 'HYMNS TO THE SILENCE' (1991) both reached the UK Top 5. The latter's title could be used to describe the music that has made up a large part of MORRISON career, songs of love and devotion unique in rock'n'roll. While more recent releases like 'TOO LONG IN EXILE' (1993) and 'DAYS LIKE THIS' (1995) have lacked just such inspiration, VAN's live work was again re-energised and the live 'A NIGHT IN SAN FRANCISCO' (1994) was roundly praised, one of the record's many highlights an electric run through of 'GLORIA' with old jamming mate, JOHN LEE HOOKER. VAN had also taken to playing with jazz maestro, GEORGIE FAME, a breezy live set recorded at Ronnie Scott's in Soho, released as 'HOW LONG HAS THIS BEEN GOING ON' (1996). 'THE HEALING GAME' in 1997 saw the man return to Top 10 territory and a subsequent tour with BOB DYLAN helped maintain his profile; a 'Basement Tapes'-type of double CD set 'THE PHILOSOPHER'S STONE' (1998) saw a slight connection still, while VAN recorded a cover of 'MULESKINNER BLUES' on DYLAN's new imprint, 'Egyptian'. VAN's final album of the 90's, 'BACK ON TOP' was his first for Virgin offshoot 'Pointblank', the transatlantic Top 30 long-player even supplying his first Top 40 single in years, 'PRECIOUS TIME'. A grumpy curmudgeon to some, a Celtic visionary to others, VAN MORRISON remains as much of an enigma as his best work. While that album occasionally offered glimpses of the pained soul searching we haven't heard from the man in years (especially 'HIGH SUMMER'), MORRISON relaxed back into the bonhomie of contented middle age with 'THE SKIFFLE SESSIONS: LIVE IN BELFAST 1998'. A glowing tribute to the music that inspired him, MORRISON lives it up with two of his oldest chums, LONNIE DONEGAN and CHRIS BARBER. You may have heard them a million times before but a sheer unbridled love of the music elevates the likes of 'ALABAMY BOUND', MIDNIGHT SPECIAL' and 'GOODNIGHT IRENE' to essential listening status. DR JOHN also guested on this knees-up tribute to skiffle and its component parts of folk, country, blues and jazz. 'YOU WIN AGAIN' (2000) was similar in spirit, a feelgood collaboration between VAN and LINDA GAIL LEWIS, JERRY LEE's kid sister. Again, this was all about the simple joys of playing music with friends, nothing more, nothing less. MORRISON has rarely sounded so at ease, knocking out vintage country, R&B and rock'n'roll with an infectious enthusiasm fired up by the pair's natural musical synergy. It seems the older VAN gets, the more he wants to resuscitate the music which inspired him in the first place, and who, after all, can really blame him. 'DOWN THE ROAD' (2002) continued his recent run of great records, an unashamed trip down memory lane, both musically and lyrically. While his songs have always been peppered with recurring autobiographical motifs, thinly veiled or otherwise, the Irishman indulges himself here, musing on his roots with candour and humour against a lovingly rendered patchwork of blues, jazz, R&B, country and folk. He namechecks the likes of PJ PROBY and SCOTT WALKER, even covering the Hoagy Carmichael chestnut, 'GEORGIA ON MY MIND'. Recording an album for 'Blue Note', 'WHAT'S WRONG WITH THIS PICTURE' (2003), meanwhile, was perhaps the logical next step for MORRISON, especially given the record's feel of an artist finally coming home, opening up his muse to the music which really fires him. And there is a definite sense of some sort of artistic unshackling: the ageing star hasn't cut such earthy blues, soul and jazz for years, whether sparring with tenor saxophonist MARTIN WINNING, or taking possession of Lightnin' Hopkins' 'STOP DRINKING'. MORRISON's latter day resurgence rolled on with 'MAGIC TIME' (2005), sustained by his continuing re-examination of the forms which originally inspired him to pick up a microphone (and a pen). Metaphysical questing replaced with blues-as-truth, the man's art rarely sounded as comfortable in its own skin; even the doubts – as on THEM-esque opener 'STRANDED' – were tempered with conviction. And given that VAN was singing about the Rat Pack as far back as the mid-70's, his swinging songbook selections (including a couple of Frank Sinatra numbers) were hardly a concession to fashion. The album's chart position (at No.3, his highest ever!) suggested the renewed enthusiasm was reflected in his fiercely partisan fanbase, one which greeted the Top 10 'PAY THE DEVIL' (2006) with as much fervour as the critics. Everyone knows that country got soul, but – save for perhaps the late RAY CHARLES – no one knows it better than MORRISON, and his first full-blown, Top 10 sojourn into country music was hardly without precedent. And given Rosanne Cash's recent revelation that her family have traced their roots right back to Fife, Scotland, VAN's Celtic-country connection (the album was recorded in Belfast rather than Nashville) felt as timely as it was natural, opening with 'THERE STANDS THE GLASS' (an early 50's hit for honky tonk pioneer Webb Pierce), and lolling through decades-deep covers of Leon Payne's GEORGE JONES signature, 'THINGS HAVE GONE TO PIECES', Hank Williams' 'YOUR CHEATIN' HEART' and Curley Williams' 'HALF AS MUCH' amongst others.

• **Songwriters:** Self-penned except covers; CALEDONIA (Fleecie Moore) / HELP ME (Sonny Boy Williamson) / BRING IT HOME TO ME (Sam Cooke) / SANTA FE (co-written w / Jackie DeShannon) / LONELY AVENUE (Doc Pomus) / GOOD MORNING LITTLE SCHOOLGIRL (Sonny Boy Williamson) / THE LONESOME ROAD (N.Shikret – G.Austin) / MOODY'S MOOD FOR LOVE (James Moody) / I'LL TAKE CARE OF YOU (Brook Benton) / BEFORE THE WORLD WAS MADE (W.B.Yeats / music; Kenny Craddock) / YOU DON'T KNOW ME (hit; Ray Charles) / I'LL NEVER BE FREE (Benjamin-Weiss) / THAT OLD BLACK MAGIC (hit; Sammy Davis Jnr).

Album rating: BLOWIN' YOUR MIND (*5) / ASTRAL WEEKS (*10) / MOONDANCE (*9) / HIS BAND AND THE STREET CHOIR (*6) / TUPELO HONEY (*8) / SAINT DOMINC'S PREVIEW (*9) / HARD NOSE THE HIGHWAY (*7) / IT'S TOO LATE TO STOP NOW (*9) / VEEDON FLEECE (*9) / A PERIOD OF TRANSITION (*5) / WAVELENGTH (*7) / INTO THE MUSIC (*8) / COMMON ONE (*6) / BEAUTIFUL VISION (*6) / INARTICULATE SPEECH OF THE HEART (*6) / LIVE AT THE GRAND OPERA HOUSE, BELFAST (*7) / A SENSE OF WONDER (*6) / NO GURU, NO METHOD, NO TEACHER (*7) / POETIC CHAMPIONS COMPOSE (*7) / IRISH HEARTBEAT with the Chieftains (*8) / AVALON SUNSET (*7) / THE BEST OF VAN MORRISON compilation (*9) / ENLIGHTENMENT (*7) / HYMNS TO THE SILENCE (*7) / THE BEST OF VAN MORRISON, VOLUME TWO compilation (*6) / TOO LONG IN EXILE (*6) / A NIGHT IN SAN FRANCISCO (*7) / DAYS LIKE THIS (*6) / HOW LONG HAS THIS BEEN GOING ON with Georgie Fame & Friends (*4) / THE HEALING GAME (*6) / THE PHILOSOPHER'S STONE (THE UNRELEASED TAPES VOL.1) collection (*6) / BACK ON TOP (*6) / YOU WIN AGAIN with Linda Gail Lewis (*5) / DOWN THE ROAD (*7) / WHAT'S WRONG WITH THIS PICTURE? (*6) / MAGIC TIME (*6) / PAY THE DEVIL (*6)

VAN MORRISON – vocals, guitar, saxophone (ex-THEM) with loads of session persons.

		London	Bang
Jun 67.	(7") *(HLZ 10150)* *<545>* **BROWN EYED GIRL. / GOODBYE BABY (BABY GOODBYE)**		10
	(re-iss. Mar71 on 'President'; PT 328) (re-iss. Apr74; HLM 10453)		
Sep 67.	(7") *<552>* **RO RO ROSEY. / CHICK-A-BOOM**	–	
Nov 67.	(7") *<585>* **SPANISH ROSE / MIDNIGHT ROSE**	–	

Feb 68. (lp; mono/stereo) *(HA-Z 8346) <BLP/+S 218>*
BLOWIN' YOUR MIND Sep67
– Brown eyed girl / He ain't give you none / T.B. sheets / Spanish rose / Goodbye baby (baby goodbye) / Ro Ro Rosey / Who drove the red sports car? / Midnight special. *(cd-iss. Jul95 on 'Epic';) (re-iss. Nov98 on 'Simply Vinyl'; SVLP 49)*

— now with **LARRY FALLON** – conductor, arranger / **JAY BERLINER** – guitar / **RICHARD DAVIS** – bass / **CONNIE KAY** – drums / **JOHN PAYNE** – flute, sporano sax / **WARREN SMITH JR** – percussion, vibraphone

Warners Warners

Sep 69. (lp) *(<WS 1768>)* **ASTRAL WEEKS** Nov68
– In the beginning: Astral weeks / Beside you / Sweet thing / Cypress avenue / Afterwards: Young lovers do / Madame George / Ballerina / Slim slow rider. *(re-iss. Aug 71; K 46024) (cd-iss. May87; K 246024)*

— now with **JOHN PLATANIA** – guitar / **JEFF LABES** – keys / **JACK SHROER** – sax / **GARY MALLABER** – drums / **JOHN KLINGBERG** – bass

Mar 70. (lp) *(<WS 1835>)* **MOONDANCE** 32 29
– And it stoned me / Moondance / Crazy love / Into the mystic / Caravan / Come running / These dreams of you / Brand new day / Everyone / Glad tidings. *(re-iss. Aug71; K 46040) (cd-iss. Jan86; K 246040)*

May 70. (7") *(WB <7383>)* **COME RUNNING. / CRAZY LOVE** Apr70 39

Dec 70. (lp) *(<WS 1884>)* **HIS BAND AND THE STREET CHOIR** Nov70 32
– Domino / Crazy face / I've been working / Call me up in Dreamland / I'll be your lover, too / Blue money / Virgo clowns / Gypsy queen / Sweet Janine / If I ever needed someone / Street choir. *(re-iss. Aug71; K 46066) (cd-iss. Feb93;)*

Dec 70. (7") *(WB <7434>)* **DOMINO. / SWEET JANINE** Oct70 9
(re-iss. Jul71; K 16044)

Feb 71. (7") *<7462>* **BLUE MONEY. / SWEET THING** – 23

Apr 71. (7") *<7488>* **CALL ME UP IN DREAMLAND. / STREET CHOIR** – 95

— now with **MALLABER, SHROER + BILL CHURCH** – bass / **RONNIE MONTROSE** – guitar / **RICK SCHLOSSER** – drums + **CONNIE KAY** – drums

Sep 71. (7") *<7518>* **WILD NIGHT. / WHEN THAT EVENING SUN GOES DOWN** – 28

Nov 71. (lp) *(K 46114) <WS 1950>* **TUPELO HONEY** Oct 71 27
– Wild night / (Straight to your heart) Like a cannonball / Old old Woodstock / Starting a new life / You're my woman / Tupelo honey / I wonna roo you / When that evening sun goes down / Moonshine whiskey. *(re-iss. Aug89 & Feb94 on 'Polydor' lp/c/cd; 839161-1/-4/-2) (re-iss. Apr98 on 'Polydor'; 537450-2)*

Dec 71. (7") *(7543>* **TUPELO HONEY. / STARTING A NEW LIFE** – 47

Mar 72. (7") *<7573>* **(STRAIGHT TO YOUR HEART) LIKE A CANNONBALL. / OLD OLD WOODSTOCK** –

— **LEROY VINNEGAR** – bass repl. CHURCH (who later joined MONTROSE) / **ROY ELLIOT** – guitar + **MARK NAFTALIN** – piano repl. SCHOSSLER + MALLABER

Jul 72. (7") *(K 16210) <7616>* **JACKIE WILSON SAID (I'M IN HEAVEN WHEN YOU SMILE). / YOU'VE GOT THE POWER** 61

Aug 72. (lp) *(K 46172) <WS 2633>* **SAINT DOMINIC'S PREVIEW** 15
– Jackie Wilson said (I'm in Heaven when you smile) / Gypsy / I will be there / Listen to the lion / Saint Dominic's preview / Redwood tree / Almost Independance day. *(re-iss. Aug89 on 'Polydor' lp/c/cd; 839162-1/-4/-2) (cd-iss. Apr95;)*

Oct 72. (7") *(7638>* **REDWOOD TREE. / SAINT DOMINIC'S PREVIEW** – 98

Jan 73. (7") *<7665>* **GYPSY. / SAINT DOMINIC'S PREVIEW** –

— RONNIE now formed MONTROSE went through various session personnel: **DAVID HAYES** – bass and most of new band.

Jul 73. (7") *(K 16299) <7706>* **WARM LOVE. / I WILL BE THERE** Jun73

Jul 73. (lp) *(K 46242) <WS 2712>* **HARD NOSE THE HIGHWAY** 22 27
– Snow in San Anselmo / Warm love / Hard nose the highway / Wild children / The great deception / Green / Autumn song / Purple heather. *(re-iss. Aug89 on 'Polydor' lp/c/cd; 839163-1/-4/-2) (cd-iss. Apr95;)*

Sep 73. (7") *<7744>* **GREEN. / WILD CHILDREN** –

Feb 74. (7") *<7797>* **AIN'T NOTHING YOU CAN DO. / WILD CHILDREN** –

Feb 74. (d-lp) *(K 86007) <WS 2760>* **IT'S TOO LATE TO STOP NOW (live)** 53
– Ain't nothing you can do / Warm love / Into the mystic / These dreams of you / I believe to my soul / I've been working / Help me / Wild children / Domino / I just wanna make love to you / Bring it on home to me / Saint Dominic's preview / Take your hand out of my pocket / Listen to the lion / Here comes the night / Gloria / Caravan / Cypress Avenue. *(re-iss. Aug89 on 'Polydor' d-lp/d-c/d-cd; 839166-1/-4/-2) (cd-iss. Apr95;)*

May 74. (7") *(K 16392)* **CALDONIA (WHAT MAKES YOUR BIG HEAD HARD?). / WHAT'S UP, CRAZY PUP** –

Oct 74. (lp/c) *(K/K4 56068) <WS 2805>* **VEEDON FLEECE** 41 53
– Streets of Arklow / Country fair / Cul de sac / Linden Arden stole the highlights / Fair play / Bulbs / You don't pull no punches but you don't push the river / Comfort you / Come here my love / Who was that masked man. *(re-iss. Aug89 on 'Polydor' lp/c/cd; 839164-1/-4/-2) (cd-iss. Apr95;)*

Jul 74. (7") *<8029>* **BULBS. / CUL DE SAC** –

Nov 74. (7") *(K 16486)* **BULBS. / WHO WAS THAT MASKED MAN** –

below featured DR. JOHN – piano

Mar 77. (lp/c) *(K/K4 56322) <2987>* **A PERIOD OF TRANSITION** 23 43
– You gotta make it through the world / It fills you up / The eternal Kansas City / Joyous sound / Flamingoes fly / Heavy connection / Cold wind in August. *(re-iss. +cd.Aug89 on 'Polydor')*

Apr 77. (7") *(K 16939)* **THE ETERNAL KANSAS CITY. / JOYOUS SOUND** –

Jul 77. (7") *(K 16986)* **JOYOUS SOUND. / MECHANICAL BLISS**

Oct 77. (7") **COLD WIND IN AUGUST. / MOONDANCE** –

— **PETER VAN HOOKE** – drums / **HERBIE ARMSTRONG** – guitar etc

Oct 78. (lp/c) *(K/K4 56526) <3212>* **WAVELENGTH** 27 28
– Kingdom hall / Checkin' it out / Natalia / Venice U.S.A. / Lifetimes / Wavelength / Santa Fe / Beautiful obsession / Hungry for your love / Take it where you find it. *(re-iss. Aug89 & Feb94 on 'Polydor' lp/c/cd; 839169-1/-4/-2) (re-iss. Apr98 on 'Polydor';)*

Oct 78. (7") *(K 17254)* **WAVELENGTH. / CHECKIN' IT OUT** 42

Feb 79. (7") *(K 17322)* **NATALIA. / LIFETIMES**

Apr 79. (7") **CHECKIN' IT OUT. /** –

— now with **HOOKE, ARMSTRONG, HAYES / + MARK JORDAN** – keyboards / **MARK ISHAM** – trumpet / **PEE WEE ELLIS** – saxophone

Mercury Warners

Aug 79. (lp/c) *(9102/? 852) <3390>* **INTO THE MUSIC** 21 43
– Bright side of the road / Full force gale / Stepping out queen / Troubadours / Rolling hills / You make me feel so free / Angeliou / And the healing has begun / It's all in the game / You know what they're writing about. *(re-iss. May83 lp/c; PRICE/PRIMC 2) (re-iss. Aug89 & Feb94 on 'Polydor' lp/c/cd; 839603-1/-4/-2) (re-iss. Apr98 on 'Polydor'; 537540-2)*

Sep 79. (7") *(6001 121)* **BRIGHT SIDE OF THE ROAD. / ROLLING HILLS** 63

Dec 79. (7") **FULL FORCE GALE. / YOU MAKE ME FEEL SO FREE** –

— **JOHN ALLAIR** – keyboards + **MICK COX** – guitar repl. JORDAN + MARCUS

Sep 80. (lp/c) *(6302/7144 021) <3462>* **COMMON ONE** 53 73
– Haunts of ancient peace / Summertime in England / Satisfied / Wild honey / Spirit / When heart is open. *(re-iss. May83 lp/c; PRICE/PRIMC 1) (cd-iss. 1986; 800 043-2) (re-iss. Aug89 & Apr95 on 'Polydor' lp/c/cd; 839600-1/-4/-2) (cd re-iss. Apr98; 537541-2)*

— added **TOM DONLINGER** – drums

Feb 82. (lp/c) *(6302/7144 122) <3652>* **BEAUTIFUL VISION** 31 44
– Celtic Ray / Northern muse (solid sound) / Dweller on the threshold / Beautiful vision / She gives me religion / Cleaning windows / Vanlose stairway / Aryan mist / Scandinavia / Across the bridge where angels dwell / Scandinavia. *(re-iss. Mar85 lp/c; PRICE/PRIMC 82) (re-iss. Aug89 & Feb94 on 'Polydor' lp/c/cd; 839601-1/-4/-2) (re-iss. Apr98 on 'Polydor'; 537542-2)*

Mar 82. (7") **CLEANING WINDOWS. / SCANDINAVIA** –

Mar 82. (7") *(MER 99)* **CLEANING WINDOWS. / IT'S ALL IN THE GAME** –

Jun 82. (7") *(MER 110)* **DWELLER ON THE THRESHOLD. / SCANDINAVIA**

— **CHRIS MICHIE** – guitar repl. COX

Feb 83. (7") *(MER 132)* **CRY FOR HOME. / SUMMERTIME IN ENGLAND (live)**
(12"+=) *(MERX 132)* – All saints day.

Mar 83. (lp/c) *(MERL/+C 16) <23802>* **INARTICULATE SPEECH OF THE HEART** 14
– Higher than the world / Connswater / River of time / Celtic swing / Rave on, John Donne / Inarticulate speech of the heart No.1 / Irish heartbeat /

The street only knew your name / Cry for home / Inarticulate speech of the heart No.2 / September night. *(re-iss. Oct86 lp/c; PRICE/PRIMC 93) (cd-iss. May86; 811 140-2) (re-iss. Aug89 & Feb94 on 'Polydor'; 839604-1/-4/-2) (re-iss. Apr98 on 'Polydor'; 537543-2)*

May 83. (7") *(MER 141)* **CELTIC SWING. / MR. THOMAS** [ ] [ ]
(12"+=) *(MERX 132)* – Rave on, John Donne.

Feb 84. (lp/c) *(MERL/+C 36)* **LIVE AT THE GRAND OPERA HOUSE, BELFAST (live)** 47 –
– (intro) / Into the music / Inarticulate seech of the heart / Dweller on the threshold / It's all in the game – You know what they're writing about / She gives me religion / Haunts of ancient peace / Full force gale / Beautiful vision / Vanlose stairway / Rave on, John Donne – Rave on (part 2) / Northern muse (solid ground) / Cleaning windows. *(cd-iss. 1986; 818336-2) (re-iss. Aug89 on 'Polydor' lp/c/cd; 839602-1/-4/-2) (cd re-iss. Apr98 on 'Polydor'; 537544-2)*

Mar 84. (7") *(MER 159)* **DWELLER ON THE THRESHOLD (live). / NORTHERN MUSE (SOLID GROUND)** [ ] [ ]

Mercury Mercury

Nov 84. (7"/12") *(MER/+X 178)* **A SENSE OF WONDER. / HAUNTS OF ANCIENT PEACE (live)** [ ] [ ]

Feb 85. (lp/c)(cd) *(MERH/+C 54)(<822 895-2>)* **A SENSE OF WONDER** 25 61
– Tore down a La Rimbaud / Ancient of days / Evening meditation / The master's eyes / What would I do / A sense of wonder / Boffyflow and Spike / If you only knew / Let the slave / A new kind of man. *(re-iss. May90 & Apr95 on 'Polydor' cd/c/lp; 843116-2/-4/-1) (cd re-iss. Apr98; 537545-2)*

Jun 86. (7") *(MER 223)* **IVORY TOWER. / NEW KIND OF MAN** [ ] [ ]
(12"+=) *(MERX 223)* – A sense of wonder / Cleaning windows.

Jul 86. (lp/c)(cd) *(MERH/+C 94)(<830077-2>)* **NO GURU, NO METHOD, NO TEACHER** 27 70
– Got to go back / Oh the warm feeling / Foreign window / Town called Paradise / In the garden / Tir na nog / Here comes the night / Thanks for the information / One Irish rover / Ivory tower. *(re-iss. Sep91 & Feb94 on 'Polydor'; 849619-2/-4/-1) (re-iss. Apr98 on 'Polydor'; 537546-2)*

Aug 86. (7") *(MER 231)* **GOT TO GO BACK. / IN THE GARDEN** [ ] [ ]

— note: HOOKE + ISHAM left early '84 / **ELLIS + DONLINGER** in '85 / now new band

Sep 87. (lp/c)(cd) *(MERH/+C 110)(<832585-2>)* **POETIC CHAMPIONS COMPOSE** 26 90
– Spanish steps / The mystery / Queen of the slipstream / I forgot that love existed / Sometimes I feel like a motherless child / Celtic excavation / Someone like you / Alan Watts blues / Give me my rapture / Did ye get healed? / Allow me. *(cd re-iss. 1992 on 'Polydor'; 517217-2)*

Sep 87. (7") *(MER 254)* **DID YE GET HEALED?. / ALLOW ME** [ ] [ ]

Apr 88. (7") *(MER 261)* **QUEEN OF THE SLIPSTREAM. / SPANISH STEPS** [ ] [ ]

Jun 88. (lp/c)(cd; VAN MORRISON & THE CHIEFTAINS) *(MERH/+C 124)(<834496-2>)* **IRISH HEARTBEAT** 18 [ ]
– Star of the County Down / Irish heartbeat / Ta mo chleamhnas deanta / Raglan road / She moved through the fair / I'll tell me ma / Carrickfergus / Celtic Ray / My lagan love / Marie's wedding. *(cd re-iss. Apr98 on 'Polydor'; 537548-2)*

Jun 88. (7") *(MER 262)* **I'LL TELL ME MA. / TA MO CHLEAMHNAS DEANTA** [ ] [ ]
(12"+=/cd-s+=) *(MER X/CD 262)* – Carrickfergus.

Polydor Polydor

May 89. (lp/c/cd) *(<839262-1/-4/-2>)* **AVALON SUNSET** 13 91
– Whenever God shines his light / Contacting my angel / I'd love to write another love song / Have I told you lately (that I love you) / Coney Island / I'm tired Joey boy / When will I ever learn to live in God / Orangefield / Daring night / These are the days.

Jun 89. (7"/c-s) *(VAN S/CS 1)* **HAVE I TOLD YOU LATELY (THAT I LOVE YOU). / CONTACTING MY ANGEL** 74 [ ]
(12"+=) *(VANX 1)* – Listen to the lion.
(cd-s+=) *(VANCD 1)* – Irish heartbeat.

Nov 89. (7"/c-s; by VAN MORRISON & CLIFF RICHARD) *(VAN S/CS 2)* **WHENEVER GOD SHINES HIS LIGHT. / I'D LOVE TO WRITE ANOTHER LOVE SONG** 20 [ ]
(12"+=) *(VANX 2)* – Cry for home.
(cd-s++=) *(VANCD 2)* – ('A'-lp version).

Dec 89. (7") *(VANS 3)* **ORANGEFIELD. / THESE ARE THE DAYS** [ ] [ ]
(12"+=) *(VANX 3)* – And the healing has begun.
(cd-s++=) *(VANCD 3)* – Coney Island.

Feb 90. (7"/c-s) *(VAN S/CS 4)* **CONEY ISLAND. / HAVE I TOLD YOU LATELY THAT I LOVE YOU** [ ] [ ]
(12"+=) *(VANX 4)* – A sense of wonder.
(cd-s++=) *(VANCD 4)* – Spirit.

Mar 90. (cd/c/lp) *(<841970-2/-4/-1>)* **THE BEST OF VAN MORRISON** (compilation) 4 May90 41
– Bright side of the road / Gloria (THEM) / Moondance / Baby please don't go (THEM) / Have I told you lately / Brown eyed girl / Sweet thing / Warm love / Wonderful remark / Jackie Wilson said (I'm in Heaven when you smile) / Full force gale / And it stoned me / Here comes the night (THEM) / Domino / Did ye get healed / Wild night / Cleaning windows / Whenever God shines his light (w / CLIFF RICHARD). *(c+cd.iss.has extra tracks) (cd re-iss. Apr98; 537459-2)*

Jul 90. (7"/c-s) *(VANS/+C 5)* **GLORIA (by Them). / RAVE ON, JOHN DONNE** [ ] [ ]
(12"+=) *(VANX 5)* – Vanlose stairway.
(cd-s++=) *(VANCD 5)* – Bright side of the road.

Sep 90. (7"/c-s) *(VAN S/CS 6)* **REAL REAL GONE. / START ALL OVER AGAIN** [ ] [ ]
(12"+=/cd-s+=) *(VAN X/CD 6)* – Cleaning windows.

Oct 90. (cd/c/lp) *(<847 100-2/-4/-1>)* **ENLIGHTENMENT** 5 62
– Real real gone / Enlightenment / So quiet in here / Avalon of the heart / See me through / Youth of 1,000 summers / In the days before rock'n'roll / Start all over again / She's a baby / Memories. *(lp re-iss. Aug99 on 'Simply Vinyl'; SVLP 109)*

Nov 90. (7"/c-s) *(VAN S/CS 7)* **IN THE DAYS BEFORE ROCK'N'ROLL. / I'D LOVE TO WRITE ANOTHER LOVE SONG** [ ] [ ]
(12"+=/cd-s+=) *(VAN X/CD 7)* – Coney Island.

Jan 91. (7") *(VANS 8)* **ENLIGHTENMENT. / AVALON OF THE HEART** [ ] [ ]
(12"+=/cd-s+=) *(VAN X/CD 8)* – Jackie Wilson said.

— (VAN is credited w/ TOM JONES on his Mar91 single 'CARRYING A TORCH')

May 91. (7"/c-s; by VAN MORRISON & THE CHIEFTAINS) *(VAN S/CS 9)* **I CAN'T STOP LOVING YOU. / ALL SAINTS DAY** [ ] [ ]
(12"+=/cd-s+=) *(VAN X/CD 9)* – Carrying a torch.

Aug 91. (7"/c-s) *(VAN S/CS 10)* **WHY MUST I ALWAYS EXPLAIN?. / SO COMPLICATED** [ ] [ ]
(12"+=/cd-s+=) *(VAN X/CD 10)* – Enlightenment.

Sep 91. (d-cd/d-c/d-lp) *(<849 026-2/-4/-1>)* **HYMNS TO THE SILENCE** 5 99
– Professional jealousy / I'm not feeling it anymore / Ordinary life / Some peace of mind / So complicated / I can't stop loving you / Why must I always explain? / Village idiot / See me through part II (just a closer walk with thee) / Take me back / By his Grace / All Saints day / Hymns to the silence / On Hyndford Street / Be thou my vision / Carrying a torch / Green mansions / Pagan streams / Quality Street / It must be you / I need your kind of loving.

Feb 93. (cd/c/lp) *(<517 760-2/-4/-1>)* **THE BEST OF VAN MORRISON VOLUME 2** (compilation) 31 [ ]
– Real real gone / When will I ever learn to live in God / Sometimes I feel like a motherless child / In the garden / A sense of wonder / I'll tell me ma / Coney Island / Enlightenment / Rave on John Donne – Rave on part two live / Don't look back / It's all over now, baby blue / One Irish Rover / The mystery / Hymns to the silence / Evening meditation.

May 93. (7"/c-s; by VAN MORRISON & JOHN LEE HOOKER) *(VAN S/CS 11)* **GLORIA. / IT MUST BE YOU (live)** 31 [ ]
(cd-s+=) *(VANCD 11)* – And the healing has begun (live) / See me through (live).
(cd-s) *(VANDR 11)* – ('A'side) / Whenever God shines his light (live) / It fills you up (live) / The star of County Down (live).

Jun 93. (cd/c/lp) *(<519 219-2/-4/-1>)* **TOO LONG IN EXILE** 4 29
– Too long in exile / Big time operators / Lonely avenue / Ball & chain / In the forest / Till we get the healing done / Gloria / Good morning little schoolgirl / Wasted years / The lonesome road / Moody's mood for love / Close enough for jazz / Before the world was made / I'll take care of you – Instrumental – Tell me what you want.

Apr 94. (d-cd/d-c) *(<521 290-2/-4>)* **A NIGHT IN SAN FRANCISCO (live)** 8 [ ]
– Did ya get healed? / It's all in the game / Make it real one more time / I've been working / I forgot that love existed / Vanlose stairway / Trans-Euro train / Fool for you / You make me feel so real / Beautiful vision / See me through / Soldier of fortune / Thankyoufalettinmebemiseldagain / Ain't that lovin' you baby / Stormy Monday / Have you ever loved a woman / No

rollin' blues / Help me / Good morning little schoolgirl / Tupelo honey / Moondance / My funny valentine / Jumpin' with Symphony Sid / It fills you up / I'll take care of you / It's a man's man's man's world / Lonely avenue / 4 o'clock in the morning / So quiet in here / That's where it's at / In the garden / You send me / Allegheny / Have I told you lately that I love you / Shakin' all over / Gloria.

Jun 95. (cd-s) *(VANCD 12)* **DAYS LIKE THIS / YO** 65

(7"+=/c-s+=/cd-s+=) *(VAN/+CS/CDX 12)* – I don't want to go on without you / That old black magic.

Jun 95. (cd/c/lp) *(<527 307-2/-4/-1>)* **DAYS LIKE THIS** 5 33

– Perfect fit / Russian roulette / Rain check / You don't know me / No religion / Underlying depression / Songwriter / Days like this / I'll never be free / Melancholia / Ancient highway / In the afternoon.

Sep 95. (c-s) *(577 014-4)* **PERFECT FIT / RAINCHECK** –

(cd-s+=) *(577 015-2)* – Cleaning windows.

Nov 95. (cd-s) *(577 488-4)* **NO RELIGION / HAVE I TOLD YOU LATELY** 54 –

(cd-s+=) *(577 489-2)* – Whenever God shines his light / Gloria.

(cd-s) *(577 579-2)* – ('A'side) / Days like this / Raincheck.

below credited as VAN MORRISON with GEORGIE FAME & FRIENDS

Oct 95. (cd/c/lp) *(<529 136-2/-4/-1>)* **HOW LONG HAS THIS BEEN GOING ON (live 3 May'95 at Ronnie Scott's)** Jan96 55

– I will be there / The new symphony Sid / Early in the morning / Who can I turn to? / Sack o'woe / Moondance / Centerpiece / How long has this been going on? / Your mind is on vacation / All saint's day / Blues in the night / Don't worry about a thing / That's life / Heathrow shuffle.

Feb 96. (c-s) *(576 204-4)* **THAT'S LIFE / MOONDANCE (live)** –

(cd-s+=) *(576 205-2)* – That's life (live).

(above two releases on 'Verve', as was a credit on the 1996 GEORGIE FAME with BEN SIDRAN, VAN MORRISON and MOSE ALLISON set 'SONGS OF MOSE ALLISON')

Feb 97. (c-s) *(573 390-4)* **THE HEALING GAME / FULL FORCE GALE '96** 46 –

(cd-s+=) *(573 391-2)* – Look what the good people done / Celtic Spring.

(cd-s) *(573 393-2)* – ('A'side) / Have I told you lately / Whenever God shines his light (with CLIFF RICHARD) / Gloria (with JOHN LEE HOOKER).

Mar 97. (cd/c/lp) *(<537 101-2/-4/-1>)* **THE HEALING GAME** 10 32

– Rough God goes riding / Fire in the belly / This weight / Waiting game / Piper at the gates of dawn / Burning ground / It once was my life / Sometimes we cry / If you love me / The healing game.

Apr 97. (c-s) *(573 933-4)* **ROUGH GOD GOES RIDING / THE HEALING GAME (alt. version)** –

(cd-s+=) *(573 933-2)* – At the end of the day.

Jun 98. (d-cd/d-c) *(<531 789-2/-4>)* **THE PHILOSOPHER'S STONE** (THE UNRELEASED TAPES – VOLUME ONE) 20 87

– Really don't know / Ordinary people / Wonderful remark / Not supposed to break down / Laughing in the wind / Madame Joy / Contemplation rose / Don't worry about tomorrow / Try for sleep / Lover's prayer / Drumshanbo hustle / Twilight zone / Foggy mountain top / Naked in the jungle / There there child // The street only knew your name / John Henry / Western plain / Joyous sound / I have finally come to realise / Flamingoes fly / Stepping out queen part 2 / Bright side of the road / Street theory / Real real gone / Showbusiness / For Mr. Thomas / Crazy Jane on God / Song of being a child / High spirits. *(re-iss. Jul99; same)*

Pointblank Pointblank

Feb 99. (cd-s) *(POBD 14)* **PRECIOUS TIME / JACKIE WILSON SAID (I'M IN HEAVEN WHEN YOU SMILE) (live) / CALL ME UP IN DREAMLAND (live)** 36 –

(cd-s) *(POBDX 14)* – ('A'side) / Naked in the jungle (live) / Give me a kiss (live).

Mar 99. (cd/c) *(VPB CD/TC 50) <47148>* **BACK ON TOP** 11 28

– Goin' down Geneva / Philosopher's stone / In the midnight / Back on top / When the leaves come falling down / High summer / Reminds me of you / New biography / Precious time / Golden autumn day.

May 99. (cd-s) *(POBD 15)* **BACK ON TOP / JOHN BROWN'S BODY / I'M READY** 69 –

(cd-s) *(POBDX 15)* – ('A'side) / Tell me / Sax instrumental No.1.

Aug 99. (cd-s) *(POBD 16)* **THE PHILOSOPHER'S STONE / THESE DREAMS OF YOU / RAINCHECK** –

— in Jan'00, VAN MORRISON teamed up with LONNIE DONEGAN and CHRIS BARBER on the UK No.14 set, 'THE SKIFFLE SESSIONS – LIVE IN BELFAST' on 'Virgin' cd/lp; *CDVE/LPVE 945)*

Sep 00. (cd/c; by VAN MORRISON & LINDA GAIL LEWIS) *(VPB CD/TC 54) <50258>* **YOU WIN AGAIN** 34 Oct00

– Let's talk about us / You win again / Jambalaya / Crazy arms / Old black Joe / Think twice before you go / No way Pedro / A shot of rhythm and blues / Real gone lover / Why don't you love me / Cadillac / Baby (you got what it takes) / Boogie chillen. *(lp re-iss. Oct00 on 'Simply Vinyl'; SVLP 251)*

Polydor Universal

May 02. (cd-s) *(570596-2)* **HEY MR. DJ / SOMEONE LIKE YOU / THE BRIGHT SIDE OF THE ROAD (re-recording)** 58 –

May 02. (cd/lp) *(<589177-2/-1>)* **DOWN THE ROAD** 6 25

– Down the road / Meet me in the Indian summer / Steal my heart away / Hey Mr. DJ / Talk is cheap / Choppin' wood / What makes the Irish heart beat / All work and no play / Whatever happened to PJ Proby? / The beauty of the days gone by / Georgia on my mind / Only a dream / Man has to struggle / Evening shadows / Fast train.

Aug 02. (cd-s) *(570891-2)* **MEET ME IN THE INDIAN SUMMER / IN THE AFTERNOON / RAINCHECK (live) / IN THE MIDNIGHT (live)** –

Blue Note Blue Note

Oct 03. (cd) *(<5 90167-2>)* **WHAT'S WRONG WITH THIS PICTURE?** 43 32

– What's wrong with this picture? / Whinin boy moan / Evening June / Too many myths / Somerset / Meaning of loneliness / Stop drinking / Goldfish bowl / Once in a blue moon / Saint James infirmary / Little village / Fame / Get on with the show.

Parlophone not iss.

Dec 03. (cd-s) *(CDR 6628)* **ONCE IN A BLUE MOON / WHEN YOU'RE SMILING (live) / WALKIN' MY BABY BACK HOME (live)** –

Exile Geffen

May 05. (cd) *(9870945) <46620-2>* **MAGIC TIME** 3 25

– Stranded / Celtic new year / Keep mediocrity at bay / Evening train / This love of mine / I'm confessin' / Just like Greta / Gypsy in my soul / Lonely and blue / This lion this time / Magic time / They sold me out / Carry on regardless.

Lost Highway Lost Highway

Mar 06. (cd)(lp) *<(9876290)>(9877074)* **PAY THE DEVIL** 8 26

– There stands the glass / Half as much / Things have gone to pieces / Big blue diamonds / Playhouse / Your cheatin' heart / Don't you make me high / My bucket's got a hole in it / Back street affair / Pay the Devil / What am I living for? / This has got to stop / Once a day / More and more / Till I gain control again.

– compilations, others, etc. –

May 71. (lp) *President; (PTLS 1045) / Bang; <BLPS 222>* **THE BEST OF VAN MORRISON** 1970

(nearly a re-issue of debut '67 lp)

Mar 74. (lp) *London; (HSM 5008) / Bang; <BLPS 400>* **T.B. SHEETS** (a near re-issue of debut 1967 lp) Jan74

(cd-iss. May91 on 'Columbia'; 467827-2)

Sep 77. (lp) *Bang; (6467 625)* **THIS IS WHERE I CAME IN** –

(nearly a re-issue of debut '67 lp)

Oct 75. (d-lp) *Warners; (K 86009)* **TWO ORIGINALS OF VAN MORRISON** –

– (VAN MORRISON, HIS BAND AND STREET CHOIR / TUPELO HONEY)

Oct 77. (7") *Warners; <8450>* **MOONDANCE. / COLD WIND IN AUGUST** – 92

Oct 82. (d-c) *Warners; (K 466116)* **MOONDANCE / . . .HIS BAND AND STREET CHOIR** –

Jan 92. (c) *Moles; (MRILC 012)* **CUCHULAINN** (spoken word) –

Mar 92. (d-cd/c) *Columbia; (468309-2/-4)* **BANG MASTERS** –

Jan 93. (cd) *Movieplay Gold; (74012)* **THE LOST TAPES VOLUME 1** –

Jan 93. (cd) *Movieplay Gold; (74013)* **THE LOST TAPES VOLUME 2** –

May 94. (cd) *Charly; (CDP 8035-2)* **PAYIN' DUES (The Best Of The 1965 Studio Recordings)** –

Apr 96. (cd) *Audiophile; (APH 102805)* **BROWN EYED GIRL** –

Mar 97. (t-lp) *Get Back; (GET 501)* **NEW YORK SESSIONS 1967** –

Mar 98. (cd) *Squire; (GUV 1)* **BROWN EYED GIRL** –

Apr 98. (d-cd) *Multimedia; (7956 766664-2)* **BROWN EYED BEGINNINGS** –

Nov 98. (d-cd) *Double Classics; (DC 31014)* **BROWN EYED GIRL** –

MORRISSEY

Born: STEPHEN PATRICK MORRISSEY, 22 May'59, Manchester, England. After his bust-up with SMITHS guitarist JOHNNY MARR in August '87, MORRISSEY, one of rock music's most intellectually incisive wordsmiths, hastily embarked upon a relatively successful solo career. Remaining with 'E.M.I.', his debut effort, 'VIVA HATE', was subsequently released on the re-activated 'H.M.V.' imprint in Spring '88. With the music co-written by his new producer, STEPHEN STREET, and a backing band that numbered VINI REILLY (guitar, keyboards; ex-DURUTTI COLUMN) and ANDREW PARESI (drums), the album was a strong start, reaching No.2 in the UK charts on the back of the catchy 'SUEDEHEAD' single (incredibly, the singer's first ever Top 5 hit single). Another stand-out track was the lavish melancholy of 'EVERYDAY IS LIKE SUNDAY', arguably his best solo track to date and a song which gave him another Top 10 hit later that summer. Though the album received a relatively warm critical reception, it was, as ever, not without controversy. 'BENGALI IN PLATFORMS' was an ambiguous address to immigrants which he later unsuccessfully attempted to play down while 'MARGARET ON THE GUILLOTINE' was self explanatory, no doubt meeting with a little more empathy. Recruiting a new band composed of NEIL TAYLOR (guitar) and ex-SMITHS', CRAIG GANNON, ANDY ROURKE and MIKE JOYCE, MORRISSEY returned the following year with another couple of fine singles, the playfully coy 'LAST OF THE INTERNATIONAL PLAYBOYS' and 'INTERESTING DRUG', both records going Top 10. The line-up didn't last, however, and he brought in a completely new cast for his next single 'OUIJA BOARD, OUIJA BOARD', a song that suffered scathing reviews in the music press and barely made the Top 20. The following year, a projected album was scrapped although its title, 'BONA DRAG', was retained for an impressive career resume that appeared in late 1990. The collection also contained some new material, notably the grim 'NOVEMBER SPAWNED A MONSTER' and the contentious narrative, 'PICCADILLY PALARE', both released as singles. With a fresh backing group that included ex-MADNESS bassist BEDDERS and MORRISSEY's new writing partner, MARK E. NEVIN (ex-FAIRGROUND ATTRACTION), the singer cut the 'KILL UNCLE' opus. Released in 1991 to mixed reviews, the album failed to deliver on the promise of the earlier singles, although MORRISSEY subsequently recruited a rockabilly backing band: ALAIN WHYTE (guitar), GARY DAY (bass), BOZ BOORER (guitar, ex-POLECATS) and SPENCER COBRIN (drums), touring the album around the world, his first live appearances since the prime of The SMITHS. The tour was largely a success and, enlivened and inspired, MORRISSEY cut the 'YOUR ARSENAL' (1992) set. Produced by MICK RONSON and co-penned with WHYTE, the album took the watered down glam-rock of 'KILL UNCLE' and kickstarted it with some raw rockabilly, resulting in MORRISSEY's highest chart placing for years (No.4). Though the record failed to spawn any major hits, it contained such thoughtful material as 'I KNOW IT'S GONNA HAPPEN SOMEDAY' and 'YOU'RE THE ONE FOR ME, FATTY', the former subsequently covered by DAVID BOWIE, another of MORRISSEY's idols. The same year, MORRISSEY hit the headlines with his scathing criticism of Johnny Rogan, author of the SMITHS biography, 'Morrissey & Marr: The Severed Alliance'. It wasn't the last time the 'Oscar Wilde of Rock' would be in the news, MORRISSEY subsequently losing a well publicised court battle with MIKE JOYCE over unpaid SMITHS royalties. More controversy surrounded the singer following his disastrous appearance at the 1993 'Madstock' concert in London's Finsbury Park. Supporting headliners MADNESS, MORRISSEY was given an extremely hostile reception after coming out draped in a Union Jack, further fuelling debate over the perceived ambiguity of his motivations. Following all this strife, 'VAUXHALL AND I' (1994) resurrected MORRISSEY's career, a sympathetic production by STEVE LILLYWHITE setting the scene for his most considered and consistent album to date. The record was also MORRISSEY's first No.1, a critically acclaimed opus that was marked by more emotionally-charged lyrics, laying off the trademark caustic barbs. Moving to 'R.C.A.', MORRISSEY released 'SOUTHPAW GRAMMER' almost a year later, a bizarre album that focussed on the singer's apparent boxing fixation. Unsurprisingly, the record met with bewilderment from critics, though it consolidated his position as one of rock's few genuine mavericks. In 1997, MORRISSEY once again shifted stables, this time to 'Island' who got their chance to showcase the bard on some new work, 'MALADJUSTED'. Without a contract for around five years, MORRISSEY looked to have retired to his L.A. bachelor pad. Suited and booted, the man eventually made his grand re-entrance in 2004 with the million selling 'YOU ARE THE QUARRY', showcasing a ramped-up guitar assault and the unlikely sonic fingerprints of producer Jerry Finn (BLINK-182, GREEN DAY etc). On the back of rave reviews, with the musical climate finally in his favour, and for the first time in a decade, he almost hit the top of the British charts while no less than four singles made the Top 10: 'FIRST OF THE GANG TO DIE', 'LET ME KISS YOU', 'I HAVE FORGIVEN JESUS' and 'IRISH BLOOD, ENGLISH HEART', the highest charting track of his career and one of the most overt invectives he's yet penned. MORRISSEY's outspoken views on a number of issues – not least animal rights and American politics – generated almost as much coverage as his musical/commercial comeback. A lifelong vegetarian, he recently announced a tour boycott of Canada in protest at the country's seal culling. The tour in question was in support of 'RINGLEADER OF THE TORMENTORS' (2006), a Tony Visconti-produced UK No.1, wrapped in a mock-up of the classic Deutsche Grammophon sleeves. The Manchester wit once again went Top 3 with the single 'YOU HAVE KILLED ME', and also pulled off something of a coup by securing the services of soundtrack legend ENNIO MORRICONE (organ accompaniment on the ANTONY & THE JOHNSONS-esque 'DEAR GOD PLEASE HELP ME').

• **Covered:** THAT'S ENTERTAINMENT (Jam) / SKIN STORM (Bradford) / MOON RIVER (Henry Mancini) / REDONDO BEACH (Patti Smith).
• **Trivia:** In the late 80's, MORRISSEY made a cameo appearance in Channel 4's 'Brookside' off-shoot, 'South'.

Album rating: VIVA HATE (*9) / BONA DRAG collection (*7) / KILL UNCLE (*8) / YOUR ARSENAL (*8) / BEETHOVEN WAS DEAF (*5) / VAUXHALL AND I (*9) / WORLD OF MORRISSEY part compilation (*7) / SOUTHPAW GRAMMAR (*6) / MALADJUSTED (*6) / SUEDEHEAD (THE BEST OF . . .) compilation (*7) / MY EARLY BURGLARY YEARS collection (*5) / YOU ARE THE QUARRY (*8) / LIVE AT EARLS COURT (*7) / RINGLEADER OF THE TORMENTORS (*7)

MORRISSEY – vocals; with **STEPHEN STREET** – guitar, bass, producer, co-writer / **ANDREW PARESI** – drums / **VINI REILLY** – guitar, keyboards (of DURUTTI COLUMN)

		H.M.V.	Sire
Feb 88.	(7") *(POP 1618)* **SUEDEHEAD. / I KNOW VERY WELL HOW I GOT MY NAME**	5	–
	(12"+=) *(12POP 1618)* – Hairdresser on fire.		
	(c-s++=/cd-s++=) *(TC/CD POP 1618)* – Oh well, I'll never learn.		
Mar 88.	(cd/c/lp) *(CD/TC+/CDS 3787)* *<25699>* **VIVA HATE**	2	48

– Alsatian cousin / Little man, what now? / Everyday is like Sunday / Bengali in platforms / Angel, angel, down we go together / Late night, Maudlin Street / Suedehead / Break up the family / The ordinary boys / I don't mind if you forget me / Dial-a-cliche / Margaret on the guillotine. *(re-iss. Mar94 on 'Parlophone' cd/c; same) (cd re-iss. Mar97 on 'E.M.I.'+=; CDCNTAV 2)* – Let the right one slip in / Pashernate love / At amber / Disappointed (live) / Girl least likely to / I'd love to / Michael's bones / I've changed my plea to guilty. *(lp re-iss. Aug00 on 'Simply Vinyl'; SVLP 233)*

Jun 88. (7") *(POP 1619)* **EVERYDAY IS LIKE SUNDAY. / DISAPPOINTED** 9 –
(12"+=) *(12POP 1619)* – Sister I'm a poet.
(c-s++=/cd-s++=) *(TC/CD+/POP 1619)* – Will never marry.

— **MORRISSEY** only retained **STREET.** He brought in **NEIL TAYLOR** – guitar and re-united with (ex-SMITHS):- **CRAIG GANNON, ANDY ROURKE + MIKE JOYCE**

Feb 89. (7") *(POP 1620)* **THE LAST OF THE FAMOUS INTERNATIONAL PLAYBOYS. / LUCKY LIPS** 6 –
(12"+=/cd-s+=) *(12/CD POP 1620)* – Michael's bones.

Apr 89. (7"/etched-12") *(POP/12POPS 1621)* **INTERESTING DRUG. / SUCH A LITTLE THING MAKES SUCH A BIG DIFFERENCE** 9 –
(c-s+=/12"+=/cd-s+=) *(TC/12/CD POP 1621)* – Sweet and tender hooligan (live).

— He brought in complete new line-up:- **KEVIN ARMSTRONG** – guitar / **MATTHEW SELIGMAN** – bass / **STEVE HOPKINS** – drums and returning **ANDREW PARESI** – keyboards

Nov 89. (7") *(POP 1622)* **OUIJA BOARD, OUIJA BOARD. / YES, I AM BLIND** 18 □
(c-s+=/12"+=/cd-s+=) *(TC/12/CD POP 1622) <21424>* – East west.

— **ANDY ROURKE** returned to repl. SELIGMAN + HOPKINS / added guest **MARY MARGARET O'HARA** – vocals (up & coming solo artist)

Apr 90. (c-s/7") *(TC+/POP 1623)* **NOVEMBER SPAWNED A MONSTER. / HE KNOWS I'D LOVE TO SEE HIM** 12 □
(12"+=/cd-s+=) *(12/CD POP 1623) <21529>* – The girl least likely to.

Oct 90. (c-s/7") *(TC+/POP 1624)* **PICCADILLY PALARE. / GET OFF THE STAGE** 18 –
(12"+=/cd-s+=) *(12/CD POP 1624)* – At amber.

Oct 90. (cd/c/lp) *(CD/TC+/CSD 3788) <26221>* **BONA DRAG** 9 59
– Piccadilly palare / Interesting drug / November spawned a monster / Will never marry / Such a little thing makes such a big difference / The last of the famous international playboys / Ouija board, ouija board / Hairdresser on fire / Everyday is like Sunday / He knows I'd love to see him / Yes, I am blind / Lucky lisp / Suedehead / Disappointed. *(re-iss. Mar94 on 'Parlophone' cd/c; same)*

— He now retained **ANDREW PARESI.** Newcomers were **BEDDERS** – bass (ex-MADNESS) / **MARK E.NEVIN** – guitars, co-composer (ex-FAIRGROUND ATTRACTION) plus **STEVE HEART + SEAMUS BEAGHAN** – keyboards / **NAWAZISH ALI KHAN** – violin

Feb 91. (c-s/7") *(TC+/POP 1625)* **OUR FRANK. / JOURNALISTS WHO LIE** 26 □
(12"+=/cd-s+=) *(12/CD POP 1625) <40043>* – Tony the pony.

Feb 91. (cd/c/lp) *(CD/TC+/CSD 3789) <26514>* **KILL UNCLE** 8 Mar91 52
– Our Frank / Asian rut / Sing your life / Mute witness / King Leer / Found found found / Driving your girlfriend home / The harsh truth of the camera eye / (I'm) The end of the family line / There's a place in Hell for me and my friends.

— His tour band Spring '91; **ALAIN WHYTE** – guitar / **GARY DAY** – bass / **BOZ BOORER** – guitar (ex-POLECATS) / **SPENCER COBRIN** – drums

Apr 91. (c-s/7") *(TC+/POP 1626)* **SING YOUR LIFE. / THAT'S ENTERTAINMENT** 33 □
(12"+=/cd-s+=) *(12/CD POP 1626) <40084>* – The loop.

Jul 91. (c-s/7") *(TC+/POP 1627)* **PREGNANT FOR THE LAST TIME. / SKIN STORM** 25 –
(12"+=/cd-s+=) *(12/CD POP 1627)* – Cosmic dancer (live) / Disappointed (live).

Oct 91. (c-s/7") *(TC+/POP 1628)* **MY LOVE LIFE. / I'VE CHANGED MY PLEA TO GUILTY** 29 □
(12"+=/cd-s+=) *(12/CD POP 1628) <40163>* – There's a place in Hell for me and my friends.

Oct 91. (cd-ep) *<40184>* **AT KROQ (live)** – □
– There's a place in Hell for my friends / My love life / Sing your life.

May 92. (c-s/7") *(TC+/POP 1629)* **WE HATE IT WHEN OUR FRIENDS BECOME SUCCESSFUL. / SUEDEHEAD** 17 □
(12"+=) *(12POP 1629)* – Pregnant for the last time.
(cd-s+=) *(CDPOP 1629) <40560>* – I've changed my plea to guilty.

Jul 92. (c-s/7") *(TC+/POP 1630)* **YOU'RE THE ONE FOR ME, FATTY. / PASHERNATE LOVE** 19 –
(12"+=/cd-s+=) *(12/CD POP 1630)* – There speaks a true friend.

Jul 92. (cd/c/lp) *(CD/TC+/CSD 3790) <26994>* **YOUR ARSENAL** 4 21
– You're gonna need someone on your side / Glamorous glue / We'll let you know / The National Front disco / Certain people I know / We hate it when our friends become successful / You're the one for me, Fatty / Seasick, yet still docked / I know it's gonna happen someday / Tomorrow. *(lp re-iss. Sep00 on 'Simply Vinyl'; SVLP 244)*

Sep 92. (cd-s) *<40580>* **TOMORROW / LET THE RIGHT ONE SLIP IN / PASHERNATE LOVE** – □

Dec 92. (c-s/7") *(TC+/POP 1631)* **CERTAIN PEOPLE I KNOW. / JACK THE RIPPER** 35 –
(12"+=/cd-s+=) *(12/CD POP 1631)* – You've had her.

Parlophone E.M.I.

May 93. (cd/c/lp) *(CD/TC+/CSD 3791) <89061>* **BEETHOVEN WAS DEAF (live)** 13 □
– You're the one for me, Fatty / Certain people I know / National Front disco / November spawned a monster / Seasick, yet still docked / The loop / Sister I'm a poet / Jack the ripper / Such a little thing makes such a big difference / I know it's gonna happen someday / We'll let you know / Suedehead / He knows I'd love to see him / You're gonna need someone on your side / Glamorous glue / We hate it when our friends become successful. *(re-iss. Sep94 on 'Parlophone' cd/c; same)*

— **BOZ BOORER + ALAIN WHYTE** – guitars / **JONNY BRIDGEWOOD** – bass / **WOODIE TAYLOR** – drums

Parlophone Sire

Mar 94. (c-s/7") *(TCR/R 6372) <18207>* **THE MORE YOU IGNORE ME, THE CLOSER I GET. / USED TO BE A SWEET BOY** 8 46
(12"+=/cd-s+=) *(12R/CDR 6372)* – I'd love to.

Mar 94. (cd/c/lp) *(CD/TC+/PCSD 148) <45451>* **VAUXHALL AND I** 1 18
– Now my heart is full / Spring-heeled Jim / Billy Budd / Hold on to your friends / The more you ignore me, the closer I get / Why don't you find out for yourself / I am hated for loving / Lifeguard sleeping, girl drowning / Used to be a sweet boy / The lazy sunbathers / Speedway.

Jun 94. (c-s/7") *(TCR/R 6383)* **HOLD ON TO YOUR FRIENDS. / MOONRIVER** 47 –
(12"/cd-s) *(12R/CDR 6383)* – (extended versions).

Aug 94. (c-s/7"; by MORRISSEY and SIOUXSIE) *(TCR/R 6365)* **INTERLUDE. / ('A'extended)** 25 –
(12"+=/cd-s+=) *(12R/CDR 6365)* – ('A'mix).

Aug 94. (cd-s) *<41700>* **NOW MY HEART IS FULL / MOON RIVER / JACK THE RIPPER** – □

Jan 95. (c-s/7") *(TC+/R 6400)* **BOXERS. / HAVE-A-GO MERCHANT** 23 □
(12"+=/cd-s+=) *(12/CD R 6400) <41914>* – Whatever happens, I love you.

Feb 95. (cd/c/lp) *(CD/TC+/PCSD 163) <45879>* **WORLD OF MORRISSEY** (part compilation) 15 □
– Whatever happens, I love you / Billy Budd / Jack the ripper (live) / Have-a-go merchant / The loop / Sister I'm a poet (live) / You're the one for me, Fatty (live) / Boxers / Moon river (extended) / My love life / Certain people I know / The last of the famous international playboys / We'll let you know / Spring-heeled Jim. *(cd re-iss. Mar99 on 'EMI Gold'; CDPCSD 163)*

— **SPENCER JAMES COBRIN** – drums; repl. WOODIE

RCA Victor RCA Victor

Aug 95. (7"/c-s) *(74321 29980-7/-4)* **DAGENHAM DAVE. / NOBODY LOVES US** 26 –
(cd-s+=) *(74321 29980-2)* – You must please remember.

Aug 95. (cd/c/lp) *(74321 29953-2/-4/-1) <45939>* **SOUTHPAW GRAMMAR** 4 66
– The teachers are afraid of the pupils / Reader meet author / The boy racer / The operation / Dagenham Dave / Do your best and don't worry / Best friend on the payroll / Southpaw.

Nov 95. (7") *(74321 33294-7)* **THE BOY RACER. / LONDON (live)** 36 –
(cd-s+=) *(74321 33295-2)* – Billy Budd (live).
(cd-s) *(74321 33294-2)* – ('A'side) / Spring heeled Jim (live) / Why don't you find out for yourself (live).

Parlophone Capitol

Dec 95. (c-s/7") *(TC+/R 6243)* **SUNNY. / BLACK-EYED SUSAN** 42 –
(cd-s+=) *(CDR 6243)* – A swallow on my neck.

Island Polygram

Jul 97. (c-s/7") *(C+/IS 667)* **ALMA MATTERS. / I CAN HAVE BOTH** 16 –
(12"+=/cd-s+=) *(12IS/CID 667)* – Heir apparent.

Aug 97. (cd/c/lp) *(CID/ICT/ILPS 8059) <536036>* **MALADJUSTED** 8 61
– Maladjusted / Alma matters / Ambitious outsiders / Trouble loves me / Papa Jack / Ammunition / Wide to receive / Roy's keen / He cried / Satan rejected my soul.

Oct 97. (c-s/7") *(C+/IS 671)* **ROY'S KEEN. / LOST** [42] [–]
(12"+=/cd-s+=) *(12IS/CID 671)* – The edges are no longer parallel.
Dec 97. (c-s/7") *(C+/IS 686)* **SATAN REJECTED MY SOUL. / NOW I AM I WAS** [39] [–]
(cd-s+=/12"+=) *(CID/12IS 686)* – This is not your country.

Attack Attack

May 04. (7"/cd-s) *(ATK SI/XD 002)* **IRISH BLOOD, ENGLISH HEART. / IT'S HARD TO WALK TALL WHEN YOU'RE SMALL** [3] [–]
(cd-s) *(ATKXS 002) <06076-86000-2>* – ('A') / Munich air disaster 1958 / The never played symphonies.
May 04. (cd/lp) *(ATK CD/LP 001) <06076-86002-2/-1>* **YOU ARE THE QUARRY** [2] [11]
– America is not the world / Irish blood, English heart / I have forgiven Jesus / Come back to Camden / I'm not sorry / The world is full of crashing bores / How can anybody possibly know how I feel? / First of the gang to die / Let me kiss you / All the lazy dykes / I like you / You know I couldn't last. *(<ltd-cd w/dvd+=; ATKDX 001 / 86003-2>* – (DVD tracks). *(d-cd iss.Nov04 +=; ATKDD 013)* – Don't make fun of daddy's voice / It's hard to walk tall when you're small / Teenage dad on his estate / Munich air disaster 1958 / Friday mourning / Never played symphones / My life is a succession of people saying goodbye / I am two people / Mexico / (videos):- Irish blood, English heart / First of the gang to die / I have forgiven Jesus / Let me kiss you / (behind the scenes).
Jul 04. (7"/cd-s) *(ATK SI/XS 003)* **FIRST OF THE GANG TO DIE. / MY LIFE IS A SUCCESSION OF PEOPLE SAYING GOODBYE** [6] [ ]
(7"+=/cd-s+=) *<06076-86007-7/-2>* – Teenage dad on his estate / Mexico.
(dvd-s++=) *(ATKDX 003)* – ('A'-video).
Oct 04. (7"/cd-s) *(ATK SE/XD 008)* **LET ME KISS YOU. / DON'T MAKE FUN OF DADDY'S VOICE** [8] [ ]
(cd-s) *(ATKXS 008)* – ('A') / Friday mourning / I am two people.
Dec 04. (7"/cd-s) *(ATK SE/XS 011)* **I HAVE FORGIVEN JESUS. / NO ONE CAN HOLD A CANDLE TO YOU** [10] [–]
(cd-s) *(ATKXD 011)* – ('A') / Slum mums / The public image / ('A'-video).
Mar 05. (7") *(ATKSE 015)* **REDONDO BEACH (live). / THERE IS A LIGHT THAT NEVER GOES OUT (live)** [11] [ ]
(cd-s+=) *(ATKXD 015) <06076-86013-2>* – Noise is the best revenge (BBC Radio 2 session).
(dvd-s+=) *(ATKDX 015)* – It's hard to walk tall when you're small (BBC Radio 2 session) / ('AA'-video) / ('AA'-live from MEN).
Apr 05. (cd) *(ATKCD 014) <86021>* **LIVE AT EARLS COURT** (live 18th December 2004) [18] [ ]
– How soon is now? / First of the gang to die / November spawned a monster / Don't make fun of daddy's voice / Bigmouth strikes again / I like you / Redondo beach / Let me kiss you / Subway train – Munich air disaster 1958 / There is a light that never goes out / The more you ignore me, the closer I get / Friday mourning / I have forgiven Jesus / The world is full of crashing bores / Shoplifters of the world unite / Irish blood, English heart / You know I couldn't last / Last night I dreamt that somebody loved me.
Mar 06. (7"/cd-s) *(ATK SE/XS 017)* **YOU HAVE KILLED ME. / GOOD LOOKING MAN ABOUT TOWN** [3] [ ]
(cd-s) *(ATKXD 017)* – ('A') / Human being / I knew I was next / ('A'-video).
Apr 06. (cd/lp) *(ATK CD/LP 016) <86014-2/-1>* **RINGLEADER OF THE TORMENTORS** [1] [27]
– I will see you in far off places / Dear God please help me / You have killed me / The youngest was the most loved / In the future when all's well / The father who must be killed / Life is a pigsty / I'll never be anybody's hero now / On the streets I ran / To me you are a work of art / I just want to see the boy happy / At last I am born. *(ltd-cd w/dvd+=; ATKDX 016)* – (DVD footage).
Jun 06. (7"/cd-s) *(ATK SE/XS 018)* **THE YOUNGEST WAS THE MOST LOVED. / IF YOU DON'T LIKE ME, DON'T LOOK AT ME** [14] [–]
(cd-s) *(ATKXD 018)* – ('A') / Ganglord / A song from under the floorboards / ('A'-video).

– compilations, etc. –

on 'E.M.I.' unless mentioned otherwise
Sep 97. (cd/c/lp) *(<CD/TC+/EMC 3771>)* **SUEDEHEAD (THE BEST OF MORRISSEY)** [26] [–]
– Suedehead / Interesting drug / Boxers / Last of the famous international playboys / Sunny / Tomorrow / Interlude / Everyday is like Sunday / Hold on to your friends / My love life / Our Frank / Piccadilly palare / Ouija board, ouija board / You're the one for me, fatty / We hate it when our friends become successful / Pregnant for the last time / November spawned a monster / The more you ignore me, the closer I get / That's entertainment. *(special edition; CDEMCX 3771)*
Sep 98. (cd) *Reprise; <WR 46874-2>* **MY EARLY BURGLARY YEARS** [–] [ ]
– Sunny / At amber / Cosmic dancer / Nobody loves us / A swallow on my neck / Sister I'm a poet / Black-eyed Susan / Michael's bones / I'd love to / Reader meet author / Pashernate love / Girl least likely to / Jack the ripper / I've changed my plea to guilty / The boy racer / Boxers. *<(re-iss. +imp Jul03; same)>*
Mar 99. (cd) *EMI Gold: CDPCSD 163)* **THE WORLD OF MORRISSEY** [ ] [–]
(re-iss. Sep02 on 'Disky'; VI 649062)
Jun 00. (10xcd-s-box) *(887293-2)* **THE CD SINGLES 1988-1991** [ ] [–]
Sep 00. (3xcd-box) *(528376-2)* **BONA DRAG / KILL UNCLE / VAUXHALL AND I** [ ] [–]
Sep 01. (9xcd-s-box) *(879745-2)* **THE CD SINGLES 1991-1995** [ ] [–]
Dec 01. (cd) *Rhino/Warners-Sire; <R2 78375>* **THE BEST OF . . .** [–] [ ]
– The more you ignore me, the closer I get / Suedehead / Everyday is like Sunday / Glamorous glue / Do your best and don't worry / November spawned a monster / The last of the famous international playboys / Sing your life / Hairdresser on fire / Interesting drug / We hate it when our friends become successful / Certain people I know / Now my heart is full / I know it's gonna happen someday / Sunny / Alma matters / Hold on to your friends / Sister I'm a poet / Disappointed / Tomorrow / Lost.
Oct 02. (d-cd) *(543151-2)* **BONA DRAG / YOUR ARSENAL** [ ] [–]

□ MOTHER LOVE BONE (see under ⇒ PEARL JAM)

□ the MOTHERS (OF INVENTION) (see under ⇒ ZAPPA, Frank)

MOTLEY CRUE

Formed: Los Angeles, California, USA . . . early 1981 by NIKKI SIXX (bass, ex-LONDON) who recruited VINCE NEIL (vocals, ex-ROCK CANDY), TOMMY LEE (drums) and finally MICK MARS (guitar). In 1981, they issued their debut album, 'TOO FAST FOR LOVE', on their own US label, 'Lethur'. From its 'STICKY FINGERS'-esque, crotch-shot cover to the low-rent sleaze-rock contained within, the album announced MOTLEY CRUE's status as wannabe metal successors to the likes of AEROSMITH and The NEW YORK DOLLS. There were certainly worse reference points to have, and the record was an amateurish, minor classic, the title track and 'PIECE OF YOUR ACTION' pouting highlights. After being signed to 'Elektra', the record was re-issued the following year while the band began work on a follow-up with producer Tom Werman. 'SHOUT AT THE DEVIL' (1983) added cod-satanic imagery to their glam fixation while beefing up the guitars. But VENOM this band were not and songs like 'GOD BLESS THE CHILDREN OF THE BEAST' were downright ridiculous. If catchy pop-metal like 'TOO YOUNG TO FALL IN LOVE' was the work of the devil, then God certainly had nothing to fear. Nevertheless, after a nationwide tour supporting KISS, the album hit the US Top 20 and things were looking up for the band. However on the 8th of December '84, VINCE NEIL was involved in a serious car accident; NICK 'RAZZLE' DINGLEY (drummer with HANOI ROCKS) was killed in the crash while two others were injured. NEIL was subsequently ordered to pay $2.5 million compensation and sentenced to 20 days in jail, after being convicted of vehicle manslaughter. The tragedy overshadowed much of the 'THEATRE OF PAIN' (1985) album, a record that went on to sell more than two million copies after its cover of Brownsville Station's 'SMOKIN' IN THE BOYS ROOM' was a Top 20 hit. The album also boasted the surprisingly poignant power ballad, 'HOME SWEET HOME', an MTV favourite later that year. 'GIRLS, GIRLS, GIRLS' (1987) was a marked improvement; the lyrics cementing The 'CRUE's reputation as the 'bad' boys of metal, the music confident and cocksure. Tracks like 'WILD SIDE', showed a newfound adventurousness, the first signs that the band were capable of promotion from the metal second division. Early in 1988, MATTHEW TRIPPE sued the CRUE for royalties, alleging he masqueraded and wrote songs as NIKKI SIXX, while he recovered from a 1983 car crash. This was later proved to be false, although there is still much speculation on how SIXX's face was bloated on some mug pics. Having survived a near-death experience after a heroin o.d., SIXX and the newly cleaned up 'CRUE delivered another album, 'DR. FEELGOOD', which duly topped the US charts (while hitting Top 5 in the UK). It was to be NEIL's parting shot, the singer ousted in the early 90's following media overkill on his war of words with AXL ROSE. While he released a solo album in '93, the group recruited a new frontman, JOHN CORABI, although the subsequent album, 'MOTLEY CRUE' found few takers. NEIL and the group had patched up their differences by 1997, the album, 'GENERATION SWINE' giving them a return to the US Top 5. With VINCE back in the fold it must've seemed a good time to capture some of their rekindled stage fire; 'LIVE: ENTERTAINMENT OR DEATH' (1999) featured a clutch of latter day tracks and a far larger whack from the halcyon days of yore, we're talking early 80's here. If that wasn't enough to please the band's diehard fans then 'NEW TATTOO' (2000) saw MOTLEY CRUE returning to their bad old days in fine style. Out went the half-arsed attempts at alternative metal and serious subject matter; in came scuzz-rock and such time honoured lyrical themes as, well, sex, drugs and rock'n'roll basically, the nastier and filthier the better. They even signed off with a rendition of the Tubes' 'WHITE PUNKS ON DOPE', a somehow more appropriate choice of cover than the Beatles' 'HELTER SKELTER'. With RANDY CASTILLO (who himself had replaced LEE in 1999) passing away from cancer on 26th March 2002, the subsequent tour saw ex-HOLE stickswoman SAMANTHA MOLONEY recruited as a fill-in. The CRUE subsequently went into hiatus as NEIL performed solo and SIXX surfaced with both 58 and BRIDES OF DESTRUCTION. While 'NEW TATTOO's sales had been disappointing, all the band needed was the right cultural conditions: they came in 2004 as the post-nu-metal/80s revival climate was ripe for a full-on MOTLEY CRUE reformation. A reunion tour – featuring all four original members – cleaned up on the nostalgia market to the tune of a cool $33 million, the band's popularity boosted by best selling autobiography 'The Dirt' (published 2001). Coming on the back of a plethora of compilation albums,'RED, WHITE & CRUE' (2005) was the most high profile (US Top 10), creaming off the best of the band's albums and adding three new tracks, one of which, 'SICK LOVE SONG', scraped the UK Top 75. Available as both a hits-orientated single disc and more exhaustive double disc set, the record also featured a cover of the Rolling Stones' 'STREET FIGHTING MAN'. The inevitable live album, 'CARNIVAL OF SINS', arrived in 2006, featuring another by-numbers cover in the Sex Pistols' 'ANARCHY IN THE UK'.

• **Covered:** JAILHOUSE ROCK (Leiber-Stoller). • **Trivia:** Late 1985, TOMMY LEE married actress Heather Lockear, although it did not last. He subsequently married Baywatch actress Pamela Anderson, although domestic bliss was short-lived; the couple divorced while TOMMY faced a lengthy jail sentence for wife-beating. In December '87, MICK married one-time PRINCE girlfriend Vanity (star of 'Purple Rain'). In May '90, NIKKI was hitched to former Playboy centrefold Brandi Brandt.

Album rating: TOO FAST FOR LOVE (*5) / SHOUT AT THE DEVIL (*6) / THEATRE OF PAIN (*5) / GIRLS, GIRLS, GIRLS (*7) / DR. FEELGOOD (*5) / DECADE OF DECADENCE compilation (*7) / MOTLEY CRUE (*5) / GENERATION SWINE (*5) / THE BEST OF MOTLEY CRUE compilation (*6) / LIVE: ENTERTAINMENT OR DEATH (*4) / NEW TATTOO (*5) / GREATEST HITS compilation (*7) / MUSIC TO CRASH YOUR CAR TO – VOL.1 boxed set (*7) / LOUD AS F@*K compilation (*6) / MUSIC TO CRASH YOUR CAR TO – VOL.2 boxed set (*6) / RED, WHITE & CRUE double compilation (*7) / CARNIVAL OF SINS (*5)

VINCE NEIL (b. VINCENT NEIL WHARTON, 8 Feb'61, Hollywood, Calif.) – vocals (ex-ROCK CANDY) / **NIKKI SIXX** (b. FRANK FERRANNO, 11 Dec'58, San Jose, Calif.) – bass (ex-LONDON) / **MICK MARS** (b. BOB DEAL, 3 Apr'56, Huntington, Indiana) – guitar / **TOMMY LEE** (b. THOMAS LE BASS, 3 Oct'62, Athens, Greece) – drums (ex-SUITE 19)

not iss. Lethur

1981. (lp) *<R-123>* **TOO FAST FOR LOVE** [–] [ ]
– Live wire / Public enemy No.1 / Take me to the top / Merry-go-round / Piece of your action / Starry eyes / Come on and dance / Too fast for love / On with the show. *(UK-iss.Oct82 as 'MOTLEY CRUE' on 'Elektra' lp/c; K/K4 52425) <US re-iss. Nov83 on 'Elektra'; 60174> (cd-iss. Feb93 on 'Elektra'; 7559 60174-2)*

1982. (7"gig freebie) **TOAST OF THE TOWN. / STICK TO YOUR GUNS** [–] [ ]

Elektra Elektra

Sep 83. (lp/c) *(960 289-1/-4) <60289>* **SHOUT AT THE DEVIL** [ ] [17]
– In the beginning / Shout at the Devil / Looks that kill / Bastard / Knock 'em dead, kid / Danger / Too young to fall in love / Helter skelter / Red hot / Ten seconds 'til love / God bless the children of the beast. *(cd-iss. Jan89; 960 289-2)*

Jul 84. (7") *(E 9756) <69756>* **LOOKS THAT KILL. / PIECE OF YOUR ACTION** [ ] Jan84 [54]
(12"+=) *(E 9756T)* – Live wire.

Oct 84. (7"/12") *(E 9732/+T) <69732>* **TOO YOUNG TO FALL IN LOVE. / TAKE ME TO THE TOP** [ ] Jun84 [90]

Jul 85. (lp/c) *(EKT 8/+C) <60418>* **THEATRE OF PAIN** [36] [6]
– City boy blues / Smokin' in the boys' room / Louder than Hell / Keep your eye on the money / Home sweet home / Tonight (we need a lover) / Use it or lose it / Save our souls / Raise your hands to rock / Fight for your rights. *(cd-iss. Jul86; 960 418-2)*

Aug 85. (7"/7"sha-pic-d/12") *(EKR 16/+P/T) <69625>*
SMOKIN' IN THE BOYS' ROOM. / USE IT OR LOSE IT [71] Jul85 [16]
<US-12"> – ('A'side) / Helter skelter / Piece of your action / Live wire.

Oct 85. (7") *<69591>* **HOME SWEET HOME. / RED HOT** [–] [89]

Jan 86. (7"/7"sha-pic-d) *(EKR 33/+P)* **SMOKIN' IN THE BOYS' ROOM. / HOME SWEET HOME** [51] [–]
(12"+=) *(EKR 33T)* – Shout at the Devil.

Jun 87. (lp/c)(cd) *(EKT 39/+C)(960 725-2) <60725>* **GIRLS, GIRLS, GIRLS** [14] [2]
– The wild side / Girls, girls, girls / Dancing on glass / Bad bad boogie / Nona / Five years dead / All in the name of . . . / Sumthin' for nuthin' / You're all I need / Jailhouse rock (live).

Jul 87. (7"/7"w-poster) *(EKR 59/+P) <69465>* **GIRLS, GIRLS, GIRLS. / SUMTHIN' FOR NUTHIN'** [26] May87 [12]
(12"+=/12"pic-d+=) *(EKR 59T)* – Smokin' in the boys' room.

Sep 87. (7") *<69449>* **THE WILD SIDE. / FIVE YEARS DEAD** [–] [ ]

Nov 87. (7") *<69429>* **YOU'RE ALL I NEED. / ALL IN THE NAME OF ROCK** [–] [83]

Jan 88. (7") *(EKR 65)* **YOU'RE ALL I NEED. / WILD SIDE** [23] [–]
(12"+=/12"pic-d+=/12"boxed+=) *(EKR 65 T/+P/B)* – Home sweet home / Looks that kill.

Jul 88. (m-lp/m-cd) *<25XD 1052>* **HOME SWEET HOME (RAW TRACKS)** [–] [ ]
– Live wire / Piece of your action / Too young to fall in love / Knock 'em dead, kid / Home sweet home.

Sep 89. (lp/c)(cd) *(EKT 59/+C)(960 829-2) <60829>* **DR. FEELGOOD** [4] [1]
– Same ol' situation (S.O.S.) / Slice of your pie / Rattlesnake shake / Kickstart my heart / Without you / Don't go away mad (just go away) / She goes down / Sticky sweet / Time for a change / T.N.T. (Terror 'n' Tinseltown) / Dr. Feelgood.

Oct 89. (7"/7"sha-pic-d/c-s) *(EKR 97/+P/C) <69271>* **DR. FEELGOOD. / STICKY SWEET** [50] Aug89 [6]
(ext.12"+=/ext.3"cd-s+=) *(EKR 97 T/CD)* – All in the name of rock.

Nov 89. (c-s) *<69248>* **KICKSTART MY HEART. / SHE GOES DOWN** [–] [27]

Feb 90. (c-s) *<64985>* **WITHOUT YOU. / SLICE OF YOUR LIFE** [–] [8]

Apr 90. (7"/7"pic-d/c-s) *(EKR 109/+P/C)* **WITHOUT YOU. / LIVE WIRE** [39] [–]
(12"+=/cd-s+=) *(EKR 109 T/CD)* – Girls, girls, girls / All in the name of rock.

May 90. (c-s) *<64962>* **DON'T GO AWAY MAD (JUST GO AWAY). / RATTLESNAKE SHAKE** [–] [19]

Aug 90. (c-s) *<64942>* **SAME OL' SITUATION (S.O.S.). / WILD SIDE** [–] [78]

Nov 90. (m-cd) <*WPCP 3462*> **RAW TRACKS II** –

Aug 91. (7"/c-s) *(EKR 133/+C) <64848>* **PRIMAL SCREAM. / DANCING ON GLASS** 32 63
(12"+=/cd-s+=) *(EKR 133 T/CD)* – Red hot (live) / Dr. Feelgood (live).

Oct 91. (cd)(lp/c) *<(7559 61204-2)>(EKT 95/+C)>* **DECADE OF DECADENCE** (compilation) 20 2
– Live wire / Piece of your action / Shout at the Devil / Looks that kill / Home sweet home / Smokin' in the boys' room / Girls, girls, girls / Wild side / Dr. Feelgood / Kickstart my heart / Teaser / Rock'n'roll junkie / Primal scream / Angela / Anarchy in the UK.

Dec 91. (7") *(EKR 136) <64818>* **HOME SWEET HOME '91. / YOU'RE ALL I NEED** 37 Nov91 37
(12"+=/12"pic-d+=/cd-s+=) *(EKR 136 T/TP/CD)* – Without you / ('A'original mix).

— Had already split temporarily Apr'91 to do own projects. The group parted company with VINCE NEIL, who went solo early 1992.

— brought in **JOHN CORABI** (b.26 Apr'59, Philadelphia, Pennsylvania) – vocals (ex-SCREAM)

Feb 94. (7"yellow) *(EKR 180)* **HOOLIGAN'S HOLIDAY. / HYPNOTIZED (demo)** 36
(12"+=/cd-s+=/cd-s+=) *(EKR 180 T/CD/CDX)* – ('A'-Brown nose edit) / ('A'-album version a.k.a. The Dregs of Society – featuring – The Slime City Sinners & The Canadian Connection) / Hypnotized (demo).

Mar 94. (cd/c/d-lp) *<(7559 61534-2/-4/-1)>* **MOTLEY CRUE** 17 7
– Power to the music / Uncle Jack / Hooligan's holiday / Misunderstood / Loveshine / Poison apples / Hammered / 'Til death us do part / Welcome to the numb / Smoke the sky / Droppin' like flies / Drift away.

May 94. (7"w-drawn) *(EKR 183)* **MISUNDERSTOOD. /** – –

— **VINCE NEIL** returned to repl. CORABI

Jun 97. (cd/c) *<(7559 61901-2/-4)>* **GENERATION SWINE** 4
– Find myself / Afraid / Flush / Generation swine / Confessions / Beauty / Glitter / Anybody out there / Let us prey / Rocketship / Rat like me / Shout at the Devil '97 / Brandon.

Jul 97. (cd-s) *(E 3936CD1)* **AFRAID / AFRAID (Swine mix) / LUST FOR LIFE / WELCOME TO THE PLANET BOOM** 58
(cd-s) *(E 3936CD2)* – ('A'side) / Generation swine / Father / Bittersweet.
(cd-s) *(E 3936CD3)* – ('A'-alternative rave mix) / Shout at the Devil '97 / All in the name of . . . (live) / Girls, girls, girls (live).

Virgin Beyond

Nov 98. (cd) *(CDVIR 77) <78002>* **THE BEST OF MOTLEY CRUE** <US-title 'GREATEST HITS'> (compilation & 2 new) 20
– Bitter pill / Enslaved / Girls, girls, girls / Kickstart my heart / Wild side / Glitter (remix) / Dr. Feelgood / Same ol' situation / Home sweet home / Afraid / Don't go away mad (just go away) / Without you / Smokin' in the boys room / Primal scream / Too fast for love / Looks that kill / Shout at the Devil '97.

— **RANDY CASTILLO** (b.18 Dec'50, Albuquerque, New Mexico, USA) – drums (ex-OZZY OSBOURNE) repl. TOMMY LEE who formed METHODS OF MAYHEM

Jul 00. (cd) *(CDVIR 117) <78120>* **NEW TATTOO** Jun00 41
– Hell on high heels / Treat me like the dog I am / New tattoo / Dragstrip superstar / 1st band on the Moon / She needs rock & roll / Punched in the teeth by love / Hollywood ending / Fake / Porno star / White punks on dope.

— sadly, CASTILLO was to die of cancer complications (26th Mar'02)

— (2003) **TOMMY LEE** returned to repl. temp. SAMANTHA MOLONEY

Universal Universal

May 05. (7"pic-d) *(9871717)* **IF I DIE TOMORROW (rock mix). / I'm A LIAR (THAT'S THE TRUTH)** 63
(cd-s) *(9871754)* – ('A') / Live wire (Lethur Records version) / Stick to your guns (Lethur Records version) / ('A'-video).

Feb 05. (d-cd) *(9870344) <39090-2> <9830870>* **RED, WHITE & CRUE** (compilation) 6
– Live wire * / Piece of your action * / Toast of the town / Too fast for love / Black widow * / Looks that kill * / Too young to fall in love (remix) * / Helter skelter / Shout at the Devil * / Smokin' in the boys' room / Use it, or lose it / Girls, girls, girls * / Wild side * / All in the name of . . . / Kickstart my heart * / Without you / Don't go away mad (just go away) / Same ol' situation (S.O.S.) / Dr. Feelgood * / Anarchy in the UK / Primal scream * / Home sweet home ('91 remix) * / Hooligan's holiday * / Misunderstood / Planet boom / Bittersuite / Afraid / Beauty * / Generation swine / Bitter pill * / Enslaved / Hell on high heels * / New tattoo (single version) / If I die tomorrow * / Sick love song * / Street fighting man.

May 05. (re-cd) *(9871160) <9830870>* **RED, WHITE & CRUE** (compilation & new) 67 –
– (tracks above *).

S.P.V. Universal

May 06. (d-cd) *(SPV 9751-2) <10003>* **CARNIVAL OF SINS** (live 2005) Mar06
– Shout at the Devil / Too fast for love / Ten seconds to love / Red hot / On with the show / Too young to fall in love / Looks that kill / Louder than Hell / Live wire / Girls, girls, girls / Wild side / Don't go away mad (just go away) / Primal scream / Glitter / Without you / Home sweet home / Dr. Feelgood / Same ol' situation / Sick love song / If I die tomorrow / Kickstart my heart / Helter skelter / Anarchy in the UK.

– compilations, etc. –

Jan 00. (d-cd) *Spitfire; (SPITCD 058) / Beyond; <63985 78034>* **LIVE: ENTERTAINMENT OR DEATH** Nov99
– Looks that kill / Knock 'em dead, kid / Too young to fall in love / Live wire / Public enemy #1 / Shout at the Devil / Merry-go-round / Ten seconds to love / Piece of your action / Starry eyes / Helter skelter / Smokin' in the boys' room / Don't go away mad (just go away) / The wild side / Girls, girls, girls / Dr. Feelgood / Without you / Primal scream / Same ol' situation / Home sweet home / Kickstart my heart.

Jun 03. (cd) *Hip-O; <(038659-2)>* **GREATEST HITS** Mar03
– Bitter pill / Enslaved / Girls, girls, girls / Kickstart my heart / Wild side / Glitter (remix) / Dr. Feelgood / Same ol' situation / Home sweet home / Afraid / Don't go away mad (just go away) / Without you / Smokin' in the boys' room / Primal scream / Too fast for love / Looks that kill / Shout at the Devil '97.

Jun 03. (cd) *Hio-O; <(038671-2)>* **SUPERSONIC AND DEMONIC RELICS** Apr03

Nov 03. (d-cd+dvd) *Universal; <(9810469)>* **LOUD AS F@*K** Mar04

Dec 03. (4xcd-box) *Hip-O; <(B00014600-2)>* **MUSIC TO CRASH YOUR CAR TO – VOL.1** Nov03

Jun 04. (4xcd-box) *Hip-O; <B000283902-2>* **MUSIC TO CRASH YOUR CAR TO – VOL.2** –

Mar 05. (cd) *Spectrum; (9813713) / Hip-O; <B00010340-2>* **THE BEST OF MOTLEY CRUE** Oct03

MOTORHEAD

Formed: London, England . . . June '75 by LEMMY (aka IAN KILMISTER; vocals, bass) who decided to form his own band when, after a five year stint with hyperspace hippies HAWKWIND, he was finally given the boot. His sharp exit came after he was briefly detained in Canada on drugs charges; a notorious speed freak, his penchant for amphetamines was directly translated into MOTORHEAD's music, a synapse-crunching racket that somehow lent itself to a tune or two (the title of the band's first single, 'WHITE LINE FEVER', said it all really). Following his departure from HAWKWIND, LEMMY toyed with the name BASTARD, before opting for the MOTORHEAD moniker, the title of the last song he'd penned for his previous band. He subsequently hooked up with LARRY WALLIS (guitar, vocals) of the PINK FAIRIES and LUCAS FOX (drums), although by early '76 these two had been replaced with 'FAST' EDDIE CLARKE and PHIL 'PHILTHY ANIMAL' TAYLOR respectively. The initial line-up had recorded a relatively laid back outing, 'ON PAROLE' for 'United Artists' in 1975, although this was shelved until 1979 when the label cashed in on the band's success. The aforementioned 'WHITE LINE FEVER' single was also held back, 'Stiff' only releasing it once MOTORHEAD's commercial credentials had been established. It was the 'Chiswick' label who finally had the balls to release something, the eponymous 'MOTORHEAD' album in 1977. It was the first opus from the definitive MOTORHEAD line-up, a combination that would become one of the most infamous in the history of heavy metal and create some of the most enduring material in the band's career. Yet while MOTORHEAD were the epitome of headbanging metal, their maniacal energy also attracted hardcore punks in the same way IRON MAIDEN's early performances had a foot in both camps. Over a series of shit kicking albums, 'OVERKILL' (1979), 'BOMBER' (1979) and 'ACE OF SPADES' (1980), MOTORHEAD became a legend, laying the foundations of thrash with testosterone saturated anthems. The latter album was the landmark MOTORHEAD release, its title track the ultimate outlaw anthem and a Top 20 hit to boot. The record went to No.4, illustrating how quickly the band had risen through the metal ranks. While CLARKE and TAYLOR provided the musical fuel, LEMMY was undoubtedly the beast's engine, his dirty, propulsive bass driving MOTORHEAD ever onwards like the aural equivalent of road rage. And crucially, like all genuine badass outlaws, LEMMY was 'orrible!, yet he still got the chicks, and he had style. In bucketloads. Decked out in his white cowboy boots, bullet belt and mutton chop sideburns, he stood centre stage, rooted to the spot, head stretched up to the mike (maybe LIAM GALLAGHER clocked a few shows) like he was summoning up the God of Thunder (possibly). LEMMY didn't sing in the conventional sense, or even in the heavy metal sense, rather he rasped like a piece of industrial strength sandpaper scraped across a blackboard. He also had more charisma than most of the preening queens that passed as frontmen, his sharp wit and biting sense of humour making him quite a celebrity in his own right and ensuring that his band never fell into parody. MOTORHEAD gained further press attention when they hooked up with rock chicks, GIRLSCHOOL, for the 'ST. VALENTINE'S DAY MASSACRE' EP, released, appropriately enough, in February '81. Credited to HEADGIRL (guffaw, guffaw), the assembled n'er do wells ran through a suitably leering version of Johnny Kidd's 'PLEASE DON'T TOUCH'. Their blistering live set was finally laid down on vinyl in the form of 'NO SLEEP 'TIL HAMMERSMITH' (1981), the band's first (and only) No.1 album and deservedly so. Surely the tightest rock band on the planet at that point, MOTORHEAD ran through a hair whipping frenzy of favourites, from 'STAY CLEAN' and '(WE ARE) THE ROAD CREW' to 'IRON HORSE', LEMMY's tribute to Hell's Angel leader, Tramp. This line-up recorded a further album, the slightly disappointing 'IRON FIST' (1982), before CLARKE left to from his own outfit, FASTWAY. His replacement was BRIAN ROBERTSON (ex-THIN LIZZY, ex-WILD HORSES) who played on only one album, 1983's 'ANOTHER PERFECT DAY'. His more subtle style didn't sit well with the trademark MOTORHEAD cacophony and he soon departed for the more appropriate FRANKIE MILLER BAND, PHIL CAMPBELL and MICHAEL BURSTON (aka WURZEL) replacing him. TAYLOR also departed, PETE GILL (ex-Saxon) being recruited to fill the drum stool and complete the new look four piece MOTORHEAD. The new band made their debut on 'NO REMORSE' (1984), a compilation that collected MOTORHEAD's meanest tracks and showcased four new ones, among them the uber-grind of 'KILLED BY DEATH', possibly LEMMY and Co.'s finest hour. The band almost made the Top 20 once again with the BILL LASWELL-produced 'ORGASMATRON' (1986), LEMMY sounding almost inhuman on the brilliant title track; part android, part wild beast. TAYLOR returned to the fold the following year for the 'ROCK 'N' ROLL' album, its 'EAT THE RICH' track used on the 'Comic Strip' film of the same name, in which LEMMY made his acting debut. Another live album followed, 'NO SLEEP AT ALL' (1988), although it failed to make the same commercial impact as its predecessor. Following a move to L.A. (it had to come sooner or later), the band were back in the charts and back on form with '1916' (1991), its title track an unprecedented show of emotion from LEMMY as he narrated the tale of a young soldier lost in battle. The wart-ridden one also indulged his war fixation on the title track to 'MARCH OR DIE' (1992), while the three most recent releases, 'BASTARDS' (1993) and 'SACRIFICE' (1995) have seen MOTORHEAD content to cruise rather than let rip. Still, as long as LEMMY dons his bass and rides into onstage battle, there'll be a willing bunch of masochists ready to have their ears bled dry by the some of the loudest, filthiest rock'n'roll on the face of the earth. After the relatively disappointing 'SNAKE BITE LOVE' (1998), the remorseless sonic abusers returned to restate their claim with 'WE ARE MOTORHEAD' (2000), as loud and obnoxious as anything they'd come up with in the preceding decade. Sadly, the fine classical violin playing with which LEMMY was gracing a high profile TV ad (would we kid you on?) was notably absent. No sign of it either on 'HAMMERED' (2002), MOTORHEAD's umpteenth release but perhaps a candidate for title of the year? With no concessions whatsoever to musical fashion, even metal fashion, LEMMY and his cohorts once again showed that where MOTORHEAD are concerned, age ain't nuthin' but a number. 'INFERNO' (2004) was meat 'n' two veg for LEMMY and co, although it did feature legendary axeman STEVE VAI on a couple of tracks.

• **Covers:** LOUIE LOUIE (hit; Kingsmen) / TRAIN KEPT A-ROLLIN' (Johnny Burnette Trio) / PLEASE DON'T TOUCH (Johnny Kidd) / (I'M YOUR) HOOCHIE COOCHIE MAN (Willie Dixon) / CAT SCRATCH FEVER (Ted Nugent).

Album rating: MOTORHEAD (*5) / OVERKILL (*8) / BOMBER (*6) / ACE OF SPADES (*8) / NO SLEEP 'TIL HAMMERSMITH (*9) / IRON FIST (*5) / ANOTHER PERFECT DAY (*5) / NO REMORSE (*7) / ORGASMATRON (*6) / ROCK'N'ROLL (*5) / NO SLEEP AT ALL (*6) / 1916 (*7) / MARCH OR DIE (*5) / SACRIFICE (*5) / OVERNIGHT SENSATION (*6) / SNAKE BITE LOVE (*4) / EVERYTHING LOUDER THAN EVERYONE ELSE (*6) / WE ARE MOTORHEAD (*5) / HAMMERED (*5) / MOTORHEAD (*5)

LEMMY (b. IAN KILMISTER, 24 Dec'45, Stoke-On-Trent, England) – vocals, bass (ex-HAWKWIND, ex-OPAL BUTTERFLY, ex-SAM GOPAL'S DREAM, ROCKIN' VICKERS) / **PHIL 'ANIMAL' TAYLOR** (b.21 Sep'54, Chesterfield, England) – drums / **FAST EDDIE CLARKE** – guitar, vocals (ex-BLUE GOOSE, ex-CURTIS KNIGHT & ZEUS) (below withdrawn)

Stiff — not iss.

Dec 76. (7") *(BUY 9)* **LEAVING HERE. / WHITE LINE FEVER** — – — –
(withdrawn but iss.Dec78 in 'Stiff' box set Nos.1-10)

Chiswick — not iss.

Jun 77. (7",12") *(S 13)* **MOTORHEAD. / CITY KIDS** — — –
(re-iss. Sep79 on 'Big Beat' 7"colrd/7"pic-d; NS/+P 13)

Aug 77. (lp) *(WLK 2)* **MOTORHEAD** — 43 — –
– Motorhead / Vibrator / Lost Johnny / Iron horse – Born to lose / White line fever / Keepers on the road / The watcher / Born to lose / Train kept a-rollin'. *(re-iss. white-lp 1978; CWK 3008) (re-iss. Sep81 red-lp,clear-lp; WIK 2) (cd-iss. Jun88 & Feb 91 on 'Big Beat'; CDWIK 2)*

Bronze — not iss.

Sep 78. (7") *BRO 60)* **LOUIE LOUIE. / TEAR YA DOWN** — 68 — –

Feb 79. (7"/12") *(BRO/12BRO 67)* **OVERKILL. / TOO LATE, TOO LATE** — 39 — –

Mar 79. (lp,green-lp) *(BRON 515)* **OVERKILL** — 24 — –
– Overkill / Stay clean / Pay your price / I'll be your sister / Capricorn / No class / Damage case / Tear ya down / Metropolis / Limb for limb. *(cd-iss. Jul87 on 'Legacy'; LLMCD 3011) (re-iss. Jul90 on 'Fame' cd/c/lp; CD/TC+/FA 3236) (re-iss. Feb91 on 'Castle' cd/c/lp; CLA CD/MC/LP 178) (re-iss. cd Aug96 on 'Essential'; ESMCD 310)*

Jun 79. (7") *(BRO 78)* **NO CLASS. / LIKE A NIGHTMARE** — 61 — –

Oct 79. (lp,blue-lp) *(BRON 523)* **BOMBER** — 12 — –
– Dead men tell no tales / Lawman / Sweet revenge / Sharpshooter / Poison / Stone dead forever / All the aces / Step down / Talking head / Bomber. *(cd-iss. Jul87 on 'Legacy'; LLMCD 3012) (re-iss. Apr91 on 'Castle' cd/c/lp; CLA CD/MC/LP 227) (re-iss. Aug96 on 'Essential'; ESMCD 311)*

Nov 79. (7",7"blue) *(BRO 85)* **BOMBER. / OVER THE TOP** — 34 — –

Apr 80. (7"ep/12"ep) *(BRO/12BRO 92)* **THE GOLDEN YEARS (live)** — 8 — –
– Leaving here / Stone dead forever / Dead men don't tell tales / Too late, too late.

Bronze — Mercury

Oct 80. (7"/12") *(BRO/+X 106)* **ACE OF SPADES. / DIRTY LOVE** — 15 —

Oct 80. (lp/gold-lp) *(BRON/+G 531)* <4011> **ACE OF SPADES** — 4 —
– Ace of spades / Love me like a reptile / Shoot you in the back / Live to win / Fast and loose / (We are) The road crew / Fire, fire / Jailbait / Dance / Bite the bullet / The chase is better than the catch / The hammer. *(cd-iss.*

Aug87 on 'Legacy'; LLMCD 3013) (re-iss. cd Aug96 on 'Essential'; ESMCD 312)

Feb 81. (7"ep/10"ep; as HEADGIRL) *(BRO/+X 116)* **ST.VALENTINE'S DAY MASSACRE** 5 –
– Please don't touch (by MOTORHEAD & GIRLSCHOOL) / Emergency (by MOTORHEAD) / Bomber (GIRLSCHOOL).

Jun 81. (lp/gold-lp/c) *(BRON/+G/C 535)* **NO SLEEP 'TIL HAMMERSMITH (live)** 1 –
– Ace of spades / Stay clean / Metropolis / The hammer / Iron horse / No class / Overkill / (We are) The road crew / Capricorn / Bomber / Motorhead. *(cd-iss. Aug87 on 'Legacy'; LLMCD 3014) (re-iss. Feb90 on 'Castle' cd/c/lp; CLA CD/MC/LP 179) (re-iss. cd Aug96 on 'Essential'; ESMCD 313)*

Jul 81. (7"/7"pic-d) *(BRO/+P 124)* **MOTORHEAD (live). / OVER THE TOP (live)** 6

below, one-off (MOTORHEAD and The NOLANS)

Oct 81. (7"; as YOUNG AND MOODY BAND) *(BRO 130)* **DON'T DO THAT. / HOW CAN I HELP YOU TONIGHT** 63 –

Mar 82. (7",7"red,7"blue) *(BRO 146)* **IRON FIST. / REMEMBER ME, I'M GONE** 29 –

Apr 82. (lp/c) *(BRNA/+C 539) <4042>* **IRON FIST** 6
– Iron fist / Heart of stone / I'm the doctor / Go to Hell / Loser / Sex and outrage / America / Shut it down / Speedfreak / (Don't let 'em) Grind ya down / (Don't need) Religion / Bang to rights. *(re-iss. Mar87 on 'Castle' lp/c/cd; CLA LP/MC/CD 123) (cd re-iss. Aug96 on 'Essential'; ESMCD 372)*

Sep 82. (7"m; by LEMMY & WENDY) *(BRO 151)* **STAND BY YOUR MAN. / NO CLASS (Plasmatics) / MASTERPLAN (Motorhead)** –

— **BRIAN ROBERTSON** (b. 2 Feb'56, Clarkston, Scotland) – guitar, vocals (ex-THIN LIZZY, ex-WILD HORSES) repl. CLARKE who formed FASTWAY

May 83. (7") *(BRO 165)* **I GOT MINE. / TURN YOU AROUND AGAIN** 46
(12"+=) *(BROX 165)* – Tales of glory.

May 83. (lp/c) *(BRON/+C 546) <811365>* **ANOTHER PERFECT DAY** 20
– Back at the funny farm / Shine / Dancing on your grave / Rock it / One track mind / Another perfect day / Marching off to war / I got mine / Tales of glory / Die you bastard. *(re-iss. Feb91 on 'Castle' cd/c/lp; CLA CD/MC/LP 225) (re-iss. cd Sep96 on 'Essential'; ESMCD 438)*

Jul 83. (7") *(BRO 167)* **SHINE. / HOOCHIE COOCHIE MAN (live)** 59 –
(12"+=) *(BROX 167)* – (Don't need) Religion.

— LEMMY with **PHIL CAMPBELL** (b. 7 May'61, Pontypridd, Wales) – guitar / **WURZEL** (b. MICHAEL BURSTON, 23 Oct'49, Cheltenham, England) – guitar both replace ROBERTSON who joined FRANKIE MILLER BAND / **PETE GILL** (b.9 Jun'51, Sheffield, England) – drums (ex-SAXON) repl. TAYLOR

Aug 84. (7"/7"sha-pic-d) *(BRO/+P 185)* **KILLED BY DEATH. / UNDER THE KNIFE** 51 –
(12"+=) *(BROX 185)* – Under the knife (version).

Sep 84. (d-lp) *(PRO MOTOR 1)* **NO REMORSE** (compilation) 14
– Ace of spades / Motorhead / Jailbait / Stay clean / Killed by death / Bomber / Iron fist / Shine / Dancing on your grave / Metropolis / Snaggletooth / Overkill / Please don't touch / Stone dead forever / Like a nightmare / Emergency / Steal your face / Louie Louie / No class / Iron horse / (We are) The road crew / Leaving here / Locomotive. *(re-iss. 1988 on 'Castle' d-lp/c/cd+=; CLA LP/MC/CD 121)* – Too late, too late. *(re-iss. cd Aug96 on 'Essential'; ESDCD 371) (cd re-iss. Jul97; ESMCD 557)*

G.W.R. GWR-Profile

Jun 86. (7") *(GWR 2)* **DEAF FOREVER. / ON THE ROAD (live)** 67 –
(12"+=) *(GWT 2)* – Steal your face (live).

Aug 86. (lp/c/cd) *(GW LP/TC/CD 1) <1223>* **ORGASMATRON** 21 Nov86
– Deaf forever / Nothing up my sleeve / Ain't my crime / Claw / Mean machine / Built for speed / Riding with the driver / Doctor Rock / Orgasmatron. *(pic-lp.Aug89; GWPD 1) (re-iss. cd Mar92; CLACD 283)*

— **PHIL CAMPBELL** – drums returned to repl. GILL

Aug 87. (lp/c/cd) *(GW LP/MC/CD 14) <1240>* **ROCK'N'ROLL** 43 Oct87
– Rock'n'roll / Eat the rich / Blackheart / Stone deaf in the USA / The wolf / Traitor / Dogs / All for you / Boogeyman.

Nov 87. (7") *(GWR 6)* **EAT THE RICH. / CRADLE TO GRAVE**
(12"+=) *(GWR 6)* – Power.
(above from the soundtrack of the film 'Eat The Rich')

Oct 88. (lp/c/cd) *(GW LP/MC/CD 31)* **NO SLEEP AT ALL (live)** 79
– Dr. Rock / Stay clean / Traitor / Metropolis / Dogs / Ace of spades / Eat the rich / Built for speed / Deaf forever / Just cos you got the power / Killed by death / Overkill. *(cd+=)* – (3 extra). *(re-iss. cd Mar92 on 'Castle' cd/c; CLA CD/MC 285)*

Epic W.T.G.

Jan 91. (7"/7"sha-pic-d/c-s) *(656578-7/-0/-4)* **THE ONE TO SING THE BLUES. / DEAD MAN'S HAND** 45
(12"+=/cd-s+=) *(656578-6/-2)* – Eagle rock / Shut you down.

Jan 91. (cd/c/lp/pic-lp) *(467481-2/-4/-1) <46858>* **1916** 24 Mar91
– The one to sing the blues / I'm so bad (baby I don't care) / No voices in the sky / Going to Brazil / Nightmare – The dreamtime / Love me forever / Angel city / Make my day / Ramones / Shut you down / 1916.

— **TAYLOR** returned but was soon repl. by **MIKEY DEE** (b.31 Oct'63, Olundby, Sweden) – drums

Aug 92. (cd/c/lp) *(471723-2/-4/-1)* **MARCH OR DIE** 60
– Stand / Cat scratch fever / Bad religion / Jack the ripper / I ain't no nice guy / Hellraiser / Asylum choir / Too good to be true / You better run / Name in vain / March or die.

Nov 92. (12"ep/cd-ep) *(658809-6/-2)* **'92 TOUR (live)** 63
– Hellraiser / You better run / Going to Brazil / Ramones.

— Above 1st track co-written w / OZZY OSBOURNE

ZYX not iss.

Nov 93. (cd/lp) *(20263-2/-1)* **BASTARDS** – German –
– On your feet or on your knees / Burner / Death or glory / I am the sword / Born to raise hell / Don't let daddy kiss me / Bad woman / Liar / Lost in the ozone / I'm your man / We bring the shake / Devils.

Nov 94. (7"/c-s; by MOTORHEAD with ICE-T & WHITFIELD CRANE) *(74321 23915-7/-4)* **BORN TO RAISE HELL. / ('A'mix)** 47 –
(12"+=/cd-s+=) *(74321 23915-1/-2)* – ('A'mix).
(above from the movie, 'Airheads', on 'Fox-Arista' records)

S.P.V. C.M.C.

Apr 95. (cd/c/lp) *(SPV 085-7694-2/-4/-1) <86231>* **SACRIFICE**
– Sacrifice / Sex & death / Over your shoulder / War for war / Order – Fade to black / Dog-face boy / All gone to hell / Make 'em blind / Don't waste your time / In another time / Out of the sun.

Oct 96. (cd/c) *(SPV 085-1830-2/-4) <86207>* **OVERNIGHT SENSATION**
– Civil war / Crazy like a fox / I don't believe a word / Eat the gun / Overnight sensation / Love can't buy you money / Broken / Them not me / Murder show / Shake the world / Listen to your heart.

Mar 98. (cd) *(SPV 0851889-2) <86238>* **SNAKE BITE LOVE**
– Love for sale / Dogs of war / Snake bite love / Assassin / Take the blame / Dead and gone / Night side / Don't lie to me / Joy of labour / Desperate for you / Better off dead.

Mar 99. (d-cd) *(SPV 087-2114-2) <86268>* **EVERYTHING LOUDER THAN EVERYONE ELSE (live)**
– Iron fist / Stay clean / On your feet or on your knees / Over your shoulder / Civil war / Burner / Metropolis / Nothing up my sleeves / I'm so bad, baby I don't care / Chase I better than the catch / Take the blame / No class / Overnight sensation / Sacrifice / Born to raise hell / Lost in the ozone / One to sing the blues / Capricorn / Love for sale / Orgasmatron / Going to Brazil / Killed by death / Bomber / Ace of spades / Overkill.

May 00. (cd/lp) *(SPV 0852182-2/-1) <86292>* **WE ARE MOTORHEAD**
– See me burning / Slow dance / Stay out of jail / God save the Queen / Out to lunch / Wake the dead / One more fucking time / Stagefright – Crash & burn / (Wearing your) Heart on your sleeve / We are Motorhead.

Jul 00. (cd-s) *(SPV 0602184-3)* **GOD SAVE THE QUEEN / ONE MORE F**KING TIME / GOD SAVE THE QUEEN (enhanced video)** –

S.P.V. Metal-I

Apr 02. (cd/lp) *(SPV 0857/0787 406-2) <85229>* **HAMMERED**
– Walk a crooked mile / Down the line / Brave new world / Voices from the war / Mine all mine / Shut your mouth / Kill the world / Dr. Love / No remorse / Red raw / Serial killer. *(ltd-cd+=; SPV 0897 406-0)* – The game / Overnight sensation (live).

Jun 04. (cd) *(SPV 0856974-2) <85241>* **INFERNO**
– Terminal show / Killers / In the name of tragedy / Suicide / Life's a bitch / Down on me / In the black / Fight / In the year of the wolf / Keys to the kingdom / Smiling like a killer / Whorehouse blues. *(ltd-cd w/dvd+=; SPV 08769740)* – (videos & documentary).

– compilations, etc. –

Oct 79. (lp) *Liberty; (LBR 1004)* **ON PAROLE** 65 –
– Motorhead / On parole / Vibrator / Iron horse – Born to lose / City kids / Fools / The watcher / Leaving here / Lost Johnny. *(was to be have been released Dec75) (re-iss. May82 on 'Fame' lp/c; FA/TC-FA 3009) (cd-iss. Oct90; CD-FA 3251) (cd remastered Feb97 on 'EMI Gold'; CDGO 2070)*

Nov 80. (7"ep,7"blue-ep,7"pink-ep,7"orange-ep/12"ep,12"blue-ep,12"pink-ep,12"orange-ep) *Big Beatl (NS/SWT 61)* **BEER DRINKERS EP** 43 –
– Beer drinkers & hell raisers / On parole / Instro / I'm your witch doctor.

Mar 83. (lp/c) *Big Beat; (NED/+C 2)* **WHAT'S WORDS WORTH (live at the Roundhouse 18/2/78)** 71 –
– The watcher / Iron horse – Born to lose / On parole (in A) / White line fever / Keep us on the road / Leaving here / I'm your witchdoctor / The train kept a-rollin' / City kids. *(re-iss. Jan90; WIKM 49)*

Aug 82. (d-c) *Bronze; (3574 138)* **OVERKILL / BOMBER** –

Nov 84. (lp/c) *Astan; <2/4 0041>* **RECORDED LIVE (live)** –

Apr 86. (lp/c) *Raw Power; (RAW LP/MC 011)* **ANTHOLOGY** –
(cd-iss. Dec86; RAWCD 011)

Apr 86. (lp/c) *Dojo; (DOJO LP/TC 18)* **BORN TO LOSE** –

1986. (cd) *Legacy; (LLMCD 3004)* **ANTHOLOGY VOL.1** –

Apr 88. (lp/cd) *That's Original; (TFO LP/CD 8)* **OVERKILL / ANOTHER PERFECT DAY** –

1988. (3"cd-ep) *Special Edition; (CD3-10)* **ACE OF SPADES / BOMBER / MOTORHEAD / OVERKILL** –

Nov 89. (lp/cd) *Receiver; (RR LP/CD 120)* **BLITZKREIG ON BIRMINGHAM LIVE '77 (live)** –

Jan 90. (cd/lp) *Receiver; (RR CD/LP 123)* **DIRTY LOVE** –

Apr 90. (cd/d-lp) *Castle; (CCS CD/LP 237)* **WELCOME TO THE BEAR TRAP** –

Apr 90. (cd/c/d-lp) *That's Original; (TFO CD/MC/LP 024)* **BOMBER / ACE OF SPADES** –

Apr 90. (cd/c/lp) *G.W.R.; (GW CD/MC/LP 101)* **THE BIRTHDAY PARTY (live '85)** –
(cd+=) – (3 extra tracks). *(also on 'Roadrunner'; RR 9376-1)*

Jun 90. (cd/c/lp) *Receiver; (RR CD/MC/LP 130)* **LOCK UP YOUR DAUGHTERS (live 1977)** –

Jul 90. (cd) *Marble Arch; (cd)* **GRIND YA DOWN** –
(re-iss. Jul94 on 'Success';)

Jul 90. (cd/c) *Action Replay; (ARLC/CDAR 1014)* **THE BEST OF THE REST OF MOTORHEAD** –
(re-iss. Jul93 cd/c; CDAR/ARLC 1032)

Nov 90. (cd/c/lp) *Knight; (NEX CD/MC/LP 136)* **FROM THE VAULTS** –

Jul 91. (3xcd-box/3xlp-box) *Essential; (ESB CD/LP 146)* **MELTDOWN** –

Feb 92. (3xcd-box) *Castle; (CLABX 901)* **3 ORIGINALS** –
– (NO REMORSE / ACE OF SPADES / NO SLEEP 'TIL HAMMERSMITH)

Feb 92. (cd/lp) *Receiver; (RR CD/LP 005)* **LIVE JAILBAIT (live)** –

Sep 92. (cd/c/lp) *Roadrunner; (RR 9125-2/-4/-1)* **THE BEST OF MOTORHEAD** –

Apr 93. (c/cd) *Tring; (MC+/JHD 081)* **LIVE (live)** –

Jun 93. (4xcd-box) *Receiver; (RRZCD 501)* **MOTORHEAD BOX SET** –

Aug 93. (c-s/12"/cd-s) *W.G.A.F.; (MC/12/CD WGAF 101)* **ACE OF SPADES (THE C.C.N.remix). / ('A'mixes)** 23 –

Nov 93. (cd/c/lp) *Castle TV; (CTV CD/MC/LP 125)* **ALL THE ACES** –

Mar 94. (cd/c/lp) *Roadrunner; (RR 9009-2/-4/-1)* **LIVE AT BRIXTON ACADEMY (live)** –

Aug 94. (cd) *Spectrum; (550 724-2)* **ACES HIGH** –

Sep 94. (cd) *Cleopatra; (CLEO 94132)* **IRON FIST AND THE HORDES FROM HELL** –

May 95. (cd) *Spectrum; ()* **ULTIMATE METAL** –

Jul 95. (2xcd-box) *Griffin; (GCD 2192)* **FISTFUL OF ACES / THE BEST OF MOTORHEAD** –

Oct 95. (cd) *Elite; (ELITE 019CD)* **HEADBANGERS** –

Apr 96. (cd/c) *Hallmark; (30369-2/-4)* **MOTORHEAD – LIVE** –

Nov 96. (cd) *Emperio; (EMPRCD 692)* **LIVE** –

Nov 96. (cd) *Steamhammer; (CD 0857694-2)* **WE'RE MOTORHEAD AND WE'RE GONNA KICK YOUR ASS** –

Feb 97. (cd) *Receiver; (RRCD 238)* **STONE DEAD FOREVER** –

May 97. (d-cd) *Snapper; (SMDCD 127)* **TAKE NO PRISONERS** –

Jul 97. (cd) *Going For A Song; (GFS 073)* **MOTORHEAD** –

Aug 97. (4xcd-box) *Essential; (ESBCD 562)* **PROTECT THE INNOCENT** –

Nov 97. (cd) *Rialto; (RMCD 221)* **ARCHIVES** –

Mar 98. (cd/c) *Select-Castle; (SEL CD/MC 502)* **DEAF FOREVER – THE BEST OF MOTORHEAD** –

Apr 98. (cd) *Cleopatra; (<CLP 203>)* **THE SINGLES COLLECTION**

Apr 98. (cd) *King Biscuit; <(KBFHCD 002)>* **KING BISCUIT PRESENTS . . .**

Oct 98. (3xcd-box) *Essential; (ESMBX 304)* **OVERKILL / BOMBER / ACE OF SPADES**

Oct 98. (d-cd) *Essential; (ESSCD 668)* **ALL THE ACES – THE BEST OF MOTORHEAD / THE MUGGER'S TAPES**

Jun 99. (cd) *Cleopatra; <(CLP 0497-2)>* **GOLDEN YEARS: THE ALTERNATIVE VERSIONS** –

Jul 00. (cd) *S.P.V.; (06021843)* **GOD SAVE THE QUEEN** –

Aug 00. (d-cd/t-lp) *Metal-Is; (MIS DD/LP 002)* **THE BEST OF MOTORHEAD** 52 –

Oct 00. (cd; by LEMMY, SLIM JIM & DANNY B) *S.P.V.; (085-2198-2)* **LEMMY & SLIM JIM / DANNY B** –

Oct 00. (10xcd-box) *Raw Power; (RAWBX 140)* **BORN TO LOSE / LIVE TO WIN**

MOTT THE HOOPLE

Formed: Hereford, England . . . Jun '69 by OVEREND WATTS, DALE GRIFFIN, VERDEN ALLEN and MICK RALPHS, who were part of The SHAKEDOWN SOUND with singer STAN TIPPINS. With new manager and producer Guy Stevens placing an ad in a music paper, the group found a replacement frontman in IAN HUNTER (he had once guested on a 45 by CHARLIE WOLFE). Naming themselves MOTT THE HOOPLE (after a novel by Willard Manus), they signed to Chris Blackwell's burgeoning 'Island' label. Their eponymous debut gained a minor chart placing, the record introducing HUNTER's bluesy DYLAN-esque delivery over a tentative set of earthy rock'n'roll. Although three more lacklustre albums were completed in quick succession, the group split in 1972 after the last of them, 'BRAIN CAPERS' failed to match its predecessors' Top 50 status. Fortunately for them, a young DAVID BOWIE was re-establishing himself in the songwriting stakes, the ascending glamster offering the band a lifeline in the form of 'ALL THE YOUNG DUDES'. Securing a new contract with 'C.B.S.', MOTT THE HOOPLE roared into the UK Top 3 with a new lease of life, although VERDEN had departed soon after the recording of the similarily-titled hit parent album. Using the glam-rock craze as their launch pad, the band straddled the widening gap between the teen-pop market and the college circuit. A trio of Top 20 hits in 1973, 'HONALOOCHIE BOOGIE', 'ALL THE WAY FROM MEMPHIS' and 'ROLL AWAY THE STONE' proved that the group were no overnight sensations, although the last of these had been recorded without RALPHS who joined BAD COMPANY. Together with VERDEN's deputy MICK BOLTON, he was replaced by ARIEL BENDER and MORGAN FISHER, two veterans of the British music scene. Releasing 'THE HOOPLE' album as a follow-up to 1973's 'MOTT', the band once again hit the UK and US charts, although the critical tide was turning against glam and everyone connected with it (i.e. SWEET, SLADE, GLITTER, QUATRO, etc). With BENDER (aka LUTHER GROSVENOR) opting to join heavyweights WIDOWMAKER, the band (with ex-BOWIE sidekick, MICK RONSON, now taking on guitar duties) also opted for a harder-edged direction after a single, 'SATURDAY GIGS', failed to scrape into the Top 40. Suffering from exhaustion, HUNTER was eager to follow a less high-profile solo career, RONSON also taking the same route, the pair, in addition touring together as The HUNTER-RONSON BAND. The remainder (OVEREND, DALE and MORGAN) re-grouped in 1975 as MOTT, enlisting the services of new frontman NIGEL

BENJAMIN and guitarist RAY MAJORS for a new album, 'DRIVE ON'. Another uninspiring set, 'SHOUTING AND POINTING' was to appear in 1976, the band soon giving up amid general disinterest, although they did resurface as the more overtly hard-rockin' BRITISH LIONS.

• **Songwriters:** HUNTER or others wrote most except; YOU REALLY GOT ME (Kinks) / LAUGH AT ME (Sonny Bono) / CROSSROADS (Sir Douglas Quintet) / KEEP A KNOCKIN' (Little Richard) / WHOLE LOTTA SHAKIN' GOIN' ON (Jerry Lee Lewis) / LAY DOWN (Melanie) / COME ON BABY, LET'S GO DOWNTOWN (Crazy Horse) / YOUR OWN BACKYARD (Dion) / etc.

Album rating: MOTT THE HOOPLE (*6) / MAD SHADOWS (*5) / WILD LIFE (*4) / BRAIN CAPERS (*6) / ALL THE YOUNG DUDES (*7) / MOTT (*8) / THE HOOPLE (*7) / LIVE (*4) / DRIVE ON (*3) / SHOUTING AND POINTING (*2) THE BALLAD OF MOTT THE HOOPLE – A RETROSPECTIVE compilation (*8)

IAN HUNTER (b. 3 Jun'46, Shrewsbury, England) – vocals, guitar, piano / **MICK RALPHS** (b.31 May'44) – guitar, vocals / **VERDEN ALLEN** (b.26 May'44, Crynant, Neath, Wales) – organ / **OVEREND WATTS** (b.13 May'49, Birmingham, England) – bass, vocals / **DALE 'BUFFIN' GRIFFIN** (b.24 Oct'48, Hereford) – drums, vocals

Island / Atlantic

Oct 69. (7") *(WIP 6072)* **ROCK AND ROLL QUEEN. / ROAD TO BIRMINGHAM** [ ] [–]

Nov 69. (lp) *(ILPS 9108)* <8258> **MOTT THE HOOPLE** [66] [ ]
– You really got me / At the crossroads / Laugh at me / Backsliding fearlessly / Rock and roll queen / Rabbit foot and Toby time / Half Moon Bay / Wrath and wroll. *(cd-iss. Jul97 on 'Going For A Song'; GFS 065) (cd re-iss. Sep03 on 'Angel Air'+=; SJPCD 157)* – Ohio / Find your way (backtrack demo).

Jan 70. (7") **ROCK AND ROLL QUEEN. / BACKSLIDING FEARLESSLY** [–] [ ]

Sep 70. (lp) *(ILPS 9119)* <8272> **MAD SHADOWS** [48] [ ]
– Thunderbuck ram / No wheels to ride / You are one of us / Walkin' with a mountain / I can feel / Threads of iron / When my mind's gone.

Feb 71. (lp) *(ILPS 9144)* <8284> **WILDLIFE** [44] [ ]
– Whisky woman / Angel of 8th avenue / Wrong side of the river / Waterloo / Lay down / It must be love / Original mixed-up lad / Home is where I want to be / Keep a knockin'.

Sep 71. (lp) *(ILPS 9178)* <8304> **BRAIN CAPERS** [ ] [ ]
– Death maybe your Santa Claus / Darkness darkness / Your own backyard / Journey / Sweet Angeline / Wheel of the quivering meat conception / Second love / Moon upstairs.

Oct 71. (7") *(WIP 6105)* **MIDNIGHT LADY. / THE DEBT** [ ] [ ]

Dec 71. (7") *(WIP 6112)* **DOWNTOWN. / HOME IS WHERE I WANT TO BE** [ ] [ ]

C.B.S. / Columbia

Jul 72. (7") *(8271)* <45673> **ALL THE YOUNG DUDES. / ONE OF THE BOYS** [3] [37]

Sep 72. (lp/c) *(CBS/40 65184)* <31750> **ALL THE YOUNG DUDES** [21] Nov72 [89]
– Sweet Jane / Momma's little jewel / All the young dudes / Sucker / Jerkin' crocus / One of the boys / Soft ground / Ready for love – After lights / Sea diver. *(cd-iss. Aug98 on 'Columbia'; 491691-2)*

Jan 73. (7") <45754> **ONE OF THE BOYS. / SUCKER** [–] [96]

Mar 73. (7") <45784> **SWEET JANE. / JERKIN' CROCUS** [–] [ ]

— **MICK BOLTON** – keyboards filled in for departing VERDEN who went solo

May 73. (7") *(1530)* <45882> **HONALOOCHIE BOOGIE. / ROSE** [12] [ ]

Jul 73. (lp/c) *(CBS/40 69038)* <32425> **MOTT** [7] Aug73 [35]
– All the way from Memphis / Whizz kid / Hymn for the dudes / Honaloochie boogie / Violence / Drivin' sister / Ballad of Mott The Hoople (March 26, 1972 – Zurich) / I'm a Cadillac – El Camino Dolo Roso / I wish I was your mother. *(cd-iss. 1988 on 'Castle'; CLACD 138X) (cd-iss. Mar95 on 'Rewind'; 467402-2)*

Aug 73. (7") *(1764)* **ALL THE WAY FROM MEMPHIS. / BALLAD OF MOTT THE HOOPLE (MARCH 26, 1972 – ZURICH)** [10] [–]

Sep 73. (7") <45920> **ALL THE WAY FROM MEMPHIS. / I WISH I WAS YOUR MOTHER** [–] [ ]

— **ARIEL BENDER** (b. LUTHER GROSVENOR, 23 Dec'49, Evesham, England) – guitar (ex-SPOOKY TOOTH) replaced RALPHS who joined BAD COMPANY / **MORGAN FISHER** – keyboards (ex-LOVE AFFAIR) repl. BOLTON (above 2 with HUNTER, WATTS and GRIFFIN.)

Nov 73. (7") *(1895)* **ROLL AWAY THE STONE. / WHERE DO YOU ALL COME FROM** [8] [–]

Mar 74. (7") *(2177)* <46035> **THE GOLDEN AGE OF ROCK'N'ROLL. / REST IN PEACE** [16] May74 [96]

Mar 74. (lp/c) *(CBS/40 69062)* <32871> **THE HOOPLE** [11] Apr74 [28]
– The golden age of rock'n'roll / Marionette / Alice / Crash Street kidds / Born late '58 / Trudi's song / Pearl 'n' Roy (England) / Through the looking glass / Roll away the stone.

Apr 74. (7") <46076> **ROLL AWAY THE STONE. / THROUGH THE LOOKING GLASS** [–] [ ]

Jun 74. (7") *(2439)* **FOXY FOXY. / TRUDI'S SONG** [33] [–]

— **BLUE WEAVER** – organ on tour (ex-AMEN CORNER)

Nov 74. (lp/c) *(CBS/40 69093)* <33282> **LIVE** (live; Broadway – Nov73 / Hammersmith – May74) [32] [23]
– All the way from Memphis / Sucker / Rest in peace / All the young dudes / Walkin' with a mountain / Sweet Angeline / Rose / Medley:- (a) Jerkin' crocus – (b) One of the boys – (c) Rock'n'roll queen – (d) Get back – (e) Whole lotta shakin' – (f) Violence.

— **MICK RONSON** – guitar, vocals (Solo artist, ex-DAVID BOWIE; SPIDERS FROM MARS) repl. ARIEL who formed WIDOWMAKER

Oct 74. (7") *(2754)* **SATURDAY GIGS. / MEDLEY; JERKIN' CROCUS – SUCKER (live)** [41] [–]

Dec 74. (7") <10091> **ALL THE YOUNG DUDES (live). / ROSE** [–] [ ]

— Split Dec'74. HUNTER and RONSON formed duo and went solo.

MOTT

(OVEREND, DALE and **MORGAN**) were joined by **NIGEL BENJAMIN** – vocals (ex-ROYCE) / **RAY MAJORS** – guitar (ex-HACKENSHACK)

C.B.S. / Columbia

Aug 75. (7") *(3528)* **MONTE CARLO. / SHOUT IT ALL OUT** [ ] [ ]

Sep 75. (lp/c) *(CBS/40 69154)* <33705> **DRIVE ON** [45] [ ]
– By tonight / Monte Carlo / She does it / I'll tell you something / Stiff upper lip / Love now / Apologies / The great white wall / Here we are / It takes one to know one / I can show you how it is.

Oct 75. (7") *(3741)* **BY TONIGHT. / I CAN SHOW YOU HOW IT IS** [ ] [ ]

Feb 76. (7") *(4055)* **IT TAKES ONE TO KNOW ONE. / I'LL TELL YOU SOMETHING** [ ] [ ]

Jun 76. (lp/c) *(CBS/40 81289)* <34236> **SHOUTING AND POINTING** [ ] [ ]
– Shouting and pointing / Collision course / Storm / Career (no such thing as rock'n'roll) / Hold on, you're crazy / See you again / Too short arms (I don't care) / Broadside outcasts / Good times. *(cd-iss. Jan98 on 'Columbia'; SMDCD 312)*

– compilations, etc. –

Oct 72. (lp) *Island; (ILPS 9215) / Atlantic; <7297>* **ROCK'N'ROLL QUEEN** [ ] Jul74 [ ]

Feb 76. (7") *C.B.S.; (3963)* **ALL THE YOUNG DUDES. / ROLL AWAY THE STONE** [ ] [–]
(re-iss. Apr83 on 'Old Gold'; OG 9312)

Mar 76. (lp/c) *C.B.S.; (CBS/40 81225) <34368>* **GREATEST HITS** [ ] [ ]
– All the way from Memphis / Honaloochie boogie / Hymn for the dudes / Born late '58 / All the young dudes / Roll away the stone / Ballad of Mott The Hoople / Golden age of rock'n'roll / Foxy lady / Saturday gigs. *(re-iss. Jun81 lp/c; CBS/40 32007) (cd-iss. Apr89; CD 32007)*

Mar 81. (lp) *Island; (IRSP 8)* **TWO MILES FROM HEAVEN** [ ] [–]

Mar 81. (lp/c) *Hallmark; (SHM 3055)* **ALL THE WAY FROM MEMPHIS** [ ] [–]

Jul 84. (7") *C.B.S.; (A 4581)* **ALL THE YOUNG DUDES. / HONALOOCHIE BOOGIE** [ ] [–]

1988. (cd) *Castle; (CCSCD 174)* **THE COLLECTION** [ ] [–]

Jun 90. (cd) *Island; (IMCD 87)* **WALKING WITH A MOUNTAIN (BEST OF 1969-1972)** [ ] [ ]
– Rock and roll queen / At the crossroads / Thunderbuck ram / Whiskey woman / Waterflow / The Moon upstairs / Second love / The road to Birmingham / Black scorpio (mama's little jewel) / You really got me / Walking with a mountain / No wheels to ride / Keep a knockin' / Midnight lady / Death may be your Santa Claus / Darkness darkness / Growing man blues / Black hills.

Jun 92. (7"/c-s) *Columbia; (658177-7/-4)* **ALL THE YOUNG DUDES. / ONCE BITTEN TWICE SHY (by Ian Hunter)** [ ] [ ]
(cd-s+=) *(658177-2)* – Roll Away The Stone.

Dec 92. (cd) *Edsel; (EDCD 361)* **MOOT THE HOOPLE / MAD SHADOWS** [ ] [–]
Jun 93. (cd) *See For Miles; (SEECD 7)* **MOTT THE HOOPLE FEATURING STEVE HYAMS** [ ] [–]
Nov 93. (d-cd) *Legacy; (CD 46973)* **THE BALLAD OF MOTT THE HOOPLE – A RETROSPECTIVE** [ ] [–]
(re-iss. Jun96 on 'Coulmbia'; 474420-2)
Jun 96. (cd-s) *Old Gold; (126236380-2)* **ALL THE YOUNG DUDES / ONE OF THE BOYS** [ ] [–]
Jul 96. (cd) *Windsong; (WINCD 064)* **THE ORIGINAL MIXED UP KIDS – THE BBC SESSIONS 1970-71** [ ] [–]
Apr 97. (cd) *BR Music; (RM 1547)* **ALL THE YOUNG DUDES** [ ] [–]
Sep 98. (cd) *Spectrum; (554600-2)* **THE BEST OF MOTT THE HOOPLE – THE ISLAND YEARS 1969-1972** [ ] [–]
Nov 98. (cd) *Angel Air; (<SJPCD 029>)* **ALL THE WAY FROM STOCKHOLM TO PHILADELPHIA (live 1971-1972)** [ ] [ ]
Jun 99. (d-cd; by MOTT) *Angel Air; <(SJPCD 025)>* **LIVE OVER HERE AND OVER THERE 1975-1976** [ ] [ ]
Oct 99. (d-cd; with Various Artists) *Eagle; (EDGCD 104)* **FRIENDS AND RELATIVES** [ ] [–]
Apr 00. (cd; with Various Artists) *Connoisseur; (VSOPCD 283)* **MOTT THE HOOPLE FAMILY ALBUM** [ ] [–]
Jul 00. (cd) *Angel Air; <(SJPCD 061)>* **ROCK'N'ROLL CIRCUS (live in Wolverhampton 6/4/72)** [ ] [ ]
Jul 00. (cd; by MOTT) *Angel Air; <(SJPCD 054)>* **THE GOOSEBERRY SESSIONS AND RARITIES** [ ] [ ]
Sep 00. (d-cd) *Recall; (SMDCD 312)* **A TALE OF TWO CITIES** [ ] [–]
Sep 02. (cd) *Angel Air; (SJPCD 121)* **HOOPLING (BEST OF LIVE)** [ ] [–]

— In Feb'80, MOTT THE HOOPLE tracks were included on double album 'SHADES OF IAN HUNTER – THE BALLAD OF IAN HUNTER & MOTT THE HOOPLE' on 'CBS'; *(88476)*

□ Bob MOULD (see under ⇒ HUSKER DU)

the MOVE

Formed: Birmingham, England ... early 1966 by ROY WOOD, CARL WAYNE, TREVOR BURTON, ACE KEFFORD and BEV BEVAN. By that summer, they had found manager Tony Secunda, who helped them sign to 'Deram'. Early the next year, their debut 45, 'NIGHT OF FEAR' (based on the 1812 Overture), had crashed into the UK Top 3. After another Top 5 hit, their third single, 'FLOWERS IN THE RAIN' (the first record to be played on the newly launched BBC Radio 1), was another to make the Top 3 in October '67 on the recently formed 'Regal Zonophone' label. Their fourth successive Top 5 hit arrived in early '68 with 'FIRE BRIGADE', quickly followed by the Top 20 self-titled album. The aforementioned singles were, for the most part, classy bubblegum psychedelia penned by the multi-talented WOOD. After a surprise flop, they scored their first No.1 early in '69 with the single, 'BLACKBERRY WAY'. They never emulated this, WOOD becoming increasingly involved with his new project, The ELECTRIC LIGHT ORCHESTRA, in 1970. He subsequently departed, JEFF LYNNE taking over the leadership, while he ended The MOVE on a high-note in mid-'72 with the Top 10 hit, 'CALIFORNIA MAN'. Remaining at 'Harvest' records, WOOD formed the 50's pastiche rock'n'roll/glam outfit, WIZZARD (the band making their live debut at Wembley's Rock'n'roll festival in June '72). They hit the Top 10 with their first 45, 'BALL PARK INCIDENT', following it with two chart toppers, 'SEE MY BABY JIVE' and 'ANGEL FINGERS'. Around the same time (mid-'73), WOOD disgarded his WIZZARD attire (tartan troosers, multi-coloured robe, tooped with face-paint and a multi-coloured hair-do), entering the album charts with his solo (in every sense of the word), 'BOULDERS' album. He continued to work on both projects simultaneously, scoring many Top 20 chart hits. Following his signing to the 'Jet' label in 1975, the hits (bar a few minor ones) duly dried up.

• **Covered;** LOVELY RITA + POLYTHENE PAM (Beatles). • **Trivia:** ROY also produced and wrote for DARTS, etc.

Album rating: THE MOVE (*7) / SHAZAM! (*9) / LOOKING ON (*5) / MESSAGE FROM THE COUNTRY (*7) / GREAT MOVE! THE BEST OF THE MOVE compilation (*8) / Roy Wood: BOULDERS (*7) / MUSTARD (*7) / ON THE ROAD AGAIN (*5) / STARTING UP (*4) / THROUGH THE YEARS – THE BEST OF ROY WOOD compilation (*7) / Wizzard: WIZZARD BREW (*4) / INTRODUCING EDDY & THE FALCONS (*5) / SUPER ACTIVE WIZZO (*4)

ROY WOOD (b. ULYSSES ADRIAN WOOD, 8 Nov'46) – guitar, vocals (ex-MIKE SHERIDAN & NIGHTRIDERS, ex-GERRY LEVENE & THE AVENGERS) / **TREVOR BURTON** (b. 9 Mar'44) – guitar, vox (ex-DANNY KING & THE MAYFAIR SET) / **CARL WAYNE** (b.18 Aug'44) – vocals (ex-CARL WAYNE & THE VIKINGS) / **CHRIS "ACE" KEFFORD** (b.10 Dec'46) – bass, vox (ex-CARL WAYNE & THE VIKINGS) / **BEV BEVAN** (b.24 Nov'44) – drums (ex-CARL WAYNE & THE VIKINGS, ex-DENNY LAINE & THE DIPLOMATS)

Deram / Deram

Dec 66. (7") *(DM 109) <7504>* **NIGHT OF FEAR. / THE DISTURBANCE** [2] [ ]
Apr 67. (7") *(DM 117) <7506>* **I CAN HEAR THE GRASS GROW. / WAVE THE FLAG, STOP THE TRAIN** [5] [ ]

Regal Zonophone / A&M

Sep 67. (7") *(RZ 3001)* **FLOWERS IN THE RAIN. / (HERE WE GO ROUND) THE LEMON TREE** [2] [–]
Feb 68. (7") *(RZ 3005)* **FIRE BRIGADE. / WALK UPON THE WATER** [3] [ ]
Mar 68. (lp; stereo/mono) *(S+/LRZ 1002)* **THE MOVE** [15] [–]
– Yellow rainbow / Kilroy was here / (Here we go round) The lemon tree / Weekend / Walk upon the water / Flowers in the rain / Useless information / Zing went the strings of my heart / The girl outside / Fire brigade / Mist on a Monday morning / Cherry blossom clinic. *(cd-iss. Nov92 & Feb98 on 'Repertoire'+=; REP 4690)* – Night of fear / The disturbance / I can hear the grass grow / Wave the flag, stop the train / Vote for me / (+ 3 others).

— quartet, (**BURTON** – bass, vocals) when KEFFORD formed ACE KEFFORD STAND

Jul 68. (7") *(RZ 3012)* **WILD TIGER WOMAN. / OMNIBUS** [ ] [–]
Sep 68. (7"ep) *(TRZ 2001)* **SOMETHING ELSE FROM THE MOVE** [ ] [–]
– Stephanie knows who / So you want to be a rock 'n' roll star / Something else / It'll be me / Sunshine help me.
Sep 68. (7") *<966>* **SOMETHING. / YELLOW RAINBOW** [–] [ ]

— added **RICHARD TANDY** – hapsicord, keyboards (of The UGLYS)

Jan 69. (7") *(RZ 3015) <1020>* **BLACKBERRY WAY. / SOMETHING** [1] [ ]

— **RICK PRICE** (b.10 Jun'44) – bass (ex-SIGHT'N'SOUND) repl. BURTON + TANDY whom became part of The UGLYS

Aug 69. (7") *(RZ 3021) <1119>* **CURLY. / THIS TIME TOMORROW** [12] [ ]
Feb 70. (lp) *(SLRZ 1012) <SP 4259>* **SHAZAM** [ ] [ ]
– Hello Susie / Beautiful daughter / Cherry blossom clinic revisted / Fields of people / Don't make my baby blue / The last thing on my mind. *(re-iss. 1982 on 'Cube';) (cd-iss. Mar93 & Nov00 on 'Repertoire' +=; REP 4691)* – Stephanie knows who / So you want to be a rock'n'roll star / Something else / It'll be me / Sunshine help me.

— now trio of **WOOD, PRICE + BEVAN** (WAYNE became a cabaret singer)

Mar 70. (7") *(RZ 3026) <1197>* **BRONTOSAURUS. / LIGHTNING NEVER STRIKES TWICE** [7] [ ]

— added **JEFF LYNNE** (b.30 Dec'47) – vocals, guitar, keys (ex-IDLE RACE)

Fly / Capitol

Sep 70. (7") *(BUG 2)* **WHEN ALICE COMES BACK TO THE FARM. / WHAT?** [ ] [ ]
Oct 70. (lp) *(HIFLY 1) <ST 658>* **LOOKING ON** [ ] [ ]
– Looking on / Turkish tram conductor blues / What? / When Alice comes back to the farm / Open up said the world at the door / Brontosaurus / Feel too good. *(cd-iss. Mar93 & Nov00 on 'Repertoire'+=; REP 4692)* – Blackberry way / Something / Curly / This time tomorrow / Lightning never strikes twice.

Harvest / Capitol

May 71. (7"; unissued) *(HAR 5036)* **ELLA JAMES. / NO TIME** [–] [–]
Jun 71. (7") *(HAR 5038) <3126>* **TONIGHT. / DON'T MESS ME UP** [11] [ ]

Jul 71. (lp) *(SHSP 4013)* <*ST 811*> **MESSAGE FROM THE COUNTRY**
– Message from the country / Ella James / No time / Don't mess me up / Until your moma's gone / It wasn't my idea to dance / The minister / Ben Crawley Steel Company / The words of Aaron / My Marge. *(cd-iss. Jul94 on 'Beat Goes On'; BGOCD 238) (cd re-iss. Sep01 on 'E.M.I.'+=; 535212-2)* – Tonight / Chinatown / Down on the bay / Do ya / California man / Don't mess me up / Words of Aaron / Do ya (BBC version).

Harvest U.A.

Oct 71. (7") *(HAR 5043)* <*50876*> **CHINATOWN. / DOWN ON THE BAY** 23

— (Aug'71) now a trio when RICK PRICE left to go solo. The other three (WOOD, LYNNE and BEVAN) continued with The MOVE although they formed ELECTRIC LIGHT ORCHESTRA. The MOVE made one more single below before ROY WOOD also undertook solo career and formed WIZZARD.

May 72. (7"m) *(HAR 5050)* <*50928*> **CALIFORNIA MAN. / DO YA / ELLA JAMES** 7

– (selective) compilations, etc. –

Mar 71. (lp) *Fly; (TON 3)* **THE BEST OF THE MOVE** –
(cd-iss. Nov00 on 'Repertoire'; REP 4686)

Sep 74. (7") *Harvest; (HAR 5086) / United Artists; <50928>* **DO YA. / NO TIME** Oct72 93

Oct 74. (lp) *Harvest; (SHSP 4035)* **CALIFORNIA MAN** –

Mar 91. (cd/c) *Music Club; (MC CD/TC 009)* **THE BEST OF THE MOVE** –

Mar 95. (cd) *Band Of Joy; (BOJCD 011)* **THE BBC SESSIONS** –
(re-iss. Jul98 on 'Strange Fruit'; SFRSCD 69)

Oct 99. (d-cd) *Repertoire; (REP 4665)* **SINGLES A'S & B'S**

Oct 00. (cd) *Metro; (METRCD 031)* **THE VERY BEST OF THE MOVE**

May 01. (cd) *Disky; (SI 64613-2)* **FLOWERS IN THE RAIN** –

Jun 03. (3xcd-box) *Westside; (WESX 302)* **MOVEMENTS: 30th ANNIVERSARY ANTHOLOGY** –

ROY WOOD

in two bands (MOVE and ELO) had also gone solo. ROY played mostly every instrument himself.

Harvest U.A.

Feb 72. (7") *(HAR 5058)* **WHEN GRAN'MA PLAYS THE BANJO. / WAKE UP**

— ROY WOOD solo (although he continued with his new band WIZZARD, see below)

Jun 73. (lp) *(SHVL 803)* <*VALA 168*> **BOULDERS** 15
– Songs of praise / Wake up / Rock down low / Nancy sing me a song / Dear Elaine / a) All the way over the hill, b) Irish loafer (and his hen) / Miss Clarke and the computer / When gran'ma plays the banjo / Rock medley: a) Rockin' shoes, b) She's too good for me, c) Locomotive. *(re-iss. Oct77; RI 2021) (cd-iss. Mar94 on 'Beat Goes On'; BGOCD 219)*

Sep 73. (7") *(HAR 5074)* **DEAR ELAINE. / SONGS OF PRAISE** 18

Nov 73. (7") *(HAR 5078)* **FOREVER. / MUSIC TO COMMIT SUICIDE BY** 8

Jun 74. (7") *(HAR 5083)* **GOING DOWN THE ROAD. / THE PREMIUM BOND THEME** 13

Jet U.A.

May 75. (7") *(JET 754)* **OH WHAT A SHAME. / BENGAL JIM** 13

Nov 75. (7") *(JET 761)* **LOOK THRU' THE EYES OF A FOOL. / STRIDER**

Dec 75. (lp) *(JETLP 12)* <*LA 575*> **MUSTARD**
– Mustard / Any old time will do / The rain came down on everything / You sure got it now / Why does such a pretty girl sing those sad songs / The song / Look thru' the eyes of a fool / Interlude / Get on down home / Rock'n'roll winter. *(re-iss. as 'THE WIZZARD – ROY WOOD')*

Mar 76. (7"; as ROY WOOD'S WIZZARD) *(JET 768)* **INDIANA RAINBOW. / THE THING IS THIS (THIS IS THE THING)** –

May 76. (7") *(JET 785)* **ANY OLD TIME WILL DO. / THE RAIN CAME DOWN ON EVERYTHING** –

May 76. (7") **ANY OLD TIME WILL DO. / WHY DOES SUCH A PRETTY GIRL SING THOSE SAD SONGS** –

— In Oct77, ROY WOOD made a duo single with ANNIE HASLAM of RENAISSANCE 'I NEVER BELIEVED IN LOVE. / INSIDE MY LIFE'. (from HASLAM's lp 'ANNIE IN WONDERLAND')

WIZZARD

(were formed August 1972 by **ROY WOOD** with **RICK PRICE**, plus other ex-MONGREL musicians) **CHARLIE GRIMA** – drums and **KEITH SMART** – drums also **HUGH McDOWELL** – cello and **BILL HUNT** – keyboards (both ex-ELO) and **NICK PENTELOW** – saxophone and **MICK BURNEY** – saxophone (ex-DALTONS)

Harvest U.A.

Nov 72. (7") *(HAR 5062)* **BALL PARK INCIDENT. / THE CARLSBERG SPECIAL** 6

Apr 73. (7") *(HAR 5070)* **SEE MY BABY JIVE. / BEND OVER BEETHOVEN** 1

Apr 73. (lp) *(SHSP 4025)* <*LA 042*> **WIZZARD BREW** 29
– You can dance the rock & roll / Meet me at the jailhouse / Jolly cup of tea / Buffalo station – Get down to Memphis / Gotta crush / Wear a fast gun.

Aug 73. (7") *(HAR 5076)* **ANGEL FINGERS. / YOU GOT THE JUMP ON ME** 1

— (Sep73) trimmed slightly when McDOWELL returned to ELECTRIC LIGHT ORCH. (Nov73) **BOB BRADY** – keyboards (ex-APPLEJACKS) repl. HUNT

Nov 73. (7") *(HAR 5173)* **I WISH IT COULD BE CHRISTMAS EVERY DAY. / ROB ROY'S NIGHTMARE** 4

Warners U.A.

Apr 74. (7") *(K 16357)* **ROCK'N'ROLL WINTER. / DREAM OF UNWIN** 6

Aug 74. (7") *(K 16434)* **THIS IS THE STORY OF MY LOVE (BABY). / MIXTURE** 34

Aug 74. (lp) *(K 56029)* <*LA 219*> **INTRODUCING EDDY AND THE FALCONS** 19
– (intro) / Eddy's rock / Brand new '88' / You got me runnin' / I dun lotsa cryin' over you / This is the story of my love / Everyday I wonder / Crazy jeans / Come back Karen / We're gonna rock & roll tonight.

Oct 74. (7") *(K 16466)* **YOU'VE GOT ME RUNNIN'. / IT'S JUST MY IMAGINATION**

Dec 74. (7") *(K 16497)* **ARE YOU READY TO ROCK. / MARATHON MAN** 8

— (Feb75) **WOOD** was just left with **PRICE** and **BURNEY**, and sessioners (BRADY joined FAIRPORT CONVENTION) (SMART joined ROCKIN BERRIES)

Jet not iss

Oct 75. (7") *(JET 758)* **RATTLESNAKE ROLL. / CAN'T HELP MY FEELINGS** –

ROY WOOD'S WIZZO BAND

(**ROY** only retained stalwart **RICK PRICE** now on pedal steel) also **GRAHAM GALLERY** – bass / **DAVE DONOVAN** – drums / **PAUL ROBBINS** – keyboards **BILLY PAUL** – alto sax / **BOB WILSON** – trombone

Warners Warne

Aug 77. (7") *(WB 16961)* **THE STROLL. / JUBILEE**

Sep 77. (lp) *(K 56388)* <*3065*> **SUPERACTIVE WIZZO**
– Life is wonderful / Waitin' at the door / Another wrong night / Sneakin' Giant footsteps (jubilees) / Earthrise.

ROY WOOD

Feb 78. (7") *(K 17094)* **DANCIN' AT THE RAINBOW'S END. / WAITING AT THE DOOR** –

Nov 78. (7") *(K 17248)* **KEEP YOUR HANDS ON THE WHEEL. / JUBILEE** –

May 79. (7"/7"pic-d) *(K/KP 17459)* **(WE'RE) ON THE ROAD AGAIN. / SAXMANIACS** –

Aug 79. (lp) *(BSK 3247)* **ON THE ROAD AGAIN**
– (We're) On the road again / Wings over the sea / Keep your hands o the wheel / Colourful lady / Road rocket / Backtown sinner / Jimmy lad Dancin' at the rainbow's end / Another night / Way beyond the rain.

ROY WOOD'S HELICOPTERS

with **MIKE DEACON** (ex-DARTS) / + members of RENAISSANCE & MAGNUM

Cheapskate not is

Nov 80. (7") *(CHEAP 6)* **GIVIN' YOUR HEART AWAY. / ROCK CITY** –

E.M.I. not is

Mar 81. (7") *(EMI 5156)* **GREEN GLASS WINDOWS. / DRIVING SONG** –

ROY WOOD

Jun 81. (7") *(EMI 5203)* **DOWN TO ZERO. / OLYMPIC FLYER** -
Jan 82. (7") *(EMI 5261)* **IT'S NOT EASY. / MOONRISER** -

Cheapskate not iss.

Dec 82. (7") *(CHEAP 12)* **SING OUT THE OLD. / WATCH THIS SPACE** -

Legacy not iss.

May 85. (7"/12") *(LGY/+T 24)* **UNDERFIRE. / ON TOP OF THE WORLD** -
Nov 85. (7"/12") *(LGY/+T 32)* **SING OUT THE OLD . . . BRING IN THE NEW. / ('A'instrumental)** -
Oct 86. (7") *(LGY 53)* **RAINING IN THE CITY. / ('A'instrumental)** -
Feb 87. (lp/c) *(LLP/LLK 106)* **STARTING UP** -
– Red cars are after me / Raining in the city / Under fire / Turn your body to the light / Hot cars / Starting up / Keep it steady / On top of the world / Ships in the night. *(cd-iss. May93 on 'Castle'; CLACD 387)*

— WOOD had earlier (late '86) featured on DOCTOR & THE MEDICS Top 50 version of ABBA's 'Waterloo'.

Woody not iss.

Dec 95. (c-s/cd-s; as The ROY WOOD BIG BAND) *(WOODY 001 CD/MC)* **I WISH IT COULD BE CHRISTMAS EVERYDAY /** -

— late in 2000, ROY returned to the UK charts (albeit alongside the WOMBLES) with the song, 'I WISH IT COULD BE A WOMBLING CHRISTMAS'

– (selective WOOD) compilations, etc. –

Apr 76. (d-lp) *Harvest; (SHDW 408)* **THE ROY WOOD STORY** (solo unless stated) -
– Ball park incident (WIZZARD) / Until you moma's gone / Dear Elaine / Ella James (MOVE) / First movement (ELECTRIC LIGHT ORCHESTRA) / California man (MOVE) / Whisper in the night / Chinatown (MOVE) / You can dance your rock'n'roll / Forever / Angel fingers (WIZZARD) / Look at me now (ELECTRIC LIGHT ORCHESTRA) / Tonight (MOVE) / See me baby jive (WIZZARD). *(re-iss. 1979 as 'YOU CAN DANCE THE ROCK'N'ROLL (THE ROY WOOD YEARS 1971-73)' lp/c; SHSM/TC-SHSM 2030) (re-iss. Jul89; CZ 177)* – Wake up / It wasn't my idea to dance / Nancy, sing me a song / Songs of praise.
Jul 82. (lp) *Speed; (SPEED 1000)* **THE SINGLES** (all his bands' work) 37 -
– See my baby jive / Are you ready to rock / Oh what a shame / Fire brigade / Forever / I can hear the grass grow / O.T.T. / Blackberry way / Angel fingers / We're on the road again / Flowers in the rain / Green grass windows / Keep your hands on the wheel / Rock & roll winter / This is the story of my love (baby).
Oct 96. (cd) *EMI Gold; (CDGOLD 1070)* **THROUGH THE YEARS**
Nov 97. (cd) *Rialto; (RMCD 219)* **ROY WOOD & WIZZARD ARCHIVE** -
Sep 99. (d-cd) *Repertoire; (REP 4744)* **EXOTIC MIXTURE**
Aug 01. (cd) *Armoury; (ARMCD 44)* **ROY WOOD & WIZZARD** -

□ the MOVING SIDEWALKS (see under ⇒ ZZ TOP)

MUDHONEY

Formed: Seattle, Washington, USA ... 1988 by MARK ARM (vocals, guitar), STEVE TURNER (guitar), MATT LUKIN (bass) and DAN PETERS (drums). A band boasting impeccable credentials, ARM and TURNER had both graduated from the seminal GREEN RIVER (and The THROWN UPS), while LUKIN had previously been a member of Seattle noisemongers, The MELVINS. With as much a claim to the 'Godfathers of Grunge' crown as labelmates NIRVANA, MUDHONEY released the definitive 'Sub Pop' single in 1988 with 'TOUCH ME I'M SICK'. Arguably one of the few tracks to ever match the primal howl of The STOOGES, the single was a revelation, a cathartically dumb three chord bludgeon with ARM shrieking over the top like a man who was, erm, very sick indeed. A mini-album followed shortly after, the wonderfully titled 'SUPERFUZZ BIGMUFF' (rather disappointingly named after STEVE TURNER's favourite effects pedals, apparently). Visceral, dirty, fuzz-drenched rock'n'roll, this was one of the seminal records of the 80's and the blueprint for "grunge", a term that would later become bastardised to represent a glut of snooze-worthy, sub-metal toss. There was also a deep, underlying sense of unease and melancholy to these songs (especially 'NO ONE HAS' and 'NEED') that gave MUDHONEY an edge over most of their contemporaries, a subsequent cover of SONIC YOUTH'S 'HALLOWEEN' (released as a split single with SONIC YOUTH covering 'TOUCH ME..') sounding positively evil. Given all this, then, the debut album proper, 'MUDHONEY', was regarded as something of a disappointment when it was finally released in late '89. Nevertheless, 'THIS GIFT' and 'HERE COMES SICKNESS' were worth the price of admission alone. By summer '91, MUDHONEY had modified their sound somewhat, releasing the 'LET IT SLIDE' EP as a taster for the forthcoming 'EVERY GOOD BOY DESERVES FUDGE' album (a UK Top 40 hit). The intensity of the EP harked back to 'SUPERFUZZ..', this time with more of a retro garage-punk feel on the blistering 'PAPERBACK LIFE' and 'OUNCE OF DECEPTION'. The album continued in this direction, adding funky (in the loosest sense of the term) hammond organ and harmonica to the mutant guitar buzz. Hell, they even came close to a pop song with 'GOOD ENOUGH'. Following a financial dispute with 'Sub Pop', MUDHONEY followed NIRVANA into the big league, signing with 'Reprise' and releasing the lacklustre 'PIECE OF CAKE' (1992). Having sold their souls to the corporate 'devil', it seemed MUDHONEY had had the life sucked out of them, the rough edges smoothed into a major production gloss. The mini-album, 'FIVE DOLLAR BOB'S MOCK COOTER STEW' (1993) was an improvement but it took Seattle legend, Jack Endino to summon forth the raw spontaneity of old on 'MY BROTHER THE COW' (1995), a return to form of sorts, notably on 'INTO YOUR SCHTIK' and 'GENERATION SPOKESMODEL'. MUDHONEY subsequently took a few years hiatus in which ARM went on tour with his side-project, BLOODLOSS, while TURNER continued with his label, 'Super-Electro' (MUDHONEY were allowed dual output for the imprint) and PETERS guested for solo MIKE JOHNSON (DINOSAUR JR). In the Autumn of '98, the quartet were back once again, although the album, TOMORROW HIT TODAY', disappointed most of their hardcore fanbase. Recorded in just over a week, emboldened by blasts of neo-free jazz horns and adrenalised by an undertow of twisted gutter-funk, 'SINCE WE'VE BECOME TRANSLUCENT' (2002) was the sound of MUDHONEY rediscovering that mutant garage gene that made them so seminal in the first place. The only 'Sub Pop' originals still kicking out the jams, MUDHONEY – much like PRIMAL SCREAM – have never given up on the transgressive power of rock'n'roll, and MARK ARM is about the only frontman around who barks with as much malice as BOBBY GILLESPIE. 'UNDER A BILLION SUNS' (2006) still found them spitting venomous sludge, if tending to favour mid-tempo workouts over breakneck garage-punk. And on the lyrical evidence of laments like 'I SAW THE LIGHT' and 'HARD-ON FOR WAR', ARM's exasperation with human folly was just as acidic, a political awakening hardly unique for the times but welcome all the same.

• **Covers:** HATE THE POLICE (Dicks) / EVOLUTION (Spacemen 3) / OVER THE TOP (Motorhead) / PUMP IT UP (Elvis Costello) / TONIGHT I THINK I'M GONNA GO DOWNTOWN (Jimmie Dale Gilmore) / BUCKSKIN STALLION BLUES (Townes Van Zandt). MARK ARM solo:- MASTERS OF WAR (Bob Dylan).

Album rating: SUPERFUZZ BIGMUFF mini (*7) / MUDHONEY (*6) / BOILED BEEF & ROTTING TEETH (*6) / EVERY GOOD BOY DESERVES FUDGE

(*7) / PIECE OF CAKE (*5) / MY BROTHER THE COW (*5) / TOMORROW TODAY (*5) / MARCH TO FUZZ compilation (*7) / SINCE WE'VE BECOME TRANSLUCENT (*6) / UNDER A BILLION SUNS (*7)

MARK ARM (b.MARK McLAUGHLIN, 21 Feb'62, California) – vocals, guitar (ex-GREEN RIVER, ex-THROWN UPS) / **STEVE TURNER** (b.28 Mar'65, Houston, Texas) – guitar (ex-GREEN RIVER, ex-THROWN UPS) / **MATT LUKIN** (b.16 Aug'64, Aberdeen, Washington) – bass (ex-MELVINS) / **DAN PETERS** (b.18 Aug'67) – drums

Glitterhouse | Sub Pop

Aug 88. (7",7"brown) *<SP 18>* **TOUCH ME I'M SICK. / SWEET YOUNG THING AIN'T SWEET NO MORE** [–] [ ]

Oct 88. (12"ep) *(GR 0034) <SP 21>* **SUPERFUZZ BIGMUFF** [ ] [ ]
– No one has / If I think / In 'n' out of grace / Need / Chain that door / Mudride. *(cd-iss. Mar00; same as US)*

Jan 89. (7",7"clear) *<SP 26>* **('A'side by 'Sonic Youth'). / TOUCH ME I'M SICK** [–] [ ]

Jun 89. (7",7"white) *(GR 060) <SP 33>* **YOU GOT IT (KEEP IT OUTTA MY FACE). / BURN IT CLEAN / NEED (demo)** [ ] [ ]
(re-iss. May93; same)

Oct 89. (7",7"purple,12") *(GR 0070) <SP 44AA>* **THIS GIFT. / BABY HELP ME FORGET / REVOLUTION** [ ] [ ]
(re-iss. May93; same)

Oct 89 (lp/c/cd) *(GR 0069) <SP 44/+A/B>* **MUDHONEY** [ ] [ ]
– This gift / Flat out f***ed / Get into yours / You got it / Magnolia caboose babyshit / Come to mind / Here comes sickness / Running loaded / The further I go / By her own hand / When tomorrow hits / Dead love. *(cd re-iss. Mar00; same as US)*

Jun 90. (7",7"pink) *(GR 0102) <SP 63>* **YOU'RE GONE. / THORN / YOU MAKE ME DIE** [60] [ ]
(re-iss. May93; same)

Sub Pop | Sub Pop

Jul 91. (7",12"grey) *(SP 15154) <SP 95>* **LET IT SLIDE. / OUNCE OF DECEPTION / CHECKOUT TIME** [60] [ ]
(cd-s+=) *(SP 95B)* – Paperback life / The money will roll right in.

Aug 91. (lp/c/cd) *<(SP 160/+A/B)>* **EVERY GOOD BOY DESERVES FUDGE** [34] [ ]
– Generation genocide / Let it slide / Good enough / Something so clear / Thorn / Into the drink / Broken hands / Who you drivin' now / Move out / Shoot the Moon / Fuzzgun '91 / Poking around / Don't fade IV / Check out time.

1991. (7") *<scale 36>* **MOD SHOWDOWN!** [–] [ ]
– She's just fifteen / (track by HALO OF FLIES)
(above issued on 'Amphetamine Reptile' + below on 'eMpTy')

1991. (7") *<MT 166>* **YOU STUPID ASSHOLE. / (w/ Gas HUFFER)** [–] [ ]

—— MARK + STEVE took up time in MONKEYWRENCH, and DAN joined SCREAMING TREES, after below album.

Warners | Reprise

Oct 92. (7"/c-s) *(W 0137/+C)* **SUCK YOU DRY. / DECEPTION PASS** [65] [–]
(12"+=/cd-s+=) *(W 0137 T/CD)* – Underride / Over the top.

Oct 92. (cd/c) *<(4509 90073-2/-4)>* **PIECE OF CAKE** [39] [ ]
– No end in sight / Make it now / Suck you dry / Blinding sun / Thirteenth floor opening / Youth body expression explosion / I'm spun / Take me there / Living wreck / Let me let you down / Ritzville / Acetone.

Jan 93. (cd-ep) *<40741>* **BLINDING SUN / DECEPTION PASS / KING SANDBOX / BABY O BABY** [–] [ ]

Oct 93. (m-cd/m-c/m-lp) *<(9362 45439-2/-4)>* **FIVE DOLLAR BOB'S MOCK COOTER STEW** [ ] [ ]
– In the blood / No song III / Between you & me kid / Six two one / Make it now again / Deception pass / Underide.

—— In Mar'94, MUDHONEY released a collab with JIMMIE DALE GILMOUR; 7"yellow/cd-ep 'BUCKSKIN STALLION BLUES' for 'Sub Pop' *(SP 124/305/+CD)* Also a single, 'PUMP IT UP, was released by 'Fox' in April '94

Reprise | Reprise

Mar 95. (cd/c/lp) *<(9362 45840-2/-4/-1)>* **MY BROTHER THE COW** [70] [ ]
– Judgement, rage, retribution and thyme / Generation spokesmodel / What moves the heart? / Today, is a good day / Into yer schtik / In my finest suit / F.D.K. (Fearless Doctor KIllers) / Orange ball-pen hammer / Crankcase blues / Execution style / Dissolve / 1995.

Apr 95. (7") *(SE 708)* **INTO YOUR SCHTIK. / YOU GIVE ME THE CREEPS** [ ] [ ]
(above single on 'Super Electro')

May 95. (7"colrd/c-s) *(W 0292/+C)* **GENERATION SPOKESMODEL. / NOT GOING DOWN THAT ROAD AGAIN** [ ] [ ]
(cd-s+=) *(W 0292CD)* – What moves the heart live) / Judgement, rage, retribution and thyme (live).

Amphetam. Reptile | Amphetam. Reptile

Aug 95. (7") *<scale 76>* **GOAT CHEESE. / (w/ Strapping Fieldhands)** [–] [ ]
(above on 'Amphetamine Reptile' and below on 'Super Electro')

May 98. (ltd-7") *(SE 716)* **NIGHT OF THE HUNTED. / BRAND NEW FACE** [ ] [ ]

Sep 98. (cd) *<(9362 47054-2)>* **TOMORROW HIT TODAY** [ ] [ ]
– A thousand forms of mind / I have to laugh / Oblivion / Try to be kind / Poisoned water / Real low vibe / This is the life / Night of the hunted / Move with the wind / Ghost / I will fight no more forever / Beneath the valley of the underdog.

—— MATT LUKIN departed in '99; GUY MADDISON – bass (replaced him)

Sub Pop | Sub Pop

Aug 02. (lp/cd) *<(SP 555/+CD)>* **SINCE WE'VE BECOME TRANSLUCENT** [ ] [ ]
– Baby, can you dig the light / The straight life / Where the flavor is / In the winner's circle / Our time is now / Dyin' for it / Inside job / Take it like a man / Crooked and wide / Sonic infusion.

Sep 02. (7") *(SP 603)* **SONIC INFUSION. / A LONG WAY TO GO** [ ] [–]

Mar 06. (lp/cd) *<(SP/+CD 700)>* **UNDER A BILLION SUNS** [ ] [ ]
– Where is the future? / It is us / I saw the light / Endless yesterday / Empty shells / Hard-on for war / A brief celebration of indifference / Let's drop in / On the move / In search of . . . / Blindspots.

May 06. (7") *(SP 716)* **IT IS US. / DIG THOSE TRENCHES** [ ] [–]

– compilations, etc. –

Nov 89. (cd-ep) *Tupelo; (TUPCD 009) / Sub Pop; <SP 62>* **BOILED BEEF AND ROTTING TEETH** [ ] [ ]

Jan 00. (cd) *Strange Fruit; (SFRSCD 090)* **THE RADIO SESSIONS** [ ] [–]

Mar 00. (t-lp/d-cd) *Sub Pop; <(SP/+CD 500)>* **MARCH TO FUZZ** [ ] [ ]
– In 'n' out of grace / Suck you dry / I have to laugh / Sweet young thing ain't sweet no more / Who you drivin' now / You got it / Judgement, rage, retribution and thyme / Into the drink / A thousand forms of mind / Generation genocide / If I think / Here comes sickness / Let it slide / Touch me I'm sick / This gift / Good enough / Blinding sun / Into your shtik / Beneath the valley of the underdog / When tomorrow hits / Make it now again / Hate the police / Hey sailor / Twenty four / Baby help me forget / Revolution / You stupid asshole / Who is who / Stab yor back / Pump it up / The money will roll right in / Fix me / Dehumanized / She's just 15 / Baby o baby / Over the top / You goive me the creeps / March to fuzz / Ounce of deception / Paperback life / Bushpusher man / Fuzzbeater / Overblown / Run shithead run / King sandbox / Tonight I think I'm gonna go downtown / Holden / Not going down that road again / Brand new face / Drinking for two / Butterfly stroke / Editions of you.

MUDVAYNE

Formed: Peoria, Illinois, USA . . . 1996 by KUD aka CHAD GRAY, GURRG aka GREG TRIBBETT and sPaG aka MATT McDONOUGH. Following a self-financed debut mini-set, 'KILL, I OUGHTA' (1997), the band were signed to 'Epic' for the recording of 'L.D. 50' (2000), by which time the line-up had been completed by RYKNOW aka RYAN MARTINIE. Sporting a disturbing line in face paint (although they maintain their image comes second to the music) and favouring a fairly pedestrian thrash sound tempered by the odd funky nu-metal flourish, MUDVAYNE have been compared to the likes of FEAR FACTORY, KORN and especially SLIPKNOT with whom they maintain a close working relationship. At their most palatable when KUD substitutes his death growl for a curiously KURT COBAIN-like vocal fragility, MUDVAYNE might be better off leaving the rock theatre stuff to their contemporaries. The release of an expanded version of their mini-debut under the title, 'THE BEGINNING OF ALL THINGS TO COME' (2001), saw them treading dirty water until second album proper, the appropriately-titled riposte, 'THE END OF ALL THINGS TO COME' (2002). While the name of the album predicted the inevitable fate of nu-metal in general, MUDVAYNE themselves wallowed in the glow of a US Top 20 placing. Discarding the grease-paint and revealing their humdrum christian names only seemed to accentuate the lack of ideas on 'LOST AND FOUND' (2005), a near US No.1 which confirmed America's addiction to sub-standard, doom-mongering metal.

Album rating: L.D. 50 (*6) / THE BEGINNING OF ALL THINGS TO END (*5) re- KILL, I OUGHTA / THE END OF ALL THINGS TO COME (*6) / LOST AND FOUND (*5)

KUD (b. CHAD GRAY) – vocals / **GURRG** (b. GREG TRIBBETT) – guitar / **sPaG** (b. MATT McDONOUGH, 7 Nov'68) – drums

not iss. — own label

1997. (m-cd) <none> **KILL, I OUGHTA** [–] demo [–]
– Poop loser / Seed / Cultivate / Some assembly required / I.D.I.O.T. / Central disposal / Coal. *<re-iss. Nov01 as 'THE BEGINNING OF ALL THINGS TO END' on 'Sony'+=; 85995-2>* – Fear / Dig (future evolution remix) / Dig (everything and nothing remix) / L.D. 50.

—— **RYKNOW** (b. RYAN MARTINIE) – bass; repl. original

Epic — Epic

Oct 00. (cd) *(500588-2) <63821>* **L.D. 50** [ ] Aug00 [85]
– Monolith / Dig / Internal primates forever / – 1 / Death blooms / Golden ratio / Cradle / Nothing to Gein / Mutatis mutandis / Everything and nothing / Severed / Recombinant resurgence / Prod / Pharmaecopia / Under my skin / (K)now (F)orever / Lethal dosage. *(re-iss. May02; same)*

Nov 02. (10"red) *<3E 79821>* **NOT FALLING. / PROD (live in Peoria)** [–] [ ]

Nov 02. (cd) *(509938-2) <86487-2>* **THE END OF ALL THINGS TO COME** [ ] [17]
– Silenced / Trapped in the wake of a dream / Not falling / (Per)version of a truth / Mercy, severity / World so cold / The patient mental / Skyring / Solve et coagula / Shadow of a man / 12:97:24:99 / The end of all things to come / A key to nothing. *(ltd-cd w/dvd+=; 509938-3)* – (DVD tracks). *(re-iss. Dec04; same)*

Apr 05. (cd) *(519353-2) <90784>* **LOST AND FOUND** [ ] [2]
– Determined / Pushing through / Happy? / I.M.N. / Fall into sleep / Rain. sun. gone. / Choices / Forget to remember / TV radio / Just / All that you are / Pulling the string.

May 05. (-) *<radio>* **HAPPY?** [–] [89]

□ MUGGS (see under ⇒ CYPRESS HILL)

□ MURDERDOLLS (see under ⇒ SLIPKNOT)

MUSE

Formed: Teignmouth, Devon, England . . . 1997 by MATTHEW BELLAMY, CHRIS WOLSTENHOLME and drummer DOMINIC HOWARD. After playing dingey pubs and damp basements, the 3-piece from the south-west arose when they debuted at the 'In The City' A&R field day in 1998. HOWARD's THOM YORKE-esque vox impressed record pedallers so much that they took the group to America to showcase them for MADONNA's record label 'Maverik' – home to DEFTONES, ALANIS MORISSETTE and, erm, WANK. The 20-something indie kids released a John Leckie (knob-twiddler for RADIOHEAD, the STONE ROSES and somebody called JOHN LENNON) produced EP entitled 'MUSE' at the beginning of 1999, which was only pressed on 999 copies (it can nowadays fetch up to £30). The EP sounded like many earlier RADIOHEAD efforts, with a little MY BLOODY VALENTINE twist thrown in for good measure. MUSE proceeded with the 'MUSCLE MUSEUM' EP and two singles 'UNO' and 'CAVE' before unveiling their debut set 'SHOWBIZ' in late '99. The album boasted nothing special (bar say, the track 'SUNBURN'), except that it may have contained some of the most melodramatic tracks since OASIS's 'WHAT'S THE STORY . . .'. It unleashed a new brand of genre that had the same ideology as Brit Pop: MOR – where have I heard this before? – rock. 2001 saw MUSE go from strength to strength via two major UK hit singles, 'PLUG IN BABY' and 'NEW BORN', both taken from their celebrated Top 3 sophomore set, 'ORIGIN OF SYMMETRY'. 2002 saw the release of the obligatory live/B-sides collection, 'HULLABALOO SOUNDTRACK', documenting a French concert performance and collecting various odd'n'sods for obsessives and completists. BELLAMY and Co returned once again in September 2003 with UK chart-topper 'ABSOLUTION', a jaded, spiky rock affair that bore all of the usual MUSE trademarks, but this time with a change of production (Rich Costey replaced regular John Leckie). In turn, the set proved to be more clean-cut, but all of the recognisable traits still remained in the band's agit (sometimes angular) – BELLAMY's soaring falsetto at the forefront of the gloomy, doom-laden music.

• **Note:** The MUSE who released the CD in '97 entitled 'Innocent Voices' were not the same band.

Album rating: SHOWBIZ (*7) / ORIGIN OF SYMMETRY (*7) / HULLABALOO SOUNDTRACK (*6) / ABSOLUTION (*7)

MATTHEW BELLAMY (b. 9 Jun'78, Cambridge, England) – vocals, lead guitar, piano / **CHRIS WOLSTENHOLME** (b. 2 Dec'78, Rotherham, Yorkshire, England) – bass, vocals / **DOMINIC HOWARD** (b. 7 Dec'77, Stockport, England) – drums

Dangerous — not iss.

May 98. (cd-ep) *(DREXCDEP 103)* **MUSE EP** [ ] [–]
– Overdue / Cave / Coma / Escape.

Jan 99. (cd-ep) *(DREXCDEP 104)* **MUSCLE MUSEUM EP** [ ] [–]
– Muscle museum / Sober / Uno / Unintented / Instant messenger / Muscle museum #2.

Mushroom — Warners

Jun 99. (7"clear) *(MUSH 50S)* **UNO. / AGITATED** [73] [–]
(cd-s) *(MUSH 50CDS)* – ('A') / Jimmy Kane / Forced in.

Sep 99. (7"clear) *(MUSH 58S)* **CAVE / CAVE (instrumental remix)** [52] [ ]
(cd-s+=) *(MUSH 58CDS)* – Twin.
(cd-s) *(MUSH 58CDX)* – ('A') / Host / Coma.

Oct 99. (cd/md/c/lp) *(MUSH 59 CD/MC/LP) <47382>* **SHOWBIZ** [69] [ ]
– Sunburn / Muscle museum / Fillip / Falling down / Cave / Showbiz / Unintended / Uno / Sober / Escape / Overdue / Hate this & I'll love you. *(re-iss. Feb00; same)*

Nov 99. (7") *(MUSH 66S)* **MUSCLE MUSEUM. / ('A'live acoustic)** [43] [ ]
(cd-s+=) *(MUSH 66CDS)* – Do we need this?
(cd-s) *(MUSH 66CDSX)* – ('A'-extended) / Pink ego box / Con-science.

Feb 00. (7") *(MUSH 68S)* **SUNBURN. / ('A'live)** [22] [ ]
(cd-s+=) *(MUSH 68CDS)* – Ashamed.
(cd-s) *(MUSH 68CDSX)* – ('A') / Yes please / Uno (live).

Jun 00. (7"/c-s) *(MUSH 72 S/MCS)* **UNINTENDED. / RECESS** [20] [ ]
(cd-s+=) *(MUSH 72CDS)* – Falling down (live acoustic) / ('A'-CD-ROM).
(cd-s) *(MUSH 72CDSX)* – ('A') / Nishe / Hate this & I'll love you (live).

Oct 00. (7") *(MUSH 84S)* **MUSCLE MUSEUM. / SOBER (The Saint remix)** [25] [–]
(cd-s+=) *(MUSH 84CDS)* – Sunburn (Timo Maas sunstroke remix).

Mushroom — Mushroom

Mar 01. (c-s) *(MUSH 89MCS)* **PLUG IN BABY / NATURE 1** [11] [–]
(cd-s+=) *(MUSH 89CDS)* – Execution commentary.
(cd-s) *(MUSH 89CDSX)* – ('A') / Spiral static / Bedroom acoustics.

Jun 01. (7") *(MUSH 92)* **NEW BORN. / SHRINKING UNIVERSE** [12] [–]
(cd-s+=) *(MUSH 92CDS)* – Piano thing / ('A'-video).
(cd-s) *(MUSH 92CDSX)* – ('A') / Map of your head / Plug in baby (live).
(12") *(MUSH 92T)* – ('A'-Perfecto remix) / Sunburn (Timo Maas sunstroke remix).

Jun 01. (cd/c/lp) *(MUSH 93 CD/MC/LP) <40093>* **ORIGIN OF SYMMETRY** [3] Jul01 [ ]
– New born / Bliss / Space dementia / Hyper music / Plug in baby / Citizen erased / Micro cuts / Screenager / Dark shines / Feeling good / Megalomania.

Aug 01. (7") *(MUSH 96S)* **BLISS. / THE GALLERY** [22] [–]
(cd-s+=) *(MUSH 96CDS)* – Screenager (live) / ('A'-video).
(cd-s) *(MUSH 96CDSX)* – ('A') / Hyper chondriac music / New born (live) / ('A'-making of the video).

Nov 01. (7") *(MUSH 97S)* **HYPER MUSIC. / FEELING GOOD (live)** [24] [–]
(cd-s+=) *(MUSH 97CDS)* – Shine / ('A'-video).
(cd-s) *(MUSH 97CDSX)* – ('A'-live) / ('B'-studio) / Please, please, please let me get what I want / ('B'-video).

Jun 02. (7") *(MUSH 104S)* **IN YOUR WORLD. / DEAD STAR** [13] [–]
(cd-s+=) *(MUSH 104CDS)* – Futurism / Dead star (video).
(cd-s+=) *(MUSH 104CDSX)* – Can't take my eyes off you / In your world (video).

Jul 02. (d-cd) *(MUSH 105CD) <65021>* **HULLABALOO SOUNDTRACK** (compilation + live) [10] [ ]
– Forced in / Shrinking universe / Recess / Yes please / Map of your head / Nature 1 / Shine acoustic / Ashamed / The gallery / Hyper chondriac music // Dead star / Micro cuts / Citizen erased / Showbiz / Megalomania / Dark shines / Screenager / Space dementia / In your world / Muscle museum / Agitated.

East West — Taste Media

Sep 03. (7"clear) *(EW 272)* **TIME IS RUNNING OUT. / THE GROOVE** [8] [–]
(cd-s+=) *(EW 272CD)* – Stockholm syndrome (video).
(dvd-s) *(EW 272DVD)* – ('A') / ('A'-video) / (making of..).

Sep 03. (cd/d-lp) *(5046 68587-2/-1) <48733>* **ABSOLUTION** [1] [ ]
– Intro / Apocalypse please / Time is running out / Sing for absolution / Stockholm syndrome / Falling away with you / Interlude / Hysteria / Blackout / Butterflies and hurricanes / The small print / Endlessly / Thoughts of a dying atheist / Ruled by secrecy.

Dec 03. (7"clear/cd-s) *(EW 278/+CD)* **HYSTERIA. / ETERNALLY MISSED** [17] [–]
(dvd-s) *(EW 278DVD)* – ('A'-video) / ('A') / ('A'-live MTV2 video) / (making of video).

May 04. (7"clear/cd-s) *(EW 285/+CD)* **SING FOR ABSOLUTION. / FURY** [16] [–]
(dvd-s) *(EW 285DVD)* – ('A'-video) / ('A') / (making of video) / Big day off (video).

Atlantic — Taste Media

Sep 04. (7"clear) *(ATUK 003)* **BUTTERFLIES AND HURRICANES** [14] [–]
(cd-s) *(ATUK 003)* – ('A') / Sing for absolution (live BBC Radio 2 acoustic version) / U-Myx technology.
(dvd-s) *(ATUK 003DVD)* – ('A'-remix) / ('A'-video) / The groove in the States documentary & (raw video footage).

Warners — Warners

Jun 06. (7"pic-d/cd-s) *(HEL 3001/+CD)* **SUPERMASSIVE BLACK HOLE. / CRYING SHAME** [4] [ ]
(dvd-s) *(HEL 3001DVD)* – ('A'-video) / ('A') / ('A'-making of..)
Jul'06, above taken from 4th set, 'BLACK HOLES & REVELATIONS'

the MUSIC

Formed: Kippax, nr. Leeds, England ... 1999 by STUART COLEMAN, ADAM NUTTER, ROBERT HARVEY and PHIL JORDAN. Barely out of their teens, and with very little money, this impressive quartet issued a demo EP entitled 'TAKE THE LONG ROAD AND WALK IT' in 2001, which led Radio 1 DJ Steve Lamacq to give the group almost unlimited airtime on his evening shows. On the strengh of this demo, tiny label 'Fierce Panda' bought the rights to the EP and re-issued it on a limited run of 1,000 copies – they sold out in almost a fortnight. With COLEMAN's intense swagger and vocals to match, he seemed like the new generation's BEZ, only with a few more brain cells. The MUSIC's music, well, it wasn't as almighty as the ensemble's moniker would have you believe; rough, early VERVE came to mind along with, traces of JOY DIVISION and even MOGWAI on the track 'WALLS GET SMALLER' – basically a fusion of good old Northern glum. 'Hut' records eventually won the bidding war for the band in 2001, prompting them to issue their first EP proper 'YOU MIGHT AS WELL TRY TO FUCK ME', followed by 'THE PEOPLE' EP and eventually their cracking self-titled debut album in 2002. Coming out of a similar blooze-myth, jack-beat headspace as soon-to-be headspinners KASABIAN, the album made the UK Top 5, trailed by Top 20 single, 'TAKE THE LONG ROAD AND WALK IT', and Top 30/Top 20 follow-ups, 'GETAWAY' and 'THE TRUTH IS NO WORDS'. Decamping to Atlanta, Georgia under the supervision of Brendan O 'Brien (PEARL JAM, etc.), the MUSIC made an even unwieldier behemoth of an album in 'WELCOME TO THE NORTH' (2004), HARVEY's antediluvian wail of a voice drawing yet more comparisons to PERRY FARRELL. Despite heaviness taking precedence over grooviness, the record failed to whet Stateside rawk appetites, although it did make the UK Top 10, spawning the Top 20 single, 'BREAKIN'.

Album rating: THE MUSIC (*8) / WELCOME TO THE NORTH (*7)

ROBERT HARVEY – vocals / **ADAM NUTTER** – guitar / **STUART COLEMAN** – bass / **PHIL JORDAN** – drums

Fierce Panda — not iss.

May 01. (ltd-7") *(NING 107)* **TAKE THE LONG ROAD AND WALK IT. / THE WALLS GET SMALLER** [ ] [–]

Hut — Capitol

Nov 01. (12"ep/cd-ep) *(HUT T/CD 145) <546066>* **THE MUSIC EP** [ ] Jan02 [ ]
– You might as well try to fuck me / Karma / Treat me right on / Too high.

Apr 02. (12"ep/cd-ep) *(HUT T/CD 152)* **THE PEOPLE EP** [ ] [–]
– The people / Let love be the healer / Life / Jag tune.

Hut — Virgin

May 02. (cd-ep) *<68381>* **THE MUSIC** [–] [ ]
– Take the long road and walk it / The walls get smaller / You might as well try to fuck me / Karma / Too high / New instrumental (live).

Hut — Capitol

Aug 02. (7"pic-d) *(HUT 158) <546023>* **TAKE THE LONG ROAD AND WALK IT. / ALONE** [14] Jan02 [ ]
(cd-s+=) *(HUTCD 158)* – Raindance / ('A'-video).
(12"++=) *(HUTT 158)* – The walls get smaller.
(cd-s) *(HUTDX 158)* – ('A'side) / The walls get smaller / New instrumental / ('A'-original).

Sep 02. (cd/d-lp) *(CDHUT/HUTDLP 76)* **THE MUSIC** [4] [–]
– The dance / Take the long road and walk it / Human / The truth is no words / Float / Turn out the light / The people / Getaway / Disco / Too high.

Nov 02. (7"pic-d) *(HUT 162)* **GETAWAY. / DRAGON SONG** [26] [–]
(cd-s+=) *(HUTCD 162)* – ('A'-video).

Feb 03. (7"pic-d) *(HUT 164)* **THE TRUTH IS NO WORDS. / WHAT'S IT FOR** [18] [–]
(cd-s+=) *(HUTCD 164)* – Turn out the light (live) / ('A'-video).

Virgin — Capitol

Sep 04. (7") *(VS 1883)* **FREEDOM FIGHTERS. / GETAWAY (slow version)** [15] [–]
(cd-s) *(VSCDT 1883)* – ('A') / Come what may.
(cd-s) *(VSCDX 1883)* – ('A') / So low / The people (Nick McCabe remix) / ('A'-video).

Sep 04. (cd/d-lp) *(CD+/V 2989) <78516>* **WELCOME TO THE NORTH** [8] Oct04 [ ]
– Welcome to the north / Freedom fighters / Bleed from within / Breakin' / Cessation / Fight the feeling / Guide / Into the night / I need love / One way in, no way out / Open your mind.

Jan 05. (7") *(VS 1894)* **BREAKIN'. / FREEDOM FIGHTERS (Jo Whiley 'live lounge' session)** [20] [–]
(cd-s) *(VSCDT 1894)* – ('A') / Middle of nowhere.
(cd-s) *(VSCDX 1894)* – ('A') / Bleed from within (live at Liverpool Academy) / Bleed from within (Thin White Duke mix).

MY BLOODY VALENTINE

Formed: Dublin, Ireland . . . 1984 by KEVIN SHIELDS and COLM O'CIOSOIG. Later the same year, the pair travelled to Germany where they hooked up with DAVE CONWAY and TINA to record a mini-lp, 'THIS IS YOUR BLOODY VALENTINE', for the small 'Tycoon' records. This was issued the following year although only 50 copies seem to have emerged (now very rare!). They subsequently moved to London, DEBBIE GOODGE replacing TINA for the recording of the 'GEEK!' EP on 'Fever'. After more 45's for 'Kaleidoscope' then 'Lazy' (home of The PRIMITIVES), the band really began to move away from their early twanging, IGGY POP-style sound following a move to 'Creation' in 1988 (masterminded by SLAUGHTER JOE FOSTER, ex-TV PERSONALITIES). With co-"vocalist", BILINDA BUTCHER now also on board, SHIELDS and Co. finally made the breakthrough in 1990 when the 'GLIDER' EP nearly went Top 40 in the UK, hot on the heels of the acclaimed 'ISN'T ANYTHING' (1988) album. The full extent of their pioneering guitar manipulation – responsible for a whole scene of "shoegazing" musical admirers, stand up RIDE, MOOSE, LUSH etc., etc. – was revealed as MBV released their most challenging and inventive track to date in 'TO HERE KNOWS WHEN' (from the Top 30 'TREMOLO' EP). Creating a whole new concept and language of sound, the song either enveloped the listener in blissful noise or just seemed out of bloody tune, there was no middle ground. 'LOVELESS' (1991), MBV's long awaited and much heralded follow-up, was a revelation. Its hypnotic, undulating noisescapes sounded not-of-this-earth and 'Creation' were saddled with an astronomical studio bill to match, almost going bankrupt as a result. They subsequently signed to 'Island' records, and 12(!!!) years on, fans are still awaiting some new product. Although MY BLOODY VALENTINE have arguably been the most influential indie band of the last decade and few doubt their potential to return with a masterpiece, their reclusive silence makes the late Stanley Kubrick appear prolific. Nevertheless, SHIELDS has surfaced occasionally as a remixer, notably for the single release of PRIMAL SCREAM's 'Stuka' and many more; he subsequently joined them in 2000. Of late, SHIELDS has contributed several tracks to the Sofia Coppola feature fulm, 'Lost In Translation' (2004).

• **Songwriters:** SHIELDS writes most of material, with words after 1987 by BILINDA. Covered MAP REF 41 (Wire). • **Trivia:** A track, 'SUGAR', was given away free with 'The Catalogue' magazine of February '89.

Album rating: THIS IS YOUR BLOODY VALENTINE (*5) / ISN'T ANYTHING (*8) / ECSTASY AND WINE compilation (*7) / LOVELESS (*9) / Kevin Shields & V/A: LOST IN TRANSLATION soundtrack (*7)

KEVIN SHIELDS (b.21 May'63, Queens, New York) – guitar, vocals, occasional bass / **DAVE CONWAY** – vocals / **COLM CUSACK** (b. COLM MICHAEL O'CIOSOIG, 31 Oct'64) – drums / **TINA** – keyboards

Tycoon | not iss.

1985. (m-lp) *(ST 7501)* **THIS IS YOUR BLOODY VALENTINE** [-] German [-]
– Forever and again / Homelovin' guy / Don't cramp my style / Tiger in my tank / The love gang / Inferno / The last supper.

— **DEBBIE GOOGE** (b.24 Oct'62, Somerset, England) – bass; repl. TINA

Fever | not iss.

Apr 86. (12"ep) *(FEV 5)* **GEEK!** [ ] [-]
– No place to go / Moonlight / Love machine / The sandman never sleeps.

Jun 86. (7") *(FEV 5X)* **NO PLACE TO GO. / MOONLIGHT** [ ] [-]

Kaleidoscope Sound | not iss.

Oct 86. (12"ep) *(KS 101)* **THE NEW RECORD BY MY BLOODY VALENTINE** [ ] [-]
– Lovelee sweet darlene / By the danger in your eyes / On another rainy Sunday / We're so beautiful.

Lazy | not iss.

Feb 87. (7") *(LAZY 04)* **SUNNY SUNDAE SMILE. / PAINT A RAINBOW** [ ] [-]
(12"+=) *(LAZY 04T)* – Kiss the eclipse / Sylvie's head.

— **BILINDA BUTCHER** (b.16 Sep'61, London, England) – vocals, guitar; repl. CONWAY

Nov 87. (m-lp) *(LAZY 08)* **ECSTASY** [ ] [-]
– (Please) Lose yourself in me / The things I miss / I don't need you / Clair / (You're) Safe in your sleep / She loves you no less / Strawberry wine / Lovelee sweet darlene.

Nov 87. (12"m) *(LAZY 07)* **STRAWBERRY WINE. / NEVER SAY GOODBYE / CAN I TOUCH YOU** [ ] [-]

Creation | Relativity

Jul 88. (7") *(CRE 055)* **YOU MADE ME REALISE. / SLOW** [ ] [-]
(12"+=) *(CRE 055T)* – Thorn / Cigarette in your bed / Drive it all over me. *(re-iss. Mar90 as cd-ep; CRECD 55)*

Oct 88. (7") *(CRE 061)* **FEED ME WITH YOUR KISSES. / EMPTINESS INSIDE** [ ] [-]
(12"+=) *(CRE 061T)* – I believe / I need no trust. *(re-iss. Mar90 as cd-ep; CRECD 61)*

Nov 88. (lp/cd)(c) *(CRELP 040/+CD)(C-CRELP 040) <1006>* **ISN'T ANYTHING** [ ] [ ]
– Soft as snow (but warm inside) / Lose my breath / Cupid come / (When you wake) You're still in a dream / No more sorry / All I need / Feed me with your kiss / Sue is fine / Several girls galore / You never should / Nothing much to lose / I can see it (but I can't feel it). *(free 7"w/ lp)* – INSTRUMENTAL. / INSTRUMENTAL *<US cd re-iss. 1993 on 'Warners'; 45231> (cd re-iss. Jan01; same)*

Creation | Sire

Apr 90. (7"ep/12"ep)(cd-ep) *(CRE 73/+T)(CRESCD 73) <26313>* **GLIDER** [41] [ ]
– Soon / Glider / Don't ask why / Off your face.

Feb 91. (7"ep/12"ep)(cd-ep) *(CRE 085/+T)(CRESCD 085) <40024>* **TREMOLO** [29] Apr91 [ ]
– To here knows when / Swallow / Honey power / Moon song.

Nov 91. (cd/lp)(c) *(CRE CD/LP 060)(C-CRELP 060) <26759>* **LOVELESS** [24] [ ]
– Only shallow / Loomer / Touched / To here knows when / When you sleep / I only said / Come in alone / Sometimes / Blown a wish / What you want / Soon. *(cd re-iss. Jan01; same)*

— During their long hiatus, KEVIN SHIELDS contributed (1996) to an album 'Beyond The Pale' by EXPERIMENTAL AUDIO RESEARCH. It also featured SONIC BOOM (ex-SPACEMEN 3), KEVIN MARTIN (of GOD) & EDDIE PREVOST (of AMM). Meanwhile, DEBBIE GOOGE teamed up with KATHERINE GIFFORD and MAX CORRADI to form SNOWPONY. In 2000, COLM finally reappeared in HOPE SANDOVAL & THE WARM INVENTIONS (she of MAZZY STAR fame).

– compilations, others, etc. –

Feb 89. (lp/cd) *Lazy; (LAZY 12/+CD)* **ECSTASY AND WINE** [ ] [-]
– Strawberry wine / Never say goodbye / Can I touch you / She loves you no less / The things I miss / I don't need you / Safe in your sleep / Clair / You've got nothing / Lose yourself in me.

KEVIN SHIELDS

Emperor Norton | Emperor Norton

Feb 04. (cd) *(<ENR 7068-2>)* **LOST IN TRANSLATION** (soundtrack w/ Various Artists plus Brian Reitzell & Roger Joseph Manning Jr) [ ] Sep03 [ ]
– (other artists) / City girl / Goodbye / Ikebana / Sometimes (MY BLOODY VALENTINE) / Are you awake? / (other artists).

MY CHEMICAL ROMANCE

Formed: New Jersey, USA . . . post-9/11, 2001 by half-Scottish/half-Italian animator GERARD WAY and mechanic MATT PELISSIER. Unusually for an American outfit, MY CHEMICAL ROMANCE gleaned their moniker from the work of a Scottish author, namely Irvine Welsh. Setting the gloomy tone for the rest of their career, the WAY-penned 'SKYLINES AND TURNSTILES', was inspired by a first-hand view of the Twin Towers terrorist strike. Consolidating the band with the arrival of half-Portuguese/half-Puerto Rican RAY TORO, FRANK IERO and MIKEY WAY, MCR put their chemistry to work on debut set, 'I BROUGHT YOU MY BULLETS, YOU BROUGHT ME YOUR LOVE' (2002). Trying but failing to escape comparisons with emo types THURSDAY (singer GEOFF RICKLY produced them at this stage), reeling off BRIAN MAY-esque riffs and, on the likes of 'HONEY, THIS MIRROR ISN'T BIG ENOUGH FOR THE BOTH OF US', referencing legendary weirdos SPARKS, MCR polarised opinion but attracted the backing of veteran imprint 'Reprise'. A sparer, cleaner production (by Howard Benson) and tighter marshalling of the arrangements, if not any compromise on the lyrics, broke 'THREE CHEERS FOR SWEET REVENGE' (2004) into the US Top 30. A year later it was Top 40 in Britain, spurred on by a clutch of catalytic singles: 'I'M NOT OKAY (I PROMISE)' (twice!), 'HELENA' and 'THE GHOST OF YOU'. By this time, drummer PELISSIER had made way for BOB BRYAR.

Album rating: I BROUGHT YOU MY BULLETS, YOU BROUGHT ME YOUR LOVE (*5) / THREE CHEERS FOR SWEET REVENGE (*7)

GERARD WAY (b. 9 Apr'77, Newark, NJ) – vocals / **RAY TORO** (b. RAYMOND TORO-ORTIZ, 15 Jul'77, Kearny, NJ) – lead guitar, vocals / **FRANK IERO** (b.31 Oct'81) – rhythm guitar, vocals / **MIKEY WAY** (b.10 Sep'80) – bass / **MATT PELISSIER** – drums

20:20 Eyeball

Jul 02. (cd) *<EB 022>* **I BROUGHT YOU MY BULLETS, YOU BROUGHT ME YOUR LOVE** [–] [ ]
– Romance / Honey, this mirror isn't big enough for the two of us / Vampires will never hurt you / Drowning lessons / Our lady of sorrows / Headfirst for halos / Skylines and turnstiles / Early sunsets over Monroeville / This is the best day ever / Cubicles / Demolition lovers.

Dec 03. (7") *(TWENTY-7S 003)* **HONEY, THIS MIRROR ISN'T BIG ENOUGH FOR THE TWO OF US. / THIS IS THE BEST DAY EVER** [ ] [–]

Apr 04. (7"/cd-s) *(TWENTY 7S/CDS 004)* **HEADFIRST FOR HALOS. / OUR LADY OF SORROWS (live)** [ ] [–]

Apr 04. (re-cd) *(9866233)* **I BROUGHT YOU MY BULLETS, YOU BROUGHT ME YOUR LOVE** [ ] [–]

Reprise Reprise

Sep 04. (cd) *<(9362 48615-2)>* **THREE CHEERS FOR SWEET REVENGE** [ ] Jun04 [28]
– Helena / Give 'em hell kid / To the end / You know what they do to guys like us in prison / I'm not okay (I promise) / The ghost of you / The jetset life is gonna kill you / Interlude / Thank you for the venom / Hang 'em high / It's not a fashion statement, it's a deathwish / Cemetery drive / I never told you what I do for a living.

Dec 04. (7") *(W 661)* **THANK YOU FOR THE VENOM** [71] [–]

Feb 05. (7"red) *(W 666)* **I'M NOT OKAY (I PROMISE). / BURY ME IN BLACK (demo)** [19] Dec04 [86]
(cd-s+=) *<24279-2>* – You know what they do to guys like us in prison (live) / ('A'-video).

Apr 05. (re-cd) *(as prev.)* **THREE CHEERS FOR SWEET REVENGE** [34] [–]
(re-iss. Nov05; same)

Jun 05. (7"pic-d/cd-s) *(W 671/+CD1)* **HELENA. / I'M NOT OKAY (I PROMISE) (live AOL session)** [20] Aug05 [33]
(cd-s) *(W 671CD2) <2802>* – ('A') / ('A'-video) / I'm not okay (I promise) (video).

Aug 05. (7"pic-d/cd-s) *(W 683/+CD1)* **THE GHOST OF YOU. / HELENA (live)** [27] [84]
(cd-s) *(W 683CD2)* – ('A') / I'm not okay (live) / Cemetery drive (live).

Sep 05. (dl-s; w/ the USED) *<online>* **UNDER PRESSURE** [–] [41]
(above for the Hurricane Katrina relief effort)

Nov 05. (cd-s) *(W 692CD1)* **I'M NOT OKAY (I PROMISE) / YOU KNOW WHAT THEY DO TO GUYS LIKE US IN PRISON (BBC session)** [28] [–]
(cd-s+=) *(W 692CD2)* – ('A'-MTV $3 bill).

—— (mid-2004) **BOB BRYAR** (b.31 Dec'80, Chicago, Illinois, USA) – drums; repl. PELISSIER who returned to his old job

– compilations, others, etc. –

Mar 06. (multimedia) *<(9362 49476-2)>* **LIFE ON THE MURDER SCENE** [ ] [ ]

MYSTERY JETS

Formed: Eel Pie Island, Twickenham, England ... 2000 (or thereabouts) by BLAINE HARRISON (then drummer), his dad! HENRY on bass (at least initially), WILLIAM REES on guitar, TAMARA on keyboards and KAI FISH on bass. Save for CAT STEVENS and SPIRIT, father and son isn't usually a combination associated with rock'n'roll, yet MYSTERY JETS proved that the generation gap wasn't an obstacle, even exchanging their respective roles in the band (BLAINE on lead vocals, etc, WILLIAM on guitar) with the departure of TAMARA and arrival of new drummer KAPIL TRIVEDI. After a couple of early demos had done the rounds, the 'JETS cruised into the review pages circa 2005 with a couple of well-received 45's, 'ZOO TIME' and 'ON MY FEET'. Subsequently signing to '679 Recordings' ('WEA' in the US), BLAINE and co scored their first UK Top 50 entry, 'YOU CAN'T FOOL ME DENNIS'. As quirky and quintessentially Eel Pie-ish as subsequent hit singles, 'ALAS AGNES' and 'THE BOY WHO RAN AWAY', the song whetted headspace for the eccentric pleasures of debut album, 'MAKING DENS' (2006). Dad-rock took on a whole new meaning as critics raved over their provincial-cum-metropolitan charms, fueling demand for the timely re-release of '.. DENNIS'.

Album rating: MAKING DENS (*7)

BLAINE HARRISON – vocals, keyboards, percussion, effects / **HENRY HARRISON** – guitar, vocals, keyboards, percussion / **WILLIAM REES** – guitar, vocals, percussion / **KAI FISH** – bass, vocals / **KAPIL TRIVEDI** – drums; repl. TAMARA (keyboards)

Transgressive not iss.

Feb 05. (7") *(Trans 004)* **ZOO TIME. / LIZZIE'S LION** [ ] [–]

Good&Evil – 679 Record not iss.

Jul 05. (7") *(679GE 01)* **ON MY FEET. / DROWNING NOT WAVING** [ ] [–]
(cd-s+=) *(679GE 01CD)* – The tale.

679 Record 679 Record

Sep 05. (7") *(679L 109)* **YOU CAN'T FOOL ME DENNIS. / QUITE A DELIGHT** [44] [–]
(cd-s) *(679L 109CD)* – ('A') / Ageless.
(7") *(679L 109X)* – ('A'-Justice mix) / ('A'-acoustic).
(12") *(MYSTJ 01)* – ('A'-Justice remix) / ('A'-Straight bat version) / Zoo time (Erol Alkan rework).

Dec 05. (7") *(679L 115)* **ALAS AGNES. / ELECTRIC FIRE** [34] [–]
(cd-s) *(679L 115CD)* – ('A') / The last bench.
(7"m) *(679L 115X)* – ('A'-live at the Astoria) / Rastamadeus (live at Eel Pie) / Lizzie's lion (live at Eel Pie).

Feb 06. (7") *(679L 122)* **THE BOY WHO RAN AWAY. / SANDY DRAKE** [23] [–]
(cd-s) *(679L 122CD)* – ('A') / Yellow springs.
(7") *(679L 122X)* – ('A'-Riton re-dub) / ('A'-The Noisettes pin'n'mix labotomy mix).

Mar 06. (cd) *(<2564 63210-2>)* **MAKING DENS** [32] [ ]
– You can't fool me Dennis / Purple prose / Soluble in air / The boy who ran away / Horse drawn cart / Zoo time / Little bag of hair / Diamonds in the dark / Alas Agnes / Making dens. *(ltd-cd w/dvd+=; 2564 63209-2)* – (DVD tour documentary).

Apr 06. (cd-ep) *<679L 126CD>* **FLOTSAM AND JETSAM EP** [–] [ ]
– You can't fool me Dennis / Zoo time / Lizzie's lion / The tale / Electric fires.

May 06. (7"/cd-s) *(679L 129/+CD)* **YOU CAN'T FOOL ME DENNIS. / FOUR WALLS** [41] [–]
(7") *(679L 129X)* – ('A'-good books mix) / Under the pews.

N

NAS

Born: NASIR JONES, 14 Sep'73, Queensbridge, New York, USA. Raised by a jazz-performing father, he cut his rapping teeth at the age of ten, developing his lyrical skills in local hip-hop posse, The DEVASTIN' SEVEN. By the end of the 80's, having made attempts at TV work, he was introduced to MAIN SOURCE producer, LARGE PROFESSOR, for whom he made a demo tape. NAS subsequently featured on their debut album, 'Breaking Atoms', making a noted guest appearance on the track 'Live At The BBQ'. With his personal life in crisis (i.e. death of friend and shooting of his brother), NAS's recording career was put on hold for a few years in the early 90's. That is, until he contributed a track, 'HALF TIME' for the 'Zebra Head' movie late in 1992, 'Columbia' subsequently impressed enough to give the precocious young rapper a sizeable deal. Guided by some of New York's most respected producers (including Q-TIP – A Tribe Called Quest, PREMIER – Gang Starr and PETE ROCK), he crafted 1994's acclaimed 'ILLMATIC' album. Two years on, NAS smashed into the US chart at No.1 with his follow-up, 'IT WAS WRITTEN', which spawned the hit singles, 'IF I RULED THE WORLD' and the crossover Eurythmics-inspired 'STREET DREAMS'. In the Autumn of '97, he collaborated with FOXY BROWN, AZ & NATURE, releasing the chart-topping 'THE FIRM – THE ALBUM', although for American ears only (so far that is). Two sets of differing quality were released before the century was out, the hard-hitting and absorbing 'I AM . . .' (1999) and the below par, 'NAStradamus' (1999). NAS was back after a two-year hiatus from the music industry via the largely disappointing 'STILLMATIC' (2001). Not even a patch on his classic breakthrough set 'ILLMATIC' the NAS man concentrated solely on rhymes and beats, letting his music wander into dangerously 'Old-Skool' territory (without a deliberate hint of irony or retro-revival). Also, it seemed the self-styled 'King of New York' had a bit of an inferiority complex, no thanks to West Coast player JAY-Z, who dissed NAS onstage and issued the venomous 'Super Ugly'. NAS struck back, but missed his target due to shoddy aiming; the anti-JAY-Z track 'ETHER' just sounded like a feeble playground taunt. But there were moments of greatness on the set, with the fantastic Big-Up to Brooklyn 'DESTROY AND REBUILD', and the chilled-out loop of 'YOU'RE DA MAN'. But the fact remained that NAS, humbled by the multi-millionaire JAY-Z, was perhaps too angry to write and produce a clever response to the rapper's comments. The album still entered the US Top Ten in 2001. 'GOD'S SON' (2002), was something of a return to form, albeit an uncomfortably personal one, probing the depths of his soul and considerable ego. Informed in part by the death of his mother, the record found NAS rising above the humdrum to concentrate on the essential. The Top 5 'STREET'S DISCIPLE' (2004) was another sprawling bulletin from the soul, namedropping Marvin Gaye, taking issue with Condaleeza Rice and sampling LIGHTNIN' ROD. Over 25-plus tracks, NAS again proved himself an alchemical orator, eloquently railing against the usual targets and turning the air a deeper shade of blue with his carnal reminiscences. Critics bowed before his lyrical gas while being in general agreement that the record would've made a killer single disc rather than an overweight double.

Album rating: ILLMATIC (*6) / IT WAS WRITTEN (*7) / I AM . . . (*8) / NAStradamus (*5) / STILLMATIC (*5) / GOD'S SON (*6) / STREET'S DISCIPLE (*6)

NAS – rapping, etc (with various producers, etc)

not iss. Sony

Nov 92. (c-s/12"; as NASTY NAS) *<74777>* **HALF TIME (mixes)** [–] [ ]

Columbia Columbia

Apr 94. (cd/c/lp) *(475959-2/-4/-1) <57684>* **ILLMATIC** [ ] [12]
– The genesis / N.Y. state of mind / Life's a bitch / The world is yours / Halftime / Memory lane (sittin' in da park) / One love / One time 4 your mind / Represent / It ain't hard to tell.

May 94. (c-s) *(660470-4) <77385>* **IT AIN'T HARD TO TELL / ('A'instrumental)** [64] Mar94 [91]
(12"+=) *(660470-6)* – (2 other mixes).
(cd-s++=) *(660470-2)* – ('A'mixes).

1994. (c-s/12") *<77513>* **THE WORLD IS YOURS (mixes)** [–] [ ]

1995. (c-s/12"/cd-s) *<77673>* **ONE LOVE (mixes)** [–] [ ]

Jul 96. (c-s) *(663402-4) <78327>* **IF I RULED THE WORLD (IMAGINE THAT) / ('A'instrumental)** [12] Jun96 [53]
(12"/cd-s) *(663402-6/-2)* – ('A'mixes).

Jul 96. (cd/c/lp) *(484196-2/-4/-1) <67015>* **IT WAS WRITTEN** [38] [1]
– Intro / Message / Street dreams / I gave you power / Watch dem niggas / Take it in blood / Nas is coming / Affirmative action / Set up / Black girl lost / Suspect / Shootouts / Live nigga rap / If I ruled the world (imagine that).

Jan 97. (c-s/12"/cd-s) *(664130-4/-6/-2) <78409>* **STREET DREAMS / AFFIRMATIVE ACTION / (+ bonus mixes)** [12] Nov96 [22]

—— In Mar'97, NAS featured on ALLURE's Top 40 hit, 'Head Over Heels'

Jul 97. (12") *<6642>* **AFFIRMATIVE ACTION (mixes)** [–] [ ]

Dec 97. (cd-s) *<2303>* **ESCOBAR 97** [–] [ ]
(above lifted from the 'Men In Black' movie)

Mar 99. (12"/cd-s) *<79113>* **NAS IS LIKE / (+ 2 mixes) / DR. KNOCKABOOT (3 versions)** [–] [86]

Apr 99. (cd/c/lp) *(489419-2/-4/-1) <68773>* **I AM . . .** [31] [1]
– (intro) / N.Y. state of mind / Hate me now / Small world / Favor for a favor / We will survive / Ghetto prisoners / You won't see me tonight / I want to talk to you / Dr. Knockaboot / Life is what you make it / Big things / Nas is like / K-I-SS-I-N-G / Money is my bitch / Undying love. *(cd re-iss. Aug01; same)*

May 99. (c-s; NAS featuring PUFF DADDY) *(667256-4) <79070>* **HATE ME NOW / ('A'mix)** [14] Apr99 [62]
(cd-s) *(667256-2)* – ('A'mix) / If I ruled the world (with LAURYN HILL) / Street dreams (with R. KELLY).
(cd-s) *(667256-5)* – ('A'-side) / ('A'-Callout hook 1 & 2).

—— NAS featured on MISSY "MISDEMEANOR" ELLIOTT's hit single, 'Hot Boyz'

Aug 99. (12"/cd-s; as NAS & NATURE) *<79216>* **IN TOO DEEP / (+ 2 mixes) / THE SPECIALIST (2 mixes)** [–] [ ]

Nov 99. (cd/c/lp) *(495312-2/-4/-1) <63930>* **NAStradamus** [ ] [7]
– Prediction / Life we choose / NAStradamus / Angels intro / Some of us have angels / Project windows / Naheim / Big girl / Hydro drops / Shoot 'em up / Last words / Hustler's and killers / Science / God love us / Quiet niggas / Come get me / Count down to 2000 / New world / You owe me / Outcome. *(cd re-iss. Dec01; same)*

Jan 00. (12"/cd-s) *(668557-6/-2)* <79299> **NAStradamus / (clean) / (instrumental) / SHOOT 'EM UP (album + instrumental)** [24] Oct99 [92]

Mar 00. (cd-s; by NAS featuring GINUWINE) *<radio cut>* **YOU OWE ME** [–] [59]

—— in Apr'01, NAS featured on QB FINEST's hit, 'Oochie Wally'

Dec 01. (cd) *(504176-9)* <85736> **STILLMATIC** [ ] [5]
– Stillmatic (intro) / Ether / Got ur self a . . . / Smokin' / You're da man / Rewind / One mic / 2nd childhood / Destroy and rebuild / The flyest / Braveheart party / Rule / My country / What goes around. *(bonus track+=)* – Every ghetto.

Dec 01. (cd-s) <79676> **GOT UR SELF A . . . / YOU'RE DA MAN** [–] [87]

Jan 02. (cd-s) *(672302-2)* **GOT UR SELF A . . . / DOO RAGS / BLACK ZOMBIE / ('A'video)** [30] [–]
(12") *(672302-6)* – ('A'side) / Ether.

Apr 02. (12"/cd-s) <79723> **ONE MIC (remix with BRAINPOWER) / MADE YOU LOOK (clean version) / ONE MIC (instrumental) / MADE YOU LOOK (instrumental) / ONE MIC (album version)** [–] [43]

Dec 02. (cd/d-lp) *(509811-2/-1)* <86930-2/-1> **GOD'S SON** [67] [12]
– Get down / The cross / Made you look / Last real nigga alive / Zone out (with BRAVEHEARTS) / Hey Nas (with KELIS & CLAUDETTE ORTIZ) / I can / Book of rhymes / Thugz mansion (N.Y.) (with 2 PAC & J. PHOENIX) / Mastermind / Warrior song (with ALICIA KEYS) / Revolutionary warfare (with LAKE) / Dance / Heaven (with JULLY BLACK).

Jan 03. (12"/cd-s) *(673479-6/-2)* <79845> **MADE YOU LOOK / MADE YOU LOOK (instrumental without guns) / ONE MIC** [27] Feb03 [32]

Mar 03. (12"/cd-s) *(673738-6/-2)* <673695> **I CAN / I CAN (Juliano Creatror explicit mix) / I CAN (instrumental)** [19] [12]
(cd-s) *(673738-5)* – ('A'side) / If I ruled the world (imagine that) (with LAURYN HILL) / Street dreams (with R. KELLY).

Nov 04. (12"/cd-s; NAS / OLU DARA) *(675468-6/-2)* **BRIDGING THE GAP / DOO RAGS (explicit). / THE WORLD IS YOURS / ('A'-instrumental)** [18] [94]

Nov 04. (d-cd) *(517724-9)* <92065> **STREET'S DISCIPLE** [45] [5]
– (intro) / A message to the feds; sincerely, we the people / Nazareth savage / American way (feat. KELIS) / Coon picnic (there are our heroes) / Disciple / Sakou story (feat. SCARLETT) / Live now (feat. SCARLETT) / Rest of my life / Just a moment (feat. QUAN) / Reason (feat. EMILY). *(bonus+=)* – You know my style // Suicide bounce (feat. BUSTA RHYMES) / Street's disciple (feat. OLU DARA) / U.B.R. (Unauthorized Biography of Rakim) / Virgo (feat. LUDACRIS & DOUG E. FRESH) / Remember the times / The makings of a perfect bitch / Getting married / No one else in the room (feat. MAXWELL) / Bridging the gap (feat. OLU DARA) / War (feat. KEON BRYCE) / Me & you (dedicated to destiny). *(bonus+=)* – Thief's theme.

– others, etc. –

Dec 01. (12"; by NAS & KOOL G RAP) *Archives; (ARC 778)* **FAST LIFE (remixes) / SILENT MURDER / LIFE'S A BITCH (mixes) / STREET DREAMS** [ ] [–]

Jan 02. (cd) *Sony; <71>* **THE BEST OF NAS** [–] [ ]

Sep 02. (cd/d-lp) *Columbia; (509362-2/-1)* <85275> **THE LOST TAPES VOL.1** [ ] [10]

☐ Graham NASH
(see under ⇒ CROSBY, STILLS, NASH & YOUNG)

☐ Dave NAVARRO (see under ⇒ JANE'S ADDICTION)

☐ the NAZZ (see under ⇒ RUNDGREN, Todd)

☐ NEARLY GOD (see under ⇒ TRICKY)

N.E.R.D.

Formed: Virginia Beach, Virginia, USA . . . late 90's by NEPTUNES men CHAD HUGO and PHARRELL WILLIAMS along with longtime buddy SHAY. Inevitably and irrevocably overshadowed by an avalanche of inspired NEPTUNES productions, the trio's independent project was nevertheless a fascinating diversion from their day jobs. Initially released on 'Virgin' in Europe, 'IN SEARCH OF . . .' (2001) plied the relatively uncharted waters of alternative hip hop, ingeniously salvaging and recycling the genre's root sources and cultural detritus with studied post-millennial cool and sly humour. Ever the sonic perfectionists, the N*E*R*D posse subsequently decided they didn't actually like it after all, re-recording the whole shebang with live instrumentation and finally issuing it for US and worldwide consumption in 2002. Lacking the profile and branding of the NEPTUNES' pop outings (although the trio no doubt hoped that some of that glamour would rub off), singles 'LAPDANCE' and 'ROCK STAR' made a great impact on the UK chart. The NEPTUNES production successes continued apace however, while PHARRELL released a solo, soul-centric single, 'FRONTIN'', in summer 2003. N.E.R.D. (No One Ever Really Dies) returned with a much anticipated sophomore set, 'FLY OR DIE' (2004). This was an even more esoteric dig through dog-eared vinyl, keeping the overriding PRINCE/SLY STONE/BEATLES sensibilities, paying homage to the Godfather on opener 'DON'T WORRY ABOUT IT', and generally making the kind of album that the 'CHILI PEPPERS might have made had they been born black; one of the most 'CHILI-soulful tracks, 'SHE WANTS TO MOVE', was lead single, making the UK Top 5. There's no argument that 'FLY..' was one of the most sussed – if indulgent – transatlantic Top 10 albums of late, and the fact that GOOD CHARLOTTE's BENJI and JOEL MADDEN guested on the hyperactive 'JUMP' shouldn't put you off.

Album rating: IN SEARCH OF . . . (*7) / FLY OR DIE (*6)

PHARRELL WILLIAMS (b. 5 Apr'73) – vocals, multi / **CHAD HUGO** – multi / **SHAY** – vocals

Virgin — Astralwerks

May 01. (c-s/cd-s; by N*E*R*D featuring LEE HARVEY & VITA) *(VUSC/+D 196)* **LAPDANCE / LIL' SUZY (with Kelis) / WHAT'S WRONG WITH ME** [33] [–]
(12"+=) *(VUST 196)* – ('A'-instrumental).

Aug 01. (cd) *(CDVUS 192)* <12622> **IN SEARCH OF . . .** [ ] Mar02 [56]
– Lapdance (with LEE HARVEY & VITA) / Things are getting better / Brain / Provider / Truth or dare (with KELIS & PUSHA T) / Tape you / Run to the sun / Baby doll / Am I high (with MALICE) / Rock star / Bobby James. *(re-iss. Mar02 cd+=/d-lp+=; CDVUS/+LP 216)* – Stay together. *(cd re-iss. Aug02 +=; CDVUSX 216)* – Rock star (Nevins' classic blaster). *(hit UK No.42) (d-lp re-iss. Mar03 +=; VUSLPX 216)* – Run to the sun (original). *(cd re-dist.Jun03)* – (hit UK No.28)

Jul 02. (cd-s) *(VUSTD 253)* **ROCK STAR (original / Jason Nevins' remix / Jason Nevins' classic club blaster)** [15] [–]
(12"+=) *(VUST 253)* – ('A'-Jason Nevins' classic instrumental).

Mar 03. (12") *(VUST 262)* **PROVIDER / PROVIDER (Zero 7 remix) / LAPDANCE (Freeform reform)** [20] [–]
(cd-s+=) *(VUSCD 262)* – ('A'-video).

Virgin — Virgin

Mar 04. (cd-s) *(VUSCD 284)* **SHE WANTS TO MOVE / ROCK STAR (Jason Nevins remix)** [5] [ ]
(12") *(VUST 284)* – ('A') / ('A'-DFA remix) / ('A'-Mac & Toolz remix).
(cd-s++=) *(VUSDX 284)* – ('A'-video).

Mar 04. (cd) *(CDVUS 250)* <91457> **FLY OR DIE** [4] [6]
– Don't worry about it / Fly or die / Jump / Backseat love / She wants to move / Breakout / Wonderful place / Drill sergeant / Thrasher / Maybe / The way she dances / Chariot of fire.

Jun 04. (cd-s) *(VUSCD 291)* **MAYBE / SHE WANTS TO MOVE (Native Tongue remix)** [25] [ ]
(12"+=) *(VUST 291)* – ('A'-SA-RA remix) / ('B'-Basement Jaxx remix).
(cd-s++=) *(VUSDX 291)* – ('A'-video).

PHARRELL WILLIAMS

Arista Arista

Aug 03. (12"; as PHARRELL WILLIAMS & JAY-Z) *(82876 55333-1)* <53004> **FRONTIN'. / HOT DAMN (with Ab Liva) / ('A'-instrumental)** 6 Jun03
(cd-s) *(82876 55333-2)* <58647> – (first 2 tracks) / Popular thug (by Kelis & Nas) / ('A'-video).

NEW FOUND GLORY

Formed: Coral Springs, Florida, USA . . . 1997 as A NEW FOUND GLORY by JORDAN PUNDIK, STEVE KLEIN, CHAD GILBERT, IAN GRUSHKA and CYRUS BOLOOKI. Fired by the success of their Xmas '97 sell-out debut EP, 'IT'S ALL ABOUT THE GIRLS', this Southern punk-pop quintet put all the twenty-something, hard earned wisdom and romantic regret they could muster into debut long player, 'NOTHING GOLD CAN STAY' (1999). 'M.C.A.' were impressed enough to offer them a major-label deal, promptly re-releasing the album later that year (1999), and following up with the rather contrived covers mini-set, 'FROM THE SCREEN TO YOUR STEREO' (2000). We really could have done without yet another airing of Aerosmith's 'I DON'T WANT TO MISS A THING' or Bryan Adams' 'EVERYTHING I DO..', and we most definitely could have done without tedious, pointless and gratingly upbeat American "punk" versions of already overplayed and overly saccaharine songs. The eponymous 'NEW FOUND GLORY' followed in 2000, another hackneyed if professional and listenable set of overly enthusiastic so-called punk. Ditto 2002's 'STICKS AND STONES', which nevertheless cracked the Top 10 and provided us with smash hit, 'MY FRIEND'S OVER YOU'. If the kids are united, they'll buy punky records to over-populate the charts. 'CATALYST' (2004) maintained the NFG/Emo formula that wasn't too far from BUSTED, SIMPLE PLAN or GOOD CHARLOTTE – only recommended are 'I DON'T WANNA KNOW', 'ALL DOWNHILL FROM HERE' and 'I'D KILL TO FALL ASLEEP' for some reason. Grow up lads!

• **Covered:** THAT THING YOU DO! (Adam Schlesinger) / THE NEVERENDING STORY THEME SONG (Limahl) / THE GOONIES 'R' GOOD ENOUGH (Cyndi Lauper) / THE GLORY OF LOVE (Peter Cetera) / MY HEART WILL GO ON (Celine Dion).

Album rating: NOTHING GOLD CAN STAY (*7) / FROM THE SCREEN TO YOUR STEREO mini (*5) / NEW FOUND GLORY (*6) / STICKS AND STONES (*6) / CATALYST (*5)

JORDAN PUNDIK (b.12 Oct'79) – vocals / **CHAD GILBERT** – lead guitar (ex-HAZEN STREET) / **STEVE KLEIN** – rhythm guitar / **IAN GRUSHKA** – bass / **CYRUS BOLOOKI** (b.27 Feb'80) – drums

not iss. Fiddler

Dec 97. (cd-ep; as A NEW FOUND GLORY) <FR 004CD> **IT'S ALL ABOUT THE GIRLS E.P.** –
– Shadow / My solution / Scraped knees / J.B. / Standstill. *(UK-iss.May01; same as US)*

drive-thru drive-thru

Mar 00. (cd; as A NEW FOUND GLORY) *(DRIVETHRU 013CD)* <112114> **NOTHING GOLD CAN STAY** Oct99
– Hit or miss / Never snows in Florida / 3rd and long / You've got a friend in Pennsylvania / The blue stare / 2's and 3's / Tell-tale heart / Winter of '95 / Passing time / Broken sound / Never sometimes / The good-bye song. *(re-iss. Jul01; same)*

M.C.A. M.C.A.

Mar 00. (m-cd; as A NEW FOUND GLORY) <112245CD> **FROM THE SCREEN TO YOUR STEREO** –
– That thing you do! / Never ending story theme song / I don't want to miss a thing / The Goonies 'R' good enough / The glory of love / (Everything I do) I do it for you / My heart will go on. *(UK-iss.Jul01; same) (re-iss. Jul03 on 'Eat Sleep'; EAT 029CD)*

Apr 01. (cd) <(112338-2)> **NEW FOUND GLORY** Sep00
– Better off dead / Dressed to kill / Sincerely me / Hit or miss / Second to last / Eyesore / Vegas / Sucker / Black and blue / Boy crazy / All about her / Ballad for the lost romantics.

Jun 01. (cd-s) <(155823-2)> **HIT OR MISS (WAITED TOO LONG) / SO MANY WAYS / YOU'VE GOT A FRIEND IN PENNSYLVANIA / HIT OR MISS (video)** 58 Aug01

Jun 02. (cd) <(112945-2)> **STICKS AND STONES** 10 4
– Understatement / My friends over you / Sonny / Something I call personality / Head on collision / It's been a summer / Forget my name / Never give up / The great Houdini / Singled out / Belated / The story so far (joke skits). *(special cd+=; 112972-2)* – Anniversary / Forget everything / The story so far (acoustic). *(d-cd-iss. Nov02 +=; AA88113123-2)* – Head on collision / Forget everything / Pride war (FURTHER SEEMS FOREVER) / What it is to burn (FINCH) / Roundabout (TSUNAMI BOMB) / Static (H20) / Lonely man's wallet (The EXIT) / Best of me (The STARTING LINE) / On my own (DON'T LOOK NOW).

Jun 02. (cd-s) <155965> **MY FRIENDS OVER YOU / IT'S BEEN A SUMMER** – 85

Jul 02. (7"pic-d) *(MCS 40286)* **MY FRIENDS OVER YOU. / SUCKER (live)** 30 –
(cd-s+=) *(MCSTD 40286)* – Hit or miss (live) / ('A'-video).
(cd-s) *(MCSXD 40286)* – ('A') / Eyesore (live) / Dressed to kill (live).

Oct 02. (cd-s) *(MCSTD 40298)* **HEAD ON COLLISION / EX-MISS / HEAD ON COLLISION (version)** 64 –
(cd-s) *(MCSXD 40298)* – ('A') / Something I call personality / Broken sound.

Geffen-MCA drive-thru

May 04. (cd) *(9862440)* <B00023831-2> **CATALYST** 27 3
– Intro / All downhill from here / This disaster / Truth of my youth / I don't wanna know / Your biggest mistake / Doubt full / Failure's not flattering / Over the head, below the knees / Ending in tragedy / At least I'm known for something / I'd kill to fall asleep / No news is good news / Who am I?

Jun 04. (7"pic-d) *(MCS 40367)* **ALL DOWNHILL FROM HERE. / BROKEN SOUND** 58
(cd-s+=) *(9862523)* – The minute I met you / ('A'-video).

Sep 04. (7"pic-d) *(MCS 40380)* **FAILURE'S NOT FLATTERING (WHAT'S YOUR PROBLEM). / HEAD ON COLLISION (live AOL session)** 67 –
(cd-s) *(MCSTD 40380)* – ('A') / All downhill from here (live AOL session) / Doubt full (live AOL session) / ('A'-video).

Feb 05. (7"pic-d) *(MCS 40404)* **I DON'T WANNA KNOW. / FORGET MY NAME (live from the Forum, August 2004)** 48 –
(cd-s+=) *(210397-2)* – ('A'-live from the Forum, August 2004) / ('A'-video).

NEW ORDER

Formed: Manchester, England . . . mid 1980, from the fragments of JOY DIVISION following the death of frontman IAN CURTIS on the 18th of May 1980. The remaining JOY DIVISION members, vocalist/guitarist BERNARD ALBRECHT (now SUMNER), bassist PETER HOOK and drummer STEPHEN MORRIS remained with 'Factory' records, subsequently adopting the NEW ORDER moniker at the suggestion of manager Rob Gretton. With SUMNER taking over vocal duties, the group gigged around Manchester, eventually releasing a debut single, 'CEREMONY' in 1981. This broke the Top 40, as did the Martin Hannett-produced follow-up, 'PROCESSION' / 'EVERYTHING'S GONE GREEN' although in reality, these releases weren't much of a departure from the rumbling, melodic bass sound of old, critics unimpressed with SUMNER's weak vocals. With their debut album, 'MOVEMENT' (1981), however, NEW ORDER were beginning to crystallise their own unique sound, new recruit GILLIAN GILBERT embellishing the music with cutting keyboard swathes. A subtle dance feel was also edging it's way in and with the release of 'TEMPTATION' the following year, NEW ORDER had begun experimenting openly with sequencing technology. The single married the raw cut 'n' thrust of alternative rock to danceable rhythms, echoing hip-hop's similar experimentation with European electronica (see AFRIKA

BAMBAATAA's seminal KRAFTWERK-sampling 'Planet Rock') and creating sonic waves that would ripple through the eclectic musical free-for-all of the 90's and beyond. Fittingly then, NEW ORDER's tour de force, 'BLUE MONDAY' was produced by cult US hip-hop producer, Arthur Baker. The best selling 12 inch single in the history of rock, the record was dominated by compelling, almost militaristic dancefloor beats behind SUMNER's introspective, melancholy vocal musings and HOOK's insidious bass melody. A true crossover single, the record appealed to indie fans, B-boys and club posers alike, cementing NEW ORDER's reputation as one of the UK's most street-cred acts. The accompanying album (an inferior demo version of 'BLUE MONDAY', '5-8-6' was included at the expense of the original single), 'POWER, CORRUPTION AND LIES' (1983) made the Top 5, confirming NEW ORDER's commitment to electronic experimentation via a hypnotic, slightly hazy set. A further Arthur Baker-produced 12 inch single followed, 'CONFUSION', the New Yorker also collaborating on the 1984 follow-up, 'THIEVES LIKE US'. But it wasn't until the acclaimed 'LOW LIFE' the following year that NEW ORDER successfully integrated the various strands which made up their inimitable sound. Previewed by the affecting 'PERFECT KISS' single and arguably the most consistently listenable NEW ORDER long player, the record convincingly welded driving, bass-heavy rock onto dance rhythms as well as featuring some interesting stylistic diversions. 'BROTHERHOOD' (1986) was a harder-edged affair, enjoyable enough and boasting the brilliant 'BIZARRE LOVE TRIANGLE', although hardly breaking new ground. 'TRUE FAITH' was another landmark NEW ORDER single; co-written and produced by STEPHEN HAGUE (who'd worked wonders on the PET SHOP BOYS' early material), the single was a hauntingly infectious piece of dance-pop, possibly the most commercial material NEW ORDER had ever released. Following the release of the best selling compilation, 'SUBSTANCE (1980-1987)' later that summer, the band went to ground, finally resurfacing in 1989 with 'TECHNIQUE' and quashing rumours of an imminent split. Heavily influenced by the house explosion of the late 80's and partly recorded on the Balearic Island of Ibiza, the album fully indulged the band's dancier leanings with a verve and passion that's missing from much of their later work. Deservedly, the album rode into the No.1 spot on the back of the club zeitgeist, a scene NEW ORDER had a major hand in creating. The single, 'FINE TIME', almost made the Top 10, an uncharacteristically humorous ditty featuring parodic mock-medallion man, BARRY WHITE-esque vocal rumblings. The following year, NEW ORDER were back at No.1 with their World Cup theme tune, 'WORLD IN MOTION'. Nationalist prejudice aside, this song seemed to set the trend for the nauseous, 'Enger-land'-lite that the LIGHTNING SEEDS would update six years later for the European championships. Maybe NEW ORDER felt the same way, as the various members soon drifted away to their respective side projects; HOOK to the muscular REVENGE (subsequently stiffing with the 'ONE TRUE PASSION' album), GILBERT and MORRIS to The OTHER TWO (1993's 'THE OTHER TWO AND YOU' album getting lost in the ether when 'Factory' went belly-up) and SUMNER hooking up with JOHNNY MARR (ex-SMITHS) and occasionally NEIL TENNANT (PET SHOP BOYS) to form ELECTRONIC. By far the most successful NEW ORDER-offshoot, the group scored three Top 20 hit singles, including the pop wistfulness of 'GETTING AWAY WITH IT'. They also narrowly missed No.1 with their 1991 eponymous album, their sound akin to a breezier NEW ORDER, fusing house and indie-pop with wry, intelligent lyrics. With 'Factory' going bust following HAPPY MONDAYS' bank-breaking 'SUNSHINE AND LOVE' debacle, a belated NEW ORDER follow-up, 'REPUBLIC' (1993), was subsequently released on 'London' records. A strangely muted collection, the record nevertheless spawned a succession of Top 30 singles including the aptly named Top 5 hit, 'REGRET'. Rumours of tensions within the group persisted and after a final appearance at the 1993 Reading Festival, the various members soon went off to do their own thing once more. ELECTRONIC charted with another set, 'RAISE THE PRESSURE' in 1996 and HOOK came up with the highly-NEW ORDER-esque MONACO project (with SUMNER-like DAVID POTTS) the following year. In 1999, ELECTRONIC returned with a third set, 'TWISTED TENDERNESS' – featuring the UK hit 'VIVID' – while MONACO again delighted the pop world with their eponymous follow-up in 2000. Few could've predicted NEW ORDER would return at all, never mind return with as good an album as 'GET READY' (2001). Rather than cater to the whims of contemporary club tastes, SUMNER, HOOK et al unashamedly made a record on their own terms. As a taster single, 'CRYSTAL' was perfect, a keening slice of classic NEW ORDER with the constituent parts (HOOKY's all-consuming bassline, SUMNER's little-boy-lost vocals, a melody to die for) all present and correct. Even the collaborative efforts of BOBBY GILLESPIE and BILLY CORGAN were subsumed under the record's driving focus. As the 80's revival kicked into gear – and any number of young, skinny-tied turks owing HOOK and co a debt – the release of 'WAITING FOR THE SIRENS' CALL' (2005) was timely enough, with lead single 'KRAFTY', going Top 10. The album itself made the Top 5 and while there was nothing new on the table – save for the quasi-white reggae of 'I TOLD YOU SO' and blooze-chops of 'WORKING OVERTIME' – the record did spawn a couple of further hits: a more obvious choice might've been the classicist 'DRACULA'S CASTLE', but both the title track and 'JETSTREAM' hovered around the Top 20. With NEW ORDER phase 2 now well underway, 'SINGLES' (2005) updated previous hits set, 'SUBSTANCE' (1987), with largely post-millennial material.

• **Songwriters:** All group compositions except; TURN THE HEATER ON (Keith Hudson). • **Trivia:** In 1987, they contributed some tracks to the movie, 'Salvation'.

Album rating: MOVEMENT (*8) / POWER, CORRUPTION AND LIES (*9) / LOW-LIFE (*8) / BROTHERHOOD (*8) / SUBSTANCE 1980-1987 compilation (*10) / TECHNIQUE (*9) / REPUBLIC (*6) / ? (THE BEST OF) compilation (*9) / THE REST OF NEW ORDER compilation (*7) / GET READY (*6) / WAITING FOR THE SIRENS' CALL (*6) / SINGLES compilation (*8) / Electronic: ELECTRONIC (*8) / RAISE THE PRESSURE (*6) / TWISTED TENDERNESS (*6)

BERNARD SUMNER (b. BERNARD DICKEN, 4 Jan'56) – vocals, guitar / **PETER HOOK** (b.13 Feb'56) – bass / **STEPHEN MORRIS** (b.28 Oct'57, Macclesfield, England) – drums

		Factory		Streetwise
Mar 81.	(7"/ext.12") *(FAC 33/+T)* **CEREMONY. / IN A LONELY PLACE** *(re-iss. Jul81 re-recorded; FAC 33-12)*	34		–

—— added **GILLIAN GILBERT** (b.27 Jan'61) – keyboards, synth.

		Factory		Streetwise
Sep 81.	(7") *(FAC 53)* **PROCESSION. / EVERYTHING'S GONE GREEN**	38		–
Nov 81.	(lp) *(FACT 50)* **MOVEMENT** – Dreams never end / Truth / Senses / Chosen time / I.C.B. / The him / Doubts even here / Denial. *(re-iss. Nov86 c)(cd; FACT 50C)(FACD 50) (re-iss. Jul93 on 'Centredate' cd/c; 520018-2/-4)*	30		–
Dec 81.	Factory Benelux; (12"m) *(FBN 8)* **EVERYTHING'S GONE GREEN (extended). / MESH / CRIES AND WHISPERS** *(re-iss. cd-ep Jul90; FBN 8CD)*	–	Belg.	–
May 82.	(7"/ext.12") *(FAC 63/+T)* **TEMPTATION. / HURT**	29		–
Nov 82.	Factory Benelux; (m-lp) *(FACTUS 8)* **NEW ORDER 1981-82** (compilation)	–	Belg.	–
Mar 83.	(12") *(FAC 73)* **BLUE MONDAY. / THE BEACH**	9		
May 83.	(lp)(c) *(FACT 75)(FACTUS 12C)* <25308> **POWER, CORRUPTION AND LIES** – Your silent face / Ultraviolence / Ecstasy / Leave me alone / Age of consent / We all stand / The village / 5-8-6. *(re-iss. Nov86 c)(cd; FACT 75C)(FAC 75CD)* – Blue Monday / The beach. *(re-iss. Jul93 on 'Centredate' cd/c; 520019-2/-4)*	4		

Aug 83. (12"ep) *(FAC 93)* **CONFUSION. / CONFUSED BEATS / CONFUSION (instrumental & Rough mixes)** 12 [ ]

Apr 84. (12") *(FAC 103)* **THIEVES LIKE US. / LONESOME TONIGHT** 18 [ ]

May 84. Factory Benelux; (12") *(FBN 22)* **MURDER. / THIEVES LIKE US (instrumental)** – Belg. –

Factory Qwest

May 85. (7") *(FAC 123)* **THE PERFECT KISS. / THE KISS OF DEATH** 46 –

(12"+=) *(FAC 123-12)* – Perfect pit.

Jun 85. (7") **THE PERFECT KISS. / PERFECT PIT** – [ ]

May 85. (lp/c)(cd) *(FACT 100/+C)(FACD 100)* <25289> **LOW-LIFE** 7 94

– Sooner than you think / Sub-culture / Face up / Love vigilantes / Elegia / The perfect kiss / This time of the night / Sunrise. *(c+=)* – The perfect kiss / The kiss of death / Perfect pit. *(re-iss. Jul93 on 'Centredate' cd/c; 520020-2/-4)*

Nov 85. (7"/ext.12") *(FAC 133/+T)* **SUB-CULTURE. / DUB-CULTURE** 63 –

Mar 86. (7") *(FAC 143)* **SHELLSHOCK. / THIEVES LIKE US (instrumental)** 28 –

(12") *(FAC 143T)* – ('A'extended) / Shellshock (dub).

Sep 86. (ext.12"/7") *(FAC 153/+7)* **STATE OF THE NATION. / SHAME OF THE NATION** 30 –

Oct 86. (lp/c/s-lp)(cd) *(FACT 150/+C/SP)(FACD 150)* <25511> **BROTHERHOOD** 9 [ ]

– Paradise / Weirdo / As it was when it was / Broken promise / Way of life / Bizarre love triangle / All day long / Angel dust / Every little counts. *(cd+=)* – State of the nation. *(re-iss. Jul93 on 'Centredate' cd/c; 520021-2/-4)*

Nov 86. (ext.12"/7") *(FAC 163/+7)* **BIZARRE LOVE TRIANGLE. / BIZARRE DUB TRIANGLE** 56 –

Mar 87. (7") **BIZARRE LOVE TRIANGLE. / EVERY LITTLE COUNTS** – [ ]

Jul 87. (ext-12"/7") *(FAC 183/+7)* <28271> **TRUE FAITH. / 1963** 4 Oct87 32

(remix-12"+=) *(FAC 183R)* – True dub.

Aug 87. (d-lp/d-c)(d-cd) *(FACT 200/+C)(FACD 200)* <25621> **SUBSTANCE (1980-1987)** (compilation) 3 36

– Ceremony / Everthing's gone green / Temptation / Blue Monday / Confusion / Thieves like us / Perfect kiss / Subculture / Shellshock / State of the nation / Bizarre love triangle / True faith. *(d-c+=)* – Procession / Mesh / Hurt / In a lonely place / The beach / Confused / Murder / Lonesome tonight / Kiss of death / Shame of the nation / 1963. *(cd++=)* – Cries and whispers / Dub culture / Shellcock / Bizarre dub triangle. *(re-iss. Jul93 on 'Centredate' cd/c; 520008-2/-4); hit UK No.32) (d-cd re-iss. Jun98; 520008-2)*

Dec 87. (ext.12"/7") *(FAC 193/+7)* **TOUCHED BY THE HAND OF GOD. / TOUCHED BY THE HAND OF DUB** 20 –

(cd-s) *(FACD 193)* – ('A'extended) / Confusion (dub '87) / Temptation (original).

Mar 88. (7") **TOUCHED BY THE HAND OF GOD. / BLUE MONDAY 1988** – [ ]

Dec 88. (7") *(FAC 223-7)* **FINE TIME. / DON'T DO IT** 11 [ ]

(12"+=) *(FAC 223)* – Fine line.

(cd-s+=) *(FACCD 223)* – ('A'-Silk mix) / ('A'-Messed around mix).

Jan 89. (cd)(lp/c/dat) *(FACD 275)(FACT 275/+C/D)* <25845> **TECHNIQUE** 1 32

– Fine time / All the way / Love less / Round & round / Guilty partner / Run / Mr. Disco / Vanishing point / Dream attack. *(re-iss. Jul93 on 'Centredate' cd/c; 520011-2)*

Mar 89. (ext.12"/7") *(FAC 263/+7)* <27524> **ROUND & ROUND. / BEST AND MARSH** 21 64

(ext.& club-12"+=) *(FAC 263R)* – ('A'-Detroit mix).

(cd-s+=) *(FACD 263)* – Vanishing point (instrumental 'Making Out' mix) / ('A'-12"mix).

(3"cd-s) *(FACD 263R)* – ('A'-Detroit) / ('A'-12") / ('A'-club).

Sep 89. (7") *(FAC 273-7)* **RUN 2. / MTO** 49 –

(12"+=) *(FAC 273)* – ('A'extended) / ('B'-Minus mix).

May 90. (12"/7"/c-s; as ENGLAND / NEW ORDER) *(FAC 293/+7/C)* **WORLD IN MOTION . . .. / THE B SIDE** 1 –

(cd-s+=) *(FACD 293)* – No alla violenzia / ('A'-Subbuteo mix).

(12") *(FAC 293R)* – ('A'-Subbuteo mix) / ('A'-Subbuteo dub) / No alla violenzia mix / ('A'-Carabinieri mix).

— Around the late 80's/early 90's, all members splintered to do own projects

Centredate Qwest

Apr 93. (7"/c-s) *(NUO/+C 1)* <18586> **REGRET. / ('A'mix)** 4 28

(cd-s+=) *(NUOCD 1)* – ('A'-Fire Island mix) / ('A'-Junior's dub mix).

(12") *(NUOX 1)* – ('A'-Fire Island mix) / ('A'-Junior's dub mix) / (2-'A' Sabres mixes)

May 93. (cd/c/lp) *(828413-2/-4/-1)* <45250> **REPUBLIC** 1 11

– Regret / World / Ruined in a day / Spooky / Everyone everywhere / Young offender / Liar / Chemical / Times change / Special / Avalanche.

Jun 93. (7"/c-s) *(NUO/+C 2)* **RUINED IN A DAY. / VICIOUS CIRCLE (mix)** 22 –

(cd-s+=) *(NUOCD 2)* – ('A'mixes).

(cd-s) *(NUOCDX 2)* – ('A'mixes).

(12") *(NUOX 2)* – ('A'side) / World (the price of dub mix).

Aug 93. (c-s) *(NUOC 3)* <18432> **WORLD (THE PRICE OF LOVE) / ('A'mixes)** 13 –

(12"+=/cd-s+=) *(NUOX/NUOCD 3)* – ('A'-Perfecto + sexy club mixes).

(cd-s) *(NUOCDX 3)* – ('A'-Brothers in rhythm mix) / ('A'dubstramental mix) / ('A'-World in action mix) / ('A'-Pharmacy dub).

Sep 93. (c-s,cd-s) <18432> **WORLD (THE PRICE OF LOVE) / RUINED IN A DAY** – 92

Dec 93. (c-s/12"/cd-s) *(NUO MC/X/CD 4)* **SPOOKY. / (3 'A' mixes-magimix-minimix-moulimix)** 22 [ ]

(cd-s) *(NUCDP 4)* – ('A'-Out of order mix) / ('A'-Stadium mix) / ('A'-In Heaven mix) / ('A'-Boo-dub mix) / ('A'-Stadium instrumental).

Nov 94. (7"/c-s) *(NUO/+MC 5)* **TRUE FAITH '94. / ('A'-Perfecto mix)** 9 [ ]

(12"+=) *(NUOX 5)* – ('A'-sexy disco dub mix) / ('A'-TWA Gim Up North mix).

(cd-s++=) *(NUOCD 5)* – ('A'radio mix).

Nov 94. (cd/c/d-lp) *(828 580-2/-4/-1)* <45794> **? (THE BEST OF)** (compilation) 4 78

– True faith '94 / Bizarre love triangle '94 / 1963 / Regret / Fine time / The perfect kiss / Shellshock / Thieves like us / Vanishing point / Run (2) / Round and round '94 / World (price of love) / Ruined in a day / Touched by the hand of God / Blue Monday '88 / World in motion.

Jan 95. (c-s) *(NUOMC 6)* **NINETEEN63 (Arthur Baker remix) / ('A'-'94 album version) / ('A'-Lionrock full throttle mix) / ('A'-Joe T Venelli remix)** 21 [ ]

(12") *(NUOX 6)* – ('A'-Lionrock & Joe T mixes / True faith (Eschreamer mix)/ ('A'-Eschreamer dub).

(cd-s) *(NUOCD 6)* – ('A'-Arthur Baker remix) / Let's go/ Spooky (Nightstripper mix)/ True faith '87 (Shep Pettibone mix).

Jul 95. (c-s) *(NUOMC 7)* **BLUE MONDAY '95 / ('A'-original)** 17 –

(12"+=/cd-s+=) *(NUO X/CD 7)* – ('A'-Hardfloor mix) / ('A'-Jam & Spoon mix).

Jul 95. (cd-ep) <20546> **BIZARRE LOVE TRIANGLE (2 mixes) / STATE OF THE NATION (2 mixes)** – 98

Aug 95. (cd/c) *(828 661-2/-4)* **THE REST OF NEW ORDER** (remixes, etc) 5 [ ]

Aug 01. (cd-s) *(NUCDP 8)* **CRYSTAL / CRYSTAL (Digweed & Muir bedrock remixes)** 8 –

(cd-s/d12") *(NUO CD/X 8)* – ('A'-Lee Coombs remix & dub) / ('A'-John Creamer & Stephane K mixes) / Behind closed doors.

(12") *(NUOXX 8)* – (some 'A'-mixes above).

(12") *(NUOXXX 8)* – (some 'A'-mixes above).

Aug 01. (cd/c/lp) *(<8573 89621-2/-4/-1>)* **GET READY** 6 Oct01 41

– Crystal / 60 miles an hour / Turn my way / Vicious streak / Primitive notion / Slow jam / Rock the shack / Someone like you / Close range / Run wild.

Nov 01. (cd-s) *(NUOCD 9)* **60 MILES AN HOUR / SABOTAGE / SOMEONE LIKE YOU (Funk D'void mix)** 29 [ ]

(cd-s) *(NUODP 9)* – ('A'side) / ('A'-Supermen lovers remix) / Someone like you (James Holden dub) / Someone like you (Future Shock mix).

Dec 01. (12") *(NUOX 10)* **SOMEONE LIKE YOU (mixes; futureshock vocal / Gabriel & Dresden 911 vocal / futureshock stripdown / Gabriel & Dresden voco-tech dub)** [ ] –

(12") *(NUOXX 10)* – ('A'-mixes; James Holden heavy dub / Funk d'Void).

Apr 02. (cd-s; as NEW ORDER & THE CHEMICAL BROTHERS) *(NUOCD 11)* **HERE TO STAY / HERE TO STAY (mix) / PLAYER IN THE LEAGUE** 15 –

(cd-s) *(NUCDP 11)* – ('A'mixes; radio / Felix Da Housecat – thee extended glitz / the scumfrog dub).

(12") *(NUOX 11)* – ('A'mixes) / Crystal (original).

Jun 02. (cd-s; as ENGLAND NEW ORDER) *(NUOCD 12)* **WORLD IN MOTION (mixes) / SUCH A GOOD THING** 43 –

— in Sep'03, PETER HOOK feat. on HYBRID's 'True To Form' hit

Mar 05. (cd-s) *(NUOCD 13)* **KRAFTY / KRAFTY (version)** [8] [ ]
(cd-s+=) *(NUCDP 13)* – ('A'-The Glimmers extended) / ('A'-Phones Reality mix) / ('A'-Andy Green mix) / ('A'-video).
(12") *(NUOX 13)* – ('A') / (first 2 mixes) / ('A'-Glimmers dub).
(d12"+=/cd-s+=) *<42800-1/-2>* – ('A'-mixes above +) / ('A'-Pink noise vocal) / ('A'-DJ Dan vocal) / ('A'-Eric Kupper club) / ('A'-Riton re-dub remix).

Mar 05. (cd/d-lp) *(2564 62202-2/-1) <49307>* **WAITING FOR THE SIRENS' CALL** [5] Apr05 [46]
– Who's Joe / Hey now what you doing / Waiting for the sirens' call / Krafty / I told you so / Morning night and day / Dracula's castle / Jetstream / Guilt is a useless emotion / Turn / Working overtime.

May 05. (cd-s; NEW ORDER feat. ANA MANTRONIC) *(NUOCD 14)* **JETSTREAM / (Richard X remix)** [20] [ ]
(12"+=) *(NUOX 14)* – ('A'-Jacques Lu Cont / Tom Neville mixes).
(cd-s++=) *(NUCDP 14)* – ('A'-mixes; Arthur Baker / Ana Bridge vox / video).
(12"+=/cd-s+=) *<42813-1/-2>* – (all mixes +) / Krafty (mixes).

Sep 05. (7") *(NUO 15V1)* **WAITING FOR THE SIRENS' CALL (Rich Costey radio edit). / TEMPTATION (Secret Machines remix)** [21] [–]
(7") *(NUO 15V2)* – ('A'-band mix) / Everything's gone green (Cicada remix).
(7"/cd-s) *(NUO/+CD 15V3)* – ('A'-Jacknife Lee remix) / Bizarre love triangle (Richard X remix).

Oct 05. (d-cd) *(2564 62690-2) <73304>* **SINGLES** (compilation) [14] [ ]
– Ceremony / Procession / Everything's gone green / Temptation / Blue Monday / Confusion / Thieves like us / The perfect kiss / Sub-culture / Shellshock / State of the nation / Bizarre love triangle / True faith / 1963 / Touched by the hand of God // Blue Monday '88 / Fine time / Round and round / Run 2 / World in motion / Regret / Ruined in a day / World (price of love) / Spooky / Crystal / 60 miles an hour / Here to stay / Krafty / Jetstream / Waiting for the sirens' call / Turn.

– compilations, etc. –

Sep 86. (12"ep) *Strange Fruit; (SFPS 001)* **PEEL SESSIONS** (1.6.82.) [54] [–]
– Turn the heater on / We all stand / 586 / Too late. *(re-iss. Jul87 c-ep; SFPSC 001) (re-iss. Mar88 cd-ep; SFPSCD 001)*

Oct 87. (12"ep) *Strange Fruit; (SFPS 039)* **PEEL SESSIONS** (26.1.81.) [ ] [–]
– Truth / Senses / I.C.B. / Dreams never end. *(re-iss. May88 cd-ep; SFPSCD 039)*

Mar 88. (7"/12") *Factory; (FAC 73-7/R) / Qwest; <27979>* **BLUE MONDAY 1988. / BEACH BUGGY** [3] [68]
(cd-s+=) *(FACD 73)* – ('A'original).

Sep 90. (m-cd/m-c/m-lp) *Strange Fruit; (SFR CD/C/LP 110)* **PEEL SESSIONS** (2 ep's combined) [ ] [–]

Feb 92. (cd/c/lp) *Windsong; (WIN CD/MC/LP 011)* **BBC RADIO 1 LIVE IN CONCERT (live June '87)** [33] [–]
– Touched by the hand of God / Temptation / True faith / Your silent face / Every second counts / Bizarre love triangle / Perfect kiss / Age of consent / Sister Ray.

Sep 97. (12") *Touch; (502780314769)* **TOUCH TONE 7.1** [ ] [–]

—— In Mar'89, they issued two 5"cd-vids of TRUE FAITH + BLUE MONDAY '88

Jul 02. (12") *Factory USA; (2054-6)* **BIZARRE LOVE TRIANGLE** [ ] [ ]

Nov 02. (12"; as BAKER vs. NEW ORDER) *Whacked; (WACKT 002)* **CONFUSION (2002 remixes; Koma & Bones / Larry T's)** [64] [–]
(12") *(WACKT 002R)* – ('A'mixes; Junior Sanchez vocal / Arthur Baker / Asto's).
(cd-s) *(WACKT 002CD)* – (all mixes above).

Dec 02. (4xcd-box) *London; (0927 49499-2) <73834>* **RETRO** [ ] [ ]

ELECTRONIC

BERNARD SUMNER – vocals, guitar / **JOHNNY MARR** – guitar (ex-SMITHS) + both programmers / also with **NEIL TENNANT** – vocals (of PET SHOP BOYS)

Factory Warners

Dec 89. (7"/c-s) *(FAC 257-7/-C) <19880>* **GETTING AWAY WITH IT. / LUCKY BAG** [12] [38]
(12"+=/cd-s+=) *(FAC 257 T/CD)* – ('A'extended).
(12"+=) *(FAC 257X)* – ('A'extra mixes).

—— added further guests **CHRIS LOWE, DONALD JOHNSON, DAVID PALMER, DENISE JOHNSON, HELEN POWELL + ANDREW ROBINSON** (on same track)

Apr 91. (7"/c-s) *(FAC 287-7/-C)* **GET THE MESSAGE. / FREE WILL** [8] [ ]
(cd-s+=) *(FACD 287)* – ('A'-DNA groove mix).
(12"+=) *(FAC-12 287)* – ('A' 2 other mixes).

May 91. (cd)(lp/c) *(FACD 290)(FACT 290/+C) <26387>* **ELECTRONIC** [2] [ ]
– Idiot country / Reality / Tighten up / The patience of a saint / Gangster / Soviet / Get the message / Try all you want / Some distant memory / Feel every beat. *(re-iss. Feb94 on 'Parlophone' cd/c; CD/TC PRG 1012)*

Sep 91. (7"/c-s) *(FAC 328-7/-C)* **FEEL EVERY BEAT. / LEAN TO THE INSIDE** [39] [ ]
(12"+=) *(FAC-12 328)* – ('A'dub version).
(cd-s+=) *(FACD 328)* – Second to none / ('A' DNA mix)

—— next with NEIL TENNANT again

Parlophone Warners

Jun 92. (c-s/7") *(TC+/R 6311)* **DISAPPOINTED. / IDIOT COUNTRY TWO** [6] [ ]
(12"+=/cd-s+=) *(12R/CDR 6311)* – ('A'-808 State mix) / ('B'-Ultimatum mix).

Jun 96. (c-s/7") *(TC+/R 6436)* **FORBIDDEN CITY. / IMITATION OF LIFE** [14] [ ]
(cd-s+=) *(CDR 6436)* – A new religion.

Jul 96. (cd/c) *(CD/TC+/PCS 7382) <45955>* **RAISE THE PRESSURE** [8] [ ]
– Forbidden city / For you / Dark angel / One day / Until the end of time / Second nature / If you've got love / Out of my league / Interlude / Freefall / Visit me / How long / Time can tell.

Sep 96. (c-s) *(TCR 6445)* **FOR YOU / ALL THAT I NEED** [16] [ ]
(cd-s+=) *(CDR 6445)* – I feel alright.
(cd-s) *(CDRS 6445)* – ('A'side) / Free will (12"mix) / Disappointed / Get the message (DNA mix).

Feb 97. (c-s) *(TCR 6455)* **SECOND NATURE / TURNING POINT** [35] [ ]
(cd-s+=) *(CDRS 6455)* – Feel every beat (12"remix).
(cd-s) *(CDR 6455)* – ('A'side) / ('A'-Plastik mix) / ('A'-Trance Atlantic dub) / ('A'-Sweet remix).

Apr 99. (12") *(12R 6514)* **VIVID. / PRODIGAL SON (mixes; Two Lone Swordsmen & Harvey's)** [17] [–]
(cd-s) *(CDR 6514)* – ('A'side) / Radiation / Prodigal son (inch mix).
(cd-s) *(CDRS 6514)* – ('A'side) / Haze (alternative mix) / Prodigal son (Harvey's a star in your mind mix).

Apr 99. (cd/c) *(<498345-2/-4>)* **TWISTED TENDERNESS** [9] [ ]
– Make it happen / Haze / Vivid / Vivid / Breakdown / Can't find my way home / Twisted tenderness / Like no other / Late at night / Prodigal son / When she's gone / Flicker.

Jul 99. (12") *(12R 6519)* **LATE AT NIGHT. / MAKE IT HAPPEN / MAKE IT HAPPEN (Darren Price mix)** [ ] [–]
(cd-s) *(CDR 6519)* – ('A'side) / King for a day / Come down now (Cevin Fisher mix).
(cd-s) *(CDRS 6519)* – ('A'side) / Warning sign / Make it happen (Darren Price mix).

□ the NEW POWER GENERATION (see under ⇒ PRINCE)

NEW YORK DOLLS

Formed: New York City, New York, USA . . . late '71 by JOHNNY THUNDERS, DAVID JOHANSEN, BILLY MURCIA, ARTHUR KANE and RICK RIVETS. In March the following year, RIVETS left to form the BRATS, being swiftly replaced by SYLVAIN SYLVAIN. After a promising start as support act on a FACES British tour, the 'DOLLS' first casualty was MURCIA who died on the 6th of November '72 after drowning in his own bath (not, as widely believed, from a drug overdose). With JERRY NOLAN as a replacement, they signed to 'Mercury' in March '73 and promptly began work on an eponymous debut album with TODD RUNDGREN producing. Released in the summer of that year, 'NEW YORK DOLLS' was a proto-punk revelation, a way cool schlock of visceral rock'n'roll which combined the more essential moments of MC5, the PRETTY THINGS, PINK FAIRIES and the SHANGRI-LAS. The ROLLING STONES were another obvious reference point, JOHANSEN a dead-ringer for MICK JAGGER in terms of both vocal style and mascara'd looks. Inevitably, then, THUNDERS was the glam-punk KEITH RICHARDS, Glitter Twins to the JAGGERS/RICHARDS Glimmer coupling. The 'DOLLS' trashy transvestite attire also borrowed heavily from the 'STONES (circa '66 'Have You Seen Your Mother . . .'), although being American they'd obviously taken it to almost cartoon-esque proportions. The likes of 'PERSONALITY CRISIS', 'TRASH' and 'JET BOY' were seminal squalls of guitar abuse, making up in attitude what they lacked in musical ability. Although the record had the critics salivating, commercial success wasn't forthcoming and, unhappy with the record's production, the band opted for SHANGRI-LA's producer, GEORGE MORTON to work on 'TOO MUCH TOO SOON' (1974). Though the album had its moments, again the band had been paired with the wrong producer and the music press were emphatically unimpressed. The lukewarm reviews heightened inter-band tension and the 'DOLLS demise was swift and inevitable. Early the following year, Londoner MALCOLM McLAREN made a last-ditch attempt to save the band, revamping their image to no avail. THUNDERS was the first to leave, departing in 1975 to form the HEARTBREAKERS, while JOHANSEN and SYLVAIN subsequently sacked KANE before finally calling it a day the following Christmas. While THUNDERS went on to most acclaim with his HEARTBREAKERS (dying from an overdose on 23rd April '91), JOHANSEN recorded a number of solo albums, 'DAVID JOHANSEN' (1978), 'IN STYLE' (1979) and 'HERE COMES THE NIGHT' (1981) as well as releasing a 1988 set under the pseudonym of BUSTER POINDEXTER. NOLAN also met an untimely death (14th January, 1992), almost a year on from THUNDERS, the man suffering a fatal stroke while undergoing treatment for meningitis and pneumonia. A pivotal reference point for not only punk, but the US sleaze/glam metal movement of the mid-80's (FASTER PUSSYCAT, L.A. GUNS, GUNS N' ROSES, et al), the NEW YORK DOLLS influence remains hugely disproportionate to their relatively slim recorded legacy. One of the band's longest and most unlikely champions has been former SMITHS bard MORRISSEY. With his own solo career back on track and the distinction of curating the South Bank's 2004 'Meltdown Festival', he valiantly rounded up the surviving 'DOLLS (who hadn't spoken to each other for more than a decade) and persuaded them to get out the greasepaint one more time. On 16th June, 2004, the trio – augmented with keyboard player BRIAN KOONIN, guitarist STEVE CONTE and LIBERTINES drummer GARY POWELL – took to the stage for the first time in 30 years. No one knew it was to be the last stand of bassist ARTHUR KANE, who was diagnosed with leukaemia just under a month later on July 15th, passing away the same day. Not just any old live set, then, 'RETURN OF THE NEW YORK DOLLS: LIVE FROM ROYAL FESTIVAL HALL, 2004', was more a tribute to KANE, alive with the unfettered joy of being on the same stage once more. Nor was it just a one-off: the NEW YORK DOLLS are once more a going concern, having signed to 'Roadrunner', and – at the time of writing – on the verge of releasing what will be a heroically belated – 32 years and counting – third album.

• **Songwriters:** JOHANSEN with THUNDERS or SYLVAIN. Covered PILLS (Bo Diddley) / DON'T START ME TALKIN' (Sonny Boy Williamson) / SHOWDOWN (Archie Bell) / SOMETHIN' ELSE (Eddie Cochran) / etc.
• **Trivia:** Two songs 'PERSONALITY CRISIS' & 'WHO ARE THE MYSTERY GIRLS', appeared on the 1977 Various Artists compilation 'New Wave'.

Album rating: NEW YORK DOLLS (*8) / TOO MUCH TOO SOON (*7) / LIPSTICK KILLERS exploitation (*5) / ROCK & ROLL compilation (*7) / THE RETURN OF . . . LIVE FROM ROYAL FESTIVAL HALL (*6)

DAVID JOHANSEN (b. 9 Jan'50, Staten Island, N.Y.) – vocals / **JOHNNY THUNDERS** (b. JOHN GENZALE, 15 Jul'52) – guitar, vocals / **SYLVAIN SYLVAIN** (b. SIL MIZRAHI) – guitar, vocals repl. RICK RIVETS / **ARTHUR KANE** (b. 3 Feb'51) – bass / **JERRY NOLAN** (b. 7 May'51) – drums repl. BILLY MURCIA who died.

Mercury Mercury

Jul 73. (7") *<73414>* **TRASH. / PERSONALITY CRISIS** –
Aug 73. (lp) *(6338 270) <SRM 675>* **NEW YORK DOLLS** Jul73
– Personality crisis / Looking for a kiss / Vietnamese baby / Lonely planet boy / Frankenstein / Trash / Bad girl / Subway train / Pills / Private world / Jet boy. *<US re-iss. 1984; same>*
Nov 73. (7") *(6052 402)* **JET BOY. / VIETNAMESE BABY** –
Jul 74. (lp) *(6338 498) <SRM 1001>* **TOO MUCH TOO SOON** May74
– Babylon / Stranded in the jungle / Who are the mystery girls? / (There's gonna be a) Showdown / It's too late / Puss 'n' boots / Chatterbox / Bad detective / Don't start me talkin' / Human being. *<US re-iss. 1984; same>*
Jul 74. (7") *(6052 615) <73478>* **STRANDED IN THE JUNGLE. / WHO ARE THE MYSTERY GIRLS?**
Sep 74. (7") *<73615>* **(THERE'S GONNA BE A) SHOWDOWN. / PUSS 'N' BOOTS** –

not iss. Trash

1974. (fan club-7"ep) *<TR 001>* **LOOKING FOR A KISS (live). / WHO ARE THE MYSTERY GIRLS? (live) / SOMETHIN' ELSE (live)** –

— **PETER JORDAN** – bass (the roadie filled in on stage when KANE was drunk)

— Disbanded mid-1975, after **BOBBY BLAIN** – keyboards repl. CHRIS ROBINSON who had repl. THUNDERS (he formed The HEARTBREAKERS with NOLAN). **TOMMY MACHINE** (was last drummer). The NEW YORK DOLLS reformed again with JOHANSEN and SYLVIAN but only toured until late '76. SYLVIAN later formed The CRIMINALS. DAVID JOHANSEN went solo in 1978.

— NEW YORK DOLLS reformed for live show:- **JOHANSEN, SYLVAIN + KANE** plus **STEVE CONTE** – guitar / **GARY POWELL** – drums / **BRIAN KOONIN** – keyboards (THUNDERS had died 1992, NOLAN absent)

Attack Attack

Sep 04. (cd) *(ATKCD 009) <86008>* **THE RETURN OF THE NEW YORK DOLLS: LIVE FROM ROYAL FESTIVAL HALL** (live)
– Looking for a kiss / Puss n' boots / Subway train / Bad girl / You can't put your arms around a memory – Lonely planet boy / Private world / Vietnamese baby / Pills / Mystery girls / Frankenstein / Out in the street / Babylon / Trash / Jet boy / Personality crisis / Human being.

— ARTHUR KANE died of leukemia shortly after recordings

– compilations, others, etc. –

Jun 77. (7"m) *Mercury; (6160 008)* **JET BOY. / BABYLON / WHO ARE THE MYSTERY GIRLS?** –
Jul 77. (d-lp) *Mercury; (6641 631)* **NEW YORK DOLLS / TOO MUCH TOO SOON** –
(re-iss. Apr86; PRID 12)
Nov 81. (c) *R.O.I.R.; <A 104>* **LIPSTICK KILLERS – MERCER ST. SESSIONS** –
(re-iss. May90 on 'Danceteria' cd/lp; DAN CD/LP 038) (re-iss. cd Feb95 & Jun97 on 'ROIR Europe'; 885615027-2) (cd re-iss. Aug00 on 'R.O.I.R.'; RUSCD 8266)
Sep 82. (12"ep) *Kamera; (ERA 13-12)* **PERSONALITY CRISIS / LOOKING FOR A KISS. / SUBWAY TRAIN / BAD GIRL** –
(re-iss. Jul90 on 'See For Miles' cd-ep; SEACD 3)
Sep 84. (red-m-lp) *Fan Club; (FC 007)* **RED PATENT LEATHER (rec. 75)** – France –
– Girls / Downtown / Private love / Personality crisis / Pills / Something else / Daddy rollin' stone / Dizzy Miss Lizzy. *(cd-iss. Oct88; FC 007CD) (UK cd-iss. Feb93 on 'Receiver'+=; RRCD 173) (cd re-iss. Apr97 on 'Last Call'; 42241-2)*
Oct 84. (7"white) *Fan Club; (NYD 1)* **PILLS (live). / DOWN, DOWN, DOWN TOWN (live)** – France –
1985. (lp) *Mercury; <8260 941>* **NIGHT OF THE LIVING DOLLS** –
Feb 86. (7",12"pic-d,12"red) *Antler; (DOLLS 1)* **PERSONALITY CRISIS. / SUBWAY TRAIN** –
Feb 86. (7",12"pic-d,12"blue) *Antler; (DOLLS 2)* **LOOKING FOR A KISS. / BAD GIRL** –

1986. (lp; one-side by SEX PISTOLS) *Receiver; (RRLP 102)* **AFTER THE STORM** [ ] [–]
(cd-iss. Jul93; RRCD 102)

Jul 93. (cd) *Receiver; <(RRCD 163)>* **SEVEN DAY WEEKEND** [ ] [ ]

Jul 93. (cd) *Receiver; <(RRCD 173)>* **IN NYC 1975** [ ] [ ]

Oct 94. (cd) *Mercury; (522 129-2)* **ROCK'N'ROLL** [ ] [ ]

Mar 96. (cd) *Skydog; <(62256-2)>* **PARIS BURNING** [ ] [ ]

Mar 96. (cd) *Skydog; <(62257-2)>* **NEW YORK TAPES 1972-1973** [ ] [ ]
<(re-iss. Feb00 on 'Munster'; MR 167/+CD)>

Oct 97. (cd) *Red Star; <(RS 7006)>* **TEENAGE NEWS** [ ] [ ]

Nov 98. (cd; shared w/ JOHNNY THUNDERS) *Recall; <(SMDCD 207)>* **STREET TRASH** [ ] [ ]

Nov 98. (cd) *Receiver; <(RRCD 260)>* **I'M A HUMAN BEING (live)** [ ] [ ]

Sep 98. (cd) *Red Star; <(RSR 7006)>* **LIVE IN CONCERT PARIS 1974** [ ] [ ]
<(re-iss. Jun99 on 'Essential'; ESMCD 734)>

Jul 99. (cd) *Big Ear; (109634022-2)* **GLAMOROUS LIFE – LIVE** [ ] [ ]

Apr 00. (lp/cd) *Get Back; (GET 60/+CD)* **THE BIRTH OF THE NEW YORK DOLLS** [ ] [ ]

NICKELBACK

Formed: Hanna, Calgary, Canada . . . 1995 by CHAD KROEGER, who played in a covers band but got fed up and wrote a handful of songs before cutting a demo tape in Vancouver. He invited his brothers MIKE and BRANDON KROEGER and a bassist friend RYAN PEAKE to play in the band and after a short time rehearsing, the group recorded and independently issued EP 'HERSHER' (1996) and managed to raise enough cash to fund a cross-country 'toilet' tour across Canada before releasing their debut set 'CURB' (1997). After two years of squabbling and disagreeing with their management, KROEGER decided that it would be best if the group managed themselves, thus adding pressure for the other members whose job it was to distribute and advertise their debut long-player. KROEGER came up with the ingenious way of creating airplay for themselves by getting friends and family members to phone up radio stations and request their songs. By this time NICKELBACK had quite a cult following in the US and in North America. They independently produced and distributed 'THE STATE' (2000), the sophomore album which held the group's hard-edged rock ethos intact but lacked the punch of their first. The set proved to be highly successful, with a sell-out tour and a growing popularity, the trio soon found themselves playing for larger audiences, supporting the likes of CREED and FUEL. Not surprisingly, 'THE STATE' was bought by various different companies for major distribution all over the globe; 'E.M.I.' for the Canadian release and 'Roadrunner' elsewhere. It also broke them into the US Top 200 later in the year. 'SILVER SIDE UP' was released the following year and spawned the massive hit single 'HOW YOU REMIND ME', a PEARL JAM-esque rock-out, with big riffs and an even bigger chorus. The soon-to-be Top 3 album and the single put NICKELBACK on the musical map, with the aforementioned single being officially claimed as 'The Most Played Song On American Radio'. It topped the charts in both America and Canada at the same time, a feat not accomplished since the GUESS WHO's 'American Woman' (me thinks?). Although whether people will still be listening to NICKELBACK three decades hence is open to question. 2002 brought another sizeable hit in 'HERO', a duet with SALIVA frontman JOSEY SCOTT which had previously appeared on the soundtrack to the 'Spiderman' movie. 'THE LONG ROAD' (2003) was another constipated collection of meat and potatoes hard rock, with just enough tortuous whining to have it labelled alternative. Grunge might have long gone but bands like NICKELBACK are still hanging around, propagating a sound that approximates to a decade's worth of bad beard days. And yes, KROEGER was still hawking up his guts on 'ALL THE RIGHT REASONS' (2005), and Americans were still buying it in mystifying quantities – enough to see it become their first US No.1 album (UK Top 20). Dewy-eyed powerballad, 'PHOTOGRAPH', found him ruminating on his high school days, memories apparently interesting enough to make No.2 (UK Top 30). Subsequent singles stalled much further down the listings, with only 'FAR AWAY' making the UK Top 40.

• **Covers:** SATURDAY NIGHT'S ALRIGHT (FOR FIGHTING) (Elton John) / WE WILL ROCK YOU (Queen).

Album rating: HESHER mini (*5) / CURB (*5) / THE STATE (*6) / SILVER SIDE UP (*7) / THE LONG ROAD (*4) / ALL THE RIGHT REASONS (*4)

CHAD KROEGER (b.15 Nov'74) – vocals, guitar / **RYAN PEAKE** (b. 1 Mar'73) – guitar, vocals / **MIKE KROEGER** (b.25 Jun'72) – bass / **BRANDON KROEGER** – drums

not iss. / own label

1996. (m-cd) *<none>* **HESHER EP** [–] Canada [–]
– Where? / Windowshopper / Fly / Truck / Left / In front of me / D.C.

1997. (cd) *<none>* **CURB** [–] Canada [–]
– Little friend / Pusher / Detangler / Curb / Where? / Falls back on / Sea groove / Fly / Just four / Left / Windowshopper / I don't have. *<(re+UK-iss.Jun02; RR 8440-2)>*

—— **RYAN VIKEDAL** (b. 9 May'75) – drums; repl. BRANDON who had repl. MITCH GUINDON

Roadrunner / Roadrunner

Mar 00. (cd) *<8586>* **THE STATE** [–] [ ]
– Breathe / Cowboy hat / Leader of men / Old enough / Worthy to say / Diggin' this / Deep / One last run / Not leavin' yet / Hold out your hand. *<cd-bonus+=>* – Leader of men (acoustic) / Worthy to say (acoustic).

Sep 01. (cd) *(120 8485-2) <61 8485>* **SILVER SIDE UP** [1] [2]
– Never again / How you remind me / Woke up this morning / Too bad / Just for / Hollywood / Money bought / Where do I hide / Hangnail / Good times now. *(lp-iss.Sep02 on 'Simply Vinyl'; S 160001) (re-iss. Mar06 w/dvd+=; RR 8095-5)* – (DVD tracks).

Oct 01. (cd-s) *(2320332-3) <012053>* **HOW YOU REMIND ME / LEADER OF MEN (acoustic)** [ ] Aug01 [1]

Feb 02. (c-s) *(2320332-4)* **HOW YOU REMIND ME / (acoustic)** [4] [–]
(cd-s+=) *(2320332-0)* – Learn the hard way / ('A'-video).
(cd-s) *(2320332-5)* – ('A') / (gold mix) / Yanking out my / Leader of men / Leader of men (video).

Jun 02. (c-s; as CHAD KROEGER & JOSEY SCOTT) *(RR 2046-4)* **HERO / HERO (superhero mix)** [4] May02 [3]
(cd-s+=) *(RR 2046-3)* – (track by THEORY OF A DEADMAN) / ('A'-video).
(above from the movie, 'Spider-Man'

Aug 02. (c-s) *(RR 2037-4)* **TOO BAD / HOW YOU REMIND ME (live)** [9] Mar02 [42]
(cd-s+=) *(RR 2037-3) <2051-3>* – Woke up this morning (live) / ('A'video).
(cd-s) *(RR 2037-5)* – ('A') / Never again (live) / Leader of men (live) / ('A'-live video).

Nov 02. (cd-s) *(RR 2025-3)* **NEVER AGAIN / ONE LAST RUN (live) / WORTHY TO SAY (live) / ('A'-video)** [30] [–]
(cd-s) *(RR 2025-5)* – ('A'-full length) / Breathe (live) / Old enough (live).

Sep 03. (cd-s) *(RR 2008-8) <55302-5>* **SOMEDAY / SLOW MOTION / SOMEDAY (acoustic) / SOMEDAY (video)** [6] [7]

Sep 03. (cd) *(RR 8400-2) <RRD 618400>* **THE LONG ROAD** [5] [6]
– Flat on the floor / Do this anymore / Someday / Believe it or not / Feelin' way too damn good / Because of you / Figured you out / Should've listened / Throw yourself away / Another hole in the head / See you at the show. *(special-cd+=; RR 8400-5)* – Yanking out my heart / Learn the hard way / Saturday night's alright (for fighting).

Feb 04. (cd-s) *<20013>* **FIGURED YOU OUT / TOO BAD (live unplugged) / WHERE DO I HIDE (live)** [–] [65]

Mar 04. (cd-s) *<(RR 3998-3)>* **FEELIN' WAY TOO DAMN GOOD / WHERE DO I HIDE (live) / ('A'-album) / ('A'-video)** [39] Apr04 [48]

—— **DANIEL ADAIR** (b.19 Feb'75) – drums (ex-3 DOORS DOWN) repl. VIKEDAL

Sep 05. (cd-s) *<(RR 3955-3)>* **PHOTOGRAPH / (version) / WE WILL ROCK YOU / (video)** [29] [2]

Oct 05. (cd) <(RR 8300-2)> **ALL THE RIGHT REASONS** 13 1
– Follow you home / Fight for all the wrong reasons / Photograph / Animals / Savin' me / Far away / Next contestant / Side of a bullet / If everyone cared / Someone that you're with / Rockstar.
Feb 06. (-) <radio> **ANIMALS** – 99
Feb 06. (cd-s) *(RR 3948-2)* **FAR AWAY / MISTAKE (live) / PHOTOGRAPH (acoustic)** 40 –
Apr 06. (cd-s) <RR 3944-3> **SAVIN' ME / (version)** – 19

NICO

Born: CHRISTA PAFFGEN, 16 Oct'38, Cologne, Germany. Her father died in a concentration camp, and, as a girl, she travelled throughout Europe with her mother. Developing a fondness for opera, she learned to play classical piano and harmonium. In 1959, while vacationing in Italy, she was introduced by new friends to film director Federico Fellini and following a bit-part in 'La Dolce Vita', she became a top model, appearing in Vogue magazine. In the early 60's, while working in films, she became the girlfriend of French actor Alain Delon. She later give birth to his son, having already borne a daughter to actor/dancer Eric Emerson. In 1963, she fell in love with up and coming folk-star BOB DYLAN, who wrote a song for her, 'I'LL KEEP IT WITH MINE'. In 1965, at his suggestion, she moved to London and signed for Andrew Loog Oldham's new label, 'Immediate'. A single, 'I'M NOT SAYING' (written by GORDON LIGHTFOOT) was issued, although the record subsequently flopped, even after an appearance on 'Ready Steady Go'. She then moved to New York, where she met pop-artist ANDY WARHOL. He asked her to feature in an avant-garde film, 'Chelsea Girl', also asking her to join LOU REED, JOHN CALE, MO TUCKER, etc. in his managerial group, The VELVET UNDERGROUND. Together they made one glorious late 1966 album, 'THE VELVET UNDERGROUND AND NICO', NICO leaving soon after for a return to solo work. Decribed as 'The Edith Piaf of the Blank Generation', she was an avant-garde, moody songstress who was anti-pop music in every sense. After a liaison with BRIAN JONES of The ROLLING STONES, she became the opposite number of teenager and new pensmith JACKSON BROWNE who wrote songs for her debut 1968 album, 'CHELSEA GIRL' (notebly 'THESE DAYS'). Regarded as an artistic triumph, she nevertheless disagreed with producer Tom Wilson's string arrangements. Subsequently moving to Los Angeles, she started writing material for her follow-up 'Elektra' album, 'THE MARBLE INDEX'. She travelled constantly between America and Europe, starring in another underground film, 'La Cicatrice Interieupe' for Philippe Garrel. In 1971, she cut the JOHN CALE-produced DESERTSHORE', the track 'Le Petit Chevalier' featuring her son. Fleeing New York for France after she was involved in a bottle fight with a female Black Panther member, she later appeared at The Rainbow, London on 1st of June '74 alongside JOHN CALE, ENO and KEVIN AYERS. A track, 'THE END', was recorded, and Island' records promptly signed her for an album of the same name, with ENO and PHIL MANZANERA at the production helm. That year, she also contributed vocals to KEVIN AYERS' album, Confessions Of Dr. Dream', although she subsequently retired from music to live between Berlin, Los Angeles and Spain. In 1981, she made a comeback album, appropriately titled 'DRAMA OF EXILE', but after poor audience response on a SIOUXSIE & THE BANSHEES support slot, she again went AWOL, shacking up in Manchester, England with her live-in-boyfriend and poet JOHN COOPER CLARKE. After another dismissed vinyl return in 1985, she again retired, only to reappear at a 1987 ANDY WARHOL tribute. Tragically, on the 18th of July '88, on a holiday in Ibiza with CLARKE, she fell off her bike and died of a brain hemorrhage.

• **Songwriters:** As said, and other covers; THE END (Doors) / DEUTSCHLAND UBER ALLES (German national anthem) / HEROES (David Bowie) / etc. Plus there are obviously a number of VELVET UNDERGROUND renditions littered about. • **Trivia:** In 1974, she joined LOU REED and JOHN CALE for a French filmed VELVET UNDERGROUND reunion.

Album rating: CHELSEA GIRL (*8) / THE MARBLE INDEX (*7) / DESERTSHORE (*7) / THE END (*5) / DRAMA OF EXILE (*4) / CAMERA OBSCURA (*4) / THE BLUE ANGEL collection (*6) / BEHIND THE IRON CURTAIN (*4) / LIVE IN TOKYO (*5) / posthumous:- HANGING GARDENS (*6) / HEROINE (*4) / INNOCENT & VAIN: AN INTRODUCTION TO NICO compilation (*7)

NICO – vocals (plus session people)

Immediate / not iss.
Aug 65. (7") *(IM 003)* **I'M NOT SAYIN'. / THE LAST MILE** –
(re-iss. May82; IMS 003) (re-iss. Apr03 on 'Munster'; 7173)
(above 'B'side featured JIMMY PAGE as guitarist/writer)

— In 1966, she teamed up with The VELVET UNDERGROUND on their eponymous lp. Breaking from them the following year, she returned to solo work, augmented by JOHN CALE + LOU REED. Her beau JACKSON BROWNE at the time also became her main songwriter.

not iss. / Verve
Feb 68. (lp) <2353 025> **CHELSEA GIRL** –
– The fairest of the seasons / These days / Little sister / Winter song / It was a pleasure then / Chelsea girls / I'll keep it with mine / Somewhere there's a father / Wrap your troubles in dreams / Eulogy to Lenny Bruce. *(UK-iss.Sep71 on 'MGM Select'; 2353 025) (re-iss. 1974 on 'Polydor'; same) (cd-iss. May88 & Apr94; 835 209-2)*

— Retained JOHN CALE as producer, etc.

Elektra / Elektra
Jul 69. (lp) <(EKL 4029)> **THE MARBLE INDEX**
– Prelude / Lawns of dawns / No one is there / Ari's song / Facing the wind / Julius Caesar (memento Hodie) / Frozen warnings / Evening of light. *(cd-iss. Apr91 on 'WEA'+=; 7559 61096-2)* – Roses in the snow / Nibelungen.

Reprise / Reprise
Jan 71. (lp) <(RSLP 6424)> **DESERTSHORE**
– Janitor of lunacy / Falconer / My only child / Le petit chevalier / Abschied / Afraid / Mutterlein / All that is my own. *(re-iss. 1974; K 44102) (cd-iss. Apr91 on 'WEA'; 7599 25870-2)*

— She retained **CALE** and brought in **ENO** – synthesizer / **PHIL MANZANERA** – guitar / **STERLING MORRISON** – guitar

Island / not iss.
Oct 74. (lp) *(ILPS 9311)* **THE END** –
– It has not taken long / Secret side / You forgot to answer / Innocent and vain / Valley of the kings / We've got the gold / The end / Das lied der Deutschen. *(cd-iss. Apr94; IMCD 174)*

— now with **ANDY CLARKE** – keyboards / **MUHAMMED HADI** – guitar / **DAVEY PAYNE** – sax / **STEVE CORDONA** – drums / **PHILIPPE QUILICHINI** – bass

Aura / not iss.
Jul 81. (lp) *(AUL 715)* **DRAMA OF EXILE** –
– Genghis Khan / Purple lips / One more chance / Henry Hudson / I'm waiting for the man / Sixty forty / The sphinx / Orly flight / Heroes. *(cdiss.Mar88 on 'Line'; LILP 400106) (cd re-iss. Jul92 on 'Great Expectations'; PIPCD 037) (cd re-iss. Aug96 on 'See For Miles'; SEECD 449)*

Flicknife / not iss.
Sep 81. (7") *(FLS 206)* **VEGAS. / SAETA** –

Half / not iss.
Jul 82. (7") *(1/2 1)* **PROCESSION. / ALL TOMORROW'S PARTIES** –
(12"+=) *(1/2 1-12)* – Secret side (live) / Femme fatale (live).

Aura / not iss.
Jun 83. (7") *(AUS 137)* **HEROES. / ONE MORE CHANCE** –

— with **JAMES YOUNG** – keyboards / **GRAHAM DIDS** – percussion

Beggars Banquet / not iss.
Jun 85. (7"/12"; as NICO & THE FACTION) **MY FUNNY VALENTINE. / MY HEART IS EMPTY** –
Jun 85. (lp/c/cd; as NICO & THE FACTION) *(BEG A/C/CD 63)* **CAMERA OBSCURA** –
– Camera obscura / Tananore / Win a few / My funny valentine / Das lied von einsamen Madchens / Fearfully in danger / My heart is empty / Into the arena / Konig. *(re-iss. Jan89 on 'Beggars Banquet-Lowdown' lp/c)(cd; BBL/+C 63)(BBL 63CD)*

— added **ERIC RANDOM** – percussion, etc / **TOBY TOMAN** – drums

Dojo not iss.

Apr 86. (d-lp/c/cd) *(DOJO LP/TC/CD 27)* **BEHIND THE IRON CURTAIN (live 1985)** [ ] [-]
– All saints night from a Polish motorway / One more chance / Frozen warnings / The song of the lonely girl / Win a few / Konig / Purple lips / All tomorrow's parties / Fearfully in danger / The end / My funny valentine / 60-40 / Tananoori / Janitor of lunacy / My heart is empty / Femme fatale.

1987. (lp) *(DOJOLP 50)* **LIVE IN TOKYO, JAPAN (live)** [ ] [-]
– My heart is empty / Purple lips / Tananore / Janitor of lunacy / You forgot to answer / 60-40 / My funny valentine / Sad lied von einsannen madchens / All tomorrow's parties / Femme fatale / The end. *(cd-iss. 1988 & Jun95; DOJOCD 50)*

— NICO died 18th Jul'88 (see info above)

– compilations, others, etc. –

1983. (c) *R.O.I.R.; <A 117>* **DO OR DIE** [-] [ ]
(cd-iss. May93 & Nov94; RE 117CD) <(cd re-mast.Apr00; RUSCD 8261)>

Sep 85. (lp/c/cd) *Aura; (AU L/C/CD 731)* **THE BLUE ANGEL** (best of) [ ] [ ]
– Femme fatale / All tomorrow's parties / I'll keep it with mine / Chelsea girls / Janitor of lunacy / Heroes / One more chance / Sixty forty / Waiting for the man / The end.

Oct 85. (7") *Aura; (AUS 147)* **I'M WAITING FOR THE MAN. / PURPLE LIPS (live)** [ ] [-]

Feb 87. (12"ep) *Archive 4; (TOF 110)* **LIVE (live)** [ ] [-]

Mar 87. (pic-lp) *V.U.; (NICO 1)* **LIVE IN DENMARK (live)** [ ] [-]

May 88. (c) *Half; (1/2 CASS 2)* **EN PERSONNE EN EUROPE** [ ] [-]

Nov 88. (12"ep/cd-ep) *Strange Fruit; (SFPS/+CD 064) / Dutch East India; <DEI 8314>* **NICO / PEEL SESSIONS** (2/2/71) [ ] [ ]
– Secret side / No one is there / Janitor of lunacy / Frozen warnings.

Jun 89. (lp/cd) *Performance; (PERF 385/+CD)* **LIVE HEROES (live)** [ ] [-]

Nov 90. (cd/c/lp) *Emergo; (EM 9349-2/-4/-1)* **HANGING GARDENS** [ ] [-]

Jul 92. (cd) *Great Expectations; (PIPCD 039)* **CHELSEA GIRL LIVE (live)** [ ] [-]
(re-iss. Jun94 on 'Cleopatra'; CLEO 61062) (cd re-iss. Nov96 on 'See For Miles'; SEECD 461)

Sep 94. (cd) *Anagram; <(CDMGRAM 85)>* **HEROINE (live)** [ ] 1995 [ ]
(lp-iss.Oct00 on 'Get Back'; GET 68) (re-iss. Mar02; CDMGOTH 16)

Apr 96. (cd) *Cleopatra; <CLP 9709>* **ICON** [-] [ ]

Sep 96. (cd) *Visionary; (VICD 008)* **JANITOR OF LUNACY** [ ] [-]
(re-iss. Jun01 on 'Anagram'; CDGOTH 7)

Sep 96. (cd) *S.P.V.; (SPV 0849620-2)* **NICO'S LAST CONCERT (FATA MORGANA – DESERTSOUNDS IN THE PLANETARIUM) (live)** [ ] [-]
(<re-iss. Feb02; SPV 0769620-2>)

Sep 98. (cd) *Island; <565185>* **THE CLASSIC YEARS** [-] [ ]

Aug 99. (cd) *Koch World; <(34042-2)>* **COSMOS** [ ] [ ]

Feb 02. (cd) *Verve; (589421-2)* **INNOCENT & VAIN: AN INTRODUCTION TO NICO** [ ] [-]
– I'll keep it with mine / All tomorrow's parties / You forgot to answer / Wrap your troubles in dreams / Valley of the kings / Femme fatale / Eulogy to Lenny Bruce / Secret side / Little sister / It was a pleasure then / Innocent and vain / The end (live).

Apr 02. (cd) *Jungle; (FREUDCD 069)* **FEMME FATALE: THE AURA ANTHOLOGY** [ ] [-]

May 03. (d-cd) *Castle; (CMDDD 732)* **WAITING FOR THE MAN** (same as above) [ ] [-]

NILSSON

Born: HARRY EDWARD NELSON, 15 Jun'41, Brooklyn, New York, USA. Subsequently raised in California, he started a career as a supervisor at the Security First National Bank in Van Nuys. By day he was developing his songwriting and piano playing talents, eventually placing three of his tracks with PHIL SPECTOR (who duly recorded two with The RONETTES and one with the MODERN FOLK QUARTET). After a couple of early singles on the 'Tower' label, the budding singer/songwriter secured a contract with 'R.C.A.'. In the process of recording his debut album, 'PANDEMONIUM SHADOW SHOW' (1968), NILSSON's 'CUDDLY TOY' was covered by fellow 'R.C.A.' act, the MONKEES, finally persuading him to leave his job at the bank and concentrate on music full-time. There was a distinct BEATLES-esque feel to much of the debut, not merely down to a faithful cover of 'SHE'S LEAVING HOME' but in the orchestrated pop of 'WITHOUT HER' and 'IT'S BEEN SO LONG', NILSSON's rich voice and immaculate phrasing belying the fact he was American. Not much of a surprise then, that LENNON, McCARTNEY and Co. raved over the record, soon becoming good friends with the singer. The album also gained considerable praise from the critics, although NILSSON would have to wait until the summer of '69 before he gained any widespread commercial recognition. This came with his definitive reading of Fred Neil's 'EVERYBODY'S TALKIN'', the wistful country-folk number used as the theme tune for the acclaimed 'Midnight Cowboy' movie and becoming a mainstay of the US Top 10 in 1969. The success of the single spurred on sales of 'ARIEL BALLET' (1968), while also creating interest for NILSSON's third album, 'HARRY' (1969). The same year, NILSSON's 'ONE' (from the debut) became a million seller for American rockers, THREE DOG NIGHT. Bizarrely enough, despite all this success, NILSSON never performed in front of a paying audience, while TV appearances were rare. The early 70's saw the singer record a critically acclaimed but poor selling album of RANDY NEWMAN covers, 'NILSSON SINGS NEWMAN' (1970) while the following year he wrote, narrated and sang the soundtrack for children's fantasy film, 'THE POINT!' (1971). NILSSON really made his breakthrough in early '72 with a hauntingly intense version of PETE HAM and TOM EVANS' (of BADFINGER) 'WITHOUT YOU', the song latterly assuming an added poignancy following the suicides of both its writers. The accompanying album, 'NILSSON SCHMILSSON' (1972) subsequently went platinum, again showing the singer's penchant for diverse stylistic territory. 'SON OF SCHMILSSON' (1972) was a generally inferior version of its predecessor while 'A LITTLE TOUCH OF SCHMILSSON IN THE NIGHT' (1973) was a semi-successful attempt at pre-war schmaltz. NILSSON subsequently took another radical stylistic shift with 'PUSSY CATS' (1974), a darkly intense album of classic pop/rock covers recorded with, and produced by, drinking buddy JOHN LENNON. Recorded during the former BEATLES' 'lost' period (when he split from YOKO), the opus was a proverbial dark night of the soul for both artists. Following a further series of inconsistent albums throughout the late 70's including 'NILSSON . . . THAT'S THE WAY IT IS' (1976) and 'KNNILLSSONN' (1977), the singer virtually retired from the music business in the early 80's, raising a family and setting up an L.A.-based film distribution company. In the early 90's, NILSSON threw himself afresh into recording and writing following a heart attack. Tragically, he suffered a fatal attack on the 15th of January '94, just days after completing a new long player. The following year, the music business paid tribute with the album, 'FOR THE LOVE OF HARRY: EVERYBODY SINGS NILSSON', featuring contributions from the likes of BRIAN WILSON and RANDY NEWMAN.

• **Covered:** YOU CAN'T DO THAT + MOTHER NATURE'S SON (Beatles) RIVER DEEP, MOUNTAIN HIGH (Phil Spector) to name but a few NILSSON's songs that have been hits for others:- ONE (Three Dog Night) THE STORY OF ROCK AND ROLL (Turtles) / THE PUPPY SONG (David Cassidy) / etc. • **Trivia:** Early in 1969, he wrote first film score, 'Skidoo', and even had a bit part as a security guard. In 1974, he provided the score and starred alongside RINGO STARR for the film, 'Son Of Dracula'.

Album rating: PANDEMONIUM SHADOW SHOW (*6) / ARIEL BALLET (*6) HARRY (*6) / NILSSON SINGS NEWMAN (*7) / THE POINT! soundtrack (*7) NILSSON SCHMILSSON (*8) / SON SCHMILSSON (*6) / A LITTLE TOUCH OF SCHMILSSON IN THE NIGHT (*5) / SON OF DRACULA soundtrack (*4) PUSSY CATS (*6) / DUIT ON MON DEI (*4) / SANDMAN (*4) / . . .THAT'

THE WAY IT IS (*4) / KNNILLSSONN (*4) / GREATEST HITS compilation (*7) / FLASH HARRY (*4) / ALL THE BEST compilation (*7) / PERSONAL BEST: THE HARRY NILSSON ANTHOLOGY (*8)

NILSSON – vocals, piano with session people and orchestra

not iss. Spindle Top

1963. (7"; as JOHNNY NILES) *<1929>* **DONNA I UNDERSTAND. / WIG JOB** –
<re-iss. 1963 on 'Mercury'; 72132>

not iss. Crusader

1964. (7"; as BO-PETE) *<103>* **BAA BAA BLACKSHEEP. / (part 2)** –

not iss. Try

1964. (7"; as BO-PETE) *<TRY 501>* **DO YOU WANNA (HAVE SOME FUN). / GROOVY LITTLE SUZIE** –

not iss. Foto-Fi

1964. (7"; by FOTO-FI FOUR) *<107>* **STAND UP AND HOLLER (THE BEATLES ARRIVE IN AMERICA). / ISMAEL** –

not iss. Tower

1964. (7") *<103>* **I'M GONNA LOSE MY MIND. / 16 TONS** –

1965. (7") *<136>* **YOU CAN'T TAKE YOUR LOVE AWAY FROM ME. / BORN IN GRENADA** –

1966. (7") **GROWING UP. / SHE'S YOURS** –

1966. (lp) *<ST 5095>* **SPOTLIGHT ON NILSSON** –
<re-iss. 1967; ST 5165>

R.C.A. R.C.A.

Jun 67. (7") *<47-9206>* **WITHOUT HER. / FRECKLES** –

Sep 67. (7") *(RCA 1632) <47-9298>* **YOU CAN'T DO THAT. / TEN LITTLE INDIANS**

Dec 67. (7") *<47-9383>* **RIVER DEEP, MOUNTAIN HIGH. / SHE BANGS HYMNS OUT OF TUNE** –

Mar 68. (lp) *(RD/SF 7928) <LSP 3874>* **PANDEMONIUM SHADOW SHOW**
– Ten little Indians / 1941 / Cuddly toy / She sang hymns out of tune / You can't do that / Sleep late, my lady friend / She's leaving home / There will never be / Without her / Freckles / It's been so long / River deep, mountain high.

Mar 68. (7") *(RCA 1675) <47-9462>* **ONE. / SISTER MARIE**

Aug 68. (lp) *(RD/SF 7973) <LSP 3956>* **AERIAL BALLET**
– Good old desk / Don't leave me / Mr. Richland's favorite song / Little cowboy / Together / Everybody's talkin' / I said goodbye to me / Mr. Tinker / One / The wailing of the willow / Bath.

Apr 69. (lp) *(SF 8010)* **SKIDOO (soundtrack)** –
– The cast and crew / I will take you there / Skidoo – Commercials / Goodnight Mr. Banks – Let's get the hardware – Murder in the car wash / Angie's suite / The tree / Garbage can ballet / Tony's trip / Escape: Impossible – Green Bay Packers march / Man wasn't meant to fly / Escape: possible / Skidoo – Goodnight Mr. Banks (CAROL CHANNING).

—— (Below 'A'side was now used in the film 'Midnight Cowboy')

Aug 69. (7") *(RCA 1707) <47-9544>* **EVERYBODY'S TALKIN'. / DON'T LEAVE ME** 6

Sep 69. (lp) *(SF 8046) <4197>* **HARRY** Aug69
– The puppy song / Nobody cares about the railroads anymore / Open your window / Mother nature's son / Fairfax rag / City life / Mournin' glory story / Marchin' down Broadway / I guess the Lord must be in New York City / Rainmaker / Mr. Bojangles / Simon Smith & his amazing dancing bear.

Sep 69. (7") *<9675>* **RAINMAKER. / I WILL TAKE YOU THERE** –

Oct 69. (7") *(RCA 1864)* **MAYBE. / THE PUPPY SONG** –

Oct 69. (7") *(RCA 1913) <74-0261>* **I GUESS THE LORD MUST BE IN NEW YORK CITY. / GOOD OLD DESK** Nov69 34

Feb 70. (7") *(RCA 1935) <74-0310>* **I'LL BE HOME. / WAITING**

Mar 70. (lp) *(SF 8166) <LSP 4289>* **NILSSON SINGS NEWMAN**
– Vine Street / Love story (you and me) / Yellow man / Caroline / Cowboy / The beehive state / I'll be home / Living without you / Dayton Ohio, 1903 / So long, dad. *(re-iss. Sep77; PL 42304) (cd-iss. Feb89; ND 90305)*

Nov 70. (7") *(RCA 1987) <74-0362>* **DOWN TO THE VALLEY. / BUY MY ALBUM**

Mar 71. (7") *<74-0443>* **ME AND MY ARROW. / ARE YOU SLEEPING?** – 34

Jun 71. (7") *<74-0524>* **WITHOUT HER. / GOOD OLD DESK** –

Jan 72. (lp) *(SF 8166) <LSP 4417>* **THE POINT!** (soundtrack) 46 Feb71 25
– Everything's got 'em / The town (narration) / Me and my arrow / The game (narration) / Poli high / The trial and banishment (narration) / Think about your troubles / The pointed man (narration) / Life line / The birds (narration) / P.O.V. waltz / The clearing in the woods (narration) / Are you sleeping? / Oblio's return (narration). *(re-iss. Jan78 on 'M.C.A.'; MCF 2826) (re-iss. Aug91 on 'Edsel' lp+=/cd+=; ED/+CD 340)* – Down to the valley / Buy my album.

Jan 72. (7") *(RCA 2165) <74-0604>* **WITHOUT YOU. / GOTTA GET UP** 1 Dec71 1
(re-iss. Feb79 on 'RCA Gold')

Jan 72. (lp) *(SF 8242) <LSP 4515>* **NILSSON SCHMILSSON** 4 Nov71 3
– Gotta get up / Driving along / Early in the morning / Moonbeam / Down / Without you / Coconut / Let the good times roll / Jump into the fire / I'll never leave you. *(re-iss. Apr80; INTS 5002) (re-iss. Nov84 lp/c/cd; NL/NK/ND 83464) (re-iss. Sep86 on 'Fame' lp/c; FA/TCFA 3166) (cd re-iss. Oct87; ND 83464)*

Mar 72. (7") *<74-0673>* **JUMP INTO THE FIRE. / MOONBEAM** – 27

May 72. (7") *(RCA 2214)* **COCONUT. / MOONBEAM** 42 –

Jun 72. (7") *<74-0718>* **COCONUT. / DOWN** – 8

Jul 72. (lp) *(SF 8297) <LSP 4717>* **SON OF SCHMILSSON** 41 12
– Take 54 / Remember (Christmas) / Joy / Turn on your radio / You're breakin' my heart / Spaceman / The lottery song / At my front door / Ambush / I'd rather be dead / The most beautiful girl in the world.

Oct 72. (7") *(RCA 2266) <74-0788>* **SPACEMAN. / YOU'RE BREAKIN' MY HEART** Sep72 23

Dec 72. (7") *(RCA 2300) <74-0855>* **REMEMBER (CHRISTMAS). / THE LOTTERY SONG** 53
<re-iss. Nov75; PB 10130>

Jul 73. (lp) *(SF 8371) <APL-1 0097>* **A LITTLE TOUCH OF SCHMILSSON IN THE NIGHT** 20 46
– Lazy Moon / For me and my gal / It had to be you / Always / Makin' whoopee / You made me love you (I didn't want to do it) / Lullaby in ragtime / I wonder who's kissing her now / What'll I do / Nevertheless (I'm in love with you) / This is all I ask / As time goes by. *(cd-iss. Aug91; ND 90582)*

Jul 73. (7") *(RCA 2395)* **AS TIME GOES BY. / MAKIN' WHOOPEE!** –

Aug 73. (7") *<APBO 0039>* **AS TIME GOES BY. / LULLABY IN RAGTIME** – 86

Apr 74. (7") *(APBO 0238) <APBO 0246>* **DAYBREAK. / DOWN** 39

May 74. (lp) *<(APL-1 0220)>* **SON OF DRACULA (Soundtrack)** Apr74
– It is he who will be King / Daybreak / At my front door / Count Down meets Merlin and Amber / Moonbeam / Perhaps this is all a dream / Remember (Christmas) / Intro: Without you / The Count's vulnerability / Down / Frankenstein, Merlin and the operation / Jump into the fire / The abdication of Count Down / The end (moonbeam).
(above was jointly issued on 'Rapple' & is a part compilation)

Sep 74. (7") *(RCA 2459) <PB 10001>* **MANY RIVERS TO CROSS. / DON'T FORGET ME**

Sep 74. (lp) *<(APL-1 0570)>* **PUSSY CATS** 60
– Many rivers to cross / Subterranean homesick blues / Don't forget me / All my life / Old forgotten soldier / Save the last dance for me / Mucho Mungo – Mt. Elga / Loop de loop / Black sails / Rock around the clock. *(cd-iss. Jan92 on 'Edsel'; EDCD 337)*

Nov 74. (7") *<PB 10078>* **MUCHO MUNGO – MT. ELGA. / SUBTERRANEAN HOMESICK BLUES** –

Jan 75. (7") *(RCA 2504)* **SAVE THE LAST DANCE FOR ME. / ALL MY LIFE** –

Feb 76. (7") *<PB 10139>* **DON'T FORGET ME. / LOOP DE LOOP** –

Mar 75. (lp) *(RS 1008) <APL-1 0817>* **DUIT EN MON DEI**
– It's a jungle out there / Down by the sea / Kojak Columbo / Easier for me / Turn out the light / Salmon falls / Puget sound / What's your sign / Home / Good for God.

Jun 75. (7") *(RCA 2565) <PB 10183>* **KOJAK COLOMBO. / TURN OUT THE LIGHT**

Sep 75. (lp) *(RS 1015) <APL-1 1031>* **SANDMAN**
– I'll take a tango / Something true / Pretty soon there'll be nothing left for everybody / The ivy covered walls / Here's why I did not go to work today / How to write a song / The flying saucer song / Will she miss me / Jesus Christ you're tall.

Jan 76. (7") *(RCA 2649)* **SOMETHING TRUE. / PRETTY SOON THERE'LL BE NOTHING** –

May 76. (7") *(RCA 2687) <10634>* **SAIL AWAY. / MOONSHINE BANDIT**

Jul 76. (lp) *(RS 1062)* <1119> **NILSSON . . . THAT'S THE WAY IT IS**
– That is all / Just one look – Baby I'm yours / Moonshine bandit / I need you / A thousand miles away / Sail away / She sits down on me / Daylight has caught me / Zombie jambouree (back to back) / That is all (reprise).

Aug 76. (7"; as LYNDA LAWRENCE & NILSSON) *<10759>* **THAT IS ALL. / JUST ONE LOOK – BABY I'M YOURS** –

Jan 77. (7") *<11059>* **WHO DONE IT. / PERFECT DAY** –

Mar 77. (7") *(PB 9048)* **MOONSHINE BANDIT. / SHE SITS DOWN ON ME** –

Jun 77. (7") *<11144>* **ALL I THINK ABOUT IS YOU. / I NEVER THOUGHT I'D GET THIS LONELY** –

Jun 77. (7") *(PB 9104)* **ALL I THINK ABOUT IS YOU. / OLD BONES** 43 –

Jul 77. (lp/c) *(PL/PK 12276)* <2276> **KNNILLSSONN**
– All I think about is you / I never thought I'd get this lonely / Who done it / Lean on me / Goin' down / Old bones / Sweet surrender / Blanket for a sail / Laughin' man / Perfect day.

Nov 77. (7") *<11193>* **AIN'T IT KINDA WONDERFUL. / I'M BRINGING A RED RED ROSE** –

Nov 77. (7") *(PB 9177)* **LEAN ON ME. / WILL SHE MISS ME** –

HARRY NILSSON

Mercury not iss.

Sep 80. (7") *(MER 40)* **I DON'T NEED YOU. / IT'S SO EASY** –

Sep 80. (lp) *(6302 022)* **FLASH HARRY** –
– Harry / Cheek to cheek / Best move / Old dirt road / I don't need you / Rain / I've got it / It's so easy / How long can disco go on / Bright side of life.

Nov 80. (7") *(MER 44)* **RAIN. / BRIGHT SIDE OF LIFE** –

—— late in 1980, he provided the score for the film musical, 'POPEYE'

Polydor not iss.

Aug 84. (7") *(POSP 703)* **LONELINESS. / SILVER HORSE**

R.C.A. not iss.

Dec 88. (lp/c) *(PL/PK 90251)* **A TOUCH MORE SCHMILSSON IN THE NIGHT** –
– Intro / I'm always chasing rainbows / Make believe / You made me love you (I didn't want to do it) / Trust in me / Lullaby in ragtime / All I think about is you / Perfect day / Always / It's only a paper moon / It had to be you / Thanks for the memory / Outro / Over the rainbow.

—— HARRY virtually retired from the music business and was still a gun-control advocate after the death of his friend, JOHN LENNON. NILSSON died of a heart attack on the 15th January '94 at his home Agoura Hills, California.

– compilations, etc. –

on 'RCA' unless mentioned otherwise

1969. (7") *Tower; <518>* **GOOD TIME. / GROWING UP** –

Feb 73. (lp) *(SF 8326)* <4543> **AERIAL PANDEMONIUM BALLET** Jun71

Sep 76. (7"m) *(RCA 2733)* **WITHOUT YOU. / EVERYBODY'S TALKIN' / KOJAK, COLOMBO** 22 –

Jan 77. (7") *<11318>* **ME AND MY ARROW. / SPACEMAN** –

Jan 77. (7") *(PB 9000)* **ME AND MY ARROW. / THURSDAY** –

Oct 77. (lp) *D.J.M.; (22075)* **EARLY TYMES** –

Jun 78. (lp/c) *(PL/PK 42728)* <2798> **GREATEST HITS**
(re-iss. Nov82; INTS 5233) (cd-iss. Jan84; PD 89081)

Oct 79. (lp) *K-Tel; (NE 1050)* **HARRY AND . . .** –

Jul 81. (7") *(RCA GOLD 9630)* **WITHOUT YOU. / EVERYBODY'S TALKIN'** –
(re-iss. Oct86 on 'Old Gold'; OG 9630)

Sep 81. (lp/c) *(RCA LP/K 3029)* **NILSSON'S GREATEST MUSIC** –

Feb 82. (c) *Orchid; (ORC 005)* **ALL FOR YOUR LOVE** –

Apr 88. (cd) *RCA Diamond;* **NILSSON** –

Oct 90. (cd) *(ND 90502)* **WITHOUT HER – WITHOUT YOU: THE VERY BEST OF NILSSON VOL.1** –

Jun 92. (cd) *(ND 90652)* **LULLABY IN RAGTIME: THE VERY BEST OF NILSSON**

Oct 92. (cd-ep) *Old Gold;* **WITHOUT YOU / EVERYBODY'S TALKIN' / COCONUT** –

Sep 93. (cd/c) *Music Club; (MCCD/MCMC 129)* **ALL THE BEST** –
– Without you / Everybody's talkin' / Mother nature's son / It's been so long / Good old desk / Without her / Mournin' glory story / Mr. Richland's favourite song / Mr.Bojangles / She's leaving home / Lulaby in ragtime / Makin' whoopee! / Cuddly toy / River deep, mountain high / Little cowboy / As time goes by.

Feb 94. (7"/c-s) *(74321 19309-7/-4)* **WITHOUT YOU. / EVERYBODY'S TALKIN'** 47
(cd-s+=) *(74321 19309-2)* – Over the rainbow.

1994. (d-cd) *<66354-2>* **PERSONAL BEST: THE HARRY NILSSON ANTHOLOGY** –

Oct 94. (cd) *(74321 22315-2)* **THE BEST OF NILSSON** –

Oct 95. (cd) *R.P.M.; (RETRO 804)* **NILSSON '62 – THE DEBUT SESSIONS** –

Aug 00. (cd) *Camden; (74321 75743-2)* **SKIDOO / THE POINT!** –

NINE INCH NAILS

Formed: San Francisco, California, USA . . . 1989 by classically trained pianist, TRENT REZNOR. He turned his attention to the darker textures of 'PRETTY HATE MACHINE' in the late 80's following a stint working in a recording studio. A solo effort – the album was written and played wholly by REZNOR – its despair and bitter self-pity were set against walls of churning synths and industrial rhythms, the compelling 'HEAD LIKE A HOLE' subsequently becoming a minor hit thanks to heavy MTV rotation. Around the same time, REZNOR recruited a band and struck out on that year's Lollapolooza trek, previewing a harder hitting, guitar influenced sound. Although the debut album was equal parts DEPECHE MODE/MINISTRY, REZNOR's follow-up, the mini-album, 'BROKEN' (1992), followed the metal/industrial fusion of the live shows. REZNOR seemed more tormented than ever on the likes of 'HELP ME I AM IN HELL', an explicitly masochistic video for the 'HAPPINESS IN SLAVERY' single courting not inconsiderable controversy. A punishing album of remixes, 'FIXED' followed a couple of months later, featuring such good-time party favourites as 'FIST FUCK' and 'SCREAMING SLAVE'. Clearly, REZNOR was rather discontented with his lot, his scary reputation heightened when it was revealed that he'd rented the L.A. pad where Charles Manson and Family had murdered Sharon Tate and her friends back in 1969. While REZNOR was allegedly unaware of this spook factor when he rented the property, it nevertheless gave 'THE DOWNWARD SPIRAL' (1994) a grim new resonance (the album was recorded in said abode). The consummation of everything REZNOR had been working towards, the record was a masterful alternative metal/industrial landmark, exploring the depths of human despair and depravity in its multifarious forms. REZNOR's tormented musings obviously struck a chord with the American populace, the album making No.2 in the US charts while NIN were given a rapturous reception at that year's Woodstock anniversary festival. Another album of remixes, 'FURTHER DOWN THE SPIRAL' (featuring remixer CHARLIE CLOUSER), appeared the following year, while REZNOR set up his own 'Nothing' label, nurturing such famous talent as the equally scary MARILYN MANSON. It had been five long years since the emergence of any new NINE INCH NAILS material (apart from TRENT producing the soundtrack to Oliver Stone's movie, 'Natural Born Killers', however REZNOR and his nihilistic NIN completed their comeback set, 'THE FRAGILE' (1999). Packed with over twenty apocalyptic tracks it hit the top of the US charts (scraped Top 10 in the UK), doom, gloom and then boom, it was all here for America's forgotten youth of today. The subsequent tour was at least partly documented on live set 'AND ALL THAT COULD HAVE BEEN' (2002), an ironically appropriate title for a record which somehow failed to communicate the frenzy of NIN in full, furious flow. After another interminable wait, 'WITH TEETH' (2005) finally saw REZNOR – with DAVE GROHL battering the drums – coming out of his shell (and allegedly his battle with the demon drink) on a record that harked back to the sinuous, splattergrind-groove of his early 90s landmarks. He was still railing at the world, if not with quite as much outrage as before, veering between expletive-filled tantrum-thrash and synth-syncopation: both the title track and UK Top 20 single 'ONLY', came on like an unholy PRINCE. Needless to say the album was a straight US No.1 and his highest ever UK chart showing at No.3, while politically-themed lead single 'THE HAND THAT FEEDS', was another first for REZNOR: the only time a NIN single has breached the UK Top 10.

• **Songwriters:** 'The Terminator' REZNOR penned except PHYSICAL YOU'RE SO (Adam Ant). • **Trivia:** REZNOR appeared in the 1987 film 'LIGHT OF DAY'.

Album rating: PRETTY HATE MACHINE (*7) / BROKEN (*7) / THE DOWNWARD SPIRAL (*8) / FURTHER DOWN THE SPIRAL (*5) / THE FRAGILE (*6) / THINGS FALLING APART remix-set (*7) / AND ALL THAT COULD HAVE BEEN (*5) / WITH TEETH (*7)

TRENT REZNOR (b.17 May'65, Mercer, Pennsylvania, USA) – vocals, guitar, keyboards, bass, drums, programming / **JAMES WOOLEY** – keyboards / **RICHARD** – guitar / **CHRIS VRENNA** – drums

Island | Nothing-TVT

Nov 90. (12"ep/cd-ep) *(12IS/CID 482)* **DOWN IN IT (skin). / TERRIBLE LIE (mix) / DOWN IN IT (shred – demo)** [ ] [ ]
(cd-ep re-iss. Oct01 on 'TVT'; TVT 2611)

Sep 91. (7"/10") *(IS/10ISP 484)* **HEAD LIKE A HOLE. / ('A'-Copper mix)** [45] [ ]
(12"+=/cd-s+=) *(12IS/CID 484)* – ('A'-Opal mix).

Sep 91. (cd/c/lp) *(CID/ICT/ILPS 9973)* *<2610>* **PRETTY HATE MACHINE** [67] Nov90 [75]
– Head like a hole / Terrible lie / Down in it / Sanctified / Something I can never have / Kinda I want to / Sin / That's what I get / The only time / Ringfinger.

Nov 91. (c-s/7") *(C+/IS 508)* **SIN. / GET DOWN MAKE LOVE** [35] [ ]
(10"+=/cd-s+=) *(10IS/CID 508)* – Sin (dub).

Sep 92. (m-cd/m-c/m-lp) *(IMCD/ICM/ILPM 8004)* *<92246>* **BROKEN** [18] [7]
– Pinion / Wish / Last / Help me I am in Hell / Happiness is slavery / Gave up. *(free 7"+/cd+=)* – Physical (you're so) / Suck.

Nov 92. (m-cd/m-c/m-lp) *(IMCD/ICM/ILPM 8005)* **FIXED** (remixes) [ ] [–]
– Gave up / Wish / Happiness is slavery / Throw this away / Fist fuck / Screaming slave.

— Below was controversally recorded at the house of the Charles Manson murders (some produced by /with FLOOD). Guests on 1 track each were **ADRIAN BELEW + DANNY LOHNER** – guitar / **CHRIS VRENNA + STEPHEN PERKINS + ANDY KUBISZEWSKI +** – drums (live:- **VRENNA, LOHNER, WOOLLEY + ROBIN FINCK**)

Mar 94. (cd/c/d-lp) *(CID/ICT/ILPSD 8012)* *<92346>* **THE DOWNWARD SPIRAL** [9] [2]
– Mr. Self destruct / Piggy / Heresy / March of the pigs / Closer / Ruiner / The becoming / I do not want this / Big man with a gun / A warm place / Eraser / Reptile / The downward spiral / Hurt.

Mar 94. (cd-ep) *<95938>* **MARCH OF THE PIGS / REPTILLIAN / ALL THE PIGS, ALL LINED UP / A VIOLET FLUID / UNDERNEATH THE SKIN** [–] [59]

Mar 94. (etched-7") *(IS 592)* **MARCH OF THE PIGS. / A VIOLENT FLUID** [45] [–]
(9"+=) *(9IS 592)* – All the pigs, all lined up / Underneath the skin.
(cd-s) *(CID 592)* – ('A'side) / Underneath the skin / Reptillian.
(cd-s+=) *(CIDX 592)* – All the pigs, all lined up / Big man with a gun.

Jun 94. (12"ep/cd-ep) *(12IS/CID 596)* **CLOSER / CLOSER TO GOD / MARCH OF THE FUCKHEADS / HERESY (BLIND) / MEMORABILIA** [25] [–]
(12"ep/cd-ep) *(12ISX/CIDX 596)* – ('A'side) – (deviation) – (further away) / ('A'original) / ('A'-Precursor) / ('A'-Internal).

Jun 94. (c-s) *<98263>* **CLOSER / MARCH OF THE PIGS (live)** [–] [41]

— added **CHARLIE CLOUSER** – keyboards, remixer

Jun 95. (cd/c) *(IMCD/IMA 8041)* *<INTDM-95811>* **FURTHER DOWN THE SPIRAL** (remixes) [ ] [23]
– Piggy (nothing can stop me now) / The art of self destruction, part one / Self destruction, part two / Heresy (version) / The downward spiral (the bottom) / Hurt (quiet) / Eraser (denial; realization) / At the heart of it all / Eraser (polite) / Self destruction, final / The beauty of being numb / Erased, over, out.

Sep 97. (cd-ep) *(IND 95542)* *<9554>* **THE PERFECT DRUG (mixes; original / Meat Beat Manifesto / Plug / Nine Inch Nails / Spacetime Continuum / The Orb)** [43] May97 [46]
(above – & solo material from REZNOR – from the movie 'Lost Highway' on the 'Interscope' imprint)

Aug 99. (c-s/cd-s) *<97026>* **THE DAY THE WORLD WENT AWAY** [–] [17]

Sep 99. (d-cd/d-c/t-lp) *(CIDD/ICT/ILPST 8091)* *<490473>* **THE FRAGILE** [10] [1]
– Somewhat damaged / The day the world went away / Frail / Wretched / We're in this together / The fragile / Just like you imagined / Even deeper / Pilgrimage / No you don't / La mer / Great below / Way out i through / Into the void / Where is everybody / Mark has been made / Please / Starfuckers Inc. / Complication / I'm looking forward to joining you finally / Pilgrimage / Big come down / Underneath it all.

Nov 99. (cd-s) *(497140-2)* **WE'RE IN THIS TOGETHER / THE DAY THE WORLD WENT AWAY (quiet version) / THE DAY THE WORLD WENT AWAY (Porter Ricks mix)** [39] [ ]
(cd-s) *(497141-2)* – ('A'side) / 10 miles high / The new flesh.
(cd-s) *(497183-2)* – ('A'side) / Complication / The perfect drug.

Nov 00. (cd) *(CID 8102)* *<490744>* **THINGS FALLING APART** (mixes, etc.) [ ] [67]
– Slipping away / The great collapse / The wretched / Starfuckers Inc. / The frail / Where is everybody? / Metal.

Mar 02. (cd) *(CID 8113)* *<493185>* **AND ALL THAT COULD HAVE BEEN** (live) [54] Jan02 [26]
– Terrible lie / Sin / March of the pigs / Piggy / The frail / Wretched / Gave up / The great below / The mark has been made / Wish / Suck / Closer / Head like a hole / The day the world went away / Starfuckers, Inc. / Hurt. *(d-cd+=; CIDD 8113)* **STILL** – Something I can never have / Adrift and at peace / Fragile / Becoming / Gone still / The day the world went away / And all that could have been / Persistence of loss / Leaving hope.

— CLOUSER went on to become involved with soundtracks

Apr 05. (9") *(9IS 888)* **THE HAND THAT FEEDS. / (Photek dub)** [7] [31]
(cd-s+=//dvd-s+=) *(CID 888)* – (Photek straight remix) // (video).
(cd-s+=) *<00602498815045>* – (video).
(12"++=) *<B0005127-11>* – ('A'-Ruff mix).
(12") *<B0005129-11>* – ('A'-DFA mixes).
(10"pic-d) *<HALO 18>* – ('A') / Home.

May 05. (cd) *(CID 8155)* *<45530-2>* **WITH TEETH** [3] [1]
– All the love in the world / You know what you are? / The collector / The hand that feeds / Love is not enough / Every day is exactly the same / With teeth / Only / Getting smaller / Sunspots / The line begins to blur / Beside you in time / Right where it belongs.

Jul 05. (9") *(9IS 903)* **ONLY. / THE HAND THAT FEEDS (DFA remix)** [20] [ ]
(cd-s+=) *(CID 903)* – Love is not enough (live).
(dvd-s) *(CDIV 903)* – ('A'-video) / ('A') / Love is not enough (live).
(12") *<B0005465-11>* – ('A'-mixes; Richard X / EL-P / Richard X dub / Richard X edit / EL-P instrumental).

□ the NIPS / the NIPPLE ERECTORS
(see under ⇒ POGUES)

NIRVANA

Formed: Aberdeen, Washington, USA . . . 1987 by singer/songwriter/guitarist KURT COBAIN and bassist KRIST NOVOSELIC. Recruiting drummer CHAD CHANNING, they soon became a talking point and pivotal band in nearby Seattle where the likes of SOUNDGARDEN and MUDHONEY were major players in the emerging grunge scene. Whereas those bands dealt in raw garage punk/metal, NIRVANA immediately stood out from the pack by dint of the subtle pop melodies which COBAIN craftily incorporated into his songs. They also fast gained a reputation for their ferocious live shows which drew comparisons with early WHO, if only for their sheer nihilistic energy, invariably ending in trashed equipment. Signing, of course, with the hub of the

Kurt Cobain of NIRVANA

Seattle scene, 'Sub Pop', NIRVANA released their debut single, 'LOVE BUZZ' in October 1988, the album, 'BLEACH', following a year later. One of the seminal 'Sub Pop' releases alongside, MUDHONEY's 'SUPERFUZZ BIGMUFF' and TAD's 'GOD'S BALLS', this was a darkly brooding, often savagely angry collection, driven by bass and fuzz and interspersed with pockets of melody. The likes of 'SCHOOL' and the throbbing 'NEGATIVE CREEP' saw COBAIN lapse into his trademark howl, an enraged, blood curdling shriek, almost primal in its intensity. Conversely, 'ABOUT A GIRL' was an achingly melodic semi-acoustic shuffle, as steeped in hurt as the rest of the album but more resigned than angry. New guitarist JASON EVERMAN had contributed to the record's sonic bludgeon as well as paying for recording costs, although he soon parted ways (he went on to play with the much hyped MINDFUNK) with COBAIN and NOVOSELIC over the ever reliable, 'musical differences'. 'BLEACH' was heartily received by the indie/metal press, NIRVANA embarking on a heavy round of touring, first in the States, then Europe. Following the departure of CHANNING, MUDHONEY's DAN PETERS joined briefly and was involved with the 'SLIVER' single, a brilliant chunk of pop-noise which further enhanced NIRVANA's underground kudos and raised expectations for a follow-up album to fever pitch. 'NEVERMIND' (1991) let down no-one, except possibly the anally-retentive sad-kids who accused the band of selling out to a major label ('Geffen'). Released immediately after a blinding set at England's Reading festival (where NIRVANA, who probably drew the most frenetic crowd reaction of the day, had to make do with a paltry afternoon slot; the following year they'd be headlining), and with appetites whetted via import copies of 'SMELLS LIKE TEEN SPIRIT', the record was met with an ecstatic press reaction. While the album brought the grunge phenomenon into the mainstream, NIRVANA had already moved on to a blistering power pop/punk sound, best evidenced in the sardonic fury of the aforementioned 'SMELLS . . .'. Here was an anthem for the blank generation, for all the people who'd given up before even starting; COBAIN had condensed the collective frustration/despair/apathy into an incendiary slice of pop genius not witnessed since The SEX PISTOLS' heyday. 'COME AS YOU ARE' was another piece of semi-acoustic bruised beauty while 'TERRITORIAL PISSINGS' was as extreme as the record went, a rabid blast of hardcore punk introduced with a sarcastic send-up pilfered from The YOUNGBLOOD's 60's love 'n' peace classic, 'GET TOGETHER'. Most of the other tracks lay somewhere in between, COBAIN never letting up the intensity level for a minute, whether on the deceptively breezy 'IN BLOOM' or the stinging 'BREED'. For a three piece (the drum seat had now been filled by DAVE GROHL, ex-SCREAM), the group made one hell of a racket, but it was a racket which was never less than 100% focused, the GROHL/NOVOSELIC rhythmic powerhouse underpinning every track with diamond-edged precision. It's fair to say that 'NEVERMIND' literally changed the face of music, American indie bands coming to dominate the scene until the arrival of OASIS in the mid-90's. COBAIN was heralded as the spokesman of a generation, although it was a role he was both unwilling and unable to cope with. As the inevitable, punishing round of touring ensued, the singer's health began to suffer once more; never the healthiest of people, COBAIN suffered from a chronic stomach complaint as well as narcolepsy, a condition which causes the sufferer to sleep for excessive periods of time. What's more, he was concerned that the irony of his lyrics was lost on his growing legions of fans (which now included the macho 'jocks' whom COBAIN so despised) who now doted on his every word. Amid all this confusion, COBAIN was married to HOLE's COURTNEY LOVE on the 24th February '92, the couple almost losing custody of their newborn child, Frances, later that summer following revelations of drug abuse. The end of the year saw the release of a compilation of rare material, 'INCESTICIDE', including two storming VASELINES' (obscure but brilliant Scottish punk-popsters) covers, 'MOLLY'S LIPS' and 'SON OF A GUN'. Rumours of COBAIN's heroin abuse were rife, however, and the singer overdosed twice the following year. 'IN UTERO' (1993) reflected the turmoil, an uncompromising wall of noise (courtesy of STEVE ALBINI) characterising most of the album. The melodies were still there, you just had to dig deeper in the sludge to find them. Despite 'Geffen's misgivings, the record was a transatlantic No.1, its success engendering another round of live work. After a final American show in January, the group set off for Europe, taking a break at the beginning of March. COBAIN remained in Rome, where, on the 4th March, LOVE found him unconscious in their hotel room, the result of an attempted tranquilizer overdose. Although COBAIN eventually recovered, the tour was abandoned and the couple returned to their Seattle home. Though it didn't come as a complete surprise, the music world was stunned nonetheless when, on the 8th April, news broke that COBAIN had finally killed himself, blowing his own head off with a shotgun. The most widely mourned rock'n'roll death since JOHN LENNON, COBAIN's suicide even sparked off a series of 'copycat' incidents in America by obsessive fans. Posthumously released later that year, the acoustic 'UNPLUGGED IN NEW YORK' (1994) live set was heavy going, a tragic poignancy underpinning the spare beauty of tracks like 'DUMB' and 'PENNYROYAL TEA' (from 'IN UTERO') while the heart-rendingly resigned 'ALL APOLOGIES' sounds like COBAIN's final goodbye to a world that he could no longer bear to be a part of. Eventually picking up the pieces, GROHL formed The FOO FIGHTERS, turning his hand to guitar playing/songwriting and recruiting ex-GERM, PAT SMEAR. After time spent campaigning for his native, war torn Yugoslavia, NOVOSELIC returned with his own band, SWEET 75, a collaboration with diminutive Venezuelan lesbian folk-singer, YVA LAS VEGAS. They finally released one unstartling eponymous set in 1997, which just might be their only outing. The man can now be found in indie supergroup, EYES ADRIFT, alongside CURT KIRKWOOD (Meat Puppets) and BUD GAUGH (Sublime). It was a long time in coming but the inevitable box-set, 'WITH THE LIGHTS OUT', finally arrived in late 2004, a compelling, painstakingly compiled and annotated (by SONIC YOUTH's THURSTON MOORE) trawl of unreleased material including early demos, sketches COBAIN recorded before his death, 'NEVERMIND' outtakes, b-sides and compilation tracks. For those with a more casual interest in the band, a slimmed down version was released the following year: 'SLIVER: THE BEST OF THE BOX' (2005), increasing its marketability with a further three unreleased tracks including a pre-NIRVANA demo of 'SPANK THRU'. Both sets made the US charts, sitting either side of the Top 20.

• **Songwriters:** COBAIN wrote late 80's work. In the 90's, the group were credited with COBAIN lyrics. Covers; LOVE BUZZ (Shocking Blue) / HERE SHE COMES NOW (Velvet Underground) / DO YOU LOVE ME? (Kiss) / TURNAROUND (Devo) / JESUS WANTS ME FOR A SUNBEAM (Vaselines) / D7 (Wipers) / THE MAN WHO SOLD THE WORLD (David Bowie) / WHERE DID YOU SLEEP LAST NIGHT (Leadbelly).

Album rating: BLEACH (*8) / NEVERMIND (*10) / INCESTICIDE collection (*7) / IN UTERO (*10) / UNPLUGGED IN NEW YORK (*9) / FROM THE MUDDY BANKS OF THE WISHKAH (*8) / NIRVANA compilation (*10) / WITH THE LIGHTS OUT boxed collection (*7) / SLIVER: THE BEST OF THE BOX condensed collection (*6) / Sweet 75: SWEET 75 (*4)

KURT COBAIN (b.20 Feb'67, Hoquaim, Washington) – vocals, guitar / **KRIST NOVOSELIC** (b.16 May'65) – bass / **CHAD CHANNING** (b.31 Jan'67, Santa Rosa, Calif.) – drums

		Tupelo	Sub Pop
Oct 88.	(7") *<SP 23>* **LOVE BUZZ. / BIG CHEESE**	–	

— Early '89, added **JASON EVERMAN** – guitar Also guest drummer on 2 tracks **DALE CROVER**

Aug 89. (lp,white or green-lp/cd) *(TUP LP/CD 6)* *<SP 34>*
BLEACH Jun89
– Blew / Floyd the barber / About a girl / School / Paper cuts / Negative creep / Scoff / Swap meet / Mr.Moustache / Sifting / Big cheese. *(cd+=)* – Love buzz / Downer. *<US re-iss. Dec91 hit 89> (re-iss. Feb92 on 'Geffen'; GEFD 24433) (hit UK No.33) (c+=)* – Big cheese. *(re-iss. Oct95 on 'Geffen' cd/c; GFLD/GFLC 19291) (lp re-iss. Aug01 on 'Sub Pop';* **SP 34)** *(re-iss. Oct01 on 'Warners' cd/lp; 9878 40034-2/-1)*

Dec 89. (12"ep/cd-ep) *(TUP EP8/CD8)* **BLEW / LOVE BUZZ. / BEEN A SON / STAIN** –

— **DAN PETERS** – drums (of MUDHONEY) repl. CHANNING (Apr90)

Jan 91. (7",7"green) *(TUP 25)* **SLIVER. / DIVE** Sep 90
(12"+=) *(TUP EP25)* – About a girl (live). *(US-iss.7"blue; SP 72)*
(cd-s++=) *(TUP CD25)* – Spank thru (live).

Feb 91. (7",7"green) *<SP 97>* **MOLLY'S LIPS. / ('Candy' by FLUID)** –

not iss. Communion

Mar 91. (7"colrd) *<Communion 25>* **HERE SHE COMES NOW. / ('Venus In Furs' by MELVINS)** –

— (Apr'91 trio) **DAVE GROHL** (b.14 Jan'69, Warren, Ohio) – drums, vocals (ex-SCREAM) repl. PETERS and EVERMAN, who joined MIND FUNK

Geffen Geffen

Sep 91. (lp/c/cd) *<(DGC/+C/D 24425)>* **NEVERMIND** 7 1
– Smells like teen spirit / In bloom / Come as you are / Breed / Lithium / Polly / Territorial pissings / Drain you / Lounge act / Stay away / On a plain / Something in the way. *(cd+=)* – Endless nameless. *(lp re-iss. Nov98 on 'Simply Vinyl'; SVLP 38)*

Oct 91. (c-s/cd-s) *<19050>* **SMELLS LIKE TEEN SPIRIT / EVEN IN HIS YOUTH** – 6

Nov 91. (7"/c-s) *(DGC/+C 5)* **SMELLS LIKE TEEN SPIRIT. / DRAIN YOU** 7 –
(12"pic-d+=) *(DGCTP 5)* – Aneurysm.
(cd-s++=) *(DGCCD 5)* – Even in his youth.
(12") *(DGCT 5)* – ('A'side) / Even in his youth / Aneurysm.

Mar 92. (c-s/cd-s) *<19120>* **COME AS YOU ARE. / DRAIN YOU (live)** – 32

Mar 92. (7"/c-s) *(DGC/+C 7)* **COME AS YOU ARE. / ENDLESS NAMELESS** 9 –
(12"+=/12"pic-d+=) *(DGCT/+P 7)* – School (live).
(cd-s++=) *(DGCTD 7)* – Drain you (live).

Jul 92. (7"/c-s) *(DGCS/+C 9)* **LITHIUM. / CURMUDGEON** 11 –
(12"pic-d+=) *(DGCTP 9)* – Been a son (live).
(cd-s++=) *(DGCSD 9)* – D7 (Peel session).

Jul 92. (c-s,cd-s) *<19134>* **LITHIUM / BEEN A SON (live)** – 64

Nov 92. (7"/c-s) *(GFS/+C 34)* **IN BLOOM. / POLLY** 28 –
(12"pic-d+=/cd-s+=) *(GFST P/D 34)* – Sliver (live).

Dec 92. (cd/c/lp) *<(GED/GEC/GEF 24504)>* **INCESTICIDE** (rare material) 14 39
– Dive / Sliver / Stain / Been a son / Turnaround / Molly's lips / Son of a gun / (New wave) Polly / Beeswax / Downer / Mexican seafood / Hairspray queen / Aero zeppelin / Big long now / Aneurysm.

— In Feb'93, NIRVANA's 'OH, THE GUILT' appeared on double'A'side with JESUS LIZARD's 'Puss'. Issued on 'Touch & Go' 7"blue/cd-s; *(TG 83/+CD).* It had UK No.12, and crashed out of the Top 60 the following week!.

— GOODBYE MR MACKENZIE's BIG JOHN played guitar for them in mid'93.

— In Aug'93, KURT COBAIN and WILLIAM S.BURROUGHS narrated 'The Priest, They Call Him By' on 10"lp/cd 'Tim Kerr'; *(92 10/CD 044)*

Aug 93. (7"/c-s) *(GFS/+C 54)* **HEART-SHAPED BOX. / MARIGOLD** 5 –
(12"+=/cd-s+=) *(GFST/+D 54)* – Milk it.

Sep 93. (cd/c/lp)<clear-lp> *<(GED/GEC/GEF 24536)><DGC 24607>* **IN UTERO** 1 1
– Serve the servants / Scentless apprentice / Heart-shaped box / Rape me / Frances Farmer will have her revenge on Seattle / Dumb / Very ape / Milk it / Penny royal tea / Radio friendly unit shifter / Tourette's / All apologies. *(cd+=)* – Gallons of rubbing alcohol flow through the strip. *(lp re-iss. Nov98 on 'Simply Vinyl'; SVLP 48)*

Dec 93. (7"/c-s) *(GFS/+C 66)* **ALL APOLOGIES. / RAPE ME** 32 –
(12"+=/cd-s+=) *(GFST/+D 66)* – MV.

— On the 4th March '94, KURT overdosed while on holiday in Italy and went into a coma. A month later, on the 8th April he committed suicide, by shooting himself through the mouth. He was only 27, and this was certainly the biggest rock star death since JOHN LENNON. For more details see HOLE and the COURTNEY LOVE story.

below album featured **LORI GOLDSTON** – cello + **MEAT PUPPETS' Curt & Cris Kirkwood** on 3rd, 4th & 5th last songs.

Nov 94. (cd/c/white-lp) *<(GED/GEC/GEF 24727)>*
UNPLUGGED IN NEW YORK (live acoustic) 1 1
– About a girl / Come as you are / Jesus doesn't want me for a sunbeam / Dumb / The man who sold the world / Pennyroyal tea / Polly / On a plain / Something in the way / Plateau / Oh me / Lake of fire / All apologies / Where did you sleep last night. *(lp re-iss. Nov98 on 'Simply Vinyl'; SVLP 53)*

— GROHL (now vox, guitar) formed FOO FIGHTERS with ex-GERMS guitarist PAT SMEAR; meanwhile NOVOSELIC formed the trio SWEET 75

– posthumous compilations, etc. –

on 'Geffen' unless mentioned otherwise

Jul 95. (d-cd) *<(GES 00001)>* **BLEACH / INCESTICIDE**

Nov 95. (6xcd-s-box) *<(GED 24901)>* **6 CD SINGLE BOXED SET**

Oct 96. (cd/c/lp) *<(GED/GEC/GEF 25105)>* **FROM THE MUDDY BANKS OF THE WISHKAH** (live) 4 1
– Intro / School / Drain you / Aneurysm / Smells like teen spirit / Been a son / Lithium / Sliver / Spank thru / Scentless apprentice / Heart-shaped box / Milk it / Negative creep / Polly / Breed / Tourette's / Blew.

Oct 02. (-) *<radio>* **YOU KNOW YOU'RE RIGHT** – 45

Oct 02. (cd) *Geffen; <(493507)>* **NIRVANA** 3 3
– You know you're right / About a girl / Been a son / Sliver / Smells like teen spirit / Come as you are / Lithium / In bloom / Heart-shaped box / Pennyroyal tea / Rape me / Dumb / All apologies (live) / The man who sold the world (live).

Nov 04. (3xcd-box w/dvd) *(9864838) <372700>* **WITH THE LIGHTS OUT** (live, demos, etc.) 56 19

Oct 05. (cd) *(9886718) <56170-2>* **SLIVER: THE BEST OF THE BOX** 56 21
– Spank thru (Fecal Matter demo) / Heartbreaker (live) / Mrs. Butterworth (rehearsal demo) / Floyd the barber (live) / Clean up before she comes (live demo) / About a girl (home demo) / Blandest (demo) / Ain't it a shame (demo) / Sappy (1990 demo) / Opinion / Lithium / Sliver (home demo) / Smells like teen spirit (boom box version) / Come as you are (boom box version) / Old age / Oh the guilt / Rape me (home demo) / Rape me (demo) / Heart shaped box (demo) / Do re mi (home demo) / You know you're right (home demo) / All apologies (home demo).

SWEET 75

KRIST NOVOSELIC – guitar / **YVA LAS VEGAS** – vocals, bass / **ADAM WADE** – drums

Geffen Geffen

Aug 97. (cd/c) *<(GED/GEC 25140)>* **SWEET 75**
– Fetch / Lay me down / Bite my hand / Red dress / La vida / Six years / Take another stab / Poor Kitty / Ode to Dolly / Dogs / Cantos de Pilon / Nothing / Japan trees / Oral health.

— late in 2002, NOVOSELIC was part of EYES ADRIFT

NO DOUBT

Formed: Orange County, California, USA ... 1987 by JOHN SPENCE, TOM DUMONT, TONY KANAL and ADRIAN YOUNG (SPENCE rocking the band by committing suicide the following year). Having gone to ground for a while, they returned in the early 90's with new blonde-bombshell frontwoman, GWEN STEFANI. Her brother, ERIC STEFANI, was also a member at this stage, although he eventually departed, having landed a job working on 'The Simpsons' TV cartoon series. After two albums for 'Trauma', an eponymous debut and 'BEACON STREET COLLECTION' they were licensed to 'Interscope' in 1995. The following year, NO DOUBT finally cracked the American market with 'TRAGIC KINGDOM', a slow starter which eventually topped the charts. Produced by MATTHEW WILDER, the record was an 80'-esque amalgam of soft-metallic ska-pop/rock, fusing elements of The POLICE and MADNESS hand in hand with tasty MADONNA lookalike, GWEN STEFANI's cutesie-pie vocal pouting. The album boasted the MTV friendly hit singles, 'JUST A GIRL' and the massive selling ballad, 'DON'T SPEAK', which boosted long term

UK sales of the album in 1997. Heavy-metal mag Kerrang!, also inconceivably took gorgeous GWEN to their leather-clad hearts (lending new weight to accusations of cock-rock inclinations). Having milked 'TRAGIC KINGDOM' dry of hits, NO DOUBT eventually returned in 1999, the 'NEW' singles UK Top 30 placing suggesting they hadn't been forgotten just yet. A year on they released the much anticipated long player, 'RETURN OF SATURN' (2000), lead track – and UK Top 40 hit – 'EX-GIRLFRIEND' setting the tone of the record as GWEN hits those twenty-something blues. Their defiant attempts at sparking a new wave revival remain undimmed and with 80's mania looming on the horizon like a particularly flint-eyed vulture, they may just pull it off. While structured with an underlying rock foundation, the aforementioned comeback set, 'RETURN TO SATURN' was an attempt to update the American New Wave sound so beloved of STEFANI and Co. While its lovingly crafted textures and 20-something restlessness of the lyrics conceivably appealed to an older audience, it's unclear exactly what market this record was aimed at. Its relatively short-lived residence in the charts prompted a link-up with all manner of name producers in an attempt to revitalise their approach. Thus the likes of SLY & ROBBIE, NELLEE HOOPER and even PRINCE were recruited to shape the reggae influenced, dancefloor pop of 'ROCK STEADY' (2001). 'THE SINGLES 1992-2003' (2003) meanwhile, deftly summed up the group's legacy over fifteen surprisingly consistent tracks, from 'TRAPPED IN A BOX' (taken from their eponymous debut) to the alluring 'UNDERNEATH IT ALL' (from their last studio set), their recent, 80's throwback cover of Talk Talk's 'IT'S MY LIFE' and all the exuberant, craftily contemporary hits in between. Having already vamped up her image with the Grammy winning, DR DRE-produced EVE collaboration, 'LET ME BLOW YA MIND' (a monster hit in 2001), STEFANI primed herself for the club-queen superstar league with transatlantic Top 5 solo album, 'LOVE.ANGEL.MUSIC.BABY' (2004). Gratuitously a product of its era, the record rounded up pace-setters past and present – the NEPTUNES, NELLEE HOOPER, ANDRE 3000, even JIMMY JAM & TERRY LEWIS – for a bling-pop, diamond-knuckled trawl through noughtiesville. 'WHAT YOU WAITING FOR', was the girls-together lead single, a HAZEL O'CONNOR-warbling, hopelessly new romantic UK Top 5 in late 2004. Co-written by LINDA PERRY, it wasn't exactly indicative of the record as a whole, but then how could it be given the diversity of its input. Follow-up 'RICH GIRL', was another DRE/EVE job (and another UK Top 5-US Top 10), living out the usual catwalk-of-life fantasies. Coming on like a syncopated spin on KELIS' 'Milkshake', the NEPTUNES-masterminded 'HOLLABACK GIRL' topped the American charts in summer 2005 (and made the UK Top 10), an album standout and the third in a release schedule that was to eventually stretch to six singles: 'COOL' was a CARS-esque 80s chugger, and another transatlantic Top 20, but the R&B-dull 'LUXURIOUS' was really milking it, and 'CRASH' stalled just inside the US Top 50.

• **Songwriters:** STEFANI w/ TOM or TONY or ERIC (perm any three).
• **Trivia:** GWEN was known to "hang out" with Scottish born GARBAGE singer SHIRLEY MANSON.

Album rating: NO DOUBT (*5) / THE BEACON STREET COLLECTION (*6) / TRAGIC KINGDOM (*7) / RETURN OF SATURN (*6) / ROCK STEADY (*6) / THE SINGLES 1992-2003 compilation (*8) / Gwen Stefani: LOVE.ANGEL.MUSIC.BABY (*7)

GWEN STEFANI (b. 3 Oct'69, Fullerton, Calif.) – vocals / **TOM DUMONT** – guitar / **TONY KANAL** – bass / **ADRIAN YOUNG** – drums / **ERIC STEFANI** – piano, keyboards

Interscope Interscope

Mar 92. (cd) *<IND 92109>* **NO DOUBT** [–] [ ]
– BND / Let's get back / Ache / Get on the ball / Move on / Sad for me / Doormat / Big city train / Trapped in a box / Sometimes / Sinking / A little something refreshing / Paulina / Brand new day. *(UK-iss.Jul96; same)*

Feb 95. (cd) *<BS 03>* **THE BEACON STREET COLLECTION** (out-takes) [–] [ ]
– Open the gate / Total hate 95 / Stricken / Greener pastures / By the way / Snakes / That's just me / Squeal / Doghouse / Blue in the face. *(UK-is.Apr97; same)*
(above album on 'Beacon Street')

—— now without ERIC (see above)

Jun 96. (cd/c) *(IND/INC 90003) <92580>* **TRAGIC KINGDOM** [ ] Feb96 [1]
– Spiderwebs / Excuse me Mr. / Just a girl / Happy now? / Different people / Hey you / The climb / Sixteen / Sunday morning / Don't speak / You can do it / World go 'round / End it on this / Tragic kingdom. *(re-dist.Jan97 hit UK No.3)*

Jun 96. (c-s) *(INC 80034) <98116>* **JUST A GIRL / DIFFERENT PEOPLE** [ ] Dec95 [23]
(cd-s+=) *(IND 80034)* – Open the gate.
(re-iss. Oct96, hit UK 38)

Feb 97. (7"pic-d/c-s/cd-s) *(INSP/INC/IND 95515)* **DON'T SPEAK / DON'T SPEAK (alternate) / HEY YOU (acoustic) / GREENER PASTURES** [1] [–]

Jun 97. (c-s) *(INC 95539)* **JUST A GIRL / HEY YOU (live) / OB-LA-DI OB-LA-DA (live)** [3] [–]
(cd-s+=) *(INDX 95539)* – Different people.
(cd-s) *(IND 95539)* – ('A'side) / Open the gate / ('A'live) / End it on this (live).

Sep 97. (c-s) *(INC 95551)* **SPIDERWEBS / DJ'S (live)** [16] [–]
(cd-s+=) *(IND 95551)* – Let's get back / Excuse me sir (cd-rom version).
(cd-s) *(INDX 95551)* – ('A'side) / The climb (live) / Doghouse / Spiderwebs (cd-rom version).

Dec 97. (c-s) *(INC 95566)* **SUNDAY MORNING / SUNDAY MORNING (live)** [50] [–]
(cd-s+=) *(IND 95566)* – Oi to the world / By the way (live).
(cd-s) *(INDX 95566)* – (virtually the same tracks).

May 99. (7") *(HIGHS 22S)* **NEW. / NEW (new and approved remix)** [30] [ ]
(c-s) *(HIGHS 22)* – ('A'side) / (A'-New Doubt club mix)
(cd-s+=) *(HIGHS 22T)* – (all three above).
(above issued on 'Higher Ground')

Mar 00. (c-s) *(497298-4)* **EX-GIRLFRIEND / LEFTOVERS** [33] [–]
(cd-s+=) *(497298-2)* – ('A'-CD-Rom).
(cd-s) *(497299-2)* – ('A'side) / Big distraction / Full circle.

Apr 00. (cd/c) *(490638-2/-4) <490441>* **RETURN OF SATURN** [31] [2]
– Ex-girlfriend / Simple kind of life / Bathwater / Six feet under / Magic's in the make up / Artificial sweetener / Marry me / New / Too late / Comforting lie / Suspension without suspense / Staring problem / Home now / Dark blue. *(cd+=)* – Big distraction. *(UK cd re-iss. Oct00 +=; 490797-2)* – Ex-girlfriend (video) / Simple king of life (video).

Sep 00. (c-s) *(497416-4) <490365>* **SIMPLE KIND OF LIFE / BEAUTY CONTEST** [69] May00 [38]
(cd-s+=) *(497417-2)* – Under construction / ('A'-CD-ROM video).
(cd-s) *(497416-2)* – ('A'side) / Ex-girlfriend / Cellophane boy.

—— in Jan'01, GWEN featured on MOBY's US-only hit, 'South Side'

—— in Apr'01, she also featured on EVE's hit, 'Let Me Blow Ya Mind'

Dec 01. (cd/d-lp) *<(493158-2/-1)>* **ROCK STEADY** [43] [9]
– (intro) / Hella good / Hey baby (with BOUNTY KILLER) / Making out / Underneath it all (with LADY SAW) / Detective / Don't let me down / Start the fire / Running / In my head / Platinum blonde life / Waiting room / Rock steady.

Feb 02. (c-s; by NO DOUBT feat. BOUNTY KILLER) *(497668-4) <radio cut>* **HEY BABY / EX-GIRLFRIEND (Philip Steir remix)** [2] Nov01 [5]
(cd-s+=) *(497668-2)* – ('A'-Fabian mix) / ('A'-video).

Jun 02. (c-s) *(497736-4) <497720>* **HELLA GOOD / HELLA GOOD (Roger Sanchez release yourself mix)** [12] May02 [13]
(cd-s+=) *(497736-2)* – ('A'-skank remix with OUTKAST) / ('A'-video).
(12") *(497736-1)* – ('A'-skank remix with OUTKAST) / ('A'-Roger's release dub).

Sep 02. (c-s; by NO DOUBT feat. LADY SAW) *(497780-4) <497779>* **UNDERNEATH IT ALL / UNDERNEATH IT ALL (live acoustic)** [18] [3]
(cd-s+=) *(497779-2)* – Just a girl (live acoustic) / ('A'video).

Jul 03. (cd-s) *<980767>* **RUNNING / HELLA GOOD (live) / UNDERNEATH IT ALL (live) / HEY BABY (live)** [–] [62]

Nov 03. (cd-s) *(9813724)* **IT'S MY LIFE / ROCK STEADY (live) / BATHWATER (live)** [20] [–]

Nov 03. (cd) *(986138-2) <014950-2>* **THE SINGLES 1992-2003** (compilation) [5] [2]
– Just a girl / It's my life / Hey baby (with BOUNTY KILLER) / Bathwater /

Sunday morning / Hella good / New / Underneath it all (with LADY SAW) / Excuse me Mr. / Running / Spiderwebs / Simple kind of life / Don't speak / Ex-girlfriend / Trapped in a box. *(UK+=)* – Girls get the bass in the back (Hey baby remix with BOUNTY KILLER) / Underneath it all (live).

Mar 04. (cd-s) *(9861993)* **IT'S MY LIFE / BATHWATER (Invincible Overlord remix) / IT'S MY LIFE (Jacques Lu Cont Thin White Duke mix) / IT'S MY LIFE (Chocolate O'Brien remix) / (videos for 2)** [17] [–]

GWEN STEFANI

with numerous collaborations

Interscope Interscope

Nov 04. (cd-s) *(9864986)* **WHAT YOU WAITING FOR? / (mixes; Jacques Lu Cont / instrumental / video)** [4] [47]
(12") *<B0003645-11>* – (mixes; Armand Van Helden / the Rude Ho mix by Felix Da Housecat / Armand Van Helden dub).

Nov 04. (cd)<d-lp> *(9866851)* *<34690-2><B0003829-01>* **LOVE.ANGEL.MUSIC.BABY** [4] [5]
– What you waiting for? / Rich girl / Hollaback girl / Cool / Bubble pop electric / Luxurious / Harajuku girls / Crash / The real thing / Serious / Danger zone / Long way to go. *(ltd-cd+=; 2103177)*

Mar 05. (cd-s) *(9880219)* **RICH GIRL / WHAT YOU WAITING FOR? (live) / HARAJUKU GIRLS (live) / ('A'-video)** [4] [7]
(12") *<B0003978-11>* – ('A'-Get Rich mixes & instrumentals).

Jun 05. (cd-s) *(9882326)* **HOLLABACK GIRL / (mixes; Hollatronix remix by Diplo / instrumental / video).**
(d12"+=) *<B0004970-11>* – (Dancehollaback mixes).

Sep 05. (cd-s) *(9884356)* **COOL / COOL (Photek remix) / HOLLABACK GIRL (Dancehollaback remix by Tony Kanal) / (video)** [11] [13]
(12") *<B0005480-11>* – (mixes; Richard X / Richard X dub / Photek DJ / Photek).

Dec 05. (cd-s) *(9888344)* **LUXURIOUS / LUXURIOUS (remix feat. Slim Thug) / COOL (Richard X remix) / LUXURIOUS (video)** [44] [21]
(12") *<B0005823-11>* – (first 2) / (acappella) / (instrumental).

Feb 06. (-) *<radio>* **CRASH** [–] [49]

the NOTORIOUS B.I.G.

Born: CHRISTOPHER WALLACE, 21 May'72, Brooklyn, New York, USA. Under the moniker BIGGIE SMALLS, WALLACE's talent as an NYC rapper caught the attention of east coast hip hop guru/owner of 'Bad Boy' records, Sean 'Puffy' Combs, who in turn brought the rising star to greater prominence through guest spots on records by the likes of MARY J. BLIGE. SMALLS' own recording debut (as NOTORIOUS B.I.G.), the US Top 30 single, 'JUICY', found him marking out his own territory at the slicker R&B/swing end of the gangsta rap spectrum. Arrested many times for robbery, assault and weapon offenses, he at least knew what he was singing about, tackling the usual subjects of 'bitches', guns and money on the accompanying album, 'READY TO DIE' (1994). A string of Top 10 hits followed, inlcuding a collaboration with METHOD MAN and even a joint effort with west coast star TUPAC SHAKUR, soon to become a sworn enemy. What had started out as a simmering east/west rivalry between 'Bad boy' and L.A. label, 'Death Row', turned into a bitter feud with 2PAC and SMALLS at its epicentre. Amid defiant threats exchanged both in the press and on vinyl, things spiralled out of control as 2PAC was gunned down by unknown assailants in Las Vegas on the 13th of September '96. The B.I.G. man's follow-up album, 'LIFE AFTER DEATH', dealt with the violence head on; the sense of fatalism running through many of the tracks was only compounded by the needless murder of BIGGIE himself, also gunned down (drive-by shooting in L.A.) on the 9th March 1997, only days before the album's release. Though the perpetrator of the crime remains unknown (a Crips gang member was said to be prime suspect), the incident only served to fan the flames of the dispute even higher. Every cynic knows that death sells; the massive transatlantic publicity surrounding this particular death ensured that the posthumously released record sold multi-millions. Two singles, 'HYPNOTIZE' and 'MO MONEY MO PROBLEMS', both topped the US charts, as did the tribute single, 'I'LL BE MISSING YOU', a joint effort of Puffy and SMALLS' wife, Faith Evans. In little more than six months, an already ailing rap scene had lost two of its most talented figureheads, a worrying sign of the genre's increasing inability to distinguish the boundary between art and reality. B.I.G. was back to haunt the airwaves from beyond the grave courtesy of posthumous packages: 'BORN AGAIN' (1999) and 'DUETS: THE FINAL CHAPTER' (2005), as star-studded as they were inevitable. Many of the same faces appeared on both sets – stand up EMINEM, SNOOP DOGG, MISSY ELLIOTT, NAS – and while second time around the idea wasn't quite so novel – 'DUETS' failed to make No.1 (stalling at No.3) – it did make for a surprising Top 20 entry in Britain, even if fans were critical of its hastily cobbled together feel.

Album rating: READY TO DIE (*8) / LIFE AFTER DEATH (*7) / BORN AGAIN (*6) / THE FINAL CHAPTER (*5)

the NOTORIOUS B.I.G. – vocals / with various producers, etc.

not iss. Life

Oct 93. (c-s/cd-s; as BIGGY SMALLZ) *<79008>* **CRUISIN' (mixes)** [–] [ ]

Arista Arista

Oct 94. (c-s) *(74321 24010-4)* *<7-9004>* **JUICY / UNBELIEVABLE** [72] [27]
(12"+=/cd-s+=) *(74321 24010-1/-2)* – (2-'A'mixes).

Oct 94. (cd/c) *<(78612 73000-2/-4)>* **READY TO DIE** [ ] [15]
– Intro / Things done changed / Gimme the loot / Machine gun funk / Warning / Ready to die / One more chance / F*** me (interlude) / The what / Juicy / Everyday struggle / Me and my bitch / Big poppa / Respect / Friend of mine / Unbelievable / Suicidal thoughts. *(cd re-iss. May97; same)*

Mar 95. (12"/cd-s) *(74321 26341-1/-2)* *<79015>* **BIG POPPA. / WHO SHOT YA? / WARNING / BIG POPPA (mix)** [63] [6]

— In Apr'95, the man featured on the TOTAL single, 'Can't You See'.

Jun 95. (12",cd-s; The NOTORIOUS B.I.G. and METHOD MAN) *<79031>* **ONE MORE CHANCE – STAY WITH ME / THE WHAT** [–] [2]

— In Jan'97, The NOTORIOUS B.I.G. collaborated with 2PAC, RADIO, DRAMACYDAL & STRETCH on Top 100 US single, 'RUNNIN'.

Mar 97. (d-cd/c/q-lp) *<(78612 73011-2/-4/-1)>* **LIFE AFTER DEATH** [23] [1]
– Life after death / Somebody's gotta die / Hypnotize / Mad rapper / Kick in the door / Lovin' you tonight / Last day / Dice / I love the dough / What's beef / B.I.G. / I'm coming out (more money) / Niggaz bleed / Story to tell / Notorious thugs / Interlude / Missing you / Another man / Cali (interlude) / Goin' back to Cali / 10 crack commandments / Playa later / Interlude / Nasty boy / Interlude / Sky's the limit / The world is filled / Interlude / My downfall / Long kiss goodnight / You're nobody. *(best bits re-iss. Nov97 cd/c; 78612 73019-22/-46) (re-iss. Feb98; same)*

— B.I.G. was shot dead on the 9th March, 1997

Apr 97. (c-s) *(74321 46641-4)* *<79092>* **HYPNOTIZE / I GOT A STORY TO TELL** [10] [1]
(12"+=/cd-s+=) *(74321 46641-1/-2)* – ('A'mixes).

Jul 97. (c-s) *(74321 49249-4)* *<79100>* **MO MONEY MO PROBLEMS / LOVIN' YOU TONIGHT** [6] [1]
(12"+=/cd-s+=) *(74321 49249-1/-2)* – ('A'mixes; instrumental / Razor-n-go).
(above credited in the States with PUFF DADDY & MASE)

Feb 98. (c-s; NOTORIOUS B.I.G. featuring 112) *(74321 56199-4)* *<79131>* **SKY'S THE LIMIT / GOIN' BACK TO CALI** [35] Nov97 [26]
(12"+=/cd-s+=) *(74321 56199-1/-2)* – Kick in the door.

— In Mar'98, the B.I.G. man featured with BUSTA RHYMES on PUFF DADDY & THE FAMILY's Top 20 (US) hit, 'Victory'.

Dec 99. (cd/c/d-lp) *(74321 71718-2/-4/-1)* *<73023>* **BORN AGAIN** [70] [1]
– Born again intro / The Notorious B.I.G. (w/ LIL' KIM & PUFF DADDY) / Dead wrong (w/ EMINEM) / Hope you niggas sleep (w/ HOT BOYS & BIG TIMER) / Dangerous MC's (w/ MARK CURRY, SNOOP DOGG & BUSTA RHYMES) / Biggie (w/ JUNIOR M.A.F.I.A.) / Niggas

Big booty hoes (w/ TOO SHORT) / Would you die for me (w/ TOO SHORT) / Come on (w/ SADAT) / Rap phenomenom (w/ REDMAN & METHOD MAN) / Let me get down (w/ G-DEP, CRAIG MACK & MISSY ELLIOTT) / Tonight (w/ MOBB DEPP & JOE HOOKER) / If I should die before I wake (w/ BLACK ROB, ICE CUBE & BEANIE SIGEL) / Who shot ya / Can I get witcha (w/ LIL' CEASE) / I really want to show you (w/ K-CI, JOJO & NAS) / Ms. Wallace (outro).

Jan 00. (c-s/12"/cd-s; as The NOTORIOUS B.I.G. featuring PUFF DADDY & LIL' KIM) *(74321 73731-4/-1/-2)* *<radio cut>* **NOTORIOUS B.I.G. (mixes; radio / club / instrumental) / DEAD WRONG (main without Eminem) / ONE MORE CHANCE – STAY WITH ME (remix)** 16 Nov99 67

— in Jan'04, a posthumous single w/ TUPAC, 'Runnin' (Dying To Live') hit the Top 20

Atlantic Atlantic

Jan 06. (cd-s) *(AT 0229CD)* **NASTY GIRL / WANT THAT OLD THING BACK (w/ JA RULE & RALPH TRESVANT)** 3 Nov05 43
(12"+=) *(AT 229T)* – Hold ya head (w/ BOB MARLEY) / ('A'-instrumental).
(cd-s) *(AT 229CDX)* – ('A'-mixes/toneRings).
(above 'A' credited DIDDY, NELLY, JAGGED EDGE & AVERY STORM)

Jan 06. (cd) *<(7567 83885-2)>* **DUETS: THE FINAL CHAPTER** 17 Dec05 3
– B.I.G. live in Jamaica (intro) / It has been said / Spit your game / Whatchu want / Get your grind on / Living the life / The greatest rapper (interlude) / 1970 somethin' / Nasty girl / Living in pain / I'm with whateva / Beef / My dad (interlude) / Hustler's story / Breakin' old habits / Ultimate rush / Mi casa / Little homie (interlude) / Hold ya head / Just a memory / Wake up / Love is everlasting (outro).

□ the NOTTING HILLBILLIES
(see under ⇒ DIRE STRAITS)

Gary NUMAN

Born: GARY WEBB, 8 Mar'58, Hammersmith, London, England. Inspired by 70's glam icons such as BOLAN and BOWIE as well as synthmeisters like KRAFTWERK, NUMAN formed punk outfit, MEAN STREET in 1977, subsequently appearing on the Various Artists compilation, 'Live At The Vortex'. To end the year, he set up TUBEWAY ARMY, basically his solo project although he was accompanied on live work by PAUL GARDINER and his uncle, GERALD LIDYARD. The debut vinyl outing, 'THAT'S TOO BAD', was issued by indie punk label, 'Beggars Banquet' in early '78. An eponymous debut album passed virtually unnoticed, although things changed dramatically in June '79, when they/he had a first No.1 with the monotonic synth-noir of 'ARE FRIENDS ELECTRIC', spurred on by a compelling appearance on UK's 'Top Of The Pops'. Its parent album, 'REPLICAS', also shot to the top the same month. A busy year for NUMAN, in addition to collaborating with ROBERT PALMER, of all people (he was initially part of offshoot outfit, DRAMATIS), he found time to record a second No.1 album, 'THE PLEASURE PRINCIPLE'. This collection was previewed with the hypnotic, sweeping electronica of the 'CARS' single, by far his most well known track and one that enjoyed a rejuvenation in 1996 after it was used in a British TV advert. NUMAN scored yet another No.1 album with 'TELEKON' (1980) the following year, his futuristic synth-based pop/rock gracing the upper reaches of the singles chart in the form of 'WE ARE GLASS' and 'I DIE: YOU DIE'. By this point, however, NUMAN was well on his way to becoming perhaps one of most visible targets of critical derision in the whole of the music industry, his neo-futurist posturing, dalek vocals, pretentious lyrics and worst of all, his vocal support of Margaret Thatcher raising the not inconsiderable ire of the music press. Nevertheless, NUMAN had a fiercely loyal grassroots following of clone-like fans (second only to NUMAN himself as figures of fun among rock circles) who ensured most of his subsequent output made the Top 50 at least. Despite the presence of such luminaries as MICK KARN (JAPAN), ROGER TAYLOR (QUEEN) and erm, NASH THE SLASH (solo artist from Canada, apparently), 'DANCE' (1981) was a decidedly ungroovy set of steely electronica and his last to achieve mainstream success. NUMAN released two further, increasingly pompous albums, 'I, ASSASSIN' (1982) and 'WARRIORS' (1983) before forming his own label, 'Numa', in 1984 to issue his own product along with material by his brother JOHN's outfit, HOHOKAM. 80's albums like 'THE FURY' (1985), 'STRANGE CHARM' (1986), 'METAL RHYTHM' (1988) and 'AUTOMATIC' (1989) continued to appeal mainly to hardcore fans although 'OUTLAND' (1991) managed to nudge into the Top 40. However, since the awful 'MACHINE AND SOUL' (1992), NUMAN has fallen further into cult status, his releases failing to even break the Top 100. Come the new millennium, NUMAN was still churning out the albums, the harsh industrialised textures of 'PURE' (2000) suggesting that he could easily give the young pretenders of goth electronica a run for their money. It also suggested that after years in the musical wilderness, NUMAN may have found a creatively profitable niche for himself. Together with producer/multi-instrumentalist, ACE FENTON, GARY leant on the side of industrial goth for 2006 comeback album, 'JAGGED' – NUMAN INCH NAILS anyone?

• **Songwriters:** Wrote own material, with inspiration from psi-fi writers (i.e. WILLIAM S. BURROUGHS). Covered 1999 + U GOT THE LOOK (Prince).
• **Trivia:** In the early 80's, he took up flying planes and bought his own aircraft (mainly warplanes).

Album rating: Tubeway Army: TUBEWAY ARMY (*4) / REPLICAS (*7) / Gary Numan: THE PLEASURE PRINCIPLE (*7) / TELEKON (*6) / LIVING ORNAMENTS 1979 (*4) / LIVING ORNAMENTS 1980 (*4) / DANCE (*4) / I, ASSASSIN (*5) / WARRIORS (*4) / BERSERKER (*4) / WHITE NOISE (*4) / THE FURY (*4) / STRANGE CHARM (*3) / EXHIBITION compilation (*7) / METAL RHYTHM (*4) / AUTOMATIC (*3; as Sharpe & Numan) / THE SKIN MECHANIC (*4) / OUTLAND (*4) / MACHINE AND SOUL (*4) / THE BEST OF . . . compilation (*7) / DREAM CORROSION (*4) / DARL LIGHT (*4) / DARK LIGHT (*4) / HUMAN (*4) / EXILE (*3) / PURE (*6) / JAGGED (*6)

TUBEWAY ARMY

GARY NUMAN – vocals, guitar, synthesizer, keyboards (ex-MEAN STREET) / **PAUL 'Scarlett' GARDINER** – bass / **GERALD 'Rael' LIDYARD** – drums

Beggars Banquet Atco

Feb 78. (7") *(BEG 5)* **THAT'S TOO BAD. / OH! DIDN'T I SAY** –

— **BARRY BENN** – drums repl. BOB SIMMONDS who had repl. LIDYARD / added **SEAN BURKE** – guitar

Jul 78. (7"m) *(BEG 8)* **BOMBERS. / O.D. RECEIVER. / BLUE EYES** –

Aug 78. (lp,blue-lp) *(BEGA 4)* **TUBEWAY ARMY** –
– Listen to the sirens / My shadow in vain / The life machine / Friends / Something's in the house / Every day I die / Steal and you / My love is a liquid / Are you real / The dream police / Jo the waiter / Zero bass. *(re-iss. Aug79 lp/c; BEGA/BEGC 4); hit No.14) (re-iss. May83 on 'Fame' lp/c; FA/TC-FA 3060) (re-iss. Jul88 lp/c; BBL/+C 4)*

— **JESS LIDYARD** – drums returned to replace BARRY and SEAN

Mar 79. (7") *(BEG 17)* **DOWN IN THE PARK. / DO YOU NEED THE SERVICE?** –
(12"+=) *(BEG 17T)* – I nearly married a human 2.

May 79. (7"/7"pic-d) <US-7"/c-s> *(BEG 18/+P)* **ARE 'FRIENDS' ELECTRIC?. / WE ARE SO FRAGILE?** 1

Jun 79. (lp/c) <credited as GARY NUMAN & TUBEWAY ARMY> *(BEGA/BEGC 7)* <117> **REPLICAS** 1
– Me I disconnect from you / Are 'friends' electric? / The machman / Praying to the aliens / Down in the park / You are in my vision / Replicas / It must have been years / When the machines rock / I nearly married a human. *(re-iss. +cd.Sep88) (re-iss. cd/c Apr95 on 'Music Club')*

GARY NUMAN

— solo retaining **PAUL GARDINER** – bass / **CEDRIC SHARPLEY** – drums / **CHRIS PAYNE** – synth, viola / **BILLY CURRIE** – keyboards

Aug 79. (7") *(BEG 23)* **CARS. / ASYLUM** 1 –

Sep 79. (lp/c) *(BEGA/BEGC 10)* *<38120>* **THE PLEASURE PRINCIPLE** 1 Jan80 16
– Airplane / Metal / Complex / Films / M.E. / Tracks / Observer / Conversation / Cars / Engineers. *(re-iss. Sep88 lp/c; BBL/+C 10)*

Nov 79. (7") *(BEG 29)* **COMPLEX. / BOMBERS (live)** 6
(12"+=) *(BEG 29T)* – Me I disconnect from you (live).

Jan 80. (7") *<7211>* **CARS. / METAL** – 9

— **DENNIS HAINES** – keyboards repl. CURRIE who returned to ULTRAVOX and VISAGE; added **RUSSELL BELL** – guitar (on tour) .

May 80. (7") *(BEG 35)* **WE ARE GLASS. / TROIS GYMNPEDIES (1st MOVEMENT)** 5

Aug 80. (7") *(BEG 46)* **I DIE: YOU DIE. / DOWN IN THE PARK (piano version)** 6 –

Sep 80. (lp/c) *(BEGA/BEGC 19)* *<32103>* **TELEKON** 1 64
– This wreckage / The aircrash bureau / Telekon / Remind me to smile / Sleep by windows / I'm an agent / I dream of wires / Remember I was a vapour / Please push no more / The joy circuit. *(free-7"w/ lp)* – REMEMBER I WAS A VAPOUR. / ON BROADWAY *(re-iss. Jul88 lp/c; BBL/+C 19)*

Sep 80. (7") **I DIE: YOU DIE. / SLEEP BY WINDOWS** –

Dec 80. (7") **REMIND ME TO SMILE. /** –

Dec 80. (7") *(BEG 50)* **THIS WRECKAGE. / PHOTOGRAPH** 20

Apr 81. (d-lp/c) *(BOX/C 1)* **LIVING ORNAMENTS 1979-1980 (live)** 2 –

Apr 81. (lp) *(BEGA 24)* **LIVING ORNAMENTS 1979 (live)** 47 –
– Airplane / Cars / We are so fragile? / Films / Something's in the house / My shadow in vain / Conversation / The dream police / Metal.

Apr 81. (lp) *(BEGA 25)* **LIVING ORNAMENTS 1980 (live)** 39 –
– This wreckage / I die: you die / M.E. / Everyday I die / Down in the park / Remind me to smile / The joy circuit / Tracks / Are 'friends' electric? / We are glass.

— GARY now recruited famous stars to replace BELL, SHARPLEY, HAINES and PAYNE. They became DRAMATIS. Jul'81 he guested on PAUL GARDINER single 'STORMTROOPER IN DRAG' *(BEG 61/+T)*, which hit UK No.49. Next with stars **MICK KARN** – bass (of JAPAN) / **ROGER TAYLOR** – drums (of QUEEN) + **NASH THE SLASH** – violin (Canadian solo artist)

Aug 81. (7") *(BEG 62)* **SHE'S GOT CLAWS. / I SING RAIN** 6
(12"+=) *(BEG 62T)* – Exhibition.

Sep 81. (lp/c) *(BEGA/BEGC 28)* *<38-143>* **DANCE** 3
– Slowcar to China / Night talk / A subway called you / Cry the clock said / She's got claws / Crash / Boys like me / Stories / My brother's time / You are you are / Moral. *(re-iss. Jan89 lp/c; BBL/+C 28)*

Nov 81. (7"; by GARY NUMAN and DRAMATIS) *(BEG 68)* **LOVE NEEDS NO DISGUISE. / TAKE ME HOME** 33
(12"+=) *(BEG 68T)* – Face to face.

— GARY NUMAN now used session people.

Feb 82. (7") *(BEG 70)* **MUSIC FOR CHAMELEONS. / NOISE NOISE** 19
(ext.12"+=) *(BEG 70T)* – Bridge? what bridge.

Jun 82. (7") *(BEG 77)* **WE TAKE MYSTERY (TO BED). / THE IMAGE IS** 9
(ext.12"+=) *(BEG 77T)* – ('A'early version).

Aug 82. (7") *(BEG 81)* **WHITE BOYS AND HEROES. / WAR GAMES** 20
(ext.12"+=) *(BEG 81T)* – Glitter and ash.

Sep 82. (lp/c) *(BEGA/BEGC 40)* *<900141>* **I, ASSASSIN** 8
– White boys and heroes / War songs / A dream of Siam / Music for chameleons / This is my house / I, assassin / The 1930's rust / We take mystery (to bed). *(re-iss. Jan89 lp/c; BBL/+C 40)*

Aug 83. (7"/7"sha-pic-d) *(BEG 95/+P)* **WARRIORS. / MY CAR SLIDES (1)** 20 –
(ext.12"+=) *(BEG 95T)* – My car slides (2).

Sep 83. (lp/c) *(BEGA/BEGC 47)* **WARRIORS** 12 –
– Warriors / I am render / The iceman comes / This prison moon / My centurion / Sister surprise / The tick tock man / Love is like clock law / The rhythm of the evening. *(re-iss. Jan89 lp/c; BBL/+C 47)*

Oct 83. (7") *(BEG 101)* **SISTER SUPRISE. / POETRY AND POWER** 32 –
(ext.12"+=) *(BEG 101T)* – Letters.

Numa not iss.

Oct 84. (7"/7"sha-pic-d) *(NU/+P 4)* **BERSERKER. / EMPTY BED, EMPTY HEART** 32 –
(12"+=) *(NUM 4)* – ('A'extended).

Nov 84. (lp/c) *(NUMA/+C 1001)* **BERSERKER** 45 –
– Berserker / This is new love / The secret / My dying machine / Cold warning / Pump it up / The God film / A child with the ghost / The hunter. *(c+=)* – (6 extra tracks). *(cd-iss. Dec95; NUMACD 1001)*

Dec 84. (7") *(NU 6)* **MY DYING MACHINE. / HERE I AM** 66 –
(ext.12"+=) *(NUM 6)* – She cries.

— next 45 with BILL SHARPE of SHAKATAK; and on 'Polydor' album 'Famous People'.

Feb 85. (7"/7"pic-d; by SHARPE & NUMAN) *(POSP/+P 722)* **CHANGE YOUR MIND. / REMIX, REMAKE, REMODEL** 17 –
(ext.12"pic-d+=) *(POSPX 722)* – Fools in a world of fire.

Apr 85. (d-lp/c) *(NUMA D/C 1002)* **WHITE NOISE (live)** 29 –
– (intro) / Berserker / Metal / Me, I disconnect from you / Remind me to smile / Sister surprise / Music for chameleons / The iceman comes / Cold warning / Down in the park / This prison moon / I die; you die / My dying machine / Cars / We take mystery (to bed) / We are glass / This is new love / My shadow in vain / Are 'friends' electric?. *(d-cd-iss. May93; NUMACD 1002)*

May 85. (7"ep/12"ep,12"blue-ep,12"white-ep) *(NU/+M 7)* **THE LIVE EP (live)** 27 –
– Are 'friends' electric? / Berserker / Cars / We are glass.

Jul 85. (7"/7"pic-d) *(NU/+P 9)* **YOUR FASCINATION. / WE NEED IT** 46 –
(ext.12"+=/ext.12"pic-d+=) *(NUM/+P 9)* – Anthem.

Sep 85. (7") *(NU 11)* **CALL OUT THE DOGS. / THIS SHIP COMES APART** 49 –
(ext.12"+=) *(NUM 11)* – No shelter.

Sep 85. (lp/pic-lp/c) *(NUMA/+P/K 1003)* **THE FURY** 24 –
– Call out the dogs / This disease / Your fascination / Miracles / The pleasure skin / Creatures / Tricks / God only knows / Creatures / I still remember. *(c+)* – (all tracks extended). *(cd-iss. 1986; CDNUMA 1003) (re-iss. cd Nov96; NUMACDX 1003)*

Nov 85. (7",7"red,7"white/ext-12",ext-12"red,ext-12"white) *(NU/+M 13)* **MIRACLES. / THE FEAR** 49 –

Apr 86. (7"/7"pic-d/ext-12"/ext-12"pic-d) *(NU/+P/M/MP 16)* **THIS IS LOVE. / SURVIVAL** 28 –
(all w/ free 7"flexi)
(d12"+=) *(NUMX 16)* – Call out the dogs (extended) / No shelter / This ship comes apart.

Jun 86. (7"/7"sha-pic-d/ext-12"/picture-12"pic-d/club-10") *(NU/+P/M/MP/DJ 17)* **I CAN'T STOP. / FACES** 27 –
(all w/ free 7"flexi)

Sep 86. (7"/7"pic-d/ext-12"/ext-12"pic-d; as SHARPE & NUMAN) *(NU/+P/M/MP 19)* **NEW THING FROM LONDON TOWN. / TIME TO DIE** 52 –

Oct 86. (lp/c)(cd) *(NUMA/+C 1005)(CDNUMA 1005)* **STRANGE CHARM** 59 –
– My breathing / Unknown and hostile / The sleep room / New thing from London Town / I can't stop / Strange charm / The need / This is love. *(re-iss. cd Nov96; NUMACDX 1005)*

Nov 86. (7"/7"pic-d/ext-12"/ext-12"pic-d) *(NU/+P/M/MP 21)* **I STILL REMEMBER. / PUPPETS** 74 –

— early in 1987, he teamed up with RADIO HEART (see further below)

Polydor not iss.

Jan 88. (7",7"white,7"blue,7"clear/ 7"pic-d/ext-12"/ext-12"pic-d; as SHARPE & NUMAN) *(POSP/+P/X/PX 894)* **NO MORE LIES. / VOICES** 34 –
(cd-s+=) *(POCD 894)* – ('A'extended) / Change your mind.

Illegal I.R.S.

Sep 88. (7"/7"w-poster) *(ILS/+P 1003)* **NEW ANGER. / I DON'T BELIEVE** 46 –
(12"+=/12"g-f+=) *(ILST/ILSG 1003)* – Children.
(cd-s+=) *(ILSCD 1003)* – Creatures (live) / I can't stop (live).

Oct 88. (lp/c/cd) *(ILP/+C/CD 035)* *<IRS/+D 82005>* **METAL RHYTHM** 48
– Respect / Don't call my name / New anger / America / Hunger / Voix / Young heart / Cold metal rhythm / This is emotion. *(pic-lp iss.Mar89; ILPX 035)*

Nov 88. (7"/7"pic-d) *(ILS/+PD 1004)* **AMERICA (remix). / RESPECT (live)** 49 –
(12"+=) *(ILST 1004)* – New anger (live).
(cd-s++=) *(ILSCD 1004)* – Call out the dogs (live).

— again with **ROGER ODELL** – drums / **TESSA MILES** + **LINDA TAYLOR** – backing vocals

SHARPE & NUMAN

Polydor not iss.

May 89. (7"/7"pic-d) *(PO/+PD 43)* **I'M ON AUTOMATIC. / LOVE LIKE A GHOST** 44 –
(ext.12"+=/ext.12"pic-d+=) *(PZ/+PD 43)* – Voices ('89 remix).
(7"w-poster) *(POPB 43)* – ('A'side) / No more lies (new version).
(cd-s+=) *(POCD 43)* – (all 4 above).

Jun 89. (lp/c/cd) *(839520-1/-4/-2)* **AUTOMATIC** 59 –
– Change your mind / Turn off the world / No more lies / Breathe in emotion / Some new game / I'm on automatic / Rip it up / Welcome to love / Voices / Nightlife. *(cd+=)* – No more lies (12"version) / I'm on automatic (12"version).

GARY NUMAN

— solo with **RUSSELL BELL** – guitar / **CHRIS PAYNE** – keyboards, violin / **ADE ORANGE** – keyboards / **CEDRIC SHARPLY** – drums / **JOHN WEBB** – saxophone / **ANDY COUGHLAN** – bass / **VAL CHALMERS** + **EMMA CHALMER** – backing vocals

I.R.S. Capitol

Oct 89. (lp/cd) *(EIRSA/+CD 1019)* **THE SKIN MECHANIC (live Sep88)** 55 –
– Survival / Respect / Call out the dogs / Cars / Hunger / Down in the park / New anger / Creatures / Are 'friends' electric / Young heart / We are glass / I die: you die.

Mar 91. (7",7"red/c-s) *(NUMAN 1/+C)* **HEART. / SHAME** 43 –
(12") *(NUMAN 1T)* – ('A') / Icehouse.
(cd-s) *(NUMAN 1CD)* – ('A') / Tread careful.
(12") *(NUMAN 1TX)* – ('A') / Are 'friends' electric?.

Mar 91. (lp/c/cd) *(EIRSA/+MC/CD 1039)* <13077> **OUTLAND** 39
– Confession / My world storm / Interval 1 / From Russia infected / Interval 2 / They whisper you / Dark Sunday / Heart / Devotion / Outland / Interval 3 / 1999 / Dream killer.

Numa not iss.

Sep 91. (7"/c-s) *(NUD/NUC 22)* **EMOTION. / IN A GLASSHOUSE** –
(12"+=) *(NUM 22)* – Hanoi.
(cd-s++=) *(NUCD 22)* – ('A'-different mix).

Mar 92. (7"/c-s) *(NU/+C 23)* **THE SKIN GAME. / DARK MOUNTAIN** 68 –
(12"+=/cd-s+=) *(NUM/NUCD 23)* – U got the look / ('A'-digi mix).

Jul 92. (7") *(NU 24)* **MACHINE + SOUL. / ('A'-promo mix)** 72 –
(cd-s+=) *(NUCD1 24)* – Cry baby / Wonder eye.
(cd-s+=) *(NUCD2 24)* – 1999 / The hauntings.
(12"+=) *(NUM1 24)* – Your fascination (live) / Outland (live) / Respect (live).
(12") *(NUM2 24)* – ('A') / Soul protection (live) / Confession (live) / From Russia infected (live).

Jul 92. (lp/c/cd) *(NUMA/+C/CD 1009)* **MACHINE + SOUL** 42 –
– Machine + soul / Generator / The skin game / Poison / I wonder / Emotion / Cry / U got the look / Love isolation. *(ext.cd re-iss. Sep93)*

— Apr 94; He guested for GENERATOR on their version of 'ARE FRIENDS' ELECTRIC'.

— NUMAN & DADAGANG; Apr 94 12"/cd-s LIKE A REFUGEE (I WON'T CRY) on 'Record Label', re-iss. Aug 94 as GARY NUMAN & FRIENDS

Aug 94. (12"ep/cd-ep) *(NU M/CD 25)* **DREAM CORROSION (THE LIVE EP)** –
– Noise, noise / It must have been years / I'm an agent / Jo the waiter.

Aug 94. (t-lp/d-c/d-cd) *(NUMA/+C/CD 1010)* **DREAM CORROSION (live)** –
– Mission / Machine and soul / Outland / Me, I disconnect from you / We are so fragile / Respect / Shame / Films / Dream killer / Down in the park / My world storm / Machman / Generator / Noise, noise / Cars / Voix / You are in my vision / It must have been years / That's too bad / Remind me to smile / I'm an agent / Are 'friends' electric / My breathing / I don't believe / Bombers / Jo the waiter / We are glass.

Oct 94. (12"ep/cd-ep) *(NU M/CD 26)* **A QUESTION OF FAITH** –
– A question of faith (agnostic edit) / Play like God / Whisper of truth / A question of faith (devout edit).

Mar 95. (cd/c/lp) *(NUMA/+C/CD 1011)* **SACRIFICE**
– Pray / Deadliner / A question of faith / Desire / Scar / Love and napalm / You walk in my soul / Magic / Bleed / The seed of life.

Mar 95. (12"/12"pic-d/cd-s/pic-cd-s) *(NU/+MP/CD/CDP 27)* **ABSOLUTION. / MAGIC (trick mix) / MAGIC (extended)** –

Jun 95. (12"ep/cd-ep) *(NUM/+CD 28)* **DARK LIGHT LIVE E.P. (live)** –
– Bleed / Everyday I die / The dream police / Listen to the sirens.

Jul 95. (d-cd/d-c) *(NUMA CD/C 1012)* **DARK LIGHT (live)**
– Pray / A question of faith / I dream of wires / Noise noise / Listen to the sirens / Everyday I die / Desire / Friens / Scar / Magic / Praying to the aliens / Replicas I / Mean street / Stormtrooper in drag / Dead liner / Bleed / The dream police / I die, you die / The hunter / Remind me to smile / Are friends "electric"? / Do you need the service? / Love and napalm / Jo the waiter / I'm an agent.

Nov 95. (d-c/d-cd; with MICHAEL R. SMITH) *(NUMA C/CD 1013)* **HUMAN** –
– Navigators / Bombay / We fold space / Cry in the dark / Manic / Empire / Little lost soul / Visitor / Magician / Undercover / Halloween / Embryo / Elm Street / Harmonos / Big alten / Blind faith / New life / Fairy tales / Disease / Tidal wave / Alone and afraid / Sahara / Cold / Do you wonder / Betrayal / Suspicion / Unborn / Lethal injection / Frantic / Mother / Black heart / Thunder road / Law and order / Needles / Climax / Inferno.

Eagle Spitfire

Oct 97. (cd/c) *(EAG CD/MC 008)* **EXILE** 48 –
– Dominion day / Prophecy / Dead heaven / Dark / Innocence bleeding / The angel wars / Absolution / An alien cure / Exile.

Apr 98. (c-s) *(EAGCS 008)* **DOMINION DAY / ANGEL WARS (extended)** –
(cd-s) *(EAGXS 008)* – ('A'side) / Voix (20th anniversary) / Dead heaven (extended) / Cars (live).
(cd-s) *(EAGXA 008)* – ('A'side) / Metal (20th anniversary) / Down in the park (20th anniversary) / Dominion day (live).

— now with **STEVE HARRIS** – guitar / **ROB HOLIDAY** – guitar, keyboards / **MONTI** – drums, prog / **RICHARD BEASLEY** – drums

Oct 00. (cd) *(EAGCD 078)* <15088> **PURE** 58 Nov00
– Pure / Walking with shadows / Rip / One perfect lie / My Jesus / Fallen / Listen to my voice / A prayer for the unborn / Torn / Little Invitro / I can't breathe. *(d-cd+=; EAGTE 078)* – (live):- Pure / My Jesus / Rip / Cars / Replicas / A prayer for the unborn (Greyed up remix) / Listen to my voice (Greyed up remix).

Jagged Halo Universal

May 02. (d-cd) *(JHCD 001)* <400008> **EXPOSURE – THE BEST OF GARY NUMAN 1977-2002** (compilation) 44
– Films / I die: you die / Are 'friends' electric? / Pure / Dead Heaven / Down in the park / Me! I disconnect from you / Metal / She's got claws / Magic / We are glass / Music for chameleons / My shadow in vain (new version) / Everyday I die (new version) / My Jesus / Cars / Dominion day / Complex / We are so fragile / Rip / M.E. / We take mystery (to bed) / Dark / Remember I was a vapour / Listen to my voice / Deadliner / Exposure / Voix / A prayer for the unborn.

Jul 02. (cd-s) *(JHCDS 1)* **RIP / A PRAYER FOR THE UNBORN / M.E. (new version) / ('A'-video)** 29 –
(cd-s) *(JHCDSX 1)* – ('A') / This wreckage / Are 'friends' electric?

Jun 03. (cd-s; as GARY NUMAN Vs RICO) *(JHCDV 6)* <40000> **CRAZIER / LISTEN TO MY VOICE / ANCIENTS / CRAZIER (dub)** 13 Jul03
(cd-s) *(JHCDX 6)* – ('A') / Big black sea / Garden man / ('A'dub).
(cd-s) *(JHCDS 6)* – ('A') / Ancients (version) / A prayer for the unborn / A prayer for the unborn (dub).

Mortal Metropolis

Mar 06. (cd/d-lp) *(MORTAL CD/LP 001)* <413> **JAGGED**
– Pressure / Fold / Halo / Slave / In a dark place / Haunted / Blind / Before you want it / Melt / Scanner / Jagged.

– compilations, etc. –

on 'Beggars Banquet' unless otherwise mentioned / * = TUBEWAY ARMY

Aug 79. (d7"*) *(BACK 2)* **THAT'S TOO BAD. / OH! I DIDN'T SAY/ / BOMBERS. / O.D. RECEIVER / BLUE EYES** –

Apr 81. (c-s*) *WEA; (SPC 4)* **ARE 'FRIENDS' ELECTRIC? / WE ARE SO FRAGILE? / DOWN IN THE PARK** –

Nov 82. (lp/c) *TV-Virgin; (TVA/TVC 7)* **NEW MAN NUMAN – THE BEST OF GARY NUMAN** 45 –

Apr 83. (12"ep,12"yellow-ep*) *(BEG 92E)* **TUBEWAY ARMY '78 VOL.1** –
– That's too bad (alternate mix) / Oh! didn't I say / Bombers / O.D. receiver / Blue eyes / Do you need the service.

Sep 84. (lp/pic-lp*) *(BEGA 55/+P)* **THE PLAN** 29 –
(re-iss. Jul88 lp/c; BBL/+C 55)

Dec 84. (12"ep,12"red-ep*) *(BEG 123E)* **TUBEWAY ARMY '78-'79 VOL.2** ☐ –
– Fade out / 1930 / The crazies / Only a downstate / We have a technical.

Dec 84. (12"ep,12"blue-ep*) *(BEG 124E)* **TUBEWAY ARMY '78-'79 VOL.3** ☐ –
– The Monday troup / Crime of assikon / The life machine / A game called Echo / Random / Oceans.

Aug 87. (12"ep/c-ep;*) *Strange Fruit; (SFPS/+C 032)* **THE PEEL SESSIONS** ☐ –
– Me I disconnect from you / Down in the park / I nearly married a human.

Aug 87. (7"/7"pic-d) *(BEG 199/+P)* **CARS (E-REG MODEL). / ARE FRIENDS ELECTRIC?** 16 ☐
(c-s+=/ext-12"+=) *(BEG 199 C/T)* – We are glass / I die: you die.
(ext-12"+=) *(BEG 199TR)* – ('A'-Motorway mix).

Sep 87. (d-lp/d-cd) *(BEGA 88/+CD)(BEGC 88)* **EXHIBITION** 43 –
– Me, I disconnect from you / That's too bad / My love is a liquid / Music for chameleons / We are glass / Bombers / Sister Surprise / Are 'friends' electric / I dream of wires / Complex / Noise noise / Warriors / Everyday I die / Cars / We take mystery to bed / I'm an agent / My centurion / Metal / You are in my vision / I die: you die / She's got claws / This wreckage / My shadow in vain / Down in the park / The iceman comes. *(d-cd+=)* – (11 trks)

Dec 87. (cd) *(BEGA 4CD)* **REPLICAS / THE PLAN** ☐ –
(re-iss. d-cd Dec93; BEGA 152CD)

Dec 87. (cd) *(BEGA 7CD)* **TUBEWAY ARMY / DANCE** ☐ –
(re-iss. d-cd Dec93; BEGA 151CD)

Dec 87. (cd) *(BEGA 10CD)* **THE PLEASURE PRINCIPLE / WARRIORS** ☐ –
(re-iss. d-cd Dec93; BEGA 153CD)

Dec 87. (cd) *(BEGA 19CD)* **TELEKON / I, ASSASSIN** ☐ ☐
(re-iss. d-cd Dec93; BEGA 154CD)
(above series of cd's, omitted some tracks on each)

Oct 89. (d-lp/cd) *Castle; (CCS LP/CD 229)* **THE GARY NUMAN COLLECTION** ☐ –

Dec 89. (m-lp/cd) *Strange Fruit; (SFPMA/+CD 202)* **DOUBLE PEEL SESSIONS** ☐ –

1990. (pic-cd-ep) **THE SELECTION** ☐ –
– Cars ('E' reg.model) / Down in the park / I die: you die / Are 'friends' electric? / We are glass / Music for chameleons.

1990. (7") *Old Gold; (OG 9917)* **ARE FRIENDS ELECTRIC?. / I DID YOU** ☐ –

1990. (7") *Old Gold; (OG 9919)* **CARS. / WE ARE GLASS** ☐ –

Mar 92. (lp/c/cd) *Numa; (NUMA/+C/CD 1008)* **ISOLATE** ☐ –

Oct 92. (d-cd) *Numa; (NUMACD 1007)* **GHOST** ☐ –

Oct 92. (cd/lp) *Receiver; (RR CD/LP 170)* **THE OTHER SIDE OF GARY NUMAN** ☐ –

Dec 92. (cd) *Connoisseur; (CSAPCD 113)* **DOCUMENT SERIES PRESENTS . . .** ☐ –

Aug 93. (7"/c-s) *(BEG 264/+C)* **CARS. / ('A'mix)** 53 ☐
(12"sha-pic-d+=/cd-s+=) *(BEG 264 L/CD)* – Cars ('93 sprint mix) / Cars (Top Gear mix).

Sep 93. (d-cd)(c) *(BEGA 150CD)(BEGC 150)* **THE BEST OF GARY NUMAN 1978-1983** 70 –

Jul 94. (cd) *Receiver; (RRCD 186)* **HERE I AM** ☐ –

Mar 95. (cd/c) *Polygram TV; (531 149-2/-4)* **GREATEST HITS** ☐ –

Feb 96. (cd) *When!; (WHENCD 006)* **TECHNO ARMY** ☐ –

Mar 96. (7"/c-s/cd-s) *Premier; (PRM/+MC/CD 1)* **CARS (premier mix) / ARE FRIENDS ELECTRIC (live) / DOWN IN THE PARK (live)** 17 ☐

Mar 96. (cd/c) *Premier;* **THE PREMIER HITS** (compilation) 21 –

Jul 96. (3xcd) *Receiver; (RRXCD 505)* **THE STORY SO FAR** ☐ –

Sep 96. (cd/c) *Emporio; (EMPR CD/MC 666)* **THE BEST OF GARY NUMAN** ☐ –

Oct 97. (12") *Random; (RANDOM 2.1)* **METAL (remixes). / DANS LE PARC** ☐ –

Nov 97. (12"green) *Random; (RANDOM 2.2)* **I DIE YOU DIE (Greenhaus mix) / CARS (Mike Dearborn mix) / CARS (Dave Clarke mix)** ☐ –

Jan 98. (12"blue) *Random; (RANDOM 2.3)* **WARRIORS (Dave Angel mix). / ARE 'FRIENDS' ELECTRIC (Liberator DJ's mix) / REMEMBER I WAS VAPOUR (Steve Stoll mix)** ☐ –

Feb 98. (12") *Random; (RANDOM 2.4)* **WE ARE GLASS (Claude Young mix) / FILMS (Alex Hazzard remix) / THE ICEMAN COMES (Peter Lazonby mix)** ☐ –

Feb 02. (d-cd) *Snapper; (SMDCD 372)* **DARK WONDERS** ☐ –

Apr 02. (3xcd-box) *Castle; (CNETD 466) / Sanctuary; <81214>* **DISCONNECTION** ☐ Oct02 ☐

— GARY has also contributed to other DRAMATIS recordings as well as joining RADIO HEART for one eponymous set

N.W.A.

Formed: NIGGAZ WITH ATTITUDE, Compton, L.A., California, USA . . . mid-80's by EAZY-E (aka ERIC WRIGHT and son of 70's soulman/funk guru, CHARLES WRIGHT) who set up his own label, 'Ruthless Records', in 1985. Allegedly founded with illegal profits, the label was a pivotal player in the burgeoning West Coast rap scene along with 24-hour hip hop radio station, KDAY. Hooking up with WORLD CLASS WRECKING CRU members, DR. DRE (aka ANDRE YOUNG) and DJ YELLA (ANTOINE CARRABY) as well as ex-STEREO CREW rapper, ICE CUBE, EAZY-E formed the core of what would become NWA. Along with the likes of ARABIAN PRINCE and The DOC, this loose affiliation recorded a promising debut set, 'NWA AND THE POSSE' (1987). EAZY-E's brutally frank 'BOYZ 'N' THE HOOD' was a sobering taster of what was to come. With MC REN (aka LORENZO PATTERSON) on board, a more compact posse of DRE, YELLA, CUBE and EAZY crafted the epochal 'STRAIGHT OUTTA COMPTON' (1989). Opening with an ominous 'You are now about to witness the strength of street knowledge . . .', the record slammed into the savage bass crunch of the title track, expletives rattled off like bullets from the proverbial AK. Next up was the infamous 'F*** THA POLICE', the boys leering their way through a defiant two-fingured salute to L.A.'s finest. The F.B.I. were sufficiently worried about the track to send the group a written warning, although they should've been more concerned with 'GANGSTA GANGSTA', a track which engendered a generation of violent, crime-obsessed albums and 'Gangsta' artists. While the rest of the set failed to maintain the vicious intensity of the opening three tracks, the damage had been done; violence-obsessed mysogynists or documenters of social realism?, the debate is still raging almost a decade on. While the record was initially isssed as a low key domestic release, word soon got round and a distribution deal was signed with 'Priority' records, the album going on to to notch up sales of 750,000 before NWA had even toured. Like PUBLIC ENEMY before them, it was obvious that a fair portion of their audience were middle class white kids out for some vicarious thrills, a theory compounded when N.W.A.'s follow-up, 'EFIL4ZAGGIN' (1991) scaled the US charts. By this point, however, the posse were in dissaray; ICE CUBE had left after falling out with manager JERRY HELLER over royalty payments while DRE left soon after the record's release, accusing HELLER of turning EAZY-E against him. This in-fighting was set against a backdrop of UK obscenity charges aimed at 'EFIL..', copies of the album siezed by British customs officials. Among the tracks which raised the authorities ire were such inimitable ditties as 'TO KILL A HOOKER' and 'FINDUM, FUCKUM and FLEE'; although the group eventually won the case, the mindless nihilism of the bulk of the album indicated that NWA had crossed the line between commentary and hilarious, often dangerous self-parody. Which is a pity, as DRE turned in another fine production. No surprise then, that as NWA imploded, DRE's solo output towered over the likes of REN's 'KIZZ MY BLACK AZZ' (1992) and EAZY's 'REAL MUTHAPHUCKIN' G's' (1994), the latter an acerbic response to DRE's G-funk innovations. With 'THE CHRONIC' (1993), DRE traded in the ever popular JAMES BROWN for the more laid back GEORGE CLINTON, pioneering the use of FUNKADELIC/PARLIAMENT samples amid a haze of marijuana references. The record was released on his new 'Death

Row' records, a joint project (you could say) with 'Interscope' and itself the subject of much recent controversy following the murder of rapper TUPAC SHAKUR and the much touted feud between the rival rap factions of east and west. While DRE's debut went triple platinum, influencing the likes of SNOOP DOGGY DOGG and his half-brother, WARREN G, the rapper was charged with battery (assault) in September '94 and sentenced to 8 months in prison. In March '95, EAZY-E succumbed to AIDS, his death finally seeing a reconciliation between DRE and ICE CUBE, the latter having gone on to even greater success. Yes, NWA sent shockwaves both through the rap scene and the white authorities and yes, 'STRAIGHT OUTTA COMPTON' remains one of the most visceral listening experiences of the 80's, but given the current bloodstained state of hip hop, the advent of 'gangsta' seems less and less like a bold step forward and more like a self-destructive blind alley. DR. DRE's album, '2001' (actually issued at the tail end of '99) was another commercial success, rumours abounded of a NWA reformation. While that never actually materialised, DRE's work on EMINEM's 'The Slim Shady' album ensured that both his production and recording career would continue to have relevance in the new millennium, something not to be sniffed at in the fast changing world of hip hop.

• **Trivia:** Album 'EFIL4ZAGGIN' is actually NIGGAZ4LIFE spelt backwards (as seen on sleeve).

Album rating: N.W.A. AND THE POSSE (*6) / STRAIGHT OUTTA COMPTON (*9) / 100 MILES AND RUNNIN' mini (*6) / EFIL4ZAGGIN (*5) / GREATEST HITS compilation (*7) / Dr Dre: THE CHRONIC (*7) / 1ST ROUND KNOCKOUT (*6) / DR. DRE – 2001 (*6) / THE CHRONICLE: THE BEST OF THE WORKS . . . productions (*7) / Eazy-E: EAZY-DUZ-IT (*7) / 5150 HOME 4 THA SICK mini (*4) / IT'S ON (DR. DRE 187UM) KILLA mini (*5) / ETERNAL E compilation (*7) / STR8 OFF THA STREETZ OF MUTHAPHUKKIN COMPTON (*5) / MC Ren: KISS MY BLACK AZZ (*5) / SHOCK OF THE HOUR (*4) / THE VILLAIN IN BLACK (*4) / RUTHLESS FOR LIFE (*4) / THE N.W.A. LEGACY VOLUME 1 1988-1998 compilation (*7)

ICE CUBE (b. O'SHEA JACKSON, 15 Jun'69) – vocals (ex-C.I.A.) / **DR DRE** (b. ANDRE YOUNG, 18 Feb'65) – producer (also of WORLD CLASS WRECKIN' CREW) / **EAZY-E** (b. ERIC WRIGHT, 7 Sep'73) – vocals / **M.C. REN** (b. LORENZO PATTERSON, 16 Jun'??) – vocals / **DJ YELLA** (b. ANTOINE CARRABY, 11 Dec'??) – turntables

not iss. Macola

1987. (lp; Various Artists) **N.W.A. AND THE POSSE** [–] [ ]
(UK-iss.Oct89 on 'Rams Horn'; RHR 5134)

4th & Broad Ruthless

Aug 89. (7"/c-s) *(BRW/BRCA 144)* **EXPRESS YOURSELF. / STRAIGHT OUTTA COMPTON** [50] [ ]
(ext;12"+=/cd-s+=) *(12BRW/BRCD 144)* – ('A'-Bonus beats) / A bitch iz a bitch. *(re-iss. May90; same)* – hit UK No.26

Aug 89. (lp/c/cd) *(BR LP/CA/CD 534)* *<SL/4XL/CDL 57102>* **STRAIGHT OUTTA COMPTON** [41] [37]
– Straight outta Compton / Fu** the police / Gangsta gangsta / If it ain't ruff / Parental discretion iz advised / 8 ball (remix) / Something like that / Express yourself / Compton's in the house (remix) / I ain't tha 1 / Dopeman (remix) / Quiet on the set / Something to dance to. *(cd re-iss. Sep02 on 'E.M.I.'; 537936-2)* – (hit UK No.35 in Jul03)

Aug 90. (7"/c-s) *(BRW/BRCA 191)* **GANGSTA, GANGSTA / IF IT AIN'T RUFF** [70] [ ]
(12"+=/cd-s+=) *(12BRW/BRCD 191)* – Dopeman (remix).

— now without ICE CUBE who was now solo

Oct 90. (7"/c-s) *(BRW/BRCA 200)* *<7224>* **100 MILES AND RUNNIN'. / REAL NIGGAZ** [38] Aug90 [27]
(12"/cd-s) *(12BRW/BRCD 200)* – ('A'side) / Just don't bite it / Sa prize (pt.2) / Kamurshoi.

Apr 91. (12"/cd-s) **F*** THE POLICE. / ('A'mixes)** [–] [ ]
(above written for RODNEY KING, the black motorist beat up by police. The court case instigated the race riots all around America.

Jun 91. (cd/c/lp) *(BR CD/CA/LP 552)* *<57126>* **EFIL4ZAGGIN** [25] [1]
– Prelude / Real niggaz don't die / Real niggaz 4 life / Protest / Appetite for destruction / Don't drink that wine / Alwayz into somethin' / Message to B.A. / Real niggaz / To kill a hooker / One less bitch / Findum, f***um and flee / Automobile / She swallowed it / I'd rather f*** you / Approach to danger / 1-900-2 Compton / The dayz of wayback.

Nov 91. (7"/c-s) *(BRW/BRCA 238)* **ALWAYZ INTO SOMETHIN'. / EXPRESS YOURSELF** [60] [ ]
(12"+=/cd-s+=) *(12BRW/BRCD 238)* – Something 2 dance 2.

— disbanded and all went solo

– compilations, etc. –

Aug 96. (cd/c) *Priority; (CDPTY 126) / Ruthless; <50561>* **GREATEST HITS** [56] Jul96 [48]
– Live intro (1989) / Arrested / angsta gangsta / F*** tha police / Compton's in the house (live) / Break out / Straight outa Compton (extended mix) / If it ain't ruff / Real niggaz / I ain't tha 1 / Alwayz into something / Don't drink that wine / Just don't bite it / Cash money / Express yourself (remix) / 100 miles & runnin' / A bitch iz a bitch / Real niggaz don't die.

Mar 99. (d-cd/d-c; Various Artists) *Priority; <51111>* **THE N.W.A. LEGACY 1988-1998** [–] [77]

EAZY-E

4th & Broad Ruthless

Sep 89. (lp/c/cd) *(BR LP/CA/CD 535)* *<57100>* **EAZY-DUZ-IT** [ ] Dec88 [41]
– (Prelude) Still talkin' / Nobody move / 2 Hard muthas (featuring MC REN) / Boyz-n-the-hood (remix) / Eazy-duz-it / We want Eazy / Eazy-er said than dunn / Radio / No more ?'s / Imma break it down / Eazy – Chapter 8, verse 10. *(re-iss. Jun91 on 'Island' lp/c)(cd; ILPM/ICM 2070)(IMCD 124)*

Jan 93. (m-cd) *<53815>* **5150 HOME FOR THA SICK** [–] [70]
– Neighbourhood sniper / Niggaz my height don't fight / Merry mutha***** Xmas / Only if you want it.

Oct 93. (m-cd) *<5503>* **IT'S ON (DR.DRE) 187 UM KILLA** [ ] [5]
– Any last werdz / Real muthaphuckin G's / Still a nigga / Exxtra special thankz / Boyz-n-the-hood / Gimme that nutt / It's on.

Jan 94. (c-s,cd-s) *<5508>* **REAL MUTHAPHUCKIN' G'S / ANY LAST WERDZ** [–] [42]

— Early in 1995, EAZY-E featured on BONE THUGS N HARMONY's hit single, 'Foe Tha Love Of'.

— EAZY-E died of AIDS on the 26th March 1995 after only being diagnosed HIV a month earlier.

Dec 95. (c-s) *(662 816-4)* *<5532>* **JUST TAH LET U KNOW / THE MUTHAPHU**IN' REAL** [30] [45]
(12"+=/cd-s+=) *(662 816-6/-2)* – ('A'-Ruthless "G" mix) / ('A'-Ba-da-ba-do acappella mix).
(above issued on 'Epic')

Jan 96. (cd/c) *(CDPTY/PTYMC/PTYLP 122)* *<50544>* **ETERNAL E** (compilation) [ ] Dec95 [84]
– Automobile / Eazy-duz-it / Boyz-in-the-hood / Eazy-er said than dunn / Neighbourhood sniper / Radio / We want Eazy / Only if you want it / Nobody move / I'd rather funk you / 8 ball / Eazy street / Niggaz my height don't fight / No more ?'s.

Ruthless Ruthless

Feb 96. (cd/c) *(483 576-2/-4)* *<5504>* **STR8 OFF THA STREETZ OF MUTHAPH**IN – E.W. COMPTON** [66] [3]
– Just tah let u know / Lickin' smokin' phuckin' / What would you do / Sorry Louie / Nutz on ya chin / Ole school shit / Slippin on a 4 / My baby'z mama / Muthaphuckin' real / Hit the hoods / Gangsta beat 4 tha street / Eternal E / Creep n crawl.

MC REN

Ruthless Ruthless

Jul 92. (cd,c) *<53802>* **KIZZ MY BLACK AZZ** [–] [12]
– Check it out y'all / Behind the scenes / Hound dogz / Kiss my black azz / Right up my alley / Final frontier.

Nov 93. (cd,c) *<5505>* **SHOCK OF THE HOUR** [–] [22]
– Fuck what ya hear / All bullshit aside / Attack on Babylon / Shock of the hour / Still the same nigga / You wanna fuck her / Same ol' shit / Mr. Fuck up / One false move / Mayday on the front line / 11.55 / Do you believe.

Nov 93. (c-s,12") *<5510>* **SAME OL' SHIT. / (radio version)** [–] [90]

— Above sampled; LET'S GET IT ON (Marvin Gaye) / I GOT A GOOD THING (James Brown) / LAD DI DA DI (Doug E.Fresh).

Apr 96. (cd/c) *(483900-2/-4)* *<5544>* **THE VILLAIN IN BLACK** [ ] [31]
– Bitch made nigga killa / Bring it on / Mad scientist / Mind blown / Still the same nigga / Muhammed speaks / Live from Compton 'Saturday night' / It's like that / Keep it real / Great elephant.

Apr 98. (cd-s) *<78901>* **RUTHLESS FOR LIFE (mixes; LP / clean radio / instrumental)** [–] [ ]
(12"+=) *<78902>* – ('A'-A cappella).

Jun 98. (cd/c) *<69313>* **RUTHLESS FOR LIFE** [–] [100]
– Ruthless for life / Who in the f*** / N***a called Ren / Comin' after you / Voyage to Compton / Must be high / So whatcha want / Shot caller / All the same / Who got that street s*** / Pimpin' is free / CPT all day.

DR. DRE

Interscope | Death Row

May 92. (cd-s) *<74547>* **DEEP COVER / (instrumental)** [–] [ ]
(above from the film of the same name on 'Epic')

Feb 93. (cd/c) *(7567 92233-2/-4) <57128>* **THE CHRONIC** [ ] [3]
– The chronic / Fuck wit Dre day (and everybody's celebrating) / Let me ride / The day the niggaz took over / Nuthin' but a "G" thang / Dreeez nuuuts / Bitches ain't shit / Lil' ghetto boy / A nigga witta gun / Rat-tat-tat-tat / The $20 sack pyramid / Lyrical gangbang / High powered / The doctor's office / Stranded on death row / The roach (the chronic outro). *(cd re-iss. Feb97; IND 57128) (re-iss. Aug00)* – hit UK No.52

Mar 93. (c-s) *<53819>* **NUTHIN' BUT A "G" THANG. / ('A'mix)** [ ] Jan93 [2]
(club-12"+=)(cd-s+=) – ('A'-freestyle mix).

May 93. (7"/c-s) *<53827>* **DRE DAY. / ('A'-flavour mix)** [ ] [8]
(cd-s+=) – ('A'extended club) / ('A'-UK Flavour mix) / ('A'instrumental) / ('A'again).
(12") – (A+B) / (above 2) / Puffin' on blunts and drinkin' tanqueray.

Aug 93. (c-s,cd-s,12") *<53839>* **LET ME RIDE / ('A'mixes)** [–] [34]

Jan 94. (c-s) *(A 8328C)* **NUTHIN' BUT A G THANG (club) / ('A'mix)** [31] [–]
(12") *(A 8328T) - ('A'-version) / Let me ride (extended club mix).*
(cd-s) *(A 8328CD)* – (their club mixes).

Aug 94. (7"/c-s) *(A 8292/+C)* **DRE DAY. / ('A'-UK radio mix)** [59] [–]
(12"+=) *(A 8292T)* – (4-'A'-Puffin' on blunts and drinkin' tanqueray mixes).
(cd-s+=) *(A 8292CD)* – ('A'-radio remix) / ('A'instrumental) / ('A'-2 other mixes).

—— In Sep'94, DR.DRE was convicted of battery (assault) and sentenced to 8 months in prison

Interscope | Hitman

Oct 94. (cd,c) *<51170>* **CONCRETE ROOTS – ANTHOLOGY** (compilation of various artists) [ ] [43]

—— DR. DRE & ICE CUBE; below from the film/video 'Murder Was The Case'.

Mar 95. (7"/c-s) *(A 8197/+C)* **NATURAL BORN KILLAZ / THA DOGG POUND: What Would U Do?** [45] [–]
(cd-s+=) *(A 8197CD)* – (2 'A'versions).

May 95. (c-s) *(PTYSC 103) <53188>* **KEEP THEIR HEADS RINGIN'. / TAKE A HIT (mix)** [25] Mar95 [10]
(12"+=/cd-s+=) *(PTY ST/CD 103)* – (other mixes).
above from the film 'Friday' on the label 'Priority')

Jun 98. (c-s/12"/cd-s; DR. DRE & LL COOL J) *(INC/INT/IND 95594)* **ZOOM / (instrumental)** [15] [–]

—— in Aug'99, DRE was credited on EMINEM's hit, 'Guilty Conscience'

Nov 99. (cd/d-lp) *<(4 90486-2/-1)>* **DR. DRE 2001** [4] [2]
– Lolo (w/ XZIBIT & TRAY-D) / The watcher / Fuck you (w/ THE DUDE & SNOOP DOGG) / Still D.R.E. (w/ SNOOP DOGG) / Big ego's (w/ HITTMAN) / Xplosive (w/ HITTMAN) / What's the difference (w/ EMINEM & XZIBIT) / Bar one (w/ TRACY NELSON, MS ROQ & EDDIE GRIFFIN) / Light speed (w/ EMINEM) / The next episode (w/ SNOOP DOGG) / Let's get high (w/ HITTMAN, KURUPT & MS ROQ) / Bitch niggaz (w/ SNOOP DOGG, HITTMAN & SIX-TWO) / Car bomb (w/ MEL-MAN & SHARI HENRY) / Education (w/ HITTMAN & MS ROQ) / Murderlink (w/ HITTMAN & MS ROQ) / Some L.A. niggaz (w/ DEFARI, XZIBIT, KNOCKTURNAL, TIMEBOMB, KING T, MC REN & KOKANE) / Pause 4 promo (w/ JAKE STEED) / Housewife (w/ KURUPT & HITTMAN) / Acrite (w/ HITTMAN) / Bang bang (w/ KNOCKTURNAL & HITTMAN) / The message (w/ MARY J. BLIGE & REIL). *(re-iss. Mar00; same)* – hit UK No.8 in Jan'01

Mar 00. (c-s/cd-s; as DR. DRE featuring SNOOP DOGG) *(497274-4/-2) <497192>* **STILL D.R.E. / THE MESSAGE (with MARY J. BLIGE & REIL)** [6] Nov99 [93]
(12")(cd-s) *(497274-1)(497286-2)* – ('A'side) / The next episode.

May 00. (c-s/cd-s; as DR. DRE featuring EMINEM) *(497341-4/-2)* **FORGET ABOUT DRE / STILL D.R.E. (mixes)** [7] Jan00 [25]
(12"/cd-s) *(497341-1/-2)* – ('A'side) / The next episode.

Jan 01. (c-s/12"; by DR. DRE featuring SNOOP DOGG) *(497476-4/-1) <497333>* **THE NEXT EPISODE. / BAD GUYS ALWAYS DIE (with EMINEM)** [3] May00 [23]
(cd-s+=) *(497476-2)* – ('A'instrumental) / ('A'-video).

—— late in 2001, DR. DRE was the mastermind behind a largely collective V/A set soundtrack, 'The Wash', featuring SNOOP DOGG, etc.

Jan 02. (c-s/12"; by DR. DRE featuring KNOC-TURN'AL) *(497393-4/-1)* **BAD INTENTIONS. / THE WATCHER / THE NEXT EPISODE (with SNOOP DOGG)** [4] [–]
(cd-s+=) *(497393-2)* – ('A'-video).

– compilations, etc. –

Jun 96. (cd,c) *Triple X; <51226>* **1ST ROUND KNOCKOUT** (compilation) [–] [52]
– Bridgette (D.O.C.) / It's not over (ROSE ROYCE) / Nicety / Sex is on / Turn off the lights / Nickel slick nigga / Juice / Funky flute / The fly / Deep cover / He's bionic.

—— In Oct'96, he featured on hit single by BLACKSTREET; 'No Diggity'.

—— In Dec'96, DR. DRE PRESENTS . . . THE AFTERMATH was the name of a Various Artists album for Interscope' <(IND/INC 90044)>

Nov 01. (cd) *Death Row; (DRE 1004) <239419>* **THE CHRONICLE: THE BEST OF THE WORKS . . .** [ ] May02 [ ]

OASIS

Formed: Manchester, England ... summer 1992, by frontman LIAM GALLAGHER, rhythm guitarist PAUL 'BONEHEAD' ARTHURS, bassist PAUL McGUIGAN and drummer TONY McCARROLL. Initially called RAIN, they were soon joined by LIAM's older brother NOEL who had worked as a roadie for The INSPIRAL CARPETS. He was also a budding songwriter/guitarist with a concrete self-belief and after a year of rehearsals and occasional local gigs, they were signed by Creation's ALAN McGEE, after the eagle-eared Scotsman clocked them at a Glasgow gig in mid-1993. With a groundswell of interest not witnessed since the heady early days of The STONE ROSES, OASIS secured a near UK Top 30 placing with 'SUPERSONIC', a sneering, leering anthem with lyrics that SHAUN RYDER would've been proud to call his own. Later that summer the band released the follow-up, 'SHAKER MAKER', a rather tame effort in comparison which appeared to be modelled on the NEW SEEKERS' chestnut, 'I'd Like To Teach The World To Sing'. Nevertheless, what the single lacked in originality, it made up for in controversy and the stage was set for OASIS' first Top 10 hit, the classic 'LIVE FOREVER'. A life-affirming rush celebrating the strength of the human spirit, the song was lauded as single of the year, closely followed by the epochal debut album, 'DEFINITELY MAYBE' (1994). There were no maybes about it, this album defined an era in the same way that The SEX PISTOLS (an obvious influence) focused the frustrations of a generation with 'Never Mind The Bollocks', it's just a pity that the dubious 'Britpop' era spawned an interminable glut of production line indie chancers. The record opens on the same wave of freefall exhilaration as say, 'Exile On Main Street', (The ROLLING STONES were another oft cited influence), 'ROCK'N'ROLL STAR' alive with a palpable sense of what it actually means to want fame that badly. The feeling that this was "for real, man", never lets up until the last track fades, a visceral, exhaustive listen and one of the most consistent debut albums ever released. Another highlight from the album, the T.REX-esque nihilism of 'CIGARETTES AND ALCOHOL' was the next single, peaking at No.7 in late '94. Basically, OASIS were like all your favourite bands rolled into one, a kind of potted history of rock, NOEL having a unique talent for constructing classic songs that seemed somehow familiar yet annoyingly difficult to pin down. On top of this, LIAM was a natural, his piercing stare and cooly motionless stage presence coupled with his inimitably lethargic sneer a vital component of OASIS' rock'n'roll juggernaut. That Christmas the band narrowly missed No.1 with the string-laden, overtly BEATLES-esque 'WHATEVER', a poppier effort that hinted at the band's future direction. By this point, OASIS were a headline act, the scramble for tickets that accompanied any announcement of a gig becoming all too familiar over the next few years. As would the brothers' press profile, their loudmouth self-aggrandising and embarrassingly public fisticuffs becoming a regular feature of OASIS' increasingly cartoonish image. The first casualty of the well documented in-fighting was McCARROLL, his place in the drum seat subsequently filled by ALAN WHITE. The boasting was backed up by consistently strong material, however, and in the Spring of '95, OASIS deservedly scored their first No.1 with the soaring, yearning 'SOME MIGHT SAY'. The band's single releases had always been good value for money, the B-sides usually better than most indie bands' half-arsed lead tracks. This release was no exception, containing the affecting 'TALK TONIGHT' (NOEL on vocals) and the brilliant melodic noise of 'ACQUIESCE', arguably one of the group's finest tracks. Thus the stage was set for the media-created battle with the recently revitalised BLUR, both bands releasing a single simultaneously that August. In the event, despite the verbal jousting, BLUR took the top spot with 'Country House', OASIS forced to bite their tongue and, erm, 'ROLL WITH IT' at No.2. The Mancs had the last laugh, however, when their follow-up album '(WHAT'S THE STORY) MORNING GLORY' (1995) proceeded to sell multi-millions, catapulting OASIS into the musical stratosphere alongside U2 etc., something unheard of for a group who started out as, basically, another guitar band from Manchester. While the album lacked the serrated edge and amphetamine rush of the debut, the songwriting was once again faultless, tracks like 'WONDERWALL' (almost a Christmas No.1), 'DON'T LOOK BACK IN ANGER', and 'CHAMPAGNE SUPERNOVA' reflecting a newfound maturity and a more coffee-table friendly pop-rock sound. The rapid ascent of the GALLAGHER's continued the following year, with awards galore and a significant dent into the US market. The latter wasn't achieved without some cost to the band, however, as LIAM and NOEL had their most serious and most widely reported fracas to date, LIAM flying home midway through a US tour amid rumours that the band had split. It was merely a case of another day, another fight however, and the band went on to break British concert attendance records with two sell-out shows at Knebworth in August ('96). Early the following year, NOEL was the featured vocalist on The CHEMICAL BROTHERS' chart-topper, 'Setting Sun', effective psychedelia and right on. Return single in '97, 'D'YOU KNOW WHAT I MEAN?' hit No.1 and was reputed to have amassed UK sales of 162,000 copies on its first day of release (19th July). Shortly afterwards, their third album 'BE HERE NOW' was finally in the shops, the hype and media attention the record (and the brothers) received paying off big-time with a massive selling chart topper (No.2 in America). Probably its finest four minutes, 'STAND BY ME', surprisingly failed to make No.1, the album was also marked as a disappointment by some and was considered underwhelming to say the least. The posturing and epic feel of '(WHAT'S THE STORY) . . .' were still there but the record sounded like a parody of OASIS, if that's not a contradiction in terms. While the album broke records with its first day sales figures, it has hardly achieved the same momentum as its predecessor. A stop-gap collection of B-sides and rarities, 'THE MASTERPLAN' (1998), did little for any obsessed fan who already owned all the singles. In May '99, former drummer TONY McCARROLL won an out of court settlement of half a million – £18m for unpaid royalties was the figure he originally wanted. The old band took time out for the rest of the

Liam Gallagher of OASIS

90's (BONEHEAD and GUIGSY also bailed out), although the GALLAGHER brothers were never far away from controversy and the tabloids. 'STANDING ON THE SHOULDER OF GIANTS' (2000) proved that OASIS were in for the long haul, a studied, immaculately professional effort which indulged NOEL's passion for classic psychedelia while grafting on just enough contemporary flourishes to make it relevant. Hardly the rebellious ball of sonic phlegm we all knew and loved, then, but no doubt the first in a series of passable 30-something efforts designed to please their already ageing fanbase. Live set 'FAMILIAR TO MILLIONS' (2000) merely confirmed the fact, a Wembley Stadium gig which underlined the band's stodgy reliability. Even LIAM's wildcard rantings have become somewhat predictable if no less amusing. Previewed by the regal, spring-coiled riffing of 'THE HINDU TIMES', the much heralded 'HEATHEN CHEMISTRY' (2002) held few surprises save perhaps LIAM's charming, countrified 'SONGBIRD'. The rest was NOEL putting in a solid day at the office with reasonably efficient results; the requisite careworn ballad, 'LITTLE BY LITTLE' hit No.2, while the album itself hit No.1; yet big brother's insistence on a bombastic production did the band few favours. Sharing out the songwriting pie (with BELL and ARCHER) and marking the debut of one ZAK STARKEY (son of RINGO), 'DON'T BELIEVE THE TRUTH' (2005) returned OASIS to their place at the top of Brit-rock's pecking order, elbowing its way straight in at No.1 (No.12 in America, their highest Stateside placing to date). Lead single 'LYLA' sized up SWEET stomp and 'STONES swagger at No.1, restaking – and at least partly vindicating – their claim as inheritors of a classicist lineage, while 'THE IMPORTANCE OF BEING IDLE' was the most self-consciously 60's referencing UK chart topper since BLUR's 'Beetlebum' almost a decade earlier. Critics were in general agreement that NOEL's songwriting was much improved, and that LIAM had finally come into his own, the GALLAGHER brothers pooling their talents on acoustic guitar'n'piano album closer (and near No.1), 'LET THERE BE LOVE'.

• **Songwriters:** NOEL, except I AM THE WALRUS + HELTER SKELTER (Beatles) / CUM ON FEEL THE NOIZE (Slade) / STREET FIGHTING MAN (Rolling Stones) / FEELIN' LONELY by Noel (Small Faces) / HEY HEY MY MY (INTO THE BLACK) (Neil Young). • **Trivia:** NOEL wrote 'SLIDE AWAY' on a Les Gibson guitar, which he bought from friend JOHNNY MARR (ex-Smiths) and which was once the property of PETE TOWNSHEND (The Who). After a long on-off relationship, LIAM married actress/singer, PATSY KENSIT. He has since divorced and is the beau of NICOLE APPLETON (of ALL SAINTS).

Album rating: DEFINITELY MAYBE (*10) / (WHAT'S THE STORY) MORNING GLORY? (*10) / BE HERE NOW (*7) / THE MASTERPLAN compilation (*7) / STANDING ON THE SHOULDER OF GIANTS (*6) / FAMILIAR TO MILLIONS (*5) / HEATHEN CHEMISTRY (*7) / DON'T BELIEVE THE TRUTH (*8)

LIAM GALLAGHER (b.21 Sep'72) – vocals / **NOEL GALLAGHER** (b.29 May'67) – guitar / **PAUL 'BONEHEAD' ARTHURS** (b.23 Jun'65) – guitar / **PAUL McGUIGAN** (b.19 May'71) – guitar / **TONY McCARROLL** – drums

Creation Epic

Apr 94. (7") *(CRE 176) <55332>* **SUPERSONIC. / TAKE ME AWAY** 31 Jul94 [ ]
(12"+=) *(CRE 176T)* – I will believe (live).
(cd-s++=) *(CRECD 176)* – Columbia (demo).
(re-iss. Nov96 c-s repl.7" as so below; same); hit No.47)
(re-iss. Mar00 on 'Big Brother'; RKIDSCD 010)

Jun 94. (7"/c-s) *(CRE/+CS 182)* **SHAKERMAKER. / D'YER WANNA BE A SPACEMAN?** 11 –
(12"+=) *(CRE 182T)* – Alive (demo).
(cd-s++=) *(CRECD 182)* – Bring it on down (live).
(re-iss. Nov96; same); hit No.48)
(re-iss. Mar00 on 'Big Brother'; RKIDSCD 011)

Aug 94. (7"/c-s) *(CRE/+CD 185)* **LIVE FOREVER. / UP IN THE SKY (acoustic)** 10 –
(12"+=) *(CRE 185T)* – Cloudburst.
(cd-s++=) *(CRECD 185)* – Supersonic (live).
(re-iss. Nov96; same); hit No.42)
(re-iss. Mar00 on 'Big Brother'; RKIDSCD 012)

Aug 94. (cd/c/d-lp) *(CRE CD/MC/LP 169) <66431>*
DEFINITELY MAYBE 1 Jan95 58
– Rock'n'roll star / Shakermaker / Live forever / Up in the sky / Columbia / Supersonic / Bring it down / Cigarettes and alcohol / Digsy's dinner / Slide away / Married with children. *(d-lp+=)* – Sad song. *(re-iss. Nov96 as '. . .SINGLES BOX – SILVER' cd/5xcd-s-box; CREDM 001/002); hit No.23) (cd re-iss. Feb00; same) (re-iss. Mar00 on 'Big Brother' cd/md/c/lp; RKID CD/MC/MC/LP 006)*

Oct 94. (7"/c-s) *(CRE/+CS 190)* **CIGARETTES AND ALCOHOL. / I AM THE WALRUS (live)** 7 –
(12"+=) *(CRE 190T)* – Fade away.
(cd-s++=) *(CRECD 190)* – Listen up.
(re-iss. Nov96; same); hit No.38)
(re-iss. Mar00 on 'Big Brother'; RKIDSCD 013)

Dec 94. (7"/c-s) *(CRE/+CS 195)* **WHATEVER. / (IT'S GOOD) TO BE FREE** 3 –
(12"+=) *(CRE 195T)* – Slide away.
(cd-s++=) *(CRECD 195)* – Half the world away.
(re-iss. Nov96; same); hit No.34)
(re-iss. Mar00 on 'Big Brother'; RKIDSCD 014)

— after a punch-up McCARROLL left and was replaced by drummer **ALAN WHITE** (b.26 May'72, London) (ex-IDHA) and brother of STEVE WHITE (long-time sticksman with PAUL WELLER)

Apr 95. (7"/c-s) *(CRE/+CS 204)* **SOME MIGHT SAY. / TALK TONIGHT** 1 –
(12"+=) *(CRE 204T)* – Acquiesce.
(cd-s++=) *(CRECD 204)* – Headshrinker.
(re-iss. Nov96; same); hit No.40)
(re-iss. Mar00 on 'Big Brother'; RKIDSCD 015)

— their first 5 singles also re-entered UK Top 60 in Jun'95

Aug 95. (7"/c-s) *(CRE/+CS 212)* **ROLL WITH IT. / IT'S BETTER, PEOPLE** 2 –
(12"+=) *(CRE 212T)* – Rockin' chair.
(cd-s+=) *(CRECD 212)* – Live forever (live).
(re-iss. Nov96; same)hit No.55)
(re-iss. Mar00 on 'Big Brother'; RKIDSCD 016)

Oct 95. (cd/c/d-lp) *(CRE CD/MC/LP 189) <67351>* **(WHAT'S THE STORY) MORNING GLORY?** 1 4
– Hello / Roll with it / Wonderwall / Don't look back in anger / Hey now! / Some might say / Cast no shadow / She's electric / Morning glory / Champagne supernova. *(d-lp+=)* – Bonehead's bank holiday. *(re-iss. Nov96 as '. . .SINGLES BOX – GOLD' cd/5xcd-s-box; CREMG 001/002); hit No.24) (re-iss. Mar00 on 'Big Brother' cd/md/c/lp; RKID CD/MD/MC/LP 007)*

Oct 95. (7"/c-s) *(CRE/+CS 215)* **WONDERWALL / ROUND ARE WAY** 2 –
(12"+=) *(CRE 215T)* – The swamp song.
(cd-s+=) *(CRECD 215)* – The masterplan.
(re-iss. Nov96; same); hit No.36)
(re-iss. Mar00 on 'Big Brother'; RKIDSCD 017)

Jan 96. (cd-s) *<49K 78216>* **WONDERWALL / ROUND ARE WAY / TALK TONIGHT / ROCKIN' CHAIR / I AM THE WALRUS (live)** – 8

— NOEL also part of one-off supergroup The SMOKIN' MOJO FILTERS alongside PAUL WELLER and PAUL McCARTNEY. They had Top 20 hit with 'COME TOGETHER'.

Feb 96. (7"/c-s) *(CRE/+CS 221)* **DON'T LOOK BACK IN ANGER. / STEP OUT** 1 –
(12"+=) *(CRE 221T)* – Underneath the sky.
(cd-s++=) *(CRECD 221)* – Cum on feel the noize.
(re-iss. Nov96; same); hit No.53)
(re-iss. Mar00 on 'Big Brother'; RKIDSCD 018)

Jul 96. (cd-s) *<34K 78356>* **DON'T LOOK BACK IN ANGER / CUM ON FEEL THE NOIZE** – 55

— NOEL met up with great pensmith and fan! BURT BACHARACH who wanted to do a collaboration. He also refused to accept his Ivor Novello award for best songwriter of the year, after he was told it would be shared with rivals BLUR. In Aug'96, NOEL objected to The SMURFS releasing 'WONDERWALL' on their album.

Jul 97. (7"/c-s) *(CRE/+CS 256)* **D'YOU KNOW WHAT I MEAN? / STAY YOUNG** 1 –
(12"+=) *(CRE 256T)* – Angel child (demo).
(cd-s++=) *(CRESCD 256)* – Heroes.
(re-iss. Mar00 on 'Big Brother'; RKIDSCD 019)

Aug 97. (cd/c/lp) *(CRECD/CCRE/CRELP 219)* <68530> **BE HERE NOW** 1 2
– D'you know what I mean? / My big mouth / Magic pie / Stand by me / I hope I think I know / Girl in the dirty shirt / Fade in-out / Don't go away / Be here now / All around the world / It's gettin' better (man) / All around the world (reprise). *(re-iss. Mar00 on 'Big Brother' cd/md/c/lp; RKID CD/MD/MC/LP 008)*

Sep 97. (7"/c-s) *(CRE/+CS 278)* **STAND BY ME. / (I GOT) THE FEVER** 2 –
(12"+=) *(CRE 278T)* – My sister lover.
(cd-s++=) *(CRESCD 278)* – Going nowhere.
(re-iss. Mar00 on 'Big Brother'; RKIDSCD 020)

Jan 98. (7"/c-s) *(CRE/+CS 282)* **ALL AROUND THE WORLD. / THE FAME** 1 –
(12"+=) *(CRE 282T)* – Flashbox.
(cd-s++=) *(CRESCD 282)* – Street fighting man.
(re-iss. Mar00 on 'Big Brother'; RKIDSCD 021)

Nov 98. (cd/d-lp)(c) *(CRE CD/LP 241)(C-CRE 241)* <69647> **THE MASTERPLAN** (compilation) 2 51
– Acquiesce / Underneath the sky / Talk tonight / Going nowhere / Fade away / The swamp song / I am the walrus / Listen up / Rockin' chair / Half the world away / (It's good) To be free / Stay young / Headshrinker / The masterplan. *(cd re-iss. Feb00; same) (re-iss. Mar00 on 'Big Brother' cd/md/c/lp; RKID CD/MD/MC/LP 009)*

— now without BONEHEAD who left after supplying his part to the forthcoming album (GUIGSY also bailed out, his replacement being **ANDY BELL** (ex-HURRICANE #1, ex-RIDE)

— In Oct'99, LIAM GALLAGHER was credited with STEVE CRADDOCK (of OCEAN COLOUR SCENE) on the UK Top 10 (JAM) tribute double-A side single, 'CARNATION' (flipped with BUFFALO TOM and 'Going Underground')

— added **GEM ARCHER** – guitar (ex-HEAVY STEREO)

Big Brother Epic

Feb 00. (7"/c-s) *(RKID/+CS 001)* **GO LET IT OUT. / LET'S ALL MAKE BELIEVE** 1 –
(12"+=)(cd-s+=) *(RKID 001T)(RKIDSCD 001)* – As long as they've got) Cigarettes in Hell.

Feb 00. (cd/c/lp) *(RKID CD/MC/LP 002)* <63586> **STANDING ON THE SHOULDER OF GIANTS** 1 Mar00 24
– Fuckin' in the bushes / Go let it out / Who feels love? / Put yer money where your mouth is / Little James / Gas panic! / Where did it all go wrong? / Sunday morning call / I can see a liar / Roll it over.

Apr 00. (7"/c-s) *(RKID/+CS 003)* **WHO FEELS LOVE? / ONE WAY ROAD** 4 –
(12"+=)(cd-s+=) *(RKID 003T)(RKIDSCD 003)* – Helter skelter (live).

Jul 00. (7"/c-s) *(RKID/+CS 004)* **SUNDAY MORNING CALL. / CARRY US ALL** 4 –
(12"+=)(cd-s+=) *(RKID 004T)(RKIDSCD 004)* – Full on.

Nov 00. (d-cd/c/t-lp) *(RKID CD/MC/LP 005)* <85267> **FAMILIAR TO MILLIONS (live)** 5
– Fuckin' in the bushes / Go let it out / Who feels love? / Supersonic / Shakermaker / Acquiesce / Step out / Gas panic! / Roll with it / Stand by me / Wonderwall / Cigarettes and alcohol / Don't look back in anger / Live forever / Hey hey, my my (into the black) / Champagne supernova / Rock'n'roll star / Helter skelter. *(cd re-iss. Oct01; RKIDCD 005X)*

Apr 02. (7") *(RKID 23)* **THE HINDU TIMES. / JUST GETTING OLDER** 1 –
(12"+=)(cd-s+=) *(RKID 23T)(RKIDSCD 23)* – Idler's dream.
(dvd-s) *(RKIDSDVD 23)* – ('A') / ('A'-demo) / 10 minutes of noise and confusion part 1 (video documentary).

Jun 02. (7") *(RKID 24)* **STOP CRYING YOUR HEART OUT. / THANK YOU FOR THE GOOD TIMES** 2 –
(12"+=)(cd-s+=) *(RKID 24T)(RKIDSCD 24)* – Shout it out loud.
(dvd-s) *(RKIDSDVD 24)* – ('A') / ('A'-demo) / 10 minutes of noise and confusion pt.2 (video documentary).

Jul 02. (cd/c/d-lp) *(RKID CD/MC/LP 25)* <86586> **HEATHEN CHEMISTRY** 1 23
– The Hindu times / Force of nature / Hung in a bad place / Stop crying your heart out / Songbird / Little by little / A quick peep / (Probably) All in the mind / She is love / Born on a different cloud / Better man.

Sep 02. (7") *(RKID 26)* **LITTLE BY LITTLE. / SHE IS LOVE** 2 –
(cd-s+=) *(RKIDSCD 26)* – My generation.
(dvd-s) *(RKIDSDVD 26)* – ('A'-demo) / ('A') / (documentary).

Feb 03. (7") *(RKID 27)* **SONGBIRD. / (YOU'VE GOT) A HEART OF A STAR** 3 –
(12"+=)(cd-s+=) *(RKID 27T)(RKIDSCD 27)* – Columbia (live).
(dvd-s) *(RKIDSDVD 27)* – ('A') / ('A'-demo) / (interview, etc.)

— **ZAK STARKEY** – drums; repl. ALAN WHITE

May 05. (7") *(RKID 29)* **LYLA. / EYEBALL TICKLER** 1 –
(cd-s+=) *(RKIDSCD 29)* – Won't let you down.
(dvd-s) *(RKIDSDVD 29)* – ('A'-video) / ('A'-demo) / (mini docu).

May 05. (cd/lp) *(RKID CD/LP 30)* <94493> **DON'T BELIEVE THE TRUTH** 1 12
– Turn up the sun / Mucky fingers / Lyla / Love like a bomb / The importance of being idle / The meaning of soul / Guess God thinks I'm Abel / Part of the queue / Keep the dream alive / A bell will ring / Let there be love. *(ltd-cd w/dvd+=; RKIDCD 30X)* – (interviews & the making of) / Lyla (video).

Aug 05. (7") *(RKID 31)* **THE IMPORTANCE OF BEING IDLE. / PASS ME DOWN THE WINE** 1 –
(cd-s+=) *(RKIDSCD 31)* – The quiet ones.
(dvd-s) *(RKIDSDVD 31)* – ('A') / ('A'-demo) / ('A'-video) / (the making of . . . documentary).

Nov 05. (10") *(RKID 32)* **LET THERE BE LOVE. / SITTIN' HERE IN SILENCE (ON MY OWN)** 2 –
(cd-s+=) *(RKIDSCD 32)* – Rock'n'roll star (live at the City of Manchester Stadium 2nd July 2005).
(dvd-s) *(RKIDSDVD 32)* – ('A') / ('A'-demo) / Lord don't let me slow down (excerpts from the forthcoming film) / ('A'-video).

– compilations, etc. –

Mar 00. (cd) *Chrome Dreams; (ABCD 047)* **MAXIMUM OASIS (AN AUDIO BIOGRAPHY)** –

OCEAN COLOUR SCENE

Formed: Moseley, Birmingham, England . . .mid-'89 out of The FANATICS, by SIMON FOWLER, DAMON MINCHELLA and OSCAR HARRISON, who released a one-off '45 for the 'Chapter 22' label before recruiting BOYS' guitarist STEVE CRADOCK. In the summer of 1990, OCS found manager JOHN MOSTYN, who signed them to his new '!Phffft' stable. A debut track, 'SWAY', helped secure a joint venture with 'Phonogram' for a follow-up, 'YESTERDAY TODAY'. The latter track breeched the Top 50 in March '91, and, just when it seemed as if a breakthrough was imminent, '!Phffft' was sold during the recording of their JIMMY MILLER-produced debut album. Now on 'Fontana', the momentum was lost as they re-recorded the whole project, a 1992 re-issue of 'SWAY' and the follow-up, 'GIVING IT ALL AWAY' sinking without trace. In April, the aforementioned eponymous album finally surfaced, although it brought criticism for its over-cooked production. After another 45, 'DO YOURSELF A FAVOUR' bombed, the group subsequently found themselves without a recording contract and up to their necks in debt. Aided by lawyer, Michael Thomas, they were successful in persuading Fontana's DAVE BATES to waive the million £'s they were still owing. OCS returned with a support slot to their newfound mate, PAUL WELLER, CRADOCK and FOWLER guested on his Autumn '93 classic 'Wildwood' album; CRADOCK subsequently became an integral part of WELLER's band over the course of the next year. Meanwhile in the summer of '94, OCEAN COLOUR SCENE supported OASIS and completed a 'Fontana' tour of the States supporting HOUSE OF LOVE and The CATHERINE WHEEL. A year later, all group members played for WELLER at some point, with CRADOCK and MINCHELLA guesting on his No.1 album, 'Stanley Road'. 1995 also saw the band recording their long-awaited follow-up album, having earlier signed to 'M.C.A.'. Early in '96 (with WELLER on organ), they scored their first of many Top 20 hits with 'THE RIVERBOAT SONG' (later chosen for Chris Evans' TFI Friday Show theme song). Dropping the indie-dance trappings of old, OCS adopted a heavier, funkier, white-soul/mod sound and a retro image to boot, dominating the charts in the wake of WELLER's massively successful return to a rootsier sound. 'YOU'VE GOT

IT BAD' fared even better, followed by a BRENDAN LYNCH-produced album, 'MOSELEY SHOALS' (name of their own studio), which hit the UK Top 3. The record inevitably featured WELLER on a few other tracks and the man augmented the group on their 'Later With Jools Holland' spot. Two further Top 10 smashes, 'THE DAY WE CAUGHT THE TRAIN' (their classiest so far) and 'THE CIRCLE' were culled from the album, an odds'n'sods collection, 'B-SIDES, SEASIDES & FREERIDES' keeping their profile high prior to the release of new material. A couple of Top 5 hits, 'HUNDRED MILE HIGH CITY' and 'TRAVELLERS TUNE', preceded an Autumn '97 album, 'MARCHIN' ALREADY', a lesser work which nevertheless reached the top of the UK charts. An easy target for the critics, only time will tell whether OCS's retro-lite and almost wholly teenage audience can stay the course. 'ONE FROM THE MODERN' (1999), was the next Top 5 album on the retro production line, OCS defiantly standing by their Mod roots while opener and hit single, 'PROFITS IN PEACE', showed they were a caring type of band. 'SO LOW' was the next single. Enough said. Yet one suspects that while there is still an audience for OASIS there will still be an audience for OCEAN COLOUR SCENE, so indistinguishable are their respective markets. No surprise then that the admittedly fairly intoxicating 'UP ON THE DOWNSIDE' single made the UK Top 20, pushing the rather more workmanlike 'MECHANICAL WONDER' (2001) album into the Top 10. After ending the year on this relative high, the band released the obligatory festive period compilation which also reached the UK Top 20. While the release of a new OCS album is hardly the news that it once was, 'NORTH ATLANTIC DRIFT' (2003) demonstrated that they're at least consistent in their hard-graft, no-nonsense rock. While not exactly a departure, the album was a far less oppressive listen than its predecessor, perhaps signalling that they've grown content in their middle age. Subsequent live set, 'ONE FOR THE ROAD' (2004), said exactly what it said on the tin and marked time until the release of a fresh batch with newcomers DAN SEALEY (who replaced DAMON) and ANDY BENNETT. Top 30 entry, 'A HYPERACTIVE WORKOUT FOR THE FLYING SQUAD' (2005), their 7th long-player was classicist rock at its funky best, reminiscent of 70s stalwarts TRAFFIC or HUMBLE PIE and recorded in the wilds of Glenrothes, Scotland the previous year. 'LIVE AT THE JAM HOUSE' (2006) was an acoustic addition to their catalogue featuring four new songs and none of their early classics.

• **Songwriters:** FOWLER lyrics / group music; except DO YOURSELF A FAVOUR (Stevie Wonder & Syreeta) / DAYTRIPPER (Beatles) / ANYWAY ANYHOW ANYWHERE (Who) / ON THE WAY HOME (Neil Young) / etc.

Album rating: OCEAN COLOUR SCENE (*6) / MOSELEY SHOALS (*8) / B-SIDES, SEASIDES & FREERIDES collection (*5) / MARCHIN' ALREADY (*6) / ONE FROM THE MODERN (*5) / MECHANICAL WONDER (*5) / SONGS FROM THE FRONT ROW – THE BEST OF . . . (*7) / NORTH ATLANTIC DRIFT (*6) / ANTHOLOGY double compilation (*7) / ONE FOR THE ROAD (*5) / A HYPERACTIVE WORKOUT FOR THE FLYING SQUAD (*5) / LIVE AT THE JAM HOUSE (*5)

SIMON FOWLER (b.25 May'65) – vocals, acoustic guitar, harmonica / **DAMON MINCHELLA** (b. 1 Jun'69) – bass / **PAUL WILKES** – guitar / **OSCAR HARRISON** (b.15 Apr'65) – drums, piano, vocals (ex- ECHO BASE) who repl. CAROLINE BULLOCK

Chapter 22 — not iss.

Mar 89. (12"ep; as the FANATICS) *(12CHAP 38)* **SUBURBAN LOVE SONGS** [ ] [–]
– Suburban love songs / 1.2.3.4. / My brother Sarah / Tight rope.

— now as OCEAN COLOUR SCENE:- **STEVE CRADOCK** (b.22 Aug'69) – guitars, piano, vocals (ex-BOYS; late 80's mods) repl. WILKES

!Phffft — not iss.

Sep 90. (7") *(FIT 001)* **SWAY. / TALK ON** [ ] [–]
(ext-12"+=/ext-cd-s+=) (FITX/FITCD 001) – One of these days.

Mar 91. (7") *(FIT 002)* **YESTERDAY TODAY. / ANOTHER GIRL'S NAME / FLY ME** [49] [ ]
(12"+=/cd-s+=) *(FITX/FITCD 002)* – No one says.

Fontana — not iss.

Feb 92. (7") *(OCSS 1)* **SWAY. / MY BROTHER SARAH** [ ] [–]
(12"+=/cd-s+=) *(OCS 112/CD1)* – Mona Lisa eyes / Bellechoux.

Apr 92. (7") *(OCSS 2)* **GIVING IT ALL AWAY. / THIRD SHADE OF GREEN** [ ] [–]
(12"+=/cd-s+=) *(OCS 212/CD2)* – Flowers / Don't play.

Apr 92. (cd/c/lp) *(<512269-2/-4/-1>)* **OCEAN COLOUR SCENE** [ ] Sep92 [ ]
– Talk on / How about you / Giving it all away / Justine / Do yourself a favour / Third shade of green / Sway / Penny pinching rainy Heaven days / One of these days / Is she coming home / Blue deaf ocean / Reprise. *(re-iss. Sep96, hit UK 54)*

May 92. (7") *(OCSS 3)* **DO YOURSELF A FAVOUR. / THE SEVENTH FLOOR** [ ] [–]
(12"+=/cd-s+=) *(OCS 312/CD3)* – Patsy in green / Suspended motion.

M.C.A. — M.C.A.

Feb 96. (7"/c-s) *(MCS/+C 40021)* **THE RIVERBOAT SONG. / SO SAD** [15] [–]
(cd-s+=) *(MCSTD 40021)* – Charlie Brown says.

Apr 96. (c-s) *(MCSTD 40036)* *<55217>* **YOU'VE GOT IT BAD / I WANNA STAY ALIVE WITH YOU** [7] Jul96 [ ]
(cd-s+=) (MCSTD 40036) – Robin Hood / Huckleberry Grove.
(cd-s) (MCSXD 40036) – ('A'demo) / Here in my heart / Men of such opinion / Beautiful losers.

Apr 96. (cd/c/d-lp) *(<MCD/MCC/MCA 60008>)* **MOSELEY SHOALS** [2] [ ]
– The riverboat song / The day we caught the train / The circle / Lining your pockets / Fleeting mind / Forty past midnight / One for the road / It's my shadow / Policeman and pirates / Downstream / You've got it bad / Get away.

Jun 96. (c-s) *(MCSC 40046)* **THE DAY WE CAUGHT THE TRAIN / THE CLOCK STRUCK 15 HOURS AGO** [4] [–]
(cd-s+=) *(MCSTD 40046)* – I need a love song / Chicken bones and stones.
(cd-s) *(MCSXD 40046)* – ('A'acoustic) / Travellers tune / Justine.

Sep 96. (c-s) *(MCSC 40077)* **THE CIRCLE / MRS JONES** [6] [–]
(cd-s+=) *(MCSTD 40077)* – Cool cool water / Top of the world.
(cd-s) *(MCSXD 40077)* – ('A'acoustic) / Chelsea walk / Alibis / Daytripper (live).

Mar 97. (cd/c/d-lp) *(<MCD/MCC/MCA 60034>)* **B SIDES • SEASIDES & FREERIDES** (compilation) [4] [ ]
– Huckleberry grove / The day we caught the train (acoustic) / Mrs Jones / Top of the world / Here in my heart / I wanna stay alive with you / Robin Hood / Chelsea walk / Outside of a circle / The clock struck 15 hours ago / Alibis / Chicken bones and stones / Cool cool water / Charlie Brown says / Day tripper / Beautiful losers.

Jun 97. (7"/c-s) *(MCS/+C 40133)* **HUNDRED MILE HIGH CITY. / THE FACE SMILES BACK EASILY** [4] [–]
(cd-s+=) *(MCSTD 40133)* – Falling to the floor / Hello Monday.

Aug 97. (7"/c-s) *(MCS/+C 40144)* *<Alex 6055>* **TRAVELLERS TUNE / SONG FOR THE FRONT ROW** [5] Apr98 [ ]
(cd-s+=) *(MCSTD 40144)* – On the way home / All God's children need travelling shoes.

Sep 97. (cd/c/d-lp) *(<MCD/MCC/MCA 60048>)* **MARCHIN' ALREADY** [1] [ ]
– Hundred mile high city / Better day / Travellers tune / Big star / Debris road / Besides yourself / Get blown away / Tele he's not talking / Foxy's folk faced / All up / Spark and Cindy / Half a dream away / It's a beautiful thing. *(<also enhanced-cd; MCD 60053>)*

Nov 97. (7"/c-s) *(MCS/+C 40151)* **BETTER DAY. / THE BEST BET ON CHINASKI** [9] [–]
(cd-s+=) *(MCSTD 40151)* – On and on.

Feb 98. (7"/c-s) *(MCS/+C 40157)* **IT'S A BEAUTIFUL THING. / MARINERS WAY** [12] [ ]
(cd-s+=) *(MCSTD 40157)* – Going nowhere for a while / Expensive chair.
(above featured singer, P.P. ARNOLD)

Island — Ark 21

Aug 99. (c-s/7") *(C+/IS 757)* **PROFIT IN PEACE. / IF YOU GET YOUR WAY** [13] [–]
(cd-s+=) *(CID 757)* – Flood tide rising.

Sep 99. (cd/c/d-lp) *(CID/ICT/ILPS 8090)* **ONE FROM THE MODERN** [4] [–]
– Profit in peace / So low / I am the news / No one at all / Families / Step by step / July / Jane she got excavated / Emily Chambers / Soul driver / The waves / I won't get grazed.

— In Oct'99, STEVE CRADDOCK was credited with LIAM GALLAGHER (of OASIS) on UK Top 10 (JAM) tribute double-A single, 'CARNATION' (flipped with 'Going Underground' by BUFFALO TOM)

Nov 99. (c-s/7") *(C+/IS 759)* **SO LOW. / HOPING YOU'RE MAKING IT TOO** 34 –
(cd-s+=) *(CID 759)* – The inheritors.
(cd-s+=) *(CIDX 759)* – Soul driver / Jane she got excavated.

Jun 00. (c-s/7") *(C+/IS 763)* **JULY. / I AM THE NEWS** 31 –
(cd-s+=) *(CID 763)* – ('A'-forza moderna mix).
(cd-s+=) *(CIDX 763)* – This understanding.

Mar 01. (c-s/7") *(C+/IS 774)* **UP ON THE DOWNSIDE. / THESE ARE THE ONES** 19 –
(cd-s+=) *(CID 774)* – Take you back.

Apr 01. (cd/lp) *(CID/ILPS 8104)* *<81007-2>* **MECHANICAL WONDER** 7 May01
– Up on the downside / In my field / Sail on my boat / Biggest thing / We made it more / Give me a letter / Mechanical wonder / You are amazing / If I gave you my heart / Can't get back to the bassline. *(UK+=)* – Something for me.

Jul 01. (7") *(IS 779)* **MECHANICAL WONDER. / FIRE ON THE WIND** 49 –
(cd-s+=) *(CID 779)* – I was.

Nov 01. (cd/d-lp) *(CID/ILPS 8111)* *<810077>* **SONGS FOR THE FRONT ROW – THE BEST OF OCEAN COLOUR SCENE** (compilation) 16
– The riverboat song / The day we caught the train / One for the road / Circle / You've got it bad / Hundred mile high city / Better day / Travellers tune / Get blown away / It's a beautiful thing / Profit in peace / So low / July / Up on the downside / Mechanical wonder / Huckleberry grove / Robin Hood (live) / Crazy lowdown ways. *(d-cd+=; CIDD 8111)* – LIVE AT STIRLING CASTLE

Dec 01. (7") *(IS 787)* **CRAZY LOWDOWN WAYS. / BEST FRIENDS AND LOVERS** 64 –
(cd-s+=) *(CID 787)* – Come home.

Sanctuary Sanctuary

Jun 03. (7") *(SANXD 159E)* **I JUST NEED MYSELF. / I WANNA SEE THE BRIGHT LIGHTS TONIGHT** 13 –
(cd-s+=) *(SANXD 159X)* – Questions.
(cd-s) *(SANXD 159)* – ('A'side) / Will you take her love / Me I'm left unsure.

Jul 03. (cd/lp) *(SAN CD/LP 160)* *<84623>* **NORTH ATLANTIC DRIFT** 14 Aug03
– I just need myself / Oh collector / North Atlantic drift / Golden Hate Bridge / Make the deal / For every corner / On my way / Second hand car / She's been writing / The song goes on / When evil comes. *<US cd+=>* – Will you take her love / Me, I'm left unsure / Questions / I want to see the bright lights.

Aug 03. (7") *(SANSE 219)* **MAKE THE DEAL. / I JUST NEED MYSELF (remix)** 35 –
(cd-s) *(SANXD 219)* – ('A') / Perfect strangers / I never believed it too.
(cd-s) *(SANXD 219X)* – ('A') / We rise / St. Cecelia.

Jan 04. (7") *(SANSE 244)* **GOLDEN GATE BRIDGE. / THE DAY WE CAUGHT THE TRAIN (live)** 40 –
(cd-s) *(SANXD 244)* – ('A') / Get away (live) / Riverboat song (live).
(dvd-s) *(SANDV 244)* – ('A'-video) / Second hand car (live) / The day we caught the train (live) / (behind the scenes).

Sep 04. (cd) *(SANCD 310)* *<84733>* **ONE FOR THE ROAD** (live) Oct04
– Riverboat song / You've got it bad / The circle / Oh collector / Golden Gate bridge / I just need myself / Wham bam thank you mama / North Atlantic drift / This day should last forever / Mechanical wonder / I love you / Foxy folk face / Travellers tune / Profit in peace / It's my shadow / One for the road / Hundred mile high city / The day we caught the train / Robin Hood.

— now without DAMON who was sacked in 2003

— added **DAN SEALEY** – bass + **ANDY BENNETT** – guitar

Mar 05. (7"/cd-s) *(SAN SE/XS 344)* **FREE MY NAME. / BETTER THAN BEFORE** 23 –
(cd-s) *(SANXD 344)* – ('A') / Make it better / Another time to stay (acoustic live) / ('A'-video & U-Myx format).

Mar 05. (cd/lp) *(SAN CD/LP 332)* *<84746>* **A HYPERACTIVE WORKOUT FOR THE FLYING SQUAD** 30
– Everything comes at the right time / Free my name / Wah wah / Drive away / I love you / This day should last forever / Move things over / Waving not drowning / God's world / Another time to stay / Have you got the right / Start of the day / My time.

Jun 05. (7") *(SANSE 380)* **THIS DAY SHOULD LAST FOREVER. / MOVE THINGS OVER (acoustic)** 53 –
(cd-s) *(SANXS 380)* – ('A') / Last December.

Kenyonrise not iss.

May 06. (cd) *(OCSCD 2)* **LIVE AT THE JAM HOUSE** (live acoustic) 73 –
– Second hand car / She's been writing / The word / This day should last forever / Beautiful thing / Won't get grazed / Great man in waiting / Here in my heart / Matilda's England / God's world / Foxy's folk face / Make the deal / Still trying / My time / Fleeting mind.

– compilations, etc. –

Sep 03. (d-cd) *M.C.A.; (077360-2)* **ANTHOLOGY** 75 –
– One of those days / Sway / Yesterday today / Giving it all away / Do yourself a favour / The riverboat song / You've got it bad / The day we caught the train / The circle / Hundred mile high city / Traveller's tune / Better day / It's a beautiful thing / Profit in peace / So low / July (new version) / I am the new (new version) / Up on the down side / Mechanical wonder / Crazy lowdown ways // Another girls name / My brother Sarah / Mona Lisa eyes / The seventh floor / Robin Hood / The face smiles back easily / Falling to the floor / Hello Monday / Song for the front row / On the way home / The best bet on Chinaski / On and on / Mariners way / Expensive chair / If you get your way / Flood tide rising / Free on the wind / I was / Come home / Best friends & lovers. *(t-cd+=; 980721-0)* – You've got it bad (demo) / Men of such opinion (demo) / Going nowhere for a while / The inheritors / July (Forenza Moderna mix) / These are the ones / Take you back / Anyway, anyhow, anywhere / Travellers tune (acoustic live) / Better day (acoustic live).

the OFFSPRING

Formed: Orange County, California, USA . . . 1984 out of MANIC SUBSIDAL and CLOWNS OF DEATH, by main songwriter DEXTER HOLLAND and GREG KRIESEL. With the addition of JAMES LILJA and KEVIN 'NOODLES' WASSERMAN they adopted THE OFFSPRING moniker, releasing a debut 45, 'I'LL BE WAITING' on the self-financed 'Black' label. With RON WELTY subsequently replacing LILJA, the band began working on demo material, eventually going into the studio with Thom Wilson. The results eventually surfaced in the form of the eponymous 'OFFSPRING' (1989), issued on the 'Nitro' label. An ambitious and experimental fusion of exotic hardcore, its schizoid ramblings not endearing the band to many outside the scene. The next few years were tough for the band as they struggled to find a steady record deal, even tougher for NOODLES who was stabbed at a benefit concert. They eventually found a sympathetic ear in the form of BRAD GUREWITZ (ex-BAD RELIGION) and his burgeoning 'Epitaph' operation, releasing a much improved follow-up album, 'IGNITION' in 1992. However, it wasn't until 1994 and their follow-up, 'SMASH', that OFFSPRING pogo'd into the US charts. Hard on the heels of GREEN DAY's phenomenal worldwide success, the 4-piece found a very successful niche in the larger than life, lads-together ska-core punk rock complete with dayglo choruses and brutally addictive hooklines. The album went on to sell over a million copies in the States and finally gained deserved recognition in Britain, especially after the 'SELF ESTEEM' track became a Top 40 smash early '95! Over the course of the ensuing two years, OFFSPRING almost became part of 'Columbia's roster, although in the end a follow-up, 'INXAY ON THE HOMBRE' appeared on 'Epitaph' in 1997. Building on the winning formula of its predecessor, the album scored another transatlantic Top 20. The dreadlocked DEXTER subsequently teamed up with JELLO BIAFRA (ex-DEAD KENNEDYS) to play some charity gigs under the banner of F.S.U. in aid of the homeless, human rights, etc. Album No.5 'AMERICANA' was delivered late in '98, nobody in their right minds prophecising it would unearth a UK chart-topper in the shape of fun novelty 45, 'PRETTY FLY (FOR A WHITE GUY)'. More of the same was to follow, British hits, 'THE KIDS AREN'T ALRIGHT' and 'SHE'S GOT ISSUES', boosting sales of an otherwise flagging album – a pretty fly move, indeed!

Now in the major league of nu-punk heroes, OFFSPRING served up more metallic mania for the masses with 'CONSPIRACY OF ONE', a record which contained precious little in the way of sonic innovation but plenty of shoutalong riffage for longtime fans and the newly converted alike. Ditto 'SPLINTER' (2003), the veteran punks probably getting just a little bit too long in the tooth to care that much about making their music fit in with anyone's agenda but their own.

• **Covered:** HEY JOE (hit; Jimi Hendrix) / SMASH IT UP (Damned) / KILLBOY POWERHEAD (Didjits).

Album rating: THE OFFSPRING (*4) / IGNITION (*6) / SMASH (*7) / IXNAY ON THE HOMBRE (*5) / AMERICANA (*5) / CONSPIRACY OF ONE (*5) / SPLINTER (*4) / GREATEST HITS compilation (*6)

DEXTER HOLLAND (b. BRYAN HOLLAND, 1966) – vocals, guitar / **NOODLES** (b. KEVIN WASSERMAN, 4 Feb'63, L.A.) – guitar / **GREG KRIESEL** (b.20 Jan'65, Glendale, Calif.) – bass / **JAMES LILJA** – drums

not iss. / Black

1987. (7") *<none>* **I'LL BE WAITING. / BLACKBALL** [–] [ ]

— **RON WELTY** (b. 1 Feb'71) – drums (ex-FQX) repl. LILJA

not iss. / Nemesis

Aug 88. (7"ep) *<NEX 21>* **BAGHDAD EP** [–] [ ]
– Get it right / Hey Joe / Baghdad / The blurb.

1989. (cd) *<NECDX 44>* **THE OFFSPRING** [–] [ ]
– Jennifer lost the war / Elders / Out on patrol / Crossroads / Demons / Beheaded / Tehran / A thousand days / Black ball / I'll be waiting / Kill the president. *(UK-iss.Nov95 on 'Epitaph' cd/c; E 86460-2/-4) (cd re-iss. Jun00 on 'Nitro'; 15803-2)*

Epitaph / Epitaph

Oct 92. (cd/c/lp) *<(E 86424-2/-4/-1)>* **IGNITION** [ ] [ ]
– Session / We are one / Kick him when he's down / Take it like a man / Get it right / Dirty magic / Hypodermic / Burn it up / No hero / L.A.P.D. / Nothing from something / Forever and a day.

Sep 94. (cd/c/lp) *<(E 86432-2/-4/-1)>* **SMASH** [21] Apr94 [4]
– Time to relax / Nitro (youth energy) / Bad habit / Gotta get away / Genocide / Something to believe in / Come out and play / Self esteem / It'll be a long time / Killboy powerhead / What happened to you / So alone / Not the one / Smash.

Sep 94. (12"/c-s/cd-s) *(EPUK/+MC/CD 001)* **COME OUT AND PLAY. / SESSION / ('A'acoustic)** [ ] [–]

Oct 94. (7") *<IGN 3H)* *<65572>* **COME OUT AND PLAY. / COME OUT AND PLAY** [ ] [ ]
(above on 'Ignition'/<'Phantom'> (below ltd. on 'Flying')

Dec 94. (10"ep) *(GOD 008)* **COME OUT AND PLAY EP** [ ] [–]

Feb 95. (7"/c-s/12"/cd-s) *(7/MC/12/CD HOLE 001)* **SELF ESTEEM. / JENNIFER LOST THE WAR / BURN IT UP** [37] [–]

Aug 95. (7"/c-s/cd-s) *(WOOS 2/+CS/CDS)* **GOTTA GET AWAY. / SMASH** [43] [–]
(above single on 'Out Of Step' UK)

— In the Spring of '96, they were fighting Epitaph and boss BRETT GUREWITZ for the right to sign with another label 'Columbia' in the US-only.

Jan 97. (7"m/cd-s) *(6495-7/-2)* **ALL I WANT. / WAY DOWN THE LINE** [31] [–]
(12"+=/cd-s+=) *(6491-1/-2)* – Smash it up.

Feb 97. (cd/lp) *(6487-2/-1)* *<67810>* **IXNAY ON THE HOMBRE** [17] [9]
– Disclaimer / Meaning of life / Mota / Me and my old lady / Cool to hate / Leave it behind / Gone away / I choose / Intermission / All I want / Way down the line / Don't pick it up / Amazed / Change the world.

Apr 97. (7"/cd-s) *(6504-7/-2)* **GONE AWAY. / D.U.I.** [42] [–]
(cd-s+=) *(6498-2)* – Cool to hate / Hey Joe.

Columbia / Columbia

Nov 98. (cd/c) *(491656-2/-4)* *<69661>* **AMERICANA** [10] [2]
– Welcome / Have you ever / Staring at the sun / Pretty fly (for a white guy) / The kids aren't alright / Feelings / She's got issues / Walla walla / End of the line / No brakes / Why don't you get a job? / Americana / Pay the man. *(pic-lp-iss.May99; 491656-0) (cd re-iss. Feb01; same)*

Jan 99. (7"/c-s) *(666880-7/-4)* *<41579>* **PRETTY FLY (FOR A WHITE GUY). / ('A'-The Geek mix)** [1] Nov98 [53]
(cd-s+=) *(666880-2)* – All I want (live).

Apr 99. (c-s) *(667354-4)* *<radio cut>* **WHY DON'T YOU GET A JOB? / BEHEADED 1999** [2] Mar99 [74]
(cd-s+=) *(667354-2)* – ('A'remix by Baka Boyz) / Pretty fly (for a white guy) (CD-ROM).
(cd-s) *(667354-5)* – ('A'remixes).

Aug 99. (c-s) *(667763-4)* **THE KIDS AREN'T ALRIGHT / PRETTY FLY (FOR A WHITE GUY) (live)** [11] [–]
(cd-s+=) *(667763-2)* – Why don't you get a job? (live).
(cd-s) *(667763-5)* – ('A'side) / Walla walla (live) / Pretty fly (for a white guy) (video).

Nov 99. (c-s) *(668377-4)* *<4274>* **SHE'S GOT ISSUES / PRETTY FLY (Baka Boyz Low Rider mix)** [41] [ ]
(cd-s+=) *(668377-2)* – ('A'side) / Kids aren't alright (Wise Guys mix) / Kids aren't alright (Wise Guys instrumental).
(cd-s) *(667377-5)* – ('A'side) / All I want (live in Vegas) / Kids aren't alright (CD-Rom video).

Nov 00. (c-s) *(669997-4)* *<radio cut>* **ORIGINAL PRANKSTER / DAMMIT, I CHANGED AGAIN** [6] [70]
(cd-s+=) *(669997-2)* – Gone away (live).
(cd-s) *(669997-5)* – ('A'side) / Come out swinging / Staring at the sun (live).

Nov 00. (cd/c/lp) *(498481-2/-4/-1)* *<61419>* **CONSPIRACY OF ONE** [12] [9]
– Intro / Come out swinging / Original prankster / Want you bad / Million miles away / Dammit, I change again / Living in chaos / Special delivery / One fine day / All along / Denial, revisited / Vultures / Conspiracy of one.

Mar 01. (c-s) *(670929-4)* **WANT YOU BAD / THE KIDS AREN'T ALRIGHT (live)** [15] [–]
(cd-s+=) *(670929-2)* – 80 times.
(cd-s) *(670929-5)* – ('A'side) / The kids aren't alright (live) / Autonomy.

Jun 01. (c-s) *(671408-4)* **MILLION MILES AWAY / STARING AT THE SUN (live)** [21] [–]
(cd-s+=) *(671408-2)* – Sin city / ('A'video).
(cd-s) *(671408-5)* – ('A'side) / Dammit, I changed again (live) / Bad habit (live).

Dec 01. (cd-s) *<672212>* **DEFY YOU / ONE HUNDRED PUNKS / SELF ESTEEM / WANT YOU BAD** [–] [77]

Dec 03. (cd/lp) *(512201-2)* *<SNY 89026-2/-1>* **SPLINTER** [27] [30]
– Neocon / The noose / Long way home / Hit that / Race against myself / (Can't get my) Head around you / The worst hangover ever / Never gonna find me / Lightning rod / Spare me the details / Da hui / When you're in prison. *(ltd-cd w/dvd+=; 512201-3)* – (the making of..).

Jan 04. (7"pic-d) *(674547-7)* **HIT THAT. / (CAN'T GET MY) HEAD AROUND YOU (live)** [11] [64]
(cd-s) *(674547-2)* – ('A') / ('A'-USC marching band).
(cd-s+=) *(674547-5)* – The kids aren't alright (BBC1 radio session) / Long way home (live) / ('A'-video).

May 04. (7"pic-d) *(674826-7)* **(CAN'T GET MY) HEAD AROUND YOU. / (live)** [48] [–]
(cd-s) *(674826-2)* – ('A') / Hit that (live) / Come out and play (live) / Gotta get away (live) / The kids aren't alright (live).

Jul 05. (cd) *(518746-2)* *<93459>* **GREATEST HITS** (compilation) [14] Jun05 [8]
– Can't repeat / Come out and play (keep 'em separated) / Self esteem / Gotta get away / All I want / Gone away / Pretty fly (for a white guy) / Why don't you get a job? / The kids aren't alright / Original prankster / Want you bad / Defy you / Hit that / (Can't get my) Head around you. *(ltd-cd w/dvd+=; 5187463)* – The kids aren't alright (Wiseguys mix) / Next to you / (documentary).

Jul 05. (cd-s) *(675981-2)* **CAN'T REPEAT / 100 PUNKS / (CAN'T GET MY) HEAD AROUND YOU (live) / ('A'-video)** [ ] [–]

Mike OLDFIELD

Born: 15 May'53, Reading, England. He started playing guitar at the age of seven, and by 1968, had formed SALLYANGIE with sister SALLY. They signed to folk-orientated label, 'Transatlantic', who issued the lp, 'CHILDREN OF THE SUN'. After releasing a single, 'TWO SHIPS' / 'COLOURS OF THE WORLD', in September '69, they split their partnership to concentrate on other projects. Following a spell in the short-lived BAREFOOT, MIKE became the bassist for KEVIN AYERS' band, The WHOLE WORLD, in March 1970, subsequently appearing on two albums, 'SHOOTING AT THE MOON' and 'WHATEVERSHEBRINGSWESING', between

1971 and 1972. Around this time, MIKE started work on his own solo project, gaining financial support in 1972 from Richard Branson's newly formed 'Virgin' label (the same year, he also contributed session work for EDGAR BROUGHTON BAND and DAVID BEDFORD). 'TUBULAR BELLS' finally saw the light of day in May '73, immediately garnering critical acclaim from the music press. A near 50-minute concept piece, overdubbed many times by multi-instrumentalist, MIKE, it went into the Top 3 a year later. Aided by a surprise US Top 10 single (an album excerpt) used in the horror movie, 'The Exorcist', 'TUBULAR BELLS' repeated the feat Stateside. In September '74, his follow-up, 'HERGEST RIDGE', was completed, going straight in at No.1. Critically lambasted by some commentators as "Son of Tubular Bells", it only managed to hit No.87 in America, OLDFIELD coming in for further flak as an orchestral Tubular Bells (conducted by DAVID BEDFORD) was panned by the rock press. The period between 1975 and 1978 saw him branch into African and folk-type origins on the albums, 'OMMADAWN' and 'INCANTATIONS', although at the same time, he embarrassed his rock following by releasing mainly festive hit 45's. Nevertheless, his contribution to the 70's, in terms of both the classical and rock fields, was arguably only matched by PINK FLOYD. The early 80's brought OLDFIELD a succession of more mainstream pop/rock albums, culminating with 1983's Top 10 'CRISES' album, which spawned his biggest ever hit single, 'MOONLIGHT SHADOW' (it featured the celestial vocal chords of MAGGIE REILLY, a member of his band and new co-writing team). Surprisingly, his next single, 'SHADOW ON THE WALL', bombed, although it did succeed in raising the profile of ex-FAMILY frontman, ROGER CHAPMAN. OLDFIELD continued to achieve reasonable chart success throughout the remainder of the decade, even scoring the soundtrack to classic Vietnam movie, 'THE KILLING FIELDS' (1984). Although he never quite regained the ground he had broken with his debut, he nevertheless returned in 1992 with a belated "follow-up" in the form of the almost identical, but still appealing, 'TUBULAR BELLS II'. This seemed to breathe more life into OLDFIELD's flagging career, 1996's 'VOYAGER' taking on the "space-race" theme. Another update of his most famous work, 'TUBULAR BELLS III' (1998), even returned him to the UK Top 5, Eastern-styled vocalist, AMAR, lending a soothing touch to a handful of tracks. Two further offerings in 1999, 'GUITARS' and 'THE MILLENNIUM BELL', were equally new age and thematic. The instrumental wizard attempted to wring yet more mileage out of his most famous work with 'TUBULAR BELLS 2003', a largely unnecessary revision of the original with endless, misguided thematic variations (from "Latin" to "Thrash" to "Jazz") on Part One. The variations on Part Two were admittedly more interesting, while John Cleese added his dry, dulcet tones. 'LIGHT AND SHADE' (2005) featured two discs, one easy-listening, the other sombre and moody, his instruments now forsaken for computerised chill-outs.

• **Covered:** SAILOR'S HORNPIPE (trad.) / IN DULCE JUBILO (R.L. Pearsall) / WILLIAM TELL OVERTURE (Korsokov) / BLUE PETER (BBC copyright) / ARRIVAL (Abba) / WONDERFUL LAND (Shadows) / ETUDE (Franscisco Tarrega). • **Trivia:** In the mid-70's, MIKE also had time to session on albums by Virgin artists; DAVID BEDFORD (Star's End) / ROBERT WYATT (Rock Bottom) / TOM NEWMAN (Fine Old Tom). MIKE's sister, SALLY, also went on to have a UK Top 20 hit with, 'MIRRORS' (late '78).

Album rating: TUBULAR BELLS (*10) / HERGEST RIDGE (*7) / THE ORCHESTRAL TUBULAR BELLS (*6) / OMMADAWN (*8) / INCANTATIONS (*8) / EXPOSED (*4) / PLATINUM (*4) / QE2 (*4) / FIVE MILES OUT (*6) / CRISES (*6) / DISCOVERY (*4) / THE KILLING FIELDS soundtrack (*6) / THE COMPLETE MIKE OLDFIELD compilation (*7) / ISLANDS (*4) / EARTH MOVING (*4) / HEAVEN'S OPEN (*4) / TUBULAR BELLS II (*6) / ELEMENTS: THE BEST OF MIKE OLDFIELD compilation (*7) / THE SONGS OF DISTANT EARTH (*4) / VOYAGER (*4) / XXV: THE BEST OF MIKE OLDFIELD compilation (*6) / TUBULAR BELLS III (*5) / GUITARS (*4) / THE MILLENNIUM BELL (*3) / TUBULAR BELLS 2003 (*4) / LIGHT AND SHADE (*4) / THE PLATINUM COLLECTION boxed (*7)

MIKE OLDFIELD – guitar, bass, multi / except **TOM NEWMAN** – guitar / **JON FIELD** – flute / **STAN BROUGHTON** – drums / **LINDSAY COOPER** – wind; plus master of ceremonies, **VIVIAN STANSHALL** (ex-BONZO DOG BAND)

Virgin Virgin

May 73. (lp/c) *(T/TCV 2001)* <105> **TUBULAR BELLS** [1] Nov73 [3]
– Tubular bells (side 1) / Tubular bells (side 2). *(hit top Oct74) (iss.quad-lp.Jul74; QV 2001) (pic-lp Dec78; VP 2001) (cd-iss. Jun83; CDV 2001); hit UK No.28) (re-iss. Feb97 on 'E.M.I.'; LPCENT 18) (cd re-mast.May98; CDVX 2001)*

Feb 74. (7") <55100> **TUBULAR BELLS (edit). / TUBULAR BELLS (excerpt)** [-] [7]

Jun 74. (7") *(VS 101)* **MIKE OLDFIELD'S SINGLE (theme from Tubular Bells). / FROGGY WENT A-COURTIN'** [31] [-]

— now with **TERRY OLDFIELD** – wind / etc.

Sep 74. (lp/c) *(V/TCV 2013)* <109> **HERGEST RIDGE** [1] [87]
– Hergest ridge (side 1) / Hergest ridge (side 2). *(re-iss. Apr86 lp/c; OVED/+C 163) (cd-iss. Apr86; CDV 2013)*

Jan 75. (lp/c) *(V/TCV 2026)* **THE ORCHESTRAL TUBULAR BELLS (WITH THE ROYAL PHILHARMONIC ORCHESTRA)** (live & conducted by DAVID BEDFORD with guitar by OLDFIELD) [17] [-]
– The orchestral Tubular Bells part 1 / The orchestral Tubular Bells part 2. *(cd-iss. Jul87; CDV 2026) (re-iss. Sep89 on 'VIP-Virgin' lp/c/cd; VVIP/+C/D 101)*

Feb 75. (7") *(VS 112)* **DON ALFONSO. / IN DULCE JUBILO** [ ] [-]

— back-up were **JUBULA** (African musicians) / **PIERRE MOERLEN** (of GONG) / backing vocals by sister **SALLY OLDFIELD** + **CLODAGH SIMMONDS**

Nov 75. (lp/c) *(V/TCV 2043)* <33913> **OMMADAWN** [4] [ ]
– Ommadawn (side 1) / Ommadawn (side 2). *(quad-lp Feb76; QV 2043) (cd-iss. 1986; CDV 2043) (cd re-iss. Apr97 on 'Virgin-VIP'; CDVIP 185)*

Nov 75. (7") *(VS 131)* **IN DULCI JUBILO. / ON HORSEBACK** [4] [-]

Nov 75. (7") <9508> **OMMADAWN (excerpt). / ON HORSEBACK** [-] [ ]

Oct 76. (7") *(VS 163)* **PORTSMOUTH. / SPEAK (THO' YOU ONLY SAY FAREWELL)** [3] [-]

Nov 76. (7") <9510> **PORTSMOUTH. / ALGIERS** [-] [ ]

Feb 77. (7") *(VS 167)* **THE WILLIAM TELL OVERTURE. / ALGIERS** [ ] [-]

Dec 77. (7") *(VS 198)* **THE CUCKOO SONG. / PIPE TUNE** [ ] [-]

— added from last album; (see most musicians from following live album)

Nov 78. (d-lp/d-c) *(VDT/TCVDT 101)* **INCANTATIONS** [14] [-]
– Incantations (part 1) / Incantations (part 2) / Incantations (part 3) / Incantations (part 4). *(cd-iss. Feb87; CDVD 101); omits last of 4 minutes side 3) (re-iss. Apr92 cd/c; OVED CD/C 417)*

Apr 79. (7") *(VS 245)* **GUILTY. / INCANTATIONS (excerpt)** [22] [-]
(12"blue) *(VS 245-12)* – ('A'side) / Guilty (live).

— MIKE with **PIERRE MOERLEN** – drums, percussion / **RINGO McDONOUGH** – bodhran / **MIKE FRYE, BENOIT MOERLEN, DAVID BEDFORD** (also string arrangements) / **NICO RAMSDEN** – guitar / **PHIL BEER** – guitar, vocals / **PEKKA POHJOLA** – bass / **RAY GAY, RALPH IZEN, SIMO SALMINEN, COLIN MOORE** – trumpets / **SEBASTIAN BELL, CHRIS NICHOLLS** – flutes / **PETE LEMER, TIM CROSS** – keyboards / **MADDY PRIOR** – vocals / **JONATHAN KAHAN, DICK STUDT, BEN CRUFT, JANE PRYCE, LIZ EDWARDS, NICOLA HURTON** – violins / **VANESSA PARK, DAVID BUCKNALL, JESSICA FORD, NIGEL WARREN-GREEN** – cellos / **NICK WORTERS, JOE KIRBY** – bass / **DON McVAY, PAULINE MACK, DANNY DAGGERS, MELINDA DAGGERS, LIZ BUTLER, ROSS COHEN** – vocals, plus 11 piece choir.

Aug 79. (d-lp/d-c) *(VD/TCVD 2511)* **EXPOSED (live)** [16] [-]
– Incantations (parts 1 and 2) / Incantations (parts 3 and 4) / Tubular bells (part 1) / Tubular bells (part 2) / Guilty. *(d-cd-iss. Jul86; CDVD 2511)*

— trimmed backing group down.

Nov 79. (7") *(VS 317)* **BLUE PETER. / WOODHENGE** [19] [-]

Dec 79. (lp/c) *(V/TCV 2141)* **PLATINUM** [24] [-]
– Platinum:- Airborne – Platinum – Charleston North star – Platimun finale / Woodhenge / Sally / Punkadiddle / I got rhythm. *(cd-iss. 1986; CDV 2141) (re-iss. 1989 lp/c; OVED/C 233)*

— next featured **PHIL COLLINS** – drums

Virgin / Epic

Sep 80. (7") *(VS 374)* **ARRIVAL. / POLKA** [ ] [–]

Oct 80. (lp/c) *(V/TCV 2181)* <FE 37358> **QE2** [27] [ ]
– Taurus I / Sheba / Conflict / Arrival / Wonderful land / Mirage / QE2 / Celt / Molly. *(cd-iss. 1986; CDV 2181) (re-iss. 1989 lp/c; OVED/+C 235)*

Nov 80. (7") *(VS 387)* **SHEBA. / WONDERFUL LAND** [ ] [–]

Dec 80. (d-lp/d-c) <13143> **AIRBORNE** [–] [ ]
– (see PLATINUM tracks, except 'Guilty' repl. – / / Tubular bells live part 1 / Incantations (segue of 20+ mins. studio and live recordings)

— MIKE brought in **MAGGIE REILLY** – vocals (ex-CADO BELLE) / **TIM CROSS** – keyboards / **MORRIS PERT** – percussion, drums (ex-BRAND X) / **RICK FENN** – bass, guitar / **PIERRE MOERLEN** – drums, percussion returned to repl. MIKE FRYE / added **TIM RENWICK** – bass, guitar

Mar 82. (7"/7"pic-d) *(VS/+Y 464)* **FIVE MILES OUT. / LIVE PUNKADIDDLE** [43] [ ]

Mar 82. (lp/c) *(V/TCV 2222)* <FE 37983> **FIVE MILES OUT** [7] [ ]
– Taurus II / Family man / Orabidoo / Mount Teidi / Five miles out. *(cd-iss. 1983; CDV 2222) (re-iss. Apr90 lp/c; OVED/+C 293) (re-iss. Oct94 on 'Virgin-VIP' cd/c;)*

Virgin / Virgin

Jun 82. (7"/7"pic-d) *(VS/+Y 489)* <02877> **FAMILY MAN. / MOUNT TEIDI** [45] [ ]

Sep 82. (7"/7"pic-d) *(VS/+Y 541)* **MISTAKE. / WALDBERG (THE PEAK)** [ ] [–]

— MIKE retained REILLY + MOERLEN. New members were **SIMON PHILLIPS** – drums / **PHIL SPALDING** – bass / **GRAEME PLEETH** – keyboards / **SIMON HOUSE** – violin

May 83. (7"/7"pic-d)(12") *(VS/+Y 586)(VS 586-12)* **MOONLIGHT SHADOW. / RITE OF MAN** [4] [ ]

May 83. (cd/c/lp) *(CD/TC+/V 2262)* **CRISES** [6] [–]
– Crises / Moonlight shadow / In high places / Foreign affair / Taurus III / Shadow on the wall. *(re-iss. Mar91 cd/c; OVED CD/C 351) (re-iss. May94 on 'Virgin-VIP' cd/c; CD/TC VIP 118)*
(below vocals by ROGER CHAPMAN, ex-FAMILY)

Sep 83. (7"/ext.12") *(VS 625/+12)* **SHADOW ON THE WALL. / TAURUS III** [ ] [ ]

Jan 84. (7"/ext.12") *(VS 648/+12)* **CRIME OF PASSION. / JUNGLE GARDENIA** [61] [ ]

— retained **REILLY, PHILLIPS + SPALDING** – adding guitar / plus **BARRY PALMER** – vocals / **MICKEY SIMMONDS** – keyboards / **HAROLD ZUSCHRADER** – synth.

Jun 84. (7") *(VS 686)* **TO FRANCE. / IN THE POOL** [48] [ ]
(ext.12"+=) *(VS 686-12)* – Bones.

Jul 84. (cd/c/lp) *(CD/TC+/V 2308)* **DISCOVERY** [15] [–]
– To France / Poison arrows / Crystal gazing / Tricks of the light / Discovery / Talk about your life / Saved by a bell / The lake. *(re-iss. Apr92 cd/c; OVED CD/C 421)*

Sep 84. (7") *(VS 707)* **TRICKS OF THE LIGHT. / APEMAN** [ ] [ ]
(12"+=) *(VS 707-12)* – ('A'instrumental).

Nov 84. (7"/ext.12") *(VS 731/+12)* **ETUDE. / EVACUATION** [ ] [ ]

Dec 84. (cd/c/lp) *(CD/TC+/V 2328)* <86009> **THE KILLING FIELDS** (soundtrack) [97] [ ]
– Pran's theme / Requiem for a city / Evacuation / Pran's theme 2 / Capture / Execution / Bad news / Pran's departure / Worksite / The year zero / Blood sucking / The year zero 2 / Pran's escape – The killing fields / The trek / Boy's burial – Pran sees the Red Cross / Good news / Etude. *(re-iss. Jun88 lp/c; OVED/+C 183) <US cd-iss. 1990; 90591-2> (UK cd-iss. Jul00 on 'Virgin-VIP'; MIKECD 12)*

— **ANITA HEGERLAND + ALED JONES** – vocals; repl. REILLY

Nov 85. (7") *(VS 836)* **PICTURES IN THE DARK. / LEGEND** [50] [ ]
(ext.12") *(VS 836-12)* – The trap.

Apr 86. (7"/7"sha-pic-d)(ext.12") *(VS/+S 863)(VS 863-12)* **SHINE. / THE PATH** [ ] [ ]

May 87. (7") *(VS 955)* **IN HIGH PLACES. / POISON ARROWS** [ ] [–]
(12"+=) *(VS 955-12)* – Jungle Gardenia.

— vocalists – **JON ANDERSON / KEVIN AYERS / BONNIE TYLER**

Sep 87. (7") *(VS 990)* **ISLANDS. / THE WIND CHIMES (part one)** [ ] [ ]
(c-s+=/ext.12"+=)(cd-s+=) *(VS/+C 990-12)(CDEP 6)* – When the night's on fire.

Oct 87. (cd/c/lp) *(CD/TC+/V 2466)* <90645> **ISLANDS** [29] [ ]
– The wind chimes (parts 1 & 2) / Islands / Flying start / North point / Magic touch / The time has come. *(cd+=)* – When the night's on fire. *(re-iss. Apr92 cd/c; OVED CD/C 418)*

Nov 87. (7") *(VS 1013)* **THE TIME HAS COME. / (final extract from) THE WIND CHIMES** [ ] [–]
(12"+=) *(VS 1013-12)* – ('A'original mix).

Nov 87. (7") **MAGIC TOUCH. / THE WIND CHIMES (part 1)** [–] [ ]

Feb 88. (7"/12") *(VS 1047/+12)* **FLYING START. / THE WIND CHIMES (part 2)** [ ] [ ]

Jul 89. (7") *(VS 1189)* **EARTHMOVING. / BRIDGE TO PARADISE** [ ] [ ]
(12"+=/cd-s+=) *(VS T/CD 1189)* – ('A'disco mix).

Jul 89. (cd/c/lp) *(CD/TC+/V 2610)* **EARTHMOVING** [30] [–]
– Holy / Hostage / Far country / Innocent / Runaway son / See the light / Earthmoving / Blue night / Nothing but – Bridge to Paradise. *(re-iss. Apr92 cd/c; OVED CD/C 420) (cd re-iss. Apr97 on 'Virgin-VIP'; CDVIP 169)*

Oct 89. (7") *(VS 1214)* **INNOCENT. / EARTHMOVING (club mix)** [ ] [ ]
(12"+=/cd-s+=) *(VS T/CD 1214)* – ('A'extended).

Jun 90. (cd/c/lp) *(CD/TC+/V 2640)* **AMAROK** [49] [–]
– Amarok (part 1) / Amarok (part 2). *(re-iss. Apr92 cd/c; OVED CD/C 422)*

— with **SIMON PHILLIPS** – drums / **DAVE LEVY** – bass / **MICKEY SIMMONDS** – keyboards / **ANDY LONGHURST** – keyboards / **COURTNEY PINE** – sax

Jan 91. (7"/12"/cd-s; as MICHAEL OLDFIELD) **HEAVEN'S OPEN. / EXCERPT FROM AMAROK** [ ] [–]

Feb 91. (cd/c/lp; as MICHAEL OLDFIELD) *(CD/TC+/V 2653)* **HEAVEN'S OPEN** [ ] [–]
– Make make / No dream / Mr. Shame / Gimme back / Heaven's open / Music from the balcony. *(re-iss. Apr92 cd/c; OVED CD/C 419)*

— solo playing most instruments, except some guests & a bagpipe band.

W.E.A. / Reprise

Sep 92. (cd)(lp/c) *(4509 90618-2)(WX 2002/+C)* <45041> **TUBULAR BELLS II** [1] [ ]
– Sentinel / Dark star / Clear light / Blue saloon / Sunjammer / Red dawn / The bell / Weightless / The great pain / Sunset door / Tattoo / Altered state / Maya gold / Moonshine.

Sep 92. (7"/c-s/cd-s) *(YZ 698/+C/CD)* **SENTINEL (SINGLE RESTRUCTION). / EARLY STAGES** [10] [–]

Dec 92. (7"/c-s) *(YZ 708/+C)* **TATTOO. / SILENT NIGHT / SENTINEL (live)** [33] [–]
(cd-ep+=) *(YZ 708CD)* – Live At Edinburgh Castle:- Moonshine / Reprise / Maya gold.

Apr 93. (7"/c-s) *(YZ 737/+C)* **THE BELL. / SENTINEL** [50] [–]
(cd-s+=) *(YZ 737CD)* – ('A'-3 mixes).
(cd-s) *(YZ 737CDX)* – (5-'A'mixes).

Nov 94. (cd/c) *(<4509 98581-2/-4>)* **THE SONGS OF DISTANT EARTH** [24] Jan96 [ ]
– In the beginning / Let there be light / Supernova / Magellan / First landing / Oceania / Only time will tell / Prayer for the Earth / Lament for Atlantis / The chamber / Hibernaculum / Tubular world / The shining ones / Crystal clear / The sunken forest / Ascension / A new beginning. *(re-iss. Oct95; same)*

Dec 94. (c-s) *(YZ 871C)* **HIBERNACULUM / MOONSHINE** [47] [–]
(cd-s+=) *(YZ 871CDX)* – Solution hoedown / Jungle.
(cd-s) *(YZ 871CD)* – ('A'side) / The spectral army / The song of the boat men.

Aug 95. (c-s) *(YZ 880C)* **LET THERE BE LIGHT (Indian Lake mix) / LET THERE BE LIGHT (BT's entropic dub)** [51] [–]
(12") *(YZ 880T)* – ('A'-BT's pure luminescence remix) / ('A'-Hardfloor mix) / ('A'club mix).
(cd-s) *(YZ 880CD)* – (above club mix) repl.by – ('A'-Ultraviolet mix).

Sep 96. (cd/c) *(0630 15896-2/-4)* <46487> **VOYAGER** [12] [ ]
– The song of the sun / Celtic rain / The hero / Women of Ireland / The voyager / She moves through the fair / Dark island / Wild goose flaps its wings / Flowers of the forest / Mont St Michel.

Mar 97. (c-s) *(WEA 093C)* **WOMEN OF IRELAND / ('A'mix)** [ ] [–]
(12"+=/cd-s+=) *(WEA 093 T/CD)* – Mike's reel.
(re-iss. Nov97 hit No.70; same)

Nov 97. (cd/c) *(3984 21218-2/-4)* **XXV (THE BEST OF MIKE OLDFIELD)** (compilation) [ ] [–]
– Tubular bells / Hergest ridge / Ommadawn / Incantation / Moonlight shadow / Portsmouth / The killing fields / Sentinel (Tubular bells II) / The bell / Let there be light / Only time will tell / The voyager / Women of Ireland.

Aug 98. (cd/c) *(<3984 24349-2/-4>)* **TUBULAR BELLS III** [4] Sep98 [ ]
– The source of secrets / The watchful eye / Jewel in the crown / Outcast / Serpent dream / The inner child / Man in the rain / The top of the morning / Moonwatch / Secrets / Far above the clouds.

Oct 98. (c-s) *(WEA 194C)* **MAN IN THE RAIN / THE INNER CHILD (live)** [ ] [–]
(cd-s+=) *(WEA 194CD)* – Serpent's dream (live).

Apr 99. (12"/cd-s) *(WEA 206 T/CD1)* **FAR ABOVE THE CLOUDS / (mixes)** [53] [–]
(cd-s) *(WEA 206CD2)* – ('A'mixes).

May 99. (cd) *(<3984 27401-2>)* **GUITARS** [40] [ ]
– Muse / Cochise / Embers / Summit day / Out of sight / B blues / Four winds / Enigmatism / Out of mind / From the ashes.

Nov 99. (cd/c) *(<8573 80885-2/-4>)* **THE MILLENNIUM BELL** [ ] [ ]
– Peace on Earth / Pacha mama / Santa Maria / Sunlight shining through cloud / Doge's palace / Lake Constance / Mastermind / Broad sunlit uplands / Liberation / Amber light / The millennium bell.

May 03. (cd) *<(2564 60204-2)>* **TUBULAR BELLS 2003** [51] [ ]
– Part one: Introduction / Fast guitars / Basses / Latin / A minor tune / Blues / Thrash / Jazz / Ghost bells / Russian / Finale / Part two: Harmonics / Peace / Bagpipe guitars / Caveman / Ambient guitars / The sailor's hornpipe. *(ltd-cd w/dvd+=; 0927 49921-2)* – (mixes + video).

Mercury not iss.

Sep 05. (d-cd) *(987364-2)* **LIGHT AND SHADE** [ ] [–]
– Angelique / Blackbird / The gate / First steps / Closer / Our father / Rocky / Sunset / Pres de toi / Quicksilver – Our father – Slipstream – Angelique // Quicksilver / Resolution / Slipstream / Surfing / Tears of an angel / Romance / Ringscape / Nightshade / Lakme (fruity loops).

– compilations, etc. –

—— on 'Virgin' unless otherwise mentioned

Nov 76. (4xlp-box) *(VBOX 1)* **BOXED** [22] [–]
– (TUBULAR BELLS / HERGEST RIDGE / OMMADAWN / + COLLABORATIONS (singles, etc.) *(re-iss. 1985 4xlp/4xc; VBOX/TCVX 1) (4xcd-box Jul87; CDBOX 1)*

Dec 78. (7"ep/12"ep) *(VS/+T 238)* **TAKE 4** [72] [–]
– Portsmouth / In dulce jubilo / Wrekorder wrondo / Sailor's hornpipe.

Oct 85. (cd/c/d-lp) *(CD/C+/MOC 1)* **THE COMPLETE MIKE OLDFIELD** [36] [–]
– Arrival / In dulce jubilo / Portsmouth / Jungle gardenia / Guilty / Blue Peter / Waldberg (the peak) / Etude / Wonderful land / Moonlight shadow / Family man / Mistake / Five miles out / Crime of passion / To France / Shadow on the wall / Excerpt from Tubular Bells / Sheba / Mirage / Platinum / Mount Tiede / Excerpt from Ommadawn / Excerpt from Hergest Ridge / Excerpt from Incantations / Excerpt from Killing Fields.

Jun 88. (3"cd-ep) *(CDT 7)* **MOONLIGHT SHADOW (extended) / RITE OF MAN / TO FRANCE / JUNGLE GARDENIA** [ ] [–]

Jun 88. (cd-video) *(080446-1)* **THE WIND CHIMES (Soundtrack 1986)** [ ] [–]

Nov 90. (3xcd-box) *(TPAK 15)* **COLLECTORS' EDITION** [ ] [–]
– (THE ORCHESTRAL TUBULAR BELLS / OMMADAWN / HERGEST RIDGE)

Nov 90. (3xcd-box) *(TPAK 16)* **COLLECTORS' EDITION** [ ] [–]
– (QE2 / PLATINUM / FIVE MILES OUT)

Dec 90. (7"/c-s) **ETUDE. / GAKKAEN** [ ] [–]
(12"+=/cd-s+=) – ('A'extended) (with "ONO GAGUKU KAI").

—— (The above 'A'side was now used on TV ad for 'Nurofen'.)

Sep 93. (cd/c/d-lp) *(VT CD/MC/LP 18)* **ELEMENTS: THE BEST OF MIKE OLDFIELD** [5] [ ]
– Tubular bells – opening theme / Family man / Moonlight shadow / Heaven's open / Five miles out / To France / Foreign affair / In dulce jubilo / Shadow on the wall / Islands / Etude / Sentinel / Ommadawn – excerpt / Incantations part four – excerpt / Amarok – excerpt / Portsmouth.

Sep 93. (4xcd-box) *(CDBOX 2)* **ELEMENTS – MIKE OLDFIELD 1973-1991** [ ] [ ]
– (all TUBULAR BELLS & other album excerpts, plus singles to 1991)

Oct 93. (c-s) *(VSC 1477)* **MOONLIGHT SHADOW / MOONLIGHT SHADOW (extended version)** [52] [ ]
(cd-s+=) *(VSCDT 1477)* – In The Pool (Instrumental) / Bones (Instrumental).

Nov 93. (c-ep/cd-ep) **THE MIKE OLDFIELD CHRISTMAS EP** [ ] [–]
– In dulci jubilo / Portsmouth / etc.

Mar 99. (3xcd-box) *Disky; (HR 85458-2)* **MIKE OLDFIELD VOL.1** [ ] [ ]

Mar 99. (3xcd-box) *Disky; (HR 85459-2)* **MIKE OLDFIELD VOL.2** [ ] [ ]

Jun 01. (cd) *(CDV 2936)* **THE BEST OF TUBULAR BELLS** [60] [–]
– Tubular bells (part 1) / Sentinel / The bell / Far above the clouds / The millennium bell / Tubular bells (part 2).

Mar 06. (t-cd) *(MIKECDX 17)* **THE PLATINUM COLLECTION** [36] [–]

Will OLDHAM

Born: 24 Dec'70, Louisville, Kentucky, USA. OLDHAM was raised by a large family (later his brothers would join him in the PALACE BROTHERS) and began his dark, revered career as an actor in John Sayles' 1987 mining vehicle 'Matewan'. After a few more made-for-TV movies, and a role in another bleedin' mining film, the repressed hillbilly for the 90's (at times compared to BECK!) photographed the front cover for SLINT's 'Spiderland', and for his troubles was awarded the assistance of McMAHAN and WALFORD on his debut album 'THERE IS NO ONE WHAT WILL TAKE CARE OF YOU' (1993). A deep crooner by nature, OLDHAM, eased his way (however unsteady he sounds on guitar), into insular tales of death, sex and er . . . death in a small town community. Several country/gospel/folk albums appeared around 1992/3; the return to basics, 'PALACE' (1994) and 'VIVA LAST BLUES' (1995), showed a marked improvement in song structure and production value. Having drifted between 'Drag City' in the US and 'Domino' in the UK, PALACE made one last attempt at sounding sadder and deeper than LEONARD COHEN ('ARISE THEREFORE'), before OLDHAM persevered under his own name, releasing the, at times, unlistenable 'JOYA' (1997) and the rarities collection 'LOST BLUES AND OTHER SONGS' (also '97). Perhaps his most remarkable contribution to the music scene, 'I SEE A DARKNESS' (1999), was issued under the alias BONNIE 'PRINCE' BILLY, and saw OLDHAM take comic twists and turns throughout the set (sending his image up on an alarming scale). The album, recorded in a nondescript house, played like a beautiful ode to the Greek tragedy, whilst managing to substain a 'live' feel throughout. 'DEATH TO EVERYONE', possibly the finest track, was so bleak and sombre that it could quite literally make one roll around the ground with laughter by its sheer piss-take alone. His humour was further in evidenced on the sharp and commercially viable 'EASE DOWN THE ROAD' (2001), under the aforementioned BONNIE 'PRINCE' BILLY nom de plume. The set, mainly comprised of melancholy love songs, boasting a tight collective of musicians (namely CATHERINE IRWIN, DAVID PAJO, JON THEODORE and arty film-maker HARMONY KORINE) to accompany an even brighter, if not mellower interpretation of OLDHAM's troubled persona. Stand-out tracks included the poetic 'A KING AT NIGHT', 'JUST TO SEE MY HOLLY HOME', which sounded suspiciously like a church choir jamboree and the fleeting title track, with its banjos et al. A new lyrical direction was also present; gone were the morbid Sunday afternoon trials and tribulations of OLDHAM's psyche, these being replaced with affectionate, if not downright rude stanzas heir to ARAB STRAP or the POGUES. No wonder JOHNNY CASH was a fan. The BONNIE PRINCE returned triumphant in 2003 with the stripped-bare 'MASTER AND EVERYONE', arguably his greatest achievement in music to date. Consisting of ten skeletal songs, OLDHAM's Kentucky neo-romantic alter-ego was beginning to make sense; it's rare to find an album of near perfection where every track is outstanding, and it was certainly true in this case. From the lush opener 'THE WAY' to the graceful backwoods haunt of 'WOLF AMONG WOLVES', musically and lyrically the album was in every way a finely-tuned masterpiece. Recruiting LAMBCHOP's guitarist and producer MARK NEVERS, plus roots singer MARY SLAYTON, it was equally about the subtle atmosphere created (especially NEVERS' weird spacy guitar effects) as it was about OLDHAM's beautifully poetic lyrics and flawless musical ark. We hear musicians creeping around in the background, OLDHAM tapping his foot on the floor to keep time, the deep wheezing of a pump organ – there's even a song dedicated to PJ HARVEY. All in all, a majestic and intrinsically sublime set, and, even though it may be foolish to compare BILLY to NICK DRAKE, this is the closest thing we'll get to the spare melodic greatness of 'Pink Moon' this side of the new century. More prolific than ever, OLDHAM faced down the mid-00s with a blizzard of often bizarre and unexpected (even for him) albums, beginning with 'SINGS GREATEST PALACE MUSIC' (2004), an idiosyncratic roadtrip down to Nashville and back through some of his most fevered, fan club-picked reveries (as well as a cover of the Mekons' 'HORSES'); kind of like BOB DYLAN hitting Music City after the arcania of 'JOHN WESLEY HARDING'. Recorded with the cream of the city's sessioneers, the record was a million country miles removed from OLDHAM's early mumblings, finally dressing his best songs up in the kind of creamy production and arrangements (pedal steel and fiddle to the fore) they perhaps weren't designed for, but fit like a foxglove all the same. Critics were understandably suspicious, questioning his intentions; fans accepted it for what it was, a sterling modern country album (and there ain't too many of those around). 'SUPERWOLF' (2005), by contrast, was an album length pairing with sometime collaborator MATT SWEENEY, a return to a more familiar OLDHAM sound, and roundly hailed as one of the most consistent albums of his career. The backwoods jacobite performed another volte face late that year with the live 'SUMMER IN THE SOUTHEAST' (2005), cranking up the amps for a back catalogue visitation every bit as hair-shirted and barroom-ragged as 'SINGS GREATEST..' was demure. 'THE BRAVE AND THE BOLD' (2006) took a different tack again, a full blown, TORTOISE-partnered covers set tackling the genius of everyone from Brazilian balladeer Milton Nascimento ('CRAVO E CANELA'; in brave Kentucky via Minas Gerais Portuguese no less!), folk statesman Richard Thompson ('CALVARY CROSS') and new wave nutters Devo ('THAT'S PEP!) to Elton John ('DANIEL') and Bruce Springsteen himself ('Thunder Road').

Album rating: Palace: THERE IS NO-ONE WHAT WILL TAKE CARE OF YOU (*8) / PALACE – DAYS IN THE WAKE (*6) / VIVA LAST BLUES (*7) / ARISE THEREFORE (*7) / LOST BLUES AND OTHER SONGS collection (*8) / Will Oldham: JOYA (*6) / ODE MUSIC mini soundtrack (*4) / GUARAPERO: LOST BLUES 2 collection (*5) / SLITCH MUSIC mini soundtrack w/ Continental Op (*5) / SEAFARERS MUSIC mini soundtrack (*5) / Bonnie "Prince" Billy: I SEE A DARKNESS (*8) / EASE DOWN THE ROAD (*8) / MORE REVERY mini (*6) / MASTER AND EVERYONE (*9) / sings GREATEST PALACE MUSIC (*6) / SUPERWOLF with Matthew Sweeney (*7) / THE BRAVE AND THE BOLD w/ Tortoise (*6)/ SUMMER IN THE SOUTHEAST (*7)

the PALACE BROTHERS

WILL OLDHAM – vocals, guitar / with **BRIAN McMAHAN** – guitar (of SQUIRREL BAIT and SLINT) / **BRITT WALFORD** – drums (of SLINT)

Big Cat / Drag City

May 93. (7") *(ABB 51S)* <*DC 25*> **OHIO RIVER BOAT SONG. / DRINKING WOMAN**

Jun 93. (lp/cd) *(ABB/+CD 050)* <*DC 34*> **THERE IS NO-ONE WHAT WILL TAKE CARE OF YOU**
– Idle hands are the Devil's playthings / Long before / I tried to stay healthy for you / The cellar song / Pulpit / There is no-one what will take care of you / O Lord are you in need / Merida / King me / I had a good mother and father / Riding / O Paul. *(UK-lp re-iss. Jun97; same as US) (cd re-iss. Jan01 on 'Domino'; REWIGCD 008)*

— now OLDHAM completely solo

Domino / Drag City

Dec 93. (7") <*DC 37*> **COME IN. / TRUDY LIES** –

May 94. (7") <*DC 47*> **HORSES. / STABLE WILL** –

Jun 94. (cd-ep) *(RUG 21CD)* **COME IN / HORSES / STABLE WILL / TRUDY DIES** –

Sep 94. (cd/c/lp) *(WIG CD/MC/LP 14)* <*DC 50*> **PALACE** <aka 'DAYS IN THE WAKE'> Aug94
– You will miss me when I burn / Pushkin / Come a little dog / I send my love to you / Meaulnes / No more workhouse blues / All is grace / Whither thou goest / (Thou without) Partner / I am a cinemagrapher. <*(re-iss. Dec97 as 'DAYS IN THE WAKE'; same)*>

Jan 95. (m-cd/m-lp; as PALACE SONGS) *(WIG CD/LP 18)* <*DC 57*> **HOPE** Nov94
– Agnes, queen of sorrow / Untitled / Winter lady / Christmastime in the mountains / All gone, all gone / Werner's last blues to blokbuster.

— with **PAUL OLDHAM** – guitar / **HAYDEN** + **JOHN STITH** – bass / **GORDON TOWNSEND** – drums

Mar 95. (7") <*DC 61*> **WEST PALM BEACH. / GULF SHORES** –

Jul 95. (7") <*DC 71*> **MOUNTAIN LOW. / (END OF) TRAVELING** –

Aug 95. (12"ep/cd-ep; as PALACE SONGS) *(RUG 35 T/CD)* **THE MOUNTAIN EP** –
– Mountain low / Gulf shores / (End of) Traveling / West Palm Beach.

— now with **BRYAN RICH** – guitar / **LIAM HAYES** – organ / **JASON LOWENSTEIN** – bass

Aug 95. (cd/c/lp; as PALACE MUSIC) *(WIG CD/MC/LP 21)* <*DC 65 – PR 4*> **VIVA LAST BLUES**
– More brothers rides / Viva ultra / Brute choir / Mountain low / Tonight's decision (and thereafter) / Work hard – play hard / New partner / Cat's blues / We all, us three, will ride / Old Jerusalem.

Oct 95. (7") <*DC 64 – PR 1*> **O HOW I ENJOY THE LIGHT. / MARRIAGE** –

— now simply as PALACE; with **NED OLDHAM** – bass / **DAVID GRUBBS** – piano / **MAYA TONE** – percussion, drums

Apr 96. (cd/c/lp) *(WIG CD/MC/LP 24)* <*DC 88*> **ARISE THEREFORE**
– Stablemate / Sucker's evening / Arise therefore / You have cum / Kid of Harith / Sun highlights / the lack in each / No gold digger / Disorder / Group of women / Give me children / Weaker soldier. *(also on ltd-cd; RUG 46CD)*

not iss. / Palace

Jun 96. (7") <*PR 13*> **FOR MEKONS ET AL. / STABLE WILL** –

Drag City / Drag City

Dec 96. (7"; as PALACE MUSIC) <*(DC 91)*> **LITTLE BLUE EYES. / THE SPIDER'S DUDE IS OFTEN THERE**

WILL OLDHAM

— now under his own moniker

Jan 96. (7") <*DC 83*> **EVERY MOTHER'S SON. / NO MORE RIDERS** –

Mar 97. (7") <*(DC 118)*> **PATIENCE. / TAKE HOWEVER LONG YOU WANT**

Domino / Drag City

Nov 97. (cd/lp) *(WIG CD/LP 39)* <*DC 107*> **JOYA** Oct97
– O let it be / Antagonism / New gypsy / Under what was oppression / The gator / Open your heart / Richer / Be still and know God (don't be shy) / Apocalypse, no! / I am still what I meant to be / Bolden boke boy / Idea and deed.

Palace / Acuarela

Oct 97. (cd-ep) *(WILL 1CD)* <*AFF 002*> **WESTERN MUSIC** Mar98
– Always bathing in the evening / Western songs for J.L.L. / Three photographs / Jump in jump in, come in come in.

Drag City / Drag City

Jun 98. (12"/cd-s) <*(DC 100/+CD)*> **BLACK/RICH MUSIC**
– Do what you will do / Do what you will do / Risen Lord / Allowance / Allowance / Black/rich tune / Black/rich / Do what you will do.

Jun 98. (cd-ep) <*(DC 107X)*> **LITTLE JOYA**
– Prologue / Joya / Exit music for a dick.

Jan 00. (m-lp/m-cd) <*(DC 183/+CD)*> **ODE MUSIC** (soundtrack to film 'Ode')
– Ode #1 / Ode #2 / Ode #3 / Ode #4 / Ode #1a / Ode #1b / Ode #2a / Ode #5 / Ode #3a / Ode #4a. <*(re-iss. Apr04; same)*

below with **DAVID PAJO**

Oct 02. (m-lp; as CONTINENTAL OP) <*(DC 195)*> **SLITCH MUSIC** (soundtrack) Sep02
– Faster / La la la / Glock / Heavy minor / Fantasy / Acoustic minor / James tired / Magnifico. <*(m-cd w/ dvd+=; DC 195CD)*> – (the short film). <*(re-iss. Jun04; same)*

Feb 04. (m-lp/m-cd) <*(DC 261/+CD)*> **SEAFARERS MUSIC** (soundtrack)
– Sapele / Lars / Bogo / Emmanuel.

– compilations, etc. –

Apr 97. (cd/d-lp; as PALACE MUSIC) *Domino; (WIG CD/LP 33) / Drag City; <DC 110>* **LOST BLUES AND OTHER SONGS**
– Ohio river boat song / Riding / Valentine's day / Trudy dies / Come in / Little blue eyes / Horses / Stable will / Untitled / O how I enjoy the light / Marriage / West Palm Beach / Gulf shores / (End of) Travelling / Lost blues.

Oct 97. (7") *Skingraft; (GR 26)* **SIDES 5-6** – –

Feb 00. (cd/lp) *Domino; (WIG CD/LP 74) / Drag City; <40111>* **GUARAPERO: LOST BLUES 2**
– Drinking woman / The spider's dude is often there / Gezundheit / Let the wires ring / Big balls / For the mekons et all / Stable Will / Every mother's son / No more rides / The risen Lord / Boy, have you cum / Patience / Take however long you want / Sugarcane juice drinker / Call me a liar / O Lord are you in need?

Jan 02. (one-sided-10"ep+book) *Konkurrent; (907538040-2)* **FOREST TIME** –

Oct 02. (7") *Isota; (SODY 005)* **WE ALL US THREE WILL RIDE. / BARCELONA** –

BONNIE 'PRINCE' BILLY

with **BOB ARELLANO, COLIN GAGON, PAUL OLDHAM + PETER TOWNSEND**

—— session people provided the backing for OLDHAM

not iss. | All City Nomad

Apr 98. (ltd-7"+purple) *<AC 7>* **BLACK DISSIMULATION. / NO SUCH AS WHAT I WANT** –
(UK-iss.Feb00; same as US)

Domino | Palace

May 98. (cd-s; tour) *(RUG 67CD)* **I AM DRINKING AGAIN / DREAMING MY DREAMS** –

Nov 98. (cd-ep) *(RUG 81CD)* **BLUE LOTUS FEET** –
– One with the birds / Southside of the world / When die song / I am the sky / Blue lotus feet / Pole star / Door of my heart.

Jan 99. (cd/lp) *(WIG CD/LP 59) <PR 22>* **I SEE A DARKNESS**
– A minor place / Nomadic revery (all around) / I see a darkness / Another day full of dread / Death to everyone / Knockturne / Madeleine- Mary / Song for the new breed / Today I was an evil one / Black / Raining in darling.

Jun 99. (7") *<PR 20>* **ONE WITH THE BIRDS. / SOUTHSIDE OF THE WORLD** –

1999. (7"blue) *<SP 462>* **LET'S START A FAMILY (BLACKS). / A WHOREHOUSE IN ANY HOUSE** –

1999. (7") *<LF 075>* **I CONFESS** –

—— <above 2 on 'Sub Pop' & 'Lowfly' – below on 'Western'>

Jul 00. (7"m; as BONNIE "BLUE" BILLY) *(West 009)* **LITTLE BOY BLUE** –
– Little boy blue I / Little boy blue II / Blue boy.

Sep 00. (cd-s; as BONNIE PRINCE BILLY & THE MARQUIS DE TREN) *(RUG 109CD) <PR 24>* **GET ON JOLLY**
– 2/15 / 25 / 81 / 86 / 64 / 66.

—— MARQUIS DE TREN included **MICK TURNER** (of DIRTY THREE)

Dec 00. (12"ep/cd-ep; as WILL OLDHAM & RYAN MURPHY) *(RUG 117) <DC 123>* **ALL MOST HEAVEN**
– Fall again / Fall and raise it on / Song of most / Song of all.

Mar 01. (cd) *(WIGCD 89) <PR 26>* **EASE DOWN THE ROAD** Apr01
– May it always be / Careless love / A king at night / Just to see my holly home / At break of day / After I made love to you / Ease down the road / the lion lair / Mrs William / Sheep / Grand dark feeling of emptiness / Rich wife full of happiness. *(w/ free cd-ep+=; WIGCD 89X)* **BONNIE 'PRINCE' BILLY WITH MIKE FELLOWS, JAMES LO, AND MATT SWEENEY** – What's wrong with a zoo / I send my love to you / Stablemate.

Temporary Residence | Temporary Residence

Jun 01. (m-cd; as BONNY BILLY) *<(TRR 37)>* **MORE REVERY** 2000
– Someone's sleeping / Sweeter than anything / Same love that made me laugh / A dream of the sea / Strange things / Just to see you smile.

Domino | Palace

2001. (cd-ep) *<MAP 001>* **GET THE FUCK ON JOLLY LIVE** –
– XXV / II-XV / LXXXI / LXXXVI / LXIV / LXVI / XIII / CII.

Jan 03. (cd) *(WIGCD 121) <pr 29cd>* **MASTER AND EVERYONE** 48
– The way / Ain't you wealthy, ain't you wise? / Master and everyone / Wolf among wolves / Joy and jubilee / Maundering / Lessons from what's poor / Even if love / Three questions / Hard life.

Domino | Drag City

Mar 04. (cd) *(WIGCD 140) <DC 252CD>* **sings GREATEST PALACE MUSIC** 63
– New partner / Ohio river boat song / Gulf shores / You will miss me when I burn / The brute choir / I send my love to you / More brother rides / Agnes, queen of sorrow / Viva ultra / Pushkin / Horses / Riding / West Palm beach / No more workhorse blues / I am a cinematographer.

Aug 04. (7") *(RUG 185)* **AGNES, QUEEN OF SORROW. / PUSSYFOOTING** 69 –
(cd-s+=) *(RUG 185CD)* – Werner last blues to blokbuster / ('A'-video).

Oct 04. (7") *(RUG 189)* **NO MORE WORKHORSE BLUES. / THE COLOR OF MY DREAMS, IF I HAD DREAMS** –
(cd-s) *(RUG 189CD)* – ('A') / Ruby / Kiss / ('A'-video).

Jan 05. (cd/lp; as MATT SWEENEY / BONNIE "PRINCE" BILLY) *(WIG CD/LP 150) <DC 279CD>* **SUPERWOLF**
– My home is the sea / Beast for thee / What are you? / Goat and ram / Lift us up / Rudy foolish / Bed is for sleeping / Only someone running / Death in the sea / Blood embrace / I gave you.

Jul 05. (7"; as BONNY / SWEENEY) *(RUG 209)* **I GAVE YOU. / FOUR SCREAMS**
(cd-s+=) *(RUG 209CD) <DC 298CD>* – My circle / Birch ballad / ('A'-video).

Sea Note | Sea Note

Nov 05. (d-lp/cd) *<(SN 11/+CD)>* **SUMMER IN THE SOUTHEAST** (live)
– Master and everyone / Pushkin / Blokbuster / Wolf and wolves / May it always be / Break of day / A sucker's evening / Nomadic revery (all around) / I see a darkness / O let it be / Beast for thee / Death to everyone / Even if love / I send my love to you / Take however long you want / Madeleine Mary / Ease down the road.

Domino | Overcoat

Jan 06. (cd; by TORTOISE & BONNIE "PRINCE" BILLY) *(WIGCD 167) <27>* **THE BRAVE AND THE BOLD**
– Cravo e canela / Thunder road / It's expected I'm gone / Daniel / Love is love / Pancho / That's pep! / Some say (I got devil) / Calvary Cross / On my own.

□ OL' DIRTY BASTARD (see under ⇒ WU-TANG CLAN)

□ OPERATION IVY (see under ⇒ RANCID)

□ ORANGE JUICE (see under ⇒ COLLINS, Edwyn)

the ORB

Formed: South London, England . . . 1989 by remix supremo and ex-KILLING JOKE roadie Dr. ALEX PATERSON. Working as an A&R bod for ambient label EG (home to he likes of BRIAN ENO), PATTERSON began recording similar ambient sounds in his spare time. He hooked up with the KLF's JIMMY CAUTY in 1988 and recorded an EP, 'KISS', using samples from NEW YORK's Kiss FM. The duo traded under the ORB moniker (which PATERSON had taken from the WOODY ALLEN sci-fi film 'Sleepers') and released the record the following year on the 'WAU!Mr Modo' label, a joint venture between PATERSON and ex-KILLING JOKE bassist YOUTH. Around this time the multi-talented PATTERSON was doing a spot of DJ'ing in the chill-out room of PAUL OAKENFOLD's Land of Oz club, where, in a well documented incident, he met STEVE HILLAGE (ex-GONG). The two struck up an immediate friendship (HILLAGE no doubt impressed by the fact that PATERSON had been spinning one of his old tracks at the time) and a series of mutual collaborations ensued. Meanwhile, the ORB carved out a place in the cobwebbed corners of music history by making what was arguably the first ever ambient dance track, entitled, pause for breath, 'A HUGE EVER GROWING PULSATING BRAIN THAT RULES FROM THE CENTRE OF THE ULTRAWORLD'. The psychedelic/progressive rock influence was glaringly obvious, not only in the overblown title but in the slowly shifting rhythms and tripped-out dub effects. The ORB's heavy use of samples continued, this time running into trouble with Minnie Riperton's 'LOVING YOU'. Come 1990, the band found themselves in the enviable position of being in-demand remixers and amid their growing reputation released another single, the celestial 'LITTLE FLUFFY CLOUDS'. This time penned by PATERSON/YOUTH, the single saw the ORB run into sample trauma again, with RICKIE LEE JONES reportedly none too happy that her, frankly, out-of-it sounding tones were used on the single. During the sessions for the single, PATERSON met a young engineer, THRASH, who would go on to become a fully fledged ORB member in late '91 as a replacement for the recently departed CAUTY. The much anticipated debut album, 'ADVENTURES BEYOND THE ULTRAWORLD', released in April '91 on Big Life, was a sprawling double set of blissed-out almost-beats and shimmering ambience. It was also a catalyst for the burgeoning ambient scene that would spawn the likes of MIXMASTER MORRIS and the APHEX TWIN, the music spilling out of chill-out rooms across the country into fully paid-up ambient club nights. In June '92, the ORB stormed into the top 10 with the 'BLUE ROOM' single. At a record breaking 39 minutes long, it wasn't exactly radio-friendly although the band 'performed' it on Top Of The Pops, sitting nonchalantly playing chess and the act's cult popularity saw the subsequent album, 'UFORB', go straight in at No.1. Following a dispute with YOUTH, PATERSON signed with Island, fighting a protracted battle for the ORB name which he eventually won. His first release for the label was a live album, imaginatively titled 'LIVE '93', and culled from the legendary ORB stage show at various locations around the globe. A collaboration with German techno exponent THOMAS FEHLMAN resulted in the harder sounding 'POMMEFRITZ' album which included such wonderfully titled tracks as 'MORE GILLS, LESS FISHCAKES'. Another two albums, 'ORBUS TERRARUM' (1995) and 'ORBLIVION' (1997) ploughed similarly obscure furrows and divided critical opinion, although both hit top 20. Along with the likes of PRIMAL SCREAM, the ORB helped define an era, bringing overt psychedelia back into the pop charts and updating the genre for the 90's. The ORB saw a welcome return to their usual spacy laid-back cosmic meanderings via the 2001 release 'CYDONIA' (named after a divison of Mars which astronauts believed was once inhabited by civilisation, mmmm). The only real difference between this and 'ORBLIVION' was the fact that PATERSON recruited two female vocalists; AKI OMORI and NINA WALSH. OMORI took the vocal duties on opener (and Top 40 single) 'ONCE MORE', while WALSH crooned over the spacy lullaby 'PLUM ISLAND'. The album was once again peppered with PATERSON's weirdness and THOMAS FEHLMANN and ANDY HUGHES' floating, almost mainstream production. FEHLMANN was once again on board – alongside old partner in chime JIMMY CAUTY – for 'BICYCLES & TRICYCLES' (2004), a record that followed on from the 'Kompakt' EP's, 'KOMPASSION' and 'KOMPLOTT' (released in '03/'04 respectively), and two of whose best tracks – 'GEE STRINGS' and 'DILMUN' – were in fact recycled from those EPs. Critics generally welcomed PATERSON's latest adventures in sound, which found him juggling with familiar dubscapes, randomly sourced vocals, exponential ambience and a rattling toolbox of beat options. Subsequently signing to 'Kompact' full time, PATERSON continued to work with label veteran FEHLMANN on 'OKIE DOKIE IT'S THE ORB ON KOMPAKT' (2005), drawing together previous excursions for the imprint with original material.

• **Songwriters:** Most by WESTON and PATERSON. • **Trivia:** The ORB have remixed many including 'Mute' label stars; DEPECHE MODE / ERASURE & WIRE. In 1992, they caused upset in the Asian community by using their religious chants.

Album rating: ADVENTURES BEYOND THE ULTRAWORLD (*9) / U.F.ORB (*9) / LIVE 1993 (*6) / POMMEFRITZ (*6) / ORBUS TERRARUM (*5) / ORBLIVION (*7) / U.F.OFF – THE BEST OF THE ORB compilation (*7) / CYDONIA (*5) / BICYCLES & TRICYCLES (*5) / F.F.W.D.: F.F.W.D. collaboration (*6)

ALEX PATERSON – synthesizer, keyboards / with **JIM CAUTY**

Wau! Mr Modo — not iss.

May 89. (ltd.12"ep; as ROCKMAN ROCK & LX DEE) *(MWS 010T)* **KISS EP** — –
– Kiss your love / Suck my kiss mix / The roof is on fire / Ambiorix mix.

Oct 89. (12"ep) *(MWS 017T)* **A HUGE EVER GROWING PULSATING BRAIN THAT RULES FROM THE CENTRE OF THE ULTRAWORLD: LOVIN' YOU (Orbital mix). / ('A'bucket and spade mix) / WHY IS 6 SCARED OF 7?** — –

Big Life — Mercury

Jun 90. (12"ep) *(BLR 270T)* **(above with new vocals)** — –
(cd-ep) *(BLR 270CD)* – (above) / Loving you (ambient house).

Jul 90. (12"ep/cd-ep) *(BLR 27 T/CD)* **(above remixed) / ('A'-9 a.m. radio mix) / ('A'-Aubrey mix I)** — –

Nov 90. (7") *(BLR 33)* **LITTLE FLUFFY CLOUDS. / ('A'-Ambient mix Mk.1)** — –
(dance mix-12"ep+=/cd-ep+=) *(BLR 33 T/CD)* – Into the fourth dimension (Essenes beyond control).
(12"ep) *(BLR 33R)* – ('A'side) / ('A'-drum & vox version) / Into the fourth dimension.

— In Nov90, they collaborated on STEVE HILLAGE's SYSTEM 7 release 'Sunburst'.

— CAUTY was replaced by **STEVE HILLAGE** – guitar (ex-Solo artist, ex-GONG) / **MIQUETTE GIRAUDY** (ex-GONG) / **ANDY FALCONER**

Apr 91. (d-cd/d-c/d-lp) *(BLR CD/MC/LP 5)* <511034> **ADVENTURES BEYOND THE ULTRAWORLD** — 29 — Nov91
– Little fluffy clouds / Earth (Gaia) / Supernova at the end of the universe / Back side of the Moon / Spanish castles in space / Perpetual dawn / Into the fourth dimension / Outlands / Star 6 & 7 8 9 / A huge ever growing pulsating brain that rules from the centre of the Ultraworld.

Jun 91. (7"/c-s) *(BLR 46/+C)* **PERPETUAL DAWN (SOLAR YOUTH). / STAR 6&789 (phase II)** — 61 — –
(cd-ep+=) *(BLR 46CD)* – Perpetual dawn: Solar flare.
(12"ep+=) *(BLRT 46)* – (above version) / ('B'side) / ('A'-Ultrabass 1 mix).
(12"ep) *(BLR 46R)* – ORB IN DUB: Towers of dub (ambient mix) / Perpetual dawn (ultrabass II). *(re-iss. Jan94; same)* – (hit No.18)

— In Nov91, SYSTEM 7 issued another release on '10-Virgin'; 'Miracle'.

Dec 91 (cd/c/lp) *(BLR CD/MC/LP 14) / Caroline; <CAROL 1717>* **THE AUBREY MIXES: THE ULTRAWORLD EXCURSIONS** (deleted after 1 day) — 44
– Little fluffy clouds / (Pal Joey mix) / Black side of the moon (Steve Hillage remix) / Spanish castles in Spain (Youth remix) / Outlands (Ready made remix) / A huge ever growing pulsating brain (Jim Caldy & Dr. Alex Patterson remix).

— **PATERSON** now with **THRASH (KRISTIAN WESTON)** – guitars, synthesizers, samplers, percussion, plus guests **YOUTH, STUART McMILLAN, GUY PRATT, JAH WOBBLE, STEVE HILLAGE, MIQUETTE GIRAUDY, THOMAS FEHLMANN, GREG HUNTER, ORDE MEIKLE, TOM GREEN, MARNEY PAX.**

Jun 92. (12"ep) *(BLRT 75)* **THE BLUE ROOM (part 1). / (part 2)** — 8 — –
(cd-ep) *(BLRDA 75)* – The blue room (40 minute version).
(cd-ep) *(BLRDB 75)* – The blue room (radio 7) / The blue room (excerpt 605) / Towers of dub (Mad Professor mix).

Jul 92. (d-cd/d-c/t-lp) *(BLR CD/MC/LP 18)* <513749> **UF ORB** — 1
– O.O.B.E. / U.F. Orb / Blue room / Towers of dub / Close encounters / Majestic / Sticky end. *(free live lp at some shops 'Soundtrack To The Film: ADVENTURES BEYOND THE ULTRAWORLD: PATTERNS & TEXTURES') (re-iss. Apr96 on 'Island; (cd)(c) IMCD 219)(ICM 8033)*

Oct 92. (c-s) **ASSASSIN (the oasis of rhythm mix)** — 12
(12"ep+=/cd-ep+=) *(BLR T/DA 81)* – U.F. ORB (Bandulu remix).
(cd-ep) *(BLRDB 81)* – ('A'-radio 7 mix) / ('A'-another live version) / ('A'-Chocolate hills of Bohol mix).

Nov 93. (c-ep/12"ep/cd-ep) *(BLR C/T/D 98)* **LITTLE FLUFFY CLOUDS. / ('A'mixes)** — 10 — –

Island Island

Nov 93. (d-cd/d-c/q-lp) *(CIDD/ICTT/ILPSQ 8022)* <535004> **LIVE 93 (live)** 23 □
– Plateau / The valley / Oobe / Little fluffy clouds / Star 6, 7, 8 & 9 / Towers of dub / Spanish castles in space / The blue room / Perpetual dawn / Assassin / Outlands / A huge ever pulsating brain that rules from the centre of the ultraworld. *(d-cd-iss. Mar97; IMCD 245)*

Jun 94. (cd/c/lp) *(ORB CD/MC/LP 1)* <535007> **POMMEFRITZ** 6 □
– Pommefritz / More gills less fishcakes / We're paste to be grill you / Banger'n'chips / Allers ist schoen / His immortal logness.

— now w /out KRIS WESTON, who was repl. (after 1995 recording by) **ANDY HUGHES**

Mar 95. (cd/cd/c/d-lp) *(CID/CIDX/ICT/ILPSD 8037)* <524099> **ORBUS TERRARUM** 20 Apr95 □
– Valley / Plateau / Oxbow lakes / Montagne d'or (der gute berg) / White river junction / Occidental / Slug dub.

May 95. (c-s) *(CIS 609)* **OXBOW LAKES / ('A'-Everglades mix)** 38 –
(12"+=) *(12IS/CID 609)* – ('A'-Sabres No.1 mix).
(12") *(12ISX 609)* – ('A'-Carl Craig psychic pals family wealth plan mix) / ('A'-Evensong string arrangement mix).
(cd-s) *(CIDX 609)* – (all 5 mixes above).

— In Jul'96, the label 'Deviant' released various artists compilation of their mixes 'AUNTIE AUBREY'S EXCURSIONS BEYOND THE CALL OF DUTY'.

— line-up **LX PATERSON / ANDY HUGHES / THOMAS FEHLMANN**

Jan 97. (12"/cd-s) *(12IS/CID 652)* <854907> **TOXYGENE. / DELTA Mk.II** 4 □
(cd-s) *(CIDX 652)* – ('A'side) / Rose tinted.

Feb 97. (cd/c/d-lp) *(CID/ICT/ILPSD 8055)* <524347> **ORBLIVION** 19 □
– Delta mk II / Ubiquity / Asylum / Bedouin / Molten love / Pi / S.A.L.T. / Toxygene / Log of deadwood / Secrets / Passing of time / 72.

May 97. (12"/cd-s) *(12IS/CID 657)* **ASYLUM. / ('A'-Blood Sugar's mix 1) / ('A'-Andrea Parker's Bezirkskrankenhaus mix)** 20 □
(cd-s) *(CIDX 657)* –

Oct 98. (cd/d-lp) *(CID/ILPSD 8078)* <524565> **U.F.OFF – THE BEST OF** (compilation) 38 □
– A huge ever growing pulsating brain rule from the centre of the world / Little fluffy clouds / Perpetual dawn / Blue room / Assassin / Pomme Fritz / Toxygene / Outlands / DJ Asylum / Mickey Mars / Towers of dub (part 1) / Oxbow lakes. *(d-cd+=; CIDD 8078)* – (other mixes).

Nov 98. (d12"ep) *(12ISD 729)* **LITTLE FLUFFY CLOUDS (mixes:- Danny Tenaglia's downtempo groove / Danny Tenaglia's detour mix / Adam Freeland Tsunami one mix / Cumulo nimbus mix / One True Parker mix)** – -non –

Feb 01. (12"/cd-s) *(12IS/CID 767)* **ONCE MORE . . . / ONCE MORE (Bedrock edit 2) / LITTLE FLUFFY CLOUDS (Danny Tenaglia's detour mix)** 38 –
(cd-s) *(CIDX 767)* – ('A'-Mark Pritchard mixes).

Feb 01. (cd/d-lp) *(CID/ILPSD 8100)* <548206> **CYDONIA** □ □
– Once more . . . / Promise / Ghostdancing / Turn it down / Egnable / Firestar / A mile long lump of lard / Centuries / Plum island / Hamlet of kings / 1,1,1 / Thursday's keeper / Terminus.

Cooking Vinyl Sanctuary

May 04. (cd) *(COOKCD 298)* <84704> **BICYCLES & TRICYCLES** □ Jul04 □
– Orb is / Aftermath / The land of green ginger (remix) / Hell's kitchen / Gee strings / Prime evil / Abstractions (trance Pennine express) / From a distance / Tower twenty three / Rompania / Dilmun.

Kompakt not iss.

Nov 04. (12") *(KOMPAKT 106)* **KOMPLOTT** – German –
– Linik / Captain Korma / Falkenbruck.

Nov 05. (cd) *(KOMPAKT 45)* **OKIE DOKIE: IT'S THE ORB ON KOMPAKT** (compilation 2002-05) – German –
– Komplikation / Lunik TM / Ripples / Captain Korma / Kan kan / Rolo / Beatitude / Cool harbour / Traumvogel / Because – Before (Sibirische musik) / Tin kan / Kompagna (Zandic mix) / Falkenbruck / Snowbow.

– compilations, others, etc. –

Nov 91. (cd/c/lp) *Strange Fruit; (SFR CD/MC/LP 118)* **THE PEEL SESSIONS** □ –
– A huge ever growing brain that rules from the centre of the ultraworld. *(re-iss. Apr96; same)*

F.F.W.D.

aka **ROBERT FRIPP** – guitar / **THOMAS FEHLMANN** – electronics / **KRIS WESTON** – electronics / **DR. ALEX PATERSON**

Intermodo not iss.

Aug 94. (cd/c/d-lp) *(INTA 001 CD/TC/LP)* **F.F.W.D.** 48 –
– Hidden / Lucky saddle / Drone / Hempire / Collosus / What time is clock / Can of bliss / Elauses / Meteor storm / Buckwheat and grits / Klangtest / Suess wie eine nuss.

Roy ORBISON

Born: 23 Apr'36, Vernon, Texas, USA. After stints with local hillbilly groups The WINK WESTERNERS and The TEEN KINGS, he cut a solo single for the 'Jewel' label in 1955 before successfully auditioning for Sam Phillips' 'Sun' records. Written by two college friends, WADE MOORE and DICK PENNER, 'OOBY DOOBY' gave him his first Top 60 hit in 1956. Subsequent 50's rockabilly/pop singles for 'Sun' and 'R.C.A.' all failed, and after moving to Nashville with his wife, ORBISON focused his attentions on songwriting. 'CLAUDETTE' (written for his wife), was placed in the capable hands of The EVERLY BROTHERS who took the uptempo song into the US Top 30 (another, 'DISTANT DRUMS', was a massive hit for JIM REEVES, reaching No.1 after his untimely death in '66). In 1959, his solo career was re-activated when 'Monument' took the reins, ORBISON embracing a more ballad-esque approach which highlighted his lyrical genius, dramatic falsetto voice and trademark tearful crescendos. It was an approach which was to make the country boy a bonafide star; the following year, 'ONLY THE LONELY' was first of many million sellers throughout the early to mid sixties period. Classic after classic saw ROY O become a regular chart fixture, the likes of 'RUNNING SCARED', 'CRYING', 'DREAM BABY', 'IN DREAMS', 'BLUE BAYOU', 'IT'S OVER' and 'OH PRETTY WOMAN' transcending the era while his contemporaries sounded somewhat dated. His ubiquitous dark glasses were initially worn in 1963 after his regular spectacles were misplaced on a plane. In November '64, at the height of his success, ORBISON divorced Claudette due to her infidelity. Reconciled, they remarried in August '65, although tragedy struck ten months later when she was killed as her motorcycle hit a truck. Later that year, ROY O began a short-lived acting career, although his initial movie experience, 'The Fastest Guitar Alive', did poorly at the box-office. Nevertheless his solo career was still flourishing, especially in the UK, where his more countrified material was going down reasonably well. However, another tragedy befell him on the 14th September '68; while on tour, ORBISON's house caught fire, killing his two oldest sons, Roy Jr. and Tony. Understandably, perhaps, he subsequently semi-retired in 1970 to Bielefeld, Germany with his remaining son and new German-born wife, Barbara Wellhonen; together they reared another son, Roy Kelton. ORBISON's recording career went through a minor comeback (i.e. a cameo in the film 1980, 'Roadie', with Emmylou Harris duetting 'You've Lost That Lovin' Feelin') before he sued Wesley Rose (head of 'Monument') for $50m in backdated royalties. In 1987, his career finally got back on track as he signed to 'Virgin' and began making new inroads into world popularity. The following year, he joined the TRAVELING WILBURYS, alongside other superstars, BOB DYLAN, GEORGE HARRISON, JEFF LYNNE and TOM PETTY. Their 'VOLUME 1' album became a US Top 3 and UK Top 20 later in the year, although tragically ROY O was to die of a heart attack on the 6th of December. The legend had just completed a tremendous comeback album, 'MYSTERY GIRL', which posthumously peaked in the British and American Top 5 (would've anyway!). One of the record's highlights, 'YOU GOT IT', gave the man his first entry into the US Top 10 for nearly 25 years. His 1987 concert, 'A BLACK & WHITE NIGHT', featured guest appearances by the cream of the roots-rock aristocracy including k.d. LANG (on a duet of 'CRYING' which became a UK Top 10 hit), BRUCE SPRINGSTEEN, TOM WAITS, BONNIE RAITT, JACKSON BROWNE and ELVIS COSTELLO among others . . .

• **Songwriters:** A brilliant poet of our time, ROY wrote most of the songs himself, at times collaborating in the 60's with JOE MELSON (1960-1963 + 1967) and BILL DEES (1964-66). His final material in the late 80's, was co-written w / JEFF LYNNE & TOM PETTY. Covered CANDY MAN (Fred Neil) / MEAN WOMAN BLUES (Elvis Presley) / LET THE GOOD TIMES ROLL (Shirley & Lee) / THE COMEDIANS (Elvis Costello) / SHE'S A MYSTERY TO ME (U2) / I DROVE ALL NIGHT (Cyndi Lauper) / AFTER THE LOVE HAS GONE (Earth, Wind & Fire). His songs, 'BLUE BAYOU' and 'CRYING', were huge hits for LINDA RONSTADT and DON McLEAN respectively.

Best CD compilation: THE VERY BEST OF ROY ORBISON (*9)

ROY ORBISON – vocals with early **BOB MOORE** – bass / **BILLY PAT ELLIS** – drums

not iss. — Je-Wel

Jan 56. (7",78; by TEEN KINGS) <101> **OOBY DOOBY. / TRYING TO GET TO YOU** [–]

Sun — Sun

May 56. (7",78; ROY ORBISON & The TEEN KINGS) <242> **OOBY DOOBY. / GO! GO! GO!** [–] [59]

Sep 56. (7",78; ROY ORBISON & The TEEN KINGS) <251> **ROCK HOUSE. / YOU'RE MY BABY** [–]
(UK-iss.1964 on 'Ember'; EMBS 197)

Nov 56. (7",78; ROY ORBISON & The ROSES) <265> **SWEET AND EASY TO LOVE. / DEVIL DOLL** [–]

Dec 57. (7",78) <284> **CHICKEN HEARTED. / I LIKE LOVE** [–]

May 58. (7",78) <353> **SWEET AND EASY TO LOVE. / DEVIL DOLL** [–]

not iss. — RCA Victor

Sep 58. (7",78) <7381> **SWEET AND INNOCENT. / SEEMS TO ME** [–]

Dec 58. (7",78) <7447> **ALMOST 18. / JOLIE** [–]

London — Monument

Jul 59. (7",78) <409> **PAPER BOY. / WITH THE BUG** [–]

Dec 59. (7",78) <412> **UPTOWN. / PRETTY ONE** [–] [72]

Jun 60. (7",78) *(HLU 9149)* <421> **ONLY THE LONELY. / HERE COMES THAT SONG AGAIN** [1] May60 [2]

Oct 60. (7") *(HLU 9207)* <425> **BLUE ANGEL. / TODAY'S TEARDROPS** [11] Sep60 [9]

1961. (lp) *(HA-U 2342)* <14002> **LONELY AND BLUE** Dec60
– Only the lonely / Bye bye love / Cry / Blue avanue / I can't stop loving you / Come back to me (my love) / Blue angel / Raindrops / (I'd be) A legend in my time / I'm hurtin' / Twenty-tow days / I'll say it's my fault. *(UK re-dist.May63, hit No.15)*

Mar 61. (7") *(HLU 9307)* <433> **I'M HURTIN'. / I CAN'T STOP LOVING YOU** Dec60 [27]

May 61. (7") *(HLU 9342)* <438> **RUNNING SCARED. / LOVE HURTS** [9] Apr61 [1]
(re-iss. 1975 on 'Monument')

Sep 61. (7") *(HLU 9405)* <447> **CRYING. / CANDY MAN** [25] [2] Aug61 [25]
(re-iss. 1975 on 'Monument')

Feb 62. (7") *(HLU 9511)* <456> **DREAM BABY. / THE ACTRESS** [2] [4]

May 62. (lp) *(HA-U 2437)* <4007> **CRYING** Apr62 [21]
– Crying / The great pretender / Love hurts / She wears my ring / Wedding day / Summersong / Dance / Lana / Loneliness / Let's make a memory / Nite life / Running scared. *(UK re-dist.Jun63, hit No.17)*

Jun 62. (7") *(HLU 9561)* <461> **THE CROWD. / MAMA** [40] [26]

Aug 62. (lp) <4009> **ROY ORBISON'S GREATEST HITS** (compilation) [–] [14]
– The crowd / Love star / Crying / Evergreen / Running scared / Mama / Candy man / Only the lonely / Dream baby / Blue angel / Uptown / I'm hurtin'. *(UK-iss.Sep67; 5007)* – hit No.40

Oct 62. (7") *(HLU 9607)* <467> **WORKIN' FOR THE MAN. / LEAH** [50] [33] [25]
(re-iss. 1975 on 'Monument')

Feb 63. (7") *(HLU 9676)* <806> **IN DREAMS. / SHAHDOROBA** [6] [7]

May 63. (7") *(HLU 9727)* <815> **FALLING. / DISTANT DRUMS** [9] [22]

Sep 63. (7") *(HLU 9777)* <824> **BLUE BAYOU. / MEAN WOMAN BLUES** [3] [29] [5]
(re-iss. 1975 on 'Monument')

Nov 63. (lp) *(HA-U/SH-U 8180)* <18003> **IN DREAMS** [6] Aug 63 [35]
– In dreams / Lonely wine / Shahdaroba / No one will ever know / Sunset / House without windows / Dream / Blue bayou / (They call you) Gigolette / All I have to do is dream / Beautiful dreamer / My prayer.

Dec 63. (7") <830> **PRETTY PAPER. / BEAUTIFUL DREAMER** [–] [15]
(UK-iss.1975 on 'Monument')

Feb 64. (7") *(HLU 9845>* **BORNE ON THE WIND. / WHAT'D I SAY** [15] [–]

Apr 64. (7") *(HLU 9882)* <837> **IT'S OVER. / INDIAN WEDDING** [1] [9]

Aug 64. (7") *(HLU 9919)* <851> **OH PRETTY WOMAN. / YO TE AMO MARIA** [1] [1]

—— (above featured/credited The CANDYMEN)

Sep 64. (lp) <18024> **MORE OF ROY ORBISON'S GREATEST HITS** (compilation) [–] [19]
(UK-iss.1968; SMO 5014)

Nov 64. (7") <HLU 9930> **PRETTY PAPER. / SUMMER SONG** [6] [–]

Nov 64. (lp) *(HA-U 8207)* **OH PRETTY WOMAN** (compilation) [4] [–]
– Oh pretty woman / It's over / Falling / Indian wedding / Borne on the wind / Distant drums / The crowd / Yo te amo / Maria / Candy man / Mama.

Feb 65. (7") *(HLU 9951)* <873> **GOODNIGHT. / ONLY WITH YOU** [14] [21]

Jul 65. (7") *(HLU 9978)* <891> **(SAY) YOU'RE MY GIRL. / SLEEPY HOLLOW** [23] [39]

London — M.G.M.

Aug 65. (7") *(HLU 9986)* <13386> **RIDE AWAY. / WONDERIN'** [34] [25]

Sep 65. (lp) *(HA-U/SH-U 8252)* <4308> **THERE IS ONLY ONE ROY ORBISON** [10] [55]
– Ride away / You fool you / Two of a kind / This is your song / I'm in a blue, blue mood / If you can't say something nice / Claudette / Afraid to sleep / Sugar and honey / Summer love / Big as I can dream / Wondering.

Oct 65. (7") *(HLU 10000)* <13410> **CRAWLIN' BACK. / IF YOU CAN'T SAY SOMETHING NICE** [19] [46]

Jan 66. (7") *(HLU 10015)* <13446> **BREAKIN' UP IS BREAKIN' MY HEART. / WAIT** [22] [31]

Feb 66. (lp) *(HA-U/SH-U 8279)* <4322> **THE ORBISON WAY** [11]
– Crawling back / It ain't no big thing / Time changed everything / This is my land / The loner / Maybe / Breakin' up is breakin' my heart / Go away / A new star / Never / It wasn't very long ago / Why hurt the one who loves you.

Mar 66. (7") *(HLU 10034)* <13498> **TWINKLE TOES. / WHERE IS TOMORROW** [29] [39]

Jun 66. (7") *(HLU 10051)* **LANA. / HOUSE WITHOUT WINDOWS** [15] [–]
(above 45 an older 'Monument' recording)

Jul 66. (7") *(HLU 10067)* <13549> **TOO SOON TO KNOW. / YOU'LL NEVER BE SIXTEEN AGAIN** [–] [68]

Aug 66. (7") *(HLU 10067)* **TOO SOON TO KNOW. / YOU'LL NEVER BE SIXTEEN AGAIN** [3] [–]

Sep 66. (lp) *(HA-U/SH-U 8279)* <4379> **THE CLASSIC ROY ORBISON** [12]
– You'll never be sixteen again / Pantomine / Twinkle toes / Losing you / City life / Wait / Growing up / Where is tomorrow / I'll never get over you / Going back to Gloria / Never love again / Just another name for rock'n'roll. *(re-iss. +c+cd.Apr89 on 'Ocean'UK / 'Rhino'US)*

Nov 66. (7") *(HLU 10096)* **THERE WON'T BE MANY COMING HOME. / GOING BACK TO GLORIA** [18] [–]

Dec 66. (7") <13634> **COMMUNICATION BREAKDOWN. / GOING BACK TO GLORIA** [–] [60]

Feb 67. (7") *(HLU 10113)* <13685> **SO GOOD. / MEMORIES** [32]

1967. (lp) *(HA-U 8318)* <4424> **SINGS DON GIBSON**
– A legend in my time / I'm hurtin' / The same street / Far far away / Big hearted me / Sweet dreams / Oh, such a stranger / Blue blue day / What about me / Give myself a party / Too soon to know / Lonesome number one.

Aug 67. (7") *(HLU 10143)* <13764> **CRY SOFTLY, LONELY ONE. / PISTOLERO** [52]

Sep 67. (lp) *(HA-U/SH-U 8357) <4514>* **CRY SOFTLY, LONELY ONE**
– She / Communication breakdown / Cry softly, lonely one / Girl like me / It takes one to know one / That's a no-no / Just let me make believe / Here comes the rain baby / Memories / Time to cry / Only alive / Just one time.

Oct 67. (7") *(HLU 10159) <13817>* **SHE. / HERE COMES THAT SONG AGAIN**

Jan 68. (7") *(HLU 10176) <13889>* **BORN TO BE LOVED BY YOU. / SHY AWAY**

Jan 68. (lp; mono/stereo) *(HA-U/SH-U 8358) <E/SE 4475>* **THE FASTEST GUITAR ALIVE (Soundtrack)**
– Whirlwind / Medicine man / River / The fastest guitar alive / Rollin' on / Pistolero / Good time party / Heading south / Best friend / There won't be many coming home. *(re-iss. Jan89 on 'M.C.A.' lp/c; MCA/+C 1437) <cd-iss. 1985 on 'Columbia'; AK 45405> (cd-iss. Apr90 on 'M.G.M.'+=; CDMGM 18)* – Your Cheatin' Heart (HANK WILLIAMS JR.)

Jul 68. (7") *(HLU 10206) <13950>* **WALK ON. / FLOWERS** 39

Sep 68. (7") *(HLU 10222) <13991>* **HEARTACHE. / SUGARMAN** 44

1969. (lp) *<4559>* **GREAT SONGS** –

Apr 69. (7") *(HLU 10261) <14039>* **MY FRIEND. / SOUTHBOUND JERICO PATHWAY** 35

May 69. (lp) *<4636>* **MANY MOODS** –
– Truly, truly, true / Unchained melody / I recommend her / More / Heartache / Amy / Good morning, dear / What now my love / Walk on / Yesterday's child / Try to remember.

Aug 69. (7") *(HLU 109285) <14079>* **PENNY ARCADE. / TENNESSEE OWNS MY SOUL** 27

1969. (lp) *<4683>* **HANK WILLIAMS – THE ROY ORBISON WAY** –
– Kaw-liga / Jambalaya (on the bayou) / (Last night) I heard you crying in your sleep / You win again / Your cheatin' heart / Cold, cold heart / A mansion on the hill / I can't help it (if I'm still in love with you) / There'll be no teardrops tonight / I'm so lonesome I could cry.

Nov 69. (7") *(HLU 10294)* **BREAK MY MIND. / HOW DO YOU START OVER** –

Nov 69. (lp) *(HA-U/SH-U 8406)* **THE BIG 'O'** –
– Break my mind / Help me Rhonda / Money / Only you / Down the line / When I stop dreaming / Living touch / Land of 1000 dances / Scarlet ribbons / She won't head her love out / Casting spell / Penny arcade. *(UK iss.Oct75 & 1982 on 'Charly') (re-iss. +cd.May89 on 'Pickwick') (cd-iss. Feb93)*

—— (above credited The ART MOVEMENT)

1970. (7") *<14105>* **SHE CHEATS ON ME. / HOW DO YOU START OVER** –

Apr 70. (7") *(HLU 10310) <14121>* **SO YOUNG. / IF I HAD A WOMAN LIKE YOU**

Aug 71. (7") *(HLU 10339) <14293>* **(LOVE ME LIKE YOU DID IT) LAST NIGHT. / CLOSE AGAIN**

Feb 72. (7") *(HLU 10358) <14358>* **GOD LOVE YOU. / CHANGES**

1972. (7") *<14413>* **REMEMBER THE GOOD. / HARLEM WOMAN (or) IF ONLY FOR A WHILE** –

Sep 72. (7") *(HLU 10358) <14441>* **MEMPHIS TENNESSEE. / I CAN READ BETWEEN THE LINES**

1973. (lp) *(SH-U 8445) <4867>* **MEMPHIS**
– Memphis, Tennessee / Why a woman cries / Run baby run (back into my arms) / Take care of your woman / I'm the man on Susie's mind / I can't stop loving you / Run the engines up high / It ain't no big thing / I fought the law / The three bells / Danny boy.

1973. (7") *<14552>* **BLUE RAIN (COMING DOWN). / SOONER OR LATER** –

1973. (7") *<14626>* **I WANNA LIVE. / YOU LAY EASY ON MY MIND** –

1974. (lp) *<4934>* **MILESTONES** –

Mercury Mercury

Sep 74. (7") *(6167014) 73610>* **SWEET MAMA BLUE. / HEARTACHE**

Apr 75. (7") *(6167067) <73652>* **HUNG UP ON YOU. / SPANISH NIGHTS**

1975. (7") *<73705>* **IT'S LONELY. / STILL** –

1976. (lp) *<SRMI 1045>* **I'M STILL IN LOVE WITH YOU** –
– Pledging my love / Rainbow love / Heartache / Still / Circle / All I need is time / Spanish nights / It's lonely / Crying time / Hung up on you / Sweet mama blue. *(cd-iss. Aug89)*

Monument Monument

May 76. (7") *(MNT 4247) <8690>* **BELINDA. / NO CHAIN AT ALL**

Nov 76. (7") *(MNT 4797) <200>* **(I'M A) SOUTHERN MAN. / BORN TO LOVE ME**

Feb 77. (lp) *(81809) <7600>* **REGENERATION**
– (I'm a) Southern man / N chain at all / Old love song / Can't wait / Born to love me / Blues in my mind / Something they can't take away / Under suspicion / I don't really want you / Belinda.

Apr 77. (7") *(MNT 5151) <215>* **DRIFTING AWAY. / UNDER SUSPICION**

—— In 1978, he underwent major heart surgery, but steadily recovered.

Asylum Asylum

May 79. (7") *(K 13153) <46048>* **EASY WAY OUT. / TEARS**

Jul 79. (lp/c) *(K/K4 53092) <6E 198>* **LAMINAR FLOW**
– Easy way out / Love is a cold wind / Lay it down / I care / We're into something good / Movin' / Poor baby / Warm spot hot / Tears / Friday night / Hound dog man. *(cd-iss. Feb93)*

Sep 79. (7") *<46541>* **LAY IT DOWN. / POOR BABY** –

Nov 79. (7") *(K 12391)* **LAY IT DOWN. / WARM SPOT HOT** –

—— (below duet with **EMMYLOU HARRIS** from the film 'Roadie')

Warners Warners

Jun 80. (7") *<49262>* **THAT LOVING YOU FEELING AGAIN. / (b-by Craig Hindley)** – 55

Apr 81. (7") *(K 18432)* **UNTIL THE NIGHT IS OVER. / LONG WAY BACK TO LOVE** –

ZTT-Island Island

Aug 85. (7") *(ZTAS 9)* **WILD HEARTS (TIME). / WILD HEARTS (VOICELESS)**
(d7"+=) *(DZTAS 9)* – Ooby dooby (revive) / Crying (live).
(12"+=) *(12ZTAS 9)* – Ooby dooby / Wild hearts (and time again).

Virgin Virgin

Jun 87. (7") *(ROY 1) <99434>* **IN DREAMS. / LEAH**

Jul 87. (d-lp/c/cd) *(VGD/+C/CD 3524) <90604>* **IN DREAMS: THE GREATEST HITS** 86 Jan 89 95
– (new versions of old songs) Only the lonely / Leah / In dreams / Uptown / It's over / Crying / Dream baby / Blue angel / Working for the man / Candy man / Running scared / Falling / I'm hurtin' / Claudette / Oh pretty woman / Mean woman blues / Ooby dooby / Lana / Blue bayou.

—— In the fall of 1988, he teamed up with DYLAN, PETTY, HARRISON and LYNNE to form The TRAVELING WILBURYS. Tragedy struck on the 7th Dec'88, when ORBISON died of a heart attack. He had coincidentally just released comeback solo album.

Dec 88. (7") *(VS 1166) <99245>* **YOU GOT IT. / THE ONLY ONE** 3 9
(12"+=/3"cd-s+=) *(VS T/CD 1166)* – Crying (with k.d. LANG).

Jan 89. (cd/c/lp) *(CD/TC+/V 2576) <91058>* **MYSTERY GIRL** 2 5
– You got it / In the real world / (All I can do is) Dream you / A love so beautiful / California blue / She's a mystery to me / The comedians / The only one / Windsurfer / Careless heart.

Feb 89. (7") *(VS 1173)* **SHE'S A MYSTERY TO ME. / CRYING** 27
(12"+=/cd-s+=) *(VS T/CD 1173)* – Dream baby (live).

Feb 89. (7") *<99227>* **SHE'S A MYSTERY TO ME. / DREAM BABY** –

Jul 89. (7") *(VS 1193) <99202>* **CALIFORNIA BLUE. / BLUE BAYOU (live with k.d. LANG)**
(12"+=) *(VST 1193)* – Leah (live).
(3"cd-s++=) *(VSCD 1193)* – In dreams (live).

Nov 89. (cd/c/lp; as ROY ORBISON & FRIENDS) *(CD/TC+/V 2601) <91295>* **A BLACK & WHITE NIGHT (live Sep'87)** 51
– Only the lonely / In dreams / Dream baby (how long must I dream) / Leah / Move on down the line / Crying / Mean woman blues / Running scared / Blue bayou / Candy man / Uptown / Ooby dooby / The comedians / (All I can do is) Dream you / It's over / Oh, pretty woman. *(re-iss. c+cd.Aug91; same) (cd re-iss. Mar03 on 'Orbison'; ROBW 7891)*

Nov 89. (7") *(VS 1224) <99159>* **OH PRETTY WOMAN ('87 version). / CLAUDETTE**
(12"+=/cd-s+=) *(VS T/CD 1224)* – ('A'-lp version).

– (selective) compilations, etc. –

Jul 64. (lp) *Ember; (NR 5013)* **THE EXCITING SOUNDS OF ROY ORBISON** 17 –

Oct 65. (7") *Monument; <906>* **LET THE GOOD TIMES ROLL. / DISTANT DRUMS** – 81

Dec 65. (lp) *Monument; (SMO 5004)* **ORBISONGS**
(UK-iss.Jul67) – hit No.40 *(cd-iss. Dec95)*

Date	Release	UK	US
Sep 66.	(lp) *Monument; <6622>* **THE VERY BEST OF ROY ORBISON**		94
Jan 73.	(d-lp) *Monument; (MNT 67290)* **ALL-TIME GREATEST HITS** *(cd-iss. Jan89) (re-iss. +cd.Dec88 on 'Skyline')*	39	
Nov 75.	(lp) *Arcade; (ADEP 19)* **THE BEST OF ROY ORBISON**	1	–
Jul 81.	(lp/c) *Monument-CBS; (MNT/40 10026)* **GOLDEN DAYS** *(cd-iss. Jun92 & Jul98; 4715559)*	63	
Sep 84.	(d-lp) *Charly; (CDX 4)* **THE SUN YEARS 1956-1958: THE DEFINITIVE COLLECTION** *(cd-iss. Apr89 on 'Bear Family'; BCD 15461)*		–
Oct 88.	(lp/c/cd) *Telstar; (STA R/C/TCD 2330)* **THE LEGENDARY ROY ORBISON** – It's over / Only the lonely / Goodnight / Lana / The crowd / All I have to do is dream / Dream baby / Mean woman blues / Oh pretty woman / Love hurts / My prayer / Falling / Blue angel / In dreams / Blue bayou / The great pretender / Pretty paper.	1	–
Oct 90.	(cd/c/lp) *Telstar; (STA TCD/C/R 2441)* **BALLADS – 22 CLASSIC LOVE SONGS**	38	–
1991.	(cd) *Magnum Force; (CDMF 079)* **LEGEND IN HIS TIME**		–
Jun 92.	(7"/c-s) *M.C.A.; (MCS/+MC 1652) <54287>* **I DROVE ALL NIGHT. / FOREVER FRIENDS (with SHEENA EASTON)** (cd-s+=) *(MCSCD 1652)* – Trickster:- Line of fire.	7	
Aug 92.	(7"/c-s; ROY ORBISON & k.d. LANG) *Virgin America; (VUS/+CS 63)* **CRYING. / FALLING** (cd-s+=) *(CDVUS 63)* – Oh pretty woman / She's a mystery to me. (cd-s+=) *(CDXVUS 63)* – Only the lonely / It's over.	13	
Oct 92.	(7"/c-s) *Virgin America; (VUS/+CS 68)* **HEARTBREAK RADIO. / CRYING (with k.d. LANG)** (cd-s) *(CDVUS 68)* – ('A'side) / In dreams / You got it / Dream baby. (cd-s) *(CDVUSX 68)* – ('A'side) / Blue angel / Claudette / Lana.	36	
Nov 92.	(lp/c/cd) *Virgin; (VUSLP/VUSMC/CDVUS 58)* **KING OF HEARTS** (1988 recordings) – You're the one / Heartbreak radio / We'll take the night / Crying (with k.d.LANG) / After the love has gone / Love in time / I drove all night / Wild hearts run out of time / Coming home / Careless heart (original demo).	23	
Jun 93.	(3xcd-box) *Sequel; (NXTCD 246)* **THE GOLDEN DECADE 1960-1969**		–
Nov 93.	(cd) *Monument; (4749562)* **LONELY AND BLUE / CRYING**		
Nov 93.	(cd) *Monument; (4749572)* **IN DREAMS / ORBISONGS**		
Nov 93.	(7"/c-s) *Virgin America; (VUS/+CS 79)* **I DROVE ALL NIGHT. / CRYING** (cd-s+=) *(CDVUS 79)* – Oh pretty woman / After the love has gone.	47	
Oct 95.	(3xcd-box) *K-Box; (KBOX 344)* **ROY ORBISON**		
Jun 96.	(cd) *Charly; (CPCD 8180)* **ROCKER: THE SUN YEARS** *(re-iss. Jun01 on 'Snapper'; SNAP 023CD)*		
Nov 96.	(cd/c) *Virgin; (CDV/TCV 2804)* **THE VERY BEST OF ROY ORBISON**	18	
Dec 97.	(cd) *Institute Of Art; (RTD 3970023CD)* **MY BOOK OF DREAMS**		
Mar 98.	(cd) *Eagle; (EABCD 095)* **THE MASTERS**		
Jul 98.	(cd/c) *Columbia; (463350-2/-4)* **THE BEST OF ROY ORBISON**		
Jul 98.	(cd) *Monument; (480570-2)* **THE DEFINITIVE COLLECTION**		
Oct 98.	(cd/c) *Monument; (492743-2/-4)* **THE BIG O: THE ORIGINAL SINGLES COLLECTION**		
Aug 99.	(d-cd) *Snapper; (SMDCD 181)* **THE ESSENTIAL SUN COLLECTION**		
Sep 99.	(cd) *Platinum; (PLATCD 503)* **THE ROCK'N'ROLL BALLADS**		
Oct 99.	(cd) *Castle Pie; (PIESD 147)* **DOMINO – ROY ROCKS**		
Jan 00.	(cd/c) *Monument; (466712-2/-4)* **LOVE SONGS**		
May 00.	(cd) *Music; (CD 41003)* **THE SUN YEARS: ORIGINAL SUN RECORDINGS**		
Jul 00.	(3xcd-box) *Goldies; (GLD 3540-2)* **OH PRETTY WOMAN**		
Jul 00.	(cd) *Members Edition; (UAE 31212)* **ROY ORBISON & FRIENDS**		
Sep 00.	(cd/c) *Castle Pulse; (PLS CD/MC 373)* **ROCK'N'ROLL**		
Nov 00.	(cd) *Disky; (SI 99892-2)* **GOLD**		
Jan 01.	(cd/c) *Virgin TV; (VTD CD/MC 360)* **LOVE SONGS**	4	–
Aug 01.	(7xcd-box) *Bear Family; (BCD 16423)* **ORBISON**		
Feb 02.	(cd) *Mercury; (838433-2)* **I'M STILL IN LOVE WITH YOU**		
Feb 02.	(cd) *Virgin; (CDV 2958)* **THE LOVE ALBUM**		
Mar 02.	(cd) *Sony; (506214-2)* **SINGS THE TEARJERKERS**		
Oct 02.	(cd/c) *Music Club; (MCCD/MCTC 507)* **BIG HITS FROM THE BIG O**		
Nov 02.	(cd) *Planet Media; (PML 1087)* **HITS LIVE**		
Feb 03.	(cd) *Metro; (METRCD 100)* **THE ESSENTIAL SUN YEARS**		
Mar 03.	(cd) *Orbison; (HCC 19650)* **COMBO CONCERT**		
Jun 03.	(cd) *Traditional Line; (TL 1316)* **BLUE BAYOU**		
Aug 04.	(t-cd) *Virgin; (VTDCDX 632) <571436>* **THE PLATINUM COLLECTION**	16 Oct04	

ORBITAL

Formed: Seven Oaks, London, England . . . late 80's by brothers PHIL and PAUL HARTNOLL. United by a shared love of electro and punk, they were inspired by the outdoor party scene of '89 and named themselves after the infamous circular motorway which ravers used in delirious pursuit of their next E'd-up shindig. A home produced 4-track demo, 'CHIME', brought the band almost instant fame and remains one of their best loved songs. Originally released on the small 'Oh-Zone' label, the track was given a full release in March 1990 on 'London' offshoot 'Ffrr', it's subtly euphoric charms elevating 'CHIME' into the top 20 and the brothers onto a memorable 'Top Of The Pops' appearance where they sported defiant 'No Poll Tax' t-shirts. Although dance culture has since become increasingly politiscized as a result of heavy handed legislation, it was unusual at the time for a techno act to be so passionately anti-establishment, an ethos the HARTNOLL brothers had carried over from their punk days and which would become a recurring theme throughout their career. Meanwhile, ORBITAL followed their debut with a trio of largely instrumental, synth-driven singles, the highlight being the pounding white noise of the BUTTHOLE SURFERS-sampling 'SATAN'. The track reached No.31 upon its release in August '91 although a subsequent live version stormed into the top 5 earlier this year. Their untitled debut album, released in September of the same year, showcased cerebral electronic soundscapes which nevertheless retained a melancholy, organic warmth while their live shows moved feet and minds en masse. Alongside events like the Shamen's Synergy, which attempted to mix the spectacle of rock 'n' roll with the communal energy of house, ORBITAL were pivotal in pioneering dance music in the live evironment. Rather than reproducing the songs live on stage, they improvised, restructuring tracks which had been pre-set into sequencers. This spontaneity was enhanced by an innovative light show utilising state of the art technology, a heady combination that saw ORBITAL headline the Glastonbury festival two years running during the mid-90's. They were no less effective in the studio and their second untitled album was a finely tuned extension of the debut, encompassing such exotica as a sample from an Australian pedestrian crossing (!) With their third long player, 1994's cynically titled 'SNIVILISATION', the music took on an uneasy paranoia, seething with a bitter undercurrent that railed against the state of humanity in general, as well as issues closer to home such as the much hated Criminal Justice Bill. The record also introduced elements of drum 'n' bass, a dalliance that continued with their 'IN SIDES' album. Preceded by the near-half hour strangeness of 'THE BOX' single, the record marked the pinnacle of ORBITAL's sonic explorations, a luminous trip to the final frontiers of electronica. In spite of their experimentalism, a loyal following ensures that the duo are never short of chart success, the 'IN SIDES' album reaching No.5, while 1997 saw ORBITAL go top 3 in the singles chart twice (first with the aforementioned live version of 'SATAN' and then with their celebrated remake of 'THE SAINT'). After a slight delay, ORBITAL were back in circulation with a fifth set, 'THE MIDDLE OF NOWHERE' (1999), a happier affair that was premiered by hit single, 'STYLE'; the album also saw POOKA singers NATASHA JONES and SHARON LEWIS collaborate on the track, 'OTONO'. Not content with sticking to their staple, ORBITAL tried to cross the boundaries on their 2001 album 'THE ALTOGETHER', a strange mix of the group's previous six albums tempered by the arrival of guest vocalists et al. Prog rockers TOOL were sampled by the group on the swirling 'SURFIN' BIRD', while the duo tried desperately to jump on the indie bandwagon courtesy of the awful DAVID GRAY collaboration 'ILLUMINATE'. ORBITAL even attempted to pull off a remix of the DR. WHO theme, with hilarious consequences, whereas tracks 'OI!' and 'SHADOWS' saw a warm return to the group's previous works. 2002 saw the release of both the Top 40 'REST AND PLAY' EP, and the greatest hits set, 'WORK 1989-2002'. While the latter featured most of the essential tracks from the band's early period, the inclusion of the aforementioned 'ILLUMINATE' only served to highlight the glaring quality differential. The 'OCTANE' (2003) soundtrack was also slightly below par, suitably atmospheric in its TANGERINE DREAM-esque meandering but lacking the dark menace and rhythmic celebration of their best work. It wasn't so much of a shock when the group announced their own demise in summer 2004, signing off with the backwards glance of 'BLUE ALBUM' (2004). A largely dark, motorik revisitation of techno's formative years and salad days, the album sounded out of place in the mid-00s but then that was probably the point. Guests included SPARKS on the old skool 808 rave-up, 'ACID PANTS' and DEAD CAN DANCE chanteuse turned soundtrack composer LISA GERRARD on the luminous wand-waving nostalgia of 'ONE PERFECT SUNRISE', a UK Top 30 hit. The album itself languished just outside the Top 40, a far cry from the days when a new HARTNOLL brothers record was guaranteed Top 5. A more concise compilation, 'HALCYON', finally bookended the band's discography in 2005.

• **Songwriters:** The duo, except cover of THE SAINT (E. Astley) and noted samples; O EUCHARI (performed by Emily Van Evera). • **Trivia:** Vox on tracks 'SAD BUT TRUE' & 'ARE WE HERE?' by ALISON GOLDFRAPP.

Album rating: UNTITLED (ORBITAL 1) (*7) / UNTITLED (ORBITAL II) (*7) / SNIVILIZATION (*8) / IN SIDES (*9) / EVENT HORIZON soundtrack w/ Michael Kamen (*5) / THE MIDDLE OF NOWHERE (*8) / THE ALTOGETHER (*6) / WORK 1989-2002 compilation (*8) / OCTANE soundtrack (*5) / BLUE ALBUM (*4) / HALCYON compilation (*6)

PHIL HARTNOLL (b. 9 Jan'64) – keyboards / **PAUL HARTNOLL** (b.19 May'68) – keyboards

Oh-Zone — not iss.

Jan 90. (12"ep) *(ZONE 001)* **CHIME. / DEEPER (full version)** [ ] [–]

Ffrr-London — Ffrr-London

Mar 90. (7"/c-s) *(F/+CS 135)* **CHIME. / DEEPER** [ ] [–]
(cd-ep+=) *(FCD 135)* – ('A'version).
(12"ep) *(FX 135)* – ('A'-JZM remix) / ('A'-Bacardi mix).

Jul 90. (7"ep) *(F 145)* **OMEN. / 2 DEEP / OPEN MIND** [ ] [–]
(cd-ep) *(FCD 145)* – (1st & 3rd track) / ('A'edit)
(12"ep) *(FX 145)* – Omen: The chariot / The tower / Wheel of fortune / The fool.
(12"ep) *(FXR 145)* – ('A'remixes).

Jan 91. (7") *(F 149)* **SATAN. / BELFAST** [31] [–]
(12"ep+=/cd-ep+=) *(FX/FCD 149)* – L.C.1. *(cd-ep re-iss. Aug95 on 'Internal'; LIECD 25)*
(12"ep) *(FXR 149)* – ('A'-rhyme & reason mix) / L.C.2 (outer limits mix) / Chime.

Aug 91. (12"/c-s) *(FX/FCS 163)* **MIDNIGHT. / CHOICE** [ ] [–]
(cd-s+=) *(FCD 163)* – Analogue test 90. *(re-iss. Aug95 on 'Internal'; LIECD 26)*
(12") *(FX 163)* – Midnight (Sasha mix) / Choice (Orbital & Eye & I mix).
(cd-s+=) *(FXCD 163)* – Analogue test 90 (remix).

Sep 91. (cd/c/lp) *(828248-2/-4/-1)* <351001> **UNTITLED (ORBITAL 1)** [71] [ ]
– The moebius / Speed freak / Oolaa / Desert storm / Fahrenheit 303 / Steel cube idolatry / High rise / Chime (live) / Midnight (live) / Belfast / Macrohead. *(cd w-out last track, repl. by)* – I think it's disgusting. *(c+=)* – Untitled. *(re-iss. Apr96 & Apr97 on 'Internal' cd/c; TRU CD/MC 9) (re-iss. Apr99 on 'London' cd/c; 828248-2/-4) (cd re-iss. Oct00 on 'Warners'; 3984 28230-2)*

Feb 92. (12"ep) *(FX 181)* **MUTATIONS (I): OOLAA (Joey Beltram remix) / OOLAA (Meat Beat Manifesto mix) / CHIME (Joey Beltram). / SPEED FREAK (Moby mix)** [24] [–]
(12"ep) *(FXR 181)* – MUTATIONS (II): Chime (Ray Keith mix) / Chime (Crime remix) / Steel cube idolatory / Farenheit 303.
(cd-ep) *(FCD 181)* – Oolaa (Joey Beltram mix) / Chime (Ray Keith mix) / Speed freak / Fahrenheit 303.

Internal — Ffrr-London

Sep 92. (12"ep/cd-ep) *(LIARX/LIECD 1)* **RADICCIO EP** [37] [–]
– Halycon / The naked and the dead.
(cd-ep) *(LIECD 2)* – The naked and the dead / Sunday.
(cd-ep re-iss. Aug95; LIECD 27)

Apr 93. (12"ep/c-ep) *(LIARX/LIEMC 7)* **LUSH 3-1. / LUSH 3-2 / LUSH 3-3 (Underworld mix)** [ ] [–]
(12"ep) *(LIAXR 7)* – LUSH 3-4 (Psychick Warriors Ov Gaia) / LUSH 3-5 (CJ Bollard).
(cd-ep) *(LIECD 7)* – (all 5 tracks).

Jun 93. (cd/c/lp) *(TRU CD/MC/LP 2)* <351026> **UNTITLED (ORBITAL II)** [28] [ ]
– Time becomes / Planet of the shapes / Lush 3-1 / Lush 3-2 / Impact (the Earth is burning) / Remind / Walk now . . . / Monday / Halycon + on + on / Input out. *(re-iss. Aug95; same) (re-iss. Apr99 on 'London' cd/c; 828386-2/-4) (cd re-iss. Oct00 on 'Warners'; 3942 28231-2)*

Mar 94. (cd-ep/12"ep) *(LIECD/LIARX 12)* **THE JOHN PEEL SESSIONS EP** [ ] [–]
– Lush (Euro-tunnel disaster '94) / Walk about / Semi detached / Attached.
(cd-ep) **DIVERSIONS EP** *(LIEDC 12)* – Impact USA / Lush 3 (Euro-Tunnel disaster '94) / Walkabout / Lush 3-5 (CJ Bolland) / Lush 3-4 (Warrior drift) / Lush 3-4 (Underworld).

Aug 94. (cd/c/d-lp) *(TRU CD/MC/LP 5)* <124027> **SNIVILIZATION** [4] [ ]
– Forever / I wish I had duck feet / Sad but true / Crash and carry / Science friction / Philosophy by numbers / Kein trink wasser / Quality seconds / Are we here? / Attached. *(re-iss. Aug95 & Apr97; same) (re-iss. Apr99 on 'London' cd/c; 828536-2/-4) (cd re-iss. Oct00 on 'Warners'; 3984 28233-2)*

Sep 94. (12"ep/c-ep) *(LIARX/LIEMC 15)* **ARE WE HERE? EP** [33] [–]
– Are we here?: Who are they? – Do they here? – They did it (mix).
(cd-ep+=/s-cd-ep+=) *(LIE CD/DC 15)* – Are we here?: What was that? – Criminal Justice bill? – Industry standard?.

— In May'95, they issued 'Belfast'/'Wasted (vocal mix)' on special cd-s which hit UK No.53. THERAPY? was on flip side with 'Innocent X'.

Aug 95. (d7"ep/12"ep/cd-ep/s-cd-ep) *(LIE/LIARX/LIECD/LIEDP 23)* **UNTITLED EP** [ ] [–]
– Times fly (slow) / Sad but new / Times fly (fast) / The tranquilizer.
(above was not eligible for UK chart position due to it's length)

Apr 96. (12"/cd-s) *(LIARX/LIECD 30)* **THE BOX. / THE BOX** [11] [–]
(cd-s+=) *(LICDP 30)* – (2 extra mixes).

Apr 96. (cd/cd/c/3x12"lp) *(TRU DC/CD/MC/LP 10)* <124087> **IN SIDES** [5] [ ]
– The girl with the sun in her head / P.E.T.R.O.L. / The box / Dwr budr / Adnan's / Out there somewhere? *(cd re-iss. Apr97 on 'Dutch East India' 124129CD) (cd re-iss. Apr99 on 'London'; 828881-2) (cd re-iss. Oct00 on 'Warners'; 3984 28232-2)*

Jan 97. (cd-s) *(LIECD 37)* <850990> **SATAN (live at New York) / OUT THERE SOMEWHERE (live at New York)** [3] Sep97 [ ]
(cd-s) *(LICDP 37)* – ('A'-live at Chelmsford) / Lush 3 (live at Boston) / The girl with the sun in her head (live at Boston).
(cd-s) *(LICDD 37)* – ('A'-Industry standard edit) / Chime (live at Chelmsford) / Impact (live at Chelmsford).

— (due to length of above it also hit No.48 in the UK album charts)

ffrr-London — ffrr-London

Apr 97. (c-s/12"/cd-s) *(FCS/FX/FCD 296)* **THE SAINT / THE SINNER** [3] [ ]
(cd-s+=) *(FCDP 296)* – Belfast (live) / Petrol (live).

Sep 97. (cd/c; by MICHAEL KAMEN & ORBITAL) *(<828939-2/-4>)* **EVENT HORIZON** (soundtrack) ☐ Oct97 ☐
– The foward decks: a) Lewis and Clark, b) Neptune, c) Claire, d) First containment, e) Core, f) Metal, g) Second containment, h) Airlock / The main access corridor: a) Singularity, b) Ducts, c) Turbulence, d) Medical, e) Gravity drive / Engineering: a) Tomb, b) Blood, c) Countdown, d) Outer door, e) Bio scan / The Event Horizon: a) Weir, b) Event Horizon.

Mar 99. (12") *(FX 358)* **STYLE. / OLD STYLE / BIG PIPE STYLE / NEW STYLE** 13 –
(cd-s) *(FCD 358)* – (first 2 tracks) / Mock Tudor.
(cd-s) *(FCDP 358)* – (third & fourth tracks) / An fhomhair.

Apr 99. (cd/c/d-lp) *(556076-2/-4/-1) <31065>* **THE MIDDLE OF NOWHERE** 4 ☐
– Way out – > / Spare parts express / Know where to run / I don't know you people / Otono / Nothing left 1 / Nothing left 2 / Style. *(cd re-iss. Oct00 on 'Warners'; 3984 27194-2)*

Jul 99. (cd-s) *(FCDP 365)* **NOTHING LEFT / (mixes; Way Out West / Schizoid man)** 32 –
(cd-s) *(FCD 365)* – Much ado about nothing left / Nothing left out / Nothing left (Tsunami one remix).

Feb 00. (12"/cd-s; by ORBITAL & ANGELO BADALAMENTI) *(FX/FCD 377)* **BEACHED / BEACHED (long) / DOCTOR LOOK OUT** 36 –

Apr 01. (cd-s) *(FCD 395)* **FUNNY BREAK (ONE IS ENOUGH) / (mixes; weekend ravers / Up mix by Layo & Bushwacka)** 21 –
(cd-s) *(FCDP 395)* – Beelzebeat / ('A'mix by Plump DJ's) / ('A'-Down mix by Layo & Bushwacka).
(12") *(FX 395)* – ('A'-weekend ravers + Plump DJ mixes).
(12") *(FXX 395)* – ('A'-Layo & Bushwacka Up & Down mixes).

Apr 01. (cd) *(8573 87782-2) <31167>* **THE ALTOGETHER** 11 May01 ☐
– Tension / Funny break (one is enough) / Oi! / Pay per view / Tootled / Last thing / Doctor? / Shadows / Waving not drowning / Illuminate / Meltdown.

May 02. (cd-ep) *(FCD 407)* **REST AND PLAY EP** 33 –
– Frenetic / Illuminate (with DAVID GRAY) / Chime (live style mix).
(cd-s) *(FCDP 407)* – (first 2 track/versions) / Monorail.
(12") *(FX 407)* – Frenetic (mix) / Chime (live style mix).

ffrr Rhino

Jun 02. (cd/d-lp) *(0927 46190-2/-1) <74493>* **WORK 1989-2002** (compilation) 36 Aug02 ☐
– Chime / Choice / Illuminate (with DAVID GRAY) / Satan / Nothing left / Halcyon and on and on / Impact / Are we here? / Style / The box / Frenetic (with LISA BILLSON) / Lush 3.1 / Funny break / Belfast.

E.M.I. not iss.

Oct 03. (cd/lp) *(593784-2/-1)* **OCTANE** (soundtrack) ☐ –
– Octane / Through the night / Strangeness in the night / Preacher / Moments of crisis / Frantic / Breaking and entering / Chasing the tanker / Total paranoia / Confrontation / Initiation / Meet the father / Blood is thicker / The road ahead.

Orbital A.T.O.

Jun 04. (cd) *(ORBITALCD 001) <21527>* **BLUE ALBUM** 44 Aug04 ☐
– Transient / Pants / Tunnel vision / Lost / You lot / Bath time / Acid pants / Easy serv / One perfect sunrise.

Jul 04. (cd-s) *(ORBITALCD 03)* **ONE PERFECT SUNRISE / WHAT HAPPENS NEXT?** 29 –
(12") *(ORBITALV 003)* – ('A'-Phil Hartnoll mix) / Acid pants (JDS mix).
(cd-s+=) *(ORBITALCD 003X)* – You lot (radio edit).

– compilations, etc. –

Sep 05. (cd) *WEA; (5101 10414-2)* **HALCYON** ☐ –
– Moebius / Chime / Belfast / Halcyon / Nothing left / Frenetic / Fahrenheit 303 / Box / Philosophy by numbers / Oi / Doctor.

the ORDINARY BOYS

Formed: Worthing, nr. Brighton, England ... 2002 (originally as NEXT IN LINE) by songwriter PRESTON, WILLIAM J. BROWN, JAMES GREGORY and CHARLES "Chuck" STANLEY, embodying their no-nonsense ethos with a name filched from a MORRISSEY song. Producer Stephen Street furthered the Mozzer connection, helming debut single, 'MAYBE SOMEDAY', in early 2004. 'Warners' took over the reins for the hit follow-ups, 'WEEK IN WEEK OUT' and 'TALK TALK TALK', very WELLER-esque titles which gave some indication of the group's blue collar Brit-pop credentials: the JAM, MADNESS, the BEAT and even GENE. The snappily titled UK Top 20 debut set, 'OVER THE COUNTER CULTURE' (2004), confirmed their love of uncomplicated, terrace-friendly song structures. After they re-grouped (with new drummer SIMON GOLDRING) in 2005, the crop-headed quartet unveiled the Two-Tone-centric Top 20 single, 'BOYS WILL BE BOYS', at least partly authenticated with the presence of BEAT offspring RANKING JUNIOR. The accompanying sophomore album, 'BRASSBOUND' (2005), repeated the Top 20 success of their debut, a cover of Locomotive's late 60s ska obscurity, 'RUDI'S IN LOVE', emphasising the album's Kingston-via-London soundclash. Yet the group might've languished in anonymity had it not been for PRESTON's well-timed arrival in the Celebrity Big Brother household (early January 2006), where he wooed – and subsequently paired-off with – non-celebrity housemate (and eventual victor) Chantelle. With PRESTON acquiting himself surprisingly well enough to excite the media gossip columns, 'Warners' took the opportunity to re-chart both the anthemic 'BOYS WILL..' single and 'BRASSBOUND' album.

• **Covers:** SUMMERTIME BLUES (Eddie Cochran) / THE KKK TOOK MY BABY AWAY (Ramones) / BABYLON'S BURNING (Ruts) / THIS COULD BE THE NIGHT (Burt Bacharach) / SET ME FREE (Kinks) / A PLACE IN THE SUN (Stevie Wonder) / MY GIRL (Madness).

Album rating: OVER THE COUNTER CULTURE (*7) / BRASSBOUND (*7)

(SAMUEL) PRESTON (b.16 Jan'82) – vocals, guitar / **WILLIAM J. BROWN** – guitar / **JAMES GREGORY** – bass / **CHARLES "CHUCK" STANLEY** – drums

B-Unique WEA

Feb 04. (7") *(BUN 0757)* **MAYBE SOMEDAY. / IN AWE OF THE AWFUL** ☐ –
(cd-s) *(BUN 075CDS)* – ('A') / Laughing from the sidelines.

WEA WEA

Apr 04. (7") *(WEA 372)* **WEEK IN WEEK OUT. / LIES** 36 –
(cd-s) *(WEA 372CD)* – ('A') / Hand in hand.

Jun 04. (7") *(WEA 377)* **TALK TALK TALK. / DREAMING IN COLOUR (dub)** 17 –
(cd-s+=) *(WEA 377CD2)* – Summertime blues / ('A'-video).
(cd-s) *(WEA 377CD1)* – ('A') / (Little) Bubble.

Jul 04. (cd/lp) *(2564 61674-2/-1) <674543>* **OVER THE COUNTER CULTURE** 19 Aug04 ☐
– Over the counter culture / The list goes on / Week in week out / Talk talk talk / Little bitch / Settle down / Weekend revolution / Maybe someday / Just a song / Seaside / In awe of awful / Robots and monkeys. *(ltd-cd w/free cd-ep+=; 5046 74543-2)* – live at the Carling Academy Birmingham 4th June 2004:- Life goes on / Little bubble / Talk talk talk / Maybe someday.

Sep 04. (7") *(WEA 379)* **SEASIDE. / HOW DO YOU SLEEP** 27 –
(cd-s) *(WEA 379CD1)* – ('A') / Nip it in the bud.
(cd-s) *(WEA 379CD2)* – ('A') / My love's coming down / All the things she said (live Radio 1 session) / ('A'-video).

— **SIMON GOLDRING** – drums; repl. CHARLES

Jun 05. (7"white) *(WEA 389)* **BOYS WILL BE BOYS. / THE KKK TOOK MY BABY AWAY** 16 –
(cd-s) *(WEA 389CD1)* – ('A') / We soldier on.
(cd-s) *(WEA 389CD2)* – ('A') / Quarter life crisis / ('A'-Lady Sovereign remix) / ('A'-video).

Jun 05. (cd) *(5046 79182-2)* **BRASSBOUND** 31 –
– Brassbound / Boys will be boys / Life will be the death of me / Thanks to the girl / On an island / One step forward (two steps back) / Skull and bones / Don't live too fast / Call to arms / A few home truths / Rudi's in love / Red letter day. *(ltd-cd w/dvd+=; 5046 79195-2)* – (DVD tracks).

Aug 05. (7") *(WEA 394)* **LIFE WILL BE THE DEATH OF ME. / BABYLON'S BURNING** 50 –
(cd-s) *(WEA 394CD1)* – ('A') / A place in the sun.
(cd-s) *(WEA 394CD2)* – ('A') / This could be the night / Set me free / ('A'-video).

— in Aug'05, LADY SOVEREIGN (featuring the ORDINARY BOYS) had a UK No.33 hit with '9 TO 5'

Jan 06. (re-7"/cd-s/cd-s) *(as prev.)* **BOYS WILL BE BOYS** 3 –

Jan 06. (re-cd) *(as prev.)* **BRASSBOUND** 11 –
B-Unique not iss.

May 06. (7"; as the ORDINARY BOYS Vs. LADY SOVEREIGN) *(BUN 1057)* **NINE2FIVE. / 9 TO 5 (the Ordinary Boys remix)** 6 –
(7") *(BUN 1057X)* – ('A') / On an island (live at Brixton Academy).
(cd-s) *(BUN 105CD)* – ('A') / My girl (featuring SUGGS live at Brixton Academy).

☐ ORGANISATION (see under ⇒ KRAFTWERK)

ORSON

Formed: Hollywood, California, USA ... 2000 by JASON PEBWORTH and GEORGE ASTASIO, naming themselves after acting giant, Orson Welles. Subsequently based in London, England, Texas-raised songwriter JASON and GEORGE enlisted other like-minded musicians KEVIN ROENTGEN, JOHNNY LONELY and CHRIS CANO to boost their Philly-inspired rawk; JASON's background was in the theatre. Their first major break came in October 2005 via In The City gig in Manchester which led to them inking a deal with 'Universal' that November. Downloaded to the max at iTunes, debut single, 'NO TOMORROW', went into the UK charts at No.5 the following February; it would be No.1 in March. Appearances around the country at various mini-festivals (i.e. Dundee, Falkirk, etc.) helped the hook-laden sunshine boys from across the pond get a foothold with the "real" music buying public who liked their blend of HALL & OATES meets 'CHILI PEPPERS fusion. A second single, 'BRIGHT IDEA', charted in May, and with their album, also called 'BRIGHT IDEA' (2006) topping the UK charts, it seemed there was no stopping ORSON.

• **Covered:** I CAN'T GO FOR THAT (NO CAN DO) (Hall & Oates).

Album rating: BRIGHT IDEA (*6)

JASON PEBWORTH – vocals, piano / **GEORGE ASTASIO** – guitar / **KEVIN ROENTGEN** – guitar / **JOHNNY LONELY** – bass / **CHRIS CANO** – drums
Universal Universal

Feb 06. (7") *(9876829)* **NO TOMORROW. / THE OKAY SONG** 1 –
(cd-s) *(9876828)* – ('A') / Everything / Jessie / ('A'-video).

May 06. (7") *(9857277)* **BRIGHT IDEA. / YOURS TRULY** 11 –
(cd-s) *(9856127)* – ('A') / I can go for that (no can do) / Last night (live at Konk).

May 06. (cd) *(9858366)* **BRIGHT IDEA** 1 –
– Bright idea / No tomorrow / Happiness / Already over / Downtown / Tryin' to help / So ahead of me / Last night / Look around / Save the world / The okay song.

Beth ORTON

Born: 14 Dec'70, East Dereham, Norfolk, England. A one-time Buddhist nun (after her mother died of cancer), she was discovered in 1991/2 by WILLIAM ORBIT who saw her performing in a play. Her collaborative work with ORBIT (on the Japanese-only 'SUPERPINKYMANDY' CD) was subsequently heard by The CHEMICAL BROTHERS and RED SNAPPER, the former act employing her downbeat but poignant vocals on the 1995 'Exit Planet Dust' album track, 'Alive Alone'. The following year, she found herself on the books of 'Heavenly' records, delivering her debut album, 'TRAILER PARK' soon after. An affecting blend of fragile folk and subtle lo-fi trip-hop rhythms, it won praise from such diverse camps as Folk Roots magazine and Mixmag (it was even nominated for the 1997 Mercury Music Prize). The same year (1997), BETH's four singles scored successively higher chart placings, the re-released 'SHE CRIES YOUR NAME', revealing the melancholy depths of her NICK DRAKE/SANDY DENNY-esque muse. The lanky ORTON (she's 6 feet tall) ended the year on a high note, collaborating with her long-time hero, TERRY CALLIER on the Top 40 EP 'BEST BIT'. The princess of bedsitter music served up a second helping of rich, thought-provoking tunes in the shape of 1999's 'CENTRAL RESERVATION'. A deserved UK Top 20 success (with guest appearances from BEN WATT, BEN HARPER, DAVE ROBACK and DR. JOHN), BETH also made some headway in the States where she had befriended BECK (to namecheck but a few). Songs such as 'STOLEN CAR', the title track (both Top 40 hits) and 'STARS ALL SEEM TO WEEP' were emotionally and lyrically attuned like paintings set on the deepest canvas taking every colour imaginable from palettes of silver. 'DAYBREAKER' (2002) paired ORTON's girl-next-door lilt with yet more A-list artists: RYAN ADAMS on 'CONCRETE SKY', and both ADAMS and EMMYLOU HARRIS harmonising on 'GOD SONG'; while the CHEMICAL BROTHERS returned to electro-fi the title track, and the swooning production came courtesy of EVERYTHING BUT THE GIRL's BEN WATT, there was the sense that the girlish folkie was finally outgrowing the growing pains. While critics were divided on its sombre merits, the record made the UK Top 10, the highest charting record of her career. 'THE COMFORT OF STRANGERS' (2006), with its end-of-the-rainbow sleeve art, was an altogether brighter sounding record. Produced by the ubiquitous JIM O'ROURKE, it found ORTON finally taking on the singer-songwriter mantle she'd been skirting throughout her career. While its UK Top 30 chart placing was perhaps a little disappointing, the album marked her first entry in the US Top 100, appropriate enough given the critical comparisons to classic Topanga Canyon.

• **Songwriters:** Most with rhythm section FRIEND and BARNES, except SHE CRIES YOUR NAME; she co-wrote this with WILLIAM ORBIT. Covered IT'S NOT THE SPOTLIGHT (Goffin – Goldberg) / I WISH I NEVER SAW THE SUNSHINE (Spector – Greenwich – Barry) / DON'T WANNA KNOW 'BOUT EVIL (John Martyn) / DOLPHINS (Fred Neil).

Album rating: SUPERPINKYMANDY (*5) / TRAILER PARK (*8) / CENTRAL RESERVATION (*8) / DAYBREAKER (*6) / PASS IN TIME compilation (*8) / COMFORT OF STRANGERS (*7)

BETH ORTON – vocals, acoustic guitar (ex-SPILL); with **TED BARNES** – guitar (of JUNCTIONS) / **ALI FRIEND** – double bass (of RED SNAPPER) / **WILL BLANCHARD** – drums (of SANDALS) / guest **DAVID BOULTER** – harmonium / + string section
not iss. Toshiba

1993. (cd) *(TOC 7984)* **SUPERPINKYMANDY** – Japan –
– Don't wanna know about evil / Faith will carry / Yesterday's gone / She cries your name / When you wake / Roll the dice / City blue / The prisoner / Where do you go / Release me.
Heavenly Dedicated

Jul 96. (7"one-sided) *(HVN 56)* **I WISH I NEVER SAW THE SUNSHINE** ☐ –

Sep 96. (10"ep/cd-ep) *(HVN 60 10/CD)* **SHE CRIES YOUR NAME / TANGENT. / SAFETY / IT'S NOT THE SPOTLIGHT** ☐ –

Oct 96. (cd/c/lp) *(HVNLP 17 CD/MC/LP)* <44007> **TRAILER PARK** 68 ☐
– She cries your name / Tangent / Don't need a reason / Live as you dream / Sugar boy / Touch me with your love / Whenever / How far / Someone's daughter / I wish I never saw the sunshine / Galaxy of emptiness.

Jan 97. (10"ep/cd-ep) *(HVN 64 10/CD)* **TOUCH ME WITH YOUR LOVE. / PEDESTAL / GALAXY OF EMPTINESS** 60 –

Mar 97. (c-ep/10"ep/cd-ep) *(HVN 65 CS/10/CD)* **SOMEONE'S DAUGHTER. / I WISH I NEVER SAW THE SUNSHINE / IT'S THIS I AM I FIND** 49 –

Jun 97. (c-s) *(HVN 68CS)* **SHE CRIES YOUR NAME (1997 version) / IT'S NOT THE SPOTLIGHT** 40 –
(10"+=/cd-s+=) *(HVN 68-10/CD)* – Bullet / Best bit.
Heavenly Heavenly

Dec 97. (c-ep; BETH ORTON featuring TERRY CALLIER) *(<HVN 72CS>)* **BEST BIT EP** 36 ☐
– Best bit / Skimming stone / Dolphins.
(12"ep+=/cd-ep+=) *(<HVN 72 12/CD>)* – Lean on me.

— next with guitarist **BEN HARPER**

Mar 99. (c-s) *(HVN89CS)* **STOLEN CAR / PRECIOUS MAYBE** [34] [ ]
(cd-s+=) *(HVN 89CD)* – I love how you love me.
(cd-s) *(HVN 89CD2)* – ('A'side) / Stars all seem to weep (shed version) / Touch me with your love (live).

Mar 99. (d-lp/c/cd) *(HVNLP 22/+MC/CD)* <19038> **CENTRAL RESERVATION** [17] [ ]
– Stolen car / Sweet decline / Couldn't cause me harm / So much more / Pass in time / Central reservation / Stars all seem to weep / Love like laughter / Blood red river / Devil song / Feel to believe / Central reservation.

Sep 99. (cd-s) *(HVN 92CD1)* **CENTRAL RESERVATION. / CENTRAL RESERVATION (Spiritual Life – Ibadan remix) / CENTRAL RESERVATION (William Orbit remix)** [37] [–]
(cd-s) *(HVN 92CD2)* – ('A'-Deep dish modern red rock mixes; remix edit / remix / 2000 dub).
(12") *(HVN 92-12)* – ('A'-Spiritual Life – Ibadan remix) / ('A'-Deep dish modern red rock 2000 dub).

Jul 02. (cd-ep) *(HVN 115CD)* **CONCRETE SKY EP** [ ] [–]
– Concrete sky / Ali's waltz / Bobby Gentry / Carmella (Four Tet remix).

Jul 02. (lp/cd) *(HVNLP 37/+CD)* <39918> **DAYBREAKER** [8] [ ]
– Paris train / Concrete sky / Mount Washington / Anywhere / Daybreaker / Carmella / God song / This one's gonna bruise / Ted's waltz / Thinking about tomorrow. *(ltd-cd-iss. Oct02; HVNLP 37CDX)*

Nov 02. (cd-s) *(HVN 125CDS)* **ANYWHERE / BEAUTIFUL WORLD / ANYWHERE (Two Lone Swordsmen remix) / ANYWHERE (video)** [55] [–]

Nov 02. (d12") *<ASW 77821>* **ANYWHERE (remixes)** [–] [ ]
– Anywhere (mixes; Two Lone Swordsmen / instrumental / Adrian Sherwood / instrumental) / Carmella (Four Tet remix) / Daybreaker / Daybreaker (instrumental).

Mar 03. (cd-s) *(HVN 129CD)* **THINKING ABOUT TOMORROW / DAYBREAKER (Roots Manuva mix) / DAYBREAKER (Four Tet mix)** [57] [–]

Sep 03. (cd) *<92266>* **THE OTHER SIDE OF DAYBREAK** (remixes) [–] [ ]

Sep 03. (d-cd) *(HVNLP 45CD) <56163>* **PASS IN TIME – THE DEFINITIVE COLLECTION** (compilation) [45] Oct03 [ ]
– She cries your name / Someone's daughter / Touch me with your love / Sugar boy / Galaxy of emptiness / I wish I never saw the sunshine / Best bit / The same day / Stolen car / Sweetest decline / Pass in time / Central reservation / Concrete sky / Thinking about tomorrow / Central reservation (Ibaden remix) / Where do I begin (with CHEMICAL BROTHERS) / Stars all seem to weep / Safety / Pedestal / Dolphins (with TERRY CALLIER) / It's not the spotlight / Don't wanna know 'bout evil / Where do you go / Water from a vine leaf (with WILLIAM ORBIT).

E.M.I. Astralwerks

Jan 06. (7") *(EM 681)* **CONCEIVED. / RECTIFY #2** [44] [–]
(cd-s) *(CDEM 681)* – ('A'-Michael Brauer mix) / Endless day.

Feb 06. (cd) *(353400-2)* <49847> **COMFORT OF STRANGERS** [24] [92]
– Worms / Countenance / Heartlandtruckstop / Rectify / Comfort of strangers / Shadow of a doubt / Conceived / Absinthe / A place aside / Safe in your arms / Shopping trolley / Feral / Heart of soul / Pieces of sky. *(ltd-cd w/cd+=; 353401-2)* – What we begin / On my way home / Comfort of strangers (alt. take #9) / Did somebody make a fool of you / Northern sky.

– compilations, others, etc. –

Sep 05. (d-cd) *Heavenly; (82876 71870-2)* **TRAILER PARK / CENTRAL RESERVATION** [ ] [–]

Ozzy OSBOURNE

Born: JOHN MICHAEL OSBOURNE, 3 Dec'48, Aston, Birmingham, England. After eleven years as frontman for BLACK SABBATH, OSBOURNE was given his marching orders, forming his own BLIZZARD OF OZZ in 1980 alongside LEE KERSLAKE (drums, ex-URIAH HEEP), BOB DAISLEY (bass, ex-RAINBOW, ex-CHICKEN SHACK), DON AVERY (keyboards) and guitar wizard, RANDY RHOADS (ex-QUIET RIOT). Signing to Don Arden's 'Jet' label, OZZY and the band released their self-titled debut in 1980, hitting the UK Top 10 and narrowly missing the US Top 20. Hailed as OZZY's best work since 'SABBATH's heyday, the unholy alliance of RHOADS's music and OSBOURNE's lyrics (which, if anything, looked even more to the 'dark side' than the 'SABBATH material) produced such wonderfully grim fare as 'CRAZY TRAIN', 'SUICIDE SOLUTION' (later the subject of much JUDAS PRIEST-style courtroom controversy) and the epic 'MR. CROWLEY', inspiring multitudes of schoolkids to raise their pinkie and forefinger in cod-satanic salutation. The record went double platinum in the States, as did the follow-up, 'DIARY OF A MADMAN' (1981) (credited to OZZY solo), a cross-Atlantic Top 20 hit. Proving once and for all that the music industry is peopled by hard-bitten control freaks, OZZY proceeded to chomp on a live dove at a record company meeting later that year. Another infamous incident occurred only a few months later when the singer gnashed the head off a bat thrown onstage by a fan at a concert in Des Moines, cementing his reputation as heavy metal monster extraordinaire and public enemy No.1. 1982 proved to be an eventful year for 'the Oz', tragedy striking when his close friend and right hand man, RHODES, died in a plane crash in March. Consolation and a modicum of much needed stability came with his subsequent marriage to Don Arden's daughter, Sharon, on the 4th of July '82, the brave lass subsequently becoming his manager. BRAD GILLIS replaced RHODES for the live album of BLACK SABBATH covers, 'TALK OF THE DEVIL' (1982), before JAKE E. LEE was brought in as a more permanent fixture prior to 'BARK AT THE MOON' (1983). The rhythm section had also undergone numerous personnel changes with a final line-up of TOMMY ALDRIDGE (drums, ex-BLACK OAK ARKANSAS,etc.) and BOB DAISLEY. Another double platinum smash, the release of the record saw OZZY undertaking a mammoth US tour during which he unwittingly relieved himself on a wall of the Alamo monument in San Antonio, consequently being charged and banned from playing there. OZZY had always been a hard drinker and drug user, Sharon finally forcing him to attend the first of many unsuccessful sessions at the Betty Ford Clinic in 1984. His albums continued to sell consistently, particularly in America, despite constant line-up changes. 1988 saw the arrival of guitarist ZAKK WYLDE, heralded as a true successor to the revered RHODES. The late 80's also saw OSBOURNE retiring to his Buckinghamshire mansion with Sharon and his three kids, eventually kicking the booze and re-emerging in 1991 after being cleared of causing the death of three fans. In three separate, well documented cases, parents claimed OZZY's 'SUICIDE SOLUTION' had driven their siblings to kill themselves. 'NO MORE TEARS' (1991) was a triumphant comeback, OSBOURNE claiming the album would be his last and subsequently embarking on a farewell tour. The last two shows of the jaunt were opened by a ROB HALFORD (of JUDAS PRIEST)-fronted BLACK SABBATH, RONNIE JAMES DIO refusing to perform. Talks of a 'SABBATH reunion came to nothing although OZZY couldn't resist another tour and eventually an album, OZZMOSIS (1995). The record made the Top 5 in America where he's still regarded as something of a Metal Godfather; maybe it's the Brummie accent. OZZY has since stunned the metal world by rejoining BLACK SABBATH for concerts and a reunion album in 1998. A true grandaddy of the metal scene and one of its most enduring celebrities, OZZY was nearing double figures with the release of 'DOWN TO EARTH' (2001). Backed up a by a band of sterling metal pedigree (ZAKK WYLDE, ROBERT TRUJILLO and MIKE BORDIN), OZZY barked out another helping of, well, OZZY, spiced up with a few contemporary production touches. How many other 70's metal gods can be assured of a Top 5 US chart placing with a new record (Top 20 UK). In fact, such an icon is our OZZ that, in a kind of Big Brother in leather keks kinda stylee, a fly on the wall TV documentary, 'The Osbournes', was about to give American viewers an often hilarious insight into the man's (and his family's) domestic life. The OSBOURNES in fact – well KELLY and her dad – scored a UK No.1 in 2003/4 with a version of Black Sabbath's 'CHANGES', and the resurrection of OZZY was complete. 'PRINCE OF DARKNESS' (2005), was the appropriately titled boxed set that included all his greats and even a few weird and wonderful failures; this Prince certainly wore his heart on his sleeve. The last disc in the box was utilised for his subsequent 'UNDER COVER' set, OZZY breaking out the karaoke machine for all his favourite rock tunes including new hit, 'IN MY LIFE'.

• **Songwriters:** OZZY lyrics, RHOADS/band music. OZZY later collaborated with BOB DAISLEY. Covered: ROCKY MOUNTAIN WAY (Joe Walsh) / IN MY LIFE (Beatles) / MISSISSIPPI QUEEN (Mountain) / GO NOW (Moody Blues) / WOMAN + WORKING CLASS HERO (John Lennon) / 21ST CENTURY SCHIZOID MAN (King Crimson) / FOR WHAT IT'S WORTH (Buffalo Springfield) / GOOD TIMES (Eric Burdon & the Animals) / SUNSHINE OF YOUR LOVE (Cream) / FIRE (Crazy World Of Arthur Brown) / SYMPATHY FOR THE DEVIL (Rolling Stones). • **Trivia:** In 1987, he played a bible-punching preacher in the film 'Trick Or Treat'.

Album rating: OZZY OSBOURNE'S BLIZZARD OF OZZ (*7) / DIARY OF A MADMAN (*6) / TALK OF THE DEVIL (*6) / BARK AT THE MOON (*5) / THE ULTIMATE SIN (*5) / TRIBUTE (*8) / NO REST FOR THE WICKED (*5) / JUST SAY OZZY (*5) / NO MORE TEARS (*7) / LIVE & LOUD (*6) / OZZMOSIS (*6) / THE OZZMAN COMETH – THE BEST OF . . . compilation (*8) / DOWN TO EARTH (*6) / THE ESSENTIAL OZZY OSBOURNE compilation (*8) / PRINCE OF DARKNESS boxed compilation (*6) / UNDER COVER (*5)

OZZY OSBOURNE'S BLIZZARD OF OZZ

OZZY OSBOURNE – vocals / **RANDY RHOADS** – guitar (ex-QUIET RIOT) / **LEE KERSLAKE** – drums (ex-URIAH HEEP) / **BOB DAISLEY** – bass (ex-RAINBOW, ex-CHICKEN SHACK) / **DON AVERY** – keyboards

Jet | Jet-CBS

Sep 80. (7") *(JET 197)* **CRAZY TRAIN. / YOU LOOKING AT ME LOOKING AT YOU** 49 | –

Sep 80. (lp/c) *(JET LP/CA 234)* *<36812>* **OZZY OSBOURNE'S BLIZZARD OF OZZ** 7 | Mar81 21
– I don't know / Crazy train / Goodbye to romance / Dee / Suicide solution / Mr. Crowley / No bone movies / Revelation (Mother Earth) / Steal away (the night). *(re-iss. Nov87 on 'Epic' lp/c; 450453-1/-4) (cd-iss. Nov87 on 'Jet'; CDJET 234) (re-iss. cd Nov95 on 'Epic'; 481674-2)*

Nov 80. (7") *(JET 7-003)* *<37640>* **MR. CROWLEY (live). / YOU SAID IT ALL (live)** 46 | Apr82
(12"+=/12"pic-d+=) *(JET/+P 12-003)* – Suicide solution (live).

Apr 81. (7") *<02079>* **CRAZY TRAIN. / STEAL AWAY (THE NIGHT)** – |

OZZY OSBOURNE

(same line-up, except AVERY)

Oct 81. (lp/c) *(JET LP/CA 237)* *<37492>* **DIARY OF A MADMAN** 14 | 16
– Over the mountain / Flying high again / You can't kill rock and roll / Believer / Little dolls / Tonight / S.A.T.O. / Diary of a madman. *(cd-iss. May87; CDJET 237) (re-iss. Apr91 on 'Epic' cd/c; 463086-2/-4) (re-iss. cd Nov95 on 'Epic'; 481677-2)*

Nov 81. (7"/12") *(JET 7/12 017)* **OVER THE MOUNTAIN. / I DON'T KNOW** | –

Nov 81. (7") *<02582>* **FLYING HIGH AGAIN. / I DON'T KNOW** – |

Feb 82. (7") *<02707>* **LITTLE DOLLS. / TONIGHT** – |

—— (Nov'81) **RUDY SARZO** – bass (ex-QUIET RIOT) repl. DAISLEY (to URIAH HEEP) **TOMMY ALDRIDGE** – drums (ex-BLACK OAK ARKANSAS, etc) repl. KERSLAKE

—— (Apr'82) **BRAD GILLIS** – guitar (of NIGHT RANGER) repl. RANDY RHOADS who was killed in a light aeroplane crash on 19th Mar'82.

Nov 82. (d-lp/d-c) *(JET DP/CD 401)* *<38350>* **TALK OF THE DEVIL** (live at Ritz Club, NY) <US-title 'SPEAK OF THE DEVIL'> 21 | 14
– Symptom of the universe / Snowblind / Black sabbath / Fairies wear boots / War pigs / The wizard / N.I.B. / Sweet leaf / Never say die / Sabbath bloody sabbath / Iron man – Children of the grave / Paranoid. *(re-iss. Sep87 on 'Epic' d-lp/d-c; 451124-1/-4) (cd-iss. Jun89; 451124-2)* – (omits dialogue). *(re-iss. cd/d-lp complete.Jul91 on 'Castle'; CCS CD/LP 296) (re-iss. cd Nov95 as 'SPEAK OF THE DEVIL' on 'Epic'; 481679-2)*

Dec 82. (7"/7"pic-d) *(JET/+P 7-030)* **SYMPTOM OF THE UNIVERSE (live). / N.I.B. (live)** | –
(12"+=) *(JET 12-030)* – Children of the grave (live).

Feb 83. (7") *<03302>* **IRON MAN (live). / PARANOID (live)** – |

—— (Dec'82) **JAKE E. LEE** (b.JAKEY LOU WILLIAMS, San Diego, California, USA) – guitar (ex-RATT) repl. GILLIS who returned to NIGHT RANGER / **DON COSTA** – bass repl. PETE WAY (ex-UFO) who had deputised for the departing RUDY SARZO who had returned to QUIET RIOT. (He later joined WHITESNAKE)

—— **OZZY, JAKE E + TOMMY** re-recruited **BOB DAISLEY** to repl. COSTA

Epic | CBS Assoc.

Nov 83. (7"/12",12"silver/12"pic-d) *(A/TA/WA 3915)* **BARK AT THE MOON. / ONE UP ON THE B-SIDE** 21 |

Dec 83. (7") *<04318>* **BARK AT THE MOON. / SPIDERS** – |

Dec 83. (lp/c) *(EPC/40 25739)* *<38987>* **BARK AT THE MOON** 24 | 19
– Rock'n'roll rebel / Bark at the Moon / You're no different / Now you see it (now you don't) / Forever / So tired / Waiting for darkness / Spiders. *(re-iss. Apr86 lp/c; EPC/40 32780) (cd-iss. Oct88; CD 32780) (re-iss. cd Nov95; 481678-2)*

Mar 84. (7") *(A 4260)* *<04383>* **SO TIRED. / FOREVER (live)** |
(12"+=/d7"+=) *(TA/DA 4260)* – Waiting for darkness / Paranoid (live).

—— ALDRIDGE was briefly replaced (Mar-May84) on tour by CARMINE APPICE.

May 84. (7") *(A 4452)* **SO TIRED. / BARK AT THE MOON (live)** 20 |
(12"+=,12"gold+=) *(WA 4452)* – Waiting for darkness / Suicide solution (live) / Paranoid (live).

—— **PHIL SOUSSAN** – bass repl. DAISLEY / **RANDY CASTILLO** (b.18 Dec'50, Albuquerque, New Mexico, USA) – drums (ex-LITA FORD BAND) repl. ALDRIDGE

Jan 86. (7"/7"w-poster/12") *(A/QA/TA 6859)* **SHOT IN THE DARK. / ROCK'N'ROLL REBEL** 20 | –

Feb 86. (lp/c) *(EPC/40 26404)* *<40026>* **THE ULTIMATE SIN** 8 | 6
– Lightning strikes / Killer of giants / Thank God for the bomb / Never / Shot in the dark / The ultimate sin / Secret loser / Never know why / Fool like you. *(cd-iss. Jul86; CD 26404) (pic-lp Aug86; EPC 11-26404) (re-iss. Feb89 on 'C.B.S.' lp/c/cd; 462496-1/-4/-2) (re-iss. Nov95; 481680-2)*

Mar 86. (7") *<05810>* **SHOT IN THE DARK. / YOU SAID IT ALL** – | 68

Jul 86. (7"/12") *(A/TA 7311)* **THE ULTIMATE SIN. / LIGHTNING STRIKES** 72 | –

1988. (7") *<08463>* **SHOT IN THE DARK. / CRAZY TRAIN** – |

—— (Aug'88) **ZAKK WILDE** (b.ZACH ADAMS, 14 Jan'66) – guitar repl. JAKE who formed BADLANDS. / **DAISLEY** returned to repl. SOUSSAN (to BILLY IDOL) / added **JOHN SINCLAIR** – keyboards

Oct 88. (lp/c/cd) *(46258-1/-4/-2)* *<44245>* **NO REST FOR THE WICKED** 23 | 13
– Miracle man / Devil's daughter / Crazy babies / Breaking all the rules / Bloodbath in Paradise / Fire in the sky / Tattooed dancer / The demon alcohol. *(cd+=)* – Hero. *(re-iss. Jun94 & Nov95; cd/c; 481681-2)*

Oct 88. (7"/7"sha-pic-d) *(653063-0/-9)* **MIRACLE MAN. / CRAZY BABIES** | –
(12"+=/12"w-poster/cd-s+=) *(653063-6/-8/-2)* – The liar.

Dec 88. (7") *<08516>* **MIRACLE MAN. / MAN YOU SAID IT ALL** – |

Feb 89. (7") *<68534>* **CRAZY BABIES. / THE DEMON ALCOHOL** – |

—— Earlier in the year OZZY had accompanied LITA FORD on 45 'CLOSE MY EYES FOREVER'. In Apr'89, it was to reach UK/US Top50.

—— **TERRY 'GEEZER' BUTLER** – bass was used for tour work late 1988.

Feb 90. (cd/c/lp) *(465940-1/-4/-2)* *<45451>* **JUST SAY OZZY (live)** 69 | 58
– Miracle man / Bloodbath in Paradise / Shot in the dark / Tattooed dancer / Sweet leaf / War pigs. *(re-iss. cd Nov95; 481517-2)*

—— In the late 80's, OZZY retired to his Buckinghamshire mansion with his manager/wife Sharon Arden and 3 kids. He had also kicked his alcohol addiction. Returned 1991 after being cleared of causing death of fan. See last studio line-up. Augmented also by **MICHAEL INEZ** – bass, inspiration repl. BUTLER

Epic / Epic Assoc

Sep 91. (7") *(657440-7)* <73973> **NO MORE TEARS. / S.I.N.** [32] [71]
(c-s+=/12"+=/12"pic-d+=/cd-s+=) *(657440-8/-6/-?/-2)* – Party with the animals.

Oct 91. (cd/c/lp) *(467859-2/-4/-1)* <46795> **NO MORE TEARS** [17] [7]
– Mr. Tinkertrain / I don't want to change the world / Mama I'm coming home / Desire / No more tears / S.I.N. / Hellraiser / Time after time / Zombie stomp / A.V.H. / Road to nowhere. *(re-iss. cd Nov95; 481675-2)*

Nov 91. (7") *(657617-7)* <74093> **MAMA I'M COMING HOME. / DON'T BLAME ME** [46] Feb92 [28]
(12"+=) *(657617-8)* – I don't know / Crazy train.
(cd-s+=) *(657617-9)* – (Ozzy on the Steve Wright show)
(12"+=) *(657617-6)* – Time after time / Goodbye to romance.
<US-cd-ep+=> *<74265>* – Party with the animals.

Jun 93. (d-cd) *(473798-2)* <46795> **LIVE & LOUD (live)** [ ] [22]
– Intro / Paranoid / I don't want to change the world / Desire / Mr. Crowley / I don't know / Road to nowhere / Flying high again / Guitar solo / Suicide solution / Goodbye to romance / Shot in the dark / No more tears / Miracle man / Drum solo / War pigs / Bark at the Moon / Mama, I'm coming home / Crazy train / Black sabbath / Changes. *(re-iss. Nov95; 481676-2)*

Jun 93. (12"/cd-s) *(659340-6/-2)* **CHANGES (live). / CHANGES / NO MORE TEARS / DESIRE** [ ] [ ]

— next featured **MIKE INEZ** – bass (of ALICE IN CHAINS)

— CASTILLO left and later joined MOTLEY CRUE

Oct 95. (cd/c/lp) *(481022-2/-4/-1)* <67091> **OZZMOSIS** [22] [4]
– Perry Mason / I just want you / Ghost behind my eyes / Thunder underground / See you on the other side / Tomorrow / Denial / My little man / My Jekyll doesn't hide / Old LA tonight. *(re-iss. Apr99; same)*

Nov 95. (7"pic-d) *(662639-7)* **PERRY MASON. / LIVING WITH THE ENEMY** [23] [ ]
(cd-s+=) *(662639-2)* – The whole world's falling down.
(cd-s) *(662639-5)* – ('A'side) / No more tears / I don't want to change the world / Flying high again.

— **ROBERT TRUJILLO** – bass (ex-SUICIDAL TENDENCIES) – bass; repl. INEZ

Aug 96. (12") *(663570-6)* **I JUST WANT YOU. / AIMEE / VOODOO DANCER** [43] [ ]
(cd-s) *(663570-2)* – ('A'side) / Aimee / Mama, I'm coming home.
(cd-s) *(663570-5)* – ('A'side) / Voodoo dancer / Iron man (with THERAPY?).

Oct 01. (cd) *(498474-2)* <63580> **DOWN TO EARTH** [19] [4]
– Gets me through / Facing hell / Dreamer / No easy way out / That I never had / You know (part 1) / Junkie / Running out of time / Black illusion / Alive / Can you hear them?

May 02. (cd-s) *(672412-2)* **DREAMER / GETS ME THROUGH / BLACK SKIES / DREAMER (video)** [18] [–]

— in Dec'03, KELLY and OZZY OSBOURNE hit UK No.1 with a version of 'CHANGES'

– compilations, others, etc. –

on 'Epic' UK / 'CBS Assoc.' unless otherwise stated

May 87. (d-lp/c/cd) *(450475-1/-4/-2)* <40714> **TRIBUTE (live 1981 with RANDY RHOADS)** [13] [6]
– I don't know / Crazy train / Revelation (Mother Earth) / Believer / Mr. Crowley / Flying high again / No bone movies / Steal away (the night) / Suicide solution / Iron man – Children of the grave / Goodbye to romance / Paranoid / Dee *[not on cd]*. *(re-iss. Apr93 cd/c;) (re-iss. cd Nov95; 481516-2)*

Jun 87. (7"/12") *(650943-7/-6)* <07168> **CRAZY TRAIN (live 1981). / CRAZY TRAIN (live 1981)** [ ] [ ]

Jul 88. (12"ep/cd-ep) *(652 875-6/-2)* **BACK TO OZZ** [76] [–]
– The ultimate sin / Bark at the Moon / Mr. Crowley / Diary of a madman.

Aug 90. (cd) *Priority;* <57129> **TEN COMMANDMENTS** (rare) [–] [ ]

Mar 93. (d-cd) *(465211-2)* **BARK AT THE MOON / BLIZZARD OF OZZ** [ ] [ ]

Nov 97. (cd/c) *(487260-2/-4)* **THE OZZMAN COMETH – THE BEST OF** [68] [13]
– Black sabbath / War pigs / Goodbye to romance (live) / Crazy train (live) / Mr. Crowley (live) / Over the mountain (live) / Paranoid (live) / Bark at the moon / Shot in the dark / Crazy babies / No more tears / Mama, I'm coming home (live) / I just want you / I don't want to change the world / Back on earth. *(cd+=)* – Fairies wear boots / Beyond the wall of sleep.

Nov 98. (3xcd-box) *Epic; (492655-2)* **DIARY OF A MADMAN / BARK AT THE MOON / THE ULTIMATE SIN** [ ] [–]
(re-iss. Sep01; same)

May 03. (d-cd) *Sony TV; (510840-2)* <86812> **THE ESSENTIAL OZZY OSBOURNE** [21] Feb03 [81]
– Crazy train / Mr. Crowley / I don't know (live) / Suicide solution / Goodbye to romance / Over the mountain / Flying high again / Diary of a madman / Paranoid (live) / Bark at the Moon / You're no different / Rock'n'roll rebel / Crazy babies / Miracle man / Fire in the sky / Breakin' all the rules / Mama, I'm coming home / Desire / No more tears / Time after time / Road to nowhere / I don't want to change the world (live) / Perry Mason / I just want you / Thunder underground / See you on the other side / Gets me through / Dreamer / No easy way out.

Mar 05. (4xcd-box) *(518900-2)* *<92960>* **PRINCE OF DARKNESS** [ ] [36]

— (note: most of tracks below feat. on above)

Nov 05. (cd) *(82876 74314-2)* *<97750>* **UNDER COVER** (covers past & present) [67] [ ]
– Rocky mountain way / In my life / Mississippi queen / Go now / Woman / 21st Century schizoid man / All the young dudes / For what it's worth / Good times / Sunshine of your love / Fire / Working class hero / Sympathy for the Devil.

Dec 05. (cd-s) *(82876 74317-2)* **IN MY LIFE / DREAMER (acoustic) / IN MY LIFE (video)** [63] [–]

OUTKAST

Born: Atlanta, Georgia, USA … 1993 by ANDRE "DRE" BENJAMIN and ANTOINE "BIG BOI" PATTON, who came to realise their lyrical talents after a playground 'rap-battle' in high school. Things happened extremely fast for this pair of highly innovative rappers when they formed OUTKAST whilst still in education. They were subsequently signed by 'LaFace' when they were barely out of their teens. OUTKAST issued 'PLAYER'S BALL' in 1993 and watched their status, as little-known mavericks of the underground to hip-hop's brightest hopes as the song topped the singles chart and became gold in a matter of weeks. OUTKAST prepared for what was to become their debut album, the annoyingly titled 'SOUTHERNPLAYALISTICADILLIACMUZIK' (1994), which earned them a 'Best Newcomer' Gong at the 1995 Source awards. This was not hard to debate, as DRE and BIG BOI's lyrical panache had a certain ebb and flow that could not be imitated by anybody else. Like KOOL KEITH and DEL THA FUNKY HOMOSAPIEN, their rhymes weaved in and out of a spectacular production which boasted eclectic instruments and sharp beats, reminiscent of the UK's own House scene. 'ATLIENS' was delivered in 1996 to critical acclaim in the Hip-Hop world and spawned two massive singles 'ELEVATORS (ME AND YOU)' and 'ATLIENS' which both climbed to the top of the rap charts and demonstrated both artists' abilities to rap around each other in a sonic-style whilst never allowing time for a collision. 'AQUEMINI' (1998), which was voted one of the most essential Hip-Hop albums by Q magazine, was much the same thing, only tighter with a better production and a more left-field sound. If 'ATLIENS' was their 'Nevermind', then this was the collective's 'In Utero', with big, brash and inventive songs, the set was lyrically more important then a dozen other aggressive rappers. However, OUTKAST's best work was to arrive in 2000, in the form of 'STANKONIA'. A masterpiece from beginning to end, 'STANKONIA' was one of the freshest and dance-orientated hip-hop records ever released. The frightful pace of single 'B.O.B', with its tribal, DR JOHN-esque call of female backing vocalists in the chorus swept you off your feet with the sheer adrenaline of the track. While Top 3 single 'MISS JACKSON' had everybody singing "I'm sorry Miss Jackson, ooooooooooohhhhh!" and 'FRESH AND CLEAN' was the ultimate player's anthem for a Saturday night on the pull. Intricate, important, untouchable were three words to describe OUTKAST; a truly remarkable group who

OUTKAST

showed us there was so much more to Hip-hop than bouncing cars, blunts and bitches. While the cannily timed best of, 'BIG BOI AND DRE PRESENT . . . OUTKAST' (2001), sought to educate the new fans with classic oldies and tantalise both old and new afficionados with a handful of fiendishly funky new tracks, 'SPEAKERBOXXX / THE LOVE BELOW' (2003) defied convention for such a hotly anticipated follow-up. Recording and releasing two separate solo albums on one CD under the OUTKAST banner might have been dismissed as a gimmick had the music itself not been among the most spontaneous, charismatic and downright funky to be released under the aegis of hip hop – never mind pop – in the last few years. Endlessly inventive with an unfailing vision, BIG BOI's 'SPEAKERBOXXX' once again drew from the wealth of black music's heritage in order to create something new and take the music forward. 'THE LOVE BELOW' was an altogether different beast, jazzier but no less creative, mapping out ANDRE's diverse reference points with the same unfettered spirit. Considered individually, the albums surpassed the one-dimensional re-run of most of what passes for hip hop these days; taken together, this million selling US No.1 (featuring the catchy 'HEY YA' smash hit) threw down the gauntlet for the very future of the genre.

Album rating: SOUTHERNPLAYALISTICADILLACMUZIK (*8) / ATLIENS (*7) / AQUEMINI (*8) / STANKONIA (*9) / BIG BOI AND DRE PRESENT . . . compilation (*8) / SPEAKERBOXXX – THE LOVE BELOW (*8)

ANDRE "DRE" BENJAMIN (b.27 May'75) – vocals / **ANTOINE "BIG BOI" PATTON** (b. 1 Feb'75, Savannah, Georgia) – vocals

La Face-Arista La Face-Arista

May 94. (7"/c-s) *(74322 09422-7/-4)* <2-4060> **PLAYERS BALL. / (instrumental)** Nov93 37
(12"+=) *(74322 09422-1)* – (3-'A'mixes).
(cd-s++=) *(74322 09422-2)* – ('A'mix).

May 94. (cd/c) <*(73008 26010)*> **SOUTHERNPLAYALISTICADILLACMUZIK** 20
– Peaches (intro) / Myintrotoletuknow / Ain't no thang / Welcome to Atlanta (interlude) / Southernplayalisticadillacmuzik / Call of da wild (featuring The GOODY MOB) / Player's ball (original) / Claimin' true / Club donkey ass (interlude) / Funky ride / Flim flam (interlude) / Git up, git out (featuring The GOODY MOB) / True dat (interlude) / Crumblin' erb / Hootie hoo / D.E.E.P. / Player's ball (reprise). *(cd re-iss. Sep98; same)*

Jul 94. (cd-s) <2-4070> **SOUTHERNPLAYALISTICADILLACMUZIK / (instrumental)** – 74

Oct 94. (cd-s) <2-4085> **GIT UP, GIT OUT (mixes)** –

Jul 96. (cd-s) <2-4177> **ELEVATORS (ME & YOU) / (instrumental)** – 12

Sep 96. (cd/c) <*(73008 26032-2/-4)*> **ATLIENS** 2
– U may die / Two dope boyz in a Cadillac / Atliens / Wheelz of steel / Jazzy Belle / Elevators (me & you) / Ova da woods / Babylon / Wailin' / Mainstream / Decateur psalm / Millennium / E.T. / 13th floor – Growin' old / Elevators (reprise). *(cd re-iss. Jan01; same)*

Nov 96. (cd-s) <2-4196> **ATLIENS / WHEELZ OF STEEL** – 35

Apr 97. (cd-s) <2-4224> **JAZZY BELLE / (Swift C's remix)** – 52

— In Jun'98, OUTKAST were credited on US hit, 'Black Ice (Sky High)' with the GOODIE MOB

Sep 98. (cd/c/d-lp) <*(73008 26053-2/-4/-1)*> **AQUEMINI** 2
– Chonkyfire / Rosa Parks / Aquemini / Da art of storytellin' (part 1 & 2) / Y'all scared / Synthesizer / Slump / Liberation / Skew it on the bar-b / Mamasita / West Savannah / Spottieottiedopalicious / Return of the G. *(cd re-iss. Jan01; same)*

Nov 98. (cd-s) <64013> **ROSA PARKS / (instrumental) / SKEW IT ON THE BAR-B** – 55

— early '99, OUTKAST featured on COOL BREEZE's hit 'Watch For The Hook'

Apr 00. (cd-s) <66478> **DA ART OF STORYTELLIN' / (part 2)** –

Nov 00. (cd/d-lp) <*(73008 26072-2/-1)*> **STANKONIA** 10 2
– Intro / Gasoline dreams (with KHUJO GOODIE) / I'm cool (interlude) / So fresh so clean (with DUNGEON FAMILY) / Ms Jackson / Snappin' and trappin' / DF (interlude) / Spaghetti junction / Kim and Goodie (interlude) / I'll call B 4 I cum (with GANGSTA BOO & ECO) / B.O.B. / Xplosion / We love deez hoez / Humble mumble (with ERYKAH BADU) / Drinkin' again (interlude) / Horror / Red velvet / Gangsta shit (with SLIMM CALHOUN & C-BONE) / Cruisin' in the ATL (interlude) / Toilet tisha / Slum beautiful / Pre nump (interlude) / Stankonia (stanklove) / Good hair (interlude).

Dec 00. (12"/cd-s) *(74321 82294-1/-2)* <2-4500> **B.O.B. (BOMBS OVER BAGHDAD) / (instrumental) / ('A'video)** 61 Sep00
(cd-s) *(74321 82174-2)* – ('A'mixes).

— the import of 'MS. JACKSON' originally hit UK No.48

Feb 01. (12"/c-s) *(74321 83682-1/-4)* <24516> **MS. JACKSON. / ('A'-Blacksmith club mix) / ('A'-Blacksmith instrumental)** 2 Jan01 1
(cd-s) *(74321 83682-2)* – ('A'-CD-Rom).

May 01. (c-s) *(74321 86340-4)* <24537> **SO FRESH SO CLEAN / SO FRESH SO CLEAN (Fatboy Slim remix)** 16 Feb01 30
(cd-s+=) *(74321 86340-2)* – Ms Jackson (Mr Drunk remix).
(12"+=) *(74321 86340-1)* – ('A'-instrumental).

Jan 02. (cd) <*(73008 26093-2)*> **BIG BOI AND DRE PRESENT . . . OUTKAST** Dec01 18
– Camp fire intro / Funkin' around / Ain't no thang / So fresh, so clean / Rosa Parks / The whole world (with KILLER MIKE) / Aquemini / B.O.B. / Southernplayalisticadillacmusik / Crumblin' erb / Ms. Jackson / Player's ball / Elevators (me and you) / Spottieottiedopaliscious / Git up, git out / Movin' cool (the after party).

Mar 02. (c-s; by OUTKAST featuring KILLER MIKE) *(74321 91759-4)* <*radio*> **THE WHOLE WORLD / ROSA PARKS** 19 Dec01 19
(cd-s+=) *(74321 91759-2)* – B.O.B. / ('A'video).
(12") *(74321 91759-1)* – ('A'side) / ('A'-instrumental).

Jul 02. (cd-s; by OUTKAST featuring KILLER MIKE & SLEEPY BROWN) *(AT 0134CD)* <85355> **LAND OF A MILLION DRUMS / (explicit version) / IT'S A MYSTERY** 46
(12") *(AT 134T)* – ('A'side) / One track Mike / ('A'-instrumental).
(above issued on 'Atlantic')

— in May'03, BIG BOI featured on KILLER MIKE's hit, 'Adidas'

Sep 03. (12"/cd-s) *(82876 56723-1/-2)* **GHETTO MUSICK / (Benny Benassi club mix)** 55 –

Sep 03. (d-cd/d-lp) <*(82876 52905-2/50133-1)*> **SPEAKERBOXXX / THE LOVE BELOW** 8 1
– Intro / Ghetto musick / Unhappy / Bowtie (with SLEEPY BROWN & JAZZE PHA) / The way you move (with SLEEPY BROWN) / The rooster / Bust / War / Church / Bamboo (interlude) / Tomb of the boom (with KONKRETE, BIG GIPP & LUDACRIS) / E-Mac (interlude) / Knowing / Flip flop rock (with KILLER MIKE & JAY-Z) / Interlude / Reset (with KHUJO GOODIE & CEE LO) / D-Boi (interlude) / Last call (with SLIMM CALHOUN & LIL JON) / Bowtie (postlude) // The love below (intro) / Love hater / God (interlude) / Happy Valentine's day / Spread / Where are my panties? / Prototype / She lives in my lap (with ROSARIO DAWSON) / Hey ya! / Roses / Good day, good sir / Behold a lady / Pink & blue / Love in war / She's alive / Dracula's wedding (with KELIS) / My favorite things (with NORAH JONES) / Take off your cool / Vibrate / A day in the life of Benjamin Andre.

Nov 03. (cd-s) <*(82876 57953-2)*> **HEY YA! / GOOD DAY, GOOD SIR** 3 1
(12") *(82876 57953-1)* – ('A') / Ghetto musick / My favorite things.
(cd-s++=) *(82876 58010-2)* – ('A'-video).

Mar 04. (cd-s; feat. SLEEPY BROWN) <*(82876 60567-2)*> **THE WAY YOU MOVE / JOHNNY TOO BAD (radio mix)** 7 1
(cd-s) *(82876 60560-2)* – ('A'-club mix) / Johnny too bad (extended) / ('A'-Full Phatt radio mix) / ('A'-video).

Jun 04. (12"pic-d/cd-s) <*(82876 62439-1/-2)*> **ROSES / CHURCH** 4 9

Nov 04. (12"/cd-s) *(82876 65530-1/-2)* **PROTOTYPE / GHETTOMUSICK. / UNHAPPY / PROTOTYPE (instrumental)** –

☐ Jimmy PAGE / PAGE & PLANT
(see under ⇒ LED ZEPPELIN)

☐ PALACE MUSIC (see under ⇒ OLDHAM, Will)

Robert PALMER

Born: ALAN ROBERT PALMER, 19 Jan'49, Batley, Yorkshire, England. From the age of 3, PALMER lived with his family in Malta (his father being in the services), moving to London in 1969 after having his first musical experience in semi-pro group, MANDRAKE PADDLE STEAMER. Replacing the solo bound JESS RODEN, PALMER joined the ALAN BROWN SET, singing on the 'Deram' 45, 'GYPSY GIRL', later that year. The following year, he hooked up with jazz-rockers DADA, who boasted vocalist ELKIE BROOKS on their eponymous 'Atco' debut long player. Come 1971, the act had evolved into VINEGAR JOE, although after three poor selling albums for 'Island' (VINEGAR JOE / ROCK'N'ROLL GYPSIES / SIX-STAR GENERAL), they eventually split in March '74. After nearly replacing LOWELL GEORGE in LITTLE FEAT, PALMER was retained by 'Island' on a solo basis. His debut release, The LITTLE FEAT and METERS-enhanced 'SNEAKIN' SALLY THROUGH THE ALLEY' (1974), stiffed in the UK, although US sales almost resulted in a Top 100 placing. As well as a seamless cover of LITTLE FEAT's 'SAILIN' SHOES', the album's highlight was the ALLEN TOUSSAINT-penned title track although many of the collection's songs suffered from a characterlessness that coloured much of PALMER's subsequent output. The following year, he relocated to New York with his wife, subsequently flirting with reggae on his follow-up album, 'PRESSURE DROP'. Following a support slot on a LITTLE FEAT tour, the singer again relocated, this time to Nassau, Bahamas to consummate his love affair with the music of the Carribbean. The culmination of this period in PALMER's career was 1978's 'DOUBLE FUN', wherein the singer sauntered through a mellow, sun-bleached cover of ANDY FRASER's (ex-FREE) 'EVERY KINDA PEOPLE', subsequently PALMER's first US Top 20 hit. 'SECRETS' (1979) was a radical stylistic departure, anchored on balls-out rock and furnishing PALMER with a second Top 20 hit in MOON MARTIN's 'BAD CASE OF LOVING YOU (DOCTOR, DOCTOR)'. The immaculately attired crooner gained a deserved commercial leap in the early 80's with the 'CLUES' album, his polished-oak vocals combining surprisingly well with GARY NUMAN's synth-pop noodlings on the likes of 'JOHNNY AND MARY'. In 1982, the very ROD (STEWART)-ish 'SOME GUYS HAVE ALL THE LUCK' single gave PALMER some belated UK Top 20 success, the singer enjoying further British exposure three years later when he became frontman for the DURAN DURAN/CHIC offshoot, The POWER STATION. An often predictably derivative affair, they were also blatantly commercial, scoring with the likes of 'SOME LIKE IT HOT' and a cover of MARC BOLAN's 'GET IT ON'. Soon back on the solo trail, PALMER carried on in a hard rock stylee for his biggest album to date, 'RIPTIDE' (1985), a record which featured the Transatlantic Top 5 (US No.1) smash, 'ADDICTED TO LOVE'. An antiseptically raunchy piece of poppy-cock-rock, the single was accompanied by a semi-ironic video featuring PALMER surrounded by a troupe of blonde bombshells rocking in formation. Now an accomplished worldwide artist, PALMER emigrated to Lugano, Switzerland prior to releasing 'HEAVY NOVA' (1988). Another big seller, PALMER showed off his mastery of diverse styles, taking in everything from suave balladeering ('SHE MAKES MY DAY') to Swiss yodelling ('CHANGE HIS WAYS') as well as scoring another massive US hit with the cliched rock of 'SIMPLY IRRESISTIBLE'. A surprisingly endearing collaboration with UB40 on BOB DYLAN's 'I'LL BE YOUR BABY TONIGHT' powered the 'DON'T EXPLAIN' (1990) album into the UK Top 10 while 'RIDIN' HIGH' (1992) was a passable tribute to the Tin Pan Alley era. Though possessed of smoothly soulful, impressively adaptable vocal chords and an often faultless choice in material, PALMER's work invariably suffers from a lack of cohesion. That said, you can't go wrong with his greatest hits' set, 1989's 'ADDICTIONS VOL.1'. After an extended absence PALMER returned with 'RHYTHM AND BLUES' (1999), a limp set of coffee-table pop that yet again undersold his talent, or rather smothered it in a sterile production. Lone highlight was a cover of Lowell George's 'TWENTY MILLION THINGS' (a fitting tribute to the great man on the 20th anniversary of his death) which survived the worst of the studio excess. PALMER, sadly, too, passed away after suffering a heart attack in his Paris home on the 26th of September, 2003; a few months earlier he had released his final set, 'DRIVE'.

• **Songwriters:** PALMER penned, except FROM A WHISPER TO A SCREAM (Allen Toussaint) / PRESSURE DROP (Lee Perry) / YOU REALLY GOT ME (Kinks) / JEALOUS + THE SILVER GUN (Alan Powell) / YOU ARE IN MY SYSTEM (System) / CAN WE STILL BE FRIENDS (Todd Rundgren) / SOME GUYS HAVE ALL THE LUCK (Persuaders) / I DIDN'T MEAN TO TURN YOU ON (hit; Cherrelle) / EARLY IN THE MORNING (Gap Band) / I'LL BE YOUR BABY TONIGHT (Bob Dylan) / MERCY MERCY ME (THE ECOLOGY) – I WANT YOU (Marvin Gaye) / WITCHCRAFT (hit; Frank Sinatra) / GIRL U WANT (Devo) / RESPECT YOURSELF (Staple Singers) / TV DINNERS (ZZ Top) / etc. • **Trivia:** PALMER produced many artists including The COMSAT ANGELS, DESMOND DEKKER and PETER BAUMANN.

Album rating: SNEAKIN' SALLY THROUGH THE ALLEY (*6) / PRESSURE DROP (*5) / SOME PEOPLE CAN DO WHAT THEY LIKE (*5) / DOUBLE FUN (*5) / SECRETS (*5) / CLUES (*5) / MAYBE IT'S LIVE (*4) / PRIDE (*4) / RIPTIDE (*7) / HEAVY NOVA (*5) / ADDICTIONS VOL.1 compilation (*7) / DON'T EXPLAIN (*4) / RIDIN' HIGH (*3) / ADDICTIONS 2 compilation (*5) / HONEY (*5) / THE VERY BEST OF ROBERT PALMER compilation (*8) / RHYTHM AND BLUES (*3) / LIVE AT THE APOLLO, NEW YORK CITY (*5) / AT HIS VERY BEST compilation (*8) / DRIVE (*5)

ROBERT PALMER – vocals with various session people

		Island	Island
Sep 74.	(lp) *(<ILPS 9294>)* **SNEAKIN' SALLY THROUGH THE ALLEY**	☐	May75 ☐

– Sailing shoes / Hey Julia / Sneakin' Sally through the alley / Through it all there's you / Get outside / Blackmail / How much fun / From a whisper to a scream / Through it all there's you. *(re-iss. Jan87 lp/c/cd; ILPM/ICM/CID 9294) (cd-iss. Aug89; IMCD 20)*

Nov 74. (7") *<006>* **SNEAKIN' SALLY THROUGH THE ALLEY. / EPIDEMIC** [–] [ ]

Oct 75. (7") *(WIP 6250) <042> (WIP 6250)* **WHICH OF US IS THE FOOL. / GET OUTSIDE** [ ] [ ]

Feb 76. (7") *(WIP 6272) <049>* **GIMME AN INCH. / PRESSURE DROP** [ ] [ ]

Mar 76. (lp/c) *(<ILPS/ICT 9372>)* **PRESSURE DROP** [ ] Nov75 [ ]
– Give me an inch / Work to make it work / Back in my arms / Riverboat / Pressure drop / Here with you tonight / Trouble / Fine time / Which of us is the fool. *(re-iss. Jan87 lp/c/cd; ILPM/ICM/CID 9372) (cd-iss. Aug89; IMCD 24)*

Oct 76. (7") *(WIP 6345)* **MAN SMART, WOMAN SMARTER. / FROM A WHISPER TO A SCREAM** [ ] [–]

Oct 76. (lp/c) *(<ILPS/ICT 9420>)* **SOME PEOPLE CAN DO WHAT THEY LIKE** [46] [68]
– One lost look / Keep in touch / Man smart, woman smarter / Spanish moon / Have mercy / Gotta get a grip on you (part II) / What can you bring me / Hard head / Off the bone / Some people can do what they like. *(cd-iss. Nov89; IMCD 69)*

Oct 76. (7") *<075>* **MAN SMART, WOMAN SMARTER. / KEEP IN TOUCH** [–] [63]

Mar 77. (7") *<081>* **SOME PEOPLE CAN DO WHAT THEY LIKE. / ONE LOST LOOK** [–] [ ]

Jan 78. (lp/c) *(<ILPS/ICT 9476>)* **DOUBLE FUN** [ ] Mar78 [45]
– Every kinda people / Best of both worlds / Come over / Where can it go / Night people / Love can run faster / You overwhelm me / You really got me / You're gonna get what's coming. *(re-iss. Jan87 lp/c/cd; ILPM/ICM/CID 9476) (cd-iss. Aug89; IMCD 23)*

Mar 78. (7") *<100>* **EVERY KINDA PEOPLE. / HOW MUCH FUN** [–] [16]

Mar 78. (7") *(WIP 6425)* **EVERY KINDA PEOPLE. / KEEP IN TOUCH** [53] [–]

May 78. (7") *<105>* **COME OVER. / YOU OVERWHELM ME** [–] [ ]

Jun 78. (7") *(WIP 6445)* **BEST OF BOTH WORLDS. / ('A'dub version)** [ ] [ ]
(12"+=) *(WIP12 6445)* – Pressure drop.

May 79. (7") *(WIP 6481) <49016>* **BAD CASE OF LOVIN' YOU (DOCTOR, DOCTOR). / LOVE CAN RUN FASTER** [61] Jul79 [14]

Jun 79. (lp/c) *(<ILPS/ICT 9544>)* **SECRETS** [54] Jul79 [19]
– Bad case of loving you (doctor, doctor) / Too good to be true / Can we still be friends / In walks love again / Mean old world / Love stop / Jealous / Under suspicion / Woman you're wonderful / What's it take / Remember to remember. *(re-iss. Jan87 lp/c/cd; ILPM/ICM/CID 9544) (cd-iss. Aug89; IMCD 26)*

Jul 78. (7") *<8697>* **YOU'RE GONNA GET WHAT'S COMING. / WHERE CAN IT GO** [–] [ ]

Aug 79. (7") *(WIP 6515)* **JEALOUS. / WOMAN YOU'RE WONDERFUL** [ ] [–]

Sep 79. (7") *<49094>* **JEALOUS. / IN WALKS LOVE AGAIN** [–] [ ]

Nov 79. (7") *(WIP 6549)* **CAN WE STILL BE FRIENDS. / BACK IN MY ARMS** [ ] [–]

Dec 79. (7") *<49137>* **CAN WE STILL BE FRIENDS. / REMEMBER TO REMEMBER** [–] [52]

Aug 80. (7") *<49554>* **JOHNNY AND MARY. / STYLE KILLS** [–] [ ]

Aug 80. (7") *(WIP 6638)* **JOHNNY AND MARY. / WHAT'S IT TAKE** [44] [–]
(12"+=) *(WIP12 6638)* – Remember to remember.

Aug 80. (lp/c) *(<ILPS/ICT 9595>)* **CLUES** [31] Oct80 [59]
– Looking for clues / Sulky girl / Johnny and Mary / What do you care / I dream of wires / Woke up laughing / Not a second time / Found you now. *(re-iss. Jan87 lp/c/cd; ILPM/ICM/CID 9595) (cd-iss. Jan89; IMCD 21)*

Oct 80. (7") *<49620>* **LOOKING FOR CLUES. / WOKE UP LAUGHING** [–] [ ]

Nov 80. (7") *(WIP 6651)* **LOOKING FOR CLUES. / IN WALKS LOVE AGAIN** [33] [–]
(12") *(WIP12 6651)* – ('A'side) / Good care of you / Style kills.

Jun 81. (7") *(WIP 6678)* **NOT A SECOND TIME. / WOKE UP LAUGHING** [ ] [–]

Jan 82. (7"pic-d) *(WIP 6754) <50042>* **SOME GUYS HAVE ALL THE LUCK. / TOO GOOD TO BE TRUE** [16] [ ]
(12"pic-d) *(WIP12 6754)* – ('A'side) / Style kills / Si Chatouillieux / What do you care.

Mar 82. (lp/c) *(<ILPS/ICT 9665>)* **MAYBE IT'S LIVE (live)** [32] May82 [ ]
– Sneakin' Sally through the alley / What's it take / Best of both worlds / Every kinda people / Bad case of loving you (doctor, doctor) / Some guys have all the luck / Style kills / Si Chatouillieaux / Maybe it's you / What do you care. *(re-iss. Apr91 c; ICM 9665) (re-iss. May93 on 'Spectrum' cd/c; 550068-2/-4)*

Nov 82. (7"pic-d) *(WIP 6833)* **PRIDE. / PRIDE (instrumental)** [ ] [–]
(12") *(WIP 6833)* – ('A'side) / Parade of the obliterators.

Mar 83. (7"/12")*(IS/12IS 104) <99866>* **YOU ARE IN MY SYSTEM. / DEADLINE** [53] Jun83 [78]

Apr 83. (lp/c) *(ILPS/ICT 9720) <90065>* **PRIDE** [37] [ ]
– Pride / Deadline / Want you more / Dance for me / You are in my system / It's not difficult / Say you will / You can have it (take my heart) / What you waiting for / The silver gun. *(re-iss. Jan87 lp/c/cd; ILPM/ICM/CID 9720) (cd-iss. Jun89; IMCD 22)*

Jun 83. (7"pic-d) *(IS 121)* **YOU CAN HAVE IT (TAKE MY HEART). / THE SILVER GUN** [66] [–]

— From early '85, PALMER became lead singer of DURAN DURAN off-shoot band The POWER STATION. Their eponymous lp, hit both UK + US Top 20's, and spawned a few hits 'SOME LIKE IT HOT', 'GET IT ON' & 'COMMUNICATION'. (see DURAN DURAN ⇒)

Oct 85. (7") *(IS 242) <99597>* **DISCIPLINE OF LOVE. / DANCE FOR ME** [ ] [82]
(12"+=) *(12IS 242)* – Woke up laughing.

Nov 85. (lp/c/cd) *(ILPS/ICT/CID 9801) <90471>* **RIPTIDE** [5] [8]
– Riptide / Hyperactive / Addicted to love / Trick bag / Get it through your heart / I didn't mean to turn you on / Flesh wound / Discipline of love / Riptide (reprise). *(cd-iss. 1988; CID 130) (re-iss. Apr91 lp/c; ILPM/ICM 9801)*

Dec 85. (7") *(IS 256)* **RIPTIDE. / BACK IN MY ARMS** [ ] [–]
(12") *(12IS 256)* – ('A'side) / No not much (live) / Trick bag (live)
(d7"++=) *(ISD 256)* – (12"tracks) / Johnny and Mary.

Feb 86. (7") *<99570>* **ADDICTED TO LOVE. / LET'S FALL IN LOVE TONIGHT** [–] [1]

Apr 86. (7"/12") *(IS/12IS 270)* **ADDICTED TO LOVE. / REMEMBER TO REMEMBER** [5] [–]
(7"sha-pic-d) *(ISP 270)* – ('A'side) / More.

May 86. (7") *<99545>* **HYPERACTIVE. / WOKE UP LAUGHING** [–] [33]

Jun 86. (7"/12") *(IS/12IS 283) <99537>* **I DIDN'T MEAN TO TURN YOU ON. / GET IT THROUGH YOUR HEART** [9] Aug86 [2]
(d7"+=) *(ISD 283)* – You are in my system / Johnny and Mary.

Oct 86. (7") *(IS 242)* **DISCIPLINE OF LOVE. / DANCE FOR ME** [68] [–]
(12"+=) *(12IS 242)* – Riptide (medley).
(d12"+=) *(12ISX 242)* – Remember to remember / Addicted to love.

Mar 88. (7") *(IS 352) <99377>* **SWEET LIES. / WANT YOU MORE** [ ] [94]
(12"+=) *(12IS 352)* – Riptide.
(cd-s++=) *(CID 352)* – ('A'extended).

E.M.I. Manhattan

Jun 88. (7"/7"pic-d) *(EM/+P 61) <50133>* **SIMPLY IRRESISTIBLE. / NOVA** [44] [2]
(12"+=/cd-s+=) *(12/CD EM 61)* – ('A'extended) / ('A'instrumental).

Jun 88. (cd/c/lp) *(CD/TC+/EMD 1007) <48057>* **HEAVY NOVA** [17] [13]
– Simply irresistible / More than ever / Change his ways / Disturbing behaviour / Early in the morning / It could happen to you / She makes my day / It could happen to you / Tell me I'm not dreaming / Between us / Casting a spell. *(re-iss. Mar94 cd/c; CD/TC EMD 1007)*

Oct 88. (7") *(EM 65)* **SHE MAKES MY DAY. / DISTURBING BEHAVIOUR** [6] [–]
(12"+=/cd-s+=) *(12/CD EM 65)* – Simply irresistible (extended).

Oct 88. (7") *<50157>* **EARLY IN THE MORNING. / DISTURBING BEHAVIOR** [–] [19]

May 89. (7"/7"pic-d) *(EM/+PD 85)* **CHANGE HIS WAYS. / MORE THAN EVER** [28] [ ]
(12") *(12EM 85)* – (2 different mixes).
(cd-s++=) *(CDEM 85)* – She makes my day.

Jun 89. (7") *<50206>* **TELL ME I'M NOT DREAMING (2 versions) / MORE THAN EVER** [–] [60]

Aug 89. (c-s/7") *(TC+/EM 99)* **IT COULD HAPPEN TO YOU. / CHANGE HIS WAYS** [71] [ ]
(12"+=) *(12EM 99)* – Early in the morning (get up mix).
(cd-s++=) *(CDEM 99)* – Casting a spell.

E.M.I. E.M.I.

Oct 90. (c-s/7"; ROBERT PALMER & UB40) *(TC+/EM 167)* **I'LL BE YOUR BABY TONIGHT. / DEEP END** [6] [ ]
(12"+=/cd-s+=) *(12/CD EM 167)* – ('A'version).

Nov 90. (cd/c/d-lp) *(CD/TC+/EMD 1018) <93935>* **DON'T EXPLAIN** [9] [88]
– Your mother should have told you / Light-years / You can't get enough

of a good thing / Dreams to remember / You're amazing / Mess around / Happiness / History / I'll be your baby tonight / Housework / Mercy mercy me – I want you / Don't explain / Aeroplane / People will say we're in love / Not a word / Top 40 / You're so desirable / You're my thrill.

Nov 90. (c-s,cd-s) <50338> **YOU'RE AMAZING / SO EMBOLDENED** – 28

Dec 90. (c-s/7") *(TC+/EM 173)* <50344> **MERCY MERCY ME (THE ECOLOGY) – I WANT YOU. / OH YEAH** 9 Feb91 16
(12"+=/cd-s+=) *(12/CD EM 173)* – (2-'A'&'B'versions).

Apr 91. (c-s/7") **HAPPINESS. / ALL SHOOK UP**
(12"+=/cd-s+=) – ('A'extended).

Jun 91. (c-s/7") *(TC+/EM 193)* **DREAMS TO REMEMBER. / MESS AROUND** 68 –
(12"+=) *(12EM 193)* – Happiness.
(cd-s+=) *(CDEM 193)* – Mercy mercy me (the ecology) – I want you.

Oct 92. (c-s/7") *(TC+/EM 251)* **WITCHCRAFT. / CHANCE** 50 –
(cd-s) *(CDEM 251)* – ('A'side) / She makes my day / Mercy mercy me – I want you.

Oct 92. (cd/c/d-lp) *(CD/MC+/EMD 1038)* <98923> **RIDIN' HIGH** 32
– Love me or leave me / (Love is) The tender trap / You're my thrill / Want you more / Baby it's cold outside / Aeroplane / Witchcraft / What a little moonlight can do / Don't explain / Chance / Goody goody / Do nothin' till you hear from me / Honeysuckle rose / No not much / Ridin' high / Hard head.
(above featured many 40's + 50's covers)

Jul 94. (c-s/7") *(TC+/EM 331)* **GIRL U WANT. / NO FUSS** 57 –
(cd-s+=) *(CDEMS 331)* – ('A'mixes).

Aug 94. (c-s/7") *(TC+/EM 343)* **KNOW BY NOW. / MERCY MERCY ME – I WANT YOU** 25 –
(cd-s+=) *(CDEM 343)* – Simply irresistible.
(cd-s) *(CDEMS 343)* – ('A'side) / ('A'mixes) / In the stars / She makes my day.

Sep 94. (cd/c/lp) *(CD/TC+/EMD 1069)* <30301> **HONEY** 25
– Honey A / Honey B / You're mine / Know by now / Nobody but you / Love takes time / Honeymoon / You blow me away / Close to the edge / Closer to the edge / Girl u want / Wham bam boogie / Big trouble / Dreams come true.

Dec 94. (c-s/7") *(TC+/EM 350)* **YOU BLOW ME AWAY. / SIMPLY IRRESISTIBLE** 38
(cd-s) *(CDEM 350)* – ('A'side) / No control / ('A'mix) / Know by now.
(cd-s) *(CDEMS 350)* – ('A'side) / ('A'mixes) / Change his ways.

Sep 95. (c-s) *(TCEM 399)* **RESPECT YOURSELF / YOU BLOW ME AWAY** 45
(cd-s+=) *(CDEM 399)* – Girl u want / Race to the end of the set medley:- Bad case of loving you (doctor, doctor) – Simply irrisistible – Some guys have all the luck – I didn't mean to turn you on – Looking for clues – Addicted to love – You are in my system – Know by now – Some like it hot – I want you – Every kinda people.
(cd-s) *(CDEMS 399)* – ('A'side) / Get it on (45 mix) / Some like it hot (7"mix) / Respect yourself (FX mix).

Oct 95. (cd/c) *(CD/TC EMD 1088)* <55312> **THE VERY BEST OF ROBERT PALMER** (compilation) 4
– Addicted to love / Bad case of loving you (doctor, doctor) / Simply irresistible / Get it on (POWER STATION) / Some guys have all the luck / I didn't mean to turn you on / Looking for clues / You are in my system / Some like it hot (POWER STATION) / Respect yourself / I'll be your baby tonight (w/ UB40) / Johnny & Mary / She makes my day / Know by now / Every kinda people / Mercy mercy me – I want you (medley).

Eagle Pyramid

Apr 99. (cd/c) *(EAG CD/MC 063)* <75865> **RHYTHM AND BLUES** Jul99
– True love / No problem / Let's get it on '99 / Stone cold / Sex appeal / Work to make it work '99 / All the will in the world / You're not the only one / Mr. Wise guy / I choose you / Dance for me / Twenty million things.

May 01. (cd) *(EAGCD 174)* <20005> **LIVE AT THE APOLLO, NEW YORK CITY (live 2000)**
– Some like it hot / Hyperactive / Discipline of love / Tell me I'm not dreaming / I didn't mean to turn you on / Looking for clues / Change his ways / Pride / Woke up laughing / Johnny & Mary / Riptide / Between us / Flesh wound / More than ever / Simply irresistible / Casting a spell / Addicted to love.

— in Jan'03, SHAKE B4 USE vs ROBERT PALMER hit the UK Top 50 with a version of 'ADDICTED TO LOVE'

Universal Compendia

May 03. (cd) *(038098-2)* <4886> **DRIVE**
– Mama talk to your daughter / Why get up? / Who's fooling who? / Am I wrong? / TV dinners / Lucky / Stella / Dr. Zhivago's train / Ain't that just like a woman / Hound dog / Crazy cajun cake walk band / I need your love so bad.

— on the 26th of September 2003, PALMER died of a heart attack

– compilations, etc. –

on 'Island' unless mentioned otherwise

Jul 87. (lp/c) *C5; (C5/+K 501)* **THE EARLY YEARS** –
– (above featured before solo work with The ALAN BOWN SET)

Nov 89. (7") *(IS 438)* **BAD CASE OF LOVING YOU (DOCTOR, DOCTOR). / SWEET LIES**
(12"+=/cd-s+=) *(12IS/CID 438)* – What's it take.

Nov 89. (lp/c/cd) *(ILPS/ICT/CID 9944)* <91318> **ADDICTIONS VOL.1** 7 79
– Bad case of loving you (doctor, doctor) / Pride / Addicted to love / Sweet lies / Woke up laughing / Looking for clues / Some guys have all the luck / Some like it hot (POWER STATION) / What's it take? / Every kinda people / Johnny & Mary / Simply irresistible / Style kills.

Feb 92. (c-s/cd-s/7") *(CIS/CID/IS 498)* **EVERY KINDA PEOPLE. / ('A'radio mix)** 43 –

Mar 92. (cd/c) *(CID/ICT TV 4)* <510345> **ADDICTIONS VOL.2** 12
– Remember to remember / Sneakin' Sally through the alley / Maybe it's you / You are in my system / I didn't mean to turn you on / Can we still be friends / Man smart, woman smarter / Too good to be true / Every kinda people / She makes my day / Best of both worlds / Give me an inch / You're gonna get what's coming / I dream of wires / The silver gun.

Jun 92. (c-s/cd-s/7") **YOU ARE IN MY SYSTEM. / YOU'RE GONNA GET WHAT'S COMING / TOO GOOD TO BE TRUE** –

Nov 95. (d-cd) *(ISDCD 2)* **ADDICTIONS VOL.1 & 2** –

May 99. (cd) *E.M.I.; (493575-2)* **WOKE UP LAUGHING (ADVENTURE IN TROPICAL MUSIC 1977-1997)** –

Sep 00. (cd) *EMI Gold; (CDGOLD 1054)* **THE ESSENTIAL COLLECTION** –

Jan 01. (cd) *Universal; (542267-2)* **THE UNIVERSAL MASTERS COLLECTION** –

Nov 02. (cd) *Universal TV; (069781-2)* <069946> **AT HIS VERY BEST** 40
– Every kinda people / Bad case of loving you (doctor, doctor) / Johnny and Mary / Looking for clues / Some guys have all the luck / You are in my system / You can have it (take my heart) / Some like it hot (POWER STATION) / Addicted to love / I didn't mean to turn you on / Sweet lies / Simply irresistible / She makes my day / I'll be your baby tonight (with UB40) / Mercy mercy me (the ecology) – I want you (medley) / Sneakin' Sally through the alley / Riptide *[UK-only]* / I need your love so bad / TV dinners. *(re-dist.Oct03)* – hit UK No.38 *(re-iss. Nov03 +=dvd; 9814155)*

Mar 03. (cd) *Universal; (AA314 546556-2)* **20th CENTURY MASTERS** –

Aug 03. (t-cd) *Spectrum; (9808976)* **CLUES / DOUBLE FUN / SOME GUYS HAVE ALL THE LUCK** –

PANIC! AT THE DISCO

Formed: Las Vegas, Nevada, USA ... early 2005 by childhood friends BRENDON URIE and RYAN ROSS, completing the line-up with rhythm section BRENT WILSON and SPENCER SMITH. Growing out of a BLINK-182 fixation, the quartet secured a deal with label of the moment, 'Fueled By Ramen', with the help of FALL OUT BOY's PETE WENTZ. The connection didn't end there as RYAN seemed to have inherited FOB's penchant for snappy song titles and Kidulthood tunes. Their moniker on the other hand ultimately originated from the more credible source of a SMITHS song ('Panic'), if by way of NAME TAKEN's version. 'A FEVER YOU CAN'T SWEAT OUT' (2005), was an archetypal slow burner of a debut album, eventually hitting the US Top 20 as well as the UK equivalent in 2006. A couple of the less long-winded tracks, 'I WRITE SINS NOT TRAGEDIES' and 'BUT IT'S BETTER IF YOU DO' hit the charts, although these were to be the swansong for BRENT.

Album rating: A FEVER YOU CAN'T SWEAT OUT (*6)

BRENDON URIE (b.12 Apr'87) – vocals, guitar, keyboards / **RYAN ROSS** – guitar, keyboards, vocals / **BRENT WILSON** – bass / **SPENCER SMITH** – drums

Fueled By Ramen — Fueled By Ramen

Feb 06. (cd) *(5101 12334-2)* *<FBR 77CD>* **A FEVER YOU CAN'T SWEAT OUT** [17] Sep05 [16]
– Introduction / The only difference between martyrdom and suicide is press coverage / London beckoned songs about money written by machines / Nails for breakfast, tacks for snacks / Camisado / Time to dance / Lying is the most fun a girl can have without taking her clothes off / Intermission / But it's better if you do / I write sins not tragedies / I constantly thank God for Esteban / There's a good reason these tables are numbered honey, you just haven't thought of it yet / Build God, then we'll talk.

Atlantic — Atlantic

Feb 06. (etched-7") *(ATUK 024)* **I WRITE SINS NOT TRAGEDIES** [ ] [17]
(cd-s+=) *(ATUK 024CD)* – Nails for breakfast, tacks for snacks (demo).

Mar 06. (-) *<radio>* **THE ONLY DIFFERENCE BETWEEN MARTYRDOM AND SUICIDE IS PRESS COVERAGE** [–] [77]

May 06. (7") *(AT 0242)* **BUT IT'S BETTER IF YOU DO. / THE ONLY DIFFERENCE BETWEEN MARTYRDOM AND SUICIDE IS PRESS COVERAGE (Tommie Sunshine Brooklyn fire remix)** [23] [–]
(7"maroon) *(AT 0242X)* – ('A') / I write sins not tragedies (iTunes session).
(cd-s) *(AT 0242CD)* – ('A') / I write sins not tragedies (91X acoustic session).

— (May'06) now without BRENT

PANTERA

Formed: Arlington, Texas, USA ... 1981 by TERRY GLAZE, 'DIAMOND' DARRELL, VINCE ABBOTT and REX ROCKER, taking their name from the Spanish word for panther. Initially a vaguely glam-influenced hard-rock band in the packet-bulging tradition of KISS and AEROSMITH, PANTERA began their career with 'METAL MAGIC' (1983), issued on their own homegrown 'Metal Magic' label. The album was fairly well-received Stateside and saw the band gain a firm foothold on the lower rungs of the hair-rock ladder. With subsequent releases like 'PROJECTS IN THE JUNGLE' (1984) and 'I AM THE NIGHT' (1985), however, the group began to adopt a more muscular approach, consolidated with the arrival of PHIL ANSELMO (as a replacement for GLAZE) on 1988's 'POWER METAL'. With a growing reputation and the help of a recommendation from JUDAS PRIEST's ROB HALFORD, the band secured a major label deal with 'Atco'. The resulting album, 'COWBOYS FROM HELL' (1990) was a dramatic turnaround, gone was the 80's metal garb and cheesy choruses; check shirts, tattoos and a brutally uncompromising thrash-based groove had forcibly taken their place. Clearly, something had made these boys angry and 'A VULGAR DISPLAY OF POWER' (1992) was arguably the most articulate and succinct fix of metallic aggression to be had that year; the likes of 'F**KING HOSTILE' said it all. The record also gave PANTERA their first taste of chart success, the 'WALK' single making the UK Top 40. So it was, then, that the stage was set for PANTERA to both consolidate their position as one of the most unrelentingly intense groups in the nu-metal hierarchy and smash into the UK album chart at pole position with 'FAR BEYOND DRIVEN' (1994). Incredibly their seventh album, the group were now virtually unrecognisable from their rather tame origins, the record's grim vignettes (select 'I'M BROKEN' and 'THROES OF REJECTION' for that ultimate feel-bad factor) were accompanied by a suitably severe Black Sabbath cover, 'PLANET CARAVAN'. The set also saw PANTERA climb to the uppermost regions of the American charts, their services sought out for a contribution to 'The Crow' soundtrack (a cover of Poison Idea's 'THE BADGE'). Silent for most of 1995 (bar ANSELMO who moonlighted with DOWN; sole album, 'NOLA'), PANTERA returned with a vengeance the following year, releasing 'THE GREAT SOUTHERN TRENDKILLERS' (1996). Easing back a little on the speed pedal, the group achieved an even more savagely focused intensity, ANSELMO raging from the depths of his tortured soul. It may have lent his lyrics and delivery a stark harshness, but surviving on the very precipice of existence eventually caught up with ANSELMO when, later that summer (13th July), the singer narrowly escaped death from a heroin overdose, later admitting to being dead for five minutes. Shaken but hardly beaten, PANTERA returned the following year with a well-overdue concert set, 'OFFICIAL LIVE – 101 PROOF', proving that there are still few to match the sheer, unadulterated heaviness of their impact. 'REINVENTING THE STEEL' in 2000 kept them high in profile as it returned ANSELMO and Co to the US Top 5. PANTERA split into many factions soon afterwards, DIMEBAG and VINNIE PAUL sticking together through it all to become DAMAGEPLAN, recruiting BOB ZILLA and PAT LACHLAN in the process. In February 2004, the quartet released their debut album, 'NEW FOUND POWER', the buzz they had already created at gigs around the US making it a Top 40 entry. However, by the end of the year, tragedy had struck the rock world yet again. On the night of December 8th (the same day JOHN LENNON was shot!), while performing at the Alrosa Village rock club in Columbus, Ohio, DIMEBAG – and three others in the audience including bodyguard Jeff "Mayhem" Thompson – were shot dead by a disgruntled, homicidal fan. All fans of PANTERA, metal and music in general mourned the loss of another great musician.

• **Covered:** HOLE IN THE SKY (Black Sabbath) / CAT SCRATCH FEVER (Ted Nugent).

Album rating: METAL MAGIC (*5) / PROJECTS IN THE JUNGLE (*5) / I AM THE NIGHT (*5) / POWER METAL (*4) / COWBOYS FROM HELL (*6) / A VULGAR DISPLAY OF POWER (*8) / FAR BEYOND DRIVEN (*7) / THE GREAT SOUTHERN TRENDKILLERS (*6) / OFFICIAL LIVE 101 PROOF (*6) / REINVENTING THE STEEL (*6) / THE BEST OF PANTERA: FAR BEYOND THE GREAT SOUTHERN COWBOYS' VULGAR HITS compilation (*7) / Damageplan: NEW FOUND POWER (*6)

TERRY GLAZE – vocals, guitar / **DARRELL ABBOTT** (b.20 Aug'66, Dallas, Texas) – guitar / **REX ROCKER** (b. REX BROWN, 27 Jul'64, Graham, Texas) – bass / **VINCENT PAUL ABBOTT** (b.11 Mar'64, Dallas) – drums

not iss. — Metal Magic

1983. (lp) *<MMR 1983>* **METAL MAGIC** [–] [ ]
– Ride my rocket / I'll be alright / Tell me if you want it / Latest lover / Biggest part of me / Metal magic / Widowmaker / Nothin' on (but the radio) / Sad lover / Rock out!.

— GLAZE became TERRENCE LEE, DARRELL prefixed the word DIMEBAG and VINCE was now VINNIE PAUL

1984. (lp) *<MMR 1984>* **PROJECTS IN THE JUNGLE** [–] [ ]
– All over tonite / Out for blood / Blue lite turnin' red / Like fire / In over my head / Projects in the jungle / Heavy metal rules! / Only a heartbeat away / Killers / Takin' my life.

1985. (lp) *<MMR 1985>* **I AM THE NIGHT** [–] [ ]
– Hot and heavy / I am the night / Onward we rock! / D.S.G.S.T.S.T.S.M. / Daughters of the queen / Down below / Come-on eyes / Right on the edge / Valhalla / Forever tonight.

— **PHILIP ANSELMO** (b.30 Jun'68, New Orleans, Louisiana) – vocals repl. TERRY

May 88. (lp) *<MMR 1988>* **POWER METAL** [–] [ ]
– Rock the world / Power metal / We'll meet again / Over and out / Proud to be loud / Down below / Death trap / Hard ride / Burnnn! / P*S*T*88.

Atco — Atco

Jul 90. (cd/c/lp) *<(7567 91372-2/-4/-1)>* **COWBOYS FROM HELL** [ ] [ ]
– Cowboys from Hell / Primal concrete sledge / Psycho holiday / Heresy / Cemetery gates / Domination / Shattered / Clash with reality / Medicine man / Message in blood / The sleep / The art of shredding.

Feb 92. (cd/c/lp) *<(7567 91758-2/-4/-1)>* **A VULGAR DISPLAY OF POWER** [64] [44]
– Mouth for war / A new level / Walk / F**king hostile / This love / Rise / No good (attack the radical) / Live in a hole / Regular people (conceit) / By demons be driven / Hollow.

Sep 92. (7"/c-s) *(A 5845/+C)* **MOUTH FOR WAR. / RISE** [73] [ ]
(cd-s+=) *(A 5845CD)* – Cowboys from Hell / Heresy.
(12") *(A 5845T)* – ('A'side) / ('A'-superloud mix) / Domination / Primal concrete sledge.

Feb 93. (12"m) *(B 6076T)* **WALK. / COWBOYS FROM HELL / PSYCHO HOLIDAY (live)** [34] [ ]
(cd-ep) *(B 6076CD)* – ('A'side) / Fucking hostile / By demons be driven.
(cd-ep) *(B 6076CDX)* – ('A'side) / No good (attack the radical)/ A new level / Walk (extended remixes by Jim 'Foetus' Thirlwell).

East West Atco

Mar 94. (12"/cd-s) *(B 5932 T/CD1)* **I'M BROKEN. / SLAUGHTERED** [19] [ ]
(cd-s+=) *(B 5932CD2)* – Domination (live) / Primal concrete sledge.
(cd-s) *(B 5932CD3)* – ('A'side) / Cowboys from Hell (live) / Psycho holiday (live).
(12") *(B 5932X)* – ('A'side) / Walk (cervical edit) / Fuckin' hostile.

Mar 94. (cd/c/lp) *<(7567 92302-2/-4/-1)>* **FAR BEYOND DRIVEN** [3] [1]
– Strength beyond strength / Becoming / 5 minutes alone / I'm broken / Good friends and a bottle of pills / Hard lines, sunken cheeks / Slaughtered / 25 years / Shedding skin / Use my third arm / Throes of rejection / Planet Caravan.

May 94. (7"white) *(A 8293)* **5 MINUTES ALONE. / THE BADGE** [ ] [ ]

Oct 94. (7") *(A 5836)* **PLANET CARAVAN. / 5 MINUTES ALONE** [26] [ ]
(12") *(A 5836T)* – ('A'side) / Cowboys from Hell / Heresay.
(cd-s) *(A 5836Cd1)* – ('A'side) / The badge / New level / Becoming.
(cd-s) *(A 5836CD2)* – ('A'side) / Domination / Hollow.

May 96. (cd/c/lp) *<(7559 61908-2/-4/-1)>* **THE GREAT SOUTHERN TRENDKILLERS** [17] [4]
– Drag the waters / War nerve / It can't destroy my body / 13 steps to nowhere / Sandblasted skin / Underground in America / Suicide note (part 1) / Suicide note (part 2).

—— On 13th Jul'96, ANSELMO luckily survived a heroin overdose in which he was reported to be dead for five minutes.

Aug 97. (cd/c/lp) *<(7559 62068-2/-4/-1)>* **OFFICIAL LIVE – 101 PROOF (live)** [54] [15]
– New level / Walk / Becoming / 5 minutes alone / Sandblasted skin / Suicide note (part 2) / War nerve / This love / Dom – Hollow / Strength beyond strength / I'm broken / Cowboys from Hell / Cemetery gates / Fuckin' hostile / Where you come from / I can't hide.

Mar 00. (cd/c) *<(7559 62451-2/-4)>* **REINVENTING THE STEEL** [33] [4]
– Hellbound / Goddamn electric / Yesterday don't mean shit / You've got to belong to it / Revolution is my name / Death rattle / We'll grind that axe for a long time / Uplift / It makes them disappear / I'll cast a shadow.

Oct 01. (cd-ep) *<7261>* **REVOLUTION IS MY NAME EP** [–] [ ]
– Revolution is my name / Hole in the sky / Immortal insane / Cat scratch fever.

—— when PANTERA split, ANSELMO continued with side-projects, VIKING CROWN, SOUTHERN ISOLATION, SUPERJOINT RITUAL and DOWN

– compilations, etc. –

Sep 03. (cd+dvd) *Elektra; (8122 73729-2) <73932-2>* **THE BEST OF PANTERA: FAR BEYOND THE GREAT SOUTHERN COWBOYS' VULGAR HITS!** (UK title 'REINVENTING HELL') [ ] [38]

DAMAGEPLAN

DIMEBAG DARRELL – guitar / **VINNIE PAUL** – drums / **PAT LACHMAN** – vocals (ex-HALFORD, ex-DIESEL MACHINE) / **BOB ZILLA** (aka KAKAHA) – bass

Elektra Elektra

Feb 04. (cd) *<(7559 62939-2)>* **NEW FOUND POWER** [ ] [38]
– Wake up / Breathing new life / New found power / Pride / Fuck you / Reborn / Explode / Save me / Cold blooded / Crawl / Blink of an eye / Blunt force trauma / Moment of truth / Soul bleed.

—— tragically, DIMEBAG was murdered playing a concert (on 7 December 2004) by a homicidal "fan"

□ PAPA M (see under ⇒ SLINT)

PAPA ROACH

Formed: Vacaville, North California, USA . . . 1993 by schoolmates JACOBY SHADDIX aka COBY DICK, DAVE BUCKNER, JERRY HORTON and WILL JAMES, taking the inspiration for their moniker from the PONCHO SANCHEZ album, 'Papa Gato'. Influenced by Bay Area mavericks such as FAITH NO MORE and PRIMUS, the band set out playing a funk/hip-hop hybrid and rapidly built up a loyal local following while making a tentative start to their recording career with 'CACA BONITA' (1995). In 1996, WILL JAMES was replaced by the band's teenage roadie TOBIN ESPERANCE and the lads cut a sophomore album, 'OLD FRIENDS FROM YOUNG YEARS' (1997) on a miniscule budget. Playlisted by many local radio stations, the record – again released on their own 'Onion Hardcore Recordings' imprint – was instrumental in raising PAPA ROACH's profile and before long the Californian upstarts were playing on the same bill as SUICIDAL TENDENCIES, HUMAN WASTE PROJECT, WILL HAVEN etc. 1998's '5 TRACKS DEEP' EP sharpened their rap-metal chops and paved the way for a major label deal with 'Dreamworks'. The Hollywood-based label released the 'INFEST' album in 2000, a record that crept unannounced into the US Top 20 and finally established PAPA ROACH as major league contenders alongside KORN, LIMP BIZKIT, DEFTONES etc. Reliable if not exactly innovative exponents of the increasingly over subscribed nu-metal agenda, P-ROACH (as their fans know and love them) can safely regard themselves as fully paid up members of America's new rock establishment. 'LOVEHATETRAGEDY' (2002) found the 'ROACH crew largely laying off the more groove based elements of their sound in favour of a more straight up alt-metal approach although lyrically JACOBY SHADDIX was as reliably despondent as ever. The transformation from nu-metal to mid-00s metal was completed by 'GETTING AWAY WITH MURDER' (2004), a flailing set of straight-down-the-line corporate angst dovetailing nicely with the currently fashionable emo scene, as heard on US Top 20 single, 'SCARS'. The album itself – complete with gratuitously tasteless cover art – also made the US Top 20, Top 30 in the UK.

Album rating: OLD FRIENDS FROM YOUNG YEARS (*5) / INFEST (*6) / LOVEHATETRAGEDY (*6) / GETTING AWAY WITH MURDER (*4)

COBY DICK (b. JACOBY SHADDIX) – vocals / **JERRY HORTON** – guitar / **WILL JAMES** – bass / **DAVE BUCKNER** – drums

not iss. own label

Dec 94. (cd-ep) **POTATOES FOR CHRISTMAS** [–] [ ]
– Coffee thoughts / Mama's dress / Lenny's / Lulu Espidachi / Cheez-z-fux / I love babies / Dendrilopis.

1995. (cd-s) **CACA BONITA** [–] [ ]

—— **TOBIN ESPERANCE** – bass; repl. WILL

1997. (cd) **OLD FRIENDS FROM YOUNG YEARS** [–] [ ]
– Intro / Orange drive palms / Liquid diet / GrrBrr / iSEDuF**nDie / Dirty cut freak / Living room / 829 / Peewagon / Hedake / Shut up n die (reprise). *(hidden track+=)* – thanx.

1998. (cd-ep) **5 TRACKS DEEP** [–] [ ]
– Revenge in Japanese / My bad side / July / Tambienemy / Thrown away.

1999. (cd-ep) **LET 'EM KNOW** [–] [ ]
– Walking thru barbed wire / Legacy / Binge / Snakes / Tightrope.

Dreamworks Dreamwo

Aug 00. (cd) *<(450223-2)>* **INFEST** [9] Apr00 [5]
– Infest / Last resort / Broken home / Dead cell / Between angels and insects / Blood brothers *[on explicit version]* / Legacy *[on clean version]* / Revenge / Snakes / Never enough / Binge / Thrown away. *(hidden track+=)* – Tight rope. *(UK re-iss. Feb01 cd/cd+=; 45031 6-2/7-2)* – Dead cell (live) / Last resort (video).

Feb 01. (c-s) *(450920-4) <album cut>* **LAST RESORT / BROKEN HOME (session)** [3] May00 [57]
(cd-s+=) *(450920-2)* – Dead cell (session) / ('A'-CD-ROM).

(cd-s) *(450921-2)* – ('A'side) / ('A'session) / Between angels and insects (session).

Apr 01. (c-s) *(450908-4)* **BETWEEN ANGELS AND INSECTS / LAST RESORT (radio)** 17 –
(cd-s) *(450908-2)* – ('A'side) / Last resort (live) / Binge (live) / ('A'-CD-ROM).
(cd-s) *(450909-2)* – ('A'side) / Tight rope (live) / Barbed wire (live).

Jun 02. (c-s) *(450818-4)* *<450820>* **SHE LOVES ME NOT / NAKED IN FRONT OF THE COMPUTER** 14 76
(cd-s+=) *(450818-2)* – Blood brothers / ('A'-video).
(cd-s) *(450817-2)* – ('A'side) / Life is a bullet (live BBC1 version) / Lovehatetragedy (live BBC1 version).

Jun 02. (cd) *<(450389-2)>* **LOVEHATETRAGEDY** 4 2
– M-80 (explosive energy movement) / Life is a bullet (explicit) / Time and time again / Walking thru barbed wire / Decompression period / Born with nothing, die with everything (explicit) / She loves me not (explicit) / Singular indestructable droid / Black clouds / Code of energy (explicit) / Lovehatetragedy. *(UK+=)* – Gouge away / Never said it. *(special cd+=; 450367-2)* – Between angels and insects (video) / The last resort (video).

Oct 02. (7") *(450805-7)* *<450809>* **TIME AND TIME AGAIN. / SHE LOVES ME NOT (live)** 54
(cd-s+=) *(450805-2)* – Code of energy (live) / ('A'-video).
(cd-s) *(450804-2)* – ('A'live) / Singular indestructable droid (live) / The last resort (live) / ('A'-video).

Geffen Geffen

Jul 04. (cd-s) *<9882137>* **SCARS / SCARS (acoustic) / GETTING AWAY WITH MURDER (live Napster version)** – 15

Aug 04. (cd) *(9863643)* *<B00031421-2>* **GETTING AWAY WITH MURDER** 30 17
– Blood (empty promises) / Not listening / Stop looking – Start seeing / Take me / Getting away with murder / Be free / Done with you / Scars / Sometimes / Blanket of fear / Tyranny normality / Do or die.

Sep 04. (7"pic-d) *(9863646)* **GETTING AWAY WITH MURDER. / ANXIETY (featuring the Black Eyed Peas)** 45 69
(cd-s+=) *(9863647)* – Harder than a coffin nail / ('A'-video).

□ PARLIAMENT/s (see under ⇒ CLINTON, George)

Gram PARSONS

Born: CECIL INGRAM CONNOR, 5 Nov'46, Winter Haven, Florida, USA. Through a privileged but traumatic childhood in Waycross, Georgia, during which his father, Coon Dog, committed suicide and his mother died of alcohol-related illness (on the day he graduated from high school), GRAM diverted himself with music; although his first love was country, the traditional preserve of white Southerners, GRAM was inspired to get up on stage after witnessing the hip-swivelling suave of ELVIS PRESLEY. Developing his talents in high-school covers outfits such as The PACERS and The LEGENDS, he was also sidelining with solo gigs and, through manager, Buddy Freeman, secured an appearance on a Greenville, South Carolina, TV Station. This in turn led to GRAM forming The SHILOS (having previously sang as a duo with KENT LAVOIE – aka hitmaker, LOBO), a fairly staid folk outfit who recorded a session for a Greenville campus radio station (released in 1979 on 'Sundown' as 'GRAM PARSONS – THE EARLY YEARS 1963-65') and with whom PARSONS penned his most fully realised song to date, 'ZAH'S BLUES'. Inevitably, the band fell by the wayside following GRAM's enrolment at Harvard in 1965; bypassing classes for the lure of the local music scene, he barely lasted six months, hooking up with local musicians, IAN DUNLOP, JOHN NUESE and MICKEY GAUVIN to form the LIKE and pioneering a synthesis of R&B, rock'n'roll and country which would would inform the remainder of PARSON's relatively short career. Around this time, GRAM spoke of having a deal with 'R.C.A.' and although it's widely believed he never recorded for the label, two tracks, 'CAN'T TAKE IT ANYMORE' and 'REMEMBER', have recently been unearthed (thanks to eagle-eyed archives man, Ron Maharg) from the label's vaults. The former a BYRDS-esque jangle calling to mind 'Chimes Of Freedom' and the latter a version of 'NOVEMBER NIGHTS' (a staple of The LIKE's live set never recorded under its original title but subsequently covered by actor Peter Fonda), these tracks may well have been recorded at the same time as the legendary lost Brandon De Wilde session, which GRAM & Co. are rumoured to have played on (the actor was a close confidante of the band and a regular at their new communal home in The Bronx, New York); through the continuing efforts of GP obsessive and all-round top man, Keith Munro, the songs might just be given an official release – subject to legal complexities – in the near future through 'B.M.G.'. Whatever, they're certainly more representative of the direction PARSONS was headed than the lame film theme, 'THE RUSSIANS ARE COMING', which served as a debut single in Spring '67. By this point trading under The INTERNATIONAL SUBMARINE BAND moniker, GRAM & Co. were encouraged by the experimentation of renegade country artists like BUCK OWENS and the hard-driving B-side, 'TRUCK DRIVING MAN' was a truer taste of what was to come. After another flop single for 'Columbia', 'SUM UP BROKE', the group relocated to L.A., where the West Coast scene was sending out cultural shockwaves around the world. Hobnobbing with the likes of the aforementioned Peter Fonda, the group blagged a cameo role in hippy flick, 'The Trip', for which they also recorded a track, 'LAZY DAYS' (it belatedly turned up on the second FLYING BURRITO BROTHERS album). As country wasn't yet hip with the L.A. set, the song was rejected and the band ended up lip-synching to music by the more suitably psychedelic ELECTRIC FLAG. Bearing out such iniquities with their heads held high, the group eventually secured a contract with L.A. producer LEE HAZLEWOOD's 'L.H.I.' records. But the INTERNATIONAL SUBMARINE BAND that signed up wasn't the same beast that had moved to California only a matter of months earlier. DUNLOP and GAUVIN, tired of waiting around and eager to move in a more R&B/rock direction, hooked up with BARRY TASHIAN and BILLY BRIGGS for the first, short-lived incarnation of The FLYING BURRITO BROTHERS. PARSONS and NUESE, meanwhile, pursued their idea of a pure country sound; JON CORNEAL, BOB BUCHANAN (co-writer of PARSONS' classic 'HICKORY WIND') and CHRIS ETHRIDGE all played on the resulting album, 'SAFE AT HOME' (1968) alongside Nashville veteran, EARL 'LES' BALL and pedal steel player, J.D. MANESS. While half the album was out and out country (including covers of Johnny Cash's 'I STILL MISS SOMEONE' and Merle Haggard's 'SOMEBODY ELSE YOU'VE KNOWN'), PARSONS was already in the process of creating something fresh and exciting with his original material; the little-boy-lost charm of 'BLUE EYES' was irresistible while the chugging 'LUXURY LINER' became something of a country-rock standard covered by EMMYLOU HARRIS amongst others, the whole record characterised by GRAM's quavering, frail but emotional depth-charge singing. Retrospectively hailed as the first ever country-rock album, it was nevertheless ignored at the time and to all intents and purposes, The BYRDS' 'Sweetheart Of The Rodeo' (1968) was the record which really introduced the concept to a wider public and more significantly, the rock and country establishments. With sales of 'SAFE AT HOME' barely registering, GRAM wasn't slow in taking up an invitation to join the band (The BYRDS), and, along with CHRIS HILLMAN, formed the main thrust of their move away from folk-rock to stone country. An album consisting almost wholly of cover versions, 'Sweetheart..'s only two originals were penned by PARSONS, the poignant 'ONE HUNDRED YEARS FROM NOW' and the aforementioned autumnal beauty of 'HICKORY WIND'. Ironically, GRAM's distinctive vocals were erased (in favour of ROGER McGUINN) on all but the latter track prior to release, the controversial reason given that PARSONS was still contracted to

HAZLEWOOD (note-the original versions were belatedly released as part of The BYRDS' 1990 'C.B.S.' box set). Despite shaking up the Grand Ole Opry, drawing critical acclaim and setting in motion a return to roots music that would reverbate well into the 70's, GRAM, in what was already becoming a familiar career pattern, was quickly tiring of life as a BYRD. Following a messy departure on the eve of a South African tour (newfound buddies The ROLLING STONES were instrumental in persuading GRAM that such a venture was really like, not a hip thing to do, man), PARSONS flew back to L.A. and mused upon his fabled vision of a "Cosmic American Music". HILLMAN soon joined him and along with pedal steel maestro, SNEAKY PETE KLEINOW and old cohorts CORNEAL and ETHRIDGE, realised that vision and then some, with The FLYING BURRITO BROTHERS. Taking the name from the brief project put together by DUNLOP, GAUVIN etc, the group blended country, soul, R&B and rock into a seamless strand of Americana that to this day has never been bettered. Yet after only two albums (see The FLYING BURRITO BROTHERS section for the full lowdown on the band's trailblazing, hellraising heyday), PARSONS again bailed out, spending more and more time with KEITH RICHARDS; PARSONS influence on The 'STONES was obvious, from the reworked hoedown of 'Honky Tonk Woman' ('Country Honk') to the stoned backwoods bliss of their finest album, 'Exile On Main Street'. Although he was never credited, GRAM is rumoured to be floating around somewhere in the murk of the latter masterpiece, certainly spending enough time at RICHARDS' French villa/makeshift recording studio to lend the claims some weight. With his career in limbo, PARSONS eventually returned to L.A. in 1972 and began recording his first fully fledged solo album; unable to secure the production services of his hero, MERLE HAGGARD, GRAM did the next best thing and hired the man's recording engineer, Hugh Davies, leaving the lion's share of the knob-twiddling to another English friend, RIK GRECH (erstwhile FAMILY member and part of the short-lived BLIND FAITH). Employing ELVIS stalwarts such as JAMES BURTON and GLEN D. HARDIN, GRAM assembled a crack band with the angel-voiced EMMYLOU HARRIS at its epicentre; a struggling folk singer when PARSONS met her, HARRIS was the musical other half that he'd been searching for all his life and vice versa. PARSONS schooled her in the ways of cosmic country and her crystal pure soprano ringing against GRAM's flawed but impassioned holler remains one of the most sublime sounds ever laid down on vinyl. Grand claims perhaps, but the pairing's magic transformed well-worn standards like 'STREETS OF BALTIMORE' and 'WE'LL SWEEP OUT THE ASHES IN THE MORNING' into bittersweet soul food, highlights – along with the fragile 'A SONG FOR YOU' – of 'G.P.' (1973). Again the critics frothed (at least the ones who could recognise the talent, others were more sceptical of what PARSONS was trying to achieve) and again the public remained indifferent. Undeterred, GRAM, EMMYLOU and manager, Eddie Tickner, took advantage of Warner's (GRAM was now signed to 'Reprise') enthusiasm for a bonafide tour and set about forming a road band, The FALLEN ANGELS. Despite managing only eight shows in an incident-packed month which saw GRAM falling further into drug oblivion, the tour was by all accounts a freewheeling success if not exactly an effective promotional tool; fans still in their nappies when GRAM's ragged country roadshow came to town can get at least some idea of what the fuss was about via a live set recorded for broadcast over a Long Island, NY radio station; 'LIVE 1973 (live with The FALLEN ANGELS)' (1994). Back in L.A., his personal life continuing to unravel with each passing month, GRAM got it together one last time and, as he eagerly told his friends upon its completion, finally made the album he'd been hearing in his head for years. Although a hotch-potch of old and new, borrowed and blue, the songs on 'GRIEVOUS ANGEL' (1974) resonate as deeply as any in the history of country, or rock for that matter. GRAM's voice had taken on a new lease of life, his duets with HARRIS, 'HEARTS ON FIRE' and 'LOVE HURTS' blessed with the kind of spiritual intensity normally found in gospel music. Similarly, the PARSONS/HARRIS pairing transformed 'HICKORY WIND' from a wistful country ballad into a transcendant country ballad (despite its cheesy mock-live setting), while 'RETURN OF THE GRIEVOUS ANGEL' combined a Beat-cowboy narrative with soaring harmonies and a swooning chorus to mesmerising effect. If 'BRASS BUTTONS' and '$1000 WEDDING' were GRAM at his most intimately confessional, then closing track, 'IN MY HOUR OF DARKNESS', read like both a prayer of hope and an uncanny portent of GRAM's own death. Within a matter of weeks, road manager/professional nanny/best friend, Phil Kaufman, was driving out to the Joshua Tree monument, Arizona desert in a ramshackle hearse, GRAM's lifeless body in the back. GRAM PARSONS died on the 19th of September '73, officially from a drugs overdose although suspicion still surrounds the events that took place in the Joshua Tree Inn that night, where the singer was taking a break with friends prior to a scheduled tour. True to the pact they'd made (at the funeral of revered country picker, CLARENCE WHITE), Kaufman burned GRAM's body in the desert heat, a fitting end perhaps, for an artist who'd blazed his way through the musical consciousness like a comet. 'GRIEVOUS ANGEL' was finally issued posthumously in early '74, although seemingly (at least initially) not even GRAM's death could spark interest in his music. While EMMYLOU HARRIS went on to an impressive and successful career of her own, belatedly popularising some of GRAM's songs, the GRAM PARSONS legend has since taken on such mythical proportions that there's even an annual event held at Joshua Tree each year. Yet while the myth threatens to obscure the actual music, a cursory glance around the country/alt-country scene of today is proof enough that GRAM's vision has endured. The Brandon De Wilde tapes mentioned above have apparently been discovered, although their exact content remains unclear at present.

Album rating: International Submarine Band: SAFE AT HOME (*5) / Gram Parsons: G.P. (*8) / GREVIOUS ANGEL (*8) / posthumous:- SLEEPLESS NIGHTS (*5) / GRAM PARSONS & THE FALLEN ANGELS (*6) / WARM EVENINGS, PALE MORNINGS, BOTTLED BLUES (*6) / COSMIC AMERICAN MUSIC demos (*4)

GRAM PARSONS – vocals, guitar / with **EMMYLOU HARRIS** – vocals / **JAMES BURTON** – guitar / **GLEN D.HARDIN** – piano / **RIK GRECH** – bass / etc.

		Reprise	Reprise
Jan 73.	(7") *<1139>* **SHE. / THAT'S ALL IT TOOK**	–	
Mar 73.	(lp) *(K 44228) <MS 2123>* **G.P.** – Still feeling blue / We'll sweep out the ashes in the morning / A song for you / Streets of Baltimore / She / That's all it took / The new soft shoe / Kiss the children / Cry one more time / How much I've lied / Big mouth blues.		
Mar 73.	(7") *(K 14245)* **THE NEW SOFT SHOE. / SHE**		–
Jan 74.	(lp) *(K 54018) <MS 2171>* **GREVIOUS ANGEL** – Return of the grevious angel / Hearts on fire / I can't dance / Brass buttons / $1000 wedding / Medley live from Northern Quebec:- (a) Cash on the barrelhead – (b) Hickory wind / Love hurts / Ooh Las Vegas / In my hour of darkness.		
Jan 74.	(7") *<1192>* **LOVE HURTS. / IN MY HOUR OF DARKNESS**	–	

— GRAM died on the 19th September '73 after recording 90% of above LP

– compilations, etc. –

May 76.	(lp; GRAM PARSONS with The FLYING BURRITO BROTHERS) *A&M; (AMLH 64578) <4578>* **SLEEPLESS NIGHTS**		
Mar 79.	(lp) *Shiloh; <SLP 4088>* **GRAM PARSONS** (with The INTERNATIONAL SUBMARINE BAND)	–	
May 79.	(lp) *Shiloh; <SRS 8702>* **GRAM PARSONS – THE EARLY YEARS 1963-65** *(UK-iss.May84 on 'Sundown'; SDLP 1010)*	–	

Dec 81. (7") *Warners; <50013>* **THE RETURN OF THE GREVIOUS ANGEL (alt.take). / HEARTS ON FIRE**

Jun 82. (lp) *Warners; (K 57008) <WS 5321>* **GRAM PARSONS**

Feb 83. (7"ep; GRAM PARSONS with EMMYLOU HARRIS & The FALLEN ANGELS) *Sundown; <GPEP 104>* **THE BIG FINISH**

1983. (7") *Sierra; <GP 105>* **LOVE HURTS (live). / THE NEW SOFT SHOE (live)**

Nov 83. (lp; GRAM PARSONS with The FALLEN ANGELS & EMMYLOU HARRIS) *Sundown; (SDLP 003) / Sierra; <GP 1973>* **LIVE 1973 (live)** Apr82
(cd-iss. Jun94; CDSD 003) <(re-iss. Mar97 on 'Rhino'; 8122 72726-2)> <(cd re-iss. Jun99 on 'Sierra'; SXCD 6002)>

May 84. (lp/c) *Sundown; (SD LP/C 008)* **MELODIES**

Nov 89. (cd) *Warners; (7599 26108-2)* **G.P. / GREVIOUS ANGEL**
(re-iss. Nov93; same)

Aug 92. (lp) *Raven;* **WARM EVENINGS, PALE MORNINGS, BOTTLED BLUES**

Jun 95. (cd) *Sundown; (CDSD 077)* **COSMIC AMERICAN MUSIC: THE GRECH TAPES 1972**

Nov 00. (cd/lp) *Sundazed; <(SC/+LP 11092)>* **ANOTHER SIDE OF THIS LIFEL THE LOST RECORDINGS OF GRAM PARSONS 1965-1966**

INTERNATIONAL SUBMARINE BAND

PARSONS / + IAN DUNLOP – bass, sax / **MICKEY GAUVIN** – drums / **JOHN NUESE** – guitar

not iss. Ascot

1967. (7") *<2218>* **THE RUSSIANS ARE COMING. / TRUCK DRIVING MAN**

not iss. Columbia

1967. (7") *<43935>* **SUM UP BROKE. / ONE DAY WEEK**

not iss. L.H.I.

1967. (7") *<LHI 1205>* **LUXURY LINER. / BLUE EYES**

Apr 68. (lp) *<LHIS 12001>* **SAFE AT HOME**
– Blue eyes / I must be somebody else you've known / A satisfied mind / Polson Prison blues / That's all right / Miller's cave / I still someone / Luxury liner / Strong boy / Do you know how it feels to be lonesome. *(re-iss. 1985 on 'Statik'; STATLP 26) <re-iss. 1985 on 'Rhino'; RNLP 069> (cd-iss. Feb91 on 'Sundown'; CDSD 071)*

1968. (7") *<LHI 1217>* **MILLER'S CAVE. / SOMEBODY ELSE YOU'VE KNOWN**

❑ PASSENGERS (see under ⇒ U2)

PAVEMENT

Formed: Stockton, California, USA ... 1989 by frontman STEPHEN MALKMUS and longtime friend/guitarist, SCOTT KANNBERG. They were soon joined by drummer GARY YOUNG (although this was initially a loose arrangement), the band recording their early US-only EP's at YOUNG's home studio, the first of which, 1989's 'SLAY TRACKS', was released on the self-financed 'Treble Kicker' label. A further two EP's, 'DEMOLITION PLOT J-7' and 'SUMMER BABE', together with a mini-lp, PERFECT SOUND FOREVER', were subsequently issued on the US indie, 'Drag City' over the course of the ensuing two years. The lo-fi, shambling charm of the likes of 'SUMMER BABE' eventually secured the band a UK deal with 'Big Cat' records, PAVEMENT consistently hitting the charts in Britain throughout their career. The debut album, 'SLANTED AND ENCHANTED' was finally released amid much anticipation in early 1992, its covertly melodic, avant-indie drawing inevitable but favourable comparisons with PIXIES, the VELVET UNDERGROUND and even KING CRIMSON! Masterfully combining chaotic dischord and shards of crystalline harmony, the record's most compelling moments lay in the lazy melancholia of 'TRIGGER CUT' or ZURICH IS STAINED'. MALKMUS' brilliantly cryptic lyrics and offhand phrasing together with the twisted beauty of their music saw the band consistently dubbed as an American FALL. No bad thing, and besides, the band were carving out their own niche on the live circuit, by now augmented with extra sticksman, BOB NASTANOVICH and bassist MARK IBOLD, wildman YOUNG's infamous onstage antics an added attraction. The debut reached the lower reaches of the UK chart while a compilation of the early EP's, 'WESTING (BY MUSKET & SEXTANT)' (1993) made the Top 30. Prior to the release of the follow-up proper, 'CROOKED RAIN CROOKED RAIN' (1994), the band parted company on less than amicable terms with YOUNG, his replacement being STEVE WEST. This folk-ish record marked the band's most enticingly melodic affair to date, the keening 'CUT YOUR HAIR' single almost making the Top 40, the record itself reaching No.15 and cementing PAVEMENT's position as the crown kings of lo-fi. Although PAVEMENT failed to breach the Billboard chart, they built up a loyal following on the US underground scene on the back of constant touring, the defiantly experimental and diverse 'WOWEE ZOWEE!' (1995) proving that the band were making no concessions to radio programmers. There were still perfect PAVEMENT moments of stark beauty, as on the single, 'FATHER TO A SISTER OF THOUGHT'. While the album may have put off those after the immediate pop fix of 'CROOKED ...', PAVEMENT's next release, the meditative 'BRIGHTEN THE CORNERS' (1997) took a different tack again. It was clear that MALKMUS' songwriting was fast maturing, his work taking on a new depth and resonance that eschewed the stylistic grab-bag of old for a more straightforwardly direct approach. Feted by the likes of BLUR, who had previously pooh-pooh'd the American scene, PAVEMENT remain one of music's most resolutely individual bands. In 1999 and with drummer GARY YOUNG back into the fray, the band scored their first Top 30 single, 'CARROT ROPE', one of highlights on their Top 20 album, 'TERROR TWILIGHT'. Unfortunately, they bowed out towards the end of the decade. The break-up of PAVEMENT hadn't effected MALKMUS that much, as in 2001 he issued his solo set 'STEPHEN MALKMUS'. Like a lost PAVEMENT album, this is probably the direction the band would have headed in, considering the tone of the joyful 'TERROR TWILIGHT' compared with that of the stuffy, cynically serious 'BRIGHTEN THE CORNERS'. The songs were delightful, with MALKMUS' half-spoken soft vocals matching that of the jangling, uptempo songs such as 'JO JO'S JACKET' and the irresistible 'TROUBBBLE'. There were still dark overtones; 'BLACK BOOK' had the slightly singular twang of a PAVEMENT song circa 'WOWEE ZOWEE', whilst 'CHURCH ON WHITE' saw MALKMUS sing his first love song since 'MAJOR LEAGUES' with beautiful integrity. It certainly wasn't Swedish Reggae, but whatever ideas MALKMUS had up in that head of his were faithfully communicated onto this album. Credited to STEPHEN MALKMUS & THE JICKS, the man's sophomore solo effort, 'PIG LIB' (2003), wasn't quite so immediate, with less of the spontaneity and mishap of classic PAVEMENT and more of the musical bonhomie which characterises a more fruitful working relationship. It was certainly MALKMUS' most polished and rounded effort to date, although it could've done with a bit more edge and a bigger injection of the man's legendary wit. The man's third solo set, 'FACE THE TRUTH' (2005) was a drawing together of the multitudinous musical arcana that drives his art, a bracing, pendulous tour through the caverns of the MALKMUS mind. Kicking off with the halter-reined, zebra-crossing electro of 'PENCIL ROT', centered with the epic 'NO MORE SHOES' – all eight oddly plangent minutes of it – and scattershot with bleeping wild cards like 'BABY C'MON', the record issued a bracing riposte to those who'd predicted a pipe-and-slippers ease into middle age.

• **Covered:** THE CLASSICAL (Fall) / THE KILLING MOON (Echo & The Bunnymen) / CAMERA (R.E.M.). • **Trivia:** MALKMUS produced early 90's album 'Eyes Wide Smile' for FAITH OVER REASON. BOB and STEVEN played on SILVER JEW's (David Berman) album 'Starlite Walter'.

Album rating: PERFECT SOUND FOREVER mini (*5) / SLANTED AND ENCHANTED (*7) / WESTING (BY MUSKET & SEXTANT) compilation (*8) / CROOKED RAIN CROOKED RAIN (*7) / WOWEE ZOWEE (*8) / BRIGHTEN THE CORNERS (*7) / TERROR TWILIGHT (*8) / Stephen Malkmus: STEPHEN MALKMUS (*8) / PIG LIB (*6) / FACE THE TRUTH (*6)

STEPHEN MALKMUS (b. 30 May'66, Santa Monica, California) – vocals, guitar / **SCOTT "SPIRAL STAIRS" KANNBERG** – guitar, vocals

not iss. | Treble Kicker

1989. (7"ep) *<TK 001>* **SLAY TRACKS 1933-1969** [–] [ ]
– You're killing me / Box elder / Maybe maybe / She believes / Price yeah!.

—— added **GARY YOUNG** (b.1953, Stockton) – drums

not iss. | Drag City

1990. (7"ep) *<DC 2>* **DEMOLITION PLOT J-7** [–] [ ]
– Forklift / Spizzle trunk / Recorder grot / Internal K-dart / Perfect depth / Recorder grot (rally).

—— (Aug90) added **BOB NASTANOVICH** – drums

1991. (10"m-lp) *<DC 4>* **PERFECT SOUND FOREVER** [–] [ ]
– Heckler spray / From now on / Angel carver blues – Mellow jazz docent / Drive by fader / Debris slide / Home / Krell vid-user.

—— (mid '91) added **MARK IBOLD** (b. New York) – bass (ex-DUSTDEVILS)

Jan 92. (7"ep) *<DC 9>* **SUMMER BABE (Winter version) / MERCY: THE LAUNDROMAT. / BAPTISS BLACKTICK / MY FIRST MINE / MY RADIO** [–] [ ]

Big Cat | Matador

Mar 92. (lp/c/cd) *(ABB 034/+C/CD) <OLE 038-2>* **SLANTED AND ENCHANTED** [72] [ ]
– Summer babe (winter version) / Trigger cut – Wounded – Kite at: 17 / No life singed her / In a mouth of a desert / Conduit for sale / Chesleys little wrists / Loretta's scars / Here / Two states / Perfume-V / Fame throwa / Jackals, false grails – The lonesome era / Our singer / Zurich is stained. *<(re-iss. d-cd Nov02 on 'Matador'+=; OLE 557-2)>* – (34 bonus tracks, etc.)

Jul 92. (7"/12"/cd-s) *(ABB 35 S/T/SCD) <OLE 042>* **TRIGGER CUT. / SUE ME JACK / SO STARK (YOU'RE A SKYSCRAPER)** [ ] [ ]

Nov 92. (12"ep/12"pic-d-ep/cd-ep) *(ABB 38 T/P/SCD) <OLE 044>* **WATERY, DOMESTIC EP** [58] [ ]
– Texas never whispers / Frontwards / Feed 'em to the (Linden) lions / Shoot the singer (1 sick verse).

Mar 93. (lp/c/cd) *(ABB 40/+C/CD) <Drag City; DC 14>* **WESTING (BY MUSKET & SEXTANT)** (first 4 US singles material) [30] [ ]
(cd/lp re-iss. Sep98/Jan99 on 'Drag City'; same as US)

—— **STEVE WEST** (b. Richmond, Virginia) – drums; repl. GARY YOUNG – solo (single; 'PLANET MAN' 94)

Jan 94. (7"/12"/cd-s) *(ABB 55 S/T/CD) <OLE 082>* **CUT YOUR HAIR. / CAMERA / STARE** [52] [ ]

Feb 94. (lp/c/cd) *(ABB 56/+C/CD) <OLE 079>* **CROOKED RAIN CROOKED RAIN** [15] [ ]
– Silence kit / Elevate me later / Stop breathin / Cut your hair / Newark wilder / Unfair / Gold sound Z / 5-4 = unity / Range life / Heaven is a truck / Hit the plane down / Fillmore jive. *(s-lp w/free 7"; OLE 087)* – HAUNT YOU DOWN. / JAM KIDS *(cd re-iss. Feb02 on 'Domino';* **REWIGCD 010)** *<(re-iss. d-cd Oct04 on 'Matador'+=; OLE 610-2)>* – (37 bonus tracks from 'L.A.'s DESERT ORIGINS')

Jul 94. (7") *(ABB 70S)* **GOLD SOUNDZ. / KNEELING BUS** [ ] [–]
(12"+=/cd-s+=) *(ABB 70 T/SCD)* – Strings of Nashville / The exit theory.

—— line-up= **STEPHEN MALKMUS / MARK IBOLD / ROBERT NASTANOVICH / STEVE WEST / SPIRAL STAIRS (KANNEBERG) + FATAH RUARK**

Jan 95. (7") *(ABB 77S)* **RANGE LIFE. / COOLIN' BY SOUND** [ ] [–]
(12"+=/cd-s+=) *(ABB 77 T/SCD)* – Raft.

Mar 95. (7"/12") *(ABB 86 S/T) <OLE 134>* **RATTLED BY THE RUSH. / FALSE SKORPION / EASILY FOOLED** [ ] [ ]
(cd-s+=) *(ABB 86SCD)* – Brink of the clouds.

Apr 95. (3-sided d-lp/c/cd) *(ABB 84/+C/CD) <OLE 130>* **WOWEE ZOWEE!** [18] [ ]
– We dance / Rattled by the rush / Black out / Brinx job / Grounded / Serpentine pad / Motion suggests / Father to a sister of thought / Extradition / Best friends arm / Grave architecture / At & t / Flux = rad / Fight this generation / Kennel district / Pueblo / Half a canyon / Western homes.

Jun 95. (7"ep/12"ep/cd-ep) *(ABB 91 S/T/SCD) <OLE 169>* **FATHER TO A SISTER OF THOUGHT. / KRIS KRAFT / MUSSLE ROCK (IS A HORSE IN TRANSITION)** [ ] [ ]

Aug 95. (7") *<3G-08>* **DANCING WITH THE ELDERS. / (other artist)** [–] [ ]

—— <above released on 'Third Gear'>

Jan 96. (cd-ep) *(ABB 110SCD) <OLE 188CD>* **PACIFIC TRIM EP:- GIVE IT A DAY / GANGSTERS & PRANKSTERS / SAGANAW** [ ] [ ]
(7"ep+=) *(ABB 110S) <OLE 188>* – I love Perth.

—— now without FATAH

Domino | Capitol

Jan 97. (7") *(RUG 51)* **STEREO. / BIRDS IN THE MAJIC INDUSTRY** [48] [–]
(cd-s) *(RUG 51CD)* – ('A') / Westie can drum / Winner of the . . .

Feb 97. (cd/c/lp) *(WIG CD/MC/LP 31) <55226>* **BRIGHTEN THE CORNERS** [27] [70]
– Stereo / Shady lane / Transport is arranged / Date with IKEA / Old to begin / Type slowly / Embassy row / Blue Hawaiian / We are underused / Passat dream / Starlings of the slipstream / Infinite spark.

Domino | Matador

Apr 97. (7") *(RUG 53) <OLE 266>* **SHADY LANE (KROSSFADER). / UNSEEN POWER OF THE PICKET FENCE** [40] Jun97 [ ]
(cd-s) *(RUG 53CD)* – ('A') / Slowly typed / Cherry area.
(cd-s) *(RUG 53CDX)* – ('A') / Wanna mess you around / No tan lines.

—— drummer **GARY YOUNG** returned

May 99. (7") *(RUG 90)* **CARROT ROPE. / AND THEN** [27] [–]
(cd-s) *(RUG 90CD1)* – ('A') / Harness your hopes / Roll with the wind.
(cd-s) *(RUG 90CD2)* – ('A') / Porpoise and the hand grenade / Rooftop rambler.

Jun 99. (cd/c/lp) *(WIG CD/MC/LP 66) <OLE 260>* **TERROR TWILIGHT** [19] [95]
– Spit on a stranger / Folk jam / You are a light / Cream of gold / Major leagues / Platform blues / Ann don't cry / Billie / Speak, see, remember / The hexx / Carrot rope.

Sep 99. (cd-s) *(RUG 96CD1)* **MAJOR LEAGUES / YOUR TIME TO CHANGE / STUB YOUR TOE / THE CLASSICAL** [ ] [–]
(cd-s) *(RUG 96CD2)* – ('A') / The killing moon / ('A'-demo) / Decouvert de soleil.
(d7"set) *(RUG 96)* – (all above).

—— KANNEBERG/STAIRS went on to form PRESTON SCHOOL OF INDUSTRY

STEPHEN MALKMUS

—— solo with **JOHN MOEN** – percussion, drums

Domino | Matador

Feb 01. (cd/lp) *(WIG CD/LP 090) <OLE 444>* **STEPHEN MALKMUS** [49] [ ]
– Black book / Phantasies / JoJo's jacket / Church on white / The hook / Discretion grove / Troubbble / Pink India / Trojan curfew / Vague space / Jenny & the ess-dog / Deado.

Apr 01. (7") *(RUG 123)* **DISCRETION GROVE. / SIN TAX** [60] [–]
(cd-s+=) *(RUG 123CD)* – Leisurely poison.

Jul 01. (7") *(RUG 128)* **JENNY & THE ESS-DOG. / ALIEN BOY** [ ] [–]
(cd-s+=) *(RUG 128CD)* – Keep the faith / That's what mama said.

Dec 01. (7") *(RUG 133)* **JO JO'S JACKET. / OPEN AND SHUT CASES** [ ] [–]
(cd-s) *(RUG 133CD)* – ('A') / Polish mule / The hook (live) / ('A' video).

—— now with **JOHN MOEN** – drums, vocals

Domino | Matador

Mar 03. (cd/lp; as STEPHEN MALKMUS & the JICKS) *(WIG CD/LP 122) <OLE 572>* **PIG LIB** [63] [97]
– Water and a seat / Ramp of death / (Do not feed the) Oyster / Vanessa from Queens / Sheets / Animal midnight / Dark wave / Witch mountain bridge / Craw song / 1% of one / Us. *<US w/ free EP>* – Dynamic calories / Fractions and feelings / Old Jerry / The poet and the witch (live) / Shake it around (live).

May 03. (10"ep/cd-ep; as STEPHEN MALKMUS & the JICKS) *(RUG 158 T/CD)* **DARK WAVE** [ ] [–]

– Dark wave / Dynamic calories / Fractions and feelings / Old Jerry / The poet and the witch (live) / Shake it around (live).

May 05. (cd/lp) *(WIG CD/LP 156)* *<OLE 650>* **FACE THE TRUTH** ☐ ☐

– Pencil rot / It kills / I've hardly been / Freeze the saints / Loud cloud crowd / No more shoes / Mama / Kindling for the master / Post-paint boy / Baby c'mon / Malediction.

Sep 05. (7") *(RUG 208)* **BABY C'MON. / WOW-ASS JEANS** ☐ -

PEARL JAM

Formed: Seattle, Washington, USA ... 1991 by JEFF AMENT and STONE GOSSARD, who, together with MARK ARM, STEVE TURNER and ALEX VINCENT had previously played in pivotal Seattle band, GREEN RIVER (ARM and TURNER went on to form the noisier, and some still argue, superior MUDHONEY). Widely held to be the first ever "Grunge" act, GREEN RIVER's distortion-heavy mash-up of punk and metal is best sampled on the 'DRY AS A BONE' EP (1987), one of the first releases on the seminal 'Sub Pop' label. Following the band's demise, GOSSARD, AMENT and BRUCE FAIRWEATHER (who had replaced TURNER in GREEN RIVER) recruited vocalist ANDREW WOOD (ex-MALFUNKSHUN) and drummer GARY GILMOUR to form the short lived MOTHER LOVE BONE. After an EP and a cult debut album, 'APPLE' (1990), WOOD overdosed on heroin (March '90), effectively bringing the band to an untimely end. However, it was within these 70's influenced grooves that AMENT and GOSSARD laid the musical foundations for what would later become PEARL JAM. The group evolved from a tribute project for the dead WOOD put together by SOUNDGARDEN frontman, CHRIS CORNELL. Also featuring GOSSARD, AMENT, guitarist MIKE McCREADY, and SOUNDGARDEN sticksman MATT CAMERON, this loose aggregation released 'TEMPLE OF THE DOG' in 1991, a critically acclaimed opus that laid further groundwork for PEARL JAM's sound. With vocalist EDDIE VEDDER and drummer DAVE KRUSEN (subsequently superceded by DAVE ABBRUZZESE) replacing the SOUNDGARDEN boys, the outfit gradually evolved into PEARL JAM, the band still something of a cult act when their 'Epic' debut was released in America at the tail end of '91. 'TEN' eventually reached No.2 in the US chart and a hefty media buzz ensured a steady flow of UK imports, the record making the British Top 20 upon its February '92 release. With VEDDER penning the lyrics and GOSSARD and AMENT writing the music, 'TEN' was a powerfully assured debut, transforming the grunge monster into a sleekly melodic rock beast. VEDDER's soulful bellow was a key factor, the singer wringing emotion from every note of the anthemic 'ALIVE' and the affecting 'JEREMY'. Granted, comparisons to LED ZEPPELIN were a little unfair, but the band's lumbering sound seemed the antithesis of the cathartic rush with which NIRVANA had revolutionised a stale music scene and KURT COBAIN was spot on with his infamous criticisms, despite cries of sour grapes. While their intentions may have been honourable, PEARL JAM ushered in a tidal wave of dull as dishwater, sub-metal masquerading as grunge, most of it, funnily enough, released on major labels. Nevertheless, the kids loved it, especially the American ones, and the band embarked on a punishing touring schedule, finding time to make a cameo appearance as Matt Dillon's band in 'Singles', the Cameron Crowe film based on the Seattle music scene. As well as standing in for JIM MORRISON when The DOORS were eventually inducted into the Rock 'n' Roll Hall Of Fame, VEDDER performed a heart stopping version of BOB DYLAN's 'Masters Of War' (playing mandolin) at the veteran's anniversary concert in 1993. The same year also saw the release of a PEARL JAM follow-up, 'VS', the band's fiercely loyal fanbase propelling the album straight in at No.1 in the US charts. A more ragingly visceral affair, 'GO' gave VEDDER something to get his teeth into while the more reflective 'DAUGHTER' proved how affecting the band (and particularly VEDDER) could be when they dropped the derivative hard rock assault. Along with their mate NEIL YOUNG, PEARL JAM seemingly have an abiding love of vinyl, releasing 'VITALOGY' (1994) initially on record only, something which didn't prevent the band scaling the US chart once again. While not exactly vital, as the title might suggest, the record saw PEARL JAM going back to basics and injecting their behemoth-rock with a bit of stripped down energy. The following year saw PEARL JAM backing NEIL YOUNG on the so-so 'MIRROR BALL' (1995) album, the fruition of their musical partnership that had begun some years previous. In 1995, each member (except ABBRUZZESE), took time to carry out other projects, although the following year they returned to full force with 'NO CODE', an album that showed a lighter, acoustic side. Unfortunately if not predictably, the fans were not best impressed by the album's more experimental turn and it quickly faded from view after a relatively brief stay at the US No.1 spot and the UK Top 3. More newsworthy was the band's feud with the Ticketmaster agency, a spat which precluded a full-scale tour. While the 'YIELD' (1998) album heralded a return to meatier fare, PEARL JAM records were beginning to follow the time-honoured heavy metal pattern of an initial high chart placing followed by a rapid descent into obscurity. All the signs were of a cult, diehard fanbase and one which lapped up both the mammoth US arena tour of summer '98 and its spin-off album, 'LIVE ON TWO LEGS' (1998). Bizarrely enough, the band then proceeded to score their biggest hit in years with a cover of the J.FRANK WILSON chestnut, 'LAST KISS'. Originally part of a fan-club only covers series, the single was given a full release due to popular demand and ended up narrowly missing the US No.1 slot in summer '99. The Tched Blake-produced 'BINAURAL' resumed normal service as PEARL JAM entered the new millennium seemingly oblivious to changing fads and fashions. A GRATEFUL DEAD for the post-grunge generation may be a comparison not too far off the mark although PEARL JAM adopted a slightly different attitude to bootlegging. While the late JERRY GARCIA and crew seemingly encouraged their fans to tape away to their hearts content, VEDDER's mob made a stubborn attempt to out-bootleg the bootleggers by recording every single date of their European and British tours and subsequently releasing them as a series of 72 double-CD sets. JERRY'll be turning in his grave and I was pulling the rest of my hair out updating this discography. VEDDER and Co were back in studio business come 2002, reading the 'RIOT ACT' to anyone who hadn't already had their fill with the interminable live sets. Musically, little had changed and it seemed PEARL JAM are determined to make as few concessions to contemporary musical mores as possible, probably a good thing, especially when it resulted in one of the more palatable albums of their stodgy oeuvre. Finally run to the end of their 'Epic' contract, the 'JAM released the self explanatory 'LOST DOGS: RARITIES AND B-SIDES' (2003), a selective, rather than exhaustive, rake through the archive with the not inconsiderable incentive of eleven unreleased tracks. Unusually – or perhaps not in PEARL JAM's case – the band's first release for 'R.C.A.' was yet another (!) live album, an acoustic set recorded at a charity gig, with VEDDER running through Dylan's 'MASTERS OF WAR' one more time (almost as compelling as the Bob Dylan tribute version) as well as Victoria Williams' 'CRAZY MARY', the Ramones' 'I BELIEVE IN MIRACLES' and Shel Silverstein's gallows humour "classic", '25 MINUTES TO GO'. Unlike their spate of concert doubles, the album went Top 20 in America, as did the inevitable 'Epic' anthology, 'REARVIEWMIRROR: GREATEST HITS 1991-2003' (2004), featuring spruced up mixes of early monster hits like 'ALIVE'. The band finally released a set of new material in 'PEARL JAM' (2006), its eponymous title reflecting both a new beginning and a forthright, back-to-the-roots sound. Again just missing out (to TOOL's 'Days') on US pole position, the album was trailed with the Bush-berating 'WORLD WIDE SUICIDE', a near Top 40 miss, but a pointer to a renewed sense of purpose.

• **Songwriters:** VEDDER wrote lyrics / GOSSARD and AMENT the songs except F***IN' UP (Neil Young). GREEN RIVER covered AIN'T NOTHIN' TO DO (Dead Boys) / QUEEN BITCH (David Bowie). • **Trivia:** Backed actor MATT DILLON's band CITIZEN DICK in the 1992 film 'Singles'. VEDDER co-wrote and sang on 2 tracks; 'THE LONG ROAD' + 'THE FACE OF LOVE' on the 1996 movie 'Dead Man Walking'.

Album rating: Green River: REHAB DOLL – DRY AS A BONE (*7) / Mother Love Bone: STARDOG CHAMPION collection (*8) / Pearl Jam: TEN (*10) / VS (*8) / VITALOGY (*7) / NO CODE (*8) / YIELD (*7) / LIVE ON TWO LEGS (*6) / BINAURAL (*7) / RIOT ACT (*6) / LIVE bootleg series (*?) / LOST DOGS: B-SIDES & RARITIES collection (*6) / BENAROYA HALL live (*4) / REARVIEWMIRROR: GREATEST HITS 1991-2003 compilation (*8) / PEARL JAM (*5)

GREEN RIVER

MARK ARM (b.21 Feb'62, California) – vocals / **STEVE TURNER** (b.28 Mar'65, Houston, Texas) – guitar / **STONE GOSSARD** (b.20 Jul'66) – guitar / **JEFF AMENT** (b.10 Mar'63, Big Sandy, Montana) – bass / **ALEX VINCENT** – drums

not iss. Homestead

Sep 85. (12"ep) *<HMS 031>* **COME ON DOWN** [–] [ ]
– New god / Swallow my pride / Ride of your life / Corner of my eye / Tunnel of love. *(cd-ep-iss.May94; same)*

—— **BRUCE FAIRWEATHER** – guitar repl. TURNER who later joined MUDHONEY

not iss. I.P.C.

Nov 86. (7"green) *<ICP 01>* **TOGETHER WE'LL NEVER. / AIN'T NOTHIN' TO DO** [–] [ ]

Glitterhouse Sup Pop

Jun 87. (12"ep) *<SP 11>* **DRY AS A BONE** [–] [ ]
– Unwind / Baby takes / This town / PCC / Ozzie. *(UK-iss.Mar91 on 'Tupelo'; TUPLP 17) (cd-iss. May94; same)*

Feb 89. (12"ep) *(GR 0031) <SP 15>* **REHAB DOLL** [ ] May88 [ ]
– Searchin' / Ain't nothin' to do / Forever means / Rehab girl / Swallow my pride / Together we'll never / Smilin' and dyin' / Porkfist / Take a dive / One more stitch. (c-ep+=) *<SP 15A>* – Queen bitch. *(US re-iss. c+cd-lp Jul88 as 'DRY AS A BONE' / 'REHAB DOLL')*

—— MARK ARM formed MUDHONEY

MOTHER LOVE BONE

formed by **AMENT, GOSSARD + FAIRWEATHER** plus **ANDREW WOOD** (b.1966) – vocals (ex-MALFUNKSHUN) / **GARY GILMOUR** – drums

Polydor Stardog

Mar 89. (m-lp) *<839011-2>* **SHINE** [–] [ ]
– Thru fade away / Midshaker meltdown / Halfass monkey boy / Medley:- Chloe dancer / Lady Godiva blues.

Jul 90. (cd/c/lp) *<(843191-2/-4/-1)>* **APPLE** [ ] Mar90 [ ]
– This is Shangri-la / Stardog champion / Holy roller / Bone China / Come bite the apple / Stargazer / Heartshine / Captain hi-top / Man of golden words / Mr.Danny boy / Capricorn sister / Crown of thorns. *(above 2 re-iss. cd as 'STAR DOG CHAMPION' Sep92 on 'Polydor'; 514177-2 / <314512 884-2>) (hit US No.77)*

—— ANDREW WOOD died on the 19th March '90 after a heroin overdose. AMENT and GOSSARD paid tribute to him by joining with SOUNDGARDEN ⇒ members in off-shoot outfit TEMPLE OF THE DOG. After this project was finished . . . PEARL JAM were formed

PEARL JAM

AMENT + GOSSARD with **EDDIE VEDDER** (b.23 Dec'66, Evanson, Illinois) – vocals / **MIKE McCREADY** (b. 5 Apr'65) – lead guitar / **DAVE ABBRUZZESE** (b.17 May'??) – drums repl. DAVE KRUZON

Epic Epic

Feb 92. (cd/c/lp/pic-lp) *(468884-2/-4/-1/-0) <47857>* **TEN** [18] Dec91 [2]
– Once / Even flow / Alive / Why go / Black / Jeremy / Oceans / Porch / Garden / Deep / Release. *(re-dist.Dec92 yellow-cd+=/m-d; 468884-5/-3)* – Alive (live) / Wash / Dirty Frank. *(lp re-iss. Feb99 on 'Simply Vinyl'; SVLP 68)*

Feb 92. (7"white/c-s) *(657572-7/-4)* **ALIVE. / WASH** [16] [ ]
(12"+=/pic-cd-s+=) *(657572-6/-5)* – Once.

Apr 92. (7"/c-s) *(657857-7/-4)* **EVEN FLOW (remix). / OCEANS** [27] [ ]
(12"white+=/cd-pic-s+=) *(657857-8/-2)* – Dirty Frank.

Sep 92. (7"white/c-s) *(658258-7/-4)* **JEREMY. / ALIVE (live)** [15] [ ]
(12"pic-d+=) *(658258-6)* – Footsteps (live).
(pic-cd-s+=) *(658258-4)* – Yellow Ledbetter.

Oct 93. (cd/c/lp) *(474549-2/-4/-1) <53136>* **VS** [2] [1]
– Go / Animal / Daughter / Glorified G / Dissident / W.M.A. / Blood / Rearviewmirror / Rats / Elderly woman behind the counter in a small town / Leash / Indifference.

Oct 93. (12"ep/cd-ep) *(659795-6/-2)* **GO. / ALONE / ELDERLY WOMAN BEHIND THE COUNTER IN A SMALL TOWN (acoustic)** [ ] [ ]
(free c-s+=) *(659795-4)* – Animal (live).

Dec 93. (7"red/c-s) *(660020-7/-4)* **DAUGHTER. / BLOOD (live)** [18] [ ]
(12"+=/cd-s+=) *(660020-6/-2)* – Yellow ledbetter (live).

May 94. (7"/c-s) *(660441-7/-4)* **DISSIDENT. / REARVIEWMIRROR (live)** [14] [ ]
(cd-s+=) *(660441-2)* – Release / Even flow (versions).
(cd-s) *(660441-5)* – ('A'side) / Deep / Even flow / Why go (versions).

—— ABBRUZZESE departed and was repl. after below album by **JACK IRONS** (ex-RED HOT CHILI PEPPERS)

Nov 94. (7"/c-s/cd-s) *(661036-7/-4/-2) <77771>* **SPIN THE BLACK CIRCLE. / TREMOR CHRIST** [10] [58] [18]

Dec 94. (cd/c/d-lp) *(477861-2/-4/-1) <66900>* **VITALOGY** [6] [1]
– Last exit / Spin the black circle / Not for you / Tremor Christ / Nothingman / Whipping / Pry, to / Corduroy / Bugs / Satan's bed / Better man / Aye davanita / Immortality / Stupid mop.

—— McCREADY now also moonlighted for MAD SEASON (see under ALICE IN CHAINS) – lead singer being LAYNE STALEY. Meanwhile, STONE GOSSARD set up own record label 'Loosegroove' and signed MALFUNKSHUN, DEVILHEAD, WEAPON OF CHOICE, BRAD and PROSE AND CONCEPTS.

Feb 95. (7"colrd/c-s/cd-s) *(661203-7/-4/-2)* **NOT FOR YOU. / OUT OF MY MIND (live)** [34] [–]

Dec 95. (7"/cd-s) *(662716-7/-2) <78199>* **MERKINBALL** [25] [7]
– I got I.D. / Long road.
(above both recorded w/ NEIL YOUNG)

—— Group had already featured on NEIL YOUNG's album 'MIRRORBALL'. GOSSARD featured on THERMIDOR's 1996 album 'Monkey On Rico'.

—— mid-96; JEFF AMENT featured for minor supergroup THREE FISH

Aug 96. (7"/c-s/cd-s) *(663539-7/-4/-2) <78389>* **WHO YOU ARE. / HABIT** [18] [31]

Sep 96. (cd/c/d-lp) *(484448-2/-4/-1) <67500>* **NO CODE** [3] [1]
– Sometimes / Habit / Who you are / In my tree / Smile / Hail hail / I'm open / Red mosquito / Lukin / Mankind / Black & red & yellow / Allnight. *(cd re-iss. Aug00; same)*

Jan 98. (7"/c-s) *(665394-7/-4) <78797>* **GIVEN TO FLY. / PILATE** [12] [21]
(cd-s+=) *(665394-2)* – Leatherman.

Feb 98. (cd/c/lp) *(489365-2/-4/-1) <68164>* **YIELD** [7] [2]
– Brain of J. / Faithfull / No way / Given to fly / Wishlist / Pilate / Do the evolution / • / MFC / Low light / In hiding / Push me, pull me / All those yesterdays.

May 98. (7"/c-s) *(665790-7/-4) <SNY 78896>* **WISHLIST. / U** [30] [47]
(cd-s+=) *(665790-2)* – Brain of J. (live).

—— **MATT CAMERON** – drums (ex-SOUNDGARDEN) repl. IRONS

Nov 98. (cd/c/d-lp) *(429859-2/-4/-1) <69752>* **LIVE ON TWO LEGS (live)** [68] [15]
– Corduroy / Given to fly / Hail hail / Daughter / Elderly woman behind the counter in a small town / Untitled / MFC / Go / Off he goes / Even flow / Red mosquito / Nothingman / Do the evolution / Better man / Black / F*ckin' up.

Aug 99. (7"red/cd-s) *(667479-7/-2) <79197>* **LAST KISS. / SOLDIER OF LOVE** [42] May99 [2]

May 00. (7"blue) *(669374-7) <79416>* **NOTHING AS IT SEEMS. / INSIGNIFICANCE** [22] Apr00 [49]
(cd-s+=) *(669374-2)* – ('A'side) / Better man (live) / Footsteps (live).

May 00. (cd/c/lp) *(494590-2/-4/-1) <63665>* **BINAURAL** [5] [2]
– Breakerfall / God's dice / Evacuation / Light years / Nothing as it seems /

Date	Release	UK	US
	Thin air / Insignificance / Of the girl / Grievance / Rival / Sleight of hand / Soon forget / Parting ways.		
Jul 00.	(7"yellow) *(669628-7)* *<79452>* **LIGHT YEARS. / SOON FORGET (live)**	52	
	(cd-s+=) *(669628-2)* – Grievance (live).		
Oct 02.	(7") *(673308-7)* *<SNY 79809>* **I AM MINE. / DOWN**	26	43
	(cd-s) *(673308-2)* – ('A'side) / Bushleaguer / Undone.		
Nov 02.	(cd) *(510000-2)* *<86825>* **RIOT ACT**	34	5
	– Can't keep / Save you / Love boat captain / Cropduster / Ghost / I am mine / Thumbing my way / You are / Get right / Green disease / Help help / Bushleaguer / 1/2 full / Arc / All or none.		
		R.C.A.	R.C.A.
Jul 04.	(d-cd) *(82876 63571-2)* *<63424>* **BENAROYA HALL: OCT 22 2003** (live)		18
	– Of the girl / Low light / Thumbing my way / Thin air / Fatal / Nothing as it seems / Man of the hour / Immortality / Off he goes / Around the bend / I believe in miracles / Sleight of hand / All or none / Lukin / Parting ways / Down / (encore break) / Can't keep / Dead man / Masters of war / Black / Crazy Mary / 25 minutes to go / Daughter / (encore break) / Yellow Ledbetter.		
		J	J
Apr 06.	(-) *<radio>* **WORLD WIDE SUICIDE**	–	41
May 06.	(cd) *<(82876 71467-2)>* **PEARL JAM**	5	2
	– Life wasted / World wide suicide / Comatose / Severed hand / Marker in the sand / Parachutes / Unemployable / Big wave / Gone / Wasted (reprise) / Army reserve / Come back / Inside job.		

– others, etc. –

on 'Epic' records unless mentioned otherwise

Date	Release	UK	US
Jul 95.	(cd-ep) *Epic; <77935>* **JEREMY / YELLOW LEDBETTER / FOOTSTEPS**	–	79
Jan 96.	(cd-ep) *Epic; <77938>* **DAUGHTER / YELLOW LEDBETTER (live) / BLOOD (live)**	–	97
Sep 00.	(d-cd) *(499623-2)* **LIVE: Palau Sant Jordi, Barcelona, Spain – May 25th, 2000**		–
Sep 00.	(d-cd) *(499624-2)* **LIVE: Parkbuhne, Wuhlheide, Berlin – June 25th, 2000**		–
Sep 00.	(d-cd) *(499626-2)* **LIVE: Spodek Arena, Katowice, Poland – June 16th, 2000**		–
Sep 00.	(d-cd) *(499628-2)* **LIVE: The Point Theater, Dublin, Ireland – June 1st, 2000**		–
Sep 00.	(d-cd) *(499629-2)* **LIVE: SECC Arena, Glasgow, Scotland – June 3rd, 2000**		–
Sep 00.	(d-cd) *(499630-2)* *<85073>* **LIVE: Sporthalle, Hamburg, Germany – June 26th, 2000**		
Sep 00.	(d-cd) *(499631-2)* *<85052>* **LIVE: Spodek Arena, Katowice, Poland – June 15th, 2000**		
Sep 00.	(d-cd) *(499632-2)* **LIVE: International Arena, Cardiff, Wales – June 6th, 2000**		–
Sep 00.	(d-cd) *(499633-2)* **LIVE: Rock Am Ring Eifel, Nurberg, Germany – June 9th, 2000**		–
Sep 00.	(d-cd) *(499634-2)* **LIVE: Estadio Do Restelo, Lisbon, Portugal – May 23rd, 2000**		–
Sep 00.	(d-cd) *(499635-2)* **LIVE: Hala Tivoli, Llubljana, Slovenia – June 19th, 2000**		–
Sep 00.	(d-cd) *(499636-2)* **LIVE: Wembley Arena, London, England – May 29th, 2000**		–
Sep 00.	(d-cd) *(499637-2)* *<85012>* **LIVE: Wembley Arena, London, England – May 30th, 2000**		
Sep 00.	(d-cd) *(499638-2)* **LIVE: Pinkpop, Heerden, Holland – June 12th, 2000**		–
Sep 00.	(d-cd) *(499639-2)* **LIVE: Evening News Arena, Manchester, England – June 4th, 2000**		–
Sep 00.	(d-cd) *(499640-2)* *<85064>* **LIVE: FILA Forum, Milan, Italy – June 22nd, 2000**		
Sep 00.	(d-cd) *(499641-2)* **LIVE: Rock In Park, Nurnberg, Germany – June 11th, 2000**		–
Sep 00.	(d-cd) *(499642-2)* **LIVE: Spectrum, Oslo, Norway – June 29th, 2000**		–
Sep 00.	(d-cd) *(499643-2)* **LIVE: Paegas Arena, Prague, Czechoslovakia – June 14th, 2000**		–
Sep 00.	(d-cd) *(499644-2)* **LIVE: Bercy, Paris, France – June 8th, 2000**		–
Sep 00.	(d-cd) *(499646-2)* **LIVE: City Square, Salzburg, Austria – June 18th, 2000**		–
Sep 00.	(d-cd) *(499647-2)* **LIVE: Velodromo Anaeta, San Sebastian, Spain – May 26th, 2000**		–
Sep 00.	(d-cd) *(499648-2)* **LIVE: Naval Museum, Stockholm, Sweden – June 28th, 2000**		–
Sep 00.	(d-cd) *(499649-2)* *<85061>* **LIVE: Arena, Verona, Italy – June 20th, 2000**		
Sep 00.	(d-cd) *(499650-2)* **LIVE: Hallenstadion, Zurich, Switzerland – June 23rd, 2000**		–
Feb 01.	(d-cd) *(501989-2)* *<E2K 85551>* *LIVE: Boston, Massachusetts Vol.1 – August 29th, 2000*		
Feb 01.	(d-cd) *(501990-2)* *<E2K 85545>* **LIVE: Jones Beach, New York, Vol.3 – August 25th, 2000**		
Feb 01.	(d-cd) *(501991-2)* *<E2K 85542>* **LIVE: Jones Beach, New York, Vol.2 – August 24th, 2000**		
Feb 01.	(d-cd) *(501992-2)* *<E2K 85536>* **LIVE: Columbus, Ohio – August 21st, 2000**		
Feb 01.	(d-cd) *(501993-2)* *<E2K 85518>* **LIVE: Tampa, Florida – August 12th, 2000**		
Feb 01.	(d-cd) *(501994-2)* *<E2K 85509>* **LIVE: Atlanta, Georgia – August 7th, 2000**		
Mar 01.	(d-cd) *<(E2K 85208)>* **LIVE: Virginia Beach, Virginia – August 3rd, 2000**		
Mar 01.	(d-cd) *<(E2K 85503)>* **LIVE: Charlotte, North Carolina – August 4th, 2000**		
Mar 01.	(d-cd) *<(E2K 85506)>* **LIVE: Greensboro, North Carolina – August 6th, 2000**		
Mar 01.	(d-cd) *<(E2K 85512)>* **LIVE: West Palm Beach, Florida. Vol.1 – August 9th, 2000**		
Mar 01.	(d-cd) *<(E2K 85515)>* **LIVE: West Palm Beach, Florida, Vol.2 – August 10th, 2000**		
Mar 01.	(d-cd) *<(E2K 85521)>* **LIVE: New Orleans, Louisiana – August 14th, 2000**		
Mar 01.	(d-cd) *<(E2K 85524)>* **LIVE: Memphis, Tennessee – August 15th, 2000**		
Mar 01.	(d-cd) *<(E2K 85527)>* **LIVE: Nashville, Tennessee – August 17th, 2000**		
Mar 01.	(d-cd) *<(E2K 85530)>* **LIVE: Indianapolis, Indiana – August 18th, 2000**		
Mar 01.	(d-cd) *<(E2K 85533)>* **LIVE: Cincinatti, Ohio – August 20th, 2000**		
Mar 01.	(d-cd) *<(E2K 85539)>* **LIVE: Jones Beach, New York, Vol.1 – August 23rd, 2000**		
Mar 01.	(d-cd) *<(E2K 85548)>* **LIVE: Saratoga, New York – August 27th, 2000**		
Mar 01.	(d-cd) *<(E2K 85554)>* **LIVE: Boston, Massachusetts Vol.2 – August 30th, 2000**		
Mar 01.	(d-cd) *<(E2K 85557)>* **LIVE: Philadelphia, Pennsylvania, Vol.1 – September 1st, 2000**		
Mar 01.	(d-cd) *<(E2K 85560)>* **LIVE: Philadelphia, Pennsylvania, Vol.2 – September 2nd, 2000**		
Mar 01.	(d-cd) *<(E2K 85563)>* **LIVE: Washington DC – September 4th, 2000**		
Mar 01.	(d-cd) *<(E2K 85566)>* **LIVE: Pittsburgh, Pennsylvania – September 5th, 2000**		
Mar 01.	(d-cd) *<(E2K 85572)>* **LIVE: Toronto, Canada – October 5th, 2000**		
Mar 01.	(d-cd) *<(E2K 85599)>* **LIVE: Dallas, Texas – October 17th, 2000**		
Mar 01.	(cd) *(502165-2)* *<E2K 85575>* **LIVE: Detroit, Michigan – October 7th, 2000**		
Mar 01.	(cd) *(502166-2)* *<E2K 85581>* **LIVE: Chicago, Illinois – October 9th, 2000**		
Mar 01.	(cd) *(502167-2)* *<E2K 85611>* **LIVE: Las Vegas, Nevada (10th Anniversary Show) – October 22nd, 2000**		
Mar 01.	(cd) *(502168-2)* *<E2K 85617>* **LIVE: San Diego, California – October 25th, 2000**		
Mar 01.	(cd) *(502169-2)* *<E2K 85635>* **LIVE: Boise, Idaho – November 3rd, 2000**		
Mar 01.	(t-cd) *(502170-2)* *<E2K 85641>* **Seattle, Washington – 6th November, 2000**		98
Apr 01.	(cd) *<(E2K 85569)>* **LIVE: Montreal, Canada – October 4th, 2000**		
Apr 01.	(cd) *<(E2K 85578)>* **LIVE: East Troy, Wisconsin – October 8th, 2000**		
Apr 01.	(cd) *<(E2K 85584)>* **LIVE: St. Louis, Missouri – October 11th, 2000**		
Apr 01.	(cd) *<(E2K 85587)>* **LIVE: Kansas City, Missouri – October 12th, 2000**		

Apr 01. (cd) *<(E2K 85590)>* **LIVE: Houston, Texas, Vol.1 – October 14th, 2000**

Apr 01. (cd) *<(E2K 85593)>* **LIVE: Houston, Texas, Vol.2 – October 15th, 2000**

Apr 01. (cd) *<(E2K 85602)>* **LIVE: Lubbock, Texas – October 18th, 2000**

Apr 01. (cd) *<(E2K 85608)>* **LIVE: Phoenix, Arizona – October 21st, 2000**

Apr 01. (cd) *<(E2K 85614)>* **LIVE: Los Angeles, California – October 24th, 2000**

Apr 01. (cd) *<(E2K 85620)>* **LIVE: Fresno, California – October 27th, 2000**

Apr 01. (cd) *<(E2K 85623)>* **LIVE: San Bernadino, California – October 28th, 2000**

Apr 01. (cd) *<(E2K 85623)>* **LIVE: Sacramento, California – October 30th, 2000**

Apr 01. (cd) *<(E2K 85629)>* **LIVE: San Francisco, California – October 31st, 2000**

Apr 01. (cd) *<(E2K 85632)>* **LIVE: Portland, Oregon – November 2nd, 2000**

Apr 01. (cd) *<(E2K 85638)>* **LIVE: Seattle, Washington – November 5th, 2000**

Apr 01. (d-cd) *<(E2K 85805)>* **LIVE: Albuquerque, New Mexico – October 20th, 2000**

Jun 03. (d-cd) *(512222-2) <90128>* **RIOT ACT WORLD TOUR VOL.10: Perth, Australia – February 23rd 2003 (live)**

Jun 03. (d-cd) *(512223-2) <90336>* **RIOT ACT WORLD TOUR VOL.13: Tokyo, Japan – March 3rd 2003 (live)**

Jul 03. (t-cd) *<90500>* **RIOT ACT WORLD TOUR: State College, Pennsylvania – May 3rd 2003 (live)** [–]

Nov 03. (t-cd) *(510510-2) <90702>* **RIOT ACT WORLD TOUR No.66: New York, New York – July 8th 2003 (live)**

Nov 03. (d-cd) *(513638-2) <90662>* **RIOT ACT WORLD TOUR No.67: New York, New York – July 9th 2003 (live)**

Nov 03. (t-cd) *(513639-2) <90721>* **RIOT ACT WORLD TOUR No.68: Mansfield, Massachusetts – July 11th 2003 (live)**

Nov 03. (d-cd) *(513640-2) <85738>* **LOST DOGS: B-SIDES & RARITIES** [15]
– All night / Sad / Down / Hitchhiker / Don't gimme no lip / Alone / In the moonlight / Education / Black, red, yellow / U / Leaving here / Gremmie out of control / Whale song / Undone / Hold on / Yellow Ledbetter / Fatal / Other side / Hard to imagine / Footsteps / Wash / Dead man walking / Strangest tribe / Drifting / Let me sleep / Last kiss / Street lew / Dirty Frank / Brother / Bee girl.

Nov 04. (d-cd) *(519113-2) <93535>* **REARVIEWMIRROR: GREATEST HITS 1991-2003** [58] [16]
– Once / Alive / Even flow / Jeremy / State of love and trust / Animal / Go / Dissident / Rearviewmirror / Spin the black circle / Corduroy / Not for you / I got I.D. / Hail hail / Do the evolution / Save you / Black / Breath / Daughter / Elderly woman behind the counter in a small town / Immortality / Betterman / Nothingman / Who are you / Off he goes / Given to fly / Wishlist / Last kiss / Nothing as it seems / LIght years / I am mine / Man of the hour / Yellow Ledbetter.

□ PELICAN CITY (see under ⇒ GNARLS BARKLEY)

PERE UBU

Formed: Cleveland, Ohio, USA . . . September '75 out of ROCKET FROM THE TOMBS, by DAVID THOMAS (aka CROCUS BEHEMOTH; his alter-ego) and PETER LAUGHNER. Along with CHARLIE WEINER (guitar), GLEN 'THUNDERHAND' HACH (guitar) and TOM 'FOOLERY' CLEMENTS (drums), they became residents at THOMAS's workplace, the Viking Saloon; he was apparently a bouncer! A revamped RFTT saw THOMAS and LAUGHNER being joined by CRAIG BELL (bass), GENE 'CHEETAH CHROME' O'CONNOR (guitar) and 'JOHNNY BLIZ' MADANSKY, and it was this line-up who recorded sessions for WMMS radio stations, later to surface as a posthumous 1990 cd, 'LIFE STINKS'. A few embryonic UBU tracks, 'FINAL SOLUTION' and '30 SECONDS OVER TOKYO', plus covers of 'SATISFACTION' (Rolling Stones) and 'SEARCH AND DESTROY' (Stooges), featured on these rare master tapes. Even 'SONIC REDUCER' was hijacked by The DEAD BOYS bound, CHEETAH and BLITZ, the pair being united with STIV BATORS, who replaced THOMAS before the ROCKETS split. Meanwhile, PERE UBU (THOMAS and LAUGHNER) recruited other musicians; TIM WRIGHT, ALLEN RAVENSTINE, TOM HERMAN plus SCOTT KRAUSS, and took their name from a play by French writer, Alfred Jarry. The large-framed THOMAS formed his own 'Hearthan' label, issuing a classic debut, '30 SECONDS OVER TOKYO', which led to gigs at (New York's) Max's Kansas City in early '76. Another gem, 'FINAL SOLUTION', was unleashed soon after, although LAUGHNER departed (at this stage the line-up numbered THOMAS, RAVENSTINE, HERMAN, KRAUSE and newcomer, TONY MAIMONE) prior to the release of their third and fourth rare 45's, 'STREET WAVES' and 'THE MODERN DANCE'. The latter subsequently became the name of their debut album which gained a release early in 1978 on the obscure US 'Blank' label (a few months later it surfaced in the UK on 'Mercury'). The sound was clearly a break from the "New Wave", echoing as it did a revival of the avant-garde (CAPTAIN BEEFHEART and ENO-era ROXY MUSIC). On the strength of this masterwork, they signed to the major 'Chrysalis' label and, six months later, wowed the music world with another abstract beauty, 'DUB HOUSING' (1978). After the disappointing 'NEW PICNIC TIME' (1979), however, they were unceremoniously dropped by their label, the band's wayward eccentricity floating right over the average pop picker's head. PERE UBU (who had replaced HERMAN with veteran, MAYO THOMPSON – formerly of RED CRAYOLA) subsequently found a home with UK indie, 'Rough Trade', although they split after two poorly-received studio sets, 'THE ART OF WALKING' (1980) and 'SONG OF THE BAILING MAN' (1982), the latter boasting the drumming talents of ANTON FIER. Over the course of the next five years, having released a debut album, 'THE SOUND OF THE SAND' early in '82, THOMAS embarked on an equally weird and anti-commercial solo career with albums, the live 'WINTER COMES HOME' (1983), 'VARIATIONS ON A THEME' (1983), 'MORE PLACES FOREVER; (1985), 'MONSTER WALKS THE WINTER LAKE' (1986) and 'BLAME THE MESSENGER' (1987). PERE UBU released a belated comeback album, 'THE TENEMENT YEARS', in 1988, a record which gathered together old UBU men, THOMAS, RAVENSTINE, MAIMONE and KRAUSE, while retaining CHRIS CUTLER and JIM JONES (previously part of THOMAS' solo band). For the 1989 set, 'CLOUDLAND', the group sought out former CAPTAIN BEEFHEART employee, ERIC DREW FELDMAN, who remained for a further two albums, 'WORLDS IN COLLISION' (1991) and 'STORY OF MY LIFE' (1993). Subsequently signing to 'Cooking Vinyl' (also now the rest home of BILLY BRAGG and The WEDDING PRESENT), PERE UBU cut one final effort, 'RAY GUN SUITCASE' (1995), before THOMAS once again opted for solo pastures with 'EREWHON' (1996). Sidestepping between solo and PERE UBU releases, THOMAS continued to create his own creative pop. UBU's 'PENNSYLVANIA' (1998) found him in a reflective mood – he had been living in England for some time now – while the solo DAVID THOMAS AND TWO PALE BOYS release 'MIRROR MAN' (1999) was pure rock-opera mixed with readings. To start the millennium, DAVID THOMAS AND FOREIGNERS (mainly Danish musicians!) got together for improv live set, 'BAY CITY' (2000); THOMAS AND TWO PALE BOYS (aka ANDY DIAGRAM and KEITH MOLINE) delivered a second batch of songs, 'SURF'S UP!', the following year. PERE UBU returned in the summer of 2002 via 'ST. ARKANSAS', their body of sound now over a quarter of a century old but still viable and conscious of today's discerning and fickle market. Together with the TWO PALE BOYS, DAVID

THOMAS delivered another brave set of weird and wonderful tracks, '18 MONKEYS ON A DEAD MAN'S CHEST' (2004).

• **Songwriters:** All group compositions. THOMAS collaborated with others on solo work and covered SLOOP JOHN B. (Beach Boys).

Album rating: THE MODERN DANCE (*9) / DUB HOUSING (*7) / NEW PICNIC TIME (*7) / THE ART OF WALKING (*6) / 390 DEGREES OF SIMULATED STEREO (*4) / SONG OF THE BAILING MAN (*5) / TERMINAL TOWER: AN ARCHIVAL COLLECTION compilation (*9) / THE TENEMENT YEAR (*6) / ONE MAN DRIVES WHILE THE OTHER MAN SCREAMS early live (*5) / CLOUDLAND (*6) / WORLDS IN COLLISION (*6) / STORY OF MY LIFE (*6) / RAYGUN SUITCASE (*7) / DATAPANIK IN THE YEAR ZERO boxed collection (*8) / PENNSYLVANIA (*6) / APOCALYPSE NOW live (*6) / ST. ARKANSAS (*6) / David Thomas: THE SOUND OF THE SAND . . . (*6) / WINTER COMES HOME (*5) / VARIATIONS ON A THEME (*6) / MORE PLACES FOREVER (*5) / MONSTER WALKS THE WINTER LAKE (*4) / BLAME THE MESSENGER (*5) / MIRROR MAN (*7) / BAY CITY (*5) / SURF'S UP! (*6) / 18 MONKEYS ON A DEAD MAN'S CHEST (*7) / Rocket From The Tombs: THE DAY THE EARTH MET THE . . . (*6)

DAVID THOMAS (b.14 Jun'53) – vocals / **PETER LAUGHNER** (b.1953) – guitar / **TIM WRIGHT** – bass, guitar / **TOM HERMAN** (b.19 Apr'49) – guitar, bass / **SCOTT KRAUSE** (b.19 Nov'50) – drums / **ALLEN RAVENSTINE** (b. 9 May'50) – synthesizer

not iss. Hearthan

Dec 75. (7"ltd) *<HR 101>* **30 SECONDS OVER TOKYO. / HEART OF DARKNESS** –

— **DAVE TAYLOR** – synthesizer repl. RAVENSTINE

Mar 76. (7"ltd) *<HR 102>* **FINAL SOLUTION. / CLOUD 149** –

— **ALLEN RAVENSTINE** – synthesizer returned to repl. TAYLOR / **ALAN GREENBLATT** – guitar; repl. LAUGHNER who formed FRICTION (he died of drug & alcohol abuse 22nd June '77)

— **TONY MAIMONE** (b.27 Sep'52) – bass, piano repl. WRIGHT who joined DNA. (GREENBLATT left also) (were now a quintet with **THOMAS, HERMAN, KRAUSE, MAIMONE + RAVENSTINE**)

Nov 76. (7"ltd) *<HR 103>* **STREET WAVES. / MY DARK AGES** –

Aug 77. (7"ltd) *<HR 104>* **THE MODERN DANCE. / HEAVEN** –

Mercury Blank

Apr 78. (lp) *(9100 052) <001>* **THE MODERN DANCE** Jan78
– Non-alignment pact / The modern dance / Laughing / Street waves / Chinese radiation / Life stinks / Real world / Over my head / Sentimental journey / Humor me. *(re-iss. Jan81 on 'Rough Trade'; ROUGH 22) (re-iss. Feb88 on 'Fontana' lp/cd; SF LP/CD 3) (cd re-iss. Jun98 on 'Cooking Vinyl'; COOKCD 141) <US cd-iss. Jun98 on 'Geffen'; 25206> (lp re-iss. May99 on 'Get Back'; GET 054)*

Radar not iss.

Apr 78. (12"ep) *(RDAR 1)* **DATAPANIK IN THE YEAR ZERO (remixes compilation)** –
– Heart of darkness / 30 seconds over Tokyo / Cloud 149 / Untitled / Heaven.

Chrysalis Rough Trade

Nov 78. (lp) *(CHR 1207) <ROUGH-US 14>* **DUB HOUSING**
– Navy / On the surface / Dub housing / Cagliari's mirror / Thriller / I will wait / Drinking wine Spodyody / Ubu dance party / Blow daddy-o / Codex. *(cd-iss. Mar89 on 'Rough Trade'; ROUGHCD 6002) (cd re-iss. Mar99 on 'Cooking Vinyl'; COOKCD 170) (lp re-iss. Feb00 on 'Get Back'; GET 58)*

Sep 79. (lp) *(CHR 1248) <ROUGH-US 20>* **NEW PICNIC TIME**
– One less worry / Make hay / Goodbye / The voice of the sand / Jehovah's kingdom comes / Have shoes will walk / 49 guitars and 1 girl / A small dark cloud / Small was fast / All the dogs are barking. *(cd-iss. Mar89 on 'Rough Trade'; ROUGHCD 6003) (cd re-iss. Mar99 on 'Cooking Vinyl'; COOKCD 171) (lp re-iss. Feb00 on 'Get Back'; GET 59)*

Oct 79. (7"m) *(CHS 2372)* **THE FABULOUS SEQUEL (HAVE SHOES WILL WALK). / HUMOR ME (live). / THE BOOK IS ON THE TABLE** –

— **MAYO THOMPSON** (b.26 Feb'44) – guitar, vocals (ex-RED CRAYOLA) repl. HERMAN who went solo

Rough Trade not iss.

Jun 80. (7") *(RT 049)* **FINAL SOLUTION. / MY DARK AGES** –

Sep 80. (lp) *(ROUGH 14)* **THE ART OF WALKING** –
– Go / Rhapsody in pink / Arabia * / Miles * / Misery goats / Loop / Rounder / Birdies / Lost in art / Horses / Crush this horn. *(re-iss. 1981; same)* – Arabian nights / Tribute to Miles; repl. *) *(cd-iss. Apr89 tracks as re-issue; ROUGHCD 14)<US = ROUGH-US-4CD> (cd re-iss. Nov99 on 'Cooking Vinyl'; COOKCD 157) <US cd re-iss. Nov99 on 'Thirsty Ear'; 57079> (lp re-iss. Sep01 on 'Get Back'; GET 81)*

Feb 81. (7") *(RT 066)* **NOT HAPPY. / LONESOME COWBOY DAVE** –

May 81. (lp) *(ROUGH 23)* **390° OF SIMULATED STEREO – UBU LIVE: VOLUME 1 (live 76-79)** –
– Can't believe it / Over my head / Sentimental journey / 30 seconds over Tokyo / Humor me / Real world / My dark ages / Street waves / Laughing / Non-alignment pact / Heart of darkness / The modern dance. *(cd-iss. Apr89; ROUGHCD 23)*

— added **ANTON FIER** (b.20 Jun'56) – drums, percussion (ex-FEELIES) / guest **EDDIE THORNTON** – trumpet

Jun 82. (lp) *(ROUGH 33)* **SONG OF THE BAILING MAN** –
– The long walk home / Use of a dog / Petrified / Stormy weather / West Side story / Thoughts that go by steam / Big Ed's used farms / A day such as this / The vulgar boatman bird / My hat / Horns are a dilemma. *(cd-iss. Apr89; ROUGHCD 33) (cd re-iss. Nov99 on 'Cooking Vinyl'; COOKCD 158) <US cd-iss. Nov99 on 'Thirsty Ear'; 57080> (lp re-iss. Jun02 on 'Get Back'; GET 90)*

— split mid 1982. MAYO returned to RED CRAYOLA (which also incl. most UBU's). KRAUSE + WRIGHT formed HOME & GARDEN, who released one album for 'Dead Man's Curve', 'HISTORY & GEOGRAPHY' (1986)

DAVID THOMAS & THE PEDESTRIANS

Rough Trade Recommended

Dec 81. (12"ep; by DAVID THOMAS) *(TRADE 5-12)* **VOCAL PERFORMANCES** –

— included **THOMPSON, KRAUSE, FIER & RAVENSTINE** plus **CHRIS CUTLER** (b. 4 Jan'47) – drums / **JOHN GREAVES** – bass (both ex-HENRY COW) / **PHILIP MOXHAM** – multi (ex-YOUNG MARBLE GIANTS) / **RICHARD THOMPSON** – guitar

Jan 82. (lp) *(ROUGH 30)* **THE SOUND OF THE SAND AND OTHER SONGS OF THE PEDESTRIANS**
– The birds are good ideas / Yiki Tiki / The crickets in the flats / Sound of the sand / The new atom mine / Big dreams / Happy to see you / Crush this horn – part 2 / Confuse did / Sloop John B. / Man's best friend.

Oct 82. (7") **PETRIFIED. /** –

— w/ **CHRIS CUTLER & LINDSAY COOPER** – bassoon (ex-MIKE OLDFIELD)

Feb 83. (lp; DAVID THOMAS & HIS LEGS) *(DTLP)* **WINTER COMES HOME (live Munich, 1982)** –
– A day such as this / Winter comes home / West side story / Sunset / Stormy weather / Poetic license / Rhapsody in pink / Dinosaurs like me / Petrified / Bones in action / Contrasted views of the archaeopterix.

— added **RICHARD THOMPSON** etc. (CUTLER, COOPER)

Dec 83. (lp) *(ROUGH 60)* **VARIATIONS ON A THEME** –
– A day at the Botanical Gardens / Pedestrians walk / Bird town / The egg and I / Who is it / Song of hoe / Hurry back / The ram / Semaphore.

— **TONY MAIMONE** – bass repl. GREAVES who joined The FLYING LIZARDS

Rough Trade Twin/Tone

May 85. (lp) *(ROUGH 80) <TTR 8551>* **MORE PLACES FOREVER**
– Through the magnifying glass / Enthusiastic / Big breezy day / About true friends / Whale head king / Song of the bailing man / The farmer's wife / New broom.

DAVID THOMAS & THE WOODEN BIRDS

(**DAVID** retained **MAIMONE** and **CUTLER**) brought in **RAVENSTINE** again. (**DAVID HILD** – accordion of LOS LOBOS guested)

Apr 86. (lp/cd) *(ROUGH 90) <TTR/+CD 8667>* **MONSTER WALKS THE WINTER LAKE**
– My theory of similtanious similtude – Red tin bus / What happened to me / Monster walks the winter lake / Bicycle / Coffee train / My town / Monster Magge king of the seas / Monster thinks about the good days / What happened to us.

— **JIM JONES** (b.12 Mar'50) – guitar was added

Mar 87. (lp) *(ROUGH 120) <TTR 87105>* **BLAME THE MESSENGER**
– The long rain / My town / King Knut / A fact about trains / When love is uneven / Storm breaks / Having time / Velikovsky / The two-step.

PERE UBU

(THOMAS, RAVENSTINE, MAIMONE, CUTLER, JONES and **KRAUSE)**

Fontana Enigma

Mar 88. (lp/c)(cd) *(SF LP/MC 5)(834 537-2) <73343>* **THE TENEMENT YEAR**
– Something's gotta give / George had a hat / Talk to me / Busman's honeymoon / Say goodbye / Universal vibration / Miss you / Dream the Moon / Rhythm kind / The hollow Earth / We have the technology.

Jul 88. (7") *(UBU 1)* **WE HAVE THE TECHNOLOGY. / THE B-SIDE** –
(12"+=/cd-s+=) *(UBU 1-12/CD1)* – The postman drove a caddy / ('A'-different mix).

—— **ERIC DREW FELDMAN** (b.16 Apr'55) – drums (ex-CAPTAIN BEEFHEART) repl. RAVENSTINE + CUTLER

Fontana not iss.

Mar 89. (7") *(UBU 2)* **WAITING FOR MARY (WHAT ARE WE DOING HERE?). / WINE DARK SPARKS** –
(12"+=/cd-s+=) *(UBU 2-12/CD2)* – Flat.

May 89. (lp/c/cd) *(838 237-1/-4/-2)* **CLOUDLAND** –
– Breath / Bus called happiness / Race the sun / Waiting for Mary / Cry / Flat * / Ice cream truck / Lost nation road / Monday night / Pushin' / The wire * / The waltz. *(cd+= *)*

Jun 89. (7") *(UBU 3)* **LOVE LOVE LOVE. / FEDORA SATELLITE** –
(cd-s+=) *(UBUCD 3)* – Say goodbye.
(12") *(UBU 3-12)* – ('A'-cajun house mix) / ('A'132 bpm mix) / ('A'side).

Oct 89. (7") *(UBU 4)* **BREATH. / BANG THE DRUM** –
(12"+=) *(UBU 4-12)* – Over my head (live) / Universal initiation (live).
(cd-s+=) *(UBUCD 4)* – Humor me (live).

Mar 91. (7") *(UBU 5)* **I HEAR THEY SMOKE THE BARBEQUE. / INVISIBLE MAN** –
(12"+=/cd-s+=) *(UBU 5-12/CD5)* – Around the fire.

May 91. (cd/c/lp) *(848 564-2/-4/-1)* **WORLDS IN COLLISION** –
– Oh Catherine / I hear they smoke the barbeque / Turpentine / Goodnight Irene / Mirror man / Cry cry / World's in collision / Life of Riley / Over the Moon / Don't look back / Playback / Nobody knows / Winter in the Netherlands.

May 91. (7") *(UBU 6)* **OH CATHERINE. / LIKE A ROLLING STONE** –
(12"+=/cd-s+=) *(UBU 6-12/CD6)* – Down by the river.

Fontana Imago

Jan 93. (cd/c) *(514159-2/-4) <21024>* **STORY OF MY LIFE**
– Wasted / Come home / Louisiana train wreck / Fedora satellite II / Heartbreak garage / Postcard / Kathleen / Honey Moon / Sleep walk / The story of my life / Last will and testament.

—— **THOMAS / KRAUSS / JONES / TEMPLE / YELLIN**

Cooking Vinyl Tim/Kerr

Aug 95. (cd) *(COOKCD 089) <TK 100>* **RAY GUN SUITCASE**
– Folly of youth / Electricity / Beach Boys / Turquoise fins / Vacuum in my head / Memphis / Three things / Horse / Don't worry / Ray gun suitcase / Surfer girl / Red sky / Montana / My friend is a stooge for the media priests / Down by the river II.

Oct 95. (cd-ep) *(FRYCD 043) <TK 111-2>* **FOLLY OF YOUTH / BALL 'N' CHAIN (jam) / DOWN BY THE RIVER II (demo) / MEMPHIS (demo)** Feb96

Mar 96. (cd-ep) *<TK 830121>* **BEACH BOYS SEE DEE +** –
– Beach Boys / Down by the river / Louisiana train wreck / Montana.

DAVID THOMAS

—— with **ANDY DIAGRAM** – trumpet (ex-PALE FOUNTAINS) / **PAUL HAMANN** – upright bass / **JIM JONES** – backing vocals

Cooking Vinyl Tim/Kerr

Sep 96. (cd; DAVID THOMAS & TWO PALE BOYS) *(COOKCD 105) <TK 145>* **EREWHON**
– Obsession / Planet of fools / Nowheresville / Fire / Lantern / Morbid sky / Weird cornfields / Kathlen / Highway 61 revisited.

PERE UBU

—— **THOMAS** with **TOM HERMAN** + **JIM JONES** newcomer + **ROBERT WHEELER** – synthesizer / **MICHELE TEMPLE** – bass

Mar 98. (cd) *(COOKCD 139) <TK 155>* **PENNSYLVANIA**
– Woolie bullie / Highwaterville / Sad. TXT / Urban lifestyle / Drive / Indiangiver / Monday morning / Perfume / Silent spring / Mr. Wheeler / Muddy waters / Slow / Fly's eye / The duke's Saharan ambitions / Wheelhouse.

DAVID THOMAS

—— with **ANDY DIAGRAM, LINDA THOMPSON, JACKIE LEVEN,** etc

Cooking Vinyl Thirsty Ear

Mar 99. (cd; by the PALE ORCHESTRA conducted by DAVID THOMAS) *(COOKCD 175) <57068>* **MIRROR MAN**
– Mirror man sees / Mirror man speaks – Lost nation road / The flying Dutchman of the interstate / Ballad of Florida – Montana / Ribbons on the road / Morbid sky / Nowheresville / Shadows on the face – Memphis / Over the moon – If the deer blinks / Bus called happiness / Weird cornfields.
next with **JORGEN TELLER** – guitar, organ / **PER BUHL ACS** – clarinet, bass / **P.O. JORGENS** – percussion

Hearpen Thirsty Ear

Aug 00. (cd; as DAVID THOMAS AND FOREIGNERS) *(HR 111) <57085>* **BAY CITY**
– Clouds of you / White room / Black coffee dawn / Salt / Nobody lives on the moon / Charlotte / The doorbell / 15 seconds / The radio talks to me / Shaky hands / Black rain / Turpentine / Untitled track.

DAVID THOMAS & TWO PALE BOYS

—— back with **DIAGRAM** + **KEITH MOLINE** – guitar

Glitterhouse Thirsty Ear

Mar 01. (cd) *(GRCD 519) <57096>* **SURF'S UP!** Feb01
– Runaway / Man in the dark / Night driving / Surf's up / River / Ghosts / Spider in my stew / Come home – Green river.

Mar 04. (cd) *(GRCD 596)* **18 MONKEYS ON A DEAD MAN'S CHEST** –
– New Orleans fuzz / Numbers man / Little sister / Habeas corpus / Brunswick parking lot / Nebraska alcohol abuse / Sad eyed lowlands / Golden surf / Prepare for the end.

– compilations, etc. –

Jun 97. (5xcd-box) *Hearpen; (HR 110)* **MONSTER** –
(compilation of all his solo work)
(re-iss. Oct02; same)

PERE UBU

Glitterhouse SpinArt

May 02. (cd) *(GRCD 554) <SPART 108>* **ST. ARKANSAS** Jun02
– The fevered dream of Hernando DeSoto / Slow walking daddy / Michele / 333 / Hell / Lisbon / Steve / Phone home Jonah / Where's the truth / Dark.

– compilations, others, etc. –

Nov 85. (lp/cd) *Rough Trade; (ROUGH 83) / Twin/Tone; <TTR/+CD 8561>* **TERMINAL TOWER: AN ARCHIVAL COLLECTION** (early work)
– Heart of darkness / 30 seconds over Tokyo / Final solution / Cloud 149 / Untitled / My dark ages / Heaven / Humor me / The book is on the table / Not happy / Lonesome cowboy Dave. *(cd re-iss. Jun98 on 'Cooking Vinyl'; COOKCD 142) <US cd re-iss. Jun98 on 'Geffen'; 25207> (lp re-iss. Feb01 on 'Get Back'; GET 73)*

Mar 89. (cd) *Rough Trade; (ROUGHCD 93)* **ONE MAN DRIVES WHILE THE OTHER MAN SCREAMS – LIVE VOL.2: PERE UBU ON TOUR** –

Nov 95. (4x7"box) *Cooking Vinyl; (FRY 045) / Tim/Kerr; <TK 107>* **THE HEARTHAN SINGLES**

Nov 95. (d-cd) *Movieplay Gold; (MPG 74178)* **THE MODERN DANCE / TERMINAL TOWER** –

Sep 96. (5xcd-box) *Cooking Vinyl; (COOKCD 098) / Geffen; <24969>* **DATAPANIK IN THE YEAR ZERO**
– (first 5 albums + 1 free rarities album)

Aug 99. (cd) *Cooking Vinyl; (COOKCD 185) / Thirsty Ear; <57074>* **APOCALYPSE NOW (live in Chicago 1991)**

Mar 03. (cd) *Hearthan; <(HR 113)>* **THE SHAPE OF THINGS** (live, April 7, 1976) Oct00

ROCKET FROM THE TOMBS

CROCUS BEHEMOTH (aka DAVID THOMAS) – vocals, guitar / **PETER LAUGHNER** – guitar, vocals / **CHEETAH CHROME** (b. GENE O'CONNOR) – guitar, organ / **CRAIG "C.W." BELL** – bass / **JOHNNY BLITZ** (b. JOHNNY MADANSKY) – drums

they released no singles during their lifespan (Jan-Aug 1975); CHEETAH + BLITZ helped to form The DEAD BOYS

– compilations, etc. –

Mar 02. (cd) *Glitterhouse; (GRCD 549)* **THE DAY THE EARTH MET THE . . . ROCKET FROM THE TOMBS** ☐ ⊟
– Raw power / So cold / What love is / Ain't it fun / Transfusion / Life stinks / Muckraker / 30 seconds over Tokyo / Satisfaction / Sonic reducer / Never gonna kill myself again / Final solution / Foggy notion / Amphetamine / Read it and weep / Seventeen / Frustration / Down in flames / Search and destroy.
—— (some tracks were initially from 1990 bootleg, 'LIFE STINKS')

☐ a PERFECT CIRCLE (see under ⇒ TOOL)

PET SHOP BOYS

Formed: London, England . . . August '81 by assistant editor of Smash Hits, NEIL TENNANT, together with architecture student CHRIS LOWE (ex-DUST). After two years spent plugging away at demos, they met disco producer Bobby 'O' Orlando, subsequently working together on the debut 1984 'Epic' single, 'WEST END GIRLS'. After the track flopped in Britain (it was a French & Belgian hit), they signed with manager Tom Watkins, who secured them a deal with 'Parlophone' early in 1985. Their first effort for the label, the sardonic 80's critique of 'OPPORTUNITIES (LET'S MAKE LOTS OF MONEY)' failed to make an impact, a Stephen Hague produced re-make of 'WEST END GIRLS' finally giving them a major breakthrough early the following year, hitting No.1 in many countries including Britain and the States. The debut album, 'PLEASE' (1986) was a Transatlantic Top 10 success, a classy collection of intelligent synth-pop, infectious melodies and wryly observant lyrics becoming the campy duo's trademark. 'OPPORTUNITIES' was hastily re-released in clanking, mechanically remixed form, almost making the Top 10, while a further single from the album, 'SUBURBIA', made No.8. Visually, the band were akin to a more stylish SPARKS or ERASURE, sharing the latter's sizeable gay following, while ironically also being idolised by thuggish football 'casuals' for their immaculate taste in designer wear. The 'BOYS even penned a song about the Italian strain of the expensively kitted out thug, 'PANINARO', featured on their mini remix album, 'DISCO' (1986). 'IT'S A SIN' gave the act their second No.1 later that summer while the duo teamed up with 60's songstress DUSTY SPRINGFIELD for 'WHAT HAVE I DONE TO DESERVE THIS', a Transatlantic No.2 hit. The fact that the Americans had taken so keenly to The PET SHOP BOYS was odd, given that nation's notorious inability to appreciate irony; it's arguably a testament to the group's finely honed melodic mastery and perfectionist production that they broke the US market where other quintessentially English pop bands have consistently failed. 'ACTUALLY' (1987) was another successful slice of sophisticated pop nous, containing the aforementioned two singles as well as the poignant 'RENT' and two further No.1 singles in 'HEART' and a flamboyant synth/strings remake of Elvis' 'ALWAYS ON MY MIND'. The group further indulged their penchant for remix albums with 'INTROSPECTIVE' (1988), which included a version of the track they'd produced for EIGHTH WONDER (featuring a pre-LIAM Patsy Kensit), 'I'M NOT SCARED'. The following year saw The PET SHOP BOYS working with such diverse artists as LIZA MINNELLI (who subsequently hit the charts with their melodramatic, collaborative cover of Stephen Sondheim's 'LOSING MY MIND') and ELECTRONIC, while the next group project, 'BEHAVIOUR' (1990), was uncharacteristically introspective, spawning a solitary hit single, the wistful 'BEING BORING'. Only the PET SHOP BOYS could get away with splicing U2's 'Where The Streets Have No Name' and FRANKIE VALLI's 'Can't Take My Eyes Off You', a masterstroke of tongue-in-cheek pop genius that reached No.4 in Spring '91. It would be another two years before 'VERY', a consummate distillation of the PET SHOP BOYS' unique grasp of pure pop, previewed by their celebratory cover of The Village People's 'GO WEST'. A limited edition dance CD, 'RELENTLESS', was included with initial copies of 'VERY', The PET SHOP BOYS proving they were hip to a music style they had helped to create. TENNANT and LOWE have maintained a fairly low profile of late, releasing a second volume of 'DISCO' remixes in 1994 and a B-sides collection in '95, 'ALTERNATIVE'. 'BILINGUAL' (1996) boasted the usual spread of UK hit singles, although The PET SHOP BOYS were getting old hat while wearing many of them in the process. Nearing the end of the millennium (aarrgghh!), credible pop music was now big fashion again, it was just that TENNANT and LOWE were losing themselves in the mire of mediocrity; the 1999 album 'NIGHTLIFE' (which featured the appallingly camp 'NEW YORK CITY BOY') the proof that they were losing the place. A few years on, the 'BOYS were back on the town with a collaborative effort, 'CLOSER TO HEAVEN'; all very high-brow but definitely low-key, outside the West End, that is. That the PET SHOP BOYS – a band so closely aligned with the 80's and, to a lesser extent, the 90's – should even choose to keep on recording into the millennium was a brave step although thankfully, 'RELEASE' (2002) made few concessions to musical fashion. Instead, it cast a knowing, wary eye over contemporary music without getting hung up on it. With JOHNNY MARR lending a seasoned hand and messrs TENNANT and LOWE freed from the role of uber-hip cultural commentators, the songs were given unprecedented room to breathe. The result was an aesthetic makeover of sorts, a record more befitting of their age. It seems incredible that such a modernist act have been recording for two decades yet that was the story which the highly entertaining 'POP ART' (2003) had to tell, a more complete anthology than 1991's 'DISCOGRAPHY' if no less playful. Ever the highbrow playboys, PSB subseqently collaborated with Dresden Sinfoniker to recreate the score to Sergei Eisenstein's early Soviet-era silent classic, 'BATTLESHIP POTEMKIN', complete with new lyrics. Not only that but they performed it at a free concert in London's Trafalgar Square in autumn 2004, releasing an album a year later. As indicated by its title and choice of producer (Trevor Horn), 'FUNDAMENTAL' (2006) was a back-to-basics effort, all the easier and more convenient given that electro-poppy 80's material was back in vogue. Back in the Thatcher era, the duo rarely dabbled in politics; in 2006, the state of the world – and more specifically the nature of Anglo-American relations – had moved them to craft their lyrics accordingly on the likes of lead hit single 'I'M WITH STUPID' (video courtesy of 'Little Britain' duo Matt Lucas and David Walliams).

• **Covers:** SOMEWHERE (Leonard Bernstein & Stephen Sondheim) / etc.

Album rating: PLEASE (*6) / DISCO remixes (*5) / ACTUALLY (*7) / INTROSPECTIVE mixes (*5) / BEHAVIOUR (*7) / DISCOGRAPHY – THE COMPLETE SINGLES COLLECTION compilation (*8) / VERY (*7) / DISCO 2 remixes (*5) / ALTERNATIVE collection (*5) / BILINGUAL (*6) / NIGHTLIFE (*6) / RELEASE (*6) / DISCO 3 remixes (*4) / POPART: THE HITS compilation (*7) / BATTLESHIP POTEMKIN soundtrack (*6) / FUNDAMENTAL (*6)

NEIL TENNANT (b.10 Jul'54, Gosforth, Northumberland, England) – vocals / **CHRIS LOWE** (b. 4 Oct'59, Blackpool, England) – keyboards, synthesizers

Epic Bobcat 12"

Apr 84. (7"/ext.12") *<A/TA 4292>* **WEST END GIRLS. / PET SHOP BOYS** ☐ ⊟

Parlophone EMI America

Jun 85. (7") *(R 6097) <8321>* **OPPORTUNITIES (LET'S MAKE LOTS OF MONEY). / IN THE NIGHT** ☐ Mar86 ☐
(12") *(12R 6097)* – ('A'dance mix) / ('B'extended).
(12") *(12RA 6097)* – ('A' Latin version). / ('B'dub for money).

Nov 85. (7") *(R 6115) <8307>* **WEST END GIRLS. / A MAN COULD GET ARRESTED** [1] Jan86 [1]
(10") *(10R 6115)* – ('A'remixed) / ('B'extended).
(12"+=) *(12R 6115)* – ('A'dance mix).
(12") *(12EA 6115)* – ('A'-Shep Pettibone mix) / (A'dub mix) / ('B'extended).

Mar 86. (7") *(R 6116) <8338>* **LOVE COMES QUICKLY. / THAT'S MY IMPRESSION** [19] Aug86 [62]
(10"/12") *(10R/12R 6116)* – ('A'dance mix) / ('B'disco mix).

Mar 86. (lp/c)(cd) *(PSB/TCPSB 1)(CDP 7-46271-2) <17193>* **PLEASE** [3] [7]
– Two divide by zero / West End girls / Opportunities (let's make lots of money) / Love comes quickly / Suburbia / Tonight is forever / Violence / I want a lover / Later tonight / Why don't we live together / Opportunities (reprise).

May 86. (7") *(R 6129) <8330>* **OPPORTUNITIES (LET'S MAKE LOTS OF MONEY) (remix). / WAS THAT WHAT IT WAS** [11] [10]
(12") *(12R 6129)* – ('A'&'B'-Shep Pettibone mastermixes) / Opportunities (original dance mix) / Opportunities (reprise Shep Pettibone mix).

Sep 86. (7") *(R 6140) <8355>* **SUBURBIA. / PANINARO** [8] Nov86 [70]
('A'-Full horror mix-12") *(12R 6140)* – Jack the lad.
(c-s++=) *(TR 6140)* – Love comes quickly (Shep Pettibone remix).
(c-s) *(TCR 6140)* – ('A'-J.Mendelsohn remixed).
(d7"+=) *(RD 6140)* – Suburbia pt.2.

Nov 86. (lp/c)(cd) *(PRG/TCPRG 1001)(CDP 7-46450-2) <17246>* **DISCO** (The 12"mixes) [15] [95]
– In the night / Suburbia / Opportunities / Paninaro / Love comes quickly / West end girls.

Jun 87. (7") *(R 6158) <43027>* **IT'S A SIN. / YOU KNOW WHERE YOU WENT WRONG** [1] Aug87 [9]
(12"+=/c-s+=/cd-s+=) *(12R/TCR/CDR 6158)* – ('A'disco mix).
(12") *(12RX 6158)* – ('A'-Ian Levene remix) / ('B'-rough mix).

Aug 87. (7"; PET SHOP BOYS & DUSTY SPRINGFIELD) *(R 6163) <50107>* **WHAT HAVE I DONE TO DESERVE THIS? / A NEW LIFE** [2] Dec87 [2]
(ext;12"+=/c-s+=/cd-s+=) *(12R/TCR/CDR 6163)* – ('A'disco mix).

Sep 87. (cd/c/lp) *(CD/TC+/PCSD 104) <46972>* **ACTUALLY** [2] [25]
– One more chance / What have I done to deserve this? / Shopping / Rent / Hit music / It couldn't happen here / It's a sin / I want to wake up / Heart / King's Cross. *(re-iss. May88; PCSDX 104) (w/free US 12" or cd-s)* – Always on my mind.

Oct 87. (7") *(R 6168)* **RENT. / I WANT A DOG** [8] [ ]
(ext;12"+=/c-s+=/cd-s+=) *(12R/TCR/CDR 6168)* – Rent (dub).

Nov 87. (7") *(R 6171) <50123>* **ALWAYS ON MY MIND. / DO I HAVE TO?** [1] Mar88 [4]
(12"+=/c-s+=/cd-s+=) *(12R/TCR/CDR 6171)* – ('A'extended dance).
('A'-Phil Harding remix-12") *(12RX 6171)* – ('A'dub).

Mar 88. (7") *(R 6177)* **HEART. / I GET EXCITED (YOU GET EXCITED TOO)** [1] [ ]
('A'disco mix-12"+=/c-s+=/cd-s+=) *(12R/TCR/CDR 6177)* – ('A'dance mix).
('A'-J.Mendelsohn mix-12"+=) *(12RX 6177)* – ('A'dub).

Jun 88. (12"/cd-s) **ACTUALLY. / ALWAYS ON MY MIND** [–] [ ]

Sep 88. (7"/7"s) *(R/RS 6190) <50161>* **DOMINO DANCING. / DON JUAN** [7] [18]
(disco;12"+=/c-s+=/cd-s+=) *(12R/TCR/CDR 6190)* – ('A'alternative mix).
(demo-12"+=) *(12RX 6190)* – ('A'remix).

Oct 88. (cd/c/lp) *(CD/TC+/PCS 7325) <90868>* **INTROSPECTIVE** (12"mixes) [2] [34]
– Left to my own devices / I want a dog / Domino dancing / I'm not scared / Always on my mind – In my house / It's alright. *(re-iss. Mar89, 3x12"; PCSX 7325) (re-iss. Mar94)*

Nov 88. (7"/7"s) *(R/RS 6198) <50171>* **LEFT TO MY OWN DEVICES. / THE SOUND OF THE ATOM SPLITTING** [4] Jan89 [84]
(12"+=/c-s+=/cd-s+=) *(12R/TCR/CDR 6198)* – ('A'disco mixes).

Jun 89. (7"/c-s/ext.12"/ext.cd-s) *(R/TCR/12R/CDR 6220)* **IT'S ALRIGHT. / ONE OF THE CROWD / YOUR FUNNY UNCLE** [5] [ ]
(10") *(10R 6220)* – ('A'alternative mix) / ('A'extended dance).
(12") *(12RX 6220)* – ('A'-Tyree mix) / ('A'-Sterling Void mix).

— NEIL and CHRIS had guested late '89-91 for BERNARD SUMNER & JOHNNY MARR on their ELECTRONIC project. (see ⇒ NEW ORDER)

— On tour augmented by **COURTNEY PINE / PETE GLEADALAS / DANNY CUMMINGS**

— next featured **JOHNNY MARR** – guitar

Sep 90. (c-s/7") *(TC+/R 6269) <50329>* **SO HARD. / IT MUST BE OBVIOUS** [4] [62]
(12"+=) *(12R 6269)* – ('A'dub mix).
(cd-s++=) *(CDR 6269)* – ('A'dance mix).

Oct 90. (cd/c/lp) *(CD/TC+/PCSD 113) <94310>* **BEHAVIOUR** [2] [45]
– Being boring / This must be the place I waited years to leave / To face the truth / How can you expect to be taken seriously? / Only the wind / My October symphony / So hard / Nervously / The end of the world / Jealousy.

Nov 90. (c-s/7") *(TC+/R 6275)* **BEING BORING. / WE ALL FEEL BETTER IN THE DARK** [20] [ ]
(12"+=/cd-s+=) *(12R/CDR 6275)* – ('A'&'B'extended mixes).

Feb 91. (c-s,cd-s) *<50343>* **HOW CAN YOU EXPECT TO BE TAKEN SERIOUSLY? / WHAT HAVE I DONE TO DESERVE THIS?** [–] [93]

Mar 91. (c-s/7") *(TC+/R 6285)* **WHERE THE STREETS HAVE NO NAME (I CAN'T TAKE MY EYES OFF YOU). / HOW CAN YOU EXPECT TO BE TAKEN SERIOUSLY? (remix)** [4] [–]
(ext;12"+=/cd-s+=) *(12R/CDR 6285)* – But she's not your girlfriend.
(12"+=) *(12RX 6285)* – ('B'classical).

May 91. (c-s,cd-s) *<50351>* **WHERE THE STREETS HAVE NO NAME (I CAN'T TAKE MY EYES OFF YOU) / BET SHE'S NOT YOUR GIRLFRIEND** [–] [72]

May 91. (c-s/7") *(TC+/R 6283)* **JEALOUSY. / LOSING MY MIND** [12] [–]
(12"+=/cd-s+=) *(12R/CDR 6283)* – ('A'&'B'extended).
(cd-s+=) *(CDRS 6283)* – This must be the place / Waited for the years to leave (extended) / So hard (eclipsed mix).

Oct 91. (c-s/7") *(TC+/R 6301)* **DJ CULTURE. / MUSIC FOR BOYS** [13] [–]
(12"+=/cd-s+=) *(12R/CDR 6301)* – ('A'-II version).

Nov 91. (cd/c/lp) *(CD/TC+/PMTV 3) <97097>* **DISCOGRAPHY – THE COMPLETE SINGLES COLLECTION** (compilation) [3] [ ]
– West End girls / Love comes quickly / Opportunities (let's make lots of money) / Suburbia / It's a sin / What have I done to deserve this? / Rent / Always on my mind / Heart / Domino dancing / Left to my own devices / It's alright / So hard / Being boring / Where the streets have no name (I can't take my eyes off you)/ Jealousy / DJ culture / Was it worth it?

Dec 91. (c-s/7") *(TC+/R 6306)* **WAS IT WORTH IT? / MISERABLISM** [24] [ ]
(12"+=/cd-s+=) *(12R/CDR 6306)* – ('A'remixes).

Jun 93. (c-s/7") *(TC+/R 6348)* **CAN YOU FORGIVE HER? / HEY, HEADMASTER** [7] [ ]
(12"+=/cd-s+=) *(12R/CDR 6348)* – ('A'-Rollo remix) / ('A'-Rollo dub).
(cd-s) *(CDRS 6348)* – ('A'remix) / I want to wake up (Johnny Marr remix) / What keeps mankind alive? / ('A' MK dub).

Sep 93. (c-s/7") *(TC+/R 6356)* **GO WEST. / SHAMELESS** [2] [ ]
(12"+=/cd-s+=) *(12R/CDR 6356)* – ('A'mixes; movements).

Oct 93. (cd/c/lp) *(CD/TC+/PCSD 143) <89721>* **VERY** [1] [20]
– Can you forgive her? / I wouldn't normally do this kind of thing / Liberation / A different point of view / Dreaming of the Queen / Yesterday, when I was mad / The theatre / One and one make five / To speak is a sin / Young offender / One in a million / Go west. *(free-cd) (CDPSDX 143)* **VERY RELENTLESS** – My head is spinning / Forever is love / KDX 125 / We came from outer space / The man who has everything / One thing leads to another.

Dec 93. (c-s/7") *(TC+/R 6370)* **I WOULDN'T NORMALLY DO THIS KIND OF THING. / TOO MANY PEOPLE** [13] [ ]
(cd-s+=) *(CDR 6370)* – Violence (Hacienda mix) / West End girls (Sasha mix).
(cd-s) *(CDRS 6370)* – ('A'side) / ('A'mixes).

— re-issued all 14 singles from 1987-1992 on cd-ep's Nov93.

Apr 94. (c-s/7") *(TC+/R 6377)* **LIBERATION. / DECADENCE** [14] [ ]
(cd-s+=) *(CDR 6377)* – ('A'-E Smoove mix).
(cd-s/d12") *(CDRS/12RD 6377)* – ('A'-Murk mix) / ('B'unplugged mix) / Young offender (jam & spoon mix).

— Below a second Comic Relief charity single, featuring vox from the TV series of that name; JENNIFER 'Edina' SAUNDERS and JOANNA 'Patsy' LUMLEY.

May 94. (c-s/7"; as ABSOLUTELY FABULOUS) *(TC+/R 6382)* **ABSOLUTELY FABULOUS. / ('A'mix)** [6] [–]
(cd-s+=) *(CDR 6382)* – ('A'mixes).

Sep 94. (c-s) *(TCR 6386)* **YESTERDAY, WHEN I WAS MAD. / EUROBOY** [13] [ ]

(cd-s) *(CDR 6386)* – ('A'side) / If love were all / Can you forgive her? (swing version) / ('A'-Jam & Spoon mix).
(cd-s) *(CDRS 6386)* – ('A'-Coconut 1 remix) / ('A'-Junior Vasquez dub & RAF zone mix) / Some speculation.
(12") *(12R 6386)* – ('A'-Jam & Spoon mix) / ('A'-Junior Vasquez dub & RAF zone mix).

Sep 94. (cd/c/lp) *(CD/TC+/PCSD 159) <28105>* **DISCO 2** (remixes) [6] [75]

Jul 95. (c-s) *(TCR 6414)* **PANINARO '95 / IN THE NIGHT** [15] [ ]
(cd-s+=) *(CDR 6414)* – Girls and boys (live in Rio).
(12") *(12R 6414)* – ('A'-Tracy's mix) / ('A'-Sharon's Sexy Boyz dub) / ('A'-Tin Tin Out mix) / ('A'extended).
(12") *(12RS 6414)* – ('A'-Angel Morales deep dance mix) / ('A'-Girls Boys in dub mix) / ('A'-Hot'n'spicy dub mix).

Aug 95. (d-cd/d-c/t-lp) *(CD/TC+/PCSD 166) <34023>* **ALTERNATIVE** (B-sides) [2] [ ]
– In the night / A man could get arrested / That's my impression / Was that what it was? / Paninaro / Jack the lad / You know where you went wrong / A new life / I want a dog / Do I have to? / I get excited (you get excited too) / Don Juan / The sound of the atom splitting / One of the crowd / Your funny uncle / / It must be obvious / We all feel better in the dark / Bet she's not your girlfriend / Losing my mind / Music for boys / Miserablism / Hey, headmaster / What keeps mankind alive? / Shameless / Too many people / Violence (Hacienda version) / Decadence / If love were all / Euroboy / Some speculation.

Apr 96. (c-s) *(TCR 6431)* **BEFORE / THE TRUCK-DRIVER AND HIS MATE** [7] [ ]
(cd-s+=) *(CDR 6431)* – Hit and miss / In the night 1995 ('New Clothes Show').
(cd-s/3x12") *(12R/CDRS 6431)* – ('A'remixes by; Love To Infinity / Joey Negro / Danny Tenaglia).

— TENNANT now back with ELECTRONIC on hit single 'FORBIDDEN CITY'.

Aug 96. (c-s/12"pic-d) *(TCR/12RD 6443)* **SE A VIDA E (THAT'S THE WAY LIFE IS) / BETRAYED** [8] [ ]
(cd-s+=) *(CDR 6443)* – How I learned to hate rock'n'roll.
(cd-s) *(CDRS 6443)* – (mixes by; Mark Picchiotti / Deep Dish / Pink Noise).

Sep 96. (cd/c) *(CD/TC PCSD 113) <31088>* **BILINGUAL** [4] [39]
– Discoteca / Single / Metamorphosis / Electricity / Se a vida e (that's the way life is) / It always comes as a surprise / A red letter day / Up against it / The survivors / Before / To step aside / Saturday night forever.

Nov 96. (c-s) *(TCR 6452)* **SINGLE – BILINGUAL / DISCOTECA** [14] [ ]
(cd-s+=) *(CDR 6452)* – Confidential (demo) / ('A'mix).
(cd-s+=) *(CDRS 6452)* – ('A'mix) / The calm before the storm.

Mar 97. (12") *(12R 6460)* **A RED LETTER DAY. / THE BOY WHO COULDN'T KEEP HIS CLOTHES ON** [9] [ ]
(cd-s+=) *(CDR 6460)* – Delusions of grandeur.
(cd-s) *(CDRS 6460)* – ('A'mixes).

Jun 97. (c-s) *(TCR 6470)* **SOMEWHERE / THE VIEW FROM YOUR BALCONY** [9] [ ]
(cd-s+=) *(CDR 6470)* – To step aside (Ralphi's old school dub) / ('A'-Forthright vocal mix).
(cd-s) *(CDRS 6470)* – ('A'-orchestral) / Disco potential / ('A'-Trouser Enthusiasts mix) / ('A'-Forthright dub).

Jul 99. (c-s/cd-s) *(TCR/CDRS 6523)* **I DON'T KNOW WHAT YOU WANT BUT I CAN'T GIVE IT ANYMORE / SILVER AGE / SCREAMING** [15] [ ]
(cd-s) *(CDR 6523)* – ('A'-David Morales mix) / ('A'-Thee Maddkatt 80 Coutship Witness mix) / Je t'aime . . . moi non plus.

Oct 99. (c-s/cd-s) *(TCR/CDRS 6525)* **NEW YORK CITY BOY / THE GHOST OF MYSELF / NEW YORK CITY (almighty definite mix)** [14] [ ]
(cd-s) *(CDR 6525)* – ('A'side) / Casting a shadow / ('A'-Superchumbo's uptown mix).

Oct 99. (cd/c/lp) *(521847-2/-4/-1) <31086>* **NIGHTLIFE** [7] Nov99 [84]
– For your own good / Closer to Heaven / I don't know what you want but I can't give it any more / Happiness is an option / You only tell me you love me when you're drunk / Vampires / Radiophonic / The only one / Boy strange / In denial / New York city boy / Footsteps.

Jan 00. (12"/cd-s) *(12R/CDR 6533)* **YOU ONLY TELL ME YOU LOVE ME WHEN YOU'RE DRUNK (mixes)** [8] [–]
(cd-s) *(CDRS 6533)* – ('A'side) / Lies / Sail away.
(cd-s) *(CDRX 6533)* – ('A'mixes) / ('A'-CD-rom) / Always on my mind (live video) / Being boring (live video).

— in Oct'01, The PET SHOP BOYS worked with the original cast of 'Closer To Heaven', a musical collaboration with playwright Jonathan Harvey

Mar 02. (cd-s) *(CDRS 6572)* **HOME AND DRY / SEXY NORTHERNER / ALWAYS** [14] [–]
(cd-s) *(CDR 6572)* – ('A'-ambient mix) / Break 4 love (with PETER RAUHOFER) / Break 4 love (Friburn & Urik hi pass remix with PATER RAUHOFER).

Apr 02. (cd) *(538150-2) <541486>* **RELEASE** [7] [73]
– Home and dry / I get along / Birthday boy / London / E mall / Samurai in autumn / Love is a catastrophe / Here / The night I fell in love / You choose. *(special cd+=; 538598-2)* – Home and dry (ambient mix) / Sexy northerner / Always / Closer to Heaven (slow version) / Nightlife / Friendly fire / Break 4 love (radio edit) / Home and dry / Home and dry (video).

Jul 02. (cd-s) *(CDRS 6581)* **I GET ALONG / SEARCHING FOR THE FACE OF JESUS / BETWEEN TWO ISLANDS** [18] [–]
(cd-s) *(CDR 6581)* – ('A'live) / Red letter day (live) / Love comes quickly (live).

Feb 03. (cd) *(582140-2) <84595>* **DISCO 3** (remixes) [36] [ ]
– Time on my hands / Positive role model / Try it (I'm in love with a married man) / London (Three Radikal Blaklite edit) / Somebody else's business / Here (PSB new extended mix) / If looks could kill / Sexy northerner (Superchumbo remix) / Home and dry (Blank & Jones remix) / London (Genuine piano mix). *(3xlp+=; 581458-1)* – (varied tracks).
(above issued on 'Sanctuary' US)

Nov 03. (cd-s) *(CDR 6620)* **MIRACLES / WE'RE THE PET SHOP BOYS / MIRACLES (Eric Prydz remix)** [10] [–]
(12") *(12R 6620)* – ('A'-12" version) / ('A'-Lemon Jelly remix).
(cd-s+=) *(CDRS 6620)* – Transparent.

Nov 03. (d-cd/t-lp) *(593884-2/-1) <594837>* **POPART: THE HITS** (compilation) [30] [ ]
– Go west / Suburbia / Se a vida E (that's the way life is) / What have I done to deserve this? / Always on my mind / I wouldn't normally do this kind of thing / Home and dry / Heart / Miracles / Love comes quickly / It's a sin / Domino dancing / Before / New York City boy / It's alright / Where the streets have no name (I can't take my eyes off you) / A red letter day / Left to my own devices / I don't know what you want but I can't give it any more / Flamboyant / Being boring / Can you forgive her? / West End girls / I get along / So hard / Rent / Jealousy / DJ culture / You only tell me you love me when you're drunk / Liberation / Paninaro '95 / Opportunities (let's make lots of money) / Yesterday, when I was mad / Single – Bilingual / Somewhere. *(ltd-t-cd+=; 595093-2)* – (bonus mixes).

Mar 04. (cd-s) *(CDR 6629)* **FLAMBOYANT / I DIDN'T GET WHERE I AM TODAY** [12] [–]
(12") *(12R 6629)* – ('A'-DJ Hell remix) / ('A'-Scissor Sisters silhouettes and shadows mix) / West End girls (DJ Hell remix).
(cd-s) *(CDRS 6629)* – ('A'-mixes; Tomcraft extended / Scissor Sisters.. / DJ Hell / original demo / video).

Sep 05. (cd) *(874450-2)* **BATTLESHIP POTEMKIN** (live soundtrack revisited) [ ] [–]
– "Comrades!" / Men and maggots / Our daily bread / Drama in the harbour / Nyet / To the shore / Odessa / No time for tears / To the battleship / After all (the Odessa staircase) / Stormy meetings / Night falls / Full steam ahead / The squadron / For freedom.

May 06. (7"pic-d) *(R 6690)* **I'M WITH STUPID. / GIRLS DON'T CRY** [8] [ ]
(cd-s) *(CDR 6690)* – ('A') / The resurrectionist.
(dvd-s++=) *(DVDR 6690)* – ('A'-video).

May 06. (ltd-12") *(3647811)* **FUNDAMENTALISM** [ ] [–]
– Fugitive (Richard X extended mix) / Sodom (Trentemoller remix) / Psychological (alter ego remix) / Flamboyant (Michael Mayer Kompakt mix).

May 06. (cd/lp) *(<362859-2/-1>)* **FUNDAMENTAL** [5] [ ]
– Psychological / The Sodom and Gomorrah show / I made my excuses and left / Minimal / Numb / God willing / Luna park / I'm with stupid / Casanova in Hell / Twentieth century / Indefinite leave to remain / Integral. *(ltd d-cd+=; 362860-2)* – Fugitive (Richard X extended mix) / Sodom (Trentemoller mix) / Psychological (Alter Ego remix) / Flamboyant (Michael Mayer mix) / Minimal (Tiga remix) / I'm with stupid (Melnyk heavy petting mix) / Gomorrah (Dettinger remix) / In private (Stuart Crichton club mix).

Tom PETTY

Born: 20 Oct'52, Gainesville, Florida, USA. In 1968, he formed school band The SUNDOWNERS, who later became The EPICS. By 1971, this outfit had evolved into MUDCRUTCH which also comprised guitarists MIKE CAMPBELL, TOMMY LEADON (brother of EAGLES man BERNIE) and drummer RANDALL MARSH. Their demo tape eventually came to the attention of Denny Cordell (co-owner of 'Shelter' records with LEON RUSSELL), who was suitably impressed enough to sign the band in 1975. They released a solitary single, 'DEPOT STREET', an album's worth of material lurking in the vaults due to the band's subsequent demise. PETTY was retained by Shelter and in 1976 he instigated The HEARTBREAKERS together with CAMPBELL, keyboardist BENMONT TENCH, bassist RON BLAIR and drummer STAN LYNCH. Later that year, the band released the eponymous 'TOM PETTY & THE HEARTBREAKERS', a raw statement on the future of roots rock'n'roll (The BYRDS, BOB DYLAN and ROLLING STONES are the most frequently cited influences) which initially flopped in the States. Perversely, the album was relatively successful in the UK and Europe, PETTY and Co. capitalising on the interest with a European tour that eventually wound its way back to the US during the summer of '77. They had already hit the UK Top 40 with two classic singles, 'ANYTHING THAT'S ROCK'N'ROLL' and 'AMERICAN GIRL' and in May '78, their first US Top 40 hit, 'BREAKDOWN', was used on the movie, 'FM'. At last there was a Stateside buzz surrounding the band and two months later their second album, 'YOU'RE GONNA GET IT', hit both the US & UK Top 40. Despite the ensuing critical and commercial success, PETTY filed for bankruptcy the following year, owing more than half a million dollars after Shelter was sold to 'ABC' and then 'MCA', the latter company duly suing him for breach of contract. Fortunately, the warring parties came to an agreement when MCA decided to put his band on their Danny Bramson-run 'Backstreet' label. The late 1979 major label debut, 'DAMN THE TORPEDOES', sold only moderately in the UK, although it smashed into the US Top 3, sales of the album boosted by harder rocking tracks like 'REFUGEE' and 'DON'T DO ME LIKE THAT'. By this point PETTY was a major league star and he could afford to challenge his record company yet again, this time over the cover price of his forthcoming album, 'HARD PROMISES' (1981), which PETTY deemed too expensive. His persistence eventually won out and the album reached No.5 in the US, subsequently going platinum. The early 80's also saw PETTY hooking up with the delectable STEVIE NICKS on the 'STOP DRAGGIN' MY HEART AROUND' single (a US No.3) and producing DEL SHANNON's 'Drop Down And Get Me', with backing from The HEARTBREAKERS. Co-produced by PETTY, together with Jimmy Iovine and EURYTHMICS guitarist Dave Stewart, the acclaimed 'SOUTHERN ACCENTS' (1985) marked a newfound maturity, both lyrically and musically, the brooding 'DON'T COME AROUND HERE NO MORE' furnishing PETTY with his biggest UK hit single to date. Following a prolonged bout of touring and a further studio album, 'LET ME UP (I'VE HAD ENOUGH)', PETTY found himself in the company of rock's oldster hierarchy alongside BOB DYLAN, GEORGE HARRISON, JEFF LYNNE and ROY ORBISON in The TRAVELLING WILBURYS (who subsequently released two albums, rather confusingly titled 'TRAVELLING WILBURYS VOLUME 1' (1988) and 'TRAVELLING WILBURYS VOLUME 3' (1990). Around this time, PETTY also released his highly successful debut solo album, 'FULL MOON FEVER' (1989), with backing from a collection of HEARTBREAKERS and WILBURYS. One of his most overtly commercial outings, the record spawned the soaring 'FREE FALLIN' (a US Top 10) and contained what could be PETTY's signature tune, the defiant 'I WON'T BACK DOWN'. The album seemed to have breathed fresh life into PETTY's musical partnership with the HEARTBREAKERS and they teamed up once more for 1991's 'INTO THE GREAT WIDE OPEN', another highly melodic opus previewed by the impassioned 'LEARNING TO FLY' single. A follow-up PETTY solo set, 'WILDFLOWERS' (1994), was his first release for 'Warners', the singer having been back in the spotlight again after allegedly keeping the deal secret fom 'M.C.A.'. Much like NEIL YOUNG, PETTY remains a stubborn maverick, refusing to play record company games and staying true to his muse. Post-mid 90's PETTY once again gathered together The HEARTBREAKERS for the recording of 'SHE'S THE ONE' (1996), the soundtrack to the Ed Burns film of the same name. In the age of multi-artist, blockbusting soundtracks, PETTY's effort was something of a rarity as well as a pleasant, loose-limbed diversion from the craft and precision of his regular stuff. The record's chart placings (UK Top 40/US Top 20) confirmed that many fans simply regarded this as another – albeit slightly different – TOM PETTY album. Normal service was resumed on the harder rocking 'ECHO' (1999), Rick Rubin adding a bit of production muscle to another HEARTBREAKERS outing. Come the new millennium, PETTY and his HEARTBREAKERS sounded somewhat desperate on 'THE LAST DJ' (2002), clutching at rather bitter lyrical straws berating the worst aspects of the business which he's been an integral part of for so many years. While the record made the Top 10 in the US, it failed to register in the UK chart, the first such absence in many years.

• **Covered:** SO YOU WANT TO BE A ROCK'N'ROLL STAR (Byrds) / NEEDLES AND PINS (Searchers) / FEEL A WHOLE LOT BETTER (Byrds) / SOMETHING IN THE AIR (Thunderclap Newman). • **Trivia:** PETTY made his major acting debut in 1997 via the Kevin Kostner epic, 'The Postman'; ten years earlier he made a brief appearance in 'Made In Heaven'.

Album rating: TOM PETTY & THE HEARTBREAKERS (*6) / YOU'RE GONNA GET IT (*7) / DAMN THE TORPEDOES (*8) / HARD PROMISES (*6) / LONG AFTER DARK (*5) / SOUTHERN ACCENTS (*6) / PACK UP THE PLANTATION – LIVE! (*4) / LET ME UP (I'VE HAD ENOUGH) (*5) / FULL MOON FEVER (*7) / INTO THE GREAT WIDE OPEN (*6) / GREATEST HITS compilation (*9) / WILDFLOWERS (*7) / SHE'S THE ONE soundtrack (*5) / ECHO (*5) / ANTHOLOGY – THROUGH THE YEARS double compilation (*8) / THE LAST DJ (*4)

TOM PETTY AND THE HEARTBREAKERS

TOM PETTY – vocals, guitar (ex-MUDCRUTCH) / **MIKE CAMPBELL** (b. 1 Feb'54, Panama City, Florida) – guitar (ex-MUDCRUTCH) / **BELMONT TENCH** (b. 7 Sep'54, Gainesville) – keyboards (ex-MUDCRUTCH) / **RON BLAIR** (b.16 Sep'52, Macon, Georgia) – bass / **STAN LYNCH** (b.21 May'55, Gainsville) – drums

		Island	Shelter
Jan 77.	(7") *<62006>* **BREAKDOWN. / THE WILD ONE, FOREVER**	–	
Feb 77.	(7") *(WIP 6377)* **AMERICAN GIRL. / THE WILD ONE, FOREVER**		–
May 77.	(lp/c) *(ILPS/ICT 5014) <52006>* **TOM PETTY AND THE HEARTBREAKERS**	24	55
	– Rockin' around (with you) / Breakdown / Hometown blues / The wild one, forever / Anything that's rock'n'roll / Strangered in the night / Fooled again (I don't like it) / Mystery man / Luna / American girl. *(cd-iss. Jul87 on 'M.C.A.'; MCAD 37143) (re-iss. Nov90 cd/c; DMCL/MCLC 1715) (re-iss. 1991 cd/c; MCAD/MCA 10135) (re-iss. Apr92 cd/c; MCLD/MCLC 19012)*		
May 77.	(7") *(WIP 6377) <62007>* **AMERICAN GIRL. / FOOLED AGAIN (I DON'T LIKE IT)**	–	
Jun 77.	(7"/12") *(WIP/+12 6369)* **ANYTHING THAT'S ROCK'N'ROLL. / FOOLED AGAIN (I DON'T LIKE IT)**	36	
Jul 77.	(7"/12") *(WIP/+12 6403)* **AMERICAN GIRL. / LUNA**	40	–
Oct 77.	(7") *<62008>* **BREAKDOWN. / FOOL AGAIN (I DON'T LIKE IT)**	–	40

May 78. (lp/c) *(ISA/ISC 5017)* <52029> **YOU'RE GONNA GET IT** [34] [23]
– When the time comes / You're gonna get it / Hurt / Magnolia / Too much ain't enough / I need to know / Listen to her heart / No second thoughts / Restless / Baby's a rock'n'roller. *(cd-iss. Jun88 on 'M.C.A.'; MCAD 31171) (re-iss. Apr92 cd/c; MCLD/MCLC 19013)*

Jun 78. (7"/12") *(WIP/+12 6426)* <62010> **I NEED TO KNOW. / NO SECOND THOUGHTS** [ ] [41]

Sep 78. (7"/12") *(WIP/+12 6455)* <62011> **LISTEN TO HER HEART. / I DON'T KNOW WHAT TO SAY TO YOU** [ ] [59]

M.C.A. Backstreet

Nov 79. (lp/c) *(MCF/+C 3044)* <5105> **DAMN THE TORPEDOES** [57] [2]
– Refugee / Here comes my girl / Even the losers / Century city / Don't do me like that / Shadows of a doubt (a complex kind) / What are you doin' in my life? / Louisiana rain / You tell me. *(cd-iss. 1985; DMCA 108) (cd re-iss. Oct87; MCAD 5105) (cd re-iss. Jul88; DMCL 1872) (re-iss. Apr92 cd/c; MCLD/MCLC 19014)*

Nov 79. (7") *(MCA 539)* <41227> **HERE COMES MY GIRL. / DON'T BRING ME DOWN** [ ] Apr80 [59]
(12"+=) *(MCAT 539)* – Casa Dega.

Feb 80. (7"/7"pic-d) *(MCA/+P 559)* <41169> **REFUGEE. / IT'S RAINING AGAIN** [ ] Jan80 [15]

Jul 80. (7") *(MCA 596)* <41138> **DON'T DO ME LIKE THAT. / CENTURY CITY** [ ] Nov79 [10]
(d7"+=) *(MCAD 596)* – Somethin' else / Stories we can tell.

— **DONALD DUNN** – bass; repl. RON BLAIR

Apr 81. (7") *(MCA 699)* <51100> **THE WAITING. / NIGHTWATCHMAN** [ ] [19]

May 81. (lp/c) *(MCF/+C 3098)* <5160> **HARD PROMISES** [32] [5]
– The waiting / A woman in love (it's not me) / Nightwatchman / Something big / King's road / Letting you go / A thing about you / Insider / The criminal kind / You can still change your mind. *(cd-iss. May86; CMCAD 31006) (cd re-iss. 1988; DIDX 344) (re-iss. Oct91 cd/c; MCLD/MCLC 19077)*

Jul 81. (7") *(MCA 730)* <51136> **A WOMAN IN LOVE (IT'S NOT ME). / GATOR ON THE LAWN** [ ] [79]

— PETTY and his band then were credited with backing STEVIE NICKS of FLEETWOOD MAC on a single 'Stop Draggin' My Heart Around' Aug81 hit US No.3.

Jul 82. (7") *(MCA 788)* <41169> **REFUGEE. / THE INSIDER ("with STEVIE NICKS")** [ ] [ ]

— **HOWARD EPSTEIN** (b.21 Jul'55) – bass repl. DUNN

Nov 82. (7") *(MCA 801)* <52144> **YOU GOT LUCKY. / BETWEEN TWO WORLDS** [ ] [20]

Nov 82. (lp/c) *(MCF/+C 3155)* <5360> **LONG AFTER DARK** [45] [9]
– A one story town / You got lucky / Deliver me / Change of heart / Finding out / We stand a chance / Straight into darkness / The same old you / Between two worlds / A wasted life. *(re-iss. May86; MCAD 5360) (cd re-iss. Oct87; CMCAD 31027) (re-iss. Oct90 cd/c; DMCL/MCLC 1818) (re-iss. Jun92 cd/c; MCLD/MCLC 19078)*

Dec 82. (7") *(MCA 805)* **STRAIGHT INTO DARKNESS. / HEARTBREAKERS BEACH PARTY** [ ] [–]

Apr 83. (7") *(MCA 814)* <52181> **CHANGE OF HEART. / HEARTBREAKERS BEACH PARTY** [ ] Feb83 [21]

Apr 85. (7"/12") *(MCA/+T 926)* <52496> **DON'T COME AROUND HERE NO MORE. / TRAILER** [50] Mar85 [13]

Apr 85. (lp/c) *(MCF/+C 3260)* <5486> **SOUTHERN ACCENTS** [23] [7]
– Rebels / It ain't nothin' to me / Don't come around here no more / Southern accents / Make it better (forget about me) / Spike / Dogs on the run / Mary's new car / The best of everything. *(cd-iss. 1986; MCAD 5486) (cd re-iss. Jan90; DMCL 1896) (re-iss. Nov90 cd/c; MCLD/MCLC 19079)*

Jun 85. (7") *(MCA 983)* <52605> **MAKE IT BETTER (FORGET ABOUT ME). / CRACKING UP** [ ] [54]
(12") *(MCAT 983)* – ('A'side) / ('A'instrumental).

Aug 85. (7") <52658> **REBELS. / SOUTHERN ACCENTS (live)** [–] [74]

Jan 86. (d-lp/d-c) *(MCMD/+C 7001)* <8021> **PACK UP THE PLANTATION (live)** [ ] Dec85 [22]
– So you want to be a rock'n'roll star / Needles and pins / The waiting / Breakdown / American girl / It ain't nothin' to me / Insider / Rockin' around (with you) / Refugee / I need to know * / Southern accents / Rebels / Don't bring me down / You got lucky * / Shout / The stories we can tell. *(cd-iss. Oct87; MCAD 8021)* – (omits *) *(re-iss. Nov91 cd/c; MCLD/MCLC 19142)*

Jan 86. (7") <52772> **NEEDLES AND PINS (live). / SPIKE (live)** [–] [37]

Feb 86. (7") *(MCA 1028)* **SO WANT TO BE A ROCK'N'ROLL STAR (live). / AMERICAN GIRL (live)** [ ] [–]
(12"+=) *(MCAT 1028)* – Spike (live).

Aug 86. (7"/12"; BOB DYLAN & THE HEARTBREAKERS) *(MCA/+T 1076)* **BAND OF THE HAND. / THEME FROM 'JOE'S DEATH'** [ ] [–]

Apr 87. (7") *(MCA 1148)* <53065> **JAMMIN' ME. / LET ME UP (I'VE HAD ENOUGH)** [ ] [18]
(12"+=) *(MCAT 1148)* – Make that connection.

Apr 87. (lp/c/cd) *(MCG/MCGC/DMCG 6014)* <5836> **LET ME UP (I'VE HAD ENOUGH)** [59] [20]
– Jammin' me / Runaway trains / The damage you've done / It'll all work out / My life – Your world / Think about me / All mixed up / A self made man / Ain't love strange / How many more days / Let me up (I've had enough). *(cd re-iss. Aug90; DMCL 1905) (re-iss. Nov92 cd/c; MCLD/MCLC 19141)*

Sep 87. (7") *(MCA 1190)* <53153> **ALL MIXED UP. / LET ME UP (I'VE HAD ENOUGH)** [ ] [ ]
(12"+=) *(MCAT 1190)* – Little bit of soul.

Nov 87. (7") *(MCA 1217)* **THINK ABOUT ME. / MY LIFE – YOUR WORLD** [ ] [–]
(12"+=) *(MCAT 1217)* – The damage you've done.

In 1988, before he went solo, TOM PETTY teamed up with BOB DYLAN, GEORGE HARRISON, JEFF LYNNE and ROY ORBISON in The TRAVELING WILBURYS

TOM PETTY

solo with **JEFF LYNNE** – guitar, bass keyboards, vocals, co-writer / **MIKE CAMPBELL** – guitar, bass mandolin, keyboards, co-writer / **PHIL JONES** – drums, percussion / +guests **GEORGE HARRISON, ROY ORBISON, BENMONT TENCH, JIM KELTNER, HOWIE EPSTIEN, KELSEY CAMPBELL.**

M.C.A. M.C.A.

Apr 89. (7") *(MCA 1334)* <53369> **I WON'T BACK DOWN. / THE APARTMENT SONG** [28] [12]
(12"+=/cd-s+=) *(MCAT/DMCAX 1334)* – Don't treat me like a stranger.

Jun 89. (lp/c/cd) *(MCG/MCG/DMCG 6034)* <6253> **FULL MOON FEVER** [8] May89 [3]
– Free fallin' / I won't back down / Love is a long road / A face in the crowd / Runnin' down a dream / Feel a whole lot better / Yer so bad / Depending on you / The apartment song / Alright for now / A mind with a heart of it's own / Zombie zoo. *(cd re-iss. Dec98 on 'Mobile Fidelity'; UDCD 735)*

Aug 89. (7"/c-s) *(MCA/+C 1359)* <53682> **RUNNIN' DOWN A DREAM. / ALRIGHT FOR NOW** [55] Jul89 [23]
(12"+=/cd-s+=) *(MCAT/DMCAX 1359)* – Down the line.

Nov 89. (7") <53748> **FREE FALLIN'. / DOWN THE LINE** [–] [7]

Nov 89. (7") *(MCA 1381)* **FREE FALLIN'. / LOVE IS A LONG ROAD** [64] [–]
(12"+=/cd-s+=) *(MCAT/DMCAX 1381)* – ('A'live version).

Feb 90. (7"/c-s) <79030><53833> **YER SO BAD. / LOVE IS A LONG ROAD** [–] [ ]

Feb 90. (7") *(MCA 1428)* **YER SO BAD. / A MIND WITH A HEART OF IT'S OWN** [ ] [–]
(12"+=/cd-s+=) *(MCAT/DMCAT 1428)* – Free fallin' (live).

Jul 90. (7") *(MCA 1449)* <53781> **A FACE IN THE CROWD. / A MIND WITH A HEART OF IT'S OWN** [ ] Feb90 [46]
(12"+=/cd-s+=) *(MCAT/DMCAT 1449)* – Refugee (live) / So you want to be a rock'n'roll star (live).

TOM PETTY AND THE HEARTBREAKERS

— (originals reformed)

M.C.A. M.C.A.

Jun 91. (7"/c-s) *(MCS/+CS 1555)* <54124> **LEARNING TO FLY. / TOO GOOD TO BE TRUE** [46] [28]
(12"/cd-=) *(MCST/+D 1555)* – ('A'side) / Baby's a rock'n'roller / I need to know.

Jul 91. (lp/c/cd) *<(MCA/+C/D 10317)>* **INTO THE GREAT WIDE OPEN** [3] [13]
– Learning to fly / Into the great wide open / Two gunslingers / The dark of the Sun / All or nothin' / All the wrong reasons / Too good to be true / Out in the cold / You and I will meet again / Makin' some noise / Built to last.

Aug 91. (7"/c-s) *(MCS/+C 1570)* <54131> **INTO THE GREAT WIDE OPEN. / MAKIN' SOME NOISE** [ ] Oct91 [92]
(cd-s+=) *(MSCTD 1570)* – Strangered in the night / Listen to her heart.

Jan 92. (7"/c-s) *(MCS/+C 1610)* **KING'S HIGHWAY. / LEARNING TO FLY** [ ] [–]
(cd-s+=) *(MCSTD 1610)* – Into the great wide open / I won't back down.

Jan 92. (c-s) *<54357>* **KING'S HIGHWAY / ALL OR NOTHIN'** [–] [ ]

Mar 92. (7"/c-s) *(MCS/+CS 1616)* **TOO GOOD TO BE TRUE. / THE DARK SIDE OF THE SUN** [34] [–]
(cd-s+=) *(MCSTD 1616)* – Hurt / Don't come around here no more.
(cd-s+=) *(MCSXD 1616)* – Psychotic reaction / I'm tired / Lonely.

May 92. (cd-s) *<54436>* **PEACE IN L.A. / (peace mix)** [–] [ ]

Oct 93. (7"/c-s) *(MCS/+CS 1945)* **SOMETHING IN THE AIR. / THE WAITING** [53] [–]
(cd-s+=) *(MCSTD 1945)* – American girl.

Nov 93. (cd/c/lp) *(MCD/MCC/MCA 10964) <10813>* **GREATEST HITS** (compilation) [10] [8]
– American girl / Breakdown / Anything that's rock'n'roll / Listen to her heart / I need to know / Refugee / Don't do me like that / Even the losers / Here comes my girl / The waiting / You got lucky / Don't come around here no more / I won't back down / Runnin' down a dream / Free fallin' / Learning to fly / Into the great wide open / Mary Jane's last dance / Something in the air.

Dec 93. (c-s,cd-s) *<54732>* **MARY JANE'S LAST DANCE / THE WAITING** [–] [14]

Feb 94. (c-s) *(MCSCS 1966)* **MARY JANE'S LAST DANCE / KING'S HIGHWAY (live)** [52] [–]
(cd-s+=) *(MCSTD 1966)* – Make that connection (live) / Take out some insurance (live).
(cd-s) *(MCSXD 1966)* – ('A'side) / Casa dega / Gator on the lawn / Down the line.

TOM PETTY

—— with backing from HEARTBREAKERS, plus **STEVE FERRONE** – drums (ex-AVERAGE WHITE BAND, etc) repl. LYNCH

Warners Warners

Oct 94. (c-s) *(W 0272C) <18030>* **YOU DON'T KNOW HOW IT FEELS / GIRL ON L.S.D.** [ ] [ ]
(cd-s+=) *(W 0272CD)* – House in the woods.

Nov 94. (c-s,cd-s) *<18030>* **YOU DON'T KNOW HOW IT FEELS / GIRL ON L.S.D.** [–] [13]

Nov 94. (cd/c/lp) *<(9362 45792-2/-4/-1)>* **WILDFLOWERS** [36] [8]
– Wildflowers / You don't know how it feels / Time to move on / You wreck me / It's good to be king / Only a broken heart / Honey bee / Don't fade on me hard on me / Cabin down below / To find a friend / A higher place / House in the woods / Crawling back to you / Wake up time.

Feb 95. (c-s) *(W 0283C)* **YOU WRECK ME / CABIN DOWN BELOW (acoustic)** [ ] [–]
(cd-s+=) *(W 0283CD)* – Only a broken heart.

Apr 95. (c-s,cd-s) *<17925>* **IT'S GOOD TO BE KING / CABIN DOWN BELOW (acoustic)** [–] [68]

Aug 95. (c-s/cd-s) *<18026>* **A HIGHER PLACE / ONLY A BROKEN HEART (acoustic)** [–] [ ]

TOM PETTY AND THE HEARTBREAKERS

Aug 96. (cd/c) *<(9362 46285-2/-4)>* **SHE'S THE ONE** (soundtrack) [37] [15]
– Walls (circus) / Grew up fast / Zero from outer space / Climb that hill / Change the locks / Angel dream (No.4) / Hope you never / Asshole / Supernatural radio / California / Hope on board / Walls (No.3) / Angel dream (No.2) / Hung up and overdue / Airport.

Sep 96. (c-s,cd-s) *<17593>* **WALLS (CIRCUS) / WALLS (NO.3)** [–] [69]

Mar 97. (c-s) *(W 0371C)* **WALLS (CIRCUS) / HUNG UP AND OVERDUE** [ ] [–]
(cd-s+=) *(W 0371CD)* – Walls (No.3).

—— now a quartet

Apr 99. (cd/c) *<(9362 47294-2/-4)>* **ECHO** [43] [10]
– Room at the top / Swingin' / Counting on you / Free girl now / Lonesome sundown / Accused of love / Echo / Won't last long / Billy the kid / I don't wanna fight / This one's for me / No more / About to give out / Rhino skin / One more day, one more night.

Nov 02. (cd) *<(9362 47955-2)>* **THE LAST DJ** [ ] Oct02 [9]
– The last DJ / Money becomes king / Dreamville / Joe / When a kid goes bad / Like a diamond / Lost children / Blue Sunday / You and me / The man who loves women / Have love will travel / Can't stop the sun.

– compilations, others, etc. –

on 'M.C.A.' unless mentioned otherwise

Sep 84. (d-c) *(MCA2 105)* **DAMN THE TORPEDOES. / HARD PROMISES** [ ] [–]

Apr 86. (12"ep) *(MCAT 1047)* **REFUGEE / DON'T DO ME LIKE THAT. / HERE COMES MY GIRL / THE WAITING** [ ] [–]

Nov 95. (6xcd-box) *(MCAD 611375)* **PLAYBACK** [ ] [ ]

Jun 01. (d-cd) *<(170177-2)>* **THROUGH THE YEARS – ANTHOLOGY** [14] Nov00 [ ]
– Breakdown / American girl / Hometown blues / The wild one, forever / I need to know / Listen to her heart / Too much ain't enough / Refugee / Here comes my girl / Don't do me like that / Even the losers / The waiting / Woman in love (it's not me) / Stop draggin' my heart around (with STEVIE NICKS) / You got lucky / Straight into darkness / Change of heart // Rebels / Don't come around here no more / The best of everything / So want to be a rock'n'roll star (live) / Jammin' me / It'll all work out / Love is a long road / Free fallin' / Yer so bad / I won't back down / Runnin' down a dream / Learning to fly / Into the great wide open / Two gunslingers / Mary Jane's last dance / Waiting on tonight / Surrender.

Apr 02. (cd) *Traditional Line; <(TL 1338)>* **LIVE IN OAKLAND (live)** [ ] [ ]

□ the P-FUNK ALL STARS
(see under ⇒ CLINTON, George)

Wilson PICKETT

Born: 18 Mar'41, Prattville, Alabama, USA. Moving to Detroit with his family when still in his teens, PICKETT initially honed his vocal chops in a gospel act before joining The FALCONS. Comprising MACK RICE and EDDIE FLOYD amongst others, this R&B act were already famous for their US Top 20 hit, 'YOU'RE SO FINE'; with PICKETT on vocals, they scraped a further Top 75 in summer '62 with 'I FOUND A LOVE'. The singer subsequently went solo and after a one-off single on the 'Cub' label, signed to LLOYD PRICE's 'Double L' imprint. There, he scored a trio of respectable PRICE-penned R&B hits which also made their way into the lower regions of the pop chart, yet it took a deal with soul giant 'Atlantic' to see the 'wicked' PICKETT really earn his famous nickname. Although his first two singles for the company were unequivocal flops, producer JERRY WEXLER duly directed him to the 'Stax' studios in Memphis where he hooked up with house band BOOKER T & THE MG's. In summer '65, he emerged with 'IN THE MIDNIGHT HOUR' (written with ace MG's guitarist STEVE CROPPER), netting him his first major US chart hit (UK Top 20 a few months later). As well as unleashing his super-stud nails'n'whisky growl, this sweaty, shuffling, groin-grinding classic also assured PICKETT a place in soul history. The man's feral, dancefloor-rooted style was based on some of the MG's tightest ever playing, engendering a series of vital US (and to a lesser extent, UK) hits: '634-5789 (SOULSVILLE, U.S.A.)', 'LAND OF 1000 DANCES', 'MUSTANG SALLY', 'FUNKY BROADWAY' etc. In 1968, PICKETT found a kindred spirit in BOBBY WOMACK whose 'I'M A MIDNIGHT MOVER' he took into the Top 30 and who would continue to be a source of inspiration for him. He also worked with DUANE ALLMAN on an unlikely cover of The Beatles' 'HEY JUDE' (the album of the same name even saw him running through Steppenwolf's 'BORN TO BE WILD'!), one of the PICKETT's biggest UK hits (Top 20). An even more unlikely cover of The Archies' 'SUGAR SUGAR' suggested that he was running out of ideas; a temporary solution came in the form of rising Philly production prodigies, GAMBLE & HUFF, with whom he recorded 1970's 'WILSON PICKETT IN PHILADELPHIA' album. The record's 'ENGINE No.9' hit the Top 20 as did further early 70's G&H productions, 'DON'T KNOCK MY

LOVE' and 'DON'T LET THE GREEN GRASS FOOL YOU'. These efforts marked his last stand as a major-league artist and amid the usual succession of label changes and personal problems (infamous for his volatile off-stage temperament and heavy drinking bouts, he was arrested on 21st November '74 for threatening behaviour with a gun), PICKETT made a living on the supper club cabaret circuit. He did, however, hit the charts one more time (in '87) with the obligatory remix of 'IN THE MIDNIGHT HOUR'. The 90's, meanwhile, saw him give up recording completely; the man's alcohol problem brought tragedy in 1993 when he was found guilty of knocking down and killing a pensioner while drink driving, receiving a one year jail sentence. PICKETT returned to the recording front in 1999 with the tellingly titled 'IT'S HARDER NOW', while post-millennium he was still performing. However, having retired because of ill-health during the fall of 2004, PICKETT died of a heart attack on the 19th of January, 2006.

• **Covered:** LAND OF A 1000 DANCES (c. Chris Kenner) / MUSTANG SALLY (Mack Rice; of The Falcons) / EVERYBODY NEEDS SOMEBODY TO LOVE (Solomon Burke) / FUNKY BROADWAY (Dyke & The Blazers) / STAG-O-LEE (Lloyd Price) / HEY JOE (Jimi Hendrix) / YOU KEEP ME HANGIN' ON (Supremes) / FIRE AND WATER (Free) / MAMA TOLD ME NOT TO COME (Randy Newman) / etc.

Best CD compilation: A MAN AND A HALF: THE BEST OF . . . (*8)

WILSON PICKETT – vocals (with session people)

not iss. Lupine

1962. (7") *<003>* **ANNA. / YOU'RE ON MY MIND** [–] [ ]

not iss. Cub

1963. (7") *<9113>* **MY HEART BELONGS TO YOU. / LET ME BE YOUR BOY** [–] [ ]
<re-iss. 1963 on 'Correctone'; 501>

Liberty Double L

May 63. (7") *<713>* **IF YOU NEED ME. / BABY CALL ON ME** [–] [64]

Aug 63. (7") *(LIB 10115) <717>* **IT'S TOO LATE. / I'M GONNA LOVE YOU** [ ] Jul63 [49]

Oct 63. (7") *<724>* **I'M DOWN TO MY LAST HEARTBREAK. / I CAN'T STOP** [–] [95]

Atlantic Atlantic

1964. (7") *<2233>* **I'M GONNA CRY. / FOR BETTER OR WORSE** [–] [ ]

1964. (7") *<2271>* **COME HOME BABY. / TAKE A LITTLE LOVE** [–] [ ]

Sep 65. (7") *(AT 4036) <2289>* **IN THE MIDNIGHT HOUR. / I'M NOT TIRED** [12] Jul65 [21]

Nov 65. (7") *(AT 4052) <2306>* **DON'T FIGHT IT. / IT'S ALL OVER** [29] [53]

Dec 65. (lp) *(ATL 5037) <SD 8114>* **IN THE MIDNIGHT HOUR** [ ] Oct65 [ ]
– In the midnight hour / Teardrops will fall / Take a little love / For better or worse / I found a love / That;s a man's way / I'm gonna cry / Don't fight it / Take this love I've got / Come home baby / I'm not tired / Let's kiss and make up. *(cd-iss Aug93 on 'Rhino'; 8122 71275-2)*

Feb 66. (7") *(AT 4072) <2320>* **634-5789 (SOULSVILLE, U.S.A.). / THAT'S A MAN'S WAY** [36] Jan66 [13]

Jun 66. (7") *(584 023) <2334>* **NINETY-NINE AND A HALF (WON'T DO). / DANGER ZONE** [ ] May66 [53]

Aug 66. (7") *(584 039) <2348>* **LAND OF A 1000 DANCES. / YOU'RE SO FINE** [22] Jul66 [6]

Sep 66. (lp) *(587/588 029) <SD 8129>* **THE EXCITING WILSON PICKETT** [ ] Aug66 [21]
– Land of 100 dances / Something you got / 634-5789 / Barefootin' / Mercy, mercy / You're so fine / In the midnight hour / 99 and a half (won't do) / Danger zone / I'm drifting / It's all over / She's so good to me. *(re-iss. Jun88) (cd-iss. Aug93 on 'Rhino')*

Nov 66. (7") *(584 066) <2365>* **MUSTANG SALLY. / THREE TIME LOSER** [28] [23]

Feb 67. (7") *(584 101) <2381>* **EVERYBODY NEEDS SOMEBODY TO LOVE. / NOTHING YOU CAN DO** [ ] [29]

Feb 67. (lp; mono/stereo) *(587/588 057) <SD 8138>* **THE WICKED PICKETT** [ ] Jan67 [42]
– Mustang Sally / New Orleans / Sunny / Everybody needs somebody to love / Ooh poo pah doo / She ain't gonna do right / Knock on wood / Time is on my side / Up tight good woman / You left the water running / Three time loser / Nothing you can do.

Mar 67. (7") *<2394>* **I FOUND A LOVE (pt.1). / (pt.2)** [–] [32]

May 67. (7") *(584 107)* **NEW ORLEANS. / SOUL DANCE NUMBER THREE** [ ] [–]

May 67. (7") *<2412>* **SOUL DANCE NUMBER THREE. / YOU CAN'T STAND ALONE** [–] [55] [70]

Aug 67. (lp; mono/stereo) *(587/588 057) <SD 8145>* **THE SOUND OF WILSON PICKETT** [ ] [54]
– Soul dance number three / Funky Broadway / I need a lot of loving every day / I found a love (part 1) / I found a love (part 2) / You can't stand alone / Mojo mamma / I found the one / Something within me / I'm sorry about that / Love is a beautiful thing.

Sep 67. (7") *(584 130) <2430>* **FUNKY BROADWAY. / I'M SORRY ABOUT THAT** [43] Aug67 [8]

Oct 67. (lp; mono/stereo) *(587/588 092) <SD 8151>* **THE BEST OF WILSON PICKETT** (compilation) [ ] [35]
– In the midnight hour / I found a love / 634-5789 / If you need me / Mustang Sally / Don't fight it / Everybody needs somebody to love / It's too late / Ninety-nine and a half (won't do) / Funky Broadway / Soul dance number three / Land of 1000 dances. *(re-iss. Apr82 lp/c; 780170-1/-4) (cd-iss. Jul87; 781737-2) (cd re-iss. Aug93; 7567 81737-2)*

Oct 67. (7") *(584 142) <2448>* **STAGGER-LEE. / I'M IN LOVE** [ ] [22] [45]

Feb 68. (7") *<2484>* **JEALOUS LOVE. / I'VE COME A LONG WAY** [–] [50]

Mar 68. (7") *(584 173)* **THAT KIND OF LOVE. / I'VE COME A LONG WAY** [ ] [–]

Apr 68. (lp; mono/stereo) *(587/588 107) <SD 8175>* **I'M IN LOVE** [ ] Feb68 [70]
– Jealous love / Stagger lee / That kind of love / I'm in love / Hello sunshine / Don't cry no more / We've got to have love / Bring it on home to me / She's looking good / I've come a long way. *(cd-iss. Jan96; 7567 80375-2)*

May 68. (7") *(584 183) <2504>* **SHE'S LOOKIN' GOOD. / WE'VE GOT TO HAVE LOVE** [ ] Apr68 [15]

Aug 68. (7") *(584 203) <2528>* **I'M A MIDNIGHT MOVER. / DEBORAH** [38] Jun68 [24]

Sep 68. (lp; mono/stereo) *(587/588 111) <SD 8183>* **THE MIDNIGHT MOVER** [ ] Jul68 [91]
– I'm a midnight mover / It's a groove / Remember, I been good to you / I'm gonna cry / Deborah / I found a true love / Down by the sea / Trust me / Let's get an understanding / For better or worse.

Nov 68. (7") *(584 221) <2558>* **I FOUND A TRUE LOVE. / FOR BETTER OR WORSE** [ ] Sep68 [42]

Nov 68. (7") *<2575>* **A MAN AND A HALF. / PEOPLE MAKE THE WORLD (WHAT IT IS)** [–] [42]

Dec 68. (7") *(584 236)* **HEY JUDE. / NIGHT OWL** [16] [–]

Jan 69. (7") *<2591>* **HEY JUDE. / SEARCH YOUR HEART** [–] [23]

Feb 69. (lp) *(588 170) <SD 8215>* **HEY JUDE** [ ] [97]
– Save me / Hey Jude / Back in your arms / Toe hold / Night owl / My own style of loving / A man and a half / Sit down and talk this over / Search your heart / Born to be wild / People make the world (what it is). *(cd-iss. Jan96; 7567 80375-2)*

Mar 69. (7") *(584 261) <2611>* **MINI SKIRT MINNIE. / BACK IN YOUR ARMS** [ ] [50]

Apr 69. (lp) *(2465 002) <SD 8250>* **RIGHT ON** [ ] [ ]
– Groovy little woman / Funky way / Sugar sugar / Sweet inspiration / This old town / You keep me hangin' on / Lord pity us all / It's still good / Woman likes to hear that / She said yes / Hey Joe / Steal away.

May 69. (7") *<2631>* **BORN TO BE WILD. / TOE HOLD** [–] [64]

Jul 69. (7") *<2648>* **HEY JOE. / NIGHT OWL** [–] [59]

Jan 70. (7") *(584 313) <2682>* **YOU KEEP ME HANGIN' ON. / NOW YOU SEE ME, NOW YOU DON'T** [ ] Nov69 [92]

May 70. (7") *(2091 005) <2722>* **SUGAR SUGAR. / COLE, COOKE AND REDDING** [ ] [25] [91]

Jul 70. (7") *(584 281)* **HEY JOE. / BORN TO BE WILD** [ ] [–]

Aug 70. (7") *<2753>* **SHE SAID YES. / IT'S STILL GOOD** [–] [68]

Oct 70. (7") *(2091 032) <2765>* **ENGINE No.9. / INTERNATIONAL PLAYBOY** [ ] [14]

Mar 71. (7") *<2781>* **DON'T LET THE GRASS FOOL YOU. / AIN'T NO DOUBT ABOUT IT** [–] [ ]

Apr 71. (7") *(2091 086)* **FIRE AND WATER. / DON'T LET THE GREEN GRASS FOOL YOU** [ ] [–]

Apr 71. (lp) *(2400 026) <SD 8270>* **ENGINE NO.9** <US title 'WILSON PICKETT IN PHILADELPHIA'> [ ] Sep70 [64]

– Run Joey run / Help the needy / Come right here / Bumble bee (sting me) / Don't let the green grass fool you / Get me back on time, engine number 9 (part 1) / Get me back on time, engine number 9 (part 2) / Days go by / International playboy / Ain't no doubt about it. *(cd-iss. US-title Jan96; 8122 72219-2)*

Jun 71. (lp) *(K 20078)* *<8290>* **THE BEST OF WILSON PICKETT, VOL.II** (compilation) May71 73
– Don't let the green grass fool you / Sugar sugar / Get me back on time, engine No.9 / I'm a midnight mover / A man and a half / Born to be wild / She's lookin' good / I'm in love / Hey Joe / Cole, Cooke & Redding / Hey Jude / You keep me hangin' on / I found a true love.

Oct 71. (7") *(2091 153)* *<2824>* **CALL MY NAME, I'LL BE THERE. / WOMAN LET ME BE DOWN HOME** Aug71 52

Dec 71. (7") *<2852>* **FIRE AND WATER. / PLEDGING MY LOVE** – 24

Jan 72. (lp) *(K 40319)* *<8300>* **DON'T KNOCK MY LOVE** Dec71
– Fire and water / (Your love has brought me) A mighty long way / Covering the same old ground / Don't knock my love (part 1) / Don't knock my love (part 2) / Call my name, I'll be there / Hot love / Not enough love to satisfy / You can't judge a book by its cover / Pledging my love / Mama told me not to come / Woman let me be down home.

Feb 72. (7") *(2091 124)* *<2797>* **DON'T KNOCK MY LOVE. / (part 2)** Apr71 13

Apr 72. (7") *(K 10166)* **DON'T LET THE GREEN GRASS FOOL YOU. / COVERING THE SAME OLD GROUND** Jan71 17

Jun 72. (7") *(K 10181)* *<2878>* **FUNK FACTORY. / ONE STEP AWAY** May72 58

Oct 72. (7") *<2909>* **MAMA TOLD ME NOT TO COME. / COVERING THE SAME OLD GROUND** – 99

1973. (7") *<2961>* **INTERNATIONAL PLAYBOY. / COME RIGHT HERE** –

R.C.A. R.C.A.

Mar 73. (7") *<74 0898>* **MR. MAGIC MAN. / I SHO' LOVE YOU** 98

Mar 73. (lp) *(SF 8390)* *<0312>* **MIZ LENA'S BOY** <US title 'MR. MAGIC MAN'>
– Take a closer look at the woman you're with / Memphis, Tennessee / Soft spoul boogie woogie / Help me make it through the night / Never my love / You lay'd it on me / Is your love life better / Two women and a wife / Why don't you make up your mind / Take the pollution out your throat.

Nov 73. (7") *(RCA 2430)* *<0049>* **TAKE A CLOSER LOOK AT THE WOMAN YOU'RE WITH. / TWO WOMEN AND A WIFE** Sep73 90

Feb 74. (7") *<(APB 0174)>* **SOFT SOUL BOOGIE WOOGIE. / TAKE THE POLLUTION OUT OF YOUR THROAT**

May 74. (lp) *(SF 8344)* *<4858>* **TONIGHT I'M MY BIGGEST AUDIENCE**
– Mr. Magic man / Only I can sing this love / Love is beautiful / I sure love you / Baby man / Sin was the blame / What it is / If you need me / I can't slip my true love away / I keep walking straight ahead.

Aug 74. (7") *(RCA 2450)* *<0309>* **TAKE YOUR PLEASURE WHERE YOU FIND IT. / WHAT GOOD IS A LIE**

Sep 74. (lp) *<APL1 0495>* **PICKETT IN THE POCKET** –
– Iron it out / Isn't that so / Take a look / I was too nice / Don't pass me by / What good is a lie / Young boy blues / Take your pleasure where you find it / You're the one.

Nov 74. (7") *<10067>* **I WAS TOO NICE. / ISN'T THAT SO** –

Dec 74. (d-lp) *<APL2 0669>* **LIVE IN JAPAN (live)** –
– T.S.O.P. (The Sound Of Philadelphia) / Proud Mary / People make the world / Sugar sugar / Don't let the green grass fool you / I'm in love / In the midnight hour / Fire and water / I found a love / Never my love / Glory hallelujah / Mustang Sally / Land of a 1000 dances / Soft soul boogie / Mr.Magic man / Don't knock my love / Goodnight my love.

Jul 75. (lp) *(SF 8439)* *<APL1 0856>* **JOIN ME AND LET'S BE FREE**
– Join me and let's be free / Let's make love right / I've got a good friend / Smokin' in the United Nations / Gone / Good things / Higher consciousness / Bailin' hay on a rainy day / Mighty mouth.

D.J.M. Wicked

Nov 76. (7") *<8101>* **HOW WILL I EVER KNOW. / THE BEST PART OF A MAN** –

Nov 76. (lp) *(DJSL 064)* *<26064>* **PEACE BREAKER**

Feb 77. (7") *<8107>* **LOVE WILL KEEP US TOGETHER. / IT'S GONNA BE GOOD** –

Atlantic Big Tree

Aug 78. (7") *<16121>* **WHO TURNED YOU ON. / DANCE YOU DOWN**

Aug 78. (lp) *(K 50528)* *<76011>* **A FUNKY SITUATION**
– Dance with me / She's so tight / The night we called a day / Dance you down / Hold on to your hiney / Groovin' / Lay me like you hate me / Funky situation / Time to let the sunshine on me / Who turned you on.

Dec 78. (7") *<16129>* **GROOVIN'. / TIME TO LET THE SUNSHINE ON ME** –

EMI America EMI America

Nov 79. (7") *<8027>* **I WANT YOU. / LOVE OF MY LIFE** –

Nov 79. (lp) *(AML 3007)* *<17019>* **I WANT YOU**
– I want you / Love of my life / Shameless / Live with me / Groove city / Superstar / Granny.

Dec 79. (7"/12") *(EA/+12 104)* **GROOVE CITY. / YOU ARE THE LOVE OF MY LIFE** –

Jan 80. (7") *<8034>* **LIVE WITH ME. / GRANNY** –

Apr 80. (7") *(EA 107)* **SHAMELESS. / SUPERSTAR** –

Feb 81. (7") *(EA 120)* *<8070>* **DON'T UNDERESTIMATE THE POWER OF LOVE. / AIN'T GONNA GIVE YOU NO MORE**
(12"+=) *(EA12 120)* – I want you.

Mar 81. (lp) *(AML 3016)* *<17043>* **THE RIGHT TRACK**
– Back on the right track / If you can't beat 'em join 'em / Help me be without / I ain't gonna give you no more / Maybe this time / Don't underestimate the power of love / It's you.

May 81. (7") *<8082>* **BACK ON THE RIGHT TRACK. / IT'S YOU** –

not iss. Erva

1985. (7") *<318>* **LOVE DAGGER. / TIME TO LET THE SUNSHINE ON ME** –

not iss. Precision

1986. (7") *<703>* **MUSTANG SALLY (THE BOSS IS BACK). / ('A'instrumental)** –

Motown Motown

Jun 87. (7") *<1898>* **DON'T TURN AWAY. / CAN'T STOP NOW** –

Sep 87. (7") *<1916>* **IN THE MIDNIGHT HOUR (remix). / JUST LET HER KNOW** –

Oct 87. (7") *(ZB 41583)* **IN THE MIDNIGHT HOUR (remix). / ('A'original)** 62 –
(12"+=) *(ZT 41584)* – ('A'dub version).

Oct 87. (lp/c/cd) *(ZL/ZK/ZD 72615)* **AMERICAN SOUL MAN**
– A thing called love / When your heart speaks / Love never let me down / A man of value / (I wanna) Make love to you / In the midnight hour / Don't turn away / Just let her know / Can't stop now. *(re-iss. Mar94 on 'Spectrum' cd/c; 550178-2/-4)*

Dec 87. (7") *<1938>* **LOVE NEVER LET ME DOWN. / JUST LET HER KNOW** –
<re-iss. 1988 on 'M.C.A.'; 53407>

New York Catawba

Feb 88. (7"/12"; by WILSON PICKETT & JACKIE MOORE) *(NY/+T 101)* *<100>* **SECONDS. / SECONDS (instrumental)**

not iss. Montage

1988. (7"; by WILSON PICKETT & JACKIE MOORE) *<1218>* **PRECIOUS, PRECIOUS. /** –

—— In October '93, PICKETT was given a 1-year jail sentence after being found guilty of drunk driving and killing a pensioner.

Bullseye Bullseye

Sep 99. (cd) *<(CDBB 9625)>* **IT'S HARDER NOW**
– Outskirts of town / Taxi love / What's under that dress / Soul survivor / It's harder now / It ain't easy / Bad people / All about sex / Better him than me / Stone crazy world.

– (selective) compilations, etc. –

Jun 93. (cd) *Rhino-Atlantic;* *<(8122 71212-2)>* **THE VERY BEST OF WILSON PICKETT**

Jul 93. (d-cd) *Rhino-Atlantic;* *<(8122 70287-2)>* **A MAN AND A HALF: THE BEST OF WILSON PICKETT** Apr92
– I found a love (the FALCONS) / Let me be your boy / If you need me / It's too late / I'm gonna cry (cry baby) / Come home baby / In the midnight hour / Don't fight it / I'm not tired / That's a man's way / 634-5789 (Soulsville U.S.A.) / Ninety-nine and a half (won't do) / Land of 1000 dances / Mustang Sally / Three-time loser / Everybody needs somebody to love / Soul dance number three / You can't stand alone / Funky Broadway / I'm in love / Stagger Lee / Jealous love / I've come a long way / In the midnight hour (live & burnin') / I'm a midnight mover / I found a true

love / She's looking good / A man and a half / Hey Jude / Mini-skirt Minnie / Toe hold / Hey Joe / You keep me hangin' on / She said yes / Cole, Cooke & Redding / Sugar sugar / Get me back on time engine number 9 / Don't let the green grass fool you / Don't knock my love (part 1) / Call my name, I'll be there / Fire and water / (Your love has brought me) A mighty long way / Funk factory / Funky Broadway. *(re-iss. Aug93; same)*

Jul 96. (cd) *Javelin; (CWNCD 2018)* **IF YOU NEED ME** ☐ [-]
(re-iss. Jul98 on 'Prestige'; CDSGP 0392)

Jun 98. (cd) *Camden; (74321 58814-2)* **TAKE YOUR PLEASURE WHERE YOU FIND IT (THE BEST OF THE R.C.A. YEARS)** ☐ [-]

Jul 01. (cd) *Cleopatra; (CLP 1010CD)* **THE BEST OF WILSON PICKETT** ☐ ☐

PINK FLOYD

Formed: London, England ... 1965 initially as The ABDABS by ROGER WATERS, RICHARD WRIGHT and NICK MASON, (with others; CLIVE METCALFE – bass, KEITH NOBLE and JULIETTE GALE on vocals). The latter three were dismissed, when the band enlisted SYD BARRETT and adopted the moniker PINK FLOYD (the name taken from bluesmen PINK ANDERSON and FLOYD COUNCIL). In March '66, they secured a residency at the Marquee Club, where their Sunday afternoon gigs were described as "spontaneous underground". Having played the UFO club late in 1966, they were subsequently signed to EMI's 'Columbia' records by their new management team of Peter Jenner and Andrew King. PINK FLOYD's March '67 debut outing, 'ARNOLD LAYNE' (about a transvestite washing-line thief), surprisingly escaped a BBC ban. One of the first missives from the psychedelic underground to reach the Top 20, it was characterised by SYD's whimsically affected vocals. On the 29th of April, they were top of the bill at Alexandria Palace's 14-hour Technicolour Dream, one of the psychedelic era's most infamous events. Their follow-up, 'SEE EMILY PLAY' (originally titled 'GAMES FOR MAY'), hit the Top 10, preceding their classic debut album, 'THE PIPER AT THE GATES OF DAWN' (a pioneering work in the sense that it contained no singles). The collection dominated by BARRETT's eccentric songwriting, it featured the cosmic 'ASTRONOMY DOMINE' alongside the acid-fuelled space-rock of 'INTERSTELLAR OVERDRIVE'. These were contrasted with idiosyncratic ramblings like 'BIKE', 'MATILDA MOTHER' and 'SCARECROW'. Their third 45, 'APPLES AND ORANGES', suprisingly flopped late in 1967, BARRETT's mental condition deteriorating rapidly due to his excessive use of LSD. He increasingly missed shows and studio sessions, PINK FLOYD bringing in DAVE GILMOUR (an old school-friend of SYD's) to compensate. In the April '68, BARRETT was asked to leave the group, retreating to a life of reclusiveness in his mother's Cambridge home. It was widely speculated that PINK FLOYD would be creatively bankrupt without SYD, especially after a further single, 'IT WOULD BE SO NICE', flopped. However, WATERS and WRIGHT took up the reins on the bulk of the songwriting duties, the band soon unleashing their second, more percussive effort, 'A SAUCERFUL OF SECRETS'. Released to ecstatic reviews, the album repeated the debut's success. The tracks, 'SET THE CONTROLS FOR THE HEART OF THE SUN', 'LET THERE BE MORE LIGHT' and SYD's harrowing farewell, 'JUGBAND BLUES' being the undisputed highlights. On the 29th of June, they played their first free concert at London's Hyde Park, alongside JETHRO TULL and ROY HARPER. They finished the year with another flop single, 'POINT ME AT THE SKY', their last in the UK for 11 years. They now concentrated on albums, releasing the under par soundtrack to the Barbet Schroeder- directed 'MORE'. It was basically an instrumental set, 'CIRRUS MINOR' being the standout track of the Top 10 album. Later in '69, they moved to EMI's new 'Harvest' label, issuing the part live, part solo, double album, 'UMMA GUMMA'. Each member contributed a piece of individually credited material, the best being WATERS' bizarre creation, 'SEVERAL SPECIES OF SMALL FURRY ANIMALS GATHERED TOGETHER IN A CAVE AND GROOVING WITH A PICT'. The live disc combined the cream of their sprawling stage improvisations, 'CAREFUL WITH THAT AXE, EUGENE' making its first album appearance. In the autumn of 1970, they released their fifth album, 'ATOM HEART MOTHER' (their first No.1), a record consisting of one patchy, experimental, side of more conventionally structured songs, while the other was a side-long collage with RON GEESIN playing on the title track. The trumpeter was to collaborate with ROGER WATERS the same year, on a soundtrack for the Roy Battersby documentary film, 'THE BODY'. On the 15th of May '71, PINK FLOYD played at the Crystal Palace Garden Party, introducing a new piece of music, 'RETURN TO THE SUN OF NOTHING', which, in six months time, became 'ECHOES'. This composition subsequently took up a whole side of their Top 3 album, 'MEDDLE', which also featured 'ONE OF THESE DAYS', 'A PILLOW OF WINDS' and 'FEARLESS' (the latter notable for its sample of the Anfield Kop). The following year, their most recent recordings were used on another Schroeder film, 'La Vallee', the album being released as 'OBSCURED BY CLOUDS', and although disappointing many die hard FLOYD fans, it cracked the Top 50 in the States. The same year, the group premiered their own music film, 'LIVE AT POMPEII', in Edinburgh. In March 1973, after its spectacular January showing at the Planetarium, the masterpiece, 'DARK SIDE OF THE MOON', was unveiled. A meticulous concept set which the band had worked on for over a year, it dealt with such taboo themes as lunacy, depression and death. These subjects were dealt with on such compelling tracks as 'US AND THEM', 'BREATHE', 'TIME' and the Top 20 US hit 'MONEY'. Scaling both the UK and US charts, the album went on to amass sales of over 10 million, incredibly residing in the chart for nearly 300 consecutive weeks. It has subsequently become regarded by many as the greatest album of all time, breathing new life into stereo headphones. They returned to London's Earl's Court for a spectacular laser show, featuring the albums' all-girl backing singers, The BLACKBERRIES. In 1974, they did a benefit gig, raising £10,000 for their recently disabled friend, ROBERT WYATT (NICK MASON also producing his 'Rock Bottom' album). In the summer of '75, their majestic Knebworth Festival performance previewed another best selling album and subsequent chart-topper, 'WISH YOU WERE HERE'. The record featured some of PINK FLOYD's most enduring songs including the space-jazz ode to SYD BARRETT, 'SHINE ON YOU CRAZY DIAMOND', the oppressive futurism of 'WELCOME TO THE MACHINE', the ROY HARPER-sung 'HAVE A CIGAR' and the wistful melancholy of the title track. It was rounded off by a reprised version of 'SHINE ON', the recording sessions blessed with a rare visit by the song's subject, SYD. Late in 1976, they let loose their 40-foot inflatable pig after a promotional session for their forthcoming 'ANIMALS' album sleeve shot. The Civil Aviation Authority was alerted to warn pilots of the danger, but it was never found. However, the Top 3 album was sighted in shops early the following year. While MASON had produced albums for The DAMNED ('Music For Pleasure') and STEVE HILLAGE ('Green'), GILMOUR and WRIGHT released their own solo albums in 1978, 'DAVID GILMOUR' and 'WET DREAM' respectively. FLOYD returned in late 1979 with a new ROGER WATERS-penned concept double, 'THE WALL', which spawned a decidedly unfestive Christmas chart topper in the lugubrious 'ANOTHER BRICK IN THE WALL (PART II)'. This was another unrelentingly cynical concept piece, centering on the life of PINK, a disillusioned pop star. The next few years were spent making it into a film, directed by Alan Parker

Syd Barrett of PINK FLOYD

and issued in 1982 (BOB GELDOF played the main character). By the time of its release, WRIGHT had already left the band after quarrelling with WATERS. In Spring 1983, they/WATERS issued a comeback album of sorts, 'THE FINAL CUT', which again hit UK No.1. However, it was found overbearingly depressing, derided by critics as a poor "son of The Wall". The year ended with WATERS recording a solo album, 'THE PROS AND CONS OF HITCH HIKING', subsequently fighting GILMOUR and MASON in court for the use of the PINK FLOYD name. In 1984, GILMOUR released his second solo album, 'ABOUT FACE', followed a year later by a NICK MASON / RICK FENN set, 'PROFILES'. With WATERS finally leaving in 1986, WRIGHT returned a year later to boost their ever-impressive live shows (which helped them win the court battle with WATERS). PINK FLOYD returned with an extended GILMOUR-led line-up in 1987 on the Top 3 album, 'A MOMENTARY LAPSE OF REASON', which produced a couple of minor hit singles, 'ON THE TURNING AWAY' and 'ONE SLIP'. A live double album, 'THE DELICATE SOUND OF THUNDER' (which, ironically enough, sounded more PINK FLOYD than ever before). A seven year studio hiatus was broken in 1994 with the release of chart-topper 'THE DIVISION BELL', regarded by long-time fans as a return to form. Following this one-off, PINK FLOYD have continued to keep their name alive purely on the back of concert and compilation sets. The huge transatlantic success of 1995's 'PULSE' was followed five years later by 'IS THERE ANYBODY OUT THERE? THE WALL: LIVE 1980-1981' (2000), a belated document of the band's live performances inspired by their famous 1979 album. 'ECHOES: THE BEST OF PINK FLOYD' (2001), meanwhile, attempted a more broad overview of the band's long and complex career. Given the man's open ended approach to recording, a DAVID GILMOUR solo album was almost as much of an event as new 'FLOYD material, and 'ON AN ISLAND' (2006) was effectively a follow-up to 'THE DIVISION BELL', with a guaranteed No.1 chart placing (US Top 10) and GILMOUR's wife Polly Samson once again heavily involved in the songwriting. The sleeve might've looked like an airbrushed still from 'Castaway', but at least it advertised the record's full-moon intimacy, its spiritual kinship with 'SMALL HOURS' JOHN MARTYN. Perambulating far from '..BELL's typically dystopian themes, GILMOUR delineated the languor of close, cloudless nights with those tactile, long-range solos (on guitar and sax as 'RED SKY AT NIGHT' exquisitely demonstrates) that made latter period PINK FLOYD so haunting. Embellishing them were the understated string arrangements of Polish modernist Zbigniew Preisner, who headed a guest roll call of elder statesmen including fellow 'FLOYD-ian RICK WRIGHT, DAVID CROSBY, GRAHAM NASH, GEORGIE FAME, PHIL MANZANERA, ROBERT WYATT and B.J. COLE.

• **Trivia:** MASON also made a 30-minute autobiographical film, 'Life Could Be A Dream' with his other outlet, racing driving, the main feature. In 1995, GILMOUR featured on JOHN 'RABBIT' BUNDRICK's ambient album, 'Dream Jungle'.

Album rating: THE PIPER AT THE GATES OF DAWN (*9) / A SAUCERFUL OF SECRETS (*8) / MORE soundtrack (*5) / UMMA GUMMA (*7) / ATOM HEART MOTHER (*7) / RELICS collection (*7) / MEDDLE (*8) / OBSCURED BY CLOUDS soundtrack to 'La Vallee' (*6) / THE DARK SIDE OF THE MOON (*10) / WISH YOU WERE HERE (*10) / ANIMALS (*8) / THE WALL (*9) / A COLLECTION OF GREAT DANCE SONGS collection (*4) / THE FINAL CUT (*5) / WORKS collection (*5) / A MOMENTARY LAPSE OF REASON (*5) / THE DELICATE SOUND OF THUNDER (*7) / THE DIVISION BELL (*6) / PULSE (*4) / IS THERE ANYBODY OUT THERE? THE WALL LIVE 1980-1981 live (*5) / ECHOES: THE BEST OF PINK FLOYD compilation (*8) / David Gilmour: DAVID GILMOUR (*5) / ABOUT FACE (*5) / ON AN ISLAND (*6) / Richard Wright: WET DREAM (*4) / BROKEN CHINA (*6) / Nick Mason: FICTITIOUS SPORTS (*4) / PROFILES with Rick Fenn (*4)

SYD BARRETT (b. ROGER KEITH BARRETT, 6 Jan'46) – vocals, guitar / **RICHARD WRIGHT** (b.28 Jul'45, London) – keyboards / **ROGER WATERS** (b. GEORGE WATERS, 9 Sep'44, Surrey, England) – bass, vocals, percussion / **NICK MASON** (b.27 Jan'45, Birmingham, England) – drums, percussion

Columbia Tower

Mar 67. (7"; as the PINK FLOYD) *(DB 8156)* <333> **ARNOLD LAYNE. / CANDY AND THE CURRANT BUN** [20] [ ]

Jun 67. (7"; as the PINK FLOYD) *(DB 8214)* <356> **SEE EMILY PLAY. / SCARECROW** [6] [ ]

Aug 67. (lp; mono/stereo) *(SX/SCX 6157)* **THE PIPER AT THE GATES OF DAWN** [6] [–]
– Astronomy domine / Lucifer Sam / Matilda mother / Flaming / Pow R. Toc H. / Take up thy stethoscope and walk / Interstellar overdrive / The gnome / Chapter 24 / Scarecrow / Bike. *(re-iss. May83 on 'Fame' lp/c; FA/TCFA 3065) (cd-iss. Feb87; CDP 746384-2) (re-iss. Oct94 on 'E.M.I.' cd/c; CD/TC EMD 1073) (re-iss. Aug97 on 'E.M.I.' cd/lp hit UK No.44; CD+/EMD 1110)*

Nov 67. (lp) <ST 5093> **PINK FLOYD** (similar to above set) [–] [ ]

Nov 67. (7") *(DB 8310)* **APPLES AND ORANGES. / PAINTBOX** [ ] [–]

Jan 68. (7") <378> **FLAMING. / THE GNOME** [–] [ ]

— added **DAVID GILMOUR** (b. 6 Mar'44, Cambridge, England) – guitar; who soon repl. BARRETT who later went solo

Apr 68. (7") *(DB 8401)* <426> **IT WOULD BE SO NICE. / JULIA DREAM** [ ] [ ]

Jun 68. (lp; mono/stereo) *(SX/SCX 6258)* <ST 5131> **A SAUCERFUL OF SECRETS** [9] [ ]
– Let there be more light / Remember a day / Set the controls for the heart of the sun / Corporal Clegg / A saucerful of secrets / See saw / Jugband blues. *(re-iss. Aug86 on 'Fame' lp/c; FA/TCFA 3163) (cd-iss. Feb87; CDP 746383-2) (re-iss. Jul94 on 'E.M.I.' cd/c; CD/TC EMD 1063)*

Jul 68. (7") <440> **LET THERE BE MORE LIGHT. / REMEMBER A DAY** [–] [ ]

Dec 68. (7") *(DB 8511)* **POINT ME AT THE SKY. / CAREFUL WITH THAT AXE, EUGENE** [ ] [–]

Jul 69. (lp/c) *(SCX/TCSCX 6346)* <ST 5169> **MORE (soundtrack)** [9] [ ]
– Cirrus minor / The Nile song / Crying song / Up the Khyber / Green is the colour / Cymbaline / Party sequence / Main theme / Ibiza bar / More blues / Quicksilver / A Spanish piece / Dramatic theme. *(cd-iss. Apr87; CDP 746386-2) (re-iss. Sep95 on 'E.M.I.' cd/c; CD/TC EMD 1084)*

Harvest Harvest

Nov 69. (d-lp)(d-c) *(SHDW 1-2)(TC2SHWD 4501)* <388> **UMMA GUMMA** (live */ others solo) [5] [74]
– Astronomy domine * / Careful with that axe, Eugene * / Set the control for the heart of the sun * / A saucerful of secrets * / RICHARD WRIGHT:- Sysyphus (parts 1-4) / ROGER WATERS:- Grantchester Meadows / Several species of small furry animals gathered together in a cave and grooving with a pict / DAVID GILMOUR: – The narrow way (parts 1-3) / NICK MASON:- The Grand Vizier's garden party – part 1; Entrance – part 2; Entertainment / part 3; Exit. *(d-cd-iss. Mar87; CDS 746404-2) (re-iss. Oct94 on 'E.M.I.' d-cd/d-c; CD/TC EMD 1074)*

Oct 70. (lp/c) *(SHVL/TCSHVL 781)* <382> **ATOM HEART MOTHER** [1] [55]
– Atom heart mother; (a) Father's shout – (b) Breast milky – (c) Mother fore – (d) Funky dung – (e) Mind your throats please – (f) Remergence / If / Summer '68 / Fat old Sun / Alan's psychedlic breakfast / Rise and shine / Sunny side up / Morning glory. *(cd-iss. Mar87; CDP 746381-2) (re-iss. Oct94 on 'E.M.I.' cd/c; CD/TC EMD 1072)*
(above featured **RON GEESIN** – horns, co-writer)

Nov 71. (lp/c) *(SHVL/TCSHVL 795)* <832> **MEDDLE** [3] [70]
– One of these days / A pillow of winds / Fearless (interpolating 'You'll never walk alone') / San Tropez / Seamus / Echoes. *(re-iss. Nov83 on 'Fame' lp/c; ATAK/TCATAK 35) (cd-iss. Aug84; CDP 746034-2) (re-iss. cd Apr89 on 'Mobile Fidelity'; UDCD 518) (re-iss. Aug94 on 'E.M.I.' cd/c; CD/TC EMD 1061)*

Dec 71. (7") <3240> **ONE OF THESE DAYS. / FEARLESS** [–] [ ]

Jun 72. (lp/c) *(SHVL/TCSHVL 4020)* <11078> **OBSCURED BY CLOUDS** [6] [46]
– Obscured by clouds / When you're in / Burning bridges / The gold it's in the . . . / Wots . . . uh the deal / Mudmen / Childhood's end / Free four / Stay / Absolute curtains. *(cd-iss. Apr87; CDP 746385-2) (re-iss. Sep95 on 'E.M.I.' cd/c; CD/TC EMD 1083)*

Jul 72. (7") <3391> **FREE FOUR. / STAY** [–] [ ]

Mar 73. (lp/c) *(SHVL/TCSHVL 804)* <11163> **THE DARK SIDE OF THE MOON** [2] [1]
– Speak to me / Breathe / On the run / Time / The great gig in the sky / Money / Us and them / Any colour you like / Brain damage / Eclipse. *(cd-iss. Aug84; CDP 746001-2) (re-iss. cd.Mar93; same); hit UK No.4) (re-*

iss. Jul94 on 'E.M.I.' cd/c; CD/TC EMD 1064) (re-iss. Feb97 on 'E.M.I.'; LPCENT 11)

May 73. (7") *<3609>* **MONEY. / ANY COLOUR YOU LIKE** [–] [13]

Oct 73. (7") *<3832>* **US AND THEM. / TIME** [–] [ ]

Harvest Columbia

Sep 75. (lp/c) *(SHVL/TCSHVL 814) <33453>* **WISH YOU WERE HERE** [1] [1]
– Shine on you crazy diamond (parts 1-5) / Welcome to the machine / Have a cigar / Wish you were here / Shine on you crazy diamond (parts 6-9). *(cd-iss. Aug84; CDP 746035-2) (re-iss. Jul94 on 'E.M.I.' cd/c; CD/TC EMD 1062)*

Oct 75. (7") *<10248>* **HAVE A CIGAR. / SHINE ON YOU CRAZY DIAMOND (excerpt)** [–] [ ]

Jan 77. (lp/quad-lp/c) *(SHVL/Q4SHVL/TCSHVL 815) <34474>* **ANIMALS** [2] Feb77 [3]
– Pigs on the wing (part 1) / Dogs / Pigs (three different ones) / Sheep / Pigs on the wing (part 2). *(cd-iss. Jul86; CDP 746128-2) (re-iss. Jul94 on 'E.M.I.' cd/c; CD/TC EMD 1060)*

Nov 79. (7") *(HAR 5194) <11187>* **ANOTHER BRICK IN THE WALL (PART 2). / ONE OF MY TURNS** [1] Jan80 [1]

Dec 79. (d-lp/d-c) *(SHWD/TC2SHWD 411) <36183>* **THE WALL** [3] [1]
– In the flesh / The thin ice / The happiest days of our lives / Another brick in the wall (part 2) / Mother / Goodbye blue sky / Empty spaces / Young lust / One of my turns / Don't leave me now / Another brick in the wall (part 3) / Goodbye cruel world / Hey you / Is there anybody out there? / Nobody home / Vera / Comfortably numb / The show must go on / Run like hell / Waiting for the worms / Stop / The trial / Outside the wall. *(d-cd-iss. Sep84; CDS 746036-2) (re-iss. UK & US Jul90;) (re-iss. Oct94 on 'E.M.I.' cd/c; CD/TC EMD 1071)*

Apr 80. (7") *<11265>* **RUN LIKE HELL. / DON'T LEAVE ME NOW** [–] [53]

Jun 80. (7") *<11311>* **COMFORTABLY NUMB. / HEY YOU** [–] [ ]

Jun 82. (7") *<03118>* **ONE OF MY TURNS. / ANOTHER BRICK IN THE WALL (part 2)** [–] [ ]

Jul 82. (video) **THE WALL (soundtrack)** [–] [–]
– (tracks from above + new singles)

Aug 82. (7") *(HAR 5222) <01342>* **WHEN THE TIGERS BROKE FREE. / BRING THE BOYS BACK HOME** [39] [ ]

—— now just main trio **WATERS, GILMOUR, MASON.**(WRIGHT left to form ZEE) guests on lp were **ANDY BROWN** – organ, **RAY COOPER** – perc., **MICHAEL KAMEN** – piano, **RALPH RAVENSCROFT** – saxophone.

Mar 83. (lp/c) *(SHPF/TCSHPF 1983) <38243>* **THE FINAL CUT** [1] [6]
– The post war dream / Your possible pasts / One of the few / The hero's return / The gunners dream / Paranoid eyes / Get your filthy hands off my desert / The Fletcher memorial home / Southampton dock / The final cut / Not now John / Two suns in the sunset. *(cd-iss. Jul86; CDP 746129-2) (re-iss. Oct94 on 'E.M.I.' cd/c; CD/TC EMD 1070)*

May 83. (7") *(HAR 5224) <03905>* **NOT NOW JOHN. / THE HERO'S RETURN (pts.1 & 2)** [30] [ ]
(12"+=) *(12HAR 5224)* – ('A'version).

—— **MASON** and **GILMOUR** recruited new members below to replace WATERS who went solo. **TIM RENWICK** – guitar (ex-SUTHERLAND BROTHERS & QUIVER, ex-TV SMITH) / **GUY PRATT** – bass (ex-KILLING JOKE, ex-ICEHOUSE) / **SCOTT PAGE** – saxophone / **RICK WRIGHT** – keyboards also returned p/t.

E.M.I. Columbia

Sep 87. (lp/c/cd) *(EMD/TCEMD/CDEMD 1003) <40599>* **A MOMENTARY LAPSE OF REASON** [3] [3]
– Signs of life / Learning to fly / The dogs of war / One slip / On the turning away / Yet another movie / Round and around / A new machine (part 1) / Terminal frost / A new machine (part 2) / Sorrow.

Sep 87. (12"pink-ep) *(EMP 26) <07363>* **LEARNING TO FLY (edit) / ONE SLIP (edit). / TERMINAL FROST (lp version)** [ ] [70]
(cd-ep+=) *(CDEM 26)* – Terminal frost (DYOL version).

Dec 87. (7"/7"pink) *(EM/+P 34) <07660>* **ON THE TURNING AWAY. / RUN LIKE HELL (live)** [55] [ ]
(12"+=/cd-s+=) *(12/CD EM 34)* – ('A'live).

Jun 88. (7"/7"pink) *(EM/+G 52)* **ONE SLIP. / TERMINAL FROST** [50] [ ]
(12"+=/12"w-poster+=)(cd-s+=) *(12EM/+P 52)(CDEM 52)* – Dogs of war (live).

Nov 88. (d-lp/d-c/d-cd) *(EQ/TCEQ/CDEQ 5009) <44484>* **THE DELICATE SOUND OF THUNDER (live)** [11] [11]
– Shine on you crazy diamond / Learning to fly / Yet another movie / Round and around / Sorrow / The dogs of war / On the turning away / One of these days / Time / Wish you were here / Us and them * / Money / Another brick in the wall (part 2) / Comfortably numb / Run like hell. *(d-cd+= *)*

—— with **GILMOUR, MASON + WRIGHT** plus **GUY PRATT / TIM RENWICK / BOB EZRIN** – keyboards, percussion / **DICK PARRY** – tenor sax / **GARY WALLIS** – percussion / **JON CARIN** – programming + add.keyboards / + backing vocalists

Apr 94. (cd/c/lp) *(CD/TC+/EMD 1055) <64200>* **THE DIVISION BELL** [1] [1]
– Cluster one / What do you want from me / Poles apart / Marooned / A great day for freedom / Wearing the inside out / Take it back / Coming back to life / Keep talking / Lost for words / High hopes.

May 94. (c-s/7"colrd) *(TC+/EMS 309) <77493>* **TAKE IT BACK. / ASTRONOMY DOMINE (live)** [23] [73]
(cd-s+=) *(CDEMS 309)* – ('A'mix).

Oct 94. (c-s/7") *(TC+/EMS 342)* **HIGH HOPES. / KEEP TALKING** [26] [ ]
(12"+=/cd-s+=) *(12/CD EMS 342)* – One of these days.

Jun 95. (d-cd/d-c/q-lp)(video) *(CD/TC+EMD 1078)(MVD 4914363) <67065>* **PULSE (live)** [1] [1]
– Shine on you crazy diamond / Astronomy domine / What do you want from me / Learning to fly / Keep talking / Coming back to life / Hey you / A great day for freedom / Sorrow / High hopes / Another brick in the wall (part 2) / One of these days *[not on cd]* / Speak to me / Breathe / On the run / Time / The great gig in the sky / Money / Us and them / Any colour you like / Brain damage / Eclipse / Wish you were here / Comfortably numb / Run like hell.

– compilations, etc. –

May 71. (lp) *Starline; (SRS 5071) / Harvest; <759>* **RELICS** [32] [ ]
– Arnold Layne / Interstellar overdrive / See Emily play / Remember a day / Paintbox / Julia dream / Careful with that axe, Eugene / Cirrus minor / The Nile song / Biding my time / Bike. *(re-iss. Oct78 on 'Music For Pleasure' lp/c; MFP/TCMFP 50397) (re-iss. Feb96 on 'E.M.I.' cd/c; CD/TC EMD 1082) (lp re-iss. Aug97 on 'E.M.I.'; EMD 1113)*

Jan 74. (d-lp)(d-c) *Harvest; (SHDW 403)(TC2EXE 1013) <11257>* **A NICE PAIR** [21] Dec73 [36]
– (THE PIPER AT THE GATES OF DAWN / A SAUCERFUL OF SECRETS)

Dec 79. (11xlp-box) *Harvest; (PF 11)* **THE FIRST XI (67-77)** [ ] [ ]

Nov 81. (lp/c) *Harvest; (SHVL/TCSHVL 822) <37680>* **A COLLECTION OF GREAT DANCE SONGS** (remixes) [37] [31]
– One of these days / Money / Another brick in the wall (part 2) / Wish you were here / Shine on you crazy diamond / Sheep. *(re-iss. 1985 on 'Fame' lp/c; ATAK/TCATAK 31) (cd-iss. Nov88; CDP 790732-2)*

Nov 81. (7"w-drawn) *Harvest; (HAR 5217)* **MONEY. / LET THERE BE MORE LIGHT** [–] [–]

Jun 83. (lp) *Capitol; <12276>* **WORKS (68-73)** [–] [68]

Nov 91. (12"/cd-s) *See For Miles; (SEA/+CD 4)* **TONITE LET'S ALL MAKE LOVE IN LONDON** [ ] [–]

Nov 92. (9xcd-box) *E.M.I.; (PFBOX 1) <53180>* **SHINE ON** [ ] [ ]
– (A SAUCERFUL OF SECRETS – MOMENTARY LAPSE . . . + rare singles) *(re-iss. Sep98; CDS 780557-2)*

Nov 93. (cd) *See For Miles; (SFM 2)* **TONITE LET'S ALL MAKE LOVE IN LONDON . . . PLUS** [ ] [–]
– Interstellar overdrive / Nick's boogie / (interviews with David Hockney & Lee Marvin).

Nov 95. (cd) *See For Miles; (SFMCD 3)* **LONDON '66-'67** [ ] [–]
– Interstellar overdrive / Nick's boogie.

Mar 00. (d-cd/d-c) *E.M.I.; (523562-2/-4) <62055>* **IS THERE ANYBODY OUT THERE? – THE WALL LIVE 1980-1981 (live)** [15] May00 [19]
– (master of ceremonies) / In the flesh / The thin ice / Another brick in the wall (part 1) / The happiest days of our lives / Another brick in the wall (part 2) / Mother / Goodbye blue sky / Empty spaces / What shall we do now? / Young lust / One of my turns / Don't leave me now / Another brick in the wall (part 3) / The last few bricks / Goodbye cruel world / Hey you / Is there anybody out there? / Nobody home / Vera / Bring the boys back home / Comfortably numb / The show must go on / (master of ceremonies) / In the flesh / Run like hell / Waiting for the worms / (stop) / The trial / Outside the wall.

Nov 01. (d-cd/d-c/q-lp) *(<5 36111-2/-4/-1>)* **ECHOES: THE BEST OF PINK FLOYD** [2] [2]
– Astronomy domine / See Emily play / The happiest days of our lives /

Another brick in the wall (part 2) / Echoes / Hey you / Marooned / The great gig in the sky / Set the controls for the heart of the sun / Money / Keep talking / Sheep / Sorrow / Shine on you crazy diamond (parts 1-7) / Time / The Fletcher memorial home / Comfortably numb / When the tigers broke free / One of these days / Us and them / Learning to fly / Arnold Layne / Wish you were here / Jugband blues / High hopes / Bike.

DAVID GILMOUR

solo with **MICK WEAVER** – keyboards / **RICK WILLIS** – bass / **JOHN WILLIE WILSON** – drums

Harvest Columbia

Jun 78. (lp/c) *(SHVL/TCSHVL 817)* <35388> **DAVID GILMOUR** [17] [29]
– Mihalis / There's no way out of it / Cry from the street / So far away / Short and sweet / Raise my rent / No way / Deafinitely / I can't breathe anymore. *(re-iss. 1983 on 'Fame' lp/c; FA/TCFA 4130791)*

Jun 78. (7") *(HAR 5167)* <10803> **THERE'S NO WAY OUT OF IT. / DEAFINITELY** [ ] [ ]

— with various on session incl. STEVE WINWOOD, JEFF PORCARO & JON LORD

Feb 84. (7"/ext.12") *(HAR/12HAR 5226)* <04378> **BLUE LIGHT. / CRUISE** [ ] [62]

Mar 84. (lp/c)(cd) *(SHSP 24-0079-1/-4)(CDP 746031-2)* <39296> **ABOUT FACE** [21] [32]
– Until we sleep / Murder / Love on the air / Blue light / Out of the blue / All lovers are deranged / You know I'm right / Cruise / Let's get metaphysical / Near the end. *(re-iss. Mar87 on 'Fame' lp/c; FA/TCFA 3171)*

May 84. (7"/7"pic-d) *(HAR/+P 5229)* **LOVE ON THE AIR. / LET'S GET METAPHYSICAL** [ ] [–]

E.M.I. Sony

Mar 06. (cd/lp) *(355695-2/-1)* <80280-2> **ON AN ISLAND** [1] [6]
– Castellorizon / On an island / The blue / Take a breath / Red sky at night / This heaven / Then I close my eyes / Smile / A pocketful of stones / Where we start.

RICHARD WRIGHT

solo with **SNOWY WHITE** – guitar / **MEL COLLINS** – saxophone / **LARRY STEELE** – bass / **REG ISADORE** – drums

Harvest Columbia

Sep 78. (lp/c) *(SHVL/TCSHVL 818)* <35559> **WET DREAM** [ ] [ ]
– Medterranean c / Against the odds / Cat cruise / Summer elegy / Waves / Holiday / Mad Yannis dance / Drop in from the top / Pink's song / Funky deux.

— In 1984, he formed ZEE duo, and returned to FLOYD later in the 80's.

— with **DAVE HARRIS** – guitar, vocals, keyboards, synth (ex-FASHION)

Apr 84. (7"/ext.12"; by ZEE) *(HAR/12HAR 5227)* **CONFUSION. / EYES OF A GYPSY** [ ] [–]

Apr 84. (lp/c; by ZEE) *(SHSP 240101/-1/-4)* **IDENTITY** [ ] [–]
– Confusion / Voices / Private person / Strange rhythm / Cuts like a diamond / By touching / How do you do it / Seems we are dreaming.

E.M.I. Capitol

Oct 96. (cd/c) *(CD/TC+/EMD 1098)* <53645> **BROKEN CHINA** [61] Nov96 [ ]
– Breaking water / Night of a thousand furry toys / Hidden fear / Runaway / Underground / Satellite / Woman of custom / Interlude / Black cloud / Far from the harbour wall / Drowning / Reaching for the rail / Blue room in Venice / Sweet July / Along the shoreline / Breakthrough.

NICK MASON

solo with **CARLA BLEY** and **ROBERT WYATT**

Harvest Columbia

May 81. (lp/c) *(SHSP/TCSHSP 4116)* <37307> **FICTITIOUS SPORTS** [ ] [ ]
– Can't get my motor to start / I was wrong / Siam / Hot river / Boo to you too / Do ya / Wervin' / I'm a mineralist.

Aug 85. (lp; by NICK MASON & RICK FENN) *(MAF 1)* <40142> **PROFILES** [ ] [ ]
– Malta / Lie for a lie / Rhoda / Profiles (part 1 & 2) / Israel / And the address / Mumbo jumbo / Zip code / Black ice / At the end of the day / Profiles (part 3).

Sep 85. (7"; by NICK MASON & RICK FENN) *(HAR 5238)* **LIE FOR A LIE. / AND THE ADDRESS** [ ] [–]
(12"+=) *(12HAR 5238)* – Mumbo jumbo.

PIXIES

Formed: Boston, Massachusetts, USA ... 1986 by L.A. born frontman and self-confessed UFO freak, BLACK FRANCIS (real name, deep breath ... CHARLES MICHAEL KITRIDGE THOMPSON IV) along with guitarist JOEY SANTIAGO. Famously placing a newspaper ad requesting musicians with a penchant for PETER, PAUL AND MARY and HUSKER DU, the only taker was KIM DEAL who subsequently brought in drummer DAVID LOVERING. Originally trading under the moniker PIXIES IN PANOPLY, the band soon trimmed this down to the punchier PIXIES and began kicking up a storm on the Boston music scene with their spiky, angular noise-pop (that's two thirds noise, one third pop) and wilfully cryptic lyrics. Along with fellow Bostonians THROWING MUSES, the band were signed to '4 a.d.' by a suitably impressed Ivo Watts-Russell, the label releasing The PIXIES' debut 'COME ON PILGRIM' in late '87. Stunningly different, the record galvanised the early PIXIES sound, a bizarre hybrid of manic, strangulated vocals (often sung in Spanish), searing melodic noise and schizophrenic, neo-latin rhythms. The album drew an early core of believers but it wasn't until the release of 'SURFER ROSA' (1988) that the band were hailed as the saviours of indie rock. Taking the formula of the debut to its brain splintering conclusion, the likes of 'BONE MACHINE', the incendiary 'SOMETHING AGAINST YOU' and careering 'BROKEN FACE' were utterly compelling in their blistering intensity. The sheer unhinged abandon with which BLACK FRANCIS threw himself into these songs has to be heard to be believed. You begin to fear that the man really has lost it when he asks 'WHERE IS MY MIND' in his inimitable melancholy howl. DEAL was equally affecting on the gorgeous 'GIGANTIC', the track building from a metaphorical whisper to a scream. Truly essential, 'SURFER ROSA' remains one of the most pivotal alternative rock records of the last fifteen years. Following their first headline UK tour, the band hooked up with producer Gil Norton for the 'DOOLITTLE' (1989) album. Previewed by the haunting 'MONKEY GONE TO HEAVEN', the record showcased a cleaner, more pop-friendly sound, most notably on (then) upcoming single, 'HERE COMES YOUR MAN'. Swoonfully poptastic, this song was guaranteed to have even the most miserable SMITHS fan grinning ear to ear, putting the toss that passes for modern 'indie-pop' to eternal shame. The demented 'DEBASER' was another highlight, becoming a dependable fixture at indie discos for oh, aeons. As well as a mammoth world tour, DEAL found time for her side project, The BREEDERS. A collaboration with the delectable TANYA DONELLY (ex-THROWING MUSES), the pair released the acclaimed 'POD' album in 1990. Later that year came 'BOSSANOVA', another breathtaking collection that had the music press in rapture. Lyrically, BLACK was in his element, losing himself in science fiction fantasy while the band raged and charmed in equal measure. The album reached No.3 in the UK charts and the PIXIES could apparently do no wrong, consolidating their position as one of the biggest American acts in Europe. Yet the critics turned on them with the release of 'TROMPE LE MONDE' (1991), in keeping with the times a decidedly grungier affair. Accusations of "Heavy Metal" were way off the mark. In reality, the record was still chokka with stellar tunes, you just had to dig deeper to find them. 'PLANET OF SOUND', 'SPACE (I BELIEVE IN)' and 'MOTORWAY TO ROSWELL' were all quintessential PIXIES, FRANCIS as endearingly fascinated as ever with the mysteries of the universe. Sadly, the singer was soon to turn his obsession into a solo venture, the PIXIES gone almost as quickly as they had arrived, leaving behind a brief but rich sonic legacy. With

PIXIES

FRANCIS changing his name to the rather dull FRANK BLACK, he went on to release a moderately successful eponymous solo debut in 1993 and a wryly titled follow-up, 'TEENAGER OF THE YEAR' (1994), DEAL going on to make a further album with The BREEDERS. Inevitably, none of these projects approached the deranged genius of the PIXIES (Rock will never see their like again). The frontman continued to surface periodically and three albums, 'THE CULT OF RAY' (1996), 'FRANK BLACK AND THE CATHOLICS' (1998) and 'PISTOLERO' (1999), have all met with diminishing fanbase response. 'DOG IN THE SAND' followed in 2001, a more down home effort which featured some of his best songwriting for years. The fact that SANTIAGO was back on board was hardly a hindrance while occasional glimpses of FRANK's legendary lyrical genius suggested there was life in the old (black) dog yet. The man's feverish creativity continued apace with the simultaneous release, in 2002, of both 'DEVIL'S WORKSHOP' and 'BLACK LETTER DAYS'. Rarely, if ever, can an artist sustain quality over such a protracted format, especially bearing in mind that the latter disc stretches to almost 20 tracks. While this, at least, might conceivably have been more focused had it been edited down to size, there's a ramshackle continuity about the record that makes for strangely addictive listening. While '. . .WORKSHOP' was the more sonically adrenalised of the two, both albums found BLACK's inimitable, impenetrable muse travelling America's stranger side roads. Reportedly inspired by a stint in therapy, 'SHOW ME YOUR TEARS' (2003) was perhaps the singer's most honest and uninhibitedly emotional set of songs. While these aren't adjectives one would normally associate with BLACK's oblique musical charms, and while there was still enough lyrical weirdness to placate longtime fans, the self-analysis seemed to have done his creative juices no end of good. And thus it arrived, the great spastic exploding inevitable that was the PIXIES reunion; to coincide with the band's return, the good folks at '4 a.d.' released another compilation (UK Top 20), 'WAVE OF MUTILATION: THE BEST OF PIXIES' (2004), although longtime fans were much more interested in concert document, 'LIVE IN MINNEAPOLIS, MN – 04.13.04' (2004). For evidence that FRANK/FRANCIS, KIM DEAL, DAVID LOVERING and JOEY SANTIAGO could still shred a gorgeous melody with more lovingly gratuitous spite than any band that ever walked the planet, those who missed the shows could try and get their hands on the latter, or any other of the PEARL JAM-style official bootlegs which the band sold in frustratingly limited quantities through their website. The rest of us mere mortals had to make do with another FRANK BLACK solo set, 'HONEYCOMB' (2005). Cut live in Nashville in such hallowed company as SPOONER OLDHAM and STEVE CROPPER, the record saw BLACK the tenacious troubadour still wrestling with end-of-marriage fallout, spilling quirky yet revealing tears over rootsy originals and covers, from the obligatory ('DARK END OF THE STREET') to the revealing (Doug Sahm's 'SUNDAY SUNNY MILL VALLEY GROOVE DA') to the whimsical ('SONG OF THE SHRIMP', most famously rendered by ELVIS on the 'King Creole' soundtrack). Almost a year on, in June 2006, FRANK delivered another set, this time a double 'FAST MAN, RAIDER MAN'.

• **Songwriters:** BLACK FRANCIS penned except; WINTERLONG + I'VE BEEN WAITING FOR YOU (Neil Young) / EVIL HEARTED YOU (Yardbirds) / HEAD ON (Jesus & Mary Chain) / CECILIA ANN (Surftones) / BORN IN CHICAGO (Paul Butterfield's Blues Band) / I CAN'T FORGET (Leonard Cohen). FRANK BLACK solo:- JUST A LITTLE (Beau Brummels) / RE-MAKE, RE-MODEL (Roxy Music) / HANG ON TO YOUR EGO (Beach Boys) / DIRTY OLD TOWN (Ewan MacColl) / THE END OF THE SUMMER (Faure) / FARE THEE WELL (trad.).

Album rating: COME ON PILGRIM mini (*7) / SURFER ROSA (*10) / DOOLITTLE (*9) / BOSSANOVA (*8) / TROMPE LE MONDE (*7) / DEATH TO THE PIXIES compilation (*8) / WAVE OF MUTILATION: BEST OF compilation (*9) / Frank Black: FRANK BLACK (*8) / TEENAGER OF THE YEAR (*8) / THE CULT OF RAY (*5) / FRANK BLACK & THE CATHOLICS (*5) / PISTOLERO (*5) / DOG IN THE SAND (*6) / DEVIL'S WORKSHOP (*5) / BLACK LETTER DAYS (*5) / SHOW ME YOUR TEARS (*6) / HONEYCOMB (*6) / FAST MAN, RAIDER MAN (*6)

BLACK FRANCIS (b. CHARLES MICHAEL KITRIDGE THOMPSON IV, 1965, Long Beach, Calif.) – vocals, guitar / **JOEY SANTIAGO** (b.10 Jun'65, Manila, Philippines) – lead guitar / **KIM DEAL** (Mrs.JOHN MURPHY) (b.10 Jun'61, Dayton, Ohio) – bass, vocals / **DAVE LOVERING** (b. 6 Dec'61) – drums

		4.a.d.	Elektra
Oct 87.	(m-lp) *(MAD 709)* *<61296>* **COME ON PILGRIM**		
	– Caribou / Vamos / Islade encounter / Ed is dead / The holiday song / Nimrod's son / I've been tried / Levitate me.		
Mar 88.	(lp/c)(cd) *(CAD/+C 803)(CAD 803CD)* *<61295>* **SURFER ROSA**		
	– Bone machine / Break my body / Something against you / Broken face / Gigantic / River Euphrates / Where is my mind? / Cactus / Tony's theme / Oh my golly! / Vamos / I'm amazed / Brick is red. *(cd+=)* – COME ON PILGRIM (m-lp)		
Aug 88.	(12"ep/cd-ep) *(BAD 805/+CD)* **GIGANTIC. / RIVER EUPHRATES. / VAMOS. / IN HEAVEN (LADY IN THE RADIATOR SONG)**		–
Mar 89.	(7") *(AD 904)* **MONKEY GONE TO HEAVEN. / MANTA RAY**	60	
	(12"+=/cd-s+=) *(BAD 904/+CD)* – Weird at my school / Dancing the manta ray.		
Apr 89.	(lp/c)(cd) *(CAD/+C 905)(CAD 905CD)* *<60856>* **DOOLITTLE**	8	98
	– Debaser / Tame / Wave of mutilation / I bleed / There goes my gun / Here comes your man / Dead / Monkey gone to Heaven / La la love you / Mr. Grieves / Crackity Jones / #13 baby / Silver / Hey / Gouge away.		
Jun 89.	(7") *(AD 909)* *<66694>* **HERE COMES YOUR MAN. / INTO THE WHITE**	54	
	(12"+=/cd-s+=) *(BAD 909/+CD)* – Wave of mutilation (UK surf) / Bailey's walk.		
——	KIM DEAL was also part of amalgamation The BREEDERS		
Jul 90.	(7"/c-s) *(AD/+C 0009)* *<66616>* **VELOURIA. / I'VE BEEN WAITING FOR YOU**	28	
	(12"+=/cd-s+=) *(BAD 0009/+CD)* – Make believe / The thing.		
Aug 90.	(cd)(lp/c) *(CAD 0010CD)(CAD/+C 0010)* *<60963>* **BOSSANOVA**	3	70
	– Cecilia Ann / Rock music / Velouria / Allison / Is she weird / Ana / All over the world / Dig for fire / Down to the wall / The happening / Blown away / Hang wire / Stormy weather / Havalina.		
Oct 90.	(7"/c-s) *(AD/+C 0014)* *<66596>* **DIG FOR FIRE. / VELVETY (instrumental)**	62	
	(12"+=/cd-s+=) *(BAD 0014/+CD)* – Winterlong / Santo.		
May 91.	(7") *(AD 1008)* **PLANET OF SOUND. / BUILD HIGH**	27	
	(c-s+=)(12"+=/cd-s+=) *(BADC 1008)(BAD 1008/+CD)* – Evil hearted you / Theme from Narc.		
Sep 91.	(cd)(lp/c) *(CAD 1014CD)(CAD/+C 1014)* *<61118>* **TROMPE LE MONDE**	7	92
	– Trompe de Monde / Planet of sound / Alec Eiffel / The sad punk / Head on / U-mass / Palace of the brine / Letter to Memphis / Bird dream Of the Olympus mons / Space (I believe in) / Subbacultcha / Distance equals rate times time / Lovely day / Motorway to Roswell / The Navajo know.		
Nov 91.	(7") *(AD 1999)* **ALEC EIFFEL. / MOTORWAY TO ROSWELL**		–
	(12"+=)(cd-s+=) *(BAD 1999)(PIX 1999CD)* – Planet of sound (live) / Tame (live).		
Feb 92.	(12"ep) *<66444>* **ALEC EIFFEL / LETTER TO MEMPHIS (instrumental). / BUILD LIFE / EVIL HEARTED YOU**	–	
——	disbanded late in '92, with BLACK FRANCIS going solo as FRANK BLACK.		

– compilations, etc. –

on '4 a.d.' / 'Elektra' unless otherwise mentioned

Sep 97.	(7") *(AD 7010)* **DEBASER (demo). / #13 BABY**	23	
	(cd-s) *(BAD 7010CD)* – ('A'studio) / Bone machine / Gigantic / Isla de Encanta.		
	(cd-s) *(BADD 7010CD)* – ('A'live) / Holiday song (live) / Cactus (live) / Nimrod's son (live).		
Oct 97.	(d-cd/d-c) *(DAD/+C 7011)* / *<62118>* **DEATH TO THE PIXIES**	28	
	– Cecilia Ann / Planet of sound / Tame / Here comes your man / Debaser /		

Wave of mutilation / Dig for fire / Caribou / Holiday song / Nimrod's son / U mass / Bone machine / Gigantic / Where is my mind / Velouria / Gouge away / Monkey gone to Heaven / Debaser / Rock music / Broken face / Isla De Encanta / Hangfire / Dead / Into the white / Monkey gone to Heaven / Gouge away / Here comes your man / Alidon / Hey / Gigantic / Crackity Jones / Something against you / Tame / Wave of mutilation / Where is my mind / Ed is dead / Vamos / Tony's theme. *(de-luxe version hit No.20 q-lp/d-cd; DADD 7011/+CD)*

Jul 98. (cd) *(GAD 8013)* *<62185>* **PIXIES AT THE BBC (live)** [45] [ ]
– Wild honey pie / There goes my gun / Dead / Subbacultcha / Manta Ray / Is she weird? / Ana / Down to the well / Wave of mutilation / Letter to Memphis / Levitate me / Caribou / Monkey gone to Heaven / Hey / In Heaven (lady in the radiator song).

Jul 02. (cd) *Cooking Vinyl; (COOKCD 234) / SpinArt; <109>*
PIXIES (demos, etc. 1987..) [ ] [ ]
– Broken face / Build high / Rock a my soul / Down to the well / Break my body / I'm amazed / Here comes your man / Subbacultcha / In Heaven.

May 04. (cd) *(CAD 2406CD)* *<72406>* **WAVE OF MUTILATION: BEST OF PIXIES** [16] [ ]
– Bone machine / Nimrod's son / Holiday song / Caribou / Broken face / Gigantic / Vamos / Hey / Monkey gone to Heaven / Debaser / Gouge away / Wave of mutilation / Here comes your man / Tame / Where is my mind? / Into the white / Velouria / Allison / Dig for fire / U-mass / Alec Eiffel / Planet of sound / Winterlong.

FRANK BLACK

— with **ERIC DREW FELDMAN** – bass, keyboards, synthetics (ex-CAPTAIN BEEFHEART) / **NICK VINCENT** – drums, percussion / + extra guitars **SANTIAGO, MORRIS TEPPER + DAVID SARDY**

4 a.d. Elektra

Mar 93. (lp/cd)(c) *(CAD 3004/+CD)(CADC 3004)* *<61467>*
FRANK BLACK [9] [ ]
– Los Angeles / I heard Ramona sing / Hang on to your ego / Fu Manchu / Places named after numbers / Czar / Old black dawning / Ten percenter / Brackish boy / Two spaces / Tossed (instrumental version) / Parry the wind high, low / Adda Lee / Every time I go around here / Don't ya rile 'em. *(cd re-iss. Jul98; GAD 3004CD)*

Apr 93. (7") *(AD 3005)* *<8782-2>* **HANG ON TO YOUR EGO. / THE BALLAD OF JOHNNY HORTON** [ ] [ ]
(cd-s+=) *(BAD 3005CD)* – Surf epic.

— same trio augmented by **SANTIAGO, TEPPER + LYLE WORKMAN** – guitar

May 94. (7") *(AD 4007)* **HEADACHE. / ('A'mix)** [53] [–]
(10"/cd-s) *(BADD 4007/+CD)* – ('A'side) / Men in black / At the end of the world / Oddball.
(cd-s) *(BAD 4007CD)* – ('A'side) / Hate me / This is where I belong / Amnesia.

May 94. (d-lp/cd)(c) *(DAD 4009/+CD)(DADC 4009)* *<61618>*
TEENAGER OF THE YEAR [21] [ ]
– Whatever happened to Pong? / Thalassocracy / (I want to live on an) Abstract plain / Calistan / The vanishing spies / Speedy Marie / Headache / Sir Rockaby / Freedom rock / Two reelers / Fiddle riddle / Ole Mulholland / Fazer eyes / I could stay here forever / The hostess with the mostest / Superabound / Big red / Space is gonna do me good / White noise maker / Pure denizen of the citizens band / Bad, wicked world / Pie in the sky. *(re-iss. Jul98; GAD 4009CD)*

— FRANK BLACK had earlier in the year teamed up with ex-SEX PISTOL; GLEN MATLOCK to form tribute band FRANK BLACK & THE STAX PISTOLS

Noise Annoys not iss.

Dec 95. (cd/d-lp) *(ANAN CD/V 7)* **THE BLACK SESSIONS (live in Paris)** [ ] [–]
– Two spaces / (I want to live on an) Abstact plain / Headache / Old black dawning / Superabound / Calistan / The vanishing spies / Sir Rockaby / Big red / The Jacques Tati / Oddball / Men in black / Czar / Freedom rock / (Whatever happened to) Pong / Thalasocracy / White noise maker / Los Angeles / Handyman / Modern age / Jumping beans / (I want to live on an) Abstact plain (acoustic). *(re-iss. Oct97; same)*

— now w/ **LYLE WORKMAN** – lead guitar / **DAVID McCAFFREY** – bass / **SCOTT BOUTIER** – drums

Epic Warners

Dec 95. (ltd-7") *(662 671-7)* **THE MARXIST. / BETTER THINGS** [ ] [–]

Jan 96. (7") *(662 786-7)* **MEN IN BLACK. / JUST A LITTLE** [37] [–]
(cd-s+=) *(662 786-2)* – Re-make, re-model.
(cd-s) *(662 786-5)* – ('A'side) / You never heard of me / Pray a little faster / Announcement.

Jan 96. (cd/c/lp) *(481 647-2/-4/-1)* *<43070>* **THE CULT OF RAY** [39] [ ]
– The Marxist / Men in black / Punk rock city / You ain't me / Jesus was right / I don't want to hurt you (every single time) / Mosh, don't pass the guy / Kicked in the taco / Creature crawling / Adventure and the resolution / Dance war / The cult of Ray / Last stand of Shazeb Andleeb. *(cd re-iss. Oct01 on 'Cooking Vinyl'; COOKCD 221)*

Jul 96. (7") *(663 463-7)* **I DON'T WANT TO HURT YOU (EVERY SINGLE TIME). / YOU AIN'T ME (live)** [63] [–]
(cd-s+=) *(663 463-2)* – The Marxist / Better things.
(cd-s) *(663 463-5)* – ('A'live) / Men in black (live) / Village of the sun (live) / The last stand of Shazeb Andleeb (live).

FRANK BLACK AND THE CATHOLICS

with **LYLE WORKMAN, DAVE McCAFFREY + SCOTT BOUTIER**

Play It Again Sam SpinArt

Apr 98. (7"ep/cd-ep) *(BIAS 347 7/CD)* **ALL MY GHOSTS / LIVING ON SOUL / HUMBOULDT COUNTY MASSACRE / CHANGING OF THE GUARDS** [ ] [–]

May 98. (cd/c/lp) *(BIAS 370 CD/MC/LP)* *<SPART 067CD>*
FRANK BLACK AND THE CATHOLICS [61] [ ]
– All my ghosts / Back to Rome / Do you feel bad about it / Dog gone / I gotta move / I need peace / King and Queen of Siam / Six sixty six / Solid gold / Steak 'n' sabre / Suffering / The man who was too loud. *(ltd-cd+=; BIAS 370CDX)* – All my ghosts / Living on soul / Humboldt county massacre / Changing of the guards. *(cd re-iss. Jul00 on 'SpinArt'; same as US)*

— **RICK GILBERT** – guitar; repl. WORKMAN

Mar 99. (cd) *(CDBIAS 390CD)* *<SPART 070CD>* **PISTOLERO** [ ] [ ]
– Bad harmony / I switched you / Western star / Tiny heart / You're such a wire / I loved your brain / Smoke up / Billy Radcliffe / So hard to make things out / Eighty five weeks / I think I'm starting to lose it / I want to rock and roll / Skeleton man / So bay. *(lp-iss.Nov99 on 'SpinArt'; SPART 70)*

— added **ERIC DREW FELDMAN** – keyboards + **JOEY SANTIAGO** – guitar / **DAVE PHILIPS** – guitar / **MORRIS TEPPER** – guitar

Cooking Vinyl What Are?

Jan 01. (cd) *(FRYCD 098)* **ROBERT ONION / PAN AMERICAN HIGHWAY / ANGST** [ ] [–]

Jan 01. (cd) *(COOKCD 200)* *<4833>* **DOG IN THE SAND** [ ] [ ]
– Blast off / I've seen your picture / St. Francis dam disaster / Robert Onion / Stupid me / Bullet / The swimmer / Hermaphroditos / I'll be blue / Llano del Rio / If it takes all night / Dog in the sand.

Feb 01. (cd-s) *(FRYCD 099)* **ST. FRANCIS DAM DISASTER / CONSTANT SORROW MAN / SLEEP** [ ] [–]

Aug 02. (cd) *(COOKCD 243)* *<SPART 112>* **DEVIL'S WORKSHOP** [ ] [ ]
– Velvety / Out of state / His kingly cave / San Antonio, TX / Bartholomew / Modern age / Are you headed my way? / Heloise / The scene / Whiskey in your shoes / Fields of marigold.

Aug 02. (cd) *(COOKCD 240)* *<SPART 113>* **BLACK LETTER DAYS** [ ] [ ]
– The black rider / California bound / Chip away boy / Cold heart of stone / Black letter day / Valentine and Garuda / How you went so far / End of miles / 1826 / The farewell bend / Southbound bevy / I will run after you / True blue / Jane the queen of love / Jet black river / 21 reasons / Whispering weeds / The black rider.

Aug 03. (cd-s) *(FRYCD 161)* **EVERYTHING IS NEW / TAKE WHAT YOU WANT / DOWN IN THE HOLE** [ ] [–]

Sep 03. (cd) *(COOKCD 262)* *<SPART 129>* **SHOW ME YOUR TEARS** [ ] [ ]
– Nadine / Everything is new / My favorite kiss / Jaina blues / New house of the Pope / Horrible day / Massif centrale / When will happiness find me again? / Goodbye Lorraine / This old heartache / The snake / Coastline / Manitoba.

FRANK BLACK

sessions with **ANTON FIG, STEVE CROPPER + SPOONER OLDHAM**

Cooking Vinyl Back Porch

Jul 05. (cd) *(COOKCD 341)* *<77293>* **HONEYCOMB** [ ] [ ]
– Selkie bride / I burn today / Lone child / Another velvet nightmare / The

dark end of the street / Go find your saint / Song of the shrimp / Strange goodbye / Sunday sunny mill valley groove day / Honeycomb / My life is in storage / Atom in my heart / Violet / Sing for joy.

Jun 06. (d-cd) *(COOKCD 376)* <875> **FAST MAN, RAIDER MAN** [ ] [ ]
– If your poison gets you / Johnny Barleycorn / Fast man / You can't crucify yourself / Dirty old town / Wanderlust / Seven days / Raider man / The end of the summer / Dog sleep / When the paint grows darker still / I'm not dead (I'm in Pittsburgh) / Golden shore // In the time of my ruin / Down to you / Highway to lowdown / Kiss my ring / My terrible ways / Fitzgerald / Elijah / It's just not your moment / The real el Rey / Where the wind is going / Holland town / Sad old world / Don't cry that way / Fare thee well.

– compilations, etc. –

Jul 95. (12"ep/cd-ep) *Strange Fruit; (SFPS/+CD 091)* **PEEL SESSION** [ ] [–]
– Handyman / The man who was too loud / The Jacques Tati / Sister Isabel.

Nov 97. (cd-ep; with TEENAGE FANCLUB) *Strange Fruit; (SFRSCD 042)* **THE JOHN PEEL SESSION** [ ] [–]

Mar 01. (cd) *4 a.d.; (GAD 2103CD)* **THE COMPLETE B-SIDES** [53] [–]

☐ PIZZAMAN (see under ⇒ COOK, Norman)

PLACEBO

Formed: South London, England … October '94 by the cosmopolitan pair of BRIAN MOLKO (son of American and Scottish – Dundee – parents) and STEFAN OLSDAL, who had attended the same school in Luxembourg. They met up again in a London tube having spent time in the States and Sweden respectively. Early the following year, they recruited Swedish drummer, ROBERT SCHULTZBERG, the trio subsequently becoming joint winners of the 'In The City' Battle Of The Bands competition. Late in '95, PLACEBO shared a one-off single, 'BRUISE PRISTINE', with the band, SOUP, on 'Fierce Panda' records. After only a handful of gigs, they signed for 'Deceptive' (home of ELASTICA), leading to tours with ASH, BUSH and WHALE. A solitary single later ('COME HOME'), MOLKO and Co., hit the proverbial jackpot via a deal with Virgin/Hut subsidiary, 'Elevator'. The openly bisexual, cross-dressing MOLKO, drew comparisons with 70's glam idols like BOLAN and BOWIE, the music, however, traded in the glitter for a darker listening experience. Taking the fast lane out of the post-grunge pile-up, they fused elements of avant-garde rock and cerebral metal, MOLKO's paint-stripping shrill drawing comparisons with Rush's GEDDY LEE and DAVID SURKAMP of the more obscure Pavlov's Dog. Their eponymous debut album was released in mid-'96 to a fawning music press, metal-mag Kerrang's strong support helping the record dent the UK Top 40. Hit singles 'TEENAGE ANGST' and the Top 5 'NANCY BOY', helped regenerate sales of a collection which many hailed as one of the years' best. In addition to the more incendiary tracks, the album also contained such hauntingly reflective songs as 'LADY OF THE FLOWERS' and 'HANG ON TO YOUR IQ'. PLACEBO – with STEVE HEWITT replacing SCHULTZBERG – were back with a bang (so to speak!) in the Autumn of '98, two blistering UK Top 5 singles in quick succession, 'PURE MORNING' and 'YOU DON'T CARE ABOUT US', premiering their equally superb sophomore set, 'WITHOUT YOU I'M NOTHING' – 'EVERY YOU EVERY ME' and collaborative title track with MOLKO's idol BOWIE, kept the band in high profile the following year. With 'BLACK MARKET MUSIC' (2000), MOLKO took his brooding sexual vision to its twisted climax on an album which ranks as one of PLACEBO's most darkly satisfying to date. Longtime fans will be glad to know that the ever androgynous frontman is still wrestling with his soiled demons, content to provide a mascara-smeared foil to the bloke-rock clogging up the music biz. Still going strong after three albums, PLACEBO issued their fourth, the hauntingly titled 'SLEEPING WITH GHOSTS' (2003). It saw a more mature MOLKO letting down his glam-rock snottiness, in favour of dark rock in the vein of MUSE and The COOPER TEMPLE CLAUSE. As always, his high-pitched whine was ever present as were the complex guitar rhythms and the off-kilter backbeat by the ever reliable OLSDAL and HEWITT. Add to the mix some dark electronica and the occasional ballad ('ENGLISH SUMMER RAIN') and what emerged was a deliciously brash and delicately dark pop-rock record that would be hard not to impress the rock fraternity. Following on from the Top 10 anthology, 'ONCE MORE WITH FEELING: SINGLES 1996-2004' (2004), 'MEDS' (2006) stripped it back even further, dispensing with any lingering production frippery on an album which returned the band to the scabrous, dirty rock thrills of their debut. On a record which followed the greatest hits set into the Top 10, Frenchman Dimitri Tikovoi was charged with the sonic reduction (achieved over an impressively concise two months), surpassing himself with the garish grind of 'INFRA RED'. Guests included an unobtrusive MICHAEL STIPE (on 'BROKEN PROMISE'), and the KILLS' ALISON MOSSHART, who sassed-up the title track.

• **Songwriters:** Group, except BIGMOUTH STRIKES AGAIN (Smiths) / 20TH CENTURY BOY (T.Rex) / JOHNNY & MARY (Robert Palmer).

Album rating: PLACEBO (*9) / WITHOUT YOU I'M NOTHING (*8) / BLACK MARKET MUSIC (*6) / SLEEPING WITH GHOSTS (*6) / ONCE MORE WITH FEELING: SINGLES 1996-2004 compilation (*8) / MEDS (*7)

BRIAN MOLKO (b.10 Dec'72, Brussels, Belgium) – vocals, guitars, bass / **STEFAN OLSDAL** (b.31 Mar'74, Sweden) – bass, guitars, keyboards / **ROBERT SCHULTZBERG** – drums, percussion, didgeridoo

Fierce Panda — not iss.

Nov 95. (7") *(NING 13)* **BRUISE PRISTINE. / (Soup: 'Meltdown')** [ ] [–]

Deceptive — not iss.

Feb 96. (7") *(BLUFF 024)* **COME HOME. / DROWNING BY NUMBERS** [ ] [–]
(cd-s+=) *(BLUFF 024CD)* – Oxygen thief.

Elevator — Caroline

Jun 96. (7") *(FLOOR 001)* **36 DEGREES. / DARK GLOBE** [ ] [–]
(cd-s+=) *(FLOORCD 001)* – Hare Krishna.

Jun 96. (cd/c/lp) *(CD/MC/LP FLOOR 002)* <7575> **PLACEBO** [40] Jul96 [ ]
– Come home / Teenage angst / Bionic / 36 degrees / Hang on to you IQ / Nancy boy / I know / Bruise pristine / Lady of the flowers / Swallow. *(re-dist.Jan97 hit UK No.5; same)*

Sep 96. (7"/cd-s) *(FLOOR/+CD 003)* **TEENAGE ANGST. / BEEN SMOKING TOO LONG / HUG BUBBLE** [30] [–]
(7"m) *(FLOORX 003)* – ('A'-V.P.R.O. radio session) / Flesh mechanic (demo) / HK farewell.

Jan 97. (7") *(FLOOR 004)* **NANCY BOY. / SLACKERBITCH** [4] [ ]
(cd-s+=) *(FLOORCD 004)* – Bigmouth strikes again / Hug bubble.
(cd-s) *(FLOORCDX 004)* – ('A'side) / Eyesight to the blind / Swallow (Brad Wood mix) / Miss Moneypenny.

May 97. (c-s/cd-s) *(FLOOR MC/CD 005)* **BRUISE PRISTINE / THEN THE CLOUDS WILL OPEN FOR ME / BRUISE PRISTINE (One Inch Punch remix)** [14] [–]
(cd-s) *(FLOORCDX 005)* – ('A'side) / Waiting for the sun of man / Serenity (Lionrock remix).

— **STEVE HEWITT** (b.22 Mar'71, Northwich, Manchester, England) – drums; repl. SCHULTZBERG

Elevator — Hut

Aug 98. (cd-ep) *(FLOORCD 6)* **PURE MORNING / MARS LANDING PARTY / LEELOO** [4] [–]
(cd-ep) *(FLOORCDX 6)* – ('A'-lp version) / Needledick / The innocence of sleep.

Sep 98. (c-s/cd-s) *(FLOOR C/CD 7)* <95363> **YOU DON'T CARE ABOUT US / 20TH CENTURY BOY / ION** [5] [ ]
(cd-s) *(FLOORDX 7)* – ('A'side) / ('A'-Les Rhythmes Digitales remix) / ('A'-Howie B remix).

Oct 98. (cd/c/lp) *(CDFLOOR/FLOORMC/FLOORLP 8) <46531>* **WITHOUT YOU I'M NOTHING** 7 Nov98
– Pure morning / Brick shithouse / You don't care about us / Ask for answers / Without you I'm nothing / Allergic (to thoughts of Mother Earth) / The crawl / Every you every me / My sweet prince / Summer's gone / Scared of girls / Burger queen.

Jan 99. (7") *(FLOORLH 9)* **EVERY YOU EVERY ME. / NANCY BOY (Blue Amazon remix)** 11 –
(c-s+=/cd-s+=) *(FLOORCD 9)* – ('A'-Jimmy Cauty remix).
(cd-s) *(FLOORDX 9)* – ('A'side) / ('A'-Sneaker Pimps version) / ('A'-Brothers In Rhythm remix).

Aug 99. (cd-ep; featuring DAVID BOWIE) *(FLOORCD 10)* **WITHOUT YOU I'M NOTHING / ('A'-Unkle remix) / ('A'-Americruiser remix) / ('A'-Brothers In Rhythm remix)** – nochart –

Jul 00. (c-s/cd-s) *(FLOOR C/CD 11)* **TASTE IN MEN / THEME FROM FUNKY REVEREND / TASTE IN MEN (Alpinestars Kamikaze skimix)** 16 –
(cd-s) *(FLOORDX 11)* – ('A'side) / Johnny & Mary / Taste in men (Adrian Sherwood Go Go dub mix).
(12"++=) *(FLOORT 11)* – (all above).

Sep 00. (c-s/cd-s) *(FLOOR C/CD 12)* **SLAVE TO THE WAGE / LENI / BUBBLEGUM** 19 –
(cd-s/12"+=) *(FLOOR DX/X 12)* – ('A'-album version) / Holocaust / ('A'-Les Rythmes Digitales new wave mix).

Oct 00. (cd/c/lp) *(CDFLOOR/FLOORMCX/FLOORLP 13) <10316>* **BLACK MARKET MUSIC** 6
– Taste in men / Days before you came / Special K / Spite & malice / Passive aggressive / Black-eyed / Blue American / Slave to the wage / Commercial for Levi / Haemoglobin / Narcoleptic / Peeping Tom.

Mar 01. (cd-s) *(CDFLOOR 14)* **SPECIAL K / DUB PSYCHOSIS / PASSIVE AGGRESSIVE (Brothers In Rhythm remix)** –
(12"+=) *(TFLOOR 14)* – Little Mo / Slave to the wage (I can't believe it's a remix).
(cd-s) *(CDFLOORX 14)* – ('A'-Timo Maas remix) / (above 2).

Elevator Astralwerks

Mar 03. (7") *(FLOOR 16)* **THE BITTER END. / DADDY COOL** 12 –
(cd-s+=) *(FLOORCD 16)* – Teenage angst (piano version) / ('A'-video).
(cd-s) *(FLOORDX 16)* – ('A'side) / Evalia / Drink you pretty.

Mar 03. (cd/lp) *(CDFLOOR/FLOORLP 17) <81936>* **SLEEPING WITH GHOSTS** 11 Apr03
– Bulletproof Cupid / English summer rain / This picture / Sleeping with ghosts / The bitter end / Something rotten / Plasticine / Special needs / I'll be yours / Second sight / Protect me from what I want / Centrefolds.

Jun 03. (7") *(FLOOR 18)* **THIS PICTURE. / WHERE IS MY MIND (XFM live)** 23 –
(cd-s+=) *(FLOORCD 18)* – Soulmates.

Sep 03. (7") *(FLOOR 19)* **SPECIAL NEEDS. / ENGLISH SUMMER RAIN (freelance hellraiser remix)** 27 –
(cd-s+=) *(FLOORCD 19)* – Plasticine (lounge version).

Feb 04. (7") *(FLOOR 21)* **ENGLISH SUMMER RAIN. / THIS PICTURE (Junior Sanchez remix)** 23 –
(cd-s+=) *(FLOORCDX 21)* – ('A'-Ecstasy Of St. Theresa remix) / ('A'-animated video).
(cd-s) *(FLOORCD 21)* – ('A') / I'll be yours (version 4 am).

Oct 04. (7") *(FLOOR 24)* **TWENTY YEARS. / DETOX FIVE** 18 –
(cd-s+=) *(FLOORCDX 24)* – ('A'-Osymyso's birthday mix) / ('A'-video).
(cd-s) *(FLOORCD 24)* – ('A') / ('A'-Fathom refix).

Oct 04. (cd) *(CDFLOOR 23) <66886>* **ONCE MORE WITH FEELING: SINGLES 1996-2004** (compilation) 8 Nov04
– 36 degrees / Teenage angst / Nancy boy / Bruise pristine / Pure morning / You don't care about us / Every you every me / Without you I'm nothing / Taste in men / Slave to the wage / Special K / Black-eyed / The bitter end / This picture / Special needs / English summer rain / Protege moi / I do / Twenty years. *(d-lp iss.Dec04; LPFLOOR 23) (ltd-cd w/cd+=; CDFLOORX 23)* – (remixes).

Mar 06. (7") *(FLOOR 25)* **BECAUSE I WANT YOU. / (Ladytron remix)** 13 –
(cd-s+=) *(FLOORCDX 25)* – 36 degrees 2005 / ('A'-video) / (making of video).
(cd-s) *(FLOORCD 25)* – ('A') / ('A'-Russell Lissack from Bloc Party remix).

Mar 06. (cd/lp) *(CD+/FLOOR 26) <53035-2>* **MEDS** 7 May06
– Meds / Infra-red / Drag / Space monkey / Follow the cops back home / Post blue / Because I want you / Blind / Pierrot the clown / Broken promise / One of a kind / In the cold light of morning / Song to say goodbye. *(ltd-cd w/dvd+=; CDFLOORX 26)* – (videos).

– compilations, etc. –

Sep 03. (d-cd) *Elevator; (591967-2)* **PLACEBO / BLACK MARKET MUSIC** –

□ Robert PLANT (see under ⇒ LED ZEPPELIN)

□ the PLASTIC ONO BAND (see under ⇒ LENNON, John)

□ PM (see under ⇒ EMERSON, LAKE & PALMER)

P.O.D.

Formed: San Ysidro, San Diego, California, USA ... 1992 by guitarist MARCOS and drummer WUV. A year later, the full line-up comprised vocalist SONNY (WUV's cousin) and bass player TRAA. Marked out a Christian metal/hard-rock act in the mould of RAGE AGAINST THE MACHINE (with dub, reggae, hip-hop and hardcore punk all thrown in), P.O.D. – PAYABLE ON DEATH were soon supporting the likes of the VANDALS, PENNYWISE and GREEN DAY, which helped them shift over 40,000 copies of four independent CD's ('SNUFF THE PUNK', 'BROWN', 'LIVE' and the EP 'WARRIORS'). These were mainly released on their own 'Rescue' records before they were snapped up by 'Atlantic' in 1998. Their first official release, 'THE FUNDAMENTAL ELEMENTS OF SOUTHTOWN' went platinum in 1999 and at that year's San Diego Music Awards, P.O.D. earned top honors for Best Hard Rock or Metal Group. The following year, they toured with Ozzfest and also played alongside STAIND and CRAZY TOWN for the MTV Campus Invasion Tour. The band released a follow-up, 'SATELLITE' in the autumn of 2001, a record that sold even better than their previous effort. The band were subsequently dealt a serious blow with the departure of founder member MARCOS, and it was initially unclear whether his replacement by former LIVING SACRIFICE man JASON TRUBY would result in a radically different sound. If the eponymous title perhaps suggested a new beginning, in reality 'PAYABLE ON DEATH' (2003) was a departure only in the sense that it was more coherent and streamlined than the band's previous efforts. Produced by Glen Ballard (he of ALANIS MORISSETTE fame), 'TESTIFY' (2006) continued the Christian rockers' rap-metal battle with the darker side, while it also gave them another US Top 10 entry.

Album rating: THE FUNDAMENTAL ELEMENTS OF SOUTHTOWN (*6) / SATELLITE (*7) / PAYABLE ON DEATH (*5) / TESTIFY (*7)

P.O.D. PAYABLE ON DEATH

SONNY (b. PAUL JOSHUA SANDOVAL, 16 May'74) – vocals / **MARCOS** (CURIEL) – guitar / **TRAA** (b. MARK DANIELS) – bass; repl. GABE PORTILLO / **WUV** (b. NOAH BERNARDO) – drums

not iss. Chula Vista

1994. (cd) *<8887>* **SNUFF THE PUNK** –
– Coming back / Let the music do the talking / Draw the line / Who is right? / Get it straight / Run / Snuff the punk / Can you feel it? / Three in the power of one / Every knee. *<re-iss. Apr00 on 'Diamante'+=; 5621>* – Abortion is murder.

not iss. Rescue

1996. (cd) **BROWN** –
– Intro / Know me / Selah / Visions / Brown / One day / Punks rock / Breathe Babylon / Funk jam / Preach / Reggae jam / Full color / Seeking the wise / Live and die / Outro. *<re-iss. Aug00 on 'Diamante'; 5628> (UK-iss.Jun03 on 'Butterfly'; 885120)*

1998. (m-cd) **PAYABLE ON DEATH LIVE** (live) –
– One day / Draw the line / Selah / Know me / Punk-reggae jam / Breath Babylon / Preach / Full color. *<re-iss. Jun01 on 'Diamante'; 5636>*

not iss. — Tooth & Nail

May 99. (cd-ep) *<71148>* **THE WARRIORS EP** –
– Intro / Southtown / Breathe Babylon / Rosa Linda / Draw the line / Full color / Sabbath.

P.O.D.

Atlantic — Atlantic

Mar 00. (cd) *<(7567 83216-2)>* **THE FUNDAMENTAL ELEMENTS OF SOUTHTOWN** Aug99 51
– Greetings / Hollywood / Checkin' levels / Rock the party / Lie down / Set your eyes to Zion / Lo siento / Bullet the blue sky / Psalm 150 / Image / Shouts / Tribal / Freestyle / Follow me / Outkast.

Jan 02. (cd) *<(7567 83475-2)>* **SATELLITE** 16 Sep01 6
– Set it off / Alive / Boom / Youth of the nation / Celestial / Satellite / Ridiculous (with EEK-A-MOUSE) / The messenjah / Guitarras de amor / Anything right (with CHRISTIAN LINDSKOG of BLINDSIDE) / Ghetto / Masterpiece conspiracy / Without jah, nothin' (with HR) / Thinking about forever / Portrait. *(UK+=)* – Whatever it takes. *(cd re-iss. Sep02 w/dvd+=; 7567 83597-2)*

Jan 02. (c-s) *(AT 0119C)* **ALIVE / CALL-OUT HOOK #1** 19 Nov01 41
(cd-s+=) *(AT 0119CD) <85165>* – Call-out hook #2.

May 02. (c-s) *(AT 0127C)* **YOUTH OF THE NATION / ALIVE (semi-acoustic)** 36 28
(cd-s+=) *(AT 0127CD) <85249>* – Sabbath.

Aug 02. (7"pic-d)<cd-s> *(AT 0135) <85340>* **BOOM. / SET IT OFF (Tweaker remix) / HOLLYWOOD (live)** Jul02

Oct 02. (cd-s) *(AT 0139CD) <85363>* **SATELLITE / CRITIC / YOUTH OF THE NATION**

—— **JASON TRUBY** – guitar (ex-LIVING SACRIFICE) repl. MARCOS

May 03. (7") *(W 608)* **SLEEPING AWAKE. / BRUISE** 42
(cd-s+=) *(W 608CD) <101094>* – The passportal.
(above from 'The Matrix: Reloaded' & issued on 'Warners')

Nov 03. (cd) *(7567 96220-2) <83661>* **PAYABLE ON DEATH** 9
– Wildfire / Will you / Change the world / Execute the sounds / Find my way / Revolution / The reasons / Freedom fighters / Waiting on today / I and identify / Asthma / Eternal.

Jun 04. (10"pic-d) *(AT 0169TE)* **WILL YOU. / (Chris Vrenna remix)** 68 Nov03
(cd-s+=) *(AT 0169CD) <88220>* – Cain / ('A'-video).

Nov 05. (cd-ep) **THE WARRIORS EP, VOLUME 2** (demos) –
– If it wasn't for you / Teachers / Ya mama / Why wait? / Eyes of a stranger / Boom (live at Cornerstone) / Wildfire (live at Cornerstone).

Jan 06. (cd) *<(7567 83857-2)>* **TESTIFY** 9
– Roots in stereo / Lights out / If you could see me now / Goodbye for now / Sounds like war / On the grind / This time / Mistakes & glories / Let you down / Teachers / Strength of my life / Say hello / Mark my words.

Jan 06. (-) *<radio>* **GOODBYE FOR NOW** – 47

the POGUES

Formed: North London, England … late 1983 by Tipperary-raised SHANE MacGOWAN, SPIDER STACEY and JEM FINER. MacGOWAN had earlier been part of punk outfit, The NIPPLE ERECTORS through 1978-1981; this motley crew released a solitary single, 'KING OF THE BOP' before shortening their name to The NIPS. A further few singles appeared and even an album, 'ONLY AT THE END OF THE BEGINNING', recommended for diehard POGUES fiends only. POGUE MAHONE (Gaelic for "kiss my arse") was subsequently formed by MacGOWAN and JAMES FEARNLEY (also a NIP), adding drinking buddies, ANDREW RANKEN, plus female singer/bassist CAIT O'RIORDAN. By Spring '84, they'd formed their own self-titled label, issuing a classic debut single, 'DARK STREETS OF LONDON'. Boasting all the Celtic melancholy, romance and gritted-teeth attitude which marked the best of the band's work, the track rather unfairly but predictably received an official BBC radio ban (apparently after the beeb managed to translate their name). A month later they secured a deal with 'Stiff', opting instead for The POGUES. Their Stan Brennan-produced debut album, 'RED ROSES FOR ME', broke into the UK Top 100 as they acquired growing support from live audiences the length and breadth of the country. Whether interpreting trad Irish folk songs or reeling off brilliant originals, the POGUES were apt to turn from high-spirited revelry ('STREAMS OF WHISKEY') to menacing threat ('BOYS FROM THE COUNTY HELL') in the time it took to neck a pint of guinness (in MacGOWAN's case, not very long at all). April '85 saw the release of perhaps their finest single (and first Top 20 hit), the misty-eyed, ELVIS COSTELLO-produced 'A PAIR OF BROWN EYES'. COSTELLO also oversaw the accompanying album, 'RUM, SODOMY & THE LASH' (1985), a debauched, bruisingly beautiful classic which elevated The POGUES to the position of modern day folk heroes. MacGOWAN's gift for conjuring up a feeling of time and place was never more vivid than on the likes of the aforementioned 'A PAIR..', the rousing 'SALLY MacLENNANE' and the cursing malice of 'THE SICK BED OF CUCHULAINN', while O'RIORDAN put in a spine-tingling performance as a Scottish laird on the traditional 'I'M A MAN YOU DON'T MEET EVERY DAY'. On the 16th of May '86, the latter married COSTELLO and when she subsequently left that November (after writing the Top 50 hit 'HAUNTED' for the Alex Cox film, 'Sid & Nancy'), a vital component of POGUES chemistry went with her. Around the same time, the group played 'The McMahon Gang' in Cox's movie 'Straight To Hell', meeting ex-CLASH singer JOE STRUMMER on the set: the veteran punk would subsequently deputise for the absent MacGOWAN on an early 1988 US tour. This period also saw them peak at No.3 in the album charts with 'IF I SHOULD FALL FROM GRACE WITH GOD', an album which spawned an unlikely No.2 Christmas 1987 hit in 'FAIRY TALE OF NEW YORK'. A drunken duet with KIRSTY MacCOLL, the track was certainly more subversive than the usual Yuletide fodder and for a brief period, The POGUES were bonafide pop stars, their rampant collaboration with The DUBLINERS on 'IRISH ROVER' earlier that year having already breached the Top 10. Live, the band were untouchable, MacGOWAN's errant, tin-tray wielding genius the stuff of legend, particularly for many who witnessed their storming Glasgow Barrowlands performances (needless to say, Rangers fans were mercifully thin on the ground at these celebratory Celtic shindigs). Inevitably, MacGOWAN's hard-drinking ways were beginning to affect his writing and 'PEACE AND LOVE' (1989) signalled a slow slide into mediocrity. 1990's 'HELL'S DITCH' carried on in much the same vein, although this was to be MacGOWAN's final album under The POGUES banner, his failing health incompatible with the demands of a successful major label band. While the gap-toothed frontman eventually got a solo career together, The POGUES bravely soldiered on with a surprisingly impressive hit single, 'TUESDAY MORNING', lifted from their 1993 UK Top 20 "comeback" album, 'WAITING FOR HERB'. Two years on, a nostalgically titled follow-up set, 'POGUE MAHONE', failed to rekindle their former glory, while MacGOWAN continued to dominate the limelight. In 1999, some of the POGUES (SPIDER, HUNT + RANKIN) got together as the WISEMEN, while FINER has emerged with the band LONGPLAYER. Following his messy departure from the POGUES in the early 90's, the Irish Keith Richards (though even Richards' mythical debauchery would struggle to match MacGOWAN's self-destructiveness in terms of sheer dogged determination) threatened to form his own outfit, the POPES; sceptics who doubted the man could even form an opinion were at least partly silenced by MacGOWAN's late '92 duet with fellow maverick, NICK CAVE, on a brilliantly skewed cover of Louis Armstrong's 'WONDERFUL WORLD'. Two years on and much press rumination later, the POPES' debut single, 'THE CHURCH OF THE HOLY SPOOK', finally put an end to the speculation and announced that MacGOWAN's muse was as darkly fertile as ever. Released on 'Z.T.T.', the song's uptempo thrash recalled the unholy spirit of the POGUES' classic 'SICK BED OF CUCHULAINN', scraping into the UK Top 75. Follow-up single, 'THAT WOMAN'S

Shane MacGowan of The POGUES

GOT ME DRINKING' (excuses, excuses), made the Top 40, while Hollywood hearthrob, JOHNNY DEPP, played guitar on their debut Top Of The Pops appearance. The accompanying album, 'THE SNAKE', was the best album the POGUES never recorded in the last decade, finding MacGOWAN back at his cursing, doomed romantic best. Alongside the obligatory traditional songs ('THE RISING OF THE MOON' and 'NANCY WHISKEY'), the record featured an amusingly appropriate cover of Gerry Rafferty's 'HER FATHER DIDN'T LIKE ME ANYWAY', while 'HAUNTED' was a collaboration with SINEAD O'CONNOR which made the Top 30 when released as a single in spring '95. CLANNAD's MAIRE BRENNAN also hooked up with MacGOWAN for 'YOU'RE THE ONE', underlining the depth of respect afforded the wayward genius, even among his more conventional peers. The live appearances which followed the record's release mightn't have matched the ferocious abandon of the POGUES in full flow but came damn near it, while MacGOWAN followed in SID VICIOUS' footsteps (the man's love of the SEX PISTOLS was revealed to the nation via a barely coherent admission on Jo Whiley's Channel 4 TV show) by recording a version of 'MY WAY' in gloriously two-fingered style. 1997 saw the release of a disappointing follow-up set, 'THE CROCK OF GOLD', a record that was at times easier on the ear but hardly threatened to set the pulse racing. Surely only SHANE MacGOWAN could perform at two St. Patrick's Day shows on the trot, given that they took place on opposite sides of the Atlantic Ocean. Yet, due to a quirk of fate, that was exactly what he did, the cream of both performances collected together on 'ACROSS THE BROAD ATLANTIC: LIVE ON PADDY'S DAY' (2002). As anticipated, the atmosphere is raucous, the banter paints the air blue and the set list is primed for maximum, whiskey-soaked celebration.

• **Songwriters:** Group compositions, except; THE BAND PLAYED WALTZING MATILDA (Eric Bogle) / DIRTY OLD TOWN (Ewan MacColl) / WILD ROVER + MADRA RUM (trad.) / MAGGIE MAY (Rod Stewart) / HONKY TONK WOMAN (Rolling Stones) / WHISKEY IN THE JAR (Thin Lizzy) / MISS OTIS REGRETS (Cole Porter) / GOT A LOT O' LIVIN' TO DO (Elvis Presley) / HOW COME (Ronnie Lane) / WHEN THE SHIP COMES IN (Bob Dylan). FINER became main writer in the mid-90's with others contributed some material. MacGOWAN covered CRACKLIN' ROSIE (Neil Diamond) / THE RISING OF THE MOON + NANCY WHISKEY (trad).

Album rating: RED ROSES FOR ME (*8) / RUM, SODOMY & THE LASH (*9) / STRAIGHT TO HELL part soundtrack (*6) / IF I SHOULD FALL FROM GRACE WITH GOD (*8) / PEACE AND LOVE (*6) / HELL'S DITCH (*6) / THE BEST OF THE POGUES compilation (*9) / THE BEST OF THE REST OF THE POGUES compilation (*7) / WAITING FOR HERB (*6) / POGUE MAHONE (*5) / THE VERY BEST OF THE POGUES compilation (*8) / THE ULTIMATE COLLECTION double compilation (*8) / Shane MacGowan & the Popes: THE SNAKE (*8) / THE CROCK OF GOLD (*5) / THE RARE OUL' STUFF (*5) / ACROSS THE BROAD ATLANTIC (*4)

the NIPS

SHANE MacGOWAN (b.25 Dec'57, Kent, England) – vocals, guitar / **ADRIAN THRILLS** – guitar (NME journalist) / **SHANE 'HASLER' BRADLEY** – bass / **ARCANE** – drums / + others

Soho | not iss.

Jun 78. (7"; as NIPPLE ERECTORS) *(SH 1/2)* **KING OF THE BOP. / NERVOUS WRECK** ☐ | –

— **LARRY HINDRICKS** – guitar; repl. THRILLS

— **MARK HARRIS** – drums repl. ARCANE

Aug 79. (7") *(SH 4)* **ALL THE TIME IN THE WORLD. / PRIVATE EYES** ☐ | –

— **GAVIN DOUGLAS** – drums repl. LARRY

— **JAMES FEARNLEY** (b.10 Oct'54, Manchester, England) – accordion (appeared on album)

Feb 80. (7") *(SH 9)* **GABRIELLE. / VENGEANCE** ☐ | –
(re-iss. 1980 on 'Chiswick'; CHIS 119)

Oct 80. (lp) *(HOHO 1)* **ONLY AT THE END OF THE BEGINNING** ☐ | –
– Love to make you cry / Vengeance / Gabrielle / King of the bop / Ghost town / Fuss 'n' bother / Venus in bovver boots / Happy song / Stupid cow / I don't want nobody to love / Infatuation / Maida Ada / Hit parade / Can't say no.

Test Press | not iss.

Oct 81. (7") *(TP 5)* **HAPPY SONG. / NOBODY TO LOVE** ☐ | –

— split in 1982. HASLER was soon to join MEN THEY COULDN'T HANG.

– compilation –

Nov 87. (m-lp) *Big Beat; (WIKM 66)* **BOPS, BABES, BOOZE & BOVVER** ☐ | –
– King of the bop / Nervous wreck / So pissed off / Stavordale Rd. N5 / All the time in the world / Private eye / Gabrielle / Vengeance.

the POGUES

MacGOWAN + FEARNLEY plus **SPIDER STACEY** (b.PETER, 14 Dec'58, Eastbourne, England) – tin whistle (ex-NIPS) / **JEM FINER** (b.JEREMY, 29 Jul'55, Stoke, England) – banjo, guitar / **CAIT O'RIORDAN** – bass, vocals / **ANDREW RANKEN** (b.13 Nov'53, London) – drums

Pogue Mahone | not iss.

May 84. (7"; as POGUE MAHONE) *(PM 1)* **DARK STREETS OF LONDON. / THE BAND PLAYED WALTZING MATHILDA** ☐ | –
(re-iss. Jun84 as The POGUES on 'Stiff'; BUY 207)

Stiff | not iss.

Sep 84. (lp) *(SEEZ 55)* **RED ROSES FOR ME** 89 | –
– Transmetropolitan / The battle of Brisbane / The auld triangle / Waxie's dargle / Boys from the county Hell / Sea shanty / Dark streets of London / Streams of whiskey / Poor daddy / Dingle regatta / Greenland whale fisheries / Down in the ground where the dead men go / Kitty. *(cd-iss. May87; CDSEEZ 55) (re-iss. Jan89 on 'WEA' lp/c; WX 240/+C)* (cd re-iss. Jan89; *244494-2)*

Oct 84. (7") *(BUY 212)* **BOYS FROM THE COUNTY HELL. / REPEALING OF THE LICENSING LAWS** ☐ | –
(d7"+=) *(BUY 212 – 207)* – (see debut 45).

Mar 85. (7"/7"pic-d) *(BUY/DBUY 220)* **A PAIR OF BROWN EYES. / WHISKEY YOU'RE THE DEVIL** 72 | –
(12"+=) *(BUYIT 22)* – Muirshin Durkin.

— added p/t **PHIL CHEVRON** (b. RYAN, 17 Jun'57, Dublin, Ireland) – guitar, producer (ex-RADIATORS FROM SPACE)

Jun 85. (7",7"green/7"sha-pic-d) *(BUY/PBUY 224)* **SALLY MacLENNANE. / WILD ROVER** 51 | –
(12"+=) *(BUYIT 224)* – The leaving of Liverpool.
(c-s++=) *(BUYC 224)* – Wild cats of Kilkenny.

Aug 85. (lp/c/cd) *(SEEZ/CSEEZ/CDSEEZ 58)* **RUM, SODOMY & THE LASH** 13 | –
– The sick bed of Cuchulainn / The old main drag / Wild cats of Kilkenny / I'm a man you don't meet every day / A pair of brown eyes / Sally MacLennane / Dirty old town / Jesse James / Navigator / Billy's bones / The gentleman soldier / And the band played waltzing Matilda. *(cd+=)* – A pistol for Paddy Garcia. *(re-iss. Jan89 on 'WEA' lp/c; WX 241/+C) (cd-iss. Jan89; 244495-2)*

Aug 85. (7"/7"pic-d) *(BUY/PBUY 229)* **DIRTY OLD TOWN. / A PISTOL FOR PADDY GARCIA** 62 | –
(12"+=) *(BUYIT 229)* – The parting glass.

Feb 86. (7"ep/12"ep/c-ep/7"pic-ep) *(BUY/BUYIT/BUYC/PBUY 243)* **POGUETRY IN MOTION** 29 | –
– A rainy night in Soho / The body of an American / London girl / Planxty Noel Hill.

Aug 86. (7") *(MCA 1084)* **HAUNTED. / JUNK THEME** 42 | –
(12"+=) *(MCAT 1084)* – Hot dogs with everything.
(above single from the motion picture, 'Sid & Nancy' on 'M.C.A.')

— **DARRYL HUNT** (b. 4 May'50, Bournemouth, England) – bass (ex-PRIDE O' THE CROSS) repl. CAIT

Mar 87. (7"; by the POGUES & the DUBLINERS) *(BUY 258)* **THE IRISH ROVER. / THE RARE OLD MOUNTAIN DEW** 8 | –
(12"+=) *(BUYIT 258)* – The Dubliners fancy.

— added **TERRY WOODS** (b. 4 Dec'47, Dublin) – banjo (now 8-piece)

Hell-Stiff | Enigma

Jun 87. (cd/c/lp) *(C/Z/+DIABLO 1)* <D2/4XJE 73308> **STRAIGHT TO HELL** (soundtrack w/ Various Artists) ☐ | Nov87 ☐
– The good, the bad and the ugly / Rake at the gates of Hell / If I should

fall from grace with God / Rabinga / Danny boy / (other artists). *(cd re-iss. Aug91 on 'Repertoire'; REP 4224-WY)* *(<cd re-iss. Jun04 as 'STRAIGHT TO HELL – RETURNS' on 'Big Beat'+=; CDWIKD 239>)* – Long cool day in Hell / Bolero del perro listo (aka Bolero) / Night on Bald Mountain / Harmonicas / Big question mark / L'amoria / Obsession / Quiet day in Blanco town / Taranta del fuente / (+ other artists).

Pogue Mahone-EMI — Island

Nov 87. (7"; The POGUES featuring KIRSTY MacCOLL) *(NY 7)* **FAIRYTALE OF NEW YORK. / BATTLE MARCH MEDLEY** [2] [ ]
(12"+=)(cd-s+=) *(NY 12)(CDNY 1)* – Shanne Bradley.

Jan 88. (cd/c/lp) *(CD/TC+/NYR 1)* *<90872>* **IF I SHOULD FALL FROM GRACE WITH GOD** [3] [88]
– If I should fall from grace with God / Turkish song of the damned / Bottle of smoke / Fairytale of New York (featuring KIRSTY MacCOLL) / Metropolis / Thousands are sailing / Fiesta / Medley:- The recruiting sergeant – The rocky road to Dublin – Galway races / Streets of Sorrow – Birmingham Six / Lullaby of London / Sit down by the fire / The broad majestic Shannon / Worms. *(cd+=)* – South Australia / The battle march medley. *(re-iss. Jan89 on 'WEA' lp/c; WX 243/+C) (cd-iss. Jan89; 244494-2)*

Feb 88. (7") *(FG 1)* **IF I SHOULD FALL FROM GRACE WITH GOD. / SALLY MacLENNANE (live)** [58] [ ]
(12"red-ep)(cd-ep+=) **ST. PATRICK'S NIGHT** *(SGG 1-12)(CDFG 1)* – A pair of brown eyes (live) / Dirty old town (live).

Jul 88. (7") *(FG 2)* **FIESTA. / SKETCHES OF SPAIN** [24] [–]
(12"+=)(cd-s+=) *(FG 2-12)(CDFG 2)* – South Australia.

WEA — Island

Dec 88. (7") *(YZ 355)* **YEAH, YEAH, YEAH, YEAH, YEAH. / THE LIMERICK RAKE** [43] [–]
(12"+=/cd-s+=) *(YZ 355 T/CD)* – ('A'extended) / Honky tonk woman.

Jun 89. (7"/c-s) *(YZ 407/+C)* **MISTY MORNING, ALBERT BRIDGE. / COTTON FIELDS** [41] [–]
(12"+=) *(YZ 407T)* – Young ned of the hill.
(3"cd-s++=) *(YZ 407CD)* – Train of love.

Jul 89. (lp/c)(cd) *(WX 247/+C)(246086-2)* *<91225>* **PEACE AND LOVE** [5] [ ]
– White City / Young ned of the hill / Misty morning, Albert Bridge / Cotton fields / Blue heaven / Down all the days / U.S.A. / Lorelei / Gartloney rats / Boat train / Tombstone / Night train to Lorca / London you're a lady / Gridlock.

Aug 89. (7"/c-s) *(YZ 409/+C)* **WHITE CITY. / EVERY MAN IS A KING** [ ] [–]
(12"+=) *(YZ 409TX)* – Maggie May (live).
(cd-s+=) *(YZ 409CD)* – The star of the County Down.

May 90. (7"/c-s; The POGUES & The DUBLINERS) *(YZ 500/+C)* **JACK'S HEROES. / WHISKEY IN THE JAR** [63] [–]
(12"+=/cd-s+=) *(YZ 500 T/CD)* – ('B'extended).

— (theme song used by Eire in World Cup; manager Jack Charlton)

Aug 90. (7") *(YZ 519)* **SUMMER IN SIAM. / BASTARD LANDLORD** [64] [–]
(12"+=/cd-s+=) *(YZ 519 T/CD)* – Hell's ditch (instrumental) / The Irish rover.

Sep 90. (cd)(lp/c) *(9031 72554-2)(WX 366/+C)* *<422846>* **HELL'S DITCH** [12] [ ]
– The sunnyside of the street / Sayonara / The ghost of a smile / Hell's ditch / Lorca's novena / Summer in Siam / Rain street / Rainbow man / The wake of the Medusa / House of the gods / Five green onions and Jean / Maidria Rua / Six to go.

Apr 91. (cd-s) **SAYONARA / CURSE OF LOVE / INFINITY** [–] [ ]

Sep 91. (7") *(YZ 603)* **A RAINY NIGHT IN SOHO (remix). / SQUID OUT OF WATER** [67] [–]
(12"+=) *(YZ 603)* – Infinity.
(cd-s+=) *(YZ 603CD)* – POGUETRY IN MOTION (ep).

Sep 91. (cd)(lp/c) *(9031 75405-2)(WX 430/+C)* **THE BEST OF THE POGUES** (compilation) <US-title 'ESSENTIAL POGUES'> [11] [ ]
– Fairytale of New York / Sally MacLennane / Dirty old town / The Irish rover / A pair of brown eyes / Streams of whiskey / A rainy night in Soho / Fiesta / Rain street / Misty morning, Albert Bridge / White City / Thousand are sailing / The broad majestic Shannon / The body of an American.

Dec 91. (7") *(YZ 628)* **FAIRYTALE OF NEW YORK. / FIESTA** [36] [–]
(12"+=/cd-s+=) *(YZ 628 T/CD)* – A pair of brown eyes / Sick bed of Cuchulainn / Maggie May.

— p/t JOE STRUMMER is deposed by member SPIDER who takes over vox.

May 92. (7"/c-s) *(YZ 673/+C)* **HONKY TONK WOMAN. / CURSE OF LOVE** [56] [–]
(12"+=) *(YZ 673T)* – Infinity.
(cd-s+=) *(YZ 673CD)* – The parting glass.

Jun 92. (cd)(lp/c) *(9031 77341-2)(WX 471/+C)* **THE BEST OF THE REST OF THE POGUES** (compilation out-takes) [ ] [–]
– If I should fall from grace with God / The sick bed of Cuchulainn / The old main drag / Boys from the County Hell / Young Ned of the hill / Dark streets of London / The auld triangle / Repeal of the licensing laws / Yeah yeah yeah yeah yeah / London girl / Honky tonk women / Summer in Siam / Turkish song of the damned / Lullaby of London / The sunnyside of the street / Hell's ditch.

— (Sep'91) MacGOWAN left when his health deteriorated (JOE STRUMMER deputised for him on tour)

— added 8th member & producer **MICHAEL BROOK** – infinite guitar

WEA — Chameleon

Aug 93. (7"/c-s) *(YZ 758/+C)* **TUESDAY MORNING. / FIRST DAY OF FOREVER** [18] [ ]
(cd-s+=) *(YZ 758CD)* – Turkish song of the damned (live).
(cd-s) *(YZ 758CDX)* – ('A'side) / London calling / I fought the law (both live with JOE STRUMMER).

Sep 93. (cd/c/lp) *(4509 93463-2/-4/-1)* *<61598>* **WAITING FOR HERB** [20] Oct98 [ ]
– Tuesday morning / Smell of petroleum / Haunting / Once upon a time / Sitting on top of the world / Drunken boat / Big city / Girl from the Wadi Hammamat / Modern world / Pachinko / My baby's gone / Small hours.

Jan 94. (7"/c-s) *(YZ 771/+C)* **ONCE UPON A TIME. / TRAIN KEPT ROLLING ON** [66] [–]
(12"+=/cd-s+=) *(YZ 771 T/CD)* – Tuesday morning / Paris St. Germain.

— FEARNEY and WOODS departed, apparently due to the brief Christmas comeback of SHANE MacGOWAN

— **SPIDER / JEM / DARRYL + RANKEN** added **JAMIE CLARKE** – banjo / **JAMES McNALLY** – accordion, uilleann pipes / **DAVID COULTER** – mandolin, tambourine

Sep 95. (7"colrd/c-s) *(WEA 011 X/C)* **HOW COME. / EYES OF AN ANGEL** [ ] [–]
(cd-s+=) *(WX 011CD)* – Tuesday morning (live) / Big city (live).

Oct 95. (cd/c/lp) *(0630 11210-2/-4/-1)* **POGUE MAHONE** [ ] [–]
– How come / Living in a world without her / When the ship comes in / Anniversary / Amadie / Love you 'till the end / Bright lights / Oretown / Pont Mirabeau / Tosspint / Four o'clock in the morning / Where that love's been gone / The sun and the moon.

— the POGUES split in 1996

— note:- the POGUES also appeared on the flip side to KIRSTY MacCOLL's Cole Porter tribute single, 'Miss Otis Regrets' on the track 'JUST ONE OF THOSE THINGS'.

– compilations, etc. –

Mar 01. (cd/c) *Warners ESP; (<8573 87459-2/-4>)* **THE VERY BEST OF . . .** [18] Jun01 [ ]
– Dirty old town / The Irish rover / Sally MacLennane / Fiesta / A pair of brown eyes / Fairytale of New York / The body of an American / Streams of whiskey / The sick bed of Cuchulainn / If I should fall from grace with God / Misty morning, Albert Bridge / Rain street / White City / A rainy night in Soho / London girl / Boys from the County Hell / The sunnyside of the street / Summer in Siam / Hell's ditch / The old main drag / The band played Waltzing Matilda.

Jan 02. (cd) *Castle; (CMRCD 388)* **STREAMS OF WHISKEY** (live in Leysin, Switzerland 1991) [ ] [–]

Mar 05. (d-cd) *Warners; (2564 62254-2)* **THE ULTIMATE COLLECTION** [15] [ ]
– THE ULTIMATE POGUES: Rainy night in Soho / Sally MacLennane / The Irish rover / Dirty old town / Fairytale of New York (feat. KIRSTY MacCOLL) / Streams of whiskey / If I should fall from grace with God / Fiesta / Body of an American / Misty morning Albert Bridge / Repeal of the licensing laws / Boys from the County Hell / Sunnyside of the street / A pair of brown eyes / Summer in Siam / The sickbed of Cuchulainn / London girl / Tuesday morning / White city / Hell's ditch / Young ned of the hill / Thousands are sailing // LIVE AT BRIXTON ACADEMY: Streams of whiskey / If I should fall from grace with God / Boys from the County Hell / Broad majestic Shannon / Ned of the hill / Turkish song of the damned / Rainy night in Soho / Tuesday morning / Rain street / Pair of brown eyes / Repeal of the licensing laws / Old man drag / Thousands are

sailing / Body of an American / Lullaby of London / Dirty old town / Bottle of smoke / The sickbed of Cuchulainn / Sally MacLennane / Fairytale of New York / Fiesta / Irish rover.

Dec 05. (7") *Warners; (WEA 400CD)* **FAIRYTALE OF NEW YORK. / THE BATTLE MARCH MEDLEY** [3] [–]
(cd-s) *(WEA 400CD)* – ('A') / ('A'-instrumental).
(cd-s) *(WEA 400DVD)* – ('A') / ('A'-video) / ('A'-Top Of The Pops performance 1987).

SHANE MacGOWAN & THE POPES

SHANE MacGOWAN – vocals / **PAUL McGUINNESS** – guitar / **BERNIE FRANCE** – bass / **DANNY POPE** – drums / **TOM NcMANAMON** – banjo

Z.T.T. Warners

Sep 94. (7"/c-s/cd-s) *(ZANG 57/+C/CD)* **THE CHURCH OF THE HOLY SPOOK. / RAKE AT THE GATES OF HELL** [74] [–]
(cd-s+=) *(ZANG 57CDX)* – King of the bop / Nancy Whiskey.

Oct 94. (c-s) *(ZANG 56C)* **THAT WOMAN'S GOT ME DRINKING / HER FATHER DIDN'T LIKE ME ANYWAY** [34] [–]
(12"+=/cd-s+=) *(ZANG 56 T/CD)* – Roddy McCorley / Minstrel boy.

Oct 94. (cd/c/lp) *(4509 98104-2/-4/-1)* <45821> **THE SNAKE** [37] Jan95 [ ]
– The church of the holy spook / That woman's got me drinking / The song with no name / Aisling / I'll be your handbag / Her father didn't like me anyway / A Mexican funeral in Paris / The snake with the eyes of Garnet / Donegal express / Victoria / The rising of the moon / Bring down the lamp. *(re-iss. Jun95 cd/c; 0630 10402-2/-4)* – Haunted (with SINEAD O'CONNOR) / You're the one (with MAIRE BRENNAN) / Cracklin' Rosie / Bring down the lamp. *(cd re-iss. Nov98; MACG 004CD)*

Dec 94. (c-s) *(ZANG 60C)* **THE SONG WITH NO NAME / NANCY WHISKEY** [ ] [–]
(12"+=/cd-s+=) *(ZANG 60 T/CD)* – Cracklin' Rosie.

Apr 95. (c-s; SHANE MacGOWAN & SINEAD O'CONNOR) *(ZANG 65C)* **HAUNTED. / THE SONG WITH NO NAME** [30] [–]
(cd-s+=) *(ZANG 65CD)* – Bring down the lamp / Cracklin' Rosie.

Jun 95. (c-s; SHANE MacGOWAN & MAIRE BRENNAN) *(ZANG 68C)* **YOU'RE THE ONE / AISLING** [ ] [–]
(cd-s) *(ZANG 68CD)* – Victoria.

Apr 96. (c-s; SHANE MacGOWAN) *(ZANG 79C)* **MY WAY / SONG WITH NO NAME** [29] [–]
(cd-s+=) *(ZANG 79CD)* – Aisling / My way (your way).

— **LUCKY DOWLING** – bass; repl. BERNIE

— added **KIERAN KIELY** – accordions, whistles, vocals + **JOHN MYERS** – fiddle, whistle, guitar

Oct 97. (cd-s) *(MACG 001CD)* **LONESOME HIGHWAY /** [ ] [–]

Oct 97. (cd/c) *(MACG 002 CD/C)* **THE CROCK OF GOLD** [59] [–]
– Paddy rolling stone / Rock'n'roll Paddy / Paddy public enemy No.1 / Back in County Hell / Lonesome highway / Come to the bower / Ceilidh cowboy / More pricks than kicks / Truck drivin' man / Joey's in America / B&I ferry / Mother mo chroi / Spanish lady / St. John of gods / Skipping rhymes / Maclennan / Wanderin' star.

Mar 98. (cd-s) *(MACG 003CD)* **ROCK'N'ROLL PADDY / SHE MOVES THROUGH THE FAIR** [ ] [–]

Jan 02. (cd) *(ZTT 178CD)* <18036> **THE RARE OUL' STUFF** [ ] Feb 02 [ ]
– You're the one / The song with no name / Nancy Whiskey / Roddy McCorley / Rock'n'roll Paddy / Christmas lullaby / Danny boy / Monstrel boy / Rake at the gates of Hell / Victoria / Donegal express / Ceilidh cowboy / Paddy rolling stone / Paddy public enemy No.1 / Back in the county hell / The snakes with eyes of garnet / Cracklin' Rosie / Aisling / Spanish lady / Come to the bower / St. John of gods.

Eagle Red Ink

Feb 02. (cd; as SHANE MacGOWAN'S POPES) *(EAGCD 192)* <57068> **ACROSS THE BROAD ATLANTIC: LIVE ON PADDY'S DAY – NEW YORK – DUBLIN (live)** [ ] [ ]
– If I should fall from grace with God / Rock & roll Paddy / Nancy Whiskey / A rainy night in Soho / Poor Paddy works on the railway / The broad majestic Shannon / Popes' instrumental:- My Ballyvourney love – The limpin' general – Bag of chips / Dirty old town / Mother MO Chroi / Body of an American / Granuaille / More pricks than kicks / Aisling / A pair of brown eyes / Streams of whiskey / Lonesome highway / Angel of death / Sick bed of Cuchulainn / The Irish rover / Fairytale of New York.

the POLICE

Formed: London, England . . .early 1977 by drummer STEWART COPELAND, vocalist/bassist STING (b. GORDON SUMNER) and guitarist HENRY PADOVANI. In May '77, this line-up released a debut punk single, 'FALL OUT', for Miles Copeland's (brother of STEWART) indie label, 'Illegal'. Immediately after the record's release, they were invited by GONG member MIKE HOWLETT to join veteran guitarist ANDY SUMMERS in live band, STRONTIUM 90. Following PADOVANI's departure in August of the same year (to form the brilliantly monikered FLYING PADOVANI BROTHERS), SUMMERS took his place in The POLICE, this modified line-up initially sessioning on EBERHARD SCHOENER's 'Video Flashback' album. Like all the best 'punk' bands of the time, the POLICE weren't actually punk at all, the members all coming from some kind of 'muso' background, SUMMERS having noodled for the likes of KEVIN AYERS and KEVIN COYNE while COPELAND had drummed for prog-rock merchants, CURVED AIR and STING had plucked his bass for the jazzy LAST EXIT. Not exactly the best credentials for the 'anyone can play' ethos of punk but the POLICE succeeded by infusing their complex reggae-tinged pop/rock with insidiously catchy hooks and radio friendly melodies while keeping most of their songs down to an acceptable post-hippy playing time. They also cultivated a trendy bleached haired image, sporting their new blonde barnets on a Wrigley's Spearmint Gum TV ad. After supporting SPIRIT of all people, the group signed to 'A&M', releasing their debut single, 'ROXANNE', soon after. Initially, this paeon to a lady of the night failed to score a chart position, although it was subsequently released a year later, reaching No.12 in the UK charts. The follow-up, 'CAN'T STAND LOSING YOU', was a minor chart hit as was the debut album, 'OUTLANDOS D'AMOUR' (1978). An impressive collection with a strong rhythmic thrust and a few token nods to punk, the album was finally given its due when it was resurrected the following year, reaching the Top 10 in the Spring of '79. Later that summer the POLICE captured their first No.1 single with the power pop of the 'MESSAGE IN A BOTTLE' single, swiftly followed by a No.1 album in 'REGATTA DE BLANC' (aka WHITE REGGAE; 1979). Again the record illustrated the band's masterful grasp of dynamics, using time changes to enhance rather than detract from the pop appeal of their songs. From the space reggae of 'WALKING ON THE MOON' to the melodic lament of 'THE BED'S TOO BIG WITHOUT YOU', The POLICE were continually charting new musical territory. It was only a matter of time before the group broke through worldwide, including the lucrative American market. That break came with the 'ZENYATTA MONDATTA' (1980) album and its attendant hits, 'DON'T STAND SO CLOSE TO ME' and the lyrically rhythmic genius of 'DE DO DO DO, DE DA DA DA'. By the release of 'GHOSTS IN THE MACHINE' (1981), The POLICE were now a world beating act, once more delivering the goods with a more instrumentally diverse opus best sampled on the exotically effervescent 'EVERY LITTLE THING SHE DOES IS MAGIC'. STING's lyrics were also taking on a new depth, notably on 'INVISIBLE SUN', wherein the singer commented on the strife-torn Northern Ireland. Bearing in mind that STING's songs formed the bulk of the band's output – leading to simmering discontentment in the ranks – it's surprising how well the trio gel on their final release and undisputed masterpiece, 'SYNCHRONICITY' (1983). The brooding atmospherics of 'EVERY BREATH YOU TAKE' (a massive worldwide No.1) formed the album's centrepiece while the melancholy 'WRAPPED AROUND YOUR FINGER' and the pummelling 'SYNCHRONICITY 2' illustrated the band's ability to craft a consistently satisfying but varied musical palate. The aforementioned tensions ultimately led to the band's demise, although an official announcement wasn't made until 1986, the trio working on solo projects in the meantime. Predictably, STING was the only member who went on to any commercial success – massive success in the event – while COPELAND and SUMMERS lingered in relative obscurity. The former had already released a string of 7"s under the KLARK KENT moniker at the turn of the decade as well as scoring the soundtrack for cult film 'Rumblefish' (featuring vocals of ex-WALL OF VOODOO man, STAN RIDGWAY). During the mid-80's, he went on to make an album of African music, 'THE RHYTHMATIST' (1985) for 'A&M' and a one-off 7" with ADAM ANT, 'OUT OF BOUNDS'. More recently, COPELAND has scored various films including 'Talk Radio', 'Wall Street' and 'First Power', going on to form ANIMAL LOGIC with bassist STANLEY CLARKE and vocalist DEBORAH HOLLAND. SUMMERS, meanwhile, continued his collaboration with ROBERT FRIPP (they'd released the 'I ADVANCE MASKED' album in 1982) on 'BEWITCHED' (1984) before going on to release a series of eclectic solo albums.

Album rating: OUTLANDOS D'AMOUR (*8) / REGATTA DE BLANC (*7) / ZENYATTA MONDATTA (*7) / GHOST IN THE MACHINE (*7) / SYNCHRONICITY (*8) / EVERY BREATH YOU TAKE – THE SINGLES compilation (*9) / GREATEST HITS compilation (*9) / LIVE! collection (*4)

STING (b. GORDON SUMNER, 2 Oct'51, Wallsend, England) – vocals, bass (ex-LAST EXIT) / **HENRY PADOVANI** (b. Corsica) – guitar, vocals / **STEWART COPELAND** (b.19 Jul'52, Alexandria, Egypt) – drums, vocals (ex-CURVED AIR)

Illegal | not iss.

May 77. (7") *(IL 1)* **FALL OUT. / NOTHING ACHIEVING** [ ] [–]
(re-act.Dec79 reached UK No.47)

—— **ANDY SUMMERS** (b. ANDREW SOMERS, 31 Dec'42, Blackpool, England) – guitar (ex-KEVIN AYERS, ex-KEVIN COYNE, ex-ERIC BURDON, ex-SOFT MACHINE) soon repl. HENRY (after brief spell as 4-piece) left to form his FLYING PADOVANI BROTHERS

A&M | A&M

Apr 78. (7",12") *(AMS 7348)* **ROXANNE. / PEANUTS** [ ] [–]
(re-iss. Apr79; same) – hit UK No.12

Aug 78. (7",7"sha-pic-d,7"in most colours) *(AMS 7381)* **CAN'T STAND LOSING YOU. / DEAD END JOB** [42] [–]
(re-iss. Jun79; same) – hit UK No.2

Oct 78. (lp/blue-lp/c) *(AMLH/AMLN/CAM 68502)* <4753> **OUTLANDOS D'AMOUR** [ ] Feb79 [23]
– Next to you / So lonely / Roxanne / Hole in my life / Peanuts / Can't stand losing you / Truth hits everybody / Born in the 50's / Be my girl – Sally / Masoko tanga. *(resurrected Apr79 made No.6) (cd-iss. Mar89; CDA 68502) (re-iss. Oct92 cd/c; CD/C MID 126)*

Oct 78. (7") *(AMS 7402)* **SO LONELY. / NO TIME THIS TIME** [ ] [ ]
(re-dist.Feb80; same) – hit UK No.6

Jan 79. (7") <2096> **ROXANNE. / DEAD END JOB** [–] [32]

Apr 79. (7") <2147> **CAN'T STAND LOSING YOU. / NO TIME THIS TIME** [–] [ ]

Sep 79. (7",7"green,7"sha-pic-d) *(AMS 7474)* <2190> **MESSAGE IN A BOTTLE. / LANDLORD** [1] Nov79 [74]

Oct 79. (lp/c) *(AMLH/CAM 64792)* <4792> **REGGATTA DE BLANC** [1] [25]
– Message in a bottle / Reggata de blanc / It's alright for you / Bring on the night / Deathwish / Walking on the Moon / On any other day / The bed's too big without you / Contact / Does everyone stare / No time this time. *(cd-iss. Mar89; CDA 64792) (re-iss. Oct92 cd/c; CD/C MID 127)*

Nov 79. (7"/12") *(AMS/+P 7494)* **WALKING ON THE MOON. / VISIONS OF THE NIGHT** [1] [–]

Jan 80. (7") **BRING ON THE NIGHT. / VISIONS OF THE NIGHT** [–] [ ]

Sep 80. (7"/7"sha-pic-d) *(AMS/+P 7564)* **DON'T STAND SO CLOSE TO ME. / FRIENDS** [1] [–]

Oct 80. (lp/c) *(AMLH/CAM 64831)* <4831> **ZENYATTA MONDATTA** [1] [5]
– Don't stand so close to me / Driven to tears / When the world is running down, you make the best of what's still around / Canary in a coalmine / Voices in my head / Bombs away / De do do do, de da da da / Behind my camel / Man in a suitcase / Shadows in the rain / The other way of stopping. *(cd-iss. Sep86; CDA 64831)*

Oct 80. (7") <2275> **DE DO DO DO, DE DA DA DA. / FRIENDS** [–] [10]

Dec 80. (7"/7"pic-d) *(AMS/+P 7578)* **DE DO DO DO, DE DA DA DA. / A SERMON** [5] [–]

Feb 81. (7") <2301> **DON'T STAND SO CLOSE TO ME. / A SERMON** [–] [10]

Sep 81. (7") *(AMS 8164)* **INVISIBLE SUN. / SHAMELLE** [2] [–]

Sep 81. (7") <2371> **EVERY LITTLE THING SHE DOES IS MAGIC. / SHAMBELLE** [–] [3]

Oct 81. (lp/c) *(AMLK/CKM 63730)* <3730> **GHOST IN THE MACHINE** [1] [2]
– Spirits in the material world / Every little thing she does is magic / Invisible sun / Hungry for love / emolition man / Too much information / Rehumanize yourself / One world (not three) / Omega man / Darkness / Omega man / Secret journey / Darkness. *(cd-iss. 1983; CDA 63730)*

Oct 81. (7"/7"pic-d) *(AMS/+P 8174)* **EVERY LITTLE THING SHE DOES IS MAGIC. / FLEXIBLE STRATEGIES** [1] [–]

Dec 81. (7") *(AMS 8194)* **SPIRITS IN THE MATERIAL WORLD. / LOW LIFE** [12] [–]

Jan 82. (7") <2390> **SPIRITS IN THE MATERIAL WORLD. / FLEXIBLE STRATEGIES** [–] [11]

Apr 82. (7") <2408> **SECRET JOURNEY. / DARKNESS** [–] [46]

May 83. (7"/7"pic-d) *(AM/+SP 117)* <2542> **EVERY BREATH YOU TAKE. / MURDER BY NUMBERS** [1] [1]
(d7"+=) *(AM 117)* – Truth hits everybody / Man in a suitcase.

Jun 83. (lp/c/cd) *(AMLX/CXM/CDA 63735)* <3735> **SYNCHRONICITY** [1] [1]
– Synchronicity / alking in your footsteps / O my God / Mother / Miss Gradenko / Synchronicity II / Every breath you take / King of pain / Wrapped around your finger / Tea in the sahara. *(c+=/cd+=)* – Murder by numbers. *(re-iss. Mar93 cd/c; CD/C MID 186)*

Jul 83. (7"/7"pic-d-x3) *(AM/+P 127)* **WRAPPED AROUND YOUR FINGER. / SOMEONE TO TALK TO** [7] [–]
(12"+=/12"pic-d+=) *(AMX/+P 127)* – Message in a bottle (live) / I burn for you.

Aug 83. (7") <2569> **KING OF PAIN. / SOMEONE TO TALK TO** [–] [3]

Oct 83. (7") *(AM 153)* <2571> **SYNCHRONICITY II. / ONCE UPON A DAYDREAM** [17] [16]

Jan 84. (7"/12") *(AM/+X 176)* **KING OF PAIN. / TEA IN THE SAHARA (live)** [17] [–]

Jan 84. (7") <2614> **WRAPPED AROUND YOUR FINGER. / TEA IN THE SAHARA (live)** [–] [8]

—— Split up although not officially, until 1986. STING, ANDY SUMMERS and STEWART COPELAND

– compilations, etc. –

on 'A&M' unless otherwise mentioned

Jun 80. (6x7"box) *(AMPP 6001)* **SIX PACK** [17] [ ]
– (first 5 – A&M singles re-issued in blue vinyl, plus added 45 below) **THE BED'S TOO BIG WITHOUT YOU. / TRUTH HITS EVERYBODY**

Sep 86. (7"/12") *(AM/+Y 354)* <2879> **DON'T STAND SO CLOSE TO ME '86. / (live version)** [24] [46]

Nov 86. (lp/c/cd) *(EVERY/EVERC/EVECD 1)* <3902> **EVERY BREATH YOU TAKE – THE SINGLES** [1] [7]
– Roxanne / Can't stand losing you / Message in a bottle / Walking on the Moon / Don't stand so close to me '86 / De do do do, de da da da / Every little thing she does is magic / Invisible Sun / Spirits in the material world / Every breath you take / King of pain / Wrapped around your finger. *(c+=/cd+=)* – So lonely. *(re-iss. UK Mar92 hit No.31)*

Nov 86. (7"/12") *(AM/+Y 363)* **ROXANNE '86. / SYNCHRONICITY II** [ ] [–]

Jan 87. (7") **WALKING ON THE MOON. / MESSAGE IN A BOTTLE** [–] [ ]

Apr 88. (3"cd-ep) *(AMCD 905)* **COMPACT HITS** [ ] [–]
– Roxanne / Can't stand losing you / Canary in a coalmine / Bed's too big without you.

Jun 89. (d-c) *(AMC 24103)* **REGATTA DE BLANC / SYNCHRONICITY** [ ] [–]

Oct 92. (cd/c/lp) *(540030-2/-4/-1)* **THE POLICE: GREATEST HITS** (like above) [10] [–]

Oct 93 (4xcd-box) *<0150>* **MESSAGE IN A BOX: THE COMPLETE RECORDINGS** [–] [79]

May 95. (7"sha-pic-d/12") *(581037-7/-1)* **CAN'T STAND LOSING YOU (live). / VOICES IN MY HEAD (mix)** [27] [ ]
(cd-s+=) *(581037-2)* – Roxanne live).
(d12") *(581061-1)* – Voices in my head (8 remixes).

May 95. (d-cd/d-c) *(540222-2/-4)* *<0222>* **THE POLICE LIVE! (live)** 25 86
– Next to you / So lonely / Truth hits everybody / Walking on the Moon / Hole in my life / Fall out / Bring on the night / Message in a bottle / The bed's too big without you / Peanuts / Roxanne / Can't stand losing you / Landlord / Born in the 50's / Be my girl – Sally / Synchronicity I / Synchronicity II / Walking in your footsteps / Message in a bottle / O my God / De do do do, de da da da / Wrapped around your finger / Tea in the Sahara / Spirits in the material world / King of pain / Don't stand so close to me / Every breathe you take / Roxanne / Can't stand losing you / So lonely.

— see also STING (GRD-only) for combined STING & THE POLICE releases

the POLYPHONIC SPREE

Formed: Dallas, Texas, USA ... 2000 by frontman/lyricist TIM DELAUGHTER in a bizarre postscript to the ill-fated TRIPPING DAISY outfit after the death of his bandmate WES BERGGREN. The aforementioned TRIPPING DAISY began in 1991 by DeLAUGHTER, BERGGREN, MARK PIRRO and BRYAN WAKELAND and signing to 'Island', the band debuted with the 'BILL' album in 1994. Sporting a psychedelic punk/hard-rock sound similar to JANE'S ADDICTION (DELAUGHTER's whining vocals a bizarre cross between PERRY FARRELL and LIAM GALLAGHER!), the group soon attracted a growing following on the American alternative scene. With media coverage also gathering strength, the band released a follow-up set, 'i am an ELASTIC FIRECRACKER' (complete with sleevework by deceased artist, Gugliemo Achille Cavellini) in early '96. The record was their most successful to date, scraping into the lower regions of the US Top 100, while the swaggering 'PIRANHA' single made the Top 75. A third album, 'JESUS HITS US LIKE AN ATOM BOMB' (1998), was a slightly disappointing set and sadder still was the untimely death of BERGGREN who o.d'd in 1999. With its twenty or so members (including PIRRO) and DELAUGHTER's loose open-door policy, the Dallas congregation were established when they issued a cassette-only mini-LP 'THE BEGINING STAGES OF . . .' (2000), before playing countless live shows around Texas. The independent label 'Good' issued the set, and, with their white sinuous robes, uplifting dreamy psychedelic gospel and quasi-religious overtones ("Jesus is love", and all that), the collective were soon becoming uber cult. It wasn't long before the British music press got their grubby little hands on the band – after all, they were still filthy with the overt favouritism and lazy handling of certain garage rock groups, it was refreshing to see around 23 robe-wearing happy Texans don the cover of a publication. The group added new material to their already existing mini-album and re-issued it as their debut LP 'THE BEGINNING STAGES OF . . .' (2002). The music it contained – all in sections – was that of strange, breezy psychedelic pop in the vein of MERCURY REV or the FLAMING LIPS, but with the general communal ethos applied by the likes of LAMBCHOP (who'd also boasted quite a line-up). After the clever pop/rock of TRIPPING DAISY, DeLAUGHTER obviously had strong intentions of creating joyful Americana; a sometimes ecstatic blend of gospel, pop and lo-fi with warm instrumentation and DELAUGHTER's cracked vocals floating over the whole thing, the POLYPHONIC SPREE were a ray of sunshine that blasted into the often bleak world of American alt-rock. Slightly less shiny-happy-people and more you've-got-a-friend, 'TOGETHER WE'RE HEAVY' (2004) saw the robed revival continue while making at least some concession to life's darker side. The phantoms of PINK FLOYD and post-GABRIEL GENESIS were haunting the SPREE's sonic rafters alongside longtime 'REV/'LIPS residents; "You've gotta be strong, you've gotta be two thousand places at once", counselled DELAUGHTER, and he could have been referring to the denseness of the songs' structures, interlocking in organised chaos and delicious harmony. The man subsequently turned his talents to film, composing the soundtrack to Mike Mills' high school comedy, 'THUMBSUCKER' (2005), a set which also included songs by the late ELLIOTT SMITH.

• **Covered:** HAPPY XMAS (WAR IS OVER) (John & Yoko).

Album rating: BILL (*5) / i am an ELASTIC FIRECRACKER (*8) / JESUS HITS US LIKE AN ATOM BOMB (*5) / Polyphonic Spree: THE BEGINNING STAGES OF . . . (*8) / TOGETHER WE'RE HEAVY (*7) / THUMBSUCKER soundtrack w/ Various (*8)

TRIPPING DAISY

TIM DELAUGHTER – vocals, guitar / **WES BERGGREN** – guitar / **MARK PIRRO** – bass / **BRYAN WAKELAND** – drums, percussion

Island Red Dragon St.

Jul 94. (cd/c/lp) *(CIRD/IRCT/IRLP 1001)* *<70392>* **BILL** Nov92
– My umbrella / One through four / Lost and found / Change of mind / On the ground / The morning / Blown away / Brown-eyed pickle boy / Miles and miles of pain / Triangle. *<cd re-iss. 1997 on 'Polygram'; 555002>*

Jul 94. (12"ep/cd-ep) *(12IR/CIRD 102)* **MY UMBRELLA / IT'S SAFE, IT'S SOCIAL (live). / GET IT ON (live) / WE'RE ONLY GONNA DIE (live)** –

Island Island

Feb 96. (c-s/7") *(C+/IS 636)* **I GOT A GIRL. / MARGARITA TROPENZANDO** –
(12"+=/cd-s+=) *(12IS/CID 636)* – Cause tomb shop / Noose.

Feb 96. (cd/lp) *(CIRD/IRLP 1004)* *<314-524 112-2>* **i am an ELASTIC FIRECRACKER** Aug95 95
– Rocket pop / Bang / I got a girl / Piranha / Motivation / Same dress new day / Trip along / Raindrop / Step behind / Noose / Prick / High.

Mar 96. (7") *(IS 638)* **PIRANHA. / CREATURE** 72 –
(12"+=/cd-s+=) *(12IS/CID 638)* – High.

1997. (m-cd) *<531095>* **TIME CAPSULE** –
– Rise / Cause tomb shop / Creature / Boobie the clown / I'm a fish / Blue train.

— added **ERIC DREW FELDMAN** – producer, multi (ex-CAPTAIN BEEFHEART, ex-FRANK BLACK)

Jul 98. (cd) *<(524518-2)>* **JESUS HITS US LIKE AN ATOM BOMB**
– Field day jitters / Waited a light year / Sonic bloom / Bandaids for Mire / Mechanical breakdown / Your socks have no name / Geeareohdoubleyou / New plains medicine / Our drive to the sun – Can a man mark / Human contact / Pillar / 8 ladies / About the movies / Tiny men / Indian poker (pt.2 & 3).

not iss. Good

1999. (cd-s) *<GR 002>* **BEDHEAD. / (other by Centro-Matic)** –

— when WES died of a drug o.d. in 1999, TIM, MARK and BRYAN formed . . .

the POLYPHONIC SPREE

TIM DELAUGHTER – vocals / **MARK PIRRO** – bass / **BRYAN WAKELAND** – drums / **RYAN FITZGERALD** – guitar / **EVAN HISEY** – organ / **TOBY HALBROOKS** – theremin, electronics, whistle / **MARK McKEEVER** – keyboards, trumpet / **JEFF BOUCK** – percussion / **MIKE MELENDI** – percussion / **ANDREW TINKER** – french horn / **AUDREY EASLEY** – flute, piccolo / **JAMES REIMER** – trombone / **RICK RASURA** – classic harp / **LOGAN REESE** – trumpet / **RICK NELSON** – violin / **JENNIFER JOBE** – vocals / **MICHAEL TURNER** + **ROY IVY** + **JOHN VINEYARD** + **CHRISTY STEWART** + **JENNIE KELLY** + **KELLY REPKA** + **JESSICA JORDAN** + **JULIE DOYLE** – backing vocals

Good Good

Jul 02. (cd) *<(GR 004CD)>* **THE BEGINNING STAGES OF . . .** Jun02
– Section 1 (Have a day – Celebratory) / Section 2 (It's the sun) / Section 3 (Days like this keep me warm) / Section 4 (La la) / / Section 5 (Middle of the day) / Section 6 (Hanging around the day – part one) / Section 7 (Hanging around the day – part two) / Section 8 (Soldier girl) / Section 9 (Light and day – Reach for the sun) / Section 10 (A long day).

Fierce Panda — not iss.

Aug 02. (cd-s) *(NING 123CD)* **SOLDIER GIRL / SUN (section 2) / SOLDIER GIRL (string version) / SOLDIER GIRL (radio) / SOLDIER GIRL (section 8)** [ ] [–]

679 Recordings — not iss.

Sep 02. (cd/lp; re-) *(5046 60918-2/-2)* **THE BEGINNING STAGES OF . . .** [ ] [–]

Oct 02. (7") *(679L 012)* **HANGING AROUND. / FIVE YEARS** [39] [–]
(cd-s+=) *(679L 012CD1)* – ('A'version) / ('A'-Video).
(cd-s) *(679L 012CD2)* – ('A'live) / What will be will be (live) / Soldier girl (live).

— now with **JOE BUTCHER** – sho-bud pedal steel, synths

Feb 03. (12") *(679L 015T2)* **LIGHT AND DAY. / SOLDIER GIRL (instrumental) / THE MARCH (symphonic version)** [40] [–]
(cd-s+=) *(679L 015CD1)* – ('A'-video).
(cd-s) *(679L 015CD2)* – ('A'side) / Have a day / Days like this keep me warm / ('A'-video).

Jun 03. (cd w/dvd+=; re-) *(2564 60352-5)* **THE BEGINNING STAGES OF . . .** [70] [–]
– (videos).

Jul 03. (12"/cd-s) *(679L 014 X/CD)* **SOLDIER GIRL. / IT'S THE SUN (new version) / SOLDIER GIRL (Death In Vegas remix)** [26] [–]

Good — Hollywood

Jul 04. (cd/d-lp) *(POLY CD/LP 1)* <2061 62423-2> **TOGETHER WE'RE HEAVY** [61] [ ]
– A long day continues – We sound amazed / Hold me now / Diamonds – Devotion to majesty / Two thousand places / Ensure your reservation / One man show / Suitcase calling / Everything starts at the seam / When the food becomes a king / Together we're heavy. *<US cd w/dvd+=; 2061 62455-2>* – (videos).

Jul 04. (cd-s) *(CDPOLY 1)* **HOLD ME NOW / (version) / WORKING OUT THE KINKS** [72] [–]

Nov 04. (7") *(7POLY 2)* **TWO THOUSAND PLACES. / THE BEST PART** [ ] [–]
(cd-s+=) *(CDPOLY 2)* – Happy Xmas (war is over).

Jul 05. (7") *(BMR 053-7)* **THE MARCH. / (flip by Grandaddy)** [ ] [–]
(above issued on 'Birdman')

Hollywood — Hollywood

Oct 05. (cd) *(342742-2)* <2061 62542-2> **THUMBSUCKER** (soundtrack) [ ] Sep05 [ ]
– The crash / Scream & shout / Slow halls / What would you let go / Empty rooms / Wonderful for you / The Rebecca fantasy / Thirteen (*) / Pink trash dream / The green lights / Debate montage / Trouble (*) / Skinny dip / Sourness makes it right / Some of the parts / Matt Schraam / Let's get lost (*) / Justin's hypnosis / The call of the wild / Wait and see / Move away and shine / Acceptance / Move away and shine – In A Dream version.

— note:- tracks * by ELLIOTT SMITH

Iggy POP

Born: JAMES JEWEL OSTERBERG, 21 Apr'47, Ypsilanti, Michigan, USA. The son of an English father and American mother, he joined The IGUANAS as a drummer in 1964. They issued a cover of Bo Diddley's 'MONA', which was limited to 1,000 copies sold at gigs. The following year, he became IGGY POP and joined The PRIME MOVERS with bassist RON ASHETON, although they folded, IGGY subsequently moving to Chicago. In 1967, he returned to Michigan and formed The (PSYCHEDELIC) STOOGES with RON and his drummer brother SCOTT. They were soon joined by DAVE ALEXANDER, IGGY making his celluloid debut in the avant-garde film, 'Francois De Moniere' with girlfriend NICO. In 1968, the band gigged constantly, on one occasion IGGY being charged with indecent exposure. The following year, A&R man Danny Fields, while looking to sign MC5, instead signed The STOOGES to 'Elektra', furnishing them with a $25,000 advance. Their eponymous debut (produced by JOHN CALE – another VELVET UNDERGROUND connection), later proved to be way ahead of its time. Tracks such as 'NO FUN', '1969' and 'I WANNA BE YOUR DOG', were howling proto-punk, garage classics, later covered by The SEX PISTOLS, SISTERS OF MERCY and SID VICIOUS! respectively. The album just failed to secure a Top 100 placing, the second album faring even worse commercially, although it was hailed by the more discerning critics of the day as a seminal work. From the primal nihilism of 'DIRT', to the psychedelic kiss-off, 'I FEEL ALRIGHT (1970)', it seemed, to The STOOGES at least, as if flower-power had never happened. They were subsequently dropped by their label, following drug-related problems and dissension in the ranks. IGGY moved to Florida, becoming a greenkeeper while taking up golf more seriously, a healthier pastime than his penchant for self-mutilation. In 1972, he had a chance meeting with DAVID BOWIE and manager TONY DeFRIES, who persuaded IGGY to reform his STOOGES and sign a MainMan management deal, this in turn leading to a 'C.B.S.' contract. After his/their flawed classic, 'RAW POWER' (not one of BOWIE's best productions), they folded again, citing drugs as the cause. It was, however, even more of an embryonic punk record, the amphetamine rush of 'SEARCH AND DESTROY' highly influential on the "blank generation" that would trade-in their STEELY DAN albums for anything with two chords and a sneering vocal. In 1975, IGGY checked in to a psychiatric institute, weaning himself off heroin. His only true friend, BOWIE, who regularly visited him in hospital, invited him to appear on his 'LOW' album. He signed to 'R.C.A.' (home of BOWIE) in 1977, issuing the BOWIE-produced debut solo album, 'THE IDIOT', which, due to the recent "new wave" explosion, broke him into the UK Top 30 and US Top 75. It contained the first BOWIE/POP collaboration, 'CHINA GIRL', later a smash hit for BOWIE. His second solo release, 'LUST FOR LIFE' (also produced by BOWIE in '77), was another gem, again deservedly reaching the UK Top 30 (the title track was later resurrected in 1996 after appearing on the soundtrack to the cult Scottish movie, 'Trainspotting'). In 1979, IGGY moved to 'Arista' records, shifting through various infamous personnel, although his commercial appeal was on the wane. The first half of the 80's saw IGGY desperately trying to carve out a successful solo career while combating his continuing drug problems. Albums such as, 'SOLDIER' (1980), 'PARTY' (1981) and 'ZOMBIE BIRDHOUSE' (1982) marking the nadir of POP's chequered career. Finally teaming up again with BOWIE for 1986's 'BLAH BLAH BLAH', the proclaimed "Godfather Of Punk" at last gained some belated recognition, his revival of a 1957 Johnny O'Keefe hit, 'REAL WILD CHILD', giving IGGY his first Top 10 hit (UK). Still with 'A&M' records and adding ex-SEX PISTOLS guitarist STEVE JONES, he consolidated his recovery with 'INSTINCT' (1988). His new lease of life prompted 'Virgin America' to give IGGY (who had recently taking up acting) a new contract, the 1990 set, 'BRICK BY BRICK' featuring the GN'R talents of SLASH and DUFF McKAGAN. To end the year, IGGY showed his caring side by duetting with former punkette, DEBORAH HARRY, on AIDS benefit single, 'WELL DID YOU EVAH!' (a bigger hit for NANCY Sinatra & LEE Hazlewood in 1971). He resurfaced once again in 1993 with 'AMERICAN CAESAR', a full-length set which contained some of his raunchiest tracks for some time, including 'WILD AMERICA', 'F*****' ALONE' and Richard Berry's 'LOUIE LOUIE'. Busying himself with more film work, he eventually broke his recording silence with an umpteenth album, 'NAUGHTY LITTLE DOGGIE' (1996). Mr. POP was back on song in the Autumn of '99, the album 'AVENUE B' delivering his usual raw power with all the finesse of a man taking a motorcycle ride to Hell. 'NAZI GIRLFRIEND', 'LONG DISTANCE' and even a cover of Johnny Kidd's 'SHAKIN' ALL OVER', all testament to a guy not yet ready to get out his pipe and slippers. Seeing as he's only ever enjoyed fleeting run-ins with the pop charts, it probably didn't bother the IG one iota that 'BEAT 'EM UP' (2001) didn't come within sniffing distance of the Top 40. Still, he'd always got plenty of other subjects to rail against and his next record was no exception. Apart from anything else, 'BEAT 'EM UP' should surely scoop the most gratuitously tasteless sleeve of the year award. In 2003, IGGY brought out yet another dose of high-octane retro-punk via 'SKULL RING', backing courtesy of the TROLLS, the STOOGES, GREEN DAY, SUM 41 and PEACHES. The man's subsequent decision to reunite the STOOGES was one of the best he ever made, finally slaying global audiences with the best music he ever made. 'TELLURIC CHAOS' (2005) was a veritable STOOGE-fest recorded in Japan; for those unlucky not to get one of the hottest tickets of the last few years, this live set wiped the floor with most the of the bootlegs which had been doing the rounds since the band's heyday. Despite the title, 'THE BEST OF IGGY POP' (2005) actually did a decent job of covering his post-'IDIOT' period, when he briefly recorded for 'Arista', while 'A MILLION IN PRIZES: THE ANTHOLOGY' (2005), was a far more comprehensive review of the IG's wild, scattershot career, beginning appropriately enough with '1969' and running right through to his unlikely collaboration with jazz-groovers, MEDESKI, MARTIN & WOOD.

• **IGGY covered;** SOMETHING WILD (John Hiatt) / LIVIN' ON THE EDGE OF THE NIGHT (Rifkin / Rackin) / SEX MACHINE (James Brown). • **Trivia:** In 1987, IGGY made a cameo appearance in the film, 'The Color Of Money'. In 1990, his film & TV work included, 'Cry Baby', 'Shannon's Deal', Tales From The Crypt' & 'Miami Vice'. In 1991, he starred in the opera! 'The Manson Family' and five years later, 'The Crow'.

Album rating: the Stooges: THE STOOGES (*8) / FUN HOUSE (*10) / RAW POWER as Iggy & the Stooges (*7) / METALLIC K.O. (*5) / Iggy Pop: THE IDIOT (*9) / LUST FOR LIFE (*9) / TV EYE (*3) / NEW VALUES (*5) / SOLDIER (*5) / PARTY (*4) / ZOMBIE BIRDHOUSE (*4) / BLAH-BLAH-BLAH (*6) / INSTINCT (*5) / BRICK BY BRICK (*7) / AMERICAN CAESAR (*6) / NAUGHTY LITTLE DOGGIE (*5) / NUDE & RUDE: THE BEST OF IGGY POP compilation (*8) / AVENUE B (*7) / BEAT 'EM UP (*5) / SKULL RING (*6) / THE BEST OF IGGY POP compilation (*5) / A MILLION IN PRIZES: THE ANTHOLOGY double compilation (*8) / Iggy And The Stooges: TELLURIC CHAOS (*6)

the STOOGES

IGGY POP – vocals / **RON ASHETON** (b. RONALD RANKLIN ASHETON JR., 17 Jul'48, Washington, D.C.) – guitar / **DAVE ALEXANDER** (b. DAVID MICHAEL ALEXANDER, 3 Jun'47, Ann Arbor) – bass / **SCOTT ASHETON** (b. SCOTT RANDOLPH ASHETON, 16 Aug'49, Washington) – drums

Elektra Elektra

Sep 69. (lp) *<(EKS 74051)>* **THE STOOGES** Aug69
– 1969 / I wanna be your dog / We will fall / No fun / Real cool time / Ann / Not right / Little doll. *(re-iss. Mar77; K 42032) <US cd-iss. 1988; 74051-2> (cd-iss. Nov93; 7559 60667-2)*

Oct 69. (7") *<EK 45664>* **I WANNA BE YOUR DOG. / 1969** –

— added guests **STEVE MACKAY** – saxophone / **BILL CHEATHAM** – 2nd guitar

Dec 70. (lp) *<(EKS 74071)>* **FUN HOUSE**
– Down on the street / Loose / T.V. eye / Dirt / I feel alright (1970) / Fun house / L.A. blues. *(re-iss. Mar77; K 42051) <US cd-iss. 1988; 74071-2> (cd-iss. Nov93; 7559 60669-2)*

Dec 70. (7") *<EKM 45695>* **I FEEL ALRIGHT (1970). / DOWN ON THE STREET** –

— broke-up in 1972. **IGGY** re-formed the group with **SCOTT** and **RON** (now bass)

IGGY AND THE STOOGES

— **JAMES WILLIAMSON** – guitar repl. DAVE (died 10 Feb'75)

C.B.S. Columbia

Jun 73. (lp) *(CBS 65586) <KC 32111>* **RAW POWER** May73
– Search and destroy / Gimme danger / Hard to beat * / Penetration / Raw power / I need somebody / Shake appeal / Death trip. *(re-iss. May77 on 'CBS-Embassy'; 31464)*, hit UK No.44, *track repl. by – Your pretty face is going to Hell. *(re-iss. Nov81; CBS 32081) <US cd-iss. 1988 on 'Columbia'; > (UK re-iss. May89 on 'Essential' cd/c/lp; ESS CD/MC/LP 005) (cd-iss. all tracks) (re-iss. May94 & Apr97 on 'Columbia' cd/c; 485176-2/-4) (lp re-iss. Jul98 on 'Simply Vinyl'; SVLP 33)*

Jun 73. (7") *<45877>* **SEARCH AND DESTROY. / PENETRATION** –

— added **SCOTT THURSTON** – keyboards (on last 1974 tour, before disbanding) The ASHETONS formed The NEW ORDER (US version), with RON moving on to DESTROY ALL MONSTERS who had three 45's for UK label 'Cherry Red' in the late 70's.

– compilations, others, etc. –

1977. (white-d-lp) *Visa; <IMP 1015>* **METALLIC K.O.** –
– Raw power / Head on / Gimme danger / Rich bitch / Cock in my pocket / Louie Louie. *(originally issued 1976 on French 'Skydog'; SGIS 008) (re-iss. May88 as 'METALLIC KO x 2' on 'Skydog' lp/cd; 62232-1/2) (cd-iss. Sep94; same) (re-iss. Sep96 & May98 on 'Dressed To Kill'; DTKLP 001)*

1977. (7"ep) *Bomp; <EP 113>* **I'M SICK OF YOU** –
– I'm sick of you / Tight pants / Scene of the crime.

1977. (7"ep; by IGGY POP & JAMES WILLIAMSON) *Bomp; <EP 114>* **JESUS LOVES THE STOOGES** –
– Jesus loves the Stooges / Consolation prizes / Johanna. *(re-iss. 10"ep.Nov94;)*

1977. (7") *Siamese; <PM 001>* **I GOT A RIGHT. / GIMME SOME SKIN** –
(UK-iss.Dec95 on 'Bomp'; REVENGE 2)

Feb 78. (lp,green-lp; as IGGY POP with JAMES WILLIAMSON) *Radar; (RAD 2) / Bomp; <BLP 4001>*
KILL CITY Nov77
– Sell your love / Kill city / I got nothin' / Beyond the law / Johanna / Night theme / Night theme reprise / Master charge / No sense of crime / Lucky monkeys / Consolation prizes. *(re-iss. ! on 'Elektra';) (cd-iss. Feb89 on 'Line'; LICD 9.00131) (cd-iss. Jan93;) (re-iss. 10"lp Feb95 on 'Bomp'; BLP 4042-10) (cd-iss. ; BCD 4042)*

Apr 78. (7") *Radar; (ADA 4)* **KILL CITY. / I GOT NOTHIN'** –

1978. (7"ep) *Skydog; (SGIS 12)* **(I GOT) NOTHING** – France –
– I got nothing / Gimme danger / Heavy liquid.

Aug 80. (lp/c) *Elektra; (K/K4 52234) <EF 7095>* **NO FUN**
(1969-70 best of THE STOOGES)

1983. (lp) *Invasion; <E 1019>* **I GOT A RIGHT** –

1987. (lp) *Revenge; (MIG 2)* **I GOT A RIGHT** – France –

1987. (7") *Revenge; (SS 1)* **I GOT A RIGHT. / NO SENSE OF CRIME** – France –

1987. (7") *Revenge; (BF 50) KILL CITY. / I'M SICK OF YOU* – France –

Dec 87. (lp) *Fan Club; (FC 037)* **RUBBER LEGS** – France –
– Rubber legs / Open up and bleed / Johanna / Cock in my pocket / Head on the curb / Cry for me. *(free 7")* – GIMME DANGER (live). / I NEED SOMEBODY (live) *(cd-iss. Apr97 on 'Last Call'; 422248)*

1988. (cd-ep) *Revenge; (CAX 1)* **PURE LUST** – France –
– I got a right / Johanna / Gimme some skin / I got nothing.

1988. (cd-ep) *Revenge; (CAX 2)* **RAW POWER** – France –
– Raw power / Head on the curb / Purple haze / Waiting for the man.

1988. (12"pink-ep,cd-ep) *Revenge; (CAX 3)* **GIMME DANGER** – France –
– Gimme danger / Open up and bleed / Heavy liquid / I got nothing / Dynamite boogie.

1988. (7") *Revenge; (SS 6)* **JOHANNA. / PURPLE HAZE** – France –

Sep 88. (pic-lp; as IGGY & THE STOOGES) *Revenge; (LPMIG 6)* **DEATH TRIP** – France –

May 88. (cd; as IGGY & THE STOOGES) *Revenge; (HTM 16)*
OPEN UP AND BLEED – France –
(re-iss. Feb96 on 'Bomp' cd/lp; BCD/BLP 4051) (cd re-iss. Jul96; 890016)

Dec 88. (lp; as IGGY & THE STOOGES) *Revenge; (MIG 7)*
LIVE AT THE WHISKEY A GO-GO –
(cd-iss. Nov94 & Feb97; 895104F)

Dec 88. (lp; as IGGY & THE STOOGES) *Electric; (190069)*
RAW STOOGES VOL.1 – German –

Dec 88. (lp; as IGGY & THE STOOGES) *Electric; (190070)*
RAW STOOGES VOL.2 – German –

May 92. (cd) *Line; (LICD 921175)* **I'M SICK OF YOU / KILL CITY** –

Jun 94. (cd; IGGY & THE STOOGES) *New Rose; (890028)* **MY GIRL HATES MY HEROIN** –
(re-iss. Feb97 on 'Wrote Music'; 7890028) (re-iss. Sep97 on 'Revenge'; MIG 28)

Jul 94. (cd; IGGY & THE STOOGES) *New Rose; (642100)*
NIGHT OF DESTRUCTION –
(re-iss. as 6xcd-s-box on 'Wind'; WM 375)

Jul 94. (cd; IGGY & THE STOOGES) *New Rose; (642042)* **TILL THE END OF THE NIGHT** –
(re-iss. Apr97; same) (re-iss. Sep97 on 'Revenge'; MIG 42)

Sep 94. (cd; IGGY & THE STOOGES) *New Rose; (642011)* **LIVE 1971 & EARLY LIVE RARITIES (live)** [ ] [–]
(re-iss. Apr97; same)

Sep 94. (cd; IGGY & THE STOOGES) *New Rose; (895002)* **RAW MIXES VOL.1** [ ] [–]

Sep 94. (cd; IGGY & THE STOOGES) *New Rose; (895003)* **RAW MIXES VOL.2** [ ] [–]

Sep 94. (cd; IGGY & THE STOOGES) *New Rose; (895004)* **RAW MIXES VOL.3** [ ] [–]

Feb 95. (10"lp/cd) *Bomp; (BLP/BCD 4049)* **ROUGH POWER** [ ] [–]

— Also in France; **THE STOOGES**(12"ep) / **SHE CREATURES OF HOLLYWOOD HILLS**

Jul 96. (cd) *Revenge; (642050)* **WILD ANIMAL (live 1977)** [ ] [–]

Jul 96. (cd) *Revenge; (893334)* **PARIS HIPPODROME 1977 (live)** [ ] [–]

Jul 96. (cd; as IGGY & THE STOOGES) *Trident; (PILOT 008)* **YOUR PRETTY FACE IS GOING TO HELL** [ ] [–]

Mar 97. (cd; IGGY & THE STOOGES) *Bomp; (BCD 4063)* **YEAR OF THE IGUANA** [ ] [–]

Apr 97. (cd; STOOGES) *Arcade; (301563-2)* **THE COMPLETE RAW MIXES** [ ] [–]

Sep 97. (cd/lp; IGGY & THE STOOGES) *Bomp; (BCD/BLP 4069)* **CALIFORNIA BLEEDING** [ ] [–]

Nov 97. (cd) *King Biscuit; (88003)* **KING BISCUIT FLOWER HOUR** [ ] [–]

Mar 98. (cd) *Snapper; (SMMCD 528)* **LIVE IN L.A. 1973 (live)** [ ] [–]

Apr 98. (cd) *King Biscuit; (KBFHCD 001)* **KING BISCUIT PRESENTS . . .** [ ] [–]

May 88. (12"ep; IGGY & THE STOOGES) *Revenge; (CAX 8MAXI)* **I GOT NOTHING. / SEARCH AND DESTROY / COCK IN MY POCKET** [ ] [–]

Jun 98. (lp; IGGY & THE STOOGES) *Get Back; (GET 33LP)* **RUBBER** [ ] [–]

Nov 99. (7"pic-d; as IGGY & THE STOOGES) *Munster; (MR 7125)* **I GOT NOTHING. /** [ ] [ ]

IGGY POP

— had already gone solo, augmented by **DAVID BOWIE** – producer, keyboards / **RICKY GARDINER** – guitar / **TONY SALES** – bass / **HUNT SALES** – drums (latter 2; ex-TODD RUNDGREN) / guest **CARLOS ALOMAR** – guitar

R.C.A. R.C.A.

Feb 77. (7") *<10989>* **SISTER MIDNIGHT. / BABY** [–] [ ]

Mar 77. (lp/c) *(PL/PK 12275) <2275>* **THE IDIOT** [30] [72]
– Sister midnight / Nightclubbing / Fun time / Baby / China girl / Dum dum boys / Tiny girls / Mass production. *(re-iss. Apr90 on 'Virgin' lp/c/cd; OVED/OVEDC/CDOVD 277)*

May 77. (7") *(PB 9093)* **CHINA GIRL. / BABY** [ ] [ ]

— **STACEY HEYDON** – guitar / **SCOTT THURSTON** – keyboards repl. BOWIE + ALOMAR

Sep 77. (lp/c) *(PL/PK 12488) <2488>* **LUST FOR LIFE** [28] [ ]
– Lust for life / Sixteen / Some weird sin / The passenger / Tonight / Success / Turn blue / Neighbourhood threat / Fall in love with me. *(re-iss. 1984 lp/c; NL/NK 82488) (re-iss. Apr90 on 'Virgin' lp/c/cd; OVED/OVEDC/CDOVD 278) (lp re-iss. Nov97 on 'Virgin'; LPCENT 40)*

Oct 77. (7") *(PB 9160)* **SUCCESS. / THE PASSENGER** [ ] [ ]

— **IGGY** retained **THURSTON**, and recruited **SCOTT ASHETON** – drums / **FRED 'SONIC' SMITH** – guitar (ex-MC5) / **GARY RAMUSSEN** – bass (The SALES brothers later to BOWIE's TIN MACHINE)

Apr 78. (7") *(PB 9213)* **I GOT A RIGHT (live). / SIXTEEN (live)** [ ] [ ]

May 78. (lp/c) *(PL/PK 12796)* **TV EYE (live 1977)** [ ] [ ]
– T.V. eye / Funtime / Sixteen / I got a right / Lust for life / Dirt / Nightclubbing / I wanna be your dog. *(cd-iss. Jul94 on 'Virgin'; CDOVD 448)*

— **IGGY / THURSTON** now with **JAMES WILLIAMSON** – guitar, producer / **JACKIE CLARKE** – bass (ex-IKE & TINA TURNER) / **KLAUS KREUGER** – drums (ex-TANGERINE DREAM) / **JOHN HORDEN** – saxophone

Arista Arista

Apr 79. (lp/c) *(SPART/TC-SPART 1092) <4237>* **NEW VALUES** [60] [ ]
– Tell me a story / New values / Girls / I'm bored / Don't look down / The endless sea / Five foot one / How do ya fix a broken part / Angel / Curiosity / African man / Billy is a runaway. *(re-iss. Mar87; 1201144) (re-iss. Oct90 cd/lp; 260/210 997)*

May 79. (7") *(ARIST 255) <0438>* **I'M BORED. / AFRICAN MAN** [ ] [ ]

Jul 79. (7"/7"pic-d) *(ARIP/+D 274)* **FIVE FOOT ONE. / PRETTY FLAMINGO** [ ] [–]

— **IGGY / KREUGER** recruited **IVAN KRAL** – guitar (ex-PATTI SMITH) / **PAT MORAN** – guitar / **GLEN MATLOCK** – bass (ex-SEX PISTOLS, ex-RICH KIDS) / **BARRY ANDREWS** – keyboards (ex-XTC, ex-LEAGUE OF GENTLEMEN) (THURSTON formed The MOTELS)

Jan 80. (lp/c) *(SPART/TC-SPART 1117) <4259>* **SOLDIER** [62] [ ]
– Knockin' 'em down (in the city) / I'm a conservative / I snub you / Get up and get out / Ambition / Take care of me / I need more / Loco mosquito / Mr. Dynamite / Play it safe / Dog food. *<US re-iss. Oct87; 201160> (cd-iss. Apr91; 251 160)*

Jan 80. (7") *(ARIST 327)* **LOCO MOSQUITO. / TAKE CARE OF ME** [ ] [–]

— **IGGY / KRAL** now with **ROB DuPREY** – guitar / **MICHAEL PAGE** – bass / **DOUGLAS BROWNE** – drums (BARRY ANDREWS formed SHRIEKBACK)

May 81. (7") *(ARIST 407)* **BANG BANG. / SEA OF LOVE** [ ] [–]

Jun 81. (lp/c) *(SPART/TC-SPART 1158) <9572>* **PARTY** [ ] [ ]
– Pleasure / Rock and roll party / Eggs on plate / Sincerity / Houston is hot tonight / Pumpin' for Jill / Happy man / Bang bang / Sea of love / Time won't let me. *(re-iss. Jan87 lp/c; 203/403 806) (cd-iss. Sep89 on 'R.C.A.'; 253 806)*

— **IGGY / DuPREY** found new people **CHRIS STEIN** – guitar, producer (ex-BLONDIE) / **CLEM BURKE** – drums (ex-BLONDIE)

Animal-Chrysalis Animal

Aug 82. (7") *(CHFLY 2634)* **RUN LIKE A VILLAIN. / PLATONIC** [ ] [ ]

Sep 82. (lp/c) *(CHR/ZCHR 1399) <APE 6000>* **ZOMBIE BIRDHOUSE** [ ] [ ]
– Run like a villain / The villagers / Angry hills / Life of work / The ballad of Cookie McBride / Ordinary bummer / Eat to be eaten / Bulldozer / Platonic / The horse song / Watching the news / Street crazies.

— In 1984, he sang the title song on Alex Cox's movie 'REPO MAN'. For the same director, he appeared in the 1985 film 'SID & NANCY' about SID VICIOUS.

— **IGGY** now with **ERDAL KIZILCAY** – drums, bass, synthesizers / **KEVIN ARMSTRONG** – guitar / **BOWIE + STEVE JONES** (guest writers)

A&M A&M

Sep 86. (7"/12") *(AM/+Y 358) <2874>* **CRY FOR LOVE. / WINNERS & LOSERS** [ ] [ ]

Oct 86. (lp/c/cd) *<(AMA/AMC/CDA 5145)>* **BLAH-BLAH-BLAH** [43] [75]
– Real wild child (wild one) / Baby, it can't fail / Shades / Fire girl / Isolation / Cry for love / Blah-blah-blah / Hideaway / Winners and losers. *(cd+=)* – Little Miss Emperor. *(cd re-iss. 1989; 395 145-2) (re-iss. Jun91 cd/c; CD/C+/MID 159)*

Nov 86. (7"/12") *(AM/+Y 368) <2909>* **REAL WILD CHILD (WILD ONE). / LITTLE MISS EMPEROR** [10] [ ]

Feb 87. (7") *(AM 374)* **SHADES. / BABY IT CAN'T FAIL** [ ] [ ]
(12"+=) *(AMY 374)* – Cry for love.

Apr 87. (7"/12") *(AM/+Y 392)* **FIRE GIRL. / BLAH-BLAH-BLAH (live)** [ ] [ ]

Jun 87. (7") *(AM 397)* **ISOLATION. / HIDEAWAY** [ ] [ ]
(12"+=) *(AMY 397)* – Fire girl (remix).

— **IGGY** now with **STEVE JONES** – guitar / **PAUL GARRISTO** – drums (ex-PSYCHEDELIC FURS) / **SEAMUS BEAGHEN** – keyboards / **LEIGH FOXX** – bass

Jul 88. (lp/c/cd) *<(AMA/AMC/ADA 5198)>* **INSTINCT** [61] [ ]
– Cold metal / High on you / Strong girl / Tom tom / Easy rider / Power & freedom / Lowdown / Tuff baby / Squarehead.

Aug 88. (7") *(AM 452)* **COLD METAL. / INSTINCT** [ ] [ ]
(12"+=/12"pic-d+=) *(AM Y/P 452)* – Tuff baby.

Nov 88. (7") *(AM 475)* **HIGH ON YOU. / SQUAREHEAD** [ ] [ ]
(12"+=) *(AMY 475)* – Tuff baby (remix).

— **ALVIN GIBBS** – guitar (ex-UK SUBS) repl. STEVE JONES (continued solo) / **ANDY McCOY** – bass (ex-HANOI ROCKS) repl. FOXX (to DEBORAH HARRY)

Nov 88. (lp/c/cd) **LIVE AT THE CHANNEL (live 17.9.88)** [–] [ ]
– Instinct / Kill city / 1969 / Penetration / Power & freedom / Your pretty face / High on you / 5 foot 1 / Johanna / Easy rider / Tuff baby / 1970 / Search & destroy / Squarehead / No fun / I wanna be your dog. *(UK-iss.May94 on 'New Rose'; 642005) (re-iss. cd Sep97 on 'Revenge'; MIG 40-41)*

— now with **SLASH** – guitar / **DUFF McKAGAN** – bass (both of GUNS N' ROSES) / **KENNY ARONOFF** – drums

Virgin America Virgin America

Jan 90. (7"/c-s) *(VUS/+C 18) <VSC 1228>* **LIVIN' ON THE EDGE OF THE NIGHT. / THE PASSENGER** [51] [ ]
(12"+=/12"pic-d+=/cd-s+=) *(VUS T/TE/CD 18)* – Nightclubbing / China girl.

Jun 90. (7"/c-s) *(VUS/+C 22)* **HOME. / LUST FOR LIFE** [ ] [ ]
(12"+=/cd-s+=) *(VUS T/CD 22)* – Pussy power / Funtime.

Jul 90. (cd/c/lp) *(CDVUS/VUSMC/VUSLP 19) <91381>* **BRICK BY BRICK** [50] [90]
– Home / Main street eyes / I won't crap out / Candy / Butt town / The undefeated / Moonlight lady / Something wild / Neon forest / Stormy night / Pussy power / My baby wants to rock & roll / Brick by brick / Livin' on the edge of the night. *(c re-iss. Apr92; OVEDC 426)*
(below 'A'side featured **KATE PIERSON** – vox (of B-52's)

Oct 90. (7"/c-s) *(VUS/+C 29) <98900>* **CANDY. / PUSSY POWER (acoustic demo)** [67] [28]
(10"+=/cd-s+=) *(VUS 29)* – My baby wants to rock'n'roll (acoustic demos).
(12"/cd-s) *(VUS T/CD 29)* – ('A'side) / The undefeated / Butt town (acoustic demo).

— Oct 90, IGGY dueted with DEBORAH HARRY on UK Top 50 single 'DID YOU EVAH'; *Chrysalis; CHS 3646)*

— with **LARRY MULLEN** (U2) – drums, percussion / **HAL CRAGIN** – bass / **ERIC SCHERMERHORN** – guitar plus guests **MALCOLM BURN** – guitars, etc

Aug 93. (7"ep/c-ep/12"ep/cd-ep) *(VUS/+C/T/CD 74)* **THE WILD AMERICA EP** [63] [ ]
– Wild America / Credit card / Come back tomorrow / My angel.

Sep 93. (cd/c/d-lp) *(CDVUS/VUSMC/VUSLP 64) <39002>* **AMERICAN CAESAR** [43] [ ]
– Character / Wild America / Mixin' the colors / Jealousy / Hate / It's our love / Plastic & concrete / F***in' alone / Highway song / Beside you / Sickness / Boogie boy / Perforation / Problems / Social life / Louie Louie / Caesar / Girls of N.Y

May 94. (10"ep) *(VUS A/C 77)* **BESIDE YOU / EVIL CALIFORNIA. / HOME (live) / FUCKIN' ALONE** [47] [–]
(cd-ep) *(VUSCD 77)* – ('A'side) / Les amants / Louie Louie (live) / ('A'acoustic).

Feb 96. (cd/c/lp) *(CDVUS/VUSMC/VUSLP 102) <41327>* **NAUGHTY LITTLE DOGGIE** [ ] [ ]
– I wanna live / Pussy walk / Innocent world / Knucklehead / To belong / Keep on believing / Outta my head / Shoeshine girl / Heart is saved / Look away.

Sep 99. (cd) *(CDVUS 163) <48216>* **AVENUE B** [ ] [ ]
– No shit / Nazi girlfriend / Avenue B / Miss Argentina / Afraid to get close / Shakin' all over / Long distance / Corruption / She called me daddy / I felt the luxury / Espanol / Motorcycle / Facade.

Oct 99. (7") *(VUS 155)* **CORRUPTION. / ROCK STAR GRAVE** [ ] [–]
(cd-s+=) *(VUSCD 155)* – Hollywood affair.

Jun 01. (cd) *(CDVUS 200) <10574>* **BEAT 'EM UP** [ ] Jul01 [ ]
– Mask / L.O.S.T. / Howl / Football / Saviour / Beat 'em up / Talking snake / The jerk / Death is certain / Go for the throat / Weasels / Drink new blood / It's all shit / Ugliness / V.I.P.

— backed by **the TROLLS, the STOOGES, SUM 41, GREEN DAY, PEACHES**

Sep 03. (cd) *(CDVUS 246) <80774>* **SKULL RING** [ ] Nov03 [ ]
– Little electric chair / Perverts in the sun / Skull ring / Superbabe / Loser / Private hell / Little know it all / Whatever / Dead rock star / Rock show / Here comes the summer / Motor Inn / Inferiority complex / Supermarket / Til wrong feels right / Blood on your cool.

— early in '04, IGGY feat. on PEACHES hit, 'Kick It'

IGGY AND THE STOOGES

IGGY POP, the ASHETON's plus **MIKE WATT** – bass (ex-MINUTEMEN) / **STEVE MacKAY** – saxophone

Skydog Skydog

Jun 05. (cd) *<(SK 20053)>* **TELLURIC CHAOS** [ ] May05 [ ]
– Loose / Down on the street / 1969 / I wanna be your dog / TV eyes / Dirt / Real cool time / No fun / 1970 / Fun house / Skull ring / Rock star / Electric chair (encore) / Little doll / Idea of fun / I wanna be your dog / Not right.

– (IGGY POP) compilations, etc. –

May 82. (7") *RCA Gold; (GOLD 549)* **THE PASSENGER. / NIGHTCLUBBING** [ ] [–]

Sep 84. (lp/c) *R.C.A.; (PL/PK 84597)* **CHOICE CUTS** [ ] [ ]

Apr 88. (cd-ep) *A&M; (AMCD 909)* **COMPACT HITS** [ ] [–]
– Real wild child (the wild one) / Isolation / Cry for love / Shades.

Jan 92. (cd) *Arista; (262 178)* **POP SONGS** [ ] [–]

Jan 93. (3xcd-box) *Virgin; (TPAK 21)* **LUST FOR LIFE / THE IDIOT / BRICK BY BRICK** [ ] [ ]

Jun 93. (cd) *Revenge; (642044)* **LIVE NYC RITZ '86 (live)** [ ] [–]

Aug 93. (cd/c) *Revenge; (642/644 050)* **SUCK ON THIS!** [ ] [–]

Aug 95. (cd) *Skydog;* **WE ARE NOT TALKING ABOUT COMMERCIAL SHIT** [ ] [–]

Aug 95. (cd) *Skydog;* **WAKE UP SUCKERS** [ ] [–]

Aug 96. (cd) *M.C.A.; (MCD 84021)* **THE BEST OF IGGY POP LIVE (live)** [ ] [ ]

Sep 96. (cd) *Camden RCA; (74321 41503-2)* **POP MUSIC** [ ] [–]

Oct 96. (cd/c/d-lp) *Virgin; (CDVUS/VUSMC/VUSLP 115) <42351>* **NUDE & RUDE: THE BEST OF IGGY POP** [ ] [ ]
– I wanna be your dog / No fun / Search & destroy / Gimme danger / I'm sick of you / Funtime / Nightclubbing / China girl / Lust for life / The passenger / Kill city / Real wild child / Cry for love / Cold metal / Candy / Home / Wild America.

Nov 96. (7"colrd/c-s) *Virgin; (VUS/+C 116)* **LUST FOR LIFE / (GET UP I FEEL LIKE BEING A) SEX MACHINE** [26] [–]
(cd-s+=) *(VUSCD 116)* – ('A'live) / I wanna be your dog (live).

Dec 96. (cd) *The Network; (3D 013)* **IGGY POP** [ ] [–]

Apr 97. (cd) *Wotre; (642007)* **LIVE IN BERLIN '91** [ ] [–]

Sep 97. (d-cd) *Snapper; (SMDCD 142)* **HEAD ON** [ ] [–]

Nov 97. (cd) *Other People's Music; (OPM 2116CD)* **HEROIN HATES YOU** [ ] [–]

Nov 97. (cd) *Eagle; (EABCD 011)* **THE MASTERS** [ ] [–]

Feb 98. (c-s) *Virgin; (VSC 1689)* **THE PASSENGER / LUST FOR LIFE** [22] [–]
(12"+=/cd-s+=) *(VS T/CDT 1689)* – Nightclubbing.

Aug 98. (cd) *A&M; (540943-2)* **BLAH BLAH BLAH / INSTINCT** [ ] [–]

Jul 05. (cd) *Sony BMG; (82876 70840-2)* **THE BEST OF IGGY POP** [ ] [–]
– Loco mosquito / Bang bang / Tell me a story / Pumpin' for Jill / Take care of me / I need more / I'm bored / Knocking 'em down / I snub you / Sea of love / Play it safe / Dog food / Happy man / Time won't let me / Five foot one / Angel / Girls / New values / Pleasure / Houston is hot tonight.

Jul 05. (d-cd) *Virgin; (CDVUSD 266) <96105>* **A MILLION IN PRIZES: AN ANTHOLOGY** [ ] [ ]
– 1969 / No fun / I wanna be your dog / Down on the street / I got a right! / Gimme some skin / I'm sick of you / Search and destroy / Gimme danger / Raw power / Kill city / Nightclubbing / Funtime / China girl / Sister midnight / Tonight / Success / Lust for life / The passenger / Some weird sin / I'm bored / I need more / Pleasure / Run like a villain / Cry for love / Real wild child (wild one) / Cold metal / Home / Candy / Well, did you evah! / Wild America / T.V. eye (live) / Loose (live) / Look away / Corruption / I felt the luxury / Mask / Skull ring.

2005. (7") *Sundazed; <S 173>* **SEARCH AND DESTROY. / (Bowie mix)** [–] [ ]

☐ PORNO FOR PYROS (see under ⇒ JANE'S ADDICTION)

PORTISHEAD

Formed: Bristol, England . . . 1993 by duo GEOFF BARROW and BETH GIBBONS, who took their name from a local coastal town. After working as MASSIVE ATTACK's studio runner and writing one of the better songs on NENEH CHERRY's 'HOMEBREW' album, BARROWS recruited covers band stalwart GIBBONS and the band signed to 'Go! Discs' off-shoot 'Go! Beat'. Named after BARROW's faded seaside resort hometown of Portishead near Bristol, the group debuted with a short film, 'TO KILL A DEAD MAN'. A retro spy movie pastiche, the film (which starred PORTISHEAD in an acting capacity) and its accompanying soundtrack were indicative of the cinematic melodrama which would characterise the band's groundbreaking debut. Released in August '94 amid much anticiption, and preceeded by the singles 'NUMB' and 'SOUR TIMES', 'DUMMY' was a wracked, claustrophobic melange of painfully slow hip hop rhythms, droning hammond, knife-edge guitar and rumbling bass. Spiced with a sprinkling of obscure samples and topped off by the sublime lament of GIBBONS' vocals, the sound PORTISHEAD had created was one of the most striking definitions of the phenomena that would come to be known as 'Trip Hop'. Along with MASSIVE ATTACK, TRICKY et all, the band insisted the label was a lazy attempt at pigeonholing but what really set PORTISHEAD apart was simply the otherness of their sound, a strange grace that made the unrelenting lyrical bleakness and despair bearable. Who knows, winning the Mercury Music Prize in 1995 may have cheered them up a bit, although it would be a long before they would resurface (meanwhile, BARROW guested on EARTHLING's 'Radar' set). During the summer of '97, PORTISHEAD delivered their first product in over two years, albeit a limited-edition 12"-only single, 'COWBOYS'. Nevertheless, the track was indeed a modern day classic, subsequently appearing on the flip of their Top 10 single, 'ALL MINE' – BETH was never better. As for their sophomore parent album, 'PORTISHEAD' (1997) – which made No.2 and nearly the Top 20 in America! – people would have been better not to compare it with their debut. Just when the fans thought it would take until the year 2000 for a third set, a live stop-gap, 'PNYC', came out the following year. BETH GIBBONS eventually returned with 'OUT OF SEASON' (2002), backed up by RUSTIN MAN (the nom de plume of PAUL WEBB, ex-TALK TALK) and shorn of the cinematic production which framed her vocals in PORTISHEAD. The result was as disarming as it was natural, the sorrowful songstress finally having her voice accompanied (by sympathetic, restrained, jazz-folksy instrumentation) rather than providing the final layer in an aural collage.

• **Songwriters:** BARROW-GIBBONS, but most with UTLEY. Sample; MORE MISSION IMPOSSIBLE (Lalo Schifrin) / SPIN IT JIG (Smokey Brooks) / ELEGANT PEOPLE (Weather Report) / MAGIC MOUNTAIN (War) / I'LL NEVER FALL IN LOVE AGAIN (Johnnie Ray; at slow speed!) / ISAAC MOODS (Isaac Hayes). • **Trivia:** Have remixed for the likes of DEPECHE MODE (In Your Room) / RIDE (I Don't Know Where It Comes From) / GRAVEDIGGAZ (Nowhere To Run).

Album rating: DUMMY (*10) / PORTISHEAD (*8) / PNYC (*6) / Beth Gibbons & Rustic Man: OUT OF SEASON (*8)

BETH GIBBONS – vocals / **GEOFF BARROW** (b.1971) – programming, synthesizer with **ADRIAN UTLEY** – guitar, bass / **CLIVE DEAMER** – drums / **DAVE McDONALD** – nose flute / **RICHARD NEWELL** – drum programme / **NEIL SOLMAN** – synthesizers, organ / **ANDY HAGUE** – trumpet

Go Beat | Polygram

Jun 94. (c-s) *(GODMC 114)* <857561> **NUMB / NUMBED IN MOSCOW** [ ] [ ]
(12"+=/cd-s+=) *(GOD X/CD 114)* – Revenge of the numbed / Numb: Earth – Linger / Extra numb
(cd-s++=) *(GOLCD 114)* – A tribute to Monk and Cantella.

Aug 94. (c-s) *(GODMC 116)* **SOUR TIMES / SOUR SOUR TIMES** [57] [–]
(12"+=) *(GODX 116)* – Lot more / Sheared times.
(re-iss. Apr95, hit UK No.13)
(cd-s++=) *(GODCD 116)* – Airbus reconstruction.
(cd-s) *(GOLCD 116)* – ('A'side) / It's a fire / Pedestal / Theme from 'To Kill A Dead Man'.

Aug 94. (cd/c/lp) *(<828552-2/-4/-1>)* **DUMMY** [2] Jan95 [79]
– Mysterons / Sour times / Strangers / It could be sweet / Wandering star / Numb / Roads / Pedestal / Biscuit / Glory box.

Oct 94. (c-s) *(GODMC 120)* **GLORY BOX / TOY BOX** [13] [ ]
(12"+=/cd-s+=) *(GOD X/CD 120)* – Scorn / Sheared box.

Jan 95. (cd-s) <857816> **SOUR TIMES (NOBODY LOVES ME) / AIRBUS RECONSTRUCTION** [–] [53]

Jun 97. (12"ltd) *(571277-1)* **COWBOYS. / COWBOYS (instrumental)** [ ] [–]

Sep 97. (c-s) *(571597-4)* <871881> **ALL MINE / COWBOYS** [8] [ ]
(12"+=/cd-s+=) *(571597-1-2)* – Cowboys (instrumental).

Oct 97. (cd/c) *(<539189-2/-4>)* **PORTISHEAD** [2] [21]
– Cowboys / All mine / Undenied / Half day closing / Over / Humming / Mourning air / Seven months / Only you / Elysium / Western eyes.

Nov 97. (12"/cd-s) *(571993-1/-2)* **OVER. / OVER (remix) / OVER (instrumental)** [25] [ ]
(cd-s) *(571995-2)* – ('A'side) / Half day closing (live) / Humming (live).

Mar 98. (c-s) *(569474-4)* **ONLY YOU / ELYSIUM (Parlour Talk remix)** [35] [ ]
(12"+=/cd-s+=) *(569475-1/-2)* – Only you (NYC) / Only you.

Nov 98. (cd/c/d-lp) *(<559424-2/-4/-1>)* **PNYC (live)** [40] [ ]
– Humming / Cowboys / All mine / Mysterons / Only you / Half day closing / Over / Glory box / Sour times / Roads / Strangers.

— UTLEY moonlighted with the MOUNT VERNON ARTS LAB via a collaborative mini-set, 'WARMINSTER' (1999).

BETH GIBBONS & RUSTIN MAN

BETH – vocals / with **PAUL WEBB** (RUSTIN MAN) – multi (ex-TALK TALK) / plus **ADRIAN UTLEY** – multi / + ex-TALK TALK members

Go Beat | Sanctuary

Oct 02. (cd/lp) *(066574-2/-1)* *<94648>* **OUT OF SEASON** [28] [ ]
– Mysteries / Tom the model / Show / Romance / Sand river / Spider monkey / Resolve / Drake / Funny time of year / Rustin man. *<US+=>* – Candy says (live) / (hidden track).

Mar 03. (7") *(GOB 55)* **TOM THE MODEL. / SPIDER MONKEY (live)** [70] [–]
(cd-s+=) *(GOBCD 55)* – ('A'-live) / ('A'video).

□ the POSTAL SERVICE
(see under ⇒ DEATH CAB FOR CUTIE)

□ the POWER STATION (see under ⇒ DURAN DURAN)

Elvis PRESLEY

Born: ELVIS AARON PRESLEY, 8 Jan'35, Tupelo, Mississippi, USA. One of twin sons (the other Jesse was stillborn), he was raised in Memphis, Tennessee. Between the summer of '53 and '54, he spent time in Sam Phillips' 'Sun' studios, cutting demos. With the arrival of back-up session players, SCOTTY MOORE and BILL BLACK, his first single, a rousing cover of Arthur Crudup's 'THAT'S ALL RIGHT MAMA', gained local airplay even before its release on the 'Sun' label. After a brief flirtation with country, he opted for R&B after his young audiences lapped up his pelvic action. Although Sam Phillips initially thought ELVIS was a black blues singer, he still chose to feature ELVIS's country recordings on the flip sides. Colonel Tom Parker became his manager in 1955, soon securing a large 5-figure deal with 'R.C.A.', who also bought out his contract with 'Sun' records; the attention ELVIS's riotous stage shows had received prompted an intense bidding war. His major debut, 'HEARTBREAK HOTEL', sparked off a new phenomenom at the start of 1956 which soon gave him a massive selling No.1. PRESLEY appeared on many TV shows around this time, the newfound star going on to appear in his first feature film, 'Love Me Tender' (named after his song, see also further film discography). The constant demand for ELVIS's records saw many simultaneous releases clogging the charts; he scored a further nine US No.1's in the States (namely 'I WANT YOU, I NEED YOU, I LOVE YOU', 'DON'T BE CRUEL', 'HOUND DOG', 'LOVE ME TENDER', 'TOO MUCH', 'ALL SHOOK UP', 'LET ME BE YOUR TEDDY BEAR', 'JAILHOUSE ROCK' and 'DON'T'), before being controversially drafted into the army on the 24th of March '58. While serving his country over a two-year period, ELVIS suffered the death of his mother, Gladys, something which was to deeply affect him in the years to come. During this period, several singles were issued, the records (including chart-topping 'HARD

ELVIS PRESLEY

HEADED WOMAN' and 'A BIG HUNK O LOVE') recorded just prior to his draft. After being promoted to Sergeant, his army time expired in March 1960, another US No.1, 'STUCK ON YOU', celebrating his return to "civvie" street. ELVIS returned to the Nashville studios and began working on a new ballad-esque style backed with an uptempo beat, a sound that was only vaguely reminiscent of his pre-army days. His films too, (around three a year in the 60's), contained a sort of manufactured pop, guided no doubt by the vast sums of money it stimulated. However, in spells between 1960 and 1965, ELVIS did create some truly wonderful pop records including 'IT'S NOW OR NEVER', 'ARE YOU LONESOME TONIGHT?', 'WOODEN HEART', 'RETURN TO SENDER', 'DEVIL IN DISGUISE', 'VIVA LAS VEGAS' and 'CRYING IN THE CHAPEL' to name but a few. In 1965, he also released the first of a series of gospel albums, 'HIS HAND IN MINE', while on the 1st of May '67, he married long-time girlfriend, Priscilla Beaulieu. After she bore him a child, Lisa Marie, in 1968, they separated in 1972 and divorced a year later (she subsequently became an actress, most notably on the 'Dallas' soap). In the late '60's, ELVIS revived a somewhat commercially declining singles career when 'IN THE GHETTO' then 'SUSPICIOUS MINDS' hit the Top 3. His work in the 70's showed him moving into the money-spinning cabaret circuit as his live appearances were mainly in Las Vegas and Hawaii. While "The King" was still a top performer, as loyal fans old and new flocked to see his larger frame (squeezing out of a white glitzy suit) churn out another exhaustive show, he was barely a shadow of the rock'n'roll hero he once was. A combination of a special diet, prescribed drugs, junk food (binges) and alcohol eventually proved too much for ailing heart and tragically on the 16th of August 1977, he was found dead in his Graceland home by girlfriend, Ginger Alden. His funeral saw over 75,000 fans/mourners flocking to the gates of his home in Gracelands. The King Of Rock was dead. Following the death of ELVIS, many tabloids reported sightings of a living Elvis and speculation about his doomed life has been catapulted into the ridiculous. The King should've been laid to rest in peace, his music the only thing to live on. In fact, ELVIS went on to have numerous hit compilations and the odd hit single, none more so than when JUNKIE XL sent his updated remixed version of 'A LITTLE LESS CONVERSATION' (taken from the movie, 'Ocean's Eleven') to the top of the UK charts in summer 2002. The PAUL OAKENFOLD twist on ELVIS's 'RUBBERNECKIN' nearly followed suit in '03, both giving the King crossover dance hits a quarter of a century after his death! After 'THAT'S ALL RIGHT' hit the UK Top 3 in October 2004, his label kept the ELVIS gravy train rolling early the following year with a weekly series of cannily-marketed re-issues, primed to break PRESLEY's record of No.1 singles but just falling short as the schedule progressed.

• **Songwriters:** Covered (singles only mentioned):- THAT'S ALL RIGHT MAMA + MY BABY LEFT ME (Arthur 'Big Boy' Crudup) / BLUE MOON OF KENTUCKY (Bill Monroe) / BABY LET'S PLAY HOUSE (Arthur Gunter) / BLUE SUEDE SHOES (Carl Perkins) / TUTTI FRUTTI + RIP IT UP (Little Richard) / HOUND DOG (Freddie Bell . . . & Big Mama Thornton) / ALL SHOOK UP (Otis Blackwell) / ONE BROKEN HEART FOR SALE (Blackwell-Scott) / ONE NIGHT (Smiley Lewis) / A FOOL SUCH AS I (Hank Snow) / MY WISH CAME TRUE (Ivory Joe White) / IT'S NOW OR NEVER + SURRENDER + ASK ME (Italian trad.) / ARE YOU LONESOME TONIGHT? (Vaughn Deleath) / I FEEL SO BAD (Chuck Willis) / WITCHCRAFT (Spiders) / WHAT'D I SAY (Ray Charles) / BOSSA NOVA BABY (Lieber-Stoller) / SUCH A NIGHT (Johnnie Ray) / FRANKIE & JOHNNY (?) / LOVE LETTERS (Dick Haymes) / BIG BOSS MAN (Jimmy Reed) / U.S. MALE (Jerry Reed) / YOU'LL NEVER WALK ALONE (hit. Gerry & The Pacemakers) / IN THE GHETTO (Mac Davis) / SUSPICIOUS MINDS (Mark James) / THE WONDER OF YOU (Ray Peterson) / KENTUCKY RAIN (Eddie Rabbit) / YOU DON'T HAVE TO SAY YOU LOVE ME (Dusty Springfield) / THERE GOES MY EVERYTHING (Engelbert Humperdink) / I REALLY WANT TO KNOW (Les Paul & Mary Ford) / RAGS TO RICHES (Tony Bennett) / I JUST CAN'T HELP BELIEVIN' (B.J.Thomas) / UNTIL IT'S TIME FOR YOU TO GO (Buffy Sainte-Marie) / AN AMERICAN TRILOGY (Mickey Newbury) / BURNING LOVE (Arthur Alexander) / STEAMROLLER BLUES (James Taylor) / POLK SALAD ANNIE (Tony Joe White) / I'VE GOT A THING ABOUT YOU BABY (Billy Lee Riley) / PROMISED LAND (Chuck Berry) / MY BOY (hit. Richard Harris) / HURT (Timi Yuro) / GREEN, GREEN GRASS OF HOME (Tom Jones) / MY WAY (Paul Anka) / TOMORROW'S A LONG TIME (Bob Dylan) / etc. • **Filmography:** LOVE ME TENDER (1956) / LOVING YOU (1957) / JAILHOUSE ROCK (1957) / KING CREOLE (1958) / G.I. BLUES (1960) / FLAMING STAR (1960) / WILD IN THE COUNTRY (1961) / BLUE HAWAII (1961) / FOLLOW THAT DREAM (1962) / KID GALAHAD (1962) / GIRLS! GIRLS! GIRLS! (1962) / IT HAPPENED AT THE WORLD'S FAIR (1963) / FUN IN ACAPULCO (1963) / KISSIN' COUSINS (1964) / VIVA LAS VEGAS (1964) / ROUSTABOUT (1964) / GIRL HAPPY (1965) / TICKLE ME (1965) / HAREM HOLIDAY (1965, 'HARUM SCARUM'-US title) / FRANKIE AND JOHNNY (1966) / PARADISE, HAWAIIAN STYLE (1966) / CALIFORNIA HOLIDAY (1966, 'SPINOUT'-US title) / EASY COME, EASY GO (1966) / DOUBLE TROUBLE (1967) / CLAMBAKE (1968) / STAY AWAY, JOE (1968) / SPEEDWAY (1968) / LIVE A LITTLE, LOVE A LITTLE (1968) / CHARRO (1969) / THE TROUBLE WITH GIRLS (1969) / CHANGE OF HABIT (1970) / (This was his last feature film, but many concerts were recorded)

Best CD compilation: PRESLEY – THE ALL-TIME GREATEST HITS (*10)

ELVIS PRESLEY – vocals with **SCOTTY MOORE** – guitar / **BILL BLACK** – bass / + session drummers

not iss. | Sun

Aug 54. (7") *<209>* **THAT'S ALL RIGHT MAMA. / BLUE MOON OF KENTUCKY** [–] [ ]
<re-iss. Nov55 on 'R.C.A.'; 6380>

Oct 54. (7") *<210>* **GOOD ROCKIN' TONIGHT. / I DON'T CARE IF THE SUN DON'T SHINE** [–] [ ]
<re-iss. Nov55 on 'R.C.A.'; 6381>

Jan 55. (7") *<215>* **MILK COW BLUES BOOGIE. / YOU'RE A HEARTBREAKER** [–] [ ]
<re-iss. Nov55 on 'R.C.A.'; 6382>

May 55. (7") *<217>* **I'M LEFT, YOU'RE RIGHT, SHE'S GONE. / BABY LET'S PLAY HOUSE** [–] [ ]
<re-iss. Nov55 on 'R.C.A.'; 6383>

Aug 55. (7") *<223>* **MYSTERY TRAIN. / I FORGOT TO REMEMBER TO FORGET** [–] [ ]
<re-iss. Nov55 on 'R.C.A.'; 6357>
(all UK rel.Feb59 & Mar64 on 'RCA')

— added **D.J. FONTANA** – drums (on tour and then on session)

— now adding on session **FLOYD CRAMER** – piano / **CHET ATKINS** – guitar / **HANK GARLAND** – guitar / **'BOOTS' RANDOLPH** – saxophone

— He was also backed and at times credited with **The JORDANAIRES; GORDON STOKER, HOYT HAWKINS, NEAL MATTHEWS** and **HUGH JARRETT.**

H.M.V. | R.C.A.

Mar 56. (7")(78) *(7M 385)(POP 182) <47-6420>* **HEARTBREAK HOTEL. / I WAS THE ONE** [2] [1]
Feb56 [19]

Mar 56. (lp) *<LPM 1254>* **ELVIS PRESLEY** [–] [1]
– Blue suede shoes* / I'm counting on you* / Money honey* / I got a sweetie (I got a woman)* / One sided love affair* / I'm gonna sit right down and cry over you* / Tryin' to get to you* / I love you because / Just because / Blue moon / I'll never let you go / Tutti frutti. (tracks * =on next album too) *(UK-iss.Oct56;) (re-iss. Mar85 on 'R.C.A.' lp/c/cd; (NL/NK/ND 89046) (pic-lp.Oct88 on 'R.C.A.'; PD 81254)*

May 56. (7")(78) *(7M 405)(POP 213)* **BLUE SUEDE SHOES. / TUTTI FRUTTI** [9] [–]

Jul 56. (7")(78) *(7M 424)(POP 235) <47-6540>* **I WANT YOU, I NEED YOU, I LOVE YOU. / MY BABY LEFT ME** [14] [1]
May56 [31]

Sep 56. (7",78) *(POP 249) <47-6604>* **HOUND DOG. / DON'T BE CRUEL** [2] Jul56 [1]
(re-iss. Jun78 on 'R.C.A.'; PB 9265) – (hit UK No.24)

Sep 56. (7",78) *(POP 253) <476643>* **LOVE ME TENDER. / ANYWAY YOU WANT ME (THAT'S HOW I WILL BE)** [11] [1]
Oct56 [20]

Nov 56. (lp) *(CLP 1093) <LPM 1382>* **ROCK'N'ROLL NO.1**
<US title 'ELVIS'> [*] [1]
– That's all right / Lawdy Miss Clawdy / Mystery train / Playing fpr keeps /

Poor boy / Money honey / I'm counting on you / My baby left me / I was the one / Shake rattle and roll / I'm left, you're right, she's gone / You're a heartbreaker / Tryin' to get to you / Blue suede shoes. *(re-iss. Mar59 as 'ELVIS'; CLP 1093)* – (hit No.4) *(re-iss. May72 as 'ROCK'N'ROLL' on 'R.C.A.'; SF 8233)* – (hit No.34) *(re-iss. Sep81 on 'R.C.A.' lp/c; NL/NK 89125)*

Nov 56. (7",78) *(POP 272)* **BLUE MOON. / I DON'T CARE IF THE SUN DON'T SHINE** | 9 | – |

Feb 57. (7",78) *(POP 295)* **MYSTERY TRAIN. / LOVE ME** | 25 | – |

Mar 57. (7",78) *(POP 305)* **RIP IT UP. / BABY LET'S PLAY HOUSE** | 27 | – |

Apr 57. (lp) *(CLP 1105)* **ROCK'N'ROLL NO.2** | * | – |
– Rip it up / When my blue moon turns to gold again / Love me / Long tall Sally / First in line / Old Shep / So glad you're mine / How's the world treating you / Any place is Paradise / Paralysed / Ready Teddy / How do think I feel. *(re-iss. 1962 on 'R.C.A.' mono/stereo; RD/SF 7528) (re-iss. Jan84 on 'R.C.A.' lp/c; NL/NK 81382) (cd-iss. May90; ND 81382)*

May 57. (7",78) *(POP 330)* *<47-6800>* **TOO MUCH. / PLAYING FOR KEEPS** | 6 | 1 | Jan57 | 21 |

Jun 57. (7",78) *(POP 359)* *<47-6870>* **ALL SHOOK UP. / THAT'S WHEN YOUR HEARTACHES BEGIN** | 1 | 1 | Mar57 | 58 |

— ELVIS was now backed by a variety of session men. SCOTTY and BILL left. In Jun'58, **BOB MOORE** – bass / **HANK GARLAND** – guitar repl. them

R.C.A. R.C.A.

Jul 57. (7",78) *(RCA 1013)* *<47-7000>* **(LET ME BE YOUR) TEDDY BEAR. / LOVING YOU** | 3 | 1 | Jun57 | 20 |

Aug 57. (10"lp) *(RC 24001)* *<LPM 1515>* **LOVING YOU** (soundtrack) | * | Jul57 | 1 |
– Mean woman blues / (Let me be your) Teddy bear / Loving you / Got a lot o' livin' to do / Lonesome cowboy / Hot dog / Party / Blueberry hill / True love / Don't leave me now / Have I told you lately that I love you / I need you so. *(re-iss. Sep77 lp/c +=; PK/PL 42358)* – (hit UK No.24) *(re-iss. Aug81 on 'R.C.A. Int.' INTS 5109) (re-iss. Jan84 lp/c; NL/NK 81515) (cd-iss. Oct87; ND 81515) <cd-iss. Feb98 +=; 07863 67452-2>* – Tell me why / Is it so strange / One night of sin / When it rains, it really pours / I beg of you (alt.) / Party (alt.) / Loving you (uptempo) / Got a lot of livin' to do (finale). *(lp re-iss. Jan02 on 'Castle'+=; ELVIS 110)* – (7" singles).

Oct 57. (7",78) *(RCA 1020)* **PARTY. / GOT A LOT OF LIVIN' TO DO** | 2 | – |

Nov 57. (7",78) *(RCA 1025)* **SANTA BRING MY BABY BACK TO ME. / SANTA CLAUS IS COMING TO TOWN** | 7 | – |

Nov 57. (lp) *(RD 27052)* *<LOC 1035>* **ELVIS' CHRISTMAS ALBUM** | * | 1 |
– Santa Claus is coming to town / White Christmas / Precious Lord it is no secret (what God can do) / Blue Christmas / Santa bring my baby back to me / I'll be home for Christmas / Here comes Santa Claus (right down Santa Claus lane) / O little town of Bethlehem / Silent night / Take my hand / I believe / (There'll be) Peace in the valley (for me). *(re-iss. Nov58; same) (re-iss. Nov71 on 'RCA International; INTS 1126)* – (hit No.7) *(re-iss. Jan84 lp/c; NL/NK 89116) (re-iss. Nov85; PL 85486) (re-iss. Oct79 on 'RCA-Camden' lp/c; CDS/CAM 1155) (re-iss. Nov75 on 'Pickwick' diff; CAM 462)*

Jan 58. (7",78) *(RCA 1028)* *<47-7035>* **JAILHOUSE ROCK. / TREAT ME NICE** | 1 | 1 | Oct57 | 18 |
(re-iss. May77; PB 2695) – (hit UK No.44 Aug77) *(re-iss. Jan83, hit No.27, also on 7"pic-d diff B-side THE ELVIS MEDLEY)*

Feb 58. (7",78) *(RCA 1043)* *<47-7150>* **DON'T. / I BEG OF YOU** | 2 | 1 | Jan58 | 8 |

— ELVIS was served US army draft notice in Dec'57. He finally – after much fan/film producer protest – joined army on 24 Mar'58. He has had enough time to record many songs and appeared on celluloid once again (aka KING CREOLE film).

Apr 58. (7",78) *(RCA 1058)* *<47-7240>* **WEAR MY RING ROUND YOUR NECK. / DON'T CHA THINK IT'S TIME** | 3 | 2 | Jun58 | 15 |

Jul 58. (7",78) *(RCA 1070)* *<47-7280>* **HARD HEADED WOMAN. / DON'T ASK ME WHY** | 2 | 1 | Jun58 | 25 |

Sep 58. (7",78) *(RCA 1081)* **KING CREOLE. / DIXIELAND ROCK** | 2 | – |

Oct 58. (lp) *(RD 27088)* *<LPM 1884>* **KING CREOLE** (soundtrack) | 4 | Sep58 | 2 |
– King Creole / As long as I have you / Hard headed woman / Trouble / Dixieland rock / Don't ask me why / Lover doll / Crawfish / Young dreams / Steadfast, loyal and true / New Orleans. *(re-iss. 1963 & Feb69; same) (re-iss. Aug81 on 'RCA Int.'; INTS 5013) (re-iss. Jan84 lp/c; NL/NK 83733) (cd-iss. Oct87; ND 83733) <cd re-iss. Feb98 +=; 07863 67454-2>* – King Creole (alt. take 18) / As long as I have you (movie version take 4) / Danny / Lover doll (undubbed) / Steadfast, loyal and true (alt.) / As long as I have you (movie version take 8) / King Creole (alt. take 3). *(lp re-mast.Jan02 on 'Castle'++=; ELVIS 112)* – (bonus 7" singles).

Jan 59. (7",78) *(RCA 1100)* *<47-7410>* **ONE NIGHT. / I GOT STUNG** | 1 | 4 | Oct58 | 8 |
(re-iss. May77; PB 2696)

Apr 59. (7",78) *(RCA 1113)* *<47-7506>* **(NOW AND THEN THERE'S) A FOOL SUCH AS I. / I NEED YOUR LOVE TONIGHT** | 1 | 2 | Mar59 | 4 |
(re-iss. May77; PB 2697)

Jul 59. (7",78) *(RCA 1136)* *<47-7600>* **A BIG HUNK O' LOVE. / MY WISH CAME TRUE** | 4 | 1 | Jun59 | 12 |
(all singles from Jul'57 were re-iss. Mar60)

— ELVIS was now demobbed from the army 5 Mar'60. His session men now are **FLOYD CRAMER** – piano / **SCOTTY MOORE** – guitar

Mar 60. (7",78) *(RCA 1187)* *<47-7740>* **STUCK ON YOU. / FAME AND FORTUNE** | 3 | 1 | 17 |

Jun 60. (mono-lp)(stereo-lp) *(RD 27171)(SF 5060)* *<LSP 2231>* **ELVIS IS BACK!** | 1 | May60 | 2 |
– Make me no it / The girl of my best friend / Dirty dirty / I will be home again / The thrill of your love / Feeling / Soldier boy / Such a night / It feels so right / Like a baby / Fever / Reconsider baby / The girl next door. *(re-iss. Apr84 lp/c; NL/NK 89013) (cd-iss. Jul89; ND 89013)*

Jul 60. (7") *(RCA 1194)* **A MESS OF BLUES. / THE GIRL OF MY BEST FRIEND** | 2 | – |

Jul 60. (7") *<47-7777>* **IT'S NOW OR NEVER. / A MESS OF BLUES** | – | 1 | 32 |

Oct 60. (7") *(RCA 1207)* **IT'S NOW OR NEVER. / MAKE ME KNOW IT** | 1 | – |
(re-iss. May77; PB 2698) – (hit UK No.39 in Aug77)

Dec 60. (mono-lp)(stereo-lp) *(RD 27192)(SF 5078)* *<LSP 2256>* **G.I. BLUES** (soundtrack) | 1 | Oct60 | 1 |
– Tonight is so right for love / What's she really like / Frankfurt special / Wooden heart / G.I. blues / Pocketful of rainbows / Shoppin' around / Big boots / Didja' ever / Blue suede shoes / Doin' the best I can. *(re-iss. Sep77; same)* – (hit UK No.14) *(re-iss. Aug81 on 'RCA Int.'; INTS 5104) (re-iss. Jan84 lp/c; NL/NK 83735) (cd-iss. Oct87; ND 83735) <cd-iss. Feb98 +=; 07863 66960-2>* – (alternate bonus tracks). *(lp re-mast.Sep01 on 'Castle'++=; ELVIS 106)* – (bonus 7"ep).

Jan 61. (7") *(RCA 1216)* *<47-7810>* **ARE YOU LONESOME TONIGHT? / I GOTTA KNOW** | 1 | 1 | Nov60 | 20 |
(re-iss. May77; PB 2699) – (hit UK No.46 Aug77)

Mar 61. (7") *(RCA 1226)* **WOODEN HEART. / TONIGHT IS SO RIGHT FOR LOVE** | 1 | – |
(re-iss. May77; PB 2700) – (hit UK No.49 Aug77)

May 61. (mono-lp)(stereo-lp) *(RD 27211)(SF 5094)* *<LSP 2328>* **HIS HAND IN MINE** | 3 | Jan61 | 13 |
– His hand in mine / I'm gonna walk dem golden stairs / Milky white way / My father's house / Known only to him / Mansions over the hilltop / I believe in the sky / If we never meet again / Working on the building / Jesus knows what I need / Joshua fit the battle / Swing low sweet chariot. *(re-iss. Aug81 on 'RCA International'; INTS 5105) (re-iss. Jan84 lp/c; NL/NK 83935) (cd-iss. Oct88; ND 83935)*

May 61. (7") *(RCA 1227)* *<47-7850>* **SURRENDER (TORNA A SURRIENTO). / LONELY MAN** | 4 | 1 | Feb61 | 32 |
(re-iss. May77; PB 2701)

Aug 61. (7") *(RCA 1244)* *<47-7880>* **WILD IN THE COUNTRY. / I FEEL SO BAD** | 1 | 26 | May61 | 5 |

Oct 61. (7") *(RCA 1258)* *<47-7908>* **(MARIE'S THE NAME) HIS LATEST FLAME. / LITTLE SISTER** | 4 | 26 | Aug61 | 5 |
(re-iss. May77; PB 2702)

Oct 61. (mono-lp)(stereo-lp) *(RD 27224)(SF 5106)* *<LSP 2370>* **SOMETHING FOR EVERYBODY** | 2 | Jul61 | 1 |
– There's always me / Give me the right / Gently / It's a sin / Sentimental

me / Starting today / I'm coming home / I slipped I stumbled I fell / Put the blame on me / I want you with me / Judy / In your arms. *(re-iss. Jan84 lp/c; NL/NK 84116) (cd-iss. Dec90;)*

Dec 61. (mono-lp)(stereo-lp) *(RD 27238)(SF 5115) <LSP 2426>* **BLUE HAWAII** (soundtrack) 1 Oct61 1
– Blue Hawaii / Almost always true / Aloha oe / No more / Can't help falling in love / Rock-a-hula baby / Moonlight swim / Ku-u-i-po (Hawaiian sweetheart) / Ito eats / Slicin' sand / Hawaiian sunset / Beach boy blues / Island of love / Hawaiian wedding song. *(re-iss. Sep77; SF 8145)* – (hit UK No.26) *(re-iss. Aug84 lp/c; NL/NK 83683) (cd-iss. Oct87; ND 83683) <(cd re-iss. Feb98 +=; 07863 66959-2)>* – (bonus film tracks). *(lp re-mast.Sep01 on 'Castle'++=; ELVIS 107)* – (bonus 7" tracks).

Jan 62. (7") *(RCA 1270) <47-7968>* **ROCK-A-HULA-BABY. / CAN'T HELP FALLING IN LOVE** 1 23
Nov61 2
(re-iss. May77; PB 2703)

May 62. (7") *(RCA 1280) <47-7992>* **GOOD LUCK CHARM. / ANYTHING THAT'S PART OF YOU** 1 1
Mar62 31
(re-iss. May77; PB 2704)

Jun 62. (mono-lp)(stereo-lp) *(RD 27265)(SF 5135) <LSP 2523>* **POT LUCK** 1 4
– Kiss me quick / Just for old times sake / Fountain of love / Gonna get back home somehow / Such an easy question / Night rider / Suspicion / Stepping out of line / I fell I've known you forever / That's someone you never forget / Something blue / I'm yours. *(re-iss. Apr81 on 'RCA International'; INTS 5074) (re-iss. Jul84 lp/c; NL/NK 89098) (cd-iss. Apr88; ND 89098)*

Aug 62. (7") *(RCA 1303) <47-8041>* **SHE'S NOT YOU. / JUST TELL HER JIM SAID HELLO** 1 5
Jul62 55
(re-iss. May77; PB 2705)

Nov 62. (7") *(RCA 1320) <47-8100>* **RETURN TO SENDER. / WHERE DO YOU COME FROM** 1 2
Oct62 99
(re-iss. May77; PB 2706) – (hit UK No.42 Aug77)

Jan 63. (lp; mono/stereo) *(RD/SF 7534) <LSP 2621>* **GIRLS! GIRLS! GIRLS!** (soundtrack) 2 Dec62 3
– Girls! girls! girls! / I don't wanna be tied / Where do you come from / I don't want to / We'll be together / A boy like me, a girl like you / Earth boy / Return to sender / Because of love / Thanks to the rolling stone / Song of the shrimp / The walls have ears / We're coming in loaded. *(re-iss. Oct79; lp/c; PL/PK 42354) (re-iss. Aug81 on 'RCA International'; INTS 5107) (re-iss. Jun84 lp/c; NL/NK 89048) (re-iss. Sep86 on 'RCA-Camden' lp/c; CDS/CAM 1221)*

Feb 63. (7") *(RCA 1337) <47-8134>* **ONE BROKEN HEART FOR SALE. / THEY REMIND ME TOO MUCH OF YOU** 12 11
53

May 63. (lp; mono/stereo) *(RD/SF 7565) <LSP 2697>* **IT HAPPENED AT THE WORLD'S FAIR** (soundtrack) 4 Apr63 4
– Beyond the bend / Relax / Take me to the fair / They remind me too much of you / One broken heart for sale / I'm falling in love tonight / Cotton candy land / A world of our own / How would you like to be? / Happy ending. *(re-iss. Aug81 on 'RCA Int.'; INTS 5033) (re-iss. Jan84 lp/c; NL/NK 82568) <(cd/c-iss.Mar93 +=; 74321 13431-2/-4)>* – Fun In Acapulco (tracks). *(cd re-iss. Apr03 on 'Follow That Dream'+=; FTD 23)* – (bonus takes).

Jun 63. (7") *(RCA 1355) <47-8188>* **(YOU'RE THE) DEVIL IN DISGUISE. / PLEASE DON'T DRAG THAT STRING AROUND** 1 3
(re-iss. May77; PB 2707)

Oct 63. (7") *(RCA 1374) <47-8243>* **BOSSA NOVA BABY. / WITCHCRAFT** 13 8
32

Dec 63. (7") *(RCA 1375) <447-0639>* **KISS ME QUICK. / SOMETHING BLUE** 14 Apr64 34

Dec 63. (lp; mono/stereo) *(RD/SF 7609) <LSP 2756>* **FUN IN ACAPULCO** (soundtrack) 9 Mar64 3
– Fun in Acapulco / Vino, dinero y amor / Mexico / El toro / Marguerita / The bullfighter was a lady / (There's) No room to rhumba in a sports car / I think I'm gonna like it here / Bossa nova baby / You can't say no in Acapulco / Guadalajara / Love me tonight * / Slowly but surely *. *(re-iss. Oct79 lp/c; PL/PKM 42357) (re-iss. Aug81 on 'RCA Int.'; INTS 5106) <(cd/c-iss.Mar93 [* not on cd] +=; 74321 13431-2/-4)>* – It Happened At The World's Fair (tracks). *(cd re-iss. Apr03 on 'Follow That Dream'+=; FTD 24)* – (bonus takes).

Mar 64. (7") *(RCA 1390) <47-8360>* **VIVA LAS VEGAS. / WHAT'D I SAY** 17 29
May64 21

Jun 64. (7") *(RCA 1404) <47-8307>* **KISSIN' COUSINS. / IT HURTS ME** 10 12
Feb64 29

Jun 64. (lp; mono/stereo) *(RD/SF 7645) <LSP 2894>* **KISSIN' COUSINS** (soundtrack) 5 Apr64 6
– Catchin' on fast / Tender feeling / Anyone (could fall in love with you) / Barefoot ballad / Once is enough / Kissin' cousins / Echoes of love / (It's a) Long, lonely highway / Smokey mountain way / There's gold in the mountains / One boy, two little girls / Kissin' cousins (reprise). *(re-iss. Oct79 lp/c; PL/PK 42355) (re-iss. Aug81 on 'RCA International'; INTS 5108) (re-iss. Nov84 lp/c; NL/NK 84115) (re-iss. Sep86 on 'RCA Camden' lp/c; CDS/CAM 1222)*

Aug 64. (7") *(RCA 1411) <47-8400>* **SUCH A NIGHT. / NEVER ENDING** 13 Jul64 16

Oct 64. (7") *(RCA 1422) <47-8440>* **AIN'T THAT LOVIN' YOU BABY. / ASK ME** 15 16
12

Nov 64. (7") *(RCA 1430) <HO-0808>* **BLUE CHRISTMAS. / WHITE CHRISTMAS** 11

Jan 65. (lp; mono/stereo) *(RD/SF 7678) <LSP 2999>* **ROUSTABOUT** (soundtrack) 12 Nov64 1
– Roustabout / Little Egypt / Poison Ivy league / Hard knocks / It's a wonderful world / Big love big heartache / One track heart / It's carnival time / Carny town / There's a brand new day on the horizon / Wheels on my heels. *(re-iss. Oct79 lp/c; PL/PK 42356) (re-iss. Aug81 on 'RCA Int.'; INTS 5110) (re-iss. Nov84 lp/c; NL/NK 89049)*

Mar 65. (7") *(RCA 1443) <47-8500>* **DO THE CLAM. / YOU'LL BE GONE** 19 Feb64 21

Apr 65. (lp; mono/stereo) *(RD/SF 7714) <LSP 3338>* **GIRL HAPPY** (soundtrack) 8 8
– Girl happy / Spring fever / Fort Lauderdale chamber of commerce / Startin' tonight / Wolf call / Do not disturb / Cross my heart and hope to die / The meanest girl in town / Do the clam / Puppet on a string / I've got to find my baby. *(re-iss. Aug81 on 'RCA International'; INTS 5034) (re-iss. Nov84 lp/c; NL/NK 83338) (cd-iss. Apr03 on 'Follow That Dream'; FTD 25)*

May 65. (7") *(RCA 1455) <447-0643>* **CRYING IN THE CHAPEL. / I BELIEVE IN THE MAN IN THE SKY** 1 3
(re-iss. May77; PB 2708) – (hit UK No.43 Aug77)

Jun 65. (7") *<47-8585>* **(SUCH AN) EASY QUESTION. / IT FEELS SO RIGHT** – 11
55

Sep 65. (7") *<47-8657>* **I'M YOURS. / (IT'S A) LONG LONELY HIGHWAY** – 11

Sep 65. (mono-lp) *(RD 7723)* **FLAMING STAR AND SUMMER KISSES** 11 –
– (compilation of 'FLAMING STAR' Film soundtrack EP + 'LOVING YOU' lp) *(re-iss. Jun69 as 'FLAMING STAR' on 'RCA Int.'; INTS 1012)* – (hit UK No.2) *(re-iss. Apr79 on 'RCA Camden' lp/c; CDS/CAM 1185)*

Nov 65. (7") *<447-0650>* **PUPPET ON A STRING. / WOODEN HEART** – 14

Nov 65. (7") *(RCA 1489)* **TELL ME WHY. / PUPPET ON A STRING** 15 –

Nov 65. (lp; mono/stereo) *(RD/SF 7752) <LSP 3450>* **ELVIS FOR EVERYONE!** 8 Sep65 10
– Your cheatin' heart / Summer kisses / Winter tears / For the millionth and the last time / Finders keepers losers weepers / In my way / Tomorrow night / Forget me never / Met her tonight / Memphis Tennessee / Sound advice / Santa Lucia / When it rains it really pours. *(re-iss. 1972; SF 8232) (re-iss. Apr84 lp/c; NL/NK 84232) (cd-iss. Apr95;)*

Jan 66. (7") *<47-8740>* **TELL ME WHY. / BLUE RIVER** – 33
95

Jan 66. (lp; mono/stereo) *(RD/SF 7767) <LSP 3468>* **HAREM HOLIDAY** (soundtrack) <US title 'HARUM SCARUM'> 11 Nov65 8
– Harem holiday / My desert serenade / Go east young man / Mirage / Kismet / Shake that tambourine / Hey little girl / Golden coins / So close, yet so far (from paradise) / Animal instinct / Wisdom of the ages. *(re-iss. Aug80 on 'RCA Int.'; INTS 5035) (re-iss. Apr84 lp/c; NL/NK 82558) (cd-iss. Nov03 on 'Follow That Dream'+=; FTD 1006)* – (extra takes).

Feb 66. (7") *(RCA 1504)* **BLUE RIVER. / DO NOT DISTURB** 22 –

Mar 66. (7") *(RCA 1509) <47-8780>* **FRANKIE AND JOHNNY. / PLEASE DON'T STOP LOVING ME** 21 25

Apr 66. (lp; mono/stereo) *(RD/SF 7793) <LSP 3553>* **FRANKIE AND JOHNNY** (soundtrack) 11 20
– Frankie and Johnny / Come along / Petunia, the gardener's daughter /

Chesay / What every woman lives for / Look out Broadway / Beginner's luck / Down by the riverside / When the saints go marching in / Shout it out / Hard luck / Please don't stop loving me / Everybody come aboard. *(re-iss. Aug80 on 'RCA Int.'; INTS 5036) (re-iss. Apr84 lp/c; NL/NK 82559) (cd-iss. Jul04 on 'Follow That Dream'+=; FTD 1005)* – (extra takes).

Jun 66. (7") *(RCA 1526) <47-8870>* **LOVE LETTERS. / COME WHAT MAY** [6] [19]

Jul 66. (lp; mono/stereo) *(RD/SF 7810) <LSP 3643>* **PARADISE, HAWAIIAN STYLE** (soundtrack) [7] [15]
– Paradise, Hawaiian style / Queenie Wahine's papaya / Scratch my back (then I'll scratch yours) / Drums of the islands / Datin' / A dog's life / House of sand / Stop where you are / This is my heaven / Sand castles. *(re-iss. Aug80 on 'RCA Int.'; INTS 5037) (re-iss. Apr84 lp/c; NL/NK 89010) (cd-iss. Jul04 on 'Follow That Dream'+=; FTD 1009)* – (extra takes).

Oct 66. (7") *(RCA 1545) <47-8941>* **ALL THAT I AM. / SPINOUT** [17] B-side [40]

Nov 66. (lp; mono/stereo) *(RD/SF 7820) <LSP 3702>* **CALIFORNIA HOLIDAY** (soundtrack) <US-title 'SPINOUT'> [17] [18]
– Stop, look and listen / Adam and evil / All that I am / Never say yes / Am I ready / Beach shack / Spinout / Smorgasbord / I'll be back / Tomorrow is a long time / Down in the alley / I'll remember you. *(re-iss. Aug80 on 'RCA Int.' lp/c; INT S/K 5038) (cd-iss. Jul04 on 'Follow That Dream'+=; FTD 1008)* – (extra takes).

Nov 66. (7") *(RCA 1557) <47-8950>* **IF EVERY DAY WAS LIKE CHRISTMAS. / HOW WOULD YOU LIKE TO BE** [13] [ ]

Feb 67. (7") *(RCA 1565) <47-9056>* **INDESCRIBABLY BLUE. / FOOLS FALL IN LOVE** [21] [33]

Apr 67. (lp; mono/stereo) *(RD/SF 7867) <LSP 3758>* **HOW GREAT THOU ART** [11] [18]
– How great thou art / In the garden / Without him / By and by / Somebody bigger than you and I / Stand by me / Farther along / Where could I go to but the Lord / Crying in the chapel / If the Lord wasn't by my side / So high / Run on / Where no one stands alone. *(re-iss. Jul84 lp/c; NL/NK 83758) (cd-iss. Apr88; ND 83758)*

May 67. (7") *(RCA 1593)* **YOU GOTTA STOP. / LOVE MACHINE** [38] [–]

Aug 67. (7") *(RCA 1616) <47-9115>* **LONG-LEGGED GIRL (WITH THE SHORT DRESS ON). / THAT'S SOMEONE YOU NEVER FORGET** [49] [63] [92]

Aug 67. (lp; mono/stereo) *(RD/SF 7892) <LSP 3787>* **DOUBLE TROUBLE** (soundtrack) [34] Jun67 [47]
– Double trouble / Baby, if you'll give me all your love / Could I fall in love / Long legged girl (with the short dress on) / City by night / Old MacDonald / I love only one girl / There is so much world to see / It won't be long / Never ending / Blue river / What now, what next, where to. *(re-iss. Aug80 on 'RCA Int.'; INTS 5039) (cd-iss. Oct04 on 'Follow That Dream'+=; FTD 1010)* – (extra takes).

Sep 67. (7") *(RCA 1628) <47-9287>* **THERE'S ALWAYS ME. / JUDY** [ ] [56] [78]

Nov 67. (7") *(RCA 1642) <47-9341>* **BIG BOSS MAN. / YOU DON'T ME** [ ] Oct67 [38]

Feb 68. (7") *(RCA 1663) <47-9425>* **GUITAR MAN. / HI-HEEL SNEAKERS** [19] [43]

Apr 68. (lp; mono/stereo) *(RD/SF 7917) <LSP 3893>* **CLAMBAKE** (soundtrack) [19] Feb68 [40]
– Clambake / Who needs money / A house that has everything / Confidence / Hey, hey, hey / You don't know me / The girl I never loved / How can you lose what you never had / Big boss man / Singing tree / Just call me lonesome / Guitar man. *(re-iss. Aug80 on 'RCA Int.'; INTS 5040) (re-iss. Jan84 lp/c; NL/NK 82565)*

May 68. (7") *(RCA 1688) <47-9465>* **U.S. MALE. / STAY AWAY** [15] [28] Mar68 [67]

Jul 68. (7") *(RCA 1714) <47-9547>* **YOUR TIME HASN'T COME YET BABY. / LET YOURSELF GO** [22] [72] Jun68 [71]

Aug 68. (lp; mono/stereo) *(RD/SF 7957) <LSP 3989>* **SPEEDWAY** (soundtrack) [ ] Jun68 [82]
– Speedway / There ain't nothing like a song / Your time hasn't come yet baby / Who are you (who am I?) / He's your uncle, not your dad / Let yourself go / Your groovy self (by NANCY SINATRA) / Five sleepyheads / Western union / Mine / Goin' home / Suppose. *(re-iss. Aug81 on 'RCA International'; INTS 5041) (re-iss. Jan84 lp/c; NL/NK 85012)*

Oct 68. (7") *(RCA 1747) <47-9600>* **YOU'LL NEVER WALK ALONE. / WE CALL ON HIM** [44] Apr68 [90]

Nov 68. (7") *<47-9670>* **IF I CAN DREAM. / EDGE OF REALITY** [–] [12]

Dec 68. (7") *(RCA 1768) <47-9610>* **A LITTLE LESS CONVERSATION. / ALMOST IN LOVE** [ ] [69] Sep68 [95]

Feb 69. (7") *(RCA 1795)* **IF I CAN DREAM. / MEMORIES** [11] [–]

Mar 69. (7") *<47-9731>* **MEMORIES. / CHARRO** [–] [35]

Jun 69. (7") *(RCA 1831) <47-9741>* **IN THE GHETTO. / ANY DAY NOW** [2] May69 [3]

Aug 69. (lp; mono/stereo) *(RD/SF 8029) <LSP 4155>* **FROM ELVIS IN MEMPHIS** [1] Jun69 [13]
– Wearin that loved-in look / Only the strong survive / I'll hold you in my heart / Long black limousine / It keeps right on a-turnin' / I'm moving on / Power of my love / Gentle on my mind / After loving you / True love travels on a gravel road / Any day now / In the ghetto. *(cd-iss. Mar91;) (re-iss. Mar94 cd/c;)*

Aug 69. (7") *(RCA 1869) <47-9747>* **CLEAN UP YOUR OWN BACK YARD. / THE FAIR IS MOVING ON** [21] Jul69 [35]

Nov 69. (7") *(RCA 1900) <47-9764>* **SUSPICIOUS MINDS. / YOU'LL THINK OF ME** [2] Sep69 [1]

Feb 70. (7") *(RCA 1916) <47-9768>* **DON'T CRY DADDY. / RUBBERNECKIN'** [8] Nov69 [6]

—— His live band mid '69 for album **JAMES BURTON** – lead guitar / **JOHN WILKINSON** – guitar / **CHARLIE HODGE** – guitar / **JERRY SCHEFF** – bass / **LARRY MUHOBERAC** – keyboards / **RONNIE TUTT** – drums back up groups were The IMPERIALS and also The SWEET INSPIRATIONS

Mar 70. (d-lp) *(SF 8080-1) <LSP 6020>* **FROM MEMPHIS TO VEGAS – FROM VEGAS TO MEMPHIS** [3] Nov69 [12]
– FROM MEMPHIS TO VEGAS (live at the International, Vegas) – Blue suede shoes / Johnny B. Goode / All shook up / Hound dog / Are you lonesome tonight / I can't stop loving you / Me babe / Medley; Mystery train – Tiger man / Words / In the ghetto / Suspicious minds / Can't help falling in love. FROM VEGAS TO MEMPHIS (studio sessions) – Elvis back in Memphis / Inherit the wind / This is the story / Stranger in my hometown / A little bit of green / The fair's moving on / And the grass don't pay no mind / From a jack to a king / You'll think of me / Without love (there's nothing). *(re-iss. Jun84; NL 89068) (cd-iss. Dec91;)* – (first lp only)

—— **GLEN D. HARDIN** – piano (ex-CRICKETS) repl. TOTT

May 70. (7") *(RCA 1949) <47-9701>* **KENTUCKY RAIN. / MY LITTLE FRIEND** [21] Feb70 [16]

Jul 70. (7") *(RCA 1974) <47-9835>* **THE WONDER OF YOU. / MAMA LIKED THE ROSES** [1] May70 [9]
(re-iss. May77; PB 2709) – (hit UK No.48)

Jul 70. (lp) *(SF 8128) <LSP 4362>* **ON STAGE – FEBRUARY 1970 (live)** [2] Jun70 [13]
– See see rider blues / Release me (and let me live again) / Sweet Caroline / Runaway / The wonder of you / Polka salad Annie / Yesterday / Proud Mary / Walk a mile in my shoes / Let it be me (je't appartiens). *(re-iss. Mar91 cd/c/lp;)*

Nov 70. (7") *(RCA 1999) <47-9873>* **I'VE LOST YOU. / THE NEXT STEP IS LOVE** [9] Aug70 [32]

Jan 71. (7") *(RCA 2046) <47-9916>* **YOU DON'T HAVE TO SAY YOU LOVE ME. / PATCH IT UP** [9] Oct70 [11]

Jan 71. (lp) *(SF 8162) <LSP 4445>* **THAT'S THE WAY IT IS (live Las Vegas)** [12] Dec70 [21]
– I just can't help believin' / Twenty days and twenty nights / How the web was woven / Patch it up / Mary in the morning / You don't have to say you love me / You've lost that lovin' feeling / I've lost you / Just pretend / Stranger in the crowd / The next step is love / Bridge over troubled water. *(re-iss. Jan84 lp/c; NL/NK 84114) <(cd-iss. Jul93; 74321 14690-2)> (5xlp-box iss.Aug00 on 'Castle'+=; ELVIS 102)* – (extra tracks). *<(3xcd-box iss.Mar01 +=; 07863 67938-2)>*

Mar 71. (7") *(RCA 2060) <47-9960>* **THERE GOES MY EVERYTHING. / I REALLY DON'T WANT TO KNOW** [6] Dec70 [21]

Mar 71. (lp) *(SF 8172) <LSP 4460>* **ELVIS COUNTRY (I'M 10,000 YEARS OLD)** [6] Jan71 [12]
– Snowbird / Tomorrow never comes / Little cabin on the hill / Whole lotta shakin' goin' on / Funny how time slips away / I really don't want to know / There goes my everything / It's your baby / You rock it / Fool / Faded love / I washed my hands in muddy water / Make the world go away / I was born about 10,000 years ago *(re-iss. Aug84)(re-iss. cd+c Jul93)*

May 71. (7") *(RCA 2084) <47-9980>* **RAGS TO RICHES. / WHERE DID THEY GO, LORD** [9] Mar71 [33]

May 71. (7") *<47-9985>* **LIFE. / ONLY BELIEVE** [–] [53]

Jul 71. (lp) *(SF 8202)* *<LSP 4530>* **LOVE LETTERS FROM ELVIS** [7] Jun71 [33]
– Love letters / When I'm over you / I'll never know / Got my mojo working / Heart of Rome / It ain't no big thing (but it's growing) / Only believe / This is our dance / Cindy Cindy / Life. *(re-iss. Aug81 on 'RCA International'; INTS 5081) (re-iss. Nov84 lp/c; NL/NK 89011) (cd-iss. Jun88; ND 89011)*

Sep 71. (7") *(RCA 2125)* *<47-9998>* **I'M LEAVIN'. / HEART OF ROME** [23] Aug71 [36]

Oct 71. (7") *<48-1017>* **IT'S ONLY LOVE. / THE SOUND OF YOUR CRY** [–] [51]

Nov 71. (7") *(RCA 2158)* **I JUST CAN'T HELP BELIEVIN'. / HOW THE WEB WAS WOVEN** [6] [–]

Nov 71. (7") *<74-0572>* **MERRY CHRISTMAS BABY. / O COME, ALL YE FAITHFUL** [–] [ ]

Mar 72. (7") *(RCA 2188)* *<74-0619>* **UNTIL IT'S TIME FOR YOU TO GO. / WE CAN MAKE THE MORNING** [5] Feb72 [40]

May 72. (lp) *(SF 8266)* *<LSP 4671>* **ELVIS NOW** [12] Jan72 [43]
– Help me make it through the night / Miracle of the rosary / Hey Jude / Put your hand in the hand / Until it's time for you to go / We can make the morning / Early mornin' rain / Sylvia / Fools rush in (where angels feared to tread) / I was born about ten thousand years ago. *(re-iss. Jul93 cd/c;)*

Jun 72. (7") *(RCA 2229)* *<74-0672>* **AN AMERICAN TRILOGY. / THE FIRST TIME EVER I SAW YOUR FACE** [8] Apr72 [66]

Jul 72. (lp) *(SF 8296)* *<LSP 4776>* **ELVIS AS RECORDED AT MADISON SQUARE GARDEN (live)** [3] [11]
– Introduction; / Theme from 2001 – a space odyssey / That's all right / Proud Mary / Never been to Spain / You don't have to say you love me / You've lost that lovin' feelin' / Polk salad Annie / Love me / All shook up / Heartbreak hotel / Medley; / (Let me your) Teddy bear – Don't be cruel – Love me tender – The impossible dream / Hound dog / Suspicious minds / For the good times / An American trilogy / Funny how time slips away / I can't stop loving you / Can't help falling in love.

Aug 72. (lp/c) *(SF 8275)* *<LSP 4690>* **HE TOUCHED ME** (gospel) [38] Apr72 [79]
– He touched me / I've got confidence / Amazing Grace / Seeing is believing / He is my everything / Bosom of Abraham / An evening prayer / Lead me, guide me / There is no god but God / Thing called love / I, John / Reach out to Jesus.

Sep 72. (7") *(RCA 2267)* *<74-0769>* **BURNING LOVE. / IT'S A MATTER OF TIME** [7] Aug72 [2]

Dec 72. (7") *(RCA 2304)* *<74-0815>* **ALWAYS ON MY MIND. / SEPARATE WAYS** [9] B-side [20]

Feb 73. (d-lp) *(DPS 2040)* *<VPSX 6089>* **ALOHA FROM HAWAII VIA SATELLITE** (TV special rec. 14th Jan '73) [11] [1]
– Theme from 2001 (a space odyssey) / See see rider / Burning love / Something / You gave me a mountain / Steamroller blues / My way / Love me Johnny B. Goode / It's over / I can't stop loving you / Blue suede shoes / I'm so lonesome I could cry / Hound dog / What now my love / Fever / Welcome to my world / Suspicious minds / I'll remember you / Medley; Long tall Sally – Whole lotta shakin goin' on – An American trilogy – A big hunk o' love – I can't help falling in love. *(re-iss. Aug84 lp/c; PL/PK 82642) (cd-iss. Sep86; PD 82642)* (cd re-iss. Oct95;)

May 73. (7") *(RCA 2359)* **POLK SALAD ANNIE. / SEE SEE RIDER** [23] [–]

Jul 73. (7") *(RCA 2393)* *<74-0910>* **FOOL. / STEAMROLLER BLUES** [16] [17]

Sep 73. (lp) *(SF 8378)* *<APL 0283>* **ELVIS** [16] [52]
– Fool / Where do I go from here / Love me, love the life I lead / I'm still here / It's impossible / (That's what you get) For lovin' me / Padre / I'll take you home again Kathleen / I will be true / Don't think twice, it's alright. *(re-iss. Mar94;)*

Nov 73. (7") *(RCA 2435)* *<APBO 0088>* **RAISED ON ROCK. / FOR OL' TIMES SAKE** [36] [ ]

Nov 73. (lp) *<(APL1 0388)>* **RAISED ON ROCK** [ ] [50]
– Raised on rock / Are you sincere / Find out what's happening / I miss you / Girl of mine / For 'ol times sake / If you don't come back / Just a little bit / Sweet Angeline / Three corn patches. *(re-iss. Mar94 cd/c;)*

Mar 74. (7") *<(APBO 0196)>* **TAKE GOOD CARE OF HER. / I'VE GOT A THING ABOUT YOU BABY** [33] Mar74 [39]

May 74. (lp) *<(APL1 0475)>* **GOOD TIMES** [42] [90]
– Take good care of her / Loving arms / I got a feeling in my body / If that isn't love / She wears my ring / I've got a thing about you baby / My boy / Spanish eyes / Talk about the good times / Good time Charlie got the blues. *(re-iss. Mar94 cd/c;)*

Jun 74. (7") *<(APBO 0280)>* **IF YOU TALK IN YOUR SLEEP. / HELP ME** [40] [17]

Aug 74. (lp) *<(APL1 0606)>* **ELVIS AS RECORDED LIVE ON STAGE (live in Memphis)** [44] [33]
– See see rider / I got a woman / Love me / Trying to get to you / Medley; Long tall Sally – Whole lotta shakin' goin on / Mama don't dance / Flip flop and fly / Jailhouse rock / Hound dog / Why me Lord / How great thou art / Blueberry hill / Can't stop loving you / Help me / An American trilogy / Let there be me / My baby left me / Lawdy Miss Clawdy / Can't help falling in love / Closing vamp.

Oct 74. (7") *(RCA 2458)* **MY BOY. / LOVING ARMS** [5] [–]

Dec 74. (7") *<(PB 10074)>* **PROMISED LAND. / IT'S MIDNIGHT** [9] Oct74 [14]

Jan 75. (7") *<PB 10191>* **MY BOY. / THINKING ABOUT YOU** [–] [20]

Feb 75. (lp) *<(APL1 0873)>* **PROMISED LAND** [21] [47]
– Promised land / There's a honky tonk angel (who will take me back in) / Help me / Mr. Songman / Love song of the year / It's midnight / Your love's been a long time comin' / If you talk in your sleep / Thinking about you / You ask me to. *(cd-iss. Dec91;)*

May 75. (7") *(RCA 2562)* *<PB 10278>* **T-R-O-U-B-L-E. / MR. SONGMAN** [31] [35]

Jun 75. (lp) *(RS 1011)* *<APL1 1039>* **TODAY** [48] [57]
– T.R.O.U.B.L.E. / And I love you so / Susan when she tried / Woman without love / Shake a hand / Pieces of my life / Fairy tale / I can help / Bringin' it back / Green green grass of home.

Oct 75. (7") *<PB 10401>* **BRINGING IT BACK. / PIECES OF MY LIFE** [–] [65]

Nov 75. (7") *(RCA 2635)* **GREEN GREEN GRASS OF HOME. / THINKING ABOUT YOU** [29] [–]

Apr 76. (7") *(RCA 2674)* *<PB 10601>* **HURT. / FOR THE HEART** [37] [28]

Jun 76. (lp) *(RS 1060)* *<APL1 1506>* **FROM ELVIS PRESLEY BOULEVARD, MEMPHIS, TENNESSEE** [29] [41]
– Hurt / Never again / Blue eyes crying in the rain / Danny boy / The last farewell / For the heart / Bitter they are, harder they fall / Solitaire / Love coming down / I'll never fall in love again. *(re-iss. Jan85 lp/c; PL/PK 89266) (re-iss. Jul93 cd/c;)*

Feb 77. (7") *(PB 857)* *<PB 10857>* **MOODY BLUE. / SHE THINKS I STILL CARE** [6] [31]

Jul 77. (7") *(PB 998)* *<PB 10998>* **WAY DOWN. / PLEDGING MY LOVE** [1] [18]

— On the 16th August 1977, ELVIS died of heart failure. Below are songs he recorded just prior to death.

Aug 77. (lp/c) *(PL/PK 12428)* *<AFL 2428>* **MOODY BLUE** (some live) [3] [3]
– Unchained melody / If you love me (let me know) / Little darlin' / He'll have to go / Let me be there / Way down / Pledging my love / Moody blue / She thinks I still care. *(re-iss. Sep81 lp/c; RCA LP/K 3021) (re-iss. Jan85 lp/c; NL/NK 90252) (cd-iss. Oct88; ND 90252)*

– (selective) posthumous comps, etc. –

all below releases were issued on 'R.C.A.' unless stated otherwise

Aug 77. (lp/c) *(PL/PK 12274)* *<APL 2274>* **WELCOME TO MY WORLD** [7] [44]
– Welcome to my world / Help me make it through the night / Release me (and let me love again) / I really don't know what to know / For the good times / Make the world go away / Gentle on my mind / I'm so lonesome I could cry / Your cheatin' heart / I can't stop loving you. *(re-iss. Sep81 lp/c; RCA LP/K 3020)*

Sep 77. (lp/c) *RCA Starcall; (HY/+C 1023)* **PICTURES OF ELVIS** [52] [–]

Oct 77. (lp) *Charly;* **THE SUN YEARS** [31] [–]

Nov 77. (d-lp/d-c) *(PL/PK 02587)* *<APL1 2587>* **ELVIS IN CONCERT (live)** [13] Oct77 [5]
– (Elvis' fans comment, and opening riff to 2001) / See see rider / That's alright / Are you lonesome tonight? / You gave me a mountain / Jailhouse rock / How great thou art / I really don't want to know / (Elvis introduces his father) / Hurt. *(re-iss. Jul93 cd/c;)*

Nov 77. (7") *(PB 1165)* *<11165>* **MY WAY (live). / AMERICA, THE BEAUTIFUL (live)** [9] [22]

Apr 78. (lp/c) *(PL/PK 12772)* *<AFL 2772>* **HE WALKS BESIDE ME** (gospel) [37] [ ]
– He is my everything / Miracle of the rosary / Where did they go Lord / Somebody bigger than you and I / An evening prayer / The impossible dream / If I can dream / Padre / Known only to him / Who am I / How great thou art.

May 78. (lp/c) *(PL/PK 42101)* **THE '56 SESSIONS VOL.1** [47] [–]
(re-iss. Sep81 lp/c; RCA LP/K 3025)

Nov 78. (lp) *<KKL 7065>* **ELVIS – A CANADIAN TRIBUTE** [–] [86]

Jan 79. (lp/c) *(PL/PK 13082) <CPL 3082>* **A LEGENDARY PERFORMER VOL.3** [43] [ ]

Apr 79. (lp/c) *(PL/PK 13279) <AQL 3279>* **OUR MEMORIES OF ELVIS** [72] [ ]

Sep 79. (lp/c) *(PL/PK 13448) <AQL 3448>* **OUR MEMORIES OF ELVIS VOL.2** [ ] [ ]

Nov 79. (d-lp/d-c) *K-Tel; (NE 1062)* **LOVE SONGS** [4] [–]

Dec 79. (7"/12") *(PB/PC 9464)* **IT WON'T SEEM LIKE CHRISTMAS (WITHOUT YOU). / MERRY CHRISTMAS BABY** [13] [–]

Jun 80. (lp/c) *(INTS/INTK 5031)* **ELVIS PRESLEY SINGS LEIBER AND STOLLER** [32] [–]
(re-iss. Apr84 lp/c; NL/NK 89099)

Aug 80. (8xlp-box) *(ELVIS 25) <CPL 3699>* **ELVIS AARON PRESLEY** [21] [27]
– (AN EARLY LIVE PERFORMANCE / AN EARLY BENEFIT PERFORMANCE / COLLECTOR'S GOLD FROM THE MOVIE YEARS / THE TV SPECIALS / THE LAS VEGAS YEARS / LOST SINGLES / ELVIS AT THE PIANO – THE CONCERT YEARS (PART 1) / THE CONCERT YEARS (concluded).

Aug 80. (7") *(RCA 4)* **IT'S ONLY LOVE. / BEYOND THE REEF** [3] [–]

Nov 80. (lp/c) *K-Tel; (NE 1101/CE 2101)* **INSPIRATION** (gospel) [6] [–]

Nov 80. (7") *(RCA 16)* **SANTA CLAUS IS BACK IN TOWN. / I BELIEVE** [41] [–]

Feb 81. (7") *(RCA 43) <PB 12158>* **GUITAR MAN (remix). / FADED LOVE** [43] [28]

Mar 81. (lp/c) *(RCA LP/K 5010) <AAL 3917>* **GUITAR MAN** [33] [49]
– Guitar man / After loving you / Too much monkey business / Just call me lonesome / Lovin' arms / You asked me to / Clean up your own backyard / She thinks I still care / Faded love / I'm movin' on.

Apr 81. (7") *(RCA 48)* **LOVING ARMS. / YOU ASKED ME TO** [47] [–]

May 81. (d-lp/d-c) *(RCA LP/K 5029) <CPL 4031>* **THIS IS ELVIS** (soundtrack) [47] Apr81 [ ]
– (Marie's the name) His latest flame / Moody blue / That's all right / Shake, rattle & roll / Flip, flop and fly / Heartbreak hotel / Hound dog / (excerpt from Hy Gardner interview) / My baby left me / Merry Christmas baby / Mean woman blues / Don't be cruel / (Let me be your) Teddy bear / Jailhouse rock / (army swearing in) / G.I. blues / (excerpt from departure for Germany press conference) / Too much monkey business / Love me tender / I've got a thing about you baby / I need your love tonight / Blue suede shoes / Viva Las Vegas / Suspicious minds (excerpt from J.C.'s award to Elvis) / Promised land / (excerpt from Madison Square Garden press conference) / Always on my mind / Are you lonesome tonight? / My way / An American trilogy / Memories. *(re-iss. May84 d-lp/d-c; BL/BK 84031)*

Nov 81. (lp/c) *K-Tel; (NE 1141)* **THE ULTIMATE PERFORMANCE** [45] [–]

Feb 82. (lp/c) *(RCA LP/K 3060)* **THE SOUND OF YOUR CRY** [31] [–]

Feb 82. (7") *(RCA 196)* **ARE YOU LONESOME TONIGHT? (live version). / FROM A JACK TO A KING (live)** [25] [–]

Mar 82. (11x7"ep-box) *(EP 1)* **THE EP COLLECTION** [97] [–]

Jun 82. (7"/7"pic-d) *(RCA/+P 232)* **THE SOUND OF YOUR CRY. / I'LL NEVER KNOW** [59] [–]

Aug 82. (d-lp/d-c) *(RCA LP/K 1000)* **ROMANTIC ELVIS 20 LOVE SONGS – ROCKIN' ELVIS 60's** [62] [–]
(re-iss. May84 lp/c; PL/PK 89124)

Nov 82. (7",7"pic-d) *<PB 13351>* **THE ELVIS MEDLEY: Jailhouse Rock-Teddy Bear-Hound Dog-Don't Be Cruel-Burning Love-Suspicious Minds. / JAILHOUSE ROCK** [–] [71]

Dec 82. (lp/c) *(NL/NK 89025)* **IT WON'T SEEM LIKE CHRISTMAS WITHOUT YOU** [80] [–]
(re-dist.Nov84; same)

Apr 83. (pic-lp) *(RCALP 9020)* **JAILHOUSE ROCK / LOVE IN LAS VEGAS** [40] [–]
– (compilation of music from the 2 films)

Apr 83. (7") *(RCA 332)* **(YOU'RE SO SQUARE) BABY, I DON'T CARE. / TRUE LOVE** [61] [–]
(12"pic-d) *(RCAP 332)* – ('A'side) / One-sided love affair / Tutti frutti.

Aug 83. (lp/c) *(RCA LP/K 3105) <AHL 4678>* **I WAS THE ONE** [83] May83 [ ]

Nov 83. (7") *(RCA 369)* **I CAN HELP. / THE LADY LOVES ME (w/ ANN-MARGARET)** [30] [–]
(10"pic-d+=) *(RCAP 369)* – If every day was like Christmas.

Nov 83. (lp/c) *(PL/PK 84848)* **A LEGENDARY PERFORMER VOL.4** [91] [–]

Mar 84. (lp/c) *(PL/PK 89287)* **I CAN HELP** [71] [–]

Apr 84. (lp/c) *(PG/PH 89387) <3601>* **ELVIS – THE FIRST LIVE RECORDINGS** [69] Mar84 [ ]

Oct 84. (7") *(RCA 459)* **THE LAST FAREWELL. / IT'S EASY FOR YOU** [48] [–]
(12"+=) *(RCAT 459)* – Shake, rattle and roll / Flip, flop and fly / That's all right (mama) / My heart cries for you.

Nov 84. (6xlp-box/6xc-box) *(PL/PK 85172) <5172>* **ELVIS – A GOLDEN CELEBRATION** [ ] [80]

Jan 85. (7") *(RCA 476)* **THE ELVIS MEDLEY. / BLUE SUEDE SHOES** [51] [–]

May 85. (lp/c/cd) *(PL/PK/PD 85418)* **RECONSIDER BABY** [92] [–]

Jul 85. (7") *(PB 49943)* **ALWAYS ON MY MIND. / TOMORROW NIGHT** [59] [–]
(12"+=) *(PT 49943)* – Ain't that loving you baby / Dark moon.

Oct 85. (lp/c/cd) *Telstar; (STA R/C/TCD 2264)* **BALLADS** [23] [–]

Mar 87. (7") *(ARON 1)* **BOSSA NOVA BABY (remix). / AIN'T THAT LOVIN' YOU BABY** [47] [–]
(12"+=) *(ARONT 1)* – I'm coming home / Rock-a-hula baby.
(12") *(PT 49745)* – ('A'side) / ('A'-Stretch mix) / I'm coming home.

Aug 87. (d-lp/d-c/d-cd) *(PL/PK/PD 90100) <6382>* **PRESLEY – THE ALL TIME GREATEST HITS** <US title 'THE TOP TEN HITS'> [4] [ ]
– Heartbreak Hotel / Blue suede shoes / Hound dog / Love me tender / Too much / All shook up / Teddy bear / Paralysed / Party / Jailhouse rock / Don't / Wear my ring around your neck / Hard headed woman / King Creole / One night / A fool such as I / Big hunk o' love / Stuck on you / Girl of my best friend / It's now or never / Are you lonesome tonight? / Wooden heart / Surrender / His latest flame / Can't help falling in love / Good luck charm / She's not you / Return to sender / Devil in disguise / Crying in the chapel / Love letters / If I can dream / In the ghetto / Suspicious minds / Don't cry daddy / The wonder of you / I just can't help believing / American trilogy / Burning love / Always on my mind / My boy / Suspicion / Moody blue / Way down / It's only love.

Aug 87. (d-lp/d-c/cd) *(PL/PK/PD 86414)* **THE COMPLETE SUN SESSIONS** [ ] [–]

Aug 87. (7") *(ARON 2)* **LOVE ME TENDER. / TEDDY BEAR** [56] [–]
(12"+=) *(ARONT 2)* – If I can dream / Bossa nova baby (extended).

Jan 88. (7"/12"/cd-s) *(PB 49595)* **STUCK ON YOU. / ANYWAY YOU WANT ME** [58] [–]

Jan 89. (lp/c/cd) *(PL/PK/PD 90250)* **ESSENTIAL ELVIS VOLUME 2: STEREO '57** [60] [–]

Jul 90. (cd/c/lp) *(PD/PK/PL 90486)* **ESSENTIAL ELVIS – VOLUME 3: HITS LIKE NEVER BEFORE** [71] [–]

Aug 90. (cd/c/lp) *(PD/PK/PL 82227)* **THE GREAT PERFORMANCES** [62] [ ]

Jul 91. (7") *(PB 49177)* **ARE YOU LONESOME TONIGHT? (live '69). / RUNAWAY (live)** [68] [–]
(12"+=/cd-s+=) *(PT/PD 49177)* – Baby, What You Want Me To Do (Live) / Reconsider Baby (Live)

Aug 91. (3xcd/3xc/3xlp) *(PD/PK/PL 90574)* **COLLECTOR'S GOLD** [57] [ ]

Feb 92. (cd/c/d-lp) *(PD/PK/PL 90642)* **FROM THE HEART – HIS GREATEST LOVE SONGS** [4] [ ]

Aug 92. (7"/c-s) *(74321 11077-7/-4)* **DON'T BE CRUEL. / ALL SHOOK UP** [42] [–]
(cd-s+=) *(74321 11077-2)* – Jailhouse rock / I need your love tonight.

Mar 93. (cd) *(74321 13430-2)* **KID GALAHAD / GIRLS! GIRLS! GIRLS!** [ ] [ ]

Mar 93. (cd) *(74321 13431-2)* **IT HAPPENED AT THE WORLD'S FAIR / FUN IN ACAPULCO** [ ] [ ]

Mar 93. (cd) *(74321 13432-2)* **VIVA LAS VEGAS / ROUSTABOUT** [ ] [ ]

Mar 93. (cd) *(74321 13433-2)* **HARUM SCARUM / GIRL HAPPY** [ ] [ ]

Jun 94. (cd/c) *(07863 66360-2/-4)* **FRANKIE & JOHNNY / PARADISE, HAWAIIAN STYLE** [ ] [ ]

Jun 94. (cd/c) *(07863 66361-2/-4)* **SPINOUT / DOUBLE TROUBLE** [ ] [ ]

Jun 94. (cd/c) *(07863 66362-2/-4)* **KISSIN' COUSINS / CLAMBAKE / STAY AWAY, JOE** [ ] [ ]

Sep 94. (cd/c/d-lp) *(74321 22871-2/-4/-1)* **THE ESSENTIAL COLLECTION** [6] [ ]

Oct 95. (cd-ep) *(74321 32012-2)* **TWELTH OF NEVER / BURNING LOVE / WALK A MILE IN MY SHOES** [21] [–]

May 96. (cd-ep) *(74321 33686-2)* **HEARTBREAK HOTEL / I WAS THE ONE** [45] [–]
May 97. (c-s) *(74321 48541-4)* **ALWAYS ON MY MIND / SEPARATE WAYS** [13] [ ]
(cd-s) *(74321 48541-2)* – ('A'side) / Are you lonesome tonight? / Moody blue / Way down.
Jun 97. (cd/c) *(74321 48984-2/-4)* **ALWAYS ON MY MIND – ULTIMATE LOVE SONGS** [3] [ ]
Jul 97. (4xcd-box) *<(07863 67469-2)>* **PLATINUM: A LIFE IN MUSIC** [ ] [80]
Feb 98. (cd/c) *(74321 55628-2/-4)* **BLUE SUEDE SHOES (The Ultimate Rock'n'roll Collection)** [39] [ ]
Jul 99. (3xcd-box/3xc-box) *<(07863 67732-2/-4)>* **ARTIST OF THE CENTURY** [ ] [ ]
Nov 00. (d-cd/c) *(74321 81102-2/-4)* **THE 50 GREATEST HITS** [8] [–]
Mar 01. (cd) *(74321 84708-2)* **THE LIVE GREATEST HITS (live)** [50] [–]
Apr 01. (cd-s) *(74321 84844-2)* **SUSPICIOUS MINDS (live) / SUSPICIOUS MINDS (studio)** [15] [–]
(cd-s) *(74321 85582-2)* – ('A'side) / The wonder of you.
Oct 01. (cd-s) *(74321 90402-2)* **AMERICA THE BEAUTIFUL / IF I CAN DREAM / AMAZING GRACE / IF I CAN DREAM (video)** [69] [ ]
Nov 01. (d-cd) *(74321 90075-2)* **THE 50 GREATEST LOVE SONGS** [21] [–]
Jun 02. (c-s; as ELVIS VS. JXL) *(74321 94357-4)* *<060575>* **A LITTLE LESS CONVERSATION. / (original)** [1] [50]
(12"+=/cd-s+=) *(74321 94357-1/-2)* – ('A'-version).
(above featured JUNKIE XL)
Sep 02. (cd/c/d-lp) *(07863 68079-2/-4/-1)* **ELV1S – 30 NO.1 HITS** [1] [1]
– Heartbreak hotel / Don't be cruel / Hound dog / Love me tender / Too much / All shook up / Teddy bear / Jailhouse rock / Don't / Hard headed woman / One night / Now and then there's a fool such as I / Big hunk o' love / Stuck on you / It's now or never / Are you lonesome tonight / Wooden heart / Surrender / (Marie's the name) His latest flame / Can't help falling in love / Good luck charm / She's not you / Return to sender / You're the Devil in disguise / Crying in the chapel / In the ghetto / Suspicious minds / The wonder of you / Burning love / Way down / A little less conversation (JXL remix).
Sep 03. (12") *(82876 54218-1)* **RUBBERNECKIN' (remix with Paul Oakenfold) / (extended)** [5] [94]
(cd-s+=) *(82876 54341-2)* *<54218>* – (original).
Oct 03. (cd/c/d-lp) *(82876 57008-2/-4/-1)* *<51108>* **ELVIS – 2ND TO NONE** [4] [3]
– That's all right / I forgot to remember to forget / Blue suede shoes / I want you, I need you, I love you / Love me / Mean woman blues / Loving you / Treat me nice / Wear my ring around your neck / King Creole / Trouble / I got stung / I need your love tonight / A mess of blues / I feel so bad / Little sister / Rock-a-hula baby / Bossa nova baby / Viva Las Vegas / If I can dream / Memories / Don't cry daddy / Kentucky rain / You don't have to say you love me / An American trilogy / Always on my mind / Promised land / Moody blue / I'm a roustabout / Rubberneckin' (with PAUL OAKENFOLD).
Nov 03. (cd) *(82876 57489-2)* *<52393>* **CHRISTMAS PEACE** (festive) [41] [ ]
Jul 04. (cd-s) *(82876 61921-2)* **THAT'S ALL RIGHT / BLUE MOON OF KENTUCKY / THAT'S ALL RIGHT (alt. Sun session)** [3] [–]
Jan 05. (cd-s) *(82876 66715-2)* **JAILHOUSE ROCK / TREAT ME NICE** [1] [–]
(10"+=) *(82876 66715-1)* – Treat me nice (alt.).
Jan 05. (cd-s) *(82876 66668-2)* **ONE NIGHT / I GOT STUNG** [1] [–]
(10"+=) *(82876 66668-1)* – One night of sin.
Jan 05. (cd-s) *(82876 66658-2)* **A FOOL SUCH AS I / I NEED YOUR LOVE TONIGHT** [2] [–]
(10"+=) *(82876 66658-1)* – A fool such as I (alt.)
Jan 05. (cd-s) *(82876 66659-2)* **IT'S NOW OR NEVER / A MESS OF BLUES** [1] [–]
(10"+=) *(82876 66659-1)* – Make me know it.
Jan 05. (cd-s) *(82876 66660-2)* **ARE YOU LONESOME TONIGHT? / I GOTTA KNOW** [2] [–]
(10"+=) *(82876 66660-1)* – Are you lonesome tonight? (alt.)
Jan 05. (cd) *(82876 67448-2)* *<67001-2>* **LOVE, ELVIS** [8] [ ]
– Are you lonesome tonight? / Can't help falling in love / Always on my mind / It's now or never / Love me tender / I want you, I need you, I love you / Don't / (Now and then there's) A fool such as I / Any way you want me (that's how I will be) / Surrender / Hawaiian wedding song / Doin' the best I can / Fever / It hurts me / I just can't help believin' / The wonder of you / Let it be me / It's impossible / For the good times / There goes my everything / And I love you so / You don't have to say you love me / Unchained melody / If I can dream.
Feb 05. (cd-s) *(82876 66661-2)* **WOODEN HEART / PUPPET ON A STRING** [2] [–]
(10"+=) *(82876 66661-1)* – Tonight is so right for love.
Feb 05. (cd-s) *(82876 66669-2)* **SURRENDER / LONELY MAN** [2] [–]
(10"+=) *(82876 66669-1)* – Lonely man (alt.)
Feb 05. (cd-s) *(82876 66670-2)* **HIS LATEST FLAME / LITTLE SISTER** [3] [–]
(10"+=) *(82876 66670-1)* – His latest flame (alt.)
Feb 05. (cd-s) *(82876 66673-2)* **ROCK-A-HULA BABY / CAN'T HELP FALLING IN LOVE** [3] [–]
(10"+=) *(82876 66673-1)* – Can't help falling in love (alt.)
Mar 05. (cd-s) *(82876 66675-2)* **GOOD LUCK CHARM / ANYTHING THAT'S PART OF YOU** [2] [–]
(10"+=) *(82876 66675-1)* – Good luck charm (alt.)
Mar 05. (cd-s) *(82876 66676-2)* **SHE'S NOT YOU / JUST TELL HER JIM SAID HELLO** [3] [–]
(10"+=) *(82876 66676-1)* – She's not you (alt.)
Mar 05. (cd-s) *(82876 66677-2)* **RETURN TO SENDER / WHERE DO YOU COME FROM** [5] [–]
(10"') *(82876 66677-1)* – Girls! girls! girls!
Mar 05. (cd-s) *(82876 66678-2)* **DEVIL IN DISGUISE / PLEASE DON'T DRAG THAT STRING AROUND** [2] [–]
(10"+=) *(82876 66678-1)* – Devil in disguise (alt.)
Apr 05. (cd-s) *(82876 66680-2)* **CRYING IN THE CHAPEL / I BELIEVE IN THE MAN IN THE SKY** [2] [–]
(10"+=) *(82876 66680-1)* – Milky white way.
Apr 05. (cd-s) *(82876 66681-2)* **THE WONDER OF YOU / MAMA LIKE THE ROSES** [4] [–]
(10"+=) *(82876 66681-1)* – Let it be me (je t'Appartiens).
Apr 05. (cd-s) *(82876 66682-2)* **WAY DOWN / PLEDGING MY LOVE** [2] [–]
(10"+=) *(82876 66682-1)* – Way down (alt.)
May 05. (d-cd) *<(82876 67883-2)>* **ELVIS BY THE PRESLEYS** (soundtrack) [13] [15]
– Trying to get to you / Heartbreak hotel / I want you, I need you, I love you / I got a woman / Got a lot o' livin' to do! / (There'll be) Peace in the valley (for me) / Trouble / Hawaiian wedding song / Indescribably blue / In the ghetto / Suspicious minds / I'll hold you in my heart (till I can hold you in my arms) / Bridge over troubled water / You've lost that loving feeling / It's over / Separate ways / Always on my mind / My way / Burning love / Welcome to my world / Steamroller blues / I got a feelin' in my body / If I can dream / A little less conversation // It wouldn't be the same without you (demo) / Jailhouse rock (alt.) / Anything that's part of you (alt.) / You'll be gone (alt.) / Too much monkey business (alt.) / Baby what you want me to do (alt.) / I'm so lonesome I could cry (alt.) / Blue Christmas (live).
Nov 05. (3xcd-box) *(82876 73952-2)* *<71247-2>* **HITSTORY** [31] [ ]

– (selective) pre-death compilations, etc. –

on 'R.C.A.' unless mentioned otherwise
Mar 56. (7"ep) *<EPA 747>* **ELVIS PRESLEY** [–] [20]
Jun 57. (7"ep) *(RCX 101)* *<EPA 4054>* **PEACE IN THE VALLEY** [ ] Apr57 [25]
– (There'll be) Peace in the valley (for me) / It is no secret / I believe / Take my hand precious Lord. *(UK re-iss. Mar60)*
Jun 57. (7"ep) *<EPA2 1515>* **LOVING YOU, VOLUME 2** [–] lp-cht [18]
Aug 57. (7"ep) *<EPA 4041>* **JUST FOR YOU** [–] lp-cht [18]
Jan 58. (7"ep) *(RCX 106)* **JAILHOUSE ROCK** [18] Nov57 [ ]
– Jailhouse rock / Young and beautiful / Don't leave me now / Baby I don't care / I want to be free. *(re-iss. Mar60 + Feb82)*
Oct 58. (lp) *(RB 16069)* *<LPM 1707>* **ELVIS' GOLDEN RECORDS** [ ] Apr58 [3]
(re-iss. 1970; (SF 8129) (re-iss. Sep81 as 'VOL.1' on 'RCA International' lp/c; INTS/INTK 5143) (re-iss. Nov84 lp/c; NL/NK 81707) (cd-iss. 1988; PD 85196)
Mar 59. (lp) *<LPM 1990>* **FOR LP FANS ONLY** [–] [19]
(UK cd-iss. Nov89; ND 90359)
Jul 59. (lp) *(RD 27128)* *<LPM 2011>* **A DATE WITH ELVIS (early Sun recordings)** [4] Sep59 [32]
– Blue Moon of Kentucky / Young and beautiful / Baby I don't care / Milk cow blues boogie / Baby let's play house / Good rockin' tonight / Is it so strange / I forgot to remember to forget. *(re-iss. Aug80 + Apr84) (cd-iss. Nov89; ND 90360)*

Feb 60. (7"ep) *(RCX 175)* **STRICTLY ELVIS** [26] Jan57 [ ]
– Old Shep / Any place is Paradise / Paralysed / Is it so strange.

Jun 60. (lp) *(RD 27159) <LPM 2075>* **50,000,000 ELVIS FANS CAN'T BE WRONG – ELVIS' GOLDEN RECORDS VOLUME 2** [4] Feb60 [31]
(re-iss. Sep81 as 'ELVIS GOLDEN VOL.2' on 'RCA International' lp/c; INTS/INTK 5144) (cd-iss. Nov84;)

Jun 62. (7"ep) *(RCX 211)* **FOLLOW THAT DREAM** [34] [15]
– Follow that dream / Angel / What a wonderful world / I'm not the marrying kind.

Jan 63. (7"ep) *(RCX 7106) <EPA 4371>* **KID GALAHAD** [16] Sep62 [30]
– King of the whole wide world / This is living / Riding the rainbow / Home is where the heart is / I got lucky / Whistling tune.

Apr 64. (lp) *(RD 7630) <LSP 2765>* **ELVIS' GOLDEN RECORDS, VOLUME 3** [6] Sep63 [3]
(re-iss. Sep81 on 'RCA International' lp/c; INTS/INTK 5145) (re-iss. Nov84 lp/c; NL/NK 82765) (cd-iss. Dec90;)

Apr 64. (7"ep) *(RCX 7141)* **LOVE IN LAS VEGAS** [ ] [92]
– If you think I don't need you / I need somebody to lean on / C'mon everybody / Today tomorrow and forever.

Jul 65. (7"ep) *(RCX 7173)* **TICKLE ME VOLUME 1** [ ] [70]
– I feel that I've known you forever / Night rider / Slowly but surely / Dirty dirty feeling / Put the blame on me.

Sep 65. (lp) *(RD 7762) <LPS 3450>* **ELVIS FOR EVERYONE!**
(UK title 'ELVIS FOR EVERYBODY') [8] [10]
(UK re-iss. +c.May72, hit No.48)

Apr 68. (lp) *(RD/SF 7924) <LSP 3921>* **ELVIS' GOLD RECORDS, VOLUME 4** [ ] [33]
(re-iss. Sep81 on 'RCA International' lp/c; (NL/NK 83921) (re-iss. Apr84 lp/c; (NL/NK 83921) (cd-iss. Dec90;)

Apr 69. (lp) *(RD 8011)* **ELVIS – N.B.C. TV SPECIAL** [2] Jan69 [8]
(re-iss. UK Aug78 hit No.50) (re-iss. Aug81 & Nov84) (cd-iss. Mar91)

Feb 70. (lp) *(RCA 555)* **PORTRAIT IN MUSIC** [36] [ ]

Nov 70. (4xlp) *(LPM 6401)* **WORLD WIDE 50 GOLD AWARD HITS** [49] [45]
(c-iss.May72 – 2 Volumes 25 hits in each)

Jul 71. (7"m) *(2104)* **HEARTBREAK HOTEL. / HOUND DOG / DON'T BE CRUEL** [10] [–]

Jul 71. (lp/c) *(INTS 1286)* **C'MON EVERYBODY** [5] [ ]

—— (above & below album were budget, below on 'RCA Camden').

Jul 71. (lp)(c) *(CDM 1088)(CAM 415)* **YOU'LL NEVER WALK ALONE** (gospel) [20] Apr71 [ ]

Sep 71. (lp/c) *(INTS 1026)* **ALMOST IN LOVE** [38] [ ]

Nov 71. (7"m) *(2153)* **JAILHOUSE ROCK. / ARE YOU LONESOME TONIGHT?. / (LET ME BE YOUR) TEDDY BEAR / STEADFAST, LOYAL AND TRUE** [42] [–]

Nov 71. (lp/c) *(PL/PK 42371)* **ELVIS SINGS THE WONDERFUL WORLD OF CHRISTMAS** [7] [ ]
(cd-iss. Nov89)

Dec 71. (lp)(c) *(CDM 1154)(CAM 496)* **I GOT LUCKY** [26] [ ]
(re-iss. Nov75 on 'RCA Camden')

Nov 72. (lp/c) *RCA Camden; <2595>* **BURNING LOVE AND HITS FROM HIS MOVIES, VOL.2** [ ] [22]

Jan 73. (lp/c) *RCA Camden; (CDS 1118/CAM 428) <2611>* **SEPARATE WAYS** [ ] [46]

Feb 74. (lp/c) *(APK1 1349)* **A LEGENDARY PERFORMER VOL.1** [20] [ ]

Dec 74. (lp/c) *(PL/PK 17527)* **HITS OF THE 70'S** [ ] [ ]
(re-iss. Sep77, hit No.30)

Jun 75. (d-lp/d-c) *Arcade; (ADEP 12)* **40 GREATEST HITS** [1] [–]
(re-iss. Nov78 on 'RCA', hit No.40)

Aug 75. (lp/c) *RCA Starcall; (NL/NK 42757)* **THE ELVIS PRESLEY SUN COLLECTION** [16] [ ]
(re-iss. Mar79) (re-iss. Oct83, cd-iss. Aug88 on 'RCA')

Sep 76. (7") *(RCA 2729)* **THE GIRL OF MY BEST FRIEND. / A MESS OF BLUES** [9] [–]

Nov 76. (7") *(RCA 2768)* **SUSPICION. / (IT'S A) LONG LONELY HIGHWAY** [9] [–]

Feb 77. (lp/c) *(PL/PK 42003)* **ELVIS IN DEMAND** [12] [ ]
(re-iss. Sep81)

May 77. (7") *(RCA 2694)* **ALL SHOOK UP. / HEARTBREAK HOTEL** [41] [ ]

the PRETENDERS

Formed: London, England ... March '78 by American singer/songwriter CHRISSIE HYNDE together with Hereford based musicians, guitarist JAMES HONEYMAN-SCOTT, bassist PETE FARNDON and drummer GERRY MACKLEDUFF. Prior to forming the band, HYNDE had spent the early 70's at Kent State University before moving to London in 1973 and securing work as an NME journalist. The following year, she relocated to Paris, to join the cringingly titled FRENCHIES, meeting CHRIS SPEDDING who invited her to contribute backing vocals on his 1977 album, 'Hurt'. Prior to this, HYNDE had returned to her home in Ohio in 1975 to join R&B group, JACK RABBIT. On the move again, she returned to London the following year to form The BERK BROTHERS (DAVE & FRED), before they replaced her with JOHNNY MOPED. Her self-penned songs were strong enough, however, to attract the attention of DAVE HILL, (then in the process of setting up his own label, 'Real') for whom she cut a demo tape in August '77. HILL subsequently asked HYNDE to form a band, and voila, The PRETENDERS were born. Their first single was a cover of The Kinks' 'STOP YOUR SOBBING', produced by NICK LOWE (ex-BRINSLEY SCHWARZ) and garnering much critical acclaim for its fresh faced new wave/ power-pop in the wake of punk overload. Another minor hit followed in the emotionally fragile 'KID' before the group hit big at the tail end of '79 with 'BRASS IN POCKET'. A simmering, swaggering slice of white pop-funk, the record became a UK No.1 and HYNDE was fast gaining a reputation as one of the finest songwriters around with an evocatively sultry voice to match. If there were any doubters then 'PRETENDERS' (1980) silenced them, a brilliant debut with a consistently engaging stylistic diversity. In addition to the singles, the album boasted the reggae-esque 'PRIVATE LIFE' and the gorgeous 'LOVERS OF TODAY', the individual musicians acquitting themselves with impressive conviction, notably the talented HONEYMAN-SCOTT. The album made The PRETENDERS a household name, the band subsequently undertaking an US stadium tour. While in America, HYNDE met her hero, RAY DAVIES (ex-KINKS), the pair duly becoming lovers (while DAVIES would eventually become her common-law husband and father of her first child, Natalie, the pair were allegedly refused a marriage certificate when the registrar became annoyed by their constant arguing!). The much anticipated follow-up, 'PRETENDERS II' (1981), was eventually released in August '81 to mixed reviews. The singles, 'MESSAGE OF LOVE' and the pop jangle of 'TALK OF THE TOWN' along with the steamy 'THE ADULTRESS' were highlights, although overall the album lacked the energy and verve of the debut. Later that summer, FARNDON was kicked out due to his spiralling drug use, narcotics also to blame for the death of HONEYMAN-SCOTT, found dead in his London flat two days later. Picking up the pieces, HYNDE went back into the studio with temporary replacements, guitarist BILLY BREMNER (ex-DAVE EDMUNDS' ROCKPILE) and bassist TONY BUTLER (future BIG COUNTRY) to record the driving melancholy of 'BACK ON THE CHAIN GANG' (written for HONEYMAN-SCOTT). With semi-permanent members ROBBIE McINTOSH and MALCOLM FOSTER brought in on guitar and bass respectively, the band began a new chapter in early '83. Incredibly, tragedy struck again almost immediately with PETE FARNDON becoming another fatal drugs casualty. A single eventually surfaced towards the end of the year, the undulating '2,000 MILES', while a third album, 'LEARNING TO CRAWL', appeared in early '84. Though the album contained some stellar PRETENDERS moments, it once more met with mixed reviews and performed better in America than Britain. The following year was to be an eventful one for HYNDE, meeting and subsequently marrying JIM KERR (SIMPLE MINDS) as well as playing Live Aid and topping the UK charts via her UB40 collaboration, a remake of the old SONNY & CHER chestnut, 'I GOT YOU BABE'. HYNDE eventually re-emerged with a slightly modified PRETENDERS line-up and a new deal with 'WEA' in late '86, the group scoring their first Top 10 hut in years with the infectiously chugging 'DON'T GET ME WRONG'. This was swiftly followed by the 'GET CLOSE' (1986) album, a warmer sounding affair with HYNDE singing to her new daughter (born to KERR) on the lovely 'HYMN TO HER', while revealing an increasing political awareness with 'HOW MUCH DID YOU GET FOR YOUR SOUL'. Indeed, 1988 saw her billed on the Nelson Mandela concert alongside UB40 at Wembley Stadium (she also scored another Top 10 collaboration with the band that summer, 'BREAKFAST IN BED'), while also becoming involved in various animal rights activities. HYNDE eventually turned her hand to The PRETENDERS once more at the turn of the decade, now virtually solo with a revolving cast of musicians backing her on 'PACKED' (1990) and 'LAST OF THE INDEPENDENTS' (1994). While not scaling the giddy heights of old, these releases proved HYNDE was still capable of writing affectingly melodic pop/rock. The unplugged set was inevitable really, HYNDE releasing 'THE ISLE OF VIEW' in 1995, a collection of spartan reworkings of old classics. The PRETENDERS return album proper, 'VIVA EL AMOR!' (1999), saw CHRISSIE and her band find old favour with her 80's fanbase (it reached the UK Top 40), the opening track 'POPSTAR' truly a single that deserved better airplay. With 'GREATEST HITS' (2000) marking the end of the band's lengthy tenure with Warners, 'LOOSE SCREW' (2002) became The PRETENDERS' first release for 'Eagle' records ('Artemis' in the States). Not that this downscaling had any kind of marked effect on their approach, except perhaps that HYNDE's lyrics were more coruscating than ever, whether the target was errant lovers or her own shortcomings.

• **Songwriters:** Group compositions, except as said plus; MAY THIS BE LOVE (Jimi Hendrix) / IF THERE WAS A MAN (co-w/ John Barry) / I'M NOT IN LOVE (10cc) / NOT A SECOND TIME (Beatles) / CREEP (Radiohead).
• **Trivia:** CHRISSIE caused controversy in June '89, when she attended a Greenpeace Rainbow Warriors press conference, telling how she (a staunch vegetarian) once firebombed McDonalds burger shop. The day after, one of their shops in Milton Keynes was firebombed and CHRISSIE was asked/told to sign a retracting statement, or be taken to court.

Album rating: PRETENDERS (*8) / PRETENDERS II (*7) / LEARNING TO CRAWL (*8) / GET CLOSE (*5) / THE SINGLES compilation (*8) / PACKED! (*4) / LAST OF THE INDEPENDENTS (*6) / THE ISLE OF VIEW (*5) / VIVA EL AMOR (*6) / GREATEST HITS compilation (*8) / LOOSE SCREW (*5)

CHRISSIE HYNDE (b. 7 Sep'51, Akron, Ohio) – vocals, guitar / **JAMES HONEYMAN-SCOTT** (b. 4 Nov'57, Hereford, England) – guitar, keyboards (ex-CHEEKS) / **PETE FARNDON** (b.1953, Hereford) – bass / **GERRY MACKLEDUFF** – drums

Real / Sire

Jan 79. (7") *(ARE 6)* **STOP YOUR SOBBING. / THE WAIT** [34] [–]

— **MARTIN CHAMBERS** (b. 4 Sep'51, Hereford) – drums repl. GERRY

Jun 79. (7") *(ARE 9)* **KID. / TATTOOED LOVE BOYS** [33] Jul 80 [ ]

Nov 79. (7") *(ARE 11)* **BRASS IN POCKET. / SWINGING LONDON** [1] [–]
(12"+=) *(ARET 11)* – Nervous but shy. *(c-ep-iss.Apr81; SPC 5)*

Jan 80. (lp/c) *(RAL/+C 3)* *<6083>* **PRETENDERS** [1] [9]
– Precious / The phone call / Up the neck / Tattooed love boys / Space invader / The wait / Stop your sobbing / Kid / Private life / Brass in pocket / Lovers of today / Mystery achievement. *(cd-iss. 1983 on 'WEA'; 256774-2)*

Feb 80. (7") *<49181>* **BRASS IN POCKET. / SPACE INVADER** [–] [14]

Apr 80. (7") *(ARE 12)* **TALK OF THE TOWN. / CUBAN SLIDE AND SLIDE** [8] [ ]

May 80. (7") *<49506>* **STOP YOUR SOBBING. / PHONE CALL** [–] [65]

Feb 81. (7") *(ARE 15)* **MESSAGE OF LOVE. / PORCELAIN** [11] Apr81 [ ]

Aug 81. (lp/c) *(RAL/+C 3)* *<3572>* **PRETENDERS II** [7] [10]
– The adultress / Bad boys get spanked / Message of love / I go to sleep / Birds of Paradise / Talk of the town / Pack it up / Waste not, want not / Day after day / Jealous dogs / Waste not want not / English rose / Louie Louie. *(cd-iss. Nov86 & Jul93 on 'WEA'; 256774-2)*

Aug 81. (7") *<49819>* **LOUIE LOUIE. / IN THE STICKS** [–] [ ]

Aug 81. (7") *(ARE 17)* **DAY AFTER DAY. / IN THE STICKS** [45] [–]
(12"+=) *(ARE 17a)* – The adultress.

Nov 81. (7") *(ARE 18)* **I GO TO SLEEP. / THE ENGLISH ROSE** [7] [–]
(12"+=) *(ARE 18T)* – Waste not, want not.

Jan 82. (7") **I GO TO SLEEP. / WASTE NOT, WANT NOT** [–] [ ]

— (Sep'82) **BILLY BREMNER** – guitar (ex-NICK LOWE, ex-DAVE EDMUNDS' ROCKPILE) repl. HONEYMAN-SCOTT who died of drug overdose 16 Jun'82 / **TONY BUTLER** – bass (of BIG COUNTRY) repl. FARNDON (died o.d. 14 Apr'83)

Sep 82. (7") *(ARE 19)* *<29840>* **BACK ON THE CHAIN GANG. / MY CITY WAS GONE** [17] Nov82 [5]
(12"+=) *(ARE 19T)* – ('A'-part 2).

— (Feb'83) **HYNDE** and **CHAMBERS** brought in new members **ROBBIE McINTOSH** (25 Oct'57) – guitar (ex-MANFRED MANN'S EARTH BAND, ex-NIGHT) repl. BREMNER who rejoined NICK LOWE etc. / **MALCOLM FOSTER** (b.13 Jan'56) – bass repl. BUTLER who rejoined BIG COUNTRY

Nov 83. (7") *(ARE 20)* **2000 MILES. / THE LAW IS THE LAW** [15] [–]
('A'fast or slow versioned 12"+=) *(ARE 20T)* – Money (live).

Nov 83. (7") *<29444>* **MIDDLE OF THE ROAD. / 2,000 MILES** [–] [19]

Jan 84. (lp/c)(cd) *(WX 2/+C)(923980-2)* *<23980>* **LEARNING TO CRAWL** [11] [5]
– Middle of the road / Back on the chain gang / Time the avenger / Watching the clothes / Show me / Thumbelina / My city was gone / Thin line between love and hate / I hurt you / 2000 miles.

Feb 84. (7"/12") *(ARE 21/+T)* **MIDDLE OF THE ROAD. / WATCHING THE CLOTHES** [ ] [–]

— added **PAUL CARRACK** – keyboards (ex-ACE, ex-ROXY MUSIC, ex-solo artist)

Mar 84. (7") *<29317>* **SHOW ME. / FAST OR SLOW (THE LAW IS THE LAW)** [–] [28]

Apr 84. (7") *(ARE 22)* *<29249>* **THIN LINE BETWEEN LOVE AND HATE. / TIME THE AVENGER** [49] Jun84 [83]
(12"+=) *(ARE 22T)* – Bad boys get spanked.

— Sep 85, CHRISSIE HYNDE guests on UB40's 'I Got You Babe' which hits No.1. Three years later the same team hit no.6 with 'Breakfast In Bed'. PRETENDERS regroup with **HYNDE, McINTOSH** and **TIM STEVENS** – bass / **BLAIR CUNNINGHAM** – drums (ex-HAIRCUT 100) repl. CHAMBERS (on some) and **BERNIE WORRELL** – keyboards

W.E.A. / Warners

Sep 86. (7") *(YZ 85)* *<28630>* **DON'T GET ME WRONG. / DANCE** [10] [10]
(12"+=) *(YZ 85T)* – ('A'extended).

Oct 86. (lp/c)(cd) *(WX 34/+C)(240976-2)* *<25488>* **GET CLOSE** [6] [25]
– My baby / When I change my life / Light of the Moon / Dance * / Tradition of love / Don't get me wrong / I remember you / How much did you get for your soul / Chill factor / Hymn to her / Room full of mirrors. *(c+=/cd+= *)*

Nov 86. (7") *(YZ 93)* **HYMN TO HER. / ROOM FULL OF MIRRORS** [8] [–]
(12"+=) *(YZ 93T)* – Stop your sobbing (demo).

Feb 87. (7") *<28496>* **MY BABY. / ROOM FULL OF MIRRORS** [–] [64]

Mar 87. (7") *(YZ 110)* **MY BABY. / TRADITION OF LOVE (remix)** [ ] [–]
(12"+=) *(YZ 110T)* – Thumbelina.
(7"ep+=) *(YZEP 110)* – Private life / Middle of the road.

Apr 87. (7") **HYMN TO HER. / TRADITION OF LOVE** [–] [ ]

Aug 87. (7"; as PRETENDERS 007) *(YZ 149)* *<28259>* **IF THERE WAS A MAN. / INTO VIENNA** [49] [ ]
(12"+=) *(YZ 149T)* – Where has everybody gone.

Oct 87. (lp/c)(cd) *(WX 135/+C)(242229-2)* *<25664>* **THE SINGLES** (compilation) [6] [69]
– Stop your sobbing / Kid / Brass in pocket / Talk of the town / I go to sleep / Day after day / Message of love / Back on the chain gang / Middle of the road / 2000 miles / Show me / Thin line between love and hate / Don't get me wrong / Hymn to her / My baby / I got you babe (w / UB40) / What you gonna do about it.

Oct 87. (7") *(YZ 156)* **KID (remix). / STOP YOUR SOBBING (original)** [ ] [–]

(12"+=/cd-s+=) *(YZ 156 T/CD)* – ('B' 1978 demo) / What you gonna do about it ('87 remix).
Jun'88, she guested again with UB40 on hit single 'BREAKFAST IN BED'.

— added guest **JOHNNY MARR** – guitar (ex-SMITHS) repl. McINTOSH

Apr 89. (7"/12"/3"cd-s) *(PRE/+T/CD 69)* **WINDOWS OF THE WORLD. / 1969** –

— (above from the film '1969', a one-off on label 'Polydor')

— now virtually **CHRISSIE** solo, augmented by **BLAIR CUNNINGHAM** – drums / **BILLY BREMNER** + **DOMINIC MILLER** – guitar / **JOHN McKENZIE** – bass / plus others

May 90. (7"/c-s) *(YZ 469/+C) <19820>* **NEVER DO THAT. / NOT A SECOND TIME**
(12"+=) *(YZ 469T)* – The wait.
(cd-s++=) *(YZ 469CD)* – Spirit of life.

May 90. (cd)(lp/c) *(9031 71403-2)(WX 346/+C) <26219>* **PACKED!** 19 48
– Never do that / Let's make a pact / Millionaires / May this be love / No guarentee / When will I see you / Sense of purpose / Downtown (Akron) / How do I miss you / Hold a candle to this / Criminal. *(cd re-iss. Nov94; 9031 71403-2)*

Oct 90. (7") *(YZ 507)* **SENSE OF PURPOSE. / SPIRIT OF LIFE** –
(12"+=) *(YZ 507T)* – Brass in pocket.
(cd-s++=/c-s++=) *(YZ 507 CD/C)* – Not a second time.

— Oct 91, CHRISSIE's vox was credited on single 'SPIRITUAL HIGH', by MOOD SWINGS. It finally hit UK no. 47 early '93.

— She wrote most with B. STEINBERG + T.KELLY. Covered; FOREVER YOUNG (Bob Dylan).

— **CHRISSIE** + main band **MARTIN CHAMBERS** – drums / **ADAM SEYMOUR** – guitar / **ANDY HOBSON** – bass

Apr 94. (7"/c-s) *(YZ 815/+C) <18160>* **I'LL STAND BY YOU. / REBEL ROCK ME** 10 Aug94 16
(cd-s+=) *(YZ 815CD1)* – Bold as love.
(cd-s) *(YZ 815CD2)* – ('A'side) / Message of love / Brass in pocket / Don't get me wrong.

May 94. (cd/c) *(4509 95822-2/-4/-1) <45572>* **LAST OF THE INDEPENDENTS** 8 41
– Hollywood perfume / Night in my veins / Money talk / 977 / Revolution / All my dreams / I'll stand by you / I'm a mother / Tequila / Every mother's son / Rebel rock me / Love colours / Forever young.

May 94. (c-s,cd-s) *<18163>* **NIGHT IN MY VEINS / ANGEL OF THE MORNING** – 71

Jun 94. (7"/c-s) *(YZ 825/+C)* **NIGHT IN MY VEINS. / BAD BOYS GET SPANKED** 25 –
(cd-s+=) *(YZ 825CD)* – My city was gone / Tattooed love boys.

Oct 94. (7"/c-s) *(YZ 848/+C)* **977. / I'LL STAND BY YOU (live)** 66 –
(cd-s+=) *(YZ 848CD1)* – Hollywood perfume (live) / Kid (live).
(cd-s) *(YZ 848CD2)* – ('A'side) / Back on the chain gang (live) / Night in my veins (live) / Precious (live).

Sep 95. (c-s) *(WEA 014C)* **KID (acoustic) / THE ISLE OF VIEW (acoustic)** 73 –
(cd-s+=) *(WEA 014CD)* – Creep (acoustic).

Oct 95. (cd/c) *(0630 12059-2/-4) <46085>* **THE ISLE OF VIEW (live acoustic)** 23 100
– Sense of purpose / Chill factor / Private life / Back on the chain gang / Kid / I hurt you / Criminal / Brass in pocket / 2000 miles / Hymn to her / Lovers of today / The phone call / I go to sleep / Revolution. *(cd+=)* – The Isle of View.

Nov 95. (c-s/cd-s) *(WEA 024 C/CD)* **2000 MILES (acoustic) / TEQUILA** –
(cd-s+=) *(WEA 024CDX)* – Happy Christmas / Night in my veins.

Apr 97. (c-s/12"/cd-s) *(NEG 104 C/T/CD)* **GOIN' BACK. / (other track by The LA'S)** –
(above issued on 'Blanco Y Negro')

May 99. (c-s) *(WEA 207C)* **HUMAN / THE HOMECOMING (Street version)** 33 –
(cd-s+=) *(WEA 207CD)* – ('A'-Glass mix).

May 99. (cd/c) *(<3984 27152-2/-4>)* **VIVA EL AMOR!** 32
– Popstar / Nails in the road / Human / From the heart down / Who's who / Dragway 42 / Baby's breath / One more time / Legalise me / Biker / Samurai / Rabo de nube.

Aug 99. (c-s) *(WEA 219C)* **POPSTAR / THE NEEDLE AND THE DAMAGE DONE** –
(cd-s+=) *(WEA 219CD)* – Samurai.

— in Jun'00, CHRISSIE HYNDE featured on HYBRID's No.32 hit version of 'KID 2000'

Sep 00. (cd/c) *(<8573 84607-2/-4>)* **GREATEST HITS** (compilation) 21 Nov00
– Brass in pocket / Message of love / Don't get me wrong / Kid / Human (Tin Tin Out remix) / I go to sleep / Forever young / I got you babe (UB40 & CHRISSIE HYNDE) / Night in my veins / Spiritual high (state of independence) (MOODSWINGS & CHRISSIE HYNDE) / Talk of the town / Stop your sobbing / Hymn to her / 2000 miles / Breakfast in bed (UB40 & CHRISSIE HYNDE) / Popstar / Middle of the road / Thin line between love and hate / Back on the chain gang / I'll stand by you. *(re-dist.Apr02)* – hit No.29

Eagle Artemis

May 03. (cd-s) *(EAGXS 257)* **YOU KNOW WHO YOUR FRIENDS ARE / COMPLICADA (complex person Spanish version)** –

May 03. (cd) *(EAGCD 256) <751153>* **LOOSE SCREW** 55 Nov02
– Lie to me / Time / You know who you're friends are / Complex person / Fools must die / Kinda nice, I like it / Nothing breaks like a heart / I should of / Clean up woman / The losing / Saving grace / Walk like a panther.

Aug 03. (cd-s; promo) *(EAGXS 261)* **SAVING GRACE** –

Oct 03. (cd-s) *(EAGXS 268)* **THE LOSING / DON'T GET ME WRONG (live)** –

– compilations, etc. –

Jul 94. (cd/c) *Carlton; (4509 91885-2/-4)* **DON'T GET ME WRONG** –

the PRETTY THINGS

Formed: Dartford, Kent, England . . . 1963 by DICK TAYLOR and PHIL MAY. The former had once been a member of LITTLE BOY BLUE & THE BLUE BOYS, an embryonic version of The ROLLING STONES. The pair added BRIAN PENDLETON, JOHN STAX and PETE KITLEY, the latter being replaced by drummer VIV PRINCE. Taking their name from a BO DIDDLEY song, they soon signed to 'Fontana', employing the management team of Bryan Morrison and James Duncan, the latter of whom wrote their summer '64 debut Top 50 hit, 'ROSALYN'. Their pure roots/R&B follow-up, 'DON'T BRING ME DOWN' (which drew inspiration from black American blues artists of the 50's) dented the UK Top 10, preceding their eponymous Top 10 album in early '65. Unlike the STONES (of whom they were dubbed by the press as uglier cousins), their hits had dried up by 1967, due to a misguided foray into psychedelia. Later that year, they moved to 'Columbia' records, releasing two flop 45's, before they embarked on their most ambitious project so far, 'S.F. SORROW'. It was the first ever "rock opera", inspiring PETE TOWNSHEND (The Who) to write his legendary 'Tommy'. The album was a commercial flop and critically lambasted by the press, although it has since become regarded as an innovative piece of work that was essential to the development of "rock" music. During its recording, TAYLOR left to become a producer, the band folding but regrouping for a heavier 'Harvest' set, 'PARACHUTE' (1970). They struggled on regardless, subsequently signing for LED ZEPPELIN's heavyweight 'Swan Song' label in '74. Two mediocre albums followed before they the band split in '76 after their remaining founder member, MAY, departed. They re-formed many times and still tread the boards on the blues circuit alongside members of The YARDBIRDS. A more or less original line-up of the band inevitably came together for a late 90's reunion although few might've predicted that they'd attempt a recording of the classic 'S.F. SORROW' in its entirety live in the studio. The result was 'RESURRECTION' (1999), which hardly improved upon the original although was notable for the inimitable narration of ARTHUR BROWN. Presumably buoyed up by the project, they proceeded to record a bonafide new album,

'RAGE . . . BEFORE BEAUTY' (1999), albeit with a raft of covers including Jagger/Richard's 'PLAY WITH FIRE' and P.F. Sloan's 'EVE OF DESTRUCTION'.

• **Songwriters:** Most by PHIL MAY, except covers; PRETTY THING + ROADRUNNER + MONA (Bo Diddley) / CRY TO ME (Bert Berns) / A HOUSE IN THE COUNTRY (Ray Davies; Kinks) / REELIN' AND ROCKIN' (Chuck Berry) / I'M A KING BEE (Muddy Waters) / SHAKIN' ALL OVER (Johnny Kidd & The Pirates) / etc. • **Trivia:** The group made cameo appearances in the films, 'What's Good For The Goose' (1969 w /Norman Wisdom) and 'The Monster Squad' (1980 w /Vincent Price). They were given a tribute by BOWIE in 1973, when he covered their first two hits on his 'PIN-UPS' album.

Album rating: THE PRETTY THINGS (*7) / GET THE PICTURE (*6) / EMOTIONS (*6) / S.F. SORROW (*7) / PARACHUTE (*6) / FREEWAY MADNESS (*6) / SILK TORPEDO (*5) / SAVAGE EYE (*5) / CROSSTALK (*4) / LIVE AT THE HEARTBREAK HOTEL (*4) / OUT OF THE ISLAND (*4) / THE PRETTY THINGS 1967-1971 compilation (*7) / . . .RAGE BEFORE BEAUTY (*4) / RESURRECTION (*5)

PHIL MAY (b. 9 Nov'44, Kent, England) – vocals / **DICK TAYLOR** (28 Jan'43) – lead guitar / **BRIAN PENDLETON** (b.13 Apr'44, Wolverhampton, England) – rhythm guitar / **JOHN STAX** (b.JOHN FULLEGAR, 6 Apr'44) – bass / **VIV PRINCE** (b. 9 Aug'44, Loughborough, Leicestershire, England) – drums (PETE KITLEY, then VIV ANDREWS sessioned on 1st-two 45's)

Fontana / Fontana

Jun 64. (7") *(TF 469)* <1916> **ROSALYN. / BIG BOSS MAN** — 41 — Oct64

Oct 64. (7") *(TF 503)* <1941> **DON'T BRING ME DOWN. / WE'LL BE TOGETHER** — 10 — Jan65

Feb 65. (7") *(TF 537)* <1508> **HONEY I NEED. / I CAN NEVER SAY** — 13

Mar 65. (lp) *(TL 5239)* <67544> **THE PRETTY THINGS** — 6
– Roadrunner / Judgement day / 13 Chester street / Honey I need / Big city / Unkown blues / Mama, keep your big mouth shut / Oh baby doll / She's fine she's mine / Don't you lie to me / The Moon is rising / Pretty thing. *(re-iss. Jul90 lp/c/cd; 646054-1/-4/-2) (lp re-iss. Nov01 on 'Norton'; ED 282) (cd re-iss. Jul02 on 'Repertoire'+=; REP 4927)* – Rosalyn / Big boss man / Don't bring me down / We'll be together / I can never say / Get yourself home. *(cd re-iss. Feb03 on 'Snapper'; SDPCD 115)*

Jul 65. (7") *(TF 585)* <1518> **CRY TO ME. / JUDGEMENT DAY** — 28

Dec 65. (7") *(TF 647)* <1540> **MIDNIGHT TO SIX MAN. / CAN'T STAND THE PAIN** — 46

Dec 65. (lp) *(TL 5280)* <5280> **GET THE PICTURE**
– You don't believe me / Buzz the jerk / Get the picture? / Can't stand the pain / Rainin' in my heart / We'll play house / You'll never do it baby / I had a dream / I want your love / London town / Cry to me / Gonna find me a substitute. *(re-iss. Mar84; 6438 214) (cd-iss. Jul90; 846459-2) (cd re-iss. Apr98 on 'Snapper'+=; SMMCD 549)* – Get a buzz / Sittin' all alone / Midnight to six man / Come see me / L.S.D. / Me needing you. *(lp re-iss. Nov01 on 'Norton'; ED 283) (cd re-mast.Sep02 on 'Repertoire'+=; REP 4928) (cd re-iss. Jan03 on 'Snapper'+=; SDPCD 114)*

—— **SKIP ALAN** (b. ALAN ERNEST SKIPPER, 11 Jun'44) – drums repl. PRINCE on some

Fontana / Blue Thumb

Apr 66. (7") *(TF 688)* **COME SEE ME. / l.s.d.** — 43

Jul 66. (7") *(TF 722)* **A HOUSE IN THE COUNTRY. / ME NEEDING YOU** — 50

Dec 66. (7") *(TF 773)* **PROGRESS. / BUZZ IN THE JERK**

Apr 67. (7") *(TF 829)* **CHILDREN. / MY TIME**

May 67. (lp; stereo/mono) *(S+/TL 5425)* **EMOTIONS** — –
– Death of a socialite / Children / The sun / There will never be another day / House of ten / Out in the night / One long glance / Growing in my mind / Photographer / Bright lights of the city / Tripping / My time. *(re-iss. Apr91 +=; 846705-2) (cd re-iss. Apr98 on 'Snapper'+=; SMMCD 550)* – A house in the country / Me needing you / Progress. *(cd re-iss. Jan03 on 'Snapper'++=; SDPCD 111)* – Photographer / There will never be another day / My time / The sun / Progress. *(cd re-mast.Sep02 on 'Repertoire'+++=; REP 4929)* – Death of a socialite (single version) / Photographer (undubbed).

—— **PHIL + DICK** were left to recruit new members **JOHN POVEY** (b.20 Aug'44) – keyboards, vocals (ex-FENMEN) repl. PENDLETON / **WALLY ALLEN** – bass, vocals (ex-FENMEN) repl. SKIP / **MITCH MITCHELL** – (session) drums repl. SKIP

Columbia / Rare Earth

Nov 67. (7") *(DB 8300)* **DEFLECTING GREY. / MR. EVASION** — –

—— **BOBBIE GRAHAM** – drums (also on session) repl. MITCHELL

Feb 68. (7") *(DB 8353)* **TALKIN' ABOUT THE GOOD TIMES. / WALKING THROUGH MY DREAMS** — –

—— **JOHN 'TWINK' ADLER** – percussion, vocals (ex-TOMORROW, etc) repl. GRAHAM

Nov 68. (7") *(DB 8494)* <5005> **PRIVATE SORROW. / BALLOON BURNING**

Dec 68. (lp; mono/stereo) *(SX/SCX 6306)* <506> **S.F. SORROW** — Feb70
– S.F. sorrow / Bracelets of fingers / She says good morning / Private sorrow / Balloon burning / Death / Baron Saturday / I see you / The journey / Well of destiny / Trust / Old man going / Loneliest person. *(re-press.1970; same) (re-iss. Oct87 on 'Edsel'; XED 236) (cd-iss. Oct90; EDCD 236) (lp re-iss. Jun00 on 'Snapper'; SMMLP 565) (cd re-iss. Feb03 on 'Snapper'+=; SDPCD 109)* – Defecting grey / Mr. Evasion / Talkin' about the good times / Walking through my dreams. *(cd re-mast.Sep02 on 'Repertoire'++=; REP 4930)* – Private sorrow / Balloon burning / Defecting grey (acetate).

—— **SKIP ALAN** – drums, vocals (returned from SUNSHINE) repl. TWINK who joined PINK FAIRIES (new one joining MAY, POVEY and ALLEN plus below) **VICTOR UNITT** – guitar, vocals (ex-EDGAR BROUGHTON) repl. TAYLOR (⇒ producer)

Harvest / Rare Earth

Apr 70. (7") *(HAR 5016)* **THE GOOD MR. SQUARE. / BLUE SERGE BLUES**

Jun 70. (lp) *(SHVL 774)* <515> **PARACHUTE** — 43
– Scene one / The good Mr. Square / She was tall, she was high / In the square / The letter / Rain / Miss Fay regrets / Cries from the midnight circus / Grass / Sickle clowns / She's a lover / What's the use / Parachute. *(re-iss. Sep88 on 'Edsel' lp/cd; ED/+CD 289) (cd re-iss. Jun99 on 'Snapper'+=; SMDCD 566)* – Blue Serge blues / October 26 / Cold stone / Stone-hearted mama / Summer time / Circus mind. *(lp re-iss. DEc01 on 'Rare Earth'; same as US) (cd re-mast.Sep02 on 'Repertoire'+=; REP 4931) (cd re-iss. Jan03 on 'Snapper'+=; SDPCD 110)*

—— **PETER TOLSON** (b.10 Sep'51, Bishops Stortford, England) – guitar, vocals (ex-EIRE APPARANT) repl. UNITT (who returned to EDGAR BROUGHTON BAND)

Oct 70. (7") *(HAR 5031)* **OCTOBER 26. / COLD STONE**

May 71. (7"m) *(HAR 5037)* **STONE-HEARTED MAMA. / SUMMERTIME / CIRCUS MIND**

—— **STUART BROOKS** – bass, vocals repl. WALLY who went into producing

Warners / Warners

Dec 72. (lp) *(K 46190)* <2680> **FREEWAY MADNESS**
– Love is good / Havana bound / Peter / Rip off train / Over the moon / Religion's dead / Country road / All night sailor / Onion soup / Another bowl? *(cd-iss. Sep00 on 'Snapper'+=; SMMCD 603)* – Religion's dead (live) / Havana bound (live) / Love is good (live) / Onion soup (live). *(cd re-mast.Sep02 on 'Repertoire'++=; REP 4932)* – Over the moon (single version) / Havana bound (single version). *(cd re-iss. Jan03 on 'Snapper'+=; SDPCD 117)*

Jan 73. (7") **OVER THE MOON. / HAVANA BOUND** — –

—— added **GORDON EDWARDS** (b.26 Dec'46, Southport, England) – keyboards (to **MAY, ALAN, POVEY, TOLSON and BROOKS)**

Swan Song / Swan Song

Oct 74. (lp) *(SSK 59400)* <8411> **SILK TORPEDO**
– Dream – Joey / Maybe you tried / Atlanta / L.A.N.T.A. / Is it only love / Come home momma / Bridge of God / Singapore silk torpedo / Belfast cowboys / Bruise in the sky. *(cd-iss. Nov98 on 'Snapper'+=; SMMCD 559)* – Singapore silk torpedo (live) / Dream – Joey (live). *(cd re-mast.Sep02 on 'Repertoire'++=; REP 4933)* – Joey (single version) / I'm keeping (single version). *(cd re-iss. Jan03 on 'Snapper'+=; SDPCD 112)*

Dec 74. (7") *(K 19401)* **JOEY. / IS IT ONLY LOVE**

Jun 75. (7") *(K 19403)* **I'M KEEPING. / ATLANTA**

—— **JACK GREEN** (b.12 Mar'51, Glasgow, Scotland) – bass, vocals (also as EDWARDS, ex-SUNSHINE) repl. BROOKS

Aug 75. (7") *(K 19404)* <70107> **JOEY. / COME HOME MOMMA**

Feb 76. (7") *(K 19405)* **SAD EYE. / REMEMBER THAT BOY** — –

Apr 76. (7") **REMEMBER THAT BOY. / IT ISN'T ROCK'N'ROLL** — –

May 76. (lp) *(SSL 59401)* <8414> **SAVAGE EYE** — Feb 76
– Under the volcano / My song / Sad eye / Remember that boy / It isn't rock'n'roll / I'm keeping / It's been so long / Drowned man / Theme for Michelle. *(cd-iss. Sep98 on 'Snapper'+=; SMMCD 560)* – Tonight (single

version) / Love me a little (demo) / Dance all night (demo). *(cd re-mast.Sep02 on 'Repertoire'+=; REP 4934) (cd re-iss. Jan03 on 'Snapper'+=; SDPCD 113)*

May 76. (7") *(K 19406)* **TONIGHT. / IT ISN'T ROCK'N'ROLL** ☐ ☐

—— Last original PHIL MAY went solo augmented by the FALLEN ANGELS (see below). POVEY also departed leaving only 4 (SKIP, PETER, JACK and GORDON) calling themselves METROPOLIS between mid '76-late'77. JACK also joined T.REX and GORDON went to The KINKS.

PHIL MAY & THE FALLEN ANGELS

with **MICKEY FINN** – guitar (ex-T.REX) / **BILL LOVELADY** – guitar / **BRIAN JOHNSTON** – keyboards (ex-STREETWALKERS) / **WALL ALLEN** – bass / **CHICO GREENWOOD** – drums / etc.

Philips not iss.

1978. (lp) *(6410 969)* **PHIL MAY & THE FALLEN ANGELS** ☐ Dutch ☐
– Fallen angels / California / 13 floor suicide / Dance again / Shine on baby / My good friend / Cold wind / I keep on / Dogs of war / Girl like you. *(UK-iss.1982;) (re-iss. Feb85;)*

the PRETTY THINGS

—— re-formed ex-members in 1980. (**PHIL MAY, DICK TAYLOR, JOHN POVEY, PETER TOLSON, WALLY ALLEN** and **SKIP ALAN**)

Warners Warners

Aug 80. (lp) *(K 56842)* <3466> **CROSS TALK** ☐ ☐
– I'm calling / Edge of the night / Sea of blue / Office love / Lost that girl / Bitter end / Falling again / It's so hard / She don't / No future. *(cd-iss. Sep00 on 'Snapper'+=; SMMCD 602)* – Wish fulfillment / Sea about me / The young pretenders. *(cd re-mast.Sep02 on 'Repertoire'+=; REP 4935) (cd re-iss. Jan03 on 'Snapper'+=; SDPCD 116)*

Aug 80. (7") *(K 17670)* **I'M CALLING. / SEA OF BLUE** ☐ ☐

—— Disbanded 1981, but re-formed briefly as . . .

ZAC ZOLAR AND ELECTRIC BANANA

Butt not iss.

1984. (7") **TAKE ME HOME. / JAMES MARSHALL** ☐ ☐

—— (above appeared on 'Minder' TV series) *(re-iss. Aug86 on 'Shanghai'; MGLS 2)*

the PRETTY THINGS

re-formed by **MAY** + **TAYLOR** in 1984. Now with **JOE SHAW** – guitar / **DAVE WINTOUR** – bass / **KEVIN FLANAGAN** – saxophone / **JOHN CLARKE** – drums

Big Beat not iss.

Aug 84. (lp) *(WIK 24)* **LIVE AT THE HEARTBREAK HOTEL (live)** ☐ ☐
– Big boss man / Midnight to six man / I'm a king bee / Honey I need / Shakin' all over / Rosalyn / Roadrunner / Mama keep your big mouth shut / Raining in my heart / Reelin' and rockin' / Don't bring me down / Mona.

—— **ROLF TER VELD** – bass + **BERTRAM ENGEL** – drums (ex-UDO LINDENBERG, ex-PANIKORCHESTER) repl.WINTOUR, FLANAGAN + CLARKE

In-Akustik not iss.

Jun 88. (cd) *(INAK 8708)* **OUT OF THE ISLAND** ☐ ☐
– Cry to me / Baby doll / She's fine, she's mine / Get the picture / Havana bound / Can't stop / Loneliest person / £.s.d. / Private sorrow / The moon is rising / Big city / Cause and effect / Well known blues / You don't believe me / Judement day. *(re-iss. May95; same)*

—— **MAY** + **TAYLOR** again re-formed them again in 1989, with new **GLEN MATLOCK** – bass, vocals (ex-SEX PISTOLS, ex-RICH KIDS) / **FRANK HOLLAND** – guitar, keyboards / **BOBBY WEBB** – keyboards, vocals / **MARK ST. JOHN** – drums, bass, vocals

Trax not iss.

Sep 89. (7") *(7TX 12)* **EVE OF DESTRUCTION. / GOIN' DOWNHILL** ☐ ☐
(12"+=) *(12TX 12)* – Can't stop.

—— (on tour) **STEVE BROWNING** – bass repl. MATLOCK

—— Re-formed again in 1991, with **PHIL MAY** / **DICK TAYLOR** (ex-MEKONS) / **JIMMY McCARTY** (ex-YARDBIRDS) / **RICHARD HITE** (ex-CANNED HEAT)

PRETTY THINGS & THE YARDBIRD BLUES BAND

Super-blues-group / collab with ex-YARDBIRDS and plenty covers

Demon not iss.

Oct 91. (cd) *(FIENDCD 708)* **CHICAGO BLUES JAM 1991** ☐ ☐
– Can't judge the book / Down in the bottom / Hush hush / Can't hold out / Spoonful / She fooled me / Time is on my side / Scratch my back / Long tall Shorty / Diddley daddy / Ain't got you / Caress my baby / Here's my picture / Chain of fools / Don't start crying now.

Feb 94. (cd) *(FIENDCD 748)* **WINE, WOMEN & WHISKEY** ☐ ☐
– Wine, women and whiskey / Sure look good to me / No questions / The amble / It's all over now / Bad boy / Spoonful (bare bones remix) / French champagne / My back scratcher / Can't hold out (big city remix) / Diddley daddy (street corner remix) / I'm cryin' / Gettin' all wet.

the PRETTY THINGS 'N MATES (WITH MATTHEW FISHER)

featuring a plethora of famous cover versions

Kingdom not iss.

May 94. (cd) *(CDKVL 9031)* **A WHITER SHADE OF DIRTY WATER** ☐ ☐
– He's waitin' / Strychnine / Pushing too hard / Kicks / Candy / Louie, Louie / 96 tears / Let's talk about girls / Sometimes good guys don't wear black / I'm a man / Red river rock / Midnight to 6 man '93.

the PRETTY THINGS

—— re-formed again 1995, **MAY, TAYLOR, POVEY, ALLEN, ALAN + HOLLAND**

Jun 96. (7"pic-d) *(FRPS 006)* **EVE OF DESTRUCTION. / ROSALYN / PASSION OF LOVE** ☐ ☐

Snapper Madfish

Mar 99. (cd) *(SMACD 814)* <128142> **. . .RAGE BEFORE BEAUTY** ☐ ☐
– Passion of love / Vivian Prince / Everlasting flame / Love keeps hanging on / Eve of destruction / Not givin' in / Pure cold stone / Blue turns to red / Goodbye, goodbye / Goin' downhill / Play with fire / Fly away / Mony mony / God give me the strength (to carry on). *(re-iss. Apr01; SMDCD 626) (cd re-mast.Sep02 on 'Repertoire'; REP 4936)*

Snapper Snapper

Apr 01. (cd) *(<SMMCD 624>)* **RESURRECTION** (S.F. SORROW live in the studio 6th September, 1998) ☐ ☐

– (selective) compilations, etc. –

Mar 82. (lp/c) *See For Miles; (CM/+K 103)* **THE PRETTY THINGS 1967-1971** ☐ ☐
(cd-iss. Oct89; SEECD 103)

Jun 84. (lp) *Edsel; (ED 139)* **LET ME HEAR THE CHOIR SING** ☐ ☐

Feb 86. (lp) *Bam Caruso; (KIRI 032)* **CLOSED RESTAURANT BLUES** ☐ ☐

May 86. (lp/c) *Harvest; (EMS/TCEMS 1119)* **CRIES FROM THE MIDNIGHT CIRCUS** (1968-1971) ☐ ☐

Nov 88. (cd) *Radioactive; (HORN 004)* **THE PRETTY THINGS** ☐ ☐

Aug 91. (cd) *Repertoire; (REP 4089WZ)* **MORE ELECTRIC BANANA** ☐ ☐

Apr 92. (cd) *Band Of Joy; (BOJCD 3)* **ON AIR** ☐ ☐

Oct 95. (d-cd) *Fragile; (FRA 005D)* **UNREPENTANT – BLOODY BUT UNBOWED** ☐ ☐
(re-iss. Mar98 on 'Snapper'; SSDCD 002)

Jun 97. (cd) *See For Miles; (SEECD 476)* **THE EP COLLECTION** ☐ ☐

May 01. (cd) *Snapper; (<SMMCD 625>)* **LATEST WRITS GREATEST HITS** ☐ ☐

Jul 01. (d-cd) *Snapper; (<SMDCD 343>)* **THE RHYTHM & BLUES YEARS** ☐ ☐

Oct 01. (d-cd) *Snapper; (<SMDCD 344>)* **THE PSYCHEDELIC YEARS 1966-1970** ☐ ☐

Mar 02. (d-cd) *Snapper; (<SMDCD 390>)* **CROSSTALK / FREEWAY MADNESS** ☐ ☐

Sep 02. (t-cd) *Repertoire; (<REP 4937>)* **SINGLES A's & B's** ☐ ☐

Nov 02. (10"m-lp) *Norton; (TED 1001)* **DEFECTING GREY** ☐ ☐

Apr 03. (d-cd) *Snapper; (<SMDCD 415>)* **S.F. SORROW / RESURRECTION** ☐ ☐

Jun 03. (cd) *Repertoire; (<REP 4990>)* **THE VERY BEST OF THE PRETTY THINGS**
Aug 03. (d-cd) *Repertoire; (<REP 4938>)* **THE BBC SESSIONS**

PRIMAL SCREAM

Formed: Glasgow, Scotland . . . summer 1984 by the JESUS & MARY CHAIN drummer BOBBY GILLESPIE. Signing to JAMC's label, 'Creation', in 1985, they cut two singles, GILLESPIE leaving The 'MARY CHAIN after the debut, 'ALL FALL DOWN' (1985). The first album, 'SONIC FLOWER GROOVE' (1987), was recorded by the current band line-up core of ANDREW INNES, ROBERT 'THROB' YOUNG and MARTIN DUFFY (save MANI, ex-STONE ROSES, who joined up in 1996) along with an ever-changing array of additional musicians. Released on 'Creation' boss ALAN McGEE's 'WEA' subsidiary label, 'Elevation', the album saw the band pretty much live up to their name, a primitive take on raw ROLLING STONES, STOOGES etc. with a bit of BYRDS jingle jangle thrown in. This sound served the band well through their second album, PRIMAL SCREAM (1989) until the release of 'LOADED' in early 1990. Back at 'Creation' and enamoured with the Acid House explosion, the band had enlisted the esteemed ANDREW WEATHERALL to remix 'I'M LOSING MORE THAN I'LL EVER HAVE' from the second lp. More a revolution than a remix, WEATHERALL created the stoned funk shuffle of 'LOADED', in the process bringing indie and rave kids together on the same dancefloor for the first time. PRIMAL SCREAM were now set on pushing the parameters of rock, releasing a trio of singles that defined an era, 'COME TOGETHER' (1990) was 90's style hedonist gospel that converted even the most cynical of rock bores while 'HIGHER THAN THE SUN' (1991) was perhaps the 'SCREAM's stellar moment, a narcotic lullaby beamed from another galaxy. Combining all the aforementioned tracks with a trippy 13TH FLOOR ELEVATORS cover, a heavyweight dub workout and a clutch of STONES-like beauties, 'SCREAMADELICA' (1991) was flawless. Opening with the euphoric 'MOVIN' ON UP' (the best song the 'STONES never wrote), the album effortlessly proved that dance and rock were essentially carved out of the same soulful root source, a seam that's been mined by any artist that's ever mattered. A landmark album, 'SCREAMADELICA' was awarded the Mercury Music prize in 1992 and for sheer breadth of vision the record has yet to meet its match. Inevitably, then, the GEORGE DRAKOULIAS-produced follow-up, 'GIVE OUT BUT DON'T GIVE UP' (1994) was a disappointment in comparison. Recorded in MEMPHIS, the record saw PRIMAL SCREAM trying far too hard to achieve a roughshod R&B grit. Where before they had made The STONES' sound their own, now they came across as mere plagiarists, and over-produced plagiarists at that. Granted, the likes of 'JAILBIRD' and 'ROCKS' were funkier than any of the insipid indie competition around at the time and GILLESPIE's epileptic handclap routine was always more endearing than the run-of-the-mill rock posturing. Rumours of severe drug abuse abounded at this point and few were shocked when, in January 1994, it emerged that DUFFY had survived a near fatal stabbing in America. For the next couple of years, the band kept a fairly low profile, only a contribution to the 'Trainspotting' soundtrack and an unofficial Scottish 'Euro '96' single confirmed the 'SCREAM were still in existence. But while Scotland stumbled to defeat (again!!), PRIMAL SCREAM cleaned up their act and recorded the wonderful 'VANISHING POINT' (1997). Apparently cut as an alternative soundtrack to cult 70's road movie 'Kowalski', this album was the true follow-up/comedown to the psychedelic high of 'SCREAMADELICA'. 'OUT OF THE VOID' was the band's darkest moment to date while the title track and 'STUKA' were fractured, paranoid psych-outs. Only the vintage screenshow of 'GET DUFFY' and the mellow 'STAR' offered any respite. Big on dub and low on derivation, the album was a spirited return to form for one of Scotland's most enduring and groundbreaking bands. The year of 2000 saw the 'SCREAM return with all guns blazing for the destructive release of 'EXTERMINATOR'. An aptly titled album, this was worrying music for the post Millennium tensions of anti-capitalist marches and technology protests. It shaped its own poisonous force as the listener ventured further into the set: 'KILL ALL HIPPIES' was certainly a phrase derived from the punk movement, while 'SWASTIKA EYES' had a morbid, self-asserting ring to it. GILLESPIE mixed in exuberant styles such as hip-hop ('PILLS'), trance ('ACCELERATOR') and a bit of old MY BLOODY VALENTINE tones into the devilish bru. One could describe 'EXTERMINATOR' as a disjointed soundtrack to a Jean Luc Godard horror pic, if he, er, did a horror that is. All in all, PRIMAL SCREAM were wise to return to wigged-out psychedelia – a style they were criticised for getting out of – with the self-indulgent 'VANISHING POINT'. 'EXTERMINATOR' is a valuable lesson in the art of punk: it's loud, it has balls, it's offensive, it's not all tuneful, and most importantly, it makes sense. This method was also applied to The 'SCREAM's seventh album proper, 'EVIL HEAT' (2002) which delved even deeper into GILLESPIE's obsession with dark, throbbing soundscapes. Possibly the musical equivalent to being repeatedly run over by a tank and then turned into a metal blob, the set curiously explored the avant-metal punk scene a little bit closer, with single 'MISS LUCIFER' spitting and bubbling like an unsteady jar of boiling acid. Basslines thrashed (especially on 'SKULL X'), keyboards sounding like they were being set on fire and GILLESPIE pumped up his frontman image by turning a piece of deadpan vocal into a plethora of screams. Apart from the SUICIDE connections, and the screeching, industrial electro-clash of it all, 'EVIL HEAT' (complete with sinister homemade, cut'n'paste album jacket) included some cringe-worthy moments: the lazy, drugged-up slur of nu-blues number 'THE LORD IS MY SHOTGUN', supermodel KATE MOSS' dreary rendition of the Lee Hazlewood song 'SOME VELVET MORNING' and the re-working of 'RISE' (originally entitled 'BOMB THE PENTAGON', but shamelessly re-titled for fears of American distribution). Former MY BLOODY VALENTINE casualty KEVIN SHIELDS took on the recording duty, doing his damndest to make it sound as dirty and as translucent as possible. PRIMAL SCREAM exist to be one of the globe's truest punk-rawk bands – a rare thing in these money spinning, 3-chord, pop-producing times. Like the BBC, they educate, entertain and inform . . . they also make one hell'uva racket too. PRIMAL SCREAM were back in the headlines in summer 2005 following oor BOB's crowd-baiting shenanigans at Glastonbury. He mightn't have much time for hippies but to GILLESPIE, rock'n'roll's unquiet urge has always traced its lineage way back beyond the 1976 year zero championed by the current crop of young post-punk turks. Critics feted many of these bands, but decided to take issue with PRIMAL SCREAM over their latest retro binge, 'RIOT CITY BLUES' (2006). In reality, its bar stool-wielding sleaze-rawk was no more derivative than contemporary neo-new wave clatter, just a few years older. They'd been there already but when you believe so fervently (even after all these years, a forty-something GILLESPIE is still the most feral frontman in the West), why not go there again? It was certainly a place where the fans felt at home, carrying the album into the Top 5 with them and making leading single, 'COUNTRY GIRL', the highest charting 'SCREAM single ever.

• **Songwriters:** GILLESPIE, YOUNG and BEATTIE, until the latter's replacement by INNES. Covered CARRY ME HOME (Dennis Wilson) / UNDERSTANDING (Small Faces) / 96 TEARS (? & The Mysterians) / KNOW YOUR RIGHTS (Clash) / MOTORHEAD (Motorhead) / GIMME

SOME TRUTH (John Lennon) / TO LIVE IS TO FLY (Townes Van Zandt).

Album rating: SONIC FLOWER GROOVE (*5) / PRIMAL SCREAM (*6) / SCREAMADELICA (*10) / GIVE OUT BUT DON'T GIVE UP (*7) / VANISHING POINT (*8) / ECHO DEK (*6) / EXTERMINATOR (*8) / EVIL HEAT (*6) / DIRTY HITS compilation (*9) / RIOT CITY BLUES (*7)

BOBBY GILLESPIE (b.22 Jun'64) – vocals (ex-WAKE, also drummer of JESUS & MARY CHAIN) / **JIM BEATTIE** – guitar / **ROBERT YOUNG** – bass / **TOM McGURK** – drums / **MARTIN ST. JOHN** – tambourine

Creation not iss.

May 85. (7") *(CRE 017)* **ALL FALL DOWN. / IT HAPPENS** [ ] [–]

— added **PAUL HARTE** – rhythm guitar (GILLESPIE left JESUS & MARY)

Apr 86. (7") *(CRE 026)* **CRYSTAL CRESCENT. / VELOCITY GIRL** [ ] [–]
(12"+=) *(CRE 026T)* – Spirea X.

— **STUART MAY** – rhythm guitar (ex-SUBMARINES) repl. HARTE (Dec'86) / **ANDREW INNES** – rhythm guitar (of REVOLVING PAINT DREAM) repl. MAY / Guest drummers **PHIL KING** (studio) + **DAVE MORGAN** (tour) repl. McGURK

Elevation not iss.

Jun 87. (7") *(ACID 5)* **GENTLE TUESDAY. / BLACK STAR CARNIVAL** [ ] [–]
(12"+=) *(ACID 5T)* – I'm gonna make you mine.

Sep 87. (7") *(ACID 5)* **IMPERIAL. / STAR FRUIT SURF RIDER** [ ] [–]
(12"+=/s12"+=) *(ACID 5T/+W)* – So sad about us / Imperial (demo).

Oct 87. (lp/c)(cd) *(ELV 2/+C)(242-182-2)* **SONIC FLOWER GROOVE** [62] [ ]
– Gentle Tuesday / Treasure trip / May the sun shine bright for you / Sonic sister love / Silent spring / Imperial / Love you / Leaves / Aftermath / We go down slowly. *(re-iss. Jul91; same)*

— (Jun'87) **GAVIN SKINNER** – drums; repl. ST. JOHN

— (Feb'88) Now a trio **GILLESPIE, YOUNG + INNES** augmented by **JIM NAVAJO** – guitar (BEATTIE formed SPIREA X; SKINNER also left)

— (Feb'89) added **HENRY OLSEN** – bass (ex-NICO) / **PHILIP 'TOBY' TOMANOV** – drums (ex-NICO, ex-DURUTTI COLUMN, ex-BLUE ORCHIDS)

Creation Mercenary

Jul 89. (7") *(CRE 067)* **IVY IVY IVY. / YOU'RE JUST TOO DARK TO CARE** [ ] [–]
(12"+=)(cd-s+=) *(CRE 067T)(CRESCD 067)* – I got you split wide open over me.

Sep 89. (lp/c/cd) *(CRE LP/C/CD 054)* *<2100>* **PRIMAL SCREAM** [ ] [ ]
– Ivy Ivy Ivy / You're just dead skin to me / She power / You're just too dark to care / I'm losing more than I'll ever have / Gimme gimme teenage head / Lone star girl / Kill the king / Sweet pretty thing / Jesus can't save me. *(free 7"ltd.)* – SPLIT WIDE OPEN (demo). / LONE STAR GIRL (demo) *(cd re-iss. Jan01; same)*

— trimmed to a trio again (**GILLESPIE, YOUNG + INNES**)

Creation Sire

Feb 90. (7") *(CRE 070)* **LOADED. / I'M LOSING MORE THAN I'LL EVER HAVE** [16] [–]
(ext.12"+=/'A'Terry Farley remix-12"+=)(ext.cd-s+=) *(CRE 070 T/X)(CRESCD 070)* – Ramblin' Rose (live).

Jul 90. (7"/c-s)(ext.12")(ext.cd-s) *(CRE/+CS 078)(CRE 078T(CRESCD 078)* *<26384>* **COME TOGETHER (Terry Farley mix). / COME TOGETHER (Andrew Weatherall mix)** [26] Aug90 [ ]
(12") *(CRE 078X)* – ('A'-HypnotoneBrainMachine mix) / ('A'-BBG mix).

Jun 91. (7"/ext.12") *(CRE 096/+T)* **HIGHER THAN THE SUN. / ('A' American Spring mix)** [40] [–]
(cd-s+=) *(CRESCD 096)* – Higher than the Orb.

— guest spot on above from **JAH WOBBLE** – bass

Aug 91. (7"/ext.12")(c-s) *(CRE 110/+T)(CRECS 110)* **DON'T FIGHT IT, FEEL IT. / ('A'scat mix featuring Denise Johnson)** [41] [–]
(cd-s+=) *(CRESCD 110)* – ('A'extended version).

Sep 91. (cd/c/d-lp) *(CRE CD/C/LP 076)* *<26714>* **SCREAMADELICA** [8] [ ]
– Movin' on up / Slip inside this house / Don't fight it, feel it / Higher than the Sun / Inner flight / Come together / Loaded / Damaged / I'm comin' down / Higher than the Sun (a dub symphony in two parts) / Shine like stars. *(cd re-iss. Jan01; same) (lp-iss.Jun01 on 'Simply Vinyl'; SVLP 344)*

Jan 92. (7"ep/c-ep) *(CRE/+CS 117)* *<40193>* **DIXIE-NARCO EP** [11] [ ]
– Movin' on up / Carry me home / Screamadelica.
(12"ep+=)(cd-ep+=) *(CRE 117T)(CRESCD 117)* – Stone my soul.

— In Jan'94, MARTIN DUFFY was stabbed in Memphis, although he recovered soon after.

— line-up:- **GILLESPIE, YOUNG, INNES, DUFFY + DAVID HOOD + DENISE JOHNSON** + guest **GEORGE CLINTON** – vocals

Mar 94. (7"/c-s) *(CRE/+CS 129)* *<18189>* **ROCKS. / FUNKY JAM** [7] Apr94 [ ]
(12")(cd-s) *(CRE 129T)(CRESCD 129)* – ('A'side) / Funky jam (hot ass mix) / Funky jam (club mix).

Apr 94. (cd/c/lp) *(CRE CD/C/LP 146)* *<45538>* **GIVE OUT, BUT DON'T GIVE UP** [2] [ ]
– Jailbird / Rocks / (I'm gonna) Cry myself blind / Funky jam / Big jet plane / Free / Call on me / Struttin' / Sad and blue / Give out but don't give up / I'll be there for you. *(cd re-iss. Feb00 & Jan01; same)*

Jun 94. (7"/c-s) *(CRE/+CS 145)* **JAILBIRD. / ('A'-Dust Brothers mix)** [29] [–]
(12"+=) *(CRE 145T)* – ('A'-Toxic Trio stay free mix) / ('A'-Weatherall dub chapter 3 mix).
(cd-s++=) *(CRESCD 145)* – ('A'-Sweeney 2 mix).

Nov 94. (7"/c-s) *(CRE/+CS 183)* **(I'M GONNA) CRY MYSELF BLIND (George Drakoulias mix). / ROCKS (live)** [51] [–]
(cd-s+=) *(CRESCD 183)* – I'm losing more than I'll ever have (live) / Struttin' (back in our minds) (Brendan Lynch remix).
(10") *(CRE 183X)* – ('A'side) / Struttin' (back in our minds) (Brendan Lynch remix) / Give out, but don't give up (Portishead remix) / Rockers dub (Kris Needs mix).

Jun 96. (c-s/cd-s; PRIMAL SCREAM, IRVINE WELSH AND ON-U SOUND PRESENT . . .) *(CRECS-CRESCD 194)* **THE BIG MAN AND THE SCREAM TEAM MEET THE BARMY ARMY UPTOWN (mixes:- full strength fortified dub / electric soup dub / a jake supreme)** [17] [–]

— In Oct'96, GILLESPIE, INNES, YOUNG & DUFFY were joined by **MANI MOUNFIELD** – bass (ex-STONE ROSES)

Creation Reprise

May 97. (c-s) *(<CRECS 245>)* **KOWALSKI / 96 TEARS** [8] [ ]
(cd-s+=) *(<CRESCD 245>)* – Know your rights / ('A'-Automator mix).

Jun 97. (c-s) *CRECS 263)* **STAR / JESUS** [16] [–]
(cd-s+=) *(CRESCD 263)* – Rebel dub / How does it feel to belong.
(12"+=) *(CRE 263T)* – ('A'mixes).

Jul 97. (cd/d-lp)(c) *(CRE CD/LP 178)(CCRE 178)* *<46559>* **VANISHING POINT** [2] [ ]
– Burning wheel / Get Duffy / Kowalski / Star / If they move, kill 'em / Out of the void / Stuka / Medication / Motorhead / Trainspotting / Long life. *(cd re-iss. Jan01; same)*

Oct 97. (7") *(CRE 272)* **BURNING WHEEL. / HAMMOND CONNECTION** [17] [–]
(12"+=)(cd-s+=) *(CRE 272T)(CRESCD 272)* – ('A'-Chemical Brothers remix) / Higher than the sun (original).

Oct 97. (cd/7"box) *(CRE CD/L7 224)* **ECHO DEK** (remixes) [43] [–]
– Duffed up / Revolutionary / Ju-87 / First name unknown / Vanishing dub / Last train / Wise blood / Dub in vain. *(cd re-iss. Feb00 & Jan01; same)*

Feb 98. (7") *(CRE 284)* **IF THEY MOVE, KILL 'EM. / BADLANDS** [ ] [–]
(12"+=)(cd-s+=) *(CRE 284T)(CRESCD 284)* – ('A'-My Bloody Valentine Arkestra mix) / ('A'-Darklands 12"disco mix).

— added on 1998 tour **JIM HUNT** – saxophone / **DUNCAN MACKAY** – trumpet / **DARREN MOONEY** – drums

Creation Astralwerks

Nov 99. (c-s) *(CRECS 326)* **SWASTIKA EYES / ('A'mix)** [22] [–]
(12"/cd-s) *(CRE 326T)(CRESCD 326)* – ('A'-Chemical Brothers mix) / ('A'-Spectre mix) / ('A'side).

Jan 00. (cd/md/c/d-lp) *(CRECD/CREMD/CCRE/CRELP 239)* *<49260>* **EXTERMINATOR** [3] May00 [ ]
– Kill all hippies / Accelerator / Exterminator / Swastika eyes / Pills / Blood money / Keep your dreams / Insect royalty / MBV Arkestra (if they move kill 'em) / Swastika eyes / Shoot speed – Kill light / I'm 5 years ahead of my time. *(cd re-iss. Jan01; same)*

Mar 00. (7") *(CRE 332)* *<8169>* **KILL ALL HIPPIES. / EXTERMINATOR (Massive Attack remix)** [24] Nov00 [ ]
(cd-s+=) *(CRESCD 332)* – The revenge of the Hammond connection.
(12"+=) *(CRE 332T)* – ('A'mixes).

Sep 00. (12")(cd-s) *(CRE 333T)(CRESCD 333)* **ACCELERATOR / I'M 5 YEARS AHEAD OF MY TIME / WHEN THE KINGDOM COMES** 34 –

Columbia Astralwerks

Jul 02. (12"/cd-s) *(672825-6/-2)* **MISS LUCIFER / (mixes: panther / hip to hip / bone to bone)** 23 –

Aug 02. (cd/lp) *(508923-2/-1)* *<87027>* **EVIL HEAT** 9

– Deep hit of morning sun / Miss Lucifer / Autobahn 66 / Detroit / Rise / The Lord is my shotgun / City / Some velvet morning / Skull X / A scanner darkly / Space blues number 2.

Oct 02. (cd-s) *(673312-2)* **AUTOBAHN 66 / AUTOBAHN 66 (alter ego remix) / SUBSTANCE D** 44 –

(12") *(673312-6)* – (first & third tracks + alter ego instr).

(cd-s) *(673312-5)* – ('A'side) / ('A'live) / Shoot speed kill light.

Nov 03. (cd/lp) *(513603-2/-1)* *<594300>* **DIRTY HITS** (compilation) 25 Dec03

– Loaded / Movin' on up / Come together / Higher than the sun (Orb remix) / Rocks / Jailbird / I'm gonna cry myself blind / Burning wheel / Kowalski / Long life / Swastika eyes / Kill all hippes / Accelerator / Shoot speed – Kill light / Miss Lucifer / Deep hit of morning sun / Some velvet morning (with KATE MOSS) / Autobahn 66. *(ltd d-cd+=; 5136039)* – (remixes of all tracks).

Nov 03. (12"; by PRIMAL SCREAM & KATE MOSS) *(674402-6)* **SOME VELVET MORNING. / COUNTRY BLUES 1 / ('A'-disco hater dub)** 44 –

(cd-s+=) *(674402-2)* – ('A'-video).

May 06. (7") *(82876 83427-7)* **COUNTRY GIRL. / GIMME SOME TRUTH** 5 –

(cd-s+=) *(82876 83428-2)* – Stone ya to the bone / ('A'-video).

(cd-s) *(82876 83427-2)* – ('A') / To live is to fly.

Jun 06. (cd) *(82876 83165-2)* **RIOT CITY BLUES** 5

– Country girl / Nitty gritty / Suicide Sally & Johnny Guitar / When the bomb drops / Little death / The 99th floor / Boogie disease / Dolls (sweet rock n roll) / Hell's comin' down / Sometimes I feel so lonely.

– others, etc. –

Nov 97. (12") *Creation; (PSTLS 1)* **STUKA (Two Lone Swordsmen mixes)** –

PRINCE

Born: PRINCE ROGERS NELSON, 7 Jun'58, Minneapolis, Minnesota, USA. Named after his father JOHN's jazz band, The PRINCE ROGER TRIO (which featured his mother Mattie on vocals), one of the young PRINCE's earliest musical experiences was witnessing JAMES BROWN in concert at the age of ten, a performer whose approach to music would heavily influence PRINCE's future career. By the time (1972) he was invited to play in his cousin CHARLES SMITH'S high school band, GRAND CENTRAL, alongside ANDRE ANDERSON (by whose family PRINCE had been adopted), the musical prodigy had already mastered guitar and piano, in addition to writing his own material. The following year, the band evolved into CHAMPAGNE as PRINCE became the leader following the replacement of SMITH by MORRIS DAY. Being in control was something PRINCE would make central to his steep career trajectory as he grew older, although he was wise enough to learn the ropes first. His initial studio experience came when he played session guitar for Sound 80 Studios' PEPE WILLIE, subsequently cutting a demo with the help of CHRIS MOON who guided him in the ways of recording. MOON also introduced him to OWEN HUSNEY whose hustling skills eventually secured PRINCE a groundbreaking solo deal with 'Warners' in 1978, allowing him complete control over every step of the creative process. His debut effort, 'FOR YOU' was released in October, a fairly conventional collection of slinky soul that spawned an American R&B hit in 'SOFT AND WET', the lewdness of the lyrics fairly tame in light of what was to come. While PRINCE played all the instruments and produced the record himself, for the eponymous 'PRINCE' (1980), the diminutive one brought in a cast of musicians for a more rock-based approach, namely guitarist DEZ DICKERSON, keyboardist GAYLE CHAPMAN, bassist ANDRE CYMONE (the same ANDRE of PRINCE's childhood who had by now changed his name), drummer BOBBY Z and MATT FINK on more keyboards. The result was a US Top 20 single with the playful funk-pop of 'I WANNA BE YOUR LOVER', a song addressed to singer Patrice Rushen. Following the album's relative success, PRINCE took his new band out on the road for the first time, meeting with consistently positive reviews. CHAPMAN was soon ousted in favour of LISA COLEMAN as the band previewed songs from the new album, 'DIRTY MIND' (1980), the first PRINCE release in which he gave free reign to his frequently sexually explicit lyrical muse. 'HEAD' was self-explanatory while 'SISTER' rather dodgily put forward the case for incest, the music moving ever further from the R&B of the debut and flirting with synth-heavy new wave. The album's lyrical frankness precluded any mainstream coverage although The ROLLING STONES were impressed enough to invite PRINCE to support them the following year. In the event, the shows were calamitous, The 'STONES infamously partisan crowd not taking too kindly to PRINCE's soulful androgyny. November of the same year saw the release of 'CONTROVERSY', an aptly titled album which divided the critics. While PRINCE once again dabbled with different styles and explored human desire on the likes of 'JACK U OFF', the record lacked the melodic immediacy of its predecessor. On a more positive note, PRINCE embarked on his most successful tour to date, building up a grassroots fanbase that would help make '1999' (1983) the biggest album of his career thus far. By the time of the record's release, PRINCE's backing band had evolved in to The REVOLUTION with a couple of personnel changes along the way; the questionably named BROWN MARK replaced ANDRE who had departed for a solo career while WENDY MELVOIN was recruited in place of DICKERSON. '1999's synth-throb of a title track gave PRINCE his first real UK success while the infectiously commercial 'LITTLE RED CORVETTE' (his first Top 10 hit, boosted by heavy MTV rotation) proved PRINCE could write top pop material to rival any stars of the day. While the album's best moments could've probably been squeezed onto a single record, there was a marked maturity in the songwriting which reached fruition with 'PURPLE RAIN' (1984), arguably the most fully realised record of PRINCE's career. The album was actually the soundtrack to the near-autobiographical film of the same name, the first single to be lifted from it, 'WHEN DOVES CRY', giving PRINCE his first No.1 in May '84. This poignant portrayal of family strife also gave PRINCE his biggest UK hit to date, reaching No.4 later that summer. Other highlights of the album included the epic title track and the loose-limbed soul-rock of 'LET'S GO CRAZY', the latter complete with a searing HENDRIX-style guitar climax. The purple-clad genius' career subsequently went stratospheric, a Purple Rain tour breaking box office records with sales of the album running into the millions worldwide. As well as furnishing CHAKA KHAN with her first hit in years ('I FEEL FOR YOU), PRINCE also wrote the controversial 'Sugar Walls' for Scottish-born SHEENA EASTON, a US Top 10 hit which further incensed the moral minority. Never the most communicative of stars, the mystique surrounding PRINCE grew deeper with the release of 'AROUND THE WORLD IN A DAY' (1985), a largely esoteric collection of psychedelic pop interspersed with the melodic brilliance of 'RASPBERRY BERET', possibly the finest song PRINCE has yet penned. This was also the album upon which PRINCE began attempting to reconcile the carnal with the spiritual, a preoccupation which would dominate his music in the years to come. 'AROUND THE WORLD . . .' was released on PRINCE's newly formed, Minneapolis-based record company (and lavish recording complex), 'Paisley Park', also home to friends like The FAMILY, SHEILA E. (who had also become part of

PRINCE

PRINCE's touring band), GEORGE CLINTON etc. Concentrating on his new baby, PRINCE announced, BEATLES-style, that he was retiring from live work, only to later backtrack on his decision and undertake a tour in support of the 'PARADE' (1986) album. Another soundtrack, this time for PRINCE's derided 'Under The Cherry Moon', the music stood apart from the movie, taking the blueprint of its predecessor as a starting point and embroidering it with pop nous (notably on the sensuous 'GIRLS AND BOYS'). The record also provided PRINCE with his third No.1 single in the shape of 'KISS', a supple, teasing funk workout later famously covered by TOM JONES. At the end of the tour, PRINCE disbanded The REVOLUTION, going solo for the next few albums while recruiting a new band for live work. 'SIGN O' THE TIMES' (1987) was PRINCE's most thorough exploration of sex and religion, a satisfyingly diverse double set that marked the maturation of everything the artist had been working toward up to that point. While the gloriously dirty funk of the title track incorporated a comment on the degradation of the social fabric, the muted musical foreplay of 'IF I WAS YOUR GIRLFRIEND', and indeed the vast majority of tracks found PRINCE back on familiar lyrical territory. 'The BLACK ALBUM' concentrated almost solely on the mechanics of sex via some visceral uncut funk yet allegedly, PRINCE considered the album was 'immoral' (!) and recalled it from 'Warners' German pressing plant at the last minute. Officially released late in 1994, the album remained a favourite talking point for years among PRINCE obsessives and casual observers alike, bootleggers no doubt making a fortune. Presumably his white album, then, 'LOVESEXY' (1988) was the flipside to its predecessor's libidinous funk, the insistent pop of the title track a UK No.1. Though the album sold relatively poorly in the States, PRINCE's commercial fortunes were revived with the 'BATMAN' soundtrack, a multi-million seller which topped the charts on both sides of the Atlantic. If not exactly the most profound of his albums, it was certainly more listenable than the weak 'GRAFFITI BRIDGE' (1990). Thankfully, PRINCE seems to have let up on his film aspirations in recent years, though his musical output doesn't seem to have benefited that much. Nevertheless, the 90's started on a high note with the massive 'DIAMONDS AND PEARLS' (1991) album, credited to PRINCE & THE NEW POWER GENERATION. This band had already backed PRINCE on the 'GRAFFITI BRIDGE' project, this time around their playing injecting a more spontaneous live feel to proceedings. The sexy strut of 'CREAM' and the more intense funk lewdness of 'GET OFF' dominated the set (a remixed import single of the former hit the UK Top 40!), while 'MONEY DON'T MATTER 2 NIGHT' was deeply affecting, soul baring stuff. Following the release of the (1992) 'symbol' album – a patchy collection partly redeemed by the jazzy leer of 'SEXY M.F.' – PRINCE bizzarely announced he was changing his name to , followed by yet more rumours that he wished to be known as VICTOR, then finally T.A.F.K.A.P. (The Artist Formerly Known As PRINCE). More controversy followed with revelations that PRINCE wanted out of his contract with 'Warners', unhappy that he was restricted to one album a year. In protest, he took to wearing a mask onstage and painting the word 'Slave' on his face, subsequently releasing the lush charm of 'THE MOST BEAUTIFUL GIRL IN THE WORLD' on independent labels worldwide. Fulfilling his contract, T.A.F.K.A.P. released a further couple of largely uninspired albums, 'THE GOLD EXPERIENCE' (1995) and 'CHAOS AND DISORDER' (1996), before disbanding the N.P.G. and retreating into silence. 'RAVE UN2 THE JOY FANTASTIC' did little to regain his diminishing audience as he indulged himself with a covered of Sheryl Crow's(!) 'EVERYDAY IS A WINDING ROAD'... sexfunk looked to be dead. Still, by the turn of the decade things were looking up: ignore the Jehovah's Witness sentiments and gimmicky processed vocals, and 'THE RAINBOW CHILDREN' (2001) was blessed with enough uncut polyrhythm and pop revelation (check '1 + 1 + 1 iIS 3' and 'SHE LOVES ME 4 ME') to suggest a new dawn around the corner. Needless to say, the jam-centric 'N.E.W.S.' (2003) wasn't it, but finally, in spring 2004, the forgotten seer acquiesced to major-label distribution: 'MUSICOLOGY' (2004) actually sounded like a major label album (and as a transatlantic Top 3, sold like one), to many critics and fans his best since the late 80's. Musically, it pretty much carried on where PRINCE left off, instantly redrawing his wilderness period as a sabbatical that never was. Nor could his comeback's timing have been better, with all things 80s back in vogue; as one of the few real geniuses from that decade, he once again proved his mettle with flirtatious call-and-response funk, flab-sheared soul and – on minor hit 'CINNAMON GIRL' – the kind of anthemic pop-rock that radio programmers would've died 4 back in the mid-80s. While 'ILLUSION, COMA, PIMP & CIRCUMSTANCE' came closest to 'DIAMONDS AND PEARLS'-era sauce, and the SLY STONE-esque 'ON THE COUCH' wasn't far behind, the forty-something married man largely laid off the explicitness of old for more socially-pointed lyrics. The revival rolled on with '3121' (2006); the superstar was back where he'd spent most of his career, at the top of the American charts. Contemporary R&B touches lent balance but lock-tight 80s throwbacks turned up the heat: 'LOLITA' and 'BLACK SWEAT' fronted some of the sharpest, sultriest synth-rock in decades, leaving the young pretenders gawping in his slipstream. It's official: raunchfunk is not dead.

• **Songwriters:** A prolific pensmith, he also wrote songs under pseudonyms CAMILLE, JAMIE STARR, CHRISTOPHER, etc., and has written hits especially for SHEENA EASTON (Sugar Walls) and BANGLES (Manic Monday). Note: WENDY AND LISA wrote 'MOUNTAINS' before departing for own duo. In 1996, he covered; BETCHA BY GOLLY WOW! (Stylistics) / I CAN'T MAKE YOU LOVE ME (Bonnie Raitt) / LA LA MEANS I LOVE YOU (Delfonics) / ONE OF US (hit; Joan Osborne). • **Trivia:** In 1988, his sister TYKA NELSON signed for 'Chrysalis', although her album failed to take off.

Album rating: FOR YOU (*5) / PRINCE (*6) / DIRTY MIND (*7) / CONTROVERSY (*6) / 1999 (*8) / PURPLE RAIN soundtrack (*8) / AROUND THE WORLD IN A DAY (*6) / PARADE soundtrack (*7) / SIGN 'O' THE TIMES (*9) / LOVESEXY (*8) / BATMAN soundtrack (*6) / GRAFFITI BRIDGE soundtrack (*6) / DIAMONDS AND PEARLS (*8) / (*8) / THE HITS 1 compilation (*9) / THE HITS 2 compilation (*9) / EXODUS (*5; as New Power Generation) / THE BEAUTIFUL EXPERIENCE mini (*5) / COME (*4) / THE GOLD EXPERIENCE (*6) / GIRL 6 soundtrack (*6) / CHAOS AND DISORDER (*5) / EMANCIPATION (*4) / NEW POWER SOUL (*5; as New Power Generation) / CRYSTAL BALL boxed-set (*5) / THE VAULT – OLD FRIENDS 4 SALE collection (*4) / RAVE UN2 THE JOY FANTASTIC (*5) / THE VERY BEST OF PRINCE compilation (*8) / THE RAINBOW CHILDREN (*5) / N.E.W.S. (*3) / MUSICOLOGY (*6) / 3121 (*5)

PRINCE – vocals, multi-instrumentalist, synthesizers, producer, everything

Warners Warners

Oct 78. (lp,c) *<3150>* **FOR YOU** – [ ]
– For you / In love / Soft and wet / Crazy you / Just as long as we're together / Baby / My love is forever / So blue / I'm yours. *(UK-iss.Sep86 lp/c; K/K4 56989) (cd-iss. Oct87; K2 56989)*

Nov 78. (7") *<8619>* **SOFT AND WET. / SO BLUE** – 92

Jan 79. (7") *<8713>* **JUST AS LONG AS WE'RE TOGETHER. / IN LOVE** – [ ]

— **PRINCE** – vocals, guitar live back-ups **DEZ DICKERSON** – guitar / **GAYLE CHAPMAN** – keyboards / **ANDRE CYMONE** – bass / **MATT FINK** – keyboards / **BOBBY Z** – drums

Nov 79. (7") *<49050>* **I WANNA BE YOUR LOVER. / MY LOVE IS FOREVER** – 11

Dec 79. (7") *(K 17537)* **I WANNA BE YOUR LOVER. / JUST AS LONG AS WE'RE TOGETHER** 41 –

Jan 80. (lp/c) *(K/K4 56772) <3366>* **PRINCE** [ ] Oct79 22
– I wanna be your lover / Why you wanna treat me so bad? / Sexy dancer / When we're dancing close and slow / With you / Bambi / Still waiting / I feel for you / It's gonna be lonely. *(cd-iss. 1986; K2 56772)*

Feb 80. (7") *<49178>* **WHY YOU WANNA TREAT ME SO BAD?. / BAD** – [ ]

— (Feb80) live **LISA COLEMAN** – keyboards repl. GAYLE

Apr 80. (7"/12") *(K 17590/+T)* **SEXY DANCER. / BAMBI** [ ] [–]
May 80. (7") *<49226>* **STILL WAITING. / BAMBI** [–] [ ]
Sep 80. (7") *<49559>* **UPTOWN. / CRAZY YOU** [–] [ ]
Oct 80. (lp/c) *(K/K4 56862) <3478>* **DIRTY MIND** [ ] [45]
– Dirty mind / When you were mine / Do it all night / Gotta broken heart again / Uptown / Head / Sister / Party up. *((re-iss. 1989) (cd-iss. Dec85; K2 56862)*
Nov 80. (7") *<49638>* **DIRTY MIND. / WHEN WE'RE DANCING CLOSE AND SLOW** [–] [ ]
Mar 81. (7"/12") *(K 17768/+T)* **DO IT ALL NIGHT. / HEAD** [ ] [–]
Jun 81. (7") *(K 17819)* **GOTTA STOP (MESSIN' ABOUT). / UPTOWN (live)** [ ] [–]
(12"+=) *(K 17819T)* – Head (live).
(12") *(K 17819TX)* – ('A'side) / I wanna be your lover (live).

—— (mid'81) live **BROWN MARK** – bass repl. ANDRE who ventured solo

Oct 81. (7"/12") *(K 17866/+T) <49808>* **CONTROVERSY. / WHEN YOU WERE MINE** [ ] [70]
Nov 81. (lp/c) *(K/K4 56950) <3601>* **CONTROVERSY** [ ] [21]
– Controversy / Sexuality / Do me, baby / Private joy / Ronnie talk to Russia / Let's work / Annie Christian / Jack u off. *(cd-iss. 1984; K2 56950)*
Apr 82. (7"/12") *(K 17922/+T) <50002>* **LET'S WORK. / RONNIE TALK TO RUSSIA** [ ] [ ]
(12") *<50028>* – ('A'side) / Gotta stop.
Jun 82. (7") *<29942>* **DO ME, BABY. / PRIVATE JOY** [–] [ ]

PRINCE & THE REVOLUTION

—— live **WENDY MELVOIN** – guitar repl. DEE

Jan 83. (7") *(W 9896) <29896>* **1999. / HOW COME U DON'T CALL ME ANYMORE** [25] Oct82 [44]
(free c-s w/7") *(W 9896C)* – 1999 / Controversy / Dirty mind / Sexuality.
(12"+=) *(W 9896T)* – D.M.S.R. *<US re-dist.Jun83 hit No.12>*
Feb 83. (lp/c) *(W 3809/+C) <23720>* **1999** [ ] [26]
– 1999 / Little red Corvette / Delirious / Let's pretend we're married / D.M.S.R. * / Delirious / Automatic / Something in the water / Free / Lady cab driver / All the critics love u in New York / International lover. *(re-iss. Nov83 as d-lp/d-c; 923720-1/-4)* – hit UK No.30. *(cd-iss. Sep84; 923720-2)* – (omits *)
Feb 83. (7") *<29746>* **LITTLE RED CORVETTE. / ALL THE CRITICS LOVE U IN NEW YORK** [–] [6]
Apr 83. (7") *<29548>* **LET'S PRETEND WE'RE MARRIED. / IRRESISTIBLE BITCH** [–] [52]
Apr 83. (7") *(W 9688)* **LITTLE RED CORVETTE. / LADY CAB DRIVER** [54] [–]
(12") – ('A'extended) / Automatic lover / International lover.
Sep 83. (7") *<29503>* **DELIRIUS. / HORNY TOAD** [–] [8]
Nov 83. (7") *(W 9436)* **LITTLE RED CORVETTE. / HORNY TOAD** [66] [–]
(ext.12"+=) *(W 9436)* – D.M.S.R.
Jun 84. (7"/12") *(W 9296/+T) <29286>* **WHEN DOVES CRY. / 17 DAYS** [4] May84 [1]
(d12"+=/c-s+=) *(W 9296 T/C)* – 1999 / D.M.S.R.
Jul 84. (lp,purple-lp/c/cd) *(925110-1/-4/-2) <25110>* **PURPLE RAIN** (soundtrack) [7] [1]
– Let's go crazy / Take me with U / The beautiful ones / Computer blue / Darling Nikki / When doves cry / I would die 4 U / Baby I'm a star / Purple rain. *<US-iss.as d-lp, w/ += tracks by The TIME + APOLLONIA 6> (re-iss. Jan92 hit UK No.59) (re-iss. cd/c Feb95; 925110-2/-4) (lp re-iss. Jun99; same)*
Jul 84. (7") *<29216>* **LET'S GO CRAZY. / EROTIC CITY** [–] [1]
Sep 84. (7"/7"sha-pic-d) *(W 9174/+P) <29174>* **PURPLE RAIN. / GOD** [8] [2]
(12") *(W 9174T)* – ('A'side) / ('A'vocal + instrumental).
Nov 84. (7") *(W 9121) <29121>* **I WOULD DIE 4 U. / ANOTHER LONELY CHRISTMAS** [58] [8]
(12"+=) *(W 9121T)* – Free.
(12") *(W 9121TE)* – ('A'&'B' US remixes).
Jan 85. (7"/12") *(K 1999/+T)* **1999. / LITTLE RED CORVETTE** [2] [–]
(free c-s w/7"+=) *(W 1999C)* – 1999 / Uptown / Controversy / D.M.S.R. / Sexy dancer.
Feb 85. (7") *(K 2000)* **LET'S GO CRAZY. / TAKE ME WITH U** [7] [–]
(ext.12"+=) *(K 2000T)* – Erotic city.
Feb 85. (7") *<29079>* **TAKE ME WITH U. / BABY I'M A STAR** [–] [25]

—— added live **SHEILA E.** (b.ESCOVEDO) – percussion, vocals / **ERIC LEEDS** – saxophone

Paisley Park Paisley Park

Apr 85. (lp/c/cd) *(925286-1/-4/-2) <25286>* **AROUND THE WORLD IN A DAY** [5] [1]
– Around the world in a day / Paisley Park / Condition of the heart / Raspberry beret / Tambourine / America / Pop life / The ladder / Temptation.
May 85. (7"/7"sha-pic-d) *(W 9052/+P)* **PAISLEY PARK. / SHE'S ALWAYS IN MY HAIR** [18] [–]
(12"+=) *(W 9052T)* – ('A'extended).
May 85. (7") *<28972>* **RASPBERRY BERET. / SHE'S ALWAYS IN MY HAIR** [–] [2]
Jul 85. (7"/12") *(W 8929/+T)* **RASPBERRY BERET. / HELLO** [25] [–]
Jul 85. (7") *<28998>* **POP LIFE. / HELLO** [–] [7]
Oct 85. (7") *<28999>* **AMERICA. / GIRL** [–] [46]
Oct 85. (7"/ext-12") *(W 8858/+T)* **POP LIFE. / GIRL** [60] [–]
Feb 86. (7"/7"pic-d/ext-12") *(W 8751/+P/T) <28751>* **KISS. / LOVE OR MONEY** [6] [1]
Apr 86. (lp,pic-lp/c/cd) *(925395-1/-4/-2) <25395>* **PARADE** (UNDER THE CHERRY MOON soundtrack) [4] [3]
– Christopher Tracy's parade / New position / I wonder U / Under the cherry moon / Girls and boys / Life can be so nice / Venus de Milo / Mountains / Do U lie? / Kiss / Anotherloverholenyohead / Sometimes it snows in April.
May 86. (7") *(W 8711) <28711>* **MOUNTAINS. / ALEXA DE PARIS** [45] [23]
(10"white/12") *(W 8711 TW/T)* – ('A'&'B'extended).
Aug 86. (7"/7"sha-pic-d) *(W 8586/+P)* **GIRLS AND BOYS. / UNDER THE CHERRY MOON** [11] [–]
(12"+=) *(W 8586T)* – Erotic city.
(d7"+=) *(W 8586F)* – She's always in my hair / 17 days.
Oct 86. (7") *<28620>* **ANOTHERLOVERHOLENYOHEAD. / GIRLS AND BOYS** [–] [63]
Oct 86. (7"/ext-12"/ext-12"pic-d) *(W 8521/+T/TP)* **ANOTHERLOVERHOLENYOHEAD. / I WANNA BE YOUR LOVER** [36] [–]
(d7"+=) *(W 8521F)* – Mountains / Alexa de Paris.

PRINCE

—— solo, without WENDY & LISA who formed own duo. He retained live **FINK, LEEDS & SHEILA E.** adding **MICO WEAVER** – guitar / **BONI BOYER** – keyboards / **LEVI STEACER JR.** – bass / **CAT GLOVER** – dancer, vocals

Mar 87. (7") *(W 8399) <28399>* **SIGN 'O' THE TIMES. / LA LA LA HE HE HE HE** [10] [3]
(12"/12"pic-d) *(W 8399/+T/TP)* – ('A'&'B'extended).
Mar 87. (d-lp/c)(cd) *(WX 88/+C)(925577-2) <25577>* **SIGN 'O' THE TIMES** [4] [6]
– Sign 'o' the times / Play in the sunshine / Housequake / Ballad of Dorothy Parker / It / Starfish and coffee / Slow love / Hot thing / Forever in my life / U got the look / If I was your girlfriend / Strange relationship / I could never take the place of your man / The cross / It's gonna be a beautiful night / Adore.
Jun 87. (7"/7"peach/c-s/ext-12"/ext-12"pic-d) *(W 8334/+E/C/T/TP) <28334>* **IF I WAS YOUR GIRLFRIEND. / SHOCKADELICA** [20] May87 [ ]

—— (next 'A'side featured backing vocals by solo artist SHEENA EASTON now living in California with all her well-invested millions!)

Aug 87. (7"/c-s) *(W 8289/+C) <28289>* **U GOT THE LOOK. / HOUSEQUAKE** [11] Jul87 [2]
('B'ext-12"+=/12"pic-d+=) *(W 8289 T/TP)* – ('A'long version).
Nov 87. (7"/c-s) *(W 8288/+C) <28288>* **I COULD NEVER TAKE THE PLACE OF YOUR MAN. / HOT THING** [29] [10] [63]
(12"+=/12"pic-d+=) *(W 8288 T/TP)* – ('B'extended).
Apr 88. (7"/c-s) *(W 7900/+C) <27900>* **ALPHABET ST. / THIS IS NOT MUSIC, THIS IS A TRIP** [9] [8]
(12"/cd-s) *(W 7900 T/CD)* – ('A'&'B'extended).
May 88. (lp/c)(cd) *(WX 164/+C)(925720-2) <25720>* **LOVESEXY** [1] [11]
– I no / Alphabet St. / Glam slam / Anna Stesia / Dance on / Lovesexy / When 2 r in love / I wish U Heaven / Positivity. *(re-iss. cd/c Feb95)*
Jul 88. (7"/12") *(W 7806/+T)* **GLAM SLAM. / ESCAPE** [29] [–]
(cd-s+=) *(W 7806CD)* – Escape (free yo mind from this rat race).
Oct 88. (7") *(W 7745)* **I WISH U HEAVEN. / SCARLET PUSSY (by 'Camille')** [24] [–]
(12"+=/cd-s+=) *(W 7745 T/CD)* – ('A' pts.2 & 3).

Jun 89. (7"/c-s/ext-12"/ext-12"pic-dcd-s/3"cd-s) *(W 2924/+C/T/TP/CD/CDX)* <22924> **BATDANCE. / 200 BALLOONS** 2 1
('A'-Batmix-12"+=) *(W 2924TX)* – ('A'-Vicki Vale mix).

Jun 89. (lp/c)(cd/pic-cd) *(WX 281/+C)(925 936-2/489-2)* <25936> **BATMAN** (soundtrack) 1 1
– The future / Electric chair / The arms of Orion / Partyman / Vicki waiting / Trust / Lemon crush / Scandalous / Batdance. *(re-iss. cd/c Feb95; same)*

Aug 89. (7"/c-s/remix-12"/ext-12") *(W 2814/+C/T/TX)* <22814> **PARTYMAN. / FEEL U UP** 14 18
(12"pic-d/cd-s) *(W 2814 TP/CD)* – ('A'video mix). / ('B'long stroke mix).

Oct 89. (7"/c-s; PRINCE with SHEENA EASTON) *(W 2757/+C)* <22757> **THE ARMS OF ORION. / I LUV U IN ME** 27 36
(12"+=/cd-s+=/12"pic-d+=) *(W 2757 T/CD/TP)* – ('A'extended).

— live **PATRICE RUSHDEN** – keyboards (solo artist) repl. BOYER + GLOVER / **MICHAEL BLAND** – drums repl. SHEILA E. / **CANDY DULFER** – saxophone repl. LEEDS

Jul 90. (7"/c-s) *(W 9751/+C)* <19751> **THIEVES IN THE TEMPLE. / (Part 2)** 7 6
('A'remix; 12"+=/cd-s+=/12"pic-d+=) *(W 9751 T/CD/TP)* – ('A'dub).

Aug 90. (cd)(d-lp/c) *(927493-2)(WX 361/+C)* <27493> **GRAFFITI BRIDGE** (soundtrack) 1 6
– Can't stop this feeling I got / New power generation / Release it (the TIME) / The question of U / Elephants and flowers / Round and round (TEVIN CAMPBELL) / We can funk (GEORGE CLINTON & PRINCE) / Joy in repetition / Love machine (the TIME) / Tick, tick, bang / Shake! (the TIME) / Thieves in the temple / The latest fashion (the TIME & PRINCE) / Melody Cool (MAVIS STAPLES) / Still would stand all time / Graffiti bridge (MAVIS STAPLES & TEVIN CAMPBELL) / New power generation (pt.II) (MAVIS STAPLES, TEVIN CAMPBELL, T.C. ELLIS & ROBIN POWER).

Oct 90. (7"/c-s) *(W 9525/+C)* <19525> **NEW POWER GENERATION. / (Part 2)** 26 64
(12"+=/cd-s+=/12"pic-d+=) *(W 9525 T/CD/TP)* – Melody Cool (extended remix).

PRINCE & THE NEW POWER GENERATION

— with **LEVI SEACER JR.** – guitar, vox / **TOMMY BARBARELLA** – keys, synths / **SONNY T.** – bass, vox / **ROSIE GAINES** – co-vocals, organ, synths / **MICHAEL B.** – drums / **TONY M.** – rap/vox / **KIRKY JOHNSON** – perc., vox / **DAMON DICKSON** – perc., vox

Aug 91. (7"/c-s) *(W 0056/+C)* <19225> **GETT OFF (remix). / HORNY PONY** 4 21
(12"+=) *(W 0056T)* – ('A'-Thrust mix).
(cd-s+=) *(W 0056CD)* – ('A'-Purple pump mix).
(above: as a m-lp, its US import hit UK chart! at No.33)

Sep 91. (7"/c-s) *(W 0061/+C)* <19175> **CREAM. / HORNY PONY** 15 1
(12"+=/cd-s+=) *(W 0061 T/CD)* – Gangster glam.

Sep 91. (cd)(d-lp/c) *(925379-2)(WX 432/+C)* <25379> **DIAMONDS AND PEARLS** 2 3
– Thunder / Daddy pop / Diamonds and pearls / Cream / Strollin' / Willing and able / Gett off / Walk don't walk / Jughead / Money don't matter 2 night / Push / Insatiable / Live 4 love. *(re-iss. cd/c Feb95)*

Nov 91. (7"/c-s) *(W 0075/+C)* <19083> **DIAMONDS AND PEARLS. / LAST DANCE** 25 4
(cd-s+=) *(W 0075CD)* – 2 the wire (Grammy instrumental) / Do you dance (remix).

Dec 91. (c-s,cd-s) <19090> **INSATIABLE / I LOVE U IN ME** – 77

Mar 92. (7"/c-s/cd-s) *(W 0091/+C/CD)* <19020> **MONEY DON'T MATTER 2 NIGHT. / CALL THE LAW** 19 23
(12"+=) *(W 0091T)* – Push.

Jun 92. (7"/c-s) *(W 0113/+C)* **THUNDER. / VIOLET THE ORGAN DRIVER** 28 –
(12"+=/cd-s+=/12"pic-d+=) *(W 0113 T/CD/TP)* – Gett off (thrust dub).

— **MAYTE** – vocals; repl. ROSIE

Jul 92. (7"/c-s) *(W 0123/+C)* <18817> **SEXY M.F. / STROLLIN'** 4 66
(12"+=/cd-s+=) *(W 0123 T/CD)* – Daddy Pop.

Sep 92. (7"/c-s) *(W 0132/+C)* **MY NAME IS PRINCE. / 2 WHOM IT MAY CONCERN** 7 –
(12"+=) *(W 0132T)* – Sexy mutha.
(cd-s++=) *(W 0132CD)* – ('A'extra mix).

Sep 92. (c-s,cd-s) <18707> **MY NAME IS PRINCE / SEXY MUTHA** – 36

Nov 92. (12"/cd-s) *(W 0142 T/CD)* **MY NAME IS PRINCE (remixes). / (other mixes)** 51 –

Oct 92. (cd)(d-lp/c) *(9362 45037-2)(WX 490/+C)* <45037> [symbol] 1 5
– My name is Prince / Sexy MF / Love 2 the 9's / The morning papers / The Max / Segue / Blue light / I wanna melt with U / Sweet baby / The continental / Dawn U / Arrogance / The flow / 7 / And God created woman / 3 chains o' gold / Segue / The sacrifice of Victor.

Nov 92. (7"/c-s) *(W 0147/+C)* <18824> **7. / 7 (acoustic)** 27 7
(cd-s+=) *(W 0147CD)* – ('A'other mixes).

Mar 93. (7"/c-s) *(W 0162/+C)* <18583> **THE MORNING PAPERS. / LIVE 4 LOVE** 52 44
(cd-s+=) *(W 0162CD)* – Love 2 the 9's.

Sep 93. (cd/c/d-lp) <*(9362 45431-2/-4/-1)*> **THE HITS 1** (compilation) 5 46
– When doves cry / Pop life / Soft and wet / I feel for you / Why you wanna treat me so bad? / When you were mine / Uptown / Let's go crazy / 1999 / I could never take the place of your man / Nothing compares 2 U / Adore / Pink cashmere / Alphabet St. / Sign 'o' the times / Thieves in the temple / Diamonds and pearls / 7.

Sep 93. (cd/c/d-lp) <*(9362 45435-2/-4/-1)*> **THE HITS 2** (compilation) 5 54
– Controversy / Dirty mind / I wanna be your lover / Head / Do me, baby / Delirious / Little red Corvette / I would die 4 U / Raspberry beret / If I was your girlfriend / Kiss / Peach / U got the look / Sexy M.F. / Gett off / Cream / Pope / Purple rain.

Sep 93. (3xcd/3xc) <*(9362 45440-2/-4)*> **THE HITS / THE B-SIDES** 4 19
– (all of above plus corresponding 'B'sides)
+ Hello / 200 ballooons / Escape / Gotta stop (messin' about) / Horny toad / Feel U up / Girl / I love U in me / Erotic city / Shockadelica / Irresistable bitch / Scarlet pussy / La, la, la, he, he, hee / She's always in my hair / 17 days / How come U don't call me anymore / Another lonely Christmas / God / Tears in your eyes / Power fantastic.

Sep 93. (c-s,cd-s) <18371> **PINK CASHMERE / SOFT AND WET (remix)** – 50

Oct 93. (7"/c-s) *(W 0210/+C)* **PEACH. / WISH U HEAVEN** 14 –
(cd-s+=) *(W 0210CD)* – Girls & boys / My name is Prince.
(cd-s) *(W 0210CD2)* – ('A'side) / Money don't matter 2 nite / Partyman / Mountains.

Dec 93. (7"pic-d/c-s) *(W 0215 P/C)* **CONTROVERSY. / THE FUTURE** 5 –
(cd-s) *(W 0215CD1)* – ('A'side) / The future (remix) / Glam slam / D.M.S.R.
(cd-s) *(W 0215CD2)* – ('A'side) / Paisley Park / Anotherloverholenyohead / New power generation.

Warners Bellmark

Mar 94. (7"/c-s) *(NPG 60155/+C)* <72514> **THE MOST BEAUTIFUL GIRL IN THE WORLD. / BEAUTIFUL** 1 3
(12"+=/cd-s+=) *(NPG 60155 T/CD)* – ('A'mixes).

May 94. (12"ep/c-ep/cd-ep) *(NPG 60212 T/C/CD)* <71003> **THE BEAUTIFUL EXPERIENCE** 18 92
– (7 versions of last single)

— Musicians: **PRINCE / MICHAEL B. / SONNY T. / TOMMY BARBARELLA / MR.HAYES / MAYLE**

Warners Warners

Aug 94. (cd/c/lp) <*(9362 45700-2/-4/-1)*> **COME** 1 15
– Come / Space / Pheromone / Loose! / Papa / Race / Dark / Solo / Letitgo / Orgasm.

Aug 94. (7"pic-d/c-s) *(W 0260/+C)* <18074> **LETITGO. / SOLO** 30 31
(cd-s+=) *(W 0260CD)* – Alexa de Paris / Pope.

Mar 95. (cd-ep) *(W 0289CD)* <17903> **PURPLE MEDLEY / PURPLE MEDLEY (extended) / PURPLE MEDLEY (Kirk J's B-side remix)** 33 84

the NEW POWER GENERATION

N.P.G. N.P.G.

Mar 95. (7"ep/c-ep/12"ep/cd-ep) *(NPG 0061045/+C/T/CD)* **GET WILD / BEAUTIFUL GIRL (sax version) / HALLUCINATION RAIN** 19 –

Apr 95. (cd/c/lp) *(NPG 6103-2/-4/-1)* **EXODUS** 11 –
– N.P.G. operator intro / Get wild / Segue / DJ gets jumped / New power soul / DJ seduces Sonny / Segue / Count the days / The good life / Cherry, Cherry / Segue / Return of the bump squad / Mashed potato girl intro / Segue / Big fun / New power day / Segue / Hallucination rain / N.P.G. bum rush the ship / The exodus has begun / Outro.

Aug 95. (cd-s) *<17859>* **THE GOOD LIFE / GET WILD** –
Aug 95. (c-s) *(NPG 0061515C)* **THE GOOD LIFE / FACE THE MUSIC** 29 –
(cd-s+=/12") *(NPG 0065151 CD/T)* – ('A'-mixes; Bullets go bang / Big city / etc). *(re-iss. Jun97; hit UK No.15; 006151 9/5/0 NPG)*
Oct 95. (c-s) *(NPG 6133-9)* **COUNT THE DAYS / (album)** –
(cd-s+=) *(NPG 6133-5)* – New power soul.

or T.A.F.K.A.P. (The Artist Formerly Known As PRINCE)

Warner-NPG Warner-NPG

Sep 95. (c-s) *(W 0315C) <17811>* **EYE HATE U / ('A'mix)** 20 12
(cd-s) *(W 0315CD)* – ('A'mixes).
Sep 95. (cd/c/lp) *<(9362 45999-2/-4/-1)>* **THE GOLD EXPERIENCE** 4 6
– P control / npq operator / Endorphinmachine / Shhh / We march / npq operator / The most beautiful girl in the world / Dolphin / npq operator / Now / npq operator / 319 / npq operator / Shy / Billy Jack bitch / Eye hate u / npq operator / Gold.
Nov 95. (c-s) *(W 0325C) <17715>* **GOLD / ROCK AND ROLL IS ALIVE! (AND IT LIVES IN MINNEAPOLIS)** 10 58
(cd-s+=) *(W 0325CD)* – Eye hate U (extended remix).
Mar 96. (cd/c; as PRINCE) *<(9362 46239-2/-4)>* **GIRL 6** (soundtrack / part compilation) 75
– She spoke to me / Pink cashmere / Count the days (NEW POWER GENERATION) / Girls and boys / The screams of passion (the FAMILY) / Nasty girl (VANITY 6) / Erotic city / Hot thing / Adore / The cross / How come U don't call me anymore? / Don't talk 2 strangers / Girl 6 (NEW POWER GENERATION).

— now performed by New Power Generation; **MR. HAYES, TONY BARBARELLA, SONNY T, MICHAEL B** plus **KIRK JOHNSON, ROSIE GAINES + NPG HORNS**

Jul 96. (cd/c) *<(9362 46317-2/-4)>* **CHAOS AND DISORDER** 14 26
– Chaos and disorder / Dinner with Dolores / The same December / Right the wrong / Zannalee / I rock, therefore I am / Into the light / I will / Dig u better dead / Had u.
Jul 96. (c-s) *(9362 43742-4)* **DINNER WITH DOLORES / HAD U** 36 –
(cd-s+=) *(9362 43742-2)* – Right the wrong.

the ARTIST with the NEW POWER GENERATION

E.M.I. NPG-Warner

Nov 96. (t-cd/t-c) *(CD/TC EMD 1102) <NPG 54982>* **EMANCIPATION** 18 11
– Jam of the year / Right back here in my arms / Somebody's somebody's / Get yo groove on / Courtin' time / Betcha by golly wow / We gets up / White mansion / Darned if I do / I can't make U love me / Mr. Happy / In this bed I scream / Sex in the summer / One kiss at a time / Soul sanctuary / Emale / Curious child / Dreamin' about U / Joint 2 joint / The holy river / Let's have a baby / Saviour / The plan / Friend lover sister mother-wife / Slave / New world / The human body / Face down / La la la means I love you / Style / Sleep around / Da da da / My computer / One of us / The love we make / Emancipation.
Dec 96. (c-s/cd-s) *(TC/CD EM 463)* **BETCHA BY GOLLY WOW! / RIGHT BACK HERE IN MY ARMS** 11 –
(cd-s) *(CDEMS 463)* – ('A'mix).
Mar 97. (c-s/cd-s) *(TC/CD EM 467)* **THE HOLY RIVER / SOMEBODY'S SOMEBODY / THE MOST BEAUTIFUL GIRL IN THE WORLD** 19
(cd-s) *(CDEMS 467)* – ('A'side) / The most beautiful girl in the world (Mustang mix) / Somebody's somebody / On sale now!

NPG NPG

Mar 98. (4xcd-box) *<(BCT 9871CD)>* **CRYSTAL BALL** (out-takes & 4th cd new) 62
– Crystal ball / Dream factory / Acknowledge me / Ripopgodazippa / Lovesign (Shock G remix) / Hide the bone / 2morrow / So dark / Movie star / Tell me how u wanna be done // Interactive / Da bang / Calhoun Square / What's my name / Crucial / An honest man / Sexual suicide / Cloreen bacon skin / Good love / Strays of the world // Days of wild / Last heart / Poom poom / She gave her angels / 18 & over / The ride / Get loose (remix) / P. control (club mix) / Make your mama hapy / Goodbye // The truth / Don't play me / Circle of amour / 3rd eye / Dionne / Man in a uniform / Animal kingdom / The other side of the pillow / Fascination / One of your tears / Comeback / Welcome 2 the dawn (acoustic). *<US mail-order cont.5th cd+=>* – KAMASUTRA (instrumental ballet score).

the NEW POWER GENERATION

— now with **CHAKA KHAN, LARRY GRAHAM + DOUG E FRESH**

NPG-RCA NPG

Jul 98. (cd/c) *(74321 60598-2/-4) <9872>* **NEWPOWER SOUL** 38 22
– New power soul / Mad sex / Until u're in my arms again / When U love somebody / Shoo-bed-ooh / Push it up / Freaks on this side / Come on / The one / (I like) Funky music.
Nov 98. (c-s) *(74321 63472-4)* **COME ON / COME ON (late night mix)** 65
(cd-s+=) *(74321 63472-2)* – Come on (The Artist remix).

the ARTIST

Arista Arista

Nov 99. (cd) *(74321 72574-2) <14624>* **RAVE UN2 THE JOY FANTASTIC** 18
– Rave un2 the joy fantastic / Undisputed / The greatest romance ever sold / Segue / Hot wit U / Tangerine / So far so pleased / The sun and the moon and the stars / Everyday is a winding road / Segue / Man o war / Baby knows / I love you but I don't trust you anymore / Silly game / Strange but true / Wherever U go whatever U do / 1800 new funk ad.
Feb 00. (cd-s) *(74321 74500-2) <13749>* **THE GREATEST ROMANCE EVER SOLD (mixes)** 65 Oct99 63

PRINCE

Redline Redline

Jan 03. (cd) *<(RDL 70004-2)>* **THE RAINBOW CHILDREN** Nov01
– Rainbow children / Muse 2 the pharaoh / Digital garden / The work (pt.1) / Everywhere / The sensual everafter / Mellow / 1 + 1 + 1 is 3 / DEconstruction / Wedding feast / She loves me 4 me / Family name / The everlasting now / Last December. *(re-iss. Mar03 on 'Wagram'; 308150-2)*

NPG not iss.

Jul 03. (cd) *(NPGNEWS 1)* **N.E.W.S.** –
– North / East / West / South.

Sony Columbia

Apr 04. (-) *<radio>* **CALL MY NAME** – 75
Apr 04. (cd) *(5171659) <92560>* **MUSICOLOGY** 3 3
– Musicology / Illusion, coma, pimp & circumstance / A million days / Life 'o' the party / Call my name / Cinnamon girl / What do U want me 2 do? / The marrying kind / If eye was the man in Ur life / On the couch / Dear Mr. Man / Reflection.
May 04. (cd-s) *(6749231)* **MUSICOLOGY / ON THE COUCH** –
Oct 04. (cd-s) *(675142-2) <17481>* **CINNAMON GIRL / ('A'video) / ('A'-xposed – footage)** 43

Universal Universal

Mar 06. (12"pic-d) *(MCST 40457) <B0006371-11>* **BLACK SWEAT. / BEAUTIFUL, LOVED AND BLESSED (feat. TAMAR)** 43 60
(cd-s+=) *(MCSTD 40457)* – ('A'-video).
Mar 06. (cd) *(985207-2) <B00062960-2>* **3121** 9 1
– 3121 / Lolita / Te amo corazon / Black sweat / Incense and candles / Love / Satisfied / Fury / The word / Beautiful, loved and blessed / The dance / Get on the boat.
May 06. (12"pic-d) *(MCST 40462)* **FURY. / TE AMO CORAZON – FURY (live from Brits 2006)** ?? –
(cd-s+=) *(MCSTD 40462)* – ('A'-video from Brits 2006).

– compilations, others, etc. –

on 'WEA/Warners' unless mentioned otherwise

Oct 88. (cd-s) *(921186-2)* **WHEN DOVES CRY / PURPLE RAIN**
Oct 88. (cd-s) *(921787-2)* **LET'S GO CRAZY (extended) / TAKE ME WITH U**
Oct 88. (cd-s) *(921842-2)* **LITTLE RED CORVETTE (dance mix) / 1999 (extended)**
Oct 88. (cd-s) *(921188-2)* **KISS / GIRLS AND BOYS / UNDER THE CHERRY MOON**
Nov 94. (cd/c) *<(45793)>* **THE BLACK ALBUM** (finally released!) 36 47
– Le grind / Cindy C. / Dead on it / When 2 R in love / Bob George / Superfunkycalifragisexy / 2 nigs united for West Compton / Rockhard in a funky place.

Dec 98. (c-s) *(W 467C)* **1999 / HOW COME U DON'T CALL ME ANYMORE** [10] [ ]
(12"+=/cd-s+=) *(W 467 T/CD)* – DMSR.
(re-iss. Dec99; same) – hit No.51

Feb 99. (m-cd) *<1999>* **1999: THE NEW MASTERS EP** [–] [ ]

Aug 99. (cd/c) *<(9362 47522-2/-4)>* **THE VAULT . . . OLD FRIENDS 4 SALE** (out-takes 1985-1994) [47] [85]
– The rest of my life / It's about that walk / She spoke 2 me / 5 women / When the lights go down / My little pill / There is lonely / Old friends 4 sale / Sarah / Extraordinary.

Nov 99. (d-cd) *Charly; (CDVAL 1112)* **THE EARLY YEARS ('94 EAST)** [ ] [–]

Jul 01. (cd/c) *Warners-ESP; <(8122 74272-2/-4)>* **THE VERY BEST OF PRINCE** [2] [66]
– I wanna be your lover / 1999 / Little red Corvette / When doves cry / Let's go crazy / Purple rain / I would die 4 U / Raspberry beret / Kiss / Sign 'O' the times / U got the look / Alphabet St. / Thieves in the temple / Gett off / Cream / Diamonds and pearls / Money don't matter 2 night.

□ PROBOT (see under ⇒ FOO FIGHTERS)

PROCOL HARUM

Formed: Southend, Essex, England ... 1959 as The PARAMOUNTS, by five schoolboys; BOB SCOTT, GARY BROOKER, ROBIN TROWER, CHRIS COPPING and MICK BROWNLEE. They played a number of local gigs, BROOKER soon taking over vocal chores when SCOTT failed to show. In 1962, they left school and acquired manager Peter Martin. The following year, with a few personnel changes, the band signed to EMI's 'Parlophone' label, soon hitting the UK Top 40 with an R&B cover of The COASTERS' 'POISON IVY'. Their follow-up, a re-working of THURSTON HARRIS's 'LITTLE BITTY PRETTY ONE', failed to emulate their minor earlier success, and, after a few more covers, they folded in late summer '66. Other covers were I FEEL GOOD ALL OVER (Drifters) / I'M THE ONE WHO LOVES YOU (Major Lance) / BAD BLOOD (Coasters) / BLUE RIBBONS (Jackie DeShannon) / CUTTIN' IN (Johnny Guitar Watson) / YOU'VE NEVER HAD IT SO GOOD (P.F.Sloan). In 1967, BROOKER and lyricist KEITH REID advertised in the Melody Maker for musicians, soon settling with MATTHEW FISHER, RAY ROYER, DAVE KNIGHTS and BOBBY HARRISON. They became PROCOL HARUM (taking the name from the Latin "procul", meaning "far from these things"), and with help from producer Denny Cordell, they unleashed their mesmeric debut 45, 'A WHITER SHADE OF PALE', for 'Deram'. Adapted from a classical suite by BACH (No.3 in d major; 'Air On A G String'), its neo-gothic/baroque organ refrain combined with REID's extremely surreal lyrics to create a quasi-psychedelic million seller (stayed at No.1 for 6 weeks in the UK charts). With record company pressures to tour, ROYER and HARRISON departed from the group, replaced by former PARAMOUNTS; TROWER and WILSON. Later that year, they moved with producer CORDELL to 'Regal Zonophone', having another major stab at the Top 10 with 'HOMBURG'. The increasingly enjoyed greater success Stateside and by 1970, the band's line-up was identical to the earlier PARAMOUNTS of '63 (see above). In 1972, with their live album riding high in the charts, they resurrected their old 1967 number, 'CONQUISTADOR', subsequently a major hit on both sides of the Atlantic. PROCOL HARUM continued to gain respect from US and Canadian audiences, although the single, 'PANDORA'S BOX', in 1975, gave them a renewed UK chart thrust. Its parent album, 'PROCOL'S NINTH', also returned them to The Top 50, including a cover of The BEATLES' 'EIGHT DAYS A WEEK'. After another patchy album, BROOKER split the band, joining the ERIC CLAPTON BAND before going solo. Like many other rock dinosaurs, the band reformed for a one-off album in the early 90's, surprising many with its inclusion of ROBIN TROWER (he had already established himself as a guitar hero in the 70's & 80's). The band returned once more in 2003 with 'THE WELL'S ON FIRE', a back to basics effort which, while not graced by TROWER's timeless class, managed to recreate the spirit of their best work while simultaneously flourishing selective contemporary influences.

Album rating: PROCOL HARUM (*6) / SHINE ON BRIGHTLY (*6) / A SALTY DOG (*6) / HOME (*6) / BROKEN BARRICADES (*7) / PROCOL HARUM LIVE IN CONCERT WITH THE EDMUNTON SYMPHONY ORCHESTRA (*6) / GRAND HOTEL (*6) / EXOTIC BIRDS AND FRUIT (*6) / PROCOL'S NINTH (*6) / SOMETHING MAGIC (*4) / THE PRODIGAL STRANGER (*3) / GREATEST HITS compilation (*7) / THE WELL'S ON FIRE (*6)

the PARAMOUNTS

GARY BROOKER (b.29 May'45) – vocals, keyboards / **ROBIN TROWER** (b. 9 Mar'45) – guitar / **DIZ DERRICK** – bass repl. CHRIS COPPING who went to Leicester University (Sep63) / **B.J. WILSON** (b.18 Mar'47) – drums repl. MICK BROWNLEE (Jan63).

Parlophone | not iss.

Dec 63. (7") *(R 5093)* **POISON IVY. / I FEEL GOOD ALL OVER** [35] [–]

Feb 64. (7") *(R 5107)* **LITTLE BIT PRETTY ONE. / A CERTAIN GIRL** [ ] [–]

Jun 64. (7") *(R 5155)* **I'M THE ONE WHO LOVES YOU. / IT WON'T BE LONG** [ ] [–]

Nov 64. (7") *(R 5187)* **BAD BLOOD. / DO I** [ ] [–]

Mar 65. (7") *(R 5272)* **BLUE RIBBONS. / CUTTIN' IN** [ ] [–]

Oct 65. (7") *(R 5351)* **YOU'VE NEVER HAD IT SO GOOD. / DON'T YA LIKE MA LOVE** [ ] [–]

PROCOL HARUM

BROOKER with also **MATTHEW FISHER** (b. 7 Mar'46) – organ (ex-SCREAMING LORD SUTCH) / **RAY ROYER** (b. 8 Oct'45) – guitar / **DAVE KNIGHTS** (b.28 Jun'45) – bass / **BOBBY HARRISON** (b.28 Jun'43) – drums / **KEITH REID** (b.10 Oct'46) – lyrics

Deram | Deram

May 67. (7") *(DM 126) <7507>* **A WHITER SHADE OF PALE. / LIME STREET BLUES** [1] [5]
<US re-iss. Jan73 on 'A&M'; 1389>

— **ROBIN TROWER** – guitar (ex-PARAMOUNTS) repl. ROYER who formed FREEDOM / **B.J. WILSON** – drums (ex-PARAMOUNTS) repl. HARRISON who also formed FREEDOM

Regal Zonophone | A&M

Sep 67. (7") *(RZ 3002) <885>* **HOMBURG. / GOOD CAPTAIN CLACK** [6] [34]
(re-iss. Oct75 on 'Fly'; BUG 2)

Dec 67. (lp) *(LRZ 1001) <18008>* **PROCOL HARUM** [ ] Sep67 [47]
– Conquistador / She wandered through the garden fence / Something following me / Mabel / Cerdes (outside the gate of) / Homburg / Christmas camel / Kaleidoscope / Salad days / Good Captain Clack / Repent Walpurgis / A whiter shade of pale. *(re-iss. May85 as 'A WHITER SHADE OF PALE' on 'Sierra' lp/c; FEDB/CFEDB 5008) (cd-iss. Jun97 as 'A WHITER SHADE OF PALE' on 'Repertoire'; RR 4666) (cd re-mast.May01 on 'Westside'+=; WESM 527)* – Lime Street blues / Homburg / Salad days (are here again) / Mabel / Cerdes (outside the gates of) / Something following me / Magdalene (my regal zonophone) / Quite rightly so / Shine on brightly.

Apr 68. (7") *(RZ 3007) <927>* **QUITE RIGHTLY SO. / IN THE WEE SMALL HOURS OF SIXPENCE** [50] [ ]

Dec 68. (lp; stereo/mono) *(S+/LRZ 1004) <SP 4151>* **SHINE ON BRIGHTLY** [ ] Oct68 [24]
– Quite rightly so / Shine on brightly / Skip softly (my moonbeams) / Wish me well / Rambling on / Magdalene (my regal zonophone) / In held twas I:- a) Glimpses of Nirvana – (b) Twas tea-time at the circus – (c) In the Autumn of my madness – (d) Look to your soul – (e) Grand finale. *(re-iss. Sep85 on 'Sierra' lp/c; FEDB/CFEDB 5026) (cd-iss. Nov92 on 'Castle'; CLACD 321) (<cd re-iss. Jun97 on 'Repertoire'+=; RR 4667>)* – In the wee small hours of sixpence / In the wee small hours of sixpence (alt.) / Quite rightly so (take 4) / Quite rightly so (extended mono) / Il tuo diamante. *(cd re-mast.May01 on 'Westside'+=; WESM 533)*

May 69. (lp) *(SLRZ 1009) <SP 4179>* **A SALTY DOG** [27] [32]

– A salty dog / The milk of human kindness / Too much between us / The Devil came from Arkansas / Boredom / Juicy John Pink / Wreck of the Hesperus / All this and more / Crucifiction Lane / Pilgrim's progress. *(re-iss. 1971 on 'Music For Pleasure'; MFP 5275) (re-iss. May85 on 'Sierra' lp/c; FEDB/CFEDB 5012) (cd-iss. 1986 on 'Mobile Fidelity'; MFCD 823) (cd re-iss. Jul92 on 'Castle'; CLACD 289) (<cd re-iss. Sep97 on 'Repertoire'+=; REP 4668>)* – Long gone geek. *(cd re-mast.May01 on 'Westside'; WESM 534)*

Jun 69. (7") *(RZ 3019)* **A SALTY DOG. / LONG GONE CREEK** [44] [–]

Jul 69. (7") *<1111>* **THE DEVIL CAME FROM KANSAS. / BOREDOM** [–] [ ]

— **CHRIS COPPING** – organ, bass (ex-PARAMOUNTS) repl. FISHER + KNIGHTS

Jun 70. (7") *<1218>* **WHISKEY TRAIN. / ABOUT TO DIE** [–] [ ]

Jun 70. (lp) *(SLRZ 1014) <SP 4261>* **HOME** [49] [34]

– Whiskey train / Dead man's dream / Still there'll be more / Nothing that I didn't know / About to die / Barnyard story / Piggy pig pig / Whaling stories / Your own choice. *(re-iss. Apr89 on 'Castle' lp/c/cd; CLA LP/MC/CD 142) (<cd re-iss. Sep97 on 'Repertoire'; REP 4669>) (cd re-mast.May01 on 'Westside'+=; WESM 535)* – Rockin' warm-up – Go go go / The dead man's dream (take 7) / Still there'll be more (instrumental take 3) / About to die / Barnyard story / Piggy pig pig / Your own choice / Whaling stories (take 2).

Chrysalis A&M

Jun 71. (lp) *(ILPS 9158) <SP 4294>* **BROKEN BARRICADES** [42] May71 [32]

– Simple sister / Broken barricades / Memorial drive / Luskus Delph / Power failure / Song for a dreamer / Playmate of the mouth / Poor Mohammed. *(re-iss. 1974 lp/c; CHS/ZCHS 1057) (<cd re-mast.Sep02 on 'Repertoire'+=; REP 4980>)* – Broken barricades (single version) / Power failure (single version) / Simple sister (mono).

Jun 71. (7") *<1264>* **BROKEN BARRICADES. / POWER FAILURE** [–] [ ]

Oct 71. (7") *<1287>* **SIMPLE SISTER. / SONG FOR A DREAMER** [–] [ ]

— **DAVE BALL** (b.30 Mar'50) – guitar repl. ROBIN TROWER (later solo) / added **ALAN CARTWRIGHT** (b.10 Oct'45) – bass (to **BROOKER, COPPING, WILSON, REID + BALL**)

Apr 72. (lp) *(CHR 1004) <SP 4335>* **PROCOL HARUM IN CONCERT WITH THE EDMUNTON SYMPHONY ORCHESTRA (live)** [48] [5]

– Conquistador / Whaling stories / A salty dog / All this and more / In held 'twas I; a) Glimpses of Nirvana – (b) 'Twas teatime at the circus – (c) In the Autumn of my madness – (d) I know if I'd been wiser – (e) Grand finales. *(<cd re-mast.Sep02 on 'Repertoire'; REP 4981>)*

May 72. (7") *<1347>* **CONQUISTADOR (live). / A SALTY DOG (live)** [–] [16]

Jul 72. (7") *(CHR 2003)* **CONQUISTADOR (live). / LUSKUS DELPH** [22] [–]

Chrysalis Chrysalis

Mar 73. (lp/c) *(<CHR/ZCHR 1037>)* **GRAND HOTEL** [ ] [21]

– Grand hotel / Toujours l'amour / A rum tale / T.V. Ceaser / A souvenir of London / Bringing home the bacon / Robert's box / For licorice John / Fires (which burnt brightly) / Robert's box. *(cd-iss. Oct95 on 'Essential'; ESMCD 290) (<cd re-mast.Apr01 on 'Repertoire'+=; REP 4916>)* – Grand hotel (single version) / Robert's box (single version).

Apr 73. (7") *(CHS 2010)* **ROBERT'S BOX. / A RUM TALE** [ ] [–]

Apr 73. (7") *<2011>* **BRINGING HOME THE BACON. / TOUJOURS L'AMOUR** [–] [ ]

Aug 73. (7") *<2013>* **GRAND HOTEL. / FIRE'S (WHICH BURNT BRIGHTLY)** [–] [ ]

Aug 73. (7") *(CHS 2015)* **A SOUVENIR OF LONDON. / TOUJOURS L'AMOUR** [ ] [–]

— **MICK GRABHAM** – guitar (ex-PLASTIC PENNY, ex-COCHISE) repl. BALL to BEDLAM

Apr 74. (lp/c) *(<CHR/ZCHR 1058>)* **EXOTIC BIRDS AND FRUIT** [ ] [86]

– Nothing but the truth / Beyond the pale / As strong as Samson / The idol / The thin edge of the wedge / Monsieur R. Monde / Fresh fruit / Butterfly boys / New lamps for old. *(cd-iss. Oct95 on 'Essential'; ESMCD 291) (<cd re-mast.Mar01 on 'Repertoire'+=; REP 4791>)* – Drunk again / As strong as Samson (single version).

Apr 74. (7") *(CHS <2032>)* **NOTHING BUT THE TRUTH. / DRUNK AGAIN** [ ] [ ]

Jul 75. (7") *(CHS <2073>)* **PANDORA'S BOX. / THE PIPER'S TUNE** [16] [ ]

Aug 75. (lp/c) *(<CHR/ZCHR 1080>)* **PROCOL'S NINTH** [41] [52]

– Pandora's box / Fools gold / Taking the time / The unquiet zone / The final thrust / I keep forgetting / Without a doubt / The piper's tune / Typewriter torment / Eight days a week. *(cd-iss. Oct95 on 'Essential'; ESMCD 292) (<cd re-mast.Mar01 on 'Repertoire'; REP 4919>)*

Oct 75. (7") *(CHS 2079)* **THE FINAL THRUST. / TAKING THE TIME** [ ] [–]

Jan 76. (7") *(CHS 2084)* **AS STRONG AS SAMSON. / THE UNQUIET ZONE** [ ] [–]

— **PETE SOLLEY** – keyboards (ex-ARTHUR BROWN, ex-SNAFU, ex-CHRIS FARLOWE) repl. CARTWRIGHT (COPPING now bass only)

Jan 77. (7") *<2115>* **WIZARD MAN. / SOMETHING MAGIC** [–] [ ]

Feb 77. (7") *(CHS 2138)* **WIZARD MAN. / BACKGAMMON** [ ] [–]

Mar 77. (lp/c) *(<CHR/ZCHR 1130>)* **SOMETHING MAGIC** [ ] [ ]

– Something magic / Skating on thin ice / Wizard man / The mark of the claw / Strangers in space / The worm and the tree (part 1 – Introduction – Menace – Occupation / part 2 – Enervation – Expectancy – Battle / part 3 – Regeneration – Epilogue). *(cd-iss. Oct95 on 'Essential'; ESMCD 293) (<cd re-mast.Mar01 on 'Repertoire'+=; REP 4918>)* – Wizard man (single version) / Backgammon (single version).

— Disbanded mid-77. WILSON joined JOE COCKER. GRABHAM to MICKEY JUPP. GARY BROOKER joined ERIC CLAPTON band and went solo. PROCOL HARUM re-formed Oct'91, TIM RENWICK instead of TROWER.

— re-formed in 1991. **BROOKER** – vocals, piano / **KEITH REID** – words / **ROBIN TROWER** – lead guitar / **MATTHEW FISHER** – hammond organ / with guests **DAVE BRONZE** – bass / **MARK BRZEZICKI** – drums (of BIG COUNTRY) / **JERRY STEVENSON** – mandolin, guitar

Zoo-B.M.G. Zoo

Feb 92. (cd/c/lp) *(HH CD/MC/LP 90589)* **THE PRODIGAL STRANGER** [ ] [ ]

– The truth won't fade away / Holding on / Man with a mission / (You can't) Turn back the page / One more time / A dream in ev'ry home / The hand that rocks the cradle / The king of hearts / All our dreams are sold / Perpetual motion / Learn to fly / The pursuit of happiness.

— in Jul'95, PROCOL HARUM members guested on a classical album, 'THE LONG GOODBYE' with The London Philharmonic Orchestra

— re-formed with **BROOKER, REID, FISHER + GEOFF WHITEHORN** plus rhythm **MATT PEGG + MARK BRZEZICKI**

Eagle Red

Mar 03. (cd) *(EAGCD 209) <20006>* **THE WELL'S ON FIRE** [ ] [ ]

– An old English dream / Shadow boxed / A robe of silk / The blink of an eye / The VIP room / The question / The world is rich / Fellow travellers / Wall Street blues / The emperor's new clothes / So far behind / Every dog will have his day / Weisselklenzenacht (the signature).

– compilations, others, etc. –

Mar 64. (7"ep) *Parlophone; (GEP 8908)* **THE PARAMOUNTS** [ ] [–]

– Little bitty pretty one / A certain girl / Poison Ivy / I feel good all over.

1971. (lp) *Fly; (TON 4)* **THE BEST OF PROCOL HARUM** [ ] [–]

<US-iss.Oct73 on 'A&M'; 4401>

Apr 72. (7"m) *MagniFly; (ECHO 101)* **A WHITER SHADE OF PALE. / HOMBURG / A SALTY DOG** [13] [–]

Apr 72. (d-lp/d-c) *Cube; (TOOFA 7)* **PROCOL HARUM – A WHITER SHADE OF PALE / A SALTY DOG** [26] [–]

(re-iss. Jan75, Mar78, Oct81; same)

Mar 76. (lp) *Decca; (ROOTS 4)* **ROCK ROOTS** [ ] [–]

Mar 78. (7") *Fly; (BUG 77)* **A WHITER SHADE OF PALE. / CONQUISTADOR** [ ] [ ]

(re-iss. Mar79; HBUG 77) (re-iss. Aug82 on 'Dakota'; BAK 1)

Mar 78. (d-lp/d-c) *Cube; (TOOFA/ZCTOF 10)* **SHINE ON BRIGHTLY / HOME** [ ] [–]

May 78. (lp) *Hallmark; (SHM 956)* **PROCOL HARUM'S GREATEST HITS** [ ] [–]

Aug 78. (7") *Chrysalis; (CHS 2244)* **CONQUISTADOR. / A SALTY DOG** [ ] [–]

Aug 78. (7"ep) *E.M.I.; (NUT 2834)* **THE PARAMOUNTS** [ ] [–]

– Poison Ivy / I feel glad all over / Blue ribbons / Cuttin' in.

Oct 81. (d-lp/c) *Cube; (PLAT/ZCPLT 1003)* **THE PLATINUM COLLECTION** [ ] [–]

Apr 82. (lp) *Ace; (6886555)* **PROCOL HARUM** (67-69) [ ] [–]

(re-iss. Apr82 on 'Impact'; 7486 552) (re-iss. Oct82 on 'Dakota'; COUNT/ZCCNT 13)

Aug 82. (7") *Dakota; (BAK 2)* **HOMBURG. / A SALTY DOG** [ ] [–]

Apr 83. (lp; by PARAMOUNTS) *Edsel; (ED 112)* **WHITER SHADES OF R'N'B** [ ] [–]

(cd-iss. Aug87 + Sep91; EDCD 112)

Oct 84. (d-lp/c) *Sierra; (FEDD/CFEDD 1004)* **OFF THE RECORD WITH PROCOL HARUM**

Apr 86. (d-lp/d-c/cd) *Castle; (CCS LP/MC/CD 120)* **THE COLLECTION**
– A whiter shade of pale / Homburg / Too much between us / A salty dog / The Devil came back from Kansas / Whaling stories / Good Captain Clack / All this and more / Quite rightly so / Shine on brightly / Grand hotel / Bringing home the bacon / Toujours l'armour / Broken barricades / Power failure / Conquistador (live) / Nothing but the truth / Butterfly boys / Pandora's box / Simple sister.

Feb 87. (7") *Old Gold; (OG 9692)* **CONQUISTADOR. / PANDORA'S BOX**

Mar 88. (d-lp/c/cd) *That's Original; (TFO LP/MC/CD 5)* **SHINE ON BRIGHTLY. / A SALTY DOG**

Mar 88. (cd-ep) *Special Edition; (CD 3-14)* **A WHITER SHADE OF PALE / HOMBURG / CONQUISTADOR / A SALTY DOG**

Jun 88. (7") *Old Gold; (OG 9225)* **A WHITER SHADE OF PALE. / HOMBURG**

Jun 88. (cd) *A&M; (CD 2515)* **CLASSICS**

Jul 88. (lp/c/cd) *Knight; (KN LP/MC/CD 10005)* **NIGHTRIDING: PROCOL HARUM**

Dec 88. (lp/c/cd) *Fun; (FUN/+C/CD 9028)* **20 GREATEST HITS**

1991. (cd)(c/lp) *Chrysalis; (MPCD 1638)(Z+/CNW 4)* **PORTFOLIO**

Feb 92. (cd-box) *Castle; (CLABX 910)* **3 ORIGINALS**
– (HOME / A SALTY DOG / A WHITER SHADE OF PALE).

Jun 92. (cd) *Dojo; (EARLD 6)* **THE EARLY YEARS**

Oct 94. (cd) *Disky; (CUCD 05)* **PROCOL HARUM**

Jan 95. (cd) *B.R.Music; (BRCD 106)* **BEST OF PROCOL HARUM**

Jul 95. (cd-ep) *Essential;* **A WHITER SHADE OF PALE / A SALTY DOG / REPENT WALPURGIS**

Sep 95. (cd/c) *Essential; (ESS CD/MC 295)* **HOMBURG & OTHER HITS – THE BEST OF PROCOL HARUM**

Jun 97. (3xcd-box) *Westside; (<WESX 301>)* **30th ANNIVERSARY COLLECTION**

Jul 99. (cd) *Strange Fruit; (SFRSCD 089)* **LIVE IN CONCERT**

Nov 99. (cd) *Westside; (WESA 821)* **PANDORA'S BOX: THE PROCOL HARUM STEREO VERSIONS**

Oct 00. (cd) *Metro; (METRCD 038)* **GREATEST HITS**

Feb 02. (d-cd) *Metro; (<METRDCD 502>)* **CLASSIC TRACKS AND RARITIES: AN ANTHOLOGY**

Jul 02. (cd) *Beat Goes On; (<BGOCD 556>)* **PROCOL HARUM / SHINE ON BRIGHTLY**

Jul 02. (d-cd) *Repertoire; (<REP 4680>)* **THE BEST OF PROCOL HARUM: 22 CLASSIC TRACKS**

Sep 02. (3xcd-box) *Repertoire; (REP 4971)* **SINGLES A'S & B'S**

Sep 02. (cd) *Repertoire; (<REP 4982)* **LIQUORICE JOHN DEATH** Nov03

Mar 03. (cd) *Beat Goes On; (<BGOCD 558>)* **A SALTY DOG / HOME**

Jun 03. (d-cd) *Metro; (<METRDCD 521>)* **THE FIRST FOUR ALBUMS**

Aug 03. (cd) *Repertoire; (<REP 4791>)* **THE ESSENTIAL COLLECTION (1967-1991)**

the PRODIGY

Formed: Braintree, Essex, England ... early 90's by LIAM HOWLETT together with MC MAXIM REALITY, LEEROY THORNHILL and KEITH FLINT. With their roots in hip hop, this irrepressible quartet of techno terrorists spread their first waves of discontent through the harder end of the rave scene, releasing the 'WHAT EVIL LURKS' EP in March '91 on the (then) fledgling 'XL' label. One track, the rave call to arms of 'EVERYBODY IN THE PLACE' would rocket to No.2 the following Christmas, hot on the heels of the PRODIGY's seminal debut hit (No.3), 'CHARLY'. A masterstroke of genius, HOWLETT sampled a veteran Government TV ad warning children off playing with fire (a recurring lyrical obsession) and welded it to fuck-off, hoover synths and a juggernaut breakbeat. The mixed result: proof that ravers had a sense of humour/irony and a string of low-rent imitations sampling everything from 'Sesame Street' to 'Rhubarb and Custard'. Borrowing from ARTHUR BROWN's hoary old chestnut of the same name, 'FIRE' gave the PRODIGY their third Top 20 hit in a row, closely followed by 'THE PRODIGY EXPERIENCE' (1992). More assured and inventive than most of the weak cash-in albums to come out of the 12" dominated rave scene, the record proffered alternate versions of the hits and killer new tracks like the brilliant breakbeat-skank, 'OUT OF SPACE'. By this point the group were also making waves with their formidable live show, still largely gracing raves yet a far cry from your average P.A. featuring a scantily clad diva miming to a 15-minute set. By 1993, HOWLETT was extending his horizons; a much in demand remixer, he worked on material for such diverse acts as DREAM FREQUENCY and FRONT 242 as well as poring over new PRODIGY tracks. The first of these, the wailing 'ONE LOVE' was initially realeased as a white label, apparently to keep in touch with their underground roots. The record still charted of course, going Top 10 in late '93 after a full release. 'NO GOOD START THE DANCE' was the sound of a group in transition, a speeded-up female vocal alternating with a thundering techno assault. The single made the Top 5 in Spring '94, but it was hardly representative of what lay in store on 'MUSIC FOR THE JILTED GENERATION' later that summer. Opening with a sinister tap-tapping typewriter and spoken word intro, then slamming into a dark, twisting techno groove, it was clear HOWLETT was no longer "luvved up". The album was breathtaking in its sweep, mapping out the future of techno, PRODIGY style, incorporating heavy riffing (on the two fingered salute to the Criminal Justice Bill, 'THEIR LAW', a collaboration with POP WILL EAT ITSELF), 70's style funky flute (the evocative '3 KILOS') and even a trio of tracks, 'THE NARCOTIC SUITE', climaxing the album in blistering form. Obvious highlights were the utterly compelling 'VOODOO PEOPLE' (riffs AND funky flute!; arguably The PRODIGY's finest moment to boot) and the military stomp of 'POISON' (complete with techno-gothic video; a must-see). The album was a UK No.1, establishing the band as major contenders who had far outstripped the narrow confines of 'dance', as was evidenced at their shows over the ensuing two years. White-gloved ravers blew their whistles hopefully, waiting in vain for 'CHARLY' or 'NO GOOD START THE DANCE', while more recent converts contorted and thrashed wildly to the new material (when, that is, they weren't threatening to shove the raver's eardrum-rupturing whistles where the sun doesn't shine!). By late '95/early '96, The PRODIGY were also showcasing new material at live gigs, including an incendiary little ditty entitled 'FIRESTARTER'. Primarily KEITH's baby, the 'song' was released as a single in Spring '96, giving The PRODIGY their first No.1. FLINT had, by now, fashioned his once flowing locks into a formidable luminous green mohican and had also developed a stage act that made IGGY POP (circa The STOOGES) look like a librarian. The fine, upstanding British public were subsequently treated to the new improved KEITH via the brilliant video (claustrophobically shot in the London Underground) on Top Of The Pops, resulting in an avalanche of complaints. Of course, the kids loved it, even toddlers were heard to garble 'I'm a twisted firestarter' while dragging their hapless mums into Woolies to bag a copy. As for the song itself, FLINT took a starring role, spitting out his demented cockney threats over depth charge beats. The next single, 'BREATHE', was even better, an ominous JOY DIVISION-esque guitar riff segueing into the hardest funkiest breakbeats this side of The CHEMICAL BROTHERS. Arguably the single of the year, the track raised expectations for the forthcoming PRODIGY opus to fever pitch. Almost inevitably, then, 'THE FAT OF THE LAND' (1997) was something of a letdown. There was nothing to match the dark majesty of 'BREATHE' (included on the album along with 'FIRESTARTER'), but there were plenty of other tracks to 'melt some brains' as HOWLETT put it. The insistent techno-hop of 'DIESEL POWER' (with KOOL KEITH guesting) attested to the group's love of hardcore rap, while the BEASTIE BOYS-sampling 'FUNKY SHIT' and MC MAXIM-led 'MINDFIELDS' were high-octane PRODIGY crowd pleasers. Minus points, however, for the dull collaboration with CRISPIAN MILLS (KULA SHAKER), 'NARAYAN' and the pointless cover of L7's 'FUEL MY FIRE'. Far more compelling was the insidiously funky 'CLIMBATIZE'. But it was the album's opener which had the nation's moral guardians and pro-women groups in a tizzy; whatever the inspiration for 'SMACK MY BITCH UP', the PRODIGY were as defiant and unapologetic as ever. Politics aside, the album may not have fully met expectations but it still trampled on the competition. Live, the PRODIGY remain a revelation, an electric maelstrom of colour and sound (and grimacing!), with an ability to mobilise a crowd unmatched in the musical spectrum. In saying that, if they rely on punk cliches without pushing the boundaries of dance music – which is what they do best – they risk becoming a caricature of themselves. Following the universally panned 'BABY'S GOT A TEMPER' single (a UK Top 5 in summer 2002), the PRODIGY's comeback was put on ice as HOWLETT went it alone on his trusty laptop. The result was the UK chart conquering 'ALWAYS OUTNUMBERED, NEVER OUTGUNNED' (2004), a defiant avowal of the man's guiding influences – industrial gurn, punk and new wave, beatbox hip hop – without too much recourse to the cyberhooks which made them lords of the late 90's festival scene. Naturally, samples were still his raw material, filched from fashionably electro-fied sources and hotwired into the likes of lead single (UK Top 20), 'GIRLS' and the belly dancing brutality of 'SPITFIRE'. HOWLETT also dug deeper for the heavily 'Love Buzz'-reliant 'PHOENIX', a good idea if NIRVANA hadn't already been there. And make what you will of Hollywood babe Juliette Lewis foxing her way through 'HOT RIDE', a grungy rewrite of the Jimmy Webb-penned Fifth Dimension hit, 'UP, UP & AWAY'. Even LIAM GALLAGHER was hauled out for a fairly anonymous turn on 'SHOOT DOWN'.

• **Songwriters:** HOWLETT except samples of BABY D ('Casanova') on 'BREAK & ENTER', and KELLY CHARLES on 'YOU'RE NO GOOD FOR ME'. 'FULL THROTTLE' is also reminiscent of JOAN ARMATRADING's 'Me Myself I'.

Album rating: EXPERIENCE (*8) / MUSIC FOR THE JILTED GENERATION (*10) / THE FAT OF THE LAND (*7) / ALWAYS OUTNUMBERED, NEVER OUTGUNNED (*5) / THEIR LAW: SINGLES 1990-2005 compilation (*8)

KEITH FLINT (b.17 Sep'69) – vocals, dancer / **LIAM HOWLETT** (b.21 Aug'71) – keyboards / **MC MAXIM REALITY** (b.KEITH PALMER, 21 Mar'67) – rapper-vox, dancer / **LEEROY THORNHILL** (b.7 Oct'69) – dancer, vocals

X.L. Elektra

Mar 91. (12"ep) *(XLT 17)* **WHAT EVIL LURKS / WE GONNA ROCK. / ANDROID / EVERYBODY IN THE PLACE** [ ] [–]

Aug 91. (7"/c-s) *(XLS/XLC 21) <66411>* **CHARLY. / CHARLY (original mix)** [3] [ ]
(12"+=/cd-s+=) *(XLT/CDXLS 21)* – Pandemonium / Your love.

Dec 91. (7"/c-s) *(XLS/XLC 26)* **EVERYBODY IN THE PLACE. / G-FORCE (ENERGY FLOW)** [2] [–]
(12"+=) *(XLT 26)* – Crazy man / Rip up the sound system.
(cd-s++=) *(XLS 26CD)* – ('A'remix).

Sep 92. (7"/c-s) *(XLS/XLC 30) <66370>* **FIRE. / JERICHO (original mix)** [11] [ ]
(12"+=/cd-s+=) *(XLT/XLS 30CD)* – Fire (sunrise version) / Jericho (genaside II remix).

Oct 92. (cd/c/lp) *(XLCD/XLMC/XLLP 110) <61365>* **EXPERIENCE** [12] [ ]
– Jericho / Music reach (1/2/3/4) / Wind it up / Your love (remix) / Hyperspeed (G-Force part 2) / Charly (trip into drum and bass version) / Out of space / Everybody in the place (155 and rising) / Weather experience / Fire (sunrise version) / Ruff in the jungle bizness / Death of the Prodigy dancers (live).

Nov 92. (7"/c-s) *(XLS/XLC 35) <66346>* **OUT OF SPACE (remix). / RUFF IN THE JUNGLE BIZNESS (uplifting vibes remix)** [5] Dec92 [ ]
(12"+=)(cd-s+=) *(XLT/XLS 35CD)* – ('A'techno underworld remix) / Music reach (1,2,3,4) (live).

Apr 93. (7"/c-s) *(XLS/XLC 39) <66319>* **WIND IT UP (REWOUND). / WE ARE THE RUFFEST** [7] [ ]
(12"+=) *(XLT 39)* – Weather experience (remix).
(cd-s++=) *(XLS 39CD)* – ('A'edit).

Oct 93. (c-ep/12"ep/cd-ep) *(XLC/XLT/XLS 47CD)* **ONE LOVE / RHYTHM OF LIFE (original mix). / FULL THROTTLE (original mix) / ONE LOVE (Jonny L remix)** [8] [–]

May 94. (12"/c-s) *(XLT/XLC 51)* **NO GOOD (START THE DANCE) / NO GOOD (bad for you mix) / NO GOOD (CJ Bolland's museum mix)** [4] [–]
(cd-s+=) *(XLS 51CD)* – No Good (original mix).

below album with **PHIL BENT** – flute / **LANCE RIDDLER** – guitar

X.L. Mute

Jul 94. (cd/c/d-lp) *(XLCD/XLMC/XLLP 114) <55642>* **MUSIC FOR THE JILTED GENERATION** [1] Mar95 [ ]
– Intro / Break & enter / Their law (featuring POP WILL EAT ITSELF) / Full throttle / Voodoo people / Speedway (theme from 'Fastlane') / The heat (the energy) / Poison / No good (start the dance) / One love (edit) – The narcotic suite / 3 kilos / Skylined / Claustrophobic sting.

Sep 94. (12"ep) *(XLT 54) <67007>* **VOODOO PEOPLE (original mix) / VOODOO PEOPLE (Dust Brothers remix). / VOODOO PEOPLE (Haiti Island mix) / GOA (THE HEAT, THE ENERGY PART 2)** [13] [ ]
(cd-ep) *(XLS 54CD)* – (3rd track repl.by) ('A'edit).

Mar 95. (c-s) *(XLC 58)* **POISON ('95) / ('A'-Rat Poison mix) / SCIENIDE** [15] [ ]
(12"+=/cd-s+=) *(XLT/XLS 58CD)* – ('A'-Environmental science dub mix).

X.L. Geffen

Mar 96. (c-s) *(XLC 70) <17387>* **FIRESTARTER / MOLOTIV BITCH** [1] Jan97 [30]
(12"+=/cd-s+=) *(XLT/XLS 70CD)* – ('A'-Empiron mix) / ('A'instrumental).

—— All singles re-issued Apr96 hitting UK Top 75.

Nov 96. (c-ep/12"ep) *(XLC/XLT 80)* **BREATHE / THEIR LAW featuring PWEI (live at Phoenix fesival '96). / POISON (live at the Tourhout & Werchter festival '96)** [1] [ ]
(cd-ep+=) *(XLS 80CD)* – The trick.

Jul 97. (cd/c/lp) *(XL CD/MC/LP 121) <46606>* **THE FAT OF THE LAND** [1] [1]
– Smack my bitch up / Breathe / Diesel power / Funky shit / Serial thrilla / Mindfields / Narayan / Firestarter / Climbatize / Fuel my fire.

Nov 97. (12"/c-s) *(XLT/XLC 90) <43946>* **SMACK MY BITCH UP. / NO MAN ARMY** [8] [89]
(cd-s+=) *(XLS 90CD)* – Minefields (heavy rock dub) / ('A'-DJ Hype remix).

—— now without LEEROY

X.L. Maverick

Jul 02. (12")(cd-s) *(XLT 145)(XLS 145CD) <42456>* **BABY'S GOT A TEMPER. / (dub) / (instrumental) (acappella)** [5] [ ]

—— now just down to **HOWLETT** + guests (FLINT + MAXIM left)

Aug 04. (cd/3xlp) *(XLCD/XLLP 183) <47990>* **ALWAYS OUTNUMBERED, NEVER OUTGUNNED** [1] Sep04 [62]
– Spitfire / Girls (feat. the PING PONG BITCHES) / Memphis belles (feat. PRINCESS SUPERSTAR) / Get up get off / Hot ride (feat. JULIETTE LEWIS) / Wake up call (feat. KOOL KEITH) / Action radar / Medusa's path / Phoenix / You'll be under my wheels / The way it is / Shoot down (feat. LIAM GALLAGHER – vocals & NOEL GALLAGHER – bass).

Aug 04. (12")(cd-s) *(XLT 195)(XLS 195CD)* **GIRLS. / MORE GIRLS / UNDER MY WHEELS (original)** [19] [–]

Nov 04. (12")(cd-s) *(XLT 202)(XLS 202CD)* **HOTRIDE / HOTRIDE (El Batori mix). / GIRLS (Rez the dog remix) / WHO U FOOLIN'** [–] non-ch [–]

– compilations, others, etc. –

Nov 04. (12"ep) *(XLXV 1501)* **WHAT EVIL LURKS / WE GONNA ROCK. / ANDROID / EVERYBODY IN THE PLACE)original)** [ ] [–]

Nov 04. (12"ep) *(XLXV 1506)* **CHARLY (alley cat mix) / PANDEMONIUM. / YOUR LOVE / CHARLY (original mix)** 73 –

Oct 05. (cd-s) *(XLS 219CD)* **VOODOO PEOPLE (Pendulum mix) / OUT OF SPACE (Audio Bullys mix)** 20 –
(12") *(XLT 219)* – ('A') / Smack my bitch up (sub focus remix) / ('AA'-original).
(12") *(XLR 219)* – ('AA') / ('A'-Wonder remix).

Oct 05. (cd) *(<XLCD 190>)* **THEIR LAW: SINGLES 1990-2005** 1
– Firestarter / Their law / Breathe / Out of space / Smack my bitch up / Poison / Girls / Voodoo people / Charly / No good (start the dance) / Spitfire / Jericho / Everybody in the place / One love / Hotride. *(bonus+=)* – Out of space (Audio Bullys remix). *(ltd d-cd+=; XLCD 190X)* – Razor / Back 20 school / Voodoo people (pendulum remix) / Under my wheels (remix) / No man army / Molotov bitch / Voodoo beats / Out of space (Audio Bullys remix) / The way it is (live remix) / We are the ruffest / Your love / Spitfire (live) / Their law (live) / Breathe (live) / Serial thrills (live) / Firestarter (live).

PUBLIC ENEMY

Formed: New York, USA ... early 80's by CHUCK D, a student at Adelphi University in Long Island. MC'ing for a local DJ crew, Spectrum City, CHUCK met the outfit's mainman, HANK SHOCKLEE (who would subsequently become PUBLIC ENEMY's co-producer), the pair subsequently teaming up for BILL STEPHNEY's rap show on WBAU. Producing rough mixes and co-hosting the show, CHUCK developed his hard hitting lyrical style while SHOCKLEE undertook his earliest experiments in creating funky noise collages. The inimitable FLAVOR FLAV (b. WILLIAM DRAYTON) was an avid listener, eventually joining the show as a co-host; the stage was set for the formation of PUBLIC ENEMY. Mulling over the offer of a record deal from 'Def Jam' via Rick Rubin, CHUCK eventually formulated the concept of the group alongside co-conspirators SHOCKLEE and STEPHNEY. With a brief to combine the caustic hip hop of RUN-D.M.C. and the radical attitude of The CLASH, they appointed DJ Terminator X (b. NORMAN RODGERS), PROFESSOR GRIFF (b. RICHARD GRIFFIN) as 'Minister Of Information' and a militaristic back-up troupe named the S1W's (Security Of The First World). They also set up a formidable production team, the aptly monikered BOMB SQUAD, consisting of CHUCK, ERIC 'VIETNAM' SADLER, HANK and his brother KEITH. Taking their name from an early demo track (included in reworked form on the debut album), 'PUBLIC ENEMY No.1', the group unleashed their debut album, 'YO! BUM RUSH THE SHOW' (1987). The intent was clear from the start; the sleeve depicted the crew standing menacingly over a turntable in a darkened basement, their faces semi-submerged in shadows while the PE logo featured a sniper surrounded by a mock rifle sight. The music inside was equally uncompromising, by 1987 standards anyway. Opening with the pre-driveby fury of 'YOU'RE GONNA GET YOURS' (still arguably PE's finest moment), the record combined 70's funk samples (METERS, FRED WESLEY etc.), punishing beats, noise collages and even a guitar solo by LIVING COLOR's VERNON REID ('SOPHISTICATED BITCH'). The political campaign was kickstarted with 'RIGHTSTARTER (MESSAGE TO A BLACK MAN)', CHUCK D possessing one of the most loudest, most portentous voices in rap. This was clearly a man who meant business, not another mealy-mouthed hip hop boaster. 'IT TAKES A NATION OF MILLIONS TO HOLD US BACK' (1988) was PE's tour de force, hip hop's tour de force, even. With the BOMB SQUAD creating a multi-layered blanket of noise (a hybrid of their trademark, screeching JAMES BROWN horn stabs, incendiary political samples and dextrous scratching), CHUCK D raged through what amounted to a whole new black manifesto. In terms of emotional directness and righteous anger, this record makes even the most vicious "Gangsta" album sound like a cash-in thrown together during a lunch break. Among the highlights were 'BRING THE NOISE' (later the subject of a collaborative re-vamp with ANTHRAX), 'DON'T BELIEVE THE HYPE' and the pulsing paranoia of 'BLACK STEEL IN THE HOUR OF CHAOS'. PE even managed to make a SLAYER riff sound groovy, mangling it up on 'SHE WATCH CHANNEL ZERO' while The BOMB SQUAD seemingly provided the base material for MADONNA's 'JUSTIFY MY LOVE' with 'SECURITY OF THE FIRST WORLD'. The album went Top 10 in the UK, propelling PUBLIC ENEMY into the media spotlight. The group were already the subject of much controversy and following anti-semitic remarks made by PROFESSOR GRIFF in a newspaper interview, the media circus went into overdrive. Although GRIFF and PUBLIC ENEMY soon parted ways, these events informed much of the group's new material. CHUCK D's initial response was the inflammatory 'FIGHT THE POWER', the rapper railing against what he perceived to be a white, European conspiracy to wipe out the black race. The song was given added resonance after appearing in Spike Lee's 'Do The Right Thing' over scenes of race rioting'. 'WELCOME TO THE TERRORDOME' was the next single, an awesome, intimidating narrative. Much of 'FEAR OF A BLACK PLANET' (1990) portrayed PE as victims, hounded by a predominantly white media and while there were accusations of racism, CHUCK had previously clearly stated that the group's agenda was not anti-white. Musically, the album wasn't quite as resourcefully ambitious as its predecessor, although tracks such as '911 IS A JOKE' and 'BURN, HOLLYWOOD, BURN' were classic PUBLIC ENEMY, the record becoming PE's biggest seller to date (Top 5 UK, Top 10 US). Later that year, it came to light that the group had been mentioned in an FBI report to congress, underlining the scale of PE's influence. With SISTER SOULJAH now on board, 'APOCALYPSE '91 ...THE ENEMY STRIKES BLACK' was as militant as ever, at least lyrically. Expressing outrage at the American state's refusal to celebrate Martin Luther King's birthday, 'BY THE TIME I GET TO ARIZONA' set swathes of towering funk against SOULJAH's almost gospel tones and CHUCK's irate rapping. Elsewhere, tracks like 'NIGHTTRAIN' and '1 MILLION BOTTLEBAGS' saw the rapper railing against the self-destructiveness of his own community. More commercial and with a cleaner production than PE's previous releases, the album reached the US Top 5. In the three years prior to the next album, FLAV (who had been arrested on a domestic charge) again found himself on the wrong side of the law in late '93, following an incident with his neighbour. After a spell in rehab for drug addiction, FLAV was back in action for 'MUSE SICK-N-HOUR MESS AGE' (1994), scoring with the funky 'GIVE IT UP' and 'SO WHATCHA GONNA DO NOW' wherein CHUCK berated the pointless negativity of gangsta rap. Although the record was a relative success, PUBLIC ENEMY felt they had taken the concept to its limit, calling it a day the following year (one of their last shows was an emotional affair at England's 'Phoenix Festival'). CHUCK D had always been peerless both as an entertainer and an educator, but it was the latter route that he subsequently chose for his post-PUBLIC ENEMY activities, lecturing on the college circuit as well as writing a book and hosting a news show on America's CNN. While this one-man think tank is not on the ball 100% of time (some controversial comments on the Northern Ireland situation at a Glasgow Barrowlands gig spring to mind), he remains a fiercely articulate voice for the disenfranchised among the black community. PUBLIC ENEMY's legacy meanwhile, transcends all boundaries of race and culture, no hip hop artists have yet come close. Of late (after a final set & soundtrack, 'HE GOT GAME' for their old label), PUBLIC ENEMY have emerged on the independent, 'Play It Again Sam', although 1999's 'THERE'S A POISON GOIN' ON', was poorly received; CHUCK D's latest project CONFRONTATION CAMP looked the more promising for the future. While hip hop had long since abandoned politics for vanity and violence, PUBLIC ENEMY are still one of the sanest voices in their field, even if not as many people – especially younger people – are taking as much notice as they once did. 'REVOLVERLUTION' (2002) was at least a partial attempt to reach out to that audience with a more contemporary, user friendly batch of new tracks, remixes, interview clips, live cuts and the like. The group's legacy was finally given its due, meanwhile, with the release of greatest hits set, 'POWER TO THE PEOPLE AND THE BEATS' (2005). The gorgonzola-pungent pun of 'NEW WHIRL ODOR' (2005), didn't promise much new on the horizon, however, with critics acknowledging the need for a conscious hip-hop figurehead yet lamenting the album's one dimensional production, metal riffs and general lack of invention. 'REBIRTH OF A NATION' (2006) was a more focused attempt at updating their classic sound, written and produced in collaboration with fellow old skool traveller PARIS.

Album rating: YO! BUMRUSH THE SHOW (*8) / IT TAKES A NATION OF MILLIONS TO HOLD US BACK (*9) / FEAR OF A BLACK PLANET (*9) / APOCALYPSE 91 . . . THE ENEMY STRIKES BACK (*8) / GREATEST MISSES part compilation (*4) / MUSE SICK-N-HOUR MESS AGE (*5) / HE GOT GAME soundtrack (*6) / THERE'S A POISON GOIN' ON (*4) / REVOLVERLUTION (*5) / POWER TO THE PEOPLE AND THE BEATS: PUBLIC ENEMY'S GREATEST HITS compilation (*8) / NEW WHIRL ODOR (*3) / REBIRTH OF A NATION (*6)

CHUCK D (b. CARLTON RIDENHOUR, 1 Aug'60) – vocals / **FLAVOR FLAV** (b. WILLIAM DRAYTON, 16 Mar'59) – multi-instrumentalist, classically trained pianist / **TERMINATOR X** (b. NORMAN LEE RODGERS, 25 Aug'66) – DJ / **PROFESSOR GRIFF** (b. RICHARD GRIFFIN) – information-vocals / plus part-time **JAMES ALLEN + JAMES NORMAN**

<Please note they never released a 7" in US>

Def Jam Def Jam

Mar 87. (7") *(650497-7)* **PUBLIC ENEMY No.1. / TIMEBOMB** [ ] [ ]
(12"+=) *(650497-6) <440671-9>* – Son of Public Enemy No.1 (Flavor Whop version).

Apr 87. (lp/c/cd) *(450482-1/-4/-2) <40658>* **YO! BUMRUSH THE SHOW** [ ] [ ]
– You're gonna get yours / Sophisticated bitch / Miuzi weighs a ton / Timebomb / Too much posse / Rightstarter (message to a black man) / Public enemy No.1 / M.P.E. / Yo! bumrush the show / Raise the roof / Megablast / Terminator X speaks with his hands. *(cd re-iss. Sep93 & Jul95; 527441-2)*

Jun 87. (7") *(650975-7)* **YOU'RE GONNA GET YOURS. / MIUZI WEIGHS A TON** [ ] [ ]
(12"+=) *(650975-6) <440686-1>* – ('A'dub mix) / ('A'-Terminator X getaway mix) / Rebel without a pause.

Nov 87. (7"/7"pic-d) *(651245-7/-0)* **REBEL WITHOUT A PAUSE (vocal). / ('A'instrumental)** [37] [–]
(12"+=) *(651245-6)* – Terminator X speaks with his hands / Sophisticated bitch.
(12"+=) *(651245-8)* – Bring the noise (noise version) / Sophisticated bitch.

Dec 87. (12"; by The BLACK FLAMES) *<440749-1>* **ARE YOU MY WOMAN? / BRING THE NOISE** [–] [ ]
(12"+=) *(440754-5>* – ('A'-Noise version) / ('A'-acappella mix).

Jan 88. (7") *(651335-7)* **BRING THE NOISE. / SOPHISTICATED BITCH** [32] [–]
(12"+=/s12"+=) *(651335-6/-8)* – ('A'noise versions) / ('A'acappella version) / ('A'-instrumental).

Jun 88. (7"/s7") *(652833-7/-0)* **DON'T BELIEVE THE HYPE. / PROPHETS OF RAGE** [18] [ ]
(12"+=) *(652833-6) <4407934>* – The rhythm, the rebel (acappella) / ('B'-power version).
(cd-s+=) *(652833-2)* – Bring the noise / ('B'-power version).

Jul 88. (lp/c/cd) *(462415-1/-4/-2) <4303>* **IT TAKES A NATION OF MILLIONS TO HOLD US BACK** [8] [42]
– Countdown to armageddon / Bring the noise / Don't believe the hype / Cold lampin' with Flavor / Terminator X to the edge of panic / Mind terrorist / Louder than a bomb / Caught, can we get a witness / Show 'em whatcha got / She watch Channel Zero?! / Night of the living baseheads / Black steel in the hour of chaos / Security of the first world / Rebel without a pause / Prophets of rage / Party for your right to fight. *(re-iss. cd Jul95; 527358-2)*

Oct 88. (7"/s7") *(653046-7/-0)* **NIGHT OF THE LIVING BASEHEADS. / TERMINATOR X TO THE EDGE OF PANIC** [63] [ ]
(12"+=/cd-s+=) *(653046-8/-2)* – ('A'-Anti high blood pressure mix) / ('A'-Terminator X meets DST and Chuck Chillout instrumental mix).
(s7") *(653046-9) - ('A'side) / ('A'-Terminator X meets DST . . .).*
(US-12"+=) *<4408121>* – Cold lampin' with Flavor.

1989. (12"ep) *<4468216>* **BLACK STEEL IN THE HOUR OF CHAOS (radio version) / ('A'instrumental). / TOO MUCH POSSE / CAUGHT, CAN I GET A WITNESS (dub mix) / B-SIDE WINS AGAIN** [–] [ ]

Jun 89. (7") *(ZB 42877)* **FIGHT THE POWER. / ('A'version)** [29] [ ]
(ext.12"+=/ext.cd-s+=) *(ZT/ZD 42878) <MOT 4647>* – ('A'-Flavor meets Spike Lee mix).
(above was issued on a one-off 'Motown' deal).

Jan 90. (7"/c-s) *(655476-0/-4)* **WELCOME TO THE TERRORDOME. / ('A'-Terromental version)** [18] [ ]
(12"+=/cd-s+=) *(655476-8/-2) <4473135>* – Terrorbeat / Black steel in the hour of chaos.

— Trimmed when PROFESSOR GRIFF left permanently to go solo. He soon released debut 'PAWNS IN THE GAME' with his LAST ASIATIC DISCIPLES. A year later he followed this with second album 'KAD'S II WIZ *7* DOME'.

Apr 90. (7"/c-s) *(655837-7/-4)* **911 IS A JOKE. / REVOLUTIONARY GENERATION** [41] [ ]
(12"+=/cd-s+=) *(655837-8/-2) <4473179>* – ('A'&'B'-instrumentals).
(12") *(655837-5)* – ('A'side) / Son of Public Enemy (Flavor Whop version) / Bring the noise (no noise version) / Rebel without a pause.

Apr 90. (cd/c/lp) *(466281-2/-4/-1) <45413>* **FEAR OF A BLACK PLANET** [4] [10]
– Contract on the world love jam / Brothers gonna work it out / 911 is a joke / Incident at 66.6 FM / Welcome to the terrordome / Meet the G that killed me / Pollywanacraka / Anti-nigger machine / Burn Hollywood burn / Power to the people / Who stole the soul / Fear of a black planet / Revolutionary generation / Can't do nuttin' for ya man / Reggae Jax / Leave this off your fuckin' charts / B side wins again / War at 33 1/3 / Final count of the collision between us and the damned. *(re-iss. cd Jul95; 523446-2)*

Jun 90. (7"/c-s) *(656018-0/-4)* **BROTHERS GONNA WORK IT OUT (remix). / WAR AT 33 1/3** [46] [ ]
(12"+=/12"w-poster+=) *(656018-6/-8) <4473391-1>* – Bring the noise (no noise instrumental) / ('B'instrumental).
(cd-s+=) *(656018-2) <44K73391>* – Anti-nigger machine / Don't believe the hype.

Oct 90. (7"/c-s) *(656385-7/-4)* **CAN'T DO NUTTIN' FOR YA MAN. / ('A'-Bass in your face mix)** [53] [–]
(12"+=/cd-s+=) *(656385-6/-2)* – ('A'-dub in your face mix).
(12") *(656385-8)* – ('A'-full rub mix) / Get the f . . . out of Dodge (uncensored) / Powersave / Burn Hollywood burn.

— added **SISTER SOULIJAH** – vocals

— (May'91) FLAVOR FLAV served 30 days in jail for an earlier incident in which he was said to have hit the mother of his 3 children Karen Ross.

— Jun'91, teamed up with ANTHRAX on a hit single version of 'BRING THE NOISE'.

Sep 91. (7"/c-s) *(657530-7/-4)* **CAN'T TRUSS IT (Goree Island Conga radio mix). / ('A'-Almighty raw 125th street bootleg mix** [22] [50]
(cd-s+=) *(657530-7) <44K73869>* – Move! (censored radio mix).
(12"++=) *(657530-6)* – ('A'-instrumental).

Oct 91. (cd/c/d-lp) *(468751-2/-4/-1) <47374>* **APOCALYPSE 91 . . .THE ENEMY STRIKES BACK** [8] [4]
– Lost at birth / Rebirth / Night train / Can't truss it / I don't wanna be called yo niga / How to kill a radio consultant / By the time I get to Arizona / Move! / 1 million bottlebags / More news at 11 / Shut 'em down / A letter to the New York post / Get the f . . . outta Dodge / Bring the noise (w/ ANTHRAX). *(re-iss. cd Jul95; 523479-2)*

Jan 92. (7"/c-s) *(657761-7/-4)* **SHUT 'EM DOWN (Pe-Te rock mixx). / BY THE TIME I GET TO ARIZONA** [21] [ ]
(12"+=/12"pic-d+=/cd-s+=) *(657761-6/-8/-2) <44K74165>* – ('A'rock mixx instrumental) / ('A'bald beat acappella) / ('B'side dubbed).

Mar 92. (7"/c-s) *(657864-7/-4)* **NIGHT TRAIN (Pe-Te rock . . .mixx). / MORE NEWS AT 11 (Funk minister . . .mixx)** [55] [ ]
(12"+=/12"pic-d+=) *(657864-6/-8)* – ('A'-Pete Rock LIRR Strong island mixx).
(cd-s++=) *(657864-2) <44K74254>* – ('A'instrumental mixx).

Sep 92. (cd/c/lp) *(472031-2/-4/-1)* <*53014*> **GREATEST MISSES** (part compilation) [14] [13]
– Tie goes to the runner / Hitt da road Jack / Get off my back / Air hoodlum got ta do what I gotta do / Hazy shade of criminal megablast (remix) / Louder than a bomb (telephone groove) / How to kill a radio consultant (DJ check chillout..) / Who stole the soul (mixx) / Party for your right to fight (metromix) / You're gonna get yours (version). *(cd+=)* – Shut 'em down (live in the UK). *(re-iss. cd Jul95; 523487-2)*

Mar 93. (cd/c) *(473052-2/-4)* **THE 12" MIXES** [ ] [–]

—— PROFESSOR GRIFF, TERMINATOR X, and newcomer SISTER SOULJAH all had own releases for various labels from 1990 onwards.
FLAVOR FLAV was charged late '93, for drunkenly attempting to shoot his neighbour, after he allegedly thought his wife was committing adultery.

Jul 94. (c-s,cd-s) <*853316*> **GIVE IT UP / BEDLAM** [–] [33]

Aug 94. (c-ep/12"ep/cd-ep) *(DEFMC/12DEF/DEFCD 1)* **GIVE IT UP. / ('A'-main version) / Bedlam (instrumental)** [18] [–]
(cd-s+=) *(DEFDX 1)* – Live and undrugged (part 2) / Harry Allen interactive highway / Bedlam (instrumental).

Aug 94. (cd/c/lp) <*(523362-2/-4/-1)*> **MUSE SICK-N-HOUR MESS AGE** [12] [14]
– Whole lotta love / Theatrical / Give it up / What side you on? / Body count / Stop in the name / What kind of power we got? / So watcha gone do now? / White Heaven – black Hell / Race against time / Used to call it dope / Aintnuthin' buttersong / Live & undrugged parts I & II / I ain't madd at all / Death of carjacka / I stand accused / Gold complexx / Hitler day / Harry Allen superhighway.

Dec 94. (12"ep/cd-ep) *(12DEF/DEFCD 2)* **I STAND ACCUSED / WHAT KIND OF POWER WE GOT** [ ] [ ]
(cd-s+=) *(DEFCDX 2)* – I stand accused (Sleek'sschool of self-defence mix) / Mao Tse Tung.

—— On 26th May'95, FLAVOR was jailed for drug possession. He was sent to a rehab centre and given three years probation. While in Italy in July, he broke his leg in a motorcycle accident.

Jul 95. (c-s) *(DEFMC 5)* **SO WHATCHA GONNA DO NOW? / BLACK STEEL IN THE HOUR OF CHAOS** [50] [ ]
(12"+=/cd-s+=) *(12DEF/DEFCD 5)* – ('A'-Drive by s**t mix) / ('A'-Drive by instrumental).

Apr 98. (cd/c/d-lp) <*(558130-2/-4/-1)*> **HE GOT GAME** (soundtrack) [50] [26]
– Resurrection / He got game / Unstoppable / Shake your booty / Is your god a dog / House of the rising sun / Revelation 33 1/3 revolutions / Game face / Politics of the Sneaker Pimps / What you need is Jesus / Super agent / Go cat go / Sudden death (interlude).

May 98. (c-s) *(568985-4)* **HE GOT GAME / ('A'mix)** [16] [ ]
(12"+=/cd-s+=) *(568985-1/-2)* – Resurrection (mixes).

Play It Again Sam / Play It again Sam

Jul 99. (cd/c/d-lp) <*(PIASX CD/MC/LP 004)*> **THERE'S A POISON GOIN' ON** [55] [ ]
– Dark side of the wall: 2000 / Do you wanna go our way / LSD / Here I go / 41.19 / Crash / Crayola / First the sheep then the shepherd? / World tour sessions / Last mass of the caballeros / I / What what / Kervorkian / Swindlers list.

Sep 99. (12") *(PIASX 005T)* **DO YOU WANNA GO OUR WAY?? (extended). / (instrumental) / CRAYOLA** [66] [–]
(cd-s) *(PIASX 005CD)* – ('A'clean version) / I / ('A'video).

Def Jam / Koch

Oct 02. (cd) *(238388-2)* <*8388*> **REVOLVERLUTION** [ ] Jul02 [ ]
– Gotta give the peeps what they need / Revolverlution / Miuzi weighs a ton / Put it up / Can a woman make a man lose his mind? / (Public Enemy service announcement #1) / Fight the power / By the time I get to Arizona / Post concert Arizona / Son of a Bush / 54321 . . . boom / Welcome to the terrordome / B side wins again / Get your shit together / (Public Enemy service announcement #2) / Shut em down / Now a' daze / Public Enemy No.1. *(bonus cd+=)* – The making of Burn Hollywood Burn (with BIG DADDY KANE & FLAVOR FLAV) / Gotta give the peeps what they need / What good is a bomb (with PROFESSOR GRIFF & 7th OCTAVE).

—— in Jul'04, MOBY & PUBLIC ENEMY released 'MAKE LOVE FUCK WAR' single

Aug 05. (cd) *(9861661)* <*1923*> **POWER TO THE PEOPLE AND THE BEATS: PUBLIC ENEMY'S GREATEST HITS** (compilation) [38] [69]
– You're gonna get yours / Public enemy No.1 / Rebel without a pause / Bring the noise / Don't believe the hype / Prophets of rage / Black steel in the hour of chaos / Fight the power / Welcome to the Terrordome / 911 is a joke / Brothers gonna work it out / Can do nuttin' for ya man / Can't truss it / Shut em down / By the time I get to Arizona / Hazy shade of criminal / Give it up / He got game. *(5xlp-iss.Nov05; 9832545)*

SlamJamz / SlamJamz

Nov 05. (cd) <*(SJRN 1005CV)*> **NEW WHIRL ODOR** [ ] [ ]
– . . .And no one broadcasted louder than . . . (intro) / New whirl odor / Bring that beat back / 66.6 strikes again / MKLVFKWR / What a fool believes / Makes you blind / Preachin' to the quiet / Either we together or we ain't (SIW Stepstrumental) / Revolution / Check what you're listening in / As long as the people got something to say / Y'all don't know / Either you get it by now or you don't / Superman's black in the building.

—— next credited as PUBLIC ENEMY featuring PARIS

Guerilla Funk / Guerilla Funk

Mar 06. (cd) <*(GFR 31021-2)*> **REBIRTH OF A NATION** [ ] [ ]
– Raw shit / Hard rhymin' / Rise / Can't hold us back / Hard truth soldiers / Hannibal lecture / Rebirth of a nation / Pump the music, pump the sound / Make it hardcore / They call me Flavor / Plastic nation / Consequences / Invisible man / Hell no (we ain't alright) / Watch the door / Field nigga boogie.

PUBLIC IMAGE LTD.

Formed: London, England . . . July '78 by ex-SEX PISTOLS frontman, JOHNNY ROTTEN, who reverted to his real name, JOHN LYDON. He recruited local friends, guitarist KEITH LEVENE (ex-CLASH), bassist JAH WOBBLE and Canadian drummmer JIM WALKER, re-signing to 'Virgin' in the process. 'PUBLIC IMAGE', both the debut single and the title track of the debut album, was a raucous slice of post-PISTOLS sonic energy, the record coming wrapped in a mock-newspaper sleeve and reaching the UK Top 10 late in 1978. The album followed it into the Top 30 at the end of the year, hardly a departure from punk but a convincing statement of intent nevertheless; tracks such as 'RELIGION', 'ANNA LISA' and 'ATTACK' formed the basis for LYDON's subsequent experiments. Preceded by the bizarre 'DEATH DISCO' single, 'METAL BOX 1' (1979) was a strikingly differerent beast, its pristine packaging (three 12" 45's inside a metal film can, something much copied by record company marketing departments in the years to come) rather deceptively encasing a dark, often disturbing set of experimental, Eastern-influenced material. As far from punk as LYDON has ever ventured, the record utilised monotonic repetition, LEVENE's shards of splintered guitar dissecting the vague structures of WOBBLE's rubbery basslines while LYDON wailed and ranted like a damned soul. John Peel was a particular champion of the record, playlisting virtually all its disturbing but accessible tracks, 'CAREERING', 'POPTONES' and 'GRAVEYARD' highlighting what came to be regarded as one of the last classic "punk/alternative" albums of the 70's. Surely one of the most avant-garde releases to ever grace the Top 20, the album even hit the charts a second time (Top 50) when it was re-issued in double-album format as 'SECOND EDITION' two months later. Following a patchy live album, 'PARIS AU PRINTEMPS' (1980), WOBBLE departed on a sour note, leaving LYDON and LEVENE to mastermind 'FLOWERS OF ROMANCE' (1981). A comparatively weaker effort, the record nevertheless almost made the Top 10 and the more contrived moments were interspersed with a few gems, notably the Burundi-esque title track, a Top 30 hit single. LEVENE was also soon to leave in less than pleasant circumstances following the success of 'P.I.L.'s biggest hit single to date, the compelling 'THIS IS NOT A LOVE SONG'. LYDON subsequently completed the lacklustre 'THIS IS WHAT YOU WANT . . . THIS IS WHAT YOU GET' opus with the help of session musicians, disbanding the group around the time of the album's release in the summer of '84. By this point, LYDON had moved to Los Angeles and his career slowed up somewhat, although he subsequently reformed 'P.I.L.' in late '85. Using such respected (and glaringly un-punk) musos as STEVE VAI, RYUICHI SAKAMOTO, GINGER BAKER and RAVI SHANKAR, LYDON recorded the minimally titled 'ALBUM' (also released as 'CASSETTE' and 'COMPACT DISC', of course). The BILL LASWELL-produced effort remains his last consistent collection, the 'SINGLE', 'RISE', almost making the Top 10, a driving, resonating, infectiously commercial example of LYDON doing what he does best (although I could be wrong . . .). For the remainder of the 80's, LYDON was content to churn out formula 'JOHNNY ROTTEN'-to-order type material that often incorporated bland Americanised rock backing. This only served to further entrench him in the mire of self-parody. Albums like 'HAPPY?' (1987) and '9' (1989) achieved only minimal commercial success although LYDON was back in the Top 20 in 1990 with 'DON'T ASK ME', the punk veteran's comment on the topical subject of the environment. The single was cannily included by 'Virgin' on a best of set, the hopefully titled 'GREATEST HITS – SO FAR' (1990). Then again, LYDON proved he could still cut the mustard with his late '93 LEFTFIELD collaboration, 'OPEN UP'. When LYDON lets rip, as he does here (a blood curdling wail of 'Burn, Hollywood, burn'), he is still the most frightening man in rock, no contest. Just to prove it, he hooked up once more with the original SEX PISTOLS line-up for the aptly titled 'Filthy Lucre' tour, appearing on 'Top Of The Pops' and scaring young children all over again with his gravity-defying hairdo. In January 2004, LYDON – and his bad language! – featured in the reality TV show, 'I'm A Celebrity, Get Me Out Of Here'; he subsequently presented a documentary on spiders.

Album rating: PUBLIC IMAGE (*9) / METAL BOX 1 (*10) / FLOWERS OF ROMANCE (*5) / LIVE IN TOKYO (*5) / THIS IS WHAT YOU WANT . . . THIS IS WHAT YOU GET (*4) / ALBUM (*7) / HAPPY? (*6) / 9 (*5) / GREATEST HITS – SO FAR compilation (*8) / THAT WHAT IS NOT (*4) / PLASTIC BOX boxed set (*8) / John Lydon: PSYCHO'S PATH (*4)

JOHN LYDON (b.31 Jan'56, Finsbury Park, London, England) – vocals (ex-SEX PISTOLS) / **KEITH LEVENE** (b. London, England) – guitar (ex-CLASH) / **JAH WOBBLE** (b. JOHN WORDLE) – bass / **JIM WALKER** (b. Canada) – drums (ex-FURIES)

— (most singles just credit "PiL")

Virgin Warners

Oct 78. (7") *(VS 228)* **PUBLIC IMAGE. / THE COWBOY SONG** [9] [–]

Dec 78. (lp/c) *(V/TCV 2114) <3288>* **PUBLIC IMAGE** [22] [ ]
– Theme / Religion I / Religion II / Annalisa / Public image / Low life / Attack / Fodderstompf. *(re-iss. Apr86 lp/c; OVED/+C 160) (cd-iss. Jun88; CDV 2114)*

— **DAVE CROWE** – drums repl. WALKER who joined The PACK (with KIRK BRANDON) added **JEANNETTE LEE** – keyboards, synthesizer

Jun 79. (7") *(VS 274)* **DEATH DISCO. / NO BIRDS DO SING** [20] [–]
(12"+=) *(VS 274-12)* – Death disco megamix.

Sep 79. (7"/ext.12") *(VS 299/+12)* **MEMORIES. / ANOTHER** [60] [–]

Dec 79. (3x12"box)<lp> *(METAL 1) <3288>* **METAL BOX 1** <US-title 'SECOND EDITION'> [18] Jul80 [ ]
– Albatross / Memories / Swan lake/ / Poptones / Careering / No birds / Graveyard / / The suit / Bad baby / Socialist – Chant – Radio 4. *(re-iss. Feb80 as 'SECOND EDITION' d-lp/c; VD/TCVD 2512); hit UK No.46) (cd-iss. Jun86; CDVD 2512) (original; cd-iss. Jun90; MTLLCD 1) (d-cd-iss. Mar03 on 'E.M.I.'; 581749-2)*

— **RICHARD DUDANSKI** – drums (ex-101'ERS, ex-BASEMENT 5) repl. CROWE

— (he had joined during Apr-Sep'79) (below French titles of above songs)

Nov 80. (lp/c) *(V/TCV 2183)* **PARIS AU PRINTEMPS (live 'PARIS IN THE SPRING')** [61] [–]
– Theme / Psalmodie (Chant) / Precipitamment (Careering) / Sale bebe (Bad baby) / La vie ignoble (Low life) / Attaque (Attack) / Timbres de pop (Poptones). *(re-iss. Mar84 lp/c; OVED/+C 50)*

— (Jul'80) trimmed to a quartet when JAH WOBBLE went solo. / **MARTIN ATKINS** (b. 3 Aug'59, Coventry, England) (aka BRIAN BRAIN) – drums repl. DUDANSKI who joined RAINCOATS. (ATKINS was sacked Jul80, most of drums by LYDON and LEVENE)

Mar 81. (7") *(VS 397)* **FLOWERS OF ROMANCE. / HOME IS WHERE THE HEART IS** [24] [–]
(12"+=) *(VS 397-12)* – ('A'instrumental).

Apr 81. (lp/c) *(V/TCV 2189) <3536>* **FLOWERS OF ROMANCE** [11] [ ]
– Four enclosed walls / Track 8 / Phenagen / Flowers of romance / Under the house / Hymie's him / Banging the door / Go back / Francis massacre. *(re-iss. Mar84 lp/c; OVED/+C 51) (cd-iss. Apr90 & Mar94; CDV 2189) (cd re-iss. Jun01 on 'Disky'; VI 64642-2)*

— **KEN LOCKIE** – keyboards (ex-COWBOYS INTERNATIONAL, ex-Solo) repl. LEE / added (May82) **MARTIN ATKINS** – drums / **PETE JONES** – bass

Aug 83. (7") *(VS 529)* **THIS IS NOT A LOVE SONG. / PUBLIC IMAGE** [5] [–]
(12"+=) *(VS 529-12)* – Blue water / ('A'remix).
(re-iss. Jun88 cd-ep; CDT 14)

— LYDON + ATKINS were joined by US session people from New Jersey; **JOSEPH GUIDA** – guitar / **TOM ZVONCHECK** – keyboards / **LOUIE BERNARDI** – bass

Virgin Elektra

Sep 83. (2x12"/c) *(VGD/+C 3508)* **LIVE IN TOKYO (live)** [28] [–]
– Annalisa / Religion / Low life / Solitaire / Flowers of romance / This is not a love song / Death disco / Bad life / Banging the door / Under the house. *(cd-iss. 1986; VGDCD 3508)*

May 84. (7"/ext.12") *(VS 675/+12)* **BAD LIFE. / QUESTION MARK** [71] [–]

Jul 84. (lp/c) *(V/TCV 2309) <60365>* **THIS IS WHAT YOU WANT . . . THIS IS WHAT YOU GET** [56] [ ]
– Bad life / This is not a love song / Solitaire / Tie me to the length of that / The pardon / Where are you? / 1981 / The order of death. *(re-iss. 1986 lp/c; OVED/+C 176) (cd-iss. Apr90; CDV 2309)*

Aug 84. (lp; as KEITH LEVENE & PiL) *<XYZ 007>* **THE COMMERCIAL ZONE** [–] [ ]
– (as last album, with LEVENE's guitar parts more obvious)

— Disbanded mid'84, but reformed by LYDON late '85 with on session **STEVE VAI** – guitar (ex-ALCATRAZZ) / **RYUICHI SAKAMOTO** – keys (ex-YELLOW MAGIC ORCHESTRA) / **GINGER BAKER** (ex-CREAM, etc) / **TONY WILLIAMS** (ex-MILES DAVIES, etc) / **RAVI SHANKER** – violin

Jan 86. (7"/12") *(VS 841/+12)* **RISE. / ('A'instrumental)** [11] [–]

Feb 86. (cd/c/lp) *(CD/TC+/V 2366) <60438>* **ALBUM** [14] [ ]
– FFF / Rise / Fishing / Round / Bags / Home / Ease. *(re-iss. 1989 lp/c; OVED/+C 245)*

Apr 86. (7") *(VS 855)* **HOME. / ROUND** [75] [–]
(12"+=) *(VS 855-12)* – ('A'-lp version).
(d7"+=) *(VSD 855)* – Rise / ('A'instrumental).

— (Feb86) **LYDON** recruited **LU EDMUNDS** – guitar, keys (ex-DAMNED, ex-MEKONS) / **JOHN McGEOGH** – guitar (of ARMOURY SHOW, ex-SIOUXSIE & THE BANSHEES) / **ALAN DIAS** – bass / **BRUCE SMITH** – drums (ex-RIP, RIG & PANIC, ex-SLITS, ex-POP GROUP)

Virgin Virgin

Aug 87. (7") *(VS 988)* **SEATTLE. / SELFISH RUBBISH** [47] [–]
(12"+=/c-s+=) *(VS/+C 988-12)* – The suit.

Sep 87. (cd/c/lp) *(CD/TC+/V 2455) <90642>* **HAPPY?** [40] [ ]
– Seattle / Rules and regulations / The body / Save me / Hard times / Open and revolving / Angry / Fat chance hotel. *(re-iss. Apr90 lp/c; OVED/+C 299)*

Oct 87. (7") *(VS 1010)* **THE BODY. / RELIGION (new version)** [100] [–]
(12"+=) *(VST 1010)* – Angry.
(12") *(VSR 1010)* – ('A'extended remix) / ('A'-U.S. remix) / Angry.

— trimmed to a quartet when EDMUNDS dispersed.

Apr 89. (7") *(VS 1181)* **DISAPPOINTED. / SAME OLD STORY** [38] [–]
(ext.12"+=/12"pic-d+=/3"cd-s+=) *(VS T/TY/CD 181)* – ('A'version).

Jun 89. (cd/c/lp) *(CD/TC+/V 2588) <91062>* **9** [36] [ ]
– Happy / Disappointed / Warrior / U.S.L.S. 1 / Sand castles in the snow / Worry / Brave new world / Like that / Same old story / Armada.

Jul 89. (7"/7"g-f) *(VS 1195)* **WARRIOR. / U.S.L.S. 1** [ ] [–]
(ext.12"+=) *(VST 1195)* – ('A'instrumental).
(3"cd-s+=) *(VSCD 1195)* – ('A'extended).
(12") *(VSTX 1195)* – ('A'-Dave Dorrell remix) / ('A'instrumental).

Oct 90. (7"/c-s) *(VS/+C 1231)* **DON'T ASK ME. / RULES AND REGULATIONS** [22] [–]
(cd-s+=) *(VSCD 1231)* – Warrior (original).
(12") *(VST 1231)* – ('A'extended) / Warrior (remix).

Oct 90. (cd/c/lp) *(CD/TC+/V 2644) <86196>* **GREATEST HITS – SO FAR** (compilation) [20] [ ]
– Public image / Death disco / Memories / Careering / Flowers of romance / This is not a love song / Rise / Home / The body / Rules and regulations / Disappointed / Warrior / Don't ask me / Seattle.

— **MIKE JOYCE** – drums (ex-SMITHS, ex-BUZZCOCKS) repl. BRUCE

Feb 92. (7") *(VS 1390)* **CRUEL. / LOVE HOPE** [49] [–]
(cd-s+=) *(VSCD 1390)* – Rise (live) / Home (live).
(10"+=) *(VST 1390)* – Happy (live).

Feb 92. (cd/c/lp) *(CD/TC+/V 2681)* <86263> **THAT WHAT IS NOT** [46] [ ]
– Acid drops / Lucks up / Cruel / God / Covered / Love hope / Unfairground / Think tank / Emperor / Good things.

— In Nov'93, LYDON was credited on acclaimed dance hit & UK No.19 'Open Up' by LEFTFIELD / LYDON on 'Hard Hands' records.

— Early '96, JOHN LYDON (ROTTEN) re-grouped with The SEX PISTOLS for summer tours in Britain, Europe and America.

– compilations, etc. –

Mar 99. (4xcd-box) *Virgin; PILBOX 1)* **PLASTIC BOX** [ ] [–]

JOHN LYDON

Virgin America / Virgin America

Jun 97. (cd/c) *(CDVUS/VUSMC 130)* <44209> **PSYCHO'S PATH** [ ] [ ]
– Grave ride / Dog / Psychopath / Sun / Another way / Dis-ho / Take me / No and a yes / Stump / Armies / Open up.

Jul 97. (12"/cd-s) *(VUS T/CD 122)* **SUN. / GRAVE RIDE / PSYCHOPATH** [42] [–]

PUDDLE OF MUDD

Formed: Kansas City, Missouri, USA . . . 1998 by WES SCANTLIN, PAUL PHILLIPS, DOUG ARDITO and GREG UPCHURCH. PUDDLE OF MUDD's rise from obscurity to post-grunge kings is an intriguing story and virtually begins with a LIMP BIZKIT gig in 1999. POM's frontman and songwriter SCANTLIN apparently snuck backstage at the said gig and handed one of FRED DURST's security men a demo tape of his band. One year down the line and the struggling ensemble found themselves shellshocked when DURST himself contacted them and offered to sign SCANTLIN and his cohorts to the newly established 'Flawless' label. Now based in L.A. and augmented by JOSH FREESE (of The VANDALS), their major label debut set 'COME CLEAN' was issued in 2001. A fairly average rock record to most observers outside the mainstream metallic world, the soon-to-be US Top 10'er was helped along by singles 'BLURRY' and 'CONTROL', which displayed the usual hard-rock/grunge formula of many NIRVANA copyists. The main problem with PUDDLE OF MUDD is that they followed the same verse/chorus/verse triad (go to STAIND, NICKELBACK and TOOL for more examples). It's sometimes hard to believe that bands like PUDDLE OF MUDD even attempt to extract creative capital from such a thoroughly exhausted genre as grunge. It's even harder to believe that there are people willing to shell out money for it (it hit US Top 20!). 'LIFE ON DISPLAY' (2003) wasn't the sound of a band flogging a dead horse, it was the sound of a band flogging the skeleton of a dead horse.

Album rating: ABRASIVE (*5) / COME CLEAN (*7) / LIFE ON DISPLAY (*4)

WES SCANTLIN (b. WESLEY, 9 Jun'72) – vocals, guitars / **PAUL PHILLIPS** – guitar / **DOUG ARDITO** – bass / **GREG UPCHURCH** (b. 1 Dec'71, Houma, Louisiana, USA) – drums

not iss. / Phatt Phunk

Jul 01. (cd) <13180> **ABRASIVE** [–] [ ]
– Abrasive / Nobody told me / Streesed out / Hour glass man / Migrain / Said / All I ask for / Purple heart / Locket / Time / Piss it all away.

Interscope / Interscope

Sep 01. (cd) <(493074-2)> **COME CLEAN** [12] [9]
– Control / Drift & die / Out of my head / Nobody told me / Blurry / She hates me (explicit) / Bring me down / Never change / Basement / Said / Piss it all away. *(cd re-iss. Jan02; 493335-2) (special cd-iss. May02 +=; 493247-2)*
– Abrasive / Control (acoustic) / Control (video).

Feb 02. (7"/c-s) *(497658-7/-4)* <497397> **CONTROL. / ABRASIVE** [15] Oct01 [68]
(cd-s+=) *(497658-2)* – ('A'-acoustic) / ('A'-video).

Jun 02. (c-s) *(497735-4)* <radio> **BLURRY / ALL ASK FOR (demo)** [8] Dec01 [5]
(cd-s+=) *(497734-2)* – Out of my head (live) / ('A'-video).
(cd-s) *(497735-2)* – ('A') / Control (live) / Bring me down (live).

Sep 02. (c-s) *(497798-4)* <radio> **SHE HATES ME / SHE HATES ME (clean) / NOBODY TOLD ME (live)** [14] Oct02 [13]
(cd-s+=) *(497798-2)* – Blurry (live).
(cd-s) *(497805-2)* – ('A'-live acoustic) / Blurry (live acoustic) / ('A'-video).

Polydor / Flawless

Nov 03. (cd) *(986148-3)* <10800-2> **LIFE ON DISPLAY** [ ] [20]
– Away from me / Heel over head / Nothing left to lose / Change my mind / Spin you around / Already gone / Think / Cloud 9 / Bottom / Freak of the world / Sydney / Time flies.

Dec 03. (7") *(981481-1)* <radio> **AWAY FROM ME. / LIFE AIN'T FAIR** [55] [72]
(cd-s+=) *(981481-0)* – Blurry (live) / ('A'-video).

— **SCANTLIN** recruited **JIMMY ALLEN, SEAN SAMON** + **KENNY BURKETT** (UPCHURCH joined 3 DOORS DOWN)

PUFF DADDY

Born: SEAN COMBS, 4 Nov'70, Harlem, New York, USA. Growing up near Mt. Vernon, the up and coming millionaire MC inforced his humble quest in becoming a businessman by applying to Howard University (in Washington) and persuading his childhood chum-cum-rapper HEAVY D to employ him at 'Uptown Records'. As the months passed by, COMBS had worked his way up from dogsbody to A&R man to executive producer on FATHER MC's hit album 'FATHER'S DAY' (1990). However, his time with the company was short-lived when in 1992 (at Uptown's peak, following the success of MARY J BLIGE and HEAVY D AND THE BOYZ), COMBS was fired, shattering all images of the bigtime. He reluctantly founded a new imprint 'Bad Boy' in 1993. Working from his apartment with little more than a workforce of five, remixing the odd track here and there for various artists in the small hours of the morning. By the end of 1993 he had signed two of the record company's main artists: CRAIG MACK and old friend the NOTORIOUS B.I.G. The following year, MACK's single 'FLAVA IN YA EAR' had become a huge hit in the states, boasting guest appearances from LL COOL J, BUSTA RYMES and NOTORIOUS. The single went platinum and went on to be Bad Boy's first major success. The words of NOTORIOUS B.I.G. were spreading like wildfire through America, and, in 1995 he achieved a Top 10 spot with his single 'Big Poppa', and a double Platinum certificate for his debut album 'Ready To Die'. COMBS signed two R&B acts, FAITH EVANS (who was the B.I.G. man's wife) and TOTAL (who was also connected to the aforementioned rapper), the pair both going on to sell double platinum. After COMBS had remixed tracks for BOYZ II MEN and MARIAH CAREY, a feud between Death Row's 2PAC SHAKUR and infamous label manager SUGE KNIGHT erupted when SHAKUR was rumoured to be sleeping with FAITH EVANS. Verbal abuse was constantly spat from America's two coasts, and in September 1996, SHAKUR was shot dead. Six months later, NOTORIOUS B.I.G. was also killed, his assailants unknown. After the death of NOTORIOUS, COMBS abandoned his PUFF DADDY solo project to mourn the once great seminal rapper. However, he subsequently exploded onto the hip hop scene early '97 with the brash 'CAN'T NOBODY HOLD ME DOWN'; the worldwide No.1, 'I'LL BE MISSING YOU' (a revamp of The Police's 'EVERY BREATH YOU TAKE') was attributed to B.I.G. and featured his widow FAITH EVANS. 'NO WAY OUT' the debut album, followed in 1998 and won the Grammy award for best rap album and best performance for the aforementioned 'I'LL BE MISSING YOU'. Along with a contribution to the 'Godzilla' soundtrack, 'COME WITH ME', which hit Top 5 for him and its maker, JIMMY PAGE (of LED ZEPPELIN), PUFF DADDY issued his sophomore set

'FOREVER' in 1999. Its sharp melodies and sublime, chilled out temperament, helped it climb up the American Billboard charts, the DADDY had now come of age. The self-proclaimed 'Bad Boy' of rap returned after hiding out in his studio for two years, stepping out occasionally with his then girlfriend – Latino lovely JENNIFER LOPEZ – to go to court on charges of assault. But things all changed for Mr. COMBS when LOPEZ dumped him, forcing him back into the rap game, even changing his name to P. DIDDY (what did it mean? And what exactly did the name PUFF DADDY seriously suggest?). 'THE SAGA CONTINUES' (2001), issued by P. DIDDY and THE BAD BOY FAMILY, was just another showcase for BAD BOY rappers BLACK ROB and G. DEP, who weren't that notorious before the release of the album, and weren't that notorious after. In fact, the only thing that saved the set from near disaster was the anthemic 'BAD BOY FOR LIFE', and even in that the MCs couldn't manage to spell the word DIDDY correctly. 'THE SAGA . . .' was just another way for COMBS to remind everyone that he was still a player and not a pauper, instead of trying to convince people that his rhymes were tight and his 'family' even tighter. But like J-LO herself sang; "Try to impress me with your Bling-Bling / thought I told you love don't cost a thing". The DIDDY man launched himself back into the fray with 'WE INVENTED THE REMIX' (2002), a rather preposterous title even if the P.'s remixes were admittedly fairly radical, offering up a couple of sterling versions of 'I NEED A GIRL' and yet another remake of 'BAD BOY . . .'. Guests and hired hands included everyone from GINUWINE, USHER and IRV GOTTI to BUSTA RHYMES and KEITH MURRAY.

Album rating: NO WAY OUT (*6) / FOREVER (*6) / P. Diddy & The Bad Boy Family: THE SAGA CONTINUES . . . (*5) / WE INVENTED THE REMIX (*6)

PUFF DADDY – vocals, etc + guests

Arista Arista

Mar 97. (c-s; PUFF DADDY featuring MASE) *(74321 46455-4) <79083>* **CAN'T NOBODY HOLD ME DOWN / ('A'-instrumental club mix)** [19] Jan97 [1]
(12"+=/cd-s+=) *(74321 46455-2/-1)* – ('A'-Bad Boy mixes; clean / instrumental / extended club).

Jun 97. (c-s; PUFF DADDY & FAITH EVANS featuring 112 & THE LOX) *(74321 49910-4)* **I'LL BE MISSING YOU / ('A'instrumental)** [1] [1]
(12"+=/cd-s+=) *(74321 49910-1/-2)* – ('A'mixes).
(above was a tribute to the recently deceased NOTORIOUS B.I.G.)

Jul 97. (cd/c/d-lp; PUFF DADDY & THE FAMILY) *<(8612 73012-2/-4/-1)>* **NO WAY OUT** [10] [1]
– No way out / Victory / Been around the world / What you gonna do? / Don't stop what you're doing / If I should die tonight / Do you know? / Young G's / I love you baby / It's all about the Benjamins / Pain / Is this the end? / I got the power / Friend / Senorita / I'll be missing you / Can't nobody hold me down.

— In Jul'97, PUFF featured on SWV's cross-Atlantic hit, 'Someone'

Oct 97. (c-s; PUFF DADDY & THE FAMILY) *(74321 53944-4) <79130>* **BEEN AROUND THE WORLD / IT'S ALL ABOUT THE BENJAMINS (instrumental)** [20] [2]
(cd-s+=) *(74321 53944-2)* – ('A'mixes; gangsta mental / ain't armand).
(cd-s) *(74321 53946-2)* – ('A'side) / It's all about the Benjamins (mixes; rock remix I & II).
(12") *(74321 53944-1)* – ('A'mixes).

Jan 98. (c-s; PUFF DADDY & THE FAMILY) *(74321 56197-4)* **IT'S ALL ABOUT THE BENJAMINS / IT'S ALL ABOUT THE BENJAMINS (DJ Ming & FS Drum & Bass mix)** [18] Nov97 [2]
(cd-s+=) *(74321 56197-2)* – ('A'-original) / ('A'-Dave Grohl mix 2).

Mar 98. (c-s,cd-s; PUFF DADDY & The FAMILY featuring THE NOTORIOUS B.I.G. & BUSTA RHYMES) *<79155>* **VICTORY / (mixes; Nine Inch Nails / drama) / BEEN AROUND THE WORLD** [–] [19]

Jul 98. (cd-s; PUFF DADDY featuring JIMMY PAGE) *(666079-2) <78954>* **COME WITH ME / (extended)** [2] Jun98 [4]
(cd-s+=) *(666284-5)* – ('A'mixes; Morello / live).
(cd-s) *(666284-2)* – (4-'A'mixes) / Out there.
(above taken from the film, 'Godzilla', issued on 'Epic' records)

— In Jul'98, he featured on MASE's US Top 10 hit, 'Lookin' At Me'.

— early '99, he featured on FAITH EVANS' Top 10 hit, 'All Night Long'.

Aug 99. (c-s; by PUFF DADDY featuring HURRICANE G) *(74321 69479-4)* **PE 2000 / (radio instrumental)** [13] [ ]
(12"+=/cd-s+=) *(74321 69447-1/69479-2)* – (mixes; club / radio Spanish / club Spanish).
(cd-s) *(74321 69498-2)* – ('A'side) / Victory / Missing you / Gangsta shit.

Aug 99. (cd/c) *(74321 68906-2/-4) <73033>* **FOREVER** [9] [2]
– Forever (intro) / What you want / I'll do this for you / Do you like it . . . do you want it . . . (with JAY-Z) / Satisfy you (with R KELLY) / Is this the end, pt.2 (with TWISTA) / I hear voices (with CARL THOMAS) / Fake thugs dedication (with REDMAN) / Daddy speaks! (interlude) / Angels with dirty faces (with BIZZY BONE) / Gangsta SH*T / P.S. 112 / Pain (with G-DEP) / Reverse / Real niggas (with NOTORIOUS B.I.G. & LIL' KIM) / Journey through the life (with NAS & BEANIE SEAGAL) / Best friend (with MARIO WINANS) / Mad rapper / P.E. 2000 (with HURRICANE G). *(explicit version; 74321 68905-2/-4)*

Oct 99. (c-s; PUFF DADDY feat. MARIO WINIANS & MAD RAPPER) *(74321 71231-4) <79318>* **BEST FRIEND / (instrumental)** [24] [59]
(cd-s) *(74321 71232-2)* – ('A'side) / Satisfy you / Do you like it . . . do you want it.
(cd-s) *(74321 71231-2)* – ('A'mixes).

Feb 00. (cd-s; as PUFF DADDY featuring R. KELLY) *(74321 74559-4/-1/-2) <79283>* **SATISFY YOU / (instrumental) / PE 2000 (instrumental) / PE 2000 (rock)** [8] Sep99 [6]

P. DIDDY & THE BAD BOY FAMILY

— a slight name change!; with **BLACK ROB, MARK CURRY, G-DEP, LOON, HOODFELLAZ, FAITH EVANS, MARIO WINANS, KAIN, MARSHA,** etc

Aug 01. (c-s/cd-s) *<73013>* **THANK YOU** [–] [ ]

Sep 01. (c-s; as P. DIDDY, BLACK ROB & MARK CURRY) *(74321 88998-4) <79400>* **BAD BOY FOR LIFE / LET'S GET IT (remix)** [13] Jul01 [33]
(12"+=) *(74321 88998-1)* – ('A'-instrumental).
(cd-s++=) *(74321 88998-2)* – ('A'video).

Aug 01. (cd) *<(78612 73045-2)>* **THE SAGA CONTINUES . . .** [ ] [2]
– The saga continues / Bad boy for life / Toe game (interlude) / That's crazy / Let's get it / Shiny suit man / Diddy / Blast off / Airport (interlude) / Roll with me / On top / Where's Sean? / Child of the ghetto / Incomplete (interlude) / So complete / Smoke / Lonely / I need a girl (to Bella) / Nothing's gonna stop me now (interlude) / If you want this money / I don't like that (interlude) / Back for good now / Can't believe / The last song / Thank you.

— in Nov'01, P. DIDDY guested on JANET JACKSON's hit, 'Son Of A Gun'

Jan 02. (c-s; as P. DIDDY featuring The NEPTUNES) *(74321 91165-4) <79408>* **DIDDY / BAD BOY FOR LIFE (remix)** [19] Oct01 [66]
(12"+=) *(74321 91165-1)* – ('A'-instrumental) / Special delivery (G. Dep radio mix).
(cd-s++=) *(74321 91165-2)* – ('A'video).

May 02. (cd) *(74321 94540-2) <78612 73062-2>* **WE INVENTED THE REMIX** (remix compilation) [17] [1]
– Intro / Special delivery (mix with G. DEP, GHOSTFACE KILLAH & KEITH MURRAY) / I need a girl – part 2 (remix with GINUWINE, LOON & MARIO WINANS) / Bad boy for life (mix with BUSTA RHYMES & M.O.P) / I need a girl – part 1 (with USHER & LOON) / The remix phenomenon (interlude) / Unfoolish (remix with ASHANTI & NOTORIOUS B.I.G.) / Dance with me – Peaches and cream (remix with 112, LUDACRIS & BEANIE SIGEL) / No more drama (remix with MARY J. BLIGE) / So complete (remix with CHERI DENNIS) / Notorious B.I.G. (remix with NOTORIOUS B.I.G. & LIL' KIM) / That's crazy (remix with BLACK ROB & MISSY ELLIOTT) / Woke up in the morning (remix with CARL THOMAS & NOTORIOUS B.I.G.) / You gets no love (remix with FAITH EVANS & G. DEP).

Jul 02. (c-s; by P. DIDDY featuring USHER & LOON) *(74321 94724-4) <79436>* **I NEED A GIRL (part 1) / (part 2)** [4] [2] Apr02 [4]
(12"+=/cd-s+=) *(74321 94724-1/-2)* – ('A'-To Bella mix).
in Mar'03, P. DIDDY featured on B2K's hit, 'Bump Bump Bump'

Aug 03. (12"; by P. DIDDY & KELIS) *(MCST 40331)* **LET'S GET ILL. / LET'S GET ILL (Darren Emerson remix)** [25] [–]
(cd-s) *(MCSTD 40331)* – ('A'-version) / ('A'-Deep Dish mixes).
in Sep'03, P.DIDDY feat. on NELLY's hit, 'Shake Ya Tailfeather'
in Feb'04, he was feat. on LENNY KRAVITZ's hit 'Show Me Your Soul'
in Jun'04, DIDDY feat. on MARIO WINANS No.1, 'I Don't Wanna Know'

PULP

Formed: Sheffield, England . . . 1981 originally as ARABACUS PULP by JARVIS COCKER while still at school. Following on in the tradition of geek heart-throbs like BUDDY HOLLY, JARVIS COCKER achieved the knicker-wetting adulation he'd always aspired to through sheer hard graft and the determination of the downtrodden. His long road to stardom began in the mid-80's with the release of the 'IT' mini-lp and a prestigious JOHN PEEL session. Further releases like the 'LITTLE GIRL AND OTHER PIECES' (1985) and 'DOGS ARE EVERYWHERE' (1986) EP's saw COCKER developing as a wry and sharply observant chronicler of working class drudgery and sexual frustration, his inimitable brand of camped-up showmanship unhampered by a spell in a wheel chair (his injuries allegedly sustained after falling from a window when trying to show off to a woman!). By the release of 'FREAKS' (1987), the core of the latter day PULP was in place, violinist/guitarist RUSSELL SENIOR and keyboardist CANDIDA DOYLE beginning to move away from the band's early LEONARD COHEN/FALL hybrid to a more arty MONOCHROME SET/ULTRAVOX (John Foxx era!) type vibe. Most of the band moved to London in the late 80's, with bassist STEVE MACKAY and drummer NICHOLAS BANKS stabilising the line-up. In this incarnation, the sleek, new-look PULP recorded the 'SEPARATIONS' (1991) album, a more ambitious affair which spawned the enduringly glitter-tastic 'MY LEGENDARY GIRLFRIEND' single. The track's success encouraged PULP to set up their own label, 'Gift', through which they released a string of early 90's EP's, becoming critical darlings with some sections of the music press alongside fellow pop sculptors like SAINT ETIENNE. It wasn't long before the enigmatic JARVIS and crew were on the roster of 'Island', releasing their breakthrough 'HIS 'N' HERS' album in 1994. Previewed by the driving, tongue-in-cheek query of the 'DO YOU REMEMBER THE FIRST TIME?' single (a short film was released to tie in with the track, featuring various biz figureheads candidly talking about their "first time"), the album expertly dissected the sexual undertow of working class Britain with an incisive accuracy, mordant humour and lashings of glam posturing. The album made the UK Top 10, becoming a consistent seller and setting COCKER up as a fashion icon (Bri-Nylon, national health specs etc.). The singer was to become a star on the same scale as BRETT ANDERSON (Suede) following the success of the landmark 'COMMON PEOPLE' single. A classic pop song that almost made No.2 on the back of the Britpop zeitgeist, the single was a brilliant portrayal of the British class divide set to an almost 80's style synth-led backdrop. After the headlining act dropped out, PULP stepped in to put in one of the most acclaimed performances of their career at the 1995 Glastonbury festival, releasing the 'DIFFERENT CLASS' album in October to round off the most successful year to date in the band's career. With the social commentary as cutting as ever (the controversial 'SORTED FOR E'S AND WHIZZ') and their gift for effortlessly poignant pop intact ('DISCO 2000'), PULP consolidated their position as Britain's leading exponents of home-grown pop genius. A more downbeat COCKER returned late in '97 with the Top 10 hit, 'HELP THE AGED' (all monies going to that particular charity), while Britain awaited with much anticipation the porn-inspired 'THIS IS HARDCORE' set in '98. Another to hit the UK Top 10 (nowhere in America!), the record dabbled with the darker side of fame, set to a lounge-feel, sweaty background of a claustrophic Britain. Following up the difficult ' . . . HARDCORE' set wasn't going to be easy, but with the aid of the legendary SCOTT WALKER as producer, PULP managed to issue a new album in the form of 'WE LOVE LIFE' (2001). Nearly three years in the making, the set reverted back to early PULP material such as songs found on 'HIS 'N' HERS' or the group's commercially brilliant 'DIFFERENT CLASS'. 'WICKERMAN' and 'THE TREES' were both fine examples of a band that had withstood the wintry climate of the music industry and still maintained an ounce of dignity and professionalism. WALKER, who had never produced before, made PULP sound as intriguing and as heart-felt as anything he has ever done. The missing JARVIS (or er, DARREN SPOONER) was back again for 2003 via the mysterious RELAXED MUSCLE side-project, albeit with heavy gothic make-up et al. The 'MUSCLE featured RICHARD HAWLEY (ex-LONGPIGS) and JASON BUCKLE, while the music on one-off set, 'A HEAVY NITE WITH . . .', was decidedly on the SUICIDE-meets-CABARET VOLTAIRE front.

• **Songwriters:** COCKER + SIMON HINKLER collaborated on debut. COCKER, SENIOR, C. DOYLE, MANSELL penned, until 90's when COCKER was main contributor. • **Trivia:** COCKER and MACKAY directed videos for TINDERSTICKS and The APHEX TWIN. • **Note:** Not to be confused with other band fronted by ANDY BEAN + PAUL BURNELL, who released in 1979; LOW FLYING AIRCRAFT single.

Album rating: IT (*4) / FREAKS (*4) / SEPARATIONS (*5) / PULPINTRO – THE GIFT RECORDINGS compilation (*7) / HIS 'N' HERS (*9) / MASTERS OF THE UNIVERSE collecttion (*5) / DIFFERENT CLASS (*9) / THIS IS HARDCORE (*8) / WE LOVE LIFE (*7) / HITS compilation (*8) / Relaxed Muscle: A HEAVY NITE WITH . . . (*7)

JARVIS COCKER (b. Sep'62) – vocals, guitar, piano / **SIMON HINKLER** – keyboards, vocals repl. PETER DALTON / **PETER BOAM** – bass repl. JAMIE PINCHBECK who had repl. DAVID LOCKWOOD / **DAVID HINKLER** – keyboards, trombone / **GARY WILSON** – drums (of ARTERY) repl. WAYNE FURNISS who had repl. JIMMY SELLERS who had repl. MARK SWIFT

— plus guests **SASKIA COCKER** + **GILL TAYLOR** – b.vox / **TIMM ALLCARD** – keyboards

Red Rhino | not iss.

Apr 83. (m-lp) *(REDLP 29)* **IT** [ ] [–]
– My lighthouse / Wishful thinking / Joking aside / Boats and trains / Blue girls / Love love / In many ways. *(cd-iss. Mar94 on 'Cherry Red'; CDMRED 112 w/drawn) (cd+=)* – Looking for life / Everybody's problem / There was. *(re-iss. cd Dec94 on 'Fire'; REFIRE CD15) (cd+=)* – Looking for life. *<US cd-iss. 1997 on 'Velvel'; 79750> (cd re-iss. Nov02 on 'Fire'+=; SFIRE 004CD)*

May 83. (7") *(RED 32)* **MY LIGHTHOUSE (remix). / LOOKING FOR LIFE** [ ] [–]

Sep 83. (7") *(RED 37)* **EVERYBODY'S PROBLEM. / THERE WAS** [ ] [–]

— **RUSSELL SENIOR** – guitar, violin, vocals; repl. DAVID

— **CANDIDA DOYLE** – keyboards, vocals; repl. SIMON who joined ARTERY then the MISSION)

— **MAGNUS DOYLE** – drums repl. GARY, SASKIA, GILL + TIMM

— **PETER MANSELL** – bass repl. BOAM

Fire | not iss.

Nov 85. (12"ep) *(FIRE 5)* **LITTLE GIRL AND OTHER PIECES** [ ] [–]
– Little girl (with blue eyes) / Simultaneous / Blue glow / The will to power. *(re-iss. Oct91)*

Jun 86. (12"ep) *(BLAZE 10)* **DOGS ARE EVERYWHERE / THE MARK OF THE DEVIL. / 97 LOVERS / ABORIGINE / GOODNIGHT** [ ] [–]
(re-iss. Oct91)

Jan 87. (7"/ext.12") *(BLAZE 17/+T)* **THEY SUFFOCATE AT NIGHT. / TUNNEL** [ ] [–]

Mar 87. (7"/12") *(BLAZE 21/+T)* **MASTER OF THE UNIVERSE (sanitised version). / MANON / SILENCE** [ ] [–]
(re-iss. Oct91)

May 87. (lp) *(FIRE LP5)* **FREAKS** [ ] [–]
– Fairground / I want you / Being followed home / Master of the universe / Life must be so wonderful / There's no emotion / Anorexic beauty / The never-ending story / Don't you know / They suffocate at night. *(cd-iss. Apr93; FIRE CD5) <US cd-iss. 1997 on 'Velvel'; 79752> (cd re-iss. Jul02; SFIRE 013CD)*

Jarvis Cocker of PULP

— **STEPHEN MACKAY** – bass repl. STEPHEN HAVENLAND who had repl. PETER

— **NICHOLAS BANKS** – drums, percussion repl. MAGNUS

Sep 90. (12"ep) *(BLAZE 44T)* **MY LEGENDARY GIRLFRIEND. / IS THIS HOUSE? / THIS HOUSE IS CONDEMNED** [ ] [–]
(re-iss. Oct91)

Aug 91. (12"ep/cd-ep) *(BLAZE 51 T/CD)* **COUNTDOWN. / DEATH GOES TO THE DISCO / COUNTDOWN (edit)** [ ] [–]
(re-iss. Oct91)

Oct 91. (cd/c/lp) *(FIRE 33/22/11 026)* **SEPARATIONS** [ ] [–]
– Love is blind / Don't you want me anymore / She's dead / Separations / Down by the river / Countdown / My legendary girlfriend / Death II / This house is condemned. *(re-iss. Jun92; same) <US cd-iss. 1995 on 'Razor & Tie'; 2090-2> (cd re-iss. Apr02; SFIRE 025CD)*

Gift | not iss.

May 92. (12"ep/cd-ep) *(GIF 1/+CD)* **O.U. (GONE GONE) / SPACE / O.U. (GONE GONE) (radio edit)** [ ] [–]

Oct 92. (12"ep/cd-ep) *(GIF 3/+CD)* **BABIES. / STYLOROC (NIGHTS OF SUBURBIA) / SHEFFIELD** – SEX CITY [ ] [–]

Feb 93. (7") *(7GIF 6)* **RAZZAMATAZZ. / INSIDE SUSAN (abridged; Stacks – 59 Lynhurst Grove)** [ ] [–]
(12"ep+/cd-ep+=) *(GIF 6/+CD)* – (B-side; A STORY IN 3 PARTS).

Island | Polygram

Oct 93. (cd/c)(lp) *(IMCD/IMCT 159)(ILPM 2076) <2076-518451>* **PULPINTRO – THE GIFT RECORDINGS** (compilation) [ ] [ ]
– Space / O.U. (gone gone) / Babies / Styloroc (nights of suburbia) / Razzamatazz / Sheffield – Sex city / Medley of stacks: Inside Susan (a story in 3 songs) Stacks – Inside Susan – 59 Lyndhurst Grove.

Nov 93. (7") *(IS 567)* **LIPGLOSS. / YOU'RE A NIGHTMARE** [50] [ ]
(12"+=)(cd-s+=) *(12IS/CID 567)* – Deep fried in Kelvin. *(re-iss. Aug96) (re-iss. Oct96 on 7"red)*

Mar 94. (7"/c-s) *(IS/CIS 574)* **DO YOU REMEMBER THE FIRST TIME?. / STREET LITES** [33] [ ]
(12"+=)(cd-s+=) *(12IS/CID 574)* - **The babysitter.** *(re-iss. Aug96, hit 73) (re-iss. Oct96 7"biege)*

Apr 94. (cd/c/lp) *(CID/ICT/ILPS 8025) <524006>* **HIS 'N' HERS** [9] Jun94 [ ]
– Joyriders / Lipgloss / Acrylic afternoons / Have you seen her lately? / She's a lady / Happy endings / Do you remember the first time? / Pink glove / Someone like the Moon / David's last summer.(cd,c+=) – Babies (remix).

May 94. (7"ep/c-ep/12"ep/cd-ep) *(IS/CIS/12IS/CID 595)* **THE SISTERS EP** [19] [–]
– Babies / Your sister's clothes / Seconds / His'n'hers. *(re-iss. Aug96) (re-iss. Oct96 on white 7"ep)*

May 95. (c-s) *(CIS 613)* **COMMON PEOPLE. / UNDERWEAR** [2] [–]
(cd-s+=) *(CID 613)* – ('A'-Motiv8 mix) / ('A'-Vocoda mix). *(re-iss. Aug96) (re-iss. Oct96 7"yellow/12")*
(cd-s) *(CIDX 613)* – ('A'side) / Razzmatazz (acoustic) / Dogs are everywhere (acoustic) / Joyriders (acoustic).

— Below second side (double A) caused controversy with tabloids and parents, due to its mis-use of drugs in JARVIS's lyrics. JARVIS was to become the hero to most and villain to the few early in 1996 at a certain awards ceremony (skinny J.C. vs. St.MICHAEL & the bouncers; who won? – you decide).

Sep 95. (c-s) *(CIS 620)* **MIS-SHAPES / SORTED FOR E'S AND WIZZ** [2] [–]
(cd-s+=) *(CID 620)* – P.T.A. (Parent Teacher Association) / Common people (live at Glastonbury). *(re-iss. Oct96 7"blue/12")*
(cd-s+=) *(CIDX 620)* – Common people (Motiv8 mix). *(re-iss. Aug96)*

Oct 95. (cd/c/lp) *(CID/ICT/ILPS 8041) <524165>* **DIFFERENT CLASS** [1] [ ]
– Mis-shapes / Pencil skirt / Common people / I spy / Disco 2000 / Live bed show / Something changed / Sorted out for E's and wizz / F.E.E.L.I.N.G.C.A.L.L.E.D.L.O.V.E. / Underwear / Monday morning / Bar Italia.

Nov 95. (c-s) *(CIS 623)* **DISCO 2000 / ANSAPHONE** [7] [–]
(cd-s+=) *(CID 623)* – ('A'-Motiv8 Gimp dub & Discoid mixes). *(re-iss. Aug96) (re-iss. Oct96 7"orange/12")*
(cd-s+=) *(CIDX 623)* – Live bed show (extended).

Mar 96. (c-s) *(CIS 632)* **SOMETHING CHANGED / MILE END** [10] [–]
(cd-s+=) *(CID 632)* – F.E.E.L.I.N.G.C.A.L.L.E.D.L.O.V.E (The Moloko mix) / F.E.E.L.I.N.G.C.A.L.L.E.D.L.O.V.E. (live from Brixton Academy). *(re-iss. Aug96) (re-iss. Oct96 7"pink/12")*

— now without SENIOR, who wanted to pursue new projects

Nov 97. (c-s/7") *(C+/IS 679)* **HELP THE AGED. / LAUGHING BOY** [8] [–]
(cd-s+=) *(CID 679)* – Tomorrow never lies.

Mar 98. (c-s) *(CIS 695)* **THIS IS HARDCORE / LADIES MAN** [12] [–]
(cd-s+=) *(CID 695)* – Professional.
(cd-s) *(CIDX 695)* – ('A'mixes).

Mar 98. (cd/c/d-lp) *(ILPSD/ICT/CID 8066) <524492>* **THIS IS HARDCORE** [1] [ ]
– The fear / Dishes / Party hard / Help the aged / This is hardcore / TV movie / A little soul / I'm a man / Seductive Barry / Sylvia / Glory days / Day after the revolution.

Jun 98. (c-s) *(CIS 708)* **A LITTLE SOUL / COCAINE SOCIALISM** [22] [–]
(cd-s+=) *(CID 708)* – Like a friend.
(cd-s) *(CIDX 708)* – ('A'alternative mix) / ('A'-Lafayette Velvet revisited mix) / That boy's evil.

Sep 98. (c-s/cd-s) *(CIS/CID 719) <572418>* **PARTY HARD / WE ARE THE BOYZ / THE FEAR** [29] [ ]
(cd-s) *(CIDX 719)* – ('A'mixes by Stretch'n'Vern & All Seeing I).

Oct 01. (cd-s) *(CID 786)* **SUNRISE / THE TREES / SUNRISE (fat truckers scott free mix)** [28] [–]
(cd-s) *(CIDX 786)* – (first 2) / The trees (felled by I Monster).
(12") *(12IS 786)* – ('A'side) / The trees (felled by I Monster) / Sunrise (All Seeing I remix) / The trees (Lovejoy mix).

Oct 01. (cd/d-lp) *(CID/ILPSD 8109) <586540>* **WE LOVE LIFE** [6] [ ]
– Weeds / Weeds II (the origin of the species) / The night that Minnie Temperley died / The trees / Wickerman / I love life / The birds in your garden / Bob Lind / Bad cover version / Roadkill / Sunrise.

Apr 02. (cd-s) *(CID 794)* **BAD COVER VERSION / YESTERDAY / FOREVER IN MY DREAMS** [27] [–]
(cd-s) *(CIDX 794)* – ('A'-video mix) / Disco 2000 (by NICK CAVE) / Sorted? (by ROISON MURPHY).

Nov 02. (cd) *(CID 8126)* **HITS** (compilation) [71] [–]
– Babies / Razzmatazz / Lipgloss / Do you remember the first time? / Common people / Underwear / Sorted for E's & wizz / Disco 2000 / Something changed / Help the aged / This is hardcore / A little soul / Party hard / The trees / Bad cover version / Sunrise / Last day of the miner's strike.

– compilations, etc. –

Jun 94. (cd/c/lp) *Fire; (FIRE CD/MC/LP 36)* **MASTERS OF THE UNIVERSE – PULP ON FIRE 1985-86** [ ] [–]
– Little girl (with blue eyes) / Simultaneous / Blue glow / The will to power / Dogs are everywhere / The mark of the Devil / 97 lovers / Aborigine / Goodnight / They suffocate at night / Tunnel / Master of the universe (sanitised version) / Manon.

Mar 96. (d-cd/c/d-lp) *Nectar; (NTM CDD/C/LP 521)* **COUNTDOWN 1992-1983** [10] [–]
– Countdown / Death goes to the disco / My legendary girlfriend / Don't you want me anymore / She's dead / Down by the river / I want you / Being followed home / Master of the universe / Don't you know / They suffocate at night / Dogs are everywhere / Mark of the Devil / 97 lovers / Little girl (with blue eyes) / Blue glow / My lighthouse / Wishful thinking / Blue girls / Countdown (extended).

Jul 98. (cd) *Connoisseur; (VSOPCD 256)* **DEATH GOES TO THE DISCO** [ ] [–]

Sep 98. (cd) *E.M.I.; <79737>* **FRESHLY SQUEEZED (EARLY YEARS)** [–] [ ]

RELAXED MUSCLE

DARREN SPOONER (JARVIS) + **WAYNE MARSDEN** (RICHARD HAWLEY) + **JASON BUCKLE**

Rough Trade | not iss.

Apr 03. (7"/cd-s) *(RTRADES/+CD 073)* **THE HEAVY. / ROD OF IRON / BRANDED!** [ ] [–]

Jul 03. (7") *(RTRADES 106)* **BILLY JACK. / SEXUALIZED** [ ] [–]
(cd-s+=) *(RTRADESCD 106)* – The year of the dog.

Oct 03. (cd/lp) *(RTRADE CD/LP 131)* **A HEAVY NITE WITH . . .** [ ] [–]
– The heavy / 3 way accumulator / Beastmaster / Billy Jack / Rod of iron / Tuff it out / Sexualized / Muscle music / B-real / Previous / Battered / Mary. *(cd bonus +=)* – Sexualized (video) / Billy Jack (video).

QUEEN

Formed: London, England . . . early 1971 by guitarist BRIAN MAY, drummer ROGER TAYLOR and vocalist par excellence FREDDIE MERCURY, bassist JOHN DEACON completing the line-up. MAY had left school in 1963 (with a whopping ten O-levels), joining teen group The OTHERS who issued one single for 'Fontana' in 1965, 'OH YEAH'. Together with TAYLOR, he then went on to form SMILE in 1969, a project that met with little success although they did release one 45 for 'Mercury US', 'EARTH' / 'STEP ON ME'. The pair then hooked up with the Zanzibar-born MERCURY and formed QUEEN in 1971, JOHN DEACON subsequently recruited on bass. After spending most of 1972 in the studio, QUEEN were picked up by 'E.M.I.' when engineer John Anthony sent the company a demo tape. The group made their live debut in April '73 at London's famed Marquee club, but prior to any QUEEN release, FREDDIE MERCURY (as LARRY LUREX!) issued a one-off 'EMI' solo single that summer, 'I CAN HEAR MUSIC' / 'GOIN' BACK' (the former an old BEACH BOYS number). A month later, QUEEN simultaneously unleashed their eponymous Roy Thomas-Baker produced debut album, and single, 'KEEP YOURSELF ALIVE'. Influenced by LED ZEPPELIN and the more garish elements of glam-rock, the group had fashioned a unique, densely layered sound around MERCURY's impressive vocal acrobatics and MAY's fluid, coin-pick guitar style. Though the album didn't exactly set the charts alight, the band subsequently set out on a heavy touring schedule, supporting friends to be, MOTT THE HOOPLE, in late '73. Success eventually came with the piano-led bombast of the 'SEVEN SEAS OF RHYE' single, the track making the Top 10 in February '74 and paving the way for 'QUEEN II' the following month. The album reached No.5, consolidating QUEEN's new position as a headline act; while MERCURY was allegedly known to be fairly shy in real life, onstage he embodied everything that the word QUEEN implied with a passionate theatricality unmatched in rock music. The group really came into their own with the 'KILLER QUEEN' single, an infectious slice of jaunty high camp that reached No.2 in late '74. The following month, QUEEN released their strongest album to date, 'SHEER HEART ATTACK', an eminently listenable collage of killer hooks, neo-metal riffs, O.T.T. choruses and satin-clad dynamics that contained the likes of 'STONE COLD CRAZY' and the next single, 'NOW I'M HERE'. But QUEEN, to use a particularly crap pun, were finally crowned, commercially at least with the 'BOHEMIAN RHAPSODY' single in late 1975. Surely one of the most annoyingly overplayed singles of all time next to 'Stairway To Heaven', the song was nevertheless something of an innovation at the time, a grandiose epic that gave new meaning to the term 'rock opera'; forget concept albums, QUEEN could condense such lofty conceits into a meagre 6 minutes! The song was accompanied by what is widely regarded as the first promotional video, a quintessentially 70's affair that, in retrospect, resembles the title sequence of 'Doctor Who'. Nevertheless, the single gave QUEEN an astonishing nine week run at the top of the charts over the Christmas period, ensuring similar success for the highly ambitious 'NIGHT AT THE OPERA' (1975) album. Apparently the most expensive project recorded up to that point, the record took QUEEN's bombastic pretensions to new limits, MERCURY's multi tracked vocals setting new standards in studio mastery. While most of QUEEN's work was penned by MERCURY and MAY, TAYLOR and DEACON were also talented songsmiths, the latter contributing one of the group's loveliest songs, 'YOU'RE MY BEST FRIEND', its heartfelt simplicity counterbalancing some of the album's more excessive moments. 'NIGHT AT THE OPERA' also went Top 5 in the States, QUEEN having broken America with their irrepressible stage show earlier that year. Their ascent into world beater status continued with 'A DAY AT THE RACES' (1976), another No.1 album which spawned a further massive hit in 'SOMEBODY TO LOVE' and contained the classic camp of 'GOOD OLD FASHIONED LOVER BOY'. The anthemic double header of the 'WE ARE THE CHAMPIONS' / 'WE WILL ROCK YOU' single reached No.2 the following year, presaging QUEEN's move away from operatic artifice to more straightahead stadium rock. 'NEWS OF THE WORLD' (1977) and 'JAZZ' (1978) confirmed this, both albums selling well despite their lack of inventiveness. The riff-heavy 'FAT BOTTOMED GIRLS' could only have been recorded in the 70's, a gloriously unreconstructed paeon to shapely women that just wouldn't do in todays PC-controlled climate. While other rock monsters of the 70's were washed away on the tide of dour aggression that was punk, QUEEN looked to other musical forms to keep their sound fresh, namely 50's style rockabilly on the classic 'CRAZY LITTLE THING CALLED LOVE', MERCURY coming on like a camp ELVIS in the video, decked out in biker gear with a leather cap, of course, de rigueur. The group also flirted with disco on the bass-heavy 'ANOTHER ONE BITES THE DUST', a US No.1 that was later sampled by GRANDMASTER FLASH. Both tracks were featured on 'THE GAME' (1980), QUEEN'S most consistent album since the mid-70's and a transatlantic chart topper. After a partially successful sidestep into soundtrack work with 'FLASH GORDON' (1980), QUEEN rounded up the highlights of the preceding decade with a multi platinum greatest hits set. While the band had been selling more records of late in the States than the UK, this trend was reversed with 'UNDER PRESSURE', a collaboration with DAVID BOWIE which topped the British charts. 'HOT SPACE' (1982) ranks as one of QUEEN's dodgiest albums but with 'THE WORKS' (1984), QUEEN once again enjoyed a run of Top 10 singles with the likes of 'RADIO GA-GA' and 'I WANT TO BREAK FREE'. While these were listenable enough they lacked the pop brilliance of QUEEN's best 70's work. Live, QUEEN were still a massive draw, MERCURY's peerless ability to work a crowd evidenced on his famous Live Aid appearance in 1985. While the group's back catalogue subsequently clogged up the album charts, QUEEN returned with new material in the shape of 'A KIND OF MAGIC' (1986). Maybe Live Aid went to QUEEN's collective head, the album suffering from a kind of plodding stadium-friendly malaise that saw the group descending into self-parody. Nevertheless, the record made No.1, as QUEEN continued to tour

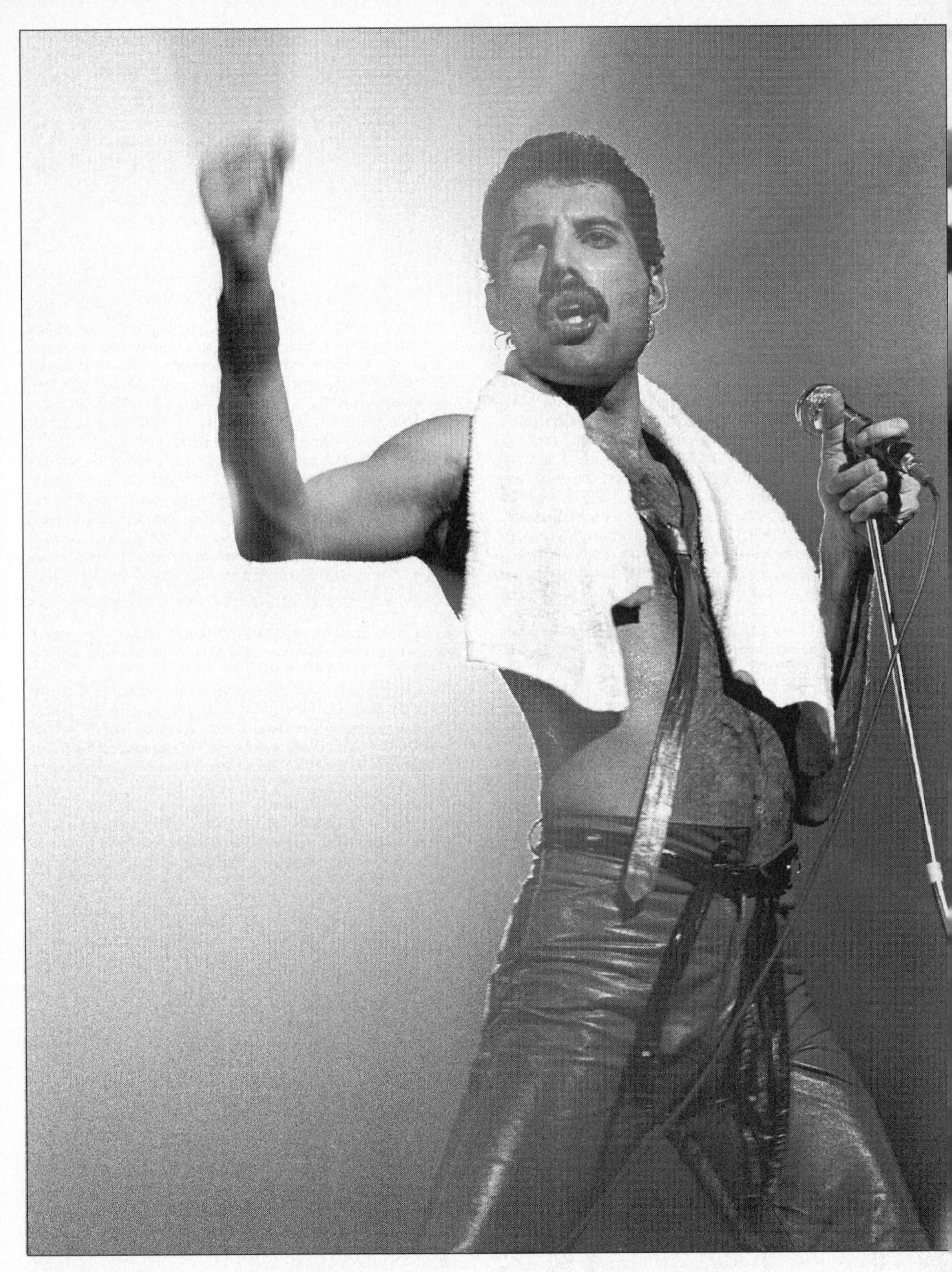

Freddie Mercury of QUEEN

the world and play to record breaking audiences. The band returned to the fray with 'THE MIRACLE' in 1989, another No.1 album that contained few surprises. Nor did 'INNUENDO' (1991), although bearing in mind MERCURY's rumoured failing health, it'd be churlish to criticise what must have been a very difficult album for the singer to finish. On the 23rd of November, 1991, a matter of months after the album's release, MERCURY succumbed to AIDS. The following month, 'BOHEMIAN RHAPSODY' was re-released and once again topped the UK charts, raising money for research into the killer disease. A tribute concert was held the following Spring at Wembley Stadium, the cream of the music world's top drawer stars paying their respects including ELTON JOHN, GUNS N' ROSES, GEORGE MICHAEL and DEF LEPPARD. Inevitably, QUEEN split although a posthumous album was released in 1995, featuring material that MERCURY had been working on prior to his death. While it didn't exactly add anything significant to QUEEN's stunning legacy, it tied up the loose ends, bringing the saga of one of music's most flamboyantly colourful bands to a dignified close. Not exactly! Just when it was thought they had all but abandoned the search for the perfect FREDDIE replacement, along came ex-FREE man PAUL RODGERS. With QUEEN and new frontman RODGERS uniting for a one-off concert in Sheffield (May 2005), it was inevitable that the pairing would release the accompanying CD, 'RETURN OF THE CHAMPIONS' (2005), complete with mostly QUEEN greats plus FREE and BAD COMPANY tracks!

• **MERCURY covered:** THE GREAT PRETENDER (Platters). The CROSS covered FOXY LADY (Jimi Hendrix), BRIAN MAY covered ROLLIN' OVER (Small Faces).

Album rating: QUEEN (*7) / QUEEN II (*6) / SHEER HEART ATTACK (*8) / A NIGHT AT THE OPERA (*7) / A DAY AT THE RACES (*5) / NEWS OF THE WORLD (*6) / JAZZ (*5) / LIVE KILLERS (*7) / THE GAME (*6) / HOT SPACE (*4) / FLASH GORDON soundtrack (*4) / THE WORKS (*4) / A KIND OF MAGIC (*5) / LIVE MAGIC (*6) / THE MIRACLE (*6) / INNUENDO (*6) / QUEEN'S GREATEST HITS compilation (*9) / GREATEST HITS II compilation (*8) / QUEEN ON FIRE – LIVE AT THE BOWL (*6) / RETURN OF THE CHAMPIONS (*4)

FREDDIE MERCURY (b. FREDERICK BULSARA, 5 Sep'46, Zanzibar, Africa. In 1959, he moved with family to Feltham, Middlesex, England) – vocals, piano / **BRIAN MAY** (b.19 Jul'47, London, England) – guitar, vocals, keyboards / **ROGER MEDDOWS-TAYLOR** (b.26 Jul'49, King's Lynn, Norfolk, England) – drums, vocals / **JOHN DEACON** (b.19 Aug'51, Leicester, England) – bass, vocals

E.M.I. Elektra

Jul 73. (7") *(EMI 2036)* <45863> **KEEP YOURSELF ALIVE. / SON AND DAUGHTER** [ ] [ ]

Jul 73. (lp/c) *(EMC/TCEMC 3006)* <75064> **QUEEN** [ ] Oct73 [83]
– Keep yourself alive / Doing all right / Great King Rat / My fairy king / Liar / The night comes down / Modern times rock'n'roll / Son and daughter / Jesus / Seven seas of rhye *[US only]. (hit UK No.24 Mar74) (re-iss. Aug82 on 'Fame' lp/c; FA/TCFA 3040) (cd-iss. Nov86; CDP 746204-2) (cd-iss. May88; CDFA 3040) <US cd-iss. Jun91 on 'Hollywood'+=; 61064-2>* – Mad the swine, keep yourself alive (long lost retake) / Liar (1991 remix) *(re-iss. Apr94 on 'Parlophone' cd/c; CD/TC PCSD 139)*

Nov 73. (7") *<45884>* **LIAR. / DOING ALL RIGHT** [–] [ ]

Feb 74. (7") *(EMI 2121)* *<45891>* **SEVEN SEAS OF RHYE. / SEE WHAT A FOOL I'VE BEEN** [10] [ ]

Mar 74. (lp/c) *(EMA/TCEMA 767)* *<75082>* **QUEEN II** [5] May74 [49]
– Procession / Father to son / White queen (as it began) / Some day one day / The loser in the end / Ogre battle / The fairy feller's master-stroke / Nevermore / The march of the black queen / Funny how love is / Seven seas of rhye. *(re-iss. Apr84 on 'Fame' lp/c; FA/TCFA 3099) (cd-iss. Nov86; CDP 746205-2) (re-iss. May88; CDFA 3099) <US cd-iss. Oct91 on 'Hollywood'+=; 61232-2>* – See what a fool I've been / Ogre battle – 1991 remix / Seven seas of rhye – 1991 remix. *(re-iss. Apr94 on 'Parlophone' cd/c; CD/TC PCSD 140)*

Oct 74. (7") *(EMI 2229)* *<45226>* **KILLER QUEEN. / FLICK OF THE WRIST** [2] Jan75 [12]

Nov 74. (lp,red-lp/c-s) *(EMC/TCEMC 3061)* *<1026>* **SHEER HEART ATTACK** [2] Dec74 [12]
– Brighton rock / Killer Queen / Tenement funster / Flick of the wrist / Lily of the valley / Now I'm here / In the lap of the gods / Stone cold crazy / Dear friends / Misfire / Bring back that Leroy Brown / She makes me (stormtrooper in stilettoes) / In the lap of the gods . . . revisited. *(re-iss. 1984 lp/c; ATAK/TCATAK 22) (cd-iss. 1984; CDP 746052-2) (cd-iss. Jun88; CDP 746206-2) <US cd-iss. Nov88 on 'Hollywood'+=; 61036-2>* – Stone cold sober – 1991 remix) *(re-iss. Aug93 on 'Parlophone' cd/c; CD/TC PCSD 129)*

Jan 75. (7") *(EMI 2256)* **NOW I'M HERE. / LILY OF THE VALLEY** [11] [–]

Apr 75. (7") *<45268>* **LILY OF THE VALLEY. / KEEP YOURSELF ALIVE** [–] [ ]

Nov 75. (7") *(EMI 2375)* *<45297>* **BOHEMIAN RHAPSODY. / I'M IN LOVE WITH MY CAR** [1] Dec75 [9]

Dec 75. (lp/c) *(EMTC/TCEMTC 103)* *<1053>* **A NIGHT AT THE OPERA** [1] [4]
– Death on two legs (dedicated to . . .) / Lazing on a Sunday afternoon / I'm in love with my car / You're my best friend / '39 / Sweet lady / Seaside rendezvous / The prophet's song / Love of my life / Good company / Bohemian rhapsody / God save the Queen. *(re-iss. 1984 lp/c; ATAK/TCATAK 27) (cd-iss. 1984; CDP 746050-2) (cd-iss. Jun88; CDP 746207-2) <US cd-iss. Aug91 on 'Hollywood'+=; 61065-2>* – I'm in love with my car – 1991 remix / You're my best friend – 1991 remix. *(re-iss. Aug93 on 'Parlophone' cd/c; CD/TC PCSD 130)*

Jun 76. (7") *(EMI 2494)* *<45318>* **YOU'RE MY BEST FRIEND. / '39** [7] May76 [16]

Nov 76. (7") *(EMI 2565)* *<45362>* **SOMEBODY TO LOVE. / WHITE MAN** [2] [13]

Dec 76. (lp/c) *(EMTC/TCEMTC 104)* *<101>* **A DAY AT THE RACES** [1] Jan77 [5]
– Tie your mother down / You take my breath away / Long away / The millionaire waltz / You and I / Somebody to love / White man / Good old fashioned lover boy / Drowse / Teo Torriate (let us cling together). *(re-iss. 1984 lp/c; ATAK/TCATAK 28) (cd-iss. 1984; CDP 746051-2) (cd-iss. Jun88; CDP 746208-2) <US cd-iss. Mar91 on 'Hollywood'+=; 61035-2>* – Tie your mother down – remix / Somebody to love – remix. *(re-iss. Aug93 on 'Parlophone' cd/c; CD/TC PCSD 131) (lp re-iss. Nov97; LPCENT 29)*

Mar 77. (7") *(EMI 2593)* **TIE YOUR MOTHER DOWN. / YOU AND I** [31] [–]

Mar 77. (7") *<45385>* **TIE YOUR MOTHER DOWN. / DROWSE** [–] [49]

May 77. (7"ep) *(EMI 2623)* **QUEEN'S FIRST EP** [17] [–]
– Good old fashioned lover boy / Death on two legs (dedicated to . . .) / Tenement funster / White Queen (as it began).

Jun 77. (7") *<45412>* **LONG AWAY. / YOU AND I** [–] [ ]

Oct 77. (7") *(EMI 2708)* *<45441>* **WE ARE THE CHAMPIONS. / WE WILL ROCK YOU** [2] [4]

Nov 77. (lp/c) *(EMA/TCEMA 784)* *<112>* **NEWS OF THE WORLD** [4] [3]
– We will rock you / We are the champions / Sheer heart attack / All dead, all dead / Spread your wings / Fight from the inside / Get down make love / Sleeping on the sidewalk / Who needs you / It's late / My melancholy blues. *(re-iss. 1984 lp/c; ATAK/TCATAK 20) (cd-iss. Jun88; CDP 746209-2) <US cd-iss. Mar91 on 'Hollywood'+=; 61037-2>* – We will rock you – 1991 remix. *(re-iss. Aug93 on 'Parlophone' cd/c; CD/TC PCSD 132)*

Feb 78. (7") *(EMI 2575)* **SPREAD YOUR WINGS. / SHEER HEART ATTACK** [34] [–]

Apr 78. (7") *<45478>* **IT'S LATE. / SHEER HEART ATTACK** [–] [74]

Oct 78. (7") *(EMI 2870)* *<45541>* **BICYCLE RACE. / FAT BOTTOMED GIRLS** [11] Nov78 [24]

Nov 78. (lp/c) *(EMA/TCEAM 788)* *<166>* **JAZZ** [2] [6]
– Mustapha / Fat bottomed girls / Jealousy / Bicycle race / If you can't beat them / Let me entertain you / Dead on time / In only seven days / Dreamer's ball / Fun it / Leaving home ain't easy / Don't stop me now / More of that jazz. *(re-iss. 1984 lp/c; ATAK/TCATAK 24) (cd-iss. Jun88; CDP 746210-2) <US cd-iss. Jun91 on 'Hollywood'+=; 61062-2>* – Fat bottomed girls – 1991 remix / Bicycle race – 1991 remix. *(re-iss. Feb94 on 'Parlophone' cd/c; CD/TC PCSD 133)*

Feb 79. (7") *(EMI 2910)* **DON'T STOP ME NOW. / IN ONLY SEVEN DAYS** [9] [–]

Feb 79. (7") *<46008>* **DON'T STOP ME NOW. / MORE OF THAT JAZZ** [–] [86]

Apr 79. (7") *<46039>* **JEALOUSY. / FUN IT** [–] [ ]

Jun 79. (d-lp/d-c) *(EMSP/TC2EMSP 330)* *<702>* **LIVE KILLERS (live)** [3] [16]
– We will rock you / Let me entertain you / Death on two legs / Killer Queen / Bicycle race / I'm in love with my car / Get down, make love / You're my best friend / Now I'm here / Dreamer's ball / '39 / Keep yourself alive / Don't stop me now / Spread your wings / Brighton rock /

Bohemian rhapsody / Tie your mother down / Sheer heart attack / We will rock you / We are the champions / God save the Queen. *(re-iss. 1984 lp/c; ATAK/TCATAK 23) (cd-iss. Jun88; CDP 746211-2) <US cd-iss. Nov88 on 'Hollywood'; 61066-2> (re-iss. Apr94 on 'Parlophone' cd/c; CD/TC PCSD 138)*

Jul 79. (7") *(EMI 2959)* **LOVE OF MY LIFE (live). / NOW I'M HERE (live)** 63 –

Aug 79. (7") *<46532>* **WE WILL ROCK YOU (live). / LET ME ENTERTAIN YOU (live)** –

Oct 79. (7") *(EMI 5001)* **CRAZY LITTLE THING CALLED LOVE. / WE WILL ROCK YOU (live)** 2 –

Dec 79. (7") *<46579>* **CRAZY LTTLE THING CALLED LOVE. / SPREAD YOUR WINGS** – 1

Feb 80. (7") *(EMI 5022)* **SAVE ME. / LET ME ENTERTAIN YOU (live)** 11 –

Jun 80. (7") *(EMI 5076) <46652>* **PLAY THE GAME. / HUMAN BODY** 14 42

Jul 80. (lp/c) *(EMA/TCEMA 795) <513>* **THE GAME** 1 1
– Play the game / Dragon attack / Another one bites the dust / Need your loving tonight / Crazy little thing called love / Rock it (prime jive) / Don't try suicide / Sail away sweet sister / Coming soon / Save me. *(re-iss. 1984 lp/c; ATAK/TCATAK 21) (cd-iss. Jun88; CDP 746213-2) <US cd-iss. Jun91 on 'Hollywood'+=; 61063-2>* – Dragon attack – 1991 remix. *(re-iss. Feb94 on 'Parlophone' cd/c; CD/TC PCSD 134)*

Aug 80. (7") *(EMI 5102)* **ANOTHER ONE BITES THE DUST. / DRAGON ATTACK** 7 –

Aug 80. (7") *<47031>* **ANOTHER ONE BITES THE DUST. / DON'T TRY SUICIDE** – 1

Oct 80. (7") *<47086>* **NEED YOUR LOVING TONIGHT. / ROCK IT (PRIME JIVE)** – 44

Nov 80. (7") *(EMI 5126) <47092>* **FLASH. / FOOTBALL FIGHT** 10 Jan81 42

Dec 80. (lp/c) *(EMC/TCEMC 795) <518>* **FLASH GORDON** (soundtrack) 10 23
– Flash's theme / In the space capsule (the love theme) / Ming's theme (in the court of Ming the Merciless) / The ring (hypnotic seduction of Dale) / Football fight / In the death cell (love theme reprise) / Execution of Flash / The kiss (Aura resurrects Flash) / Arboria (planet of the Tree Men) / Escape from the swamp / Flash to the rescue / Vultan's theme (attack of the Hawk Men) / Battle theme / The wedding march / The marriage of Dale and Ming (and Flash approaching) / Crash dive on Mingo City / Flash's theme reprise (victory celebrations) / The hero. *(re-iss. 1984 lp/c; ATAK/TCATAK 26) (cd-iss. Jun88; CDP 746214-2) <US cd-iss. Aug91 on 'Hollywood'+=; 61203-2>* – Flash's theme. *(re-iss. Apr94 on 'Parlophone' cd/c; CD/TC PCSD 137)*

Nov 81. (lp/c) *(EMTV/TCEMTC 30) <564>* **QUEEN'S GREATEST HITS** (compilation) 1 14
– Bohemian rhapsody / Another one bites the dust / Killer queen / Fat bottomed girls / Bicycle race / You're my best friend / Don't stop me now / Save me *[or US= Keep yourself alive / Under pressure]* / Crazy little thing called love / Somebody to love / Now I'm here / Good old-fashioned lover boy / Play the game / Flash / Seven seas of Rhye / We will rock you / We are the champions. *(cd-iss. Aug84; CDP 746033-2) (re-hit at No.7 – Dec91) (re-iss. Jun94 on 'Parlophone' cd/c; CD/TC PCSD 141)*

Nov 81. (7"; by QUEEN and DAVID BOWIE) *(EMI 5250) <47235>* **UNDER PRESSURE. / SOUL BROTHER** 1 29

Apr 82. (7") *(EMI 5293) <47452>* **BODY LANGUAGE. / LIFE IS REAL (SONG FOR LENNON)** 25 11

May 82. (lp/c) *(EMA/TCEMA 797) <60128>* **HOT SPACE** 4 22
– Staying power / Dancer / Back chat / Body language / Action this day / Put out the fire / Life is real (song for Lennon) / Calling all girls / Las Palabras de amor / Cool cat / Under pressure. *(cd-iss. Jun88; CDP 746215-2) (re-iss. Aug89 on 'Fame' cd/c/lp; CD/TC+/FA 3228) <US cd-iss. Mar91 on 'Hollywood'+=; 61038-2>* – Body language – 1991 remix. *(re-iss. Feb94 on 'Parlophone' cd/c; CD/TC PCSD 135)*

Jun 82. (7") *(EMI 5316)* **LAS PALABRAS DE AMOR. / COOL CAT** 17 –

Jul 82. (7") *<69981>* **CALLING ALL GIRLS. / PUT OUT THE FIRE** – 60

Aug 82. (7"/ext.12") *(EMI/12EMI 5325) <69941>* **BACKCHAT. / STAYING POWER** 40

E.M.I. Capitol

Jan 84. (7") *(QUEEN 1) <5317>* **RADIO GA GA. / I GO CRAZY** 2 16
(ext.12") *(12QUEEN 1)* – ('A'dub version).

Mar 84. (lp/c)(cd) *(WORK/TCWORK 1)(CDP 7460160-2) <12322>* **THE WORKS** 2 23
– Radio ga ga / Tear it up / It's a hard life / Man on the prowl / Machines (or back to humans) / I want to break free / Keep passing the open windows / Hammer to fall / Is his he world we created?. *<US cd-iss. Dec91 on 'Hollywood'+=; 61233-2>* – Radio Ga Ga (12"mix) / I want to break free (12"mix) / I go crazy. *(re-iss. Feb94 on 'Parlophone' cd/c; CD/TC PCSD 136)*

Apr 84. (7"/ext.12") *(QUEEN/12QUEEN 2) <5350>* **I WANT TO BREAK FREE (remix). / MACHINES (OR BACK TO HUMANS)** 3 45

Jul 84. (7"/12"pic-d) *(QUEEN/12QUEENP 3) <5372>* **IT'S A HARD LIFE. / IS THIS THE WORLD WE CREATED?** 6 72
(12"+=) *(12QUEEN 3)* – ('A'extended remix).

Sep 84. (7"/'A'-Headbangers-12") *(QUEEN/12QUEEN 4) <5424>* **HAMMER TO FALL. / TEAR IT UP** 13

Dec 84. (7"/ext.12") *(QUEEN/12QUEEN 5)* **THANK GOD IT'S CHRISTMAS. / MAN ON THE PROWL / KEEP PASSING OPEN WINDOWS** 21 –

—— In the mid 80's & before, each individual had also launched solo

Nov 85. (7"/ext-12") *(QUEEN/12QUEEN 6) <5530>* **ONE VISION. / BLURRED VISION** 7 61

Mar 86. (7") *<5568>* **PRINCES OF THE UNIVERSE. / A DOZEN RED ROSES FOR MY DARLING** –

Mar 86. (7"/ext.12"/ext.12"pic-d) *(QUEEN/12QUEEN/12QUEENP 7)* **A KIND OF MAGIC. / DON'T LOSE YOUR HEAD** 3 –

May 86. (lp/c)(cd) *(EU/TCEU 3509)(CDP 746267-2) <12476>* **A KIND OF MAGIC** 1 46
– One vision / A kind of magic / One year of love / Pain is so close to pleasure / Friends will be friends / Who wants to live forever / Gimme the prize / Don't lose your head / Princes of the universe. *(cd+=)* – A kind of 'A kind of magic – Friends will be friends – Who wants to live forever. *<US cd-iss. Jun91 on 'Hollywood'+=; 61152>* – Forever, One vision.

Jun 86. (7") *<5590>* **A KIND OF MAGIC. / GIMME THE PRIZE (KURGAN'S THEME)** – 42

Jun 86. (7"/7"pic-d) *(QUEEN/+P 8)* **FRIENDS WILL BE FRIENDS. / SEVEN SEAS OF RHYE** 14 –
(12"+=) *(12QUEEN 8)* – ('A'extended mix).

Jul 86. (7") *<5633>* **DON'T LOSE YOUR HEAD. / PAIN IS SO CLOSE TO PLEASURE** –

Sep 86. (7") *(QUEEN 9)* **WHO WANTS TO LIVE FOREVER. / KILLER QUEEN** 24 –
(12"+=) *(12QUEEN 9)* – ('A'-lp version) / Forever.

Dec 86. (d-lp/c)(cd) *(EMC/TCEMC 3519)(CDP 746413-2)* **LIVE MAGIC** (live) 3 –
– One vision / Tie your mother down / I want to break free / Hammer to fall / Seven seas of rhye / We are the champions / Another one bites the dust / Is this the world we created? / Bohemian rhasody / Radio Ga Ga / Friends will be friends / We will rock you / Under pressure / A kind of music / God save the Queen. *(re-iss. Dec91 on 'Parlophone')*

—— During this lull in QUEEN activity, FREDDIE MERCURY had released some solo singles and collaborated with MONTSERRAT CABALLE. TAYLOR had formed The CROSS

Parlophone Capitol

Apr 89. (c-s/7") *(TC+/QUEEN 10) <44372>* **I WANT IT ALL. / HANG ON IN THERE** 3 50
(12"+=/cd-s+=) *(12/CD QUEEN 10)* – ('A'album version).

May 89. (lp/c/cd) *(PCSD/TCPCSD/CDPCSD 107) <92357>* **THE MIRACLE** 1 24
– Party / Khashoggis ship / The miracle / I want it all / The invisible man / Breakthru / Rain must fall / Scandal / Was it all worth it / My baby does me. *(cd+=)* – Hang on in there / Chinese torture / The invisible man (ext). *<US cd-iss. Oct91 on 'Hollywood' ++=; 61134-2>* – Scandal (12"mix).

Jun 89. (c-s/7"/7"sha-pic-d) *(TC+/QUEEN/+PD 11)* **BREAKTHRU. / STEALIN'** 7 –
(12"+=/cd-s+=) *(12/CD QUEEN 11)* – ('A'extended).

Aug 89. (c-s/7"/7"clear) *(TC+/QUEEN/+X 12)* **INVISIBLE MAN. / HIJACK MY HEART** 12 –
(cd-s+=/12"+=/12"clear+=) *(CD/12 QUEEN/+X 12)* – ('A'extended).

Oct 89. (c-s/7") *(TC+/QUEEN 14) <44457>* **SCANDAL. / MY LIFE HAS BEEN SAVED** 25
(12"+=/cd-s+=) *(12/CD QUEEN 14)* – ('A'extended).

Dec 89. (c-s/7") *(TC+/QUEEN 15)* **THE MIRACLE. / STONE COLD CRAZY (live)** 21
(12"+=/cd-s+=) *(12/CD QUEEN 15)* – My melancholy blues (live).

Parlophone Hollywood

Jan 91. (c-s/7") *(TC+/QUEEN 16)* **INNUENDO. / BIJOU** 1
('A'-Explosion mix; cd-s+=12"+=/12"pic-d+=) *(CD/12 QUEEN/+P 16)* – Under pressure (extended).

Feb 91. (cd/c/lp) *(CD/TC+/PCSD 115)* <61020> **INNUENDO** [1] [30]
– Innuendo / I'm going slightly mad / Headlong / I can't live with you / Don't try so hard / Ride the wild wind / All God's people / These are the days of our lives / Delilah / Hit man / Bijou / The show must go on.

Mar 91. (c-s/7"/7"sha-pic-d) *(TC+/QUEEN/+P 17)* **I'M GOING SLIGHTLY MAD. / HIT MAN** [22] [ ]
(12"+=/cd-s+=) *(12/CD QUEEN 17)* – Lost opportunity.

May 91. (c-s/7") *(TC+/QUEEN 18)* **HEADLONG. / ALL GOD'S PEOPLE** [14] [ ]
(cd-s+=/12"+=/12"pic-d+=) *(CD/12 QUEEN/+P 18)* – Mad the swine.

Oct 91. (c-s/7") *(TC+/QUEEN 19)* **THE SHOW MUST GO ON. / KEEP YOURSELF ALIVE** [16] [ ]
(12"+=) *(12QUEEN 19)* – (Queen talks – interview).
(cd-s++=) *(CDQUEEN 19)* – Body language.
(cd-s) – ('A'side) / Now I'm here / Fat bottomed girls / Los Palabras de amor.

Oct 91. (cd/c/d-lp) *(CD/TC+/PMTV 2)* <61311> **GREATEST HITS II** (compilation) (US title 'CLASSIC QUEEN') [1] [4]
– A kind of magic / Under pressure / Radio Ga Ga / I want it all / I want to break free / Innuendo / It's a hard life / Breakthru / Who wants to live forever / Headlong / The miracle / I'm going slightly mad / The invisible man / Hammer to fall / Friends will be friends / The show must go on / One vision. *(hit UK No.29 in May93)* (US-version +=)– Bohemian rhapsody / Stone cold crazy / One year of love / Tie your mother down / These are the days of our lives / Keep yourself alive.

— On the 23rd November 1991, FREDDIE lost his silent 2-year battle against AIDS.

Dec 91. (c-s/12"/cd-s/7") *(TC/12/CD+/QUEEN 20)* <64794> **BOHEMIAN RHAPSODY. / THESE ARE THE DAYS OF OUR LIVES** [1] [2]

Jun 92. (12")(c-s) <64725> **WE WILL ROCK YOU. / WE ARE THE CHAMPIONS** [–] [52]

Jun 92. (d-cd) <CDPCSD 725> <61104> **QUEEN: LIVE AT WEMBLEY 1986 (live; ex-video)** [2] [53]
– One vision / Tie your mother down / In the lap of the gods / Seven seas of rhye / Tear it up / A kind of magic / Under pressure / Another one bites the dust / Who wants to live forever / I want to break free / Impromptu / Brighton rock solo / Now I'm here / Love of my life / Is this the world we created / Baby I don't care / Hello Mary Lou / Tutti frutti / Gimme some lovin' / Bohemian rhapsody / Hammer to fall / Crazy little thing called love / Big spender / Radio ga ga / We will rock you / Friends will be friends / We are the champions / God save the Queen. *(re-iss. Jun03; 591092-2)* (hit UK No.38)

Sep 92. (cd) <61265> **GREATEST HITS** [–] [11]

Apr 93. (c-ep/cd-ep/7"ep; by GEORGE MICHAEL & QUEEN) *(TC/CD+/R 6340)* <61479> **FIVE LIVE EP** [1] album [46]
– Somebody to love / Medley: Killer – Papa was a rollin' stone / These are the days of our lives (with LISA STANSFIELD) / Calling you.
(cd-ep) *(CDRS 6340)* – ('A'side) / Medley: Killer / Papa was a rollin' stone (with PM DAWN).
(12"+=) *(12RS 6340)* – Medley: Killer / Papa was a rollin' stone – instrumental.

— <In the US, the EP's main track 'SOMEBODY TO LOVE', hit No.30; <64647>

— In Feb'95, FREDDIE and BRIAN featured on EDDIE HOWELL's re-issued 1977 single 'THE MAN FROM MANHATTAN'.

Oct 95. (c-s) *(TCQUEEN 21)* **HEAVEN FOR EVERYONE / IT'S A BEAUTIFUL DAY** [2] [ ]
(cd-s+=) *(CDQUEEN 21)* – ('A'-lp version).
(cd-s) *(CDQUEENS 21)* – ('A'side) / Keep yourself alive / Seven seas of rhye / Killer queen.

Nov 95. (cd/c/lp) *(CD/TC+/PCSD 167)* <62017> **MADE IN HEAVEN** [1] [58]
– It's a beautiful day / Made in Heaven / Let me live / Mother love / My life has been saved / I was born to love you / Heaven for everyone / Too much love will kill you / You don't fool me / A winter's tale / It's a beautiful day (reprise) / Yeh / Track 13.

Dec 95. (c-s/7") *(TC+/QUEEN 22)* **A WINTER'S TALE. / THANK GOD IT'S CHRISTMAS** [6] [ ]
(cd-s+=) *(CDQUEEN 22)* – Rock in Rio blues.
(cd-s) *(CDQUEENS 22)* – ('A'side) / Now I'm here / You're my best friend / Somebody to love.

Feb 96. (c-s/7") *(TC+/QUEEN 23)* **TOO MUCH LOVE WILL KILL YOU. / WE WILL ROCK YOU / WE ARE THE CHAMPIONS** [15] [ ]
(cd-s+=) *(CDQUEEN 23)* – Spread your wings.

Jun 96. (c-s/7"pic-d) *(TCQUEEN/QUEENP 24)* **LET ME LIVE. / MY FAIRY KING / DOIN' ALRIGHT / LIAR** [9] [ ]
(cd-s) *(CDQUEEN 24)* – ('A'side) / Fat bottomed girls / Bicycle race / Don't stop me now.

Nov 96. (c-s) *(TCQUEEN 25)* **YOU DON'T FOOL ME / ('A'remix)** [17] [–]
(12") *(12QUEEN 25)* – ('A'-Freddie's club + revenge mixes).
(cd-s+=) *(CDQUEEN 25)* – ('A'-Dancing Divas mix) / ('A'-sexy club mix).

Nov 97. (cd/c/d-lp) *(823091-2/-4/-1)* <162132> **QUEEN ROCKS** [7] [ ]
– No-one but you / We will rock you / Tie your mother down / Seven seas of rhye / I can't live with you / Hammer to fall / Stone cold crazy / Fat bottomed girls / Keep yourself alive / Tear it up / One vision / Killer queen / Sheer heart attack / I'm in love with my car / Put out the fire / Headlong / It's late / I want it all. *<US-title 'ROCKS VOL.1' diff tracks; 162132>*

Jan 98. (c-s) *(TCQUEEN 27)* **NO-ONE BUT YOU / TIE YOUR MOTHER DOWN** [13] [ ]
(12"+=/cd-s+=) *(QUEENPD/CDQUEEN 27)* – We will rock you (mix) / Gimme the prize (mix).

Nov 98. (c-s; by QUEEN / WYCLEF JEAN featuring PRAS MICHEL & FREE) *(DRMC 22364)* **ANOTHER ONE BITES THE DUST / (mix)** [5] [ ]
(12"+=/cd-s+=) *(DRM T/CD 22364)* – (Wyclef Jean remix) / (Black Rock Star remix).
(above from the movie, 'Small Soldiers', released on 'Dreamworks')

Nov 99. (cd/c/d-lp) *(523452-2/-4/-1)* <162250> **GREATEST HITS III** (hits/collaborations & solo material) [5] [ ]
– The show must go on / Under pressure / Barcelona / Too much love / Somebody to love / You don't fool me / Heaven for everyone / Las palabras / Driven by you / Living on my own / Let me live / The great pretender / Princess of the universe / Another one bites the dust / No one but you / These are the days of our lives / Thank God it's Christmas.

Dec 99. (7"pic-d; QUEEN & DAVID BOWIE) *(QUEENPD 28)* **UNDER PRESSURE. / BOHEMIAN RHAPSODY** [14] [ ]
(c-s+=/cd-s+=) *(TC/CD QUEEN 28)* – Thank God it's Christmas.
(cd-s) *(CDQUEENS 28)* – ('A'mixes).

— In Jul'00, QUEEN were back at No.1 collaborating with pop group FIVE on a rendition of 'WE WILL ROCK YOU'

Nov 00. (3xcd) *(<529883-2>)* **GREATEST HITS I II & III: THE PLATINUM COLLECTION** [2] Sep01 [48]
in Mar'03, QUEEN & VANGUARD went Uk Top 20 with 'FLASH'

Aug 04. (cd) *<162465-2>* **GREATEST HITS: WE WILL ROCK YOU** [–] [42]

Oct 04. (cd) *(683211-2)* **QUEEN ON FIRE – LIVE AT THE BOWL** (live) [20] [–]

— added **PAUL RODGERS** – vocals (ex-FREE, ex-BAD COMPANY, ex-Solo)

Sep 05. (d-cd; QUEEN + PAUL RODGERS) *(336979-2)* *<62526-2>* **RETURN OF THE CHAMPIONS** (live) [12] [84]
– Reaching out / Tie your mother down / I want to break free / Fat bottomed girls / Wishing well / Another one bites the dust / Crazy little thing called love / Say it's not true / '39 / Love of my life / Hammer to fall / Feel like makin' love / Let there be drums / I'm in love with my car / Guitar solo / Last horizon / These are the days of our lives / Radio Ga Ga / Can't get enough / A kind of magic / I want it all / Bohemian rahpsody / The show must go on / All right now / We will rock you / We are the champions / God save the Queen.

– more compilations, etc. –

on 'EMI'UK / 'Capitol'US, unless otherwise mentioned.

Dec 85. (14xlp-box) *(QB 1)* **THE COMPLETE WORKS** [ ] [ ]

Nov 88. (3"cd-ep) *(QUECD 1)* **SEVEN SEAS OF RHYE / SEE WHAT A FOOL I'VE BEEN / FUNNY HOW LOVE IS** [ ] [–]

Nov 88. (3"cd-ep) *(QUECD 2)* **KILLER QUEEN / FLICK OF THE WRIST / BRIGHTON ROCK** [ ] [–]

Nov 88. (3"cd-ep) *(QUECD 3)* **BOHEMIAN RHAPSODY / I'M IN LOVE WITH MY CAR / YOU'RE MY BEST FRIEND** [ ] [–]

Nov 88. (3"cd-ep) *(QUECD 4)* **SOMEBODY TO LOVE / WHITE MAN / TIE YOUR MOTHER DOWN** [ ] [–]

Nov 88. (3"cd-ep) *(QUECD 5)* **GOOD OLD FASHIONED LOVER BOY / DEATH ON TWO LEGS (DEDICATED TO . . .) / TENEMENT FUNSTER / WHITE QUEEN (AS IT BEGAN)** [ ] [–]

Nov 88. (3"cd-ep) *(QUECD 6)* **WE ARE THE CHAMPIONS / WE WILL ROCK YOU / FAT BOTTOMED GIRLS** [ ] [–]

Nov 88. (3"cd-ep) *(QUECD 7)* **CRAZY LITTLE THING CALLED LOVE / SPREAD YOUR WINGS / FLASH** [ ] [–]

Nov 88. (3"cd-ep) *(QUECD 8)* **ANOTHER ONE BITES THE DUST / DRAGON ATTACK / LAS PALABRAS DE AMOR** [ ] [–]
Nov 88. (3"cd-ep) *(QUECD 9)* **UNDER PRESSURE / SOUL BROTHER / BODY LANGUAGE** [ ] [–]
Nov 88. (3"cd-ep) *(QUECD 10)* **RADIO GA GA / I GO CRAZY / HAMMER TO FALL** [ ] [–]
Nov 88. (3"cd-ep) *(QUECD 11)* **I WANT TO BREAK FREE / MACHINES (OR BACK TO HUMANS) / IT'S A HARD LIFE** [ ] [–]
Nov 88. (3"cd-ep) *(QUECD 12)* **A KIND OF MAGIC / A DOZEN RED ROSES FOR MY DARLING / ONE VISION** [ ] [–]
Dec 89. (lp/c/cd) *Band Of Joy; (BOJ LP/MC/CD 001)* **QUEEN AT THE BEEB (live)** [67] [–]
Oct 94. (d-cd/d-c) *Parlophone; (CD/TC PCSD 161)* **GREATEST HITS 1 & 2** [37] [ ]
Dec 95. (20xcd-box) *E.M.I.; (QUEENBOX 20)* **ULTIMATE QUEEN** [ ] [ ]
Apr 06. (cd) *()* *<6206-2>* **STONE COLD CLASSICS** [ ] [45]

FREDDIE MERCURY

C.B.S. Columbia

Sep 84. (7"/7"pic-d/ext.12") *(A/WA/TA 4375)* *<04606>* **LOVE KILLS. / (other by Giorgio Moroder)** [10] [69]
(above from the re-score for the film 'Metropolis')
Apr 85. (7"/ext.12") *(A/TA 6019)* *<04869>* **I WAS BORN TO LOVE YOU. / STOP ALL THE FIGHTING** [11] [76]
(d7"+=) *(DA 6019)* – Love kills (extended) / Stop all the fighting (extended).
May 85. (lp/c/cd) *(CBS/+40/CD 86312)* *<40071>* **MR. BAD GUY** [6] [ ]
– Let's turn it on * / Made in Heaven / I was born to love you * / Foolin' around / Mr. Bad guy / Man made Paradise / There must be more to life than this / Living on my own * / Your kind of lover / My love is dangerous / Love me like there's no tomorrow. *(c+cd+=)* – (* extended tracks).
Jul 85. (7"/7"sha-pic-d) *(A/WA 6413)* **MADE IN HEAVEN (remix). / SHE BLOWS HOT AND COLD** [57] [–]
(ext.12"+=) *(TA 6413)* – ('A'extended).
Sep 85. (7"/12"/12"g-f) *(A/TA/GA 6555)* *<05455>* **LIVING ON MY OWN. / MY LOVE IS DANGEROUS** [50] [–]
Oct 85. (7") **LIVING ON MY OWN. / SHE BLOWS HOT AND COLD** [–] [ ]
Nov 85. (7"/ext.12") *(A/TA 6725)* **LOVE ME LIKE THERE IS NO TOMORROW. / LET'S TURN IT ON** [ ] [–]
(below from Dave Clark musical 'Time')

E.M.I. not iss.

May 86. (7"/ext.12") *(EMI/+12 5559)* **TIME. / TIME (instrumental)** [ ] [–]

Parlophone Capitol

Feb 87. (7"/7"sha-pic-d) *(R/RP 6151)* *<5696>* **THE GREAT PRETENDER. / EXERCISES IN FREE LOVE** [4] [ ]
(12"+=) *(12R 6151)* – ('A'extended).

FREDDIE MERCURY with MONTSERRAT CABALLE

— (with female Spanish opera star)

Polydor Hollywood

Oct 87. (7") *(POSP 887)* **BARCELONA. / EXERCISES IN FREE LOVE** (her version) [8] [ ]
(c-s+=/12"+=/12"pic-d+=/cd-s+=) *(POSP C/X/P/CD 887)* – ('A'extended).
Oct 88. (lp/c)(cd) *(POLH/+C 44)(<837277-2>)* **BARCELONA** [25] [ ]
– Barcelona / La Japonaise / The fallen priest / Ensueno / The golden boy / Guide me home / How can I go on / Overture piccante. *(re-iss. Aug92, hit UK No.15)*
Oct 88. (7") *(POSP 23)* **THE GOLDEN BOY. / THE FALLEN PRIEST** [ ] [ ]
(12"+=)(cd-s+=) *(POSPX 23)(PZ 23CD)* – ('A'instrumental).
Jan 89. (7"/7"pic-d) *(POSP/POSX 29)* **HOW CAN I GO ON. / OVERTURE PICCANTE** [ ] [ ]
(12"+=)(cd-s+=) *(POSPX 29)(PZ 29CD)* – Guide me home.
(below were posthumous releases)
Jul 92. (7"/c-s/cd-s) *(PO/+CS/CD 221)* **BARCELONA. / EXCERCISES IN FREE LOVE** [2] [ ]
(12"+=) *(P 221)* – ('A'extended).
Oct 92. (7"/c-s) **HOW CAN I GO ON. / THE GOLDEN BOY** [ ] [ ]
(cd-s+=) – The fallen priest.
(12"+=/cd-s+=) – Guide me home / Overture piccante.

Parlophone not iss.

Nov 92. (cd/c/lp) *(CD/TC+/PCSD 124)* **THE FREDDIE MERCURY ALBUM** (compilation) [4] [–]
– The great pretender / Foolin' around / Time / Your kind of love / Exercises in free love / In my defence / Mr. Bad guy / Let's turn it on / Living on my own / Love kills / Barcelona (w / MONSERRAT CABALLE).
Dec 92. (c-s/7") *(TC+/R 6331)* **IN MY DEFENCE. / LOVE KILLS (original)** [8] [–]
(cd-s+=) *(CDR 6331)* – Mr. Bad guy / Living on my own (mix).
Jan 93. (c-s/7") *(TC+/R 6336)* **THE GREAT PRETENDER. / STOP ALL THE FIGHTING** [29] [–]
(cd-s+=) *(CDR 6336)* – Exercises in free love / ('A'-Malouf mix).
Jul 93. (c-s/7") *(TC+/R 6355)* **LIVING ON MY OWN. / ('A'mix)** [1] [–]
(12"+=/cd-s+=) *(12R/CDR 6355)* – ('A'mixes).

– compilations, etc. –

Oct 00. (3xcd-box) *Parlophone; (528047-2)* **SOLO** [13] [–]
– (MR. BAD GUY / BARCELONA / bonus)
Oct 00. (9xcd-box) *Parlophone; (527964-0)* **THE SOLO COLLECTION** [ ] [–]
— **JOHN DEACON** played bass on The IMMORTALS May'86 'M.C.A.' single 'NO TURNING BACK', from the film 'Biggles'.

BRIAN MAY

— with **EDDIE VAN HALEN** – guitar / **PHIL CHEN** – bass / **FRED MANDEL** – keyboards / **ALAN GRATZER** – drums etc.

E.M.I. Capitol

Oct 83. (7"; as BRIAN MAY & FRIENDS) *(EMI 5436)* **STARFLEET. / SON OF STARFLEET** [65] [–]
Oct 83. (7"; as BRIAN MAY & FRIENDS) *<B-5278>* **STARFLEET. / STARFLEET (extended)** [–] [ ]
Oct 83. (m-lp/c; as BRIAN MAY & FRIENDS) *(SFLT 107806-1/-4)* *<15014>* **STARFLEET PROJECT** [35] [ ]
– Starfleet / Let me out / Bluesbreakers.
— In the Autumn of'89, BRIAN MAY wrote the song 'WHO WANTS TO LIVE FOREVER' and gave it to charity for single by youngsters IAN MEESON & BELINDA GHILETT; 'EMI' 7"/12"*(ODO/12ODO 112)*

Parlophone Hollywood

Nov 91. (7"/c-s) *(R/TCR 6304)* **DRIVEN BY YOU. / JUST ONE LIFE (dedicated to the memory of Philip Sayer)** [6] [–]
(b-guitar version; 12"+=/cd-s+=) *(12R/CDR 6034)* – Driven by you (Ford Ad version).
Sep 92. (7"/c-s) *(R/TCR 6320)* **TOO MUCH LOVE WILL KILL YOU. / I'M SCARED** [5] [–]
(cd-s+=/s-cd-s+=) *(CDR/+S 6320)* – Driven by you (feat. COZY POWELL + NEIL MURRAY).
Oct 92. (cd/c/lp) *(CD/C+/PCSD 123)* *<61404>* **BACK TO THE LIGHT** [6] [ ]
– The dark / Back to the light / Love token / Resurrection / Too much love will kill you / Driven by you / Nothin' but blue / I'm scared / Last horizon / Let your heart rule your head / Just one life / Rollin' over. *(re-iss. Jun93 in gold-cd; CDPCSDX 123)*
— In Oct'92, BRIAN featured on HANK MARVIN's (Shadows) version of QUEEN's song 'WE ARE THE CHAMPIONS'.
Nov 92. (7"/c-s) *(R/TCR 6329)* **BACK TO THE LIGHT. / NOTHING BUT BLUE (guitar version)** [19] [–]
(B-guitar cd-s+=) *(CDR 6329)* – Blues breaker.
(cd-s) *(CDRX 6329)* – ('A'side) / Star fleet / Let me out.

Parlophone Elektra

Apr 93. (c-s) *<64642>* **DRIVEN BY YOU** [–] [ ]
Jun 93. (c-s; by BRIAN MAY with COZY POWELL) *(TCR 6351)* **RESURRECTION / LOVE TOKEN** [23] [–]
(12"pic-d+=/cd-s+=) *(12RPF/CDRS 6351)* – Too much love will kill you (live).
(cd-s) *(CDR 6351)* – ('A'side) / Driven by you (two) / Back to the light (live) / Tie your mother down (live).
Dec 93. (7"/c-s) *(R/TCR 6371)* **LAST HORIZON. / LET YOUR HEART RULE YOUR HEAD** [51] [–]
(cd-s/s-cd-s) *(CDR/+S 6371)* – ('A'side) / ('A'live) / We will rock you (live) / ('A'album mix).

— **MAY** – vox, guitar with **COZY POWELL** – drums / **NEIL MURRAY** – bass / **SPIKE EDNEY** – keyboards / **JAMIE MOSES** – guitar, vocals / **CATHY PORTER** + **SHELLEY PRESTON** – vox

Feb 94. (cd/c/d-lp; by BRIAN MAY BAND) *(CD/C+/PCSD 150)* **LIVE AT THE BRIXTON ACADEMY (live London, 15th June 1993)** 20 –
– Back to the light / Driven by you / Tie your mother down / Love token / Headlong / Love of my life / '39 – Let your heart rule your head / Too much love will kill you / Since you've been gone / Now I'm here / Guitar extravagance / Resurrection / Last horizon / We will rock you / Hammer to fall.

May 98. (7") *(R 6498)* **THE BUSINESS (Rock On Cozy mix). / MAYBE BABY** 51 –
(cd-s+=) *(CDR 6498)* – (Brian talks) / ('A'-CD-Rom video).

Jun 98. (cd/c/lp) *(494973-2/-4/-1)* <162103> **ANOTHER WORLD** 23
– Space / The business / China belle / Why don't we try again / On my way up / Cyborg / Guv'nor / Wilderness / Slow down / One rainy wish / All the way from Memphis / Another world.

Aug 98. (c-s/cd-s) *(TCR/CDR 6504)* **WHY DON'T WE TRY AGAIN / ONLY MAKE BELIEVE / F.B.I.** 44 –
Liberty not iss.

Nov 00. (cd) *(5 28585-2)* **FURIA** (soundtrack) –
– Furia theme – Opening titles / First glance (solo flute) / Landscape / Tango: 'Cuesta abajo' (MANUEL CEDRON) / The meeting (solo guitar) / First kiss / Storm / Phone / Pursuit / Diner / Apparition / Arrest / Father and son / Aaron / Fire / Gun (solo violin) / Reggae: 'Bird in hand' (LEE 'SCRATCH' PERRY) / Killing / Escape / Go on / Dream of thee / Alternative gun. *(re-iss. Jan03 on 'E.M.I.' France; 528321-2)*

– (MAY) compilations, etc. –

Nov 95. (cd) *Javelin; (HADCD 190)* **THEMES AND DREAMS** –
Dec 95. (cd-s) *Koch; (34337-2)* **BLACK WHITE HOUSE** –

— with APPICE (veteran drummer) + SLASH (of Guns N' Roses)

Feb 96. (cd-s; by BRIAN MAY with CARMINE APPICE'S GUITAR ZEUS) **NOBODY KNEW (BLACK WHITE HOUSE) / NOBODY KNEW (BLACK WHITE HOUSE) (long version)** –

QUEENS OF THE STONE AGE

Formed: Palm Springs, California, USA . . . 1991 as KYUSS by JOHN GARCIA, JOSH HOMME, SCOTT REEDER and ALFREDO HERNANDEZ. Initially playing bluesy punk, the group's rather lacklustre debut, 'WRETCH', was followed up by the blinding intensity of 'BLUES FOR THE RED SUN' (1992). Seemingly coming from out of nowhere, it had taken MASTERS OF REALITY retro guru CHRIS GOSS to develop the band's latent genius. A smouldering slab of frazzled flare-rock, the band had dragged garage-psych stoned and stumbling into the 90's, carving a new benchmark for would-be sonic archivists. Live, most commentators were in agreement that KYUSS were peerless, the group soon finding themsleves playing on the same bill as the likes of DANZIG and METALLICA. 'Elektra' were sufficiently impressed to offer the band a deal when their label went belly-up, KYUSS once again working with GOSS on the fuzzed-up bludgeon of 'WELCOME TO SKY VALLEY' (1994). Despite the critical raving, the group's label were unsure how to market their hippy-rock sound with the result that KYUSS' record sales were less than impressive. So it was then, that after a final masterpiece, 'AND THE CIRCUS LEAVES TOWN' (1995), the group decided to call it a day. The fact that KYUSS were just obviously beginning to reach their full potential was illustrated with the 'QUEENS OF THE STONE AGE' (1997) set. A combination of unreleased KYUSS material and a clutch of new, even more mind-altering tracks from HOMME's similarly titled new outfit (also numbering GOSS, VAN CONNER and VIC THE STICK), the album was a disorientatingly heavy testament (including a suitably trippy cover of Black Sabbath's 'INTO THE VOID') to one of the most criminally ignored bands of the 90's. Meanwhile, KYUSS' former frontman, GARCIA, was making his name with a new outfit, UNIDA. QUEENS OF THE STONE AGE carried the KYUSS flag into the new millennium courtesy of a new major label deal with 'Interscope' and the highly acclaimed 'RATED R' (2000) album. A record that featured highly in many end of year polls and finally saw HOMME, OLIVERI and Co gain the popular rock god homages that their music had always begged, 'RATED R' started as it meant to go on with 'FEEL GOOD HIT OF THE SUMMER' gratuitously reeling off a list of narcotics ad nauseam. While markedly more hallucinogenically swinging than its predecessor with more elaborate instrumentation and arrangements, the California stoners proved their desert-grunge could still scorch at a hundred paces on the likes of the demented 'TENSION HEAD'. 'LEG OF LAMB', meanwhile, recalled MASTERS OF REALITY at their trippy best. QOTSA returned in the summer of 2002 to issue their much anticipated follow-up to 'RATED R', but this time with MARK LANEGAN on full-time guitar duties and ex-NIRVANA and FOO FIGHTERS frontman DAVE GROHL on drumming duties. 'SONGS FOR THE DEAF' was all the better for it, and although the band weren't necessarily moving in new circles, their music was still punctuated with the same jaded desert rock vibe that had made those early KYUSS albums so enjoyable. GROHL, hammering away like a madman, reminded people of how good he still was on the drums and DEAN WEEN cranked up the tension even higher with his impeccable guitar playing. Meanwhile HOMME and OLIVERI began working on the soundtrack to the film 'Dangerous Lives Of Altar Boys' and dabbled in a brand new project – HEADBAND – with ex-MARILYN MANSON bassist TWIGGY RAMIREZ and CASEY CHAOS from heavy rockers AMEN. To add to HOMME's vast and varied canon was The DESERT SESSIONS, a side project born from the ashes of KYUSS' "generator parties". Including all that was cool in the LA rock scene, The DESERT SESSIONS played out like the Robert Altman of rock, enlisting everybody from PJ HARVEY to TWIGGY RAMIREZ. Their first releases were issued in an approximate one year period (1998-99) via whopping six volumes on the alternative label 'Man's Ruin'. However, the best of the bunch was collected by the 'Southern Lord' imprint who delivered 'VOL. 7-8' in 2001, featuring the insane desert-stomp 'UP IN HELL', not to mention collaborations by BEN SHEPARD (of SOUNDGARDEN), JOHN McBAIN (MONSTER MAGNET), BRANT BJORK (KYUSS), CHRIS GOSS (MASTERS OF REALITY) and QUEENS regular MARK LANEGAN to name but a few. 'VOL. 9 & 10' were released in 2003 and featured guests DEAN WEEN (WEEN), JOEY CASTILLO (DANZIG) and NATASHA SCHNIEDER (ELEVEN) as well as a ballad with PJ HARVEY 'CRAWL HOME' (which hit the Top 40 in the UK). As confusing as the KYUSS and QOTSA output may be (see below for further and more rigorous inspection), it is hard to ignore their diverse and varied musical ambitions especially with tracks as brilliant as 'HANGING TREE' and 'AVON'; they also made it onto the 'SONGS FOR THE DEAF' set. Prior to the release of 'LULLABIES TO PARALYZE', all the talk was of OLIVERI's departure and how it was going to affect the QUEENS' sound. When the album finally arrived in spring 2005, the overwhelming concensus was that HOMME was more than capable of howling down the wind on his own. Accurately titled, 'LULLABIES..' was at odds with almost every single rock album that charted that year (and there weren't that many that managed transatlantic Top 5): aural ether for the decadent of heart, blues for a dethroned desert magus. No one outside of MASTERS OF REALITY have disseminated those dark-siren melodies as alluringly as HOMME does on 'BURN THE WITCH' (abetted by BILLY GIBBONS no less). 'OVER THE YEARS AND THROUGH THE WOODS' (2005) was their requisite contribution to the CD/DVD double-pack fad, but QOTSA fans had more interesting extra-curricular fare on offer from EAGLES OF DEATH METAL, a tongue-in-cheek side project from HOMME (aka CARLO VON SEXRON) and falsetto-firing sidekick JESSE HUGHES. Formed in 1998, the EAGLES made their debut on Vols 3 and 4 of the 'DESERT SESSIONS', finally releasing debut album, 'PEACE LOVE DEATH METAL', in spring 2004. Its solo cover, Stealers Wheel's 'STUCK IN THE MIDDLE WITH YOU', was a hint at the record's looser, more humorous and gratuitously degenerate – if no less (ironically) 70s fixated – vibe, to which HOMME made his unlikely debut on the drum stool. 'DEATH BY SEXY' (2006) was even more lascivious, welcoming to the party JACK BLACK, MARK LANEGAN and onetime DANZIG drummer JOEY CASTILLO amongst others.

• **Covered:** EVERYBODY'S GONNA BE HAPPY + WHO'LL BE THE NEXT IN LINE (Kinks) / NEVER SAY NEVER (Romeo Void) / THE MOST EXALTED POTENTATE OF LOVE (Cramps). Desert Sessions covered: ECCENTRIC MAN (Groundhogs).

Album rating: Kyuss: WRETCH (*7) / BLUES FOR THE RED SUN (*9) / WELCOME TO SKY VALLEY (*8) / . . .AND THE CIRCUS LEAVES TOWN (*8) / QUEENS OF THE STONE AGE (*8) / MUCHAS GRACIAS compilation (*8) / Queens Of The Stone Age: QUEENS OF THE STONE AGE (*8) / RATED R (*9) / SONGS FOR THE DEAF (*8) / LULLABIES TO PARALYZE (*8) / OVER THE YEARS AND THROUGH THE WOODS compilation dvd/cd (*7) / Desert Sessions: VOL.I/II (*7) / VOL.III/IV (*6) / VOL.V/VI (*6) / 7 & 8 (*7) / 9 & 10 (*7) / Eagles Of Death Metal: PEACE LOVE DEATH METAL (*6) / DEATH BY SEXY . . . (*7)

KYUSS

JOHN GARCIA – vocals / **JOSH HOMME** (b. 1973) – guitar / **SCOTT REEDER** – bass; repl. NICK OLIVERI (b. 1971) who joined the DWARVES / **ALFREDO HERNANDEZ** (b. 1966) – drums

Dali-Chameleon Dali-Chameleon

Nov 91. (cd) *<61256-2>* **WRETCH** [–] [ ]
– HWY 74 (beginning of what's about to happen) / Love has passed me by / Son of a bitch / Black widow / Katzenjammer / Deadly kiss / The law / Isolation / I'm not / Big bikes / Stage III. *(UK-iss.Feb98; same as US)*

Feb 93. (cd/c) *<(3705 61340-2/-4)>* **BLUES FOR THE RED SUN** [ ] [ ]
– Thumb / Green machine / Molten universe / 50 million years trip / (Downside up) / Thong song / Apothecaries' weight / Catepillar march / Freedom run / 800 / Writhe / Capsized. *(cd+=)* – Allen's wrench / Mondo generator / Yeah.

Elektra Warners

Jun 94. (cd/c/lp) *<(7559 61571-2/-4/-1)>* **WELCOME TO SKY VALLEY** [ ] [ ]
– I / Gardenia / Asteroid / Supa scoopa and mighty scoop / II / 100 degrees / Space cadet / Demon cleaner / III / Odyssey / Conan troutman / N.O. / Whitewater. *(lp-iss.Nov99 on 'White & Black'; WB 7524)*

Sep 94. (7"blue) *(EKR 192)* **DEMON CLEANER. / FREEDOM RUN (live)** [ ] [ ]
(cd-s) *(EKR 192CD1)* – ('A'side) / Day one (to Dave & Chris) / El rodeo / Hurricane.
(cd-s) *(EKR 192CD2)* – ('A'side) / Gardenia (live) / Thumb (live) / Conan trout man (live).

Feb 95. (cd-s) *(EKR 197CD)* **GARDENIA / U.N. SANDPIPER / CONAN TROUT MAN (live)** [ ] [ ]

Jun 95. (cd/c) *<(7559 61811-2/-4)>* **. . .AND THE CIRCUS LEAVES TOWN** [ ] [ ]
– Hurricane / One inch man / Thee of boozeroony / Gloria Lewis / Phototropic / El rodeo / Jumbo blimp jumbo / Tango zizzle / Size queen / Catamarran / Spaceship landing.

— split in 1995 leaving some recordings below. HOMME formed QUEENS OF THE STONE AGE, which was released by below label as KYUSS' epitaph album. He was joined by **VAN CONNER** – bass (SCREAMING TREES) / **CHRIS GOSS** (MASTER OF REALITY) / **VIC THE STICK** – drums

Mans Ruin Mans Ruin

Jul 97. (10") *(MR 015)* **INTO THE VOID. / FATSO FORGETSO** [ ] [ ]

Dec 97. (cd) *<(MR 063)>* **QUEENS OF THE STONE AGE** [ ] [ ]
– KYUSS: Into the void / Fatso forgotso / Fatso Forgotso phase II / QUEENS OF THE STONE AGE: If only everything / Born to hula / Spiders and vinegaroons. *(re-iss. Aug00; same)*

QUEENS OF THE STONE AGE

— **JOSH HOMME** – vocals, guitar / **NICK OLIVERI** – bass / **ALFREDO HERNANDEZ** – drums

Mans Ruin Mans Ruin

Jan 96. (7"; as GAMMA RAY) *<MR 036>* **GAMMA RAY. / IF ONLY EVERYTHING / BORN TO HULA** [–] [ ]

Sep 98. (10"ep/cd-ep) *<(MR 141/+CD)>* **QUEENS OF THE STONE AGE / BEAVER EP** [ ] [ ]
– The bronze / These aren't the droids you're looking for / BEAVER: Absence without leave / Morocco.

Roadrunner Mans Rui

Oct 98. (cd) *(RR 8674-2)* *<MR 151CD>* **QUEENS OF THE STONE AGE** [ ] [ ]
– Regular John / Avon / If only / Walkin' on the sidewalks / You would know / How to handle a rope / Mexicola / Hispanic impressions / You can't quit me baby / Give the mule what he wants / I was a teenage hand model.

— added **DAVE CATCHING** – guitar, steel guitar, piano / **NICKY LUCERO** – drums

Interscope Interscop

Jun 00. (cd) *<(490683-2)>* **RATED R** [54] [ ]
– Feel good hit of the summer / The lost art of keeping a secret / Leg of lamb / Auto pilot / Better living through chemistry / Monsters in the parasol / Quick and to the pointless / In the fade / Tension head / Lightning song / I think I lost my headache. *(lp-iss.Nov00+=; 490864-1)* – Ode to Clarissa. *(cd re-iss. Nov00 w/ free cd+=; same)* – FEEL GOOD HIT OF THE SUMMER EP

Aug 00. (7") *<(497387-7)>* **THE LOST ART OF KEEPING A SECRET. / ODE TO CLARISSA** [31] [ ]
(cd-s+=) *<(497392-2)>* – Monsters in the parasol (live).
(cd-s) *<(497391-2)>* – ('A'side) / Born to hula / ('A'-CD-Rom).

Nov 00. (cd-ep) *(497455-2)* *<497443-2>* **FEEL GOOD HIT OF THE SUMMER EP** [ ] [–]
– Feel good hit of the summer / Never say never / You're so vague / Who'll be the next in line / Feel good hit of the summer (CD-ROM video).

— **OLIVERI** + **HOMME** recruited **DAVE GROHL** – drums (of FOO FIGHTER) / **MARK LANEGAN** – vocals (ex-SCREAMING TREES) / **DEAN WEEN** – guitar (of WEEN)

Aug 02. (cd) *<(493435-2)>* **SONGS FOR THE DEAF** [4] [17]
– You think I ain't worth a dollar, but I feel like a millionaire / No one knows / First it giveth / A song for the deaf / The sky is fallin' / Six shooter / Hangin' tree / Go with the flow / Gonna leave you / Do it again / God is on the radio / Another love song / A song for the deaf. *(UK+=)* – Mosquito song *[hidden US]* / The lost art of keeping a secret (live) / Everybody's gonna be happy. *(cd w/dvd+=; 493444-0) (d-lp-iss.Sep02; 439435-1)*

Nov 02. (7"colrd) *(497812-7)* *<radio>* **NO ONE KNOWS. / TENSION HEAD (live)** [15] [51]
(cd-s+=) *(497812-2)* – Gonna leave you (Spanish version).
(cd-s) *(497808-2)* – ('A'side) / A song for the deaf (live) / Avon (live) / ('A'video).

Apr 03. (12"clear) *(497869-0)* **GO WITH THE FLOW. / NO ONE KNOWS (Unkle reconstruction)** [21] [–]
(cd-s+=) *(497869-2)* – Hanging tree (live) / ('A'-video).
(cd-s) *(497870-2)* – ('A'side) / Regular John (live) / Do it again (live).

Aug 03. (7"red) *(9810506)* **FIRST IT GIVETH. / THE MOST EXALTED POTENTATE OF LOVE** [33] [–]
(cd-s+=) *(9810505)* – A song for the deaf (the blind can goes get fucked remix) / ('A'-video).
(cd-s) *(9810507)* – ('A'side) / Wake up screaming / You think I ain't worth a dollar, but I feel like a millionaire (Troy mix).

Mar 05. (7"pic-d) *(9880671)* **LITTLE SISTER. / (Contradiktator remix)** [18] [88]
(cd-s+=) *(9880670)* – The blood is love (Contradiktator remix).
(dvd-s) *(9880672)* – ('A'-video) / ('A'-montage) / (Lullabies To Paralyze snippets).

Mar 05. (cd) *(9880297)* *<41860-2>* **LULLABIES TO PARALYZE** [4] [5]
– This lullaby / Medication / Everybody knows that you are insane / Tangled up in plaid / Burn the witch / In my head / Little sister / I never came / Someone's in the wolf / The blood is love / Skin on skin / Broken box / You got a killer scene / Long slow goodbye. *(UK+=)* – Like a

drug / Precious and grace. *(ltd-cd w/dvd+=; 9880313)* – (studio, videos & interview).

Jul 05. (7"pic-d) *(9883542)* **IN MY HEAD. / I THINK I LOST MY HEADACHE (live)** [44] [–]
(cd-s+=) *(9883541)* – God is on the radio (live) / ('A'-video).

Nov 05. (dvd/+cd) *(9887615)* *<5718>* **OVER THE YEARS AND THROUGH THE WOODS** (compilation) [ ] [ ]
– (DVD tracks) // Go with the flow / Regular john / Monsters in the parasol / Tangled up in plaid / Little sister / You can't quit me, baby / I wanna make it wit chu / Leg of lamb / I think I lost my headache / Mexicola / Burn the witch / Song for the deaf / No one knows / Long slow goodbye.

Jan 06. (7"pic-d) *(9879191)* **BURN THE WITCH. / BROKEN BOX (fixed the box remix by Peaches)** [–] non-ch [–]
(cd-s) *(9879554)* – ('A') / No one knows (live) / I wanna make it wit chu (live) / Monsters in the parasol (live) / ('A'-Unkle remix) / ('A'-video).

– KYUSS compilation –

Oct 00. (cd) *Elektra;* *<(7559 62571-2)>* **MUCHAS GRACIAS – THE BEST OF KYUSS** [ ] [ ]
– U.N. sandpiper / Shine / 50 million year trip (downside up) / Mudfly / Demon cleaner / A day early and a dollar extra / I'm not / Hurricane / Flip the phrase / Fatso forgotso / El rodeo / Gardenia (live) / Thumb (live) / Conan Troutman (live) / Freedom run (live).

DESERT SESSIONS

JOSH HOMME with **PETER STAHL** – vocals (ex-WOOL, of EARTHLINGS) / **FRED DRAKE** – guitar (of EARTHLINGS) / **DAVE CATCHINGS** – bass (of EARTHLINGS) / **BEN SHEPHERD** – bass (ex-SOUNDGARDEN, of WELLWATER CONSPIRACY) / **ALFREDO HERNANDEZ** – drums

not iss. Man's Ruin

Nov 97. (d10"lp) *<MR 81>* **VOL.1: INSTRUMENTAL DRIVING MUSIC FOR FELONS** [–] [ ]
– Girl boy Tom / Monkey in the middle / Cowards way out / Robotic lunch.

— added **BRANT BJORK** – percussion, drums (of FU MANCHU) / **JOHN McBAIN** (WELLWATER CONSPIRACY)

Feb 98. (d10"lp/cd) *<MR 82>* **VOL.II: STATUS, SHIPS COMMANDER BUTCHERED** [–] [ ]
– Johnny the boy / Screamin' eagle / Cake (who shit on the?). *<cd+=>* – VOL.1

May 98. (d10"lp) *<MR 111>* **VOL.III: SET CO-ORDINATES FOR THE WHITE DWARF!!!** [–] [ ]
– Nova / At the helm of Hell's ships / Avon / Sugar rush.

— **HOMME + HERNANDEZ + NICK OLIVERI** recruited **CHRIS GOSS** – vocals (of MASTERS OF REALITY) / **MARIO LALLI** – guitar (of FATSO JETSON) / **TONY TONRAY** – drums (of FATSO JETSON) / **LARRY LALLI** – bass / **T. FRESH** – turntables / etc.

Sep 98. (lp/cd) *<MR 112>* **VOL.IV: HARD WALLS AND LITTLE TRIPS** [–] [ ]
– The gosso king of Crater Lake / Monster in the parasol / Jr. high love / Eccentric man / Hohleg. *<cd+=>* – VOL.III

Sep 99. (lp) *<MR 121>* **VOL.V: POETRY FOR THE MASSES** [–] [ ]
– You think I ain't worth a dollar, but I . . .. / Punk rock caveman living in a prehistoric . . .. / Going to a hanging / Letters to mommy / The day I die.

Sep 99. (lp/cd) *<MR 122/123>* **VOL.VI: POETRY FOR THE MASSES** [–] [ ]
– A #1 / Like a drug / Take me to your leader / Teens of Thailand / Rickshaw / Like a drug (instrumental). *<cd+=>* – VOL.V

— **HOMME** with **MARK LANEGAN, CHRIS GOSS, ALAIN JOHANNES, BRENDON McNICHOL, FRED DRAKE + SAMANTHA MALONEY**

not iss. Southern Lord

Oct 01. (cd; as JOSH HOMME & FRIENDS) *<12>* **DESERT SESSIONS 7 & 8** [–] [ ]
– Don't drink poison / Hanging tree / Winners / Polly wants a crack rock / Up in Hell / Nenada / The idiots guide / Interpretive reading / Covousier / Cold sore super stars / Making a cross. *<hidden tracks+=>* – Ending / Piano bench breaks.

— with **PJ HARVEY, JOSH FREESE, TWIGGY RAMIREZ, TROY VAN LEEUWEN, JOEY CASTILLO, DEAN WEEN, DAVE CATCHING, ALAIN JOHANNES**, etc

Island Ipecac

Oct 03. (cd) *(9865704)* *<44>* **DESERT SESSIONS 9: I SEE YOU HEARIN ME / DESERT SESSIONS 10: I HEART DISCO** [ ] [ ]
– Dead in love / I wanna make it wit chu / Covered in punks blood / There will never be a better time / Crawl home / I'm here for your daughter / Powered wig machine / In my head . . . or something / Holey dime / A girl like me / Creosote / Subcutaneous phat. *(d-lp iss.Nov03 +=; 9865812)* – Bring it back gentle / Shepherd's pie.

Nov 03. (7"; as JOSH HOMME & PJ HARVEY) *(IS 835)* **CRAWL HOME. / WHORES HUSTLE AND HUSTLERS WHORE** [41] [–]
(cd-s+=) *(CID 835)* – It / ('A'-video).

EAGLES OF DEATH METAL

CARLO VON SEXRON (aka JOSH HOMME) – drums / **JESSE HUGHES** – vocals, guitar

Ant Acid Audio Ant Acid Audio

Apr 04. (cd/lp) *<(AAA 999)>* **PEACE LOVE DEATH METAL** [ ] Mar04 [ ]
– I only want you / Speaking in tongues / So easy / Flames go higher / Bad dream mama / English girl / Stacks o' money / Midnight creeper / Stuck in the metal / Already died / Kiss the Devil / Whorehoppin (shit, goddamn) / San Berdoo sunburn / Wastin' my time / Miss Alissa.

not iss. Downtown

Apr 06. (cd/lp) *<70001>* **DEATH BY SEXY . . .** [–] [ ]
– I want you so hard (boy's bad news) / I gotta feeling (just nineteen) / Cherry cola / I like to move in the night / Solid gold / Don't speak (I came to make a bang!) / Keep your head up / The ballad of Queen Bee and Baby Duck / Poor doggie / Chase the Devil / EAgles goth / Shasta beast / Bag o' miracles.

□ the RACONTEURS (see under ⇒ WHITE STRIPES)

RADIOHEAD

Formed: Oxford, England . . . 1988 by frontman THOM YORKE, guitarist ED O'BRIEN and bassist COLIN GREENWOOD with drummer PHIL SELWAY completing the line-up. Dubbing themselves ON A FRIDAY, the band began gigging around Oxford, subsequently boasting a triple guitar attack following the addition of COLIN's brother, JONNY. Initially, the group also fleshed out their sound with a couple of saxaphone players (though it's now difficult to imagine what that must have sounded like). With the various members trooping off to complete their respective educations, the RADIOHEAD story really began in the summer of '91 when the band got back together and adopted the aforesaid moniker (after a TALKING HEADS song). Signed to the ever vigilant 'Parlophone', the band enjoyed some airplay with their first release, a spring '92 EP with 'PROVE YOURSELF' as the lead track. Next up was the seminal 'CREEP', an incendiary anthem for anyone who'd ever felt rejected/alienated (and let's face it, that's most of the population), the song stiffing first time round but subsequently kickstarting RADIOHEAD's career. The track also used the group's trademark soft bit/quiet bit dynamics to stunning effect, a method which would come to form the basis for some of the band's best tracks. In the meantime, RADIOHEAD eventually scraped in to the lower regions of the Top 40 with the abrasive 'ANYONE CAN PLAY GUITAR', the debut album, 'PABLO HONEY' making the UK Top 30 around the same time in early '93. Though it had its moments, the album lacked consistency with YORKE seemingly searching for some kind of vocal identity. While the record found enthusiastic champions in some sections of the music press, by and large, RADIOHEAD were passed over. All that changed, however, when 'CREEP' exploded in the States, the record obviously striking a deep chord with the multitudes who weren't part of the 'American Dream'. Taking the first flight over there, RADIOHEAD capitalised on this surprise success, the band treated like homecoming heroes and selling out concerts night after night. In a bizarre reversal of the standard process, this US success laid the groundwork for the re-release of 'CREEP' in the UK, where it became a Top 10 hit, sales of the album also enjoying a healthy re-invigoration. With such a universal theme, it was no surprise that the track was also a massive hit all over the world, RADIOHEAD finding themselves in the strange position of being international pop stars yet at the same time, regarded merely as a competent indie band in their home country. 'THE BENDS' (1995) convincingly silenced the doubters once and for all, a groundbreaking album with a spectral musical vision which rarely failed to take the breath away. Opening with the searing, reverbating 'PLANET TELEX' the record proceeded to juxtapose howling guitar menace against bleakly beautiful melodies, echoing synth and acoustic strumming, YORKE painting piercingly vivid images with his tortured musings on the nature of the human psyche. The fragile majesty of 'FAKE PLASTIC TREES' was RADIOHEAD at their most sublime, YORKE's ability to hit those high notes pivotal to the resigned melancholy of his vocals. The churning claustrophobia of 'BLACK STAR' sounded like the final fling of a condemned man, positively revelling in its own pain and misery, while the funereal 'STREET SPIRIT' was a ghostly coda, its award-winning video perfectly evoking the track's haunting feeling of time standing still. Basically, the album wiped the floor with the competition, laying waste to the snot-nosed chaff of Brit-pop and confirming that there was indeed a thinking man's alternative to OASIS. R.E.M. felt the same way, inviting the band to support them on tour later that year, something of a dream come true for RADIOHEAD who had long been massive fans of STIPE & Co. The summer of '95 also saw the release of the 'HELP' album, a project involving the cream of the British music scene with proceeds from album sales donated to the War Child charity (which raised money for war torn Bosnia). RADIOHEAD contributed 'LUCKY', a song apparently written about the band's newfound position as one of the most highly regarded group's in the world. Stunning though the track is, it sounds more like a dirge than a celebration, the searing guitar line evoking a feeling of utter desolation and emptiness. Probably the best example of YORKE's self-acknowledged struggle to sound anything other than melancholy, the track was one of many highlights on 'OK COMPUTER' (1997), RADIOHEAD's feverishly anticipated follow-up to the poll-topping 'THE BENDS'. A densely complex, almost initially impenetrable album, 'OK..' was a demanding beast, previewed by the wildly ambitious 'PARANOID ANDROID', a kind of post-prog symphony in three parts. The oscillating guitar vibration of 'AIRBAG' kicked off proceedings in much the same fashion as 'PLANET TELEX', but then things started getting weird. 'SUBTERRANEAN HOMESICK ALIEN' was truly adrift in space, the guitars twinkling and shimmering like tiny constellations, while with 'EXIT MUSIC (FOR A FILM)' (written for closing sequence of the revamped 'Romeo And Juliet' movie), YORKE's vocal was so eerily intimate, it sounded as if he was in the same room, the song building to a majestic climax via unearthly choral parts and swooning synths. 'LET DOWN' was an almost BYRDS-esque follow-up to 'CREEP', its pealing guitar and infectious melody framing a similar theme and creating what was conceivably the nearest the record came to conventional rock. Much of the album was vaguely reminiscent of the more cerebral moments on U2's 'Unforgettable Fire', although YORKE has never come so close to sounding like BONO as on 'CLIMBING THE WALLS', for once managing to avoid the bruised resignation that normally colours his voice. With 'NO SURPRISES', RADIOHEAD cleverly contrasted an almost child-like musical lullaby with lyrics expressing a hopeless world weariness. Of their contemporaries, only SPIRITUALIZED and MOGWAI were making music this far out, RADIOHEAD once again almost sweeping the board at the end of year polls and bravely taking rock music into the future rather than fawning over a Union Jack-clad past. With 'KID A' (2000) they took the music into the future with a vengeance; whether this was a brave new sonic world or a sterile wasteland of short-circuit experimentation remains a moot point. Maybe it should've been

Thom Yorke of RADIOHEAD

titled 'All That You CAN Leave Behind', YORKE and Co putting to bed the bruised beauty of their best work with brutal determination. The oblique, serrated electronica and disjointed dirgescapes offered up nothing in the way of redemptive miserabilism never mind a hook or a melody. Perseverance dragged brief snatches of genius screaming petulantly from the broodingly dense mix yet the effort was hardly relative to the meagre rewards on offer. More, YORKE's vocal, previously a thing of exotic desolation, begins to grate against the unremitingly bleak backdrop, reduced to one of the dismal whole's gratuitously mechanical constituent parts – in other words a classic! 'AMNESIAC' (2001) was an equally daunting if not quite so wilfully oppressive listen, its material drawn from the same sessions as its predecessor. Despite featuring the studio debut of established live favourites 'KNIVES OUT' and 'YOU AND WHOSE ARMY?', the album merely confirmed that RADIOHEAD had absolutely no intention of resuming normal service anytime soon. On the contrary, they kept up their new adrenaline-paced release schedule with 'I MIGHT BE WRONG: LIVE RECORDINGS' (2001), a clipped concert set again inspired by the template of 'KID A'. Whether they'd taken the not inconsiderable criticism to heart or whether they really were making a conscious effort to put some kind of discernible structure back into the music, 'HAIL TO THE THIEF' (2003) did at least make some concessions to convention. The likes of opener '2 + 2 = 5' possessed some familiar reference points, while the sinister 'SAIL TO THE MOON' ranked as perhaps the most discomfortingly effective piece of music they've written in years.

Album rating: PABLO HONEY (*7) / THE BENDS (*10) / OK COMPUTER (*10) / KID A (*9) / AMNESIAC (*7) / I MIGHT BE WRONG: LIVE RECORDINGS mini (*5) / HAIL TO THE THIEF (*7) / COM LAG (2PLUS2ISFIVE) collection (*5) / Jonny Greenwood: BODYSONG soundtrack (*6)

THOM YORKE (b. 7 Oct'68) – vocals, guitar / **ED O'BRIEN** (b.15 Apr'68) – guitar, vocals / **JON GREENWOOD** (b. 5 Nov'71) – guitar / **COLIN GREENWOOD** (b.26 Jun'69) – bass / **PHIL SELWAY** (b.23 May'67) – drums

Parlophone | Capitol

May 92. (c-ep/12"ep/cd-ep) *(TCR/12R/CDR 6312)* **DRILL EP** [ ] [ ]
– Prove yourself / Stupid car / You / Thinking about you.

Sep 92. (c-ep/12"ep/cd-ep) *(TCR/12R/CDR 6078)* **CREEP / LURCEE. / INSIDE MY HEAD / MILLION $ QUESTION** [ ] [–]

Feb 93. (c-ep/12"ep/cd-ep) *(TCR/12R/CDR 6333)* **ANYONE CAN PLAY GUITAR. / FAITHLESS, THE WONDER BOY / COKE BABIES** [32] [–]

Feb 93. (cd/c/lp) *(CD/TC+/PCS 7360)* *<81409>* **PABLO HONEY** [25] Jun93 [32]
– You / Creep / How do you? / Stop whispering / Thinking about you / Anyone can play guitar / Ripcord / Vegetable / Prove yourself / I can't / Lurgee / Blow out.

Apr 93. (c-s,cd-s) *<44932>* **CREEP / FAITHLESS, THE WONDER BOY** [–] [34]

May 93. (c-ep/12"ep/cd-ep) *(TCR/12R/CDR 6345)* **POP IS DEAD / BANANA CO. (acoustic). / CREEP (live) / RIPCORD (live)** [42] [–]

Sep 93. (7") *(RS 6359)* **CREEP. / YES I AM** [7] [–]
(cd-s+=) *(CDR 6359)* – Blow out (remix) / Inside my head (live).
(12"clear) *(12RG 6359)* – ('A'-acoustic KROQ) / You (live) / Vegetable (live) / Killer cars (live).

Oct 94. (c-ep/12"ep) *(TCR/12R 6984)* *<58274>* **MY IRON LUNG / THE TRICKSTER / LEWIS (mistreated) / PUNCHDRUNK LOVESICK SINGALONG** [24] [ ]
(cd-s) *(CDRS 6394)* – (1st & 4th track) / Lozenge of love.
(cd-s) *(CDR 6394)* – (1st & 2nd track) / Permanent daylight / You never wash up after yourself.

Mar 95. (c-s) *(TCR 6405)* *<58537>* **HIGH & DRY / PLANET TELEX** [17] Feb96 [ ]
(cd-s+=) *(CDR 6405)* – Killer cars / Planet Telex (LFO JD mix).
(cd-s+=) *(CDRS 6405)* – Maquiladora / Planet Telex (hexadecimal mix).
(12") *(12R 6405)* – Planet Telex (hexadecimal mix) / Planet Telex (LFO JD mix) / Planet Telex (hexadecimal dub) / High & dry.

Mar 95. (cd/c/lp) *(CD/TC+/PCS 7372)* *<29626>* **THE BENDS** [6] [88]
– Planet Telex / The bends / High & dry / Fake plastic trees / Bones (nice dream) / Just / My iron lung / Bulletproof . . .I wish I was / Black star / Sulk / Street spirit (fade out).

May 95. (c-ep/cd-ep) *(TCR/CDRS 6411)* *<58424>* **FAKE PLASTIC TREES / INDIA RUBBER / HOW CAN YOU BE SURE?** [20] Jul95 [ ]
(cd-s) *(CDR 6411)* – ('A'side) / ('A'acoustic) / Bulletproof..I wish I was (acoustic) / Street spirit (fade out) (acoustic).

Aug 95. (c-ep/12"ep) *(TCR/12R 6415)* **JUST / PLANET TELEX (Karma Sun Ra mix) / KILLER CARS (mogadon mix)** [19] [–]
(cd-s) *(CDR 6415)* – ('A'side) / Bones (live) / Planet Telex (live) / Anyone can play guitar (live).

Jan 96. (7"white) *(R 6419)* *<82523>* **STREET SPIRIT (FADE OUT). / BISHOP'S ROBES** [5] [ ]
(cd-s+=) *(CDRS 6419)* – Talk show host.
(cd-s) *(CDR 6419)* – ('A'side) / Banana co. / Molasses.

Feb 96. (c-s,cd-s) *<58537>* **HIGH AND DRY / FAKE PLASTIC TREES** [–] [78]

Jun 97. (7") *(NODATA 01)* **PARANOID ANDROID. / POLYETHYLENE (PARTS 1 & 2)** [3] [–]
(cd-s+=) *(CDNODATAS 01)* – Pearly.
(cd-s) *(CDNODATA 01)* – ('A'side) / A reminder / Melatonin.

Jun 97. (cd/c/d-lp) *(CD/TC+/NODATA 02)* *<55229>* **OK COMPUTER** [1] [21]
– Airbag / Paranoid android / Subterranean homesick alien / Exit music (for a film) / Karma police / Electioneering / Climbing up the walls / No surprises / Lucky / The tourist.

Aug 97. (cd-s) *(CDNODATA 03)* **KARMA POLICE / CLIMBING UP THE WALLS (Fila Brazillia & Zero 7 mixes)** [8] [ ]
(12"+=) *(12NODATA 03)* – Meeting in the aisle.
(cd-s) *(CDNODATAS 03)* – ('A'side) / Meeting in the aisle / Lull.

Jan 98. (12") *(12NODATA 04)* **NO SURPRISES. / PALO ALTO** [4] [ ]
(c-s+=/cd-s+=) *(TC/CD NODATA 04)* – How I made my millions.
(cd-s) *(CDNODATAS 04)* – ('A'side) / Airbag (live) / Lucky (live).

Apr 98. (m-cd) *(858701-2)* **AIRBAG / PEARLY (remix) / MEETING IN THE AISLE / A REMINDER / POLYTHENE (parts 1 & 2) / MELATONIN / PALO ALTO** [ ] [–]
(above wasn't legitimate to chart in Britain)

Apr 98. (m-cd) *<58071>* **AIRBAG / HOW AM I DRIVING (EP)** [–] [56]

Oct 00. (cd/c) *(<2435 27753-2/-4>)* **KID A** [1] [1]
– Everything in its right place / Kid A / The national anthem / How to disappear completely / Treefingers / Optimistic / In limbo / Idioteque / Morning bell / Motion picture soundtrack.

May 01. (12") *(12FHEIT 45102)* **PYRAMID SONG. / THE AMAZING SOUNDS OF ORGY / FAST TRACK** [5] [–]
(cd-s) *(CDSHEIT 45102)* – (first 2 tracks) / Trans Atlantic drawl.
(cd-s) *(CDFHEIT 45102)* – (first & third tracks) / Kinetic.

Jun 01. (cd/c/d-lp) *(CD/TC/LP FHEIT 45101)* *<32764>* **AMNESIAC** [1] [2]
– Packt like sardines in a crushd tin box / Pyramid song / Pulk-pull revolving doors / You and whose army? / I might be wrong / Knives out / Morning bell / Amnesiac / Dollars & cents / Hunting bears / Like spinning plates / Life in a glasshouse.

Aug 01. (12"/cd-s) *(12/CD FHEIT 45103)* **KNIVES OUT / CUTTOTH. / LIFE IN A GLASSHOUSE (extended)** [13] [–]
(cd-s) *(CDSFHEIT 45103)* – ('A'side) / Worrywort / Fog.

Nov 01. (m-cd/m-lp) *(CD/12 FHEIT 45104)* *<36616>* **I MIGHT BE WRONG: LIVE RECORDINGS** (live) [23] [44]
– The national anthem / I might be wrong / Morning bell / Like spinning plates / Idioteque / Everything in its right place / Dollars and cents / True love waits.

May 03. (12"/cd-s) *(12R/CDR 6608)* **THERE THERE. / PAPERBAG WRITER / WHERE BLUEBIRDS FLY** [4] [–]

Jun 03. (cd/d-lp) *(584543-2/-1)* *<84543>* **HAIL TO THE THIEF** [1] [3]
– 2 + 2 = 5 / Sit down. stand up / Sail to the Moon / Backdrifts / Go to sleep / Where I end and you begin / We suck young blood / The gloaming / There there / I will / A punchup at a wedding / Myxomatosis / Scatterbrain / A wolf at the door.

Aug 03. (cd-s) *(CDRS 6613)* **GO TO SLEEP / I AM CITIZEN INSANE / FOG** [12] [–]
(12") *(12R 6613)* – (first 2 tracks) / I am a wicked child.
(cd-s) *(CDR 6613)* – ('A') / I am a wicked child / Gagging order.

Nov 03. (cd-s) *(CDRS 6623)* **2 + 2 = 5 / MYXOMATOSIS (Christian Vogel remix) / THERE THERE (demo)** [15] [–]
(cd-s) *(CDRS 6623)* – ('A') / Skttrbrain (Four Tet remix) / I will (1st mix).

(12") *(12R 6623)* – ('A') / Myxomatosis (Cristian Vogel remix) / Skttrbrain (Four Tet remix).

May 04. (cd) *(TOCP 66280)* *<44058-2>* **COM LAG (2PLUS2ISFIVE)** (collection) | 37 Apr04 | □
– 2 + 2 = 5 (live at Earls Court) / Remyxomatosis (Cristian Vogel remix) / I will (Los Angeles version) / Paperbag writer / I am a wicked child / I am citizen insane / Skttrbrain (Four Tet remix) / Gagging order / Fog (again) (live) / Where bluebirds fly / 2 + 2 = 5 (live at Belfort Festival – video).

JONNY GREENWOOD

with **COLIN GREENWOOD + GRAEME STEWART**

E.M.I. E.M.I.

Oct 03. (cd) *(<5 95147-0>)* **BODYSONG** (soundtrack) □ □
– Moon trills / Moon mall / Trench / Iron swallow / Clockwork tin soldiers / Convergence / Nudnik headache / Peartree / Splitter / Bode radio – Glass light – Broken hearts / 24 hour Charleston / Milky drops from Heaven / Tehellet.

in Jul'06, THOM YORKE will release a solo set, 'THE ERASER'

□ RAEKWON (see under ⇒ WU-TANG CLAN)

Gerry RAFFERTY

Born: 16 Apr'47, Paisley, Scotland. In 1968, he joined the HUMBLEBUMS, alongside TAM HARVEY and future comedian, BILLY CONNOLLY. The trio signed up to folk label, 'Transatlantic', recording two albums, 'HUMBLEBUMS' (1969) & 'OPEN UP THE DOOR' (1970), together before parting ways. RAFFERTY subsequently released a debut solo album, 'CAN I HAVE MY MONEY BACK', in 1971 before moving to London and forming STEALERS WHEEL with RAB NOAKES and JOE EGAN. Signed to 'A&M', the band went through some major personnel upheaval prior to the release of their eponymous album in late '72, PAUL PILNICK, TONY WILLIAMS and ROB COOMBES replacing RAB NOAKES, IAN CAMPBELL and ROGER BROWN respectively. Overseen by veteran production duo, LEIBER & STOLLER, the album was characterised by gentle, folky harmonies and an unerring ear for pop melody, the haunting 'NEXT TO ME' resonating long after the first listen. Then of course, there was the 'Dylanesque' shuffle of 'STUCK IN THE MIDDLE OF YOU', a transatlantic Top 10 upon its original 1973 release and later an integral, ingeniously effective part of Quentin Tarantino's infamous 'Reservoir Dogs' movie. There was almost as much confusion surrounding the identity of the STEALERS WHEEL line-up as there was among Tarantino's panicked criminal pros, RAFFERTY leaving for a couple of months before returning in time for a follow-up. By this point, all the original members (who themselves had been temporarily replaced!) were gone and the core duo of EGAN and RAFFERTY roped in a crew of session players to complete 'FERGUSLIE PARK' (1973). Another set of consummate folk-pop, the record was nevertheless a commercial disappointment save for a minor Top 30 hit, 'STAR'. Disillusioned, the pair completed one further set, the equally impressive 'RIGHT OR WRONG' (1975), before permanently parting company and embarking on respective solo careers. After a number of years grappling with business problems, RAFFERTY emerged in early '78 with the 'CITY TO CITY' album. Changing tack to a more contemporary, MOR style, RAFFERTY scored a massive international hit (and a US No.1) with the 'BAKER STREET' single, RAPHAEL RAVENSCROFT's famous sax riff forming the basis of this world-weary classic. The track's success saw album sales go through the roof, RAFFERTY becoming something of a reluctant overnight superstar. Shunning the limelight and choosing not to promote the album in America (where it went platinum), RAFFERTY instead began work on a follow-up, 'NIGHT OWL' (1979). While failing to scale the commercial heights of its predecessor, the record was a sizeable success nonetheless, RAFFERTY's inimitably understated approach again delighting fans who put it into the UK Top 10. Subsequent albums such as 'SLEEPWALKING' (1982) and 'NORTH AND SOUTH' (1988) weren't quite as inspired, RAFFERTY taking a sabbatical during the mid-80's (although he did contribute to MARK KNOPFLER's 'Local Hero' soundtrack and produce The PROCLAIMERS' 1987 single, 'Letter From America'). He continued to record in the 90's, if sporadically, such seasoned hands as pedal steel player, B.J. COLE, lending their expertise to 1993's 'ON A WING AND A PRAYER', the record also featuring the backing vocal and co-writing talents of brother JIM.

• **Songwriters:** STEALER'S WHEEL was virtually a writing partnership for RAFFERTY and EGAN. GET OUT OF MY LIFE WOMAN (Allen Toussaint).

Album rating: CAN I HAVE MY MONEY BACK? (*6) / Stealers Wheel: STEALERS WHEEL (*7) / FERGUSLIE PARK (*7) / RIGHT OR WRONG (*6) / Gerry Rafferty: CITY TO CITY (*8) / NIGHT OWL (*7) / SNAKES AND LADDERS (*6) / SLEEPWALKING (*4) / NORTH AND SOUTH (*4) / RIGHT DOWN THE LINE – THE BEST OF GERRY RAFFERTY compilation (*6) / ON A WING & A PRAYER (*4) / OVER MY HEAD (*4) / ONE MORE DREAM – THE VERY BEST OF GERRY RAFFERTY compilation (*8)

GERRY RAFFERTY – vocals, guitar (with session people including future STEALERS WHEEL members)

Transatla. Blue Thumb

1971. (lp) *(TRA 241)* *<BTS 58>* **CAN I HAVE MY MONEY BACK** □ □
– New street blues / Didn't I / Mr. Universe / Mary Skeffington / Long way round / Can I have my money back / Sign on the dotted line / Make you break you / To each and everyone / One drink down / Don't count me out / Half a chance / Where I belong. *<US re-iss. 1978; 6031> (re-iss. Sep81 lp/c; TRS/KTRS 112) (re-iss. Apr85 on 'Autograph' c; ASK 769) (re-iss. cd+c Apr93 on 'Ariola Express') (cd re-iss. Oct98 on 'Wooded Hill'; HILLCD 3)*

Oct 71. (7") *(BIG 139)* **CAN I HAVE MY MONEY BACK. / SO SAD THINKING** □ –

Jan 72. (7") **CAN I HAVE MY MONEY BACK. / SIGN ON THE DOTTED LINE** – □

STEALERS WHEEL

GERRY with **JOE EGAN** – vocals, keyboards / **PAUL PILNICK** – guitar (ex-BIG THREE) repl. RAB NOAKES who went solo / **TONY WILLIAMS** – bass repl. IAN CAMPBELL / **ROD COOMBES** – drums repl. ROGER BROWN

A&M A&M

Oct 72. (7") *(AMS 7033)* **LATE AGAIN. / I GET BY** □ –

Nov 72. (7") *(AMS 7036)* *<1416>* **STUCK IN THE MIDDLE WITH YOU. / JOSE** □ Feb73 6
(re-dist.May73, hit UK No.8)

Dec 72. (lp) *(AMLH 68121)* *<4377>* **STEALER'S WHEEL** □ 50
– Late again / Stuck in the middle with you / Another meaning / I get by / Outside looking in / Johnny's song / Next to me / Jose / Gets so lonely / You put something better inside of me.

Feb 73. (7") *(AMS 7046)* **YOU PUT SOMETHING BETTER INSIDE OF ME. / NEXT TO ME** □ –

— Group had disbanded when RAFFERTY had been replaced by **LUTHER GROSVENOR** (ex-SPOOKY TOOTH) for 2 months. **DELISLE HARPER** – bass repl. others

— By mid'73, they were a basic duo (**RAFFERTY & EGAN**) augmented by **BERNIE HOLLAND** – guitar / **CHRIS MERCER** – saxophone / **ANDREW STEELE** – drums / **CHRIS NEILL** – harmonica and loads more sessioners.

Aug 73. (7") *(AMS 7079)* **EVERYTHING'L TURN OUT FINE. / JOHNNY'S SONG** 33 –

Aug 73. (7") *<1450>* **EVERYONE'S AGREED THAT EVERYTHING WILL TURN OUT FINE. / NEXT TO ME** – 49

Nov 73. (lp) *(AMLH 68209)* *<4419>* **FERGUSLIE PARK** □ □
– Good businessman / Star / Wheelin' / Waltz (you know it makes sense!) / What more could you want / Over my head / Blind faith / Nothing's gonna change my mind / Steamboat row / Back on my feet again / Who cares / (Everyone's agreed that) Everything will turn out fine.

Dec 73. (7") *(AMS 7094)* *<1483>* **STAR. / WHAT MORE COULD I WANT** 25 29

Apr 74. (7") <1529> **WHEELIN'. / YOU PUT SOMETHING BETTER INSIDE OF ME** [–] [ ]
Feb 75. (7") *(AMS 7152)* **RIGHT OR WRONG. / THIS MORNING** [ ] [–]
Feb 75. (lp) *(AMLH 68293)* <4517> **RIGHT OR WRONG** [ ] [ ]
– Benediction / Found my way to you / This morning / Let yourself go / Home from home / Go as you please / Wishbone / Don't get me wrong / Monday morning / Right or wrong.
May 75. (7") *(AMS 7170)* **FOUND MY WAY TO YOU. / WISHBONE** [ ] [–]
May 75. (7") <1675> **FOUND MY WAY TO YOU. / THIS MORNING** [–] [ ]
—— Broke up again later in the year. JOE EGAN went solo, as did GERRY.

– compilations, etc. –

Sep 78. (lp) *A&M; (AMLH 64708)* <4708> **THE BEST OF STEALERS WHEEL** [ ] [ ]
– Stuck in the middle with you / Nothing's gonna change my mind / Star / This morning / Steamboat row / Next to me / Right or wrong / Go as you please / Benediction / Waltz (you know it makes sense!) / Blind faith / Late again / Wheelin' / Jose. *(re-iss. 1981 on 'Music For Pleasure'; MFP 50501) (cd/c-iss.Jun90 on 'Connoisseur'; CSAP CD/MC 106)*
Sep 78. (7") *A&M;* <2075> **(EVERYONE AGREED THAT) EVERYTHING'L TURN OUT FINE. / WHO CARES** [–] [ ]
Mar 82. (7") *Old Gold; (OG 9148)* **STUCK IN THE MIDDLE WITH YOU. / STAR** [ ] [–]
Sep 98. (cd) *Spectrum; (552496-2)* **STUCK IN THE MIDDLE** [ ] [–]

GERRY RAFFERTY

with many session people.

U.A. U.A.

Oct 77. (7") *(UP 36278)* **CITY TO CITY. / MATTIE'S RAG** [ ] [ ]
Jan 78. (lp/c) *(UAS/TCK 30104)* <840> **CITY TO CITY** [6] [1]
– he ark / Baker Street / Right down the line / City to city / Stealin' time / Mattie's rag / Whatever's written in your heart / Home and dry / Island / Waiting for the day. *(re-iss. Mar85 on 'Fame' lp/c; FA/TC-FA 3119) (cd-iss. Jul89; CDFA 3119) (cd re-iss. Apr99 on 'D.C.C.'; GZS 1075)*
Feb 78. (7") *(UP 36346)* <1192> **BAKER STREET. / BIG CHANGE IN THE WEATHER** [3] Apr78 [2]
above featured **RAPHAEL RAVENSCROFT** – saxophone
May 78. (7") *(UP 36403)* **WHATEVER'S WRITTEN IN YOUR HEART. / WAITING FOR THE DAY** [ ] [–]
Aug 78. (7") <1233> **RIGHT DOWN THE LINE. / WAITING FOR THE DAY** [–] [12]
Sep 78. (7") *(UP 36445)* **RIGHT DOWN THE LINE. / ISLAND** [ ] [–]
Nov 78. (7") <1266> **HOME AND DRY. / MATTIE'S RAG** [–] [28]
May 79. (7") *(UP 36512)* **NIGHT OWL. / WHY DON'T YOU TALK TO ME** [5] [–]
May 79. (lp/c) *(UAK/TCK 30238)* <958> **NIGHT OWL** [9] [29]
– Days gone down (still got the light in your eyes) / Night owl / The way that you do it / Why won't you talk to me / Get it right next time / Take the money and run / Family tree / Already gone / The tourist / It's gonna be a long night. *(re-iss. 1985 on 'Liberty' lp/c; ATAK/TC-ATAK 37) (re-iss. Jul86 on 'Fame' lp/c; FA/TC-FA 3147) (cd-iss. Jul89; CDFA 3147)*
May 79. (7") <1298> **DAYS GONE DOWN (STILL GOT THE LIGHT IN YOUR EYES). / WHY WON'T YOU TALK TO ME?** [–] [17]
Aug 79. (7") *(BP 301)* <1316> **GET IT RIGHT NEXT TIME. / IT'S GONNA BE A LONG NIGHT** [30] [21]
Mar 80. (7") *(BP 340)* **BRING IT ALL HOME. / IN TRANSIT** [54] [ ]
Mar 80. (lp/c) *(UAK/TCK 30298)* <1039> **SNAKES AND LADDERS** [15] [61]
– The Royal Mile / I was a boy scout / Welcome to Hollywood / Wastin' away / Look at the Moon / Bring it all home / The garden of England / Johnny's song / Didn't I / Syncopatin' Sandy / Cafe le Cabotin / Don't close the door. *(cd-iss. Mar89 on 'Liberty'; CZ 162)*
Oct 80. (7") *(BP 354)* <1366> **THE ROYAL MILE (SWEET DARLIN'). / WASTIN' AWAY** [67] Jul80 [54]

Liberty Liberty

Aug 82. (7") *(BP 413)* **SLEEPWALKING. / WHEN I REST** [ ] [ ]
Sep 82. (lp/c) *(LEG/TCG 30352)* <51132> **SLEEPWALKING** [39] [ ]
– Standing at the gates / Good intentions / A change of heart / On the way / Sleepwalking / Cat and mouse / The right moment / As wise as a serpent. *(re-iss. Sep84 on 'Fame' lp/c; FA/TC-FA 3113) (re-iss. Aug86 on 'E.M.I.' lp/c; ATAK/TC-ATAK 84) (cd-iss. Mar89; CZ 163) (cd re-iss. Feb01 on 'EMI Plus'; 576089-2)*
Nov 82. (7") *(BP 415)* **A CHANGE OF HEART. / GOOD INTENTIONS** [ ] [–]
Nov 82. (7") **STANDING AT THE GATES. / GOOD INTENTIONS** [–] [ ]
—— he took some time off, although he did appear on MARK KNOPFLER's 'Local Hero' 1983 soundtrack and in 1987 produced 'Letter From America' by the PROCLAIMERS.

London Polydor

Apr 88. (7") *(LON 170)* **SHIPYARD TOWN. / HEARTS DESIRE** [ ] [–]
(12"+=/cd-s+=) *(LON X/CD 170)* – ('A'lp version).
May 88. (lp/c)(cd) *(LON LP/C 55)(828089-2)* <835449> **NORTH AND SOUTH** [43] Jun88 [ ]
– North and south / Moonlight and gold / Tired of talking / Hearts run dry / A dangerous age / Shipyard town / Winter's come / Nothing ever happens down here / On a night like this / Unselfish love. *(re-iss. Apr91; same)*
—— now with **PAVEL ROSAK** – keyboards, drums, bass, percussion, programming / **HUGH BURNS** – electric guitars, co-producer / **MEL COLLINS** – sax / **B.J. COLE** – pedal steel / **ARRAN AHMUN** – percussion / **MO FOSTER** – bass / **BRYN HAWORTH** – bottleneck guitar / etc. Note: Brother **JIM RAFFERTY** also provided backing vocals & co-songwriting.

A&M Avalanche

Nov 92. (7"/c-s/cd-s) **I COULD BE WRONG. / BAKER STREET / LIFE GOES ON** [ ] [–]
Feb 93. (cd/c) *(517495-2/-4)* <0016> **ON A WING & A PRAYER** [73] [ ]
– Time's caught up on you / I see red / It's easy to talk / I could be wrong / Don't speak of my heart / Get out of my life woman / Don't give up on me / Hang on / Love and affection / Does he know what he's taken on / The light of love / Life goes on. *(cd re-iss. Jul02 on 'Spectrum'; 517238-2)*

Polydor Avalanche

Jun 95. (cd) *(523599-2)* <0017> **OVER MY HEAD** [ ] [ ]
– Bajan moon / The waters of forgetfulness / Down and out / Over my head / The girl's got no confidence / Wrong thinking / Lonesome polecat / Right or wrong / Late again / Clear day / Out the blue / A new beginning / Her father didn't like me anyway.

– (his) compilations, others, etc. –

Apr 74. (lp) *Transatlantic; (TRA 270)* **GERRY RAFFERTY REVISITED** [ ] [–]
Jul 87. (cd) *Transatlantic; (TRACD 601)* **THE COLLECTION** [ ] [–]
Apr 78. (7") *Logo; (GO 314)* **MARY SKEFFINGTON. / SHOESHINE BOY** [ ] [–]
Sep 78. (lp) *Logo; (VISA 7006)* **GERRY RAFFERTY** [ ] [–]
Apr 84. (lp/c) *Cambra; (CR/+T 132)* **THE FIRST CHAPTER** [ ] [–]
Jun 88. (lp) *Demon; (TRANDEM 3)* **BLOOD AND GLORY** [ ] [–]
Nov 89. (cd/c/lp) *E.M.I.; (CD/TC+/UAG 30333)* **RIGHT DOWN THE LINE – THE BEST OF GERRY RAFFERTY** [ ] [–]
– Baker Street / Whatever's written in your heart / Bring it all home / Right down the line / Get it right next time / Night owl / A dangerous age / Family tree / Shipyard town / The right moment / Look at the Moon. *(cd+=)* – The way that you do it / Tired of talking / The garden of England / Sleepwalking / As wise as a serpent.
Feb 90. (7") *E.M.I.; (EM 132)* **BAKER STREET (remix). / NIGHT OWL (remix)** [53] [–]
(12"+=) *(12EM 132)* – ('A'extended).
(cd-s++=) *(CDEM 132)* – Bring it all home (remix).
Apr 95. (cd) *Castle; (CCSCD 428)* **THE TRANSATLANTIC YEARS** [ ] [–]
Oct 95. (cd/c) *Polygram TV; (529279-2/-4)* **ONE MORE DREAM – THE VERY BEST OF . . .** [17] [–]
– Get it right next time / The garden of England / Baker street / Moonlight and gold / Stuck in the middle with you / Night owl / Waiting for the day / Right down the line / Tired of talkin' / Bring it all home / The girl's got no confidence / Days gone down / Everyone's agreed that everything will turn out fine / Over my head / Shipyard town / Whatever's written in your heart.
Feb 96. (cd/c) *True Trax; (TRT CD/MC 196)* **THE EARLY YEARS** [ ] [–]
Mar 97. (d-cd) *Raven;* <63> **CLOWNS TO THE LEFT, JOKERS TO THE RIGHT: 1970-1982** [–] [ ]
Jun 98. (cd) *EMI Gold; (494941-2)* **BAKER STREET** [ ] [–]
Oct 98. (cd) *Castle Select; (SELCD 547) / Phantom;* <21864-2> **DON'T COUNT ME OUT: THE VERY BEST OF THE TRANSATLANTIC YEARS** [ ] [ ]
Dec 99. (cd) *Disky;* <85442> **BAKER STREET** [–] [ ]
May 00. (cd) *Essential; (ESMCD 879)* **CAN I HAVE MY MONEY BACK – THE BEST OF GERRY RAFFERTY** [ ] [–]

RAGE AGAINST THE MACHINE

Formed: Los Angeles, California, USA . . . 1992 by rapper/vocalist ZACK DE LA ROCHA and guitarist TOM MORELLO along with bassist TIMMY C and drummer BRAD WILK. Signed to 'Epic' partly on the strength of their infamous live reputation, the band divebombed their way into the UK charts after performing the incendiary 'KILLING IN THE NAME OF' on cult 'yoof' TV show (now sadly missed), 'The Word'. One of the most visceral, angry and overtly political records of the 90's, the song formed the centrepiece of their pivotal 1993 eponymous debut album. A revelatory hybrid of monster riffing and knotty hip hop rhythms, the album was venom-spewing and utterly defiant. While detractors argued that the band's position on the roster of a major corporation was untenable, RATM countered that they had to get their message across to as wide an audience as possible. The vital point was that this was one SERIOUSLY angry young man, raging against all kinds of injustice, mainly the ruling white American capitalist system. Most of the tracks (highlights being 'BOMBTRACK', BULLET IN THE HEAD' and 'KNOW YOUR ENEMY') were positively seething with anger but crucially, they were also funky as hell and this is where RATM scored over their square-jawed copyists. Music aside, how many bands in the 90's have had the balls to be openly political?, or rather, how many bands even know the meaning of protest? In a music world of drug-inspired vacancy, RATM provided a vital injection of reality. Putting their money where their mouth was, or rather putting their modesty thereabouts, the band walked on stage naked at a show in Philadelphia, the initials PMRC (Parent Music Resource Centre) scrawled across their respective chests in defiance of the risible censorship organisation. Political dissent was nothing new to either TOM or ZACK, MORELLO's father being a member of the Mau Mau's (Kenyan Guerrillas) who fought for an end to British colonialism while his uncle JOMO KENYATTA was imprisoned, later becoming the Kenyan president. LA ROCHA's father, meanwhile, was a noted L.A. muralist and political activist. While the band continued to stir up controversy with their live work (including a sold out 1993 UK tour and blinding set at the 1994 Glastonbury Festival), a follow-up album wasn't released until 1996. When it eventually surfaced, 'EVIL EMPIRE' was something of a disappointment, lacking the focus and some of the funkiness of the debut, although it did hit US No.1. The cover art too, lacked the impact of the first album (a powerful photo of a buddhist monk setting himself on fire in protest at the Vietnam war). Nevertheless, the group put in a brilliant performance at that year's Reading Festival, whipping the crowd into a frenzy and almost upstaging headliners, The PRODIGY. The impressively talented and ever inventive MORELLO subsequently hooked up with the Essex electro-punks on the acclaimed 'NO MAN ARMY' track. Three years in the making (as per usual), the third album, 'THE BATTLE OF LOS ANGELES' (1999), once again pulled no punches and deservedly topped the US chart (only Top 30 in Britain!). Tracks such as the single, 'GUERRILLA RADIO', 'MIC CHECK' and 'NEW MILLENNIUM HOMES', were certainly the highlights as the band undertook an extensive world tour. After the 'RENEGADES' covers set late in 2000, DE LA ROCHA departed – rumours were subsequently rife that CYPRESS HILL's frontman B-REAL would take his place. In the event no-one took his place. Or at least someone took his place – that someone being former SOUNDGARDEN frontman CHRIS CORNELL – but the group morphed into an altogether different entity, AUDIOSLAVE. Like most so-called supergroup amalgamations, this much heralded project failed to fully live up to the hype: pitting CORNELL's 70's sludge predilections against the militant sonic efficiency of RAGE was never going to result in fireworks although admittedly it didn't end in tears. The group's eponymous debut, released in late 2002, was a curious beast, coming together definitively on the single 'COCHISE' but otherwise sounding only partly realised, lacking either the sting of RATM or the grand designs of CORNELL. RAGE fans were given a last-gasp blast of the band's fury with 'LIVE AT THE GRAND OLYMPIC AUDITORIUM' (2003), a belated concert set documenting the band's final couple of shows in autumn 2000, and featuring a couple of covers (MC5's 'KICK OUT THE JAMS' and EPMD's 'I'M HOUSIN'') from their final studio set. AUDIOSLAVE returned a couple of years later with 'OUT OF EXILE' (2005), a disarmingly straight-down-the-line rock album which did a lot to dissolve any remaining suspicions attached to the supergroup tag. A chart topper in America and a UK Top 5, the record's more holistic, melodic approach precluded any real pigeonholing but if anything, there was a distinct PEARL JAM-esque lustre – admittedly much of it to do with CORNELL's increasingly VEDDER-esque tones – to such wholesomely laid back fare as 'DANDELION' and 'DOESN'T REMIND ME' (a minor US hit).

Album rating: RAGE AGAINST THE MACHINE (*9) / EVIL EMPIRE (*7) / THE BATTLE OF LOS ANGELES (*7) / RENEGADES (*8) / LIVE AT THE GRAND OLYMPIC AUDITORIUM posthumous (*5) / Audioslave: AUDIOSLAVE (*6) / OUT OF EXILE (*7)

ZACK DE LA ROCHA (b.1970, Long Beach, Calif.) – vocals (ex INSIDE OUT) / **TOM MORELLO** (b.1964, New York City, NY) – guitars / **TIMMY C.** (b. TIM COMMERFORD) – bass / **BRAD WILK** (b.1968, Portland, Oregon) – drums

Epic — Epic

Feb 93. (7"/12"white/cd-s) *(658492-7/-6/-2)* **KILLING IN THE NAME. / CLEAR THE LANE / DARKNESS OF GREED** — 25 — –

Feb 93. (cd/c/lp) *(472224-2/-4/-1) <52959>* **RAGE AGAINST THE MACHINE** — 17 — Nov92 45
– Bombtrack / Killing in the name / Take the power back / Settle for nothing / Bullet in the head / Know your enemy / Wake up / Fistful of steel / Township rebellion / Freedom. *(lp re-iss. Feb99 on 'Simply Vinyl'; SVLP 69)*

Apr 93. (7") *(659258-7)* **BULLET IN THE HEAD. / BULLET IN THE HEAD (remix)** — 16 — –
(12"/cd-s) *(659258-6/-2)* – Bullet in the head / Settle for nothing.

Sep 93. (7") *(659471-7)* **BOMBTRACK. / ('A'mix)** — 37 — –
(12"+=/cd-s+=) *(659471-6/-2)* – ('A'version).

Feb 94. (cd-s; w-drawn) *(659821-2)* **FREEDOM** — – — –

Apr 96. (7"colrd/cd-s) *(663152-7/-2)* **BULLS ON PARADE. / HADDA BE PLAYING ON THE JUKEBOX** — 8 — –

Apr 96. (cd/c/lp) *(481026-2/-4/-1) <57523>* **EVIL EMPIRE** — 4 — 1
– People of the sun / Bulls on parade / Vietnow / Revolver / Snakecharmer / Tire me / Down rodeo / Without a face / Wind below / Roll right / Year of tha boomerang.

Aug 96. (7"orange) *(663628-7)* **PEOPLE OF THE SUN. / ZAPATA'S BLOOD (live)** — 26 — –
(cd-s+=) *(663628-2)* – Without a face (live).
(cd-s) *(663628-5)* – ('A') / Killing in the name (live) / Bullet in the head (live).

— TIMMY C. now as **Y.tim.K**

Oct 99. (7") *(668314-7) <79720>* **GUERRILLA RADIO. / THE GHOST OF TOM JOAD** — 32 — 69
(cd-s+=) *(668314-2)* – No shelter.
(cd-s) *(668314-5)* – ('A') / F*** tha police (live) / Freedom (live).

Nov 99. (cd/c) *(491993-2/-4) <69630>* **THE BATTLE OF LOS ANGELES** — 23 — 1
– Testify / Guerrilla radio / Calm like a bomb / Mic check / Sleep now in the fire / Born of a broken man / Born as ghosts / Maria / Voice of the voiceless / New millennium homes / Ashes in the fall / War within a breath.

Apr 00. (7"colrd) *(669136-7)* **SLEEP NOW IN THE FIRE. / ('A'-live)** — 43 — –
(cd-s) *(669136-2)* – ('A') / Bulls on parade (live) / ('A'-video).
(cd-s) *(669136-5)* – ('A') / Guerilla radio (live) / Freedom (live).

Nov 00. (cd/c/lp) *(499921-2/-4/-1)* *<85289>* **RENEGADES** (covers) 71 14
– Microphone fiend / Pistol grip pump / Kick out the jams / Renegades of funk / Beautiful world / I'm housin' / In my eyes / How could I just kill a man / The ghost of Tom Joad / Down on the street / Street fighting man / Maggie's farm. *(ltd-cd+=; 499921-0/-9/-8/-7)* – Kick out the jams (live) / How could I just kill a man.

— RATM split in October 2000

– compilations, etc. –

Apr 97. (10"ep) *Revelation; (REV 056)* **PEOPLE OF THE SUN (live) / WITHOUT A FACE (live) / INTRO BLACK STEEL IN THE HOUR OF CHAOS (live). / ZAPATA'S BLOOD (live) / BULLS ON PARADE / HADDA BE PLAYING ON THE JUKEBOX (live)** [ ] –

Nov 03. (cd) *Epic; (509544-2)* *<85114>* **LIVE AT THE GRAND OLYMPIC AUDITORIUM** (live) [ ] 94
– Bulls on parade / Bullet in the head / Born of a broken man / Killing in the name / Calm like a bomb / Testify / Bombtrack / War with a breath / I'm housin' / Sleep now in the fire / People of the sun / Guerrilla radio / Kick out the jams / Know your enemy / No shelter / Freedom.

Dec 03. (d-cd) *Epic; (509507-2)* **RAGE AGAINST THE MACHINE / EVIL EMPIRES / THE BATTLE OF LOS ANGELES** [ ] [ ]

AUDIOSLAVE

CHRIS CORNELL – vocals (ex-SOUNDGARDEN) / **TOM MORELLO, TIM COMMERFORD + BRAD WILK**

Epic Sony

Nov 02. (cd) *(510130-2)* *<86968>* **AUDIOSLAVE** 19 7
– Cochise / Show me how to live / Gasoline / What you are / Like a stone / Set it off / Shadow on the sun / I am the highway / Exploder / Hypnotize / Bring em back alive / Light my way / Getaway car / The last remaining light. *<lp-iss.Feb03; E 286968>*

Jan 03. (cd-s) *(673276-2)* **COCHISE / WE GOT THE WHIP / GASOLINE (live on Letterman) / ('A'-video)** 24 69

Apr 03. (7") *(673788-7)* **LIKE A STONE. / SET IT OFF (live on Letterman)** 31 –
(cd-s+=) *(673788-5)* – ('A'-live Radio 1 session).
(cd-s) *(673788-2)* – ('A') / Super stupid (live Radio 1 session) / Gasoline (live Radio 1 session) / ('A'-video).

Dec 03. (7"red) *<674148>* **SHOW ME HOW TO LIVE. / SUPER STUPID (live at the BBC)** – 67

May 05. (7"pic-d) *(9882598)* **BE YOURSELF. / SUPER STUPID** 40 Jul05 32
(cd-s+=) *<(9882599)>* – Show me how to live (remix by T Ray) / ('A'-video).

May 05. (cd/blue-d-lp) *(9882468)* *<B0004603-02/-01>* **OUT OF EXILE** 5 1
– Your time has come / Out of exile / Be yourself / Doesn't remind me / Drown me slowly / Heaven's dead / The worm / Man or animal / Yesterday to tomorrow / Dandelion / #1 zero / The curse. *(UK+=)* – Like stone (live).

Oct 05. (7") *(9885536)* **DOESN'T REMIND ME. / (live & acoustic AOL session)** [ ] Nov05 68
(cd-s) *<(9885099)>* – ('A') / Out of exile (live & acoustic AOL session) / ('A'-radio edit) / ('A'-video).

☐ RAIN TREE CROW (see under ⇒ JAPAN)

RAINBOW

Formed: 1975 . . . by former DEEP PURPLE guitar guru, RITCHIE BLACKMORE. Recruiting New York band ELF wholesale, including the esteemed metal warbler RONNIE JAMES DIO, BLACKMORE recorded the eponymous debut album ('RITCHIE BLACKMORE'S RAINBOW') in the summer of '75. While 'PURPLE lumbered towards imminent implosion, BLACKMORE took the Brontosaurus-rock blueprint to mystical new heights, the classic 'MAN ON THE SILVER MOUNTAIN' being the prime example. By the release of the seminal 'RAINBOW RISING' (1976), the ubiquitous COZY POWELL was on the drum stool. The record (released under the slightly clipped moniker of BLACKMORE'S RAINBOW) featured such enduring BLACKMORE stage favourites as 'TAROT WOMAN', 'STARGAZER' and 'A LIGHT IN THE BLACK', arguably the most cohesive set of the guitarist's career. After a live album, more line-up changes ensued, BOB DAISLEY finally stepping in for MARK CLARKE, who had temporarily replaced BAIN (DAVID STONE was now the new keyboard man in place of TONY CAREY). Although 'LONG LIVE ROCK'N'ROLL' (1978) was another hard-rock classic, it wasn't until DIO had departed for BLACK SABBATH that the band enjoyed their greatest success. Recruiting ex-MARBLES vocalist, GRAHAM BONNET, as a replacement, and surprisingly enlisting old 'PURPLE mucker ROGER GLOVER on bass, the band hit the UK Top 10 twice in a row at the turn of the decade with 'SINCE YOU BEEN GONE' and 'ALL NIGHT LONG'. Watertight, marvellously crafted melodic rock, both songs featured on the 'DOWN TO EARTH' (1979) album. POWELL left the following year, as did BONNET, BLACKMORE recruiting JOE LYNN TURNER as frontman. Their next single, 'I SURRENDER', was their biggest hit to date, an epic slice of American-influenced rock that stands among metal's greatest moments. The album, 'DIFFICULT TO CURE' (1981) made the UK Top 5 although it was clear RAINBOW had adopted a more commercial approach in an attempt to break America, subsequent efforts failing to make much impact, however. With no pot of gold at the end of this particular rainbow, BLACKMORE eventually folded the band in 1984, with plans to resurrect the classic Mk.II DEEP PURPLE line-up. Ten years on, BLACKMORE (again leaving 'PURPLE) resurrected another version of RAINBOW, a 1995 album, 'STRANGER IN US ALL', purely for BLACKMORE diehards. The veteran guitarist took a radically different tack on 'SHADOW OF THE MOON' (1998), the first recorded fruits of his collaboration with musical partner/fiancee, CANDICE NIGHT. Released under the moniker of BLACKMORE'S NIGHT (apparently not an awful pun on the old DP chestnut but a reference to the happy couple . . .), the album found RITCHIE and his young vocalist exploring Renaissance-era music via elements of new age, world, rock and folk. Such distinctly un-rock'n'roll instrumentation as pennywhistle, hurdy gurdy and mandolin contributed to the ambience while IAN ANDERSON even made an appearance with a blast of his trademark flute. Written with the anticipation of a full stage tour, 'UNDER A VIOLET MOON' (1999) was similar if less restrained, BLACKMORE again demonstrating his mastery of the acoustic guitar. In a hitherto unprecedented burst of creativity, the man continued his immersion in archaic motifs with 2001's 'FIRES AT MIDNIGHT' (although how Bob Dylan's 'THE TIMES THEY ARE A-CHANGIN' fit into the latter's medieval tapestry is anyone's guess), 2003's live (for a select, olde English-attired audience) 'PAST TIME WITH GOOD COMPANY' (within which Rainbow's '16th CENTURY GREENSLEEVES' was an admittedly better fit) and yet another studio set, 'GHOST OF A ROSE' (2003). The pattern was continued for 2006's renaissance-inspired 'THE VILLAGE LANTERNE', a record which even includes music from ye olde Deep Purple ('CHILD IN TIME') and Rainbow ('STREET OF DREAMS').

Album rating: RITCHIE BLACKMORE'S RAINBOW (*6) / RAINBOW RISING (*8) / LIVE ON STAGE (*4) / LONG LIVE ROCK'N'ROLL (*6) / DOWN TO EARTH (*6) / DIFFICULT TO CURE (*5) / THE BEST OF RAINBOW compilation (*7) / STRAIGHT BETWEEN THE EYES (*5) / BENT OUT OF SHAPE (*4) / FINAL VINYL (*4) / STRANGER IN US ALL (*4) / THE VERY BEST OF RAINBOW compilation (*6) / Blackmore's Night: SHADOW OF THE MOON (*4) / UNDER A VIOLET MOON (*4) / FIRES AT MIDNIGHT (*6) / PAST TIMES WITH GOOD COMPANY (*5) / GHOST OF A ROSE (*4) / BEYOND THE SUNSET: THE ROMANTIC COLLECTION (*5) / THE VILLAGE LANTERNE (*6)

RITCHIE BLACKMORE'S RAINBOW

RITCHIE BLACKMORE (b.14 Apr'45, Weston-Super-Mare, England) – guitar with (ex-ELF) men **RONNIE JAMES DIO** (b.10 Jul'49, Portsmouth, New Hampshire, USA) – vocals / **MICKEY LEE SOULE** – keyboards / **CRAIG GRUBER** – bass / **GARY DRISCOLL** – drums

Oyster Oyster

Aug 75. (lp/c) *(OYA 2001)* <6049> **RITCHIE BLACKMORE'S RAINBOW** [11] [30]
– Man on the silver mountain / Self portrait / Black sheep of the family / Catch the rainbow / Snake charmer / Temple of the king / If you don't like rock'n'roll / Sixteenth century Greensleeves / Still I'm sad. *(re-iss. Aug81 on 'Polydor'; 2490 141) (re-iss. Aug83 on 'Polydor' lp/c; SPE LP/MC 7) (cd-iss. 1988 & Jan93 on 'Polydor'; 825089-2) (cd re-iss. Jun99; 547360-2)*

Oct 75. (7") *(OYR 103)* <14290> **MAN ON THE SILVER MOUNTAIN. / SNAKE CHARMER** [ ] [ ]

— RITCHIE only retained **DIO,** recruiting new members **TONY CAREY** – keyboards / **JIMMY BAIN** – bass / **COZY POWELL** – drums

Polydor Oyster

May 76. (lp/c; as BLACKMORE'S RAINBOW) *(2490 137)* <1601> **RAINBOW RISING** [11] [48]
– Tarot woman / Run with the wolf / Starstruck / Do you close your eyes / Stargazer / A light in the black. *(re-iss. Aug83 lp/c; SPE LP/MC 35) (cd-iss. Nov86; 823089-2) (cd re-iss. Jun99; 547361-2)*

RAINBOW

Jul 77. (d-lp) *(2657 016)* <1801> **RAINBOW ON STAGE (live)** [7] [65]
– Kill the king: (a) Man on a silver mountain, (b) Blues, (c) Starstruck / Catch the rainbow / Mistreated / Sixteenth century Greensleeves / Still I'm sad. *(re-iss. Jan84; SPDLP 6) (cd-iss. Nov86; 823656-2)*

Aug 77. (7") *(2066 845)* **KILL THE KING: MAN ON THE SILVER MOUNTAIN. / MISTREATED** [44] [–]
(re-iss. Jul81; same) ; reached UK No.41

— **MARK CLARKE** – bass (ex-COLOSSEUM, ex-URIAH HEEP) repl. BAIN who joined WILD HORSES / **BOB DAISLEY** – bass (ex-WIDOWMAKER, ex-CHICKEN SHACK) repl. CLARKE / **DAVID STONE** – keyboards (ex-SYMPHONIC SLAM) repl. CAREY

Polydor Polydor

Mar 78. (7") *(2066 913)* <14481> **LONG LIVE ROCK'N'ROLL. / SENSITIVE TO LIGHT** [33] [ ]
(re-iss. Jul81; same)

Apr 78. (lp/c) *(POLD/+C 5002)* <6143> **LONG LIVE ROCK'N'ROLL** [7] [89]
– Long live rock'n'roll / Lady of the lake / L.A. connection / Gates of Babylon / Kill the king / The shed (subtle) / Sensitive to light / Rainbow eyes. *(re-iss. Aug83 lp/c; SPE LP/MC 34) (cd-iss. Jan93; 825090-2) (cd re-iss. Jun99; 547363-2)*

Sep 78. (7"red) *(2066 968)* **L.A. CONNECTION. / LADY OF THE LAKE** [40] [–]
(re-iss. 7"black Jul81; same)

— **BLACKMORE** retained only **COZY POWELL / GRAHAM BONNET** – vocals (ex-Solo artist, ex-MARBLES) repl. DIO who went solo / **ROGER GLOVER** – bass, vocals (ex-DEEP PURPLE) repl. DAISLEY / **DON AIREY** – keyboards repl. STONE

Aug 79. (clear-lp/c) *(POLD/+C 5023)* <6221> **DOWN TO EARTH** [6] [66]
– All night long / Eyes of the world / No time to lose / Makin' love / Since you been gone / Love's no friend / Danger zone / Lost in Hollywood. *(re-iss. Apr84 lp/c; SPE LP/MC 69) (cd-iss. Dec86; 823705-2) (cd re-iss. Jun99; 547364-2)*

Aug 79. (7") *(POSP 70)* <2014> **SINCE YOU BEEN GONE. / BAD GIRLS** [6] Oct79 [57]
(re-iss. Jul81; same)

Feb 80. (7") *(POSP 104)* <2060> **ALL NIGHT LONG. / WEISS HEIM** [5] [ ]
(re-iss. Jul81; same)

— **JOE LYNN TURNER** (b. 2 Aug'51, Hackensack, New Jersey, USA) – vocals, repl. BONNET who continued solo career. / **BOBBY RONDINELLI** – drums repl. POWELL who later joined E.L.P.

Jan 81. (7") *(POSP 221)* **I SURRENDER. / MAYBE NEXT TIME** [3] [–]
(re-iss. Jul81; same)

Feb 81. (lp/c) *(POLD/+C 5036)* <6316> **DIFFICULT TO CURE** [3] [50]
– I surrender / Spotlight kid / No release / Vielleicht das nachster zeit (Maybe next time) / Can't happen here / Freedom fighter / Midtown tunnel vision / Difficult to cure. *(re-iss. Aug84 lp/c)(cd; SPE LP/MC 76)(800-018-2) (cd re-iss. Jun99; 547365-2)*

Jun 81. (7") *(POSP 251)* **CAN'T HAPPEN HERE. / JEALOUS LOVER** [20] [–]

Nov 81. (m-lp) <502> **JEALOUS LOVER** [–] [ ]
– Jealous lover / Can't happen here / I surrender / Weiss Helm.

— **DAVE ROSENTHAL** – keyboards; repl. AIREY who joined OZZY OSBOURNE

Polydor Mercury

Mar 82. (7"blue/ext-12"blue) *(POSP/+X 421)* <76146> **STONE COLD. / ROCK FEVER** [34] [40]

Apr 82. (lp/c) *(POLD/+C 5056)* <4041> **STRAIGHT BETWEEN THE EYES** [5] [30]
– Death alley driver / Stone cold / Bring on the night (dream chaser) / Tite squeeze / Tearin' out my heart / Power / Miss Mistreated / Rock fever / Eyes of fire. *(cd-iss. Nov83; 800-028-2) (cd re-iss. Apr94; 521709-2) (cd re-iss. Jun99; 547366-2)*

— **BLACKMORE** still had in his ranks **GLOVER, TURNER, ROSENTHAL, /** and **CHUCK BURGI** – drums (ex-BRAND X) repl. RONDINELLI

Aug 83. (7"/7"pic-d) *(POSP/+P 631)* <815660> **STREET OF DREAMS. / IS ANYBODY THERE** [52] [60]
(12"+=) *(POSPX 631)* – Power (live).

Sep 83. (lp/c)(cd) *(POLD/+C 5116)(<815-305-2>)* **BENT OUT OF SHAPE** [11] [34]
– Stranded / Can't let you go / Fool for the night / Fire dance / Anybody there / Desperate heart / Street of dreams / Drinking with the devil / Snowman / Make your move. *(cd re-iss. Jun99; 547367-2)*

Oct 83. (7"/7"sha-pic-d) *(POSP/+P 654)* **CAN'T LET YOU GO. / ALL NIGHT LONG (live)** [43] [ ]
(12"+=) *(POSPX 654)* – Stranded (live).

— Split late '83 . . . BLACKMORE and GLOVER reformed DEEP PURPLE

RITCHIE BLACKMORE'S RAINBOW

— re-formed for comeback concerts & an album. His new band:- **DOOGIE WHITE** – vocals / **PAUL MORRIS** – keyboards / **GREG SMITH** – bass / **JOHN O'REILLY** – drums

Arista Beacon

Sep 95. (cd/c) *(74321 30337-2/-4)* <51565> **STRANGER IN US ALL** [ ] 1996 [ ]
– Wolf to the Moon / Cold hearted woman / Hunting humans (insatiable) / Stand and fight / Ariel / Too late for tears / Black masquerade / Silence / Hall of the mountain king / Still I'm sad.

– compilations, etc. –

Sep 78. (d-lp) *Polydor; (268 3078)* **RITCHIE BLACKMORE'S RAINBOW / RAINBOW RISING** [ ] [–]

Nov 81. (d-lp/d-c) *Polydor; (POLDV/PODVC 2)* **THE BEST OF RAINBOW** [14] [ ]
– All night long / Man on the silver mountain / Can't happen here / Lost in Hollywood / Since you been gone / Stargazer / Catch the rainbow / Kill the king / 16th century Greensleeves / I surrender / Long live rock'n'roll / Eyes of the world / Starstruck / A light in the black / Mistreated. *(cd-iss. 1983; 800-074-2)*

Feb 83. (d-c) *Polydor; (3574 141)* **DOWN TO EARTH / DIFFICULT TO CURE** [ ] [–]

Feb 86. (d-lp/d-c)(d-cd) *Polydor; (PODV/+C 8)(<827-987-2>)* **FINYL VINYL** (live 80's material) [ ] [87]
– Spotlight kid / I surrender / Miss mistreated / Jealous lover / Can't happen here / Tearin' out my heart / Since you been gone / Bad girl / Difficult to cure / Stone cold / Power / Man on the silver mountain / Long live rock'n'roll / Weiss heim. *(d-cd re-iss. Jun99; 547368-2)*

Feb 88. (7") *Old Gold; (OG 9772)* **SINCE YOU BEEN GONE. / ALL NIGHT LONG** [ ] [–]

Oct 89. (d-lp/c/cd) *Connoisseur; (RPVSOP LP/MC/CD 143)* **ROCK PROFILE VOL.1** [ ] [–]
(above credited to RITCHIE BLACKMORE contains early sessions and PURPLE work) (cd.omits interview tracks + 1 song)

Dec 90. (d-cd/c/d-lp) *Connoisseur; (DPVSOP CD/MC/LP 155)* **LIVE IN GERMANY 1976 (live)** [ ] [–]

Jul 91. (cd/d-lp) *Connoisseur; (RPVSOP CD/LP 157)* **ROCK PROFILE VOLUME 2** [ ] [–]
(above also credited to RITCHIE BLACKMORE cont. RAINBOW material, etc.)

Jun 93. (cd-s) *Old Gold; (OG)* **I SURRENDER / SINCE YOU BEEN GONE / ALL NIGHT LONG** –
Jan 94. (cd) *R.P.M.; (RPM 120)* **SESSION MAN** –
Jun 94. (cd) *R.P.M.; (PRM)* **TAKE IT! – SESSIONS 63-68** –
Aug 97. (cd) *Polydor; (537687-2)* **THE VERY BEST OF RAINBOW**
Feb 02. (cd) *Spectrum; (544651-2)* **POT OF GOLD** –
May 02. (cd) *Polydor; (589652-2)* **ALL NIGHT LONG: AN INTRODUCTION TO RAINBOW**
May 03. (d-cd) *Polydor; (065538-2)* **CATCH THE RAINBOW: THE ANTHOLOGY**
Oct 05. (d-cd) *Castle; (CMEDD 1029)* **GETAWAY: 60s GROUPS & SESSIONS**

BLACKMORE'S NIGHT

RITCHIE with **CANDICE NIGHT** (b. 8 May'71, Hauppauge, Long Island, New York) – vocals / **LADY GREEN** – violin / etc

Edel Edeltone

Oct 97. (cd) *(0099022WHE)* *<3755>* **SHADOW OF THE MOON** Feb98
– Shadow of the Moon / The clock ticks on / Be mine tonight / Play minstrel play / Ocean gypsy / Minstrel hall / Magical world / Writing on the wall / Renaissance faire / Memmingen / No second chance / Mond tanz / Spirit of the sea / Greensleeves / Wish you were here. *(re-iss. May98 on 'H.T.D.'; HTDCD 84) (cd re-iss. May00 on 'Candlelight'; LIGHTCD 1)*

—— added **JOHN FORD** – bass / **KEVIN DUNNE** – drums / **JENS JOHANSSON** – keyboards / etc.

Pony Canyon Intersound

Jun 99. (cd) *(PCCY 01377) <3741>* **UNDER A VIOLET MOON** Jul99
– Under a violet moon / Castles and dreams / Past time with good company / Morning star / Avalon / Possum goes to Prague / Wind in the willows / Gone with the wind / Beyond the sunset / March the heroes home / Spanish nights (I remember it well) / Catherine Howard's fate / Durch den wald zum balch haus / Fool's gold / Now and then / Self portrait.

S.P.V. S.P.V.

Aug 01. (cd) *(<SPV 085-7243-2>)* **FIRES AT MIDNIGHT** Jul01
– Written in the stars / The times they are a-changin' / I still remember / Home again / Crowning of the king / Fayre thee well / Fires at midnight / Hanging tree / The storm / Mid winter's night / All because of you / Waiting just for you / Praetorius (courante) / Benzai-ten / Village on the sand / Again someday.
Oct 02. (d-cd) *(<SPV 092-7449-2>)* **PAST TIMES WITH GOOD COMPANY** (live) Feb03
– Shadow of the Moon / Play minstrel play / Minstrel hall / Past times with good company / Fires at midnight / Under a violet moon / Soldier of fortune / 16th Century Greensleeves / Beyond the sunset / Morning star / Home again / Renaissance faire / I still remember / Durch den wald zum bachhaus / Writing on the wall. *(ltd-cd+=; 095-7449-0)* – Fires at midnight / Mid winter's night.
Jun 03. (cd) *(<SPV 085-7499-2>)* **GHOST OF A ROSE**
– Way to Mandalay / 3 black crows / Diamonds and rust / Cartouche / Queen for a day (part 1) / Queen for a day (part 2) / Ivory tower / Nur eine minute / Ghost of a rose / Mr. Peagram's Morris and sword / Loreley / Where are we going from here / Rainbow blues / All for one / Dandelion wine. *(ltd-cd+=; SPV 085-7499-0)* – Just one minute.
Sep 04. (cd) *(<SPV 087-6990-2>)* **BEYOND THE SUNSET: THE ROMANTIC COLLECTION**
– Once in a million years / Be mine tonight / Wish you were here / Waiting just for you / Durch den wald zum bach haus / Ghost of a rose (new version) / Spirit of the sea / I still remember / Castles and dreams / Beyond the sunset / Again someday / Diamonds and rust / Now and then / All because of you. *(ltd-cd w/dvd+=; SPV 087-6990-0)* – (video tracks).
Apr 06. (cd) *<SPV 087-9970-2>* **THE VILLAGE LANTERNE** –
– 25 years / Village lanterne / I guess it doesn't matter / The messenger / World of stone / Faerie queen / St. Teresa / Village dance / Mond tanz – Child in time / Streets of London / Just call my name / Olde mill inn / Windmills / Street of dreams.

Bonnie RAITT

Born: 8 Nov'49, Burbank, California, USA. Brought up in a Quaker family (her dad John was also an actor!), she learned guitar as a young child, receiving the instrument as a Christmas present and subsequently catching the blues bug at college in Cambridge, Massachusetts (reading African studies). Branching out from her love of folk music (JOAN BAEZ was a favourite) to records by JOHN LEE HOOKER, SON HOUSE and MISSISSIPPI FRED McDOWELL, the young RAITT became a well known blues performer on the Northeastern circuit alongside bassist, DAN 'FREEBO' FRIEDBERG (sometimes sharing a stage with her idols, MISSISSIPPI JOHN HURT, HOWLIN' WOLF and SIPPIE WALLACE). Her boyfriend, Dick Waterman, became her manager and, influenced by BOB DYLAN, MUDDY WATERS and JOHN HAMMOND, RAITT began recording for 'Warner Brothers' in 1971. Establishing her own individual blend of country blues and LA-style soft rock, her eponymous debut album set the tone for her later work with a combination of self penned songs and carefully selected covers (by the likes of JACKSON BROWNE, ROBERT JOHNSON and RANDY NEWMAN). Her second set, 'GIVE IT UP', followed in 1972 and featured the lusty Chris Smithers' cover, 'LOVE ME LIKE A MAN', Jackson Browne's 'UNDER THE FALLING SKY' and Eric Katz's 'LOVE HAS NO PRIDE'. Recorded after RAITT's relocation to LA, 1973's 'TAKIN' MY TIME' (with contributions from TAJ MAHAL, JIM KELTNER, BILL PAYNE and LOWELL GEORGE) featured such outstanding tracks as 'KOKOMO BLUES'. Over the ensuing decade, RAITT moved towards an out and out rock direction, exemplified in 1977's 'SWEET FORGIVENESS' (her most successful 'Warner Brothers' album, peaking at US 25), recorded with her regular touring band of WILL McFARLANE (guitar), JEFF LABES (keyboards), DENNIS WHITTED (drums), FREEBO (bass) and vocalists MICHAEL McDONALD and JOHN DAVID SOUTHER. The record provided RAITT with her first US Top 60 hit single, a rocking version of Del Shannon's 'RUNAWAY'. 1982's 'GREEN LIGHT' (a US Top 40 album) featured a new backing outfit, The BUMP BAND, which numbered ex-FACES keyboard man, IAN McLAGAN, drummer RICKY FATAAR (ex-BEACH BOYS), bassist RAY OHARA and guitarist JOHNNY LEE SCHELL. RAITT subsequently disappeared from the scene to undergo drugs and alcohol rehabilitation, resurfacing in 1985 when she took part in the ARTISTS AGAINST APARTHEID project. Her last album for 'Warners' was 'NINE LIVES', a modest selling record which included songs by KARLA BONOFF, TOM SNOW, BRYAN ADAMS, WILL JENNINGS, RICHARD KERR and ERIC KATZ. It also featured her old friend and blues mentor, SIPPIE WALLACE, singing on their version of Toots & The Maytals' 'TRUE LOVE IS HARD TO FIND'. In 1987, RAITT joined a programme for recovering alcoholics and after recovering, spent two days recording with PRINCE in Minneapolis. Her benefit work also increased in 1987 when she took part in The July Fourth Disarmament Festival in the Soviet Union, Stop Contra Aid, Amnesty International, Farm Aid and a film about homeless awareness. Real success had been a long time coming, although she bounced back with 'BABY OF MINE' (a duet recorded with DON WAS) from the Disney covers album, 'Stay Awake' (1988); the single's release led to a new recording deal with 'Capitol'. Her first album for her new company, 1989's DON WAS-produced 'NICK OF TIME', (highlights being the self-penned title track, 'THE ROAD'S MY MIDDLE NAME' and JOHN HIATT's 'THING CALLED LOVE') was aimed at the AOR market, subsequently netting her three Grammy's and gave her a UK chart debut at number No.51 (a chart topper in America). This elevated her into the superstar bracket, leading to guest spots on projects by the likes of DAVID CROSBY, EMMYLOU HARRIS and B.B. KING to name but a few. RAITT's next album, 'LUCK OF THE DRAW' (1991), was an even bigger seller (US Top 3 and UK Top 40), although the songs (from the likes of JOHN HIATT, PAUL BRADY and herself) weren't quite as strong. RAITT's personal life became stable following her marriage to actor, MICHAEL O'KEEFE, in 1991 after years of singing about broken hearts and no-good men. 1994 saw a return to previous highs with 'LONGING IN THEIR HEARTS', an album that reaped more Grammy's and went deservedly multi-platinum. A concert set, 'ROAD TESTED' (1995), was incredibly her first such outing despite her legendary live status. Featuring duets with JACKSON BROWNE and BRUCE HORSNBY, it also contained a disappointing collaboration with BRYAN ADAMS, although excellent versions of Talking Heads' 'BURNING DOWN THE HOUSE' and John Prine's 'ANGEL FROM MONTGOMERY' were enough to save the album. Having started out in her long career using an acoustic, thumb-picking style of playing and progressing to slide guitar, she has become perhaps the only woman in the "rock" world to be recognised as a guitar virtuoso (RAITT was initially tutored by the late, great LOWELL GEORGE of LITTLE FEAT). For 1998's 'FUNDAMENTAL', RAITT ditched Don Was and brought in producers of the moment Mitchell Froom and Tchad Blake. Unfortunately, the latter pair's more adventurous studio techniques sat particularly uncomfortably with RAITT's earthy style, experiments with cajun, reggae and caribbean music falling particularly flat. Production duties back within her own remit on 'SILVER LINING' (2002), RAITT turned in one of her most engaging albums in years, guest spots from the likes of STEVE CROPPER and ROY ROGERS adding texture and colour. While her guitar playing was never less than dazzling, the spotlight fell squarely on RAITT's ever maturing vocals, showcased to particularly heart-rending effect on 'WOUNDED HEART'. Her increasingly high profile as a quality adult contemporary artist was reflected in another US Top 20 placing. At a few years short of 60, RAITT proved herself as defiant an individualist as ever, assuming both the bulk of the production responsibilities and the weight of life's iniquities on 'SOULS ALIKE' (2005), another US Top 20 success heralded with unyielding adult contemporary hit, 'I WILL NOT BE BROKEN'. Among the various collaborators it was ex-pat New Orleans pianist JON CLEARY who supplied RAITT with the loosest grooves, harking back to the second line spirit of her early 70s work with LOWELL GEORGE on the likes of 'LOVE ON ONE CONDITION' and 'UNNECESSARILY MERCENARY'. In the awkward funk of 'DEEP WATER', the stanky 'GOD WAS IN THE WATER' (co-penned by another 70s stalwart, RANDALL BRAMLETT) and the gnarled 'CROOKED CROWN', however, RAITT showed herself to be on a par with EMMYLOU HARRIS as an elderstateswoman unafraid of sonic replacement therapy.

• **Covered:** WALKING BLUES (Robert Johnson) / UNDER THE FALLING SKY (Jackson Browne) / LOVE HAS NO PRIDE (Eric Kaz) / GUILTY (Randy Newman) / WHAT IS SUCCESS (Allen Toussaint) / WOMEN BE WISE (Wallace-Beach) / MY FIRST NIGHT ALONE WITH YOU (. . . Vassey) / SUGAR MAMA (McClinton-Clark) / LOUISE (Paul Siebel) / NO WAY TO TREAT A LADY (Bryan Adams) / THE GLOW (. . . Hildebrand) / BUILT TO MAKE ME LEAVE HOME (. . . Randle) / WITH YA, WON'T CHAS (. . . Schell) / YOUR GOOD THING (Hayes-Porter) / YOUR GONNA GET WHAT'S COMING (Robert Palmer) / GOIN' WILD FOR YOU BABY (Snow-Batteau) / etc. In 1989 most were written by JOHN HIATT and others including SOMETHING TO TALK ABOUT (S.Eikhardt) / I CAN'T MAKE YOU LOVE ME (Reid / Shamblin).

Album rating: BONNIE RAITT (*5) / GIVE IT UP (*6) / TAKIN' MY TIME (*7) / STREETLIGHTS (*6) / HOME PLATE (*4) / SWEET FORGIVENESS (*5) / THE GLOW (*6) / GREEN LIGHT (*6) / NINE LIVES (*5) / NICK OF TIME (*8) / THE BONNIE RAITT COLLECTION compilation (*7) / LUCK OF THE DRAW (*8) / LONGING IN THEIR HEARTS (*7) / ROAD TESTED (*5) / FUNDAMENTAL (*5) / SILVER LINING (*5) / THE BEST OF BONNIE RAITT compilation (*7) / SOULS ALIKE (*6)

BONNIE RAITT – vocals, guitar, steel guitar / **FREEBO** – bass / **A.C.REID** – tenor sax / etc.

Warners Warners

Nov 71. (lp) *<(WS 1953)>* **BONNIE RAITT**
– Bluebird revisited / I'm a mighty tight woman / Thank you / Finest lovin' man / Any day woman / Big road / Walking blues / Danger heartbreak dead ahead / Since I fell for you / I ain't blue / Woman be wise. *(re-iss. Jun76; K 56255) <(cd-iss. Oct01 on 'Warner-ESP'; 8122 78377-2)>*

Dec 71. (7") *<7554>* **BLUEBIRD. / WOMAN BE WISE** –

Nov 72. (lp) *(K 46189) <BS 2643>* **GIVE IT UP** Oct72
– Give it up or let me go / Nothing seems to matter / I know / If you gotta make a fool of somebody / Love me like a man / Stayed too long at the fair / Under the falling sky / You got to know how / You told me baby / Love has no pride. *(<cd-iss. Mar02 on 'Warners-ESP'; 8122 78378-2)>*

Dec 72. (7") *(K 16226) <7645>* **STAYED TOO LONG AT THE FAIR. / UNDER THE FALLING SKY**

— now on session **LOWELL GEORGE / BILL PAYNE / JIM KELTNER + TAJ MAHAL**

Oct 73. (7") *<7758>* **YOU'VE BEEN IN LOVE TOO LONG. / EVERYBODY'S CRYIN' MERCY** –

Nov 73. (lp) *(K 46261) <BS 2729>* **TAKIN' MY TIME** Oct73 87
– You've been in love too long / I gave my love a candle / Let me in / Everybody's cryin' mercy / Cry like a rainstorm / Wah she go do / I feel the same / I thought I was a child / Write me a few of your lines – Kokomo blues / Guilty. *(re-iss. Jun76; K 56254) (cd-iss. Feb93; 7599 27275-2) <(cd re-iss. Mar02 on 'Warners-ESP'; 8122 78379-2)>*

Oct 74. (7") *<8044>* **I GOT PLENTY. / YOU GOTTA BE READY FOR LOVE (IF YOU WANNA BE MINE)** –

Nov 74. (lp) *(K 56075) <BS 2818>* **STREETLIGHTS** Oct74 80
– That song about the Midway / Rainy day man / Angel from Montgomery / I got plenty / Streetlights / What is success / Ain't nobody home / Everything that touches you / Got you on my mind / You gotta be ready for love (if you wanna be mine). *(cd-iss. 1989; 927286-2) <(cd re-iss. Oct01 on 'Warners-ESP'; 8122 78380-2)>*

Nov 75. (7") *<8166>* **MY FIRST NIGHT ALONE WITH YOU. / GOOD ENOUGH** –

Dec 75. (lp/c) *(K/K4 56160) <BS 2864>* **HOME PLATE** Oct75 43
– What do you want the boy to do / Good enough / Run like a thief / Fool yourself / My first night alone with you / Walk out the front door / Sugar mama / Pleasin' each other / I'm blowin' away / Your sweet and shiny eyes. *(cd-iss. Feb93; 7599 27292-2) <(cd re-iss. Mar02 on 'Warners-ESP'; 8122 78381-2)>*

May 76. (7") *<8189>* **WALK OUT THE FRONT DOOR. / RUN LIKE A THIEF** –

Jun 76. (7") *(K 16728)* **I'M BLOWIN' AWAY. / RUN LIKE A THIEF** –

— In 1976, she duetted w/**GEOFF MULDAUR** on single 'WHEN YOU TOUCH ME THIS WAY' / SINCE I'VE BEEN WITH YOU BABE'.

— Her touring band were **WILL McFARLANE** – guitar / **JEFF LABES** – keyboards / **DENNIS WHITTED** – drums / **FREEBO** – bass (as always) + guests **MICHAEL McDONALD + J.D. SOUTHER** on guest backing vocals

Apr 77. (lp/c) *(K/K4 56323) <BS 2990>* **SWEET FORGIVENESS** 25
– Sweet forgiveness / Gamblin' man / Two lives / Runaway / About to make me leave home / Three time loser / My opening farewell / Takin' my time / Home / Louise. *<(cd-iss. Oct01 on 'Warners-ESP'; 8122 78382-2)>*

May 77. (7") *<8382>* **RUNAWAY. / LOUISE** – 57

May 77. (7") *(K 16953)* **RUNAWAY. / HOME** –

Aug 77. (7") *<8430>* **THREE TIME LOSER. / TWO LIVES** –

Aug 77. (7") *(K 17003)* **THREE TIME LOSER. / LOUISE** –

Nov 77. (7") *<8485>* **GAMBLIN' MAN. / ABOUT TO MAKE ME LEAVE HOME** –

Oct 79. (lp/c) *(K 56706) <3369>* **THE GLOW** 30
– I thank you / Your good thing (is about to end) / Sleep's dark and silent gate / The glow / Bye bye baby / The boy can't help it / (I could have been your) Best old friend / You're gonna get what's coming / (Goin') Wild for you baby. *(cd-iss. Feb93; 7559 27403-2) <(cd re-iss. Mar02 on 'Warners-ESP'; 8122 78383-2)>*

Nov 79. (7") *<49116>* **YOU'RE GONNA GET WHAT'S COMING. / THE GLOW** – 73

Mar 80. (7") *<49185>* **(I COULD HAVE BEEN YOUR) BEST OLD FRIEND. / (GOIN') WILD FOR YOU BABY** –

— In mid-80's, she released 'Asylum' 45; 'DON'T IT MAKE YOU WANNA DANCE'. At the same time she and J.D. SOUTHER issued 'ONCE IN A LIFETIME' / 'YOU'RE ONLY LONELY'.

— next feat. **The BUMP BAND** incl. **IAN McLAGAN** – keyboards (ex-SMALL FACES) / **JOHNNY LEE SCHELL** – guitar / **RAY O'HARA** – bass / **RICKY FATAAR** – drums

Feb 82. (7") *<50022>* **CAN'T GET ENOUGH. / KEEP THIS HEART IN MIND** [–] [ ]

Feb 82. (lp/c) *(K/K4 56980) <BSK 3630>* **GREEN LIGHT** [ ] [38]
– Keep this heart in mind / River of tears / Can't get enough / Me and the boys / I can't help myself / Willya wontcha / Let's keep it between us / Baby come back / Talk to me / Green light. *<(cd-iss. Mar02 on 'Warners-ESP'; 8122 78384-2)>*

Apr 82. (7") *<29992>* **ME AND THE BOYS. / RIVER OF TEARS** [–] [ ]

Apr 82. (7") *(K 17943)* **ME AND THE BOYS. / KEEP THIS HEART IN MIND** [ ] [–]

— BONNIE semi-retired in 1982 to go through a period of drug rehabilitation and attend a form of alcoholics anonymous.

Sep 86. (lp/c/cd) *(925486-1/-4/-2) <25486>* **NINE LIVES** [ ] Aug 86 [ ]
– No way to treat a lady / Runnin' back to me / Who but a fool / Crime of passion / All day, all night / Stand up to the night / Excited / Freezin' (for a little human love) / True love is hard to find / Angel. *<(cd re-iss. Oct01 on 'Warners-ESP'; 8122 78385-2)>*

Sep 86. (7") *<28615>* **NO WAY TO TREAT A LADY. / STAND UP TO THE NIGHT** [–] [ ]

Feb 87. (7") *<28450>* **CRIMES OF PASSION. / STAND UP TO THE NIGHT** [–] [ ]

— In Oct '88, she teamed up with DON WAS of WAS (NOT WAS) on 'A&M' single 'BABY MINE'. Their vocalists **SWEAT PEA ATKINSON + SIR HARRY BOWENS** plus guests **DAVID CROSBY & GRAHAM NASH, FATAAR & SCHELL, KIM WILSON,** etc.

Capitol Capitol

Apr 89. (cd/c/lp) *(CD/TC+EST 2095) <91268>* **NICK OF TIME** [51] [1]
– Nick of time / A thing called love / Love letter / Cry on my shoulder / Real man / Nobody's girl / Have a heart / Too soon to tell / I will not be denied / I ain't gonna let you break my heart again / The road's my middle name. *(re-dist.Apr90)*

May 89. (c-s/7") *(TC+/CL 530) <44364>* **NICK OF TIME. / THE ROAD'S MY MIDDLE NAME** [ ] Aug89 [ ]
(12"+=/cd-s+=) *(12/CD CL 530)* – I ain't gonna let you break my heart again. *(re-dist.Mar90) <re-iss. May90; hit US No.92>*

Mar 90. (7") *<44501>* **HAVE A HEART. / THE ROAD'S MY MIDDLE NAME** [–] [49]

May 90. (7") *(CL 576)* **A THING CALLED LOVE. / NOBODY'S GIRL** [ ] [–]
(12"+=/cd-s+=) *(12/CD CL 576)* – The road's my middle name.

— next featured **HIATT** plus **BRUCE HORNSBY + RICHARD THOMPSON**

Jul 91. (cd/c/lp) *(CD/TC+/EST 2145) <96111>* **LUCK OF THE DRAW** [38] [2]
– Something to talk about / Good man, good woman / I can't make you love me / Tangled and dark / Come to me / No business / One part of my lover / Not the only one / Papa come quick (Jody and Chico) / Slow ride / Luck of the draw / All at once.

Jul 91. (c-s/7") *(TC+/CL 619) <44724>* **SOMETHING TO TALK ABOUT. / ONE PART OF MY LOVER** [ ] [5]
(12"+=) *(12CL 619)* – I ain't gonna let you break my heart again.
(cd-s++=) *(CDCL 619)* – Nick of time. *(re-iss. Feb92; same)*

Aug 91. (c-s/7") *(TC/+CL 627) <44764>* **NOT THE ONLY ONE. / COME TO ME** [ ] Mar92 [34]
(12"+=/cd-s+=) *(12/CD CL 627)* – Papa come quick (Jody and Chico).

Dec 91. (c-s/7") *(TC+/CL 639) <44729>* **I CAN'T MAKE YOU LOVE ME. / COME TO ME** [50] Nov91 [18]
(cd-s+=) *(CDCL 639)* – Tangled and dark.

Jun 92. (c-s/7") *(TC+/CL 666)* **GOOD MAN, GOOD WOMAN. / NICK OF TIME** [ ] [–]
(cd-s+=) *(CDCL 666)* – Thing called love / One part be my lover.

Apr 94. (c-s) *(TCCL 713) <58125>* **LOVE SNEAKIN' UP ON YOU / HELL TO PAY** [69] Mar94 [19]
(cd-s+=) *(CDCL 713)* – Nick of time / Baby be mine.

Apr 94. (cd/c) *(CD/TC EST 2227) <81427>* **LONGING IN THEIR HEARTS** [26] Mar94 [1]
– Love sneakin' up on you / Longing in their hearts / You / Cool, clear water / Circle dance / I sho do / Dimming of the day / Feeling of falling / Steal your heart away / Storm warning / Hell to pay / Shadow of doubt.

Jun 94. (c-s) *(TCCL 718)* **YOU / I CAN'T MAKE YOU LOVE ME** [31] [–]
(cd-s+=) *(CDCL 718)* – I ain't gonna let you break my heart again / All at once.
(cd-s) *(CDCLS 718)* – ('A'side) / This thing called love / Longing in their hearts / Good man, good woman.

Jul 94. (c-s) *<58195>* **YOU / FEELING OF FALLING** [–] [92]

May 95. (c-s) *(74321 26624-4) <12795>* **YOU GOT IT / FEELING OF FALLING** [ ] Feb95 [33]
(cd-s+=) *(74321 26624-2)* – Circle dance.
(above single issued on 'Arista' & from movie 'Boys On The Side')

Nov 95. (c-s; BONNIE RAITT & BRYAN ADAMS) *(TCCL 763) <58500>* **ROCK STEADY (live) / COME TO ME (live)** [50] [73]
(cd-s+=) *(CDCL 763)* – Thing called love (live with BRUCE HORNSBY).

Nov 95. (cd/c) *(CD/TC EST 2274) <33702>* **ROAD TESTED (live)** [69] [44]
– Thing called love / Something to talk about / Never make your move too soon / Shake a little / Matters of the heart / Love me like a man / The Kokomo medley: Write me a few of your lines – Kokomo blues / My opening farewell / Dimming of the day / Longing in their hearts / Love sneakin' up on you / Burning down the house / I can't make you love me / I believe I'm in love / Rock steady / Angel from Montgomery.

Apr 96. (c-s) *(TCCL 771)* **BURNING DOWN THE HOUSE (live) / SHAKE A LITTLE (live)** [ ] [–]
(cd-s+=) *(CDCL 771)* – I can't make you love me (live) / Rock steady (live).

Apr 98. (cd) *<(8 56397-2)>* **FUNDAMENTAL** [ ] [17]
– The fundamental things / Cure for love / Round & round / Spit of love / Lover's will / Blue for no reason / Meet me half way / I'm on your side / Fearless love / I need love / One belief away.

Apr 02. (cd) *<(5 31816-2)>* **SILVER LINING** [ ] [13]
– Fool's game / I can't help you now / Silver lining / Time of our lives / Gnawin' on it / Monkey business / Wherever you may be / Valley of pain / Hear me Lord / No gettin' over you / Back around / Wounded heart.

May 03. (cd) *<(5 82113-2)>* **THE BEST OF BONNIE RAITT** (compilation) [37] Sep03 [47]
– A thing called love / Nick of time / Nobody's girl *[UK-only]* / Love letter *[US-only]* / Have a heart *[US-only]* / Something to talk about / Not the only one / I can't make you love me / Love sneakin' up on you / You / Dimming of the day / Love me like a man (live) / Rock steady (live) *[UK-only]* / I believe I'm in love with you (live) *[UK-only]* / Spit of love / One belief away *[US-only]* / I can't help you now / Gnawing on it *[US-only]* / Silver lining / Time of our lives *[UK-only]* / Hear me Lord.

Jun 03. (cd-s) *(CDCL 846)* **SILVER LINING / BLUE FOR NO REASON / BURNING DOWN THE HOUSE (live)** [ ] [–]

Sep 05. (cd) *<(4 73628-2)>* **SOULS ALIKE** [ ] [19]
– I will not be broken / God was in the water / Love on one condition / So close / Trinkets / Crooked crown / Unneccesarily mercenary / I don't want anything to change / Deep water / Two lights in the nighttime / The bed I made.

– compilations, etc. –

Aug 90. (cd/c) *Warners; <(2-/4-26242)>* **THE BONNIE RAITT COLLECTION** [ ] Jun90 [61]
– Finest lovin' man / Give it up or let me go / Women be wise (live with SIPPIE WALLACE) / Under the falling sky / Love me like a man / Love has no pride / I feel the same / Guilty / Angel from Montgomery / What is success / My first night alone without you / Sugar mama / Louise / About to make me leave home / Runaway / The glow / (Goin') Wild for you baby / Willya wontcha / True love is hard to find / No way to treat a lady.

the RAKES

Formed: Whitechapel, London, England … 2002 by ALAN DONOHOE, MATTHEW SWINNERTON, LASSE PETERSEN and JAMIE HORNSMITH. London-centric heirs to FRANZ FERDINAND-esque drainpipe chic, the Rake-ish art-punks were nicely positioned in the wings for the impending implosion of fellow scenesters, the LIBERTINES. After scoring a couple of minor, and not so minor hits with 'STRASBOURG' and 'RETREAT', Richard Branson's 'V2' picked them up for third single, 'WORK, WORK, WORK (PUB, CLUB, SLEEP)'. Similar themes of digital era drudgery filled their debut long-player, 'CAPTURE/RELEASE' (2005), with future singles, '22 GRAND JOB' and 'ALL TOO HUMAN', taking cues from the STRANGLERS and bringing BLUR/PULP-era Brit-Pop to a dystopian conclusion.

Album rating: CAPTURE – RELEASE (*9)

ALAN DONOHOE – vocals / **MATTHEW SWINNERTON** – guitar / **JAMIE HORNSMITH** – bass / **LASSE PETERSEN** – drums

City Rockers not iss.

Sep 04. (7") *(ROCKERS 28)* **STRASBOURG. / JUST GOT PAID / T-BONE (demo)** 57 –
(cd-s) *(ROCKERS 28CD)* – (first 2 tracks) / Ausland mission (demo).

Moshi Moshi not iss.

Apr 05. (7") *(MOSHI 18)* **RETREAT. / DARK CLOUDS** 24 –
(cd-s+=) *(MOSHI 18CD)* – Strasbourg (live at Rough Trade).

V2 not iss.

Jul 05. (cd-s) *(VVR 503277-3)* **WORK, WORK, WORK (PUB, CLUB, SLEEP) / WISH YOU WERE HERE** 28 –
(cd-s) *(VVR 503277-8)* – ('A') / Something clicked and I feel off the edge (demo) / Retreat (phones remix).

Aug 05. (cd/lp) *(VVR 103276-2/-1)* **CAPTURE / RELEASE** 32 –
– Strasbourg / Retreat / 22 grand job / Open book / The guilt / Binary love / We are all animals / T-bone / Terror / Work, work, work (pub, club, sleep).

Oct 05. (cd-s) *(VVR 503461-8)* **22 GRAND JOB / I PROBLEM** 39 –
(cd-s) *(VVR 503461-3)* – ('A') / Pass the metro / ('A'-Filthy Dukes remix) / ('A'-video).

Feb 06. (7") *(VVR 503620-7)* **ALL TOO HUMAN. / 22 GRAND JOB (Lethal Bizzle mix)** 22 –
(cd-s) *(VVR 503620-8)* – ('A') / Watford.
(cd-s) *(VVR 503620-3)* – ('A') / Vitamin V / Terror (acoustic) / ('A'-video).

Mar 06. (re-cd+=) *(VVR 103276-8)* **CAPTURE / RELEASE** –
– (+=) All too human.

RAMMSTEIN

Formed: East Berlin & Schwerin, Germany . . . 1994 by former East German Olympic swimmer, TILL LINDEMANN, plus his 30-something long-time companions, OLIVER RIEDEL, RICHARD Z. KRUSPE-BERNSTEIN, CHRISTIAN "FLAKE" LORENZ, PAUL H. LANDERS and CHRISTOPH SCHEIDER. Naming themselves after the German airbase at Ramstein (originally went by the name of ORGASM DEATH GIMMICK), the industrial shock metallers, like a fusion of LAIBACH, MINISTRY and fellow countrymen, EINSTURZENDE NEUBAUTEN, RAMMSTEIN had five hit singles in their home country. This was due to their OTT stage extravaganzas which featured TILL singing (in his native tongue) covered in a metallic coat of fire before he unveiled to show off his muscular, naked body complete with very large dildo strapped upside his leather belt!. Meanwhile, the naked OLIVER (bar his white socks), RICHARD (wearing a white wedding dress) and the rest of the bare-cheeked crew played their aggro-rock to a backdrop of Leni Riefenstahl's (Hitler's fave!) controversial film, 'Olympiad'. A German-only released debut album was finally upstaged by a second, 'SEHNSUCHT' (1997), which went on to surprisingly sell over half a million copies in the States. In the Autumn of '98, RAMMSTEIN were at the centre of some accusations of neo Nazi-ism when English tabloids branded them with that unfortunate tag. Around the same time, the single 'DU HAST' (actually a cover of Depeche Mode's 'STRIPPED') was given a British release and it looked as if these brassnecked technoid show-offs were going to eventually invade our shores. RAMMSTEIN's long-awaited studio follow-up album, 'MUTTER', was unleashed to the public in spring 2001, the broody ensemble were now on their way to becoming Germany's best export since SCHENKER and the SCORPIONS. The techno shock troopers returned in 2004 with 'REISE, REISE', their first UK Top 40 album, if hardly a departure from the Halls-Of-Valhalla arrangements and wheat beer-curdling growl that their fans know and love. Among subjects for lyrical bulldozing were the Dalai Lama, Germany's infamous cannibal case and life in 21st century America, as heard in hilarious UK Top 40 single, 'AMERIKA' (altogether now.."We're all living in Amerika, Amerika is wunderbar!!!" – JAMES BROWN eat your heart out.

Album rating: HERZELEID (*5) / SEHNSUCHT (*7) / LIVE AUS BERLIN (*5) / MUTTER (*8) / REISE, REISE (*5) / ROSENROT (*5)

TILL LINDEMANN (b. 4 Jan'63) – vocals / **RICHARD Z. KRUSPE-BERNSTEIN** (b.24 Jun'67) – guitar / **PAUL H. LANDERS** (b. HENRY HIRSCH, 9 Dec'64) – guitar / **OLIVER RIEDEL** (b.11 Apr'71) – bass / **CHRISTIAN "FLAKE" LORENZ** (b. 6 Nov'66) – keyboards / **CHRISTOPH "DOOM" SCHNEIDER** (b.11 May'66) – drums

Ils Inter. not iss.

Jul 95. (cd-s) **DU RIECHST SO GUT / WOLLT IHR DAS BETT IN FLAMEN SEHEN? / DU RIECHST SO GUT (scal remix)** – German –

Sep 95. (c) *(529160)* **HERZELEID** – German –
– Wollt ihr das bett in flamen sehen? / Der meister / Weisses fleisch / Asche zu asche / Seeman / Du riechst so gut / Das alte leid / Heirate mich / Herzeleid / Laichzeit / Rammstein. *<US cd-iss. Dec96 on 'Slash'; 529160-2>*

Jan 96. (cd-s) **SEEMAN / DER MEISTER / RAMMSTEIN IN THE HOUSE (timewriter remix)** – German –

London Slash

Apr 97. (cd-s) *(573665)* **ENGEL / SEHNSUCHT / RAMMSTEIN (Eskimos & Egypt radio mixes x3)** – German –

Jul 97. (cd-s) **DU HAST / BUCK DICH / DU HAST (Jacob Hellner remix) / DU HAST (Clawfinger remix)** – German –
(UK-iss.Nov98; LONCD 422)

Nov 97. (cd) *(537304-2)* *<539901>* **SEHNSUCHT** Jan98 45
– Sehnsucht / Engel / Tier / Bestrafe mich / Du hast / Buck dich / Spiel mit mir / Klavier / Alter Mann / Eifersucht / Kuss mich (fellfrosch) / Engel / Du hast. *(re-iss. Mar99 on 'XIII Bis'; 18795-2)*

Nov 97. (cd-s) **DAS MODELL / KOKAIN / ALTER MANN (special version) / (CD-Rom)** – German –

May 98. (cd-s) **DU RIECHST SO GUT '98** – German –
– Du riechst so gut (remixes; Faith No More / Gunter Schulz & Hiwatt Mashall / Sascha Knoietzko / Olaf Bruhn / Sascha Moser / Jacob Hellner & Marc Stagg / Gunter Schulz / video.

Aug 99. (c)<cd> *(<547590-2>)* **LIVE AUS BERLIN (live)** –
– Spiel / mit mir / Bestrafe mich / Weisses fleisch / Sehnsucht / Asche zu asche / Wilder wein / Heirate mich / Du riechst so gut / Du hast / Buck dich / Engel / Rammstein / Laichzeit / Wollt ihr das bett in flammen sehen? / Seeman.

Universal Universal

Feb 01. (cd-s) *(587940)* **SONNE / ADIOS / SONNE (Clawfinger k.o. remix) / SONNE (Clawfinger t.k.o. remix)** – German –

Apr 01. (cd) *<(549639-2)>* **MUTTER** 77
– Mein herz brennt / Links 2 3 4 / Sonne / Ich will / Feuer frei! / Mutter / Spielurhr / Zwitter / Rein raus / Adios / Nebel. *(special cd May02 +=; 589367-2)* – Ich will (live) / Links 2 3 4 in arbelt (live) / Sonne (live) / Spleluhr (live).

May 01. (cd-s) *(587095)* **LINKS 2 3 4 / HALLELUJA / LINKS 2 3 4 (Clawfinger geradeaus remix) / LINKS 2 3 4 (Westbam technoelectro mix) / LINKS 2 3 4 (Westbam hard rock cafe mix)** – German –

Sep 01. (cd-s) *(563271)* **ICH WILL / ICH WILL (live: Berlin) / ICH WILL (Westbam mix) / ICH WILL (Paul Van Dyk mix) / PET SEMATARY (live) / ICH WILL (CD-Rom)** – German –

M.C.A. M.C.A.

May 02. (cd-s) *(MCSTD 40280)* **ICH WILL / LINKS 2 3 4 (Clawfinger Geradeaus remix) / DU HAST (remix by Jacob Hellner)** 30 –
(cd-s) *(MCSXD 40280)* – ('A'side) / Halleluja / Stripped (heavy mental mix by Charlie Clouser).

Nov 02. (cd-s) *(MCSTD 40302)* **FEUER FREI! (video) / (interview & history) / Buck dich / Du hast / (photo gallery 9 shots)** 35 –
(cd-s) *(MCSXD 40302)* – ('A'-Rammstein vs. Junkie XL remix) / Mutter / ('A'-remix 95) / (photo gallery & interview).

Aug 04. (7") *(MCS 40381)* **MEIN TEIL. / WILDER WEIN** 61
(7") *(MCSX 40381)* – ('A') / Asche zu asche (live..)
(cd-s) *(MCSTD 40381)* *<9866978>* – ('A') / Ich will orchesterlied VII / ('A'-Pet Shop Boys' you are what you eat remix) / ('A'-Arthur Baker's return to New York buffet remix).

Sep 04. (cd) *(<986815-0>)* **REISE, REISE** 37 Nov04 61
– Reise, reise / Mein teil / Dalai Lama / Keine lust / Los / Amerika / Moskau / Morgenstern / Stein un stein / Ohne dich / Amour.

Oct 04. (7") *(MCS 40394)* **AMERIKA. / WILDER WEIN** 38 –
(cd-s) *(MCSTD 40394)* – ('A') / ('A'-digital hardcore mix by Alec Empire) / Mein herz brennt (as featured on the Mercedes ad) / Ich will orchesterlied VII).
(dvd-s) *(MCSVD 40394)* – ('A'-video) / (making of video) / ('A').

Feb 05. (7"clear) *(MCS 40405)* **KEINE LUST. / DU HAST (live at Parkbuhne Wuhlheide, Berlin, August 1998)** 35 –
(cd-s) *(MCSTD 40405)* – ('A') / Ohne dich (Mina Harker's version – remixed by Laibach) / Mutter orchesterfied I.
(dvd-s) *(MCSDVD 40405)* – ('A') / Mein Teil / Mein Teil (video) / (making of 'Mein Teil' EPK).

Oct 05. (cd-s) *(987430-2)* **BENZIN** 58 –
– (combustion remix by Meshuggah) / (smallstars remix by Ad Rock) / (kerosinii remix by Apocalyptica) / (enhanced weblink).

Oct 05. (cd) *(<987458-8>)* **ROSENROT** 29 Nov05
– Benzin / Mann gegen mann / Rosenrot / Spring / Wo bist du / Stirb nicht vor mir (Don't die before I do) / Zerstoren / Hilf mir / Te quiero puta! / Feuer und wasser / Ein lied.

Mar 06. (12") *(MCST 40451)* **MANN GEGEN MANN. / ROSENROT (3am at Cosey remix by Jagz Kooner)** –
(cd-s) *(MCSTD 40451)* – ('A') / Rosenrot (the tweaker remix by Chris Vrenna).
(cd-s) *(MCSXD 40451)* – ('A') / ('A'-popular music mix by Vince Clarke) / ('A'-Musensohn remix by Sven Helbig) / Ich will (live video).

– compilations, etc. –

Mar 99. (6xcd-box) *Polygram; (569815)* **ORIGINAL SINGLES KOLEKTION** – German –
– Du riechst so gut / Seeman / Engel / Engel (fan edition) / Du hast / Das modell.

RAMONES

Formed: Forest Hills, New York, USA . . . August '74 as a trio by JOHNNY, JOEY and DEE DEE, who all took the working surname RAMONE (although they were brothers only in the loosest sense of the term). One of the prime movers (many would subsequently cite them as the first) in the emergent US punk scene, the band began a residency at the legendary NY club, CBGB's, TOMMY coming in on the drum stool in order to free JOEY up for suitably deranged vocal duties. In June '75, the band were dealt a slight setback when they failed an audition for RICK DERRINGER's 'Blue Sky' label in front of 20,000 fans at a JOHNNY WINTER concert, although later that year manager, Danny Fields, found up and coming new wave label, 'Sire' (run by Seymour Stein) considerably more receptive. Released around the same time as their pivotal (and highly influential) London Roundhouse gig, the band's eponymous summer '76 debut album presented a sound every bit as exhilaratingly juvenile and humorously warped as their leering, mop-topped scruffiness might suggest. Ripping out gloriusly dumb, two-minute buzz-saw classics on such perennial punk subjects as solvent abuse ('I WANNA SNIFF SOME GLUE'), girls (most of the album) and erm, chainsaws ('CHAIN SAW'), The RAMONES had invented themselves as larger than life, cartoon yob no-wavers well ahead of their time, their attitude alone copied by countless two-bit punk bands (and a few great ones) the length and breadth of the British Isles. Barely pausing for breath (or whatever it was these guys inhaled), the new yoik brudders followed up with 'LEAVE HOME' (1977), another strychnine-fuelled session of primitive but tuneful terrace chant anthems, RAMONES style; from this point onwards, the words 'Gabba Gabba Hey' would be forever carved in the stone of the punk lexicon. The album even managed a minor dent in the UK charts, a full scale assault led later that year with the brilliantly throwaway 'SHEENA IS A PUNK ROCKER'. The climax of the early RAMONES blitzkrieg came with 'ROCKET TO RUSSIA' (1977), the lads easing ever so slightly off the gas pedal and taking the credo of mangled, two minute surf-pop to its dayglo conclusion; the hilarious 'CRETIN HOP', 'ROCKAWAY BEACH' and 'TEENAGE LOBOTOMY' remain among the most definitive moments in the RAMONES' dog-eared catalogue. A rather disappointing Top 60 placing failed to do the record justice, although by this stage the band were beginning to make some inroads into the home market. Further evidence, if any was needed, that The RAMONES' chief writer was at the peak of his powers came with the blistering 'Chinese Rocks', a HEARTBREAKERS track co-penned by DEE DEE. With the departure of TOMMY (into production work) the following year, ex-VOID-OID MARC BELL was recruited in his place, rechristened, of course, MARKY RAMONE. Incredibly, the tried and tested formula (with a few notable exceptions, a guitar solo (!) on 'GO MENTAL' and a ballad, 'QUESTIONINGLY') continued to excite with 'ROAD TO RUIN' (1978), their first album to break into the UK Top 40 and the resting place of the legendary 'I WANNA BE SEDATED'. The riotous 'IT'S ALIVE' (1979) captured the RAMONES concert experience head-on, neatly wrapping up the first stage of the boys' career and providing a handy overview of their career to date. Every punk band coped with the scene's fragmentation in their own way, The RAMONES not so wisely choosing to indulge their love of classic 60's pop via the genre's guru, Phil Spector. The results were predictably confused, many longtime RAMONES headbangers balking at their UK Top 10 cover of The Ronettes' 'BABY I LOVE YOU'. Subsequent 80's efforts such as 'PLEASANT DREAMS' (1981) and 'SUBTERRANEAN JUNGLE' (1983) lacked the ragged glory of their earlier work although with the replacement of MARKY with RICHIE (aka RICHARD REINHARDT) in 1984, 'TOO TOUGH TO DIE' (1985) found the band sharpening their attack and presenting a united front against the hardcore pretenders of the day. They couldn't keep it up though, and the limitations of their art really began to bite deep on the bedraggled 'ANIMAL BOY' (1986) and 'HALFWAY TO SANITY' (1987). DEE DEE bailed out after 'BRAIN DRAIN' (1989), replacement C.J. effecting something of a rejuvenation on 'MONDO BIZARRO' (1992). The following year's 'ACID EATERS' saw the band pay tribute to the 60's sounds which had inspired them, while in turn, many of the younger bands who had actually been inspired by The RAMONES would soon be calling the shots at America's major labels. Yet despite this punk revival and the success of such acts as GREEN DAY and OFFSPRING, The RAMONES finally decided to call it a day in early 1996 following the release of the 'ADIOS AMIGOS' set and the accompanying tour. Fans of all ages were shocked to hear the news of JOEY's death (of lymphoma) in NY on the 15th of April, 2001. Barely a year later (5th June 2002), DEE DEE also passed away. Johnny died of cancer on 15th Sept 2004.

• **Songwriters:** DEE DEE and group, except; DO YOU WANNA DANCE (Bobby Freeman) / SURFIN' BIRD (Trashmen) / BABY I LOVE YOU (Ronettes; Phil Spector) / NEEDLES AND PINS (Searchers) / STREET FIGHTIN' MAN (Rolling Stones) / TAKE IT AS IT COMES (Doors) / R.A.M.O.N.E.S. (Motorhead) / ANY WAY YOU WANT IT (Dave Clark) / SPIDER-MAN (Harris-Webster) / etc. In '77, DEE DEE co-wrote 'CHINESE ROCKS' for The HEARTBREAKERS. • **Trivia:** The RAMONES featured in the films 'Blank Generation' (1976) & 'Rock'n'Roll High School' (1979).

Album rating: RAMONES (*9) / LEAVE HOME (*8) / ROCKET TO RUSSIA (*8) / ROAD TO RUIN (*7) / IT'S ALIVE (*6) / ROCK'N'ROLL HIGH SCHOOL soundtrack w/ Various Artists (*7) / END OF THE CENTURY (*7) / PLEASANT DREAMS (*6) / SUBTERRANEAN JUNGLE (*6) / TOO TOUGH TO DIE (*7) / ANIMAL BOY (*6) / HALFWAY TO SANITY (*4) / RAMONES MANIA compilation (*9) / BRAIN DRAIN (*4) / LOCO LIVE (*3) / MONDO BIZARRO (*3) / ACID EATERS (*3) / ADIOS AMIGOS (*5) / WE'RE OUTTA HERE (*5)

JOEY RAMONE (b. JEFFREY HYMAN, 19 May'51) – vocals (was drummer) / **JOHNNY RAMONE** (b. JOHN CUMMINGS, 8 Oct'51, Long Island, N.Y.) – guitar, vocals / **DEE DEE RAMONE** (b. DOUGLAS COLVIN, 18 Sep'52, Fort Lee, Virginia) – bass, vocals / **TOMMY RAMONE** (b. TOM ERDELYI, 29 Jan'49, Budapest, Hungary) – drums

Sire Sire

Jul 76. (lp) *(9103 253)* <7520> **RAMONES** [ ] May76 [ ]
– Blitzkrieg bop / Beat on the brat / Judy is a punk / I wanna be your boyfriend / Chain saw / Now I wanna sniff some glue / I don't wanna go down to the basement / Loudmouth / Havana affair / Listen to my heart / 53rd & 3rd / Let's dance / I don't wanna walk around with you / Today your love, tomorrow the world. *(re-iss. Sep78; SRK 6020) <(cd-iss. Oct99 on 'Rhino'; 7559 27421-2)> <(cd re-mast.Jun01 on 'Rhino'+=; 8122 74306-2)>* – (extra tracks).

Jul 76. (7") *(6078 601)* <725> **BLITZKRIEG BOP. / HAVANA AFFAIR** [ ] May76 [ ]

Oct 76. (7"m) <734> **I WANNA BE YOUR BOYFRIEND. / CALIFORNIA SUN (live) / I DON'T WANNA WALK AROUND WITH YOU (live)** [–] [ ]

Feb 77. (7"m) *(6078 603)* **I REMEMBER YOU. / CALIFORNIA SUN (live) / I DON'T WANNA WALK AROUND WITH YOU (live)** [ ] [–]

Mar 77. (lp) *(9103 254)* <7528> **LEAVE HOME** [45] Feb77 [ ]
– Glad to see you go / Gimme gimme shock treatment / I remember you / Oh oh I love her so / Babysitter * / Suzy is a headbanger / Pinhead / Now I wanna be a good boy / Swallow my pride / What's your game / California sun / Commando / You're gonna kill that girl / You should never have opened that door / California sun. *(re-iss. Jun77 'Carbona Not Glue' replaced *; other re-iss's same) (re-iss. Sep78; SRK 6031) (re-iss. Nov87 on 'Mau Mau'; MAU 602) <(cd re-iss. Oct99 on 'Rhino'; 7599 27422-2)> <(cd re-mast.Jun01 on 'Rhino'+=; 8122 74307-2)>* – (extra tracks).

May 77. (7"m,12"m) *(6078 606)* <746> **SHEENA IS A PUNK ROCKER. / COMMANDO / I DON'T CARE** [22] [81]

Jul 77. (7"m) *(6078 607)* <738> **SWALLOW MY PRIDE. / PINHEAD / LET'S DANCE (live)** [36] Mar77 [ ]

Nov 77. (7"m,12"m) *(6078 611)* **ROCKAWAY BEACH. / TEENAGE LOBOTOMY / BEAT ON THE BRAT** [ ] [–]

Nov 77. (7") <1008> **ROCKAWAY BEACH. / LOCKET LOVE** [–] [66]

Dec 77. (lp) *(9103 255)* <6042> **ROCKET TO RUSSIA** [60] Nov77 [49]
– Cretin hop / Rockaway beach / Here today, gone tomorrow / Locket love / I don't care / Sheena is a punk rocker / We're a happy family / Teenage lobotomy / Do you wanna dance? / I wanna be well / I can't give you anything / Ramona / Surfin' bird / Why is it always this way. *(re-iss. Sep78; SRK 6042) <(cd-iss. Oct99 on 'Rhino'; 7559 27424-2)> <(cd re-mast.Jun01 on 'Rhino'+=; 8122 74309-2)>* – (extra tracks).

Feb 78. (7") <1017> **DO YOU WANNA DANCE?. / BABYSITTER** [–] [86]

Mar 78. (7"m) *(6078 615)* **DO YOU WANNA DANCE? / IT'S A LONG WAY BACK TO GERMANY / CRETIN HOP** [ ] [–]

— **MARKY RAMONE** (b. MARC BELL, 15 Jul'56) – drums (ex-RICHARD HELL & THE VOID-OIDS, ex-DUST) repl. TOMMY who continued producing others.

Sep 78. (7",7"yellow,12"yellow,12"red) *(SRE 1031)* <1025> **DON'T COME CLOSE. / I DON'T WANT YOU** [38] [ ]

Oct 78. (yellow-lp) <*(SRK 6063)*> **ROAD TO RUIN** [32] [ ]
– I just want to have something to do / I wanted everything / Don't come close / I don't want you / Needles and pins / I'm against it / I wanna be sedated / Go mental / Questioningly / She's the one / Bad brain / It's a long way back. *(cd-iss. Oct99; 7559 27426-2) <(cd re-mast.Jun01 on 'Rhino'+=; 8122 74308-2)>* – (extra tracks).

Nov 78. (7") <1045> **NEEDLES AND PINS. / I WANTED EVERYTHING** [–] [ ]

Jan 79. (7") *(SIR 4009)* **SHE'S THE ONE. / I WANNA BE SEDATED** [ ] [–]

May 79. (d-lp/c) *(SRK/SRC 26074)* **IT'S ALIVE (live)** [27] [–]
– Rockaway beach / Teenage lobotomy / Blitzkrieg bop / I wanna be well / Glad to see you go / Gimme gimme shock treatment / You're gonna kill that girl / I don't care / Sheena is a punk rocker / Havana affair / Commando / Here today, gone tomorrow / Surfin' bird / Cretin hop / Listen to my heart / California sun / I don't wanna walk around with you / Pinhead / Do you wanna dance? / Chain saw / Today your love, tomorrow the world / Now I wanna be a good boy / Judy is a punk / Suzy is a headbanger / Let's dance / Oh oh I love her so / Now I wanna sniff some glue / We're a happy family. *(cd-iss. Nov93 on 'Warners'; 7599 26069-2) (cd re-iss. Jan96; 9362 46045-2)*
(above album features TOMMY on drums)

May 79. (7") <1051> **ROCK'N'ROLL HIGH SCHOOL. / DO YOU WANNA DANCE?** [–] [ ]

Sep 79. (7") *(SIR 4021)* **ROCK'N'ROLL HIGH SCHOOL. / SHEENA IS A PUNK ROCKER (live) / ROCKAWAY BEACH (live)** [67] [–]

Oct 79. (lp/c) <*(SRK/SRC 6070)*> **ROCK'N'ROLL HIGH SCHOOL** (soundtrack w/ Various Artists) [ ] May79 [ ]
– Rock'n'roll high school / I want you around / Come on let's go (w/ PALEY BROTHERS) / Blitzkrieg bop – Teenage lobotomy – California sun – Pinhead – She's the one / (others by Various Artists). *<cd-iss. May90; 2-6070> <re-iss. May02; same>*

Jan 80. (lp/c) <*(SRK/SRC 6077)*> **END OF THE CENTURY** [14] [44]
– Do you remember rock'n'roll radio? / I'm affected / Danny says / Chinese rock / The return of Jackie and Judy / Let's go / Baby I love you / I can't make it on time / This ain't Havana / Rock'n'roll high school / All the way / High risk insurance. *(re-iss. cd Mar94; 7599 27429-2) <(cd re-mast.Aug02 on 'Rhino'+=; 8122 78155-2)>* – (bonus tracks).

Jan 80. (7") *(SIR 4031)* <49182> **BABY, I LOVE YOU. / HIGH RISK INSURANCE** [8] [ ]

Apr 80. (7") <49261> **DO YOU REMEMBER ROCK'N'ROLL RADIO?. / LET'S GO** [–] [ ]

Apr 80. (7") *(SIR 4037)* **DO YOU REMEMBER ROCK'N'ROLL RADIO?. / I WANT YOU AROUND** [54] [–]

Jul 81. (7") *(SIR 4051)* <49812> **WE WANT THE AIRWAVES. / ALL'S QUIET ON THE EASTERN FRONT** [ ] [ ]

Jul 81. (lp/c) <*(SRK/SRC 3571)*> **PLEASANT DREAMS** [ ] [58]
– We want the airwaves / All's quiet on the Eastern front / The KKK took my baby away / Don't go / You sound like you're sick / It's not my place / She's a sensation / 7-11 / You didn't mean anything to me / Come on now / This business is killing me / Sitting in my room. *(re-iss. cd Mar94 & Jun00; 7599 23571-2) <(cd re-mast.Aug02 on 'Rhino'+=; 8122 78156-2)>* – (bonus tracks).

Oct 81. (7") *(SIR 4052)* **SHE'S A SENSATION. / ALL'S QUIET ON THE EASTERN FRONT** [ ] [–]

May 83. (lp/c) *(WX/+C 3800)* <23800> **SUBTERRANEAN JUNGLE** [ ] [83]
– Little bit o' soul / I need your love / Outsider / What'd ya do / Highest trails above / Somebody like me / Psycho therapy / Time has come today / My-my kind of girl / In the park / Time bomb / Everytime I eat vegetables It makes me think of you. *(re-iss. cd Mar94 & Jun00; 7599 23800-2) <(cd re-mast.Aug02 on 'Rhino'+=; 8122 78157-2)>* – (bonus tracks).

Jun 83. (7") *(W 9606)* **TIME HAS COME TODAY. / PSYCHO THERAPY** [ ] [–]
(12"+=) *(W 9606T)* – Baby I love you / Don't come close.

— **RICHIE RAMONE** (b. RICHARD REINHARDT, aka BEAU) – drums (ex-VELVETEENS) repl. MARC

Beggars Banquet Sire

Nov 84. (7") <29107> **HOWLING AT THE MOON (SHA LA LA). / WART HOG** [–] [ ]

Jan 85. (lp/c) *(BEGA/BEGC 59)* <25187> **TOO TOUGH TO DIE** [63] Oct84 [ ]
– Mama's boy / I'm not afraid of life / Too young to die / Durango 95 / Wart hog / Danger zone / Chasing the night / Howling at the Moon (sha-la-la) / Daytime dilemma (dangers of love) / Planet Earth 1988 / Human kind / Endless vacation / No go. *<(cd re-mast.Aug02 on 'Rhino'+=; 8122 78158-2)>* – (bonus tracks).

Jan 85. (7") *(BEG 128)* **HOWLING AT THE MOON (SHA-LA-LA). / CHASING THE NIGHT** [ ] [–]
(d7"+=)(12"pic-d+=) *(BEG 128D)(BEGTP 128)* – Smash you / Street fighting man.

Jun 85. (7") *(BEG 140)* **BONZO GOES TO BITBURG. / DAYTIME DILEMMA (DANGERS OF LOVE)** [ ] [–]
(12"+=) *(BEG 140T)* – Go home Annie.

Apr 86. (7") *(BEG 157)* **SOMETHING TO BELIEVE IN. / SOMEBODY PUT SOMETHING IN MY DRINK** [69] [–]
(12"+=) *(BEG 157T)* – (You) Can't say anything nice.

May 86. (lp/c) *(BEGA/BEGC 70)* <25433> **ANIMAL BOY** [38] [ ]
– Somebody put something in my drink / Animal boy / Love kills / Apeman hop / She belongs to me / Crummy stuff / My brain is hanging upside down (Bonzo goes to Bitburg) / She belongs to me / Mental hell / Eat that rat / Freak of nature / Hair of the dog / Something to believe in.

Jun 86. (7") <28599> **SOMETHING TO BELIEVE IN. / ANIMAL BOY** [–] [ ]

Jul 86. (7") *(BEG 167)* **CRUMMY STUFF. / SHE BELONGS TO ME** [ ] [–]
(12"+=,12"red+=) *(BEG 167 T)* – I don't want to live this life.

— **MARKY RAMONE** – drums returned to repl. CLEM BURKE (ex-BLONDIE) who had repl. RICKY (above now with originals JOEY, DEE DEE and JOHNNY)

Sep 87. (7") *(BEG 198)* **A REAL COOL TIME. / INDIAN GIVER** [ ] [–]
(12"+=) *(BEG 198T)* – Life goes on.

Sep 87. (lp/c) *(BEGA/BEGC 89)* *<25641>* **HALFWAY TO SANITY** [78] [ ]
– I wanna live / Bop 'til you drop / Garden of serenity / Weasel face / Go lil' Camaro go / I know better now / Death of me / I lost my mind / A real cool time / I'm not Jesus / Bye bye baby / Worm man. *(cd-iss. Dec87 +=; BEGA 89CD)* – Indian giver / Life goes on.

Nov 87. (7"/12") *(BEG 201/+T)* **I WANNA LIVE. / MERRY CHRISTMAS (I DON'T WANT TO FIGHT TONIGHT)** [ ] [ ]

Chrysalis Sire

Aug 89. (lp/c/cd) *(CHR/ZCHR/CCD 1725)* *<25905>* **BRAIN DRAIN** [75] Jun89 [ ]
– I believe in miracles / Zero zero UFO / Don't bust my chops / Punishment fits the crime / All screwed up / Palisades Park / Pet sematary / Learn to listen / Can't get you outta my mind / Ignorance is bliss / Come back, baby / Merry Christmas (I don't want to fight tonight).

Sep 89. (7") *(CHS 3423)* **PET SEMATARY. / ALL SCREWED UP** [ ] [–]
(12"+=) *(CHS12 3423)* – Zero zero UFO.

Sep 89. (7") *<22911>* **PET SEMATARY. / SHEENA IS A PUNK ROCKER** [–] [ ]

— **C.J. RAMONE** (b. CHRISTOPHER JOSEPH WARD, 8 Oct'65, Long Island, N.Y.) – bass repl. DEE DEE who became rap artist DEE DEE KING

Oct 91. (cd/c/d-lp) *(CCD/ZCHR/CHR 1901)* **LIVE LOCO (live)** [ ] [ ]
– The good, the bad and the ugly / Django 95 / Teenage lobotomy / Psycho therapy / Blitzkrieg bop / Rock'n'roll radio / I believe in miracles / Gimme gimme shock treatment / Rock'n'roll high school / I wanna be sedated / The KKK took my baby away / I wanna live / Bonzo goes to Bitzburg / Too tough to die / Sheena is a punk rocker / Rockaway beach / Pet semetary / Don't bust my shape / Palisades park / Mama's boy / Animal boy / Wart hog / Surfin' bird / Cretin hop / I don't wanna walk around with you / Today your love, tomorrow the world / Pinhead / Somebody put something in my drink / Beat on the brat / Judy is a punk / Chinese rocks / Love kills / Ignorance is bliss.

Radioactive Radioactive

Sep 92. (cd/c/lp) *<(RAR D/C 10615)>* **MONDO BIZARRO** [ ] [ ]
– Censorshit / The job that ate my brain / Poison heart / Anxiety / Strength to endure / It's gonna be alright / Take it as it comes / Main man / Tomorrow she goes away / I won't let it happen again / Cabbies on crack / Heidi is a heartache / Touring.

Chrysalis Radioactive

Nov 92. (c-s/7"yellow) *(TC+/CHS 3917)* **POISON HEART. / CENSORSHIT (live)** [69] [–]
(12"+=) *(12CHS 3917)* – Chinese rocks (live) / Sheena is a punk rocker (live).
(cd-s+=) *(CDCHS 3917)* – Rock and roll radio (live).

Dec 93. (cd/c/lp) *(CD/TC+/CHR 6052)* *<10913>* **ACID EATERS** [ ] [ ]
– Journey to the center of the mind / Substitute / Out of time / The shape of things to come / Somebody to love / When I was young / 7 and 7 is / My back pages / Can't seem to make you mine / Have you ever seen the rain / I can't control myself / Surf city.

— Album of covers; SUBSTITUTE (Who) / I CAN'T CONTROL MYSELF (Troggs) / SURF CITY (Jan & Dean) / OUT OF TIME (Rolling Stones) / THE SHAPE OF THINGS TO COME (Headboys) / etc.

Jun 95. (cd/c/lp) *(CD/TC+/CHR 6104)* *<11273>* **ADIOS AMIGOS** [62] [ ]
– I don't want to grow up / I'm makin' monsters for my friends / It's not for me to know / The crusher / Life's a gas / Take the pain away / I love you / Cretin family / Have a nice day / Scattergun / Got a lot to say / She talks to rainbows / Born to die in Berlin.

— split after tour early the following year, although they had a brief reunion on the 6th August, 1996 at The Palace, Los Angeles

Eagle Radioactive

Nov 97. (cd) *(EAGCD 010)* *<11555>* **WE'RE OUTTA HERE!** (their last show) [ ] [ ]
– Durango 95 / Teenage lobotomy / Psycho therapy / Blitzkrieg bop / Do you remember rock and roll radio / I believe in miracles / Gimme gimme shock treatment / Rock'n'roll high school / I wanna be sedated / Spider-man / The K.K.K. took my baby away / I just want to have something to do / Commando / Sheena is a punk rocker / Rockaway beach / Pet sematary / The crusher / Love kills / Do you wanna dance / Someone put something in my drink / I don't want you / Wart hog / Cretin hop / R.A.M.O.N.E.S. / Today your love, tomorrow the world / Pinhead / 53rd & 3rd / Listen to your heart / We're a happy family / Chinese rock / Beat on the brat / Any way you want it.

— after what we think is their final release, MARKY RAMONE went solo

– compilations, etc. –

Aug 80. (7") *R.S.O.; (RSO 70) / Sire; <2090 512>* **I WANNA BE SEDATED. / THE RETURN OF JACKIE AND JUDY** [ ] [ ]

— (above from Various Artists Film Soundtrack 'Rock'n'roll High School' also incl. 'Medley: Blitzkrieg bop – Teenage lobotomy – California sun – Pinhead – She's the one')

Nov 80. (7"ep) *Sire; (SREP 1)* **MELTDOWN WITH THE RAMONES** [ ] [ ]
– I just wanna have something to do / Questioningly / I wanna be your boyfriend / Here today, gone tomorrow.

Jun 88. (7") *Sire; <27663>* **I WANNA BE SEDATED. / (part 2)** [–] [ ]

Jun 88. (d-lp/c/cd) *Sire; (925709-1/-4/-2) <25709>* **RAMONES MANIA** [ ] [–]
– I wanna be sedated / Teenage lobotomy / Do you remember rock'n'roll radio? / Gimme gimme shock treatment / Beat on the brat / Sheena is a punk rocker / I wanna live / Pinhead / Blitzkrieg bop / Cretin hop / Rockaway beach / Commando / I wanna be your boyfriend / Mama's boy / Bop 'til you drop / We're a happy family / Bonzo goes to Bitburg / The outsider / Psycho therapy / Wart hog / Animal boy / Needles and pins / Howlin' at the Moon / Somebody put something in my drink / We want the airwaves / Chinese rocks / I just want to have something to do / The KKK took my baby away / Indian giver / Rock'n'roll high school.

Sep 90. (cd/c/d-lp) *Sire; (7599 26220-2/-4/-1)* **ALL THE STUFF (AND MORE)** (demos 1976-77, etc) [ ] [–]

May 99. (d-cd+book) *Megaworld; (MEGBK 02)* **BLITZKREIG BOP** [ ] [–]

Aug 99. (d-cd) *Sire; <(8122 7581-2)>* **HEY HO LET'S GO – THE RAMONES ANTHOLOGY** [ ] [ ]

Aug 00. (cd) *Burning Airlines; <(PILOT 79)>* **YOU DON'T COME CLOSE** [ ] [ ]

May 01. (d-cd) *Sire: <(8122 73557-2)>* **HEY HO LET'S GO! (THE RAMONES ANTHOLOGY)** [74] [ ]

Aug 01. (cd) *E.M.I.; (534696-2)* **MASTERS OF ROCK – THE VERY BEST OF THE RAMONES** [ ] [–]

Sep 01. (7"/cd-s) *Musical Tragedies; (EFA 12615-7/-2)* **JUDY IS A PUNK. / (other track by New York Dolls)** [ ] [–]

Apr 02. (cd) *EMI Gold; (538472-2)* **THE BEST OF THE CHRYSALIS YEARS** [ ] [–]

Aug 02. (3xcd-box) *E.M.I.; (541080-2)* **THE CHRYSALIS YEARS** [ ] [–]

Nov 02. (cd) *W.S.M.; (8122 76101-2)* **LOUD FAST RAMONES – THEIR TOUGHEST HITS** [ ] [–]

— JOEY also on "HOLLY & JOEY" 7" – 1982 'I Got You Babe' on 'Virgin'.

— In August '88, JOHNNY teamed up with DEBBIE HARRY for 7" – 'Go Lil Camara Go'. In 1994, JOEY RAMONE featured (+ on cover sleeve) of SIBLING RIVALRY's 'In A Family Way' EP for 'Alternative Tentacles'.

JOEY RAMONE

with a plethora of session players

Sanctuary Sanctuary

Dec 01. (cd-s) *<84541>* **MERRY CHRISTMAS (I DON'T WANT TO FIGHT TONIGHT)** [–] [ ]

Feb 02. (cd) *(SANC 108CD)* *<84542>* **DON'T WORRY ABOUT ME** [ ] [ ]
– What a wonderful world / Stop thinking about it / Mr. Punchy / Maria Bartiromo / Spirit in my house / Venting (it's a different world today) / Like a drug I never did before / Searching for something / I got knocked down (but I'll get up) / 1969 / Don't worry about me.

Dec 02. (cd-ep) *<84589>* **CHRISTMAS SPIRIT . . . IN MY HOUSE** [–] [ ]
– Christmas (baby please come home) / Merry Christmas (I don't want to fight tonight) / Spirit in my house / Don't worry about me / What a wonderful world.

DEE DEE RAMONE

writes with **REY**

World Dom. World Dom.

Jun 94. (cd/lp) *<(1571757-2/-1)>* **I HATE FREAKS LIKE YOU** [ ] [ ]

– I'm making monsters for my friends / Don't look in my window / Chinese bitch / It's not for me to know / Runaway / All's quiet on the Eastern Front / I hate it / Life is like a little smart Alleck / I hate creeps like you / Trust me / Curse on me / I'm seeing strawberry's again / Lass mich in Fuhe / I'm making monsters for my friends.

Other People's Music — Other People's Music

Sep 97. (cd) *<(OPM 2118CD)>* **ZONKED**
– I'm zonked, los hombres / Fix yourself up / I am seeing UFO's / Get off of the scene / Never never again / Bad horoscope / It's so bizarre / Get out of my room / Someone who don't fit in / Victim of society / My Chico / Disguises / Why is everybody always against Germany.

Blackout — Blackout

Oct 97. (7") *(BLK 5008E7)* **I AM SEEING UFO'S. / BAD HOROSCOPE** [–]

Nov 97. (cd) *(BLK 5008ECD)* **AIN'T IT FUN**
– I'm zonked los hombres / Fix yourself up / I am seeing UFO's / Get off the scene / Never never again / Bad horoscope / It's so bizarre / Get out of the room / Someone who doesn't fit in / Victim of society / My Chico / Disguises / Why is everyone always against Germany / Please kill me.

Corazong — not iss.

Mar 00. (cd) *(2000 006)* **HOP AROUND** [–]
– I don't wanna die in the basement / Mental patient / Now I wanna be sedated / Rock & roll vacation in L.A. / Get out of this house / 38th & 8th / Nothin' / Hop around / What about me? / I saw a skull instead of my head / I wanna you / Master plan / Born to lose / Hurtin' kind / I'm horrible. *(re-iss. Jul02; same)*

Eagle — Conspiracy

Sep 00. (cd) *(EAGCD 156)* *<10>* **GREATEST AND LATEST**
– Blitzkrieg bop / Timebomb / Sheena is a punk rocker / Shaking all over / I wanna be sedated / Cretin hop / Teenage lobotomy / Gimme gimme shock treatment / Motorbikin' / Come on now / Cathy's clown / Pinhead / Rockaway beach / Fix yourself up / Sidewalk surfin' / Beat on the brat. *(re-iss. Mar02; same)*

RANCID

Formed: Albany, California, USA . . . 1987 as tattooed ska-punk act, OPERATION IVY, by TIM 'LINT' ARMSTRONG and MATT FREEMAN (alias MATT McCALL), who also numbered JESSE MICHAELS and DAVE MELLO in their ranks. This quartet would become a cult act of the late 80's, although they only managed to squeeze out one album, 'ENERGY', in 1989. ARMSTRONG and FREEMAN continued to work with various outfits, including MDC, a band that they often supported at the infamous Gilman Street Club in Berkeley. In 1990, the pair were joined by BRETT REED and thus RANCID were spawned. After the release of a self-financed EP, 'I'M NOT THE ONLY ONE' in '92, the trio inked a deal with BRETT GUREWITZ's 'Epitaph' records. They subsequently added second guitarist LARS FREDERIKSON, who was to swell the ranks following the release of their well-received eponymous debut in 1993. With the early 90's resurgence of punk and youthful peers such as OFFSPRING and GREEN DAY making commercial headway, RANCID were well placed to capitalise on their particular brand of gut-level hardcore. Following the release of a 1994 EP, 'RADIO RADIO RADIO' on FAT MIKE's (NOFX) independent 'Fat Wreck Chords' label, the band cracked the elusive US Top 100 with their second album, 'LET'S GO' (1994). The following year, RANCID scored with an even higher placed album, '. . . AND OUT COME THE WOLVES', a Top 60 success. In 1998, like The CLASH over 20 years before them, RANCID adopted some roots reggae and ska into their umpteenth set, 'LIFE WON'T WAIT' (Jamaican, BUJU BANTON and MIGHTY MIGHTY BOSSTONES' mainman DICKY BARRETT guested). The results surprisingly worked as the album went Top 40 in America and Britain. In summer 2000, the mighty RANCID delivered another eponymous album which hit the UK Top 75.

• **Trivia:** ARMSTRONG also set up his own label, 'Hellcat', his best signings being DROPKICK MURPHYS, The PIETASTERS, GADJITS, HEPCAT and US BOMBS.

Album rating: Operation Ivy: ENERGY (*6) / Rancid: RANCID (*7) / LET'S GO (*6) / . . .AND OUT COME THE WOLVES (*8) / LIFE WON'T WAIT (*7) / RANCID (*6) / INDESTRUCTIBLE (*7)

OPERATION IVY

TIM ARMSTRONG – vocals, guitar / **MATT FREEMAN** (as MATT McCALL) – bass / **JESSE MICHAELS** – vocals / **DAVE MELLO** – drums

not iss. — Lookout!

Jan 88. (7"ep) *<LOOKOUT 3>* **HECTIC EP** [–]
– Junkies running dry / Here we go again / Hoboken / Yellin' in my ear / Sleep long / Healthy body.

May 89. (lp) *<LOOKOUT 10>* **ENERGY** [–]
– Knowledge / Sound system / Jaded / Take warning / The crowd / Bombshell / Unity / Vulnerability / Bankshot / One of these days / Gonna find you / Bad town / Smiling / Caution / Freeze up / Artificial life / Room without a window / Big city / Missionary. *(UK-iss.Oct94 lp/c/cd+=; LOOKOUT 10/+MC/CD)* – HECTIC EP + / Officer / I got no.

—— they split in May '89, DAVE joined SCHLONG while JESSE became a Buddhist monk! but ten years later formed COMMON RIDER with members from SQUIRTGUN. ARMSTRONG and FREEMAN worked with the DANCE HALL CRASHERS and DOWNFALL, while both joined MDC, FREEMAN more so; he featured on the group's 1990 set, 'Hey Cop, If I Had A face Like Yours'.

RANCID

ARMSTRONG + FREEMAN added **BRETT REED** – drums (ex-SMOG)

not iss. — Lookout!

Jan 92. (7"ep) *<LOOK 059>* **RANCID** [–]
– I'm not the only one / Battering ram / The sentence / Media controller / Idle hands. *(UK-iss.Dec94 & Nov00; same as US)*

Epitaph — Epitaph

May 93. (cd/c/lp) *<(E 86428-2/-4/-1)>* **RANCID**
– Adina / Hyena / Detroit / Rats in the hallway / Another night / Animosity / Otta my mind / Whirlwind / Rejected / Injury / The bottle / Trenches / Holiday sunrise / Unwritten rules / Get out of my way / (untitled).

—— added **LARS FREDERIKSON** – guitar (ex-UK SUBS)

Apr 94. (7"ep) *<FAT 509>* **RADIO, RADIO, RADIO EP**
– Radio / Dope sick girl / Just a feeling / Someone gunna die.
(above on 'Fat Wreck Chords'

Jan 95. (cd/c/d-10"lp) *<(E 86434-2/-4/-1)>* **LET'S GO** Jun94 [97]
– Nihilism / Radio / Sidekick / Salvation / Tenderloin / Let's go / As one / Burn / Ballad of Jimmy & Johnny / Gunshot / I am the one / Gave it away / Ghetto box / Harry Bridges / Black and blue / St. Mary / Dope sick girl / International cover-up / Solidarity / Midnight / Motorcycle ride / Name / 7 years down.

Feb 95. (cd-s) *<8645-2>* **ROOTS RADICALS / I WANNA RIOT** [–]

Aug 95. (cd/c/lp) *<(E 86444-2/-4/-1)>* **. . .AND OUT COME THE WOLVES** [55] [45]
– Maxwell murder / 11th hour / Roots radicals / Time bomb / Olympia Wa. / Lock, step and gone / Junkie man / Listed M.I.A. / Ruby Soho / Daly city train / The way I feel / Avenues and alleyways / As wicked / You don't care nothin' / Wars end / Disorder and disarray / Old friend / She's automatic / Journey to the end of the East Bay.

Oct 95. (7"ep/cd-ep) *(WOOS 8 S/CDS)* **TIME BOMB / THE WAR'S END / BLAST 'EM** [56] [–]
(above issued on 'Out Of Step')

May 96. (7"ep/cd-ep) *(86464-7/-2)* **RUBY SOHO. / THAT'S ENTERTAINMENT / DISORDER AND DISARRAY** [–]

Jun 98. (d-cd/d-c/d-lp) *(6497-2/-4/-1)* *<86497>* **LIFE WON'T WAIT** [32] [35]
– Intro / Bloodclot / Black lung / Life won't wait / New dress / Warsaw / Hooligan / Crane fist / Leicester Square / Backslide / Who would've thought / Cas culture and violence / Wolf / 1998 / Lady Liberty / Wrongful suspicion / Turntable / Something in the world today / Corazon de oro / Coppers.

Aug 98. (7"ep/cd-ep) *(1005-7/-2)* **BLOODCLOT. / ENDRINE / STOP**

Dec 98. (7"ep/cd-ep) *(1009-7/-2)* **HOOLIGANS / CASH, CULTURE AND VIOLENCE (bass drop mix) / THINGS TO COME (dance hall mix)**

Jul 00. (cd/c/lp) *(0427-2/-4/-1)* <*80427*> **RANCID** 68 68
– Don Giovanni / Disgruntled / It's quite alright / Let me go / I am forever / Poison / Loki / Blackhawk down / Rwanda / Corruption / Antennas / Rattlesnake / Not to regret / Radio Havana / Axiom / Black derby jacket / Meteor of war / Dead bodies / Fuck you / Young Al Capone / Golden gate fields / Churchill Downs.

Nov 00. (7"/cd-s) *(1040-7/-2)* **LET ME GO. / BEN ZANOTTO / DEAD AND GONE** –

Warners Warners

Aug 03. (cd) <*(9362 48529-2)*> **INDESTRUCTIBLE** 29 15
– Indestructible / Fall back down / Red hot moon / David Courtney / Start now / Out of control / Django / Arrested in Shanghai / Travis Bickle / Memphis / Spirit of '87 / Ghost band / Tropical London / Roadblock / Born frustrated / Back up against the wall / Ivory Coast / Stand your ground / Otherside. *(red-d-lp+=; 9362 48529-1)* – Killing zone.

Sep 03. (7") *(W 618)* **FALL BACK DOWN. / KILLING ZONE** 42 –
(cd-s+=) *(W 618CD)* – Stranded.

– compilations, others, etc. –

Mar 02. (lp/cd; split w/ NOFX) *B.Y.O.;* <*(BYO 079/+CD)*> **BYO SPLIT SERIES VOL.3** 75
– (tracks by NOFX) / (covers of NOFX by RANCID)

☐ RAPHAELS (see under ⇒ BIG COUNTRY)

the RAPTURE

Formed: New York City, New York, USA . . . early 1998 by VITO ROCCOFORTE and LUKE JENNER. This experimental punk group released their debut album, 'MIRROR', in 1999 – think TELEVISION, TALKING HEADS and PiL. The band's blistering three-minute sonic assaults may not have been to everyone's taste but they could not fail to grab your attention. In 2001 the group recruited bass player MATT SAFER and released the mini-set, 'OUT OF THE RACES AND ONTO THE TRACKS' (for 'Sub Pop'), which had critics championing them as leaders of the post-New Wave revival. The following year the band became a four-piece with the inclusion of multi-instrumentalist, GABRIEL ANDRUZZI, and released their finest collection of songs on the 'HOUSE OF JEALOUS LOVERS' EP. The RAPTURE finally delivered the album 'ECHOES' in 2003, which displayed their funk-punk rock minimalism even further. Not as brilliant as the hype suggested, the group still managed to maintain a spiritual GANG OF FOUR appeal and tracks such as 'OPEN UP YOUR HEART' and 'THE COMING OF SPRING' drew those TALKING HEADS comparisons in even closer. Although the album was spiky and often relentlessly abrasive, final track 'INFATUATION' was a little bit of a disappointment, and on some of the album's weaker moments you could almost hear them try too hard, sometimes lost in the syncopation. This said, 'ECHOES' was a great reminder that the post-punk vehicle had still got enough fuel in it to keep running for a good decade yet.

• **Covered:** DUMB WAITERS (Psychedelic Furs).

Album rating: MIRROR mini (*5) / OUT OF THE RACES AND ONTO THE TRACKS mini (*5) / ECHOES (*6)

LUKE JENNER – vocals, guitar / **VITO ROCCOFORTE** – drums / + bassist

not iss. Gold Standard

1998. (7") <*GSL 36*> **THE CHAIR THAT SQUEAKS. / DUMB WAITERS** –
(UK-iss.Jul01 & Jul02; same as US)

Gravity Gravity

Jan 99. (m-lp/m-cd) <*(GRAVITY 36/+CD)*> **MIRROR**
– In finite clock! / Notes . . . / Olio / Frames frames frames / Mirror / Alienation / Dusk at Maureen's / Kid 606 in love with the underground.

—— **MATT SAFER** – bass; repl. original

Sub Pop Sub Pop

Jun 01. (10"white-m-lp/m-cd) <*(SP/+CD 505)*> **OUT OF THE RACES AND ONTO THE TRACKS** May01
– Out of the races and onto the tracks / Modern romance / Caravan / The jam / The pop song / Confrontation. *(re-iss. Oct02; same)*

Output not iss.

Apr 02. (12") *(OPRDFA 001)* **HOUSE OF JEALOUS LOVERS. / HOUSE OF JEALOUS LOVERS (Morgan Geist remix) / SILENT MORNING** –
(re-iss. Mar03; same)

Jul 02. (12") *(OPRDFA 003)* **OLIO. / (mixes)** –

—— added **GABRIEL ANDRUZZI** – multi

Aug 03. (12") *(OPRDFA 005)* **HOUSE OF JEALOUS LOVERS (Maurice Fulton remix). / KILLING (original)** –

Mercury Universal

Aug 03. (7") *(9811125)* **HOUSE OF JEALOUS LOVERS. / ALABAMA SUNSHINE** 27
(cd-s+=) *(9810767)* – ('A'-Maurice Fulton mix).
(cd-s) *(9810768)* – ('A') / ('A'-Tom Middleton remix) / Killing (ends remix). *(re-iss. Sep03 on 'Output'+=; OPRDFA 006)*

Sep 03. (cd) *(9865447)* <*128302*> **ECHOES** 32
– Olio / Heaven / Open up your heart / I need your love / The coming of spring / House of jealous lovers / Echoes / Killing / Sister savior / Love is all / Infatuation. *(lp-iss.on 'Output'; OPRDFA 007)*

Dec 03. (7") *(9814183)* **SISTER SAVIOUR. / ECHOES (DFA remix)** 51
(cd-s) *(9814181)* – ('A'-Blackstrobe remix) / ('A'-DFA vocal remix).
(12"/12") *(OPRDFA 008/+X)* – ('A'mixes).

Feb 04. (7"red/cd-s) *(981680 9/8)* **LOVE IS ALL. / I NEED YOUR LOVE** 38 –
(cd-s) *(9816876)* – ('A'-live) / ('B'-live) / Sister saviour (live) / ('A'-video).

the RASMUS

Formed: Helsinki, Finland ... late 1994 as SPUTNIK, then ANTILLA by LAURI YLONEN, PAULI RANTASALMI, EERO HEINONEN and JANNE HEINONEN. Signed to 'Warners' in their homeland, RASMUS (as they were known at the time) quickly established themselves as one of Finland's most high profile bands. A trio of domestic albums, 'PEEP' (1996), 'PLAYBOYS' (1997) and 'HELL OF A TESTER' (1998), generated award after award before they were even out of their teens. An enforced change of name (prefixing their title with the definite article) was effected at the turn of the decade in order to avoid any misunderstanding with a similarly monikered Swedish DJ. What did it mean, anyway? Apparently a splicing of the Finnish words for "trash" and "mosh" respectively, at least partly symbolising their melodic pop-metal style. New drummer AKI HAKALA replaced JANNE on 4th studio set, 'INTO' (2001), named not for an English word but actually the Finnish term for "enthusiasm". Yet it must have been difficult for anyone over the age of twenty to summon up much "into" for their early 2004 UK debut, 'DEAD LETTERS' (2003; in Finland), an album which nevertheless hit the Top 10 and produced both a Top 3 monster, 'IN THE SHADOWS' and Top 20 breaker, 'GUILTY'. The latter title might have referred to their "guilty" listening pleasures, which by the sounds of it, may well have included DEF LEPPARD, EUROPE and BRYAN ADAMS. Six albums in and still on the RAS (well, not as RAS'd as the crowd at the previous year's Reading Festival, who'd unceremoniously bottled them off), the Hell-sinki crew sink-ied all the way down to the lower regions of the charts with 'HIDE FROM THE SUN' (2005).

Album rating: PEEP (*7) / PLAYBOYS (*5) / HELL OF A TESTER (*5) / INTO (*6) / HELL OF A COLLECTION compilation (*6) / DEAD LETTERS (*6) / HIDE FROM THE SUN (*4)

RASMUS

LAURI YLONEN (b.23 Apr'79) – vocals / **PAULI RANTASALMI** (b. 1 May'79) – guitar / **EERO HEINONEN** (b.27 Nov'79) – bass / **JANNE HEINONEN** – drums

Warners — not iss.

1995. (cd-ep) **1st** — [–] Fin [–]
– Frog / Funky jam / Myself / Rakkauslaulu.

1996. (cd-s) **2nd** — [–] Fin [–]
– Myself / Postman.

1996. (cd) *(0630 14882-2)* **PEEP** — [–] Fin [–]
– Ghostbusters / Postman / Fool / Shame / P.S. / Julen ar har igen / Peep / Frog / Funky jam / Outflow / Myself / Life 705 / Small. *(UK-iss.Jul04 on 'WEA'; same)*

1996. (cd-s) **GHOSTBUSTERS / FOOL** — [–] Fin [–]

1997. (cd-s) **KOLA** — [–] Fin [–]

1997. (cd-s) **BLUE / KOLA** — [–] Fin [–]

1997. (cd) *(0630 19923-2)* **PLAYBOYS** — [–] Fin [–]
– Playboys / Blue / Ice / Sophia / Wicked moments / Well well / Sold / Carousel / Jailer / Kola / Raggatip / Violence / Panda. *(UK-iss.Jul04 on 'WEA'; same)*

1997. (cd-s) **PLAYBOYS** — [–] Fin [–]

1998. (cd-s) **ICE / UFOLAULA / WELL WELL – KOLA (live)** — [–] Fin [–]

1998. (cd-s) **LIQUID** — [–] Fin [–]

1998. (cd) *(3984 25728-2)* **HELL OF A TESTER** — [–] Fin [–]
– Every day / Dirty moose / Swimming in the street / Man in the street / Tonight, tonight / City of the dead / Liquid / Pa-pa / Vibe / Help me sing / Tempo. *(UK-iss.Jul04 on 'WEA'; same)*

the RASMUS

—— **AKI HAKALA** (b.28 Oct'79, Espoo, Finland) – drums; repl. JANNE

Playground — not iss.

2001. (cd-s) **SWIMMING WITH THE KIDS / TEMPO (DJ Midas remix) / LIFE 705 (1999 version)** — [–] Fin [–]

2001. (cd-s) **F-F-F-FALLING / (making of Into)** — [–] Fin [–]

2001. (cd) *(PGMCD 2)* **INTO** — [–] Fin [–]
– Madness / Bullet / Chill / F-F-F-Falling (2001 version) / Heartbreaker / Smash / Someone else / Small town / One & only / Last waltz. *(UK-iss.Nov04 on 'Universal'+=; E 986702-2)* – F-F-F-Falling (video).

2001. (cd-s) **CHILL / CAN'T STOP ME / F-F-F-FALLING (acoustic)** — [–] Fin [–]

2001. (cd-s) **MADNESS / PLAY DEAD / USED TO FEEL BEFORE / CHILL (video)** — [–] Fin [–]

2002. (cd-s) **HEARTBREAKER / DAYS / ('A'-rock radio mixes) / ('A'-pop radio mixes)** — [–] Fin [–]

Mar 03. (cd-s) **IN THE SHADOWS / IN THE SHADOWS (revamped) / FIRST DAY OF MY LIFE (acoustic)** — [–] Fin [–]

Mar 03. (cd) *(PGMCD 14)* **DEAD LETTERS** — [–] Fin [–]
– In the shadows / Guilty / First day of my life / Still standing / In my life / Time to burn / Not like the other girls / The one I love / Back in the picture / Funeral song.

2003. (cd-s) **IN MY LIFE / WHAT EVER** — [–] Fin [–]

2003. (cd-s) **FIRST DAY OF MY LIFE / IN THE SHADOWS / WHAT EVER / ('A'-video)** — [–] Fin [–]

M.C.A. — Universal

Feb 04. (re-cd) *(9806934)* *<A00022691-2>* **DEAD LETTERS** — [10] [ ]
– (+=) F-F-F-Falling / If you ever / What ever.

Apr 04. (7"pic-d) *(MCS 40351)* **IN THE SHADOWS. / IF YOU EVER** — [3] [ ]
(cd-s) *(MCSXD 40351)* – ('A') / Everything you say / Days / ('A'-video).

Aug 04. (7"pic-d) *(MCS 40376)* **GUILTY. / FIRST DAY OF MY LIFE (live xfm session)** — [15] [–]
(cd-s) *(MCSTD 40376)* – ('A') / Play dead / Used to feel before / ('A'-video).

Nov 04. (7") *(MCS 40391)* **FIRST DAY OF MY LIFE. / STILL STANDING (live acoustic at xfm)** — [50] [–]
(cd-s) *(MCSTD 40391)* – ('A') / Guilty (live acoustic at xfm) / Since you've been gone / ('A'-video).

Sep 05. (cd-s) *(MCSTD 40429)* **NO FEAR / NO FEAR (freelance hellraiser remix)** — [43] [–]
(cd-s) *(MCSXD 40429)* – ('A') / Immortal / Dancer in the dark / ('A'-Vrenna remix) / ('A'-video).

Sep 05. (cd) *(987369-2)* **HIDE FROM THE SUN** — [65] [–]
– Shot / Night after night (out of the shadows) / No fear / Lucifer's angel / Last generation / Dead promises / Immortal / Sail away / Keep your heart broken / Heart of misery / Don't let go / Open my eyes (*). *(ltd-cd w/out * +=; 987361-2)* – Dancer in the dark.

Nov 05. (cd-s) *(MCSTD 40441)* **SAIL AWAY / LUCIFER'S ANGEL (alt. version)** — [ ] [–]
(cd-s) *(MSCXD 40441)* – ('A') / Lucifer's angel (acoustic live) / No fear (rehearsal room version) / ('A'-Benztown chill out mix) / ('A'-video).

Apr 06. (cd-s) **SHOT / KEEP YOUR HEART BROKEN (live) / SHOT (live) / LAST GENERATION (live)** — [–] Fin [–]

– compilations, etc. –

Apr 05. (cd) *Warners; (2564 62027-2)* **HELL OF A COLLECTION** — [ ] [–]
– F-F-F-Falling / Chill / Liquid / Every day / City of the dead / Help me sing / Playboys / Blue / Ice / Sophia / Wicked moments / Ghostbusters / Funky jam / Myself / P.S. / Rakkauslaulu / Life 705 / Liquid (demo).

RAZORLIGHT

Formed: London, England ... 2002 by JOHNNY BORRELL and Swedish ex-pat BJORN AGREN, who soon added rhythm section CARL DALEMO and CHRISTIAN SMITH-PANCORVO (the latter was superseded by ANDY BURROWS early 2004). Unlike many of their spiky compadres, RAZORLIGHT went straight to a major label deal with recently re-activated 'Mercury' offshoot, 'Vertigo', scoring a minor hit with debut single, 'ROCK N ROLL LIES'. A further couple of singles ('RIP IT UP' and 'STUMBLE AND FALL') rose progressively higher through late 2003/early 2004 before the classic 'GOLDEN TOUCH' went Top 10 later that summer. With a rhythm suspiciously derivative of '10:15 Saturday Night', the track played like a festival-friendly reincarnation of the CURE, becoming a center-piece of their live show. As their Steve Lillywhite-produced UK Top 3 album, 'UP ALL NIGHT' (2004) showed however, the street poetry and serrated thrash of PATTI SMITH or RICHARD HELL was likely closer to BORRELL's heart, or maybe just contemporary raves the STROKES. While the press made the most of BORRELL's posturing, no one could accuse the man of lacking a certain iconic passion, even if he did strain to sound like a CBGB's old-hand. Both the 'Horses'-esque 'VICE' and a re-recording of 'RIP IT UP' made the Top 20, while the previously unreleased (and subsequent re-promoted album addition) 'SOMEWHERE ELSE' had a close shave with the top of the charts. Inevitably, BORRELL's chest-beating charisma ensured RAZORLIGHT's summer 2005 performance at Live 8 was one of the concert's talking points, while an appearance on cult BBC3 TV show, 'The Mighty Boosh', proved the band didn't take themselves too seriously.

Album rating: UP ALL NIGHT (*8)

JOHNNY BORRELL – vocals, guitar / **BJORN AGREN** (b. Sweden) – guitars, vocals / **CARL DALEMO** – bass / **CHRISTIAN SMITH-PANCORVO** – drums

Vertigo — not iss.

Aug 03. (cd-s) *(9800413)* **ROCK N ROLL LIES / ACTION! / YEAH YEAH YEAH** — [56] [–]
(7"ep+=) *(9800414)* – In the city.

Nov 03. (cd-s) *(9814044)* **RIP IT UP / SPIRIT / YES, YOU SHOULD KNOW** — [42] [–]
(7"ep+=) *(9814045)* – When he was twenty / Heartbreak soup / Here it comes.

Jan 04. (cd-s) *(9816398)* **STUMBLE AND FALL / FOR GEORGIA (live)** — [27] [–]
(cd-s) *(9816397)* – ('A') / Control / Rip it up (Toerag demo).
(7"ep++=) *(9816396)* – (all above) / We all get up.

—— **ANDY BURROWS** – drums; repl. CHRISTIAN

Jun 04. (cd-s) *(9866836)* **GOLDEN TOUCH / YOU & ME AND ALCOHOL** — [9] [–]
(7"ep+=) *(9866834)* – Dean take your time / Losing your mind / If you know what I mean.

Jun 04. (cd/lp) *(986694 4/3)* **UP ALL NIGHT** — [3] [–]
– Leave me alone / Rock n roll lies / Vice / Up all night / Which way is out / Rip it up / Dalston / Golden touch / Stumble and fall / Get it and go / In the city / Hang by, hang by / To the sea. *(lp w/ 7") (cd w/ live-dvd+=)* – Rip it up / Stumble and fall / Bright lights / To the sea / In the city / Rock n roll lies. *(cd re-iss. Apr05 +=; 9871043)* – Somewhere else.

Sep 04. (cd-s) *(9867758)* **VICE / HEY YA! (Jo Whiley sessions)** [18] [–]
(cd-s) *(9867759)* – ('A'-full version) / Believe in me / Anabelle says (4-track).
(7"ep++=) *(9867757)* – (above tracks) / Golden touch.
Nov 04. (cd-ep) *(9869076)* **RIP IT UP (re-recording) / FAIRY TALE OF NEW YORK (the Lamacq session) / STUMBLE AND FALL (live)** [20] [–]
(7"ep+=) *(9869078)* – Just can't explain / Don't go back to Dalston.
Apr 05. (cd-s) *(9869892)* **SOMEWHERE ELSE / KEEP THE RIGHT PROFILE** [2] [–]
(7"ep+=) *(9869894)* – Hang by, hang by / Up all night (live).
(cd-s) *(9869893)* – ('A') / (2 above).
in Jul'06, the single 'IN THE MORNING' will be released from forthcoming 'RAZORLIGHT'

the RED HOT CHILI PEPPERS

Formed: Hollywood, California, USA . . . 1983 after four years as ANTHEM, by schoolfriends ANTHONY KIEDIS (aka ANTWAN THE SWAN), Israeli-born HILLEL SLOVAK, MICHAEL 'FLEA' BALZARY and JACK IRONS. This motley bunch of funky funsters then proceeded to sign with 'E.M.I.' stark naked as part of a now famous publicity stunt. The exhibitionist streak was to be a mainstay of their early career, most famously on the cover for the ABBEY ROAD EP (1988), the lads wearing nought but one sock, strategically placed (no prizes for guessing where!) in a send-up of the classic Beatles' album of the same name. With IRONS and SLOVAK under contractual obligations to their own group, WHAT IS THIS?, drummer JACK SHERMAN (ex-CAPTAIN BEEFHEART) and guitarist CLIFF MARTINEZ (ex-WEIRDOS, ex-TEENAGE JESUS & THE JERKS) filled in on the 1984 eponymous debut album, a promising start which introduced the band's mutant funk-punk hybrid. Taking their cue from the cream of 70's funk (obvious reference points were SLY STONE, JAMES BROWN, the METERS, etc.) and injecting it with a bit of L.A. hardcore mayhem, the CHILI PEPPERS came up with such gonzoid grooves as 'GET UP AND JUMP' and 'POLICE HELICOPTER', although the most interesting track was the haunting 'GRAND PAPPY DU PLENTY', a kind of pre-'Twin Peaks' slice of instrumental noir. The GEORGE CLINTON-produced follow-up, FREAKY STYLEY (1985) sounded more cohesive, most impressively on the galvanising defiance of the hypnotic title track. Alongside fairly faithful covers of Sly Stone's 'IF YOU WANT ME TO STAY' and The Meters' 'HOLLYWOOD (AFRICA)', the group "got down" with their own groove thang on the likes of 'JUNGLE MAN' and 'AMERICAN GHOST DANCE'. 'CATHOLIC SCHOOL GIRLS RULE' and 'SEX RAP', meanwhile, left no doubt as to the CHILI PEPPERS' feminist-baiting agenda. While these records were American-only affairs, the band's manic reputation was beginning to reach across the Atlantic, 'UPLIFT MOFO PARTY PLAN' (1988) intoducing the band to a receptive UK audience. Tougher than their earlier releases, the record consolidated the group's place at the forefront of the burgeoning funk-metal explosion, their brash, kaleidoscopic sound injecting a bit of colour and excitement to Blighty's rather dour rock scene. The party was cut somewhat short, however, with the death of SLOVAK in June, yet another victim of a heroin overdose. With KEIDIS also a heroin addict, IRONS (who subsequently formed the band, ELEVEN) obviously didn't like the way things were going and decided to bail out. Eventual replacements were found in guitarist JOHN FRUSCIANTE and drummer CHAD SMITH, the group throwing themselves into the recording of 'MOTHER'S MILK' (1989). Unfairly criticised in some quarters, the album contained some of the CHILI PEPPERS' finest moments to date. 'KNOCK ME DOWN' was an impassioned plea for sanity in the face of drugs hell, the group enjoying MTV exposure for the first time with the video. A brilliant, celebratory cover of Stevie Wonder's 'HIGHER GROUND' also scored with MTV, easing the band slowly out of cultdom. 'TASTE THE PAIN' was an uncharacteristically introspective (by the CHILI's standards anyhow) song, no doubt also borne of the band's recent troubles and showing a newfound maturity in songwriting. More trouble was to follow in April '90, when that young scamp, KIEDIS, was given a 60-day jail sentence for sexual battery and indecent exposure to a female student (the following year, FLEA and SMITH were both charged with offences of a similar nature). As well as clearly possessing red hot libidos, by the early 90's the band had become red hot property following the release of the RICK RUBIN-produced 'BLOOD SUGAR SEX MAGIK' (1991). Their first release for new label, 'Warners', at last the band had fulfilled their potential over the course of a whole album (a US Top 3). With another series of striking videos, the CHILI PEPPERS almost scored a US No.1 with the aching ballad, 'UNDER THE BRIDGE' while the body-jerk funk-rock of 'GIVE IT AWAY' made the UK Top 10. A multi million seller, the album catapulted the RED HOT CHILI PEPPERS into the big league, the band subsequently securing a prestigious headlining slot on the 1992 Lollapalooza tour. Always an utterly compelling live proposition, the group's hyperactive stage show is the stuff of legend, what with KEIDIS' manic athletics and FLEA's (possibly) JIMI HENDRIX-inspired upside down bass playing, hanging feet-up by a rope!!!. By the release of 'ONE HOT MINUTE' (1995), a transatlantic Top 5, FRUSCIANTE had been replaced with DAVE NAVARRO (ex-JANE'S ADDICTION), adding a new dimension to the band's sound. For many, the album was the 'CHILI PEPPERS' peak achievement, from the dreamy 'WALKABOUT' to the japery of 'AEROPLANE', the latter becoming a UK hit single. While many of the group's funk-rock contemporaries folded or fell by the wayside when that scene went out of fashion, the RED HOT CHILI PEPPERS developed into one of America's most entertaining, and biggest selling 'alternative' acts through a combination of sheer hard work, talent and concrete self belief (and no doubt a hefty dose of shagging!). Never the most stable of bands, rumours of a 'PEPPERS split were rife in 1997, although they still managed to hit the UK Top 10 with their fantastic cover of The Ohio Players' 'LOVE ROLLERCOASTER' (straight from the Beavis & Butt-Head Do America movie). With the returning FRUSCANTE out from the bench to replace NAVARRO, the band were back with a bang on 1999's 'CALIFORNICATION'. Meanwhile, another stab at the singles chart paid off with a transatlantic Top 20 hit, 'SCAR TISSUE'. With the release of 2002's 'BY THE WAY', the RED HOT CHILI PEPPERS proved themselves to be one of the few acts in popular music to carry off almost twenty years' worth of consistently wonderful music. Incredibly, the band still look great, still sound fresh and still have that edge of danger that almost all rock artists lose along with their figures as middle age looms. Granted, their hooks and melodies may be sounding that bit more wistful, and their words that bit more wise these days, but if that translates into songs as gorgeous as single 'BY THE WAY', growing old can only be a good thing. Two decades of keeping the funk flame alive was marked with the release of 2003's 'GREATEST HITS', largely covering the post-'MOTHERS MILK' era. 'LIVE IN HYDE PARK' (2004) was a concert document testifying to the band's enduring popularity on British shores, a straight to No.1 record not even released in America. The quartet's global superstardom was such that they could record a sprawling double set, call it 'STADIUM ARCADIUM' (2006) and fill it with the kind of ruminatory pop that's surfaced with increasing frequency as they've hit middle age. IGGY POP aside, KIEDIS is still the most energetic 40-something in the business but he finally sounded like he was tiring of the chipper-hop which kineticised 'TELL ME

BABY' (the second track to be lifted from the album), issuing the lower-gear 'DANI CALIFORNIA' as a lead single instead, one that became the subject of speculation after some commentators pointed out its similarity to TOM PETTY's 'Mary Jane's Last Dance'; the fact that it became the fastest selling in their career (US Top 10, UK No.2) suggested that slowing down didn't mean turning off or tuning out. KIEDIS even compared the album – their first transatlantic No.1, and first time they'd gone straight to the top of the US charts – to the band's early-mid 80's releases, yet it was difficult to divine that manic energy in the careworn balladry that filled most of 'STADIUM..'s grooves, even if the record did explore territory previously foreign to the 'CHILIs – check out the spacey 'IF', for example, a song that veered into FRUSCIANTE-esque solo soundscapes.

• **Songwriters:** Group compositions except other covers; SUBTERRANEAN HOMESICK BLUES (Bob Dylan) / FIRE + CASTLES MADE OF SAND (Jimi Hendrix) / MOMMY WHERE'S DADDY (Frank Zappa) / THEY'RE RED HOT (Robert Johnson) / SEARCH AND DESTROY (Iggy Pop) / SUFFRAGETTE CITY (David Bowie) / WHY DON'T YOU LOVE ME (Hank Williams) / TINY DANCER (Elton John) / TEENAGER IN LOVE (Dion & The Belmonts) / I FEEL LOVE (Donna Summer) / BRANDY (Looking Glass) / RIGHT ON TIME (Joy Division) / BLACK CROSS (45 Grave).

Album rating: THE RED HOT CHILI PEPPERS (*5) / FREAKY STYLEY (*5) / THE UPLIFT MOFO PARTY PLAN (*6) / MOTHER'S MILK (*7) / BLOOD SUGAR SEX MAGIK (*8) / WHAT HITS!? compilation (*7) / PLASMA SHAFT collection (*4) / OUT IN L.A. collection (*3) / ONE HOT MINUTE (*6) / CALIFORNICATION (*6) / BY THE WAY (*8) / GREATEST HITS compilation (*8) / LIVE IN HYDE PARK (*6) / STADIUM ARCADIUM (*6)

ANTHONY KIEDIS (ANTWAN THE SWAN) (b. 1 Nov'62, Grand Rapids, Michigan) – vocals / **HILLEL SLOVAK** (b.13 Apr'62, Haifa, Israel) – guitar / **MICHAEL 'FLEA' BALZARY** (b.16 Oct'62, Melbourne, Australia) – bass / **JACK IRONS** (b.18 Jul'62, Los Angeles, California) – drums

EMI America — EMI America

1984. (lp/c/cd) *<790616-1/-4/-2>* **THE RED HOT CHILI PEPPERS** [–] [ ]
– True men don't kill coyotes / Baby appeal / Buckle down / Get up and jump / Why don't you love me / Green heaven / Mommy where's daddy? / Out in L.A. / Police helicopter / You always sing / Grand pappy du plenty. *(UK-iss.Aug90 on 'EMI Manhattan' cd/c/lp; CD/TC+/MTL 1056) (re-iss. Jun93 on 'Fame' cd/c; CD/TC FA 3297) (lp re-iss. Dec99 on 'Simply Vinyl'; SVLP 156)*

— (Due to contractual reasons, SLOVAK and IRONS couldn't play on debut. They were deputised by session men **JACK SHERMAN** – guitar (ex-CAPTAIN BEEFHEART) / & **CLIFF MARTINEZ** – drums (ex-WEIRDOS, ex-TEENAGE JESUS & THE JERKS)

— **HILLEL SLOVAK** returned from WHAT IS THIS? to repl. SHERMAN guests included **MACEO PARKER + FRED WESLEY** (of FUNKADELIC / PARLIAMENT)

1985. (lp/c/cd) *<790617-1/-4/-2>* **FREAKY STYLIE** [–] [ ]
– Jungle man / Hollywood (Africa) / American ghost dance / If you want me to stay / Never mind / Freaky stylie / Blackeyed blonde / The brothers cup / Battle ship / Lovin' and touchin' / Catholic school girls rule / Sex rap / Thirty dirty birds / Yertle the turtle. *(UK-iss.Aug90 on 'EMI Manhattan' cd/c/lp; CD/TC+/MTL 1057) (re-iss. Dec94 on 'Fame' cd/c; CD/TC FA 3309)*

Aug 85. (7") *(EA 205)* **HOLLYWOOD (AFRICA). / NEVER MIND** [ ] [ ]
(remixed-12"+=) *(12EA 205)* – ('A'dub version).

— **JACK IRONS** returned from WHAT IS THIS? to repl. MARTINEZ who joined the DICKIES; he also went into soundtracks

Jan 88. (7") *(EA 241)* **FIGHT LIKE A BRAVE. / FIRE** [ ] [ ]
(12"+=/12"pic-d+=) *(12EA/+P 241)* – ('A'-Mofo mix) / ('A'-Knucklehead mix).

EMI Manhattan — EMI Manhattan

Mar 88. (cd/c/lp) *(CD/TC+/AML 3125) <48036>* **THE UPLIFT MOFO PARTY PLAN** [ ] Nov87 [ ]
– Fight like a brave / Funky crime / Me and my friends / Backwoods / Skinny sweaty man / Behind the sun / Subterranean homesick blues / Special secret song inside / No chump love sucker / Walkin' on down the road / Love trilogy / Organic anti-beat box band. *(lp re-iss. Aug00 on 'Simply Vinyl'; SVLP 242)*

May 88. (7"ep) *(MT 41)* **THE ABBEY ROAD EP** [ ] [–]
– Backwoods / Hollywood (Africa) / True men don't kill coyotes.
(12"ep+=) *(12MT 41)* – Catholic school girls rule.

— **ANTWAN & FLEA** (now adding trumpet) brought in new lads **JOHN FRUSCIANTE** (b. 5 Mar'70, New York City) – guitar repl. HILLEL who died (of heroin OD) 25 Jun'88. **CHAD SMITH** (b.25 Oct'62, St. Paul, Minnesota) – drums repl. IRONS who later formed ELEVEN and joined PEARL JAM

E.M.I. USA — E.M.I.

Aug 89. (7"/7"sha-pic-d/12"pic-d) *(MT/MTPD/12MTPD 70)* **KNOCK ME DOWN. / PUNK ROCK CLASSIC / PRETTY LITTLE DITTY** [ ] [ ]
(12") *(12MT 70)* – (first 2 tracks) / Special secret song inside / Magic Johnson.
(cd-s) *(CDMT 70)* – (first 2 tracks) / Jungle man / Magic Johnson.

Aug 89. (cd/c/lp) *(CD/TC+/MTL 3125) <92152>* **MOTHER'S MILK** [ ] [52]
– Good time boys / Higher ground / Subway to Venus / Magic Johnson / Nobody weird like me / Knock me down / Taste the pain / Stone cold bush / Fire / Pretty little ditty / Punk rock classic / Sexy Mexican maid / Johnny kick a hole in the sky. *(lp-iss.Apr01 on 'Simply Vinyl'; SVLP 328)*

Dec 89. (7") *(MT 75)* **HIGHER GROUND. / MILLIONAIRES AGAINST HUNGER** [55] [ ]
('A'-Munchkin mix-cd-s+=) *(CDMT 75)* – Mommy where's daddy / Politician (mini rap).
(12") *(12MT 75)* – ('A'-Munchkin mix) / ('A'dub mix) / Politician (mini rap) / Mommy where's daddy.
(12") *(12MTX 75)* – ('A'side) / ('A'-Munchkin mix) / ('A'dub mix) / Politician (mini rap).

Jun 90. (c-s/7") *(TC+/MT 85)* **TASTE THE PAIN. / SHOW ME YOUR SOUL** [29] [ ]
(12"+=/9"square-pic-d+=) *(12/10 MT 85)* – Castles made of sand (live).
(cd-s++=) *(CDMT 85)* – Never mind.
(remixed-12"+=) *(12MTX 85)* – If you want me to stay / Never mind.

Aug 90. (c-s/7") *(TC+/MT 88)* **HIGHER GROUND. / FIGHT LIKE A BRAVE** [54] [ ]
(12"+=/12"pic-d+=) *(12MT/+PD 88)* – ('A'-Daddy-O mix).
(cd-s+=) *(CDMT 88)* – Behind the sun / Out in L.A.

Warners — Warners

Sep 91. (cd)(d-lp/c) *(7599 26681-2)(WX 441/+C) <26681>* **BLOOD SUGAR SEX MAGIK** [25] [3]
– The power of equality / If you have to ask / Breaking the girl / Funky monks / Suck my kiss / I could have lied / Mellowship slinky in B major / The righteous & the wicked / Give it away / Blood sugar sex magik / Under the bridge / Naked in the rain / Apache Rose peacock / The greeting song / My lovely man / Sir psycho sexy / They're red hot. *(re-iss. Mar92 cd/c; same)*

Dec 91. (c-s,cd-s) *<19147>* **GIVE IT AWAY / SEARCH AND DESTROY** [–] [73]

Mar 92. (c-s,cd-s) *<18978>* **UNDER THE BRIDGE / THE RIGHTEOUS AND THE WICKED** [–] [2]

Mar 92. (7"/s7"/c-s) *(W 0084/+W/C)* **UNDER THE BRIDGE. / GIVE IT AWAY** [26] [–]
(12"/cd-s) *(W 0084 T/CD)* – ('A'side) / Search and destroy / Soul to squeeze / Sikamikanico.

— (the last track also featured on 'Wayne's World' film/single)

— **ZANDER SCHLOSS** (THELONIUS MONSTER) – guitar; repl. FRUSCANTE who went solo 'TO CLARA' in 1994 on 'American'

Aug 92. (7"/c-s) *(W 0126/+C)* **BREAKING THE GIRL. / FELA'S COOK** [41] [ ]
(12"+=/cd-s+=) *(W 0126 T/CD)* – Suck my kiss (live) / I could have lied (live).

— (Aug'92) **ARIK MARSHALL** (b.13 Feb'67, Los Angeles) – guitar (ex-MARSHALL LAW) repl. SCHLOSS

Jun 93. (c-s) *(W 188C)* **GIVE IT AWAY / IF YOU HAVE TO ASK (Friday night fever blister mix)** [ ] [–]
(12"+=/cd-s+=) *(W 188 TP/CD1)* – ('A'-extended + Rasta mixes).
(cd-s) *(W 188CD2)* – ('A'side) / ('A'-Disco Krisco mix) / ('A'-Scott & Garth mix).

Aug 93. (c-s,cd-s) *<18401>* **SOUL TO SQUEEZE / NOBODY WEIRD LIKE ME** [–] [22]

— **DAVE NAVARRO** (b. 7 Jun'67, Santa Monica, Calif.) – guitar (ex-JANE'S ADDICTION) repl. MARSHALL

Jan 94. (c-s) *(W 0225C)* **GIVE IT AWAY / SOUL TO SQUEEZE** [9] [–]
(cd-s+=) *(W 0225CD1)* – ('A'-extended & Rasta mixes).
(cd-s) *(W 0225CD2)* – ('A'side) / If you have to ask (Friday night fever blister mix) / ('A'-Scott & Garth mix) / Nobody weird like me (live).

(12") *(W 0225T)* – ('A'extended) / ('A'-Rasta mix) / If you have to ask (disco krisco mix).

Apr 94. (7"blue/c-s) *(W 0237/+C)* **UNDER THE BRIDGE. / SUCK MY KISS (live)** [13] [–]
(cd-s+=) *(W 0237CD)* – Sikamikanico / Search and destroy (live).
(cd-s) *(W 0237CDX)* – ('A'side) / I could have lied (live) / Fela's cock / Give it away (in progress; demo).

Aug 95. (c-s) *(W 0316C)* **WARPED / PEA** [31] [–]
(cd-s+=) *(W 0316CD)* – Melancholy mechanics.

Sep 95. (cd/c/lp) *<(9362 45733-2/-4/-1)>* **ONE HOT MINUTE** [2] [4]
– Warped / Aeroplane / Deep kick / My friends / Coffee shop / Pea / One big mob / Walkabout / Tearjerker / One hot minute / Falling into grace / Shallow be thy name / Transcending.

Oct 95. (c-s) *(W 0317C)* **MY FRIENDS / LET'S MAKE EVIL** [29] [–]
(12"+=/cd-s+=) *(W 0317 TX/CD)* – Coffee shop / Stretch.

Feb 96. (c-s) *(W 0331C)* **AEROPLANE / SUFFRAGETTE CITY (live)** [11] [–]
(cd-s+=) *(W 0331CD)* – Suck my kiss (live).
(cd-s) *(W 0331CDX)* – ('A'side) / Backwoods (live) / Transcending (live) / Me and my friends (live).

— FLEA + CHAD splintered with THERMIDOR, which was formed by ROBBIE ALLEN and DAVID KING. An album 'MONKEY ON RICO' was released in the Spring.

Jun 97. (7"/c-s/cd-s) *(GFS/+C/TD 22188)* **LOVE ROLLERCOASTER. / (other by Engelbert Humperdinck)** [7] [–]
(above from the 'Beavis & Butt-Head Do America' film; on 'Geffen')

— (Apr'98) **JOHN FRUSCANTE** returned to repl. NAVARRO (who formed SPREAD)

May 99. (c-s) *(W 490C)* *<16913>* **SCAR TISSUE / GONG LI** [15] [9]
(cd-s+=) *(W 490CD2)* – Instrumental No.1.

Jun 99. (cd/c) *<(9362 47386-2/-4)>* **CALIFORNICATION** [5] [3]
– Around the world / Parallel universe / Scar tissue / Otherside / Get on top / Californication / Easily / Porcelain / Emit remmus / Velvet glove / Savoir / Purple stain / Right on time / Road trippin'.

Aug 99. (c-s) *(W 500C)* **AROUND THE WORLD / YERTLE TRILOGY** [35] [ ]
(cd-s+=) *(W 500CD2)* – Me and my friends.
(cd-s) *(W 500CD1)* – ('A'side) / Parallel universe / Teatro jam.

Jan 00. (cd-s) *(W 510CD1)* *<album cut>* **OTHERSIDE / HOW STRONG / ROAD TRIPPIN' (without strings) / OTHERSIDE (CD-Rom)** [33] [14]
(cd-s) *(W 510CD2)* – ('A'side) / My lovely man / Around the world (CD-Rom).

Aug 00. (c-s/cd-s) *(W 534 C/CD)* *<album cut>*
CALIFORNICATION / END OF THE SHOW (live) / I COULD HAVE LIED (live) / END OF SHOW (live) [16] May00 [69]

Jan 01. (c-s) *(W 546C)* **ROAD TRIPPIN' / CALIFORNICATION (live)** [30] [–]
(cd-s+=) *(W 546CD1)* – BloodSugarSexMagick (live) / ('A'-CD-ROM).
(cd-s) *(W 546CD2)* – ('A'side) / Under the bridge (live) / If you have to ask (live).

Jul 02. (7") *(W 580)* **BY THE WAY. / TIME** [2] [34]
(cd-s+=) *(W 580CD1)* *<42459>* – Teenager in love.
(cd-s) *(W 580CD2)* – Search and destroy (live).

Jul 02. (cd/c/lp) *<(9362 48140-2/-4/-1)>* **BY THE WAY** [1] [2]
– By the way / Universally speaking / This is the place / Dosed / Don't forget me / The zephyr song / Can't stop / I could die for you / Midnight / Throw away your television / Cabron / Tear / On Mercury / Minor thing / Warm tape / Venice queen.

Oct 02. (7") *(W 592)* **THE ZEPHYR SONG. / OUT OF RANGE** [11] [49]
(cd-s+=) *(W 592CD2)* *<radio>* – Rivers of Avalon.
(cd-s) *(W 592CD1)* – ('A') / Body of water / Someone.

Feb 03. (7"red) *(W 599)* **CAN'T STOP. / CHRISTCHURCH FIREWORKS MUSIC (live)** [22] [57]
(cd-s+=) *(W 599CD1)* – If you have to ask (live).
(cd-s) *(W 599CD2)* – ('A'mix) / Right on time (live) / Nothing to lose (live).

Jun 03. (cd-s) *(W 609CD1)* **UNIVERSALLY SPEAKING / SLOWLY DEEPLY** [27] [–]
(cd-s) *(W 609CD2)* – ('A') / By the way (live acoustic) / Don't forget me (live).

Nov 03. (cd-s) *(W 630CD)* **FORTUNE FADED / ESKIMO / BUNKER HILL** [11] [–]

Nov 03. (cd) *<(9362 48545-2)>* **GREATEST HITS** (compilation) [4] [18]
– Under the bridge / Give it away / Californication / Scar tissue / Soul to squeeze / Otherside / Suck my kiss / By the way / Parallel universe / Breaking the girl / My friends / Higher ground / Universally speaking / Road trippin' / Fortune faded / Save the population. *(cd w/dvd+=; 9362 48956-2)*

Jul 04. (d-cd) *(9362 48863-2)* **LIVE IN HYDE PARK** (live) [1] [–]
– (intro) / Can't stop / Around the world / Scar tissue / By the way / Fortune faded / I feel love / Otherside / Easily / Universally speaking / Get on top / Brandy / Don't forget me / Rolling Sly Stone / Throw away your television / Leverage of space / Purple stain / The zephyr song / Californication / Right on time / Parallel universe / Drum homage medley / Under the bridge / Black cross / Flea's trumpet treated by John / Give it away.

Apr 06. (7"pic-d) *(W 715)* **DANI CALIFORNIA. / WHATEVER WE WANT** [2] [6]
(cd-s+=) *(W 715CD2)* – Lately.
(cd-s) *(W 715CD1)* – ('A') / Million miles of water.

May 06. (d-cd) *<(9362 44222-2)>* **STADIUM ARCADIUM** [1] [1]
– 'Jupiter':- Dani California / Snow (hey oh) / Charlie / Stadium arcadium / Hump de bump / She's only 18 / Slow cheetah / Torture me / Strip my mind / Especially in Michigan / Warlocks / C'mon girl / Wet sand / Hey // 'Mars':- Desecration smile / Hard to concentrate / 21st century / She looks to me / Readymade / If / Make you feel better / Animal bar / So much I / Storm in a teacup / We believe / Turn it again / Death of a Martian. *<(ltd d-cd w/dvd+=; 9362 49997-2)>* – Dani California (video) / (interviews) / (making of).

– compilations, others, etc. –

Oct 92. (cd/c/d-lp) *EMI USA; (CD/TC+/MTL 1071)* *<94762>* **WHAT HITS!?** [23] [22]
– Higher ground / Fight like a brave / Behind the Sun / Me & my friends / Backwoods / True men don't kill coyotes / Fire / Get up and jump / Knock me down / Under the bridge / Show me your soul / If you want me to stay / Hollywood / Jungle man / The brothers cup / Taste the pain / Catholic school girls rule / Johnny kick a hole in the sky. *(cd re-dist.Mar03)* – hit UK No.44

Oct 94. (d-cd) *Warners; (9362 45649-2)* **PLASMA SHAFT** (rare mixes/live) [ ] [ ]

Nov 94. (cd/c/lp) *E.M.I.; (CD/TC+/MTL 1062)* **OUT IN L.A.** (rare remixes, demos & live) [61] [82]

Nov 95. (3xcd-box) *E.M.I.; (CDOMB 004)* **THE RED HOT CHILI PEPPERS / FREAKY STYLIE / THE UPLIFT MOFO PARTY PLAN** [ ] [ ]

Apr 98. (cd/c) *EMI-USA; <72434-94139-2/-4>* **ESSENTIAL RED HOT CHILI PEPPERS: UNDER THE COVERS** [–] [ ]

Jun 00. (cd) *E.M.I.; (527294-2)* **MOTHER'S MILK / THE UPLIFT MOFO PARTY PLAN / FREAKY STYLEY** [ ] [–]

Otis REDDING

Born: 9 Sep'41, Dawson, Georgia, USA. Singing in a gospel choir as a child and later winning a succession of talent contests with LITTLE RICHARD covers, REDDING's prescient abilities were noted by PHIL WALDEN who, at the time, was managing local R&B outfit, JOHNNY JENKINS & THE PINETOPPERS. OTIS soon became a driver/occasional singer with the act, his/their first release being the 'SHOUT BAMALAMA' single released on the 'Confederate' label in 1960. The following year, after OTIS' marriage to ZELDA, they issued 'GETTIN' HIP' on 'Alshire', while 1962 saw the release of a further single, 'LOVE TWIST' on 'Gerald' records. During this time, OTIS was only given the odd vocal spot, although this changed following the group's 'Atlantic'-sponsored recording session at the burgeoning 'Stax' studios. REDDING was allotted the time left over from JENKINS' session, putting it to good use and cutting two tracks, a soul shouter, 'HEY HEY BABY' and a ballad, 'THESE ARMS OF MINE'. Impressed, 'Stax' released the two tracks as a single on their subsidiary, 'Volt', the latter song becoming a minor US hit in mid '63. By mutual agreement and a special contract, 'Atlantic (aka Atco)' decided to allow the label to continue releasing REDDING material. Backed by 'Stax' house band, BOOKER T & THE MG's, the singer scored another minor hit with the lovesick ballad, 'PAIN IN MY HEART', releasing a similarly titled album the following year. REDDING led the way in 'Stax's back to basics soul crusade, the singer being widely credited with altering the sound of black music with his radically inventive horn parts. Though he wasn't an accomplished musician, he had an intuitive feel for rhythm and melody which he'd translate to his backing band, most of his material recorded spontaneously with a minimal number of takes. Co-written with MG, STEVE CROPPER, 'MR PITIFUL' was a slightly self-mocking caricature of REDDING as the king of soul heartbreak, its driving, emotive delivery overshadowing the baleful 'THAT'S HOW STRONG MY LOVE IS' when it was released as the B-side of the latter in the Spring of '65. REDDING's first real breakthrough, however, came with another poignant ballad, 'I'VE BEEN LOVING YOU TOO LONG', a near-Top 20 hit later that summer. After a follow-up album, 'THE GREAT OTIS REDDING SINGS SOUL BALLADS' (1965) failed to chart, REDDING had a surprise UK Top 20 hit towards the end of the year with a cover of The Temptations' 'MY GIRL', paving the way for the success of his seminal third album, 'OTIS BLUE (OTIS REDDING SINGS SOUL)', one of the most revered records in the soul canon. As well as featuring the enduring, much covered classic, 'RESPECT', the album boasted three SAM COOKE covers, including the uplifting 'CHANGE GONNA COME', as well as his famous cover of The Rolling Stones' 'I CAN'T GET NO SATISFACTION'. Though REDDING continued to sell respectably in the States, he was a massive crossover success in the UK, his profile heightened by an ecstatically received performance on hip 60's TV Show, 'Ready Steady Go'. By all accounts, REDDING was an inspirational live performer, his frenetic delivery and magnetic enthusiasm drawing rave reviews and striking fear into the heart of any act unlucky enough to have to follow him. REDDING returned to the UK in 1967, following the release of 'OTIS REDDING'S DICTIONARY OF SOUL' (which included the soul sophistication of 'TRY A LITTLE TENDERNESS and a follow-up of sorts to 'MR. PITIFUL', the rhythmic punch of 'FA-FA-FA-FA-FA (SAD SONG)'), he and his band given a rapturous reception with many stars of the day present in the audience. In June, REDDING was the first black soul singer to perform at a predominantly white rock event, namely the Monterey Pop Festival. His acclaimed performance finally saw the singer gaining the Stateside respect that had long been his due. Later that summer, an album of duets with fellow 'Stax' artist, CARLA THOMAS, 'KING AND QUEEN' dented the US Top 40. Lifted from the record, the brilliant 'TRAMP', in which OTIS' backwoods country hick was pitted against the worldly wise THOMAS, gave REDDING another American Top 30 single. Following an operation for throat problems, REDDING went back into the studio late in '67 and cut a final series of tracks, one song in particular, (SITTIN' ON) THE DOCK OF THE BAY', becoming his epitaph; on the 10th of December, 1967, REDDING's private plane crashed into Lake Monona, Madison, the singer and four members of his backing band, The BAR-KAYS subsequently drowning. As a stunned music world tried to come to terms with the tragedy, thousands attended REDDING's funeral in his hometown of Macon, the aforementioned 'SITTIN'..' subsequently scaling the American charts upon its posthumous release early in '68. REDDING's voice honey-sweet and fragile in contrast to the earthiness of old, the song was a heart-rendingly wistful acoustic folk/soul hybrid, the singer's death adding to its poignancy. The song reflected a new found maturity (also evident in the subsequent album of the same name) which indicated that REDDING was only beginning to realise his full potential, his contribution incalculable to not only black soul but music in general.

• **Covered:** DOCK OF THE BAY (c. Steve Cropper) / MY GIRL (Temptations) / PAIN IN MY HEART (Irma Thomas) / DAY TRIPPER (Beatles) / SHAKE! (Sam Cooke) / KNOCK ON WOOD (Eddie Floyd) / PAPA'S GOT A BRAND NEW BAG (James Brown) / A LOVER'S QUESTION (Clyde McPhatter) / AMEN (Impressions) / etc. • **Trivia:** Late in 1973, his son DEXTER issued single GOD BLESS. In the early 80's, he was joined by other son OTIS and their cousin MARK LOCKET who transpired as The REDDINGS. All on vocals and instruments, they released 2 albums THE AWAKENING and CLASS on the 'Believe' label.

Album rating: PAIN IN MY HEART (*7) / THE GREAT OTIS REDDING SINGS SOUL BALLADS (*7) / OTIS BLUE – OTIS REDDING SINGS SOUL (*9) / THE SOUL ALBUM (*6) / COMPLETE & UNBELIEVABLE . . . THE OTIS REDDING DICTIONARY OF SOUL (*8) / KING AND QUEEN with Carla Thomas (*7) / OTIS REDDING LIVE IN EUROPE (*7) / HISTORY OF OTIS REDDING compilation (*8) / posthumous:- THE DOCK OF THE BAY (*6) / THE IMMORTAL OTIS REDDING (*5) / . . .IN PERSON AT THE WHISKY A GO GO (*6) / LOVE MAN compilation (*5) / THE BEST OF OTIS REDDING compilation (*7) / PURE OTIS (*5) / THE VERY BEST OF OTIS REDDING compilation (*7) / OTIS! THE DEFINITIVE OTIS REDDING compilation (*9)

OTIS REDDING – vocals (solo with session people)

London | Volt

Oct 62. (7") <103> **THESE ARMS OF MINE. / HEY HEY BABY** [–] [85]

Jul 63. (7") <109> **THAT'S WHAT MY HEART NEEDS. / MARY'S LITTLE LAMB** [–] [ ]

Nov 63. (7") *(HLK 9833)* <112> **PAIN IN MY HEART. / SOMETHING IS WORRYING ME** [ ] [61]

— His backing included BOOKER T. & THE MG'S plus JOHNNY JENKINS.

Mar 64. (7") *(HLK 9876)* <116> **COME TO ME. / DON'T LEAVE ME THIS WAY** [ ] [69]

Apr 64. (lp) <161> **PAIN IN MY HEART** [–] [ ]
– Pain in my heart / The dog / Stand by me / Hey hey baby / You send me / I need your lovin' / Louie Louie / These arms of mine / Something is worrying me / Security / That's what my heart needs / Lucille. *(UK-iss.Apr67 on 'Atlantic', hit No.28) (cd-iss. Aug93)*

May 64. (7") *(2091020)* **SECURITY. / WONDERFUL WORLD** [ ] [–]

Jun 64. (7") <117> **SECURITY. / I WANT TO THANK YOU** [–] [97]

Oct 64. (7") <121> **CHAINED AND BOUND. / YOUR ONE AND ONLY MAN** [–] [70]

Atlantic | Volt

Apr 65. (7") *(4024)* <124> **MR.PITIFUL. / THAT'S HOW STRONG MY LOVE IS** [ ] [41] Feb65 [74]

May 65. (7") <126> **I'VE BEEN LOVING YOU TOO LONG (TO STOP NOW). / I'M DEPENDING ON YOU** [–] [21]

Aug 65. (7") *(2091062)* **I'VE BEEN LOVING YOU TOO LONG. / RESPECT** [ ] [–]

Sep 65. (lp) *(SD 33248)* <411> **THE GREAT OTIS REDDING SINGS SOUL BALLADS** [ ] Mar65 [ ]
– That's how strong my love is / Chained and bound / A woman, a lover, a friend / Your one and only man / Nothing can change this love / It's too late / For your precious love / I want to thank you / Come to me / Home in your heart / Keep your arms around me / Mr. Pitiful. *(hit UK chart No.30, Apr66) (re-iss. Jun88 on 'Atco', cd-iss. Jul91) (cd-iss. May93)*

Sep 65. (7") <128> **RESPECT. / OLE MAN TROUBLE** [–] [35]

Nov 65. (7") *(4050)* **MY GIRL. / DOWN IN THE VALLEY** [11] [–]

Nov 65. (7") <130> **JUST ONE MORE DAY. / I CAN'T TURN YOU LOOSE** [–] [85]

Feb 66. (lp) *(ATL 5041)* <412> **OTIS BLUE (OTIS REDDING SINGS SOUL)** [6] Oct 65 [75]
– My girl / (I can't get no) Satisfaction / Respect / Shake! / I've been loving you too long / You don't miss your water / Rock me baby / Wonderful world / Down in the valley / Change gonna come / Ole man trouble. *(UK re-iss. Jan67, hit No.7) (re-iss. 1974 + Dec83 +c) (cd-iss. Jun91 on 'Atco')*

Mar 66. (7") *(4080)* <132> **(I CAN'T GET NO) SATISFACTION. / ANY OLE WAY** [33] [31]

Jul 66. (7") *(584019)* <136> **MY LOVER'S PRAYER. / DON'T MESS WITH CUPID** [37] Jun66 [61]

Jul 66. (lp) *(587-011)* <413> **THE SOUL ALBUM** [22] Apr66 [54]
– Just one more day / It's growing / Cigarettes and coffee / Chain gang / Nobody knows you (when you're down and out) / Good to me / Scratch my back / Treat her right / Everybody makes a mistake / Any ole way / 634-5789. *(cd-iss. Jul91 on 'Atco') (cd-iss. Jun93)*

Aug 66. (7") *(584030)* **I CAN'T TURN YOU LOOSE. / JUST ONE MORE DAY** [29] [–]

Nov 66. (7") *(584049)* <138> **FA FA FA FA FA (SAD SONG). / GOOD TO ME** [23] Sep66 [29]

Jan 67. (lp) *(588-050)* <415> **OTIS REDDING'S DICTIONARY OF SOUL** [23] Nov 66 [73]
– Fa-fa-fa-fa-fa (sad song) / I'm sick y'all / Tennessee waltz / Sweet Lorene /

Try a little tenderness / Day tripper / My lover's prayer / She put the hurt on me / Ton of joy / You're still my baby / Hawg for you / Love have mercy. *(re-iss. Jun88, cd-iss. Jul91 on 'Atco') (cd-iss. Jun93)* (US-title 'COMPLETE AND UNBELIEVABLE . . . THE OTIS REDDING DICTIONARY OF SOUL')

Jan 67. (7") *(584070)* *<141>* **TRY A LITTLE TENDERNESS. / I'M SICK Y'ALL** 46 Dec 66 25

Mar 67. (7") *(K 10051)* **RESPECT. / THESE ARMS OF MINE** –
(re-iss. Feb72)

Stax Volt

Mar 67. (7") *(601005)* **DAY TRIPPER. / SHAKE!** 43 –

Apr 67. (7") *(601007)* *<146>* **LET ME COME ON HOME. / I LOVE YOU MORE THAN WORDS CAN SAY** 48 B-side 78

May 67. (7"; by OTIS REDDING & CARLA THOMAS) *<216>* **TRAMP. / TELL IT LIKE IT IS** – 26

Jun 67. (7") *(601011)* **SHAKE (live). / 634-5789 (live)** 28 –

Jun 67. (7") *<149>* **SHAKE. / YOU DON'T MISS YOUR WATER** –

—— Some releases on 'Stax' now with CARLA THOMAS, daughter of singer RUFUS.

Jun 67. (lp; as OTIS REDDING & CARLA THOMAS) *(589-007)* *<716>* **KING AND QUEEN** 18 Apr67 36
– Knock on wood / Let me be good to you / Tramp / Tell it like it is / When something is wrong with my baby / Lovey dovey / New Year's resolution / It takes two / Are you lonely for me baby / Bring it on home to me / Ooh Carla, Ooh Otis. *(re-iss. Jun88) (cd-iss. Jul91; 7567 82256-2)*

Jul 67. (7"; by OTIS REDDING & CARLA THOMAS) *(601 012)* **TRAMP. / OOH CARLA OOH OTIS** 18 –

Aug 67. (7") *(601 017)* *<152>* **GLORY OF LOVE. / I'M COMING HOME** Jul67 60

Sep 67. (lp) *<416>* **LIVE IN EUROPE (live)** – Aug67 32
– Respect / Can't turn you loose / I've been loving you too long / My girl / Shame / Satisfaction / Fa-fa-fa-fa-fa (sad song) / These arms of mine / Day tripper / Try a little tenderness. *(UK-iss.Mar68; 589 016)* – hit No.2 *(re-iss. Aug69 on 'Atco'; 228 017) (cd-iss. Aug93) (cd-iss. Feb95 & Sep95 on 'Warners')*

Oct 67. (7"; as OTIS REDDING & CARLA THOMAS) *(601 021)* *<228>* **KNOCK ON WOOD. / LET ME BE GOOD TO YOU** 35 Aug67 30

Nov 67. (7") *(601027)* **SATISFACTION. / I'VE BEEN LOVING YOU TOO LONG** –

—— on the 10th of December '67, OTIS was killed in a plane crash

– (selective) compilations, etc. –

Dec 67. (lp/c) *Volt; <(418)>* **THE HISTORY OF OTIS REDDING** 2 9
(re-iss. 1969 on 'Atco'; 228 001)
below released on 'Volt'/ 'Stax' unless mentioned otherwise

Feb 68. (7") *(601 031)* *<157>* **(SITTIN' ON) THE DOCK OF THE BAY. / MY SWEET LORENE** 3 Jan68 1

Mar 68. (7"; by OTIS REDDING & CARLA THOMAS) *(601 033)* *<244>* **LOVEY DOVEY. / NEW YEAR'S RESOLUTION** Feb68 68

May 68. (lp) *(230 001)* *<419>* **DOCK OF THE BAY** (late 1967 sessions) 1 Mar68 4
– The dock of the bay / Home in your heart / I want to thank you / Your one and only man / Nothing can change this love / It's too late / For your precious love / Keep your arms around me / Come to me / A woman, a lover, a friend / Chained and bound / That's how strong my love is. *(re-iss. Jul69 on 'Atco'; 228 022) (re-iss. Nov71)*

May 68. (7") *(601 040)* *<163>* **THE HAPPY SONG (DUM DUM). / OPEN THE DOOR** 24 Apr68 25
below released on 'Atlantic' UK/ 'Atco' US unless mentioned

Feb 68. (7") *(K 10111)* **MY GIRL. / MR. PITIFUL** 36
(re-iss. 1972, 1980 & Mar84)

Jul 68. (7") *(584199)* *<6592>* **HARD TO HANDLE. / AMEN** 15 B-side 36

Aug 68. (lp) *<252>* **THE IMMORTAL OTIS REDDING** 19 Jul68 58
(re-iss. Jan72 on 'Atco') (cd-iss. Aug93; 7567 80270-2)

Sep 68. (7") *<6612>* **I'VE GOT DREAMS TO REMEMBER. / NOBODY'S FAULT BUT MINE** – 41

Oct 68. (7") *(584220)* **I'VE GOT DREAMS TO REMEMBER. / CHAMPAGNE AND WINE** –

Nov 68. (lp) *(587148)* *<265>* **OTIS REDDING IN PERSON AT THE WHISKEY A GO-GO (live 1966)** 82
– I can't turn you loose / Pain in my heart / Just one more day / Mr.Pitiful / (I can't get no) Satisfaction / I'm depending on you / Any ole way / These arms of mine / Papa's got a brand new bag / Respect. *(cd-iss. Dec94 & Sep95 on 'Warners')*

Dec 68. (7") *(584234)* *<6636>* **PAPA'S GOT A BRAND NEW BAG (live). / DIRECT ME** Nov68 21
Below released on 'Atco' unless mentioned.

Mar 69. (7") *(584249)* *<6654>* **A LOVER'S QUESTION. / YOU MADE A MAN OUT OF ME** Feb69 48

May 69. (7") *<6677>* **LOVE MAN. / CAN'T TURN YOU LOOSE** – 72

Jun 69. (7") *(226001)* **LOVE MAN. / THAT'S HOW STRONG MY LOVE IS** 43 –

Jun 69. (lp) *(228 025)* *<289>* **LOVE MAN** 46
(re-iss. Nov71 on 'Atlantic') (cd-iss. Jul92 on 'Rhino')

Jan 71. (lp) *(2400 018)* *<333>* **TELL THE TRUTH** (rec.1967) Aug70
– Demonstration / Tell the truth / Out of sight / Give away none of my love / Wholesale love / I got the will / Johnny's heartbreak / Snatch a little piece / Slippin' and slidin' / The match game / A little time / Swingin' on a string. *(cd-iss. Jul92 on 'Rhino'; 8122 70295-2)*

Jul 73. (lp/c) *(K/K4 60016)* *<801>* **THE BEST OF OTIS REDDING** Sep72 76
(cd-iss. Mar87)

Jul 87. (lp/c/cd) *(241118-1/-4/-2)* **DOCK OF THE BAY – THE DEFINITIVE COLLECTION**

Jul 92. (cd/c) *Castle; (CCS CD/MC 339)* **THE COLLECTION** –
– My girl / Stand by me / Higher and higher / The happy song / I love you more than words can say / Amen / Fa-fa-fa-fa-fa (sad song) / I've been losing you too long / The glory of love / I've got dreams to remember / Love man / Free me / Papa's got a brand new bag / (Sittin' on) The dock of the bay.

Mar 93. (3xcd-box) *<(7567 81762-2)>* **THE OTIS REDDING STORY**

Oct 93. (4xcd-box) *<(8122 71439-2)>* **OTIS: THE DEFINITIVE OTIS REDDING**

May 98. (cd) *Rhino; <(8122 72955-2)>* **LOVE SONGS**

Oct 98. (d-cd) *Rhino; <(8122 75471-2)>* **THE OTIS REDDING ANTHOLOGY: DREAMS TO REMEMBER**

Oct 00. (d-cd/d-c) *Atlantic; <(9548 38087-2/-4)>* **THE VERY BEST OF OTIS REDDING** 26

Lou REED

Born: LOUIS FIRBANK, 2 Mar'42, Freeport, Long Island, New York, USA. In 1958, he formed The JADES, who released two REED-penned singles, 'LEAVE HER FOR ME' / 'SO BLUE' and 'LEAVE HER FOR ME' / 'BELINDA' for 'Time' and 'Dot' respectively. Late in '64, he joined the 'Pickwick' stable of writers, achieving a local minor hit when The PRIMITIVES issued his 'The Ostrich' / 'Sneaky Pete' 45. Later in the year, he helped for the seminal VELVET UNDERGROUND. An integral part of the group's songwriting prowess, he departed in September 1970, going solo and signing to 'R.C.A.'. His eponymous 1972 debut (with Richard Robinson on production), scraped into the US Top 200, gaining nothing in renewed respect. Later that year, helped by stablemates DAVID BOWIE and MICK RONSON, he unleashed 'TRANSFORMER', gaving him his first major triumph when it reached the Top 30 on both sides of the Atlantic. It was boosted by 'WALK ON THE WILD SIDE' (a superb Top 20 single), the piano-led melancholy of 'PERFECT DAY', the raw glam of 'VICIOUS' and one-that-got-away 'SATELLITE OF LOVE'. His next album, 'BERLIN' (1973), although unfairly panned by US critics, still managed a Top 10 placing in Britain. On reflection, its subject matter of suicide and child neglect ('THE BED' and 'THE KIDS') didn't help win any new friends and it still stands as one of the most unrelentingly bleak listens in the history of rock. After the claustrophobic confessions of 'BERLIN', the live 'ROCK 'N' ROLL ANIMAL' (1974) album must have come as something of a relief to R.C.A. A technically faultless back-up band roared through a selection of old VELVETS numbers with REED hollering over the top, and while the set represented something of a concession to commercial credibility (by REED's standards anyway) it captured little of the VELVET UNDERGROUND's subtlety. It also saw REED sinking further into self-parody, hamming up his studied image of sleazy decadence to the max. 'SALLY CAN'T DANCE', released later the same year, was REED in full emotionless flight, an icy collection of biting cynicism that included the infamous 'ANIMAL LANGUAGE' track. But laughing LOU hadn't played his ace card yet, that musical two fingered salute fell to 1975's 'METAL MACHINE MUSIC', the one everyone talks about but have never had the will or mental endurance to listen to the whole way through. A double album of impenetrable feedback noise interspersed with inhuman screams, hums etc., the record successfully alienated most of REED's long suffering fans amid critical meltdown. In true contrary style, he sashayed sweetly back with the mellow 'CONEY ISLAND BABY' (1976), although the lyrics remained as brutally frank as ever. His first record for 'Arista', 'ROCK 'N' ROLL HEART' (1976) was indeed as vacantly awful as the title suggests, though the punk-inspired 'STREET HASSLE' (1978) showcased a re-energised REED, most impressively on the malicious guitar workout of 'DIRT' and the swaggering title track. After a tedious live album, REED started to show uncharacteristic signs of maturity in both his music and lyrics with 'THE BELLS' (1979) and 'GROWING UP IN PUBLIC' (1980). At the turn of the 80's, he hooked up with former Void-Oid, ROBERT QUINE, a partnership that resulted in one of the most consistent and accomplished sets in REED's solo career, 'THE BLUE MASK'. Newly married and back at his original stable, 'R.C.A.', REED proffered more domestic lyrical fare alongside darker musings. QUINE remained for one more studio album, the similarly focused 'LEGENDARY HEARTS', before breaking ranks. 1984's 'NEW SENSATIONS' was fairly low-key while 'MISTRIAL' (1986) saw REED introduce a few drum machine tracks in typical 80's style. These were competent albums but hardly essential and only the most devout REED believer could've predicted the creative, commercial and critical renaissance that would ensue with 1989's 'NEW YORK' album. A skeletal strum-athon, this was LOU REED in the raw with the sparsest of musical accompaniment. Back on familiar territory, his sardonic tales of the Big Apple's seedier side made for compelling listening. 'SONGS FOR DRELLA' (1990), a collaboration with JOHN CALE, was a heartfelt tribute to ANDY WARHOL, while 'MAGIC AND LOSS' (1992) was a sincere series of stark meditations on life and death. Despite an ill-advised VELVET UNDERGROUND reunion, REED retained critical favour, going on to release another well-received album in 1996, 'SET THE TWILIGHT REELING'. Rather than relying on the cosy reflections of an ageing iconic life, REED entered his fourth decade as a solo artist with more contrary perversity than most young bucks can muster these days. The aptly titled 'ECSTASY' (2000) found the cantankerous ex-VELVET fearlessly analysing the more uncomfortable dimensions of man's primal urges. He may be reaching pensionable age but his visceral guitar work still throbbed with the energy of misspent youth, REED aided and abetted by the rhythm section of FERNANDO SAUNDERS and TONY 'THUNDER' SMITH. 'THE RAVEN' (2003), meanwhile, has to rank as one of the more unconventional projects REED has undertaken in recent years. In setting the works of Edgar Allan Poe to music at the request of theatre director Robert Wilson, REED exorcised some of his own demons in line with Poe's dark imaginings. The resulting album – the double-set version of which came complete with the production's spoken word performances from the likes of Willem Dafoe and Steve Buscemi – ran the gamut of REED's stylistic arsenal, while musical guests included everyone from DAVID BOWIE and ORNETTE COLEMAN to the FIVE BLIND BOYS OF ALABAMA. Neither this nor his subsequent live album, 'ANIMAL SERENADE' (2004) did much chart wise, despite generally glowing reviews. Featuring familiar faces FERNANDO SAUNDERS and MIKE RATHKE, as well as cellist JANE SCARPANTONI, the drum-free '..SERENADE' was hailed as REED's most revelatory concert set in years, its unusual arrangements stripping away the bluster and magnifying the feral bite of his lyrics. Some commercial consolation came the old trooper's way later that year when he finally had a hit with old 'TRANSFORMER' perennial, 'SATELLITE OF LOVE', after it was remixed into the UK Top 10.

• **Songwriters:** REED compositions except, SEPTEMBER SONG (Kurt Weill) / SOUL MAN (Sam & Dave). In 1979 and 1980, he co-wrote with MICHAEL FORFARA plus other group members. The single, 'CITY LIGHTS', was co-written with NILS LOFGREN. • **Trivia:** Surprisingly in 1973, WALK ON THE WILD SIDE was not banned from airplay. It contained lyrics "giving head", which had been overlooked by unstreet-wise cred. radio producers. LOU has been married twice, first to cocktail waitress, Betty on the 9th of January '73, then to Sylvia Morales on the 14th of February '80. He played guitar and composed four tracks on NICO's 'Chelsea Girl' lp in 1967. Nine years later he produced NELSON SLATER's 'Wild Angel' album, also contributing guitar, piano and vocals. In 1979 and 1981 he co-composed with NILS LOFGREN and KISS on their 'NILS' and 'THE ELDER' albums respectively. In the late 80's, he guested for RUBEN BLADES and his old friend MAUREEN TUCKER. He was also backing vocalist on SIMPLE MINDS' 'This is Your Land' / DION's 'King of The New York Streets' and TOM TOM CLUB's version of 'Femme Fatale'.

Album rating: LOU REED (*5) / TRANSFORMER (*10) / BERLIN (*8) / ROCK'N'ROLL ANIMAL (*6) / SALLY CAN'T DANCE (*5) / LOU REED LIVE (*5) / METAL MACHINE MUSIC (*1) / CONEY ISLAND BABY (*7) / ROCK AND ROLL HEART (*4) / WALK ON THE WILD SIDE – THE BEST OF LOU REED compilation (*7) / STREET HASSLE (*7) / LIVE – TAKE NO PRISONERS (*3) / THE BELLS (*5) / GROWING UP IN PUBLIC (*4) / ROCK AND ROLL DIARY 1967-1980 compilation (*6) / THE BLUE MASK (*6) / LEGENDARY HEARTS (*6) / LIVE IN ITALY (*4) / NEW SENSATIONS (*7) / MISTRIAL (*5) / NEW YORK (*8) / RETRO compilation (*7) / SONGS FOR DRELLA with John Cale (*7) / MAGIC AND LOSS (*7) / BETWEEN THOUGHT AND EXPRESSION: THE LOU REED ANTHOLOGY boxed-compilation (*7) / SET THE TWILIGHT REELING (*6) / PERFECT NIGHT LIVE IN LONDON (*6) / ECSTASY (*8) / NYC MAN compilation (*8) / THE RAVEN (*6) / ANIMAL SERENADE (*7)

LOU REED – vocals, guitar (ex-VELVET UNDERGROUND) / with **STEVE HOWE** – guitar / **RICK WAKEMAN** – keyboards (both of YES) / **CLEM CATTINI** – drums (ex-TORNADOES)

R.C.A. R.C.A.

Jun 72. (7") <0727> **GOING DOWN. / I CAN'T STAND IT** –

Jul 72. (lp) *(SF 8281)* <4701> **LOU REED** Jun72

– I can't stand it / Going down / Walk and talk it / Lisa says / Berlin / I love you / Wild child / Love makes you feel / Ride into the Sun / Ocean. *(cd-iss. Feb00 on 'RCA-Camden'; 74321 72712-2)*

Aug 72. (7") *(RCA 2240)* <0784> **WALK AND TALK IT. / WILD CHILD**

— now with **MICK RONSON** – guitar / **HERBIE FLOWERS** + **KLAUS VOORMANN** – bass / **JOHN HALSEY** + **RITCHIE DHARMA** + **BARRY DE SOUZA** – drums / **RONNIE ROSS** – saxophone / **DAVID BOWIE** – backing vocals, producer

Nov 72. (lp) *(LSP 4807)* <4807> **TRANSFORMER** 13 29

– Vicious / Andy's chest / Perfect day / Hangin' round / Walk on the wild side / Make up / Satellite of love / Wagon wheel / New York telephone conversation / I'm so free / Goodnight ladies. *(re-iss. Feb81 lp/c; INT S/K 5061); hit UK No.91) (re-iss. 1984 lp/c; NL/NK 83806) (cd-iss. 1985 & Oct87 & Aug95; PD 83806) (re-iss. Sep98 cd/c; 74321 60181-2/-4) (lp re-iss. Nov98 on 'Simply Vinyl'; SVLP 58) (lp re-iss. Mar99; NL 83806) (re-dist.Sep01)* – hit UK No.16

Nov 72. (7") *(RCA 2303)* <0887> **WALK ON THE WILD SIDE. / PERFECT DAY** 10 16

(re-iss. May79 on 'RCA Gold'; GOLD 5)

Feb 73. (7") <0964> **SATELLITE OF LOVE. / WALK AND TALK IT** –

Mar 73. (7") *(RCA 2318)* **SATELLITE OF LOVE. / VICIOUS** –

Apr 73. (7") <0054> **VICIOUS. / GOODNIGHT LADIES** –

— all new band **DICK WAGNER** + **STEVE HUNTER** – guitar (both ex-ALICE COOPER) / **STEVE WINWOOD** – keyboards / **JACK BRUCE** – bass / **AYNSLEY DUNBAR** – drums / etc.

Oct 73. (7") <0172> **HOW DO YOU THINK IT FEELS. / LADY DAY** –

Oct 73. (lp) *(RS 1002)* <0207> **BERLIN** 7 98

– Berlin / Lady day / Men of good fortune / Caroline says I / How do you think it feels / Oh Jim / Caroline says II / The kids / The bed / Sad song. *(re-iss. Oct81 lp/c; INT S/K 5150) (re-iss. 1984 lp/c; NL/NK 84388) (cd-iss. Jun86; PD 84388) (cd re-iss. Mat98; 7863 67489-2) (lp re-iss. Feb99 on 'Simply Vinyl'; SVLP 66) (lp re-iss. Mar99; 7863 67489-1)*

Feb 74. (7") *(APBO 0221)* **CAROLINE SAYS I. / CAROLINE SAYS II** [ ] [–]

— **PRAKASH JOHN** – bass (ex-ALICE COOPER) repl. TONY LEVIN / **JOSEF CHIROWSKY** – keyboards / **WHITNEY GLEN** – drums (ex-ALICE COOPER)

Feb 74. (lp/c) *(APL 1/4 0472) <0472>* **ROCK'N'ROLL ANIMAL (live)** [26] [45]
– (intro) – Sweet Jane / Heroin / White light – white heat / Lady day / Rock and roll. *(re-iss. May81 lp/c; INT S/K 5086) (re-iss. 1984 lp/c; NL/NK 83664) (cd-iss. Jun86; PD 83664)*

Apr 74. (7") *<(APBO 0238)>* **SWEET JANE (live). / LADY DAY (live)** [ ] [ ]

— **MICHAEL FORFARA** – keyboards repl. JOSEF

Aug 74. (7") *<10053>* **SALLY CAN'T DANCE. / VICIOUS** [–] [ ]

Sep 74. (lp/c) *(APL 1/4 <0611>)* **SALLY CAN'T DANCE** [ ] [10]
– Ride Sally ride / Animal language / Baby face / N.Y. stars / Kill your sons / Billy / Sally can't dance / Ennui. *(cd-iss. Mar87; PD 80611) (re-iss. cd Feb89; ND 90308)*

Oct 74. (7") *(RCA 2467) <10081>* **SALLY CAN'T DANCE. / ENNUI** [ ] [ ]

Mar 75. (lp) *(RS 1007) <0959>* **LOU REED LIVE (live)** [ ] [62]
– Walk on the wild side / I'm waiting for the man / Vicious / Oh Jim / Satellite of love / Sad song. *(re-iss. Feb81 lp/c; INT S/K 5071) (cd-iss. Mar87 + Feb90; ND 83752)*

— LOU now used synthesizer only.

Jul 75. (d-lp) *<(CPL2 1101)>* **METAL MACHINE MUSIC – (THE AMINE B RING)** [ ] [ ]
– Metal machine music A1 / A2 / A3 / A4. *(re-iss. Mar91 on 'Great Expectations' cd/d-c/d-lp; PIPD C/M/L 023) (cd re-iss. Jan01; 74465 99752-2)*

— Band now featured **MICHAEL SUCHORSKY** – percussion / **BOB KULICK** – guitar / **BRUCE YAW** – bass

Jan 76. (lp) *(RS 1035) <0915>* **CONEY ISLAND BABY** [52] [41]
– Crazy feeling / Charley's girl / She's my best friend / Kicks / A gift / Oooh baby / Nobody's business / Coney Island baby. *(re-iss. Mar81 lp/c; INT S/K 5082) (re-iss. 1984 lp/c; NL/NK 83807) (cd-iss. Dec86 & Sep89; PD 83807)*

Mar 76. (7") *(RCA 2666) <10573>* **CHARLEY'S GIRL. / NOWHERE AT ALL** [ ] [ ]

May 76. (7") *<10648>* **CRAZY FEELING. / NOWHERE AT ALL** [–] [ ]

Arista Arista

Nov 76. (lp/c) *(ARTY/TC-ARTY 142) <4100>* **ROCK AND ROLL HEART** [ ] [64]
– I believe in love / Banging on my drum / Follow the leader / You wear it so well / Ladies pay / Rock and roll heart / Temporary thing. *(cd-iss. Feb93; 262271)*

Nov 76. (7") *<0215>* **I BELIEVE IN LOVE. / SENSELESSLY CRUEL** [–] [ ]

Apr 77. (7") *(105)* **ROCK AND ROLL HEART. / SENSELESSLY CRUEL** [ ] [–]

— **STUART HEINRICH** – guitar, vocals repl. KULICK / **MARTY FOGEL** – saxophone repl. YAW

Apr 78. (lp/c) *(SPART/TC-SPART 1045) <4169>* **STREET HASSLE** [ ] [89]
– Gimme some good times / Dirt / Street hassle / I wanna be black / Real good time together / Shooting star / Leave me alone / Wait. *(cd-iss. Feb93; 262270)*

Apr 78. (12") **STREET HASSLE. / (same track)** [–] [ ]

Jul 78. (12"ep) *(ARIST12 198)* **STREET HASSLE. / Waiting For The Man + Venus In Furs (by "The VELVET UNDERGROUND")** [ ] [–]

— **ELLARD BOLES** – bass, guitar repl. HEINRICH. (Below released 'RCA' UK)

Mar 79. (d-lp)<red,blue-lp> *(XL 03066) <8502>* **LIVE – TAKE NO PRISONERS (live)** [ ] Nov78 [ ]
– Sweet Jane / I wanna be black / Satellite of love / Pale blue eyes / Berlin / I'm waiting for the man / Coney Island baby / Street hassle / Walk on the wild side / Leave me alone.

— **REED** now with **FORFARA, BOLES, SUCHORSKY, FOGEL** and **DON CHERRY** – trumpet

Oct 79. (lp/c) *(SPART/TC-SPART 1093) <4229>* **THE BELLS** [ ] May 79 [ ]
– Stupid man / Disco mystic / I want to boogie with you / With you / Looking for love / City lights / All through the night / Families / The bells. *(cd-iss. Aug92; 262 918)*

Jun 79. (7") *<0431>* **CITY LIGHTS. / I WANT TO BOOGIE WITH YOU** [–] [ ]

Oct 79. (7") *(ARIST 308)* **CITY LIGHTS. / SENSELESSLY CRUEL** [ ] [–]

— **CHUCK HAMMER** – synthesizer, guitar repl. FOGEL & CHERRY

May 80. (lp/c) *(SPART/TC-SPART 1131) <9522>* **GROWING UP IN PUBLIC** [ ] [ ]
– How do you speak to an angel / My old man / Keep away / Growing up in public / Standing on ceremony / So alone / Love is here to stay / The power of positive drinking / Smiles / Think it over / Teach the gifted children. *(cd-iss. Aug92; 262 917)*

Jun 80. (7") *<0535>* **THE POWER OF POSITIVE DRINKING. / GROWING UP IN PUBLIC** [–] [ ]

— now with **ROBERT QUINE** – guitar / **FERNANDO SAUNDERS** – bass, vocals / **DOANE PERRY** – drums

R.C.A. R.C.A.

Mar 82. (lp/c) *(RCA LP/K 6028) <4221>* **THE BLUE MASK** [ ] Feb82 [ ]
– My house / Women / Underneath the bottle / The gun / The blue mask / Average guy / The heroine / Waves of fear / The day John Kennedy died / Heavenly arms. *(cd-iss. Feb98; ND 84780)*

Mar 83. (lp/c) *(RCA LP/K 6071) <4568>* **LEGENDARY HEARTS** [ ] [ ]
– Legendary hearts / Don't talk to me about work / Make up mind / Martial law / The last shot / Turn out the light / ow wow / Betrayed / Bottoming out / Home of the brave / Rooftop garden. *(re-iss. Oct86 lp/c; NL/NK 89843) (re-iss. Apr91 cd/c; ND/NK 89843)*

Apr 83. (7") *<13558>* **MARTIAL LAW. / DON'T TALK TO ME ABOUT WORK** [–] [ ]

Jan 84. (d-lp/c) *(PL/PK 89156)* **LIVE IN ITALY (live)** [ ] [–]
– Sweet Jane / I'm waiting for the man / Martial law / Satellite of love / Kill your sons / Betrayed / Sally can't dance / Waves of fear / Average guy / White light – white heat / Some kinda love / Sister Ray / Walk on the wild side / Heroin / Rock and roll.

— line-up now **SAUNDERS** plus **FRED MAHER** – drums / **PETER WOOD** – piano, synthesizer, accordion / **L. SHANKER** – electric violin

Mar 84. (7") *<13841>* **I LOVE YOU SUZANNE. / MY FRIEND GEORGE** [–] [ ]

May 84. (12") *<13849>* **MY RED JOY STICK. / ('A' remix)** [–] [ ]

May 84. (lp/c) *(PL/PK 84998) <4998>* **NEW SENSATIONS** [92] [56]
– I love you, Suzanne / Endlessly jealous / My red joystick / Turn to me / New sensations / Doin' the things that we want to / What becomes a legend most / Fly into the Sun / High in the city / My friend George / Down at the arcade. *(cd-iss. Jul86; PD 84998)*

May 84. (7") *(RCA 417)* **I LOVE YOU, SUZANNE. / VICIOUS** [ ] [–]
(12"+=) *(RCAT 417)* – Walk on the wild side.

1985. (7") *<7-89468>* **MY LOVE IS CHEMICAL. / PEOPLE HAVE TO MOVE** [–] [ ]
(above issued on 'Atlantic' and taken from 'White Nights' movie)

Apr 86. (12") *<14427>* **THE ORIGINAL WRAPPER. / (2 'A' versions)** [–] [ ]

Apr 86. (lp/c/cd) *(PL/PK/PD 87190) <7190>* **MISTRIAL** [69] [47]
– Mistrial / No money down / Outside / Don't hurt a woman / Video violence / Spit it out / The original wrapper / Mama's got a lover / I remember you / Tell it to your heart. *(re-iss. Oct88 lp/c/cd; NL/NK/ND 90253)*

Jun 86. (7") *(RCA 501) <14368>* **NO MONEY DOWN. / DON'T HURT A WOMAN** [ ] [ ]
(12"+=) *(RCAT 501) <14388>* – ('A'dub version).

— Next from the film 'Soul Man'.

A&M A&M

Jan 87. (7"; LOU REED & SAM MOORE) *(AM 364)* **SOUL MAN. / Sweet Sarah (by 'Tom Scott')** [30] Nov86 [ ]
<US-12"+=> *<364>* – My love is chemical.

— new band **MIKE RATHKE** – guitar / **ROB WASSERMAN** – bass / **FRED MAHER** – drums / **MAUREEN TUCKER** – drums on 2 (ex-VELVET UNDERGROUND)

Sire Sire

Jan 89. (lp/c)(cd) *(WX 246/+C)(925 829-2) <25829>* **NEW YORK** [14] [40]
– Romeo had Juliette / Halloween parade / Dirty Blvd. / Endless cycle / There is no time / The last great American whale / Beginning of a great adventure / Busload of faith / Sick of you / Hold on / Good evening Mr. Waldheim / Xmas in February / Strawman / Dime store mystery. *(re-iss. Feb95 cd/c;)*

Feb 89. (7") *<9 22875-7>* **ROMEO HAD JULIETTE. / BUSLOAD OF FAITH (live)** [–] [ ]

Feb 89. (7") *(W 7547)* **DIRTY BLVD. / THE LAST GREAT AMERICAN WHALE** [ ] [–]
(12"+=) *(W 7547T)* – The room.

Apr 90. (cd)(lp/c; by LOU REED / JOHN CALE) *(7599 <26140-2>)(WX 345/+C)* **SONGS FOR DRELLA** [22] [ ]
– Smalltown / Open house / Style it takes / Work / Trouble with classicists / Starlight / Faces and names / Images / Slip away (a warning) / It wasn't me / I believe / Nobody but you / A dream / Forever changed / Hello it's me. *(re-iss. Feb91 & Jan97; same)*
(above re-united the two VELVET UNDERGROUND members, tributing the recently deceased ANDY WARHOL)

— **MICHAEL BLAIR** – percussion, drums, vocals repl. MAHER

Jan 92. (cd/lp/c) *(7599 <26662-2>)(WX 435/+C)* **MAGIC AND LOSS** [6] [80]
– Dorita – the spirit / What's good – the thesis / Power and glory – the situation / Magician – internally / Sword of Damocles – eternally / Goodby mass – in a chapel bodily termination / Cremation – ashes to ashes / Dreamin' – escape / No chance – regret / Warrior king – revenge / Harry's circumcision – reverie gone astray / Gassed and stoked – loss / Power and glory part II – magic transformation / Magic and loss – the summation. *(cd re-iss. Jan97; same)*

Mar 92. (c-s) *(W 0090C)* **WHAT'S GOOD. / THE ROOM** [ ] [–]
(12"+=/cd-s+=) *(W 0090 T/CD)* – Harry's circumcision / A dream.

— now with just **FERNANDO SAUNDERS** – basses / **TONY 'Thunder' SMITH** – drums / **MIKE RATHKE** – guitars / + guest **LAURIE ANDERSON** – backing vocals

Reprise Reprise

Feb 96. (cd/c) *<(9362 46159-2/-4)>* **SET THE TWILIGHT REELING** [26] [ ]
– Egg cream / NYC man / Finish line / Trade in / Hang on to your emotions / Sex with your parents (motherfucker) part II (live) / Hooky wooky / The proposition / Adventurer / Riptide / Set the twilight reeling.

May 96. (c-s) *(W 0351C)* **HOOKY WOOKY / ON THE RUN** [ ] [ ]
(cd-s) *(W 0351CD)* – ('A'side) / This magic moment / You'll never know you loved.

Apr 98. (cd/c) *<(9362 46917-2/-4)>* **PERFECT NIGHT LIVE IN LONDON (live)** [ ] [ ]
– I'll be your mirror / Perfect day / The kids / Vicious / Busload of faith / Kicks / Talking book / Into the divine / Coney Island baby / New sensations / Why do you talk / Riptide / Original wrapper / Sex with your parents / Dirty Blvd.

Apr 00. (cd/c) *<(9362 47425-2/-4)>* **ECSTASY** [54] [ ]
– Paranoia key of E / Mystic child / Mad / Ecstasy / Modern dance / Tatters / Future farmers of America / Turning time around / White prism / Rock minuet / Baton rouge / Like a possum / Rouge / Big sky.

Feb 03. (cd) *<(9362 48372-2)>* **THE RAVEN** [ ] Jan03 [ ]
– The conqueror worm * / Overture / Old Poe * / Prologue (Ligiea) * / Edgar Allan Poe / The valley of unrest * / Call on me (with LAURIE ANDERSON) / The city in the sea – Shadow * / A thousand departed friends / Change / The fall of the House of Usher * / The bed / Perfect day / The raven (with WILLEM DaFOE) / Balloon / Broadway song (with STEVE BUSCEMI) / The tell-tale heart part 1 * / Blind rage / The tell-tale heart part 2 * / Burning embers / Imp of the perverse * / Vanishing act / The cask * / Guilty * / Guilty (with ORNETTE COLEMAN) / A wild being from birth * / I wanna know (the pit and the pendulum) (with BLIND BOYS OF ALABAMA) / Science of the mind / Annabel Lee – The bells * / Hop frog (with DAVID BOWIE) / Every frog has his day * / Tripitena's speech / Who am I? (Tripitena's song) / Courtly orangutans * / Fire music * / Guardian angel. *<(ltd d-cd+= *; 9362 48373-2)>*

Mar 04. (d-cd) *<(9362 48678-2)>* **ANIMAL SERENADE** (live) [ ] [ ]
– Advice / Smalltown / Tell it to your heart / Men of good fortune / How do you think it feels / Vanishing act / Ecstasy / The day John Kennedy died / Street hassle / The bed / Revein Cherie / Venus in furs / Dirty blvd. / Sunday morning / All tomorrow's parties / Call on me / The raven / Set the twilight reeling / Candy says / Heroin.

– compilations, others, etc. –

— Below releases issued on 'RCA' unless mentioned otherwise

Apr 77. (lp/c) *(PL/PK 12001)* *<2001>* **WALK ON THE WILD SIDE – THE BEST OF LOU REED** [ ] [ ]
(cd-iss. Mar87 & Oct91; PD 83753)

Jan 79. (lp/c) *(NL/NK 42731)* **VICIOUS** [ ] [ ]

Dec 80. (d-lp) *Arista; (DARTY 8)* **ROCK AND ROLL DIARY 1967-1980** [ ] [ ]
– (above featured 8 tracks by Velvet Underground)

Aug 81. (7") *RCA Gold; (GOLD 523)* **WALK ON THE WILD SIDE. / VICIOUS** [ ] [–]
(re-iss. Oct86 & Mar89 on 'Old Gold'; OG 9635)

Sep 82. (lp) *(SF 8281)* **I CAN'T STAND IT** [ ] [ ]

Oct 85. (7") *A&M; (AM 283)* **SEPTEMBER SONG. / Oh Heavenly Action (by 'Mark Bingham with Johnny Adams & Aaron Neville')** [ ] [ ]

May 86. (c) *(NK 89895)* **MAGIC MOMENTS** [ ] [–]

Sep 86. (lp/c) *Fame; (FA/TC-FA 3164)* **NEW YORK SUPERSTAR** [ ] [–]

Feb 89. (3"cd-ep) *(PD 49453)* **WALK ON THE WILD SIDE / PERFECT DAY / SATELLITE OF LOVE / VICIOUS** [ ] [ ]

Sep 89. (lp/c/cd) *(PL/PK/PD 90389)* **RETRO** [29] [ ]
– Walk on the wild side / Satellite of love / I love you Suzanne / Wild child / How do you think it feels / Lady day / Coney Island baby / Sweet Jane (live) / Vicious / Sally can't dance / Berlin / Caroline says II / Kill your sons / White light – white heat (live). *(cd+=)* – I'm waiting for the man (VELVET UNDERGROUND) / Heroin (VELVET UNDERGROUND).

Mar 92. (3xcd-box/3xc-box) *(PD/PK 90621)* **BETWEEN THOUGHT AND EXPRESSION: THE LOU REED ANTHOLOGY** [ ] Apr92 [ ]

Jan 95. (d-cd) *(74321 29209-2)* **STREET HASSLE / THE BELLS** [ ] [ ]

Jan 95. (d-cd) *(74321 29210-2)* **TRANSFORMER / BERLIN** [ ] [ ]

Oct 95. (cd/c; by LOU REED & VELVET UNDERGROUND) *Global TV; (RAD CD/MC 21)* **LOU REED & VELVET UNDERGROUND** [ ] [–]

Aug 96. (cd) *(07863 66864-2)* **DIFFERENT TIMES – LOU REED IN THE 70'S** [ ] [–]

Oct 96. (cd) *Camden-RCA; (74321 43157-2)* **LOU REED LIVE IN CONCERT (live)** [ ] [–]

Sep 97. (cd/c) *Camden-RCA; (74321 52375-2/-4)* **PERFECT DAY** [ ] [ ]

Nov 97. (cd) *Eagle; (EABCD 012)* **THE MASTERS** [ ] [–]

Apr 99. (cd/c) *RCA-Camden; (74321 66046-2/-4)* **THE VERY BEST OF LOU REED** [ ] [–]

May 01. (cd) *Burning Airlines; (PILOT 083)* **HAMPSTEAD NEW YORK 26.12.72 (live)** [ ] [ ]

Aug 02. (cd) *Superior; (SU 29025)* **AMERICAN POET** [ ] [–]

May 03. (d-cd) *(82876 50131-2)* *<50564>* **NYC MAN** [31] Jun03 [ ]
– Who am I (Tripitena's song) / Sweet Jane (VELVET UNDERGROUND) / Rock and roll (VELVET UNDERGROUND) / I'm waiting for the man (VELVET UNDERGROUND) / White light – white heat (VELVET UNDERGROUND) / Street hassle / Berlin / Caroline says II / The kids / Walk on the wild side / Kill your sons / Vicious / Blue mask / I'll be your mirror / Magic and loss / Ecstasy / I wanna be black / Temporary thing / Shooting star / Legendary hearts / Heroin / Coney Island baby / Last shot / The bells / Perfect day / Sally can't dance / NYC man / Dirty Blvd. / Rocket minuet / Pale blue eyes (VELVET UNDERGROUND).

Jul 04. (12"/cd-s) *(82876 63647-1/-2)* **SATELLITE OF LOVE '04** [10] [–]
– (mixes:- Dab hands re touch radio / Dab hands re touch / Groovefinder / video).

Jul 04. (cd) *(82876 63112-2)* **NYC MAN – GREATEST HITS** (best of +) [43] [ ]

☐ RELAXED MUSCLE (see under ⇒ PULP)

R.E.M.

Formed: Athens, Georgia, USA ... spring 1980 by MICHAEL STIPE and PETER BUCK, MIKE MILLS and BILL BERRY, who soon played at a local party under the name TWISTED KITES. In 1981, through manager Jefferson Holt, they released their debut MITCH EASTER-produced 45, 'RADIO FREE EUROPE'. With its soaring melody and jangly guitar playing off STIPE's low-key vocals, the sound was unique and caught the ears of 'I.R.S.' label boss, MILES COPELAND. The latter duly signed them up and retained EASTER for the mini-lp 'CHRONIC TOWN' (1982). The five-song set was received with gushing enthusiasm and set the scene for R.E.M.'s first album proper, 'MURMUR' (1983). Co-produced by EASTER and DON DIXON, the album was a stunning debut which

REM

sharpened the hooks, honed the pealing guitar sound and generally engendered a compelling air of mystique. Much of this was down to STIPE's impenetrable lyrics and vague execution which enhanced rather than detracted from the melodic melancholy of songs like 'TALK ABOUT THE PASSION'. While this inventiveness wasn't quite consolidated with 'RECKONING' (1984), the album was slightly more accessible, leading to a Top 30 placing in the American charts. Boasting the ambling country poignancy of '(DON'T GO BACK TO) ROCKVILLE', what the record lacked in innovation it made up for in songwriting skill. Never content to tread water, the band recorded 'FABLES OF THE RECONSTRUCTION' (1985) in London with veteran folk producer JOE BOYD, an interesting pairing which made for a trippy, heavily atmospheric sound. Even the poppier 'DRIVER 8' wasn't free of the edginess which characterised the record. Dextrously combining sonic exploration and heart-melting melodies, 'LIFE'S RICH PAGEANT' (1986) was a bold step forward. Tracks like 'FALL ON ME', 'I BELIEVE' and 'CUYAHOGA' showed an assured poise which the band were undoubtedly developing through their ceaseless touring and snowballing critical acclaim. 'DOCUMENT' (1987) was even more focused, STIPE actually beginning to sound comprehensible. The sardonic, brooding 'THE ONE I LOVE' single gave R.E.M. their first US Top 10 hit, while the band's 'Warners' debut, 'GREEN' (1988), finally saw the band become a mainstream act, in terms of commercial success at least. The unashamed jaunty pop of 'STAND' (1989) gave the band their biggest hit to date while 'ORANGE CRUSH' (1989) echoed the muted moodiness of 'THE ONE I LOVE'. Elsewhere, gems like 'WORLD LEADER PRETEND' were artful examples of that rare ability to create subtle, intelligent songs that were still annoyingly hummable. After 'GREEN's release, R.E.M. undertook a mammoth world tour with the result that the next album, 'OUT OF TIME', didn't hit the shelves until 1991. For most people it was well worth the wait. Preceded by the starkly melancholy 'LOSING MY RELIGION' with its mournful mandolin refrain, 'OUT OF TIME' was a multi-million seller, hitting the top spot on both sides of the Atlantic. While 'SHINY HAPPY PEOPLE' was a mite sickly sweet after 10,000 listens, and 'RADIO' was an ill-advised foray into rap, acoustic flavoured diamonds like 'HALF A WORLD AWAY', 'COUNTRY FEEDBACK' and 'ME IN HONEY' rendered the album a classic. Equally successful but much harder going, 1992's 'AUTOMATIC FOR THE PEOPLE' was a moody masterpiece. Focusing on the more painful aspects of human existence, the album wasn't as immediate as its predecessor but the lucid beauty of tracks like 'NIGHTSWIMMING' and 'MAN ON THE MOON' (written about their tragic comic-hero, Andy Kaufman and later made into a film starring Jim Carrey, c.1999) soon slipped insidiously into your subconscious. Silencing rumours that MICHAEL STIPE was suffering from Aids, R.E.M. bounced back with the grungy 'MONSTER' (1994) album. Despite confident hits like 'WHAT'S THE FREQUENCY KENNETH' and 'CRUSH WITH EYELINER', R.E.M. were capable of more imaginative fare. The subsequent tour (the first since the late 80's) came to a premature halt when BILL BERRY suffered a brain haemorrhage. After a successful recovery, the band reconvened to record 1996's 'NEW ADVENTURES IN HI-FI' (sadly, the last with BERRY). Written mainly on the road, the album was a return to more familiar R.E.M. territory, rich in imagery and possessed of all the qualities that make R.E.M. one of rock's most respected bands. Between '. . .HI-FI' and 98's slightly disappointing Top 3 set 'UP', BUCK took up posts in MINUS 5 (with YOUNG FRESH FELLOWS' SCOTT McCAUGHEY) and lounge-pop/jazz supergroup, TUATARA. The aforementioned 'UP' was certainly their most pensive and melancholy record to date, UK Top 30 singles such as 'DAYSLEEPER', 'LOTUS' and 'AT MY MOST BEAUTIFUL', sitting alongside their use of LEONARD COHEN lyrics on 'HOPE'. Come the new millennium, R.E.M. were looking back as well as forward on the shiny, happy but ultimately unfulfilled 'REVEAL' (2001), attempting a marriage of their classic songcraft with the more recent experimentalism. Despite moments of lush, summery abandon, it doesn't quite come off, STIPE and Co sounding like they're still grappling with that sonic mid-life crisis. Another crisis was on hand in April 2001 when PETER BUCK allegedly got into some serious mischief while on a BA flight; his case would take until early the following year to settle. The ruminatory, intricately crafted 'AROUND THE SUN' (2004) saw the band back at the top of the UK chart for the first time in over a decade, powered by the Top 5 success of lead single – and opening track – 'LEAVING NEW YORK', their most R.E.M.-esque in almost as many years.

• **Songwriters:** Group compositions except 'B'side covers; THERE SHE GOES AGAIN + PALE BLUE EYES + FEMME FATALE (Velvet Underground) / TOYS IN THE ATTIC (Aerosmith) / KING OF THE ROAD (Roger Miller) / CRAZY (Pylon) / AFTER HOURS (Lou Reed) / LOVE IS ALL AROUND (Troggs) / FIRST WE TAKE MANHATTAN (Leonard Cohen) / LAST DATE (Floyd Cramer) / TIGHTEN UP (Booker T. & The MG's) / SEE NO EVIL (Television) / ACADEMY EIGHT SONG (Mission of Burma) / WALL OF DEATH (Richard Thompson) / FUNTIME (Iggy Pop) / SUMMERTIME (Gershwin) / BABY BABY (Vibrators) / WHERE'S CAPTAIN KIRK? (Spizz) / PARADE OF WOODEN SOLDIERS (Tchaikovsky) / TOM'S DINER (Suzanne Vega) / MOON RIVER (Henry Mancini) / THE ARMS OF YOU (Robyn Hitchcock) / THE LION SLEEPS TONIGHT (Tokens) / DARK GLOBE (Syd Barrett) / SPONGE (Vic Chesnutt) / FAVORITE WRITER (Magnapop) / OUT IN THE COUNTRY (Nichols-Williams). • **Trivia:** R.E.M. stands for Rapid Eye Movement.

Album rating: CHRONIC TOWN mini (*6) / MURMUR (*9) / RECKONING (*9) / FABLES OF THE RECONSTRUCTION (*8) / LIFE'S RICH PAGEANT (*8) / DEAD LETTER OFFICE compilation (*7) / DOCUMENT (*8) / EPONYMOUS compilation (*7) / GREEN (*8) / THE BEST OF R.E.M. compilation (*9) / OUT OF TIME (*9) / AUTOMATIC FOR THE PEOPLE (*10) / MONSTER (*7) / NEW ADVENTURES IN HI-FI (*8) / UP (*7) / REVEAL (*7) / IN TIME: THE BEST OF R.E.M. 1988-2003 compilation (*8) / AROUND THE SUN (*5) / Hindu Love Gods: HINDU LOVE GODS (*5)

MICHAEL STIPE (b. JOHN MICHAEL STIPE, 4 Jan'60, Decatur, Atlanta) – vocals / **PETER BUCK** (b. 6 Dec'56, Oakland, Calif.) – guitar / **MIKE MILLS** (b.17 Dec'58, Orange County, Calif.) – bass, keyboards, vocals / **BILL BERRY** (b.31 Jul'58, Duluth, Minnesota) – drums, vocals

not iss. Hib-Tone

Jul 81. (7") *(HT-0001)* **RADIO FREE EUROPE. / SITTING STILL** [–] [ ]

I.R.S. I.R.S.

Aug 82. (m-lp) *<SP 70502>* **CHRONIC TOWN** [–] [ ]
– Wolves, lower / 1,000,000 / Gardening at night / Stumble / Carnival of sorts (box cars). *(re-iss. Feb85; IRS 70502)*

Aug 83. (7") *(PFP 1017) <9916>* **RADIO FREE EUROPE. / THERE SHE GOES AGAIN** [ ] Jul83 [78]

Aug 83. (lp/c) *(SP/CS 70604) <70604>* **MURMUR** [ ] May83 [36]
– Radio free Europe / Pilgrimage / Laughing / Talk about the passion / Moral kiosk / Perfect circle / Catapult / Sitting still / 9-9 / Shaking through / We walk / West of the fields. *(cd-iss. 1988; CDA 7014) (cd re-iss. Mar91 ++; CDMID 129)* – There she goes again / 9-9 (live) / Gardening at night (live) / Catapult (live).

Nov 83. (7") *(PFP 1026)* **TALK ABOUT THE PASSION. / SHAKING THROUGH** [ ] [–]
(12"+=) *(PFSX 1026)* – Carnival of sorts (box cars) / 1,000,000.

Mar 84. (7") *(IRS 105) <9927>* **S). CENTRAL RAIN (I'M SORRY). / KING OF THE ROAD** [ ] Jun84 [85]
(12") *(PFSX 105)* – ('A'side) / Voice of Harold / Pale blue eyes.

Apr 84. (lp/c) *(IRS A/C 7045) <70044>* **RECKONING** [91] [27]
– Harborcoat / 7 Chinese Bros. / So. central rain (I'm sorry) / Pretty persuasion / Time after time (Annelise) / Second guessing / Letter never sent / Camera / (Don't go back to) Rockville / Little America. *(cd-iss. 1988 on 'A&M'; CDA 7045) (re-iss. Oct94 on 'A&M' cd/c;)*

Jun 84. (7") *(IRS 107)* **(DON'T GO BACK TO) ROCKVILLE. / WOLVES** [ ] [–]
(12"+=) *(IRSX 107)* – 9 minus 9 (live) / Gardening at night (live).

Jun 84. (7") *<IR 9931>* **(DON'T GO BACK TO) ROCKVILLE. / CATAPULT (live)** [–] [ ]

Jul 85. (7") *(IRM 102)* **CAN'T GET THERE FROM HERE. / BANDWAGON** [ ] [–]
(12"+=) *(IRT 102)* – Burning Hell.

Jul 85. (lp/c) *(MIR F/C 1003)* *<5592>* **FABLES OF THE RECONSTRUCTION – RECONSTRUCTION OF THE FABLES** [35] Jun85 [28]
– Feeling gravitys pull / Maps and legends / Driver 8 / Life and how to live it / Old Man Kensey / Can't get there from here / Green grow the rushes / Kokoutek / Auctioneer (another engine) / Good advices / Wendell Gee. *(cd-iss. Apr87; DMIRF 1003) (re-iss. cd Jan90; DMIRL 1503) (lp re-iss. Dec99 on 'Simply Vinyl'; SVLP 151)*

Oct 85. (7") *<52678>* **DRIVER 8. / CRAZY** [–] [ ]

Oct 85. (7") *(IRM 105)* **WENDELL GEE. / CRAZY** [ ] [–]
(d7"+=) *(IRMD 105)* – Ages of you / Burning down.
(12"+=) *(IRT 105)* – Driver 8.

Aug 86. (7") *(IRM 121)* *<52883>* **FALL ON ME. / ROTARY TEN** [ ] [94]
(12"+=) *(IRMT 121)* – Toys in the attic.

Aug 86. (lp/c) *(MIRG/+C 1014)* *<5783>* **LIFE'S RICH PAGEANT** [43] [21]
– Begin the begin / These days / Fall on me / Cuyahoga / Hyena / Underneath the bunker / The flowers of Guatemala / I believe / What if we give it away? / Just a touch / Swan swan H / Superman. *(cd-iss. Dec86; DMIRG 1014) (re-iss. cd Sep91; DMIRL 1507)*

Mar 87. (7") *(IRM 128)* **SUPERMAN. / WHITE TORNADO** [ ] [–]
(12"+=) *(IRMT 128)* – Femme fatale.

Aug 87. (7") *(IRM 145)* **IT'S THE END OF THE WORLD AS WE KNOW IT (AND I FEEL FINE). / THIS ONE GOES OUT (live)** [ ] [–]
(12"+=) *(IRMT 145)* – Maps and legends (live).

Sep 87. (7") *<53171>* **THE ONE I LOVE. / MAPS AND LEGENDS (live)** [–] [9]

Oct 87. (lp/c/cd) *(MIRG/MIRGC/DMIRG 1025)* *<42059>* **DOCUMENT** [28] Sep87 [10]
– Finest worksong / Welcome to the occupation / Exhuming McCarthy / Disturbance at Heron House / Strange / It's the end of the world as we know it (and I feel fine) / The one I love / Fireplace / Lightnin' Hopkins / King of birds / Oddfellows local 151. *(cd re-iss. Sep91 +=; DMIRL 1508)* – Finest worksong (other mix) / Last date / The one I love (live) / Time after time etc. (live) / Disturbance at the Heron house (live) / Finest worksong (lengthy club mix). *(lp re-iss. Apr99; 499466-1)*

Nov 87. (7") *(IRM 146)* **THE ONE I LOVE. / LAST DATE** [51] [–]
(12"+=/cd-s+=) *(IRMT/DIRM 146)* – Disturbance at the Heron House (live).

Jan 88. (7") *(IRM 161)* **FINEST WORKSONG. / TIME AFTER TIME, ETC.** [50] [–]
(12"+=) *(IRMT 161)* *<23850>* – ('A'-lengthy club mix).
(cd-s+=) *(DIRM 161)* – It's the end of the world and we know it (and I feel fine).

Jan 88. (7") *<53220>* **IT'S THE END OF THE WORLD AS WE KNOW IT (AND I FEEL FINE). / LAST DATE** [–] [69]

Warners Warners

Nov 88. (lp/c)(cd) *(WX 234/+C)<(7599-25795-2)>* **GREEN** [27] [12]
– Pop song '89 / Get up / You are the everything / Stand / World leader pretend / The wrong child / Orange crush / Turn you inside-out / Hairshirt / I remember California / Untitled song. *(lp re-iss. Jul99; same)*

Jan 89. (7"/s7") *(W 7577/+X)* *<27688>* **STAND. / MEMPHIS TRAIN BLUES** [51] [6]
(12"+=/3"cd-s+=/3"s-cd-s+=) *(W 7577 T/CD/CDX)* – (The eleventh untitled song).

Mar 89. (7"/s7"/7"box/c-s) *(W 2960/+X/B/C)* **ORANGE CRUSH. / GHOST RIDERS** [28] [–]
(12"+=/3"cd-s+=) *(W 2960 T/CD)* – Dark globe.

Jun 89. (7") *<27640>* **POP SONG '89 / ('A'acoustic)** [–] [86]

Jul 89. (7"/s7") *(W 2833/+W)* **STAND. / POP SONG '89 (acoustic)** [48] [–]
(12"+=/3"cd-s+=/3"s-cd-s+=) *(W 2833 T/CD/CDX)* – Skin tight (live).

—— (all above 7"singles were re-iss. in 4xbox Dec89)

Sep 89. (7") *(7-22791)* **GET UP. / FUNTIME** [–] [ ]

—— R.E.M. toured early '91 as BINGO HAND JOB.

Feb 91. (7"/c-s) *(W 0015/+C)* *<19392>* **LOSING MY RELIGION. / ROTARY ELEVEN** [19] Mar91 [4]
(12"+=/cd-s+=) *(W 0015 T/CD)* – After hours (live).
(cd-s) *(W 0015CDX)* – ('A'side) / Stand (live) / Turn you inside-out (live) / World leader pretend (live).

Mar 91. (cd/c/lp) *<(7599 26496-2/-4/-1)>* **OUT OF TIME** [1] [1]
– Radio song / Losing my religion / Low / Near wild Heaven / Endgame / Shiny happy people / Belong / Half a world away / Texarkana / Country feedback / Me in honey. *(lp re-iss. Jul99; same)*

—— (the album feat. PETER HOLSAPPLE – guitar (ex-DB'S) / KRS-1 – rapper) MICHAEL STIPE released album with KRS-1 'CIVILIZATION VS.TECHNOLOGY' Oct91.

May 91. (7"/c-s) *(W 0027/+C)* *<19242>* **SHINY HAPPY PEOPLE. / FORTY SECOND SONG** [6] Jul91 [10]
(12"+=/cd-s+=) *(W 0027 T/CD)* – Losing my religion (live acoustic).
(cd-s) *(W 0027CDX)* – ('A') / I remember California (live) / Get up (live) / Pop song '89 (live).
(above 'A'side feat. KATE PIERSON of The B-52'S)

Aug 91. (7"/c-s) *(W 0055/+C)* **NEAR WILD HEAVEN. / POP SONG '89** [27] [–]
(12"+=) *(W 0055T)* – Half a world away (live).
(cd-s) *(W 0055CDX)* – ('A') / Tom's diner (live) / Low (live) / Endgame (live).

Nov 91. (7"/c-s) *(W 0072/+C)* **RADIO SONG. / LOVE IS ALL AROUND (live)** [28] [–]
(12"+=) *(W 0072T)* – Shiny happy people (music mix).
(cd-s) *(W 0072CDX)* – ('A'side) / You are my everything (live) / Orange crush (live) / Belong (live).

Oct 92. (7"/c-s) *(W 0136/+C)* **DRIVE. / WORLD LEADER PRETEND** [11] [–]
(cd-s+=) *(W 0136CD)* – First we take Manhattan.
(cd-s) *(W 0136CDX)* – ('A') / It's a free world, baby / Winged mammal theme / First we take Manhattan.

Oct 92. (c-s,cd-s) *<18729>* **DRIVE / WINGED MAMMAL THEME** [–] [28]

Oct 92. (cd)(lp/c) *<(9362 45055)>(WX 488/+C)* **AUTOMATIC FOR THE PEOPLE** [1] [2]
– Drive / Try not to breathe / The sidewinder sleeps tonight / Everybody hurts / New Orleans instrumental No.1 / Sweetness follows / Monty got a raw deal / Ignoreland / Star me kitten / Man on the Moon / Nightswimming / Find the river.

Nov 92. (7"/c-s) *(W 0143/+C)* **MAN ON THE MOON. / TURN YOU INSIDE-OUT** [18] [–]
(cd-s+=) *(W 0143CD)* – Arms of love.
(cd-s) *(W 0143CDX)* – ('A') / Fruity organ / New Orleans instrumental #2 / Arms of love.

Jan 93. (c-s,cd-s) *<18642>* **MAN ON THE MOON / NEW ORLEANS INSTRUMENTAL #2** [–] [30]

Feb 93. (7"/c-s) *(W 0152/+C)* **THE SIDEWINDER SLEEPS TONIGHT. / GET UP** [17] [–]
(cd-s) *(W 0152CD1)* – ('A') / The lion sleeps tonight (live) / Fretless.
(cd-s) *(W 0152CD2)* – ('A') / Organ song / Star me kitten (demo).

Apr 93. (7"/c-s) *(W 0169/+C)* **EVERYBODY HURTS. / POP SONG '89** [7] [–]
(cd-s) *(W 0169CD1)* – ('A') / Mandolin strum / New Orleans instrumental No.1 (long version).
(cd-s) *(W 0169CD2)* – ('A') / Dark globe / Chance (dub).

Jul 93. (7"/c-s) *(W 0184/+C)* **NIGHTSWIMMING. / LOSING MY RELIGION (live)** [27] [–]
(one-sided-12"pic-d/cd-s) *(W 0184 TP/CD)* – ('A'side) / World leader pretend (live) / Low (live) / Belong (live).

Aug 93. (c-s) *<18638>* **EVERYBODY HURTS / MANDOLIN STRUM** [–] [29]
(12"orange+=) *<9362 40989-04>* – Belong / Orange crush (live).
(12"white or blue)(cd-ep) *<9362 40992-08>* – ('A'side) / Star me kitten (demo) / Losing my religion (live) / Organ song.

Dec 93. (7"/c-s) *(W 0211/+C)* **FIND THE RIVER. / EVERYBODY HURTS (live)** [54] [–]
(cd-s+=) *(W 0211CD1)* – World leader pretend (live).
(cd-s+=) *(W 0211CD2)* – Orange crush (instrumental).

Sep 94. (7"/c-s) *(W 0265/+C)* *<18050>* **WHAT'S THE FREQUENCY, KENNETH? / ('A'instrumental)** [9] [21]
(cd-s) *(W 0265CD)* – ('A') / Monty got a raw deal (live) / Everybody hurts (live) / Man on the Moon (live).

Oct 94. (cd/c/lp) *<(9362 45740-2/-4/-1)>* **MONSTER** [1] [1]
– What's the frequency, Kenneth? / Crush with eyeliner / King of comedy / I don't sleep I dream / Star 69 / Strange currencies / Tongue / Bang and blame / I took your name / Let me in / Circus envy / You.

Nov 94. (7"/c-s) *(W 0275/+C)* *<17994>* **BANG AND BLAME / ('A'instrumental)** [15] [19]
(cd-s) *(W 0275CD)* – ('A') / Losing my religion (live) / Country feedback (live) / Begin the begin (live).

Jan 95. (7"/c-s) *(W 0281 X/C)* **CRUSH WITH EYELINER. / ('A'instrumental)** [23] [–]

(cd-s) *(W 0281CD)* – ('A') / Calendar bag / Fall on me (live) / Me in honey (live) / Finest worksong (live).

— On 1st March, 1995, BILL BERRY suffered a brain haemorrhage, after collapsing during a concert in Switzerland. Thankfully, he steadily recovered during the following few months.

Apr 95. (7"/c-s) *(W 0290 X/C)* <17900> **STRANGE CURRENCIES. / ('A'instrumental)** [9] [47]
(cd-s) *(W 0290CD)* – ('A') / Drive (live) / Funtime (live) / Radio free Europe (live).

Jul 95. (c-s) *(W 0308 X/C)* **TONGUE / ('A'-instrumental)** [13] [–]
(cd-s) *(W 0308CD)* – ('A') / Bang and blame (live) / What's the frequency, Kenneth? (live) / I don't sleep, I dream (live).

Aug 96. (c-s) *(W 0369C)* <17529> **E-BOW THE LETTER / TRICYCLE** [4] [49]
(cd-s+=) *(W 0369CD)* – Wall of death / Departure.

Sep 96. (cd/c/d-lp) *<(9362 46320-2/-4/-1)>* **NEW ADVENTURES IN HI-FI** [1] [2]
– How the west was won and where it got us / The wake-up bomb / New test leper / Undertow / E-bow the letter / Leave / Departure / Bittersweet me / Be mine / Binky the doormat / Zither / So fast, so numb / Low desert / Electrolite.

Oct 96. (c-s) *(W 0377C)* <17490> **BITTERSWEET ME / UNDERTOW (live)** [19] [46]
(cd-s+=) *(W 0377CD)* – Wichita lineman (live) / New test leper (acoustic).

Dec 96. (c-s) *(W 0383C)* <43810> **ELECTROLITE / THE WAKE-UP BOMB (live)** [29] [96]
(cd-s+=) *(W 0383CD)* – King of comedy (808 State mix) / Binky the doormat (live).

— now without BERRY whose place was taken up by guests

Oct 98. (c-s) *(W 0455C)* <17129> **DAYSLEEPER / EMPHYSEMA** [6] [57]
(cd-s+=) *(W 0455CD)* – Why not smile (Oxford American version).
(3"cd-s) *(W 0466CDX)* – Daysleeper / Sad professor (live in the studio).

Oct 98. (cd/c/lp) *(9362 47151-2/-4/-1)* <47112> **UP** [2] [3]
– Airportman / Lotus / Suspicion / Hope / At my most beautiful / The apologist / Sad professor / You're in the air / Walk unafraid / Why not smile / Daysleeper / Diminished / Parakeet / Falls to climb.

Dec 98. (c-s) *(W 466C)* **LOTUS / SURFING THE GANGES** [26] [–]
(cd-s+=) *(W 466CD)* – Lotus (weird mix).
(3"cd-s) *(W 466CDX)* – Lotus / Suspicion (live in the studio).

Mar 99. (cd-s) *(W 477CD)* **AT MY MOST BEAUTIFUL / THE PASSENGER (live at 'Later With Jools Holland') / COUNTRY FEEDBACK (live at 'Later With Jools Holland')** [10] [–]
(3"cd-s) *(W 477CDX)* – ('A'-live) / So. central rain (live at 'Later With Jools Holland').

Jun 99. (cd-s) *(W 488CD)* **SUSPICION / ELECTROLITE ('Later With Jools Holland' version) / MAN ON THE MOON ('Later With Jools Holland' version)** [–] tour [–]
(3"cd-s+=) *(W 488CDX)* – ('A'-live) / Perfect circle ('Later With Jools Holland' version).

Jan 00. (c-s) *(W 516C)* *<radio cut>* **THE GREAT BEYOND / MAN ON THE MOON (live)** [3] Dec99 [57]
(cd-s) *(W 516CD)* – ('A') / Everybody hurts (live) / The one I love (live).
(above was taken from the movie/soundtrack, 'Man On The Moon', in which they contributed several other tracks)

Apr 01. (c-s) *(W 559C)* <42365> **IMITATION OF LIFE / THE LIFTING** [6] May01 [83]
(cd-s+=) *(W 559CD)* – Beat a drum (Dalkey demo) / 2JN.

May 01. (cd/c/lp) *<(9362 47946-2/-4/-1)>* **REVEAL** [1] [6]
– The lifting / I've been high / All the way to Reno (you're gonna be a star) / She just wants to be / Disappear / Saturn return / Beat a drum / Imitation of life / Summer turns to high / The chorus and the ring / I'll take the rain / Beachball.

Jul 01. (c-s) *(W 568C)* **ALL THE WAY TO RENO (YOU'RE GONNA BE A STAR) / 165 HILLCREST (instrumental)** [24] [–]
(cd-s) *(W 568CDX)* – ('A') / Yellow river / Imitation of life (live) / Imitation of life (live – video).

Nov 01. (c-s) *(W 573C)* **I'LL TAKE THE RAIN / 32 CHORD SONG** [44] [–]
(cd-s+=) *(W 573CD1)* – I've been high (CD-Rom video).
(cd-s++=) *(W 573CD2)* – She just want to be (live).

Oct 03. (7") *(W 624)* **BAD DAY. / FAVORITE WRITER** [9] [–]
(cd-s+=) *(W 624CD1)* – ('A'-video).
(cd-s)<cd-s+=> *(W 624CD2)* <42668> – ('A') / Out in the country / Adagio.

Oct 03. (cd) *<(9362 48381-2)>* **IN TIME: THE BEST OF R.E.M. 1988-2003** (compilation) [1] [8]
– Man on the moon / The great beyond / Bad day / What's the frequency, Kenneth? / All the way to Reno (you're gonna be a star) / Losing my religion / E-bow the letter / Orange crush / Imitation of life / Daysleeper / Animal / The sidewinder sleeps tonite / Stand / Electrolite / All the right friends / Everybody hurts / At my most beautiful / Nightswimming. *<(ltd d-cd+=; 9362 48602-2)>* – Pop song '89 (acoustic) / Turn you inside out (live) / Fretless / Chance (dub) / It's a free world baby / Drive (live) / Star me kitten / Revolution / Leave / Why not smile / The lifting (demo) / Beat a drum (demo) / 2JN / The one I love (live) / Country feedback (live).

— (hit UK No.36 + US No.16 separately)

Jan 04. (cd-s) *(W 633CD)* **ANIMAL / PRETTY PERSUASION (live) / Losing my religion (live video)** [33] [–]

Sep 04. (7"pic-d/cd-s) *(W 654/+CD1)* **LEAVING NEW YORK. / DON'T GO BACK TO ROCKVILLE (live)** [5] [ ]
(cd-s) *(W 654CD2)* – ('A') / You are the everything (live) / These days (live).

Oct 04. (cd) *<(9362 48894-2)>* **AROUND THE SUN** [1] [13]
– Leaving New York / Electron blue / The outsiders (feat. Q-TIP) / Make it all okay / Final straw / I wanted to be wrong / Wanderlust / Boy in the well / Aftermath / High speed train / The worst joke ever / The ascent of man / Around the sun. *(re-iss. Feb05 w/dvd+=; 9362 49315-2)* – (videos).

Nov 04. (cd-s) *(W 658CD1)* **AFTERMATH / HIGH SPEED TRAIN (live)** [41] [–]
(cd-s) *(W 658CD2)* – ('A') / So fast, so numb (live) / All the right friends (live).

Feb 05. (7"blue/cd-s) *(W 665/+CD1)* **ELECTRON BLUE. / WHAT'S THE FREQUENCY, KENNETH? (live)** [26] [–]
(cd-s) *(W 665CD2)* – ('A') / Sweetness follows (live) / Leaving New York (live in Helsinki video).

Jul 05. (7"red) *(W 676)* **WANDERLUST. / THE OUTSIDERS (feat. Q-TIP)** [27] [–]
(cd-s+=) *(W 676CD2)* – Bad day (live video from Spain 2003).
(cd-s) *(W 676CD1)* – ('A') / Low (alt.).

– compilations, others, etc. –

— on 'I.R.S.' unless mentioned otherwise

May 87. (lp/c/cd) *<(SP/CS/CDA 70054)>* **DEAD LETTER OFFICE** (b-sides, rarities, etc.) [60] [52]
– Crazy / There she goes again / Burning down / Voice of Harold / Burning Hell / White tornado / Toys in the attic / Windout / Ages of you / Pale blue eyes / Rotary ten / Bandwagon / Femme fatale / Walters theme / King of the road. *(cd+=)* – CHRONIC TOWN *(re-iss. Oct94 on 'A&M' cd/c; CD/C MID 195)*

Oct 88. (lp/c/cd) *(MIRG/MIRGC/DMIRG 1038)* <6262> **EPONYMOUS** [69] [44]
– Radio free Europe / Gardening at night / Talk about the passion / So. central rain / (Don't go back to) Rockville / Can't get there from here / Driver 8 / Romance / Fall on me / The one I love / Finest worksong / It's the end of the world as we know it (and I feel fine).

Oct 88. (7") *(IRM 173)* **THE ONE I LOVE. / FALL ON ME** [ ] [–]
(12"+=/cd-s+=) *(IRMT/DIRM 173)* – So. central rain (I'm sorry).

May 90. (c) *A&M; (AMC 24109)* **MURMUR / RECKONING** [ ] [ ]

Sep 91. (cd/c/lp) *(DMIRH/MIRHC/MIRH 1)* **THE BEST OF R.E.M.** [7] [–]
– Carnival of sorts / Radio free Europe / Perfect circle / Talk about the passion / So. central rain / (Don't go back to) Rockville / Pretty persuasion / Green grow the rushes / Can't get there from here / Driver 8 / Fall on me / I believe / Cuyahoga / The one I love / Finest worksong / It's the end of the world as we know it (and I feel fine).

Sep 91. (7"/c-s) *(IRM/+C 178)* **THE ONE I LOVE. / CRAZY** [16] [ ]
(cd-s) *(DIRMT 178)* – ('A'side) / This one goes out (live) / Maps and legends (live).
(cd-s) *(DIRMX 178)* – ('A'side) / Driver 8 (live) / Disturbance at the Heron House (live).

Dec 91. (7"/c-s) *(IRM/+C 180)* **IT'S THE END OF THE WORLD (AS WE KNOW IT). / RADIO FREE EUROPE** [39] [ ]
(cd-s+=) *(DIRMT 180)* – Time after time, etc. (live).

— When MICHAEL STIPE went off guesting for groups incl. GOLDEN PALOMINOS; others splintered off into . . .

HINDU LOVE GODS

not iss. I.R.S.

Sep 85. (7") *<IRS-52867>* **NARRATOR. / GONNA HAVE A GOOD TIME TONIGHT** [–] [ ]

— with **WARREN ZEVON** – vocals (they guested on his late '89 album, 'Sentimental Hygene')

Reprise Giant

Nov 90. (7") *(W 9502)* **RASPBERRY BERET. / WANG DANG DOODLE** [ ] [-]
(12"+=/cd-s+=) *(W 9502 T/CD)* – Mannish boy.

Nov 90. (cd/c/lp) <*(7599 24406-2/-4/-1)*> **HINDU LOVE GODS** [ ] [ ]
– Walkin' blues / Travelin' riverside blues / Raspberry beret / Crosscut saw / Junco pardner / Mannish boy / Wang dang doodle / Battleship chains / I'm a one woman man / Vigilante man.

the REPLACEMENTS

Formed: Minneapolis, Minnesota, USA . . . 1980 originally as the IMPEDIMENTS by the STINSON brothers – TOMMY and BOB – along with CHRIS MARS and chief songwriter/frontman, PAUL WESTERBERG. Legendary purveyors of ramshackle three-chord punk rock, the REPLACEMENTS' early efforts were so lo-fi they were off the end of the scale. Signed to Minneapolis indie stalwart, 'Twin Tone', the band debuted with 'SORRY MA, FORGOT TO TAKE OUT THE TRASH' (1981), the record's raw-nerve attitude, cathartic melodies and twisted humour shining through the garden shed (and a particularly dilapidated one at that) production. The following year's 'STINK' stepped on the gas and upped the nihilism ('GIMME NOISE', 'FUCK SCHOOL') although 'HOOTENANNY' (1983) and 'LET IT BE' (1984) used the hormonal energy to more satisfying and constructive ends. The latter set, especially, saw WESTERBERG's breathtakingly intuitive way with a melody reach fruition; granted, the likes of 'GARY'S GOT A BONER' didn't suggest another ELVIS COSTELLO in the ascendant but the bruised beauty of 'SIXTEEN BLUE' put WESTERBERG head and shoulders above most of his contemporaries (with the honourable exception of, perhaps, HUSKER DU). The record's charms were powerful enough to attract the major label attentions of 'Sire' and in late '85, the REPLACEMENTS released the Tommy Erdelyi (formerly TOMMY RAMONE)-produced 'TIM'. Furnished with a bigger budget, the group tempered their ragged sound while retaining much of the threadbare authenticity, the hooks as razor sharp as ever. It was to be the last album to feature the departing BOB, the band's notoriously shambolic live appearances robbed of the man's more erm, eccentric tendencies (playing in a dress – radical for the time! – or indeed in the nude, was not uncommon). With ROBERT 'SLIM' DUNLAP brought in as a replacement (ha!), the band recorded what many fans and critics alike regard as their finest hour, 'PLEASED TO MEET ME' (1987). More musically adventurous in line with their growing eclecticism, the album also found WESTERBERG's songwriting prowess at its unprecedented best, 'SKYWAY' soaring heavenward while 'CAN'T HARDLY WAIT' was the killer pop song he'd been threatening to pen since the band's inception. Criminally, the rave reviews and positive momentum surrounding the album's release failed to translate into sales, The REPLACEMENTS sounding strangely muted on 1989's 'DON'T TELL A SOUL'. While the minor concessions to commerciality resulted in a Top 60 US chart entry, the band were on their last legs and 1990's 'ALL SHOOK DOWN' was a WESTERBERG solo effort in all but name. The split eventually came in 1992, TOMMY forming BASH & POP (who released an album, 'FRIDAY NIGHT IS KILLING ME' the following year), while WESTERBERG worked on his solo debut proper, '14 SONGS' (1993). Although the writing was faultless, the record lacked the unkempt charm of old, any chance of a full REPLACEMENTS reunion suffering a serious setback as BOB succumbed to a drugs overdose the following year. In the latter half of the 90's (while MARS was also delivering the odd album), WESTERBERG found acceptance – in the way of US chart fame – via two further sets, 'EVENTUALLY' (1996) and 'SUICAINE GRATIFACTION' (1999). You couldn't disguise the fact (well, you could for a while!) that his next project, GRANDPABOY, was just what WESTERBERG needed – a return to basic, anthemic rock with a twist of punk. Early in 2002, the mysterious (until now) GRANDPABOY unleashed his 'MONO' album (recorded in er, mono), most fans however opted for his simultaneous release 'STEREO', although this set was billed under his proper PAUL WESTERBERG name. While 'MONO' was obviously raw and retrofied harking back to say, The Stones' "Exile . . ." days, 'STEREO' was the complete article and returned him into the US Top 100. The following year saw a similar, simultaneous release of a solo set, 'COME FEEL ME TREMBLE' and a blues set, 'DEAD MAN SHAKE', credited to WESTERBERG's alter-ego GRANDPABOY. Both were pretty much in line with his recent studio tinkerings, the former reeling out a patchy collection of heads-down guitar mangling (its best moment coming with a singular cover of Jackson Browne's 'THESE DAYS') and the latter consisting of an equally lo-fi clutch of bluesy songwriting experiments and engaging covers, among them Jimmy Reed's 'TAKE OUT SOME INSURANCE', John Prine's 'SOUVENIRS' and Hank Williams' 'I'M SO LONESOME I COULD CRY'.

• **Songwriters:** Penned by WESTERBERG, except; I WILL DARE (Kiss) / ROUTE 66 (Bobby Troupe) / 20TH CENTURY BOY (T-Rex) / HEY GOOD LOOKING (Hank Williams) / CRUELLA DE VILLE (from '101 Dalmations'). • **Trivia:** Were quoted after a tour as saying 'Better hours, 9 to 5; 9 at night to 5 in the morning, that is'. Their '87 single 'ALEX CHILTON', was dedicated to legendary BOX TOPS leader.

Album rating: SORRY MA, FORGOT TO TAKE OUT THE TRASH (*6) / STINK mini (*5) / HOOTENANNY (*6) / LET IT BE (*9) / TIM (*7) / BOINK!! compilation (*8) / PLEASED TO MEET ME (*8) / DON'T TELL A SOUL (*7) / ALL SHOOK DOWN (*6) / ALL FOR NOTHING – NOTHING FOR ALL compilation (*8) / DON'T YOU KNOW WHO I THINK I WAS compilation (*8) / Paul Westerberg: 14 SONGS (*7) / EVENTUALLY (*6) / SUICAINE GRATIFACTION (*5) / STEREO (*7) / COME FEEL ME TREMBLE (*5) / Grandpaboy: MONO (*6) / DEAD MAN SHAKE (*6) / Chris Mars: HORSESHOES AND HAND GRENADES (*6) / 75% LESS FAT (*5) / TENTERHOOKS (*6) / ANONYMOUS BOTCH (*4)

PAUL WESTERBERG (b.31 Dec'60) – vocals, rhythm guitar / **BOB STINSON** (b.17 Dec'59) – lead guitar / **TOMMY STINSON** (b. 6 Oct'66, San Diego, Calif.) – bass / **CHRIS MARS** (b.26 Apr'61) – drums

not iss. Twin Tone

Aug 81. (7") <*TTR 8120*> **I'M IN TROUBLE. / IF ONLY YOU WERE LONELY** [-] [ ]

Aug 81. (lp) <*TTR 8123*> **SORRY MA, FORGOT TO TAKE OUT THE TRASH** [-] [ ]
– Takin' a ride / Careless / Customer / Hanging downtown / Kick your door down / Otto / I bought a headache / Rattlesnake / I hate music / Johnny's gonna die / Shiftless when idle / More cigarettes / Don't ask why / Something to do / I'm in trouble / Love you till Friday / Shut up / Raised in the city. *(UK-iss.Mar88 on 'What Goes On'; GOES ON 017) (cd-iss. Apr93 on 'Roadrunner'; RR 9089-2) (cd re-iss. Mar95; TTR 8123-2) <(cd re-mast.Aug02 on 'Restless'; REST 7376-2)>*

Jun 82. m-(lp) <*TTR 8228*> **STINK** [-] [ ]
– Kids don't follow / Fuck school / Stuck in the middle / God damn job / White and lazy / Dope smokin' moron / Go / Gimme noise. *(UK-iss.Mar88 on 'What Goes On'; GOES ON 020) (cd-iss. Apr93 on 'Roadrunner'; RR 9090-2) (cd re-iss. Mar95; 8228-2) <(cd re-iss. Aug02 on 'Restless'; REST 73763)>*

Apr 83. (lp) <*TTR 8332*> **HOOTENANNY** [-] [ ]
– Hootenanny / Run it / Color me impressed / Will power / Take me down to the hospital / Mr. Whirly / Within your reach / Buck hill / Lovelines / You lose / Hayday / Treatment bound. *(UK-iss.Mar88 on 'What Goes On'; GOES ON 021) (cd-iss. Apr93 on 'Roadrunner'; RR 9091-2) (cd re-iss. Feb95; TTR 8332-2) <(cd re-mast.Aug02 on 'Restless'; REST 73760)>*

Aug 84. (12") <*TTR 8440*> **I WILL DARE. / 20TH CENTURY BOY / HEY GOOD LOOKING (live)** [-] [ ]

Zippo Twin Tone

Oct 84. (lp) *(ZONG 002)* <*TTR 8441*> **LET IT BE** [ ] [ ]
– I will dare / We're comin' out / Tommy gets his tonsels out / Black diamond / Androgynous / Unsatisfied / Seen your video / Gary's got a boner / Sixteen blue / Answering machine. *(cd-iss. Apr93 on 'Roadrunner'; RR 9092-2) (cd-iss. Mar95 & Sep98 on 'R.C.A.'; 74321 60574-2) <(cd re-mast.Aug02 on 'Restless'; REST 73761)>*

1985. (c) **THE SHIT HITS THE FAN (live bootleg)** –

Sire Sire

Nov 85. (lp/c) *(K 925330-1/-4) <25330>* **TIM**
– Hold my life / I'll buy / Kiss me on the bus / Dose of thunder / Waitress in the sky / Swingin' party / Bastards of young / Lay it down clown / Left of the dial / Litle mascara / Here comes a regular. *(cd-iss. Jul93; 7599 25330-2)*

Mar 86. (7") *(W 8727)* **SWINGIN' PARTY. / LEFT OF THE DIAL** –

May 86. (7") *(W 8679)* **KISS ME ON THE BUS. / LITTLE MASCARA** –

— **ROBERT 'SLIM' DUNLAP** (b.14 Aug'51, Plainview, Minnesota) – guitar; repl. BOB (he was to die on the 18th of February 1995 o.d.)

Apr 87. (lp/c/cd) *(K 925557-1/-4/-2) <25557>* **PLEASED TO MEET ME**
– I.O.U. / Alex Chilton / I don't know / Nightclub jitters / The ledge / Never mind / Valentine / Shooting dirty pool / Red red wine / Skyway / Can't hardly wait. *(cd re-iss. Jul93; 7599 25557-2)*

Jun 87. (7") *(W 8297)* **ALEX CHILTON. / ELECTION DAY** –
(12"+=) *(W 8297T)* – Nightclub jitters / Route 66.

Jul 87. (7") *<28151>* **CAN'T HARDLY WAIT. / COOL WATER** –

Jan 89. (lp/c/cd) *(K 925721-1/-4/-2) <25721>* **DON'T TELL A SOUL** 57
– Talent show / Back to back / We'll inherit the Earth / Achin' to be / They're blind / Anywhere's better than here / Asking me lies / I won't / Rock'n'roll ghost / Darlin' one. *(cd re-iss. Jul93; 7559 25831-2)*

Apr 89. (7") *<22992>* **I'LL BE YOU. / DATE TO CHURCH (with TOM WAITS)** – 51
(below w/ guests **STEVE BERLIN / MICHAEL BLAIR / BELMONT TENCH / JOHN CALE** / etc.

Sep 90. (cd/c/lp) *<(7599 26298-2/-4/-1)>* **ALL SHOOK DOWN** 69
– Merry go round / One wink at a time / Nobody / Bent out of shape / Sadly beautiful / Someone takes the wheel / When it began / All shook down / Attitude / Happy town / Torture / My little problem / The lost. *(cd re-iss. Jul93 & Feb95; same)*

— (Mar'91) **STEVE FOLEY** – drums; repl. MARS who went solo

— disbanded late in 1991, TOMMY formed BASH & POP, while WESTERBERG and MARS went solo

– compilations, others, etc. –

Apr 86. (m-lp/m-c) *Glass; (MGA LP/MC 016)* **BOINK!!** –
– Color me impressed / White and lazy / Within your reach / If only you were lonely / Kids don't follow / Nowhere is my home / Take me down to the hospital / Go.

Nov 97. (d-cd) *Reprise; <(9362 46807-2)>* **ALL FOR NOTHING / NOTHING FOR ALL**
– Left of the dial / Kiss me on the bus / Bastards of young / Here comes a regular / Skyway / Alex Chilton / The ledge / Can't hardly wait / I'll be you / Achin' to be / Talent show / Anywhere's better than here / Merry-go-round / Sadly beautiful / Nobody / Someone take the wheel / Can't hardly wait (the TIM version) / Birthday gal / Beer for breakfast / Till we're nude / Election day / Jungle rock / All he wants to do is fish / Date to church / Cruella De Ville / We know the night / Portland / Wake up / Satellite / Like a rolling pin / Another girl, another planet / Who knows / All shook down.

Jun 06. (cd) *Rhino; <(8122 70013-2)>* **DON'T YOU KNOW WHO I THINK I WAS – THE VERY BEST OF THE REPLACEMENTS**

PAUL WESTERBERG

Sire Warners

Jun 93. (cd/c) *<(9362 45255-2/-4)>* **14 SONGS** 44
– Knockin' on mine / First glimmer / World class fad / Runaway wind / Dice behind your shades / Even here we are / Silver naked ladies / A few minutes of silence / Someone I once knew / Black eyed Susan / things / Something is me / Mannequin shop / Down love.

Jul 93. (7"/c-s) *(W 0183/+C)* **WORLD CLASS FAD. / SEEING HER**
(12"/cd-s) *(W 0183 T/CD)* – ('A'side) / Men without ties / Down love.

Oct 93. (7"/c-s) *(W 0209/+C)* **WORLD CLASS FAD. / CAN'T HARDLY WAIT (live)**
(cd-s+=) *(W 0209CD1)* – Left of the dial (live) / Another girl another planet (live).
(cd-s) *(W 0209CD2)* – ('A'side) / Waiting for somebody / Dyslexic heart / Answering machine (live).

Apr 96. (cd/c) *(9362 46251-2/-4) <46176>* **EVENTUALLY** 50
– These are the days / Century / Love untold / Ain't got me / You've had it with you / Mamadaddydid / Hide n seekin' / Once around the weekend / Trumpet clip / Angels walk / Good day / Time flies tomorrow.

Capitol Capitol

Apr 99. (cd/c) *(499145-2/-4) <59004>* **SUICAINE GRATIFACTION** Mar99
– It's a wonderful lie / Self defence / The best thing that ever happened / Lookin' out forever / Born for me / The final hurrah / Tears rolling up our sleeves / The fugitive kind / Sunrise always listens / Whatever makes you happy / Actor in the street / Bookmark.

GRANDPABOY

— aka **PAUL WESTERBERG**

not iss. Monolyth

1997. (7") *<7 1313>* **I WANT MY MONEY BACK. / UNDONE** –

1997. (cd-ep) *<1315>* **GRANDPABOY** –
– Hot un / Ain't done much / Psychopharmacology / Lush and green / Homelessexual.

Vagrant Vagrant

Apr 02. (cd) *<(VR 368CD)>* **MONO** Feb02
– High time / Anything but that / Let's not belong together / Silent film star / Knock it right out / 2 days 'til tomorrow / Eyes like sparks / Footsteps / Kickin' the stall / Between love and like / AAA.

PAUL WESTERBERG

Vagrant Vagrant

Apr 02. (cd) *<(VAG 369CD)>* **STEREO** 81
– Baby learns to crawl / Dirt to mud / Only lie worth telling / Got you down / No place for you / Boring enormous / Nothing to no one / We may be the one / Don't want never / Mr. Rabbit / Let the bad times roll / Call that gone? / (untitled). *(re-iss. Jun02 on 'B-Unique'+=; BUN 025)* – MONO

Oct 03. (cd) *<VAG 387CD>* **COME FEEL ME TREMBLE** –
– Dirty diesel / Making me go / Hillbilly junk / Soldier of misfortune / My daydream / What a day (for a night) / Wild & lethal / Crackle & drag (original take) / Crackle & drag (alt. version) / Never felt like this before / Knockin' em back / Pine box / Meet me down in the alley / These days.

GRANDPABOY

Fat Possum Fat Possum

Oct 03. (cd/lp) *<(0377-2/-1)>* **DEAD MAN SHAKE**
– MPLS / Do right in your eyes / Vampires & failures / No matter what you say / Take out some insurance / Cleaning house / Natural mean lover / Get a move on / Bad boy blues / Souvenirs / I'm so lonesome I could cry / O.D. blues / Dead man shake / What kind of fool am I?

☐ Martin REV (see under ⇒ SUICIDE)

☐ Gruff RHYS (see under ⇒ SUPER FURRY ANIMALS)

Damien RICE

Born: 7 Dec'73, Celbridge, County Kildare, Ireland. Spending his childhood growing up near the River Liffey, DAMIEN formed the indie-rock outfit JUNIPER in the mid-90's and was signed to 'Polygram' records in 1997, however contractual disagreements eventually split the band. RICE subsequently moved to Tuscany before travelling across Europe, busking his own songs before returning to Ireland in 1999. He had written a handful of tracks which he demo'd to movie composer and uber-producer DAVID ARNOLD (the man responsible for the new James Bond movies). ARNOLD encouraged RICE to record an album and donated enough money so that he could set up his own studio. He issued the single 'THE BLOWER'S DAUGHTER' which became a moderate hit in his native country, before releasing the critically lauded debut album 'O' in 2002. Much more rewarding and interesting than the troubadour winge of DAVID GRAY, RICE fell somewhere between 'Tea For The Tillerman'-era CAT STEVENS, LEONARD COHEN and even MERCURY REV during their 'See You On The Other Side' period. Hushed vocals, wind-swept pianos and floating melodies were all present on what was perhaps the most gentle acoustic release of the year. Missed by many first time around, it received a second life in 2003 via massive radio play and a more aggressive advertising campaign which led to a UK Top 40 placing for the album and classy single, 'CANNONBALL'.

• **Covered:** SILENT NIGHT (trad).

Album rating: O (*8)

DAMIEN RICE – vocals, multi / with **LISA HANNIGAN** – vocals / **TOMO** – drums, percussion / **VYVIENNE LONG** – cello / **SHANE FITZSIMMONS** – bass

Damien Rice Music — not iss.

Sep 01. (cd-s) *(drm 001cd)* **THE BLOWER'S DAUGHTER / THE PROFESSOR & LA FILLE DANSE / MOODY MOODAY – THE BLOWER'S DAUGHTER (original demo)** [–] Irish [–]

May 02. (cd-s) *(drm 003cd)* **CANNONBALL / LONELILY (original demo) / WOMAN LIKE A MAN (live unplugged) / CANNONBALL (instrumental)** [–] Irish [–]

Oct 02. (cd-s) *(drm 004cd)* **VOLCANO / DELICATE (live acoustic) / VOLCANO (instrumental) / (hidden demo & CD-ROM track)** [–] Irish [–]
(UK-iss.Feb04; dr 04cd1/2)

14th Floor — Vector

Mar 03. (cd-ep) *(dr 01)* **WOMAN LIKE A MAN EP** [ ] [–]
– Woman like a man / Delicate / Lonelily / The professor.

Jul 03. (cd) *(505046-64788-5-6)* <48507> **O** [8] Jun03 [ ]
– Delicate / Volcano / The blower's daughter / Cannonball / Older chests / Amie / Cheers darlin' / Cold water / I remember / Eskimo. *(hidden tracks+=)* – Prague / Silent night. *(orig.Ire Feb02; drm 02cd) (cd re-iss. Jun04 w/dvd+=; 2564 61495-2)* – Cannonball (live) / The blower's daughter (live) / Volcano (live).

Oct 03. (cd-s) *(dr 03cd1)* <69532> **CANNONBALL / MOODY MOODAY / ('A'-video)** [32] Dec03 [ ]

Jul 04. (cd-s) *(dr 03cd2)* **CANNONBALL (live) / AMIE (live) / THE BLOWER'S DAUGHTER (live)** [19] [–]
(dvd-s) *(dr 03dvd)* – ('A'-radio) / ('A'-remix) / (dialogue).

Aug 04. (m-cd) *(5046 75006-2)* <48830> **B-SIDES** [ ] Aug04 [ ]
– The professor & la fille danse (live at Cornucopia) / Lonelily (demo) / Woman like a man (live unplugged) / Moody Mooday / Delicate (live in Dublin) / Volcano (instrumental) / Volcano (1997 demo). *(UK+=)* – Cannonball (radio remix). *<re-iss. Jan05 on 'WEA'+=; 675006>*

14th Floor — WEA

Dec 04. (7"white/cd-s) *(dr 06 v/cd2)* <676515> **THE BLOWER'S DAUGHTER. / SILENT NIGHT** [27] Jan05 [ ]
(cd-s) *(dr 06cd1)* <676515> – ('A') / The Professor & la fille danse (live at Cornucopia) / Moody Mooday (remix).

Apr 05. (7"toffee) *(dr 07v)* <677788> **VOLCANO. / LONELY SOLDIER (live)** [29] Jul05 [ ]
(cd-s+=) *(dr 07cd2)* – ('A'-live from Shortlist awards) / ('A'-video).
(cd-s) *(dr 07cd1)* – ('A') / The blower's daughter.

Jul 05. (7"/cd-s; as DAMIEN RICE & LISA HANNIGAN) *(dr 08 v/cd)* **UNPLAYED PIANO (Chris Lord-Alge mix) / (instrumental)** [24] [–]

□ Keith RICHARDS (see under ⇒ ROLLING STONES)

Jonathan RICHMAN

Born: 16 May'51, Boston, Massachusetts, USA. After a period in the late 60's working as a contributor for local music papers, 'Vibrations' & 'Fusion', he formed his first real band, MODERN LOVERS, in 1971. With the help of producer KIM FOWLEY, they recorded a successful demo for 'Warners' in 1972, although the label subsequently shelved their JOHN CALE-produced debut album and soon dropped the group. RICHMAN & Co. finally split in late '74, only to re-form again six months later and record a debut single, 'ROADRUNNER', for 'United Artists'. They then moved to West Coast label 'Beserkley', who bought the unreleased Warners tapes and finally packaged the songs as an eponymous album in 1976. Featuring the classic MODERN LOVERS line-up of JERRY HARRISON, ERNIE BROOKS and DAVID ROBINSON, the album was one of the more genuine efforts to lay claim to the vastly oversubscribed 'first punk album' tag. Carrying on where his heroes The VELVET UNDERGROUND left off, RICHMAN fashioned an idiosyncratic update of late 60's garage-rock, his REED-y vocals carrying epistles of adolescent angst over a simplistic but effective musical backing. While UK Top 20 hit, 'ROADRUNNER', may have whetted fans appetites for more of the same, a belated follow-up album, 'JONATHAN RICHMAN & THE MODERN LOVERS' (1977) was a different beast altogether. While HARRISON and BROOKS were now tending greener new wave pastures with The TALKING HEADS and The CARS respectively, the revamped MODERN LOVERS line-up of ROBINSON, LEROY RADCLIFFE and GREG KERANEN were following RICHMAN's more whimsically eccentric path, cutting retro pop, acoustic-based tracks about aliens, insects and erm, abominable snowmen. A second album that year, 'ROCK'N'ROLL WITH THE MODERN LOVERS', confirmed RICHMAN's new strategy, hitting the British Top 50 despite itself and spawning a second hit (Top 5) in the bizarre instrumental, 'EGYPTIAN REGGAE'. Critics were divided, some hailing the man as a wayward genius, some confounded at what they perceived as a waste of good talent. Whatever, after a late 70's lay-off, RICHMAN continued to plow his singular furrow throughout the following decade with an ever changing cast of musicians and different labels. Amid the grating childishness, the man was still capable of a wistful charm and the occasional sting of biting poignancy, fans and critics alike generally agreed that 'JONATHAN SINGS!' (1984) remains his finest release from this period. Towards the end of the decade, he recruited BRENDAN TOTTEN and JOHNNY AVILA for the leaner 'MODERN LOVERS '88' before abandoning the backup for good and going it alone. His 1989 eponymous solo debut was followed up with a misguided attempt at C&W, 'JONATHAN GOES COUNTRY' (1990), while a Spanish-language set, '!JONATHAN, TE VAS A EMOCIONAR!' (1994) surely tested the patience of even his most loyal fans. Much more promising were 1995's 'YOU MUST ASK THE HEART' and the following year's 'SURRENDER TO JONATHAN', the latter his first for a major label ('WEA') after years in the commercial wilderness. During the latter half of the 90's, RICHMAN stuck to his task of coming up with the odd album, 1999's 'I'M SO CONFUSED', a slight return to the old fun JONNO of yore. Fans however were disappointed with RICHMAN's US-only issued 'HER MYSTERY NOT OF HIGH HEELS AND EYE SHADOW' (2001), which showcased two instrumentals and four songs sung in Spanish. However, live, the old Modern Lover still packed a retro punch. He might be less prolific these days but he continues to bless the faithful with an album every three or so years. 'NOT SO MUCH TO BE LOVED AS TO LOVE' (2004) was met with fears that RICHMAN might finally be sloughing off his whimsy for weightier matters; 'MUMIA ABU-JAMAL' was the kind of protest song more likely to have been delivered from the pen of ASIAN DUB FOUNDATION, yet on the likes of 'THE WORLD IS SHOWING ITS HAND' he still sounded as enchanted with nature's detail as he ever did. Singing in no less than three languages (Spanish, French and Italian), he also gave lesser talents a lesson in global pop.

• **Trivia:** JOHN CALE (ex-Velvet Underground), went on to record his brilliant 'PABLO PICASSO'.

Album rating: THE MODERN LOVERS (*8) / JONATHAN RICHMAN & THE MODERN LOVERS (*7) / ROCK'N'ROLL WITH THE MODERN LOVERS (*6) / THE MODERN LOVERS LIVE (*5) / BACK IN YOUR LIFE (*6) /

THE JONATHAN RICHMAN SONGBOOK compilation (*7) / JONATHAN SINGS! (*6) / ROCKIN' AND ROMANCE (*5) / IT'S TIME FOR JONATHAN RICHMAN & THE MODERN LOVERS (*5) / MODERN LOVERS '88 (*5) / JONATHAN RICHMAN (*4) / JOHNATHAN GOES COUNTRY (*4) / 23 GREAT RECORDINGS BY JONATHAN RICHMAN & THE MODERN LOVERS compilation (*8) / HAVING A PARTY WITH JONATHAN RICHMAN collection (*4) / I, JONATHAN (*6) / JONATHAN, TE VAS A EMOCIONAR! (*5) / YOU MUST ASK THE HEART (*5) / SURRENDER TO JONATHAN (*6) / I MUST BE KING: THE BEST OF JONATHAN RICHMAN compilation (*6) / I'M SO CONFUSED (*6) / HER MYSTERY NOT OF HIGH HEELS AND EYE SHADOW (*5) / NOT SO MUCH TO BE LOVED AS TO LOVE (*5)

the MODERN LOVERS

were formed by **RICHMAN** – vocals, guitar / with **JERRY HARRISON** – keyboards, vocals / **ERNIE BROOKS** – bass, vocals / **DAVID ROBINSON** – drums (left Nov73 to DMZ, after recording debut)

U.A. U.A.

Jun 75. (7") *(UP 36006)* **ROADRUNNER. / IT WILL STAND**

Beserkley Beserkley

Oct 76. (7") *<5701>* **ROADRUNNER. / Friday On My Mind (by Earthquake)** –

Oct 77. (lp/c) *(BSERK/BSERC 1) <BZ/+CA 0050>* **THE MODERN LOVERS** (1972 demos) Oct76
– Roadrunner / Astral plane / Old world / Pablo Picasso / I'm straight / She cracked / Hospital / Someone I care about / Girlfriend / Modern world. *(re-iss. Nov87; same> <re-iss. Nov89 on 'Rhino'; RNLP 70091> (cd-iss. Feb93 on 'Rev-Ola'+=; CREV 007CD)* – (3 extra tracks). *(lp re-iss. Jun00 on 'Get Back'; GET 66)*

— HARRISON (also to TALKING HEADS) and BROOKS joined ELLIOTT MURPHY

JONATHAN RICHMAN & THE MODERN LOVERS

with also **LEROY RADCLIFFE** – guitar, vox / **GREG KERANEN** – bass, vox / **DAVID ROBINSON** – drums

Feb 77. (7") *<5743>* **NEW ENGLAND. / HERE COME THE MARTIAN MARTIANS** –

Jun 77. (7") *(BZZ 1)* **ROADRUNNER (once). / ROADRUNNER (twice)** 11 –
(re-iss. Jul82 on 'Old Gold'; OG 9113)

Oct 77. (lp/c) *(BSERK/BSERC 2) <BZ/+CA 0048>* **JONATHAN RICHMAN & THE MODERN LOVERS** Jan77
– Rockin' shopping center / Back in the U.S.A. / Important in your life / New England / Lonely financial zone / Hi dear / Abominable snowman in the market / Hey there little insect / Here comes the Martian Martians / Springtime / Amazing Grace. *<re-iss. Nov87; same> (cd-iss. Feb93 on 'Rev-Ola'; CREV 008CD)*

Aug 77. (lp/c) *(BSERK 9) <BZ/+CA 0053>* **ROCK'N'ROLL WITH THE MODERN LOVERS** 50 Feb77
– The sweeping wind (kwa ti feng) / Ice cream man / Rockin' rockin' leprechauns / Summer morning / Afternoon / Fly into the mystery / South American folk song / Roller coaster by the sea / Dodge veg-o-matic / Egyptian reggae / Coomyah / The wheels on the bus / Angels watching over you. *<re-iss. Nov87; same> (cd-iss. Feb93 on 'Rev-Ola'; CREV 009CD)*

Sep 77. (7") *(BZZ 2)* **EGYPTIAN REGGAE. / ROLLER COASTER BY THE SEA** 5

— **D.SHARPE** – drums repl. ROBINSON / **ASA BREMNER** – bass repl. KERANEN

Dec 77. (lp/c) *(BSERK/BSERC 12) <BZ/+CA 055>* **THE MODERN LOVERS LIVE (live)**
– I'm a little airplane / Hey there little insect / Egyptian reggae / Ice cream man / I'm a little dinosaur / My little kookenhaken / South American folk song / New England / Morning of our lives. *<re-iss. Nov87; same> (cd-iss. Feb93 on 'Rev-Ola'; CREV 010CD) (cd re-iss. Apr97 on 'Wooded Hill'; HILLCD 15)*

Jan 78. (7"; as MODERN LOVERS) *(BZZ 7)* **MORNING OF OUR LIVES (live). / ROADRUNNER (thrice) (live)** 28

Apr 78. (7"; as MODERN LOVERS) *(BZZ 14)* **NEW ENGLAND. / ASTRAL PLANE (live)** –

Jul 78. (7") *(BZZ 19)* **ABDUL & CLEOPATRA. / OH CAROL**

Dec 78. (7") *(BZZ 25)* **BUZZ BUZZ BUZZ. / HOSPITAL (live)**

Feb 79. (lp/c) *(BSERK/BSERC 17) <BZ/+CA 0060>* **BACK IN YOUR LIFE**
– Abdul and Cleopatra / (She's gonna) Respect me / Lover please / Affection / Buzz buzz buzz / Back in your life / Party in the woods tonight / My love is a flower (just beginning to bloom) / I'm nature's mosquito / Emaline / Lydia / I hear you calling me. *<re-iss. Nov86; same> (cd-iss. Feb93 on 'Rev-Ola'; CREV 011CD) (cd re-iss. Apr97 on 'Wooded Hill'; HILLCD 14)*

Mar 79. (7") *(BZZ 28)* **LYDIA. / IMPORTANT IN YOUR LIFE**

JONATHAN RICHMAN

Jan 80. (lp) *(DSERK 19)* **JONATHAN RICHMAN SONGBOOK – THE BEST OF . . .** (compilation)

— JONATHAN retired in the late 70's, until 1982. Joining him were **KEN FORFIA** – keyboards / **BETH HARRINGTON** – guitar / **GREG KERANEN** – bass, vocals / **MICHAEL GUARDABASCIO** – drums, vocals / **ELLIE MARSHALL** – backing vocals

Rough Trade Sire

Aug 84. (lp/c) *(ROUGH/+C 52)* **JONATHAN SINGS!**
– That summer feeling / This kind of music / The neighbors / Somebody to hold me / These conga drums / Stop this car / Not yet three / Give Paris one more chance / You're the one for me / When I'm walking.

May 85. (7") *(RT 152)* **THAT SUMMER FEELING. / THIS KIND OF MUSIC**
(12"+=) *(RTT 152)* – The tag game.

— re-formed again with **JONATHAN, ELLIE, MICHAEL** and newcomer **ANDY PALEY** – toy piano

Jun 85. (lp/c) *(ROUGH/+C 72)* **ROCKIN' AND ROMANCE**
– The beach / My jeans / Bermuda / The U.F.O. man / Down in Bermuda / V. Van Gogh / Walter Johnson / I'm just beginning to live / The fenway / Chewing gum wrapper / The Baltimores / Up in the sky sometime / Now is better than before.

Aug 85. (7") *(RT 154)* **I'M JUST BEGINNING TO LIVE. / CIRCLE I**
(12"+=) *(RTT 154)* – Shirin & Fahrad.

JONATHAN RICHMAN & THE MODERN LOVERS

Feb 86. (lp/c) *(ROUGH/+C 92)* **IT'S TIME FOR JONATHAN RICHMAN & THE MODERN LOVERS**
– It's you / Let's take a trip / This love of mine / Neon sign / Double chocolate malted / Just about seventeen / Corner store / The desert / Yo Jo Jo / When I dance / Shirin & Fahrad / Ancient and long ago.

— **JONATHAN** recruited complete new line-up **BRENDAN TOTTEN** – guitar / **JOHNNY AVILA** – drums

Demon Rounder

Feb 88. (lp/cd) *(FIEND/+CD 106) <ROUNDER/+CD 9014>* **MODERN LOVERS '88**
– Dancin' late at night / When Harpo played his harp / Gail loves me / New kind of neighborhood / African lady / I love hot nights / California desert party / Everything's gotta be right / Circle 1 / I have come out to play / The theme from 'Moulin Rouge'!.

JONATHAN RICHMAN

Special Delivery Rounder

Aug 89. (lp/c/cd) *<(SPD/+C/CD 1024)>* **JONATHAN RICHMAN**
– Malagueno de Jojo / Action packed / Everyday clothes / Fender Stratocaster / Blue Moon / Closer / I eat with Gusto / Damn!! you bet / Miracles will start to happen / Sleepwalk / Que reste t'll de nos amours / A mistake today for me / Cerca.

— now with **TOM BRUMLEY** – guitar

Aug 90. (lp/c/cd) *<(SPD/+C/CD 1037)>* **JONATHAN GOES COUNTRY**
– Since she started to ride / Reno / You're the one for me / Your good girl's gonna go bad / I must be king / You're crazy for takin' the blues / Rodeo wind / Corner store / The neighbours / Men walks among us / I can't stay mad at you / Satisfied mind.

Rounder Rounder

Dec 92. (cd/c) *<(ROU CD/C 9036)>* **I, JONATHAN**
– Parties in the U.S.A. / Tandem jump / You can't talk to the dude / Velvet underground / I was dancing in the lesbian bar / Rooming house on Venice beach / That summer feeling / Grunion run / A higher power / Twilight in Boston.

May 94. (cd) *<(ROUCD 9040)>* **JONATHAN, TE VAS A EMOCIONAR!**
– Pantomima de el amor Brujo / Harpo en su Harpa / No te oye / No mas por fun / Papel de chicle / Los vecinos / Compadrito corazon / Melodia tradicional Ecuadoriana / Shirin y Farad / Reno / Cerca / El U.F.O. man / Ahora es Mejor / Sabor A.Mi / Una Fuerza alla.

May 95. (cd/c) *<(ROU CD/C 9047)>* **YOU MUST ASK THE HEART**
– To hide a little thought / The heart of Saturday night / Vampire girl / Just because I'm Irish / That's how I feel / Let her go into darkness / The rose / You must ask the heart / Nothing can change this love / Amorcito corazon / City vs. country / Walter Johnson / Nishi.

Vapor – Warners — Vapor – Warners

Sep 96. (cd/c) *<(9362 46296-2/-4)>* **SURRENDER TO JONATHAN**
– Just look at me / That little sleeper car / Not just a plus list on the guest list anymore / My little girl's got a full time daddy now / Rock'n'roll drummer straight from the hospy-tel / atisfy / When she kisses me / Egyptian reggae / To hide a little thought / I was dancing in the lesbian bar / Surrender / Floatin' / French style.

—— next with **DARRYL JENIFER** – bass / **TOMMY LARKINS** – drums

Feb 99. (cd) *<(9362 47086-2/-4)>* **I'M SO CONFUSED**
– When I dance / Nineteen in Naples / I'm so confused / True love is not nice / Love me like I love / Hello from Cupid / If she don't love me / The lonely little thrift store / Affection / I can hear her fighting with herself / The night is still young / I can't find my best friend.

not iss. — Vapor

Oct 01. (cd) *<48216>* **HER MYSTERY NOT OF HIGH HEELS AND EYE SHADOW**
– Her mystery not of high heels and eye shadow / Springtime in New York / Me and her got a good thing goin' baby / Couples must fight / I took a chance on her / Maybe a walk home from Natick High School / Give Paris one more chance / My love for her ain't sad / Leaves on the sidewalk after the rain / Tonight / Yo tengo una novia / El joven se estremece / Con el merengue / Vampiresa mujer (Vampire girl).

Sanctuary — Sanctuary

Jun 04. (cd) *(SANCD 290) <89404>* **NOT SO MUCH TO BE LOVED AS TO LOVE**
– Not so much to be loved as to love / Sunday afternoon / Vincent Van Gogh / Cosi veloce / He gave us the wine to taste / Salvador Dali / My baby love love loves me / In che mondo viviamo / Behold the lillies of the field / Les etoilles / The world is showing its hand / Abu Jamal / On a du soleil.

– compilations, etc. –

Oct 81. (lp) *Bomp; <LBOM 1>* **THE ORIGINAL MODERN LOVERS**
(UK-iss.Jun87 on 'Link'; 400.310) <re-iss. 1991 on 'Ubik'; BAKTUN 004> <(UK-iss.Feb97 & Nov00 on 'Bomp'; BLP 4021)>

Jul 82. (7") *Old Gold; (OG 9112)* **EGYPTIAN REGGAE. / MORNING OF OUR LIVES (live)**

1987. (cd) *Rhino; <RNCD 75889>* **THE BEST OF JONATHAN RICHMAN AND THE MODERN LOVERS**

1988. (cd) *Rounder; (CDS1)* **JONATHAN RICHMAN & BARRENCE WHITFIELD**

Feb 91. (cd/c/lp) *Essential; (ESS CD/MC/LP 128)* **23 GREAT RECORDINGS BY JONATHAN RICHMAN AND THE MODERN LOVERS**
– Roadrunner / Dignified & old / Pablo Picasso / I'm straight / Astral plane / Girl friend / Government centre / New teller / It will stand / Morning of our lives / Abominable snowman in the market / Important in your life / My little kookenhaken / Dodge veg-o-matic / Lonely financial zone / Roller coaster by the sea / New England / Egyptian reggae / Ice cream man / Buzz buzz buzz / Abdul & Cleopatra / Roadrunner (twice). *(c+=)* – She cracked / Hospital. *(re-iss. cd Sep93 on 'Castle'; CSCD 397)*

Nov 91. (cd) *Cheree; (CHEREE 22)* **HAVING A PARTY WITH JONATHAN RICHMAN (live US tour in '83)**
– The girl stands up to me now / Cappuccino bar / my career as a homewrecker / She doesn't laugh at my jokes / When she kisses me / They're not tryin' on the dance floor / At night / When I say wife / 1963 / Monologue about bermuda / Our swingin' pad / Just for fun.

Apr 94. (cd) *Castle; (CCSCD 397)* **THE COLLECTION**

May 94. (cd) *New Rose; (422439)* **LIVE AT THE LONGBRANCH SALOON (live)**
<(US+re-iss. Aug98 on 'Last Call'; 303821)>

Apr 95. (cd; by MODERN LOVERS) *Rounder; (ROUCD 9042)* **PRECISE MODERN LOVERS ORDER**
(originally issued in 1992 on French 'Fan Club'; 422439)

Jun 95. (cd) *Nectar; (NPMCD 506)* **A PLEA FOR TENDERNESS**

Jul 97. (cd) *Snapper; (SMDCD 115)* **RADIO ON / STOP AND SHOP**

Aug 98. (cd) *Castle; (SELCD 521)* **ROADRUNNER**

Nov 98. (cd) *Cooking Vinyl; (COOKCD 166)* **I MUST BE KING: THE BEST OF JONATHAN RICHMAN**
– That summer feeling / Fender stratocaster / Foggy notion / No mas po fun (Just for fun) / You're the one for me / Girls stand up to me now / Satisfied mind / Velvet underground / Pablo Picasso / A plea for tenderness / Corner stone / Neighbours / Dignified and old / Parties in the USA / I must be king / El UFO man / Action packed / Roadrunner.

Sep 00. (cd) *Target; (47038)* **BUZZ BUZZ BUZZ: AN INTROSPECTIVE**

Feb 02. (cd) *Rounder; <(ROUCD 11596)>* **ACTION PACKED: THE BEST OF JONATHAN RICHMAN**

☐ RIFF RAFF (see under ⇒ BRAGG, Billy)

☐ Chris ROBINSON (see under ⇒ BLACK CROWES)

☐ Rich ROBINSON (see under ⇒ BLACK CROWES)

☐ ROCKET FROM THE TOMBS (see under ⇒ PERE UBU)

☐ Omar A. RODRIGUEZ-LOPEZ (see under ⇒ AT THE DRIVE-IN)

the ROLLING STONES

Formed: London, England ... mid-1962 by JONES, JAGGER and RICHARDS. After a residence at Richmond blues club, 'The Crawdaddy', the band were signed by A&R man DICK ROWE to 'Decca', who had just rejected The BEATLES. Their debut single, a cover of Chuck Berry's 'COME ON ', almost hit top 20, and the band were well on the way to crystallising their image as the original bad boys of rock. Hairier, uglier and more rebellious (publicly anyway) than The BEATLES, manager/hustler extrordinaire, ANDREW LOOG OLDHAM, wasted no time in playing the outlaw card for all it was worth. Working the press like a true pro, he elicited a string of publicity grabbing headlines, culminating with the infamous "Would you let your daughter marry a ROLLING STONE?" Which, of course, made the band even more desirable in the eyes of those self same teenage daughters and as The 'STONES snaked their way across the country the following year on a joint headlining tour with The RONETTES, what had begun as hysteria and isolated fisticuffs had escalated into full-on rioting with promoters quaking in their boots. That summer, they scored their first No.1 single with a cover of Buddy Holly's 'NOT FADE AWAY', now beginning to usurp The BEATLES as the UK's premier knicker-wetting phenomenon. As for the music, the early 'STONES' sound was a fairly derivative take on black America yet it possessed a primal, sexual intensity that made their Merseyside rivals sound like choirboys. Rhythm was everything and in full flight WATT's fluid, unswerving backbeat locked in perfect unholy union with WYMAN's bass and RICHARDS' demonic guitar grooves. JONES, meanwhile, casually lashed out searing slide guitar and JAGGER, the blueprint for decades of wannabe's to come, pouted, preened and snarled in equal measure. The first three albums, 'THE ROLLING STONES' (1964), '12 x 5' (1964) and 'THE ROLLING STONES NOW' (1965) were made up largely of R&B and blues covers, the latter

The ROLLING STONES

marginally topping the other two with the most focused number JAGGERS/RICHARDS had come up with by that point, 'HEART OF STONE' and an electrifying reading of Willie Dixon's 'LITTLE RED ROOSTER'. Apparently revealed to KEITH RICHARDS in a dream, one of the most recognisable and famous riffs in rock history formed the core of The 'STONES' breakthrough hit, '(I CAN'T GET NO) SATISFACTION'. Despite the controversial lyrics which earned a boycott from US radio and further enhanced their reputation as leering malcontents, the record hit the top of the charts on both sides of the Atlantic during the summer of '65. This opened the floodgates for a wave of No.1 singles: 'GET OFF MY CLOUD' (1965), '19TH NERVOUS BREAKDOWN' (1966) and 'PAINT IT BLACK' (1966), the latter a brooding psychedelic-tinged stampede that featured some nifty sitar playing by a cross-legged BRIAN JONES. 'AFTERMATH' (1966) was a huge step forward with JONES adding exotic touches in line with his growing admiration for the JouJouka musicians of Morocco. Meanwhile, the JAGGER/RICHARDS songwriting partnership was blossoming, tackling social issues with trenchant ease; 'MOTHER'S LITTLE HELPER' as well as the usual sexual politics; 'UNDER MY THUMB'. It was around this time that JAGGER began assuming the multitude of different masks he would use onstage and off, as one journalist aptly pointed out; "MICK JAGGER was an interesting bunch of guys". His cocky, chameleon-like affectations stood in stark contrast to KEITH RICHARDS' sullen, slightly aloof distance but it was exactly this homo-erotic chemistry that fuelled The STONES and fashioned the decadent legend of 'The Glimmer Twins' as they'd come to be known in the 70's. 'BETWEEN THE BUTTONS' (1967) contained another salacious rebel anthem in 'LET'S SPEND THE NIGHT TOGETHER' alongside the ebb and flow wistfulness of 'RUBY TUESDAY'. By this time, though, the powers that be had had just about enough of these unkempt subversives and their dubious morals. The infamous Redlands drug bust in February '67 was probably the most famous of all The 'STONES' run-in's with the law, although by no means the most serious and in the end, RICHARDS' conviction was quashed on appeal while JAGGER was given a year's probation. Yet only a few days later, MICK talked defiantly to the press about revolution and The 'STONES recorded their acerbic reply to The BEATLES' 'All You Need Is Love'. With LENNON and McCARTNEY collaborating, the band cut 'WE LOVE YOU'. Allegedly written by JAGGER in jail as a tribute to the fans who had stood by him, it came out sounding like a deliciously snide riposte to the authorities, complete with the sounds of heavy footsteps and a cell door clanging shut. While they were successful with occasional ventures into warped psychedelia, The 'STONES remained first and foremost a rock'n'roll band and their attempt at a psychedelic concept album, 'THEIR SATANIC MAJESTIES REQUEST' (1967) was always destined to sound half-baked at best. The stellar '2000 LIGHT YEARS FROM HOME' and 'SHE'S A RAINBOW' saved the album from being a complete failure although it didn't even come close to rivalling 'Sgt. Pepper'. A more honest response to The BEATLES' magnum opus, 'BEGGARS BANQUET' (1968) was the first album in a staggering burst of creativity that would see The ROLLING STONES release four of the best albums in the history of rock over a five year period. Preceded by the much needed No.1 hit, 'JUMPIN' JACK FLASH', (which marked the beginning of a fruitful partnership with JIMMY MILLER), the album saw the band realign themselves with roots music to startling effect. At this point The 'STONES' were not simply imitating their heroes of the American South, they had made the music truly their own. Inspired by Mikhail Bulgakov's novel, 'The Master And Margarita', 'SYMPATHY FOR THE DEVIL' was pure malevolent genius, MICK casting himself gleefully in the role of Beelzebub over an irresistible voodoo funk. Similarly controversial were the topical 'STREET FIGHTIN' MAN' and the leering 'STRAY CAT BLUES' which centred on a rock star and an obliging 15 year old groupie, the grinding rhythm oozing illicit sex. These subversive broadsides were alternated with threadbare country blues numbers that, save for JAGGER's barrow boy via Louisiana vocals, sounded so authentic you could almost smell the corn bread. During sessions for the follow-up, 'LET IT BLEED' (1969), BRIAN JONES had left the band and was found dead in controversial circumstances a month later on the 3rd of July, 1969, at his Pooh Corner home. He had never really recovered from having control of the band wrestled from him and his unstable personality buckled under a frightening drug intake. Preceded by The 'STONES' last No.1 single, 'HONKY TONK WOMAN', 'LET IT BLEED' was eventually released the same fateful month as the Altamont disaster and possessed a vivid essence of brooding portent, most obvious on the opening track 'GIMME SHELTER', with its thundering rhythm and near-hysterical urging. 'MIDNIGHT RAMBLER' was equally chilling while RICHARDS made his vocal debut on 'YOU GOT THE SILVER', his voice a ragged sliver of emotive simplicity that stood in direct contrast to MICK's affectations. Closing with the aching desolation of 'YOU CAN'T ALWAYS GET WHAT YOU WANT', the album was another example, if one was needed at all, that The 'STONES' preferred harsh realism to dopey idealism and had never really embraced the hippy philosophy. Perhaps it was fitting then, that The 'STONES' were, quite literally, centre stage when that hopeful euphoria of the 60's finally came to an end during the last bitterly cold days of 1969. As the band played a free gig at a barren speedway track in Altamont, Northern California, poor organisation and delays contributed to bad vibes which were exacerbated by brutal, acid-crazed Hell's Angels. Supposedly acting in a security capacity, one of their number ended up stabbing an innocent fan to death while many others were beaten up, The 'STONES' ferried out by helicopter in fear of their lives. By the release of 'STICKY FINGERS' (1971), the dark potency of the previous albums had gone, save for a few tracks, notably MARIANNE FAITHFUL's bleakly beautiful 'SISTER MORPHINE'. The band had pushed things to the limit and from here on in they retreated. Nevertheless, the best was yet to come, and 'STICKY FINGERS' kept 'up the momentum. 'DEAD FLOWERS' was a rollicking country hoedown shot through with typically twisted humour while JAGGER assumed his inimitable Delta Bluesman mantle for the inspired cover of Mississippi Fred McDowell's 'YOU GOT TO MOVE'. Elsewhere, tracks like 'BROWN SUGAR' and 'BITCH' were quintessential 'STONES, revelling in their own mythology. This was also the first stuio material to feature ex-BLUESBREAKER, MICK TAYLOR, who'd joined in '69 as a replacement for BRIAN JONES. Athough his distinctive style was an integral part of the band's early 70's sound, he'd later leave amid growing disatisfaction with the JAGGER/RICHARDS domination of the band. 'EXILE ON MAIN STREET' (1972) remains one of the best double album ever released and quite possibly staking a claim for the best album, bar none, ever released. Big claims, yet this was the pure, unadulterated essence of that cliched thing called rock'n'roll, no cobwebbed history lecture, but a living, breathing, sweating justification for white boys playing the blues. Recorded in a dank, humid basement in RICHARDS' villa in the South of France, the production is so murky that JAGGER's vocals verge on the indecipherable at points and the whole thing seems continually on the brink of collapse. Yet this only serves to enhance the unerringly strong material and elegantly wasted mood of the record. From the aural massage of 'TUMBLING DICE' to the raggedy-assed beauty of 'LOVING CUP', the down home gospel of 'SHINE A LIGHT' to KEITH RICHARDS' off-the-cuff anthem 'HAPPY', The 'STONES, or rock music, for that matter, would never sound so spiritually debauched again. In comparison, 'GOAT'S HEAD SOUP' (1973) was inevitably a let down, the band sounding tired and listless, although JAGGER at least sounded half-convincing on his tender ballad, 'ANGIE'. MICK TAYLOR's last album, 'IT'S ONLY ROCK'N'ROLL' (1974) was 'STONES by numbers and didn't bode well for the coming decade. 'BLACK AND BLUE' (1976) saw ex-FACE, RON WOOD brought into the fold and a half hearted attempt at reggae stylings. By this point, the band were a massive live draw but often sloppy on stage due in no small part to the band's collosal drug intake. It came as little surprise to even the most casual 'STONES observer when, in February 1977, RICHARDS was busted in Toronto holding serious amounts of Class A. Amid alleged rumours of a huge pay-off, KEITH was eventually let off fairly leniently and yet again, the 'STONES lived to fight another day, another 20 years in fact, and counting. Too long some might say, as 'SOME GIRLS' (1978) was the last 'STONES album that actually sounded like they meant it. Although the disco experimentalism of 'MISS YOU' was rather lukewarm, the album contained the last great JAGGER/RICHARDS song, 'BEAST OF BURDEN'. 'EMOTIONAL RESCUE' (1980) was dull and formulaic while 1981's 'TATTOO YOU' redeemed itself slightly with a rawer sound and the sprightly, if cliched hit 'START ME UP'. THE ROLLING STONES were, by now, one of the biggest acts on the stadium rock circuit, particularly in the U.S.A. and although their studio output was stagnating, the band's live show was still worth the admission price, especially now that KEITH had cleaned up his act and could get through a whole set without falling asleep on stage. 'UNDERCOVER' (1984) was a typically ill-advised 80's attempt at experimentation and as such, an unmitigated disaster, while 'DIRTY WORK' (1986) was only marginally less tedious. After a brief lull, the band returned with 1989's 'STEEL WHEELS' and while the single 'MIXED EMOTIONS' was their best in a decade, the album favoured glossy production and slick professionalism over content. With a move to 'Virgin' amid million pound deals, 'VOODOO LOUNGE' (1994) was touted as a dangerous return to form, although it was their first as a quartet as WYMAN departed. In the event, it was as flaccid and cliched as anything the band had done. The pared down, semi-acoustic 'STRIPPED' (1995) was listenable although as the prospect of a creative rebirth grows ever more remote, maybe one more album would suffice. This came in the shape of 1997's 'BRIDGES TO BABYLON', another commercial success that spawned a few minor hits, the near 60 year olds still drawing the crowds (not in Britain though as the taxman became their enemy once again). JAGGER was back in the new millennium with another instalment in his intermittent solo career although 'GODDESS IN THE DOORWAY' (2001) was hardly anything to write home about. It nevertheless cracked the US and UK Top 50, helped no doubt by a UK TV documentary about its making. After rolling for a staggering forty years, it was inevitable some kind of compilation would be unveiled to celebrate such an admittedly impressive landmark. 'FORTY LICKS' (2002), found the 'STONES bring their catalogue up to date, creaming off choice cuts from each of the four decades without even beginning to exhaust the wealth and depth of that incredible legacy. The obligatory concert set, 'LIVE LICKS' (2004), featured lean, mean (at least, leaner and meaner than their years) stage versions of the rolled gold, wrapped in the kind of cock-rock cover art last seen in the mid-80s. While this barely scraped the Top 50, the long awaited, DON WAS-produced 'A BIGGER BANG' (2005) was hailed as the band's best for decades; sounds familiar, non? Yet, in a five year period that's seen twilight, back-to-roots "comebacks" released by everyone from BOB DYLAN and VAN MORRISON to ELTON JOHN and PAUL McCARTNEY, the 'STONES' latest opus was apparently the real thing, scoring a UK Top 20 hit with classicist opener 'ROUGH JUSTICE', resuscitating JAGGER's blues masque on 'BACK OF MY HAND' and harking back – successfully – to the highwire funk of the late 70's on Top 40 single, 'RAIN FALL DOWN'. And it's surely a testament to the polarising power of the Bush regime that they managed to inspire a rare political jibe – 'SWEET NEO CON' – from the original 24-hour hedonists. The album itself narrowly missed No.1, and the 'STONES topped off a profitable winter season with a world news-making free concert on Rio De Janeiro's Copacabana beach.

• **Trivia:** JAGGER's relationship with singer MARIANNE FAITHFULL ended in 1970, when he met Nicaraguan model, Bianca Rosa Perez-Mora and later married her on the 12th of May '71. They split in 1978, probably over Marsha Hunt's allegations that MICK was the father of her child. After a long relationship with Jerry Hall (formerly Bryan Ferry's girlfriend), he later married her on the 21st November '90. WYMAN's marriage (since 1959) ended abruptly in the mid-80's, after his 2-year relationship with 16 year-old, Mandy Smith, was revealed in the News Of The World. They married relatively quietly on the 2nd of June '89, but controversially divorced in 1992, with the now famous Mandy allegedly sueing for half a million. • **Songwriters:** JAGGER-RICHARDS mostly except covers; NOT FADE AWAY (Buddy Holly) / ROUTE 66 (Nelson Riddle Orchestra) / I JUST WANT TO MAKE LOVE TO YOU (Willie Dixon) / HONEST I DO (Jimmy Reed) / I NEED YOU BABY (Bo Diddley) / POISON IVY (Coasters) / NOW I'VE GOT A WITNESS . . . (Gene Pitney) / LITTLE BY LITTLE (Pitney / Spector) / COME ON + CAROL + YOU CAN'T CATCH ME + TALKIN' 'BOUT YOU + LITTLE QUEENIE + AROUND AND AROUND + BYE BYE JOHNNY (Chuck Berry) / CAN I GET A WITNESS (Holland-Dozier-Holland) / MONEY (Barrett Strong) / I WANNA BE YOUR MAN (Beatles) / LITTLE BY LITTLE (w/Spector) / YOU CAN MAKE IT IF YOU TRY (Gene Allison; hit) / WALKING THE DOG (Rufus Thomas) / SUSIE Q (Dale Hawkins) / UNDER THE BOARDWALK (Drifters) / I CAN'T BE SATISFIED + MANNISH BOY (Muddy Waters) / DOWN HOME GIRL (Jerry Butler) / IT'S ALL OVER NOW (Valentinos) / LITTLE RED ROOSTER (Willie Dixon) / PAIN IN MY HEART + MY GIRL (Otis Redding) / EVERYBODY NEEDS SOMEBODY TO LOVE (Solomon Burke) / DOWN THE ROAD APIECE (Will Bradley) / TIME IS ON MY SIDE (Irma Thomas) / SHE SAID YEAH (Jackson/Christy) / I DON'T KNOW WHY (Stevie Wonder) / MERCY, MERCY (Don Covay) / GOOD TIMES (Sam Cooke) / CRY TO ME (Betty Harris; hit) / HITCH HIKE (Marvin Gaye) / THAT'S HOW STRONG MY LOVE IS (Otis Redding) / OH BABY (WE GOT A GOOD THING GOIN') (Gonzales Ozen) / PRODIGAL SON (Robert Wilkins) / YOU BETTER MOVE ON (Arthur Alexander) / LOVE IN VAIN (Robert Johnson; trad.) / AIN'T TOO PROUD TO BEG + JUST MY IMAGINATION (Temptations) / I'M A KING BEE + SHAKE YOUR HIPS (Slim Harpo) / CHERRY OH BABY (? reggae) / GOING TO A GO-GO (Smokey Robinson / Miracles) / HARLEM SHUFFLE (Bob & Earl) / TWENTY FLIGHT ROCK (Eddie Cochran) / CORRINA (Taj Mahal) / etc. KEITH RICHARDS solo wrote with JORDAN. RONNIE WOOD covered TESTIFY (Parliaments) / AM I GROOVIN' YOU (Bert Berns) / SEVEN DAYS (Bob Dylan) / SHOW ME (J. Williams).

Album rating (UK): THE ROLLING STONES (*8) / THE ROLLING STONES NO.2 (*8) / OUT OF OUR HEADS (*7) / AFTERMATH (*7) / BIG HITS (HIGH TIDE AND GREEN GRASS) compilation (*8) / GOT LIVE IF YOU WANT IT (*5) / BETWEEN THE BUTTONS (*7) / THEIR SATANIC MAJESTIES REQUEST (*5) / BEGGARS BANQUET (*10) / THROUGH THE PAST, DARKLY (BIG HITS VOL.2) compilation (*8) / LET IT BLEED (*9) / GET YER YA-YA'S OUT! (*7) / STONE AGE exploitation (*7) / STICKY FINGERS (*8) / GIMME SHELTER exploitation (*6) / HOT ROCKS 1964-1971 compilation US (*10) / MILESTONES exploitation (*6) / EXILE ON MAIN ST. (*10) / ROCK 'N' ROLLING STONES exploitation (*5) / GOATS HEAD SOUP (*6) / IT'S ONLY ROCK'N'ROLL (*6) / MADE IN THE SHADE compilation (*6) / METAMORPHOSIS exploitation (*5) / ROLLED GOLD – THE VERY BEST OF THE ROLLING STONES compilation (*10) / BLACK AND BLUE (*6) / LOVE YOU LIVE (*5) / GET STONED exploitation (*7) / SOME GIRLS (*7) / EMOTIONAL RESCUE (*5) / TATTOO YOU (*6) / STILL LIFE (AMERICAN CONCERTS 1981) (*3) / STORY OF THE STONES exploitation (*6) / UNDERCOVER (*5) / REWIND 1971-1984 (THE BEST OF THE ROLLING STONES) compilation (*7) / DIRTY WORK (*6) / STEEL WHEELS (*6) / FLASHPOINT (*4) / JUMP BACK – THE BEST OF THE ROLLING STONES 1971-1993 compilation (*8) / VOODOO LOUNGE (*8) / STRIPPED (*6) / BRIDGES TO BABYLON (*6) / NO SECURITY (*5) / FORTY LICKS compilation (*10) / LIVE LICKS (*6) / A BIGGER BANG (*7) / Mick Jagger: SHE'S THE BOSS (*5) / PRIMITIVE COOL (*4) / WANDERING SPIRIT (*6) / GODDESS IN THE DOORWAY (*5) / ALFIE soundtrack w/ Dave Stewart (*6) / Keith Richards: TALK IS CHEAP (*8) / . . .LIVE AT THE HOLLYWOOD PALLADIUM (*5) / MAIN OFFENDER (*5)

MICK JAGGER (b.26 Jul'43, Dartford, Kent, England) – vocals, harmonica / **KEITH RICHARDS** (b.18 Dec'43, Dartford) – rhythm guitar / **BRIAN**

JONES (b.28 Feb'43, Cheltenham, England) – lead guitar / **CHARLIE WATTS** (b. 2 Jun'41, Islington, London) – drums (ex-BLUES INC.) / **BILL WYMAN** (b.WILLIAM PERKS, 24 Oct'36, Lewisham, London) – bass repl. DICK TAYLOR who later joined PRETTY THINGS / **IAN STEWART** – piano (was 6th member, pushed to the background by manager)

Decca London

Jun 63. (7") *(F 11675)* **COME ON. / I WANT TO BE LOVED** 21 –

Nov 63. (7") *(F 11764)* *<9641>* **I WANNA BE YOUR MAN. / STONED** 12 Jan64

Feb 64. (7") *(F 11845)* **NOT FADE AWAY. / LITTLE BY LITTLE** 3 –

Mar 64. (7") *<9657>* **NOT FADE AWAY. / I WANNA BE YOUR MAN** – 48

Apr 64. (lp) *(LK 4605)* *<375>* **THE ROLLING STONES** (US-title 'ENGLAND'S NEWEST HITMAKERS – THE ROLLING STONES) 1 Jun64 11
– (Get your kicks on) Route 66 / I just want to make love to you / Honest I do / I need you baby (Mona) / Now I've got a witness (like uncle Phil and uncle Gene) / Little by little / I'm a king bee / Carol / Tell me (you're coming back) / Can I get a witness / You can make it if you try / Walking the dog. *(US)* – Not fade away. / – Mona *(re-iss. Jul84 lp/c; LKD/KSDC 4605) (cd-ss.1985 on 'London'; 820 047-2) (re-iss. Jun95 on 'London' cd/c/lp; 844460-2/-4/-1)*

Jun 64. (7") *(F 11934)* *<9687>* **IT'S ALL OVER NOW. / GOOD TIMES, BAD TIMES** 1 Aug64 26

Jul 64. (7") *<9682>* **TELL ME (YOU'RE COMING BACK). / I JUST WANT TO MAKE LOVE TO YOU** – 24

Oct 64. (7") *<9708>* **TIME IS ON MY SIDE. / CONGRATULATIONS** – 6

Nov 64. (7") *(F 12014)* **LITTLE RED ROOSTER. / OFF THE HOOK** 1 –

Nov 64. (lp) *<402>* **12 x 5** – 3
– Around and around / Confessin' the blues / Empty heart / Time is on my side / Good times bad times / It's all over now / 2120 South Michigan Avenue / Under the boardwalk / Congratulations / Grown up wrong / If you need me / Susie Q. *(UK-iss.Aug84 lp/c; LKD/KDKHAC 5335) (cd-iss. Nov84 on 'London'; 820 048-2) (re-iss. Jun95; 844461-2/-4/-1)*

Jan 65. (lp) *(LK 4661)* **THE ROLLING STONES No.2** 1 –
– Everybody needs somebody to love / Down home girl / You can't catch me / Time is on my side / What a shame / Grown up wrong / Down the road apiece / Under the boardwalk / I can't be satisfied / Pain in my heart / Off the hook / Susie Q. *(re-iss. 1986;)*

Jan 65. (7") *<9725>* **HEART OF STONE. / WHAT A SHAME** – 19

Feb 65. (7") *(F 12104)* *<9741>* **THE LAST TIME. / PLAY WITH FIRE** 1 9
Mar65 96

Mar 65. (lp) *<420>* **THE ROLLING STONES NOW!** – 5
– Everybody needs somebody to love / Down home girl / You can't catch me / Heart of stone / I need you baby (Mona) / Down the road apiece / Off the hook / Pain in my heart / Oh baby (we got a good thing goin') / Little red rooster / Surprise surprise. *(UK-iss.Aug88 cd; 820133-2) (re-iss. Jun95 on 'London' cd/c/lp; 844462-2/-4/-1)*

May 65. (7") *(F 12220)* **(I CAN'T GET NO) SATISFACTION. / THE SPIDER AND THE FLY** 1 –

Jun 65. (7") *<9766>* **(I CAN'T GET NO) SATISFACTION. / THE UNDER ASSISTANT WEST COAST MAN** – 1

Sep 65. (lp; mono/stereo) *(LK/SKL 473)* *<429>* **OUT OF OUR HEADS** 2 Aug 65 1
– She said yeah * / Mercy, mercy / Hitch hike / That's how strong my love is / Good times / Gotta get away * / Talkin' 'bout you * / Cry to me / Oh baby (we got a good thing going) * / Heart of stone / The under assistant west coast man / I'm free. *<UK tracks above * were repl. by in US>* – I'm alright (live) / (I can't get no) Satisfaction / Play with fire / The spider and the fly / One more try. *(re-iss. Jul84 lp/c)(cd; LKD/LSLSC 5336)(820 049-2) (re-iss. Jun95 on 'London' cd/c/lp; 844463-2/-4/-1)*

Sep 65. (7") *<9792>* **GET OFF OF MY CLOUD. / I'M FREE** – 1

Oct 65. (7") *(F 12263)* **GET OFF OF MY CLOUD. / THE SINGER NOT THE SONG** 1 –

Nov 65. (lp) *<451>* **DECEMBER'S CHILDREN (AND EVERYBODY'S)** – 4
– She said yeah / Talkin' 'bout you / You better move on / Look what you've done / The singer not the song / Route 66 (live) / Get off of my cloud / I'm free / As tears go by / Gotta get away / Blue turns to grey / I'm movin' on (live). *(UK-iss.Aug88 cd; 820 135-2) (re-iss. Jun95 on 'London' cd/c/lp; 844464-2/-4/-1)*

Dec 65. (7") *<9808>* **AS TEARS GO BY. / GOTTA GET AWAY** – 6

Feb 66. (7") *(F 12331)* **19th NERVOUS BREAKDOWN. / AS TEARS GO BY** 1 –

Feb 66. (7") *<9823>* **19th NERVOUS BREAKDOWN. / SAD DAY** – 2

Apr 66. (lp; mono/stereo)(c) *(LK/SKL 4786)(KSKC 4786) <451>* **AFTERMATH** 1 Jul66 2
– Mother's little helper / Stupid girl / Lady Jane / Under my thumb / Doncha bother me / Goin' home / Flight 505 / High and dry / Out of time / It's not easy / I am waiting / Take it or leave it / Think / What to do. *(US version+=)* – Paint it black. *(re-iss. May85 lp/c)(cd; SKLD/ 4786)(820 050-2) (re-iss. Jun95 on 'London' cd/c/lp; 844466-2/-4/-1)*

May 66. (7") *<901>* **PAINT IT BLACK. / STUPID GIRL** – 1

May 66. (7") *(F 12395)* **PAINT IT BLACK. / LONG LONG WHILE** 1 –

Jul 66. (7") *<902>* **MOTHER'S LITTLE HELPER. / LADY JANE** – 8
24

Sep 66. (7") *(F 12497)* *<903>* **HAVE YOU SEEN YOUR MOTHER BABY, STANDING IN THE SHADOW?. / WHO'S DRIVING YOUR PLANE?** 5 9

Nov 66. (lp; mono/stereo)(c) *(TXL/TXS 101)(KSKC 101) <1>* **BIG HITS (HIGH TIDE AND GREEN GRASS)** (compilation) 4 Apr 66 3
– Have you seen your mother baby, standing in the shadows? / Paint it black / It's all over now / The last time / Heart of stone / Not fade away / Come on / (I can't get no) Satisfaction / Get off my cloud / As tears go by / 19th nervous breakdown / Lady Jane / Time is on my side / Little red rooster. *(re-iss. Jun95 on 'London' cd/c/lp; 844465-2/-4/-1)*

Dec 66. (lp) *<493>* **GOT LIVE IF YOU WANT IT (live, Royal Albert Hall)** – 6
– Under my thumb / Get off of my cloud / Lady Jane / Not fade away / I've been loving you too long (to stop now) (studio) / Fortune teller (studio) / The last time / 19th nervous breakdown / Time is on my side / I'm alright / Have you seen your mother baby, standing in the shadow? / (I can't get no) Satisfaction. *(UK-iss.Aug88 cd; 820 137-2) (re-iss. Jun95 on 'London' cd/c/lp; 844467-2/-4/-1)*

Jan 67. (7") *(F 12546)* *<904>* **LET'S SPEND THE NIGHT TOGETHER. / RUBY TUESDAY** 3 55
1

Jan 67. (lp; mono/stereo)(c) *(LK/SKL 4852)(KSKC 4852) <499>* **BETWEEN THE BUTTONS** 3 Feb67 2
– Yesterday's papers / My obsession / Back street girl* / Connection / She smiled sweetly / Cool, calm and collected / All sold out / Please go home* / Who's been sleeping here? / Complicated / Miss Amanda Jones / Something happened to me yesterday. *(US version*; = tracks repl. by)*
– Let's spend the night together / Ruby Tuesday. *(cd-iss. Jul85; 820 138-2) (re-iss. lp/cd. Dec91 on 'UFO' with free booklet) (re-iss. Jun95 on 'London' cd/c/lp; 844468-2/-4/-1)*

Jul 67. (lp) *<509>* **FLOWERS** (compilation) – 3
(UK cd-iss. Aug88; 820 139-2) (re-iss. cd Jun95 on 'London')

Aug 67. (7") *(F 12654)* *<905>* **WE LOVE YOU. / DANDELION** 8 50
14

Nov 67. (7") *<906>* **SHE'S A RAINBOW. / 2,000 LIGHT YEARS FROM HOME** – 25

Dec 67. (lp; mono/stereo)(c) *(TXL/TXS 103)(KTXC 103) <2>* **THEIR SATANIC MAJESTIES REQUEST** 3 2
– Sing this all together / Citadel / In another land / 2,000 man / Sing this all together (see what happens) / She's a rainbow / The lantern / Gomper / 2,000 light years from home / On with the show. *(re-iss. Feb86 lp/c/cd; 820 129-1/-4/-2) (re-iss. Jun95 on 'London' cd/c/lp; 844469-2/-4/-1)*

Dec 67. (7"; by BILL WYMAN) *<907>* **IN ANOTHER LAND. / THE LANTERN** – 87

May 68. (7") *(F 12782)* *<908>* **JUMPIN' JACK FLASH. / CHILD OF THE MOON** 1 3

Aug 68. (7") *<909>* **STREET FIGHTING MAN. / NO EXPECTATIONS** – 48

Dec 68. (lp; mono/stereo)(c) *(LK/SKL 4955)(KSKC 4955) <539>* **BEGGARS BANQUET** 3 5
– Sympathy for the Devil / No expectations / Dear doctor / Parachute woman / Jigsaw puzzle / Street fighting man / Prodigal son / Stray cat blues / Factory girl / Salt of the Earth. *(cd-iss. Jan83; 800 084-2) (re-iss. Jul84 lp/c; SKDL/KSKC 4955) (re-iss. Jun95 on 'London' cd/c/lp; 844471-2/-4/-1)*

— (Jun'69) **MICK TAYLOR** (b.17 Jan'48, Hertfordshire, England) – lead guitar (ex-JOHN MAYALL's BLUESBREAKERS) repl. BRIAN JONES who was found dead by his girlfriend on 3 Jul'69, after a heavy drink/drugs binge.

Jul 69. (7") *(F 12952)* *<910>* **HONKY TONK WOMEN. / YOU CAN'T ALWAYS GET WHAT YOU WANT** 1 1

Sep 69. (lp; mono/stereo)(c) *(LK/SKL 5019)(KSKC 5019) <3>* **THROUGH THE PAST DARKLY (BIG HITS VOL.2)** (compilation) 2 2
– Jumping Jack Flash / Mother's little helper / 2,000 light years from home / Let's spend the night together / You'd better move on / Street fighting man / She's a rainbow / Ruby Tuesday / Dandelion / Sittin' on the fence / Honky tonk women. *(re-iss. Jun95 on 'London' cd/c/lp; 844472-2/-4/-1)*

— (all UK singles so far were re-iss. Mar82)

Dec 69. (lp/c) *(SLK/KSKC 5025) <4>* **LET IT BLEED** 1 3
– Gimme shelter / Love in vain / Country honk / Live with me / Let it bleed / Midnight rambler / You got the silver / Monkey man / You can't always get what you want. *(cd-iss. Feb86; 820 052-2) (re-iss. Jun95 UK+US on 'London' cd/c/lp; 844473-2/-4/-1)*

Sep 70. (lp/c) *(SKL/KSKC 5065) <5>* **GET YER YA YA'S OUT** (live, New York, Nov'69) 1 Oct69 6
– Jumpin' Jack Flash / Carol / Stray cat blues / Love in vain / Midnight rambler / Sympathy for the Devil / Live with me / Little Queenie / Honky tonk women. *(cd-iss. Aug88; 820 131-2) (re-iss. Jun95 on 'London' cd/c/lp; 844474-2/-4/-1)*

— In 1970, MICK JAGGER starred in his second feature film 'Performance'. Below single was his first solo 45 from the film.

Nov 70. (7"; by MICK JAGGER) *(F 13067)* **MEMO FROM TURNER. / ('B'side by 'Jack Nitzsche')** 32

Apr 71. (lp/c) *(SKL/KSKC 5084)* **STONE AGE** (compilation) 4 –
– Look what you've done / It's all over now / Confessin' the blues / One more try / As tears go by / The spider and the fly / My girl / Paint it black / If you need me / The last time / Blue turns to grey / Around and around.

Rolling Stones Rolling Stones

Apr 71. (7"m) *(RS 19100)* **BROWN SUGAR. / BITCH / LET IT ROCK** 2 –

Apr 71. (lp/c) *(<COC/KCOC 59100>)* **STICKY FINGERS** 1 1
– Brown sugar / Sway / Wild horses / Can't you hear me knocking? / You gotta move / Bitch / I got the blues / Sister Morphine / Dead flowers / Moonlight mile. *(re-iss. Nov79 on 'E.M.I.'; CUN 59100) <US re-iss. 1980; MFSL 1-060> (cd-iss. Nov86 on 'C.B.S.; CK 40488) (re-iss. Nov89 on 'CBS' UK/US lp/c/cd; 450 195-1/-4/-2) (re-iss. cd Jun94 on 'Virgin' UK+US; 7243-8-39504-2-3) (re-iss. Aug94 on 'Virgin' cd/c; CDV/TCV 2730) (lp re-iss. Nov97 on 'Virgin'; LPCENT 38)*

Apr 71. (7") *<19100>* **BROWN SUGAR. / BITCH** – 1

Jun 71. (7") *<RS 19101>* **WILD HORSES. / SWAY** – 28

Apr 72. (7") *(<RS 19103>)* **TUMBLING DICE. / SWEET BLACK ANGEL** 5 7

Jun 72. (d-lp/c) *(COC/KCOC 69100) <2900>* **EXILE ON MAIN ST.** 1 1
– Rocks off / Rip this joint / Shake your hips / Casino boogie / Tumbling dice / Sweet Virginia / Torn and frayed / Sweet black angel / Loving cup / Happy / Turd on the run / Ventilator blues / I just want to see his face / Let it loose / All down the line / Stop breaking down / Shine a light / Soul survivor. *(re-iss. Nov79 on 'E.M.I.'; CUNSP 69100) (re-iss. Nov89 on 'CBS' lp/c/cd UK/US; 450 196-1/-4/-2) (re-iss. Aug94 on 'Virgin' cd/c; CDV/TCV 2731)*

Jun 72. (7") *<19104>* **HAPPY. / ALL DOWN THE LINE** – 22

Aug 73. (7") *(RS <19105>)* **ANGIE. / SILVER TRAIN** 5 1

Sep 73. (lp/c) *(<COC/KCOC 59101>)* **GOATS HEAD SOUP** 1 1
– Dancing with Mr.D / 100 years ago / Coming down again / Doo doo doo doo doo (heartbreaker) / Angie / Silver train / Hide your love / Winter / Can you hear the music / Star star. *(re-iss. Nov79 on 'E.M.I.'; CUN 59101) (re-iss. Nov89 on 'CBS' UK/US; 450 207-1/-4/-2) (re-iss. Aug94 on 'Virgin' cd/c; CDV/TCV 2735)*

Jan 74. (7") *<19109>* **DOO DOO DOO DOO DOO (HEARTBREAKER). / DANCING WITH MR.D** – 15

Jul 74. (7") *(RS 19114) <19304>* **IT'S ONLY ROCK'N'ROLL. / THROUGH THE LONELY NIGHTS** 10 16

Oct 74. (lp/c) *(COC/KCOC 59103) <79101>* **IT'S ONLY ROCK'N'ROLL** 2 1
– If you can't rock me / Ain't too proud to beg / It's only rock'n'roll / Till the next goodbye / Time waits for no one / Luxury / Dance little sister / If you really want to be my friend / Short and curlies / Fingerprint file. *(re-iss. Nov79 on 'E.M.I.'; CUN 59103) (re-iss. Nov89 on 'CBS' UK/US lp/c/cd; 450 202-1/-4/-2) (re-iss. Aug94 on 'Virgin' cd/c; CDV/TCV 2733)*

Oct 74. (7") *(19302>* **AIN'T TOO PROUD TO BEG. / DANCE LITTLE SISTER** – 17

Jun 75. (lp/c) *(COC/KCOC 59104) <79102>* **MADE IN THE SHADE** (compilation) 14 6
– Brown sugar / Tumbling dice / Happy / Dance little sister / Wild horses / Angie / Bitch / It's only rock'n'roll (but I like it) / Doo doo doo doo doo (heartbreaker) / Rip this joint. *(re-iss. Nov89 on 'CBS' UK/US lp/c/cd; 450 201-1/-4/-2)*

— (Apr-Dec75) **RON WOOD** – lead guitar (ex-FACES, ex-CREATION, etc) repl. MICK TAYLOR who left Dec74 and later joined JACK BRUCE BAND

Apr 76. (7") *(RS 19121)* **FOOL TO CRY. / CRAZY MAMA** 6 –

Apr 76. (7") *<19304>* **FOOL TO CRY. / HOT STUFF** – 10 49

May 76. (lp/c) *(COC/KCOC 59106) <79104>* **BLACK AND BLUE** 2 1
– Hot stuff / The hand of fate / Cherry oh baby / Memory motel / Hey Negrita / Melody / Fool to cry / Crazy mama. *(re-iss. Nov79 on 'E.M.I.; CUN 59106) (re-iss. Nov89 on 'C.B.S.' UK/US; 450 203-1/-4/-2) (re-iss. Aug94 on 'Virgin' cd/c; CDV/TCV 2736)*

Sep 77. (d-lp/d-c) *(COC/KCOC 89101) <9001>* **LOVE YOU LIVE (live)** 3 5
– Fanfare for the common man / Honky tonk woman / If you can't rock me / Get off of my cloud / Happy / Hot stuff / Star star / Tumbling dice / Fingerprint file / You gotta me / You can't always get what you want / Mannish boy / Crackin' up / Little red rooster / Around and around / It's only rock'n'roll / Brown sugar / Jumpin' Jack Flash / Sympathy for the Devil. *(re-iss. Nov79 on 'E.M.I.'; CUNSP 69101) (re-iss. Nov89 on 'C.B.S.' UK/US d-lp/c/cd; 450 208-1/-4/-2) (cd re-iss. Apr98 on 'Virgin'; CDV 2857)*

May 78. (7"/ext.12"pink) *(EMI/12EMI 2802) <19307>* **MISS YOU. / FARAWAY EYES** 3 1

Jun 78. (lp/c) *(<CUN/TCCUN 39108>)* **SOME GIRLS** 2 1
– Miss you / When the whip comes down / Just my imagination / Some girls / Lies / Far away etes / Respectable / Before they make me run / Beast of burden / Shattered. *(re-iss. Nov89 on 'C.B.S' UK/US lp/c/cd; 450 197-1/-4/-2) (re-iss. Aug94 on 'Virgin' cd/c;)*

Sep 78. (7") *<19309>* **BEAST OF BURDEN. / WHEN THE WHIP COMES DOWN** – 8

Sep 78. (7") *(EMI 2861)* **RESPECTABLE. / WHEN THE WHIP COMES DOWN** 23 –

Dec 78. (7") *<19310>* **SHATTERED. / EVERYTHING IS TURNING TO GOLD** – 31

Jun 80. (7") *(RSR 105) <20001>* **EMOTIONAL RESCUE. / DOWN IN THE HOLE** 9 3

Jul 80. (lp/c) *(CUN/TCCUN 39111) <16015>* **EMOTIONAL RESCUE** 1 1
– Dance (pt.1) / Summer romance / Send it to me / Let me go / Indian girl / Where the boys go / Down in the hole / Emotional rescue / She's so cold / All about you. *(re-iss. Nov89 on 'C.B.S.' UK/US; 450 206-1/-4/-2) (re-iss. Aug94 on 'Virgin' cd/c; CDV/TCV 2737)*

Sep 80. (7") *(RSR 106) <21001>* **SHE'S SO COLD. / SEND IT TO ME** 33 26

Mar 81. (lp/c) *(CUN/TCCUN 39112) <16028>* **SUCKING IN THE 70'S** (compilation + new) 15
– Shattered / Everything is turning to gold / Hot stuff / Time waits for no one / Fool to cry / Mannish boy / When the whip comes down (live) / I was a dancer (part 2) / Crazy mama / Beast of burden. *(re-iss. Nov89 on 'C.B.S.' UK/US; 450 205-1/-4/-2)*

Aug 81. (7") *(RSR 108) <21003>* **START ME UP. / NO USE IN CRYING** 7 2

Sep 81. (lp/c) *(CUN/TCCUN 39114) <16052>* **TATTOO YOU** 2 1
– Start me up / Hang fire / Slave / Little T & A / Black limousine / Neighbours / Worried about you / Tops / Heaven / No use in crying / Waiting on a friend. *(re-iss. Nov89 on 'C.B.S.' UK/US; 450 198-1/-4/-2) (re-iss. Aug94 on 'Virgin' cd/c; CDV/TCV 2732)*

Nov 81. (7") *(RSR 109) <21004>* **WAITING ON A FRIEND. / LITTLE T & A** 50 13

Mar 82. (7") *<21300>* **HANG FIRE. / NEIGHBORS** – 20

Jun 82. (7") *(RSR 110) <21301>* **GOING TO A GO-GO (live). / BEAST OF BURDEN (live)** 26 25

Jun 82. (lp/pic-lp/c) *(CUN/CUNP/TCCUN 39115) <39113>* **STILL LIFE (AMERICAN CONCERTS 1981)** 4 5
– Under my thumb / Let's spend the night together / Shattered / Twenty flight rock / Going to a go-go / Let me go / Time is on my side / Just my imagination / Start me up / (I can't get no) Satisfaction / Take the A train / Star-spangled banner. *(re-iss. Nov89 on 'C.B.S.' UK/US lp/c/cd; 450 204-1/-4/-2) (cd re-iss. Apr98 on 'Virgin'; CDV 2856)*

Sep 82. (7") *(RSR 111) <99978>* **TIME IS ON MY SIDE (live). / TWENTY FLIGHT ROCK (live)** 62
(12"+=) *(12RSR 111)* – Under my thumb (live).

Nov 83. (7") *(RSR 113) <99813>* **UNDERCOVER OF THE NIGHT. / ALL THE WAY DOWN** 11 9
(ext.12"+=) *(12RSR 113)* – Feel on baby (instrumental dub).

Nov 83. (lp/c/cd) *(CUN 165436-1/-4/-2)* <90120>
UNDERCOVER [3] [4]
– Undercover of the night / She was hot / Tie you up / Wanna hold you / Feel on baby / Too much blood / Pretty beat up / Too tough / All the way down / It must be hell. *(re-iss. Nov89 on 'C.B.S.' UK/US; 450 200-1/-4/-2) (re-iss. Aug94 on 'Virgin' cd/c; CDV/TCV 2741)*

Jan 84. (7"/12"sha-pic-d) *(RSR/+P 114)* <99788> **SHE WAS HOT. / I THINK I'M GOING MAD** [42] [44]

Apr 84. (7") <99724> **TOO TOUGH. / MISS YOU** [–] [ ]

Jul 84. (lp/c/cd) *(CUN 1)* <90176> **REWIND 1971-1984 (THE BEST OF THE ROLLING STONES)** (compilation) [23] [86]
– Brown sugar / Undercover of the night / Start me up / Tumbling dice / It's only rock'n'roll (but I like it) / She's so cold / Hang fire / Miss you / Beast of burden / Fool to cry / Waiting on a friend / Angie / Emotional rescue. *(cd+= 2 extra) (re-iss. Nov89 on 'C.B.S.' UK/US; 450 199-1/-4/-2)*

— In 1984, JAGGER guested dual vocals w / MICHAEL JACKSON on The JACKSONS' 'State Of Shock'. He also recorded debut solo album 'She's The Boss', which was released 1985. Later mid'85, he appeared at LIVE AID with DAVID BOWIE duetting on (Martha & The Vandellas) song 'DANCING IN THE STREET'. When issued as a charity single, it made UK No.1 / US No.7 (see BOWIE ⇒).

— 12th Dec'85, IAN STEWART their long-serving 6th member died of a heart attack.

C.B.S. — Rolling Stones

Mar 86. (7"/7"w-poster) *(A/QA 6864)* <05802> **HARLEM SHUFFLE. / HAD IT WITH YOU** [13] [5]
('A'-New York mix; 12"+=/12"w-poster+=) *(TA/QTA 6864)* – ('A'-London mix).

Mar 86. (lp/c/cd) *(CUN/40/CD 86321)* <40250> **DIRTY WORK** [4] [4]
– One hit (to the body) / Fight / Harlem shuffle / Hold back / Too rude / Winning ugly / Back to zero / Dirty work / Had it with you / Sleep tonight. *(re-iss. Nov89 on 'C.B.S.' UK/US; 465 953-1/-4/-2) (re-iss. Aug94 on 'Virgin' cd/c; CDV/TCV 2743)*

May 86. (7"/'A'-London mix-12") *(A/TA 7160)* <05906> **ONE HIT (TO THE BODY). / FIGHT** [ ] [28]

— During this lull in group activity, JAGGER and RICHARDS ventured solo amidst rumours of disbandment. In 1989, they re-surfaced.

Aug 89. (7"/c-s) *(655 193-7/-4)* <69008> **MIXED EMOTIONS. / FANCY MAN BLUES** [36] [5]
(cd-s+=) *(655 193-2)* – Tumbling dice / Miss you.
(cd-s+=) *(655 214-2)* – Shattered / Waiting on a friend.
(12"+=) *(655 193-8)* – ('A'-Chris Kimsey's mix).

Sep 89. (lp/c/cd) *(465 752-1/-4/-2)* <45333> **STEEL WHEELS** [2] [3]
– Sad sad sad / Mixed emotions / Terrifying / Hold on to your hat / Hearts for sale / Blinded by love / Rock and a hard place / Can't be seen / Almost hear you sigh / Continental drift / Break the spell / Slipping away. *(cd re-iss. Dec92;) (re-iss. Aug94 on 'Virgin' cd/c; CDV/TCV 2742)*

Nov 89. (7"/c-s) *(655 422-7/-4)* <73057> **ROCK AND A HARD PLACE. / COOK COOK BLUES** [63] [23]
('A'dance-12"+=) *(655 422-8)* – ('A'-Oh-oh hard dub mix).
(cd-s+=) *(655 448-2)* – It's only rock'n'roll / Rocks off.
(cd-s+=) *(655 448-5)* – Emotional rescue / Some girls.
(12") *(655 422-5)* – ('A'-Michael Brauer mix) / ('A'side) / ('A'-bonus beats mix).

Jun 90. (7") <73093> **ALMOST HEAR YOU SIGH. / BREAK THE SPELL** [–] [50]

Jun 90. (7"/c-s) *(656 065-7/-4)* **ALMOST HEAR YOU SIGH. / WISH I'D NEVER MET YOU** [31] [–]
(c-s+=) *(656 065-2)* – Mixed emotions.
(cd-s+=) *(656 065-5)* – Miss you / Waiting on a friend.
(12")(cd-s) – ('A'side) / Beast of burden / Angie / Fool to cry.

Aug 90. (7"/c-s) *(656 122-7/-4)* **TERRIFYING (remix). / ROCK AND A HARD PLACE (remix)** [ ] [ ]
('A'-dance-12"+=) *(656 122-6)* – Harlem shuffle (London mix).
(cd-s) *(655 122-5)* – ('A'side) / Start me up / Shattered / If you can't rock me.

Sony — Sony

Mar 91. (7"/c-s) *(656 756-7/-4)* <73742> **HIGHWIRE. / 2000 LIGHT YEARS FROM HOME (live)** [29] [57]
(12"+=/cd-s+=) *(656 756-6/-2)* – Sympathy for the Devil (live) / I just want to make love to you (live).
(cd-s+=) *(656 756-5)* – Play with fire (live) / Factory girl (live).

Apr 91. (d-cd/cd/c/lp) *(468 135-9/-2/-4/-1)* <47456>
FLASHPOINT (live) [6] [16]
– Start me up / Sad sad girl / Miss you / Ruby Tuesday / Tou can't always get what you want / Factory girl / Little red rooster / Paint it black / Sympathy for the Devil / Brown sugar / Jumpin' Jack Flash / (I can't get no) Satisfaction / Sexdrive (studio) / High wire (studio). *(cd+=)* – Rock and a hard place / Can't be seen. *(cd re-iss. Apr98 on 'Virgin'; CDV 2855)*

May 91. (7"/c-s) *(656 892-7/-4)* **RUBY TUESDAY (live). / PLAY WITH FIRE (live)** [59] [–]
(12"+=) *(656 892-6)* – You can't always get what you want (live) / Rock and a hard place (live).
(3"cd-s+=) *(656 892-1)* – You can't always get what you want (live) / Undercover of the night (live).
(cd-s) *(656 892-5)* – ('A'side) / Harlem shuffle / Winning ugly London mix).

— In Nov'91, The STONES signed to 'Virgin', and BILL WYMAN soon quit.

Virgin — Virgin

Nov 93. (d-lp/c/cd) *(V/TCV/CDV 2726)* **JUMP BACK: THE BEST OF THE ROLLING STONES 1971-1993** (compilation) [16] [–]
– Start me up / Brown sugar / Harlem shuffle / It's only rock'n'roll (but I like it) / Mixed emotions / Angie / Tumbling dice / Fool to cry / Rock and a hard place / Miss you / Hot stuff / Emotional rescue / Respectable / Beast of burden / Waiting on a friend / Wild horses / Bitch / Undercover of the night. *(re-iss. Oct94 & Jun95;)*

— WYMAN replaced by sessioners **DARRYL JONES** – bass / **CHUCK LEAVELL** – piano

Jul 94. (7"/c-s) *(VS/+C 1503)* <38446> **LOVE IS STRONG. / THE STORM** [14] [91]
(cd-s+=) *(VSCDT 1503)* – So young / ('A'-Bob Clearmountain mix).
(cd-s) *(VSCDX 1503)* – ('A'-Teddy Riley mixes; 5 mixes + other).

Jul 94. (cd/c/d-lp) *(8397821-2/-4/1)* <39782> **VOODOO LOUNGE** [1] [2]
– Love is strong / You got me rocking / Sparks will fly / The worst / New faces / Moon is up / Out of tears / I go wild / Brand new car / Sweethearts together / Suck on the jugular / Blinded by rainbows / Baby break it down / Thru and thru. *(cd-rom-iss.Jun95; VMED 2)*

Oct 94. (7"/c-s) *(VS/+C 1518)* **YOU GOT ME ROCKING. / JUMP ON TOP OF ME** [23] [ ]
(cd-s+=) *(VSCDG 1518)* – ('A'-Perfecto mix) / ('A'-sexy dub mix).
(12") *(VST 1518)* – ('A'-Perfecto mix) / ('A'-sexy dub) / ('A'-trance).

Dec 94. (7"/c-s) *(VS/+C 1524)* <38459> **OUT OF TEARS. / I'M GONNA DRIVE** [38] Oct94 [60]
(cd-s+=/s-cd-s+=) *(VSCD T/X 1524)* – Sparks will fly / ('A'-Bob Clearmountain remix).

Jul 95. (7"/c-s) *(VSP/VSC 1539)* **I GO WILD. / ('A'-Scott Litt remix)** [29] [–]
(cd-s+=) *(VSCDX 1539)* – ('A'version) / ('A'-Luis Resto straight vocal mix).

Nov 95. (c-s) *(VSC 1562)* **LIKE A ROLLING STONE / BLACK LIMOUSINE / ALL DOWN THE LINE** [12] [–]
(cd-s+=) *(VSCDT 1562)* – ('A'edit).

Nov 95. (cd/c/d-lp) *(CD/TC+/V 2801)* <41040> **STRIPPED (live)** [9] [9]
– Street fighting man / Like a rolling stone / Not fade away / Shine a light / The spider and the fly / I'm free / Wild horses / Let it bleed / Dead flowers / Slipping away / Angie / Love in vain / Sweet Virginia / Little baby.

Sep 97. (7"pic-d/c-s) *(VS/+C 1653)* **ANYONE SEEN MY BABY? / ('A'-Soul Solution remix)** [22] [ ]
(12"+=/cd-s+=) *(VSCDT 1653)* – ('A'-Armand's Rolling Steelo).

Oct 97. (cd/c) *(CD/TC+/V 2840)* <44712> **BRIDGES TO BABYLON** [6] [3]
– Flip the switch / Anybody seen my baby? / Low down / Already over me / Gunface / You don't have to mean it / Out of control / Saint of me / Might as well get juiced / Always suffering / Too tight / Thief in the night / How can I stop.

Jan 98. (7"pic-d) *(VSY 1667)* <38626> **SAINT OF ME. / ANYWAY YOU LOOK AT IT** [26] Feb98 [94]
(cd-s+=) *(VSCDX 1667)* – ('A'-Deep Dish grunge garage remix).
(cd-s) *(VSCDT 1667)* – Gimme shelter (live) / Anybody seen my baby? (Phil Jones remix) / ('A'-Deep Dish grunge garage remix).
(d12"+=) *(VSTX 1667)* – ('A'mixes incl. Armand's Rolling Steelo mix of 'B'side).
(d12"+=) *(VSTDT 1667)* – ('A'mixes; Deep Dish & Garage).

Aug 98. (7"pic-d) *(VSY 1700)* **OUT OF CONTROL. / ('A'-In Hand With Fluke mix)** [51] [–]
(cd-s+=) *(VSCDT 1700)* – ('A'-In hand with Fluke instrumental).
(pic-cd-s) *(VSCDX 1700)* – ('A'-Saber final mix) / ('A'-Bi-Polar At The Controls mix) / ('A'-Bi-Polar's Fat Controller mix).

— next featured guests, DAVE MATTHEWS and TAJ MAHAL

Nov 98. (cd/c/lp) *(CD/TC+/V 2880)* <46740> **NO SECURITY (live 1997)** [67] [34]

– (intro) / You got me rocking / Gimme shelter / Flip the switch / Memory hotel / Corinna / Saint of me / Waiting on a friend / Sister morphine / Live with me / Respectable / Thief in the night / The last time / Out of control.

— In Dec'99, a VARIOUS ARTISTS version of 'IT'S ONLY ROCK'N'ROLL' made the UK Top 20

Oct 02. (d-cd/d-c) *(CDVD/TCVD 2964)* <13378> **FORTY LICKS** (compilation) [2] [2]
– Street fighting man / Gimme shelter / (I can't get no) Satisfaction / The last time / Jumpin' Jack Flash / You can't always get what you want / 19th nervous breakdown / Under my thumb / Not fade away / Have you seen your mother, baby (standing in the shadows) / Sympathy for the Devil / Mother's little helper / She's a rainbow / Get off my cloud / Wild horses / Ruby Tuesday / Paint it black / Honky tonk women / It's all over now / Let's spend the night together / Start me up / Brown sugar / Miss you / Beast of burden / Don't stop / Happy / Angie / You got me rocking / Shattered / Fool to cry / Love is strong / Mixed emotions / Keys to your love / Anybody seen my baby? / Stealing my heart / Tumbling dice / Undercover of the night / Emotional rescue / It's only rock'n'roll (but I like it) / Losing my touch.

Dec 02. (7") *(VS 1838)* <546821> **DON'T STOP. / DON'T STOP (new rock remix)** [36] [ ]
(cd-s+=) *(VSCDT 1838)* – Miss you (remix).

Nov 04. (d-cd) *(CDVD 3000)* <75183> **LIVE LICKS** (live 2002) [38] [50]
– Brown sugar / Street fighting man / Paint it black / You can't always get what you want / Start me up / It's only rock'n'roll (but I like it) / Angie / Honky tonk women / Happy / Gimme shelter / (I can't get no) Satisfaction / Neighbours / Monkey man / Rocks off / Can't you hear me knocking / That's how strong my love is / The nearness of you / Beast of burden / When the whip comes down / Rock me baby / You don't have to mean it / Worried about you / Everybody needs somebody to love.

Sep 05. (7"red/cd-s) *(VS/+CDT 1905)* **STREETS OF LOVE. / ROUGH JUSTICE** [15] [–]

Sep 05. (cd/d-lp) *(CD+/V 3012)* <30067> **A BIGGER BANG** [2] [3]
– Rough justice / Let me down slow / It won't take long / Rain fall down / Streets of love / Back of my hand / She saw me coming / Biggest mistake / This place is empty / Oh no not you again / Dangerous beauty / Laugh, I nearly died / Sweet neo con / Look what the cat dragged in / Driving too fast / Infamy. *(cd re-iss. Nov05 w/dvd+=; CDVX 3012)* – (video tracks).

Dec 05. (12") *(VST 1907)* **RAIN FALL DOWN (Will.I.Am remix) / (Ashley Beedle's 'Heavy Disco' radio edit)** [33] [–]
(7"+=/cd-s+=) *(VS/+CDT 1907)* – ('A'-radio mix).

– (selective) compilations, etc. –

below releases issued on 'Decca' UK/ 'Abkco' US unless mentioned

Jul 71. (7"m) *(F 13195)* **STREET FIGHTING MAN. / SURPRISE SURPRISE / EVERYBODY NEEDS SOMEBODY TO LOVE** [21] [–]

Aug 71. (lp/c) *(SLK/KSKC 5101)* **GIMME SHELTER** [19] [–]

Jan 72. (d-lp/c) <606-7> **HOT ROCKS 1964-1971** [–] [4]
(UK cd-iss. 1983 on 'Decca'; 800 083-2) (re-iss. Jul90 cd/c/lp; 820 140-2/-4/-1) <US cd-iss. 1989 on 'Abko'> (re-iss. Jun95 on 'London' cd/c/d-lp; 844475-2/-4/-1)

Feb 72. (lp/c) *(SKL/KSKC 5098)* **MILESTONES** [14] [–]

Nov 72. (lp/c) *(SKL/KSKC 5149)* **ROCK'N'ROLLING STONES** [41] [–]

Dec 72. (lp/c) <626-7> **MORE HOT ROCKS (BIG HITS & FAZED COOKIES)** [–] [9]
(UK cd-iss. Aug88; 820 515-2) (re-iss. cd Nov90;) (re-iss. Jun95 on 'London' cd/c; 844478-2/-4)

Apr 73. (7") *(F 13404)* **YOU CAN'T ALWAYS GET WHAT YOU WANT. / SAD DAY** [ ] [42]

May 75. (7") *(F 13584)* **I DON'T KNOW WHY. / TRY A LITTLE HARDER** [ ] [42]

Jun 75. (lp/c) *(SKL/KSKC 5212)* **METAMORPHISIS** (early demos) [45] [8]

Sep 75. (7") *(F 13597)* **OUT OF TIME. / JIVING SISTER FANNY** [45] [81]

Nov 75. (d-lp)(d-c) *(ROST 1-2)(K2R 26)* **ROLLED GOLD – (THE VERY BEST OF THE ROLLING STONES)** [7] [–]
– Come on / I wanna be your man / Not fade away / Carol / It's all over now / Little red rooster / Time is on my side / The last time / (I can't get no) Satisfaction / Get off my cloud / 19th nervous breakdown / As tears go by / Under my thumb / Lady Jane / Out of time / Paint it black / Have you seen your mother baby, standing in the shadows? / Let's spend the night together / Ruby Tuesday / Yesterday's papers / We love you / She's a rainbow / Jumpin' Jack Flash / Honky tonk women / Sympathy for the Devil / Street fighting man / Midnight rambler / Gimme shelter.

Oct 77. (lp/c) *Arcade; (ADE P/C 32)* **GET STONED** [13] [–]

Oct 82. (d-lp/d-c) *K-Tel; (NE2/CE2 201)* **THE STORY OF THE STONES** [24] [–]

Sep 89. (d-lp/d-c/d-cd) *(820 900-1/-4/-2) / Abkco; <1218>* **SINGLES COLLECTION: THE LONDON YEARS** [ ] [91]
(re-iss. Jun95)

Jun 90. (7") *(LON/+CS 264)* **PAINT IT BLACK. / HONKY TONK WOMAN** [61] [–]
(12"+=/remix-12"+=) *(LONX/+R 264)* – Sympathy for the Devil.

Jul 90. (3xcd-box) *Columbia; (466918-2)* **COLLECTOR'S EDITION** [ ] [ ]

May 99. (cd/c) *Deram; (526771-2/-4) / Abkco; <1268>* **ROCK AND ROLL CIRCUS** (soundtrack with others) [ ] Oct96 [92]
– (Mick Jagger's introduction to Rock And Roll Circus – tracks by JETHRO TULL / The WHO / TAJ MAHAL, MARIANNE FAITHFULL, DIRTY MAC, YOKO ONO & IVRY GITILIS/DIRTY MAC – John Lennon's introduction of The ROLLING STONES):- Jumpin' Jack Flash / Parachute woman / No expectations / You can't always get what you want / Sympathy for the Devil / Salt of the earth.

Sep 03. (7") *Mercury; (981061-3)* **SYMPATHY FOR THE DEVIL (2003 remix by The Neptunes). / (Full Phatt remix)** [14] [ ]
(12"+=) *(981061-5)* – (Fatboy Slim remix).
(cd-s++=) *(981059-9)* – (Neptunes full mix) / (original).

Nov 05. (cd/d-lp) *Virgin; (CDVX/V 3015)* **RARITIES 1971-2003** [ ] [76]

– solo releases –

MICK JAGGER

(see also other single late 1970)

C.B.S. Columbia

Feb 85. (7") *(A 4722)* <04743> **JUST ANOTHER NIGHT. / TURN THE GIRL LOOSE** [32] [12]
('A'extended-12"+=) *(TA 4722)* – ('A'dub version).

Mar 85. (lp/c/cd) *(CBS/40/CD 86310)* **SHE'S THE BOSS** [6] [13]
– Lonely at the top / Half a loaf / Hard woman / Lucky in love / Secrets / Just another night / She's the boss / Running out of luck / Turn the girl loose. *(re-iss. cd Aug95 on 'East West'; 7567 82553-2)*

Apr 85. (7"/12") *(A/TA 6213)* <04893> **LUCKY IN LOVE. / RUNNING OUT OF LUCK** [ ] [38]

Jul 86. (7") <34-06211> **RUTHLESS PEOPLE. / I'M RINGING** [–] [51]
(above from the film 'Ruthless People', issued on 'Epic' records)

Aug 87. (7"/s7") *(651028-7/-0)* <07306> **LET'S WORK. / CATCH US CATCH CAN** [31] [39]
(12"+=) *(651028-6)* – ('A'dance mix).

Sep 87. (lp/c/cd) *(460 123-1/-4/-2)* **PRIMITIVE COOL** [26] [41]
– Throwaway / Let's work / Radio control / Say you will / Primitive cool / Kow Tow / Shoot off your mouth / Party doll / War baby. *(re-iss. cd Aug95 on 'East West'; 7567 82554-2)*

Nov 87. (7"/7"pic-d) *(THROW/+P 1)* <07653> **THROWAWAY. / PEACE FOR THE WICKED** [ ] [67]
('A'remixed; 12"+=/cd-s+=) *(THROW T/C 1)* – ('A'vocal dub mix).

Feb 88. (7") <07703> **SAY YOU WILL. / SHOOT OFF YOUR MOUTH** [–] [ ]

Atlantic Atlantic

Jan 93. (7"/c-s) *(A 7401/+C)* <87410> **SWEET THING. / WANDERING SPIRIT** [24] [84]
(12"+=/cd-s+=) *(A 7410 T/CD)* – ('A'dub mix).

Feb 93. (cd/c/lp) *(<7567 82436-2/-4/-1>)* **WANDERING SPIRIT** [12] [11]
– Wired all night / Sweet thing / Out of focus / Don't tear me up / Put me in the trash / Use me / Evening gown / Mother of a man / think / Wandering spirit / Hang on to me tonight / I've been lonely for so long / Angel in my heart / Handsome Molly. *(re-iss. cd Aug95 on 'East West'; same)*

Apr 93. (7"/c-s) *(A 7368/+C)* **DON'T TEAR ME UP. / EVERYBODY KNOWS ABOUT MY GOOD THING** [ ] [–]
(12"+=/cd-s+=) *(A 7368 T/CD)* – Sweet thing (funky guitar edit).

Jul 93. (7"/c-s) *(A 7332/+C)* **OUT OF FOCUS. / HIPGRASS** [ ] [ ]
(12"+=/cd-s+=) *(A 7332 T/CD)* – ('A'mix).

Virgin Virgin

Nov 01. (cd/d-lp) *(CDVUS/VUSLP 214)* <11288> **GODDESS IN THE DOORWAY** [44] [39]
– Visions of paradise / Joy / Dancing in the starlight / God gave me everything / Hide away / Don't call me up / Goddess in the doorway / Lucky day / Everybody getting high / Gun / Too far gone / Brand new set of rules.

Mar 02. (7") *(VUSP 240)* **VISIONS OF PARADISE. / GOD GAVE ME EVERYTHING (Dan The Automator remix)** 43
(cd-s) *(VUSCD 240)* – ('A'side) / If things could be different / Blue.

MICK JAGGER & DAVE STEWART

DAVE STEWART ex-EURYTHMICS

Oct 04. (cd-s) *(VSCDT 1887)* **OLD HABITS DIE HARD / NEW YORK HUSTLE** 45 –
(cd-s+=) *(VSCDX 1887)* – ('A'-L.A.-acoustic session) / ('A'-footage of recording session).

Oct 04. (cd) *(CDV 2992)* <63934> **ALFIE** (soundtrack)
– Old habits die hard / Blind leading the blind (live acoustic) / New York hustle / Let's make it up / Wicked time (JOSS STONE & NADIRAH "NADZ" featuring MICK JAGGER) / Lonely without you (this Christmas) (MICK JAGGER & JOSS STONE) / Darkness of your love (GARY "MUDBONE" COOPER & DAVE STEWART) / Jack the lad / Oh Nikki / Blind leading the blind / Standing in the rain / Counting the days / Old habits reprise / Alfie (JOSS STONE) / Old habits die hard (with SHERYL CROW).

KEITH RICHARDS

(covers 'A'side= Chuck Berry / 'B'= Jimmy Cliff)

Rolling Stones Rolling S.

Nov 78. (7") *(RSR 102)* <19311> **RUN RUDOLPH RUN. / THE HARDER THEY COME**

Virgin Virgin

Oct 88. (lp/c/cd) *(V/TCV/CDV 2554)* <90973> **TALK IS CHEAP** 37 24
– Talk is cheap / Take it so hard / Struggle / I could have stood you up / Make no mistake / You don't move me / It means a lot / Whip it up / How I wish / Rock awhile / Locked away. *(re-iss. Sep90 on 'Virgin' lp/c/cd; OVED/+C/CD 338)*

Oct 88. (7") *(VS 1125)* <99297> **TAKE IT SO HARD. / I COULD HAVE STOOD YOU UP**
(12"+=/3"cd-s+=) *(VST/VSCD 1125)* – It means a lot.

Apr 89. (7") *(VS 1179)* <99240> **MAKE NO MISTAKE. / IT MEANS A LOT**
(12"+=/cd-s+=) *(VST/VSCD 1179)* – ('A'extended).

Virgin Virgin

Nov 91. (cd/c/lp) *(CDVUS/VUSMC/VUSLP 45)* <91808> **KEITH RICHARDS AND THE X-PENSIVE WINOS LIVE AT THE HOLLYWOOD, PALLADIUM, DECEMBER 15, 1988 (live)** Dec91
– Take it so hard / How I wish / I could have stood you up / Too rude / Make no mistake / Time is on my side / Big enough / Whip it up / Locked away / Struggle / Happy / Connection / Rockawhile.

Oct 92. (cd/c/lp) *(CDVUS/VUSMC/VUSLP 59)* <86499> **MAIN OFFENDER** 45 99
– 999 / Wicked as it seems / Eileen / Words of wonder / Yap yap / Bodytalks / Hate it when you leave / Runnin' too deep / Will but you don't / Demon.

☐ Francis ROSSI (see under ⇒ STATUS QUO)

☐ ROSSINGTON-COLLINS BAND (see under ⇒ LYNYRD SKYNYRD)

☐ Kevin ROWLAND (see under ⇒ DEXYS MIDNIGHT RUNNERS)

ROXY MUSIC

Formed: Newcastle, England . . . 1970 by art school graduate and teacher, BRYAN FERRY alongside GRAHAM SIMPSON. Early in 1971, they invited ANDY MACKAY and electronic wizard BRIAN ENO to join, finally settling with the debut album line-up a year later, when they added PHIL MANZANERA and PAUL THOMPSON. The concept of ROXY MUSIC was the brainchild of FERRY, who attempted to realise his vision of a musical equivalent to the pop art he'd become fascinated with at college. Fashioning the band in an outlandish hybrid of decadent glamour and future shock experimentalism, FERRY made sure ROXY MUSIC would be hot property after only a handful of gigs. At this point, the other prime mover behind ROXY MUSIC was BRIAN ENO, who shaped the band's pioneering sound by wrenching all manner of bizarre electronic noises from his mini-moog, feeding the rest of the instruments through an EMS modular synth and masterminding pre-recorded special effects. Signed to 'Island', the band released their self-titled debut in the summer of 1972. Produced by PETE SINFIELD (the KING CRIMSON lyricist), the album effortlessly fused FERRY's suave crooning, a pulsing rhythm section and ENO's inspired electronic experimentation, garnering rave reviews and defying any attempts to pigeonhole the band's sound. But it was the follow-up single, 'VIRGINIA PLAIN' (1972), which launched the band into pop stardom. A careering blast of avant-pop that managed to incorporate a lyric focusing on one of FERRY's surrealist paintings, the single breached the upper echelons of the charts. By this juncture, SIMPSON had been given his marching orders and the band went through a bewildering succession of personnel changes, FERRY retaining strict control throughout. After another top ten hit with 'PJAMARAMA' in 1973, ROXY MUSIC released their second album, 'FOR YOUR PLEASURE' later the same year. Juxtaposing the ironic wig-out of tracks like 'DO THE STRAND' and 'BEAUTY QUEEN' with the vivid desolation of 'IN EVERY DREAM HOME A HEARTACHE', the album distilled the essence of FERRY's original vision. ENO left soon after, his more extreme experimental leanings at odds with the direction in which FERRY wanted to take the band. FERRY also began a solo career around this time which he ran in tandem with the band, releasing an album of covers, 'THESE FOOLISH THINGS', in 1973. ROXY MUSIC, meanwhile, released their third masterpiece, 'STRANDED', a month later. The first album to feature new recruit EDDIE JOBSON (ex-CURVED AIR), the record was less confrontational but more assured in terms of songwriting, FERRY excelling himself with the haunted romanticism of 'MOTHER OF PEARL' and the sweeping grandeur of 'A SONG FOR EUROPE'. A typically ROXY slice of ambiguous, discordant pop, the single, 'STREET LIFE', gave the band yet another Top 10 hit. By the following summer, FERRY had another solo album on the shelves; 'ANOTHER TIME, ANOTHER PLACE' saw him revelling in the role of slicked-back sophisticate, while ROXY's 'COUNTRY LIFE' saw the band in rock-out mode on tracks like 'THE THRILL OF IT ALL', while still buffing the sound with an ironic sheen. Despite a promising single, 'LOVE IS THE DRUG', 'SIREN' (1975) found FERRY's studied musings sounding jaded. Less then a year later, the band split, with McKAY and MANZANERA off to work on solo projects while JOBSON joined FRANK ZAPPPA. FERRY, meanwhile, concentrated on his burgeoning solo career, hitting Top 5 with the funky 'LET'S STICK TOGETHER', following it up with the good-time album of the same name, for once going a bit easier on the irony. 'IN YOUR MIND' (1977) kept up the momentum, spawning the hit, 'TOKYO JOE', and seeing FERRY branch out into original material. Recorded in L.A. with aging session musicians,

ROXY MUSIC

the sober tones of 'THE BRIDE STRIPPED BARE' (1978) was never going to gain much headway during the height of the punk explosion, yet it remains one the more accessible of FERRY's solo albums. The same year, he cannily reformed ROXY MUSIC, 'MANIFESTO' (1979) heralding a smoother, cleaner sound with the emphasis on FERRY's wistful crooning. The singles 'ANGEL EYES' and 'DANCE AWAY' were the first in a string of tortured pop nuggets that breached the upper reaches of the charts at the turn of the decade, the band finally reaching No.1 with their sublime cover of JOHN LENNON's 'JEALOUS GUY' in 1981. 'FLESH AND BLOOD' (1980) and 'AVALON' (1982) were commercial but finely honed and exquisitely melodic, the latter a quintessentially 80's piece of synthesizer sophistication which inspired many 'New wave-futurist' bands of the 80's. On this high note, FERRY disbanded ROXY MUSIC finally in 1982 and resumed his solo career, carving out a niche as a purveyor of refined, complex adult orientated pop on albums 'BOYS AND GIRLS' (1985) and 'BETE NOIR' (1987). TAXI (1993) saw him return to covers material while 'MAMOUNA' (1994) was an accomplished, mature set of original material. FERRY's first solo album of the new millennium was the ROBIN TROWER-produced 'FRANTIC' (2002), featuring a satisfying combination of choice covers (including a Bob Dylan double header, 'DON'T THINK TWICE IT'S ALRIGHT' and 'IT'S ALL OVER NOW, BABY BLUE') and originals co-written with both DAVE STEWART and BRIAN ENO.

• **Songwriters:** FERRY / MANZANERA with contributions from MACKAY and ENO, until the latter bailed out. They covered; IN THE MIDNIGHT HOUR (Wilson Pickett) / EIGHT MILES HIGH (Byrds) / JEALOUS GUY (John Lennon) / LIKE A HURRICANE (Neil Young). • **FERRY's solo covers:**- A HARD RAIN'S A-GONNA FALL (Bob Dylan) / SYMPATHY FOR THE DEVIL (Rolling Stones) / DON'T EVER CHANGE (Crickets) / THESE FOOLISH THINGS (Col Porter?) / PIECE OF MY HEART (hit; Janis Joplin) / I LOVE HOW YOU LOVE ME (Paris Sisters) / DON'T WORRY BABY (Beach Boys) / TRACKS OF MY TEARS (Miracles) / IT'S MY PARTY (Leslie Gore) / BABY I DON'T CARE (Leiber-Stoller) / WALK A MILE IN MY SHOES (Joe South) / THE IN-CROWD (Dobie Gray) / WHAT A WONDERFUL WORLD (Sam Cooke) / YOU ARE MY SUNSHINE (Ray Charles) / SMOKE GETS IN YOUR EYES (Platters) / HELP ME MAKE IT THROUGH THE NIGHT (Kris Kristofferson) / FINGERPOPPIN' (Hank Ballard) / FUNNY HOW TIME SLIPS AWAY (Jimmy Ellidge) / LET'S STICK TOGETHER (Wilbert Harrison) / THE PRICE OF LOVE (Everly Brothers) / IT'S ONLY LOVE (Barry White) / SHAME SHAME SHAME (Shirley & Company) / HEART ON MY SLEEVE (Gallagher & Lyle) / SHE'S LEAVING HOME + YOU WON'T SEE ME (Beatles) / WHEN SHE WALKS IN THE ROOM (Searchers) / TAKE ME TO THE RIVER (Al Green) / YOU DON'T KNOW (Sam & Dave) / PARTY DOLL (Buddy Knox) / FEEL THE NEED (Detroit Emeralds). Note:- JOHNNY MARR (ex-Smiths) co-wrote THE RIGHT STUFF with him. FERRY returned in 1993 with a covers album 'TAXI'. • **Trivia:** FERRY married model, Lucy Helmore, on the 26th of June '82 after a 70's relationship with Jerry Hall had finished. He was said to have turned down the Keith Forsey-penned song, 'DON'T YOU FORGET ABOUT ME', a No.1 for SIMPLE MINDS.

Album rating: ROXY MUSIC (*8) / FOR YOUR PLEASURE (*9) / STRANDED (*8) / COUNTRY LIFE (*7) / SIREN (*6) / VIVA! ROXY MUSIC (*5) / GREATEST HITS compilation (*8) / MANIFESTO (*6) / FLESH + BLOOD (*5) / AVALON (*7) / THE HIGH ROAD mini (*4) / THE ATLANTIC YEARS 1973-1980 compilation (*8) / Bryan Ferry: THESE FOOLISH THINGS (*7) / ANOTHER TIME, ANOTHER PLACE (*5) / LET'S STICK TOGETHER (*6) / IN YOUR MIND (*5) / THE BRIDE STRIPPED BARE (*6) / BOYS AND GIRLS (*7) / BETE NOIRE (*5) / TAXI (*4) / MAMOUNA (*5) / AS TIME GOES BY (*3) / FRANTIC (*6) / Bryan Ferry & Roxy Music compilations:- STREET LIFE: 20 GREAT HITS (*9) / THE ULTIMATE COLLECTION (*8) / MORE THAN THIS – THE BEST OF . . . (*8) / THE PLATINUM COLLECTION boxed (*9)

BRYAN FERRY (b.26 Sep'45, Washington, Durham, England) – vocals, piano / **ANDY MACKAY** (b.23 Jul'46, London, England) – saxophone, oboe, wind inst. / (BRIAN) **ENO** (b.15 May'48, Woodbridge, Suffolk, England) – synthesizers-keyboards / **GRAHAM SIMPSON** – bass, vocals / **PHIL MANZANERA** (b. PHILIP TARGETT-ADAMS, 31 Jan'51, London) – guitar (ex-QUIET SUN) repl. DAVID O'LIST (ex-NICE) who had repl. original ROGER BUNN (Jul'71). / **PAUL THOMPSON** (b.13 May'51, Jarrow, Northumberland, England) – drums repl. original DEXTER LLOYD (Jul'71).

Island Reprise

Jun 72. (lp/c) *(ILPS/ICT 9200)* *<RS 2114>* **ROXY MUSIC** [10] [ ]
– Re-make/re-model / Ladytron / If there is something / 2 H.B. / The bob (medley) / Chance meeting / Would you believe? / Sea breezes / Bitters end. *(re-iss. Feb77 on 'Polydor' lp)(c; 2302 048)(3100 348) (re-iss. Jan87 & Sep91 on 'EG' lp/c/cd+=; EG LP/MC/CD 6)* – Virginia plain.

— (May'72) **RIK KENTON** (b.31 Oct'45) – bass; repl. SIMPSON

Aug 72. (7") *(WIP 6144)* *<1124>* **VIRGINIA PLAIN. / THE NUMBERER** [4] [ ]

— (Jan'73) **JOHN PORTER** – bass; repl. KENTON who went solo

Island Warners

Mar 73. (7") *(WIP 6159)* **PJAMARAMA. / THE PRIDE AND THE PAIN** [10] [ ]

Mar 73. (lp/c) *(ILPS/ICT 9232)* *<2696>* **FOR YOUR PLEASURE** [4] [ ]
– Do the strand / Beauty queen / Strictly confidential / Editions of you / In every dream home a heartache / The bogus man / Grey lagoons / For your pleasure. *(re-iss. Feb77 on 'Polydor' lp)(c; 2302 049)(3100 349) (re-iss. Jan87 on 'E.G.' lp/c/cd; EG LP/MC/CD 8) (cd+c.Sep91 on 'EG') (re-iss. Feb97 on 'E.M.I.'; LPCENT 19)*

Jul 73. (7") *<7719>* **DO THE STRAND. / EDITIONS OF YOU** [–] [ ]

— (Jul'73) **EDDIE JOBSON** (b.28 Apr'55, Billingham, Teeside, England) – keyboards, violin (ex-CURVED AIR) repl. ENO who went solo

— session bassmen incl. **JOHN GUSTAFSON** (studio) / **SAL MAIDA** (tour) repl. PORTER (other 5= **FERRY, MANZANERA, MACKAY, JOBSON & THOMPSON)**

Island Atco

Nov 73. (7") *(WIP 6173)* **STREET LIFE. / HULA KULA** [9] [–]

Nov 73. (lp/c) *(ILPS/ICT 9252)* *<7045>* **STRANDED** [1] [ ]
– Street life / Just like you / Amazona / Psalm / Serenade / A song for Europe / Mother of pearl / Sunset. *(re-iss. Feb77 on 'Polydor' lp)(c; 2302 050)(3100 350) (re-iss. Jan87 on 'E.G.' lp/c/cd; EG LP/MC/CD 10) (cd+c. Sep91 on 'EG')*

— brought in **JOHN WETTON** (b.1949, Derby, England) – tour bass (ex-FAMILY, ex-KING CRIMSON, etc.) repl. MAIDA

Oct 74. (7") *(WIP 6208)* **ALL I WANT IS YOU. / YOUR APPLICATIONS FAILED** [12] [–]

Nov 74. (lp/c) *(ILPS/ICT 9303)* *<106>* **COUNTRY LIFE** [3] Jan75 [37]
– The thrill of it all / Three and nine / All I want is you / Out of the blue / If it takes all night / Bitter-sweet / Triptych / Casanova / A really good time / Prairie rose. *(re-iss. Feb77 on 'Polydor' lp)(c; 2302 051)(3100 351) (re-iss. Jan87 on 'E.G.' lp/c/cd; EG LP/MC/CD 16) (cd+c.Sep91 on 'EG')*

Nov 74. (7") *<7018>* **THE THRILL OF IT ALL. / YOUR APPLICATIONS FAILED** [–] [ ]

Sep 75. (7") *(WIP 6248)* **LOVE IS THE DRUG. / SULTANESQUE** [2] [–]

Oct 75. (lp/c) *(ILPS/ICT 9344)* *<127>* **SIREN** [4] [50]
– Love is the drug / End of the line / Sentimental fool / Whirlwind / She sells / Could it hapen to me / Both ends burning / Nightingale / Just another high. *(re-iss. Feb77 on 'Polydor' lp)(c; 2302 052)(3100 352) (re-iss. Jan87 on 'E.G.' lp/c/cd; EG LP/MC/CD 20) (cd+c.Sep91 on 'EG')*

Dec 75. (7") *(WIP 6262)* **BOTH ENDS BURNING. / FOR YOUR PLEASURE** [25] [ ]

Dec 75. (7") *<7042>* **LOVE IS THE DRUG. / BOTH ENDS BURNING** [–] [30]

— **RICK WILLS** – tour bass repl. WETTON who stayed on with FERRY

— Disbanded officially mid'76, leaving behind one more album

Jul 76. (lp/c) *(ILPS/ICT 9400)* *<139>* **VIVA! ROXY MUSIC (live 1973-1975)** [6] [81]
– Out of the blue / Pjamarama / The bogus man / Chance meeting / Both ends burning / If there is something / In every dream home a heartache / Do the strand. *(re-iss. Feb77 on 'Polydor' lp)(c; 2302 053)(3100 353) (re-iss. Jan87 on 'E.G.' lp/c/cd; EG LP/MC/CD 25) (cd+c.Sep91 on 'EG')*

— After split ANDY MACKAY continued solo work, as did PHIL MANZANERA. EDDIE JOBSON joined FRANK ZAPPA.

BRYAN FERRY

also had simultaneous solo career. (same labels). He used various session people, including many members of ROXY MUSIC.

Sep 73. (7") *(WIP 6170)* **A HARD RAIN'S GONNA FALL. / 2 HB** 4 [ ]

Oct 73. (lp/c) *(ILPS/ICT 9249)* *<7304>* **THESE FOOLISH THINGS** 5 [ ]
– A hard rain's a-gonna fall / River of salt / Don't ever change / Piece of my heart / Baby I don't care / It's my party / Don't worry baby / Sympathy for the Devil / Tracks of my tears / You won't see me / I love how you love me / Loving you is sweeter than ever / These foolish things. *(re-iss. Aug84 on 'Polydor' lp/c;) (re-iss. Jan87 on 'E.G.' lp/c/cd; EG LP/MC/CD 9)*

May 74. (7") *(WIP 6196)* **THE IN-CROWD. / CHANCE MEETING** 13 –

Jul 74. (lp/c) *(ILPS/ICT 9284)* *<18113>* **ANOTHER TIME, ANOTHER PLACE** 4 [ ]
– The in-crowd / Smoke gets in your eyes / Walk a mile in my shoes / Funny how time slips away / You are my sunshine / (What a) Wonderful world / It ain't me babe / Fingerpoppin' / Help me make it through the night. *(re-iss. Aug84 on 'Polydor' lp/c;) (re-iss. Jan87 on 'E.G.' lp/c/cd; EG LP/MC/CD 14)*

Aug 74. (7") *(WIP 6205)* **SMOKE GETS IN YOUR EYES. / ANOTHER TIME, ANOTHER PLACE** 17 –

Jun 75. (7") *(WIP 6234)* **YOU GO TO MY HEAD. / RE-MAKE RE-MODEL** [ ] –

— Solo again, with ex-ROXY MUSIC men **PAUL THOMPSON** + **JOHN WETTON**. Added **CHRIS SPEDDING** – guitar (ex-SHARKS)

Island Atlantic

Jun 76. (7") *(WIP 6307)* **LET'S STICK TOGETHER. / SEA BREEZES** 4 [ ]

Aug 76. (7"ep) *(IEP 1)* **EXTENDED PLAY** 7 –
– The price of love / Shame shame shame / Heart on my sleeve / It's only love.

Sep 76. (lp/c) *(ILPS/ICT 9367)* *<18187>* **LET'S STICK TOGETHER** 19 [ ]
– Let's stick together / Casanova / Sea breeze / Shame shame shame / 2HB / The price of love / Chance meeting / It's only love / You go to my head / Re-make/re-model / Heart on my sleeve. *(re-iss. Aug84 on 'Polydor' lp/c/cd;) (re-iss. Jan87 on 'E.G.' lp/c/cd; EG LP/MC/CD 24)*

Nov 76. (7") *<3364>* **HEART ON MY SLEEVE. / RE-MAKE/RE-MODEL** – 86

— added **PHIL MANZANERA** – guitar / **ANN ODELL** – keyboards / **MEL COLLINS** – sax / plus many backing singers.

Polydor Atlantic

Jan 77. (7") *(2001 704)* **THIS IS TOMORROW. / AS THE WORLD TURNS** 9 [ ]

Feb 77. (lp/c) *(2302/3100 055)* *<18216>* **IN YOUR MIND** 5 [ ]
– This is tomorrow / All night operator / One kiss / Love me madly again / Tokyo Joe / Party doll / Rock of ages / In your mind. *(re-iss. Jan87 on 'E.G.' lp/c/cd; EG LP/MC/CD 27)*

Apr 77. (7") *(2001 711)* **TOKYO JOE. / SHE'S LEAVING HOME** 15 –

Jun 77. (7") **TOKYO JOE. / AS THE WORLD TURNS** – [ ]

— FERRY continued to use many different musicians, too many to mention.

Apr 78. (7") *(POSP 3)* **WHAT GOES ON. / CASANOVA** 67 [ ]

Apr 78. (lp/c) *(POLD/+C 5003)* **THE BRIDE STRIPPED BARE** 13 [ ]
– Sign of the times / Can't let go / Hold on (I'm coming) / The same old blues / When she walks in the room / Take me to the river / What goes on / Carrickfergus / That's how strong my love is / This island Earth. *(re-iss. Jan87 on 'E.G.' lp/c/cd; EG LP/MC/CD 36)*

Jul 78. (7") *(2001 798)* **SIGN OF THE TIMES. / FOUR LETTER LOVE** 37 –

Nov 78. (7") **SIGN OF THE TIMES. / CAN'T LET GO** – [ ]

Nov 78. (7") *(2001 834)* **CARRICKFERGUS. / WHEN SHE WALKS IN THE ROOM** [ ] [ ]

ROXY MUSIC

re-formed with **FERRY, MANZANERA, MACKAY, THOMPSON,** plus **PAUL CARRACK** – studio keyboards (ex-ACE) / **DAVID SKINNER** – tour keyboards / **GARY TIBBS** – bass (ex-VIBRATORS)

Polydor-EG Atco

Feb 79. (7") *(POSP 32)* **TRASH. / TRASH 2** 40 –

Mar 79. (lp/c)(pic-lp) *(POLH/+C 001)(EGPD 001)* *<114>* **MANIFESTO** 7 23
– Manifesto / Trash / Angel eyes / Still falls the rain / Stronger through the years / Ain't that so / My little girl / ance away / Cry cry cry / Spin me round. *(re-iss. Jan87 on 'E.G.' lp/c/cd+=; EG LP/MC/CD 38)* – Angel eyes (12"disco version).

Apr 79. (7") *(POSP 44)* **DANCE AWAY. / CRY CRY CRY** 2 –

Apr 79. (7") *<7100>* **DANCE AWAY. / TRASH 2** – 44

Aug 79. (7"/ext.12") *(POSP/+X 67)* **ANGEL EYES. / MY LITTLE GIRL** 4 [ ]

May 80. (7") *(POSP 93)* **OVER YOU. / MANIFESTO** 5 –

May 80. (lp/c) *(POLH/+C 002)* *<102>* **FLESH + BLOOD** 1 35
– In the midnight hour / Oh yeah (on the radio) / Same old scene / Flesh and blood / My only love / Over you / Eight miles high / Rain rain rain / No strange delight / Running wild. *(re-iss. Jan87 on 'E.G.' lp/c/cd; EG LP/MC/CD 46)*

May 80. (7") *<7301>* **OVER YOU. / MY ONLY LOVE** – 80

Jul 80. (7") *(2001 972)* **OH YEAH (ON THE RADIO). / SOUTH DOWNS** 5 [ ]

Nov 80. (7") *(ROXY 1)* **SAME OLD SCENE. / LOVER** 12 –

Dec 80. (7") **IN THE MIDNIGHT HOUR. /** – [ ]

— Earlier 1980, CARRACK joined SQUEEZE, and TIBBS joined ADAM & THE ANTS. Session men used at the time **NEIL HUBBARD** – guitar / **ALAN SPENNER** – bass / **ANDY NEWMARK** – drums repl. THOMPSON

E.G. Warners

Feb 81. (7") *(ROXY 2)* *<7329>* **JEALOUS GUY. / TO TURN YOU ON** 1 [ ]

Apr 82. (7"/12") *(ROXY/+X 3)* **MORE THAN THIS. / INDIA** 6 –

May 82. (lp/c) *(EGHP/+C 50)* *<23686>* **AVALON** 1 53
– More than this / The space between / India / While my heart is still beating / Main thing / Take a chance with me / Avalon / To turn you on / True to life / Tara. *(re-iss. Jan87 on 'E.G.' lp/c/cd; EG LP/MC/CD 50) (re-iss. Apr92 on 'Virgin' lp/c; OVED/+C 397)*

Jun 82. (7") *(ROXY 4)* **AVALON. / ALWAYS UNKNOWING** 13 [ ]

Sep 82. (7"/12") *(ROXY/+X 5)* **TAKE A CHANCE WITH ME. / THE MAIN THING** 26 –

Sep 82. (7") *<29978>* **TAKE A CHANCE ON ME. / INDIA** – [ ]

Nov 82. (7") *<29912>* **MORE THAN THIS. / ALWAYS UNKNOWING** – [ ]

— added **GUY FLETCHER** + **JIMMY MAELEN** – keyboards / **MICHELLE COBBS** + **TAWATHA AGEE**

Mar 83. (m-lp/c) *(EGM LP/MC 1)* *<23808>* **THE HIGH ROAD (live)** 26 67
– Can't let go / My only love / Like a hurricane / Jealous guy.

— Had already disbanded again late 1982. MANZANERA and MACKAY became The EXPLORERS, and FERRY went solo again.

BRYAN FERRY

E.G. Warners

May 85. (7") *(FERRY 1)* **SLAVE TO LOVE. / VALENTINE (instrumental)** 10 [ ]
(12"+=) *(FERRYX 1)* – ('A'instrumental).

Jun 85. (lp/c/cd) *(EG LP/MC/CD 62)* *<25082>* **BOYS AND GIRLS** 1 63
– Sensation / Slave to love / Don't stop the dance / A wasteland / Windswept / The chosen one / Valentine / Stone woman / Boys and girls. *(re-iss. Jan87; same) (re-iss. cd+c.Sep91)*

Aug 85. (7") *(FERRY 2)* **DON'T STOP THE DANCE. / NOCTURNE** 21 [ ]
(12"+=) *(FERRYX 2)* – Windswept (instrumental).

Nov 85. (7"/7"pic-d) *(FERRY/FEREP 3)* **WINDSWEPT. / CRAZY LOVE** 46 [ ]
(12"+=) *(FERRYX 3)* – Feel the need / Broken wings.

Mar 86. (7") *(FERRY 4)* **IS YOUR LOVE STRONG ENOUGH. / WINDSWEPT (instrumental)** 22 [ ]
(12"+=) *(FERRYX 4)* – ('A'mix).

Jul 86. (7") **HELP ME. / BROKEN WINGS** – [ ]

Virgin Reprise

Sep 87. (7"/12") *(VS 940/+12)* **THE RIGHT STUFF. / ('A'instrumental)** 37 [ ]
(c-s+=) *(VSC 940)* – ('A'extended) / ('A'dub version).

Nov 87. (cd/c/lp) *(CD/TC+/V 2474)* *<25598>* **BETE NOIRE** 9 63
– Limbo / Kiss and tell / New town / Day for night / Zamba / The right stuff / Seven deadly sins / The name of the game / Bete noire. *(cd re-iss. Dec88; CDVP 2474)*

Feb 88. (7") *(VS 1034)* *<28117>* **KISS AND TELL. / ZAMBA** 41 31
(12"+=)(cd-s+=) *(VST 1034)(CDEP 19)* – ('A'&'B'remixes).

Jun 88. (7") *(VS 1066)* **LIMBO (Latin mix). / BETE NOIRE (instrumental)** [ ] [ ]
(12"+=/cd-s+=) *(VS T/CD 1066)* – ('A'mix).
Feb 93. (7"/c-s) *(VS/+C 1400)* **I PUT A SPELL ON YOU. / THESE FOOLISH THINGS** [18] [ ]
(cd-s+=) *(VSCDX 1400)* – Ladytron (live) / While my heart is still beating (live).
(cd-s) *(VSCDG 1400)* – ('A'-5 mixes).
Mar 93. (cd/c/lp) *(CD/TC+/V 2700)* <45246> **TAXI** [2] [79]
– I put a spell on you / Will you love me tomorrow / Answer me / Just one look / Rescue me / All tomorrow's parties / Girl of my best friend / Amazing Grace / Taxi / Because you're mine.
May 93. (7"/c-s) *(VS/+C 1455)* **WILL YOU LOVE ME TOMMOROW. / A HARD RAIN'S A-GONNA FALL** [23] [ ]
(cd-s+=) *(VSCDT 1455)* – A wasteland (live) / Windswept (live).
(cd-s) *(VSCDG 1455)* – ('A'side) / Crazy love / Feel the need / When she walks in the room.
Aug 93. (c-s) *(VSC 1468)* **GIRL OF MY BEST FRIEND / NOCTURNE** [57] [ ]
(cd-s+=) *(VSCDT 1468)* – Are you lonesome tonight? / Valentine.
(cd-s) *(VSCDG 1468)* – Let's stick together / Boys and girls (live) / The bogus man (live).

—— now with a plethora of musicians

Virgin Virgin
Sep 94. (cd/c/lp) *(CD/TC+/V 2751)* <39838> **MAMOUNA** [11] [94]
– Don't want to know / N.Y.C. / Your painted smile / Mamouna / The only face / The 39 steps / Which way to turn / Wildcat days / Gemini Moon / Chain reaction.
Oct 94. (7"/c-s) *(VS/+C 1508)* **YOUR PAINTED SMILE. / DON'T STOP THE DANCE** [ ] [ ]
(cd-s+=) *(VSCDG 1508)* – In every dream home a heartache (live) / Bete noire (live).
Feb 95. (c-s) *(VSC 1528)* **MAMOUNA / THE 39 STEPS (Brian Eno mix)** [57] [ ]
(cd-s+=) *(VSCDG 1528)* – Jealous guy (live) / Slave to love (live).
Oct 99. (cd/c) *(CD/TC VIR 89)* <48270> **AS TIME GOES BY** [16] [ ]
– As time goes by / The way you look tonight / Easy living / I'm in the mood for love / Where or when / When somebody thinks you're wonderful / Sweet and lovely / Miss Otis regrets / Time on my hands / Lover, come back to me / Falling in love again / Love me or leave me / You do something to me / Just one of those things / September song.
Apr 02. (cd) *(CDVIR 167)* <812138> **FRANTIC** [6] [ ]
– It's all over now, baby blue / Cruel / Goin' down / Goddess of love / Don't think twice, it's alright / Nobody loves me / Ja nun hons pris / A fool for love / Goodnight Irene / Hiroshima (Ash Howes mix) / San Simeon / One way love / I thought.
May 02. (cd-s) *(DINSCD 238)* **GODDESS OF LOVE / WHICH WAY TO TURN / SMOKE DREAMS OF YOU** [ ] [–]

– (FERRY) compilations, others, etc. –

Jun 88. (3"cd-ep) *E.G.; (CDT 10)* **LET'S STICK TOGETHER / SHAME SHAME SHAME / CHANCE MEETING / SEA BREEZES** [ ] [–]
Oct 88. (7") *E.G.; (EGO 44)* **LET'S STICK TOGETHER ('88 remix). / TRASH** [12] [ ]
(12"+=) *(EGOX 44)* – Shame shame shame / Angel eyes.
(cd-s+=) *(EGOCD 44)* – Casanova / Sign of the times.
Nov 88. (lp/c/cd/pic-cd; BRYAN FERRY & ROXY MUSIC) *E.G.; (EG TV/MTV/CTV/CPTV 2)* **THE ULTIMATE COLLECTION** [6] [ ]
– Let's stick together ('88 remix) / The in-crowd / Angel eyes (ROXY MUSIC) / He'll have to go / Tokyo Joe / All I want is you (ROXY MUSIC) / Jealous guy (ROXY MUSIC) / The price of love / Don't stop the dance / Love is the drug (ROXY MUSIC) / This is tomorrow / Slave to love / Help me / Avalon (ROXY MUSIC) / Dance away (ROXY MUSIC).
Feb 89. (7") *E.G.; (EGO 46)* **THE PRICE OF LOVE (R&B mix). / LOVER** [49] [ ]
(12"+=) *(EGOX 46)* – Don't stop the dance (remix) / Nocturne.
(cd-s+=) *(EGOCD 46)* – Don't stop the dance (remix) / Slave to love (remix).
Apr 89. (7") *E.G.; (EGO 48)* **HE'LL HAVE TO GO. / CARRICKFERGUS** [63] [ ]
(cd-s+=) *(EGOCD 48)* – Take me to the river / Broken wings.
(12") *(EGOX 48)* – ('A'side) / Windswept / Is your love strong enough.
Dec 89. (3xc-box/3xcd-box) *E.G.; (EGBM/EGBC 5)* **THESE FOOLISH THINGS / LET'S STICK TOGETHER / BOYS AND GIRLS** (free w / Island Various Artists compilations) [ ] [–]
Oct 95. (cd/c/d-lp) *Virgin; (CD/TC+/V 2791)* **MORE THAN THIS – THE BEST OF BRYAN FERRY & ROXY MUSIC** [15] [ ]
Jul 00. (cd/c) *Virgin; (CDV/TCV 2921)* **SLAVE TO LOVE** [11] [–]
– (with also ROXY MUSIC tracks).

– (ROXY MUSIC) compilations, etc. –

—— on 'E.G.' unless mentioned otherwise
Oct 77. (7") *Polydor; (2001 739)* **VIRGINIA PLAIN. / PJAMARAMA** [11] [ ]
Nov 77. (lp)(c) *Polydor; (2303 073)(3100 407)* **GREATEST HITS** [20] [ ]
– Virginia Plain / Do the strand / All I want is you / Out of the blue / Pjamarama / Editions of you / Love is the drug / Mother of pearl / Song for Europe / Thrill of it all / Street life. *(re-iss. Jan87 on 'E.G.' lp/cd; EG LP/CD 31)*
Jan 78. (7") *Polydor; (2001 756)* **DO THE STRAND. / EDITIONS OF YOU** [ ] [–]
Dec 81. (7xlp-box/7xc-box) *(EG BS/BC 1)* **THE FIRST SEVEN ALBUMS** [ ] [–]
– (ROXY MUSIC / FOR YOUR PLEASURE / STRANDED / COUNTRY LIFE / SIREN / MANIFESTO / FLESH AND BLOOD).
Nov 83. (lp/c)(cd) *(EG LP/MC 54)(815 849-2) / Atco; <90122>* **THE ATLANTIC YEARS 1973-1980** [23] [ ]
Apr 86. (d-lp/c)(cd) (BRYAN FERRY & ROXY MUSIC) *(EGTV/EGMTV/EGCTV 1)* <25857> **STREET LIFE: 20 GREAT HITS** [1] Aug89 [100]
– Virginia plain / A hard rain's a-gonna fall (BRYAN FERRY) / Pjamarama / Do the strand / These foolish things (BRYAN FERRY) / Street life / Let's stick together (BRYAN FERRY) / Smoke gets in your eyes (BRYAN FERRY) / Love is the drug / Sign of the times (BRYAN FERRY) / Dance away / Angel eyes / Oh yeah / Over you / Same old scene / The midnight hour / More than this / Avalon / Slave to love (BRYAN FERRY) / Jealous guy.
Jun 88. (3"cd-ep) *(CDT 8)* **JEALOUS GUY / LOVER / SOUTHDOWN** [ ] [ ]
Dec 89. (3xc-box/3xcd-box) *(EGBM/EGBC 3)* **ROXY MUSIC – THE EARLY YEARS** [ ] [ ]
– (ROXY MUSIC / FOR YOUR PLEASURE / STRANDED)
Dec 89. (3xc-box/3xcd-box) *(EGBM/EGBC 4)* **ROXY MUSIC – THE LATER YEARS** [ ] [ ]
– (MANIFESTO / FLESH AND BLOOD / AVALON)
Oct 90. (cd/c/d-lp) *(EG CD/MC/LP 77)* **HEART STILL BEATIN' (live in France '82)** [ ] [ ]
Oct 90. (7") **LOVE IS THE DRUG (live). / EDITIONS OF YOU (live)** [ ] [–]
(12"+=/cd-s+=) – Do the strand (live).
Oct 94. (3xcd-box) **THE COMPACT COLLECTION** [ ] [ ]
Nov 95. (4xcd-box) *Virgin; (CDBOX 5)* **THE THRILL OF IT ALL – ROXY MUSIC 1972-1982** [ ] [ ]
Apr 96. (c-ep/12"ep/cd-ep) *Virgin; (VS C/T/CDT 1580)* **LOVE IS THE DRUG (Rollo & Sister Bliss Monster mixes; 3) / ('A'-original version)** [33] [ ]
Jun 01. (cd) *Virgin; (CDV 2939)* **THE BEST OF ROXY MUSIC** [12] [–]
Jun 04. (t-cd; as BRYAN FERRY / ROXY MUSIC) *Virgin; (BFRM 1)* <71224> **THE PLATINUM COLLECTION** [17] [ ]

ROYKSOPP

Formed: Tromso, Norway ... early 90's by TORBJORN BRUNDTLAND and his collegue SVIEN BERGE. The pair, who met in college and began recording in the twilight years of the millennium, were signed to R&S offshoot label 'Appolo' (where they issued the 'TRAVELLER'S DREAM' LP under the moniker AEDENA CYCLE), but as their partnership collapsed, so did the deal. They spent years apart, finally re-emerging in 1998 for a few low-key singles, until influential dance label 'Wall Of Sound' snapped them up and released the sublime 'EPLE' EP (2001). Also featuring the track 'POOR LENO', the downbeat, breezy chillout electronica gave many an excuse to dig up their old ENO records (and buy a few rip-off "chill-out" compilation albums while they were at it). The same year ROYKSOPP delivered their debut album 'MELODY A.M.', a multi-textured album full of swirling musical landscapes and stoned sublimeness akin to the likes of FOUR TET, but less experimental than, say, BOARDS OF CANADA. The album, in all its technicoloured glory went on to be nominated for many awards including MTV's "best dance album", although there wasn't really much dancing to be done. Ultimately, ROYKSOPP appealed to those exhausted clubbers, detoxing themselves on a beach somewhere after a night/morning out, or the hard-house freak who thought it was avant garde to listen to something this mellow and strange. As popularity beckoned and the group's music was used in a (shudder) car advert, much was in doubt about the individuality of their music. However, it will take a genius to recreate and reproduce an album that matches the emotional intensity of 'MELODY A.M.'. 'THE UNDERSTANDING' (2005) wasn't quite sophomore slump but critics fudged on the merits of their great leap sideways (onto the nearest dancefloor). A UK Top 20 entry, the beats were faster, crisper, trendier, especially on the likes of coo-ing UK Top 40 single, 'ONLY THIS MOMENT'. While both the hi-hat hiss of the CHELONIS R JONES-featuring '49 PERCENT' and 'WHAT ELSE IS THERE?' (BJORK-y vocals courtesy of the KNIFE's KARIN DREIJER) were also minor British hits, fans of their more abstract impulses could take heart in the MORODER-esque communique, 'SOMBRE DETUNE' or the MICHAEL NYMAN-meets-AIR melancholia of opener 'TRIUMPHANT'.

Album rating: MELODY A.M. (*8) / THE UNDERSTANDING (*6)

TORBJORN BRUNDTLAND + SVEIN BERGE – electronics

Wall Of Sound | Wall Of Sound

Jul 01. (12"/cd-s) *(WALL T/D 071) <5071>* **EPLE / EPLE (Bjorn Torske mix) / ROYKSOPP'S NIGHT OUT** [ ] [ ]

Oct 01. (cd/lp) *(WALL CD/LP 027) <90148>* **MELODY A.M.** [ ] [ ]
– So easy / Eple / Sparks / In space / Poor Leno / A higher place / Royksopp's night out / Remind me / She's so / 40 years back / Come.

Dec 01. (12"/cd-s) *(WALL T/D 073)* **POOR LENO (mixes; edit / Sander Kleinenberg northern beach / Istanbul forever)** [59] [ ]
(12") *(WALLT 073Y)* – ('A'album) / ('A'-Silicone Soul hypno house mix).

Wall Of Sound | Astralwerks

Aug 02. (cd-s) *(WALLD 074X)* **REMIND ME (mixes; radio / James Zabela / SO EASY** [21] [–]
(12") *(WALLT 074X)* – ('A'mixes; Tom Middleton cosmos / Ernest St. Laurent moonfish / someone else's).
(cd-s/12") *(WALL D/T 074R)* – ('A'mixes).

Aug 02. (cd+=; re-) *(as prev) <13352>* **MELODY A.M.** [9] Oct02 [ ]
– mixes:- Remind me (2 mixes + dub) / Poor Leno (2 mixes + dub) / Eple (dub).

Nov 02. (cd-s) *(WALLD 079)* **POOR LENO / POOR LENO (Jakatta mix) / POOR LENO (Royksopp's Istanbul forever mix)** [38] [–]
(cd-s) *(WALLD 079V)* – ('A') / ('A'-Silicone Soul's hypno beat mix) / So easy / ('A'-video).
(12") *(WALLT 079)* – ('A'-Jakatta mix) / ('A'-Silicone Soul's hypno beat mix) / ('A'album version).

Feb 03. (cd-s/12") *(WALL D/T 080)* **EPLE / EPLE (Fatboy Slim remix) / EPLE (shakedown remix)** [16] [–]
(cd-s/12") *(WALL D/T 080 V/X)* – (mises; edit / Boris & Michi's eplistic-scratch-attack / Black strobe).

Jun 03. (cd-s) *(WALLD 084)* **SPARKS / DON'T GO / SO EASY (Derrick Carter so BHQ remix)** [41] [–]
(12") *(WALLT 084)* – (Roni Size remixes).
(12") *(WALLT 084Y)* – ('A') / So easy (Derrick Carter so BHQ remix) / ('A'-Murk downtown Miami mix).
(cd-s) *(WALLD 084V)* – ('A'-Murk downtown Miami mix) / REmind me (someone else's mix) / ('A'-video).

Jul 05. (7") *(WALLS 104)* **ONLY THIS MOMENT. / WHAT ELSE IS THERE (edit)** [33] [–]
(cd-s) *(WALLD 104X)* – ('A') / ('A'-Royksopp's hissage) / Sombre detune.

Jul 05. (cd/d-lp) *(WALL CD/LP 035) <11352>* **THE UNDERSTANDING** [13] [ ]
– Triumphant / Only this moment / 49 percent / Sombre detune / Follow my ruin / Beautiful day without you / What else is there / Circuit breaker / Alpha male / Someone like me / Dead to the world / Tristesse globale. *(ltd d-cd+=; WALLCD 035X)* – Go away / Clean sweep / Boys / Head / Looser now.

Sep 05. (7"pic-d) *(WALLS 107)* **49 PERCENT. / GO AWAY** [55] [–]
(cd-s) *(WALLD 107)* – ('A') / ('A'-Angello & Ingrosso remix) / Curves.
(12") *(WALLT 107)* – ('A'-mixes; Angello & Ingrosso / Ewan Pearson glass half full / M.A.N.D.Y. / original).

Dec 05. (7") *(WALLS 111)* **WHAT ELSE IS THERE. / CLEAN SWEEP** [32] [–]
(cd-s) *(WALLD 111)* – ('A') / ('A'-Thin White Duke edit) / Alpha male (live from Roskilde) / ('A'-video).
(12") *(WALLT 111)* – ('A'-Thin White Duke mix) / ('A'-TRentemoller mix).

RUN-D.M.C.

Formed: Hollis, New York, USA . . . 1982 by JOE SIMMONS (aka RUN) and MC D. (aka DARRYL McDANIELS) along with DJ JAM-MASTER JAY (aka JASON MIZEL) These schoolboy friends had persuaded JOE's brother, RUSSELL (owner of 'Rush' productions and future co-chairman of the seminal 'Def Jam' label) to let them make a record, the result being the seminal 1983 single, 'IT'S LIKE THAT' / 'SUCKER M.C.'S'. Oft quoted as the record which kickstarted modern hip-hop, 'SUCKER M.C.'S' substituted the conventional live backing band of the day for stripped down, pulverising drum machine beats. RUN-D.M.C. also had attitude aplenty, their leather-clad, sneaker-obsessed B-Boy image more accurately reflecting street culture and what was going down in the underground clubs. With the help of RUSSELL, they signed to 'Profile', releasing their eponymous debut the following year. Underscoring their uncompromising vision, the record introduced the group's pioneering marriage of metal and rap on the stinging 'ROCK BOX', subsequently going gold. 1985 saw the group make an appearance in the film, 'Krush Groove' (based on the life of RUSSELL) alongside the likes of KURTIS BLOW and The BEASTIE BOYS as well as releasing a follow-up album, 'KING OF ROCK' (1985), taking their rock/rap hybrid to new extremes. But it was 'RAISING HELL' (1986) which really put RUN-D.M.C. on the map, their genius collaborative effort with AEROSMITH (then in a career trough) on the latter's 'WALK THIS WAY' making them chart stars (Top 5 UK, Top 10 US). From the style frenzy of 'MY ADIDAS' to the vocal wordplay of 'PETER PIPER' and 'IT'S TRICKY' the record led the mid-80's hip hop zeitgeist, becoming the first rap album to go platinum. The BEASTIE BOYS' 1986 debut, 'License To Ill' followed suit, a multi-million seller which topped the US chart and an anarchic joint tour with the BEASTIE's further consolidated RUN-D.M.C.'s reputation as the kings of rap. A year is a long time in hip hop, and by the release of 'TOUGHER THAN LEATHER' (1988), hard hitting young upstarts like PUBLIC ENEMY were crossing over to the lucrative white audience with a vengeance. Although tracks like 'RUN'S HOUSE' and 'BEATS TO THE RHYME' stood up among the best of their earlier work, the record lacked the fire of old, while a film of the same name failed miserably at the box office. 'BACK FROM HELL' (1990) barely scraped into the US charts and though the record had its moments, it failed to remedy the group's critical and commercial decline. A difficult period for them, SIMMONS and McDANIELS had undergone various personal problems, the latter suffering from alcoholism while SIMMONS was accused of rape. They eventually re-emerged three years later on 'DOWN WITH THE KING' (1993), its title a reference to their recent religious conversion. With contributions from the cream of the rap fraternity, the album was a reasonable success, their first foray into the US Top 10 in five years. However, along with the likes of the once mighty JUNGLE BROTHERS,

RAKIM etc., RUN-D.M.C. have failed to re-invent themselves (like old buddies The BEASTIE BOYS), their sound now somewhat dated in a hip hop scene which thrives on constant flux. Although they did finally re-emerge in the new millennium, 'CROWN ROYAL' (2001; although it was scheduled for '99) sounded as tired as their image looked. One time grandmasters of the rock crossover track, RUN-DMC did that legacy few favours on the featured collaborations with LIMP BIZKIT ('THEM GIRLS') and KID ROCK ('THE SCHOOL OF OLD') while even the contributions of NAS and METHOD MAN failed to inject any passion.

Album rating: RUN-D.M.C. (*8) / KING OF ROCK (*7) / RAISING HELL (*8) / TOUGHER THAN LEATHER (*6) / BACK FROM HELL (*6) / RUN-D.M.C.'S GREATEST HITS TOGETHER FOREVER 1983-1991 compilation (*8) / DOWN WITH THE KING (*6) / CROWN ROYAL (*4) / GREATEST HITS compilation (*8)

RUN (b. JOSEPH SIMMONS, 14 Nov'64) – vocals / **D.M.C.** (b. DARRYL McDANIELS, 31 May'64) – vocals / **JAM-MASTER JAY** (b. JASON MIZELL, 21 Jan'65) – turntables, programming

4th & Broad Profile

1983. (7") **IT'S LIKE THAT. / SUCKER M.C.'s** [–] [ ]

Jun 84. (lp) *(1202>* **RUN-D.M.C.** [–] [53]
– Hard times / Rock box / Jam-master Jay / Hollis Crew (krush-groove 2) / Sucker M.C.'s (krush-groove 1) / It's like that / Wake up / 30 days / Jay's game. *(UK-iss.May85 lp/c; BR LP/CA 506) (cd-iss. 1990 on 'London'; 846 561-2) (re-iss. Apr91 on 'Profile' cd/c/lp; FILE CD/CT/R 202) (cd re-iss. Sep99 on 'Arista'; 07822 16406-2)*

Jun 84. (7") *(BRW 8)* **ROCK BOX. / ('A'vocal dub)** [ ] [ ]
(12"+=) *(12BRW 8)* – ('A'dub version).

Sep 84. (7") **30 DAYS. / (instrumental)** [–] [ ]

Jan 85. (7") **HOLLIS CREW. / (instrumental)** [–] [ ]

Feb 85. (lp/c)(pic-lp) *(BR LP/CA 504)(PBRLP 504) <1205>*
KING OF ROCK [ ] [52]
– Rock the house / King of rock / You talk too much / Jam-master jammin' / Roots, rap, reggae / Can you rock it like this / You're blind / It's not funny / Daryll and Joe (krush-groove 3). *(cd-iss. May88; BRCD 504) (re-iss. Apr91 on 'Profile' cd/c; FILE CD/CT 205) (cd re-iss. Sep99 on 'Arista'; 07822 16407-2)*

Mar 85. (7") *(BRW 21)* **KING OF ROCK. / JAM MASTER JAMMIN'** [ ] [ ]
(12"+=) *(12BRW 21)* – You talk too much.

Mar 86. (7") *(BRW 25)* **YOU TALK TOO MUCH. / DARRYL AND JOE (KRUSH-GROOVE 3)** [ ] [ ]
(12"+=) *(12BRW 25)* – ('A'instrumental) / Sucker M.C.'s (krush-groove 1).

Apr 86. (7") **JAM-MASTER JAMMIN'. / (part 2)** [–] [ ]

May 86. (7") **CAN YOU ROCK IT LIKE THIS. / TOGETHER FOREVER** [–] [ ]

London Profile

Jun 86. (7") *(LON 101)* **MY ADIDAS. / PETER PIPER** [62] [ ]
(12"+=) *(LONX 101)* – ('A'instrumental).

Jul 86. (lp/c)(cd) *(LON LP/C 21)(828018-2) <1217>* **RAISING HELL** [41] Jun86 [3]
– Peter Piper / It's tricky / My Adidas / Walk this way / Is it live / Perfection / Hit it run / Raising hell / You be illin' / Dumb girl / Son of Byford / Proud to be black. *(cd re-iss. Sep99 on 'Arista'; 07822 16408-2) (lp re-iss. Jun01 on 'Simply Vinyl'; SVLP 347)*

Jul 86. (7") *<5112>* **WALK THIS WAY. / KING OF ROCK** [–] [4]

Aug 86. (7"; RUN-D.M.C. featuring AEROSMITH) *(LON 104)*
WALK THIS WAY. / ('A'instrumental) [8] [–]
(12"+=) *(LONX 104)* – My Adidas.

Feb 87. (7") *(LON 118) <5119>* **YOU BE ILLIN'. / HIT IT RUN** [42] Oct86 [29]
(12"+=) *(LONX 118)* – ('A'instrumental).

May 87. (7") *(LON 130) <5131>* **IT'S TRICKY. / PROUD TO BE BLACK** [16] Feb87 [57]
(12"+=) *(LONX 130)* – ('A'club tempo mix) / ('A'-Scratchappella) / ('A'reprise).

Sep 87. (7") *(LON 154)* **PETER PIPER. / MY ADIDAS** [ ] [–]
(12"+=) *(LONX 154)* – Walk this way / King of rock.

Nov 87. (7"/7"g-f) *(LON/+G 163)* **XMAS IN HOLLIS. / PETER PIPER** [56] [–]
(12"+=) *(LONX 163)* – My Adidas / Walk this way / King of rock.

Apr 88. (7"/7"pic-d) *(LON/+P 177)* **RUN'S HOUSE. / BEATS TO THE RHYME** [37] [ ]
(12"+=/cd-s+=) *(LON X/CD 177)* – ('A'&'B'instrumental).

Jun 88. (lp/c)(cd) *(LON LP/C 38)(828070-2) <1265>*
TOUGHER THAN LEATHER [13] May88 [9]
– Run's house / Mary, Mary / They call us Run DMC / Beats to the rhyme / Radio station / Papa crazy / Tougher than leather / I'm not going out like that / How d'ya do it Dee? / Miss Elaine / Soul to rock and roll / Ragtime. *(re-iss. Nov92 on 'Profile' cd/c; PCD/PCT 1265) (cd re-iss. Sep99 on 'Arista'; 07822 16409-2)*

Jul 88. (7") *<5211>* **MARY, MARY. / ROCK BOX** [–] [75]

Aug 88. (7"/7"s) *(LON/+S 191)* **MARY, MARY. / RAISING HELL** [ ] [–]
(12"+=) *(LONX 191)* – ('A'instrumental).

M.C.A. Profile

Aug 89. (7"/c-s) *(MCA/+C 1360) <PROF 262>*
GHOSTBUSTERS THEME II. / ('A'instrumental) [65] [ ]
(12"+=/cd-s+=) *(MCA T/CD 1360) <PRO FT/CD 262>* – Pause.

Profile Profile

Nov 90. (7"/c-s) *<(PROF/+C 315)>* **WHAT'S IT ALL ABOUT. / THE AVE** [48] [ ]
(12"+=) *<(PROFT 315)>* – ('A'&'B'instrumentals).
(cd-s+=) *<(PROCD 315)>* – ('A'instrumental) / ('A'version).

Nov 90. (cd/c/lp) *<(FILE CD/CT/R 1401)>* **BACK FROM HELL** [ ] [81]
– Back from hell / Bob your head / Livin' in the city / Sucker DJs / What's it all about / Word is born / Pause / Not just another groove / P upon a tree / Party time / Naughty / Kick the frama lama lama / Groove to the sound / Don't stop. *(cd re-iss. Sep99 on 'Arista'; 07822 16410-2)*

Mar 91. (7"/c-s) **FACES. / BACK FROM HELL (remix)** [ ] [ ]
(12"+=) – ('A'radio mix) / ('A'instrumental).
(cd-s) – (2 'A'versions see above) / (2 'B'versions).
(12") – (4 'A'mixes – 3 above).

Nov 91. (cd/c/lp) *<(FILE CD/CT/R 1419)>* **RUN DMC GREATEST HITS TOGETHER FOREVER 1983-1991** (compilation) [ ] [ ]
– Sucker M.C.'s (krush groove 1) / Walk this way / Together forever (krush groove 4) (live at Hollis Park '84) / King of rock / Run's house / It's tricky / Pause / You be illin' / My Adidas / Here we go (live at The Funhouse) / Rock box / What's it all about / Hard times / Beats to the rhyme / Jam-master Jay / Peter Piper / It's like that / Christmas in Hollis.

Mar 93. (12"/cd-s) *(PROF T/CD 39) <5391>* **DOWN WITH THE KING. / ('A'instrumental)** [69] [21]
(re-iss. Nov93 UK; same)

May 93. (cd/c/lp) *<(FILE CD/CT/R 1440)>* **DOWN WITH THE KING** [44] [7]
– Down with the king / C'mon everybody / Can I get it to yo / Hit 'em hard / To the maker / In the head / Ooh, what ya gonna do / Big Willie / Three little Indians / In the house / Kick it (can I get a witness) / Get open / What's next / Wreck shop / For ten years. *(cd re-iss. Sep99 on 'Arista'; 07822 16412-2)*

Jul 93. (c-s)(12") *(5400)(7400)* **OOH, WHATCHA GONNA DO. / ('A'mixes)** [ ] [–]

Apr 94. (12")(cd-s) *(5405)(7405)* **WHAT'S NEXT. / CAN I GET IT, YO / PIED PIPER** [ ] [–]

Sep 97. (cd-s; RUN-DMC VS JASON NEVINS) *Smile; (SM 9065-2)* **IT'S LIKE THAT (mixes)** [ ] [ ]

Feb 98. (12"/cd-s; RUN-DMC VS JASON NEVINS) *Columbia; <665293-6/-2>* **IT'S LIKE THAT (mixes)** [63] [ ]
(yes! the above version actually hit the UK charts! before it gained another official release)

Mar 98. (10"/c-s/12"/cd-s; RUN-DMC VS JASON NEVINS)
Smile (SM 9065/+4/1/2) **IT'S LIKE THAT (mixes)** [1] [ ]

May 98. (cd) *(FILECD 474)* **TOGETHER FOREVER – GREATEST HITS 1983-1998** (compilation) [31] [–]
– (same as earlier compilation + add recent hit remixes).

Arista Arista

Mar 01. (7") *(74321 84805-7)* **ROCK SHOW. / WALK THIS WAY (with AEROSMITH)** [ ] [–]
(cd-s+=) *(74321 84805-2)* – Peter Piper.

Apr 01. (cd/c/d-lp) *(74321 84063-2/-4/-1) <16400>* **CROWN ROYAL** [ ] [37]
– It's over (with JERMAINE DUPREE) / Queens day (with NAS & The PRODIGY) / Crown royal / Them girls (with FRED DURST) / The school of old (with KID ROCK) / Take the money and run (with EVERLAST) / Rock show (with STEPHAN JENKINS) / Here we go 2001 (with SUGAR RAY) / Ahhh (with CHRIS DAVIS) / Let's stay together (together forever) (with JAGGED EDGE) / Ay papi (with FAT JOE) / Simmons incorporated (with METHOD MAN).

— disbanded November 2002

Apr 03. (12"/cd-s; as RUN DMC featuring JACKNIFE LEE) *(82876 51371-1/-2)* **IT'S TRICKY 2003 (mixes)** 20 –

Apr 03. (cd) *(74321 98060-2)* **GREATEST HITS** (compilation) 15 –
– It's like that (feat. JASON NEVINS) / Walk this way (feat. AEROSMITH) / Sucker MC's / My Adidas / King of rock / It's tricky / Can you rock it like this / You be illin' / Rock box / Run's house / Peter Piper / Bounce / Beats to the rhyme / Jam Master Jay / Hard times / Down with the king / Mary Mary / What's it all about / It's tricky 2003 (feat. JACKNIFE LEE).

– others, etc. –

Sep 86. (7") *4th & Broadway; (BRW 56)* **KING OF ROCK. / ROCK BOX (vocal)** –
(12"+=) *(12BRW 56)* – Jam master Jay.
(12"+=) *(12BRWX 56)* – ('A'-Cut-up version) / Jay's game / Rock box.

Nov 95. (10x12"box) *Profile; (1004)* **12" SINGLES BOX SET** –

Mar 98. (12"; RUN-DMC VS JASON NEVINS) *Time; (TIME 094)* **IT'S LIKE THAT (mixes)** –

May 98. (12"; RUN-DMC VS JASON NEVINS) *Epidrome; (EPD 66665698)* **IT'S TRICKY (mixes)**

Sep 02. (cd) *Arista; <10607>* **GREATEST HITS** (diff. to UK) –

Todd RUNDGREN

Born: 22 Jun'48, Upper Darby, Pennsylvania, USA. In 1967, he and another ex-WOODY'S TRUCK STOP member, CARSTEN VAN OSTEN, formed The NAZZ (taking the name from a YARDBIRDS b-side). In 1968, after supporting The DOORS a year previously, they signed to 'Screen Gems/Columbia'. An eponymous debut album sold moderately, RUNDGREN leaving the band in the middle of '69, after the completion of two further albums of psychedelic metal. In 1970, he became an in-house producer for Albert Grossman's 'Bearsville', his first job being for The AMERICAN DREAM. Later in the year, he formed his own band, RUNT (his nickname), releasing an album of the same name which spawned his first Top 20 hit, 'WE GOTTA GET YOU A WOMAN'. Following a further RUNT album, he decided to use his own name for future releases. In 1972, after taking over the production duties from GEORGE HARRISON on BADFINGER's 'Straight Up' set, he unleashed a truly wonderful solo debut, 'SOMETHING / ANYTHING?'. The double album reached the Top 30, a cut from it, 'I SAW THE LIGHT', making the US Top 20 (a year later Top 40 in the UK). Playing every instrument himself, it encompassed almost every style in the pop/rock pantheon. Among the many highlights were; the aforementioned single, 'HELLO IT'S ME', 'MARLENE', COULDN'T I JUST TELL YOU' and 'COLD MORNING LIGHT'. His next effort, 'A WIZARD, A TRUE STAR' was a wildly ambitious concept piece that attempted to reconstruct psychedelia. Although the record overreached itself, failing commercially as a result, it nevertheless contained a smattering of RUNDGREN gems including 'JUST ONE VICTORY'. Prolific in his songwriting, he returned after only nine months with yet another double set, 'TODD', an unrelentingly snooze-worthy affair. To complement his wide ranging solo work under many styles, TODD formed a band, UTOPIA, who were a much more free flowing, progressive rock/jazz outfit. Their first self-titled outing was released at the end of '74, while RUNDGREN himself worked on his monumental 'INITIATION'. Released in '75, it was largely lambasted by the press, although inside the hour-long lp was the minor classic hit, 'REAL MAN' and the 30-odd minute 'A TREATISE ON COSMIC FIRE' (which was split into three parts). RUNDGREN increasingly seemed to lose his penchant for experimentalism, although UTOPIA's 'RA' album was the exception. The album, 'OOPS! WRONG PLANET' (also 1977), took a more commercial direction, while at the same time, TODD was painstakingly producing MEAT LOAF's grandiose 'Bat Out Of Hell'. For the remainder of the 70's and throughout the first half of the 80's, TODD combined his solo output with UTOPIA releases. Most of these were well-received commercially, although critically, he was often unfairly savaged by the music press. Following UTOPIA's ultimate demise in 1986, RUNDGREN spent a few years studio-bound working on other people's projects before recruiting ex-JOURNEY bassist ROSS VALORY and former TUBES drummer PRAIRIE PRINCE for the impressive, soul-centric live-in-the-studio set, 'NEARLY HUMAN' (1989), featuring an unlikely cover of Elvis Costello's 'TWO LITTLE HITLERS'. While 90's sets like 'NO WORLD ORDER' (1994) and the quasi-lounge revisionism of 1997's 'WITH A TWIST' (which featured makeovers of 'I SAW THE LIGHT' and 'THE DREAM GOES ON FOREVER' amongst others) kept him busy, he increasingly channelled his creative energies into the musical possibilities of the internet. 'ONE LONG YEAR' (2000) gathered together bits and pieces he'd already previewed online, although on the evidence of 'I HATE MY FRICKIN' I.S.P.', RUNDGREN's cyberspace adventures weren't without mishap. Impatient fans waiting for a return to form, greeted 'LIARS' (2004) like a sermon from the mount, TODD's back-to-basics formula evident on tracks such as 'PAST', 'TRUTH' and closer 'LIAR'; his best album for 20 years, no question.

• **Songwriters:** Phenomenal pensmith, although he did fit in a number of near perfect covers; DO YA (Move) / GOOD VIBRATIONS (Beach Boys) / LOVE OF THE COMMON MAN (from West Side Story?) / MOST LIKELY TO GO YOUR WAY (Bob Dylan) / TIN SOLDIER (Small Faces) / STRAWBERRY FIELDS FOREVER + RAIN (Beatles) / IF SIX WAS NINE (Jimi Hendrix) / HAPPENINGS TEN YEARS TIME AGO (Yardbirds) / etc? • **Trivia:** In 1983, TODD co-wrote the Top 20 hit 'KISSING WITH CONFIDENCE' for WILL POWERS (see under Carly SIMON). TODD's others major productions have included GRAND FUNK (1973) / HALL & OATES (1974) / TOM ROBINSON (1978) / TUBES (1979) / PSYCHEDELIC FURS (1982) / etc. Note:- TODD has just released in 1992 a compilation album of his production work.

Album rating: Nazz: NAZZ (*6) / NAZZ NAZZ (*5) / NAZZ III (*5) / compilation:- THE BEST OF NAZZ (*7) / Todd Rundgren: RUNT (*6; as Runt) / THE BALLAD OF TODD RUNDGREN (*7; as Runt) / SOMETHING – ANYTHING? (*9) / A WIZARD, A TRUE STAR (*6) / TODD (*4) / TODD RUNDGREN'S UTOPIA (*4; as Todd Rundgren's Utopia) / INITIATION (*8) / ANOTHER LIVE (*4; as Todd Rundgren's Utopia) / FAITHFUL (*6) / RA (*7; as Utopia) / OOPS! WRONG PLANET (*6; as Utopia) / HERMIT OF MINK HOLLOW (*8) / BACK TO THE BARS (*5) / ADVENTURES IN UTOPIA (*6; as Utopia) / DEFACE THE MUSIC (*6; as Utopia) / HEALING (*5) / SWING TO THE RIGHT (*4; as Utopia) / UTOPIA (*4; as Utopia) / THE EVER POPULAR TORTURED ARTIST EFFECT (*7) / OBLIVION (*4; as Utopia) / POV (*4; as Utopia) / A CAPPELLA (*4) / NEARLY HUMAN (*6) / SECOND WIND (*4) / REDUX '92: LIVE IN JAPAN (*4; as Utopia) / NO WORLD ORDER – LITE (*3) / THE INDIVIDUALIST (*5) / WITH A TWIST (*4) / ONE LONG YEAR (*5) / LIARS (*7) / greatest compilation:- THE BEST OF TODD RUNDGREN "GO AHEAD, IGNORE ME." (*9)

the NAZZ

TODD RUNDGREN – lead guitar, vocals, composer / **ROBERT 'Stewkey' ANTONI** (b.17 Nov'47, Rhode Island, N.Y.) – vocals, piano / **CARSTEN VAN OSTEN** (b.24 Sep'46, New Jersey) – bass, vocals / **THOM MOONEY** (b. 5 Jan'48, Pennsylvania) – drums

Screen Gems | Screen Gems

Sep 68. (7") *(SGC 219 001) <001>* **HELLO IT'S ME. / OPEN MY EYES** 66

Apr 69. (lp) *(SGC 221 001) <SD 5001>* **NAZZ** Oct68
– Open my eyes / See what you can be / Back of your mind / Hello it's me / Wildwood blues / If that's the way you feel / When I get my plane / The lemming song / Crowded / She's goin' down. *<US re-iss. Oct83 on 'Rhino'; 109> <Cd-iss.1990's; R2 70109>*

Apr 69. (7") *(SGC 219 002) <002>* **HELLO IT'S ME. / CROWDED** –

May 69. (lp,red-lp) *<SD 5002>* **NAZZ NAZZ** – 80
– Forget all about it / Not wrong long / Rain rider / Gonna cry today / Meridian Leeward / Under the ice / Hang on Paul / Kiddie boy / Featherbedding lover / Letters don't count / A beautiful song. *<US re-iss. Oct83 on 'Rhino'; RNLP 110> <cd-iss. 1990's; R2 70110>*

May 69. (7") *(SGC 219 003)* <006> **NOT WRONG LONG. / UNDER THE ICE**

Nov 70. (7") <009> **SOME PEOPLE. / MAGIC ME** –

Dec 70. (lp,green-lp) <SD 5003> **NAZZ III** –
– Some people / Only one winner / Kicks / It's not that easy / Old time lovemaking / Magic me / Loosen up / Take the hand / How can you call that beautiful / Plenty of lovin' / Christopher Colombus / You are my window. <*US re-iss. Nov83 on 'Rhino'; RNLP 111*> <*cd-iss. 1990's; 70111*>

—— Had already disbanded early 1970, after completion of III'rd album.

RUNT

—— was formed by **RUNDGREN** now on – lead vocals, guitar / **TONY SALES** – bass / **HUNT SALES** – drums

not iss. Ampex

Nov 70. (7") <31001> **WE GOTTA GET YOU A WOMAN. / BABY LET'S SWING** – 20

Dec 70. (lp) <10105> **RUNT** –
– Broke down and busted / Believe in me / We gotta get you a woman / Who's that man / Once burned / Devil's bite / I'm in the cliche / There are no words / Baby let's swing / The last thing you said / Don't tie my hands / Birthday carol. *(UK-iss.Apr72 on 'Bearsville'; K 44505)* <*US re-iss. Oct87 on 'Rhino'; 70686*> *(cd-iss. May93 on 'Rhino-Bearsville'; 812270686-2)*

—— **N.D.SMART** – drums repl. HUNT who later joined IGGY POP then TIN MACHINE

May 71. (7") <31002> **BE NICE TO ME. / BROKE DOWN AND BUSTED** – 71

May 71. (lp) <10116> **THE BALLAD OF TODD RUNDGREN** –
– Long flowing robe / The ballad / Bleeding / Wailing wall / The range war / Chain letter / A long time, a long way to go / Boat on the Charles / Be nice to me / Hope I'm around / Parole / Remember me. *(UK-iss.Apr72 on 'Bearsville'; K 45506)* <*US re-iss. Oct87 on 'Rhino'; 71109*> *(cd-iss. May93 on 'Rhino-Bearsville'; 812271109-2)*

Aug 71. (7") <31004> **A LONG TIME, A LONG WAY TO GO. / PAROLE** – 92

TODD RUNDGREN

—— now completely solo except for one side of the d-lp which was frequented by session people.

Bearsville Bearsville

Mar 72. (d-lp) *(K 65501)* <2066> **SOMETHING / ANYTHING?** 29
– I saw the light / It wouldn't have made any difference / Wolfman Jack / Cold morning light / It takes two to tango (this is for the girls) / Sweeter memories / (intro) Breathless / The night the carousel burned down / Saving grace / Marlene / Song of the Viking / I went to the mirror / Black Maria / One more day (one word) / Couldn't I just tell you / Torch song / Little red lights / Dust in the wind / Piss Aaron / Hello it's me / Some folks is even whiter than me / You left me sore / Slut. <*US re-iss. Nov87 on 'Rhino'; *> *(re-iss. Jul89 on 'Essential' d-lp/c/cd; ESD LP/MC/CD 007) (re-iss. Jun93 on 'Rhino-Bearsville'; 812271107-2)*

Mar 72. (7") <0003> **I SAW THE LIGHT. / BLACK MARIA** – 16

Mar 72. (7") *(K 15502)* **I SAW THE LIGHT. / MARLENE** –

Jul 72. (7") <0007> **COULDN'T I JUST TELL YOU. / WOLFMAN JACK** – 93

May 73. (7"m) *(K 15506)* **I SAW THE LIGHT. / BLACK MARIA / LONG FLOWING ROBE** 36 –
(re-iss. Nov76)

Jun 73. (lp) *(K 45513)* <213> **A WIZARD, A TRUE STAR** 86
– International feel / Never never land / Tic tic tic it wear off / You need your head / Rock and roll pussy / Dogfight giggle / You don't have to camp around / Flamingo / Zen archer / Just another onionhead – Da da Dali / When the shit hits the fan – Sunset Blvd. / Le feel internacionale / Sometimes I don't know what to feel / Does anybody love you? / I'm so proud – Ooh ooh baby – La la means I love you – Cool jerk / Is it my name? / Just one victory. *(re-iss. Nov80 on 'Island'; IRSP 10) (re-iss. Apr89 on 'Castle' lp/c/cd; CLA LP/MC/CD 134) (re-iss. May93 on 'Rhino-Bearsville' cd; 812270864-2)*

Oct 73. (7") *(K 15509)* **WE GOTTA GET YOU A WOMAN. / COULDN'T I JUST TELL YOU** –

Dec 73. (7") *(K 15513)* <0009> **HELLO IT'S ME. / COLD MORNING LIGHT** Sep73 5

Dec 73. (7") <0015> **SOMETIMES I DON'T KNOW WHAT TO FEEL. / DOES ANYONE LOVE YOU?** –

—— He now used many musicians that were to appear as first UTOPIA incarnation

Mar 74. (d-lp) *(K 85501)* <6952> **TODD** 54
– How about a little fanfare? / I think you know / The spark of life / An elpee's worth of toons / A dream goes on forever / Lord Chancelor's nightmare song / Drunken blue rooster / The last ride / Everybody's going to Heaven / King Kong reggae / Number one lowest common denominator / Useless begging / Sidewalk cafe / Izzat love / Heavy metal kids / In and out of Chakras we go / Don't you ever learn / Sons of 1984. *(re-iss. Dec89 on 'Castle' d-lp/c/cd; CLD LP/MC/CD 177) (re-iss. May93 on 'Rhino-Bearsville' cd; 812271108-2)*

May 74. (7") *(K 15515)* <0020> **A DREAM GOES ON FOREVER. / HEAVY METAL KIDS** 69

—— **TODD** formed UTOPIA with **MOODY KLINGMAN** – keyboards / **RALPH SHUCKETT** – bass / **JOHN SIEGLER** – bass, cello / **M.FROG LABAT** – synthesizers (TODD also released solo material)

Nov 74. (lp; by TODD RUNDGREN'S UTOPIA) *(K 55501)* <6954> **TODD RUNDGREN'S UTOPIA** 34
– Utopia (theme) / Freak parade / Freedom fighter / The ikon. *(re-iss. cd May93 on 'Rhino-Bearsville'; 812270865-2)*

Feb 75. (7") *(K 15519)* <0301> **WOLFMAN JACK. / BREATHLESS** 1974

Jun 75. (lp) *(K 55504)* <6981> **INITIATION** 86
– Real man / Born to synthesize / The death of rock and roll / Eastern intrigue / Initiation / Fair warning / A treatise on cosmic fire: Intro-Prana, (ii) The fire of mind – or solar fire, (iii) The fire of spirit – or electric fire, (i) The internal fire – or fire by friction (Muladhara – The dance of Kundalini / Svadhishthana – Bam, bham, mam, yam, ram, lam, thank you mahm / Manipura – seat of fire / Anahata – the hals of air / Vishudda – sounds beyond ears / Anja – sights beyond eyes / Brahmarandhra – nirvana shakti) / Outro-Prana. *(cd-iss. May93 on 'Rhino-Bearsville'; 812270866-2)*

Sep 75. (7") *(K 15521)* <0304> **REAL MAN. / PRANA** 83

—— trimmed slightly when LABAT departed.

Oct 75. (lp; as TODD RUNDGREN'S UTOPIA) *(K 55508)* <6961> **ANOTHER LIVE (live)** 66
– Another life / The wheel / The seven rays / (intro) – Mister Triscuts / West Side Story theme / Something's coming / Just one victory / Heavy metal kids / Do ya / Just one victory. *(cd-iss. Aug93 on 'Rhino-Bearsville'; 812270867-2)*

Apr 76. (lp) *(K 55510)* <6963> **FAITHFUL** 54
– Happenings ten years time ago / Good vibrations / Rain / Most likely you go your way and I'll go mine / If six was nine / Strawberry fields forever / Black and white / Love of the common man / When I pray / Cliche / The verb "to love" / Boogies (hamburger hell). *(cd-iss. Jun93 on 'Rhino-Bearsville'; 812270868-2)*

Jun 76. (7") <0309> **GOOD VIBRATIONS. / WHEN I PRAY** – 34

Jun 76. (7") *(K 15524)* **LOVE OF THE COMMON MAN. / GOOD VIBRATIONS** –

Nov 76. (7") <0310> **LOVE OF THE COMMON MAN. / BLACK AND WHITE** –

UTOPIA

with **TODD** now completely changed line-up into **ROGER POWELL** – keyboards (from late '75) / **JOHN 'Willie' WILCOX** – drums / **KASIM SULTON** – bass

Jan 77. (lp) *(K 55514)* <6965> **RA** 27 79
– (overture) / Communion with the sun / Magic dragon theatre / Jealousy / Eternal love / Sunburst finish / Hiroshima / Singing and the glass guitar. *(cd-iss. May93 on 'Rhino-Bearsville'; 812270869-2)*

Feb 77. (7") *(K 15531)* <0317> **COMMUNION WITH THE SUN. / SUNBURST FINISH**

—— TODD played/produced 'BAT OUT OF HELL' album for MEAT LOAF, which included some UTOPIANS and was massive seller from 1978 onwards.

Sep 77. (lp) *(K 55517)* <6970> **OOPS! WRONG PLANET** 59 73
– Trapped / Windows / Love in action / Crazy lady blue / Back on the street / Marriage of Heaven and Hell / The martyr / Abandon city / Gangrene / My angel / Rape of the young / Love is the answer. *(cd-iss. Jun93 on 'Rhino-Bearsville'; 812270870-2)*

Oct 77. (7") *(K 15536)* <0321> **LOVE IS THE ANSWER. / THE MARRIAGE OF HEAVEN AND HELL**

TODD RUNDGREN

Apr 78. (lp) *(K 55521)* <6981> **HERMIT OF MINK HOLLOW** 42 36
– All the children sing / Can we still be friends / Hurting for you / Too far gone / Onomatopoeia / Determination / Bread / Bag lady / You cried wolf / Lucky guy / Out of control / Fade away. *(cd-iss. May93 on 'Rhino-Bearsville'; 812270784-2)*

May 78. (7") *(K 15539) <0324>* **CAN WE STILL BE FRIENDS. / DETERMINATION** [ ] [29]
<some US copies had 'OUT OF CONTROL' on B-side>

Jul 78. (7") *<0330>* **YOU CRIED WOLF. / ONOMATOPOEIA** [–] [ ]

Nov 78. (7") *(K 15543)* **ALL THE CHILDREN SING. / BAG LADY** [ ] [–]

Dec 78. (d-lp) *(K 65511) <6986>* **BACK TO THE BARS (live)** [ ] [75]
– Real man / Love of the common man / The verb "to love" / Love in action / A dream goes on forever / Sometimes I just don't know what to think / The range war / Black and white / The last ride / Cliche / Don't you ever learn / Never never land / Black Maria / Zen archer / Medley: I'm so proud – Ooh ooh baby – La la means I love you / I saw the light / It wouldn't have made any difference / Eastern intrigue / Initiation / Couldn't I just tell you / Hello it's me. *(cd-iss. Jun93 on 'Rhino-Bearsville'; 812271109-2)*

Feb 79. (7") *<0335>* **IT WOULDN'T HAVE MADE ANY DIFFERENCE. / DON'T YOU EVER LEARN** [–] [ ]

UTOPIA

Island / Bearsville

Jan 80. (lp/c) *(ILPS/ZCI 9602) <6991>* **ADVENTURES IN UTOPIA** [57] [32]
– The road to Utopia / You make me crazy / Second nature / Set me free / Caravan / Last of the new wave riders / Shot in the dark / The very last time / Love alone / Rock love. *<(cd-iss. May93 on 'Rhino'; 8122 70872-2)>*

Mar 80. (7") *(WIP 6581) <49180>* **SET ME FREE. / UMBRELLA MAN** [ ] [27]

May 80. (7") *<49247>* **THE VERY LAST TIME. / LOVE ALONE** [–] [76]

Oct 80. (lp) *(ILPS 9642) <3487>* **DEFACE THE MUSIC** [ ] [65]
– I just want to touch you / Crystal ball / Where does the world go to hide / Silly boy / Alone / That's not right / Take it home / Hoi poloi / Life goes on / Feel too good / Always late / All smiles / Everybody else is wrong. *(cd-iss. May93 on 'Rhino-Bearsville'; 812270873-2)*

Oct 80. (7") *<49545>* **SECOND NATURE. / YOU MAKE ME CRAZY** [–] [ ]

Nov 80. (7"ep) *(IEP 12)* **I JUST WANT TO TOUCH YOU EP** [ ] [–]
– I just want to touch you / Silly boy / Life goes on / All smiles.

Dec 80. (7") *<49579>* **I JUST WANT TO TOUCH YOU. / ALWAYS LATE** [–] [ ]

TODD RUNDGREN

Feb 81. (7") *<49696>* **TIME HEALS. / TINY DEMONS** [–] [ ]

Feb 81. (lp) *(ILPS 9567) <3522>* **HEALING** [ ] [48]
– Healer / Pulse / Flesh / Golden goose / Compassion / Shine / Healing (part 1, 2 & 3). *(free-7"ltd.w.a.)* – TIME HEALS. / TINY DEMONS *(re-iss. Dec81 on 'Avatar' lp/c; AALP/BHS 3522) (cd-iss. May93 on 'Rhino-Bearsville'; 812270874-2)*

Jan 82. (7") *<49771>* **COMPASSION. / HEALING** [–] [ ]

UTOPIA

Avatar / Bearsville

Mar 82. (lp) *(BRK <3666>)* **SWING TO THE RIGHT** [ ] [ ]
– Swing to the right / Lysistrata / The up / Junk rock (million monkeys) / Shinola / For the love of money / Last dollar on Earth / Fahrenheit 451 / Only human / One world. *(cd-iss. Mar93 on 'Rhino-Bearsville'; 812270785-2)*

Apr 82. (7") *<50062>* **ONE WORLD. / SPECIAL INTEREST** [–] [ ]

May 82. (7") *(AAA 126)* **ONE WORLD. / JUNK ROCK (MILLION MONKEYS)** [ ] [–]

Jun 82. (7") *<29947>* **LYSISTRATA / JUNK ROCK (MILLION MONKEYS)** [–] [ ]

Nov 82. (7"ep) *(AVAB 1)* **TIME HEALS / TINY DEMONS / I SAW THE LIGHT / CAN WE STILL BE FRIENDS** [ ] [–]

Epic / Network

Nov 82. (7") *(EPCA 2972) <69859>* **FEET DON'T FAIL ME NOW. / FORGOTTEN BUT NOT GONE** [ ] [82]

Nov 82. (lp/c) *(EPC/40 25207) <60183>* **UTOPIA** [ ] [84]
– Libertine / Bad little actress / Feet don't fail me now / Neck on up / Say yeah / Call it what you will / I'm looking at you but I'm talking to myself / Hammer in the heart / Burn three times / There goes my inspiration. *(w/ free UK+US m-lp)* – Princess of the universe / Infrared and ultraviolet / Forgotten but not gone / Private Heaven / Chapter and verse. *(cd-iss. Aug93 on 'Rhino-Bearsville'; 812270713-2)*

Jan 83. (7") *<69859>* **HAMMER IN MY HEART. / I'M LOOKING AT YOU BUT I'M TALKING TO MYSELF** [–] [ ]

TODD RUNDGREN

Lambourghini / Bearsville

Mar 83. (7") *<29686>* **BANG THE DRUM ALL DAY. / CHANT** [–] [63]

Aug 83. (lp/c) *(LMGLP/ZCLMG 2000) <23732>* **THE EVER POPULAR TORTURED ARTIST EFFECT** [ ] Feb83 [66]
– Hideaway / Influenza / Don't hurt yourself / There goes my baybay / Tin soldier / Emperor of the highway / Bang the drum all day / Drive / Chant. *(cd-iss. Jun93 on 'Rhino-Bearsville'; 812270876-2)*

Aug 83. (7") *(LMG 1)* **BANG THE DRUM ALL DAY. / DRIVE** [ ] [–]

Sep 83. (7") *<29759>* **HIDEAWAY. / EMPEROR OF THE HIGHWAY** [–] [ ]

UTOPIA

W.E.A. / Passport

Apr 84. (lp/c) *(WX 4/+C) <6029>* **OBLIVION** [ ] [74]
– Itch in my brain / Love with a thinker / Bring me my longbow / If I didn't try / Too much water / Maybe I could change / Crybaby / Welcome to my revolution / Winston Smith takes it on the jaw / I will wait.

May 84. (7") *(YZ 5) <7923>* **CRYBABY. / WINSTON SMITH TAKES IT ON THE JAW** [ ] [ ]

Jul 84. (7") *(YZ 11)* **LOVE WITH A THINKER. / WELCOME TO MY REVOLUTION** [ ] [–]

Food For Thought / Passport

Jun 85. (lp/c) *(GRUB 5) <6044>* **POV** [ ] May 85 [ ]
– Play this game / Style / Stand for something / Secret society / Zen machine / Mated / Wildlife / Mimi gets mad / Mystified / More light.

Jun 85. (7") *(YUM 107)* **MATED. / MAN OF ACTION** [ ] [–]

Jun 85. (7") *<7927>* **MATED. / STAND FOR SOMETHING** [–] [ ]

—— (Oct85) TODD is credited on duet with BONNIE TYLER on single 'LOVING YOU IS A DIRTY JOB'.

TODD RUNDGREN

Warners / Warners

Oct 85. (7") *(W 8852) <28821>* **SOMETHING TO FALL BACK ON. / LOCKJAW** [ ] [ ]
(12"+=) *(WT 8862)* – ('A'dance mix).

Nov 85. (lp/c) *(925128-1/-4) <25128>* **A CAPPELLA** [ ] [ ]
– Blue Orpheus / Johnee Jingo / Pretending to care / Hodja / Lost horizon / Something to fall back on / Miracle in the bazaar / Lockjaw / Honest work / Mighty love.

—— Early in 1986, UTOPIA split and ROGER POWELL went solo. TODD returned to solo work in 1988 augmented by **ROSS VALORY** – bass (ex-JOURNEY) / **PRAIRIE PRINCE** – drums (ex-TUBES) (same label)

May 89. (lp/c/cd) *(K 92588-1/-4/-2) <25881>* **NEARLY HUMAN** [ ] [ ]
– The want of a nail / The waiting game / Parallel lines / Can't stop running / Unloved children / Fidelity / Feel it / Hawking / I love my life. *(cd+=)* – Two little Hitlers.

May 89. (7") *<22868>* **PARALLEL LINES. / I LOVE MY LIFE** [–] [ ]

Feb 91. (cd/c/lp) *(7599-26478-2/-4/-1) <26478>* **SECOND WIND** [ ] [ ]
– Change myself / Love science / Who's sorry now / The smell of money / If I have to be alone / Love in disguise / Kindness / Public servant / Goya's eyes / Second wind.

Jun 93. (cd/c) *<(8122-71185-2/-4)>* **REDUX '92: LIVE IN JAPAN (Utopia live)** [ ] [ ]
– Fix your gaze / Zen machine / Trapped / Princess of the universe / Abandon city / Hammer in my heart / Swing to the right / Ikon / Hiroshima / Back on the street / Only human / Love in action / Caravan / Last of the new wave riders / One world / Love is the answer.

Food For Thought / Rhino

Sep 94. (d-cd/d-c) *(CD/C+/GRUB 30) <R2/R4 71266>* **NO WORLD ORDER / LITE** [ ] Jul93 [ ]
– Worldwide epiphany / No world order / Worldwide epiphany / Day job / Property / Fascist Christ / Love thing / Time stood still / Proactivity / No world order / World epiphany / Time stood still / Love thing / Time stood still / World made flesh / Fever broke. *(d-cd+=)* – (10 different versions of above).

not iss. / Pony Canyon

1995. (cd; as TR-i) *<00720>* **THE INDIVIDUALIST** [–] [ ]
– Tables will turn / If not now, when? / Family values / The ultimate crime /

Espresso (all jacked up) / The individualist / Cast the first stone / Beloved infidel / Temporary sanity / Woman's world.

E.M.I. E.M.I.

Oct 97. (cd) <(859866-2)> **WITH A TWIST** (re-workings in acoustic/lounge style)
– I saw the light / Influenza / Can we still be friends / Mated / It wouldn't have made any difference / Love is the answer / Fidelity / Never neverland / Hello it's me / I want you / The dream goes on forever.

Artemis Artemis

Jun 00. (cd) <(69967 75104-2)> **ONE LONG YEAR**
– I hate frickin I.S.P. / Buffalo grass / Jerk / Bang on the ukulele daily / Where does the time go? / Love of the common man / Mary and the holy ghost (instrumental) / Yer fast (and I like it) / Hit me like a train / The surf talks.

Sanctuary Sanctuary

Apr 04. (cd) *(SANCD 277)* <86357> **LIARS**
– Truth / Sweet / Happy anniversary / Soul brother / Stood up / Mammon / Future / Past / Wondering / Flaw / Afterlife / Living / God said / Liar.

– compilations, etc. –

1984. (lp; by NAZZ) *Rhino;* <RNLP 116> **THE BEST OF NAZZ** –

Nov 87. (lp/c/cd; UTOPIA) *Passport;* <PB/+C/CD 6053> **TRIVIA** –

Feb 88. (d-lp/c/cd; by TODD RUNDGREN) *Raw Power; (RAW LP/TC/CD 035)* **ANTHOLOGY** 1989
– Can we still be friends / All the children sing / Too far gone / Sweet memories / It wouldn't have made any difference / Hello it's me / I saw the light / Just one victory / Love of the common man / The verb 'to love' / Sometimes I don't know what to feel / Couldn't I just tell you / Tiny demons / Initiation / Real man / A long time a long way to go / Long flowing robe / Compassion / We gotta get you a woman / A dream goes on forever / The last ride / Don't you ever learn / Bang the drum all day / Zen archer.

Mar 88. (d-lp/d-c/d-cd; by RUNT /+/ TODD RUNDGREN) *That's Original; (TFO LP/MC/CD 3)* **RUNT / HERMIT OF MINK HOLLOW** –

Mar 88. (d-lp/d-c/d-cd; by UTOPIA) *That's Original; (TFO LP/MC/CD 9)* **OOPS! SORRY WRONG PLANET / ADVENTURES IN UTOPIA** –

Jun 88. (d-lp/d-c/d-cd; by UTOPIA) *Castle; (CCS LP/MC/CD 181)* **THE UTOPIA COLLECTION** –
– Where does the world go to hide / Freedom fighters / All smiles / Lysistrata / Always late / Love in action / Rock love / Set me free / The seven rays / Traped / Swing to the right / One world / Heavy metal kids / The very last time / Crazy lady blue / Feel too good / Love alone / Love is the answer.

Sep 88. (cd-ep) *Special Edition; (CD 3-6)* **BANG THE DRUM ALL DAY / I SAW THE LIGHT / CAN WE STILL BE FRIENDS / ALL THE CHILDREN SING** –

Oct 88. (7") *Old Gold; (OG)* **I SAW THE LIGHT. / (other artist)** –

1989. (d-lp; by TODD RUNDGREN) *Rhino;* <R1 71491> **ANTHOLOGY (1968-1985)** –
(UK-iss.d-cd Aug93 on 'Rhino-Bearsville';)

Apr 92. (cd) *Rhino;* <R2> **AN ELPEE'S WORTH OF PRODUCTIONS** (various) –

May 95. (cd; by UTOPIA) *Rhino; (8122 70892-2)* **ANTHOLOGY**

Jul 96. (cd; as UTOPIA) *Rhino; (8122 72287-2)* **THE PASSPORT COLLECTION**

Apr 98. (cd) *Canyon; (PCCY 01121)* **UP AGAINST IT**

RUSH

Formed: Toronto, Canada . . . 1969 by ALEX LIFESON, GEDDY LEE and JOHN RUTSEY. Initially a hard-rock power outfit in the classic British mould of CREAM and LED ZEPPELIN, they toured local bars and clubs, culminating in a hometown support slot with the NEW YORK DOLLS. Immediately prior to this (1973), RUSH formed their own label, 'Moon', issuing a cover of Buddy Holly's 'NOT FADE AWAY' as their debut 45. An eponymous debut followed in early '74 and was soon picked up by DJ, Donna Halper, who sent a copy to Cliff Burnstein at 'Mercury' records. The company signed RUSH for a 6-figure sum, re-mixing (courtesy of Terry 'Broon' Brown) and re-releasing the record to minor US success (bubbled under the Top 100). Although a tentative start, GEDDY's helium-laced shrill was employed to stunning effect on tracks such as 'WORKING MAN', 'FINDING MY WAY' and 'WHAT YOU'RE DOING'. However, with drummer NEIL PEART replacing RUTSEY, RUSH began to develop the unique style which would characterise their classic 70's work. As well as being a consummate sticksman, PEART masterminded the band's lyrical flights of fantasy, beginning with 'FLY BY NIGHT' (1975). With the conceptually similar YES still world-beating favourites, RUSH found it difficult to progress commercially. Creatively however, the trio attempted to wrestle the symphonic-rock crown from their transatlantic neighbours with such mystical, grandiose fare as 'BY-TOR AND THE SNOW DOG'. Later the same year, they released the under par 'CARESS OF STEEL', which featured the self-indulgently lengthy 'FOUNTAIN OF LAMNETH'. This stage of RUSH's career reached its zenith in 1976 with the concept album, '2112', based on the work of novelist and philosopher Ayn Rand. Boasting a spectacular side-long 20-minute title track/overture, this feted prog-rock/sci-fi classic gave RUSH their long-awaited breakthrough, the record almost achieving a US Top 60 placing. In the course of the previous three years, the band's fanbase had swelled considerably, enabling them to get away with releasing a live double set, 'ALL THE WORLD'S A STAGE'. Featuring electrifying renditions of RUSH's most exquisite material to date, the album was hailed as an instant classic, its Top 40 success in the States leading to massive import sales in Europe. This persuaded the band to bring their live show to Britain/Europe, their wildly enthusiastic reception encouraging them to stay on in Wales and record 'A FAREWELL TO KINGS'. Not surprisingly, the album made the UK (& US) Top 40, its success boosted by a UK Top 40 hit/EP, 'CLOSER TO THE HEART' early the following year. 1978's 'HEMISPHERES' set was the last to feature PEART's trademark epics, the album consolidating the band's growing UK support, while their native Canada lavished upon them the title, 'Ambassadors Of Music'. While many bands of their ilk floundered critically, RUSH began the 80's on a high note, scoring a rare UK Top 20 hit single with 'THE SPIRIT OF RADIO'. Taken from their million-selling 'PERMANENT WAVES' opus, the track was characteristic of the shorter, leaner sound that RUSH would pursue throughout the coming decade. Not escaping the increasing technological influence of 80's music, the band adopted a more keyboard-orientated approach on albums such as 'MOVING PICTURES' (1981), 'SIGNALS' (1982), 'GRACE UNDER PRESSURE' (1984) and 'POWER WINDOWS' (1985). Finally parting company with their longstanding producer, TERRY BROWN, they further refined their sound on the 1987 album, 'HOLD YOUR FIRE', which spawned a near UK Top 40 single, 'TIME STAND STILL' (credited AIMEE MANN of 'TIL TUESDAY). After the compulsory live set, 'A SHOW OF HANDS', the band opted for a fresh start with 'Atlantic', 'PRESTO' (1989) being the first fruits of this new alliance. Incredibly, despite regular critical derision from the trendier sections of the music press, RUSH went on to even greater success in the 90's, both 'ROLL THE BONES' (1991) and 'COUNTERPARTS' (1993) making the US Top 5 (now only Top 30 in Britain!). Certainly, PRIMUS' well-documented admiration has done the band no harm, LIFESON even bringing in the latter band's LES CLAYPOOL for a guest spot on his ill-advised VICTOR project. The same year (1996), RUSH released their umpteenth set, 'TEST FOR ECHO', the band looking good for their 30th anniversary just prior to the millennium. Of late (November 2000 to be exact), GEDDY LEE has become a solo artist, releasing his debut solo album 'MY FAVOURITE HEADACHE' to lukewarm reviews. Despite a traumatic time for PEART in his personal life, losing both his wife and daughter within a year of each other, RUSH re-emerged in 2002 with 'VAPOR TRAILS'. Solid and thoughtful, it proved the Canadians were still relevant in the new millennium even if they were long past their 30th anniversary. With 'RUSH IN RIO' (2003), moreover, they not only proved they could still push boundaries on stage, they also proved that there's still a huge, wildly appreciative audience for their work. PEART especially, can be heard going for broke here, both feeding on, and thriving off, the kind of energy that perhaps can only be generated by the exuberance of a Latin audience. Also to mark over 30 years in the business, RUSH chose to get their Prog teeth into covering songs written prior to their conception. 'FEEDBACK' (2004), an EP/mini-set showed GEDDY and Co at ease with such gems as SUMMERTIME BLUES (Eddie Cochran), HEART FULL OF SOUL + SHAPES OF THINGS (Yardbirds), FOR WHAT IT'S WORTH + MR. SOUL (Buffalo Springfield), THE SEEKER (the Who), SEVEN AND SEVEN IS (Love) and Robert Johnson's CROSSROADS, better known to Cream fans.

• **Trivia:** Early in 1982, GEDDY guested for BOB & DOUG McKENZIE (aka Rick Moranis & Dave Thomas) on their US Top 20 single 'Take Off'.

Album rating: RUSH (*6) / FLY BY NIGHT (*6) / CARESS OF STEEL (*5) / 2112 (*8) / ALL THE WORLD'S A STAGE (*8) / A FAREWELL TO KINGS (*7) / HEMISPHERES (*6) / PERMANENT WAVES (*6) / MOVING PICTURES (*7) / EXIT . . . STAGE LEFT (*5) / SIGNALS (*6) / GRACE UNDER PRESSURE (*5) / POWER WINDOWS (*5) / HOLD YOUR FIRE (*5) / A SHOW OF HANDS (*5) / PRESTO (*5) / CHRONICLES compilation (*7) / ROLL THE BONES (*5) / COUNTERPARTS (*4) / TEST FOR ECHO (*5) / DIFFERENT STAGES live compilation (*5) / VAPOR TRAILS (*5) / RUSH IN RIO (*7) / THE SPIRIT OF RADIO: GREATEST HITS 1974-1987 compilation (*8) / FEEDBACK mini (*6) / Alex Lifeson: VICTOR (*3) / Geddy Lee: MY FAVOURITE HEADACHE (*5)

GEDDY LEE (b. GARY LEE WEINRIB, 29 Jul'53, Willowdale, Toronto, Canada) – vocals, bass, keyboards / **ALEX LIFESON** (b. ALEX ZIVOJINOVICH, 27 Aug'53, Surnie, British Columbia, Canada) – lead guitar / **JOHN RUTSEY** – drums

not iss. | Moon

1973. (7") **NOT FADE AWAY. / YOU CAN'T FIGHT IT** [–] [ ]

Mercury | Mercury

Aug 74. (7") *<73623>* **FINDING MY WAY. /** [–] [ ]

Feb 75. (lp) *(9100 011) <1011>* **RUSH** [ ] Jul74 [ ]
– Finding my way / Need some love / Take a friend / Here again / What you're doing / In the mood / Before and after / Working man. *(c-iss.Apr82; 7142 365) (re-iss. Jun83 lp/c; PRICE/PRIMC 18) (cd-iss. Apr87; 822 541-2)*

Feb 75. (7") *<73647>* **WHAT YOU'RE DOING. / IN THE MOOD** [–] [ ]

—— (Autumn '74) **NEIL PEART** (b.12 Sep'52, Hamilton, Ontario, Canada) – drums, vocals, lyrics repl. RUTSEY

Apr 75. (lp) *(9100 013) <1023>* **FLY BY NIGHT** [ ] Feb75 [ ]
– Anthem / Best I can / Beneath, between and behind / By-Tor & the snowdog: (i) At the tobes of Hades – (ii) Across the Styx – (iii) Of the battle – (iv) Epilogue / Fly by night / Making memories / Rivendell / In the end. *(c-iss.Apr82; 7142 389) (re-iss. Jun83 lp/c; PRICE/PRIMC 19) (cd-iss. Apr87; 822 542-2)*

May 75. (7") *<73681>* **FLY BY NIGHT. / ANTHEM** [–] [ ]
<re-iss. Dec77; 73990>

Nov 75. (7") *<73737>* **BASTILLE DAY. / LAKESIDE PARK** [–] [ ]

Mar 76. (lp) *(9100 018) <1046>* **CARESS OF STEEL** [ ] Oct75 [ ]
– Bastille day / I think I'm going bald / Lakeside Park / The necromancer: (I) Unto darkness – (II) Under the shadow – (III) REturn of the prince / In the valley / Didacts and narpets / No one at the bridge / Panacea / Bacchus plateau / The fountain. *(c-iss.Apr82; 7142 421) (re-iss. Jun83 lp/c; PRICE/PRIMC 20) (cd-iss. Apr87; 822 543-2)*

Jun 76. (lp) *(9100 039) <1079>* **2112** [ ] Apr76 [61]
– Overture / The temples of Syrinx / Discovery / Presentation / Oracle. The dream / Soliliquy / Grand finale / A passage to Bangkok / The twilight zone / Lessons / Tears / Something for nothing. *(re-iss. Jan85 lp/c; PRICE/PRIMC 79) (cd-iss. Apr87; 822 545-2)*

Jun 76. (7") *<73803>* **LESSONS. / THE TWILIGHT ZONE** [–] [ ]

Mar 77. (d-lp) *(6672 015) <7508>* **ALL THE WORLD'S A STAGE (live)** [ ] Sep76 [40]
– Bastille day / Anthem / Fly by night / In the mood / Something for nothing / Lakeside park / Overture / The temple of Syrinx / Presentation / Soliloquy / Grand finale / By-Tor and the snowdog / In the end / Working man / Finding my way / What you're doing. *(c-iss.Apr78; 7553 047) (re-iss. Sep84 d-lp/d-c; PRID/+C 1) (cd-iss. Apr87 – = a few tracks; 822 552-2)*

Dec 76. (7") *<73873>* **FLY BY NIGHT (live). / IN THE MOOD (live) / SOMETHING FOR NOTHING (live)** [–] [88]

Feb 77. (7") *<73912>* **THE TEMPLES OF SYRINX. / MAKING MEMORIES** [–] [ ]

Sep 77. (lp) *(9100 042) <1184>* **A FAREWELL TO KINGS** [22] [33]
– A farewell to kings / Xanadu / Closer to the heart / Cinderella man / Madrigal / Cygnus X-1. *(re-iss. Apr86 lp/c; PRICE/PRIMC 92) (cd-iss. Apr87; 822 546-2)*

Nov 77. (7") *<73958>* **CLOSER TO THE HEART. / MADRIGAL** [–] [76]

Jan 78. (7"ep) *(RUSH 7)* **CLOSER TO THE HEART. / BASTILLE DAY / THE TEMPLES OF SYRINX** [36] [–]
(12"ep+=) *(RUSH 12)* – Anthem.

Nov 78. (lp)(c)<US-pic-lp> *(9100 059)(7142 647) <3743>* **HEMISPHERES** [14] [47]
– Prelude / Apollo (bringer of wisdom) Hemispheres / Dionysus (bringer of love) / Armageddon (the battle of heart and mind) / Cygnus (bringer of balance) / The sphere (a kind of dream) / Circumstances / The trees / La villa Strangiato. *(cd-iss. Apr87; 822 547-2) (re-iss. Mar88 lp/c; PRICE/PRIMC 118)*

Jan 79. (7") *<74051>* **CIRCUMSTANCES. / THE TREES** [–] [ ]

Jan 80. (lp)(c) *(9100 071)(7142 720) <4001>* **PERMANENT WAVES** [3] [4]
– Spirit of radio / Freewill / Jacob's ladder / Entre nous / Different strings / Natural science. *(cd-iss. Apr87; 822 548-2)*

Feb 80. (7") *<76044>* **SPIRIT OF RADIO. / CIRCUMSTANCES** [–] [51]

Feb 80. (7") *(RADIO 7)* **SPIRIT OF RADIO. / THE TREES** [13] [–]
(12"+=) *(RADIO 12)* – Working man.

Apr 80. (7") *<76060>* **DIFFERENT STRINGS. / ENTRE NOUS** [–] [ ]

Feb 81. (7") *<76095>* **LIMELIGHT. / XYZ** [–] [55]

Feb 81. (lp/c) *(6337/7141 160) <4013>* **MOVING PICTURES** [3] [3]
– Tom Sawyer / Red Barchetta / XYZ / Limelight / The camera eye / Witch hunt (part III of fear) / Vital signs. *(cd-iss. 1983; 800 048-2)*

Mar 81. (7") *(VITAL 7)* **VITAL SIGNS. / IN THE MOOD** [41] [–]
(12"+=) *(VITAL 12)* – A passage to Bangkok / Circumstances.

May 81. (7") *<76109>* **TOM SAWYER. / WITCH HUNT** [–] [44]

Oct 81. (7") *<76124>* **FREEWILL (live). / CLOSER TO THE HEART (live)** [–] [ ]

Oct 81. (d-lp/d-c) *(6619/7558 053) <7001>* **EXIT . . . STAGE LEFT (live)** [6] [10]
– The spirit of radio / Red Barchetta / YYZ / A passage to Bangkok *[not on cd]* / Closer to the heart / Beneath, between and behind / Jacob's ladder / Broon's bane / The trees / Xanadu / Freewill / Tom Sawyer / La villa Strangiato. *(cd-iss. Apr87; 822 551-2)*

Oct 81. (7") *(EXIT 7)* **TOM SAWYER (live). / A PASSAGE TO BANGKOK (live)** [25] [–]
(12"+=) *(EXIT 12)* – Red Barchetta (live).

Dec 81. (7") *(RUSH 1) <76124>* **CLOSER TO THE HEART (live). / THE TREES (live)** [ ] [69]

Aug 82. (7") *(RUSH 8) <76179>* **NEW WORLD MAN. / VITAL SIGNS (live)** [42] [21]
(12"+=) *(RUSH 8-12)* – Freewill (live).

Sep 82. (lp/c) *(6337/7141 243) <403>* **SIGNALS** [3] [10]
– Subdivisions / The analog kid / Chemistry / Digital man / The weapon / New world man / Losing it / Countdown. *(cd-iss. 1983; 810 002-2)*

Oct 82. (7") *<76196>* **SUBDIVISIONS. / COUNTDOWN** [–] [ ]

Oct 82. (7"/7"pic-d) *(RUSH/+P 9)* **SUBDIVISIONS. / RED BARCHETTA (live)** [53] [–]
(12"+=) *(RUSH 9-12)* – Jacob's ladder (live).

Apr 83. (7"/7"sha-pic-d) *(RUSH 10/+PD)* **COUNTDOWN. / NEW WORLD MAN** [36] [ ]
(12"+=) *(RUSH 10-12)* – Spirit of radio (live) / (interview excerpts).

Apr 84. (lp/c)(cd) *(VERH/+C 12)(818 476-2) <818476>* **GRACE UNDER PRESSURE** [5] [10]
– Distant early warning / After image / Red sector A / The enemy within / The body electric / Kid gloves / Red lenses / Between the wheels.

May 84. (7") *(RUSH 11)* **THE BODY ELECTRIC. / THE ANALOG KID** [56] [ ]
(10"red+=/12"+=) *(RUSH 11 10/12)* – Distant early warning.

Oct 85. (7") *(RUSH 12) <884191>* **THE BIG MONEY. / TERRITORIES** [ ] [45]
(12"+=) *(RUSH 12-12)* – Red sector A (live).

(d7"+=) *(RUSHD 12)* – Closer to the heart / Spirit of radio.
(7"g-f) *(RUSHG 12)* – ('A'side) / Middletown dreams.

Nov 85. (lp/pic-lp/c)(cd) *(VERH/+P/C 31)(826 098-2) <826098>* **POWER WINDOWS** [9] Oct85 [10]
– The big money / Grand designs / Manhattan project / Marathon / Territories / Middletown dreams / Emotion detector / Mystic rhythms.

Oct 87. (7") *(RUSH 13)* **TIME STAND STILL. / FORCE TEN** [41] [ ]
(12"pic-d+=) *(RUSHP 13-12)* – The enemy within (live).
(12"++=) *(RUSH 13-12)* – Witch hunt (live).

Nov 87. (lp/c)(cd) *(VERH/+C 47)(832 464-2) <832464>* **HOLD YOUR FIRE** [10] Sep87 [13]
– Force ten / Time stand still / Open secrets / Second nature / Prime mover / Lock and key / Mission / Turn the page / Tai Shan / High water.

Mar 88. (7") *(RUSH 14)* **PRIME MOVER. / TAI SHAN** [ ] [ ]
(12"+=) *(RUSH 14-12)* – Open secrets.
(12"++=) *(RUSHR 14-12)* – New world man (live).
(cd-s+=) *RUSHCD 14)* – Distant early warning (live) / New world man (live).
(7"white) *(RUSHR 14)* – ('A'side) / Distant early warning (live).

Jan 89. (d-lp/c/cd) *(836 346-1/-4/-2) <836346>* **A SHOW OF HANDS (live)** [12] [21]
– (intro) / The big money / Subdivisions / Marathon / Turn the page / Manhattan project / Mission / Distant early warning / Mystic rhythms / Witch hunt (part III of fear) / The rhythm method / Force ten / Time stand still / Red sector A / Closer to the heart.

Atlantic Atlantic

Dec 89. (lp/c)(cd) *(WX 327/+C)(782 040-2) <82040-1/-4/-2>* **PRESTO** [27] Nov89 [16]
– Show don't tell / Chain lightning / The pass / War paint / Scars / Presto / Superconductor / Anagram (for Mongo) / Red tide / Hand over fist / Available light.

Jan 90. (7") **SHOW DON'T TELL. /** [–] [ ]

Sep 91. (cd)(lp/c) *<7567 82293-2>(WX 436/+C)* **ROLL THE BONES** [10] [3]
– Dreamline / Bravado / Roll the bones / Face up / Where's my thing? (part IV 'Gangster Of Boats' trilogy) / The big wheel / Heresy / Ghost of a chance / Neurotica / You bet your life.

Feb 92. (7") *(A 7524)* **ROLL THE BONES. / SHOW DON'T TELL** [49] [ ]
(cd-s+=) *(A 7524CD)* – (interviews) / Anagram.
(7"sha-pic-d) *(A 7524TE)* – ('A'side) / The pass / It's a rap part 1.

Apr 92. (7") *(A 7491)* **GHOST OF A CHANCE. / DREAMLINE** [ ] [ ]
(cd-s+=) *(A 7491CD)* – Chain lightning / Red tide.

Oct 93. (cd/c/lp) *<(7567 82528-2/-4/-1)>* **COUNTERPARTS** [14] [2]
– Animate / Stick it out / Cut to the chase / Nobody's hero / Between sun & moon / Alien shore / The speed of love / Double agent / Leave that thing alone / Cold fire / Everyday glory.

Sep 96. (cd/c) *<(7567 82925-2/-4)>* **TEST FOR ECHO** [25] [5]
– Test for echo / Driven / Half the world / The color of right / Time and motion / Totem / Dog years / Virtuality / Resist / Limbo / Carve away the stone.

Nov 98. (t-cd/d-c) *(7567 80921-2/-4) <83122>* **DIFFERENT STAGES** (live history) [ ] [35]
– Dreamline / Limelight / Driven / Bravado / Animate / Show don't tell / The trees / Nobody's hero / Closer to the heart / 2112: i) Overture, ii) Temples in Syrinx, iii) Discovery, iv) Presentation, v) Oracle: the dream, vi) Soliloquy, vii) Grand finale // Test for echo / Analog kid / Freewill / Roll the bones / Stick it out / Resist / Leave that thing alone / The rhythm method / Natural science / The spirit of radio / Tom Sawyer / XYZ // Bastille day / By Tor and the snow dog / Xanadu / A farewell to kings / Something for nothing / Cygnus X-1 / Anthem / Working man / Fly by night / In the mood / Cinderella man.

May 02. (cd) *<(7567 83531-2)>* **VAPOR TRAILS** [38] [6]
– One little victory / Ceiling unlimited / Ghost rider / Peaceable kingdom / The stars look down / How it is / Vapor trail / Secret touch / Earthshine / Sweet miracle / Nocturne / Freeze (Fear part 4) / Out of the cradle.

Nov 03. (t-cd) *<(7567 83672-2)>* **RUSH IN RIO** (live) [ ] Oct03 [33]
– Tom Sawyer / Distant early warning / New world man / Roll the bones / Earthshine / YYZ / The pass / Bravado / The big money / The trees / Freewill / Closer to the heart / Natural science / One little victory / Driven / Ghost rider / Secret touch / Dreamline / Red sector 'A' / Leave that thing alone / O baterista / Resist / 2112 / Limelight / La villa strangiato / The spirit of radio / By-Tor and the snow dog / Cygnus X-1 / Working man / Between sun & moon / Vital signs.

Jul 04. (m-cd) *<(7567 83728-2)>* **FEEDBACK** [68] Jun04 [19]
– Summertime blues / Heart full of soul / For what it's worth / The seeker / Mr. Soul / Seven and seven is / Shapes of things / Crossroads.

– compilations, others, etc. –

on 'Mercury' unless otherwise mentioned

May 78. (t-lp)(d-c) *(6641 779)(7649 103) <9200>* **ARCHIVES** [ ] Apr78 [ ]
– (RUSH / FLY BY NIGHT / CARESS OF STEEL)

Sep 81. (lp/c) *<6337/7141 171)* **RUSH THROUGH TIME** [–] [ ]

Feb 88. (7") *Old Gold; (OG 9767)* **THE SPIRIT OF RADIO. / CLOSER TO THE HEART** [ ] [–]

Oct 90. (d-cd/d-c/t-lp) *Vertigo; (838 936-2/-4/-1) / Mercury; <838936>* **CHRONICLES** [42] Sep90 [51]
– Finding my way / Working man / Fly by night / Anthem / Bastille day / Lakeside park / 2112: a) Overture, b) The temples of Syrinx / What you're doing (live) / A farewell to kings / Closer to the heart / The trees / La villa Strangiato / Freewill / Spirit of radio// Tom Sawyer / Red barchetta / Limelight / A passage to Bangkok (live) / Subdivisions / New world man / Distant early warning / Red sector A / The big money / Manhattan project / Force ten / Time stand still / Mystic rhythms (live) / Show don't tell.

Feb 03. (cd+dvd) *Universal; <(063335-2)>* **THE SPIRIT OF RADIO: GREATEST HITS 1974-1987** [ ] [62]
– Working man / Fly by night / 2112 overture – The temples Syrinx / Closer to the heart / The trees / The spirit of radio / Freewill / Limelight / Tom Sawyer / Red barchetta / New world man / Subdivisions / Distant early warning / The big money / Force ten / Time stand still.

VICTOR

ALEX LIFESON – guitar, bass, keyboards / **BILL BELL** – wobble & slide guitar, co-writer / **PETER CARDINALI** – bass / **BLAKE MANNING** – drums / + guests EDWIN – vocals (of I MOTHER EARTH) + LES CLAYPOOL – bass (of PRIMUS)

Atlantic Atlantic

Feb 96. (cd/c) *<(7567-82852-2/-4)>* **VICTOR** [ ] Jan96 [99]
– Don't care / Promise / Start today / Mr. X / At the end / Sending a warning / Shut up shuttin' up / Strip and go naked / The big dance / Victor / I am the spirit.

GEDDY LEE

with **BEN MONK** – guitar, violin (ex-FM) / **MATT CAMERON** – drums (ex-SOUNDGARDEN)

Atlantic Atlantic

Nov 00. (cd) *<(7567 83384-2)>* **MY FAVOURITE HEADACHE** [ ] [ ]
– My favourite headache / The present tense / Window to the world / Working at perfekt / Runaway train / The angels' share / Moving to Bohemia / Home on the strange / Slipping / Still / Grace to grace.

□ RZA (see under ⇒ WU-TANG CLAN)

SALIVA

Formed: Memphis, Tennessee, USA . . . September 1996 by vocalist JOSEY SCOTT, CHRIS D'ABALDO, DAVE NOVOTNY, WAYNE SWINNY and PAUL CROSBY. Their career got off to a flyer in '97 when they made the finals of a Grammy sponsored showcase competition, creating a groundswell of support for a subsequent debut set, 'SALIVA' (1997). Plying straight-up post-Grunge with scattershot pseudo rapping, the Memphis quintet weren't exactly in the grand old tradition of their famous hometown, instead getting lumped in with the likes of CREED, KORN and NICKELBACK. They subsequently made the first of several canny diversions into soundtrack work, recording a one-off song, 'YOUR DISEASE', for the Hollywood feature 'Dracula 2000'. Taking up with 'Island' records, SALIVA didn't have the American market drooling just yet, but 'EVERY SIX SECONDS' (2001) – judging by the sleeve art, a reference to man's famous tendency for regular carnal thoughts – made a respectable No.56. The impressively bearded JOSEY SCOTT was headhunted the following year for the hit theme tune ('HERO') to box-office blockbuster 'Spider-Man', cut in collaboration with NICKELBACK's CHAD KROEGER. Like the nu garage-rock revolution never happened, SALIVA lumbered on to even greater success with US Top 20 albums, 'BACK INTO YOUR SYSTEM' (2003) and 'SURVIVAL OF THE SICKEST' (2004).

Album rating: SALIVA (*6) / EVERY SIX SECONDS (*6) / BACK INTO YOUR SYSTEM (*7) / SURVIVAL OF THE SICKEST (*5)

JOSEY SCOTT (b. 3 May'71) – vocals, acoustic guitar / **WAYNE SWINNY** – lead guitar / **CHRIS D'ABALDO** – guitar / **DAVE NOVOTNY** – bass / **PAUL CROSBY** – drums

not iss. | Rocking Chair

Aug 97. (cd) *<1107>* **SALIVA** [–] [ ]
– Beg / Sink / Call it something / Spitshine / Greater than less than / Cellophane / Tongue / Pin cushion / Sand castle / Groovy / I want it / Suffocate / 800.

Island | Island

Jun 01. (cd) *<(542959-2)>* **EVERY SIX SECONDS** [ ] Mar01 [56]
– Superstar / Musta been wrong / Click click boom / Your disease / After me / Greater than – Less than / Lackluster / Faultline / Beg / Hollywood / Doperide / My goodbyes.

— in early summer '02, JOSEY SCOTT featured on CHAD KROEGER (of NICKELBACK) Top 5 single, 'Hero', taken from the 'Spider-Man' movie

Mar 03. (cd) *(77147-2) <063153-2>* **BACK INTO YOUR SYSTEM** [ ] Nov02 [19]
– Superstar II / Weight of the world / Always / Back into your system / All because of you / Raise up / Separated self / Rest in pieces / Storm / Holdin' on / Pride / Famous monsters. *<US bonus+=>* – Warcraft III: Reign of chaos. *(UK bonus+=)* – Click click boom / Click click boom (MK version – video) / Your disease (video).

Mar 03. (cd-s) *(063708-2)* **ALWAYS / CLICK CLICK BOOM / YOUR DISEASE** [47] [–]

Sep 03. (cd-s) *<11913-2>* **REST IN PIECES / (acoustic) / BLEED FOR ME** [–] [ ]

Sep 04. (cd) *(9863534) <B00029570-2>* **SURVIVAL OF THE SICKEST** [ ] Aug04 [20]
– Rock & roll revolution / Bait & switch / One night only / Survival of the sickest / No regrets, Vol.2 / Two steps back / Open eyes / Fuck all y'all / I want you / Carry on / Razor's edge / No hard feelings / (second of silence) / Sex, drugs & rock'n'roll.

— now without D'ABALDO

☐ Richie SAMBORA (see under ⇒ BON JOVI)

SANTANA

Formed: San Francisco, California, USA ... October '66 as The SANTANA BLUES BAND, by Mexican-born/Tijuana-raised CARLOS SANTANA. The guitarist's distinctly pure, fluid sound was backed by a constantly changing personnel over the years, though the best work was driven by the powerhouse rhythm section of drummer, MICHAEL SHRIEVE, and percussionist JOSE 'CHEPITO' AREAS. A compelling fusion of Latin stylings and psychedelic-tinged blues jamming, the band's early work has often been copied but rarely equalled. In 1968, the BLUES BAND part of the name was jettisoned and under the more effective moniker of SANTANA they played San Francisco's Fillmore West. Later the same year, CARLOS guested on the album, 'THE LIVE ADVENTURES OF AL KOOPER AND MIKE BLOOMFIELD' which brought him to the attention of 'Columbia' records. Following a show-stopping performance at The Woodstock Festival, their long-awaited eponymous debut album cracked the US Top 5 in late '69. The record, together with their next two follow-up albums, 'ABRAXAS' (1970) and 'SANTANA III' (1971), secured SANTANA's position as one of US rock's leading lights, the latter two sets hitting No.1 in America as well as spawning the hits 'BLACK MAGIC WOMAN', 'EVERYBODY'S EVERYTHING' and a dazzling, frenetic cover of TITO PUENTE's 'OYE COMO VA'. Following an indulgent live set featuring BUDDY MILES, SANTANA released 'CARAVANSERAI' in 1972, a transitional piece that signalled a tentative move away from blues towards the jazz-fusion that would come to characterise most of the band's later 70's output. Around this time CARLOS became a devotee of Indian guru, Sri Chinmoy, recording the 'LOVE DEVOTION SURRENDER' (1973) album with the similarly converted JOHN McLAUGHLIN. A contemplative piece of ethereal jazz, it had a spiritual partner in the following year's 'ILLUMINATIONS', recorded with fellow Chinmoy disciple and jazz composer ALICE COLTRANE. Meanwhile, the SANTANA band released 'WELCOME' (1973) and 'BORBOLETTA' (1974), which further explored complex jazz textures, although 1976's 'AMIGOS' returned to a more grounded Latin-rock sound. It was short-lived though, and late 70's albums such as 'MOONFLOWER' (1977) and 'INNER SECRETS' (1978) bordered on the snooze-worthy with their directionless experimentation. 'ZEBOP' (1981) began the new decade on a high note, a masterful set that spawned the US hit single, 'WINNING'. The 80's also saw a solo effort, 'HAVANA MOON' (1983) and the grammy-award winning 'BLUES FOR SALVADOR' (1987) as well as a film score for 'La Bamba'. Following a deal with

'Island', SANTANA has continued his prolific output, releasing the 'BROTHERS' album in 1994 – a collaboration with sibling JORGE. When the phrase "re-inventing yourself" was thought up, they must have had CARLOS SANTANA in mind because what happened by the end of the decade transformed the SANTANA we once knew into Latino Blues stars of the new millennium. The record in question, 'SUPERNATURAL' (1999), was a record inspired by the gods and only CARLOS could hand-pick a team of guest singers/musicians (DAVE MATTHEWS, EVERLAST, LAURYN HILL, WYCLEF JEAN, EAGLE EYE CHERRY and ERIC CLAPTON) to complement this "tight" masterwork. However, it would be matchbox20's ROB THOMAS who stole some of the spotlight, providing cooler than cool vocal chords on multi-million selling single, 'SMOOTH'; it would be no surprise when SANTANA cleaned up most of the top awards in next years' Grammys. From the cover art to the minimalist title to the range of tasteful guest stars, 'SHAMAN' (2002) was basically an attempt to repeat the phenomenal success of its predecessor. While THOMAS was still on board, he concentrated on writing this time around, tailoring songs to both MUSIQ and SEAL, although the pick of the collaborations was arguably 'THE GAME OF LOVE', fronted by MICHELLE BRANCH. After helping out HERBIE HANCOCK on the pianist's collaborative set, 'Possibilities', CARLOS was back with 'ALL THAT I AM' (2005), inviting yet another crop of major label guests – among them STEVEN TYLER, MARY J BLIGE, JOSS STONE, SEAN PAUL, the BLACK EYED PEAS' WILL.I.AM, and welcome back MICHELLE BRANCH – on a collection whose writing credits threw up a bewildering array of names. There was plenty of Latinate pop but, for longtime fans, probably not enough Mexicali blues, and certainly no hits on a par with this album's predecessors; less a case of third time lucky (it just missed being his third US album in a row, peaking at No.2) than third time around the block.

• **Songwriters:** CARLOS penned with group, except covers:- JIN-GO-LA-BA (Michael Babatunde Olatunji) / BLACK MAGIC WOMAN (Fleetwood Mac) / GYPSY WOMAN (Curtis Mayfield) / PEACE ON EARTH (Alice Coltrane) / STORMY (Classics IV) / SHE'S NOT THERE (Zombies) / WELL ALL RIGHT (Buddy Holly) / ONE CHAIN (Four Tops) / WINNING (Russ Ballard) / THIRD STONE FROM THE SUN (Jimi Hendrix) / WHO'S THAT LADY (Isley Brothers) / FULL MOON (Paola Rustichelli) / RIGHT ON (Marvin Gaye) / I'VE BEEN TO THE MOUNTAIN TOP (. . . King) / etc. • **Trivia:** In the mid-70's, Bill Graham took over the management of SANTANA. For lovers of anything SANTANA, his brother JORGE (in Latin-rock band MALO) had success in April '72 with an eponymous album, which hit US No.14. A single lifted from it, 'SALI VECITO', made No.18. MALO went on to release three more 'Warner Bros.' albums; DOS (1972) / EVOLUTION (1973) + ASCENSION (1974).

Album rating: SANTANA (*7) / ABRAXAS (*8) / SANTANA III (*7) / CARLOS SANTANA & BUDDY MILES! LIVE! solo/collaboration with Buddy Miles (*4) / CARAVANSERAI (*8) / LOVE DEVOTION SURRENDER solo/collaboration with Mahavishnu John McLaughlin (*6) / WELCOME (*6) / ILLUMINATIONS solo/collaboration with Turiya Alice Coltrane (*4) / SANTANA'S GREATEST HITS compilation (*8) / BORBOLETTA (*6) / LOTUS (*6) / AMIGOS (*7) / FESTIVAL (*6) / MOONFLOWER (*6) / INNER SECRETS (*4) / ONENESS: SILVER DREAMS – GOLDEN REALITY solo as Devadip (*5) / MARATHON (*5) / THE SWING OF DELIGHT solo (*4) / ZEBOP! (*6) / SHANGO (*5) / HAVANA MOON solo (*5) / BEYOND APPEARANCES (*4) / FREEDOM (*6) / BLUES FOR SALVADOR solo (*6) / VIVA! SANTANA boxed-compilation (*8) / SPIRITS DANCING IN THE FLESH (*5) / MILAGRO (*5) / SACRED FIRE – LIVE IN SOUTH AMERICA (*4) / BROTHERS as Santana Brothers (*4) / DANCE OF THE RAINBOW SERPENT boxed-set (*7) / SUPERNATURAL (*7) / SHAMAN (*5) / ALL THAT I AM (*4)

CARLOS SANTANA (b.20 Jul'47, Autlan de Navarro, Mexico) – lead guitar / **GREGG ROLIE** (b.17 Jun'47, Seattle, Washington) – keyboards, vocals / **DAVID BROWN** (b.15 Feb'47, New York) – bass repl. GUS RODRIGUES (in 1967) / **MIKE SHRIEVE** (b. 6 Jul'49, San Francisco) – drums repl. BOB LIVINGSTONE (in '67). He had repl. ROD HARPER / **JOSE CHEPITO AREAS** (b.25 Jul'46, Leon, Nicaragua) – percussion / **MIKE CARABELLO** (b.18 Nov'47, San Francisco) – congas repl. TOM FRAZER – guitar

C.B.S. | Columbia

Oct 69. (7") *(CBS 4593)* **PERSUASION. / SAVOR** [ ] [–]

Oct 69. (7") *<45010>* **JIN-GO-LA-BA. / PERSUASION** [–] [56]

Nov 69. (lp) *(CBS 63015) <9781>* **SANTANA** [26] Sep69 [4]
– Waiting / Evil ways / Shades of time / Savor / Jin-go-la-ba / Persuasion / Treat / You just don't care / Soul sacrifice. *(re-iss. Mar70; CBS 63815) (re-iss. Mar81 lp/c; CBS/40 32003) (cd-iss. May87; CD 63815) (cd re-iss. May92 & Apr98 on 'Columbia'; 489542-2)*

Jan 70. (7") *<45069>* **EVIL WAYS. / WAITING** [–] [9]

Apr 70. (7") *(CBS 4940)* **EVIL WAYS. / JIN-GO-LA-BA** [ ] [–]

Nov 70. (lp) *(CBS 64087) <30130>* **ABRAXAS** [7] Sep 70 [1]
– Singing winds, crying beasts / Black magic woman – Gypsy queen / Oyo como va / Incident at Neshabur / Se a cabo / Mother's daughter / Samba pa ti / Hope you're feeling better / El Nicoya. *(re-iss. Mar81 lp/c; CBS/40 32032) (cd-iss. Mar86; CD 64087) (cd re-iss. Mar91; CD 32032) (cd re-iss. Apr98 on 'Columbia'; 489543-2)*

Dec 70. (7") *(CBS 5325) <45270>* **BLACK MAGIC WOMAN. / HOPE YOU'RE FEELING BETTER** [ ] Nov70 [4]

Mar 71. (7") *(CBS 7046) <45330>* **OYE COMO VA. / SAMBA PA TI** [ ] Feb71 [13]

—— added **NEAL SCHON** (b.27 Feb'54) – guitar / **COKE ESCOVEDO** (b. THOMAS ESCOVEDO, 30 Apr'41, Calif.) – percussion

Oct 71. (lp) *(CBS 69015) <30595>* **SANTANA III** [6] [1]
– Batuka / No one to depend on / Taboo / Toussaint l'overture / Everybody's everything / Guajira / Everything's coming our way / Jungle strut / Para los rumberos. *(re-iss. Mar82 lp/c; CBS/40 32058) (cd-iss. Mar87; CD 69015) (re-iss. Jun94 on 'Columbia' cd/c; 476830-2) (cd re-iss. Apr98; 489554-2)*

Nov 71. (7") *(CBS 7546) <45472>* **EVERYBODY'S EVERYTHING. / GUAJIRA** [ ] Oct71 [12]

Mar 72. (7") *(CBS 7842) <45552>* **NO ONE TO DEPEND ON. / TABOO** [ ] Feb72 [36]

Jul 72. (lp; by CARLOS SANTANA & BUDDY MILES) *(CBS 65142) <31308>* **CARLOS SANTANA & BUDDY MILES! LIVE! (live)** [29] [8]
– Marbles / Lava / Evil ways / Faith interlude / Them changes / Free form funkafide filth. *(re-iss. Sep84 lp/c; CBS/40 32271)*

Oct 72. (7"; by CARLOS SANTANA & BUDDY MILES) *(CBS 8338) <45666>* **EVIL WAYS (live). / THEM CHANGES (live)** [ ] Aug72 [84]

—— **ARMANDO PERAZA** – percussion repl. CARABELLO and ESCOVEDO (latter died 30 Apr'85) / **TOM RUTLEY** – bass repl. BROWN

Nov 72. (lp) *(CBS 65299) <31610>* **CARAVANSERAI** [6] [8]
– Eternal caravan of reincarnation / Waves within / Look up (to see what's coming down) / Just in time to see the sun / Song of the wind / All the love of the universe / Future primitive / Stone flower / La fuente del ritmo / Every step of the way. *(re-iss. Nov81 lp/c; CBS/40 32060) (cd-iss. 1988; CD 65299)*

Jan 73. (7") *<45753>* **LOOK UP (TO SEE WHAT'S COMING DOWN). / ALL THE LOVE OF THE UNIVERSE** [–] [ ]

Jul 73. (lp; by CARLOS DEVADIP SANTANA AND MAHAVISHNU JOHN McLAUGHLIN) *(CBS 69073) <32034>* **LOVE DEVOTION SURRENDER** [7] [14]
– A love supreme / Naima / The lie divine / Let us go into the house of the Lord / Meditation. *(re-iss. Oct92 & Jun94 on 'Columbia' cd/c; 982830-2/-4)*
(above album featured below newcomers (**RAUCH + LEWIS**) + **PERAZA, JAN HAMMER** – keyboards / **BILLY COBHAM** – drums / **LARRY YOUNG** – keyboards)

—— **CARLOS** retained **AREAS, PERAZA + SHRIEVE** and brought in newcomers **TOM COSTER** – keyboards, vocals repl. ROLIE who formed JOURNEY / **RICHARD KERMODE** – keyboards repl. SCHON who also formed JOURNEY / **DOUG RAUCH** – bass repl. RUTLEY / added **LEON THOMAS** – vocals / **JAMES MINGO LEWIS** – congas

Nov 73. (lp) *(CBS 69040) <32445>* **WELCOME** [8] [25]
– Going home / Love, devotion and surrender / Samba de sausalito / When I look into your eyes / Yours is the light / Mother Africa / Light of life / Flame-sky / Welcome. *(re-iss. 1984 lp/c; CBS/40 32194)*

Nov 73. (7") *(CBS 1925) <45999>* **WHEN I LOOK INTO YOUR EYES. / SAMBA DE SAUSALITO** [ ] [ ]

Sep 74. (lp; by TURIYA ALICE COLTRANE & DEVADIP CARLOS SANTANA) *(CBS 69063) <32900>* **ILLUMINATIONS** [40] [79]
– Guru Sri Chimnoy aphorism / Angel of air – Angel of water / Bliss: The eternal now / Angel of sunlight / Illuminations. *(cd-iss. Mar96 on 'Columbia; 483810-2)*
above w/ **ALICE** – keyboards, etc.

— **GREG WALKER** – vocals + sessioners repl. KERMODE, LEWIS and THOMAS

Nov 74. (lp/c) *(CBS/40 69084)* *<33135>* **BORBOLETTA** [18] Oct74 [20]
– Spring manifestations / Canto de los flores / Life is anew / Give and take / One with the Sun / Aspirations / Practice what you preach / Mirage / Here and now / Flor de canela / Promise of a fisherman / Borboletta. *(re-iss. Nov83 lp/c; CBS/40 32157) (re-iss. cd Nov93 on 'Sony Collectors';)*

Nov 74. (7") *(CBS 2829)* **PRACTICE WHAT YOU PREACH. / CANTO DE LOS FLORES** [ ] [-]

Jan 75. (7") *(CBS 3005)* *<10073>* **MIRAGE. / FLOR DE CANELA** [ ] [ ]

Mar 75. (7") *<10088>* **GIVE AND TAKE. / LIFE IS ANEW** [-] [ ]

— (Below triple album was issued initially in Japan 1973)

Dec 75. (t-lp) *(CBS 66325)* **LOTUS (live)** [ ] [-]
– Meditation / Going home / A-1 funk / Every step of the way / Black magic woman – Gypsy queen / Oye como va / Yours is the light / Batuka / Xibaba (she-ba-ba) / Savor / Stone flower / (introduction) / Castillos de arena (pt.1) / Waiting / Se a cabo / Samba pa ti / Toussaint l'overture / Incident at Neshabur. *(re-iss. Dec90 d-cd/d-c; 467943-2/-4)*

— **LEON NDUGU CHANCLER** – drums repl. SHRIEVE and AREAS / **IVORY STONE** – bass repl. RAUCH

Mar 76. (7") *(CBS 4143)* *<10421>* **EUROPA. / TAKE ME WITH YOU** [ ] Nov76 [ ]

Apr 76. (lp/c) *(CBS/40 86005)* *<33576>* **AMIGOS** [21] [10]
– Dance sister dance (baila mi Hermana) / Take me with you / Let me / Gitano / Tell me are you tired / Europa (Earth's cry, Heaven's smile) / Let it shine. *(re-iss. Jun84 lp/c; CBS/40 32476) (cd-iss. Mar87; CD 86005) (re-iss. cd Jun92)*

May 76. (7") *(CBS 4335)* *<10336>* **LET IT SHINE. / TELL ME ARE YOU TIRED** [ ] [77]

Aug 76. (7") *(CBS 4512)* *<10353>* **DANCE SISTER DANCE (BAILA MI HERMANA). / LET ME** [ ] [ ]

— **JOSE AREAS** returned to repl. PERAZA / **PABLO TELEZ** – bass repl. STONE

Dec 76. (lp/c) *(CBS/40 86020)* *<34423>* **FESTIVAL** [27] [27]
– Carnaval / Let the children play / Jugando / Carnival / Give me love / Verao Vermelho / Let the music set you free / Revelations / Reach up / The river / Try a little harder / Maria Caracoles.

Jan 77. (7") *(CBS 4927)* **REVELATIONS. / REACH UP** [ ] [-]

Jan 77. (7") *<10524>* **REVELATIONS. / GIVE ME LOVE** [-] [ ]

Mar 77. (7") *(CBS 5102)* *<10481>* **LET THE CHILDREN PLAY. / CARNAVAL** [ ] [ ]

— Trimmed slightly when CHANCLER vacated

Sep 77. (7") *(CBS 5671)* *<10616>* **SHE'S NOT THERE. / ZULU** [11] [27]

Oct 77. (d-lp/c) *(CBS/40 88272)* *<34914>* **MOONFLOWER (live + studio)** [7] [10]
– Dawn – Go within / Carnaval / Let the children play / Jugando / I'll be waiting / Zulu / Bahia / Black magic woman – Gypsy queen / Dance sister dance (baila mi Hermana) / Europa (Earth's cry, Heaven's smile) / She's not there / Flor de Luna (Moonflower) / Soul sacrifice / Heads, hands & feet / El Morocco / Transcendance / Savor / Toussaint l'overture. *(re-iss. Apr85 d-lp/c; CBS/40 86098) (cd-iss. Apr89; CD 33280) (re-iss. cd Jun96; 463370-2)*

Jan 78. (7") *(CBS 6055)* **BLACK MAGIC WOMAN (live). / TRANSCENDANCE** [ ] [-]

Jan 78. (7") *<10677>* **BLACK MAGIC WOMAN (live). / I'LL BE WAITING (live)** [-] [ ]

Aug 78. (7"; by CARLOS SANTANA) *(CBS 6520)* **I'LL BE WAITING. / FLOR DE LUNA (MOONFLOWER)** [ ] [-]

— **CARLOS** retained only **WALKER + COSTER** and introduced **ARMANDO PERAZA** returned to repl. AREAS / **DAVID MARGEN** – bass repl. TELLEZ / added **GRAHAM LEER** – drums / **CHRIS RHYME** – keyboards / **RAUL REKOW** – percussion / **CHRIS SOLBERG** – guitar, keyboards, vocals

Oct 78. (7") *<10839>* **WELL ALL RIGHT. / JERICHO** [-] [69]

Oct 78. (7") *(CBS 6755)* **WELL ALL RIGHT. / WHAM!** [53] [-]
(12"+=) *(CBS12-6755)* – Life is a lady – Holiday.

Nov 78. (lp/c) *(CBS/40 86075)* *<35600>* **INNER SECRETS** [17] [27]
– Dealer / Spanish rose / Well all right / One chain (don't make no prison) / Stormy / Open invitation / Wham! / The facts of love / Life is a lady – Holiday / Move on. *(cd-iss. 1986 & Jun92; CD 86075)*

Jan 79. (7") *(CBS 6998)* **ONE CHAIN (DON'T MAKE NO PRISON). / MOVE ON** [ ] [-]

Jan 79. (7") *<10873>* **STORMY. / MOVE ON** [-] [32]

Mar 79. (lp/c; as DEVADIP) *(CBS/40 86037)* *<35686>* **ONENESS: SILVER DREAMS, GOLDEN REALITY** [55] [87]
– The chosen hour / Arise awake / Light versus darkness / Jim Jeannie / Transformation day / Victory / Silver dreams golden smiles / Cry of the wilderness / Guru's song / Oneness / Life is just a passing parade / Golden dawn / Free as the morning sun / Song for Devadip. *(cd-iss. Mar97 on 'Columbia'; 487238-2)*

Apr 79. (7") *<10938>* **ONE CHAIN (DON'T MAKE NO PRISON). / LIFE IS A HOLIDAY** [-] [59]

— **ALEX LIGERTWOOD** (b.18 Dec'46, Glasgow, Scotland) – vocals (ex-BRIAN AUGER) repl. WALKER / **ALAN PASQUE** – keyboards, vocals repl. COSTER + RHYME

Oct 79. (7") *(CBS 7971)* *<11144>* **YOU KNOW THAT I LOVE YOU. / AQUA MARINE** [ ] [35]

Oct 79. (lp/c) *(CBS/40 86098)* *<36154>* **MARATHON** [28] [25]
– Marathon / Lightning in the sky / Aqua marine / You know that I love you / All I ever wanted / Stand up – Runnin' / Summer lady / Love / Stay / Hard times. *(cd-iss. May87; CD 86098)*

Feb 80. (7") *(CBS 8160)* **ALL I EVER WANTED. / LOVE** [57] [-]

Feb 80. (7") *<11218>* **ALL I EVER WANTED. / LIGHTNING IN THE SKY** [-] [ ]

Jun 80. (7") *(CBS 8649)* **AQUA MARINE. / STAND UP – RUNNIN'** [ ] [-]

Sep 80. (d-lp/d-c; by CARLOS SANTANA) *(CBS/40 84514)* *<36590>* **THE SWING OF DELIGHT** [65] [65]
– Swapan tari / Love theme from 'Sparticus' / Phuler Matan / Song for my brother / Jharna kala / Gardenia / La Llave / Golden hours / Shere Khan, the tiger.
(above featured The MILES DAVIS QUINTET of the 60's)

— added **ORESTES VILATO** – percussion / **RICHARD BAKER** – keyboards

Apr 81. (7") *(A-1139)* *<01050>* **WINNING. / BRIGHTEST STAR** [ ] [17]

Apr 81. (lp/c) *(CBS/40 84946)* *<37158>* **ZEBOP!** [33] [9]
– Changes / E papa re / Primera invasion / Searchin' / Over and over / Winning / Tales of Kilimanjaro / The sensitive kind / American gypsy / I love you much too much / Brightest star / Hannibal. *(cd-iss. Dec85; CD 84946)*

Jun 81. (7") *(A-1388)* **CHANGES. / AMERICAN GYPSY** [ ] [-]

Sep 81. (7") *(A-1556)* *<02178>* **THE SENSITIVE KIND. / AMERICAN GYPSY** [ ] Jul81 [56]

Jan 82. (7") *<02519>* **SEARCHIN'. / TALES OF KILIMANJARO** [-] [ ]

— **CARLOS** retained only **LEAR, MARGEN, BAKER + VILATO**

Aug 82. (lp/c) *(CBS/40 85915)* *<38122>* **SHANGO** [35] [22]
– The Nile / Hold on / Night hunting time / Nowhere to run / Nueva York / Oxun / Body surfing / What does it take / Let me inside / Warrior / Shango. *(cd-iss. 1983; CD 85914)*

Aug 82. (7") *<03160>* **HOLD ON. / OXUN** [-] [15]

Nov 82. (7") *<03376>* **NOWHERE TO RUN. / NUEVA YORK** [-] [66]

CARLOS SANTANA

solo, featuring **WILLIE NELSON, BOOKER T.JONES & The FABULOUS THUNDERBIRDS**

Apr 83. (7") *<03925>* **WATCH YOUR STEP. / TALES OF KILIMANJARO** [-] [ ]

Apr 83. (7") *(A-3330)* **WATCH YOUR STEP. / LIGHTNIN'** [ ] [-]

Apr 83. (lp/c) *(CBS/40 25350)* *<38642>* **HAVANA MOON** [84] [31]
– Watch your step / Lightnin' / Who do you love / Mudbone / One with you / Ecuador / Tales of Kilimanjaro / Havana Moon / Daughter of the night / They all went to Mexico / Vereda tropical. *(cd-iss. May87' CD 25350)*

May 83. (7") *(A-3359)* **THEY ALL WENT TO MEXICO. / MUDBONE** [ ] [-]

Jun 83. (7") *<04034>* **HAVANA MOON. / LIGHTNIN'** [-] [ ]

SANTANA

CARLOS only retained **VILATO** plus sessioners

Mar 85. (7") *(A-4514)* *<04758>* **SAY IT AGAIN. / TOUCHDOWN RAIDERS** [ ] Feb85 [46]
(12"+=) *(TA-4514)* – She's not there / ('A'instrumental).

Mar 85. (lp/c) *(CBS/40 86307)* *<39527>* **BEYOND APPEARANCES** [58] [50]
– Breaking out / Written in sand / How long / Brotherhood / Spirit / Say it again / Who loves you / I'm the one who loves you / Touchdown raiders / Right now. *(cd-iss. Mar86; CD 86307)*

May 85. (7") *(A-6284)* **HOW LONG. / RIGHT NOW** [ ] [-]
(12"+=) *(TA-6284)* – She's not there.

May 85. (7") *<04912>* **I'M THE ONE WHO LOVES YOU. / RIGHT NOW** [-] [ ]

— **CARLOS** re-united **GREGG ROLIE, MIKE SHRIEVE, JOSE AREAS** +sessioners

Feb 87. (lp/c/cd) *(450 500-1/-4/-2)* *<40272>* **FREEDOM** [ ] [95]
– Vera Cruz / She can't let go / Once it's gotcha / Love is you / Songs of freedom / Deeper, dig deeper / Praise / Mandela / Before we go / Victim of circumstance.

May 87. (7"/12") *(650417-7/-6)* *<06654>* **VERA CRUZ. / MANDELA** [ ] Mar87 [ ]

May 87. (7") *<07038>* **VERA CRUZ (remix). / MANDELA** [–] [ ]

Jul 87. (7") *<07140>* **PRAISE. / LOVE IS YOU** [–] [ ]

— SANTANA touring band **ROLIE, CHESTER THOMPSON** – keyboards / **TOM COSTER** – synthesizers / **ALFONSO JOHNSON** – bass / **GRAHAM LEER** – drums / **BUDDY MILES** – vocals / **ARMANDO PERAZA, PAUL REKOW + ORESTES VILATO** – percussion

Nov 87. (lp/c/cd; by CARLOS SANTANA) *(460 258-1/-4/-2)* *<40875>* **BLUES FOR SALVADOR** [ ] [ ]
– Bailando / Aquatic park / Bella / I'm gone / 'Trane / Deeper, dig deeper / Mingus / Now that you know / Hannibal / Blues for Salvador.
(above featured mainly session people)

— **CARLOS** retained **THOMPSON + PERAZA,** plus recruited **BENNY RIETVELD** – bass / **ALEX LIGERTWOOD** – vocals, guitar / **WALFREDO REYES** – drums, timbales, perc with host of guests (over 15).

Jun 90. (cd/c/lp) *(466913-2/-4/-1)* *<46065>* **SPIRITS DANCING IN THE FLESH** [68] [85]
– Let there be light – Spirits dancing in the flesh / Gypsy woman / It's a jungle out there / Soweto (African libre) / Choose / Peace on Earth . . . Mother Earth . . . Third stone from the Sun / Full Moon / Who's that lady / Jin-go-la-ba / Goodness and mercy.

Jun 90. (7") *(656027-7)* **GYPSY WOMAN. / GOODNESS AND MERCY** [ ] [ ]
(12"+=/cd-s+=) *(656027-6/-2)* – Black magic woman (live) / Oye como va (live) / She's not there (live).

— Next with samples from MILES DAVIS and JOHN COLTRANE.

Polydor Polydor

Apr 92. (cd/c/d-lp) *(513197-2/-4/-1)* *<513197>* **MILAGRO** [ ] [ ]
– Medley:- Introduction by BILL GRAHAM – Milagro / Medley:- I've been to the mountain top – Somewhere in Heaven / Medley:- Saja – Right on / Your touch / Life is for living / Red prophet / Aqua que va ceer / Make somebody happy / Free all the people (South Africa) / Medley:- Gypsy – Grajoonca / We don't have to wait / Adios.

Nov 93. (cd/c) *<(521082-2/-4)>* **SACRED FIRE** (live in South America) [ ] [ ]
– Angels all around us / Vive le Vada (life is for living) / Esperando / No one to depend on / Black magic woman – Gypsy queen / Oye como va / Samba pa ti / Guajira / Make somebody happy / Toussaint l'overture / Soul sacrifice / Don't try this at home / Europa / Jingo-la-ba.

— with brother **JORGE** – guitar (ex-MALO) + **CARLOS HERNANDEZ**

Island Island

Sep 94. (cd/c; by SANTANA BROTHERS) *(CID/ICT 8034)* *<523677>* **BROTHERS** [ ] [ ]
– Transmutation industrial / Thoughts / Luz amor y vida / En aranjouz con tu amour / Contigo / Blues Latino / La olaza / Brujo / The trip / Reflections / Morning in Marin.

Arista Arista

Aug 99. (cd/c) *<(07822 19080-2/-4)>* **SUPERNATURAL** [1] Jun99 [1]
– (Da le) Yaleo / Love of my life (w/ DAVE MATTHEWS) / Put your lights on (w/ EVERLAST) / Africa bamba / Smooth (w/ ROB THOMAS) / Do you like the way (w/ LAURYN HILL) / Maria Maria (w/ WYCLEF JEAN) / Migra / Corazon Espinado / Wishing it was (w/ EAGLE EYE CHERRY) / El farol / Primavera / The calling (w/ ERIC CLAPTON).

Oct 99. (c-s/cd-s; SANTANA featuring ROB THOMAS) *(74321 70949-4/-2)* *<13718>* **SMOOTH / EL FAROL** [75] Jul99 [1]
(re-iss. Mar00 c-s/cd-s; 74321 74876-4/-2) – hit No.3

Jul 00. (c-s/cd-s; as SANTANA featuring the PRODUCT G&B) *(74321 76937-4/-2)* *<13773>* **MARIA MARIA / (mixes; Wyclef + Pumpin' Dolls)** [6] Jan00 [1]

Oct 02. (cd/c) *(74321 95938-2/-4)* *<14737>* **SHAMAN** [15] [1]
– Adouma / Nothing at all (with MUSIQ) / The game of love (with MICHELLE BRANCH) / You are my kind (with SEAL) / Amore (sexo) (with MACY GRAY) / Foo foo / Victory is won / Since Supernatural (with GOVERNOR WASHINGTON & MELKIE JEAN) / America (with P.O.D.) / Sideways (with CITIZEN COPE) / Why don't you & I (with CHAD KROEGER) / Feels like fire (with DIDO) / Aye aye aye / Hoy es adios (with ALEJANDRO LERNER) / One of these days (with OZOMATLI) / Novus (with PLACIDO DOMINGO).

Nov 02. (c-s; by SANTANA & MICHELLE BRANCH) *(74321 95944-4)* **THE GAME OF LOVE / COME TO MY WORLD** [16] [5]
(cd-s+=) *(74321 95944-2)* *<radio>* – Curacion / ('A'video).

Sep 03. (cd-s) *<54071>* **WHY DON'T YOU & I** [–] [8]

Oct 05. (cd-s; SANTANA feat. MICHELLE BRANCH & THE WRECKERS) *<73544>* **I'M FEELING YOU / CALL OUT HOOK** [–] [55]

Oct 05. (cd) *(82876 69620-2)* *<59773>* **ALL THAT I AM** [36] [2]
– Hermes / El fuego / I'm feeling you (with MICHELLE BRANCH & the WRECKERS) / My man (with MARY J. BLIGE & BIG ROI) / Just feel better (with STEVEN TYLER) / I am somebody (with WILL.I.AM) / Con Santana / Twisted (with ANTHONY HAMILTON) / Trinity (with KIRK HAMMETT & ROBERT RANDOLPH) / Cry baby cry (with SEAN PAUL & JOSS STONE) / Brown skin girl (with BO BICE) / I don't wanna lose your love (with LOS LONELY BOYS) / Da tu amor.

Nov 05. (cd-s; SANTANA & STEVEN TYLER) *(82876 75191-2)* **JUST FEEL BETTER / SMOOTH (with ROB THOMAS)** [ ] [–]

– compilations, others, etc. –

on 'CBS/ Columbia' until mentioned otherwise.

Mar 73. (7") *(CBS 1155)* **OYE COMO VA. / BLACK MAGIC WOMAN** [ ] [–]
(re-iss. Feb76; CBS 3950)

Aug 74. (lp/c) *(CBS/40 69081)* *<3050>* **SANTANA'S GREATEST HITS** [14] Jul74 [17]
– Evil ways / Jin-go-la-ba / Hope you're feeling better / Samba pa ti / Persuasion / Black magic woman / Oye como va / Everything's coming up roses / Se a cabo / Everybody's everything. *(cd-iss. Jun87; CD 69081) (re-iss. Feb88 lp/c; CBS/40 32386) (cd re-iss. Jul99 on 'Columbia'; CDZ 32386)*

Sep 74. (7") *(CBS 2561)* *<46067>* **SAMBA PA TI. / INCIDENT AT NESHABUR** [27] [ ]
(re-iss. Feb79; CBS 7063)

Oct 80. (t-lp) *(CBS 66354)* **BOX SET** (first 3 albums) [ ] [ ]

Jul 84. (7") *(A-4587)* **SHE'S NOT THERE. / SAMBA PA TI** [ ] [–]

Feb 86. (12"ep) *Old Gold; (OG 4005)* **SAMBA PA TI / JIN-GO-LA-BA. / SHE'S NOT THERE / EVIL WAYS** [ ] [–]

Oct 86. (lp/c/cd) *K-Tel; (NE1/CE2/NCD3 338)* **VIVA! SANTANA – THE VERY BEST OF SANTANA** [50] [–]

Jan 88. (7") *Old Gold; (OG 9753)* **SAMBA PA TI. / SHE'S NOT THERE** [ ] [–]

May 88. (cd) *Arcade; (ADEHCD 828-0)* **THE VERY BEST OF SANTANA – VOLUME ONE** [ ] [–]

May 88. (cd) *Arcade; (ADEHCD 828-1)* **THE VERY BEST OF SANTANA – VOLUME TWO** [ ] [–]

Jun 88. (d-lp/c/d-cd) *That's Original; (TFO LP/MC/CD 14)* **WELCOME / CARLOS SANTANA & BUDDY MILES LIVE** [ ] [–]

Oct 88. (t-lp/d-c/d-cd) *(462500-1/-4/-2)* *<44344>* **VIVA! SANTANA** (best + live) [ ] [ ]
– Everybody's everything / Black magic woman – Gypsy queen / Guajira / Jungle strut / Jingo / Ballin' / Bambara / Angel Negro / Incident at Neshabur / Just let the music speak / Super boogie – Hong Kong blues / Song of the wind / Abi cama / Vitalo / Paris finale / Brotherhood / Open invitation / Aqua marine / Dance, sisters, dance / Europa / Peraza 1 / She's not there / Bambele / Evil ways / Daughter of the night / Peraza II / Black magic woman – Gypsy woman (live) / Oyo como va / Persuasion / Soul sacrifice. *(d-cd re-iss. Jun97; same)*

May 89. (3"cd-ep) **BLACK MAGIC WOMAN / SAMBA PA TI / OYE COMO VA / JIN-GO-LA-BA** [ ] [–]

Jun 89. (lp/cd) *Thunderbolt; (THBVL/CDTB 071)* **PERSUASION** [ ] [–]
(cd re-iss. Apr98 on 'MagMid'; MM 003)

Jan 90. (lp/cd) *Thunderbolt; (THBVL/CDTB 079)* **LATIN TROPICAL** [ ] [–]
(cd re-iss. Jun98 on 'MagMid'; MM 007)

Oct 90. (cd) *Thunderbolt; (CDTB 087)* **ACAPULCO SUNRISE** [ ] [–]
(re-iss. May97 on 'C.M.C.'; 100182) (re-iss. Mar99 on 'MagMid'; MM 024)

May 92. (cd) *Traditional Line; (TL 1315)* **LIVE IN MONTREUX 1971 (live)** [ ] [–]

Jun 92. (cd/c) *(468267-2/-4)* **THE BEST OF SANTANA** [ ] [ ]
(re-iss. Oct94; same)

Mar 93. (d-cd) *(465221-2)* **SANTANA / ABRAXAS** [ ] [ ]

May 93. (cd) *F.N.A.C.;* **NINETEEN SIXTY EIGHT** [ ] [–]

Sep 93. (cd/c) *Sony Collectors; (983259-2/-4)* **SALSA, SAMBA & SANTANA** [ ] [–]

Nov 93.	(d-cd) *Sound Wings; (ACD 23057-2)* **SAMBA PA TI**		–
Feb 94.	(cd) *Thunderbolt; (CDTB 502)* **EVOLUTION**		–
Mar 94.	(cd) *Charly; (CDCD 1168)* **SOUL SACRIFICE**		–
Apr 94.	(3xcd) *Pulsar; (PULS 302)* **THE SUPER COLLECTION**		–
Nov 96.	(cd/c) *Tring; (QED 056)* **AS YEARS GO BY**		–
Jul 94.	(cd/c) *Success; (1348)* **SANTANA JAM**		–
Jul 94.	(cd/c) *Success;* **EVERY DAY I HAVE THE BLUES**		–
Jul 94.	(cd/c) *Success;* **WITH A LITTLE HELP FROM MY FRIENDS**		–
Oct 94.	(cd) *Charly; (CDCD 1187)* **LATIN ROCK FUSIONS**		–
Feb 95.	(cd/c) *B.A.M.;* **PEARLS OF THE PAST**		–
Apr 95.	(cd/c) *Muskateer; (MU 5/4 025)* **THE EARLY YEARS**		–
Sep 95.	(3xcd-box) *Legacy-Columbia; (C3K 64605)* **DANCE OF THE RAINBOW SERPENT**		
Oct 95.	(cd/c) *Collectors Choice; (462563-2/-4)* **SAMBA PA TI**		–
Nov 95.	(3xcd-box) *The Collection; (KBOX 346)* **THE COLLECTION**		–
Mar 97.	(d-cd) *Legacy; (485106-2)* **LIVE ROCK . . . AT FILLMORE (live)**		–
Apr 97.	(cd) *(CDX 32386)* **THE VERY BEST**		–
May 97.	(cd) *C.M.C.; (101182)* **LIVE**		–
May 97.	(d-cd) *Laserlight; (24359)* **SANTANA**		–
May 97.	(cd) *Experience; (EXP 027)* **SANTANA VOL.1**		–
May 97.	(cd) *Experience; (EXP 028)* **SANTANA VOL.2**		–
Mar 98.	(d-cd) *Charly; (CPCD 83312)* **AWAKENING**		–
Apr 98.	(cd) <65561> **THE BEST OF SANTANA**	–	82
Aug 98.	(d-cd/d-c) *Sony TV; (SONYTV 47 CD/MC)* **THE ULTIMATE COLLECTION** *(re-dist.Mar00)* – hit No.12	23	–
Jun 99.	(cd) *Columbia: (494678-2)* **BLACK MAGIC WOMAN – THE BEST OF SANTANA**		
Jul 99.	(cd) *Akarma; (AK 068CD)* **SF MISSION DISTRICT LIVE (live)**		–
Jul 99.	(d-cd) *Yeaah; (YEAAH 4)* **FRIED NECKBONES AND HOME FRIES**		–

— Note: Most albums up to 1974 were also issued on quad-lp. SUCH IS LIFE album late '93, must have been by other band of same name.

SCISSOR SISTERS

Formed: New York City, New York, USA . . . 2001 as DEAD LESBIAN AND THE FIBRILLATING SCISSOR SISTERS by JAKE SHEARS (aka JASON SELLARDS), ANA MATRONIC (aka ANA LYNCH), BABYDADDY (aka SCOTT HOFFMAN), DEL MARQUIS (aka DEREK GRUEN) and PADDY BOOM (aka PATRICK SECORD) – "Scissor Sisters" is a lesbian sex position. Like the NEW YORK DOLLS before them, SCISSOR SISTERS coalesced around the the Big Apple's gender-bending club scene. Unlike the 'DOLLS, their influences include ELTON JOHN (who collaborated with the band on their forthcoming sophomore album), the BEE GEES, the Rocky Horror Picture Show and PINK FLOYD, whose 'Comfortably Numb' they brazenly reinvented (in 2004) as a UK dancefloor anthem (and Top 10 hit). Previous to this, they'd scraped the lower rungs of the British chart with soul-powered debut single, 'LAURA', a song which eventually made No.12 on its post-album re-release. With no genre or 70's/80's melodic honeypot off-limits, their sleazy, pseudonymous arch-glam and guilt-free cherry picking saw them run away with the best selling long player of 2004: 'SCISSOR SISTERS' (2004) topped the British album chart, released on 'Universal' and wrapped in the kind of cod-ethereal cover art unwitnessed since the heyday of 80's prog-metal. Talismanically performed at the 2005 Brit Awards, the Stonesy, 'Saturday Night's All Right'-y buck and grind of 'TAKE YOUR MAMA' deserved more than Top 20, even if the raunchier 'FILTHY/GORGEOUS' subsequently went Top 5. The awards saw them breaking records and sweeping the board in the global category, scooping Best International Group, Best International Breakthrough and Best International Album. For trivia-amenable, surrealistically inclined British fans of a certain age, however, perhaps the most fascinating thing about SCISSOR SISTERS is the fact that their sometime live keyboard player is JOHN 'JJ' GARDEN, son of none other than Graeme Garden of determinedly non-glamourous – and still underrated – 70's buffoons, 'The Goodies'. Would a disco cover of the Goodies' theme tune be too much to ask?

• **Covered:** TAKE ME OUT (Franz Ferdinand).

Album rating: SCISSOR SISTERS (*8)

JAKE SHEARS (b. JASON SELLARDS, 3 Oct'77, Arizona, USA) – vocals / **ANA MATRONIC** (b. ANA LYNCH, 14 Aug'74, San Francisco, Calif.) – vocals / **DEL MARQUIS** (b. DEREK GRUEN) – guitar / **BABY DADDY** (b. SCOTT HOFFMAN) – bass / **PADDY BOOM** (b. PATRICK SECORD) – drums

		A Touch Of Class	not iss.
Oct 02.	(12") *(ATOC 008)* **ELECTROBIX (mixes; 12" / radio / hungry wives depressive) / Comfortably numb**		–
		Polydor	Universal
Oct 03.	(12"pic-d) *(9812787)* **LAURA. / ('A'-City hi-fi vocal mix) / AVAILABLE FOR YOU**	54	–
	(cd-s+=) *(9812788)* – ('A'-video).		
Jan 04.	(cd-s) *(9815883)* **COMFORTABLY NUMB / (Fatboy Slim extended mix) / ROCK MY SPOT / ('A'-video)**	10	–
	(12") *(9815884)* – ('A') / (Hughes & Spier remix) / (Tommie's sunshine remix).		
	(12") *(9815885)* – ('A'-Fatboy Slim remix) / ('A'-Paper Faces remix).		
Feb 04.	(cd/lp) *(98660 58/77)* <27720-2> **SCISSOR SISTERS** – Laura / Take your mama / Comfortably numb / Mary / Lovers in the backseat / Tits on the radio / Filthy/Gorgeous / Music is the victim / Better luck / It can't come quickly enough / Return to Oz. *(bonus +=)* – The skins / Get it get it.	1	May04
Mar 04.	(cd-s) *(9866277)* **TAKE YOUR MAMA / BACKWOODS DISCOTHEQUE II**	17	–
	(12") *(9866283)* – ('A'-National forest remix) / ('B').		
	(12") *(9866278)* – ('A'-Hot chip remix) / ('A'-acappella).		
Jun 04.	(cd-s) *(9866832)* **LAURA / LAURA (Craig C's vocal dub workout)**	12	–
	(cd-s) *(9866833)* – ('A') / Borrowed time / Laura (Riton re-dub).		
Oct 04.	(12"pic-d) *(986828-0)* **MARY. / LAURA (City Hi Fi remix)**	14	–
	(12") *(986828-1)* – ('A') / ('A'-Junkie XL radio mix).		
	(cd-s+=) *(986828-2)* – Take me out (Jo Whiley session).		
Jan 05.	(12"pic-d) *(986980-1)* **FILTHY/GORGEOUS. / FILTHY/GORGEOUS – I LOVE YOU (See You Next Tuesday mix) / FILTHY/GORGEOUS (Paper Faces main mix)**	5	–
	(cd-s+=) *(986979-9)* – ('A'-video).		

– others, etc. –

Dec 03.	(12") *(efa 590636)* **COMFORTABLY NUMB (remixes)**		–

□ Mike SCOTT (see under ⇒ the WATERBOYS)

Gil SCOTT-HERON

Born: 1 Apr'49, Chicago, Illinois, USA. The son of a footballer father, Gil Heron "Black Arrow" (who enjoyed a spell with Glasgow Celtic F.C.) and a librarian mother, SCOTT-HERON spent the bulk of his childhood in Jackson, Tennessee, raised by his grandmother following his parents' separation. By the time GIL was back living with his mother in New York and attending high school, he had already began to master piano, his precocious talent for writing subsequently recognised by one of his teachers and leading to SCOTT-HERON completing his studies at noted private school, Fieldston. From there he moved on to Lincoln University, following in the footsteps of his literary hero, Langston Hughes, and subsequently taking a year out to write his first novel, 'The Vulture' (recently republished by the illustrious Canongate Books imprint, Payback Press!). Musically,

SCOTT-HERON cited influences as diverse as RICHIE HAVENS, BILLIE HOLIDAY, OTIS REDDING and JOSE FELICIANO; more obvious was the radical style of THE LAST POETS (whom after witnessing at a show in Ohio, allegedly inspired SCOTT-HERON to take up performing) as well as the melting pot of African and Latin sounds that echoed through the Chelsea district of New York where he lived. GIL made his recording debut with 'SMALL TALK AT 125th AND LENOX' (1972), a set largely comprised of poems set to a sparse percussive backing, released on Bob Thiele's 'Flying Dutchman' label. Updating the tradition of the African griot, SCOTT-HERON laid out an uncompromising manifesto for the black man, executed with mordant humour and sly wit and railing against consumerism, drug addled hippies, false prophets and white oppression. The record's worth hearing for the brilliant 'WHITEY ON THE MOON' alone, that's if you can stomach the rampant homophobia of 'THE SUBJECT WAS FAGGOTS'; clearly, SCOTT-HERON's vision of a brighter tomorrow had no place for gay men. Nevertheless, 'PIECES OF A MAN' (1973) was a stunning, often tenderly poignant follow-up, benefitting from a fuller sound courtesy of keys player/co-writer, BRIAN JACKSON along with such notable players as BERNARD PURDIE, RON CARTER and flautist HUBERT LAWS. 'LADY DAY AND JOHN COLTRANE' remains one of GIL's most uplifting songs, the singer stepping off the soapbox for once and celebrating the power of music. In stark contrast, 'THE REVOLUTION WILL NOT BE TELEVISED' was SCOTT-HERON at his most glaringly effective, ominously intoning the death knell for white, middle class inertia over a hypnotic, stinging bassline. Often cited as one of the earliest prototype rap tracks, its most readily identifiable antecedant was 'Television, Drug Of The Nation' by THE DISPOSABLE HEROES OF HIP HOPRISY, a group closer in spirit to SCOTT-HERON's work than many rap acts. But the man was most affecting when he addressed the everyday tragedies of human experience; any listener not moved by the likes of 'PIECES OF A MAN' and 'HOME IS WHERE THE HATRED IS' must have a heart of steel. Following his departure from 'Flying Dutchman', SCOTT-HERON recorded 'WINTER IN AMERICA' (1974) on the US independent, 'Strata East'. As well as the atmospheric lament of the title track, the album featured one of the singer's most famous tracks, 'THE BOTTLE' a much covered, funky, flute-driven testament to the dangers of alcohol. The following year, he signed to the newly formed 'Arista', scoring a Top 30 album with 'THE FIRST MINUTE OF A NEW DAY' (1975). Co-credited to BRIAN JACKSON, the album was the first to feature The MIDNIGHT BAND, a backing troupe which the pair led right through into the 80's with varying line-ups. The record also provided a minor US R&B hit with the disco influenced 'JOHANNESBURG', once again conclusively proving that dancefloor didn't necessarily mean braindead. Throughout the latter part of the 70's and on into the early 80's, SCOTT-HERON maintained an impressively consistent, unusually prolific recording schedule, his coffee-rich vocals and enduring blend of jazz, blues and soul providing an often lone voice of sanity in the decadent, coke-fuelled music scene of the time. As well as documenting the very real threat of nuclear power ('WE ALMOST LOST DETROIT', 'SHUT 'EM DOWN'), he continued to address the concerns of working class blacks ('INNER CITY BLUES', 'BLUE COLLAR') and the contentious issue of drugs ('ANGEL DUST'). His scathing political commentary also continued apace, 'B-MOVIE', from the acclaimed 'REFLECTIONS' (1981) set, nailing the newly elected REAGAN with pinpoint accuracy. It's all the more ironic, then, that SCOTT-HERON releases petered out after the early 80's, the singer falling prey to the drug and alcohol abuse he'd spoken out so militantly against throughout his career. Maybe the state of politics (US and British) was just too much for him to take, after all, if SCOTT-HERON's articulate defense of humanist principles was ever needed at all, it was in the moral wasteland of that vilified decade. Though a belated comeback album, 'SPIRITS' (1994) failed to impress many fans, SCOTT-HERON continued to tour, his live shows highly impressive if you were lucky enough to catch him on a good night. Though his golden period may be over, arguably, GIL has nothing left to prove, his back catalogue standing up amongst the cream of black music history. Post-millennium, the great poet was fighting drug addiction, culminating in 2001 when he was sentenced to three years imprisonment for cocaine possession; stop press:- on 5th July 2006, he was given two-to-four years for violating a plea deal through a previous drug possession charge.

• **Covered:** INNER CITY BLUES (Marvin Gaye) / GRANDMA'S HANDS (Bill Withers). GIL was the original voice-over for the "You know you've been Tangoed" TV ad. LaBELLE covered his song 'THE REVOLUTION WILL NOT BE TELEVISED' in 1974.

Album rating: SMALL TALK AT 125th AND LENOX (*6) / FREE WILL (*7) / PIECES OF A MAN (*7) / WINTER IN AMERICA (*7) / THE REVOLUTION WILL NOT BE TELEVISED compilation (*8) / THE FIRST MINUTE OF A NEW DAY with Brian Jackson (*7) / FROM SOUTH AFRICA TO SOUTH CAROLINA with Brian Jackson (*6) / IT'S YOUR WORLD with Brian Jackson (*7) / BRIDGES with Brian Jackson (*6) / SECRETS with Brian Jackson (*6) / 1980 with Brian Jackson (*6) / REAL EYES (*6) / REFLECTIONS (*7) / MOVING TARGET (*5) / THE BEST OF GIL SCOTT-HERON compilation (*7) / THE TALES OF GIL SCOTT-HERON AND THE AMNESIA EXPRESS (*6) / SPIRITS (*8) / GHETTO STYLE compilation (*8) / ANTHOLOGY: MESSAGES compilation with Brian Jackson (*7)

GIL SCOTT-HERON – vocals, piano, guitar

Philips | Flying Dutchma

1970. (lp) *<10131>* **SMALL TALK AT 125th AND LENOX** (rap poems) [–] [ ]
– Introduction – The revolution will not be televised / Omen / Brother / Comment #1 / Small talk at 125th & Lenox / The subject was faggots / Evolution (and flashback) / Plastic pattern people / Whitey on the moon / The vulture / Enough / Paint it black / Who'll pay reparations on my soul? / Everyday. *(cd-iss. Jun97 on 'RCA Victor'; 07863 66611-2)*

1972. (lp) *<10153>* **FREE WILL** [–] [ ]
– Free will / The middle of your day / The get out of the ghetto blues / Speed kills / Did you hear what they said? / The King Alfred plan / No knock / Wiggy / Ain't no new thing / Billy Green is dead / Sex education: ghetto style / . . .And then he wrote "meditations". *<cd-iss. Nov01 on 'B.M.G.'+=; 74321 85161-2>* – Free will (alt.) / Speed kills (alt.) / The King Alfred plan (alt.) / No knock (alt.) / Wiggy (alt.) / Ain't no new thing / Billy Green is dead / Free will.

— added **BRIAN JACKSON** – keyboards / **DANNY BOWENS** – bass / **BOB ADAMS** – drums

Apr 73. (lp) *(6369 415) <10143>* **PIECES OF A MAN** [ ] [ ]
– Lady Day and John Coltrane / When you are who you are / The revolution will not be televised / Home is where the hatred is / I think I'll call it morning / Save the children / The needle's eye / Pieces of a man / A sign of the ages / Or down you fall / The prisoner.

Apr 73. (7") *(6073 705)* **WHEN YOU ARE WHO YOU ARE. / LADY DAY AND JOHN COLTRANE** [ ] [ ]

R.C.A. | Flying Dutchma

Jul 75. (lp) *(SF 8428) <BXL1-0613>* **THE REVOLUTION WILL NOT BE TELEVISED** [ ] Mar74 [ ]
– The revolution will not be televised / Sex education: ghetto style / The get out of the ghetto blues / No knock / Lady Day and John Coltrane / Pieces of a man / Home is where the hatred is / Brother / Save the children / Did you hear what they said? *(cd-iss. May89 on 'Bluebird-RCA' lp/c/cd+=; NL/NK/ND 86994)* – (extra track).

not iss. | Stata Eas

1974. (lp) *<19742>* **WINTER IN AMERICA** [–] [ ]
– Peace go with you brother / Rivers of my father / A very precious time / Back home / The bottle / Song for Bobby Smith / Your daddy loves you / H2o gate blues / Peace go with you brother. *(cd-iss. Sep92; 66051015) (cd re-iss. Mar99 on 'Charly'; CDGR 225)*

GIL SCOTT-HERON & BRIAN JACKSON

— next featured The MIDNIGHT BAND

— **JOSEF BLOCKER + REGGIE BRISBANE** – drums repl. ADAMS

Arista Arista

Jul 75. (lp) *(ARTY 106)* *<4030>* **THE FIRST MINUTE OF A NEW DAY** Jun75 **30**
– Offering / The liberation song (red, black and green) / Must be something / Ain't no such thing as Superman / Pardon our analysis (we beg your pardon America) / Winter in America / Guerilla / Western sunrise / Alluswe. *(cd-iss. Feb99 on 'TVT'; 4350)*

Jul 75. (7") *<0117>* **AIN'T NO SUCH THING AS SUPERMAN. / WE BEG YOUR PARDON AMERICA** –

Oct 75. (7") *(ARIST 23)* *<0152>* **(WHAT'S THE WORD) JOHANNESBURG. / FELL TOGETHER**

Jan 76. (lp) *(ARTY 121)* *<4044>* **FROM SOUTH AFRICA TO SOUTH CAROLINA** Oct75
– (What's the word) Johannesburg / A toast to the people / The summer of '42 / Beinnings (first minute of a new day) / South Carolina (Barnwell) / Essex / Fell together / A lovely day.

Nov 76. (7") *<0225>* **THE BOTTLE. /** –

Nov 76. (lp) *(DARTY 1)* *<5001>* **IT'S YOUR WORLD (live)**
– Seventeenth street / Tomorrow's trane (gospel trane) / Must be something / It's your world / New York City / The bottle / Possum Slim / Home is where the hatred is / Bicentennial blues / Sharing.

— **JOSEF BLOCKER + REGGIE BRISBANE** – drums repl. ADAMS

Dec 77. (lp) *(SPARTY 1031)* *<4147>* **BRIDGES** Oct77
– Hello Sunday! hello road! / Song of the wind / Racetrack in France / Vildgolia (deaf, dumb and blind) / Under the hammer / We almost lost Detroit / Tuskeegee No.626 / Delta man (where I'm coming from) / 95 South (all of the places we've been).

Dec 77. (7") *(ARIST 169)* **HELLO SUNDAY, HELLO ROAD. / THE BOTTLE (live)** –

Dec 77. (7") *<0285>* **HELLO SUNDAY, HELLO ROAD. / SONG OF THE WIND** –

Mar 78. (7") *<0317>* **UNDER THE HAMMER. / RACETRACK IN FRANCE** –

— **GREG PHILLINGANES** – keyboards repl. BOWENS

Jul 78. (7") *<0366>* **ANGEL DUST. / THIRD WORLD REVOLUTION** –

Sep 78. (lp) *(SPARTY 1073)* *<4189>* **SECRETS** **61**
– Angel dust / Madison Avenue / Cane / Third world revolution / Better days ahead / Three miles down / Angola, Louisiana / Show bizness / A prayer for everybody / To be free.

Oct 78. (7") *(ARIST 215)* *<0390>* **SHOW BIZNESS. / BETTER DAYS AHEAD**

— retained only **JACKSON** + recruited **ED GRADY** – guitar / **KENNY POWELL** – drums / **GLEN TURNER** – keyboards / **CARL CORNWALL + VERNON JAMES** – tenor sax, flute / **KENNY SHEFFIELD** – trumpet

Feb 80. (lp) *<9514>* **1980** – **82**
– Shut 'um down / Alien / Willing / Corners / 1980 / Push comes to shove / Shah mot / Late last night. *(UK-iss.Jul85; 201733)*

Mar 80. (7"/ext-12") *<0488>* **SHUT 'UM DOWN. / BALTIMORE** –

May 80. (7") *<0505>* **WILLING. /** –

GIL SCOTT-HERON

Dec 80. (lp) *<9540>* **REAL EYES** –
– The train from Washington / Not needed / Waiting for the axe to fall / Combinations / A legend in his own mind / You could be my brother / The Klan / Your daddy loves you.

Dec 80. (7") *<0583>* **LEGEND IN HIS OWN MIND. /** –

Aug 81. (7") *<0634>* **STORM MUSIC. /** –

Oct 81. (7") *<0647>* **B-MOVIE. /** –

Dec 81. (lp) *(SPARTY 1180)* *<9566>* **REFLECTIONS**
– Storm music / Grandma's hands / Is that jazz? / Morning thoughts / Inner city blues (poem – The siege of New Orleans) / Gun / B-movie. *(cd-iss. Feb97; 254094)*

Feb 82. (7") *(ARIST 452)* **STORM MUSIC. / B-MOVIE** –
(12"+=) *(ARIST12 452)* – Gun.

Sep 82. (7") **FAST LANE. / BLUE COLLAR** –

Sep 82. (lp) *(204921)* *<9606>* **MOVING TARGET**
– Fast lane / Washington D.C. / No exit / Blue collar / Ready or not / Explanations / Black history – The word. *(cd-iss. Feb97; 254921)*

May 83. (7") *(ARIST 527)* **(WHAT'S THE WORD) JOHANNESBURG. / WAITING FOR THE AXE TO FALL**
(12"+=) *(ARIST12 527)* – B-Movie (intro, poem, song).

Aug 84. (7") *(ARIST 573)* **RE-RON. / B-MOVIE**
(12") *(ARIST12 573)* – Re-Ron (the missing brain mix). / B-Movie (intro, poem, song).

Sep 84. (lp/c) *(206/406 618)* **THE BEST OF GIL SCOTT-HERON** (compilation)
– The revolution will not be televised / The bottle / Winter in America / Ain't no such thing as Superman / Re-Ron / Shut 'em down / Angel dust / B-movie. *(cd-iss. Apr88; 256 618)*

Nov 85. (7"/10") *(ARIST/+10 643)* **WINTER IN AMERICA. / JOHANNESBURG**

— now with **ROBBIE GORDON** – bass, percussion / **RON HOLLOWAY** – saxophone

Essential Rykodisc

Mar 90. (7") *(GILL 003)* **SPACE SHUTTLE (vocal). / ('A'original mix)**
(12"+=) *(GILT 003)* – ('A'deep club mix) / Pieces of gold – medley.
(12"+=) *(GILTY 003)* – ('A'deep club dub) / War is very ugly.
(cd-s+=) *(GILTX 003)* – The bottle / Pieces of gold – medley.

Mar 90. (cd/c/d-lp) *(ESD CD/MC/LP 201)* **THE TALES OF GIL SCOTT-HERON AND HIS AMNESIA EXPRESS (live)**
– Washington DC / Save the children / Angel dust / Gun / Blue collar / Amen (hold on to your dream) / Three miles down / The bottle.

Mother T.V.T.

Jul 94. (cd/c) *(MUM CD/C 9415)* *<TVT 43102>* **SPIRITS**
– Message to the messengers / Spirits / Give her a call / Laly's song / Spirits past / The other side (parts 1-3) / Work for peace / Don't give up. *(lp-iss.Mar99 on 'TVT'; same as US)*

Oct 94. (12"/cd-s) **DON'T GIVE UP. / MESSAGE TO THE MESSENGERS / THE BOTTLE (live)**

– others, etc. –

Jul 80. (7"/12"; GIL SCOTT-HERON & BRIAN JACKSON) *Inferno; (HEAT 23/+12)* **THE BOTTLE (drunken mix). / THE BOTTLE (sober mix)**
(re-iss. Jan81 on 'Champagne' 7"/12"; VAT/+S 302)

1981. (lp) *Audio Fidelity; (1017)* **THE BOTTLE** (1973) –

Mar 88. (12"m) *Old Gold; (OG 4054)* **THE BOTTLE. / JOHANNESBURG / WINTER IN AMERICA** –

Nov 90. (d-cd) *Arista; (353913)* **GLORY (THE GIL SCOTT-HERON COLLECTION)**

Apr 94. (cd/c) *Castle; (CCS CD/MC 403)* **MINISTRY OF INFORMATION (live)** –
– Winter in America / Alien / The bottle / Is that jazz / Washington DC / Gun / B-movie.

Nov 98. (cd) *Camden-BMG; (74321 628062)* **GHETTO STYLE** –
– The revolution will not be televised / Or down you fall / The needle's eye / I think I'll call it morning / When you are who you are / Save the children / Did you hear what they said? / Free will / Speed kills / Middle of your day / Pieces of a man / A sign of the ages / The get out of the ghetto blues / Lady day & John Coltrane / Home is where the hatred is / No knock / The revolution will not be televised (early version) / Sex education ghetto style / Small talk at 125th & Lenox / King Alfred plan / Billy Green is dead.

Feb 99. (cd) *R.C.A.; <63141>* **EVOLUTION: THE VERY BEST OF GIL SCOTT-HERON** –

Oct 99. (12")(cd-s) *Joeboy; (JBV 008)(JBCD 017)* **THE BOTTLE** –

Jul 05. (cd; GIL SCOTT-HERON AND BRIAN JACKSON) *Soul Brother; <(CDSBP 26)>* **ANTHOLOGY: MESSAGES**
– The bottle / Johannesburg / Winter in America / Liberation (red, black & green) / It's your world / Home is where the hatred is (live) / Racetrack in France / Hello Sunday hello road / We almost lost Detroit / Delta man (where I'm coming from) / Angel dust / Show bizness / Madison Avenue / Shut 'em down / Alien (hold on to your dreams).

SCREAMING TREES

Formed: Ellensburg, Washington, USA ... 1985 by girthsome brothers VAN and GARY LEE CONNER along with frontman MARK LANEGAN and drummer MARK PICKEREL. Following early effort, 'CLAIRVOYANCE' (1986) for the tiny 'Velvetone' label, the group signed to respected US indie, 'S.S.T.', making their debut with the convincing 'EVEN IF AND ESPECIALLY WHEN' (1987). Fuelled by raging punk, The SCREAMING TREES were nevertheless characterised by the spectral hue of 60's psychedelia running through much of their music, LANEGAN's exotic, JIM MORRISON-esque vocals adding an air of brooding mystery on the likes of fans' favourite, 'TRANSFIGURATION'. Another couple of stirring sets, 'INVISIBLE LANTERN' (1988) and 'BUZZ FACTORY' (1989), followed before the group released a one-off EP for 'Sub Pop'. With the emerging grunge phenomenon in nearby Seattle on the cusp of world domination, The SCREAMING TREES were obviously a promising prospect for major label A&R and it came as little surprise when they signed for 'Epic'. That same year, prior to their debut for the label, the various 'TREES occupied themselves with solo projects, GARY LEE forming PURPLE OUTSIDE and releasing 'MYSTERY LANE', while brother VAN issued the eponymous 'SOLOMON GRUNDY' set the same year, both appearing on 'New Alliance'. Best of the lot, however, was LANEGAN's windswept 'WINDING SHEET', an intense, largely acoustic collection featuring a cover of Leadbelly's 'WHERE DID YOU SLEEP LAST NIGHT' (as later covered in frightening style by KURT COBAIN). Co-produced by CHRIS CORNELL, the subsequent SCREAMING TREES effort, 'UNCLE ANAESTHESIA' (1991), saw the group moving towards a more overt 70's rock sound, while 'SWEET OBLIVION' (1992) saw PICKEREL replaced with BARRETT MARTIN on a more low-key set which stood at odds with the grunge tag unwillingly forced on the band. Augmented by such Seattle "luminaries" as TAD and DAN PETERS (MUDHONEY) along with DINOSAUR JR.'s J. MASCIS, LANEGAN cut an acclaimed solo follow-up, 'WHISKEY FOR THE HOLY GHOST' (1993), before beginning the long and arduous work on the material which would eventually come to make up 'DUST' (1996). Widely held up as the group's most affecting work to date, the George Drakoulias-produced album perfectly captured their threadbare grit and world-weary mysticism, the disparate elements of their sound finally fusing in harmony and exorcising the lingering spirit of grunge. During the latter part of the 90's, LANEGAN was again a solo artist, two albums for 'Sub Pop' ('Beggars Banquet' in Britain), 'SCRAPS AT MIDNIGHT' (1998) and 'I'LL TAKE CARE OF YOU' (1999), being released to mixed response and sliding out of the hard/grunge-rock circle. Meanwhile, VAN CONNOR was back in action via GARDENER, a collaborative duo that also featured Seaweed's AARON STAUFFER. In mid '99, this supergroup of sorts delivered their Lo-Fi psychedelic album for 'Sub Pop', 'NEW DAWNING TIME'. LANEGAN continued to nurse his alt-country blues on his fifth solo effort, 'FIELD SONGS' (2001), his grainy narratives given added muscle by such alt-rock notables as BEN SHEPHERD, BILL RIEFLIN, DUFF McKAGEN and MIKE JOHNSON. Mini-set, 'HERE COMES THAT WEIRD CHILL' (2003), meanwhile, featured guest spots from various MASTERS OF REALITY and AFGHAN WHIGS personnel, the perfect company for LANEGAN's brooding, coruscating narratives and an appropriately twisted cover of Captain Beefheart's 'CLEAR SPOT'. McKAGEN and MASTERS OF REALITY man CHRIS GOSS guested on the gutter balladeering 'BUBBLEGUM' (2004), GOSS co-producing on an album that also featured GREG DULLI, PJ HARVEY and IZZY STRADLIN. Having been a proxy member of the QUEENS OF THE STONE AGE for most of the first half of the 00s, LANEGAN was also joined by mainmen JOSH HOMME and NICK OLIVERI. The legacy of his former band was under the spotlight on anthology, 'OCEAN OF CONFUSION: SONGS OF SCREAMING TREES 1989 – 1996' (2005), albeit on a set which necessarily passed over the 'S.S.T.' years. One of LANEGAN's most unlikely collaborators of recent years has been ISOBEL CAMPBELL, latterly of BELLE & SEBASTIAN. With CAMPBELL laying down her weary tunes in Glasgow and LANEGAN adding his ravaged baritone in L.A., the pair came up with the WAITS-ian clatter of 'RAMBLIN' MAN' as a prepatory EP in early 2006, closely followed by the full length 'BALLAD OF THE BROKEN SEAS' (2006). Essential for fans of the NANCY/LEE, STAPLES/MAGNUSON, CAVE/MINOGUE school of double acts, the album made sweet/sour music of a rare beauty, marrying its inspirations with tough love rather than a shotgun wedding; even B&S fans must've appreciated the symphonic pop shuffle of 'HONEY CHILD WHAT CAN I DO?'.

• **Covered:** SLIDE MACHINE (13th Floor Elevators). • **Note:** Not to be confused with the English band on 'Native' records.

Album rating: OTHER WORLDS mini (*4) / EVEN IF AND ESPECIALLY WHEN (*7) / INVISIBLE LANTERN (*5) / BUZZ FACTORY mini (*5) / UNCLE ANAESTHESIA (*6) / ANTHOLOGY – THE S.S.T. YEARS 1985-1989 compilation (*7) / SWEET OBLIVION (*7) / DUST (*9) / OCEANS OF CONFUSION: SONGS OF SCREAMING TREES 1989-1996 compilation (*8) / Mark Lanegan: THE WINDING SHEET (*6) / WHISKEY FOR THE HOLY GHOST (*7) / SCRAPS AT MIDNIGHT (*6) / I'LL TAKE CARE OF YOU (*8) / FIELD SONGS (*6) / HERE COMES THAT WEIRD CHILL mini (*6) / BUBBLEGUM (*7)

MARK LANEGAN (b.25 Nov'64) – vocals / **GARY LEE CONNER** (b.22 Aug'62, Fort Irwin, Calif.) – guitar, vocals / **VAN CONNER** (b.17 Mar'67, Apple Valley, Calif.) – bass, vocals / **MARK PICKEREL** – drums, percussion

not iss. Velveton

1986. (m-lp) *<none>* **CLAIRVOYANCE** [–] [ ]
– Orange airplane / You tell me all these things / Standing on the edge / Forever / Seeing and believing / I see stars / Lonely girl / Strange out here / The turning / Clairvoyance.

S.S.T. S.S.T.

Feb 87. (m-lp/m-cd) *<SST/+C/CD 105>* **OTHER WORLDS** [–] [ ]
– Like I said / Pictures in my mind / Turning / Other worlds / Barriers / Now your mind is next to mine. *(UK-iss.May93; same as US)*

Sep 87. (lp/cd) *<(SST 132/+CD)>* **EVEN IF AND ESPECIALLY WHEN** [ ] [ ]
– Transfiguration / Straight out to any place / World painted / Don't look down / Girl behind the mask / Flying / Cold rain / Other days and different planets / The pathway / You know where it's at / Back together / In the forest. *(cd re-iss. May93; same)*

Jul 88. (12"ep; shared w/ BEAT HAPPENING) *(AGARR 020)* *<110>* **POLLY PEREGUIN E.P.** [ ] [–]
(above issued on UK '53rd & 3rd') <US-iss.on 'Positive'>

Sep 88. (lp/c/cd) *<(SST 188/+C/CD)>* **INVISIBLE LANTERN** [ ] [ ]
– Ivy / Walk through to the other side / Line & circles / Shadow song / Grey diamond desert / Smokerings / The second I awake / Invisible lantern / Even if / Direction of the sun / Night comes creeping / She knows.

Mar 89. (m-lp/m-cd) *<(SST 248/+CD)>* **BUZZ FACTORY** [ ] [ ]
– Where the twain shall meet / Windows / Black sun morning / Too far away / Subtle poison / Yard trip / Flower web / Wish bringer / Revelation revolution / The looking glass cracked / End of the universe.

Glitterhouse Sub Pop

Dec 89. (d7"w /1-white) *(GR 80)* *<SP 48B>* **CHANGE HAS COME. / DAYS / / FLASHES. / TIME SPEAKS HER GOLDEN TONGUE** [ ] [ ]
(re-iss. Dec90 cd-ep+=; GRCD 80) – I've seen you before. *(re-iss. May93; same)*

— LEE CONNER also formed PURPLE OUTSIDE in 1990, releasing 'MYSTERY LANE'. Brother VAN with SOLOMON GRUNDY issued eponymous same year also for 'New Alliance'.

Epic Epic

Oct 90. (12"ep) *<73539>* **UNCLE ANAESTHESIA / WHO LIES IN DARKNESS. / OCEAN OF CONFUSION / SOMETHING ABOUT TODAY (numb inversion version)** [–] [ ]

Jun 91. (cd/c/lp) *(467 307-2/-4/-1)* *<EK 46800>* **UNCLE ANAESTHESIA** [ ] Mar91 [ ]
– Beyond this horizon / Bed of roses / Uncle anaesthesia / Story of her fate / Caught between / Lay your head down / Before we arise / Something about today / Alice said / Time for light / Disappearing / Ocean of confusion / Closer.

— **BARRETT MARTIN** (b.14 Apr'67, Olympia, Washington) – drums repl. PICKEREL who later joined TRULY

Oct 92. (cd/c/lp) *(471 724-2/-4/-1)* *<48996>* **SWEET OBLIVION** [ ] [ ]
– Shadow of the season / Nearly lost you / Dollar bill / More or less / Butterfly / For celebrations past / The secret kind / Winter song / Troubled times / No one knows / Julie Paradise.

Feb 93. (12"ep/pic-cd-ep) *(658 237-6/-2)* **NEARLY LOST YOU. / E.S.K. / SONG OF A BAKER / WINTER SONG (acoustic)** 50 –

Apr 93. (7"pic-d) *(659 179-7)* **DOLLAR BILL. / (THERE'LL BE) PEACE IN THE VALLEY FOR ME (acoustic)** 52 –
(12"colrd+=/cd-s+=) *(659 179-6/-2)* – Tomorrow's dream.

Jul 96. (cd/c/lp) *(483 980-2/-4/-1)* *<64178>* **DUST** 32
– Halo of ashes / All I know / Look at you / Dying days / Make my mind / Sworn and broken / Witness / Traveler / Dime western / Gospel plow.

Sep 96. (7") *(663 351-7)* **ALL I KNOW. / WASTED TIME**
(cd-s+=) *(663 351-2)* – Silver tongue.
(cd-s) *(663 351-5)* – ('A'side) / Dollar bill / Nearly lost you / Winter song (acoustic).

Nov 96. (7"white) *(663 870-7)* **SWORN AND BROKEN. / BUTTERFLY** –
(cd-s+=) *(663 870-2)* – Dollar bill (U.S. radio session) / Caught between – The secret kind (U.S. radio session).

— on a long holiday from each other, maybe for ever, VAN CONNER moonlighted in VALIS with DAN PETERS of MUDHONEY, while BARRETT played on tour with R.E.M., while joining PETER BUCK's supergroup, TUATARA. LANEGAN continued solo (see below)

– compilations, others, etc. –

Nov 91. (d-lp/d-cd) *<(SST 260/+CD)>* **ANTHOLOGY . . . THE S.S.T. YEARS 1985-1989**

May 05. (cd) *Epic; (518901-2)* *<92852>* **OCEAN OF CONFUSION: SONGS OF SCREAMING TREES 1989-1996**
– Who lies in the darkness / Alice said / Disappearing / Ocean of confusion / Shadows of the season / Nearly lost you / Dollar bill / More or less / For celebrations past / Julie Paradise / Butterfly / E.S.K. / Watchpocket blues / Paperback bible / Make my mind / Dying days / Sworn and broken / Witness / Traveler.

MARK LANEGAN

— with on first **MIKE JOHNSON** – guitar / **JACK ENDINO** – bass, guitar / **KURT COBAIN** – guitar, vocals / **CHRIS NOVOSELIC** – bass / **MARK PICKEREL** – drums / **STEVE FISK** – keyboards

Glitterhouse Sub Pop

May 90. (red-lp/cd) *(GR 085/+CD)* *<SP 61>* **THE WINDING SHEET**
– Mockingbirds / Museum / Undertow / Ugly Sunday / Down in the dark / Wild flowers / Eyes of a child / The winding sheet / Woe / Ten feet tall / Where did you sleep last night? / Juarez / I love you little girl. *(c+cd+=)* – I love you little girl. *(re-iss. Apr94 & Oct99; same) (cd re-iss. Jun01; SP 618)*

Sep 90. (7") *(GR 0101)* **DOWN IN THE DARK. / LOVE YOU LITTLE GIRL** –

— next w / **J.MASCIS** + **MARK JOHNSON** (Dinosaur Jr.) / **TAD DOYLE** (Tad) / **DAN PETERS** (Mudhoney) / **KURT FEDORA** (Gobblehoof)

Sub Pop Sub Pop

Jan 94. (lp/cd) *<(SP/+CD 78249)>* **WHISKEY FOR THE HOLY GHOST**
– The river rise / Borracho / House a home / Kingdoms of rain / Carnival / Riding the nightingale / El Sol / Dead on you / Shooting gallery / Sunrise / Pendulum / Jesus touch / Beggar's blues. *(cd re-iss. Oct99 & Jun01; SPCD 132)*

May 94. (cd-ep) *<(SPCD 131-327)>* **HOUSE A HOME / SHOOTING GALLERY / UGLY SUNDAY / SUNRISE**

Beggars Banquet Sub Pop

Jul 98. (cd) *(BBQCD 204)* *<SP 419>* **SCRAPS AT MIDNIGHT**
– Hospital roll call / Hotel / Stay / Black bell ocean / Last one in the world / Wheels / Waiting on a train / Day and night / Praying ground / Because of this.

Sep 98. (7"colrd) *(BBQ 328)* **STAY. / SLIDE MACHINE** –
(cd-s+=) *(BBQ 328CD)* – Death don't have no mercy.

Sep 99. (cd/lp) *(BBQ CD/LP 215)* *<SP 445>* **I'LL TAKE CARE OF YOU**
– Carry home / I'll take care of you / Shiloh town / Creeping coastline of lights / Ba dee da / Consider me / On Jesus program / Little Sadie / Together again / Shanty man's life / Boogie boogie.

Jun 01. (cd) *(BBQCD 224)* *<SP 502>* **FIELD SONGS** May01
– One way street / No easy action / Miracle / Pill hill serenade / Don't forget me / Kimiko's dream house / Resurrection song / Field song / Love / Blues for D / She done too much / Fix.

MARK LANEGAN BAND

— now with **DEAN WEEN** – guitar (of WEEN) / **JOSH HOMME** – bass, guitar, drums (of QUEENS OF THE STONE AGE) / **NICK OLIVERI** – organ, synthesizer (of QUEENS OF THE STONE AGE) / **DAVE CATCHING** – guitar / **CHRIS GOSS** – bass, guitar, vocals (ex-MASTERS OF REALITY) GREG DULLI – drums (ex-AFGHAN WHIGS)

Nov 03. (10"m-lp/m-cd) *(BBQ 373 TT/CD)* *<81373>* **HERE COMES THAT WEIRD CHILL**
– Methamphetamine blues / On the steps of the cathedral / Clear spot / Message to mine / Lexington slow down / Skeletal history / Wish you well / Sleep with me (version).

Aug 04. (cd) *(BBQCD 237)* *<80237>* **BUBBLEGUM**
– When your number isn't up / Hit the city / Wedding dress / Methamphetamine blues / One hundred days / Bombed / Strange religion / Sideways in reverse / Come to me / Like Little Willie John / Can't come down / Morning glory wine / Head / Driving Death Valley blues / Out of nowhere.

Nov 04. (7"/cd-s) *(BBQ 381/+CD)* **HIT THE CITY. / MUD PINK SKAG / MIRRORED** –

— in Mar'06, LANEGAN collaborated with ISOBEL CAMPBELL (ex-BELLE AND SEBASTIAN) on the album, 'BALLAD OF THE BROKEN SEAS'

SCRITTI POLITTI

Formed: London, England . . . late '77 by Leeds art student (and former Young Communist), 'GREEN' GARTSIDE, along with NIAL JINKS and TOM MORLEY. Politically motivated punks, their first release, 'SKANK BLOC BOLOGNA' (issued on their own 'St. Pancras' label) created enough interest for a John Peel session, the tracks subsequently released on 'Rough Trade' in 1979. By the release of the classic 'SWEETEST GIRL' single in summer '81, only MORLEY remained from the original line-up, GREEN now steering the band in an altogether more endearing new-wave art-pop/white reggae vein. The track (which featured the piano talents of ROBERT WYATT) was a minor chart hit, likewise the follow-up singles, 'FAITHLESS' and 'JERUSALEM'. All three were included on the much anticipated debut set, 'SONGS TO REMEMBER' (1982), GREEN's dreamy falsetto, musical eclecticism and unerring way with an insidious pop hook (not to mention clever-clever lyric) making him – by this juncture SCRITTI POLITTI were basically a studio vehicle for GREEN – a critical darling and one of 'Rough Trade's most unlikely success stories; the album almost made the UK Top 10, becoming the label's biggest selling release to date. Subsequently relocating to New York and moving up to 'Virgin', GREEN sought out such accomplished US musicians as MARCUS MILLER (former bassist for MILES DAVIS), who accompanied him on his first (UK) Top 10 hit, 'WOOD BEEZ (PLAY LIKE ARETHA FRANKLIN)' in 1984. A succession of different sessioners played on subsequent singles, 'ABSOLUTE', 'HYPNOTISE' and 'THE WORD GIRL', although FRED MAHER and DAVID GAMSON went on to augment GREEN on the follow-up album, 'CUPID AND PSYCHE '85' (1985). Again including all the singles, this slick set of Arif Mardin-produced dancefloor pop-soul also included 'PERFECT WAY', the track which broke SCRITTI POLITTI (albeit briefly) in the States and was later given the honour of a cover by aforementioned jazz legend, MILES DAVIS. The trumpeter also contributed to 'OH PATTI (DON'T FEEL SORRY FOR LOVERBOY)', GREEN's first single after three years of beavering away in the studio. The accompanying album, 'PROVISION' (1988), further refined the man's luxuriant pop vision with an altogether more straightforward approach, GAMSON again providing the lush synth textures. Despite the quality, further singles, 'FIRST BOY IN TOWN (LOVESICK)' and 'BOOM! THERE SHE WAS' lingered in the lower regions of the singles chart. After another interminable lay-off, GREEN returned in 1991 for a Top 20 collaborative cover of The Beatles' 'SHE'S A WOMAN' with ragga loveman, SHABBA RANKS, a further duet with SWEETIE IRIE (a version of Gladys Knight's hit, 'TAKE ME IN YOUR ARMS') not quite so successful. With no album forthcoming in the 90's so far, it does seem as if GREEN had finally abandoned SCRITTI POLITTI as a front for his musical activities although it's likely that this pop maverick will emerge at one point in one form or another. Ah, to see a prophecy come true. Re-inventing himself as a bearded rapper type (well his backing group were anyhow), GREEN and SCRITTI POLITTI came storming back from oblivion on the long-awaited fourth set, 'ANOMIE AND BONHOMIE' (1999). Not the most prolific artist by any means, GREEN returned from a long leave of absence to release acclaimed comeback set, 'WHITE BREAD BLACK BEER' (2006).

• **Trivia:** SCRITTI POLITTI is nearly Italian for political writing. MADNESS had a 1986 hit with 'THE SWEETEST GIRL'. That year also saw GREEN and GAMSON write the title track for AL JARREAU's album, 'L Is For Lover'.

Album rating: SONGS TO REMEMBER (*8) / CUPID & PSYCHE (*7) / PROVISION (*4) / ANOMIE AND BONHOMIE (*6) / EARLY compilation (*8) / WHITE BREAD BLACK BEER (*7)

GREEN GARTSIDE (b. PAUL JULIAN STROHMEYER, 22 Jun'56, Cardiff, Wales) – vocals, guitar / **TOM MORLEY** – linn drum / **MATTHEW 'K'** – programme organiser / **NIAL JINKS** – bass

St.Pancras — not iss.

Nov 78. (7") *(SCRIT 1)* **SKANC BLOG BOLOGNA. / IS AND OUGHT OF THE WESTERN WORLD** [ ] [–]

Rough Trade — not iss.

Sep 79. (12"ep) *(RT 027T)* **4 A SIDES** [ ] [–]
– Doubt beat / Confidences / Bibbly O'tek / P.A.'s.

Nov 79. (7"ep) *(SCRIT 2 – RT 034)* **WORK IN PROGRESS (PEEL SESSIONS)** [ ] [–]
– Hegamony / Scritlocks door / Opec-Immac / Messthetics.

—— added **MIKE MacEVOY** – synthesizers, vocoder / **MGOTSE** – d.bass / guest **ROBERT WYATT** – piano

Aug 81. (7"/12") *(RT 091/+T)* **THE SWEETEST GIRL. / LIONS AFTER SLUMBER** [64] [–]

—— **JOE CANG** – bass repl. NIAL / **STEVE SIDWELL** – trumpet / **JAMIE TALBOT** – saxophone repl. MGOTSE

Apr 82. (7"/12") *(RT 107/+T)* **FAITHLESS. / FAITHLESS PART II (instrumental)** [56] [–]

Jul 82. (7"/7"pic-d) *(RT 111/+P)* **ASYLUMS IN JERUSALEM. / JAQUES DERRIDA** [43] [–]
(12"+=) *(RT 111T)* – ('A'extended).

Aug 82. (lp) *(ROUCH/+C 20)* **SONGS TO REMEMBER** [12] [–]
– Asylums in Jerusalem / A slow soul / Jacques Derrida / Lions after slumber / Faithless / Sex / Rock-a-boy blue / Gettin' havin' & holdin' / The sweetest girl. *(cd-iss. May87; ROUGH/+CD 20) (cd re-iss. Oct01 on 'Virgin'; CDV 2944)*

—— **GREEN** recruited US musicians **MARCUS MILLER** – bass (ex-MILES DAVIS) / **STEVE FERRONE** – drums (ex-BRIAN AUGER) / **PAUL JACKSON Jnr.** – guitar / (MORLEY went solo and released one 1985 single for 'Zarjazz', 'WHO BROKE THE LOVE?')

Virgin — Warners

Mar 84. (7"/7"pic-d) *(VS 657/+P)* <28811> **WOOD BEEZ (PLAY LIKE ARETHA FRANKLIN). / ('A'dub)** [10] Jan86 [91]
(12"+=) *(VS 657T)* – ('A'extended).

—— **GREEN** with **ROBBIE BUCHANAN** + **DAVID FRANK** – keyboards / **FRED MAHER** – drums

Jun 84. (7"/7"pic-d) *(VS 680/+P)* **ABSOLUTE. / ('A'version)** [17] [ ]
(12"+=) *(VS 680T)* – ('A'extended).

—— **GREEN** now with **DAVID GAMSON** – keyboards / **ALLAN MURPHY** – guitar

Nov 84. (7"/7"pic-d) *(VS 725/+P)* **HYPNOTISE. / ('A'version)** [68] [ ]
(12"+=) *(VS 725T)* – ('A'extended).

—— **NICK MOROCH** – guitar was added to above guests for album below.

May 85. (7"/7"sha-pic-d) *(VS 747/+P)* **THE WORD GIRL. / FLESH AND BLOOD** [6] [ ]
(12"+=) *(VS 747-12)* – ('A'&'B'versions).

Jun 85. (lp/c/cd) *(V/TCV/CDV 2350)* <25302> **CUPID AND PSYCHE '85** [5] [50]
– The word girl / Small talk / Absolute / A liitle knowledge / Don't work that way / Perfect way / Lover to fall / Wood beez (pray like Aretha Franklin) / Hypnotize. *(cd+=)*– (other versions). *(re-iss. Apr90 lp/c; OVED/C 294)*

Aug 85. (7") *(VS 780)* <28949> **PERFECT WAY. / ('A'version)** [48] [11]
(12"+=) *(VS 780-12)* – ('A'extended).

—— **GREEN** with numerous session people, + guest MILES DAVIS

Apr 88. (7") *(VS 1006)* **OH PATTI (DON'T FEEL SORRY FOR LOVERBOY). / ('A'instrumental)** [13] [ ]
(12"+=/12"pic-d+=) *(VST/+P 1006)* – ('A'extended).
(cd-s+=) *(VSCD 1006)* – Best thing ever.
(c-s++=) *(VSTC 1006)* – ('A'-Drumless mix).

Jun 88. (lp/c/cd) *(V/TCV/CDV 2515)* <25686> **PROVISION** [8] [ ]
– Boom! there she was / Overnite / First boy in this town / All that we are / Best thing ever / Oh Patti (don't feel sorry for loverboy) / Bam salute / Sugar and spice / Philosophy now. *(cd+=)* – Oh Patti (extended) / Boom! . . . (dub). *(re-iss. Aug91 cd/c;)*

Jul 88. (7") *(VS 1082)* **FIRST BOY IN TOWN (LOVESICK). / WORLD COME BACK TO LIFE** [63] [–]
(12"+=) *(VST 1082)* – ('A'instrumental).
(cd-s+=) *(VSCD 1082)* – ('A'extended remix).

Oct 88. (7") *(VS 1143)* <27973> **BOOM! THERE SHE WAS. / PHILOSOPHY NOW** [55] Jun88 [53]
(12"+=/3"cd-s+=) *(VS T/CD 1143)* – ('A'mix) / ('A'dub version).

Mar 91. (7"/c-s; SCRITTI POLITTI & SHABBA RANKS) *(VS/+C 1333)* **SHE'S A WOMAN. / LITTLE WAY (different)** [20] [–]
(12"+=) *(VST 1333)* – ('A'-Apollo 440 remix).
(cd-s+=) *(VSCD 1333)* – Wood beez (pray like Aretha Franklin).
(12") *(VSTX 1333)* – ('A'-William Orbit remix) / ('A'-Tutology business mix).

Jul 91. (7"/c-s) *(VS/+C 1346)* **TAKE ME IN YOUR ARMS. / ('A'instrumental) / ('A'mix)** [47] [–]
(12"+=/cd-s+=) *(VS T/CD 1346)* – She's a woman.
above single credited SWEETIE IRIE on the sleeve. GREEN abandoned SCRITTI although he still writes for and with others until . . .

Jul 99. (cd-s) *(VSCDT 1731)* **TINSEL TOWN TO THE BOOGIEDOWN / DEAD CERTAINTY** [46] [–]
(12"/cd-s) *(VST/VSCDX 1731)* – ('A'mixes).

Jul 99. (cd/c) *(CDV/TCV 2884)* <8 47488> **ANOMIE AND BONHOMIE** [33] [ ]
– Umm / Tinsel town to the boogiedown / First goodbye / Die alone / Mystic handyman / Smith n' slappy / Born to be / World you understand is over and over / Here come July / Prince among men / Brushed with oil dusted with powder.

Rough Trade — Nonesuch

May 06. (7") *(RTRADS 345)* **THE BOOM BOOM RAP. / HANDS UP** [ ] [–]
(cd-s+=) *(RTRADSCD 345)* – Last time I looked /

May 06. (cd/lp) *(RTRAD CD/LP 270)* <79966> **WHITE BREAD BLACK BEER** [ ] [ ]
– The boom boom rap / No fine lines / Snow in sun / Cooking / Throw / Dr. Abernathy / After six / Petrococadollar / E eleventh nuts / Window wide open / Road to no regret / Mrs. Hughes / Robin Hood.

– compilations, others, etc. –

on 'Virgin' unless mentioned otherwise

Jun 88. (3"cd-ep) *(CDT 13)* **THE WORD GIRL / FLESH AND BLOOD / ('A'-Turntable mix)** [ ] [–]

Nov 88. (3"cd-ep) *(CDT 34)* **WOOD BEEZ (PRAY LIKE ARETHA FRANKLIN) / ('A'dub) / SMALL TALK** [ ] [–]

Apr 90. (3"cd-ep) *(VVCS 1)* **ABSOLUTE / (3 tracks by other artists)** [ ] [–]

Feb 05. (cd) *Rough Trade; (RTRADCD 188)* <30054> **EARLY** [ ] [ ]

☐ SEAHORSES (see under ⇒ STONE ROSES)

SEETHER

Formed: South Africa . . . 2000 as SARON GAS by SHAUN MORGAN, NICK ANNIS, DALE STEWART and DAVE COHOE, releasing a self-financed LP, 'FRAGILE' (2000), under this moniker. More than a decade after 'Nevermind', young bands were still trying to nail NIRVANA's singular chemistry. And they don't come much more COBAIN-like than Springbok wannabe MORGAN, just as his companions DALE STEWART and new drummer NICK OSHIRO, did their best to approximate the melodic crunch of GROHL and NOVOSELIC. Still, as 'Epic' records debut 'DISCLAIMER' (2002) proved, even enthusiastic imitation was better than the current crop of colourless GREEN DAY acolytes. Criticised in many quarters as a cash-in, remix set 'DISCLAIMER II' (2004), surprisingly charted even higher than the original. Hot on its heels was a collaborative US hit single, 'BROKEN', featuring MORGAN's belle AMY LEE (of EVANESCENCE), a track licensed for the soundtrack to 'The Punisher'. Yet more personnel changes (the addition of PAT CALLAHAN and JOHN HUMPHREY for OSHIRO) were effected prior to the release of second album proper, 'KARMA AND EFFECT' (2005), a Top 10 American breaker which suggested SEETHER weren't going to get over their NIRVANA fixation any time soon, even if they varied their sound with some STAIND-patented growling.

• **Covered:** SOMETHING IN THE WAY (Nirvana).

Album rating: FRAGILE (*5) / DISCLAIMER (*6) / DISCLAIMER II (*5) / KARMA AND EFFECT (*6)

SHAUN MORGAN (b. WELGEMOED) – vocals, guitar / **NICK ANNIS** – guitar / **DALE STEWART** – bass, vocals / **DAVE COHOE** – drums

not iss. | cocaberry

Nov 00. (cd; as SARON GAS) **FRAGILE** [–] Africa [–]
– Beer / 69 tea / Pride / Fine again / Empty / Tied my hands / Take me away / Driven under / Stay and play / Your bore / Pig / Dazed and abused / Gasoline / Tied my hands / Senseless tragedy.

— (Mar'02) **NICK OSHIRO** – drums; repl. COHOE and ANNIS

Epic | Wind-Up

Aug 02. (cd-ep) *<20014-2>* **SEETHER EP** [–] [ ]
– Needles / Fine again / Gasoline / Pig / Driven under.

Aug 02. (cd) *<13068-2>* **DISCLAIMER** [–] [92]
– Gasoline / 69 tea / Fine again / Needles / Driven under / Pride / Sympathetic / Your bore / Fade away / Pig / F**k it / Broken.

Jun 04. (cd) *(5095735) <13100-2>* **DISCLAIMER II** (remixes) [ ] [53]
– Gasoline / 69 tea / Fine again / Needles / Driven under / Pride / Sympathetic / Your bore / Fade away / Pig / Fuck it / Broken / Sold me / Cigarettes / Love her / Take me away / Got it made / Out of my way / Hang on / Broken (feat. AMY LEE). *<US+=>* – (DVD tracks).

Aug 04. (cd-s; SEETHER feat. AMY LEE) *(675105-2) <radio>* **BROKEN / SOMETHING IN THE WAY (live X session at 99x Atlanta) / OUT OF MY WAY / ('A'-video)** [ ] [20]

— (2003) **JOHN HUMPHREY** – drums; repl. OSHIRO

— added **PAT CALLAHAN** – guitar

May 05. (-) *<radio>* **REMEDY** [–] [70]

Sep 05. (cd) *(520105-2) <13115-2>* **KARMA AND EFFECT** [ ] May05 [8]
– Because of me / Remedy / Truth / The gift / Burrito / Given / Never leave / World falls away / Tongue / I'm the one / Simplest mistake / Diseased / Plastic man / Interlude – Outro.

Nov 05. (-) *<radio>* **FINE AGAIN** [–] [61]

Bob SEGER

Born: 6 May'45, Dearborn, Michigan, USA. Coming from an impoverished working class background, SEGER began developing his hard hitting brand of rock'n'roll in the early 60's, eventually joining (DOUG BROWN &) THE OMENS as a keyboard player. Tha material was co-written by SEGER and BROWN, the pair even managing a spoof of BARRY SADLER's 'The Ballad Of The Green Berets' under the pseudonym of The BEACH BUMS in early '66. The OMENS subsequently became BOB SEGER & THE LAST HEARD, the hard gigging troupe garnering a hardcore local following and releasing a handful of singles on the small 'Hideout' and 'Cameo' labels. Early in '68, Eddie 'Punch' Andrews became their manager as the band were now billed as The BOB SEGER SYSTEM; with a 'Capitol' contract in hand, a line-up of SEGER, DAN HONAKER, TONY NEME, BOB SCHULTZ and PEP PERRINE scored a US Top 20 hit with the blistering white R&B of 'RAMBLIN' GAMBLIN' MAN', a fitting title track for the freewheeling 1969 debut album. The group's Motor City following helped place the record in the lower reaches of the American chart although subsequent singles failed to build on this initial success. Disbanding The SYSTEM, SEGER replaced the departing SCHULTZ and NEME with DON WATSON, recording his solo debut set, 'MONGREL' (1970). The musical chairs continued as the singer hooked up with musicians DAVE TEEGARDEN, SKIP VANWINKLE KNAPE and MICHAEL BRUCE for 72's 'SMOKIN' O.P.'s', a set of eclectic covers with the added bluster of a revamped 'HEAVY MUSIC' and the distinction of being SEGER's first album issued on his own label, 'Palladium'. The rootsy 'BACK IN '72' (1973), despite boasting the backing talents of JJ CALE and one MARCY LEVY (later reborn as MARCELLA DETROIT of SHAKESPEAR'S SISTER fame), failed to raise SEGER above cult acclaim. Likewise 'SEVEN' (1974), although it did spawn a minor hit in the brawny 'GET OUT OF DENVER'. SEGER's hard-bitten determination finally began to pay off in the mid-70's as he formed his finest backing unit to date in The SILVER BULLET BAND (namely DREW ABBOTT, ROBIN ROBBINS, CHRIS CAMPBELL, ALTO REED and CHARLIE ALLEN MARTIN) and returned to 'Capitol' for the 'BEAUTIFUL LOSER' album. Combining his trademark JOHN FOGERTY-esque grit with a newfound maturity and precision, SEGER was hailed in some quarters as the new BRUCE SPRINGSTEEN; certainly, in America at least, the singer's hard driving, pretension-free nuggets of everyday wisdom went down a storm and with the superior 'NIGHT MOVES' (1977), SEGER at last found himself in the Top 10. Proving that he was now as equally adept at delivering more sensitive material as high-octane rock'n'roll, the singer breached the US Top 5 with the album's moving title track. 'STRANGER IN TOWN' (1978) kept up the momentum, again, like its predecessor, utilising The MUSCLE SHOALS' rhythm section for added authenticity. Brushing aside the new wave pretenders, SEGER was now something of an American institution, finally topping the charts in 1980 with the ballad-heavy 'AGAINST THE WIND' album. The record also saw him making the UK Top 30 for the first time, although his British sales would never match the multi-platinum success afforded him in the States. Though hardly prolific in the 80's, his two studio albums, 'THE DISTANCE' (1982) and 'LIKE A ROCK' (1986) both made the US Top 5, dependable million sellers which satisfied his loyal fans if not exactly breaking any new ground. SEGER was naturally in his element in the live environment, a scathing in-concert cover of Creedence Clearwater Revival's 'FORTUNATE SON' making the latter set an essential purchase. With The SILVER BULLET BAND whittled away to its barest bones throughout the 80's, SEGER's work may lack the intensity of old, though his two latter-day albums, 'THE FIRE INSIDE' (1991) and 'IT'S A MYSTERY' (1995) illustrated that SEGER himself was far from a spent force.

• **Songwriters:** SEGER wrote most except, RIVER DEEP MOUNTAIN HIGH + NUTBUSH CITY LIMITS (Ike & Tina Turner) / BO DIDDLEY (Bo Diddley) / IF I WERE A CARPENTER (Tim Hardin) / LOVE THE ONE YOU'RE WITH (Stephen Stills) / BLIND LOVE + 16 SHELLS FROM A 30.6 (Tom Waits) / SHE CAN'T DO ANYTHING WRONG (C. Davis-Richmond) / C'EST LA VIE (Chuck Berry) / etc. • **Trivia:** SEGER's songs have been covered by many including ROSALIE (Thin Lizzy) / GET OUT OF DENVER (Eddie & The Hot Rods) / WE'VE GOT TONITE (Kenny Rogers & Sheena Easton).

Album rating: RAMBLIN' GAMBLIN' MAN (*6) / NOAH (*6) / MONGREL (*5) / BRAND NEW MORNING (*5) / BACK IN '72 (*5) / SMOKIN' O.P.'s (*6) / SEVEN (*6) / BEAUTIFUL LOSER (*7) / 'LIVE' BULLET (*7) / NIGHT MOVES (*8) / STRANGER IN TOWN (*7) / AGAINST THE WIND (*6) / NINE TONIGHT (*6) / THE DISTANCE (*6) / LIKE A ROCK (*6) / THE FIRE INSIDE (*6) / THE FIRE INSIDE (*5) / GREATEST HITS compilation (*8) / IT'S A MYSTERY (*5) / GREATEST HITS 2 compilation (*7)

BOB SEGER & THE LAST HEARD

BOB SEGER – vocas, guitar with **DAN HONAKER** – bass, guitar, vocals / **PEP PERRINE** – drums, vocals / **DOUG BROWN** – keyboards

not iss. Hideout

May 66. (7") *<1013>* **EAST SIDE STORY. / EAST SIDE SOUND** [–] [ ]

—— <above & below 45's, were soon distributed by 'Cameo' 438 + 465>

Jul 66. (7") *<1014>* **PERSECUTION SMITH. / CHAIN SMOKIN'** [–] [ ]

not iss. Cameo

Dec 66. (7") *<444>* **SOCK IT TO ME, SANTA. / FLORIDA TIME** [–] [ ]

1967. (7") *<473>* **VAGRANT WINTER. / VERY FEW** [–] [ ]

1967. (7") *<494>* **HEAVY MUSIC (part 1). / HEAVY MUSIC (part 2)** [–] [ ]

BOB SEGER SYSTEM

—— repl. BROWN with **BOB SCHULTZ** – keyboards, saxophone / **TONY NEME** – guitar, keyboards

Capitol Capitol

Jan 68. (7") *<2145>* **2 + 2 = WHAT?. / DEATH ROW** [–] [ ]

Dec 68. (7") *(CL 15574) <2297>* **RAMBLIN' GAMBLIN' MAN. / TALES OF LUCY BLUE** [ ] [17]

Jan 69. (lp) *<172>* **RAMBLIN' GAMBLIN' MAN** [–] [62]
– Ramblin' gamblin' man / Tales of Lucy Blue / Ivory / Gone / Down home / Train man / White wall / Black eyed girl / 2 + 2 = what? / Doctor Fine / The lost song (love needs to be loved). *(UK-iss.Nov77; CAPS 1013) (re-iss. Jun81 on 'Greenlight'; GO 2018)*

May 69. (7") *<2480>* **IVORY. / LOST SONG (LOVE NEEDS TO BE LOVED)** [–] [97]

Jan 70. (7") *<2576>* **LENNIE JOHNSON. / NOAH (or) OUT LOUD** [–] [ ]

Mar 70. (7") *<2640>* **INNERVENUS EYES. / LONELY MAN** [–] [ ]

Apr 70. (lp) *<236>* **NOAH** [–] [ ]
– Noah / Innervenus eyes / Lonely man / Loneliness is a feeling / Cat / Jumpin' humpin' hip hypocrite / Follow the children / Lennie Johnson / Paint them a picture Jane / Death row.

May 70. (7") *(CL 15642) <2748>* **LUCIFER. / BIG RIVER** [ ] Mar70 [84]

Oct 70. (lp) *<499>* **MONGREL** [–] [ ]
– Song to Rufus / Evil Edna / Highway child / Big river / Mongrel / Lucifer / Teachin' blues / Leavin' on my dream / Mongrel too / River deep mountain high. *(UK-iss.Nov77; CAPS 1010) (re-iss. Jun81 on 'Greenlight'; GO 2022) (re-iss. Jul83 on 'Fame' lp/c; FA/TC-FA 3072)*

BOB SEGER

—— added **DON WATSON** – keyboards to repl SCHULTZ + NEME

—— now with **DAVE TEEGARDEN** – drums / **SKIP VANWINKLE KNAPE** – keyboards, bass / **MICHAEL BRUCE** – guitar

Nov 71. (lp) *<731>* **BRAND NEW MORNING** [–] [ ]
– Brand new morning / Maybe today / Sometimes / You know who you are / Railroad days / Louise / Song for him / Something like.

Nov 71. (7") *<3187>* **LOOKIN' BACK. / HIGHWAY CHILD** [–] [96]

Reprise Palladium

Jul 72. (7") *<1079>* **IF I WERE A CARPENTER. / JESSE JAMES** [–] [76]

Aug 72. (lp) *(K 44214) <2109>* **SMOKIN' O.P.'s** [ ] Jul72 [ ]
– Bo Diddley / Love the one you're with / If I were a carpenter / Hummingbird / Let it rock / Turn on your love light / Jesse James / Someday / Heavy music. *(re-iss. Apr80; 11746)*

Nov 72. (7") *<1117>* **TURN ON YOUR LOVE LIGHT. / Bo Diddley: BO DIDDLEY** [–] [ ]

—— SEGER's back-up back included **DICK SIMS** – keyboards / **TOM CARTMELL** – sax / **JAMIE OLDAKER** – drums / **SERGIO PASTORA** – percussion / **MARCY LEVY** – backing vocals

Mar 73. (lp) *(K 44227) <2126>* **BACK IN '72** [ ] [ ]
– Midnight rider / So I wrote you a song / Stealer / Rosalie / Turn the page / Back in '72 / Neon sky / I've been working / I've got time.

Apr 73. (7") *<1143>* **ROSALIE. / NEON SKY** [–] [ ]

Nov 73. (7") *(K 14243)* **ROSALIE. / BACK IN '72** [ ] [–]

—— His band all left to join ERIC CLAPTON. Newcomers **KENNY BUTTREY** – drums / **RANDY MEYERS** – drums / **RICK MANSKA** – keyboards / **TOMMY COGBILL** – bass / + guitars.

Jun 74. (7") *<1171>* **NEED YA. / SEEN A LOT OF FLOORS** [–] [ ]

Jul 74. (lp) *(K 44262) <2184>* **SEVEN / CONTRASTS** [ ] [ ]
– Get out of Denver / Long song comin' / Need ya / School teacher / Cross of gold / U.M.C. (Upper Middle Class) / Seen a lot of floors / 20 years from now / All your love. *(re-iss. Apr80; 11748) (re-iss. Jun81 on 'Greenlight'; GO 2006)*

Aug 74. (7") *(K 14364) <1205>* **GET OUT OF DENVER. / LONG SONG COMIN'** [ ] [80]

Nov 74. (7") *<1316>* **U.M.C. (UPPER MIDDLE CLASS). / THIS OLD HOUSE** [–] [ ]

—— new line-up consisted of **DREW ABBOTT** – guitar / **ROBIN ROBBINS** – keyboards / **CHRIS CAMPBELL** – bass / **ALTO REED** – saxophone / **CHARLIE ALLEN MARTIN** – drums

Capitol Capitol

May 75. (7") *<4062>* **BEAUTIFUL LOSER. / FINE MEMORY** [–] [ ]

Aug 75. (lp/c) *<(EST/TC-EST 11378)>* **BEAUTIFUL LOSER** [ ] Apr75 [ ]
– Beautiful loser / Black night / Katmandu / Jody girl / Travellin' man / Momma / Nutbush city limits / Sailing nights / Fine memory. *(re-iss. Jun85 on 'Fame'; FA41 3117-1)*

Aug 75. (7") *(CL 15831) <4116>* **KATMANDU. / BLACK NIGHT** [ ] [43]

Nov 75. (7") *<4183>* **NUTBUSH CITY LIMITS. / TRAVELIN' MAN** [–] [ ]

BOB SEGER & THE SILVER BULLET BAND

Aug 76. (d-lp/d-c) *(ESTSP/TC-ESTSP 16) <11523>* **LIVE BULLET (live Detroit)** [ ] Apr76 [34]
– Nutbush city limits / Travellin' man / Beautiful loser / Jody girl / Lookin' back / Get out of Denver / Let it rock / I've been workin' / Turn the page / U.M.C. (Upper Middle Class) / Bo Diddley / Ramblin' gamblin' man / Heavy music / Katmandu. *(cd-iss. Oct88; CDP 746085-2) (cd re-iss. Feb95; CDP 746085-2)*

Jun 76. (7") *<4269>* **NUTBUSH CITY LIMITS (live). / LOOKIN' BACK** [–] May76 [69]

Aug 76. (7") *CL 15884) <4300>* **TRAVELLIN' MAN (live). / BEAUTIFUL LOSER (live)** [ ] [ ]

—— Next 2 albums also credited The MUSCLE SHOALS RHYTHM SECTION on one side apiece. They were **DAVID HOOD** – bass / **ROGER HAWKINS** – drums / **BARRY BECKETT + JIMMY JOHNSON** – horns / **DOUG RILEY** – keyboards / **PETE CARR** – guitar / + **GLENN FREY**

Nov 76. (7") *(CL 15895)* **MAINSTREET. / COME TO POPPA** [ ] [–]

Mar 77. (lp/c) *<(EST/TC-EST 11557)>* **NIGHT MOVES** [ ] Nov76 [8]
– Rock and roll never forgets / Night moves / The fire down below / Sunburst / Sunspot baby / Mainstreet / Come to poppa / Ship of fools / Mary Lou. *(re-iss. May82 on 'Fame' lp/c; FA/TC-FA 3022) (cd-iss. Oct88 & Feb95; CDP 746075-2)*

Mar 77. (7") *(CL 15904) <4369>* **NIGHT MOVES. / SHIP OF FOOLS** [ ] Dec76 [4]

Apr 77. (7") *<4422>* **MAINSTREET. / JODY GIRL** [–] [24]

Jul 77. (7") *<4449>* **ROCK AND ROLL NEVER FORGETS. / THE FIRE DOWN BELOW** [–] [41]

Sep 77. (7") *(CL 15938)* **ROCK AND ROLL NEVER FORGETS. / SHIP OF FOOLS** [ ] [–]

—— **DAVE TEEGARDEN** – drums (ex-STK) repl. CHARLIE (was paralysed from car crash)

May 78. (silver-lp/c) *<(EST/TC-EST 11698)>* **STRANGER IN TOWN** [31] [4]
– Hollywood nights / Still the same / Old time rock & roll / Till it shines / Feel like a number / Ain't got no money / We've got tonite / Brave strangers / The famous final scene. *(cd-iss. Oct88 & Feb95; CDP 746074-2)*

May 78. (7") *(CL 15990) <4581>* **STILL THE SAME. / FEEL LIKE A NUMBER** [ ] [4]

Jul 78. (7") *<4618>* **HOLLYWOOD NIGHTS. / BRAVE STRANGERS** [–] [ ]

Aug 78. (7"silver) *(CL 16004)* **HOLLYWOOD NIGHTS. / OLD TIME ROCK & ROLL** [42] [–]
Jan 79. (7") *(CL 16028)* <4653> **WE'VE GOT TONITE. / AIN'T GOT NO MONEY** [41] Oct78 [13]
Mar 79. (7") *(CL 16073)* **TILL IT SHINES. / BEAUTIFUL LOSER** [ ] [–]
(12"+=) *(12CL 16073)* – Get out of Denver.
Apr 79. (7") <4702> **OLD TIME ROCK & ROLL. / SUNSPOT BABY** [–] [28]
Mar 80. (7") *(CL 16130)* <4836> **FIRE LAKE. / LONG TWIN SILVER LINE** [ ] Feb80 [6]
Mar 80. (lp/c) *<(EST/TC-EST 12041)>* **AGAINST THE WIND** [26] [1]
– The horizontal bop / You'll accomp'ny me / Her strut / No man's land / Long twin silver line / Against the wind / Good for me / Betty Lou's getting out tonight / Fire Lake / Shinin' brightly. *(cd-iss. 1986 & Feb95; CDP 746060-2) <cd re-mast.Jun03; CAP 84316>*
May 80. (7") *(CL 16143)* <4863> **AGAINST THE WIND. / NO MAN'S LAND** [ ] Apr80 [5]
Aug 80. (7") *(CL 16163)* <4904> **YOU'LL ACCOMP'NY ME. / BETTY LOU'S GETTING OUT TONIGHT** [ ] Jul80 [14]
Oct 80. (7"m) *(CL 16174)* **AGAINST THE WIND. / GET OUT OF DENVER / NUTBUSH CITY LIMITS** [ ] [–]
Nov 80. (7") <4951> **THE HORIZONTAL BOP. / HER STRUT** [–] [42]
Sep 81. (d-lp/d-c) *(ESTSP/TC2-ESTSP 23)* <12182> **NINE TONIGHT (live)** [24] [3]
– Nine tonight / Tryin' to live my life without you / You'll accomp'ny me / Hollywood nights / Old time rock & roll / Mainstreet / Against the wind / The fire down below / Her strut / Feel like a number / Fire Lake / Betty Lou's gettin' out tonight / We've got tonight / Night moves / Rock and roll never forgets / Let it rock. *(cd-iss. Feb95; CDP 746086-2)*
Sep 81. (7") <5042> **TRYIN' TO LIVE MY LIFE WITHOUT YOU (live). / BRAVE STRANGERS (live)** [–] [5]
Oct 81. (7"/12") *(CL/12CL 223)* **HOLLYWOOD NIGHTS (live). / BRAVE STRANGERS (live)** [49] [–]
Dec 81. (7") *(CL 235)* **WE'VE GOT TONIGHT (live). / FEEL LIKE A NUMBER (live)** [60] [–]
(12"+=,12"red+=) *(12CL 235)* – Brave strangers (live).
Dec 81. (7") <5077> **FEEL LIKE A NUMBER (live). / HOLLYWOOD NIGHTS (live)** [–] [48]

— **SEGER** retained **CHRIS CAMPBELL + ALTO REED,** and recruited **ROY BITTAN** – keyboards (of BRUCE SPRINGSTEEN's E-STREET BAND) / **RUSS KUNKEL** – drums / **WADDY WACHTEL** – guitar / **CRAIG FROST** – keyboards (ex-GRAND FUNK RAILROAD)

Dec 82. (7") *(CL 275)* <5187> **SHAME ON THE MOON. / HOUSE BEHIND A HOUSE** [ ] [2]
Dec 82. (lp/c) *<(EST/TC-EST 12254)>* **THE DISTANCE** [45] [5]
– Even now / Makin' Thunderbirds / Boomtown blues / Shame on the Moon / Love's the last to know / Roll me away / House behind a house / Comin' home / Little victories. *(cd-iss. Oct88; CDP 746 005-2)*
Mar 83. (7") *(CL 284)* <5213> **EVEN NOW. / LITTLE VICTORIES** [73] [12]
(d7"+=/c-s+=) *(CLD/TCCL 284)* – We've got tonight / Brave strangers.
Jun 83. (7") *(CL 297)* <5235> **ROLL ME AWAY. / BOOMTOWN BLUES** [ ] May83 [27]
(below 'A'side was used on the film 'Teachers')
Jan 85. (7") *(CL 350)* <5413> **UNDERSTANDING. / EAST L.A.** [ ] Nov84 [11]
(12"+=) *(12CL 350)* – We've got tonite.

— **DON BREWER** – drums (ex-GRAND FUNK RAILROAD) repl. KUNKEL

Mar 86. (7") *(CL 396)* <5532> **AMERICAN STORM. / FORTUNATE SON (live)** [ ] [13]
(12"+=) *(12CL 396)* – Hollywood nights (live).
(d7"++=) *(CLD 396)* – Hollywood nights.
Apr 86. (lp/c) *(EST/TC-EST 2011)* <12398> **LIKE A ROCK** [35] [3]
– American storm / Like a rock / Miami / The ring / Tightrope / The aftermath / Sometimes / It's you / Somewhere tonight. *(cd-iss. Oct88 +=; CDP 746195-2)* – Living inside my heart / Like a rock (edit) / Fortunate son (live).
Jul 86. (7") *(CL 408)* <5592> **LIKE A ROCK. / LIVING INSIDE MY HEART** [ ] May86 [12]
(12"+=) *(12CL 408)* – Katmandu.
Aug 86. (7") <5623> **IT'S YOU. / THE AFTERMATH** [–] [52]
Nov 86. (7") <5658> **MIAMI. / SOMEWHERE TONIGHT** [–] [70]
(below solo 45 from the 'Beverly Hills Cop II' film on 'M.C.A.')
Aug 87. (7"/12") *(MCA/T 1172)* <53094> **SHAKEDOWN. / THE AFTERMATH** [ ] May87 [1]
Sep 91. (cd/c/lp) *(CD/TC+/EST 2149)* <91134> **THE FIRE INSIDE** [54] [7]
– Take a chance / The real love / Sightseeing / Real at the time / Always in my heart / The fire inside / Which way / New coat of paint / The mountain / The long way home / Blind love / She can't do anything wrong.
Aug 91. (c-s,cd-s) <44743> **THE REAL LOVE / THE MOUNTAIN** [–] [24]
Sep 91. (7") **THE REAL LOVE. / WHICH WAY** [ ] [–]
(12"+=) – The mountain.
(cd-s++=) – Hollywood nights.
Mar 92. (c-s/cd-s/7") *(TC/CD+/648)* **THE FIRE INSIDE. / THE REAL LOVE** [ ] [ ]
Jan 95. (7") *(CL 734)* **WE'VE GOT TONIGHT. / HOLLYWOOD NIGHTS** [22] [–]
(c-s+=/cd-s+=) *(TC/CD+/CL 734)* – C'est la vie.
(cd-s) *(CDCLS 734)* – ('A'side) / Night moves (live) / Nutbush city limits (live).
Feb 95. (cd/c/lp) *(CD/TC+/EST 2241)* <30334> **GREATEST HITS** (compilation) [6] Nov94 [8]
– Roll me away / Night moves / Turn the page / You'll accomp'ny me / Hollywood nights / Still the same / Old time rock & roll / We've got tonight / Against the wind / Main street / The fire inside / Like a rock / C'est la vie / In your time.
Apr 95. (c-s) *(TCCL 741)* **NIGHT MOVES / EVEN NOW / WE'VE GOT TONIGHT (live)** [50] [–]
(cd-s+=) *(CDCL 741)* – American storm.
(cd-s) *(CDCLS 741)* – ('A'side) / Katmandu (live) / The fire down below / The famous final scene.
Jul 95. (c-s/cd-s) *(TC/CD CL 749)* **HOLLYWOOD NIGHTS / ROCK AND ROLL NEVER FORGETS / HOLLYWOOD NIGHTS (live)** [52] [–]
(cd-s) *(CDCLS 749)* – ('A'side) / Come to poppa / Fire lake.
Nov 95. (cd/c) *(CD/TC EST 2271)* <99774> **IT'S A MYSTERY** [ ] [27]
– Rite of passage / Lock and load / By the river / Manhattan / I wonder / It's a mystery / Revisionism street / Golden boy / I can't save you, Angelene / 16 shells from a 30.6 / West of the Moon / Hands in the air.
Feb 96. (c-ep/cd-ep) *(TC/CD CL 765)* **LOCK AND LOAD / THE FIRE INSIDE / LIKE A ROCK / MANHATTAN** [57] [ ]
(cd-ep) *(CDCLS 765)* – ('A'side) / It's a mystery / Roll me away / Mainstreet.

– compilations, etc. –

on 'Capitol' unless mentioned otherwise

Jun 77. (7"ep) *Reprise; (K 14476)* **EXTENDED PLAY** [ ] [–]
– Get out of Denver / Back in '72 / Midnight rider / Rosalie.
Nov 77. (7"m) *(CL CL 15956)* **TURN THE PAGE. / GET OUT OF DENVER (live) / HEAVY MUSIC (live)** [ ] [–]
Sep 83. (7") <5276> **OLD TIME ROCK & ROLL. / TILL IT SHINES** [–] [48]
Mar 84. (7") *(CL 326)* **OLD TIME ROCK & ROLL. / ROLL ME AWAY** [ ] [–]
(12"+=) *(12CL 326)* – Makin' Thunderbirds.
Nov 03. (cd) <5277-2> **GREATEST HITS 2** [–] [23]
– Understanding (from 'Teachers' soundtrack) / The fire down below / Her strut / Beautiful loser / Sunspot baby / Katmandu / Shame on the moon / Fire lake / Tryin' to live my life without you (live) / Shakedown (from 'Beverly Hills Cop II' soundtrack) / Manhattan / New coat of paint / Chances are (with MARTINA McBRIDE from 'Hope Floats' soundtrack) / Rock and roll never forgets. *<bonus +=>* – Satisfied / Tomorrow / Turn the page (video).

SEPULTURA

Formed: Belo Horizonte, Brazil . . . 1983 by brothers MAX and schoolboy IGOR CAVALERA alongside JAIRO T. and PAOLO JR., taking the name SEPULTURA from the MOTORHEAD song, 'Dancing On Your Grave' (Sepultura meaning 'grave' in Portuguese). Influenced largely by black metal bands such as VENOM, as well as British punk, SEPULTURA's earliest release was a split album with fellow Brazilian death metallers, OVERDOSE, entitled 'BESTIAL DEVASTATION' (1984). Another rudimentary thrash effort followed in 'MORBID VISIONS' (1985), again released on the small 'Cogumelo' label. It was nevertheless enough to see the band snapped up by 'Roadrunner', who released the 'SCHIZOPHRENIA' set in early '87. With ANDREAS KISSER replacing JAIRO T, SEPULTURA at last began to focus some of their unbridled sonic savagery, MAX's trademark growl assuming the bowel quaking chill it had always threatened as the ubiquitous Scott Burns worked his magic at the mixing desk. With BURNS in a production capacity, the masterful 'BENEATH THE REMAINS' (1989) finally signalled the arrival of a major force on the international metal scene. Breathtakingly dynamic, the album twisted and turned like a joyrider on speed, switching from breakneck thrash to pummeling sludge-riffing with untrammelled ferocity. Though you still couldn't actually make out what CAVALERA was saying, the unearthly roar of his voice was a revelation, almost an instrument in itself with its own rhythmic thrust. And while many thrash acts gave the impression of playing aggressively purely because that's what was expected of them, the likes of 'INNER SELF' and 'STRONGER THAN HATE' reeked of the genuine frustration, despair and disillusionment of growing up in an impoverished third world country. One of the last great thrash albums of the 80's, the record marked the end of the first stage in SEPULTURA's development; the next album, 'ARISE' (1991), was released as the scene was in its death throes and on this showing it was clear they weren't going to be left behind. On many tracks, the pace was slowed to a seismic turbo-Sabbath grind, gut-wrenchingly heavy and immensely powerful; SEPULTURA were redefining the boundaries of metal with each successive release. Already massive in Brazil (SEPULTURA had played the huge 'Rock In Rio' festival in 1990), the group narrowly missed the UK Top 10 with 'CHAOS A.D.' (1993). Taking the more basic approach of its predecessor even further, the record adopted a markedly more political lyrical stance than anything they'd released to date, the anger ferociously focused into bitter diatribes like 'SLAVE NEW WORLD'. Having previously injected a malignant power into MOTORHEAD's 'Orgasmatron' (which even LEMMY couldn't muster) a couple of years back, here SEPULTURA steamrollered NEW MODEL ARMY's 'The Hunt', proving that punk was as close as metal, if not more so, to the group's charred heart. But SEPULTURA really guaranteed their place in the rock hall of fame with 'ROOTS' (1996), voted by Kerrang! magazine as one of the best metal albums ever released. Stunning in both its stylistic breadth and unrelenting intensity, this was the masterpiece SEPULTURA had been working towards from the beginning of their career. Leaving most of their peers banging their heads on the starting post, the record embraced the cultural heritage of their native Brazil (with the help of rainforest tribe, the Xavantes) to concoct a haunting fusion of ethno-metal and hypnotic tribal spiritualism. The rock world was stunned when SEPULTURA disbanded early in 1997, one of the few metal acts to quit while they were on top (MAX has since formed SOULFLY, taking up where 'ROOTS' more rhythmic sound left off). However, that was certainly not the end, as SEPULTURA regrouped the following year complete with new frontman, DERRICK GREEN. An excellent comeback set, 'AGAINST', astonished most hardcore fans, GREEN's earthy vocal chords giving the group another dimension. While its lack of commercial chart success might've suggested otherwise, 'NATION' (2001) – the band's first album recorded in Brazil for over a decade – was the sound of a band finally rediscovering itself after the upheavals of the late 90's. A quasi concept set with cold war-style cover art, the record found GREEN, CAVALERA and Co wielding a focused anger that many modern metal acts either can't muster or fail to articulate, the presence of JELLO BIAFRA on 'POLITRICKS' heightening the sense of seething injustice. With concert set 'UNDER A PALE GREY SKY' (2002), SEPULTURA fans were transported back to the turbulent period immediately prior to MAX's departure. Deeply emotionally wounded from the death of his stepson, the singer poured every ounce of his battered soul into this blistering tour de force of live performance. The brutal, electrifying charge of SEPULTURA Mk.1 in full flight was a tall order to follow, even for the band CAVALERA left behind. Yet with 'ROORBACK' (2003), they again proved themselves committed to giving it their best shot. Ugly, hostile and uncompromising are some of the best compliments anyone can give in relation to the kind of metal SEPULTURA continue to deal in, and their latest set merited all three. Best of all though, was a murderous makeover of U2's 'BULLET THE BLUE SKY', DERRICK GREEN extracting the lyrics' true horror like a demented dentist. 'LIVE IN SAO PAULO' (2005) offered a concert document of the GREEN era, adding Public Enemy's 'BLACK STEEL IN THE HOUR OF CHAOS' to their litany of inspired covers. 'DANTE XXI' (2006) looked to the famous Italian visionary of its title for lyrical inspiration, specifically 'The Divine Comedy' (a work that also gave its name to NEIL HANNON's arch-pop combo). SEPULTURA's inspiration was naturally less tongue-in-cheek, more concerned with the man's traversal of purgatory and bleak assessment of humanity, even bringing in baroque strings for that authentic medieval vibe.

• **Songwriters:** Group penned, except DRUG ME (Dead Kennedys) / SYMPTOM OF THE UNIVERSE (Black Sabbath) / CLENCHED FIST (Ratos De Porao) / INTO THE CRYPT OF RAYS + PROCREATION (OF THE WICKED) (Celtic Frost) / GENE MACHINE – DON'T BOTHER ME (Bad Brains) / BELA LUGOSI'S DEAD (Bauhaus) / ANNIHILATION (Crucifix) / RISE ABOVE (Black Flag) / MESSIAH (Hellhammer) / ANGEL (Massive Attack) / BLACK STEEL IN THE HOUR OF CHAOS (Public Enemy) / MONGOLOID (Devo) / MOUNTAIN SONG (Jane's Addiction) / PIRANHA (Exodus).

Album rating: MORBID VISIONS (*4) / SCHIZOPHRENIA (*7) / BENEATH THE REMAINS (*9) / ARISE (*6) / CHAOS A.D. (*7) / ROOTS (*9) / BLOOD-ROOTED compilation (*7) / AGAINST (*8) / NATION (*6) / UNDER A PALE GREY SKY (*7) / ROORBACK (*7) / LIVE IN SAO PAOLO (*6) / DANTE XXI (*6)

MAX CAVALERA (b. MASSIMILANO A. CAVALERA, 4 Aug'69) – vocals, guitar / **JAIRO GUEDEZ** – guitar / **PAULO JR.** (b. PAULO XISTO PINTO JR., 30 Apr'69) – bass / **IGOR CAVALERA** (b.4 Sep'70) – drums

Cogumelo — not iss.

Nov 84. (m-lp; shared with OVERDOSE) *(803248)* **BESTIAL DEVASTATION** [–] Brazil [–]
– Bestial devastation / Antichrist / Necromancer / Warriors of death. *(cd-iss. Mar97 on 'Bestial'; SBD 001)*

Nov 85. (lp) **MORBID VISIONS** [–] [–]
– Morbid visions / Mayhem / Troops of doom / War / Crucifixion / Show me the wrath / Funeral rites / Empire of the damned / The curse. *(UK-iss.Apr89 on 'Shark' German; SHARK 004) (UK-iss.Nov91 on 'Roadracer' w/ 'BESTIAL DEVASTATION' cd/c/lp; RO 9276-2/-4/-1) (re-iss. Apr94 + Aug95 on 'Roadrunner'; same)*

—— **ANDREAS KISSER** (b.24 Aug'68, Sao Bernado Do Campo, Brazil) – lead guitar; repl. JAIRO T

Shark — New Renaissance

Feb 88. (lp/cd) *(SHARK/+CD 006)* **SCHIZOPHRENIA** [–] German [ ]
– Intro / From the past comes the storms / To the wall / Escape to the void / Inquisition symphony / Screams behind the shadows / Septic schizo / The abyss / R.I.P. (Rest In Pain). *(c+=/cd+=)* – Troops of doom. *(re-iss. cd/c/lp Apr94 & Aug95 & May00 on 'Roadrunner'; RR 8764-2)*

Roadracer — Roadracer

Apr 89. (lp/c/cd) *<(RO 9511-1/-4/-2)>* **BENEATH THE REMAINS** [ ] [ ]
– Beneath the remains / Inner self / Stronger than hate / Mass hypnosis / Sarcastic existence / Slaves of pain / Lobotomy / Hungry / Primitive future. *(re-iss. Apr94 & Aug95 on 'Roadrunner'; same)*

Mar 91. (cd/c/lp/pic-lp) *<(RO 9328-2/-4/-1/-8)>* **ARISE** [40] [ ]
– Arise / Dead embryonic cells / Desperate cry / Murder / Subtraction / Altered state / Under siege (regnum Irae) / Meaningless movements / Infected voice. (pic-lp+=) – Orgasmatron. *(re-iss. Apr94 & Aug95 on 'Roadrunner'; same)*

Mar 91. (c-ep/12"ep/cd-ep) *(RO 2424-4/-6/-3)* **UNDER SIEGE (REGNUM IRAE). / TROOPS OF DOOM (re-recorded) / ORGASMATRON** [ ] [ ]

Feb 92. (c-ep/12"ep/cd-ep) *(RO 2406-4/-6/-3)* **ARISE. / INNER SELF (live) / TROOPS OF DOOM (live)** [ ] [ ]

Roadrunner Epic

Sep 93. (7"pic-d-ep/c-ep/12"ep/cd-ep) *(RR 2382-7/-4/-6/-3)* **TERRITORY. / POLICIA / BIOTECH IS GODZILLA** [66] [ ]

Oct 93. (cd/c/lp) *(RR 9000-2/-4/-1)* *<57458>* **CHAOS A.D.** [11] [32]
– Refuse-Resist / Territory / Slave new world / Amen / Kaiowas / Propaganda / Biotech is Godzilla / Nomad / We who are not as others / Manifest / The Hunt / Clenched fist *(cd-tin-box.Mar94; 9000-0) (+=)* – Policia / Inhuman nature. *(re-iss. Aug95+=; same)* – Chaos B.C. / Kaiowas (tribal jam) / Territory (live) / Amen – Inner self (live). *(re-iss. Oct96; same)*

—— Early in '94, MAX was arrested and fined for stamping on the Brazilian flag. He is said to have done it accidentally.

Feb 94. (7"ep/c-ep/12"ep/12"purple-ep/cd-ep/s-cd-ep) *(RR 2377-7/-4/-6/-8/-3/-5)* **REFUSE – RESIST. / INHUMAN NATURE / PROPAGANDA** [51] [ ]

May 94. (cd-s) *(RR 2374-3)* **SLAVE NEW WORLD / DESPERATE CRY** [46] [ ]
(c-ep/etched-12"ep/cd-ep) *(RR 2374-4/-8/-5)* – ('A'side) / Crucificados Pelo systema / Drug me / Orgasmatron (live).

Feb 96. (7"colrd) *(RR 2320-7)* **ROOTS BLOODY ROOTS. / SYMPTOM OF THE UNIVERSE** [19] [ ]
(cd-s) *(RR 2320-2)* – ('A'side) / Procreation (of the wicked) / Refuse – resist (live) / Territory (live).
(cd-s) *(RR 2320-5)* – ('A'side) / Propaganda (live) / Beneath the remains (live) / Escape to the void (live).

Feb 96. (cd/c/lp) *<(RR 8900-2/-4/-1)>* **ROOTS** [4] [27]
– Roots bloody roots / Attitude / Cut-throat / Ratamahatta / Breed apart / Straighthate / Spit / Lookaway / Dusted / Born stubborn / Jasco / Itsari / Ambush / Endangered species / Dictatorshit. *(cd+=)* – Chaos B.C. / Symptom of the universe / Kaiowas (live). *(re-iss. Oct96 as 'THE ROOTS OF SEPULTURA' cd w/cd of 20 unreleased + rare tracks; RR 8900-8)*

Aug 96. (7") *(RR 2314-7)* **RATAMAHATTA. / MASS HYPNOSIS (live)** [23] [ ]
(cd-s) *(RR 2314-2)* – ('A'side) / War / Slave new world (live) / Amen – Inner self (live).
(cd-s) *(RR 2314-5)* – ('A'side) / War / Roots bloody roots (demo) / Dusted (demo).

Dec 96. (7") *(RR 2299-7)* **ATTITUDE. / DEAD EMBRYONIC CELLS (live)** [46] [ ]
(cd-s) *(RR 2299-2)* – ('A'side) / Lookaway (master vibe mix) / Mine.
(cd-s) *(RR 2299-5)* – ('A'side) / Kaiowas (tribal jam) / Clenched fist (live) / Biotech is Godzilla (live).

—— split late '96, when MAX was told he was no longer wanted. He subsequently formed SOULFLY, while SEPULTURA went to ground for a year. They returned with a new singer **DERRICK GREEN** (ex-ALPHA JERK)

Oct 98. (cd/c/lp) *(<RR 8700-2/-4/-1>)* **AGAINST** [40] [82]
– Against / Choke / Rumors / Old earth / Floaters in mud / Boycott / Tribus / Common bonds / F.O.E. / Reza / Unconscious / Kamaitachi / Drowned out / Hatred aside / T3rcermillennium.

Nov 98. (cd-s) *(RR 2219-3)* **CHOKE / GENE MACHINE (demo) / DON'T BOTHER ME (demo) / AGAINST (demo)** [ ] [ ]

Jul 99. (cd-s) *(RR 2169-3)* **AGAINST / THE WASTE / TRIBUS / COMMON BONDS (alternate mix)** [ ] [ ]

Mar 01. (cd) *(<RR 8560-2>)* **NATION** [ ] [ ]
– Sepulnation / Revolt / Border wars / One man army / Vox populi / The ways of faith / Uma cura / Who must die? / Saga / Tribe to a nation / Politricks / Human cause / Reject / Water / Valtio. *(special-cd+=; RR 8560-5)* – Bela Lugosi's dead / Annihilation / Rise above / Revolt (demo) / Roots bloody roots (live).

S.P.V. S.P.V.

May 03. (cd) *<(SPV 085-7483-2)>* **ROORBACK** [ ] Aug03 [ ]
– Come back alive / Godless / Apes of God / More of the same / Urge / Corrupted / As it is / Mind war / Leech / The rift / Bottomed out / Activist / Outro. *(UK bonus+=)* – Bullet the blue sky / Bullet the blue sky (video). *(ltd-d-cd+=; SPV 092 7483-0)* – REVOLUSONGS EP:- Messiah / Angel / Black steel in the hour of chaos / Mongloid / Mountain song / Bullet the blue sky / Piranha.

Nov 05. (d-cd) *<(SPV 9952-2)>* **LIVE IN SAO PAOLO** (live) [ ] [ ]
– Intro / Apes of God / Slave new world / Propaganda / Attitude / Choke / Innerself – Beneath the remains / Escape to the void / Mindwar / Troops of doom / Necromancer / Sepulnation / Refuse – Resist / Territory / Black steel in the hour of chaos / Bullet the blue sky / Reza / Biotech is Godzilla / Arise – Dead embryonic cells / Come back alive / Roots bloody roots.

Mar 06. (cd) *(SPV 9981-2)* *<239981>* **DANTE XXI** [ ] [ ]
– Lost (intro) / Dark wood of error / Convicted in life / City of dis / False / Fighting on / Limboi (intro) / Ostia / Buried words / Nuclear seven / Repeating the horror / Eunoe (intro) / Crown and miter / Primium mobile (intro) / Still flame.

—— **ROY MAYORGA** – drums (of SOULFLY) repl. IGOR (on tour only)

– compilations, etc. –

Nov 89. (cd) *Shark; (CDSHARK 012)* **MORBID VISIONS / CEASE TO EXIST** [–] German [–]

May 90. (c) *Shark; (SHARKMC 017)* **SCHIZOPHRENIA / MORBID VISIONS** [–] German [–]

Aug 97. (cd) *Roadrunner; (<RR 8821-2>)* **BLOOD ROOTED** [ ] [ ]
– Procreation (of the wicked) / Inhuman nature / Policia / War / Criucificados pelo sistema / Symptom of the universe / Mine / Lobotomy / Dusted / Roots bloody roots / Drug me / Refuse – resist / Slave new world / Propaganda / Beneath the remains / Escape to the void / Kaiowas / Clenched fist / Biotech is Godzilla. *(re-iss. May00; same)*

May 00. (cd) *Roadrunner; <(RR 8765-2)>* **MORBID VISIONS / BESTIAL DEVASTATION** [ ] [ ]

Sep 02. (d-cd) *Roadrunner; <(RR 8436-2)>* **UNDER A PALE GREY SKY** [ ] [ ]
– Itsari (intro) / Roots bloody roots / Spit / Territory / Monologo ao pe do ouvido / Breed apart / Attitude / Cut-throat / Troops of doom / Beneath the remains – Mass hypnosis / Born stubborn / Desperate cry / Necromancer / Dusted / Endangered species / We who are not as others / Straighthate / Dictatorshit / Refuse – Resist / Arise – Dead embryonic cells / Slave new world / Biotech is Godzilla / Inner self / Policia / We gotta know / Kaiowas / Ratamahatta / Orgasmatron.

☐ Will SERGEANT
(see under ⇒ ECHO & THE BUNNYMEN)

the SEX PISTOLS

Formed: London, England ... summer 1975 out of The SWANKERS by PAUL COOK, STEVE JONES and GLEN MATLOCK, the latter two regular faces at MALCOLM McLAREN's 'Sex' boutique on the capital's King's Road. With the NEW YORK DOLLS already on his CV, McLAREN was well qualified to mastermind the rise and fall of The SEX PISTOLS as he dubbed his new plaything, the entrepreneur/svengali installing another 'Sex' customer, the green-haired JOHN LYDON, as a suitably sneering frontman. JONES soon renamed the latter JOHNNY ROTTEN, informing his farting rear-end, "You're rotten, you are"; the tone of the SEX PISTOLS was set. After a few local gigs, the group supported JOE STRUMMER's 101'ers in April '76, their bedraggled, low-rent bondage chic troupe of followers including the likes of SIOUXSIE SIOUX (later of BANSHEES fame) and one SID VICIOUS, allegedly the perpetrator behind the infamous glass-throwing incident at the 100 Club punk all-dayer in which a girl was partially blinded. Controversy, intentional or otherwise, hung around the group like a bad smell and made The SEX PISTOLS into minor legends with barely one single under their belts. Signed to 'E.M.I.' for £40,000, their debut release, 'ANARCHY IN THE U.K.' (having already shocked those of a sensitive disposition after being aired on the 'So It Goes' TV pop show) was finally released in November '76. An inflammatory slice of primal nihilism which surpassed even The STOOGES' finest efforts, the track initially climbed into the Top 40 before being unceremoniously withdrawn following the band's riotous appearance on a local chat/news programme, 'Today'. With JONES swearing copiously at presenter Bill Grundy, the tabloids had a field day, stirring up the moral majority and prompting more "must we subject our pop kids to this filth" editorials than you could shake a snotty stick at. 'E.M.I.' of course, bailed out (writing off the advance as a particularly bad debt) early the following year, while MATLOCK was fired around the same time for being,

Johnny Rotten of The SEX PISTOLS

well, er . . . too nice. His replacement was the aforementioned VICIOUS, a suitably violent and abusive character who duly became more of a punk anti-hero/caricature than McLAREN could ever have dreamed. After a short period in label limbo, The 'PISTOLS signed to 'A&M' in March '77 for another six figure sum; the honeymoon period was probably the shortest in recording history as the band's infamous antics at the post-signing party, together with protests from other artists on the label saw the UK's foremost punk band once again minus a recording contract. Once again, the band retained the loot from the advance and once again, a single, 'GOD SAVE THE QUEEN', was withdrawn (some copies did find their way into circulation and now fetch considerably more than the original 50p price tag). Arguably The SEX PISTOLS' defining moment, this jaw-clenching two-fingured salute to the monarchy and everything it represented was to truly make the band public enemy No.1, its release coinciding sweetly with her highness' silver jubilee year. Re-released by new label 'Virgin' (virtually the only company willing to take the band on for a meagre £15,000 advance), the single was predictably banned by the BBC, though that didn't prevent it from outselling the official No.1 at the time, Rod Stewart's 'I Don't Want To Talk About It'. That long, hot summer also saw the band hiring a boat and sailing up and down the Thames in a publicity stunt which ended in chaos; cue yet more controversy and howls of derision from the nation's moral guardians. Knuckle-headed English royalists decided to take matters into their own hands, both COOK and ROTTEN attacked in separate incidents as another blankly brilliant single, 'PRETTY VACANT', gatecrashed the Top 10. Previewed by the seething, squalling outrage of 'HOLIDAYS IN THE SUN', the legendary debut album, 'NEVER MIND THE BOLLOCKS, HERE'S THE SEX PISTOLS' was finally released at the end of the year. While the record undeniably contained some filler, it remains the classic punk statement, the blistering 'BODIES' and the gleeful kiss-off to their former employers, 'E.M.I.', almost standing up against the intensity of the singles (included in their entirety). As ever, controversy clouded its release, the album reaching No.1 in spite of the word 'Bollocks' – a near contravention of the 1889 Indecent Advertisements Act(!) – resulting in boycotts from many major outlets. Constantly on the verge of falling apart, the band subsequently flew to America for a string of chaotic dates, the final round of blanks in The SEX PISTOLS' depleted armoury. Amid sporadic showdowns with Deep South cowboys and SID's ever worsening heroin problem, ROTTEN (bowing out on stage in San Francisco with the immortal phrase "Ever get the feeling you've been cheated") effectively ended the whole sorry affair with his departure after the final gig. While LYDON (the name he now reverted back to) went on to form PUBLIC IMAGE LTD., McLAREN had other ideas for the splintered remains of the band, namely jetting off to Rio De Janeiro to record a single with exiled trainrobber, RONNIE BIGGS. The result, 'NO ONE IS INNOCENT (A PUNK PRAYER BY RONNIE BIGGS)', made the Top 10 in summer '78, although VICIOUS was absent from the recording, holed up in New York with his similarly addicted girlfriend, Nancy Spungeon. He did find time to record a peerless rendition of Paul Anka's 'MY WAY', the single taking on an added poignancy following his untimely but hardly surprising death early the following year; out on bail after being charged with the murder of Spungeon in October, VICIOUS succumbed to a fatal heroin overdose on the 2nd of February '79. The following month saw the belated release of McLAREN's pet project, an artistically licensed celluloid account of The SEX PISTOLS' history entitled 'THE GREAT ROCK'N'ROLL SWINDLE'. Widely criticised for its blatant exclusion of GLEN MATLOCK, the glaring absence of ROTTEN as an active participant and its paper-thin storyline, the movie was nevertheless an occasionally exhilarating, often hilarious trip through the misspent youth of Britain's best-loved punk band. While a perfunctory cover of Eddie Cochran's 'C'MON EVERYBODY' (a posthumous VICIOUS recording) made the Top 10 later that summer and 'Virgin' continued to flog The SEX PISTOLS' dead corpse with a variety of exploitation jobs, COOK and JONES formed the short-lived PROFESSIONALS. Although they didn't invent punk, The SEX PISTOLS certainly helped popularise it and while they were at least partly responsible for an avalanche of unlistenably amateurish shit, the band's uncompromising approach permanently altered the machinations of the music industry and took three-chord rock'n'roll to its ultimate conclusion. Despite the fact original fans had long since given up on the UK ever descending into anarchy, the original 'PISTOLS line-up of LYDON, MATLOCK, JONES and COOK reformed in summer '96 for a handful of outdoor gigs and an accompanying live album. Opinion was divided as to whether this blatantly commercial venture (billed as "The Filthy Lucre Tour") was in keeping with the original punk spirit; probably not, although few paying punters complained about what was subsequently hailed as one of the events of the summer and it was certainly a safer bet than the new GREEN DAY album . . .

• **Songwriters:** Group compositions, until COOK & JONES took over in 1978. They also covered; NO FUN (Stooges) / ROCK AROUND THE CLOCK (Bill Haley) / JOHNNY B. GOODE (Chuck Berry) / STEPPING STONE (Boyce-Hart) / etc. • **Trivia:** In 1979, they took McLAREN to court for unpaid royalties. In 1986, the official receiver, through McLAREN paid a 7-figure out of court settlement to LYDON, JONES, COOK and SID's mother.

Album rating (selective): NEVER MIND THE BOLLOCKS, HERE'S THE SEX PISTOLS (*10) / THE GREAT ROCK'N'ROLL SWINDLE soundtrack (*8) / FLOGGING A DEAD HORSE compilation (*8) / KISS THIS compilation (*8) / FILTHY LUCRE LIVE (*6) / THE FILTH AND THE FURY soundtrack compilation w/ V/A (*8) / JUBILEE compilation (*8)

JOHNNY ROTTEN (b. JOHN LYDON, 31 Jan'56) – vocals / **STEVE JONES** (b. 3 Sep'55) – guitar / **GLEN MATLOCK** (b.27 Aug'56) – bass / **PAUL COOK** (b.20 Jul'56) – drums

E.M.I. — not iss.

Nov 76. (7") *(EMI 2566)* **ANARCHY IN THE U.K. / I WANNA BE ME** — 38 — –

— (Feb'77) **SID VICIOUS** (b.JOHN RITCHIE, 10 May'57) – bass, vocals (ex-SIOUXSIE & THE BANSHEES) repl. MATLOCK who soon formed RICH KIDS

A&M — not iss.

Mar 77. (7"w-drawn) *(AMS 7284)* **GOD SAVE THE QUEEN. / NO FEELINGS** — – — –

— Were soon paid off yet again. Above copies filtered through and soon became a collectors item).

Virgin — Warners

May 77. (7") *(VS 181)* **GOD SAVE THE QUEEN. / DID YOU NO WRONG** — 2 — –

— (above was banned by the BBC, and outsold the official No.1 at the time; Rod Stewart's 'I Don't Want To Talk About It'.)

Jul 77. (7") *(VS 184)* **PRETTY VACANT. / NO FUN** — 6 — –

Oct 77. (7") *(VS 191)* **HOLIDAYS IN THE SUN. / SATELLITE** — 8 — –

Nov 77. (7") **PRETTY VACANT. / SUBMISSION** — – —

Nov 77. (lp/c) *(V/TCV 2086)* <3147> **NEVER MIND THE BOLLOCKS, HERE'S THE SEX PISTOLS** — 1 — 106
– Holidays in the sun / Bodies / No feelings / Liar / God save the Queen / Problems / Seventeen / Anarchy in the UK / Submission / Pretty vacant / New York / E.M.I. *(7" free w/some copies of 'Submission'; SPOTS 001)* – **SUBMISSION** (one-sided). *(pic-lp Jan78; VP 2086) (re-iss. Oct86 lp/c; OVED/+C 136) (cd-iss. Oct86; CDV 2086) (re-iss. cd May93; CDVX 2086) (re-iss. 1996 on cd w/ free 'SPUNK' bootleg tracks) <cd-iss. Jul96 on 'Alex; 5695>*

— ROTTEN left, reverted to JOHN LYDON and created new band PUBLIC IMAGE LTD. His place was temporarily taken by **RONNIE BIGGS** (the Great Train Robber escapee now exiled in Brazil) 'A'-side vocals / **SID VICIOUS** – 'B'side vocals

Jun 78. (7") *(VS 220)* **NO ONE IS INNOCENT (A PUNK PRAYER BY RONNIE BIGGS). / MY WAY** — 7 — –
(12") *(VS 220-12 A1/2)* – The biggest blow (a punk prayer by Ronnie Biggs) / My way.
(12"+=) *(VS 220-12 A3)* – (above listing) / (interview).

— On 11 Oct'78, SID was charged with the murder of girlfriend NANCY SPUNGEON. MALCOLM McLAREN/'Virgin' bailed him out, but he died 2 Feb'79 of drug overdose. The 1979/80 singles were all taken from THE GREAT ROCK'N'ROLL SWINDLE film.

Feb 79. (7") *(VS 240)* **SOMETHING ELSE. / FRIGGIN' IN THE RIGGIN'** 3 –

Mar 79. (d-lp/d-c) *(VD/TCV 2510) <45083>* **THE GREAT ROCK'N'ROLL SWINDLE** (soundtrack) 7
– God save the Queen symphony / Johnny B. Goode / Roadrunner / Anarchy in the UK / Don't give me no lip child / Stepping stone / L'anarchie pour le UK / Silly thing / My way / Watcha gonna do about it / Something else / We're gonna rock around the clock (TENPOLE TUDOR) / Lonely boy / E.M.I. (orchestral) / Great rock'n'roll swindle / Friggin' in the riggin' / You need hands (MALCOLM McLAREN) / Who killed Bambi (TEMPOLE TUDOR) / Belsen was a gas (live) / Black arabs (BLACK ARABS) / Substitute / No one is innocent (RONNIE BIGGS) / C'mon everybody / Belsen was a gas (RONNIE BIGGS). *(re-iss. 1-lp May80; V 2168) (re-iss. Apr89 lp/c; OVED/+C 234) (d-cd iss.Jul86; CDVD 2510) (re-iss. cd May93; CDVDX 2510)*

Apr 79. (7") *(VS 256)* **SILLY THING. / WHO KILLED BAMBI?** 6

— (above 'A'vocals – **STEVE JONES**, 'B'vocals – **EDDIE TENPOLE TUDOR**) (below 'A'vocals – **SID VICIOUS**)

Jun 79. (7") *(VS 272)* **C'MON EVERYBODY. / GOD SAVE THE QUEEN SYMPHONY / WATCHA GONNA DO ABOUT IT** 3

Aug 79. (lp/c) *(VR/ 2)* **SOME PRODUCT: CARRI ON SEX PISTOLS** 6 –
– The very name (the Sex Pistols) / From beyond the grave / Big tits across America / The complex world of Johnny Rotten / Sex Pistols will play / Is the Queen a moron / The fuckin' rotter. *(cd-iss. May93; CDVR 2)*

Oct 79. (7") *(VS 290)* **THE GREAT ROCK'N'ROLL SWINDLE. / ROCK AROUND THE CLOCK** 21

Dec 79. (lp/c; by SID VICIOUS) *(V/TCV 2144)* **SID SINGS** 30 –
– Born to lose / I wanna be your dog / Take a chance on me / (I'm not your) Stepping stone / My way / Belsen was a gas / Somethin' else / Chatterbox / Search and destroy / Chinese rocks / My way. *(re-iss. Aug88 lp/c; OVED/+C 85)* (cd-iss. Feb89; *CDV 2144)*

— There were other SID VICIOUS exploitation releases later.

Feb 80. (lp/c) *(V/TCV 2142)* **FLOGGING A DEAD HORSE** 23 –
– (singles compilation) *(re-iss. Apr86 lp/c; OVED/+C 165) (cd-iss. Oct86; CDV 2142)*

Jun 80. (7") *(VS 339)* **(I'M NOT YOUR) STEPPING STONE. / PISTOLS PROPAGANDA** 21 –

— COOK and JONES were now the PROFESSIONALS

— The original SEX PISTOLS re-formed at the back end of '95. Messrs LYDON, JONES, COOK + MATLOCK finally returned live on 24th June 1996, with packed out Finsbury Park concert. Embarked on their 'Filthy Lucre' tour soon after.

Virgin America | Caroline

Jul 96. (7"silver) *(VUS 113)* **PRETTY VACANT – LIVE. / BODIES – lIVE** 18 –
(cd-s+=) *(VUSCD 113)* – No fun (live) / Problems (live).

Aug 96. (cd/c/lp) *(41926) <7541>* **FILTHY LUCRE LIVE (live)** 26
– Seventeen / New York / Did you no wrong / God save the Queen / Liar / Satellite / (I'm not your) Stepping stone / Holidays in the sun / Submission / No feelings / Pretty vacant / E.M.I. / Problems / Anarchy in the UK / No fun.

— JONES was also part-member of transatlantic supergroup, NEUROTIC OUTSIDERS, alongside DUFF McKAGAN and MATT SORUM (Guns N' Roses) and JOHN TAYLOR (Duran Duran). They released an eponymous album for 'Maverick' in August '96 and from it they lifted the single, 'JERK'.

– compilations, exploitation releases –

Note; on 'Virgin' until mentioned otherwise.

Jan 80. (lp) *Flyover; (YX 7247)* **THE BEST OF . . . AND WE DON'T CARE** –

Dec 80. (6x7"box) *(SEX 1)* **PISTOLS PACK** –
– GOD SAVE THE QUEEN. / PRETTY VACANT / / HOLIDAYS IN THE SUN. / MY WAY / / SOMETHING ELSE. / SILLY THING / / C'MON EVERYBODY. / THE GREAT ROCK'N'ROLL SWINDLE / / STEPPING STONE. / ANARCHY IN THE U.K. / / BLACK LEATHER. / HERE WE GO AGAIN
(below 45 credited EDDIE TENPOLE TUDOR)

Sep 81. (7") *(VS 443)* **WHO KILLED BAMBI?. / ROCK AROUND THE CLOCK** –

1983. (7") *(VS 609)* **ANARCHY IN THE UK. / NO FUN** –
(12"+=) *(VS 609-12)* – E.M.I.

Jan 85. (7"/7"pic-d)(12") *Cherry Red; (PISTOL 76P)(12PISTOL 76)* **LAND OF HOPE AND GLORY. ("EX-PISTOLS") / FLOWERS OF ROMANSK** 69 –

Jan 85. (m-lp) *Chaos; (MINI 1)* **THE MINI-ALBUM** –
(pic-m-lp.Jan86; AMPL 37) (cd-iss. Mar89; APOCA 3)

Mar 87. (7",7"yellow,7"pink) *Chaos; (DICK 1)* **SUBMISSION. / NO FEELINGS** –
(12",12"colrd) *(EXPORT 1)* – ('A'side) / Anarchy in the U.K.

Feb 85. (lp) *Receiver; (RRLP 101)* **THE ORIGINAL PISTOLS LIVE (live)** –
(pic-lp Jun86 on 'American Phono.'; APKPD 13) (re-iss. Jan89 on 'Dojo'; DOJOLP 45) (re-iss. May86 on 'Fame' lp/c; FA 41-3149-1/-4) (cd-iss. Jul89; CDFA 3149)

1985. (lp) *Receiver; (RRLP 102)* **AFTER THE STORM** –
(above with tracks by NEW YORK DOLLS) (cd-iss. Jul91; RRCD 102)

Aug 85. (lp) *Konnexion;* **LIVE WORLDWIDE (live)** –

Nov 85. (lp) *Receiver;* **WHERE WERE YOU IN '77** –

Nov 85. (lp/pic-lp) *Bondage;* **BEST OF SEX PISTOLS LIVE (live)** –

Nov 85. (lp) *Hippy;* **NEVER TRUST A HIPPY** –

Nov 85. (lp) *'77 Records;* **POWER OF THE PISTOLS** –

Feb 86. (lp) *McDonald-Lydon; (JOCK 1)* **THE LAST SHOW ON EARTH (live)** –

Apr 86. (12") *McDonald-Lydon; (JOCK 1201)* **ANARCHY IN THE U.K. (live). / FLOGGING A DEAD HORSE** –

Aug 86. (lp) *McDonald-Lydon; (JOCKLP 3)* **THE SEX PISTOLS 10th ANNIVERSARY ALBUM** –

Aug 86. (12"ep) *Archive 4; (TOF 104)* **ANARCHY IN THE UK / I'M A LAZY SOD. / PRETTY VACANT / SUBSTITUTE** –

Jan 87. (6xlp-box) *McDonald-Lydon; (JOCK BOX1)* **THE FILTH AND THE FURY** –
– FILTH & THE FURY / LAST SHOW ON EARTH / 10th ANNIVERSARY ALBUM / ITALIAN DEMOS / NO FUTURE USA / THE REAL SID & NANCY

May 88. (lp/cd) *Restless; <72255-1/-2>* **BETTER LIVE THAN DEAD (live)** –

Jun 88. (cd/lp) *M.B.C.; (JOCK/+LP 12)* **IT SEEMED TO BE THE END UNTIL THE NEXT BEGINNING** –

Jun 88. (3"cd-s) *(CDT 3)* **ANARCHY IN THE U.K. / E.M.I. / NO FUN** –

Oct 88. (m-lp) *Specific; (SPAW 101)* **ANARCHY WORLDWIDE** –

Oct 88. (cd-ep) *Specific; (SPCFC 102)* **CASH FOR CHAOS** –
– Submission (live) / God save the Quen / Liar.

Oct 88. (cd-ep) *Classic Tracks; (CDEP 13C)* **THE ORIGINAL PISTOLS (live)** –
– Anarchy in the U.K. / Pretty vacant / No fun / Substitute.

Dec 88. (3"cd-s) *(CDT 37)* **GOD SAVE THE QUEEN / DID YOU NO WRONG / DON'T GIVE ME NO LIP CHILD** –

Jun 89. (lp,pink-lp,green-lp/c) *Link; (LINK LP/MC 063)* **LIVE AND LOUD (live)** –
(cd-iss. Oct92; LINKCD 063)

Dec 89. (lp/c/cd,pic-cd) *Receiver; (RR LP/MC/CD 117)* **NO FUTURE U.K.?** –

Feb 90. (cd/c) *Action Replay; (CDAR/ARLC 1008)* **THE BEST OF AND THE REST OF THE SEX PISTOLS** –

1990. (12"blue-ep) *Receiver; (REPLAY 3012)* **THE EARLY YEARS LIVE** –
– Anarchy in the U.K. / Pretty vacant / Liar / Dolls (aka 'New York').

Jan 91. (d-lp) *Receiver; (RRLD 004)* **PRETTY VACANT** –
(d-cd-iss. Jul93; RRDCD 004)

Sep 92. (7"/c-s) *(VS/+C 1431)* **ANARCHY IN THE U.K. / I WANNA BE ME** 33
(cd-s+=/s-cd-s+=) *(VSCD T/X 1431)* – ('A'demo).

Oct 92. (cd) *Streetlink; (STRCD 019)* **EARLY DAZE – THE STUDIO COLLECTION** –
(re-iss. May93 on 'Dojo'; DOJOCD 119)

Oct 92. (cd/c/d-lp) *(V/TC/CDV 2702) / Alex; <2931>* **KISS THIS** 10
– Anarchy in the UK / God save the Queen / Pretty vacant / Holidays in ther Sun / I wanna be me / Did you no wrong / No fun / Satellite / Don't give me no lip child / (I'm not your) Stepping stone / Bodies / No feelings / Liar / Problems / Seventeen / Submission / New York / E.M.I. / My way /

Silly thing. // (*cd w/bonus cd+=*) **LIVE IN TRONDHEIM 21st JULY 1977** :- Anarchy in the UK / I wanna be me / Seventeen / New York / E.M.I. / No fun / No feelings / Problems / God save the Queen.

Nov 92. (7") (*VS 1448*) **PRETTY VACANT. / NO FEELINGS (demo)** 56 –
(12"+=) (*VST 1448*) – Satellite (demo) / Submission (demo).
(cd-s+=) (*VSCDG 1448*) – E.M.I. (demo) / Satellite (demo).
(cd-s) (*VSCDT 1448*) – ('A'side) / Seventeen (demo) / Submission (demo) / Watcha gonna do about it?

Mar 93. (cd) *Dojo; (DOJOCD 66)* **LIVE AT CHELMSFORD PRISON** –

Nov 93. (cd) *Dojo; (DOJOCD 73)* **BETTER LIVE THAN DEAD** –

Jul 95. (cd) *Dojo; (DOJOCD 216)* **WANTED – THE GOODMAN TAPES** –

Oct 95. (d-cd) *Essential; (ESDCD 321)* **ALIVE** –

Jan 96. (cd) *Dojo; (DOJOCD 222)* **PIRATES OF DESTINY** –

Jan 97. (7") *Man's Ruin; (MR 053)* **split with the UGLYS** –

Mar 97. (7") *Man's Ruin; (MR 056)* **split with the SOPHISTICATES** –

Jun 97. (cd) *Emporio; (EMPRCD 716)* **RAW** –

May 00. (d-cd; w/ Various Artists) *(CDVD 2909)* <72703> **THE FILTH AND THE FURY** (soundtrack)
– God save the Queen – symphony / (other artists) / Submission / Don't gimme no lip child / Roadrunner / Substitute / Seventeen // Anarchy in the UK / Pretty vacant / Did you no wrong / Liar / E.M.I. / No feelings / I wanna be me / God save the Queen / Problems / (other artists) / Holidays in the sun / Bodies / My way / No fun.

May 02. (7") (*VS 1832*) **GOD SAVE THE QUEEN. / GOD SAVE THE QUEEN (Neil Barnes & Sex Pistols extended mix)** 15 –
(12"+=/cd-s+=) (*VST/VSCDT 1832*) – ('A'-Neil Barnes dance mix).

Jun 02. (cd) *(CDV 2961)* <812566> **JUBILEE** 29
– God save the Queen / Anarchy in the UK / Pretty vacant / Holidays in the sun / No one is innocent / My way / Somethin' else / Friggin' in the riggin' / Silly thing / C'mon everybody / The great rock'n'roll swindle / (I'm not your) Steppin' stone / Pretty vacant (live) / E.M.I. (unlimited edition) / God save the Queen (video) / Anarchy in the UK (video) / Pretty vacant (video).

the SHADOWS

Formed: London, England . . . 1958 as THE FIVE CHESTERNUTS by HANK MARVIN, BRUCE WELCH and PETE CHESTER (son of comedian Charlie Chester) along with GERALD HURST and NEIL JOHNSON. Following a one-off flop single, 'TEENAGE LOVE', for 'Columbia' in Autumn of that year, they were spotted by CLIFF RICHARD manager, John Foster, who needed a replacement for guitarist KEN PAVEY. Six-string wizard MARVIN agreed to join on the condition that WELCH was also hired, the susbsequent addition of IAN SAMWELL and TERRY SMART fleshing out a unit which was now trading under The DRIFTERS moniker. In November '58, CLIFF replaced SAMWELL (who became their manager in 1959) with JET HARRIS and the new-look beat combo backed up RICHARD on his famous 'LIVIN' LOVIN' DOLL' single. More upheaval followed at the tail end of the year as TONY MEEHAN replaced SMART (who went off to join the merchant navy!). By this point, the quartet had managed a further couple of singles in their own right, 'FEELIN' FINE' and 'JET BLACK'. Neither was successful and to compound their problems, the band had an injuction slapped on them by the US soul/R&B outfit of the same name. After a final flop 45 at the tail end of the year (featuring a rare vocal) things took a serious turn for the better the following summer as the rumbling Wild West-style guitar atmospherics of 'APACHE' saw them topping the UK chart. A benchmark track that saw the bespectacled MARVIN embraced by many young wannabe guitar heros as a role model, the song was subsequently turned into a 70's funk/breakbeat classic by MICHAEL VINER'S INCREDIBLE BONGO BAND. It also signalled the beginning of an incredible (largely instrumental) chart run that lasted right through until the hippy revolution of the mid-late 60's. 'MAN OF MYSTERY', 'F.B.I.', 'FRIGHTENED CITY', 'THE SAVAGE' and 'KON TIKI' all went Top 10 over 1960/'61, the latter track giving them their second No.1 while their eponymous album also topped the charts. A more laid-back, quintessentially English counterpoint to the surf instrumentals sweeping the American West Coast, the SHADOWS sound was hugely influential on many young guitarists who snapped up their records in droves; 1962 saw the band score three No.1's in a row with 'WONDERFUL LAND', the 'OUT OF THE SHADOWS' album and 'DANCE ON', topping it with another No.1 in '63, 'FOOT TAPPER'. By this point JET HARRIS and TONY MEEHAN had both been replaced (by BRIANs, BENNETT and LOCKING respectively), the pair going on to score three 1963 UK Top 5 singles in their own right (i.e. 'DIAMONDS', 'SCARLETT O'HARA' and 'APPLEJACK'). While still a regular fixture on the chart, The SHADOWS' began losing their identity as they added more vocals to their repertoire towards the middle of the decade. By 1967, their (lone) star was really beginning to fade and after the October '68 release of joint CLIFF RICHARD set, 'ESTABLISHED 1958', the band split to concentrate on solo projects. While BENNETT's material failed to spark much interest, MARVIN's eponymous 1969 solo set made the UK Top 20. 1969 also saw MARVIN duetting with CLIFF on Top 10 hit, 'THROW DOWN A LINE', following it up in 1970 with 'JOY OF LIVING'. The SHADOWS also returned that year on 'Parlophone' with a flop album of pop/rock standards, 'SHADES OF ROCK', only to disband the same year. MARVIN and WELCH then got together with Aussie guitarist, JOHN FARRAR to form a vocal trio although the project again proved relatively short-lived and commercially unsuccessful. The SHADOWS re-formed for a second time in 1973 with a line-up of MARVIN, WELCH, FARRAR and BENNETT, WELCH undertaking vocal duties for their 1975 Eurovision entry (!), 'LET ME BE THE ONE'. Although the song was runner-up it did furnish them with a much needed Top 20 hit. This pushed the brilliantly titled 'SPECS APPEAL' (1975) album into the Top 30. The late 70's brought another mini-revival with a Top 5 cover of 'DON'T CRY FOR ME ARGENTINA' (from the musical, 'Evita'), a Top 10 reading of 'THEME FROM THE DEER HUNTER (CAVATINA)', a Top 5 CLIFF collaboration, 'THANK YOU VERY MUCH' and a No.1 album of covers from all walks of musical life (everything from Blondie's 'HEART OF GLASS' to Art Garfunkel's 'BRIGHT EYES'). Though they wouldn't hit the singles chart again, the SHADOWS stepped into middle-age with a winning formula of fine but not specy-tacular (sorry) renditions of classics from every genre and era of music history, making regular appearances in the Top 10 album chart throughout the 80's. MARVIN also carried his solo career into the 80's/90's with occasional success, working alongside the likes of BRIAN MAY and MARK KNOPFLER.

• **Songwriters:** First songs written by/with PETE CHESTER or IAN SAMWELL. The group, mainly MARVIN and WELCH pen some, but mainly use other worldly sources; JERRY LORDAN wrote APACHE / WONDERFUL LAND / etc. His wife PETRINA penned A PLACE IN THE SUN. Their producer NORRIE PARAMOUR wrote THE FRIGHTENED CITY + THE SAVAGE. MAN OF MYSTERY + KON-TIKI (Michael Carr). They also covered ('A'singles only, their were loads more); DANCE ON (Avons) / DON'T MAKE MY BABY BLUE (hit; Frankie Laine) / THE WARLORD (Jerome Moross) / MAROC 7 + LET ME BE THE ONE (Paul Ferris; a friend) / SLAUGHTER ON 10th AVENUE (Richard Rodgers) / DON'T CRY FOR ME ARGENTINA (Tim Rice-Andrew Lloyd Webber) / DEER HUNTER (John Williams) / RODRIGO'S GUITAR CONCERTO (Manuel; Geoff Love) / RIDERS IN THE SKY (Stan Jones; hit, Ramrods) / EQUINOXE V (Jean-Michel Jarre) / MOZART FORTE (Mozart; hit, Waldo De La Rios) / TELSTAR (Tornados) / TREAT ME NICE (Elvis Presley) / MISSING (Vangelis) / GOIN' HOME (Mark Knopfler) / MOONLIGHT SHADOW (Mike Oldfield) / DANCING IN THE DARK (Bruce Springsteen) / EASTENDERS-HOWARD'S WAY + PULASKI (TV themes) / SNOWMAN (hit; Aled Jones) / etc, etc, etc. • **Trivia:** WELCH was married in 1959, although he left his wife eight years later for singer OLIVIA NEWTON JOHN. The group appeared in CLIFF's films; THE YOUNG ONES / SUMMER HOLIDAY (title track penned by MARVIN & BENNETT) / WONDERFUL LIFE / ALADDIN . . . + CINDERELLA (wrote and performed the pantomines).

Best CD compilation: LIFE STORY – THE VERY BEST OF.. (*8)

HANK MARVIN (b. BRIAN RANKIN, 28 Nov'41, Newcastle, England) – lead guitar / **BRUCE WELCH** (b.CRIPPS, 2 Nov'41, Bognor Regis, England) – rhythm guitar / **GERALD HURST** – vocals / **PETER CHESTER** – drums / **NEIL JOHNSON** – bass

Columbia | not iss.

Aug 58. (7",78; as FIVE CHESTERNUTS) *(DB 4165)* **TEENAGE LOVE. / JEAN DOROTHY** [ ] [–]

—— (Oct'58) they were also the backing for CLIFF RICHARD

—— **IAN SAMWELL** – bass + **TERRY SMART** – drums; repl. all bar **MARVIN** + **WELCH** (Oct-Dec'58) / **JET HARRIS** (b.TERRENCE, 6 Jul'39, London) – bass (ex-VIPERS) repl. IAN SAMWELL who became their manager in 1959) / **TONY MEEHAN** (b. DANIEL, 2 Mar'43, London) – drums (ex-VIPERS) repl. TERRY SMART who joined the merchant navy

Feb 59. (7",78; as DRIFTERS) *(DB 4263)* **FEELIN' FINE. / DON'T BE A FOOL WITH LOVE** [ ] [–]

Jul 59. (7"; as DRIFTERS) *(DB 4325)* **JET BLACK. / DRIFTIN'** [ ] [ ]
(above single released in the US as "The FOUR JETS")

—— the SHADOWS name was taken to avoid confusion with American soul/R&B group, they also remained as CLIFF RICHARD's backers

Columbia | Atlantic

Dec 59. (7",78) *(DB 4387)* **SATURDAY DANCE. / LONESOME FELLA** [ ] [–]
(above 'A'side featured vocals by BRUCE)

Jul 60. (7") *(DB 4484)* **APACHE. / QUARTERMASTER'S STORES** [1] [–]

Oct 60. (7") *(DB 4530)* **MAN OF MYSTERY. / THE STRANGER** [5] [ ]

Jan 61. (7") *(DB 4580)* **F.B.I. / MIDNIGHT** [6] [–]

May 61. (7") *(DB 4637)* **FRIGHTENED CITY. / BACK HOME** [3] [–]

Jun 61. (7") **FRIGHTENED CITY. / F.B.I.** [–] [ ]

Aug 61. (7") *(DB 4698)* **KON TIKI. / 36-24-36** [1] [ ]

Sep 61. (lp; mono/stereo) *(33SX 1374/SCX 3414)* **THE SHADOWS** [1] [–]
– Shadoogie / Nivram / Blue star / Theme from a filletted plaice / Sleepwalk / See you in my dreams / Stand up and say that / All my sorrows / That's my desire / Find me a golden street / Big boy / Gonzales / My resistance is low / Baby my heart. *(re-iss. +c.May83 on 'Fame')*

—— **BRIAN BENNETT** (b. 9 Feb'40, London) – drums; repl. MEEHAN

Nov 61. (7") *(DB 4726)* **THE SAVAGE. / PEACE PIPE** [10] [–]

Feb 62. (7") *(DB 4790)* **WONDERFUL LAND. / STARS FELL ON STOCKTON** [1] [ ]

—— **BRIAN 'Licorice' LOCKING** – bass; repl. JET HARRIS (who still featured on next LP's tracks) to own duo with MEEHAN

Jul 62. (7") *(DB 4870)* **GUITAR TANGO. / WHAT A LOVELY TUNE** [4] [ ]

Oct 62. (lp; mono/stereo) *(33SX 1458/SCX 3449)* **OUT OF THE SHADOWS** [1] [–]
– The rumble / The bandit / Perfidia / Cosy / Some are lonely / Little B / Spring is nearly here / Bo Diddley / Kinda cool / 1861 / South of the border / Are they all like you / Tales of a raggy tramline. *(re-iss. +c.Aug86 on 'Awareness')*

Dec 62. (7") *(DB 4948)* **DANCE ON. / ALL DAY** [1] [–]

Dec 62. (7") **DANCE ON. / RUMBLE** [–] [ ]

Mar 63. (7") *(DB 4984)* **FOOT TAPPER. / THE BREEZE AND I** [1] [–]

May 63. (7") *(DB 7047)* **ATLANTIS. / I WANT YOU TO BUY ME** [2] [–]

Jun 63. (lp) *(33SX 1522)* **GREATEST HITS** (compilation) [2] [–]
– Apache / Man of mystery / F.B.I. / Midnight / Frightened city / Kon-tiki / 36-24-36 / The savage / Peace pipe / Wonderful land / Stars fell on Stockton / Guitar tango / The boys / Dance on / The stranger. *(re-iss. Aug71 / re-iss. May74, hit No.48) (cd-iss. May89 on 'E.M.I.')*

Sep 63. (7") *(DB 7106)* **SHINDIG. / IT'S BEEN A BLUE DAY** [6] [–]

—— **JOHN ROSTILL** (b.16 Jun'42, Birmingham, England) – bass (ex-INTERNS) repl. LOCKING; they shared duties on below album

Nov 63. (7") *(DB 7163)* **GERONIMO. / SHAZAM** [11] [–]

Feb 64. (7") *(DB 7231)* **THEME FOR YOUNG LOVERS. / THIS HAMMER** [12] [–]

May 64. (7") *(DB 7261)* **THE RISE & FALL OF FLINGEL BUNT. / IT'S A MAN'S WORLD** [5] [–]

May 64. (lp; mono/stereo) *(33SX 1619/SCX 3511)* **DANCE WITH THE SHADOWS** [2] [–]
– Chattanooga choo choo / Blue shadows / Fandango / Tonight / That's the way it goes / Don't it make you feel good / Big 'B' / Dakota / In the mood / The lonely bull / French dressing / The high and the mighty / Zambesi / Temptation.

Jun 64. (7") **THE RISE AND FALL OF FLINGEL BUNT. / THEME FOR YOUNG LOVERS** [–] [ ]

Aug 64. (7") *(DB 7342)* **RHYTHM AND GREENS. / THE MIRACLE** [22] [ ]

Nov 64. (7") *(DB 7416)* **GENIE WITH THE LIGHT BROWN LAMP. / PRINCESS** [17] [–]

—— Next with vocals as was alternate singles until MAROC 7 instrumental

—— **HANK** + **BRIAN** also added keyboards to repertoire

Feb 65. (7") *(DB 7476)* **MARY ANNE. / CHU-CHI** [17] [–]

May 65. (7") *(DB 7588)* **STINGRAY. / ALICE IN SUNDERLAND** [19] [–]

Jul 65. (lp; mono/stereo) *(33SX 1736/SCX 3554)* **SOUND OF THE SHADOWS** [4] [–]
– A little bitty tear / Five hundred miles / Let it be me / Brazil / Lost city / Blue sky, blue sea, blue me / Bossa roo / Cotton pickin' / Santa Ana / The windjammer / Deep purple / Dean's theme / Breakthru / National provincial samba.

Jul 65. (7") *(DB 7650)* **DON'T MAKE MY BABY BLUE. / MY GRANDFATHER** [10] [–]

Nov 65. (7") *(DB 7769)* **WARLORD. / WISH I COULD SHIMMY** [18] [–]

Dec 65. (lp; mono/stereo) *(33SX 1791/SCX 3578)* **MORE HITS!** (compilation) [ ] [–]
– Foot tapper / Atlantis / Shindig / Theme for young lovers / Geronimo / Shazam / The rise and fall of Flingel Bunt / Genie with the light brown lamp / Mary-Anne / Stingray / Rhythms and greens / Don't make my baby blue / Lute number / Drum number. *(re-iss. Aug85) (cd-iss. May89 on 'E.M.I.')*

Mar 66. (7") *(DB 7853)* **I MET A GIRL. / LATE LAST NIGHT** [22] [–]

May 66. (lp; mono/stereo) *(33SX/SCX 6041)* **SHADOW MUSIC** [5] [–]
– Razzamatazz / I only want to be with you / Babes in the wood / Only one way to love / Stay around / In the past / Bento-San / Fly me to the Moon / 4th street / A sigh (un sospero) / Don't stop now / March to Drina / The magic doll / Now that you're gone / Maid Marion's theme.

Jun 66. (7") *(DB 7952)* **A PLACE IN THE SUN. / WILL YOU BE THERE** [24] [–]

Oct 66. (7") *(DB 8034)* **THE DREAMS I DREAM. / SCOTCH ON THE SOCKS** [42] [–]

Mar 67. (7") *(DB 8170)* **MAROC 7. / BOMBAY DUCK** [24] [–]

Jul 67. (lp) *(SCX 6148)* **JIGSAW** [8] [–]
– Prelude in E major / Jigsaw / Waiting for Rosie / With a hym hym on my knee / Chelsea boot / Winchester cathedral / Green eyes / Stardust / Marie Elena / Tennessee waltz / Trains and boats and planes / Cathy's clown / Semi-detached Mr.James / Friday on my mind. *(re-iss. Apr90 on 'Beat Goes On';)*

Sep 67. (7") *(DB 8264)* **TOMORROW'S CANCELLED. / SOMEWHERE** [ ] [–]

Dec 67. (lp) *(SCX 6199)* **FROM HANK, BRUCE, BRIAN AND JOHN** [ ] [–]
– Snap, crackle and how's your dad / Evening glow / A thing of beauty / Naughty Nippon nights / The wild roses / The letter / San Francisco / The day I met Marie / Holy cow / I'm a believer. *(re-iss. Apr90 on 'Beat Goes On';)*

Jan 68. (7"; as HANK MARVIN & THE SHADOWS) *(DB 8326)* **LONDON'S NOT TOO FAR. / RUNNING OUT OF THE WORLD** [ ] [–]

Mar 68. (7") *(DB 8372)* **DEAR OLD MRS. BELL. / TRYING TO FORGET THE ONE YOU LOVE** [ ] [–]

—— The SHADOWS split late '68, after release in October of shared lp 'ESTABLISHED 1958' with CLIFF RICHARD.

—— re-formed in mid'69. **ALAN HAWKSHAW** – guitar, keyboards repl. WELCH (see further below)

Parlophone | not iss.

Oct 69. (7"; by HANK MARVIN) **SLAUGHTER ON 10th AVENUE. / MIDNIGHT COWBOY** [ ] [–]

—— augmented by bassmen; **HERBIE FLOWERS, DAVE RICHMOND** + **BRIAN HODGES**

Oct 70. (lp) *(SCX 6420)* **SHADES OF ROCK** [ ] [–]

– Proud Mary / My babe / Lucille / Johnny B.Goode / Paperback writer / (I can't get no) Satisfaction / Bony Moronie / Get back / Something / River deep, mountain high / Memphis / What'd I say.

— they disbanded again in 1970; ROSTILL rejoined the TOM JONES band but was tragically electrocuted on the 26th November '73 when playing guitar in his home

MARVIN, WELCH & FARRAR

— formed trio (**FARRAR** – b. Australia), augmented by **HAWKSHAW, RICHMOND / CLEM CATTINI** – drums / **PETER VINCE** – organ

Regal Zonophone — not iss.

Jan 71. (7") *(RZ 3030)* **FAITHFUL. / MR. SUN** –

Feb 71. (lp) *(SRZA 8502)* **MARVIN, WELCH & FARRAR** 30 –
– You're burning bridges / A thousand conversations / Brownie Kentucky / My home town / Silvery rain / Throw down a line / Baby I'm calling you / Faithful / Mistress Fate & Father Time / Take her away / Wish you were here / Mr. Sun / Strike a light. *(cd-iss. Aug91 on 'See For Miles';)* – (extra tracks).

— the trio now augmented by **BENNETT, HAWKSHAW + RICHMOND**

May 71. (7") *(RZ 3035)* **LADY OF THE MORNING. / TINY ROBIN** –

Nov 71. (lp) *(SRZA 8504)* **SECOND OPINION** –
– Black eyes / Tiny Robin / Ronnie / Far away falling / Lady of the morning / Let's say goodbye / Lonesome mole / The time to come / Thank Heaven's I've got you / Come back to natre / All day, all night blues. *(cd-iss. Aug91 on 'See For Miles';)* – (extra tracks)

Apr 72. (7") *(RZ 3048)* **MARMADUKE. / STRIKE A LIGHT** –

— early in 1972, when WELCH's girlfriend (OLIVIA NEWTON-JOHN) broke off engagement, he attempted suicide. The remaining 5 members became part of

MARVIN & FARRAR

E.M.I. — not iss.

Aug 73. (7") *(EMI 2044)* **MUSIC MAKES MY DAY. / SKIN DEEP** –

Aug 73. (lp) *(EMA 755)* **HANK MARVIN AND JOHN FARRAR** –
– So hard to live with / Music makes my day / Skin deep / If I rewrote yesterdays / Galadrie / Love oh love / Help me into your wagon / Small and lonely night / You never can tell / Nobody cares / Lord how it's hurting. *(cd-iss. Aug91 on 'See For Miles' with extra tracks)*

the SHADOWS

— re-formed (**MARVIN, WELCH, FARRAR + BENNETT**)

E.M.I. — not iss.

Nov 73. (7") *(EMI 2081)* **TURN AROUND AND TOUCH ME. / JUNGLE JAM** –

— added **ALAN TARNEY** – bass

Dec 73. (lp/c) *(EMA/TCEMA 762)* **ROCKIN' WITH CURLY LEADS** 45 –
– Pinball wizard – See me, feel me / Years away / Deep roots / Humbucker / Jungle jam / Gracie / Good vibrations / Rockin' with curly leads / Turn around and touch me / Wide mouthed frog / Gutbucket / Jumpin' Jack input.

Apr 74. (7"; by BRUCE WELCH) *(EMI 2141)* **PLEASE MR. PLEASE. / SONG OF YESTERDAY** –

— same 5-piece, but **WELCH** now vocals, **TARNEY** – piano

Mar 75. (7") *(EMI 2269)* **LET ME BE THE ONE. / STAND UP LIKE A MAN** 12 –

Apr 75. (lp/c) *(EMC/TCEMC 3066)* **SPECS APPEAL** 30 –
– God only knows / Cool clear air / Rose, Rose / This house runs on sunshine / Colarado songbird / No no Nina / Don't throw it all away / Honourable puff-puff / Spider juice / Let me be the one / Like strangers / Stand up like a man.

Jun 75. (7") *(EMI 2310)* **RUN BILLY RUN. / HONOURABLE PUFF-PUFF** –

Oct 75. (7"; as MARVIN & FARRAR) **SMALL AND LONELY NIGHT. / GALADRIEL (SPIRIT OF STARLIGHT)** –

Nov 75. (lp) *(EMC 3095)* **LIVE AT THE PARIS OLYMPIA (live April'75)** –
– The rise and fall of Flingel Bunt / Man of mystery / Lady of the morning / Nivram / Tiny Robin / Sleepwalk / Guitar tango / Honourable puff-puff / Apache / Shadoogie / Marmaduke / Somewhere / Little 'B' / Medley (Lucille – Rip it up – Blue suede shoes). *(re-iss. Apr81 on 'M.F.P.', w/free other live at Sankei Hall) (cd-iss. Feb92)*

Jun 76. (7") *(EMI 2461)* **IT'LL BE ME BABE. / LIKE STRANGERS** –

— In Jan'77, the TV advertised compilation '20 GOLDEN GREATS' hit No.1

— **FRANCIS MONKMAN** – keyboards repl. FARRAR who went to solo & Australia. / **ALAN JONES** – bass repl. TARNEY

Jul 77. (7") *(EMI 2660)* **ANOTHER NIGHT. / CRICKET BAT BOOGIE** –

Aug 77. (lp/c) *(EMC/TCEMC 3195)* **TASTY** –
– Cricket bat boogie / Return to the Alamo / Another night / Goodbye yellow brick road / Honky tonk woman / Montezuma's revenge / Walk don't run / Superstar / Bermuda triangle / The most beautiful girl in the world / Creole nights.

Aug 78. (7") *(EMI 2838)* **LOVE DE LUXE. / SWEET SATURDAY NIGHT** –

— **CLIFF HALL** – keyboards (ex-CLIFF RICHARD Band) repl. MONKMAN to SKY They were now virtually a trio of **MARVIN, WELCH & BENNETT**

Nov 78. (7") *(EMI 2890)* **DON'T CRY FOR ME ARGENTINA. / MONTEZUMA'S REVENGE** 5 –

— In Feb79, their album with CLIFF 'THANK YOU VERY MUCH' hit No.5.

Apr 79. (7") *(EMI 2939)* **THEME FROM 'THE DEER HUNTER'. / BERMUDA TRIANGLE** 9 –

Sep 79. (lp/c) *(EMC/TCEMC 3310)* **STRING OF HITS** 1 –
– Riders in the sky / Parisienne walkways / Heart of glass / Classical gas / You're the one that I want / Theme from 'The Deer Hunter' / Bridge over troubled water / Don't cry for me Argentina / Song for Duke / Bright eyes / Rodrigo's guitar de Aranjuez / Baker street. *(re-iss. Sep85 on 'M.F.P.', cd-iss. Sep88) (cd-iss. Oct87)*

Oct 79. (7") *(EMI 5004)* **RODRIGO'S GUITAR CONCERTO. / SONG FOR DUKE** –

Jan 80. (7") *(EMI 5027)* **RIDERS IN THE SKY. / RUSK** 12 –

Jul 80. (7") *(EMI 5083)* **HEART OF GLASS. / RETURN OF THE ALAMO** –

Polydor — not iss.

Aug 80. (7") *(POSP 148)* **EQUINOXE V. / FENDER BENDER** 50 –

Sep 80. (lp)(c) *(2442 179)(3184 147)* **CHANGE OF ADDRESS** 17 –
– Mozart forte / Midnight creeping / Change of address / Just the way you are / Indigo-Outdigo / Arty's party / Albatross / Hello Mr. W.A.M. / Temptation / If you leave me now / Equinoxe V. *(re-iss. Aug83)*

Nov 80. (7") *(POSP 187)* **MOZART FORTE. / MIDNIGHT CREEPING** –

Apr 81. (7") *(POSP 255)* **THE THIRD MAN. / THE FOURTH MAN** 44 –

Sep 81. (7") *(POSP 316)* **TELSTAR. / SUMMER LOVE '59** –

Sep 81. (lp/c) *(POLD/+C 5046)* **HITS RIGHT UP YOUR STREET** 15 –
– Telstar / Chi Mai (theme from 'The Life & Times Of David Lloyd George') / We don't talk anymore / Imagine; Woman / Hats off to Wally / One day I'll fly away / Summer love '59 / Misty / This ole house / The winner takes all / Sailing / Nut rocker / Thing-me-jig / More than I can say / Cowboy cafe / The third man.

Nov 81. (7") *(POSP 376)* **IMAGINE; WOMAN. / HATS OFF TO WALY** –

May 82. (7") *(POSP 439)* **TREAT ME NICE. / SPOT THE BALL** –

Jul 82. (7") *(POSP 485)* **THE THEME FROM 'MISSING'. / THE SHADY LADY** –

Sep 82. (2xlp/d-c) *(SHAD S/C 1)* **LIFE IN THE JUNGLE** 24 –
– Life in the jungle / High noon / The theme from 'Missing' / Treat me nice / Cat'n'mouse / Chariots of fire / No dancing / Riders of the range / The old romantics / You rescue me / Lili Marlene / Raunchy. *(re-iss. as lp Jan85) (cd-iss. May89)* **LIVE AT ABBEY ROAD (live)** – The third man / Thing-me-jig / Runaway / All I have to do is dream / It doesn't matter anymore / Johnny B.Goode / Over in a flash / Summer love '59 / Oh! boy / Crying in the rain / Arty's party. *(cd-iss. May89)*

Aug 83. (7") *(POSP 629)* **DIAMONDS. / ELEVEN IS** –

Oct 83. (lp/c) *(POLD/+C 5120)* **XXV** 34 –
– Africa / Goin' home (theme from 'Local Hero') / Up where we belong / You don't have to say you love me / The modern way / Diamonds / Time is tight / Memory / Liverpool days / Queen of hearts / A whiter shade of pale. *(cd-iss. 1988)*

Oct 83. (7") *(POSP 647)* **GOIN' HOME. / CAT'N'MOUSE** –

Aug 84. (7") *(POSP 694)* **ON A NIGHT LIKE THIS. / THING-ME-JIG** –

Nov 84. (lp/c) *(POLD/+C 5169)* **GUARDIAN ANGEL** 98 –

– How do I love thee / Hammerhead / The Saturday western / On a night like this / Look back on love / Johnny Staccato / I will return / (I'm gonna be your) Guardian angel / Can't play your game / Turning point / Our Albert. *(cd-iss. Nov86; 823797-2)*

May 86. (7") *(POSP 792)* **MOONLIGHT SHADOW. / JOHNNY STACCATO** [ ] [–]

May 86. (lp/c)(cd) *(PRO LP/MC 8)(829358-2)* **MOONLIGHT SHADOWS** [6] [–]
– Moonlight shadow / Walk of life / I just called to say I love you / Hello / Every breath you take / Nights in white satin / The power of love / Three times a lady / Against all odds / Hey Jude / Dancing in the dark / Imagine / I know him so well / Memory / Sailing / A whiter shade of pale. *(re-iss. cd/c Apr95)*

Aug 86. (7") *(POSP 808)* **DANCING IN THE DARK. / TURNING POINT** [ ] [–]
(12"+=) *(POSPX 808)* – ('A'version).

Nov 86. (7") *(POSP 847)* **EASTENDERS; HOWARD'S WAY. / NO DANCING!** [ ] [–]

Oct 87. (7") *(POSP 886)* **PULASKI. / CHANGE OF ADDRESS** [ ] [–]

Oct 87. (lp/c)(cd) *(SHAD/+C 1)(833682-2)* **SIMPLY SHADOWS** [11] [–]
– I knew you were waiting (for me) / We don't need another hero / Theme from 'The Snowman' / Careless whisper / Don't give up / I guess that's why they call it the blues / A heart will break tonight / The lady in red / Pulaski / Take my breath away / Eastenders / I want to know what love is / Skye boat song / Jealous guy / Chain reaction / Howard's way.

Nov 87. (7") *(POSP 898)* **THEME FROM THE SNOWMAN. / OUTDIGO** [ ] [–]

Apr 89. (7") *(PO 47)* **MOUNTAINS OF THE MOON. / STACK-IT** [ ] [–]
(cd-s+=) *(PZCD 47)* – Turning point.

May 89. (lp/c)(cd) *(SHAD/+C 30)(839357-2)* **STEPPIN' TO THE SHADOWS** [11] [–]
– You win again / I wanna dance with somebody (who loves me) / He ain't heavy, he's my brother / Candle in the wind / Farewell my lovely / Mountains of the Moon / Nothing's gonna change my love for you / Heaven is a place on Earth / When the going gets tough / Alone / All I ask of you / Stack-it / Shoba / You keep me hangin' on / Some people / One moment in time. *(re-iss. cd+c May93 on 'Spectrum')*

Oct 90. (cd/c/lp) *(847120-2/-4/-1)* **REFLECTION** [6] [–]
– Eye of the tiger / Crockett's theme / Right here waiting / Every little thing she does is magic / Sealed with a kiss / Uptown girl / Strawberry fields forever / Riders in the sky '90 / Flashdance / Something's gotten hold of my heart / Love changes everything / Nothing's gonna stop us now / Bilitis / You'll never walk alone / Always on my mind / Megamix.

Oct 91. (cd/c/lp) *(511374-2/-4/-1)* **THEMES AND DREAMS** [21] [–]
– Crockett's theme / Up where we belong / Take my breath away / Theme from The Deerhunter / Walking in the air / If you leave me now / One day I'll fly away / Africa / Every breath you take / Memory / Nights in white satin / Candle in the wind / You win again / Sailing / Just the way you are / Moonlight shadow.

Eagle — not iss.

Nov 04. (d-cd) *(EDGCD 283)* **THE FINAL TOUR: TOGETHER AGAIN FOR THE LAST TIME** (live) [ ] [–]
– Intro – Apache medley / Riders in the sky / The frightened city / Theme for young lovers / Peace pipe / The savage / Let me be the one / The stranger / Kon Tiki / Going home (theme from 'Local Hero') / Dance on / Nivram / Lady of the morning / My home town / Guitar tango / Geronimo / Sleepwalk / 36-24-36 / Shazam / Don't cry for me Argentina / Equinox V // Mountains of the Moon / Shadoogie / Gonzales / Don't make my baby blue / The rise and fall of Flingel Bunt / Atlantis / Shindig / Man of mystery / Foot tapper / Please don't tease / In the country / I could easily fall / The day I met Marie / Gee whiz it's you / Summer holiday / Bachelor boy / Little B / Theme from The Deer Hunter / Wonderful land / F.B.I. / Apache.

– (selective) compilations, etc. –

Jan 77. (lp/c) *E.M.I.; (EMTV/TCEMTV 3)* **20 GOLDEN GREATS** [1] [–]
– Apache / Frightened city / Guitar tango / Kon-tiki / Genie with the light brown lamp / The warlord / A place in the Sun / Atlantis / Wonderful land / F.B.I. / The savage / Geronimo / Shindig / Stingray / Theme for young lovers / The rise and fall of Flingel Bunt / Maroc 7 / Dance on / Man of mystery / Foot tapper. *(cd-iss. Aug87; CDP 746243-2)*

Nov 86. (cd; as MARVIN, WELCH & FARRAR) *See For Miles; (SEE 78)* **STEP FROM THE SHADOWS** [ ] [–]
(cd-iss. Nov89; SEECD 78) (re-iss. cd/lp Apr93)

Jan 89. (lp/c/cd) *See For Miles; (SEE/+K/CD 246)* **THE EP COLLECTION** [ ] [–]

Dec 89. (lp/c/cd) *Polydor; (841520-1/-4/-2)* **AT THEIR VERY BEST** [ ] [–]

Dec 89. (7"ep/cd-ep) *Polydor; (PD/PZCD 61)* **SHADOWMIX** [ ] [–]
– Apache – Wonderful land – Rise and fall of Flingel Bunt – Kon Tiki – F.B.I. – Man of mystery – Apache.

Feb 90. (d-cd/d-c/d-lp) *E.M.I.; CD/TC+/EM 1354)* **THE ORIGINAL CHART HITS 1960-1980** [ ] [–]
(d-cd+=) – (11 tracks).

Sep 90. (lp/c/cd) *See For Miles; (SEE/+K/CD 296)* **THE EP COLLECTION VOL.2** [ ] [–]

Mar 91. (cd) *E.M.I.; (CZ 378)* **THE SHADOWS / OUT OF THE SHADOWS** [ ] [–]

Sep 91. (6xcd-box) *E.M.I.; (CDSHAD 1)* **THE EARLY YEARS** [ ] [–]

Feb 92. (cd) *E.M.I.; (CZ 477)* **SHADOW MUSIC / SHADES OF ROCK** [ ] [–]

May 93. (cd/c) *Polygram TV; (843798-2/-4)* **SHADOWS IN THE NIGHT – 16 CLASSIC TRACKS** [22] [–]

Oct 93. (cd) *See For Miles; (SEECD 375)* **THE EP COLLECTION VOLUME 3** [ ] [–]

Oct 94. (cd/c) *Polygram TV; (523821-2/-4)* **THE BEST OF HANK MARVIN & THE SHADOWS** [19] [–]

May 95. (3xcd-box) *E.M.I.; (CDSHAD 2)* **THE FIRST 20 YEARS AT THE TOP – 75 ORIGINALS 1959-1979** [ ] [–]

Oct 97. (cd) *E.M.I.; (CDABBEY 104)* **AY ABBEY ROAD** [ ] [ ]

Nov 98. (cd; as HANK MARVIN & THE SHADOWS) *Polygram TV; (559211-2/-4)* **THE FIRST 40 YEARS** [56] [–]

Dec 98. (3xcd-box) *Disky; (HR 85328-2)* **GOOD VIBRATIONS** [ ] [ ]

Jul 00. (cd/c) *E.M.I.; (527586-2/-4)* **50 GOLDEN GREATS** [35] [–]

May 03. (cd) *E.M.I.; (583110-2)* **A'S, B'S & EP'S** [ ] [ ]

Apr 04. (d-cd) *Universal TV; (9817819)* **LIFE STORY – THE VERY BEST OF THE SHADOWS** [7] [–]
– Apache / Man of mystery / Shadoogie '83 / Shindig / Wonderful land / The rise of fall of Flingel Bunt / The boys / The theme from "The Deer Hunter" (Cavatina) / The frightened city / Theme for young lovers / Dance on / The savage / Albatross / F.B.I. / Guitar boogie / Genie with the light brown lamp / Atlantis / Foot tapper / Don't cry for me Argentina / Kon-tiki / Telstar / The Third Man / Geronimo / Equinoxe (part V) / The stranger / Riders in the sky // Mountains on the Moon / Moonlight shadow / You win again / Memory (from 'Cats') / I guess that's why they call it the blues / Thing-me-jig / Life story / Johnny Stacatto / Summer love 59 / Turning point / This old house / Chariots of fire / Crockett's theme (from 'Miami Vice') / Midnight creepin' / Going home (theme from 'Local Hero') / Every breath you take / Africa / Walk of life / Dancing in the dark.

Aug 05. (d-cd) *E.M.I.; (334938-2)* **THE PLATINUM COLLECTION** [30] [–]

□ Pete SHELLEY (see under ⇒ BUZZCOCKS)

□ Kevin SHIELDS (see under ⇒ MY BLOODY VALENTINE)

SIGUR ROS

Formed: Reykjavik, Iceland . . . early 1994 by guitarist and squeaky vocalist JON POR BIRGISSON and GEORG HOLM, later recruiting ORRI PALL DYRASON and keyboardist KJARTAN SVEINSSON. The original 3-piece line-up (consisting of BIRGISSON, HOLM and then drummer AGUST) entered a downtrodden studio and managed to record one track before their shoestring budget expired. The song was sent to 'Smekkleyse' records and was subsequently included on a compilation featuring various other artists signed to the label. The first set 'VON' (1997) – 'HOPE' – was quickly delivered, pointing the road to success for these experimental debutants. At their peak, keyboard and piano player SVEINSSON was added, who arguably became a vehicle for the group's stark, uplifting and eerie sound. From 'VON BRIGOI' (translated: 'HOPE ALTERATION'), 'LEIT AF LIFI' was released as a single in summer 1998. The band had underestimated their widespread acclaim when the single rocketed to the Icelandic No.1 and stayed a further 8 weeks at the top spot! But with the good came the bad: the departure of lifelong friend and original drummer AGUST. This major setback almost put the band's future into jeopardy when they returned to the studio and came to near collapse during the recording sessions of 'AGAETIS BYRJUN' (1999) – AN ALL RIGHT START'. DYRASON was added to the line-up following a spectacular radio broadcasted show in the Icelandic Opera House. At the same time, SIGUR ROS had struck a deal with London based 'Fat Cat', who issued the 'SVEFN-G-ENGLAR' EP in 1999. In Iceland 'AGAETIS BYRJUN' was doing the same thing to crowds as RADIOHEAD's 'OK Computer' did when it was released on these shores. Which, in all circumstances, is not hard to see why, since SR had (practically) the same ideals as RADIOHEAD did. Cresendos of earth quaking guitars (that didn't really sound like guitars at all), soft piano and BIRGISSON's uniquely high falsetto vocals that reminisced of the COCTEAU TWINS' 'Baby talk'. Not surprising then that multi-instrumentalists GODSPEED YOU BLACK EMPEROR! invited the 'ROS to join them on tour. The result: The greatest show on earth, quite possibly! After selling loads of albums in their native Iceland, including a soundtrack collaboration, 'ANGELS OF THE UNIVERSE' with composer HILMAR ORN HILMARSSON in 2000, and regretfully donating 'SVEFN-G-ENGLAR' to the 'Vanilla Sky' OST, SIGUR ROS engrossed themselves in the mimbars of northern Iceland and recorded the wistful '()' in 2002. Yes, that's right – '()'. Just as The Beatles' eponymous album was christened 'The White Album' by fans, SIGUR ROS' effort became known as 'The Untitled Album', as no information was provided in the album sleeve and all tracks were, well, untitled. If it all sounded a bit pretentious, that's because it was, with BIRGISSON bordering on the line of childishness and pure musical poetry; '()' was an album that could not be ignored. From its grandiose opening, through to the set's middle section and coda, this was really music you could eat. Some of it sounded like GODSPEED, although slowed down to 25rpm, and BIRGISSON's promise of singing in English was missing. However, musically the LP was an elegant and mysterious journey heavily featuring the quartet's scrawled signature of falsetto vocals, eerie organ drones, sparse arrangements, plus a newly added string section to boot. 'TAKK' (2004) went even further critically and commercially ('E.M.I.' UK and 'Geffen' US just might've been responsible), highlights on the transatlantic Top 30 entry being 'SEAGLOPUR' and hit single, 'HOPPIPOLLA'.

Album rating: VON (*6) / VON BRIGOI remixes (*5) / AGAETIS BYRJUN (*8) / ANGELS OF THE UNIVERSE soundtrack w/ Hilmar Orn Hilmarsson (*7) / () (*7) / TAKK . . . (*8)

JON POR BIRGISSON – vocals, guitar / **GEORG HOLM** – bass / **AGUST** – drums

Smekkleysa not iss.

1997. (cd) *(SM 67CD)* **VON (HOPE)** [–] Iceland [–]
– Sigur Ros / Dogun / Hun joro . . . / Leit ao lifi / Myrkur / 18 sekundur fyrir solaruppras / Hafsol / Verold ny og oo / Von / Mistur / Syndir Guos (opinberun frelsarans) / Rukrym. *(UK-iss.Sep04; same)*

— added **KJARTAN SVEINSSON** – keyboards

1998. (cd) *(SM 67CDR)* **VON BRIGOI (RECYCLE BIN)** (remixes/recycled) [–] Iceland [–]
– Syndir Guos (by BIOGEN) / Syndir Guos (by MUM) / Leit af lifi (by PLASTMIC) / Myrkur (by ILA) / Myrkur (by DIRTY-BIX) / 180 sekundur fyrir solaruppras (by CURVER) / Hun Joro (by HASSEBRAEOUR) / Von (by GUS GUS) / Leit af lifi (by SIGUR ROS). *(UK-iss.Nov04; same)*

— **ORRI PALL DYRASON** – drums; repl. AGUST

Fat Cat PIAS

Oct 99. (12"ep) *(12FAT 036)* **SVEFN-G-ENGLAR EP** [ ] [–]
– Svefn-g-englar / Vioar vel til loftarasa / Verold ny og oo.
(cd-ep) *(CDFAT 036)* – (first two tracks) / Nyjalagio (live) / Syndir Guos (live). *(re-iss. Feb00 & Apr01; same)*

Mar 00. (12"ep/cd-ep) *(12/CD FAT 039)* **NY BATTERI** [ ] [–]
– Rafmagnio buio / Ny battery / Bium bium bambalo / Danarfregnir og Jaroafarir.

Aug 00. (cd/lp) *(FAT CD/LP 11)* *<PIAS A1-2>* **AGAETIS BYRJUN** [52] [ ]
– Intro / Svefn-g-englar / Staralfur / Flugufrelsarinn / Ny batteri / Hjartao hamast (bamm bamm bamm) / Vioar vel til lofttarasa / Olsen Olsen / Agaetis byrjun / Avalon. *(issued 1999 in Iceland; SM 79CD)*

Krunk not iss.

Jan 01. (cd; by HILMAR ORN HILMARSSON & SIGUR ROS) *(CDKRU 001)* **ANGELS OF THE UNIVERSE** (soundtrack) [–] Icelan [–]
– Aoflung (Approach) – Draumer (Dream) / Minning (Memory) / Svarti hundurrin og Skoksa leikritio (The black dog and the Scottish play) / Niourlaeging (Degradation) / Y firum (Over the bend) / Litbrigol (Colours) / Stigio niour til heljar (Journey to the underworld) / Snoo (Shave) / Fero (On the road) / Onnur minning (Another memory) / Bakslag (Relapse) / Mok (Coma) / Schiller I kina (Schiller in China) / Mattleysi (Helpless) / Kveoja (Te morituri) / Bium bium bambalo / Danafregnir og jaroafarir (Death announcements and funerals). *(UK-iss.Sep01 on 'Fat Cat'; FATOSTCD 01)*

Fat Cat M.C.A.

Oct 02. (cd/lp) *(FAT CD/LP 22)* *<AA88 113091-2>* **()** [49] [51]
– () (part I) – aka 'Vaka' / () (part II) – aka 'Fyrsta' / () (part III) – aka 'Samskeyti' / () (part IV) – aka 'Njosnavelin' / () (part V) – aka 'Alafoss' / () (part VI) aka 'E-bow' / () (part VII) – aka 'Dauoalagio' / () (part VIII) – aka 'Popplagio'.

May 03. (10"/3"cd-s) *(10/CD FAT 02)* *<27111>* **()** (aka 'VAKA') [72] [ ]

E.M.I. Geffen

Mar 04. (12"/cd-s) *(549691-6/-2)* *<B000 2157-11/2158-22>* **BA BA / TI KI / DI DO** [ ] [ ]

Sep 05. (cd) *(337252-2)* *<534502>* **TAKK . . .** [16] [27]
– Takk . . . Glosoli / Hoppipolla / Meo blodnasir / Se lest / Saeglopur / Milano / Gong / Andvari / Svo hljott / Heysatan. *(t-lp iss.Dec05; 337252-1)*

Nov 05. (12"/cd-s) *(12EM/CDEM 673)* **HOPPIPOLLA. / MEO BLODNASIR / HAFSOL** [35] [–]

Apr 06. (12"/cd-s; re-) *(as prev)* **HOPPIPOLLA** [24] [–]

☐ Gene SIMMONS (see under ⇒ KISS)

☐ Paul SIMON (see under ⇒ SIMON AND GARFUNKEL)

SIMON AND GARFUNKEL

Formed: New York, USA . . . 1957 as TOM & JERRY by ART GARFUNKEL (b. ARTHUR GARFUNKEL, 5 Nov'41, Queens, New York) and PAUL SIMON (b.13 Oct'41, Newark, New Jersey). Though the pair scored their first hit in 1957 with the lightweight rock'n'roll of 'HEY SCHOOLGIRL', it would be almost a decade later before they met with any real success. In the meantime, SIMON released a series of obscure singles under various pseudonyms including TRUE TAYLOR (!) and JERRY LANDIS, wisely opting for a plain and simple PAUL SIMON as his songs began to take on a more folky hue. GARFUNKEL, meanwhile, had gone back to college, although by 1964 the duo had reunited, subsequently signing with 'C.B.S.' and recording a tentative debut album, 'WEDNESDAY MORNING 3 A.M.' The record's dismal sales figures prompted SIMON to return to Europe, where he'd been living the previous year. He duly recorded an eponymous solo album in London, the set featuring many SIMON compositions (including the evocative 'HOMEWARD BOUND', the railway station weighing so heavily on SIMON's homesick heart actually being Widnes in England) which he'd later re-record with GARFUNKEL and which would become mainstays of the S&G repertoire. Back in New York, producer Tom Wilson had taken it upon himself to revamp the acoustic 'SOUND OF SILENCE' (from 'WEDNESDAY . . .') in an electric folk-rock style, de rigeur in 1965. The result was stunning, as powerful and revelatory as the BYRDS' re-working of 'Mr. Tambourine Man', the track storming to the top

SIMON AND GARFUNKEL

of the US charts (The BACHELORS subsequently took the track to No.3 in Britain). SIMON returned from Blighty poste-haste, hooking up with GARFUNKEL once again for what would become the most commercially successful period of his career. 'SOUND OF SILENCE' the album was hurriedly released to consolidate the duo's new found fame, a set largely comprising folk-rock reworkings of SIMON's back catalogue and spawning two further US Top 5 hits in the shape of bedsit classic, 'I AM A ROCK' and the aforementioned 'HOMEWARD BOUND', a worldwide smash. 'PARSLEY, SAGE, ROSEMARY & THYME' (1966) polished up the clean-cut harmonies and witnessed SIMON's songwriting develop apace; 'SCARBOROUGH FAIR / CANTICLE' was an inventive attempt to splice two traditional songs, while '7 O'CLOCK NEWS / SILENT NIGHT' fairly effectively overlaid the traditional Christmas carol with bad tidings in the form of a grim newscast. 'FOR EMILY, WHEREVER I MAY FIND HER', meanwhile, arguably ranks as one of SIMON's most emotive and personal performances. The following summer saw SIMON play a major hand in organising the Monterey Pop Festival, SIMON & GARFUNKEL subsequently headlining the first day of the event. The summer of '68, meanwhile, finally saw S&G break big-time in Britain, both with the evergreen pop fizz of 'MRS. ROBINSON' (written as part of the soundtrack which S&G penned for 'The Graduate', a cult flick turned blockbuster starring Dustin Hoffman and Anne Bancroft) and their biggest album to date, 'BOOKENDS'. A transatlantic No.1, the record is still regarded by many as representing the peak of S&G's career, an even more ambitious set then its predecessor, encompassing everything from the autumnal melancholy of 'HAZY SHADE OF WINTER' to the BEATLES-esque 'OLD FRIENDS'. Even greater success was to come though, the duo making rock/pop history in 1970 when 'BRIDGE OVER TROUBLED WATER' simultaneously made the UK and US Top spot in both its single and album format, the latter staying in the UK chart for an incredible 300 weeks. Its title track was the album's main selling point, an epic, exquisitely arranged ballad sung by GARFUNKEL, the song becoming the group's signature tune, even more so than say, 'MRS ROBINSON'. Other highlights included the celebratory 'CECILIA', 'THE BOXER' and the adapted Peruvian folk tune, 'EL CONDOR PASA'. GARFUNKEL was dissatisfied, however, both with the direction in which SIMON was steering the group and the fact that the latter dominated the songwriting front. At the peak of their fame, then, S&G disbanded, creating a legend in their wake. While GARFUNKEL concentrated on acting, SIMON continued with the solo career he'd begun in 1965, scoring almost immediately with the buoyant pop-reggae of 'MOTHER AND CHILD REUNION', a transatlantic Top 5 hit single in early 1972. The track was released the same month as the album, his second effort to bear an eponymous title and a UK No.1 to boot. Widely acclaimed, the record proved conclusively that SIMON could fashion his own distinct musical identity, experimenting with an array of musical styles on the likes of 'ME AND JULIO DOWN BY THE SCHOOLYARD' and 'DUNCAN'. 'THERE GOES RHYMIN' SIMON' (1973) and the Grammy Award-winning 'STILL CRAZY AFTER ALL THESE YEARS' (1975) were even more successful, if more overtly commercial, the latter featuring a rare duet with GARFUNKEL, 'MY LITTLE TOWN'. SIMON suffered a critical roasting, however, with 'ONE-TRICK PONY' (1980), the ambitious soundtrack to his flop film of the same name. Reuniting briefly with GARFUNKEL in 1981, the pair gave a hugely popular free concert in New York's Central Park (released as a double album the following year), although a mooted studio project was abandoned. Left to his own devices, SIMON came up 'HEARTS AND BONES' (1983), a patchy effort which nevertheless included some of SIMON's most affecting material. With 'GRACELAND' (1986), the singer/songwriter changed tack again, looking to African rhythms and musicians for inspiration. The result was a highly infectious, exotic fusion of SIMON's innate feel for pop melody and traditional African sounds, recorded in collaboration with the likes of LADYSMITH BLACK MAMBAZO. Despite the initial fuss over SIMON's supposed breach of the anti-apartheid cultural boycott (through recording and touring the album in South Africa), the groundbreaking charm of tracks like 'THE BOY IN THE BUBBLE', 'DIAMONDS ON THE SOLES OF HER SHOES' and 'YOU CAN CALL ME AL' was eventually recognised when the album won a Grammy. The record also resurrected SIMON's UK career, making No.1, as did the follow-up, 'THE RHYTHM OF THE SAINTS' (1990), a similar project, constructed around compelling Brazilian percussion. More recently, SIMON has been working on 'SONGS FROM THE CAPEMAN', a concept project based on the life of Salvador Agron, a Puerto Rican criminal turned writer. Working with Nobel-prize winning poet/playwright, Derek Walcott, the album was one of SIMON's most ambitious recordings to date. Unfortunately for SIMON, the effort he put into 'SONGS FROM THE CAPEMAN' went largely unrewarded and come the new millennium he went back to basics with his first studio set in ten years, 'YOU'RE THE ONE' (2000). Together with veteran but youthful sounding musical accomplices BAKITHI KUMALO, VINCENT NGUINI and STEVE GADD, SIMON crafted a cerebral yet spontaneous album which inherited the rich rhythmic grace of his past work while simultaneously showcasing his insight, intelligence and lightness of touch as a singer/songwriter. On the other end of the musical scale, ART GARFUNKEL balanced his acting work with a recording career, releasing a string of albums throughout the 70's and 80's, 'ANGEL CLARE' (1973) and 'BREAKAWAY' (1975) being the most successful, the latter featuring a fine cover of Stevie Wonder's 'I BELIEVE (WHEN I FALL IN LOVE IT WILL BE FOREVER)'. The angelic voiced singer was at his best performing other people's material, his most famous hit coming in early '79 with the poignant 'BRIGHT EYES' (penned by none other than Wombling free MIKE BATT), the theme tune from animated film, 'Watership Down'. Chart success eluded GARFUNKEL in the 80's although he continued to record for 'Columbia', releasing an album, 'UP UNTIL NOW' (1993), duetting on one track with JAMES TAYLOR. Following the live 'ACROSS AMERICA' (1996), GARFUNKEL hooked up with Nashville singer/songwriter BUDDY MONDLOCK for 2002's 'EVERYTHING WAITS TO BE NOTICED'. If it was a nifty title, then the writing (a fair part of it by ART himself) and performing within was none too shabby either, SIMON's former foil showcasing some of his most engaging work for many a year. Sparked by a performance of 'THE SOUND OF SILENCE' at the annual Grammy Awards in early 2003, a fully fledged SIMON & GARFUNKEL tour got underway towards the end of the year. The results of the unexpected reunion were released as 'OLD FRIENDS: LIVE ON STAGE' (2004), presaging a belated comeback album from PAUL SIMON. 'SURPRISE' (2006) was aptly titled, produced and at least partly co-written by BRIAN ENO of all people. As many critics pointed out, this ostensibly odd couple actually had a shared passion in ethnic roots and global rhythms dating back decades. The presence of jazzbo's like STEVE GADD, HERBIE HANCOCK and BILL FRISELL might have suggested a sleepy session fest akin to 'ONE-TRICK PONY', yet while 'SURPRISE' shared some of that soundtrack's lack of hooks, it replaced them with the kind of quizzical monologues and shifting sonics that saw SIMON hailed for dragging his art into the future as many of his peers were casting fond backward glances.

• **Covered:** THE TIMES THEY ARE A-CHANGIN' (Bob Dylan) / BYE BYE LOVE (Everly Brothers). PAUL SIMON covered GO TELL IT TO THE MOUNTAIN (trad). GARFUNKEL covered loads including ALL I KNOW (Jimmy Webb) / SECOND AVENUE (Tim Moore) / BREAKAWAY

(Gallagher & Lyle) / I ONLY HAVE EYES FOR YOU (Flamingos) / WONDERFUL WORLD (Sam Cooke) / SINCE I DON'T HAVE YOU (Skyliners) / SO MUCH IN LOVE (Tymes) / MISS YOU NIGHTS (Cliff Richard) / WHEN A MAN LOVES A WOMAN (Percy Sledge) / RAG DOLL (Four Seasons) / etc. • **ART's filmography:** CATCH 22 (1970 with Alan Arkin) / CARNAL KNOWLEDGE (1971 w/ Ann-Margret, Candice Bergen & Jack Nicholson) / BAD TIMING (1979 w/ Teresa Russell) / ILLUSIONS (1980) / GOOD TO GO (1986) / MOTHER GOOSE ROCK'N'RHYME (1989 TV Disney musical with PAUL). Note PAUL cameod in the 1977 Woody Allen film 'Annie Hall'. • **Trivia:** PAUL's video for the 1986 single, 'YOU CAN CALL ME AL', featured comic actor Chevy Chase.

Album rating: WEDNESDAY MORNING 3 A.M. (*6) / SOUNDS OF SILENCE (*7) / PARSLEY, SAGE, ROSEMARY & THYME (*7) / THE GRADUATE soundtrack (*6) / BOOKENDS (*8) / BRIDGE OVER TROUBLED WATER (*9) / SIMON AND GARFUNKEL'S GREATEST HITS compilation (*10) / THE CONCERT IN CENTRAL PARK (*7) / THE DEFINITIVE SIMON AND GARFUNKEL compilation (*10) / THE ESSENTIAL . . . compilation (*8) / OLD FRIENDS – LIVE ON STAGE (*5) / Paul Simon:- THE PAUL SIMON SONGBOOK (*6) / PAUL SIMON (*8) / THERE GOES RHYMIN' SIMON (*7) / LIVE RHYMIN' (*5) / STILL CRAZY AFTER ALL THESE YEARS (*8) / GREATEST HITS, ETC compilation (*7) / ONE-TRICK PONY soundtrack (*5) / HEARTS AND BONES (*4) / GRACELAND (*8) / NEGOTIATIONS AND LOVE SONGS 1971-1986 compilation (*8) / THE RHYTHM OF THE SAINTS (*7) / PAUL SIMON'S CONCERT IN THE PARK (*7) / 1964-1993 boxed set (*6) / SONGS FROM THE CAPEMAN Broadway musical (*4) / YOU'RE THE ONE (*5) / SURPRISE (*7) / Art Garfunkel: ANGEL CLARE (*7) / BREAKAWAY (*6) / WATERMARK (*5) / FATE FOR BREAKFAST (*4) / SCISSORS CUT (*4) / LEFTY (*4) / THE ART GARFUNKEL ALBUM compilation (*6) / UP 'TIL NOW (*4) / THE VERY BEST OF – ACROSS AMERICA (*4) / SONGS FROM A PARENT TO A CHILD (*5)

TOM AND JERRY

TOM = ART GARFUNKEL / JERRY = PAUL SIMON

Gala / Big

Dec 57. (7") *<613>* **HEY! SCHOOLGIRL. / DANCIN' WILD** – 49
<US re-iss. 1960 on 'King'; 5167>

1958. (7") *<616>* **OUR SONG. / TWO TEENAGERS** –

1958. (7") *<618>* **DON'T SAY GOODBYE. / THAT'S MY STORY** –
<US re-iss. 1959 on 'Hunt' & flipped over; 319>

1959. (7") *<621>* **BABY TALK. / TWO TEENAGERS** –
<US re-iss. 1971 on 'Bell' w/ diff.B-side by RONNIE LAWRENCE; 120>

1959. (7") *(GSP 806) BABY TALK. / (b-side by PAUL SHELDON)* –

Pye Int. / Ember

May 63. (7") *(7N 25202) <1094>* **I'M LONESOME. / LOOKING AT YOU** 1962

not iss. / ABC Para..

1962. (7") *<10363>* **SURRENDER, PLEASE SURRENDER. / FIGHTING MAD** –

1966. (7") *<10788>* **THAT'S MY STORY. / TIA-JUANA BLUES** –

– PAUL SIMON under pseudonyms –

not iss. / Big

1958. (7"; as TRUE TAYLOR) *<614>* **TRUE OR FALSE. / TEENAGE FOOL** –

not iss. / M.G.M.

1959. (7"; as JERRY LANDIS) *<12822>* **ANNA BELLE. / LONELINESS** –

not iss. / Warwick

1959. (7"; as JERRY LANDIS) *<522>* **SWANEE. / TOOT, TOOT TOOTSIE GOODBYE** –

1960. (7"; as JERRY LANDIS) *<552>* **SHY. / JUST A BOY** –

1960. (7"; as JERRY LANDIS) *<588>* **ID LIKE TO BE THE LIPSTICK ON YOUR COLLAR. / JUST A BOY** –

1961. (7"; as JERRY LANDIS) *<619>* **PLAY ME A SAD SONG. / IT MEANS A LOT TO THEM** –

not iss. / Canadian A

1961. (7"; as JERRY LANDIS) *<130>* **I'M LONELY. / I WISH I WEREN'T IN LOVE** –

not iss. / Amy

Dec 62. (7"; as JERRY LANDIS) *<875>* **THE LONE TEEN RANGER. / LISA** – 97
<re-iss. 1963 on 'Jason Scott'; 2>

Oriole / Tribute

May 64. (7"; as JERRY LANDIS; in US- by PAUL KANE) *(CB 1930 <128>* **CARLOS DOMINGUEZ. / HE WAS MY BROTHER**

not iss. / Madison

Dec 61. (7"; as TICO & THE TRIUMPHS) *<169>* **MOTORCYCLE. / I DON'T BELIEVE THEM** –
<re-iss. Dec61 on 'Amy'; 835> <hit US No.99>

not iss. / Amy

1962. (7"; as TICO & THE TRIUMPHS) *<845>* **EXPRESS TRAIN. / WILDFLOWER** –

1962. (7"; as TICO & THE TRIUMPHS) *<860>* **CRY, LITTLE BOY, CRY. / GET UP & DO THE WONDER** –

Feb 63. (7"; as TICO) *<876>* **CARDS OF LOVE. / NOISE** –

ARTIE GARR

pseudonym of ART GARFUNKEL

not iss. / Warwick

1959. (7") *<515>* **DREAM ALONE. / BEAT LOVE** –

not iss. / Octavia

1960. (7") *<8002>* **PRIVATE WORLD. / FORGIVE ME** –

PAUL SIMON

C.B.S. / Columbia

May 65. (lp) *<62579>* **THE PAUL SIMON SONGBOOK**
– I am a rock / Leaves that are green / A church is burning / April come she will / The sound of silence / Patterns / A most peculiar man / He was my brother / Kathy's song / The side of a hill / A simple desultory Philippic / Flowers never bend with the rainfall. *(cd-iss. Jan88)*

Jul 65. (7") *(201797)* **I AM A ROCK. / LEAVES THAT ARE GREEN**

SIMON AND GARFUNKEL

both vocals, acoustic guitar

C.B.S. / Columbia

Oct 64. (lp) *<9049>* **WEDNESDAY MORNING 3 A.M.** –
– You can tell the world / Last night I had the strangest dream / Bleecker Street / Sparrow / Benedictus / The sound of silence / He was my brother / Peggy-O / Go tell it to the mountain / The sun is burning / The times they are a-changin' / Wednesday morning 3 a.m. *(US re-dist.Jan66, hit No.30) (UK-iss.Nov68; 63370)* – hit No.24. *(re-iss. Nov85 lp/c; CBS/40 32575) (cd-iss. Dec85; CD 63370)*

Jul 65. (7"ep) *(EP 6053)* **SIMON AND GARFUNKEL**
– Bleecker Street / Sparrow / Wednesday morning 3 a.m. / The sound of silence.

Dec 65. (7") *(201977) <43396>* **THE SOUND OF SILENCE. / WE'VE GOT A GROOVY THING GOIN'** Nov65 1

Mar 66. (lp) *(BPG 62690) <9269>* **SOUND OF SILENCE** 13 Feb66 21
– The sound of silence / Leaves that are green / Blessed / Kathy's song / Somewhere they can't find me / Anji / Homeward bound / Richard Cory / A most peculiar man / April come she will / We've got a groovy thing goin' / I am a rock. *(re-iss. Mar81 lp/c; CBS/40 32020) (cd-iss. Dec85; CD 62690)*

Mar 66. (7") *(202045) <43511>* **HOMEWARD BOUND. / LEAVES THAT ARE GREEN** 9 Feb66 5

Jun 66. (7") *(202303) <43617>* **I AM A ROCK. / FLOWERS NEVER BEND WITH THE RAINFALL** 17 May66 3
(7"ep+=) *(EP 6074)* – The sound of silence / Blessed.

Sep 66. (7") *(202285) <43728>* **THE DANGLING CONVERSATION. / THE BIG BRIGHT GREEN PLEASURE MACHINE** Aug66 25

Oct 66. (lp) *(BPG 62860) <9363>* **PARSLEY, SAGE, ROSEMARY & THYME** 4
– Dangling conversation / Scarborough fair – Canticle / Patterns / For Emily, whenever I may find her / The big bright green pleasure machine / A poem on the underground all / Cloudy / A simple desultory Philippic (or how I was Robert McNamara'd into submission) / The 59th Street Bridge song (feelin' groovy) / Flowers never bend with the rainfall / 7 o'clock news – Silent night / Parsley, sage, Rosemary and thyme. *(UK re-dist.Aug68, hit No.13) (re-iss. Mar81 lp/c; CBS/40 32031) (cd-iss. Jul87; CD 62825) (cd re-iss. Apr89; CD 32031)*

Nov 66. (7") *(202378) <43873>* **A HAZY SHADE OF WINTER. / FOR EMILY, WHENEVER I MAY FIND HER** 13

Mar 67. (7") *(202608)* *<44046>* **AT THE ZOO. / THE 59th STREET BRIDGE SONG (FEELIN' GROOVY)** [ ] [16]

Jun 67. (7"ep) *(EP 6360)* **FEELIN' GROOVY** [ ] [–]
– The 59th Street bridge song (feelin' groovy) / The big bright green pleasure machine / A hazy shade of winter / Homeward bound.

Aug 67. (7") *(2911)* *<44232>* **FAKIN' IT. / YOU DON'T KNOW WHERE YOUR INTEREST LIES** [ ] Jul67 [23]

Mar 68. (7") *(3317)* *<44465>* **SCARBOROUGH FAIR; CANTICLE. / APRIL COME SHE WILL** [ ] Feb68 [11]

Jul 68. (7") *(3443)* *<44511>* **MRS. ROBINSON. / OLD FRIENDS; BOOKENDS** [4] Apr68 [1]

Jul 68. (lp) *(BPG 63101)* *<9529>* **BOOKENDS** [1] May 68 [1]
– Bookends theme / Save the life of my child / America / Overs / (voices of old people) – Old friends / Bookends / Fakin' it / Punky's dilemma / Mrs. Robinson / A hazy shade of winter / At the zoo. *(re-iss. Nov82 lp/c; CBS/40 32073) (cd-iss. Dec85; CD 63101)*

Oct 68. (lp) *(BPG 70042)<3180>* **THE GRADUATE (Film Soundtrack; with tracks by DAVE GRUISIN *)** [3] Mar68 [1]
– The sound of silence / The singleman party foxtrot * / On the strip * / Sunporch cha-cha-cha * / Mrs.Robinson / A great effect * / Scarborough fair – Canticle / April come she will / Whew * / The folks * / The big bright green pleasure machine. *(re-iss. Feb84 lp/c; CBS/40 32359) (cd-iss. Dec85; CD 70042) (cd re-iss. Apr89; CD 32359) (cd-iss. Apr91 on 'Sequel';) (re-iss. Feb94 on 'Columbia' cd/c; CD/40 32359)*

Dec 68. (7"ep) *(EP 6400)* **MRS. ROBINSON** [9] [–]
– Mrs.Robinson / April come she will / Scarborough fair – Canticle / The sound of silence.

Apr 69. (7") *(4162)* *<44785>* **THE BOXER. / BABY DRIVER** [6] [7]

Feb 70. (7") *(4790)* *<45079>* **BRIDGE OVER TROUBLED WATER. / KEEP THE CUSTOMER SATISFIED** [1] [1]
(re-iss. Feb78 + Jul84; CBS 4596)

Feb 70. (lp) *(63699)* *<9914>* **BRIDGE OVER TROUBLED WATER** [1] [1]
– Bridge over troubled water / El Condor Pasa / Cecilia / Keep the customer satisfied / So long, Frank Lloyd Wright / The boxer / Baby driver / The only living boy in New York / Why don't you write me / Bye bye love / Song for the asking. *(re-iss. on quad 1974; CQ 30995) (cd-iss. Dec82; CD 63699) (re-iss. Sep93 cd/c; 462488-2/-4) (cd re-iss. Dec95 on 'Columbia'; 480418-2)*

Apr 70. (7") *(4916)* *<45133>* **CECILIA. / THE ONLY LIVING BOY IN NEW YORK** [ ] [4]

Sep 70. (7") *<45237>* **EL CONDOR PASA. / WHY DON'T YOU WRITE ME** [–] [18]

— both went solo, after ART wanted to concentrate on an acting career

— SIMON AND GARFUNKEL re-united for one-off concert 20 Dec'81

Geffen Warners

Mar 82. (d-lp/d-c) *(GEF/40 96008)* *<3654>* **THE CONCERT IN CENTRAL PARK (live)** [6] [6]
– Mrs. Robinson / Homeward bound / America / Scarborough fair / Me and Julio down by the schoolyard / Wake up little Susie / April come she will / Slip slidin' away / Still crazy after all these years / American tune / 50 ways to leave your lover / Late in the evening / Bridge over troubled water / A heart in New York / The 59th Street bridge song (feelin' groovy) / The sound of silence / Kodachrome / Old friends: bookends / Maybellene / The boxer. *(re-iss. May88 lp/c/cd; GEF/40/CD 96008)*

Mar 82. (7") *(GEF 2287)* **WAKE UP LITTLE SUSIE (live). / THE BOXER (live)** [ ] [–]

Mar 82. (7") *<50053>* **WAKE UP LITTLE SUSIE (live). / ME AND JULIO DOWN BY THE SCHOOLYARD (live)** [–] [27]

— the pair reunited once again for one-off tour

Columbia Warners

Nov 04. (d-cd) *(519173-2)* *<48967-2>* **OLD FRIENDS – LIVE ON STAGE** (live) [61] [ ]
– Old friends – Bookends / A hazy shade of winter / I am a rock / America / At the zoo / Baby driver / Kathy's song / Tom and Jerry story / Hey, schoolgirl / The Everly Brothers intro / Bye bye love (w/ EVERLY BROTHERS) / Scarborough fair / Homeward bound / The sound of silence // Mrs. Robinson / Slip slidin' away / El condor pasa / The only living boy in New York / American tune / My little town / Bridge over troubled water / Cecilia / The boxer / Leaves that are green. *(UK bonus+=)* – Citizen of the planet. *(ltd d-cd w/dvd+=; 519173-3)* – (DVD tracks).

– (selective) compilations, etc. –

Note; Released on 'CBS/ Columbia' unless otherwise mentioned

Jul 72. (lp/c) *(CBS/40 69003)* *<31350>* **SIMON AND GARFUNKEL'S GREATEST HITS** [2] Jun72 [5]
– Mrs. Robinson / For Emily, wherever I may find her / The boxer / Feelin' groovy / The sound of silence / I am a rock / Scarborough fair (Canticle) / Homeward bound / Bridge over troubled water / America / Kathy's song / If I could / Bookends / Cecilia. *(cd-iss. Mar87; CD 69003)*

Sep 72. (7") *(8336)* *<45663>* **AMERICA. / FOR EMILY, WHENEVER I MAY FIND HER** [25] [97] [53]

Nov 81. (lp/c) *(CBS/40 24005)* **THE SIMON AND GARFUNKEL COLLECTION** [4] [–]
– I am a rock / Homeward bound / America / 59th Street Bridge song / Wednesday morning 3 a.m. / El condor pasa / At the Zoo / Scarborough fair (Canticle) / The boxer / The sound of silence / Mrs.Robinson / Keep the customer satisfied / Song for the asking / Hazy shade of winter / Cecilia / Old friends / Bookends / Bridge over troubled water. *(cd-iss. Apr85 + 1988; CD 24005)*

1988. (cd) *(CDSG 241)* **BRIDGE OVER TROUBLED WATER / PARSLEY, SAGE, ROSEMARY & THYME** [ ] [ ]

Nov 91. (7"/c-s/cd-s) *(657 653-7/-4/-2)* **A HAZY SHADE OF WINTER. / SILENT NIGHT – SEVEN O'CLOCK NEWS (Medley)** [30] [ ]

Nov 91. (lp/c/cd) *Sony-Columbia; (MOOD/+C/D 21)* **THE DEFINITIVE SIMON & GARFUNKEL** [8] [ ]
– Wednesday morning 3 a.m. / The sound of silence / Homeward bound / Cathy's song / I am a rock / For Emily wherever I may find her / Scarborough fair (canticle) / The 59th Street bridge song (feelin' groovy) / Seven o'clock news – Silent night / A hazy shade of winter / El Condor pasa (If I could) / Mrs.Robinson / America / At the zoo / Old friends / Bookends theme / Cecilia / The boxer / Bridge over troubled water / Song for the asking. *(hit UK No.12 in Aug'97)*

Feb 92. (7") *Sony-Columbia; (657 806-7)* **THE BOXER. / CECILIA** [75] [–]
(cd-ep+=/cd-ep+=) *(657 806-2/-5)* – The only living boy in New York.

Aug 92. (2xcd-box) *(465212-2)* **PARSLEY, SAGE, ROSEMARY & THYME / BOOKENDS** [ ] [ ]

Oct 96. (3xcd-box) *(485324-2)* **BRIDGE OVER TROUBLED WATER / SOUNDS OF SILENCE / THE GRADUATE** [ ] [–]

Jan 00. (d-cd/d-c) *Sony TV; (SONYTV 81 CD/MC)* **TALES FROM NEW YORK – THE VERY BEST OF SIMON & GARFUNKEL** [9] [–]

Nov 03. (d-cd) *Sony TV; (513470-2) / Columbia; <90716>* **THE ESSENTIAL SIMON AND GARFUNKEL** <US track listing> [25] Oct03 [27]
– Wednesday morning, 3 a.m. (live) / Bleecker Street / The sound of silence / Leaves that are green (live) / A most peculiar man (live) / I am a rock / Richard Cory / Kathy's song / Scarborough fair – Canticle / Homeward bound / Sparrow (live) / The 59th Street Bridge song (feelin' groovy) / The dangling conversation / A poem on the underground wall (live) / A hazy shade of winter / At the zoo / Mrs. Robinson / Fakin' it / Old friends / Bookends theme / America / Overs (live) / El condor pasa (If I could) / Bridge over troubled water / Cecilia / Keep the customer satisfied / So long, Frank Lloyd Wright / The boxer / Baby driver / The only living boy in New York / Song for the asking / For Emily, whenever I may find her / My little town.

PAUL SIMON

(solo with session people)

C.B.S. Columbia

Feb 72. (7") *(7793)* *<45547>* **MOTHER AND CHILD REUNION. / PARANOIA BLUES** [5] [4]

Feb 72. (lp/c) *(CBS/40 69007)* *<30750>* **PAUL SIMON** [1] [4]
– Mother and child reunion / Duncan / Everything put together falls apart / Run that body down / Armistice day / Me and Julio down by the schoolyard / Peace like a river / Papa hobo / Hobo's blues / Paranoia blues / Congratulations. *(re-iss. 1974 on quad; CQ 30750) (re-iss. Dec87 on 'WEA' lp/c/cd; 925588-1/-4/-2)*

Apr 72. (7") *(7264)* *<45585>* **ME AND JULIO DOWN BY THE SCHOOLYARD. / CONGRATULATIONS** [15] [22]

Jul 72. (7") *<45638>* **DUNCAN. / RUN THAT BODY DOWN** [–] [52]

May 73. (lp/c) *(CBS/40 69035)* *<32280>* **THERE GOES RHYMIN' SIMON** [4] [2]
– Kodachrome / Tenderness / Take me to the Mardi Gras / Something so right / One man's ceiling is another man's floor / American tune / Was a sunny day / Learn how to fall / St. Judy's comet / Loves me like a rock. *(re-iss. 1974 on quad; CQ 32280) (re-iss. Dec87 on 'WEA' lp/c/cd; 925589-1/-4/-2)*

May 73. (7") *<45859>* **KODACHROME. / TENDERNESS** [–] [2]

May 73. (7") *(1578)* **TAKE ME TO THE MARDI GRAS. / KODACHROME** [7] [–]

Sep 73. (7") *(1700)* *<45907>* **LOVES ME LIKE A ROCK. / LEARN HOW TO FALL** [39] Aug73 [2]

Feb 74. (7") *(1979)* *<45900>* **AMERICAN TUNE. / ONE MAN'S CEILING IS ANOTHER MAN'S FLOOR** [ ] Nov73 [35]

— Below in concert with URUBOMBA and The JESE DIXON SINGERS.

Mar 74. (lp/c) *(CBS/40 69059)* *<32855>* **PAUL SIMON IN CONCERT / LIVE RHYMIN' (live)** [ ] [33]
– Jesus is the answer / The boxer / Duncan / El Condor pasa (if I could) / Me and Julio down by the schoolyard / American tune / Homeward bound / America / Mother and child reunion / Loves me like a rock / Bridge over troubled water / The sound of silence. *(re-iss. Dec87 on 'WEA' lp/c/cd; 925590-1/-4/-2)*

May 74. (7") *(2349)* *<46038>* **THE SOUND OF SILENCE (live). / MOTHER AND CHILD REUNION (live)** [ ] [ ]

Nov 74. (7") *(2822)* **SOMETHING SO RIGHT. / TENDERNESS** [ ] [ ]

Aug 75. (7") *<10197>* **GONE AT LAST (w/ PHOEBE SNOW). / TAKE ME TO THE MARDI GRAS** [–] [23]

Oct 75. (7"; PAUL SIMON & PHOEBE SNOW with The JESSE DIXON SINGERS) *(3594)* **GONE AT LAST. / TENDERNESS** [ ] [–]

Oct 75. (lp/c) *(CBS/40 86001)* *<33540>* **STILL CRAZY AFTER ALL THESE YEARS** [6] [1]
– Still crazy after all these years / My little town / I do it all for love / 50 ways to leave your lover / Night game / Gone at last / Some folks lives roll easy / Have a good time / You're kind / Silent eyes. *(re-iss. 1976 on quad; Q 86001) (cd-iss. Dec85; CD 86001) (re-iss. Dec87 on 'WEA' lp/c/cd; 925591-1/-4/-2)*

Oct 75. (7"; SIMON & GARFUNKEL) *<10230>* **MY LITTLE TOWN. / Art Garfunkel: RAG DOLL** [–] [9]

Nov 75. (7"m; SIMON & GARFUNKEL) *(3712)* **MY LITTLE TOWN. / Art Garfunkel: RAG DOLL / YOU'RE KIND** [ ] [–]

Dec 75. (7") *(3887)* *<10270>* **50 WAYS TO LEAVE YOUR LOVER. / SOME FOLKS LIVES ROLL EASY** [23] [1]

Apr 76. (7") *<10332>* **STILL CRAZY AFTER ALL THESE YEARS. / I DO IT FOR YOUR LOVE** [–] [40]

Apr 76. (7") *(4188)* **STILL CRAZY AFTER ALL THESE YEARS. / SILENT EYES** [ ] [–]

Nov 77. (7") *(5770)* *<10630>* **SLIP SLIDIN' AWAY. / SOMETHING SO RIGHT** [36] Oct77 [5]

Nov 77. (lp/c) *(CBS/40 10007)* *<35032>* **GREATEST HITS, ETC.** (part compilation) [6] [18]
– Slip slidin' away / Stranded in a limousine / Still crazy after all these years / Have a good time / Duncan / Me and Julio down by the schoolyard / Something so right / Kodachrome / I do it for your love / 50 ways to leave your lover / American tune / Mother and child reunion / Loves me like a rock / Take me to the Mardi Gras. *(re-iss. Nov86 lp/c; 450166-1/-4) (cd-iss. Mar87; CD 69003)*

— See ART GARFUNKEL discography further on for other single

May 78. (7") *(6290)* *<10711>* **STRANDED IN A LIMOSINE. / HAVE A GOOD TIME** [ ] [ ]

Warners Warners

Aug 80. (lp/c) *(K/K4 56846)* *<3472>* **ONE-TRICK PONY** (soundtrack) [17] [12]
– Late in the evening / That's why God made the movies / One-trick pony / How the heart approaches what it yearns / Oh, Marion / Ace in the hole / Nobody / Jonah / God bless the absentee / Long, long day. *(cd-iss. 1987; K2 56846) <(cd re-iss. Jul04 +=; 8122 78902-2)>* – Soft parachutes / All because of you / Spiral highway / Stranded in a limousine.

Aug 80. (7") *(K 17666)* *<49511>* **LATE IN THE EVENING. / HOW THE HEART APPROACHES WHAT IT YEARNS** [58] [6]

Nov 80. (7") *(K 17715)* *<49601>* **ONE-TRICK PONY. / LONG, LONG DAY** [ ] Oct80 [40]

Jan 81. (7") *(K 17745)* *<49675>* **OH, MARION. / GOD BLESS THE ABSENTEE** [ ] [ ]

— see ART GARFUNKEL discography again for duet A HEART IN NEW YORK single

— early '83, PAUL collaborated with RANDY NEWMAN on US No.51 single THE BLUES

Nov 83. (lp/c/cd) *(923942-1/-4/-2)* *<23942>* **HEARTS AND BONES** [34] [35]
– Allergies / Hearts and bones / When numbers get serious / Think too much (part 1) / Song about the Moon / Think too much (part 2) / Train in the distance / Renee and Georgette Margritte with the dog after the war / Cars are cars / The late great Johnny Ace.

Nov 83. (7") *(W 9453)* *<29453>* **ALLERGIES. / THINK TOO MUCH** [ ] [44]

Feb 84. (7") *<29333>* **SONG ABOUT THE MOON. / THINK TOO MUCH** [–] [ ]

Aug 86. (7")(12") *(W 8667)* *<28667>* **YOU CAN CALL ME AL. / GUMBOOTS** [4] [44]
<re-iss. Mar87 US, hit No.23>

Sep 86. (lp/c)(cd) *(WX 52/+C)(925477-2)* *<25447>* **GRACELAND** [1] [3]
– The boy in the bubble / Graceland / I know what I know / Gumboots / Diamonds on the sole of her shoes / You can call me Al / Under African skies / Homeless / Crazy love Vol.2 / That was your mother / All around the world of the myth of fingerprints.

Nov 86. (7") *(W 8509)* **THE BOY IN THE BUBBLE. / ('A'remix)** [33] [–]
(12"+=) *(W 8509T)* – Hearts and bones.

Dec 86. (7") *<28522>* **GRACELAND. / HEARTS AND BONES** [–] [81]
(re-iss. US 1988)

Feb 87. (7") *<28460>* **THE BOY IN THE BUBBLE. / CRAZY LOVE VOL. 2** [–] [86]

Apr 87. (7"/12") *()* *<28389>* **DIAMONDS ON THE SOLES OF HER SHOES. / ALL AROUND THE WORLD OF THE MYTH OF FINGERPRINTS** [–] [ ]

Apr 87. (7") *(W 8349)* **GRACELAND. / CRAZY LOVE VOL.2** [ ] [–]
(12"+=) *(W 8349T)* – The late great Johny Ace.

Aug 87. (7") *(W 8221)* *<28221>* **UNDER AFRICAN SKIES. / I KNOW WHAT I KNOW** [ ] [ ]
(12"+=) *(W 8221T)* – Homeless. (above w/LINDA RONSTADT)

Oct 90. (7") *(W 9549)* *<19549>* **THE OBVIOUS CHILD. / THE RHYTHM OF THE SAINTS** [15] [92]
(12"+=) *(W 9549T)* – You can call me Al.
(cd-s++=) *(W 9549CD)* – The boy in the bubble.

Oct 90. (cd)(lp/c) *<(9 26098-2)>(WX 340/+C)* **THE RHYTHM OF THE SAINTS** [1] [4]
– The obvious child / Can't run but / The coast / Proof / Further to fly / She moves on / Born at the right time / The cool cool river / Spirit voices / The rhythm of the saints.

Feb 91. (7") *(W 0003)* **PROOF. / THE OBVIOUS CHILD** [ ] [–]
(12"/cd-s) *(W 0003 T/CD)* – ('A'side) / The cool cool river / American tune.

Apr 91. (7") *(W 0026)* **BORN AT THE RIGHT TIME. / FURTHER TO FLY** [ ] [–]
(12"+=) *(W 0026T)* – You can call me Al.
(cd-s++=) *(W 0026CD)* – Me and Julio down by the schoolyard / 50 ways to leave your lover.

Nov 91. (cd)(d-lp/c) *<(9 26737-2)>(WX 448/+C)* **THE CONCERT IN THE PARK – AUGUST 15th 1991 (live)** [60] [–]
– The obvious child / The boy in the bubble / She moves on / Kodachrome / Born at the right time / Train in the distance / Me and Julio down by the schoolyard / I know what I know / Cool cool river / Bridge over troubled water / Proof / Coast / Graceland / You can call me Al / Still crazy after all these years / Loves me like a rock / Diamonds on the sole of her shoes / Hearts and bones / Later in the evening / America / The boxer / Cecelia / Sound of silence.

Nov 97. (cd/c) *<(9362 46814-2/-4)>* **SONGS FROM THE CAPEMAN** (Broadway musical) [ ] [42]
– Adios Hermanos / Born in Puerto Rico / Satin summer nights / Bernadette / The vampires / Quality / Can I forgive him / Sunday afternoon / Killer wants to go to college / Time is an ocean / Virgil / Killer wants to go to college II / Trailways bus. *<(cd re-iss. Jul04 +=; 8122 78906-2)>* – Shoplifting clothes / Born in Puerto Rico (demo) / Can I forgive him.

Oct 00. (cd/c) *<(9362 47844-2/-4)>* **YOU'RE THE ONE** [20] [19]
– That's where I belong / Darling Lorraine / Old / You're the one / The teacher / Look at that / Senorita with a necklace of tears / Pigs, sheep and wolves / Hurricane eye / Quiet.

May 06. (cd-s) *(W 719CD)* **FATHER AND DAUGHTER / ANOTHER GALAXY** [19] [ ]
(above was featured in 2002's 'The Wild Thornberrys Movie')

Jun 06. (cd) *<(9362 49982-2)>* **SURPRISE** [4] May06 [15]
– How can you live in the Northeast? / Everything about it is a love song / Outrageous / Sure don't feel like love / Wartime prayers / Beautiful / I don't believe / Another galaxy / Once upon a time there was an ocean / That's me / Father and daughter.

– (PAUL SIMON) compilations, others, etc. –

on 'Warners' unless mentioned otherwise

Nov 88. (d-lp/c/cd) *(WX 223/+C)(925789-2) <25789>* **NEGOTIATIONS AND LOVE SONGS** [17] [ ]
– Mother and child reunion / Me and Julio down by the schoolyard / Something so right / St.Judy's comet / Loves me like a rock / Have a good time / 50 ways to leave your lover / Still crazy after all these years / Late in the evening / Slip slidin' away / Hearts and bones / Train in the distance / Rene and Georgette Magritte with their dog after the war / Diamonds on the soles on her shoes / You can call me Al / Kodachrome. *(d-lp+=)* – Graceland.

Nov 88. (7") *(W 7655)* **MOTHER AND CHILD REUNION. / TRAIN IN THE DISTANCE** [ ] [ ]
(12"+=/cd-s+=) *(W 7655 T/CD)* – The boy in the bubble.

Feb 89. (c) *Venus; (VENUMC 5)* **THE MAGIC OF PAUL SIMON** [ ] [–]

May 93. (cd) *Royal; (RC 82112)* **PAUL SIMON & FRIENDS** [ ] [–]

Sep 93. (3xcd-box) *Warners; (9362 45474-2)* **1964-1993** [ ] [ ]

Sep 93. (cd/c) *Warners; (9362 45408-2/-4)* **ANTHOLOGY** [ ] [ ]

May 00. (cd/c) *Warner ESP; (9362 47721-2/-4)* **GREATEST HITS – SHINING LIKE A GUITAR** [6] [–]

ART GARFUNKEL

(solo with session people)

C.B.S. Columbia

Sep 73. (7") *(1777) <45926>* **ALL I KNOW. / MARY WAS AN ONLY CHILD** [ ] [9]

Oct 73. (lp/c) *(CBS/40 89021) <31472>* **ANGEL CLARE** [14] Sep73 [5]
– Travelling boy / Down in the willow garden / I shall sing / Old man / Feuilles oh! – Do spacemen pass dead souls on their way to the Moon? / All I know / Woyaya / Mary was an only child / Barbara Allen / Another lullaby. *(also on quad-lp; CQ 31474) (cd-iss. 1988; CD 69021) (re-iss. Jul89 on 'Pickwick'; 982185)*

Feb 74. (7") *(2013) <45983>* **I SHALL SING. / FEUILLES OH! – DO SPACEMEN PASS DEAD SOULS ON THEIR WAY TO THE MOON?** [ ] Dec 73 [38]

Sep 74. (7") *(2672) <10020>* **SECOND AVENUE. / WOYAYA** [ ] [34]

—— (above 1973/74 releases as "GARFUNKEL")

Sep 75. (7") *(3575) <10190>* **I ONLY HAVE EYES FOR YOU. / LOOKING FOR THE RIGHT ONE** [1] Aug75 [18]

Oct 75. (lp/c) *(CBS/40 86002) <33700>* **BREAKAWAY** [7] [7]
– I believe (when I fall in love it will be forever) / Rag doll / Breakaway / Disney girls / Waters of March / My little town / I only have eyes for you / Looking for the right one / 99 miles from L.A. / The same old tears on a new background. *(re-iss. Nov85 lp/c; CBS/40 32574) (cd-iss. Apr86; CD 86002) (re-iss. Sep89 on 'Pickwick' lp/c/cd; 902199-1/-4/-2) (cd re-iss. Sep93 on 'Sony Collectors';) (cd re-iss. Feb87; 468873-2)*

—— See PAUL SIMON section, for their hit duet MY LITTLE TOWN.

Dec 75. (7") *<10273>* **BREAKAWAY. / DISNEY GIRLS** [–] [ ]

Jan 76. (7") *(3888)* **BREAKAWAY. / THE SAME OLD TEARS ON A NEW BACKGROUND** [ ] [–]

May 76. (7") *(4348)* **I BELIEVE (WHEN I FALL IN LOVE IT WILL BE FOREVER). / WATERS OF MARCH** [ ] [–]

Nov 77. (7") *(5683) <10608>* **CRYING IN MY SLEEP. / MR.SHUCK'N'JIVE** [ ] [ ]

Jan 78. (7"; ART GARFUNKEL, PAUL SIMON & JAMES TAYLOR) *(6061) 19676>* **(WHAT A) WONDERFUL WORLD. / WOODEN PLANES** [ ] [17]

Feb 78. (lp/c) *(CBS/40 86054) <34975>* **WATERMARK** [25] [19]
– Crying in my sleep / Marionette / Shine it on me / Watermark / Saturday suit / All my love's laughter / (What a) Wonderful world / Mr. Shuck 'n' jive / Paper chase / She moved through the fair / Someone else (1958) / Wooden planes. *(re-iss. Jan87 lp/c; 450378-1/-4) (cd-iss. Apr94 on 'Sony')*

Apr 78. (7") *(6325)* **MARIONETTE. / ALL MY LOVE'S LAUGHTER** [ ] [–]

Feb 79. (7") *(6847)* **BRIGHT EYES. / KEHAAR'S THEME** [1] [–]
(above from animated film 'Watership Down') *(re-iss. Jul84)*

Mar 79. (7") *<10933>* **AND I KNOW. / IN A LITTLE WHILE (I'LL BE ON MY WAY)** [–] [ ]

Apr 79. (lp/c) *(CBS/40 86090) <35780>* **FATE FOR BREAKFAST** [2] [67]
– In a little while (I'll be on my way) / Since I don't have you / And I know / Sail on a rainbow / Miss you nights / Bright eyes / Finally a reason / Beyond the tears / Oh how happy / When someone doesn't want you / Take me away. *Cd-iss.Jul97 on 'Columbia'; 487946-2)*

May 79. (7") *<10999>* **SINCE I DON'T HAVE YOU. / WHEN SOMEONE DOESN'T WANT YOU** [–] [53]

Jun 79. (7") *(7371)* **SINCE I DON'T HAVE YOU. / AND I KNOW** [38] [–]

Aug 79. (7") **BRIGHT EYES. / SAIL ON A RAINBOW** [–] [ ]

Aug 81. (7"; ART GARFUNKEL & PAUL SIMON) *(A 1495) <02307>* **A HEART IN NEW YORK. / IS THIS LOVE** [ ] [66]

Sep 81. (lp/c) *(CBS/40 85259) <37392>* **SCISSORS CUT** [51] [ ]
– Scissors cut / A heart in New York / Up in the world / Hang on in / So easy to begin / Can't turn my heart away / The French waltz / The romance / In cars / That's all I've got to say.

Oct 81. (7") *(A 1708)* **SCISSORS CUT. / SO EASY TO BEGIN** [ ] [–]

—— Late 1981, he had re-united with PAUL SIMON for live one-off album.

Oct 84. (7") *(A 4674)* **SOMETIME WHEN I'M DREAMING. / SCISSORS CUT** [ ] [–]

Nov 84. (lp/c/cd) *(CBS/40/CD 10046)* **THE ART GARFUNKEL ALBUM** (compilation) [12] [–]
– Bright eyes / Break away / A heart in New York / I shall sing / 99 miles from L.A. / All I know / I only have eyes for you / Watermark / Sometimes when I'm dreaming / Travelin' boy / The same old tears on a new background / (What a) Wonderful world / I believe (when I fall in love it will be forever) / Scissors cut. *(cd re-iss. Oct90; 466333-2)*

Nov 86. (7"; with AMY GRANT) **CAROL OF THE BIRDS. / THE DECREE** [–] [ ]

Dec 86. (lp/c) *(CBS/40 26704) <40212>* **THE ANIMALS' CHRISTMAS** [ ] [ ]
– The annunciation / The creatures of the field / Just a simple little tune / The decree / Incredible phat / The friendly beasts / The song of the camel / Words from an old Spanish carol / Carol of the birds / The frog / Herod / Wild geese.

Jan 88. (7") *<07711>* **SO MUCH IN LOVE. / KING OF TONGA** [–] [ ]

Feb 88. (7") *(651 450-7)* **SO MUCH IN LOVE. / SLOW BREAKUP** [ ] [–]
(12"+=/cd-s+=) *(651 450-6/-2)* – (What a) Wonderful world / I only have eyes for you.

Mar 88. (7") *<07949>* **THIS IS THE MOMENT. / SLOW BREAKUP** [–] [ ]

Mar 88. (lp/c/cd) *(460694-1/-4/-2) <40942>* **LEFTY** [ ] [ ]
– This is the moment / I have a love / So much in love / Slow breakup / Love is the only chain / When a man loves a woman / I wonder why / King of Tonga / If love takes you away / The promise.

May 88. (7") *(651 632-7)* **WHEN A MAN LOVES A WOMAN. / KING OF TONGA** [ ] [–]

May 88. (7") *<08511>* **WHEN A MAN LOVES A WOMAN. / I HAVE A LOVE** [–] [ ]

Columbia Columbia

Nov 93. (cd/c/lp) *(474853-2/-4) <47113>* **UP 'TIL NOW** [ ] Oct93 [ ]
– Crying in the rain (w/ JAMES TAYLOR) / All I know / Just over the Brooklyn Bridge / The sound of silence / The breakup / Skywriter / The decree / It's all in the game / One less holiday / Since I don't have you / Two sleepy people / Why worry / All my love's daughter.

Virgin Virgin

Dec 96. (cd/c) *(VT CD/MC 113) <20001>* **ACROSS AMERICA (live)** [59] May97 [ ]
– Heart in New York / Crying in the rain / Scarborough fair / Poem on the underground wall / Homeward bound / All I know / Bright eyes / El condor pasa (If i could) / Bridge over troubled water / Mrs. Robinson / 59th Street Bridge song (feelin' groovy) / I will / April come she will / Sound of silence / Grateful / Goodnight my love.

Liberty Blue Note

Feb 03. (cd; as ART GARFUNKEL with MAIA SHARP & BUDDY MONDLOCK) *<(5 40990-2)>* **EVERYTHING WAITS TO BE NOTICED** [ ] Oct02 [ ]
– Bounce / The thread / The kid / Crossing lines / Everything waits to be noticed / Young and free / Perfect moment / Turn, don't turn away / Wishbone / How did you know? / What I love about rain / Every now and then / Another only one.

– (ART GARFUNKEL) compilations, etc. –

Oct 79. (3xlp-box) *C.B.S.;* **ART GARFUNKEL** [ ] [ ]
(first 3 albums)

1984. (7") *Columbia;* **BRIGHT EYES. / THE ROMANCE** [–] [ ]

Jun 97. (cd) *<67674>* **SONGS FROM A PARENT TO A CHILD** (covers) [–] [ ]

Aug 98. (cd) *Columbia; (491473-2)* **THE BEST OF ART GARFUNKEL** [ ] [–]

SIMPLE MINDS

Formed: Glasgow, Scotland ... early 1978 after four members (frontman JIM KERR, guitarists CHARLIE BURCHILL and DUNCAN BARNWELL and drummer BRIAN McGEE) had left punk band, JOHNNY & THE SELF ABUSERS. Taking the group name from a line in a BOWIE song, the band gigged constantly at Glasgow's Mars Bar, finally being signed on the strength of a demo tape by local Edinburgh music guru and record store owner, Bruce Findlay. Also becoming the band's manager, Findlay released their debut album, 'LIFE IN A DAY' (1979) on his own 'Zoom' label, the record scoring a Top 30 placing. Its minor success led to a deal with 'Arista' who released the follow-up, 'REEL TO REEL CACOPHONY' (1979), a set of post-punk, electronic experimentation best sampled on the evocative synth spirals of 'FILM THEME'. SIMPLE MINDS took another about turn with 'EMPIRES AND DANCE' (1980), an album heavily influenced by the harder end of the Euro-disco movement, the abrasive electro pulse of the 'I TRAVEL' single becoming a cult dancefloor hit. Initially released as a double set, 'SONS AND FASCINATION' / 'SISTER FEELINGS CALL' (1981), marked the first fruits of a new deal with 'Virgin' and gave the group their first major success, peaking at No.11 in the UK chart on the back of the Top 50 single, 'LOVE SONG'. SIMPLE MINDS were beginning to find their niche, incorporating their artier tendencies into more conventional and melodic song structures. This was fully realised with 'NEW GOLD DREAM (81-82-83-84)' (1982), a record which marked the pinnacle of their early career and one which arguably, they've since failed to better. Constructed with multiple layers of synth, the band crafted a wonderfully evocative and atmospheric series of undulating electronic soundscapes, often married to pop hooks, as with 'GLITTERING PRIZE' and 'PROMISED YOU A MIRACLE' (the group's first Top 20 hits), but more effectively allowed to veer off into dreamier territory on the likes of 'SOMEONE SOMEWHERE IN SUMMERTIME'. While SIMPLE MINDS and U2 were often compared in terms of their anthemic tendencies, a closer comparison could be made, in spirit at least, between 'NEW GOLD..' and U2's mid-80's experimental classic, 'The Unforgettable Fire'. The album reached No.3 in the UK charts, a catalyst for SIMPLE MINDS' gradual transformation from an obscure cult act to stadium candidates, this process helped along nicely by the success of 'SPARKLE IN THE RAIN' (1984), the band's first No.1 album. Though it lacked the compelling mystery of its predecessor, the record featured such memorable SIMPLE MINDS' moments as 'UP ON THE CATWALK', 'SPEED YOUR LOVE TO ME' and an inventive cover of Lou Reed's 'STREET HASSLE'. For better or worse, the album also boasted SIMPLE MINDS' first truly BIG anthem, the sonic bombast of 'WATERFRONT'. But the track that no doubt finally alienated the old faithful was 'DON'T YOU (FORGET ABOUT ME)', the theme tune for quintessentially 80's movie, 'The Breakfast Club' and surely one of the most overplayed records of that decade. The song had stadium-friendly written all over it, subsequently scaling the US charts and paving the way for the transatlantic success of 'ONCE UPON A TIME' (1985). Unashamedly going for the commmercial pop/rock jugular, the album was heady, radio orientated stuff, the likes of 'ALIVE AND KICKING', 'SANCTIFY YOURSELF' and 'OH JUNGLELAND' among the most definitive anthems of the stadium rock genre. Predictably, the critics were unimpressed, although they didn't really stick the knife in until the release of the overblown 'BELFAST CHILD', a UK No.1 despite its snoozeworthy meandering and vague political agenda. The accompanying album, 'STREET FIGHTING YEARS' (1989) brought more of the same, although it cemented SIMPLE MINDS' position among the coffee table elite. Down to a trio of KERR, BURCHILL and and drummer, MEL GAYNOR, the group hired a team of session players for their next album, 'REAL LIFE' (1991), the record almost spawning a Top 5 hit in the celebratory 'LET THERE BE LOVE'. Although the album narrowly missed the UK top spot, it held nothing new, nor did their next release, 'GOOD NEWS FROM THE NEXT WORLD' (1995). Although KERR and BURCHILL brought back DEREK FORBES and signed a new deal with 'Chrysalis' for 1998's 'NEAPOLIS' set, the band only managed to scrape into the UK Top 20. You couldn't help feeling a little sorry for JIM KERR (one-time spouse of CHRISSIE HYNDE), not only does a young pretender like LIAM GALLAGHER hook up with his then wife (PATSY KENSIT), but his band became something of an anachronism in the ever changing world of 90's music. This was realized come their 2002 release 'CRY', a leap backwards into the world of old SIMPLE MINDS. Granted, the group had started using loops and adding a little guitar playing here and there, but what remained was a keyboard-driven album that gave us little in the way of musical vision. While U2 have at least made an attempt to move with the times, SIMPLE MINDS' sound is so deeply rooted in the 80's that it seems inconceivable they could ever make any kind of relevant departure. Those words may well have to be eaten judging by the unheralded and unanticipated acclaim generated by 'OUR SECRETS ARE THE SAME' (2003), the much talked of but hitherto unheard set shelved in the mid to late 90's. The album's savvy pop smarts harked back to their early 80's purple period, only underlining the shortcomings of 'NEAPOLIS', while the sassy momentum of 'JEWELLER TO THE STARS' could've easily regenerated KERR and Co's contemporary credibility. SIMPLE MINDS were back in the UK Top 40, courtesy of "comeback" set, 'BLACK AND WHITE 050505' (2005), the post-Punk 80s going through something of a revival.

• **Songwriters:** All group compositions or KERR-BURCHILL. Covered BIKO (Peter Gabriel) / SIGN O' THE TIMES (Prince) / DON'T YOU FORGET ABOUT ME (Keith Forsey-Steve Chiff) / GLORIA (Them) / THE MAN WHO SOLD THE WORLD (David Bowie) / HOMOSAPIEN (Pete Shelley) / DANCING BAREFOOT (Patti Smith) / NEON LIGHTS (Kraftwerk) / HELLO I LOVE YOU (Doors) / BRING ON THE DANCING HORSES (Echo & The Bunnymen) / THE NEEDLE & THE DAMAGE DONE (Neil Young) / FOR YOUR PLEASURE (Roxy Music) / ALL TOMORROW'S PARTIES (Velvet Underground). • **Trivia:** SIMPLE MINDS played LIVE AID and MANDELA DAY concerts in 1985 and 1988 respectively.

Album rating: LIFE IN A DAY (*7) / REAL TO REAL CACOPHONY (*5) / EMPIRES AND DANCE (*8) / SONS AND FASCINATION – SISTER FEELING CALL (*8) / CELEBRATION compilation (*7) / NEW GOLD DREAM (81-82-83-84) (*8) / SPARKLE IN THE RAIN (*8) / ONCE UPON A TIME (*8) / LIVE IN THE CITY OF LIGHT (*6) / STREET FIGHTING YEARS (*5) / REAL LIFE (*5) / GLITTERING PRIZE – SIMPLE MINDS 81-92 compilation (*9) / GOOD NEWS FROM THE NEXT WORLD (*4) / NEAPOLIS (*3) / NEON LIGHTS (*4) / THE BEST OF SIMPLE MINDS compilation (*8) / CRY (*4) / OUR SECRETS ARE THE SAME "lost album" (*6) / BLACK AND WHITE 050505 (er! *4)

JOHNNY & THE SELF ABUSERS

JIM KERR (b. 9 Jul'59) – vocals / **CHARLIE BURCHILL** (b.27 Nov'59) – guitar / **BRIAN McGEE** – drums / **TONY DONALD** – bass / **JOHN MILARKY** – guitar / **ALAN McNEIL** also

	Chiswick	not iss.
Nov 77. (7") *(NS 22)* **SAINTS AND SINNERS. / DEAD VANDALS**		–

SIMPLE MINDS

— (**KERR, BURCHILL + McGEE**) recruited **MICK McNEILL** (b.20 Jul'58) – keyboards / **DEREK FORBES** (b.22 Jun'56) – bass (ex-SUBS) + **DUNCAN BARNWELL** – guitar (left before recording)

	Zoom	not iss.
Apr 79. (7") *(ZUM 10)* **LIFE IN A DAY. / SPECIAL VIEW**	62	–

Apr 79. (lp) *(ZULP 1)* **LIFE IN A DAY** [30] [–]
– Someone / Life in a day / Sad affair / All for you / Pleasantly disurbed / No cure / Chelsea girl / Wasteland / Destiny / Murder story. *(re-iss. Oct82 on 'Virgin' lp/c; VM/+C 6) (re-iss. 1985 on 'Virgin' lp/c; OVED/+C 95) (cd-iss. Jul86; VMCD 6)*

Jun 79. (7") *(ZUM 11)* **CHELSEA GIRL. / GARDEN OF HATE** [ ] [–]

Arista Arista

Nov 79. (lp/c) *(SPART/TC-SPART 1109)* **REAL TO REAL CACOPHONY** [ ] [ ]
– Real to real / Naked eye / Citizen (dance of youth) / Carnival (shelter in a suitcase) / Factory / Cacophony / Veldt / Premonition / Changeling / Film theme / Calling your name / Scar. *(re-iss. Oct82 on 'Virgin' lp/c; V/TCV 2246) (re-iss. 1985 on 'Virgin' lp/c; OVED/+C 124) (cd-iss. May88; CDV 2246)*

Jan 80. (7") *(ARIST 325)* **CHANGELING. / PREMONITION (live)** [ ] [–]

Sep 80. (lp/c) *(SPART/TC-SPART 1140)* **EMPIRES AND DANCE** [41] [ ]
– I travel / Today I died again / Celebrate / This fear of gods / Capital city / Constantinople line / Twist-run-repulsion / Thirty frames a seconds / Kant-kino / Room. *(re-iss. Oct82 on 'Virgin' lp/c; V/TCV 2247) (cd-iss. May88; CDV 2247)*

Oct 80. (7") *(ARIST 372)* **I TRAVEL. / NEW WARM SKIN** [ ] [ ]
(w/ free 7"blue flexi) – KALEIDOSCOPE. / FILM DUB THEME
(12") *(ARIST 12-372)* – ('A'side) / Film dub theme.

Feb 81. (7") *(ARIST 394)* **CELEBRATE. / CHANGELING (live)** [ ] [ ]
(12"+=) *(ARIST 12-394)* – I travel (live).

Virgin A&M

May 81. (7"/remix.12") *(VS 410/+12)* **THE AMERICAN. / LEAGUE OF NATIONS** [59] [–]

— **KENNY HYSLOP** (b.14 Feb'51, Helensburgh, Scotland) – drums (ex-SKIDS, ex-ZONES, ex-SLIK) repl. McGEE who joined ENDGAMES; in 1994 he became a songwriter for LES McKEOWN (ex-BAY CITY ROLLERS)

Aug 81. (7"/12") *(VS 434/+12)* **LOVE SONG. / THE EARTH THAT YOU WALK UPON (instrumental)** [47] [–]

Sep 81. (2xlp/d-c) *(V/TCV 2207)* **SONS AND FASCINATION / SISTER FEELINGS CALL** [11] [ ]
– SONS AND FASCINATION – In trance as mission / Sweat in bullet / 70 cities as love brings the fall / Boys from Brazil / Love song / This Earth that you walk upon / Sons and fascination / Seeing out the angels. SISTER FEELINGS CALL – Theme for great cities * / The American / 20th Century promised land / Wonderful in young life / League of nations / Careful in career / Sound in 70 cities. *(issued separately Oct81; V 2207 / OVED 2) (cd-iss. Apr86 + Apr90; CDV 2207)* – (omits tracks *)

Oct 81. (7") *(VS 451)* **SWEAT IN BULLET. / 20th CENTURY PROMISED LAND** [52] [–]
(d7"+=) *(VSD 451)* – League of nations (live) / Premonition (live).
(12"+=) *(VS 451-12)* – League of nations (live) / In trance as mission (live).

Apr 82. (7") *(VS 488)* **PROMISED YOU A MIRACLE. / THEME FOR GREAT CITIES** [13] [–]
(12"+=) *(VS 488-12)* – Seeing out the angel (instrumental mix).

— **MIKE OGLETREE** – drums (ex-CAFE JAQUES) repl. HYSLOP who formed SET THE TONE

Aug 82. (7"/12") *(VS 511/+12)* **GLITTERING PRIZE. / GLITTERING THEME** [16] [ ]

— **MEL GAYNOR** (b.29 May'59) – drums (ex-sessions) repl. MIKE who joined FICTION FACTORY

Sep 82. (lp/c)<gold-lp> *(V/TCV 2230) <4928>* **NEW GOLD DREAM (81-82-83-84)** [3] Jan83 [69]
– Someone, somewhere in summertime / Colours fly and the Catherine wheel / Promised you a miracle / Big sleep / Somebody up there likes you / New gold dream (81-82-83-84) / Glittering prize / Hunter and the hunted / King is white and in the crowd. *(cd-iss. Jul83 & Apr92; CDV 2230) (re-iss. Apr92 lp/c; OVED/+C 393)*

Nov 82. (7"/7"pic-d) *(VS/+Y 538)* **SOMEONE, SOMEWHERE IN SUMMERTIME. / KING IS WHITE AND IN THE CROWD** [36] [ ]
(12"+=) *(VS 538-12)* – Soundtrack for every Heaven.

Nov 82. (7") **PROMISED YOU A MIRACLE. / THE AMERICAN** [–] [ ]

Nov 83. (7"/12") *(VS 636/+12)* **WATERFRONT. / HUNTER AND THE HUNTED (live)** [13] [ ]

Jan 84. (7"/7"pic-d) *(VS/+Y 649)* **SPEED YOUR LOVE TO ME. / BASS LINE** [20] [ ]
(12"+=) *(VS 649-12)* – ('A'extended).

Feb 84. (cd/c/lp,white-lp) *(CD/TC+/V 2300) <4981>* **SPARKLE IN THE RAIN** [1] [64]
– Up on the catwalk / Book of brilliant things / Speed your love to me / Waterfront / East at Easter / White hot day / Street hassle / "C" Moon cry like a baby / The kick inside of me / Shake off the ghosts. *(re-iss. cd Mar91; same)*

Mar 84. (7"/7"pic-d)(12") *(VS/+Y 661)(VS 661-12)* **UP ON THE CATWALK. / A BRASS BAND IN AFRICA** [27] [ ]

Apr 85. (7"/7"sha-pic-d)(12") *(VS/+S 749)(VS 749-12) <2703>* **DON'T YOU (FORGET ABOUT ME). / A BRASS BAND IN AFRICA** [7] Feb85 [1]
(re-iss. Jun88 cd-s; CDT 2)

— **KERR, BURCHILL, McNEILL + GAYNOR** brought in new member **JOHN GIBLING** – bass (ex-PETER GABRIEL sessions) to repl. FORBES

Oct 85. (7"/12") *(VS 817/+12)* **ALIVE AND KICKING. / ('A'instrumental)** [7] [–]
(12"+=) *(VS 817-13)* – Up on the catwalk (live).

Oct 85. (cd/c/lp,pic-lp) *(CD/TC+/V 2364) <5092>* **ONCE UPON A TIME** [1] [10]
– Once upon a time / All the things she said / Ghost dancing / Alive and kicking / Oh jungleland / I wish you were here / Sanctify yourself / Come a long way. *(lp re-iss. Mar01 on 'Simple Vinyl'; SVLP 312)*

Oct 85. (7") *<2783>* **ALIVE AND KICKING. / UP ON THE CATWALK (live)** [–] [3]

Jan 86. (7") *(SM 1) <2810>* **SANCTIFY YOURSELF. / ('A'instrumental)** [10] [14]
(d7"+=) *(SMP 1)* – Love song (live) / Street hassle (live).
(12") *(SM 1-12)* – ('A'mix). / ('A'dub instrumental).

Apr 86. (7") *(VS 860) <2828>* **ALL THE THINGS SHE SAID. / DON'T YOU (FORGET ABOUT ME)** [9] [28]
(12"+=) *(VS 860-12)* – Promised you a miracle (US mix).

Nov 86. (7") *(VS 907)* **GHOSTDANCING. / JUNGLELAND (instrumental)** [13] [ ]
(12"+=/cd-s+=) *(VS/MIKE 907-12)* – ('A'instrumental) / ('B'instrumental).

May 87. (d-cd/d-c/d-lp) *(CDVSM/SMDCX/SMDLX 1) <6850>* **LIVE IN THE CITY OF LIGHT (live)** [1] Jul87 [96]
– Ghostdancing / Big sleep / Waterfront / Promised you a miracle / Someone somewhere in summertime / Oh jungleland / Alive and kicking / Don't you (forget about me) / Once upon a time / Book of brilliant things / East at Easter / Sanctify yourself / Love song / Sun City – Dance to the music / New gold dream (81-82-83-84).

Jun 87. (7"/10") *(SM 2/+10)* **PROMISED YOU A MIRACLE (live). / BOOK OF BRILLIANT THINGS (live)** [19] [ ]
(12"+=/c-s+=) *(SM/+C 2-12)* – Glittering prize (live) / Celebrate (live).

— **KERR, BURCHILL + McNEILL** were basic trio, w/other 2 still sessioning.

Feb 89. (7") *(SMX 3)* **BELFAST CHILD. / MANDELA DAY** [1] [ ]
(c-s+=/12"ep+=/12"box-ep+=/cd-ep+=) **BALLAD OF THE STREETS** *(SMX C/T/C/CD 3)* – Biko.

Apr 89. (7") *(SMX 4)* **THIS IS YOUR LAND. / SATURDAY GIRL** [13] [ ]
(c-s+=/12"+=/12"g-f+=/3"cd-s+=) *(SMX C/T/TG/CD 4)* – Year of the dragon.

May 89. (cd/c/lp) *(MIND D/C/S 1) <3927>* **STREET FIGHTING YEARS** [1] [70]
– Soul crying out / Wall of love / This is your land / Take a step back / Kick it in / Let it all come down / Biko / Mandela day / Belfast child / Street fighting years. *(re-iss. Dec89 box-cd/c +=; SMBX D/C 1)* – (interview cassettes).

Jul 89. (7"/c-s) *(SMX/+C 5)* **KICK IT IN. / WATERFRONT ('89 mix)** [15] [ ]
(12"+=/cd-s+=) *(SMX T/CD 5)* – Big sleep (live).
(12"g-f+=) *(SMXTG 5)* – ('A'mix).

Dec 89. (7"ep/c-ep/12"ep/cd-ep) *(SMX/+C/T/CD 6)* **THE AMSTERDAM EP** [18] [ ]
– Let it all come down / Sign o' the times / Jerusalem.
(12"ep+=/cd-ep+=) *(SMX TR/X 6)* – Sign o' the times (mix).

— **KERR, BURCHILL + GAYNOR** brought in sessioners **MALCOLM FOSTER** – bass / **PETER JOHN VITESSE** – keyboards / **STEPHEN LIPSON** – bass, keyboards / **ANDY DUNCAN** – percussion / **GAVIN WRIGHT** – string leader / **LISA GERMANO** – violin

Mar 91. (7"/c-s) *(VS/+C 1332)* **LET THERE BE LOVE. / GOODNIGHT** [6] [ ]
(12"+=) *(VST 1332)* – Alive and kicking (live).
(cd-s++=) *(VSCD 1332)* – East at Easter (live).

Apr 91. (cd/c/lp) *(CD/TC+/V 2660) <5352>* **REAL LIFE** 2 74
– Real life / See the lights / Let there be love / Woman / Stand by love / African skies / Let the children speak / Ghostrider / Banging on the door / Travelling man / Rivers of ice / When two worlds collide.

May 91. (7"/c-s) *(VS/+C 1343)* **SEE THE LIGHTS. / THEME FOR GREAT CITIES ('91 edit)** 20 –
(12"+=/cd-s+=) *(VS T/CD 1343)* – Soul crying out (live).

May 91. (c-s,cd-s) *<1553>* **SEE THE LIGHTS / GOODNIGHT** – 40

Aug 91. (7"/c-s) *(VS/+C 1358)* **STAND BY LOVE. / KING IS WHITE AND IN THE CROWD (live)** 13
(12"+=/cd-s+=) *(VS T/CD 1358)* – Let there be love (live).

Oct 91. (7"/c-s) *(VS/+C 1382)* **REAL LIFE. / SEE THE LIGHTS** 34
(ext.12"+=) *(VST 1382)* – Belfast child (extended).
(cd-s++=) *(VSCD 1382)* – Ghostrider.

Oct 92. (7"/c-s) *(VS/+C 1440)* **LOVE SONG. / ALIVE AND KICKING** 6
(ext.cd-s+=) *(VSCDG 1440)* – ('B'instrumental).
(cd-s+=) *(VSCDX 1440)* – Travelling man / Oh jungleland.

Oct 92. (cd/c/lp) *(SMTV D/C/S 1)* **GLITTERING PRIZE – SIMPLE MINDS 81-92** (compilation) 1 –
– Waterfront / Don't you (forget about me) / Alive and kicking / Sanctify yourself / Love song / Someone somewhere in summertime / See the lights / Belfast child / The American / All the things she said / Promised you a miracle / Ghostdancing / Speed your love to me / Glittering prize / Let there be love / Mandela Day. *(lp re-iss. Oct00 on 'Simply Vinyl'; SVLP 258)*

—— **KERR + BURCHILL** with guests MARK BROWNE, MALCOLM FOSTER, MARCUS MILLER + LANCE MORRISON – bass / MARK SCHULMAN, TAL BERGMAN + VINNIE COLAIUTA – drums

Virgin Virgin

Jan 95. (7"/c-s/cd-s) *(VS/+C/+DG 1509) <38467>* **SHE'S A RIVER. / E55 / ('A'mix)** 9 52
(cd-s) *(VSCDX 1509)* – ('A'side) / Celtic strings / ('A'mix).

Jan 95. (cd/c/lp) *(CD/TC+/V 2760) <39922>* **GOOD NEWS FROM THE NEXT WORLD** 2 87
– She's a river / Night music / Hypnotised / Great leap forward / 7 deadly sins / And the band played on / My life / Criminal world / This time.

Mar 95. (7"/c-s) *(VS/+C 1534)* **HYPNOTISED. / #4** 18 –
(cd-s+=) *(VSCDX 1534)* – ('A'-Tim Simenon extended remixes) / ('A'-Malfunction mix).
(cd-s) *(VSCDT 1534)* – ('A'side) / Up on the catwalk (live) / And the band played on (live) / She's a river (live).

—— **KERR + BURCHILL** brought back **DEREK FORBES** – bass / **MEL GAYNOR** – drums / also **HAMI LEE** – additional programming

Chrysalis not iss.

Mar 98. (c-s) *(TCCHS 5078)* **GLITTERBALL / WATERFRONT (Union Jack mix)** 18 –
(cd-s+=) *(CDCHSS 5078)* – Love song (Philadelphia Bluntz mix).
(cd-s) *(CDCHS 5078)* – ('A'side) / Don't you forget about me (Jam & Spoon mix) / Theme for great cities (Fila Brazillia mix).

Mar 98. (cd/c) *(493712-2/-4)* **NEAPOLIS** 19 –
– Song for the tribes / Glitterball / War babies / Tears of a guy / Superman v supersoul / Lightning / If I had wings / Killing Andy Warhol / Androgyny.

May 98. (ext;c-s/7") *(TC+/CHS 5088)* **WAR BABIES. / I TRAVEL (Utah Saints mix)** 43 –
('A'-Bascombe mix;cd-s+=) *(CDCHS 5088)* – Theme for great cities '98 (Fluke's Atlantis mix) / ('A'-Johnson Somerset extended mix).

Eagle Red Ink

Sep 01. (cd-ep) *(EAGEP 198)* **DANCING BAREFOOT EP** –
– Dancing barefoot / Gloria / Being boiled / Love will tear us apart.

Sep 01. (cd) *(EAGCD 194) <55944>* **NEON LIGHTS** Oct01
– Gloria / The man who sold the world / Homosapien / Dancing barefoot / Neon lights / Hello I love you / Bring on the dancing horses / The needle & the damage done / For your pleasure / All tomorrow's parties.

Dec 01. (12") *(REMOTE 016)* **HOMOSAPIEN (Malcolm Duffy mix). / HOMOSAPIEN (Malcolm Duffy dub mix)** –
(cd-s+=) *(REMOTE 016CD)* – ('A'-Malcolm Duffy edit).
(above issued on 'Remote')

—— in Feb'02, SIMPLE MINDS featured/vs on JOHN '00' FLEMING's single 'Belfast Trance' (i.e. 'Belfast Child')

Mar 02. (cd-s) *(EAGXA 218)* **CRY / LEAD THE BLIND / HOMOSAPIEN (Vince Clarke remix)** 47 –
(cd-s) *(EAGXS 218)* – ('A'side) / For what it's worth / The garden.

Apr 02. (cd) *(EAGCD 196) <59145>* **CRY**
– Cry / Spaceface / New sunshine morning / One step closer / Face in the sun / Disconnected / Lazy lately / Sugar / Sleeping girl / Cry again / Slave nation / The floating world.

Jun 02. (cd-s) *(EAGXS 232)* **SPACEFACE / NEW SUNRISE** –

—— in Jun'02, LIQUID PEOPLE vs. SIMPLE MINDS had a hit with 'Monster' which sampled 'CHANGELING'

Absolute not iss.

Sep 02. (12") *(ABR 014)* **CRY (phunk investigation club mix). / CRY (dub mix) / CRY (radio)** –
(cd-s) *(ABR 015)* – ('A'-Tazz Glasgoal vocal + tech-house dub).

Dec 02. (12") *(ABR 027)* **SPACEFACE (remixes)** –

Feb 03. (12") *(ABR 036)* **SPACEFACE (remixes)** –

Mar 03. (12") *(ABR 041)* **DON'T YOU (FORGET ABOUT ME) (remixes)** –

—— **EDDIE DUFFY** – bass + **MARK TAYLOR** – keyboards; repl. HAMI

Sanctuary Sanctuary

Sep 05. (cd-s) *(SANXD 388)* **HOME / BIRD ON A WIRE** 41 –
(cd-s) *(SANXS 388)* – ('A') / Mighty Joe Moon / ('A'-Trixton Porteno mix) / ('A'-video).

Sep 05. (cd) *(SANCD 390) <84769>* **BLACK AND WHITE 050505** 37 –
– Stay visible / Home / Stranger / Different world / Underneath the ice / Jeweller / Black and white / Kiss the ground / Dolphin. *(bonus+=)* – Home (video).

Nov 05. (cd-s) *(SANXD 415)* **STRANGER (London mix) / BIRD ON A WIRE / TOO MUCH TV / STRANGER** –

– compilations, others, etc. –

on 'Virgin' unless otherwise mentioned

Jan 82. (7") *Arista; (ARIST 448)* **I TRAVEL. / THIRTY FRAMES A SECOND (live)** –
(12"+=) *(ARIST12 448)* – ('A'live).

Feb 82. (lp/c) *Arista; (SPART/TCSPART 1183)* **CELEBRATION** 45
(re-iss. Oct82 on 'Virgin' lp/c; V/TCV 2248) (re-iss. Apr89 on 'Virgin' lp/c; OVED/+C 275) (cd-iss. Aug89; CDV 2248)

Apr 83. (12") *(VS 578-12)* **I TRAVEL (mix). / FILM THEME** –

Aug 90. (5xcd-box-ep) *(SMTCD 1)* **THEMES – VOLUME ONE** –
– (Apr79 – LIFE IN A DAY – Apr82 – PROMISED YOU A MIRACLE singles)

Sep 90. (5xcd-box-ep) *(SMTCD 2)* **THEMES – VOLUME TWO** –
– (Aug82 – GLITTERING PRIZE – Apr85 – DON'T YOU (FORGET ABOUT ME) singles)

Oct 90. (5xcd-box-ep) *(SMTCD 3)* **THEMES – VOLUME THREE** –
– (Oct85 – ALIVE AND KICKING – Jun87 – PROMISED YOU A MIRACLE (live) singles)

Nov 90. (5xcd-box-ep) *(SMTCD 4)* **THEMES – VOLUME FOUR** –
– (Feb89 – BELFAST CHILD, Dec89 – THE AMSTERDAM EP)

Nov 90. (3xcd-box) *(TPAK 2)* **COLLECTOR'S EDITION** –
– (LIFE IN A DAY / REEL TO REAL CACOPHONY / EMPIRES AND DANCE)

Nov 01. (d-cd) *(CDVD 2953)* **THE BEST OF SIMPLE MINDS** 34 –

Jun 03. (cd) *(SIMCD 13)* **OUR SECRETS ARE THE SAME** –
– Swimming towards the sun / Jeweller to the stars / Space / Death by chocolate / Waiting for the end of the world / Neon city cowboys / She knows / Hello / Happy is the man / Sleeping.

SIOUXSIE & THE BANSHEES

Formed: London, England . . . September '76 by SIOUXSIE SIOUX and STEVE SEVERIN, both members of the infamous 'Bromley Contingent' punk troupe who religiously followed The SEX PISTOLS during the turbulent early years of their career; an early incarnation of The BANSHEES even featured future PISTOL, SID VICIOUS on drums, the outfit mangling the Lord's Prayer at the legendary 100 Club punk all-dayer in summer '76. SIOUX gained further notoriety following her appearance (as a fan) on the fateful edition of Bill Grundy's 'Today' programme wherein his tete-a-tete with the 'PISTOLS outraged the country's more upstanding citizens. Cutting a striking dash through the punk scene with her Nazi chic and proto-goth garb, SIOUXSIE and her BANSHEES (who, after much to-ing and fro-ing, were eventually completed by JOHN McKAY amd KENNY MORRIS) toured constantly throughout 1977, eventually signing to 'Polydor' the following year after their original label, 'Track', went bust. A debut single, 'HONG KONG GARDEN' was a sprightly slice of oriental flavoured post-punk which hit the Top 10 with ease and introduced the band outwith the confines of the London scene. 'THE SCREAM' (1978) was instantly hailed as a classic upon its release a few months later, the record's queasy, churning goth-psychedelia breaking new ground and spearheading a new direction for many bands inspired by a movement already dying on its feet. For many recent converts, then, 'JOIN HANDS' (1979) was a disappointment, a turgid affair which lacked the bite of its predecessor and presaged a band breakdown; McKAY and MORRIS upped sticks and left mid-tour, ROBERT SMITH (The CURE) briefly deputising before a new guitarist was eventually found in erstwhile MAGAZINE man, JOHN McGEOGH. The drum seat, meanwhile, was taken by ex-SLITS man, BUDGIE, who would subsequently become SIOUXSIE's beau and eventual husband. The revamped line-up bounced back in 1980 with the enchanting 'HAPPY HOUSE' (a Top 20 hit that Spring) and an accompanying Top 5 album, 'KALEIDOSCOPE', investing their sound with a newly acquired accessibility and ensuring a degree of crossover success for SIOUXSIE's icy sensuality. 'JU JU' (1981) further refined the group's subtle gothic tapestries, again taking the band into the UK Top 10 and spawning a clutch of minor hits while 'ONCE UPON A TIME – THE SINGLES' neatly rounded up the first instalment in The BANSHEES' career. More overtly experimental was the following year's 'A KISS IN THE DREAMHOUSE', utilising strings and flirting with club sounds. 1983 saw a flurry of side project activity as SIOUXSIE and BUDGIE formed the CREATURES, releasing 'FEAST', the first of two albums together (they also had a major hit with Mel Torme's 'RIGHT NOW'). SEVERIN, meanwhile, formed The GLOVE with SMITH (who had also rejoined the BANSHEES ranks as a part-time, temporary replacement for the departing McGEOGH), releasing the 'BLUE SUNSHINE' album the same year. No new BANSHEES material surfaced, although an atmospheric cover of The Beatles' 'DEAR PRUDENCE' hit No.3 and gave them their biggest selling single to date. The track featured on 1983's live set, 'NOCTURNE', while the following year's 'HYAENA', saw SMITH making his presence felt over the course of a haunting set that was unfairly panned by the critics. With SMITH subsequently finding the demands of a dual lifestyle too tiring, ex-CLOCKDVA man, JOHN CARRUTHERS was drafted in for 'TINDERBOX' (1986), an album which carried on in much the same vein, spawning a sizeable hit with the infectious 'CITIES IN DUST'. Perhaps the band really were running out of ideas as their detractors suggested, a suitably gothic Top 20 rendition of Bob Dylan's 'THIS WHEEL'S ON FIRE' trailing a whole album's worth of competent but hardly inspiring cover versions. Featuring yet another guitarist, JON KLEIN, 1988's 'PEEPSHOW' was a much more compelling proposition, a perversely eclectic selection best sampled on the mutant dancefloor hit, 'PEEK-A-BOO'. Now something of an alternative institution, SIOUXSIE & THE BANSHEES cruised into the 90's with their most chart-friendly original material to date, the swooning 'KISS THEM FOR ME' (the band's first – and to date only – major US hit) single and attendant 'SUPERSTITION' (1991) album. Despite the latter set's commercial and critical success, the group reached the end of its natural lifespan in the mid-90's, bowing out on a high with the majestic 'THE RAPTURE'. Officially splitting in April '96, SIOUXSIE was working on new CREATURES material with spouse BUDGIE, while SEVERIN scored the soundtrack for the movie, 'Visions Of Ecstasy'. The aforementioned CREATURES finally resurfaced via 'ANIMA ANIMUS' (1999), an album that boasted a few minor hits; SIOUXSIE was now looking rather Elizabeth Taylor-ish although when she wailed and her BUDGIE drummed it was safe there was no lasting comparison. Getting back-to-basics (much in the same way as 'BOOMERANG'), the duo chose to explore the art of Japanese sounds via 4th set, 'HAI!' (2003), recorded in under 24 hours. Around the same period, SIOUXSIE guested for BASEMENT JAXX on their hit single, 'Cish Cash', before releasing a solo DVD, DREAMSHOW' (2005).

• **Songwriters:** All written by SIOUXSIE / SEVERIN except; HELTER SKELTER (Beatles) / 20th CENTURY BOY (T.Rex) / IL EST NE LE DIVIN ENFANT (French festive song) / ALL TOMORROW'S PARTIES (Velvet Underground). THROUGH THE LOOKING GLASS was a covers album containing THE PASSENGER (Iggy Pop) / YOU'RE LOST LITTLE GIRL (Doors) / GUN (John Cale) / THIS TOWN AIN'T BIG ENOUGH FOR THE BOTH OF US (Sparks) / SEA BREEZES (Roxy Music) / STRANGE FRUIT (Billie Holiday) / WALL OF MIRRORS (Kraftwerk) / LITTLE JOHNNY JEWEL (Television) / TRUST IN ME ('Jungle Book' animated film). • **Trivia:** SEVERIN produced ALTERED IMAGES debut 45 'Dead Pop Stars'.

Album rating: THE SCREAM (*9) / JOIN HANDS (*7) / KALEIDOSCOPE (*7) / JU JU (*7) / ONCE UPON A TIME – THE SINGLES compilation (*9) / A KISS IN THE DREAMHOUSE (*7) / NOCTURNE (*5) / HYAENA (*7) / TINDERBOX (*7) / THROUGH THE LOOKING GLASS (*5) / PEEP SHOW (*5) / SUPERSTITION (*5) / TWICE UPON A TIME compilation (*7) / THE RAPTURE (*5) / THE BEST OF SIOUXSIE & THE BANSHEES compilation (*6) / the Creatures: FEAST (*5) / BOOMERANG (*4) / ANIMA ANIMUS (*6) / HAI! (*5) / the Glove: BLUE SUNSHINE (*5)

SIOUXSIE SIOUX (b. SUSAN DALLION, 27 May'57) – vocals / **STEVEN SEVERIN** (b. STEVEN BAILEY, 25 Sep'55) – bass / **JOHN McKAY** – guitar; repl. PT FENTON; who had repl. MARCO PIRRONI (he joined The MODELS and later ADAM & THE ANTS) / **KENNY MORRIS** – drums repl. SID VICIOUS who later became bassman for SEX PISTOLS

Polydor Polydor

Aug 78. (7") *(2059 052)* **HONG KONG GARDEN. / VOICES** 7 –

Oct 78. (7") **HONG KONG GARDEN. / OVERGROUND** –

Nov 78. (lp/c) *(POLD/+C 5009) <6207>* **THE SCREAM** 12
– Pure / Jigsaw feeling / Overground / Carcass / Helter skelter / Mirage / Metal postcard / Nicotine stain / Suburban relapse / Switch. *(cd-iss. Mar89 & Mar95 on 'Wonderland'; 839 008-2) (cd re-iss. Mar95)*

Mar 79. (7") *(POSP 9)* **THE STAIRCASE (MYSTERY). / 20th CENTURY BOY** 24 –

Jun 79. (7") *(POSP 59)* **PLAYGROUND TWIST. / PULLED TO BITS** 28 –

Sep 79. (lp/c) *(POLD/+C 5024)* **JOIN HANDS** 13 –
– Poppy day / Regal zone / Placebo effect / Icon / Premature burial / Playground twist / Mother / Oh mein papa / The Lord's prayer. *(cd-iss. Mar89 & Mar95 on 'Wonderland'; 839004-2)*

Sep 79. (7") *(2059 151)* **MITTAGEISEN (METAL POSTCARD). / LOVE IN A VOID** 47 –

—— **BUDGIE** (b.PETER CLARK, 21 Aug'57, St.Helens, England) – drums (ex-SLITS, ex-PLANETS, ex-BIG IN JAPAN, etc.) repl. MORRIS who bailed out (he subsequently released a solo 12", 'LA MAIN MORTE', for 'Temple' records in '86) / **JOHN McGEOGH** (b. 1955, Greenock, Scotland) – guitar (of MAGAZINE) finally repl. ROBERT SMITH (of The CURE) + JOHN CARRUTHERS who repl. McKAY (he finally formed ZOR GABOR in 1986 – with vocalist LINDA CLARK – and released one single, 'TIGHTROPE', for 'In-Tape' early '87)

Mar 80. (7") *(POSP 117)* **HAPPY HOUSE. / DROP DEAD** 17 –

May 80. (7") *(2059 249)* **CHRISTINE. / EVE WHITE EVE BLACK** 24 –

Aug 80. (lp)(c) *(2442 177)(3184 146)* **KALEIDOSCOPE** 5 –
– Happy house / Tenant / Trophy / Hybrid / Lunar camel / Christine / Desert kisses / Red light / Paradise place / Skin. *(cd-iss. Mar89 & Mar95 on 'Wonderland'; 839006-2)*

Nov 80. (7"/dance-12") *(POSP/+X 205)* **ISRAEL. / RED OVER WHITE** 41 –

May 81. (7") *(POSP 273)* **SPELLBOUND. / FOLLOW THE SUN** 22 –
(12"+=) *(POSPX 273)* – Slap dash snap.

Jun 81. (lp/c) *(POLS/+C 1034)* **JU JU** 7 –
– Spellbound / Into the light / Arabian knights / Halloween / Monitor / Night shift / Sin in my heart / Head cut / Voodoo dolly. *(cd-iss. Mar89 & Mar95 on 'Wonderland'; 839005-2)*

Jul 81. (7") *(POSP 309)* **ARABIAN KNIGHTS. / SUPERNATURAL THING** [32] [–]
(12"+=) *(POSPX 309)* – Congo conga.

— SIOUXSIE & BUDGIE as The CREATURES hit Top 30 with WILD THINGS EP.

Dec 81. (lp/c) *(POLS/+C 1056)* **ONCE UPON A TIME – THE SINGLES** [21] [–]
– Hong Kong garden / Mirage / The staircase (mystery) / Playground twist / Happy house / Christine / Israel / Spellbound / Arabian knights / Fireworks. *(cd-iss. Mar89 on 'Wonderland'; 831542-2)*

May 82. (7") *(POSPG 450)* **FIREWORKS. / COAL MIND** [22] [–]
(12"+=) *(POSPX 450)* – We fall.

Sep 82. (7") *(POSP 510)* **SLOWDIVE. / CANNIBAL ROSES** [41] [–]
(12"+=) *(POSPX 510)* – Obsession II.

Nov 82. (lp/c) *(POLD/+C 5064)* **A KISS IN THE DREAMHOUSE** [11] [–]
– Cascade / Green fingers / Obsession / She's a carnival / Circle / Melt! / Painted bird / Cocoon / Slowdive. *(cd-iss. Apr89 & Mar 95 on 'Wonderland'; 839007-2)*

Nov 82. (7") *(POSP 539)* **MELT! / IL EST NE LE DIVIN ENFANT** [49] [ ]
(12"+=) *(POSPX 539)* – A sleeping rain.

— **ROBERT SMITH** – guitar (of The CURE) returned part-time to repl. McGEOGH who later joined The ARMOURY SHOW.

— In 1983, SMITH and SEVERIN had also splintered into The GLOVE, with SIOUXSIE and BUDGIE re-uniting as The CREATURES (see further on).

Wonderland – Polydor / Geffen

Sep 83. (7") *(SHEG 4)* **DEAR PRUDENCE. / TATTOO** [3] [–]
(12"+=) *(SHEX 4)* – There's a planet in my kitchen.

Nov 83. (d-lp/c) *(SHAH/+C 1)* **NOCTURNE (live)** [29] [–]
– Intro – The rite of Spring / Israel / Dear Prudence / Paradise place / Melt! / Cascade / Pulled to bits / Night shift / Sin in my heart / Slowdive / Painted bird / Happy house / Switch / Spellbound / Helter skelter / Eve white eve black / Voodoo dolly. *(cd-iss. Apr89 & Mar95; 839009-2)*

Mar 84. (7") *(SHE 6)* **SWIMMING HORSES. / LET GO** [28] [–]
(12"+=) *(SHEX 6)* – The humming wires.

May 84. (7") *(SHE 7)* **DAZZLE. / I PROMISE** [33] [–]
(12"+=) *(SHEX 7)* – Throw them to the lions / ('A'mix).

Jun 84. (lp/c)(cd) *(SHEH P/C 1)(821510-2) <24030>* **HYAENA** [15] [ ]
– Dazzle / We hunger / Take me back / Belladonna / Swimming horses / Bring me the head of the preacher man / Running town / Pointing bone / Blow the house down. *(re-iss. cd Mar95; same)*

— **JOHN CARRUTHERS** – guitar (ex-CLOCKDVA, ex-JEFFREY LEE PIERCE) returned to repl. SMITH who had CURE commitments.

Oct 84. (12"ep) *(SHEEP 8)* **THE THORN (live)** [47] [–]
– Voices / Placebo effect / Red over white / Overground.

Oct 85. (7") *(SHE 9)* **CITIES IN DUST. / AN EXECUTION** [21] [–]
(12"+=) *(SHEX 9)* – Quarter drawing of the dog.

Feb 86. (7") *(SHE 10)* **CANDYMAN. / LULLABY** [34] [–]
(12"+=) *(SHEX 10)* – Umbrella.

Apr 86. (lp/c)(cd) *(SHE LP/MC 3)(829145-2) <24092>* **TINDERBOX** [13] [88]
– Candyman / The sweetest chill / This unrest / Cities in dust / Cannons / Partys fall / 92° / Lands End. *(cd+=)* – An execution / Quarter drawing of the dog / Lullaby / Umbrella / Candyman (extended). *(re-iss. cd Mar95; same)*

Jan 87. (7") *(SHE 11)* **THIS WHEEL'S ON FIRE. / SHOOTING SUN** [14] [–]
(12"+=) *(SHEX 11)* – Sleepwalking (on the high wire).

Feb 87. (lp/c)(cd) *(SHE LP/MC 3)(831474-2) <24134>* **THROUGH THE LOOKING GLASS** [15] [ ]
– Hall of mirrors / Trust in me / This wheel's on fire / Strange fruit / This town ain't big enough for the both of us / You're lost little girl / The passenger / Gun / Sea breezes / Little Johnny Jewel. *(re-iss. cd Mar95; same)*

Mar 87. (7") *(SHE 12)* **THE PASSENGER. / SHE'S CUCKOO** [41] [–]
(12"+=) *(SHEX 12)* – Something blue.

— **JON KLEIN** (b. 9 May'??, Bristol, England) – guitar (ex-SPECIMEN) repl. CARRUTHERS / added **MARTIN McCARRICK** (b.29 Jul'??) – cello, keyboards (ex-MARC ALMOND, ex-The GLOVE) (to SIOUXSIE, SEVERIN, BUDGIE + KLEIN)

Jul 87. (7"/7"pic-d/c-s) *(SHE/+P/+PC 13)* **SONG FROM THE EDGE OF THE WORLD. / THE WHOLE PRICE OF BLOOD** [59] [–]
(12"+=) *(SHEX 13)* – Mechanical eyes.

Jul 88. (7"/7"g-f) *(SHE/+G 14) <27760>* **PEEK-A-BOO. / FALSE FACE** [16] [53]
(c-s+=/cd-s+=) *(SHE CS/CD 14)* – Catwalk / ('A'-Big suspender mix).
(12"+=) *(SHEXR 14)* – ('A'-2 other mixes).

Sep 88. (lp/c)(cd) *(SHE LP/MC 5)(837240-2) <24205>* **PEEPSHOW** [20] [68]
– Peek-a-boo / Killing jar / Scarecrow / Carousel / Burn-up / Ornaments of gold / Turn to stone / Rawhead and bloodybones / The last beat of my heart / Rhapsody. *(re-iss. cd Mar95; same)*

Sep 88. (7"/7"g-f/7"pic-d) *(SHE/+G/P 15)* **KILLING JAR. / SOMETHING WICKED (THIS WAY COMES)** [41] [–]
(12"+=/cd-s+=) *(SHE X/CD 15)* – Are you still dying, darling.

Nov 88. (7"/7"g-f) *(SHE/+G 16)* **THE LAST BEAT OF MY HEART. / EL DIABLO LOS MUERTOS** [44] [ ]
(12"+=) *(SHEX 16)* – Sunless.
(cd-s++=) *(SHECD 16)* – ('B'mix).

— In Autumn'89, The CREATURES issued singles and 'BOOMERANG' album.

May 91. (7"/c-s) *(SHE/+CS 19) <19031>* **KISS THEM FOR ME. / RETURN** [32] [23]
(ext-12"+=/12"pic-d+=) *(SHE X/XD 19)* – Staring back.
(cd-s++=) *(SHECD 19)* – ('A'side).

Jun 91. (cd/c/lp) *(847731-2/-4/-1)) <24387>* **SUPERSTITION** [25] [65]
– Kiss them for me / Fear (of the unknown) / Cry / Drifter / Little sister / Shadowtime / Silly thing / Got to get up / Silver waterfalls / Softly / The ghost in you. *(re-iss. cd Mar95; same)*

Jul 91. (7"/c-s) *(SHE/+CS 20)* **SHADOWTIME. / SPIRAL TWIST** [57] [ ]
(12"+=/cd-s+=) *(SHE X/CD 20)* – Sea of light. / ('A'-Eclipse mix).

— Below single from the film 'Batman Returns'.

Jul 92. (7"/c-s) *(SHE/+CS 21)* **FACE TO FACE. / I COULD BE AGAIN** [21] [ ]
(cd-s+=) *(SHECD 21)* – ('A'-catatonic mix) / Hothead.
(12") *(SHEX 21)* – ('A'side) / ('A'-catatonic mix) / Hothead.

Oct 92. (cd/c/lp) *(517160-2/-4/-1)* **TWICE UPON A TIME – THE THING** [26] [ ]
– Fireworks / Slowdive / Melt / Dear Prudence / Swimming horses / Dazzle / Overground (from The Thorn) / Cities in dust / Candyman / This wheel's on fire / The passenger / Peek-a-boo / The killing jar / The last beat of my heart / Kiss them for me / Shadowtime / Fear (of the unknown) / Face to face. *(re-iss. cd Mar95; same)*

— In Aug 94, SIOUXSIE partnered MORRISSEY on his single, 'INTERLUDE'.

Dec 94. (c-s) *(SHECS 22)* **O BABY. / OURSELVES** [34] [–]
(cd-s+=) *(SHECD 22)* – ('A'-Manhattan mix).
(cd-s) *(SHECDX 22)* – ('A'side) / Swimming horses (live) / All tomorrow's parties (live).

Jan 95. (cd/c/lp) *(523725-2/-4/-1) <24630>* **THE RAPTURE** [33] [ ]
– O baby / Tearing apart / Stargazer / Fall from grace / Not forgotten / Sick child / The lonely one / Falling down / Forever / The rapture / The double life / Love out me.

Feb 95. (7"/c-s) *(SHE/+CS 23)* **STARGAZER. / HANG ME HIGH** [64] [ ]
(cd-s+=) *(SHECD 23)* – Black Sun.
(cd-s) *(SHECDX 23)* – ('A'-Mambo sun) / ('A'-Planet queen mix) / ('A'-Mark Saunders mix).

— Split Apr'96 although SIOUXSIE and BUDGIE recorded a third album as The CREATURES. SEVERIN has written for the film 'Visions Of Ecstacy'.

– compilations, etc. –

Feb 87. (12"ep) *Strange Fruit; (SFPS 012)* **THE PEEL SESSIONS (29.11.77)** [ ] [–]
– Love in a void / Mirage / Suburban relapse / Metal postcard. *(c-ep-iss.Jun87; SFPSC 012) (cd-ep-iss.Mar88; SFPSCD 012)*

Feb 89. (12"ep/cd-ep) *Strange Fruit; (SPPS/+CD 066)* **THE PEEL SESSIONS** (Feb'78) [ ] [–]
– Hong Kong garden / Carcass / Helter skelter / Overground.

Sep 02. (cd) *Universal; (<065152-2>)* **THE BEST OF SIOUXSIE & THE BANSHEES** [ ] Nov02 [ ]
– Dear Prudence / Hong Kong garden / Cities in dust / Peek-a-boo / Happy house / KIss them for me / Face to face / Dizzy / Israel / Christine / Spellbound / Stargazer / Arabian knights / The killing jar / This wheel's on fire. *(<d-cd+=; 065150-2>)* – (bonus mixes).

the CREATURES

(SIOUXSIE & BUDGIE)

Polydor not iss.

Sep 81. (d7"ep/d7"gf-ep) *(POSP D/G 354)* **WILD THINGS** 24 –
– Mad-eyed screamer / So unreal / But not them / Wild thing / Thumb.

Wonderland Geffen

May 83. (7") *(SHE 1)* **MISS THE GIRL. / HOT SPRING IN THE SNOW** 21 –

May 83. (lp/c) *(SHE LP/MC 1)* **FEAST** 17 –
– Morning dawning / Inoa 'ole / Ice house / Dancing on glass / Gecko / Sky train / Festival of colours / Miss the girl / A strutting rooster / Flesh.

Jul 83. (7") *(SHE 2)* **RIGHT NOW. / WEATHERCADE** 14 –
(12"+=) *(SHEX 2)* – Festival of colours.

Oct 89. (7") *(SHEP 17)* **STANDING THERE. / DIVIDED** 53 –
(12"+=/cd-s+=) *(SH X/CD 17)* – Solar choir / ('A'-Andalucian mix).
('A'-La Frontera mix-10"+=) *(SHET 17)* – Solar choir.

Nov 89. (lp/c/cd) *(841463-1/-4/-2)* <24275> **BOOMERANG**
– Standing there / Manchild / You! / Pity / Killing time / Willow / Pluto drive / Solar choir * / Speeding * / Fury eyes / Fruitman / Untiedundone * / Simoom * / Strolling wolf / Venus sands / Morriha. *(extra tracks on cd= *)*

Feb 90. (7"/7"box) *(SHE/+B 18)* **FURY EYES. / ABSTINENCE** –
(12"/cd-s) *(SHE P/CD 18)* – ('A'-20/20 mix) / ('A'dub) / ('A'-Fever mix).

Sioux Record Of Substance

Jun 98. (7") *(SIOUX 1)* **SAD CUNT. / SAD CUNT (chix'n'dix mix)** –

Aug 98. (10"ep/cd-ep) *(SIOUX 2 V/CD)* <1> **ERASER CUTS**
– Pinned down / Guillotine / Thank you / Slipping away.

Oct 98. (7"green) *(SIOUX 3V)* **2ND FLOOR. / TURN IT ON** –
(12"on 'Hydrogen Jukebox'+=)(cd-s+=) *(DUKE 044DJV)(SIOUX 3CD)* – ('A'-Girl eats boy mix) / ('A'-Emperor Sly mix).

Dec 98. (cd-ep) *(SIOUX 5CD)* **EXTERMINATING ANGEL** – mail-o –
– Exordium (one night in France) / Interim (NYC & Paris) / Remake (the James Hardway) / Remodel (album mix).

Sioux Instinct

Feb 99. (cd/c/2x10"lp) *(SIOUX 4 CD/C/V)* <413> **ANIMA ANIMUS**
– 2nd floor / Disconnected / Turn it on / Take mine / Say / I was me / Prettiest thing / Exterminating angel / Another planet / Don't go to sleep without me.

Mar 99. (7"clear) *(SIOUX 6V)* **SAY. / ALL SHE COULD ASK FOR** 72 –
(cd-s) *(SIOUX 6CD)* – ('A'side) / Broken.
(cd-s) *(SIOUX 6CDX)* – ('A'-Witchman remix) / ('A'-Justice & Endemic void remix).

Mar 99. (12"ltd) *(DUKE 055DJV)* **SAY (Witchman 4x4 mix). / THANK YOU (Dub Pistols brings you joy mix)** –

Jul 99. (12"ltd) *(DUKE 064DJV)* **DISCONNECTING (Beloved's mix). / PRETTIEST THING (Super Chumbo's mix)** –
(above singles on 'Hydrogen Dukebox')

Sep 99. (10"blue/cd-s) *(SIOUX 9 V/CD)* **PRETTIEST THING (Super Chumbo's waking dream mix) / TURN IT ON (Emperor Sly's elemental mix) / GUILLOTINE (bitten by the black dog)** –
(cd-s) *(SIOUX 9CDX)* – ('A'-mixes; Howie B hormonal / album / subsonic legacy).

Nov 99. (cd/d-lp) *(DUKE 066 CD/DJV)* <433> **HYBRIDS** (remixes)
(re-iss. Aug01; same)

Dec 00. (m-cd) <516> **U.S. RETRACE** (compilation) –
– Pinned down / Guillotine / Turn it on (bound 'n' gagged mix) / All she could ask for / Broken / Turn it on (Emperor Sly's elemental mix) / Thank you / Slipping away.

Sioux Sioux

Jun 01. (cd) <79611> **SEQUINS IN THE SUN** (compilation) –
– All she could ask for / Disconnected / Turn it on / Take mine / Pinned down / Guillotine / 2nd floor / Pluto drive – Nightclubbing / Prettiest thing / Exterminating angel.

Oct 03. (cd-s) *(SIOUX 14)* **GODZILLA! / (instrumental) / (video)** 53 –

Oct 03. (d-cd) *(SIOUXDCD 15)* **HAI!** –
– Say yes! / Around the world / Seven tears / Godzilla! / Imagoro / Tourniquet / Further nearer / City island / Tantara! // (instrumental versions). *(cd re-iss. Sep05 w/dvd; SIOUX 18CD)* – (drumming session video).

the GLOVE

(SEVERIN & ROBERT SMITH) also incl. **MARTIN McCARRICK** – cello / **ANNE STEPHENSON** + **GINNY HEWES** – strings / **ANDY ANDERSON** – drums / (JEANETTE) **LANDRAY** – dual vocals w/**SMITH**

Wonderland Rough Trade

Aug 83. (7") *(SHE 3)* **LIKE AN ANIMAL. / MOUTH TO MOUTH** 52 –
(12"+=) *(SHEX 3)* – Animal (club mix).

Aug 83. (lp/c) *(SHE LP/MC 2)* <ROUGHUS 85> **BLUE SUNSHINE** 35
– Like an animal / Looking glass girl / Sex-eye-make-up / Mr. Alphabet says / A blues in drag / Punish me with kisses / This green city / Orgy / Perfect murder / Relax. *(re-iss. Sep90 lp/c/cd+=; 815019-1/-4/-2)* – Mouth to mouth / The tightrope / Like an animal (club mix).

Nov 83. (7") *(SHE 5)* **PUNISH ME WITH KISSES. / THE TIGHTROPE** –

the SISTERS OF MERCY

Formed: Leeds, England ... 1980 by frontman/lyricist extraordinaire, ANDREW ELDRITCH along with guitarist, GARY MARX. The original "goth" combo, ELDRITCH and Co. were among the first acts to define the genre in its lasting image of black-clad, po-faced rockers meditating on dark, impenetrable lyrics, decipherable only for those willing to substitute make-up for flour or wear pointy boots (and, more importantly, never to emerge in daylight!). For their early releases, the group employed a drum machine, christened Doktor Avalanche, issuing material on their self-financed label, 'Merciful Release'. Following the debut single, 'DAMAGE DONE', ELDRITCH and MARX recruited guitarist BENN GUNN and bassist CRAIG ADAMS, fleshing out the sound on a further series of 7 and 12 inchers, the 'ALICE' EP drawing widespread interest with its goth/alternative/dance fusion. GUNN was then replaced with ex-DEAD OR ALIVE guitarist, WAYNE HUSSEY, for the piledriving theatrics of 'TEMPLE OF LOVE'. During this time, the group had also built up a live reputation, supporting the likes of the BIRTHDAY PARTY and the PSYCHEDELIC FURS as well as appearing at the Leeds Futurama festival. Word was spreading, and in 1984, the SISTERS OF MERCY and their label were signed to a worldwide deal with 'WEA'. A debut album, 'FIRST AND LAST AND ALWAYS', appeared the following year, a worthwhile effort which saw the group almost break into the UK Top 10. Yet only a month after the record's release, the band announced they were to split, tension between ELDRITCH and MARX resulting in the latter leaving the group first. After a final concert at London's Royal Albert Hall, a bitter legal battle ensued between ELDRITCH and ADAMS/HUSSEY. At stake was the SISTERS OF MERCY moniker, ELDRITCH eventually winning out, though not before he'd hastily released a single and album, 'GIFT' (1986), under The SISTERHOOD, primarily to prevent ADAMS and HUSSEY using the title. The latter two subsequently formed The MISSION while ELDRITCH relocated to Berlin/Hamburg, retaining ex-GUN CLUB bassist, PATRICIA MORRISON (who'd played on 'GIFT') and recording 'FLOODLAND' (1987) with the help of his ever-faithful drum machine. The preceding single, 'THIS CORROSION' was suitably grandiose, all ominous vocals and OTT production courtesy of JIM STEINMAN, the single giving ELDRITCH his first UK Top 10 hit. The album achieved a similar feat, incorporating a more overtly rhythmic feel to create a kind of doom-disco sound (perfect for goths who couldn't dance anyway!). MORRISON subsequently left, ELDRITCH recruiting an array of diverse musicians including TIM BREICHENO, ANDREAS BRUHN and punk veteran, TONY JAMES (ex-SIGUE SIGUE SPUTNIK, ex-GENERATION X) to record 'VISION THING' (1990). Employing a more commercial hard rock sound, 'MORE' was one of The SISTERS' most effective singles to date while again the album was a Top 20 success. Further acclaim came in 1992 with the surprisingly consistent retrospective, 'SOME GIRLS WANDER BY MISTAKE' (1992), and its attendant single, a brilliant re-vamp of 'TEMPLE OF LOVE', Israeli warbler, OFRA HAZA, adding that extra mystical touch. After a 1991 joint tour with PUBLIC ENEMY (nice idea, but probably taking the Lollapollooza ethic a bit too far) was abandoned after poor ticket sales, not much has been heard from The SISTERS OF MERCY. ELDRITCH remains an enigmatic figure, any significant activity normally resulting in intense interest from the music press. The odds are that he'll return, though whether in the guise of The SISTERS OF MERCY remains to be seen.

• **Covered:** EMMA (Hot Chocolate) / 1969 (Stooges) / GIMME SHELTER (Rolling Stones) / KNOCKIN' ON HEAVEN'S DOOR (Bob Dylan).

Album rating: FIRST AND LAST AND ALWAYS (*8) / GIFT (*7; as Sisterhood) / FLOODLAND (*8) / VISION THING (*7) / SOME GIRLS WANDER BY MISTAKE compilation (*8) / GREATEST HITS VOLUME 1 – A SLIGHT CASE OF OVERBOMBING compilation (*7)

ANDREW ELDRITCH (b. ANDREW TAYLOR, 15 May'59, East Anglia, England) – vocals / **GARRY MARX** (b. MARK PEARMAN) – guitar / + drum machine DOKTOR AVALANCHE

Merciful Release | not iss.

1980. (7"m) *(MR 7)* **THE DAMAGE DONE. / WATCH / HOME OF THE HITMAN** [ ] [–]

— added **BEN GUNN** (b. BENJAMIN MATTHEWS) – guitar / **CRAIG ADAMS** (b. 4 Apr'62) – bass (ex-EXPELAIRES)

C.N.T. | not iss.

Feb 82. (7") *(CNT 002)* **BODY ELECTRIC. / ADRENOCHROME** [ ] [–]

Merciful | BrainEater

Nov 82. (7") *(MR 015)* **ALICE. / FLOORSHOW** [ ] [–]
Mar 83. (7") *(MR 019)* **ANACONDA. / PHANTOM** [ ] [–]
Apr 83. (12"ep) *(MR 021)* **ALICE. / FLOORSHOW / 1969 / PHANTOM** [ ] [ ]
May 83. (12"ep) *(MR 023)* **THE REPTILE HOUSE** [ ]
– Kiss the carpet / Lights / Valentine / Burn / Fix. *(re-iss. Apr94)*

— **WAYNE HUSSEY** (b. JERRY LOVELOCK, 26 May'58, Bristol, England) – guitar (ex-DEAD OR ALIVE, ex-HAMBI & THE DANCE) repl. BEN

Oct 83. (7") *(MR 027)* **TEMPLE OF LOVE. / HEARTLAND** [ ] [–]
(ext.12"+=) *(MRX 027)* – Gimme shelter.
Jun 84. (7"; as The SISTERS) *(MR 029)* **BODY AND SOUL. / TRAIN** [46] [–]
(12"+=) *(MR 029T)* – After hours / Body electric.

Merciful Release | Elektra

Oct 84. (7") *(MR 033)* **WALK AWAY. / POISON DOOR** [45] [–]
(above w/free 7"flexi) *(MR 033 – SAM 218)* – Long Train.
(12"+=) *(MR 033T)* – On the wire.
Feb 85. (7") *(MR 035)* **NO TIME TO CRY. / BLOOD MONEY** [63] [–]
(12"+=) *(MR 035T)* – Bury me deep.
Mar 85. (lp/c) *(MR 337 L/C)* <60405> **FIRST AND LAST AND ALWAYS** [14] [ ]
– Black planet / Walk away / No time to cry / A rock and a hard place / Marian / First and last and always / Possession / Nine while nine / Amphetamine logic / Some kind of stranger. *(cd-iss. Jul88; 240616-2) (re-iss. re-mastered.Jul92 on 'East West' lp/c; MR 571 L/C) (cd re-mast.Jun92; 9031 77379-2)*

— disbanded mid-'85 ... GARRY MARX helped form GHOST DANCE. HUSSEY and ADAMS formed The MISSION after squabbles with ANDREW over use of group name.

— **ELDRITCH** with ever faithful drum machine adopted

the SISTERHOOD

— recruited **PATRICIA MORRISON** (b.14 Jan'62) – bass, vocals (ex-FUR BIBLE, ex-GUN CLUB) / **JAMES RAY** – guitar / **ALAN VEGA** – synthesizers (ex-SUICIDE) / **LUCAS FOX** – drums (ELDRITCH moved to Berlin, Germany)

Merciful | not iss.

Feb 86. (7") *(SIS 001)* **GIVING GROUND (remix). / GIVING GROUND (album version)** [ ] [–]
Jul 86. (lp/c) *(SIS 020/+C)* **GIFT** [90] [–]
– Jihad / Colours / Giving ground / Finland red, Egypt white / Rain from Heaven. *(cd-iss. Sep89; SIS 020CD) (re-iss. Jul94 cd/c; 1131684-2/-4)*

— JAMES RAY went solo (backed with The PERFORMANCE), subsequently issuing a couple of 45's, 'MEXICO SUNDOWN BLUES' and 'TEXAS', for 'Merciful Release'. At the turn of the decade, he and his new outfit, JAMES RAY'S GANGWAR, issued a few more, 'DUSTBOAT' and 'WITHOUT CONSCIENCE', the former from a part compilation set, 'A NEW KIND OF ASSASSIN' (1989). In 1992 and '93, the band delivered two more, 'DIOS ESTA DE NUESTRO LADO' and 'THIRD GENERATION'.

the SISTERS OF MERCY

— were once again **ELDRITCH + MORRISON** obtaining rights to name

Merciful-WEA | Elektra

Sep 87. (7") *(MR 39)* **THIS CORROSION. / TORCH** [7] [ ]
(c-s+=/12"+=/cd-s+=) *(MR 39 C/T/CD)* – Colours.
Nov 87. (lp/c)(cd) *(MR 441 L/C)(242246-2)* <60762> **FLOODLAND** [9] [ ]
– Dominion / Mother Russia / Flood I / Lucretia my reflection / 1959 / This corrosion / Flood II / Driven like the snow / Neverlan. *(c+=)*– Torch. *(cd-s++=)* – Colours.
Feb 88. (7") *(MR 43)* **DOMINION. / SANDSTORM / UNTITLED** [13] [–]
(d12"+=) *(MR 43TB)* – Emma.
(c-s+=/3"cd-s+=) *(MR 43 C/CD)* – Ozy-Mandias.
May 88. (7"/ext.12"/ext.3"cd-s) *(MR 44/+T/CD)* **LUCRETIA MY REFLECTION. / LONG TRAIN** [20] [ ]

— (Feb'90) **ELDRITCH** w/drum machine, recruited complete new line-up / **TONY JAMES** (b.1956) – bass, vocals (ex-SIGUE SIGUE SPUTNIK, ex-GENERATION X) / **ANDREAS BRUHN** (b. 5 Nov'67, Hamburg, Germany) – guitar / **TIM BRICHENO** (b. 6 Jul'63, Huddersfield, England) – guitar (ex-ALL ABOUT EVE) / guests were **MAGGIE REILLY** – b.vocals (ex-MIKE OLDFIELD) / **JOHN PERRY** – guitar (ex-ONLY ONES)

Oct 90. (7"/c-s) *(MR 47/+C)* <66595> **MORE. / YOU COULD BE THE ONE** [21] [ ]
(cd-s+=/cd-s+=) *(MR 47CD/+X)* – ('A'extended).
Oct 90. (cd)(c/lp) *(9031 72663-2)(MR 449 C/L)* <61017> **VISION THING** [11] [ ]
– Vision thing / Ribons / Destination Boulevard / Something fast / When you don't see me / Doctor Jeep / More / I was wrong. *(cd re-iss. Jul00; same)*
Dec 90. (7") *(MR 51)* **DOCTOR JEEP. / KNOCKIN' ON HEAVEN'S DOOR (live)** [37] [ ]
(12"+=/cd-s+=) *(MR 51 T/CD)* – ('A'extended).
(ext.12") *(MR 51TX)* – Burn (live) / Amphetamine logic (live).

— (Oct91) **TONY JAMES** split from ELDRITCH amicably.

— Next featured vocals by **OFRA HAZA**

East West | Elektra

Apr 92. (7") *(MR 53)* **TEMPLE OF LOVE (1992). / I WAS WRONG (American fade)** [3] [ ]
(ext.12"+=) *(MR 53T)* – Vision thing (Canadian club mix).
(cd-s+=) *(MR 53CD)* – When you don't see me (German release).
Apr 92. (cd)(c/d-lp) *(9031 76476-2)(MR 449 C/L)* <61306> **SOME GIRLS WANDER BY MISTAKE** (1980-1983 material) [5] [ ]
– Alice / Floorshow / Phantom / 1969 / Kiss the carpet / Lights / Valentine / Fix / Burn / Kiss the carpet (reprise) / Temple of love / Heartland / Gimme shelter / Damage done / Watch / Home of the hitmen / Body electric / Adrenochrome / Anaconda.

— now just **ANDREW ELDRITCH** on own with guests

Aug 93. (7"/c-s) *(MR 59/+C)* **UNDER THE GUN. / ALICE (1993)** [19] [–]
(12"+=/cd-s+=) *(MR 59 T/CD)* – ('A'-Jutland mix).
Aug 93. (cd/c/d-lp) *(4509 93579-2/-4/-1)* <61399-2/-4> **GREATEST HITS VOLUME 1 – A SLIGHT CASE OF OVERBOMBING** (compilation) [14] [ ]
– Under the gun / Temple of love (1992) / Vision thing / Detonation boulevard / Doctor Jeep / More / Lucretia my reflection / Dominion – Mother / This corrosion / No time to cry / Walk away / Body and soul.

— ELDRITCH and his gang seem to have split from the music scene

– compilations, etc. –

Jan 94. (cd) *Cleopatra;* <(CLEO 6642CD)> **FIRST, LAST FOREVER** [ ] [ ]

SLADE

Formed: Wolverhampton, Midlands, England ... 1964 as the VENDORS, by DAVE HILL and DON POWELL, becoming the IN-BE-TWEENS the following year and recording a demo EP for French label, 'Barclay'. Their official debut 45, 'YOU BETTER RUN' (with newcomers NODDY HOLDER and JIMMY LEA), flopped late in '66, the group retiring from studio activity until 1969 when they became AMBROSE SLADE at the suggestion of Fontana's Jack Baverstock. A belated debut album, 'BEGINNINGS', sold poorly although ex-ANIMALS bass player, CHAS CHANDLER, recognised the band's potential after spotting them performing in a London night club (the band now residing in the capital) and subsequently became their manager/producer. Kitted out in bovver boots, jeans, shirt and braces, SLADE topped their newly adopted 'ard look with skinheads all round, CHANDLER moulding the band's image and sound in an attempt to distance them from the fading hippy scene. Although they attracted a sizable grassroots following, SLADE's appropriately titled first album, 'PLAY IT LOUD' (on 'Polydor') failed to translate into sales. However, they finally cracked the UK Top 20 in May 1971 via a rousing cover of Bobby Marchan's 'GET DOWN AND GET WITH IT', the track bringing SLADE into the living rooms of the nation through a Top Of The Pops appearance. By this point, HOLDER and Co. had grown some hair, painted their boots sci-fi silver and initiated the roots of "Slademania" (foot-stomping now all the rage). The noisy, gravel-throated HOLDER (complete with tartan trousers, top hat and mutton-chop sideburns), the bare-chested, glitter-flecked HILL and the not so flamboyant LEA and POWELL, became part of the glam-metal brigade later in the year, 'COZ I LUV YOU' hitting the top of the charts for 4 weeks. Competing with the likes of GARY GLITTER, T. REX and SWEET, the lads amassed a string of anthemic UK chart toppers over the ensuing two years, namely 'TAKE ME BACK 'OME', 'MAMA WEER ALL CRAZEE NOW', 'CUM ON FEEL THE NOIZE', 'SKWEEZE ME PLEEZE ME' and the perennial festive fave 'MERRY XMAS EVERYBODY'. The noize level was markedly lower on the pop-ballad, 'EVERYDAY' (1974), a song that only hit No.3, glam-rock/pop shuddering to a halt around the same time. Their chart-topping albums, 'SLAYED?' (1972), 'SLADEST' (1973) and 'OLD NEW BORROWED AND BLUE' (1974) were now shoved to the back of people's record collections, PINK FLOYD, MIKE OLDFIELD and GENESIS now vying for the attention of the more discerning rock fan. Late '74 saw the release of a film/rockumentary 'FLAME'; issued as an album, it only managed a Top 10 placing. SLADE found it even harder to compete with the burgeoning punk/new wave scene, only re-emerging into the Top 10 in 1981 with 'WE'LL BRING THE HOUSE DOWN', released on their own 'Cheapskate' records. Three years later, the loveable rogues with the 'Bermingim' accent scored yet again, 'MY OH MY' just narrowly missing the No.1 spot, while the follow-up, 'RUN RUNAWAY' made the Top 10. Both records surprised observers by cracking the elusive US charts, the former hitting No.37, the latter No.20; a year previously, metal act, QUIET RIOT had taken Slade's 'CUM ON FEEL THE NOIZE' into the US Top 5 and subsequently charted with another, 'MAMA WEER ALL CRAZEE NOW'. SLADE continued on their merry way, untroubled by the fashion crimes of the 80's. The following decade saw the band chart once more, 'RADIO WALL OF SOUND' blasting out HOLDER's frantic yell to an appreciative Kerrang!- friendly audience. The jovial HOLDER has regained his footing as a celebrity in the 90's, VIC REEVES and BOB MORTIMER giving him and SLADE the highest accolade by inventing a whole series of irreverent sketches based around the band. OASIS, too, have contributed to the cult of NODDY, regularly performing 'CUM ON FEEL THE NOIZE' on stage.

• **Songwriters:** HOLDER-LEA or LEA-POWELL penned except IN-BETWEENS:- TAKE A HEART (Sorrows) / CAN YOUR MONKEY DO THE DOG (Rufus Thomas) / YOU BETTER RUN (Rascals). AMBROSE SLADE:- BORN TO BE WILD (Steppenwolf) / AIN'T GOT NO HEAT (Frank Zappa) / IF THIS WORLD WERE MINE (Marvin Gaye) / FLY ME HIGH (Justin Hayward) / MARTHA MY DEAR (Beatles) / JOURNEY TO THE CENTER OF MY MIND (Ted Nugent). SLADE:- THE SHAPE OF THINGS TO COME (Max Frost & The Troopers; Mann-weill) / ANGELINA (Neil Innes) / COULD I (Griffin-Royer) / JUST A LITTLE BIT (?) / DARLING BE HOME SOON (Lovin' Spoonful) / LET THE GOOD TIMES ROLL (Shirley & Lee) / MY BABY LEFT ME – THAT'S ALL RIGHT (Elvis Presley) / PISTOL PACKIN' MAMA (Gene Vincent) / SOMETHIN' ELSE (Eddie Cochran) / OKEY COKEY (seasonal; trad) / HI HO SILVER LINING (Jeff Beck) / STILL THE SAME (Bob Seger) / YOU'LL NEVER WALK ALONE (Rogers-Hammerstein) / AULD LANG SYNE (trad.) / SANTA CLAUS IS COMING TO TOWN (festive) / LET'S DANCE (Chris Montez) / etc.

Album rating: Ambrose Slade: BEGINNINGS (*4) / Slade: PLAY IT LOUD (*4) / SLADE ALIVE! (*5) / SLAYED? (*6) / SLADEST compilation (*7) / OLD, NEW, BORROWED AND BLUE (*5) / FLAME soundtrack (*7) / NOBODY'S FOOLS (*5) / WHATEVER HAPPENED TO SLADE (*4) / SLADE ALIVE VOL.2 (*5) / RETURN TO BASE (*4) / WE'LL BRING THE HOUSE DOWN (*5) / TILL DEAF US DO PART (*4) / ON STAGE (*5) / THE AMAZING KAMIKAZE SYNDROME (*4) / ROGUES GALLERY (*4) / YOU BOYZ MAKE BIG NOIZE (*4) / WALL OF HITS compilation (*6) / FEEL THE NOIZE: THE VERY BEST OF SLADE compilation (*8)

the IN-BE-TWEENS

JOHNNY HOWELLS – vocals / **MICKEY MARSTON** – guitar / **DAVE HILL** (b. 4 Apr'52, Fleet Castle, Devon, England) – guitar / **DAVE JONES** – bass / **DON POWELL** (10 Sep'50, Bilston, Staffordshire) – drums

Barclay | not iss.

1965. (7"ep) **TAKE A HEART / LITTLE NIGHTINGALE. / (2 tracks by 'The Hills')** – France –

1965. (7"ep) **TAKE A HEART. / CAN YOUR MONKEY DO THE DOG / OOP OOP I DO** – France –

— **NODDY HOLDER** (b. NEVILLE HOLDER, 15 Jun'50, Walsall, England) – vox, guitar repl. HOWELLS / **JIM LEA** (b.14 Jun'52, Wolverhampton) – bass, piano repl. MARSTON + JONES

Columbia | not iss.

Nov 66. (7"; as N' BETWEENS) *(DB 8080)* **YOU BETTER RUN. / EVIL WITCHMAN** –

AMBROSE SLADE

(HOLDER, HILL, LEA + POWELL)

Fontana | Fontana

Apr 69. (lp) *(STL 5492) <67592>* **BEGINNINGS**
– Genesis / Everybody's next one / Knocking nails into my house / Roach daddy / Ain't got no heat / Pity the mother / Mad dog Cole / Fly me high / If this world were mine / Martha my dear / Born to be wild / Journey to the centre of my mind. *(re-iss. Jun91 & Jun99 on 'Polydor' cd/c; 849 185-2/-4)*

May 69. (7") *(TF 1015)* **GENESIS. / ROACH DADDY** –

SLADE

(same line-up + label)

Oct 69. (7") *(TF 1056)* **WILD WINDS ARE BLOWING. / ONE WAY HOTEL** –

Mar 70. (7") *(TF 1079)* **SHAPE OF THINGS TO COME. / C'MON C'MON** –

Polydor | Cotillion

Sep 70. (7") *(2058 054)* **KNOW WHO YOU ARE. / DAPPLE ROSE** –

Nov 70. (lp) *(2383 026) <9035>* **PLAY IT LOUD**
– Raven / See us here / Dapple rose / Could I / One way hotel / The shape of things to come / Know who you are / I remember / Pouk Hill / Angelina / Dirty joker / Sweet box. *(re-iss. Jun91 cd/c; 849 178-2/-4)*

May 71. (7"m) *(2058 112) <44128>* **GET DOWN AND GET WITH IT. / DO YOU WANT ME / THE GOSPEL ACCORDING TO RASPUTIN** 16

Polydor Polydor

Oct 71. (7") *(2058 155)* **COZ I LUV YOU. / LIFE IS NATURAL** [1] [-]
Jan 72. (7") *(2058 195)* <15041> **LOOK WOT YOU DUN. / CANDIDATE** [4] [ ]
Jan 72. (7") <15044> **COZ I LOVE YOU. / GOTTA KEEP A-ROCKIN' (live)** [-] [ ]
Mar 72. (lp) *(2383 101)* <5508> **SLADE ALIVE! (live)** [2] [ ]
– Hear me calling / In like a shot from my gun / Darling be home soon / Know who you are / Gotta keep on rockin' / Get down and get with it / Born to be wild. *(re-iss. Nov84 lp/c; SPE LP/MC 84) (re-iss. Jun91 cd/c; 841 114-2/-4)*
May 72. (7") *(2058 231)* <15046> **TAKE ME BAK 'OME. / WONDERIN'** [1] Sep72 [97]
Aug 72. (7") *(2058 274)* <15053> **MAMA WEER ALL CRAZEE NOW. / MAN WHO SPEAKS EVIL** [1] Nov72 [76]
Nov 72. (7") *(2058 312)* <15060> **GUDBUY T'JANE. / I WON'T LET IT 'APPEN AGAIN** [2] Mar73 [68]
Dec 72. (lp)(c) *(2383 163)* <5524> **SLAYED?** [1] [69]
– How d'you ride / The whole world's goin' craze / Look at last nite / I won't let it 'appen again / Move over / Gudbuy t'Jane / Gudbuy gudbuy / Mama weer all crazee now / I don't mind / Let the good times roll. *(cd-iss. May91; 849 180-2)*
Feb 73. (7") *(2058 339)* <15069> **CUM ON FEEL THE NOIZE. / I'M MEE, I'M NOW AN' THAT'S ORL** [1] May73 [98]
Jun 73. (7") *(2058 377)* **SKWEEZE ME PLEEZE ME. / KILL 'EM AT THE HOT CLUB TONITE** [1] [-]
Jul 73. (7") <15080> **LET THE GOOD TIMES ROLL. / FEEL SO FINE – I DON' MINE** [-] [ ]

Polydor Reprise

Sep 73. (7") *(2058 407)* **MY FRIEND STAN. / MY TOWN** [2] [-]
Sep 73. (lp) *(2442 119)* <2173> **SLADEST** (compilation) [1] [ ]
– Wild things are blowing / Shape of things to come / Know who you are / Pounk Hill / One way hotel / Get down and get with it / Coz I luv you / Look wot you dun / Tak me bak ome / Mama weer all crazee now / Gudbuy t'Jane / Look at last night / Cum on feel the noize / Skweeze me pleeze me. *(cd-iss. Mar93; 837 103-2)*
Sep 73. (7") <1182> **SKWEEZE ME PLEEZE ME. / MY TOWN** [-] [ ]

Polydor Warners

Dec 73. (7") *(2058 422)* <7759> **MERRY XMAS EVERYBODY. / DON'T BLAME ME** [1] [ ]
(re-iss. Dec80, Dec81 (No.32), Dec82 (No.67), Dec83 (No.20), Dec84 (No.47).
Feb 74. (lp) *(2383 261)* <2770> **OLD NEW BORROWED AND BLUE** <US title 'STOMP YOUR HANDS, CLAP YOUR FEET'> [1] [ ]
– Just want a little bit / When the lights are out / My town / Find yourself a rainbow / Miles out to sea / We're really gonna raise the roof / Do we still do it / How can it be / Don't blame me / My friend Stan / Everyday / Good time gals. *(cd-iss. May91; 849 181-2)*
Mar 74. (7") *(2058 453)* <7777> **EVERYDAY. / GOOD TIME GALS** [3] [ ]
Jun 74. (7") *(2058 492)* **THE BANGIN' MAN. / SHE DID IT TO ME** [3] [-]
Jul 74. (7") <7808> **WHEN THE LIGHTS ARE OUT. / HOW CAN IT BE** [-] [ ]
Oct 74. (7") *(2058 522)* **FAR FAR AWAY. / O.K. YESTERDAY WAS YESTERDAY** [2] [-]
Nov 74. (lp) *(2442 126)* <2865> **FLAME** (soundtrack) [6] [93]
– How does it feel? / Them kinda monkeys can't swing / So far so good / Summer song (wishing you were here) / O.K. yesterday was yesterday / Far far away / This girl / Lay it down / Heaven knows / Standin' on the corner. *(re-iss. Nov82 on 'Action Replay'; REPLAY 1000) (cd-iss. May91; 849 182-2)*
Feb 75. (7") *(2058 547)* **HOW DOES IT FEEL? / SO FAR SO GOOD** [15] [-]
Apr 75. (7") <8134> **HOW DOES IT FEEL. / O.K. YESTERDAY WAS YESTERDAY** [-] [ ]
May 75. (7") *(2058 585)* **THANKS FOR THE MEMORY (WHAM BAM THANK YOU MAM). / RAINING IN MY CHAMPAGNE** [7] [-]
Nov 75. (7") *(2058 663)* **IN FOR A PENNY. / CAN YOU JUST IMAGINE** [11] [-]
Jan 76. (7") *(2058 690)* **LET'S CALL IT QUITS. / WHEN THE CHIPS ARE DOWN** [11] [-]
Mar 76. (lp) *(2383 377)* <2936> **NOBODY'S FOOLS** [14] [ ]
– Nobody's fools / Do the dirty / Let's call it quits / Pack up your troubles / In for a penny / Get on up / L.A. jinx / Did your mama ever tell ya / Scratch my back / I'm a talker / All the world is a stage. *(cd-iss. May91; 849 183-2)*
Apr 76. (7") *(2058 716)* **NOBODY'S FOOL. / L.A. JINX** [ ] [-]
Apr 76. (7") <8185> **NOBODY'S FOOL. / WHEN THE CHIPS ARE DOWN** [-] [ ]

Barn-Polydor not iss.

Feb 77. (7") *(2014 105)* **GYPSY ROADHOG. / FOREST FULL OF NEEDLES** [48] [-]
Mar 77. (lp) *(2314 103)* **WHATEVER HAPPENED TO SLADE** [ ] [-]
– Be / Lightning never strikes twice / Gypsy roadhog / Dogs of vengeance / When fantasy calls / One eyed Jacks with moustaches / Big apple blues / Dead men tell no tales / She's got the lot / It ain't love but it ain't bad / The soul, the fall and the motion. *(cd-iss. May93; 849 184-2)*
Apr 77. (7") *(2014 106)* **BURNING IN THE HEAT OF LOVE. / READY STEADY KIDS** [ ] [-]
Oct 77. (7") *(2014 114)* **MY BABY LEFT ME – THAT'S ALL RIGHT (Medley). / O.H.M.S.** [32] [-]
Mar 78. (7") *(2014 121)* **GIVE US A GOAL. / DADDIO** [ ] [-]
Oct 78. (7") *(2014 127)* **ROCK'N'ROLL BOLERO. / MY BABY'S GOT IT** [ ] [-]
Nov 78. (lp) *(2314 106)* **SLADE ALIVE VOL.2** [ ] [-]
– Get on up / Take me bak 'ome / Medley: My baby left me – That's all right / Be / Mama weer all crazee now / Burning in the heat of love / Everyday / Gudbuy t' Jane / One-eyed Jacks with moustaches / C'mon feel the noize. *(cd-iss. May93; 849 179-2)*

Barn not iss.

Mar 79. (7"yellow) *(BARN 002)* **GINNY GINNY. / DIZZY MAMA** [ ] [-]
Oct 79. (7") *(BARN 010)* **SIGN OF THE TIMES. / NOT TONIGHT JOSEPHINE** [ ] [-]
Oct 79. (lp) *(NARB 003)* **RETURN TO BASE** [ ] [-]
– Wheels ain't coming down / Hold on to your hats / Chakeeta / Don't waste your time / Sign of the times / I'm a rocker / Nuts, bolts and screws / My baby's got it / I'm mad / Lemme love into ya / Ginny, Ginny.
Dec 79. (7") *(BARN 011)* **OKEY COKEY. / MY BABY'S GOT IT** [ ] [-]

Cheapskate not iss.

Sep 80. (7"ep) *(CHEAP 5)* **SLADE ALIVE AT READING '80 (live)** [44] [-]
– When I'm dancing I ain't fightin' / Born to be wild / Somethin' else / Pistol packin' mama / Keep a rollin'.
Nov 80. (7") *(CHEAP 11)* **MERRY XMAS EVERYBODY. / OKEY COKEY / GET DOWN AND GET WITH IT** [70] [-]
Jan 81. (7") *(CHEAP 16)* **WE'LL BRING THE HOUSE DOWN. / HOLD ON TO YOUR HATS** [10] [-]
Mar 81. (lp/c) *(SKATE/KAT 1)* **WE'LL BRING THE HOUSE DOWN** [25] [-]
– Night starvation / Wheels ain't coming down / I'm a rocker / Nuts, bolts and screws / We'll bring the house down / Dizzy mama / Hold on to your hats / Lemme love into ya / My baby's got it / When I'm dancing I ain't fightin'. *(cd-iss. Nov96 on 'Castle'; CLACD 418) (cd re-iss. Sep99; 547412-2)*
Mar 81. (7") *(CHEAP 21)* **WHEELS AIN'T COMING DOWN. / NOT TONIGHT JOSEPHINE** [60] [-]
May 81. (7") *(CHEAP 24)* **KNUCKLE SANDWICH NANCY. / I'M MAD** [ ] [-]

R.C.A. CBS-Assc

Sep 81. (7") *(RCA 124)* **LOCK UP YOUR DAUGHTERS. / SIGN OF THE TIMES** [29] [-]
Nov 81. (lp/c) *(RCA LP/K 6021)* **TILL DEAF US DO PART** [ ] [-]
– Rock and roll preacher (hallelujah I'm on fire) / Ruby red / Lock up your daughters / Till deaf us do part / That was no lady that was my wife / She brings out the devil in me / A night to remember / M'hat m'coat / It's your body not your mind / Let the rock and roll out of control / Knuckle sandwich Nancy / Till deaf resurrected. *(cd-iss. Apr93 & Nov96 on 'Castle'; CLACD 377 & 415) (cd re-iss. Sep99, 547407-2)*
Mar 82. (7") *(RCA 191)* **RUBY RED. / FUNK PUNK AND JUNK** [51] [-]
(d7"+=) *(RCAD 191)* – Rock'n'roll preacher (live) / Take me back 'ome (live).
Nov 82. (7") *(RCA 291)* **(AND NOW – THE WALTZ) C'EST LA VIE. / MERRY XMAS EVERYBODY (ALIVE & KICKIN')** [50] [-]
Dec 82. (lp/c) *(RCA LP/K 3107)* **ON STAGE (live)** [ ] [-]
– Rock and roll preacher / When I'm dancing I ain't fightin' / Tak me bak 'ome / Everyday / Lock up your daughters / We'll bring the house down / A night to remember / Mama weer all crazee now / Gudbuy t'Jane / You'll never walk alone. *(cd-iss. Jul93 & Nov96 on 'Castle'; CLACD 380 & 420) (cd re-iss. Sep99; 547413-2)*

Nov 83. (7"m) *(RCA 373)* **MY OH MY. / MERRY XMAS EVERYBODY (live) / KEEP YOUR HANDS OFF MY POWER SUPPLY** 2 –

Dec 83. (lp/c) *(PL/PK 70116)* **THE AMAZING KAMIKAZE SYNDROME** 49 –
– Slam the hammer down / In the doghouse / Run runaway / High and dry / My oh my / Cocky rock boys / Ready to explode / (And now – The waltz) C'est la vie / Cheap 'n' nasty love / Razzle dazzle man. *(cd-iss. Apr93 & Nov96 on 'Castle'; CLACD 381 & 419) (cd re-iss. Sep99; 547411-2)*

Jan 84. (7"/12") *(RCA/+T 385)* **RUN RUNAWAY. / TWO TRACK STEREO, ONE TRACK MIND** 7 –

Apr 84. (lp) *<39336>* **KEEP YOUR HANDS OFF MY POWER SUPPLY** – 33
<cd-iss. 1988; ZK 3936>

Apr 84. (7") *<04398>* **RUN RUNAWAY. / DON'T TAME A HURRICANE** – 20

Jul 84. (7") *<04528>* **MY OH MY. / HIGH AND DRY** – 37

Nov 84. (7") *(RCA 455)* **ALL JOIN HANDS. / HERE'S TO . . . (THE NEW YEAR)** 15 –
(12"+=) *(RCAT 455)* – Merry xmas everybody (live & kickin').

Jan 85. (7") *(RCA 475)* **7 YEAR (B)ITCH. / LEAVE THEM GIRLS ALONE** 60 –
(12"+=) *(RCAT 475)* – We'll bring the house down (live).

Mar 85. (lp/c) *(PL/PK 70604) <39976>* **ROGUES GALLERY**
– Hey ho wish you well / Little Sheila / Harmony / Myzsterious Mizster Jones / Walking on water, running on alcohol / 7 year (b)itch / I'll be there / I win, you lose / Time to rock / All join hands. *(cd-iss. Sep99; 547406-2)*

Mar 85. (7",7"pic-d) *(PB 40027)* **MYZSTERIOUS MIZSTER JONES. / MAMA NATURE IS A ROCKER** 50 –
(ext.12"+=) *(PT 40028)* – My oh my (piano and vocal version).

Apr 85. (7") *<04865>* **LITTLE SHEILA. / LOCK UP YOUR DAUGHTERS** – 86

Nov 85. (7") *(PB 40449)* **DO YOU BELIEVE IN MIRACLES. / MY OH MY (swing version)** 54 –
(d7"+=) *(PB 40549)* – (see below d12" for extra tracks)
(12"+=) *(PT 40450)* – Time to rock.
(12"++=) *(PT 40550)* – Santa Claus is coming to town / Auld lang syne / You'll never walk alone.

Feb 87. (7"/12") *(PB 4113 7/8)* **STILL THE SAME. / GOTTA GO HOME** 73 –
(d7"+=) *(PB 41147D)* – The roaring silence / Don't talk to me about love.

Apr 87. (7") *(PB 41271)* **THAT'S WHAT FRIENDS ARE FOR. / WILD WILD PARTY** –
(12"+=) *(PT 41272)* – Hi ho silver lining / Lock up your daughters (live).

Apr 87. (lp/c/cd) *(PL/PK/PD 71260)* **YOU BOYZ MAKE BIG NOIZE** –
– Love is like a rock / That's what friends are for / Still the same / Fools go crazy / She's heavy / We won't give in / Won't you rock with me / Ooh la la in L.A. / Me and the boys / Sing shout (knock yourself out) / The roaring silence / It's hard having fun nowadays / You boyz make big noize / Boyz (instrumental). *(cd re-iss. Apr93 & Nov96 on 'Castle'; CLACD 379 & 417) (cd re-iss. Sep99; 547408-2)*

Cheapskate-RCA — not iss.

Jun 87. (7") *(BOYZ 1)* **YOU BOYZ MAKE BIG NOIZE. / ('A'instrumental)** –
(12"+=) *(TBOYZ 1)* – ('A'-USA mix).

Nov 87. (7") *(BOYZ 2)* **WE WON'T GIVE IN. / LA LA IN L.A.** –

Nov 88. (7") *(BOYZ 3)* **LET'S DANCE (1988 remix). / STANDING ON THE CORNER** –
(cd-s+=) *(BOYZCD 3)* – Far far away / How does it feel.

Polydor — not iss.

Oct 91. (7"/c-s) *(PO/+CS 180)* **RADIO WALL OF SOUND. / LAY YOUR LOVE ON THE LINE** 21 –
(cd-s+=) *(PZCD 180)* – Cum on feel the noize.

Nov 91. (cd/c/lp) *(511 612-2/-4/-1)* **WALL OF HITS** (compilation & new hits) 34
– Get down and get with it / Coz I luv you / Look wot you dun / Take me bak 'ome / Gudbuy t'Jane / Cum on feel the noize / Skweeze me pleeze me / My friend Stan / Everyday / Bangin' man / Far far away / Let's call it quits / My oh my / Run run away / Radio wall of sound / Universe / Merry Xmas everybody. *(cd/c+=)* – How does it feel / Thanks for the memory (wham bam thank you mam).

Nov 91. (7"/c-s) **UNIVERSE. / MERRY CHRISTMAS EVERYBODY** –
(12"+=/cd-s+=) – Gypsy roadhog.

— SLADE continued to do the odd gig/concert

– compilations, etc. –

on 'Polydor' unless stated otherwise

Jun 80. (12"ep) *Six Of The Best; (SUPER45 3)* **SIX OF THE BEST** –
– Night starvation / When I'm dancing I ain't fightin' / I'm a rocker / Don't waste your time / Wheels ain't coming down / Nine to five.

Nov 80. (lp) *(POLTV 13)* **SLADE SMASHES** 21 –

Apr 81. (d-lp/d-c) *(2689/3539 101)* **THE STORY OF SLADE** –
(cd-iss. VOL.1 & VOL.2 Nov90 on 'Bear Tracks'; BTCD 97941-1/-2)

Dec 81. (7"ep) *(POSP 399)* **CUM ON FEEL THE NOIZE / COZ I LUV YOU. / TAKE ME BAK 'OME / GUDBUY T'JANE** –
(12"ep+=) *(POSPX 399)* – Coz I luv you.

Dec 82. (7"/7"pic-d) *Speed; (SPEED/+P 201)* **THE HOKEY COKEY. / GET DOWN AND GET WITH IT** –

May 84. (lp/c) *(SLAD/+C 1)* **SLADE'S GREATS** –

Nov 85. (7"/12") *(POSP/+X 780)* **MERRY CHRISTMAS EVERYBODY (remix). / DON'T BLAME ME** 48 –
(re-iss. Dec86, hit No.71)

Nov 85. (lp/c) *Telstar; (STAR/STAC 2271)* **CRACKERS – THE SLADE CHRISTMAS PARTY ALBUM** 34 –

1988. (cd-ep) *Counterpoint; (CDEP 12C)* **HOW DOES IT FEEL / FAR FAR AWAY / (2 tracks by Wizzard)** –

Mar 89. (3"cd-ep) *R.C.A.; (PD 42637)* **MY OH MY / KEEP YOUR HANDS OFF MY POWER SUPPLY / RUNAWAY / ONE TRACK STEREO, ONE TRACK MIND** –

Apr 91. (cd/c/lp) *R.C.A.; (ND/NK/NL 74926)* **COLLECTION 81-87** –
(re-iss. Apr93 on 'Castle' cd/c; CCS CD/MC 372) (cd re-iss. Sep99 on 'Polydor'; 547410-2)

Dec 95. (c) *Prestige; (CASSGP 0253)* **KEEP ON ROCKIN'** –

Jan 97. (cd/c) *(537 105-2/-4)* **GREATEST HITS – FEEL THE NOIZE** 19 –
– Get down and get with it / Coz I luv you / Look wot you dun / Take me bak 'ome / Mama weer all crazee now / Gudbuy t'Jane / Cum on feel the noize / Skweeze me pleaze me / My friend Stan / Everyday / Bangin' man / Far far away / How does it feel to feel / In for a penny / We'll bring the house down / Lock up your daughters / Oh my my / Run run away / All join hands / Radio wall of sound / Merry Xmas everybody. *(re-iss. Dec99 as 'GREATEST HITS – FEEL THE NOIZE'; same)*

Mar 97. (cd) *Music Corp; (TMC 9606)* **THE GENESIS OF SLADE** –

Dec 98. (c-s; SLADE VS FLUSH) *Polydor; (563352-4)* **MERRY XMAS EVERYBODY '98 REMIX / ('A'remix)** 30 –
(12"+=) *(563353-1)* – ('A'mix).
(cd-s+=) *(563353-2)* – Cum on feel the noize.

□ SLASH'S SNAKEPIT (see under ⇒ GUNS N' ROSES)

□ Grace SLICK (see under ⇒ JEFFERSON AIRPLANE)

SLINT

Formed: Louisville, Kentucky, USA . . . 1988 by former SQUIRREL BAIT partners, BRIAN McMAHAN and BRITT WALFORD, who had already teamed up with DAVID PAJO and ETHAN BUCKLER prior to the latter band's division into BASTRO and SLINT. The influential noiseniks made their debut the following year with the self-financed, STEVE ALBINI-produced album, 'TWEEZ', a willfully weird clutch of mainly instrumental guitar/bass-led creations named after their family members (including a dog!). While WALFORD (aka SHANNON DOUGHTY) moonlighted on The BREEDERS first album, 'Pod', BUCKLER would subsequently leave to form KING KONG, replacement TODD BRASHER installed as work commenced on a BRIAN PAULSON-produced follow-up set, 'SPIDERLAND'. Upon its release (on 'Touch & Go') in '91, the album generated a healthy amount of column inches praising its uncategorisable guitar-scapes, Scotland's own MOGWAI later citing the record as a pivotal reference point. While rumours circulated that the album's recording had almost sent

SLINT over the edge, the individual members were obviously sane enough to work on various projects including WILL OLDHAM's PALACE BROTHERS (WALFORD, McMAHAN and BRASHER) and TORTOISE (PAJO). A final postscript to the SLINT story came in 1993 with the release of double-A side ("untitled") single, 'GLENN' / 'RHODA' (the latter a cut from '89), with McMAHAN, however, embarking on his own adventure, the FOR CARNATION with SLINT buddy PAJO; other members DOUGLAS McCOMBS, GRANT BARGER and JOHN HERNDON. This quintet released the EP, 'FLIGHT SONGS' (1995), while the mini-set 'MARSHMALLOWS' (1996) was without the much in-demand PAJO. Not released in Britian, it finally surfaced in 1997 as 'PROMISED WORKS', containing the debut EP tracks. Like in SLINT, McMAHAN enforced the dizzy guitars and whispering sung/spoken vocals that made the aforementioned group sound so interesting, GALAXIE 500 and GASTR DEL SOL were also names that were thrown in as noteworthy comparisons. Adding LEONARD COHEN-esque incoherence to the mix, a slightly surreal view of life encouraged McMAHAN's lyrics and influence to reach higher dynamic points within his sound and vision. With his brother MICHAEL on guitar, BOB BRUNO, TODD COOK and moonlighting RADAR BROS drummer STEVE GOODFRIEND, The FOR CARNATION were reborn for an album which was scheduled for release early 2000. Meanwhile, following PAJO's stint with avant-jazz combo, TORTOISE, the musical Jack-of-all trades followed a similar dusty path to the aforementioned WILL OLDHAM, on his eponymous 1997 debut solo set (released under the AERIAL-M moniker), foregoing vocals in favour of backporch strumming. Licensed from 'Drag City' to 'Domino' in the UK, the rootsy homegrown affair showed a mellower side to the normally uncompromising guitarist and paved the way for two further releases over the course of the following year, EP's 'M IS . . .' and 'OCTOBER'. PAJO's increasingly interesting full-time project AERIAL M reached a peak with the release of his remix album 'POST-GLOBAL MUSIC' (1999), a record which saw single 'WEDDING SONG NO.3' get the mixing treatment from DJ YOUR FOOD, FLACCO and BUNDY K. BROWN. A back-to-roots move, and a transformation had PAJO change what was once M, AERIAL M and M IS THE THIRTEENTH LETTER to the new post-rock infused PAPA M. He issued his best to date under this moniker, the sweeping, placid and intimately creepy 'LIVE FROM A SHARK CAGE' at the end of 1999. A slow-burning blend of echoing guitars, badly recorded keyboards and lo-fi stoned beats, the album began with the sweet chamber drone of 'ARUNDAL' moving into the xylophone driven, wintery 'ROADRUNNER'. Elsewhere on the set, PAJO advanced into the quiet eerie proportions of songwriting; the brooding atmosphere on 'CROWD OF ONE' (in which PAJO's recently deceased grandfather's answering machine messages are played over a floating ambient guitar) matches that of some of TORTOISE's more experimental works, where 'KNOCKING THE CASKET' was a banjo-laden lament, PAJO himself knocking on his acoustic guitar, to keep a beat while stomping his foot on a wooden floor. This was to ultimately lead the way for his next outing, the EP 'PAPA M SINGS', in which he put his voice to the test by singing songs in a country style, similar to friend and PALACE man WILL OLDHAM. PAJO recorded the EP on a four-track and passed it around friends. Luckily they liked it. The EP was issued on MOGWAI's 'Rock Action' in Febuary 2001 and boasted the hugely satisfying bitter-sweet/drunk love song 'JADED LOVER'. 'PISSING IN THE WIND', a donkey-paced front porch banjo track had him singing sarcastically about the 'Drag City' imprint, while the slide-guitar rambling in ode-to-a-lover 'TRUE LOVE' reminded listeners of how talented a guitarist PAJO actually was. Sure, his voice was a bit flat, but that all added to the folksy, Kentucky image honed by OLDHAM et al. Later that year, PAJO began work on his follow-up to ' . . .SHARK CAGE' and appeared as a guest on MOGWAI's 'Rock Action' album. PAJO sang again on the 2002 release 'SONGS FOR MAC' where this time PAPA M took two songs by unknowns, MAC FINLEY and AUBREY ROZIER, and covered them knowing most of his audience hadn't heard the originals. A brief and well laid-out EP, the two songs that featured were competent and displayed PAJO's trademark Louisville drawl. The set also saw a switch to the little known label 'Western Vinyl'. Meanwhile PAJO was said to be switching to the mainstream; an unlikely pairing with BILLY CORGAN and his new supergroup ZWAN. 'Drag City' subsequently collected togther the singles ouptut of PAJO's various aliases on 'HOLE OF BURNING ALMS' (2004), a collection whose sleepy extemporising stretched right back to the mid-90s. Highlights included a wickedly pastoral re-envisioning of the Misfits' brutal 'LAST CARESS', more famously covered by METALLICA (on the classic '$5.98 EP – Garage Days Revisited'), as well as an instrumental saunter through Pete Seeger's 'TURN! TURN! TURN!', a predictably more abstract take on the folk legend than the recent BRUCE SPRINGSTEEN tribute and a damn sight longer – PAJO and co famously vowed to improvise till the studio tape ran out. A further PAPA M EP, 'FIVE', appeared in 2004, closely followed by 'SIX'.

Album rating: TWEEZ (*7) / SPIDERLAND (*8) / For Carnation: PROMISED WORKS collection of US EP's (*6) / THE FOR CARNATION (*8) / Aerial-M: AS PERFORMED BY . . . (*7) / POST-GLOBAL MUSIC (*7) / Papa M: LIVE FROM A SHARK CAGE (*8) / WHATEVER, MORTAL (*7) / HOPE OF BURNING ALMS collection (*8)

BRIAN McMAHAN – vocals, guitar (ex-SQUIRREL BAIT) / **DAVID PAJO** – guitar / **ETHAN BUCKLER** – bass / **BRITT WALFORD** – drums (ex-SQUIRREL BAIT)

Jennifer Hartman Jennifer Hartman

Sep 89. (lp) <*(JHR 136)*> **TWEEZ**
– Ron / Nan ding / Carol / Kent / Charlotte / Darlene / Warren / Pat / Rhoda. <*(re-iss. May93 on 'Touch & Go' lp/cd; TG 138/+D)*>

— **TODD BRASHER** – bass; BUCKLER who formed KING KONG

Touch & Go Touch & Go

Mar 91. (lp/cd) <*(TGLP 64/+cd)*> **SPIDERLAND**
– Breadcrumb trail / Nosferatu man / Don, Aman / Washer / For dinner . . . / Good morning, captain. *(re-iss. Sep98; same)*

Sep 94. (10"/cd-s) <*(TG 132/+cd)*> **SLINT**
– Glenn / Rhoda.

— had already disbanded in 1992, WALFORD + McMAHAN later joined the PALACE BROTHERS; the latter also formed The FOR CARNATION. PAJO (a part-timer with TFC) subsequently joined TORTOISE before forming AERIAL-M.

the FOR CARNATION

BRIAN McMAHAN with **DAVID PAJO** – guitar / **DOUGLAS McCOMBS** – bass / **JOHN HERNDON** – drums / **GRANT BARGER** – engineer, co-writer

Matador Matador

Jun 95. (cd-ep) <*(OLE 131-2)*> **FIGHT SONGS EP** Apr95
– Grace beneath the pines / How I beat the Devil / Get and stay get March.

— **BRAD WOOD, JOHN WEISS + TIM RUTH**; repl. PAJO

Mar 96. (m-cd/m-lp) <*OLE 172-2/-1*> **MARSHMALLOWS** –
– On the swing / I wear the gold / Imyr, marshmallow / Winter lair / Salo / Preparing to receive you.

Runt not iss.

Jun 97. (cd) *(RUNT 30)* **PROMISED WORKS** (compilation of the EP and mini-set) –

— **McMAHAN** recruited his brother **MICHAEL McMAHAN** – guitar / **BOBBY BRUNO** – guitar, sampler, keyboards / **TODD COOK** – bass / **STEVE GOODFRIEND** – drums / forthcoming set in March 2000 also incl. **KIM DEAL** – vocals (ex-PIXIES) / **RACHEL HAYDEN** – vocals (of that dog.) + **JOHN McENTIRE** – (who else?, on production)

Domino Touch & Go

Mar 00. (cd/lp) *(WIG CD/LP 77)* <*TG 214*> **THE FOR CARNATION**
– Empowered man's blues / A tribute to / Being held / Smoother / Tales (live from the crypt) / Moonbeams.

AERIAL-M

DAVID PAJO – guitars (with **LATETIA SADIER** on first)

not iss. Palace

Dec 95. (7"; as M IS THE THIRTEENTH LETTER) *<PR 11>* **SAFELESS. / NAPOLEON** [–] [ ]

not iss. All City

Dec 96. (7") **VOL DE NUIT. / (other track by MONADE)** [–] [ ]

Domino Drag City

Sep 97. (cd/lp) *(WIG CD/LP 037)* *<DC 114>* **AS PERFORMED BY . . . AERIAL-M** [ ] Aug97 [ ]
– Dazed and awake / Aass / Wedding song No.2 / Rachmaninoff / Skrak theme / Compassion for M / Always farewell.

Feb 98. (7"m)<cd-ep> *(RUG 062)<DC 144CD>* **M IS . . . / WEDDING THEME NO.3 / MOUNTAINS HAVE EARS** [ ] Dec97 [ ]

Jun 98. (7") *(RUG 070)* *<DC 155>* **OCTOBER** [ ] Feb99 [ ]
– Vivea / Last caress.

Feb 99. (cd/lp) *(WIG CD/LP 63)* *<DC 170>* **POST-GLOBAL MUSIC** [ ] Jan99 [ ]
– Wedding song No.3 (FLACCO mix) / Wedding song (TIED + TICKLED TRIO remix) / Wedding song No.3 (BUNDY K. BROWN mix) / Attention span deficit disorder disruption a journey wherein (. . . seeks the gateway out of the world of red dust and learns that running between the raindrops won't save you from the chocolate thunder) (DJ YOUR FOOD mix).

PAPA M

— aka **DAVID PAJO**

Nov 99. (cd/d-lp) *(WIG CD/LP 71)* *<DC 170>* **LIVE FROM A SHARK CAGE** [ ] Oct99 [ ]
– Arundel / Roadrunner / Pink holler / Plastic energy man / Drunken spree / Bups / Crowd of one / I am not lonely with cricket / Knocking the casket / Up north kids / Arundel.

Jul 00. (cd-ep) *<MTOURCD 1>* **1999 TOUR EP** [–] [ ]
– Up north kids No.2 / She said yes.

Rock Action Sea Note

Apr 01. (cd-ep)<12"ep> *(ROCKACTCD 7)* *<SN 8>* **PAPA M SINGS** [ ] Jan01 [ ]
– Jaded lover / Pissing in the wind / I of mine / Who am I / True love / London homesick blues.

Awkward Awkward

Nov 01. (7") *<(AWKWARD 10)>* **MAMA YOU BEEN ON MY MIND. / (other by UNHOME)** [ ] [ ]

— now augmented by **BRITT WALFORD** – drums (ex-SLINT) **WILL OLDHAM** – guitars, etc / + TARA JANE O'NEIL – guitar (ex-RODAN)

Domino Drag City

Nov 01. (cd/d-lp) *(WIG CD/LP 103)* *<DC 194>* **WHATEVER, MORTAL** [ ] [ ]
– Over Jordan / Beloved woman / Roses in the snow / Sorrow reigns / Krusty / The lass of Roch Royal / Many splendored thing / Glad you're here with me / Tamu / Sabotage / Purple eyelid / The unquiet grave / Northwest passage.

Western Vinyl Western Vinyl

Mar 02. (cd-ep) *<(WV 014)>* **SONGS OF MAC** [ ] [ ]
– So warped / The person and the skeleton.

— PAJO subsequently joined ZWAN (yes, BILLY CORGAN's outfit)

Tiger Style Tiger Style

Mar 03. (7") *<(TS 041)>* **ORANGE WORLD. / (other by ENTRANCE)** [ ] [ ]

Drag City Drag City

Mar 03. (cd-ep) *<DC 241>* **ONE** [–] [ ]
– Flashlight tornado / Beloved woman / I am the light of this world.

Apr 03. (cd-ep) *<(DC 242)>* **TWO** [ ] [ ]
– (untitled) / (untitled) / (untitled).

Jul 03. (cd-ep) *<(DC 243)>* **THREE** [ ] [ ]
– Wild mountain thyme / Truckstop girl / Who knows.

Nov 03. (cd-ep) *<(DC 247)>* **FOUR** [ ] [ ]
– Long may you burn / Red curtains / Local boy makes good.

Jan 04. (cd-s) *<DC 258>* **FIVE** [–] [ ]
– Petals weep / Nickel song.

Domino Drag City

Mar 04. (cd/d-lp) *(WIG CD/LP 139)* *<DC 231>* **HOPE OF BURNING ALMS** (compilation) [ ] Feb04 [ ]
– Safeless / Napoleon / Vol de nuit / Wedding song No.3 / Mountains have ears / Vivea / Last caress / Travels in constants / Up north kids No.2 / She said yes / Turn turn turn / Xmas 1997.

Mar 04. (cd-ep) *<DC 259>* **SIX** [–] [ ]
– The trees do grow so high / Lovely room / Foreign hotel garden.

SLIPKNOT

Formed: Des Moines, Iowa, USA . . . 1995 by members 0, 1, 2, 3, 4, 5, 6, 7 and 8 – aka DJ SID WILSON, JOEY JORDISON, PAUL GRAY, CHRIS FEHN, JAMES ROOT, CRAIG JONES, SHAWN CRAHAN, MIC THOMPSON and singer (or screamer) COREY TAYLOR. The menacing 9-piece recorded and released the now rare album 'MATE. FEED. KILL. REPEAT' in 1996, receiving mass attention from record labels in the process. The ensemble signed with 'Roadrunner' in 1997 and released their self-titled debut album in 1999. The album (predictably) gained a huge cult following from the widespread majority of dysfunctional teens all over the globe. In a way, it's not hard to describe SLIPKNOT's music: fast, heavy, vicious, ferocious, venomous and crude – in fact a few journos made them out to be Rock's answer to 'The Texas Chainsaw Massacre'. The mask-clad spooksters have found their niche within the flow of sports metal in the US; bands such as KORN and white chumps LIMP BIZKIT thrive off the money made from these double-bass drum pedallers. But as a band, the angsty punk-metallers are not bad, mixing in a blend of tricky, thumping and downright blastferic lyrics along with the pounding guitars and drums. It's what grandmothers have nightmares about. During the months touring to promote their self-titled debut album, the group of intensely intense metallers – for some obscure reason – became hugely popular with the amount of 'KNOT followers exceeding that of a huge, sinister American cult. Soon the troupe of rubber monsters were featured on every T-shirt worn by every prepubescent kid who, just two weeks ago, thought the Kylie Minogue album was a classic (hence the alleged statement by TAYLOR that all SLIPKNOT fans were "maggots"). Sick of this worrying sight and worried themselves over the musical direction in which the record company wanted the follow-up album to go, the group cut and issued the dark, theatrical and utterly insane sophomore set 'IOWA' (2001). More Black Metal than early BLACK SABBATH, the group were slightly in danger of turning into G.G. ALLIN's backing band. 'LEFT BEHIND' tore the speakers apart with its emotional apathy accumulating in thrash guitar noise that was the musical equivalent of being fisted by a robot. The end result was the creeping 15-minute epitaph to their home town, 'IOWA', in which TAYLOR was said to be (whilst recording the track) "puking, bleeding, trampling on glass and being burnt by hot wax" . . . Hot wax?! You have been warned. For those still not satiated after such sonic torture, there was the re-emergence of STONE SOUR, the band with which TAYLOR and ROOT had first begun to terrorize the metal scene. After seeking out fellow conspirators SEAN ECONOMAKI and JOSH RAND, together with new faces JOEL EKMAN and SID WILSON, the band contributed 'BOTHER' for the soundtrack to the 2002 'Spiderman' remake. As a taster for their eponymous album, released the same year, it heralded a promise that was pretty much fulfilled. Leaving behind the theatrics of SLIPKNOT and actually vocalising to the best of his not inconsiderable abilities, TAYLOR pretty much stole the show on a set of songs all the better for taking their foot off the gas. MURDERDOLLS, the side project of JORDISON and his compadre TRIPP EISEN (of STATIC-X), was a different matter altogether, a self-indulgent, splattercore shamble through various strands of moribund metal going by the tongue-in-cheek title 'BEYOND THE VALLEY OF THE MURDER DOLLS' (2002). One of SLIPKNOT's most unlikely and least successful extra curricular projects was TO

MY SURPRISE, the brainchild of SHAWN CRAHAN, SLIPKNOT DJ BRANDON DARNER and fellow Des Moines vocalist/guitarist STEVEN ROBINSON. Released on 'Roadrunner' and produced by Rick Rubin no less, their eponymous 2003 debut album left behind the puke and grimace of CRAHAN's day job for a pleasant, mildly trippy retro vibe referencing the likes of the MONKEES and the DOORS. Rubin stuck around to work his beardy magic on 'VOL.3: THE SUBLIMINAL VERSES' (2004), widely hailed as the most adventurous album of SLIPKNOT's career. Like SLAYER on 'South Of Heaven', the band fattened up their sound by going on a speed diet, putting on the brakes and opening their masks to ideas that would've been heresy only a few years ago: the cantering monologue of opener 'PRELUDE 3.0' and especially the pastoral acoustica of 'VERMILLION, PT.2' – OK, it was "a stalker's love song", but it sounded pretty. The more traditionally throat-ripping 'BEFORE I FORGET' ended up as a UK Top 40 single, while the album itself was another transatlantic Top 5. Many of the tracks made it onto '9.0: LIVE' (2005), a US Top 20 concert set with the added woaarrgh! factor of the band's infamously partisan fans in full voice.

Album rating: MATE. FEED. KILL. REPEAT (*5) / SLIPKNOT (*8) / IOWA (*8) / VOL.3 (THE SUBLIMINAL VERSES) (*7) / 9.0: LIVE (*6) / Stone Sour: STONE SOUR (*7) / Murderdolls: BEYOND THE VALLEY OF THE MURDERDOLLS (*6) / To My Surprise: TO MY SURPRISE (*5)

COREY TAYLOR – vocals / **MIC THOMPSON** – guitar / **JIM ROOT** – guitar / **PAUL GRAY** – bass / **JOEY JORDISON** – drums / **CHRIS FEHN** – percussion / **SHAWN CRAHAN** – percussion / **CRAIG JONES** – samples, programmes / **SID WILSON** – DJ

not iss. ismist

Jul 97. (cd) <*ismCD 0032*> **MATE. FEED. KILL. REPEAT** [–] [ ]
– Slipknot / Gently / Do nothing – Bitchslap / Only one / Tattered and torn / Confessions / Some feel / Killers are quite.

Roadrunner Roadrunner

Jun 99. (cd) <*(RR 8655-2)*> **SLIPKNOT** [37] [51]
– 74261000027 / Eyel ESS / Wait and bleed / Surfacing / Spit it out / Tattered and torn / Frail limb nursery / Purity / Liberate / Prosthetics / No life / Diluted / The only one. *(other cd+=; RR 8655-5)* – Me inside / Get this / Interloper (demo) / Despise (demo). *(pic-lp iss.Aug00; RR 8655-6)*

Feb 00. (cd-s) *(RR 2112-5)* **WAIT AND BLEED / SPIT IT OUT (overcaffeinated hyper-molt mix) / SIC (Spaceship Console mix) / WAIT AND SEE (live promo video)** [27] [–]

Sep 00. (7") *(RR 2090-7)* **SPIT IT OUT. / SURFACING (live)** [28] [–]
(cd-s+=) *(RR 2090-3)* – Wait and bleed (live) / ('A'-video).

Aug 01. (cd/d-lp) *(1208564-2/-1)* <*618564*> **IOWA** [1] [3]
– (515) / People = shit / Disasterpiece / My plague / Everything ends / The heretic anthem / Gently / Left behind / The shape / I am hated / Skin ticket / New abortion / Metabolic / Iowa.

Oct 01. (7"pic-d) *(2320335-7)* **LEFT BEHIND. / LIBERATE (live)** [24] [–]
(cd-s+=) *(2320335-5)* – Surfacing (live) / ('A'-video).

Jul 02. (cd-s) *(RR 2045-3)* **MY PLAGUE (new abuse mix) / SIC (live) / HERETIC ANTHEM (live) / MY PLAGUE (explicit video)** [43] [–]
(above from the movie, 'Resident Evil')

May 04. (cd) *(RR 8388)* <*618388*> **VOL.3 (THE SUBLIMINAL VERSES)** [5] [2]
– Prelude 3.0 / The blister exists / Three nil / Duality / Opium of the people / Circle / Welcome / Vermilion / Pulse of the maggots / Before I forget / Vermilion (part 2) / The nameless / The virus of life / Danger – keep away.

Jun 04. (7"pic-d)<7"red> *(RR 3988-7)* <*16861 3984-7*> **DUALITY. / DON'T GET CLOSE** [15] [ ]
(cd-s+=) *(RR 3988-0)* – Disasterpieces (live) / ('A'-uncensored video).

Oct 04. (7"pic-d) *(RR 3977-7)* **VERMILION. / SCREAM** [31] [ ]
(cd-s+=) *(RR 3977-0)* – Danger, keep away / ('A'-video).

May 05. (7") *(RR 3968-7)* **BEFORE I FORGET. / THE BLISTER EXISTS (live)** [35] [–]
(7"pic-d) *(RR 3968-8)* – ('A') / Three nil (live).

Oct 05. (d-cd) *(RR 8115-2)* <*618115*> **9.0: LIVE** (live) [53] [17]
– The blister exists / (Sic) / Disasterpiece / Before I forget / Left behind / Liberate / Vermilion / Pulse of the maggots / Purity / Eyeless / Drum solo / Eeyore // Three nil / The nameless / Skin ticket / Everything ends / The heretic anthem / Iowa / Duality / Spit it out / People = shit / Get this / Wait and bleed / Surfacing.

STONE SOUR

COREY TAYLOR – vocals / **JIM ROOT** – guitar / **JOSH RAND** – guitar / **SEAN ACONOMAKI** – bass / **JOEL EKMAN** – drums / **SID WILSON** – DJ

Roadrunner Roadrunner

Aug 02. (cd) <*(RR 8425-2)*> **STONE SOUR** [41] [46]
– Get inside / Orchids / Cold reader / Blotter / Choose / Monolith / Inhale / Bother (by COREY TAYLOR) / Blue study / Take a number / Idle hands / Tumult / Omega.

Mar 03. (cd-s) <*(RR 2024-3)*> **BOTHER / RULES OF EVIDENCE / WICKED / BOTHER (video)** [28] Jan04 [56]

Jul 03. (cd-s) *(RR 2009-3)* **INHALE / INSIDE THE CYNIC / INHALE (rough mix) / INHALE (video)** [63] [–]

MURDERDOLLS

JOEY JORDISON – guitar / **TRIPP EISEN** – guitar, vocals (of STATIC-X) / **WEDNESDAY 13** – vocals, guitar / **ERIC GRIFFIN** – bass / **BEN GRAVES** – drums

Roadrunner Roadrunner

Aug 02. (cd) <*(RR 8426-2)*> **BEYOND THE VALLEY OF THE MURDERDOLLS** [40] [ ]
– Slit my wrist / Twist my sister / Dead in Hollywood / Love at first fright / People hate me / She was a teenage zombie / Die my bride / Grave robbing U.S.A. / 197666 / Dawn of the dead / Let's go to war / Dressed to depress / Kill Miss America / B-movie scream queen / Motherfucker, I don't care. *(re-iss. Jul03 +=; RR 8426-8)* – Crash crash / Hit and . . . / Let's fuck / I take drugs / White wedding / I love to say fuck / Dead in Hollywood (video) / White wedding (video) / Love at first fright (video).

Jul 03. (cd-s) *(RR 2015-3)* **WHITE WEDDING / I LOVE TO SAY FUCK / I TAKE DRUGS / WHITE WEDDING (video)** [24] [–]

Nov 03. (cd-s) *(RR 2022-3)* **DEAD IN HOLLYWOOD / CRASH CRASH / LET'S FUCK / DEAD IN HOLLYWOOD (director's cut video)** [54] [–]

TO MY SURPRISE

SHAWN CRAHAN – percussion / **BRANDON DARNER** – vocals, guitar / **STEVAN ROBINSON** – lead guitar, bass

Roadrunner Roadrunner

Oct 03. (cd) *(RR 8396-2)* <*618396*> **TO MY SURPRISE** [ ] [ ]
– The world's too small / Get it to go / In the mood / Blue / Say goodbye / Easy or not / Turn it back around / This life / Come with me / Sunday / Who's to say.

the SLITS

Formed: London, England . . . early 1977 as the foremost all-girl outfit on the punk scene (until BUDGIE joined that is) and initially comprising ARI UP (aka ARIANNA FOSTER), KATE KORUS, SUZI GUTSY and PALMOLIVE. By the time the group had secured a support slot on The CLASH's Spring 1977 tour, KORUS and GUTSY had been replaced by VIV ALBERTINE and TESSA POLLITT respectively, the band's infamously amateurish approach compensated by their bolshy hardline feminist attitude. Although they had two John Peel sessions under their belts, the SLITS didn't actually sign a deal until 1979, having turned down the 'Real' label (home to The HEARTBREAKERS and PRETENDERS) the previous year. In the event the not-so "TYPICAL GIRLS" signed with 'Island' and set to work on a debut album with reggae producer, Dennis Bovell, the aforementioned BUDGIE (PETER CLARK) coming in as a replacement for PALMOLIVE who departed midway through the recording sessions. A Top 30 hit upon its release in late '79, the seminal 'CUT' showcased ARI's distinctive vocal phrasing against a compelling backdrop of unorthodox tribal rhythms and raw guitar abrasion, the sleeve's cover shot of the lasses getting butt naked and muddy generating almost as much interest as the music. With

The SLITS

BUDGIE decamping to SIOUXSIE & THE BANSHEES, BRUCE SMITH was recruited in his place and despite the presence of respected jazz trumpeter, DON CHERRY (father of NENEH), a dreadful untitled bootleg/jam affair did the band no favours. Much more enjoyable was the subsequent cover of John Holt's 'MAN NEXT DOOR', released as a single a couple of months later in the summer of 1980. A further single followed on the 'Human' label before the SLITS signed to 'C.B.S.' for a final disappointing patchy album, 'RETURN OF THE GIANT SLITS' (1981), the group disbanding in early '82. While SMITH joined Bristolian avant-funk collective RIP, RIG & PANIC, the remaining members (minus POLLITT) went on to be part of colossus ensemble, The NEW AGE STEPPERS.

• **Songwriters:** Group compositions, except I HEARD IT THROUGH THE GRAPEVINE (Marvin Gaye). • **Trivia:** Early in 1978, they were sighted in the punk film, 'Jubilee'.

Album rating: CUT (*9) / UNTITLED (*1) / RETURN OF THE GIANT SLITS (*6) / IN THE BEGINNING collection (*4) / THE PEEL SESSIONS collection (*7)

ARI UP (b. ARIANNA FOSTER) – vocals / **VIVIEN ALBERTINE** – guitar (ex-FLOWERS OF ROMANCE) repl. KATE KORUS to KLEENEX (Feb77) / **TESSA POLLITT** – bass repl. SUZI GUTSY who formed The FLICKS. / **PALMOLIVE** – drums (ex-FLOWERS OF ROMANCE) was repl. (Oct78) by **BUDGIE** (b. PETER CLARK, 21 Aug'??, St.Helens, England) – percussion, drums (ex-BIG IN JAPAN, ex-SECRETS,etc)

Island / Antilles

Sep 79. (lp/c) *(ILPS/ZC1 9573)* *<7072>* **CUT** [30] [ ]
– Instant hit / So tough / Spend spend spend / Shoplifting / FM / Newtown / Ping pong affair / Love and romance / Typical girls / Adventures close to home. *(cd-iss. Apr90; IMCD 89) (cd re-mast.Oct00 +=; IMCD 275)* – I heard it through the grapevine / Liebe and romanza (slow version).

Sep 79. (7") *(WIP 6505)* **TYPICAL GIRLS. / I HEARD IT THROUGH THE GRAPEVINE** [60] [ ]
(12"+=) *(12WIP 6505)* – Typical girls (brink style) / Liebe and romanze.

—— **BRUCE SMITH** – drums (of POP GROUP) repl. BUDGIE to SIOUXSIE & BANSHEES jazz-trumpeter **DON CHERRY** guested

Y – Rough Trade / not iss.

Mar 80. (7") *(Y1 – RT 039)* **IN THE BEGINNING THERE WAS RHYTHM. / (B-side by the Pop Group)** [ ] [-]

May 80. (lp) *(Y3LP)* **UNTITLED (Y3LP)** (bootleg demo jam) [ ] [-]
– A boring life / Slime / Or what it is / No.1 enemy / Once upon a time in a living room / Bongos on the lawn / Face place / Let's do the split / Mosquitos / Vaseline / No more rock and roll for you.

Jun 80. (7") *(Y4 – RT 044)* **MAN NEXT DOOR. / MAN NEXT DOOR (dub version)** [ ] [-]

—— added guest **STEVE BERESFORD** – keyboards, guitar (of FLYING LIZARDS)

Human / not iss.

Nov 80. (7") *(HUM 4)* **ANIMAL SPACE. / ANIMAL SPACIER** [ ] [-]

C.B.S. / Epic

1981. (12"m) **ANIMAL SPACE. / ANIMAL SPACIER / IN THE BEGINNING THERE WAS RHYTHM** [-] [ ]

Aug 81. (7") *(A 1498)* **EARTHBEAT. / BEGIN AGAIN RHYTHM** [ ] [-]
(12"+=) *(A13 1498)* – Earthdub.

Oct 81. (lp/c) *(CBS/40 85269)* **RETURN OF THE GIANT SLITS** [ ] [ ]
– Earthbeat / Or what it is? / Face place / Walkabout / Difficult fun / Animal space – Spacier / Improperly dressed / Life on Earth. *(free-7"w/ lp) (XPS 125)* – AMERICAN RADIO INTERVIEW (Winter 1980). / FACE DUB

Dec 81. (7") *(49-02567>* **EARTHBEAT. / OR WHAT IT IS?** [-] [ ]

—— Parted ways early 1982. BRUCE joined RIP, RIG & PANIC. All except TESSA were part of colossus band NEW AGE STEPPERS.

– compilations, others, etc. –

on 'Strange Fruit' unless otherwise mentioned

Feb 87. (12"ep) *(SFPS 021)* **THE PEEL SESSION** (27.9.77) [ ] [-]
– Love and romance / Vindictive / Newtown / Shoplifting.

Nov 88. (m-lp/m-cd) *(SFPMA/+CD 207)* **THE DOUBLE PEEL SESSIONS** (27.9.77 + 22.5.78) [ ] [-]
– (THE PEEL SESSION) + So tough / Instant hit / FM.

Aug 97. (cd) *Jungle; (FREUDCD 057) / Cleopatra; <65>* **IN THE BEGINNING (live)** [ ] [ ]
– Vindictive / A boring life / Slime / New town / Love and romance / Shoplifting / Number one enemy / Number one enemy (acoustic) / In the beginning / New town / Man next door / I heard it through the grapevine / Typical girls / Fade away / In the beginning.

Feb 98. (cd) *(SFRCD 052) <8304>* **THE PEEL SESSIONS** [ ] [ ]
– (THE DOUBLE PEEL SESSIONS) + Difficult fun / In the beginning / Earthbeat – Wedding song.

Feb 05. (cd) *Castle; <36213>* **LIVE AT THE GIBUS CLUB** [-] [ ]

SLY & THE FAMILY STONE

Formed: San Francisco, California, USA . . . 1966, initially as The STONERS by former DJ/Producer, SLY STONE (born SYLVESTER STEWART) with brother FREDDIE, sister ROSEMARY and cousin LARRY GRAHAM. They adopted the name SLY & THE FAMILY STONE after gigging around local bars/clubs in Oakland and in 1967 they signed to 'Epic', releasing their debut album, 'A WHOLE NEW THING'. The record introduced the superfly new sound created by one of the first inter-racial, inter-gender and inta-drugs outfits to emerge between the rock/soul divide. With SLY casting himself HENDRIX-like in the role of Afro-American uber-hippie, he and his family were pioneers of the "Psychedelic Soul" movement, re-influencing old hands like The TEMPTATIONS and The ISLEY BROTHERS. Their breakthrough came with the 1968 single, 'DANCE TO THE MUSIC', a skilfully honed melange of doo-wop, soul and acid-funk that shook even the most stoned of hippy asses. The album of the same name followed later that year, crystallising the bands distinctive cross-over sound. Possibly their finest moment, the irresistible swing of 'EVERYDAY PEOPLE' was almost gospel-like in its passionate intensity. The single's B-side, 'SING A SIMPLE SONG', was similarly evangelical and illustrated that musically, at least, in The FAMILY STONE all the soul brothers and sisters were born equal. Each family member was given a fair deal in the mix, both instrumentally and vocally, and along with the band's unique hyrid of styles, this musical equanimity defined their sound. The classic 'STAND' (1969) album fully captured this collective, celebratory fanfare, including the aforementioned tracks as well as the 15-minute bass-heavy pulse of 'SEX MACHINE'. It also introduced SLY's penchant for mordant humour with 'DON'T CALL ME NIGGER, WHITEY'. As the 60's dream turned sour, this penchant would become ever more pronounced, 'HOT FUN IN THE SUMMERTIME' (1969) a wry observation on America's summer of discontent. Come 1970, SLY had moved to L.A. where he immersed himself in cocaine and the vacuum of the back-slapping Hollywood elite. 'THANK YOU (FALLETTINME BE MICE ELF AGIN)' (1970) was an edgy piece of taut funk that indicated the way SLY was headed. Partly composed in SLY's infamous drug den of a motorhome, where he lived gypsy-style around L.A., 'THERE'S A RIOT GOIN' ON' finally appeared in 1971. Reflecting the drug-induced paranoia and detachment of the recording sessions, most of the tracks were blurred snatches of dirty, slow burning funk, topped off by SLY's ravaged vocal chords. The deceptively laid-back groove of 'FAMILY AFFAIR' belied a grim lyrical content which extended to the whole album. From his embalming cocoon of Grade-A narcotics, SLY gave a hazily cynical commentary on the decline of American civilisation and the album remains a darkly brooding classic. With drug busts, financial pressures and hassles from militant black nationalists who didn't care for SLY's racially mixed philosophy, it was two years before 'FRESH' (1973) was released. While the sound recalled the band's effervescent charisma

SLY & THE FAMILY STONE

of old, a distinct edginess remained in the watertight grooves. The cool pop-funk of 'IF YOU WANT ME TO STAY' (1973) was the 'FAMILY STONE's last top 20 single. 'SMALL TALK' (1974) was almost overwhelmingly bland save for the title track and from there on in, SLY lost it big time. A drug casualty of the saddest order, SLY's latter 70's output was unremarkable at best.

• **Songwriters:** All by SLY and group except; I CAN'T TURN YOU LOOSE (Otis Redding) / YOU REALLY GOT ME (Kinks). • **Trivia:** On the 5th of June '74, SLY married Kathy Silva on stage at Madison Square Garden. Two months earlier, she had borne him his first child, Bubb Ali (all three pictured on the album cover of 'SMALL TALK'). She divorced SLY in '75, and he filed for bankruptcy early '76.

Album rating: A WHOLE NEW THING (*5) / DANCE TO THE MUSIC (*6) / LIFE (*6) / STAND! (*9) / GREATEST HITS compilation (*8) / THERE'S A RIOT GOIN' ON (*9) / FRESH (*7) / SMALL TALK (*6) / HIGH ON YOU (*5; by Sly Stone) / HEARD YA MISSED ME, WELL I'M BACK (*4) / BACK ON THE RIGHT TRACK (*4) / AIN'T BUT THE ONE WAY (*4) / TAKIN' YOU HIGHER – THE BEST OF SLY & THE FAMILY STONE compilation (*8)

SLY STONE

SLY STONE's early US recordings under various pseudonyms

— first 2 with brother FREDDIE and sister ROSE? (most doo-wop sound)

1959. (7"; by STEWART BROTHERS) <*Ensign; 4032*> **THE RAT. / RA RA ROO** –

1960. (7"; by STEWART BROTHERS) <*Keen; 2113*> **SLEEP ON THE PORCH. / YUM YUM YUM** –

1961. (7"; by DANNY STEWART) <*Luke 1008*> **A LONG TIME ALONE. / I'M JUST A FOOL** –

1961. (7"; by SYLVESTER STEWART) <*G&P; 901*> **A LONG TIME ALONE. / HELP ME WITH MY BROKEN HEART** –

1961. (7"; by the VISCANES) <*Tropo; 101*> **STOP WHAT YOU ARE DOING. / I GUESS I'LL BE** –

1961. (7"; by the VISCANES) <*VPM; 1006*> **YELLOW MOON. / UNCLE SAM NEEDS YOU** –

1961. (7"; by SLY STEWART) **YELLOW MOON. / HEAVENLY ANGEL** –

1964. (7"; by SLY STEWART) <*Autumn; 3*> **I JUST LEARNED HOW TO SWIM. / SCAT SWIM** –

1965. (7"; by SLY) <*Autumn; 14*> **BUTTERMILK. / (part 2)** –

1965. (7"; by SLY) <*Autumn; 26*> **TEMPTATION WALK. / (part 2)** –

— SLY at this time was producing Autumn acts The BEAU BRUMMELS, BOBBY FREEMAN and The MOJO MEN. He also became well-known local DJ for K-DIA.

SLY & THE FAMILY STONE

SLY STONE (b. SYLVESTER STEWART, 15 Mar'44, Dallas, Texas) – vox, guitar, keyboards (ex-SLY & THE MOJO MEN) / **FREDDIE STONE** (b. FRED STEWART, 5 Jun'46, Dallas) – guitar / **CYNTHIA ROBINSON** (b.12 Jan'46, Sacramento, Calif.) – trumpet / **ROSEMARY STONE** (b. ROSEMARY STEWART, 21 Mar'45, Vallejo, Calif.) – vocals, piano / **LARRY GRAHAM** (b.14 Aug'46, Beaumont, Texas) – bass / **JERRY MARTINI** (b. 1 Oct'43, Colorado) – saxophone / **GREG ERRICO** (b. 1 Sep'46) – drums

not iss. — Loadstone

1966. (7") <*3951*> **I AIN'T GOT NOBODY. / I CAN'T TURN YOU LOOSE** –

Columbia — Epic

1967. (lp) <*30333*> **A WHOLE NEW THING** –
– Underdog / If this room could talk / Run run run / Turn me loose / Let me hear it from you / Advice / I cannot make it / Trip to your heart / I hate to love her / Bad risk / That kind of person / Day. *(cd-iss. Jul95 on 'Epic'; EK 66424)*

1967. (7") <*10229*> **(I WANT TO TAKE YOU) HIGHER. / UNDERDOG** –

Mar 68. (7") *(DB 8369)* <*10256*> **DANCE TO THE MUSIC. / LET ME HEAR IT FROM YOU** Jan68 8

Direction — Epic

Jun 68. (7") *(58-3568)* **DANCE TO THE MUSIC. / LET ME HEAR IT FROM YOU** 7 –

Sep 68. (lp) *(8-63412)* <*26371*> **DANCE TO THE MUSIC** Apr68
– Dance to the music / (I want to take you) Higher / I ain't got nobody (for real) / Dance to the medley: Music is alive – Dance in – Music lover / Ride the rhythm / Color me true / Are you ready / Don't burn baby / I'll never fall in love again. *(re-iss. Oct73 on 'Embassy'; EMB 31030) (cd-iss. Jul94 on 'Epic'; 480906-2)*

Sep 68. (7") *(58-3707)* <*10353*> **M'LADY. / LIFE** 32 93
Jun68 93

Jan 69. (lp) *(8-63461)* <*26397*> **M'LADY** (US-title 'LIFE') Nov68
– Dynamite! / Chicken / Plastic Jim / Fun / Into my own thing / Harmony / Life / Love city / I'm an animal / M'lady / Jane is a groupie.

Mar 69. (7") *(58-3938)* <*10407*> **EVERYDAY PEOPLE. / SING A SIMPLE SONG** 36 1
Nov68 89

May 69. (7") *(58-4279)* <*10450*> **STAND!. / I WANT TO TAKE YOU HIGHER** 22
Apr69 60
<re-prom.May70 but flipped over, hit US No.38>

Jul 69. (lp) *(8-63655)* <*26456*> **STAND!** Apr69 13
– Stand! / Don't call me nigger, Whitey / I want to take you higher / Somebody's watching you / Sing a simple song / Everyday people / Sex machine / You can make it if you try. *(cd-iss. Feb95 on 'Epic'; EK 64422)*

Aug 69. (7") *(58-4471)* <*10497*> **HOT FUN IN THE SUMMERTIME. / FUN** 2

Feb 70. (7") *(58-4782)* <*10555*> **THANK YOU (FALLETTINME BE MICE ELF AGIN). / EVERYBODY IS A STAR** Dec69 1

C.B.S. — Epic

May 70. (7") *(5054)* **I WANT TO TAKE YOU HIGHER. / YOU CAN MAKE IT IF YOU TRY** –

Jan 71. (lp) *(EPC 69002)* <*30325*> **GREATEST HITS** (compilation) Oct70 2
– I want to take you higher / Everybody is a star / Stand / Life / Fun / You can make it if you try / Dance to the music / Everyday people / Hot fun in the summertime / M'lady / Sing a simple song / Thank you (falletinme be mice elf agin). *(<quad-lp 1975; EQ 30325>) (re-iss. Mar81 on 'Epic'; EPC 32029) (re-iss. Jun90 on 'Epic' cd/c/lp; EPC 462524-2/-4/-1)*

Epic — Epic

Nov 71. (7") *(EPC 7632)* <*10805*> **FAMILY AFFAIR. / LUV 'N' HAIGHT** 15 Oct71 1

Jan 72. (lp/c) *(EPC/40 64613)* <*30986*> **THERE'S A RIOT GOIN' ON** 31 Nov71 1
– Luv 'n' haight / Just like a baby / Poet / Family affair / Africa talks to you 'The Asphalt Jungle' / Brave & strong / Smilin' / Time / Spaced cowboy / Runnin' away / Thank you for talkin' to me Africa. *(UK-iss.w/free ltd.7"ep & newspaper) (re-iss. Feb86 on 'Edsel' lp/c; XED/CED 165) (cd-iss. Jan91; EDCD 165) (re-iss. May94 cd/c; 467063-2/-4)*

Mar 72. (7") *(EPC 7810)* <*10829*> **RUNNIN' AWAY. / BRAVE & STRONG** 17 Jan72 23

Apr 72. (7") <*10850*> **SMILIN'. / LUV 'N' HAIGHT** – 42

— (Jan73) **RUSTEE ALLEN** – bass repl. LARRY (formed GRAHAM CENTRAL STATION) **ANDY NEWMARK** – drums repl. ERRICO. / added **PAT RICCO** – saxophone

Jun 73. (lp/c) *(EPC/40 69039)* <*32134*> **FRESH** 7
– In time / If you want me to stay / Let me have it all / Frisky / Thankful 'n' thoughtful / The skin I'm in / I don't know (satisfaction) / Keep on dancin' / Que sera sera / If it were left up to me / Babies makin' babies. *(re-iss. May87 on 'Edsel' lp/c/cd; XED/CED/EDCD 232) (cd re-iss. Sep96 on 'Columbia'; 485170-2)*

Aug 73. (7") *(EPC 1655)* <*11017*> **IF YOU WANT ME TO STAY. / THANKFUL 'N' THOUGHTFUL** Jun73 12

Oct 73. (7") <*11060*> **FRISKY. / IF IT WERE LEFT UP TO ME** – 79

Jan 74. (7") *(EPC 1981)* **QUE SERA SERA. / IF IT WERE LEFT UP TO ME** –

— **BILL LORDAN** – drums repl. NEWMARK who became session man

Jul 74. (lp/c) *(EPC/40 69070)* <*32930*> **SMALL TALK** 15
– Small talk / Say you will / Mother beautiful / Time for livin' / Can't strain my brain / Loose booty / Holdin' on / Wishful thinking / Better thee than me / Livin' while I'm livin' / This is love.

Jul 74. (7") *(EPC 2530)* <*11140*> **TIME FOR LIVIN'. / SMALL TALK** 32

Jan 75. (7") *(EPC 1882)* <*50033*> **LOOSE BOOTY. / CAN'T STRAIN MY BRAIN** Oct84 84

SLY STONE

Oct 75. (lp/c) *<EPC/40 69165> <33835>* **HIGH ON YOU** [ ] [45]
– I get high on you / Crossword puzzle / That's lovin' you / Who do you love / Green-eyed monster girl / Organize / Le lo li / My world / So good to me / Greed.

Oct 75. (7") *(EPC 3596) <50135>* **I GET HIGH ON YOU. / THAT'S LOVIN' YOU** [ ] Sep75 [52]

Dec 75. (7") *<50175>* **LE LO LI. / WHO DO YOU LOVE** [–] [ ]

Mar 76. (7") *<50201>* **CROSSWORD PUZZLE. / GREED** [–] [ ]

SLY & THE FAMILY STONE

—— reformed with last line-up

Dec 76. (lp/c) *(EPC/40 81641) <33698>* **HEARD YA MISSED ME, WELL I'M BACK** [ ] [ ]
– Heard ya missed me, well I'm back / What was I thinkin' / In my head / Sexy situation / Blessing in disguise / Everything in you / Mother is a hippie / Let's be together / The thing / Family again.

Feb 77. (7") *<50331>* **FAMILY AGAIN. / NOTHING LESS THAN HAPPINESS** [–] [ ]

Warners Warners

Sep 79. (7") *(K 17474) <49062>* **REMEMBER WHO YOU ARE. / SHEER ENERGY** [ ] [ ]

Oct 79. (lp/c) *(K/K4 56640) <3303>* **BACK ON THE RIGHT TRACK** [ ] [ ]
– Remember who you are / Back on the right track / If it's not addin' up . . . / The same thing (makes you laugh, makes you cry) / Shine it on / It takes all kinds / Who's to say / Sheer energy. *(cd-iss. Jan96; 7599 26858-2)*

Dec 79. (7") *<49132>* **THE SAME THING (MAKES YOU LAUGH, MAKES YOU CRY). / WHO'S TO SAY** [–] [ ]

—— In 1981, SLY guested on album 'THE ELECTRIC SPANKING OF WAR BABIES' by George Clinton's FUNKADELIC.

– compilations, etc. –

—— on 'Epic' unless stated otherwise

1972. (lp; by SLY STONE) *Sculpture; <SCP 2001>* **RECORDED IN SAN FRANCISCO: 1964-67** [–] [ ]

Mar 73. (7") *(EPC 1148)* **FAMILY AFFAIR. / DANCE TO THE MUSIC** [ ] [–]

Feb 75. (7"ep) *(EPC 3048)* **DANCE TO THE MUSIC / COLOUR ME TRUE. / STAND! / RIDE THE RHYTHM** [ ] [–]

May 75. (d-lp) *(EPC 22004) <33462>* **HIGH ENERGY** [ ] [ ]
– (A WHOLE NEW THING / LIFE)

1975. (7") *<50119>* **HOT FUN IN THE SUMMERTIME. / FUN** [–] [ ]

1975. (7") *(152282)* **DANCE TO THE MUSIC. / LIFE** [ ] [–]

1975. (7") *(152302)* **HOT FUN IN THE SUMMERTIME. / M'LADY** [ ] [–]

1975. (7") *(152317)* **FAMILY AFFAIR. / RUNNIN' AWAY** [ ] [–]

1975. (7") *(152331)* **IF YOU WANT ME TO STAY. / FRISKY** [ ] [–]

Jan 77. (7") *(EPC 4879)* **DANCE TO THE MUSIC. / I WANT TO TAKE YOU HIGHER** [ ] [–]

Mar 79. (7") *(EPC 7070)* **DANCE TO THE MUSIC. / STAND!** [ ] [–]

Nov 79. (7") *(EPC 8017) <50795>* **DANCE TO THE MUSIC. / SING A SIMPLE SONG** [ ] [ ]

Jan 80. (lp) *(EPC 83640) <35974>* **TEN YEARS TOO SOON** [ ] [ ]
(disco remixes)

Aug 80. (7") *(EPC 8853)* **DANCE TO THE MUSIC. / EVERYDAY PEOPLE** [ ] [–]
(re-iss. Jul82 on 'Old Gold'; OG 9188)

May 82. (d-lp) *(EPC 22119) <37071>* **ANTHOLOGY** [ ] Dec81 [ ]
(re-iss. Sep87 lp/c; 460175-1/-4)

Sep 87. (7") *Portrait; (SLY 1)* **DANCE TO THE MUSIC. / FAMILY AFFAIR** [ ] [ ]
(12"+=) *(SLYT 1)* – Everyday people / Runnin' away.

Apr 91. (cd/c) *Thunderbolt; (CDTB/THBC 119)* **FAMILY AFFAIR** [ ] [–]

Nov 91. (cd/c) *Castle; (CCS CD/MC 307)* **THE COLLECTION** [ ] [–]

Dec 91. (cd) *Thunderbolt; (CDTB 129)* **IN THE STILL OF THE NIGHT** [ ] [–]

Jul 92. (cd/c) *Sony; (471758-2/-4)* **TAKIN' YOU HIGHER – THE BEST OF SLY & THE FAMILY STONE** [ ] [ ]
– Dance to the music / I want to take you higher / Family affair / Thank you (falletinme be mice elf agin) / I get high on you / Stand / M'lady / Skin I'm in / Everyday people / Sing a simple song / Hot fun in the summertime / Don't call me nigger, Whitey / Brave & strong / Life / Everybody is a star / If you want me to stay / (You caught me) Smilin' / Que sera sera / Running away / Family affair (remix). *(cd re-iss. Oct94 on 'Epic'; 477506-2)*

Feb 94. (cd/c) *Javelin; (HAD CD/MC 119)* **SPOTLIGHT ON SLY & THE FAMILY STONE** [ ] [–]

Mar 94. (cd) *Charly;* **REMEMBER WHO YOU ARE** [ ] [–]

Sep 94. (cd) *Ace; (CDCHD 539)* **PRECIOUS STONE: IN THE STUDIO WITH SLY STONE** (rec.1963-65) [ ] [–]

Dec 94. (cd/c) *Prestige; (CD/CAS SGP 0125)* **EVERY DOG HAS IT'S DAY** [ ] [–]

Feb 95. (cd; by SLY STONE & THE MOJO MEN) *(KLMCD 005)* **PEARLS FROM THE PAST** [ ] [–]

—— Thunderbolt records issued 2 albums of SLY STONE productions in Apr87 + Oct87 respectively, named 'DANCE TO THE MUSIC' & 'FAMILY AFFAIR'.

SLY STONE

Warners Warners

Mar 83. (lp) *(923700-1) <23700-1>* **AIN'T BUT THE ONE WAY** [ ] [ ]
– L.O.V.I.N.U. / One way / Ha ha, hee hee / Hobo Ken / Who in the funk do you think we are / You really got me / Sylvester / We can do it / High, y'all. *(cd-iss. Jan96; 7599 23700-2)*

—— In 1984, SLY joined BOBBY WOMACK on tour. He later guested on JESSE JOHNSON's 'A&M' US No.53 hit single 'Crazay' (Oct86) *AM 360 /<2878>.*

not iss. A&M

Oct 86. (7") *<2890>* **EEK-A-BO-STATIK. / BLACK GIRLS (RAE DAWN CHONG)** [–] [ ]

Dec 86. (7"w/ MARTHA DAVIS) **STONE LOVE AND AFFECTION. / BLACK GIRLS (RAE DAWN CHONG)** [–] [ ]

the SMALL FACES

Formed: East London, England . . . mid '65 by RONNIE LANE, KENNY JONES and JIMMY WINSTON, who subsequently found lead singer and ex-child actor, STEVE MARRIOTT. After a successful residency at Leicester Square's Cavern Club, the band were snapped up by 'Decca' records as potential usurpers to The WHO's mod crown. Their debut single, 'WHATCHA GONNA DO ABOUT IT' (1965) graced the Top 20 with its roughshod R&B and amid the ensuing attention the band received, WINSTON was kicked out after shamelessly trying to promote himself as the lynchpin of the group. With IAN McLAGAN drafted in as a replacement, the band hit Top 3 with the 'SHA LA LA LA LEE' (1966) single. Despite the cliched boy-meets-girl lyric, the record was a wildly exhilarating rush of amphetamine pop and suddenly The SMALL FACES were big news. After another Top 10 single and a critically acclaimed eponymous debut album, the band were being mentioned in the same breath as The BEATLES and The ROLLING STONES. Indeed, in August '66 they deposed The Fab Four's 'ELEANOR RIGBY' at the top of the charts with 'ALL OR NOTHING'. Come 1967, the band had left 'Decca' and signed with ANDREW LOOG-OLDHAM's 'Immediate' label, releasing 'HERE COMES THE NICE'. The single marked a change in direction and in keeping with the times, was vaguely psychedelic. After a similarly adventurous second album that bore a decidedly unadventurous title ('SMALL FACES' yet again), the band released their most well-known track, the slightly twee, deeply dippy 'ITCHYCOO PARK' (later reduced to dross by M-PEOPLE). Next came the abrasive 'TIN SOLDIER' (1967) single after which the band began working on their psychedelic masterpiece, 'OGDEN'S NUT GONE FLAKE' (1968). An engaging blend of trippy R&B and cockney charm, the album's influence was far reaching and it gets re-issued with the same tireless regularity as 'OCEAN WELLER SCENE' namedrop the band. Timeless as it was, the record proved to be the group's swansong and after a few singles, including the

The SMALL FACES

gorgeous 'AFTERGLOW (OF YOUR LOVE)' (1969), the band split with MARRIOTT flouncing off to form HUMBLE PIE. Meanwhile JONES, LANE and McLAGAN ditched the psychedelic overtones, recruited RON WOOD and ROD STEWART, renaming the band The FACES; lad-rock was born! The FACES peddled a distinctive strain of ramshackle, boozy, bluesy rock that was apparently best heard in a live setting surrounded by sweaty males. Their debut, 'FIRST STEP' (1970), was a boisterous statement of intent which included the ragged charm of 'THREE BUTTON HAND ME DOWN' and a raw cover of DYLAN's 'WICKED MESSENGER'. 'LONG PLAYER' (1971) was equally ballsy, while 'A NOD IS AS GOOD AS A WINK ...TO A BLIND HORSE' (1971) saw the band in full flight, WOOD going hell for leather on 'MISS JUDY'S FARM' and the gloriously un-PC raunch of 'STAY WITH ME'. The McLAGAN/LANE penned 'YOU'RE SO RUDE' was a leering gem and LANE excelled himself with the lovely 'DEBRIS'. As STEWART's solo career skyrocketed, the band began to splinter, unbalanced by ROD's high profile. After the slightly disappointing 'OOH LA LA' (1973) album, LANE left to go solo, The FACES basically becoming STEWART's backing band and after a final below par live album, RON WOOD left for The ROLLING STONES. There was a brief SMALL FACES reunion (minus LANE) in the late 70's and although the band had a deal with 'Atlantic', no commercial success was forthcoming. JONES went on to join The WHO, while MARRIOTT re-formed HUMBLE PIE but any chances of a further reunion were dealt a fatal blow in 1991 when MARRIOTT tragically died in a fire at his Essex home. After a respectable, if hardly commercial solo career, RONNIE LANE finally succumbed to Multiple Sclerosis in 1997. A sad end for two pioneering musicians who, through both The FACES and The SMALL FACES, heavily influenced the course of popular music; stand up BLUR, PULP, OASIS, PRIMAL SCREAM, The BLACK CROWES etc.

• **Songwriters:** MARRIOTT and LANE except; WHATCHA GONNA DO ABOUT IT (Ian Samwell-Smith; their early producer) / SHA-LA-LA-LA-LEE (c.Kenny Lynch & Mort Schuman) / EVERY LITTLE BIT HURTS (Brenda Holloway) / TAKE THIS HURT OFF ME (Don Covay) / YOU'VE REALLY GOT A HOLD ON ME (Miracles) / etc. The FACES covered MAYBE I'M AMAZED (Paul McCartney) / I WISH IT WOULD RAIN (Temptations) / etc. • **Trivia:** The FACES had come together initially as the supergroup, QUIET MELON, which included ART WOOD, LONG JOHN BALDRY and JIMMY HOROWITZ.

Album rating: THE SMALL FACES (*6) / FROM THE BEGINNING out-takes (*6) / SMALL FACES (*5) / THERE ARE BUT FOUR SMALL FACES (*7) / OGDENS' NUT GONE FLAKE (*8) / THE AUTUMN STONE collection (*5) / Faces: FIRST STEP (*6) / LONG PLAYER (*7) / A NOD'S AS GOOD AS A WINK (TO A BLIND HORSE) (*7) / OOH LA LA (*6) / COAST TO COAST – OVERTURE FOR BEGINNERS (*5; as Rod Stewart & The Faces) / SNAKES AND LADDERS: THE BEST OF THE FACES compilation (*7) / Small Faces: PLAYMATES (*3) / 78 IN THE SHADE (*4) / ULTIMATE COLLECTION compilation (*8)

STEVE MARRIOTT (b.30 Jan'47, Bow, London) – vocals, guitar (ex-solo artist) / **JIMMY WINSTON** (b. JAMES LANGWITH, 20 Apr'45, Stratford, London) – organ / **RONNIE LANE** (b. 1 Apr'45, Plaistow, London) – bass, vocals / **KENNY JONES** (b.16 Sep'48, Stepney, London) – drums

Decca / Press

Aug 65. (7") *(F 12208)* *<45-9794>* **WHATCHA GONNA DO ABOUT IT?. / WHAT'S A MATTER, BABY** — 14 Jan66

— **IAN McLAGAN** (b.12 May'45, Hounslow, England) – keyboards repl. WINSTON who went solo

Nov 65. (7") *(F 12276)* **I'VE GOT MINE. / IT'S TOO LATE** — –

Jan 66. (7") *(F 12317)* *<45-9826>* **SHA-LA-LA-LA-LEE. / GROW YOUR OWN** — 3 Apr66

May 66. (7") *(F 12393)* *<45-5007>* **HEY GIRL. / ALMOST GROWN** — 10 Jul66

May 66. (lp) *(LK 4790)* **SMALL FACES** — 3 –
– Shake / Come on children / You better believe it / It's too late / One night stand / Whatcha gonna do about it? / Sorry she's mine / E to D / You need loving / Don't stop what you're doing / Own up / Sha-la-la-la-lee. *(cd-iss. Jul88 on 'London'+= 820 572-2)* – What's a matter baby / I've got mine / Grow your own / Almost grown.

Decca / RCA Victor

Aug 66. (7") *(F 12470)* *<47-8949>* **ALL OR NOTHING. / UNDERSTANDING** — 1 Sep66

Nov 66. (7") *(F 12500)* *<47-9055>* **MY MIND'S EYE. / I CAN'T DANCE WITH YOU** — 4 Dec66

Feb 67. (7") *(F 12565)* **I CAN'T MAKE IT. / JUST PASSING** — 26 –

Apr 67. (7") *(F 12619)* **PATTERNS. / E TO D** — –

May 67. (lp) *(LK 4879)* **FROM THE BEGINNING** (out-takes, demos, etc) — 17 –
– Runaway / My mind's eye / Yesterday, today and tomorrow / That man / My way of giving / Hey girl / Tell me have you ever seen me? / Come back and take this hurt off me / All or nothing / Baby don't do it / Plum Nellie / Sha-la-la-la-lee / You really got a hold on me / What'cha gonna do about it? *(re-iss. Aug84; DOA 2) (cd-iss. Jan89 on 'London'+=; 820 766-2) (cd re-iss. Jun03 on 'Deram'+=; 844633-2)* – My mind's eye (French EP version) / Hey girl (French EP version) / Take this hurt off me (version) / Baby don't you do it (version) / What'cha gonna do about it (BBC session).

Immediate / Immediate

Jun 67. (7") *(IM 050)* *<1902>* **HERE COMES THE NICE. / TALK TO YOU** — 12

Jun 67. (lp; mono/stereo) *(IMLP/IMSP 008)* **SMALL FACES** — 12 –
– Green circles / Become like you / Get yourself together / All our yesterdays / Talk to you / Show me the way / Up the wooden hills to Bedfordshire / Eddie's dreaming / (Tell me) Have you ever seen me / Something I want to tell you / Feeling lonely / Happy boys happy / Things are going to get better / My way of giving. *(cd-iss. May91 as 'GREEN CIRCLES (FIRST IMMEDIATE ALBUM)' on 'Sequel'; NEXCD 163) (+=)* – Green circles (take 2) / Donkey rides, a penny, a glass / Have you ever seen me (take 2). *(cd re-iss. Apr97 on 'Essential'; ESMCD 476)*

Aug 67. (7") *(IM 052)* *<501>* **ITCHYCOO PARK. / I'M ONLY DREAMING** — 3 Nov67 16

Nov 67. (7") *(IM 062)* *<5003>* **TIN SOLDIER. / I FEEL MUCH BETTER** — 9 Mar68 73
(re-iss. May75; IMS 100)

Feb 68. (lp) *<Z12-52-002>* **THERE ARE BUT FOUR SMALL FACES** — –
– Here comes the nice / All or nothing / Lazy Sunday / Sha-la-la-la-lee / Collibosher / The Autumn stone / Whatcha gonna do about it? / My mind's eye / Itchycoo Park / Hey girl / The universal / Runaway / Call it something nice / I can't make it / Afterglow (of your love) / Tin soldier. (

Apr 68. (7") *(IM 064)* *<5007>* **LAZY SUNDAY. / ROLLIN' OVER** — 2
(re-iss. Oct82; same)

Jun 68. (lp; mono/stereo) *(IMLP/IMSP 012)* *<Z12-52-008>* **OGDENS' NUT GONE FLAKE** — 1
– Ogden's nut gone flake / Afterglow (of your love) / Long agos and worlds apart / Rene / Son of a baker / Lazy Sunday / Happiness Stan / Rollin' over / The hungry intruder / The journey / Mad John / Happy days / Toy town. *<US re-iss. Mar73 on 'Abkco'; 4225> (re-iss. Dec75; IML 1001) (re-iss. Jun77; IML 2001) (re-iss. export Aug78 on 'Charly'; CR 300015) (re-iss. Mar80 on 'Virgin'; V 2159) (re-iss. Oct86 on 'Castle' lp/cd+=; CLA LP/CD 116)* – Tin soldier (live). *(re-cd-iss. in box Feb91 on 'Castle'; CLACT 016) (cd re-iss. Feb97 on 'Original Recordings'; ORRLP 001) (cd re-iss. Apr97 on 'Essential'; ESMCD 477)*

Jul 68. (7") *(IM 069)* *<5009>* **THE UNIVERSAL. / DONKEY RIDES, A PENNY, A GLASS** — 16

Nov 68. (7") *<5012>* **THE JOURNEY. / MAD JOHN** — –

Mar 69. (7") *(IM 077)* *<5014>* **AFTERGLOW (OF YOUR LOVE). / WHAM BAM, THANK YOU MAM** — 36

Mar 69. (d-lp) *(IMAL 01/02)* **THE AUTUMN STONE** (rarities, live, etc)
– Here comes the nice / The Autumn stone / Collibosher / All or nothing / Red balloon / Lazy Sunday / Rollin' over / If I were a carpenter / Every little bit hurts / My mind's eye / Tin soldier / Just asking / Call it something nice / I can't make it / Afterglow (of your love) / Sha-la-la-la-lee / The universal / Itchycoo Park / Hey girl / Wide eyed girl / On the wall / What'cha gonna do about it / Wham bam thank you mam. *(re-iss. Jul84; IMLD 1) (re-iss. May86 on 'Castle' lp/c/cd; CLA LP/MC/CD 114) (re-iss. 1991) (cd re-mast.Apr97 on 'Essential'+=; ESMCD 478)* – Donkey rides a peeny a glass / All or nothing (live) / Tin soldier (live) / Rollin' over (live). *(cd re-iss. Mar03 on 'Snapper'; SNIP 404CD) (cd re-iss. May03 on 'Sunspot'; SPOT 536)*

— disbanded Mar'69 when STEVE MARRIOTT formed HUMBLE PIE. The remaining members became The FACES

the FACES

alongside **ROD STEWART** (b.10 Jan'45, London) – vocals (also Solo artist, ex-JEFF BECK) / **RON WOOD** (b. 1 Jun'47, Hillingdon, England) – guitar (ex-JEFF BECK GROUP, ex-CREATION)

(note: in the US, debut lp still credited to The SMALL FACES)

Warners Warners

Feb 70. (7") *(WB 8005)* **FLYING. / THREE-BUTTON HAND-ME-DOWN** [ ] [–]

Mar 70. (lp) *(WS 3000)* **FIRST STEP** [45] [–]
– Wicked messenger / Devotion / Shake, shudder, shiver / Stone / Around the plynth / Flying / Pineapple and the monkey / Nobody knows / Looking out the window / Three-button hand-me-down. *(re-iss. Dec71 lp/c; K/K4 46053) (re-iss. Jul87 on 'Edsel'; ED 240) (cd-iss. Sep91; EDCD 240) (cd re-iss. Sep93; 7599 26376-2)*

Mar 71. (7") *(WB 8018)* **HAD ME A REAL GOOD TIME. / REAR WHEEL SKID** [ ] [–]

Mar 71. (lp) *(WS 3011) <1892>* **LONG PLAYER** [31] [29]
– Bad 'n' ruin / Tell everyone / Sweet lady Mary / Richmond / Maybe I'm amazed / Had a real good time / On the beach / I feel so good / Jerusalem. *(re-iss. Dec71 lp/c; K/K4 46064) (cd-iss. Sep93; 7599 26191-2)*

Apr 71. (7") **MAYBE I'M AMAZED. / OH LORD I'M BROWNED OFF** [–] [ ]

Nov 71. (7") *(K 16136)* **STAY WITH ME. / DEBRIS** [6] [–]

Nov 71. (lp/c) *(K/K4 56006) <2574>* **A NOD IS AS GOD AS A WINK . . . TO A BLIND HORSE** [2] [6]
– Miss Judy's farm / You're so rude / Love lives here / Last orders please / Stay with me / Debris / Memphis / Too bad / That's all I need. *(cd-iss. Sep93; 7599 25929-2)*

Dec 71. (7") *<7545>* **STAY WITH ME. / YOU'RE SO RUDE** [–] [17]

Feb 73. (7") *(K 16247) <7681>* **CINDY INCIDENTALLY. / SKEWIFF** [2] [48]

Apr 73. (lp/c) *(K/K4 56011) <2665>* **OOH LA LA** [1] [21]
– Silicone grown / Cindy incidentally / Flags and banners / My fault / Borstal boys / Fly in the ointment / If I'm on the late side / Glad and sorry / Just another monkey / Ooh la la. *(cd-iss. Sep93; 7599 26368-2)*

May 73. (7") **OOH LA LA. / BORSTAL BOYS** [–] [ ]

—— **TETSU YAMAUCHI** (b.21 Oct'47, Fukuoka, Japan) – bass (ex-FREE) repl. RONNIE LANE who went solo

Nov 73. (7") *(K 16341)* **POOL HALL RICHARD. / I WISH IT WOULD RAIN** [8] [ ]

ROD STEWART & THE FACES

due to ROD's solo successes

Mercury Mercury

Jan 74. (lp) *(9100 011) <1-697>* **COAST TO COAST – OVERTURE FOR BEGINNERS (live)** [3] [63]
– It's all over now / Cut across Shorty / Too bad / Every picture tells a story / Angel / Stay with me / I wish it would rain / I'd rather go blind / Borstal boys / Amazing Grace / Jealous guy. *(cd-iss. Nov87; 832 128-2)*
(above also featured ROD's songs from solo career)

Warners Warners

Nov 74. (7") *(K 16494)* **YOU CAN MAKE ME DANCE SING OR ANYTHING. / AS LONG AS YOU TELL HIM** [12] [ ]

—— Late '75, crumbled again, as ROD STEWART enjoyed overwhelming solo stardom. RON WOOD went off to join The ROLLING STONES.

– (FACES) compilations, etc. –

Oct 75. (d-lp) *Warners; (K 66027)* **TWO ORIGINALS OF THE FACES** [ ] [–]
– (FIRST STEP / LONG PLAYER)

Apr 77. (lp/c) *Riva; (K/K4 56172) <2897>* **SNAKES AND LADDERS – THE BEST OF THE FACES** [24] [ ]
– Pool hall Richard / Cindy incidentally / Ooh la la / Sweet Lady Mary / Flying / Pineapple and the monkey / You can make me dance, sing or anything / Had me a real good time / Stay with me / Miss Judy's farm / Silicone grown / That's all you need.

May 77. (7"ep) *Riva; (RIVA 8)* **THE FACES** [41] [ ]
– Cindy incidentally / Stay with me / Memphis / You can make me dance, sing or anything.

Sep 80. (lp/c) *Pickwick; (SSP/SSC 3074)* **THE FACES FEATURING ROD STEWART** [ ] [–]

Nov 92. (cd/c) *Mercury; (514 180-2/-4)* **THE BEST OF ROD STEWART & THE FACES** [58] [–]

May 93. (cd/c; ROD STEWART & THE FACES) *Spectrum; (550026-2/-4)* **AMAZING GRACE** [ ] [–]

the SMALL FACES

SMALL FACES re-formed by **JONES, McLAGAN** + reinstated **MARRIOTT** incomer **RICKY WILLS** – bass (ex-Peter FRAMPTON'S CAMEL, ex-ROXY MUSIC, etc)

Atlantic Atlantic

Jul 77. (7") *(K 10983)* **LOOKIN' FOR A LOVE. / KO'D (BY LUV)** [ ] [ ]

Aug 77. (lp/c) *(K/K4 50375) <SD 19113>* **PLAYMATES** [ ] [ ]
– High and happy / Never too late / Tonight / Say larvee / Find it / Lookin' for a love / Playmates / Drive in romance / This song's just for you / Smilin' in tune. *(cd-iss. Jun92 on 'Repertoire';)*

Nov 77. (7") *(K 11043)* **STAND BY ME (STAND BY YOU). / HUNGRY AND LOOKING** [ ] [ ]

—— added on tour **JIMMY McCULLOCH** (b.1953, Glasgow, Scotland) – guitar (of WINGS)

Jun 78. (7") *(K 11173)* **FILTHY RICH. / OVER TOO SOON** [ ] [ ]

Sep 78. (lp/c) *(K/K4 50468) <SD 19171>* **78 IN THE SHADE** [ ] [ ]
– Over too soon / Too many crossroads / Let me down gently / Thinkin' about love / Stand by me (stand by you) / Brown man do / Soldier / Reel sour / You ain''t seen nothin' yet / Filthy rich. *(cd-iss. Nov93 on 'Repertoire';)*

—— Disbanded again mid'78. KENNY JONES joined The WHO. McCULLOCH died 27th Sep'79. MARRIOTT re-formed HUMBLE PIE. He was to tragically die in his Essex home after it went on fire 20 Apr'91. Founder member RONNIE LANE finally died in June '97 after 18 years suffering from multiple sclerosis.

– (selective) compilations, etc. –

Nov 75. (7") *Immediate; (IMS 102)* **ITCHYCOO PARK. / MY MIND'S EYE** [9] [–]

Mar 76. (7") *Immediate; (IMS 106)* **LAZY SUNDAY. / (TELL ME) HAVE YOU EVER SEEN ME** [36] [–]

May 90. (cd/c/d-lp) *Castle TV; (CTV CD/MC/LP 004)* **THE ULTIMATE COLLECTION** [ ] [–]
(cd re-iss. Dec91 as 'THE COMPLETE COLLECTION'; CCSCD 302)

Jun 90. (cd/c/lp) *See For Miles; (SEE 293/+C/CD)* **THE SINGLES A's & B's** [ ] [–]

Nov 95. (4xcd-box) *Charly; (IMMBOX 1)* **THE IMMEDIATE YEARS** [ ] [–]

May 96. (d-cd/d-c/d-lp) *Deram; (844583-2/-4/-1)* **THE DECCA ANTHOLOGY 1965-1967** [66] [–]

Nov 96. (d-cd) *Charly; (CPCD 82602)* **THE VERY BEST OF THE SMALL FACES** [ ] [–]

Oct 98. (3xcd-box) *Essential; (ESMBX 302)* **SMALL FACES / OGDEN'S NUT GONE FLAKE / THE AUTUMN STONE** [ ] [ ]

Apr 99. (d-cd) *Sequel; (NEECD 311)* **THE DARLINGS OF THE WAPPING WHARF** [ ] [ ]

Nov 99. (cd/lp) *Strange Fruit; (SFRS CD/LP 087)* **THE BBC SESSIONS** [ ] [ ]

Jan 00. (cd) *Universal; (E 844942-2)* **UNIVERSAL MASTERS COLLECTION** [ ] [–]

Feb 00. (d-cd) *Charly; (CDVAL 1152)* **THE ULTIMATE COLLECTION** [ ] [–]

Apr 00. (cd) *Disky; <(SI 99078-2)>* **THE BEST OF THE 60'S** [ ] [ ]

Sep 01. (cd) *Decca; (882973-2)* **THE BEST OF THE SMALL FACES** [ ] [ ]

May 03. (d-cd) *Sanctuary; (TDSAN 004) <27977>* **ULTIMATE COLLECTION** [24] [ ]
– What'cha gonna do about it? / I've got mine / It's too late / Sha-la-la-la-lee / Grow your own / Hey girl / Shake / Come on children / You better believe it / One night stand / Sorry she's mine / Own up time / You need loving / Don't stop what you are doing / E too D / All or nothing / Understanding / My mind's eye / I can't dance with you / I can't make it / Just passing / Patterns / Yeasterday today and tomorrow / That man / Baby don't do it / Here comes the nice / Talk to you / Tell me have you ever seen me / Things are going to get better / My way of giving / Green circles / Get yourself together / Up the wooden hills to Bedfordshire / Eddie's dreaming / Itchycoo Park / I'm only dreaming / Tin soldier / I feel much better / Ogden's nut gone flake / Afterglow of your love / Song of a baker / Lazy Sunday / Rollin' over / Mad John / Happy days toy town / The universal / Donkey rides a penny a glass / Wham bam thank you mam / Don't burst my bubble / The autumn stone.

the SMASHING PUMPKINS

Formed: Chicago, Illinois, USA . . . late 80's by BILLY CORGAN, JAMES IHA, D'ARCY WRETZKY. The son of a jazz guitarist and former member of local goth band, the MARKED, CORGAN initiated the SMASHING PUMPKINS as a three piece using a drum machine, before the band recruited sticksman, JIMMY CHAMBERLAIN. After a debut single for a local label, 'I AM ONE', and the inclusion of two tracks on a local compilation album, the group came to the attention of influential Seattle label, 'Sub Pop'. After only one single, 'TRISTESSA', the SMASHING PUMPKINS moved once more, signing to Virgin subsidiary, 'Hut', in the UK, 'Caroline' in America. Produced by BUTCH VIG, a debut album, 'GISH', was released in early '92, its grunge pretensions belying a meandering 70's/psychedelic undercurrent which distanced the band from most of their contemporaries. Nevertheless, the group amassed a sizable student/grassroots following which eventually saw the debut go gold in the States, a re-released 'I AM ONE' sneaking into the UK Top 75 later that year. With the masterful 'SIAMESE DREAM' (1993), the band went from underground hopefuls to alternative rock frontrunners, the album fully realising the complex 'PUMPKINS sound in a delicious wash of noise and gentle melody. Influenced by acoustic LED ZEPPELIN fused with slices of 70's PINK FLOYD, CORGAN's croaky but effective voice was at its best on the pastel, NIRVANA-esque classics, 'TODAY' and 'DISARM', while the 'PUMPKINS went for the jugular on the likes of 'CHERUB ROCK', 'ROCKET' and 'GEEK U.S.A.'. The album made the Top 5 in Britain, Top 10 in the States, selling multi-millions and turning the band into a 'grunge' sensation almost overnight, despite the fact that their mellotron stylings and complex arrangements marked them out as closer in spirit to prog-rock than punk. Amidst frantic touring, the band released the outtakes/B-sides compilation, 'PISCES ISCARIOT' (1994), the next album proper surfacing in late '95 as the sprawling double set, 'MELLON COLLIE AND THE INFINITE SADNESS'. Dense and stylistically breathtaking, the album veered from all-out grunge/thrash to acoustic meandering and avant-rock doodlings, a less cohesive whole than its predecessor but much more to get your teeth into. Inevitably, there were criticisms of self-indulgence, though for a two-hour set, there was a surprising, compelling consistency to proceedings; among the highlights were 'BULLET WITH BUTTERFLY WINGS', 'TONIGHT, TONIGHT' and the visceral rage of '1979'. The record scaled the US charts, where the SMASHING PUMPKINS were almost reaching the commercial and critical heights of NIRVANA, the group also taking Britain by storm, headlining the 1995 Reading Festival. Never the most stable of bands, disaster struck the following year when new boy (keyboard player) JONATHAN MELVOIN died of a drugs overdose and heroin addict CHAMBERLAIN was finally kicked out. More recently (early 1998), IHA released an acclaimed solo album of acoustic strumming ('LET IT COME DOWN') while the others recorded fresh songs with a drum machine, taking things full circle. That summer, the 'PUMPKINS showed a softer side to their character when the mournful but still effective album, 'ADORE', hit the Top 5. 1999 saw two major personnel changes via the return of CHAMBERLAIN and the departure of D'ARCY (who was replaced by ex-HOLE bassist MELISSA AUF DER MAUR); one last set would appear in 2000, 'MACHINA – THE MACHINES OF GOD'. In a postscript to the messy break-up of the SMASHING PUMPKINS, BILLY CORGAN began putting together a supergroup, hand-picking musicians such as DAVID PAJO (ex-SLINT and currently PAPA M), MATT SWEENEY (of post-rockers CHAVEZ) and A PERFECT CIRCLE bassist PAZ LENCHANTIN. Along with PUMPKINS drummer JIMMY CHAMBERLAIN the group emerged as ZWAN, playing a handful of gigs in America during 2001. Buzz was now circling CORGAN's new mantle, with some critics dismissing it purely as a vanity project. They were pleasantly surprised then, when the quintet issued 'MARY STAR OF THE SEA' in 2003 to rave reviews and massive sales. Like a lost PUMPKINS record, with PAJO firmly replacing IHA on guitar duties and CHAMBERLAIN's thunderous backbone still intact, it was ultimately CORGAN's record and solid proof of his majestic songwriting skills. ZWAN was however shortlived, as CORGAN disbanded the project shortly after the album's release. Finally going on his ownsome, CORGAN poured his insecurities, mopes and fears into 'THE FUTURE EMBRACE' (2005), an album that actually looked to the past – more specifically, surprise, surprise, the 80s – in order to go forward. The album's razor-jawed synth pulse, industrial-mascara shadings and neo-gothic navel-gazing was a far cry from the SMASHING PUMPKINS, but at least it was in step with contemporary sensibilities, right down to an ethereal, post-pop cover the Bee Gees' 'TO LOVE SOMEBODY' (featuring ROBERT SMITH). A Top 40 entry in the US, the album also generated a very minor UK hit in 'WALKING SHADE'.

• **Songwriters:** CORGAN, except several with IHA. Covered; A GIRL NAMED SANDOZ (Eric Burdon & The Animals) / LANDSLIDE (Fleetwood Mac) / DANCING IN THE MOONLIGHT (Thin Lizzy) / NEVER LET ME DOWN (Depeche Mode) / YOU'RE ALL I'VE GOT TONIGHT (Cars) / CLONES (WE'RE ALL) (Alice Cooper) / DREAMING (Blondie) / A NIGHT LIKE THIS (Cure) / DESTINATION UNKNOWN (Missing Persons) / SAD PETER PAN with Red Red Meat (Vic Chesnutt). • **Miscellaneous:** IHA and D'ARCY set up their own label, 'Scratchie', for whom the outfit, FULFLEJ recorded an album ('Wack-Ass Tuba Riff') in 1996 with the pair making guest appearances.

Album rating: GISH (*6) / SIAMESE DREAM (*9) / MELLON COLLIE AND THE INFINITE SADNESS (*9) / PISCES ISCARIOT compilation (*5) / THE AEROPLANE FLIES HIGH boxed set (*6) / ADORE (*5) / MACHINA – THE MACHINES OF GOD (*5) / (ROTTEN APPLES) GREATEST HITS compilation (*7) / EARPHORIA (*6) / James Iha: LET IT COME DOWN (*5) / Zwan: MARY STAR OF THE SEA (*7) / Billy Corgan: THE FUTURE EMBRACE (*5)

BILLY CORGAN (b.17 Mar'67) – vocals, guitar / **JAMES IHA** (b.26 Mar'68, Elk Grove, Illinois) – guitar / **D'ARCY (WRETZKY)** (b. 1 May'68, South Haven, Michigan) – bass, vocals / **JIMMY CHAMBERLIN** (b.10 Jun'64, Joliet, Illinois) – drums

		not iss.	Limited Potential
Apr 90.	(7") *<Limp 006>* **I AM ONE. / NOT WORTH ASKING**	–	
		Glitterhouse	Sub Pop
Dec 90.	(7",7"pink) *<SP 90>* **TRISTESSA. / LA DOLLY VITA** (UK-12"+=; May93) *(SP 10-137)* – Honeyspider.	–	
		Hut	Caroline
Aug 91.	(12") *(HUTT 6)* **SIVA. / WINDOW PAINE**		–
Feb 92.	(12"ep/cd-ep) *(HUTT/CDHUT 10)* **LULL EP** – Rhinoceros / Blue / Slunk / Bye June (demo).		–
Feb 92.	(cd/c/lp) *(HUT CD/MC/LP 002)* *<1705>* **GISH** – I am one / Siva / Rhinoceros / Bury me / Crush / Suffer / Snail / Tristessa / Window paine / Daydream. *(re-iss. May94; diff.versions cd/lp; HUT CDX/LPX 002)*		Aug91
Jun 92.	(c-ep/12"ep/cd-ep) *(HUT C/T/CD 17)* **PEEL SESSIONS** – Siva / A girl named Sandoz / Smiley.		–
Aug 92.	(12"ep/cd-ep) *(HUTT/CDHUT 18)* **I AM ONE. / PLUME / STARLA** (10"ep) *(HUTTEN 18)* – ('A'side) / Terrapin (live) / Bullet train to Osaka.	73	–
Jun 93.	(7"clear) *(HUT 31)* **CHERUB ROCK. / PURR SNICKETY** (12"/cd-s) *(HUTT/CDHUT 31)* – ('A'side) / Pissant / French movie theme / (Star spangled banner).	31	–
Jul 93.	(cd/c/d-lp) *(HUT CD/MC/LP 011)* *<88267>* **SIAMESE DREAM** – Cherub rock / Quiet / Today / Hummer / Rocket / Disarm / Soma / Geek U.S.A. / Mayonaise / Spaceboy / Silverfuck / Sweet sweet / Luna. *(d-lp re-iss. Dec99 on 'Caroline'; CAROL 17401)*	4	10
Sep 93.	(7"red) *(HUT 37)* **TODAY. / APATHY'S LAST KISS** (c-s/12"/cd-s) *(HUTC/HUTT/CDHUT 37)* – ('A'side) / Hello kitty kat / Obscured.	44	–

Feb 94. (7"purple) *(HUT 43)* **DISARM. / SIAMESE DREAM** [11] [–]
(12"/cd-s) *(HUT T/CD 43)* – ('A'side) / Soothe (demo) / Blew away.
(cd-s) *(HUTDX 43)* – ('A'side) / Dancing in the moonlight / Landslide.

Oct 94. (cd/c/gold-lp) *<39834>* **PISCES ISCARIOT**
(compilation of B-sides & rarities) [–] [4]
– Soothe / Frail and bedazzled / Plume / Whir / Blew away / Pissant / Hello Kitty Kat / Obscured / Landslide / Starla / Blue / A girl named Sandoz / La dolly vita / Spaced. *<w/ free gold-7"; CAR 1767-7>* **NOT WORTH ASKING. / HONEY SPIDER II** *(UK-iss.Oct96 cd/c/lp; HUT CD/MC/LP 41)*

Hut Virgin

Dec 94. (7"peach) *(HUTL 48)* **ROCKET. / NEVER LET ME DOWN** [ ] [–]
(4x7"box-set) *(SPBOX 1)* **SIAMESE SINGLES** – (last 3 singles 1993-94 + above)

Oct 95. (c-s/cd-s) *(HUT C/CD 63)* *<38522>* **BULLET WITH BUTTERFLY WINGS / . . .SAID SADLY** [20] [25]

Oct 95. (d-cd/d-c) *(CD/TC HUTD 30)* *<40861>* **MELLON COLLIE AND THE INFINITE SADNESS** [4] [1]
– DAWN TO DUSK:- Mellon Collie and the infinite sadness / Tonight, tonight / Jellybelly / Zero / Here is no why / Bullet with butterfly wings / To forgive / An ode to no one / Love / Cupid de Locke / Galapogos / Muzzle / Porcelina of the vast oceans / Take me down. // TWILIGHT TO STARLIGHT:- Where boys fear to tread / Bodies / Thirty-three / In the arms of sleep / 1979 / Tales of a scorched Earth / Thru the eyes of Ruby / Stumbleine / X.Y.U. / We only come out at night / Beautiful / Lily (my one and only) / By starlight / Farewell and goodnight. *(re-iss. Apr96 as t-lp+=; HUTTLP 30)* – Tonight reprise / Infinite sadness.

— added on tour **JONATHAN MELVOIN** – keyboards (ex-DICKIES) (brother of WENDY; ex-WENDY & LISA, ex-PRINCE)

Jan 96. (c-ep/12"ep/cd-ep) *(HUT C/T/CD 67)* *<38547>* **1979 / UGLY. / BELIEVE / CHERRY** [16] [12]
(12"ep/cd-ep; Mar96) *(HUT TX/CDX 67)* – 1979 REMIXES: Vocal / Instrumental / Moby / Cement.

May 96. (c-ep) *(HUTC 69)* *<38547>* **TONIGHT, TONIGHT / MELADORI MAGPIE / ROTTEN APPLES** [7] Jun96 [36]
(cd-ep+=) *(HUTCD 69)* – Medellia of the gray skies.
(cd-ep) *(HUTDX 69)* – ('A'side) / Jupiter's lament / Blank / Tonite (reprise).

— On 12th Jul'96, MELVOIN died of a heroin overdose. CHAMBERLIN, who found him dead, was charged with drug offences and sacked by the remaining trio who were said to sick of his long-lasting drug addiction. In August, they were replaced for tour by **DENNIS FLEMION** – keyboards (ex-FROGS) + **MATT WALKER** – drums (of FILTER)

Sep 96. (m-cd) *(HUTCD 73)* *<38545>* **ZERO EP** [ ] May96 [46]
– Zero / God / Mouths of babes / Tribute to Johnny / Marquis in spades / Pennies / Pastichio medley: (excerpts).

Nov 96. (cd-ep) *(HUTCD 78)* *<38574>* **THIRTY THREE / THE LAST SONG / THE AEROPLANE FLIES HIGH (TURNS LEFT, LOOKS RIGHT) / TRANSFORMER** [21] [39]
(cd-ep) *(HUTDX 78)* – ('A'side) / The bells / My blue Heaven.

Nov 96. (5xcd-ep;box) *<SPBOX 2>* **THE AEROPLANE FLIES HIGH** [–] [42]
– (BULLET WITH BUTTERFLY WINGS / 1979 / TONIGHT, TONIGHT / THIRTY THREE / ZERO)

— late in '96, CORGAN (with WALKER) provided six songs for the 'RANSOM' film soundtrack credited to conductor JAMES HORNER

Jun 97. (c-s) *(W 0404C)* **THE END IS THE BEGINNING IS THE END / THE BEGINNING IS THE END IS THE BEGINNING** [10] [–]
(cd-s+=) *(W 0404CD)* – The ethers tragic / The guns of love disastrous.
(12"/cd-s) *(W 0410 T/CD)* – ('A'mixes; 2 Fluke mixes / 2 Rabbit in The Moons mixes / Hallucination Gotham mix).
(above from the film 'Batman & Robin' on 'Warners')

May 98. (7") *(HUT 101)* *<38647>* **AVA ADORE. / CZARINA** [11] Jun98 [42]
(c-s+=/cd-s+=) *(HUT C/CD 101)* – Once in a while.

Jun 98. (cd/c/d-lp) *(CDHUT/TCHUT/HUTDLP 51)* *<45879>* **ADORE** [5] [2]
– To Sheila / Ava adore / Perfect / Daphne decends / Once upon a time / Tear / Crestfallen / Appels + oranjes / Pug / The tale of Dusty and Pistol Pete / Annie-dog / Shame / Behold! the night mare / For Martha / Blank page / 17.

Sep 98. (c-s/cd-s) *(HUT C/CD 106)* *<38650>* **PERFECT / SUMMER / PERFECT (Nellee Hooper mix)** [24] [54]
(cd-s) *(HUTDX 106)* – ('A'side) / Daphne descends (Oakenfold Perfecto mix) / Daphne descends (Kerry B mix).

— **CHAMBERLAIN** was now back in the fold

— **MELISSA AUF DER MAUR** – bass (ex-HOLE) repl. D'ARCY

Feb 00. (c-s/cd-s) *(HUT C/CD 127)* **STAND INSIDE YOUR LOVE / SPEED KILLS** [23] [–]

Feb 00. (cd/c/d-lp) *(CDHUT/HUTMC/HUTDLP 59)* *<48936>* **MACHINA / THE MACHINES OF GOD** [7] [3]
– The everlasting gaze / Rain drops & sun showers / Stand inside your love / I of the mourning / The sacred and profane / Try, try, try / Heavy metal machine / This time / The imploding voice / Glass and the ghost children / Wound / The crying tree of Mercury / With every light / Blue skies bring tears / Age of innocence.

Sep 00. (cd-s) *(HUTCD 140)* **TRY, TRY, TRY / HERE'S TO THE ATOM BOMB** [73] [–]

— the band split in November 2000; CORGAN was back with ZWAN in '03

– compilations, etc. –

on 'Hut' UK / 'Virgin' America unless stated otherwise

Nov 01. (cd) *(CDHUT 70)* *<11316>* **(ROTTEN APPLES) GREATEST HITS** [28] [31]
– Siva / Rhinoceros / Drown / Cherub rock / Today / Disarm / Bullet with butterfly wings / 1979 / Zero / Tonight, tonight / Eye / Ava adore / Perfect / The everlasting gaze / Stand inside your love / Try, try, try / Real love / Untitled. *(d-cd+=; CDHUTD 70)* – Lucky 13 / Aeroplane flies high (turns left looks right) / Because you are / Slow down / Believe / My mistake / Marquis in spades / Here's to the atom bomb / Sparrow / Waiting / Saturnine / Rock on / Set the ray to Jerry / Winterlong / Soot and stars / Blissed and gone.

Nov 02. (cd) *(CDHUT 79)* *<42706>* **EARPHORIA (live)** [ ] [ ]
– Sinfony / Quiet / Disarm / Cherub rock / Today / Bugg superstar / I am one / Pulseczar / Soma / Slunk / French movie theme / Geek U.S.A. / Mayonnaise / Silverfuck / Why am I so tired.

ZWAN

BILLY CORGAN – vocals, guitar / **JIMMY CHAMBERLIN** – drums / **MATT SWEENEY** – guitar (ex-CHAVEZ, ex-SKUNK) / **DAVID PAJO** – guitar, bass (ex-SLINT, ex-TORTOISE) / **PAZ LENCHANTIN** – bass (of A PERFECT CIRCLE)

Reprise Reprise

Feb 03. (cd/d-lp) *<(9362 48436-2/-1)>* **MARY STAR OF THE SEA** [33] Jan03 [3]
– Lyric / Settle down / Declarations of faith / Honestly / El sol / Of a broken heart / Ride a black swan / Heartsong / Endless summer / Baby let's rock! / Ywah! / Desire / Jesus, I – Mary star of the sea / Come with me. *(ltd cd w/dvd+=; 9362 48425-2)* – My life and times / Rivers we can't cross / Mary star of the sea / Love lies in ruin / For your love / Down down down / New poetry / W.P. / Jesus, I / God's gonna set this world on fire / To love you / Consumed / My life and times / Danger boy / Spilled milk.

Feb 03. (7") *(W 600)* **HONESTLY. / NUMBER OF THE BEAST** [28] [–]
(cd-s+=) *(W 600CD)* – Freedom ain't what it used to be.

Jun 03. (7") *(W 607)* **LYRIC. / NOBODY 'CEPT YOU (live)** [44] [–]
(cd-s+=) *(W 607CD)* – Autumn leaves.

— split mid September 2003

BILLY CORGAN

not iss. Hollywood

Nov 96. (cd/c) *<162086-2/-4>* **RANSOM** (soundtrack w/ JAMES HORNER) [–] [ ]
– (tracks by JAMES HORNER) / Rats / Worms / Spiders / Lizards / Worms part 2 / Squirrels with tails.

Virgin Virgin

Sep 99. (cd) *(CDVUS 161)* *<7243 8 47753-2>* **STIGMATA** (soundtrack w/ MIKE GARSON & Various Artists) [ ] Aug99 [ ]
– (other artists) / Identify / Pop pop – Await – Reflect (pretty) / Reflect (clouds) – Truth / Of square waves – Random though / Reflection – Possession / Reflect (gray) – Of sine waves / Distrbnce (after sckhausen) – Reflect (pause) – Orah / Sustain – Identify (affectation) / All answers revealed – Reflect (devotion) / Purge – 10,000,000 voices – Reflect (purity) – Identify (peace) / Reflect (time) – Tree whispers.

Warners Warners

Jun 05. (dvd-s) *(W 673DVD)* **WALKING SHADE (video) / WALKING SHADE /)interviews from 'There')** [74] [–]

Jun 05. (cd) *<(9362 48712-2)>* **THE FUTURE EMBRACE** [ ] [31]
– All things change / Mina Loy (M.O.H.) / Thecameraeye / To love somebody (feat. ROBERT SMITH) / A100 / D.I.A. / Now (and then) / I'm ready / Walking shade / Sorrows (in blue) / Pretty, pretty star / Strayz.

JAMES IHA

JAMES IHA – vocals, guitar / **NEAL CASAL** – guitar / **ADAM SCHLESINGER** – piano (of FOUNTAINS OF WAYNE) / **GREG LEISZ** – steel guitar / **JOHN GINTY** – hammond organ / **SOLOMON SNYDER** – bass / **MATT WALKER** – drums / **NINA GORDON** (of VERUCA SALT) also a part of initial basement set-up

Feb 98. (cd/c/lp) *(CDHUT/HUTMC/HUTLP 47)* *<45411>* **LET IT COME DOWN** [ ] [ ]
– Be strong now / Sound of love / Beauty / See the sun / Country girl / Jealousy / Lover, lover / Silver string / Winter / One and two / No one's gonna hurt you.

Feb 98. (12"ep/cd-ep) *(HUT T/CD 99)* **BE STRONG NOW / MY ADVICE. / TAKE CARE / FALLING** [ ] [–]

Elliott SMITH

Born: STEVEN PAUL SMITH, 6 Aug'69, Omaha, Nebraska, USA, although raised from a young age by his father in Portland, Oregon, after his parents divorced. The singer/songwriter relocated to university digs in Brooklyn, New York, playing in mid-90's noisy alternative rock band, HEATMISER. They released four rare albums, 'DEAD AIR' (1993), 'YELLOW NO.5' (1994; a mini-set), 'COP AND SPEEDER' (1995) and 'MIC CITY SONS' (1996), while ELLIOTT, meantime had opted for a more sedate solo career. He delivered three very well received albums for the 'Kill Rock City' imprint', namely 'ROMAN CANDLE' (1994), 'ELLIOTT SMITH' (1995) and 'EITHER/OR' (1997) – all licensed in 1998 to the UK arm of 'Domino' – before he inked a deal with 'DreamWorks'. This was due to the plaudits heaped upon him after appearing on stage alongside CELINE DION and TRISHA YEARWOOD at the "Oscars" ceremony! An unlikely story you may think, although the truth is, he provided part of the soundtrack to one of the best films of the year, 'Good Will Hunting'. His unfashionable (especially his taste in clothing and headgear – sometimes a tammy) approach was slightly reminiscent of SIMON & GARFUNKEL, BIG STAR or the lo-fi RICHARD DAVIES (of CARDINAL). His fourth album, 'XO', hit the shops later in 1998 and ELLIOTT looked certain to make his impact on the music scene. Sounding very much at home in his new big budget environment, 'FIGURE 8' (2000) found SMITH taking the opportunity to imbue his songcraft with the luxurious feel of classic BEATLES-meets-CS&N-meets-ERIC MATTHEWS while never relinquishing the skid row wisdom of his lyrical genius. ELLIOT was still in the process of recording his next album, 'FROM A BASEMENT ON A HILL', when he unexpectedly commited suicide on 21st October 2003. The record was posthumously collated and mixed by longtime producer Rob Schnapf and former girlfriend JOANNA BOLME (of MINDERS, STEPHEN MALKMUS & THE JICKS fame), and released in October 2004, almost exactly a year after his passing. While there was controversy over the fact that producer David McConnell wasn't involved with the record, despite presiding over the sessions prior to ELLIOTT's death, the end result was generally well received by both fans and critics. Darker and harder-edged than anything he'd previously released, the record (a US Top 20) inevitably saw comment focused on the lyrics and their relationship to SMITH's fate.

Album rating: Heatmiser: DEAD AIR (*6) / COP AND SPEEDER (*7) / MIC CITY SONS (*6) / Elliott Smith: ROMAN CANDLE (*7) / ELLIOTT SMITH (*7) / EITHER/OR (*8) / XO (*7) / FIGURE 8 (*7) / FROM A BASEMENT ON THE HILL (*8)

HEATMISER

ELLIOTT SMITH – vocals / **NEIL GUST** – guitar, vocals / **SAM COOMES** – bass / **TONY LASH** – drums

not iss. own label

1992. (c) **THE MUSIC OF HEATMISER** [–] [ ]
– Lowlife / Bottle rocket / Buick / Just a little prick / Dirt / Mightier than you.

not iss. Wake

1993. (7") **STRAY. / CAN'T BE TOUCHED** [–] [ ]
<re-iss. 1995 on 'Cavity Search'; CSR 02>

Frontier Frontier

Jul 93. (cd/c) *<(31057-2/-4)>* **DEAD AIR** [ ] Jun93 [ ]
– Still / Candyland / Mock up / Dirt / Bottle rocket / Blackout / Stray / Can't be touched / Cannibal / Don't look down / Sands hotel / Low life / Buick / Dead air.

Jul 94. (m-cd) *<(31062-2)>* **YELLOW NO.5** [ ] [ ]
– Wake / Fortune 500 / The corner seat / Idler / Junior mint / Yellow No.5.

Apr 95. (cd) *<(31063-2)>* **COP AND SPEEDER** [ ] [ ]
– Disappearing ink / Bastard John / Flamel / Temper / Why did I decide to stay? / Collect to NYC / Hitting on the waiter / Busted lip / Antonio Carlos Jobim / It's not a prop / Something to lose / Sleeping pill / Trap door / Nightcap.

Caroline Cavity Search

Jun 95. (7") *<CSR 7>* **SLEEPING PILL. / TEMPER** [–] [ ]

Apr 96. (7") *<CSR 25>* **EVERYBODY HAS IT. / DIRTY DREAM** [–] [ ]

Oct 96. (cd) *(CAR 75402)* *<CSR 35-2>* **MIC CITY SONS** [ ] [ ]
– Get lucky / Plainclothes man / Low flying jets / Rest my head against the wall / Fix is in / Eagle eye / Cruel reminder / You gotta move / Pop in G / Blue highway / See you later.

— split after SMITH was already making a name for himself as a solo act, while COOMES was in a duo with JANET WEISS called QUASI.

ELLIOTT SMITH

- vocals, drums, bass, saxophones, etc.

not iss. Cavity Search

Dec 94. (cd) *<CSR 13-2>* **ROMAN CANDLE** [–] [ ]
– Roman candle / Condor avenue / No name #I / No name #II / No name #III / Drive all over town / No name #IV / The last call / Kiwi mad-dog 20-20. *(UK-iss.Mar98 on 'Cavity Search'; same as US) (re-iss. Aug98 & Dec04 on 'Domino' cd/lp; REWIG CD/LP 002)*

Kill Rock Stars Kill Rock Stars

Feb 95. (7"m) *<(KRS 239)>* **NEEDLE IN THE HAY. / ALPHABET TOWN / SOME SONG** [ ] [ ]

Jul 95. (lp/cd) *<KRS 246/+CD>* **ELLIOTT SMITH** [–] [ ]
– Needle in the hay / Christian brother / Clementine / Southern belle / Single file / Coming up roses / Satellite / Alphabet town / St.Ides heaven / Good to go / White lady loves you more / Biggest lie. *(UK-iss.Mar98; same) (re-iss. Aug98 & Dec04 on 'Domino' cd/lp; REWIG CD/LP 001)*

Oct 96. (7"m) *<(KRS 266)>* **SPEED TRIALS. / ANGELES / I DON'T THINK I'M EVER GONNA FIGURE IT OUT** [ ] [ ]

Mar 97. (lp/cd) *<(KRS 269/+CD)>* **EITHER/OR** [ ] [ ]
– Speed trials / Alameda / Ballad of big nothing / Between the bars / Pictures of me / No name No.5 / Rose parade / Punch and Judy / Angeles / Cupid's trick / 2:45 am / Say yes. *(UK-iss.Jun98 & Dec04 on 'Domino' cd/lp; WIG CD/LP 51)*

1997. (7"; by ELLIOTT SMITH & PETE KREBS) **NO CONFIDENCE MAN. / SHIPTOWN** [–] [ ]
(below issued on 'Suicide Squeeze')

1997. (cd-s) *<S 005CD>* **DIVISION DAY. / NO NAME #6** [–] [ ]
(UK-iss.May00; same as US; re-Feb00)

Jun 98. (7") *(RUG 74)* **BALLAD OF BIG NOTHING. / SOME SONG / DIVISION DAY** [ ] [ ]
(cd-s+=) *(RUG 74CD)* – Angeles.

— now with a plethora of session people + strings

DreamWorks DreamWorks

Aug 98. (cd/c) *<(DRD/DRC 50048)>* **XO** [ ] [ ]
– Sweet Adeline / Tomorrow tomorrow / Waltz #2 (XO) / Baby Britain / Pitseleh / Independence day / Bled white / Waltz #1 / Amity / Oh well, okay / Bottle up and explode! / A question mark / Everybody cares, everybody understands / I didn't understand. *<(lp-iss.on 'Bongload'; BL 35)>*

Dec 98. (c-s) <*(DRMS 22347)*> **WALTZ #2 (XO) / OUR THING** 52 Feb99
(cd-s+=) *(DRMCD 22347)* – How to take a fall.

Apr 99. (7") *(DRMS7 50953)* **BABY BRITAIN. / WALTZ No.1** 55 –
(cd-s+=) *(DRMDM 50950)* – The enemy is you.
(cd-s) *(DRMDM 50951)* – ('A'side) / Some song / Bottle up and explode.

Jan 00. (7"/cd-s) <459037> **HAPPINESS. / SON OF SAM** –

Apr 00. (cd) <*(4 50225-2)*> **FIGURE 8** 37 99
– Son of Sam / Somebody that I used to know / Junk bond trader / Everything reminds me of her / Everything means nothing to me / LA / In the lost and found (honky Bach) – The roost / Stupidity tries / Easy way out / Wouldn't mama be proud? / Color bars / Happiness – The gondola man / Pretty Mary K / I better be quiet now / Can't make a sound / Bye. *<(lp-iss.Jul00 on 'Bongload'; BL 48)>*

Jun 00. (7") *(450949-7)* **SON OF SAM. / A LIVING WILL** 55 –
(cd-s+=) *(450949-2)* – Figure 8.

not iss. Suicide Squeeze

Aug 03. (7") **PRETTY (UGLY BEFORE). / A DISTORTED REALITY IS NOW A NECESSITY TO BE FREE** –
(UK-iss.Dec04 on 'Domino'; RUG 175)

— ELLIOTT died in L.A. on 21st October, 2003 – final recordings below

Domino Anti

Oct 04. (cd) *(WIGCD 147)* <86741> **FROM A BASEMENT ON THE HILL** 41 19
– Coast to coast / Let's get lost / Pretty (ugly before) / Don't go down / Strung out again / A fond farewell / King's crossing / Ostrich & chirping / Twilight / A passing feeling / The last hour / Shooting star / Memory lane / Little one / A distorted reality is now a necessity to be free.

Patti SMITH

Born: PATTI LEE SMITH, 31 Dec'46, Chicago, Illinois, USA. She started to write for New York magazine 'Rock' in 1969, having earlier being shipped around by her family between Paris and London. In the early 70's, PATTI began writing poetry full-time and met fellow rock-scribe, LENNY KAYE, who provided guitar accompaniment for her beat-poet monologues at readings/gigs. By 1971 she was writing for 'Creem' magazine and soon developed a professional musical partnership with playwright, SAM SHEPHERD. A prolific time for SMITH, come Christmas '72 she had two books of poetry, 'Witt' and '7th Heaven' in the stores and, after contributing to TODD RUNDGREN's 'A WIZARD, A TRUE STAR' album, he credited her for nicknaming him 'Runt'. RICHARD SOHL was recruited alongside SMITH and KAYE for a one-off single in 1974, 'HEY JOE / PISS FACTORY' on the small 'MER' label. A suitably caustic slice of proto-punk, it later gained airplay after being picked up by 'Sire' records. Meanwhile, SMITH completed the line-up of what would become The PATTI SMITH GROUP with IVAN KRAAL and JAY DEE DAUGHERTY, signing to 'Arista' and starting work on the 'HORSES' (1975) album with JOHN CALE producing. From the monochrome androgyny of the cover shot to the DIY three chord thrash which formed the bulk of the musical backing, the album was a blueprint for a generation of both American and British punk/new wave artists. Although SMITH's vocals were something of an acquired taste, her distinctive intonation was a perfect vehicle for the image rich symbolism of her free flowing lyrics. 'GLORIA' and 'LAND OF 1,000 DANCES' were transformed into wired, beat-inspired flashes of nervous energy, while quieter moments like the intro to 'REDONDO BEACH' and 'FREE MONEY' possessed a stark beauty. After this alternative tour de force, the follow-up, 'RADIO ETHIOPIA' (1976), came as something of a departure. Possessing a more straightforward hard-rock approach save for the chaotic feedback-drenched exploration of the title track, the album received mixed reviews. After SMITH survived breaking her neck after falling from the stage at a gig, it was to be another two years before the release of her next album. 'EASTER' (1978) was a confident comeback which moved even further into commercial rock territory without extinguishing the livewire spark that had made 'HORSES' so compelling. The record contained an unlikely collaboration with BRUCE SPRINGSTEEN, 'BECAUSE THE NIGHT', which saw SMITH breach the upper reaches of the singles charts on both sides of the Atlantic and propelled the album to similar success. 'WAVE' (1979) sounded slightly unfocused although it attained a higher chart placing Stateside than its predecessor. After a final tour in 1979, SMITH bowed out of the music business for domestic bliss with her new husband FRED 'SONIC' SMITH (ex-MC5). Together with her spouse, SOHL and DOUGHERTY, she recorded a low-key comeback album in 1988, 'DREAM OF LIFE', although tragedy struck in the 90's when both SOHL and her husband died from heart failure. With many artists namechecking her as an influence, SMITH recorded 'GONE AGAIN' (1996) amid a mini-renaissance. A tribute to FRED, it was filled with a sense of loss and yearning, echoing the intensity of her earlier work. 'PEACE AND NOISE' (1997), was surprisingly released only a year later than its predecessor and showed signs she could easily get back to her poetic past. Three years later, 'GUNG HO' (2000), delivered all sorts of emotions, from its opener, 'ONE VOICE' (a tribute to the work of Mother Teresa) to the heartbreaking 'LO AND BEHOLDEN', all marked a fine return to form for the former goddess of punk. PATTI came roaring back in spring 2004 with 'TRAMPIN', a record hailed by many as one of her best since 'HORSES'. Singing/declaiming/prophesying in as many timbral variants as the humanist icons she drew strength from, SMITH led her own, defiantly personal yet irremediably universal take on her post-9/11 homeland, backed up by a LENNY KAYE-dominated band. Recounting the luminous revelations of 'MY BLAKEAN YEAR', hurting for the slow hum of a 'PEACEABLE KINGDOM' and strafing US foreign policy on the epic 'RADIO BAGHDAD', SMITH articulated what it perhaps still might have meant to be American in 2004, echoed by her own daughter JESSE LEE on the title track.

• **Songwriters:** Lyrics PATTI, some music KAYE. Covered HEY JOE (Jimi Hendrix) / LAND OF A THOUSAND DANCES (Cannibal & The Headhunters) / MY GENERATION (The Who) / GLORIA (Them) / SO YOU WANNA BE A ROCK'N'ROLL STAR (Byrds) / 5-4-3-2-1 (Manfred Mann) / DOWNTOWN TRAIN (Tom Waits) / WICKED MESSENGER (Bob Dylan) / WHEN DOVES CRY (Prince). • **Trivia:** In 1974, she co-wrote with ex-boyfriend ALLEN LANIER, his groups' (BLUE OYSTER CULT) 'Career Of Evil'. Her albums were produced by JOHN CALE (1st) / JACK DOUGLAS (2nd) / JIMMY IOVINE (3rd) / TODD RUNDGREN (4th) / FRED SMITH and JIMMY IOVINE (1988).

Album rating: HORSES (*9) / RADIO ETHIOPIA (*7) / EASTER (*7) / WAVE (*6) / DREAM OF LIFE (*5) / GONE AGAIN (*6) / PEACE AND NOISE (*6) / GUNG HO (*6) / LAND (1975-2002) compilation (*8) / TRAMPIN' (*6)

PATTI SMITH – vocals, poetry / with **LENNY KAYE** – guitar / **RICHARD SOHL** – piano

not iss. M.E.R.

Aug 74. (7") <601> **HEY JOE. / PISS FACTORY** –
(UK-iss.Mar78 on 'Sire'; SRE 1009)

— added **IVAN KRAL** – bass, guitar, piano / **JAY DEE DAUGHERTY** – drums

Arista Arista

Dec 75. (lp) *(ARTY 122)* <4066> **HORSES** 47
– Gloria / Redondo Beach / Birdland / Free money / Kimberly / Break it up / Land: Horses – Land of a thousand dances – La mer (de) / Elegie. *(re-iss. Aug88 lp/c/cd; 201/401/252-112) (cd re-iss. Jul96+=; 18827-2)* – My generation (live).

Apr 76. (7") *(ARIST 47)*<*AS 0171*> **GLORIA. / MY GENERATION (live)**
(re-iss. 12"-Sep77; ARIST 12135)

Oct 76. (lp/c) *(SPARTY/TCSPARTY 1001)* <4097> **RADIO ETHIOPIA**
– Ask the angels / Ain't it strange / Poppies / Pissing in the river / Pumping

PATTI SMITH

(my heart) / Distant fingers / Radio Ethiopia / Abyssinia. *(re-iss. Aug88 lp/c/cd; 201/401/251-117) (re-iss. cd Jul96; 18825-2)*

— Her tour featured **LEIGH FOXX** – bass repl. SOHL. Others augmenting at the time **ANDY PALEY** (ex-ELLIOT MURPHY) + **BRUCE BRODY** – keyboards (ex-JOHN CALE)

PATTI SMITH GROUP

with **KAYE, KRAAL, DAUGHERTY, BRODY + SOHL**

Mar 78. (7") *(ARIST 181) <AS 0318>* **BECAUSE THE NIGHT. / GOD SPEED** [5] [13]

Mar 78. (lp/c) *(SPARTY/TCSPARTY 1043) <4171>* **EASTER** [16] [20]
– Till victory / Space monkey / Because the night / Ghost dance / Babelogue / Rock'n'roll nigger / Privilege (set me free) / We three / 25th floor / High on rebellion / Easter. *(re-iss. Jan83 on 'Fame' lp/c; FA/TCFA 3058) (re-iss. Aug88 lp/c/cd; 201/401/251-128) (re-iss. cd Jul96; 18826-2)*

Jun 78. (7") *(ARIST 191)* **PRIVILEGE (SET ME FREE). / ASK THE ANGELS** [72] [–]
(12"+=) *(ARIST 12191)* – 25th floor (live) / Bablefield (live).

— **FRED 'Sonic' SMITH** – drums (ex-MC5) repl. DAUGHERTY to TOM VERLAINE

May 79. (7") *(ARIST 264)* **FREDERICK. / FIRE OF UNKNOWN ORIGIN** [63] [–]

May 79. (lp/c) *(SPART/TCART 1086) <4221>* **WAVE** [41] [18]
– Frederick / Dancing barefoot / Citizen ship / Hymn / Revenge / So you want to be a rock'n'roll star / Seven ways of going / Broken flag / Wave. *(re-iss. Aug88 lp/c/cd; 201/401/251-139) (re-iss. cd Jul96; 18829-2)*

Jun 79. (7") *<AS 0427>* **FREDERICK. / FREDERICK (live)** [–] [90]

Jul 79. (7") *(ARIST 281)* **DANCING BAREFOOT. / 5-4-3-2-1 (live)** [ ] [–]

Aug 79. (7"m) *<AS 0453>* **SO YOU WANT TO BE A ROCK'N'ROLL STAR. / 5-4-3-2-1 / FIRE OF UNKNOWN ORIGIN** [–] [ ]

Sep 79. (7") *(ARIST 291)* **SO YOU WANT TO BE A ROCK'N'ROLL STAR. / FREDERICK (live)** [ ] [–]

— PATTI retired Mar'80 with her new husband FRED SMITH to bring up children. BRUCE BRODY was another vacate to ex-TELEVISION singer TOM VERLAINE's band; he later joined LONE JUSTICE

PATTI SMITH

re-appeared in 1988 with **SOHL, DAUGHERTY & SONIC**

Fierce Fierce

Feb 88. (7"m) *(white label)* **BRIAN JONES. / STOCKINGED FEET / JESUS CHRIST** [ ] [–]

Arista Arista

Jul 88. (7")<US-c-s> *(109877) <AS1/CAS 9689>* **PEOPLE HAVE THE POWER. / WILD LEAVES** [ ] [ ]
(12"+=) *(609877)<AD1 9688>* – Where duty calls.
(cd-s++=) *(659877)* – ('A'-album version).

Jul 88. (lp/c/cd) *(209/409/259-172) <8453>* **DREAM OF LIFE** [70] [65]
– People have the power / Going under / Up there, down there / Paths that cross / Dream of life / Where duty calls / (I was) Looking for you / The Jackson song. *(re-iss. cd.Apr92;) (cd re-iss. Jul96; 18828-2)*

— RICHARD SOHL was to die from a cardiac arrest on 3 Jun'90. PATTI returned to reciting and recording her poetry in 1995. Now with some of her original group (**DAUGHERTY + KAYE**), **TONY SHANAHAN** – bass / **LUIS RESTO** – keyboards and on some **TOM VERLAINE** – guitar (ex-TELEVISION) / **OLIVER RAY** – guitars. Album featured guest spots from JOHN CALE, JEFF BUCKLEY and JANE SCARPANTONI – cello

Jul 96. (cd/c) *(74321 38474-2/-4) <18747>* **GONE AGAIN** [44] [55]
– Gone again / Beneath the Southern Cross / About a boy / My madrigal / Summer cannibals / Dead to the world / Wing / Ravens / Wicked messenger / Fireflies / Farewell reel.

Aug 96. (cd-ep) *(74321 40168-2)* **SUMMER CANNIBALS / COME BACK LITTLE SHEEBA / GONE AGAIN (live) / PEOPLE HAVE THE POWER** [ ] [–]
(cd-ep) *(74321 40299-2)* – ('A'side) / People have the power (live) / Beneath the Southern cross / Come in my kitchen.

— **OLIVER RAY** ; repl. RESTO

Nov 97. (cd/c) *<(07822 18986-2/-4)>* **PEACE AND NOISE** [ ] Sep97 [ ]
– Waiting underground / Whirl away / 1959 / Spell / Don't say nothing / Dead city / Blue poles / Death singing / Memento Mori / Last call.

Mar 00. (cd) *<(07822 14618-2)>* **GUNG HO** [ ] [ ]
– One voice / Lo and beholden / Boy cried wolf / Persuasion / Gone pie / China bird / Glitter in their eyes / Strange messengers / Grateful / Upright come / New party / Libbie's song / Gung ho.

Columbia Columbia

Apr 04. (cd) *(515215-2) <90330>* **TRAMPIN'** [70] [ ]
– Jubilee / Mother Rose / Stride of the mind / Cartwheels / Gandhi / Trespasses / My Blakean year / Cash / Peaceable kingdom / Radio Baghdad / Trampin'.

– compilations, others, etc. –

Apr 83. (7") *Arista; (ARIST 513)* **BECAUSE THE NIGHT. / GLORIA** [ ] [–]
(12") *(ARIST 12513)* – ('A'side) / Redondo beach / Dancing barefoot / Free money.

Jul 84. (7") *Old Gold; (OG 9458)* **BECAUSE THE NIGHT. / GLORIA** [ ] [–]

Sep 91. (3xcd-box) *R.C.A.; (354.226)* **BOX SET** [ ] [ ]
– (RADIO ETHIOPIA / HORSES / WAVE albums)

Apr 02. (cd) *Arista; <(07822 14708-2)>* **LAND (1975-2002)** [ ] Mar02 [ ]
– Dancing barefoot / Babelogue / Rock'n'roll nigger / Gloria / Pissing in a river / Free money / People have the power / Because the night / Frederick / Summer cannibals / Ghost dance / Ain't it strange / 1959 / Beneath the southern cross / Glitter in their eyes / Paths that cross / When doves cry. *(free cd+=)* – Piss factory (version) / Redondo beach (demo) / Distant fingers (demo) / 25th floor (live) / Come back little Sheba (version) / Wander I go (version) / Dead city (live) / Spell (live) / Wing (live) / Boy cried wolf (live) / Birdland (live) / Higher learning (live) / Notes to the future (live).

the SMITHS

Formed: Manchester, England ... late '82 by (STEPHEN PATRICK) MORRISSEY and JOHNNY MARR. An intellectually intense, budding pop scholar and music journalist, MORRISSEY had previously had a book, 'James Dean Isn't Dead', published by 'Babylon' and had served a stint as UK president of The NEW YORK DOLLS fan club. MARR, meanwhile, had cut his six-string teeth in a variety of Manc beat combos, the pair initially forming a songwriting partnership and subsequently bringing in drummer MIKE JOYCE and bassist ANDY ROURKE to realise their vision of The SMITHS. Kicking off at The Ritz in Manchester, the group played a series of debut gigs around the country, earning rave reviews and attracting the interest of indie label, 'Rough Trade'. Turning down a deal with the local 'Factory', The SMITHS recorded a one-off single for 'Rough Trade', 'HAND IN GLOVE', the track championed by John Peel and subsequently topping the indie charts. Wooed by the majors, MORRISSEY and Co. stuck to their principals and inked a long-term contract with 'Rough Trade'. Later that year saw the release of the Top 30 hit, 'THIS CHARMING MAN', the first real glimpse of the The SMITHS' strange allure, MARR's rhythmic exuberance buoying MORRISSEY's morose verbal complexities. This was also the first time the Great British public were treated to the legendary sight of MORRISSEY sashaying and shimmying across the Top Of The Pops stage sporting a hearing aid and a back pocketfull of gladioli. Defiantly original, The SMITHS rapidly amassed a large, fiercely partisan fanbase with MORRISSEY as chief deity, MARR running a close second. A follow-up single, 'WHAT DIFFERENCE DOES IT MAKE', narrowly missed the Top 10 in early '84 with the breathlessly anticipated debut, 'THE SMITHS', hitting the shelves the following month. It didn't disappoint, a darkly ruminating kick in the eye for the tosspot music scene of the mid-80's and a compelling showcase for the unbounded potential of the MORRISSEY/MARR writing partnership. While the album missed the No.1 slot by a whisker, a high profile scrape with the tabloids followed soon after, the press hounds rounding on what they supposed to be ambiguous references to child abuse. The highly

The SMITHS

articulate MORRISSEY vocally put matters to right, the singer finally vindicated when a mother of one of the Moors murder victims openly supported the 'SUFFER THE LITTLE CHILDREN' track, another target of press speculation. The SMITHS were nothing if not controversial, MORRISSEY's pro-miserablist, anti-royalist and openly celibate stance making him the first real 'bedsit' non-pop star and drawing more and more attention to the group. No bad thing of course, when the music was as good as 'HEAVEN KNOWS I'M MISERABLE NOW' and 'WILLIAM, IT WAS REALLY NOTHING', another couple of fine Top 20 singles released later that summer. Both were included on the brilliant 'HATFUL OF HOLLOW' (1984) set along with a number of BBC session recordings and a few new tracks, notably the haunting 'PLEASE PLEASE PLEASE LET ME GET WHAT I WANT' and one of The SMITHS' trump cards, 'HOW SOON IS NOW' (previously released as a B-side to 'WILLIAM . . .' and subsequently as a single in its own right in early '85), a churning mantra presumably laying bare the depths of MORRISSEY's tortured soul with its bitter lyrical plea; that pop/dance outfit SOHO later managed to incorporate its ominous guitar reverb into a club hit is surely one of the great wonders of modern music. The following month saw the release of the acclaimed 'MEAT IS MURDER', MORRISSEY partly substituting the navel gazing of old for a more socially-pointed stance; slap happy headmasters, teenage thugs, child abusers and of course, those partial to a bit of steak, being the prime targets of the frontman's razor-sharp lyrical barbs. MORRISSEY wasn't hogging all the limelight, however, MARR's nimble fingered genius on the likes of 'THAT JOKE ISN'T FUNNY ANYMORE' seeing him touted as the greatest British guitarist since ERIC CLAPTON. The album gave the group their first No.1, solidifying their position as the biggest "indie" band of the decade, The SMITHS now at the peak of their powers. Next up was the irrepressible 'THE BOY WITH THE THORN IN HIS SIDE' and the scathing wit of 'BIGMOUTH STRIKES AGAIN', both featured on, and acting as preludes to 'THE QUEEN IS DEAD' (1986). Though the album was delayed due to record company hassles, with personnel difficulties (ROURKE briefly kicked out for heroin abuse, the addition of CRAIG GANNON) also arising, it remains The SMITHS' magnum opus and, for many, the album of the decade. Effortlessly segueing from the darkly claustrophobic (the stinging social commentary of the title track and to a lesser extent, the lugubrious 'NEVER HAD NO ONE EVER') to the whimsically witty ('VICAR IN A TUTU') and on to the heartbreakingly poignant ('THERE IS A LIGHT THAT NEVER GOES OUT'), the album was breathtaking in its emotional sweep and musical focus. Though they would never quite reach those heights again, The SMITHS' highly prolific recording schedule continued apace with the anthemic 'PANIC' (indie kids delighting in its clarion call of 'Hang the DJ') and the breezy 'ASK', probably The SMITHS most commercial moment. The fact that, like most of their singles, it failed to break the Top 10, led to the group announcing a split with 'Rough Trade' and a new deal with 'E.M.I.'. Further controversy followed around this time as CRAIG GANNON was sacked, the guitarist duly sueing the group. Early '87 saw the release of another semi-compilation of old and new material, 'THE WORLD WON'T LISTEN', essential if only for the classic MORRISSEY angst of 'HALF A PERSON' and the sublime 'OSCILLATE WILDLY'. Though the wellspring of the MORRISSEY/MARR muse was seemingly bottomless, relations between the pair were reaching breaking point and by the release of the 'STRANGEWAYS HERE WE COME' (1987) opus, The SMITHS had already split. The album's morbid, fractured sound apparently confirmed the growing musical differences between the group's main protaganists, an inevitability perhaps, for such a consistently intense and perfectionist band. A posthumous live album, 'RANK' (1988) appeared the following year, documenting the London stop on The SMITHS' final frenzied tour of 1986. Various compilations were released in successive years, especially after 'Warners' secured the rights to The SMITHS' back catalogue in 1992, heralding a period when, ironically, most of the material was only available on US import! While MARR sessioned for the likes of The PRETENDERS and BRYAN FERRY before working with THE THE and forming ELECTRONIC with NEW ORDER's BERNARD SUMNER, MORRISSEY went on to a relatively successful, if comparitively drab solo career. As is so often the case, the sum of The SMITHS parts was always less than the whole, the group's influence on modern rock music incalculable, their unique sound echoing through the strains of countless indie success stories and untold hopefuls alike.

• **Songwriters:** Lyrics – MORRISSEY / music – MARR, except HIS LATEST FLAME (Elvis Presley) / GOLDEN LIGHTS (Twinkle).

Album rating: THE SMITHS (*10) / HATFUL OF HOLLOW part compilation (*9) / MEAT IS MURDER (*10) / THE QUEEN IS DEAD (*10) / THE WORLD WON'T LISTEN part compilation (*8) / STRANGEWAYS HERE WE COME (*8) / LOUDER THAN BOMBS import (*8) / RANK (*7) / BEST . . . I compilation (*10) / BEST II compilation (*9) / THE VERY BEST OF THE SMITHS compilation (*8)

MORRISSEY (b. STEPHEN PATRICK MORRISSEY, 22 May'59) – vocals (ex-NOSEBLEEDS) / **JOHNNY MARR** (b. JOHN MAHER, 31 Oct'63) – guitar, harmonica, mandolins, piano / **ANDY ROURKE** (b.1963) – bass / **MIKE JOYCE** (b. 1 Jun'63) – drums

Rough Trade | Sire

May 83. (7") *(RT 131)* **HAND IN GLOVE. / HANDSOME DEVIL** [ ] [–]

Nov 83. (7") *(RT 136)* **THIS CHARMING MAN. / JEANE** [25] [–]
(12") *(RTT 136)* – ('A'side) / Accept yourself / Wonderful woman.

Jan 84. (7") *(RT 146)* **WHAT DIFFERENCE DOES IT MAKE?. / BACK TO THE OLD HOUSE** [12] [–]
(12"+=) *(RTT 146)* – These things take time.

Feb 84. (lp/c) *(ROUGH/+C 61) <25065>* **THE SMITHS** [2] [ ]
– Reel around the fountain / You've got everything now / Miserable lie / Pretty girls make graves / The hand that rocks the cradle / Still ill / Hand in glove / What difference does it make? / I don't owe you anything / Suffer little children. *(cd-iss. May87; ROUGHCD 61) (cd re-iss. 1989 on 'Line'; LICD 9.00308) (re-iss. cd/c)(ltd-10"lp Nov93 on 'WEA'; 4509 91892-2/-4)(SMITHS 1)*

May 84. (7") *(RT 156)* **HEAVEN KNOWS I'M MISERABLE NOW. / SUFFER LITTLE CHILDREN** [10] [ ]
(12"+=) *(RTT 156)* – Girl afraid.

Aug 84. (7") *(RT 166)* **WILLIAM, IT WAS REALLY NOTHING. / PLEASE PLEASE PLEASE LET ME GET WHAT I WANT** [17] [ ]
(12"+=) *(RTT 166)* – How soon is now?

Nov 84. (lp/c) *(ROUGH/+C 76)* **HATFUL OF HOLLOW** (with BBC sessions *) [7] [–]
– William, it was really nothing / What difference does it make? * / These things take time * / This charming man * / How soon is now? / Handsome devil * / Hand in glove / Still ill * / Heaven knows I'm miserable now / This night has opened my eyes * / You've got everything now * / Accept yourself * / Girl afraid / Back to the old house * / Reel around the fountain * / Please please please let me get what I want. *(cd-iss. May87; ROUGHCD 76) (re-iss. cd/c)(ltd-d10"lp Nov93 on 'WEA'; 4509 91893-2/-4)(SMITHS 2)*

Jan 85. (7") *(RT 176)* **HOW SOON IS NOW?. / WELL I WONDER** [24] [–]
(12"+=) *(RTT 176)* – Oscillate wildly.

Feb 85. (7") **HOW SOON IS NOW?. / THE HEADMASTER RITUAL** [–] [ ]

Feb 85. (lp/c) *(ROUGH/+C 81) <25269>* **MEAT IS MURDER** [1] [ ]
– The headmaster ritual / Barbarism begins at home / Rusholme ruffians / I want the one I can't have / What she said / Nowhere fast / That joke isn't funny anymore / Nowhere fast / Well I wonder / Meat is murder. *(cd-iss. May87; ROUGHCD 81) (re-iss. cd/c)(ltd-d10"lp Nov93 on 'WEA'; 4509 91895-2/-4)(SMITHS 3)*

Mar 85. (7") *(RT 181)* **SHAKESPEARE'S SISTER. / WHAT SHE SAID** [26] [ ]
(12"+=) *(RTT 181)* – Stretch out and wait.

Jul 85. (7") *(RT 186)* **THAT JOKE ISN'T FUNNY ANYMORE. / MEAT IS MURDER (live)** [49] [ ]
(12"+=) *(RTT 186)* – Nowhere fast / Shakespeare's siste / Stretch out and wait (all live).

Sep 85. (7") *(RT 191)* **THE BOY WITH THE THORN IN HIS SIDE. / ASLEEP** [23] [ ]
(12"+=) *(RTT 191)* – Rubber ring.

— added **CRAIG GANNON** – guitar, bass (ex-AZTEC CAMERA, ex-BLUEBELLS)

May 86. (7") *(RT 192)* **BIGMOUTH STRIKES AGAIN. / MONEY CHANGES EVERYTHING** [26] [ ]
(12"+=) *(RTT 192)* – Unloveable.

Jun 86. (lp/c) *(ROUGH/+C 96)* *<25426>* **THE QUEEN IS DEAD** [2] [70]
– Frankly Mr. Shankly / I know it's over / Never had no one ever / Cemetery gates / Big mouth strikes again / Vicar in a tutu / There is a light that never goes out / Some girls are bigger than others / The queen is dead / The boy with the thorn in his side. *(cd-iss. May87; ROUGHCD 96) (re-iss. cd/c)(ltd-d10"lp Nov93 on 'WEA'; 4509 91896-2/-4)(SMITHS 4)*

Jul 86. (7") *(RT 193)* **PANIC. / VICAR IN A TUTU** [11] [ ]
(12"+=) *(RTT 193)* – The draize train.

Oct 86. (7") *(RT 194)* **ASK. / CEMETRY GATES** [14] [ ]
(12"+=/c-s+=) *(RTT 194/+C)* – Golden lights.

— Reverted to a quartet, when GANNON left to join The CRADLE.

Feb 87. (7") *(RT 195)* **SHOPLIFTERS OF THE WORLD UNITE. / HALF A PERSON** [12] [ ]
(12"+=) *(RTT 195)* – London.

Feb 87. (lp/c/cd) *(ROUGH/+C/CD 101)* **THE WORLD WON'T LISTEN** (part compilation) [7] [–]
– Panic / Ask / London / Big mouth strikes again / Shakespeare's sister / There is a light that never goes out / Shoplifters of the world unite / The boy with the thorn in his side / Asleep / Unloveable / Half a person / Stretch out and wait / That joke isn't funny anymore / Oscillate wildly / You just haven't earned it yet baby / Rubber ring. *(c+=)* – Money changes everything. *(re-iss. cd/c)(ltd-d10"lp Nov93 on 'WEA'; 4509 91898-2/-4)(SMITHS 5)*

Apr 87. (7") *(RT 196)* **SHEILA TAKE A BOW. / IS IT REALLY SO STRANGE?** [10] [ ]
(12"+=) *(RTT 196)* – Sweet and tender hooligan.

Jun 87. (d-lp/d-c/d-cd) *(ROUGH/+C/CD 255)* *<25569>* **LOUDER THAN BOMBS** (compilation) [38] Apr87 [62]
– Is it really so strange? / Sheila take a bow / Sweet and tender hooligan / Shoplifters of the world unite / Half a person / London / Panic / Girl afraid / Shakespeare's sister / William, it was really nothing / You just haven't earned it yet, baby / Golden lights / Ask / Heaven knows I'm miserable now / Unloveable / Asleep / Oscillate wildly / These things take time / Rubber ring / Back to the old house / Hand in glove / Stretch out and wait / This night has opened my eyes / Please, please, please, let me get what I want. *(cd re-iss. Feb95 on 'WEA'; 4509 93833-2)*

Aug 87. (7") *(RT 197)* **GIRLFRIEND IN A COMA. / WORK IS A FOUR-LETTER WORD** [13] [ ]
(12"+=/c-s+=) *(RTT 197/+C)* – I keep mine hidden.

Sep 87. (lp/c/cd) *(ROUGH/+C/CDR 106)* *<25649>* **STRANGEWAYS HERE WE COME** [2] [55]
– A rush and a push and the land is ours / I started something I couldn't finish / Death of a disco dancer / Girlfriend in a coma / Stop me if you think you've heard this one before / Last night I dreamt that somebody loved me / Unhappy birthday / Paint a vulgar picture / Death at one's elbow / I won't share you. *(re-iss. cd/c)(ltd-d10"lp Nov93 on 'WEA'; 4509 91899-2/-4)(SMITHS 6)*

Oct 87. (7") **STOP ME IF YOU THINK YOU'VE HEARD THIS ONE BEFORE. / I KEEP MINE HIDDEN** [–] [ ]

Nov 87. (7") *(RT 198)* **I STARTED SOMETHING I COULDN'T FINISH. / PRETTY GIRLS MAKE GRAVES** [23] [ ]
(12"+=) *(RTT 198)* – Some girls are bigger than others (live).
(c-s++=) *(RTT 198C)* – What's the world (live).

Dec 87. (7") *(RT 200)* **LAST NIGHT I DREAMT THAT SOMEBODY LOVED ME. / NOWHERE FAST (BBC version)** [30] [ ]
(12"+=) *(RTT 200)* – Rusholme Russians (BBC version).
(cd-s++=) *(RTT 200CD)* – William, it was really nothing (BBC version).

— they broke-up in August '87, ROURKE and JOYCE splintered with ADULT NET before joining MORRISSEY when he went solo.

– compilations, etc. –

Note; on 'Rough Trade' UK / 'Sire' US, unless otherwise mentioned.

Aug 88. (lp/c/cd/dat) *(ROUGH/+C/CD 126)* *<25786>* **RANK (live October '86)** [2] [77]
– The queen is dead / Panic / Vicar in a tutu / Ask / Rusholme ruffians / The boy with the thorn in his side / What she said / Is it really so strange? / Cemetry gates / London / I know it's over / The draize train / Still ill / Bigmouth strikes again / (Marie's the name) His latest flame – Take me back to dear old blighty. *(re-iss. cd/c)(ltd-d10"lp Nov93 on 'WEA'; 450991900-2/-4)(SMITHS 7)*

Nov 88. (3"cd-ep) *(RTT 215CD)* **THE HEADMASTER RITUAL / NOWHERE FAST (live) / MEAT IS MURDER (live) / STRETCH OUT AND WAIT (live)** [ ] [–]

Nov 88. (3"cd-ep) *(RTT 171CD)* **BARBARISM BEGINS AT HOME / SHAKESPEARE'S SISTER / STRETCH OUT AND WAIT** [ ] [–]

— (Note:- 12"singles from Jan84 / May84 / Sep85 / Jul86 / Oct86 were issued on 3"cd-ep Nov88 – add suffix of CD to cat no.).

Oct 88. (12"ep/cd-ep) *Strange Fruit; (SFPS/+CD 055)* **THE PEEL SESSIONS** (18.5.83) [ ] [–]
– What difference does it make? / Reel around the fountain / Miserable lie / Handsome devil.

— Note; Below on 'WEA' UK/ 'Sire' US unless otherwise mentioned.

Jul 92. (7"/c-s) *(YZ 0001/+C)* **THIS CHARMING MAN. / WONDERFUL WOMAN / ACCEPT YOURSELF** [8] [–]
(cd-s+=) *(YZ 0001CD)* – Jeane.

Aug 92. (cd)(lp/c) *(4509 90044-2)(SMITHS 8/+C)* *<45042>* **BEST . . . 1** [1] [ ]
– This charming man / William, it was really nothing / What difference does it make / Stop me if you think you've heard it before / Girlfriend in a coma / Half a person / Rubber ring / How soon is now? / Hand in glove / Shoplifters of the world unite / Sheila take a bow / Some girls are bigger than others / Panic / Please please please let me get what I want.

Sep 92. (7"/c-s) *(YZ 0002/+C)* **HOW SOON IS NOW. / HAND IN GLOVE** [16] [–]
(cd-s+=) *(YZ 0002CD1)* – The queen is dead / Handsome devil / I started something I couldn't finish.
(cd-s+=) *(YZ 0002CD2)* – I know it's over / Suffer little children / Back to the old house.

Oct 92. (7"/c-s) *(YZ 0003/+C)* **THERE IS A LIGHT THAT NEVER GOES OUT. / HANDSOME DEVIL (live)** [25] [ ]
(cd-s+=) *(YZ 0003CD1)* – I don't owe you anything / Hand in glove / Jeane.
(cd-s+=) *(YZ 0003CD2)* – Money changes everything (live) / Some girls are bigger than others (live) / Hand in glove (live).

Nov 92. (cd)(lp/c) *(4509 90406-2)(SMITHS 9/+C)* **BEST II** [29] [ ]
– The boy with a thorn in his side / The headmaster ritual / Heaven knows I'm miserable now / Ask / Osciliate wildly / Nowhere fast / Still ill / That joke isn't funny anymore / Shakespeare's sister / Girl afraid / Reel around the fountain / Last night I dreamt somebody loved me / There is a light that never goes out.

Feb 95. (7"/c-s) *(YZ 0004/+C)* **ASK. / CEMETARY GATES** [62] [–]
(cd-s+=) *(YZ 0004CD)* – Golden lights.

Mar 95. (cd/c) *(4509 99090-2/-4)* **"SINGLES"** [5] [ ]
– Hand in glove / This charming man / What difference does it make? / Heaven knows I'm miserable now / William, it was really nothing / How soon is now? / Shakespeare's sister / That joke isn't funny anymore / The boy with the thorn in his side / Bigmouth strikes again / Panic / Ask / Shoplifters of the world unite / Sheila take a bow / Girlfriend in a coma / I started something I couldn't finish / Last night I dreamt that somebody loved me / There is a light that never goes out.

Jun 01. (cd) *(8573 88948-2)* **THE VERY BEST OF THE SMITHS** [30] [–]

SNOOP DOGG

Born: CALVIN BROADUS, 20 Oct'72, Long Beach, California, USA; he was given his nickname – SNOOP DOGGY DOGG – by his mother(!). Unleashed in 1993 when his debut DR. DRE (ex-N.W.A.) produced album 'DOGGYSTYLE' created furore amongst the moral majority in America, SNOOP swaggered his way to the forefront of the new G-funk strain of Gangsta-rap like a doberman on heat. Signed to DRE's 'Death Row' label (he also guested on the man's 'Nuthin' But A G Thang'), the canine sensation sniffed out a Top 10 position for the 'WHAT'S MY NAME' single before notching up record-breaking sales of his chart-topping debut album. Before the record's release (August '93), however, SNOOP (a convicted teenage drug dealer) was arrested when a local hood was killed; shots were allegedly fired by his bodyguard MALIK out of SNOOP's car. The rapper was released after being bailed for a $1m and early in 1994, he hit London under a storm of protest, not least from tabloid press; The Daily Star's memorable front page headline ran; 'KICK THIS EVIL BASTARD OUT!'. Of course, this only spurred on Brit youngsters' enthusiasm, especially after he was premiered on C4's 'The Word', complete with interview; a film 'Murder Was The Case' (based around a track SNOOP was famous for) hit Stateside No.1 in November '94. Never out of the headlines on drug charges SNOOP stood trial for murder on the 13th of January '95. That October, SNOOP'S trial finally got underway due to his attorney Johnnie Cochran being slightly busy with the O.J. Simpson case!. THA DOGG POUND album hit US No.1 in November '95 and soon afterwards he was cleared of murder and attempted manslaughter. While on bail, he had guested on 2 PAC's 'All Eyez on Me' album and other credits were with NATE DOGG on his late 1996 US Top 40 single, 'Never Leave Me Alone'. Later that year, the rapper delivered his sophomore set, 'THA DOGGFATHER', another chart-topper (Top 20 in the UK). SNOOP DOGG was indeed back on the prowl, the man even delighting his pop fans with a hit cover of the Gap Band's 'Snoop's UPSIDE YOUR HEAD'. From 1997-1999, SNOOP was never far from some sort of controversial headlines (either drug busts, shootings or whatever) and it was amazing he found the time to deliver two further long-players, 'DA GAME IS TO BE TOLD, NOT TO BE SOLD' (1998) and 'TOP DOGG' (1999). 'THA LAST MEAL' (2000) featured a whole host of up-and-coming producers such as JELLY ROLL, MEECH WELLS and SOOPAFLY. Although sounding as if it was entirely produced by DR. DRE (who actually produced three tracks), "tha set" failed because of SNOOP alone, who's half-baked half rhymes sounded more and more like a stoned old man with each release. Add this to the fact that SNOOP had nothing left to rap about (he did bitches, blunts and bouncy cars about three albums ago) and that he basically regurgitated his old material said something about the mainstream West Coast scene. SNOOP subsequently went into making a soft-core porn video available through tha intanet. The canine one redeemed himself to a certain degree with 'PAID THA COST TO BE DA BO$$' (2002), the JAMES BROWN reference of the title not the only nod to the past with a stodgy update of Parliament classic 'Flashlight', imaginatively entitled 'STOPLIGHT'. A rehash of Robert Palmer's 'I DIDN'T MEAN TO TURN YOU ON' was equally uninspired although SNOOP was in his element on the sleaze-hop of 'LOLLIPOP' and the two NEPTUNES productions, 'FROM THA CHUUUCH TO DA PALACE' and 'BEAUTIFUL' were probably the strongest tracks he's put his name to in many a year. Trailed by (US) No.1 single, 'DROP IT LIKE IT'S HOT', the US Top 10, NEPTUNES-centric 'R&G (RHYTHM & GANGSTA): THE MASTERPIECE' (2004) saw a thirty something SNOOP showing few signs of mellowing with age. While there was nothing to match the robotic cool of the single (a quintessential NEPTUNES pop miniature), the man with the most horizontal flow in hip hop proved himself unperturbable in both his love of 70s/80s grooves (RICK JAMES/late FUNKADELIC synth mewling especially) and his misogynistic lyrical tendencies. 'CAN U CONTROL YO HOE' saw him laying down the usual macho ground rules, and everyone from NELLY ('GIRL LIKE YOU') to BOOTSY COLLINS (the Hi-Tek-produced 'NO THANG ON ME', a virtual cover of the CURTIS MAYFIELD song) came along for the ride (subsequently issued in the UK in 2005, the album went Top 20). 'THE BEST OF SNOOP DOGG' (2005) covered his latter period albums from the later 90s through to the early 00s, while 'WELCOME TO THA CHUUCH: DA ALBUM' (2005) was SNOOP's official contribution to the underground mixtape phenomenon.

Album rating: DOGGYSTYLE (*7) / THA DOGGFATHER (*7) / DA GAME IS TO BE TOLD, NOT TO BE SOLD (*6) / TOP DOGG (*8) / THA LAST MEAL (*5) / BONES soundtrack w/ Various Artists (*5) / DEATH ROW'S SNOOP DOGGY DOGG GREATEST HITS compilation (*7) / PAID THA COST TO BE THA BO$$ (*7) / R & G (RHYTHM & GANGSTA): THE MASTERPIECE (*7) / THE BEST OF SNOOP DOGG compilation (*7)

SNOOP DOGGY DOGG

- vocals / with Tha DOGG POUND & The DRAMATICS plus **WARREN G / KURUPT / NANCY FLETCHER / DAT NIGGA DAZ / D.O.C. RBX / THE LADY OF RAGE / LIL HERSHEY LOC (MALIK) / NATE DOGG**

Death Row-East West | Death Row-Interscope

Dec 93. (7"/c-s) *(A 8337/+C)* *<98340>* **WHAT'S MY NAME? / ('A'club mix)** 20 Nov93 8
(12"+=/cd-s+=) *(A 8337 T/CD)* – ('A'-Explicit mix) / ('A'instrumental) / Who am I (what's my name?).

Dec 93. (cd/c) *<(IND/INC 92279)>* **DOGGYSTYLE** 38 Nov93 1
– Bathtub / G funk intro / Gin and juice / Tha shiznit / Lodi dodi / Murder was the case / Seria killa / Who am I (what's my name)? / For all my niggaz & bitches / Aint no fun (if the homies cant have none) / Doggy Dogg world / GZ and hustlas / Pump pump. *(cd re-iss. Apr01 on 'Death Row'; DROW 116) (d-lp iss.Jul01; DROW 116LP)*

Feb 94. (7"/c-s) *(A 8316/+C)* *<98318>* **GIN AND JUICE / ('A'-Laid back mix)** 39 8
(12"+=/cd-s+=) *(A 8316 T/CD)* – (2-'A'mixes).

Aug 94. (c-s) *(A 8289C)* **DOGGY DOGG WORLD / ('A'-Perfecto mix)** 32 –
(12"+=/s12"+=/cd-s+=) *(A 8289 T/TX/CD)* – ('A'-Dr.Dre mix) / ('A'-Perfecto x-rated mix).

— In Oct'94, SNOOP provided a handful of songs for his movie/video, 'Murder Was The Case'

Nov 96. (cd/c/lp) *<(IND/INC/INTLP 90038)>* **THA DOGGFATHER** 15 1
– Intro / Tha Doggfather / Ride 4 me / Up jump tha boogie / Freestyle conversation / When I grow up / Snoop bounce / Gold rush / (Tear 'em off) Me & my doggz / You thought / Vapors / Groupie / 2001 / Sixx minutes / (O.J.) Wake up / Snoops upside ya head / Blueberry / Traffic jam / Doggyland / Downtown assassins / Outro. *(cd re-iss. Apr01 on 'Death Row'; DROW 117)*

Dec 96. (c-s) *(INC 95520)* **SNOOPS UPSIDE YA HEAD / ('A'mix)** 12 –
(cd-s+=) *(IND 95520)* – ('A'mixes).
(12"+=) *(INT 95520)* – ('A'mixes).

— In Apr'97, SNOOP partnered the late 2PAC on a UK Top 20 single, 'WANTED DEAD OR ALIVE'.

Apr 97. (c-s/12"/cd-s) *(INC/INT/IND 95530)* **VAPORS. / ('A'live) / SNOOPS UPSIDE YA HEAD** 18

Sep 97. (c-s/cd-s) *(664990-4/-5)* **WE JUST WANNA PARTY WITH YOU (feat. JD) / (track by NAS)** 21
(cd-s+=) *(664990-2)* – (track by BUCKSHOT LEFONQUE).
(above on 'Columbia' and from the movie, 'Men In Black')

Jan 98. (c-s) *(INC 95550)* **THA DOGGFATHER / ('A'mix)** 36
(cd-s) *(IND 95550)* – ('A'mixes).
(cd-s) *(INT 95550)* – ('A'mixes).

— shortened his moniker to SNOOP DOGG

Priority | No Limit

Aug 98. (cd/d-lp) *(CDPTY/PTYLP 153)* *<50000>* **DA GAME IS TO BE SOLD, NOT TO BE TOLD** 28 1
– Snoop worls / Slow down / Woof! / Gin & juice II / Show me love / Hustle & ball / Don't let go / Tru tank dogs / Whatcha gon do? / Still a G thang / 20 dollars to my name / D.O.G.'s get lonely 2 / Ain't nut'in personal / DP gangsta / Game of life / See ya when I get there / Pay for P / Picture this / Doggz gonna get ya / Hoes, money & clout / Get 'bout it & rowdy.

Aug 98. (c-s/cd-s) *<53450>* **STILL A G THANG / FULL FLEDGED PIMPIN** – 19

— In Oct'98, SNOOP was credited on the massive US hit (minor UK one in November) for KEITH SWEAT, 'Come And Get With Me'.

Dec 98. (c-s/cd-s; as SNOOP DOGG featuring MYSTIKAL & FIEND) *<53462>* **WOOF / WOOF (instrumental) / IT'S ALL A T*T** – 62

May 99. (cd) *(CDPTY 171)* *<50052>* **TOP DOGG** 48 2
– Dolomite (intro) / Buck 'em (with STICKY FINGERS) / Trust me (with SYLK E. FINE & SUGA FREE) / My heart goes boom / Dolomite / Snoopafella / In love with a thug / 6 bedtime stories / Down 4 my N's (with C-MURDER & MAGIC) / Betta days / Somethin bout yo bidness (with RAPHAEL) / B- please (with XZIBIT & NATE DOGG) / Doin' too much / Gangsta ride (with SILKK THE SHOCKER) / Ghetto symphony (with

MIA X & FIEND) / Party with a D.P.G. / Buss 'n rocks / Just dippin' (with DR. DRE & JEWELL) / Don't tell (with WARREN G & MAUSEBURG) / 20 minutes (with GOLDIE LOC) / I love my momma.

Sep 99. (-; as SNOOP DOGG featuring XZIBIT & NATE DOGG) *<radio cut>* **B-PLEASE** [-] [77]

— In Jun'00, SNOOP featured on MARIAH CAREY's US Top 30 hit, 'Crybaby'

— SNOOP DOGG was also part of the team augmenting DR. DRE (i.e. on the hit single, 'The Next Episode')

Dec 00. (cd) *(CDPTY 199) <23225>* **THA LAST MEAL** [ ] [4]
– (intro) / Hennesey n Buddah / Snoop Dogg (what's my name part 2) / True lies / Wrong idea / Go away / Set it off / Stacey Adams / Lay low / Bring it on / Game court (skit) / Issues / Brake fluid (biiitch pump yo brakes) / Ready 2 ryde / Loosen' control / I can't swim / Leave me alone / Back up off me / Y'all gone miss me. *(re-iss. Mar01 cd/d-lp; CDPTYX/ PTYLP 199)* – hit No.62

Apr 01. (cd-s) *(PTYCD 134) <radio cut>* **SNOOP DOGG / Y'ALL GONE MISS ME** [13] Jan01 [77]
(12") *(PTYST 134)* – ('A'side) / ('A'-instrumental).
(c-s) *(PTYC 134)* – ('A'-clean) / Y'all gone miss me (clean) / Back up ho (clean).

Jul 01. (cd-s; by SNOOP DOGG featuring TYRESE & MR. TAN) *<158986>* **JUST A BABY BOY** [-] [90]

Aug 01. (12"/cd-s; by SNOOP DOGG featuring MASTER P, NATE DOGG, BUTCH CASSIDY & THA EASTSIDAZ) *(PTY T/CD 133) <radio cut>* **LAY LOW. / BRING IT ON / TRUE LIES** [ ] Mar01 [50]
(c-s) *(PTYC 133)* – ('A'-clean) / Bring it on (clean).

— in Oct'01, SNOOP featured with R.L. & LIL' KIM on the hit single, 'Do U Wanna Roll (Dolittle Theme)'

Oct 01. (cd) *(CDPTY 223) <50227>* **BONES** (soundtrack w/ Various Artists) [ ] [39]
– Birth of Jimmy Bones / Legend of Jimmy Bones (w/ MC REN & RBX) / (other artists) / Dogg named Snoop (w/ TREY DEEE) / (other artists) / Death of Snow White (w/ BAD AZZ, CHAN & CONLYAC) / If you came here to party (w/ EASTSIDAZ & KOLA) / (other artist) / Jimmy's revenge (w/ SOOPAFLY) / (other artist) / Gangsta wit it (w/ NATE DOGG & BUTCH CASSIDY) / (other artist) / Endo (w/ OUTKAST) / Fresh and clean (w/ OUTKAST).

Nov 01. (cd) *(CDPTY 218) <50030>* **DEATH ROW'S SNOOP DOGGY DOGG GREATEST HITS** (compilation) [ ] [28]
– Nuthin' but a "G" thang (with DR. DRE) / Head doctor (with SWOOP G) / Gin and juice / Eastside party (with NATE DOGG) / Murder was the case (remix) / Ain't no fun (if the homies can't have none) (with WARREN G, KURUPT & NATT DOGG) / Doggfather (remix) / Midnight love (with RAPHAEL SAADIQ & DAZ DILLINGER) / Eastside / Who am I (what's my name)? / Doggy Dogg world (with THA DOGG POUND & DRAMATICS) / Too high (poly high) (with DAZ DILLINGER & BIG PIMPIN') / Vapors / Usual suspects (with THREAT) / Keep it real (with MACK 10, BAD AZZ & TECHNIEC) / Snoop bounce (with TIM COMMERFORD & TOM MORELLO).

Capitol Capitol

Nov 02. (12"/cd-s) *(12CL/CDCL 841)* **FROM THA CHUUUCH TO DA PALACE. / (instrumental) / PAPER'D UP (clean)** [27] [77]

Nov 02. (cd/d-lp) *<(5 39157-0/-1)>* **PAID THA COST TO BE DA BO$$** [ ] [12]
– Don Doggy / Da bo$$ would like to see you / Stoplight / From tha chuuuch to da palace (with PHARRELL) / I believe in you (with LATOIYA WILLIAMS) / Lollipop (with JAY-Z, SOOPAFLY & NATE DOGG) / Ballin' (with DRAMATICS & LIL' HALF DEAD) / Beautiful (with PHARRELL & UNCLE CHARLIE WILSON) / Paper'd up (with MR. KANE & TRACI NELSON) / Wasn't your fault / Bo$$ playa (with ARCH BISHOP DON MAGIC JUAN) / Hourglass (with MR. KANE & GOLDIE LOC) / The one and only / I miss that bitch (with E-WHITE) / From Long Beach 2 Brick City (with REDMAN, NATE DOGG & WARREN G) / Suited n booted / You got what I want (with LUDACRIS & GOLDIE LOC) / Batman & Robin (with LADY OF RAGE & RBX) / A message 2 Fat Cuzz / Pimp slapp'd. *(re-dist.Apr03)* – hit UK No.64

— in Feb'03, SNOOP & NATE DOGG featured on WC's hit, 'The Streets'

Mar 03. (12"; by SNOOP DOGG featuring PHARRELL & UNCLE CHARLIE WILSON) *(12CL 842)* **BEAUTIFUL. / (instrumental) / BALLIN' (clean version)** [23] [6]
(cd-s+=) *(CDCL 842)* – ('A'-video).

— in Feb & Aug'04, SNOOP feat. on CHINGY's hits, 'Holidae In' & 'I Wanna Thank Ya'

Geffen Geffen

Nov 04. (cd/d-lp) *(9864841) <37630-2/-1>* **R & G (RHYTHM & GANGSTA): THE MASTERPIECE** [12] [6]
– (intro) I love to give you light / Bang out / Drop it like it's hot (feat. PHARRELL WILLIAMS) / Can I get a flicc witchu (feat. BOOTSY COLLINS) / Ups & downs (feat. BEE GEES) / The bidness / Snoop D.O. double G. / Let's get blown / Step ya game up (feat. LIL JON & TRINA) / Perfect (feat. CHARLIE WILSON) / Wballz interlude / Fresh pair of panties on / Promise I / Oh no (feat. 50 CENT) / Can U control yo hoe / Signs (feat. CHARLIE WILSON & JUSTIN TIMBERLAKE) / I'm threw witchu (feat. SOOPAFLY) / Pass it pass it / Girl like U (feat. NELLY) / No thang on me (feat. BOOTSY COLLINS). *(cd re-iss. Jun05 w/dvd+=; 2103813)* – (DVD tracks).

Nov 04. (12"; SNOOP DOGG & PHARRELL) *(2103504) <GEF 357411>* **DROP IT LIKE IT'S HOT. / GET TO KNOW YA / DROP IT LIKE IT'S HOT (instrumental)** [10] Sep04 [1]
(cd-s+=) *(2103461)* – ('A'-video).

Feb 05. (12"; SNOOP DOGG & PHARRELL) *<(9880426)>* **LET'S GET BLOWN / UPS & DOWNS / LET'S GET BLOWN (instrumental)** [13] [54]
(cd-s+=) *(9880425)* – ('A'-video).

Apr 05. (12"; SNOOP DOGG feat. CHARLIE WILSON & JUSTIN TIMBERLAKE) *<(9881783)>* **SIGNS / PASS IT PASS IT / SIGNS (instrumental)** [2] [46]
(cd-s+=) *(9881781)* – ('A'-video).

Aug 05. (12"; feat. BEE GEES) *(988373-6)<B0004927-11>* **UPS & DOWNS / BANG OUT** [36] [ ]
(cd-s+=) *(988373-2)* – ('A'-video).

— in Jun'06, SNOOP feat. on PUSSYCAT DOLLS hit, 'Buttons'

– compilations, others, etc. –

Aug 99. (cd-book) *Star Profile; (8246)* **STAR PROFILE** [ ] [-]

Dec 00. (cd) *Death Row; <(33349-2)>* **DEAD MAN WALKING** [ ] Nov00 [24]
(re-iss. Apr01; DROW 115)

Apr 01. (12"; by SNOOP DOGGY DOGG & 2PAC) *ZYX; (JIG 50201-2)* **FATHA FIGGA. /** [ ] [-]

Oct 02. (d-cd) *Virgin; (812882-2)* **THA LAST MEAL / TOPP DOGG** [ ] [ ]

Oct 05. (cd) *Priority; <(333957-2)>* **THE BEST OF SNOOP DOGG** [50] [ ]
– Beautiful / Snoop Dogg (what's my name, pt.2) / Woof! / Lay low / Down 4 my N's / From the chuuuch to da palace / Bitch please / Still a G thang / Just dippin' / Wrong idea / Stoplight / Snoopafella / The one and only / Loosen' control / Gin & juice II / Stacey Adams / Ride on – Caught up! / G bedtime stories / Hell yeah (stone cold Steve Austin theme).

tha EASTSIDAZ

SNOOP DOGG, TRAY DEEE + GOLDIE LOC

not iss. Dogg House – TVT

Jan 00. (cd-s) *<2041>* **G'D UP (mixes)** [-] [47]

Feb 00. (cd) *<2040>* **SNOOP DOGG PRESENTS THA EASTSIDAZ** [-] [8]

Jun 00. (cd-s; by SNOOP DOGG presents THA EASTSIDAZ featuring JAYE FELONY & BLAQTHOVEN) *<2004>* **GOT BEEF** [-] [99]

Aug 01. (cd) *<2230>* **SNOOP DOGG PRESENTS THA EASTSIDAZ** [-] [4]

SNOW PATROL

Formed: Glasgow, Scotland . . . 1996 as POLARBEAR by Belfast-born Dundee University students GARY LIGHTBODY and MARK McCLELLAND; RICHARD COLBURN (with the assistance of BELLE & SEBASTIAN's STUART MURDOCH) augmented early on. Unfortunately, after only one single, 'STARFIGHTER PILOT' (for Glasgow's Stow College label, 'Electric Honey'), and due to the already established US outfit POLAR BEAR (note the space!) getting the dry hump – so to speak, they changed their moniker. Subsequently inking a deal with 'Jeepster' (home to BELLE . . .), SNOW PATROL gently breezed into the ears and minds of their audience via two singles, 'LITTLE HIDE' and ONE HUNDRED THINGS YOU SHOULD HAVE DONE IN BED', both highlights from the brittle guitar-pop band's debut long-player, 'SONGS FOR POLAR BEARS' (1998). Still located somewhere around Glasgow (with some sidelining with Scotland's indie conglomorate, REINDEER SECTION), the dreamy SNOW PATROL collected themselves together for a second set, 'WHEN IT'S ALL OVER WE STILL HAVE TO CLEAR UP' (2001). Bedsitter music, indeed. Another brilliant addition to GARY LIGHTBODY's already impressive CV came in the form of 'FINAL STRAW' issued in 2003. A strange mixture of rocky power ballads (in a good way!), PINK FLOYD-infused psychedelia and soft, melodic folk, the set pleased indie fan-boy types and rock/pop lovers alike. As diverse as it comes, switching from one musical genre to the next, LIGHTBODY maintained the casual instrumentation of the likes of his other project the REINDEER SECTION and even gave COLDPLAY a run for their money with the excellent rock-out of 'SOMEWHERE A CLOCK IS TICKING'. While other bands strive to be emo – emotional harcore – GARY LIGHTBODY proved that real emotions could be equally as subtle on soft, unwinding tracks such as 'SAME' as they could be on audacious guitar-led wig-outs. In short, a triumph in the ever confusing world of indie rock. Everyone's favourite dirge-rockers returned with more of the dirge and even more of the rock on 'EYES OPEN' (2006), a UK No.1 album trailed by the roiling Top 10 single, 'YOU'RE ALL I HAVE'. LIGHTBODY still sounded like the most lovelorn man in Christendom, ceding little ground to contemporary musical trends and – save for playing at a slightly rockier clip (especially on the riff-churning 'HEADLIGHTS ON DARK ROADS') – all but sticking with the Celtic hugeness that the band's Scots-Irish blend generates so well. Guests included MARTHA WAINWRIGHT, who joined in on 'SET THE FIRE TO THE THIRD BAR', while the album's US Top 40 entry suggested the American market was theirs for the conquering.

• **Covers:** CRAZY IN LOVE (Beyonce).

Album rating: SONGS FOR POLAR BEARS (*6) / WHEN IT'S ALL OVER WE STILL HAVE TO CLEAR UP (*6) / FINAL STRAW (*9) / EYES OPEN (*6)

GARY LIGHTBODY (b. 1976) – guitar, vocals / **MARK McCLELLAND** – bass, keyboards / **RICHARD COLBURN** – drums, keyboards (of BELLE & SEBASTIAN) / with **STUART MURDOCH** – piano (of BELLE & SEBASTIAN)

Electric Honey — not iss.

Jun 97. (cd-s; as POLARBEAR) *(EHRCD 007)* **STARFIGHTER PILOT / HOLY COW / SAFETY** [ ] [-]

—— **JOHN QUINN** – drums; repl. COLBURN

—— added live contributor: **TOM SIMPSON** – turntables

Jeepster — Imprint

Feb 98. (7") *(JPR7 004)* **LITTLE HIDE. / STICKY TEENAGE TWIN** [ ] [-]
(cd-s+=) *(JPRCDS 004)* – Limited edition / JJ.

May 98. (7") *(JPR7 005)* **ONE HUNDRED THINGS YOU SHOULD HAVE DONE IN BED. / MY LAST GIRLFRIEND** [ ] [-]
(cd-s+=) *(JPRCDS 005)* – T.M.T. / I could stay away forever.

Aug 98. (cd/lp) *(JPR CD/LP 004)* <113141> **SONGS FOR POLAR BEARS** [ ] [ ]
– Downhill from here / Starfighter pilot / The last shot ringing in my ears / Absolute gravity / Get balsamic vinegar . . . quick you fool / Mahogany / NYC / Little hide / Make up / Velocity girl / Days without paracetamol / Fifteen minutes old / Favourite friend / One hundred things you should have done in bed. *<US cd re-iss. 1999 on 'Never'; 4039> (cd re-iss. Apr06 +=; JPRCD 004X)* – Sticky teenage twin / Limited edition / JJ / My last girlfriend / T.M.T. / Could I stay away forever / When you're right, you're right (Darth Vader bringing in his washing mix) / Raze the city / Riot, please.

Nov 98. (7") *(JPR7 007)* **VELOCITY GIRL. / ABSOLUTE GRAVITY** [ ] [-]
(cd-s+=) *(JPRCDS 007)* – When you're right, you're right.

Jun 99. (cd-s) *(JPRCDS 013)* **STARFIGHTER PILOT (the Spynci new radio edit) / RAZE THE CITY / RIOT, PLEASE** [ ] [-]
(cd-s) *(JPRCDS 013R)* – (remixes; Cut La Roc and Belle & Sebastian).

Jeepster — Jeepster

Nov 00. (cd-s) *(JPRCDS 020)* **ASK ME HOW I AM / IN COMMAND OF CARS / TALK TO THE TREES** [ ] [-]

Mar 01. (cd-s) *(JPRCDS 021)* **ONE NIGHT IS NOT ENOUGH / MONKEY MOBE / WORKWEAR SHOP** [ ] [-]

Mar 01. (cd/lp) *(JPR CD/LP 012)* *<4052>* **WHEN IT'S ALL OVER WE STILL HAVE TO CLEAR UP** [ ] [ ]
– Never gonna fall in love again / Ask me how I am / Making enemies / Black and blue / Last ever lone gunman / If I'd found the right words to say / Batten down the hatch / One night is not enough / Chased by . . . I don't know what / On-off / An olive grove facing the sea / When it's all over we still have to clear up / Make love to me forever / Firelight. *(cd re-iss. Apr06 +=; JPRCD 012E)* – In command of cars / Talk to the trees / Monkey mobe / Workwear shop / Ask me how I am (video).

—— added **NATHAN CONNOLLY** – guitar

—— IAN ARCHER was also touring guitarist/co-songwriter (2001-2003)

Fiction — Universal

Aug 03. (cd) *(9865408)* **FINAL STRAW** [ ] [-]
– How to be dead / Wow / Gleaming auction / Whatever's left / Spitting games / Chocolate / Run / Grazed knees / Ways & means / Tiny little fractures / Somewhere a clock is ticking / Same.

Sep 03. (7") *(980935-1)* **SPITTING GAMES. / STEAL** [54] [-]
(cd-s+=) *(980935-0)* – Brave / ('A'-video).

Jan 04. (7"white) *(9816354)* **RUN. / POST PUNK PROGRESSION** [5] [-]
(cd-s+=) *(9816353)* – Spitting games (2001 country version) / ('A'-video).
(ltd-10"clear) *(FICTION 001)* – ('A'-Jacknife Lee remix) / ('A'-Freelance Hellraiser remix).

Feb 04. (cd+=; re-) *(as prev)* *<237636>* **FINAL STRAW** [3] Mar04 [91]
– (+=) We can run away now they're all dead and gone / Half the fun.

Apr 04. (7"orange) *(9866356)* **CHOCOLATE. / ONE NIGHT IS NOT ENOUGH (live)** [24] [-]
(cd-s+=) *(9866355)* – Run (Jacknife Lee remix) / ('A'-video).

Jul 04. (7") *(9867127)* **SPITTING GAMES. / WOW (acoustic)** [23] [-]
(cd-s) *(9867126)* – ('A') / Crazy in love (BBC live version) / New partner (BBC live version) / ('A'-video).

Oct 04. (7") *(9868778)* **HOW TO BE DEAD. / YOU ARE MY JOY (live at Somerset House)** [39] [-]
(cd-s+=) *(9868777)* – Chocolate (Grand National remix).

—— **PAUL WILSON** – bass (ex-TERRA DIABLO) repl. McCLELLAND

—— added (now full-time) **TOM SIMPSON** – keyboards

Apr 06. (7") *(9853868)* **YOU'RE ALL I HAVE. / (Minotaur Shock remix)** [7] [-]
(cd-s) *(9853867)* – ('A') / The only noise / Perfect little secret / ('A'-video).
(cd-s) *(9857184)* – ('A'-live from Koko 12/4/06) / Run (live from Koko 12/4/06).

May 06. (cd)(lp) *(9852908)(9853626)* *<66750-2>* **EYES OPEN** [1] [34]
– You're all I have / Hands open / Chasing cars / Shut your eyes / It's beginning to get to me / You could be happy / Make this go on forever / Set the fire to the third bar / Headlights on dark roads / Open your eyes / The finish line. *(ltd-cd w/dvd+=; 9853361)* – (DVD tracks).

□ SOFT CELL (see under ⇒ ALMOND, Marc)

□ SONIC BOOM (see under ⇒ SPACEMEN 3)

SON VOLT

Formed: Belleville, Illinois, USA . . . 1994 by JAY FARRAR and his former UNCLE TUPELO compadre, MIKE HEIDORN; JIM and DAVE BOQUIST joined soon afterwards. Fans yearning for the down-at-heel spirit of UNCLE TUPELO's moodier moments were comforted by the fact that FARRAR himself was still treading the dirt-road backstreets of country's dark underbelly with SON VOLT, releasing 'TRACE' in 1994 and 'STRAIGHTAWAYS' in late '96; 'WIDE SWING TREMELO' (1998) was their most recent set. While some critics railed against what they perceived as the unrelenting miserabilism of FARRAR's approach (especially with regards to the SON VOLT live experience), there was no disputing the quality or honesty of the writing. After 'STRAIGHTAWAYS', FARRAR took time out from SON VOLT (they split 1999) to record 'SEBASTAPOL' (2001) an album of self-conscious beauty, but of beauty all the same. Acoustic numbers such as the whispering 'CLEAR DAY THUNDER' and 'OUTSIDE THE DOOR' evoked that folksy UNCLE TUPELO formula, where as 'BARSTOW' and 'DAMN SHAME' had FARRAR's own personalised stamp. Elsewhere on the set, he had trouble dealing with the process alone (after all he was always best with a collaborator), although the man proved he was still a great contender in the American alt country scene. FARRAR was still meandering down his own ragged path, cutting soundtrack set, 'THE SLAUGHTER RULE' (2003) and the austere 'TERROIR BLUES' in 2003. The latter record found him paring back the arrangements with a ruthlessness unwitnessed since his split from TWEEDY, resulting in one of the most intimate yet exploratory works of his career. While 'STONE, STEEL & BRIGHT LIGHTS' (2004) was the sound of FARRAR in the raw, showcasing the cream of his post-SON VOLT work and tearing through a couple of explosive interpretations in Syd Barrett's 'LUCIFER SAM' and Neil Young's 'LIKE A HURRICANE (those who witnessed 'TUPELO era set closers like CCR's 'EFFIGY' will know what to expect), 'A RETROSPECTIVE: 1995-2000' (2005) drew on the archives for a SON VOLT summary, spicing up the package with more obscure covers such as Alex Chilton's 'HOLOCAUST', Leadbelly's 'AIN'T NO MORE CANE' and Townes Van Zandt's 'REX'S BLUES' amongst others. For reasons known only to himself, FARRAR resurrected the SON VOLT moniker for 'OKEMAH AND THE MELODY OF RIOT' (2006), even though he was the band's sole remaining member. Whether that made it a solo set in all but name is debateable but the album – recorded with ex-WHISKEYTOWN guitarist BRAD RICE, who's since rumoured to have departed – showcased some of FARRAR's sharpest, hardest-rocking material since his country-punk beginnings. Named for WOODY GUTHRIE's home town and boasting iconic, neo-socialist artwork, it was also as politically charged as anything he's put his pen to, with 'JET PILOT' even referencing the Who's 'WON'T GET FOOLED AGAIN' and Gil Scott-Heron's 'THE REVOLUTION WILL NOT BE TELEVISED'.

• **Songwriters:** FARRAR except covers I'VE GOT TO KNOW (Woody Guthrie) / REX'S BLUES (Townes Van Zandt) / LOOKING AT THE WORLD THROUGH A WINDSHIELD (Jerry Chesnut) / TULSA COUNTY (Pamela Polland) / HOLOCAUST (Alex Chilton) / OPEN ALL NIGHT (Bruce Springsteen).

Album rating: TRACE (*7) / STRAIGHTAWAYS (*6) / WIDE SWING TREMELO (*7) / A RETROSPECTIVE (1995-2000) compilation (*7) / Jay Farrar: SEBASTAPOL (*6) / THE SLAUGHTER RULE soundtrack w/ Various (*7) / TERROIR BLUES (*6) / STONE, STEEL & BRIGHT LIGHTS (*6) / Son Volt: OKEMAH AND THE MELODY OF RIOT (*7)

JAY FARRAR – vocals, guitar, organ, harmonica / **DAVE BOQUIST** – guitars, fiddle, banjo, lap steel / **JIM BOQUIST** – bass, backing vocals / **MIKE HEIDORN** – drums

Warners Warners

Oct 95. (cd/c) *<(9362-46010-2/-4)>* **TRACE** ☐ Sep95 ☐
– Windfall / Live free / Tear stained eye / Route / Ten second news / Drown / Loose string / Out of the picture / Catching on / Too early / Mystifies me.

— with guests **ERIC HEYWOOD** – pedal steel, mandolin / **PAULI RYAN** – tambourine

Aug 97. (cd) *<(9362-46518-2/-4)>* **STRAIGHTAWAYS** ☐ May97 44
– Caryatid easy / Back into the world / Picking up the signal / Left a slide / Creosote / Cemetery savior / Last minute shakedown / Been set free / No more parades / Way down Watson.

Oct 98. (cd/c) *<(9362 47059-2/-4)>* **WIDE SWING TREMELO** ☐ 93
– Straightface / Driving the view / Jodel / Medicine hat / Strands / Flow / Dead man's clothes / Right on through / Chanty / Carry you down / Question / Streets that time walks / Hanging blue side / Blind hope.

– compilations, etc. –

May 05. (cd) *Rhino; <(8122 74619-2)>* **A RETROSPECTIVE (1995-2000)** ☐ ☐
– Drown / Windfall / Route / Rex's blues / Looking at the world through a windshield / Too early / Back into your world / Picking up the signal / I've got to know / Creosote / Straightface / Tulsa county / Driving the view / Ain't no more cane / Flow / Holocaust / Tear stained eye (demo) / Loose string (demo) / Medicine hat (live) / Open all night.

JAY FARRAR

with **DAVID RAWLINGS, TOM RAY, MATT PENCE, JON WURSTER, DADE FARRAR, JOHN AGNELLO, KELLY JOE PHELPS + GILLIAN WELCH**

Epic Artemis

Oct 01. (cd) *(504570-2) <751093>* **SEBASTAPOL** ☐ Sep01 ☐
– Feel free / Clear day thunder / Voodoo candle / Barstow / Damn shame / Damaged son / Prelude (make it alright) / Dead promises / Feedkill chain / Make it alright / Fortissimo wah / Drain / Different eyes / Outside the door / Equilibrium / Direction / Vitamins.

Nov 02. (cd-ep) *<751138>* **THIRDSHIFTGROTTOSLACK** – ☐
– Greenwich time / Damn shame / Station to station / Kind of madness / Dues.

Bloodshot Bloodshot

Jun 03. (cd) *<(BS 087)>* **THE SLAUGHTER RULE** (soundtrack w/ Various Artists) – Mar03 ☐
– Open ground / Gather / Rank stranger / Frost heaves / Highwood / Augusta / Buffalo jump / Freight / Dark early / Cold chimes / Gumption / Hangman / Blue eyes (UNCLE TUPELO) / Open ground – reprise / (+ other artists).

Artemis Artemis

Jun 03. (cd) *<(ATMCD 51172)>* **TERROIR BLUES** ☐ ☐
– No rolling back / Space junk I / Hard is the fall / Fool king's crown / Space junk II / Hanging on to you / Cahokian / Heart on the ground / Out on the road / All of your might / Space junk III / California / Walk you down / Space junk IV / Dent county / Fish fingers Norway / Space junk V / Hanging on to you II / Hard is the fall II / Jam / Heart on the ground II / No rolling back II / Space junk VI.

Jun 04. (cd) *<(ATMCD 51523)>* **STONE, STEEL & BRIGHT LIGHTS** ☐ ☐
– Doesn't have to be this way / Greenwich time / 6 string belief / Feel free / Make it alright / No rolling back / Damn shame / All of your might / Cahokian / Heart on the ground / California / Fool king's crown / Vitamins / Voodoo candle / Damaged son / Freed kill chain / Clear day thunder / Lucifer Sam / Like a hurricane.

SON VOLT

JAY FARRAR – vocals, guitar, harmonica / **BRAD RICE** – guitar / **ANDREW PuPLANTIS** – bass, vocals / **DAVE BRYSON** – drums

Sony Sony

Jul 05. (cd) *(520313-2) <96469>* **OKEMAH AND THE MELODY OF RIOT** ☐ 89
– Bandages and scars / Afterglow 61 / Jet pilot / Atmosphere / Ipecac / Who / Endless war / Medication / 6 string belief / Gramophone / Chaos streams / World waits for you / World waits for you – reprise.

Oct 05. (cd-ep) *(520539-2) <94830>* **AFTERGLOW 61 EP** ☐ Jun05 ☐
– Afterglow 61 / Joe Citizen blues (live) / Bandages and scars (live) / Medication (live) / Gramophone (acoustic).

SONIC YOUTH

Formed: New York City, New York, USA ... early 1981 by THURSTON MOORE and KIM GORDON. They replaced an early embryonic rhythm section with LEE RANALDO and RICHARD EDSON. After numerous releases on various US indie labels (notably Glenn Branca's 'Neutral' records), they signed to 'Blast First'in the U.K. First up for the label was 'BAD MOON RISING' in 1985, showing them at their most menacing and disturbing, especially on the glorious 'DEATH VALLEY 69' (a macabre reference to killer Charles Manson) with LYDIA LUNCH providing dual vox. They subsequently secured a US deal with 'S.S.T.', heralding yet another socially passionate thrash effort with 'EVOL'. A sideline project, CICCONE YOUTH, saw KIM and the lads plus MIKE WATT (of fIREHOSE), take off MADONNA's 'INTO THE GROOVE(Y)', which became a surprise dancefloor fave. Two more classic pieces, 'SISTER' (1987) & 'DAYDREAM NATION' (1988), finally secured them a major deal with 'D.G.C.' (David Geffen Company). In the early 90's, they smashed into the UK Top 40 with the album 'GOO', featuring a cameo by CHUCK D (of PUBLIC ENEMY) on the track/single 'KOOL THING'. The album, which sweetened their garage-punk/art-noise collages with melodic hooks, also included their deeply haunting tribute to KAREN CARPENTER, 'TUNIC (SONG FOR KAREN)'. They supported PUBLIC ENEMY that year, also stepping out with NEIL YOUNG on his 'Ragged Glory' tour in '91 (much to the distaste of YOUNG's more conservative fans!). In 1992, many thought 'DIRTY' to be a disappointment, the record being overproduced and overtaken by their new rivals and labelmates NIRVANA. By the mid-late 90's, they had returned to ground roots with acoustic psychedelia and the albums, 'EXPERIMENTAL JET SET' (1994), 'WASHING MACHINE' (1995) and 'A THOUSAND LEAVES' (1998) were again lauded by the alternative music press. All members had also taken on side solo projects, KIM featuring in all-star punk-grunge affair, FREE KITTEN. SONIC YOUTH returned towards the end of the decade with an appropriately-titled set, 'GOODBYE 20th CENTURY' (1999), a record in which they took on the works of avant-garde composers CHRISTIAN WOLFF, JOHN CAGE and CORNELIUS CARDEW. 'NYC GHOSTS & FLOWERS' (2000) was also a tribute of sorts, inspired by the beat poets who once upon a time fed their wayward muse on the Big Apple's mean streets. Featuring an Allen Ginsberg-derived title and William Burroughs cover art, the album was only partly successful in capturing the wild-eyed passion of the era. Their first straight up rock'n'roll album (if SONIC YOUTH could ever be described as dealing in straight up rock'n'roll) in almost five years, 'MURRAY STREET' (2002) found RANALDO and Co (with JIM O'ROURKE now a fully paid up member) reining in much of their tendency to free-form noise experimentation with a refreshingly prudent approach to their too often wearingly familiar craft. The playfully titled 'SONIC NURSE' (2004) offered up more music therapy for hopeless noise-pop addicts on a record that witnessed the resurgence of KIM GORDON. Having taken a back seat over the last half decade, she restated her hip-queen credentials on contemporary-culture shredding standouts like opener 'PATTERN RECOGNITION'. Yet it was on the acclaimed 'RATHER RIPPED' (2006) that GORDON really came back into her own, heralding the album's open-plan, aggravated pop sympathy on opener 'REENA'. With O'ROURKE having departed to continue his soundtrack career, and the band pared down to the original unit that recorded their late 80's/early 90's masterworks, there was a definite sense of coming full circle without abandoning their avant-garde template.

• **Songwriters:** MOORE / RANALDO / GORDON compositions, except I WANNA BE YOUR DOG (Stooges) / TICKET TO RIDE + WITHIN YOU WITHOUT YOU (Beatles) / BEAT ON THE BRAT + others (Ramones) / TOUCH ME, I'M SICK (Mudhoney) / ELECTRICITY (Captain Beefheart) / COMPUTER AGE (Neil Young). Their off-shoot CICCONE YOUTH covered INTO THE GROOVE (Madonna) / ADDICTED TO LOVE (Robert Palmer) / IS IT MY BODY (Alice Cooper) / PERSONALITY CRISIS (New York Dolls) / CA PLANE POUR MOI (Plastic Bertrand) / MOIST VAGINA = (MV) (Nirvana). FREE KITTEN covered: OH BONDAGE UP YOURS (X-Ray Spex). • **Trivia:** Early in 1989, they were featured on hour-long special TV documentary for Melvyn Bragg's 'The South Bank Show'.

Album rating: CONFUSION IS SEX (*6) / KILL YR IDOLS (*4) / BAD MOON RISING (*8) / EVOL (*8) / SISTER (*9) / DAYDREAM NATION (*9) / GOO (*9) / DIRTY (*7) / EXPERIMENTAL JET SET, TRASH AND NO STAR (*6) / MADE IN U.S.A. soundtrack rec. 1986 (*4) / WASHING MACHINE (*8) / SCREAMING FIELDS OF SONIC LOVE compilation (*6) / A THOUSAND LEAVES (*6) / GOODBYE 20th CENTURY (*7) / NYC GHOSTS & FLOWERS (*4) / MURRAY STREET (*6) / SONIC NURSE (*7) / HIDROS 3 (TO PATTI SMITH) with Mats Gustafsson (*5) / RATHER RIPPED (*7)

THURSTON MOORE (b.25 Jul'58, Coral Gables, Florida) – vocals, guitar / **KIM GORDON** (b.28 Apr'53, Rochester, N.Y.) – vocals, bass / **LEE RANALDO** (b. 3 Feb'56, Glen Cove, N.Y.) – vocals, guitar repl. ANN DEMARIS / **RICHARD EDSON** – drums repl. DAVE KEAY

Neutral — not iss.

Feb 84. (m-lp) *(ND 01)* **SONIC YOUTH (live)** [–] German [–]
– The burning spear / I dreamt I dreamed / She's not alone / I don't want to push it / The good and the bad. *(re-iss. cd Oct87 on 'S.S.T.'; SSTCD 097)*

—— **JIM SCLAVUNOS** – drums repl. EDSON

Feb 84. (lp) *(ND 02)* **CONFUSION IS SEX** [–] German [–]
– Inhuman / The world looks red / Confusion is next / Making the nature scene / Lee is free / (She's in a) Bad mood / Protect me you / Freezer burn / I wanna be your dog / Shaking Hell. *(re-iss. cd Oct87 on 'S.S.T.'; SSTCD 096)*

—— **BOB BERT** – drums repl. SCLAVUNOS (still featured on 2 tracks)

Zensor — not iss.

Oct 83. (m-lp) *(ZENSOR 10)* **KILL YR. IDOLS** [–] German [–]
– Protect me you / Shaking Hell / Kill yr. idols / Brother James / Early American.

not iss. — Ecstatic Peace

1984. (c) *<none>* **SONIC DEATH (SONIC YOUTH LIVE)** [–] [ ]
– Sonic Death (side 1) / Sonic Death (side 2). *(UK cd-iss. Jul88 on 'Blast First'; BFFP 32CD>*

not iss. — Iridescence

Dec 84. (12"; by SONIC YOUTH & LYDIA LUNCH) *<1-12>*
DEATH VALLEY '69. / BRAVE MEN (RUN IN MY FAMILY) [–] [ ]

Blast First — Homestead

Mar 85. (lp) *(BFFP 1) <HMS 016>* **BAD MOON RISING** [ ] [ ]
– Intro / Brave men rule / Society is a hole / I love her all the time / Ghost bitch / I'm insane / Justice is might / Death valley '69. *(cd-iss. Nov86+=; BFFP 1CD)* – Satan is boring / Flower / Halloween. *<US cd re-iss. 1995 on 'Geffen'; 24512>*

Jun 85. (12"ep; by SONIC YOUTH & LYDIA LUNCH) *(BFFP 2) <HMS 012>* **DEATH VALLEY '69. / I DREAMT I DREAMED / INHUMAN / BROTHER JAMES / SATAN IS BORING** [ ] [ ]

Jan 86. (12",12"yellow) *(BFFP 3)* **HALLOWEEN. / FLOWER** [–] [ ]

Jan 86. (7") *(BFFP 3)* **FLOWER. / REWOLF (censored)** [ ] [–]
(12") – ('A'side) / Satan is boring (live).

Mar 86. (etched-12") *(BFFP 3-B)* **HALLOWEEN II** [ ] [–]

—— **STEVE SHELLEY** (b.23 Jun'62, Midland, Michigan) – drums repl. BOB BERT who joined PUSSY GALORE

Blast First — S.S.T.

May 86. (lp/c) *(BFFP 4/+C) <SST/+C/CD 059>* **EVOL** [ ] [ ]
– Green light / Star power / Secret girl / Tom Violence / Death to our friends / Shadow of a doubt / Marilyn Moore / In the kingdom / Madonna, Sean and me. *(cd-iss. Nov86+=; BFFP 4CD)* – Bubblegum. *<US cd re-iss. 1995 on 'Geffen'; 24513>*

Jul 86. (7") *(BFFP 7) <SST 80>* **STAR POWER. / BUBBLEGUM** [ ] [ ]
(12"+=) *(BFFP 7T) <SST 80-12>* – Expressway.

—— added guest **MIKE WATT** – bass (of fIREHOSE)

Nov 86. (12"; as CICCONE YOUTH) *(BFFP 8)* **INTO THE GROOVE(Y). / TUFF TITTY RAP / BURNIN' UP** [ ] [ ]

Jun 87. (lp/c/cd) *(BFFP 20/+C/CD) <SST/+C/CD 134>* **SISTER** [ ] [ ]
– White cross / (I got a) Catholic block / Hot wire my heart / Tuff gnarl / Kotton crown / Schizophrenia / Beauty lies in the eye / Stereo sanctity / Pipeline – killtime / PCH. *(cd+=)* – Master-Dik (original). *<US cd re-iss. 1995 on 'Geffen'; 24514>*

Jan 88. (m-lp) *(BFFP 26T) <SST 155>* **MASTER-DIK** [ ] [ ]
– Master-Dik / Beat on the brat / Under the influence of the Jesus & Mary Chain: Ticket to ride / Ringo – He's on fire – Florida oil / Chines jam / Vibrato – Guitar lick – Funky fresh / Our backyard / Traffik.

Blast First — Capitol

Jan 88. (lp/c/cd; as CICCONE YOUTH) *(BFFP 28/+C/CD) <C1/C4/C2 75402>* **THE WHITEY ALBUM** [63] [ ]
– Needle-gun (silence) / G-force / Platoon II / Macbeth / Me & Jill / Hendrix Cosby / Burnin' up / Hi! everybody / Children of Satan / Third fig / Two cool rock chicks / Listening to Neu! / Addicted to love / Moby-

Dik / March of the Ciccone robots / Making the nature scene / Tuff titty rap / Into the groovey. <US cd re-iss. 1995 on 'Geffen'; 24516>

Feb 88. (d-one-sided-7"on 'Fierce') *(FRIGHT 015-016)* **STICK ME DONNA MAGICK MOMMA / MAKING THE NATURE SCENE (live)** [ ] [–]
(also soon issued as normal-7")

Blast First — Torso

Oct 88. (d-lp/c/cd) *(BFFP 34/+C/CD)* <2602339> **DAYDREAM NATION** [99] [ ]
– Teenage riot / Silver rocket / The sprawl / 'Cross the breeze / Eric's trip / Total trash / Hey Joni / Providence / Candle? / Rain king / Kissability / Trilogy: The wonder – Hyperstation – Eliminator Jr.

— Late in '88, KIM teamed up with LYDIA LUNCH and SADIE MAE to form one-off project HARRY CREWS. Their live appearences were issued in Apr 90 as 'NAKED IN GARDEN HILLS' for 'Big Cat' UK + 'Widowspeak' US.

Feb 89. (12") *(BFFP 46)* **TOUCH ME, I'M SICK. / (Halloween; by MUDHONEY)** [ ] [ ]

W.E.A. — D.G.C.

Jun 90. (cd/c/lp) <(7599 24297-2/-4/-1)> **GOO** [32] [96]
– Dirty boots / Tunic (song for Karen) / Mary-Christ / Kool thing / Mote / My friend Goo / Disappearer / Mildred Pierce / Cinderella's big score / Scooter + Jinx / Titanium expose. *(re-iss. cd Oct95 on 'Geffen'; GFLD 19297)*

Geffen — Geffen

Sep 90. (7") *(GEF 81)* **KOOL THING. / THAT'S ALL I KNOW (RIGHT NOW)** [ ] [–]
(12"+=) *(GEF 81T)* – ('A'demo version).
(cd-s++=) *(GEF 81CD)* – Dirty boots (rock & roll Heaven version).

— In autumn '90, THURSTON was part of 'Rough Trade' supergroup VELVET MONKEYS.

D.G.C. — D.G.C.

Apr 91. (m-lp/m-c/m-cd) *(DGC/+C/D 21634)* **DIRTY BOOTS** [69] [–]
(all live, except the title track)
– Dirty boots / The bedroom / Cinderella's big scene / Eric's trip / White kross. *(re-iss. cd Apr92; DGLD 19060)*

— Early in '92, THURSTON and STEVE also teamed up with RICHARD HELL's off-shoot group The DIM STARS.

Jun 92. (7") *(DGCS 11)* **100%. / CREME BRULEE** [28] [–]
(10"orange+=/12"+=) *(DGC V/T 11)* – Hendrix necro.
(cd-s++=) *(DGCTD 11)* – Genetic.

Jul 92. (d-lp/c/cd) <(DGC/+C/D 24485)> **DIRTY** [6] [83]
– 100% / Swimsuit issue / Theresa's sound-world / Drunken butterfly / Shoot / Wish fulfillment / Sugar Kane / Orange rolls, angel's spit / Youth against fascism / Nic fit / On the strip / Chapel Hill / JC / Purr / Creme brulee. *(d-lp+=)* – Stalker. *(re-iss. cd Oct95; GFLD 19296)*

Geffen — D.G.C.

Oct 92. (7") *(GFS 26)* **YOUTH AGAINST FASCISM. / PURR** [52] [–]
(10"colrd+=) *(GFSV 26)* – ('A'version).
(12"++=/cd-s++=) *(GFST/+D 26)* – The destroyed room (radio version)

Apr 93. (7"/c-s) *(GFS/+C 37)* **SUGAR KANE. / THE END OF THE END OF THE UGLY** [26] [–]
(10"blue+=/cd-s+=) *(GFS V/TD 37)* – Is it my body / Personality crisis.

Apr 94. (10"silver/c-s/cd-s) *(GFS V/C/TD 72)* **BULL IN THE HEATHER. / RAZORBLADE** [24] [–]

May 94. (cd/c/blue-lp) <(GED/GEC/GEF 24632)> **EXPERIMENTAL JET SET, TRASH AND NO STAR** [10] [34]
– Winner's blues / Bull in the heather / Starfield road / Skink / Self-obsessed and sexxee / Bone / Androgynous mind / Quest for the cup / Waist / Doctor's orders / Tokyo eye / In the mind of the bourgeois reader / Sweet shine.

— In Sep 94; 'A&M' released CARPENTERS tribute album, which contained their single 'SUPERSTAR'. It was combined with also another cover from REDD KROSS, and reached UK No.45.

Oct 95. (cd/c/d-lp) <(GED/GEC/GEF 24925)> **WASHING MACHINE** [39] [58]
– Becuz / Junkie's promise / Saucer-like / Washing machine / Unwind / Little trouble girl / No queen blues / Panty lies / Becuz coda * / Skip tracer / The diamond sea. *(cd+= *)*

Apr 96. (12"/cd-s) *(GRS T/D 22132)* **LITTLE TROUBLE GIRL. / MY ARENA / THE DIAMOND SEA (edit)** [ ] [–]

Feb 98. (12"ep/cd-ep; SONIC YOUTH & JIM O'ROURKE) *<(SYR 003/+CD)>* **INVITO AL CIELO EP** [ ] [ ]
– Invito al cielo / Hungara vivo / Radio-Amatoroj.
(above issued on own 'Sonic Youth Records')

May 98. (d-cd/d-lp) *<(GED/GEF 25203)>* **A THOUSAND LEAVES** [38] [85]
– Contre le sexisme / Sunday / Female mechanic now on duty / Wildflower soul / Hoarfrost / French tickler / Hits of sunshine (for Allen Ginsberg) / Karen Koltrane / The ineffable me / Snare / Girl / Heather angel.

Jun 98. (7") *(GFS 22332)* **SUNDAY. / MOIST VAGINA** [72] [–]
(cd-s+=) *(GFSTD 22332)* – Silver panties / ('A'edit).

— THURSTON collaborated with DON FLEMING and JIM DUNBAR on the freeform/experimental project, FOOT, releasing 'S/T' for 'God Bless'

Sonic Youth — Sonic Youth

Nov 99. (d-lp/d-cd) *<(SYR 04/+CD)>* **GOODBYE 20th CENTURY** [ ] [ ]
– Edges / Six / Six for new time for Sonic Youth / + – / Voice piece for soprano / Pendulum music // Having never written a note for percussion / Six / Burdocks / Four / Piano piece #3 / Enfantine / Treatise.

Geffen — Geffen

May 00. (cd/lp) *<(490665-2/-1)>* **NYC GHOSTS AND FLOWERS** [ ] [ ]
– Free city rhymes / Renegade princess / Nevermind (what was it anyway) / Small flowers crack concrete / Side 2 side / Streamsonik subway / NYC ghosts and flowers / Lightnin'.

— added **JIM O'ROURKE** – guitars, etc. (Solo artist)

Jun 02. (cd) *<(493319-2)>* **MURRAY STREET** [ ] [ ]
– The empty page / Disconnection notice / Rain on tin / Karen revisited / Radical adults lick godhead style / Plastic sun / Sympathy for the strawberry.

Apr 03. (7") *<NACK 002>* **MARIAH CAREY AND THE ARTHUR DOYLE HANDCREAM. / (other by ERASE ERRATA)** [–] [ ]
(above on 'NarNack')

Jun 04. (cd) *(9862547)* *<25491-2>* **SONIC NURSE** [ ] [64]
– Pattern recognition / Unmade bed / Dripping dream / Kim Gordon and the Arthur Doyle hand cream / Stones / Dude ranch nurse / New Hampshire / Paper cup exit / I love you golden blue / Peace attack. *(bonus+=)* – Kim chords.

— now without O'ROURKE

Jun 06. (cd) *(9878304)* *<757>* **RATHER RIPPED** [ ] [71]
– Reena / Incinerate / Do you believe in rapture? / Sleepin' around / What a waste / Jams run free / Rats / Turquoise boy / Lights out / The neutral / Pink steam / Or.

– compilations, others, etc. –

Feb 92. (cd) *Sonic Death;* *<(SD 13001)>* **GOO DEMOS LIVE AT THE CONTINENTAL CLUB (live)** [ ] Nov89 [ ]

Mar 95. (cd/c) *Blast First; (BFFP 113 CD/C)* **CONFUSION IS SEX / KILL YR IDOLS** [ ] [–]

Mar 95. (cd) *Warners-Rhino;* *<(8122 71591-2)>* **MADE IN U.S.A.** (1988 soundtrack; rec.late 1986) [ ] [ ]
– Mackin' for Doober / Full chrome logic / Secret girls / Cork mountain incident / Moustache riders / Tuck n Dar / Moon in the bathroom / Thought bubbles / Rim thrusters / Lincoln's gout / Coughing up tweed / Pre-poured wood / Hairpiece lullaby 1 & 2 / Pocketful of Sen-Sen / Smoke blisters 1 & 2 / The velvet plug / Giggles / Tulip fire 2 / The dynamics of bulbing / Smoke blisters 3 & 4 / O.J.'s glove or what? / Webb of mud 1, 2 & 3 / Bachelors in fur!

Apr 95. (cd) *Blast First; (BFFP 119CD) / Geffen;* *<24809>* **SCREAMING FIELDS OF SONIC LOVE** [ ] [ ]
– Teen age riot / Kissability / Eric's trip / Candle / Into the groove(y) / Macbeth / Beauty lies in the eye / Kotton krown / Shadow of a doubt / Expressway to yr. skull / Star power / Death Valley '69 / Halloween / Inhuman / Making the nature scene / Brother James / I dreamed I dreamed.

May 97. (pic-lp) *Sonic Death; (SYLB 1)* **LIVE IN BREMEN** (live) [ ] [–]

Jun 97. (12"ep/cd-ep) *Sonic Youth; (SYR 1/+CD)* **SYR VOL.1** [ ] [ ]
– Anagrama / Improvisation ajout'e / Tremens / Mieux: de corrosion.

Jul 98. (cd) *S.Y.R.; (SYR 1)* **SILVER SESSION FOR JASON KNUTH** [ ] [ ]

Aug 98. (cd) *Goofin' (GOO 2CD)* **HOLD THAT TIGER** (live 1987) [ ] [ ]

2000. (cd) *Sonic Youth;* *<SYR 5>* **SYR 5** [–] [ ]
– Olive's horn / International spy / Neu adult / Paperbag – Orange laptop / Stuck on gum / Fried mushroom / What do you want? (Kim) / Lemonade / We are the princesses / Take me back / Take it to the hit.
(above credited to KIM GORDON, DJ OLIVE & IKUE MORI)

Jul 00. (cd; by SONIC YOUTH & YAMATSUKA EYE) *Ecstatic Peace; <(E 38CD)>* **TV SHIT** [ ] [ ]

Sep 04. (cd; with MATS GUSTAFSSON) *Smalltown Supersound; <80>* **HIDROS 3 (TO PATTI SMITH)** [–] [ ]
– (parts 1 – 9).

□ SONNY & CHER (see under ⇒ CHER)

SOUNDGARDEN

Formed: Seattle, Washington, USA … 1984 by lead singer CHRIS CORNELL, guitarist KIM THAYIL and bassist HIRO YAMAMOTO. With the addition of drummer MATT CAMERON in '86, the band became one of the first to record for the fledgling 'Sub Pop' label, releasing the 'HUNTED DOWN' single in summer '87. Two EP's, 'SCREAMING LIFE', and 'FOPP' followed, although the group signed to 'S.S.T.' for their debut album, 'ULTRAMEGA OK' (1988). Despite its lack of focus, the record laid the foundations for what was to follow; a swamp-rich miasma of snail-paced, bass-crunch uber-riffing, wailing vocals and punk attitude shot through with bad-trip psychedelia (i.e. not something to listen to last thing at night). And with the Grammy-nominated 'LOUDER THAN LOVE' (1989), the group's major label debut for 'A&M', SOUNDGARDEN harnessed their devilish wares onto infectious melodies and fuck-off choruses; one listen to the likes of 'HANDS ALL OVER', 'LOUD LOVE' and the tongue-in-cheek brilliance of 'BIG DUMB SEX' was enough to convince you that these hairy post-metallers were destined for big, grunge-type things. Success wasn't immediate however, the album failing to make a dent beyond the Sub-Pop in-crowd and a few adventurous metal fans. YAMAMOTO departed soon after the record's release, his replacement being ex-NIRVANA guitarist JASON EVERMAN, who was succeeded in turn by BEN SHEPHERD. CORNELL and CAMERON subsequently got together with future PEARL JAM mambers, EDDIE VEDDER, STONE GOSSARD and JEFF AMENT to form TEMPLE OF THE DOG, releasing an eponymous album in early '91 to critical acclaim. SOUNDGARDEN, meanwhile, finally got their break later that year when 'BADMOTORFINGER' broke the US/UK Top 40. An even more accessible proposition, the record combined a tighter, more driven sound with pop/grunge hooks and their trademark cerebral lyrics to create such MTV favourites as 'JESUS CHRIST POSE' and 'OUTSHINED'. 'RUSTY CAGE' was another juggernaut riffathon, while 'SEARCHING WITH MY GOOD EYE CLOSED' meted out some of the most brutal psychedelia this side of MONSTER MAGNET. A high profile support slot on GUNS N' ROSES' 'Lose Your Illusion' tour afforded the band valuable exposure in the States, their crossover appeal endearing them to the metal hordes on both sides of the Atlantic. Previewed by the Top 20 'SPOONMAN' single, SOUNDGARDEN's masterful fourth set, 'SUPERUNKNOWN' (1994), finally gave the group long overdue success, scaling the US charts and going Top 5 in Britain. Constructed around a head-spinning foundation of acid-drenched retro-rock and JIM MORRISON-esque doom, this epic album spawned the Grammy-winnning 'BLACK HOLE SUN' while 'FELL ON BLACK DAYS' stands as one of their most realised pieces of warped psychedelia to date. Following a world tour with the likes of The SMASHING PUMPKINS, the group began work on 'DOWN ON THE UPSIDE' (1996). Another marathon set boasting sixteen tracks, the record inevitably failed to garner the plaudits of its predecessor; the claustrophobia of old had given way to a marginally more straightforward melodic grunge sound, evidenced to best effect on the likes of 'BURDEN IN MY HAND'. Subversiveness was still the key word; 'TY COBB's mutant country-punk and gonzoid expletive-filled attitude was reminiscent of MINISTRY's seminal 'Jesus Built My Hotrod'. The album ultimately proved to be their swan song, SOUNDGARDEN subsequently pushing up the daisies as of April '97. CORNELL (now in his mid-30's!) returned as a solo artist a few years later, although a largely timid soft-rock debut, 'EUPHORIA MORNING' (1999) – featuring the JEFF BUCKLEY tribute, 'WAVE GOODBYE' – saw the man lose his "metal" credentials. However, the frontman resurfaced – on and off – via post-RAGE AGAINST THE MACHINE project, AUDIOSLAVE; their eponymous debut hitting the Top 20 late 2002.

• **Songwriters:** Most by CORNELL and group permutations. Covered SWALLOW MY PRIDE (Ramones) / FOPP (Ohio Players) / INTO THE VOID tune only (Black Sabbath) / BIG BOTTOM (Spinal Tap) / EARACHE MY EYE (Cheech & Chong) / I CAN'T GIVE YOU ANYTHING (Ramones) / HOMOCIDAL SUICIDE (Budgie) / I DON'T CARE ABOUT YOU (Fear) / CAN YOU SEE ME (Jimi Hendrix) / COME TOGETHER (Beatles).

Album rating: ULTRAMEGA OK (*7) / LOUDER THAN LOVE (*8) / BADMOTORFINGER (*9) / SUPERUNKNOWN (*9) / DOWN ON THE UPSIDE (*6) / A-SIDES compilation (*8) / Chris Cornell: EUPHORIA MORNING (*4) / Temple Of The Dog: TEMPLE OF THE DOG (*7)

CHRIS CORNELL (b.20 Jul'64) – vocals, guitar / **KIM THAYIL** (b. 4 Sep'60) – lead guitar / **HIRO YAMAMOTO** (b.13 Apr'61) – bass / **MATT CAMERON** (b.28 Nov'62, San Diego, Calif.) – drums, percussion

not iss. Sub Pop

Jun 87. (7"blue) *<SP 12a>* **NOTHING TO SAY. / HUNTED DOWN** [–] [ ]

Oct 87. (12"ep,orange-12"ep) *<SP 12>* **SCREAMING LIFE** [–] [ ]
– Hunted down / Entering / Tears to forget / Nothing to say / Little Joe / Hand of God.

Aug 88. (12"ep) *<SP 17>* **FOPP** [–] [ ]
– Fopp / Fopp (dub) / Kingdom of come / Swallow my pride.

S.S.T. S.S.T.

Nov 88. (m-lp/c/cd) *<(SST 201/+C/CD)>* **ULTRAMEGA OK** [ ] [ ]
– Flower / All your lies / 665 / Beyond the wheel / 667 / Mood for trouble / Circle of power / He didn't / Smokestack lightning / Nazi driver / Head injury / Incessant mace / One minute of silence. *(re-iss. Oct95;)*

May 89. (12"ep/c-ep/cd-ep) *<(SST 231/+C/CD)>* **FLOWER. / HEAD INJURY / TOY BOX** [ ] [ ]

A&M A&M

Sep 89. (lp/c/cd) *<(AMA/AMC/CDA 5252)>* **LOUDER THAN LOVE** [ ] [ ]
– Ugly truth / Hands all over / Gun / Power trip / Get on the snake / Full on Kevin's mom / Loud love / I awake / No wrong no right / Uncovered / Big dumb sex / Full on (reprise).

Apr 90. (10"ep/cd-ep) *(AM X/CD 560)* **HANDS ALL OVER** [ ] [–]
– Hands all over / Heretic / Come together / Big dumb sex.

Jul 90. (7"ep/12"ep) *(AM/+Y 574)* **THE LOUD LOVE E.P.** [ ] [–]
– Loud love / Fresh deadly roses / Big dumb sex (dub) / Get on the snake.

—— **JASON EVERMAN** (b.16 Aug'67) – bass (ex-NIRVANA) repl. HIRO who later formed TRULY after working in a bike shop.

Oct 90. (7",7"purple/green) *<SP 83>* **ROOM A THOUSAND YEARS WIDE. / H.I.V. BABY** [–] [ ]
(above issued on 'Sub Pop')

—— **BEN SHEPHERD** (b. HUNTER SHEPHERD, 20 Sep'68, Okinawa, Japan) – bass repl. JASON

Oct 91. (cd/c/lp) *(395374-2/-4/-1) <5374>* **BADMOTORFINGER** [39] [39]
– Rusty cage / Outshined / Slaves & bulldozers / Jesus Christ pose / Face pollution / Somewhere / Searching with my good eye closed / Room a thousand years wide / Mind riot / Drawing flies / Holy water / New damage.

Mar 92. (7") *(AM 862)* **JESUS CHRIST POSE. / STRAY CAT BLUES** [30] [–]
(cd-s+=) *(AMCD 862)* – Into the void (stealth).

Jun 92. (7"pic-d) *(AM 874)* **RUSTY CAGE. / TOUCH ME** [41] [–]
(12"+=/cd-s+=) *(AM Y/CD 874)* – Show me.
(cd-s+=) *(AMCDX 874)* – Big bottom / Earache my eye.

Nov 92. (7") *(AM 0102)* **OUTSHINED. / I CAN'T GIVE YOU ANYTHING** [50] [–]
(12"+=/cd-s+=) *(AM 0102 T/CD)* – Homocidal suicide.
(cd-s+=) *(AM 0102CDX)* – I don't care about you / Can't you see me.

Feb 94. (7"pic-d/c-s) *(580 538-7/-4)* **SPOONMAN. / FRESH TENDRILS** [20] [–]
(12"clear+=/cd-s+=) *(580 539-1/-2)* – Cold bitch / Exit Stonehenge.

Mar 94. (cd/c/orange-d-lp) *(540215-2/-4/-1) <0198>* **SUPERUNKNOWN** | 4 | 1
– Let me drown / My wave / Fell on black days / Mailman / Superunknown / Head down / Black hole Sun / Spoonman / Limo wreck / The day I tried to live / Kickstand / Fresh tendrils / 4th of July / Half / Like suicide / She likes surprises.

Apr 94. (7"pic-d/c-s) *(580594-7/-4)* **THE DAY I TRIED TO LIVE. / LIKE SUICIDE (acoustic)** | 42 | –
(12"etched+=/cd-s+=) *(580595-1/-2)* – Kickstand (live).

Aug 94. (7"pic-d/c-s) *(580736-7/-4)* **BLACK HOLE SUN. / BEYOND THE WHEEL (live) / FELL ON BLACK DAYS (live)** | 12 | –
(pic-cd-s+=) *(580753-2)* – Birth ritual (demo).
(cd-s) *(580737-2)* – ('A'side) / My wave (live) / Jesus Christ pose (live) / Spoonman (remix).

Jan 95. (7"pic-d/c-s) *(580947-7/-4)* **FELL ON BLACK DAYS. / KYLE PETTY, SON OF RICHARD / MOTORCYCLE LOOP** | 24 | –
(cd-s) *(580947-2)* – ('A'side) / Kyle Petty, son of Richard / Fell on black days (video version).
(cd-s) *(580947-5)* – ('A'side) / Girl u want / Fell on black days (early demo).

May 96. (7"red/cd-s) *(581620-7/-4)* **PRETTY NOOSE. / JERRY GARCIA'S FINGER** | 14 | –
(cd-s) *(581620-2)* – ('A'side) / Applebite / An unkind / (interview with Eleven's Alain and Natasha).

May 96. (cd/c/d-lp) *(540526-2/-4/-1) <0526>* **DOWN ON THE UPSIDE** | 7 | 2
– Pretty noose / Rhinosaur / Zero chance / Dusty / Ty Cobb / Blow up the outside world / Burden in my hand / Never named / Applebite / Never the machine forever / Tighter & tighter / No attention / Switch opens / Overfloater / An unkind / Boot camp.

Sep 96. (7"/cd-s) *(581854-7/-2)* **BURDEN IN MY HAND. / KARAOKE** | 33 | –
(cd-s) *(581855-2)* – ('A'side) / Bleed together / She's a politician / (Chris Cornell interview).

Dec 96. (7") *(581986-7)* **BLOW UP THE OUTSIDE WORLD. / DUSTY** | 38 | –
(cd-s+=) *(581987-2)* – Gun.
(cd-s) *(581986-2)* – ('A'side) / Get on the snake / Slice of spacejam.

— split on the 9th of April 1997

– compilations, etc –

Oct 93. (cd) *A&M; (CDA 24118)* **LOUDER THAN LOUD / BADMOTORFINGER** | |

Oct 93. (c/cd) *Sub Pop; (SP/+CD 12)* **SCREAMING LIFE / FOPP** | |

Nov 97. (cd) *A&M; (540833-2) <0833>* **A-SIDES** | | 63
– Nothing to say / Flower / Loud love / Hands all over / Get on the snake / Jesus Christ pose / Outshined / Rusty cage / Spoonman / The day I tried to live / Black hole sun / Fell on black days / Pretty noose / Burden in my hand / Blow up the outside world / Ty Cobb / Bleed together.

CHRIS CORNELL

Sep 99. (cd/c) *<(490412-2/-4)>* **EUPHORIA MORNING** | 31 | 18
– Can't change me / Flutter girl / Preaching the end of the world / Follow my way / When I'm down / Mission / Wave goodbye / Moonchild / Sweet euphoria / Disappearing one / Pillow of your bones / Steel rain.

Oct 99. (7") *(497173-7)* **CAN'T CHANGE ME. / FLUTTER GIRL** | 62 | –
(cd-s+=) *(497173-2)* – Nowhere but you.
(cd-s) *(497174-2)* – ('A'side) / When I'm down / ('A'-video).

TEMPLE OF THE DOG

splinter-group feat. **CORNELL + CAMERON** plus **STONE GOSSARD / JEFF AMENT** (both ex-MOTHER LOVE BONE, future PEARL JAM)

A&M A&M

Jun 92. (cd/c/lp) *(395 350-2/-4/-1) <5350>* **TEMPLE OF THE DOG** | | 5
– Say hello to Heaven / Reach down / Hunger strike / Pushing forward back / Call me a dog / Times of trouble / Wooden Jesus / Your saviour / 4-walled world / All night thing.

Oct 92. (7"pic-d/c-s) *(AM 0091/+C)* **HUNGER STRIKE. / ALL NIGHT THING** | 51 |
(12"+=/cd-s+=) *(AM 0091 T/CD)* – Your saviour.

□ the SOUTHERN DEATH CULT (see under ⇒ CULT)

SPACEMEN 3

Formed: Rugby, Warwickshire, England ... 1983 by SONIC BOOM (PETE KEMBER) and JASON PIERCE. They enlisted PETE BAINES and ROSCO as a rhythm section and through their manager, Gerald Palmer, they signed to indie label, 'Glass'. In 1986, they debuted with 'SOUND OF CONFUSION', a primal embryo for "shoegazers" to come. Their follow-up, 'THE PERFECT PRESCRIPTION', set the world alight (well! the indie world anyway), with some clever pulsating, psychedelic garage-noise intertwined with melancholy bursts of beauty and experimentation, i.e 'WALKIN WITH JESUS' (again!), 'TRANSPARENT RADIATION' and 'TAKE ME TO THE OTHER SIDE'. In 1989, they were back again with a third set, 'PLAYING WITH FIRE', featuring the 10-minute squall of 'SUICIDE', and 'REVOLUTION' (later covered by MUDHONEY). SONIC BOOM's heroin addiction was taking its toll during the early 90's and with JASON having founded SPIRITUALIZED, the group were heading for their own proverbial rocketship to oblivion. Their final outing, 'RECURRING' (1991), recorded amid escalating tension, was a slight disappointment. By this time, SONIC had gone solo, subsequently going under the guise of SPECTRUM. His debut was followed by two albums of patchy, yet somewhat appealing albums, 'SOUL KISS (GLIDE DIVINE)' (1992) and 'HIGH LOWS AND HEAVENLY BLOWS' (1994). The ever prolific KEMBER went on play with mid 90's outfit, JESSAMINE, who to date have released a string of albums including 1997's 'ANOTHER FICTIONALIZED HISTORY'. Around the same time, KEMBER/SONIC simultaneously resurfaced with a SPECTRUM set, 'FOREVER ALIEN', released on the '3rd Stone' imprint. The SPECTRUM posse subsequently indulged their passion for prehistoric analog synth by hooking up with legendary early electronic experimentalists SILVER APPLES. The resulting 'LAKE OF TEARDROPS' (1998) was pretty much what you'd expect from such a collaboration with the respective parties' dedication to retroactivity precluding any startling intergalactic innovation. During the 90's, SONIC BOOM was also part of indie noisesters, EXPERIMENTAL AUDIO RESEARCH alongside (initially) KEVIN SHIELDS (of MY BLOODY VALENTINE) and EDDIE PREVOST (of AMM). EAR – as they were known for short – were primarily concerned with exploring the boundaries where stark ambience meets uncompromising guitar manipulation/noise, making their first lunar mission via a US-only debut CD-album, 'MESMERISED' (1994). Reflecting his love of collectable vinyl, SONIC BOOM decided to release a 5" single, 'POCKET SYMPHONY' a few months later. Subsequently securing a UK deal with 'Big Cat', EAR finally got round to issuing their first studio venture (actually recorded during their formative year), 'BEYOND THE PALE', in 1996. Over the course of the ensuing two years or so, the group were surprisingly prolific, completing a trio of long-players, 'PHENOMENA 256' (1996), 'THE KONER EXPERIMENT' (1997) and 'MILLENNIUM MUSIC' (1998) for three separate labels. Of late, the avant-garde troupe (who had now lost SHIELDS and MARTIN) introduced a revolutionary technique called "circuit bending" on their sixth album, 'DATA RAPE' (1998). 'VIBRATIONS' (2000) continued to tweak the listener into submission, EAR opening their musical account on this occasion with the spaced-out 'KALIMBELL'.

• **Songwriters:** KEMBER or PIERCE material until the 90's when KEMBER penned all. Covered; LITTLE DOLL (Stooges) / TRANSPARENT RADIATION (Red Krayola) / IT'S ALRIGHT (Bo Diddley) / CHE + ROCK'N'ROLL IS KILLING MY LIFE (Suicide) / WHEN TOMORROW

HITS (Mudhoney) / COME TOGETHER + STARSHIP (MC5) / MARY-ANNE (Juicy Lucy) / ROLLER COASTER (13th Floor Elevators).

Album rating: SOUND OF CONFUSION (*7) / THE PERFECT PRESCRIPTION (*8) / PLAYING WITH FIRE (*8) / RECURRING (*8) / PERFORMANCE posthumous (*7) / DREAM WEAPON – ECSTASY IN SLOW MOTION posthumous: (*7) / TAKING DRUGS TO MAKE MUSIC TO TAKE DRUGS TO posthumous (*5) / SPACEMEN ARE GO! posthumous (*3) / FOR ALL THE FUCKED UP CHILDREN IN THE WORLD posthumous (*4) / TRANSLUCENT FLASHBACKS collection (*6) / Sonic Boom: SPECTRUM (*5) / Spectrum: SOUL KISS (GLIDE DIVINE) (*6) / HIGH LOWS AND HEAVENLY BLOWS (*6) / FOREVER ALIEN (*6)

SONIC BOOM (b. PETE KEMBER, 19 Nov'65) – vocals / **JASON PIERCE** (b.19 Nov'65) – guitar / **STEWART (ROSCO) ROSSWELL** – keyboards / **PETE (BASSMAN) BAINES** – bass

Glass / not iss.

Jun 86. (lp) *(GLA 018)* **SOUND OF CONFUSION** [ ] [–]
– Losing touch with my mind / Hey man / Roller coaster / Mary Anne / Little doll / 2:35 / O.D. catastrophe. *(re-iss. Sep89 on 'Fire' lp/c/cd; REFIRE CD/MC/LP 5) <US cd-iss. 1994 on 'Taang!'; 93>*

Dec 86. (12"m) *(GLAEP 105)* **WALKIN' WITH JESUS (SOUND OF CONFUSION). / ROLLERCOASTER / FEEL SO GOOD** [ ] [–]

Jul 87. (12"m) *(GLAEP 108)* **TRANSPARENT RADIATION / ECSTASY SYMPHONY / TRANSPARENT RADIATION (FLASHBACK). / THINGS'LL NEVER BE THE SAME / STARSHIP** [ ] [–]

Aug 87. (lp/c) *(GLA LP/MC 026)* **THE PERFECT PRESCRIPTION** [ ] [–]
– Take me to the other side / Walking with Jesus / Ode to street hassle / Ecstasy – Symphony / Feel so good / Things'll never be the same / Come down easy / Call the doctor / Soul 1 / That's just fine. *(re-iss. Dec89 on 'Fire' lp/c/cd; REFIRE LP/MC/CD 6) <US cd-iss. 1994 on 'Taang!'; 94>*

Mar 88. (12") *(GLASS 12-054)* **TAKE ME TO THE OTHER SIDE. / SOUL 1 / THAT'S JUST FINE** [ ] [–]

Jul 88. (lp/cd) *(GLA LP/CD 030)* **PERFORMANCE** (live 1988 Holland) [ ] [–]
– Mary-Anne / Come together / Things'll never be the same / Take me to the other side / Roller coaster / Starship / Walkin' with Jesus. *(re-iss. May91 & Apr02 on 'Fire' cd/c/lp; REFIRE CD/MC/LP 11)*

— **WILLIE B. CARRUTHERS** – bass / **JON MATLOCK** – drums repl. ROSCO + BAINES who formed The DARKSIDE

Fire / not iss.

Nov 88. (7") *(BLAZE 29S)* **REVOLUTION. / CHE** [ ] [–]
(12"+=/cd-s+=) *(BLAZE 29 T/CD)* – May the circle be unbroken.

Feb 89. (lp/c/cd) *(FIRE LP/MC/CD 16)* **PLAYING WITH FIRE** [ ] [–]
– Honey / Come down softly to my soul / How does it feel? / I believe it / Revolution / Let me down gently / So hot (wash away all my tears) / Suicide / Lord can you hear me. *(free-12"ep/cd-ep+=)* – Starship / Revolution / Suicide (live) / Repeater / Live intro theme (xtacy). *<US cd-iss. 1994 on 'Taang'; 97> <d-lp-iss.Sep99 on 'Space Age'; ORBIT 011LP)*

Jul 89. (7") *(BLAZE 36S)* **HYPNOTIZED. / JUST TO SEE YOU SMILE HONEY (part 2)** [ ] [–]
(12"+=/3"cd-s+=) *(BLAZE 36 T/CD)* – The world is dying.
(free 7"flexi w.a) *(CHEREE 5)* – EXTRACTS FROM A CONTEMPORARY SITAR EVENING (with other artists).

Jan 91. (7") *(BLAZE 41)* **BIG CITY. / DRIVE** [ ] [–]
(12"+=/cd-s+=) *(BLAZE 41 T/CD)* – Big City (everybody I know can be found here).
(12"w-drawn) *(BLAZE 41TR)* – ('A'remix) / I love you (remix).

Feb 91. (cd/lp)(s-lp) *(FIRE CD/LP 23)(FIRELP 23S)* **RECURRING** [46] [–]
– Big city (everybody I know can be found here) / Just to see you smile (orchestral) / I love you / Set me free – I've got the key / Set me free (reprise) / Feel so bad (reprise) / Hypnotized / Sometimes / Feelin' just fine (head full of shit) / Billy Whizz – blue 1. *(cd+=)* – When tomorrow hits / Why couldn't I see / Just to see you smile (instrumental) / Feel so sad (demo) / Drive.

— they had already folded June '90.

– compilations, etc. –

Dec 90. (cd/d-lp) *Fierce; (FRIGHT 042/+CD)* **DREAM WEAPON / ECSTASY IN SLOW MOTION** [ ] [–]
(re-iss. Nov95 on 'Space Age' cd/d-lp; ORBIT 001 CD/LP) (cd re-iss. May02 on 'Sympathy For The Record Industry'; SFTRI 211)

Jun 94. (cd/lp) *Taang!; <TAANG 96 CD/LP>* **THE SINGLES** [–] [ ]

Nov 94. (cd) *Bomp; (<BCD 4047>)* **TAKING DRUGS TO MAKE MUSIC TO TAKE DRUGS TO** (demos of 1986) [ ] [ ]
(re-iss. Mar00 on 'Space Age'; ORBIT 023CD)

May 95. (cd/lp) *Sympathy For The Record Industry; (<SFTRI 136 CD/B>)* **FOR ALL FUCKED UP CHILDREN OF THE WORLD WE GIVE YOU . . .** (debut recording session) [ ] [ ]
(cd re-iss. Jun00 & May02; SFTRI 368CD)

May 95. (cd) *Bomp; (<BCD 4044>)* **SPACEMEN ARE GO!** [ ] [ ]
(re-iss. Jun00; same)

Jun 95. (cd/d-lp) *Fire; (FLIP CD/DLP 003)* **TRANSLUCENT FLASHBACKS (THE GLASS SINGLES)** [ ] [–]
(cd re-iss. Aug01; same)

Sep 95. (cd) *Taang; <TAANG 95CD>* **LIVE AT THE MILKWEG 6/2/88 (live)** [–] [ ]
– Mary Ann / Come together / Things'll never be / Take me to the other side / Rollercoaster / Walking with Jesus / Repeater / Starship / Revolution / Suicide.

Oct 95. (cd) *Fierce; (FRIGHT 063)* **THE CHOICE IS REVOLUTIONORHERION** [ ] [–]

Nov 95. (cd/d-lp) *Space Age; (ORBIT 002 CD/LP)* **LIVE IN EUROPE 1989 (live)** [ ] [–]

Mar 97. (d-cd) *Nectar; (NTMCDD 534)* **1 + 1 = 3** [ ] [–]

SONIC BOOM

(**PETE KEMBER** solo with **WILLIE B. CARRUTHERS** and also **PHIL PARFITT + JO WIGGS** of PERFECT DISASTER)

Silvertone / Sympathy

Oct 89. (12"ep/cd-ep) *(ORE T/CD 11)* **ANGEL. / ANGEL (version) / HELP ME PLEASE** [ ] [–]

Feb 90. (cd/c/lp) *(ORE CD/MC/LP 506)* **SPECTRUM** [65] [–]
– Pretty baby / If I should die / Lonely avenue / Help me please / Angel / Rock'n'roll is killing my life / You're the one. *(free 10" w-lp) (SONIC 1)* – DRONE DREAM EP: OCTAVES. / TREMELOS *<US-iss.Oct97 as 'WHEN CAME BEFORE AFTER' on 'Sympathy For The Record Industry'; SFTRI 493>*

Apr 91. (7"colrd) *<SFTRI 75>* **TREMELOS. / ECSTACY (IN SLOW MOTION)** [–] [ ]

Apr 91. (7"; gig freebie) *(SONIC 2)* **(I LOVE YOU) TO THE MOON AND BACK. / CAPO WALTZ (live)** [–] [–]

— SONIC BOOM has now featured in E.A.R. (EXPERIMENTAL AUDIO RESEARCH), who after first low-key album 'MESMERISED' in 1994 on 'Sympathy For The Record Industry', released for 'Big Cat' the 1996 lp/cd 'BEYOND THE PALE' *(ABB 96/+CD)*. It featured KEVIN SHIELDS (of; we still think; MY BLOODY VALENTINE), KEVIN MARTIN (of GOD) and EDDIE PREVOST. SONIC BOOM and E.A.R. released a split 7" in Jul'98 on 'Earworm' (WORM 22)

— In Mar 92, HONEY TONGUE (aka MATTOCK + WIGGS) released lp 'NUDE NUDES' on 'Playtime'; *AMUSE 012CD)*

SPECTRUM

KEMBER, CARRUTHERS, etc

Silvertone / Warners

Jun 92. (7") *(ORE 41)* **HOW YOU SATISFY ME. / DON'T GO (instrumental 2)** [ ] [–]
(12"clear+=/cd-s+=) *(ORE 41 T/CD)* – My life spins around your every smile / Don't go (instrumental 1).

Jun 92. (cd/c/lp) *(ORE CD/C/LP 518) <41501>* **SOUL KISS (GLIDE DIVINE)** [ ] [ ]
– How you satisfy me / Lord I don't even know my name / The drunk suite (overture) / Neon sigh / Waves wash over me / (I love you) To the Moon and back / My love for you never died away but my soul gave out and wit / Sweet running water / Touch the stars / Quicksilver glide divine / The drunk suite / Phase me out (gently). *(re-iss. Apr95; same)*

Sep 92. (7") *(ORE 44)* **TRUE LOVE WILL FIND YOU IN THE END. / MY LIFE SPINS AROUND YOUR EVERY SMILE** [70] [–]
(12"/cd-s) *(ORE T/CD 44)* – ('A'side) / To the moon and back / Waves wash over me.

— now w/ **KEVIN COWAN** – guitar (ex-DARKSIDE) repl. FORMBY

Sep 92. (d7") *<SFTRI 188>* **TRUE LOVE WILL FIND YOU IN THE SUN. / TASTE THE OZONE // DON'T GO (PLEASE STAY). / DRUNK SUITE – QUICKSILVER GLIDE DIVINE** [-] [ ]

Nov 92. (7") *<SFTRI 209>* **SANTA CLAUS (as the Sonics). / CHRISTMAS MESSAGE FROM SONIC BOOM** [-] [ ]

Aug 93. (7") *(ORE 56)* **INDIAN SUMMER. / BABY DON'T YOU WORRY (California lullabye)** [ ] [-]
(12"+=/cd-s+=) *(ORE T/CD 56)* – It's alright / True love will find you in the end.

Oct 94. (12"ep/cd-ep) *(ORE T/CD 65)* **UNDO THE TABOO / IN THE FULLNESS OF TIME. / TURN THE TIDE (SUB AQUA) / GO TO SLEEP** [ ] [-]

Nov 94. (cd/lp) *(ORE CD/LP 532)* **HIGHS, LOWS AND HEAVENLY BLOWS** [ ] [-]
– Undo the taboo / Feedback / Then I just drifted away / Take your time / Soothe me / All night long / Don't pass me by / I know they say / Take me away.

not iss. Sympathy F

Oct 96. (10"ep) *<SFTRI 278>* **SPECTRUM 10** [-] [ ]
– California lullabye / It's alright / Indian summer / True love . . . (alt. version) / Through the rhythm.

— SONIC BOOM also became part of JESSAMINE, an outfit who released a few albums including 'Another Fictionalized History' in '97.

— now with **ALF HARDY** – synthesizers

3rd Stone Reprise

Oct 96. (cd-ep) *<46303>* **SONGS FOR OWSLEY** [-] [ ]
– Owsley / Liquid intentions / Feels like I'm slipping away / Sine study #1 / The new Atlantis.

Aug 97. (d-lp/cd) *(ORBIT 008/+CD) <46715>* **FOREVER ALIEN** [ ] [ ]
– Feels like I'm slipping away / The stars are so far (how does it feel?) / Close your eyes and you'll see / Delia Derbyshire / Owsley / Forever alien / Matrix / Like . . . / The new Atlantis / The end. *(UK+=)* – Sounds for a thunderstorm (for Peter Zinovieft) / Liquid intentions / Sine study.

Sep 97. (cd-ep) *(ORBIT 010CD)* **FEELS LIKE I'M SLIPPING AWAY** [ ] [-]
– Feels like I'm slipping away / Forever alien / Dream time / What comes before after? *<US-iss.Jun00; same>*

Oct 98. (cd/lp; as SPECTRUM & SILVER APPLES) *(ORBIT 016 CD/LP)* **A LAKE OF TEARDROPS** [ ] [-]
– Streams of sorrow / Sixth sense / The edge / Second sight / Whirlwind / (I don't care if you) Never come back.

Jun 99. (cd; split w/ IMAJINARY FRIENDS) *(ORBIT 017CD)* **INTERFACE / COME OUT TO PLAY** [ ] [-]
– Against the grain / Taste the night / (5 by other group).

SPARKS

Formed: Los Angeles, California, USA . . . 1968 as HALFNELSON by brothers RON and RUSSELL MAEL. TODD RUNDGREN was sufficiently impressed with a demo tape to get them signed up for Albert Grossman's 'Bearsville' label where he worked as an in-house producer. With EARLE MANKEY, RALPH OSWALD and JOHN HENDERSON completing the line-up, the outfit recorded the eponymous 'HALFNELSON' (1972) under RUNDGREN's guidance. The record sold poorly, however, and the duo changed their name to SPARKS, replacing the rhythm section with JIM MANKEY and HARVEY FEINSTEIN. The resulting 'A WOOFER IN TWEETER'S CLOTHING' (1973) was equally unsuccessful and following an encouraging UK live reception, the brothers relocated to London in 1974, signing to 'Island'. Recruiting a new troupe of backing musicians, RON and RUSSELL were a massive hit (No.2) almost immediately with the pseudo-operatic glam melodrama of 'THIS TOWN AIN'T BIG ENOUGH FOR THE BOTH OF US'. Strikingly eccentric, both visually (RON's unnerving Hitler-esque moodiness and RUSSELL's flouncing, near-falsetto androgyny was quite a match) and musically, it was small wonder the duo were doomed to failure in the States. With Muff Winwood at the controls, the accompanying 'KIMONO MY HOUSE' (1974) developed their arch glam-pop over a whole album and drew inevitable if somewhat inaccurate comparisons with ROXY MUSIC. 'PROPAGANDA' (1974) carried on in the same vein, another Top 10 success which spawned a further two Top 20 hit singles in 'NEVER TURN YOUR BACK ON MOTHER EARTH' and 'SOMETHING FOR THE GIRL WITH EVERYTHING'. By the release of the Tony Visconti-produced 'INDISCREET' (1975), the formula was wearing thin and an expensively disastrous attempt at sub-metal posturing with 'BIG BEAT' (1976) marked the end of the brothers' tenure with 'Island' and a move back to Los Angeles. Meeting electro disco guru, GIORGIO MORODER in Germany the following year, SPARKS collaborated with him on comeback set, 'NUMBER ONE IN HEAVEN' (1979). Released by their new bosses, 'Virgin', the album spawned a couple of major UK hits in 'THE NUMBER ONE SONG IN HEAVEN' and the itchy disco-funk of 'BEAT THE CLOCK', despite barely scraping into the Top 75 itself. Although many 80's outfits owed an obvious debt to SPARKS' innovations, the decade saw them confined to the margins; while they were popular in France, the brothers failed to notch up any hits at all in Britain during this period. Bizarrely enough, SPARKS enjoyed some belated success in the States with the warbling 'ANGST IN MY PANTS' (1982) and 'SPARKS IN OUTER SPACE' (1983) sets. The MAELS' influence on the late 80's/early 90's house scene saw them release a one-off 12" for Scotland's very own 'Finflex' label, 'NATIONAL CRIME AWARENESS WEEK' with dance imprint, 'Logic' subsequently picking them up for the oh-so-cleverly titled 'GRATUITOUS SAX & SENSELESS VIOLINS' (1994). The latter opus actually spawned two minor Top 40 hits, 'WHEN DO I GET TO SING "MY WAY"' and 'WHEN I KISS YOU (I HEAR CHARLIE PARKER PLAYIN')'. With a career incredibly spanning almost thirty years, SPARKS are still showing no signs of pulling the plug, a collaborative revamp (with the late FAITH NO MORE) of the enduring 'THIS TOWN..' making the Top 40 in late '97. The new millennium saw the old SPARKS rekindle once more via a new set, 'BALLS' (2000) – it says it all really. 'LIL' BEETHOVEN' (2002), meanwhile, gathered up various textural strands and ideas from the group's lengthy career, tying them all up with the kind of quasi-classical arrangements suggested by the title. All in, it was their most realised and rewarding release in years, with enough sly humour, wry commentary, chameleon-like energy and musical invention to stake their claim among the cream of contemporary experimentalists. Followers of SPARKS had seen their fair share of hits and misses throughout their long musical tenure; 2006's 'HELLO YOUNG LOVERS' (their 20th studio set!) was definitely a hit. From the mischievous 'DICK AROUND' to the quirky 'METAPHOR', the effervescent RON and RUSS were back in vogue.

• **Songwriters:** RON MAEL wrote lyrics / music, and they also covered; I WANT TO HOLD YOUR HAND (Beatles) / FINGERTIPS (Stevie Wonder) / etc. • **Trivia:** In 1979, they produced NOEL'S album 'Is There More To Life Than Dancing'. They also worked for ADRIAN MUSSEY, BIJOU + TELEX.

Album rating: HALFNELSON (*4; as Halfnelson) / A WOOFER IN TWEETER'S CLOTHING (*5) / KIMONO MY HOUSE (*7) / PROPAGANDA (*6) / INDISCREET (*5) / BIG BEAT (*4) / THE BEST OF SPARKS compilation (*7) / INTRODUCING SPARKS (*3) / NUMBER ONE IN HEAVEN (*5) / TERMINAL JIVE (*4) / WHOMP THAT SUCKER (*4) / ANGST IN MY PANTS (*5) / SPARKS IN OUTER SPACE (*4) / INTERIOR DESIGN (*3) / MAEL INTUITION: THE BEST OF SPARKS 1974-1976 compilation (*7) / GRATUITOUS SAX AND SENSELESS VIOLINS (*4) / PLAGIARISM (*4) / BALLS (*5) / LIL' BEETHOVEN (*6) / HELLO YOUNG LOVERS (*8)

RUSSELL MAEL (b. 5 Oct'55, Santa Monica, Calif.) – vocals, bass / **RON MAEL** (b.12 Aug'50, Culver City, Calif.) – keyboards / **EARLE MANKEY** – guitar / with **RALPH OSWALD** – bass / **JOHN HENDERSON** – drums

Bearsville Bearsville

Feb 72. (lp; as HALFNELSON) *<2048>* **HALFNELSON** [-] [ ]
– Wonder girl / Fa la fa lee / Roger / High C / Fletcher Honorama / Simple ballet / Slowboat / Biology 2 / Saccharin and the war / Big bands / Mr.Nice guys. *(UK-iss.Oct74 as 'SPARKS'; K 45511) (UK cd-iss. Aug93 on 'Rhino'; 8122 71300-2)*

— **JIM MANKEY** – bass + **HARVEY FEINSTEIN** – drums repl. RALPH and JOHN

Nov 72. (7") *(K 15505)* **WONDER GIRL. / (NO MORE) MR.NICE GUYS** [ ] [ ]

Feb 73. (lp) *(K 45510)* **A WOOFER IN TWEETER'S CLOTHING** [ ] [ ]
– Girl from Germany / Beaver O'Lindy / Nothing is sacred / Here comes Bob / Moon over Kentucky / Do re mi / Argus desire / Underground / The louvre / Batteries not incuded / Whippings and apologies. *(cd-iss. Aug91 on 'Repertoire'; REP 4051)*

— The **MAELS** moved to London and recruited British musicians **ADRIAN FISHER** – guitar / **MARTIN GORDON** – bass, vocals / **DINKY DIAMOND** – drums / **PETER OXENDALE** – keyboards

Island Island

May 74. (7") *(WIP 6193)* *<IS 001>* **THIS TOWN AIN'T BIG ENOUGH FOR THE BOTH OF US. / BARBECUTIE** [2] Aug74 [ ]

May 74. (lp/c) *<(ILPS/ICT 9272)>* **KIMONO MY HOUSE** [4] [ ]
– This town ain't big enough for the both of us / Amateur hour / Falling in love with myself again / Here in Heaven / Thank God it's not Christmas / Hasta manana Monsieur / Talent is an asset / Complaints / In the family / Equator. *(cd-iss. Aug94; IMCD 198)*

Jul 74. (7") *(WIP 6203)* **AMATEUR HOUR. / LOST AND FOUND** [7] [–]

Oct 74. (7") *<IS 009>* **TALENT IS AN ASSET. / LOST AND FOUND** [–] [ ]

— **TREVOR WHITE** – guitar repl. PETER / **IAN HAMPTON** – bass (ex-JOOK) repl. MARTIN who joined JET

Oct 74. (7") *(WIP 6211)* **NEVER TURN YOUR BACK ON MOTHER EARTH. / ALABAMY NIGHT** [13] [–]

Nov 74. (lp/c) *<(ILPS/ICT 9312)>* **PROPAGANDA** [9] Feb75 [63]
– Propaganda / At home, at work, at play / Reinforcements / B.C. / Thanks but no thanks / Don't leave me alone with her / Never turn your back on Mother Earth / Something for the girl with everything / Achoo / Who don't like kids / Bon voyage. *(cd-iss. Aug94; IMCD 199)*

Jan 75. (7") *(WIP 6221)* **SOMETHING FOR THE GIRL WITH EVERYTHING. / MARRY ME** [17] [–]

Mar 75. (7") *<IS 023>* **SOMETHING FOR THE GIRL WITH EVERYTHING. / ACHOO** [–] [ ]

Jul 75. (7") *(WIP 6236)* **GET IN THE SWING. / PROFILE** [27] [–]

Sep 75. (7") *(WIP 6249)* **LOOKS, LOOKS, LOOKS. / PINEAPPLE** [26] [–]

Oct 75. (lp/c) *<(ILPS/ICT 9345)>* **INDISCREET** [18] [ ]
– Hospitality on parade / Happy hunting ground / Without using hands / Get in the swing / Under the table with her / How are you getting home / Pineapple / Tits / It ain't 1918 / The lady is lingering / In the future / Looks, looks, looks / Miss the start, miss the end. *(cd-iss. Aug94; IMCD 200)*

Nov 75. (7") *<IS 043>* **LOOKS, LOOKS, LOOKS. / THE WEDDING OF JACQUELINE KENNEDY TO RUSSELL MAEL** [–] [ ]

Mar 76. (7"; w-drawn) *(WIP 6282)* **I WANT TO HOLD YOUR HAND. / ENGLAND** [ ] [–]

— The **MAELS** used session people incl. **SAL MAIDA** – bass (ex-ROXY MUSIC)

Oct 76. (7") *(WIP 6337)* **BIG BOY. / FILL 'ER UP** [ ] [–]

Oct 76. (lp/c) *<(ILPS/ICT 9445)>* **BIG BEAT** [ ] [ ]
– Big boy / I want to be like everybody else / Nothing to do / I bought the Mississippi River / Fill 'er up / Everybody's stupid / Throw her away / Confusion / Screwed up / White women / I like girls. *(cd-iss. Aug94; IMCD 201)*

Dec 76. (7") *(WIP 6377)* **I LIKE GIRLS. / ENGLAND** [ ] [–]

C.B.S. Columbia

Sep 77. (7") *(CBS 5593)* **A BIG SURPRISE. / FOREVER YOUNG** [ ] [ ]

Oct 77. (lp/c) *(CBS/40 82284)* **INTRODUCING SPARKS** [ ] [ ]
– A big surprise / Occupation / Ladies / I'm not / Forever young / Goofing off / Girls on the brain / Over the summer / Those mysteries.

— augmented by **GIORGIO MORODER** – electronics, producer

Virgin Elektra

Mar 79. (7",7"green/12"red,12"blue) *(VS 244/+12)* **THE NUMBER ONE SONG IN HEAVEN. / ('A'-long version)** [14] [–]

Mar 79. (lp/c) *(V/TCV 2115)* **NO.1 IN HEAVEN** [73] [ ]
– Tryouts for the human race / Academy award performance / La dolce vita / Beat the clock / My other voice / The number one song in Heaven. *(re-iss. Aug82 on 'Fame' lp/c; FA/TCFA 3035)* *<(cd-iss. Mar00 on 'Repertoire'; REP 4768)>*

Jul 79. (7"/12",12"various colrd) *(VS 270/+12)* **BEAT THE CLOCK. / ('A'-long version)** [10] [–]

Oct 79. (7"/12",12"colrd pic-d) *(VS 289/+12)* **TRYOUTS FOR THE HUMAN RACE. / ('A'-long version)** [ ] [–]

Nov 79. (7") **TRYOUTS FOR THE HUMAN RACE. / NO. 1 SONG IN HEAVEN** [–] [ ]

Jan 80. (7") *(VS 319)* **WHEN I'M WITH YOU. / ('A'-long version)** [ ] [–]

Feb 80. (lp/c) *(V/TCV 2137)* **TERMINAL JIVE** [ ] [–]
– When I'm with you / Just because you love me / Rock and roll people in a disco world / When I'm with you (instrumental) / Young girls / Noisy boys / Stereo / The greatest show on Earth.

Apr 80. (7"/ext.12") *(VS 343/+12)* **YOUNG GIRLS. / JUST BECAUSE YOU LOVE ME** [ ] [–]

— added (ex-BATES MOTEL members) **BOB HAAG** – guitar / **LESLIE BOHEM** – bass / **DAVID KENDRICK** – drums

Why-Fi R.C.A.

Apr 81. (7"/12") *(WHY/+T 1)* **TIPS FOR TEENS. / DON'T SHOOT ME** [ ] [–]

May 81. (lp) *(WHO 1)* *<4091>* **WHOMP THAT SUCKER** [ ] [ ]
– Tips for teens / Funny face / Where's my girl / Upstairs / I married a Martian / The willys / Don't shoot me / Suzie safety / That's not Nastassia / Wacky women.

Sep 81. (7") *(WHY 4)* **FUNNY FACE. / THE WILLYS** [ ] [–]

— the **MAELS** + **MORODER** added **JAMES GOODWIN** – synths

Atlantic Atlantic

Jun 82. (7") *(K 11740)* *<4030>* **I PREDICT. / MOUSTACHE** [ ] May82 [60]

Jun 82. (lp/c) *(K/K4 50888)* *<19347>* **ANGST IN MY PANTS** [ ] [ ]
– Angst in my pants / I predict / Sextown U.S.A. / Sherlock Holmes / Nicotina / Mickey mouse / Moustache / Instant weight loss / Tarzan and Jane / The decline and fall of me / Eaten by the monster of love.

1982. (7") **EATEN BY THE MONSTER OF LOVE. / MICKEY MOUSE** [–] [ ]

Jun 83. (7"; SPARKS & JANE WIEDLIN) *<89866>* **COOL PLACES. / SPORTS** [ ] Apr83 [49]

Jun 83. (lp/c) *(K 780055-1/-4)* *80055>* **SPARKS IN OUTER SPACE** [ ] [88]
– Cool places / Popularity / Prayin' for a party / All you ever think about is sex / Please, baby please / Rockin' girls / I wish I looked a little better / Lucky me, lucky you / A fun bunch of guys from Outer Space / Dance godammit.

Nov 83 (7") *<86990>* **ALL YOU EVER THINK ABOUT IS SEX. / I WISH I LOOKED A LITTLE BETTER** [–] [ ]
(12") *<86990>* – ('A'club) / Dance goddamit (club version) / With all my might (extended club).

Jun 84. (lp/c) *<7-80160-1/-4>* **PULLING RABBITS OUT OF A HAT** [–] [ ]

— MORODER moved on to produce PHIL OAKEY

Jun 84 (7") *<7-89616>* **PRETENDING TO BE DRUNK. / KISS ME QUICK** [–] [ ]

London Curb-MC

Jun 85. (7"/12") *(LON/+X 69)* **CHANGE. / THIS TOWN AIN'T BIG ENOUGH FOR THE BOTH OF US (acoustic)** [ ] [ ]

— **JOHN THOMAS** – keyboards repl. GOODWIN

Consolidated M.C.A.

Nov 86. (7"/ext.12") *(TOON/+T 2)* **MUSIC THAT YOU CAN DANCE TO. / FINGERTIPS** [ ] [ ]

Nov 86. (lp/c) *(TOONLP 2)* *<MCA 5780>* **MUSIC THAT YOU CAN DANCE TO** [ ] Aug86 [ ]
– Music that you can to / Rosebud / Fingertips / Armies of the night / The scene / Shopping mall of love / Modesty plays (new version) / Let's ge funky. *<US version; 'Armies of the night'; repl. Change>*

Feb 87. (7") *(TOON 4)* **ROSEBUD. / ('A'-Cinematic version)** [ ] [–]
(12") *<TOONT 4>* – ('A'extended) / ('A'-FM mix).

— The **MAELS** retained **THOMAS** + **DAVID KENDRICK** introducing **SPENCER SIRCOMBE** – guitar / **HANS CHRISTIAN REUMSCHUSSEL** – bass / **PAMELA STONEBROOK** – vocals

Carrere Fine A

Jul 88. (7") *(CAR 427)* **SO IMPORTANT. / BIG BRASS RING** [ ] [ ]
(12"+=) *(CART 427)* – ('A'extremely important mix).
(cd-s++=) *CARCD 427)* – Madonna.

SPARKS

— In Aug 88, SPARKS collaborated on 'SINGING IN THE SHOWER'. / 'SMOG' single by French husband and wife duo LES RITA MITSOUKO on 'Virgin' label.

Carrere Rhino

Jul 88. (lp/c/cd) <R1/R4/R2 70841> **INTERIOR DESIGN** Aug88
– So important / Just got back from Heaven / Lots of reasons / You got a hold of my heart / Love o rama / The toughest girl in town / Let's make love / Stop me if you've heard this before / A walk down memory lane / Madonna. *(cd+=)* – Madonna (French – German – Spanish; versions) / The big brass ring / So important. *(UK-iss.cd Aug92 on 'Thunderbolt'; CDTB 141)*

Aug 89. (7") *(CAR 431)* **SO IMPORTANT. / JUST GOT BACK FROM HEAVEN** –
(12"+=) *(CART 431)* – ('A'-Extremely Important mix).

— In 1991, the MAELS were working on own feature film 'Mai The Psychic Girl',

Fineflex Fineflex

Nov 93. (12") *(FF 1004)* **NATIONAL CRIME AWARENESS WEEK. / (13 MINUTES OF HEAVEN) / ('A'-Perkins playtime mix)**
(cd-s) *(FFCD 1004)* – ('A'side) / (3 other mixes).

Logic-BMG BMG

Oct 94. (12"/c-s/cd-s) *(74321 3446-1/-4/-2)* **WHEN DO I GET TO SING MY WAY. / ('A'-Grid mix) / ('A'-Rapino Brrothers mix)** 38
(cd-s) *(74321 3447-2)* – ('A'side) / ('A'-Vince Clarke mixes).

Nov 94. (cd/c) <(74321 23267-2/-4)> **GRATUITOUS SAX & SENSELESS VIOLINS**
– Gratutous sex / When do I get to sing 'My Way' / (When I kiss you) I hear Charlie Parker playing / Frankly Scarlett I don't give a damn / I thought I told you to wait in the car / Hear no evil, see no evil, speak no evil / Now that I own the BBC / Tsui Hark (featuring TSUI HARK & BILL KONG) / The ghost of Liberace / Let's go surfing / Senseless violins.

Feb 95. (c-s) *(74321 26427-4)* **WHEN I KISS YOU (I HEAR CHARLIE PARKER PLAYIN') / ('A'-Beatmasters mix)** 36
(cd-s+=) *(74321 26428-2)* – This town ain't big enough for the both of us.
(12"+=/cd-s+=) *(74321 26427-1/-2)* – ('A'-Bernard Butler mix).

May 95. (c-s) *(74321 27400-4)* **WHEN DO I GET TO SING 'MY WAY' / ('A'-the Grid mix)** 32
(12"+=) *(74321 27400-1)* – National crime awareness week.
(cd-s++=) *(74321 27400-2)* – (2 extra 'A'-mixes).

Feb 96. (c-s) *(74321 34867-4)* **NOW THAT I OWN THE BBC / BEAT THE CLOCK (live)** 60
(cd-s) *(74321 34867-2)* – ('A') / ('A'-mixes) / She's an anchorman.

Roadrunner Roadrunner

Oct 97. (12"/cd-s) *(RR 2262-6/-9)* **THE NUMBER ONE SONG IN HEAVEN. / ('A'mix)** 70 –
(cd-s) *(RR 2262-3)* – ('A'remixes with Jimmy Somerville).

Oct 97. (cd) <*(RR 8791-2)*> **PLAGIARISM** (remixes)
– Pulling rabbits out of a hat / This town ain't big enough for the both of us / The number one song in Heaven / Funny face / When do I get to sing 'My Way' / Angst in my pants / Change / Popularity / Something for the girl with everything / This town ain't big enough for the both of us / Beat the clock / Big brass ring / Amateur hour / Propaganda / When I'm with you / Something for the girl with everything / Orchestral collage / The number one song in Heaven / Never turn your back on Mother Earth.

Dec 97. (cd-ep; as SPARKS VS FAITH NO MORE) *(RR 2251-3)* **THIS TOWN AIN'T BIG ENOUGH FOR THE BOTH OF US / ('A'version) / SOMETHING FOR THE GIRL WITH EVERYTHING / THE GREAT LEAP FORWARD** 40 –

Recognition Oglio

Aug 00. (cd) *(CDREC 5108 B/R/Y/G)* <89119> **BALLS**
– Balls / More than a sex machine / Scheherazade / Aeroflot / The calm before the storm / How to get your ass kicked / Bullet train / It's a knockoff / Irreplaceable / It's educational / The angels.

Artful Palm Pics

Nov 02. (cd) *(LILBCD 1)* <400009> **LIL' BEETHOVEN**
– The rhythm thief / How do I get to Carnegie Hall? / What are all these bands so angry about? / I married myself / Ride 'em cowboy / My baby's taking me home / Your call's very important to us. Please hold / Ugly guys with beautiful girls / Suburban homeboy.

Gut In The Red

Feb 06. (cd-s) *(CDGUT 77)* **PERFUME / CAN I INVADE YOUR COUNTRY (alt take) / PERFUME (Clor's Eu De Perfume mix)** –

Feb 06. (cd/lp) *(GUT CD/LP 53)* <ITR 131> **HELLO YOUNG LOVERS** Mar06
– Dick around / Perfume / The very next fight / (Baby, baby) Can I invade your country / Rock, rock, rock / Metaphor / Waterproof / Here Kitty / There's no such thing as aliens / As I sit to play the organ at the Notre Dame Cathedral.

– compilations, others, etc. –

Jul 74. (7") *Bearsville; (K 15516)* **GIRL FROM GERMANY. / BEAVER O'LINDY** –

Mar 76. (d-lp) *Bearsville; (K 85505)* **TWO ORIGINALS OF SPARKS** –
– (the albums from 1972 + 1973)

Mar 77. (lp/c) *Island; (ILPS/ICT 9493)* **THE BEST OF SPARKS** –
– This town ain't big enough for the both of us / Hasta manana monsieur / Tearing the place apart / At home, at work, at play / Never turn your back on Mother Earth / Get in the swing / Amateur hour / Looks, looks, looks / Thanks but no thanks / Gone with the wind / Something for the girl with everything / Thank God it's not Christmas. *(re-iss. Sep79; same) (cd-iss. Feb90; CID 9493)*

Sep 79. (7") *Island; (WIP 6532)* **THIS TOWN AIN'T BIG ENOUGH FOR THE BOTH OF US. / LOOKS, LOOKS, LOOKS** –

May 83. (12"ep) *Virgin; (VS 590-12)* **THE NUMBER ONE SONG IN HEAVEN / BEAT THE CLOCK. / WHEN I'M WITH YOU / YOUNG GIRLS** –

Nov 81. (lp) *Underdog;* **THE HISTORY OF THE SPARKS** – French –

May 90. (cd) *Island; (IMCD 88)* **MAEL INTUITION** –

Jun 91. (d-cd) *Rhino;* <R2 70731> **PROFILE: IT'S A MAEL MAEL MAEL WORLD**
(above was re-issue of BEST OF SPARKS)

May 93. (cd/c) *Spectrum; (550065-2/-4)* **IN THE SWING** –

Oct 93. (cd) *Sony;* **THE HEAVEN COLLECTION** –

Oct 93. (cd) *Sony; (473516-2)* **THE HELL COLLECTION** –
(above also issued both as d-cd)

Mar 94. (cd) *Loma; (LOMACD 23)* **SPARKS / A WOOFER IN TWEETER'S CLOTHING** –
(re-iss. Mar99 on 'Essential'; ESMCD 677)

Jul 94. (cd/c) *Success;* **JUST GOT BACK FROM HEAVEN** –

Oct 95. (cd) *Laserlight; (12571)* **SO IMPORTANT** –

Jul 02. (cd) *Repertoire;* <*(REP 4906)*> **THE BEST OF SPARKS**

Sep 02. (cd) *Music Club; (MCCD 503)* **THIS ALBUM'S BIG ENOUGH: THE BEST OF SPARKS** –

□ SPARTA (see under ⇒ AT THE DRIVE-IN)

the SPECIALS

Formed: Coventry, Midlands, England ... 1978 by keyboardist JERRY DAMMERS, guitarist LYNVAL GOULDING and bassist HORACE GENTLEMAN. After a brief spell with CLASH manager, Bernie Rhodes, DAMMERS formed the seminal '2-Tone' label in in 1979, releasing a debut single, 'GANGSTERS' (based on the Prince Buster track, 'Al Capone') under The SPECIAL A.K.A. moniker. By this point, the line-up had widened to include frontman TERRY HALL, vocalist/percussionist NEVILLE STAPLES, guitarist RODDY RADIATION and drummer JOHN BRADBURY. Issued as a split single with fellow ska revivalists, The SELECTER, the track almost made the UK Top 5 in the summer of '79, the label – with its unmistakable rude boy logo – quickly becoming the hippest namedrop in Britain as MADNESS debuted with 'The Prince' later that summer. Adding trombonist RICO RODRIGUEZ, the group released a follow-up, 'A MESSAGE TO YOU, RUDY', the mellow warmth of RICO's brass virtually making the track, a socially aware message, as ever, belying the song's easy going feel. An eponymous ELVIS COSTELLO-produced album was released the same month, the record blowing a breath of fresh air through the ashes of the punk scene and heralding one of the most exciting periods in

The SPECIALS

British music since the SEX PISTOLS' heyday. The stand-out track was 'TOO MUCH TOO YOUNG', a frenetic stomp railing against teenage pregnancies and showcasing perfectly the compelling mash-up of reggae, ska, punk and pop which became synonymous with the '2-Tone' label. The song formed part of a live EP released early the following year along with a number of covers including Harry J. All Stars' 'LIQUIDATOR' and Symarip's wonderfully titled 'SKINHEAD MOONSTOMP', the record giving the group their first No.1. Two further Top 10 hits followed in 1980 with 'RAT RACE' and 'STEREOTYPES', along with a second album, 'MORE SPECIALS'. The group's defining moment, however, came during the long hot summer of '81, with the eerily evocative 'GHOST TOWN', the track's plea of "why must the youth fight among themselves?" echoing against a backdrop of inner city rioting in both London and Liverpool. Though the track was easily the best No.1 single released that year, the band splintered soon after, GOULDING, STAPLES and HALL forming The FUN BOY THREE, while RADIATION formed The TEARJERKERS and RICO went solo. DAMMERS and BRADBURY re-adopted the SPECIAL A.K.A. moniker, recruiting RHODA DAKAR, NICKY SUMMERS, JOHN SHIPLEY and DICK CUTHELL. After a couple of minor hits with 'The BOILER' and 'RACIST FRIEND', DAMMERS & Co. were back in the Top 10 with 'FREE NELSON MANDELA' (1984), arguably one of the best pop singles of the 80's, an incredibly inspiring, heartfelt plea for the imprisoned ANC leader, almost gospel-like in its intensity and funky as hell to boot. The accompanying album, 'IN THE STUDIO', wasn't so successful and DAMMERS subsequently split the band, putting his creative talent into political activism. In 1985 he turned up on the 'STARVATION' reggae charity project, formed Artists Against Apartheid in 1986 and played a major role in oraganising the Nelson Mandela 70th Birthday concert at Wembley Stadium in 1988. While a re-formed SPECIALS appeared in 1995, the absence of both DAMMERS (who retired from live work after developing tinnitus) and HALL meant the project lacked credibility. Though they recorded a relatively small body of work, The SPECIALS remain one of the most influential and pivotal bands of the last 20 years.

• **Covered:** GUNS OF NAVARONE (Skatelites) / CONCRETE JUNGLE (Bob Marley) / LONG SHOT KICK DE BUCKET (Pioneers) / MONKEY MAN (Maytals) / MAGGIE'S FARM (Bob Dylan).

Album rating: THE SPECIALS (*8) / MORE SPECIALS (*6) / IN THE STUDIO (*6) / THE SPECIALS SINGLES compilation (*9) / TODAY'S SPECIALS (*3)

TERRY HALL (b.19 Mar'59) – vocals / **NEVILLE STAPLES** – vocals, percussion / **LYNVAL GOULDING** (b.24 Jul'51) – guitar, vocals / **JOHN BRADBURY** – drums / **JERRY DAMMERS** (b. GERALD DANKIN, 22 May'54, India) – keyboards / **RODDY RADIATION** (b. RODERICK BYERS) – guitar / **HORACE GENTLEMAN** (b. HORACE PANTER) – bass

2-Tone | not iss.

Jul 79. (7"; SPECIAL A.K.A.) *(TT 1 – TT2)* **GANGSTERS. / The Selecter: THE SELECTER** [6] [–]

— added (on some) guest **RICO RODRIQUEZ** – trombone

Chrysalis – 2-Tone | Chrysalis

Oct 79. (7") *(CHSTT 5)* **A MESSAGE TO YOU RUDY. / NITE CLUB** [10] [ ]

Oct 79. (lp/c) *(CDLTT/ZCDTL 5001) <1265>* **SPECIALS** [4] [84]
– A message to you Rudy / Do the dog / It's up to you / Nite club / Doesn't make it alright / Concrete jungle / Too hot / Monkey man / (Dawning of a) New era / Blank expression / Stupid marriage / Too much too young / Little bitch / You're wondering now. *(US-version with +=)* – Gangsters. *(re-iss. Nov84 on 'Fame' lp/c; FA41 3116-1/-4) (cd-iss. 1991; CCD 5001) (cd re-iss. Mar94; CD25CR 02)*

Jan 80. (7"ep) *(CHSTT 7)* **THE SPECIAL A.K.A. LIVE EP (live)** [1] [ ]
– Too much too young / Guns of Navarone / Long shot kick de bucket / The liquidator / Skinhead moonstomp.

May 80. (7") *(CHSTT 11)* **RAT RACE. / RUDE BOYS OUTA JAIL** [5] [ ]

Sep 80. (7") *(CHSTT 13)* **STEREOTYPES (part 1). / INTERNATIONAL JET SET** [6] [ ]

Sep 80. (lp/c) *(CHRTT/ZCHRT 5003) <1303>* **MORE SPECIALS** [5] [98]
– Enjoy yourself (it's later than you think) / Man at C & A / Hey little rich girl / Do nothing / Pearl's cafe / Sock it to 'em J.B. / Stereotypes / Stereotypes (part 2) / Holiday fortnight / I can't stand it / International jet set / Enjoy yourself (reprise). *(with free 7"; TT 999)* – Roddy Radiation & The Specials: BRAGGIN' AND TRYIN' NOT TO LIE. / Judge Roughneck: RUDE BUOYS OUTA JAIL *(cd-iss. 1991; CCD 5003)*

Jan 81. (7") *(CHSTT 16)* **DO NOTHING. / MAGGIE'S FARM** [4] [ ]

Jun 81. (7"m/12"m) *(CHSTT/+12 17)* **GHOST TOWN. / WHY / FRIDAY NIGHT, SATURDAY MORNING** [1] [ ]

— Only two originals (DAMMERS & BRADBURY) remained, as GOULDING, STAPLES & HALL formed The FUN BOY THREE. RADIATION formed TEARJERKERS. RICO went solo. All repl. by **RHODA DAKAR** – vocals + **NICKY SUMMERS** – bass (ex-BODYSNATCHERS) / **JOHN SHIPLEY** – guitar / **DICK CUTHELL** – saxophone

Jan 82. (7"; RHODA with The SPECIAL A.K.A.) *(CHSTT 18)* **THE BOILER. / THEME FROM THE BOILER** [35] [–]

the SPECIAL A.K.A.

— **HORACE PANTER** – bass returned to repl. SUMMERS who joined The BELLE STARS / **STAN CAMPBELL** (b. 2 Jan'62) – vocals / **NICK PARKER** – violin repl. CUTHELL (same label)

Dec 82. (7"/10") *(CHSTT/+10 23)* **WAR CRIMES (THE CRIME IS STILL THE SAME). / WAR CRIMES** [ ] [ ]

— **RODDY RADIATION** – guitar returned with newcomer **EGIDIO NEWTON** – vox

Aug 83. (7"/7"pic-d) *(CHSTT/CHSTPTT 25)* **RACIST FRIEND. / BRIGHT LIGHTS** [60] [ ]

— **GARY McMANUS** – bass repl. PANTER who joined GENERAL PUBLIC guested on album **DICK CUTHELL** – cornet / **ANDY ADERINTO** – saxophone

Mar 84. (7"/12") *(CHSTT/+12 26)* **NELSON MANDELA. / BREAK DOWN THE DOOR** [9] [ ]

Jun 84. (lp/c) *(<CHRTT/ZCHRT 5008>)* **IN THE STUDIO** [34] [ ]
– Bright lights / Lonely crowd / House bound / War crimes / What I like most about you is your girlfriend / Night on the tiles / Nelson Mandela / War crimes / Rascist friend / Alcohol / Break down the door. *(cd-iss. 1991; CCD 5008)*

Aug 84. (7"/12") *(CHSTT/+12 27)* **WHAT I LIKE MOST ABOUT YOU IS YOUR GIRLFRIEND. / CAN'T GET A BREAK** [51] [ ]

— Folded late '84, STAN CAMPBELL went solo and BRADBURY formed The JB's ALL STARS. DAMMERS turned up on a charity single by STARVATION early 1985.

— In Oct'93, SPECIALS were credited on DESMOND DEKKER single 'Jamaica Sky'.

— re-form with **GOLDING, STAPLES + RADIATION** + featuring **SHEENA STAPLE + KENDELL**

Kuff | not iss.

Jan 96. (c-s/12"/cd-s) *(KUFF C/T/D 3)* **HYPOCRITE / (mixes)** [66] [–]
above a Bob Marley cover and below a Toots & The Maytals number.

Mar 96. (c-s/cd-s) *(KUFF C/D 4)* **PRESSURE DROP / (mixes)** [ ] [–]

Apr 96. (cd/c) *(KUFF CD/MC 2)* **TODAY'S SPECIALS** [ ] [–]
– Take five / Pressure drop / Hypocrite / Goodbye girl / Little bit / The time has come / Somebody got murdered / 007 / Simmer down / Maga dog / Bad boys.

– compilations, etc. –

on 'Chrysalis' unless mentioned otherwise

Dec 82. (d-c) *(ZCDP 104)* **SPECIALS / MORE SPECIALS** [ ] [–]

Feb 87. (12"ep) *Strange Fruit; (SFPS 018)* **THE PEEL SESSIONS (23.5.79)** [ ] [–]
– Gangsters / Too much too young / Concrete jungle / Monkey man.

Feb 87. (7"0 *Old Gold; (OG 9683)* **TOO MUCH TOO YOUNG (live). / RAT RACE** [ ] [–]

Feb 87. (7") *Old Gold; (OG 9686)* **GHOST TOWN. / RAT RACE** [ ] [–]

Jun 88. (7"/12") *(CHS/+12 3276)* **FREE NELSON MANDELA – 70th Birthday re-make). / ('A'original)** [ ] [–]

Aug 91. (cd/c/lp) *(CHRTT/ZCHRT/CCD 5010)* **THE SPECIALS SINGLES** 10
– Gangsters / A message to you Rudy / Nite club / Too much too young – Guns of Navarone / Rat race / Rude boys outta jail / Stereotype / International jet set / Do nothing / Ghost town / Why? / Friday night, Saturday morning / Racist friend / Free Nelson Mandela / What I like most about you is your girlfriend.
Oct 91. (7"/cd-s) **GHOST TOWN (REVISITED. / ('A'dub version)** –
(12"+=) – Why / ('A'demo version).
Apr 92. (cd/c/lp) *(CCD/ZCHRITT/CHRITT 5011)* **LIVE AT THE MOONLIGHT CLUB (live)** –
Apr 92. (cd/c/lp) *Receiver;* **TOO MUCH TOO YOUNG** –
—— next shared with The SELECTER.
Dec 92. (cd) *Windsong; (WINCD 030)* **BBC RADIO 1 LIVE IN CONCERT (live)** –
Sep 93. (12"ep/c-ep/cd-ep; Various) *(CHS TT/TC/CD)* **THE TWO-TONE EP** 30 –
– Gangsters (SPECIAL AKA) / The Prince (MADNESS) / On my radio (SELECTER) / Tears of a clown (BEAT).
Sep 93. (cd) *Receiver; (RR CD/LP 178)* **DAWNING OF A NEW ERA** –
May 96. (cd/c) *EMI Gold; (CD/TC GOLD 1022)* **TOO MUCH TOO YOUNG** –

☐ SPECTRUM (see under ⇒ SPACEMEN 3)

☐ the SPIDERS (see under ⇒ COOPER, Alice)

SPIRIT

Formed: Los Angeles, California, USA ... 1964 as The RED ROOSTERS, by RANDY CALIFORNIA and his middle-aged, shaven-headed stepfather, ED CASSIDY. The band split in late '65 and later reformed as SPIRITS REBELLIOUS in the Spring of '67, CALIFORNIA returning from New York where he'd traded axe licks with, and been heavily influenced by, a young JIMI HENDRIX. Along with ex-ROOSTERS, MARK ANDES, JOHN LOCKE and JAY FERGUSON, the band became SPIRIT and signed to LOU ADLER's 'Ode' records. Their eponymous debut was released soon after, a mellow melange of jazz and trippy, bluesy rock that marked the band out from the bulk of the folk-rock pack in the L.A. of 1968. SPIRIT also looked different, CASSIDY resembling some ageing hippy Kojak. With the exuberant 'I GOT A LINE ON YOU' single from the follow-up album, 'THE FAMILY THAT PLAYS TOGETHER' (1969), the band scored an unexpected Top 30 hit, although the bulk of the record explored the grey area where jazz, rock and psychedelia met. 'CLEAR SPIRIT' (1969) displayed a harder-edged sound but the band didn't really come into their own until they were paired with NEIL YOUNG producer DAVID BRIGGS and recorded the psychedelic masterwork, 'TWELVE DREAMS OF DR. SARDONICUS' (1971). From the pastoral psychedelia of 'NATURE'S WAY' to the more direct approach of 'MORNING WILL COME' and 'MR. SKIN', this was CALIFORNIA at his most creative in terms of both songwriting and guitar playing. Although it was critically acclaimed upon release, it failed to sell in any great quantity and FERGUSON left shortly after to form JO JO GUNNE. With CALIFORNIA laid up after a road accident and ED CASSIDY the only original remaining member involved in the 'FEEDBACK' (1972) album, it came as no surprise when the record was a resounding failure, creatively, critically and commercially. This was, in effect, the end of the line for the band although a bogus SPIRIT sprang up to haunt them, fronted by the STAEHELY brothers who'd played on 'FEEDBACK'. Meanwhile, CALIFORNIA recorded a minor classic of a solo album, 'KAPT. KOPTER AND THE (FABULOUS) TWIRLYBIRDS'. A rough-hewn set of psychedelic garage-rock, the record featured some inspired covers including The BEATLES' 'RAIN ' and 'DAY TRIPPER'. The original SPIRIT line-up reformed in the mid-70's and recorded a series of albums for 'Mercury', which tried and failed to capture the original vibe. After yet another split and reformation, the band resurrected Kapt. Kopter and recorded a cod-concept album, 'JOURNEY TO POTATOLAND', in 1981 before breaking up again. In the way of these things, the band reformed with differing line-ups throughout the 80's, CALIFORNIA also recording two solo albums. The long 'SPIRIT'-ual journey finally came to an end when CALIFORNIA was tragically drowned off the coast of the Hawaiian island of Molokai, on the 3rd of January, 1997.

• **Songwriters:** CALIFORNIA and group, except YESTERDAY (Beatles) / HEY JOE (hit; Jimi Hendrix; c.William Roberts). CALIFORNIA covered solo:- MOTHER AND CHILD REUNION (Paul Simon) / ALL ALONG THE WATCHTOWER (Bob Dylan) / WILD THING (Troggs). • **Trivia:** MARK ANDES played on BORIS PICKETT & THE CRYPT KICKER 5's hit single, 'Monster Mash'. LED ZEPPELIN (Jimmy Page), must have listened to 1968 track, 'TAURUS', before writing 'Stairway To Heaven' (listen?).

Album rating: SPIRIT (*7) / THE FAMILY THAT PLAYS TOGETHER (*7) / CLEAR SPIRIT (*7) / TWELVE DREAMS OF DR SARDONICUS (*8) / FEEDBACK (*4) / THE BEST OF SPIRIT compilation (*8) / SPIRIT OF '76 (*5) / SON OF SPIRIT (*5) / FARTHER ALONG (*5) / FUTURE GAMES (A MAGICAL KAHUANA DREAM) (*4) / SPIRIT LIVE (*3) / JOURNEY TO POTATOLAND (*8) / THE THIRTEENTH DREAM remixes (*4) / Randy California: KAPTAIN KOPTER AND THE (FABULOUS) TWIRLY BIRDS (*5) / EURO AMERICAN (*4) / RESTLESS (*5) / SHATTERED DREAMS (*4) / Randy California's Spirit: RAPTURE IN THE CHAMBERS (*4) / TENT OF MIRACLES (*4) / LIVE AT LA PALOMA (*5) / CALIFORNIA BLUES (*4)

RANDY CALIFORNIA (b. RANDALL CRAIG WOLFE, 20 Feb'51) – guitar, vox / **JAY FERGUSON** (b. JOHN ARDEN FERGUSON, 10 May'47, Burbank, Calif.) – vocals / **MARK ANDES** (b.19 Feb'48, Philadelphia) – bass (ex-YELLOW BALLOON, w /JAY) / **ED CASSIDY** (b. 4 May'22, Chicago, Illinois) – drums (ex-NEW JAZZ TRIO) / **JOHN LOCKE** (b.25 Sep'43) – keyboards (ex-NEW WORLD JAZZ CO.)

C.B.S. Ode

Jun 68. (lp) *(63278) <44004>* **SPIRIT** Jan68 31
– Fresh garbage / Uncle Jack / Mechanical world / Taurus / Straight arrow / Topango windows / Gramophone man / Water woman / Great canyon fire in general / Elijah / Girl in your eyes. *(re-iss. Apr79 as 'THE FIRST OF SPIRIT' on 'CBS-Embassy'; 31693) (re-iss. Apr89 on 'Edsel' lp/c/cd; ED/+MC/CD 311) (re-iss. cd Aug95; 480965-2)*
Jun 68. (7") *(3523) <257-108>* **UNCLE JACK. / MECHANICAL WORLD**
Feb 69. (7") *(3880) <257-115>* **I GOT A LINE ON YOU. / SHE SMILED** Dec68 25
Apr 69. (lp) *(63523) <44014>* **THE FAMILY THAT PLAYS TOGETHER** Jan69 22
– I got a line on you / Poor Richard / Aren't you glad / It shall be / The drunkard / It's all the same / Dream within a dream / Jewish / So little to say / Silky Sam. *<US re-iss. Jul72; > (re-iss. Mar86 on 'Edsel' lp/c/cd+=; XED/CED/EDCD 162)* – She smiles / Darlin'. *(cd re-iss. Sep94 on 'Rewind';)*
Aug 69. (7") *(4511)* **DARK EYED WOMAN. / ICE** –
Sep 69. (7") *(4565) <257-122>* **DARK EYED WOMAN. / NEW DOPE AT TOWN**
Oct 69. (lp) *(63729) <44016>* **CLEAR SPIRIT** Jul69 55
– Dark eyed woman / Apple orchard / So little time to fly / Groundhog / Cold wind / Policeman's ball / Ice / Give a life, take a life / I'm truckin' / Clear / Caught / New dope in town. *(re-iss. Mar88 on 'Edsel' lp/cd; ED/+CD 268)*
Jan 70. (7") *(4773) <257-128>* **1984. / SWEET STELLA BABY** Dec69 69

C.B.S. Epic

Sep 70. (7") *(5149) <10648>* **ANIMAL ZOO. / RED LIGHT, ROLL ON** Aug70 97
Oct 70. (7") *<10685>* **MR. SKIN. / SOLDIER** –

Epic Epic

Feb 71. (lp) *(EPC 64191) <30267>* **TWELVE DREAMS OF DR. SARDONICUS** Dec70 63
– Nothing to hide / Nature's way / Animal zoo / Love has found a way / Why can't I be free / Mr. Skin / Space child / When I touch you / Sweet worm / Life has just begun / Morning will come / Soldier. *(re-iss. Mar81 lp/c; EPC/40 32006) (re-iss. Apr89 on 'Edsel' lp/c/cd; ED/+MC/CD 313) (re-iss. cd Aug93; 468030-2) (re-iss. cd Apr94; 476603-2)*

— (Dec70) **JOHN ARLISS** – bass repl. FERGUSON and ANDES who formed JO JO GUNNE (May71) **CASSIDY + LOCKE** recruited new men **AL STAEHELY** – bass (ex-PUMPKIN) / **J.CHRISTIAN** (b.CHRIS STAEHELY) – guitar repl. ARLISS + RANDY who went solo

May 72. (7") *(EPC 8083)* **CADILLAC COWBOYS. / DARKNESS** [ ] [–]

Jun 72. (lp) *(EPC 64507)* <31175> **FEEDBACK** [ ] Mar72 [63]
– Chelsea girl / Cadillac / Cowboys / Puesta del scam / Ripe and ready / Darkness / Earth shaker / Mellow morning / Trancas fog-out / The witch.

— (Aug72) Now a totally 'bogus' SPIRIT, fronted by The STAEHELY brothers. **STU PERRY** – drums repl. CASSIDY (see further below), and LOCKE who went solo. An album 'STA-HAY-LEE', included CASSIDY and LOCKE surfaced in US later? CHRIS was another to join JO JO GUNNE. Regarded as the 'real SPIRIT'

RANDY CALIFORNIA

(solo!) with **TIM McGOVERN** – drums, vocals / **CHARLIE BUNDY** – bass, b.vox / **HENRY MANCHOVITZ** (aka MITCH MITCHELL) – drums / **CLIT McTORIUS** (aka NOEL REDDING) – bass / guests **CASS STRANGE** (aka ED CASSIDY) – bass / **FUZZY KNIGHT** (aka ARRY WEISBER) – keyboards

Sep 72. (7") <10927> **WALKIN' THE DOG. / LIVE FOR THE DAY** [–] [ ]

Sep 72. (lp) *(EPC 65381)* <31755> **KAPTAIN KOPTER AND THE (FABULOUS) TWIRLY BIRDS** [ ] [ ]
– Downer / Devil / I don't want nobody / Day tripper / Mother and child reunion / Things yet to come / Rain / Rainbow. *(re-iss. Jun80 on 'C.B.S.' lp/c; CBS/40 31829) (re-iss. Nov85 on 'Edsel'+=; ED 164)* – Walkin' the dog / Live for the day. *(cd-iss. Aug93 & May97 on 'Edsel'; EDCD 164)*

— In 1973, CALIFORNIA attempted suicide by jumping off Chelsea Bridge.

SPIRIT

— after a few other line-up's in 1974, settled with **CASSIDY, CALIFORNIA + MARK ANDES** who repl. FUZZY KNIGHT. **JOHN LOCKE** re-joined for short spell, until he went into sessions. Also ANDES (who joined FIREFALL) were repl. by **BARRY KEANE** – bass

Mercury Mercury

Jun 75. (d-lp) *(6672 012)* <804> **SPIRIT OF '76** [ ] [ ]
– America the beautiful / The times they are a-changin' / Victim of society / Lady of the lakes / Tampa man / Mounalo / What do I have / Sunrise / Walking the dog / Joker on the run / When? / Like a rolling stone / Once again / Feeling in time / Happy / Jack Bond (part 1) / Mr. Road / Thank you Lord / Urantia / Guide me / Veruska / Hey Joe / Jack Bond (part 2) / The star spangled banner. *(re-iss. May88 on 'Edsel'; DED 251) (cd-iss. Mar93; EDCD 251)*

Aug 75. (7") <73697> **AMERICA THE BEAUTIFUL. / THE TIMES THEY ARE A-CHANGIN' / LADY OF THE LAKES** [–] [ ]

— added **MATT ANDES** – guitar (ex-JO JO GUNNE)

Oct 75. (lp) <SRM1 1053> **SON OF SPIRIT** [–] [ ]
– Holy man / Looking into darkness / Maybe you'll find / Don't go away / Family / Magic fairy princess / Circle / The other song / Yesterday / It's time now. *(UK-iss.May89 on 'Great Expectations' lp/cd; PIP LP/CD 2)*

Oct 75. (7") <73722> **HOLY MAN. / LOOKING INTO DARKNESS** [–] [ ]

Jul 76. (lp) <(SRM1 1094)> **FARTHER ALONG** [ ] [ ]
– Farther along / Atomic boogie / World eat world dog / Stoney night / Pineapple / Colossus / Mega star / Phoebe / Don't look up your door / Once with you / Diamond spirit / Nature's way.

Sep 76. (7") <73837> **FARTHER ALONG. / ATOMIC BOOGIE** [–] [ ]

— Now just a trio, when MARK re-joined FIREFALL and MATT & JOHN also left.

Apr 77. (lp) *(9100 036)* <SRM1 1133> **FUTURE GAMES (A MAGICAL KAHUANA DREAM)** [ ] [ ]
– CB talk / Stars are love / Kahouna dream / Brued my brain / Bionic unit / So happy now / All along the watchtower / Would you believe / Jack Bond speaks / Star Trek dreaming / Interlude XM / China doll / Hawaiian times / Gorn attack / Interlude 2001 / Detroit City / Freak out frog / The Romulan experiences / Monkey see, monkey do / Mt. Olympus / The journey of Nomad / Ending. *(re-iss. May89 on 'Great Expectations' lp/c/cd; PIP LP/MC/CD 3)*

May 77. (7") *(6167 519)* **ALL ALONG THE WATCHTOWER. / FURTHER ALONG** [ ] [–]

— **LARRY KNIGHT** – bass returned to repl. KEENE

Illegal Potato

Dec 78. (7") *(IL 007)* **NATURE'S WAY (live). / STONE FREE (live)** [ ] [–]

Jan 79. (lp) *(ILP 001)* <PR 2001> **SPIRIT LIVE** (live 11th Mar'78, Rainbow, London) [ ] [ ]
– Rock and roll planet / Nature's way / Animal zoo / 1984 / Looking down / It's all the same / I got a line on you / These are words / Hollywood dream.

— disbanded yet again late 1978; RANDY formed own band with **STEVE LAURA** – bass / **JACK WILLOUGHBY** – drums.

— they re-formed to re-record old unissued lost album below. **CALIFORNIA & CASSIDY** (alias KAPTAIN KOPTER & COMMANDER CASSIDY) enlisted **GEORGE VALUCK, JOHN LOCKE, MIKE BUNNELL + KARI NILE** – keys / **JEFF JARVIS, MIKE THORNBURGH + CHUCK SNYDER** – horns / **JOE GREEN** – strings

Beggars Banquet Rhino

Apr 81. (lp) *(BEGA 23)* <RNSP 303> **JOURNEY TO POTATOLAND** [40] [ ]
– We've got a lot to learn / Potatoland theme / Open up your heart / Morning light / Potatoland prelude / Potatoland intro / Turn to the right / Donut house / Fish fry road / Information / My friend. *(re-iss. 1988 += on 'Chord' lp/c/cd; CHORD/+TC/CD 010) (re-iss. cd Jan91 on 'Line'; LICD 90009-2)*

Apr 81. (7") *(BEGA 45)* **WE'VE GOT A LOT TO LEARN. / FISH FRY ROAD** [ ] [–]

Jun 81. (7") *(BEGA 56)* **TURN TO THE RIGHT. / POTATOLAND THEME** [ ] [–]

— Band toured 1981:- **CALIFORNIA, CASSIDY, VALUCK + STEVE LAURA** (aka LIBERTY)

RANDY CALIFORNIA

— solo including all present SPIRIT members and some past.

Apr 82. (lp) *(BEGA 36)* **EURO-AMERICAN** [ ] [–]
– Easy love / Fearless leader / Five in the morning / Skull and crossbones / Breakout / Hand gun (toy guns) / This is the end / Mon ami / Rude reaction / Calling you / Wild thing. *(free w/7") (RAN 1)* – SHATTERED DREAMS. / MAGIC WAND

Apr 82. (7") *(BEG 76)* **HAND GUNS (TOY GUNS). / THIS IS THE END** [ ] [–]

Aug 82. (7") *(BEG 82)* **ALL ALONG THE WATCHTOWER. / RADIO MAN** [ ] [–]
(12"+=) *(BEG 82T)* – Breakout / Killer weed.

SPIRIT

— originals re-formed re-recording material from that era.

Mercury not iss.

Jan 84. (7") *(MER 151)* **1984. / ELIJAH** [ ] [–]
(12"+=) *(MERX 151)* – I got a line on you.

Mar 84. (lp) *(MERL 35)* **THE THIRTEENTH DREAM** (remixes) [ ] [–]
– Black satin nights / Mr. Skin / Mechanical world / Pick it up / All over the world / 1984 / Uncle Jack / Natures way / Fresh garbage / I got a line on you. *(c+=)* – Elijah. *(cd-iss. Jul84; 818 514-2)*

Apr 84. (7"/6") *(MER 162/+6)* **FRESH GARBAGE. / MR. SKIN** [ ] [–]

RANDY CALIFORNIA

— solo with live + studio **MIKE SHEPHERD** – bass / **NEIL MURRAY + ADRIAN LEE + NEAL DOUGHTY** – keyboards / **CURLY SMITH** – drums live: **SCOTT MONAHAN** – keys / **LES WARNER** – drums

Vertigo not iss.

May 85. (7") *(VER 16)* **RUN TO YOUR LOVER. / SECOND CHILD** [ ] [–]
(12"+=) *(VERX 16)* – Shane.

Jun 85. (lp/c) *(VERL 19)* **RESTLESS** [ ] [–]
– Run to your lover / Restless nights / Second child / Jack Rabbit / Shane / One man's Heaven / Murphy's law / Camelot / Battle march of the overlords / Childhood's end.

Jun 85. (7") *(VER 21)* **JACK RABBIT. / SUPER CHILD** [ ] [–]

Line not iss.

1986. (lp) *(LCD 197)* **SHATTERED DREAMS** [–] German [–]
– Hey Joe (live) / Shattered dreams / All along the watchtower / Don't bother me / Downer / Second child / Man at war / Killer weed / Hand guns (toy guns) / Radio man / Run to your lover.

— In Apr'89, RANDY appeared on Various Artists live d-lp,c,cd,video 'NIGHT OF THE GUITAR', which was on next label.

RANDY CALIFORNIA'S SPIRIT

— gigged with various line-ups, until in 1989 settled with **RANDY, ED + SCOTT** plus **MIKE BUNNELL** – bass

I.R.S. I.R.S.

Jun 89. (7") *(EIRS 117)* **HARD LOVE. / THE PRISONER** [ ] [–]
(12"+=) *(EIRST 117)* – Hey Joe.

Aug 89. (lp/c/cd) *(EIRS A/C/CD 1014)* <13007> **RAPTURE IN THE CHAMBERS** [ ] [ ]
– Hard love / Love tonight / Thinking of / Rapture in the chambers / Mojo man / Contact / The prisoner / One track mind / Enchanted forest / Human sexuality / Shera, princess of power / End suite.

— now without BUNNELL, repl. by **MIKE NILE**

not iss. Dolphin

1991. (cd) <*DRG 22001*> **TENT OF MIRACLES** [–] [ ]
– Borderline / Zandu / Love from here / Ship of fools / Burning love / Tent of miracles / Logical answers / Old black magic / Neglected emotion / Imaginary mask / Stuttgart says good-bye / Deep in this land.

not iss. Phantom

1995. (cd) <*22003*> **LIVE AT LA PALOMA (live)** [–] [ ]
– Life has just begun / Sadana / Mr. Skin / Hey Joe / I got a line on you / Prelude – Nothin' to hide / Like a rolling stone / Going back to Jones / Living in this world / Magic wand / Give a life take a life / La Paloma jam / 1984 / Jamaica jam / Super la Paloma jam / Nature's way.

— SCOTT repl. by **MATT ANDES** – slide guitar / **STEVE LORIA** – bass / **RACHEL ANDES** (daughter of MATT) – vocals

not iss. C.R.E.W.

Dec 96. (cd) <*2204*> **CALIFORNIA BLUES** [–] [ ]
– California blues / Look over yonder / The river / Call on me / Crossroads / Song for Clyde / Pawn shop blues / Sigar mama / Red house / Gimme some lovin' / We believe / One world / Like a dog / oem for John Lennon / Shoes back on (live '67) / Tell everyone (live '67) / Soundtrack for a moth (live '67).

— On the 3rd of January '97, RANDY was drowned while surfing

– compilations, others, etc. –

— on 'Epic' unless mentioned otherwise

Aug 73. (d-lp) <*31457*> **SPIRIT. / CLEAR SPIRIT** [–] [ ]

Oct 73. (7") *(EPC 7082)* <*10701*> **MR. SKIN. / NATURE'S WAY** [ ] [92]

Oct 73. (lp) *(EPC 65585)* <*32271*> **THE BEST OF SPIRIT** [ ] Jul73 [ ]
(re-iss. Sep84; EPC 32516) <US re-iss. May89; >

Dec 91. (d-cd/d-c) *Columbia; (471268-2/-4)* **TIME CIRCLE (1968-72)** [ ] [ ]
– (first 4 albums)

Jan 92. (cd/c) *Castle; (CCS CD/MC 319)* **THE COLLECTION** [ ] [–]

Feb 92. (cd) *Outline; (OLCD 991133)* **CHRONICLES 1967-1982** [ ] [–]

Mar 94. (cd) *Line; (LICD 9000920)* **ADVENTURES OF KAPTAIN KOPTER & COMMANDER CASSIDY IN POTATOLAND** [ ] [–]

Aug 02. (d-cd; by RANDY CALIFORNIA & SPIRIT) *Acadia;* <*(ACAD 8017)*> **SEA DREAM** [ ] [ ]

SPIRITUALIZED

Formed: Rugby, England, 1990 ... initially as a side project for JASON 'SPACEMAN' PIERCE, who was soon to split from SONIC BOOM and SPACEMEN 3. He retained JON MATTOCK and WILLIE B. CARRUTHERS from the latter outfit and set about getting to grips with a new 90's psychedelia. Their first release was a version of The Troggs' 'ANYWAY THAT YOU WANT ME', which squeezed into the UK Top 75. The debut album, 'LAZER GUIDED MELODIES', was awash with VELVET-tones, recycled, and heavily distorted. A three year hiatus did not deter the British buying public, who also assured the follow-up, 'PURE PHASE', of a Top 30 placing in 1995. It was blessed with a more soulful vibe, while the majestic, lo-fi rhythm lifted it from an ambient crypt. In June '97, they returned to the fold (albeit a month after schedule) with their third album, 'LADIES AND GENTLEMEN WE ARE FLOATING IN SPACE B P'. The delay was due to ELVIS PRESLEY's team of whatnots objecting to the sample of 'Can't Help Falling In Love'. Nevertheless, the album, complete with bizarre prescription pill cd packaging, duly floated into the UK Top 5. Described by one reviewer as 'album of the decade', the record met with almost universal praise while its blissful melange of retro-psych, ambient noise and gospel was a heady tonic for the Dad-rock by numbers peddled by most 'indie' bands. PIERCE and his massive assembly/band gave listeners the chance to hear what it felt like to witness the grandiose SPIRITUALIZED in concert on a double vinyl LP entitled 'ROYAL ALBERT HALL OCTOBER 10 1997' (1998). After firing his band (yes, that's right) and going through a difficult and much publicised drug problem, PIERCE took to writing and recording his next magnum opus; 'LADIES AND GENTLEMEN . . .' part 2, if you will – the brilliant 'LET IT COME DOWN' (2001). Featuring huge gospel choirs and a plethora of musicians, the set boasted fragile songs from the SPIRITUALIZED camp as well as lush orchestrations and sometimes sentimental odes; example the album's finale 'LORD CAN YOU HEAR ME'. Ambitious not just in scope, but also in lyrical content and emotional content, PIERCE would follow this mini-masterpiece in 2003 with a surprisingly stripped-down 'AMAZING GRACE', an album in stark comparison to the lushly orchestrated 'LET IT COME DOWN'. Apparently influenced by the garage rock trashiness of BLACK REBEL MOTORCYCLE CLUB and the bare-bones guitar playing of JACK WHITE, PIERCE ditched the 50-strong choirs and orchestras in favour of aggressive rock, with only the weep-core lament 'THE BALLAD OF RICHIE LEE' and 'LORD LET IT RAIN ON ME' displaying the usual SPIRITUALIZED archetypes. Nevertheless, 'AMAZING GRACE' was undoubtably a JASON PIERCE album and shifted the rock riffage into overdrive on tracks 'CHEAPSTER' and 'SHE KISSED ME (IT FELT LIKE A HIT)'. Superb stuff from a man who never fails to impress.

• **Songwriters:** PIERCE, except more covers; BORN NEVER ASKED (Laurie Anderson) / WALKING WITH JESUS (Spacemen 3) / OH HAPPY DAY (Edwin Hawkins Singers). • **Trivia:** In the early 90's, they headlined at the ICA Rock Week sponsored by Irn Bru.

Album rating: LAZER GUIDED MELODIES (*8) / PURE PHASE (*8) / LADIES AND GENTLEMEN WE ARE FLOATING IN SPACE B P (*10) / ROYAL ALBERT HALL OCTOBER 10 1997 (*8) / LET IT COME DOWN (*8) / THE COMPLETE WORKS VOLUME ONE compilation (*7) / AMAZING GRACE (*7)

JASON PIERCE – guitar / **WILLIE B. CARRUTHERS** – bass / **JON MATTOCK** – drums / plus girlfriend **KATE RADLEY** – organ, keyboards, vocals / **MARK REFOY** – guitar, dulcimer

Dedicated R.C.A.

Jun 90. (7") *(ZB 43783)* **ANYWAY THAT YOU WANT ME. / STEP INTO THE BREEZE** [75] [–]
(12"+=/cd-s+=) *(ZT/ZD 43784)* – ('B'-part 2).
(12") *(ZT 43780)* – ('A'remix) / ('B'-parts 2-3) / ('A'demo).

Jun 91. (7") *(FRIGHT 053)* **FEEL SO SAD. / I WANT YOU** [ ] [–]
(above is a gig freebie given away by 'Fierce' re-iss. Apr97)

Aug 91. (7"clear) *(SPIRIT 002)* **RUN. / I WANT YOU** [59] [–]
(12"+=/cd-s+=) *(SPIRIT 002 T/CD)* – Luminescence (stay with me) / Effervescent (chimes).

Nov 91. (7") *(SPIRIT 003)* **WHY DON'T YOU SMILE NOW. / SWAY** [ ] [–]
(12"/cd-s) *(SPIRIT 003 T/CD)* – ('A'extended) / Sway.

Mar 92. (7"ep/cd-ep) *(SPIRIT 004/+CD)* **I WANT YOU. / YOU KNOW IT'S TRUE (instrumental) / 100 BARS (flashback)** [ ] [–]

Apr 92. (cd/c/2x12"lp) *(DED CD/MC/LP 004)* <*66035-2/-4*> **LAZER GUIDED MELODIES** [27] [ ]
– You know it's true / If I were with her now / I want you / Run / Smiles / Step into the breeze / Symphony space / Take your time / Shine a light / Angel sigh / Sway / 200 bars. *(free-7" at 'Chain With No Name' shops)* – ANY WAY THAT YOU WANT ME / WHY DON'T YOU SMILE NOW *(re-iss. Jul97; same)*

Jul 92. (7"red) *(SPIRIT 005)* **MEDICATION. / SMILES (Peel session)** [55] [–]
(12") *(SPIRIT 005T)* – ('A'side) / Feel so sad (Peel session) / Angel sigh.
(cd-s++=) *(SPIRIT 005CD)* – Space (instrumental).

Jun 93. (7"flexi) *(SPIRIT 006)* **SMILES (live). / 100 BARS (acappella)** [–] [–]

Jun 93. (mail-order cd) *(DEDLP 008)* **F***ED UP INSIDE** [–] [–]

Oct 93. (7"yellow) *(SPIRIT 007)* **GOOD TIMES / LAY BACK IN THE SUN** [49] [–]
(12"ep+=/cd-ep+=) *(SPIRIT 008 T/CD)* – Electric Mainline 1 + 2.

—— now without REFOY, who formed SLIPSTREAM. They issued two albums for 'Che' in 1995; 'SLIPSTREAM' & 'SIDE EFFECTS'.

SPIRITUALIZED ELECTRIC MAINLINE

—— **SPACEMAN (JASON)** + **KATE RADLEY** – keyboards, vox / **SEAN COOK** – bass, harmonica / plus **MARK REFOY** – guitar (guest only) / **JON MATTOCK** – percussion / **LEON HUNT** – banjo / **STEWART GORDON** – violin / **THE BALANESCU QUARTET** – strings / + others on wind instruments

Dedicated Arista

Jan 95. (cd-ep) *(SPIRIT 009CD)* **LET IT FLOW / DON'T GO / STAY WITH ME / DON'T GO / STAY WITH ME (THE INDIVIDUAL)** [30] [–]
(cd-ep) *(SPIRIT 009CD2)* – ('A'side) / Take good care of it / Things will never be the same / Clear rush.
(cd-ep) *(SPIRIT 009CD3)* – ('A'side) / Medication / Take your time / Smile.
(3xbox-cd-ep/10"ep) *(SPIRIT 009BOX/T)* – (all above).

Feb 95. (cd/c/d-lp) *(DED CD/MC/LP 017)* <26035> **PURE PHASE** [20] Mar95 [ ]
– Medication / The slide song / Electric phase / All of my tears / These blues / Let it flow / Take good care of it / Born never asked / Electric mainline / Lay back in the sun / Good times / Pure phase / Spread your wings / Feel like goin' home. *(re-iss. Jul97; same)*

Nov 95. (cd-ep) *(74321 31178-2)* **LAY BACK IN THE SUN / THE SLIDE SONG / SPREAD YOUR WINGS (instrumental) / LAY BACK IN THE SUN (instrumental)** [ ] [–]

Feb 96. (12") *(SPIRT 101T)* **PURE PHASE TONES FOR DJs** [ ] [–]

SPIRITUALIZED

—— **DAMON REECE** – percussion + guests, repl. MATTOCK, HUNT + GORDON

Jun 97. (cd/c/lp) *(DED CD/MC/LP 034)* <18974> **LADIES AND GENTLEMEN WE ARE FLOATING IN SPACE** [4] [ ]
– Ladies and gentlemen we are floating in space / Come together / I think I'm in love / All of my thoughts / Stay with me / Electricity / Home of the brave / The individual / Broken heart / No god only religion / Cool waves / Cop shoot cop . . . *(re-iss. Jan98 as 12xcd-s box; DEDCD 034A)*

Jul 97. (7") *(SPIRIT 012)* **ELECTRICITY. / COOL WAVES (instrumental)** [32] [–]
(cd-s+=) *(SPIRIT 012CD1)* – Take your time (live) / All of my tears (live).
(cd-s) *(SPIRIT 012CD2)* – ('A'album version) / Cop shoot cop (live) / Shine a light (live) / Electric mainline (live).

Feb 98. (7") *(SPIRIT 014)* **I THINK I'M IN LOVE. / ('A'version)** [27] [–]
(12"+=/cd-s+=) *(SPIRIT 014 T/CD)* – ('A'-Chemical Brothers vocal & instrumental mixes).

May 98. (7") *(SPIRIT 015)* <13508> **THE ABBEY ROAD EP** [39] [ ]
– Come together / Broken heart.
(cd-s+=) *(SPIRIT 015CD)* – Broken heart (instrumental).
(12"++=) *(SPIRIT 015T)* – ('A'-Richard Fearless remix) / ('A'-Two Lone Swordsmen remix).

—— **J(ASON) SPACEMAN, DAMON REECE, SEAN COOK, MICHAEL MOONEY, THIGHPAULSANDRA + RAYMOND (MOONSHAKE) DICKATY**

Oct 98. (d-cd/d-lp) *(74321 62285-2/-1)* <19032> **ROYAL ALBERT HALL OCTOBER 10 1997 (live)** [38] Nov98 [ ]
– Intro / Shine a light / Electric mainline / Electricity / Home of the brave / The individual / Medication / Walking with Jesus / Take your time / No God only religion / Broken heart / Come together / I think I'm in love / Cop shoot cop / Oh happy day.

—— COOK, REECE + MOONEY were sacked in June '99 and subsequently formed their own "real" band, LUPINE HOWL, who signed to 'Vinyl Hiss' for releases in early 2000

Spaceman – Arista Arista

Sep 01. (12") *(OPM 003)* **STOP YOUR CRYING. / ANYTHING MORE (instrumental) / ROCK'N'ROLL** [18] [–]
(cd-s+=) *(OPM 002)* – ('A'-video).

Sep 01. (cd/d-lp) *(OPM 001 CD/LP)* <14722> **LET IT COME DOWN** [3] [ ]
– On fire / Do it all over again / Don't just do something / Out of sight / The twelve steps / The straight and the narrow / I didn't mean to hurt you / Stop your crying / Anything more / Won't get to Heaven (the state I'm in) / Lord can you hear me.

Nov 01. (12") *(OPM 006)* **OUT OF SIGHT. / DIDN'T MEAN TO HURT YOU (instrumental) / GOING DOWN SLOW** [65] [–]
(cd-s+=) *(OPM 005)* – ('A'-video)>

Feb 02. (7") *(OPM 008)* **DO IT ALL OVER AGAIN. / ROCK AND ROLL (instrumental)** [31] [–]
(cd-s) *(OPM 004)* – ('A'side) / On fire (evening session version) / Amazing grace (peace on earth).
(cd-s) *(OPM 007)* – ('A'side) / Come together (Steve Lamacq session) / Going down slowly / ('A'-video).

Sanctuary Sanctuary

Aug 03. (12"ep) *(SANEV 220)* **AMAZING GRACE EP 1** [ ] [–]
– Cheapster / Hold on / Never goin' back / Power and the glory.

Aug 03. (12"ep) *(SANEV 221)* **AMAZING GRACE EP 2** [ ] [–]
– Lord let it rain on me / Oh baby / Rated X / Lay it down slow.

Sep 03. (12"ep) *(SANEV 222)* **AMAZING GRACE EP 2** [ ] [–]
– She kissed me (it felt like a hit) / This little life of mine / The ballad of Richie Lee.

Sep 03. (cd-s) *(SANXD 222)* **SHE KISSED ME (IT FELT LIKE A HIT) / (video)** [38] [–]

Sep 03. (cd/lp) *(SAN CD/LP 214)* <84634> **AMAZING GRACE** [25] [ ]
– This little life of mine / She kissed me (it felt like a hit) / Hold on / Oh baby / Never goin' back / The power and the glory / Lord let it rain on me / The ballad of Richie Lee / Cheapster / Rated X / Lay it down low.

– compilations, others, etc. –

Mar 03. (d-cd) *Spaceman; (OPM 009CD) / Arista; <50325>* **THE COMPLETE WORKS VOLUME ONE** [ ] [ ]
– Anyway that you want me / Step into the breeze (part 1) / Feel so sad (7" single version) / Feel so sad (rhapsodies) / Feel so sad (glides and chimes) / Run (single version) / Luminescence (stay with me) / I want you / Effervescent (chimes) / Why don't you smile now / Sway / 100 bars (acappella) / I want you (instrumental) / Medication / Smiles / Angel sigh / Feel so sad (Medication EP version) / Good dope – Good fun / Lay back in the sun / Good times / Electric mainline (part 1) / Electric mainline (part 2) / 100 bars (flashback).

Feb 04. (d-cd) *Spaceman; / Arista; <59131>* **THE COMPLETE WORKS VOLUME TWO** [ ] [ ]

☐ SPLIT ENZ (see under ⇒ CROWDED HOUSE)

Bruce SPRINGSTEEN

Born: 23 Sep'49, Freehold, New Jersey, USA. While still attending college, SPRINGSTEEN formed the short-lived STEEL MILL, three members ('LITTLE STEVEN' VAN ZANDT, DANNY FEDERICI and VINI LOPEZ) subsequently becoming part of his 10-piece back-up group. In May '72, the singer signed to 'Columbia' with the help of legendary A&R man, John Hammond, who had previously signed BOB DYLAN to the same label a decade earlier. The connection didn't stop there, SPRINGSTEEN duly heralded as the latest successor to ZIMMERMAN's singer/songwriter mantle upon the release of his debut album, 'GREETINGS FROM ASBURY PARK, N.J.' Released in early '73, it originally sold poorly, as did the follow-up, 'THE WILD, THE INNOCENT & THE E-STREET SHUFFLE'. Following the latter set's completion, SPRINGSTEEN concentrated on heavy touring with the newly formed E-STREET BAND, the subsequent exposure resurrecting, to some degree, the commercial fortunes of his first two releases, both hitting the US Top 60 in mid-75. It was with much anticipation, then, that a

BRUCE SPRINGSTEEN

third album, 'BORN TO RUN', eventually hit the shelves later that year. Co-producer and future manager, Jon Landau, had steered the project towards a suitably grandise sound, the starry-eyed romanticism of SPRINGSTEEN's lyrical themes complementing the lavish arrangements. The title track best summed up the mood of the album, teenage rebels following their dreams on the open road; not exactly an original take on rock'n'roll but one which the singer would refine and subvert as his career unfolded. Reaching Top 3 in the USA, the album gave SPRINGSTEEN his first real breakthrough, in the States at least, 'The Boss' (as the Americans soon took to calling him) undertaking a full scale US tour. It would be almost three years before another album as SPRINGSTEEN became embroiled in a legal battle with his former manager, Mike Appel. The latter had attempted to prevent his client working with Landau, an out of court settlement eventually bringing matters to a close and allowing the beleaguered singer to begin recording 'DARKNESS ON THE EDGE OF TOWN' (1978). As the title suggested, the album was an altogether more bleak affair, no doubt inspired by the legal traumas of the preceding few years. Yet it remains one of SPRINGSTEEN's most enduring efforts, establishing him as a sympathetic and cuttingly accurate observer of the gritty realities, hopes and dreams facing ordinary Americans. The spartan echoes of tracks like 'ADAM RAISED A CAIN' would resonate through SPRINGSTEEN's more introspective work throughout his subsequent career. Though the record again made the US Top 5, consolidating SPRINGSTEEN's position as a firm critics' favourite, he only really made a substantial breakthrough with 'THE RIVER' (1980), his first US No.1. A double set, the record could easily have been trimmed down to a single album, brimming as it was with workaday rockers centering on cars, girls, cars and, erm ... more cars (see 'CADILLAC RANCH', 'RAMROD', 'CRUSH ON YOU', 'DRIVE ALL NIGHT' etc). One of the record's few redeeming factor's was the title track, an aching ode to doomed love which indicated the direction of SPRINGSTEEN's next effort, 'NEBRASKA' (1982). Arguably one of the most darkly powerful modern folk albums of the past twenty years, the record's stark, sublime beauty stood in glaring contrast to the banal excess of its predecessor and could've conceivably been recorded by a different man. Accompanied by a lone acoustic guitar and occasional wailing harmonica, SPRINGSTEEN explored the boundaries between good and evil, right and wrong, through a series of deeply affecting character studies, his whisky throated voice wracked with doubt, frustration and pain. Although the record was a transatlantic Top 3 hit, it somewhat predictably failed to spawn any successful singles. Nevertheless, any readers basing their opinion of 'The Boss' solely on 'BORN IN THE U.S.A.' (1984) and suchlike are urged to give 'NEBRASKA' a spin. 'BORN ...' saw SPRINGSTEEN's career finally go stratospheric, a record that came to define 80's America as much as it came to define the singer's stadium sound and blue collar image. Though SPRINGSTEEN had simplified his dark musings on the American dream for a wider audience, the message still wasn't clear enough for some people, Ronald Reagan included. Following the latter's attempt to hijack the supposed patriotic sentiments of the record, SPRINGSTEEN made his political allegiances public by supporting environmental and civil right groups. He'd also previously played a number of benefits for Vietnam war veterans, a subject he addressed in the album's raging title track. Elsewhere, songs like 'DOWNBOUND TRAIN' and 'I'M ON FIRE' centred on familiar SPRINGSTEEN themes of human suffering while 'DANCING IN THE DARK' gave him his biggest US hit to date. Despite the lyrical content, however, the bulk of the album was upbeat, infectious and highly commercial, a multi-million seller which precipitated the most extensive touring of SPRINGSTEEN's career. The massive selling live boxed set, 'LIVE 1977-1985' neatly chalked out the end of an era, a markedly different SPRINGSTEEN surfacing in 1987 with 'TUNNEL OF LOVE'. With his marriage under strain, the album was a more personal affair exploring the vagaries of romance. While the likes of 'TOUGHER THAN THE REST' were touchingly direct, overall the album lacked the fire of old. Despite finally parting ways with the E STREET BAND, the concurrently released 'HUMAN TOUCH' and 'LUCKY TOWN' (1992) sets failed to satisfy critics or fans with their formulaic material. More endearing was the poignant 'STREETS OF PHILADELPHIA', which SPRINGSTEEN contributed to the film, 'Philadelphia', a subsequent Grammy Award winner and the singer's biggest hit single for over a decade. The following year saw the low key release of 'THE GHOST OF TOM JOAD' (1995). This was SPRINGSTEEN back doing what he does best, strumming desolate tales of America's lost underclass. With a title taken from Steinbeck's 'Grapes Of Wrath', WOODY GUTHRIE was mentioned in more than one review. It's a comparison not too far off the mark, SPRINGSTEEN never giving up the ghost on documenting the trials of the downtrodden. Many rank the stripped down, one-man shows that accompanied the album's release as among the best of SPRINGSTEEN's career, the singer achieving a newfound authority and maturity. 'LIVE IN NEW YORK CITY' (2001) was a wholly different proposition, a document of SPRINGSTEEN's much lauded millennial reunion with The E STREET BAND. Rather than relying on the big hits, the album featured a clutch of more obscure classics from the late 70's and early 80's such as 'BADLANDS' and 'MANSION ON THE HILL', songs that sound as vital today as they did back then. Of all the American artists who undertook some serious soul-searching after 9/11 – and there were many – it was perhaps SPRINGSTEEN who emerged with the most cohesive, honest and perceptive set of songs. Unlikely as this may have seemed to some, the man's ability to tap into the substrata of American culture and consciousness has been ably demonstrated in the past. Nor did the fact that 'THE RISING' (2002) marked a reunion with The E STREET BAND, detract from the depth and simplicity of the writing. While the band have rarely sounded so powerfully unfettered, it was the hushed grace and spiritual intensity of tracks such as 'MY CITY OF RUINS' which lent the album its root sense of painful catharsis. SPRINGSTEEN subsequently retreated to make his once-a-decade folk record: that 'DEVILS & DUST' (2005) traced its lineage back through the closely observed desperadoes and down and outs of '..TOM JOAD' and 'NEBRASKA' hardly needs reiterating, but the most revelatory aspect of the album was BRUCE's falsetto, a thing of fleet-sinewed wonder; why has he been hiding it under a stubble-chinned bushel all these years? In the wider horn stakes, 'MARIA'S BED' and 'ALL I'M THINKIN' ABOUT' weren't exactly MARVIN GAYE/TIM BUCKLEY, but they were arguably the most pleasurable moments on an album which topped the charts in both the UK and US. With its fiddle arrangement and ensemble feel, 'LONG TIME COMIN'' was perhaps a pointer to the man's next project, a full-tilt immersion in the work of folk legend PETE SEEGER. 'WE SHALL OVERCOME: THE SEEGER SESSIONS' (2006) rang true not just because of the relevance of the spirit of SEEGER's songs to contemporary ills, but because it was recorded straight over two days with a raggle-taggle band (so raggle-taggle they could hardly all fit on the same stage when they hit UK shores recently) and no rehearsals. While tempering SEEGER's earnestness with an irreverent spirit, the album also put the work of one of America's most famous folk singers back into the Top 3 in both his homeland and in Britain.

• **Covered:** JERSEY GIRL (Tom Waits) / WAR (Edwin Starr) / SANTA CLAUS IS COMING TO TOWN (festive trad.) / VIVA LAS VEGAS (Elvis Presley) etc. • **Trivia:** SPRINGSTEEN produced two albums by GARY U.S. BONDS 'Dedication' (1981) and 'On The Line' (1982), records that featured The BOSS's songs. He also provided songs for; SPIRIT IN THE NIGHT + BLINDED BY THE LIGHT for (Manfred Mann's Earth Band) / SANDY

(Hollies) / FIRE (Robert Gordon) + (Pointer Sisters) / BECAUSE THE NIGHT (Patti Smith) / FOR YOU (Greg Kihn) / FROM SMALL THINGS (Dave Edmunds) / DANCING IN THE DARK (Big Daddy) / THERE'S A RIOT GOIN' ON (Sly & The Family Stone) / etc.

Album rating: GREETINGS FROM ASBURY PARK, N.J. (*6) / THE WILD, THE INNOCENT & THE E-STREET SHUFFLE (*6) / BORN TO RUN (*9) / DARKNESS ON THE EDGE OF TOWN (*8) / THE RIVER (*7) / NEBRASKA (*9) / BORN IN THE U.S.A. (*8) / LIVE 1977-1985 (*6) / TUNNEL OF LOVE (*6) / HUMAN TOUCH (*5) / LUCKY TOWN (*5) / IN CONCERT – MTV PLUGGED (*5) / GREATEST HITS compilation (*8) / THE GHOST OF TOM JOAD (*7) / TRACKS early material (*5) / LIVE IN NEW YORK CITY (*5) / THE RISING (*7) / THE ESSENTIAL . . . compilation (*9) / DEVILS & DUST (*6) / WE SHALL OVERCOME: THE SEEGER SESSIONS (*7)

BRUCE SPRINGSTEEN – vocals, guitar / **DAVID SANCIOUS + DANNY FEDERICI** – keyboards / **GARRY TALLENT** – bass / **VINI LOPEZ** – drums / **CLARENCE CLEMENS** – saxophone / **STEVE VAN ZANDT** – lead guitar (left before recording of debut album)

C.B.S. Columbia

Feb 73. (7") *<45805>* **BLINDED BY THE LIGHT. / ANGEL** [–] [ ]

Mar 73. (lp/c) *(CBS/40 65480) <31903>* **GREETINGS FROM ASBURY PARK, N.J.** [ ] Jan73 [ ]
– Blinded by the light / Growin' up / Mary Queen of Arkansas / Does this bus stop at 82nd Street / Lost in the flood / The angel / For you / / Spirit in the night / It's hard to be a saint in the city. *<hit No.60 in the US; Jul75> (re-iss. Nov82 lp/c; CBS/40 32210)* – hit No.41 in Jun85) *(cd-iss. 1986; CD 65480)*

May 73. (7") *<45864>* **SPIRIT IN THE NIGHT. / FOR YOU** [–] [ ]

— For live appearances The BRUCE SPRINGSTEEN BAND now The E-STREET SHUFFLE. **ERNEST CARTER** – drums repl. LOPEZ

Feb 74. (lp/c) *(CBS/40 65780) <32432>* **THE WILD, THE INNOCENT & THE E-STREET SHUFFLE** [ ] Nov73 [ ]
– The E-Street shuffle / 4th of July, Asbury Park (Sandy) / Kitty's back / Wild Billy's circus story / Incident on 57th Street / Rosalita (come out tonight) / New York City serenade. *<hit No.59 in the US; Jul75> (re-iss. Nov83 lp/c; CBS/40 32363)* – (hit No.33 in Jun85) *(cd-iss. Apr89; CD 32363)*

— **ROY BITTAN** – piano / **MAX WEINBERG** – drums / and the returning **VAN ZANDT** repl. SANCIOUS and CARTER

Oct 75. (lp/c) *(CBS/40 69170) <33795>* **BORN TO RUN** [17] Sep75 [3]
– Thunder road / Tenth Avenue freeze-out / Night / Backstreets / Born to run / She's the one / Meeting across the river / Jungleland. *(re-iss. Jan87 boxed; BRUCE B2)* (w / free-7") **BECAUSE THE NIGHT. / SPIRIT IN THE NIGHT** *(cd-iss. 1983; CD 69170) (cd re-iss. 1988; CD 80959) (re-iss. cd.Jun93) (lp re-iss. Feb99 on 'Classic'; PC 33795)*

Oct 75. (7") *(A 3661) <10209>* **BORN TO RUN. / MEETING ACROSS THE RIVER** [ ] Sep75 [23]

Feb 76. (7") *(A 3940) <10274>* **TENTH AVENUE FREEZE-OUT. / SHE'S THE ONE** [ ] Jan76 [83]

Jun 78. (7") *(A 6424) <10763>* **PROVE IT ALL NIGHT. / FACTORY** [ ] [33]

Jun 78. (lp/c)<US-pic-d> *(CBS/40 86061) <35318>* **DARKNESS ON THE EDGE OF TOWN** [16] [5]
– Badlands / Adam raised a Cain / Something in the night / Candy's room / Racing in the street / Promised land / Factory / Streets of fire / Prove it all night / Darkness on the edge of town. *(cd-iss. Jul84; CD 66061) (re-iss. Nov84 lp/c; CBS/40 32542)*

Jul 78. (7") *<10801>* **BADLANDS. / STREETS OF FIRE** [–] [42]

Jul 78. (7") *(A 6532)* **BADLANDS. / SOMETHING IN THE NIGHT** [ ] [–]

Oct 78. (7") *(A 6720)* **PROMISED LAND. / STREETS OF FIRE** [ ] [ ]

Oct 80. (d-lp/d-c) *(CBS/40 88510) <36854>* **THE RIVER** [2] [1]
– The ties that bind / Sherry darling / Jackson cage / Two hearts / Independence day / Hungry heart / Out in the street / Crush on you / You can look (but you better not touch) / I wanna marry you / The river / Point blank / Cadillac ranch / I'm a rocker / Fade away / Stolen car / Ramrod / The price you pay / Drive all night / Wreck on the highway. *(d-cd-iss. 1985; CD 88510) (re-iss. d-cd+d-c Oct94 on 'Columbia')*

Nov 80. (7") *(A 9309) <11391>* **HUNGRY HEART. / HELD UP WITHOUT A GUN** [44] [5]

Jan 81. (7") *<11431>* **FADE AWAY. / BE TRUE** [–] [20]

Feb 81. (7") *(A 9568)* **SHERRY DARLING. / BE TRUE** [ ] [–]

May 81. (7") *(A 1179)* **THE RIVER. / INDEPENDENCE DAY** [35] [–]
(12") *(A13 1179)* – ('A'side) / Born to run / Rosalita.

Aug 81. (7") **CADILLAC RANCH. / WRECK ON THE HIGHWAY** [–] [ ]

Sep 82. (lp/c) *(CBS/40 25100) <38358>* **NEBRASKA** [3] [3]
– Nebraska / Atlantic City / Mansion on the hill / Johnny 99 / Highway patrolman / State trooper / Used cars / Open all night / My father's house / Reason to believe. *(cd-iss. 1983; CD 25100) (re-iss. Feb89 lp/c/cd; 463360-1/-4/-2)*

Oct 82. (7") *(A 2794)* **ATLANTIC CITY. / MANSION ON THE HILL** [ ] [ ]

Nov 82. (7") **OPEN ALL NIGHT. / THE BIG PAYBACK** [ ] [ ]

— **NILS LOFGREN** – lead guitar (Solo artist) repl. VAN ZANDT to solo as LITTLE STEVEN / added **PATTI SCIALFA** – backing vox (ex-SOUTHSIDE JOHNNY)

May 84. (7"/7"sha-pic-d/12") *(A/TA/WA 4436) <04463>* **DANCING IN THE DARK. / PINK CADILLAC** [28] [2]
(re-entered UK charts in Jan85, hit No.4)

Jun 84. (lp/c/cd/pic-lp) *(CBS/40/CD/11 86304) <38653>* **BORN IN THE U.S.A.** [1] [1]
– Born in the U.S.A. / Cover me / Darlington County / Working on the highway / Downbound train / I'm on fire / No surrender / Bobby Jean / I'm goin' down / Glory days / Dancing in the dark / My hometown.

Sep 84. (7") *(A 4662) <04561>* **COVER ME. / JERSEY GIRL (live)** [38] Aug84 [7]
(d7"+=) *(DA 4662)* – Dancing in the dark / Pink Cadillac.
(12"+=) *(TA 4662)* – Dancing in the dark (dub version).

Nov 84. (7") *<04680>* **BORN IN THE U.S.A. / SHUT OUT THE LIGHTS** [–] [9]

Jan 85. (7") *<04772>* **I'M ON FIRE. / JOHNNY BYE BYE** [–] [6]

Mar 85. (7"/7"sha-pic-d) *(A/WA 4662)* **COVER ME. / JERSEY GIRL (live)** [16] [–]
(12"+=) *(QTA 4662)* – Dancing in the dark (dub) / Shut out the light / Cover me (dub).

May 85. (7"/7"sha-pic-d) *(A/WA 6342)* **I'M ON FIRE. / BORN IN THE U.S.A. (Freedom mix)** [5] [–]
(12"+=) *(TA 6342)* – Rosalita / Bye Bye Johnny.

Jul 85. (7") *(A 6375) <04924>* **GLORY DAYS. / STAND ON IT** [17] May85 [5]
(12"+=) *(QTA 6375)* – Sherry darling / Racing in the street.

Aug 85. (7") *<05603>* **I'M GOIN' DOWN. / JANEY, DON'T YOU LOSE HEART** [–] [9]

Dec 85. (7") *(A 6773) <05728>* **MY HOMETOWN. / SANTA CLAUS IS COMIN' TO TOWN** [9] [6]

Nov 86. (7") *(650 193-7) <06432>* **WAR (live). / MERRY XMAS BABY (live)** [18] [8]
(12"+=) *(650 193-6)* – Incident on 57th Street (live).
(d7"+=) *(650 193-0)* – My home town (live) / Santa Claus is coming to town (live).

Dec 86. (5xlp-box/3xc-box/3xcd-box) *(450227-1/-4/-2) <40588>* **LIVE 1977-1985 (live)** [4] Nov86 [1]
– Thunder road / Adam raised a Cain / Fire / Spirit in the night / 4th of July – Asbury Park (Sandy) / Paradise by the 'C' / Growin' up / It's hard to be a saint in the city / Backstreets / Rosalita (come out tonight) / Raise your hand / Hungry heart / Two hearts / Cadillac ranch / You can look (but you better not touch) / War / Candy's room / Badlands / Because the night / Independence day / Johnny 99 / Darkness on the edge of town / Racing in the street / Nebraska / This land is your land / Working on the highway / Reason to believe / Born in the U.S.A. / Seeds / The river / Born to run / Darlington County / Jersey girl / Bobby Jean / Cover me / My hometown / No surrender / I'm on fire / The promised land.

Jan 87. (7") *<06657>* **FIRE (live). / INCIDENT ON 57TH STREET** [–] [46]

Jan 87. (7") *(650 381-7)* **FIRE (live). / FOR YOU (live)** [54] [–]
(12"+=) *(650 381-6)* – Born to run (live) / No surrender (live) / Tenth avenue freeze-out (live).

May 87. (7"/7"s) *(BRUCE/+BP 2)* **BORN TO RUN (live). / JOHNNY 99 (live)** [16] [–]
(d7"+=) *(BRUCEB 2)* – Spirit in the night / Because the night (live).
(cd-s+=) *(BRUCEC 2)* – Spirit in the night (live) / Seeds (live).

Sep 87. (7"/7"g-f/12") *(651 141-7/-0/-6) <07595>* **BRILLIANT DISGUISE. / LUCKY MAN** [20] [5]

Oct 87. (lp/c/cd/pic-lp/pic-cd) *(460 270-1/-4/-2/-0/-9) <40999>* **TUNNEL OF LOVE** [1] [1]
– Ain't got you / Tougher than the rest / All that Heaven will allow / Spare parts / Cautious man / Walk like a man / Tunnel of love / Two faces / Brilliant disguise / One step up / When you're alone / Valentine's day.

Dec 87. (7"/7"sha-pic-d) *(651 295-7/-0) <07663>* **TUNNEL OF LOVE. / TWO FOR THE ROAD** [45] [9]
(cd-s+=) *(651 295-6/-2)* – Santa Claus is comin' to town.

Mar 88. (7") *(651 442-7) <07726>* **ONE STEP UP. / ROULETTE** [ ] Feb88 [13]
(12"+=/cd-s+=) *(651 442-6/-2)* – Lucky man.

Jun 88. (7") *(BRUCE 3)* **TOUGHER THAN THE REST. / ROULETTE** [13] [–]
(12"+=) *(BRUCEQ 3)* – Born to run (live) / Be true (live).
(cd-s+=) *(BRUCEC 3)* – ('A'live) / Born to run (live).

Oct 88. (7") *(BRUCE 4)* **SPARE PARTS. / PINK CADILLAC** [32] [–]
(cd-s+=/s-cd-s+=) *(BRUCE C/B 4)* – ('A'live version) / Chimes of freedom (live).
(12") *(BRUCEQ 4)* – ('A'side) / Cover me (live) / ('A'live) / I'm on fire (live).

—— new band:- **SHANE FONTAYNE** – guitar / **ZACHERY ALFORD** – drums / **TOMMY SIMMS** – bass / **ROY BITTAN** – keyboards / **CRYSTAL TALIEFERO** – guitar, percussion, vocals / + backing vocalists

Columbia Columbia

Mar 92. (c-s,cd-s) *<74273>* **HUMAN TOUCH / BETTER DAYS** [–] [16]

Mar 92. (7"/c-s) *(657872-7/-4)* **HUMAN TOUCH. / SOULS OF THE DEPARTED** [11] [–]
(12"+=/cd-s+=/pic-cd-d+=) *(657872-1/-2/-0)* – Long goodbye.

Mar 92. (cd/c/lp) *(471423-2/-4/-1) <53000>* **HUMAN TOUCH** [1] [2]
– Human touch / Soul driver / 57 channels (and nothin' on) / Cross my heart / Gloria's eyes / With every wish / Roll of the dice / Real world / All or nothin' at al / Man's job / I wish I were blind / Long goodbye / Real man / Pony boy.

Mar 92. (cd/c/lp) *(471424-2/-4/-1) <53001>* **LUCKY TOWN** [2] [3]
– Better days / Lucky town / Local hero / If I should fall apart / Leap of faith / Big Muddy / Living proof / Book of dreams / Souls of the departed / My beautiful reward.

May 92. (7"/c-s) *(657890-7/-4)* **BETTER DAYS. / TOUGHER THAN THE REST** [34] [–]
(12"+=/cd-s+=) *(657890-1/-2)* – Part man, part monkey.

Jun 92. (c-s/cd-s) *<74273>* **57 CHANNELS (AND NOTHIN' ON). / PART MAN, PART MONKEY** [–] [68]

Jul 92. (7"/c-s) *(658138-7/-4)* **57 CHANNELS (AND NOTHIN' ON). / STAND ON IT** [32] [–]
(cd-s+=) *(658138-5)* – Janey don't you lose heart.
(cd-s) *(658138-2)* – ('A'side) / Little Steven mix version 1 / Little Steven mix version 2 / There's a riot goin' on.

Oct 92. (7"/c-s) *(658369-7/-4)* **LEAP OF FAITH. / ('A'version)** [46] [–]
(cd-s+=) *(658369-2)* – Shut out the light / The big payback.
(cd-s) *(658369-5)* – ('A'side) / 30 days out.

Apr 93. (7"/c-s) *(659228-7/-4)* **LUCKY TOWN (live). / ('A' version)** [48] [–]
(cd-s+=) *(659228-2)* – Human touch (live).

Apr 93. (cd/c/lp) *(473860-2/-4/-1)* **IN CONCERT – MTV PLUGGED (live)** [4] [–]
– Red headed woman / Better days / Atlantic city / Darkness on the edge of town / Man's job / Human touch / Lucky town / I wish I were blind / Thunder Road / Light of day / If I should fall behind / Living proof / My beautiful reward.

below from the film 'Philadelphia'

Mar 94. (7"/c-s/12") *(660065-7/-4/-1) <77354>* **STREETS OF PHILADELPHIA. / IF I SHOULD FALL BEHIND** [2] Feb94 [9]
(cd-s+=) *(660065-2)* – Growing up (live) / The big Muddy (live).

Feb 95. (cd/c/lp) *(478555-2/-4/-1) <67060>* **GREATEST HITS** (compilation) [1] [1]
– Born to run / Thunder road / Badlands / The river / Hungry heart / Atlantic city / Dancing in the dark / Born in the U.S.A. / My hometown / Glory days / Brilliant disguise / Human touch / Better days / Streets of Philadelphia / Secret garden / Murder incorporated / Blood brothers / This hard land.

Apr 95. (c-s) *(661295-4) <77847>* **SECRET GARDEN / THUNDER ROAD (plugged live version)** [44] [63]
(cd-s+=) *(661295-2)* – Murder incorporated.
(cd-s) *(661295-5)* – ('A'side) / Because the night / Pink Cadillac / 4th Of July, Asbury Park (Sandy).

Oct 95. (7"pic-d/c-s) *(662625-7/-4)* **HUNGRY HEART. / STREETS OF PHILADELPHIA** [28] [ ]
(cd-s+=) *(662 625-2)* – ('A'-Berlin '95 version) / Thunder Road.

Nov 95. (cd/c/lp) *(481650-2/-4/-1) <67484>* **THE GHOST OF TOM JOAD** [16] [11]
– The ghost of Tom Joad / Straight time / Highway 29 / Youngstown / Sinaola cowboys / The line / Balboa Park / Dry lightning / The new timer / Across the border / Galveston Bay / The best was never good enough.

Apr 96. (7"pic-d) *(663031-7)* **THE GHOST OF TOM JOAD. / STRAIGHT TIME (live)** [26] [ ]
(cd-s+=) *(663031-2)* – Sinaloa cowboys (live) / Darkness on the edge of town (live).
(cd-s) *(663031-5)* – ('A'side) / Meeting across the river / One step up / Nebraska.

Apr 97. (c-s) *(664324-4)* **SECRET GARDEN / HIGHWAY 29** [17] Jan97 [19]
(cd-s+=) *(664324-2)* – Missing / High hopes.
(cd-s) *(664324-5)* – ('A'side) / Ghost of Tom Joad / Blood brothers / Streets of Philadelphia.

Apr 00. (cd-s) *<667491>* **SAD EYES / MISSING / MAN AT THE TOP / TAKE 'EM AS THEY COME** [–] [ ]

Apr 01. (d-cd/t-lp) *(500000-2/-1) <85490>* **LIVE IN NEW YORK CITY (live)** [12] [5]
– My love will not let you down / Prove it all night / Two hearts / Atlantic city / Mansion on the hill / The river / Youngstown / Murder incorporated / Badlands / Out in the street / Tenth Avenue freeze-out / Land of hope and dreams / American skin (41 shots) / Lost in the flood / Born in the U.S.A. / Don't look back / Jungleland / Ramrod / If I should fall behind.

Sep 01. (cd-s) *<67122-2>* **AMERICAN SKIN (live)** [–] [ ]

Jul 02. (cd-s) *<79788>* **THE RISING / LAND OF HOPE AND DREAMS (live at Madison Square Garden)** [–] [52]

Jul 02. (cd/lp) *(508000-2/-1) <86600>* **THE RISING** [1] [1]
– Lonesome day / Into the fire / Waitin' for a sunny day / Nothing man / Countin' on a miracle / Empty sky / Worlds apart / Let's be friends (skin to skin) / Further on (up the road) / The fuse / Mary's place / You're missing / The rising / Paradise / My city of ruins.

Nov 02. (cd-s) *(673408-2) <67327-2>* **LONESOME DAY / LAND OF HOPE AND DREAMS** [39] Dec02 [ ]
(cd-s) *(673408-5)* – ('A') / Spirit in the night / The rising.

Nov 03. (d-cd) *(513700-2) <90773>* **THE ESSENTIAL BRUCE SPRINGSTEEN** (compilation) [28] [14]
– Blinded by the light / For you / Spirit in the night / 4th of July, Asbury Park (Sandy) / Rosalita (come out tonight) / Thunder road / Born to run / Jungleland / Badlands / Darkness on the edge of town / The promised land / The river / Hungry heart / Nebraska / Atlantic City / Born in the U.S.A. / Glory days / Dancing in the dark / Tunnel of love / Brilliant disguise / Human touch / Living proof / Lucky town / Streets of Philadelphia / The ghost of Tom Joad / The rising / Mary's place / Lonesome day / American skin (41 shots) (live) / Land of hope and dreams (live). *(ltd-3xcd+=; 513700-9)* – From small things (big things one day come) / The big paypack / Held up without a gun (live) / Trapped (live) / None but the brave / Missing / Lift me up / Viva Las Vegas / County fair / Code of silence (live) / Dead man walkin' / Countin' on a miracle (acoustic).

Apr 05. (cd/d-lp) *(520000-2) <C1/C2 93900>* **DEVILS & DUST** [1] [1]
– Devils & dust / All the way home / Reno / Long time comin' / Black cowboys / Maria's bed / Silver Palomino / Jesus was an only son / Leah / The hitter / All I'm thinkin' about / Metamoros banks. *(cd w/dvd+=)* – (tracks on video) / (acoustic versions).

Apr 06. (cd) *<(82876 83074-2)>* **WE SHALL OVERCOME: THE SEEGER SESSIONS** [3] [3]
– Old Dan Tucker / Jesse James / Mrs. McGrath / O Mary don't you weep / John Henry / Erie canal / Jacob's ladder / My Oklahoma home / Eyes on the prize / Shenandoah / Pay me my money down / We shall overcome / Froggie went a-courtin'. *(cd w/dvd+=)* – (tracks on video).

– compilations, others, etc. –

Nov 85. (4x12"box) *C.B.S.; (BRUCE 1)* **BOXED SET 12" SINGLES** [ ] [ ]

Nov 88. (d-cd) *C.B.S.; (CDBOS 241)* **NEBRASKA / BORN IN THE U.S.A.** [ ] [ ]

Mar 93. (d-cd) *Columbia: (471607-2)* **DARKNESS ON THE EDGE OF TOWN / NEBRASKA** [ ] [ ]
(re-iss. Feb95; same)

Jan 94. (d-cd/d-c/d-lp) *Dare Int.;* **PRODIGAL SON** [ ] [ ]

Oct 96. (3xcd-box) *Columbia; (485325-2)* DARKNESS ON THE EDGE OF TOWN / GREETINGS FROM ASBURY, N.J. / THE WILD, THE INNOCENT & THE E-STREET SHUFFLE [ ] [–]

Nov 98. (4xcd-box) *Columbia; (492605-2) <69475>* **TRACKS** (collection of outtakes, B-sides & rarities) [50] [27]
– Mary Queen of Arkansas / It's hard to be a saint in the city / Growin' up / Does this bus stop at 52nd Street / Bishop danced / Santa Ana / Seaside bar song / Zero & Blind Terry / Linda let me be the one / Thundercrack / Rendezvous / Give the girl a kiss / Iceman / Bring on the night / So young and in love / Hearts of stone / Don't look back // Restless nights / A good man is hard to find (Pittsburgh) / Roulette / Dollhouse / Where the bands are / Loose ends / Living on the edge of the world / Wages of sin / Take 'em as they come / Be true / Ricky wants a man of her own / I wanna be with

you / Mary Lou / Stolen car / Born in the U.S.A. / Johnny bye-bye / Shut out the light // Cynthia / My love will not let you down / This hard land / Frankie / TV movie / Stand on it / Lion's den / Car wash / Rockaway the days / Brothers under the bridges ('83) / Man at the top / Pink Cadillac / Two for the road / Janey don't you lose heart / When you need me / The wish / The honeymooners / Lucky man // Leavin' train / Seven angels / Gave it a name / Sad eyes / My lover man / Over the rise / When the lights go out / Loose change / Trouble in Paradise / Happy / Part man, part monkey / Goin' Cali / Back in your arms / Brothers under the bridge.

Apr 99. (cd/c) *(494200-2/-4)* <69476> **18 TRACKS** 23 64
– Growin' up / Seaside bar song / Rendezvous / Hearts of stone / Where the bands are / Loose ends / I wanna be with you / Born in the U.S.A. / My love will not let you down / Lion's den / Pink Cadillac / Janey don't you lose heart / Sad eyes / Part man, part monkey / Trouble river / Brothers under the bridge / The fever / The promise.

May 99. (c-s) *(667491-4)* **SAD EYES / I WANNA BE WITH YOU** ☐ ☐
(cd-s+=) *(667491-2)* – Man at the top.
(cd-s) *(667491-5)* – ('A') / Born in the USA / Pink Cadillac.

Feb 06. (d-cd) <*(82876 77995-2)*> **HAMMERSMITH ODEON LONDON 75** (live) 33 93
– Thunder road / Tenth avenue freeze-out / Spirit in the night / Lost in the flood / She's the one / Born to run / The E-Street shuffle / It's hard to be a saint in the city / Backstreets // Kitty's back / Jungleland / Rosalita (come out tonight) / 4th of July, Asbury Park (Sandy) / Detroit medley / For you / Quarter to three.

SQUEEZE

Formed: Deptford, South London, England . . . March '74 by CHRIS DIFFORD and GLENN TILBROOK, the pair initially forming a writing partnership whereby the former penned the lyrics with the latter writing the music. Their genius was subsequently incorporated into a group format as the pair recruited ace pianist, JOOLS HOLLAND, bassist HARRY KAKOULLI and drummer PAUL GUNN, forming SQUEEZE in the process. Early 1977 saw the group's vinyl debut on the independent 'B.T.M.' label with the mock-Egyptian new wave pop/rock of 'TAKE ME I'M YOURS'. Despite the single being subsequently withdrawn, the group replaced GUNN with GILSON LAVIS and proceeded to release the JOHN CALE-produced 'PACKET OF THREE' EP on the 'Deptford Fun City' label. This duly attracted the attentions of 'A&M', keen to get in on the new wave act after their abortive signing of the SEX PISTOLS earlier that year. Immediate Top 20 chart success came with the re-release of 'TAKE ME..', an eponymous debut surfacing soon after. With the addition of JOHN BENTLEY on bass as a replacement for the departing KAKOULLI, the group narrowly missed No.1 in Spring '79 with the cockney wide-boy rap of 'COOL FOR CATS', a similarly titled follow-up album almost breaking the Top 40. The record consolidated the growing reputation of the DIFFORD/TILBROOK songwriting axis; their sagely observed, often darkly amusing social commentary drew inevitable comparisons with prime RAY DAVIES, definitely more accurate than the fanciful LENNON & McCARTNEY references. 'UP THE JUNCTION' was a perfect example, a compelling, hard-bitten tale of love on the breadline leading to broken-hearted disillusionment, a swooning, deceptively melancholy keyboard refrain holding the whole thing together. The song clearly struck a chord in the populace at large, SQUEEZE once again coming within a whisker of No.1. 'ARGYBARGY' (1980) gave the group their first Top 40 album, although the comparatively lowly placings afforded SQUEEZE's long players never really reflected the enduring quality of the songs contained within. Tracks like 'PULLING MUSSELS (FROM THE SHELL)', a brilliant slice of pop genius featuring a rollicking piano break courtesy of the illustrious HOLLAND. The latter left soon after to follow his boogie-woogie muse with JOOLS HOLLAND AND THE MILLIONAIRES and more famously, to present Channel 4's legendary music show, 'The Tube', alongside a young Paula Yates. Finding a replacement in respected vocalist/pianist, PAUL CARRACK (ex-ACE, ex-FRANKIE MILLER etc.), SQUEEZE cut their most successful album to date, 'EAST SIDE STORY' (1981). Co-produced by ELVIS COSTELLO, the album had a rootsier feel, CARRACK's COCKER-esque vocals gracing the grittily soulful 'TEMPTED', while the poignant 'LABELLED WITH LOVE' proved SQUEEZE could 'do' country better than most country artists. The latter song (Top 5) marked the end of their reign as a singles band, however, with the evocative 'BLACK COFFEE IN BED' not even breaching the Top 40. By this point CARRACK had left for a solo career, DON SNOW brought in for a final, patchy album, 'SWEETS FROM A STRANGER' (1982). Though the group were at the height of their popularity, creatively they were beginning to stall and wisely decided to quit while they were still on top. Later that year, the compilation, 'THE SINGLES – 45 AND UNDER', brought the era neatly to a close, a seminal record (no household is complete without a copy!) illustrating why SQUEEZE have aged better than many "new wave" bands of the era. This wasn't the end, though, and after a solo 'DIFFORD & TILBROOK' (1984) album, the pair reunited with HOLLAND, recruiting KEITH WILKINSON on bass. A new album, 'COSI FAN TUTTI FRUTTI' appeared in summer '85, although they didn't really recapture anything resembling the old magic until 'BABYLON AND ON' (1987). That album gave SQUEEZE their first UK Top 20 hit in years with 'HOURGLASS', as well as some belated US chart action, the single reaching No.15 in the States while the album made the Top 40. 'FRANK' (1989) failed to capitalise on the momentum and SQUEEZE were subsequently dealt a double blow when HOLLAND left once again to concentrate on TV work and A&M finally let the band go. The band soldiered on, releasing a sole album, the acclaimed 'PLAY' (1991), for 'Reprise' before eventually regrouping with CARRACK and re-signing with 'A&M' for a further couple of 90's albums, 'SOME FANTASTIC PLACE' (1993) and 'RIDICULOUS' (1995). While the latter set featured at least a handful of bonafide DIFFORD/TILBROOK gems, 'DOMINO' (1998) was something of a career low. If the staleness of the record suggested the writing partnership was past its sell-by date, then 'THE INCOMPLETE GLENN TILBROOK' (2001) offered an opportunity to see what one half of it could achieve on their own. Despite having decided to record alone due to a disagreement over touring rather than writing, TILBROOK grabbed the bull by the proverbial horns nevertheless, turning out a consummately crafted, often charming effort that proved he could go it alone and then some. Although there were contributions from the likes of RON SEXSMITH and AIMEE MANN, the record had TILBROOK's trademarks stamped all over it. Although lyrics were traditionally DIFFORD's bag, TILBROOK proved he was no slouch when it came to wordsmithery. DIFFORD finally released his own solo debut, 'I DIDN'T GET WHERE I AM', in 2002, a disarmingly intimate work co-written and produced by ex-IT BITES man FRANCIS DUNNERY. Critics fell over themselves to point out how radical a departure it was from SQUEEZE (whose 'BLACK COFFEE' and PLAYING WITH ELECTRIC TRAINS' he reprised, the former in skeletal acoustic mode, the latter in full C&W garb), and how composed DIFFORD sounded, even proferring an unlikely gay love song, 'COWBOYS ARE MY WEAKNESS' (and prefiguring 'Brokeback Mountain'. TILBROOK continued in a more raucous solo vein with 'TRANSATLANTIC PING PONG' (2004), a brighter, bolshier record full of high spirits and risqué humour. Once again, TILBROOK collaborated with various songwriters – including CHRIS DIFFORD on the one-off 'WHERE I CAN BE YOUR FRIEND' – even if some of the record's best songs – including opener 'UNTOUCHABLE' and 60s vibrato fest closer 'ONE FOR THE ROAD' – emanated solely from the man himself.

• **Songwriters:** Mostly DIFFORD & TILBROOK compositions, and some by CARRACK who joined late 1980. Covered END OF THE CENTURY (Blur).

Album rating: SQUEEZE (*6) / COOL FOR CATS (*7) / ARGYBARGY (*8) / EAST SIDE STORY (*7) / SWEETS FROM A STRANGER (*4) / THE SINGLES – 45 AND UNDER compilation (*8) / DIFFORD & TILBROOK (*5; as Difford & Tilbrook) / COSI FAN TUTTI FRUTTI (*6) / BABYLON AND ON (*5) / FRANK (*4) / A ROUND AND A BOUT early live (*3) / PLAY (*5) / GREATEST HITS compilation (*8) / SOME FANTASTIC PLACE (*6) / RIDICULOUS (*7) / DOMINO (*5) / THE BIG SQUEEZE – THE VERY BEST OF SQUEEZE compilation (*8) / Glenn Tilbrook: THE INCOMPLETE.. (*6) / THE COMPLETELY ACOUSTIC.. (*5) / TRANSATLANTIC PING PONG (*6) / Chris Difford: I DIDN'T GET WHERE I AM (*5)

CHRIS DIFFORD (b. 4 Nov'54) – vocals, guitar / **GLENN TILBROOK** (b.31 Aug'57) – vocals, guitar / **JOOLS HOLLAND** (b.JULIAN, 24 Jan'58) – keyboards / **HARRY KAKOULLI** – bass / **PAUL GUNN** – drums (below 45 withdrawn from release)

B.T.M. | not iss.

Jan 77. (7"; w-drawn) *(SBT 107)* **TAKE ME I'M YOURS. / NO DISCO KID, NO** – | –

— **GILSON LAVIS** (b.27 Jun'51) – drums (ex-MUSTARD) repl. GUNN

Deptford Fun City | not iss.

Aug 77. (7"ep,12"ep) *(DFC 01)* **PACKET OF THREE** | –
– Cat on a wall / Back track / Night ride. *(re-iss. Nov79 12"ep; same)*

A&M | A&M

Feb 78. (7"/12") *(AMS/+P 7335)* **TAKE ME, I'M YOURS. / NIGHT NURSE** 19 |

Mar 78. (lp/c) *(AMLH/CAM 68465)* <4687> **SQUEEZE** |
– Sex master / Bang bang / Strong in reason / Wild sewerage tickles Brazil / Out of control / Take me, I'm yours / The call / Model / Remember what / First thing wrong / Hesitation (rool Britania) / Get smart. *(re-iss. Mar82 lp/c; AMID/CMID 122)*

May 78. (7",7"green) *(AMS 7360)* **BANG BANG. / ALL FED UP** 49 | –

— **JOHN BENTLEY** (b.16 Apr'51) – bass; repl. KAKOULLI who went solo (he released an album, 'EVEN WHEN I'M NOT', in 1980 and subsequently released a handful of singles in the first half on the 80's)

Nov 78. (7") *(AMS 7398)* **GOODBYE GIRL. / SAINTS ALIVE** 63 | –

Mar 79. (7",7"pale pink,7"pink,7"red/12"pink) *(AMS/+P 7426)* **COOL FOR CATS. / MODEL** 2 |

Apr 79. (lp/c) *(AMLH/CAM 68503)* <4759> **COOL FOR CATS** 45 |
– Slap and tickle / Revue / Touching me, touching you / It's not cricket / It's so dirty / The knack / Hop, skip and jump / Up the junction / Hard to find / Slightly drunk / Goodbye girl / Cool for cats. *(cd-iss. Mar91; CDMID 131)*

May 79. (7",7"lilac) *(AMS 7444)* **UP THE JUNCTION. / IT'S SO DIRTY** 2 | –

Jun 79. (7") <2168> **SLIGHTLY DRUNK. / GOODBYE GIRL** – |

Aug 79. (7",7"red) *(AMS 7466)* **SLAP AND TICKLE. / ALL'S WELL** 24 |

Nov 79. (7",7"white) *(AMS 7495)* **CHRISTMAS DAY. / GOING CRAZY** | –

Jan 80. (7",7"clear) *(AMS 7507)* **ANOTHER NAIL IN MY HEART. / PRETTY THING** 17 | –

Feb 80. (7") <2229> **IF I DIDN'T LOVE YOU. / PRETTY ONE** – |

Feb 80. (lp/c) *(AMLH/CAM 64802)* <4802> **ARGYBARGY** 32 | 71
– Pulling mussels (from the shell) / Another nail in my heart / Separate beds / Misadventure / I think I'm go go / Farfisa beat / Here comes that feeling / Vicky Verky / If I didn't love you / Wrong side of the Moon / There at the top.

Apr 80. (7",7"red) *(AMS 7523)* **PULLING MUSSELS (FROM THE SHELL). / WHAT THE BUTLER SAW** 44 | –

Jun 80. (7") <2247> **PULLING MUSSELS (FROM THE SHELL). / PRETTY ONE** – |

Sep 80. (7"m) <2263> **ANOTHER NAIL IN MY HEART. / GOING CRAZY / WHAT THE BUTLER SAW** – |
<re-iss. Sep82>

— **PAUL CARRACK** (b. Apr'51, Sheffield, England) – keyboards (ex-ACE, ex-FRANKIE MILLER, ex-ROXY MUSIC) repl. JOOLS who formed his own MILLIONAIRES

Apr 81. (7") *(AMS 8129)* **IS THAT LOVE. / TRUST** 35 | –

May 81. (lp/c) *(AMLH/CAM 64854)* <4854> **EAST SIDE STORY** 19 | 44
– In quintessence / Someone else's heart / Tempted / Piccadilly / There's no tomorrow / A woman's world / Is that love / F-hole / Labelled with love / Someone else's bell / Mumbo jumbo / Vanity fair / Messed around. *(cd-iss. Jan87; CDA 3253) (re-iss. cd Mar91; same)*

Jul 81. (7") *(AMS 8147)* **TEMPTED. / YAP YAP YAP** 40 | –
(free 5"w.a.) **ANOTHER NAIL IN MY HEART. / IF I DIDN'T LOVE YOU**

Jul 81. (7") <2345> **TEMPTED. / TRUST** – | 49

Sep 81. (7") *(AMS 8166)* **LABELLED WITH LOVE. / SQUABS ON FORTY FAB** 4 |

Oct 81. (7") <2377> **MESSED AROUND. / YAP YAP YAP** – |

— **DON SNOW** (b.13 Jan'57, Kenya) – keyboards (ex-VIBRATORS, ex-SINCEROS) repl. CARRACK (now solo)

Apr 82. (7",7"pic-d) *(AMS 8219)* <2424> **BLACK COFFEE IN BED. / THE HUNT** 51 | Jul82

Apr 82. (12") <2413> **WHEN THE HANGOVER STRIKES. / I'VE RETURNED** – |

May 82. (lp/c) *(AMLH/CAM 64899)* <4899> **SWEETS FROM A STRANGER** 37 | 32
– Out of touch / I can't hold on / Points of view / Stranger than the stranger on the shore / Onto the dance floor / When the hangover strikes / Black coffee in bed / I've returned / Tongue like a knife / His house her home / The very last dance / The elephant ride.

Jul 82. (7",7"pic-d) *(AMS 8237)* **WHEN THE HANGOVER STRIKES. / THE ELEPHANT RIDE** | –

Oct 82. (7") *(AMS 8259)* <2518> **ANNIE GET YOUR GUN. / SPANISH GUITAR** 43 | Feb83

Nov 82. (lp/c) *(AMLH/CAM 68552)* <4922> **SINGLES – 45 AND UNDER** (compilation) 3 | 47
– Take me I'm yours / Goodbye girl / Cool for cats / Up the junction / Slap and tickle / Another nail in my heart / Pulling mussels (from the shell) / Tempted / Is that love / Labelled with love / Black coffee in bed / Annie get your gun. *(cd-iss. Dec84; CDA 64922)*

Dec 82. (7") <2534> **ANOTHER NAIL IN MY HEART. / GOING CRAZY – WHAT THE BUTLER SAW** – |

— Split at same time of compilation.

DIFFORD & TILBROOK

— carried on as duo, augmented by **KEITH WILKINSON** (b.24 Sep'54, Southfield, England) – bass / + other musicians

Jun 84. (7"/ext.12") *(AM/+X 193)* **LOVE'S CRASHING WAVES. / WITHIN THESE WALLS OF WITHOUT YOU** 57 | –

Jun 84. (lp/c) *(AMLX/CXM 64985)* <4985> **DIFFORD & TILBROOK** 47 | 55
– Action speaks faster / Love's crashing waves / Picking up the pieces / On my mind tonight / Man for all seasons / Hope fell down / Wagon train / You can't hurt the girl / Tears for attention / The apple tree.

Jun 84. (7") <2648> **PICKING UP THE PIECES. / WITHIN THESE WALLS OF WITHOUT YOU** – |

Oct 84. (7"/12") *(AM/+X 219)* **HOPE FELL DOWN. / ACTION SPEAKS FASTER** | –

SQUEEZE

— re-formed '78 line-up except **KEITH WILKINSON** – bass (- HARRY)

Jun 85. (7"/12") *(AM/+Y 255)* **LAST TIME FOREVER. / SUITE FROM FIVE STRANGERS** 45 |

Aug 85. (lp/c/cd) *(AMLH/AMC/CDA 5085)* <5085> **COSI FAN TUTTI FRUTTI** 31 | 57
– Big bang / By your side / King George Street / I learnt how to pray / Last time forever / No place like home / Heartbreakin' world / Hits of the year / Break my heart / I won't ever go drinking again.

Sep 85. (7") <2776> **HITS OF THE YEAR. / THE FORTNIGHT SAGA** – |

Sep 85. (7") *(AM 277)* **NO PLACE LIKE HOME. / THE FORTNIGHT SAGA** | –
(12"+=) *(AMY 277)* – Last time forever.

Nov 85. (7") *(AM 291)* **HEARTBREAKING WORLD. / BIG BANG** | –
(10"+=) *(AMY 291)* – Tempted (live) / By your side (live).

Apr 86. (7") *(AM 306)* **KING GEORGE STREET. / LOVE'S CRASHING WAVES (live)** | –
(12"+=) *(AMY 306)* – Up the junction (live).

— added **ANDY METCALFE** – keyboards (ex-SOFT BOYS)

Aug 87. (7") *(AM 400)* <2967> **HOURGLASS. / WEDDING BELLS** 16 | 15
(12"+=) *(AMY 400)* – Splitting into three.

Sep 87. (lp/c/cd) *(<AMA/AMC/CDA 5161>)* **BABYLON AND ON** [14] [36]
– Hourglass / Footprints / Tough love / The prisoner / 853-5937 / In today's room / Trust me to open my mouth / Striking matches / Cigarette of a single man / Who are you? / The waiting game / Some Americans.

Sep 87. (7") *(AM 412)* **TRUST ME TO OPEN MY MOUTH. / TAKE ME, I'M YOURS (live)** [72] [–]
(12"+=) *(AMY 412)* – Black coffee in bed (live).

Nov 87. (7") *(AM 420)* **THE WAITING GAME. / LAST TIME FOREVER** [ ] [ ]
(12"+=) *(AMY 420)* – The prisoner.

Dec 87. (7") *<2994>* **853-5937. / TAKE ME I'M YOURS (live)** [–] [32]

Jan 88. (7"/ext.12") *(AM/+Y 426)* **853-5937. / TOUGH LOVE** [ ] [–]

Apr 88. (7") *<3021>* **FOOTPRINTS. / BLACK COFFEE IN BED (live)** [–] [ ]

Jun 88. (7") *(AM 450)* **FOOTPRINTS. / STRIKING MATCHES (INSTANT BUFF)** [ ] [–]
(ext.12"+=) *(AMY 450)* – In today's room.

—— reverted back to 5-piece when METCALFE departed

Sep 89. (7") *(AM 350) <1457>* **IF IT'S LOVE. / FRANK'S BAG** [ ] [–]
(12"+=/cd-s+=) *(AMY/CDEE 350)* – Vanity fair (piano version).

Sep 89. (lp/c/cd) *(<AMA/AMC/CDA 5278>)* **FRANK** [58] [ ]
– Frank / If it's love / Peyton Place / Rose I said / Slaughtered, gutted and heartbroken / (This could be) The last time / She doesn't have to shave / Love circles / Melody hotel / Can of worms / Dr. Jazz / Is it too late.

Jan 90. (7") *(AM 535)* **LOVE CIRCLES. / RED LIGHT** [ ] [–]
(12"+=/cd-s+=) *(AMY/CDEE 535)* – Who's that?

Deptford Fun City — I.R.S.

Mar 90. (cd/c/lp) *(DFC CD/MC/LP 1) <82040>* **A ROUND AND A BOUT (live 1974-1989)** [50] [ ]
– Footprints / Pulling mussels (from the shell) / Black coffee in bed / She doesn't have to shave / Is that love / Dr. Jazz / Up the junction / Slaughtered, gutted and heartbroken / Is it too late / Cool for cats / Take me, I'm yours / If it's love / Hourglass / Labelled with love / Annie get your gun / Boogie woogie country girl / Tempted. *(free 7"ep 'PACKET OF THREE')*

—— JOOLS left again to go solo and take up more TV work. In 1991 he was repl. by **MATT IRVING** + **STEVE NIEVE** – keyboards / **TONY BERG** – guitar, keyboards / **BRUCE HORNSBY** – accordion

Reprise — Reprise

Jul 91. (7"/c-s) *(W 0054/+C)* **SUNDAY STREET. / MAIDSTONE** [ ] [–]
(12"+=/cd-s+=) *(W 0054 T/CD)* – Mood swings.

Aug 91. (lp/c)(cd) *(WX 428/+C)(<7599 26644-2>)* **PLAY** [41] [ ]
– Satisfied / Crying in my sleep / Letting go / The day I get home / The truck / House of love / Cupid's toy / Gone to the dogs / Walk a straight line / Sunday street / Wicked and cruel / There is a voice. *(re-iss. cd Feb95; same)*

Nov 91. (7"/c-s) *(W 0071/+C)* **SATISFIED. / HAPPINESS IS KING** [ ] [–]
(12"+=/cd-s+=) *(W 0071 T/CD)* – Laughing in my sleep.

—— **DIFFORD** + **TILBROOK** + **WILKINSON** plus returning **PAUL CARRACK** – keyboards / **PETE THOMAS** – drums

A&M — A&M

Jul 93. (7"/c-s) *(580334-7/-4)* **THIRD RAIL. / COOL FOR CATS – STRONG IN REASON (live medley)** [39] [–]
(cd-s+=) *(580335-2)* – Take me I'm yours (Paul Dakeyne remix).
(cd-s) *(580337-2)* – ('A'side) / The truth (live) / Melody hotel (live) / Walk a straight line (live).

Aug 93. (7"/c-s) *(580376-7/-4)* **SOME FANTASTIC PLACE. / JUMPING** [73] [–]
(cd-s+=) *(580377-2)* – Dark saloons / Discipline.
(cd-s) *(580379-2)* – ('A'side) / Is that the time? / Don't be a stranger / Stark naked.

Sep 93. (cd/c/lp) *(<540140-2/-4/-1>)* **SOME FANTASTIC PLACE** [26] [ ]
– Everything in the world / Some fantastic place / Third rail / Loving you tonight / It's over / Cold shoulder / Talk to him / Jolly comes home / Images of loving / True colours (the storm) / Pinocchio.

Oct 93. (7"/c-s/12") *(580412-7/-4/-1)* **LOVING YOU TONIGHT. / ('A'edit)** [ ] [–]
(cd-s+=) *(580413-2)* – Tempted (session) / Third rail (session).

Feb 94. (7"/c-s) *(580506-7/-4)* **IT'S OVER. / IS THAT LOVE (live)** [ ] [–]
(cd-s+=) *(580507-2)* – Pulling mussels (from the shell) (live) / Goodbye girl (live).

—— they were joined by drummer **KEVIN WILKINSON** (b.1957, Swindon)

A&M — IRS-Capitol

Aug 95. (c-s) *(581189-4)* **THIS SUMMER / GOODBYE GIRL (live)** [47] [–]
(cd-s+=) *(581191-2)* – All the king's horses.
(cd-s) *(581189-2)* – ('A'side) / End of a century (live acoustic) / Periscope.

Nov 95. (c-ep/cd-ep) *(581271-4/-2)* **ELECTRIC TRAINS / CRACKER JACK / FIGHTING FOR PEACE / COLD SHOULDER (live)** [44] [–]
(cd-ep) *(581269-2)* – ('A'side) / Some fantastic place / It's over / Hour glass.

Nov 95. (cd/c) *(540440-2/-4) <38304>* **RIDICULOUS** [50] [ ]
– Electric trains / Heaven knows / Grouch of the day / Walk away / This summer / Got to me / Long face / I want you / Daphne / Lost for words / Great escape / Temptation for love / Sound asleep / Fingertips. *(re-iss. Sep97 cd/c; same)*

Jun 96. (cd-s) *(581605-2)* **HEAVEN KNOWS / GOODBYE GIRL (live) / LABELLED WITH LOVE (live) / IS THAT LOVE? (live)** [27] [–]
(cd-s) *(581607-2)* – ('A'side) / Tempted (live) / Walk away (live) / Some fantastic place (live).
(cd-s) *(581609-2)* – ('A'side) / Take me I'm yours (live) / Annie get your gun (live) / Slap and tickle (live).

Aug 96. (cd-s) *(581837-2)* **THIS SUMMER (remix) / ELECTRIC TRAINS / HEAVEN KNOWS / THIS SUMMER** [32] [–]
(cd-s) *(581839-2)* – ('A'side) / Cool for cats / Up the junction / Black coffee in bed.
(cd-s) *(581841-2)* – ('A'side) / Sweet as a nut / In another lifetime / Never there.

—— **DIFFORD**, **TILBROOK** with **CHRIS HOLLAND** – keyboards, vocals / **HILAIRE PENDA** – bass / **ASHLEY SOAN** – drums, vocals

Quixotic — Valley

May 98. (cd-s) *(QRCSQ 098)* **DOWN IN THE VALLEY / DOWN IN THE VALLEY (mixes; crowd / jug band / instrumental)** [ ] [–]

Nov 98. (cd) *(QRSQD 098) <15046>* **DOMINO** [ ] Sep99 [ ]
– Play on / Bonkers / What's wrong with this picture? / Domino / To be a dad / Donkey talk / Sleeping with a friend / Without you here / In the morning / A moving story / Little king / Short break.

—— tragedy struck, when former member KEVIN committed suicide 17 Jul'99

– compilations, etc. –

1981. (10"m-lp) *A&M; <SP 3413>* **SIX SQUEEZE SONGS CRAMMED ONTO ONE TEN INCH RECORD** [–] [ ]

Oct 83. (7") *Old Gold; (OG 9364)* **TAKE ME, I'M YOURS. / UP THE JUNCTION** [ ] [–]

Sep 85. (7") *Old Gold; (OG 9546)* **COOL FOR CATS. / LABELLED WITH LOVE** [ ] [–]

Apr 92. (7"/c-s) *A&M; (AM/+MC 860)* **COOL FOR CATS. / TRUST ME TO OPEN MY MOUTH** [62] [–]
(cd-s+=) *(AMCD 860)* – Squabs on forty fab (medley hits).

May 92. (cd/c/d-lp) *A&M' (397181-2/-4/-1)* **GREATEST HITS** [6] [ ]
– (as THE SINGLES 45 AND UNDER +) Take me, I'm yours / Goodbye girl / Cool for cats / Up the junction / Slap and tickle / Another nail in my heart / Pulling mussels (from the shell) / Tempted / Is that love / Labelled with love / Black coffee in bed / Annie get your gun / King George Street / Last time forever / No place like home / Hourglass / Trust me to open my mouth / Footprints / If it's love / Love circles.

Oct 93. (cd) *A&M; (CDA 24120)* **BABYLON AND ON / EAST SIDE STORY** [ ] [ ]

Aug 96. (cd) *A&M; <540425-2>* **PICCADILLY COLLECTION** [–] [ ]

Nov 96. (d-cd) *A&M; (540651-2)* **EXCESS MODERATION** [ ] [ ]

Oct 97. (6xcd-box) *(540801-2)* **SIX OF ONE** [ ] [ ]

Aug 00. (cd) *Spectrum; (544229-2)* **UP THE JUNCTION** [ ] [–]

Jun 02. (cd) *Universal TV; (493253-2)* **THE BIG SQUEEZE – THE VERY BEST OF SQUEEZE** [8] [–]
– Take me I'm yours / Goodbye girl / Cool for cats / Up the junction / Slap and tickle / Another nail in my heart / Pulling mussels from a shell / Is that love / Tempted / Black coffee in bed / Annie get your gun / Labelled with love / Last time forever / Hourglass / Some fantastic place / Third rail / This summer / Electric trains / Heaven knows / Domino / Suites from five strangers / Squabs on forty five / Model / Spanish guitar / Elephant girl / Trust / Yap yap yap / Fortnight saga / Wedding bells / What the butler saw / Going crazy / Introvert / Who's that / Vanity fair / Christmas day / Maidstone / Discipline / Periscope / All's well that ends well.

GLENN TILBROOK

with ANDY METCALFE, SIMON HANSON, STEPHEN LARGE, etc

Quixotic — Valley

Nov 00. (cd-s) *(QUIXCD 005)* **PARALLEL WORLD / BY THE LIGHT OF THE CASH MACHINE / PARALLEL WORLD** [ ] [–]

Apr 01. (cd-s) *(QUIXCD 006)* **THIS IS WHERE YOU AIN'T / THIS IS WHERE YOU AIN'T / SUNDAY BREAKFAST TREAT** [ ] [–]

May 01. (cd) *(QUIXCD 007)* *<15144>* **THE INCOMPLETE GLENN TILBROOK** [ ] [ ]
– This is where you ain't / Observatory / Parallel world / Morning / One dark moment / G.S.O.H. essential / Up the creek / Other world / Interviewing Randy Newman / You see me / I won't see you / We went thataway.

Nov 01. (cd) *(QUIXCD 007A)* **THE COMPLETELY ACOUSTIC GLENN TILBROOK** [ ] [–]
– Morning / I won't see you / This is where you ain't / Interviewing Randy Newman / Observatory / One dark moment / Other world / Parallel world / G.S.O.H. essential.

Quixotic — Compass

May 04. (cd-s) *(QUIXCD 009)* **UNTOUCHABLE / DOMESTIC DISTORTION (quick mix)** [ ] [–]

May 04. (cd) *(QUIXCD 010)* *<4383>* **TRANSATLANTIC PING PONG** [ ] Jun04 [ ]
– Untouchable / Lost in space / Neptune / Hostage / Hot shaved Asian teens / Ray & me / Reinventing the wheel / Domestic distortion / The genitalia of a fool / Where I can be your friend / There for her / One for the road.

CHRIS DIFFORD

Adventures In Music — Adventures In Music

Nov 02. (cd) *(ADVCD 1)* *<63203>* **I DIDN'T GET WHERE I AM** [ ] Feb03 [ ]
– Tight rope / For a change / Cowboys are my weakness / No show Jones / A world that passed me by / One day / Playing with electric trains / Lama fayre / Trafalgar Square / Parents.

Nov 02. (cd-s) *(ADVS 2)* **COWBOYS ARE MY WEAKNESS / BLACK COFFEE / LAMA FAYRE** [ ] [–]

☐ Chris SQUIRE (see under ⇒ YES)

☐ John SQUIRE (see under ⇒ STONE ROSES)

STAIND

Formed: Springfield, Massachusetts, USA . . . Xmas 1994 by vocalist AARON LEWIS and guitarist MIKE MUSHOK, the pair almost immediately hooking up with drummer JON WYSOCKI and an unknown original bassist; JOHNNY APRIL would become their 4-string plucker after their first gig in February '95. In late '96, the quartet self-financed a debut album, 'TORMENTED', its title pretty much giving the game away as to their miserabilist nu-metal approach. Spurred on by healthy sales, the band jumped at the chance to play on the same bill as LIMP BIZKIT in late 1997. While that band's ubiquitous lead singer, FRED DURST, initially took vocal exception to STAIND's quasi-Satanic cover art, an impassioned performance on the night persuaded him they were worthy of his new label. After trying and failing to contact DURST by phone, they travelled to a LIMP BIZKIT gig and left a new demo tape for the man's perusal. He was suitably impressed and soon STAIND were cutting their major label debut for the 'Elektra'-backed 'Flip' imprint with Terry Date (SOUNDGARDEN, DEFTONES, PANTERA etc.) at the production helm. 'DYSFUNCTION' arrived in Spring '99, pulling few punches and even less surprises with a solid if uninspiring set of treacle-thick post-grunge. The record went down a storm nevertheless, spawning three sizeable rock radio hits in 'JUST GO', 'MUDSHOVEL' and 'HOME'. Tours with KID ROCK, KORN and LIMP BIZKIT followed and STAIND were subsequently named as the headline act for MTV's 'Return Of The Rock' jaunt. Amid the media circus and general mayhem, a sophomore album, 'BREAK THE CYCLE', appeared in 2001, the record hitting No.1 in the States (and in Britain) but earning short shrift from the likes of Kerrang! – FRED DURST (of LIMP BIZKIT) featured on the hit track, 'OUTSIDE', while just previously 'IT'S BEEN AWHILE' hit the US Top 10. 2003's '14 SHADES OF GREY' (another US No.1) meditated upon the success of that single, putting the spotlight on LEWIS' angst-ridden navel-gazing rather than the crunching dynamics with which they made their name. The self explanatory 'CHAPTER V' (2005) was an obligatory US No.1, compulsory listening for the grunge crowd who still haven't gotten over the genre's demise. Only a few bars into opener 'RUN AWAY', LEWIS was castigating himself for being "dead inside", thus setting the regulatory troubled tone for the rest of the album. Laying off the acoustic guitars which had brushed a relatively sunnier glaze over their last album, the STAIND boys grinched and churned their way through a set overlight on hooks.

Album rating: TORMENTED (*5) / DYSFUNCTION (*6) / BREAK THE CYCLE (*6) / 14 SHADES OF GREY (*5) / CHAPTER V (*5)

AARON LEWIS (b.13 Apr'72, Rutland, Vermont, USA) – vocals, guitar / **MIKE MUSHOK** (b.10 Apr'70, Ludlow, Massachusetts, USA) – guitar / **JOHNNY APRIL** (b.27 Mar'65, Enfield, Connecticut, USA) – bass, vocals / **JON WYSOCKI** (b.17 Jan'71) – drums

not iss. — own label

Oct 96. (cd) **TORMENTED** [–] [ ]
– Tolerate / Come again / Break / Painful / Nameless / Mudshuvel / See thru / Question? / No one's kind / Self destruct / Walls.

Elektra — Elektra

Mar 00. (cd) *<7559 62356-2>* **DYSFUNCTION** [ ] Apr99 [74]
– Suffocate / Just go / Me / Raw / Mudshovel / Home / A flat / Crawl / Spleen. *(hidden track+=)* – Excess baggage.

Feb 01. (-; as AARON LEWIS of STAIND with FRED DURST) *<radio play>* **OUTSIDE** [–] [56]

Aug 01. (cd/c) *<7559 62626-2/-4>* **BREAK THE CYCLE** [1] May01 [1]
– Open your eyes / Pressure / Fade / It's been awhile / Change / Can't believe / Epiphany / Suffer / Safe place / For you / Take it.

Sep 01. (c-s) *(E 7252C)* **IT'S BEEN AWHILE / (acoustic)** [15] Apr01 [6]
(cd-s+=) *(E 7252CD1)* *<67228>* – Suffocate (version).

Oct 01. (cd-s) *<67259>* **FADE / FADE (album version) / IT'S BEEN AWHILE (live) / SPLEEN (album version)** [–] [62]

Nov 01. (c-s) *(E 7277C)* **OUTSIDE / OUTSIDE (live acoustic with FRED DURST) / MUDSHOVEL** [33] [–]
(cd-s+=) *(E 7277CD)* – ('A'-CD-Rom).

Feb 02. (c-s/cd-s) *(E 7281 C/CD)* *<67281>* **FOR YOU / FOR YOU (lp version) / SUFFER (live)** [55] [63]

May 03. (7") *(E 7417)* *<radio>* **PRICE TO PLAY. / CAN'T BELIEVE (live)** [36] [66]
(cd-s+=) *(E 7417CD)* – Let it out / ('A'-video).

May 03. (cd) *<7559 62882-2>* **14 SHADES OF GREY** [16] [1]
– Price to play / How about you / So far away / Yesterday / Fray / Zoe Jane / Fill me up / Layne / Falling down / Reality / Tonight / Could it be / Blow away / Intro.

Sep 03. (7") *(E 7464)* **SO FAR AWAY. / MUDSHOVEL** [ ] Aug03 [24]
(cd-s+=) *(E 7464CD)* *<67450>* – (home grown promo footage).

Aug 05. (cd) *<7559 62982-2>* **CHAPTER V** [ ] [1]
– Run away / Right here / Paper Jesus / Schizophrenic conversations / Falling / Cross to bear / Devil / Please / Everything changes / Take this / King of all excuses / Reply.

Mar 06. (cd-s) *<223>* **RIGHT HERE / OPEN WIDE / COME AGAIN (demo)** [–] [55]

the STANDS

Formed: Liverpool, England ... 2001 by ex-BIG KIDS frontman/songwriter HOWIE PAYNE, together with LUKE THOMPSON, DEAN RAVEA and STE PILGRIM. Gaining endorsement from NOEL and LIAM GALLAGHER, the STANDS built up a strong reputation in and around Merseyside having signed a deal with 'Echo'. If your cup of tea was retro jingle-jangle folk-rock (like a cross between the BEATLES and the BYRDS/DYLAN), then the STANDS were for you – the pity was we'd heard it all somewhere before. A series of UK Top 40 hits ('WHEN THIS RIVER ROLLS YOU OVER', 'I NEED YOU' and 'HERE SHE COMES AGAIN') preceded an equally successful debut album, 'ALL YEARS LEAVING' (2004). Heading to the West Coast (where else!) to record the country-flavoured follow-up, 'HORSE FABULOUS' (2005), drummer PILGRIM was replaced by GRAEME ROBINSON. The album couldn't match its predecessor on the commercial or critical front, with only the track 'DO IT LIKE YOU LIKE' getting a high chart placing; after recording, LUKE made way for PAUL MOLLOY. Later in 2005, HOWIE decided this was the best time for him and the band to split.

Album rating: ALL YEARS LEAVING (*7) / HORSE FABULOUS (*6)

HOWIE PAYNE – vocals, guitar / **LUKE THOMPSON** – guitar / **DEAN RAVEA** – bass / **STE PILGRIM** – drums

		Echo	WEA Int.
Aug 03.	(7") *(ECS 142)* **WHEN THIS RIVER ROLLS OVER YOU. / SHE SPEAKS OF THESE THINGS**	32	–
	(cd-s+=) *(ECSCD 142)* – In so many ways.		
Oct 03.	(7") *(ECS 146)* **I NEED YOU. / I WILL JOURNEY HOME**	39	–
	(cd-s+=) *(ECSCD 146)* – She only cares for me.		
	(cd-s) *(ECSCX 146)* – ('A') / The shape you're in / Still water / ('A'-video).		
Feb 04.	(7") *(ECS 148)* **HERE SHE COMES AGAIN. / HOW YOU SEEM TO BE**	25	–
	(cd-s+=) *(ECSCX 148)* – All years leaving (acoustic) / ('A'-video).		
	(cd-s) *(ECSCD 148)* – ('A') / Stumbling home.		
Feb 04.	(cd/lp) *(ECH CD/LP 50)* <830239-2> **ALL YEARS LEAVING**	28	Jun04
	– I've waited so long / All years leaving / Outside your door / When this river rolls over you / It's only everything / Always is the same – Shine on / Here she comes again / The big parade / The love you give / I need you / Some weekend night / The way she does.		
May 04.	(7"/cd-s) *(ECS/+CD 151)* **OUTSIDE YOUR DOOR. / WHEN THIS RIVER ROLLS OVER YOU**	49	–
	(cd-s) *(ECSCX 151)* – ('A') / All that's glass (home recording) / It takes a while (home recording).		
——	**GRAEME ROBINSON** – drums; repl. PILGRIM		
May 05.	(7") *(ECS 165)* **DO IT LIKE YOU LIKE. / A SEASON TO BE LOVED**	28	–
	(cd-s) *(ECSCD 165)* – ('A') / Into the morning / One of the millions.		
Jul 05.	(cd/lp) *(ECH CD/LP 64)* **HORSE FABULOUS**	62	–
	– Turn the world around / Soon come / Just enough love / I will journey home / Back to you / Mountains blue and the world through my window / Nearer than green / When the night falls in / Bluer than blue / Do it like you like / You said.		
Aug 05.	(dl-s) *(ECDL 177)* **WHEN THE NIGHT FALLS IN**		–
——	(May'05) **PAUL MOLLOY** – guitar (ex-SKYLARKS) repl. THOMPSON		
——	in Nov'05, the STANDS stood down		

☐ Paul STANLEY (see under ⇒ KISS)

☐ Stuart A. STAPLES (see under ⇒ TINDERSTICKS)

☐ Scott STAPP (see under ⇒ CREED)

Ringo STARR

Born: RICHARD STARKEY, 7 Jul'40, Liverpool, England. Taking up the drums professionally in his late teens, STARKEY played with various skiffle outfits before being invited into The BEATLES fold in August '62. So named due to his predeliction for wearing rings, STARR filled the band's drum stool right through till their messy demise in 1969, occasionally doing a lead vocal and finally penning his own track with the endearing 'DON'T PASS ME BY' (from 1968's classic double set, 'THE BEATLES'). Early in '69, just prior to the band's split, STARR appeared in the movie version of Terry Southern's novel, 'Candy', taking a role alongside Peter Sellers the following year in another Southern adaptation, 'The Magic Christian'. A busy year for the budding actor, STARR also released two post-BEATLES solo albums, 'SENTIMENTAL JOURNEY' and 'BEAUCOUPS OF BLUES'. While the former was a string-laden, George Martin-produced set of Tin Pan Alley standards which made the UK Top 10 (and the US Top 30), the latter was a Nashville-recorded country affair, STARR immersing himself in a genre with which he obviously felt at home (he'd previously sung the few country/rockabilly tunes The BEATLES attempted, while the honky tonk fiddle of the aforementioned 'DON'T PASS..' was an indication of the direction he was headed). Although these sets failed to spawn any hit singles, STARR scored a string of transatlantic Top 10 hits in 1971 with the hard hitting 'IT DON'T COME EASY', 'BACK OFF BOOGALOO' and 'PHOTOGRAPH'. A US chart topper, the latter was featured on the eponymous 'RINGO' (1973), his most successful solo album by a mile. Boasting the musical and songwriting talents of all three former BEATLES, the album was also STARR's most consistent, spawning a further sizeable hit in 'YOU'RE SIXTEEN'. The following year's 'GOODNIGHT VIENNA' included the Top 5 cover of Hoyt Axton's novelty number, 'NO NO SONG', while 'BLAST FROM YOUR PAST' (1975) summed up the first half of STARR's solo career. This half decade was also a purple patch for his acting career, STARR taking a lead role in 'That'll Be The Day' alongside DAVID ESSEX and even making his directing debut with 'Born To Boogie' a rockumentary of MARC BOLAN and T. REX. STARR subsequently signed with 'Atlantic' in 1976, 'RINGO'S ROTOGRAVURE' failing to match the success of his previous efforts, while 'RINGO THE 4TH' (1977) was a commercial failure. An album for 'Portrait', 'BAD BOY' (1978), failed to reverse his ailing fortunes and while he scored a Top 40 hit in 1981 with 'WRACK MY BRAIN', 1983's 'OLD WAVE' was only released in Germany. The 80's proved a difficult time for STARR as he struggled with alcohol and drug abuse, retiring completely from recording and concentrating on TV/film work; he famously narrated celebrated children's TV series, 'Thomas The Tank Engine' in 1984. STARR eventually returned to music full-time at the turn of the decade with 'RINGO STARR & HIS ALL-STARR BAND' (1990), a live set of favourites and cover versions performed with the formidable line-up of DR. JOHN, BILLY PRESTON, NILS LOFGREN, JOE WALSH, RICK DANKO, JIM KELTNER, LEVON HELM and CLARENCE CLEMONS. The collaborative spirit carried over into both 'TIME TAKES TIME' (1992) and 'VERTICAL MAN' (1998), although on the latter he was also joined by contemporary stars like ALANIS MORISSETTE. Not that the album itself was contemporary, merely an update of RINGO's offbeat, unassuming style. 'RINGORAMA' (2003), meanwhile, found the likes of WILLIE NELSON and DAVID GILMOUR pitching in with the amiable studio antics. While STARR's vocal talent may be basic, his patter and wit more often than not makes up for it, and while he displays little of the technical flash of his BEATLES heyday, he remains one of the most solidly reliable drummers in the business. The self explanatory 'TOUR 2003' was the latest offering from the ALL-STARR BAND, featuring a very 80s looking lineup of SHIELA E, JOHN WAITE, COLIN HAY (ex-MEN AT WORK) and PAUL CARRACK, the omission of whose 'TEMPTED' was chief among many criticisms. 'CHOOSE LOVE' (2005), by contrast, cut back on the stars (only CHRISSIE HYNDE and BILLY PRESTON made the session, the former duetting on 'DON'T HANG UP' and the latter pounding the keys on the salutory 'OH MY LORD') to a core of the usual RINGO sidekicks on an album buoyed by the undying spirit – and a few lyrical cues – of the BEATLES.

• **Covered:** YOU'RE SIXTEEN (Johnny Burnette) / ONLY YOU (Platters) / SNOOKEROO (Elton John / Bernie Taupin) / IT'S ALL DOWN TO GOODNIGHT VIENNA (John Lennon) / HEY BABY (Bruce Channel). His 1978 album BAD BOY was another covers album. • **Trivia:** In the early 80's, he met actress Barbara Bach, whom he married on 27th of April '81.

Album rating: SENTIMENTAL JOURNEY (*5) / BEAUCOUPS OF BLUES (*5) / RINGO (87) / GOODNIGHT VIENNA (*5) / BLAST FROM YOUR PAST compilation (*6) / RINGO'S ROTOGRAVURE (*5) / RINGO THE 4th (*4) / BAD BOY (*4) / STOP AND SMELL THE ROSES (*5) / OLD WAVE (*3) / STARRSTRUCK: RINGO'S BEST compilation (*6) / RINGO STARR AND HIS ALL-STARR BAND (*6) / TIME TAKES TIME (*6) / RINGO STARR AND HIS ALL-STARR BAND, VOL.2 – LIVE FROM MONTREUX (*5) / VERTICAL MAN (*5) / RINGORAMA (*6) / TOUR 2003 (*3) / CHOOSE LOVE (*5)

RINGO STARR – vocals, drums, etc (on first LP with session people incl. JOHN LENNON and PAUL McCARTNEY)

Apple — Apple

Mar 70. (lp) *(PCS 7101)* *<3365>* **SENTIMENTAL JOURNEY** [7] [22]
– Sentimental journey / Night and day / Whispering grass / Bye bye blackbird / I'm a fool to care / Stardust / Blue, turning grey over you / Love is a many splendoured thing / Dream / You always hurt the one you love / Have I told you lately that I love you / Let the rest of the world go by. *(cd-iss. May95; CDPCS 7101)*

Sep 70. (lp) *(PAS 10002)* *<3368>* **BEAUCOUPS OF BLUES** [ ] [65]
– Beaucoups of blues / Love don't last long / Fastest growing heartache in the west / Without her / Woman of the night / I'd be talking all the time / $15 draw / Wine, women and loud happy songs / I wouldn't have you any other way / Loser's lounge / Waiting / Silent homecoming. *(cd-iss. May95 +=; CDPAS 10002)* – Coochy coochy / Nashville jam.

Oct 70. (7") *<2969>* **BEAUCOUPS OF BLUES. / COOCHY COOCHY** [–] [87]

Apr 71. (7") *(R 5898)* *<1831>* **IT DON'T COME EASY. / EARLY 1970** [4] [4]

Mar 72. (7") *(R 5944)* *<1849>* **BACK OFF BOOGALOO. / BLINDMAN** [2] [9]

Oct 73. (7") *(R 5992)* *<1865>* **PHOTOGRAPH. / DOWN AND OUT** [8] [1]

Nov 73. (lp/c) *(PCTC 252)* *<3413>* **RINGO** [7] [2]
– You and me (babe) / I'm the greatest / Have you seen my baby / Photograph / Sunshine life for me / You're sixteen / Oh my my / Step lightly / Six o'clock * / Devil woman. *(US track *= extended) (re-iss. Nov80 on 'Music For Pleasure'; MFP 50508) (re-iss. Mar91 on 'E.M.I.' cd/c/lp; CD/TC+/EMS 1386)*

Feb 74. (7") *(R 5995)* *<1870>* **YOU'RE SIXTEEN. / DEVIL WOMAN** [4] Dec73 [8]

Mar 74. (7") *<1872>* **OH MY MY. / STEP LIGHTLY** [–] [5]

Nov 74. (7") *(R 6000)* *<1876>* **ONLY YOU. / CALL ME** [28] [6]

Nov 74. (lp) *(PCS 7168)* *<3417>* **GOODNIGHT VIENNA** [30] [8]
– It's all down to goodnight Vienna / Occapella / Oo-wee / Husbands and wives / Snookeroo / All by myself / Call me / No no song / Only you / Easy for me / Goodnight Vienna (reprise). *(re-iss. Oct92 cd/c; CD/TC EMS 1467)*

Feb 75. (7") *(R 6004)* **SNOOKEROO. / OO-WEE** [ ] [–]

Feb 75. (7") *<1880>* **NO NO SONG. / SNOOKEROO** [–] [3]

Jun 75. (7") *<1882>* **IT'S ALL DOWN TO GOODNIGHT VIENNA. / OO-WEE** [–] [31]

Dec 75. (lp/c) *(PCS 7170)* *<3422>* **BLAST FROM YOUR PAST** (compilation) [ ] [30]
– You're sixteen / No no song / It don't come easy / Photograph / Back off boogaloo / Only you / Beacoups of blues / Oh my my / Early 1970 / I'm the greatest. *(re-iss. Nov81 on 'Music For Pleasure'; MFP 50524) (cd-iss. 1987 on 'E.M.I.'; CDP 746663-2)*

Jan 76. (7") *(R 6011)* **OH MY MY. / NO NO SONG** [ ] [–]

Polydor — Atlantic

Sep 76. (7") *(2001 694)* *<3361>* **A DOSE OF ROCK'N'ROLL. / CRYIN'** [ ] [26]

Sep 76. (lp/c) *(2382 040)* *<18193>* **RINGO'S ROTOGRAVURE** [ ] [28]
– A dose of rock'n'roll / Hey baby / Pure gold / Cryin' / You don't know me at all / Cookin' / I'll still love you / This be called a song / La brisas / Lady Gaye. *(re-iss. Jun82 lp/c; 2485 235)(3201 743)*

Nov 76. (7") *(2001 699)* *<3371>* **HEY BABY. / LADY GAYE** [ ] [74]

Sep 77. (7") *<3412>* **DROWNING IN THE SEA OF LOVE. / GROWING** [–] [ ]

Sep 77. (7") *(2001 734)* **DROWNING IN THE SEA OF LOVE. / JUST A DREAM** [ ] [–]

Sep 77. (lp/c) *(2310 556)* *<19108>* **RINGO THE 4th** [ ] [ ]
– Drowning in the sea of love / Tango all night / Wings / Gave it all up / Out on the streets / Can she do it like she dances / Sneaking Sally through the alley / It's no secret / Gypsies in flight / Simple love song.

Oct 77. (lp) *(2480 429)* **SCOUSE THE MOUSE** [ ] [–]
– (8 children's songs)

Nov 77. (7") *<3429>* **WINGS. / JUST A DREAM** [–] [ ]

Polydor — Portrait

Apr 78. (lp/c) *(2310 599)* *<35378>* **BAD BOY** [ ] [ ]
– Who needs a heart / Bad boy / Lipstick traces / Heart on my sleeve / Where did our love go / Hard times / Tonight / Monkey see monkey do / Old time relovin' / A man like me.

May 78. (7"w-drawn) *(2001 782)* *<70015>* **OLD TIME RELOVIN'. / LIPSTICK TRACES (ON A CIGARETTE)** [–] [ ]

Jun 78. (7") *(2001 795)* **TONIGHT. / OLD TIME RELOVIN'** [ ] [–]

Jan 79. (7") *<70018>* **HEART ON MY SLEEVE. / WHO NEEDS A HEART** [–] [ ]

— with NILSSON as COLONEL DOUG BOGIE, he released US single 'OKEY COKEY' / 'AWAY IN A MANGER'; *<ABC Paramount; 12148>*

R.C.A. — Boardwalk

Nov 81. (7") *(RCA 166)* *<130>* **WRACK MY BRAIN. / DRUMMING IS MY MADNESS** [ ] [38]

Nov 81. (lp/c) *(LP/K 6022)* *<33246>* **STOP AND SMELL THE ROSES** [ ] [98]
– Private property / Wrack my brain / Drumming is my madness / Attention / Stop and take the time to smell the roses / Dead giveaway / You belong to me / Sure to fall (in love with you) / Nice way / Back off boogaloo.

Feb 82. (7") *<134>* **STOP AND TAKE TIME TO SMELL THE ROSES. / PRIVATE PROPERTY** [–] [ ]

Bellaphon — not iss.

Jun 83. (7") *(100.16.012)* **IN MY CAR. / AS FAR AS WE CAN GO** [–] German [–]

Jun 83. (lp) *(260.16.029)* **OLD WAVE** [–] German [–]
– In my car / Hopeless / Alibi / Be my baby / She's about a mover / Keep forgettin' / Picture show life / As far as we can go / Everybody's in a hurry but me / I'm going down.

— Retired from solo work, guesting on ex-BEATLES' (PAUL McCARTNEY & GEORGE HARRISON solo). In '84, he narrated for children TV series 'Thomas The Tank Engine'. Returned to studio for 1990 album

RINGO STARR & HIS ALL-STARR BAND

with **DR.JOHN + BILLY PRESTON** – keyboards / **NILS LOFGREN + JOE WALSH** – guitar / **RICK DANKO** – bass / **JIM KELTNER** – drums / **LEVON HELM** – percussion / **CLARENCE CLEMONS** – saxophone

E.M.I. — Arista

Nov 90. (cd/c/lp) *(CD/TC+/EMC 1375)* **RINGO STARR AND HIS ALL-STARR BAND** (live) [ ] [ ]
– It don't come easy / The no-no song / Iko Iko / The weight / Shine silently / Honey don't / You're sixteen, you're beautiful, and you're mine / Quarter to three / Raining in my heart / Will it go round in circles / Life in the fast lane / Photograph.

Arista — Private

May 92. (12") *(115392)* **WEIGHT OF THE WORLD. / AFTER ALL THESE YEARS** [74] [–]

Jun 92. (cd/c) *(262/412 902)* *<82097-2/-4>* **TIME TAKES TIME** [ ] May92 [ ]
– Weight of the world / Don't know a thing about love / Don't go where the road don't go / Golden blunders / All in the name of love / After all these years / I don't believe you / Runaways / In a heartbeat / What goes around.

Rykodisc Rykodisc

Oct 93. (cd/c) *(<RCD2/RAC 0264>)* **RINGO STARR AND HIS ALL-STARR BAND, VOL.2: LIVE FROM MONTREUX** (live)
– Really serious introduction (QUINCY JONES & RINGO) / I'm the greatest (RINGO) / Don't go where the rain don't go (RINGO) / Desperado (JOE WALSH) / I can't tell you why (TIMOTHY B.SCHMIT) / Girls talk (DAVE EDMUNDS) / Weight of the world (RINGO) / Bang the drum all day (TODD RUNDGREN) / Walking nerve (NILS LOFGREN) / Black Maria (TODD RUNDGREN) / In the city (JOE WALSH) / American woman (BURTON CUMMINGS) / Boys (RINGO) / With a little help from my friends (RINGO).

— now with **DUDAS, GRAKAL + HUDSON**

Mercury Mercury

Aug 98. (cd/c) *(558598-2/-4)* <558400> **VERTICAL MAN** Jun98 61
– One / What in the . . . world / Mindfield / King of broken hearts / Love me do / Vertical man / Drift away / I was walking / De da / Without understanding / I'll be fine anywhere / Puppet / I'm yours.

Universal Koch

Apr 03. (cd) *(E 238429-2)* <8429> **RINGORAMA** Mar03
– Eye to eye / Missouri loves company / Instant amnesia / Memphis in your mind / Never without you / Imagine me there / I think therefore I rock'n'roll / Trippin' on my own tears / Write one for me / What love wants to be / Love first, ask questions later / Elizabeth reigns / English garden. *(cd re-iss. Nov03 w/dvd+=; E 239533-2)* – (DVD tracks).

C.N.R. Koch

Jun 04. (cd) *(2299905-2)* <9549> **TOUR 2003** (live) Mar04
– It don't come easy / Honey don't / Memphis in your mind / How long / Down under / When I see you smile / Love bizarre / Boys / Don't pass me by / Yellow submarine / Living years / Missing you / Glamourous life / I wanna be your man / Who can it be now / With a little help from my friends.

Jul 05. (cd) *(229879-2)* <9550> **CHOOSE LOVE** Jun05
– Fading in fading out / Give me back the beat / Oh my Lord / Hard to be true / Some people / Wrong all the time / Don't hang up / Choose love / Me and you / Satisfied / The turnaround / Free drinks. *(ltd-cd w/dvd+=; 229879-8)* – (DVD tracks).

– compilations, etc. –

May 84. (7") *EMI Gold; (G45 13)* **IT DON'T COME EASY. / BACK OFF BOOGALOO** –

Feb 89. (lp/c/cd) *Rhino;* <R1/R4/R2 70135> **STARRSTRUCK: RINGO'S BEST** (1976-1983) –
– Wrack my brain / In my car / Cookin' (in the kitchen of love) / I keep forgettin' / Hard times / Hey baby / Attention / A dose of rock'n'roll / Who needs a heart / Private property / Can she do it like she dances / Heart on my sleeve. *(cd+=)* – Sure to fall (in love with you) / Hopeless / You belong to me / She's about a mover.

Jan 00. (t-cd) *Cleopatra; (CLP 7512)* **ANTHOLOGY: 10 YEAR ANNIVERSARY**

Mar 03. (cd) *Universal;* <*(AA314 538118-2)*> **VH-1 STORYTELLERS**

May 03. (cd) *King Biscuit; (KBCCD 143)* **KING BISCUIT PRESENTS . . .**

STARSAILOR

Formed: Wigan, England . . . late 90's by Chorley & Warrington lads JAMES WALSH, JAMES STELFOX and BEN BYRNE with the belated arrival of keyboardist BARRY WESTHEAD. All former music students, the group lifted their name from a TIM BUCKLEY album which obviously proved to be a major influence along with VAN MORRISON and TOM WAITS. The indie quintet debuted at the 'Heavenly Social' in 2000, after having only five songs, three of which were floating around on demo tapes circulating the music industry. Giants 'E.M.I.' eventually won over the band, who were still astonished by the critical response they were receiving, it being so early on in their careers. STARSAILOR were put on tour with fellow indie guitar comrades JJ72 and ALFIE and issued their debut single 'FEVER' which would then spark a sold-out, nationwide headline tour. 'GOOD SOULS', a simple guitar-jangling lullaby followed and word seemed to be spreading as the single was another to crash into the Top 20, earning them an American tour with The DOVES and a spot on nightly comic David Letterman's show. 'LOVE IS HERE' was issued the following year to mixed reviews (one of its harshest critics being MOGWAI's STUART BRAITHWAITE who bravely said: "You can just tell JAMES WALSH would sell his granny for a Brit Award") and boasted the Top 10 single 'ALCOHOLIC', a whinging but endearing lament that would've made even THOM YORKE groan. That said, STARSAILOR obviously had a general appeal and were musically talented enough to climb as high as they did (album hit UK Top 3) in such a short period of time. WALSH displayed his songwriting skills even further on the band's sophomore effort 'SILENCE IS EASY' (2003). With troubled PHIL SPECTOR producing two of the eleven songs on offer, the group weren't moving in any new directions; the soft vocals of WALSH were still present as were the beautiful guitar melodies and poignant lyrics of love and squalor. Although the album wasn't nearly as well received as their debut, perhaps because it sounded a tad over-produced (especialy the SPECTOR tracks), it tended to wear its heart firmly on its sleeve for most of the duration. STARSAILOR seemed to be treading water on third album, 'ON THE OUTSIDE' (2005), however it still sold reasonably well in the UK, as did the singles 'IN THE CROSSFIRE' (an anti-Iraq War song) and 'THIS TIME'.

Album rating: LOVE IS HERE (*8) / SILENCE IS EASY (*7) / ON THE OUTSIDE (*5)

JAMES WALSH (b. 8 Jun'01) – vocals, guitar / **BARRY WESTHEAD** – keyboards / **JAMES STELFOX** – bass / **BEN BYRNE** – drums

Chrysalis Capitol

Feb 01. (cd-s/7"/cd-s) *(CD+/CHS/+S 5123)* **FEVER. / COMING DOWN / LOVE IS HERE** 18 –

Apr 01. (c-s/7") *(TC+/CHS 5125)* **GOOD SOULS. / THE WAY YOUNG LOVERS DO** 12 –
(c-s+=) *(CDCHS 5125)* – Good souls (Echoboy remix).
(cd-s++=) *(CDCHSS 5125)* – ('A'-video).

Sep 01. (7") *(CHS 5130)* **ALCOHOLIC. / LET IT SHINE** 10 –
(cd-s+=) *(CDCHS 5130)* – ('A'-original) / ('A'-video).
(c-s+=) *(TCCHS 5130)* – Grandma's hands.
(cd-s) *(CDCHSS 5130)* – ('A') / Grandma's hands / Good souls (Soulsavers remix).

Oct 01. (cd/c/lp) *(535350-2/-4/-1)* <7243 5 36448 2 6> **LOVE IS HERE** 2 Jan02
– Tie up my hands / Poor misguided fool / Alcoholic / Lullaby / Way to fall / Fever / She just wept / Talk her down / Love is here / Good souls / Coming down.

Dec 01. (c-s) *(TCCHS 5131)* **LULLABY / FROM A WHISPER TO A SCREAM / TIE UP MY HANDS (live)** 36 –
(cd-s+=) *(CDCHS 5131)* – ('A'-video).
(dvd-s) *(DVDCHS 5131)* – ('A'-video) / From a whisper to a scream / Love is here (live at the Troubadour) / (videos & interview).

Mar 02. (c-s) *(TCCHS 5136)* **POOR MISGUIDED FOOL / BORN AGAIN** 23 –
(cd-s+=) *(CDCHS 5136)* – ('A'-soulsavers mix).
(dvd-s) *(DVDCHS 5136)* – ('A'-video) / Born again / Hot burrito #2 / (the making of..).

E.M.I. Capitol

Sep 03. (7") *(EM 625)* **SILENCE IS EASY. / SHE UNDERSTANDS** 9 –
(cd-s+=) *(CDEM 625)* – Could you be mine?
(dvd-s) *(DVDEM 625)* – ('A'-video) / (behind the scenes video) / Could you be mine? / Good souls (live 2003).

Sep 03. (cd/lp) *(590007-2/-1)* <591741> **SILENCE IS EASY** 2 Jan04
– Music was saved / Fidelity / Some of us / Silence is easy / Telling them / Shark food / Bring my love / White dove / Four to the floor / Born again / Restless heart. <*US cd+=*> – Could you be mine? / At the end of the show.

Nov 03. (cd-s/7") *(CD+/EM 632)* **BORN AGAIN. / AT THE END OF THE SHOW** 40 –
(cd-s) *(CDEMS 632)* – ('A') / White dove (original demo) / Silence is easy (live in Cardiff) / ('A'-alt. video).
(dvd-s) *(DVDEM 632)* – ('A'-video) / White dove (original demo) / (10 minute documentary).

Mar 04. (cd-s) *(CDEM 634)* **FOUR TO THE FLOOR / A MESSAGE** 24 –
(10"+=) *(10EM 634)* – ('A'-Thin White Duke mix).
(12") *(12EM 634)* – ('A'-above mix) / ('A'-Soulsavers mix).
(cd-s) *(CDEMS 634)* – ('A'-mixes above) / ('A'-video).

E.M.I. Artists Addiction

Oct 05. (cd-s/7"mustard) *(CD+/EM 671)* **IN THE CROSSFIRE. / ALWAYS** 22 –
(dvd-s) *(DVDEM 671)* – ('A'-video) / Four to the floor (live at Somerset House video) / ('A') / Empty streets.

Oct 05. (cd/lp) *(342274-2/-1)* **ON THE OUTSIDE** 13 Aug06
– In the crossfire / Counterfeit life / In my blood / Faith hope love / I don't know / Way back home / Keep us together / Get out while you can / This time / White light / Jeremiah. *(ltd-cd w/dvd+=; 343722-2)* – (DVD tracks).

Jan 06. (7"green) *(EM 679)* **THIS TIME. / BELIEVE ME** 24 –
(cd-s) *(CDEM 679)* – ('A') / Push the button (Jo Whiley Radio 1 live lounge version).
(dvd-s) *(DVDEM 679)* – ('A'-video) / In the crossfire (live from Brixton Academy video) / This time (live) / Believe me.

May 06. (7") *(EM 691)* **KEEP US TOGETHER. / KEEP US TOGETHER (tribute to Schroeder mix by Modlang)** 47 –
(cd-s) *(CDEM 691)* – ('A') / Rise up.

□ STARSHIP (see under ⇒ JEFFERSON AIRPLANE)

STATIC-X

Formed: based – Los Angeles, California, USA . . . 1996 by WAYNE STATIC and KEN JAY, who'd met while working in a Chicago record store before they briefly formed DEEP BLUE DREAM. They soon recruited Japanese-born KOICHI FUKUDA and California native TONY CAMPOS, building up a genuine grass roots fanbase in thrall to their guttural, technologically enhanced metal. A subsequent deal with 'Warners' led to the release of a debut album, 'WISCONSIN DEATH TRIP' (1999), earning a fair whack of airtime on US rock radio via the tracks, 'PUSH IT', 'I'M WITH STUPID' and 'BLED FOR DAYS'. By the time the record had gone platinum, FUKUDA had been replaced by TRIPP REX EISEN, the erstwhile DOPE guitarist making his debut on sophomore effort, 'MACHINE' (2001). By the release of 2003's hackneyed 'SHADOW ZONE' (featuring temp drummer JOSH FREESE deputising for JAY), it was hard to avoid the impression that the alternative rock/metal scene had long left the likes of STATIC-X behind. Displaying a dearth of either lyrical or musical inspiration, the album couldn't hope to compete with the restless innovation of the band's contemporaries. STATIC-X subsequently marked time by releasing a rarities collection, 'BENEATH . . . BETWEEN . . . BEYOND' (2004), including other remixes, B-sides and demos dating back a good/bad eight years. Having enticed KOICHI back to the fold, while also promoting tour drummer NICK OSHIRO into the studio, the band returned to the Top 30 courtesy of 4th set proper, 'START A WAR' (2005). However, its lack of diversion and stale lyrics (always roared), led to it being panned by some critics.

• **Covers:** BURNING INSIDE (Ministry) / BEHIND THE WALL OF SLEEP (Black Sabbath) / GIMME GIMME SHOCK TREATMENT (Ramones).

Album rating: WISCONSIN DEATH TRIP (*5) / MACHINE (*6) / SHADOW ZONE (*4) / BENEATH . . . BETWEEN . . . BEYOND rarities collection (*3) / START A WAR (*4)

WAYNE STATIC (b. WAYNE RICHARD WELLS, 4 Nov'65, Muskegon, Michigan) – vocals, guitar, programming / **KOICKI FUKUDA** – guitar / **TONY CAMPOS** – bass / **KEN JAY** – drums

Warners Warners

Nov 98. (cd-s) **3 SONG EP** –
– Push it / Bled for days / Down.

May 99. (cd/c) *<(9362 47271-2/-4)>* **WISCONSIN DEATH TRIP** Mar99
– Push it / I'm stupid / Bled for days / Love dump / I am / Otsegolation / Stem / Sweat of the bud / Fix / Wisconsin death trip / The trance is the motion / December.

Jan 00. (cd-s) *<44782>* **PUSH IT / BLED FOR DAYS (live) / PUSH IT (JB's death trance mix) / DOWN (demo) / PUSH IT (Mephisto Odyssey crucified dub mix)** –

Sep 00. (12") *(F 1114490-2)* **LOVE DUMP** –
(above issued on Higher Education')

—— **TRIPP REX EISEN** – guitar (ex-DOPE) repl. FUKUDA

Jun 01. (cd/c) *<(9362 47948-2/-4)>* **MACHINE** 56 11
– Bien venidos / Get to the gone / Permanence / Black and white / This is not / Otsego undead / Cold / Structural defect / . . .In a bag / Burn to burn / Machine / A dios alma perida.

Sep 01. (dvd-s) *(W 560DVD)* **BLACK AND WHITE / ANYTHING BUT THIS / SWEAT OF THE BUD (live)** 65 –

—— **JOSH FREESE** – drums (of A PERFECT CIRCLE) repl. JAY

Oct 03. (cd) *<(9362 48427-2)>* **SHADOW ZONE** 20
– Destroy all / Control it / New pain / Shadow zone / Dead world / Monster / The only / Kill your idols / All in wait / Otsegolectric / So / Transmission / Invincible. *<(ltd-cd w/dvd+=; 9362 48548-2)>*

—— **KOICHI FUKUDA** returned to repl. TRIPP

—— **NICK OSHIRO** – drums (ex-SEETHER) repl. temp. JOSH

Jul 05. (cd) *<(9362 49372-2)>* **START A WAR** 29
– The enemy / I'm the one / Start a war / Pieces / Dirthouse / Skinnyman / Just in case / Set it off / I want to fucking break it / Night terrors / Otsego amigo / My damnation / Brainfrog. *<(ltd-cd w/dvd+=; 9362 49301-2)>* – (DVD tracks).

– compilations, etc. –

Jul 04. (cd) *Warners; <(9362 48796-2)>* **BENEATH . . . BETWEEN . . . BEYOND . . .** (rarities)
– Breathe / Deliver me / Anything but this / S.O.M. / Down / Head / So real / Crash / Push it / I'm with stupid / Burning inside / Behind the wall of sleep / Gimme gimme shock treatment / I am (demo) / Love dump (demo) / Get to the gone (live demo) / New pain (demo) / Otsegolectric (demo).

STATUS QUO

Formed: London, England . . . 1962 as the SPECTRES, by schoolboys ALAN LANCASTER, ALAN KEY, MIKE ROSSI (aka FRANCIS) and JESS JAWORSKI. They subsequently added JOHN COGHLAN to replace BARRY SMITH, and, by the mid-60's were playing a residency at Butlin's holiday camp, where ROY LYNES took over from JESS. In July '66, they signed to 'Piccadilly' records but failed with a debut 45, a Leiber & Stoller cover, 'I (WHO HAVE NOTHING)'. They released two more flops, before they changed name in March '67 to the TRAFFIC JAM. After one 45, they chose an alternative moniker, the STATUS QUO, due to the more high profile TRAFFIC making the charts. In October '67, MIKE ROSSI reverted back to his real Christian name, FRANCIS, the band adding a second guitarist, RICK PARFITT. Now re-signed to 'Pye' records, they unleashed their first single, 'PICTURES OF MATCHSTICK MEN', giving them a breakthrough into the UK Top 10 (it also hit No.12 in the States – their only Top 50 hit). This was an attempt to cash-in on the hugely popular psychedelic scene, an enjoyable pastiche nevertheless, which remains one of their most enduring, timeless songs. The following year, they were again in the Top 10 with 'ICE IN THE SUN', another taken from the same blueprint. Soon after, the band shed their psychedelic trappings, opting instead for a blues/boogie hard rock sound a la CANNED HEAT. After two more Top 30 hits in the early 70's, their biggest and best being, 'DOWN THE DUSTPIPE', they jumped ship in 1972, signing to 'Vertigo' records. With their trademark blue jeans and (sometimes) white T-shirts, they became one of the top selling bands of the 70's. Their 3-chord-wonder barrage of rock'n'roll had few variations, a disappointing 1971 set, 'DOG OF TWO HEAD' nevertheless hiding a minor classic in 'MEAN

GIRL' (a hit two years later). Flying high once more in early '73, STATUS QUO hit the Top 10 with 'PAPER PLANE', the single lifted from the accompanying album, 'PILEDRIVER' (which featured a cover of The Doors' 'ROADHOUSE BLUES'!). The 'QUO said 'HELLO' in fine fashion nine months later, the chart-topping album widely regarded as ROSSI and Co.'s 12-bar tour de force, the hit single 'CAROLINE' also making the Top 5. The following year, another Top 10'er, 'BREAK THE RULES' (from the 'QUO' album), saw the band rather ironically sticking steadfastly to their tried and tested formula. This same formula served them well throughout the mid 70's, their commercial peak coming with 'DOWN DOWN', a No.1 single from the similarly successful 'ON THE LEVEL' album. They followed this with 'BLUE FOR YOU', a set that was lapped up by the massed ranks of the 'QUO army and featured two classy, almost credible hit singles, 'RAIN' and 'MYSTERY SONG'. A hairy eight-legged hit machine, the band just kept on rockin' oblivious to the punk upstarts; perhaps the song most readily identifiable with STATUS QUO, the cover of John Fogerty's 'ROCKIN' ALL OVER THE WORLD' "rocked" the nation in 1977, everyone from housewives to headbangers getting down with their air-guitar. Although they kept their notoriously die-hard following, the band became something of a reliable joke in the music journals as they veered more and more into R&B-by-numbers pop-rock territory, 1984's cover of Dion's 'THE WANDERER' being a prime example. Two years previous, COGHLAN departed (possibly after hearing the same three chords just once too many), the group bringing in PETE KIRCHNER until 1986 when JEFF RICH replaced him. That same year, yet another founder member, LANCASTER, bailed out, keyboard player, ANDY BOWN (a part-time member since '74) become a full-time fifth member. Hardly recognisable as a 'QUO single, the dreary 'IN THE ARMY NOW' almost took ROSSI, PARFITT and Co. back to the top of the charts in '86 (having earlier wowed the world at Live Aid). STATUS QUO's past musical misdemeanours paled dramatically against the unforgivable early 90's medley, entitled 'ANNIVERSARY WALTZ' (25th unfortunately). The song found them vying for the knees-up-Mother Brown position previously held by cockney "entertainers", CHAS & DAVE. Enough said. The band redeemed themselves to a certain degree with 'HEAVY TRAFFIC' (2002), claimed by some of their more excitable fans as their best record since the 70's. They had a point, certainly: the record's brutally stripped down, live-in-the-studio, heads down blues-rock suggested that they'd been saving it up for years. The double-disc 'RIFFS' (2003), meanwhile, carried that back-to-basics ethos forward to a lean covers/live set, with spirited interpretations of various good-time rockers. The all too familiar compilation (although it was a double), 'XS ALL AREAS: THE GREATEST HITS', hit the charts in 2004. The 'QUO returned in 2005 on new label ('Sanctuary') for umpteenth album, 'THE PARTY AIN'T OVER YET', another Top 20 entry that featured the odd hit or two and a cover of Connie Francis' 'CUPID STUPID'. Talking of the odd hit or two, ROSSI and PARFITT also made their impression (as STATUS QUO!) by "decking" Les Battersby on ITV's long-running soap, Coronation Street.

• **Songwriters:** LANCASTER (until his departure) or ROSSI and PARFITT. In the early 70's, ROSSI and tour manager BOB YOUNG took over duties. Covered; SPICKS AND SPECKS (Bee Gees) / GREEN TAMBOURINE (Lemon Pipers) / SHEILA (Tommy Roe) / ICE IN THE SUN + ELIZABETH DREAMS + PARADISE FLAT + others (Marty Wilde – Ronnie Scott) / JUNIOR'S WAILING (Steamhammer) / DOWN THE DUSTPIPE (Carl Grossman) / THE PRICE OF LOVE (Everly Brothers) / WILD SIDE OF LIFE (Tommy Quickly) / IN THE ARMY NOW (Bolland-Bolland) / RESTLESS (Jennifer Warnes) / WHEN YOU WALK IN THE ROOM (Jackie DeShannon) / FUN, FUN, FUN (Beach Boys) / I CAN HEAR THE GRASS GROW (Move) / YOU NEVER CAN TELL (Chuck Berry) / GET BACK (Beatles) / SAFETY DANCE (Men Without Hats) / RAINING IN MY HEART (Buddy Holly) / DON'T STOP (Fleetwood Mac) / PROUD MARY (Creedence Clearwater Revival) / LUCILLE (Little Richard) / JOHNNY AND MARY (Robert Palmer) / GET OUT OF DENVER (Bob Seger) / THE FUTURE'S SO BRIGHT (Timbuk 3) / ALL AROUND MY HAT (Steeleye Span) / etc.

Album rating: PICTURESQUE MATCHSTICKABLE MESSAGES FROM THE STATUS QUO (*5) / SPARE PARTS (*4) / MA KELLY'S GREASY SPOON (*4) / DOG OF TWO HEAD (*6) / PILEDRIVER (*6) / HELLO! (*7) / QUO (*6) / ON THE LEVEL (*6) / BLUE FOR YOU (*5) / STATUS QUO LIVE! (*6) / ROCKIN' ALL OVER THE WORLD (*6) / IF YOU CAN'T STAND THE HEAT (*6) / WHATEVER YOU WANT (*6) / 12 GOLD BARS compilation (*8) / JUST SUPPOSIN' (*6) / NEVER TOO LATE (*5) / 1+9+8+2 (*5) / FROM THE MAKERS OF . . . compilation/live (*6) / BACK TO BACK (*4) / 12 GOLD BARS, VOL.2 compilation (*6) / IN THE ARMY NOW (*6) / AIN'T COMPLAINING (*5) / PERFECT REMEDY (*3) / ROCKIN' ALL OVER THE YEARS compilation (*7) / ROCK 'TIL YOU DROP (*5) / LIVE ALIVE QUO (*4) / THIRSTY WORK (*4) / DON'T STOP (*3) / UNDER THE INFLUENCE (*3) / FAMOUS IN THE LAST CENTURY (*3) / HEAVY TRAFFIC (*5) / RIFFS (*4) / XS ALL AREAS: THE GREATEST HITS double compilation (*8) / THE PARTY AIN'T OVER YET (*5) / Francis Rossi: KING OF THE DOGHOUSE (*3)

MIKE ROSSI (b. FRANCIS, 29 Apr'49, Forest Hill, London) – vocals, guitar / **ROY LYNES** (b.25 Oct'43, Surrey, Kent) – organ, vocals repl. JESS JAWORSKI / **ALAN LANCASTER** (b. 7 Feb'49, Peckham, London) – bass, vocals / **JOHN COGHLAN** (b.19 Sep'46, Dulwich, London) – drums repl. BARRY SMITH

		Piccadilly	not iss.
Sep 66.	(7"; as The SPECTRES) *(7N 35339)* **I (WHO HAVE NOTHING). / NEIGHBOUR, NEIGHBOUR**		–
Nov 66.	(7"; as The SPECTRES) *(7N 35352)* **HURDY GURDY MAN. / LATICA**		–
——	(above was not the DONOVAN song)		
Feb 67.	(7"; as The SPECTRES) *(7N 35368)* **(WE AIN'T GOT) NOTHIN' YET. / I WANT IT**		–
Jun 67.	(7"; as TRAFFIC JAM) *(7N 35386)* **ALMOST THERE BUT NOT QUITE. / WAIT JUST A MINUTE**		–

the STATUS QUO

—— added **RICK PARFITT** (b. RICHARD HARRISON, 12 Oct'48, Woking, Surrey) – guitar, vocals / MIKE now **FRANCIS ROSSI**

		Pye	Cadet Concept
Nov 67.	(7") *(7N 17449)* <7001> **PICTURES OF MATCHSTICK MEN. / GENTLEMAN JOE'S SIDEWALK CAFE**	7	May68 12
Apr 68.	(7") *(7N 17497)* <7015> **BLACK VEILS OF MELONCHOLY. / TO BE FREE**		Jul69
Aug 68.	(lp) *(NSPL 18220)* <LSP 315> **PICTURESQUE MATCHSTICKABLE MESSAGES FROM THE STATUS QUO** (US-title 'MESSAGES FROM THE STATUS QUO')		

– Black veils of meloncholy / When my mind is not live / Ice in the Sun / Elizabeth dreams / Gentleman Joe's sidewalk cafe / Paradise flat / Technicolour dreams / Spicks and specks / Sheila / Sunny cellophane skies / Green tambourine / Pictures of matchstick men. *(re-iss. Oct87 on 'P.R.T.' lp/c/cd; PYL/PYM/PYC 6020) (cd re-iss. Dec89 on 'Castle'; CLACD 168)*

		Pye	Cadet Concept
Aug 68.	(7") *(7N 17581)* <7006> **ICE IN THE SUN. / WHEN MY MIND IS NOT ALIVE**	8	70
Jan 69.	(7"w-drawn) *(7N 17650)* **TECHNICOLOR DREAMS. / PARADISE FLAT**	–	–
Feb 69.	(7") *(7N 17665)* **MAKE ME STAY A BIT LONGER. / AUNTIE NELLIE**		–
Mar 69.	(7") *<7010>* **TECHNICOLOR DREAMS. / SPICKS AND SPECKS**	–	
May 69.	(7") *(7N 17728)* **ARE YOU GROWING TIRED OF MY LOVE. / SO ENDS ANOTHER LIFE**	46	–
Sep 69.	(lp) *(NSPL 18301)* **SPARE PARTS**		–

– Face without a soul / You're just what I'm looking for / Mr.Mind detector / Antique Angelique / So ends another life / Are you growing tired of my love / Little Miss Nothing / Poor old man / The clown / Velvet curtains / When I awake / Nothing at all. *(re-iss. Oct87 on 'P.R.T.' lp/c/cd; PYL/PYM/PYC 6021) (re-iss. Aug90 on 'Castle' cd/c/lp; CLA CD/MC/LP 205) (re-mast.Aug98 on 'Essential'+=; ESMCD 625)* – (extra tracks).

		Pye	Cadet Concept
Oct 69.	(7") *(7N 17825)* <7017> **THE PRICE OF LOVE. / LITTLE MISS NOTHING**		

Pye Janus

Mar 70. (7") *(7N 17907) <127>* **DOWN THE DUSTPIPE. / FACE WITHOUT A SOUL** [12] [ ]

Sep 70. (lp) *(NSPL 18344) <3018>* **MA KELLY'S GREASY SPOON** [ ] [ ]
– Spinning wheel blues / Daughter / Everything / Shy fly / (April) Spring, Summer and Wednesdays / Junior's wailing / Lakky lady / Need your love / Lazy poker blues / (a) Is it really me – (b) Gotta go home. *(re-iss. Oct87 on 'P.R.T.'; PYL/PYM/PYC 6022) (cd re-iss. Dec89 on 'Castle'; CLACD 169)*

STATUS QUO

— now a quartet of **ROSSI, PARFITT, LANCASTER + COGHLAN** when LYNES departed

Oct 70. (7") *(7N 17998) <141>* **IN MY CHAIR. / GERDUNDULA** [21] [ ]
(re-iss. Jun79)

Pye Pye

Jun 71. (7") *(7N 45077) <65000>* **TUNE TO THE MUSIC. / GOOD THINKING** [ ] [ ]

Dec 71. (lp/c) *(NSPL 18371) <3301>* **DOG OF TWO HEAD** [ ] [ ]
– Umleitung / Nanana / Something going on in my head / Mean girl / Nanana / Gerdundula / Railroad / Someone's learning / Nanana. *(cd-iss. 1986 on 'P.R.T.'; CDMP 8837) (re-iss. Oct87 on 'P.R.T.' lp/c/cd; PYL/PYM/PYC 6023) (re-iss. Aug90 on 'Castle' cd/c/lp; CLA CD/MC/LP 206) (re-mast.Aug98 on 'Essential'+=; ESMCD 626)* – (extra tracks).

Vertigo A&M

Jan 73. (7") *(6059 071)* **PAPER PLANE. / SOFTER RIDE** [8] [–]

Jan 73. (lp) *(6360 082) <4381>* **PILEDRIVER** [5] [ ]
– Don't waste my time / O baby / A year / Unspoken words / Big fat mama / Paper plane / All the reasons / Roadhouse blues. *(re-iss. May83 lp/c; PRICE/PRIMC 17) (cd-iss. Feb91; 848 176-2)*

May 73. (7") *<1425>* **DON'T WASTE MY TIME. / ALL THE REASONS** [–] [ ]

Jul 73. (7") *<1443>* **PAPER PLANE. / ALL THE REASONS** [–] [ ]

Sep 73. (7") *(6059 085)* **CAROLINE. / JOANNE** [5] [–]

Sep 73. (lp) *(6360 098) <3615>* **HELLO!** [1] [ ]
– Roll over lay down / Claudie / A reason for living / Blue eyed lady / Caroline / Softer ride / And it's better now / Forty-five hundred times. *(re-iss. May83 lp/c; PRICE/PRIMC 16) (cd-iss. Feb91; 848 172-2)*

Feb 74. (7") *<1510>* **CAROLINE. / SOFTER RIDE** [–] [ ]

Apr 74. (7") *(6059 101)* **BREAK THE RULES. / LONELY NIGHT** [8] [–]

May 74. (lp/c) *(9102/7231 001) <3649>* **QUO** [2] [ ]
– Backwater / Just take me / Break the rules / Drifting away / Don't think it matters / Fine fine fine / Lonely man / Slow train. *(re-iss. Aug83 lp/c; PRICE/PRIMC 38)*

Vertigo Capitol

Nov 74. (7") *(6059 114) <4039>* **DOWN DOWN. / NIGHT RIDE** [1] [ ]

Feb 75. (lp/c) *(9102/7231 002) <11381>* **ON THE LEVEL** [1] [ ]
– Little lady / Most of the time / I saw the light / Over and done / Nightride / Down down / Broken man / What to do / Where I am / Bye bye Johnny. *(re-iss. Aug83 lp/c; PRICE/PRIMC 39) (cd-iss. Feb91; 848 175-2)*

Apr 75. (7") *<4125>* **BYE BYE JOHNNY. / DOWN DOWN** [–] [ ]

May 75. (7"ep) *(QUO 13)* **STATUS QUO LIVE! (live)** [9] [–]
– Roll over lay down / Gerdundula / Junior's wailing.

Feb 76. (7") *(6059 133)* **RAIN. / YOU LOST THE LOVE** [7] [ ]

Mar 76. (lp/c) *(9102/7231 006) <11509>* **BLUE FOR YOU** <US title 'STATUS QUO'> [1] [ ]
– Is there a better way / Mad about the boy / Ring of a change / Blue for you / Rain / Rolling home / That's a fact / Ease your mind / Mystery song. *(re-iss. Dec83 lp/c; PRICE/PRIMC 55)*

Jul 76. (7") *(6059 146)* **MYSTERY SONG. / DRIFTING AWAY** [11] [ ]

Dec 76. (7") *(6059 153)* **WILD SIDE OF LIFE. / ALL THROUGH THE NIGHT** [9] [ ]

Mar 77. (d-lp)(d-c) *(6641 580)(7599 171) <11623>* **LIVE! (live)** [3] [ ]
– Junior's wailing / (a) Backwater, (b) Just take me / Is there a better way / In my chair / Little lady / Most of the time / Forty-five hundred times / Roll over lay down / Big fat mama / Caroline / Bye bye Johnny / Rain / Don't waste my time / Roadhouse blues. *(re-iss. Sep84; d-lp/d-c; PRID/+C 5) (d-cd-iss. Feb92 & Aug98; 510 334-2)*

Oct 77. (7") *(6059 184)* **ROCKIN' ALL OVER THE WORLD. / RING OF A CHANGE** [3] [ ]

Nov 77. (lp)(c) *(9102 014)(7231 012) <11749>* **ROCKIN' ALL OVER THE WORLD** [5] [ ]
– Hard time / Can't give you more / Let's ride / Baby boy / You don't own me / Rockers rollin' / Rockin' all over the world / Who am I? / Too far gone / For you / Dirty water / Hold you back. *(re-iss. Aug85 lp/c; PRICE/PRIMC 87) (cd-iss. Feb91; 848 173-2)*

Aug 78. (7") *(QUO 1)* **AGAIN AND AGAIN. / TOO FAR GONE** [13] [–]

Oct 78. (lp)(c) *(9102 027)(7231 017)* **IF YOU CAN'T STAND THE HEAT** [3] [–]
– Again and again / I'm giving up my worryin' / Gonna teach you to love me / Someone show me home / Long legged Linda / Oh! what a night / Accident prone / Stones / Let me fly / Like a good girl. *(cd-iss. see-compilations)*

Nov 78. (7") *(QUO 2)* **ACCIDENT PRONE. / LET ME FLY** [36] [–]

Sep 79. (7") *(6059 242)* **WHATEVER YOU WANT. / HARD RIDE** [4] [–]

Oct 79. (lp)(c) *(9102 037)(7231 025)* **WHATEVER YOU WANT** [3] [–]
– Whatever you want / Shady lady / Who asked you / Your smiling face / Living on an island / Come rock with me / Rockin' on / Runaway / High flyer / Breaking away. *(cd-iss. see-compilations)*

Nov 79. (7") *(6059 248)* **LIVING ON AN ISLAND. / RUNAWAY** [16] [–]

Apr 80. (lp/c) *(QUO TV/MC 1)* **12 GOLD BARS** (compilation) [3] [–]
– Rockin' all over the world / Down down / Caroline / Paper plane / Break the rules / Again and again / Mystery song / Roll over lay down / Rain / The wild side of life / Whatever you want / Living on an island. *(cd-iss. Nov83; 800 062-2)*

Oct 80. (7") *(QUO 3)* **WHAT YOU'RE PROPOSIN'. / AB BLUES** [2] [–]

Oct 80. (lp/c) *(6302/7144 057)* **JUST SUPPOSIN'** [4] [–]
– What you're proposin' / Run to mummy / Don't drive my car / Lies / Over the edge / The wild ones / Name of the game / Coming and going / Rock'n'roll.

Dec 80. (7") *(QUO 4)* **DON'T DRIVE MY CAR. / LIES** [11] [–]

Feb 81. (7") *(QUO 5)* **SOMETHING 'BOUT YOU BABY I LIKE. / ENOUGH IS ENOUGH** [7] [–]

Mar 81. (lp/c) *(6302/7144 104)* **NEVER TOO LATE** [2] [–]
– Never too late / Something 'bout you baby I like / Take me away / Falling in falling out / Carol / Long ago / Mountain lady / Don't stop me now / Enough is enough / Riverside. *(cd-iss. Oct83; 800 053-2)*

Nov 81. (7"m) *(QUO 6)* **ROCK'N'ROLL. / HOLD YOU BACK / BACKWATER** [8] [–]

— **PETE KIRCHNER** – drums (ex-ORIGINAL MIRRORS, ex-HONEYBUS, etc.) repl. COUGHLAN who formed PARTNERS IN CRIME

Mar 82. (7") *(QUO 7)* **DEAR JOHN. / I WANT THE WORLD TO KNOW** [10] [–]

Apr 82. (lp/c) *(6302/7144 189)* **1+9+8+2** [1] [–]
– She don't fool me / Young pretender / Get out and walk / Jealousy / I love rock and roll / Resurrection / Dear John / Doesn't matter / I want the world to know / I should have known / Big man. *(cd-iss. Oct83; 800 035-2)*

Jun 82. (7") *(QUO 8)* **SHE DON'T FOOL ME. / NEVER TOO LATE** [36] [–]

Oct 82. (7"/7"pic-d) *(QUO/+P 10)* **CAROLINE (live). / DIRTY WATER (live)** [13] [–]
(12"+=) *(QUO 10-12)* – Down down (live).

Nov 82. (t-lp/3xlp-box) *(PRO LP/BX 1)* **FROM THE MAKERS OF . . .** (compilation & 2 lp-sides live) [4] [–]
– Pictures of matchstick men / Ice in the Sun / Down the dustpipe / In my chair / Junior's wailing / Mean girl / Gerdundula / Paper plane / Big fat mama / Roadhouse blues / Break the rules / Down down / Bye bye Johnny / Rain / Mystery song / Blue for you / Is there a better way / Again and again / Accident prone / The wild side of life / Living on an island / What you're proposing / Rock and roll / Something 'bout you baby I like / Dear John / Caroline / Roll over lay down / Backwater / Little lady / Don't drive my car / Whatever you want / Hold you back / Rockin' all over the world / Over the edge / Don't waste my time.

Sep 83. (7"/7"blue) *(QUO/+B 11)* **OL' RAG BLUES. / STAY THE NIGHT** [9] [–]
(ext.12"+=) *(QUO 11-12)* – Whatever you want (live).

Oct 83. (lp/c)(cd) *(VERH/+C 10)(814 662-2)* **BACK TO BACK** [9] [–]
– A mess of blues / Ol' rag blues / Can't be done / Too close to the ground / No contrast / Win or lose / Marguerita time / Your kind of love / Stay the night / Going down town tonight. *(cd re-iss. see-compilations)*

Oct 83. (7") *(QUO 12)* **A MESS OF BLUES. / BIG MAN** [15] [–]
(ext.12"+=) *(QUO 12-12)* – Young pretender.

Dec 83. (7"/7"pic-d) *(QUO/+P 14)* **MARGUERITA TIME. / RESURRECTION** [3] [–]
(d7"+=) *(QUO 14-14)* – Caroline / Joanne.

May 84. (7") *(QUO 15)* **GOING DOWN TOWN TONIGHT. / TOO CLOSE TO THE GROUND** 20 –

Oct 84. (7"/12"clear) *(QUO/+P 16)* **THE WANDERER. / CAN'T BE DONE** 7 –

Nov 84. (d-lp/c)(cd) *(QUO TV/MC 2)(822 985-2)* **12 GOLD BARS VOL.2** (compilation) 12 –
– What you're proposing / Lies / Something 'bout you baby I like / Don't drive my car / Dear John / Rock and roll / Ol' rag blues / Mess of the blues / Marguerita time / Going down town tonight / The wanderer. / (includes VOL.1).

— **ROSSI + PARFITT** enlisted **ANDY BOWN** – keyboards (ex-HERD) (He was p/t member since 1974) / **JEFF RICH** – drums (ex-CLIMAX BLUES BAND) repl. KIRCHNER / **RHINO EDWARDS** (r.n.JOHN) – bass (ex-CLIMAX BLUES BAND) repl. LANCASTER

May 86. (7"/7"sha-pic-d) *(QUO/+PD 18)* **ROLLIN' HOME. / LONELY** 9 –
(12"+=) *(QUO 18-12)* – Keep me guessing.

Jul 86. (7") *(QUO 19)* **RED SKY. / DON'T GIVE IT UP** 19 –
(12"+=)(12"w-poster+=) *(QUO 19-12)(QUOPB 19-1)* – The Milton Keynes medley (live).
(d7"+=) *(QUOPD 19)* – Marguerita time.

Aug 86. (lp/c)(cd) *(VERH/+C 36)(830 049-2)* **IN THE ARMY NOW** 7 –
– Rollin' home / Calling / In your eyes / Save me / In the army now / Dreamin' / End of the line / Invitation / Red sky / Speechless / Overdose.

Sep 86. (7"/7"pic-d) *(QUO/PD 20)* **IN THE ARMY NOW. / HEARTBURN** 2 –
(d7"+=) *(QUODP 20)* – Marguerita time / What you're proposin'.
('A'-military mix.12"+=) *(QUO 20-12)* – Late last night.

Nov 86. (7") *(QUO 21)* **DREAMIN'. / LONG-LEGGED GIRLS** 15 –
('A'-wet mix.12"+=) *(QUO 21-12)* – The Quo Christmas cake mix.

Mar 88. (7"/7"s) *(QUO/+H 22)* **AIN'T COMPLAINING. / THAT'S ALRIGHT** 19 –
(ext.12"+=) *(QUO 22-12)* – Lean machine.
(cd-s++=) *(QUOCD 22)* – In the army now (remix).

May 88. (7"/7"s) *(QUO/+H 23)* **WHO GETS THE LOVE?. / HALLOWEEN** 34 –
(ext.12"+=) *(QUO 23-12)* – The reason for goodbye.
(cd-s++=) *(QUOCD 23)* – The wanderer (Sharon the nag mix).

Jun 88. (lp/c)(cd) *(VERH/+C 58)(834 604-2)* **AIN'T COMPLAINING** 12 –
– Ain't complaining / Everytime I think of you / One for the money / Another shipwreck / Don't mind if I do / I know you're leaving / Cross that bridge / Cream of the crop / The loving game / Who gets the love? / Burning bridges / Magic.

— (Below single was a re-working of 'ROCKIN' ALL . . . ' for Sport Aid)

Aug 88. (7") *(QUAID 1)* **RUNNING ALL OVER THE WORLD. / MAGIC** 17 –
(12"+=) *(QUAID 1-12)* – ('A'extended).
(cd-s++=) *(QUACD 1)* – Whatever you want.

Nov 88. (7") *(QUO 25)* **BURNING BRIDGES (ON AND OFF AND ON AGAIN). / WHATEVER YOU WANT** 5 –
(ext.12"+=/cd-s+=) *(QUO 25-12/CD25)* – Marguerita time.

Oct 89. (7"/c-s) *(QUO/+MC 26)* **NOT AT ALL. / GONE THRU THE SLIPS** 50 –
(12"+=)(cd-s+=) *(QUO 26-12/CD26)* – Every time I think of you.

Nov 89. (lp/c/cd) *(842 098-1/-4/-2)* **PERFECT REMEDY** 49 –
– Little dreamer / Not at all / Heart on hold / Perfect remedy / Address book / The power of rock / The way I am / Tommy's in love / Man overboard / Going down for the first time / Throw her a line / 1,000 years. *(cd re-iss. Jan06 +=; 9834123)* – Gone thru the slips / Rotten to the bone / Doing it all for you / Dirty water (live) / The power of rock (edited version) / The anniversary waltz (7" version).

Dec 89. (7"/7"pic-d/c-s) *(QUO/+P/MC 27)* **LITTLE DREAMER. / ROTTEN TO THE BONE** –
(12"+=)(12"g-f+=/cd-s+=) *(QUO 27-12)(QUO X/CD 27)* – Doing it all for you.

Oct 90. (7"/7"silver/c-s) *(QUO/+G/MC 28)* **THE ANNIVERSARY WALTZ – (PART 1). / THE POWER OF ROCK** 2 –
(12"+=/cd-s+=) *(QUO 28-12/CD28)* – Perfect remedy.

Oct 90. (cd/c/d-lp) *(846 797-2/-4/-1)* **ROCKIN' ALL OVER THE YEARS** (compilation) 2 –
– Pictures of matchstick men / Ice in the Sun / Paper plane / Caroline / Break the rules / Down down / Roll over lay down / Rain / Wild side of life / Whatever you want / What you're proposing / Something 'bout you baby I like / Rock'n'roll / Dear John / Ol' rag blues / Marguerita time / The wanderer / Rollin' home / In the army now / Burning bridges / Anniversary waltz (part 1).

Dec 90. (7"/c-s) *(QUO/+MC 29)* **THE ANNIVERSARY WALTZ – (PART 2). / DIRTY WATER (live)** 16 –
(12"+=/cd-s+=) *(QUO 29-12/CD29)* – Pictures of matchstick men – Rock'n'roll music – Lover please – That'll be the day – Singing the blues.

Aug 91. (7"/c-s) *(QUO/+MC 30)* **CAN'T GIVE YOU MORE. / DEAD IN THE WATER** 37 –
(12"+=/cd-s+=) *(QUO 30-12/CD30)* – Mysteries from the ball.

Sep 91. (cd/c/lp) *(510 341-2/-4/-1)* **ROCK 'TIL YOU DROP** 10 –
– Like a zombie / All we really wanna do (Polly) / Fakin' the blues / One man band / Rock 'til you drop / Can't give you more / Warning shot / Let's work together / Bring it on home / No problems. *(cd+=/c+=)* – Good sign / Tommy / Nothing comes easy / Fame or money / Price of love / Forty-five hundred times. *(re-iss. Feb93)*

Jan 92. (7"/c-s) *(QUO/+MC 32)* **ROCK 'TIL YOU DROP. / Awards Medley:- CAROLINE – DOWN DOWN – WHATEVER YOU WANT – ROCKIN' ALL OVER THE WORLD** 38 –
(12"+=/cd-s+=) *(QUO 32-12/CD32)* – Forty-five hundred times.

Polydor not iss.

Oct 92. (7"/c-s) *(QUO/+MC 33)* **ROADHOUSE MEDLEY (ANNIVERSARY WALTZ 25). / ('A'extended)** 21 –
(cd-s+=) *(QUOCD 33)* – (A'mix).
(cd-s+=) *(QUODD 33)* – Don't drive my car.

Nov 92. (cd/c/lp) *(517 367-2/-4/-1)* **LIVE ALIVE QUO (live)** 37 –
– Roadhouse medley:- Roadhouse blues – The wanderer – Marguerita time – Living on an island – Break the rules – Something 'bout you baby I like – The price of love – Roadhouse blues / Whatever you want / In the army now / Burning bridges / Rockin' all over the world / Caroline / Don't drive my car / Hold you back / Little lady.

— In May 94; their 'BURNING BRIDGES' tune, was used for Manchester United Football Squad's UK No.1 'Come On You Reds'.

Jul 94. (7"colrd/c-s) *(QUO/+MC 34)* **I DIDN'T MEAN IT. / WHATEVER YOU WANT** 21 –
(cd-s+=) *(QUODD 34)* – Down down / Rockin' all over the world.
(cd-s) *(QUOCD 34)* – ('A'side) / ('A'-Hooligan version) / Survival / She knew too much.

Aug 94. (cd/c/lp) *(523607-2/-4/-1)* **THIRSTY WORK** 13 –
– Goin' nowhere / I didn't mean it / Confidence / Point of no return / Sail away / Like it or not / Soft in the head / Queenie / Lover of the human race / Sherri don't fail me now! / Rude awakening time / Back on my feet / Restless / Ciao ciao / Tango / Sorry.

Oct 94. (7"colrd/c-s) *(QUO/+MC 35)* **SHERRI DON'T FAIL ME NOW!. / BEAUTIFUL** 38 –
(cd-s+=) *(QUOCD 34)* – In the army now.
(cd-s) *(QUODD 34)* – ('A'side) / Tossin' and turnin' / Down to you.

Nov 94. (7"/c-s/cd-s) *(QUO/+MC/CD 36)* **RESTLESS (re-orchestrated). / AND I DO** 39 –

PolygramTV not iss.

Oct 95. (7"/c-s) *(577 512-7/-4)* **WHEN YOU WALK IN THE ROOM. / TILTING AT THE MILL** 34 –
(cd-s+=) *(577 512-2)* – ('A'version).

Feb 96. (7"/c-s; STATUS QUO with The BEACH BOYS) *(576 262-7/-4)* **FUN FUN FUN. / MORTIFIED** 24 –
(cd-s+=) *(576 262-2)* – ('A'mix).
below album features all covers. They sued Radio One for not playing the above hit on their playlist after it charted. The QUO finally lose out in court and faced costs of over £50,000.

Feb 96. (cd/c) *(531 035-2/-4)* **DON'T STOP** 2 –
– Fun, fun, fun (with The BEACH BOYS) / When you walk in the room / I can hear the grass grow / You never can tell (it was a teenage wedding) / Get back / Safety dance / Raining in my heart (with BRIAN MAY) / Don't stop / Sorrow / Proud Mary / Lucille / Johnny and Mary / Get out of enver / The future's so bright (I gotta wear shades) / All around my hat (with MADDY PRIOR).

Apr 96. (7"/c-s) *(576 634-7/-4)* **DON'T STOP. / TEMPORARY FRIEND** 35 –
(cd-s+=) *(576 635-2)* – ('A'extended).

Oct 96. (7"/c-s; STATUS QUO with MADDY PRIOR) *(575 944-7/-4)* **ALL AROUND MY HAT. / I'LL NEVER GET OVER YOU** 47 –
(cd-s+=) *(575 945-2)* – Get out of Denver.

— FRANCIS ROSSI also issued solo releases, the album 'KING OF THE DOGHOUSE' was out in Sept'96

Eagle Spitfire

Mar 99. (c-s) *(EAGCS 075)* **THE WAY IT GOES / UNDER THE INFLUENCE** [39] [–]
(cd-s) *(EAGXS 075)* – ('A'side) / Sea cruise.

Mar 99. (cd/c) *(EAG CD/MC 076)* *<5035>* **UNDER THE INFLUENCE** [26] Jul99 [ ]
– Twenty wild horses / Under the influence / Round and round / Shine on / Little white lies / Keep 'em coming / Little me and you / Making waves / Blessed are the meek / Roll the dice / Not fade away.

May 99. (c-s) *(EAGCS 101)* **LITTLE WHITE LIES / I KNEW THE BRIDE** [47] [–]
(cd-s+=) *(EAGXS 101)* – Pictures of matchstick men (1999).

Sep 99. (c-s) *(EAGCS 105)* **TWENTY WILD HORSES / ANALYSE TIME** [53] [–]
(cd-s+=) *(EAGXS 105)* – Destruction day.

Universal Universal

Apr 00. (cd/c) *(157814-2/-4)* **FAMOUS IN THE LAST CENTURY** [19] [–]
– Famous in the last century / Old time rock'n'roll / Way down / Rave on / Roll over Beethoven / When I'm dead and gone / Memphis Tennessee / Sweet home Chicago / Crawling from the wreckage / Good golly Miss Molly / Claudette / Rock'n'me / Hound dog / Runaround Sue / Once bitten twice shy / Mony mony / Famous in the last century (reprise).

May 00. (c-s) *(158013-4)* **MONY MONY / FAMOUS IN THE LAST CENTURY (extended)** [48] [–]
(cd-s+=) *(158013-2)* – Gerundula (live).

Aug 02. (cd-s) *(019234-2)* **JAM SIDE DOWN / THE MADNESS / JAM SIDE DOWN (video)** [17] [–]
(cd-s) *(019235-2)* – ('A'side) / Down down (rec. at Top Of The Pops 2) / Rockin' all over the world (rec. at Top Of The Pops 2).

Sep 02. (cd) *(018790-2)* *<64435>* **HEAVY TRAFFIC** [15] [ ]
– Blues and rhythm / All stand up (never say never) / The Oriental / Heavy traffic / Solid gold / Green / Jam side down / Diggin' Burt Bacharach / Do it again / Another day / I don't remember anymore / Rhythm of life.

Oct 02. (cd-s) *(019487-2)* **ALL STAND UP (NEVER SAY NEVER) / YOU LET ME DOWN / ALL STAND UP (NEVER SAY NEVER) (video)** [51] [–]

Nov 03. (cd) *(9813910)* **RIFFS** (covers, etc.) [44] [–]
– Caroline / I fought the law / Born to be wild / Takin' care of business / Wild one / On the road again / Tobacco road / Centerfold / All day and all of the night / Don't bring me down / Junior's wailing / Pump it up / Down the dustpipe / Whatever you want / Rockin' all over the world. *(ltd cd w/ dvd+=; 9813909)*

Sep 04. (7"pic-d) *(9868066)* **YOU'LL COME 'ROUND. / LUCINDA** [14] [–]
(cd-s+=) *(9868038)* – Down down (live at Montreux Jazz Festival).

Sep 04. (d-cd) *(9824883)* **XS ALL AREAS – THE GREATEST HITS** (compilation) [16] [–]
– Caroline / Down down / Paper plane / Big fat mama / Roll over lay down / Softer ride / Don't waste my time / Little lady / Mystery song / Rain / Break the rules / Something about you baby I like / Hold you back / Rockin' all over the world / Whatever you want / Don't drive my car / Again and again / 4500 times / All stand up // You'll come 'round / Thinking of you / Jam side down / Creepin' up on you / Down the dustpipe / Pictures of matchstick men / Ice in the sun / In my chair / Gerdundula / Wild side of life / Rock'n'roll / What you're proposin' / The wanderer / Livin' on an island / Marguerita time / In the army now / When you walk in the room / Burning bridges / Fun fun fun / Old time rock and roll / Anniversary waltz part 1.

Nov 04. (7"pic-d) *(9825823)* **THINKING OF YOU. / SOMETHING 'BOUT YOU BABY I LIKE – BREAK THE RULES (live at Montreux)** [21] [–]
(cd-s) *(9825824)* – ('A') / Mystery medley (live at Montreux Jazz Festival) / (interview).
(dvd-s) *(9825822)* – ('A'-video) / You'll come 'round (video).

Sanctuary not iss.

Sep 05. (7") *(SANSE 400)* **THE PARTY AIN'T OVER YET. / GERDUNDULA (live)** [11] [–]
(cd-s) *(SANXS 400)* – ('A') / I'm watching over you.
(dvd-s) *(SANDX 400)* – ('A'-video) / ('A'-radio mix) / ('A').

Sep 05. (cd) *(SANCD 389)* **THE PARTY AIN'T OVER YET** [18] [–]
– The party ain't over yet / Gotta get up and go / All that counts is love / Familiar blues / The bubble / Belavista man / Nevashooda / Velvet train / Goodbye baby / You never stop / Kick me when I'm down / Cupid stupid / This is me.

Oct 05. (cd-s) *(SANXS 413)* **ALL THAT COUNTS IS LOVE / I AIN'T READY** [29] [–]
(cd-s) *(SANXD 413)* – ('A') / Belavista man (live at Emden) / The party ain't over yet (live at Emden).

– compilations, etc. –

Dec 69. (lp) *Marble Arch; (MALS 1193)* **STATUS QUOTATIONS** [ ] [–]

Mar 73. (7") *Pye; (7N 45229) / <65017>* **MEAN GIRL. / EVERYTHING** [20] [ ]

May 73. (lp/c) *Pye; (NSPL/ZCP 18402)* **THE BEST OF STATUS QUO** [32] [–]
– Down the dustpipe / Gerdundula / In my chair / Umleitung / Lakky lady / Daughter / Railroad / Tune to the music / April, Spring, Summer and Wednesdays / Mean girl / Spinning wheel blues. *(cd-iss. 1986 on 'P.R.T.'; CDNSP 7773)*

Jun 73. (lp/c) *Golden Hour; (GH/ZCGH 556)* **A GOLDEN HOUR OF . . .** [ ] [–]
(re-iss. Apr90 on 'Knight' cd/c; KGH CD/MC 110)

Jul 73. (7") *Pye; (7N 45253)* **GERDUNDULA. / LAKKY LADY** [ ] [–]

1975. (lp) *Starline;* **ROCKIN' AROUND WITH** [ ] [–]

Oct 75. (lp/c) *Golden Hour; (GH/ZCGH 604)* **DOWN THE DUSTPIPE: THE GOLDEN HOUR OF . . . VOL.2** [20] [–]

Sep 76. (lp/c) *Pye; (PKL/ZCPKB 5546)* **THE REST OF STATUS QUO** [ ] [–]

Jan 77. (lp/c) *Pye; (FILD 005)* **THE STATUS QUO FILE SERIES** [ ] [–]
(re-iss. Sep79 on 'P.R.T.';)

Apr 77. (12"ep) *Pye; (BD 103)* **DOWN THE DUSTPIPE / MEAN GIRL. / IN MY CHAIR / GERDUNDULA** [ ] [–]

Apr 78. (lp) *Hallmark; (HMA 257)* **PICTURES OF MATCHSTICK MEN** [ ] [–]

May 78. (lp)(c) *Marble Arch; (HMA 260)(HSC 322)* **STATUS QUO** [ ] [–]

Aug 78. (d-lp/d-c) *Pickwick; (PDA/PDC 046)* **THE STATUS QUO COLLECTION** [ ] [–]

May 79. (7"yellow) *Flashback-Pye; (FBS 2)* **PICTURES OF MATCHSTICK MEN. / DOWN IN THE DUSTPIPE** [ ] [–]
(re-iss. 7"black Apr83 on 'Old Gold'; OG 9298)

Jun 79. (lp,orange-lp/c) *Pye; (NPSL/ZCP 18607)* **JUST FOR THE RECORD** [ ] [–]

Jun 80. (d-lp/d-c) *P.R.T.; (SPOT/ZCSPT 1028)* **SPOTLIGHT ON . . .** [ ] [–]

Sep 80. (d-lp/d-c) *Pickwick; (SSD/+C 8035)* **STATUS QUO** [ ] [–]

Oct 81. (10"lp/c) *P.R.T.; (DOW/ZCDOW 2)* **FRESH QUOTA** (rare) [74] [–]

Jun 82. (c) *P.R.T.; (ZCTON 101)* **100 MINUTES OF . . .** [ ] [–]

Jul 82. (7") *Old Gold; (OG 9142)* **MEAN GIRL. / IN MY CHAIR** [ ] [–]

Oct 82. (lp/c) *P.R.T.; (SPOT/ZCSPT 1028)* **SPOTLIGHT ON . . . VOL.II** [ ] [–]

Apr 83. (lp/c) *Contour; (CN/+4 2062)* **TO BE OR NOT TO BE** [ ] [–]
(cd-iss. Apr91 on 'Pickwick'; PWKS 4051P)

Jul 83. (10"lp/c) *P.R.T.; (DOW/ZCDOW 10)* **WORKS** [ ] [–]

Jul 84. (lp/c) *Vertigo; (818 947-2/-4)* **LIVE AT THE N.E.C. (live)** [83] Dutch [–]
(UK cd-iss. Jul91; 818 947-2)

Sep 85. (7") *Old Gold; (OG 9566)* **CAROLINE. / DOWN DOWN** [ ] [–]

Oct 85. (lp/c) *Flashback; (FBLP/ZCFBL 8082)* **NA NA NA** [ ] [–]

Nov 85. (7") *Old Gold; (OG 9567)* **ROCKIN' ALL OVER THE WORLD. / PAPER PLANE** [ ] [–]
(re-iss. Aug89 & Sep90)

Nov 85. (d-lp/c) *Castle; (CCS LP/MC 114)* **THE COLLECTION** [ ] [–]
(cd-iss. 1988; CCSCD 114)

Oct 87. (lp/c/cd) *P.R.T.; (PYL/PYM/PYC 6024)* **QUOTATIONS VOL.1 – (THE EARLY YEARS)** [ ] [–]

Oct 87. (lp/c/cd) *P.R.T.; (PYL/PYM/PYC 6025)* **QUOTATIONS VOL.2 – (ALTERNATIVES)** [ ] [–]

Sep 88. (lp/pic-lp/c/cd) *P.R.T.; (PYZ/PYX/PYM/PYC 4007)* **FROM THE BEGINNING (1966-67)** [ ] [–]

Apr 89. (c)(cd) *Legacy; (C 903)(GHCD 3)* **C90 COLLECTOR** [ ] [–]

Sep 90. (cd/c/d-lp) *Castle; (CCS CD/MC/LP 271)* **B SIDES AND RARITIES** [ ] [–]

Dec 90. (3xcd-box/3xlp-box) *Essential; (ESS CD/LP 136)* **THE EARLY WORKS** [ ] [–]

Feb 91. (cd) *Vertigo; (848 087-2)* **WHATEVER YOU WANT / JUST SUPPOSIN'** [ ] [–]

Feb 91. (cd) *Vertigo; (848 088-2)* **NEVER TOO LATE / BACK TO BACK** [ ] [–]

Feb 91. (cd) *Vertigo; (848 089-2)* **QUO / BLUE FOR YOU** [ ] [–]
(re-iss. Sep97; same)

Feb 91.	(cd) *Vertigo; (848 090-2)* **IF YOU CAN'T STAND THE HEAT / 1+9+8+2**		-
Sep 91.	(d-cd) *Decal; (CDLIK 81)* **BACK TO THE BEGINNING**		-
Nov 91.	(cd) *Pickwick; (PWKS 4087P)* **THE BEST OF STATUS QUO 1972-1986**		-
May 93.	(cd/c) *Spectrum; (550002-2/-4)* **A FEW BARS MORE**		-
Feb 94.	(cd) *Dojo; (EARLD 8)* **THE EARLY YEARS**		-
Aug 94.	(cd/c) *Matchstick; (MAT CD/MC 291)* **STATUS QUO**		-
Sep 94.	(cd/c) *Spectrum; (550190-2/-4)* **IT'S ONLY ROCK'N'ROLL**		-
Mar 95.	(cd) *Connoisseur; (VSOPCD 213)* **THE OTHER SIDE OF STATUS QUO**		-
May 95.	(cd/c) *Spectrum; (550727-2/-4)* **PICTURES OF MATCHSTICK MEN**		-
Jun 95.	(cd/c) *Savanna; (SSL CD/MC 204)* **ICE IN THE SUN** *(re-iss. Apr97 on 'Pulse' cd/c; PLS CD/MC 206)*		-
Jul 96.	(cd/c) *Truetrax; (TRT CD/MC 198)* **THE BEST OF STATUS QUO**		-
Oct 97.	(d-cd/d-c) *Polygram TV; (553507-2/-4)* **WHATEVER YOU WANT – THE VERY BEST OF**	13	-
Mar 99.	(cd) *Castle Select; (SELCD 555)* **MATCHSTICK MEN – THE PSYCHEDELIC YEARS**		-
Mar 99.	(cd) *Spectrum; (554891-2)* **THE ESSENTIAL STATUS QUO VOL.1**		-
Aug 99.	(cd) *Spectrum; (554896-2)* **THE ESSENTIAL STATUS QUO VOL.2**		-
Aug 99.	(cd) *Castle Pie; (PIESD 005)* **ICE IN THE SUN**		-
Feb 00.	(cd) *Spectrum; (554897-2)* **THE ESSENTIAL STATUS QUO VOL.3**		-
Jul 00.	(cd) *Delta No.10; (CD 23106)* **ROCKIN' ALL OVER THE WORLD**		-
Sep 00.	(d-cd) *Castle; (CCSCD 821)* **THE SINGLES COLLECTION 1968-1972**		-

☐ STEALERS WHEEL (see under ⇒ RAFFERTY, Gerry)

STEELY DAN

Formed: New York, USA . . . by DONALD FAGEN and WALTER BECKER, initially as a writing partnership after leaving Bard's college in 1969. At the turn of the decade the pair toured with JAY & THE AMERICANS as backing musicians as well as recording a soundtrack for the movie, 'YOU GOTTA WALK IT LIKE YOU TALK IT' (starring Richard Pryor). Attempts to hawk their songs to Big Apple publishers proved fruitless however and it was only through meeting independent producer Gary Katz that the duo found their way into a staff job at L.A.'s 'Dunhill-ABC' label. Katz was also the catalyst for what would become STEELY DAN, a studio outfit comprising FAGEN, BECKER, vocalist DAVID PALMER, DENNY DIAS (a rhythm guitarist with whom they'd previously recorded early demos), ex-HOLY MODAL ROUNDERS guitarist, JEFF 'SKUNK' BAXTER and drummer JIM HODDER, famously naming themselves after a steam-powered(!) dildo in William Burroughs' novel, 'Naked Lunch'. Although a debut single, 'DALLAS', made little impact, the simmering latin-funk rock of 'DO IT AGAIN' made the US Top 10. It also introduced FAGEN's inimitable lyrical wit, a cynical DLYAN-esque worldview which mocked L.A.'s pretensions and would see STEELY DAN hailed as one of the most cuttingly accurate commentators of the 70's. 'CAN'T BUY A THRILL' (1973) nailed the point home with consummate ease, laying down the jazz-rooted, FM-slick blueprint that was endlessly tweaked, polished and perfected with each successive album. The enduring 'REELIN' IN THE YEARS' was lifted as a second single and gave the group another major hit, the track's searing guitar solo, as with 'KINGS', provided by session man, ELLIOTT RANDALL; if there was one critical niggle it was that PALMER couldn't always carry the subtle insinuations of the lyrics. BECKER and FAGEN subsequently took up the task themselves on 'COUNTDOWN TO ECSTACY' (1973), combining even more opaque themes with densely layered, immaculately executed musicianship. Without the help of a hit single, however, the record only just made the Top 40; 'RIKKI DON'T LOSE THAT NUMBER' redressed the balance in fine style, a gorgeously lovelorn Top 5 hit inspired by a HORACE SILVER piano riff and a track which formed the centrepiece of 'PRETZEL LOGIC' (1974). More obviously jazz-influenced (included was a droll cover of Duke Ellington's 'EAST ST. LOUIS TOODLE-OO', while 'PARKER'S BAND' was a tribute to be-bop legend, CHARLIE PARKER) yet more immediately accessible, the album further enhanced their reputation among rock/pop connoisseurs. And it was a reputation that mushroomed without the PR of touring, BECKER and FAGEN refusing to play live after 1974 – although a tour was planned to promote the forthcoming 'KATY LIED' (1975), the idea was abandoned in its early stages. With STEELY DAN now basically a studio entity, both HODDER and BAXTER departed, the latter joining The DOOBIE BROTHERS (ironically enough, an easy rocking, all-American, all-touring hit machine that was essentially the antithesis of the whole SD concept). Coincidentally, BAXTER's replacement was MICHAEL McDONALD, a silky voiced future DOOBIES mentor whose harmony vocals helped sweeten the bite of the aforementioned 'KATY..'. 1976's 'THE ROYAL SCAM' was even more scathing in its lyrical ferocity, taking no prisoners in its portrayal of American society's inherent hypocrisy and monetary greed. But if the sentiments were getting darker, the music was getting slicker; by this point, BECKER and FAGAN were employing the cream of the city's session musicians, recording 'AJA' (1977) in numerous different studios and endlessly remixing it prior to release. Painstakingly crafted but rarely overdone, 'AJA' – for many fans and critics alike – remains the definitive STEELY DAN opus, its dense, lush arrangements rewarding repeated listening. It was also their best seller, a transatlantic Top 5 (at the height of punk in the UK) later plundered by hip hopper's DE LA SOUL ('PEG'), Scotland's very own DEACON BLUE even taking their name from one of its tracks. With 'A.B.C.' coming under the auspices of 'M.C.A.', legal problems led to a three year wait for the final album of STEELY DAN's career, 'GAUCHO' (1980). Criticised for what many detractors saw as cloying slickness, the record was nevertheless another masterstroke of detached observation; the likes of 'BABYLON SISTERS' and 'GLAMOUR PROFESSION' were aimed squarely at the decadence of L.A.'s showbiz elite while 'THIRD WORLD MAN' remains one of the most haunting STEELY DAN compositions. After more than a decade of living in each other's pocket, BECKER and FAGAN parted company; while BECKER went into production, FAGAN penned a solo masterpiece in 'THE NIGHTFLY' (1982), trading in irony for surprisingly upbeat youthful reminiscences. The album's critical and commercial success didn't seem to spur him on to further glories, however, an incredible eleven year gap preceding a belated 90's follow-up, 'KAMAKIRIAD'. FAGAN returned BECKER's production favour on the latter's one and only solo effort, 'ELEVEN TRACKS OF WHACK' (1994), a hard-bitten affair borne of the kind of narcotic strife which would've finished a lesser talent. After appearing live as part of the New York Rock and Soul Revue in the early 90's, BECKER and FAGEN finally reformed STEELY DAN for a series of feverishly anticipated US live dates. Documented on 1995's 'ALIVE IN AMERICA' alive, the tour was an unqualified success despite the duo's misgivings. As the success of the live shows might've predicted, fresh studio set 'TWO AGAINST NATURE' (2000) was a belated comeback well worth waiting for. All the STEELY DAN trademarks – painstakingly crafted arrangements, luxuriant sonic textures, obliquely witty lyrics – were in present and correct, BECKER and FAGEN sounding like their partnership hadn't been interrupted for a single day never mind two decades. Like almost all their works, this was also an album which rewarded the repeated listening necessary to uncover the manifold layers of subtle meaning, shading and tone. Thankfully, fans didn't have to wait another generation for the release of a second latter day studio set. Basically, 'EVERYTHING MUST GO' (2003) continued in a similar vein to its predecessor (it also had nothing whatsoever to do with the MANIC STREET PREACHERS), albeit with a more relaxed vibe and production than any album in their immaculately crafted career. BECKER even made his lead vocal debut, more than thirty years after starting the band, an interesting development even if it was never going to threaten FAGEN's still masterfully insinuating croon. His average of one solo album per decade (all part of his "life trilogy") might make GUNS N' ROSES look prolific, but at least FAGEN fans know those long years have been spent ruminating, digesting, analysing and, most importantly, perfecting. On 'MORPH THE CAT' (2006) his voice sounded as creamy, his lyrics as sardonically savvy and his sophisti-funk as 70s-rooted as they'd ever done. It's this genius for delivering often heavy sentiment – the shifting reality of post-9/11 New York being an obvious source – in horizontally laid-back packaging that's kept fans on board for all these years, even if the record's US/UK Top 30/40 placings were unusually disappointing.

• **Trivia:** In 1985, BECKER produced CHINA CRISIS' album 'Flaunt The Imperfection'.

Album rating: Walter Becker & Donald Fagen: YOU GOTTA WALK IT LIKE YOU TALK IT.. soundtrack (*5) / Steely Dan: CAN'T BUY A THRILL (*8) / COUNTDOWN TO ECSTASY (*8) / PRETZEL LOGIC (*9) / KATY LIED (*8) / THE ROYAL SCAM (*6) / AJA (*8) / GREATEST HITS compilation (*9) / GAUCHO (*6) / STEELY DAN GOLD compilation (*8) / REELIN' IN THE YEARS – THE VERY BEST compilation (*9) / ALIVE IN AMERICA (*4) / TWO AGAINST NATURE (*8) / EVERYTHING MUST GO (*6) / SHOWBIZ KIDS: THE STEELY DAN STORY 1972-1980 double compilation (*8) / Donald Fagen: THE NIGHTFLY (*6) / KAMAKIRIAD (*7) / MORPH THE CAT (*7) / Walter Becker: ELEVEN TRACKS OF WHACK (*5)

WALTER BECKER & DONALD FAGEN

WALTER BECKER (b.20 Feb'50, New York) – bass, vocals / **DONALD FAGEN** (b.10 Jan'48, Passaic, New Jersey) – keyboards, vocals

Visa — not iss.

1971. (lp) *<IMP 7005>* **YOU GOTTA WALK IT LIKE YOU TALK IT** (soundtrack) [–] [ ]
– You gotta walk it like you talk it / Flotsam and jetsam / War and peace / Roll back the meaning / You gotta walk it like you talk it – reprise / Dog eat dog / Red giant – White dwarf / If it rains. *(UK-iss.Mar78 on 'Spark'; SRLP 124) (cd-iss. Sep92 on 'See For Miles'; SEECD 357)*

STEELY DAN

FAGEN + BECKER added **DAVID PALMER** – vocals (ex-MIDDLE CLASS) / **DENNY DIAS** – rhythm guitar / **JEFF BAXTER** – guitar (ex-HOLY MODAL ROUNDERS) / **JIM HODDER** – drums (ex-BEAD GAME)

Probe — A.B.C.

Sep 72. (7") *(PRO 562) <11323>* **DALLAS. / SAIL THE WATERWAY** [ ] [ ]

Nov 72. (7") *(PRO 577) <11338>* **DO IT AGAIN. / FIRE IN THE HOLE** [ ] [6]
(re-iss. Sep75 on 'A.B.C.'; 4075); hit UK No.39

Jan 73. (lp) *(SPB 1062) <758>* **CAN'T BUY A THRILL** [ ] Nov72 [17]
– Do it again / Dirty work / Kings / Midnite cruiser / Only a fool would say that / Reeling in the years / Fire in the hole / Brooklyn (owes the charmer and me) / Change of the guard / Turn that heartbreak over again. *(re-iss. Sep75 on 'A.B.C.' lp/c; ABCL/+C 5034); hit UK No.38) (re-iss. 1983 on 'M.C.A.' lp/c; MCL/+C 1769) (cd-iss. Jul88; DMCL 1769) (cd re-iss. Apr92; MCLD 19017) (cd re-iss. Mar00 on 'M.C.A.'; 111886-2)*

Mar 73. (7") *(PRO 587) <11352>* **REELING IN THE YEARS. / ONLY A FOOL WOULD SAY THAT** [ ] [11]

— **BECKER & FAGEN** now on lead vocals, when PALMER left to BIG WHA-KOO

Jul 73. (7") *(PRO 602) <11382>* **SHOWBIZ KIDS. / RAZOR BOY** [ ] [61]

Jul 73. (lp) *(SPB 1079) <779>* **COUNTDOWN TO ECSTACY** [ ] [35]
– Bodhizattva / Razor boy / The Boston rag / Your gold teeth / Showbiz kids / My old school / Pearl of the quarter / King of the world. *(re-iss. Feb82 on 'M.C.A.' lp/c; MCL/+C 1654) (re-iss. Jul83 on 'Fame' lp/c; FA/TC-FA 3069) (cd-iss. Dec88; DMCL 1654) (cd re-iss. Apr92; MCLD 19018) (cd re-iss. Mar00 on 'M.C.A.'; 111887-2)*

Oct 73. (7") *(PRO 606) <11396>* **MY OLD SCHOOL. / PEARL OF THE QUARTER** [ ] [63]

Mar 74. (lp) *(SPBA 6282) <808>* **PRETZEL LOGIC** [37] [8]
– Rikki don't lose that number / Night by night / Any major dude will tell you / Barrytown / East St.Louis toodle-oo / Parker's bad / Through with buzz / Pretzel logic / With a gun / Charlie Freak / Monkey in your soul. *(re-iss. Oct74 on 'A.B.C.' lp/c; ABCL/+C 5045) (re-iss. Feb84 on 'M.C.A.' lp/c; MCL/+C 1781) (cd-iss. Aug88 on 'M.C.A.; DIDX 371) (cd re-iss. May90; DMCL 1781) (cd re-iss. Jun92; MCLD 19081) (cd re-iss. Mar00 on 'M.C.A.'; 111917-2)*

May 74. (7") *(PRO 622) <11439>* **RIKKI DON'T LOSE THAT NUMBER. / ANY MAJOR DUDE WILL TELL YOU** [ ] [4]
(re-iss. Oct78 on 'A.B.C.'; ABC 4241); hit UK No.58

A.B.C. — A.B.C.

Oct 74. (7") *(ABC 4019) <12033>* **PRETZEL LOGIC. / THROUGH WITH BUZZ** [ ] [57]

— **MICHAEL McDONALD** (b.12 Feb'52, St. Louis, Missouri) – keyboards, vocals repl. BAXTER to DOOBIE BROTHERS / **JEFF PORCARO** (b. 1 Apr'54) – drums repl. HODDER

Apr 75. (lp/c) *(ABCL/+C 5094) <846>* **KATY LIED** [13] [13]
– Black Friday / Bad sneakers / Rose darling / Daddy don't live in that New York City no more / Doctor Wu / Everyone's gone to the movies / Your gold teeth II / Chain lightning / Any world (that I'm welcome to) / Throw back the little ones. *(re-iss. Jun84 on 'M.C.A.' lp/c; MCL/+C 1800) (cd-iss. Aug88; DIDX 373) (cd re-iss. Sep90 & Jun92; MCLD 19082) (cd re-iss. Mar00 on 'M.C.A.'; 111916-2)*

May 75. (7") *(ABC 4058) <12101>* **BLACK FRIDAY. / THROW BACK THE LITTLE ONES** [ ] [37]

Sep 75. (7") *<12128>* **BAD SNEAKERS. / CHAIN LIGHTNING** [–] [ ]

— When McDONALD joined DOOBIE BROTHERS and PORCARO left later joining TOTO, **BECKER & FAGEN** employed session people incl. **DENNY DIAS** part-time

May 76. (lp/c) *(ABCL/+C 5161)* **THE ROYAL SCAM** [11] [15]
– Kid Charlemagne / Caves of Altamira / Don't take me alive / Sign in stranger / The fez / Green earrings / Haitian divorce / Everything you did / The royal scam. *(re-iss. Sep82 on 'M.C.A.' lp/c; MCL/+C 1708) (cd-iss. Aug88; DIDX 370) (cd re-iss. Sep91 & Jun92; MCLD 19083) (cd re-iss. Apr00 on 'M.C.A.'; 811708-2)*

May 76. (7") *(ABC 4124) <12195>* **KID CHARLEMAGNE. / GREEN EARRINGS** [ ] [82]

Sep 76. (7") *<12222>* **THE FEZ. / SIGN IN STRANGER** [–] [59]

Nov 76. (7") *(ABC 4152)* **HAITIAN DIVORCE. / SIGN IN STRANGER** [17] [–]

Sep 77. (lp/c) *(ABCL/+C 5225) <1006>* **AJA** [5] [3]
– Black cow / Aja / Deacon blues / Peg / Home at last / I got the news / Josie. *(re-iss. 1983 on 'M.C.A.' lp/c; MCL/+C 1745) (cd-iss. 1985; DIDX 55) (cd re-iss. Sep91 & Jul92; MCLD 19145) (cd re-iss. Apr00 on 'M.C.A.'; 811745-2)*

Nov 77. (7") *(ABC 4207) <12320>* **PEG. / I GOT THE NEWS** [ ] [11]

Apr 78. (7"/12") *(ABC/+12 4217) <12355>* **DEACON BLUES. / HOME AT LAST** [ ] Mar78 [19]

Aug 78. (7") *<12404>* **JOSIE. / BLACK COW** [–] [26]

M.C.A. — M.C.A.

Jul 78. (7") *(MCA 374) <40894>* **FM (NO STATIC AT ALL). / FM (Reprise)** [49] May78 [22]

Nov 80. (lp/c) *(ABCD/+C 616) <6102>* **GAUCHO** [27] [9]
– Babylon sisters / Hey nineteen / Glamour profession / Gaucho / Time out of mind / My rival / Third world man. *(cd-iss. Jan85; DIDX 56) (re-iss. Sep86 lp/c; MCL/+C 1814) (cd re-iss. Sep91 & Jul92; MCLD 19146)*

Nov 80. (7") *(MCA 659) <51036>* **HEY NINETEEN. / BODHISATTVA (live)** [ ] [10]

Mar 81. (7") *(MCA 680)* **BABYLON SISTERS. / TIME OUT OF MIND** [ ] [–]

Mar 81. (7") *<51082>* **TIME OUT OF MIND. / BODHISATTVA** [–] [22]

— Parted ways after album. FAGEN went solo and BECKER to production.

STEELY DAN

DONALD FAGEN

Warners Warners

Oct 82. (lp/c) *(923696-1/-4)* <23696> **THE NIGHTFLY** [44] [11]
– New frontier / Walk between the raindrops / Maxine / Green flower street / The goodbye look / The nightfly / I.G.Y. (what a wonderful world). *(cd-iss. Jul88; 923696-2)*

Oct 82. (7") *(W 9900)* <29900> **I.G.Y. (WHAT A WONDERFUL WORLD). / WALK BETWEEN THE RAINDROPS** [ ] [26]

Jan 83. (7") *(W 9792)* <29792> **NEW FRONTIER. / MAXINE** [ ] [70]
(12"+=) *(W 9792T)* – The goodbye look.

Apr 83. (7") *(W 9674)* **RUBY BABY. / WALK BETWEEN THE RAINDROPS** [ ] [–]
(below single from the film 'Bright Lights, Big City')

Apr 88. (7") *(W 7972)* <27972> **CENTURY'S END. / SHANGHAI CONFIDENTIAL (instrumental)** [ ] Mar88 [83]
(3"cd-s+=) *(W 7972CD)* – The nightfly / The goodbye look.

— with **WALTER BECKER** – bass, solo guitar, co-writer some / **GEORGE WADENIUS** – guitar / **PAUL GRIFFIN** – hamond organ / **LEROY CLOUDEN or CHRISTOPHER PARKER** – drums / **BASHIRI JOHNSON** – percussion / **RANDY BRECKER + others** – horns

Reprise Reprise

May 93. (cd/c/lp) <(9362 45230-2/-4/-1)> **KAMAKIRIAD** [3] [10]
– Trans-island skyway / Countermoon / Springtime / Snowbound / Tomorrow's girls / Florida room / On the dunes / Teahouse on the tracks.

Jun 93. (7"/c-s) *(W 0180/+C)* **TOMORROW'S GIRL. / SHANGHAI CONFIDENTIAL** [46] [ ]
(cd-s+=) *(W 0180CDX)* – Confide in me.

Aug 93. (7"/c-s) *(WO 196/+C)* **TRANS-ISLAND SKYWAY. / BIG NOISE, NEW YORK** [ ] [ ]
(12"+=/cd-s+=) *(WO 196 T/CD)* – Home at last (live).

Nov 93. (7"/c-s) *(W 0216/+C)* **SNOWBOUND. / TRANS-ISLAND SKYWAY** [ ] [ ]
(cd-s+=) *(W 0216CD)* – ('A'mix).

WALTER BECKER

Giant-RCA Giant

Nov 94. (cd/c) <(74321 22609-2/-4)> **ELEVEN TRACKS OF WHACK** [ ] [ ]
– Down in the bottom / Junkie girl / Surf and or die / Book of liars / Lucky Henry / Hard up case / Cringemaker / Girlfriend / My Waterloo / This moody bastard / Hat too flat.

STEELY DAN

— duo re-formed for live appearances in the States. They had featured on V/A album 'Live At The Beacon' with The NEW YORK ROCK AND SOUL REVUE

Giant-RCA Giant

Oct 95. (cd/c) *(74321 28691-2/-4)* <24634> **ALIVE IN AMERICA (live 1994)** [62] [40]
– Babylon sister / Green earrings / Bodhisattva / Reelin' in the years / Josie / Book of liars / Peg / Third World man / Kid Charlemagne / Sign in stranger / Aja.

Feb 00. (cd) *(74321 62190-2)* <24719> **TWO AGAINST NATURE** [11] [6]
– Gaslighting Abbie / What a shame about me / Two against nature / Janie runaway / Almost gothic / Jack of speed / Cousin Dupree / Negative girl / West of Hollywood.

Reprise Reprise

Jun 03. (cd/lp) <(9362 48435-2/-1)> **EVERYTHING MUST GO** [21] [9]
– The last mall / Things I miss the most / Blues beach / Godwhacker / Slang of ages / Green book / Pixeleen / Lunch with Gina / Everything must go.

– compilations, others, etc. –

on 'M.C.A.' unless otherwise mentioned

Jan 78. (12"ep) *A.B.C.; (ABE 12-003)* **+ FOUR** [ ] [–]
– Do it again / Haitian divorce / Dallas / Sail the waterway.

Nov 78. (d-lp/c) *A.B.C.; (ABCD/+C 616)* <1107> **GREATEST HITS 1972-78** [41] [30]
(re-iss. Mar82 on 'M.C.A.'; MCLD/+C 608)

Apr 82. (d-c) *(MCA2 101)* **CAN'T BUY A THRILL / AJA** [ ] [–]

Jun 82. (lp/c) *(MCF/+C 3145)* <5324> **GOLD** [44] [ ]
(w/ free-12") *(re-iss. Aug91 cd/c; MCAD 10387)*

Jul 82. (7") *(MCA 786)* **FM (NO STATIC AT ALL). / FM (REPRISE)** [ ] [–]
(12"+=) *(MCAT 786)* – East St. Louis toodle-oo.

Apr 83. (7") *Old Gold; (OG 9321)* **DO IT AGAIN. / RIKKI DON'T LOSE THAT NUMBER** [ ] [–]

Oct 83. (d-c) *(MCA2 109)* **KATY LIED / THE ROYAL SCAM** [ ] [–]

Dec 83. (12"ep) *(MCAT 852)* **HAITIAN DIVORCE / DO IT AGAIN. / REELING IN THE YEARS / RIKKI DON'T LOSE THAT NUMBER** [ ] [–]

Mar 84. (lp) *Aero; <ML 8101>* **THE EARLY YEARS – WALTER BECKER & DONALD FAGEN** [–] [ ]

Sep 84. (d-c) *(MCA2 115)* **COUNTDOWN TO ECSTACY / PRETZEL LOGIC** [ ] [–]

Aug 85. (cd) *(DIDX 306)* **DECADE OF STEELY DAN – THE BEST OF STEELY DAN** [ ] [ ]

Oct 85. (lp/c) *(DAN TV/TC 1)* **REELIN' IN THE YEARS – THE VERY BEST OF STEELY DAN** [43] [–]
– Do it again / Reelin' in the years / My old school / Bodhisattva / Show biz kids / Rikki don't lose that number / Pretzel logic / Black Friday / Bad sneakers / Doctor Wu / Haitian divorce / Kid Charlemagne / The fez / Peg / Josie / Deacon blues / Hey nineteen / Babylon sisters. *(re-iss. Dec92 d-cd/c; MCLD/MCLC 19147)*

Nov 85. (7") *(MSAM 32)* **REELING IN THE YEARS. / RIKKI DON'T LOSE THAT NUMBER** [ ] [–]

Apr 86. (c) *Showcase; (SHTC 128)* **SUN MOUNTAIN** (early demos) [ ] [–]
(cd-iss. Oct92 on 'Thunderbolt'; CDTB 139)

May 86. (lp)(cd) *Bellaphon; (230-07-065)(288 07014)* **BERRYTOWN** (demos) [–] German [–]

May 87. (lp/c/cd) *Thunderbolt; (THBL/THBL/CDTB 040)* **OLD REGIME** (early material) [ ] [–]
(re-iss. Mar94 on 'Prestige' cd/c;)

Oct 87. (7") *(MCA 1214)* **RIKKI DON'T LOSE THAT NUMBER. / DO IT AGAIN** [ ] [–]

Oct 87. (lp/c/cd) *Telstar; (STAR/STAC/TCD 2297)* **DO IT AGAIN – THE VERY BEST OF STEELY DAN** [64] [–]

Apr 88. (lp)cd) *Thunderbolt; (THBL 054)(CDTB 056)* **STONE PIANO** (early material) [ ] [–]

Jun 88. (d-lp) *Castle; (CCSLP 193)* **BECKER AND FAGEN – THE COLLECTION** [ ] [–]
(cd-iss. Nov93; CLACD 365)

Jul 93. (cd/c) *Charly; (CD CD/MC 116)* **ROARING OF THE LAMB** [ ] [–]

Sep 93. (cd/c; as WALTER BECKER & DONALD FAGEN) *Remember; (RMB 7/4 5004)* **FOUNDERS OF STEELY DAN** [ ] [–]

Nov 93. (cd/c) *(MCD/MCC 10967)* **REMASTERED – THE BEST OF STEELY DAN** [49] [ ]

Dec 93. (4xcd-box) *(MCAD 410981)* **CITIZEN STEELY DAN (1972-1980)** [ ] [ ]

Feb 94. (cd/c) *Javelin; (HAD CD/MC 103)* **SPOTLIGHT ON STEELY DAN** [ ] [–]

Jun 94. (d-cd) *Thunderbolt; (CDTB 503)* **CATALYST (THE ORIGINAL RECORDINGS 1968-71)** [ ] [–]

Feb 95. (cd; BECKER & FAGEN) *B.A.M.;* **PEARLS OF THE PAST** [ ] [–]

1995. (cd/c) *O.N.N.; (ONN 54 CD/MC)* **STEELY DAN (FEATURING WALTER BECKER & DONALD FAGEN)** [ ] [–]

Mar 00. (4xcd-box) *(110981-2)* **CITIZEN 1972-1980 (THE BEST OF STEELY DAN)** [ ] [ ]

Feb 03. (cd; as WALTER BECKER / DONALD FAGEN) *Blu Mountain; <(90709)>* **COME BACK BABY** [ ] [ ]

May 05. (d-cd) *(9811741)* <112407> **SHOWBIZ KIDS: THE STEELY DAN STORY 1972-1980** [53] Nov00 [ ]
– Do it again / Dirty work / Reelin' in the years / Only a fool would say that / Changes of the guard / Bodhisattva / The Boston rag / Showbiz kids / My old school / Rikki don't lose that number / Night by night / Pretzel logic / Any major dude will tell you / Black Friday / Bad sneakers / Doctor Wu / Any world that I'm welcome to / Chain lightning // Kid Charlemagne / Don't take me alive / Haitian divorce / The fez / Here at the western world / Black cow / Aja / Deacon blues / Peg / Josie / FM / Babylon sisters / Hey nineteen / Time out of mind / Third World man.

DONALD FAGEN

Reprise Reprise

Mar 06. (cd) *<(9362 49975-2)>* **MORPH THE CAT** [35] [26]
– Morph the cat / H gang / What I do / Brite nitegown / The great pagoda of funn / Security Joan / The night belongs to Mona / Mary shut the garden door / Morph the cat (reprise). *<(ltd-cd w/dvda+=; 9362 49976-2)>* – (videos).

☐ Gwen STEFANI (see under ⇒ NO DOUBT)

STEREOLAB

Formed: South London, England … late 1990, by ex-indie stalwart/songwriter TIM GANE (mainman for McCARTHY), who invited lyricist girlfriend LAETITIA SADIER to join. They soon completed the initial line-up with MARTIN KEAN and JOE DILWORTH (other past indie veterans), subsequently forming their own label, 'Duophonic Super 45s'. The group released three 45's ('SUPER 45', 'SUPER ELECTRIC' & 'STUNNING DEBUT ALBUM') in 1991, the second of which was for the 'Too Pure' label (these have re-instated vinyl as worthy product, whether for limited edition collectors or just vinyl junkies who hate cd's). The following year, the eclectic ambient-boogie machine that was STEREOLAB topped the indie charts with their actual "stunning debut album", 'PENG!'. The record ran the gamut of the band's minimalist influences including VELVET UNDERGROUND, JOHN CAGE, NEU! and SPACEMEN 3. During this period, the couple introduced four new members; MARY HANSEN, SEAN O'HAGAN, DUNCAN BROWN and ANDY RAMSAY, who helped them with a busy touring schedule. In 1993, they signed to 'Elektra' in the States for a 6 figure-sum, while in the UK, they released several more 45's! and an album, 'TRANSIENT RANDOM-NOISE BURSTS WITH ANNOUNCEMENTS', which, like the classy single, 'JENNY ONDIOLINE', scraped into the UK charts (the track was premiered on Channel 4's "The Word" programme). 1994 saw them unsurprisingly hit the UK Top 20 with another double album, 'MARS AUDIAC QUINTET'. Two years later, with their best offering to date, 'EMPEROR TOMATO KETCHUP', they had established themselves as leaders of the "Metronomic Underground" scene, as the opening track suggested. Over the course of the last three years (including 1997's excellent 'DOTS AND LOOPS'), the band's sound had become increasingly characterised by the dreamy French-style vocals of LAETITIA (pronounced Le-ti-seaya), akin to a spacier SARAH CRACKNELL (of SAINT ETIENNE). Returning to the fold in August '99, STEREOLAB (complete with Gallic songstress, BRIGITTE FONTAINE) issued one of their special limited singles, 'CALIMERO', although it was not a feature on their accompanying album, 'COBRA AND PHASES GROUP PLAY VOLTAGE IN THE MILKY NIGHT'. Officially previewed with yet another single, 'THE FREE DESIGN' (inspired by the obscure outfit of the same name!), the album was a little too twee and lightweight for some, one slightly perturbed (or disturbed?) NME critic in particular panning it enough to give zero out of ten! (a hanging offence in anyone's book). Augmented by main protagonists of the underground post-rock scene, JIM O'ROURKE and TORTOISE leader JOHN McENTIRE, STEREOLAB – after a long gap inbetween "long-playing" records – issued the near fantastic 'SOUND-DUST' (2001), a swirling trip into the uncharted territories for the group. The set matched that of the mini-album, or largely ignored 'THE FIRST OF THE MICROBE HUNTERS' (2000), which separated the band from math-rock wizards to sci-fi pop magicians. On 'SOUND-DUST' SADIER's vocals levitated through soft guitars and echoing bass guitar. Opener 'BLACK ANTS IN SOUND-DUST' was reminiscent of previous 'LAB outings, whereas 'CAPTAIN EASYCHORD' focused on being just a great space lullaby. Tragically, on the 9th of December 2002, at the age of only 36, MARY HANSEN was killed when on a bicycle trip. The band eventually returned to the studio in autumn 2003 to record the 'INSTANT O IN THE UNIVERSE' EP, a much less diffuse affair then their recent albums. While lead track ' …SUDDEN STARS' harked back to former glories, the record had the feel of a band taking stock rather than retreating. The STEREO crew returned in 2004 with 'MARGERINE ECLIPSE', their first full length release since HANSEN's passing. More accommodating and approachable than almost anything else they'd done, and hailed as their best album since the classic 'EMPEROR TOMATO KETCHUP', '..ECLIPSE' gilded its bustling, blinking rhythms with the kind of string cascades, disco glitter and mineral-rich vocal strata that suggested STEREOLAB were still bunsen-burning their own sonic trail; they were just doing it a bit more unambiguously than in the past. 'OSCILLIONS FROM THE ANTI-SUN' (2005) rounded up some 35 single/EP cuts from the 90s and obliged the fad for CD/DVD packages by including a DVD of video promos. 'FAB FOUR SUTURE' (2006) was also a collection, albeit a more desirable one, gathering the series of limited edition EPs the band had released in the preceding six months.

Album rating: SWITCHED ON collection (*6) / PENG! (*7) / THE GROOP PLAYED "SPACE AGE BATCHELOR PAD MUSIC" (*5) / TRANSIENT RANDOM-NOISE BURSTS WITH ANNOUNCEMENTS (*8) / REFRIED ELECTOPLASM (SWITCHED ON, VOL.2) compilation (*6) / MUSIC FOR THE AMORPHOUS BODY STUDY CENTER (*8) / MARS AUDIO QUINTET (*8) / EMPEROR TOMATO KETCHUP (*9) / DOTS AND LOOPS (*8) / COBRA AND PHASES GROUP PLAY VOLTAGE IN THE MILKY NIGHT (*6) / THE FIRST OF THE MICROBE HUNTERS mini (*6) / SOUND-DUST (*5) / MARGERINE ECLIPSE (*7) / OSCILLIONS FROM THE ANTI-SUN compilation (*7) / FAB FOUR SUTURE (*7)

TIM GANE (b.12 Jul'64) – guitar, vox organ, guitar (ex-McCARTHY) / **LAETITIA SADIER** (b. 6 May'68, Paris, France) – vocals, vox organ, guitar, tambourine, moog / **GINA MORRIS** – vocals / **JOE DILWORTH** – drums (of TH' FAITH HEALERS)

Duophonic not iss.

May 91. (10"ep-mail order) *(DS45-01)* **SUPER 45** [ ] [–]
– The light (that will cease to fail) / Au grand jour / Brittle / Au grand jour!.

— added **MARTIN KEAN** (b.New Zealand) – guitar (ex-CHILLS) / **RUSSELL YATES** – live guitar (of MOOSE). **MICK CONROY** (ex-MOOSE) was also a live member early '92.

Nov 91. (7"clear,7"colrd) *(DS45-02)* **STUNNING DEBUT ALBUM: Doubt / Changer** [ ] [–]

Too Pure Slumberland

Sep 91. (10"ep) *(PURE 4)* **SUPERELECTRIC / HIGH EXPECTATION. / THE WAY WILL BE OPENING / CONTACT** [ ] [–]

Apr 92. (cd/lp) *(31022) <SLR 22>* **SWITCHED ON** (compilation) [ ] Oct92 [ ]
– Super-electric / Doubt / Au grand jour 1 / The way will be opening / Brittle / Contact / Au grand jour / High expectation / The light that will cease to fail / Changer. *(re-iss. Mar97 on 'Duophonic' cd/lp; TBC 25/24) (cd/lp re-iss. Mar99 on 'Too Pure'; PUREL 78 CD/LP)*

— GINA departed after above

Too Pure American

May 92. (cd,c,lp) *(PURE 11) <43018>* **PENG!** [ ] [ ]
– Super falling star / Orgiastic / Peng! 33 / K-stars / Perversion / You little shits / The seeming and the meaning / Mellotron / Enivrez-vous / Stomach worm / Surrealchemist.

— added **MARY HANSEN** (b. 11 Jan'66, Brisbane, Australia) – vocals, tambourine, guitar / **ANDY RAMSAY** – percussion, vox organ, bazouki; repl. DILWORTH

Sep 92. (10"ep,10"clear-ep,cd-ep) *(PURE 14)* **LOW FI** [ ] [–]
– Et de votre coeur endormi / (Varoom!) / Laisser-faire / Elektro – He held the world in his iron grip.

— added **SEAN O'HAGAN** – vox organ, guitar (ex-MICRODISNEY, ex-HIGH LLAMAS)

Feb 93. (7",7"pink) *<SLR 24>* **JOHN CAGE BUBBLEGUM. / ELOGE D'EROS** –

— added **DUNCAN BROWN** – bass, guitar, vocals

Mar 93. (cd,c,m-lp) *(PURE 19) <43013>* **THE GROOP PLAYED "SPACE AGE BACHELOR PAD MUSIC"**
– Avant-garde M.O.R. / Space age bachelor pad music (mellow) / The groop play chord X / Space age bachelor pad music (foamy) / Ronco symphony / We're not adult orientated / UHF-MFP / We're not adult orientated (new wave live).

Duophonic Elektra

Aug 93. (10"ep/cd-ep) *(DUHF D/CD 01) <8815>* **JENNY ONDIOLINE / FRUCTION / GOLDEN BALL / FRENCH DISCO** 75

Sep 93. (cd/c/2xlp) *(DUHF CD/DMC/D 02) <7559 61536-2>* **TRANSIENT RANDOM-NOISE BURSTS WITH ANNOUNCEMENTS** 62
– Tone burst / Our trinitone blast / Pack yr romantic mind / I'm going out of my way / Golden ball / Pause / Jenny Ondioline / Analogue rock / Crest / Lock-groove lullaby.

Nov 93. (7") *(D-UHF D01P)* **FRENCH DISKO (new version). / JENNY ONDIOLINE** –

— added **KATHERINE GIFFORD** – synthesizers, keyboards

Jul 94. (7"ltd) *(D-UHFD 04S)* **PING PONG. / MOOGIE WONDERLAND** 45 –
(10"+=/cd-s+=) *(D-UHF D/CD 04)* – Pain et spectacles / Transcoma (live).

Aug 94. (cd/c/d-lp) *(D-UHF CD/MC/D 05) <61669>* **MARS AUDIAC QUINTET** 16
– Three-dee melodie / Wow and flutter / Transona five / Des etoiles electroniques / Ping pong / Anamorphose / Three longers later / Nihilist assault group / International colouring contest / The stars of our destination / Transporte sans bouger / L'enfer des formes / Outer accelerator / New orthophony / Fiery yellow. *(free clear-7" w /d-lp + cd-s on cd) (DUHF D/CD 05X)* – Klang-tang / Ulaan batter.

Oct 94. (7"ltd) *(D-UHFD 07S)* **WOW AND FLUTTER. / HEAVY DENIM** 70 –
(10"+=/cd-s+=) *(D-UHF D/CD 07)* – Nihilist assault group / Narco Martenot.

Apr 95. (10"ep/cd-ep) *(D-UHF D/CD 08)* **AMORPHOUS BODY STUDY CENTRE** 59 –
– Pop quiz / The extension trip / How to explain your internal organs overnight / The brush descends the length / Melochord seventy five / Space moment.

Sep 95. (cd/c/colrd-d-lp) *(D-UHF CD/MC/D 09) / Drag City; <DC 82>* **REFRIED ECTOPLASM (SWITCHED ON – VOLUME II)** (compilation) 30
– Harmonium / Lo boob oscillator / Mountain / Revox / French disko / Exploding head movie / Eloge d'eros / Tone burst (country) / Animal or vegetable (a wonderful wooden reason) / John Cage bubblegum / Sadistic / Farfisa / Tempter. *(d-lp re-iss. May98; same as US)*

— **GANE / SADIER / HANSEN / RAMSAY + BROWN** added **MORGANE LHOTE** (guests; SEAN O'HAGAN / JOHN McENTIRE (of TORTOISE) + RAY DICKARTY)

— KATHERINE GIFFORD formed indie supergroup SNOWPONY

Feb 96. (7") *(D-UHFD 10S)* **CYBELE'S REVERIE. / BRIGITTE** 62 –
(10"+=/cd-s+=) *(D-UHF D/CD 10)* – Les yper yper sound / Young lungs.

Mar 96. (d-lp/c/cd) *(D-UHF D/MC/CD 11) <61640-2>* **EMPEROR TOMATO KETCHUP** 27 Apr96
– Metronomic underground / Cybele's reverie / Percolator / Les ypersound / Spark plug / Olv 26 / The noise of carpet / Tomorrow is already here / Emperor tomato ketchup / Monstre sacre / Motoroller scalatron / Slow fast Hazel / Anonymous collective.

Apr 96. (12"ltd.) *(DS 3311)* **SIMPLE HEADPHONE MIND. / (other track by NURSE WITH WOUND)** –
(re-iss. Jun97; same)

— now without BROWN, who was repl. by **RICHARD HARRISON**

Sep 96. (7") *(LISS 15)* **SHE USED TO CALL ME SADNESS. / (other by Fuxa)** –
(above on 'Lissys')

Nov 96. (7"ep)(12"ep/cd-ep) *(D-UHFD 14S)(D-UHF D/CD 14)* **FLUORESCENCES EP** –
– Fluorescences / Pinball / You used to call me sadness / Soop groove *2.

Dec 96. (12"; STEREOLAB & WAGON CHRIST) *(D-UHFD 15)* **METROGNOMIC UNDERGROUND. /** –

Sep 97. (7") *(D-UHFD 16S)* **MISS MODULAR. / ALLURES** 60 –
(12"+=/cd-s+=) *(D-UHF D/CD 16)* – Off-on / Spinal column.

Sep 97. (cd/c/d-lp) *(D-UHF CD/C/D 17) <62065>* **DOTS AND LOOPS** 19
– Brakhage / Miss Modular / The flower called Nowhere / Prisoner of Mars / Rainbo conversation / Refractions in the plastic pulse / Parsec / Ticker-tape of the unconscious / Contronatura.

— **SADIER, GANE, HANSEN, RAMSEY + LHOTE** were joined by **SIMON JOHNS** – bass (ex-CLEARSPOT) / **KEV HOOPER** – musical saw (ex-STUMP) / **ROB MAZUREK** – cornet / **DOMINIC MURCOTT** – marimba / plus guests **JOHN McENTIRE** (of TORTOISE) / **JIM O'ROURKE + SEAN O'HAGAN**

Aug 99. (7"/cd-s; STEREOLAB & BRIGITTE FONTAINE) *(DS45/+CD 25)* **CALIMERO. / (other track 'Cache Cache' by MONADE)** –

Sep 99. (7") *(D-UHFD 22S)* **THE FREE DESIGN. / ESCAPE POD (FROM THE WORLD OF MEDICAL OBSERVATIONS)** –
(cd-s+=) *(D-UHFCD 22)* – With friends like these / Les aimes des memes.

Sep 99. (cd) *(D-UHFCD 23)* **COBRA AND PHASES GROUP PLAY VOLTAGE IN THE MILKY NIGHT** –
– Fuses / People do it all the time / The free design / Blips drips and strips / Italian shoes continuum / Infinity girl / The spiracles / Op hop detonation / Puncture in the radah permutation / Velvet water / Blue milk / Caleidoscopic gaze / Strobo acceleration / The emergency kisses / Come and play in the milky night.

May 00. (m-lp/m-cd) *(D-UHF D/CD 25) <62537-2>* **THE FIRST OF THE MICROBE HUNTERS**
– Outer Bongolia / Intervals / Barock – plastik / Nomus et phusis / I feel the air (of another planet) / Household names / Retrograde mirror form.

— **O'ROURKE + McENTIRE** were virtually fully-fledged 'LAB techs

Jul 01. (12"/cd-s) *(D-UHF D/CD 26)* **CAPTAIN EASYCHORD / LONGLIFE LOVE. / CANNED CANDIES / MOODLES** –

Sep 01. (cd/d-lp) *(D-UHF CD/D 27) <62676-2>* **SOUND-DUST**
– Black ants in sound-dust / Space moth / Captain Easychord / Baby Lulu / The black arts / Hallucinex / Double rocker / Gus the mynah bird / Naught more terrific than man / Nothing to do with me / Suggestion diabolique / Les bons bons des raisons.

— on 9th Dec'02, MARY was killed in a bicycle accident in London

Oct 03. (3x7"ep)(m-cd) *(D-UHFD 28S)(D-UHFCD 28) <62893>* **INSTANT O IN THE UNIVERSE**
– . . .Sudden stars / Jaunty Monty and the bubbles of silence / Good is me / Microclimate / Mass riff.

Feb 04. (d-lp/cd) *(D-UHF-S/D-UHFCD 29) <62926>* **MARGERINE ECLIPSE**
– Vonal declosion / Need to be / . . .Sudden stars / Cosmic country noir / Le demeure / Margerine rock / The man with 100 cells / Margerine melodie / Hillbilly motorbike / Feel and triple / Bop scotch / Dear Marge.

Too Pure Too Pure

Sep 05. (7") *(PURE 174S)* **KYBERNETICK A BABICKA PART 1. / PART 2** –

Sep 05. (7") *(PURE 175S)* **PLASTIC MILE. / I WAS A SUNNY RAINPHASE** –

Sep 05. (7") *(PURE 176S)* **INTERLOCK. / VISIONARY ROAD MAPS** –

Mar 06. (7") *(PURE 187S)* **WHISPER PITCH. / WIDOW WEIRDO** –

Mar 06. (7") *(PURE 188S)* **EXCURSIONS INTO "OH-A-OH". / GET A SHOT OF THE REFRIGERATOR** –

Mar 06. (7") *(PURE 189S)* **EYE OF THE VOLCANO. / VODIAK** –

Mar 06. (cd/2x10"lp) *(PURE 190 CD/LP) <80190>* **FAB FOUR SUTURE** (2005-06 singles collection)

– more very limited singles, etc. –

Jun 92. (7"pink) *B.M.I.; (BMI 025)* **THE LIGHT (THAT WILL CEASE TO FAIL). / AU GRAND JOUR** –

Jul 92. (7"colrd) *Duophonic; (DS45-04)* **HARMONIUM. / FARFISA** –

Oct 93. (10"ep) *Clawfist; (Clawfist 20)* **CRUMB DUCK (with NURSE WITH WOUND)** –
– Animal or vegetable / Exploding head movie.

Oct 93. (7"clear) *Sub Pop; (<SP 107/283>)* **LE BOOB OSCILLATOR. / TEMPTER**

Nov 93. (7") *Teenbeat; <Teenbeat 121>* **MOUNTAIN. / ('B' by Unrest)** –

Feb 98. (12"ep/cd-ep; by STEREOLAB & UI) *(DS45/+CD 19)*
FIRES [ ] [-]
– St. Elmo's fire (mixes) / Less time / Impulse rah. *(re-iss/lp Aug00 on 'Bingo'; BIN 2)*

Oct 98. (d-cd/d-lp) *<DC 159>* **ALUMINIUM TUNES: SWITCHED ON VOL.3** [-] [ ]
– Pop quiz – The extension trip / How to play your internal organs / Brush descends the length / Melochord seventy-five / Space moment / Speedy car / Golden atoms / Olan bator / One small step / Iron man / Long hair of death / You used to call me sadness / New orthophony / One note samba – Surfboard / Cadriopo / Klang tone / Get Carter / 1000 miles an hour / Percolations / Seeperbold / Check and double check / Munich madness / Metronumero underground / Incredible He-woman.

Oct 02. (d-cd) *Strange Fruit; (SFRSCD 111)* **ABC MUSIC: THE RADIO 1 SESSIONS** [ ] [-]

Apr 05. (t-cd w/dvd) *Too Pure: (<PURE 160CD>)* **OSCILLIONS FROM THE ANTI-SUN** [ ] [ ]

STEREOPHONICS

Formed: Cwmaman, Mid-Glamorgan, Wales ... late 80's as the TRAGIC LOVE COMPANY by songwriter KELLY JONES, RICHARD JONES and STUART CABLE, initially treading the boards as a teenage covers band. The trio proved they were more than capable of spearheading Richard Branson's new 'V2' label with the release of debut single, 'LOOKS LIKE CHAPLIN', a melodic riffathon that had more in common with trad 70's rock and Seattle grunge than the still dominant Britpop. A Spring '97 follow-up, 'LOCAL BOY IN THE PHOTOGRAPH', came within breathing distance of the Top 50, a dizzying amalgam of the MANICS, RADIOHEAD, OASIS and BUFFALO TOM that managed to sound simultaneously contemporary and classic. JONES confirmed his newfound status as one of Britain's most promising young songwriters as STEREOPHONICS embarked on an impressive chart run with the Top 40-breaking 'MORE LIFE IN A TRAMP'S VEST'. Late summer saw them nudge closer to the Top 20 with 'A THOUSAND TREES', the opening track on debut album, 'WORD GETS AROUND'. A massive selling UK Top 10 success, the record featured in the upper reaches of many end-of-year polls, helping to net the band a Brit Award (Best New Group) in early '98. Having seen out '97 with the moody magnificence of 'TRAFFIC', JONES and Co began the new year with a Top 20 re-issue of 'LOCAL BOY' prior to a summer of heavy touring. Towards Christmas, STEREOPHONICS became a household name with Top 3 hit, 'THE BARTENDER & THE THIEF', proving that despite the continued predictions of its imminent demise, good old fashioned guitar-rock and solid songwriting was alive and well in Wales. The following year saw the trio peak both critically and commercially, three massive hits, 'JUST LOOKING', 'PICK A PART THAT'S NEW' and 'I WOULDN'T BELIEVE YOUR RADIO', all squeezed out of an excellent sophomore set, 'PERFORMANCE AND COCKTAILS' (1999). Welsh pop idol, TOM JONES, also called up the services of his fellow countrymen to duet with him on a Top 10 hit of 'Mama Told Me Not To Come'. Everyone's favourite trad-rockers returned in 2001 with 'JUST ENOUGH EDUCATION TO PERFORM', the record's title engendering an unlikely bout of controversy when the band – much to car manufacturer Daimler-Chrysler's disapproval – attempted to abbreviate it to 'J.E.E.P.'. Needless to say, this episode was more unpredictable than any of the meat and potatoes fare on offer within. Which isn't to say STEREOPHONICS are worthy but dull, just that their acoustic-laced melodic rock lends itself to daytime radio play annoyingly well. Once again, JONES proved himself a master of rock classicism , taking his inspiration from the choicest, most authentic sounding 60's/70's moments and infusing them with the deftest of rootsy flourishes. Thus, try as you might to resist, singles such as 'STEP ON MY OLD SIZE NINES' and the breezy 'HAVE A NICE DAY' slowly but surely shoehorned their way into your consciousness much like that Top Gear compilation your dad used to play. While JONES is a writer who is undoubtedly maturing with age, he still lacks that strain of rugged individuality that marks out a ROD STEWART or a JOHN FOGERTY – 'HANDBAGS & GLADRAGS' indeed. JONES did yet more growing up the hard way with 'YOU GOTTA GO THERE TO COME BACK' (2003), detailing his travails through a series of affecting if often disillusioned vignettes. With the likes of 'NOTHING PRECIOUS AT ALL' and the hit singles 'MADAME HELGA' and 'MAYBE TOMORROW', the band sounded less like they had something to prove and more like they had something to say. The first album to feature Argentinian JAVIER WEYLER on the drumstool (in place of the departed CABLE), 'LANGUAGE. SEX. VIOLENCE. OTHER?' (2005) was the sound of a rejuvenated, testosterone-taut band mitigating their primal rock instincts with contemporary 80s-centric treatments. Lead single 'DAKOTA' cruised to the top of the British charts with Dean-dream, stick-shift cool, arguable the most stylish three minutes they've ever committed to tarmac. Follow-up and album opener, 'SUPERMAN' combined falsetto vocals and an evil sounding bassline, going Top 20 as did successive spin-offs 'DEVIL' and 'REWIND', both of which reverberated to echo-chamber vocals and the latter recalling nothing so much as vintage U2. So much for the singles; the album cuts – from the brutal epiphany of 'DOORMAN' onwards – weren't so forgiving, pulverising slabs of crew-cut rock that might've been hewed raw from the glowering Welsh valleys. Many of the best tracks showed up on 'LIVE FROM DAKOTA' (2006), a double set capturing the band in their leather-clad element.

• **Covered:** SUNNY AFTERNOON (Kinks) / POSITIVELY 4th STREET (Bob Dylan) / SOMETHING IN THE WAY (Nirvana) / THE OLD LAUGHING LADY + HEART OF GOLD (Neil Young) / FIRST TIME EVER I SAW YOUR FACE (Ewan MacColl) / I'M ONLY SLEEPING + DON'T LET ME DOWN (Beatles) / HANDBAGS & GLADRAGS (Mike D'Abo).

Album rating: WORD GETS AROUND (*7) / PERFORMANCE AND COCKTAILS (*8) / JUST ENOUGH EDUCATION TO PERFORM (*7) / YOU GOTTA GO THERE TO COME BACK (*6) / LANGUAGE. SEX. VIOLENCE. OTHER? (*7) / LIVE FROM DAKOTA (*6)

KELLY JONES (b. 3 Jun'74, Aberdare, Wales) – vocals, guitar / **RICHARD JONES** (b.23 May'74, Aberdare) – bass / **STUART CABLE** (b.19 May'70, Aberdare) – drums

V2 V2

Nov 96. (7") *(SPH 1)* **LOOKS LIKE CHAPLIN. / MORE LIFE IN A TRAMP'S VEST** [ ] [-]
(cd-s+=) *(SPHD 1)* – Raymond's shop.

Mar 97. (7") *(SPH 2)* **LOCAL BOY IN THE PHOTOGRAPH. / TWO MANY SANDWICHES** [51] [ ]
(cd-s+=) *(SPHD 2)* – Buy myself a small plane.

May 97. (7") *(SPH 4)* **MORE LIFE IN A TRAMP'S VEST. / RAYMOND'S SHOP** [33] [-]
(cd-s+=) *(SPHD 4)* – Poppy day.
(cd-s) *(SPHDX 4)* – ('A'side) / Looks like Chaplin (live) / Too many sandwiches (live) / Last of the big time drinkers (live).

Aug 97. (7"/c-s) *(VVR 500044-7/-5)* **A THOUSAND TREES. / CARROT CAKE AND WINE** [22] [-]
(cd-s+=) *(VVR 500044-3)* – ('A'live).
(cd-s) *(VVR 500044-8)* – ('A'acoustic) / Home to me (acoustic) / Looks like Chaplin (acoustic) / Summertime (acoustic).

Aug 97. (cd/c/lp) *(VVR 100043-2/-4/-9)* <27006> **WORD GETS AROUND** [6] [ ]
– A thousand trees / Looks like Chaplin / More life in a tramps vest / Local boy in the photograph / Traffic / Not up to you / Check my eyelids for holes / Same size feet / Last of the big time drinkers / Goldfish bowl / Too many sandwiches / Billy Daveys daughter.

Nov 97. (7"/c-s) *(VVR 500094-7/-5)* **TRAFFIC. / TIE ME UP TIE ME DOWN** [20] [-]
(cd-s+=) *(VVR 500094-3)* – Chris Chambers / ('A'version).
(cd-s) *(VVR 500094-8)* – ('A'live) / More life in a tramp's vest (live) / A thousand trees (live) / Local boy in the photograph (live).

STEREOPHONICS

Feb 98. (7"/c-s) *(VVR 500126-7/-5)* **LOCAL BOY IN THE PHOTOGRAPH (remix). / WHO'LL STOP THE RAIN** [14] [–]
(cd-s+=) *(VVR 500126-3)* – Check my eyelids for holes / ('A'-CD-Rom video).
(cd-s) *(VVR 500126-8)* – ('A'side) / Not up to you (live in session) / The last resort / Traffic (CD-rom video live).

Nov 98. (7"/c-s) *(VVR 500467-7/-5)* **THE BARTENDER AND THE THIEF. / SHE TAKES HER CLOTHES OFF** [3] [–]
(cd-s+=) *(VVR 500465-3)* – Fiddler's green.
(cd-s) *(VVR 500466-3)* – ('A'live) / Traffic (live) / Raymond's shop (live).

Feb 99. (7"/c-s) *(VVR 500532-7/-5)* **JUST LOOKING. / POSTMEN DO NOT GREAT MOVIE HEROES MAKE (featuring Marco Migliani)** [4] [–]
(cd-s+=) *(VVR 500530-3)* – Sunny afternoon.
(cd-s) *(VVR 500530-0)* – ('A'side) / Local boy in the photograph (live) / Same size feet (live).

Mar 99. (cd/c/lp) *(VVR 100449-2/-4/-9)* <27052> **PERFORMANCE AND COCKTAILS** [1] May99 [ ]
– Roll up and shine / The bartender and the thief / Hurry up and wait / Pick a part that's new / Just looking / Half the lies you tell ain't true / I wouldn't believe your radio / T-shirt sun tan / Is yesterday, tomorrow, today? / A minute longer / She takes her clothes off / Plastic California / I stopped to fill my car up. *(special cd+=; VVR 100449-8)*

May 99. (7"/c-s) *(VVR 500677-7/-5)* **PICK A PART THAT'S NEW. / NICE TO BE OUT (demo)** [4] [–]
(cd-s+=) *(VVR 500677-3)* – Positively 4th street / ('A'-CD-Rom video).
(cd-s) *(VVR 500677-8)* – ('A'acoustic) / In my day / Something in the way.

Aug 99. (7"/c-s) *(VVR 500882-7/-5)* **I WOULDN'T BELIEVE YOUR RADIO. / THE BARTENDER AND THE THIEF (bar version)** [11] [–]
(cd-s+=) *(VVR 500882-3)* – The old laughing lady.
(cd-s) *(VVR 500882-8)* – ('A'live) / Pick a part that's new (live) / T-shirt suntan (live).

Nov 99. (7"/c-s) *(VVR 500932-7/-5)* **HURRY UP AND WAIT. / ANGIE** [11] [–]
(cd-s+=) *(VVR 500932-3)* – I wouldn't believe your radio.
(cd-s) *(VVR 500932-8)* – ('A'live) / I stopped to fill my car up (live) / Billy Davey's daughter (live) / ('A'-video).

— In Mar'00, STEREOPHONICS were credited on TOM JONES' UK Top 5 smash, 'Mama Told Me Not To Come'

May 00. (cd-ep) <70041> **T-SHIRT SUNTAN EP** [–] [ ]
– I wouldn't believe your radio / The bartender and the thief / Sunny afternoon / Positively 4th Street / Tie me up, tie me down.

— In Sep'00, KELLY JONES collaborated with MANCHILD on their UK Top 60 hit, 'The Cliches Are True'

Mar 01. (7"/c-s) *(VVR 501593-7/-5)* **MR. WRITER. / MARITIM BELLE VUE IN KIEL** [5] [–]
(cd-s+=) *(VVR 501593-3)* – An audience with Mr. Nice.
(cd-s) *(VVR 501593-8)* – ('A'-live acoustic) / Hurry up and wait (live acoustic) / Don't let me down (live acoustic).

Apr 01. (cd/c/lp) *(VVR 101583-2/-4/-1)* <27092> **JUST ENOUGH EDUCATION TO PERFORM** [1] [ ]
– Vegas two times / Lying in the sun / Mr. Writer / Step on my old size nines / Have a nice day / Nice to be out / Watch them fly Sundays / Everyday I think of money / Maybe / Caravan holiday / Rooftop. *(cd re-iss. Nov01; VVR 101829-2)*

Jun 01. (7"/c-s) *(VVR 501624-7/-4)* **HAVE A NICE DAY. / SURPRISE** [5] [–]
(cd-s+=) *(VVR 501624-3)* – Piano for a stripper (demo).
(cd-s) *(VVR 501624-8)* – ('A'live acoustic) / Heart of gold (live acoustic) / I stopped to fill my car up (live acoustic).

Sep 01. (c-s) *(VVR 501625-5)* **STEP ON MY OLD SIZE NINES / SHOESHINE BOY** [16] [–]
(cd-s+=) *(VVR 501625-3)* – I'm only sleeping / ('A'-CD-Rom).
(cd-s) *(VVR 501625-8)* – ('A'side) / Everyday I think of money / Just looking / ('A'live video).

Dec 01. (7"/c-s) *(VVR 501775-7/-5)* **HANDBAGS AND GLADRAGS. / FIRST TIME EVER I SAW YOUR FACE** [4] [–]
(cd-s+=) *(VVR 501775-3)* – How.
(cd-s) *(VVR 501775-8)* – ('A'live) / Caravan holiday (live) / Nice to be out (live).

Apr 02. (7") *(VVR 501917-7)* **VEGAS TWO TIMES. / VEGAS TWO TIMES (live)** [23] [–]
(cd-s) *(VVR 501917-3)* – ('A') / Mr Writer (live) / Watch them fly Sundays (live).

May 03. (7") *(VVR 502174-7)* **MADAME HELGA. / HIGH AS THE CEILING** [4] [–]
(cd-s+=) *(VVR 502174-3)* – Royal flush (mono demo).
(cd-s) *(VVR 502174-9)* – ('A') / ('A'-video).

Jun 03. (cd/c/d-lp) *(VVR 102190-2/-4/-1)* <80025> **YOU GOTTA GO THERE TO COME BACK** [1] [ ]
– Help me (she's out of her mind) / Maybe tomorrow / Madame Helga / You stole my money honey / Getaway / Climbing the wall / Jealousy / I'm alright (you gotta go there to come back) / Nothing precious at all / Rainbows and pots of gold / I miss you now / High as the ceiling / Since I told you it's over. *(ltd-cd+=; VVR 102190-0)* – Lying to myself again.

Jul 03. (7") *(VVR 502189-7)* **MAYBE TOMORROW. / HAVE WHEELS WILL TRAVEL** [3] [–]
(cd-s+=) *(VVR 502189-3)* – Change changes things.
(cd-s) *(VVR 502189-5)* – ('A'-demo) / Madame Helga (demo) / You stole my money honey (demo).
(dvd-s) *(VVR 502189-9)* – ('A') / (the making of..).

Nov 03. (7") *(VVR 502262-7)* **SINCE I TOLD YOU IT'S OVER. / MAYBE TOMORROW (live acoustic)** [16] [–]
(cd-s) *(VVR 502262-3)* – ('A'side) / Nothing precious at all (live acoustic) / Madame Helga (live acoustic).
(cd-s) *(VVR 502262-5)* – ('A'-demo) / Jealousy (demo) / I miss you (demo).
(dvd-s) *(VVR 502262-9)* – ('A'-video) / Maybe tomorrow (live video).

— temp. **STEVE GORMAN** – drums (ex-BLACK CROWES) repl. CABLE

Feb 04. (7") *(VVR 502465-7)* **MOVIESTAR. / MOVIESTAR (live)** [5] [–]
(cd-s) *(VVR 502465-8)* – ('A') / Local boy in the photograph (live).
(cd-s) *(VVR 502465-3)* – ('A'-live) / The bartender and the thief (live) / Help me (she's out of her mind) (live) / (behind the scenes footage).
(dvd-s) *(VVR 802465-9)* – ('A'-video) / ('A'-live video at Earls Court) / (behind the scenes) / ('A') / Climbing the walls (live).

Feb 05. (7"red/cd-s) *(VVR 503104-7/-8)* **DAKOTA. / LONG WAY ROUND** [1] [–]
(cd-s) *(VVR 503104-3)* – ('A') / ('A'-footswitch rework) / You're my soul (demo) / ('A'-video).
(dvd-s) *(VVR 803104-9)* – ('A'-rehearsal video) / ('A'-studio video) / ('A').

Mar 05. (cd/lp) *(VVR 103105-2/-1)* <27245> **LANGUAGE. SEX. VIOLENCE. OTHER?** [1] [ ]
– Superman / Doorman / Brother / Devil / Dakota / Rewind / Pedal pusher / Girl / Lolita / Deadhead / Feel.

Jun 05. (7"colrd/cd-s) *(VVR 503106-7/-8)* **SUPERMAN. / OUTSIDE** [13] [–]
(cd-s) *(VVR 503106-3)* – ('A') / I wanna be your dog / ('A'-live from Milan) / (making of video).
(dvd-s) *(VVR 803106-9)* – ('A'-video) / (tour diary, lyrics..)

Sep 05. (7"orange) *(VVR 503405-7)* **DEVIL. / DEVIL (footswitch rework)** [11] [–]
(cd-s) *(VVR 503405-8)* – ('A') / Dapper Dan (live from Tower Bridge rehearsals).
(cd-s) *(VVR 503405-3)* – ('A') / Dakota (live from New York) / Brother (live from New York) / ('A'-video).

Nov 05. (7"blue) *(VVR 503504-7)* **REWIND. / SUPERMAN (MHC remix)** [17] [–]
(cd-s) *(VVR 503504-8)* – ('A') / Hammerhead.
(cd-s) *(VVR 503504-3)* – ('A') / Maybe tomorrow (live on tour) / Ooh la la (live on Jo Whiley Radio 1 session).

V2 Nettwerk

Apr 06. (d-cd/d-lp) *(VVR 103809-8/-1)* <3056-2> **LIVE FROM DAKOTA** (live) [13] [ ]
– Superman / Doorman / A thousand trees / Devil / Mr. Writer / Pedalpusher / Deadhead / Maybe tomorrow / The bartender and the thief / Local boy in the photograph / Hurry up and wait / Madame Helga / Vegas two times / Carrot cake and wine / I'm alright (you gotta go there to come back) / Jayne / Too many sandwiches / Traffic / Just looking / Dakota.

Cat STEVENS

Born: STEVEN DEMETRI GEORGIOU, 21 Jul'47, Soho, London, England; son of Greek restaurant owner and Swedish mother. While studying at Hammersmith college in 1966 he met Mike Hurst (ex-SPRINGFIELDS). He produced first single 'I LOVE MY DOG', after which CAT was signed by Tony Hall to new Decca subsidiary label 'Deram'. It reached the UK Top 30, but was surpassed the next year when follow-up 'MATTHEW AND SON' hit No.2. His songs were soon being covered by many, including P.P. ARNOLD (First Cut Is The Deepest) & TREMELOES (Here Comes My Baby). After a barren chart spell and recuperation from TB two years previous, he signed new deal with 'Island' in 1970 (A&M in America). He scored a comeback Top 10 hit with 'LADY D'ARBANVILLE', which lent on the production skills of ex-YARDBIRD Keith Relf. He stayed for the follow-up to 'MONA BONE JAKON', the 1970 classic album 'TEA FOR THE TILLERMAN'. CAT went on to become one of the biggest stars of the 70's although his output became increasingly stale. 'TEASER AND THE FIRECAT' (1971) was another collection of pleasant but ultimately unsatisfying singer songwriter musings while 'CATCH BULL AT FOUR' (1972) and 'FOREIGNER' (1973) sounded overwrought and cluttered , a failing that marked the remainder of his output for 'Island' until his musical retirement in 1979 when he converted to the muslim faith and changed his name to YUSUF ISLAM; he also married Fouzia Ali that September. He and his large family continue to reside in London teaching his faith to a local primary school. With a compilation riding high in the UK charts at the end of 2003, and a version of 'FATHER AND SON' (featuring YUSUF) by RONAN KEATING at No.2 the following Xmas, the man formerly known as CAT STEVENS just might've been tempted to get back on the pop bandwagon – everybody else had!

• **Songwriters:** Self-penned except; MORNING HAS BROKEN (Eleanor Farjeon) / ANOTHER SATURDAY NIGHT (Sam Cooke). • **Trivia:** Other STEVENS' songs given new light were; WILD WORLD (Jimmy Cliff – 1970, Maxi Priest – 1988) / THE FIRST CUT IS THE DEEPEST (Rod Stewart) / PEACE TRAIN (10,000 Maniacs).

Album rating: MATTHEW AND SON (*6) / NEW MASTERS (*5) / MONA BONE JAKON (*6) / TEA FOR THE TILLERMAN (*8) / TEASER AND THE FIRECAT (*9) / CATCH BULL AT FOUR (*7) / FOREIGNER (*5) / BUDDHA AND THE CHOCOLATE BOX (*6) / GREATEST HITS compilation (*9) / NUMBERS (*3) / IZITSO (*4) / BACK TO EARTH (*3) / FOOTSTEPS IN THE DARK – GREATEST HITS, VOL.2 compilation (*6) / THE VERY BEST OF CAT STEVENS compilation (*9) / REMEMBER CAT STEVENS compilation (*8)

CAT STEVENS – vocals, guitar, keyboards with orchestra

Deram / Deram

Sep 66. (7") *(DM 102)* **I LOVE MY DOG. / PORTOBELLO ROAD** [28] [ ]

Dec 66. (7") *(DM 110)* **MATTHEW AND SON. / GRANNY** [2] [ ]
(re-iss. Aug81 on 'Decca')

Mar 67. (lp; mono/stereo) *(DML/SML 1004)* <18005> **MATTHEW AND SON** [7] [ ]
– Matthew and son / I love my dog / Here comes my baby / Bring another bottle baby / Portobello road / I've found a love / I see a road / Baby get your head screwed on / Granny / When I speak to the flowers / The tramp / Come on and dance / Hummingbird / Lady. *(cd-iss. Jul88 & Nov99 on 'London'; 820 560-2)*

Mar 67. (7") *(DM 118)* **I'M GONNA GET ME A GUN. / SCHOOL IS OUT** [6] [ ]

Jul 67. (7") *(DM 140)* **A BAD NIGHT. / THE LAUGHING APPLE** [20] [ ]

Dec 67. (7") *(DM 156)* **KITTY. / BLACKNESS OF THE NIGHT** [47] [ ]

Dec 67. (lp; mono/stereo) *(DML/SML 1018)* <18010> **NEW MASTERS** [ ] [ ]
– Kitty / I'm so sleepy / Northern wind / The laughing apple / Smash your heart / Moonstone / The first cut is the deepest / I'm gonna be king / Ceylon city / Blackness of the night / Come on baby / I love them all. *(re-iss. Nov84; DOA 5) (cd-iss. Apr89 +=; 820 767-2)* – Image of Hell / Lovely city / Here comes my wife / The view from the top / It's a supa dupa life / Where are you / A bad night.

Feb 68. (7") *(DM 178)* **LOVELY CITY. / IMAGE OF HELL** [ ] [ ]

— Around early 1968, CAT slowly recovered from tuberculosis.

Oct 68. (7") *(DM 211)* **HERE COMES MY WIFE. / IT'S A SUPA DUPA LIFE** [ ] [–]

Jun 69. (7") *(DM 260)* **WHERE ARE YOU. / THE VIEW FROM THE TOP** [ ] [–]

— recruited band; **ALUN DAVIES** – guitar / **JOHN RYAN** – bass / **HARVEY BURNS** – drums

Island / A&M

Jun 70. (7"m) *(WIP 6086)* **LADY D'ARBANVILLE. / TIME / FILL MY EYES** [8] [–]

Jun 70. (lp) *(ILPS 9118)* <4260> **MONA BONE JAKON** [63] [ ]
– Lady d'Arbanville / Maybe you're right / Pop star / I think I see the light / Trouble / Mona bone Jakon / I wish, I wish / Katmandu / Time – Fill my eyes / Lilywhite. *(re-iss. 1974 & Jan78; same) (cd-iss. Apr87; CID 9118) (cd re-iss. Nov89; IMCD 35) (cd re-mast.May00; IMCD 269)*

Nov 70. (lp) *(ILPS 9135)* <4280> **TEA FOR THE TILLERMAN** [20] Feb71 [8]
– Where do the children play / Hard headed woman / Wild world / Sad Lisa / Miles from nowhere / But I might die tonight / Longer boats / Into white / On the road to find out / Father and son / Tea for the tillerman. *(re-iss. 1974 & Jan78; same) (re-iss. Oct86 lp/c/cd; ILPM/ICM/CID 9135) (cd re-iss. Nov89; IMCD 36) (re-iss. lp Jan94 + May94; same) (cd re-mast.May00; IMCD 268)*

Feb 71. (7") <1231> **WILD WORLD. / MILES FROM NOWHERE** [–] [11]

— **LARRY STEELE** – bass repl. RYAN

Jun 71. (7") *(WIP 6092)* <1265> **MOON SHADOW. / FATHER AND SON** [22] [30]

Sep 71. (7") *(WIP 6102)* **TUESDAY'S DEAD. / MILES FROM NOWHERE** [ ] [–]

Sep 71. (7") <1291> **PEACE TRAIN. / WHERE DO THE CHILDREN PLAY?** [–] [7]

Sep 71. (lp) *(ILPS 9154)* <4313> **TEASER AND THE FIRECAT** [3] [2]
– The wind / Ruby love / If I laugh / Changes IV / How can I tell you / Tuesday's dead / Morning has broken / Bitterblue / Moon shadow / Peace train. *(re-iss. 1974 & Jan78; same) (re-iss. Oct86 lp/c/cd; ILPM/ICM/CID 9154) (cd re-iss. Mar90; IMCD 104) (cd re-mast.May00; IMCD 267)*

(below 'A'side featured **RICK WAKEMAN** – piano)

Dec 71. (7") *(WIP 6121)* <1335> **MORNING HAS BROKEN. / I WANT TO LIVE IN A WIGWAM** [9] Mar72 [6]

— In Apr'72, STEVENS contributed tracks to film 'Harold And Maude'.

— added **JEAN ROUSELL** – piano / **CAT** – some synthesizers repl. WAKEMAN. **ALAN JAMES** – bass repl. LARRY

Sep 72. (lp) *(ILPS 9206)* <4365> **CATCH BULL AT FOUR** [2] [1]
– Sitting / Boy with a moon and star on his head / Angel sea / Silent sunlight / Can't keep it in / 18th Avenue / Freezing steel / O Caritas / Sweet Scarlet / Ruins. *(re-iss. 1974 & Jan78; same) (cd-iss. Oct86; CID 9206) (cd re-iss. Jul89; IMCD 34) (cd re-mast.Aug00; IMCD 271)*

Nov 72. (7") *(WIP 6152)* **CAN'T KEEP IT IN. / CRAB DANCE** [13] [–]

Nov 72. (7") <1396> **SITTING. / CRAB DANCE** [–] [16]

— CAT now became a tax exile in Brazil and donated money to charity

— now w / **ROUSSEL, DAVIS, LYNCH + CONWAY** plus loads of sessioners

Jul 73. (7") *(WIP 6163)* <1418> **THE HURT. / SILENT SUNLIGHT** [ ] [31]

Jul 73. (lp) *(ILPS 9240)* <4391> **FOREIGNER** [3] [3]
– Foreigner suite / The hurt / How many times / Later / 100 I dream. *(re-iss. quad.1974) (cd-iss. Nov89; IMCD 72) (cd re-mast.Aug00; IMCE 272)*

— **BRUCE LYNCH** – bass repl. PAUL

Mar 74. (7") *(WIP 6190)* <1503> **OH VERY YOUNG. / 100 I DREAMS** [ ] [10]

Mar 74. (lp/c) *(ILPS/ICT 9274)* <3623> **BUDDAH AND THE CHOCOLATE BOX** [3] [2]
– Music / Oh very young / Sun – C79 / Ghost town / Jesus / Ready / King of trees / Bad penny / Home in the sky. *(cd-iss. Nov89; IMCD 70) (cd re-mast.Aug00; IMCD 273)*

Jun 74. (lp) <228> **SATURDAY NIGHT (live in Tokyo)** [–] [ ]
– Wild world / Oh very young / Sitting / Where do the children play? / Lady d'Arbanville / Another Saturday night / Hard-headed woman / Peace train / Father & son / King of trees / A bad penny / Bitter blue.

Aug 74. (7") *(WIP 6206)* <1602> **ANOTHER SATURDAY NIGHT. / HOME IN THE SKY** [19] [6]

Dec 74. (7") <1645> **READY. / I THINK I SEE THE LIGHT** [–] [26]

Jul 75. (7") *(WIP 6238)* <1700> **TWO FINE PEOPLE. / BAD PENNY** [ ] [33]

Jul 75. (lp/c) *(ILPS/ICT 9310)* <4519> **GREATEST HITS** (compilation) [2] [6]
– Wild world / Oh very young / Can't keep it in / Hard headed woman / Moonshadow / Two fine people / Peace train / Ready / Father and son / Sitting / Morning has broken / Another Saturday night. *(cd-iss. Apr87; CID 9310) (cd-iss. Mar93; IMCD 168)*

— now w / **ROUSSEL, DAVIS, LYNCH + CONWAY** plus loads of sessioners

Dec 75. (lp/c) *(ILPS/ICT 9370)* <4555> **NUMBERS** [ ] [13]
– Whistlestar / Novim's nightmare / Majik of majiks / Dry wood /

Banapple gas / Land o' free love and goodbye / Jzero / Home / Nomad's anthem. *(cd-iss. Mar01; IMCD 277)*

Mar 76. (7") *(WIP 6276)* *<1785>* **BANAPPLE GAS. / GHOST TOWN** [ ] Feb76 [41]

Mar 76. (7") *<1924>* **LAND O' FREE LOVE AND GOODBYE. / (I NEVER WANTED) TO BE A STAR** [–] [ ]

Apr 77. (lp/c) *(ILPS/ICT 9451)* *<4702>* **IZITSO** [18] [7]
– (Remember the days of the) Old schoolyard / Life / Killin' time / Kypros / Bonfire / To be a star / Crazy / Sweet Jamaica / Was Dog a doughnut / Child for a day. *(cd-iss. Mar01; IMCD 278)*

Jun 77. (7") *(WIP 6387)* **(REMEMBER THE DAYS OF THE) OLD SCHOOLYARD. / DOVES** [44] [–]

Jun 77. (7") *<1948>* **(REMEMBER THE DAYS OF THE) OLD SCHOOLYARD. / LAND O' FREE LOVE AND GOODBYE** [–] [33]

Nov 77. (7") *<1971>* **WAS DOG A DOUGHNUT. / SWEET JAMAICA** [–] [70]

Jan 79. (7") *<2109>* **BAD BRAKES. / NASCIMENTO** [–] [83]

Jan 79. (lp/c) *(ILPS/ICT 9565)* *<4735>* **BACK TO EARTH** [ ] Dec 78 [33]
– Just another night / Daytime / Bad brakes / Randy / The artist / Last love song / Nascimento / Father / New York times / Never. *(cd-iss. Mar01; IMCD 279)*

Feb 79. (7") *(WIP 6465)* **LAST LOVE SONG. / NASCIMENTO** [ ] [–]

Apr 79. (7") *<2126>* **RANDY. / NASCIMENTO** [–] [ ]

—— STEVENS retired from the music scene

– compilations, etc. –

Nov 70. (lp) *Decca; (SPA 93)* **THE WORLD OF CAT STEVENS** [ ] [–]

Mar 71. (d-lp) *Deram; <18005>* **MATTHEW AND SON / NEW MASTERS** [–] [ ]
(UK-iss.May75 as 'VIEW FROM THE TOP'; DPA 3019-20)

Jan 72. (lp) *Deram; <18061>* **VERY YOUNG AND EARLY SONGS** [–] [94]

Nov 73. (7") *Deram; (DM 406)* **I LOVE MY DOG. / MATTHEW AND SON** [ ] [–]
(re-iss. Oct83 on 'Old Gold'; OG 9336)

Aug 80. (7"ep) *Deram; (DM 435)* **MATTHEW AND SON / I LOVE MY DOG. / A BAD NIGHT / I'M GONNA GET ME A GUN** [ ] [–]

Aug 81. (lp/c) *Rock Echoes; (TAB/KTAB 25)* **THE FIRST CUT IS THE DEEPEST** [ ] [–]

Nov 83. (7") *Island; (IS 123)* **MORNING HAS BROKEN. / MOON SHADOW** [ ] [–]

Jan 85. (lp/c) *Island; <(ILPS/ICT 3736)>* **FOOTSTEPS IN THE DARK – GREATEST HITS VOL. 2** [ ] Dec84 [ ]
(US version +=) – (3 extra tracks). *(cd-iss. 1988; CD 3736)*

Apr 86. (d-lp/c) *Castle; (CCS LP/MC 127)* **THE COLLECTION** [ ] [–]
(cd-iss. Sep92; CCSCD 127)

Apr 86. (c) *Spot; (SPC 8574)* **CAT STEVENS** [ ] [–]

Jan 88. (cd) *Deram; (820 561-2)* **FIRST CUTS** [ ] [–]

Feb 90. (cd)(lp/c) *Island; (840 148-2)(CATV/+C 1)* **THE VERY BEST OF CAT STEVENS** [4] [ ]
– Where do the children play / Wild world / Tuesday's dead / Lady D'Arbanville / The first cut is the deepest / Oh very young / Rubylove / Morning has broken / Moonshadow / Matthew and son / Father and son / Can't keep it in / Hard headed woman / (Remember the days of the) Old school yard / I love my dog / Another Saturday night / Sad Lisa / Peace train. *(re-iss. Jul92; same)*

Nov 92. (d-cd) *Island; (ITSCD 12)* **TEA FOR THE TILLERMAN / TEASER & THE FIRECAT** [ ] [–]

Apr 93. (cd) *Pulsar;* **WILD WORLD** [ ] [–]

Sep 93. (cd/c) *Spectrum; (550108-2/-4)* **EARLY TAPES** [ ] [–]

Nov 99. (cd/c) *Island; (CID/ICT 8079) <524608>* **REMEMBER CAT STEVENS – THE ULTIMATE COLLECTION** [31] [ ]
– Moon shadow / Father and son / Morning has broken / Wild world / The first cut is the deepest / Lady d'Arbanville / Oh very young / Matthew and son / Sitting / Hard-headed woman / I love my dog / Rubylove / Don't be shy / Can't keep it in / Here comes my baby / Into white / (Remember the days of the) Old schoolyard / Where do the children play / Land o' freelove & goodbye / Another Saturday night / The Foreigner suite (excerpt) / Just another night / Peace train / If you want to sing out, sing out.

Apr 00. (cd) *A&M; <541387>* **THE VERY BEST OF CAT STEVENS** [–] [58]

Sep 03. (4xcd-box) *(<585285-2>)* **ON THE ROAD TO FIND OUT** [ ] Oct03 [ ]

Oct 03. (cd+dvd) *Universal TV; (9811208)* **THE VERY BEST OF CAT STEVENS** [6] [–]

YUSUF ISLAM

Mountain Of Light — Resurgent

Sep 95. (d-cd/d-c) *(MOL 7001 CD/MC 3)* *<70001>* **THE LIFE OF THE LAST PROPHET** (spoken word) [ ] Nov95 [ ]

Feb 99. (cd) *Mountain Of Light; (MOL 70006CD)* *<70006>* **PRAYERS OF THE LAST PROPHET** (spoken word) [ ] Sep99 [ ]

May 00. (cd/c) *(MOL 70010 CD/MC)* *<4707>* **A IS FOR ALLAH** [ ] Jul00 [ ]

Jamal — not iss.

2003. (cd; as YUSUF ISLAM, FRIENDS & CHILDREN) *<2724>* **I LOOK, I SEE** [ ] [–]

2004. (cd) *(MOL 70028)* **NIGHT OF REMEMBRANCE: LIVE AT THE ROYAL ALBERT HALL** (live) [ ] [ ]

Rod STEWART

Born: RODERICK DAVID STEWART, 10 Jan'45, Highgate, London, England. Of Scottish parentage, STEWART remains a passionate Scotland supporter and considers himself an adopted Scot. In addition to music, obviously, the singer's other passion is football, the young ROD initially biding his time as an apprentice for Brentford F.C. The lure of the itinerant lifestyle proved irresistible, however, and STEWART subsequently hooked up with folk singer, WIZZ JONES, busking/learning his trade around Europe before eventually being deported for vagrancy in 1963. Upon his return, STEWART threw himself headlong into the burgeoning Brit R&B scene as part of West Midlands group, JIMMY POWELL & The FIVE DIMENSIONS. He then took his feted harmonica blowing skills to London, playing on a live effort by JOHN BALDRY & THE HOOCHIE COOCHIE MEN. This in turn, led to ROD developing his vocal talents and releasing a one-off single for 'Decca' in 1964, 'GOOD MORNING LITTLE SCHOOLGIRL', before briefly joining BALDRY's new outfit (also featuring BRIAN AUGER, JULIE DRISCOLL and MICK WALLER, the latter a future STEWART collaborator), STEAMPACKET, the following year. After a dispute with BALDRY, STEWART then added a stint with SHOTGUN EXPRESS (alongside a star-studded line-up which boasted a young PETER GREEN and MICK FLEEETWOOD amongst others) to his increasingly impressive CV. The big break finally came in 1967, when JEFF BECK recruited him as a lead singer, ROD's vocals gracing two albums, 'TRUTH' (1968) and 'BECK-OLA' (1969). While still a member of the JEFF BECK GROUP, STEWART signed a solo deal with 'Phonogram', debuting with 'AN OLD RAINCOAT WON'T EVER LET YOU DOWN' in early 1970 (US title, 'THE ROD STEWART ALBUM'). The record was a revelation, the years of practice finally coming together with STEWART rasping his way through a rootsy solo blueprint of folk, country, blues and R&B. Rapidly establishing himself as one of the finest white soul vocalists in the history of rock, STEWART's voice was a unique, compelling combination of bourbon-throated abrasiveness and blue-eyed crooning, equally at home on choice cover material (EWAN MacCOLL's 'Dirty Old Town' and MIKE D'ABO's 'Handbags And Gladrags') as his own brilliant originals, highlights being the gritty 'CINDY'S LAMENT' and the title track. Simultaneously, ROD had joined The FACES (formerly The SMALL FACES) along with RON WOOD, the pair forming the central writing core of the band as they grew from a laddish club act into stadium headliners, WOOD also becoming STEWART's right-hand writing partner through the pioneering early years of the singer's solo career. 'GASOLINE ALLEY' (1970) was a FACES album in all but name, if a bit more downbeat, WOOD, RONNIE LANE and KENNY JONES (IAN McLAGAN absent due to a 'bus strike', apparently!) all playing on a record which launched STEWART in the States (Top 30) and musically, was a companion piece to The FACES' acclaimed 'A Nod Is As Good

As A Wink To A Blind Horse' (1971). Kicking in with the plaintive slide guitar moan and emotive reverie of the title track through a cover of ELTON JOHN's 'Country Comfort' and STEWART's own 'LADY DAY', the album also featured the first of his DYLAN cover versions, a sympathetic reading of 'ONLY A HOBO'. With the amplified acoustic double whammy of the 'MAGGIE MAY' / 'REASON TO BELIEVE' single in summer '71, ROD went from critical darling to international superstar overnight, the attendant transatlantic No.1 album, 'EVERY PICTURE TELLS A STORY' (1971) representing the creative pinnacle of his career. Featuring regular contributors such as guitarist, MARTIN QUITTENTON alongside the likes of DANNY THOMPSON and Scot, MAGGIE BELL, the album was a masterclass in roots rock boasting one of his most perfectly conceived originals in the lovely 'MANDOLIN WIND'. The choice of cover material was, as ever, impeccable, STEWART cutting a dash through ARTHUR CRUDUP's 'That's All Right' (a track originally made famous by ELVIS PRESLEY) and wringing a pathos from TIM HARDIN's aforementioned 'Reason To Believe' which even its doomed composer couldn't muster. 'NEVER A DULL MOMENT' (1972) was almost as good, the record taking STEWART's boisterous-lad-with-a-senstitive-side persona to its ultimate conclusion by interspersing a trio of worldly-wise rockers (including the classic 'TRUE BLUE') with a beautiful cover of BOB DYLAN's 'Mama You Been On My Mind', the record also spawning another UK No.1 single with 'YOU WEAR IT WELL'. By 1974, The FACES were buckling under the pressure of STEWART's massive successful solo career although, ironically, this also began to slide inexorably downhill, creatively at least, with the disappointing 'SMILER' set. This was the sound of ROD going through the motions, only 'LOCHINVAR' and 'DIXIE TOOT' approaching previous standards. Worse was to come though, as STEWART jacked in London for America, hooking up with sex bomb actress, Britt Ekland and effecting one of the most extensive and needless musical turnarounds of the 70's. Many rock artists have been accused of 'selling-out' over the years but few managed it with such thoroughness and dearth of integrity. 'ATLANTIC CROSSING' (1975) and 'A NIGHT ON THE TOWN' (1976) had their moments (a cover of DANNY WHITTEN's 'I Don't Want To Talk About It' on the former and a definitive reading of CAT STEVEN's 'The First Cut Is The Deepest' on the latter), although danger signs were on the horizon. While the engaging ballad, 'THE KILLING OF GEORGIE' saw ROD acknowledging his sizeable gay following and the lilting 'TONIGHT'S THE NIGHT' (both major hits from 'A NIGHT . . .') proved ROD could still pen a decent love song, such tasteless nonsense as 'HOT LEGS' and 'D'YA THINK I'M SEXY' saw the singer living his sexist image up to the full as well as indulging his growing passion for pseudo-disco MOR. Predictably, by the release of 'BLONDES HAVE MORE FUN' (1978), STEWART was enjoying more success in America than his home country, the singer trawling a creative trough in the early 80's with the likes of 'FOOLISH BEHAVIOUR' and 'TONIGHT I'M YOURS'. His sales figures remained relatively undiminished however, STEWART enjoying the life of the rock aristocrat, his string of relationships with high profile blondes never far from the gossip columns. Tellingly, the singer's best work of the decade came via a reunion with JEFF BECK, the pair getting together for a brilliant reworking of CURTIS MAYFIELD's 'People Get Ready' (Top 50). The 90's saw STEWART regain at least some critical ground with 'VAGABOND HEART' (1991) while the obligatory 'UNPLUGGED . . . AND SEATED' (1993) saw an entertaining reunion with WOOD. Bizarrely enough, ROD has also exhibited a penchant for covering songs by arch weirdo, TOM WAITS, the latest of which, 'HANG ON ST. CHRISTOPHER', appeared on 'A SPANNER IN THE WORKS' (1995). While this alone signals that STEWART hasn't completely lost the musical plot, the prospect of him ever returning to the downhome brilliance of old looked slimmer with each passing year. However, 1998 saw Rod The Mod turn in a fine batch of covers (bar one of his own) under the title of 'WHEN WE WERE THE NEW BOYS'. At the tender age of 56, ROD crossed over to 'Atlantic' records although things didn't get off to a flyer when the single, 'RUN BACK INTO YOUR ARMS', flopped. However, 'I CAN'T DENY IT' restored the man to the Top 30 and secured a Top 10 spot for his umpteenth set, 'HUMAN' (2001). Moving to an Americanised blend of R&B-pop (BABYFACE and EN VOGUE might've been his template), ROD suffered a backlash of sorts from the critics who thought his previous set was a step forward. Cue the entrance of industry mogul extrordinaire Clive Davis, who came up with the idea of rehabilitating ROD's failing career via an album of standards. Hardly an original concept, granted, but one guaranteed to appeal more to his ageing fanbase than a ridiculous attempt at pseudo-R&B. In the event, 'IT HAD TO BE YOU: THE GREAT AMERICAN SONGBOOK' (2002) sounded pretty much as expected, ROD bringing his battered tonsils to the likes of Gershwin's 'YOU CAN'T TAKE THAT AWAY FROM ME' and Jerome Kern's 'THE WAY YOU LOOK TONIGHT'. Suited up and sounding more at ease than he's done since ' . . . THE NEW BOYS', the singer had seemingly found his latter day vocation. So much so that a second volume was paraded a year later, CHER and QUEEN LATIFAH making unlikely – and somewhat distracting – guest appearances. Whether that famous hairdo actually goes well with a suit remains a moot point, but ROD chose to stick with his winning formula over successive transatlantic Top 3's: both 'STARDUST . . . THE GREAT AMERICAN SONGBOOK, VOL.3' (2004) and 'THANKS FOR THE MEMORY: THE GREAT AMERICAN SONGBOOK VOL.4' (2005) combed through the same easy listening archives – COLE PORTER, HOAGY CARMICHAEL, GEORGE GERSHWIN, JEROME KERN etc. – and the same concept which ELLA FITZGERALD and other famous singers pioneered fifty years earlier. Save for a bit of production tweaking (and a revolving cast of soul, jazz and country guests that included STEVIE WONDER, DAVE GRUSIN, ARTURO SANDOVAL, DIANA ROSS, DOLLY PARTON, GEORGE BENSON and CHRIS BOTTI) the song remained pretty much the same although ROD did offer a brief nod to his soul-boy roots with a – CHAKA KHAN assisted – cover of Sam Cooke's 'YOU SEND ME'.

• **Songwriters:** ROD's cover versions:- STREET FIGHTING MAN (Rolling Stones) + RUBY TUESDAY / SWEET SOUL MUSIC (Arthur Conley) / I KNOW I'M LOSING YOU (Temptations) / IT'S ALL OVER NOW (Valentinos) / MY WAY OF GIVING (Small Faces) / CUT ACROSS SHORTY (hit; Eddie Cochran) / ANGEL (Jimi Hendrix) / AMAZING GRACE (trad. / hit; Judy Collins) / I'D RATHER GO BLIND (Etta James) / ONLY A HOBO + SWEETHEART LIKE YOU (Bob Dylan) / TWISTIN' THE NIGHT AWAY + BRING IT ON HOME TO ME + YOU SEND ME + HAVING A PARTY + SOOTHE ME (Sam Cooke) / OH NO NOT MY BABY + PRETTY FLAMINGO (Manfred Mann) / COUNTRY COMFORTS + YOUR SONG (Elton John) / WHAT MADE MILWALKEE FAMOUS (hit; Jerry Lee Lewis) / SAILING (Sutherland Brothers) / THIS OLD HEART OF MINE (Isley Brothers) / GET BACK (Beatles) / YOU KEEP ME HANGIN' ON (Supremes) / I DON'T WANT TO TALK ABOUT IT (Crazy Horse member Danny Whitten) / SOME GUYS HAVE ALL THE LUCK (Robert Palmer) / HOW LONG (Ace) / SWEET LITTLE ROCK'N'ROLLER + LITTLE QUEENIE (Chuck Berry) / THE GREAT PRETENDER (Platters) / ALL RIGHT NOW (Free) / TRY A LITTLE TENDERNESS (Otis Redding) / THE MOTOWN SONG (L.J.McNally) / IT TAKES TWO (Marvin Gaye & Tammi Terrell) / DOWNTOWN TRAIN + TOM TRAUBERT'S BLUES (Tom Waits) / BROKEN ARROW (Robbie Robertson) / HAVE I TOLD YOU LATELY THAT I LOVE YOU (Van Morrison) / PEOPLE GET READY (Curtis Mayfield) / SHOTGUN WEDDING (Roy C) / WINDY TOWN (Chris Rea) / DOWNTOWN LIGHTS (Blue Nile) / LEAVE VIRGINIA ALONE (Tom Petty) / OOH LA LA (with The Faces) / CIGARETTES & ALCOHOL (Oasis) / ROCKS (Primal Scream) / SUPERSTAR (Superstar) / SECRET

HEART (Ron Sexsmith) / HOTEL CHAMBERMAID (Graham Parker) / SHELLY MY LOVE (Nick Lowe) / WEAK (Skunk Anansie) / WHAT DO YOU WANT ME TO DO (Mike Scott). SIMON CLIMIE began writing for him from 1988. YOU'RE THE STAR single written by Livesey, Lyle & Miller. • **Trivia/Blondeography:** BRITT EKLAND (marriage 5 Mar'75-1978) / ALANA HAMILTON (marriage 1979-1984) / KELLY EMBERG (1985-1990) / RACHEL HUNTER (marriage 1990-1999) / PENNY LANCASTER (1999-now).

Album rating: AN OLD RAINCOAT WILL NEVER LET YOU DOWN (*7) / GASOLINE ALLEY (*7) / EVERY PICTURE TELLS A STORY (*9) / NEVER A DULL MOMENT (*8) / SING IT AGAIN ROD (*5) / SMILER (*4) / ATLANTIC CROSSING (*7) / A NIGHT ON THE TOWN (*6) / FOOT LOOSE AND FANCY FREE (*4) / BLONDES HAVE MORE FUN (*5) / GREATEST HITS VOL.1 compilation (*8) / FOOLISH BEHAVIOUR (*3) / TONIGHT I'M YOURS (*6) / ABSOLUTELY LIVE (*3) / BODY WISHES (*3) / CAMOUFLAGE (*3) / EVERY BEAT OF MY HEART (aka ROD STEWART) (*4) / OUT OF ORDER (*5) / STORYTELLER – THE BEST OF ROD STEWART 1964-1990 compilation (*8) / VAGABOND HEART (*6) / UNPLUGGED . . . AND SEATED (*7) / A SPANNER IN THE WORKS (*6) / IF WE FALL IN LOVE TONIGHT (*6) / WHEN WE WERE THE NEW BOYS (*7) / HUMAN (*5) / THE STORY SO FAR compilation (*8) / IT HAD TO BE YOU . . . THE GREAT AMERICAN SONGBOOK (*5) / AS TIME GOES BY . . . THE GREAT AMERICAN SONGBOOK VOLUME II (*4) / CHANGING FACES: THE VERY BEST OF ROD STEWART & THE FACES compilation (*8) / STARDUST: THE GREAT AMERICAN SONGBOOK VOLUME III (*4) / THANKS FOR THE MEMORY: THE GREAT AMERICAN SONGBOOK VOLUME IV (*3)

ROD STEWART – vocals with session people

Decca Press

Oct 64. (7") *(F 11996)* **GOOD MORNING LITTLE SCHOOLGIRL. / I'M GONNA MOVE TO THE OUTSKIRTS OF TOWN** [ ] [ ]
(re-iss. Mar82)

—— in 1965, ROD joined STEAMPACKET but they issued no 45's; split Mar'66

Columbia not iss.

Nov 65. (7") *(DB 7766)* **THE DAY WILL COME. / WHY DOES IT GO ON** [ ] [–]
Apr 66. (7") *(DB 7892)* **SHAKE. / I JUST GOT SOME** [ ] [–]

—— A month previous, he had joined SHOTGUN EXPRESS who released one 45, 'I COULD FEEL THE WHOLE WORLD TURN AROUND' Oct66 on 'Columbia'.

Immediate not iss.

Nov 67. (7") *(IM 060)* **LITTLE MISS UNDERSTOOD. / SO MUCH TO SAY** [ ] [–]
(re-iss. Sep80 on 'Virgin') (re-iss. Feb83)

—— In 1968, he joined JEFF BECK GROUP, appearing on 2 albums; 'TRUTH' & 'BECK-OLA'. Similtaneously joined The FACES and returned to solo work 1969.

Vertigo Mercury

Feb 70. (lp) *(VO 4)* <61237> **AN OLD RAINCOAT WON'T EVER LET YOU DOWN** <US-title 'THE ROD STEWART ALBUM'> [ ] [ ]
– Street fighting man / Man of constant sorrow / Blind prayer / Handbags and gladrags / An old raincoat won't ever let you down / I wouldn't ever change a thing / Cindy's lament / Dirty old town. *(re-iss. Aug83 on 'Mercury' lp/c; PRICE/PRIMC 27) (cd-iss. Nov87 & Sep95; 830 572-2) (cd re-iss. Aug98; 558058-2)*
Feb 70. (7") <73009> **AN OLD RAINCOAT WON'T LET YOU DOWN. / STREET FIGHTING MAN** [–] [ ]
May 70. (7") *(73031)* **HANDBAGS AND GLADRAGS. / MAN OF CONSTANT SORROW** [–] [ ]
<re-iss. Feb72; 73031> – hit No.42.
Sep 70. (7") *(6086 002)* <73095> **IT'S ALL OVER NOW. / JO'S LAMENT** [ ] [ ]
Sep 70. (lp) *(6360 500)* <61264> **GASOLINE ALLEY** [62] Jun70 [27]
– Gasoline alley / It's all over now / My way of giving / Country comfort / Cut across Shorty / Lady day / Jo's lament / I don't want to discuss it. *(re-iss. Aug83 on 'Mercury' lp/c; PRICE/PRIMC 28) (cd-iss. Oct84 + Sep95; 824 881-2) (cd re-iss. Aug98; 558059-2)*
Nov 70. (7") <73115> **GASOLINE ALLEY. / ONLY A HOBO** [–] [ ]
Jan 71. (7") <73156> **CUT ACROSS SHORTY. / GASOLINE ALLEY** [–] [ ]
Mar 71. (7") <73175> **MY WAY OF GIVING. /** [–] [ ]
May 71. (7") <73196> **COUNTRY COMFORT. / GASOLINE ALLEY** [–] [ ]

Mercury Mercury

Jul 71. (7") *(6052 097)* <73224> **MAGGIE MAY. / REASON TO BELIEVE** [1] [1] [62]
(above was flipped over for BBC Radio One playlist. MAGGIE MAY was now the bigger played hit) *(re-iss. Oct84)*
Jul 71. (lp) *(6338 063)* <609> **EVERY PICTURE TELLS A STORY** [1] Jun71 [1]
– Every picture tells a story / Seems like a long time / That's all right / Tomorrow is such a long time / Amazing Grace / Henry / Maggie May / Mandolin wind / (I know) I'm losing you / Reason to believe. *(re-iss. May83 lp/c; PRICE/PRIMC 15) (cd-iss. Nov87 & Sep95; 822 385-2) (cd re-iss. Aug98; 558060-2)*
Nov 71. (7") <73244> **(I KNOW) I'M LOSING YOU. / MANDOLIN WIND** [–] [24]
Jul 72. (lp) *(6499 153)* <646> **NEVER A DULL MOMENT** [1] [2]
– True blue / Lost Paraguayos / Mama you been on my mind / Italian girls / Angel / Interludings / You wear it well / I'd rather go blind / Twisting the night away. *(re-iss. May83 lp/c;) (cd-iss. Nov87 & Sep95; 826 263-2) (cd re-iss. Aug98; 558061-2)*
Aug 72. (7") *(6052 171)* **YOU WEAR IT WELL. / LOST PARAGUAYOS** [1] [–]
Aug 72. (7") <73330>**YOU WEAR IT WELL. / TRUE BLUE** [–] [13]

—— Sep72, a ROD STEWART early recording with PYTHON LEE JACKSON; 'In A Broken Dream' hits UK No.3 / US No.56.

Nov 72. (7") *(6052 198)* **ANGEL. / WHAT MADE MILWAUKEE FAMOUS (HAS MADE A LOSER OUT OF ME)** [4] [–]
Nov 72. (7") <73344> **ANGEL. / LOST PARAGUAYOS** [–] [40]

—— May73, older JEFF BECK & ROD STEWART recording 'I'VE BEEN DRINKIN' ' hit 27.

Aug 73. (7") <73412> **TWISTING THE NIGHT AWAY. / TRUE BLUE – LADY DAY** [–] [59]
Aug 73. (lp)(c) *(6499 484)(7142 183)* <680> **SING IT AGAIN ROD** (compilation of covers) [1] Jul73 [31]
– Reason to believe / You wear it well / Mandolin wind / Country comforts / Maggie May / Handbags and gladrags / Street fighting man / Twisting the night away / Lost Paraguayos / (I know) I'm losing you / Pinball wizard / Gasoline alley. *(cd-iss. Oct84; 824882-2) (cd re-iss. Aug98; 558062-2)*
Aug 73. (7") *(6052 371)* <73426> **OH! NO NOT MY BABY. / JODIE** [6] Oct73 [59]
Sep 74. (7") *(6167 033)* **FAREWELL. / BRING IT ON HOME TO ME – YOU SEND ME (Medley)** [7] [–]
Oct 74. (lp)(c) *(9104 001)* <1017> **SMILER** [1] [13]
– Sweet little rock'n'roller / Lochinvar / Farewell / Sailor / Bring it on home to me – You send me (medley) / Let me be your car / A natural man / A natural man / Dixie toot / Hard road / I've grown accustomed to her face / Girl of the North Country / Mine for me. *(cd-iss. Nov87 & Sep95; 832 056-2) (cd re-iss. Aug98; 558063-2)*
Nov 74. (7") <73636> **MINE FOR ME. / FAREWELL** [–] [91]
Jan 75. (7") <73660> **LET ME BE YOUR CAR. / SAILOR** [–] [ ]

Warners Warners

Aug 75. (7") *(K 16600)* **SAILING. / STONE COLD SOBER** [1] [–]
(re-activated Sep76, hit UK No.3, re-iss. Jan84) (re-iss. Jun77 on 'Riva') (re-iss. Mar87 for Channel Ferry disaster fund, hit No.41)
Aug 75. (lp/c) *(K/K4 56151)* <2875> **ATLANTIC CROSSING** [1] [9]
– Three time loser / Alright for an hour / All in the name of rock'n'roll / Drift away / Stone cold sober / I don't want to talk about it / It's not the spotlight / This old heart of mine / Still love you / Sailing. *(re-iss. Jan78 on 'Riva' lp/c; RV LP/4 4) (cd-iss. Feb87; K2 56151) (blue-lp Jul77) (cd re-iss. Nov00 on 'WEA'; 9362 47729-2)*
Aug 75. (7") <8146> **SAILING. / ALL IN THE NAME OF ROCK'N'ROLL** [–] [58]

Riva Warners

Nov 75. (7") *(1)* **THIS OLD HEART OF MINE. / ALL IN THE NAME OF ROCK'N'ROLL** [4] [–]
Jan 76. (7") <8170> **THIS OLD HEART OF MINE. / STILL LOVE YOU** [–] [83]
May 76. (7") *(RIVA 3)* **TONIGHT'S THE NIGHT. / THE BALLTRAP** [5] [–]
Jun 76. (lp/c) *(RV LP/4 1)* <2938> **A NIGHT ON THE TOWN** [1] [2]
– Tonight's the night / The first cut is the deepest / Fool for you / The killing of Georgie (part 1 & 2) / The balltrap / Pretty flamingo / Big bayou / The wild side of life / Trade winds. *(re-iss. Jun83 on 'Warner Bros' lp/c; K/K4 56234) (cd-iss. 1989 on 'WEA'; K2*

56234) (cd re-iss. Jun93; 7599 27339-2) (cd re-iss. Nov00 on 'WEA'; 9362 47730-2)

Aug 76. (7") *(RIVA 4)* **THE KILLING OF GEORGIE. / FOOL FOR YOU** [2] [–]

Sep 76. (7") *<8262>* **TONIGHT'S THE NIGHT. / FOOL FOR YOU** [–] [1]

Nov 76. (7") *(RIVA 6)* **GET BACK. / TRADE WINDS** [11] [–]

Feb 77. (7") *<8321>* **THE FIRST CUT IS THE DEEPEST. / THE BALLTRAP** [–] [21]

Apr 77. (7") *(RIVA 7)* **THE FIRST CUT IS THE DEEPEST. / I DON'T WANT TO TALK ABOUT IT** [1] [–]

Apr 77. (7") *<8396>* **THE KILLING OF GEORGIE. / ROSIE** [–] [30]

Oct 77. (7") *(RIVA 11) <8476>* **YOU'RE IN MY HEART. / YOU GOT A NERVE** [3] [4]

Nov 77. (lp/c) *(RV LP/4 5) <3092>* **FOOT LOOSE AND FANCY FREE** [3] [2]
– Hot legs / You're insane / You're in my heart / Born loose / You keep me hangin' on / (If loving you is wrong) I don't want to be right / You got a nerve / I was only joking. *(re-iss. Jun83 on 'Warner Bros.' lp/c; K/K4 56423) (cd-iss. Jun89; K2 56423) (cd re-iss. Nov00 on 'WEA'; 9362 47731-2)*

Jan 78. (7") *(RIVA 10)* **HOT LEGS. / I WAS ONLY JOKING** [5] [–]

Feb 78. (7") *<8535>* **HOT LEGS. / YOU'RE INSANE** [–] [28]

Apr 78. (7") *<8568>* **I WAS ONLY JOKING. / BORN LOOSE** [–] [22]

May 78. (7"; by ROD STEWART with the SCOTLAND WORLD CUP SQUAD) *(RIVA 15)* **OLE OLA (MUHLER BRASILEIRA). / I'D WALK A MILLION MILES FOR ONE OF YOUR GOALS** [4] [–]

Nov 78. (7") *(RIVA 17)* **D'YA THINK I'M SEXY?. / DIRTY WEEKEND** [1] [–]

Dec 78. (7") *<8734>* **D'YA THINK I'M SEXY?. / SCARRED AND SCARED** [–] [1]

Dec 78. (lp/c)<US-pic-lp> *(RV LP/4 8) <3261>* **BLONDES HAVE MORE FUN** [3] [1]
– D'ya think I'm sexy / Dirty weekend / Ain't love a bitch / The best days of my life / Is that the thanks I get / Attractive female wanted / Blondes (have more fun) / Last summer / Standing in the shadows of love / Scarred and scared. *(re-iss. Jun83 on 'Warner Bros.' lp/c; K/K4 56572) (cd-iss. Jan91 on 'Warners'; 7599 27376-2) (cd re-iss. Nov00 on 'WEA'; 9362 47732-2)*

Jan 79. (7") *(RIVA 18)* **AIN'T LOVE A BITCH. / SCARRED AND SCARED** [11] [–]

Apr 79. (7") *<8810>* **AIN'T LOVE A BITCH. / LAST SUMMER** [–] [22]

Apr 79. (7") *(RIVA 19)* **BLONDES (HAVE MORE FUN). / THE BEST DAYS OF MY LIFE** [63] [–]

Nov 79. (lp/c) *(RODTV/+4 1) <3373>* **GREATEST HITS VOLUME 1** (compilation) [1] [22]
– Hot legs / Maggie May / a ya think I'm sexy / You're in my heart / Sailing / I don't want to talk about it / Tonight's the night / The killing of Georgie (parts 1 & 2) / Maggie May / The first cut is the deepest / I was only joking. *(re-iss. Jun83 lp/c; K/K4 56744) (cd-iss. Jan84 on 'Warner Bros.'; K2 56744)*

Dec 79. (7") *<49138>* **I DON'T WANT TO TALK ABOUT IT. / THE BEST DAYS OF MY LIFE** [–] [46]

May 80. (7") *(RIVA 23)* **IF LOVING YOU IS WRONG (I DON'T WANT TO BE RIGHT). / LAST SUMMER** [23] [–]

Nov 80. (7"/ext.12") *(RIVA 26/+T) <49617>* **PASSION. / BETTER OFF DEAD** [17] [5]

Nov 80. (lp/c) *(RV LP/4 11) <3485>* **FOOLISH BEHAVIOR** [4] [12]
– Better off dead / Foolish behaviour / My girl / She won't dance with me / Gi' me wings / So soon we change / Somebody special / Passion / Say it ain't true / Oh God, I wish I was home tonight. *(re-iss. Jun83 on 'Warner Bros.' lp/c; >)*

Dec 80. (7") *(RIVA 28)* **MY GIRL. / SHE WON'T DANCE WITH ME** [32] [–]

Mar 81. (7"/c-s) *(RIVA 29/+M)* **OH GOD, I WISH I WAS HOME TONIGHT. / SOMEBODY SPECIAL** [ ] [–]

Mar 81. (7") *<49686>* **SOMEBODY SPECIAL. / SHE WON'T DANCE WITH ME** [–] [71]

Oct 81. (7") *<49843>* **YOUNG TURKS. / SONNY** [–] [5]

Oct 81. (7") *(RIVA 33)* **TONIGHT I'M YOURS (DON'T HURT ME). / SONNY** [8] [–]

Nov 81. (lp/c) *(RV LP/4 14) <3602>* **TONIGHT I'M YOURS** [8] [11]
– Tonight I'm yours (don't hurt me) / Only a boy / Just like a woman / How long / Never give up on a dream / Jealous / Tora, Tora, Tora (out with the boys) / Young Turks / Tear it up / Sonny. *(re-iss. Jun83 lp/c; K/K4 56951) (cd-iss. Jun93 on 'Warners'; 7599 23602-2) (cd re-iss. Nov00 on 'WEA'; 9362 47717-2)*

Dec 81. (7") *(RIVA 34)* **YOUNG TURKS. / TORA, TORA, TORA (OUT WITH THE BOYS)** [11] [–]

Jan 82. (7") *<49886>* **TONIGHT I'M YOURS (DON'T HURT ME). / TORA, TORA, TORA (OUT WITH THE BOYS)** [–] [20]

Feb 82. (7") *(RIVA 35) <50051>* **HOW LONG. / JEALOUS** [41] Apr82 [49]

Nov 82. (d-lp/d-c) *(RV LP/4 17) <23743>* **ABSOLUTELY LIVE (live)** [35] [46]
– The stripper / Tonight I'm yours / Sweet little rock'n'roller / Hot legs / Tonight's the night / The great pretender / Passion / She won't dance with me / Little Queenie / You're in my heart / Rock my plimsoul / Young Turks / Guess I'll always love you / Gasoline alley / Maggie May / Tear it up / D'ya think I'm sexy / Sailing / I don't want to talk about it / Stay with me. *(re-iss. Mar84 on 'Warner Bros.' d-lp/dc; 923743-1/-4) (cd-iss. Mar87; 923743-2)*

Nov 82. (7") *<29874>* **GUESS I'LL ALWAYS LOVE YOU (live). / ROCK MY PLIMSOUL (live)** [–] [ ]

Warners Warners

May 83. (7") *(W 9608) <29608>* **BABY JANE. / READY NOW** [1] [14]
(12"+=) *(W 9608T)* – If loving you is wrong (live).

Jun 83. (lp/c) *(K 923977-1/-4) <23877>* **BODY WISHES** [5] [30]
– Dancin' alone / Baby Jane / Move me / Body wishes / Sweet surrender / What am I gonna do / Ghetto blaster / Ready now / Strangers again / Satisfied. *(cd-iss. Jul84; K 923977-2)*

Aug 83. (7"/12") *(W 9564/+T) <29564>* **WHAT AM I GONNA DO?. / DANCIN' ALONE** [3] [35]

Dec 83. (7"/67"pic-d) *(W 9440/+P)* **SWEET SURRENDER. / GHETTO BLASTER** [23] [–]
(12"+=) *(W 9440T)* – Oh God I wish I was home tonight.

May 84. (7") *<29256>* **INFATUATION. / SHE WON'T DANCE WITH ME** [–] [6]

May 84. (7") *(W 9256)* **INFATUATION. / THREE TIME LOSER** [27] [–]
(12"+=) *(W 9256T)* – Tonight's the night.

Jun 84. (lp/c/cd) *(925095-1/-4/-4) <25095>* **CAMOUFLAGE** [8] [18]
– Infatuation / All right now / Some guys have all the luck / Can we still be friends / Bad for you / Heart is on the line / Camouflage / Trouble. *(free 1-sided 7"pic-d w.a.)* – INFATUATION / (interview).

Jul 84. (7") *(W 9204) <29215>* **SOME GUYS HAVE ALL THE LUCK. / I WAS ONLY JOKING** [15] [10]
(12"+=) *(W 9204T)* – The killing of Georgie.

Nov 84. (7") *(W 9115)* **TROUBLE. / TORA, TORA, TORA (OUT WITH THE BOYS)** [ ] [–]
(12"+=) *(W 9115T)* – This old heart of mine.

Dec 84. (7") *<29112>* **ALL RIGHT NOW. / DANCIN' ALONE** [–] [72]

—— In 1985, he was credited on 45 'PEOPLE GET READY' by JEFF BECK.

Jun 86. (7") *(W 8668) <28668>* **LOVE TOUCH. / HEART IS ON THE LINE** [27] May86 [6]
(12"pic-d+=) *(W 8668TP)* – Hard lesson to learn.

Jun 86. (lp/c)(cd) *(WX 53/+C)(925446-2) <25446>* **EVERY BEAT OF MY HEART** <US-title 'ROD STEWART'> [5] [28]
– Here to eternity / Another heartache / A night like this / Who's gonna take me home / Red hot in black / Love touch / In my own crazy way / Every beat of my heart / Ten days of rain / In my life. *(cd+=)* – Every beat of my heart (remix).

Jul 86. (7") *(W 8625) <28625>* **EVERY BEAT OF MY HEART. / TROUBLE** [2] Nov86 [83]
(12"+=) *(W 8625)* – ('A'mix).
(12"pic-d+=) *(W 8625TE)* – Some guys have all the luck (live)

Sep 86. (7") *(W 8631) <28631>* **ANOTHER HEARTACHE. / YOU'RE IN MY HEART** [54] [52]
(12"+=) *(W 8631T)* – ('A'extended).

Jul 87. (7") *<28303>* **TWISTING THE NIGHT AWAY. / LET'S GET SMALL** [–] [80]
above was issued on 'Geffen' and on film 'Innerspace'.

May 88. (7")<US-c-s> *(W 7927) <27927>* **LOST IN YOU. / ALMOST ILLEGAL** [21] [12]
(12"+=/12"pic-d+=) *(W 7927 T/TP)* – ('A'extended).
(cd-s+=) *(W 7927CD)* – Baby Jane / Every beat of my heart.

May 88. (lp/c)(cd) *(WX 152/+C)(925684-2) <25684>* **OUT OF ORDER** [11] [20]
– Lost in you / The wild horse / Lethal dose of love / Forever young / My heart can't tell you no / Dynamite / Nobody loves you when you're down and out / Crazy about her / Try a little tenderness / When I was your man.

Jul 88. (7") *(W 7796) <27796>* **FOREVER YOUNG. / DAYS OF RAGE** [57] [12]
(12"+=) *(W 7796)* – ('A'extended).
(cd-s+=) *(W 7796CD)* – Every beat of my heart.

Jan 89. (7") **TRY A LITTLE TENDERNESS. / MY HEART CAN'T TELL YOU NO** – [ ]

Apr 89. (7") *(W 7729)* *<27729>* **MY HEART CAN'T TELL YOU NO. / THE WILD HORSE** 49 Nov88 4
(12"+=/12"pic-d+=/cd-s+=) *(W 7729 T/TP/CD)* – Passion (live).

May 89. (7"/c-s) *<27657>* **CRAZY ABOUT HER. / DYNAMITE** – 11

Nov 89. (7"/7"pic-d/c-s; with RONALD ISLEY) *(W 2686/+P)* *<19983>* **THIS OLD HEART OF MINE. / TONIGHT I'M YOURS (DON'T HURT ME)** 51 –
(12"+=/cd-s+=/12"pic-d+=) *(W 2686 T/TP/CD)* – Ain't love a bitch.

Nov 89. (d-lp/d-c/d-cd) *(925987-2/-4/-1)* *<25987>* **STORYTELLER – THE BEST OF ROD STEWART 1964-1990** (compilation) 3 54

— (was also issued UK on (7xlp)(4xc)(4xcd).

Jan 90. (7"/c-s) *(W 2647/+C)* *<22685>* **DOWNTOWN TRAIN. / THE KILLING OF GEORGIE (pt.1 & 2)** 10 Nov89 3
(12"/cd-s) *(W 2647 T/CD)* – ('A'side) / Hot legs.
(12"+=) *(W 2647TE)* – ('A'side) / Cindy incidentally / To love somebody.

Mar 90. (7"; with RONALD ISLEY) *<19983>* **THIS OLD HEART OF MINE. / YOU'RE IN MY HEART** – 10

Mar 90. (cd/c) *<26158>* **DOWNTOWN TRAIN – SELECTIONS FROM STORYTELLER** (compilation) – 20

Nov 90. (7"/c-s; ROD STEWART & TINA TURNER) *(ROD 1/+C)* **IT TAKES TWO. / HOT LEGS (live)** 5 [ ]
(12"+=/cd-s+=) *(ROD 1 T/CD)* – ('A'extended remix).

Mar 91. (7"/c-s) *(W 0017)* *<19366>* **RHYTHM OF MY HEART. / MOMENT OF GLORY** 3 Feb91 5
(12"+=/cd-s+=) *(W 0017 T/CD)* – I don't want to talk about it (re-recording).

Apr 91. (cd)(lp/c) *(<7599 26596-2>)(WX 408/+C)* **VAGABOND HEART** 2 10
– Rhythm of my heart / Rebel heart / Broken arrow / It takes two / When a man's in love / You are everything / The Motown song / Go out dancing / No holding back / Have I told you lately that I love you / Moment of glory / Downtown train / If only.

Jun 91. (7"/c-s) *(W 0030/+C)* *<19322>* **THE MOTOWN SONG. / SWEET SOUL MUSIC (live)** 10 10
(12"+=/cd-s+=) *(W 0030 T/CD)* – Try a little tenderness.

Aug 91. (7"/c-s) *(W 0059/+C)* **BROKEN ARROW. / I WAS ONLY JOKING** 54 –
(10"+=/cd-s+=) *(W 0059 T/CD)* – The killing of Georgie (parts 1 & 2).

Oct 91. (c-s,cd-s) *<19274>* **BROKEN ARROW / THE WILD HORSE** – 20

Apr 92. (c-s,cd-s) *<865944>* **YOUR SONG / MANDOLIN WIND** – 48

— <above issued on 'Polydor' US>

Apr 92. (7"/c-s) *(W 0104/+C)* **YOUR SONG. / BROKEN ARROW** 41 –
(12"+=/cd-s+=) *(W 0104 T/CD)* – Mandolin wind / The first cut is the deepest.

Nov 92. (7"/c-s) *(W 0104/+C)* **TOM TRAUBERT'S BLUES (WALTZING MATILDA). / NO HOLDING BACK** 6 –
(cd-s+=) *(W 0104CD)* – Downtown train.
(cd-s) *(W 0104CDX)* – ('A'side) / Sailing / I don't want to talk about it / Try a little tenderness.

Feb 93. (cd/c/lp) *(<9362 45258-2>)(WX 503/+C)* **ROD STEWART, LEAD VOCALIST** (part compilation) 3 –
– I ain't superstitious / Handbags & gladrags / Cindy incidentally / Stay with me / True blue / Sweet Mary lady / Hot legs / Stand back / Ruby Tuesday / Shotgun wedding / First I look at the purse / Tom Traubert's blues.

Feb 93. (7"/c-s) *(W 0158/+C)* **RUBY TUESDAY. / YOU'RE IN MY HEART** 11 –
(cd-s+=) *(W 0158CD)* – Out of order / Passion.
(cd-s+=) *(W 0158CDX)* – Crazy about her / Passion.

Apr 93. (7"/c-s) *(W 0171/+C)* **SHOTGUN WEDDING. / EVERY BEAT OF MY HEART** 21 –
(cd-s+=) *(W 0171CD)* – Sweet soul music (live).
(cd-s) *(W 0171CDX)* – ('A'side) / Memphis / Maybe I'm amazed / Had me a real goodtime (all 3 by ROD STEWART & THE FACES).
below with special guest **RONNIE WOOD** – guitar plus others **JEFF GOLUB** – guitar / **CARMINE ROJAS** – bass / **CHARLES KENTISS III** – piano, organ / **KEVIN SAVIGAR** – piano, organ & accordion / **JIM CREGAN** – guitar / **DON TESCHNER** – guitar, violin & mandolin / **PHIL PARLAPIANO** – accordion & mandolin / & backing singers

May 93. (cd/c/lp) *(<9362 45289-2/-4/-1>)* **UNPLUGGED . . . AND SEATED (live)** 2 2
– Hot legs / Tonight's the night / Handbags and gladrags / Cut across Shorty / Every picture tells a story / Maggie May / Reason to believe / People get ready / Have I told you lately / Tom Traubert's blues (waltzing Matilda) / The first cut is the deepest / Mandolin wind / Highgate shuffle / Stay with me / Having a party.

Jun 93. (7"/c-s) *(W 0185/+C)* *<18511>* **HAVE I TOLD YOU LATELY THAT I LOVE YOU? / GASOLINE ALLEY** 5 Apr93 5
(cd-s+=) *(W 0185CD)* –
(cd-s) *(W 0185CDX)* – ('A'side) / Love wars / One night.

Aug 93. (7"/c-s) *(W 0198/+C)* *<18427>* **REASON TO BELIEVE (unplugged). / IT'S ALL OVER NOW (unplugged)** 51 19
(cd-s+=) *(W 0198CD1)* – Love in the right hands.
(cd-s) *(W 0198CD2)* – ('A'side) / Cindy incidentally / Stay with me (both w / FACES).

— In Dec '93, ROD & STING, teamed up with BRYAN ADAMS on his US Top 5 hit 'All For Love'.

Dec 93. (7"/c-s) *(W 0226/+C)* **PEOPLE GET READY. / I WAS ONLY JOKING** 45 –
(cd-s) *(W 0226CD1)* – ('A'side) / Tonight's the night / If loving you is wrong (I don't want to be right).
(cd-s) *(W 0226CD2)* – ('A'side) / Da ya think I'm sexy / Sweet little rock'n'roller (live) / Baby Jane.

— Late '93, ROD, BRYAN ADAMS and STING teamed up on a song from 'The Three Musketeers' film; 'ALL FOR LOVE', which hit UK No.2 (early '94) + US No.1.

Dec 93. (c-s,cd-s; ROD STEWART with RONNIE WOOD) *<18427>* **HAVING A PARTY (live unplugged) / SWEET LITTLE ROCK AND ROLLER (live acoustic)** – 36

May 95. (c-s) *(W 0296C)* **YOU'RE THE STAR / SHOCK TO THE SYSTEM** 19 –
(cd-s+=) *(W 0296CD)* – Have I told you lately.

May 95. (cd/c/lp) *(<9362 45867-2/-4/-1>)* **A SPANNER IN THE WORKS** 4 35
– Windy town / Downtown lights / Leave Virginia alone / Sweetheart like you / This / Lady luck / You're the star / Muddy, Sam and Otis / Hang on St. Christopher / Delicious / Soothe me / Purple heather.

Jun 95. (c-s,cd-s) *<17847>* **LEAVE VIRGINIA ALONE / SHOCK TO THE SYSTEM** – 52

Aug 95. (c-s) *(W 0310C)* **LADY LUCK / HOT LEGS** 56 –
(cd-s+=) *(W 0310CD1)* – The groom still waiting at the altar / Young Turks.
(cd-s) *(W 0310CD2)* – ('A'side) / The killing of Georgie / Sailing / The first cut is the deepest.

Jun 96. (c-s/cd-s) *(W 0354 C/CD)* **PURPLE HEATHER / EVERY BEAT OF MY HEART** 16 [ ]

— The official song for Scotland's Euro '96 football campaign. All proceeds were donated to the families of the Dunblane tragedy.

Nov 96. (cd/c) *(<9362 46467-2/-4>)* **IF WE FALL IN LOVE TONIGHT** 8 19
– If we fall in love tonight / Sometimes when we touch / I don't want to talk about it / For the first time / When I need you / Broken arrow / Have I told you lately / Tonight / Forever young / My heart can't tell you no / First cut is the deepest / Tonight's the night / You're in my heart.

Dec 96. (c-s) *(W 0380C)* *<17459>* **IF WE FALL IN LOVE TONIGHT / TOM TRAUBERT'S BLUES (WALTZING MATILDA)** 58 Nov96 54
(cd-s) *(W 0380CD)* – ('A'side) / So far away / I was only joking / Ten days of rain.

— N-TRANCE featured ROD on their version of 'DA YA THINK I'M SEXY?', which hit UK No.7 in Nov'97.

May 98. (c-s) *(W 0446C)* *<17195>* **OOH LA LA / A NIGHT LIKE THIS** 16 Jun98 39
(cd-s+=) *(W 0446CD)* – Ten days of rain.

Jun 98. (cd/c) *(<9362 46792-2/-4>)* **WHEN WE WERE THE NEW BOYS** 2 44
– Cigarettes and alcohol / Ooh la la / Rocks / Superstar / Secret heart / Hotel chambermaid / Shelly my love / When we were the new boys / Weak / What do you want me to do?

Aug 98. (c-s) *(W 0452C)* **ROCKS / STAY WITH ME (live)** 55 –
(cd-s+=) *(W 0452CD2)* – Maggie May (live).
(cd-s) *(W 0452CD1)* – ('A'side) / Hot legs (live) / Da ya think I'm sexy? (live).

Dec 98. (c-s/cd-s; w-drawn) *(W 465 C/CD)* **SUPERSTAR** – –
Universal not iss.

Apr 99. (c-s) *(UNC 56235)* **FAITH OF THE HEART / Mark Shainman: MAIN TITLE SCORE** 60 –
(cd-s+=) *(UND 56235)* – Front porch.

Atlantic Atlantic

Oct 00. (c-s) *(AT 0088C)* **RUN BACK INTO YOUR ARMS / WHEN WE WERE THE NEW BOYS** [ ] [–]
(cd-s+=) *(AT 0088CD)* – Red hot and black.
Mar 01. (c-s) *(AT 0096C) <85018>* **I CAN'T DENY IT / PEACH** [26] [–]
(cd-s+=) *(AT 0096CD)* – Do wah diddy.
Mar 01. (cd/c) *(<7567 83411-2/-4>)* **HUMAN** [9] Feb01 [50]
– Human / Smitten / Don't come around here / Soul on soul / Loveless / If I had you / Charlie Parker loves me / It was love that we needed / To be with you / Run back into your arms / I can't deny it. *(UK+=)* – Doo wah diddy (if you want me to go) / Peach.
May 01. (c-s; as ROD STEWART & HELICOPTER GIRL) *(AT 0104C)* **DON'T COME AROUND HERE / CUPID** [ ] [–]
(cd-s+=) *(AT 0104CD)* – Charlie Parker loves me.

J – B.M.G. J – B.M.G.

Oct 02. (cd/c) *(74321 96867-2/-4) <20039>* **IT HAD TO BE YOU . . . THE GREAT AMERICAN SONGBOOK** [8] [4]
– You go to my head / They can't take that away from me / The way you look tonight / It had to be you / That old feeling / These foolish things / The very thought of you / Moonglow / I'll be seeing you / Ev'ry time we say goodbye / The nearness of you / For all we know / We'll be together again / That's all.
Oct 03. (cd) *(82876 57484-2) <55710>* **AS TIME GOES BY . . . THE GREAT AMERICAN SONGBOOK VOLUME II** [4] [2]
– Time after time / I'm in the mood for love / Don't get around much anymore / Bewitched, bothered & bewildered (with CHER) / 'Till there was you / Until the real thing comes along / Where or when / Smile / My heart stood still / Someone to watch over me (with QUEEN LATIFAH) / As time goes by (with QUEEN LATIFAH) / I only have eyes for you / Crazy she calls me / Our love is here to stay.
Oct 04. (cd) *(82876 65928-2) <62182>* **STARDUST . . . THE GREAT AMERICAN SONGBOOK VOLUME III** [3] [1]
– Embracable you / For sentimental reasons / Blue moon / What a wonderful world / Stardust / Manhattan / 'S wonderful / Isn't it romantic / I can't get started / But not for me / A kiss to build a dream on / Baby, it's cold outside / Night and day / A nightingale sang in Berkeley Square.
Oct 05. (cd) *(82876 75190-2) <69286>* **THANKS FOR THE MEMORY: THE GREAT AMERICAN SONGBOOK VOLUME IV** [3] [2]
– I've got a crush on you / I wish you love / You send me / Long ago and far away / Makin' whoopee / My one and only love / Taking a chance on love / My funny valentine / I've got my love to keep me warm / Nevertheless / Blue skies / Let's fall in love / Thanks for the memory.

– compilations, etc. –

Sep 72. (7"; by PYTHON LEE JACKSON) *Youngblood; (YB 1017) / GNP Crescendo; <449>* **IN A BROKEN DREAM. / THE BLUES** [3] [56]
(re-iss. Jul80 /12"+=) – Cloud 9. *(re-iss. Aug87 as "PYTHON LEE JACKSON / ROD STEWART" on 'Bold Reprieve')*

— PYTHON LEE JACKSON was in fact an Australian 5-piece of the late 60s, headed by keyboard player **DAVID BENTLEY**, who employed ROD to sing on 3 tracks from their lp 'IN A BROKEN DREAM'.

1979. (7") *Lightning;* **IN A BROKEN DREAM. / IF THE WORLD STOPS STILL TONIGHT** [ ] [–]
Below releases on 'Mercury' until otherwise mentioned.
Feb 76. (d-lp/c) *(6672 013)* **THE VINTAGE YEARS 1969-70** [ ] [ ]
Feb 76. (7") *(6086 02)* **IT'S ALL OVER NOW. / HANDBAGS AND GLADRAGS** [ ] [–]
1976. (7") **EVERY PICTURE TELLS A STORY. / WHAT MADE MILWAUKEE FAMOUS (HAS MADE A LOSER OUT OF ME)** [–] [ ]
Jul 76. (lp/c) **RECORDED HIGHLIGHTS AND ACTION REPLAYS** [ ] [ ]
Jun 77. (7"m) *(6160 007)* **MANDOLIN WIND. / GIRL FROM THE NORTH COUNTRY / SWEET LITTLE ROCK'N'ROLLER** [ ] [–]
Jun 77. (d-lp)(d-c) *(6643 030)(7599 141) <7507>* **THE BEST OF ROD STEWART** [18] [90]
(re-iss. Sep85 lp/c; PRID/+C 10)
Jul 77. (c) *(714506-1)* **THE MUSIC OF ROD STEWART (1970-71)** [ ] [–]
Aug 77. (d-lp/d-c) *(661903-1/-4)* **THE BEST OF ROD STEWART VOLUME 2** [ ] [ ]
Dec 78. (lp) *St.Michael;* **REASON TO BELIEVE** [ ] [–]
Nov 79. (7") *(6160 006)* **MAGGIE MAY. / YOU WEAR IT WELL** [ ] [–]
(re-iss. Apr88 on 'Old Gold';)
Sep 80. (lp) *(646306-1)* **HOT RODS** [ ] [–]
May 81. (lp) *(927913-2)* **BEST OF THE BEST** [ ] [–]
Sep 81. (lp/c) *Contour; (CN/+4 2045)* **MAGGIE MAY** [ ] [–]
(cd-iss. Jul90 on 'Pickwick'; PWKS 586)
Oct 82. (lp/c) *Contour; (CN/+4 2059)* **ROD STEWART** [ ] [–]
Jul 83. (d-c) *Cambra;* **ROD STEWART** [ ] [–]
Nov 83. (d-c) *Warners; (923955-2)* **ATLANTIC CROSSING / A NIGHT ON THE TOWN** [ ] [–]
Nov 84. (lp/c) *Astan; (2/4 0119)* **CAN I GET A WITNESS** [ ] [–]
Sep 85. (lp/c) *Contour; (CN/+4 2077)* **THE HITS OF ROD STEWART** [ ] [–]
Jan 87. (lp/c) *Contour; (CN/+4 2082)* **JUKE BOX HEAVEN (14 ROCK'N'ROLL GREATS)** [ ] [–]
Nov 87. (cd) *(925466-2)* **THE ROD STEWART ALBUM** [ ] [–]
Jul 88. (lp/c) *Knight; (KNLP/KNMC 10002)* **NIGHTRIDIN'** [ ] [–]
Feb 89. (c) *Venus; (VENUMC 3)* **THE MAGIC OF ROD STEWART** [ ] [–]
Jun 89. (lp/c/cd) *(830784-1/-4/-2)* **THE ROCK ALBUM** [ ] [–]
Jun 89. (cd) *(830785-2)* **THE BALLAD ALBUM** [ ] [–]
Oct 89. (lp/c/cd) *K-Tel;* **IN A BROKEN DREAM** [ ] 1988 [ ]
Feb 91. (cd/c) *(846 988-2/-4)* **GASOLINE ALLEY / SMILER** [ ] [–]
Oct 92. (7"/c-s) **YOU WEAR IT WELL. / I WOULD RATHER GO BLIND** [ ] [ ]
(cd-s+=) – Angel.
Dec 92. (cd/c) *M Classics; (CJES D/C 2)* **JUST A LITTLE MISUNDERSTOOD** [ ] [–]
Feb 93. (cd; ROD STEWART & STEAMPACKET) *Charly;* **THE FIRST SUPER GROUP** [ ] [–]
Jul 93. (cd/c) *Telstar; (CDSR/TCSR 014)* **THE FACE OF THE SIXTIES** [ ] [–]
Jul 94. (cd/c) *Success;* **COME HOME BABY** [ ] [–]
Jan 95. (cd/c) *K-Tel; (ECD3/EMC2 109)* **THE EARLY YEARS** [ ] [–]
Aug 95. (cd/c) *Spectrum; (551110-2/-4)* **MAGGIE MAY – THE CLASSIC YEARS** [ ] [–]
(re-iss. Sep98; same)
Oct 95. (d-cd) *Mercury; (528 823-2)* **HANDBAGS AND GLADRAGS (The Mercury Recordings 1970-1974)** [ ] [ ]
May 97. (cd) *Experience; (EXP 030)* **ROD STEWART** [ ] [–]
Jul 97. (cd) *Going For A Song; (GFS 061)* **ROD STEWART** [ ] [–]
Aug 98. (cd) *Mercury; (558873-2)* **THE VERY BEST OF ROD STEWART** [ ] [–]
Oct 99. (cd) *Spectrum; (544165-2)* **REASON TO BELIEVE** [ ] [–]
Jan 00. (cd) *Universal; (E 546836-2)* **UNIVERSAL MASTERS COLLECTION** [ ] [–]
Apr 00. (cd) *A.B.M.; (ABMMCD 1082)* **SHAKE** [ ] [–]
Jul 00. (d-cd+CD-rom) *Burning Airlines; (PILOT 044)* **ROD STEWART 1964-1969** [ ] [–]
(d-lp re-iss. Dec00 on 'Get Back'; GET 578) (re-iss. Nov01; same)
Oct 00. (d-cd) *Universal; (E 536421-2)* **EVERY PICTURE TELLS A STORY / GASOLINE ALLEY** [ ] [–]
Oct 00. (3xcd-box) *Universal; (E 546586-2)* **EVERY PICTURE TELLS A STORY / GASOLINE ALLEY / SMILER** [ ] [–]
Nov 01. (d-cd/d-c) *(8122 73581-2/-4) <78328>* **THE STORY SO FAR – THE VERY BEST OF** [7] [69]
Jun 02. (d-cd; shared w/ ERIC CLAPTON) *Delta Blue; (6305-2)* **WHITE BOY BLUES** [ ] [–]
Oct 03. (d-cd) *Universal; (<9812604>)* **CHANGING FACES: THE VERY BEST OF ROD STEWART & THE FACES** [13] Dec03 [ ]
– Maggie May / Stay with me (FACES) / Reason to believe / You wear it well / In a broken dream (PYTHON LEE JACKSON) / Cut across Shorty / Had a real good time (FACES) / Miss Judy's farm (FACES) / Angel / Oh no not my baby / What made Milwaukee famous (has made a loser out of me) / (I know) I'm losing you / Mandolin wind / Every picture tells a story / I'd rather go blind / Twistin' the night away / Sweet little rock'n'roller / Bring it on home – You send me / Handbags & gladrags / It's all over now / Cindy incidentally (FACES) / Pool hall Richard (FACES) / Street fighting man / Gasoline alley / Let me be your car / That's all right / My way of giving / Italian girls / Lost Paraguayos / True blue / Hard road / (You make me feel like) A natural man / An old raincoat won't ever let you down / Jodie / Man of constant sorrow / You can make me dance, sing or anything (FACES).

☐ Stephen STILLS / MANASSAS

(see under ⇒ CROSBY, STILLS, NASH & YOUNG)

STING

Born: GORDON MATTHEW SUMNER, 2 Oct'51, Wallsend, nr. Newcastle, England. In the early 70's he gave up his job as a primary school teacher and joined a local group, gaining his nickname in honour of his famous black and yellow hooped T-shirt. STING joined jazz combo, LAST EXIT, in 1974, where he became lead singer on a single, 'WHISPERING VOICES'. Around the same time, the man enrolled with RADA and began occasional TV ad work (he was later to become a successful actor in the 70's). Early in 1977, he formed The POLICE, one of the world's top selling outfits until their demise (and his failed marriage to actress, Frances Tomelty) in 1983. STING had earlier branched out on a solo career, starring in, and scoring the soundtrack for the Dennis Potter film, 'Brimstone & Treacle'. It wasn't until 1985, however, that he released his first solo long player, 'DREAM OF THE BLUE TURTLES'. Employing such noted musicians as BRANFORD MARSALIS and WEATHER REPORT's OMAR HAKIM, STING crafted an endearing set of jazz-influenced, infectiously off-kilter pop songs, highlights being the gaslit noir of 'MOON OVER BOURBON STREET' and the two minor hit singles, 'IF YOU LOVE SOMEBODY SET THEM FREE' and 'SEVENTH WAVE'. The record was a Transatlantic Top 3 hit, STING subsequently touring/promoting with most of the musicians who'd played on the project, 'BRING ON THE NIGHT' (1986) documenting events. Again featuring MARSALIS, in addition to contributions from such luminaries as ERIC CLAPTON, MARK KNOPFLER, GIL EVANS and former colleague, ANDY SUMMERS, 'NOTHING LIKE THE SUN' (1987) was a largely introspective, instrumentally dextrous collection dedicated to STING's recently departed mother. 'AN ENGLISHMAN IN NEW YORK' was quintessential STING, a wry observation on cultural disparity, while the likes of 'FRAGILE' saw STING's work take on a more self-consciously political hue alongside contemporaries like U2 and SIMPLE MINDS. Indeed, most of '89 saw the singer campaigning for Brazilian rainforest projects, STING also championing the efforts of human rights organisation, Amnesty International. Commendable as all this was, many factions of the music press gave the singer a roasting for what they perceived as an often lofty and self-righteous attitude, BONO also coming in for similar flak. Brushing aside such criticism, STING eventually returned to recording with 'THE SOUL CAGES' (1991), a sombre affair informed this time around by the death of his father. Again retaining MARSALIS, STING also employed folk player, KATHRYN TICKELL, her Northumbrian pipes adding to the often bleak atmospherics. Despite its dearth of hit singles, the album gave STING his second UK No.1 in succession, paving the way for the massive selling, and markedly more upbeat 'TEN SUMMONER'S TALES' (1993). As strong a set of songs as STING had yet penned, the record spawned two of his most enduring singles in 'IF I EVER LOSE MY FAITH IN YOU' and the pastoral beauty of 'FIELDS OF GOLD'. Later that year, the singer was back in the upper reaches of the singles chart with the theme tune from the film 'Demolition Man' and a three way collaboration with BRYAN ADAMS and ROD STEWART on the vomit-inducing 'ALL MY LOVE' (the theme from 'The Three Musketeers'. STING even attempted a country/reggae crossover together with PATO BANTON on 'THIS COWBOY SONG', a track culled from 94's greatest hits set, 'FIELDS OF GOLD – THE BEST OF STING 1984-1994'. Not exactly the most prolific of artists, STING's most recent release was the 'MERCURY FALLING' album in 1996. As well as being something of an older guy sex symbol, STING continues to court controversy, his recent comments on the benefits of Ecstasy coming under particular scrutiny. 'BRAND NEW DAY' (1999), was a slight return to his more conventional pop songwriting days, the Top 5 album featuring a title track hit that was certainly his finest number for a long time – it's now used on a TV ad. 'SACRED LOVE' (2003), meanwhile, summarily failed to build on the creative rediscovery of its predecessor despite – or perhaps because of – the presence of such credible guests as ANOUSHKA SHANKAR and MARY J BLIGE, preening itself on sheen over content.

• **Covered:** SPREAD A LITTLE HAPPINESS + SOMEONE TO WATCH OVER ME (George Gershwin) / TUTTI FRUTTI (Little Richard) / NEED YOUR LOVE SO BAD (Little Willie John) / MACK THE KNIFE (Bertold Brecht) / PURPLE HAZE (Jimi Hendrix) / SISTERS OF MERCY (Leonard Cohen) w/ CHIEFTAINS. • **Trivia:** In 1985, he dueted on singles MONEY FOR NOTHING (Dire Straits), which he co-wrote, plus LONG WAY TO GO (Phil Collins). That year, STING also guested on MILES DAVIS' album, 'You're Under Arrest'. He was also another one of the stars on BAND AID and LIVE AID. In 1988, STING narrated Stravinsky's 'Soldier's Tale', which was soon issued on own 'Pangaea' label. He followed this by writing score for the documentary about Quentin Crisp, 'Crisp City'.

Album rating: BRIMSTONE & TREACLE soundtrack w/ others (*5) / THE DREAM OF THE BLUE TURTLES (*6) / BRING ON THE NIGHT soundtrack (*6) / NOTHING LIKE THE SUN (*8) / THE SOUL CAGES (*7) / TEN SUMMONER'S TALES (*8) / FIELDS OF GOLD – THE BEST OF STING 1984-1994 compilation (*8) / MERCURY FALLING (*6) / THE VERY BEST OF STING & THE POLICE compilation (*8) / BRAND NEW DAY (*7) / DOLPHINS soundtrack with Steve Wood (*5) / ALL THIS TIME compilation (*8) / SACRED LOVE (*5)

STING – vocals, bass, etc. (with session people)

		A&M	A&M
Aug 82.	(7") *(AMS 8242)* **SPREAD A LITTLE HAPPINESS. / ONLY YOU**	16	
Sep 82.	(lp/c) *(AMLH/CAM 64915)* **BRIMSTONE & TREACLE** (soundtrack w/ The POLICE * & others)	67	–

– Brimstone & treacle / Narration / How stupid Mr. Bates (*) / Only you / I burn for you (*) / Spread a little happiness / You know I had the strangest dream / A kind of loving (*) / Brimstone 2. *<US cd/c-iss.1990's; 75021 3245-2/-4>*

— enlisted US musicians **KENNY KIRKLAND** – keyboards / **BRANFORD MARSALIS** – sax, percussion / **DARRYL JONES** – bass (ex-MILES DAVIS) / **OMAR HAKIM** – drums (WEATHER REPORT)

May 85.	(7") *(AM 258)* *<2738>* **IF YOU LOVE SOMEBODY SET THEM FREE. / ANOTHER DAY**	26	3

(12"+=) *(AMY 258)* – ('A'-Torch song mix) / ('A'-Jellybean dance mix).

Jun 85.	(lp)(c/cd) *(DREAM 1)(DRE MC/MD 1)* *<3750>* **THE DREAM OF THE BLUE TURTLES**	3	2

– If you love somebody set them free / Love is the seventh wave / Russians / Children's crusade / Shadows in the rain / We work the black seam / Consider me gone / The dream of the blue turtles / Moon over Bourbon Street / Fortress around your heart. *(pic-lp Jan86; DREAMP 1) (lp re-iss. Sep99 on 'Simply Vinyl'; SVLP 116)*

Aug 85.	(7"/12") *(AM/+Y 272)* **LOVE IS THE SEVENTH WAVE. / CONSIDER ME GONE (live)**	41	–
Aug 85.	(7") *<2767>* **FORTRESS AROUND YOUR HEART. / CONSIDER ME GONE (live)**	–	8
Oct 85.	(7"/12") *(AM/+Y 286)* **FORTRESS AROUND YOUR HEART. / SHADOWS IN THE RAIN**	49	–
Oct 85.	(7") *<2787>* **LOVE IS THE SEVENTH WAVE. / DREAM OF THE BLUE TURTLES**	–	17
Dec 85.	(7") *(AM 292)* *<2799>* **RUSSIANS. / GABRIEL'S MESSAGE**	12	16

(12"+=) *(AMY 292)* – I burn for you (live).

Feb 86.	(7") *(AM 305)* **MOON OVER BOURBON STREET. / MACK THE KNIFE**	44	

(12"+=) *(AMY 305)* – Fortress around your heart.

Jul 86.	(d-lp/c/cd) *(BRIN G/C/D 1)* **BRING ON THE NIGHT (live soundtrack)**	16	–

– Bring on the night – When the world is running down you make the best of what's still around / Consider me gone / Low life / We work the black seam / Driven to tears / The dream of the blue turtles – Demolition man / One world (not three) – Love is the seventh wave / Moon over Bourbon Street / I burn for you / Another day / Children's crusade / Down so long / Tea in the Sahara.

— he retained **KIRKLAND + MARSALIS,** and recruited **MANU KATCHE** – drums / **MINO CINELU** – percussion, vocoder / **ANDY NEWMARK** –

2nd drummer / plus guests **ERIC CLAPTON, MARK KNOPFLER, ANDY SUMMERS + GIL EVANS**

Oct 87. (7") *(AM 410) <2983>* **WE'LL BE TOGETHER. / CONVERSATION WITH A DOG** 41 7
(12"+=/3"cd-s+=) *(AM Y/CD 410)* – ('A'extended) / ('A'instrumental).

Oct 87. (d-lp/c/cd) *(AMA/AMC/CDA 6402) <6402>* **NOTHING LIKE THE SUN** 1 9
– The Lazarus heart / Be still my beating heart / Englishman in New York / History will teach us nothing / They dance alone (gueca solo) / Fragile / We'll be together / Straight to my heart / Rock steady / Sister Moon / Little wing / The secret marriage.

Jan 88. (7") *<2992>* **BE STILL MY BEATING HEART. / GHOST IN THE STRAND** – 15

Jan 88. (7") *(AM 431)* **ENGLISHMAN IN NEW YORK. / GHOST IN THE STRAND (instrumental)** 51 –
(12"+=/3"cd-s+=) *(AM Y/CD 431)* – Bring on the night – When the world is running down (live).

Mar 88. (7") *<1200>* **ENGLISHMAN IN NEW YORK. / IF YOU'RE THERE** – 84

Mar 88. (7") *(AM 439)* **FRAGILE. / FRAGIL (Portuguese mix)** 70 –
(12"+=/cd-s+=) *(AM Y/CD 439)* – Fragilidad (Spanish mix) / Mariposa libre.

Sep 88. (7") *(AM 458)* **THEY DANCE ALONE. / ELLAS DAMZON SOLAS (GUECA SOLO)**
(12"+=/cd-s+=) *(AM Y/CD 458)* – Si estamos juntos.

Aug 90. (7"/c-s) *(AM/+MC 580)* **ENGLISHMAN IN NEW YORK (Ben Liebrand mix). / IF YOU LOVE SOMEBODY SET THEM FREE** 15 –
(12"+=/cd-s+=/pic-cd-s+=) *(AM Y/CD/CDR 580)* – ('A'original mix) / ('A'-Jellybean dance mix).

— he retained **MARSALIS, KIRKLAND, KATCHE.** New **DOMINIC MILLER** – guitar / **DAVID SANCIOUS** – keyboards / **KATHRYN TICKELL** – pipes / **PAOLA PAPAREUE** – oboe / **RAY COOPER, VINK, BILL SUMMERS, MUNYUNGO JACKSON, SKIP BURNEY, TONY VALCA** – percussion.

Dec 90. (7"/c-s) *(AM/+MC 713)* **ALL THIS TIME. / I MISS YOU, KATE (instrumental)** 22 5
(12"+=/cd-s+=/pic-cd-s+=) *(AM Y/CD/CDR 713) <1541>* – King of pain (live).

Jan 91. (cd/c/lp) *(396 405-2/-4/-1) <6405>* **THE SOUL CAGES** 1 2
– Island of souls / All this time / Mad about you / Jeremiah blues (pt.1) / Why should I cry for you / Saint Agnes and the burning train / The wild wild sea / The soul cages / When the angels fall.

Feb 91. (7"/c-s) *(AM/+MC 721)* **MAD ABOUT YOU (remix). / TEMPTED (live)** 56
(12"+=/cd-s+=) *(AM Y/CDR 721)* – If you love somebody set them free (live).

Apr 91. (7"/c-s) *(AM/+MC 759)* **THE SOUL CAGES. / OH LA LA HUGH** 57 –
(cd-s+=) *(AMCD 759)* – Walking in your footsteps (live).
(12"++=) *(AMY 759)* – Don't stand so close to me (live).
(12") *(AMYR 759)* – ('A'side) / Walking in your footsteps (live) / The Lazarus heart (live) / Too much information (live).

Aug 92. (7"/c-s/cd-s; by STING with ERIC CLAPTON) *(AM/+MC/CD 883)* **IT'S PROBABLY ME. / ('A'-long version)** 30

— retained on album **MILLER, SANCIOUS & TICKELL** and brought in **VINNIE COLAIUTA** – drums / **LARRY ADLER + BRENDAN POWER** – chromatic harmonicas / **SIAN BELL** – cello / **DAVE HEATH** – flute / **PAUL FRANKLIN** – pedal steel / **JAMES BOYD** – viola / **KATHRYN GREELEY + SIMON FISCHER** – violins / **GUY BARKER + JOHN BARCLAY** – trumpets / **RICHARD EDWARDS + MARK NIGHTINGALE** – trombone / **DAVID ROXXE** – narration

Feb 93. (7"/c-s) *(AM/+MC 0172) <0111>* **IF I EVER LOSE MY FAITH IN YOU. / ALL THIS TIME (unplugged)** 14 17
(cd-s+=) *(AMCD 0172)* – Mad about you (live) / Every breath you take (live).
(cd-s) *(AMCDR 0172)* – ('A'side) / Message in a bottle (live) / Tea in the Sahara (live) / Walking on the moon (live).

Mar 93. (cd/c/lp) *(540 074-2/-4/-1) <0070>* **TEN SUMMONER'S TALES** 2 2
– Prologue (If I ever lose my faith in you) / Love is stronger than justice (the magnificent seven) / Fields of gold / Heavy cloud no rain / She's too good for me / Seven days / Saint Augustine in Hell / It's probably me / Everybody laughed but you / Shape of my heart / Something the boy said / Epilogue (Nothing 'bout me).

Apr 93. (7"/c-s) *(580 222-7/223-4)* **SEVEN DAYS. / JANUARY STARS** 25 –
(cd-s+=) *(580 223-2)* – Mad about you (live) / Ain't no sunshine (live).
(cd-s) *(580 225-2)* – ('A'side) / Island of souls (live) / The wild wild sea (live) / The soul cages (live).

Jun 93. (7"/c-s) *(580 301-7/302-4) <0258>* **FIELDS OF GOLD. / WE WORK THE BLACK SEAM** 16 23
(cd-s) *(580302-2)* – ('A'side) / King of pain (live) / Fragile (live) / Purple haze (live).
(cd-s) *(580303-2)* – ('A'side) / Message in a bottle (live) / Fortress around your heart (live) / Roxanne (live).

Aug 93. (7"/c-s) *(580353-7-/4)* **SHAPE OF MY HEART. / WALKING ON THE MOON** 57 –
(cd-s) *(580353-2)* – ('A'side) / The soul cages / The wild wild sea / All this time.

Nov 93. (7"/c-s) *(580450-7/-4)* **DEMOLITION MAN (live). / ('A'mix)** 21 –
(cd-s+=) *(580451-2)* – King of pain (live) / Shape of my heart (live).
(cd-s) *(580453-2)* – ('A'side) / It's probably me (live) / A day in the life of (live).
above single was the title track from the movie, 'Demolition Man'

— late 1993, he teamed up with BRYAN ADAMS & ROD STEWART to sing theme from 'The Three Musketeers'; ALL FOR LOVE, which hit UK No.2 & US No.1.

Feb 94. (7"/12"/c-s) *(580529-7/-1/-4) <0350>* **NOTHING 'BOUT ME. / IF I EVER LOSE MY FAITH IN YOU** 32 Sep93 57
(cd-s+=) *(580529-2)* – ('B'mixes) / Demolition man (soul power mix).

Oct 94. (c-s) *(580858-4)* **WHEN WE DANCE / FORTRESS AROUND YOUR HEART** 9 –
(cd-s) *(580859-2)* – ('A'side) / If you love somebody set them free (remix) / ('A'remix).
(12"/cd-s) *(580861-1/-2)* – ('A'remixes).

Oct 94. (c-s,cd-s) *<0846>* **WHEN WE DANCE / DEMOLITION MAN** – 38

Nov 94. (cd/c/d-lp) *(540307-2/-4/-1) <0269>* **FIELDS OF GOLD – THE BEST OF STING 1984-1994** (compilation) 2 7
– When we dance / If you love somebody set them free / Fields of gold / All this time / Englishman in New York / Mad about you / It's probably me / They dance alone / If I ever lose my faith in you / Fragile / We'll be together / Nothing 'bout me / Love is the seventh wave / Russians / Seven days / Demolition man / This cowboy song.

— Around same time, Spanish crooner JULIO IGLESIAS covered his 'FRAGILE', which he accompanied with STING.
(below single featured PATO BANTON)

Jan 95. (c-s) *(580957-4)* **THIS COWBOY SONG / IF YOU LOVE SOMEBODY SET THE FREE (Brothers In Rhythm mix)** 15 –
(cd-s+=) *(580957-2)* – Demolition man (Soul Power mix).
(12"++=) *(580965-2)* – If you love somebody set them free (extended).
(cd-s) *(580957-1)* – ('A'side) / ('A'extended) / When we dance (classic) / Take me to the sunshine.

May 95. (cd) *<540350-2>* **THE LIVING SEA** (soundtrack) –
– Fragile / Why should I cry for you? / Cool breeze / Mad about you / Ocean waltz / One world (not three) – Love is the seventh wave / Why should I cry for you / Saint Agnes and the burning train / Tides / Why should I cry for you? / Arrival / Jellyfish lake / Fragile (reprise).
(UK-iss.Mar99 on 'Universal'; same as US)

— Jan 96, featured on PATO BANTON's UK Top 40 version of POLICE hit 'SPIRITS IN THE MATERIAL WORLD' from the film 'Ace Ventura II'.

— with band: **MILLER, COLAIUTA / + KENNY KIRKLAND** – keyboards

Feb 96. (c-s) *(581330-4) <1456>* **LET YOUR SOUL BE YOUR PILOT / THE BED'S TOO BIG WITHOUT YOU** 15 86
(cd-s+=) *(581331-2)* – Englishman in New York.
(12") *(581527-1)* – ('A'mixes).

Mar 96. (cd/c/lp) *(540486-2/-4/-1) <0483>* **MERCURY FALLING** 4 5
– The hounds of winter / I hung my head / Let your soul be your pilot / I was brought to my senses / You still touch me / I'm so happy I can't stop crying / All four seasons / Twenty five to midnight / La belle dame sans regrets / Valparaiso / Lithium sunset.

Apr 96. (c-s/cd-s) *(581545-4/-2) <1582>* **YOU STILL TOUCH ME / TWENTY-FIVE TO MIDNIGHT** 27 60
(12"+=/cd-s+=) *(581547-1/-2)* – Lullaby to an anxious child / The pirate's bride.

Jun 96. (c-ep/cd-ep) *(581761-4/-2)* **LIVE AT TFI FRIDAY EP** 53 –
– You still touch me / Lithium sunset / Message in a bottle.

Sep 96. (c-s/cd-s) *(581890-4/-2)* **I WAS BROUGHT TO MY SENSES (Steve Lipson remix) / WHEN WE DANCE / IF I EVER LOSE MY FAITH IN YOU / IF YOU LOVE SOMEBODY SET THEM FREE** [31] [–]
(cd-s) *(581889-2)* – ('A'side) / This was never meant to be / The pirate's bride.

Oct 96. (c-s,cd-s) *<1982>* **I'M SO HAPPY I CAN'T STOP CRYING / THIS WAS NEVER MEANT TO BE** [–] [94]

Nov 96. (c-s) *(582029-4)* **I'M SO HAPPY I CAN'T STOP CRYING / FRAGILIDAD** [54] [–]
(cd-s+=) *(582029-2)* – Fields of gold / Englishman in New York.
(cd-s) *(582031-2)* – ('A'side) / Seven days / Moonlight / Giacomo's blues.

— In Dec'97, STING featured on TOBY KEITH's version of 'I'm So Happy I Can't Stop Crying'.

Sep 99. (c-s) *(497153-4)* **BRAND NEW DAY / (lp version)** [13] [ ]
(cd-s) *(497152-2)* – ('A'side) / Windmills of your mind / End of the game (long version).
(cd-s) *(497153-2)* – ('A'side) / Fields of gold / Englishman in New York.

Sep 99. (cd/c) *(490425-2/-5) <490443>* **BRAND NEW DAY** [5] [9]
– A thousand years / Desert rose / Big lie small world / After the rain has fallen / Perfect love . . . gone wrong / Tomorrow we'll see / Prelude to the end of the game / Fill her up / Ghost story / Brand new day.

Jan 00. (c-s/12"; as STING featuring CHEB MAMI) *(497240-4/-1) <497321>* **DESERT ROSE / (filter dub mix)** [15] May00 [17]
(cd-s) *(497241-2)* – ('A'side + mixes' melodic club x2 / video).
(cd-s) *(497240-2)* – ('A'side) / ('A'CD-Rom) / Fragile (live) / If you love somebody (set them free) (live).

Apr 00. (c-s) *(497325-4)* **AFTER THE RAIN HAS FALLEN / AFTER THE RAIN HAS FALLEN (Tin Tin Out mix)** [31] [ ]
(cd-s+=) *(497325-2)* – Shape of my heart / ('A'-CD-Rom).
(cd-s) *(497326-2)* – ('A'side) / Seven days (live) / Desert rose (version).

Aug 00. (cd) *(<810057-2>)* **DOLPHINS** (soundtrack w/ Steve Wood) [ ] Apr00 [ ]
– I need you like this hole in my head / Fill her up / Ghost story / When we dance / (other tracks by Steve Wood).
(above issued on 'Ark 21')

— late in 2000, STING was credited with lyrics/songs on the Walt Disney movie, 'The Emperor's New Groove' alongside David Hartley & John Debney

Nov 01. (cd) *(493180-2) <493169>* **ALL THIS TIME** (compilation) [3] [32]
– Fragile / A thousand years / Perfect love . . . gone wrong / All this time / The hounds of winter / Mad about you *[UK-only]* / Don't stand so close to me / When we dance / Dienda / Roxanne / If you love somebody set them free / Brand new day / Fields of gold / Moon over Bourbon Street / Shape of my heart *[UK-only]* / If I ever lose my faith in you / Every breath you take.

— in May'03, STING featured on CRAIG DAVID's Top 3 hit, 'Rise & Fall'

Sep 03. (cd-s) *(9810103)* **SEND YOUR LOVE / MOON OVER BOURBON STREET (Cornelius mix) / ('A'-Dave Aude remix) / ('A'-video)** [30] [ ]

Sep 03. (cd) *(9860535) <87236>* **SACRED LOVE** [3] [3]
– Inside / Send your love / Whenever I say your name (with MARY J. BLIGE) / Dead man's rope / Never coming home / Stolen car (take me dancing) / Forget about the future / This war / The book of my life / Sacred love / Send your love.

Dec 03. (cd-s; by STING & MARY J. BLIGE) *(9815304)* **WHENEVER I SAY YOUR NAME / (Will I am remix) / (Salaam Remi groove mix)** [60] [–]

May 04. (cd-s) *(9862266) <B0002699-32>* **STOLEN CAR (TAKE ME DANCING) (mixes; radio / w/ WILL I AM / B. Recluse feat. TWISTA / video)** [60] [ ]

– compilations, others, etc. –

on 'A&M' unless mentioned otherwise

Jul 88. (cd-ep) *(AMCD 911)* **COMPACT HITS** [ ] [–]
– Someone to watch over me / Englishman in New York / If you love somebody set them free / Spread a little happiness.

Feb 90. (d-c) *(AMC 24110)* **THE DREAM OF THE BLUE TURTLES / NOTHING LIKE THE SUN** [ ] [ ]

Nov 91. (cd-box) *(397 171-2)* **ACOUSTIC LIVE IN NEWCASTLE – LIMITED EDITION BOXED SET** [ ] [ ]

Nov 97. (cd/c; STING & THE POLICE) *(540428-2/-4)* **THE VERY BEST OF STING & THE POLICE** [11] [100]
– Message in a bottle / Can't stand losing you / Englishman in New York / Every breath you take / Seven days / Walking on the moon / Fields of gold / Fragile / Every little thing she does is magic / De do do do de da da da / If you love somebody set them free / Let your soul be your pilot / Russians / If I ever lose my faith in you / When we dance / Don't stand so close to me / Roxanne / Roxanne '97 (Puff Daddy remix).

Dec 97. (c-s; STING & The POLICE) *(582455-4) <582449>* **ROXANNE '97 (Puff Daddy remix) / ROXANNE (original)** [17] [59]
(12"+=/cd-s+=) *(582455-1/-2)* – Walking on the moon (Roger Sanchez mix).

Joss STONE

Born: JOSCELYN EVE STOKER, 11 Apr'87, Dover, Kent, England. Referencing a potted rawk history with her surname, and taking it to the stage in bare feet and flowing mane, STONE arrived seemingly fully formed on a pop scene plastic enough to make her classicist chic seem fresh. That her voice seemed to have weathered a good few decades more than her birth certificate endeared her to semi-legendary Miami soulstress Betty Wright (herself only 15 when she scored her first hit), brought in as a collaborator on her debut album. Naturally, recording sessions were held in the Florida capital, where some of Miami's gnarliest players – Latimore, Little Beaver etc. – dropped by to authenticate matters. The result – completed, like all the best albums, in less than a weeek – was 'THE SOUL SESSIONS' (2003), a covers set generating royalties for the relatively obscure likes of Harlan Howard, Bobby Miller, and Willie Garner right through to legends ARETHA FRANKLIN ('All The King's Horses'), the ISLEY BROTHERS ('For The Love Of You') and erm. the WHITE STRIPES, whose 'Fell In Love With A Girl' STONE gender-bent into 'FELL IN LOVE WITH A BOY'. Released as a single, it made the lower reaches of the UK Top 20, as did follow-up, 'Super Duper Love (Are You Diggin On Me?)'. Wright stuck around for a follow-up album, initiating STONE into the joys of songwriting along with Lamont Dozier and son Beau (whose relationship with the teenage star had the showbiz columns buzzing), as well as Steve Greenberg, her producer and the man who'd initially signed her up. 'MIND, BODY & SOUL' (2004) consolidated the precocity and – at least to some extent – justified the hype. If the style and attitude was still retro, the sound was contemporary enough to joss-tle with the best R&B divas. A clipped, sound-bite sneer of a lead single 'You Had Me', took STONE into the UK Top 10 for the first time, while the album itself entered the British chart at No.1, anointing her as the youngest female ever to scale such heights. Successive singles 'Right To Be Wrong', 'Spoiled' and the saucy 'Don't Cha Wanna Ride', failed to make quite so much impact but – like KT TUNSTALL – STONE appealed equally to the kind of albums-orientated demographic that goes with the hippie-soul turf. If you can judge a singer by the company she keeps, her duets with both STEVIE WONDER and JAMES BROWN (and appearance at the Grammys tribute to blonde-mohicaned namesake, SLY) speak soul-powered volumes.

Album rating: THE SOUL SESSIONS (*7) / MIND, BODY & SOUL (*6)

JOSS STONE – vocals / with various session people

Relentless S-Curve

Jan 04. (cd) *(CDREL 2) <42234>* **THE SOUL SESSIONS** [4] Dec03 [39]
– The chokin' kind / Super duper love (are you diggin' on me?) – part 1 / Fell in love with a boy / Victim of a foolish heart / Dirty man / Some kind of wonderful / I've fallen in love with you / I had a dream / All the king's horses / For the love of you.

Jan 04. (7") *(REL 3)* **FELL IN LOVE WITH A BOY. / SUPER DUPER LOVE (ARE YOU DIGGIN' ON ME?) – PART 1** [18] [–]
(cd-s) *(RELCD 3)* – ('A') / Victim of a foolish heart (live).

May 04. (7"/cd-s) *(REL/+CD 4)* **SUPER DUPER LOVE (ARE YOU DIGGIN' ON ME?) – PART 1. / IT'S A MAN'S MAN'S WORLD (live)** [18] [–]

Sep 04. (cd-s) *(RELCD 10)* **YOU HAD ME / DIRTY MAN (live)** [9] [–]

(cd-s) *(RELDX 10)* – ('A') / Holding out for a hero / Fell in love with a boy / Fell in love with a boy (video).
(dvd-s) *(RELDVD 10)* – ('A'-video) / Super duper love (video) / Fell in love with a boy (acoustic).

Sep 04. (cd) *(CDREL 04)* <94897> **MIND, BODY & SOUL** [1] [11]
– Right to be wrong / Jet lag / You had me / Spoiled / Don't cha wanna ride / Less is more / Security / Young at heart / Snakes and ladders / Understand / Don't know how / Torn and tattered / Killing time / Sleep like a child. *(re-iss. Nov05 w/ dvd+=; CDRELX 04)* – (DVD tracks).

Nov 04. (7"/cd-s) *(REL/+CD 13)* **RIGHT TO BE WRONG. / JET LAG (acoustic)** [29] [–]
(cd-s) *(RELCDX 13)* – ('A') / The player / Don't know how (live from AOL sessions).

Apr 05. (cd-s) *(RELCD 16)* **SPOILED / RIGHT TO BE WRONG (live)** [32] [–]
(cd-s) *(RELDVD 16)* – ('A'-video) / The chokin' kind (live video) / Fell in love with a boy (live).

Jul 05. (7"pic-d/cd-s) *(REL/+CD 20)* **DON'T CHA WANNA RIDE. / THE RIGHT TIME** [20] [–]
(dvd-s) *(RELDVD 20)* – ('A'-video) / Right to be wrong (live at the Brits 2005) / Spoiled (live).

□ Sly STONE (see under ⇒ SLY & THE FAMILY STONE)

the STONE ROSES

Formed: Sale & Chorley, Gtr. Manchester, England . . . 1984 by IAN BROWN, JOHN SQUIRE, RENI, ANDY COUZENS and PETER GARNER who took their name from a group called ENGLISH ROSE and The ROLLING STONES. After a MARTIN HANNETT produced 45, they signed a one-off deal with 'Black' records and in 1988, were snapped up by ANDREW LAUDER's 'Jive' subsidiary, 'Silvertone'. They soon became darlings of the music press after the indie success of the single, 'ELEPHANT STONE' (1988), a gloriously uplifting piece of pristine pop. Propelled by RENI's consummate drumming and featuring SQUIRE's dizzy, spiralling guitar, the track was a blueprint for the group's eponymous debut album, released the following year. Surely a contender for album of the decade, the record was flawless, from the ominous opening bass rumble of 'I WANNA BE ADORED' to the orgasmic finale of 'I AM THE RESURRECTION'. This life-affirming hybrid of BYRDS-style psychedelia and shuffling rhythmic flurries remains the definitive indie album, its all-pervading influence more pronounced with each successive crop of guitar bands. Incredibly, the band topped the magic of their debut with the 'FOOL'S GOLD' single, which exploded into the Top 10 later that year. A seminal guitar-funk workout, it was the crowning glory of the 'Baggy' movement with which the STONE ROSES had become so closely affiliated, and marked a creative highpoint in their career. After a few one-off shows (that have since achieved almost mythical status) and a solitary single, 'ONE LOVE', the following year, the band went to ground. In the five years that followed, the band fought a protracted court battle with 'Silvertone', eventually signing with 'Geffen' for a reported record sum of $4,000,000. After much speculation and intrigue into when or if a follow-up would finally appear, the appropriately titled 'SECOND COMING' was eventually released in 1994. A month previously, they had enjoyed a return to the singles chart with the ZEPPELIN-esque 'LOVE SPREADS'. On the album, the effervescent pop of old took second place to riff-heavy guitar workouts, alienating many of their original fans. Nevertheless, the blistering funk-rock of 'BEGGING YOU' partly made up for any excess noodling by SQUIRE. As the STONES ROSES faithful dusted down their flares and beany hats in readiness for the band's headlining spot at the 1995 Glastonbury festival, they were again bitterly disappointed. At the last minute the band pulled out, apparently due to SQUIRE breaking his collarbone, young pretenders OASIS stealing the show in their absence. They had failed to seize the moment and from here on in, it was all downhill. Despite an ecstatically received Winter tour, SQUIRE shocked the music world by departing the following spring (RENI had already quit a year earlier). BROWN and MANI bravely soldiered on for a headlining appearance at the 1996 Reading Festival but were given a critical mauling (particularly by the NME), finally splitting later that year. It was a sorry, messy end for a band that had seemed, at one point, to be on the brink of world domination and it remains a bitter irony that their duller Manchester progeny, OASIS, seem to have inherited the success that tragically eluded the 'ROSES. The SEAHORSES were formed in London 1996 by guitarist JOHN SQUIRE who allegedly "discovered" frontman CHRIS HELME busking in his native Yorkshire. With STUART FLETCHER and ANDY WATTS completing the line-up, the band hooked up with producer Tony Visconti and quickly entered a studio in L.A. to begin work on their debut set, 'DO IT YOURSELF'. In stark contrast to the infamously drawn out sessions for the final 'ROSES album, all the tracks were laid down inside a month and the record was in the shops by spring '97. Inevitably, the hype surrounding the whole thing tended to obscure the question of whether the record was actually any good or not; the bulk of critics (perhaps only too eager to get the boot in to SQUIRE, a previously unassailable indie guitar god) thought not, or at least panned the set for its inoffensive blandness. Certainly, there was nothing to match the quality of any track from the STONE ROSES sublime debut, although on its own terms, the record's vaguely enjoyable, bluesy indie-rock would've counted as a decent debut by a new band. Somewhat akin to a folk-ish cross between IAN BROWN and LIAM GALLAGHER (who, incidentally, co-penned 'LOVE ME AND LEAVE ME'), HELME's singing, as with SQUIRE's guitar flash, was as competent yet ultimately forgettable as any second division Brit-rock outfit. With the album lacking any real songwriting magic (bar say 'LOVE IS THE LAW' and 'BLINDED BY THE SUN'), some fans began to wonder just who was the mysterious X factor into the STONE ROSES, although enough people thought differently to take the album to No.2 in the UK chart. With a string of successful singles and festival appearances also now under their belt, British sales of the debut were approaching the half million mark; SQUIRE may at last be achieving the success that has long seemed his due, ironically, with the most underwhelming material of his career. However, the SEAHORSES were treading water (so to speak!) during the latter half of '98, HELME expressing to mainman SQUIRE he wanted more of a say in the music/lyrics he was to sing. Inevitably, with more of a whimper than a bang, the band were no more, speculating tabloid rumours of yet another STONES ROSES reformation; HELME was meanwhile plotting his own solo career. After the end of the SEAHORSES, SQUIRE himself disappeared for a few years before delivering his solo effort in 2002, 'TIME CHANGES EVERYTHING'. A rather mediocore album from the outset, here was a songwriter with nothing to prove, unlike RICHARD ASHCROFT (who didn't do so well). Centered around jangly guitar parts, plus the wishful-thinking folk of DYLAN and NILSSON (not to mention the impending presence of the bloody ROLLING STONES), SQUIRE had managed to uphold his brilliant and taut lyricism, adding in a few hammond organs and token slide guitars. A second solo offering came in the shape of 2004's 'MARSHALL'S HOUSE', a critical and commercial failure that only managed to deliver one minor hit, 'ROOM IN BROOKLYN'.

• **Songwriters:** Mainly SQUIRE but with other members also collaborating. NOEL GALLAGHER co-wrote 'LOVE ME AND LEAVE ME' for the SEAHORSES. • **Trivia:** Their debut album artwork was a pastiche of a Jackson Pollock splatter job painted by the multi-talented SQUIRE.

Album rating: THE STONE ROSES (*10) / TURNS INTO STONE collection (*6) / SECOND COMING (*7) / THE COMPLETE STONE ROSES compilation (*8) / GARAGE FLOWER exploitation (*5) / THE VERY BEST OF THE STONE

The STONE ROSES

ROSES compilation (*9) / the Seahorses: DO IT YOURSELF (*7) / John Squire: TIME CHANGES EVERYTHING (*6) / MARSHALL'S HOUSE (*4)

IAN BROWN (b.20 Feb'63, Ancoats, Manchester) – vocals / **JOHN SQUIRE** (b.24 Nov'62, Broadheath, Manchester) – guitar, vocals / **PETER GARNER** – rhythm guitar / **ANDY COUZENS** – bass / **RENI** (b. ALAN WREN, 10 Apr'64) – drums

Thin Line / not iss.

Sep 85. (12") *(THIN 001)* **SO YOUNG. / TELL ME** [ ] [–]

— now a quartet when PETER departed

Revolver / not iss.

May 87. (12"m) *(12REV 36)* **SALLY CINNAMON. / HERE IT COMES / ALL ACROSS THE SANDS** [ ] [–]
(re-iss. Feb89; same) (re-iss. Dec89 cd-ep+=; CDREV 36) – ('A'demo). (hit No.46) *(re-iss. Nov00; REVXD 36)*

— (1987) **GARY 'MANI' MOUNFIELD** (b.16 Nov'62, Crumpsall, Manchester) – bass, vocals repl. COUZENS who later joined The HIGH.

Silvertone / Silvertone

Oct 88. (7") *(ORE 1)* **ELEPHANT STONE. / THE HARDEST THING IN THE WORLD** [ ] [–]
(12"+=) *(ORE 1T)* – Full fathoms five. *(re-iss. Feb90 c-s/cd-s; ORE 1 C/CD); hit No.8. (cd-s re-iss. Oct96; same)*

Mar 89. (7") *(ORE 2)* **MADE OF STONE. / GOING DOWN** [ ] [–]
(12"+=) *(ORE 2T)* – Guernica. *(re-iss. Mar90 c-s/cd-s; ORE 2 C/CD); hit No.20. (cd-s re-iss. Oct96; same)*

Apr 89. (lp/c/cd) *(ORE LP/MC/CD 502) <1184-1/-4/-2>* **THE STONE ROSES** [19] [86]
– I wanna be adored / She bangs the drum / Waterfall / Don't stop / Bye bye badman / Elizabeth my dear / (Song for my) Sugar spun sister / Made of stone / Shoot you down / This is the one / I am the resurrection. *(re-iss. Aug91 as 2x12"+=; OREZLP 502)* – Elephant stone / Fool's gold. *(cd re-iss. Mar97; same) (d-cd re-iss. as 10th ANNIVERSARY EDITION; 059124-2)* – (w/ extra tracks). – (hit UK No.26)

Jul 89. (7"/7"s) *(ORE/+X 6)* **SHE BANGS THE DRUM. / STANDING HERE** [36] [–]
(12"+=/12"s+=) *(ORE T/Z 6)* – Mersey Paradise.
(c-s++=/cd-s++=) *(ORE C/CD 6)* – Simone. *(re-entered chart Mar90; hit No.34) (cd-s re-iss. Oct96; same)*

Silvertone / Jive

Nov 89. (7"/ext.12") *(ORE/+T 13) <1315-1>* **FOOL'S GOLD. / WHAT THE WORLD IS WAITING FOR** [8] Mar90 [ ]
(c-s+=/cd-s+=) *(ORE C/CD 13)* – ('A'extended). *(flipped over re-entered chart Sep90; hit No.22) (re-iss. remix May92, hit No.73) (cd-s re-iss. Oct96; same)*
(12") *(ORET 13)* – ('A'-The Top Won mix) / ('A'-The Bottom Won mix).

Nov 89. (12"ep) *<1301>* **I WANNA BE ADORED / (long version) / GOING DOWN / SIMONE** [–] [ ]

Jul 90. (7"/c-s/12"/cd-s) *(ORE/+C/T/CD 17) <1399-1/-2>* **ONE LOVE. / SOMETHING'S BURNING** [4] [ ]
(cd-s re-iss. Oct96; same)

Sep 91. (7"/c-s) *(ORE/+C 31)* **I WANNA BE ADORED. / WHERE ANGELS PLAY** [20] [–]
(12"+=/cd-s+=) *(ORE T/CD 31)* – Sally Cinnamon (live).
(cd-s re-iss. Oct96; same)

Jan 92. (7"/c-s) *(ORE/+C 35)* **WATERFALL (remix). / ONE LOVE (remix)** [27] [ ]
(12"+=/cd-s+=) *(ORE T/CD 35)* – ('A'&'B'extended versions).
(cd-s re-iss. Oct96; same)

Apr 92. (7"/c-s) *(ORE/+C 40)* **I AM THE RESURRECTION. / ('A'-Pan & scan radio version)** [33] [ ]
(12"+=) *(ORET 40)* – Fool's gold (The Bottom Won mix).
(cd-s++=) *(ORECD 40)* – ('A'-5:3 Stoned Out club mix).
(cd-s re-iss. Oct96; same)

Jul 92. (cd/c/lp) *(ORE CD/C/LP 521)* **TURNS INTO STONE** (demos & rare) [32] [–]
– Elephant stone / The hardest thing in the world / Going down / Mersey Paradise / Standing here Where angels play / Simone / Fools gold / What the world is waiting for / One love / Something's burning. *(cd re-iss. Mar97 & Mar99; same)*

Geffen / Geffen

Nov 94. (7"/c-s) *(GFS/+C 84)* **LOVE SPREADS. / YOUR STAR WILL SHINE** [2] [ ]
(cd-s+=) *(GFST 84)* – Breakout.
(12"++=) *(GFSTD 84)* – Groove harder.

Dec 94. (cd/c/lp) *<(GED/GEC/GEF 24503)>* **SECOND COMING** [4] Jan95 [47]
– Breaking into Heaven / Driving south / Ten storey love song / Daybreak / Your star will shine / Straight to the man / Begging you / Tightrope / Good times / Tears / How do you sleep? / Love spreads. *(cd+=)* – (untitled hidden track No.90). *(lp re-iss. Aug99 on 'Simply Vinyl'; SVLP 111)*

Feb 95. (7"/c-s) *(GFS/+C 87)* **TEN STOREY LOVE SONG. / RIDE ON** [11] [ ]
(12"+=/cd-s+=) *(GFST/+D 87)* – Moses.

— In Apr'95, RENI quit and was replaced by **ROBERT MADDIX** (ex-GINA GINA).

Oct 95. (c-s) *(GFSC 22060)* **BEGGING YOU / ('A'-Chic mix)** [15] [ ]
(cd-s+=) *(GFSTD 22060)* – ('A'-Stone Corporation mix) / ('A'-Lakota mix) / ('A'-Young American primitive remix).
(12") *(GFST 22060)* – ('A'-Carl Cox mix) / ('A'-Development Corporation mix).

— Late in March '96, SQUIRE left to pursue new venture, The SEAHORSES. The STONE ROSES continued and in Aug'96, they recruited **AZIZ IBRAHIM** (ex-SIMPLY RED) / **NIGEL IPPINSON** – keyboards

— they officially split in Nov'96, after MANI joined PRIMAL SCREAM. IBRAHIM would join IAN BROWN and eventually issue his solo album in 1999, thoughtfully titled 'AZIZ'.

– compilations, etc. –

on 'Silvertone' unless mentioned; who else?

Jan 92. (8xcd-s-box-set) *(SRBX 1)* **SINGLES BOX** [ ] [–]

Nov 92. (10x12"box-set) *(SRBX 2)* **SINGLES BOX** [ ] [–]

Apr 95. (c-s) *(OREC 71)* **FOOL'S GOLD '95 / ('A'extended mix)** [23] [ ]
(12"+=/cd-s+=) *(ORE T/CD 71)* – ('A'-Tall Paul remix) / (A'-Cricklewood Ballroom mix).

May 95. (cd/c/lp) *(ORE CD/C/ZLP)* **THE COMPLETE STONE ROSES** [4] [ ]

Nov 96. (cd/c/lp) *(GARAGE CD/C/LP 1)* **GARAGE FLOWER** (early demos) [58] [–]
(cd re-iss. Augg99; same)

Jun 97. (7"ep) *Fierce; (FRIGHT 044)* **SPIKE ISLAND EP** (interviews, etc.) [ ] [–]

Feb 99. (c-s/cd-s) *Jive Electro; (052309-4/-2)* **FOOL'S GOLD / FOOL'S GOLD (Grooverider mix) / RABBIT IN THE MOON** [25] [–]

Oct 00. (cd/d-lp) *(926015-2/-1)* **THE REMIXES** [41] [–]

Nov 02. (cd/d-lp) *(926037-2/-1)* **THE VERY BEST OF THE STONE ROSES** [19] [ ]
– I wanna be adored / She bangs the drums / Ten storey love song / Waterfall / Made of stone / Love spreads / What the world is waiting for / Sally Cinnamon / Fools gold / Begging you / Elephant stone / Breaking into heaven / One love / This is the one / I am the resurrection.

the SEAHORSES

JOHN SQUIRE (b.24 Nov'62, Broadheath, Lancashire, England) – guitar / **CHRIS HELME** – vocals, acoustic guitar / **STUART FLETCHER** – bass / **ANDY WATTS** – drums, vocals

Geffen / Geffen

May 97. (7"/c-s/cd-s) *(GFS/+C/TD 22243)* **LOVE IS THE LAW. / DREAMER / SALE OF THE CENTURY** [3] [–]

May 97. (cd/c/lp) *(<GED/GEC/GEF 25134>)* **DO IT YOURSELF** [2] [ ]
– I want you to know / Blinded by the sun / Suicide drive / The boy in the picture / Love is the law / Happiness is eggshaped / Love me and leave me / Round the universe / 1999 / Standing on your head / Hello.

Jul 97. (7"/c-s/cd-s) *(GFS/+C/TD 22266)* **BLINDED BY THE SUN. / KILL PUSSYCAT KILL / MOVING ON** [7] [–]

Sep 97. (7"/c-s/cd-s) *(GFS/+C/TD 22282)* **LOVE ME AND LEAVE ME. / SHINE / FALLING IS EASY** [16] [–]

Dec 97. (7"/c-s/cd-s) *(GFS/+C/TD 22297)* **YOU CAN TALK TO ME. / DON'T TRY / 3 WIDE** [15] [–]

— **MARK HEANEY** – drums; repl. WATTS

— in Feb'99, the SEAHORSES announced they had split

JOHN SQUIRE

SQUIRE – vocals, guitar + **ANDY TREACEY** – drums (of FAITHLESS) / **JONATHAN WHITE** – bass (of GROOVE ARMADA) / **JOHN ELLIS** – keyboards

North Country | not iss.

Sep 02. (cd/d-lp) *(NCCD/NCLP 001)* **TIME CHANGES EVERYTHING** 17 –
– Joe Louis / I miss you / Shine a little light / Time changes everything / Welcome to the valley / 15 days / Transatlantic near death experience / All I really want / Strange feeling / Sophia.

Oct 02. (7") *(NC 001)* **JOE LOUIS. / HOME SWEET HOME** 43 –
(cd-s+=) *(NCCDA 001)* – 15 days (home demo).
(cd-s) *(NCCDB 001)* – ('A') / See you on the other side / I miss you (home demo).

Feb 04. (7"pic-d/cd-s) *(NC/+CDA 003)* **ROOM IN BROOKLYN. / NIGHTHAWKS** 44 –

Feb 04. (cd/lp) *(NCCD/NCLP 003)* **MARSHALL'S HOUSE** –
– Summertime / Hotel room / Marshall's house / Lighthouse & buildings, Portland Head, Cape Elizabeth, Maine / Cape Cod morning / People in the sun / Tables for ladies / Automat / Yawl riding a swell / Room in Brooklyn / Gas.

☐ STONE SOUR (see under ⇒ SLIPKNOT)

STONE TEMPLE PILOTS

Formed: Los Angeles, California, USA . . . 1987 as MIGHTY JOE YOUNG by WEILAND and ROBERT DeLEO. Recruiting DeLEO's brother, DEAN and ERIC KRETZ, they opted for the less frenetic San Diego as a musical base, changing their moniker to STONE TEMPLE PILOTS (thankfully changed from the considerably more controversial SHIRLEY TEMPLE'S PUSSY). After a few years on the hard/alternative rock circuit, they finally signed to 'Atlantic', the fruits of their labour, 'CORE' released in '92. Critical raves saw the album climb up the US chart (eventually reaching Top 3), songs like 'SEX TYPE THING' and 'PLUSH' drawing inevitable comparisons with PEARL JAM; WEILAND's vocals especially, were from the EDDIE VEDDER school of gravel-throated cool. After the aforementioned tracks were issued as UK singles, the album surfaced in the British Top 30 a full year on from its original release date, WEILAND's carrot-topped mop marking him out as a distinctive focal point for the band. LED ZEPPELIN and ALICE IN CHAINS were other obvious reference points, a second album, 'PURPLE' (1994), building on these influences to create a more cerebral post-grunge sound. The fact that the album rocketed into the American charts at No.1 was a measure of the group's lofty standing in the echelons of US alt-rock. WEILAND's love of nose candy and associated pleasures was no secret in the music world, the frontman narrowly avoiding a sizeable prison stretch for possession. Early in 1996, STP delivered a third (Top 5) album, 'TINY MUSIC . . . SONGS FROM THE VATICAN GIFT SHOP', accompanying touring commitments were severely disrupted when WEILAND was ordered by the court to attend a rehab centre while awaiting trial (he was later cleared). The following year, WEILAND continued his self-destructive behaviour, STP's future looking bleak as the remaining band members formed TALK SHOW. A WEILAND solo effort, '12 BAR BLUES' (1998), was poorly received by critics and fans alike, while a long 18 months (and after more WEILAND arrests!) saw the group back together on a 'NO.4' set in 1999 – needless to say this type of music had died in Britain ages ago. It was still going strong in the US though, where 'SHANGRI-LA DEE DA' (2001) made the Top 10, a record that faithfully followed the pattern set by its predecessor and further explored their interest in retro-psych. In 2004, WEILAND made a surprise comeback as frontman for VELVET REVOLVER, a band that featured three ex-GUNS N' ROSES members.

• **Songwriters:** Lyrics: WEILAND + R. DeLEO / KRETZ most of music except covers DANCING DAYS (Led Zeppelin).

Album rating: CORE (*7) / PURPLE (*7) / TINY MUSIC . . . SONGS FROM THE VATICAN GIFT SHOP (*7) / NO.4 (*4) / Talk Show: TALK SHOW (*5) / Scott Weiland: 12 BAR BLUES (*5) / Stone Temple Pilots: SHANGRI-LA DEE DA (*6) / THANK YOU compilation (*8)

(SCOTT) WEILAND (b.27 Oct'67, Santa Cruz, Calif.) – vocals / **DEAN DeLEO** (b.23 Aug'61, New Jersey) – guitar / **ROBERT DeLEO** (b. 2 Feb'66, New Jersey) – bass / **ERIC KRETZ** (b. 7 Jun'66, Santa Cruz) – drums

Atlantic | Atlantic

Nov 92. (cd/c/lp) *<(7567 82418-2/-4/-1)>* **CORE** 3
– Dead and bloated / Sex type thing / Wicked garden / No memory / Sin / Creep / Piece of pie / Naked Sunday / Plush / Wet my bed / Crackerman / Where the river goes. *(re-dist.Sep93, hit UK No.27) (cd re-iss. Jul00; same)*

Mar 93. (12"/cd-s) *(A 5769 T/CD)* **SEX TYPE THING. / WICKED GARDEN (acoustic) / PLUSH (acoustic)** 60 –

Aug 93. (7") *(A 7349)* **PLUSH. / SIN** 23 –
(cd-s+=) *(A 7349CD)* – Sex type thing (swing version).
(12"++=) *(A 7349T)* – Plush (acoustic).

Nov 93. (7"/c-s) *(A 7293/+C)* **SEX TYPE THING. / PIECE OF PIE** 55 –
(12"+=) *(A 7293TP)* – ('A'-Dead & Bloated mix).
(cd-s++=) *(A 7293CD)* – ('A'live).
(cd-s+=) *(A 7293CDX)* – Wicked garden (live) / Sin (live).

Jun 94. (cd/c/purple-lp) *<(7567 82607-2/-4/-1)>* **PURPLE** 10 1
– Meatplow / Vasoline / Lounge fly / Interstate love song / Still remains / Pretty penny / Silvergun Superman / Big empty / Unglued / Army ants / Kitchenware & candybar!. *(cd+=/c+=)* – Gracious melodies.

Aug 94. (12"blue-ep/cd-ep) *(A 5650 T/CD)* **VASOLINE / MEATPLOW. / ANDY WARHOL (MTV unplugged) / CRACKERMAN (unplugged)** 48 –

Dec 94. (7"purple/c-s) *(A 7192 K/C)* **INTERSTATE LOVE SONG. / LOUNGE FLY** 53 –
(cd-s+=) *(A 7192CD)* – Vasoline (live) / ('A'live).
(cd-s) *(A 7192CDX)* – ('A'side) / Shotgun superman / Army ants.

— In summer '95, WEILAND was credited on a MAGNIFICENT BASTARDS single, 'Mockingbird Girl'; other tracks by Devo & Stomp.

Mar 96. (cd/c/lp) *<(7567 82871-2/-4/-1)>* **TINY MUSIC . . . SONGS FROM THE VATICAN GIFT SHOP** 31 4
– Press play / Pop's love suicide / Tumble in the rough / Big bang baby / Lady picture show / And so I know / Tripping on a hole in a paper heart / Art school girl / Adhesive / Ride the cliche / Daisy / Seven caged tigers. *(cd re-iss. Jul00; same)*

Apr 96. (c-s) *(A 5516C)* **BIG BANG BABY / ADHESIVE** –
(cd-s+=) *(A 5516CD)* – Daisy.

— the group had to cancel promotion tours due to WEILAND being ordered by a Pasadena court to attend a live-in drug rehabilitation programme. He discharged himself for a few days in July '96 and gave himself up to the LAPD who had issued a warrant for his arrest; WEILAND was subsequently cleared. The other members (ROBERT DeLEO + KRETZ) started working on a side-project VITAMIN, which became TALK SHOW after recruiting frontman DAVID COUTTS

TALK SHOW

— **ERIC KRETZ + ROBERT DeLEO + DEAN DeLEO / + DAVE COUTTS** – vocals (ex-TEN INCH MEN)

Oct 97. (cd/c) *<(7567 83040-2/-4)>* **TALK SHOW**
– Ring twice / Hello hello / Everybody loves my car / Peeling an orange / So long / Wash me down / End of the world / John / Behind / Morning girl / Hide / Fill the fields.

SCOTT WEILAND

plays nearly every instrument, SHERYL CROW guests on accordion!

May 98. (cd/c) *<(7567 83084-2/-4)>* **12 BAR BLUES** Apr98 42
– Desperation #5 / Barbarella / About nothing / Where's the man / Divider / Cool kiss / The date / Son / Jimmy was a stimulator / Lady, your roof brings me down / Mockingbird girl / Opposite octave reaction.

Jun 98. (7"pink/c-s) *(AT 0035/+C)* **BARBARELLA. / MOCKINGBIRD GIRL**
(cd-s+=) *(AT 0035CD)* – ('A'-album version).

STONE TEMPLE PILOTS

— re-formed again

Oct 99. (cd/c) *<(7567 83255-2/-4)>* **NO.4** 6
– Down / Heaven and hot rods / Pruno / Church on Tuesday / Sour girl / No way out / Sex and violence / Glide / I got you / MC5 / Atlanta.

Apr 00. (-) *<album cut>* **SOUR GIRL** – 78

Aug 00. (cd/c) <(7567 83449-2/-4)> **SHANGRI-LA DEE DA** [ ] Jun00 [9]
– Dumb love / Days of the week / Coma / Hollywood bitch / Wonderful / Black again / Hello it's late / Too cool queenie / Regeneration / Bi-polar bear / Transmissions from a lonely room / A song for sleeping / Long way home.

Sep 01. (c-s) *(AT 0113C)* **DAYS OF THE WEEK / DOWN (live)** [ ] [–]
(cd-s+=) *(AT 0113CD)* – Big empty (live) / ('A'-CD-Rom).

Nov 01. (cd-s) <7567 85200-2> **REVOLUTION / (Cd-Rom)** [–] [ ]

— WEILAND became part of GUNS N' ROSES offshoot, VELVET REVOLVER

– compilations, etc. –

Nov 03. (cd) <(7567 83586-2)> **THANK YOU** [ ] [26]
– Vasoline / Down / Wicked garden / Big empty / Plush / Big bang baby / Creep / Lady picture show / Trippin' on a hole in a paper heart / Interstate love song / All in the suit that you wear / Sex type thing / Days of the week / Sour girl / Plush (acoustic).

☐ the STOOGES (see under ⇒ POP, Iggy)

the STRANGLERS

Formed: Chiddington, Surrey, England ... autumn 1974 as the GUILDFORD STRANGLERS by ex-science teacher, HUGH CORNWELL, history graduate JEAN-JACQUES BURNEL and jazz drummer JET BLACK. Augmented by organist DAVE GREENFIELD in the Spring of '75, they commenced gigging around the pub-rock circuit, developing their boorish, black-clad brand of DOORS/ELECTRIC PRUNES/DR.FEELGOOD retro rock with scant encouragement from the press. Late in '76, after supporting the likes of The FLAMIN' GROOVIES and The RAMONES, The STRANGLERS were signed to 'United Artists' and initially lumped in with the fermenting punk/new wave scene. Released early the following year, '(GET A) GRIP (ON YOURSELF)' found the band at their sneering, leering best, GREENFIELD's churning organ characterising a sound with which they'd stick fairly closely over the early part of their career. The single stalled outside the UK Top 40 – reportedly due to a chart mistake – although its controversial follow-up, 'PEACHES', made the Top 10 and immediately brought the band into conflict with feminists and the more liberal contingent of the music press. It was also banned by the BBC (a slightly modified version was later deemed acceptable), the surrounding controversy the first of many throughout the band's career and one which certainly didn't harm sales of the classic debut album, 'STRANGLERS IV – RATTUS NORVEGICUS' (1977). A Top 5 success comprising both singles and the enduring STRANGLERS favourite, 'HANGING AROUND', the record met with enthusiastic reviews as the group enjoyed the briefest of honeymoon periods with the press. A not entirely convincing attempt at political comment, 'SOMETHING BETTER CHANGE', gave the band a second Top 10 hit later that summer, closely followed by the vicious momentum of 'NO MORE HEROES'. Also released in '77, the album of the same name narrowly missed No.1, another solid set which armed their detractors with more ammunition in the form of 'BRING ON THE NUBILES'; a notorious, stripper-enhanced gig at Battersea Park didn't help matters and The STRANGLERS' were firmly tarred as sexist yobs. Not that their fans cared, helping put a further two singles, 'FIVE MINUTES' and 'NICE 'N' SLEAZY', into the Top 20, both tracks featuring on the album, 'BLACK AND WHITE' (1978). The latter set came free with a limited edition 7" featuring the lads' interesting cover of the BACHARACH/DAVID standard, 'WALK ON BY' tastefully placed side by side with the inimitable 'TITS'. More promising and certainly more memorable was the surprisingly melodic 'DUCHESS', a Top 20 hit lifted from accompanying album, 'THE RAVEN' (1979). That year also saw the release of solo albums from both J.J. BURNEL and HUGH CORNWELL (with ROBERT WILLIAMS), the former's 'EUROMAN COMETH' barely making the Top 40 while the latter's 'NOSFERATU' failed to make any impression on the charts. Worse was to come for CORNWELL when, on the 7th of January 1980, the singer was found guilty of drug possession and sentenced to three months in prison. Later that year, the whole band fell foul of the law, this time in the South of France where they were accused of inciting a riot; although threatened with serious jail terms, they were susbsequently let off with fines, later claiming it was 'NICE IN NICE' on 1986's 'DREAMTIME' album. The STRANGLERS' commercial fortunes didn't fare much better with 'THE MEN IN BLACK' (1981), a tongue-in-cheek (but critically derided nonetheless) pseudo-concept affair about alien undercover agents. Boasting the exquisite harpsichord stylings of 'GOLDEN BROWN', 'LA FOLIE' (1981) was a considerably more successful album, if somewhat pretentious. In line with the prevailing trend, The STRANGLERS' moved perilously closer to synth-pop as the 80's wore on, 'Epic' albums such as 'FELINE' (1983) and 'AURAL SCULPTURE' (1984) seeing the band's hardcore fanbase dwindle. Even a return to their former stamping ground (and the UK Top 10) with a musclebound run-through of The Kinks' 'ALL DAY AND ALL OF THE NIGHT' couldn't rejuvenate them and the subsequent studio album, '10' (1990) was the last to feature CORNWELL. Deciding to carry on with new frontman, JOHN ELLIS, the band recorded for various indie labels in the 90's and although the likes of 'STRANGLERS IN THE NIGHT' (1992) and 'ABOUT TIME' (1995) made the Top 40, most commentators (and many fans) were agreed that the band's glory days were definitely behind them. Thirty years young, re-signed (to 'E.M.I.') rather than resigned, and reverting to the roiling bass-keys aggro of yore on 'NORFOLK COAST' (2004), the STRANGLERS returned with what many fans – and not a few critics – regarded as their best album in decades. Co-produced by Mark Wallis (U2, TRAVIS) and featuring new guitarist BAZ WARNE, the record was top heavy with terrace-ready choruses, not least on the single, 'BIG THING COMING'.

• **Songwriters:** Mostly CORNWALL-penned except some by BURNEL. They also covered; 96 TEARS (? & The Mysterians).

Album rating: STRANGLERS IV – RATTUS NORVEGICUS (*8) / NO MORE HEROES (*7) / BLACK AND WHITE (*7) / LIVE (X CERT) (*5) / THE RAVEN (*6) THE MEN-IN-BLACK (*5) / LA FOLIE (*7) / THE COLLECTION 1977-1982 compilation (*7) / AURAL SCULPTURE (*6) / DREAMTIME (*6) / ALL LIVE AND ALL OF THE NIGHT (*4) / 10 (*5) / THE STRANGLERS' GREATEST HITS compilation (*9) / STRANGLERS IN THE NIGHT (*4) / SATURDAY NIGHT SUNDAY MORNING (*3) / ABOUT TIME (*4) / WRITTEN IN RED (*4) / THE HIT MEN – THE COMPLETE SINGLES 1977-1990 compilation (*8) / COUP DE GRACE (*4) / PEACHES – THE VERY BEST OF THE STRANGLERS compilation (*8) / NORFOLK COAST (*6)

HUGH CORNWALL (b.28 Aug'48, London, England) – vocals, guitar / **JEAN-JAQUES BURNEL** (b.21 Feb'52, London; French parents) – bass, vocals / **DAVE GREENFIELD** (b.29 Mar'49, Brighton, England) – keyboards / **JET BLACK** (b. BRIAN DUFFY, 26 Aug'43, Ilford, England) – drums

U.A. A&M

Jan 77. (7") *(UP 36211)* **(GET A) GRIP (ON YOURSELF). / LONDON LADY** [44] [–]

Apr 77. (lp/c) *(UAG/UAC 30045)* <4648> **STRANGLERS IV – RATTUS NORVEGICUS** [4] [ ]
– Sometimes / Goodbye Toulouse / London lady / Princess of the streets / Hanging around / Peaches / (Get a) Grip (on yourself) / Ugly / Down in the sewer: (a) Falling – (b) Down in the sewer – (c) Trying to get out again – (d) Rats rally. *(free ltd.7"w.a.)* **CHOOSEY SUSIE. / IN THE BIG SHITTY (live)** *(re-iss. May82 on 'Fame' lp/c; FA/TC-FA 3001) (cd-iss. Apr88; CDFA 3001) (cd-iss. Feb88 on 'Liberty'; CZ 85) (lp re-iss. Jan01 on 'Simply Vinyl'; SVLP 291) (cd re-iss. Aug01 on 'EMI Gold'+=; 534406-2)* – Choosey Susie / Go buddy go / Peasant in the big shitty (live).

May 77. (7") *(UP 36248)* **PEACHES. / GO BUDDY GO** [8] [–]

— Jun77; They backed CELIA & THE MUTATIONS on cover single 'MONY MONY'.

Jul 77. (7") *(UP 36277)* **SOMETHING BETTER CHANGE. / STRAIGHTEN OUT** [9] [–]

Sep 77. (7") *(UP 36300)* **NO MORE HEROES. / IN THE SHADOWS** [8] [–]

Oct 77. (lp/c) *(UAG/UAC 30200)* <4659> **NO MORE HEROES** [2] [ ]
– I feel like a wog / Bitching / Dead ringer / Dagenham Dave / Bring on the nubiles / Something better change / No more heroes / Peasant in the big shitty / Burning up time / English towns / School mam / In the shadows. *(re-iss. 1985 lp/c; ATAK/TC-ATAK 32) (cd-iss. Feb88 on 'E.M.I.'; CDP 746613-2) (re-iss. Sep87 on 'Fame' lp/c; FA/TC-FA 3190) (cd-iss. Aug88; CDFA 3190) (cd re-iss. Aug01 on 'EMI Gold'+=; 534407-2)* – Straighten out / Five minutes / Rok it to the Moon.

Nov 77. (7"pink-ep) **SOMETHING BETTER CHANGE / STRAIGHTEN OUT. / GRIP / HANGIN' AROUND** [–] [ ]

Jan 78. (7") *(UP 36350)* **FIVE MINUTES. / ROK IT TO THE MOON** [11] [–]

Apr 78. (7") *(UP 36379)* **NICE 'N' SLEAZY. / SHUT UP** [18] Aug78 [ ]

May 78. (lp/c)<US-grey-lp> *(UAK/TCK 30222)* <4706> **BLACK AND WHITE** [2] [ ]
– Tank / Nice 'n' sleazy / Outside Tokyo / Mean to me / Hey! (rise of the robots) / Sweden (all quiet on the Eastern Front) / Toiler on the sea / Curfew / Threatened / Do you wanna? / Death and night and blood (Yukio) / Enough time. *(free ltd.7"w.a.) (FREE 9)* **WALK ON BY. / TITS / MEAN TO ME** *(re-iss. Jan86 on 'Epic' lp/c; EPC/40 26439) (cd-iss. Jul88 on 'E.M.I.'+=; CZ 109)* – (free 7" tracks). *(cd re-iss. Aug01 on 'E.M.I.'+=; 534691-2)* – Mean to me / Shut up / Walk on by / Sveridge / Old codger / Tits.

Jul 78. (7"m) *(UP 36429)* **WALK ON BY. / OLD CODGER / TANK** [21] [–]

U.A. I.R.S.

Mar 79. (lp/c) *(UAG/TCK 30224)* <70011> **X-CERT (live)** [7] [ ]
– (Get a) Grip (on yourself) / Dagenham Dave / Burning up time / Dead ringer / Hanging around / I feel like a wog / Straighten out / Do you wanna – Death and night and blood (Yukio) / Five minutes / Go buddy go. *(re-iss. 1985 lp/c; ATAK/TC-ATACK 33) (cd-iss. Jul88 +=; CZ 110)* – In the shadows / Peasant in the big shitty. *(cd re-iss. Aug01 on 'E.M.I.'++=; 534687-2)* – In the shadows / Sometimes / Mean to me / London lady / Goodbye Toulouse / Hangin' around.

Aug 79. (7") *(BP 308)* **DUCHESS. / FOOLS RUSH OUT** [14] [ ]

Sep 79. (lp/c) *(UAG/TCK 30262)* **THE RAVEN** [4] [–]
– Longships / The raven / Dead Loss Angeles / Ice / Baroque bordello / Nuclear device / Shah shah a go go / Don't bring Harry / Duchess / Meninblack / Genetix. *(re-iss. Sep85 on 'Fame' lp/c; FA/TC-FA 3131) (cd-iss. Aug88; CDFA 3131) (cd-iss. Oct87 on 'E.M.I.'+=; CZ 20)* – Bear cage. *(cd re-iss. Aug01 on 'E.M.I.'++=; 534689-2)* – Fools rush out / N'emmenes pas Harry / Yellowcake UFO.

Oct 79. (7") *(BP 318)* **NUCLEAR DEVICE (THE WIZARD OF AUS). / YELLOWCAKE UF6** [36] [–]

Nov 79. (7"ep) *(STR 1)* **DON'T BRING HARRY** [41] [–]
– Don't bring Harry / Wired / Crabs (live) / In the shadows (live).

Liberty I.R.S.

Jan 80. (7") **DUCHESS. / THE RAVEN** [–] [ ]

Jan 80. (lp) <SP 70011> **STRANGLERS IV** [–] [ ]
– (5 tracks from 'THE RAVEN', plus recent singles)
(above w/ free 7"ep) – Do The European / Choosie Suzie / Wired / Straighten out.

Mar 80. (7"/12") *(BP/12BP 344)* **BEAR CAGE. / SHAH SHAH A GO GO** [36] [–]

May 80. (7") *(BP 355)* **WHO WANTS THE WORLD. / MENINBLACK** [39] [–]

Jan 81. (7") *(BP 383)* **THROWN AWAY. / TOP SECRET** [42] [–]

Feb 81. (lp/c) *(LBG/TC-LBG 30313)* **THE MEN• IN• BLACK** [8] [–]
– Waltzinblack / Just like nothing on Earth / Second coming / Waiting for the meninblack / Turn the centuries, turn / Two sunspots / Four horsemen / Thrown away / Manna machine / Hallo to our men. *(re-iss. 1985 lp/c; ATAK/TC-ATAK 34) (re-iss. Sep88 on 'Fame' lp/c/cd; FA/TCFA/CDFA 3208)* – Top secret / Maninwhite. *(cd re-iss. Aug01 on 'E.M.I.'++=; 534690-2)* – Tomorrow was hereafter.

Mar 81. (7") *(BP 393)* **JUST LIKE NOTHING ON EARTH. / MANINWHITE** [ ] [–]

Nov 81. (7") *(BP 405)* **LET ME INTRODUCE YOU TO THE FAMILY. / VIETNAMERICA** [42] [–]

Nov 81. (lp/c) *(LBG/TC-LBG 30342)* **LA FOLIE** [11] [–]
– Non stop / Everybody loves you when you're dead / Tramp / Let me introduce you to the family / The man they love to hate / Pin up / It only takes two to tango / Golden brown / How to find true love and happiness in the present day / La folie. *(re-iss. Nov83 on 'Fame' lp/c; FA/TC-FA 3083) (cd-iss. Aug88; CDFA 3083) (cd-iss. Feb88 +=; CZ 86)* – Cruel garden. *(cd re-iss. Aug01 on 'E.M.I.'++=; 534688-2)* – Cocktail nubiles / Vietnamerica / Love 30 / You hold the key to my love in your hands / Strange little girl.

Jan 82. (7") *(BP 407)* **GOLDEN BROWN. / LOVE 30** [2] [–]

Apr 82. (7") *(BP 410)* **LA FOLIE. / WALTZINBLACK** [47] [–]

Jul 82. (7") *(BP 412)* **STRANGE LITTLE GIRL. / CRUEL GARDEN** [7] [–]

Sep 82. (lp/c) *(LBG/TC-LBG 304353)* **THE COLLECTION 1977-1982** (compilation) [12] [–]
– (Get a) Grip (on yourself) / Peaches / Hanging around / No more heroes / Duchess / Walk on by / Waltzinblack / Something better change / Nice'n'sleazy / Bear cage / Who wants the world / Golden brown / Strange little girl / La folie. *(cd-iss. 1985; CDP 746066-2) (re-iss. Aug89 on 'Fame' cd/c/lp; CD/TC+/FA 3230)*

Epic Epic

Nov 82. (7"/7"pic-d) *(EPCA/+11 2893)* **THE EUROPEAN FEMALE. / SAVAGE BEAST** [9] [–]

Jan 83. (lp/c) *(EPC/40 25237)* <38542> **FELINE** [4] [ ]
– Midnight summer dream / It's a small world / Ships that pass in the night / The European female / Let's tango in Paris / Paradise / All roads lead to Rome / Blue sister / Never say goodbye. *(free ltd.one-sided-7"w.a.)* **AURAL SCULPTURE** *(re-iss. Apr86 lp/c; EPC/40 32711) <US lp+=>* – Golden brown. *(cd-iss. Jul97; 484469-2) (cd re-iss. Oct01 +=; 504592-2)* – SAvage breast / Pawsher / Permission / Midnight summer dream / European female (live) / Vladimir and Olga / Aural sculpture manifesto.

Feb 83. (7"/12") *(A/+13 3167)* **MIDNIGHT SUMMER DREAM. / VLADIMIR AND OLGA** [35] [–]

Jul 83. (7") *(A 3387)* **PARADISE. / PAWSHER** [48] [–]
(12"+=) *(A13 3387)* – Permission.

Jul 83. (12") **MIDNIGHT SUMMER DREAM. / PARADISE** [–] [ ]

Sep 84. (7") *(A 4738)* **SKIN DEEP. / HERE AND NOW** [15] [–]
(12"+=) *(TA 4738)* – Vladimir and the beast.

Nov 84. (lp/c) *(EPC/40 26220)* <39959> **AURAL SCULPTURE** [14] [ ]
– Ice queen / Skin deep / Let me down easy / No mercy / North winds / Uptown / Punch & Judy / Spain / Laughing / Souls / Mad Hatter. *(re-iss. May87 lp/c; 450488-1/-4) (cd-iss. 1987; 450488-2) (re-iss. cd Sep93 on 'Sony Collectors'; 983285-2) (cd re-iss. Feb97; 474676-2)*

Nov 84. (7"/7"sha-pic-d) *(A/WA 4921)* **NO MERCY. / IN ONE DOOR** [37] [–]
(12"+=) *(TA 4921)* – Hot club (riot mix).
(d7"++=) *(GA 4921)* – Head on the line.

Feb 85. (7") *(A 6045)* **LET ME DOWN EASY. / ACHILLES HEEL** [48] [–]
(12"+=) *(TA 6045)* – Place des victories.
(12"++=) *(QTA 6045)* – Vladimir goes to Havana / The aural sculpture manifesto.

Aug 86. (7"/12"/7"sha-pic-d) *(650055-7/-6/-0)* **NICE IN NICE. / SINCE YOU WENT AWAY** [30] [–]

Oct 86. (7"/7"sha-pic-d) *(SOLAR/+P 1)* **ALWAYS THE SUN. / NORMAN NORMAL** [30] [–]
(12"+=) *(SOLART 1)* – Soul.
(d7"+=) *(SOLARD 1)* – Nice in Nice / Since you went away.

Oct 86. (lp/c/cd/pic-lp) *(EPC/40/CD/11 26648)* <40607> **DREAMTIME** [16] [ ]
– Always the sun / Dreamtime / Was it you? / You'll always reap what you sow / Ghost train / Nice in Nice / Big in America / Shakin' like a leaf / Mayan skies / Too precious. *(re-iss. Feb89 lp/c/cd; 463366-1/-4/-2) (cd re-iss. Oct01 +=; 504593-2)* – Since you went away / Norman normal / Dry day / Hitman / Was it you / Burnham beaches.

Dec 86. (7"/7"sha-pic-d) *(HUGE/+P 1)* **BIG IN AMERICA. / DRY DAY** [48] [–]
(12"+=) *(HUGET 1)* – Uptown.
(d7"+=) *(HUGED 1)* – Always the sun / Norman normal.

Feb 87. (7"/7"sha-pic-d) *(SHEIK/+P 1)* **SHAKIN' LIKE A LEAF. / HIT MAN** [58] [–]
('A'-Jelly mix-12"+=) *(SHEIKQ 1)* – Was it you?
('A'live-12") *(SHEIKB 1)* – (an evening with Hugh Cornwall).

Dec 87. (7"/7"sha-pic-d) *(VICE/+P 1)* **ALL DAY AND ALL OF THE NIGHT (live). / VIVA VLAD** [7] [ ]
(12"+=) *(VICET 1)* – Who wants the world (live).
(cd-s+=) *(CDVICE 1)* – Strange little girl.

Feb 88. (lp/c/cd) *(460259-1/-4/-2)* <44209> **ALL LIVE AND ALL OF THE NIGHT (live)** [12] [ ]
– No more heroes / Was it you? / Down in the sewer / Always the sun / Golden brown / North winds / The European female / Strange little girl / Nice 'n' sleazy / Toiler on the sea / Spain / London lady / All day and all of the night. *(cd re-iss. Oct01 +=; 504594-2)* – Souls / Uptown / Shakin' like

a leaf / Who wants the world / Peaches / Straighten out / Nuclear device / Punch and Judy.

Feb 90. (7"/c-s) *(TEARS/+M 1)* **96 TEARS. / INSTEAD OF THIS** 17 –
(12"+=/cd-s+=/pic-cd-s+=) *(TEARS T/C/P 1)* – Poisonality.

Mar 90. (cd/c/lp/pic-lp) *(466483-2/-4/-1/-0)* **10** 15 –
– The sweet smell of success / Someone like you / 96 tears / In this place / Let's celebrate / Man of the Earth / Too many teardrops / Where I live / Out of my mind / Never to look back. *(cd re-iss. Oct01 ++; 504595-2)* – Instead of this / Personality / Motorbike / Something / You / Viva Vlad / All day and all of the night (studio) / Always the sun (sunny side up mix).

Apr 90. (7"/c-s/7"pic-d) *(TEARS/+M/P 2)* **THE SWEET SMELL OF SUCCESS. / MOTORBIKE** 65 –
(12"+=/cd-s+=) *(TEARS T/C 2)* – Something.

Nov 90. (cd/c/lp/pic-cd) *(467541-2/-4/-1/-9)* *<47081>* **THE STRANGLERS' GREATEST HITS 1977-1990** (complation) 4
– Peaches / Something better change / No more heroes / Walk on by / Duchess / Golden brown / Strange little girl / The European female / Skin deep / Nice in Nice / Always the sun / Big in America / All day and all of the night / 96 tears / No mercy.

Dec 90. (7"/c-s) *(656 430-7/-4)* **ALWAYS THE SUN. / BURNHAM BEECHES** 29 –
(12"+=) *(656 430-6)* – Straighten out.
(cd-s) *(656 430-2)* – ('A'side) / Nuclear device (live) / All day and all of the night (live) / Punch and Judy (live).

Mar 91. (7"/c-s) *(656 761-7/-4)* **GOLDEN BROWN (re-mix). / YOU** 68 –
(cd-s+=) *(656 761-2)* – Skin deep (extended) / Peaches.

—— (late 1990) **JOHN ELLIS** (b. 1 Jun'52, London) – guitar, vocals (once p/t member) (ex-VIBRATORS, etc.) repl. CORNWALL who has already ventured solo.

—— (Jan'91) also added **PAUL ROBERTS** (b.31 Dec'59, London) – vocals (ex-SNIFF 'N' THE TEARS)

China Viceroy

Aug 92. (7") *(WOK 2025)* **HEAVEN OR HELL. / DISAPPEAR** 46 –
(12"+=/c-s+=/cd-s+=) *(WOK T/C/CD 2025)* – Brainbox / Hanging around.

Sep 92. (lp/c/cd) *(WOL/+MC/CD 1030)* *<8007>* **STRANGLERS IN THE NIGHT** 33 Feb93
– Time to die / Sugar bullets / Heaven or Hell / Laughing at the rain / This town / Brainbox / Southern mouintains / Gain entry to your soul / Grand canyon / Wet afternoon / Never see / Leave it to the dogs.

Psycho not iss.

Oct 92. (7"/c-s) *(PSY/+MC 002)* **SUGAR BULLETS. / SO UNCOOL** –
(cd-s+=) *(PSYCD 002)* – ('A'version).

—— **TIKAKE TOBE** – drums; repl. JET BLACK

Essential Viceroy

Jun 93. (cd/c/lp) *(ESS CD/MC/LP 194)* *<ESM 388>* **SATURDAY NIGHT SUNDAY MORNING (live)** Mar96
– Toiler on the sea / 96 Tears / Always the sun / No more heroes / Golden brown / Tank / Strange little girl / Something better change / Hanging around / All day and all of the night / Duchess / *Medley / Was it you? / Down in the sewer.

—— In Jun'93, old Strangler HUGH CORNWALL released album 'WIRED' on 'Transmission' label. Nearly a year earlier as CCW, he, ROGER COOK & AND WEST issued cd 'CCW FEATURING HUGH CORNWALL • ROGER COOK • ANDY WEST' on 'UFO'.

—— **JET BLACK** returned

When! Beacon

May 95. (cd/c/lp) *(WEN CD/MC/LP 001)* *<51568>* **ABOUT TIME** 31 Jan96
– Golden boy / Money / Sinister / Little blue lies / Still life / Paradise row / She gave it all / Lies and deception / Lucky finger / And the boat sails by.

Jun 95. (12"/cd-s) *(WEN T/X 1007)* **LIES AND DECEPTION. / SWIM / DANNY COOL** –
(cd-s) *(WENX 1008)* – ('A'side) / Kiss the world goodbye / Bed of nails.

Jan 97. (pic-cd/cd/c) *(WEN PD/CD/MC 009)* **WRITTEN IN RED** 52 –
– Valley of the birds / In Heaven she walks / In a while / Silver into blue / Blue sky / Here / Joy de viva / Miss you / Daddy's riding the range / Summer in the city / Wonderful land. *(cd re-iss. Mar98 on 'Eagle'; EAMCD 001)*

Feb 97. (c-s/cd-s) *(WEN N/X 1018)* **IN HEAVEN SHE WALKS / GOLDEN BROWN (live)** –
(cd-s) *(WENX 1020)* – ('A'side) / Grip (live) / Something better change (live).

Eagle Festival

Oct 98. (cd) *(EAGCD 042)* *<31965>* **COUP DE GRACE** Mar99
– God is good / You don't think that what you've done is wrong / Tonight / Jump over my shadow / Miss you / Coup de grace (S-O-S) / In the end / No reason / Known only unto God / The light.

—— **BAZ WARNE** – guitar; repl. ELLIS who went solo

Liberty Liberty

Feb 04. (7"red/cd-s) *(548069-7/-2)* **BIG THING COMING. / PEACHES 2004** 31 –
(cd-s) *(548069-0)* – ('A') / I don't agree / Tuckers grave (live at Shepherd's Bush Empire) / ('A'-video).

Feb 04. (cd) *(<596951-2>)* **NORFOLK COAST** 70 Mar04
– Norfolk coast / Big thing coming / Long black veil / I've been wild / Dutch moon / Lost control / Into the fire / Tuckers grave / I don't agree / Sanfte kuss / Mine all mine.

Apr 04. (7"red) *(548906-7)* **LONG BLACK VEIL. / WALTZINBLACK** 51 –
(cd-s+=) *(548906-2)* – Life's too short / ('A'-extended).

– compilations, etc. –

Mar 84. (7") *EMI Gold; (G45 6)* **GOLDEN BROWN. / STRANGE LITTLE GIRL** –
Sep 86. (lp/c) *Liberty; (LBG/TCLBG 5001)* **OFF THE BEATEN TRACK** 80 –
Nov 88. (lp/c) *Liberty; (EMS/TCEMS 1306)* **THE RARITIES** –
(cd-iss. Oct02 on 'E.M.I.'; 541079-2)
Jan 89. (7"/7"red) *E.M.I.; (EM/+R 84)* **GRIP '89. / WALTZINBLACK** 33 –
(12"+=) *(12EM 84)* – Tomorrow was thereafter.
(cd-s++=) *(CDEM 84)* – ('A'mix).
Feb 89. (cd/c/lp) *E.M.I.; (CD/TC+/EM 1314)* **THE SINGLES** 57 –
Jun 89. (12"ep) *Nighttracks; (SFNT/+CD 020)* **RADIO 1 SESSION (1982)** –
– The man they love to hate / Nuclear device / Genetix / Down in the sewer.
Dec 90. (3xcd-box) *Epic; (467395-2)* **FELINE / AURAL SCULPTURE / DREAMTIME**
(re-iss. Oct02; 509722-2)
Feb 92. (cd/c/d-lp) *Newspeak; (SPEAK CD/MC/LP 101)* **THE EARLY YEARS 74-75-76, RARE LIVE & UNRELEASED** –
Mar 92. (cd/c) *Epic; (471416-2/-4)* **ALL TWELVE INCHES** –
May 92. (cd/c) *(CDGO/TCGO 2033)* **LIVE AT THE HOPE AND ANCHOR (live)** –
(cd re-iss. Feb95 on 'Fame'; CDFA 3316)
Jul 92. (d-cd) *Epic; (466835-2)* **FELINE / DREAMTIME** –
Dec 92. (4xcd-box) *E.M.I.; CDS 799924-2)* **THE OLD TESTAMENT – THE U.A. STUDIO RECORDINGS (demos)** –
May 94. (cd) *Receiver; (<RRCD 187>)* **DEATH AND NIGHT AND BLOOD**
Jun 94. (cd) *Castle; (CLACD 401)* **THE EARLY YEARS 1974-76** –
Feb 95. (cd) *Receiver; (RRCD 195)* **LIVE IN CONCERT (live w/ FRIENDS)**
Nov 95. (cd) *Essential; <ESM 283>* **RADIO ONE** –
Nov 95. (cd-s) *Old Gold; (12623 6339-2)* **GOLDEN BROWN / NO MORE HEROES** –
Feb 97. (cd/c) *E.M.I.; (CD/TC EMC 3759)* **THE HIT MEN (The Complete Singles 1977-1990)** –
Apr 97. (cd) *EMI Gold; (CDGOLD 171)* **THE COLLECTION** –
Dec 97. (cd) *Rialto; (<RMCD 220>)* **STRANGLERS ARCHIVE LIVE IN LONDON (live)**
Feb 98. (cd) *Disky; (DC 88187-2)* **THE COLLECTION** –
Feb 98. (cd) *Cleopatra; <206>* **FRIDAY THE THIRTEENTH** –
Mar 98. (cd) *Eagle; (EABCD 111)* **THE MASTERS** –
Apr 98. (cd) *Stranglers; (SOF 001CD) / Voiceprint; <1>* **ACCESS ALL AREAS (live)** Jul98
May 98. (cd) *Stranglers; (SOF 002CD)* **FROM BIRTH TO BEYOND** –
Oct 98. (cd) *E.M.I.; (497773-2)* **THE BBC SESSIONS / LIVE AT THE HAMMERSMITH ODEON 1981** –
Jan 00. (cd) *Eagle; (EAGCD 006)* **FRIDAY 13TH (live at the Royal Albert Hall)** –
Feb 01. (cd) *S.P.V.; (SPV 0857105-2)* **5 LIVE VOL.1** –

Jun 01. (10xcd-s; box) *E.M.I.; (889172-2)* **THE U.A. SINGLES 1977-1979** –
Aug 01. (cd) *Armoury; (ARMCD 053)* **THE STRANGLERS** –
Oct 01. (5xcd-box) *Epic; (504596-2)* **THE EPIC YEARS** –
Jan 02. (cd) *Castle; (CMRCD 455)* **DEATH AND NIGHT AND BLOOD – THE STRANGLERS LIVE (live)** –
Jan 02. (cd) *Castle; (CMRCD 459)* **LIVE IN CONCERT (live)** –
Jan 02. (d-cd) *Snapper; (<SMDCD 373>)* **LIES AND DECEPTION (live)**
Mar 02. (cd) *Stable; (STABLE 1)* **CLUBBED TO DEATH – THE GREATEST HITS REMIXED** –
Jun 02. (cd) *Liberty; (540202-2)* **PEACHES – THE VERY BEST OF THE STRANGLERS** 21 –
– Peaches / Golden brown / Walk on by / No more heoes / Skin deep / Hanging around / All day and all of the night / Straighten out / Nice 'n' sleazy / Strange little girl / Who wants the world? / Something better change / Always the sun (sunny side up mix) / European female / Grip (1989 mix) / Five minutes / Don't bring Harry / La folie / 96 tears.
Jul 02. (12") *Tried & Twisted; (TT 2001)* **GOLDEN BROWN (earth loop remix). / GOLDEN BROWN (slipped disco remix)** –
Aug 02. (cd) *Zenith; (ZEN 0031-2)* **LAID BACK** –
Oct 02. (cd) *Epic; (487997-2)* **THE BEST OF THE EPIC YEARS** –
Oct 02. (cd) *Delta; (CD 47103)* **OUT OF THE BLACK** –
Jun 03. (cd) *Nobel Price; (220779)* **MISS YOU**
Aug 03. (cd) *Burning Airlines; (PILOT 177)* **APOLLO REVISITED (live)**

the STREETS

Formed: Birmingham, England . . . late 2000 as the brainchild of MIKE SKINNER. All decked out in a hoodie, low-slung cap and white nikes, MIKE took the British Garage scene – not to mention the actual music scene – by storm in 2002 with his debut album 'ORIGINAL PIRATE MATERIAL'. Growing up in a working class household in the suburbs of Birmingham, SKINNER became interested in keyboards at an early age, and, having been raised on a staple diet of hip-hop (apparently his brother was part of the whole VW Beetle medalion-wearing scene in the early '90's) decided to dedicate his life to making music. Setting up a makeshift studio in his bedroom, using a cupboard and a mattress as a vocal booth, the switched-on Brummie invited local MCs around to record and mix tracks. This established The STREETS. Beginning as a collective crew, many soon lost interest, which forced SKINNER to branch out on his own, mixing, recording, mutating styles and sounds, until pirate radio stations and garage DJ's picked up on his immense talent. Hence the album 'ORIGINAL PIRATE MATERIAL', a contender for best album of the year, and one of the most original urban records ever. On the single 'HAS IT COME TO THIS', SKINNER took the speedy garage beat format, mixed it with his own sardonic vocals (a kind of cross between EMINEM and the ARTFUL DODGER) and also added a bit of dancehall ragga to the deck. Standout track 'THE IRONY OF IT ALL' coupled two characters (both played by SKINNER), one being a mouthy lager lout, the other a gentle stoner debating the causes and effects of both drugs with tack-sharp wit and brilliant social observations. At the end of the day, The STREETS were massive amongst kids and students alike; here was an album devoid of the cute, self-indulgent narcissism of mainstream garage and the fake fubbery of the "bling-bling" era – MIKE was taking it back . . . back to the streets. 'A GRAND DON'T COME FOR FREE' (2004) saw SKINNER return with a No.1 album and more tales of everyday urban blandness, nailing Blair's Britain in unapologetically accented free speech. The record's days-in-the-life narrative was previewed by lead single, 'FIT BUT YOU KNOW IT', a UK Top 5 powered by a chipper guitar loop and allegedly inspired by pop star Rachel Stevens. Along with uncharacteristically lovelorn follow-up, 'DRY YOUR EYES' (a straight-to No.1), it was also about the closest the opus came to the dynamics of conventional songwriting. Third single 'BLINDED BY THE LIGHT' (Top 10), was more representative, a club-sick monologue delivered at will over blurred-vision beats. Cannily re-issued around the same time, 'ORIGINAL PIRATE MATERIAL' roared back into the Top 10, crowning SKINNER's unfazed leap into the A-list. His inevitable distancing from working class routine underpinned third album, 'THE HARDEST WAY TO MAKE AN EASY LIVING' (2006), a UK No.1 in which he got to grips with fame and its charms, caprices and paranoia. Top 10 lead single, 'WHEN YOU WASN'T FAMOUS', chronicled the vagaries of romance in the fame game, an NME Single Of The Week which generated yet more speculation on who exactly constituted its subject matter.

Album rating: ORIGINAL PIRATE MATERIAL (*9) / A GRAND DON'T COME FOR FREE (*8) / THE HARDEST WAY TO MAKE AN EASY LIVING (*7)

MIKE SKINNER (b.27 Nov'78) – vocals, electronics

Locked On — not iss.
May 01. (12") *(LOCKED 035)* **HAS IT COME TO THIS? (mixes)** –
679 Record — Atlantic
Oct 01. (12"/cd-s) *(679L 001 T/CD1)* **HAS IT COME TO THIS? (mixes; original / Jameson / Zed Bias vocal)** 18 –
(cd-s) *(679L 001CD2)* – ('A'side) / Geezers need excitement / Streets score (instrumental).
Mar 02. (cd/c/d-lp) *(0927 43568-2/-4/-1)* *<93181>* **ORIGINAL PIRATE MATERIAL** 10 Oct02
– Turn the page / Has it come to this? / Let's push things forward / Sharp darts / Same old thing / Geezers need excitement / It's too late / Too much brandy / Don't mug yourself / Who got the funk? / The irony of it all / Weak become heroes / Who dares wins / Stay positive.
Apr 02. (12") *(679 005T)* **LET'S PUSH THINGS FORWARD (mixes; Studio Gangsters / Zed Bias vocal / Mystery)** 30 –
(cd-s) *(679 005CD1)* – ('A'mixes; original / Studio Gangsters / Zed Bias dub).
(cd-s) *(679 005CD2)* – ('A'-original) / Runnins / Don't mug yourself (instrumental).
Jul 02. (12") *(679L 007TX)* **WEAK BECOME HEROES. / LET'S PUSH THINGS FORWARD (remix featuring ROLL DEEP) / GIVE ME LIGHTER BACK** 27 –
(cd-s+=) *(679L 007CD1)* – ('A'-video).
(cd-s) *(679L 007CD2)* – ('A'-Ashley Beadle's love bug vocal) / Same old thing (Outlaw breaks remix) / Same old thing (Morph resurrection remix).
Oct 02. (12") *(679L 008T)* **DON'T MUG YOURSELF. / OUT TAKES / STREETS SCORE** 21 –
(cd-s+=) *(679L 008CD1)* – ('A'-video).
(cd-s) *(679L 008CD2)* – ('A') / Weak become heroes (Royksopp's memory lane mix) / Has it come to this? (high contrast remix).
Jul 03. (12"/cd-s) *<60393/60543>* **DON'T MUG YOURSELF (Mr. Figit mix). / GIVE ME BACK MY LIGHTER (Jammer mix)** –
Apr 04. (cd-s) *(679L 071CD1)* **FIT BUT YOU KNOW IT / SOAKED BY THE ALE** 4 –
(cd-s) *(679L 071CD2)* – ('A') / ('A'-feat. the FUTUREHEADS) / ('A'-feat. KANO, DONAE'O, TINCHY STRYDER & LADY SOVEREIGN) / Don't mug yourself (remix by Donae'o) / ('A'-video).
(dvd-s) *(679L 071DVD)* – ('A'-video) / The irony of it all (video).
May 04. (cd) *(<2564 61534-2>)* **A GRAND DON'T COME FOR FREE** 1 82
– It was supposed to be so easy / Could well be in / *** Not addicted *** / Blinded by the lights / Wouldn't have it any other way / Get out of my house / Fit but you know it / Such a tw*t / What is he thinking? / Dry your eyes / Empty cans.
Jul 04. (cd-s) *(679L 077CD1)* **DRY YOUR EYES / IT'S TOO LATE (live in France)** 1
(cd-s) *(679L 077CD2)* – ('A') / Let's push things forward (live in France) / Has it come to this (live in France) / ('A'-video).
Sep 04. (cd-s) *(679L 085CD)* **BLINDED BY THE LIGHTS / (the Mitchell Brothers remix)** 10 –
(12") *(679L 085T)* – ('A') / Get out of my house (MC version) / Fit but you know it (MC version).
(dvd-s) *(679L 085DVD)* – ('A'-video) / Fit but you know it (MC version) (video).
Nov 04. (7"/cd-s) *(679L 092/+CD)* **COULD WELL BE IN. / (MC version with Bruza, D Double E, Ghetto & Scratchy)** 30 –

Mike Skinner of The STREETS

Mar 06. (7") *(679L 125)* **WHEN YOU WASN'T FAMOUS. / WHEN YOU WASN'T FAMOUS (Bromhead's jacket version)** 8 –
(cd-s) *(679L 125CD1)* – ('A') / ('A'-live from the Astoria).
(cd-s) *(679L 125CD2)* – ('A'-Professor Green mix) / ('A'-Doctor & Bearman mix) / ('A'-video).

Apr 06. (cd) *(<2564 63230-2>)* **THE HARDEST WAY TO MAKE AN EASY LIVING** 1
– Prangin out / War of the sexes / The hardest way to make an easy living / All goes out the window / Memento mori / Can't con an honest john / When you wasn't famous / Never went to church / Hotel expressionism / Two nations / Fake street hats.

Jun 06. (cd-s) *(679L 132CD1)* **NEVER WENT TO CHURCH / WHEN YOU WASN'T FAMOUS (Example MC version)** 20 –
(cd-s) *(679L 132CD2)* – ('A') / ('A'-acoustic) / ('A'-Guillemots version) / Prangin out (instrumental).
(dvd-s) *(679L 132DVD)* – ('A'-video) / ('B'-Prof. Green mix video).

the STROKES

Formed: New York City, New York, USA . . . 1998 by JULIAN CASABLANCAS (son of Elite Model Agency CEO, John Casablancas, and a one-time Miss Denmark), guitarist NICK VALENSI, bass guitarist NIKOLAI FRAITURE and drummer FABRIZIO MORETTI; ALBERT HAMMOND JR would be added later. Fed up with the recent import of Nu-metal bands such as LINKIN PARK, LIMP BIZKIT and the soft post-grunge credentials of STAIND, the NME decided to promote a new form of rock music between spring and summer 2001; and the STROKES became virtually overnight the headlining act along with fellow garage rockers the WHITE STRIPES. The question begged to be asked, however: if such publicity (and some might've called it hype) wasn't used to promote this youthful garage rock band, would the public and press still deem them to be the saviours of rock? The STROKES began playing – minus HAMMOND – in 1998 where they all attended the upper-class prep school Dwight. It was there that the group discovered their love for garage rock and quickly began pulling ideas together for songs. The sound would be halfway between LOU REED's "ostrich guitar", MC5's thrash meanderings and the tunefulness of TOM PETTY. Surprisingly, the ensemble (now playing in a plush rehearsal room in the lower east side of Manhattan and with the arrival of newcomer HAMMOND) pulled off the technical trickery of the above mentioned, and, through all of the scattered influences, began to develop a sound of their own. They debuted live in spring '99, performing in such venues as NYC's 'Baby Jupiter' and 'LUNA'. Ryan Gentles was finally brought in as manager and helped them require spots at 'Mercury Lounge' and 'Bowery Ballroom'. Things were almost reaching fever pitch for the STROKES, and, alongside the MOLDY PEACHES and ANDREW W.K., they were becoming the most talked about band in NYC. A tape, including the tracks 'SOMA', 'BARELY LEGAL' and the rip-roaring 'MODERN AGE' was sent to 'Rough Trade' in London. The label (at that time, pulling themselves out of financial difficulty) signed the band, issuing the 'MODERN AGE' EP to critical acclaim. The NME went nuts, urging the record-buying public to go out and listen to this new and exciting group. Bidding wars began in America over the STROKES distribution, with 'R.C.A.' emerging as the champions. The single 'HARD TO EXPLAIN' was issued and reached No.16 in the British charts. Now, it seemed, this group of talented young upstarts were emerging as bonafide rockstars . . . even COURTNEY LOVE wrote a song about CASABLANCAS, entitled 'But Julian, I am much older than you'. With all of the commotion, the humble and ironically titled debut album 'IS THIS IT' was premiered amid much audience anticipation in early September 2001. It reached No.2 in the UK, even with its risqué Helmut Newton-inspired cover (which was refused by Woolworth's and HMV). But as the band watched the Twin Towers collapse from their rehearsal room on September 11, they decided to pull the song 'NYC COPS' from the American release of 'IS THIS IT'. Perhaps not one of their better moves, as the above mentioned song was a blinder; perhaps the best track on the LP, and a genuine audience favourite. 'LAST NITE' appeared on single at the end of 2001, with a video accompanied by Roman Copolla, featuring a live performance from the band. Things were looking bright at the turn of the year, with the addition of a few new tracks, a sold-out tour of Britain and the re-admission of 'NYC COPS' into the live brew. Perhaps The STROKES weren't the saviours of rock, but they were sure pretty damn close. After dabbling with RADIOHEAD producer Nigel Godrich for their sophomore album, the group and Godrich departed citing musical differences, leaving the recording duties up to Gordon Raphael. They worked "soldiers hours" in his basement recording room and churned out their "difficult" sophomore record 'ROOM ON FIRE' in 2003. Going down a storm with the press, the STROKES hadn't suffered from second album syndrome, as tracks such as 'MEET ME IN THE BATHROOM' and hit single 'REPTILIA' beat the living crap out of their critics with their tightly focused arrangements. A sell out tour promptly followed, and many fans and touts (cough-NME-cough!) were sighing a breath of relief that these switched-on fellas weren't just a flash in the pan. Third album in and it was still difficult in STROKES-ville; 'FIRST IMPRESSIONS OF EARTH' (2006) had critics bemoaning both unfulfilled promise and misjudged editing, and taking CASABLANCAS at his word over the ad nauseam repitition of the line "I've got nothing to say" (on the slight nihilisitic return of 'ASK ME ANYTHING'). Then there were the birthing pains: jettisoning producer Gordon Raphael and sessions he'd overseen, the band started over with David Kahne, the man who famously K.O.'d WILCO's 'Yankee Hotel Foxtrot' for not being commercial enough (and whose CV included such garage-rock heroes as the BANGLES, TONY BENNETT and SUGAR RAY). Yet it all started so well; the opening fusillade of the upwardly mobile 'YOU ONLY LIVE ONCE', the good cop-bad cop thrash of 'JUICEBOX' (a UK Top 5 single) and the hi-toned intro of 'RAZOR BLADE' justified the album's UK No.1 (US Top 5) status, even if it ran out of puff before the finish line.

• **Covers:** CLAMPDOWN (Clash) / LIFE'S A GAS (Ramones).

Album rating: IS THIS IT (*9) / ROOM ON FIRE (*7) / FIRST IMPRESSIONS OF EARTH (*6)

JULIAN CASABLANCAS (b.23 Aug'78) – vocals / **NICK VALENSI** (b.16 Jan'81) – guitars / **NIKOLAI FRAITURE** (b.13 Nov'79) – bass / **FABRIZIO MORETTI** (b. 2 Jun'80) – drums / added **ALBERT HAMMOND, JR.** – guitars

Rough Trade R.C.A.

Jan 01. (7"/cd-s) *(RTRADES/+CD 010)* **MODERN AGE. / LAST NIGHT / BARELY LEGAL** 68 –
(above charted in Jul01 same week as below)

Jun 01. (7"/cd-s) *(RTRADES/+CD 023)* **HARD TO EXPLAIN. / NEW YORK CITY COPS** 16 –

Aug 01. (cd/lp) *(RTRADE CD/LP 030)* *<68101>* **IS THIS IT** 2 33
– Is this it / The modern age / Soma / Barely legal / Someday / Alone, together / Last nite / Hard to explain / New York City cops / Trying your luck / Take it or leave it.

Nov 01. (7"/cd-s) *(RTRADES/+CD 041)* **LAST NITE. / WHEN IT STARTED** 14
(cd-s) *(RTRADES 041X)* *<07863 60611-2>* – ('A'-live) / Trying your luck (live) / Take it or leave it (live).

Apr 02. (cd-ep) *(RTRADESCD 053)* **HARD TO EXPLAIN / THE MODERN AGE / LAST NITE / WHEN IT STARTED / TAKE IT OR LEAVE IT (live)** – Irish –

Jun 02. (7"clear) *<7863-60554-7>* **HARD TO EXPLAIN. / NEW YORK CITY COPS** –
(cd-s+=) *<60533>* – Take it or leave it / Trying your luck.

Sep 02. (7"yellow/cd-s) *(RTRADES/+CD 063)* *<07863 60623-2>* **SOMEDAY. / ALONE, TOGETHER (home recording) / IS THIS IT (home recording)** 27

The STROKES

Oct 03. (7"/cd-s) *(RTRADES/+CD 140)* <56610> **12:51. / THE WAY IT IS (home recording)** [7] [ ]

Oct 03. (cd/lp) *(RTRADE CD/LP 130)* <55497> **ROOM ON FIRE** [2] [4]
– What ever happened? / Reptilia / Automatic stop / 12:51 / You talk way too much / Between love & hate / Meet me in the bathroom / Under control / The way it is / The end has no end / I can't win.

Feb 04. (7"/cd-s) *(RTRADES/+CD 155)* <59176> **REPTILIA. / MODERN GIRLS & OLD FASHIONED MEN (duet w/ Regina Spektor)** [17] [ ]

Nov 04. (7"/cd-s) *(RTRADS/+CD 205)* **THE END HAS NO END. / CLAMPDOWN (live)** [27] [–]

Dec 05. (7"/cd-s) *(RTRADS/+CD 282)* <76418> **JUICEBOX. / HAWAII** [5] [98]
(cd-s) *(RTRADSCDX 282)* – ('A') / ('A'-live) / ('A'-video).

Jan 06. (cd/lp) *(RTRAD CD/LP 330)* <73177> **FIRST IMPRESSIONS OF EARTH** [1] [4]
– You only live once / Juicebox / Heart in a cage / Razorblade / On the other side / Vision of division / Ask me anything / Electricityscape / Killing lies / Fear of sleep / 15 minutes / Ize of the world / Evening sun / Red light.

Mar 06. (7") *(RTRADS 305)* **HEART IN A CAGE. / I'LL TRY ANYTHING ONCE ('You Only Live Once' demo)** [25] [–]
(cd-s+=) *(RTRADSCDX 305)* – ('A'-video).
(cd-s) *(RTRADSCD 305)* – ('A') / Life's gas (Radio 1 session).

☐ Joe STRUMMER (see under ⇒ CLASH)

☐ the STYLE COUNCIL (see under ⇒ WELLER, Paul)

☐ SUB SUB (see under ⇒ DOVES)

the SUBWAYS

Formed: Welwyn Garden City, Hertfordshire, England . . . 2003 as MUSTARDSEED by BILLY LUNN, his girlfriend CHARLOTTE COOPER and – regardless of different surnames – his brother JOSH MORGAN (LUNN took his mother's maiden name). The model of net-literate youth, the SUBWAYS took the mainline to success via their own website and relentless self-promotion. An off-the-cuff decision to send in one of their many demos to Glastonbury organiser, Michael Eavis, winning themselves a slot on the festival's Other Stage. Who else but John Peel would pledge solidarity with their cause by airing their classy late 2004 debut, '1 AM.'. Coming on, variously, like a younger, spunkier OASIS (primitive chemistry rather than heathen) and girl-boy acolytes of American garage-rock (the WHITE STRIPES to MUDHONEY to the STOOGES), the SUBWAYS signed to veteran US alt-rock imprint, 'Sire' ('Infectious' in the UK). After perfecting their dirty guitar grind on UK hit singles, 'OH YEAH' and 'ROCK & ROLL QUEEN' (as heard on Rimmel/Kate Moss ad), the trio won almost universal critical acclaim for their IAN BROUDIE-produced debut LP, 'YOUNG FOR ETERNITY' (2005). The group subsequently performed both of the aforementioned singles on the third series of 'The O.C.', while further 45's, 'WITH YOU' and 'NO GOODBYES', hit the UK Top 30.

Album rating: YOUNG FOR ETERNITY (*8)

BILLY LUNN – vocals, guitars / **CHARLOTTE COOPER** – vocals, bass / **JOSH MORGAN** – drums

Transgressive — not iss.

Oct 04. (ltd-7") *(58241 H1)* **1 AM. / I WANT TO HEAR WHAT YOU HAVE GOT TO SAY / YOU GOT ME** [ ] [–]

Infectious – WEA — Sire – Warners

Mar 05. (7"white) *(WEA 384)* **OH YEAH. / I AM YOUNG** [25] [–]
(cd-s) *(WEA 384CD)* – ('A') / Take me away.

Jun 05. (7"blue) *(WEA 390)* **ROCK & ROLL QUEEN. / UNDER THE SUN** [22] [–]
(cd-s) *(WEA 390CD1)* – ('A') / Automatic.
(cd-s) *(WEA 390CD2)* – ('A') / Another sense / I want to hear what you have got to say (live Zane Lowe session) / ('A'-video).

Jul 05. (cd/d-lp) *(2564 62484-2/-1)* **YOUNG FOR ETERNITY** [32] [–]
– I want to hear what you have got to say / Holiday / Rock & roll queen / Mary / Young for eternity / Lines of light / Oh yeah / City pavement / No goodbyes / With you / She sun / Somewhere / At 1 am.

Sep 05. (7"clear) *(WEA 392)* **WITH YOU. / STARING AT THE SUN** [29] [–]
(cd-s) *(WEA 392CD)* – ('A') / A plain above.
(dvd-s) *(WEA 392DVD)* – ('A') / Lost you to the city / Rock & roll queen (live from Isle Of Wight video) / ('A'-video) / (making of..)

Dec 05. (7") *(WEA 398)* **NO GOODBYES. / YOU'VE GOT TO HIDE YOUR LOVE AWAY** [27] [–]
(7") *(WEA 398X)* – ('A'-Chris Lord-Alge original mix) / Mary (live from Islington Academy).
(cd-s+=) *(WEA 398CD)* – ('A') / Road to nowhere.

Feb 06. (re-cd) *(as prev.)* <49918-2> **YOUNG FOR ETERNITY** [ ] [ ]

SUEDE

Formed: London, England . . . 1989 by BRETT ANDERSON, who, by 1992 had put together the final line-up of guitarist BERNARD BUTLER, bassist MATT OSMAN and drummer SIMON GILBERT (ELASTICA prime mover, JUSTINE FRISCHMANN, had also been an early member). After a single, 'BE MY GOD' / 'ART', failed to appear in 1990 on 'RML' (this lost recording was famous for featuring ex-SMITHS drummer, MIKE JOYCE), the band signed to 'Nude', precipitating a storm of media hype and adulation. Featured on the cover of NME before they had even released their debut single, the band became press darlings of a post-grunge/pre-Brit pop music scene desperate for a bit of cheap glamour. Widely touted as spiritual antecedents of The SMITHS, the group were actually closer in style to the camp affectations of mid-period BOWIE, although there was definitely a MORRISSEY-like archness to the lyrics, the glum one actually taking to covering 'MY INSATIABLE ONE' (the B-side of SUEDE's acclaimed debut effort, 'THE DROWNNERS') live. Another couple of singles followed, 'METAL MICKEY' and 'ANIMAL NITRATE', these scoring successively higher chart positions. The media support, together with ANDERSON's sleazy, androgynous posturing, made him, and his band, instant heroes for a new generation of crazy, mixed up kids, the eponymous 1993 debut album quickly reaching No.1. 'Nude's takeover by 'Sony' in early that year gave the act a bit of major label muscle, ironically helping them on their way to becoming one of the biggest "indie" bands in Britain. At the beginning '94, the band scored their biggest hit single to date with the epic 'STAY TOGETHER', the track peaking at No.3. Later that Spring, gay drummer SIMON bravely went to the House Of Commons to air his views on the homosexual laws of consent, which were to be lowered from 21 to either 16 (the heterosexual age) or 18, as it finally turned out. Around the same time, more controversy dogged the group when an American jazz singer called SUEDE won her lawsuit against the band in the US, the upshot of the affair being that from that point on, the band were to be known in America as LONDON SUEDE (lucky for them they didn't come from Leatherhead!). Meantime, the group had won the Mercury Music Prize for their acclaimed debut album and were well on the way to releasing a follow-up, 'DOG MAN STAR' (1994). The last album to feature the departing BUTLER (heralded by some as the UK's most promising guitarist since JOHNNY MARR, BUTLER subsequently went on to a successful, if short lived, collaboration with DAVID McALMONT before signing to 'Creation' and embarking on a solo career), it marked something of a departure in the band's sound, a dense, ambitious set which met with a mixed critical reception. Unbowed, SUEDE swaggered on, recruiting the teenage

RICHARD OAKES as BUTLER's replacement and providing a welcome diversion from the laddish excesses of Brit-pop. SUEDE's next effort, 'COMING UP' proved to be their most consistent set to date, spawning the brilliant lowlife anthem, 'TRASH' along with the similarly infectious, organic glam of 'FILMSTAR' and the dislocated melancholy of 'SATURDAY NIGHT'. A stop-gap but worthy collection of rarities and B-sides, 'SCI-FI LULLABIES' (1997) marked time before their return in the Spring of '99. 'ELECTRICITY' sparked off proceedings, the UK Top 5 single also the opening track on their No.1 Steve Osborne-produced 4th album proper, 'HEAD MUSIC' (1999). Three other retro-fied 45's ('SHE'S IN FASHION', 'EVERYTHING WILL FLOW' and 'CAN'T GET ENOUGH') were delivered to an eager kitsch fanbase who were still "into" all things glam:- BOWIE, ROXY, NUMAN, HUMAN . . . A few years in the proverbial wilderness, BRETT and his beloved SUEDE team returned on the scene in summer 2002 (with ex-STRANGELOVE drummer, ALEX LEE, replacing NEIL), releasing 'A NEW MORNING', a set that didn't go straight to No.1; or even make the Top 10, or Top 20! The reunion of BUTLER and ANDERSON has been one of the bigger stories in recent years, one which few would've forecast with any confidence. Picking up where they left off after the bitter post-'DOG MAN STAR' recriminations, 'HERE COME THE TEARS' (2005) was the opening salvo from a redeemed working relationship that became a going concern. As the TEARS, BUTLER 'N' ANDERSON both sparked each other into life and acted as a check on the other's excesses; BUTLER took the production chair, crafting his own mannered take on Wall Of Sound glam-sonics and shaping the kind of chorus-ready singles that SUEDE fans hadn't heard in years: the UK Top 10 grandeur of 'REFUGEES' and the infectious Top 30 hit, 'LOVERS'.

• **Songwriters:** ANDERSON / BUTLER, except; BRASS IN POCKET (Pretenders) / etc.

Album rating: SUEDE (*8) / DOG MAN STAR (*7) / COMING UP (*7) / SCI-FI LULLABIES collection (*6) / HEAD MUSIC (*7) / A NEW MORNING (*6) / SINGLES compilation (*8) / the Tears: HERE COME THE TEARS (*7)

BRETT ANDERSON (b.27 Sep'67, Haywards Heath, Sussex, England) – vocals / **BERNARD BUTLER** (b. 1 May'70) – guitar, piano / **MATT OSMAN** (b. 9 Oct'67) – bass / **SIMON GILBERT** (b.23 May'65) – drums

Nude | not iss.

Apr 92. (7") *(nud 1s)* **THE DROWNERS. / TO THE BIRDS** [49] [–]
(12"+=/cd-s+=) *(nud 1 t/cd)* – My insatiable one.

Sep 92. (7"/c-s) *(nud 3 s/mc)* **METAL MICKEY. / WHERE THE PIGS DON'T FLY** [17] [–]
(12"+=/cd-s+=) *(nud 3 t/cd)* – He's dead.

Nude-Sony | Columbia

Feb 93. (7"/c-s) *(nud 4 s/mc)* **ANIMAL NITRATE. / THE BIG TIME** [7] [–]
(12"+=/cd-s+=) *(nud 4 t/cd)* – Painted people.

Apr 93. (cd/c/lp) *(nude 1 cd/mc/lp)* <53792> **SUEDE** [1] [ ]
– So young / Animal nitrate / She's not dead / Moving / Pantomime horse / The drowners / Sleeping pills / Breakdown / Metal Mickey / Animal lover / The next life. *(cd re-iss. Aug02 on 'Epic'; 473735-2)*

May 93. (7"/c-s) *(nud 5 s/mc)* **SO YOUNG. / HIGH RISING** [22] [–]
(12"+=/cd-s+=) *(nud 5 t/cd)* – Dolly.

Sep 93. (cd-ep) *<44K 77172>* **THE DROWNERS / MY INSATIABLE ONE / TO THE BIRDS / THE BIG TIME / HE'S DEAD (live)** [–] [ ]

Feb 94. (7"/c-s) *(nud 9 s/mc)* **STAY TOGETHER. / THE LIVING DEAD** [3] [–]
(ext;12"+=/cd-s+=) *(nud 9 t/cd) – My dark star.*

—— An American jazz singer called SUEDE won her lawsuit against the band in the US. They are now to be called LONDON SUEDE, but thankfully only in the States.

Mar 94. (cd-ep) *<CK 64382>* **STAY TOGETHER / THE LIVING DEAD / MY DARK STAR / DOLLY HIGH RISING / STAY TOGETHER (extended)** [–] [ ]

Sep 94. (7"/c-s) *(nud 10 s/mc)* **WE ARE THE PIGS. / KILLING OF A FLASH BOY** [18] [–]
(12"+=/cd-s+=) *(nud 10 t/cd)* – Whipsnade.

Oct 94. (cd/c/d-lp) *(nude 3 cd/mc/lp)* <66769> **DOG MAN STAR** [3] [ ]
– Introducing the band / We are the pigs / Heroine / The wild ones / Daddy's speeding / The power / New generation / This Hollywood life / The 2 of us / Black or blue / The asphalt world / Still life. *<US-version +=>* – Modern boys. *(cd re-iss. Aug02 on 'Epic'; 477811-2)*

—— (July'94; after rec. album) **RICHARD OAKES** – guitar; repl. BUTLER who went solo

Nov 94. (c-s) *(nud 11mc)* **THE WILD ONES / MODERN BOYS** [18] [–]
(cd-s+=) *(nud 11cd1)* – This world needs a father.
(12") *(nud 11t)* – ('A') / Eno's introducing the band.
(cd-s) *(nud 11cd2)* – (above 2) / Asda town.

Jan 95. (7"/c-s) *(nud 12mc)* **NEW GENERATION. / TOGETHER** [21] [–]
(12"+=/cd-s+=) *(nud 12 t/cd1)* – Bentswood boys.
(cd-s) *(nud 12cd2)* – ('A') / Animal nitrate (live) / The wild ones (live) / Pantomime horse (live).

—— added new member **NEIL CODLING** – keyboards, vocals

Jul 96. (c-s) *(nud 2mc)* **TRASH / EUROPE IS OUR PLAYGROUND** [3] [–]
(cd-s+=) *(nud 21cd1)* – Every Monday morning comes.
(pic-cd-s) *(nud 21cd2)* – ('A') / Have you ever been this low? / Another no one.

Sep 96. (cd/c/lp) *(nude 6 cd/mc/lp)* <67911> **COMING UP** [1] [ ]
– Trash / Filmstar / Lazy / By the sea / She / Beautiful ones / Starcrazy / Picnic by the motorway / The chemistry between us / Saturday night. *(cd re-iss. Aug02 on 'Epic'; 485129-2)*

Oct 96. (c-s) *(nud 23mc)* **BEAUTIFUL ONES / BY THE SEA (demo)** [8] [–]
(cd-s) *(nud 23 cd1)* – ('A') / Young men / The sound of the streets.
(cd-s) *(nud 23 cd2)* – ('A') / Money / Sam.

Jan 97. (c-s) *(nud 24mc)* **SATURDAY NIGHT / PICNIC BY THE MOTORWAY (live)** [6] [–]
(cd-s) *(nud 24cd1)* – ('A') / W.S.D. / Jumble sale mums.
(cd-s) *(nud 24cd2)* – ('A') / This time / ('A'demo).
(d7") *(nud 24s)* – ('A') / This time / Beautiful ones / The sound of the streets.

Apr 97. (c-s) *(nud 27mc)* **LAZY / SHE (live)** [9] [–]
(cd-s) *(nud 27cd1)* – ('A') / These are the sad songs / Feel.
(cd-s) *(nud 27cd2)* – ('A') / Sadie / Digging a hole.

Aug 97. (7") *(nud 30s)* **FILMSTAR. / ('A'-original demo)** [9] [–]
(cd-s) *(nud 30cd1)* – ('A') / Graffiti women / Duchess. *(w/ free video footage; Beautiful ones / Coming up.*
(cd-s) *(nud 30cd2)* – ('A') / Rent / Saturday night / Saturday night (video).

Oct 97. (d-cd) *(nude 9cd)* <68857> **SCI-FI LULLABIES** (flipsides) [9] [ ]
– My insatiable one / To the birds / Where the pigs don't fly / He's dead / The big time / High rising / The living dead / My star / Killing of a flash boy / Whipsnade / Modern boys / Together / Bentswood boys / Europe is our playground // Every Monday morning comes / Have you ever been this low? / Another no one / Young men / The sound of the streets / Money / W.S.D. / This time / Jumble sale mums / These are the sad songs / Sadie / Graffiti women / Duchess. *(cd re-iss. Aug02 on 'Epic'; 488851-2)*

Apr 99. (c-s) *(nud 43mc)* **ELECTRICITY / IMPLIMENT, YEAH!** [5] [–]
(cd-s) *(nud 43cd1)* – ('A') / Popstar / Killer.
(cd-s) *(nud 43cd2)* – ('A') / See that girl / Waterloo.

May 99. (cd/c/d-lp) *(nude 14 cd/mc/lp)* <69986> **HEAD MUSIC** [1] Jun99 [ ]
– Electricity / Savoir faire / Can't get enough / Everything will flow / Down / She's in fashion / Asbestos / Head music / Elephant man / Hi-fi / Indian strings / He's gone / Crack in the Union Jack. *(cd re-iss. Aug02 on 'Epic'; 494243-2)*

Jun 99. (c-s) *(nud 44mc)* **SHE'S IN FASHION / DOWN (demo)** [13] [–]
(cd-s) *(nud 44cd1)* – ('A') / Bored / Pieces of my mind.
(cd-s) *(nud 44cd2)* – ('A') / Jubilee / God's gift.

Sep 99. (c-s) *(nud 45mc)* **EVERYTHING WILL FLOW / BEAUTIFUL ONES (live)** [24] [–]
(cd-s) *(nud 45cd1)* – ('A') / Weight of the world / Leaving.
(cd-s) *(nud 45cd2)* – ('A') / Crackhead / Seascape.

Nov 99. (cd-s) *(nud 47cd1)* **CAN'T GET ENOUGH / LET GO / SINCE YOU WENT AWAY** [23] [–]
(cd-s) *(nud 47cd2)* – ('A') / Situations / Read my mind.
(cd-s) *(nud 47cd3)* – ('A') / Everything will flow (Rollo's vocal mix) / She's in fashion (Lironi version) / ('A'-video).

—— (Mar'01) **ALEX LEE** – drums (ex-BLUE AEROPLANES, ex-STRANGELOVE) repl. NEIL

Epic Sony

Sep 02. (cd-s) *(672949-2)* **POSITIVITY / ONE LOVE / SIMON / POSITIVITY (video)** [16] [–]
(cd-s) *(672949-5)* – ('A'side) / Superstar / Cheap.
(dvd-s) *(672949-9)* – ('A'-video) / Colours / Campfire / (rehearsal footage).

Sep 02. (cd) *(508956-2) <649168>* **A NEW MORNING** [24] [ ]
– Positivity / Obsessions / Lonely girls / Lost in TV / Beautiful loser / Streetlife / Astrogirl / Untitled . . .morning / One hit to the body / When the rain falls. *(special cd+=; 508956-9)* – You belong to me / Oceans.

Nov 02. (cd-s) *(673294-2)* **OBSESSIONS / COOL THING / INSTANT SUNSHINE** [29] [–]
(cd-s) *(673294-5)* – ('A') / UFO / Rainy day girl.
(dvd-s) *(673294-9)* – ('A'-video) / Hard candy / ABC song.

Oct 03. (cd-s) *(674358-2)* **ATTITUDE / GOLDEN GUN / OXYGEN / ATTITUDE (video)** [14] [–]
(cd-s) *(6743585)* – ('A') / ('A'-demo) / Just a girl / Heroin.
(dvd-s) *(674358-9)* – ('A'-video) / We're so disco / Head music (Arthur Baker remix).

Oct 03. (cd) *(513604-2) <70011>* **SINGLES** (compilation) [31] [ ]
– Beautiful ones / Animal nitrate / Trash / Metal Mickey / So young / The wild ones / Obsessions / Filmstar / Can't get enough / Everything will flow / Stay together / Love the way you love / The drowners / New generation / Lazy / She's in fashion / Attitude / Electricity / We are the pigs / Positivity / Saturday night.

the TEARS

BRETT ANDERSON + BERNARD BUTLER

Independiente Independiente

May 05. (7"clear) *(ISOM 92S)* **REFUGEES. / BREAK AWAY** [9] [–]
(cd-s) *(ISOM 92MS)* – ('A') / Southern rain.
(cd-s) *(ISOM 92SMS)* – ('A') / Feels like Monday / Branded / ('A'-video).

Jun 05. (cd/lp) *(<ISOM 49 CD/LP>)* **HERE COME THE TEARS** [15] [ ]
– Refugees / Autograph / Co-star / Imperfection / The ghost of you / Two creatures / Lovers / Fallen idol / Brave new century / Beautiful pain / The asylum / Apollo 13 / A love as strong as death.

Jul 05. (7"green) *(ISOM 95S)* **LOVERS. / BECAUSE YOU'RE WORTHLESS** [24] [–]
(cd-s) *(ISOM 95MS)* – ('A') / Song for the migrant worker.
(cd-s) *(ISOM 95SMS)* – ('A') / Low life / The primitive / ('A'-video).

☐ SUGAR (see under ⇒HUSKER DU)

☐ the SUGARCUBES (see under ⇒ BJORK)

☐ SUGGS (see under ⇒ MADNESS)

SUICIDE

Formed: New York, USA . . . 1971 by ALAN VEGA and ex-jazz band organist MARTIN REV. After a series of sporadic, performance art-style gigs in the early 70's, the duo laid low until the emergence of the CBGB's punk/new wave scene a few years later. Signed to US independent, 'Red Star' (run by Marty Thau, former manager of The NEW YORK DOLLS), the duo released one of the most influential records of the era in 1977's eponymous 'SUICIDE'. Delivering shock screams and whispered goth-rockabilly vocals over brooding, churning Farfisa organ, the duo laid the foundations for the industrial/electro experimentation of the following decade and in 'ROCKET U.S.A.' and 'FRANKIE TEARDROPS', penned two of the most compelling compositions in the NY avant-garde pantheon. Now almost universally heralded as being ahead of their time, punters of the day weren't always so appreciative; SUICIDE performances were infamous for audience stand-off's, a tour with the CLASH running into trouble while a gig in Belgium ended in a full-on riot (the same gig documented on the 1978 "official bootleg", '24 MINUTES OVER BRUSSELS'). Unperturbed, the pair moved to 'Ze' records ('Island' in the UK) and recorded a follow-up, 'ALAN VEGA / MARTIN REV – SUICIDE' (1980). Produced by CARS mainman, RIC OCASEK, the record presented a slightly more palatable version of SUICIDE's patented synth apocalypse, although sales remained minimal. Subsequently embarking on solo careers, the pair met with little more than cult success, although VEGA's eponymous 1980 solo debut spawned a Top 5 hit in France, 'JUKEBOX BABE'. Following his eponymous 1980 solo debut, REV devoted his time to sculpture with his work exhibited in 1982-83. VEGA continued working with OCASEK, also bringing in a young AL JOURGENSEN (later of MINISTRY fame) for 1983's 'SATURN STRIP' (featuring an unlikely but entertaining cover of Hot Chocolate's 'EVERYONE'S A WINNER') and guesting for SISTERS OF MERCY re-incarnation, the SISTERHOOD in 1986. VEGA and REV eventually reformed SUICIDE in 1988 and recorded 'A WAY OF LIFE' (1989) for 'Wax Trax!' (licensed to 'Chapter 22' in the UK), a label heavily indebted to the duo's pioneering electronics. With the album afforded little interest, VEGA resumed his solo activities on through the 90's, collaborating with STEPHEN LIRONI on his REVOLUTIONARY CORPS OF TEENAGE JESUS project and also ALEX CHILTON on their 1997 set, 'Cubist Blues'. Ironically, there's been something of an upsurge of interest in SUICIDE of late, the duo receiving renewed press attention after their performances with critical darlings SPIRITUALIZED. It was no surprise then, that the inevitable comeback album would appear. The thought-provoking 'AMERICAN SUPREME' (2002), sarcastically waved the stars'n'stripes aloft through the confrontational, snidey words of VEGA and REV. Tracks such as opener 'TELEVISED EXECUTIONS', plus 'SWEARING TO THE FLAG' and 'DACHAU, DISNEY, DISCO', pounded their caustic messages from stark funky beats. Nothing's changed on both fronts then.

Album rating: SUICIDE (*8) / ALAN VEGA – MARTIN REV (*5) / HALF ALIVE exploitation (*6) / GHOST RIDERS exploitation (*5) / A WAY OF LIFE (*7) / Y.B. BLUE (*4) / AMERICAN SUPREME (*4) / Alan Vega: ALAN VEGA (*4) / COLLISION DRIVE (*5) / SATURN STRIP (*7) / JUST A MILLION DREAMS (*4) / DEUCE AVENUE (*5) / POWER ON TO ZERO HOUR (*4) / NEW RACEION (*4) / DUJANG PRANG (*3) / CUBIST BLUES with Alex Chilton & Ben Vaughn (*5) / Martin Rev: MARTIN REV (*4) / CLOUDS OF GLORY (*6) / CHEYENNE (*5) / SEE ME RIDIN' (*7) / STRANGEWORLD (*4) / TO LIVE (*3)

ALAN VEGA (b. 1948) – vocals / **MARTIN REV** – keyboards, percussion

Bronze Red Star

Nov 77. (lp) *(BRON 508) <RS 1>* **SUICIDE** [ ] [ ]
– Ghost rider / Rocket U.S.A. / Cheree / Frankie Teardrops / Johnny / Girl / Che. *(re-iss. Sep86 on 'Demon'; FIEND 74) (cd-iss. Jun88; FIENDCD 74)*

Jul 78. (7",12") *(BRO 57)* **CHEREE. / I REMEMBER** [ ] [ ]
(re-is.Nov86 on 'Demon' 12"; D 1046T)

1978. (lp-ltd; official bootleg) *(FRANKIE 1)* **24 MINUTES OVER BRUSSELS (live)** [ ] [–]

Island Ze

Nov 79. (ext.12"/7") *(12+/WIP 6543)* **DREAM BABY DREAM. / RADIATION** [ ] [–]

May 80. (lp) *(ILPS 7007) <7080>* **ALAN VEGA / MARTIN REV – SUICIDE** [ ] [ ]
– Diamonds, furcoats, champagne / Mr. Ray / Sweetheart / Fast money music / Touch me / Harlem / Be bop kid / Las Vegas man / Shadazz / Dance. *(re-iss. Jun99 on 'Blast First' d-lp/d-cd+=; BFFP 162/+CD)* – Super subway comedian / Dream baby dream / Radiation / Speed queen / Creature feature / Tough guy / Man / Sneakin' around / Too fine for you / See you around / Be my dream / Space blue mambo / Spaceship / Into my eyes / C'mon babe / New city / Do it nice.

— split partnership in the early 80's and both went solo

ALAN VEGA

with **PHIL HAWK** – guitar

not iss. P.V.C.

1980. (lp) *<PVC 7915>* **ALAN VEGA** [–] [ ]
– Jukebox babe / Fireball / Kung Foo cowboy / Love cry / Speedway / Ice drummer / Bye bye bayou / Lonely.

— w/band 81-83 **MARK KUGH** – guitar / **LARRY CHAPLAN** – bass / **SESU COLEMAN** – drums

Island Island

Nov 81. (lp) *<(ILPS 9692)>* **COLLISION DRIVE**
– Magdalena 82 / Be bop a lula / Outlaw / Raver / Ghost rider / I believe / Magdalena 83 / Rebel / Viet vet.

Nov 81. (ext.12"/7") *(12+/WIP 6744)* **JUKEBOX BABE. / LONELY** –

— added **AL JOURGENSEN** – keyboards (of MINISTRY) / **STEPHEN GEORGE** – drums / **GREG HAWKES** – synth, sax (of CARS) / **RIC OCASEK** – guitar, producer (of CARS)

Elektra Elektra

Sep 83. (lp) *(K 960259-1) <60259-1>* **SATURN STRIP**
– Saturn drive / Video babe / American dreamer / Wipeout beat / Je t'adore / Angel / Kid Congo / Goodbye darling / Every 1's a winner.

— retained **OCASEK** + added **KENNAN KEATING** – guitar / **CHRIS LORD** – synth

Oct 85. (7") *(EKR 24)* **ON THE RUN. / CRY FIRE** –
(12"+=) *(EKR 24T)* – Rah rah baby.

Dec 85. (lp/c) *(EKT 15/+C) <60434-1/-4>* **JUST A MILLION DREAMS**
– On the run / Shooting for you / Hot fox / Too late / Wild heart / Creation / Cry fire / Ra ra baby.

— In 1986, VEGA guested for SISTERS OF MERCY re-incarnation, SISTERHOOD

MARTIN REV

not iss. Infidelity

Feb 80. (lp) *<228>* **MARTIN REV** –
– Mari / Baby o baby / Nineteen 86 / Temptation / Jomo / Asia. *<(cd-iss. Nov02 on 'R.O.I.R.'; RUSCD 8279)>* – Coal train / Marvel / 5 to 5 / Wes / Daydreams.

New Rose Red Star

Mar 85. (lp) *(ROSE 52) <RS 700>* **CLOUDS OF GLORY**
– Rodeo / Clouds of glory / Metatron / Whisper / Rocking horse / Parade / Island. *(cd-iss. May98 on 'Mau Mau'; MAUCD 648) (cd re-iss. Jun00; RS 700-2>*

SUICIDE

re-formed in 1988

Chapter 22 Wax Trax!

Jan 89. (lp/cd) *(CHAP LP/CD 35) <WAX/+CS/CD 7072>* **A WAY OF LIFE**
– Wild in blue / Surrender / Jukebox baby 96 / Rain of ruin / Sufferin' in vain / Dominic Christ / Love so lonely / Devastation.

Feb 89. (12") *(12CHAP 36)* **RAIN OF RUIN. / SURRENDER** –

Brake Out Brake Out

Jun 92. (cd) *<(OUT 108-2)>* **Y B BLUE**
– Why be blue / Cheat-cheat / Hot ticket / Universe / The last time / Play the dream / Pump it / Flashy love / Chewy-chewy / Mujo.

ALAN VEGA

returned to solo work for the 90's. **LIZ LAMERA** – drums

Chapter 22 Infinite Zero

Feb 90. (cd/lp) *(CHAP CD/LP 45) <43032>* **DEUCE AVENUE**
– Body bop jive / Sneaker gun fire / Jab Gee / Bad scene / La la bola / Deuce avenue / Faster blaster / Sugee / Sweet sweet money / Love on / No tomorrow / Future sex. *(re-iss. Jun90 on 'Musicdisc' cd/c/lp; 10558-2/-4/-1)*

Musidisc Warners

Jul 91. (cd/c/lp) *(10812-2/-4/-1) <43027>* **POWER ON TO ZERO HOUR**
– Bring in the year 2000 / Sucker / Fear / Doomo dance / Automatic terror / Jungle justice / Full force of them nuclear shoes / Believe it / Cry a sea of tears / Quasi.

May 93. (cd/c) *(11012-2/-4) <43051>* **NEW RACEION**
– The pleaser / Christ dice / Gamma pop / Viva the legs / Do the job / Junior's little sister's dropped ta cheap / How many lifetimes / Holy skips / Keep it alive / Go Trane go / Just say.

— next with **LIZ LAMERE** – keyboards, vocals

Thirsty Ear Thirsty Ear

Dec 96. (cd) *<(21308)>* **DUJANG PRANG** Jul96
– Dujang prang / Hammered / Chennaroka / Saturn drive 2 (subtalk) / Jaxson gnome / Life ain't life / Flowers, candles, crucifixes / Big daddy stat's livin' on Tron / Sacrifice / Kiss.

Last Call Thirsty Ear

May 97. (cd; ALAN VEGA, ALEX CHILTON, BEN VAUGHN) *(422466) <21314>* **CUBIST BLUES** Oct96
– Fat city / Fly away / Freedom / Candyman / Come on Lord / Promised land / Lover of love / Sister / Too late / Do not do not / Werewolf / Dream baby revisited.

MARTIN REV

Marilyn Alive

Jul 92. (cd) *(FM 1006CD) <ALIVE 2>* **CHEYENNE** Jan95
– Wings of the wind / Red Sierra / Dakota / Cheyenne / River of tears / Buckeye / Little Rock / Prairie star / Mustang.

R.O.I.R. R.O.I.R.

Jan 96. (cd) *<(RUSCD 8220)>* **SEE ME RIDIN'**
– See me ridin' / Pillars / I heard your name / No one knows / Be mine / Mari go round / Small talk / Secret teardrops / I made you cry / Here we go / Ten two / Hop and scotch / Told the moon / Yours tonight / Tell me why / Post card.

Sahko Sahko

Mar 00. (cd/lp) *<(efa 50167-2/-1)>* **STRANGEWORLD**
– My strange world / Sparks / Solitude / Funny / Ramplin' / Trouble / Splinters / Cartoons / One track mind / Chalky / Reading my mind / Jacks and aces / Day and night.

not iss. File 13

Sep 03. (cd) *<46>* **TO LIVE** –
– To live / In your arms / Black ice / Gutter rock / Shimmer / Painted / Places I go / Lost in the orbits / Jaded / Our roads / Search for stone / Water / Stormy.

SUICIDE

REV + VEGA re-united

Blast First Mute

Oct 02. (lp/cd) *(BFFP 168/+CD) <9196>* **AMERICAN SUPREME**
– Televised executions / Misery train / Swearin' to the flag / Beggin' for miracles / American mean / Wrong decisions / Death machine / Power au go-go / Dachau, Disney, disco / Child, it's a new world / I don't know.

– compilations, etc. –

Dec 81. (c) *R.O.I.R.; <(A 103)>* **HALF-ALIVE (half studio)**

Oct 86. (c) *R.O.I.R.; <(A 145)>* **GHOST RIDERS (live)**
(cd-iss. Apr90 on 'Danceteria'; DANCD 029) (cd-iss. Feb95 on 'ROIR Europe'; RE 145CD)

Mar 96. (cd; by ALAN VEGA) *Infinite Zero; <43069>* **JUKEBOX BABE / COLLISION DRIVE** –

Jan 98. (12"ep) *Blast First; (BFFP 115)* **CHEREE. / HARLEM / I REMEMBER** –

— Their classic 'FRANKIE TEARDROP' was used by STEPHEN LIRONI (producer and ex- ALTERED IMAGES guy) on project REVOLUTIONARY CORPS, etc

SUM 41

Formed: Ajax, Ontario, Canada .... 41 days into summer '96. DERYCK WHIBLEY, DAVE BAKSH, MARK SPICOLUK and STEVE JOCZ all met as members of rival bands and immediately made an impact on the local scene; CONE McCASLIN joined in 1999 replacing MARK. They were signed to 'Island' that December after releasing their now infamous homemade EPK (Electronic Press Kit). SUM 41 then sharpened their colourful pop-punk aplomb on the road while touring with bands such as the OFFSPRING, BLINK 182 and the MIGHTY MIGHTY BOSSTONES. Meanwhile, a debut mini-set, 'HALF HOUR OF POWER' (2000), was unleashed to the North American public, although it made little impact initially. The following May – with producer Jerry Finn in tow – they delivered a second batch of songs, 'ALL KILLER NO FILLER' (2001). A Top 20 entry in both the US and (a little later) the UK charts, the disc featured two major UK hit singles, 'FAT LIP' and 'IN TOO DEEP'. Not content with having one of the most inane names in rock, the Canadian troupe followed on with one of the dumbest album titles of the year in 'DOES THIS LOOK INFECTED?' (2002), although the heavier LP did manage to hit the Top 40 while lead single, 'STILL WAITING' repeated the formula. The following year saw them back IGGY POP on his 2003 album, 'Skull Ring' (promoting it on The David Letterman Show), while in May 2004, the band travelled to the Congo to film some documentary footage for the War Child charity organization. However, just days after arriving at the troubled Democratic Republic, hostilities broke out again, although the lads were quickly saved by U.N. aid worker (and fellow Canadian), Chuck Pelletier. To mark this near death experience, the band showed their respect to the man by naming their fourth set, 'CHUCK' (2004). This record – clocking in at just over the half-hour – continued the group's surge to the top, well Top 10 at least. The customary live set, 'GO CHUCK YOURSELF!' (recorded in April 2005), appeared in 2006, while DERYCK was planning his wedding to pop starlet, AVRIL LAVIGNE. That May, DAVE BAKSH left to form his own punk-pop outfit, BROWN BRIGADE.

Album rating: HALF HOUR OF POWER mini (*5) / ALL KILLER NO FILLER (*7) / DOES THIS LOOK INFECTED? (*5) / CHUCK (*6) / GO CHUCK YOURSELF! (*4)

DERYCK WHIBLEY (b.21 Mar'80, Scarborough, Ontario) – vocals, guitar / **DAVE BAKSH** (b.26 Jul'80, Toronto, Ontario) – guitar / **CONE McCASLIN** (b. JASON, 3 Sep'80, Toronto) – bass; repl. MARK SPICOLUK / **STEVE JOCZ** (b.23 Jul'81) – drums

Mercury Island

Jun 00. (m-cd) <542419-2> **HALF HOUR OF POWER** [–] [ ]
– Grab the Devil by the horns and fuck him up the ass / Machine gun / What I believe / THT / Makes no difference / Summer / 32 ways to die / Second chance for Max Headroom / Dave's possessed hair / What we're all about / Ride the charlot to the Devil / Another time around. *(UK-iss.Nov01 & May02; same as US)*

Jul 01. (cd) <(548662-2)> **ALL KILLER NO FILLER** [7] May01 [13]
– Introduction to destruction / Nothing on my back / Never wake up / Fat lip / Rhythms / Motivation / In too deep / Summer / Handle this / Crazy Amanda Bunkface / All she's got / Heart attack / Pain for pleasure. *(re-iss. Oct01 +=; 548662-9)* – Makes no difference.

Oct 01. (c-s) *(588801-4)* *<radio>* **FAT LIP / CRAZY AMANDA BUNKFACE** [8] Sep01 [66]
(cd-s+=) *(588801-2)* – Machine gun / ('A'-video).
(dvd-s) *(588801-9)* – ('A'-video) / Pain for pleasure / (meet the band video).

Dec 01. (c-s) *(860982-4)* **IN TOO DEEP / FAT LIP (live)** [13] [–]
(cd-s+=) *(588898-2)* – All she's got (live) / ('A'-video).

Mar 02. (c-s) *(588945-4)* **MOTIVATION / PAIN FOR PLEASURE (live)** [21] [–]
(cd-s+=) *(588945-2)* – What I believe (version) / ('A'-video).

Jun 02. (cd-s) *(672864-2)* **IT'S WHAT WE'RE ALL ABOUT / MOTIVATION / (making of the video – video footage)** [32] [–]
(above issued on 'Columbia' & from the film, 'Spider-Man')

Nov 02. (c-s) *(63831-4)* **STILL WAITING / IN TOO DEEP (live)** [16] [–]
(cd-s+=) *(63831-2)* – Fat lip (live).
(cd-s) *(63834-2)* – ('A') / All messed up (demo) / Motivation (live) / ('A'-video).

Nov 02. (cd) *(63483-2)* *<06349-2>* **DOES THIS LOOK INFECTED?** [39] [32]
– The hell song / Over my head (better off dead) / My direction / Still waiting / A.N.I.C. / No brains / All messed up / Mr. Amsterdam / Thanks for nothing / Hyper-insomnia-para-condroid / Billy Spleen / Hooch. *(UK+=)* – Reign in pain (heavy metal jamboree) / WWVII Part II. *(w/dvd+=)* – (DVD videos).

Feb 03. (7") *(063720-7)* **THE HELL SONG. / STILL WAITING (live)** [35] [–]
(cd-s+=) *(063720-2)* – Rhythms (live) / ('A'video).
(cd-s) *(063719-2)* – ('A') / Over my head (better off dead) (demo) / My direction (demo) / ('A'-video).

Jun 03. (cd-s) *<9807997>* **OVER MY HEAD (BETTER OFF DEAD)** [–] [ ]

Oct 04. (cd) *(9864426)* **CHUCK** [59] [10]
– Intro / No reason / We're all to blame / Angels with dirty faces / Some say / The bitter end / Open your eyes / Slipping away / I'm not the one / Welcome to Hell / Pieces / There's no solution / 88. *(incl. videos & making of..).*

not iss. Aquarius

Mar 06. (cd) *<200624>* **GO CHUCK YOURSELF!** (live) [–] [ ]
– The hell song / My direction / Over my head (better off dead) / A.N.I.C. / Never wake up / We're all to blame / There's no solution / No brains / Some say / Welcome to Hell / Grab the Devil / Makes no difference / Pieces / Motivation / Still waiting / 88 / No reason / I have a question / Moron / Fat lip / Pain for pleasure.

— (May'06) DAVE BAKSH split from the band

SUPER FURRY ANIMALS

Formed: Cardiff, Wales ... 1993 by GRUFF RHYS, DAFYDD IEUAN, CIAN CIARAN, GUTO PRYCE and HUW BUNFORD. Emerging from the Welsh underground scene in the mid-90's with a wholly unpronounceable EP on their native 'Ankst' label, the band whipped up a fair bit of interest from the London-based media and industry insiders alike. Alan McGee's 'Creation' subsequently took them on with the proviso that the bulk of their work be in English, the 'FURRY's famously stipulating that they never be made to work on St. David's day. Their first single for the label, 'HOMETOWN UNICORN' appeared in early '96 and dented the Top 50, while the dayglo rampage of 'GOD! SHOW ME MAGIC' made the Top 40 a couple of months later. Hailed by critics as one of the debuts of the year, the accompanying 'FUZZY LOGIC' (1996) album thrilled jaded Brit-pop fans with its dayglo showcase of deranged prog-retro pop/rock; 'MARIO MAN' was their most definitive slice of pseudo psychedelia to date while 'HANGIN' WITH HOWARD MARKS' gave them instant cool – the record's cover art depicted the various guises of "nice guy" one-time drug smuggler, MARKS. A Top 30 hit, the album spawned a further two singles in 'SOMETHING 4 THE WEEKEND' and 'IF YOU DON'T WANT ME TO DESTROY YOU', while the blase brilliance of 'THE MAN DON'T GIVE A FUCK' (repetitive line from the STEELY DAN number, 'Showbiz Kids') drew a swaggering close to a successful but inevitably controversial year, the group having been earlier banned from the Welsh BAFTA awards after a skirmish in the crowd. 1997's follow-up set, 'RADIATOR', made the Top 10, its less intense but equally compelling shenanigans threatening to take the band into the big league (they played the festival circuit that included a return to the rainy 'T In The Park' – Muddy Waters was not even invited). In May '98, after two further Top 30 hits, 'PLAY IT COOL' and 'DEMONS', the band had their biggest hit to date (#12) via non-album cut, 'ICE HOCKEY HAIR'. To end the year, 'OUT-SPACED' (a selection of rare B-sides, etc), marked time as GRUFF RHYS and his crew plotted their return. The 'NORTHERN LITES' single (which reached No.11), previewed unquestionably their finest hour to date, 'GUERILLA' (1999), a Top 10 album that featured xylophones, Caribbean brass, steel guitars, etc over some "way-out" experimental jugband psychedelia. Following the demise of 'Creation', the SUPER FURRIES were free to pursue their own cultural peccadilloes, specifically a Welsh language album on their own 'Placid Casual' imprint. Not just any old Welsh language album though, the first Welsh language record to make the UK Top 20 no less! While the significance of this may be lost on foreign readers, the fact that 'MWNG' (2000) was discussed in the UK parliament demonstrates the precedent it set. More, it was perhaps the band's most readily accessible effort to date, not so ironic when you consider the power of say, Brazilian music; often the melodies are so strong, the lyrics' meaning is besides the point. They merely function as another instrument. So with the SUPER FURRY

ANIMALS and their patented brand of psyched-out leftfield pop exoctica; the melodies soar, the arrangements confound and the hooks reel you in. Although they recorded one of their best efforts on a miniscule budget, a subsequent deal with 'Columbia' presented an opportunity to go for broke on 'RINGS AROUND THE WORLD' (2001). A quasi-concept set based on the earth's ongoing disintegration, the record's technicolour melancholy represented a wild-eyed creative peak for RHYS and Co. Rarely has such digital-era indulgence reaped such endearing rewards. The single 'JUXTAPOSED WITH U' was among the highlights, a deceptive 80's AZTEC CAMERA-style croon which belied a despairing lyric railing against fat cats. From the industrial-strength ELO of the title track to the truly discomforting 'RUN! CHRISTIAN, RUN!', 'RINGS AROUND THE WORLD' truly ran kaleidoscopic rings around its indie competition. Inevitably perhaps, the 'FURRIES reined in the studio excess on their 2003 effort, 'PHANTOM POWER', hooking up with sometime BEASTIE BOYS producer Mario Caldato Jr. The result was a record with a much more easy going, lazy-eyed appeal, insinuating rather than showing off and showcasing a newly Americana-esque twang. 'SONGBOOK: THE SINGLES, VOL.1' (2004) was another Top 20 album, showcasing a grasp of lysergic stylistics that rivalled any other band of the 90s/00s. Caldato, Jr. stuck around for 'LOVE KRAFT' (2005), heading up a cast of interlopers that numbered HIGH LLAMA/Pop High Priest SEAN O'HAGAN and a full-on Catalan choir. From the opening electric piano notes of 'ZOOM!', it was clear this was going to be a cosmic honky tonking, life-affirming, harmonica-blowing, teaching-the-world-to-sing in Welsh harmony kinda record, possibly the 'FURRIES' most affectionate to date. Top 20 hardly reflected its philanthropic flair, nor did a mere Top 30 for the SCISSOR SISTERS-meets-MICHAEL WHITE-at-the-hootenanny vibe that was 'LAZER BEAM'. Sure, it was out of step with the 80s revival but that was never going to trouble an aggregate with the psychotronic flair of a Boyo BETA BAND. Chief FURRY, GRUFF RHYS, subsequently released a stripped-back, Welsh language solo set, 'YR ATAL GENHEDLAETH' (2005) to overwhelmingly positive reviews.

Album rating: FUZZY LOGIC (*8) / RADIATOR (*7) / OUTSPACED collection (*6) / GUERILLA (*9) / MWNG (*7) / RINGS AROUND THE WORLD (*9) / PHANTOM POWER (*7) / SONGBOOK: THE SINGLES VOLUME ONE compilation (*8) / LOVE KRAFT (*6) / Gruff Rhys: YR ATAL GENHEDLAETH (*7)

GRUFF RHYS (b.18 Jul'70, Bethesda, Gwynedd, Wales) – vocals, guitars (ex-EMILY, ex-FFA COFFI PAWB) / **CIAN CIARAN** (b.16 Jun'76, Isle of Anglesey, Wales) – keyboards / **HUW 'Bumpf' BUNFORD** (b.15 Sep'67, Bath, England) – guitars, vocals / **GUTO PRYCE** (b. 4 Sep'72) – bass / **DAFYDD IEUAN** (b. 1 Mar'69, Isle of Anglesey) – drums, percussion, vocals (ex-ANHREFN, ex-FFA COFFI PAWB)

Ankst / not iss.

Jun 95. (7"ep/cd-ep) *(ANKST 057/+CD)* **LLANFAIRPWLLGWYNGYLLGOGERYCHWYNDROBW-LLANTYSILIOGOGOGOCHOCYNYGOFOD (IN SPACE) EP** [ ] [–]
– Organ yn dy geg / Fix idris / Crys Ti / Blerwytirhwng? *(re-iss. May97; same)*

Oct 95. (7"ep/cd-ep) *(ANKST 062/+CD)* **MOOG DROOG EP** [ ] [–]
– Pam V / God! show me magic / Sali Mali / Focus pocus – Debiel. *(re-iss. May97; same)*

Creation / Sony

Feb 96. (7"/c-s) *(CRE/+CS 222)* **HOMETOWN UNICORN. / DON'T BE A FOOL, BILLY** [47] [–]
(cd-s+=) *(CRESCD 222)* – Lazy life (of no fixed identity).

Apr 96. (7"/c-s) *(CRE/+CS 231)* **GOD! SHOW ME MAGIC. / DIM BENDITH** [33] [–]
(cd-s+=) *(CRESCD 231)* – Death by melody.

May 96. (cd/lp)(c) *(CRE CD/LP 190)(CCRE 190)* <67827> **FUZZY LOGIC** [23] [ ]
– God! show me magic / Fuzzy birds / Something 4 the weekend / Frisbee / Hometown unicorn / Gathering moss / If you don't want me to destroy you / Bad behaviour / Mario man / Hangin' with Howard Marks / Long gone / For now and ever. *(cd re-iss. Feb00; same)*

Jul 96. (7"/c-s) *(CRE/+CS 235)* **SOMETHING 4 THE WEEKEND. / WAITING TO HAPPEN** [18] [–]
(cd-s+=) *(CRESCD 235)* – Arnofio / Glow in the dark.

Sep 96. (7"/c-s/cd-s) *(CRE/+CS/SCD 243)* **IF YOU DON'T WANT ME TO DESTROY YOU. / GUACAMOLE** [18] [–]
(cd-s+=) *(CRESCD 243)* – (Nid) Hon yw'r gan sy'n mynd I achub yr iaith (This song will save the Welsh language (not).

Dec 96. (one-sided-7"blue) *(CRE 247)* **THE MAN DON'T GIVE A FUCK** [22] [–]
(cd-s+=) *(CRESCD 247)* – ('A'-Matthew 'Herbert' Herbert mix) / ('A'-Howard Marks mix).
(12"++=) *(CRE 247T)* – ('A'-Darren Price mix).

Creation / Flydaddy

May 97. (7"/c-s) *(CRE/+CS 252)* **HERMANN LOVES PAULINE. / CALIMERO** [26] [–]
(cd-s+=) *(CRESCD 252)* – Trons Mr. Urdd.

Jul 97. (7"/c-s) *(CRE/+CS 269)* **THE INTERNATIONAL LANGUAGE OF SCREAMING. / WRAP IT UP** [24] [–]
(cd-s+=) *(CRESCD 269)* – Foxy music / O.K.

Aug 97. (cd/c/lp) *(CRECD/CCRE/CRELP 214)* *<FLY 34CD>* **RADIATOR** [8] [ ]
– Furryvision / The placid casual / The international language of screaming / Demons / Short painkiller / She's got spies / Play it cool / Hermann love's Pauline / Chupacabras / Torra fy ngwallt yn hir / Bass tuned to D.E.A.D. / Down a different river / Download / Mountain people.

Sep 97. (7"/c-s) *(CRE/+CS 275)* **PLAY IT COOL. / PASS THE TIME** [27] [–]
(cd-s+=) *(CRESCD 275)* – Cryndod yn dy lais.

Nov 97. (7"/c-s) *(CRE/+CS 283)* **DEMONS. / HIT AND RUN** [27] [–]
(cd-s+=) *(CRESCD 283)* – Carry the can.

May 98. (7"/c-s) *(CRE/+CS 288)* **ICE HOCKEY HAIR. / SMOKIN'** [12] [–]
(12"+=)(cd-s+=) *(CRE 288T)(CRESCD 288)* – Mu-tron / Let's quit smokin'.

Nov 98. (cd/lp) *(CRE CD/LP 229)* **OUT SPACED** (selected B-sides & rarities 1994-1998) [44] [–]
– The man don't give a fuck / Dim brys dim chwys / Smokin' / Dim bendith / Arnofio – Glo in the dark / Guacamole / Don't be a fool, Billy / Focus pocus – Debiel / Fix Idris / Pam V / Pass the time / Carry the can / Blerwytirhwng? *(ltd-cd; CRECD 229L) (cd re-iss. Sep99 & Feb00; same)*

May 99. (7"/c-s) *(CRE/+CS 314)* **NORTHERN LITES. / RABID DOG** [11] [–]
(cd-s+=) *(CRESCD 314)* – This, that and the other.

Jun 99. (cd/c/lp) *(CRECD/CCRE/CRELP 242)* *<FLY 36CD>* **GUERILLA** [10] [ ]
– Check it out / Do or die / The turning tide / Northern lites / Night vision / Wherever I lay my phone (that's my home) / A specific ocean / Some things come from nothing / The door to this house remains open / The teacher / Fire in my heart / The sound of life today / Chewing chewing gum / Keep the cosmic trigger happy. *(cd re-iss. Feb00; same)*

Aug 99. (7"/c-s) *(CRE/+CS 323)* **FIRE IN MY HEART. / THE MATTER OF TIME** [25] [–]
(cd-s+=) *(CRESCD 323)* – Mrs Spector.

Jan 00. (7"/c-s) *(CRE/+CS 329)* **DO OR DIE. / MISSUNDERSTANDING (sic)** [20] [–]
(cd-s+=) *(CRESCD 329)* – Colorblind.

Placid Casual / Flydaddy

May 00. (7") *(PC 02)* **YSBEIDIAU HEULOG. / CHARGE** [ ] [–]

May 00. (cd/c/lp)<d-cd> *(PLC 03 CD/MC/LP)* *<FLY 040>* **MWNG** [11] Jun00 [ ]
– Drygioni / Ymaelodi a'r ymylon / Y gwyneb lau / Dacw hi / Nythod cacwn / Pan ddaw'r wawr / Ysbeidiau heulog / Y teimlad / Sarn Helen / Gwreiddiau dwfn mawrth oer ar y blaned neifion. *<US cd+=>* – Cryndod yn dy lais / Trons mr urdd / Calimero / Sali Mali / (Nid) Hon yw'r gan sy'n mynd I achub yr laith.

Epic / Epic

Jul 01. (12"/c-s) *(671224-6/-4)* **JUXTAPOSED WITH U. / TRADEWINDS / HAPPINESS IS A WORN PUN** [14] [–]
(cd-s+=) *(671224-2)* – ('A'-video).

Jul 01. (cd/c/d-lp) *(<502413-2/-4/-1>)* **RINGS AROUND THE WORLD** [3] [ ]
– Alternate route to Vulcan Street / Sidewalk serfer girl / (Drawing) Rings around the world / It's not the end of the world? / Receptable for the respectable / (A) Touch sensitive / Shoot Doris Day / Miniature / No sympathy / Juxtaposed with U / Presedential suite / Run! Christian, run! / Fragile happiness.

Oct 01. (c-s/12") *(671908-4/-6)* **(DRAWING) RINGS AROUND THE WORLD / EDAM ANCHORMAN / ALL THE SHIT U DO** 28 –
(cd-s+=) *(671908-2)* – ('A'video).

Jan 02. (12"/cd-s) *(672175-6/-2)* **IT'S NOT THE END OF THE WORLD? / ROMAN ROAD / GYPSY SPACE MUFFIN** 30 –

Epic XL – Beggars

Jul 03. (7"pic-d/cd-s) *(673906-7/-2)* **GOLDEN RETRIEVER. / SUMMER SNOW / BLUE FRUIT** 13 –

Jul 03. (cd/lp) *(512375-2/-1)* *<85035>* **PHANTOM POWER** 4
– Hello sunshine / Liberty belle / Golden retriever / Sex, war & robots / The piccolo snare / Venus & Serena / Father father #1 / Bleed forever / Out of control / Cityscape skybaby / Father father #2 / Valet parking / The undefeated / Slow life.

Oct 03. (7"pic-d) *(674360-7)* **HELLO SUNSHINE. / COWBIRD** 31 –
(cd-s+=) *(674360-2)* – Sanitizzzed.

Sep 04. (one-sided-12"/cd-s) *(675304-6/-1)* **THE MAN DON'T GIVE A FUCK (live)** 16 –

Oct 04. (cd/d-lp) *(517671-2/-1)* *<85042>* **SONGBOOK: THE SINGLES VOLUME ONE** (compilation) 18 Jan05
– Something for the weekend / It's not the end of the world / Northern lites / Juxtapozed with U / Slow life / Fire in my heart / The man don't give a fuck / Herman loves Pauline / Play it cool / Ice hockey hair / Do or die / Rings around the world / God show me magic / Ysbeidiau heulog / Demons / Golden retriever / International language of screaming / Hello sunshine / Hometown unicorn / If you don't want me to destroy you / Blerwytirhwng. *(ltd-cd; 517671-9)*

Aug 05. (7") *(676011-7)* **LAZER BEAM. / SUNNY SEVILLE** 28 –
(cd-s+=) *(676011-1)* – Colonise the Moon.

Aug 05. (cd) *(520501-2)* *<85047>* **LOVE KRAFT** 19 Sep05
– Zoom! / Atomik lust / The horn / Ohio heat / Walk you home / Lazer beam / Frequency / Oi Frango / Psyclone! / Back on a roll / Cloudberries / Cabin fever.

– compilations, etc. –

Aug 04. (cd) *Placid Casual; (PLC 07CDLL)* **PHANTOM PHORCE** (remixes) –

GRUFF RHYS

Placid Casual RoughTrade

Jan 05. (cd) *(PLC 10CDLL)* *<30053>* **YR ATAL GENHEDLAETH** Mar05
– Yr atal genhedlaeth / Gwn mi wn / Epynt / Rhagluniaeth ysgafn / Pwdin wy 1 / Pwdin wy 2 / Y gwybodusion / Caerffosiaeth / Ambell waith / Ni yw y byd / Chwarae'm troi'n chwerw.

SUPERGRASS

Formed: Oxford, England ... 1991 as The JENNIFERS by schoolboy GAZ COOMBES and DANNY GOFFEY along with brother NICK and ANDY DAVIES. After a sole EP on 'Nude' (home to SUEDE), DAVIES went off to university, COOMBES and DANNY subsequently recruiting MICKEY QUINN and forming SUPERGRASS. Their raucous debut single, 'CAUGHT BY THE FUZZ', complete with a STIFF LITTLE FINGERS-like intro and a snotty, shouty vocal rampage recounting the teenage trauma of being busted for cannabis, could've conceivably come straight out of 1977. Initially released on the small 'Backbeat' label in 1994, the single was eventually re-released by 'Parlophone' after the label promptly snapped the group up in 1994. Although the track narrowly missed the Top 40, a 1995 follow-up, 'MANSIZE ROOSTER', made the Top 20, the MADNESS comparisons inevitable as SUPERGRASS wore their influences proudly on their retro sleeves. Another couple of singles followed in quick succession, 'LOSE IT' as a limited 'Sub Pop' singles club release and 'LENNY' as the group's first Top 10 hit. Few were surprised, then, when the debut album, 'I SHOULD COCO' (1995) made No.1 the following month, a proverbial grab-bag of musical styles from 60's harmony pop to sneering punk. The record's indisputable highlight was 'ALRIGHT', a perfectly formed BEACH BOYS via The YOUNG ONES' pop romp guaranteed to bring a smile to your face and proving that "Brit-pop" didn't necessarily mean second rate STRANGLERS/BLONDIE rip-offs. The song, and especially the Raleigh Chopper-riding exploits of the video, did much to crystallise The SUPERGRASS image, carefree, fun-loving lads with GAZ's wildly impressive sideburns adding to the cartoon appeal. Steven Spielberg was apparently even moved to offer the band the opportunity of starring in a 90's remake of The MONKEES! This was turned down, as was an offer for GAZ to model for Calvin Klein, the group preferring to concentrate solely on the music and downplay the novelty factor. Instead, there were two gems hidden away at the end of 'I SHOULD..' which indicated the direction SUPERGRASS were headed; the intoxicating, slow rolling 70's groove of 'TIME' and the dreamy psychedelia of 'SOFA (OF MY LETHARGY). Save a few live appearances and a solitary single, 'GOING OUT', SUPERGRASS were notably absent in 1996, tucked away once more at Sawmill Studios crafting their acclaimed follow-up, 'IN IT FOR THE MONEY'. Eventually released in Spring '97, the record was something of a departure to say the least. The impetuous buzzsaw punk-pop of old had been replaced by the dark assault of 'RICHARD III' while the bulk of the album fed off warped neo-psychedelia and stark introspection. Horn flourishes were sighted here and there, most satisfyingly on the lazy chug of the aforementioned 'GOING OUT', while parping organs and acoustic strumming were the order of the day. The enigmatic shadow of The BEATLES' 'White Album' loomed large over proceedings, especially on 'YOU CAN SEE ME' and the oom-pa-pa eccentricity of 'SOMETIMES I MAKE YOU SAD'. In fact, the only glimpse of the old SUPERGRASS came with 'SUN HITS THE SKY', a soaring, handclapping, spirit-lifting celebration of good times and faraway places. No matter though, the record's dark charm ensured the band remained a critical favourite, if not quite consolidating the commercial heights of the debut. Clearly, SUPERGRASS were looking at a long term, albums-based career, and on the strength of 'IN IT . . .', the future seemed promising. In May '99, the glam BOWIE-esque 'PUMPING ON YOUR STEREO' was the first of three hit singles, the second 'MOVING' ('Dogs' by PINK FLOYD might've been "pumping on their stereo" at the time!?) previewing their self-titled third Top 3 album. However, several critics rated this as a drop in form. ALI G (Boo-y aka SACHA BARON COHEN) subsequently demolished the er, "Super-tramp" GAZ on his cult TV show; the 'SUN HITS THE SKY', indeed. The 'GRASS returned in 2002 with the brilliant 'LIFE ON OTHER PLANETS', a sweeping pop/rock album featuring COMBS' wacky strained vocals and a couple of surefire singles to boot; the infectious 'SAVE YOUR MONEY FOR THE CHILDREN' (which was just 'PUMPING ON YOUR STEREO' reprise) and the power pop punk of 'EVENING OF THE DAY'. In short, it was great to have them back. It hardly seemed like almost a decade since 'ALRIGHT', but 'SUPERGRASS IS 10: THE BEST OF 1994-2004' (2004) told its own story of a band who forsook a brief burst of Brit-Pop fame for weightier projects. The latest of these, the Top 10 'ROAD TO ROUEN' (2005) was a punningly titled, largely introspective and unexpectedly haunting work recorded in a remodelled barn in the Gallic hinterlands of Normandy (hence the title). Opening with the heavy, piano-chord soul of a lost JOHN MARTYN classic, the album uncoiled as a mood piece rather than a pop album, tailored here and there with some stray folk influences (Eastern European as well as Anglophone; see the playful 'COFFEE IN THE POT') and peppered with the odd upbeat rocker. The overriding influence, however, was the BEATLES, looming large in both the Top 30 single, 'ST.

PETERSBURG', and the LENNON-esque closing brace of 'LOW C' and 'FIN'.

• Covered: STONE FREE (Jimi Hendrix) / ITCHYCOO PARK (Small Faces) / SOME GIRLS ARE BIGGER THAN OTHERS (Smiths).

Album rating: I SHOULD COCO (*9) / IN IT FOR THE MONEY (*8) / SUPERGRASS (*6) / LIFE ON OTHER PLANETS (*7) / SUPERGRASS IS 10 – THE BEST OF 1994-2004 compilation (*9) / ROAD TO ROUEN (*7)

GAZ COOMBES (b. GARETH, 8 Mar'76, Brighton, England) – vocals, guitar / **NICK GOFFEY** – guitar / **ANDY DAVIES** – bass / **DANNY GOFFEY** (b. DANIEL, 7 Feb'75, London, England) – drums

Nude-Sony / not iss.

Aug 92. (12"ep/cd-ep; as the JENNIFERS) *(NUD2 T/CD)* **JUST GOT BACK TODAY / ROCKS AND BOULDERS. / DANNY'S SONG / TOMORROW'S RAIN** [ ] [–]

— **MICK QUINN** (b.17 Dec'69) – guitar; repl. TARA MILTON who had repl. NICK (and now without DAVIES who went to Bristol University)

Parlophone / Capitol

Oct 94. (7"/c-s) *(R/TCR 6396)* *<81769>* **CAUGHT BY THE FUZZ. / STRANGE ONES** [43] Feb95 [ ]
(cd-s+=) *(CDR 6396)* – Caught by the fuzz (acoustic).

Feb 95. (7"/7"red/c-s) *(R/RS/TCR 6402)* *<81964>* **MANSIZE ROOSTER. / SITTING UP STRAIGHT** [20] Jun95 [ ]
(cd-s+=) *(CDR 6402)* – Odd.

Mar 95. (7"yellow) *(<SP 281>)* **LOSE IT. / CAUGHT BY THE FUZZ (acoustic)** [75] [ ]
(above on 'Sub Pop' also feat. on Jul95 box-set 'HELTER SHELTER')
(re-iss. Sep99; same)

Apr 95. (7"blue/c-s) *(RS/TCR 6401)* **LENNY. / WAIT FOR THE SUN** [9] [–]
(cd-s+=) *(CDR 6410)* – Sex!.

May 95. (cd/c/lp) *(CD/TC+/PCS 7373)* *<33350>* **I SHOULD COCO** [1] Jul95 [ ]
– I'd like to know / Caught by the fuzz / Mansize rooster / Alright / Lose it / Lenny / Strange ones / Sitting up straight / She's so loose / We're not supposed to / Time / Sofa (of my lethargy) / Time to go. *(7"free w/ ltd lp)* **STONE FREE. / ODD?**

Jul 95. (c-s/7"colrd) *(TC+/R 6413)* *<82277>* **ALRIGHT. / TIME** [2] [ ]
(cd-s+=) *(CDR 6413)* – Condition / Je suis votre papa sucre.
(cd-s+=) *(CDRX 6413)* – Lose it.

Feb 96. (c-s/7"burgundy) *(TC+/R 6428)* **GOING OUT. / MELANIE DAVIS** [5] [–]
(cd-s+=) *(CDR 6428)* – Strange ones (live).

Apr 97. (cd-s/7"yellow) *(CD/+R 6461)* *<83820>* **RICHARD III. / NOTHING MORE'S GONNA GET IN MY WAY** [2] [ ]
(cd-s+=) *(CDRS 6461)* – 20ft halo.
(cd-s) *(CDRS 6461)* – ('A'side) / Sometimes I make you very sad / Sometimes we're very sad.

Apr 97. (cd/c/lp) *(CD/TC+/PCS 7388)* *<55228>* **IN IT FOR THE MONEY** [2] May97 [ ]
– In it for the money / Richard III / Tonight / Late in the day / G-song / Sun hits the sky / Going out / It's not me / Cheapskate / You can see me / Hollow little reign / Sometimes I make you sad.

Jun 97. (c-s/7") *(TC+/R 6469)* *<84187>* **SUN HITS THE SKY. / SOME GIRLS ARE BIGGER THAN OTHERS** [10] [ ]
(cd-s+=) *(CDR 6469)* – ('A'extended).

Oct 97. (7"gold) *(R 6484)* *<84758>* **LATE IN THE DAY. / WE STILL NEED MORE (THAN ANYONE CAN GIVE)** [18] [ ]
(cd-s+=) *(CDRS 6484)* – It's not me (demo).
(cd-s) *(CDR 6484)* – ('A'side) / Don't be cruel / The animal.

— while SUPERGRASS took a break from the biz, DANNY moonlighted with the indie superband, LODGER, who issued a few singles in '98

— **GAZ, DANNY + MICK** added **ROBERT COOMBES** – keyboards

May 99. (c-s) *(TCR 6518)* **PUMPING ON YOUR STEREO / YOU'LL NEVER WALK AGAIN** [11] [ ]
(cd-s+=) *(CDRS 6518)* – Sick.
(cd-s) *(CDR 6518)* – ('A') / What a shame / Lucky (no fear).

Sep 99. (7") *(R 6524)* **MOVING. / BELIEVER** [9] [ ]
(c-s+=/cd-s+=) *(TCR/CDR 6524)* – Faraway (acoustic).
(cd-s) *(CDRS 6524)* – ('A') / You too can play alright / Pumping on your stereo (CD-Rom).

Sep 99. (cd/c) *(5 22056-2/-4)* *<542388>* **SUPERGRASS** [3] [ ]
– Moving / Your love / What went wrong (in your head) / Beautiful people / Shotover hill / Eon / Mary / Jesus came from outta space / Pumping on your stereo / Born again / Faraway / Mama & papa.

Nov 99. (7"silver) *(R 6531)* **MARY / PUMPING ON YOUR STEREO (live)** [36] [ ]
(c-s+=/cd-s+=) *(TCR/CDR 6531)* – Strange ones (live).
(cd-s+=) *(CDRS 6531)* – Richard III (live) / Sun hits the sky (live).

Parlophone / Island

Jul 02. (ltd-7"one-sided) *(R 6583)* **NEVER DONE NOTHING LIKE THAT BEFORE** [75] [–]

Sep 02. (7") *(R 6586)* **GRACE. / VELVETINE** [13] [–]
(cd-s+=) *(CDRS 6586)* – Electric cowboy.
(cd-s) *(CDR 6586)* – ('A') / Tishing in windows (kicking down doors) / That old song / ('A'-video).

Sep 02. (cd/lp) *(541800-2/-1)* *<063685>* **LIFE ON OTHER PLANETS** [9] [ ]
– Za / Rush hour soul / Seen the light / Brecon beacons / Can't get up / Evening of the day / Never done nothing like that before / Funniest thing / Grace / La song / Prophet 15 / Run.

Jan 03. (7"grey) *(R 6592)* **SEEN THE LIGHT. / THE LONER** [22] [–]
(cd-s+=) *(CDR 6592)* – I told the truth.

Aug 03. (7") *(R 6612)* **RUSH HOUR SOUL. / EVERYTIME** [ ] [–]
(cd-s+=) *(CDR 6612)* – ('A'-video).

May 04. (cd-s/7"clear) *(CD+/R 6638)* **KISS OF LIFE. / WE DREAM OF THIS** [23] [–]
(cd-s+=) *(CDRS 6638)* – ('A'-Tom Tom Club full mix) / ('A'-video) / Rob's guide to responsible flying (video).

Jun 04. (cd/d-lp) *(<570860-2/-1>)* **SUPERGRASS IS 10: THE BEST OF 1994-2004** (compilation) [4] [ ]
– Caught by the fuzz / Pumping on your stereo / Alright / Moving / Richard III / Grace / Late in the day / Seen the light / Mansize rooster / Sun hits the sky / Kiss of life / Mary / Going out / Lenny / Bullet / It's not me / Rush hour soul / Strange ones / Lose it / Time / Wait for the sun.

Sep 05. (7"red) *(R 6670)* **ST. PETERSBURG. / KISS OF LIFE (live)** [22] [–]
(cd-s+=) *(CDR 6670)* – Bullet (live).

Sep 05. (cd/lp) *(333334-2/-1)* *<38392>* **ROAD TO ROUEN** [9] [ ]
– Tales of endurance parts 4, 5 & 6 / St. Petersburg / Sad girl / Roxy / Coffee in the pot / Road to Rouen / Kick in the teeth / Low C / Fin.

Oct 05. (7"red) *(R 6675)* **LOW C. / ROXY (live & acoustic from Ronnie Scott's)** [52] [–]
(cd-s) *(CDR 6675)* – ('A') / ('A'-live & acoustic from Oxford Playhouse).
(dvd-s) *(DVDR 6675)* – ('A') / Lady Day and John Coltrane (live & acoustic from Ronnie Scott's) / ('A'-video) / St. Petersburg (video).

Jan 06. (7") *(R 6682)* **FIN. / FIN (Radio 2 session)** [ ] [–]

– compilations, etc. –

Oct 02. (d-cd) *EMI Catalogue; (541103-2)* **SUPERGRASS / I SHOULD COCO** [ ] [–]

SUPERTRAMP

Formed: London, England ... 1969 by RICHARD DAVIES. Through the sponsorship of Dutch millionaire, Stanley Miesegaes, he enlisted RICHARD PALMER, BOB MILLER and co-writer, ROBERT HODGSON through a music paper ad. Signing to 'A&M', the band released a largely ignored and directionless eponymous debut in summer 1970, the record's poor critical and commercial reception engendering a personnel reshuffle; HODGSON switched to guitar, recruiting a new rhythm section of FRANK FARRELL and KEVIN CURRIE and adding sax player, DAVE WINTHROP. The resulting album, 'INDELIBLY STAMPED' (1971) was more notable for the tasteless cover shot (a heavily tattooed bust) than any of the music contained within and the group packed it in later that summer. While WINTHROP later joined SECRET AFFAIR, DAVIES and HODGSON resurrected SUPERTRAMP a couple of years later, enlisting the rhythm section of DOUGIE THOMSON and BOB C. BENBERG along with sax/clarinet player JOHN ANTHONY HELLIWELL. The musical chemistry finally clicked and 1974's 'CRIME OF THE CENTURY' album propelled SUPERTRAMP to major league prog-rock/pop status. Complex, insidious and intelligently crafted, the record married conceptually depressing lyrical fare to infectiously melodic hooklines with surprising results. The album itself made the Top 5 while 'DREAMER' was a Top 20 hit single. 'CRISIS? WHAT CRISIS?' (1975) and 'EVEN IN THE QUIETEST MOMENTS' (1977) utilised the same musicians and carried on in much the same vein, solidifying their growing cult fanbase (especially in the US) and even spawning a transatlantic hit single in the acoustic-based 'GIVE A LITTLE BIT'. Increasingly catering to the American AOR market, SUPERTRAMP finally broke through big style with the multi-million selling (US No.1) 'BREAKFAST IN AMERICA' (1979) and its attendant US hits. A living, breathing example of all that punk set out to destroy, this perhaps remains one of the album's charms; while the vocals may have erred towards limp posturing and the lyrics towards irrelevance, there was no denying the record's lasting pop appeal, especially the pompous yet evocative title track. '. . .FAMOUS LAST WORDS' (1982) was the next studio set, carrying on in much the same inoffensive vein without the saving grace of its predecessor's charm. HODGSON left soon after (subsequently recording two mid-80's solo albums, 'IN THE EYE OF THE STORM' and 'HAI HAI'), leaving SUPERTRAMP to complete a further two studio sets, 'BROTHER WHERE YOU BOUND' (1985) and 'FREE AS A BIRD' (1987) amid increasing disinterest. Although they finally folded after a 1988 live effort, they reformed a mere eight years later and recorded an album for 'Chrysalis', 'SOME THINGS NEVER CHANGE' (1997). Unfortunately for SUPERTRAMP, the music scene had changed irrevocably and the record barely scraped a Top 75 placing. To their credit, the HODGSON-less troupe tramped on into the new millennium with 'SLOW MOTION', for the most part failing to capture the exotic, indefinable allure of their best 70's work but nevertheless crafting a passable set of songs destined to placate fans who were still listening.

• **Songwriters:** HODGSON and/or DAVIE, except I'M YOUR HOOCHIE COOCHIE MAN (John Lee Hooker). • **Trivia:** They took their name from a 1910 W.H. Davies book, 'The Autobiography Of A Supertramp'.

Album rating: SUPERTRAMP (*4) / INDELIBLY STAMPED (*4) / CRIME OF THE CENTURY (*8) / CRISIS? WHAT CRISIS? (*6) / EVEN IN THE QUIETEST MOMENTS (*6) / BREAKFAST IN AMERICA (*7) / PARIS (*5) / . . .FAMOUS LAST WORDS (*6) / BROTHER WHERE YOU BOUND (*4) / THE AUTOBIOGRAPHY OF SUPERTRAMP compilation (*8) / FREE AS A BIRD (*4) / LIVE '88 (*4) / SOME THINGS NEVER CHANGE (*5) / SLOW MOTION (*4) / RETROSPECTACLE: THE SUPERTRAMP ANTHOLOGY double compil'n (*8)

RICHARD DAVIES (b.22 Jul'44) – vocals, keyboards (ex-The JOINT) / **ROGER HODGSON** (b.21 Mar'50) – bass, keyboards, vocals / **RICHARD PALMER** – guitar / **BOB MILLER** – drums

A&M A&M

Aug 70. (lp) *(AMLS 981)* **SUPERTRAMP** [ ] [–]
– Surely / It's a long road / Aubade / And I am not like other birds of prey / Words unspoken / Maybe I'm a beggar / Home again / Nothing to show / Shadow song / Try again / Surely (reprise). *<US-iss.Mar78; 4665> (re-iss. Mar82 lp/c; AMID/CMID 123) (re-iss. May84 on 'Hallmark' lp/c; SHM/HSC 3139) (cd-iss. 1988; CDA 3129) (re-iss. c Jan93)*

— (May'71) **HODGSON** now also lead guitar, vox / **FRANK FARRELL** – bass / **KEVIN CURRIE** – drums repl. PALMER + MILLER / added **DAVE WINTHROP** (b.27 Nov'48, New Jersey) – saxophone

Jun 71. (lp/c) *(AMLS 64306)* **INDELIBLY STAMPED** [ ] [ ]
– Your poppa don't mind / Travelled / Rosie had everything planned / Remember / Forever / Potter / Coming home to see you / Times have changed / Friend in need / Aries. *(cd-iss. 1988; CDA 3149) (re-iss. c Jan93) (cd re-iss. Feb98; 393129-2)*

Oct 71. (7") *<1305>* **FOREVER. / YOUR POPPA DON'T MIND** [–] [ ]

— Disbanded late Summer 1971, WINTHROP later joined SECRET AFFAIR. **DAVIES + HODGSON** re-formed them Aug'73. Recruited **DOUGIE THOMSON** (b.24 Mar'51, Glasgow, Scotland) – bass (ex-ALAN BOWN SET) / **BOB C. BENBERG** (b. SIEBENBERG) – drums (ex-BEES MAKE HONEY) / **JOHN ANTHONY HELLIWELL** (b.15 Feb'45, Todmorden, England) – saxophone, clarinet, vocals (ex-ALAN BOWN SET)

Mar 74. (7") *(AMS 7101)* **LAND HO. / SUMMER ROMANCE** [ ] [–]

Sep 74. (lp/c) *(AMLS/CAM 68258) <3647>* **CRIME OF THE CENTURY** [4] [38]
– School / Bloody well right / Hide in your shell / Asylum / Dreamer / Rudy / If everyone was listening / Crime of the century. *(cd-iss. Apr86; CDA 68258) (cd re-iss. May97; 393647-2) (cd re-mast.Sep03; 493346-2)*

Dec 74. (7") *(AMS 7152) <1660>* **DREAMER. / BLOODY WELL RIGHT** [13] Mar75 [35]

— <above B-side was US A-side>

Nov 75. (lp/c) *(AMLH/CAM 68347) <4560>* **CRISIS? WHAT CRISIS?** [20] [44]
– Easy does it / Sister Moonshine / Ain't nobody but me / A soapbox opera / Another man's woman / Lady / Poor boy / Just a normal day / The meaning / Two of us. *(cd-iss. Apr86; CDA 4560) (cd re-iss. May97; 394560-2) (cd re-mast.Sep03; 493347-2)*

Nov 75. (7") *(AMS 7201) <1793>* **LADY. / YOU STARTED LAUGHING (WHEN I HELD YOU IN MY ARMS)** [ ] [ ]

Jun 76. (7") *<1814>* **SISTER MOONSHINE. / AIN'T NOBODY BUT ME** [–] [ ]

Apr 77. (lp/c) *(AMLK/CAM 64634) <4634>* **EVEN IN THE QUIETEST MOMENTS** [12] [16]
– Give a little bit / Lover boy / Even in the quietest moments / Downstream / Babaji / From now on / Fool's overture. *(cd-iss. Apr86; CDA 4634) (cd re-iss. May97; 394634-2) (cd re-mast.Sep03; 493348-2)*

Jun 77. (7") *(AMS 7293) <1938>* **GIVE A LITTLE BIT. / DOWNSTREAM** [29] [15]

Nov 77. (7") *<1981>* **FROM NOW ON. / DREAMER** [–] [ ]

Nov 77. (7") *(AMS 7326)* **BABAJI. / FROM NOW ON** [ ] [–]

Mar 79. (lp/c) *(AMLK/CAM 63708) <3708>* **BREAKFAST IN AMERICA** [3] [1]
– Gone Hollywood / The logical song / Goodbye stranger / Breakfast in America / Oh darling / Take the long way home / Lord is it mine / Just another nervous wreck / Casual conversations / Child of vision. *(cd-iss. 1983; CDA 63708) (cd re-iss. May97; 393708-2) (lp re-iss. Mar00 on 'Simply Vinyl'; SVLP 184) (cd re-mast.Sep03; 493349-2)*

Mar 79. (7") *(AMS 7427) <2128>* **THE LOGICAL SONG. / JUST ANOTHER NERVOUS WRECK** [7] [6]

Jun 79. (7") *(AMS 7451)* **BREAKFAST IN AMERICA. / GONE HOLLYWOOD** [9] [–]

Sep 79. (7") *(AMS 7481) <2162>* **GOODBYE STRANGER. / EVEN IN THE QUIETEST MOMENTS** [57] Jul79 [15]

Oct 79. (7") *(AMS 7560)* **TAKE THE LONG WAY HOME. / FROM NOW ON** [ ] [–]

Oct 79. (7") *<2193>* **TAKE THE LONG WAY HOME. / RUBY** [–] [10]

Sep 80. (d-lp/d-c) *(AMLM/CLM 66702) <6702>* **PARIS (live 29-11-79)** [7] [8]
– School / Ain't nobody but me / The logical song / Bloody well right / Breakfast in America / You started laughing / Hide in your shell / From now on / Dreamer / Rudy / A soapbox opera / Asylum / Take the long way home / Fool's overture / Two of us / Crime of the century. *(cd-iss. Apr86; CDD 6702) (cd re-iss. May97; 396702-2) (d-cd re-mast.Sep03; 493350-2)*

Sep 80. (7") *<2269>* **DREAMER (live). / FROM NOW ON (live)** [–] [15]

Nov 80. (7") *(AMS 7576)* **DREAMER (live). / YOU STARTED LAUGHING (live)** [ ] [–]

Nov 80. (7") *<2292>* **BREAKFAST IN AMERICA (live). / YOU STARTED LAUGHING (live)** [–] [62]

Oct 82. (7") *(AMS 8255) <2502>* **IT'S RAINING AGAIN. / BONNIE** [26] [11]

Oct 82. (lp/c) *(AMLK/CKM 63732) <3732>* **. . . FAMOUS LAST WORDS** [6] [5]
– Crazy / Put on your brown school shoes / It's raing again / Bonnie / Know who you are / My kind of lady / C'est la bon / Waiting so long / Don't leave me now. *(cd-iss. 1983; CDA 63732) (cd re-mast.Sep03; 493353-2)*

Jan 83. (7") *(AMS 8301) <2517>* **MY KIND OF LADY. / KNOW WHO YOU ARE** [ ] [31]

— (Nov82) Now a quartet when HODGSON departed to go solo. (Re-joined briefly late'86 tour). HODGSON solo albums: IN THE EYE OF THE STORM ('84) / HAI HAI ('87).

Apr 85. (7") *(AMS 248) <2731>* **CANNONBALL. / EVER OPEN DOOR** [ ] [28]

May 85. (lp/c/cd) *(<AMA/AMC/CDA 5014>)* **BROTHER WHERE YOU BOUND** [20] [21]
– Cannonball / Still in love / No inbetween / Better days / Brother where you bound / Ever open door. *(re-iss. Jan93) (cd re-mast.Sep03; 493354-2)*

Jul 85. (7") *(AMS 265) <2720>* **STILL IN LOVE. / NO INBETWEEN** [ ] Feb85 [ ]
(12"+=) *(AMY 265)* – Cannonball (dance mix).

Sep 85. (7") *<2760>* **BETTER DAYS. / NO INBETWEEN** [–] [ ]

Nov 86. (lp/c/cd) *(TRAMP/TRAMC/TRACD 1)* **THE AUTOBIOGRAPHY OF SUPERTRAMP** (compilation) [9] [–]
– Goodbye stranger / The logical song / Bloody well right / Breakfast in America / Take the long way home / Crime of the century / Dreamer / From now on / Give a little bit / It's raining again / Cannonball / Ain't nobody but me / Hide in your shell / Rudy. *(cd= 3 extra) (re-iss. cd Jan93 as 'THE VERY BEST OF SUPERTRAMP'+=)*– School.

Oct 87. (7"/12") *(AM/+Y 415) <2985>* **I'M BEGGIN' YOU. / NO INBETWEENS** [ ] [ ]

Oct 87. (lp/c/cd) *(<AMA/AMC/CDA 5181>)* **FREE AS A BIRD** [93] [ ]
– It's alright / Not the moment / It doesn't matter / Where I stand / Free as a bird / I'm beggin' you / You never can tell with friends / Thing for you / An awful thing to waste. *(cd re-mast.Sep03; 493355-2)*

Feb 88. (7") *<2996>* **FREE AS A BIRD. / THING FOR YOU** [–] [ ]

Feb 88. (7") *(AM 430)* **FREE AS A BIRD. / I'M BEGGIN' YOU** [ ] [–]

Oct 88. (lp/c/cd) *(<MA/AMC/CDA 3923>)* **LIVE '88** (live) [ ] [ ]
– You started laughing / It's alright / Not the moment / Oh darling / Breakfast in America / From now on / Just another nervous wreck / The logical song / I'm your hoochie coochie man / Crime of the century / Don't you lie to me. *(re-iss. cd Jan93)*

—— Folded after above, although they reformed 8 years later. Line-up:- **RICK DAVIES** – vocals, keyboards / **MARK HART** – vocals, keyboards, guitars / **JOHN HELLIWELL** – saxophones, woodwind / **CLIFF HUGO** – bass / **BOB SIEBENBERG** – drums / **LEE R. THORNBURG** – trumpet, trombone, vocals / **CARL VERHEYEN** – guitars / **TOM WALSH** – percussion

Chrysalis Oxygen

Apr 97. (cd/c) *(CD/TC CHR 6121) <9000-2>* **SOME THINGS NEVER CHANGE** [74] Jun97 [ ]
– It's a hard world / You win, I lose / Get your act together / Live to love you / Some things never change / Listen to me please / Sooner or later / Help me down that road / And the light / Give me a chance / C'est what? / Where there's a will.

—— **JESSE SIEBENBERG** – percussion; repl. WALSH

E.M.I. E.M.I.

Mar 02. (cd) *(<538624-2>)* **SLOW MOTION** [ ] Apr02 [ ]
– Slow motion / Little by little / Broken hearted / Over you / Tenth Avenue breakdown / A sting in the tail / Bee in your bonnet / Goldrush / Dead man's blues.

– compilations, etc. –

on 'A&M' unless mentioned otherwise

May 81. (d-c) *(CAMCR 7)* **CRISIS? WHAT CRISIS? / EVEN IN THE QUIETEST MOMENTS** [ ] [–]

Sep 85. (7") *Old Gold; (OG 9542)* **DREAMER. / GIVE A LITTLE BIT** [ ] [–]

Sep 86. (7") *(AM 357)* **THE LOGICAL SONG. / GOODBYE STRANGER** [ ] [–]

Aug 88. (cd-ep) *(AMCD 914)* **COMPACT HITS** [ ] [–]
– The logical song / Breakfast in America / Goodbye stranger / Hide in your shell.

Jul 92. (7"/c-s) *(AM/+C 0007)* **GIVE A LITTLE BIT (for Telethon). / ('A'-live)** [ ] [–]
(cd-s+=) *(AMCD 0007)* – Breakfast in America.

Aug 92. (cd/c) *(TRA CD/MC 1992)* **THE VERY BEST OF SUPERTRAMP** [24] [ ]
– Schhol / Goodbye stranger / The logical song / Bloody well right / Breakfast in America / Rudy / Take the long way home / Crime of the century / Dreamer / Ain't nobody but me / Hide in your shell / From now on / It's raining again / Give a little bit / Cannonball.

Apr 94. (cd) *Compact Club; (CCV 8919)* **THE SUPERTRAMP SONGBOOK** [ ] [–]

Sep 97. (re-cd) *(as prev.)* **THE VERY BEST OF SUPERTRAMP** [8] [–]

Apr 99. (cd) *E.M.I.; (<499390-2>)* **IT WAS THE BEST OF TIMES** [ ] [ ]

Mar 02. (d-lp) *Fruit Tree; (FT 816)* **IS EVERYBODY LISTENING** (live in Cleveland, Ohio 1976) [ ] [–]

Aug 03. (cd) *King Biscuit; (KBCCD 128)* **IN CONCERT** (live) [ ] [ ]

Oct 05. (d-cd) *(9886928) <0005490-2>* **RETROSPECTACLE: THE SUPERTRAMP ANTHOLOGY** [9] [ ]
– Surely (edit) / Your poppa don't mind / Land ho / Summer romance / School / Bloody well right / Dreamer / Rudy / Crime of the century / Sister moonshine / Ain't nobody but me / Lady / Two of us / Give a little bit / Downstream / Even in the quietest moments / From now on / Gone Hollywood / The logical song / Goodbye stranger / Breakfast in America / Oh darling / Take the long way home / You started laughing (live) / It's raining again / My kind of lady / Don't leave me now / Cannonball / Free as a bird / You win, I lose / Another man's woman (live) / Over you. [–]

Apr 06. (cd) *EMI Gold; (359044-2)* **LIVE** (live) [ ] [–]

SWEET

Formed: London, England ... early 1968 as SWEETSHOP, by BRIAN CONNOLLY and MICK TUCKER (former members of Harrow bubblegum-pop band, WAINWRIGHT'S GENTLEMEN). Completing the line-up with STEVE PRIEST and FRANK TORPY, SWEET released a one-off 45 for 'Fontana', 'SLOW MOTION', before MICK STEWART replaced TORPY. A further three throwaway pop singles (on 'Parlophone') followed with little interest, prior to the band finding a more steady guitarist in ANDY SCOTT and hooking up with the now famous hitmaking/songwriting team of (NICKY) CHINN and (MIKE) CHAPMAN through producer PHIL WAINMAN. Signing to 'R.C.A.', SWEET emerged from their sticky patch with a handful of chartbustin' pure pop nuggets between 1971/72, including 'FUNNY FUNNY', 'CO-CO', 'POPPA JOE', 'LITTLE WILLY' (also a Top 3 Stateside success!) and 'WIG WAM BAM'. One of the pivotal bands of the glam-pop era, SWEET, as with their music, took sugary fashion excess to gender-bending new limits. Early in '73, they followed in the high-heeled footstompin' steps of GARY GLITTER, SLADE, etc, by adopting a slightly harder-edged anthemic approach for the chart-topping 'BLOCKBUSTER'. They repeated this winning formula over the next twelve months, three more singles, 'HELLRAISER', 'BALLROOM BLITZ' and 'TEENAGE RAMPAGE' enjoying a tantalisingly close shave with the No.1 spot. Surprisingly banned from many British ballrooms/concert halls, SWEET subsequently toning down their OTT effeminate image for a more mature "harder" look. The resulting album, 'SWEET FANNY ADAMS' hit the UK Top 30, although no tracks were issued as singles. However, they did score a Top 10 hit later that year with 'THE SIX TEENS' (they also suffered their first flop in some years, 'TURN IT DOWN'), both songs taken from another Top 30 album, 'DESOLATION BOULEVARD'. Early in '75, now without CHINN and CHAPMAN, they particially resurrected their flagging public profile with the self-penned 'FOX ON THE RUN', the single hitting No.2 (and later in the year No.5 in America, 'BALLROOM BLITZ' having achieved a similar feat a few months previous). Alienated from most of their former teenbop fans, SWEET's career began to turn sour, that is, until 'LOVE IS LIKE OXYGEN' breathed some fresh air into their newfound AOR/hard-rock sound, the single a Top 10 transatlantic smash. The internal tensions that had simmered through SWEET's career finally boiled over in 1979, CONNOLLY (younger brother of actor, MARK 'Taggart' McMANUS) striking out on a solo career, while the remaining members recruited GARY MOBERLEY for a handful of forgettable albums, including the aptly-titled 'IDENTITY CRISIS'. The 80's were characterised by countless reformations, tussles over the group name, etc, SWEET effectively finished as a chart commodity and opting instead to trawl the cabaret circuit while SCOTT released a few records under the ANDY SCOTT'S SWEET moniker. Meanwhile, CONNOLLY's health was in terminal decline, any SWEET fans witnessing the TV documentary no doubt shocked by his ravaged appearance. Sadly, CONNOLLY died of heart failure on the 10th of February '97 (he'd previously survived a number of heart attacks) shortly after the programme was made.

Best CD compilation: BALLROOM BLITZ – THE VERY BEST OF SWEET (*8)

BRIAN CONNOLLY (b. BRIAN McMANUS, 5 Oct'49, Hamilton, Scotland) – vocals (ex-WAINWRIGHT'S GENTLEMEN) / **STEVE PRIEST** (b.23

Feb'50, Hayes, Middlesex, England) – bass / **MICK TUCKER** (b.17 Jul'49, Harlesden, London) – drums, vocals (ex-WAINWRIGHT'S GENTLEMEN) / **FRANK TORPY** – guitar

Fontana | not iss.

Jul 68. (7") *(TF 958)* **SLOW MOTION. / IT'S LONELY OUT THERE** [ ] [–]

— **MICK STEWART** – guitar repl. FRANK

Parlophone | not iss.

Sep 69. (7") *(R 5803)* **LOLLIPOP MAN. / TIME** [ ] [–]

Jan 70. (7") *(R 5826)* **ALL YOU'LL EVER GET FROM ME. / THE JUICER** [ ] [–]
(re-iss. May71 flipped over; R 5902)

Jun 70. (7") *(R 5848)* **GET ON THE LINE. / MR. McGALLAGHER** [ ] [–]

— **ANDY SCOTT** (b.30 Jun'51, Wrexham, Wales) – guitar (ex-ELASTIC BAND) repl. STEWART. (employed session people in 71-72)

R.C.A. | Bell

Mar 71. (7") *(RCA 2051)* **FUNNY FUNNY. / YOU'RE NOT WRONG FOR LOVING ME** [13] [ ]

Jun 71. (7") *(RCA 2087)* **CO-CO. / DONE ME WRONG ALRIGHT** [2] [–]

Jul 71. (7") *<45126>* **CO-CO. / YOU'RE NOT WRONG FOR LOVING ME** [–] [99]

Oct 71. (7") *(RCA 2121)* **ALEXANDER GRAHAM BELL. / SPOTLIGHT** [33] [–]

Nov 71. (lp) *(SF 8288)* **FUNNY HOW SWEET CO-CO CAN BE** [ ] [–]
– Co-Co / Chop chop / Reflections / Honeysuckle love / Santa Monica sunshine / Daydream / Funny funny / Tom Tom turnaround / Jeanie / Sunny sleeps late / Spotlight / Done me wrong all right.

Jan 72. (7") *(RCA 2164)* **POPPA JOE. / JEANIE** [11] [–]

Jun 72. (7") *(RCA 2225) <45251>* **LITTLE WILLY. / MAN FROM MECCA** [4] Jan73 [3]

Sep 72. (7") *(RCA 2260)* **WIG-WAM BAM. / NEW YORK CONNECTION** [4] Dec73 [ ]

Dec 72. (lp) *(SF 8316)* **SWEET'S BIGGEST HITS** (compilation) [ ] [–]
– Wig-wam bam / Little Willy / Done me wrong alright / Poppa Joe / Funny funny / Co-Co / Alexander Graham Bell / Chop chop / You're not wrong for loving me / Jeanie / Spotlight / Tom Tom turnaround.

Jan 73. (7") *(RCA 2305) <45361>* **BLOCKBUSTER. / NEED A LOT OF LOVIN'** [1] Jun73 [73]

Apr 73. (7") *(RCA 2357)* **HELL RAISER. / BURNING** [2] [ ]

Jul 73. (lp) *<1125>* **THE SWEET** [–] [ ]
– Little Willy / New York connection / Wig-wam bam / Done me wrong alright / Hell raiser / Blockbuster / Need a lot of lovin' / Man from Mecca / Spotlight / You're not wrong for loving me. *<re-iss. 1976 on 'Kory'; KK 3009>*

R.C.A. | Capitol

Sep 73. (7") *(RCA 2403)* **BALLROOM BLITZ. / ROCK'N'ROLL DISGRACE** [2] [–]

Jan 74. (7") *(LPBO 5004)* **TEENAGE RAMPAGE. / OWN UP, TAKE A LOOK AT YOURSELF** [2] [ ]

Apr 74. (lp) *(LPLI 5039)* **SWEET FANNY ADAMS** [27] [–]
– Set me free / Heartbreak today / No you don't / Rebel rouser / Peppermint twist / Sweet F.A. / Restless / Into the night / AC-DC.

Jul 74. (7") *(LPBO 5037)* **THE SIX TEENS. / BURN ON THE FLAME** [9] [ ]

Nov 74. (7") *(RCA 2480)* **TURN IT DOWN. / SOMEONE ELSE WILL** [41] [ ]

Nov 74. (lp) *(LPLI 5080) <11395>* **DESOLATION BOULEVARD** [ ] Jul75 [25]
– The six teens / Solid gold brass / Turn it down / Medusa / Lady Starlight / Man with the golden arm / Fox on the run / Breakdown / My generation. *<US – version incl. tracks from 'SWEET FANNY ADAMS'> (re-iss. Feb90 on 'Castle' cd/lp; CLA CD/LP 170)*

Mar 75. (7") *(RCA 2524)* **FOX ON THE RUN. / MISS DEMEANOR** [2] [–]

Jun 75. (7") *<4055>* **BALLROOM BLITZ. / RESTLESS** [–] [5]

Jul 75. (7") *(RCA 2578)* **ACTION. / SWEET F.A.** [15] [–]

Nov 75. (d-lp) *(SPC 0001)* **STRUNG UP** (live rec. Dec'73 + hits, etc.) [ ] [–]
– Hell raiser / Burning / Someone else will / Rock'n'roll disgrace / Need a lot of lovin' / Done me wrong alright / You're not wrong for loving me / The man with the golden arm / Action / Fox on the run / Set me free / Miss Deameanour / Ballroom blitz / Burn on the flame / Solid gold brass / The six teens / I wanna be committed / Blockbuster.

Nov 75. (7") *<4157>* **FOX ON THE RUN. / BURN ON THE FLAME** [–] [5]

Jan 76. (7") *(RCA 2641)* **THE LIES IN YOUR EYES. / COCKROACH** [35] [ ]

Feb 76. (7") *<4220>* **ACTION. / MEDUSA** [–] [20]

Mar 76. (lp) *(RS 1036) <11496>* **GIVE US A WINK** [ ] [27]
– The lies in your eyes / Cockroach / Keep it in / 4th of July / Action / Yesterday's rain / White mice / Healer. *(re-iss. Aug91 on 'Repertoire' cd+=)(pic-lp; REP4084WZ)(REP 2084)* – Fox on the run / Lady Starlight / Sweet Fanny Adams / Miss Demeaner.

Oct 76. (7") *(RCA 2748)* **LOST ANGELS. / FUNK IT UP** [ ] [ ]

Feb 77. (7") *(PB 5001)* **FEVER OF LOVE. / DISTINCT LACK OF ANCIENT** [ ] [–]

Mar 77. (lp/c) *(PL/PK 25072) <11636>* **OFF THE RECORD** [ ] [ ]
– Fever of love / Lost angels / Midnight to daylight / Windy city / Live for today / She gimme lovin' / Laura Lee / Hard times / Funk it up (David's song). *(pic-cd.Aug91 on 'Repertoire'+=; REP4085WZ)* – Distinct lack of ancient / Stairway to the stars / Why don't you do it to me.

Mar 77. (7") *<4429>* **FEVER OF LOVE. / HEARTBREAK TODAY** [–] [ ]

Jul 77. (7",12") *<4454>* **FUNK IT UP (DAVID'S SONG). / ('A'disco mix)** [–] [88]

Aug 77. (7") *(PB 5046)* **STAIRWAY TO THE STARS. / WHY DON'T YOU DO IT TO ME** [ ] [–]

Oct 77. (lp/c) *(PL/PK 25111)* **SWEET'S GOLDEN GREATS** (compilation) [ ] [–]
– Blockbuster / Hell raiser / Ballroom blitz / Teenage rampage / The six teens / Turn it down / Fox on the run / Action / Lost angels / The lies in your eyes / Fever of love / Stairway to the stars.

Polydor | Capitol

Jan 78. (7") *(POSP 1) <4549>* **LOVE IS LIKE OXYGEN. / COVER GIRL** [9] Feb78 [8]

Jan 78. (lp/c) *(POLD/+C 5001) <11744>* **LEVEL HEADED** [ ] [52]
– Dream on / Love is like oxygen / California nights / Strong love / Fountain / Anthem No.1 / Silverbird / Lettres d'amour / Anthem No.2 / Air on "A" tape loop. *(cd-iss. Aug91 on 'Repertoire'+=; REP 4234WP)* – Love is like oxygen (single) / Cover girl / California nights (single) / Show the way.

Jul 78. (7") *<4610>* **CALIFORNIA NIGHTS. / DREAM ON** [–] [76]

— **GARY MOBERLEY** – keyboards repl. CONNOLLY who went solo & later formed The NEW SWEET. (ANDY SCOTT was now on lead vocals)

Mar 79. (7") *(POSP 36)* **CALL ME. / WHY DON'T YOU** [ ] [–]

Apr 79. (7") *<4730>* **MOTHER EARTH. / WHY DON'T YOU** [–] [ ]

Aug 79. (7") *(POSP 73)* **BIG APPLE WALTZ. / WHY DON'T YOU** [ ] [–]

Oct 79. (lp/c) *(POLD/+C 5022) <11929>* **CUT ABOVE THE REST** [ ] Apr79 [ ]
– Call me / Play all night / Big Apple waltz / Dorian Gray / Discophony / Eye games / Mother Earth / Hold me / Stay with me.

Apr 80. (7") *(POSP 131)* **GIVE THE LADY SOME RESPECT. / TALL GIRLS** [ ] [–]

Apr 80. (lp/c) *(POLS/+C 1021) <12106>* **WATER'S EDGE** (US-title 'SWEET IV') [ ] [ ]
– Sixties man / Getting in the mood for love / Tell the truth / Own up / Too much talking / Thank you for loving me / At midnight / Water's edge / Hot shot gambler / Give the lady some respect.

Sep 80. (7") *(POSP 160)* **THE SIXTIES MAN. / OH YEAH** [ ] [–]

Sep 80. (7") *<4908>* **THE SIXTIES MAN. / WATER'S EDGE** [–] [ ]

— **MICK STEWART** – guitar returned to guest on next album.

Nov 82. (lp) *(2311 179)* **IDENTITY CRISIS** [ ] [–]
– Identity crisis / New shoes / Two into one / Love is the cure / It makes me wonder / Hey mama / Falling in love / I wish you would / Strange girl.

— They had already split Spring 1981, with PRIEST going to the States and SCOTT going into production for heavy metal bands like IRON MAIDEN. He also went solo (see further below). The SWEET re-formed in the mid-80's, with SCOTT, TUCKER plus **PAUL MARIO DAY** – vocals (ex-WILD FIRE) / **PHIL LANZON** – keyboards (ex-GRAND PRIX) / **MAL McNULTY** – bass repl. PRIEST

— CONNOLLY died of heart failure in 1997

– compilations, etc. –

Dec 70. (lp; one-side by The PIPKINS) *Music For Pleasure; (MFP 5248)* **GIMME DAT THING** [ ] [–]
Jul 78. (lp) *Camden-RCA; (CDS 1168)* **THE SWEET** [ ] [–]
Jun 80. (7"ep) *R.C.A.; (PE 5226)* **FOX ON THE RUN / HELLRAISER. / BLOCKBUSTER / BALLROOM BLITZ** [ ] [–]
Aug 81. (7") *RCA Gold; (524)* **BLOCKBUSTER. / HELLRAISER** [ ] [–]
May 82. (7") *RCA Gold; (551)* **BALLROOM BLITZ. / WIG-WAM BAM** [ ] [–]
Aug 84. (pic-lp/lp) *Anagram; (P+/GRAM 16)* **SWEET 16 – IT'S . . . IT'S . . . SWEET'S HITS** [49] [–]
Sep 84. (7") *Anagram; (ANA 27)* **THE SIX TEENS. / ACTION** [ ] [–]
(12"+=) *(12ANA 27)* – Teenage rampage.
Dec 84. (7"/12") *Anagram; (ANA/12ANA 28)* **IT'S . . . IT'S . . . THE SWEET MIX (Medley; Blockbuster – Fox on the run – Teenage rampage – Hell raiser – Ballroom blitz). / FOX ON THE RUN** [45] [–]
May 85. (7"/12") *Anagram; (ANA/12ANA 29)* **SWEET 2TH – THE WIG-WAM WILLY MIX. / THE TEEN ACTION MIX** [ ] [–]
Apr 87. (7") *Old Gold; (OG 9707)* **BLOCKBUSTER. / LITTLE WILLY** [ ] [–]
Apr 87. (7") *Old Gold; (OG 9709)* **FOX ON THE RUN. / BALLROOM BLITZ** [ ] [–]
Jul 87. (cd/lp) *Zebra; (CDM+/ZEB 11)* **HARD CENTRES – THE ROCK YEARS** [ ] [–]
(re-iss. cd Oct95; CDMZEB 11)
Jan 88. (7") *Old Gold; (OG 9760)* **WIG-WAM BAM. / CO-CO** [ ] [–]
Jan 88. (7") *Old Gold; (OG 9762)* **TEENAGE RAMPAGE. / HELLRAISER** [ ] [–]
Nov 89. (7") *R.C.A.; (PB 43337)* **WIG-WAM BAM. / LITTLE WILLY** [ ] [–]
Dec 89. (lp/c/cd) *R.C.A.; (NL/NK/ND 74313)* **BLOCKBUSTERS** [ ] [–]
– Ballroom blitz / Hell raiser / New York connection / Little Willy / Burning / Need a lot of lovin' / Wig-wam bam / Blockbuster / Rock'n'roll disgrace / Chop chop / Alexander Graham Bell / Poppa Joe / Co-Co / Funny funny.
Dec 89. (d-lp/c/cd) *Castle; (CCS LP/MC/CD 230)* **SWEET COLLECTION** [ ] [–]
Jul 92. (cd-ep) *Old Gold; (OG 6174)* **WIG-WAM BAM / CO-CO / LITTLE WILLY** [ ] [–]
Feb 93. (cd) *Receiver; (RRCD 169)* **ROCKIN' THE RAINBOW** [ ] [–]
Feb 93. Receiver; (cd) *(RRCD 171)* **LAND OF HOPE AND GLORY** [ ] [–]
Jul 93. (cd) *Repertoire; (REP 4140WZ)* **FIRST RECORDINGS 1968-1971** [ ] [–]
Dec 93. (cd) *Receiver; (RRCD 175)* **LIVE FOR TODAY** [ ] [–]
Jul 94. (cd) *Receiver; (RRCD 189)* **BREAKDOWN – THE SWEET LIVE (live)** [ ] [–]
Nov 94. (cd) *Start;* **IN CONCERT** [ ] [–]
Apr 95. (cd) *Receiver; (RRCD 198)* **SET ME FREE** [ ] [–]
Jul 95. (cd) *Aim; (AIM 1041)* **GREATEST HITS LIVE** [ ] [–]
Jan 96. (cd/c) *Polygram; (<535001-2/-4>)* **BALLROOM HITZ – THE VERY BEST OF SWEET** [15] [ ]
Jan 96. (cd) *Happy Price; (HP 9346-2)* **IN CONCERT** [ ] [–]
Jan 96. (cd) *Music De-Luxe; (MDCD 013)* **BLOCKBUSTER (live on stage)** [ ] [–]
Aug 96. (cd) *KFG; (CDEC 5)* **HITZ, BLITZ, GLITZ** [ ] [–]
Jan 05. (cd) *B.M.G.; (82876 66817-2)* **THE VERY BEST OF SWEET** [72] [–]

☐ SWEET 75 (see under ⇒ NIRVANA)

☐ David SYLVIAN (see under ⇒ JAPAN)

SYSTEM OF A DOWN

Formed: Los Angeles, California, USA . . . late '94 by expatriot Armenians, SERJ TANKIAN (looks like JELLO BIAFRA with a MICHAEL BOLTON hairdo), DARON MALAKIAN and SHAVO ODADJIAN, the trio almost immediately adding JOHN DOLMAYAN. Produced by RICK RUBIN, their '98 eponymous debut revealed them to be anthemic and politically emotional noise-merchants in the mould of COAL CHAMBER or FAITH NO MORE, stretching punk-metal into jazzy Armenian folk. Largely overlooked until the release of the single 'CHOP SUEY', SYSTEM OF A DOWN's album 'TOXICITY' (2001) smashed the barriers of modern rock, vocalist TANKIAN's scattering lyrics torn between religious connotation and just sheer madness. The group differed from the normal Nu-metal fare; some of the guitar playing was not dissimilar to MOGWAI's more sonic releases, whereas the songs blasted the barriers of popular rock, even interesting the slightly more mellow ARTHUR BAKER into including the group on a recent collection. SYSTEM OF A DOWN proved conclusively they were operating way beyond the confines of anything as restrictive as nu-metal with 'STEAL THIS ALBUM!' (2002), ostensibly an odds'n'sods collection which actually held together better than most of their contemporaries' regular albums; they were also in the process of a three-year hiatus. May 2005, saw the first slice of an ambitious, conceptual two-part package, 'MEZMERIZE', an incredible comeback of sorts that went straight to No.1. Six months later, the formula was repeated both commercially and critically with part two, 'HYPNOTIZE' – SYSTEM OF A DOWN were now America's biggest metal group with a Hard Rock Grammy further proof if we needed it.

Album rating: SYSTEM OF A DOWN (*8) / TOXICITY (*8) / STEAL THIS ALBUM! collection (*4) / MEZMERIZE (*8) / HYPNOTIZE (*8)

SERJ TANKIAN (b.21 Aug'67, Beirut, Lebanon) – vocals, keyboards, guitar / **DARON MALAKIAN** (b.18 Jul'75, Hollywood, Calif.) – guitar, vocals / **SHAVO ODADJIAN** (b. SHAVARSH, 22 Apr'74, Yerevan, Armenia) – bass / **JOHN DOLMAYAN** (b.15 Jul'73, Lebanon) – drums

American – Columbia / American Sony

Oct 98. (cd) *(491209-2) <68924>* **SYSTEM OF A DOWN** [ ] Sep98 [ ]
– Suite-pee / Know / Sugar / Suggestions / Spiders / Ddevil / Soil / War? / Mind / Peephole / CUBErt / Darts / P.L.U.C.K. *(re-iss. Aug01 & Apr06; 491209-5)*
May 99. (7") *(667478-7)* **SUGAR. / WAR? (live)** [ ] May98 [ ]
(cd-s+=) *(667478-2)* – Sugar (live) / Suite-pee (live).
Aug 01. (cd/lp) *(501534-2/-1) <62240>* **TOXICITY** [13] [1]
– Prison song / Needles / Deer dance / Jet pilot / X / Chop suey! / Bounce / Forest / Atwa / Science / Shimmy / Toxicity / Psycho / Aerials. *(bonus track +=)* – Arto. *(d-cd-iss. Jul02 +=; 508383-2)* – Toxicity (video) / Chop suey (live video) / Prison song (live) / Bounce (live).
Oct 01. (7"clear) *(672034-7) <radio>* **CHOP SUEY! / JOHNNY** [17] Dec01 [76]
(cd-s+=) *(672034-2)* – Know (live).
(cd-s) *(672034-5)* – ('A') / Sugar (live) / War (live) / ('A'-video).
Mar 02. (7"red) *(672502-7) <radio>* **TOXICITY. / STORAGED** [25] [70]
(cd-s) *(672502-2)* – ('A') / X (live) / Suggestions (live) / ('A'-video).
(cd-s) *(672502-5)* – ('A') / Marmalade / Metro (explicit).
Jul 02. (7") *(672869-7) <radio>* **AERIALS. / SNOWBLIND** [34] [55]
(cd-s+=) *(672869-5)* – Streamline / Sugar (live).
(cd-s) *(672869-2)* – ('A') / Toxicity (live) / P.L.U.C.K. (live) / ('A'-video).
Nov 02. (d-cd) *(510248-2) <87062>* **STEAL THIS ALBUM!** (demos, etc.) [56] [15]
– Chic 'n' Stu / Innervision / Bubbles / Boom! / Nuguns / A.D.D. / Mr. Jack / I-E-A-I-A-I-O / 36 / Pictures / Highway song / Fuck the system / Ego brain / Thetawaves / Roulette / Streamline.
May 05. (cd-s) *<675685-2>* **B.Y.O.B. / CIGARO** [–] [27]
May 05. (cd/pic-lp) *(519000-2/-1) <90648>* **MEZMERIZE** [2] [1]
– Soldier side (intro) / B.Y.O.B. / Revenga / Cigaro / Radio – Video / This cocaine makes me feel like I'm on this song / Violent pornography / Question! / Sad statue / Old school Hollywood / Lost in Hollywood.
Sep 05. (cd-s) *(676056-1)* **QUESTION! / SUGAR (live)** [41] [–]
(cd-s) *(676056-2)* – ('A') / Forest (live) / Prison song (live) / ('A'-live video).
Nov 05. (7") *(82876 74187-7)* **HYPNOTIZE. / FOREST (live from the Hurricane Festival)** [48] [57]
(cd-s) *(82876 74129-2)* – ('A') / Science (live from the Hurricane Festival).
(cd-s) *<(82876 74130-2)>* – ('A') / Mr. Jack (live from the Hurricane Festival) / War? (live from the Hurricane Festival).
Nov 05. (cd/pic-lp) *(82876 72611-2/-1) <93871>* **HYPNOTIZE** [11] [1]
– Attack / Dreaming / Kill rock 'n roll / Hypnotize / Stealing society / Tentative / U-fig / Holy mountains / Vicinity of obscenity / She's like heroin / Lonely day / Soldier side.

TAKING BACK SUNDAY

Formed: Amityville, New York, USA ... late 1999 by vocalist ANTONIO LONGO, JOHN NOLAN, EDDIE REYES, SHAUN COOPER and drummer STEVIE D. A series of self-financed demo EPs identified TBS as exactly the kind of emo-centric group 'Victory' records were willing to take a chance on. 'TELL ALL YOUR FRIENDS' (2002), announced the quintet as they arrived on the post-millennium hardcore/punk scene, an album recorded with new frontman ADAM LAZZARA and sticksman MARK O'CONNELL. A Mk.III line-up materialized in 2003 as yet more personnel changes saw NOLAN and COOPER making way for guitarist FRED MASCHERINO and bassist MATT RUBANO on the album, 'WHERE YOU WANT TO BE' (2004). Their genetically modified "punk-rock" proved popular enough for a surprise breakthrough into the US Top 3, tracks such as 'A DECADE UNDER THE INFLUENCE' and 'THE PHOTOGRAPH IS PROOF (I KNOW YOU KNOW)' – the latter licensed for the soundtrack of 'Spider-Man 2' – striking a chord with the younger end of the rock market. As it turned out they weren't to be 'Victory' records' biggest selling bands of all time for long as 'Warner Bros.' stepped in for third set, 'LOUDER NOW' (2006). The large part of any musical evolution was expressed in the title, as an even harder rocking TBS made inroads into the difficult (well, at least for US emo types) British market (Top 20) and almost reached the top of the pile at home.

Album rating: TELL ALL YOUR FRIENDS (*6) / WHERE YOU WANT TO BE (*7) / LOUDER NOW (*7)

ANTONIO LONGO – vocals / **JOHN NOLAN** – guitar, vocals / **EDDIE REYES** – guitar / **SHAUN COOPER** – bass / **STEVIE D.** – drums / **JESSE LACEY** (played on this; now BRAND NEW)

not iss. / own label

2001. (cd-ep) <*none*> **TAKING BACK SUNDAY** [–] [–]
– Lost and found / The things we'll never know / Eleven / Go on / One way conversation / Summer stars.

2001. (cd-ep) <*none*> **LULLABY** [–] [–]
– Lullaby / (+ others unknown)

2002. (cd-ep) <*none*> **TAKING BACK SUNDAY DEMO** [–] [–]
– Great romances of the Twentieth Century / The blue channel / Monterey peninsula bike scene / Mutual head club / Your own disaster.

— **ADAM LAZZARA** (b.22 Sep'81, Sheffield, Alabama) – vocals; repl. LONGO

— **MARK O'CONNELL** – drums, percussion; repl. STEVIE D.

Victory / Victory

Apr 02. (cd) <*(VR 176CD)*> **TELL ALL YOUR FRIENDS** [ ] Mar02 [ ]
– You know how I do / Bike scene / Cute without the 'E' (cut from the team) / There's no 'I' team / Great romances of the 20th Century / Ghost man on third / Timberwolves at New Jersey / The blue channel / You're so last summer / Head club. *(ltd d-cd-iss. May04 +=; VR 230CDD)* – The ballad of Sal Villanueva / Cute without the "E" (acoustic).

— **FRED MASCHERINO** – guitar, vocals (ex-BRODY, ex-BREAKING PANGAEA) + **MATT RUBANO** – bass; repl. NOLAN + COOPER who both formed STRAYLIGHT RUN

Jul 04. (cd) <*(VR 228CD)*> **WHERE YOU WANT TO BE** [71] [3]
– Set phasers to stun / Bonus mosh pt.II / A decade under the influence / This photograph is proof (I know you know) / The union / New American classic / I am Fred Astaire / One-eighty by summer / Number five with a bullet / Little devotional / . . .Slowdance on the inside.

Sep 04. (7") <*(VR 236)*> **A DECADE UNDER THE INFLUENCE. / LITTLE DEVOTIONAL (Mike Sapone demo)** [70] Jun04 [ ]
(cd-s+=) <*(VR 236CD)*> – ('A'-Mike Sapone demo).

Warners / Warners

Apr 06. (cd) <*(9362 49424-2)*> **LOUDER NOW** [18] [2]
– What's it feel like to be a ghost? / Liar (it takes one to know one) / MakeDamnSure / Up against (blackout) / My blue heaven / Twenty-twenty surgery / Spin / Divine intervention / Miami / Error: operator / I'll let you live.

May 06. (7"red/cd-s) *(W 716/+CD1)* **MAKEDAMNSURE. / SLEEP** [36] [48]
(cd-s) *(W 716CD2)* – ('A') / What it feels like to be a ghost? (live) / Error operator / ('A'-video).

TALKING HEADS

Formed: Manhattan, New York, USA . . . May '75 by former art & design students DAVID BYRNE, TINA WEYMOUTH and CHRIS FRANTZ. Their first gig was supporting the RAMONES at the CBGB's club in New York, circa mid '75. The band were soon spotted by Seymour Stein, who duly signed them to his new US label, 'Sire' and in late 1976 they released their debut 45, 'LOVE GOES TO A BUILDING ON FIRE'. Although this flopped, the following year's '77' album sold well enough to reach the lower regions of the album chart. The record's centerpiece was the spastic, new wave-funk of 'PSYCHO KILLER', BYRNE's compelling eccentricity making the number a live favourite. By this point the band were well established as one of the leading lights in the New York art-punk scene, firing subversively intelligent broadsides at the overblown rock establishment. The follow-up album, 'MORE SONGS ABOUT BUILDINGS AND FOOD' (1978) was produced by BRIAN ENO whom the band had met on a British tour the previous year. Sharing ENO's disregard for the workmanlike, the band were spurred on to new heights, FRANTZ and WEYMOUTH fashioning intricate but gloriously funky rhythms, BYRNE turning around Al Green's 'TAKE ME TO THE RIVER' with his wonderfully idiosyncratic vocal style. ENO stuck around for 'FEAR OF MUSIC' (1979), an album which saw them experimenting with complex ethnic rythms and instrumentation, an area that was further explored on the BYRNE/ENO collaboration, 'MY LIFE IN THE BUSH OF GHOSTS' (1981). Bolstered by a crew of esteemed session musicians, the band cut 'REMAIN IN LIGHT' (1980). Swathed in giddy funk and rooted by African polyrhythms, the album spawned the wondrous 'ONCE IN A LIFETIME' single. The band had now established themselves as a top live draw and were notching up increasing record sales, although it was to be three years before the next TALKING HEADS studio album as the band divided their time between solo projects and live work. Worth the wait, 'SPEAKING IN TONGUES' (1983) was another classy outing, spawning the trance-rock of the 'SLIPPERY PEOPLE'

(1984) single and the jittery 'BURNING DOWN THE HOUSE' (1983) which went top 10 in the UK. The Jonathon Demme-directed concert movie 'STOP MAKING SENSE' contained some of the most innovative live footage ever commited to celluloid and further increased The TALKING HEADS' burgeoning reputation. Another groundbreaking piece of film came with the video for 'ROAD TO NOWHERE' (1985), the band's biggest chart hit to date. Its parent album, 'LITTLE CREATURES' (1985), marked a return to a more basic sound. From this point on, the band began to spend an increasing amount of time on solo projects. 'TRUE STORIES' (1986) was a patchy TALKING HEADS version of the soundtrack to the DAVID BYRNE film of the same name while 'NAKED' (1986) came on like an over-produced version of 'REMAIN IN LIGHT'. Following this album, the various 'HEADS went on to do their own thing, BYRNE concentrating on his solo career. The band officially split in 1991, although the HEADS (as WEYMOUTH, FRANTZ and HARRISON were now known) made a comeback album of sorts in '96 entitled 'NO TALKING, JUST HEAD', a record that utilised an array of vocal talent including SHAUN RYDER on the minor hit single, 'DON'T TAKE MY KINDNESS FOR WEAKNESS'. One of the more recent and arguably more compelling BYRNE solo releases (apart from his near chart-topping 'LAZY' experience with dancemeisters X-PRESS 2) was 2003's 'LEAD US NOT INTO TEMPTATION', the soundtrack for the film version of Alex Trocchi's 'Young Adam'. You might say BYRNE went back to his roots in a sense, collaborating with Scottish artists such as MOGWAI and BELLE & SEBASTIAN to create a glowering, autumnal, largely instrumental song cycle perfectly suited to the movie's grainy Caledonian-noir. TOM TOM CLUB also re-emerged in 2002 with 'LIVE @ THE CLUBHOUSE', an animated concert set drawing largely from 2000's 'THE GOOD, THE BAD AND THE FUNKY'. For 'GROWN BACKWARDS' (2004), BYRNE revealed a different writing process, conceiving the lyrics first and developing the songs around them, fleshing them out with accompaniment from chamber ensemble the Tosca Strings. As ever, the results were intriguing, often mystifying and occasionally brilliant. Gorgeous opener 'GLASS, CONCRETE AND STONE' had previously aired on the soundtrack to Stephen Frears' 'Dirty Pretty Things', a plinking ethnic-orchestral hymnal which almost won its composer an Oscar. Alongside a few backwards nods to TALKING HEADS – the wry automatonata of 'TINY APOCALYPSE' – BYRNE even ventured a rare, tastefully selected cover in Lambchop's 'THE MAN WHO LOVED BEER'.

• **Songwriters:** Group compositions except; TAKE ME TO THE RIVER (Al Green) / SLIPPERY PEOPLE (Staple Singers). TOM TOM CLUB:- UNDER THE BOARDWALK (Drifters) / FEMME FATALE (Velvet Underground) / YOU SEXY THING (Hot Chocolate). DAVID BYRNE: – GREENBACK DOLLAR (Hoyt Axton) / GIRLS ON MY MIND (Toquinnho Vinicius) / DON'T FENCE ME IN (Cole Porter). • **Trivia:** FRANTZ and WEYMOUTH (later TOM TOM CLUB) married on the 18th of June '77. BYRNE produced The B-52's on their 1982 album, 'Mesopotamia' and FUN BOY THREE on their 1983, 'Waiting' album. HARRISON produced The VIOLENT FEMMES on 1986 album, 'The Blind Leading The Naked'. TOM TOM CLUB started out producing in 1988 with ZIGGY MARLEY, later working with HAPPY MONDAYS.

Album rating: TALKING HEADS '77 (*9) / MORE SONGS ABOUT BUILDINGS AND FOOD (*8) / FEAR OF MUSIC (*8) / REMAIN IN LIGHT (*8) / THE NAME OF THIS BAND IS TALKING HEADS (*6) / SPEAKING IN TONGUES (*7) / STOP MAKING SENSE (*7) / LITTLE CREATURES (*7) / TRUE STORIES (*5) / SOUNDS FROM TRUE STORIES V/A soundtrack (*5) / NAKED (*5) / ONCE IN A LIFETIME – THE BEST OF TALKING HEADS compilation (*9) / THE BEST OF compilation (*8) / Tom Tom Club: TOM TOM CLUB (*5) / CLOSE TO THE BONE (*4) / BOOM BOOM CHI BOOM BOOM (*3) / DARK SNEAK LOVE ACTION (*3) / THE GOOD, THE BAD AND THE FUNKY (*6) / LIVE @ THE CLUBHOUSE (*6) / Jerry Harrison: THE RED AND THE BLACK (*4) / CASUAL GODS (*4) / WALK ON WATER (*4) / the Heads: NO TALKING, JUST HEADS (*4) / David Byrne: SONGS FROM THE CATHERINE WHEEL theatre soundtrack (*6) / MUSIC FOR THE KNEE PLAYS (*6) / REI MOMO (*7) / THE FOREST (*4) / UH-OH (*5) / DAVID BYRNE (*4) / FEELINGS (*5) / LOOK INTO THE EYEBALL (*5) / LEAD US NOT INTO TEMPTATION soundtrack (*7) / GROWN BACKWARDS (*6)

DAVID BYRNE (b.14 May'52, Dumbarton, Scotland) – vocals, guitar / **TINA WEYMOUTH** (b.22 Nov'50, Coronado, Calif.) – bass, vocals / **CHRIS FRANTZ** (b. CHARLTON CHRISTOPHER FRANTZ, 8 May'51, Fort Campbell, Kentucky) – drums

		UK: Sire	US: Sire
Feb 77.	(7") *(6078 604)* <737> **LOVE GOES TO A BUILDING ON FIRE. / NEW FEELING**		

— added **JERRY HARRISON** (b.21 Feb'49, Milwaukee, Wisconsin) – guitar, keyboards (ex-JONATHAN RICHMAN & THE MODERN LOVERS)

Sep 77.	(lp) *(9103 328)* <SR 6306> **TALKING HEADS '77** – Uh-oh, love comes to town / New feeling / Tentative decisions / Happy day / Who is it? / No compassion / The book I read / Don't worry about the government / First week – last week . . . carefree / Psycho killer / Pulled up. *(re-iss. Sep78; SR 6036) (cd-iss. Feb87; K2 56647)*	60	97
Oct 77.	(7") <1002> **UH-OH, LOVE COMES TO TOWN. / I WISH YOU WOULDN'T SAY THAT**	–	
Dec 77.	(7") *(6078 610)* **PSYCHO KILLER. / I WISH YOU WOULDN'T SAY THAT** (12"+=) *(same)* – Psycho killer (acoustic).		–
Jan 78.	(7") <1013> **PSYCHO KILLER. / PSYCHO KILLER (acoustic)**	–	92
May 78.	(7") *(6078 620)* **PULLED UP. / DON'T WORRY ABOUT THE GOVERNMENT**		–
Jul 78.	(lp/c) *(K/K4 56531)* <SR 6058> **MORE SONGS ABOUT BUILDINGS AND FOOD** – Thank you for sending me an angel / With our love / The good thing / Warning sign / Girls want to be with the girls / Found a job / Artists only / I'm not in love / Stay hungry / Take me to the river / The big country. *(double-play cass. includes debut album) (cd-iss. Jan87; K2 56531)*	21	29
Oct 78.	(7") <1032> **TAKE ME TO THE RIVER. / THANK YOU FOR SENDING ME AN ANGEL**	–	26
Jun 79.	(7") *(SIR 4004)* **TAKE ME TO THE RIVER. / FOUND A JOB** (d7"+=) *(SAM 87)* – Love goes to a building on fire / Psycho killer.		–
Aug 79.	(lp/c) *(K/K4 56707)* <SRK 6076> **FEAR OF MUSIC** – Air / Animals / Cities / Drugs / Electric guitar / Heaven / I Zimbra / Life during wartime / Memories can't wait / Mind / Paper. *(re-iss. Sep79 lp/c; SRK/SRC 6076) (w/ free 7")* – PSYCHO KILLER (live). / NEW FEELING (live) *(cd-iss. Jul84; K2 56707)*	33	21
Oct 79.	(7") *(SIR 4027)* <49075> **LIFE DURING WARTIME. / ELECTRIC GUITAR**		80
Feb 80.	(7") *(SIR 4033)* **I ZIMBRA. / PAPER**		–
Jun 80.	(7") *(SIR 4040)* **CITIES. / CITIES (live)** (12"+=) *(SIR 4040T)* – Artists only.		–

— basic 4 added **BUSTA CHERRY JONES** – bass / **ADRIAN BELEW** – guitar / **BERNIE WORRELL** – keyboards / **STEVEN SCALES** – percussion / **DONETTE McDONALD** – backing vox

Oct 80.	(lp/c) <(SRK/SRC 6095)> **REMAIN IN LIGHT** – The great curve / Crosseyed and painless / Born under punches / Houses in motion / Once in a lifetime / Listening wind / Seen and not seen / The overlord. *(cd-iss. Mar84; K2 56867)*	21	19
Feb 81.	(7"/ext.12") *(SIR 4048/+T)* <40649> **ONCE IN A LIFETIME. / SEEN AND NOT SEEN**	14	
May 81.	(7") <49734> **HOUSES IN MOTION (remix). / THE OVERLORD**	–	
May 81.	(7") *(SIR 4050)* **HOUSES IN MOTION (remix). / AIR** (ext.12"+=) *(SIR 4050T)* – ('A'live).	50	–

— In 1981, all 4 diversed into own projects

Mar 82.	(7") *(SIR 4055)* **LIFE DURING WARTIME (live). / LIFE DURING WARTIME** (12"+=) *(SIR 4055T)* – Don't worry about the government (live).		–
Apr 82.	(d-lp/d-c) <(SRK/SRC 23590)> **THE NAME OF THIS BAND IS TALKING HEADS (live)** – I Zimbra / Drugs / Houses in motion / Life during wartime / Take me to the river / The great curve / Cross-eyed and painless / New feeling / A clean break / Don't worry about the government / Pulled up / Psycho killer / Artists only / Stay hungry / Air / Building on fire / Memories can't wait. *(cd-iss. May87; K2 66112)*	22	31
Jun 83.	(lp,clear-lp/c/cd) *(923883-1/-4/-2)* <23883> **SPEAKING IN TONGUES** – Burning down the house / Making flippy floppy / Girlfriend is better / Slippery people / I get wild – Wild gravity / Swamp / Moon rocks / Pull up the roots / This must be the place (naive melody). *(c+=/cd+=)* – (6 extra mixes).	21	15

Jul 83. (7") *(W 9565) <29565>* **BURNING DOWN THE HOUSE. / I GET WILD – WILD GRAVITY** [ ] [9]
(12"+=) *(W 9565T)* – Moon rocks.

Jan 84. (7") *(W 9451) <29451>* **THIS MUST BE THE PLACE (NAIVE MELODY). / MOON ROCKS** [51] Oct83 [62]
(ext.d12"+=) *(W 9451T / SAM 176)* – Slippery people (remix) / Making flippy floppy (remix).

E.M.I. Sire

Oct 84. (7"/ext.12") *(EMI/12EMI 5504)* **SLIPPERY PEOPLE (live). / THIS MUST BE THE PLACE (NAIVE MELODY) (live)** [68] [–]

Oct 84. (lp/c) *(TAH/+TC 1) <25121>* **STOP MAKING SENSE** (live soundtrack) [37] Sep84 [41]
– Psycho killer / Swamp / Slippery people / Burning down the house / Girlfriend is better / Once in a lifetime / What a day that was / Life during wartime / Take me to the river. *(cd-iss. Feb85; CDP 746064-2) (c+=/cd+=)* – (extra extended tracks) *(re-iss. Mar90 cd)(c/lp; CZ 289)(TC+/ATAK 147) (re-iss. Nov93 on 'Fame' cd/c; CD/TC FA 3302) (lp-iss.Apr99 on 'E.M.I.'; 499471-1) <(cd re-iss. Sep99 on 'E.M.I.'+=; 522453-2)>* – Heaven / Thank you for sending me an angel / Found a job / Making flippy floppy / This must be the place (naive melody) / Genius of love / Crosseyed and painless.

Nov 84. (7"/ext.12") *(EMI/12EMI 5509)* **GIRLFRIEND IS BETTER (live). / ONCE IN A LIFETIME (live)** [ ] [–]

Dec 84. (7") *<29080>* **GIRLFRIEND IS BETTER (live). / HEAVEN (live)** [–] [ ]

May 85. (7"/ext.12") *(EMI/12EMI 5520)* **THE LADY DON'T MIND. / GIVE ME BACK MY NAME** [ ] [–]
(d12"+=) *(12EMID 5520)* – Slippery people (live) / This must be the place (naive melody) (live).

Jun 85. (lp/c)(cd) *(TAH/+TC 2)(CDP 746158-2) <25035>* **LITTLE CREATURES** [10] [20]
– And she was / Give me back my name / Creatures of love / The lady don't mind / Perfect world / Stay up late / Walk it down / Television man / Road to nowhere. *(c+=)* – The lady don't mind (extended). *(re-iss. Mar90 cd)(c/lp; CZ 287)(TC+/ATAK 146) (re-iss. Nov93 on 'Fame' cd/c; CD/TC FA 3301) (lp-iss.Dec99 on 'Simply Vinyl'; SVLP 152)*

Jun 85. (7") *<28987>* **ROAD TO NOWHERE. / GIVE ME BACK MY NAME** [–] [ ]

Sep 85. (7") *<28917>* **AND SHE WAS. / ('A'dub)** [–] [54]

Sep 85. (7"/7"pic-d) *(EMI/+P 5530)* **ROAD TO NOWHERE. / TELEVISION MAN** [6] [–]
(d12"+=) *(12EMID 5530)* – Slippery people (extended live) / This must be the place (naive melody) (live).

Feb 86. (7") *(EMI 5543)* **AND SHE WAS. / PERFECT WORLD** [17] [–]
(12"pic-d+=) *(12EMIP 5543)* – ('A'extended).

Apr 86. (7") *<29163>* **ONCE IN A LIFETIME (live). / THIS MUST BE THE PLACE (live)** [–] [91]
(above re-generated from 1984 album & taken from 'Down And Out In Beverly Hills')

Aug 86. (7") *(EMI 5567) <28629>* **WILD WILD LIFE. / PEOPLE LIKE US (movie version)** [43] [25]
(12"+=/12"pic-d+=) *(12EMI/+P 5567)* – ('A'extended).

Sep 86. (lp/c)(cd) *(EU/TCEU 3511)(CDP 746345-2) <25512>* **TRUE STORIES** [7] [17]
– Love for sale / Puzzlin' evidence / Hey now / Papa Legba / Wild wild life / Radio head / Dream operator / People like us / City of dreams. *(cd+=)* – Wild wild life (Eric 'E.T.' Thorngren mix). *(re-iss. Sep89 on 'Fame' cd/c/lp; CD/TC+/FA 3231)*

Nov 86. (7") *<28497>* **LOVE FOR SALE. / HEY NOW** [–] [ ]

Apr 87. (7") *(EM 1)* **RADIO HEAD. / HEY NOW (movie version)** [52] [–]
(d7"+=)(12"+=/cd-s+=) *(EMD 1)(12/CD EM 1)* – ('A'remix) / ('B'-Milwaukee remix).

Mar 88. (cd/c/lp) *(CD/TC+/EMD 1005) <26654>* **NAKED** [3] [19]
– Blind / Mr. Jones / Totally nude / Ruby dear / (Nothing but) Flowers / The Democratic circus / The facts of life / Mommy daddy you and I / Big daddy / Cool water. *(other cd+=; CDP 790156-2)* – Bill. *(re-iss. Nov93 on 'Fame' cd/c; CD/TC FA 3300)*

Aug 88. (c-s/7") *(TC+/EM 68) <27948>* **BLIND. / BILL** [59] [ ]
(ext.12"+=/cd-s+=) *(12/CD EM 68)* – ('A'-Def, dub & blind mix).

Oct 88. (c-s/7") *(TC+/EM 53) <27992>* **(NOTHING BUT) FLOWERS. / RUBY DEAR** [ ] Apr88 [ ]
(10"+=) *(10EM 53)* – Facts of life / Mommy, daddy, you and I.
(12") *(12EM 53)* – ('A'extended) / ('B'-Lillywhite mix).
(cd-s) *(CDEM 53)* – ('A'side) / ('B'-bush mix) / Mommy, daddy, you and I / ('A'-Lillywhite mix).

— officially split 1991

– compilations, others, etc. –

on 'E.M.I.' UK / 'Sire' US unless mentioned otherwise

Apr 81. (c-s) *WEA; (SPC 9)* **TAKE ME TO THE RIVER / PSYCHO KILLER** [ ] [–]

1989. (3"cd-ep) *Sire; (921 135-2)* **LOVE GOES TO A BUILDING ON FIRE / PSYCHO KILLER / ONCE IN A LIFETIME / BURNING DOWN THE HOUSE** [ ] [–]

Oct 92. (c-s/7") *(TC+/EM 250)* **LIFETIME PILING UP. / ROAD TO NOWHERE** [50] [ ]
(cd-s+=) *(CDEM 250)* – Love for sale / The lady don't mind (extended).
(cd-s) *(CDEMS 250)* – ('A') / Stay up late / Radio head / Take me to the river.

Oct 92. (d-cd/d-c/d-lp) *(CD/TC+/EQ 5010) <26760>* **POPULAR FAVOURITES 1976-1992** [7] [ ]
– ONCE IN A LIFETIME:- Psycho killer / Take me to the river / Once in a lifetime / Burning down the house / This must be the place (naive melody) / Slippery people (live) / Life during wartime (live) / And she was / Road to nowhere / Wild wild life / Blind / (Nothing but) Flowers / Sax and violins / Lifetime piling up. // SAND IN MY VASELINE:- Sugar on my tongue / I want to live / Love goes to a building on fire / I wish you wouldn't say that / Don't worry about the government / The big country / No compassion / Warning sign / Heaven / Memories can't wait / I Zimbra / Crosseyed and painless / Swamp / Girlfriend is better (live) / Stay up late / Love for sale / City of dreams / Mr. Jones / Gangster of love / Popsicle.

Nov 95. (3xcd-box) *(CDOMB 003)* **THE ORIGINALS** [ ] [–]
– (STOP MAKING SENSE / LITTLE CREATURES / TRUE STORIES). *(re-iss. Mar97; same)*

Sep 00. (3xcd-box) *E.M.I.; (5283722-2)* **LITTLE CREATURES / TRUE STORIES / NAKED** [ ] [–]

Apr 01. (cd) *E.M.I.; (532569-2)* **REMIXED** [ ] [–]

Sep 01. (c-s/12"/cd-s) *(W 571 C/T/CD)* **ONCE IN A LIFETIME** [ ] [–]

Oct 04. (cd) *Rhino; <(8122 76488-2)>* **THE BEST OF** [30] [ ]
– Love goes to a building on fire / Psycho killer / Uh-oh, love comes to town / Take me to the river / Found a job / Life during wartime / Heaven / Memories can't wait / Once in a lifetime / Houses in motion / This must be the place (naive melody) / Girlfriend is better / Burning down the house / Road to nowhere / And she was / Wild wild life / Blind / (Nothing but) Flowers.

DAVID BYRNE

Early in 1981, he had collaborated with BRIAN ENO ⇒ on album 'MY LIFE IN THE BUSH OF GHOSTS'.

Sire Sire

Dec 81. (7") *(SIR 4054)* **BIG BLUE PLYMOUTH (EYES WIDE OPEN). / CLOUD CHAMBER** [ ] [–]
(12") *(SIR 4054T)* – ('A') / Leg bells / Light bath.

Jan 82. (lp/c) *(SRK/SRC 3645) <3645>* **SONGS FROM 'THE CATHERINE WHEEL'** (stage score) [ ] Dec81 [ ]
– His wife refused / Two soldiers / The red house / Eggs in a briar patch / Poison / Cloud chamber / My big hands (fall through the cracks) / Big business / What a day that was / Big blue Plymouth (eyes wide open) / Light bath. *<US d-lp+=)* – Light bath / Ade / Walking / Under the mountain / Dinosaur / Wheezing / Combat / Leg bells / The blue flame / Danse beast / Five golden sections. *<(cd-iss. May 89 & Jan93; 7599 27418-2)>*

Feb 82. (12"ep) *<50034>* **THREE BIG SONGS** [–] [ ]
– Big business (remix) / My big hands (fall through the cracks) / Big blue Plymouth (eyes wide open).

E.M.I. ECM

Sep 85. (lp/c) *(EJ 240381-1/-4) <ECM 25022>* **MUSIC FOR THE KNEE PLAYS** [ ] May85 [ ]
– Tree (today is an important occasion) / In the upper room / The sound of business / Social studies / (The gift of sound) Where the sun never goes down / Theadora is dozing / Admiral Perry / I bid you goodnight / I've tried / Winter / Jungle book / In the future.

Nov 86. (lp/c) *(ENC/TCENC 3520) <25515>* **SOUNDS FROM TRUE STORIES** (soundtrack by DAVID BYRNE & Various Artists) [ ] [ ]
– Cocktail desperado (TERRY ALLEN & THE PANHANDLE MYSTERY BAND) / Road song (MEREDITH MONK) / Freeway son (DAVID BYRNE) / Brownie's theme (DAVID BYRNE) / Mall muzak: a) Building a highway, b) Puppy polka, c) Party girls (DAVID BYRNE) / Dinner music (KRONOS QUARTET) / Disco hits! (DAVID BYRNE) / City of steel (TALKING HEADS) / Love theme from True Stories (DAVID

BYRNE) / Festa para um Rei Negro (BANDA ECLIPSE) / Buster's theme (CARL FINCH) / Soy de Tejas (STEVE JORDAN) / I love metal buildings (DAVID BYRNE) / Glass operator (DAVID BYRNE).

— BYRNE recorded a collaboration set with RYUICHI SAKAMOTO on film 'THE LAST EMPEROR'.

— BYRNE (below) now used a plethora of Brazilian musicians, after compiling various artists 'BELEZA TROPICAL', 'O SAMBA', etc.

Luaka Bop-Sire | Luaka Bop

Oct 89. (lp/c)(cd) *(WX 319/+C)(K 925990-2) <25990>* **REI MOMO** [52] [71]
– Independence day / Make believe mambo / The call of the wild / Dirty old town / The rose tattoo / The dream police / Don't want to be part of your world / Marching through the wilderness / Lie to me / Women vs. men / Carnival eyes / I know sometimes a man is wrong.

Dec 89. (7"/ext.12") **MAKE BELIEVE MAMBO. / LIE TO ME** [ ] [ ]

Jun 91. (cd/c) *<(7599 26584-2/-4)>* **THE FOREST (instrumental)** [ ] [ ]
– Ur / Kish / Dura Europus / Nineveh / Ava / Machu picchu / Teotihuaean / Asuka. *(cd+=)* – Samara / Tula. *(re-iss. Jul00; same)*

Aug 91. (m-cd) *<40177>* **FORESTRY** [–] [ ]
– Ava (nu wage remix) / Nineveh (industrial mix) / Ava (less space dance mix edit) / Ava (space dance mix) / Machu picchu (album version).

Mar 92. (cd)(lp/c) *<(7599 26799-2)>(WX 464/+C)* **UH-OH** [26] [ ]
– Now I'm your mom / Girls on my mind / Something ain't right / She's mad / Hanging upside down / Twistin' in the wind / A walk in the dark / The cowboy mambo (hey lookit me now) / Tiny town / Somebody. *(re-iss. Feb95 cd/c; same)*

Apr 92. (7"/c-s) **GIRLS ON MY MIND. / MONKEY MAN** [ ] [ ]
(12"+=/cd-s+=) – Cantode oxum.

May 92. (7"/c-s) *(W 0108/+C)* **HANGING UPSIDE DOWN. / TINY TOWN** [ ] [ ]
(cd-s) *(W 0108CD1)* – ('A'side) / Dirty old town (live) / (Nothing but) Flowers (live) / Girls on my mind (live).
(cd-s) *(W 0108CD2)* – ('A'side) / Something ain't right (live) / Who we're thinking of (live) / Rockin' in the free world (live).

Jul 92. (7"/c-s) *(W 0199/+C)* **SHE'S MAD. / SOMEBODY** [ ] [–]
(12") *(W 0199T)* – ('A'side) / Butt naked (live) / Greenback dollar (live).
(cd-s++=) *(W 0199CD)* – Now I'm your man (live).

— with **PAUL SOCOLOW** – bass, vocals / **TODD TURKISHER** – drum, percussion / **VALERIE NARANJO** – percussion, tambourine (live: MAURO REFOSCO – percussion) / **BILL WARE** – marimba / **ARTO LINDSAY** – guitar / **JOHN MEDESKI** – organ / **BASHIRI JOHNSON** – congas, bongos / **BEBEL GILBERTO** – vocals

May 94. (cd/c) *<(9362 45558-2/-4)>* **DAVID BYRNE** [44] [ ]
– A long time ago / Angels / Crash / A self-made man / Back in the box / Sad song / Nothing at all / My love is you / Lillies of the valley / You & eye / Strange ritual / Buck naked. *(cd re-iss. Jul00; same)*

Jun 94. (7"/c-s) *(W 0253/+C)* **ANGELS. / PRINCESS** [ ] [–]
(12"+=/cd-s+=) *(W 0253 T/CD)* – Ready for this world.

Sep 94. (c-s/cd-s) *(W 0263 C/CD)* **BACK IN THE BOX / GYPSY WOMAN (live) / GIRLS ON MY MIND (live)** [ ] [–]
(US cd-ep) *<41766>* – (first 2 tracks) / Back in the box (mixes) / A woman's secret / Cool water (live).

May 97. (cd/c) *<(9362 46605-2/-4)>* **FEELINGS** [ ] [ ]
– Fuzzy freaky / Miss America / A soft seduction / Dance on vaseline / The gates of Paradise / Amnesia / You don't know me / Daddy go down / Finite = alright / Wicked little doll / Burnt by the sun / The civil wars / They are in love.

Jun 97. (cd-s) *(W 0401CD)* **MISS AMERICA (mixes; clean / album / I love America)** [ ] [–]

Jan 99. (cd) *<2085>* **THE VISIBLE MAN** (remixes) [–] [ ]

Virgin America | Virgin America

May 01. (cd) *(CDVUS 189) <50924>* **LOOK INTO THE THE EYEBALL** [58] [ ]
– UB Jesus / Revolution / Great intoxication / Like humans do / Broken things / Accident / Desconocido soy / Neighbourhood / Smile / Moment of conception / Walk on water / Everyone's in love with you.

Sep 01. (cd-s) *(897529)* **LIKE HUMANS DO / ALL OVER ME / PRINCESS** [ ] [–]

2002. (m-cd) **IN SPITE OF WISHING AND WANTING** (theatre soundtrack) [–] [ ]
– Horses / Sleeping up / Speech / Said & the ants / Fear / Danceonvaselinesuperextendedremix / Idiot music.

Thrill Jockey | Thrill Jockey

Sep 03. (cd/lp) *<(THRILL 133/+LP)>* **LEAD US NOT INTO TEMPTATION: MUSIC FROM THE FILM YOUNG ADAM** (soundtrack) [ ] [ ]
– Body in a river / Mnemonic discordance / Seaside smokes / Canal life / Locks & barges / Haitian fight song (HUNG DRAWN QUARTET) / Sex on the docks / Inexorable / Warm sheets / Dirty hair / Bastard / The lodger / Ineluctable / Speechless / The Great Western Road.

Nonesuch | Nonesuch

Mar 04. (cd) *<(7559 79826-2)>* **GROWN BACKWARDS** [ ] [ ]
– Glass, concrete and stone / The man who loved beer / Au fond du temple saint / Empire / Tiny apocalypse / She only sleeps / Dialog box / The other side of this life / Why / Pirates / Civilization / Astronaut / Glad / Un di Felice, eterea. *(bonus+=)* – Lazy.

TOM TOM CLUB

CHRIS FRANTZ + **TINA WEYMOUTH** plus her 2 sisters + **STEVE SCALES** – percussion / **ALEX WEIR** – guitar / **TYRON DOWNIE** – keyboards

Island | Sire

Jun 81. (7") *(WIP 6694)* **WORDY RAPPINGHOOD. / YOU DON'T STOP (WORDY RAP)** [7] [ ]
(12"+=) *(12WIP 6694)* – L'elephant.

Sep 81. (7") *(WIP 6735) <49882>* **GENIUS OF LOVE. / LORELEI (instrumental)** [65] Jan82 [31]
(12"+=) *(12WIP 6735)* – Rappa rappa rhythm / Yella.
(re-iss. Oct82; same)

Oct 81. (lp/c) *(ILPS/ICT 9686) <SRK 3628>* **TOM TOM CLUB** [78] [23]
– Wordy rappinghood / Genius of love / Tom Tom theme / L'elephant / As above, so below / Lorelei / On, on, on, on . . . / Booming and zooming. *(re-iss. Oct86 lp/c; ILPM/ICM 9686) (cd-iss. May87; CID 9686) (re-iss. cd Apr90; IMCD 103)*

Jul 82. (7") *(WIP 6762)* **UNDER THE BOARDWALK. / ON, ON, ON, ON . . . (remix)** [22] [ ]
(12"+=) *(12WIP 6762)* – Lorelei (remix).

Jul 83. (7"/12") *(IS/12IS 117)* **THE MAN WITH THE 4-WAY HIPS. / ('A'dub version)** [ ] [ ]

Aug 83. (lp/c) *(ILPS/ICT 9738) <23916>* **CLOSE TO THE BONE** [ ] [73]
– Pleasure of love / On the line again / This is a foxy world / Bamboo town / The man with the 4-way hips / Measure up / Never took a penny / Atsababy! (life is great).

Dec 83. (7") **NEVER TOOK A PENNY. / PLEASURE OF LOVE** [–] [ ]

— **TINA** + **CHRIS** added **GARY POZNER** – keyboards / **MARK ROULE** – guitar, percussion

Fontana | Sire

Sep 88. (7") *(TCB 1)* **DON'T SAY NO. / DEVIL DOES YOUR DOG BITE?** [ ] [ ]
(12"+=) *(TCBX 1)* – ('A'version) / Beats and pieces.
(cd-s+=) *(TCBCD 1)* – Beats and pieces / Percapella.

Oct 88. (lp/c)(cd) *(SF LP/MC 8)(836 416-2) <25888>* **BOOM BOOM CHI BOOM BOOM** [ ] [ ]
– Suboceana / Shock the world / Don't say no / Challenge of the love warriors / Femme fatale / Born for love / Broken promises / She belongs to me / Little Eva / Misty teardrop.

— **KIRSTY MacCOLL** makes a guest vocal appearance on below

Jan 92. (cd/c) *<2-/4-26951>* **DARK SNEAK LOVE ACTION** [–] [ ]
– Love wave / Sunshine and ecstasy / You sexy thing / Who wants an ugly girl? / Say I am / Irrisistable party dip / Dark sneak love action / Innocent sex kiss / Dogs in the trash / My mama told me / As the disco ball turns / Daddy come home.

Rykodisc | Rykodisc

Sep 00. (12") *<R 607>* **HAPPINESS CAN'T BUY MONEY** [–] [ ]

Oct 00. (cd) *<(RCD 10603)>* **THE GOOD THE BAD AND THE FUNKY** [ ] Sep00 [ ]
– Time to bounce / Who feelin' it / Happiness can't buy money / Holy water / Soul fire / She's dangerous / She's a freak / (C'mon) Surrender / Love to love you baby / Superdreaming / Lesbians by the lake / Let there be love / Time to bounce / Dangerous dub.

Artist Direct | Artist Dire

Apr 03. (cd) *<(IMUCDD 072)>* **LIVE @ THE CLUBHOUSE (live)** [ ] Sep02 [ ]
– Suboceana / Time to bounce / Punk lolita / Soul fire / Who feelin' it / Happiness can't buy money / Sand / She's dangerous / The man with the 4-way hips / Genius of love / Band introduction / You sexy thing / Holy water / Wordy rappinghood / As above so below / 96 tears / Take me to the river.

JERRY HARRISON

Sire | Sire

Oct 81. (7") *(SIR 4053)* **THINGS FALL APART. / WORLDS IN COLLISION**

Oct 81. (lp/c) *<(SRK/SRC 3631)>* **THE RED AND THE BLACK**
– Things fall apart / Slink / The new adventure / Magic hymie / Fast karma / No questions / Worlds in collision / The red nights / No more returns / No warning no alarm. *(cd-iss. Apr96 on 'Warners'; 7599 23631-2)*

Fontana | Sire

Feb 88. (7") *(JERRY 1)* **REV IT UP. / BOBBY**
(12"+=)(12"pic-d+=)(cd-s+=) *(JERRY 1-12)(JERYP 1-12)(JERCD 1)* – ('A'versions). *(re-iss. Jul88; same)*

Feb 88. (lp/c)(cd) *(SF LP/MC 2)(832992-2) <25663>* **JERRY HARRISON: CASUAL GODS** — 78
– Rev it up / Songs of angels / Man with a gun / Let it come down / Cherokee chief / A perfect lie / Are you running? / Breakdown in the passing lane / A.K.A. love / We're always talkin' / Bobby. *(cd+=)* – Bobby (12"version).

May 88. (7") *(JERRY 2)* **MAN WITH A GUN. / ('A'radio edit)**
(12"+=)(cd-s+=) *(JERRY 2-12)(JERCD 2)* – Breakdown on the passing line / Wire always talking.

— backing incl. **BROOKS, WORRELL, BAILEY, SIEGER + WEIR**

Jun 90. (7") *(JERRY 3)* **WALK ON WATER. / MAN WITH A GUN**
(12"+=)(cd-s+=) *(JERRY 3-12)(JERCD 3)* – Racing the fire.

Jun 90. (cd/c/lp) *(846321-2/-4/-1) <25943>* **WALK ON WATER**
– Flying under radar / Cowboy's got to go / Kick start / I don't mind / Sleep angel / Confess / I cry for Iran / Never let it slip / If the rain returns / The doctor's lie.

the HEADS

HARRISON, WEYMOUTH, FRANTZ + guest vocalists & lyricists (see below)

Radioactive-MCA | M.C.A.

Oct 96. (c-s) *(MCS 48024)* **DON'T TAKE MY KINDNESS FOR WEAKNESS / ('A'mix)** — 60
(cd-s+=) *(MCSTD 48024)* – ('A'-Lunatic Calm remix).

Nov 96. (cd/c) *<(MCD/MCC 11504)>* **NO TALKING, JUST HEAD**
– Damage I've done (w/ JOHNETTE NAPOLITANO) / The king is gone (w/ MICHAEL HUTCHENCE) / No talking just head (w/ DEBBIE HARRY) / Never mind (w/ RICHARD HELL) / No big bang (w/ MARIA McKEE) / Don't take my madness for weakness (w/ SHAUN RYDER) / No more lonely nights (w/ MALIN ANNETEG) / Indie hair (w/ ED KOWALCZYK) / Punk lolita (w/ DEBBIE HARRY, JOHNETTE NAPOLITANO & TINA WEYMOUTH) / Only the lonely (w/ GORDON GANO) / Papersnow (w/ ANDY PARTRIDGE) / Blue blue moon (w/ GAVIN FRIDAY).

□ TALK SHOW (see under ⇒ STONE TEMPLE PILOTS)

TANGERINE DREAM

Formed: Berlin, Germany ... autumn 1967 by art student EDGAR FROESE, who took the name, TANGERINE DREAM, from lyrics used in The BEATLES' classic, 'Lucy In The Sky With Diamonds'. He was invited to play some classical improvisations by surrealist painter SALVADOR DALI in his Spanish villa, EDGAR subsequently going through many egotistical rock musicians before he finally met KLAUS SCHULZE in '69. Together, they soon found KONRAD SCHNITZLER and JOSEPH BEUYS, who, with other guests, worked on the sessions for the 1970 debut, 'ELECTRONIC MEDITATION'. With others going solo, EDGAR then found CHRIS FRANKE and another album, 'ALPHA CENTAURI' surfaced for UK 'Polydor'. In 1972, PETER BAUMANN joined for their third album, 'ATEM', the record heavily playlisted on John Peel's night-time Radio One show and leading to new entrepeneur, Richard Branson, signing them to his 'Virgin' label. Surprisingly, the following year, 'PHAEDRA' made it into the UK Top 40 lists, much aided by the fact 'Virgin' was now an influential part of the British/continental scene. With this album, TANGERINE DREAM made a departure from their PINK FLOYD-like experimentalism, discovering picturesque, electronic waves of sound, rhythmically haunting and repetitive. 'RUBYCON' (1975) was similarly influential, although from there on in the band started to gravitate towards soundtrack work, their atmospheric mood pieces fitting the genre with ease. Over the course of the following decade, they recorded music for such diverse screen projects as 'SORCERER' (1977), 'THIEF' (1981), 'RISKY BUSINESS' (1983) and 'FIRESTARTER' (1984), although their music increasingly verged upon "New Age" sterility. The group issued their final album for 'Virgin', 'HYPERBOREA' (1983) and, much to fans' delight, the fantastic 'LE PARC' (1985), which many believed was the band's swansong. They continued to experiment with new and exciting ideas (using more samples, loops and electronic wizzardry than before) resulting in the mainly vocal 'TYGER' (1987). SCHMOELLING departed in 1986, his replacement being PAUL HASLINGER first featured on 'UNDERWATER SUNLIGHT' (1986) and more so, 'OPTICAL RACE' (1988). However, it was HASLINGER who subsequently walked out on the group to pursue his career in scoring movies. Replaced by JEROME FROESE, TANGERINE DREAM would encounter their most celebrated album for some time, the seven-times Grammy nominated 'ROCKOON' (1992). Throughout the 90's, they issued a staggering body of work, resulting in perhaps two (new age or soundtrack) albums a year, along with remixes and soundtracks here and there. Among their latter-day work, 'L'INFERNO' (2002) was one of the most notable recordings, at least in terms of its inspiration and execution. Based on Dante's famous work of the same name, the album was recorded live within the confines of a church, incorporating religious music into their ever expansive electronica agenda. The album, 'MOTA ATMA' (2003), was in fact the score for an unreleased German film, its driving synth-led beats getting back to the TD of old; FROESE and his son JEROME also on form with 2006's 'JEANNE D'ARC'.

Album rating: ELECTRONIC MEDITATION (*4) / ALPHA CENTAURI (*5) / ZEIT (*4) / ATEM (*6) / PHAEDRA (*9) / RUBYCON (*8) / RICOCHET (*8) / STRATOSFEAR (*7) / SORCERER soundtrack (*7) / ENCORE (*4) / CYCLONE (*5) / FORCE MAJEURE (*6) / TANGRAM (*6) / QUICHOTTE (aka 'PERGAMON – LIVE AT THE PALAST DER REPUBLIK') (*5) / THIEF soundtrack (*5) / EXIT (*6) / WHITE EAGLE (*5) / LOGOS – LIVE (*5) / WAVELENGTH soundtrack (*4) / HYPERBOREA (*4) / RISKY BUSINESS (*4) / FIRESTARTER soundtrack (*4) / POLAND – THE WARSAW CONCERT (*4) / FLASHPOINT soundtrack (*4) / LE PARC (*5) / HEARTBREAKERS soundtrack (*4) / DREAM SEQUENCES compilation (*6) / LEGEND soundtrack with other artists (*3) / UNDERWATER SUNLIGHT (*4) / GREEN DESERT early work (*5) / TYGER (*5) / THREE O'CLOCK HIGH soundtrack with Silvester Levay (*3) / THE TANGERINE DREAM COLLECTION compilation (*7) / NEAR DARK soundtrack (*4) / LIVE MILES (*4) / SHY PEOPLE soundtrack (*4) / OPTICAL RACE (*5) / MIRACLE MILE soundtrack (*5) / THE BEST OF TANGERINE DREAM compilation (*6) / LILY ON THE BEACH (*4) / MELROSE (*5) / DEAD SOLID PERFECT TV soundtrack (*3) / THE PARK IS MINE TV soundtrack (*3) / ROCKOON (*6) / DEADLY CARE TV soundtrack (*3) / CANYON DREAMS soundtrack (*6) / 220 VOLT LIVE (*6) / TURN OF THE TIDES (*6) / TYRANNY OF BEAUTY (*6) / BOOK OF DREAMS collection (*6) / THE DREAM MIXES remixes (*6) / THE DREAM ROOTS COLLECTION compilation (*6) / GOBLIN'S CLUB soundtrack (*6) / OASIS soundtrack (*4) / TOURNADO (*4) / TRANS SIBERIA (*5) / WHAT A BLAST soundtrack (*5) / AMBIENT MONKEYS (*4) / QUINOA (*5) / MARS POLARIS (*7) / THE GREAT WALL OF CHINA soundtrack (*5) / THE SEVEN LETTERS FROM TIBET (*4) / L'INFERNO (*6) / MOTA ATMA soundtrack (*6) / JEANNE D'ARC (*6) / Edgar Froese: AQUA (*6) / EPSILON IN MALAYSIAN PALE (*6) / MACULA TRANSFER (*4) / AGES (*6) / STUNTMAN (*5) / KAMIKAZE 1989 soundtrack (*4) / PINNACLES (*5) / BEYOND THE STORM compilation (*5) / THE AMBIENT HIGHWAY VOL.1-4 (*5) / DALINETOPIA (*5)

EDGAR FROESE (b. 6 Jun'44, Tilsit, Germany) – guitar, piano, organ (ex-The ONES) / **VOLKER HOMBACH** – flute, violin / **KIRT HERKENBERG** – bass / (Mar69) / **SVEN JOHANNSON** – drums; repl. LANSE HAPRHASH

— In 1970, after HOMBACH became film cameraman for W.R.FASSBINDER, and brief wind instrumentalist STEVE JOLIFFE departed to join STEAMHAMMER. Group reformed **EDGAR FROESE** brought in newcomers **KLAUS SCHULTZE** (b. 4 Aug'47) – drums, percussion / **CONRAD SCHNITZLER** – cello, flute, violin. with guests **JIMMY JACKSON** – organ / **THOMAS VON KEYSERLING** – flute

Ohr — not iss.

Jun 70. (lp) *(OMM 556 004)* **ELECTRONIC MEDITATION** [–] German [–]
– Geburt (Genesis) / Reise durch ein brennendes gehirn (Journey through a burning brain) / Kalter rauch (Cold smoke) / Asche zu asche (Ashes to ashes) / Auferstehung (Resurrection). *(UK cd-iss. Jan87 on 'Jive'; CTANG 4) (cd re-iss. Feb96 on 'Essential'; ESMCD 345)*

— **FROESE** added bass to repertoire, and again supplanted new members **CHRISTOPHER FRANKE** (b. 6 Apr'53) – drums, percussion, synthesizer repl. CONRAD / **STEVE SCHROEDER** – organs repl. KLAUS SCHULTZE who went solo / added new guests **UDO DENNEBORG** – flute, words / **ROLAND PAULICK** – synthesizer

Apr 71. (lp) *(OMM 556 012)* **ALPHA CENTAURI** [–] German [–]
– Sunrise in the third system / Fly and collision of Comas Sola / Alpha Centauri. *(UK-iss.Nov73 on 'Polydor Super'; 2383 314) (cd-iss. Jan87 on 'Jive'; CTANG 5) (re-iss. cd Feb96 on 'Essential'; ESMCD 346)*

— **PETER BAUMANN** – synthesizer, organ repl. SCHROYDER (guested on below)

Feb 72. (7") *(OSS 7006)* **ULTIMA THULE (tell 1). / ULTIMA THULE (tell 2)** [–] German [–]

— More guests were added on next; **FLORIAN FRICKE** – synthesizers / cellists / **CHRISTIAN VALBRACHT / JOCKEN VON GRUMBCOW / HANS JOACHIM BRUNE / JOHANNES LUCKE**

Feb 72. (d-lp) *(OMM 2-556 021)* **ZEIT** [–] German [–]
– 1st movement: Birth of liquid plejades / 2nd movement: Nebulous dawn / 3rd movement: Origins of supernatural probabilities / 4th movement: Zeit. *(UK-iss.Jun76 on 'Virgin'; VD 2503) (cd-iss. Jan87 on 'Jive'; CTANG 3) (cd re-iss. Feb96 on 'Essential'; ESMCD 347)*

Mar 73. (lp) *(OMM 556 031)* **ATEM** [–] German [–]
– Atem / Fauni-Gena / Wahn / Circulation of events. *(UK-iss.Nov73 on 'Polydor Super'; 2383 297) (cd-iss. Jan87 on 'Jive'; CTANG 2) (re-iss. cd Feb96 on 'Essential'; ESMCD 348)*

— In Aug'73, they recorded 'GREEN DESERT' album, unreleased until 1986.

Virgin — Virgin

Mar 74. (lp/c) *(V/TCV 2010)* *<13108>* **PHAEDRA** [15] [ ]
– Phaedra / Mysterious semblance at the strand of nightmares / Movements of a visionary / Sequent 'C'. *(re-iss. Mar84 lp/c; OVED/+C 25) (cd-iss. Jul87; CDV 2010) (cd re-iss. Feb95; TAND 5)*

— **MICHAEL HOENIG** – synthesizer (ex-AGITATION FREE) repl. BAUMANN (on tours only 1974-75)

Mar 75. (lp/c) *(V/TCV 2025)* *<13166>* **RUBYCON** [12] [ ]
– Rubycon – part one / Rubycon – part two. *(re-iss. Mar84 lp/c; OVED/+C 27) (cd-iss. Jul87; CDV 2025) (cd re-iss. Feb95; TAND 6)*

Dec 75. (lp/c) *(V/TCV 2044)* **RICOCHET (live at Liverpool, Coventry & Yorkminster Cathedrals)** [40] [–]
– Ricochet (part 1) / Ricochet (part 2). *(re-iss. Mar84 lp/c; OVED/+C 26) (cd-iss. Jul87; CDV 204) (cd re-iss. Feb95; TAND 7)*

— **BAUMANN** re-united with TD to depose HOENIG who later went solo

Nov 76. (lp/c) *(V/TCV 2068)* *<34427>* **STRATOSFEAR** [39] [ ]
– Stratosfear / The big sleep in search of Hades / 3 a.m. at the border of the marsh from Okefnokee / Invisible limits. *(cd-iss. Jul87; CDV 2068) (re-iss. Aug88 lp/c; OVED/+C 70) (cd re-iss. Feb95; TAND 8)*

Jul 77. (lp/c) *(MCF/+C 2806)* *<2277>* **SORCERER** (soundtrack) [25] Jun77 [ ]
– Main title / Search / The call / Creation / Vengeance / The journey / Grind / Rain forest / Abyss / The mountain road / Impressions of Sorcerer / Betrayal (Sorcerer theme). *(re-iss. Feb82 lp/c; MCL/+C 1646) (cd-iss. Aug92; MCLD 19159) <cd-iss. 1992; 10842>*

Aug 77. (7") *<40740>* **BETRAYAL. / GRIND** [–] [ ]

Nov 77. (d-lp/d-c) *(VD/TCVD 2506)* *<35014>* **ENCORE (live)** [55] [ ]
– Cherokee lane / Moonlight / Coldwater canyon / Desert dream. *(cd-iss. Jul87; CDV 2506) (cd re-iss. Apr95; TAND 1)*

Jan 78. (7") *(VS 199)* **ENCORE. / HOBO MARCH** [ ] [–]

Mar 78. (7") *<9516>* **MOONLIGHT. / COLDWATER CANYON** [–] [ ]

— **STEVE JOLIFFE** – vocals, keyboards, wind returned after several years to repl. BAUMANN who went solo. Added **KLAUS KRIEGER** – drums

Mar 78. (lp/c) *(V/TCV 2097)* **CYCLONE** [37] [–]
– Bent cold sidewalk / Rising runner missed by endless sender / Madrigal meridian. *(cd-iss. Jul87; CDV 2097) (re-iss. Aug88 lp/c; OVED/+C 71) (cd re-iss. Apr95)*

Feb 79. (lp,clear-lp/c) *(V/TCV 2111)* **FORCE MAJEURE** [26] [–]
– Force majeure / Cloudburst flight / Thru metamorphic rocks. *(cd-iss. Jul87; CDV 2111) (re-iss. Aug88 lp/c; OVED/+C 111) cd re-iss. Apr95; TAND 10)*

— (now trio) **FROESE + FRANKE** recruited **JOHANNES SCHMOELLING** – keyboards

May 80. (lp/c) *(V/TCV 2147)* **TANGRAM** [36] [–]
– Tangram set 1 / Tangram set 2. *(cd-iss. Oct85; CDV 2147) (re-iss. Aug88 lp/c; OVED/+C 112) (cd-iss. Apr95; TAND 11)*

Virgin — Elektra

Apr 81. (lp/c) *(V/TCV 2198)* *<5E/5C 521>* **THIEF** (soundtrack) [43] [ ]
– Beach theme / Dr. Destructo / Diamond diary / Burning bar / Beach scene *[UK-only]* / Scrap yard / Trap feeling / Igneous / Confrontation *[US-only]*. *(re-iss. Aug88 lp/c; OVED/+C 72) (cd-iss. Jun88; CDV 2198) (<cd re-iss. Aug95; TAND 12>)*

Sep 81. (lp/c) *(V/TCV 2212)* *<557>* **EXIT** [43] [ ]
– Kiev mission / Pilots of purple twilight / Chronozon / Exit / Network 23 / Remote viewing. *(re-iss. Aug88 lp/c; OVED/+C 166) (cd-iss. Aug88; CDV 2212) (re-iss. cd Aug95; TAND 13)*

Sep 81. (7") *(VS 444)* **CHRONOZON. / NETWORK 23** [ ] [–]

Apr 82. (lp/c) *(V/TCV 2226)* **WHITE EAGLE** [57] [–]
– Midnight in Tulo / Convention of the 24 / White eagle / Mojave plan. *(re-iss. Aug88 lp/c; OVED/+C 150) (cd-iss. Aug88; CDV 2226) (cd re-iss. Aug95; TAND 2)*

Dec 82. (lp/c) *(V/TCV 2257)* **LOGOS – LIVE (At The Dominion)** [ ] [–]
– Logos part 1 / Logos part 2 / Dominion. *(re-iss. Apr86 lp/c; OVED 167) (cd-iss. Jun88; CDV 2257) (re-iss. cd Aug95; TAND 3)*

1983. (lp/c) *<STV/CTV 81207>* **WAVELENGTH** (soundtrack) [–] [ ]
– Alien voices / Wavelength (main title) / Desert drive / Mojave (end title) / Healing / Breakout / Alien goodbyes / Spaceship / Church theme / Sunset drive / Airshaft / Alley walk / Cyro lab / Running through the hills / Campfire theme / Mojave (end title reprise). *(UK cd-iss. Jan89 also on 'Varese Sarabande'; VCD 47223)*
(above issued on 'Silva Screen')

Oct 83. (lp/c/cd) *(V/TCV/CDV 2292)* **HYPERBOREA** [45] [–]
– No man's lannd / Hyperborea / Cinnamon road / Sphinx lightning. *(re-iss. Jun88 lp/c; OVED/+C 175) (re-iss. cd Aug95; TAND 4)*

Dec 83. (lp/c) *(V/TCV 2302)* *<098620>* **RISKY BUSINESS** (soundtrack) [ ] [ ]
– The dream is always the same / No future (get off the babysitter) / Guido the killer pimp / Lana / Love on a real train (Risky Business) / (tracks by other artists; BOB SEGER / MUDDY WATERS / JEFF BECK / PRINCE / JOURNEY / PHIL COLLINS). *(cd-iss. May87; CDV 2302) (re-iss. Apr90 lp/c; OVED/+C 2302)*

M.C.A. — Varese Sarabande

Jul 84. (lp/c) *(MCF/+C 3233)* *<VSD 5251>* **FIRESTARTER** (soundtrack) [ ] [ ]
– Crystal voice / The run / Test lab / Charley the kid / Escaping point / Rainbird's move / Burning force / Between realities / Shop territory / Flash final / Out of the heat. *(re-iss. Jan89; MCA/+C 6163) (cd-iss. Apr90; DMCL 1899)*

Jive Electro — Relativity

Sep 84. (7"/7"sha-pic-d) *(JIVE/+P 74)* **WARSAW IN THE SUN. / POLISH DANCE** [ ] [–]
(12"+=) *(JIVET 74)* – ('A'-part 2) / Rare bird.

Oct 84. (d-lp/d-pic-lp/c) *(HIP/+X/C 22)* *<826099>* **POLAND – THE WARSAW CONCERT (live)** [90] [ ]
– Poland / Tangent / Barbakane / Horizon. *(cd-iss. 1988; CHIP 22) (re-iss. cd May96 on 'Essential'; ESMCD 365)*
(below album released on 'Heavy Metal' UK / 'EMI America' US)

Feb 85. (lp/pic-lp/c) *(HM1 HP/PD/MC 29)* *<ST 17141>* **FLASHPOINT** (soundtrack) [ ] Dec84 [ ]
– Going west / Afternoon in the desert / Plane ride / Mystery tracks / Lost in the dunes / Highway patrol / Love phantasy / Madcap story / Dirty cross-roads / Flashpoint. *(cd-iss. Apr87; HM1 XD 29) (re-iss. cd Sep95 on 'One Way'; OW 18507)*

1985. (lp) Virgin; *(207 212-620)* **HEARTBREAKERS** (soundtrack) [–] German [–]
– Heartbreakers / Footbridge to Heaven / Twilight painter / Gemini / Rain

in New York City / Pastime / The loser / Breathing the night away / Desire / Thorny affair / Daybreak. *(UK cd-iss. Jun95 on 'Silva Screen'; FILMCD 163) <US cd-iss. Jun95 on 'Silva Screen'; 1039>*

Aug 85. (lp/c) *(HIP/+C 26) <8043>* **LE PARC** [ ] [ ]
– Bois de Boulogne (Paris) / Central Park (New York) / Gaudi Park (Guell Garden, Barcelona) / Tiergarten (Berlin) / Zen Garden (Myoonj, Temple Kyoto) / Le Parc (L.A. Streethawk) / Hyde Park (London) / The Cliffs of Sydney (Sydney) / Yellowstone Park (Rocky Mountains). *(cd-iss. Mar88; CHIP 26) (re-iss. cd May96 on 'Essential'; ESMCD 364)*

— guest on above album **CLARE TORY** – vocals

Aug 85. (7") *(JIVE 101)* **STREETHAWK. / TIERGARTEN** [ ] [–]
(12"+=) *(JIVET 101)* – Gaudi Park / Warsaw in the sun (part 1 & 2).

May 86. (lp/c) *M.C.A.; <MCA/+C 6165>* **LEGEND** (soundtrack) [–] [96]
– (a BRYAN FERRY track) / Opening / Cottage / Unicorn theme / Goblins / Fairies / (a JON ANDERSON track) / Blue room / The dance / Darkness / The kitchen – Unicorn theme. *(UK-iss.Jan89; same as US) (re-iss. Jan90 on 'Silva Screen' lp/c/cd; FILM/+C/CD 045)*

— **PAUL HASLINGER** – multi; repl. SCHMOELLING who went solo

Jul 86. (lp/c)(cd) *(HIP/+C 40)(CHIP 40) <8113>*
UNDERWATER SUNLIGHT [97] [ ]
– Song of the whale / From dawn . . . to dusk / Ride on the ray / Dolphin dance / Underwater sunlight / Scuba scuba. *(cd re-iss. May96 on 'Essential'; ESMCD 366)*

Aug 86. (12"ep) *<88561-8120-1>* **DOLPHIN DANCE. / DOLPHIN SMILE / SONG OF THE WHALE** [–] [ ]
Jive Caroline

Jun 87. (lp/c)(cd) *(HIP/+C 47)(CHIP 47) <CAROL 1341>*
TYGER [88] [ ]
– Tyger / London / Alchemy of the heart / Smile. *(cd+=)* – 21st century common man I & II. *(cd re-iss. May96 on 'Essential'; ESMCD 367)*

— guest vox – BERNADETTE SMITH

Jun 87. (7") *(JIVE 143)* **TYGER. / 21st CENTURY COMMON MAN II** [ ] [ ]
(12"+=) *(JIVET 143)* – ('A'extended).

Nov 87. (lp; shared w/ SYLVESTER LEVAY, etc.) *Varese Sarabande; <STV 81339>* **THREE O'CLOCK HIGH** (soundtrack) [–] [ ]
– It's Jerry's day today / 46-32-15 / No detention / Any school bully will do / Go to the head of the class / (SYLVESTER LEVAY tracks) / Big bright brass knuckles / Buying paper like it's going out of style / Dangerous trend / Who's chasing who? / Bonding by candlelight / You'll never believe it / Starting the day off right / Weak at the knees / Kill him (the football dummy) / Not so quiet in the library – Get lost in a crowd / (tracks by JIM WALKER / RICK MAROTTA & DAVID TICKLE). *(UK cd-iss. Oct90 also on 'Varese Sarabande'; VCD 47307)*

Apr 88. (lp/c)(cd) *(HIP/+C 62)(CHIP 62) <CAROL 1349>*
LIVEMILES (live) [ ] [ ]
– Live miles: (part 1) – The Albuquerque concert / Live miles: (part 2) – The West Berlin concert. *(re-iss. cd May96 on 'Essential'; ESMCD 368)*

Silva Screen Silva Screen

Feb 88. (lp/c/cd) *(<FILM/+C/CD 026>)* **NEAR DARK** (soundtrack) [ ] [Nov87]
– Caleb's blues / Pick up at high noon / Rain in the third house / Bus station / Good times / She's my sister (resurrection 1) / Mae comes back / Father and son (resurrection 2) / Severin dies / Fight at dawn / Mae's transformation. *<(cd-iss. Jun90; VSD 47309)>*

Jul 88. (lp/c/cd) *(FILM/+C/CD 027) <VCD 47357>* **SHY PEOPLE** (soundtrack) [ ] [Nov87]
– Shy people (vocals: JACQUIE VIRGIL) / Joe's place / The harbor (vocals: DIAMOND ROSS) / Nightfall / Dancing on a white moon (vocals: JACQUIE VIRGIL) / Civilized illusions / Swamp voices / Transparent days / Shy people (reprise).

— now a duo of **FROESE + HASLINGER**

Arista Private Music

Feb 89. (lp/c/cd) *(209/409/259 557) <2042-1/-4/-2 P>* **OPTICAL RACE** [ ] [Aug88]
– Marakesh / Atlas eyes / Mothers of rain / Twin soul tribe / Optical race / Cat scan / Sun gate / Turning of the wheel / The midnight trail / Ghtrezi (long song).

Jul 89. (lp/c/cd) *(209/409/259 887) <2047-1/-4/-2>* **MIRACLE MILE** (soundtrack) [ ] [ ]
– Teetering scales / One for the books / After the call / On the spur of the moment / All of a dither / Final statement / In Julie's eyes / Running out of time / If it's all over / People in the news / Museum walk. *(re-iss. cd Feb96; 260.016)*

Dec 89. (lp/c/cd) *<210/410/260 103>* **LILY ON THE BEACH** [–] [ ]
– Too hot for my chinchilla / Lily on the beach / Alaskan summer / Desert drive / Mount Shasta / Crystal curfew / Paradise cove / Twenty nine palms / Valley of the kings / Radio city / Blue mango cafe / Gecko / Long island sunset.

Dec 89. (cd/lp) *<260/210 440>* **DESTINATION BERLIN** (soundtrack) [–] [Canada] [–]
– Alexander Square (lp version) / Emperors castle / Hitchhikers point / Brandenburg gate / Wall-street / Peacock island / Down the Avus / Midnight in Bear City / Berlin summer nights / Alexander Square (reprise).

Nov 90. (cd/lp) *(<261/211 105>)* **MELROSE** [ ] [Sep90]
– Melrose / Three bikes in the sky / Dolls in the shadow / Yucatan / Electric lion / Rolling down Cahenga / Art of vision / Desert train / Cool at heart.

EMI France not iss.US

1991. (cd) *(795617-2)* **L'AFFAIRE WALLRAFF / THE MAN INSIDE** (soundtrack) [–] [French] [–]
– Wallraff's theme / Tendency of love / Addicted to the truth / World of the "standard" / Purposes of brevity / Tobel's death by the river / Taboo society / The drive to Hanover / Correlation of lies / Investigation / News and morality.

— in 1990/91, TANGERINE DREAM featured with actress KATHLEEN TURNER on the children's CD/album, 'Rumpelstiltskin', for 'Rhino'

— now a duo of **FROESE + JEROME FROESE** his son and **LINDA SPA** – sax / **ZLASLO PERICA** – synth

Essential Miramar

Feb 92. (cd/c/lp) *(ESM CD/MC/LP 403) <2802>* **ROCKOON** [ ] [ ]
– Big city dwarves / Red roadster / Touchwood / Graffiti sreeet / Funky Atlanta / Spanish love / Lifted veil / Penguin reference / Body corporate / Rockoon / Girls on Broadway. *(re-iss. cd Feb96; same) (cd re-iss. Feb00 on 'Tandream'; TDICD 017)*

Miramar Miramar

Oct 93. (cd/c) *(<MPCD/MPMC 2804>)* **220 VOLT LIVE (live)** [ ] [ ]
– Oriental haze / Two bunch palms / 220 volt / Homeless / Treasure of innocence / Sundance kid / Backstreet hero / The blue bridge / Hamlet / Dreamtime / Purple haze. *(cd re-iss. Nov99 on 'Tandream'; TDICD 018)*

CoastCoast Miramar

Nov 94. (cd) *(CTCZ 108) <2806>* **TURN OF THE TIDES** [ ] [ ]
– Pictures at an exhibition / Firetongues / Galley slave's horizon / Death of a nightingale / Twilight brigade / Jungle journey / Midwinter night / Turn of the tides. *(re-iss. Nov96; same) (cd re-iss. Nov99 on 'Tangerine Dream Int,'; TDICD 019)*

Amp Miramar

Sep 95. (cd) *(23046) <MM 137>* **TYRANNY OF BEAUTY** [ ] [ ]
– Catwalk / Birdwatcher's dream / Little blond in the park of attractions / Living in a fountain pen / Stratosfear 95 / Bride in cold tears / Haze of fame / Tyranny of beauty / Largo / (untitled). *(re-iss. Oct96 on 'Tangerine Dream Int.'; TDI 002CD) (cd re-iss. Nov99; TDICD 020)*

When! Tangerine

Sep 96. (cd) *(<WENCD 011>)* **GOBLINS CLUB** [ ] [ ]
– Towards the evening star / At Darwin's motel / On Cranes' passage / Rising haul in silence / United goblin's parade / Lamb with radar eyes / Elf June and the midnight patrol / Sad Merlin's Sunday.

Mar 97. (c-s) *(WENM 1022)* **TOWARDS THE EVENING STAR / ('A'mix)** [ ] [–]
(12"+=/cd-s+=) *(WEN T/X 1022)* – ('A'remixes).

Tandream Miramar

Jun 97. (cd) *(TDI 009CD) <63009>* **OASIS** (soundtrack) [ ] [Oct97]
– Flashflood / Zion / Reflections / Cliff dwellers / Waterborne / Cedar breaks / Summer storm / Hopi mesa heart / Chia maroon. *(re-iss. Mar00; same)*

Sep 97. (cd) *(TDI 011CD)* **TOURNADO (live in Europe)** [ ] [–]
– Flashflood / 220 volt / Firetongues / Girls on Broadway / Little blond in the park of attractions / Rising haul in silence / Lamb with radar eyes / Touchwood / Towards the evening star.

Apr 99. (cd) *(TDI 012CD) <63012>* **TRANS SIBERIA** [ ] [ ]
– Yarloslaw station / Smoky Karlow / Siberian lights / Jenissei river / Baikal sunrise / Samowar Juri / Ulan-Ude / Chingan night / Russian soul / The golden horn.

May 99. (cd) *(TDICD 015) <63015>* **WHAT A BLAST** (soundtrack) [ ] [ ]
– Stoneyard / Silver siren / Beauty of the blast / Dream sculpture / Last trumpet on 23rd Street / Art of destruction / Forced to surrender / TimeSquare (the legendary N.Y. Brix mix) / Jungle journey (the bond of ages mix).

Jul 99. (cd) *(TDI 016CD) <63016>* **MARS POLARIS** [ ] [ ]
– Comet's figure head / Rim of Schiaparelli / Pilots of the ether belt /

Deep space cruiser / Outland (the colony) / Spiral star date / Mars mission encounter / Astrophobia / Tharsis manoeuver / Dies martis (transmercury).

Mar 00. (cd) *(TDI 022CD) <63022>* **GREAT WALL OF CHINA** (new soundtrack for 1970 film) Jan00
– Meng tian / Summer in Shauxi / The south gate knights / Silence the barking monk / Zhu zhanji / Stranded without shade / No more candles burning / Lights of Beijing / Snow on dragon's peak / Cradle of prodigies / Tiger forest.

Nov 00. (cd) *(TDI 029CD) <63029>* **THE SEVEN LETTERS FROM TIBET** Aug00
– The red blood connection / The orange breath / The golden heart / The green land / The blue pearl / The indigo clouds / The purple of all curtains.

Dec 02. (cd) *(<TDICD 032>)* **L'INFERNO** (live 2001) Sep02
– Before the closing of the day / The spirit of Virgil / Minotaurae hunt at dawn / Those once broke the first word / Dante in despair / Io non mori / Vidi tre facce / At the deepest point in space / L'omperador del doloroso regno / Voices in a starless night / Fear and longing / Fallen for death / Where all light went silent / Charon, il barchere / La grey de los almas perdidas / Justice of the karma law / As the sun moves towards heaven / Beatrice, l'ame infinie.

May 03. (cd) *(<TDP 001>)* **MOTA ATMA** (soundtrack)
– The courage to lose / For the summit only / No pleasure no pain / Royal way of privacy / Phoenix burning / Prophet in chains / Snow on angels feather / A fair days wage / Brain offender / A day in Liberty Valley.

Jan 06. (cd) *(TDP 014CD) <01111>* **JEANNE D'ARC**
– La vision / La joie / La force dans l'espoir / La marche / La sagesse du destin / Le combat du sang / Le combat des epees / La liberation.

– compilations, others, etc. –

—— on 'Virgin' unless mentioned otherwise

Dec 86. (cd) *Zomba; (CTANG 1)* **GREEN DESERT** (rec.1973)
(re-iss. May89 on 'Jive' lp/c; HOP/+C 226) (re-iss. Feb96 on 'Essential'; ESMCD 349)

Mar 87. (d-lp/c/cd) *(CCS LP/MC/CD 161)* **THE TANGERINE DREAM COLLECTION**

Nov 89. (lp/c)(cd) *Jive; (HIP/+C 75)(CHIP 75)* **THE BEST OF TANGERINE DREAM**

Nov 90. (3xcd-box) *(TPAK 11)* **COLLECTORS' EDITION**
– (CYCLONE / FORCE MAJEURE / ENCORE)

Mar 91. (cd) *Silva Screen; (<FILMCD 079>)* **DEAD SOLID PERFECT** (1988 TV soundtrack)
– Theme from Dead Solid Perfect / In the pond / Beverly leaves / Of cads and caddies / (Tournament montage) / A whore in one / Sand trap / In the rough / Nine iron / US Open / My name is bad hair / In the hospital room / Welcome to Bushwood / Deja vu / Birdie / Divot / Kenny and Donny montage / Phone to Beverly / Nice shots / Sinking putts / Kenny's winning shot.

Oct 91. (cd) *(FILMCD 080) <1004-2>* **THE PARK IS MINE** (1985 soundtrack) Mar92
– The park is mine – main title / Fatal fall – Funeral / The letter (parts 1 & 2) / Taking the park (parts 1 & 2) / Swatting S.W.A.T. / Love theme / Helicopter attack / Morning / We're running out of time / The claymore mine – Stalking / The final confrontation – The park is yours / Finale – End credits.

Oct 91. (cd/c) *Music Club; (MC CD/TC 034)* **FROM DAWN . . . TILL DUSK 1973-88**

Dec 92. (cd) *Silva Screen; (<FILMCD 121>)* **DEADLY CARE** (1987 TV soundtrack)
– Main theme / Paddles – Stolen pills / A strong drink – A bad morning / Wasted and sick / Hope for future / The hospital in bed / Annie and father / More pills / In the Head nurse's – At the father's grave / Clean and sober.

Mar 93. (cd) *Silva Screen; (FILMCD 125)* **DREAM MUSIC**
– from TV films; THE PARK IS MINE / DEADLY CARE / DEAD SOLID PERFECT

Jul 93. (cd) *Miramar; (<MPCD 2801>)* **CANYON DREAMS** (1987 soundtrack) 1991
– Shadow flyer / Canyon carver / Water's gift / Canyon voices / Sudden revelation / A matter of time / Purple nightfall / Colorado dawn. *(re-iss. Nov99 on 'Tandream'+=; TDICD 021)* – Rocky Mountain hawk.

Feb 94. (cd) *Edel America; <EDS 5413-2>* **CATCH ME IF YOU CAN** (1989 soundtrack)
– Dylan's future / Sad Melissa / Fast Eddie's car / Back to the race / Melissa asks Dylan out / Dylan alone at home / Melissa needs help / The kiss / Racing montage / The clock is ticking / Widow maker / Dylan's dream / Taking the test / Back to the race again / One more chance / Melissa's challenge / Widow maker race / Dylan's triumph / Catch Me If You Can main theme.

Oct 94. (5xcd-box) *(CDBOX 4)* **TANGENTS**

Dec 95. (d-cd) *Essential; (EDFCD 353)* **BOOK OF DREAMS**
– (THE PINK YEARS: 1970-1973) // THE BLUE YEARS: 1983-1987)

Apr 96. (cd) *Tsunami; (TCI 0616)* **THE KEEP** (a compilation!)
– The Keep – main title / Glaken's quest / Brothers in death / Fisherman's morning / Evil healing / Gloria/ Crystal voice / Burning force / Heartbreakers / Twilight painter / Caleb's blues / The search / The call / Grind / Mountain road / Love on a real train.

1996. (cd) *Repertoire; (REP 4595WY)* **ZONING** (1986 soundtrack) German
– The conspiracy / Skyscraper / Headhunter / Downtown Chicago / Fading and turning / Affluent society / Stairway affair / Good choice, bad timing / Bachelor of crime / Unfit for consumption / Days of grief and glory / Eyewitness news / Missing link.

Jul 96. (cd) *Tangerine Dream Int.; (TDI 001CD)* **THE DREAM MIXES**

Nov 96. (5xcd-box) *Essential; (ESFCD 420)* **THE DREAM ROOTS COLLECTION**

1997. (cd) *bootleg; (none)* **THE KEEP** (soundtrack) German
– Puer natus est nobis (Gloria theme) / Ancient powerplant / The silver seal / Voices from a common land / Arx allemand / The night in Romania / Canzone / Sign in the dark / Weird village / Love and destiny / The challenger's arrival / Supernatural accomplice / Parallel worlds / Truth and fiction / Wardays sunrise / Heritage survival.

Oct 98. (3xcd-box) *Essential; (ESMBX 305)* **ELECTRONIC MEDITATION / ALPHA CENTAURI / ZEIT**

Mar 00. (cd) *Tandream; (TDICD 001) / Resurgent; <4250>* **AMBIENT MONKEYS (live 1997)** 1998
– Token from Birdland / Symphony in a minor / The seventh propeller of silence / Calyx calamander / Largo / Riddle of the monkey tribe / Moon marble / Concerto in a minor, adagio / Lemon vendor khaly / Campera de mon glyan / Virtue is its own reward / Pantha rhei / Myopia world.

Mar 00. (cd) *Tandream; (TDICD 004) <63004>* **DREAM ENCORES (live)** Jun99
– Order of the ginger guild / Forth Worth runway one / Eleanor Rigby / Oriental haze / Story of the brave / Thief Yang and the tangram seal / Catwalk / Purple haze / The midnight trail / Rolling down Cahuenga / Towards the evening star / Dominion.

Mar 00. (d-cd) *Tandream; (TDICD 005) <63005>* **DREAM MIXES I**

Mar 00. (cd) *Tandream; (TDICD 006) <63006>* **TIMESQUARE – DREAM MIXES II** (rec. summer 1997)
– Mobocaster / Jungle jacula / Towards the evening star / Digital sister / Pixel pirates / Culpa levis / TimesSquare.

May 00. (d-cd) *Tandream; (TDICD 026) <63026>* **TANG-GO – THE WORLD OF TANGERINE DREAM 1990-2000**

Jun 00. (cd) *(TDI 027CD) <63027>* **SOUNDMILL NAVIGATOR (live at the Philharmonics 1976)** Apr00
– Soundmill navigator.

Aug 00. (cd) *Tandream; (TDICD 028) <63028>* **ANTIQUE DREAMS**

May 01. (cd) *Tandream; (TDICD 031) <63031>* **DM3: DREAM MIXES THREE** Apr01
– Prime time / Astrophobia / Stereolight / Diamonds and dust / Blue spears / Meng tian / Girl on the stairs / The spirit of the czar / The comfort zone.

Jan 06. (cd) *Tandream; (TDP 013CD) <6462>* **ROCKING MARS** (rec.1999)

EDGAR FROESE

—— solo (all music by himself)

Virgin Virgin

Jun 74. (lp) *(V 2016) <13111>* **AQUA**
– NGC 891 / Upland / Aqua / Panorphelia. *(re-iss. Mar84; OVED 20) (cd-iss. Jun87; CDV 2016)*

Sep 75. (lp) *(V 2040)* **EPSILON IN MALAYSIAN PALE**
– Epsilon in Malaysian pale / Maroubra Bay. *(re-iss. Mar84; OVED 22) (cd-iss. Jun87; CDV 2040) (cd re-iss. Jul05 on 'Tangerine Dream'; TDP 009CD)*

1976. Brain; (lp) *(60.008)* **MACULA TRANSFER** German
– Os / Af / Pa / Quantas / If. *(re-iss. Mar82; 0060.008) (cd-iss. Nov05 on 'Tangerine Dream'; TDP 011CD)*

Jan 78. (d-lp) *(VD 2507)* **AGES** [ ] [–]
– Metropolis / Era of the slaves / Tropic of Capricorn / Nights of automatic women / Icarus / Childrens deeper study / Ode to Granny "A" / Pizarro and Atahwallpa / Golgatha and the circle closes. *(cd-iss. Jun97; CDOVD 480) (cd re-iss. Jul05 on 'Tangerine Dream'; TDP 008CD)*

Sep 79. (lp) *(V 2139)* **STUNTMAN** [ ] [–]
– Stuntman / It would be like Samoa / Detroit snackbar dreamer / Drunken Mozart in the desert / A Dali-esque sleep fuse / Scarlet score for Mescalero. *(re-iss. Mar84; OVED 21) (cd-iss. Jun87 & Mar94; CDV 2139) (cd re-iss. Nov05 on 'Tangerine Dream'; TDP 012CD)*

Oct 82. (lp) *(V 2255)* **KAMIKAZE 1989** (soundtrack) [ ] [–]
– Videophonic / Vitamin 'C' / Krismopompas / Police disco / Intuition / Police therapy center / Blue panther / Snake bath / Unexpected death / Flying kamikaze / Tower block / The 31st floor. *(re-iss. Aug88; OVED 125) (cd-iss. Aug88; CDV 2255) <cd-iss. 1992 on 'Caroline'; CAROL 1626-2>*

Aug 83. (lp) *(V 2277)* **PINNACLES** [ ] [–]
– Specific gravity of smile / The light cone / Walkabout / Pinnacles. *(re-iss. Aug88; OVED 144) (cd-iss. May88; CDV 2277) (cd re-iss. Nov05 on 'Tangerine Dream'; TDP 013CD)*

Tangerine Dream | Eastgate Music

Oct 03. (cd) *(TDP 002CD)* **AN INTRODUCTION TO AMBIENT HIGHWAY** [ ] [–]

Oct 03. (cd) *(TDP 003CD)* **THE AMBIENT HIGHWAY VOL.1** [ ] [–]
– Sahara child / Walkabout Abora / Santa Elena Marisal / Carneol / Bobcats in the sun / Afternoon on the Nile / Magic lantern / Crane routing / Tierra del fuego / Dome of yellow turtles / Car dreaming.

Oct 03. (cd) *(TDP 004CD)* **THE AMBIENT HIGHWAY VOL.2** [ ] [–]
– Stuntman pt.2 (re-rec.) / Moonlight on a crawler lane / Raindance / One fine day in Siberia / Heatwave city / Epsilon in Malaysian pale pt.2 (re-rec.) / Shores of Guam / Tropic of Capricorn pt.2 (re-rec.) / Vault of the heaven / Koala sunrise / The morning seal.

Oct 03. (cd) *(TDP 005CD)* **THE AMBIENT HIGHWAY VOL.3** [ ] [–]
– Down to Barstow / Copper coast / Days of camouflage / Macula transfer pt.2 (re-rec.) / The night at Ayers Rock / The light cone pt.2 (re-rec.) / Genesta in the afternoon glow / Drunken Mozart in the desert pt.2 (re-rec.) / Gizeh sunset / Summer in Key West / Craving for a rose.

Oct 03. (cd) *(TDP 006CD)* **THE AMBIENT HIGHWAY VOL.4** [ ] [–]
– Colorado dawn / Great Barrier riff / Bourbon street parade / Descent like a hawk / Juniper mascara / Pinnacles pt.2 / Vulcano / Metropolis pt.2 / South Dakota / Year of the falcon / Raindrops on black skin.

Jul 05. (cd) *(TDP 007CD) <604388 65612-7>* **DALINETOPIA** [ ] Aug05 [ ]
– Daleroshima / Dalozapata / Dalamuerte / DElerotica / Daliesquador / Daluminacion / Dalagalor / Daluna / Dalysisiphus / Dalinetopia.

– FROESE compilations, others –

Aug 82. (lp) *Virgin; (V 2197)* **SOLO 1974-1979** [ ] [–]
(re-iss. Mar84; OVED 21) (cd-iss. Aug88; CDV 2197)

Jun 95. (d-cd) *Ambient; (AMBT 5)* **BEYOND THE STORM** [ ] [–]

TAPROOT

Formed: Ann Arbor, Michigan, USA ... 1997 by University of Michigan students STEPHEN RICHARDS, MIKE DeWOLF, PHIL LIPSCOMB and JARROD MONTAGUE. Inspired by the likes of NIRVANA and RAGE AGAINST THE MACHINE, TAPROOT began using the internet for publicity and eventually appropriated a fan's web page as their official site. With a bit of DIY improvement, the site soon generated enough interest for the band to distribute a demo to LIMP BIZKIT mainman FRED DURST. A growing friendship ended in tears after DURST allegedly offered a below par deal and TAPROOT looked elsewhere, resulting in a now infamous answering machine message from the pissed off 'BIZKIT mainman. Undeterred, the group released their self-produced debut album, 'SOMETHING MORE THAN NOTHING' (1998) off their own steam, following it up with the 'MENTOBE' EP. Their internet endeavours together with word of mouth publicity soon attracted major label interest, the band signing with 'Atlantic' for their second album, 'GIFT' (2000). Awarded 5 stars by Kerrang!, the record bore favourable comparison with rap-influenced nu-metal pioneers such as KORN and DEFTONES with a conspicuous lack of any contrived image going in their favour. This very quality perhaps worked against them on 'WELCOME' (2002), another post-grunge by numbers set to add to the avalanche of similar albums clogging up American charts and radio. RICHARDS and TAPROOT stretched their repertoire with a long-awaited third set, 'BLUE-SKY RESEARCH' (2005), a US Top 40 entry that featured three collaborative songs with BILLY CORGAN: 'VIOLENT SEAS', 'LOST IN THE WOODS' and 'PROMISE'.

Album rating: GIFT (*7) / WELCOME (*5) / BLUE-SKY RESEARCH (*4)

STEPHEN RICHARDS – vocals, guitar / **MIKE DeWOLF** – guitar / **PHIL LIPSCOMB** – bass / **JARROD MONTAGUE** – drums

Atlantic | Atlantic

Sep 00. (cd) *<7567 83341-2>* **GIFT** [ ] Jun00 [ ]
– Smile / Again and again / Emotional times / Now / 1 nite stand / Believed / Mentobe / I / Mirror's reflection / Dragged down / Comeback / Impact.

Mar 01. (cd-s) *(AT 0099CD)* **AGAIN AND AGAIN (clean version) / DAY BY DAY / SMILE (clean version)** [ ] [–]

Sep 02. (cd) *<7567 83561-2>* **WELCOME** [ ] [17]
– Mine / Poem / Everything / Art / Myself / When / Fault / Sumtimes / Breathe / Like / Dreams / Time.

Oct 02. (cd-s) *(AT 0138CD)* **POEM / TRANSPARENT / FREE** [ ] [–]

Jun 03. (cd-s) *(AT 0153CD)* **MINE / POEM (live at Radio 1's Rockshow) / MINE (video)** [ ] [–]
(dvd-s) *(AT 0153DVD)* – ('A') / Again & again (live at Radio 1's Rockshow) / Poem (video – live in Tokyo).

Aug 05. (-) *<radio>* **CALLING** [–] [ ]

Aug 05. (cd) *<7567 83720-2>* **BLUE-SKY RESEARCH** [ ] [33]
– I will not fall for you / Violent seas / Birthday / Facepeeler / Calling / Forever endevor / April suits / Lost in the woods / So eager / She / Promise / Nightmare / Blue-sky research – What's left.

□ TASTE (see under ⇒ GALLAGHER, Rory)

James TAYLOR

Born: 12 Mar'48, Boston, Massachusetts, USA. Despite a privileged upbringing, the troubled TAYLOR admitted himself to a mental institute in 1965, aged only 17. It was during his near-year long stay that the budding singer began writing his own material although it would be early '67 before he'd get the chance to lay some of his ideas down on vinyl. This opportunity presented itself after TAYLOR moved to New York and hooked up with old friend DANNY KORTCHMAR in The FLYING MACHINE, the group subsequently recording two TAYLOR tracks, 'NIGHT OWL' and 'BRIGHTEN YOUR NIGHT WITH MY DAY'. A combination of poor sales and TAYLOR's worsening heroin addiction caused the band to splinter a few months later, the singer subsequently moving to Notting Hill in London the following year. Persuaded to send a demo to Peter Asher, then A&R man at 'Apple' (and future manager of LINDA RONSTADT), TAYLOR soon found himself recording for The BEATLES' fledgling label. His Asher-produced, eponymous debut was released at the tail end of the year, a promising collection of understated strumming and wistful introspection. Almost country-rock but not quite, such memorable originals as 'SOMETHING IN THE WAY SHE MOVES' (NOT the BEATLES song!) and the yearning 'CAROLINA IN MY MIND' marked TAYLOR out as a kind of male JONI MITCHELL, if not quite as adventurous. As it turned out, the pair found they had more in common than just music, TAYLOR and MITCHELL becoming romantically involved in the early 70's. As well as performing together, the couple guested on each other's releases with MITCHELL partly documenting the affair on her landmark 'BLUE' album. Despite its potential, 'JAMES TAYLOR' sank without trace amid the chaotic situation at 'Apple', both TAYLOR and ASHER moving back to the States. After another period in a mental institution, TAYLOR emerged to find himself with a 'Warner Bros' contract, pre-arranged by ASHER (now his manager). Surrounding himself with the likes of RUSS KUNKEL, RANDY MEISNER and CAROLE KING, TAYLOR duly cut a belated follow-up album. Though it took a while to warm up, 'SWEET BABY JAMES' (1970) became one of the best selling US albums of the early 70's as well as a blueprint of sorts for the Laurel Canyon elite (whose tortured musings would come to dominate the American rock scene). Following the Top 3 success of the enduring 'FIRE AND RAIN', the album went on to reside in the upper reaches of the US chart for more than a year, its unassuming confessionals striking at the strife-torn heart of the post-hipppie dream. Not blessed with the most striking of voices, TAYLOR nevertheless relied on it to power his songs, backed by the sparsest of accompaniment, an acoustic strum here, a hint of pedal steel there. What he lacked in impact he made up for in intimacy (although his vocals improved over time), it's just a pity he moved ever further into MOR schmooze-pop. 'MUD SLIDE SLIM AND THE BLUE HORIZON' (1971) consolidated TAYLOR's standing in the L.A. firmament, a transatlantic Top 5 which featured his rather weak reading of CAROLE KING's 'YOU'VE GOT A FRIEND', a US No.1 later that summer. Ironically, many of TAYLOR's subsequent hits would be cover versions although his original material was far more affecting, the lovely 'YOU CAN CLOSE YOUR EYES' for example. This period saw TAYLOR at the height of his fame and apart from the inevitable media attention over his marriage to CARLY SIMON on the 3rd of November '72, he subsequently avoided the spotlight. Both 'ONE MAN DOG' (1972) and 'WALKING MAN' (1974) failed to spawn any major hits, TAYLOR's only Top 5 single during this time a duet with SIMON entitled 'MOCKINGBIRD'. 'GORILLA' (1975) marked a return to form of sorts, the buoyant 'MEXICO' demonstrating what TAYLOR was capable of when he decided to step up a gear. The album's hit was a laboured cover of Marvin Gaye's 'HOW SWEET IT IS TO BE LOVED BY YOU', the song going Top 5 in the summer of '75. Two years on, TAYLOR repeated the success with yet another cover, a strident run-through of the Jimmy Jones & Otis Blackwell's R&B number, 'HANDY MAN'. The album which housed it, 'J.T.' (1977), was TAYLOR's last commercial blockbuster, subsequent releases selling respectably but failing to produce any singles. For the ensuing two years, the singer turned his talents towards collaboration; Autumn '77 saw him produce and play guitar on sister KATE TAYLOR's debut US Top 50 single, 'IT'S IN HIS KISS', while early the folowing year he was credited alongside PAUL SIMON and ART GARFUNKEL on a hit cover of SAM COOKE's 'WONDERFUL WORLD'. 'FLAG' (1979) gave him another Top 10 album although the formula was wearing a mite thin, his marriage with SIMON soon going the same way. In late '78 the couple rode into the Top 40 together with the duet 'DEVOTED TO YOU', but in 1982, CARLY filed for divorce. TAYLOR had hit the US charts the previous year with his last Top 10 album, 'DAD LOVES HIS WORK', the singer spending the first half of the 80's on a massive world tour. Though his albums didn't command the mass audience of yore, TAYLOR retained a loyal following throughout the 80's and beyond. Fans lapped up 'THAT'S WHY I'M HERE' (1986), although he only really hit the mark with 'NEW MOON SHINE' (1991), a strong set which tackled many current issues in impressive fashion and proved that TAYLOR, along with his old mucker, JACKSON BROWNE, could still cut the mustard. A (US) Top 20 live album in 1993 marked his biggest success for years and certainly, it's on a stage in lone acoustic fashion that TAYLOR really comes into his own, the singer playing some rare, warmly received Scottish dates in early '98 at the annual Celtic Connections festival in Glasgow. On the recording front, he finally broke his silence with 'OCTOBER ROAD' (2002), a rich, mellow, intimate album perfectly in tune with his advancing middle age. Unhurried and glowing with contentment without sounding smug, the likes of the title track resurrected well worn themes from his long career, laying his ghosts to rest once and for all.

• **Songwriters:** Prolific pensmith, who also covered others; LO AND BEHOLD (Bob Dylan) / MOCKINGBIRD duet (Inez & Charlie Foxx) / DEVOTED TO YOU duet (Everly Brothers) / UP ON THE ROOF (Goffin-King) / DAY TRIPPER (Beatles) / JELLY MAN KELLY (with daughter Sarah) / EVERYDAY (Buddy Holly). • **Trivia:** TAYLOR starred in the 1971 road movie, 'Two Lane Blacktop' and also acted on US TV production, 'Working' (1981).

Album rating: JAMES TAYLOR (*7) / SWEET BABY JAMES (*8) / MUD SLIDE SLIM AND THE BLUE HORIZON (*7) / ONE MAN DOG (*6) / WALKING MAN (*6) / GORILLA (*6) / IN THE POCKET (*5) / GREATEST HITS compilation (*8) / JT (*7) / FLAG (*6) / DAD LOVES HIS WORK (*5) / THAT'S WHY I'M HERE (*6) / BEST OF JAMES TAYLOR – CLASSIC SONGS compilation (*7) / NEVER DIE YOUNG (*5) / NEW MOON SHINE (*6) / (LIVE) (*6) / HOURGLASS (*6) / GREATEST HITS VOLUME 2 compilation (*7) / OCTOBER ROAD (*6) / YOU'VE GOT A FRIEND – THE BEST OF . . . compilation (*8)

JAMES TAYLOR – vocals, acoustic guitar (with session people)

Apple / Apple

Dec 68. (lp) *(SAPCOR 3)* <3352> **JAMES TAYLOR** — [ ] / Sep 70 [62]
– Don't talk now / Something's wrong / Knockin' round the zoo / Sunshine sunshine / Taking it in / Something in the way she moves / Carolina in my mind / Brighten your night with my day / Night owl / Rainy day man / Circle 'round the Sun / The blues is just a bad dream. *(re-iss. Jun71; same) (re-iss. Oct91)*

Apr 69. (7") *<1805>* **CAROLINA ON MY MIND. / SOMETHING'S WRONG** — [–] / [ ]
<re-iss. Nov70; same> – <hit No.67>

—— now with **DANNY KOOTCH** (b.KORTCHMAR) – guitar / **CAROLE KING** – piano / **RUSS KUNKEL** – drums / **RANDY MEISNER, BOBBY WEST + JOHN LONDON** – bass / **CHRIS DARROW** – fiddle / **RED RHODES** – steel guitar / **JACK BIELAN** – brass arrangement

Warners / Warners

Jul 70. (7") *<7387>* **SWEET BABY JAMES. / SUITE FOR ZOG** — [–] / [ ]

Sep 70. (7") *<7423>* **FIRE AND RAIN. / ANYWHERE LIKE HEAVEN** — [–] / [3]

Nov 70. (7") *(WB 6104)* **FIRE AND RAIN. / SUNNY SKIES** — [42] / [–]

Nov 70. (lp) *(K 46043)* <1843> **SWEET BABY JAMES** — [7] / Mar 70 [3]
– Sweet baby James / Lo and behold / Sunny skies / Steamroller / Country road / Oh, Susannah / Fire and rain / Blossom / Anywhere like Heaven / Oh baby, don't you loose your lip on me / Suite for 20 G. *(re-iss. Dec71, hit UK No.34) (re-iss. Jul88 cd/c; K2/K4 46043)*

Feb 71. (7") *<7460>* **COUNTRY ROAD. / SUNNY SKIES** — [–] / [37]

—— **LEE SKLAR** – bass repl. 3 bassmen. Guest **JONI MITCHELL** – b.vox (2 – 45's)

May 71. (lp/c) *(K/K4 46085) <2561>* **MUD SLIDE SLIM AND THE BLUE HORIZON** — [4] / [2]
– Love has brought me around / You've got a friend / Places in my past / Riding on a railroad / Soldiers / Mud slide Slim / Hey mister, that's me upon the jukebox / You can close your eyes / Machine gun Kelly / Long ago and far away / Let me ride / Highway song / Isn't it nice to be home again. *(re-iss. Mar72, hit UK No.49) (cd-iss. 1989; K2 56004)*

Aug 71. (7") *(K 16085) <7498>* **YOU'VE GOT A FRIEND. / YOU CAN CLOSE YOUR EYES** — [4] / Jun71 [1]

Sep 71. (7") *<7521>* **LONG AGO AND FAR AWAY. / LET ME RIDE** — [–] / [31]

Nov 72. (lp/c) *(K/K4 46185) <2660>* **ONE MAN DOG** — [27] / [4]
– One man parade / Nobody but you / Chili dog / Fool for you / Instrumental I / New tune / Back on the street again / Don't let me be lonely tonight / Woh, don't you know / One morning in May / Instrumental II / Someone / Hymn / Fanfare / Little David / Mescalito / Dance / Jig. *(quad-lp US Feb76) (cd-iss. Feb92)*

Nov 72. (7") *(K 16231) <7655>* **DON'T LET ME BE LONELY TONIGHT. / WOH, DON'T YOU KNOW** — [ ] / [14]

Feb 73. (7") *<7682>* **ONE MAN PARADE. / NOBODY BUT YOU** — [–] / [67]

May 73. (7") *<7695>* **HYMN. / FANFARE** — [–] / [ ]

—— In Jan'74, did duet with wife CARLY SIMON on UK No.34 / US No.5 hit MOCKINGBIRD.

Jul 74. (lp/c) *(K/K4 56042)* <2794> **WALKING MAN** [ ] [13]
– Walking man / Rock'n'roll is music now / Let it fall down / Me and my guitar / Daddy's baby / Ain't no song / Hello old friend / Migration / The promised land / Fading away.

Aug 74. (7") *<8028>* **WALKING MAN. / DADDY'S BABY** [–] [ ]

Aug 74. (7") *(K 16444)* **AIN'T NO SONG. / HELLO OLD FRIEND** [ ] [–]

May 75. (lp/c) *(K/K4 56137)* <2866> **GORILLA** [ ] [6]
– Mexico / Music / How sweet it is (to be loved by you) / Wandering / Gorilla / You make it easy / I was a fool to care / Lighthouse / Angry blues / Love song / Sarah Maria. *(cd-iss. Jul88; K 256137) (quad-lp Feb76)*

Jul 75. (7") *(K 16582)* <8109> **HOW SWEET IT IS (TO BE LOVED BY YOU). / SARAH MARIA** [ ] Jun75 [5]

Oct 75. (7") *(K 16632)* <8137> **MEXICO. / GORILLA** [ ] [49]

Apr 76. (7") *(K 16708)* **WANDERING. / ANGRY BLUES** [ ] [–]

Jun 76. (lp/c) *(K/K4 56197)* <2912> **IN THE POCKET** [ ] [16]
– Shower the people / A junkie's lament / Money machine / Slow burning love / Everybody has the blues / Daddy's all gone / Woman's gotta have it / Captain Jim's drunken dream / Don't be sad 'cause your sun is down / Nothing like a hundred miles / Family man / Golden moments.

Jun 76. (7") *(K 16776)* <8222> **SHOWER THE PEOPLE. / I CAN DREAM OF YOU** [ ] [22]

Aug 76. (7") *(K 16808)* **EVERYBODY HAS THE BLUES. / I CAN DREAM OF YOU** [ ] [–]

Oct 76. (7") *(K 16819)* **EVERYBODY HAS THE BLUES. / MONEY MACHINE** [ ] [–]

Nov 76. (7") *<8278>* **WOMAN'S GOTTA HAVE IT. / YOU MAKE IT EASY** [–] [ ]

Dec 76. (lp/c) *(K/K4 56309)* <2979> **GREATEST HITS** (compilation) [ ] [23]
– Something in the way she moves / Carolina in my mind / Fire and rain / Sweet baby James / Country roads / You've got a friend / Don't let me be lonely tonight / Walking man / How sweet it is (to be loved by you) / Mexico / Shower the people / Steamroller. *(re-iss. Mar82) (re-iss. +cd.Jan87)*

— Retained **KORTCHMAR, KUNKEL + SKLAR** and recruited **DAVID SANBORN** – sax / **CLARENCE McDONALD** – percussion

C.B.S. Columbia

Jun 77. (7") *(CBS 5363)* <10557> **HANDY MAN. / BARTENDER'S BLUES** [ ] [4]

Jul 77. (lp/c) *(CBS/40 86029)* <34811> **J.T.** [ ] [4]
– Your smiling face / There we are / Honey don't leave L.A. / Another grey morning / Bartender's blues / Secret of life / Handy man / I was only telling a lie / Looking for love on Broadway / Terra Nova / Traffic jam / If I keep my heart out of sight. *(re-iss. +cd.Feb85) (re-iss. cd+c Oct93 on 'Sony Collectors')*

Oct 77. (7") *(CBS 5737)* <10602> **YOUR SMILING FACE. / IF I KEEP MY HEART OUT OF SIGHT** [ ] Sep 77 [20]

— Autumn'77, saw him produce, play guitar, etc. for sister KATE TAYLOR's debut US Top 50 hit single IT'S IN HIS KISS. Early in 1978, he was credited on another cover hit 45; 'WHAT A WONDERFUL WORLD' with PAUL SIMON & ART GARFUNKEL.

Feb 78. (7") *<10689>* **HONEY DON'T LEAVE L.A. / ANOTHER GREY MORNING** [–] [61]

— In Sep78, another CARLY SIMON / J.T. duet 'DEVOTED TO YOU' hit US No.36.

Jun 79. (7") *(CBS 7389)* <11005> **UP ON THE ROOF. / CHANSON FRANCAISE** [ ] May 79 [28]

Aug 79. (lp/c) *(CBS/40 86091)* <36058> **FLAG** [ ] May 79 [10]
– Company man / Johnnie comes back / Day tripper / I will not lie for you / Brother Trucker / Is that the way you look / B.S.U.R. / Rainy day man / Millworker / Up on the roof / Chanson francaise / Slep come free me. *(re-iss. Feb86) (cd-iss. Sep93 on 'Sony Collectors')*

Aug 79. (7") *(CBS 7773)* **B.S.U.R. / SLEEP COME FREE ME** [ ] [ ]

Mar 81. (7"; JAMES TAYLOR & J.D. SOUTHER) *(CBS A1048)* <60514> **HER TOWN TOO. / BELIEVE IT OR NOT** [ ] Feb 81 [11]

Apr 81. (lp/c) *(CBS/40 86131)* <37009> **DAD LOVES HIS WORK** [ ] Mar 81 [10]
– Hard times / Her town too / Hour that the morning comes / I will follow / Believe it or not / Stand and fight / Only for me / Summer's here / Sugar trade / London town / That lonesome road. *(cd-iss. May87) (cd-iss. Jan94 on 'Sony Europe')*

May 81. (7") *<02093>* **HARD TIMES. / SUMMER'S HERE** [–] [72]

— Late '85, he duets on RICKY SCAGGS track 'New Star Shining', for current lp

Jan 86. (lp/c/cd) *(CBS/40/CD 25547)* <40052> **THAT'S WHY I'M HERE** [ ] Nov 85 [34]
– That's why I'm here / Song for you far away / Only a dream in Rio / Turn away / Going around one more time / Everyday / Limousine driver / Only one / Mona / The man who shot Liberty Valance / That's why I'm here (reprise).

Mar 86. (7") *(CBS A6683)* <05681> **EVERYDAY. / LIMOUSINE DRIVER** [ ] Nov85 [61]

Mar 86. (7") *<05785>* **MONA. / ONLY ONE** [–] [ ]

May 86. (7") *<05884>* **THAT'S WHY I'M HERE. / GOING AROUND ONE MORE TIME** [–] [ ]

Sep 86. (7") *<06278>* **ONLY A DREAM IN RIO. / TURN AWAY** [–] [ ]

Feb 88. (lp/c/cd) *(46043-1-4-2)* <40851> **NEVER DIE YOUNG** [ ] [25]
– Never die young / T-bone / Baby boom baby / Runaway boy / Valentine's day / Sun on the Moon / Sweet potato pie / Home by another day / Letter in the mail / First of May.

Feb 88. (7") *(651204)* <07616> **NEVER DIE YOUNG. / VALENTINE'S DAY** [ ] [80]
(12"+=) *(651 204-1/-2)* – Everyday. *(re-iss. Jun88)*

May 88. (7") *<07948>* **LETTER IN THE MAIL. / BABY BOOM BABY** [–] [ ]

Sep 88. (7") *<08493>* **FIRST OF MAY. / SWEET POTATO PIE** [–] [ ]

Sep 91. (c-s) *<74214>* **(I'VE GOT TO) STOP THINKIN' 'BOUT THAT. / SLAP LEATHER** [–] [ ]

Oct 91. (cd/c/lp) *(468977-2-4-1)* <46038> **NEW MOON SHINE** [ ] [37]
– Copperline / Down in the hole / (I've got to) Stop thinkin' 'bout that / Shed a little light / The frozen man / Slap leather / Like every one she knows / One more round to cha cha cha / Native son / Oh brother / The water is wide. *(re-iss. cd Jul94 on 'Sony Europe')*

— with **CLIFFORD CARTER** – keyboards / **DON GROLNICK** – piano / **JIMMY JOHNSON** – bass / **MICHAEL LANDALL** – guitar / **VALERIE CARTER, DAVID LASLEY, KATE MARKOWITZ & ANDREW McCULLEY** – vocals / **CARLOS VEGA** – drums

Columbia Columbia

Sep 93. (d-cd/d-c) *(474216-2)* <47056> **(LIVE)** [ ] Aug93 [20]
– Sweet baby James / Traffic jam / Handy man / Your smiling face / Secret of life / Shed a little light / Everybody has the blues / Steamroller blues / Mexico / Millworker / Country road / Fire and rain / Shower the people / How sweet it is / New hymn / Walking man / Riding on a railroad / Something in the way she moves / Sun on the Moon / Up on the roof / Don't let me be lonely tonight / She thinks I still care / Copperline / Slap leather / Only one / You make it easy / Carolina on my mind / I will follow / That lonesome road / You've got a friend.
('BEST LIVE' of above issued Apr94; *476657-2)*

Jun 97. (cd/c) *(487748-2/-4)* <67912> **HOURGLASS** [46] May97 [9]
– Line 'em up / Enough to be your way / Little more time with you / Gaia / Ananas / Jump up behind me / Another day / Up er mei / Up from your life / Yellow and rose / Boatman / Walking my baby back home / Hangnail.

Nov 00. (cd) *<85223>* **GREATEST HITS VOLUME 2** (compilation) [–] [97]
– Secret o' life / Handy man / Your smiling face / Up on the roof / Her town too / That's why I'm here / Only a dream in Rio / Everyday / Song for you far away / Never die young / (I've got to) Stop thinkin' 'bout that / Copperline / Shed a little light / Another day / Little more time with you / Enough to be on your way.

Aug 02. (cd) *(503292-2)* <63584> **OCTOBER ROAD** [39] [4]
– September grass / October road / On the 4th of July / Whenever you're ready / Belfast to Bolton / Mean old man / My travelling star / Raised up family / Carry me on my way / Caroline I see you / Baby buffalo / Have yourself a merry little Christmas. *(ltd-cd+=; 503292-9)* – Don't let me be lonely tonight / Sailing to Philadelphia / Benjamin.

– compilations, etc. –

Feb 71. (m-lp) *Euphoria;* <2> **JAMES TAYLOR & THE ORIGINAL FLYING MACHINE** (early material 1967) [–] [ ]
– Night owl / Brighten your night with my day / Kootch's song / Knocking 'round the zoo / Rainy day man / Something's wrong. *(re-iss. Nov76 as 'RAINY DAY MAN' on 'DJM'/'Trip', tracks differed slightly)*

1974. (7"ep) *Warners;* **YOU'VE GOT A FRIEND / SUNNY SKIES. / FIRE AND RAIN / SWEET BABY JAMES** [ ] [–]

Oct 75. (d-lp) *Warners; (K 66029)* **TWO ORIGINALS OF . . .** [ ] [–]
– (contains the 2 albums below)

Oct 82. (d-c) *Warners;* **SWEET BABY JAMES / MUD SLIDE SLIM & THE BLUE HORIZON** [ ] [–]
(d-cd-iss. Apr84)

Mar 86. (7") *Old Gold; (OG 9576)* **YOU'VE GOT A FRIEND. / FIRE AND RAIN** [ ] [–]

Jan 87. (7") *CBS; (YZ 105)* **UP ON THE ROOF. / FIRE AND RAIN** [ ] [–]

Mar 87. (lp/c)(cd) *CBS-WEA TV; (JTV 1/+C)(241 0892)* **THE BEST OF JAMES TAYLOR – CLASSIC SONGS** [53] [–]
– Fire and rain / Mexico / You've got a friend / How sweet it is (to be loved by you) / Carolina on my mind / Something in the way she moves / Shower the people / Sweet baby James / That's why I'm here / Everyday / Up on the roof / Your smiling face / Her town too / Handyman / Don't let me be lonely tonight / Only a dream in Rio.

Sep 03. (cd) *WEA; <(8122 73837-2)>* **YOU'VE GOT A FRIEND – THE BEST OF JAMES TAYLOR** [4] Apr03 [11]
– Something in the way she moves / Sweet baby James / Fire and rain / Country road / You've got a friend / You can close your eyes / Long ago and far away / Don't let me be lonely tonight / Walking man / How sweet it is (to be loved by you) / Mexico / Shower the people / Golden moments / Steamroller blues (live) / Carolina in my mind (1976 version) / Handy man / Your smiling face / Up on the roof / Only a dream in Rio / Bittersweet.

□ John TAYLOR (see under ⇒ DURAN DURAN)

□ TEAM SLEEP (see under ⇒ DEFTONES)

□ the TEARDROP EXPLODES (see under ⇒ COPE, Julian)

□ the TEARS (see under ⇒ SUEDE)

TEARS FOR FEARS

Formed: Bath, Avon, England . . . 1981 by ROLAND ORZABAL and CURT SMITH, childhood friends who had initially played together in ska-pop outfit, GRADUATE. Inspired by psychotherapist Arthur Janov's controversial "primal scream" therapy, ORZABAL and SMITH named the group accordingly, subsequently signing to 'Mercury' on the strength of some demos. After two early singles, 'SUFFER THE CHILDREN' and 'PALE SHELTER (YOU DON'T GIVE ME LOVE), failed to chart, the duo eventually hit the UK Top 3 with the claustrophobic synth-pop of 'MAD WORLD' (produced by CHRIS 'Merrick' HUGHES; ex-ADAM & THE ANTS, as was the debut album). They scored another Top 5 single early the following year with 'CHANGE', the subsequent album, 'THE HURTING' (1983), reaching No.1. Po-faced in true 80's style, with ORZABAL's lyrics centering on mental functioning, therapy, healing etc., the group were often accused of angst-ridden pretension despite their pin-up status. By the release of the million selling 'SONGS FROM THE BIG CHAIR' (1985), however, their focus had widened somewhat, a preceding single, 'SHOUT', surprisingly taking them to the top of the US charts (UK Top 5). The uncharacteristically breezy guitar pop of 'EVERYBODY WANTS TO RULE THE WORLD' was another massive transatlantic hit, further boosting sales of the album. Masterfully crafted, the record displayed a more considered approach to both songwriting and arranging, while ORZABAL and SMITH had more or less ditched the bedsit whine of old. It was to be almost four years before TEARS FOR FEARS released a follow-up, the much anticipated 'THE SEEDS OF LOVE' finally hitting the shelves in the Autumn of '89. A preceding single, 'SOWING THE SEEDS OF LOVE', was a clever take on The BEATLES' 'I AM THE WALRUS', pre-empting OASIS' more cumbersome efforts by a good few years. The whole album, in fact, displayed an even greater level of pop sophistication than its predecessor, boasting contributions from the likes of OLETA ADAMS and JON HASSELL. While the record initially sold well, however, it failed to generate much chart staying power, exacerbating the growing rift between SMITH and ORZABAL. The pair finally split in the early 90's, engendering a covert slanging match similar to the JOHN SQUIRE/IAN BROWN jousting. ORZABAL carried on under the TEARS FOR FEARS moniker, although subsequent releases, 'ELEMENTAL' (1993) and 'RAOUL AND THE KINGS OF SPAIN' (1995) failed to scale the heights of the group's mid-80's heyday, the latter not even breaking the Top 40. Reunions often arise out of the most unpredictable of events, and none came more unpredictable than either 'Donnie Darko' itself, or the fact that the movie's soundtrack generated a huge UK hit in Gary Jules' catatonic cover of 'MAD WORLD'. Interest peaked by the unexpected tribute, and with a musical climate once more favourable to 80s artifice, ROLAND and ORZABAL put their differences behind them and convened to record a belated follow-up to 1989's 'THE SEEDS OF LOVE'. In the event, 'EVERYBODY LOVES A HAPPY ENDING' (2004) eschewed their 80s sound for a more forthright, singer-songwriterly approach in keeping with their advancing years. All shag-pile harmonies, BEATLES-esque verve and assiduously crafted arrangements, the album was actually more successful in the States (where it made the Top 50) than Britain, although they did score a solitary UK Top 40 hit with the soaring 'CLOSEST THING TO HEAVEN'.

• **Songwriters:** All written by ORZABAL, except CREEP (Radiohead) / ASHES TO ASHES (David Bowie).

Album rating: THE HURTING (*7) / SONGS FROM THE BIG CHAIR (*7) / THE SEEDS OF LOVE (*6) / TEARS ROLL DOWN – GREATEST HITS 1982-1992 compilation (*8) / ELEMENTAL (*4) / RAOUL AND THE KINGS OF SPAIN (*4) / SATURNINE, MARSHALL & LUNATIC collection (*4) / EVERYBODY LOVES A HAPPY ENDING (*4)

GRADUATE

ROLAND ORZABAL (b. ROLAND ORZABAL DE LA QUINTANA, 22 Aug'61, Portsmouth, England) – vocals, guitar / **CURT SMITH** (b.24 Jun'61) – vocals, bass / **JOHN BAKER** – vocals, guitar / **STEVE BUCK** – keyboards, flute / **ANDY MARSDEN** – drums

Precision — not iss.

Mar 80. (7") *(PAR 100)* **ELVIS SHOULD PLAY SKA. / JULIE JULIE** [ ] [–]

May 80. (7") *(PAR 104)* **EVER MET A DAY. / SHUT UP** [ ] [–]

May 80. (10"lp) *(PART 001)* **ACTING MY AGE** [ ] [–]
– Acting my age / Sick and tired / Ever met a day / Dancing nights / Shut up / Elvis should play ska / Watching your world / Love that is bad / Julie Julie / Bad dreams. *(re-iss. Jul86 on 'P.R.T.')*

Oct 80. (7") *(PAR 111)* **AMBITION. / BAD DREAMS** [ ] [–]

Mar 81. (7") *(PAR 117)* **SHUT UP. / EVER MET A DAY** [ ] [–]

TEARS FOR FEARS

ROLAND + **CURT** with **DAVID LORD** – synthesizers (duo also on synthesizers)

Mercury — Mercury

Nov 81. (7") *(IDEA 1)* **SUFFER THE CHILDREN. / WIND** [ ] [ ]
(remixed-12"+=) *(IDEA 12)* – ('A'instrumental). *(re-iss. Aug85, 7"/12"; same); hit UK No.52)*

—— Trimmed to a basic duo of **ORZABAL & SMITH**

Mar 82. (7") *(IDEA 2)* **PALE SHELTER (YOU DON'T GIVE ME LOVE). / THE PRISONER** [ ] [ ]
(12"+=) *(IDEA 2-12)* – ('A'extended). *(re-iss. Aug85, 7"/12"; same); hit No.73)*

Sep 82. (7") *(IDEA 3)* **MAD WORLD. / IDEAS AS OPIATES** [3] [ ]
(12"+=) *(IDEA 3-12)* – Saxophones as opiates.
(d7"+=) *(IDEA 33)* – ('A'-world remix) / Suffer the children.

Jan 83. (7") *(IDEA 4)* *<812677>* **CHANGE. / THE CONFLICT** [4] Jun83 [73]
(12"+=) *(IDEA 4-12)* – ('A'extended).

—— augmented by **IAN STANLEY** – keyboards / **MANNY ELIAS** – drums

Mar 83. (lp/c) *(MERS/+C 17)* *<811039>* **THE HURTING** [1] [73]
– The hurting / Mad world / Pale shelter / Ideas as opiates / Memories fade / Suffer the children / Watch me bleed / Change / The prisoner / Start of the breakdown. *(cd-iss. Sep89; 811039-2) (cd re-mast.Jun99 +=; 558104-2)* – Pale shelter (long version) / The way you are (extended) / Mad world (world remix) / Change (extended).

Apr 83. (7"/7"red/7"green/7"white/7"blue/7"pic-d) *(IDEA 5/+R/G/W/B/P)* **PALE SHELTER. / WE ARE BROKEN** 5 ☐
(12"+=) *(IDEA 5-12)* – ('A'extended).

Nov 83. (7") *(IDEA 6)* **(THE) WAY YOU ARE. / THE MARAUDERS** 24 ☐
(ext.12"+=) *(IDEA 6-12)* – Start of the breakdown (live).
(d7"++=) *(IDEAS 6)* – Change (live).

Aug 84. (7",7"green,12"/7"clear-pic-d)(ext.12") *(IDEA/+P 7)(IDEA 7-12) <884638>* **MOTHER'S TALK. / EMPIRE BUILDING** 14 Mar86 27

Nov 84. (7"/10") *(IDEA/+C 8) <880294>* **SHOUT. / THE BIG CHAIR** 4 May85 1
(12"+=) *(IDEA 8-12)* – ('A'extended).

— added mainly on tour **WILLIAM GREGORY** – saxophone / **NICKY HOLLAND** – keyboards

Mar 85. (lp/c)(cd) *(MERH/+C 58) <(824300-2)>* **SONGS FROM THE BIG CHAIR** 2 1
– Shout / The working hour / Everybody wants to rule the world / Mother's talk / I believe / Broken / Head over heels / Broken (live) / Listen. *(c+=)* – The big chair (mix) / Empire building (mix) / The marauders (mix) / Broken revisited (mix) / The conflict (mix). *(cd re-mast.Jun99 ++=; 558106-2)* – Mothers talk (US remix) / Shout (US remix).

Mar 85. (7"/10") *(IDEA 9/+10) <880659>* **EVERYBODY WANTS TO RULE THE WORLD. / PHAROAHS** 2 1
(12"+=) *(IDEA 9-12)* – ('A'extended or urban mix).
(d7"+=) *(IDEA 9-9)* – ('A'-urban mix) / (duo interviewed).

Jun 85. (7"/7"sha-pic-d)(10") *(IDEA/+P 10)(IDEA 10-10) <880899>* **HEAD OVER HEELS (remix). / WHEN IN LOVE WITH A BLIND MAN** 12 Sep85 3
(12"+=) *(IDEA 10-12)* – ('A'preacher mix).

Oct 85. (7") *(IDEA 11)* **I BELIEVE (A soulful re-recording). / SEA SONG** 23 ☐
(10"+=) *(IDEA 11-10)* – I believe (US mix).
(12"++=) *(IDEA 11-12)* – Shout (US mix).
(d7"+=) *(IDEA 11-11)* – Shout (dub) / I believe (original).

May 86. (7"/12") *(RACE 1/+12)* **EVERYBODY WANTS TO RUN THE WORLD. / EVERYBODY . . . (Running version)** 5 ☐

— **ORZABAL + SMITH** retained **IAN** and **NICKY** and brought in sessioners **OLETA ADAMS** – some dual vocals, piano / **SIMON CLARK** – organ / **PINO PALLADINO** – bass / **ROBBIE McINTOSH, NEIL TAYLOR + RANDY JACOBS** – guitar / **PHIL COLLINS, CHRIS HUGHES + MANU KATCHE** – drums

Fontana Fontana

Aug 89. (7"/7"g-f/c-s) *(IDEA/IDEAG/IDMC 12) <874710>* **SOWING THE SEEDS OF LOVE. / TEARS ROLL DOWN** 5 2
(ext.12"+=/12"pic-d+=/3"cd-s+=) *(IDEAT/IDPT/IDCD 12)* – Shout (US mix).

Sep 89. (lp/c/cd) *(838730-1/-4/-2) <838730>* **THE SEEDS OF LOVE** 1 8
– Woman in chains / Bad man's song / Sowing the seeds of love / Advice for the young at heart / Standing on the corner of the third world / Swords and knives / Year of the knife / Famous last words. *(cd re-mast.Jun99 +=; 558105-2)* – Tears roll down / Always in the past / Music for tables / Johnny Panic and the bible of dreams.

— (next featured **OLETA ADAMS** – co-vox)

Nov 89. (7"/c-s; as TEARS FOR FEARS featuring OLETA ADAMS) *(IDEA/IDMC 13) <876248>* **WOMAN IN CHAINS. / ALWAYS IN THE PAST** 26 36
(12"+=/12"pic-d+=/cd-s+=/3"cd-s+=) *(IDEA/IDPT/IDCD/IDSTN 13)* – ('A'instrumental) / My life in the suicide ranks.

Feb 90. (7"/c-s) *(IDEA/IDMC 14) <876894>* **ADVICE FOR THE YOUNG AT HEART. / JOHNNY PANIC AND THE BIBLE OF DREAMS** 36 89
(12"+=/12"pic-d+=/cd-s+=) *(IDPT/IDPIC/IDCD 14)* – Music for tables.
(3"cd-s++=) *(IDCDS 14)* – Johnny Panic (instrumental).

Jul 90. (7") *(IDEA 15)* **FAMOUS LAST WORDS. / MOTHER'S TALK (US remix)** ☐ ☐
(c-s+=/12"+=/12"pic-d+=/cd-s+=) *(IDEMC/IDEAT/IDPIC/IDECD 15)* – Listen.

Jan 91. (7"; as JOHNNY PANIC and the BIBLE OF DREAMS) *(PANIC 1)* **JOHNNY PANIC AND THE BIBLE OF DREAMS (mix one). / (mix two)** 70 –
(12")(cd-s) *(PANIC 112)(PANCD 1)* – (extended versions).

Feb 92. (7"/c-s) *(IDEA/IDMC 17)* **LAID SO LOW. / THE BODY WAH** 17 ☐
(12"pic-d+=/cd-s+=) *(IDEAT/IDCD 17)* – Lord of the Kharma.

Mar 92. (cd/c/lp) *(<510 939-2/-4/-1>)* **TEARS ROLL DOWN – GREATEST HITS 1982-1992** (compilation) 2 53
– Sowing the seeds of love / Everybody wants to rule the world / Woman in chains / Shout / Head over heels / Mad world / Pale shelter / I beieve / Laid so low (tears roll down) / Mothers talk / Change / Advice for the young at heart. *(re-dist.Jan04; same)* – hit UK No.6 *(cd re-iss. Jun04 w/dvd+=; 981912-2)*

Apr 92. (7"/c-s; as TEARS FOR FEARS featuring OLETA ADAMS) *(IDEA/IDMC 16)* **WOMAN IN CHAINS. / BADMAN'S SONG** 57 ☐
(cd-s+=) *(IDCD 16)* – Ghost papa.

— **ROLAND ORZABAL** now sole survivor, when CURT launched solo career with his album, 'SOUL ON BOARD'.

Mercury Mercury

May 93. (7"/c-s) *(IDEA/IDMC 18) <862330>* **BREAK IT DOWN AGAIN. / BLOODLETTING GO** 20 25
(cd-s+=) *(IDECD 18)* – ('A'-mix).

Jun 93. (cd/c/lp) *(<514875-2/-4/-1>)* **ELEMENTAL** 5 45
– Elemental / Cold / Break it down again / Mr. Pessimist / Dog's a best friend's dog / Fish out of water / Gas giants / Power / Brian Wilson said / Goodnight song.

Jul 93. (7"/c-s) *(IDEA/IDMC 19)* **COLD. / NEW STAR** 72 ☐
(cd-s+=) *(IDECD 19)* – Deja vu / The sins of silence.

Epic Sony

Sep 95. (c-s) *(662 476-4)* **RAOUL AND THE KINGS OF SPAIN / QUEEN OF COMPROMISE** 31 ☐
(cd-s+=) *(662 476-2)* – All of the angels.
(cd-s) *(662 476-5)* – ('A') / Creep / The madness of Roland.

Oct 95. (cd/c) *(480 982-2/-4) <67318>* **RAOUL AND THE KINGS OF SPAIN** 41 79
– Raoul and the Kings of Spain / Falling down / Secrets / God's mistake / Sketches of pain / Los Reyes Catolicos / Sorry / Humdrum and humble / I choose you / Don't drink the water / Me and my big ideas / Los Reyes Catolicos (reprise).

Jan 96. (c-s/cd-s) *(662 797-4/-2)* **SECRETS / RAOUL AND THE KINGS OF SPAIN (acoustic) / BREAK IT DOWN AGAIN (acoustic)** ☐ ☐
(cd-s) *(662 797-5)* – ('A') / Until I drown / War of attrition.

Jun 96. (c-s/cd-s) *(663 418-4/-2)* **GOD'S MISTAKE / UNTIL I DROWN** 61 –
(cd-s) *(663 418-5)* – ('A') / Raoul and the kings of Spain (acoustic) / Break it down again (acoustic).

— **ROLAND + CURT** re-formed TFF in 2004

Gut New Door

Mar 05. (12") *(12GUT 66)* **CLOSEST THING TO HEAVEN (Brothers In Rhythm group therapy mix). / CLOSEST THING TO HEAVEN (Solasso mix)** 40 –
(cd-s+=) *(CDGUT 66)* – ('A'-radio mix) / ('A'-Solasso dub) / ('A'-Brothers In Rhythm group therapy dub).

Mar 05. (cd) *(GUTCD 37) <B000 30420-2>* **EVERYBODY LOVES A HAPPY ENDING** 45 Aug04 46
– Everybody loves a happy ending / Closest thing to heaven / Call me mellow / Size of sorrow / Who killed Tangerine? / Quiet ones / Who you are / The Devil / Secret world / Killing with kindness / Ladybird / Last days on Earth.

– compilations, etc. –

Aug 95. (d-cd) *Fontana; (528599-2)* **THE HURTING / SONGS FROM THE BIG CHAIR** ☐ –

Jun 96. (cd/c) *Fontana; (528114-2/-4)* **SATURNINE, MARSHALL & LUNATIC** (rare material) ☐ ☐

Jun 00. (cd) *Universal; <E 542492-2>* **THE BEST OF TEARS FOR FEARS: THE MILLENNIUM COLLECTION** – ☐

Oct 00. (d-cd) *Universal; (E 542789-2)* **THE HURTING / THE SEEDS OF LOVE** ☐ ☐

Jan 01. (cd) *Universal; (E 548319-2)* **THE UNIVERSAL MASTERS COLLECTION** ☐ –

May 01. (cd) *Mercury; (548515-2)* **THE WORKING HOUR: AN INTRODUCTION TO TEARS FOR FEARS** ☐ –

Oct 03. (cd) *Spectrum; (063358-2)* **THE COLLECTION** ☐ –

TEENAGE FANCLUB

Formed: Glasgow, Scotland . . . 1989 although earlier they had posed as The BOY HAIRDRESSERS. After a one-off single, 'GOLDEN SHOWERS' (1988), bassist GERRY LOVE was recruited and BRENDAN O'HARE replaced FRANCIS MACDONALD (who went off to join that other Glasgow institution, The PASTELS) on the drums. As TEENAGE FANCLUB, they cut the inspired chaos of the 'EVERYTHING FLOWS' (1990) single and followed it up with the debut album, 'A CATHOLIC EDUCATION' later the same year. The term slacker rock was surely coined with this bunch of cheeky Glaswegian wide boys in mind and if it was lazy to compare their honey-in-the-dirt melodic dischord with DINOSAUR JR., that was nothing compared to the laid back, laissez faire philosophy that fuelled (if that's not too strong a word) TEENAGE FANCLUB's ramshackle racket, both on stage and in the studio. By the release of the DON FLEMING-produced 'BANDWAGONESQUE' (1991), ('THE KING' was a sub-standard effort released to fulfil contractual obligations), the band were sounding more professional, crafting an album of langourous harmonies and chiming guitar that was a thinly veiled homage to BIG STAR as well as taking in such obvious reference points as the BYRDS, the BEACH BOYS, BUFFALO SPRINGFIELD etc. Ironically, rather than propelling TEENAGE FANCLUB into the big league, the album seemed instead to merely rekindle interest in BIG STAR's back catalogue and after a honeymoon period of being indie press darlings, the backlash was sharp and swift. The fact that the self-produced 'THIRTEEN' (1993) lacked their trademark inspired sloppiness didn't help matters any. Not that the band were overly concerned, they crafted modern retro more lovingly than most and had a loyal following to lap it up. The FANNIE's – with PAUL QUINN replacing O'HARE – further developed their niche with 'GRAND PRIX' (1995) and if it was that reliably trad, West Coast via Glasgow roots sound you were after then TEENAGE FANCLUB were your band. While they wear their influences more proudly than any other group, (O.K., so I forgot about OASIS . . .) they do it with such verve and style that it'd be churlish to write them off as mere plagiarists and they remain one of Scotland's best loved exports. Their next effort, 'SONGS FROM NORTHERN BRITAIN' (1997) was their most considered release to date, sharpening up their sound and arrangements to an unprecedented degree. But if that's what it takes to come up with something as engagingly swoonsome as 'I DON'T CARE' or 'IS THAT ENOUGH', no one's going to make much of a fuss. Now on the roster of the mighty 'Columbia' records, TEENAGE FANCLUB (complete with former BMX BANDITS man FINLAY McDONALD) returned to the fold via album No.6 proper, 'HOWDY!' (2000). Slightly back to basics and reminiscent of BIG STAR (once again!), the album only just managed to gain a UK Top 40 placing; the appropriately-titled single from it 'I NEED DIRECTION' only just dented the Top 50. Drummer and original member, FRANCIS MACDONALD, subsequently superseded QUINN for a one-off single collaboration 'DUMB DUMB DUMB' with daisy-chain hip hop stars, DE LA SOUL, although this failed miserably with the record buying public. The group were back to basics again (this time on STEPHEN PASTEL's 'Geographic' imprint) come their short but sweet set, 'WORDS OF WISDOM AND HOPE' (2002), a record that saw them collaborate with US-born songwriter JAD FAIR. Ditching their more commercial rock flair, TFC went for something a bit rougher – all thanks to FAIR – hammering out tracks 'I FEEL FINE', 'VAMPIRE'S CLAW' and 'NEAR TO YOU' (the single) to brilliant effect. A link-up with TORTOISE sound sculptor JOHN McENTIRE perhaps wasn't so eyebrow raising giving the traditionally string link between Glasgow and the American underground. And recorded at McENTIRE's Chicago studio, 'MAN-MADE' (2005) wasn't such a departure from the band's hippy-harmony sound. The main difference was the TORTOISE guru's beavering keyboard (and even harpsichord) filigree, spacing out TFC's West Coast signature to the point that it occasionally resembled 'Eight Miles High'-era BYRDS or a more adept garage-psyche combo instead of the usual BIG STAR/CS&N. A UK Top 40 entry, the album preceded the band's contribution to 'Late Great Daniel Johnston: Discovered Covered' (2006), a half covers/half originals tribute (also featuring the likes of BECK, EELS, CALVIN JOHNSON and BRIGHT EYES) where the Glaswegians performed 'MY LIFE IS STARTING OVER' along with JAD FAIR.

• **Songwriters:** BLAKE or BLAKE-McGINLEY or group compositions except; DON'T CRY NO TEARS (Neil Young) / THE BALLAD OF JOHN AND YOKO (Beatles) / LIKE A VIRGIN (Madonna) / LIFE'S A GAS (T.Rex) / FREE AGAIN + JESUS CHRIST (Alex Chilton) / HOW MANY MORE YEARS + NOTHING TO BE DONE (Pastels) / CHORDS OF FAME (Phil Ochs) / PERSONALITY CRISIS (New York Dolls) / HE'D BE A DIAMOND (Bevis Frond) / INTERSTELLAR OVERDRIVE (Pink Floyd) / FALLIN' (Tom Petty) / BAD SEEDS (Beat Happening) / HAVE YOU EVER SEEN THE RAIN? (Creedence Clearwater Revival) / BETWEEN US (Rutles) / I HEARD YOU LOOKING (Yo La Tengo) / OLDER GUYS (Gram Parsons) / FEMME FATALE (Velvet Underground). • **Trivia:** ALEX CHILTON (ex-BOX TOPS) guested on 1992 sessions and contributed some songs.

Album rating: A CATHOLIC EDUCATION (*6) / THE KING instrumental (*5) / BANDWAGONESQUE (*8) / THIRTEEN (*7) / DEEP FRIED FANCLUB collection (*4) / GRAND PRIX (*8) / SONGS FROM NORTHERN BRITAIN (*8) / HOWDY! (*6) / WORDS OF WISDOM AND HOPE with Jad Fair (*6) / FOUR THOUSAND SEVEN HUNDRED AND SIXTY-SIX SECONDS: A SHORT CUT TO TEENAGE FANCLUB compilation (*8) / MAN-MADE (*7)

NORMAN BLAKE (b.20 Oct'65, Bellshill, Scotland) – vocals, guitar (ex-BMX BANDITS) / **RAYMOND McGINLEY** (b. 3 Jan'64, Glasgow) – bass, vocals / **FRANCIS MACDONALD** (b.11 Sep'70, Bellshill, Scotland) – drums / **JOE McALINDEN** – violin / **JIM LAMBIE** – vibraphone

53rd & 3rd | not iss.

Jan 88. (12"; as BOY HAIRDRESSERS) *(AGARR 12T)* **GOLDEN SHOWERS. / TIDAL WAVE / THE ASSUMPTION AS AN ELEVATOR** [ ] [–]

—— **NORMAN + RAYMOND** – guitars, vocals plus **GERARD LOVE** (b.31 Aug'67, Motherwell, Scotland) – bass, vocals / **BRENDAN O'HARE** (b.16 Jan'70, Bellshill, Scotland) – drums; repl. MACDONALD who joined The PASTELS

Paperhouse | Matador

Jun 90. (7"m) *(PAPER 003)* **EVERYTHING FLOWS. / PRIMARY EDUCATION / SPEEEDER** [ ] [–]
(cd-ep+=) *(PAPER 003CD)* – Don't Cry No Tears. *(rel.Feb91)*

Jul 90. (cd/c/lp) *(PAP CD/MC/LP 004)* <OLE 012> **A CATHOLIC EDUCATION** [ ] Aug90 [ ]
– Heavy metal / Everything flows / A catholic education / Too involved / Don't need a drum / Critical mass / Heavy metal II / A catholic education 2 / Eternal light / Every picture I paint / Everybody's fool. *(re-iss. cd Mar95; same) (cd re-iss. Apr02 on 'Fire'; SFIRE 001CD)*

Oct 90. (one-sided-7") *(PAPER 005)* **THE BALLAD OF JOHN AND YOKO** [ ] [–]

Nov 90. (7"m) *<OLE 007-7>* **EVERYBODY'S FOOL. / PRIMAL EDUCATION / SPEEDER** [–] [ ]

Nov 90. (7") *(PAPER 007)* *<OLE 023>* **GOD KNOWS IT'S TRUE. / SO FAR GONE** [ ] Jan91 [ ]
(12"+=/cd-s+=) *(PAPER 007 T/CD)* – Weedbreak / Ghetto blaster.

Creation | Geffen

Aug 91. (cd/lp) *(CRE CD/LP 096)* **THE KING** (instrumental) [53] [–]
– Heavy metal 6 / Mudhoney / Interstellar overdrive / Robot love / Like a virgin / The king / Opal inquest / The ballad of Bow Evil (slow and fast) / Heavy metal 9.
(above originally only meant for US ears, deleted after 24 hours)

Aug 91. (7") *(CRE 105)* **STAR SIGN. / HEAVY METAL 6** [44] [–]
(12"+=)(cd-s+=) *(CRE 105T)(CRESCD 105)* – Like a virgin / ('A'demo version).
(7"ltd) *(CRE 105L)* – ('A'side) / Like a virgin.

Oct 91. (7"/c-s) *(CRE/+CS 111)* <4370> **THE CONCEPT. / LONG HAIR** [51] Jan92 [ ]
(12"+=)(cd-s+=) *(CRE 111T)(CRESCD 111)* – What you do to me (demo) / Robot love.

Nov 91. (cd)(c/lp) *(CRECD 106)(C+/CRE 106) <24461>* **BANDWAGONESQUE** [22] [ ]
– The concept / Satan / December / What you do to me / I don't know / Star sign / Metal baby / Pet rock / Sidewinder / Alcoholiday / Guiding star / Is this music?. *(cd re-iss. Jan01; same)*

Jan 92. (7"/c-s) *(CRE/+CS 115) <21708>* **WHAT YOU DO TO ME. / B-SIDE** [31] [ ]
(12"+=)(cd-s+=) *(CRE 115T)(CRESCD 115)* – Life's a gas / Filler.

Jun 93. (7"/c-s) *(CRE/+CS 130)* **RADIO. / DON'S GONE COLUMBIA** [31] [ ]
(12"+=)(cd-s+=) *(CRE 130T)(CRESCD 130)* – Weird horses / Chords of fame.

Sep 93. (7"/c-s) *(CRE/+CS 142)* **NORMAN 3. / OLDER GUYS** [50] [-]
(12"+=)(cd-s+=) *(CRE 142T)(CRESCD 142)* – Golden glades / Genius envy.

Oct 93. (cd)(c/lp) *(CRECD 144)(C+/CRE 144) <24533>* **THIRTEEN** [14] Nov93 [ ]
– Hang on / The cabbage / Radio / Norman 3 / Song to the cynic / 120 minutes / Escher / Commercial alternative / Fear of flying / Tears are cool / Ret live dead / Get funky / Gene Clark. *(cd re-iss. Jan01; same)*

— also in 1993, they made a joint single with BIG STAR, 'MINE EXCLUSIVELY' b/w 'PATTI GIRL', proceeds going towards Bosnia, etc

— In Mar'94, they teamed up with DE LA SOUL on single 'FALLIN''. This was from the rock-rap soundtrack album 'Judgment Night' on 'Epic' records (hit UK 59).

1994. (cd-ep) *<21887>* **AUSTRALIAN TOUR SAMPLER** [-] [ ]

— **PAUL QUINN** – drums (ex-SOUP DRAGONS) repl. O'HARE who later joined MOGWAI

Mar 95. (7"/c-s) *(CRE/+CS 175)* **MELLOW DOUBT. / SOME PEOPLE TRY TO FUCK WITH YOU** [34] [-]
(cd-s+=) *(CRESCD 175)* – Getting real / About you.
(cd-s) *(CRESCD 175X)* – ('A'side) / Have you ever seen the rain? / Between us / You're my kind.

May 95. (7"/c-s) *(CRE/+CS 201)* **SPARKY'S DREAM. / BURNED** [40] [-]
(cd-s+=) *(CRESCD 201)* – For you / Headstand.
(cd-s) *(CRESCD 201X)* – ('A'-alternative version) / Try and stop me / That's all I need to know / Who loves the sun.

May 95. (cd)(c/lp) *(CRECD 173)(C+/CRE 173) <24802>* **GRAND PRIX** [7] Jul95 [ ]
– About you / Sparky's dream / Mellow doubt / Don't look back / Verisinilitude / Neil Jung / Tears / Discolite / Say no / Going places / I'll make it clear / I gotta know / Hardcore – ballad. *(lp w/ free 7")* – DISCOLITE (demo). / I GOTTA KNOW (demo) *(cd re-iss. Jan01; same)*

Aug 95. (7"/c-s) *(CRE/+CS 210)* **NEIL JUNG. / THE SHADOWS** [62] [-]
(cd-s+=) *(CRESCD 210)* – My life / Every step is a way through love.
(cd-s) *(CRESCD 210X)* – ('A'side) / Traffic jam / Hi-fi / I heard you looking.

Dec 95. (7"ep/c-ep/cd-ep) *(CRE/+CS/SCD 216)* **TEENAGE FANCLUB HAVE LOST IT EP (acoustic)** [53] [-]
– Don't look back / Everything flows / Starsign / 120 mins.

— late in '96, LOVE and McGINLEY joined forces with The VASELINES' EUGENE KELLY to form ASTROCHIMP; one single 'DRAGGIN'' for 'Shoeshine'

Creation Sony

Jun 97. (cd-s) *(CRESCD 228)* **AIN'T THAT ENOUGH / KICKABOUT / BROKEN** [17] [-]
(cd-s) *(CRESCD 228X)* – ('A'side) / Femme fatale / Jesus Christ.

Jun 97. (cd/c/lp) *(CRECD/CCRE/CRELP 196) <68202>* **SONGS FROM NORTHERN BRITAIN** [3] [ ]
– Start again / Ain't that enough / Can't feel my soul / I don't want control of you / Planets / It's a bad world / Take the long way round / Winter / I don't care / Mount Everest / Your love is the place where I come from / Speed of light. *(cd re-iss. Jan01; same)*

Aug 97. (7") *(CRE 238)* **I DON'T WANT CONTROL OF YOU. / THE COUNT** [43] [-]
(cd-s+=) *(CRESCD 238)* – Middle of the road.
(cd-s) *(CRESCD 238X)* – ('A'side) / He'd be a diamond / Live my life.

Nov 97. (7") *(CRE 280)* **START AGAIN. / AIN'T THAT ENOUGH (TOTP acoustic)** [54] [-]
(cd-s+=) *(CRESCD 280)* – Take the long way round (radio).
(cd-s) *(CRESCD 280X)* – ('A'side) / How many more years / Nothing to be done.

— added **FINLAY McDONALD** – keyboards (ex-BMX BANDITS, ex-SPEEDBOAT); was p/t on tour

Jun 98. (7") *(CRE 298)* **LONG SHOT. / LOOPS AND STRINGS** [ ] [-]

Columbia Columbia

Oct 00. (7") *(669951-7)* **I NEED DIRECTION. / ON THIS GOOD NIGHT** [48] [-]
(cd-s+=) *(669951-2)* – I lied / Here comes your man.

Oct 00. (cd/lp) *(<500622-2/-1>)* **HOWDY!** [33] Nov00 [ ]
– I need direction / I can't find my way home / Accidental life / Near you / Happiness / Dumb dumb dumb / Town and the city / The sun shines from you / Straight and narrow / Cul de sac / My uptight life / If I never see you again.

— **FRANCIS MACDONALD** – drums (of Shoeshine records) repl. QUINN who quit during the middle of the last set

Jun 01. (7"; as TEENAGE FANCLUB & DE LA SOUL) *(<671213-7>)* **DUMB DUMB DUMB. / STRAIGHT AND NARROW** [ ] Jan02 [ ]
(cd-s+=) *(671213-2)* – Thaw me / One thousand lights.

TEENAGE FANCLUB & JAD FAIR

Geographic Alternative Tentacles

Feb 02. (7") *(GEOG 013)* **NEAR TO YOU. / ALWAYS IN MY HEART** [68] [-]
(cd-s+=) *(GEOG 013CD)* – Let's celebrate.

Mar 02. (cd/lp) *(GEOG 014 CD/LP) <VIRUS 274>* **WORDS OF WISDOM AND HOPE** [ ] Jan02 [ ]
– Behold the miracle / I feel fine / Near to you / Smile / Crush on you / Cupid / The power of your tenderness / Vampire's claw / Secret heart / You rock / Love's taken over / The good thing.

Nov 02. (7") *(VIRUS 278)* **ALWAYS IN MY HEART. / LET'S CELEBRATE** [ ] [-]

TEENAGE FANCLUB

Poolside not iss.

Aug 03. (7") *(POOLS 5)* **DID I SAY. / THE CABBAGE** [ ] [-]

Geographic not iss.

Aug 04. (7"; INTERNATIONAL AIRPORT & TEENAGE FANCLUB) *(GEOG 029CD)* **ASSOCIATION. / (Teenage Fanclub vocal)** [75] [-]

PeMa Merge

May 05. (cd) *(PEMA 002CD) <262>* **MAN-MADE** [34] [ ]
– It's all in my mind / Time stops / Nowhere / Save / Slow fade / Only with you / Celts / Feel / Fallen leaves / Flowing / Born under a good sign / Don't hide.

May 05. (7"/cd-s) *(PEMA 004/+CDS)* **FALLEN LEAVES. / FALLING LEAF** [ ] [-]

Nov 05. (7") *(PEMA 006S)* **IT'S ALL IN MY MIND. / PLEASE STAY** [ ] [-]

May 06. (7"; w/ JAD FAIR) *(PEMA 001)* **HAPPY SOUL. / MONKEY IN A ZOO** [ ] [-]

– compilations, others, etc. –

May 92. (7") *K; <IPU 26>* **FREE AGAIN. / BAD SEEDS** [-] [ ]

Nov 92. (12"ep/cd-ep) *Strange Fruit; (SFPS/+CD 081)* **THE JOHN PEEL SESSION** [ ] [-]
– God knows it's true / Alcoholiday / So far gone / Long hair. *(re-iss. Dec93 & Jul95; same)*

Mar 95. (cd/c) *Snapper; (FLIPCD 002)* **DEEP FRIED FANCLUB** [ ] [-]
– Everything flows / Primary education / Speeder / Critical mass (orig.) / The ballad of John and Yoko / God knows it's true / Weedbreak / So far gone / Ghetto blaster / Don't cry no tears / Free again / Bad seed. *(cd re-iss. Jan03 on 'Fire'; SFIRE 017CD)*

Jul 95. (12"ep/cd-ep; as FRANK BLACK & TEENAGE FANCLUB) *Strange Fruit; (SFPS/+CD 091)* **PEEL SESSION** [ ] [-]
– Handy man / The man who was too loud / The Jacques Tati / Sister Isabel.

Apr 97. (cd) *Nectar; (NTMCD 543)* **FANDEMONIUM** [ ] [-]

Sep 97. (7"ep) *Radiation; (RARE 033)* **TEENAGE FANCLUB EP** [ ] [-]

Jan 03. (cd/lp) *Poolside; (POOLS 3 CD/LP) / JetSet; <66>* **FOUR THOUSAND SEVEN HUNDRED AND SIXTY-SIX SECONDS** [47] [ ]
– The concept / Ain't that enough / The world'll be OK / Everything flows / Star sign / Mellow doubt / I need direction / About you / What you do to me / Empty space / Sparky's dream / I don't want control of you / Hang on / Did I say / Don't look back / Your love is the place where I come from / Neil Jung / Radio / Dumb dumb dumb / Planets / My uptight life.

TELEVISION

Formed: New York City, New York, USA based ... late '73 by TOM VERLAINE, RICHARD HELL and BILLY FICCA who had all been members of The NEON BOYS. In 1975, William Terry Ork gave them a deal on his own self-named indie label, for whom they issued a one-off flop single, 'LITTLE JOHNNY JEWEL'. By this point, HELL (who went on to form the equally seminal RICHARD HELL & THE VOID-OIDS) had been replaced by ex-MC5 man, FRED 'SONIC' SMITH, TELEVISION subsequently signing with 'Elektra' and unleashing their classic debut album, 'MARQUEE MOON'. Although virtually ignored in America (more astute British punk/new wave fans placed it in the UK Top 30) upon its 1977 release, the album has since been acknowledged as a landmark release. The hypnotic near-10 minute title track (also a UK Top 30 hit) breathtakingly showcased the driving/free-form cool guitar interplay between LLOYD and virtuoso VERLAINE (the track first debuted at their early CBGB's shows and perfected/modified over the next couple of years), while the album as a whole testified to VERLAINE's barely disguised passion for The ROLLING STONES, PINK FLOYD and the darker moments of The VELVET UNDERGROUND. While VERLAINE's tortured vocals were reminiscent of LOU REED/PATTI SMITH, his molten-spark histrionics resolutely distinguished the band from the more wilfully amateurish new wave pack and TELEVISION remain the most musically adept band of the era. Unsurprisingly, however, they found it difficult following up such a milestone and although 'ADVENTURE' (1978) contained sporadic moments of genius, TELEVISON were beginning to lose clarity. Ironically, as the New York scene was at its height, LLOYD effectively pulled the plug on the group after walking out mid-tour later that year. VERLAINE tried unsuccessfully to translate his distinctive sound into a more mainstream rock setting with his solo career, retaining his characteristic vocals and of course, his trademark guitar alchemy. TELEVISION eventually re-formed in the 90's with the classic line-up of VERLAINE, LLOYD, SMITH and FICCA, recording the acclaimed 'TELEVISION' (1992) for 'Capitol' and suggesting that what VERLAINE's solo career was lacking was the anchor and foil of LLOYD's rhythm playing. The latter kept himself busy during the 90's with guest spots for the likes of MATTHEW SWEET although parental considerations also took up much of his time. He eventually returned to solo work with 'THE COVER DOESN'T MATTER' (2001), a belated – 15 years (!) – set of pared-back alt-rock recorded with PETER STUART and CHRIS BUTLER. Finding a home at Chicago left field institution, 'Thrill Jockey', the infamously reticent VERLAINE issued not one, but two albums on the same day: 'SONGS AND OTHER THINGS' (2006) and 'AROUND (2006), a concession to both the creative impulse and the contemporary fad for double-whammy release schedules. The former was his first vocal album for more than a decade: he still sounded like a cross between a less jaundiced LOU REED and DAVID BOWIE as rendered on 'Stella Street', but it's a voice that suits those angular, emaciated songs, the best of which, 'THE DAY ON YOU', raised a swaying curtain on some of the album's thinnest, wildest guitar mercury. 'AROUND' was the instrumental arm of the package, with VERLAINE setting his phaser to mood, drip-feeding filmic, six-string sutras with assiduously anti-rock verve.

• **Songwriters:** VERLAINE lyrics / group compositions, except early live material; FIRE ENGINE (13th Floor Elevators) / KNOCKIN' ON HEAVEN'S DOOR (Bob Dylan) / SATISFACTION (Rolling Stones). • **Trivia:** VERLAINE played guitar on PATTI SMITH's 1974 single 'Hey Joe'.

Album rating: MARQUEE MOON (*10) / ADVENTURE (*6) / THE BLOW UP exploitation (*4) / TELEVISION (*5) / Tom Verlaine: TOM VERLAINE (*7) / DREAMTIME (*6) / WORDS FROM THE FRONT (*6) / COVER (*7) / FLASH LIGHT (*7) / THE WONDER (*7) / WARM AND COOL (*5) / THE MILLER'S TALE: A TOM VERLAINE ANTHOLOGY compilation (*8) / SONGS AND OTHER THINGS (*7) / AROUND (*6)

TOM VERLAINE (b. THOMAS MILLER, 13 Dec'49, Mt.Morris, New Jersey) – vocals, lead guitar / **RICHARD LLOYD** – guitar, vocals / **RICHARD HELL** (b. RICHARD MYERS, 2 Oct'49, Lexington, Kentucky) – bass, vocals / **BILLY FICCA** – drums

not iss. — Ork

Oct 75. (7") *<81975>* **LITTLE JOHNNY JEWEL. / (part 2)** [–] [ ]

— **FRED SMITH** (b.10 Apr'48) – bass, vocals (ex-BLONDIE) repl. RICHARD HELL who went solo

Elektra — Elektra

Feb 77. (lp/c) *(K/K4 52046) <7E 1098>* **MARQUEE MOON** [28] [ ]
– See no evil / Venus / Friction / Marquee moon / Elevation / Guiding light / Prove it / Torn curtain. *(cd-iss. Jun89; 960616-2) (lp re-iss. Dec02 on '4 Men With Beards'; 4M 501) <(cd re-mast.Sep03 on 'Rhino'+=; 8122 73920-2)>* – Little Johnny Jewel (pts.1 & 2) / See no evil (alt.) / Friction (alt.) / Marquee moon (alt.) / Untitled instrumental.

Mar 77. (12",2-part-7") *(K 12252)* **MARQUEE MOON (stereo). / MARQUEE MOON (mono)** [30] [–]

Jul 77. (7"/12",12"green) *(K 12262/+T)* **PROVE IT. / VENUS** [25] [–]

Apr 78. (lp,red-lp/c) *(K/K4 52072) <6E 133>* **ADVENTURE** [7] [ ]
– Glory / Days / Foxhole / Careful / Carried away / The fire / Ain't that nothin' / The dream's dream. *(cd-iss. Nov93 on 'WEA'; 7559 60523-2) <(cd re-mast.Sep03 on 'Rhino'+=; 8122 73912-2)>* – Adventure / Ain't that nothin' (single version) / Glory (early version) / Untitled.

Apr 78. (7"/12"red) *(K 12287/+T)* **FOXHOLE. / CAREFUL** [36] [–]

Jul 78. (7") *(K 12306)* **GLORY. / CARRIED AWAY** [ ] [–]

Jul 78. (7") *<45516>* **GLORY. / AIN'T THAT NOTHIN'** [–] [ ]

— broke ranks in Aug'78, FICCA joined the WAITRESSES, FRED joined The PATTI SMITH GROUP and RICHARD LLOYD went solo.

TOM VERLAINE

— went solo augmented mainly by **FRED SMITH** – bass / **JAY DEE DAUGHERTY** – drums / **BRUCE BRODY** – keyboards / **ALLAN SCHWARTZBERG** – drums, percussion

Elektra — Elektra

Sep 79. (lp/c) *(K/K4 52156) <2156>* **TOM VERLAINE** [ ] [ ]
– The grip of love / Souvenir from a dream / Kingdom come / Mr. Bingo / Yonki time / Flash lightning / Red leaves / Last night / Breakin' in my heart.

Warners — Warners

Sep 81. (lp/c) *(K/K4 56919) <BSK 3559>* **DREAMTIME** [ ] [ ]
– There's a reason / Penetration / Always / The blue robe / Without a word / Mr. Blur / Fragile / A future in noise / Down on the farm / Mary Marie.

Sep 81. (7"/12") *(K 17855/+T)* **ALWAYS. / THE BLUE ROBE** [ ] [–]

— **JIMMY RIPP** – guitar; repl. BRODY

Virgin — Warners

May 82. (lp/c) *(V/TCV 2227) <BSK 3685>* **WORDS FROM THE FRONT** [ ] [ ]
– Present arrived / Postcard from Waterloo / True story / Clear it away / Words from the front / Coming apart / Days on the mountain. *(cd-iss. Aug88; OVED 87) (re-iss. cd Jun89; CDV 2227)*

May 82. (7"/12") *(VS 501/+12)* **POSTCARD FROM WATERLOO. / DAYS ON THE MOUNTAIN** [ ] [–]

Jun 84. (7") *(VS 696)* **LET'S GO TO THE MANSION. / ('A'version)** [ ] [–]
(12"+=) *(VS 696/+12)* – Lindi Lu.

Aug 84. (7") *(VS 704)* **FIVE MILES OF YOU. / YOUR FINEST HOUR** [ ] [–]
(12"+=) *(VS 704/+12)* – Dissolve reveal.

Sep 84. (lp/c) *(V/TCV 2314) <25144>* **COVER** [ ] [ ]
– Five miles of you / Let's go to the mansion / Travelling / O foolish heart / Dissolve – Reveal / Miss Emily / Rotation / Swim. *(re-iss. Apr86 lp/c; OVED/+C 168) (cd-iss. Jun89; (CDV 2314)*

— **ANDY NEWMARK** – drums; repl. JAY DEE

Fontana — Mercury-IRS

Feb 87. (7") *(FTANA 1)* **A TOWN CALLED WALKER. / SMOOTHER THAN JONES** [ ] [–]
(12"+=) *(FTANA 1-12)* – ('A'version) / Caveman flashlight.

Feb 87. (lp/c)(cd) *(SF LP/MC 1)(830861-2) <42050>* **FLASH LIGHT** [99] [ ]
– Cry mercy, judge / Say a prayer / A town called Walker / Song / The

TELEVISION

scientist writes a letter / Bomb / 4 a.m. / The funniest thing / Annie's tellin' me / One time at sundown.

Mar 87. (7") *(FTANA 2)* **CRY MERCY JUDGE. / CALL ME THE CIRCLING** ☐ -
(12"+=) *(FTANA 2-12)* – At this moment (live) / Lover of the night (live) / Strange things happening.

Jun 87. (7") *(VLANE 3)* **THE FUNNIEST THING. / ONE TIME AT SUNDOWN** ☐ -
(12"+=) *(VLANE 3-12)* – Marquee Moon ('87 version).

Aug 87. (7") *(VLANE 4)* **THE SCIENTIST WRITES A LETTER. / ('A'-Paris version)** ☐ -

Oct 89. (7") *(VLANE 5)* **SHIMMER. / BOMB** ☐ -
(12"+=)(cd-s+=) *(VLANE 5-12)(VLACD 5)* – The scientist writes a letter.

Mar 90. (7") *(VLANE 6)* **KALEIDOSCOPIN'. / SIXTEEN TULIPS** ☐ -
(12"+=)(cd-s+=) *(VLANE 6-12)(VLACD 6)* – Vanity fair.

Apr 90. (cd/c/lp) *(842420-2/-4/-1)* **THE WONDER** ☐ -
– Kaleidoscopin' / August / Ancient Egypt / Shimmer / Stalingrad / Pillow / Storm / 5 hours from Calais / Cooleridge / Prayer.

Rough Trade Rykodisc

Apr 92. (cd/lp) *(R 288-2/-1)* <10216> **WARM AND COOL** ☐ ☐
– Those harbour lights / Sleepwalkin' / The deep dark clouds / Saucer crash / Depot (1951) / Boulevard / Harley Quinn / Sor Juanna / Depot (1957) / Spiritual / Little dance / Ore.

Thrill Jockey Thrill Jockey

Apr 06. (cd) <*(THRILL 173)*> **SONGS AND OTHER THINGS** ☐ ☐
– A parade in Littleton / Heavenly charm / Orbit / Blue light / From her fingers / Nice actress / A stroll / The Earth is in the sky / Lovebird asylum seeker / Documentary / Shingaling / All weirded out / The day on you / Peace piece.

Apr 06. (cd) <*(THRILL 174)*> **AROUND** ☐ ☐
– The O of adore / Brief description / Rain, sidewalk / Shadow walks away / Meteor beach / Mountain / Candle / Balcony / Fame / Curtains open / Eighty eights / A burned letter / Wheel broke / The suns gliding! / New / Rings.

– compilation –

Apr 96. (cd) *Virgin; (CDVDM 9034)* **A MILLER'S TALE (The Tom Verlaine Story)** ☐ -
– Kingdom come / Souvenir from a dream / Clear it away / Always / Postcard from Waterloo / Penetration / Breakin' in my heart / Marquee moon / Days on the mountain / Prove it / Venus / Glory / The grip of love / Without a word / Words from the front / Let's go to the mansion / Lindi-Lu / O foolish heart / Five miles of you / Your finest hour / Anna / Sixteen tulips / Call me the / At 4 a.m. / Stalingrad / Call Mr. Lee / No glamour for Willi / The revolution.

TELEVISION

— re-formed for one-off with **VERLAINE, LLOYD, FICCA + SMITH**

Capitol Capitol

Sep 92. (cd/c/lp) <*(CD/TC+/EST 2181)*> **TELEVISION** ☐ ☐
– 1880 or so / Shane, she wrote this / In world / Call Mr. Lee / Rhyme / No glamour for Willi / Beauty trip / The rocket / This fire / Mars. *(cd re-iss. Feb99; CDESTV 2181)*

– compilations, others, etc. –

Jan 83. (c) *R.O.I.R.;* <*A-114*> **THE BLOW UP (live)** - ☐
– The blow up / See no evil / Prove it / Elevation / I don't care / Venus de Milo / Foxhole / Ain't that nothin' / Knockin' on Heaven's door / Little Johnny Jewel / Friction / Marquee moon / Satisfaction. *(UK cd-iss. Feb90 on 'Danceteria'; DANCD 030) (cd re-iss. Nov94 on 'R.O.I.R.'; RE 114CD) <(cd-iss. Apr99; RUSCD 8249)> <(d-lp iss.May01; RUSLP 8249)>*

1979. (12"m) *Ork-WEA; (NYC 1T)* **LITTLE JOHNNY JEWEL (parts 1 & 2). / ('A'live version)** ☐ -

☐ TEMPLE OF THE DOG (see under ⇒ SOUNDGARDEN)

the TEMPTATIONS

Formed: Birmingham, Alabama, USA . . . 1960, initially as The ELGINS, by EDDIE KENDRICKS and PAUL WILLIAMS (from The PRIMES), plus MELVIN FRANKLIN and OTIS WILLIAMS (from The DISTANTS). They moved to Detroit in 1961 after two flop 45's for 'Miracle'. Securing a deal with the Berry 'Gordy' label (aka Tamla Motown), they finally scored their first US hit in 1964 with 'THE WAY YOU DO THE THINGS YOU DO'. By early 1965, 'MY GIRL' had given them their first chart topper. Penned by SMOKEY ROBINSON (who dominated most of the band's songwriting during this period), the song was the first in an incredible run of chart hits that included 'IT'S GROWING', 'SINCE I LOST MY BABY' and 'MY BABY', all released in 1965. Though the act were 'manufactured' to a certain degree by 'Motown', they possessed an impressive three-pronged vocal attack in DAVID RUFFIN's gravel-flecked rasp, EDDIE KENDRICKS' high tenor and PAUL WILLIAMS' heavy baritone. But it was RUFFIN's vocals which were pushed to the fore as producer NORMAN WHITFIELD began to lead the group's sound in a rougher direction, 'AIN'T TOO PROUD TO BEG' (1966), an early example of what was to come. As the band enjoyed a further string of hits including '(I KNOW) I'M LOSING YOU)' (1966), 'YOU'RE MY EVERYTHING' (1967) and 'I WISH IT WOULD RAIN' (1968), RUFFIN became increasingly jealous of the way DIANA ROSS was being nurtured for solo stardom by 'Motown', things coming to a head when RUFFIN failed to show for a gig. The group duly sent him packing, recruiting DENNIS EDWARDS and with the 'CLOUD NINE' (1969) single, hitched a ride on the magic roundabout of "psychedelic soul" pioneered by SLY STONE's thrilling honky hybrids. With WHITFIELD and his partner BARRETT STRONG penning most of the material, the band released a clutch of hard-hitting, socially aware classics like 'PSYCHEDELIC SHACK' (1970), 'BALL OF CONFUSION (THAT'S WHAT THE WORLD IS TODAY)' (1970), the funk getting dirtier and nastier with the hard-bitten tale of a broken home, 'PAPA WAS A ROLLING STONE' (1972). KENDRICKS departed in 1971 after his swansong for the band, 'JUST MY IMAGINATION (RUNNING AWAY WITH ME)' and PAUL WILLIAMS left later the same year, the band drafting in replacements DAMON HARRIS and RICHARD STREET. While the singles dried up, in the pop charts at least, the band still shifted albums up until the late 70's. As their creative muse began to falter, the band extricated itself from 'Motown' and despite a well-received self-produced album, 'THE TEMPTATIONS DO THE TEMPTATIONS' (1976), their two albums for 'Atlantic', 'HEAR TO TEMPT YOU' (1978) and 'BARE BACK' (1978) were marred by insipid disco stylings. EDWARDS had been absent for these albums (replaced by LOUIS PRICE), although he returned towards the end of the decade and the band hooked up with 'Motown' again for a comeback single, 'POWER' (1980) which scraped into the charts. RUFFIN and KENDRICKS returned to the fold for a short-lived reunion in 1982 and following their departure, OTIS WILLIAMS and MELVIN FRANKLIN carried the TEMPTATIONS flame through the 80's and beyond, completing studio and live work with a changing cast of musicians. Although they were inducted into the Rock'n'Roll Hall Of Fame in 1989, the band were merely retreading their 60's heyday, cabaret style. With KENDRICKS dying of cancer in 1992 and MELVIN FRANKLIN dying three years later, WILLIAMS is the sole remaining member from the original group. With a line-up that included OTIS WILLIAMS, ALI WOODSON, RON TYSON and RAY DAVIS, he cut the mid-90's set, 'FOR LOVERS ONLY' and 1998's 'PHOENIX RISING'. Incredibly perhaps, the latter album was the first of their career to hit the platinum sales bracket although it paled next to their classic work. While it's difficult to even contemplate someone coming up with such a cheesy title as 'EAR-RESISTIBLE' (yep, you read that right), this millennial effort featured a clutch of classy ballads that actually did some justice to the group's legacy, earning them a US Top 60 chart placing. 'AWESOME' (c'mon guys, get your titles sorted out!!!) followed in 2001, a pleasant if forgettable addition to their humungous back catalogue. The TEMPTATIONS continued to release (and chart!) via albums, 'LEGACY' (2004) and 'REFLECTIONS' (2006), although only OTIS WILLIAMS remained from their earliest days.

• **Covered:** THE WEIGHT (Band) / I'LL TRY SOMETHING NEW (Miracles) / I'M GONNA MAKE YOU LOVE ME (Madeleine Bell) / etc.
• **Trivia:** In 1987, actor and fan, BRUCE WILLIS, invited the TEMPTATIONS to sing back-up on his hit version of the DRIFTERS' 'Under The Boardwalk'.

Album rating: MEET THE TEMPTATIONS (*7) / THE TEMPTATIONS SING SMOKEY (*7) / TEMPTIN' TEMPTATIONS (*7) / GETTIN' READY (*7) / THE TEMPTATIONS GREATEST HITS compilation (*8) / TEMPTATIONS LIVE! (*5) / WITH A LOT OF SOUL (*6) / THE TEMPTATIONS IN A MELLOW MOOD (*6) / WISH IT WOULD RAIN (*7) / DIANA ROSS & THE SUPREMES JOIN THE TEMPTATIONS with Diana Ross & The Supremes (*6) / TCB special with Diana Ross & The Supremes (*6) / LIVE AT THE COPA (*4) / CLOUD NINE (*8) / THE TEMPTATIONS SHOW special (*6) / PUZZLE PEOPLE (*6) / TOGETHER with Diana Ross & The Supremes (*5) / ON BROADWAY special with Diana Ross & The Supremes (*5) / PSYCHEDELIC SHACK (*8) / LIVE AT LONDON'S TALK OF THE TOWN (*5) / TEMPTATIONS GREATEST HITS II compilation (*7) / SKY'S THE LIMIT (*6) / SOLID ROCK (*6) / ALL DIRECTIONS (*6) / MASTERPIECE (*6) / ANTHOLOGY compilation (*8) / 1990 (*6) / A SONG FOR YOU (*5) / HOUSE PARTY (*4) / WINGS OF LOVE (*4) / THE TEMPTATIONS DO THE TEMPTATIONS (*4) / HEAR TO TEMPT YOU (*4) / BARE BACK (*3) / POWER (*5) / ALL THE MILLION SELLERS compilation (*8) / THE TEMPTATIONS (*4) / REUNION (*6) / SURFACE THRILLS (*4) / BACK TO BASICS (*5) / TRULY FOR YOU (*5) / TOUCH ME (*4) / 25th ANNIVERSARY compilation (*7) / TO BE CONTINUED (*5) / TOGETHER AGAIN (*5) / SPECIAL (*4) / MILESTONE (*4) / MOTOWN'S GREATEST HITS compilation (*8) / FOR LOVERS ONLY (*4) / PHOENIX RISING (*5) / GREAT SONGS AND PERFORMANCES ... compilation (*7) / ALL THE MILLION SELLERS compilation (*8) / EAR-RESISTIBLE (*6) / AT THEIR VERY BEST compilation (*8) / AWESOME (*4) / LEGACY (*5) / REFLECTIONS (*5)

MELVIN FRANKLIN (b. DAVID ENGLISH, 12 Oct'42, Montgomery, Alabama) – vocals / **OTIS WILLIAMS** (b. OTIS MILES, 30 Oct'49, Texarkana, Texas) – vocals / **ELDRIDGE BRYANT** – vocals

not iss. Thelma

1960. (7"; as the DISTANTS) *<2282>* **ANSWER ME. / SAVE ME FROM THIS MISERY** –

not iss. Northern

1960. (7"; as the DISTANTS) *<3732>* **COME ON. / ALWAYS** –

not iss. Warwick

1960. (7"; as the DISTANTS) *<546>* **COME ON. / ALWAYS** –
1960. (7"; as the DISTANTS) *<577>* **ALRIGHT. / OPEN UP YOUR HEART** –

—— added **EDDIE KENDRICKS** (b.17 Dec'39, Union Springs, Alabama) – lead vocals (ex-PRIMES) / **PAUL WILLIAMS** (b. 2 Jul'39) – vocals (ex-PRIMES)

not iss. Miracle

Aug 61. (7") *<05>* **OH, MOTHER OF MINE. / ROMANCE WITHOUT FINANCE** –
Nov 61. (7") *<12>* **CHECK YOURSELF. / YOUR WONDERFUL LIFE** –

Stateside Gordy

Apr 62. (7") *<7001>* **DREAM COME TRUE. / ISN'T SHE PRETTY** –
Sep 62. (7"; as The PIRATES) *<Mel-O-Die; 105>* **MIND OVER MATTER (I'M GONNA MAKE YOY MINE). / I'LL LOVE YOU TILL I DIE** –
Jan 63. (7") *<7010>* **PARADISE. / SLOW DOWN HEART** –
Mar 63. (7") *<7015>* **I WANT A LOVE I CAN SEE. / THE FURTHER YOU LOOK THE LESS YOU SEE** –
Jul 63. (7") *<7020>* **MAY I HAVE THIS DANCE. / FAREWELL MY LOVE** –

—— **DAVID RUFFIN** (b.18 Jan'41, Meridian, Missouri) – vocals (lead in 1965) had already deposed BRYANT

Apr 64. (7") *(SS 278) <7028>* **THE WAY YOU DO THE THINGS YOU DO. / JUST LET ME KNOW** Jan64 11

—— Early 1964, they backed and were credited on LIZ LANDS 'Gordy' single 'MIDNIGHT JOHNNY'. / KEEP ME'. *<7030>*

Jul 64. (7") *(SS 319) <7032>* **I'LL BE IN TROUBLE. / THE GIRL'S ALRIGHT WITH ME** May64 33
Oct 64. (7") *(SS 348) <7035>* **GIRL (WHY YOU WANNA MAKE ME BLUE). / BABY BABY I NEED YOU** Aug64 26
Jan 65. (7") *(SS 378) <7038>* **MY GIRL. / TALKIN' 'BOUT NOBODY BUT MY BABY** 43 Dec64 1

Tamla Motown Gordy

Mar 65. (7") *(TMG 504) <7040>* **IT'S GROWING. / WHAT LOVE HAS JOINED TOGETHER** 45 18
May 65. (lp) **MEET THE TEMPTATIONS** Apr64 95
– The way you do the things you do / I want a love I can see / Dream come true / Paradise / May I have this dance / Isn't she pretty / Just let me know / Your wonderful love / The further you look the less you see / Check yourself / Slow down heart / Farewell my love. *(cd-iss. Jun99; 549513-2)*
Aug 65. (7") *(TMG 526) <7043>* **SINCE I LOST MY BABY. / YOU'VE GOT TO EARN IT** Jul65 17
Oct 65. (lp) *(TML 11016) <912>* **TEMPTATIONS SING SMOKEY** Mar65 35
– The way you do the things you do / Baby baby I need you / You'd lose a precious love / My girl / It's growing / Who's loving you / What love has joined together / What's so good 'bout goodbye. *(re-iss. Feb80 & Oct81 lp/c; STMR/CSTMR 9005) (cd-iss. Mar03; 530930-2)*
Nov 65. (7") *(TMG 541) <7047>* **MY BABY. / DON'T LOOK BABY** 13 Oct65 83
Mar 66. (lp; stereo/mono) *(S+/TML 11023) <914>* **TEMPTIN' TEMPTATIONS** Nov65 11
– Since I lost my babe / Girl's alright with me / Just another lonely night / My baby / You've got to earn it / Everybody needs love / Girl / Don't look back / I gotta know now / Born to love you / I'll be in trouble / You're the one I need. *(cd-iss. Mar03; 530931-2)*
Apr 66. (7") *(TMG 557) <7049>* **GET READY. / FADING AWAY** Feb66 29
Jun 66. (7") *(TMG 565) <7054>* **AIN'T TOO PROUD TO BEG. / YOU'LL LOSE A PRECIOUS LOVE** 21 May66 13
Sep 66. (lp; stereo/mono) *(S+/TML 11035) <918>* **GETTIN' READY** 40 Jul66 12
– Say you / Little Miss Sweetness / Ain't too proud to beg / Get ready / Lonely, lonely man am I / Too busy thinking about my baby / I've been good to you / It's a lonely world without your love / Fading away / Who you gonna run to / You're not an ordinary girl / Not now I'll tell you later. *(re-iss. Jul82 on 'Motown') (cd-iss. Jun99; 549514-2)*
Sep 66. (7") *(TMG 578) <7055>* **BEAUTY IS ONLY SKIN DEEP. / YOU'RE NOT AN ORDINARY MAN** 18 Aug66 3
Dec 66. (7") *(TMG 587) <7057>* **(I KNOW) I'M LOSING YOU. / LITTLE MISS SWEETNESS** 19 Nov66 8
May 67. (7") *(TMG 610) <7061>* **ALL I NEED. / SORRY IS A SORRY WORD** Apr67 8
Jul 67. (lp; stereo/mono) *(S+/TML 11053) <921>* **TEMPTATIONS LIVE! (live)** 20 Mar67 10
– Medley: Girl (why you wanna make me blue) – Girl's alright with me – I'll be in trouble – I want a love I can see / What love has joined together / My girl / Yesterday / What now my love / Beauty is only skin deep / Group introduction / I wish you love / Ain't too proud to beg / Ol' man river / Get ready / Fading away / My baby / Youll lose a precious love / Baby, baby I need you / Don't look back.
Sep 67. (7") *(TMG 620) <7063>* **YOU'RE MY EVERYTHING. / I'VE BEEN GOOD TO YOU** 26 Jul67 6
Oct 67. (lp; stereo/mono) *(S+/TML 11057) <922>* **WITH A LOT O' SOUL** 19 Aug67 7
– You're my everything / All I need / I'm losing you / Ain't no Sun since you've gone / No more water in the well / It's you that I need / Save my love for a rainy day / Just one last look / Sorry is a sorry word / Now that you've won me / Two sides to love / Don't send me away. *(cd-iss. Aug01; 530932-2)*
Dec 67. (7") *(TMG 633) <7065>* **(LONELINESS MADE ME REALISE) IT'S YOU THAT I NEED. / I WANT A LOVE I CAN SEE** Sep67 14
Feb 68. (7") *(TMG 641) <7068>* **I WISH IT WOULD RAIN. / I TRULY, TRULY BELIEVE** 45 Dec67 4
Mar 68. (lp; stereo/mono) *(S+/TML 11068) <924>* **IN A MELLOW MOOD** Dec67 13
– Hello young lovers / A taste of honey / For once in my life / Somewhere /

Ol' man river / I'm ready for love / Try to remember / Who can I turn to (when nobody needs needs me) / What now my love / That's life / With these hands / The impossible dream. *(cd-iss. Aug01; 530933-2)*

— **DENNIS EDWARDS** (b. 3 Feb'43) – vocals repl. RUFFIN who went solo

May 68. (7") *(TMG 658)* *<7072>* **I COULD NEVER LOVE ANOTHER (AFTER LOVING YOU). / GONNA GIVE HER ALL THE LOVE I GOT** 47 May68 13

Aug 68. (lp; stereo/mono) *(S+/TML 11079)* *<927>* **THE TEMPTATIONS WISH IT WOULD RAIN** Apr68 13
– I could never love another (after loving you) / Cindy / I wish it would rain / Please return your love to me / Fan the flame / He who picks a rose / Why did you leave me darling / I truly, truly believe / This is my beloved / Gonna give her all the love I've got / I've passed this way before / No man can love her like I do.

Jul 68. (7") *<7074>* **PLEASE RETURN YOUR LOVE TO ME. / HOW CAN I FORGET** – 26

Oct 68. (7") *(TMG 671)* **WHY DID YOU LEAVE ME DARLING. / HOW CAN I FORGET** –

Dec 68. (7") *<7082>* **RUDOLPH, THE RED-NOSED REINDEER. / SILENT NIGHT** –

— In Jan69 UK / Nov68, they teamed up with DIANA ROSS & THE SUPREMES (see ⇒) on Top 3 single I'M GONNA MAKE YOU LOVE ME. Around the same time the album DIANA ROSS AND THE SUPREMES JOIN THE TEMPTATIONS hit UK No.1 & US No.2. Throughout 1969, this combination also had Top 50 hits with I'LL TRY SOMETHING NEW / I SECOND THAT EMOTION (UK No.18) / THE WEIGHT / WHY (MUST WE FALL IN LOVE) (UK No.31). Their albums TCB (Soundtrack) hit UK No.11 + US No.1 / ON BROADWAY (TV Show) hit US No.38 / TOGETHER hit both UK + US No.38 early 1970.

Feb 69. (7") *(TMG 688)* **GET READY. / MY GIRL** 10 –

May 69. (7") *(TMG 699)* **AIN'T TOO PROUD TO BEG. / FADING AWAY** –

May 69. (lp; stereo/mono) *(S+/TML 11104)* *<938>* **LIVE AT THE COPA (live)** Dec68 15
– (Introduction) / Get ready / You're my everything / I truly, truly believe / I wish it would rain / For once in my life / I could never love another / For once in my life / I could never love another / Hello young lovers / With these hands / Swanee / The impossible dream / Please return your love to me / (I know) I'm losing you.

May 69. (7") *<7086>* **DON'T LET THE JONESES GET YOU DOWN. / SINCE I'VE LOST YOU** – 20

— line-up update:- **MELVIN FRANKLIN, OTIS WILLIAMS, EDDIE KENDRICKS, PAUL WILLIAMS + DENNIS EDWARDS**

Aug 69. (7") *(TMG 707)* *<7081>* **CLOUD NINE. / WHY DID SHE HAVE TO LEAVE ME (WHY DID SHE HAVE TO GO)** 15 Oct68 6

Sep 69. (lp; stereo/mono) *(S+/TML 11109)* *<939>* **CLOUD NINE** 32 Mar69 4
– Cloud nine / I heard it through it the grapevine / Why did she have to leave me (why did she have to go) / Runaway child, running wild / Love is a hurtin' thing / Hey girl / I need your lovin' / Don't let him take your love from me / Gonna keep on tryin' till I win your love / I gotta find away (to get you back). *(re-iss. Oct81 lp/c; STML/CSTML 5020) (cd-iss. Aug93; 530153-2)*

Nov 69. (7") *(TMG 716)* *<7084>* **RUNAWAY CHILD, RUNNING WILD. / I NEED YOUR LOVIN'** Feb69 6

Jan 70. (7") *(TMG 722)* *<7093>* **I CAN'T GET NEXT TO YOU. / RUNNING AWAY (AIN'T GONNA HELP ME)** 13 Aug69 1

Feb 70. (lp; stereo/mono) *(S+/TML 11133)* *<949>* **PUZZLE PEOPLE** 20 Oct69 5
– I can't get next to you / Hey Jude / Don't let the Joneses get you down / Message from a black man / It's your thing / Little green apples / You don't love me no more / Running away (ain't gonna help you) / Since I've lost you / Slave / That's the way love is. *(re-iss. Mar82 lp/c; STML/CSTMS 5050)*

Apr 70. (lp; stereo/mono) *(S+/TML 11141)* *<953>* **LIVE AT THE (LONDON'S) TALK OF THE TOWN (live)** Aug70 21
– I'm gonna make you love me / The impossible dream / Run away child running wild / Don't let the Joneses get you down / Love theme from Romeo & Juliet / I can't get next to you / This guy's in love with you / I've got to be me / I'm losing you / Cloud nine / Everything is going to be alright. *(re-iss. Jan79 on 'Music For Pleasure' lp/c; MFP/TCMFP 50419)*

Jun 70. (7") *(TMG 741)* *<7096>* **PSYCHEDELIC SHACK. / THAT'S THE WAY LOVE IS** 33 Jan70 7

Jun 70. (lp) *(STML 11147)* *<947>* **PSYCHEDELIC SHACK** 56 Mar70 9
– Psychedelic shack / Hum along and dance / War / It's summer / You make your own Heaven and Hell right here on Earth / You need love like I do (don't you) / Take a stroll thru your mind / Friendship train. *(re-iss. Mar82 lp/c; STMS/CSTMS 5051)*

Sep 70. (7") *(TMG 7049)* *<7099>* **BALL OF CONFUSION (THAT'S WHAT THE WORLD IS TODAY). / IT'S SUMMER** 7 May70 3

Oct 70. (7") *<7102>* **UNGENA ZA ULIMWENGU (UNITE THE WORLD). / HUM ALONG AND DANCE** – 33

Dec 70. (lp) *<951>* **CHRISTMAS CARD** (Festive songs) –
(UK-iss.1988 on 'Pickwick' lp/c; SHM/HSC 3202)

May 71. (7") *(TMG 773)* *<7105>* **JUST MY IMAGINATION (RUNNING AWAY WITH ME). / YOU MAKE YOUR OWN HEAVEN AND HELL RIGHT HERE ON EARTH** 8 Jan71 1

— **EDWARDS, FRANKLIN & WILLIAMS** recruited new members **DAMON HARRIS** (b. 3 Jul'50, Baltimore, Maryland) – vocals repl. EDDIE KENDRICKS who went solo.

Jul 71. (7") *<7109>* **IT'S SUMMER. / I'M THE EXCEPTION TO THE RULE** – 51

Aug 71. (lp) *(STML 11184)* *<957>* **SKY'S THE LIMIT** Apr71 16
– Gonna keep on tryin' till I win your love / Just my imagination / I'm the exception to the rule / Smiling faces sometimes / Man / Throw a farewell kiss / Ungenza za Ulimwenga / Love can be anything. *(re-iss. May91 cd/c; WD/WK 72743)*

Sep 71. (7") *(TMG 783)* **IT'S SUMMER. / UNGENA ZA ULIMWENGU (UNITE THE WORLD)** –

— **RICHARD STREET** (b. 5 Oct'42, Detroit) – vocals (ex-DISTANTS) repl. PAUL. He later committed suicide 17 Aug'73.

Jan 72. (7") *(TMG 800)* *<7111>* **SUPERSTAR (REMEMBER HOW YOU GOT WHERE YOU ARE). / GONNA KEEP ON TRYIN' TILL I WIN YOUR LOVE** 32 Nov71 18

Apr 72. (7") *(TMG 808)* *<7115>* **TAKE A LOOK AROUND. / SMOOTH SAILING FROM NOW ON** 13 Feb72 30

Apr 72. (lp) *(STML 11202)* *<961>* **SOLID ROCK** 34 Jan72 30
– Take a look around / Ain't no sunshine / Stop the war now / What it is / Smooth sailing / Superstar (remember how you got where you are) / It's summer / The end of our road.

Jun 72. (7") *<7119>* **MOTHER NATURE. / FUNKY MUSIC SHO NUFF TURNS ME ON** – 92

Oct 72. (7") *(TMG 832)* **MOTHER NATURE. / SMILING FACES SOMETIMES** –

Jan 73. (7") *(TMG 839)* *<7121>* **PAPA WAS A ROLLIN' STONE. / ('A'instrumental)** 14 Oct72 1

Dec 72. (lp) *(STML 11218)* *<962>* **ALL DIRECTIONS** 19 Aug72 2
– Funky music sho nuff turns me on / Run Charlie run / I ain't got nothing / Papa was a rollin' stone / Love woke me up this morning / The first time ever I saw your face / Mother nature / It's your thing. *(re-iss. Mar82 lp/c; STMS/CSTMS 5052) (cd-iss. Sep93 & Mar03; 530155-2)*

Apr 73. (7") *<TMG 854>* *<7126>* **MASTERPIECE. / ('A'instrumental)** Feb73 7

Jun 73. (lp) *(STML 11229)* *<965>* **MASTERPIECE** 28 Mar73 7
– Masterpiece / Hey girl (I like your style) / Ha / The plastic man / Law of the land / Hurry tomorrow. *(re-iss. Oct81 lp/c; STMS/CSTMS 5021) (cd-iss. Jan93; 530100-2)*

Jun 73. (7") *<7129>* **THE PLASTIC MAN. / HURRY TOMORROW** – 40

Aug 73. (7") *<7131>* **HEY GIRL (I LIKE YOUR STYLE). / MA** – 35

Aug 73. (7") *(TMG 866)* **LAW OF THE LAND. / FUNKY MUSIC SHO NUFF TURN ME ON** 41 –

Nov 73. (7") *<7133>* **LET YOUR HAIR DOWN. / AIN'T NO JUSTICE** – 27

Dec 73. (lp) *(STMA 8016)* *<966>* **1990** 19
– Let your hair down / I need you / Heavenly / You've got my soul on fire / Ain't no justice / 1990 / Zoom.

Mar 74. (7") *(TMG 887)* **HEY GIRL (I LIKE YOUR STYLE). / I NEED YOU** –

Apr 74. (7") *<7135>* **HEAVENLY. / ZOOM** – 43

Jun 74. (7") *<7136>* **YOU'VE GOT MY SOUL ON FIRE. / I NEED YOU** – 74

— **GLEN LEONARD** – vocals repl. HARRIS

Jan 75. (7") *(TMG 931)* *<7138>* **HAPPY PEOPLE. / ('A'instrumental)** 40

Feb 75. (lp) *(STMA 8021)* *<969>* **A SONG FOR YOU** 13
– Happy people / Glasshouse / Shakey ground / The prophet / Happy people (Instrumental) / A song for you / Memories / I'm a bachelor.

Apr 75. (7") *<7142>* **SHAKEY GROUND. / I'M A BACHELOR** – 26

May 75. (7") *<TMG 948>* **MEMORIES. / AIN'T NO JUSTICE** –

Aug 75. (7") *<7144>* **GLASSHOUSE. / THE PROPHET** – 37

— **LOUIS PRICE** – vocals repl. EDWARDS who went solo

Jan 76. (7") *<7146>* **KEEP HOLDING ON. / WHAT YOU NEED MOST (I DO BEST OF ALL)** [–] [54]

Feb 76. (lp) *(STML 12006) <973>* **HOUSE PARTY** [ ] Nov75 [40]
– Keep holding on / It's just a matter of time / You can't stop a man in love / World of you, love and music / What you need most (I do best of all) / Ways of a grown up man / Johnny Porter / Darling stand by me / If I don't love you this way.

Jun 76. (7") *<7150>* **UP THE CREEK (WITHOUT A PADDLE). / DARLING STAND BY ME** [–] [94]

Jun 76. (lp) *(STMA 8025) <971>* **WINGS OF LOVE** [ ] Mar76 [29]
– Sweet gypsy Jane / Sweetness in the dark / Up the creek / China doll / Mary Ann / Dream world / Paradise.

Oct 76. (7") *(TMG 1057) <7152>* **WHO ARE YOU. / LET ME COUNT THE WAYS (I LOVE YOU)** [ ] [ ]

Oct 76. (lp) *(STML 12040) <975>* **THE TEMPTATIONS DO THE TEMPTATIONS** [ ] Sep76 [53]
– Why can't you and me get together / Who are you / I'm on fire / Put your trust in me, baby / There's no stopping / Let me count the ways / Is there anybody else / I'll take you in.

Jan 77. (7") *(TMG 1063)* **SHAKEY GROUND. / I'M A BACHELOR** [ ] [–]

Atlantic Atlantic

Nov 77. (7") *<3436>* **IN A LIFETIME. / I COULD NEVER STOP LOVING YOU** [–] [ ]

Feb 78. (lp) *(K 50413) <19143>* **HEAR TO TEMPT YOU** [ ] Dec77 [ ]
– Think for yourself / In a lifetime / Can we come and share in love / She's all I've got / Snake in the grass / It's time for love / Let's live in peace / Road between the lines / I could never stop loving you.

Feb 78. (7") *<3461>* **LET'S LIVE IN PEACE. / THINK FOR YOURSELF** [–] [ ]

Aug 78. (7") *<3517>* **BARE BACK. / I SEE MY CHILD** [–] [ ]

Aug 78. (lp) *(K 50504) <19188>* **BARE BACK** [ ] [ ]
– Bare back / Mystic woman (love me over) / I just don't know how I let you go / That's when you need love / Ever ready love / Wake up to me / You're so easy to love / I see the child / Touch me again.

Sep 78. (7") *(K 11186)* **BARE BACK. / EVER READY LOVE** [ ] [–]

Sep 78. (7") *<3538>* **EVER READY LOVE. / TOUCH ME AGAIN** [–] [ ]

Jan 79. (7") *<3567>* **JUST DON'T KNOW HOW TO LET YOU GO. / MYSTIC WOMAN** [–] [ ]

Motown Gordy

May 80. (7"/12") *(TMG/+T 1186) <7183>* **POWER. / ('A'instrumental)** [ ] [43]

Jun 80. (lp/c) *(STML/CSTML 12136) <994>* **POWER** [ ] May80 [45]
– Power / Struck by lightning twice / How can I resist your love / Isn't the night fantastic / Shadow of your love / Go for it / Can't you see sweet thing / I'm coming her.

Aug 80. (7") *(TMG 1197) <7188>* **STRUCK BY LIGHTNING TWICE. / I'M COMING HOME** [ ] [ ]

Jan 81. (7") *(TMG 1216)* **TAKE ME AWAY. / THERE'S MORE WHERE THAT CAME FROM** [ ] [–]

— **DENNIS EDWARDS** returned on lead vocals

Oct 81. (7") *(TMG 1243) <7208>* **AIMING AT YOUR HEART. / LIFE OF A COWBOY** [ ] [67]

Jan 82. (lp/c) *(STML/CSTML 12159) <1006>* **THE TEMPTATIONS** [ ] Aug81 [ ]
– Aiming at your heart / Evil woman (gonna take your love) / The best of both worlds / Ready, willing and able / Oh what a night / Open their eyes / The life of a cowboy / What else / Just ain't havin' fun / Your lovin' is magic.

Feb 82. (7") *<7213>* **OH, WHAT A NIGHT. / ISN'T THE NIGHT FANTASTIC** [–] [ ]

— **OTIS WILLIAMS, MELVIN FRANKLIN, RICHARD STREET & DENNIS EDWARDS** re-united with **DAVID RUFFIN & EDDIE KENDRICKS** for one-off album

May 82. (lp) *<6008>* **REUNION** [–] Apr82 [37]
– Standing on the top / You better beware / Lock it in the pocket / I've never been to me / Backstage / More on the inside / Money's hard to get.

May 82. (7"; TEMPTATIONS featuring RICK JAMES) *(TMG 1263) <1616>* **STANDING ON THE TOP. / (part 2)** [53] [66]

Jul 82. (7") *<1631>* **MORE ON THE INSIDE. / MONEY'S HARD TO GET** [–] [ ]

Nov 82. (7") *<1654>* **SILENT NIGHT. / EVERYTHING FOR CHRISTMAS** [–] [ ]
<re-iss. Nov83; 1713>

— The quartet added **RON TYSON** (their composer in '78) – vocals

Mar 83. (7"/12") *(TMG/+T 1297) <1666>* **LOVE ON MY MIND TONIGHT. / BRING YOUR BODY HERE** [ ] [88]

Mar 83. (lp/c) *(STML/CSTML 12182) <6032>* **SURFACE THRILLS** [ ] [ ]
– Surface thrills / Love on my mind tonight / One man woman / Show me your love / The seeker / What a way to put it / Made in America / Bring your body here (exercise chant).

May 83. (7") *<1683>* **SURFACE THRILLS. / MADE IN AMERICA** [–] [ ]

Oct 83. (7") *<1707>* **MISS BUSY BODY (GET YOUR BODY BUSY). / (part 2)** [–] [ ]

Dec 83. (lp/c) *(STML/CSTML 12196) <6085>* **BACK TO BASICS** [ ] [ ]
– Miss busy body (get your body busy) / Sail away / Outlaw / Stop the world right here (I wanna get off) / The battle song (I'm the one) / Hollywood / Isn't the night fantastic / Make me believe in love again.

Apr 84. (7") *<1720>* **SAIL AWAY. / ISN'T THE NIGHT FANTASTIC** [–] [54]

— **ALI OLLIE WODSIN** – lead vocals repl. EDWARDS

Nov 84. (7"/12") *(TMG/+T 1365) <1765>* **TREAT HER LIKE A LADY. / ISN'T THE NIGHT FANTASTIC** [12] [48]

Dec 84. (lp/c) *(ZL/ZK 72342) <6119>* **TRULY FOR YOU** [75] Nov84 [55]
– Running / Treat like a lady / How can you say it's over / My life is true (truly for you) / Memories / Just to keep you in my life / Set your love right / I'll keep my light on in my window. *(re-iss. Oct88 lp/c/cd; WL/WK/WD 76244)*

Feb 85. (7") *<1781>* **MY LOVE IS TRUE (TRULY FOR YOU). / SET YOUR LOVE RIGHT** [–] [ ]

Mar 85. (7") *(TMG 1373)* **MY LOVE IS TRUE (TRULY FOR YOU). / I'LL KEEP A LIGHT ON IN MY WINDOW** [ ] [–]
(12"+=) *(TMGT 1373)* – Treat her like a lady (remix).

Jun 85. (7") *<1789>* **HOW CAN YOU SAY IT'S OVER. / I'LL KEEP MY LIGHT IN THE WINDOW** [–] [ ]

— In Sep'85, RUFFIN & KENDRICKS were credited on HALL & OATES live album 'LIVE AT THE APOLLO WITH . . . '

Nov 85. (7"/12") *(ZB/ZT 40453) <1818>* **DO YOU REALLY LOVE YOUR BABY. / I'LL KEEP A LIGHT ON IN MY WINDOW** [ ] [ ]

Nov 85. (lp/c) *(ZL/ZK 72413) <6164>* **TOUCH ME** [ ] [ ]
– Magic / Give her some attention / Deeper than love / I'm fascinated / Touch me / Don't break your promise to me / She got tired of loving me / Do you really love your baby / Oh lover.

Feb 86. (7") *<1834>* **TOUCH ME. / SET YOUR LOVE RIGHT** [–] [ ]

Mar 86. (7"/12") *(ZB/ZT 40622)* **I'M FASCINATED. / HOW CAN YOU SAY IT'S OVER** [ ] [–]

Jun 86. (7") *<1837>* **WISHFUL THINKING. / A FINE MESS** [–] [ ]

Aug 86. (7") *(ZB 40850)* **LADY SOUL. / A FINE MESS** [ ] [–]
(12"+=) *(ZT 40850)* – Papa was a rolling stone.

Sep 86. (lp/c) *(ZL/ZK 72515) <6207>* **TO BE CONTINUED** [ ] Jul86 [74]
– Lady soul / Message to the world / To be continued / Put us together again / Someone / Girls (they like it) / More love, your love / A fine mess / You're the one / Love me right.

Oct 86. (7") *<1856>* **LADY SOUL. / PUT US TOGETHER AGAIN** [–] [47]

Jan 87. (7") *<1871>* **TO BE CONTINUED. / YOU'RE THE ONE** [–] [ ]

Apr 87. (7") *<1881>* **SOMEONE. / LOVE ME RIGHT** [–] [ ]

— **DENNIS EDWARDS** returned again to repl. OTIS

Aug 87. (7") *(ZB 41431)* **PAPA WAS A ROLLIN' STONE (remix). / DON'T SAY NOTHING'S CHANGED** [31] [–]
(12"+=) *(ZT 41431)* – Papa was a rollin' stone (remix 2).

Oct 87. (lp/c/cd) *(ZL/ZK/ZD 72616) <6246>* **TOGETHER AGAIN** [ ] [ ]
– I got your number / Look what you started / I wonder who she's seeing now / 10 x 10 / Do you wanna go with me / Little things / Everytime I close my eyes / Lucky / Put your foot down.

Oct 87. (7"/12") *(ZB/ZT 41547) <1908>* **I WONDER WHO SHE'S SEEING NOW. / GIRLS (THEY LIKE IT)** [ ] [ ]

Jan 88. (7"/c-s) *(ZB/ZV 41734) <1920>* **LOOK WHAT YOU STARTED. / MORE LOVE, YOUR LOVE** [63] [ ]
(12"+=) *(ZT 41734)* – ('A'extended).

Apr 88. (7") *<1933>* **DO YOU WANNA GO WITH ME. / PUT YOUR FOOT DOWN** [–] [ ]

— Late 1987, RUFFIN & KENDRICKS released eponymous duo album on 'RCA'.

— **RON TYSON** – vocals repl. EDWARDS

Oct 89. (7") *(ZB 43233) <1974>* **ALL I WANT FROM YOU. / ('A'instrumental)** [71] [ ]
(12"+=/cd-s+=) *(ZT/ZD 43234)* – Papa was a rollin' stone / Treat her like a lady.

Oct 89. (lp/c/cd) *(ZL/ZK/ZD 72667) <6275>* **SPECIAL** [ ] [ ]
– Friends / Special / All I want from you / She's better than money / One step at a time / Fill me up / Go ahead / Loveline / Soul to soul. *(cd+=)* – O.A.A. lover.

Jan 90. (7") *<2004>* **SPECIAL. / O.A.A. LOVER** [–] [ ]

Mar 90. (7") *<2023>* **SOUL TO SOUL. / ('A'instrumental)** [–] [ ]

Jun 90. (7") *<903>* **ONE STEP AT A TIME. / ('A'instrumental)** [–] [ ]

Jan 92. (cd/c/lp) *(ZD/ZK/ZL 72768) <6331>* **MILESTONE** [ ] [ ]
– Eenie, meenie, minie moe / Any old lovin' (just won't do) / Hoops of fire / We should be makin' love / The Jones' / Get ready / Corner of my heart / Whenever you're ready / Do it easy / Wait a minute. (cd+=) – Celebrate. *(re-iss. cd Apr95; 530005-2)*

Feb 92. (7"/c-s) *(TMG/+C 1403)* **THE JONES'. / ('A'-Surgery mix)** [69] [ ]
(12"+=/cd-s+=) *(TMG T/CD 1403)* – ('A'instrumental).

— sadly, EDDIE KENDRICKS died of cancer in Oct '92

— **THEO PEOPLES** – vocals; repl. STREET

— another original, MELVIN FRANKLIN, also died on 23rd February 1995

— **OTIS WILLIAMS, PEOPLES + ALI WOODSON** with **RON TYSON** recruited **RAY DAVIS** (b.29 Mar'40, Sumter, South Carolina, USA)

Universal Motown

Sep 95. (cd/c) *<(530568-2/-4)>* **FOR LOVERS ONLY** [ ] [ ]
– Some enchanted evening / I've grown accustomed to her face / At last / Night and day / Time after time / Melvin's interlude / Life is but a dream / What a difference a day makes / I'm glad there is you / South shell interlude / That's why (I love you so) / For your love – You send me.

— **HARRY GILBERRY Jr. + BARRINGTON SCOTT** – vocals; repl. PEOPLES + WOODSON

Oct 98. (cd/c) *<(530937-2/-4)>* **PHOENIX RISING** [ ] Aug98 [44]
– Here after (interlude) / Stay / False faces / How he could hurt you / I'm calling you (interlude) / This is my promise / My love / Tempt me / If I give you my heart / Take me in your arms / That's what friends are for / Just like I told you / Stay.

Sep 00. (cd) *<(157742-2)>* **EAR-RESISTIBLE** [ ] May00 [54]
– I'll just go crazy (intro) / I'm here / Your love / Elevator eyes / Selfish reasons / Kiss me like you miss me / Party / It's alright to be wrong / Proven and true / Got to get on the road / I'll just go crazy / A little bit lonely / One love one world (interlude) / Error of our ways.

Nov 01. (cd) *<(016330-2)>* **AWESOME** [ ] [ ]
– Awesome (intro) / Hurt so bad / 4 days / Lady / Forget about it / Awesome / Race for your heart / Swept away / My baby / Open letter, my one temptation (interlude) / So easy / I want a love I can see / That's how heartaches are made / I feel good.

Jun 04. (cd) *<(AAB00025890-2)>* **LEGACY** [ ] [ ]
– Still tempting / Round here / Stay together / Fifty fifty love / Love to the music / You are necessary in my life (the wedding song) / Mr. Fix It / All the wrong people / Baby it's me / Why can't we be lovin' friends / Never let you down.

Jan 06. (cd) *<(AAB00051700-2)>* **REFLECTIONS** [ ] [80]
– Can I get a witness / Reflections / How sweet it is (to be loved by you) / Don't leave me this way / This old heart of mine (is weak for you) / Ain't nothing like the real thing / I hear a symphony / Try it baby / Ain't no mountain high enough / Ooo baby baby / What becomes of the broken hearted / Never can say goodbye / I'll be there / Neither one of us (wants to be the first to say goodbye) / Reach out and touch (somebody's hand).

– (selective) compilations, etc. –

note; on 'Tamla Motown' UK/ 'Gordy' US unless otherwise mentioned

Feb 67. (lp; stereo/mono) *(S+/TML 11042) <919>* **THE TEMPTATIONS' GREATEST HITS** [26] Dec66 [5]
– The way you do the things you do / My girl / Ain't too proud to beg / Don't look back / Get ready / Beauty is only skin deep / Since I lost my baby / The girl's alright with me / My baby / Its growing / I'll be in trouble / Girl (why you wanna make me blue). *(re-iss. Sep88 lp/c/cd; WL/WK/WD 72646)*

Aug 69. (lp) *<933>* **THE TEMPTATIONS SHOW (TV Soundtrack)** [–] [24]

Dec 70. (lp) *(STML 11170) <954>* **THE TEMPTATIONS' GREATEST HITS VOL.2** [35] Sep70 [15]
(re-iss. Sep88 lp/c/cd; WL/WK/WD 72647)

May 74. (d-lp/d-c) *(TMSP/CTMSP 6003) <974>* **ANTHOLOGY 64-73** [ ] Sep73 [65]
(re-iss. Oct82; same)

Oct 80. (d-lp/d-c) *(STML/CSTML 12140)* **20 GOLDEN GREATS** [ ] [–]
(cd-iss. 1986; ZL 72160)

Oct 81. (d-lp/d-c) *(TMSP/CTMSP 6003)* **ALL THE MILLION SELLERS** [ ] [–]
(re-iss. Apr84 lp/c; WL/WK 72096) (cd-iss. Feb86; WD 72096)

Nov 86. (cd) *(ZD 72460)* **CLOUD NINE / PUZZLE PEOPLE** [ ] [–]
(re-iss. Oct00; 159446-2)

Nov 86. (cd) *(ZD 72486)* **PSYCHEDELIC SHACK / ALL DIRECTIONS** [ ] [–]
(re-iss. Oct00; 159445-2)

Dec 86. (cd) *(ZD 72499)* **SONG FOR YOU / MASTERPIECE** [ ] [–]

Jan 87. (cd) *(ZD 72501)* **LIVE AT THE COPA / WITH A LOT O' SOUL** [ ] [–]

Jan 87. (cd) *(ZD 72525)* **ANTHOLOGY 1 & 2** [ ] [–]

Apr 89. (cd) *(WD 72365)* **COMPACT COMMAND PERFORMANCES** [ ] [–]

below from the film 'My Girl' starring McAuley Caulkin.

Feb 92. (7"/c-s/cd-s) *Epic; (657676-7/-4/-2) <74108>* **MY GIRL. / (James Newton Howard theme from 'My Girl')** [2] [ ]

Apr 92. (cd/c) *(530015-2/-4)* **MOTOWN'S GREATEST HITS** [8] [ ]
– My girl / The Jones' / Get ready (new version) / Ain't too proud to beg / Beauty is only skin deep / I wish it would rain / (I know) I'm losing you / Cloud nine / Paa was a rollin' stone / Law of the land / Just my imagination (running away with me) / Take a look around / Ball of confusion (that's what the world is today) / I can't get to you / Psychedelic shack / Treat her like a lady / Get ready / You're my everything / Superstar (remember how you got where you are) / Standing on the top (part 1).

Nov 98. (cd) *<5315>* **GREAT SONGS AND PERFORMANCES THAT INSPIRED THE MOTOWN 25th ANNIVERSARY TELEVISION SPECIAL** [–] [ ]

Feb 00. (cd) *Spectrum; (544255-2)* **PSYCHEDELIC SOUL** [ ] [ ]

Jul 00. (cd) *(153366-2)* **MOTOWN LOST AND FOUND: YOU'VE GOT TO EARN IT – 1962-1968** [ ] [ ]

Oct 00. (cd) *(157519-2)* **LET YOUR HEART BE YOUR GUIDE: AN INTRODUCTION TO THE TEMPTATIONS** [ ] [ ]

Oct 00. (cd) *(159443-2)* **MEET THE TEMPTATIONS / SING SMOKEY** [ ] [ ]

Oct 00. (cd) *(159444-2)* **LIVE AT THE COPA / WITH A LOT O' SOUL** [ ] [ ]

Oct 00. (cd) *(159510-2)* **MASTERPIECE / A SONG FOR YOU** [ ] [ ]

Oct 00. (cd) *(159511-2)* **WISH IT WOULD RAIN / IN A MELLOW MOOD** [ ] [ ]

Jan 01. (d-cd) *Universal TV; (013578-2)* **AT THEIR VERY BEST** [30] [ ]

Oct 01. (cd) *<(AA4400 14594-2)>* **THE BEST OF TEMPTATIONS CHRISTMAS** [ ] [ ]

Apr 02. (d-cd) *<017298>* **MY GIRL: THE VERY BEST OF THE TEMPTATIONS** [–] [ ]

Mar 03. (d-cd) *Universal; (E 530615-2)* **ONE BY ONE: THE BEST OF THE TEMPTATIONS** [ ] [ ]

Jun 03. (d-cd) *Universal; (AAB00005820-2)* **PSYCHEDELIC SOUL** [ ] [ ]

□ THAT PETROL EMOTION
(see under ⇒ the UNDERTONES)

the THE

Formed: Swadlincote, Derbyshire, England . . . 1979 as a studio project by MATT JOHNSON who was part of post-punk outfit The GADGETS, at the same time. JOHNSON signed to indie label, '4 a.d.' in 1980, unleashing the poignant single, 'CONTROVERSIAL SUBJECT'. JOHNSON released a further debut album for the label in summer '81, 'BURNING BLUE SOUL', although in effect it was a THE THE recording in all but name, JOHNSON being the sole permanent member of the group. Signing briefly to 'Some Bizzare',

THE THE released another three singles, 'COLD SPELL AHEAD', 'PERFECT' and the brilliant 'UNCERTAIN SMILE', before securing a deal with 'Epic'. The long awaited and much anticipated 'SOUL MINING' was eventually released in late '83, JOHNSON's critical favour and cult standing seeing the album reach the UK Top 30. An entrancing, ambitious pop record with a brooding undertow, the keening 'THIS IS THE DAY' stands among the best of JOHNSON's work, the album's claustrophobic lyrics marking out JOHNSON as a bedsit commentator par excellence. For live work, JOHNSON recruited the likes of ex-ORANGE JUICE man, ZEKE MANYIKA, JIM THIRLWELL and JOOLS HOLLAND, the latter actually having guested on the album. Three years in the making, 'INFECTED' (1986) was JOHNSON's tour de force, a scathing attack on the industrial, economic and moral wasteland that was Thatcher's Britain. Nowhere was this better articulated than the malignant power of the album's centrepiece, 'HEARTLAND', JOHNSON berating 80's material gain and America's all-pervasive influence through gritted teeth. The pumping electro-soul of the title track, meanwhile, dealt with sexual obsession and the AIDS crisis, the attendant devil-masturbating video causing a storm of controversy. Other highlights included the tortured 'OUT OF THE BLUE (INTO THE FIRE)' and the breathy duet with NENEH CHERRY, 'SLOW TRAIN TO DAWN', JOHNSON's mastery of mood and atmosphere, together with a crack troupe of guest musicians making this one of the most realised albums of the decade. Accompanied by a full-length video/film (which was aired on Channel 4), the record also gave JOHNSON some belated Top 20 success. Spurred on, the restless maverick subsequently recruited a permanent band to turn THE THE into a group proposition, namely DAVID PALMER, JAMES ELLER and ex-SMITHS guitarist JOHNNY MARR. Though the resulting album, 'MIND BOMB' (1989) was THE THE's most successful to date (Top 5), its caustic barrage of political ranting lacked the twisted pop subtlety of its predecessor and left some critics unimpressed (a guest spot from SINEAD O'CONNOR on 'KINGDOM OF RAIN' made up for the pop tones of 'THE BEAT(EN) GENERATION'). Retaining the same core of musicians while adding keyboard player, D.C. COLLARD, THE THE eventually resurfaced with a full length album in the form of 'DUSK' (1993). Previewed by the harmonica howl of 'DOGS OF LUST', the album saw JOHNSON once again wrestling with his inner demons in his disturbingly insinuating way. A mid-life dark-night-of-the-soul, JOHNSON has rarely bared his soul or expressed his despair as affectingly as on the very SMITHS-esque 'SLOW EMOTION REPLAY', MARR literally wringing the pathos from his chiming guitar. This cathartic collection of urban blues nevertheless ended on something of a more hopeful note with 'LONELY PLANET', JOHNSON coming to some kind of peace with himself and the world. The record deservedly reached No.2, becoming the most successful THE THE release to date and making up the critical and commercial ground lost with 'MIND BOMB'. Of course, the ever restless JOHNSON turned his hand to something completely different, so to speak, for his next full-length release; 'HANKY PANKY' (1995) was a tribute album to his hero, country star HANK WILLIAMS, although only the track 'I SAW THE LIGHT' was of much note. Given short shrift by critics (the same ones probably), the record saw JOHNSON going out on a limb, no doubt alienating many of his long-time fans, although he was distant from them after relocating to Sherman Oaks in California. Then again, anyone familiar with the work of this elusive genius knows to expect the unexpected. Not the most prolific of artists these days, JOHNSON emerged blinking into the harsh electronic light of the new millennium with 'NAKEDSELF' (2000). The record (released on Interscope's 'Nothing' records – home to NINE INCH NAILS) only just scraped into the UK Top 50 and featured flop single, 'SHRUNKEN MAN'.

Album rating: Matt Johnson: BURNING BLUE SOUL (*7) / The The: SOUL MINING (*7) / INFECTED (*8) / MIND BOMB (*8) / DUSK (*7) / HANKY PANKY (*4) / NAKEDSELF (*5) / 45 RPM – THE SINGLES OF . . . compilation (*8)

GADGETS

MATT JOHNSON – guitars / **COLIN TUCKER** – synthesizers / **JOHN HYDE** – synthesizers (both ex-PLAIN CHARACTERS)

Final Solution | not iss.

Dec 79. (lp) *(FSLP 001)* **GADGETREE** [ ] [–]
– Kyleaking / Making cars / Narpath / UFO import No.1 / Slippery / Singing in the rain / Only one me / Shouting 'Nispers' / There over there / Termite mound / Sleep / Devil's dyke / Six mile bottom / UFO import No.2 / Autumn 80 / Duplicate / Bog track / Thin line. *(re-iss. Jun89 on 'Plastic Head' lp/cd; PLAS LP/CD 013)*

—— They continued as a studio set-up with MATT's help.

Dec 80. (lp) *(FSLP 002)* **LOVE, CURIOSITY, FRECKLES & DOUBT** [ ] [–]
– Bodorgan / Gadget speak / Checking to make sure / Aeron / Leave it to Charlie / Prayers / Happy endido / Quatt / Pictures of you / Aaft / Railway line through blubber houses / She's queen of toyland / Sex / It wasn't that way at all / The death and resurrection of Jennifer Gloom / Bill posters will be prosecuted. *(re-iss. Jun89 on 'Plastic Head' lp/cd; PLAS LP/CD 014)*

—— next featured **PETER ASHWORTH** dubbed in instead of MATT

Glass | not iss.

Jan 83. (lp/c) *(GLA LP/C 006)* **THE BLUE ALBUM** [ ] [–]
– We had no way of knowing / Space in my heart / Bodies without heads / The boyfriend / Uneasy listening / Juice of love / Discuss the sofa / Long empty train / Bite the sawdust / Broken fall. *(re-iss. Jun89 on 'Plastic Head' lp/cd; PLAS LP/CD 016)*

Jun 83. (7"/12"; unissued) *(GLASS/+12 026)* **WE HAD NO WAY OF KNOWING. / ACID BATH** [–] [–]

the THE

MATT JOHNSON (b.15 Aug'61, Essex, England . . . raised London) – vocals, guitar, etc. (also of The GADGETS) / **KEITH LAWS** – synthesizers, drum machine / **PETER 'Triash' ASHWORTH** – drums / **TOM JOHNSTON** – bass

4 a.d. | not iss.

Jul 80. (7") *(AD 10)* **CONTROVERSIAL SUBJECT. / BLACK AND WHITE** [ ] [–]

—— next with guests **GILBERT & LEWIS** (of WIRE) on 2nd last track

Aug 81. (lp; as MATT JOHNSON) *(CAD 113)* **BURNING BLUE SOUL** [ ] [–]
– Red cinders in the sand / Song without an ending / Time again for the golden sunset / Icing up / Like a Sun risin' thru my garden / Out of control / Bugle boy / Delirious / The river flows east in Spring / Another boy drowning. *(re-iss. Sep83; same) (re-iss. credited to THE THE, Jun93 cd)(c; HAD 113CD)(HADC 113); hit UK No.65 <US cd-iss. 1993 on 'Warners'; 45266>*

Some Bizzare | not iss.

Sep 81. (7") *(BZ 4)* **COLD SPELL AHEAD. / HOT ICE** [ ] [–]
(re-iss. Aug92, 12"pic-d/cd-s;)

—— **MATT JOHNSON** was now virtually **THE THE**, although he was augmented by others on tour.

Epic | Epic

Oct 82. (7") *(EPCA 2787)* **UNCERTAIN SMILE. / THREE ORANGE KISSES FROM KAZAN** [68] [–]
(12"+=,12"yellow+=) *(EPC13 2787)* – Waiting for the upturn.

Dec 82. (7") **UNCERTAIN SMILE. / WAITING FOR THE UPTURN** [–] [ ]

Feb 83. (7") *(EPCA 3119)* **PERFECT. / THE NATURE OF VIRTUE** [ ] [–]
(12"+=) *(EPCA13 3119)* – The nature of virtue II.

Sep 83. (7") *(A 3710)* **THIS IS THE DAY. / MENTAL HEALING PROCESS** [71] [ ]
(w/ free-7") *(same)* – Leap into the wind / Absolute liberation.
(12") *(TA 3710)* – ('A'side) / I've been waiting for tomorrow (all of my life).

—— added live **ZEKE MANYIKA** – drums (of ORANGE JUICE) / **JIM THIRLWELL / JOOLS HOLLAND** – piano (ex-SQUEEZE) / **THOMAS LEER** – synthesizers, keyboards

Oct 83. (lp/c) *(EPC/40 25525)* *<EK 39266>* **SOUL MINING** [27] [ ]
– I've been waiting for tomorrow (all of my life) / This is the day / The

sinking feeling / Uncertain smile / The twilight hour / Soul mining / Giant. *(free-12"ep.w.a.)* **PERFECT. / SOUP OF MIXED EMOTIONS / FRUIT OF THE HEART** *(c+=)* – Perfect / Three orange kisses from Kazan / Nature of virtue / Fruit of the heart / Soup of mixed emotions / Waiting for the upturn. *(cd-iss. Jun87+=; CD 25525)* – Perfect. *(re-iss. Mar90 cd/c/lp; 466337-2/-4/-1) (cd re-iss. Apr02 +=; 504465-2)*

Nov 83. (7") *(A 3588)* **UNCERTAIN SMILE. / DUMB AS DEATH'S HEAD** [ ] [–]
(12") *(TA 3588)* – ('A'side) / Soul mining.

— guests for next album **ROLI MOSSIMAN / NENEH CHERRY / DAVID PALMER / STEVE HOGARTH / ANNA DOMINO / JAMIE TALBOT / WAYNE LIVESEY / ZEKE MANYIKA** / etc.

May 86. (12"m) *(TRUTH 1)* **SWEET BIRD OF TRUTH. / HARBOUR LIGHTS / SLEEPING JUICE** [ ] [–]

Jul 86. (7") *(TRUTH 2)* **HEARTLAND. / BORN IN THE NEW S.A.** [29] [–]
(12"+=) *(TRUTH T2)* – Flesh and bones.
(d12"++=) *(TRUTH D2)* – Perfect / Fruit of the heart.
(12"+=) *(TRUTH Q2)* – Sweet bird of truth.
(c-s++=) *(TRUTH C2)* – Harbour lights.

Oct 86. (7") *(TRUTH 3)* **INFECTED. / DISTURBED** [48] [ ]
(12"+=/12"uncensored+=) *(TRUTH T/Q 3)* – ('A'-energy mix).
(d12"++=) *(TRUTH D3)* – Soul mining (remix) / Sinking feeling.
(c-s+=) *(TRUTH C3)* – ('A'-Skull crusher mix) / Soul mining / Sinking feeling.

Nov 86. (lp/c/cd) *(EPC/40/CD 26770)* *<40471>* **INFECTED** [14] [89]
– Infected / Out of the blue (into the fire) / Heartland / Angels of deception / Sweet bird of truth / Slow train to dawn / Twilight of a champion / The mercy beat. *(cd+=)* – ('A'-INFECTED singles remixed) *(TA 3588) (cd re-iss. Apr02; 504466-2)*

Jan 87. (7") *(TENSE 1)* **SLOW TRAIN TO DAWN. / HARBOUR LIGHTS** [64] [ ]
(12"+=/12"w-stencil+=) *(TENSE T/D 3)* – The nature of virtue.

May 87. (7") *(TENSE 2)* **SWEET BIRD OF TRUTH. / SLEEPING JUICE** [55] [ ]
(12"+=) *(TENSE T2)* – Harbour lights.
(c-s++=)(cd-s++=) *(TENSE C2)(CDTHE 2)* – Soul mining (12"mix).

— THE THE were again a group when **MATT** with past session man **DAVID PALMER** – drums (ex-ABC) / recruited **JOHNNY MARR** – guitar (ex-SMITHS) / **JAMES ELLER** – bass (ex-JULIAN COPE)

Feb 89. (7") *(EMU 8)* **THE BEAT(EN) GENERATION. / ANGEL** [18] [ ]
(12"box+=/cd-s+=/3"cd-s+=) *(EMUB/EMUCD/CBEMU 8)* – Soul mining (mix).
(12"+=/pic-cd+=) *(EMUT/CPEMU 8)* – ('A'-Palmer mix) / ('A'-campfire mix).

May 89. (lp/c/cd) *(463319-1/-4/-2)* *<45241>* **MIND BOMB** [4] [ ]
– Good morning beautiful / Armageddon days are here (again) / The violence of truth / Kingdom of rain / The beat(en) generation / August & September / Gravitate to me / Beyond love. *(cd re-iss. Apr02; 504467-2)*

Jul 89. (7"/c-s) *(EMU/+C 9)* **GRAVITATE TO ME. / THE VIOLENCE OF TRUTH** [63] [ ]
(12"+=/cd-s+=) *(EMUT/CDEMU 9)* – I've been waiting for tomorrow (all of my life).
(etched-12") *(EMUE 9)* – ('A'dub) / I've been waiting for tomorrow.

Sep 89. (7"/c-s) *(EMU/+C 10)* **ARMAGEDDON DAYS ARE HERE (AGAIN). / ('A'orchestral)** [70] [ ]
(12"+=) *(EMUT 10)* – The nature of virtue / Perfect.
(cd-s+=) *(CDEMU 10)* – Perfect / Mental healing process.
(10"ep) *(EMUQT 10)* **THE THE V. THE WORLD EP** – ('A'side) / The nature of virtue / Perfect / Mental healing process.
(etched-12") *(EMUE 10)* – ('A'edit) / Perfect.

Feb 91. (12"/c-s) *(655 798-6/-4)* **JEALOUS OF YOUTH. / ANOTHER BOY DROWNING (live)** [54] [ ]
(cd-s+=) **SHADES OF YOUTH EP** *(655 796-8)* – Solitude / Dolphins.

— added **D.C. COLLARD** – instruments

Jan 93. (7"marble) *(658 457-7)* **DOGS OF LUST. / THE VIOLENCE OF TRUTH** [25] [ ]
(12"pic-d+=/cd-s+=) *(658 457-6/-2)* – Infected (live).
(cd-s) *(658 457-5)* – ('A'side) / Jealous of youth (live) / Beyond love (live) / Armageddon days are here (again) (D.N.A. remix).

Jan 93. (cd/c/lp) *(472468-2/-4/-1)* *<53164>* **DUSK** [2] [ ]
– True happiness this way lies / Love is stronger than death / Dogs of lust / This is the night / Slow emotion replay / Helpline operator / Sodium light baby / Lung shadows / Bluer than midnight / Lonely planet. *(cd re-iss. Apr02; 504468-2)*

Apr 93. (12"red-ep/cd-ep) *(659 077-6/-9)* **SLOW MOTION REPLAY. / DOGS OF LUST (3 mixes by Jim Thirlwell)** [35] [ ]
(cd-ep) *(659077-0)* – ('A'side) / Scenes from Active Twilight (parts I-V).

Jun 93. (12"ep/cd-ep) *(659 371-6/-2)* **LOVE IS STRONGER THAN DEATH. / THE SINKING FEELING (live) / THE MERCY BEAT (live) / ARMAGEDDON DAYS ARE HERE (AGAIN) (live)** [39] [ ]
(cd-ep) *(659 371-5)* – ('A'side) / Infected / Soul mining / Armageddon days are . . .

Jan 94. (c-ep/12"ep/cd-ep) *(659811-4/-6/-2)* **DIS-INFECTED EP** [17] [ ]
– This was the day / Dis-infected / Helpline operator (sick boy mix) / Dogs of lust (germicide mix).

Jan 95. (c-ep/10"ep/cd-ep) *(661091-0/-6/-9)* *<61119>* **I SAW THE LIGHT / I'M FREE AT LAST. / SOMEDAY YOU'LL CALL MY NAME / THERE'S NO ROOM IN MY HEART FOR THE BLUES** [31] Aug95 [ ]

Feb 95. (cd/c/10"lp) *(478139-2/-4/-0)* *<66908>* **HANKY PANKY** [28] [ ]
– Honky tonkin' / Six more miles / My heart would know / If you'll be a baby to me / I'm a long gone daddy / Weary blues from waitin' / I saw the light / Your cheatin' heart / I can't get you off of my mind / There's a tear in my beer / I can't escape from you.

Nothing – Interscope | Nothing – Interscope

Feb 00. (cd) *(<490510-2>)* **NAKEDSELF** [45] [ ]
– Boiling point / Shrunken man / The whisperers / Soul catcher / Global eyes / December sunlight / Swine fever / Diesel breeze / Weather belle / Voidy numbness / Phantom walls / Salt water.

Apr 00. (cd-ep) *(497273-2)* **THE SHRUNKENMAN EP** [ ] [–]
– Shrunken man / (mixes by DAAU / JOHN PARISH / FOETUS).

Jun 02. (cd-s) *(672855-2)* **PILLARBOX RED** [ ] [–]

– compilations, others, etc. –

Dec 88. (d-cd) *Epic; (CDTT 241)* **SOUL MINING / INFECTED** [ ] [–]

May 02. (d-cd) *Epic; (504469-2) / Sony; <86611>* **45 RPM – THE SINGLES OF . . .** [60] [ ]

Jul 02. (4xcd-box) *Epic; (507902-2)* **LONDON TOWN 1983-1993** [ ] [–]

THEM

Formed: Belfast, N. Ireland . . . 1963 by VAN MORRISON, BILLY HARRISON, ALAN HENDERSON, ERIC WRIXEN and RONNIE MELLINGS. After their debut single flopped, producers TOMMY SCOTT and BERT BERNS, recruited session men JIMMY PAGE (future LED ZEPPELIN) and PETER BARDENS (future CAMEL) to feature on their hot-wired cover of BIG JOE WILLIAMS' 'BABY PLEASE DON'T GO', the single rocketing into the Top 10 in early '65. The B-side, 'GLORIA' was even more primal, a riotous piece of garage that inspired generations of spotty youths to pick up guitars and has subsequently been covered by everyone from The SHADOWS OF KNIGHT to The DOORS and PATTI SMITH. Although the band found it difficult to equal this incredible double shot, their next single, 'HERE COMES THE NIGHT' climbed to No.2 in the UK charts. The eponymous debut album followed later that summer and although it failed to chart, it was a precocious collection of early VAN-penned originals and incendiary covers. Their fame was short-lived though, as successive singles failed to chart and the second album, 'THEM AGAIN' (1966) lacked the consistency of its predecessor. There were occasional flashes of VAN's maverick genius and it was clear he was the lynchpin holding the thing together. When he left to go solo in 1966, the band inevitably split, only to reform a number of times (minus VAN) around differing line-ups, trading on past glories but predictably producing no new material of any great note.

• **Songwriters:** MORRISON penned (until his departure), except HERE COMES THE NIGHT + (IT WON'T HURT) HALF AS MUCH + few early songs (Bert Berns). DON'T START CRYING NOW (Slim Harpo) / BABY

PLEASE DON'T GO (Big Joe Williams) / DON'T LOOK BACK (John Lee Hooker) / I PUT A SPELL ON YOU (Screaming Jay Hawkins) / IT'S ALL OVER NOW, BABY BLUE (Bob Dylan), etc.

Album rating: THEM (*7) / THEM AGAIN (*6) / NOW AND THEM (*5) / TIME OUT, TIME IN FOR THEM (*4) / THEM on 'Happy Tiger' (*4) / IN REALITY (*4) / THEM FEATURING VAN MORRISON compilation (*7) / SHUT YOUR MOUTH (*4)

VAN MORRISON (b.GEORGE IVAN, 31 Aug'45) – vocals, harmonica / **BILLY HARRISON** – guitar / **ERIC WRIXEN** – piano, keyboards / **RONNIE MELLINGS** – drums / **ALAN HENDERSON** (b.26 Nov'44) – bass

Decca Parrot

Aug 64. (7") *(F 11973)* *<9702>* **DON'T START CRYING NOW. / ONE TWO BROWN EYES**

— **JACKIE McAULEY** – organ + **PATRICK McAULEY** – organ repl. ERIC and RONNIE WRIXEN who joined The WHEELS, while MELLINGS became a milkman.

Dec 64. (7") *(F 12018)* *<9727>* **BABY PLEASE DON'T GO. / GLORIA** 10 Mar65 93
<US re-dist.Apr66, flipped over; hit 71> (re-iss. Jul73 on 'Deram'; DM 394) (re-iss. May82; F 13923) (re-iss. Oct83 on 'Old Gold'; OG 9341)

Mar 65. (7") *(F 12094)* *<9747>* **HERE COMES THE NIGHT. / ALL FOR MYSELF** 2 May65 24
(re-iss. Sep73 on 'Deram'; DM 400)

Jun 65. (lp; mono/stereo) *(LK 4700)* *<PS/PAS 6/7 1005>* **THEM** Jul65 54
– Here comes the night *[US-only]* / Mystic eyes / If you and I could be as two / Little girl / Just a little bit / I gave my love a diamond (UK-only) / Go on home baby / Gloria / You just can't win / Don't look back / I like it like that / Bright lights big city / My little baby *[UK-only]* / Route 66. *(cd-iss. Feb89 on 'London'; 820 563-2) (cd re-mast.Jun98 +=; 844824-2)*
above lp featured sessioners **PETER BARDENS** – keyboards + **JIMMY PAGE** – guitar

— **PETER BARDENS** – keyboards + **JOHN WILSON** (b. 6 Nov'47) – drums now repl. The McAULEY's who formed The BELFAST GYPSIES

Jun 65. (7") *(F 12175)* **ONE MORE TIME. / HOW LONG BABY?** –

Aug 65. (7") *(F 12215)* *<9784>* **(IT WON'T HURT) HALF AS MUCH. / I'M GONNA DRESS IN BLACK**

Nov 65. (7") *(F 12281)* *<9796>* **MYSTIC EYES. / IF YOU AND I COULD BE AS TWO** Oct65 33

— **MORRISON, HENDERSON + WILSON** were joined by **RAY ELLIOTT** (b.13 Sep'43) – piano, sax repl. BARDENS to solo & later CAMEL / **JIM ARMSTRONG** (b.24 Jun'44) – guitar repl. HARRISON

Jan 66. (lp; mono/stereo) *(LK 4751)* *<PS/PAS 6/7 1008>* **THEM AGAIN**
– Could you would you / Something you got / Call my name / Turn on your love light / I put a spell on you / I can only give you everything / My lonely sad eyes / I got a woman / Out of sight / It's all over now, baby blue / Bad or good / How long baby / Hello Josephine / Don't you know / Hey girl / Bring 'em on in. *(cd-iss. Feb89 on 'London'; 820 564-2) (cd re-mast.Jun98 +=; 844825-2)*

Mar 66. (7") *(F 12355)* *<9819>* **CALL MY NAME. / BRING 'EM ON IN**

— (Jan 66) **TERRY NOONE** – drums repl. WILSON later to TASTE (RORY GALLAGHER) Apr 66, **DAVE HARVEY** – drums repl. NOONE.

May 66. (7") *(F 12403)* *<3003>* **RICHARD CORY. / DON'T YOU KNOW**

— Disbanded mid 1966 when VAN MORRISON went solo. In 1967, they re-formed. **KEN McDOWELL** – vocals repl. him

Major Minor not iss.

1967. (7") *(MM 509)* **GLORIA. / FRIDAY'S CHILD** –
1967. (7") *(MM 513)* **THE STORY OF THEM. / (part 2)** –

not iss. Tower-Capitol

Jan 68. (lp) *<ST 5104>* **NOW AND THEM** –
– I'm your witch doctor / What's the matter baby / Truth machine / Square room / You're just what I was looking for today / Dirty old man / At the age of sixteen / Nobody loves you when you're down and out / Walking the Queen's garden / I happen to love you / Come to me. *(UK-iss.Dec88 on 'Zap!'; ZAP 6) (cd-iss. May03 on 'Rev-Ola'+=; CRREV 29)* – Walking in the Queen's garden (mono) / I happen to love you (mono).

Feb 68. (7") *<384>* **WALKING IN THE QUEEN'S GARDEN. / I HAPPEN TO LOVE YOU** –

Apr 68. (7") *<407>* **SQUARE ROOM. / BUT IT'S ALRIGHT** –

— trimmed to a quartet when ELLIOTT departed

Nov 68. (lp) *<ST 5116>* **TIME OUT! TIME IN FOR THEM** –
– Time out for time in / She put a hex on you / Bent over you / Waltz of the flees / Black widow spider / We've all agreed to help / Market place / Just one conception / Young woman / The moth. *(UK-iss.Dec88 on 'Zap!'; ZAP 7)*

Nov 68. (7") *<461>* **WALTZ OF THE FLIES. / WE ALL AGREED TO HELP** –

Mar 69. (7") *<493>* **DARK ARE THE SHADOWS. / CORINA** –

— added on session **JERRY COLE** – guitar, vocals / **JOHN STARK** – drums (tour) In 1969, ARMSTRONG, ELLIOT, McDOWELL went off to Chicago to form The TRUTH alongside bassman CURTIS BACHMAN and rummer RENO SMITH. An album 'TRUTH OF TRUTHS' surfaced in 1971 for US 'Oak'. In March '95, an exploitation cd 'OF THEM AND OTHER TALES' was released for 'Epilogue' *(EPI 003)*

not iss. Happy Tiger

1970. (lp) *<HT 1004>* **THEM** –
– I keep singing / Lonely weekends / Take a little time / You got me good / Jo Ann / Memphis lady / In the midnight hour / Nobody cares / I am waiting / Just a little.

1970. (7") *<525>* **I AM WAITING. / LONELY WEEKENDS** –
1970. (7") *<534>* **MEMPHIS LADY. / NOBODY CARES** –
1971. (lp; as THEM featuring ALAN HENDERSON) *<HT 1012>* **THEM IN REALITY** –
– Gloria / Baby please don't go / Laugh / Let my song through / California man / Lessons of the sea / Rayn / Back to the country / Can you believe.

— **THEM** re-formed originals **HENDERSON, HARRISON & WRIXEN + MEL AUSTIN** – vocals / **BILLY BELL** – drums

Decca not iss.

1979. (lp) **SHUT YOUR MOUTH** –
– Hamburg connection / I'm a lover not a worker / Shut your mouth / Needed on the farm / Streetwalking lady / Firewater / Child of the sixties / Slowdown / Losing you / Weekend entertainer / Holy roller / Cincinnati diceman.

— split 1979 after **JIM ARMSTRONG** – guitar + **BRIAN SCOTT** – keyboards, flute repl. WRIXEN + HARRISON. The latter became BILLY WHO

– (selective) compilations, etc. –

Oct 73. (d-lp; as THEM FEATURING VAN MORRISON) *(DPA 3001-2)* *<BP 71053-4>* **THEM FEATURING VAN MORRISON** Jul72
– Don't start crying now / Baby please don't go / Here comes the night / One more time / It won't hurt half as much / Mystic eyes / Call my name / Richard Cory / One two brown eyes / All for myself / If you and I could be as two / Don't you know / Friday's child / The story of Them (part 1) / Philosophy / How long baby / I'm gonna dress in black / Bring 'em on in / Little girl / I gave my love a diamond / Gloria / You just can't win / Go on home baby / Don't look back / I like it like that / Bright lights big city / My little baby / Route 66. *(re-iss. Jul82; lp/c TAB/KTBC 45) (cd-iss. 1987 on 'London'; 810 165-2)*

Aug 86. (d-lp/d-c; as THEM featuring VAN MORRISON) *Castle; (CCS LP/MC 131)* **THE COLLECTION** –
(cd-iss. Aug92; CCSCD 131)

Sep 87. (lp/c) *See For Miles; (SEE/+K 31)* **THE SINGLES** –

Jan 91. (7"/c-s) *London; (LON/+C 292)* **BABY PLEASE DON'T GO. / GLORIA** 65
(12"+=/cd-s+=) *(LON X/CD 292)* – Mystic eyes.

Apr 97. (cd) *Spalax; (14967)* **REUNION CONCERT (live)** –

THIN LIZZY

Formed: Dublin, Ireland . . . 1969 by PHIL LYNOTT and BRIAN DOWNEY together with ERIC BELL and ERIC WRIXON (the latter leaving after the first 45). After a debut single for 'Parlophone' Ireland, the group relocated to London in late 1970 at the suggestion of managers, Ted Carroll and Brian Tuite, having already signed to 'Decca'. 'THIN LIZZY' (1971) and 'SHADES OF A BLUE ORPHANAGE' (1972) passed without much notice, although the group scored a surprise one-off UK Top 10 with 'WHISKEY IN THE JAR'. A traditional Irish folk song, THIN LIZZY's highly original adaptation married plangent lead guitar and folk-rock arrangements to memorable effect. The accompanying album, 'VAGABONDS OF THE WESTERN WORLD' (1973), failed to capitalise on the song's success, although it gave an indication of where the band were headed with the hard-edged likes of 'THE ROCKER'. BELL departed later that year, his replacement being ex-SKID ROW axeman GARY MOORE, the first of many sojourns the guitarist would enjoy with 'LIZZY over the course of his turbulent career. He was gone by the Spring tour of the following year (subsequently joining COLOSSEUM II), the trademark twin guitar attack introduced on that tour courtesy of JOHN CANN and ANDY GEE. They were soon replaced more permanently by SCOTT GORHAM and BRIAN ROBERTSON, THIN LIZZY signing a new deal with 'Vertigo' and releasing the 'NIGHTLIFE' set in late '74. Neither that album nor 1975's 'FIGHTING' succeeded in realising the group's potential, although the latter gave them their first Top 60 entry on the album chart. Partly due to the group's blistering live shows and partly down to the massive success of 'THE BOYS ARE BACK IN TOWN', 'JAILBREAK' (1976) was a transatlantic Top 20 smash. One of the band's most consistent sets of their career, it veered from the power chord rumble and triumphant male bonding of 'THE BOYS . . .' to the epic Celtic clarion call of 'EMERALD'. The brooding, thuggish rifferama of the title track was another highlight, LYNOTT's rich, liquor-throated drawl sounding by turns threatening and conspiratorial. 'JOHNNY THE FOX' (1976) followed into the UK Top 20 later that year, a record which lacked the continuity of its predecessor but nevertheless spawned another emotive, visceral hard rock single in 'DON'T BELIEVE A WORD'. This is what marked THIN LIZZY out from the heavy-rock pack; LYNOTT's outlaw-with-a-broken-heart voice and the propulsive economy of the arrangements were light-years away from the warbling and posturing of 70's proto-metal. Accordingly, 'LIZZY were one of the few rock bands who gained any respect from punks and indeed, LYNOTT subsequently formed an extra curricular project with The DAMNED's RAT SCABIES as well as working with ex-SEX PISTOLS, PAUL COOK and STEVE JONES (as The GREEDIES on the Christmas 1980 single, 'A MERRY JINGLE'). A 1977 US tour saw MOORE fill in for ROBERTSON who'd injured his hand in a fight, although the Scots guitarist was back in place for a headlining spot at the 'Reading Festival' later that year. 'BAD REPUTATION' was released the following month, preceded by the R&B-flavoured 'DANCING IN THE MOONLIGHT' single and furnishing the group with their highest chart placing to date (UK Top 5). But it was through blistering live work that THIN LIZZY had made their name and they finally got around to releasing a concert set in 1978. 'LIVE AND DANGEROUS' remains deservedly revered as a career landmark, as vital, razor sharp and unrestrained as any live set in the history of rock. Later that summer, THIN LIZZY again took to the road with MOORE (ROBERTSON departed to form WILD HORSES) undertaking his third stint in the band alongside MARK NAUSEEF who was deputising for an absent DOWNEY. Previewed by the keening exhilaration of 'WAITING FOR AN ALIBI', the 'BLACK ROSE (A ROCK LEGEND)' (1979) set was the last great THIN LIZZY album. Placing all-out rockers alongside more traditionally influenced material, the set produced another two major UK hits in the defiant 'DO ANYTHING YOU WANT TO DO' and the poignant 'SARAH', a beautifully realised tribute to LYNOTT's baby daughter. MOORE, meanwhile, had been enjoying solo chart success with 'PARISIENNE WALKWAYS', the THIN LIZZY frontman guesting on vocals. By late '79, MOORE was out, however, and LYNOTT secured the unlikely services of another Scot, MIDGE URE, to fulfil touring commitments. When the latter subsequently departed to front ULTRAVOX, LYNOTT replaced him with ex-PINK FLOYD man, SNOWY WHITE. 1980 saw LYNOTT marrying Caroline Crowther (daughter of LESLIE) and releasing his first solo set, 'SOLO IN SOHO'. Although it hit the UK Top 30, the record sold poorly, a shame as it contained some of his most endearingly experimental work. The classic 'YELLOW PEARL' (co-written with URE) nevertheless scored a Top 20 placing and was later used as the theme tune for 'Top Of The Pops'. Later that year saw the release of 'CHINATOWN', the title track giving THIN LIZZY yet another hit. A further patchy album, 'RENEGADE' followed in late '81, THIN LIZZY's popularity clearly on the wane as it struggled to break the Top 40. With the addition of ex-TYGERS OF PAN TANG guitarist JOHN SYKES and keyboardist DARREN WHARTON, the group released something of a belated comeback album in 'THUNDER AND LIGHTNING' (1983). It was to be THIN LIZZY's swansong, however; by the release of live set, 'LIFE' (1983), the group had already split, LYNOTT and DOWNEY forming the short-lived GRAND SLAM. LYNOTT eventually carried on with his solo career (he'd previously released a second set, 'THE PHIL LYNOTT ALBUM' in 1982) in 1985, after settling his differences with MOORE. The pair recorded the driving 'OUT IN THE FIELDS', a UK Top 5 hit and a lesson in consummate heavy-rock for the hundreds of dismal 80's bands wielding a guitar and a poodle haircut. A follow-up single, '19', proved to be LYNOTT's parting shot, the Irishman dying from a drugs overdose on the 4th of January '86. As family, rock stars and wellwishers crowded into a small chapel in Southern Ireland for LYNOTT's low-key funeral, the rock world mourned the loss of one of its most talented, charismatic and much-loved figureheads. Towards the end of the millennium, THIN LIZZY (JOHN SYKES, SCOTT GORHAM, DARREN WHARTON, MARCO MENDOZA and TOMMY ALDRIDGE) played several LYNOTT-tribute shows, concert set 'ONE NIGHT ONLY' (2000) was evidence that their late great frontman was sadly missed.

• **Songwriters:** PHIL LYNOTT and Co and also covers of ROSALIE (Bob Seger) / I'M STILL IN LOVE WITH YOU (Frankie Miller).

Album rating: THIN LIZZY (*4) / SHADES OF A BLUE ORPHANAGE (*4) / VAGABONDS OF THE WESTERN WORLD (*5) / NIGHTLIFE (*5) / FIGHTING (*6) / JAILBREAK (*8) / JOHNNY THE FOX (*8) / BAD REPUTATION (*6) / LIVE AND DANGEROUS (*9) / BLACK ROSE – A ROCK LEGEND (*6) / CHINATOWN (*5) / ADVENTURES OF THIN LIZZY compilation (*8) / RENEGADE (*5) / THUNDER AND LIGHTNING (*7) / LIFE (*7) / DEDICATION – THE VERY BEST OF THIN LIZZY compilation (*8) / ONE NIGHT ONLY (*4) / GREATEST HITS double compilation (*9) / Phil Lynott: SOLO IN SOHO (*4) / THE PHIL LYNOTT ALBUM (*6) / THE BEST OF PHIL LYNOTT & THIN LIZZY – SOLDIER OF FORTUNE compilation (*7)

PHIL LYNOTT (b.20 Aug'51, from Brazillian + Irish parents. Raised from 3 by granny in Crumlin, Dublin) – vocals, bass (ex-ORPHANAGE, ex-SKID ROW brief) / **ERIC BELL** (b. 3 Sep'47, Belfast, N.Ireland) – guitar, vocals (ex-DREAMS) / **BRIAN DOWNEY** (b.27 Jan'51) – drums (ex-ORPHANAGE) / **ERIC WRIXON** – keyboards

Parlophone — not iss.

1970. (7"; as THIN LIZZIE) *<DIP 513>* **THE FARMER. / I NEED YOU** — [–] Ireland [–]

—— now a trio (+ without WRIXON)

Decca — London

Apr 71. (lp) *(SKL 5082) <594>* **THIN LIZZY** — [ ] [ ]
– The friendly ranger at Clontarf Castle / Honesty is no excuse / Diddy Levine / Ray-gun / Look what the wind blew in / Eire / Return of the farmer's son / Clifton Grange Hotel / Saga of the ageing orphan / Remembering. *(cd-iss. Jan89 on 'Deram'+=; 820 528-2)* – Dublin / Remembering (part 2) / Old moon madness / Things ain't working out down at the farm.

Aug 71. (7"ep) *(F 13208)* **NEW DAY** — [ ] [–]
– Things ain't working out down on the farm / Remembering pt.II / Old moon madness / Dublin.

Mar 72. (lp) *(TXS 108)* **SHADES OF A BLUE ORPHANAGE** — [ ] [–]
– The rise and dear demise of the funky nomadic tribes / Buffalo gal / I don't want to forget how to jive / Sarah / Brought down / Baby face / Chatting today / Call the police / Shades of a blue orphanage. *(cd-iss. Nov88 on 'Deram'; 820 527-2)*

Nov 72. (7") *(F 13355) <20076>* **WHISKEY IN THE JAR. / BLACK BOYS IN THE CORNER** — [6] [ ]

May 73. (7") *(F 13402) <20078>* **RANDOLPH'S TANGO. / BROKEN DREAMS** — [ ] [ ]

Sep 73. (lp) *(SKL 5170)* *<636>* **VAGABONDS OF THE WESTERN WORLD** □ □
– Mama nature said / The hero and the madman / Slow blues / The rocker / Vagabonds (of the western world) / Little girl in bloom / Gonna creep up on you / A song for while I'm away. *(cd-iss. May91 on 'Deram'+=; 820969-2)* – Whiskey in the jar / Black boys on the corner / Randolph's tango / Broken dreams.
Nov 73. (7") *(F 13467)* **THE ROCKER. / HERE I GO AGAIN** □ –

— **GARY MOORE** (b. 4 Apr'52, Belfast) – guitar, vocals (ex-SKID ROW) repl. BELL (later MAINSQUEEZE)

Apr 74. (7") *(F 13507)* *<20082>* **LITTLE DARLIN'. / BUFFALO GIRL** □ □

— (on tour May'74) **JOHN CANN** – guitar (ex-ATOMIC ROOSTER, ex-BULLITT) / + **ANDY GEE** – guitar (ex-ELLIS) both repl. GARY MOORE who joined COLOSSEUM II. These temp. guitarists were deposed by **SCOTT GORHAM** (b.17 Mar'51, Santa Monica, Calif.) + **BRIAN ROBERTSON** (b.12 Sep'56, Glasgow, Scotland)

Vertigo Vertigo

Oct 74. (7") *(6059 111)* **PHILOMENA. / SHA LA LA** □ –
Nov 74. (lp) *(6360 116)* *<SRMI 1107>* **NIGHTLIFE** □ □
– She knows / Night life / It's only money / Still in love with you / Frankie Carroll / Showdown / Banshee / Philomena / Sha-la-la / Dear heart. *(re-iss. Aug83 lp/c; PRICE/PRIMC 31) (cd-iss. Jun89; 838029-2)*
Jan 75. (7") *<202>* **SHOWDOWN. / NIGHT LIFE** – □
Jun 75. (7") *(6059 124)* **ROSALIE. / HALF CASTE** □ –
Aug 75. (lp)(c) *(6360 121)(7138 070)* *<SRMI 1108>* **FIGHTING** 60 □
– Rosalie / For those who love to live / Suicide / Wild one / Fighting my way back / King's vengeance / Spirit slips away / Silver dollar / Freedom song / Ballad of a hard man. *(re-iss. Aug83 lp/c; PRICE/PRIMC 32) (cd-iss. Jun89; 842433-2) (cd re-iss. Mar96 on 'Mercury'; 532296-2)*
Oct 75. (7") *(6059 129)* **WILD ONE. / FOR THOSE WHO LOVE TO DIE** □ –
Nov 75. (7") *<205>* **WILD ONE. / FREEDOM SONG** – □

Vertigo Mercury

Mar 76. (lp)(c) *(9102 008)(7138 075)* *<SRMI 1081>* **JAILBREAK** 10 18
– Jailbreak / Angel from the coast / Running back / Romeo and the lonely girl / Warriors / The boys are back in town / Fight or fall / Cowboy song / Emerald. *(re-iss. Oct83 lp/c; PRICE/PRIMC 50) (cd-iss. Jun89; 822785-2) (cd re-iss. Mar96 on 'Mercury'; 532294-2)*
Apr 76. (7") *(6059 139)* **THE BOYS ARE BACK IN TOWN. / EMERALD** 8 –
Apr 76. (7") *<73786>* **THE BOYS ARE BACK IN TOWN. / JAILBREAK** – 12
Jul 76. (7") *(6059 150)* **JAILBREAK. / RUNNING BACK** 31 –
Sep 76. (7") *<73841>* **THE COWBOY SONG. / ANGEL FROM THE COAST** – 77
Oct 76. (lp)(c) *(9102 012)(7138 082)* *<SRMI 1119>* **JOHNNY THE FOX** 11 52
– Johnny / Rocky / Borderline / Don't believe a word / Fools gold / Johnny the fox meets Jimmy the weed / Old flame / Massacre / Sweet Marie / Boogie woogie dance. *(re-iss. May83 lp/c; PRICE/PRIMC 11) (cd-iss. May90; 822687-2) (cd re-iss. Mar96 on 'Mercury'; 532295-2)*
Nov 76. (7") *<73867>* **ROCKY. / HALF-CASTE** – □
Jan 77. (7") *(LIZZY 1)* **DON'T BELIEVE A WORD. / OLD FLAME** 12 –
Jan 77. (7") *<73882>* **JOHNNY THE FOX MEETS JIMMY THE WEED. / OLD FLAME** – □

— BRIAN ROBERTSON became injured, GARY MOORE deputised (on 6 mths. tour only)

Aug 77. (7") *(6059 177)* *<73945>* **DANCING IN THE MOONLIGHT. / BAD REPUTATION** 14 □
Sep 77. (lp)(c) *(9102 016)(7231 011)* *<SRMI 1186>* **BAD REPUTATION** 4 39
– Soldier of fortune / Bad reputation / Opium trail / Southbound / Dancing in the moonlight (it's caught me in its spotlight) / Killer without a cause / Downtown sundown / That woman's gonna break your heart / Dear Lord. *(re-iss. May83 lp/c; PRICE/PRIMC 12) (cd-iss. Apr90; 842434-2) (cd re-iss. Mar96 on 'Mercury'; 532298-2)*
Apr 78. (7") *(LIZZY 2)* **ROSALIE; COWBOY'S SONG (live medley). / ME AND THE BOYS** 20 –

Vertigo Warners

Jun 78. (d-lp) *(9199 645)* *<3213>* **LIVE AND DANGEROUS (live)** 2 84
– Jailbreak / Emerald / South bound / Rosalie – Cowgirls' song / Dancing in the moonlight (it's caught me in its spotlight) / Massacre / Still in love with you / Johnny the fox meets Jimmy the weed / Cowboy song / The boys are back in town / Don't believe a word / Warriors / Are you ready / Suicide / Sha la la / Baby drives me crazy / The rocker. *(re-iss. Nov84; d-lp/d-c; PRID/+C 6) (cd-iss. Jun89; 838030-2) (cd re-iss. Mar96 on 'Mercury'; 532297-2)*
Jul 78. (7") *<8648>* **COWBOY SONG. / JOHNNY THE FOX (MEETS JIMMY THE WEED)** – □

— In Autumn'78 tour, DOWNEY was deputised by MARK NAUSEEF. **GARY MOORE** – guitar, vocals returned to repl. ROBERTSON who formed WILD HORSES

Feb 79. (7") *(LIZZY 3)* **WAITING FOR AN ALIBI. / WITH LOVE** 9 –
Apr 79. (lp/c) *(9102/7231 032)* *<3338>* **BLACK ROSE (A ROCK LEGEND)** 2 81
– Do anything you want to / Toughest street in town / S & M / Waiting for an alibi / Sarah / Got to give it up / Get out of here / With love / A roisin dubh (Black rose) A rock legend part 1. Shenandoah – part 2. Will you go lassy go – part 3. Danny boy – part 4. The mason's apron. *(re-iss. Sep86 lp/c; PRICE/PRIMC 90) (cd-iss. Jun89; 830392-2) (cd re-iss. Mar96 on 'Mercury'; 532299-2)*

— Apr'79, LYNOTT's vox feat. on GARY MOORE's Top 10 hit 'Parisienne Walkways'.

Jun 79. (7") *(LIZZY 4)* **DO ANYTHING YOU WANT TO. / JUST THE TWO OF US** 14 –
Jun 79. (7") *<49019>* **DO ANYTHING YOU WANT TO. / S & M** – □
Sep 79. (7") *(LIZZY 5)* **SARAH. / GOT TO GIVE IT UP** 24 –
Sep 79. (7") *<49078>* **WITH LOVE. / GO TO GIVE IT UP** – □

— (for 2 months-late'79) **MIDGE URE** (b. JAMES URE, 10 Oct'53, Glasgow) – guitar (ex-SLIK, ex-RICH KIDS) repl. GARY MOORE who went solo. URE joined ULTRAVOX when repl. by **SNOWY WHITE**

May 80. (7") *(LIZZY 6)* **CHINATOWN. / SUGAR BLUES** 21 –
Sep 80. (7") *(LIZZY 7)* **KILLER ON THE LOOSE. / DON'T PLAY AROUND** 10 –
(d7"+=) *(LIZZY 7/+701)* – Got to give it up (live) / Chinatown (live).
Oct 80. (lp/c) *(6359/7150 030)* *<3496>* **CHINATOWN** 7 □
– We will be strong / Chinatown / Sweetheart / Sugar blues / Killer on the loose / Having a good time / Genocide (the killing of buffalo) / Didn't I / Hey you. *(re-is.Sep86, cd-iss. Jun89)*
Oct 80. (7") *<49643>* **KILLER ON THE LOOSE. / SUGAR BLUES** – □
Nov 80. (7"; as The GREEDIES) *(GREED 1)* **A MERRY JINGLE. / A MERRY JANGLE** 28 –
above also featured STEVE JONES + PAUL COOK (ex-SEX PISTOLS)
Feb 81. (7") *<49679>* **WE WILL BE STRONG. / SWEETHEART** – □
Apr 81. (7"ep/12"ep) *(LIZZY 8/+12)* **LIVE KILLERS (live)** 19 –
– Are you ready / Opium trail / Dear Miss lonely heart / Bad reputation.
Jul 81. (7") *(LIZZY 9)* **TROUBLE BOYS. / MEMORY PAIN** 53 –
Nov 81. (lp/c) *(6359/7150 083)* *<3622>* **RENEGADE** 38 □
– Angel of death / Renegade / The pressure will blow / Leave this town / Hollywood (down on your luck) / No one told him / Fats / Mexican blood / It's getting dangerous. *(cd-iss. Jun90; 842435-2)*
Feb 82. (7"/7"pic-d) *(LIZZY/+PD 10)* *<50056>* **HOLLYWOOD (DOWN ON YOUR LUCK). / THE PRESSURE WILL BLOW** 53 □
(10"one-sided) *(LIZZY 10)* – ('A'side only)

— **LYNOTT + DOWNEY** recruited new members **JOHN SYKES** – guitar (ex-TYGERS OF PAN TANG) repl. GORHAM **DARREN WHARTON** – keyboards repl. SNOWY WHITE went solo + re-joined PINK FLOYD

Feb 83. (d7"/12") *(LIZZY 11 11-12/22)* **COLD SWEAT. / BAD HABITS / DON'T BELIEVE A WORD (live). / ANGEL OF DEATH (live)** 27 –
Mar 83. (lp/c) *(VERL/+C 3)* *<23831>* **THUNDER AND LIGHTNING** 4 □
– Thunder and lightning / This is the one / The sun goes down / The holy war / Cold sweat / Someday she is going to hit back / Baby please don't go / Bad habits / Heart attack. *(initial copies with free live 12")* – EMERALD / KILLER ON THE LOOSE. / THE BOYS ARE BACK IN TOWN / HOLLYWOOD *(cd-iss. Jun89; 810490-2)*
Apr 83. (7"/12") *(LIZZY 12/+12)* **THUNDER AND LIGHTNING. / STILL IN LOVE WITH YOU (live)** 39 –
Jul 83. (7") *(LIZZY 13)* **THE SUN GOES DOWN (remix). / BABY PLEASE DON'T GO** 52 –
(12"+=) *(LIZZY 13/+12)* – ('A'remix).
Nov 83. (d-lp/d-c) *(VERD/+C 6)* *<23986>* **LIFE (live)** 29 □
– Thunder & lightning / Waiting for an alibi / Jailbreak / Baby please don't

go / The holy war / Renegade / Hollywood / Got to give it up / Angel of death / Are you ready / Boys are back in town / Cold sweat / Don't believe a word / Killer on the loose / The sun goes down / Emerald / Roisin dubh (Black rose) A rock legend part 1. Shenandoah – part 2. Will you go lassy go – part 3. Danny boy – part 4. The mason's apron / Still in love with you / The rocker. *(4th side featured past members) (cd-iss. Aug90; 812882-2)*

—— Had already concluded proceedings. LYNOTT and DOWNEY formed short-lived GRAND SLAM. Tragically, PHIL LYNOTT died of heart failure due to drugs o.d. on the 4th January '86.

– compilations, others –

Aug 76. (lp/c) *Decca; (SKL/KSKC 5249)* **REMEMBERING – PART ONE** [ ] [–]

Jan 78. (7"m) *Decca; (F 13748)* **WHISKEY IN THE JAR. / SITAMOIA / VAGABOND OF THE WESTERN WORLD** [ ] [–]

Aug 79. (7"m) *Decca; (THIN 1)* **THINGS AIN'T WORKING OUT DOWN ON THE FARM. / THE ROCKER / LITTLE DARLIN'** [ ] [–]

Sep 79. (lp) *Decca; (SKL 5298)* **THE CONTINUING SAGA OF THE AGEING ORPHANS** [ ] [–]

Apr 81. (lp/c) *Vertigo; (LIZ TV/MC 001)* **ADVENTURES OF THIN LIZZY** [6] [–]
– Whiskey in the jar / Wild one / Jailbreak / The boys are back in town / Don't believe a word / Dancing in the moonlight / Waiting for an alibi / Do anything you want to / Sarah / Chinatown / Killer on the loose.

Dec 81. (lp/c) *Decca; (KTBC/TAB 28)* **ROCKERS** [ ] [–]
(re-iss. Oct93 on 'Deram' cd/c; 820 526-2/-4)

Mar 83. (cd) *Vertigo; (800 060-2)* **LIZZY KILLERS** [ ] [–]

Oct 83. (7") *Old Gold; (OG 9330)* **WHISKEY IN THE JAR. / THE ROCKER** [ ] [–]

Nov 83. (lp/c) *Contour; (CN/+4 2066)* **THE BOYS ARE BACK IN TOWN** [ ] [–]

Jan 85. (7") *Old Gold; (OG 9484)* **DANCING IN THE MOONLIGHT. / DON'T BELIEVE A WORD** [ ] [–]

Nov 85. (d-lp/c) *Castle; (CCS LP/MC 117)* **THE COLLECTION** [ ] [–]
(cd-iss. Jul87; CCSCD 117)

Nov 85. (lp/c) *Karussel Gold; (822694-1/-4)* **WHISKEY IN THE JAR** [ ] [–]

Apr 86. (lp/c) *Contour; (CN/+4 2080)* **WHISKEY IN THE JAR** [ ] [–]

Aug 86. (12"ep) *Archive 4;* **WHISKEY IN THE JAR / THE ROCKER. / SARAH / BLACK BOYS ON THE CORNER** [ ] [–]

Nov 87. (lp/c/cd) *Telstar; (STAR/STAC/TCD 2300)* **THE BEST OF PHIL LYNOTT & THIN LIZZY – SOLDIER OF FORTUNE** [55] [–]
– Whiskey in the jar / Waiting for an alibi / Sarah / Parisieene walkways / Do anything you want to / Yellow pearl / Chinatown / King's call / The boys are back in town / Rosalie (cowboy's song) / Dancing in the moonlight / Don't believe a word / Jailbreak. *(cd+=)* – Out in the fields / Killer on the loose / Still in love with you.

Feb 88. (7") *Old Gold; (OG 9764)* **THE BOYS ARE BACK IN TOWN. / ('B'by Bachman-Turner Overdrive)** [ ] [–]

Jun 89. (lp) *Grand Slam; <SLAM 4>* **LIZZY LIVES (1976-84)** [–] [ ]

Jan 91. (7"/c-s) *Vertigo; (LIZZY/LIZMC 14)* **DEDICATION. / COLD SWEAT** [35] [–]
(12"+=/cd-s+=) *(LIZZY1/LIZCD 14)* – Emerald (live) / Still in love with you.
(12"pic-d+=) *(LIZP1 14)* – Bad reputation / China town.

Feb 91. (cd/c/lp) *Vertigo; (848 192-2/-4/-1)* **DEDICATION – THE VERY BEST OF THIN LIZZY** [8] [–]
– Whiskey in the jar / The boys are back in town / Jailbreak / Don't believe a word / Dancing in the moonlight / Rosalie – Cowgirl song (live) / Waiting for an alibi / Do anything you want to / Parisienne walkways (with GARY MOORE) / The rocker / Killer on the loose / Sarah / Out in the fields (with GARY MOORE) / Dedication. *(cd+=/c+=)* – Still in love with you (live) / Bad reputation / Emerald / Chinatown.

Mar 91. (7"/c-s) *Vertigo; (LIZZY/LIZMC 15)* **THE BOYS ARE BACK IN TOWN. / SARAH** [63] [–]
(12"/cd-s) *(LIZZY1/LIZCD 15)* – ('A'side) / Johnny the fox / Black boys on the corner / Me and the boys.

Oct 92. (cd) *Windsong; (WINCD 024)* **BBC RADIO 1 LIVE IN CONCERT** [ ] [–]

Nov 94. (cd/c) *Strange Fruit; (SFR CD/MC 130)* **THE PEEL SESSIONS** [ ] [–]

Jan 96. (cd/c) *Polygram; (528113-2/-4)* **WILD ONE – THE VERY BEST OF THIN LIZZY** [18] [–]

Mar 96. (cd) *Spectrum; (552085-2/-4)* **WHISKEY IN THE JAR** [ ] [–]

Jan 00. (cd) *Universal; (E 844945-2)* **UNIVERSAL MASTERS COLLECTION** [ ] [ ]

Jun 04. (d-cd) *Universal TV; (<9821111>)* **GREATEST HITS** [3] [ ]
– The boys are back in town / Jailbreak / Don't believe a word / Dancing in the moonlight (it's caught me in it's spotlight) / Rosalie / Waiting for an alibi / Do anything you want to / Sarah / Chinatown / Killer on the loose / Trouble boys / Hollywood (down on your luck) / Cold sweat / Thunder and lightning / The sun goes down / Dedication / Still in love with you / She knows / Yellow pearl (PHIL LYNOTT) // Whiskey in the jar / Out in the fields (GARY MOORE & PHIL LYNOTT) / Parisienne walkways (GARY MOORE & PHIL LYNOTT) / Emerald / Bad reputation / Wild one / Fighting my way back / Showdown / Black rose / Dear Miss Lonely Hearts (PHIL LYNOTT) / The rocker / Are you ready / Renegade / Kings call (PHIL LYNOTT) / Angel of death / Cowboy song (live) / The boys are back in town (live). *(ltd d-cd w/dvd+=; 9833258)* – (DVD tracks).

PHIL LYNOTT

(solo) with THIN LIZZY members

Vertigo Warners

Mar 80. (7"/12") *(SOLO 1/+12)* **DEAR MISS LONELY HEARTS. / SOLO IN SOHO** [32] [–]

Apr 80. (lp)(pic-lp) *(9102 038)(PHIL 1) <3405>* **SOLO IN SOHO** [28] [ ]
– Dear Miss lonely hearts / King's call / A child's lullaby / Tattoo / Solo in Soho / Girls / Yellow pearl / Ode to a black man / Jamaican rum / Talk in '79. *(re-iss. Sep85 lp'c; PRICE/PRIMC 88) (cd-iss. Jul90; 842564-2)*

Jun 80. (7") *(SOLO 2) <49272>* **KING'S CALL. / ODE TO A BLACK MAN** [35] [ ]

Mar 81. (7"yellow) *(SOLO 3)* **YELLOW PEARL. / GIRLS** [56] [–]
(re-iss. Dec81 – 12"; SOLO 3-12)
(above was later the TV theme for 'Top Of The Pops')

Aug 82. (7") *(SOLO 4)* **TOGETHER. / SOMEBODY ELSE'S DREAM** [ ] [–]
(12"+=) *(SOLO 4-12)* – ('A'dance version).

Sep 82. (7") *(SOLO 5)* **OLD TOWN. / BEAT OF THE DRUM** [ ] [–]

Oct 82. (lp/c) *(6359/7150 117)* **THE PHIL LYNOTT ALBUM** [ ] [–]
– Fatalistic attitude / The man's a fool / Old town / Cathleen / Growing up / Together / Little bit of water / Ode to Liberty (the protest song) / Gino / Don't talk about me baby. *(cd-iss. Jul90; 842564-2)*

—— May'85, GARY MOORE & PHIL hit UK Top 5 with 'OUT IN THE FIELDS'.

Polydor not iss.

Nov 85. (7") *(POSP 777)* **19. / 19 (dub)** [ ] [–]
(12"+=) *(POSPX 777)* – A day in the life of a blues singer.
(d7"+=; 1 pic-d) *(POSPD 777)* – THIN LIZZY; Whiskey in the jar – The rocker.

– (PHIL LYNOTT) posthumous –

Jan 87. (7") *Vertigo; (LYN 1)* **KING'S CALL. / YELLOW PEARL** [68] [–]
(12"+=) *(LYN 1-12)* – Dear Miss lonely hearts (live).

THIN LIZZY

JOHN SYKES – vocals, guitar / **SCOTT GORHAM** – guitar / **DARREN WHARTON** – keyboards / **MARCO MENDOZA** – bass / **TOMMY ALDRIDGE** – drums

S.P.V. C.M.C.

Jun 00. (cd) *(SPV 085-2199-2) <86296>* **ONE NIGHT ONLY** [ ] [ ]
– Jailbreak / Waiting for an alibi / Don't believe a word / Cold sweat / The sun goes down / Are you ready / Bad reputation / Suicide / Still in love with you / Cowboy song / The boys are back in town / Rosalie / Black rose.

THIRTEEN SENSES

Formed: Cornwall, England . . . 2002 as SOUL MAGICIAN by school mates WILL SOUTH and ADAM WILSON, who were joined by TOM WELHAM and BRENDON JAMES. Compared to COLDPLAY and STARSAILOR, the quartet delivered a set of self-financed CD's, one of them, the Dare Mason-produced 'FALLS IN THE DARK', was sneaked out sometime in 2003. Having subsequently inked a deal with 'Vertigo' early 2004, THIRTEEN

SENSES issued their debut single proper, 'THRU THE GLASS', a track that would finally break the UK Top 20 a whole year later. By this time, two others – 'DO NO WRONG' and 'INTO THE FIRE' – had paved the way for an excellent Top 20 album, 'THE INVITATION' (2004), a record that was probably too similar to KEANE for its own good. Summer 2005 saw them play the festival circuit, although from that point on they've somewhat retreated from the musical spotlight.

Album rating: FALLS IN THE DARK (*6) / THE INVITATION (*8)

WILL SOUTH – vocals, rhythm guitar, piano / **TOM WELHAM** – lead guitar, vocals / **ADAM WILSON** – bass / **BRENDON JAMES** – drums

own label — not iss.

2002. (cd-ep; as SOUL MAGICIAN) *(SOULMAGCD)* **INSIDE A HEALING MIND EP** [ ] [–]
– Glow / Bittersweet / Attracting submission / The spring.

Dec 02. (cd-ep) *(none)* **NO OTHER LIFE IS ATTRACTIVE** [ ] [–]
– No other life is attractive / Little unrest / The questions / Sound / Falling to the ground.

2003. (cd) *(none)* **FALLS IN THE DARK** [ ] [–]
– Thru the glass / Gone / The salt wound routine / Lead us / No other life is attractive / Little unrest / Slightly defect hands / Exploding star / The questions / Shape / Spitting out teeth / This is an order / Do no wrong.

Vertigo — Universal

Mar 04. (7"/cd-s) *(981633 4/5)* **THRU THE GLASS. / NO OTHER LIFE IS ATTRACTIVE** [ ] [–]

May 04. (7") *(9866747)* **DO NO WRONG. / ATTRACTING SUBMISSION** [38] [–]
(cd-s) *(9866745)* – ('A') / Little unrest.
(cd-s) *(9866746)* – ('A') / The questions / Control / ('A'-video).

Sep 04. (7") *(9867847)* **INTO THE FIRE. / THIS IS AN ORDER** [35] [–]
(cd-s) *(9867849)* – ('A') / Late gazes.
(cd-s) *(9867851)* – ('A'-alt.) / Falling to the ground / Tended to break up.

Sep 04. (cd)(lp) *(9866910)(9867852) <9870153>* **THE INVITATION** [14] Jan05 [ ]
– Into the fire / Thru the glass / Gone / Do no wrong / The salt wound routine / Saving / Lead us / Last forever / History / Undivided / Angels and spies / Automatic. *(cd re-iss. Jan05; same)*

Jan 05. (7") *(9869348)* **THRU THE GLASS. / LOSERS** [18] [–]
(cd-s) *(9869346)* – ('A') / Lights out.
(cd-s) *(9869347)* – ('A') / Picture this / Turn out the light.

Mar 05. (7") *(9870782)* **THE SALT WOUND ROUTINE. / EXPECTING TO FLY** [45] [–]
(cd-s) *(9870780)* – ('A') / Sunshine illuminate.
(cd-s) *(9870781)* – ('A'-Danton edit) / Straight through your bones / You never really try to turn it back.

□ 31st FEBRUARY
(see under ⇒ ALLMAN BROTHERS BAND)

□ David THOMAS (see under ⇒ PERE UBU)

Richard THOMPSON

Born: 3 Apr'49, London, England. A founder member of FAIRPORT CONVENTION from 1967 until his departure early in 1971, THOMPSON was an important catalyst in the translation of English folk music into a rock format. He contributed many of FAIRPORT CONVENTION's finest songs including 'MEET ON THE LEDGE' and 'SLOTH'. After session work for ex-FAIRPORT friends, SANDY DENNY and IAIN MATTHEWS, the bearded guitarist finally issued his 1972 debut album, 'HENRY THE HUMAN FLY', for 'Island' records. Just prior to this, he had worked with other recent ex-FAIRPORT members ASHLEY HUTCHINGS and DAVE MATTACKS who, as The BUNCH, released the budget covers lp 'ROCK ON'. The following year, he teamed up both artistically and romantically with Glasgow-born LINDA PETERS, the couple becoming RICHARD & LINDA THOMPSON after their marriage in 1974. Their first of seven albums together, 'I WANT TO SEE THE BRIGHT LIGHTS AGAIN', was acclaimed by many, and by rights, should have provided them with a hit single in the evocative title track. During the recording of their next album, 'HOKEY POKEY' (1975), they converted to Sufism, even initiating their own Sufi community. Over the course of the next seven years, the royal couple of British folk created a string of finely crafted, harmony-laden albums, the pick of which was arguably 1982's 'SHOOT OUT THE LIGHTS'. The album featured the enduring 'WALL OF DEATH', appropriately enough the final track on their final album together, their marriage already having floundered. Picking up the pieces, RICHARD went solo again the following year, recording 'HAND OF KINDNESS' for 'Hannibal' Records, a set which included the excellent 'TWO LEFT FEET'. After finally achieving a more widespread recognition, he moved to 'Capitol' in the second half of the 80's and made significant inroads with the 1988 set, 'AMNESIA'. THOMPSON gained a belated UK Top 40 solo success with his 1991 album, 'RUMOUR AND SIGH', a wonderfully eclectic set running the gamut of THOMPSON's influences. 1994 saw the release of 'MIRROR BLUE', another critically acclaimed set including highlights such as 'MINGUS EYES' and 'THE WAY THAT IT SHOWS'. His 1996 release, 'YOU? ME? US?', introduced his son, TEDDY, to the proceedings and offered up further classic tracks in the shape of 'COLD KISSES' and 'WOODS OF DARNEY'. His home city of London was the lyrical core of THOMPSON's next work, 'MOCK TUDOR' (1999). His witty tales of the capital's downside, 'WALKING THE LONG MILES HOME' and 'SIGHTS AND SOUNDS OF LONDON TOWN', could have been written years ago (but weren't!) but somehow RICHARD gives them a modern day sheen that his contemporaries can only dream of. After finally being dropped by 'Capitol', THOMPSON took the opportunity of going back to basics on 'THE OLD KIT BAG' (2003), casting an even more economical hand over the writing, recording and production than on its predecessor. With only DANNY THOMPSON, drummer MICHAEL JEROME and singer JUDITH OWEN working alongside him in the studio, the resulting album was simultaneously more intimate and more self-possessed. Lyrically, THOMPSON was also at the top of his game, taking an unflinching look at the more extreme elements of his faith on 'OUTSIDE OF THE INSIDE'. In his time, THOMPSON (now a practising Muslim) has influenced many guitarists including Americans, FRANK BLACK (of PIXIES) and BOB MOULD (of HUSKER DU) and has come to be regarded as one of England's finest songwriting guitarists. 2005 was a relatively busy year for the guitarist with both a soundtrack to Werner Herzog's award winning documentary, 'GRIZZLY MAN', and an all-acoustic solo album, 'FRONT PARLOUR BALLADS', released within months of each other. The latter was THOMPSON's first set of wholly acoustic material since the traditional 'STRICT TEMPO', roundly praised as among the finest of his long solo career. Kicking off with the wry celebrity yarn of 'LET IT BLOW', the record was as humane as it was acerbic, resolutely English in its conception and execution despite being recorded in the man's L.A. garage. THOMPSON maintained his main inspiration was classical yet in penetrating character studies like 'A SOLITARY LIFE', the fog-bound glower of vintage folk was as pervasive as it was on the more obviously trad-influenced 'ROW, BOYS, ROW' and 'OLD THAMES SIDE'.

• **Trivia:** A RICHARD THOMPSON tribute album in 1994 featured many top stars, playing their best RT tracks.

Album rating: HENRY THE HUMAN FLY (*7) / Richard & Linda Thompson: I WANT TO SEE THE BRIGHT LIGHTS TONIGHT (*8) / HOKEY POKEY (*7) / POUR DOWN LIKE SILVER (*7) / FIRST LIGHT (*6) / SUNNYVISTA (*5) / SHOOT OUT THE LIGHTS (*9) / Richard Thompson: (guitar, vocal) collection (*4) / STRICT TEMPO! (*4) / HAND OF KINDNESS (*7) / SMALL TOWN

ROMANCE (*7) / ACROSS A CROWDED ROOM (*6) / DARING ADVENTURES (*7) / THE MARKSMAN soundtrack for TV with Peter Filleul (*4) / AMNESIA (*6) / RUMOUR AND SIGH (*7) / SWEET TALKER soundtrack (*4) / WATCHING THE DARK (THE HISTORY OF RICHARD THOMPSON 1969-1982) boxed-set (*8) / MIRROR BLUE (*6) / YOU? ME? US? (*6) / INDUSTRY with Danny Thompson (*5) / MOCK TUDOR (*7) / THE BEST OF RICHARD & LINDA THOMPSON compilation (*7) / ACTION PACKED – THE BEST OF THE CAPITOL YEARS compilation (*7) / THE OLD KIT BAG (*7) / FRONT PARLOUR BALLADS (*7) / GRIZZLY MAN soundtrack (*6) / RT: THE LIFE AND TIMES OF RICHARD THOMPSON boxed compilation (*8)

RICHARD THOMPSON – vocals, guitar (ex-FAIRPORT CONVENTION) with **LINDA PETERS / PAT DONALDSON** – bass / **TIM DONALD** – drums / plus **SANDY DENNY / ASHLEY HUTCHINGS / JOHN KIRKPATRICK / JOHN DEFERERI / BARRY DRANSFIELD / DAVID SNELL / CLAY TOYANI / ANDY ROBERTS / SUE DRAHEIM / JEFF COLE**

Island Reprise

Jun 72. (lp/c) *(ILPS/ZCI 9197)* <2112> **HENRY THE HUMAN FLY**
– Roll over Vaughn Williams / Nobody's wedding / The poor ditching boy / Shaky Nancy / The angels took my racehorse away / Wheely down / The new St. George / Painted ladies / Cold feet / Mary and Joseph / The old changing ways / Twisted. *(re-iss. Jan87 on Hannibal'; HNBL 4405) (re-iss. May87 c/cd; HNBC/HNCD 4405)*

RICHARD & LINDA THOMPSON

husband & wife duo. LINDA (nee. PETERS) (ex-ALBION COUNTRY BAND) with SOUR GRAPES: **SIMON NICOL** – dulcimer / **STEVE BORRELL** – bass / **WILLIAM MURRAY** – drums (ex-KEVIN AYERS)/ plus most of main musicians on above album

Island Island

Jan 74. (7") *(WIP 6186)* **I WANT TO SEE THE BRIGHT LIGHTS TONIGHT. / WHEN I GET TO THE BORDER**

Apr 74. (lp/c) *(<ILPS/ZCI 9266>)* **I WANT TO SEE THE BRIGHT LIGHTS TONIGHT**
– When I get to the border / The Calvery Cross / Withered and died / I want to see the bright lights tonight / Down where the drunkards roll / We sing hallelujah / Has he got a friend for me? / The little beggar girl / The end of the rainbow / The Great Valero. *(cd-iss. May88; CID 9266) (re-iss. Oct89 on 'Carthage'; CGLP 4407) (cd re-iss. Mar93 on Island')*

— **IAN WHITEMAN** – keyboards, flute / **ALY BAIN** – fiddle repl. guests

Feb 75. (7") *(WIP 6220)* **HOKEY POKEY. / I'LL REGRET IT ALL IN THE MORNING**

Mar 75. (lp/c) *(<ILPS/ZCI 9305>)* **HOKEY POKEY**
– Hokey pokey (the ice-cream song) / I'll regret it all in the morning / Smiffy's glass eye / Egypt room / Never again / Georgie on a spree / Old man inside a young man / The Sun never shines on the poor / A heart needs a home / Mole in a hole. *(re-iss. Jun86 on Hannibal'; HNBL 4408) (re-iss. May89 c/cd; HNBC/HNBD 4408)*

Nov 75. (lp/c) *(<ILPS/ZCI 9348>)* **POUR DOWN LIKE SILVER**
– Streets of Paradise / For shame of doing wrong / The poor boy is taken away / Night comes in / Jet plane in a rocking chair / Beat the retreat / Hard luck stories / Dimming of the day / Dargai. *(re-iss. Jun86 on Hannibal'; HNBL 4404) (re-iss. May89 c/cd; HNBC/HNBD 4404)*

— Their main band was:- **WILLIE WEEKS** – bass / **ANDY NEWMARK** – drums / **NEIL LARSON** – keyboards / **SIMON NICOL** – guitar, dulcimer / **JOHN KIRKPATRICK** – accordion

Chrysalis Chrysalis

Nov 78. (lp/c) *(<CHR/ZCHS 1177>)* **FIRST LIGHT**
– Restless highway / Sweet surrender / Don't let a thief steal into your heart / The choice wife / Died for love / Strange affair / Layla / Pavanne / House of cards / First light. *(cd-iss. Jun86; CCD 1177) (re-iss. May89 on 'Carthage' lp/c; CGLP/CGC 4412)*

Jan 79. (7") *(CHS 2278)* **DON'T LET A THIEF STEAL INTO YOUR HEART. / FIRST LIGHT**

— **TIM DONALD, PAT DONALSON + RABBIT BUNDRICK** repl. NEWMARK, WEEKS + LARSON / guests:- **DAVE MATTACKS** – drums / **DAVE PEGG** – bass

Sep 79. (lp/c) *(<CHR/ZCHS 1247>)* **SUNNYVISTA**
– Civilization / Borrowed time / Saturday rolling around / You're going to need somebody / Why do you turn your back / Sunnyvista / Lonely hearts / Sisters / Justice in the streets / Traces of my love. *(re-iss. May89 on 'Carthage' lp/c/cd; CGLP/CGC/CGCD 4403)*

Sep 79. (7") *(CHS 2369)* **CIVILIZATION. / GEORGIE ON A SPREE** –

Elixir not iss.

Sep 81. (lp) *(LP 1)* **STRICT TEMPO (RICHARD THOMPSON solo / instrumental)** –
– Scott Skinner medley / Banish misfortune / Dundee hornpipe / Do it for my sake / New fangled flogging reel / Vailance polka militair / Belfast polka / Rockin' in rhythm / The random jig / The grinder / Andalus / Marrakesh / The knife edge. *(re-iss. Jul89 on 'Carthage' lp/c/cd; CGLP/CGC/CGCD 4409)*

— next w / **NICOL / MATTACKS / PEGG / + bassman PETE ZORN**

Hannibal Hannibal

Apr 82. (7") *(HNS 703)* **DON'T RENEGE ON YOUR LOVE. / LIVING IN LUXURY** –

Nov 82. (lp) *(<HNBL 1303>)* **SHOOT OUT THE LIGHTS**
– Man in need / Walking on a wire / Don't renege on your love / Just the motion / Shoot out the lights / Back street slide / Did she jump or was she pushed / Wall of death. *(re-iss. Jun86 lp/c/cd+=; HNBL/HNBC/HNBD 1303)* – Living in luxury. *(cd-iss. Dec94 on 'Hannibal')*

RICHARD THOMPSON

— returned to solo work after separating with LINDA. He retained last band and label, while LINDA went on in 1985 to release an album ONE CLEAR MOMENT' for Warners'.

Jun 83. (lp) *(<HNBL 1313>)* **HAND OF KINDNESS**
– A poisoned heart and a twisted memory / Tear stained letter / How I wanted to / Both ends burning / The wrong heartbeat / Hand of kindness / Devonside / Two left feet. *(re-iss. Jun86 lp/c/cd+=; HNBL/HNBC/HNBD 1313)* – Where the wind don't whine.

Jul 83. (7") *(HNS 704)* **THE WRONG HEARTBEAT. / DEVONSIDE** –

Dec 84. (lp) *(<HNBL 1316>)* **SMALL TOWN ROMANCE (live)** –
– Time to ring some changes / Beat the retreat / A heart needs a home / Woman or a man / For shame of doin' wrong / Genesis Hall / Honky tonk blues / Small town romance / I want to see the bright lights tonight / Down where the drunkards roll / Love is bad for business / Never again / The Great Valero / Don't let a thief steal into your heart. i(re-iss. Jun86 lp/c/cd; *HNBL/HNBC/HNBD 1316)*

Polydor Polydor

Mar 85. (lp/c) *(POLD/+C 5175)* <825421> **ACROSS A CROWDED ROOM** 80
– When the spell is broken / You don't say / I ain't going to drag my feet no more / Love in a faithless country / Fire in the engine room / Walking through a wasted land / Little blue number / She twists the knife again / Ghosts in the wind. *(cd-iss. Jun86; 825421-2) (cd re-iss. Jun92 on 'Beat Goes On' cd/c/lp; BGO CD/MC/LP 139)*

Jun 85. (7") *(POSP 750)* **YOU DON'T SAY. / WHEN THE SPELL IS BROKEN**

— now with **MITCHELL FROOM** – organ / **JERRY SCHEFF** – bass / **MICKEY CURRY + JIM KELTNER** – drums / **JOHN KIRKPATRICK** – accordion / **ALEX ACUNA** – percussion

Oct 86. (lp)(cd) *(POLD 5202)(<829728-2>)* **DARING ADVENTURES** 92
– A bone through her nose / Valerie / Missie how you let me down / Dead man's handle / Long dead love / Lover''s lane / Nearly in love / Jennie / Baby talk / Cash down / Never never / How wll I ever be simple again / Al Bowly's in Heaven. *(re-iss. Jun92 on 'Beat Goes On' cd/c/lp; BGO CD/MC/LP 138)*

B.B.C. not iss.

Oct 87. (lp/c; by RICHARD THOMPSON & PETER FILLEUL) *(REB/ZCF 660)* **THE MARKSMAN (TV soundtrack)** –
– My time / Gordon / Rude health / Night school / Cornish pastiche / Crossing the water / The marksman / Kyrie / On yer eyes / Cutters on the run / Don't ever change / Up there.

Capitol Capitol

Oct 88. (cd/c/lp) *(CD/TC/+EST 2075)* <48845> **AMNESIA** 89
– Turning of the tide / Gypsy love songs / Reckless kind / Jerusalem on the jukebox / I still dream / Don't tempt me / Yankee, go home / Can't win / Waiting for dreamers / Pharoah. *(re-iss. Mar91 lp/c; ATAK/TC-ATAK 169) (cd re-iss. Aug91; CZ 399)*

Nov 88. (7") *(CL 516)* **TURNING OF THE TIDE. / PHAROAH**

Sep 89. (7") *(CL 550)* **RECKLESS KIND (live). / TURNING OF THE TIDE (live)**
(12"+=) *(12CL 550)* – Pharoah (live) / Can't win (live).
(cd-s+=) *CDCL 550)* – Jerusalem on the jukebox (live).

May 91. (cd/c/lp) *(CD/TC+/EST 2142)* **RUMOUR AND SIGH** [32] [ ]
– Read about love / I feel so good / I misunderstood / Behind grey walls / You dream too much / Why must I plead / Vincent / Backlash love affair / Mystery wind / Jimmy Shands / Keep your distance / Mother knows best / God loves a drunk / Psycho Street.

Jun 91. (7") *(CL 617)* **I FEEL SO GOOD. / HARRY'S THEME (from the film 'Sweet Talker')** [ ] [-]
(cd-s+=) *(CDCL 617)* – Backlash love affair.

Mar 92. (7") *(CL 638)* **READ ABOUT LOVE. / I MISUNDERSTOOD** [ ] [-]
(cd-s+=) *(CDCL 638)* – I feel so good / The choice wife.

May 92. (cd/c/lp) *(CD/TC/+EST 2170) <C2/C4 94490>* **SWEET TALKER** (soundtrack) [ ] [ ]
– Put your trust in me / Persuasion / Roll up / The Dune ship / Conviction / Boomtown / Harry's theme / Sweet talker / To hang a dream on / Beachport / False or true.

— with **PETE THOMAS** – drums, percussion / **JERRY SCHEFF** – bass, double bass / **MITCHELL FROOM** – keyboards, producer / **ALISTAIR ANDERSON** – concertina, pipes / **TOM McCONVILLE** – fiddle / **MARTIN DUNN** – flute / **PHIL PICKETT** – shawms / **JOHN KIRKPATRICK** – accordion, concertina / **DANNY THOMPSON** – double bass (1) / **CHRISTINE COLLISTER + MICHAEL PARKER** – backing vocals

Jan 94. (cd/c) *(CD/TC EST 2207) <81492>* **MIRROR BLUE** [23] [ ]
– For the sake of Mary / I can't wake up to save my life / MGB-GT / The way that it shows / Easy there, steady now / King of Bohemia / Shane and Dixie / Mingus eyes / I ride in your slipstream / Beeswing / Fast food / Mascara tears / Taking my business elsewhere.

Apr 96. (d-cd/d-c) *(CD/TC EST 2282) <33704>* **YOU? ME? US?** (part compilation / acoustic) [32] [97]
– Razor dance / She steers by lightning / Dark hand over my heart / Hide it away / Put it there pal / Business on you / No's not a word / Am I wasting my love on you? / Bank vault in Heaven / The ghost of you walks / Baby don't know what to do with herself / She cut off her long silken hair / Hide it away / Burns supper / Train don't leave / Cold kisses / Sam Jones / Razor dance / Woods of Darney.

Parlophone Hannibal

May 97. (cd; RICHARD & DANNY THOMPSON) *(CDPCS 7383) <1414>* **INDUSTRY** [69] [ ]
– Chorale / Sweetheart on the barricade / Children of the dark / Big chimney / Kitty "quick get up I can hear clogs going up in the street" / Drifting through the days / Lotteryland / Pitfalls / Saboteur / Mew rhythms / Last shift.

Parlophone Capitol

Aug 99. (cd) *(<4 98860-2>)* **MOCK TUDOR** [28] [ ]
– METROLAND:- Cooksferry queen / Sibella / Bathsheba smiles / Two-faced love / Hard on me / HEROES IN THE SUBURBS:- Crawl back (under my stone) / Uninhabited man / Dry me tears and move on / Walking the long miles home / STREET CRIES AND STAGE WHISPERS:- Sights and sounds of London town / That's all, amen, close the door / Hope you like the new me. *(d-lp-iss.Nov99 on 'Bongload'; BL 44)*

Cooking Vinyl Cooking Vinyl

Feb 03. (cd) *(COOKCD 251) <74651>* **THE OLD KIT BAG** [52] [ ]
– THE HAUNTED KEEPSAKE:- Gethsemane / Jealous words / I'll tag along / A love you can't survive / One door opens / First breath / THE PILGRIMS FANCY:- She said it was destiny / Got no right / Pearly Jim / Word unspoken, sight unseen / Outside of the inside / Happy days and Auld Lang Syne.

Jun 03. (cd-s) *(FRYCD 155)* **SHE SAID IT WAS DESTINY / SO BEN MI CA BON TEMPO / HARD ON ME** [ ] [-]

Aug 05. (cd) *(COOKCD 325) <4725>* **FRONT PARLOUR BALLADS** [54] [ ]
– Let it blow / For whose sake? / Miss Patsy / Old Thames side / How does your garden grow? / My soul, my soul / Cressida / Row, boys, row / The boys of Mutton Street / Precious one / A solitary life / Should I betray? / When we were boys at school.

Oct 05. (cd) *(<COOKCD 360>)* **GRIZZLY MAN** (soundtrack) [ ] Sep05 [ ]
– Tim & the bears / Main title / Foxes / Ghosts in the maze / Glencoe / Parents / Bear swim / Twilight cowboy / The kibosh / Treadwell no more / Teddy bear / Small racket / Streamwalk / That's my story / Bear fight / Big racket / Corona for Mr. Chocolate / Main title revisited / (track by DON EDWARDS).

– compilations, etc. –

(below album recorded between 1967-1976)

May 76. (d-lp) *Island; (ICD 8)* **(guitar, vocal)** <US title 'LIVE MORE OR LESS'> [ ] [-]
– A heart needs a home / Flee as a bird / Night comes in / Pitfall / Excursion / Calvery Cross / Time will show the wiser / Throw-away street puzzle / Mr. Lacy / The ballad of Easy Rider / Poor Will and the jolly hangman / Sweet little rock'n'roller / Dark end of the street / I'll be me. *(incl.Live Oxford Street concert & early demos) (re-iss. Jun86 on 'Hannibal'; HNBL 4801) cd-iss. May89; HNBD 4413)*

Apr 93. (3xcd-box) *Hannibal; (HNCD 5303)* **WATCHING THE DARK (THE HISTORY OF RICHARD THOMPSON 1969-1982)** [ ] [-]
– A man in need / Can't win / Waltzing's for dreamers / Crash the party / I still dream / Bird in God's garden / Lost and found / Now be thankful / A sailor's kife / Genesis Hall / The knife-edge / Walking on a wire / Small town romance / Shepherd's march – Maggie Cameron / Wall of death / For shame of doing wrong / Back street slide / Strange affair / The wrong heartbeat / Borrowed time / From Galway to Graceland / Tear-stained letter / Keep your distance / Bogie's bonnie / Poor wee Jockey Clarke / Jet plane in a rocking chair / Dimming of the day / Old man inside a young man / Never again / Hokey pokey (the ice cream song) / A heart needs a home / Beat the retreat / Al Bowlly's in Heaven / Walking through a wasted land / When the spell is broken / Devonside / Little blue number / I ain't going to drag my feet no more / Withered and died / Nobody's wedding / The poor ditching boy / The Great Valerio / The Calvary Cross / Twisted / Jennie / Hand of kindness / Two left feet / Shoot out the lights.

May 93. (cd) *Windsong; (WINCD 034)* **BBC LIVE IN CONCERT** [ ] [-]

Jul 00. (cd) *Capitol; <542456>* **THE BEST OF RICHARD & LINDA THOMPSON: THE ISLAND RECORD YEARS** [-] [ ]
– Roll over Vaughn Williams / The poor ditching boy / When I get to the border / Withered and died / I want to see the bright lights tonight / Down where the drunkards roll / The end of the rainbow / The great Valerio / Hokey pokey / Never again / A heart needs a home / For shame of doing wrong / Night comes in / Beat the retreat / Dimming of the day / Calvary cross (live).

Aug 00. (cd) *Island; (IMCD 271)* **END OF THE RAINBOW: AN INTRODUCTION TO RICHARD & LINDA THOMPSON** [ ] [-]

Apr 01. (cd) *Capitol; (<5 31051-2>)* **ACTION PACKED – THE BEST OF THE CAPITOL YEARS** [ ] [ ]
– Turning of the tide / Waltzing's for dreamers / 1952 Vincent black lightning / I misunderstood / I feel so good / Keep your distance / Kinf of Bohemia / I can't wake up to save my life / Beeswing / The ghost of you walks / Razor dance / Cool kisses / Bathsheba smiles / Cooksferry queen / Uninhabited man / Walking the long miles home / Persuasion / Mr. Rebound / Fully qualified to be your man. *(<d-lp-iss.Feb01 on 'Bongload'; BL 52>)*

Feb 06. (5xcd-box) *Free Reed; (<FRQCD 55>)* **RT: THE LIFE AND MUSIC OF RICHARD THOMPSON** [ ] [ ]

☐ 3 (see under ⇒ EMERSON, LAKE & PALMER)

3 DOORS DOWN

Formed: Escatawpa, nr. Biloxi, Missouri, USA … late 90's by vocalist/drummer BRAD ARNOLD, MATT ROBERTS and TODD HARRELL; added CHRIS HENDERSON soon after. Described by some pundits as bland all-American – similar in some respects to drummer/singer PHIL COLLINS – their local radio station WCPR in Biloxi frequently spun their records. Clones to CREED – i.e. big stadium rock and with God on their side; they're all believers – it looked like 3 DOORS DOWN would be another to break in the US but not the UK. After the multi-million selling success of their debut, the tediously named 3 DOORS DOWN once again appealed to the good ol' US of A's hard rocking heartland with 'AWAY FROM THE SUN' (2002), bolstered by the Top 5 success of single, 'WHEN I'M GONE'. Live EP, 'ANOTHER 700 MILES' confirmed their common man credentials and Southern rock references with a cover of Lynyrd Skynyrd's anti-drugs anthem, 'THAT SMELL'. 3 DOORS DOWN continued their passionate, post-Grunge rise to the top, courtesy of platinum-selling third album, 'SEVENTEEN DAYS' (2005); BOB SEGER even taking the time to guest on the track 'LANDING IN LONDON'.

Album rating: THE BETTER LIFE (*5) / AWAY FROM THE SUN (*5) / SEVENTEEN DAYS (*6)

BRAD ARNOLD (b.27 Sep'78) – vocals, drums / **MATT ROBERTS** (b.10 Jan'78) – lead guitar / **CHRIS HENDERSON** (b.30 Apr'71) – rhythm guitar / **TODD HARRELL** (b.13 Apr'72) – bass

Universal Universal

Jan 00. (-) *<radio play>* **KRYPTONITE** [–] [3]
Sep 00. (cd) *<(153920-2)>* **THE BETTER LIFE** [ ] Feb00 [7]
– Kryptonite / Loser / Duck and run / Not enough / Be like that / Life of my own / The better life / Down poison / By my side / Smack / So I need you.
Oct 00. (-) *<radio play>* **LOSER** [–] [55]

— added drummer **DANIEL ADAIR** (b.19 Feb'75) when BRAD took on vocal duties on stage

M.C.A. Universal

Apr 01. (cd-s) *(MCSTD 40251)* **KRYPTONITE / KRYPTONITE (acoustic sic) / KRYPTONITE (video)** [ ] [–]
Nov 01. (cd-s) *(MCSTD 40269) <radio cut>* **BE LIKE THAT / BE LIKE THAT (American pie edit) / NOT ENOUGH (live) / BE LIKE THAT (video)** [ ] Jul01 [24]
Mar 03. (cd) *(067563-2) <064396>* **AWAY FROM THE SUN** [ ] Nov02 [8]
– When I'm gone / Away from the sun / The road I'm on / Ticket to Heaven / Running out of days / Here without you / I feel you / Dangerous game / Changes / Going down in flames / Sarah yellin'. *(UK+=)* – Popsong / Kryptonite / Untitled.
Jun 03. (cd-s) *(MCSTD 40307) <19485>* **WHEN I'M GONE / LIVING A LIE / WASTED ME / WHEN I'M GONE (video)** [ ] Jan03 [4]
Nov 03. (m-cd) *<(16030-2)>* **ANOTHER 700 MILES (live)** [ ] [21]
– Duck and run / When I'm gone (intro) / When I'm gone / Kryptonite / Here without you / It's not me / That smell.
Feb 04. (-) *<radio>* **HERE WITHOUT YOU** [–] [5]
Apr 04. (-) *<radio>* **AWAY FROM THE SUN** [–] [62]

— **GREG UPCHURCH** (b. 1 Dec'71, Houma, Luoisiana, USA) – drums (ex-PUDDLE OF MUDD) repl. ADAIR who joined NICKELBACK

Jun 05. (cd-s) *(MCSXD 40423)* **LET ME GO / WHEN I'M GONE (live) / IT'S NOT ME (live) / LET ME GO (video)** [ ] [14]
Jun 05. (cd) *(9882728) <4100>* **SEVENTEEN DAYS** [ ] Feb05 [1]
– Right where I belong / It's not me / Let me go / Be somebody / Landing in London / The real life / Behind those eyes / Never will I break / Father's son / Live for today / My world / Here by me. *(UK+=)* – Here without you (acoustic) / Away from the sun (acoustic) / Let me go (acoustic).

THRICE

Formed: Irvine, California, USA ... 1998 by high school buddies DUSTIN KENSRUE, TEPPEI TERANISHI, EDDIE BRECKENRIDGE and RILEY BRECKENRIDGE. Taking the initiative by recording and distributing mini-set, 'FIRST IMPRESSIONS' (1999), out of their own pocket, they secured an independent release (by 'Sub City') of debut LP, 'IDENTITY CRISIS' (2001). The record was aptly named, swinging violently between classic 80s thrash riffing and la-la pop-punk, KENSRUE's vocals doing likewise. Although a split personality was still evident on follow-up, 'THE ILLUSION OF SAFETY' (2002), its more convincing soldering of their competing influences was enough to draw 'Island' into the equation. Producer Brian McTernan was back at the helm for their major label debut, 'THE ARTIST IN THE AMBULANCE' (2003), streamlining their emo-metallic sound for their first entry into the American Top 20. The very unlikely choice of Steve Osbourne (MASSIVE ATTACK, U2 and PETER GABRIEL) as producer on 'VHEISSU' (2005), seriously chilled the band's shoutier impulses and deepened their sound, especially on the likes of 'RED SKY' and 'OF DUST AND NATIONS'.

Album rating: FIRST IMPRESSIONS mini (*3) / IDENTITY CRISIS (*5) / THE ILLUSION OF SAFETY (*8) / THE ARTIST IN THE AMBULANCE (*7) / VHEISSU (*5)

DUSTIN KENSRUE (b.18 Nov'80) – vocals, rhythm guitar / **TEPPEI TERANISHI** (b.13 Sep'80) – lead guitar / **EDDIE BRECKENRIDGE** – bass, vocals / **RILEY BRECKENRIDGE** (b. 5 Jan'75) – drums

not iss. own label

1999. (m-cd) *<none>* **FIRST IMPRESSIONS** [–] [ ]
– All eyes / Lockdown / Opaque / T & C / Freedom / Second sight / Better days.

Golf Sub City

Apr 01. (cd) *<SC 019CD>* **IDENTITY CRISIS** [–] [ ]
– Identity crisis / Phoenix ignition / In your hands / To what end / Ultra blue / As the ruin falls / The next day / A torch to end all torches / Unquestioned answers / Madman *[on Greenflag version only]* / Under par / T & C. *(UK-iss.Jul04; same as US)*
Apr 02. (cd) *(CDHOLE 055) <SC 021CD>* **THE ILLUSION OF SAFETY** [ ] Feb02 [ ]
– Kill me quickly / A subtle dagger / See you in the shallows / Betrayal is a symptom / Deadbolt / In years to come / The red death / A living dance upon dead minds / Where idols once stood / Trust / To awake and avenge the dead / So strange I remember you / The Beltsville crucible. *(UK re-iss. May06 lp/cd; SC 021 1/22)*

Island Island

Jul 03. (cd/d-lp) *(077291-2/-1) <2950-2>* **THE ARTIST IN THE AMBULANCE** [ ] [16]
– Cold cash and colder hearts / Under a killing moon / All that's left / Silhouette / Stare at the sun / Paper tigers / Hoods on Peregrine / The melting point of wax / Blood clots and black holes / The artist in the ambulance / The abolition of man / Don't tell and we won't ask. *(UK lp+=)* – Eclipse. *<US re-iss. Nov03 ++=; 1038-2>* – Motion without meaning.
Aug 03. (7"clear) *(801246)* **UNDER A KILLING MOON. / (other by THURSDAY)** [ ] [–]

Mercury Island

Oct 03. (7") *(9811958)* **ALL THAT'S LEFT. / ECLIPSE** [69] [–]
(cd-s) *(9811957)* – ('A') / Stare at the sun (acoustic) / Motion without meaning / ('A'-video).
Mar 05. (dvd w/cd) *(8391750) <B000391750>* **IF WE COULD ONLY SEE US NOW** (videos & B-sides compilation) [–] non-ch [–]
Oct 05. (-) *<radio>* **IMAGE OF THE INVISIBLE** [–] [ ]
Oct 05. (cd) *(9885245) <5428>* **VHEISSU** [ ] [15]
– Image of the invisible / Between the end and where we lie / The earth will shake / Atlantic / For miles / Hold fast hope / Music box / Like moths to flame / Of dust and nations / Stand and feel your worth / Red sky.
Apr 06. (cd-ep) *<0006343>* **RED SKY EP** [–] [ ]
– Flags of dawn / Weight of glory / Under a killing moon (live) / For miles (live) / Red sky (live) / Of dust and nations (live).

the THRILLS

Formed: Dublin, Ireland ... summer 1999 as the CHEATING HOUSEWIVES by CONOR DEASY and DANIEL RYAN who initially recruited KEVIN HORAN, then BEN CARRIGAN and PADRAIC McMAHON. United in a love of all things musically laid back, soulful and sunkissed, the lads understandably had a bit of a fixation for the classicist sounds of the American West Coast. Though they weren't the first – and no doubt won't be the last – to be influenced by the likes of the BEACH BOYS, the BYRDS, BURT BACHARACH, NEIL YOUNG, PHIL SPECTOR etc, their rock revisionism had less zeal and more heart than the likes of say ... JET. MORRISSEY of all people – now living in sunny L.A. – took the band under his wing, securing their services for a support slot at the Royal Albert Hall. So far so good, as the band relocated to the USA and began living out the lifestyle they'd only heard about on scratchy old vinyl. A major label deal with 'Virgin' eventually resulted in the acclaimed debut album, 'SO MUCH FOR THE CITY' (2003). From the retro sleeve design to the flawless harmonies and country-tinged, banjo picking roots pop sensibilities, The THRILLS had pulled off one of the last few years' most alluring updates of that elusive 60's/70's vibe. Listening to the likes of hit singles 'BIG SUR', 'SANTA CRUZ (YOU'RE NOT THAT FAR)' and

'ONE HORSE TOWN' floating from the radio, it really was hard to believe the THRILLS weren't California born and bred. The sleeve art for the Top 10 'LET'S BOTTLE BOHEMIA' (2004) might've been more suited to a Mexican punk band but the THRILLS' follow-up album dealt in more of the same Topanga Canyon vibes that they'd so authentically transcribed on their debut. Second time around they inevitably sounded more jaded with the fringe benefits of Hollywood Babylon, while the choice of metal guru, D. Sardy (SYSTEM OF A DOWN, MARILYN MANSON) as producer was a strange, ultimately unprofitable one. On the plus side, the Irish roots-rockers had the good taste to bring in VAN DYKE PARKS for the baroque-pop UK Top 30 single, 'WHATEVER HAPPENED TO COREY HAIM?', while their seemingly second nature understanding of what remains a dyed-in-the-arrangements American art form remains remarkable.

• **Covers:** LAST NIGHT I DREAMT THAT SOMEBODY LOVED ME (Smiths) / THIS GUY'S IN LOVE WITH YOU (Bacharach-David) / VIVA LAS VEGAS (Elvis Presley).

Album rating: SO MUCH FOR THE CITY (*8) / LET'S BOTTLE BOHEMIA (*6)

CONOR DEASY – vocals / **DANIEL RYAN** – guitar, vocals, bass / **KEVIN HORAN** – keyboards / **PADRAIC McMAHON** – bass / **BEN CARRIGAN** – drums

Virgin | E.M.I.

Nov 02. (7"white) *(VS 1840)* *<546885>* **SANTA CRUZ (YOU'RE NOT THAT FAR). / DECKCHAIRS AND CIGARETTES** [ ] Dec02 [ ]
(cd-s+=) *(VSCDT 1840)* – Your love is like Las Vegas / Plans.

Mar 03. (7"yellow) *(VS 1845)* **ONE HORSE TOWN. / DON'T PLAY IT COOL** 18 –
(cd-s+=) *(VSCDT 1845)* – Car crash.

Jun 03. (7"blue) *(VS 1852)* **BIG SUR. / YOUR LOVE IS LIKE LAS VEGAS** 17 –
(cd-s) *(VSCDT 1852)* – ('A') / No one likes to be upstaged / One horse town (demo) / ('A'-video).

Jun 03. (cd/lp) *(CD+/V 2974)* *<584968>* **SO MUCH FOR THE CITY** 3 [ ]
– Santa Cruz (you're not that far) / Big Sur / Don't steal our sun / Deckchairs and cigarettes / One horse town / Old friends, new lovers / SAy it ain't so / Hollywood kids / Just travelling through / Your love is like Las Vegas / 'Til the tide creeps in.

Aug 03. (7"plum) *(VS 1862)* **SANTA CRUZ (YOU'RE NOT THAT FAR). / DON'T PLAY IT COOL (orginial version)** 33 –
(cd-s) *(VSCDT 1862)* – ('A') / Blue September.

Nov 03. (7"green) *(VS 1864)* **DON'T STEAL OUR SUN. / THE ONE I LOVE (Radio 1 version)** 45 –
(cd-s) *(VSCDT 1864)* – ('A') / One horse town (live).
(cd-s) *(VSCDX 1864)* – ('A') / Last night I dreamt that somebody loved me / Santa Cruz (acoustic) / ('A'-video).

Aug 04. (7") *(VS 1876)* **WHATEVER HAPPENED TO COREY HAIM? / A CITY OF LONG NIGHTS (acoustic)** 22 –
(cd-s) *(VSCDT 1876)* – ('A') / Big sur (Dave Sardy remix).
(cd-s) *(VSCDX 1876)* – ('A') / If I wasn't so pretty / ('A'-Zane Lowe session) / ('A'-video).

Sep 04. (cd/lp) *(CD+/V 2986)* *<64509>* **LET'S BOTTLE BOHEMIA** 9 [ ]
– Tell me something I don't know / Whatever happened to Corey Haim? / Faded beauty queens / Saturday night / Not for all the love in the world / Our wasted lives / You can't fool old friends with limousines / Found my rosebud / The curse of comfort / The Irish keep gate-crashing. *(lp w/free 7")* – A CITY OF LONG NIGHTS. / THE IRISH KEEP GATE-CRASHING (reprise)

Nov 04. (7"red) *(VS 1890)* **NOT FOR ALL THE LOVE IN THE WORLD. / SATURDAY NIGHT (acoustic)** 39 –
(cd-s) *(VSCDT 1890)* – ('A') / What a cruel trick to play upon myself.
(cd-s) *(VSCDX 1890)* – ('A') / This guy's in love with you (Ken Bruce session) / ('A'-Sebastien Tellier remix) / ('A'-video).

Mar 05. (7"pic-d) *(VS 1895)* **THE IRISH KEEP GATE-CRASHING. / NOT FOR ALL THE LOVE IN THE WORLD (acoustic)** 48 –
(cd-s) *(VSCDT 1895)* – ('A') / Viva Las Vegas (live feat. JAMES BURTON).
(dvd-s) *(VSDVD 1895)* – ('A'-video) / Movie premieres / (the making of So Much For The City: A film about the Thrills by the Thrills)

THURSDAY

Formed: New Brunswick, New Jersey, USA . . . 1997 by frontman GEOFF RICKLY, along with guitarists STEVE PEDULLA, TOM KEELEY and rhythm men TIM PAYNE and TUCKER RULE. Forging their melodious emo-core rock into the American mainstream through two CURE-esque sets, 'WAITING' (1999) and 'FULL COLLAPSE' (2001), THURSDAY delivered the 5-song EP, 'FIVE STORIES FALLING', a year later. This epitomised their uniformed, hard-edged sound via four live faves, 'AUTOBIOGRAPHY OF A NATION', 'UNDERSTANDING OF A CAR CRASH', 'STANDING ON THE EDGE OF SUMMER' and 'PARIS IN FLAMES'. It was no surprise when 'Island' records took up the reins and set the ball rolling again with their third full-set, 'WAR ALL THE TIME' (2003). With shades of U2 at their most anthemic and grandiose (example 'THIS SONG BROUGHT TO YOU BY A FALLING BOMB' and 'SIGNALS OVER THE AIR'), the critically acclaimed album raced into the US Top 10 and into the minds and souls of a new breed of American youth. Teaming up with producer DAVE FRIDMANN (and new permanent addition, ANDREW EVERDING), THURSDAY finally delivered their 4th set, 'A CITY BY THE LIGHT DIVIDED' (2006), having shelved a plan to release a double disc. Highlighted by limited edition 45, 'COUNTING 5-4-3-2-1', the album escaped from their post-hardcore Emo sound and into the US Top 20.

Album rating: WAITING (*5) / FULL COLLAPSE (*5) / WAR ALL THE TIME (*7) / A CITY BY THE LIGHT DIVIDED (*7)

GEOFF RICKLY (b. 8 Mar'79) – vocals / **STEVE PEDULLA** (b. 3 Apr'75) – guitar, vocals / **TOM KEELEY** (b.18 Mar'79) – guitar, vocals / **TIM PAYNE** (b. 4 May'79) – bass / **TUCKER RULE** (b.17 Nov'78) – drums

not iss. | Eyeball

Dec 99. (cd) *<EB 015CD>* **WAITING** – [ ]
– Porcelain / This side of brightness / Ian Curtis / Introduction / Streaks in the sky / In transmission / Dying in New Brunswick / The dotted line / Where the circle ends. *(UK-iss.Sep02; same as US)*

Victory | Victory

Apr 01. (-) *<radio>* **UNDERSTANDING IN A CAR CRASH** – [ ]

Oct 01. (lp/cd) *<(VR 145/+CD)>* **FULL COLLAPSE** [ ] [ ]
– A0001 / Understanding in a car crash / Concealer / Autobiography of a nation / A hole in the world / Cross out the eyes / Paris in flames / I am the killer / Standing on the edge of summer / Wind-up / How long is the night? / I1100.

Oct 02. (cd-ep) *<(VR 189CD)>* **FIVE STORIES FALLING** (live) [ ] [ ]
– Autobiography of a nation / Understanding in a car crash / Standing on the edge of summer / Paris in flames / Jet black New Year (studio).

Universal | Island

Aug 03. (7"clear) *(801246)* **FOR THE WORKFORCE, DROWNING. / (other by THRICE)** [ ] –

Sep 03. (cd)(lp) *(9860874)(0772931)* *<2930-2/-1>* **WAR ALL THE TIME** 62 7
– For the workforce, drowning / Between rupture and rapture / Division St. / Signals over the air / Marches and manoeuvres / Asleep in the chapel / This song brought to you by a falling bomb / Steps ascending / War all the time / M. Shepard / Tomorrow I'll be you.

Oct 03. (7") *(9812291)* **SIGNALS OVER THE AIR. / NY BATTERI** 43 [ ]
(cd-s) *<(9 812292)>* – ('A') / Division St. (acoustic) / Hole in the world (acoustic) / ('A'-video).

— added (now) full-time **ANDREW EVERDING** (b.13 Nov'79) – keyboards (was featured on last set)

Hassle | Island

May 06. (cd) *(HOFF 014CD)* *<B0006482>* **A CITY BY THE LIGHT DIVIDED** [ ] 20
– The other side of the crash – Over and out (of control) / Counting 5-4-3-2-1 / Sugar in the sacrament / At this velocity / We will overcome / Arc-lamps, signal flares, a shower of white (the light) / Running from the rain / Telegraph avenue kiss / The lovesong writer / Into the blinding light / Autumn leaves revisited.

Jun 06. (7"blue) *(HOFF 015S)* **COUNTING 5-4-3-2-1. / EVEN THE SAND IS MADE OF SEASHELLS** ☐ ☐

☐ TIGER LILY (see under ⇒ ULTRAVOX)

☐ Glenn TILBROOK (see under ⇒ SQUEEZE)

TINDERSTICKS

Formed: Nottingham, England . . . 1988 as ASPHALT RIBBONS, by STUART STAPLES, DAVE BOULTER and DICKON HINCHCLIFFE, the line-up completed by NEIL FRASER, MARK COLWILL and AL McCAULEY. Abandoning their previous TRIFFIDS/GO-BETWEENS-esque indie attempts, the group adopted a darkly brooding hybrid of faded-glamour easy listening and semi-acoustic strumming, incorporating swooning strings, mournful violin, frantic flamenco and hints of country. Surely the heartbroken, doomed romantic to top all doomed romantics, STAPLES' low-key mumblings were somehow utterly compelling, his often barely audible melange of NICK CAVE, LEE HAZLEWOOD and TOM WAITS capable of expressing every nuance in the music regardless of what he was actually saying. The TINDERSTICKS came to critical notice with only their second single, 'MARBLES', a lo-fi STAPLES monologue cosetted by an aching melody. Released on their own 'Tippy Toe' label, the track was unanimously awarded Single Of The Week by both NME and Melody Maker, creating a buzz which would eventually see the group sign to the newly formed 'This Way Up' label. Previewed by the string-drenched melancholy of the 'CITY SICKNESS' single, the eponymous 'TINDERSTICKS' was released in late '93. A dense, bleakly beautiful, seedily glamorous near 80-minute epic, the record was so strikingly different from anything else around (save for maybe GALLON DRUNK or NICK CAVE) it sounded timeless. From the edgy resignation of 'WHISKEY & WATER' to the lovelorn lament of 'RAINDROPS', this was one of the most luxuriantly dark albums of the 90's, reeking of failed relationships and nicotine-stained despair. With gushing praise from the music press, both for the album and their hypnotic live shows, The TINDERSTICKS even managed to scrape a Top 60 chart placing. Released simultaneously with the album was a cover of John Barry's 'WE HAVE ALL THE TIME IN THE WORLD' alongside GALLON DRUNK on a 'Clawfist' 7", the latter group's TERRY EDWARDS having guested on the album and subsequently adding string arrangements on their next long player. Preceded by a cover of the late Townes Van Zandt's 'KATHLEEN', 'TINDERSTICKS' (same title, different album) was finally released in Spring '95, its grainy noir narratives and downtrodden country enhanced with exquisite orchestration. There were no great stylistic leaps, just a further exploration and refinement of the blurred shadows and twilit corners that graced the debut. An undisputed highlight was the goose-bump country duet with The WALKABOUTS' CARLA TORGERSON, 'TRAVELLING LIGHT', released as a single that summer. TINDERSTICKS were also in the process of refining their live sound, or rather expanding it, with the help of a full orchestra; the gorgeous results can be heard on concert set, 'THE BLOOMSBURY THEATRE 12.3.95'. Unable to sustain such a money draining enterprise for too long, TINDERSTICKS-plus-orchestra phase reached its zenith during a hugely successful week long residency at London's ICA theatre in late '96. The same year also saw the group's first foray into soundtrack work, scoring the music for French art film, 'NENETTE ET BONI'. Largely instrumental, the piano and bass-led main theme was fleshed out with the moving 'TINY TEARS' (or 'PETITES GOUTTES D'EAU' in French) from the second album; hardly essential but a pleasant listen all the same. Following the group's own fears that the fragile balance of TINDERSTICKS' muse was becoming unworkable, the difficult third album, 'CURTAINS' was finally completed in a fevered rush of creativity and released in summer '97. Less sprawling and more cohesive than previous efforts, it was also bolder and more accessible, STAPLES actually singing comprehensibly on the bulk of the tracks. Predictably, there were also more strings than ever, HINCHCLIFFE's orchestral flourishes crescendoing majestically on 'DON'T LOOK DOWN' and achieving a pathos only previously glimpsed before on 'LET'S PRETEND', JESUS ALEMANY's mariachi-style trumpet a bittersweet counterpart. There was even another country duet, 'BURIED BONES', a brilliantly executed NANCY/LEE-style sparring match featuring the velvet tones of BONGWATER's ANN MAGNUSON. Lyrically, the themes remained reliably unchanged, tales of everyday lust and disillusionment dripping from STAPLES' lips like the honey from his claws as described in the gripping, unsettling 'BEARSUIT'. And, with 'BALLAD OF TINDERSTICKS', STAPLES indicated that they don't take this music business lark TOO seriously. After a stop-gap 'best of' album, 'DONKEYS' was released in '98, TINDERSTICKS were back to their mournful best courtesy of 1999's 'SIMPLE PLEASURE'. Opening with the minor hit, 'CAN WE START AGAIN?' and then a cover of Odyssey's dancefloor hit(!), 'IF YOU'RE LOOKING FOR A WAY OUT', it was clear to see the familiar 'STICKS territory had been given a modern day injection. Switching to another label was perhaps the best possible thing to happen to TINDERSTICKS who issued their dark melancholic set 'CAN OUR LOVE . . .' in 2001. A jazzy, but yet still tortoise speed release, STAPLES' crooning, brooding, COHEN-esque vocals reached new heights of intimacy on songs such as 'DYING SLOWLY' and 'SWEET RELEASE'. The group returned one year later to issue the soundtrack to Claire Denis' post-feminist, cannibal movie 'TROUBLE EVERY DAY', which marked the group's second collaboration with the director after her debut film 'Nenette et Boni'. As usual, the tone set was a dark one, STAPLES providing only one vocal track, to much eerie and frightening effect. If there was any justice, TINDERSTICKS would be bigger than OASIS; as it is they remain a treasured secret for anyone who's ever glimpsed the universe through the bottom of a wine glass. With 'WAITING FOR THE MOON' (2003), the band signalled both their ability and willingness to follow their dark musical whims seemingly indefinitely, with only occasional fine tuning. And if they can still create sound-lyric atmospherics as menacingly vivid as opener 'UNTIL THE MORNING COMES', that can only be a good thing. 'WORKING FOR THE MAN: THE ISLAND YEARS' (2004) was a self-explanatory rake through the 'This Way Up/Island' era, updating the previous 'DONKEYS 92-97' and sweetening the package with more rarities and covers, including Otis Redding's 'I'VE BEEN LOVING YOU TOO LONG'. With no new material on the horizon, fans desperate for their next fix of misery could take solace in a STUART STAPLES solo debut: 'LUCKY DOG RECORDINGS 03-04' (2005). Like the band's soundtrack diversions, this was never likely to deviate too much from the chamber-croon blueprint. Originating in a clutch of home-recorded sketches sans strings, the record roped in the likes of TERRY EDWARDS and YANN TIERSEN for subtle elaboration rather than any real fleshing-out. STAPLES always had a spiritual home in Nashville, but 'LEAVING SONGS' (2006), was his first time recording there. Following on from his earlier boy-girl duets, he took the opportunity to ruminate alongside alt-country girl MARIA McKEE and World-music dame LLASA DE SELA.

• **Covers:** KOOKS (David Bowie) / HERE (Pavement). • **Trivia:** JON LANGFORD of the THREE JOHNS, produced early ASPHALT RIBBONS material.

Album rating: Asphalt Ribbons: OLD HORSE & OTHER SONGS (*4) / Tindersticks: TINDERSTICKS (*8) / THE SECOND TINDERSTICKS ALBUM

(*7) / THE BLOOMSBURY THEATRE 12.3.95 (*6) / NENETTE ET BONI soundtrack (*6) / CURTAINS (*8) / DONKEYS 92-97 compilation (*7) / SIMPLE PLEASURE (*8) / CAN OUR LOVE . . . (*7) / TROUBLE EVERY DAY soundtrack (*6) / WAITING FOR THE MOON (*6) / WORKING FOR THE MAN: THE ISLAND YEARS compilation (*8) / Stuart A. Staples: LUCKY DOG RECORDINGS 03-04 (*7) / LEAVING SONGS (*7)

the ASPHALT RIBBONS

STUART STAPLES (b.14 Nov'65) – vocals, guitar / **DICKON HINCHCLIFFE** (b. 9 Jul'67) – violin, keyboards, etc. / **DAVE BOULTER** (b.27 Feb'65) – keyboards / **BLACKHOUSE** – guitar / **FRASER** – bass / **WATT** – drums

In-Tape not iss.

Oct 89. (7"ep) *(IT 063)* **THE ORCHARD** ☐ [–]
– Over again / Red sauce / Greyhound / I used to live T.

May 90. (7"m) *(IT 068)* **GOOD LOVE. / LONG LOST UNCLE / THE DAY I TURNED BAD** ☐ [–]

— (alongside new stablemates MY LIFE WITH PATRICK, their new label below issued a flexi sampler with 'Zip Code' fanzine; cat no. LILY 001)

Tiger Lily not iss.

Apr 91. (12"ep) *(LILY 002)* **PASSION, COOLNESS, INDIFFERENCE, BOREDOM, MOCKERY, CONTEMPT, DISGUST** ☐ [–]

E.T.T. not iss.

Aug 91. (m-lp) *(E 101)* **OLD HORSE & OTHER SONGS** ☐ [–]
– Rosemarie / Old horse / State inside / The distance between us / Strong hands / Downside. *(cd-iss. Apr92; E 101-2)*

TINDERSTICKS

were formed by **STUART, DICKON and DAVE**, plus Londoners **NEIL FRASER** (b.22 Nov'62) – lead guitar, vibraphone / **MARK COLWILL** (b.12 May'60) – bass / **AL McCAULEY** (b. ALASDAIR MACCAULEY, 2 Aug'65) – drums

Tippy Toe No.6

Nov 92. (7") *(TIPPY TOE 1)* **PATCHWORK. / MILKY TEETH** ☐ [–]

Mar 93. (10"ep) *(TIPPY TOE – che 2)* **MARBLES / JOE STUMBLE. / FOR THOSE . . . / BENN** ☐ [–]
below featured dual vox of **NIKI SIN** of HUGGY BEAR.

Rough Trade Sing. Club not iss.

Mar 93. (7") *(45REV 16)* **A MARRIAGE MADE IN HEAVEN. / (instrumental)** ☐ [–]

Domino No.6

Jul 93. (7"ep) *(RUG 6)* **UNWIRED E.P.** ☐ [–]
– Feeling relatively good / Rottweilers and mace / She / Kooks.

Sep 93. (7") <KAR 028> **MARBLES. / FOR THOSE NOT BEAUTIFUL** [–] ☐

This Way Up Bar None

Sep 93. (7"/cd-s) *(WAY 1811/1833)* **CITY SICKNESS. / UNTITLED / THE BULLRING** ☐ [–]

Oct 93. (cd/c/lp) *(518306-2/-4/-1)* <46> **TINDERSTICKS** [56] ☐
– Nectar tyed / Sweet, sweet man (pt.1) / Whiskey & water / Blood / City sickness / Patchwork / Marbles / The Walt blues / Milky teeth (pt.2) / Sweet, sweet man (pt.2) / Jism / Piano song / Tie dye / Raindrops / Sweet, sweet man (pt.3) / Her / Tea stain / Drunk tank / Paco de Renaldo's dream / The not knowing. *(lp+=)* – Fruitless. *(re-iss. Jun97; same)*

Oct 93. (7") *(XPIG 21)* **WE HAVE ALL THE TIME IN THE WORLD – JAMES BOND THEME. / (other by Gallon Drunk)** ☐ [–]
(above issued on 'Clawfist')

— 'Tippy Toe' also gave away 7" 'LIVE IN BERLIN' at gigs.

Jan 94. (7"ep/10"ep/cd-ep) *(WAY 2811/2888/2833)* **KATHLEEN EP** [61] [–]
– Kathleen / Summat Moon / A sweet sweet man / E-type Joe.

— In Aug'94, they appeared on Various Artists EP on 'Blue Eyed Dog'; track 'LOVE BITES', and others by STRANGELOVE / GOD MACHINE + BREED.

This Way Up London

Mar 95. (7") *(WAY 38-11)* **NO MORE AFFAIRS. / (instrumental)** [58] [–]
(cd-s+=) *(WAY 38-33)* – Fruitless.

Apr 95. (cd/c/d-lp) *(526303-2/-4/-1)* <6303> **THE SECOND TINDERSTICKS ALBUM** [13] Oct95 ☐
– El diablo en el ojo / My sister / Tiny tears / Snowy in F minor / Seaweed / Vertrauen 2 / Talk to me / No more affairs / Singing / Travelling light / Cherry blossoms / She's gone / Mistakes / Vertraven 3 / Sleepy song. *(ltd.lp w/ free one-sided-7")* – PLUS DE LIAISONS

Jun 95. (7") <SP 297> **THE SMOOTH SOUNDS OF TINDERSTICKS** [–] ☐
– Here / Harry's dilemma.

— <above issued for 'Sub Pop'>

Jul 95. (7"/cd-s) *(WAY 45-11)* **TRAVELLING LIGHT. / WAITING 'ROUND YOU / I'VE BEEN LOVING YOU TOO LONG** [51] [–]

Oct 95. (cd/d-10"lp) *(528597-2/-1)* **THE BLOOMSBURY THEATRE 12.3.95 (live)** [32] [–]
– El diablo en el ojo / A night in / Talk to me / She's gone / My sister * / No more affairs / City sickness / Vertrauen II / Sleepy song / Jism / Drunk tank / Mistakes / Tiny tears / Raindrops / For those . . . *(d-lp+= *)*

This Way Up Bar None

Oct 96. (cd/lp) *(524300-2/-1)* <99> **NENETTE ET BONI** (soundtrack) ☐ ☐
– Ma souer / La passerelle / Les gateaux / Camions / Nenette est la / Petites chiennes / Nosferatu / Petites gouttes d'eau / Les Cannes a peche / La mort de Felix / Nenette s'en va / Les bebes / Les fleurs / Rumba.

This Way Up Polygram

May 97. (12"ep/cd-ep) *(WAY 61-22/-33)* **BATHTIME. / MANALOW / SHADOWS / PACO'S THEME** [38] [–]
(cd-ep) *(WAY 61-66)* – ('A') / Kathleen / Here / Tyed.

Jun 97. (cd/c/lp) *(<524344-2/-4/-1>)* **CURTAINS** [37] ☐
– Another night in / Rented rooms / Don't look down / Dick's slow song / Fast one / Ballad of Tindersticks / Dancing / Let's pretend / Desperate man / Buried bones / Bearsuit / (Tonight) Are you trying to fall in love again / I was your man / Bathtime / Walking.

Oct 97. (7") *(WAY 65-22)* **RENTED ROOMS. / ('A'-Swing version)** [56] ☐
(cd-s+=) *(WAY 65-33)* – Make believe.
(cd-s) *(WAY 65-66)* – ('A') / Cherry blossoms (live) / She's gone (live) / Rhumba (live).

Island Island

Sep 98. (cd/lp) *(CID/ILPS 8074)* <524588> **DONKEYS 92-97 (A COLLECTION OF SINGLES ° RARITIES ° UNRELEASED RECORDINGS)** (compilation) ☐ ☐
– Patchwork / Marbles / Her / City sickness / Travelling light / I've been loving you too long / Plus de liaisons / Here / Tiny tears / Bathtime / A marriage made in Heaven / For those . . .

Aug 99. (7") *(IS 756)* **CAN WE START AGAIN? / ONE WAY STREET** [54] [–]
(cd-s+=) *(CID 756)* – A little time.
(cd-s) *(CIDX 756)* – ('A'demo) / Puppy fat / Desperate man (alternate version).

Aug 99. (cd) *(CID 8085)* <546372> **SIMPLE PLEASURE** [36] ☐
– Can we start again? / If you're looking for a way out / Pretty words / From the inside / If she's torn / Before you close your eyes / (You take) This heart of mine / I know that loving / CF GF. *(lp-iss.Sep99 on 'Simply Vinyl'; SVLP 112)*

Beggars Banquet Beggars Banquet

Dec 00. (7"/cd-s) *(SINS 001/1CD)* **WHAT IS A MAN. / (instrumental)** ☐ [–]

May 01. (cd/lp) *(BBQ CD/LP 222)* <80222> **CAN OUR LOVE . . .** [47] ☐
– Dying slowly / People keep comin' around / Tricklin' / Can our love . . . / Sweet release / Don't ever get tired / No man in the world / Chilitetime.

Oct 01. (cd/lp) *(BBQ CD/LP 225)* <80225> **TROUBLE EVERY DAY** (soundtrack) ☐ ☐
– Opening titles / Dream / Houses / Maid theme 1 / Room 321 / Computer / Notre Dame / Killing theme / Taxi to Core / Core on stairs – Love theme (Shane and June) / Maid theme (end) / Closing titles / Killing theme (alternate version) / Trouble every day.

May 03. (12"ep/cd-ep) *(BBQ 367 T/CD)* **DON'T EVEN GO THERE EP** ☐ [–]
– Trying to find a home / Sexual funk / Everything changes / I want you.

Jun 03. (cd/lp) *(BBQ CD/LP 232)* <80232> **WAITING FOR THE MOON** ☐ ☐
– Until the morning comes / Say goodbye to the city / Sweet memory / 4.48 psychosis / Waiting for the moon / Trying to find a home / Sometimes it hurts / My oblivion / Just a dog / Running wild.
below featured **LHASA DE SELA**

Jul 03. (7"/cd-s) *(BBQ 369/+CD)* **SOMETIMES IT HURTS. / MY AUTUMN'S DONE COME** [60] [–]

Oct 03. (12"/cd-s) *(BBQ 372 T/CD)* **MY OBLIVION. / NOW IT'S OVER / RUNNING WILD (instrumental)** [ ] [–]

– compilations, etc. –

Apr 04. (d-cd) *This Way Up; (9816878)* **WORKING FOR THE MAN** [ ] [–]
– City sickness / Marbles / Patchwork / Her (original) / Travelling light / Tiny tears / Bathtime / Another night in / Can we start again? / I know that loving / For those . . . (orchestral version) // Patchwork / Milky teeth / Joe stumble / For those . . . / Benn / Fruitless / Untitled / The bullring / Kathleen / Summat moon / A sweet sweet man / E-type Joe / Plus de liaisons / Waiting 'round you / I've been loving you too long / Here / Harry's dilemma.

Feb 05. (cd) *Koch; <KOCD 9679>* **WORKING FOR THE MAN: THE GREATEST HITS** [–] [ ]
– (first disc above //).

STUART A. STAPLES

with **TERRY EDWARDS** – saxophone / **YANN TIERSON** – piano / **DAVID BOULTER** – keyboards / **NEIL FRASER** – guitar / **ADRIAN STOUT** – bass / **ADRIAN HUGE** – drums

Beggars Banquet / Beggars Banquet

Jul 05. (cd) *(<BBQCD 242>)* **LUCKY DOG RECORDINGS 03-04** [ ] [ ]
– Somerset house / Marseilles sunshine / Say something now / Friday night / Shame on you / Untitled / Dark days / People fall down / She don't have to be good to me / I've come a long way.

May 06. (cd/lp) *(<BBQ CD/LP 246>)* **LEAVING SONGS** [ ] [ ]
– Goodbye to old friends / Path / Which way the wind / Road is long / One more time / Dance with an old man / That leaving feeling / Already gone / This old town / Pulling in to the sea.

☐ TIN MACHINE (see under ⇒ BOWIE, David)

☐ TO MY SURPRISE (see under ⇒ SLIPKNOT)

☐ TOM TOM CLUB (see under ⇒ TALKING HEADS)

TOOL

Formed: Hollywood, California, USA . . . 1990 by ADAM JONES, MAYNARD JAMES KEENAN, PAUL D'AMOUR and DANNY CAREY. Signing to 'Zoo' records, TOOL showcased their claustrophobic, nihilistic nu-metal on the 1992 mini-set, 'OPIATE'. Creating a buzz with high-profile supports to the likes of HENRY ROLLINS, TOOL subsequently hammered out a full album's worth of HELMET-like savage intensity with 'UNDERTOW' (1993), a record with such bluntly titled tracks as 'PRISON SEX' (also a single), 'INTOLERANCE' and 'BOTTOM' (the latter featuring the aforementioned ROLLINS). The album went on to sell over a million copies in the States, having only reached the Top 50. Three years later, after extensive touring, they resurfaced in dramatic fashion with 'AENIMA', the record bolting straight to No.2, surprising many who had yet to acquire a taste for TOOL. An ensuing legal battle with 'Freeworld Entertainment' lasted two years before the band agreed a joint deal for subsequent recordings. While TOOL then underwent a hard earned sabbatical, KEENAN hooked up with BILLY HOWERDEL (TOOL guitar tech), PAZ LENCHANTIN, TOY VAN LEEUWEN and JOSH FREESE to form A PERFECT CIRCLE. After making their debut at L.A.'s Viper Room in summer '99, the group released the 'MER DE NOMS' album in 2000. With songwriting duties shared by KEENAN and HOWERDEL, the record carried on in the dark spirit of TOOL while drawing a string-enhanced gothic cloak (or cape, even) around KEENAN's emotionally ravaged vocals. Following the release of the millennial 'SALIVAL' box set, TOOL themselves re-entered the fray in 2001 with the widely acclaimed 'LATERALUS', an ineffably complex work of shifting textures, oblique mood and inscrutable lyrics carrying the mystical torch of its predecessor into a parallel sonic universe. Kerrang! hailed it as one of the greatest albums ever recorded, grand claims which will no doubt leave those humble TOOL lads unfazed. A PERFECT CIRCLE returned in 2003 with the ominously titled 'THIRTEENTH STEP' album, featuring former MARILYN MANSON bassist JEORDIE OSBORNE WHITE (who stepped into the breach after the departure of LENCHANTIN) and guitarist DANNY LOHNER, who was the immediate stand-in for VAN LEEUWEN and was himself later replaced by ex-SMASHING PUMPKINS man JAMES IHA. Produced by HOWERDEL, the record sought to deepen and enhance the sinister atmospherics of the debut, relying on skilfully wrought, sonic light and shade rather than dynamic bludgeon. With a CV featuring not a few radical cover versions, KEENAN and his PERFECT CIRCLE of collaborators released an album's worth of interpretations under the title 'EMOTIVE' (2004), a US No.2 protest opus casting their creepy, whispered spell over sacred cows like John Lennon's 'IMAGINE', Nick Lowe's ('WHAT'S SO FUNNY 'BOUT) PEACE, LOVE AND UNDERSTANDING?' and Marvin Gaye's 'WHAT'S GOING ON'. Black Flag's 'GIMMIE GIMMIE GIMMIE', Depeche Mode's 'PEOPLE ARE PEOPLE', Devo's 'FREEDOM OF CHOICE' and Fear's 'LET'S HAVE A WAR' were perhaps more suited to the industrio-apocalyse treatment but – outside of a satisfyingly ectoplasmic rendering of Led Zeppelin's 'WHEN THE LEVEE BREAKS' – arguably the best (and most disturbing) songs on the album were the originals: 'PASSIVE', and the nerve-pulping, percussive death march of 'COUNTING BODIES LIKE SHEEP TO THE RHYTHM OF THE WAR DRUMS'. TOOL themselves finally surfaced in spring 2006 with '10,000 DAYS', another US No.1 (UK Top 5) which found KEENAN and co taking a more meditative, less didactic view of man's flawed nature.

Album rating: OPIATE mini (*5) / UNDERTOW (*6) / AENIMA (*7) / SALIVAL live (*6) / LATERALUS (*8) / 10,000 DAYS (*7) / A Perfect Circle: MER DE NOMS (*6) / THIRTEENTH STEP (*6) / eMOTIVe (*4)

MAYNARD JAMES KEENAN – vocals / **ADAM JONES** – guitar / **PAUL D'AMOUR** – bass / **DANNY CAREY** – drums

Zoo-RCA / Zoo

Jul 92. (m-cd/m-c/m-lp) *<(72445 11027-2/-4/-1)>* **OPIATE** [ ] [ ]
– Sweat / Hush / Part of me / Cold and ugly (live) / Jerk-off (live) / Opiate.

Apr 93. (cd/c) *<(72445 11052-2/-4)>* **UNDERTOW** [ ] [50]
– Intolerance / Prison sex / Sober / Bottom / Crawl away / Swamp song / Undertow / 4 degrees / Flood / Disgustipated.

Mar 94. (12"grey/cd-s) *(74321 19432-1/-2)* **PRISON SEX. / UNDERTOW (live) / OPIATE (live)** [ ] [ ]

Jul 94. (12"/cd-s) *(74321 22043-1/21849-2)* **SOBER. / INTOLERANCE** [ ] [ ]

—— **JUSTIN CHANCELLOR** – bass; repl. D'AMOUR

Oct 96. (cd/c/lp) *(61422 31144-2/-4/-1) <72445 11087-2/-4/-1>* **AENIMA** [ ] [2]
– Stinkfist / Eulogy / H. / Useful idiot / Forty six & 2 / Message to Harry Manback / Hooker with a penis / Intermission / Jimmy / Die eier von Satan / Pushit / Cesaro summability / Aenima / (-)Ions / Third eye.

a PERFECT CIRCLE

MAYNARD JAMES KEENAN – vocals / **BILLY HOWERDEL** – guitar, keyboards, programming, vocals / **PAZ LENCHANTIN** – bass / **TROY VAN LEEUWEN** – guitar (ex-FAILURE, ex-ENEMY) / **JOSH FREESE** – drums (ex-GUNS N' ROSES, ex-VANDALS)

Virgin / Virgin

May 00. (cd/lp) *(CDVUS/VUSLP 173) <49253>* **MER DE NOMS** [55] [4]
– The hollow / Magdalena / Rose / Judith / Orestes / 3 Libras / Sleeping beauty / Thomas / Renholder / Thinking of you / Brena / Over.

Jul 00. (cd-s) *(VUSCD 168)* **JUDITH / MAGDALENA (live) / BRENA (live) / ORESTES (demo)** [ ] [–]
(7"/7") *(VUS/+X 168)* – (same tracks).

Nov 00. (7"/cd-s) *(VUS/+DX 181)* **THE HOLLOW. / THE HOLLOW (Bunk mix)** [72] [-]
(cd-s) *(VUSCD 181)* – ('A'side) / ('A'-Constantly consuming mix) / Judith (Danny Lohner mix).

Jan 01. (7") *(VUS 184)* **3 LIBRAS. / MAGDALENA (live)** [49] [ ]
(cd-s) *(VUSCD 184)* – ('A'side) / ('A'-All main courses remix) / Judith (live) / ('A'-CD ROM).
(cd-s) *(VUSDX 184)* – ('A'live) / ('A'-Feel my ice dub) / Sleeping beauty (live).

TOOL

—— were back (see last line-up)

Music For Nations — Volcano

Feb 01. (cd-set; w/dvd/vhs) *(DVDMFN/VFN 18)* *<31159>* **SALIVAL** [ ] [38]
– Third eye (live) / Part of me (live) / Pushit (live) / Message to Harry Manback II / Merkarba (live) / You lied (live) / No quarter / L.A.M.C. / Sober (video) / Prison sex (video) / Aenima (video) / Stinkfist (video).

Volcano — Volcano

May 01. (cd/c) *(921013-2)* *<31160>* **LATERALUS** [16] [1]
– The grudge / Eon blue apocalypse / The patient / Mantra / Schism / Parabol / Parabola / Tricks and leeches / Lateralus / Disposition / Reflection / Triad / Faaip de Oiad.

May 01. (-) *<radio>* **SCHISM** [-] [67]

a PERFECT CIRCLE

HOWERDEL + KEENAN + FREESE recruited **DANNY LOHNER** – guitar; repl. TROY (on most) / **JEORDIE OSBORNE WHITE** (aka TWIGGY RAMIREZ) – bass (ex-MARILYN MANSON) repl. PAZ / added **JAMES IHA** – guitar (ex-SMASHING PUMPKINS)

Virgin — Virgin

Sep 03. (cd) *(CDVUS 247)* *<80918>* **THIRTEENTH STEP** [27] [2]
– The package / Weak and powerless / The noose / Blue / Vanishing / A stranger / The outsider / Crimes / The nurse who loved me / Pet / Lullaby / Gravity.

Dec 03. (cd-s) *<38888>* **WEAK AND POWERLESS (Tiling My Grave mix) / BLUE** [-] [61]

Feb 04. (-) *<radio>* **THE OUTSIDER** [-] [79]

Nov 04. (cd) *(CDVUS 257)* *<66687>* **eMOTIVe** [ ] [2]
– Annihilation / Imagine / (What's so funny 'bout) Peace, love and understanding? / What's going on / Passive / Gimmie gimmie gimmie / People are people / Freedom of choice / Let's have a war / Counting bodies like sheep to the rhythm of the war drums / When the levee breaks / Fiddle and the drum.

TOOL

—— same line-up (see previous)

May 06. (-) *<radio>* **VICARIOUS** [-] [55]

May 06. (cd) *<(82876 81991-2)>* **10,000 DAYS** [4] [1]
– Vicarious / Jambi / Wings for Marie (pt.1) / 10,000 days (Wings pt.2) / The pot / Lipan conjuring / Lost keys (blame Hofmann) / Roseta stoned / Intension / Right in two / Viginti tres.

TORTOISE

Formed: Chicago, Illinois, USA . . . 1990 by DOUGLAS McCOMBS and JOHN HERNDON, who started jamming together with JOHN McENTIRE, BUNDY K. BROWN and DAN BITNEY. This cult outfit initially crawled out of their collective shell with a series of early 90's EP's before finally unleashing their eponymous debut in '94. Remixed by STEVE ALBINI on the following year's blistering EP, 'RHYTHMS, RESOLUTIONS & CLUSTERS', the record proved TORTOISE to be the foremost purveyors of cut'n'mix avant-jazz. In 1996, their second album, 'MILLIONS NOW LIVING WILL NEVER DIE' (featuring the STEREOLAB trio of TIM, LAETITIA and MARY) was even better, opening with the psychedelic/Krautrock marathon of 'DJED'. This 20-minute track was subsequently given the 'Mo Wax' treatment, the extent of the band's appeal illustrated by their impressive run of collaborations over the course of the next year. The hard-working McENTIRE, who was also a part-time member of the RED CRAYOLA and the SEA AND CAKE, returned to the studio at the end of the year, beavering away on what was yet another classic TORTOISE set, 'TNT' (1998). A segued journey from cool avant-jazz rock that unsuspectingly flowed into complex rhythmical landscapes, the record proved a hard listen for alt-rock buffs. JOHN McENTIRE (who also sidelined with the SEA AND CAKE), subsequently found his niche in soundtrack work, although 'REACH THE ROCK' (1999) was too pretentious and complex for some. After a one-off collaboration ('IN THE FISHTANK') with Dutch indie-meisters, The EX, TORTOISE resumed their position as electronica's top groovesters via their fourth album proper, 'STANDARDS' (2001) – their first for the seminal UK imprint, 'Warp'. McENTIRE and the group "prog"-ressed with every mixed-up, well-rehearsed bass and vibraphone beat, although it didn't quite match the experimentation of their previous work. The trio of PARKER, HERNDON and BITNEY were also behind ISOTOPE 217, an inevitable TORTOISE offshoot which catered to the guys' jazzier urges. Also featuring MATT LUX, ROB MAZUREK and SARA P. SMITH, the ensemble debuted in 1997 with 'THE UNSTABLE MOLECULE', a supple, low-key excursion into the kind of fusion territory where even most Chicago outfits, never mind conventional lo-fi experimentalists, wouldn't dare to venture. 'UTONIAN AUTOMATIC' (1999) extended their intrepid musical brief while the 'COMMANDER MINDFUCK/DESIGNER' remix EP, released the same year, offered up dynamic reworkings of selected live performances. 'WHO STOLE THE I WALKMAN?' followed in 2000. TORTOISE eventually followed up 'STANDARDS' with 'IT'S ALL AROUND YOU' (2004), a largely disappointing and derivative TORTOISE-by-numbers album that did little to excite the listener. A change of tack via their 2006 collaborative covers album, 'THE BRAVE AND THE BOLD' with BONNIE "PRINCE" BILLY (i.e. WILL OLDHAM), saw the group experimenting once again.

Album rating: TORTOISE (*8) / RHYTHMS, RESOLUTIONS & CLUSTERS remixes (*6) / MILLIONS NOW LIVING WILL NEVER DIE (*9) / DIGEST COMPENDIUM OF . . . compilation (*7) / TNT (*8) / IN THE FISHTANK mini; with the Ex (*5) / STANDARDS (*7) / IT'S ALL AROUND YOU (*5) / THE BRAVE AND THE BOLD with Bonnie "Prince" Billy (*6) / John McEntire: REACH THE ROCK soundtrack (*6)

JOHN McENTIRE (b. Portland, Oregon, USA) – synthesizers, drums, vibraphone (ex-BASTRO, ex-SHRIMP BOAT) / **BUNDY K BROWN** – guitar, bass (ex-GASTR DE SOL) / **DOUGLAS McCOMBS** – bass (ex-ELEVENTH DREAM DAY) / **JOHN HERNDON** – drums, synthesizers, vibraphone (ex-POSTER CHILDREN) / **DAN BITNEY** – synthesizers, percussion, multi (ex-TAR BABIES) / 6th member **CASEY RICE** – soundman

not iss. — Torsion

1993. (7") *<003>* **MOSQUITO. / ONIONS WRAPPED IN RUBBER / GOOSENECK** [-] [ ]

not iss. — Soul Static

1994. (7") *<SOUL 7>* **WHY WE FIGHT. / WHITEWATER** [-] [ ]
(UK-iss.Jan95; same)

City Slang — Thrill Jockey

1994. (12") *<THRILL 006>* **LONESOME SOUND. / RESERVOIR / SHEETS** [-] [ ]

Jan 95. (cd/lp) *(EFA 04950-2/-1)* *<THRILL 013>* **TORTOISE** [ ] [ ]
– Magnet pulls through / Night air / Ry Cooder / Onions wrapped in rubber / Tin cans & twine / Spiderwebbed / His second story island / On noble / Flyrod / Cornpone brunch. *(cd-iss. remixed May97; TKCB 71016) (lp re-iss. Jun97 on 'Thrill Jockey'; THRILL 013)*

Apr 95. (12") *(Dodgey Beast; DS 3309)* **GAMERA. / CLIFF DWELLER SOCIETY** [ ] [ ]
(12") *(DS 3309S)* – ('A'mixes).

Jun 95. (m-cd/m-lp) *(EFA 04957-2/-1)* *<THRILL 019>* **RHYTHMS, RESOLUTIONS & CLUSTERS: REMIXED AND RARE** [ ] [ ]
– Alcohall / Your new rod / Cobwebbed / Match incident / Not quite east of the Ryan / Initial gesture protraction.

— **DAVE PAJO** – guitar (ex-SLINT) repl. BUNDY who formed DIRECTIONS IN MUSIC for one eponymous set; he and McCOMBS were also part of alt-supergroup, PULLMAN.

Jan 96. (cd/lp) *(EFA 04972-2/-1)* <*THRILL 025*> **MILLIONS NOW LIVING WILL NEVER DIE** ☐ ☐
– Djed / Glass museum / A survey / The taut and the tame / Dear grandma and grandpa / Along the banks of rivers. *(cd-iss. Japanese version May97; TKCB 70931)*

Apr 96. (12"; by TORTOISE Vs U.N.K.L.E./JOHN McENTIRE) *(SHELL 001)* <*TJ 12.1*> **DJED (bruise blood mix). / TJED** ☐ ☐

Jul 96. (12"; by TORTOISE Vs BUNDY BROWN) <*TJ 12.2*> **ROME** [-] ☐

Jul 96. (12"; by TORTOISE Vs OVAL) *(SHELL 002)* <*TJ 12.3*> **MUSIC FOR WORK GROUPS EP** ☐ ☐
– The bubble economy (mix by Marcus Popp) / Learning curve (mix by Marcus Popp).

Sep 96. (12"; by TORTOISE VS SPRING HEEL JACK) *(SHELL 003)* <*TJ 12.4*> **GALAPAGOS 1 (Spring Heel Jack remix). / REFERENCE RESISTANCE GATE (Jim O'Rourke remix)** ☐ ☐
(re-iss. Jun97 on 'Thrill Jockey'; TJ 124)

Oct 96. (12"; by TORTOISE Vs LUKE VIBERT/BUNDY K BROWN) *(SHELL 004)* <*TJ 12.5*> **THE TAUT AND THE TAME. / FIND THE ONE (WAIT, ABSTRACTION NO . . .)** ☐ ☐

— In 1996, they also shared a single with STEREOLAB, 'VAUS' / 'SPEEDY CAR', released on 'Duophonic'; *D-UHF-D12)*

— **JEFF PARKER** – guitar; repl. PAJO who formed AERIAL M

Mar 98. (cd/d-lp) *(EFA 08705-2/-1)* <*THRILL 050*> **TNT** ☐ ☐
– Swung from the gutters / Ten-day interval / I set my face to the hillside / The equator / A simple way to go faster than light that does not work / The suspension bridge at Iguazu Falls / Four-day interval / In Sarah, Mencken, Christ, and Beethoven there were women and men / Almost always is nearly enough / Jetty / Everglade.

Jul 98. (ltd-12"; TORTOISE VS. DERRICK CARTER) *(087096)* **IN SARAH, MENCKEN, CHRIST, AND BEETHOVEN THERE WERE WOMEN AND MEN** ☐ [-]
– (D's winter crazy mix) / (D's winter outtake).
(above issued on 'Rephlex') (below on 'Fishtank/Konkurrent')

May 99. (m-cd/m-lp; by TORTOISE & THE EX) *(FISH 5 CD/LP)* **IN THE FISHTANK** ☐ ☐
– Lawn of the limb / Pooh song / Central heating / Pleasure as usual / Did you comb / Huge hidden spaces. *(re-iss. Sep05; same)*

Warp — Thrill Jockey

Feb 01. (cd/lp) *(WARP CD/LP 081)* <*THRILL 089*> **STANDARDS** ☐ ☐
– Seneca / Eros / Benway / Firefly / Six pack / Eden 2 / Monica / Blackjack / Eden 1 / Speakeasy.

Thrill Jockey — Thrill Jockey

Jul 04. (cd) <*(THRILL 115)*> **IT'S ALL AROUND YOU** ☐ Apr04 ☐
– It's all around you / The lithium shifts / Crest / Stretch (you are all right) / Unknown / Dot – Eyes / On the chin / By dawn / Five too many / Salt the skies.

— early in '06, they released, 'THE BRAVE AND THE BOLD' with BONNIE "PRINCE" BILLY (aka WILL OLDHAM)

– compilations, others, etc. –

May 97. (cd) *Thrill Jockey;* <*(TKCB 70932)*> **A DIGEST COMPENDIUM OF TORTOISE'S WORLD** ☐ 1996 ☐
– Tin cans & twine / Alcohall / Night air / Gooseneck / Onions wrapped in rubber / Spiderwebbed / Cobnebbed / Your new rod / Ry Cooder (the beer incident) / Not quite east of the Ryan / Reservoir / Cornpone brunch / Whitewater / Initial gesture protraction.

Apr 98. (cd) *Thrill Jockey;* <*(TKCB 71016)*> **TORTOISE REMIXED** (all the 4 collaboration/Vs singles) ☐ 1996 ☐

Oct 01. (m-cd) *Thrill Jockey;* <*(THRILL 122-2)*> **GENTLY CUPPING THE CHIN OF THE APE** ☐ ☐
– Waihopai / Peering / Seneca (video) / Tortoise 98 (video) / Rehearsal 2001 (video).

JOHN McENTIRE

— his debut solo album (although shared with others)

Hefty — Hefty

Feb 99. (7"pic-d) <*(HEF 13)*> **split w/ SEA AND CAKE** ☐ ☐

Mar 99. (cd) <*(HEFT 14CD)*> **REACH THE ROCK** (soundtrack w/ Various Artists) ☐ ☐
– In a thimble (TORTOISE) / Criminal record / Overview / Stolen car / Drift (BUNDY K. BROWN) / Quinn goes to town / Window lights (SEA AND CAKE) / Reverse migraine (POLVO) / Lise arrives / The kiss / Main title / Dreams of being king (DIANOGAH). *(lp-iss.Nov99; HEFT 014LP)*

☐ the TOURISTS (see under ⇒ EURYTHMICS)

☐ Pete TOWNSHEND (see under ⇒ the WHO)

TRAFFIC

Formed: based Midlands, England . . . April '67, by STEVE WINWOOD, DAVE MASON, JIM CAPALDI and CHRIS WOOD. Initially, TRAFFIC purveyed musically accomplished, thinking man's psychedelia, debuting with the yearning 'PAPER SUN' (1967) single after signing to 'Island'. Utilising MASON's lilting, sitar-like guitar playing, the record perfectly anticipated the mood of the times and duly hit the Top 5. Dippy but delightful, the follow-up, 'HOLE IN MY SHOE' (1967) (later covered with great affection by NIGEL PLANER aka 'NEIL' of 'Young Ones' comedy fame) hit No.2 and after their third Top 10 hit in a row, 'HERE WE GO ROUND THE MULBERRY BUSH' (from the film of the same name), the band released their debut album, 'MR FANTASY' (1967). The record was a well crafted melting pot of ideas and genres put through the psychedelic blender and given a soulful reading by WINWOOD's wholesome vocal chords. The conspicuous absence of any of the previous hit singles, however, signalled that, as was the wont of group in those serious muso days, TRAFFIC wished to be considered an 'Albums' band. Around this time, MASON split, only to return another six months later whence the band fashioned their second album, 'TRAFFIC' (1968), a marked progression that highlighted the band's instrumental dexterity and flowering songwriting talent. Once again, MASON came up with one of the record's most memorable tunes, 'FEELIN' ALRIGHT', later covered by JOE COCKER amongst others. The ever dependable MASON upped sticks and left once more during the recording of TRAFFIC's third album, 'LAST EXIT' (1969). Aptly titled, this careless rag-bag of below par live and studio tracks did indeed mark the end of MASON's time with the band (save for a brief spell of live work in the early 70's), in fact the end of the band itself, for the time being at least. After a spell in short-lived 'supergroup', BLIND FAITH, WINWOOD went in to the studio to commence the recording of a mooted solo album with a working title of 'MAD SHADOWS'. When WOOD and CAPALDI were drafted in for work on the sessions, the project became a fully fledged TRAFFIC concern. The resulting album, re-titled 'JOHN BARLEYCORN MUST DIE' (1970) was a triumphant return to form, mixing up folk, R&B and jazz into a prog-rock classic. In the year or so before their next album, the band recruited bassist RICK GRECH (ex-FAMILY/BLIND FAITH), African percussionist REEBOP KWAKU-BAAH, drummer JIM GORDON (ex-DEREK AND THE DOMINOES) and their old mucker DAVE MASON. 'WELCOME TO THE CANTEEN' (1971) was fairly heavy going but no less self-indulgent than your average early 70's live effort, while the next studio outing, 'THE LOW SPARK OF HIGH HEELED BOYS' (1971) saw the band add to their not inconsiderable studio accomplishments despite the cringe-inducing title. DAVID HOOD and ROGER HAWKINS (both of whom had played on CAPALDI's solo project, 'OH HOW WE DANCED') replaced GRECH and GORDON for 1973's 'SHOOT OUT AT THE FANTASY FACTORY'. The 'Muscle Shoals' veterans had tightened up the rhythm section considerably, cutting it on stage and in the studio, as evidenced by the best live album of TRAFFIC's career, 'ON THE ROAD' (1973). By 1974's 'WHEN THE EAGLE FLIES', TRAFFIC were beginning to sound congested, finally stalling the following year. CAPALDI and WINWOOD both went on to successful solo careers, resurrecting TRAFFIC briefly in 1994. WINWOOD's output, in particular was undeniable coffee table rock at its shiniest, though surprisingly, he was given top billing at the 1997 Glastonbury festival. In the event he didn't show, apparently due to illness, his place taken by KULA SHAKER. Another TRAFFIC reunion – trying to catch up with the WHO, no doubt! – saw WINWOOD, CAPALDI together with newcomers RANDALL BRAMLETT, MIKE McEVOY and WALFREDO REYES get together for a series of live shows, historically documented on the now familiar CD/DVD-package, 'THE LAST GREAT TRAFFIC JAM' (2005).

• **Songwriters:** Individually or group compositions, except GIMME SOME LOVIN' (Spencer Davis Group). CAPALDI covered LOVE HURTS (Everly Brothers).

Album rating: MR. FANTASY (*8) / TRAFFIC (*9) / LAST EXIT (*5) / THE BEST OF TRAFFIC compilation (*8) / JOHN BARLEYCORN MUST DIE (*7) / WELCOME TO THE CANTEEN (*5) / THE LOW SPARK OF THE HIGH HELED BOYS (*7) / SHOOT OUT AT THE FANTASY FACTORY (*6) / ON THE ROAD (*5) / WHEN THE EAGLE FLIES (*5) / HEAVY TRAFFIC compilation (*7) / MORE HEAVY TRAFFIC compilation (*5) / SMILING PHASES compilation (*9) / FAR FROM HOME (*5) / THE LAST GREAT TRAFFIC JAM compilation (*6)

STEVE WINWOOD (b.12 May'48, Birmingham, England) – vocals, keyboards (ex-SPENCER DAVIS GROUP) / **DAVE MASON** (b.10 May'47, Worcester, England) – guitar, vocals (ex-HELLIONS) / **JIM CAPALDI** (b.24 Aug'44, Evesham, England) – drums, vocals (ex-HELLIONS) / **CHRIS WOOD** (b.24 Jun'44, Birmingham) – flute, sax (ex-SOUNDS OF BLUE)

Island U.A.

May 67. (7") *(WIP 6002)* *<50195>* **PAPER SUN. / GIVING TO YOU** 5 Aug67 94

Aug 67. (7") *(WIP 6017)* *<50218>* **HOLE IN MY SHOE. / SMILING PHASES** 2

Nov 67. (7") *(WIP 6025)* *<50232>* **HERE WE GO ROUND THE MULBERRY BUSH. / COLOURED RAIN** 8

Dec 67. (lp; mono/stereo) *(ILP/+S 9061)* *<6651>* **MR. FANTASY** 8 Apr68 88
– Heaven is in your mind / Berkshire poppies / House for everyone / No name, no face, no number / Dear Mr. Fantasy / Dealer / Utterly simple / Coloured rain / Hope I never find me there / Giving to you. *<US version +=)* – Paper sun / Hole in my shoe. *(re-iss. 1970; same) (re-iss. Feb87 lp/c; ILPM/ICM 9061) (cd-iss. Nov87; CID 9061) (cd re-iss. Sep89; IMCD 43) <US version-iss.Aug92; 3DCID 1003> (cd re-mast.Oct99 +=; IMCD 264)<546496>* – Paper sun / Dealer / Coloured rain / Hole in my shoe / No face, no name, no number / Heaven is in your mind / House for everyone / Berkshire poppies / Giving to you / Smiling phases / Dear Mr. Fantasy / We're a fade, you missed this.

Feb 68. (7") *(WIP 6030)* **NO NAME, NO FACE, NO NUMBER. / ROAMIN' IN THE GLOAMIN' WITH 40,000 HEADMEN** 40 –

Feb 68. (7") *<50261>* **NO NAME, NO FACE, NO NUMBER. / HEAVEN IS IN YOUR MIND** –

Sep 68. (7") *(WIP 6041)* *<50460>* **FEELIN' ALRIGHT. / WITHERING TREE**

Oct 68. (lp; mono/stereo) *(ILPS 9081/+T)* *<6676>* **TRAFFIC** 9 17
– You can all join in / Pearly queen / Don't be sad / Who knows what tomorrow may bring / Feelin' alright / Vagabond virgin / Forty thousand headmen / Cryin' to be heard / No time to live / Means to an end. *(re-iss. Feb87 lp/c; ILPM/ICM 9081) (cd-iss. Nov87; CID 9081) (cd re-iss. Sep89; IMCD 45) (<cd re-mast.Oct99 +=; IMCD 265>)* – Here we go 'round the mulburry bush / Am I what I was or am I what I am / Withering tree / Medicated goo / Shanghai noodle factory.

Dec 68. (7") *(WIP 6050)* **MEDICATED GOO. / SHANGHAI NOODLE FACTORY** –

Jan 69. (7") *<50500>* **MEDICATED GOO. / PEARLY QUEEN** –

— Below album was recorded before their split late 1968.

May 69. (lp; mono/stereo) *(ILP/+S 9097)* *<6702>* **LAST EXIT (some live)** 19
– Just for you / Shanghai noodle factory / Something's got a hold of my toe / Withering tree / Medicated goo / Feelin' good / Blind man. *(cd-iss. May88; CID 9097) (cd re-iss. Sep89; IMCD 41)*

Oct 69. (lp; mono/stereo) *(ILP/+S 9112)* *<5500>* **THE BEST OF TRAFFIC** (compilation) 48
– Paper Sun / Heaven is in your mind / No face, no name, no number / Coloured rain / Smiling phases / Hole in my shoe / Medicated goo / Forty thousand headmen / Feelin' alright / Shanghai noodle factory / Dear Mr. Fantasy. *(cd-iss. Mar93; IMCD 169)*

— In 1969, WINWOOD formed BLIND FAITH with ERIC CLAPTON and GINGER BAKER. WOOD also joined the latter's group AIRFORCE. WOOD, MASON and CAPALDI then formed WOODEN FROG. DAVE MASON went solo as TRAFFIC re-formed as a trio.

Jul 70. (lp) *(ILPS 9116)* *<5504>* **JOHN BARLEYCORN MUST DIE** 5 11
– Glad / Freedom rider / Empty pages / Stranger to himself / John Barleycorn / Every mother's son. *(re-iss. Sep86 lp/c/cd; ILPM/ICM/CID 9116) (cd-iss. Sep89; IMCD 40) (cd re-mast.Oct99 +=; IMCD 266)<548541>* – I just want you to know / Sittin' here thinkin' of my love / Backstage and introduction / Who knows what tomorrow may bring (live) / Glad (live).

Aug 70. (7") *<50692>* **EMPTY PAGES. / STRANGER TO HIMSELF** – 74

— added **RIC GRECH** (b. 1 Nov'46) – bass (ex-FAMILY, ex-BLIND FAITH, ex-GINGER BAKER'S AIRFORCE) / **REEBOP KWAKU-BAAH** (b. Konongo, Ghana) – percussion (ex-GINGER BAKER'S AIRFORCE) / **JIM GORDON** – drums (ex-DEREK & THE DOMINOES) / **DAVE MASON** guested on some live.

Sep 71. (lp) *(ILPS 9166)* *<5550>* **WELCOME TO THE CANTEEN (live)** 26
– Medicated goo / Sad and deep as you / 40,000 headmen / Shouldn't have took more than you gave / Dear Mr. Fantasy / Gimme some lovin'. *(cd-iss. May88; CID 9166) (cd re-iss. Sep89; IMCD 39) (<cd re-mast.Apr02 +=; 586847-2>)* – (extended tracks).

Oct 71. (7") *<50841>* **GIMME SOME LOVIN'. / (part 2)** – 68

Island Island

Dec 71. (lp/c) *(ILPS/ZCI 9180)* *<9306>* **THE LOW SPARK OF THE HIGH HEELED BOYS** 7
– Hidden treasure / The low spark of the high heeled boys / Light up or leave me alone / Rock & roll stew / Many a mile to freedom / Rainmaker. *(re-iss. Sep86 lp/c; ILPM/ICM 9180) (cd-iss. Nov87; CID 9180) (cd re-iss. Sep89; IMCD 42) (<cd re-mast.Apr02 +=; 548827-2>)* – Rock & roll stew (parts 1 & 2).

Jan 72. (7") *<1201>* **ROCK & ROLL STEW. / (part 2)** – 93

— **DAVID HOOD** – bass + ROGER HAWKINS – drums (both of JIM CAPALDI band) repl. JIM GORDON and GRECH. (The latter formed KGB)

Feb 73. (lp/c) *(ILPS/ZCI 9224)* *<9323>* **SHOOT OUT AT THE FANTASY FACTORY** 6
– Shoot out at the fantasy factory / Roll right stone / Evening blue / Tragic magic / (Sometimes I feel so) Uninspired. *(cd-iss. May88; CID 9224) (cd re-iss. Sep89; IMCD 44) (<cd re-mast.Jun03; ISL 842781>)*

— added **BARRY BECKETT** – keyboards

Oct 73. (d-lp)(d-c) *(ILSD 2)(ZCID 102)* *<9336>* **ON THE ROAD (live)** 40 29
– Glad – Freedom rider / Tragic magic / (Sometimes I feel so) Uninspired / Shoot out at the fantasy factory / Light up or leave me alone / The low spark of the high heeled boys. *(cd-iss. Jun88; CIDD 2) (cd re-iss. Aug91 & Apr94; IMCD 183) (<cd re-mast.Jun03; ISL 63434>)*

Dec 73. (7") *<50883>* **GLAD. / (part 2)** –

— **WINWOOD, CAPALDI & WOOD** enlisted **ROSKO GEE** – bass (ex-GONZALES)

Island Asylum

Sep 74. (lp/c) *(ILPS/ZCI 9273)* *<7E 1020>* **WHEN THE EAGLE FLIES** 31 9
– Something new / Dream Gerrard / Graveyard people / Walking in the wind / Memories of a rock and rolla / Love / When the eagle flies. *(cd-iss. Jun88; CID 9273) (re-iss. Aug91 cd)(c; IMCD 142)(ICM 9273) (<cd re-mast.Jun03; ISL 548826>)*

Oct 74. (7") *(WIP 6207)* **WALKING IN THE WIND. / WALKING IN THE WIND (instrumental)**

— Disbanded early 1975. STEVE WINWOOD went solo, also collaborating with STOMU YAMASHTA. WOOD and GEE took up session work. On 12 Jul'83, CHRIS WOOD died of liver failure. JIM CAPALDI continued his solo career

TRAFFIC

— **WINWOOD + CAPALDI** re-formed for the studio

Virgin Virgin

May 94. (cd/c) *(CD/TC V 2727) <39490>* **FAR FROM HOME** 29
– Riding high / Here comes a man / Far from home / Nowhere is their freedom / Holy ground / Some kinda woman / Every night, every day / This train won't stop / State of grace / Mosambique. *(cd re-iss. Nov02 on 'Disky'; VI 905179)*

May 94. (7"/c-s) *(VS/+C 1494)* **HERE COMES A MAN. / GLAD (live)** -
(cd-s+=) *(VSCDG 1494)* – ('A'mix).

Sep 94. (c-s) *(VSC 1506)* **SOME KINDA WOMAN. / FORTY THOUSAND HEADMEN (live)** -
(cd-s+=) *(VSCDX 1506)* – Low spark of high heeled boys (live)/ ('A'mix).

– compilations, etc. –

— on 'Island' unless stated otherwise

May 74. (7") **HOLE IN MY SHOE. / HERE WE GO ROUND THE MULBERRY BUSH** -

May 75. (lp) *United Artists; <4211>* **HEAVY TRAFFIC** -

Sep 75. (lp) *United Artists; <LA 526>* **MORE HEAVY TRAFFIC** -

Mar 78. (7"ep,7"pic-d-ep) *(IEP 7)* **EXTENDED PLAY** -
– I'm a man / Hole in my shoe / Gimme some lovin' / No name, no face, no number.

Jun 92. (d-cd) *(IMCCD 158)* **SMILING PHASES** -
– Paper sun / Hole in my shoe / Smiling phases / Heaven is in your mind / Coloured rain / No face, no name, no number / Here we go round the mulbury bush / Dear Mr. Fantasy / You can all join in / Feelin' alright / Pearly queen / Forty thousand headmen / Vagabond virgin / Shanghai noodle factory / Withering tree / Medicated goo / Glad / Freedom rider / Empty pages / John Barleycorn / The low spark of the high heeled boys / Light up or leave me alone / Rock & roll stew / Shoot out at the fantasy factory / Walking in the wind / When the eagle flies.

Nov 98. (cd) *(IMCD 257)* **HEAVEN IS IN YOUR MIND: AN INTRODUCTION TO TRAFFIC**

Feb 00. (cd) *What's Up; (PLG 54227-2)* **FEELIN' ALRIGHT: THE VERY BEST OF TRAFFIC** -

Jun 01. (cd) *Spectrum; (544558-2)* **THE BEST OF TRAFFIC** -

Nov 05. (cd w/dvd) *Epic; (82876 73459-2) <97688>* **THE LAST GREAT TRAFFIC JAM**
– Pearly queen / Medicated goo / Mozambique / 40,000 headmen / Glad / Light up or leave me alone / Walking in the wind / The low spark of high heeled boys / John Barleycorn (must die) / Dear Mr. Fantasy / Gimme some lovin'. *(DVD equivalents).*

TRAIN

Formed: San Francisco, California, USA . . . 1994 by PATRICK MONAHAN and ex-APOSTLES frontman ROB HOTCHKISS. The two became friends after a chance meeting and the soon began playing acoustic-driven pop in the local coffee houses of the city's Bay Area. The pair decided to invite other APOSTLE casualties, JIMMY STAFFORD, CHARLIE COLIN and percussionist SCOTT UNDERWOOD to form what would ultimately become TRAIN. After self-financing their debut recording, the eponymous 'TRAIN' in 1996, 'Columbia' records (through offshoot imprint 'Aware') took them on board, giving the record a whole new lease of life when (re-)issuing it early '98. Guitar driven ballads such as 'FREE' and 'I AM' began to receive heavy rotation on college radio, while 'MEET VIRGINIA' finally dented the US Top 20 a year later. Like the COUNTING CROWS before them, TRAIN dealt in soft, tingling American sentimentality that became overtly hyberbolated come the release of their sophomore set 'DROPS OF JUPITER' (2001). Paul Buckmaster, who was the main driving force on ELTON JOHN's recent classical/string arrangements, finely-tuned the more heart-felt tracks, whereas pop guitar songs such as 'GET AWAY' and 'HOPELESS' became a tad mundane after two or three listenings. The aforementioned album slowly climbed into the US and British Top 10, while its classy radio-friendly title track did the same. The new kings of MOR roots rock were back in 2003 with the Brendan O'Brien-produced 'MY PRIVATE NATION', another solid US Top 10 album which rarely veered from their tried and tested sound and earnest lyrical themes. The record's more interesting moments came courtesy of O'Brien, who co-wrote a handful of tracks. 'ALIVE AT LAST' (2004), transcended its rock history-referencing title for a concert set distinguished by disarmingly vibrant sound quality and a warts'n'all corps d'esprit. Love 'em or hate 'em, they could at least belt through a cover of the Faces' 'STAY WITH ME' as if their last beer depended on it. MONAHAN doesn't have the sandpaper-soul talent of a ROD STEWART but he and his roots acolytes stormed the US Top 10 once again with the dependably fashion-defying 'FOR ME, IT'S YOU' (2006), another Brendan O'Brien-tutored opus introducing ex-BLACK CROWES man JOHNNY COLT. In amongst the worthy originals was a cover of Sugar's 'IF I CAN'T CHANGE YOUR MIND', one which it's difficult to imagine their legions of fans being familiar with.

• **Covers:** RAMBLE ON (Led Zeppelin).

Album rating: TRAIN (*6) / DROPS OF JUPITER (*7) / MY PRIVATE NATION (*4) / ALIVE AT LAST (*5) / FOR ME, IT'S YOU (*5)

PATRICK MONAHAN – vocals / **ROB HOTCHKISS** – guitar / **JIMMY STAFFORD** – guitar / **CHARLIE COLIN** – bass / **SCOTT UNDERWOOD** – drums

Columbia Columbia

Feb 98. (cd) *<38052>* **TRAIN** -
– Meet Virginia / I am / If you leave / Homesick / Free / Blind / Eggplant / Idaho / Days / Rat / Swaying / Train / Heavy. *<re-dist.Jun99; same>* – hit No.76 *(UK-iss.Feb02; 496289-2)*

1999. (cd-ep) **LIVE FROM FANTASY STUDIOS** (live) -
– Eggplant / I am / Train / If you leave.

1999. (cd-ep) **ONE AND A HALF ep** -
– Counting on you / Hopeless / Ramble on (acoustic) / Sweet rain / The highway / Meet Virginia (acoustic).

Sep 99. (cd-s; promo) *<41775>* **MEET VIRGINIA / (+4 mixes)** - 20

Dec 99. (cd-s; promo) *<42830>* **I AM / (+ 2 mixes)** -

Jul 01. (c-s) *(671447-4) <radio>* **DROPS OF JUPITER (TELL ME) / THIS IS NOT YOUR LIFE** 10 Mar01 5
(cd-s) *(671447-2)* – ('A'side) / It's love / ('A'-CD-Rom).

Aug 01. (cd) *(5023069) <69888>* **DROPS OF JUPITER** 8 Apr01 6
– She's on fire / I wish you would / Drops of Jupiter (tell me) / It's about you / Hopeless / Respect / Let it roll / Something more / Whipping boy / Getaway / Mississippi.

Nov 01. (c-s) *(672041-4)* **SOMETHING MORE / I WISH YOU WOULD (live)** -
(cd-s+=) *(672041-2)* – Eggplant (live) / Free (live).

Feb 02. (c-s) *(672281-4)* **SHE'S ON FIRE / DROPS OF JUPITER (TELL ME) (live)** 49
(cd-s+=) *(672281-2)* – Meet Virginia (live) / ('A'-video).

Jun 03. (cd) *(511222-9) <86593>* **MY PRIVATE NATION** 6
– Calling all angels / All American girl / When I look to the sky / Save the day / My private nation / Get to me / Counting airplanes / Following Rita / Your every colour / Lincoln Avenue / I'm about to come alive.

Jul 03. (cd-s) *(674028-2) <radio>* **CALLING ALL ANGELS / DROPS OF JUPITER (live) / CALLING ALL ANGELS (vide)** 19

not iss. Columbia

Oct 04. (cd) *<92830>* **ALIVE AT LAST** (live) - 48
– Calling all angels / She's on fire / Meet Virginia / Save the day / Get to me / Landmine / All American girl / When I look to the sky / Latin interlude / I wish you would / Sweet rain / Free / Drops of Jupiter / Stay with me / Ordinary / New sensation.

— (earlier 2004) **BRANDON BUSH** – keyboards; repl. HOTCHKISS

— (earlier 2004) **JOHNNY COLT** – bass; repl. COLIN

Jan 06. (cd) *<94472>* **FOR ME, IT'S YOU** - 10
– All I ever wanted / Get out / Cab / Give myself to you / Am I reaching you now / If I can't change your mind / All I hear / Shelter me / Explanation / Always remember / I'm not waiting in line / Skyscraper / For me, it's you.

TRAVIS

Formed: Glasgow, Scotland . . . 1991 as GLASS ONION by ANDY DUNLOP and NEIL PRIMROSE, who'd both been members of RUNNING RED. Songwriting singer FRAN HEALY (English-born, Glasgow-raised) was invited to join the fresh-faced guitar-pop quintet (with the MARTYN brothers), replacing the original female vocalist soon after. In 1993, FRAN's mother advanced the lads some cash to cut a demo and this led to a publishing contract with 'Sony'. Winning a trip to the New Music Seminar in New York via first place in a talent contest might've given them an early break had they attended, although they did manage to squeeze out an eponymous EP the same year. With the band going nowhere fast, changes had to be made and by March '96, the MARTYN brothers had made way for FRAN's Glasgow School Of Art chum, DOUGIE PAYNE (ANDY had also been a student); TRAVIS were now in circulation. Following a self-financed debut single, 'ALL I WANT TO DO IS ROCK', the quartet were taken under the wing of (ex-Go! Discs man) Andy McDonald's 'Independiente' (still through 'Sony') early in '97. Subsequently relocating to London, TRAVIS released their controversial follow-up single, 'U16 GIRLS', apparently a paeon to the charms of underage females. A re-vamp of their hard-to-find debut single followed it into the Top 40 and suddenly TRAVIS were one of the hippest new names on the block. Though HEALY was a charismatic frontman, the Top 10 debut album, 'GOOD FEELING', illustrated at the time the one-dimensional nature of much of their material. Nevertheless, the record did spawn two further Top 40 hits, 'TIED TO THE 90's' and 'HAPPY', indicating that there was at least some potential for the future. After a relatively quiet '98 – although 'MORE THAN US' became their biggest hit to date at No.16 – TRAVIS were back the following March. Taking a softer, laid back approach (70's BREAD come to mind!), the quartet achieved a deserved second Top 20 spot with the beautiful ballad 'WRITING TO REACH YOU'. Further successes came in the shape of 'DRIFTWOOD', 'WHY DOES IT ALWAYS RAIN ON ME?' and 'TURN', all songwriting masterpieces from the critically acclaimed No.1 follow-up set, 'THE MAN WHO' (1999). TRAVIS were fast becoming the United Kingdom's No.1 band and by the start of the year 2000 they were given that accolade by winning the now prestigious Brit award. OASIS (who had been tops until recently!) invited nice guy HEALY and Co to support them on a US tour, the American audiences eventually being won over by their sheer honest enthusiasm and talent. While many critics predictably put the boot in, you could bet your bottom dollar they had a secret copy of UK chart-topper 'THE INVISIBLE BAND' (2001) hidden away for furtive listening pleasure. TRAVIS simply write great songs, occasionally something more but rarely anything less. On first listen, the deceptively simple single, 'SING' may sound trite, but its subtle, banjo inflected power deepens with every spin, enveloping you in a dizzying aura of elemental truth. Similarly the lyrics of 'SIDE' were the butt of cheap jibes yet their sentiment leaks into the consciousness like a zen koan. The band's lack of image and endearing avoidance of any flirtations with the vagaries of musical fashion merely accentuates the strength of the material. While there was nothing on the album that matched the searing melancholy of say, 'WRITING TO REACH YOU', chances are you'll still be playing this album next year, and the next, and the next . . . However, disaster struck the band on the 9th of July 2002, when drummer PRIMROSE accidently hit his upper torso on the bottom of a swimming pool in France. He underwent extensive surgery to his neck, accumulating in the cancellation of the group's entire European tour (as well as V2002). All was said to be well, with PRIMROSE making a slow but steady recovery as the band entered the studio to record their fourth album, the darker and more agitated '12 MEMORIES' in 2003. Probably hoping to match COLDPLAY's emotional, piano-driven songwriting, TRAVIS seemed to be slowly running out of steam, with HEALY's ballady content becoming more and more moot. However, for fans of TRAVIS their was much to admire here: the attack on American ignorance entitled 'THE BEAUTIFUL OCCUPATION' and the spunky UK hit 'RE-OFFENDER' were two that stood out. 'SINGLES' (2004) was just what it said on the proverbial tin, all of their hits plus a new one, 'WALKING IN THE SUN'.

• **Covered:** BE MY BABY (Ronettes) / BABY ONE MORE TIME (Britney Spears) / ALL THE YOUNG DUDES (Mott The Hoople) / HERE COMES THE SUN (Beatles).

Album rating: GOOD FEELING (*7) / THE MAN WHO (*8) / THE INVISIBLE BAND (*7) / 12 MEMORIES (*6) / SINGLES compilation (*7)

GLASS ONION

FRAN HEALY (b. FRANCIS, 23 Jul'73, Stafford, England) – vocals, guitar; repl. female / **ANDY DUNLOP** (b.16 Mar'72, Lenzie, Scotland) – guitar / **NEIL PRIMROSE** (b.20 Feb'72, Cumbernauld, Scotland) – drums / **. . . MARTYN** – bass / **. . . MARTYN** – keyboards

own label | not iss.

Nov 93. (cd-ep) *(GLASSCD 001)* **GLASS ONION** [ ] [ ]
– Dream on / The day before / Free soul / Whenever she comes around.

TRAVIS

— **DOUGIE PAYNE** (b.14 Nov'72) – bass; repl. the MARTYN brothers

Red Telephone | not iss.

Oct 96. (10"ep) *(PHONE 001)* **ALL I WANT TO DO IS ROCK. / THE LINE IS FINE / FUNNY THING** [ ] [–]

Independiente | Independiente

Mar 97. (7"pic-d/c-s) *(ISOM 1 S/CS)* **U16 GIRLS. / HAZY SHADES OF GOLD / GOOD TIME GIRLS** [40] [–]
(c-s+=/cd-s+=) *(ISOM 1MS)* – Good feeling.

Jun 97. (7") *(SOM 3S) <6080>* **ALL I WANT TO DO IS ROCK. / BLUE ON A BLACK WEEKEND** [39] Apr98 [ ]
(cd-s+=) *(ISOM 3MS)* – Combing my hair.
(cd-s) *(ISOM 3SMS)* – ('A'side) / "20" / 1922.

Aug 97. (7"/cd-s) *(ISOM 5S/+MS) <6084>* **TIED TO THE 90's. / ME BESIDE YOU** [30] Apr98 [ ]
(cd-s) *(ISOM 5MS)* – ('A') / City in the rain / Whenever she comes around / Standing on my own.

Sep 97. (cd/c/lp) *(ISOM 1 CD/MC/LP) <68239>* **GOOD FEELING** [9] Oct97 [ ]
– All I want to do is rock / U16 girls / Line is fine / Good day to die / Good feeling / Midsummer nights dreamin' / Tied to the 90's / I love you anyways / Happy / More than us / Falling down / Funny thing. *(re-iss. Nov99; same) (re-dist.Jun01)* – hit No.19

Oct 97. (c-s) *(ISOM 6CS) <6081>* **HAPPY / UNBELIEVERS** [38] Apr98 [ ]
(cd-s+=) *(ISOM 6MS)* – Everyday faces.
(cd-s) *(ISOM 6SMS)* – ('A') / When I'm feeling blue (days of the week) / Mother.

Mar 98. (7"ep/c-ep/cd-ep) *(ISOM 11 S/CS/MS)* **MORE THAN US E.P.** [16] [–]
– More than us (with Anne Dudley) / Give me some truth / All I want to do is rock (with Noel Gallagher) / Funny thing (mixed by Tim Simenon).
(cd-s) *(ISOM 11SMS)* – (lead track) / Beautiful bird (demo version) / Reason (with Susie Hug) / More than us (acoustic version).

Mar 99. (7"/c-s) *(ISOM 22 S/CS)* **WRITING TO REACH YOU. / ONLY MOLLY KNOWS** [14] [–]
(cd-s+=) *(ISOM 22MS)* – Green behind the ears.
(cd-s) *(ISOM 22SM)* – ('A') / Yeah yeah yeah yeah / High as a kite.

May 99. (c-s) *(ISOM 27CS)* **DRIFTWOOD / WRITING TO REACH YOU (Deadly Avenger remix)** [13] [–]
(cd-s+=) *(ISOM 27SMS)* – Writing to reach you (Deadly Avenger instrumental remix).
(cd-s) *(ISOM 27MS)* – ('A') / Be my baby / Where is the love.

May 99. (cd/c/lp) *(ISOM 9 CD/MC/LP) <62151>* **THE MAN WHO** [1] Apr00 [ ]
– Writing to reach you / The fear / As you are / Driftwood / The last laugh of the laughter / Turn / Why does it always rain on me? / Luv / She's so strange / Slide show. *(lp w/free 12"; ISOM 27T)* – WRITING TO REACH YOU (Deadly Avenger mixes). *(ltd-cd+=; ISOM 9CDX)* – Blue flashing light / Writing to reach you / Driftwood. *(cd re-iss. Aug02; same)*

Aug 99. (c-s) *(ISOM 33CS)* **WHY DOES IT ALWAYS RAIN ON ME? / VILLAGE MAN** [10] [–]
(cd-s+=) *(ISOM 33MS)* – Driftwood (live).
(cd-s) *(ISOM 33SMS)* – ('A') / The urge for going / Slide show (live).

Nov 99. (c-s) *(ISOM 39CS)* **TURN / DAYS OF OUR LIVES** [8] [–]
(cd-s+=) *(ISOM 39MS)* – River.
(cd-s) *(ISOM 39SMS)* – ('A') / We are monkeys / Baby one more time.

Jun 00. (7"/c-s) *(ISOM 45 S/CS)* **COMING AROUND. / CONNECTION** [5] [ ]
(cd-s+=) *(ISOM 45MC)* – Just the faces change.
(cd-s) *(ISOM 45SMS)* – ('A') / Rock'n'(salad) roll / The weight.

May 01. (7"/c-s) *(ISOM 49 S/CS)* **SING. / KILLER QUEEN** [3] [–]
(cd-s+=) *(ISOM 49MS)* – Ring out the bell.
(cd-s) *(ISOM 49SMAS)* – ('A') / You don't know what I'm like / Beautiful.

Jun 01. (cd/c/lp) *(ISOM 25 CD/MC/LP)* <85788> **THE INVISIBLE BAND** [1] [39]
– Sing / Dear diary / Side / Pipe dreams / Flowers in the window / The cage / Safe / Follow the light / Last train / Afterglow / Indefinitely / The Humpty Dumpty love song.

Sep 01. (7"/c-s) *(ISOM 54 S/CS)* **SIDE. / ALL THE YOUNG DUDES (live)** [14] [–]
(cd-s) *(ISOM 54MS)* – ('A') / Driftwood (live).
(cd-s) *(ISOM 54SMS)* – ('A') / You're a big girl now / Ancient train.

Mar 02. (c-s) *(ISOM 56CS)* **FLOWERS IN THE WINDOW / A LITTLE BIT OF SOUL** [18] [–]
(cd-s+=) *(ISOM 56MS)* – Here comes the sun.
(cd-s) *(ISOM 56SMS)* – ('A') / Central station / No cigar.
(7") *(ISOM 56S)* – ('A') / Here comes the sun.

Sep 03. (7") *(ISOM 78S)* **RE-OFFENDER. / DEFINITION OF WRONG** [7] [–]
(cd-s+=) *(ISOM 78SMS)* – Enemy.
(cd-s) *(ISOM 78MS)* – ('A') / The sea / Don't be shy.

Oct 03. (cd/c/lp) *(ISOM 40 CD/MC/LP)* <90672> **12 MEMORIES** [3] [41]
– Quicksand / The beautiful occupation / Re-offender / Peace the fuck out / How many hearts / Paperclips / Somewhere else / Love will come through / Mid-life Krysis / Happy to hang around / Walking down the hill. *(clean cd; ISOM 40CDX)*

Dec 03. (7") *(ISOM 81S)* **THE BEAUTIFUL OCCUPATION. / I DIDN'T MEAN TO GET HIGH** [48] [–]
(cd-s+=) *(ISOM 81MS)* – Score.
(cd-s) *(ISOM 81SMS)* – ('A') / Distraction / Back in the day.

Mar 04. (7") *(ISOM 84S)* **LOVE WILL COME THROUGH. / GOOD FOR NOTHING** [28] [–]
(cd-s+=) *(ISOM 84MS)* – Know nothing / ('A'-video).

Oct 04. (7") *(ISOM 88S)* **WALKING IN THE SUN. / BRING ME ROUND** [20] [–]
(cd-s) *(ISOM 88SMS)* – ('A') / I forget my name / Life and soul of the party / ('A'-video).

Nov 04. (cd) *(ISOM 46CD)* <93519> **SINGLES** (compilation) [4] [ ]
– Sing / Driftwood / Writing to reach you / Why does it always rain on me? / Re-offender / Walking in the sun / Tied to the 90's / Coming around / Flowers in the window / Love will come through / More than us / Side / U16 girls / Happy / All I want to do is rock / The beautiful occupations / Turn / The distance.

☐ T. REX (see under ⇒ BOLAN, Marc)

TRICKY

Born: ADRIAN THAWES, 27 Jan'68, Knowle West, Bristol, England. After a troubled youth growing up on one of Bristol's poorer housing estates, THAWES began spending less time lawbreaking and more time busying himself with the city's club culture, helping run sound systems and hanging out with The WILD BUNCH, a loose collective of musicians and DJ's that icluded MASSIVE ATTACK and famed producer NELLEE HOOPER. In between trips to court in OXFORD, where he was defending an assault charge, TRICKY KID (as he was nicknamed by his Bristolian cohorts) occasionally collaborated with MASSIVE ATTACK on their seminal 'BLUE LINES' album, contributing stoned raps on several tracks. He also contributed to MASSIVE's follow-up, 'PROTECTION', although his first solo effort was a 'Betty Blue'-sampling track entitled 'LOYALTY IS VALUABLE', engineered by future PORTISHEAD mainman GEOFF BARROWS and featured on the 1991 Sickle Cell charity album, 'HARD SELL', alongside the likes of MASSIVE ATTACK, SMITH & MIGHTY etc. Yet the track that brought him to the attention of a discerning public was the sublime claustrophobia of 'AFTERMATH'. Eventually released in early '94, the track had previously been recorded a couple of years earlier with TRICKY's musical partner, MARTINA, predating the trip-hop scene that TRICKY would later be lumped in with. Next came the jarring loops and nervous paranoia of 'PONDEROSA', another taster for the pioneering debut album, 'MAXINQUAYE' (1994), released later that summmer. A dense, brooding collection of slow motion beat-poetry from the darkside, the record was immediately hailed as a classic. Taking bastardised hip-hop beats as his raw material then suffocating them with layers of samples, disjointed rhythms, freak instrumental lines and obscure noises, TRICKY created music that was wired yet lethargic, with lyrics equally contradictory and ambiguous to match. Collaborating with TERRY HALL, NENEH CHERRY and ALISON MOYET amongst others, TRICKY released his 'NEARLY GOD' project in 1996. The album revisited the dark intensity of 'MAXINQUAYE' without quite the same effect, possibly a case of too many cooks (or too many spliffs) spoiling the broth. 'PRE-MILLENNIUM TENSION', released later the same year, was on a par with 'MAXINQUAYE' and if it didn't exactly break new ground, the album illustrated that TRICKY's wellspring of paranoid psychosis was far from running dry. Tracks like 'BAD THINGS', 'MAKES ME WANNA DIE' and 'MY EVIL IS STRONG' speak for themselves, and though it's a well worn cliche, it would appear that this man really does suffer for his art. Then again, maybe he shouldn't smoke so much. 1999 was a busy year for TRICKY, everything from making "real" gangster LP, 'PRODUCT OF THE ENVIRONMENT' (with Mad Frankie Fraser for one!) to delivering his final album for 'Island', 'JUXTAPOSE'. The latter – which was recorded with DJ MUGGS (of CYPRESS HILL) and GREASE – achieved the usual plaudits, its return to his experimental trip-hop roots gaining him a near UK Top 30 place. TRICKY was to fall out with his label 'Island' one year later. Comeback set, 'BLOWBACK', was finally unleashed by 'Epitaph' (once home to BAD RELIGION and their ilk) wasn't thought ready until summer 2001. A slightly disappointing set, the album displayed TRICKY's usual mix of hip-hop beats and chilled-out smoking rhymes. From the Red Hot Chili Peppers' 'GIRLS' to collaboration dabblings with HAWKMAN (a toaster from Jamaica), ED KOWALCZYK (of LIVE) and AMBERSUNSHOWER (an obscure new age diva), the album certainly had its moments. TRICKY had a commercial set back when his 2003 set, 'VULNERABLE', didn't chart.

• **Songwriters:** Self-penned & samples except; BLACK STEEL + THE MOMENT I FEARED (Public Enemy) / PONDEROSA (co-with HOWIE B) / HELL IS ROUND THE CORNER (same source that PORTISHEAD found 'Glory Box'?) / SINGING THE BLUES (Mary McReary) / POP MUZIK (M) / he also sampled a song by Billie Holiday on 'Carriage For Two'.

Album rating: MAXINQUAYE (*9) / NEARLY GOD (*7; as Nearly God) / PRE-MILLENNIUM TENSION (*7) / ANGELS WITH DIRTY FACES (*7) / JUXTAPOSE (*7) / BLOWBACK (*6) / A RUFF GUIDE compilation (*8) / VULNERABLE (*7)

TRICKY – vocals (ex-MASSIVE ATTACK) / with **MARTINE TOPLEY-BIRD** – vocals / and others

4th & Broad 4th & Broad

Jan 94. (7") *(BRW 288)* <590> **AFTERMATH. / ('A'-I could be looking for people mix)** [69] [ ]
(12"+=) *(12BRW 288)* – ('A'mix).
(cd-s++=) *(BRCD 288)* – ('A'mix).

Apr 94. (7") *(BRW 299) <595>* **PONDEROSA. / ('A'-Dobie's roll pt.1 mix)** [ ] Jul94 [ ]
(12"+=/cd-s+=) *(12BRW/BRCD 299)* – (3 'A'mixes; Ultragelic / Original / Dobie's roll pt.2).

Jan 95. (7"/c-s) *(BR W/CA 304)* **OVERCOME. / ABBA ON FAT TRACKS** [34] [–]
(12"+=/cd-s+=) *(12BRW/BRCD 304)* – ('A'-Zippy & Bungle mix).

— guests on below ALISON GOLDFRAPP + RAGGA – vocals / PETE BRIQUETTE – bass / MARK SAUNDERS – keyboards / FTV – guitar, drums / TONY WRAFTER – flute / JAMES STEVENSON – guitar

Feb 95. (cd/c/lp) *(BR CD/CA/LP 610) <524089>* **MAXINQUAYE** [3] Apr95 [ ]
– Overcome / Ponderosa / Black steel / Hell is round the corner / Pumpkin / Aftermath / Abbaon fat tracks / Brand new you're retro / Suffocated love / You don't / Strugglin' / Feed me.

Mar 95. (c-s) *(BRCA 320)* **BLACK STEEL. / ('A'-Been caught stealing mix)** [28] [–]
(12"+=/cd-s+=) *(12BRW/BRCD 320)* – ('A'live) / ('A'-In the draw mix).
(cd-s++=) *(BRCDX 320)* – ('A'edit).

Jul 95. (7"pic-d-ep/12"red-ep/cd-ep; as TRICKY VS. THE GRAVEDIGGAZ) *(BRW/12BRW/BRCD 326) <383>* **THE HELL E.P.** [12] [ ]
– Hell is round the corner (original) / ('A'-Hell and water mix) / Psychosis / Tonite is a special nite (chaos mass confusion mix).

Nov 95. (c-s) *(BRCA 330)* **PUMPKIN / MOODY BROODY BUDHIST CAMP / NEW KINGDOM** [26] [ ]
(cd-s+=) *(BRCD 330)* – Brand new you're retro (Alex Reece mix).
(12"colrd) *(12BRW 330)* – ('A'side) / (above track) / Slick 66.

NEARLY GOD

TRICKY with **TERRY HALL / MARTINE / BJORK / NENEH CHERRY / ALISON MOYET + CATH COFFEY**

Durban Poison — Island

Apr 96. (7") *(DP 003)* **POEMS / CHILDREN'S STORY** [28] [ ]
(12"+=/cd-s+=) *(DP X/CD 003)* – ('A'extended).

Apr 96. (cd/c/lp) *(DP CD/MC/LP 1001) <531064>* **NEARLY GOD** [11] [ ]
– Tattoo / Poems / Together now / Keep your mouth shut / I be the prophet / Make a chane / Black cofee / Bubbles / I sing for you / Yoga.
above was to have been under his DURBAN POISON project.

— Aug 96, TRICKY PRESENTS GRASS ROOTS 12"ep for 'Ultra'.

TRICKY

— with a plethora of musicians incl. **PATRICE CHEVALIER** – guitar / **JOHN TONKS** – drums / **PAT McMANUS** – piano, violin

4th & Broad — Island

Oct 96. (7"pic-d) *(BRW 340)* **CHRISTIANSANDS. / FLYNN** [36] [ ]
(12"+=/cd-s+=) *(12BRW/BRCD 340)* – Ghetto youth.

Nov 96. (cd/c/lp) *(BR CD/CA/LP 623) <524302>* **PRE-MILLENNIUM TENSION** [30] [ ]
– Vent / Christiansands / Tricky kid / Bad dreams / Makes me wanna die / Ghetto youth / Sex drive / Bad things / Lyrics of fury / My evil is strong / Piano. *(d-cd-iss. ; BRCDX 623)*

— late '96, featured on the hit single by GARBAGE; 'Milk'.

Dec 96. (cd-ep) *(BRCDX 341)* **TRICKY KID. / MAKES ME WANNA DIE (Tricky's extremix) / GRASS ROOTS** [28] [ ]
(12"ep+=) *(12BRW 341)* – Smoking Beagles (Sub Sub vs Tricky).
(cd-ep) *(BRCD 341)* – ('A'side) / Devils helper / Smoking Beagles (Sub Sub vs Tricky) / Suffocated love (live on 'Later with Jools').

Apr 97. (cd-s) *(BRCDX 348)* **MAKES ME WANNA DIE / MAKES ME WANNA DIE (The Weekend mix – remixed by The Stereo MC's) / PIANO (the Green sticky mix remixed by A Guy Called Gerald)** [29] [ ]
(12"clear+=) *(BRX 348)* – Here comes the aliens (AFRIKA IZLAM & TRICKY).
(cd-s) *(BRCD 348)* – ('A'side) / ('A'acoustic) / Here come the aliens (AFRIKA IZLAM & TRICKY).

Island — Island

May 98. (7"; TRICKY featuring POLLY JEAN HARVEY) *(IS 701)* **BROKEN HOMES. / MONEY GREEDY** [25] [–]
(cd-s+=) *(CID 701)* – Anti histamine / Taxi.
(cd-s+=) *(CIDX 701)* – 360 degrees.

May 98. (cd/c/d-lp) *(CID/ICT/ILPS 8071) <524520>* **ANGELS WITH DIRTY FACES** [23] Jun98 [84]
– Money greedy / Mellow / Singing the blues / Broken homes / 6 minutes / Analyze me / The moment I feared / Talk to me (angels with dirty faces) / Carriage for two / Demise / Tear out my eyes / Record companies / Peyote sings / Taxi.

Dec 98. (cd-s) *<572515>* **6 MINUTES (mixes)** [–] [ ]

Aug 99. (12"/cd-s) *(12IS/CID 753)* **FOR REAL (mixes; Hip Hop / Genaside II / Rollo)** [45] [–]
(cd-s) *(CIDX 753)* – ('A'side) / Bombing bastards / Pop muzik.

Aug 99. (cd/lp; by TRICKY with DJ MUGGS & GREASE) *(CID/ILPS 8087) <546432>* **JUXTAPOSE** [22] [ ]
– For real / Bom bom diggy / Contradictive / She said / I like the girls / Hot like a sauna / Call me / Wash my soul / Hot like a sauna (metal mix) / Scrappy love.

Anti — Hollywood

Nov 00. (12"ep/cd-ep) *(6595-1/-2)* **MISSION ACCOMPLISHED EP** [ ] [–]
– Mission accomplished / Crazy claws / Tricky versus Lynx (live) / Divine comedy.

— next with guests ED KOWALCZYK, HAWKMAN, ANTHONY KEIDIS, JOHN FRUSCIANTE, FLEA, AMBERSUNSHOWER, CYNDI LAUPER

Anti — Hollywood

Jul 01. (cd/d-lp) *(6596-2/-1) <162285>* **BLOWBACK** [34] [ ]
– Excess / Evolution revolution love / Over me / Girls / You don't wanna / 1da woman / Your name / Diss never (dig up we history) / Bury the evidence / Something in the way / Five days / Give it to 'em / Song for Yukiko. *(ltd d-cd-iss. Jul02 +=; 6645-2)* – Excess / My head / Costanza / Five days (instrumental) / Suffocating / Divine comedy / I da woman / Unofficial.

Anti — Sanctuary

May 03. (cd) *(6686-2) <84618>* **VULNERABLE** [ ] Jun03 [ ]
– Stay / Antimatter / Ice pick / Car crash / Dear God / How high / What is wrong / Hollow / Moody / Wait for God / Where I'm from / The love cats / Search, search, survive. *(cd w/ dvd+=)* – Antimatter (Jimmy & T remix) / Receive us / You don't wanna (with RADAGON).

Jul 03. (12") *(1101-1)* **ANTIMATTER / (mixes; ragga / Jimmy & T / Ollie)** [ ] [–]
(cd-s+=) *(1101-2)* – ('A'-video).

– compilations, etc. –

May 02. (cd) *Island; (CID 8114) <586872>* **A RUFF GUIDE** [ ] [ ]
– Aftermath / Poems (NEARLY GOD) / For real / Black steel / Pumpkin / Broken homes / Wash my soul / I be the prophet / Makes me wanna die / Tricky kid / Scrappy love / Ponderosa / Christiansands / Hell is around the corner / Singing the blues / Bubbles (NEARLY GOD) / Overcome / Aftermath (I could be looking for people remix) / Black steel (in the draw mix).

☐ TRIPPING DAISY (see under ⇒ POLYPHONIC SPREE)

☐ TUBEWAY ARMY (see under ⇒ NUMAN, Gary)

KT TUNSTALL

Born: KATE TUNSTALL, 23 Jun'75, Edinburgh, Scotland. Born to a Chinese mother and Irish father but adopted and raised among the dreaming spires, sloane ranger students and bracing climate of St. Andrews, KT learned to sing from an Ella Fitzgerald tape, and began writing songs and playing guitar in her mid-teens. A year's scholarship to a private American prep school was the cue for her first band, the Happy Campers, as well as her first stab at busking. Back in the UK, she studied theatre and music at London's Royal Holloway College before heading home to Fife where she hooked up with the nascent Fence Collective, starting a band with Pip Dylan and touring with the Skuobhie Dubh Orchestra. A stint in the capital saw her promoting her own Acoustic Extravaganza nights (a forerunner of the still-going-strong Acoustic Edinburgh) before a 2002 move to London and a publishing contract. Despite the disappointment of a scuppered Columbia deal, her perseverence eventually paid off with the recording of a Steve Osborne-produced debut album for 'Relentless' (also home to JOSS STONE). 'EYE TO THE TELESCOPE' (2005) announced TUNSTALL as a no-frills troubadour with a yen for cathartic, Celtic-anthemic choruses. A string of singles edged her ever closer to household name status, with both 'Suddenly I See' and the swooning 'Other Side Of The World' knocking on the Top 10. But it's as an albums artist that the lusty-lunged Fifer has made her name, attracting a Mercury nomination, selling a cool one million and seeing off the competition (and outselling even MADONNA) with a deft flick of her beloved loop pedal. Jools Holland's 'Later With..' was the first show to beam KT's foot-stomping charisma into British living rooms, followed by celebrated spots on BBC4's Bob Dylan tribute (performing 'Simple Twist Of Fate') and Edinburgh's Hogmanay shindig in Princes Street Gardens. Subsequently nominated for three Brit awards, she scooped Best British Female Solo Artist.

• **Covered:** GET UR FREAK ON (Missy Elliott) / TANGLED UP IN BLUE (Bob Dylan) / FAKE PLASTIC TREES (Radiohead).

Album rating: EYE TO THE TELESCOPE (*7)

KT TUNSTALL – vocals, acoustic guitar

Outcaste | not iss.

Mar 04. (ltd-7") *(OUT 56)* **THROW ME A ROPE. /** [ ] [–]

Relentless | E.M.I.

Oct 04. (2x7"ep/cd-ep) *(REL/+CD 12)* **FALSE ALARM EP** [ ] [–]
– False alarm / Heal over / Miniature disasters / Throw me a rope.

Jan 05. (cd/lp) *(CD/LP REL 06)* **EYE TO THE TELESCOPE** [3] [–]
– Other side of the world / Another place to fall / Under the weather / Black horse & the cherry tree / Miniature disasters / Silent sea / Universe & U / False alarm / Suddenly I see / Stoppin' the love / Heal over / Through the dark. *(ltd-cd+=; CDRELX 06)* – Black horse & the cherry tree (live).

Feb 05. (7") *(REL 14)* **BLACK HORSE & THE CHERRY TREE. / BARBIE** [28] [–]
(cd-s) *(RELCD 14)* – ('A') / One day (live).

May 05. (7"burgundy) *(REL 18)* **OTHER SIDE OF THE WORLD. / MORNING STARS** [13] [–]
(cd-s) *(RELCD 18)* – ('A') / Boo hoo.
(dvd-s) *(RELDVD 18)* – ('A'-video) / Black horse & the cherry tree (video) / Throw me a rope.

Sep 05. (7") *(REL 21)* **SUDDENLY I SEE. / MOMENT OF MADNESS (live)** [12] [–]
(cd-s) *(RELCD 21)* – ('A') / Girl and the ghost.
(dvd-s) *(RELDVD 21)* – ('A') / Miniature disasters (live at Glastonbury) / Get UR freak on (BBC Radio 1 live lounge).

Dec 05. (7") *(REL 23)* **UNDER THE WEATHER. / LITTLE FAVOURS** [39] [–]
(cd-s) *(RELCD 23)* – ('A') / Tangled up in blue (BBC4 live..)

Feb 06. (cd) *<50729>* **EYE TO THE TELESCOPE** [–] [33]

Feb 06. (-) *<radio>* **BLACK HORSE & THE CHERRY TREE** [–] [20]

Mar 06. (7") *(REL 24)* **ANOTHER PLACE TO FALL. / UNIVERSE & U (acoustic extravaganza version)** [52] [–]
(cd-s) *(RELCD 24)* – ('A') / Fake plastic trees (Radio 1 live).

TURIN BRAKES

Formed: Balham, London, England . . . 1998 by OLLIE KNIGHTS and GALE PARADJANIAN (a guy). Acting as Britain's own KINGS OF CONVENIENCE, TURIN BRAKES have been fighting the NAM (New Acoustic Movement) war since the release of their 1999 EP 'THE DOOR'. Comprising of hushed acoustic tracks with multi-talented OLLIE KNIGHTS on vocals and PARADJANIAN playing whatever took his fancy, the set helped them grab the attention of independent label 'Source', who issued two EP's 'FIGHT OR FLIGHT' and 'THE STATE OF THINGS' in 2000, whilst re-issuing 'THE DOOR'. After much attention from the music press and MTV's own 'alternative' music channel MTV2, the duo had a Top 40 chart position with their debut album 'THE OPTIMIST LP' (2001). The set, with added percussion, piano and emotive strings, spawned three further Top 40 singles, the best being the sublime 'MIND OVER MONEY', with KNIGHTS' vocal gymnastics being a particular highlight. The quietly confident duo would return in 2003 to issue possibly their best work to date, the delicate 'ETHER SONG', another to add to the post-millennium canon of soft melodic rock. Producer, Tony Hoffer, brought out the best in KNIGHTS' earnest songwriting, with tracks 'PAINKILLER' and the gorgeous 'AVERAGE MAN' setting the tone quite nicely. Elsewhere on the album 'CLEAN BLUE AIR' was TURIN BRAKES at their lo-fi indie best, while the title track soared with majestic grace, proving that the group hadn't lost the verve and reverence displayed on their earlier material. 'JACKINABOX' (2005) fused West Coast, renaissance folk-rock with a hint of 60s psychedelia (think TIM BUCKLEY or CROSBY, STILLS & NASH); highlights of the UK Top 10 set included sole hit, 'FISHING FOR A DREAM', 'RED MOON' and 'ASLEEP WITH THE FIREFLIES'.

• **Covered:** WHAT'S NEXT TO THE MOON (Ac/Dc).

Album rating: THE OPTIMIST LP (*8) / ETHER SONG (*8) / JACKINABOX (*6)

OLLIE KNIGHTS – vocals, guitar / **GALE PARADJANIAN** – multi

Anvil | not iss.

Jun 99. (ltd;7"ep/cd-ep) *(ANV 027/+CDS)* **'THE DOOR' EP** [ ] [–]
– The door / By TV light / Nowhere / The road.

Source | Astralwerks

Aug 00. (d7"ep/cd-ep) *(SOUR V/CDS 008)* **THE STATE OF THINGS EP** [ ] [–]
– The boss / Balham to Brooklyn / All away / The state of things.

Oct 00. (7"ep/cd-ep) *(SOUR V/CDS 012)* **FIGHT OR FLIGHT EP** [ ] [–]
– Mind over money / Nine to five / Emergency 72 / Christine.

Feb 01. (7"ep/cd-ep) *(SOUR V/CDS 024)* **THE DOOR EP** [67] [–]
– The door / Reach out / Boss.

Mar 01. (cd/lp) *(SOUR CD/LP 023) <30696>* **THE OPTIMIST LP** [27] May01 [ ]
– Feeling oblivion / Underdog (save me) / Emergency 72 / Future boy / The door / The state of things / By TV light / Slack / Starship / The road / Mind over money / The optimist.

Apr 01. (7") *(SOURV 015)* **UNDERDOG (SAVE ME). / BALHAM TO BROOKLYN** [39] [–]
(cd-s+=) *(SOURCDS1 015)* – The door (live).
(cd-s) *(SOURCDS2 015)* – ('A') / Nowhere / Feeling oblivion (live) / ('A'-video).

Jul 01. (7") *(SOUR 038)* **MIND OVER MONEY. / STONE** [31] [–]
(cd-s+=) *(SOURCDX 038)* – Tunnel.
(cd-s) *(SOURCD 038)* – ('A'-extended) / Road (session) / Sunjets – Heavy 2 (instrumental) / ('A'-video).

Oct 01. (7") *(SOUR 041)* **EMERGENCY 72. / EVERYBODY KNOWS** [41] [–]
(cd-s+=) *(SOURCDX 041)* – The first time / ('A'-video).
(cd-s) *(SOURCD 041)* – ('A'-extended) / The last time / Lasso.

Oct 02. (7") *(SOUR 064)* **LONG DISTANCE. / LOST AND FOUND** [22] [–]
(cd-s+=) *(SOURCD 064)* – ('A'-The Bees remix).
(cd-s) *(SOURCDX 064)* – ('A') / ('A'-Max Tundra remix) / Soul less (home recording).

Feb 03. (7") *(SOUR 068)* **PAIN KILLER. / LITTLE BROTHER (demo)** [5] [–]
(cd-s) *(SOURCD 068)* – ('A') / Where's my army (home recording) / ('A'-video).

Feb 03. (cd/d-lp) *(CDSOUR/SOURLP 054) <82407>* **ETHER SONG** [4] Mar03 [ ]
– Blue hour / Average man / Long distance / Self help / Falling down / Stone thrown / Clean blue air / Pain killer (summer rain) / Full of stars / Panic attack / Little brother / Rain city. *(hidden +=)* – Ether song. *(ltd d-cd+=; CDSOURX 054)* – Blue hour (home recording) / Self help (SBN session) / Long distance (SBN session) / Bright golden lights (home recording) / Ether song (EPK video). *(ltd d-cd-iss. Oct03 +=; CDSOURXX 054)* – 5 mile (these are the days) / The boss / Piano instrumental / Long distance (VARA Radio 3FM) / Falling down (SBN session) / Pain killer (RTL2 acoustic). *(re-iss. Nov03 +=; CDSOURY 054)* – Ether song / 5 mile (these are the days).

May 03. (7") *(SOUR 085)* **AVERAGE MAN. / WHERE I'VE BEEN (XFM acoustic session)** [35] [–]
(cd-s+=) *(SOURCD 085)* – Pain killer (Today FM acoustic).

Sep 03. (7") *(SOUR 089)* **5 MILE (THESE ARE THE DAYS). / SELF HELP (WFUV acoustic version)** [31] [–]
(cd-s) *(SOURCD 089)* – ('A') / Pain killer (RTL2 acoustic). (cd-s)

(*SOURCDX 089*) – ('A') / The door (KEXP acoustic) / Stone thrown (acoustic) / ('A'-video).

May 05. (7"/cd-s) (*SOUR/+CD 109*) **FISHING FOR A DREAM. / CRYING** [32] [–]
(cd-s) (*SOURCDX 109*) – ('A') / Atlas of the world / What's next to the Moon (live from Re:Covered) / ('A'-video).

May 05. (cd/lp) (*CDSOUR/SOUR LP 110*) *<73852>*
JACKINABOX [9] Jun05 [ ]
– They can't buy the sunshine / Red moon / Forever / Asleep with the fireflies / Fishing for a dream / Road to nowhere / Over and over / Last clown / Above the clouds / Building wraps round me / Jackinabox / Come and go. (*ltd-cd+=; CDSOURX 110*) – (DVD tracks).

Aug 05. (7"/cd-s) (*SOUR/+CD 114*) **OVER AND OVER. / (Plantlife remix)** [62] [–]
(cd-s) (*SOURCDX 114*) – ('A') / Last clown (Tony Hoffer version) / ('A'-video).

– compilations, others, etc. –

Sep 04. (d-cd) *Source; (VBX 24)* **ETHER SONG / THE OPTIMIST LP** [ ] [–]

(Ike &) Tina TURNER

Initiated: 1956-58, when billed as "IKE TURNER, CARLSON OLIVER & LITTLE ANN" they recorded a 1958 single, 'BOXTOP' for 'Tune Town' records. LITTLE ANN was renamed TINA TURNER the following year, although the couple weren't married until 1962(!), having conceived a child in '59. TINA was born ANNIE MAE BULLOCK, 26th November '38, Brownsville, Texas, USA, although she was raised in Nutbush, Tennessee and became a local choir singer. IKE TURNER was born on 5th November '31, Clarksville, Mississippi, USA where he became a regular DJ aged ony sixteen. In 1950, with solid session work behind him, the crack blues guitarist formed his own 5-piece outfit, IKE & THE KINGS OF RHYTHM (WILLIE WIZARD, EUGENE FOX, JACKIE BENSTON and one other). They made a couple of singles for 'Chess'; 'HEARTBROKEN AND WORRIED' / 'I'M LONESOME BABY' plus 'ROCKET 88' / 'COME BACK WHERE YOU BELONG' before signing to Sam Phillips management, the 'Sun' head honcho taking on the role of both producer and A&R man. Five years later, IKE flitted from Memphis to St. Louis where he was to strike up a working and loving partnership with TINA (after she persuaded him to let her have a go at fronting his band) and in 1960, now billed as IKE & TINA TURNER, they hit the US Top 30 with 'A FOOL IN LOVE'. As well as presenting a much feted stage show (which served to highlight both IKE's musical and choreographic skills alongside TINA's raunchy vocals and stunning appearance), the duo proceeded to notch up a string of R&B hits, even hitting the pop charts the following year with their Top 20 smash hit, 'IT'S GONNA WORK OUT FINE'. After one further major hit, things dried up until the mid-60's, when they were introduced to the legendary PHIL SPECTOR. He produced their magnus-opus, 'RIVER DEEP MOUNTAIN HIGH', a "wall of sound" soul classic which, although a relative flop in the States, peaked at No.3 in the UK. With varying degrees of fortune, they moved from one label to another, finally scoring a massive Top 5 US hit on 'Liberty' in early '71 with an earthy cover of JOHN FOGERTY's classic 'PROUD MARY'. The enthusiastic patronage of The ROLLING STONES did much to raise their profile (the pair performed at the ill-fated Altamont gig in 1969) and they finally broke out again in 1973 when TINA's autobiographical composition, 'NUTBUSH CITY LIMITS', was a massive seller on both sides of the Atlantic. In 1974, she landed the part of 'The Acid Queen' in The WHO's rock opera, 'TOMMY', her new-found independence giving her time to reflect on her well-documented ill-treatment by IKE. In 1976, after converting to Buddhism, she finally divorced him, in effect ending not only their marriage but their lucrative musical partnership. After a time on welfare (US equivalent of the dole), she began to make tentative moves to carving out a solo career, already having released an impressive album of covers, 'ACID QUEEN', the previous year. Yet although she remained a star attraction on the live club circuit scene, she still found it hard to sell records. Until that is, 'Capitol' contracted her late in '82 following some show-stopping support slots for The 'STONES. Following the surprise international success of her Al Green cover, 'LET'S STAY TOGETHER' in late '83, the multi-million 'PRIVATE DANCER' album was rush-recorded and released in summer '84. The record included her recent Grammy winner and US No.1, 'WHAT'S LOVE GOT TO DO WITH IT' alongside the Top 10 title track and the Top 5 'BETTER BE GOOD TO ME, going platinum in both America and Britain. It also showcased a more sophisticated, smoother approach although TURNER's range was as impressive as ever and incredibly, she was looking better than many female stars half her age. In '85, she starred in the film 'Mad Max: Beyond The Thunderdome', receiving an award by NAACP for best actress; TURNER was also reputed to have turned down the offer of a major part in the film, 'The Color Purple'. She was now arguably the most famous female Rock & Pop singer on Earth, a claim to which the 180,000 audience attending the Rio De Janeiro January '86 concert would testify. In contrast with her continuing triumphs – TURNER went on to release further million selling 80's albums, 'BREAK EVERY RULE' (1986) and 'FOREIGN AFFAIR' (1989) – IKE was unceremoniously sentenced to a year in prison in 1988 after admitting his dealings with cocaine. The troubled history of IKE and TINA's former partnership was documented in the 1993 biopic, 'WHAT'S LOVE GOT TO DO WITH IT' (based on TINA's book, 'I, Tina'), the accompanying soundtrack topping the UK charts.

• **Songwriters:** IKE wrote most of the early material, but with (selective) covers interspersed I'VE BEEN LOVING YOU TOO LONG (Otis Redding) / PLEASE PLEASE PLEASE (James Brown) / COME TOGETHER (Beatles) / I WANT TO TAKE YOU HIGHER (Sly & The Family Stone) / HONKY TONK WOMAN + LET'S SPEND THE NIGHT TOGETHER + UNDER MY THUMB (Rolling Stones) / OOH POO PAH DOO (Jesse Hill) / SAVE THE LAST DANCE FOR ME (Drifters) / etc. TINA's solo covers; ACID QUEEN + I CAN SEE FOR MILES (Who) / SOMETIME WHEN WE TOUCH (Dan Hill) / THE BITCH IS BACK (Elton John) / VIVA LA MONEY (Allen Toussaint) / EARTHQUAKE AND HURRICANE (Willie Dixon) / FIRE DOWN BELOW (Bob Seger) / WHOLE LOTTA LOVE (Led Zeppelin) / FUNNY HOW TIME SLIPS AWAY (. . . Nelson) / BACKSTABBERS (O'Jays) / HELP! + COME TOGETHER (Beatles) / TAKE ME TO THE RIVER (Al Green) / I CAN'T STAND THE RAIN (Ann Peebles) / TONIGHT I'LL BE STAYING HERE WITH YOU (Bob Dylan) / PRIVATE DANCER (Mark Knopfler) / WHAT'S LOVE GOT TO DO WITH IT? (Terry Britten, her co-producer & Graham Lyle; ex-Gallagher & Lyle) / ADDICTED TO LOVE (Robert Palmer) / IN THE MIDNIGHT HOUR (Wilson Pickett) / STEAMY WINDOWS (Tony Joe White) / IT TAKE TWO (Marvin Gaye & Tammi Terrell) / WHY MUST WE WAIT UNTIL TONIGHT (Bryan Adams – Mutt Lange) / GOLDEN EYE (U2) / etc. • **Trivia:** In the 60's, The IKETTES also had US hits with I'M BLUE (THE GONG-GONG SONG) (No.19, Feb62) / PEACHES'N'CREAM (No.36, Apr65). In 1981, TINA appeared on BEF's (HEAVEN 17) various vocalists album 'MUSIC OF QUALITY . . . ' re-actifying The Temptations number BALL OF CONFUSION.

Album rating: PROUD MARY: BEST OF IKE & TINA TURNER (best CD compilation; *7) / Tina Turner: TINA TURNS THE COUNTRY ON (*4) / ACID QUEEN (*5) / ROUGH (*4) / LOVE EXPLOSION (*4) / PRIVATE DANCER (*7) / BREAK EVERY RULE (*6) / TINA LIVE IN EUROPE (*4) / FOREIGN AFFAIR (*6) / SIMPLY THE BEST compilation (*8) / WHAT'S LOVE GOT TO DO WITH IT soundtrack (*6) / WILDEST DREAMS (*6) / TWENTY FOUR SEVEN (*5) / ALL THE BEST: THE HITS compilation (*8)

TINA TURNER

IKE & TINA TURNER

IKE TURNER – guitar, vocals / **TINA TURNER** – vocals plus sessioners & singing group The IKETTES (aka **P.P.ARNOLD, MERRY CLAYTON & BONNIE BRAMLETT** and loads more at various times).

London / Sue

Nov 60. (7") *(HLU 9226) <730>* **A FOOL IN LOVE. / THE WAY YOU LOVE ME** [ ] Aug 60 [27]
Dec 60. (7") *<735>* **I IDOLISE YOU. / LETTER FROM TINA** [–] [82]
1961. (7") **I'M JEALOUS. / YOU'RE MY BABY** [–] [ ]
1961. (lp) *<2001>* **THE SOUL OF IKE & TINA TURNER** [–] [ ]
– I'm jealous / I idolize you / If / Letter from Tina / You can't love two / I had a motion / A fool in love / Sleepless / Chances are / You're my baby / The way you love me. *(UK-iss.Apr84 on 'Kent')*
Oct 61. (7") *(HL 94510) <749>* **IT'S GONNA WORK OUT FINE. / WON'T YOU FORGIVE ME** [ ] Jul 61 [14]
Nov 61. (7") *<753>* **POOR FOOL. / YOU CAN'T BLAME ME** [–] [38]
1962. (lp) *<2005>* **DON'T PLAY ME CHEAP** [–] [ ]
– Wake up / I made a promise up above / Desire / Those ways / Mamma tell him / Pretend / Don't play me cheap / The real me / Forever mine / No amending / Love letters / My everything to me.
Mar 62. (7") *<757>* **TRA LA LA LA LA. / PUPPY LOVE** [–] [ ]
Jun 62. (7") *<765>* **YOU SHOULD'VE TREATED ME RIGHT. / SLEEPLESS** [–] [89]
1962. (lp) *<2007>* **IT'S GONNA WORK OUT FINE** [–] [ ]
– Gonna find me a substitute / Mojo queen / Kinda strange / Why should I / Tinarro / I'm gonna cut you loose / Foolish / It's gonna work out fine / I'm fallin' in love / This man's crazy / Good good lovin' / The rooster / Steel guitar rag / Trackdown twist / Going home.

Sue / Kent

Nov 62. (7") **I IDOLIZE YOU. / TINA'S DILEMMA** [–] [ ]
1963. (7") **MIND IN A WHIRL. / THE ARGUMENT** [–] [ ]
1963. (7") **PLEASE DON'T HURT ME. / WORRIED AND HURTIN' INSIDE** [–] [ ]
1963. (7") **DON'T PLAY ME CHEAP. / WAKE UP** [–] [ ]
Feb 64. (7"ep) *(IEP 706)* **THE SOUL OF IKE & TINA TURNER** [ ] [–]
Aug 64. (7") *(SR 322)* **THE ARGUMENT. / POOR FOOL** [ ] [–]
Nov 64. (7") *(SR 350) <402>* **I CAN'T BE BELIEVE WHAT YOU SAY (FOR SEEING WHAT YOU DO). / MY BABY NOW** [ ] Sep 64 [95]
Nov 64. (lp) <> **IKE & TINA TURNER REVUE!!! (live)** [–]
– Please, please, please / Feel so good / The love of my man / Think / Drown in my own tears / I love the way you love / Your precious love / All in my mind / I can't believe what you say. *(UK-iss.Jul66 on 'Ember') (re-iss. Dec72 on 'New World') (cd-iss. Jul93 on 'Kent')*
May 65. (7") *(SR 376)* **PLEASE PLEASE PLEASE. / AM I A FOOL IN LOVE** [ ] [–]

—— They had already signed to . . .

Warners / Warners

Jan 65. (7") *(WB 153)* **FINGER POPPIN'. / OOH POO PAH DOO** [ ] [ ]
Jan 65. (7"ep) *(WEP 619)* **THE IKE & TINA TURNER SHOW (live)** [ ] [ ]
Apr 65. (lp) *(W 1579) <1579>* **LIVE! THE IKE & TINA TURNER SHOW (live)** [ ] Feb 65 [ ]
– Finger poppin' / Down in the valley / Good times / You are my sunshine / Good time tonight / Twist and shout / Something's got a hold on me / I know (you don't want me no more) / (Tight pants) High heel sneakers / My man he's a loving man / I can't stop loving you / Tell the truth. *(re-iss. Jul66) (re-iss. May70 on 'Valient') (cd-iss. Apr85 on 'Edsel')*
Jan 66. (7"ep) *(WEP 620)* **SOMEBODY NEEDS YOU** [ ] [ ]

—— Warners continued to issue material after 1966 success and new dealings . . .

Jul 66. (7") *(WB 5753)* **TELL HER I'M NOT HOME. / FINGER POPPIN'** [48] [ ]
Nov 66. (7") *(WB 5766)* **SOMEBODY (SOMEWHERE) NEEDS YOU. / JUST TO BE WITH YOU** [ ] [ ]
Feb 67. (lp) *(WB 5904) <1568>* **THE IKE & TINA TURNER SHOW VOL.II (live)** [ ] [ ]
– Shake a tail feather / You must believe in me / Ooh poo pah doo / Early in the morning / All I can do is cry / Somebody somewhere needs you / Keep on pushing / It's all over / You're no good / Fool for you.

—— Signed to different labels at same time . . .

H.M.V. / Tangerine

Aug 66. (7") *(POP 1544)* **ANYTHING THAT YOU WASN'T BORN WITH. / BEAUTY IS JUST SKIN DEEP** [ ] [ ]
Mar 67. (7") *(POP 1583)* **I'M HOOKED. / DUST MY BROOM** [ ] [ ]

Stateside / Modern

Oct 66. (7") *(SS 551)* **GOODBYE, SO LONG. / HURT IS ALL YOU GAVE ME** [ ] [ ]

London / Philles

May 66. (7") *(HLU 10046) <131>* **RIVER DEEP, MOUNTAIN HIGH. / I'LL KEEP YOU HAPPY** [3] [88]
(re-iss. Dec 69 on 'A & M' US)
Sep 66. (lp) *(HAU 8396)* **RIVER DEEP MOUNTAIN HIGH** [27] [–]
– River deep, mountain high / I idolize you / A love like yours (don't come knockin' every day) / A fool in love / Make 'em wait / Hold on baby / I'll never need more than this / Save the last dance for me / Oh! baby (things ain't what they used to be) / Every day I have to cry / Such a fool for you / It's gonna work out fine. *(US-iss.Sep 69 on 'A&M', UK-re-iss. Mar70 +cd.1988) (UK re-iss. 1974 on 'Mayfair-A&M', Jan 75 on 'Hamlet-A&M', Dec79 on 'M.F.P.', re-iss. +c.May 84 on 'Spot', cd-iss. 1988 on 'Mobile Fidelity') (re-iss. cd+c Sep 93 on 'Yesterday's Gold')*
Oct 66. (7") *(HLU 10083)* **A LOVE LIKE YOURS (DON'T COME KNOCKIN' EVERY DAY). / HOLD ON BABY** [16] [ ]
Sep 67. (7") *(HLU 10155)* **I'LL NEVER NEED MORE THAN THIS. / SAVE THE LAST DANCE FOR ME** [ ] [ ]
Apr 68. (7") *(HLU 10189)* **SO FINE. / SO BLUE OVER YOU** [ ] [ ]
Aug 68. (7") *(HLU 10217)* **WE NEED AN UNDERSTANDING. / IT SHO' AIN'T ME** [ ] [ ]
Jan 69. (lp) *(SHU 8370) <6000>* **SO FINE** [ ] [ ]
– Bet'cha can't kiss me (just one time) / T'ain't nobody's business / It sho' ain't me / Too hot to hold / A fool in love / Poor little fool / I better get ta steppin' / Shake a tail feather / So fine / We need an understanding / You'e so fine / Poor Sam. *(cd-iss. Sep87 on 'Entertainer')*

—— Were again on the books of 2 labels.

Minit / Minit

Apr 69. (7") *(MLF 11016) <32060>* **I'M GONNA DO ALL I CAN (TO DO RIGHT BY MY MAN). / YOU'VE GOT TOO MANY TIES THAT BIND** [ ] [98]
Jun 69. (7") **I WISH IT WOULD RAIN. / WITH A LITTLE HELP FROM MY FRIENDS** [–] [ ]
Sep 69. (7") **I WANNA JUMP. / TREATING US FUNKY** [–] [ ]
Oct 69. (lp) *(40014) <24018>* **IN PERSON (live)** [ ] Jul 69 [ ]
– Everyday people / Gimme some lovin' / Sweet soul music / Son of a preacher man / I heard it through the grapevine / Respect / Medley: There was a time – African boo's / Funky street / A fool in love / Medley: The summit – All I could do was cry – Please, please, please – Baby I love you / Goodbye, so long.
Feb 70. (7") *(LBF 15303)* **COME TOGETHER. / HONKY TONK WOMAN** [–] [57]

Harvest / Blue Thumb

May 69. (7") *<101>* **I'VE BEEN LOVING YOU TOO LONG. / GRUMBLING** [–] [68]
Jul 69. (7") *<102>* **THE HUNTER. / CRAZY 'BOUT YOU BABY** [–] [93]
Nov 69. (7") *<104>* **BOLD SOUL SISTER. / I KNOW** [–] [59]
May 70. (7") *(HAR 5018)* **THE HUNTER. / BOLD SOUL SISTER** [ ] [–]
Sep 70. (lp) *(LBS 83350) <7637>* **COME TOGETHER** [ ] May 70 [ ]
– It ain't right / Too much woman (for a henpecked man) / Unlucky creature / Young and dumb / Honky tonk woman / Come together / Why can't we be happy / Contact high / Keep on walkin' / I want to take you higher / Evil man / Doin' it.
Sep 70. (lp) *(SHSP 4001) <11>* **THE HUNTER** [ ] Nov 69 [ ]
– The hunter / You don't love me (yes I know) / You got me running / Bold soul sister / I smell trouble / Things I used to do / Early in the morning / You're still my baby / I know.

Liberty / Blue Thumb

Jun 69. (lp) *(LBS 83241) <5>* **OUTTA SEASON** [ ] Apr 69 [ ]
– I've been loving you too long / Mean old world / 3 o'clock im the morning blues / Five long years / Dust my broom / Grumbling / I am a motherless child / Crazy 'bout your baby / Reconsider baby / Honest I do / Please love me / My babe / Rock me baby. *(re-iss. Sep73 on 'Sunset')*
Jul 69. (7") *(LBF 15223)* **CRAZY ABOUT YOU BABY. / I'VE BEEN LOVIN' YOU TOO LONG** [ ] Apr 69 [ ]

Liberty / Liberty

Jun 70. (7") *(LBF 15367) <56177>* **I WANT TO TAKE YOU HIGHER. / CONTACT HIGH** [ ] May 70 [34]
Sep 70. (7") **WORKIN' TOGETHER. / THE WAY YOU LOVE ME** [–] [ ]

Jan 71. (7") *(LBF 15432)* <56216> **PROUD MARY. / FUNKIER THAN MOSQUITA'S TWEETER** — 4

Feb 71. (lp) *(LBS 83455)* <7650> **WORKIN' TOGETHER** — Dec 70 25
– Workin' together / Get you when I want you / Get back / The way you love me / You can have it / Game of love / Funkier than a mosquito's tweeter / Ooh poo pah doo / Proud Mary / Goodbye so long / Let it be. *(cd-iss. Dec95 on 'EMI Europe')*

U.A. U.A.

Jun 71. (7") *(UP 35245)* <50782> **OOH POO PAH DOO. / I WANNA JUMP** — 60

Sep 71. (d-lp) *(UAD 600056)* <9953> **LIVE AT THE CARNEGIE – WHAT YOU HEAR IS WHAT YOU GET (live)** — Jul 71 25
– Piece of my heart / Everyday people / Doin' The Tina Turner / Sweet soul music / Ooh poo pah doo / Honky tonk women / A love like yours (don't come knockin' every day) / Proud Mary / I smell trouble / Ike's tune / I want to take you higher / I've been loving you too long / Respect / What you see is what you get.

Nov 71. (7") *(UP 35310)* **I'M YOURS. / DOIN' IT**

Jan 72. (7") *(UP 35219)* **CRAZY ABOUT YOU BABY. / I'VE BEEN LOVIN' YOU TOO LONG**

Mar 72. (lp/c) *(UAG 29256)* <5530> **'NUFF SAID** — Dec 71
– I love what you do to me / Baby (what you want me to do) / Sweet flustrations / What you don't see (is better yet) / Nuff said (part 1) / Tell the truth / Pick me up (take me where your home is) / Moving into hip style – A trip child / I love baby / Can't you hear me callin' / Nuff said (part 2).

Feb 72. (7") <50881> **UP IN HEAH. / DOO WAH DIDDY** — – 83

Jun 72. (7") *(UP 35373)* **FEEL GOOD. / OUTRAGEOUS**

Oct 72. (lp) *(UAS 29377)* <5598> **FEEL GOOD** — Jul 72
– Chopper / Kay got laid, Joe got paid / Feel good / I like it / If you can hully gully (I can hully gully too) / Black coffee / She came in through the bathroom window / If I knew then (what I know now) / You better think of something.

Oct 72. (7") *(UP 9)* **LET ME TOUCH YOUR MIND. / CHOPPER**

Feb 73. (lp) *(UAS 29423)* <5660> **LET ME TOUCH YOUR MIND**
– Let me touch your mind / Annie had a baby / Don't believe her / I had a notion / Popcorn / Early one morning / Help him / Up on the roof / Born free / Heaven help us all

Jul 73. (7") *(UP 35550)* **WORK ON ME. / BORN FREE**

Oct 73. (7") *(UP 35582)* <298> **NUTBUSH CITY LIMITS. / HELP HIM** — 4 Sep 73 22

Nov 73. (lp/c) *(UA S/C 29557)* <180> **NUTBUSH CITY LIMITS**
– Nutbush city limits / Make me over / Drift away / That's my purpose / Fancy Annie / River deep mountain high / Get it out of your mind / Daily bread / You are my sunshine / Club Manhattan.

Dec 73. (7") *(UP 35632)* **FANCY ANNIE. / RIVER DEEP MOUNTAIN HIGH**

Apr 74. (7") *(UP 35650)* **SWEET RHODE ISLAND RED. / GET IT OUT OF YOUR MIND**

Sep 74. (7") *(UP 35726)* <528> **SEXY IDA. / (part 2)** — 65

Oct 74. (lp/c) **SWEET RHODE ISLAND RED**
– Let me be there / Living for the city / I know / Mississippi rolling stone / Sugar hill / Sweet Rhode Island red / Ready for you baby / Smooth out the wrinkles / Doozie / Higher ground.

Jul 75. (7") *(UP 35766)* <598. **BABY-GET IT ON. / ('A'disco version)** — Jun 75 88

Oct 75. (7") *(UP 36028)* **DELILAH'S POWER. / THAT'S MY PURPOSE**

Mar 77. (lp/c) *(UA S/C 30040)* <707> **DELILAH'S POWER**
– Delilah's power / Never been to Spain / Unhappy birthday / (You've got to) Put something into it / Nothing comes to you when you're asleep but a dream / Stormy weather (keeps rainin' all the time) / Sugar sugar / Too much for one woman / Trying to find my mind / Pick me up (take me where your home is) / Too many women / I want to take you higher. *(cd-iss. Feb01 on 'EMI Plus'; 576099-2)*

—— Above album was already recorded mid 70's, before their divorce/split.

TINA TURNER

—— went solo in 1974 with session people

U.A. U.A.

Aug 74. (lp/c) <200> **TINA TURNS THE COUNTRY ON**
– Bayou song / Help me make it through the night / Tonight I'll be staying here with you / If you love me (let me know) / He belongs to me / Don't talk now / Long long time / I'm moving on / There'll always be music / The love that lights our way.

Oct 75. (lp/c) *(UN S/C 29875)* <495> **ACID QUEEN** — Sep75
– Under my thumb / Let's spend the night together / The Acid queen / I can see for miles / Whole lotta love / Baby git it on / Bootsey Whitelaw / Pick me tonight / Rockin' and rollin'. *(cd-iss. May96 on 'EMI Gold'; CDGOLD 1026)*

Jan 76. (7") *(UP 36043)* **THE ACID QUEEN. / ROCKIN' AND ROLLIN'**

Sep 78. (lp/c) *(UAG/UAC 30211)* **ROUGH**
– Fruits of the night / The bitch is back / The woman I'm supposed to be / Viva la money / Funny how time slips away / Earthquake & hurricane / Root toot undisputable rock'n'roller / Fire down below / Sometimes when we touch / A woman in a man's world / Night time is the right time. *(cd-iss. Aug95; CDP 795213-2)*

Feb 79. (7") *(UP 36485)* **ROOT TOOT UNDISPUTABLE ROCK'N'ROLLER. / FIRE DOWN BELOW**

Mar 79. (lp/c) *(UA G/C 30267)* **LOVE EXPLOSION**
– Love explosion / Fool for your love / Sunset on sunset / Music keeps me dancin' / I see home / Backstabbers / Just a little lovin' (early in the morning) / You get what I'm gonna get / On the radio.

Apr 79. (7") *(UP 36513)* **SOMETIMES WHEN WE TOUCH. / EARTHQUAKE AND HURRICANE**

Nov 79. (7") *(BP 322)* **BACKSTABBERS. / SUNSET ON SUNSET**

—— In May'82, she sang on BALL OF CONFUSION single by 'BEF' (aka HEAVEN 17).

Capitol Capitol

Nov 83. (7")(12")(12"pic-d) *(CL/12CL/12CLP 316)* <5322> **LET'S STAY TOGETHER. / I WROTE A LETTER** — 6 Jan 84 26

Feb 84. (7"/12"/7"pic-d) *(CL/12CL/CLP 325)* **HELP!. / ROCK'N'ROLL WIDOW** — 40

May 84. (7") <5354> **WHAT'S LOVE GOT TO DO WITH IT. / ROCK'N'ROLL WIDOW** — – 1

Jun 84. (7"/'A'ext-12"/12"pic-d) *(CL/12CL/12CLP 334)* **WHAT'S LOVE GOT TO DO WITH IT. / DON'T RUSH THE GOOD THINGS** — 3 –

Jun 84. (lp/c)(cd) *(TINA/TCTINA 1)(CDP 7460412)* <12330> **PRIVATE DANCER** — 2 3
– I might have been queen / What's love got to do with it / Show some respect / Private dancer / I can't stand the rain / Let's stay together / Better be good to me / Steel claw / Help! / 1984. *(pic-lp Apr85) (special cd-iss. Aug00 +=; CDCNTAV 1)* – (extra tracks).

Sep 84. (7")(12")(7"sha-pic-d) *(CL/12CL/CLP 338)* <5387> **BETTER BE GOOD TO ME. / WHEN I WAS YOUNG** — 45 5

Nov 84. (7"/12") *(CL/12CL 343)* <5433> **PRIVATE DANCER. / NUTBUSH CITY LIMITS** — 26 7

Feb 85. (7"/12") *(CL/12CL 352)* **I CAN'T STAND THE RAIN. / LET'S PRETEND WE'RE MARRIED** — 57

Apr 85. (7") <5461> **SHOW SOME RESPECT. / LET'S PRETEND WE'RE MARRIED** — – 37

Jun 85. (7"/12"/7"pic-d/7"sha-pic-d) (CL/12CL/CLP 364) <5491> *(CL 364)* **WE DON'T NEED ANOTHER HERO (THUNDERDOME). / ('A'instrumental)** — 3 2

—— Above + below 45s, from her film 'Mad Max: Beyond The Thunderdome'.

Sep 85. (7"/12") *(CL/12CL 376)* <5518> **ONE OF THE LIVING. / (part 2)** — 55 15

—— In Oct85, teamed up with BRYAN ADAMS on UK No.29 + US 19 hit IT'S ONLY LOVE

Aug 86. (7") *(CL 419)* <5615> **TYPICAL MALE. / DON'T TURN AROUND** — 33 2
('A'extended-12"+=) *(12CL 419)* – ('A'dub version).
(12"++=)(12"pic-d++=) *(12CLP 419,)* – ('A'dance mix).

Sep 86. (lp/c)(cd) *(EST/TCEST 2018)(CDP 7463232)* <12530> **BREAK EVERY RULE** — 2 4
– Typical male / What you get is what you see / Two people / Till the right man comes along / Afterglow / Girls / Back where you started / Break every rule / Overnight sensation / Paradise is here / I'll be thunder.

Oct 86. (7"/12") *(CL/12CL 430)* <5644> **TWO PEOPLE. / HAVIN' A PARTY** — 43 30
(d12"+=) *(12CLD 430)* – Let's stay together (live) / Private dancer (live).

Feb 87. (7"/12") *(CL/12CL 439)* <5668> **WHAT YOU GET IS WHAT YOU SEE. / TINA TURNER MONTAGE MIX – I Can't Stand The Rain – Two People – We Don't Need Another Hero – What's Love Got To Do With It – Typical Male – Let's Stay Together** — 30 13
(d7"+=) *(7CLD 439)* – ('A'live) / Take me to the river.

Apr 87. (7") *<44003>* **BREAK EVERY RULE. / TAKE ME TO THE RIVER** [–] [74]

May 87. (7"/7"sha-pic-d) *(CL/+P 452)* **BREAK EVERY RULE. / GIRLS** [43] [–]

Sep 87. (7"/12"/7"pic-d) *(CL/12CL/CLP 459)* **PARADISE IS HERE. / IN THE MIDNIGHT HOUR** [ ] [ ]

Mar 88. (7") *(CL 484)* **ADDICTED TO LOVE (live). / OVERNIGHT SENSATION (live)** [71] [ ]
(12"+=/cd-s+=) *(12CL/CDCL 484)* – Legs (live).

Mar 88. (d-c/d-cd/d-lp) *(TC/CD+/ESTD 1)* *<90126>* **TINA LIVE IN EUROPE (live)** [8] [86]
– What you get is what you see / Break every rule / I can't stand the rain / Two people / Girls * / Typical male / Back where you started * / Better be good to me / Addicted to love / Private dancer / We don't need another hero (Thunderdome) / What's love got to do with it / Let's stay together / Show some respect / Land of 1,000 dances / In the midnight hour / 634-5789 (with ROBERT CRAY) / A change is gonna come / River deep, mountain high * / Tearing us apart (with ERIC CLAPTON) / Proud Mary / Help! / Tonight + Let's dance (with DAVID BOWIE) / Overnight sensation * / It's only love (with BRYAN ADAMS) / Nutbush city limits / Paradise is here. *(c+cd+= *)*

Jun 88. (7"/12") *(CL/12CL 495)* **A CHANGE IS GONNA COME (live). / NUTBUSH CITY LIMITS (live)** [ ] [ ]

Aug 89. (7"/c-s) *(CL/TCCL 543)* *<44442>* **THE BEST. / UNDERCOVER AGENT FOR THE BLUES** [5] [15]
(12"+=)(cd-s+=) *(12CL/CDCL 543)* – Bold and reckless.

Sep 89. (c/cd/lp) *(TC/CD+/ESTU 2103)* *<91873>* **FOREIGN AFFAIR** [1] [31]
– Steamy windows / The best / You know who (is doing you know what) / Undercover agent for the blues / Look me in the heart / Be tender with me baby / You can't stop me loving you / Ask me how I feel / Falling like rain / I don't wanna lose you / Not enough romance / Foreign affair. *(re-iss. Sep94)*

Oct 89. (7"/c-s) *(CL/TCCL 553)* **I DON'T WANNA LOSE YOU. / NOT ENOUGH ROMANCE** [8] [ ]
(12"+=/12"pic-d+=) *(12CL/+P 553)* – Stronger than the wind.
(cd-s+=) *(CDCL 553)* – We don't need another hero.

Jan 90. (7") *(CL 560)* *<44473>* **STEAMY WINDOWS. / THE BEST (muscle mix)** [13] Nov89 [39]
('B'extended-cd-s+=) *(CDCL 560)* – ('A'house mix).
(12")(c-s) *(12CL/TCCL 560)* – ('A'side) / ('A'vocal mix) / ('A'house mix).

Jul 90. (c-s,cd-s) <>**LOOK ME IN THE HEART / STRONGER THAN THE WIND** [–] [ ]

Aug 90. (7"/c-s) *(CL/TCCL 584)* **LOOK ME IN THE HEART. / STEEL CLAW (live)** [31] [–]
(12"+=)(cd-s+=) *(12CL/CDCL 584)* – ('A'instrumental).
('A'remixed-cd-s) *(CDCLX 584)* – ('A'instrumental) / Tina Turner montage mix.

Oct 90. (7"/c-s/7"pic-d) *(CL/TCCL/CLP 593)* **BE TENDER WITH MY HEART. / ('A'live)** [28] [ ]
(12"+=/cd-s+=) *(12CL/CDCL 593)* – You know who is doing you know what.

— In Nov90, she teamed up with ROD STEWART on hit single IT TAKES TWO.

Sep 91. (7"/c-s) *(CL/TCCL 630)* **NUTBUSH CITY LIMITS (THE 90's VERSION). / THE BEST** [23] [ ]
(12"+=/cd-s+=) *(12/CD CL 630)* – Addicted to love (live) / Nutbush city limits ('91).

Oct 91. (cd/c/d-lp) *(CD/TC+/ESTV 1)* *<97152>* **SIMPLY THE BEST** (compilation) [1] [ ]
– The best / Better be good to me / I can't stand the rain / What's love got to do with it / I don't wanna lose you / Nutbush city limits (the 90's version) / What you get is what you see / Let's stay together / River deep – mountain high / Steamy windows / Typical male / We don't need another hero (Thunderdome) / Private dancer / Look me in the heart / It takes two / I want you near me / Way of the world / Love thing.

Nov 91. (7"/c-s) *(CL/TCCL 637)* **WAY OF THE WORLD. / I DON'T WANNA LOSE YOU** [13] [ ]
(12"+=)(cd-s+=) *(12CL/CDCL 637)* – Foreign affair.

Feb 92. (7") *(CL 644)* **LOVE THING. / I'M A LADY** [29] [ ]
(c-s+=/cd-s+=) *(TC/CD CL 644)* – It's only love / Private dancer (live).

May 92. (7"/c-s) *(CL/TCCL 659)* **I WANT YOU NEAR ME. / LET'S STAY TOGETHER** [22] [ ]
(cd-s+=) *(CDCL 659)* – Tonight + Let's dance (live with DAVID BOWIE).
(cd-s) *(CDCLX 659)* – ('A'side) / Land of a 1,000 dances / In the midnight hour / 634-5789 (live with ROBERT CRAY).

Parlophone Virgin

May 93. (7"/c-s) *(R/TCR 6346)* **I DON'T WANNA FIGHT. / THE BEST** [7] [–]
(cd-s+=) *(CDR 6346)* – I don't wanna lose you / What's love got to do with it.
(cd-s) *(CDRS 6346)* – ('A'side) / Tina's wish / ('A'urban mix).

May 93. (c-s,cd-s) *<12652>* **I DON'T WANNA FIGHT / TINA'S WISH** [–] [9]

Jun 93. (cd/c/lp) *(CD/TC+/PCSD 128)* *<88189>* **WHAT'S LOVE GOT TO DO WITH IT (soundtrack)** [1] [17]
– I don't wanna fight / Rock me baby / Disco inferno / Why must we wait until tonight? / Nutbush city limits / (Darlin') You know I love you / Proud Mary / A fool in love / It's gonna work out fine / Stay awhile / Shake a tail feather *[UK-only]* / I might have been Queen / What's love got to do with it (live) / Tina's wish *[UK-only]*.

Aug 93. (7"/c-s) *(R/TCR 6357)* **DISCO INFERNO. / I DON'T WANNA FIGHT** [12] [ ]
(12"+=/cd-s+=) *(12R/CDR 6357)* – ('A'mixes).

Oct 93. (7"/c-s) *(R/TCR 6366)* *<12683>* **WHY MUST WE WAIT UNTIL TONIGHT? / SHAKE A TAIL FEATHER** [16] [97]
(cd-s+=) *(CDR 6366)* – The best.
(cd-s++=) *(CDRS 6366)* – ('A'remix).

Nov 95. (7"/c-s) *(R/TCR 0071001)* **GOLDENEYE. / ('A'-Morales club mix)** [10] [ ]
(cd-s+=) *(CDR 0071001)* – ('A'-urban mix) / ('A'-A/C mix) / ('A'-urban A/C mix).

Mar 96. (c-s) *(TCR 6429)* **WHATEVER YOU WANT / GOLDENEYE** [23] [ ]
(cd-s+=) *(CDR 6429)* – ('A'-extended Olympic mix).
(cd-s+=) *(CDRS 6429)* – Unfinished sympathy.

Apr 96. (cd/c) *(CD/TC+/EST 2279)* *<41920>* **WILDEST DREAMS** [4] Sep96 [61]
– Missing you / In your wildest dreams / Whatever you want / Do what you do / Thief of hearts / On silent wings / Something beautiful remains / Confidential / The difference between us / All kinds of people / Unfinished symphony / Goldeneye / Dancing in my dreams.

May 96. (c-s/cd-s) *(TCR/CDR 6434)* **ON SILENT WINGS / PRIVATE DANCER / THE BEST / I DON'T WANNA LOSE YOU** [13] [ ]
(cd-s) *(CDRS 6434)* – ('A'side) / Whatever you want / Do something.

Jul 96. (c-s) *(TCR 6441)* **MISSING YOU / WHATEVER YOU WANT** [12] [–]
(cd-s+=) *(CDR 6441)* – The difference between us.
(cd-s) *(CDRS 6441)* – ('A'side) / We don't need another hero (live) / What's love got to do with it (live).

Sep 96. (c-s,cd-s) *<38553>* **MISSING YOU / DO SOMETHING** [–] [84]

Oct 96. (c-s) *(TCR 6448)* **SOMETHING BEAUTIFUL REMAINS / ADDICTED TO LOVE (live)** [27] [ ]
(cd-s) *(CDR 6448)* – ('A'side) / Steamy windows / Better be good to me.
(cd-s) *(CDRS 6448)* – ('A'mixes).

Dec 96. (c-s; by TINA TURNER featuring BARRY WHITE) *(TCR 6451)* **IN YOUR WILDEST DREAMS / WHAT'S LOVE GOT TO DO WITH IT?** [32] [ ]
(cd-s+=) *(CDR 6451)* – Goldeneye (live) / Missing you (live).
(cd-s) *(CDRS 6451)* – ('A') / ('A'-mixes).

TINA

Oct 99. (c-s) *(TCR 6529)* **WHEN THE HEARTACHE IS OVER / ('A'-Metro mix)** [10] [ ]
(cd-s+=) *(CDR 6529)* – ('A'-7th district club mix).
(cd-s) *(CDRS 6529)* – ('A'mix) / I can't stand the rain (live) / On silent wings (live).

Nov 99. (cd/c) *(523180-2/-4)* *<23180>* **TWENTY FOUR SEVEN** [9] Feb00 [21]
– Whatever you need / All the woman / When the heartache is over / Absolutely nothing's changed / Talk to my heart / Don't leave me this way / Go ahead / Without you / Falling / Will be there / Twenty four seven. *(d-cd-iss. Jul00; 527213-0)*

Jan 00. (c-s) *(TCR 6532)* **WHATEVER YOU NEED / (mix)** [27] [ ]
(cd-s) *(CDRS 6532)* – ('A') / The best (live) / River deep mountain high (live).
(cd-s) *(CDR 6532)* – ('A'-live) / What's love got to do with it (live) / Steamy windows (live).

Oct 04. (cd-s) *(CDCL 6532)* **OPEN ARMS / THE BEST** [25] [–]
(cd-s) *(CDCLS 6532)* – ('A') / Great spirits / Cose della vita (duet w/ Eros Ramazotti) / ('A'-video).

Nov 04. (cd) *(866717-2)<340186-2>* **ALL THE BEST: THE HITS** 6 Oct05 2
– I don't wanna fight / What's love got to do with it? / Proud Mary / Open arms / Private dancer / The best / Better be good to me / Let's stay together / Nutbush city limits / Missing you / Complicated disaster / It's only love / Look me in the heart / On silent wings / Two people / Typical male / We don't need another hero (Thunderdome) / What you get is what you see.

– (IKE & TINA) compilations, etc. –

Jan 69. (7") *London; (HLU 10242)* **RIVER DEEP MOUNTAIN HIGH. / SAVE THE LAST DANCE FOR ME** 33 –
May 76. (lp/c) *United Artists; (UA S/C 29948)* **THE VERY BEST OF IKE & TINA TURNER**
Feb 88. (cd) *Edsel; (ED 243)* **FINGER POPPIN' – THE WARNER BROS YEARS** –
Dec 88. (c) *Capitol; (4XLL 9191)* **PROUD MARY AND OTHER HITS** –
– A fool in love / I idolize you / I'm jealous / It's gonna work out fine / Poor fool / Tra la la la la / You shoulda treated me right / Come together / Honky tonk woman / I want to take you higher / Workin' together / Proud Mary / Funkier than a mosquito's tweeter / Ooh poo pah doo / I'm yours (use me any way you wanna) / Up in heah / River deep, mountain high / Nutbush city limits / Sweet Rhode Island red / Sexy Ida (parts 1 & 2) / Baby – Get it on / Acid queen. *(re-iss. Oct91 as 'PROUD MARY – THE BEST OF IKE & TINA TURNER' on 'EMI')*
Nov 94. (3xcd-box) *Capitol; (CDEST 2240)* **THE COLLECTED RECORDINGS** –
Jul 96. (cd) *EMI Gold; (CDGOLD 1049)* **18 CLASSIC TRACKS**
Sep 96. (3xcd-box) *Disky; (SA 87270-2)* **WORKIN' TOGETHER**
Nov 96. (3xcd-box) *Disky; (LAD 87330-2)* **THE BEST OF IKE & TINA TURNER: 18 ORIGINIAL HITS** –
Feb 97. (cd/c) *Platinum; (PLA TCD/C 211)* **BOLD SOUL SISTER**
May 97. (cd/c) *A-Play; (10176-2/-4)* **LIVING FOR THE CITY**
Oct 97. (cd/c) *Castle Pulse; (PLS CD/MC 253)* **LET THE GOOD TIMES ROLL**
Nov 97. (d-cd) *Eagle; (EDMCD 016)* **THE MASTERS**
Nov 98. (d-cd) *Disky; (HR 85303-2)* **ORIGINAL GOLD**
Dec 98. (d-cd) *Double Classics; (DC 31017)* **THE STORY OF . . .**
May 99. (cd) *Platinum; (PLATCD 507)* **THE VERY BEST OF IKE & TINA TURNER**
Aug 99. (d-cd) *K-Box; (KBOX 244)* **IKE & TINA TURNER**
Nov 99. (cd) *Laserlight; (21330)* **ROCKIN' AND ROLLIN'**
Jan 00. (cd) *Universal; (E 112167-2)* **UNIVERSAL MASTERS COLLECTION**
Apr 00. (cd) *Disky; (SI 99035-2)* **THE BEST OF THE 70'S**
May 00. (cd) *Kent; (CDKEND 182)* **THE KENT YEARS**
Jun 00. (d-cd) *Snapper; (SMDCD 290)* **TWO TOUGH**
Jun 00. (cd) *Starburst; (CDSB 017)* **LET THE GOOD TIMES ROLL**
Sep 00. (cd) *Members Edition; (UAE 31252)* **IKE & TINA TURNER**
Nov 00. (3xcd-box) *Goldies; (GLD 25407)* **RIVER DEEP MOUNTAIN HIGH**
Jan 01. (cd) *Bianco; (BIA 4043)* **LIVING FOR THE CITY**
Feb 01. (cd) *EMI Plus; (576074-2)* **WORKIN' TOGETHER**
Jul 01. (d-cd) *Laserlight; (24697)* **BABY GET IT ON**
Oct 01. (cd) *Platinum; (PLATCD 696)* **ROCKIN' AND ROLLIN': 20 HIP SHAKING FAVOURITES**
Dec 01. (cd) *Prestige; (CDSGP 058)* **IT'S ALL OVER**
Feb 02. (d-cd) *Universe; (UV 035)* **PORTRAIT IN BLUES**
Apr 02. (d-cd) *Platinum; (PLATBX 2217)* **ROCKIN' AND ROLLIN' / THE VERY BEST OF IKE & TINA TURNER**
Jun 02. (cd) *Stateside; (537960-2)* **FUNKIER THAN A MOSQUITO'S TWEETER**
Feb 03. (cd) *Mystic; (MYSCD 143)* **ULTIMATE MAXIMUM**
Mar 03. (3xcd-box) *Trilogie; (20595-2)* **I WANNA TAKE YOU HIGHER** –
Jun 03. (d-cd) *Gemini; (220444)* **I WANNA TAKE YOU HIGHER**
Jul 03. (d-cd) *Black Box; (BB 208)* **NUTBUSH CITY LIMITS**

☐ Jeff TWEEDY (see under ⇒ WILCO)

2PAC

Born: LESANE PARISH CROOKS, 16 Jun'71, Brooklyn, New York, USA. The son of a Black Panther member, after a successful start to his career as a member of West Coast rap act, DIGITAL UNDERGROUND, the "re-christened" TUPAC AMARU SHAKUR signed to 'Interscope' in 1991, making his solo debut with '2PACALYPSE NOW' (1992). A veritable journey into the heart of black inner city darkness, the record combined the bleak violence of gangsta with strong pro-Afro-American sentiments, as did the follow-up, 'STRICTLY 4 MY N.I.G.G.A.Z.' (1993), 2PAC almost breaking the US Top 10 with the 'I GET AROUND' single. He also had a penchant for getting on the wrong side of the law, running up an incredible string of charges including shooting two off-duty police officers, forceful sodomy (not with the police officers!) and attacking the co-director of the film, 'Menace II Society', Allen Hughes (2PAC had already made appearances in 'Juice', 'Under The Rim' and an acclaimed role in 'Poetic Justice'). While the shooting charge was dropped, 2PAC was subsequently sentenced to spend some time in prison for the sexual assault, ironically beginning his sentence while his third album, the aptly titled 'ME AGAINST THE WORLD' (1995) went to the top of the Billboard charts. The following year, the rapper was back at No.1 in defiant form with the landmark double set, 'ALL EYEZ ON ME', answering his many critics with 'ONLY GOD CAN JUDGE ME'. The album also spawned a No.1 single in the epochal 'CALIFORNIA LOVE', an utterly compelling 70's style pimp-rolling groove singing the praises of 2PAC's beloved home state, cut in collaboration with ex-ZAPP frontman, ROGER TROUTMAN. But if 2PAC was pro-Cali, he was viciously anti-New York, or at least its rap contingency, as witnessed on the track 'HIT 'EM UP' (included on the CD single of 'HOW DO YOU WANT IT'), a ferocious litany of hate primarily directed against his one-time friend, BIGGIE SMALLS (tried to shoot him?) but also stretching to MOBB DEEP and 'Bad Boy' records, the label at the centre of the East v West feud along with DR DRE's 'Death Row'. It had to end in tears of course, and it came as little surprise when 2PAC was shot and killed in a drive-by incident (13 September, 1996). Although no-one was subsequently charged with the murder, the rapper's list of enemies was almost as big as his police charge sheet and it was probably inevitable that a man who lived so closely by the gun wouldn't live to see 30. Violence and politics aside, there's no getting around the fact that 2PAC was an immensely talented artist, having scored his third US No.1 album in a row with 'THE DON KILLUMANATI: THE 7 DAY THEORY' (1996) under the alias MAKAVELI. His status as an American cultural icon was underlined recently when a US college introduced a 2PAC course, exploring the man's life and work. Crazy? Well, certainly no crazier than the esteem afforded the Kray Twins in Britain, and besides, did they pen anything as groovy as 'CALIFORNIA LOVE' (?!). In common with JEFF BUCKLEY, TUPAC's profile has remained high after his death through the regular release of half-finished, work in progress, the most recent being 'UNTIL THE END OF TIME' (2001). Also in common with BUCKLEY, the bulk of this material is of prime interest largely to hardcore fans who've got the time and inclination to muse over what the finished article would've sounded like. 2002's 'BETTER DAYZ' ranked as one of the more enduring posthumous releases, a sprawling double set of largely unreleased material which attempted some kind of focus by splitting the music up into one disc of hardcore and one of more accessible tracks. Of the two, the harder material perhaps left the deepest impression, the likes of 'F*** 'EM ALL' – a collaboration with OUTLAWZ – generating the kind of brooding portent that sounded all the more menacing in the light of subsequent events. One year on and fans were still being supplied with songs from beyond the grave, this time in the shape of the 'TUPAC: RESURRECTION' (2003) soundtrack. Another essential purchase for diehards, the record gathered together more obscure tracks from TUPAC's bulging back catalogue, a brace of which benefitted from EMINEM's production genius. The most poignant moment had to be the long lost collaboration with NOTORIOUS B.I.G., 'RUNNIN' (DYING TO LIVE)', an echo of happier days. The notoriously bad, sub-bootleg sound quality of '2PAC LIVE' (2004) made it superfluous for all but the most diehard of fans, even if it did make the US Top 60. Much more marketable was 'LOYAL TO THE GAME' (2004), an American chart topping (UK Top 20) reanimation of vintage 2PAC masterminded once again by EMINEM. Erasing the old backing tracks and retooling them with his own blockrocking productions, the Detroit superstar welded Elton John's 'INDIAN SUNSET' onto 'GHETTO GOSPEL' and landed TUPAC his first posthumous (US) No.1 single. 'LIVE AT THE HOUSE OF BLUES' (2005), on the other hand, was yet another archival release, catching him on top of his game but once again suffering from poor presentation.

Album rating: 2PACALYPSE NOW (*6) / STRICTLY 4 MY N.I.G.G.A.Z. (*7) / VOLUME 1 by Thug Life (*6) / ME AGAINST THE WORLD (*7) / ALL EYEZ ON ME (*7) / DON KILLUMMINATI: THE 7 DAY THEORY (*4; as Makeveli) / R U STILL DOWN (REMEMBER ME) (*5) / IN HIS OWN WORDS (*5) / GREATEST HITS compilation (*8) / UNTIL THE END OF TIME (*6) / BETTER DAYZ (*7) / NU-MIXX KLAZZICS remixes (*3) / TUPAC: RESURRECTION soundtrack (*6) / LIVE (*3) / LOYAL TO THE GAME (*5) / LIVE AT THE HOUSE OF BLUES w/ Snoop Dogg, etc. (*3)

TUPAC SHAKUR – vocals (with various guests, etc)

Interscope Interscope

Feb 92. (cd/c) *<IND/INC 91767>* **2PACALYPSE NOW** [ ] [64]
– Young black male / Trapped / Soulja's story / I don't give a fuck / Violent / Words of wisdom / Something wicked / Crooked ass nigga / If my home calls / Brenda's got a baby / Lunatic / Rebel of the underground / Part time mutha. *(cd re-iss. Feb97; same) (cd re-iss. Mar98 on 'Jive'; CHIP 199)*

Feb 93. (cd/c) *<IND/INC 92209>* **STRICTLY 4 MY N.I.G.G.A.Z.** [ ] [24]
– Holler if ya hear me / 2Pac's theme / Point the finga / Something 2 die 4 / Last wordz / Souljah's revenge / Peep game / Strugglin' / Guess who's back / Representin' / Keep ya head up / Strictly 4 my N.I.G.G.A.Z. / Streetz R deathrow / I get around / Papa'z song / Five deadly venomz. *(cd re-iss. Feb97; same) (cd re-iss. Mar98 on 'Jive'; CHIP 197)*

Jun 93. (c-s,cd-s) *<98372>* **I GET AROUND / NOTHING BUT LOVE** [–] [11]
<with free c-s+=; 96036> – KEEP YA HEAD UP *<hit No.12>*

Apr 94. (c-s,cd-s) *<98303>* **PAPA'Z SONG / ('A'instrumental)** [–] [87]

— 2PAC briefly set up THUG LIFE with **SKYE, MOPREME, MACADOSHIS + THE RATED R**

Nov 94. (cd/c; as THUG LIFE) *<(6544 92360-2/-4)>* **THUG LIFE VOLUME 1** [ ] [42]
– Bury me a G / Don't get it twisted / Shit don't stop (THUG LIFE & YNV) / Pour out a little liquor / Stay true / How long will they mourn me? (THUG LIFE & NATE DOGG) / Under pressure / Street fame / Cradle to the grave / Str8 ballin'. *(cd re-iss. Feb97; IND 92360) (cd re-iss. Mar98 on 'Jive'; CHIP 198)*

Mar 95. (cd/c/lp) *<(6544 92399-2/-4/-1)>* **ME AGAINST THE WORLD** [ ] [1]
– Intro / If I die 2nite / Me against the world / So many tears / Temptations / Young niggaz / Heavy in the game / Lord knows / Dear mama / It ain't easy / Can U get away / Old school / Fuck the world / Death around the corner / Outlaw. *(cd re-iss. Feb97; IND 92399) (cd re-iss. Mar98 on 'Jive'; CHIP 200)*

Jun 95. (c-s,cd-s) *<95748>* **SO MANY TEARS / (track by Dramacydal)** [–] [44]

Aug 95. (c-s) *(A 8156C)* **DEAR MAMA / OLD SCHOOL** [ ] Mar95 [9]
(12"+=/cd-s+=) *(A 8156 T/CD)* – ('A'mixes).
(above on 'Atlantic' UK)

Sep 95. (12",cd-s) *<98120>* **TEMPTATIONS (mixes) / ME AGAINST THE WORLD (mixes)** [–] [68]

Death Row Death Row

Mar 96. (d-cd/d-c) *(524249-2/-4) <524204>* **ALL EYEZ ON ME** [33] Feb96 [1]
– Book 1:- Ambitionz az a ridah / All bout u / Skandalouz / Got my mind made up / How do u want it / 2 of Amerikaz most wanted / No more pain / Heartz of men / Life goes on / Only God can judge me / Tradin war stories / California love / I ain't mad at cha / What'z ya phone # // Book 2:- Can't c me / Shorty wanna be a thug / Holla at me / Wonda why they call U bitch / When we ride / Thug passion / Picture me rollin' / Check out time / Ratha be ya nigga / All eyez on me / Run tha streetz / Ain't hard 2 find / Heaven ain't hard 2 find. *(d-cd-iss. Sep02)* – hit UK No.65

Apr 96. (c-s; 2PAC featuring DR.DRE) *(DRWMC 3)* **CALIFORNIA LOVE / (instrumental)** [6] [–]
(12"+=/cd-s+=) *(12DRW/DRWCD 3)* – ('A'mixes)

Jul 96. (c-s; 2PAC featuring KC and JOJO / 2PAC featuring DR.DRE and ROGER TRAUTMAN) *(DRWMC 4)* *<854652>* **HOW DO U WANT IT / CALIFORNIA LOVE** [17] [1] [6]
(12"+=/cd-s+=) *(12DRW/DRWCD 4)* – 2 of Amerikaz most wanted / Hit 'em up.

— 2PAC was shot dead on the 13th September, 1996 (below were posthumous releases)

Nov 96. (c-s) *(DRWMC 5)* **I AIN'T MAD AT CHA / SKANDALOUZ** [13] [–]
(12"+=) *(12DRW 5)* – Got my mind made up.
(cd-s++=) *(DRWCD 5)* – Heartz of men.

Jive Amaru – Death Row – Interscope

Nov 97. (d-cd/d-c) *(CHIP/HIPC 195) <41630>* **R U STILL DOWN? (REMEMBER ME)** [44] [2]
– Redemption / Open fire / R U still down? (remember me) / Hellrazor / Thug style / I wonder if Heaven got a ghetto / Nothing to lose / I'm gettin' money / Lie to kick it / Fuck all y'all / Let them thangs go / Definition of a thug nigga // Ready 4 whatever / When I get free / Hold on be strong / I'm losin' it / Fake ass bitches / Do for love / Enemies with me / Nothin' but love / 16 on death row / I wonder if Heaven got a ghetto (hip hop version) / When I get free II / Black starry night / Only fear of death.

Dec 97. (c-s) *(JIVEC 446) <42500>* **I WONDER IF HEAVEN GOT A GHETTO / WHEN I GET FREE** [21] [67]
(12"+=/cd-s+=) *(JIVE T/CD 446)* – ('A'mixes).

Jun 98. (c-s) *(051851-4) <42516>* **DO FOR LOVE / BRENDA'S GOT A BABY** [12] Mar98 [21]
(12"+=/cd-s+=) *(051851-6/-2)* – ('A'mixes; soul society / Pic-a-dil-yo!).
(above credited in the States to 2PAC featuring ERIC WILLIAMS)

Nov 98. (d-cd/d-c/q-lp) *Jive; (052266-2/-4/-1) / Amaru – Death Row – Interscope; <490307>* **GREATEST HITS** (compilation) [17] [3]
– Keep ya head up / 2 of Americaz most wanted / Temptations / God bless the dead / Hail Mary / Me against the world / How do you want it? / So many tears / Unconditional love / Trapped / Life goes on / Hit 'em up // Troublesome '96 / Brenda's got a baby / I ain't mad at cha / I get around / Changes / California love / Picture me rollin' / How long will they mourn me / Toss it up (remix) / Dear mama / All bout U (w/ TOPP DOGG) / To live & die in L.A. / Heartz of men. *(d-cd re-iss. Jul01; same)* – hit UK No.25

Feb 99. (c-s) *(052283-4) <radio cut>* **CHANGES / ('A'mix)** [3] Nov98 [32]
(12"+=/cd-s+=) *(052283-0/-2)* – ('A'mixes).

Jun 99. (c-s) *(052334-4/-2)* **DEAR MAMA / (instrumental)** [27] [–]
(cd-s) *(052370-2)* – (2-'A'mixes by Moe Z).

Dec 99. (cd/c; by 2PAC + OUTLAWZ) *<(490413-2/-4)>* **STILL I RISE** [75] [6]
– Letter to the president / Still I rise / Secretz of war / Baby don't cry (keep ya head up II) / As the world turns / Black Jesuz / Homeboyz / Hell 4 a hustler / High speed / The good die young / Killuminati / Teardrops and closed caskets / Tattoo tears / U can be touched / Y'all don't know us. *<(clean version; 490417-2)>*

Feb 00. (-; by 2PAC + OUTLAWZ) *<radio cut>* **BABY DON'T CRY (KEEP YOUR HEAD UP II)** [–] [72]

Apr 01. (d-cd) *<(490840-2)>* **UNTIL THE END OF TIME** [33] [1]
– Ballad of a dead soulja / Fuck friendz / Lil' homies / Let 'em have it / Good life / Letter 2 my unborn / Breathin' / Happy home / All out / Fuckin' wit the wrong nigga / Thug n U thug n me (remix) / Everything they owe / Until the end of time / M.O.B. / World wide mob figgaz / Big skye (intelude) / My closest roaddogz / Niggaz nature (remix) / When thugz cry / U don't have to worry / This

ain't livin' / Why U turn me on / Lastonesleft / Thug n U thug me (Hutch mix) / Words 2 my first born / Let 'em have it (committee mix) / Runnin' on E / When I get free / Until the end of time (RP remix).

Jun 01. (c-s/12") *(497581-1/-4)* *<radio cut>* **UNTIL THE END OF TIME. / THUG N THUG N ME / BABY DON'T CRY (KEEP YA HEAD UP)** [4] Apr01 [52]
(cd-s+=) *(497581-2)* – ('A'-video).

Oct 01. (c-s) *(497614-4)* **LETTER 2 MY UNBORN / UNTIL THE END OF TIME** [21] [–]
(12") *(497614-1)* – ('A'side) / Hell 4 a hustler / ('A'0instrumental).
(cd-s+=) *(497614-2)* – ('A'-video).

Nov 02. (d-cd) *<(497070-2)>* **BETTER DAYZ** [68] [5]
– Intro / Still ballin (with TRICK DADDY) / When we ride on our enemies / Changed man (with JAZZE PHA, T.I. & JOHNTA' AUSTIN) / Fuck em all (with OUTLAWZ) / Never B peace (with E.D.I. & KASTRO) / Mama's just a little girl (with KIMMY HILL) / Street fame / Whatcha gonna do (with KASTRO & YOUNG NOBLE) / Fair xchange (with JAZZE PHA) / Late night (with DJ QUIK & OUTLAWZ) / Ghetto star (with NUTSO) / Thugz mansion (with NAS & J. PHOENIX) / My block (remix) / Thugz mansion (with ANTHONY HAMILTON) / Never call U bitch again (with TYRESE) / Better dayz (with MR. BIGGS) / U can call (with JAZZE PHA) / Military minds (with CO CO BROTHERS & BUCKSHOT) / Fame (with KADAFI, KASTRO, NAPOLEON & YOUNG NOBLE) / Fair xchange (remix with MYA) / Catching feelins (with MUSSAMILL, E.D.I., NAPOLEON & YOUNG NOBLE) / There U go (with KADAFI, E.D.I., KASTRO & NAPOLEON) / This life I lead (with OUTLAWZ) / Who do U believe in (with KADAFI) / They don't give a fuck about us (with OUTLAWZ).

Feb 03. (c-s) *(497854-4)* **THUGZ MANSION / THUGZ MANSION (explicit with NAS)** [24] [19]
(12"+=) *(497854-1)* – Fuck em all (explicit).
(cd-s+=) *(497854-2)* – ('A'-video).

Universal Amaru

Nov 03. (cd) *(9861159)* *<154302>* **TUPAC: RESURRECTION** (soundtrack) [62] [2]
– Intro / Ghost / One day at a time (with EMINEM & OUTLAWZ) / Death around the corner / Secretz of war / Runnin' (dying to live) (with NOTORIOUS B.I.G.) / Holler if ya' hear me / Starin' through my rear view / Bury me a G / Same song (with DIGITAL UNDERGROUND) / Panther power / Str8 ballin / Rebel of the underground / The realist killaz (with 50 CENT).

Jan 04. (12"; with NOTORIOUS B.I.G.) *(9861687)* *<11042>* **RUNNIN' (DYING TO LIVE) / STILL BALLIN' (nitty remix) / (version)** [17] Oct03 [47]
(cd-s+=) *(9815329)* – ('A'-video).

Dec 04. (cd) *(2103291)* *<38610-2>* **LOYAL TO THE GAME** [20] [1]
– Soldier like me (aka Return of the Soulja) (w/ EMINEM) / The uppercut (w. E.D.I. & NOBIE) / Out on bail / Ghetto gospel / Black cotton (w/ EMINEM) / Loyal to the game (w/ G-UNIT) / Thugs get lonely too (w/ NATE DOGG) / N.I.G.G.A. (Never Ignorant about Getting Goals Accomplished) (w/ JADAKISS) / Who do you love? / Crooked nigga too / Don't you trust me / Hennessey (w/ OBIE TRICE) / Thug 4 life / Po nigga blues (Scott Starch remix w/ RON ISLEY) / Hennessey (Red Spyda remix w/ E.D.I. & SLEEPY BROWN) / Crooked nigga too (Raphael Saadiq remix) / Loyal to the game (DJ Quik remix w/ BIG SYKE).

Jan 05. (-) *<radio>* **THUGS GET LONELY TOO** [–] [98]

Jun 05. (cd-s; feat. ELTON JOHN) *(988303-2)* **GHETTO GOSPEL / THUGS GET LONELY TOO** [1] [–]
(12"+=) *(9882168)* – ('A'-instrumental).
(cd-s++=) *(9883048)* – ('A'-video).

– compilations, etc. –

Sep 97. (cd) *Aim; (AIM 4001CD)* **1 IN 2 1 (2PAC – A TUPAC SHAKUR STORY)** [ ] [ ]

Jun 98. (cd; as 2PAC & NOTORIOUS B.I.G.) *Cashmoneybruthas; (CMBCD 1)* **WHO SHOT YA** [ ] [ ]

Jul 98. (c-s; 2PAC & NOTORIOUS B.I.G.) *Black Jam; (BJAM 9005)* **RUNNIN'** (rec.1995) / ('A'mixes) [15] [ ]
(12"+=/cd-s+=) *(BJAM 1205/6605)* – ('A'mixes).

Jul 98. (cd/c) *Eagle; (EAG CD/MC 050)* **IN HIS OWN WORDS** [65] [ ]

Nov 98. (12"/c-s/cd-s) *Eagle; (EAG CS/12/XS 058)* **HAPPY HOME (mixes)** [17] [ ]

Sep 99. (cd; as 2PAC & The NOTORIOUS B.I.G.) *ZYX; (20531-2)* **THE HERE AFTER** [ ] [ ]

Nov 00. (cd; by TUPAC SHAKUR & Various Artists) *Polydor; <(490813-2)>* **THE ROSE THAT GREW FROM CONCRETE VOL.1** [ ] [89]

Oct 03. (cd) *Koch; <(23 9530-2)>* **NU MIXX KLAZZICS** [ ] [15]

Aug 04. (cd) *Koch; <(23 5746-2)>* **LIVE** (live) [67] [54]
– California love – So many tears / (intro) / Ambitionz az a ridah / So many tears / Troublesome / Hit em up / Tattoo tears / Heartz of men / All about you / Never call you bitch again / How do you want it / 2 of Amerikaz most wanted / California love.

Feb 05. (cd) *Street Dance; (SDR 016688-2)* **READY 2 DIE** [70] [–]

Oct 05. (cd) *Eagle; (EAGCD 209)* *<20080>* **LIVE AT THE HOUSE OF BLUES** (live w/ Snoop Dogg, etc.) [ ] Sep05 [ ]

MAKAVELI

Interscope Interscope

Nov 96. (cd/c) *<(IND/INC 90039)>* **THE DON KILLUMINATI: THE 7 DAY THEORY** [53] [1]
– (intro) – Bomb first (my second reply) / Hail Mary / Toss it up / To live & die in L.A. / Blasphemy / Life of an outlaw / Just like daddy / Krazy / White man'z world / Me and my girlfriend / Hold ya head / Against all odds. *(re-iss. Feb97 on 'Interscope' cd/c; same)*

— In Jan'97, 2PAC plus NOTORIOUS B.I.G., RADIO, DRAMACYDAL & STRETCH, released collaboration single, 'RUNNIN', which hit US No.84

Apr 97. (c-s) *(INC 95529)* **TO LIVE & DIE IN L.A. / (album mix)** [10] [ ]
(12"+=/cd-s+=) *(INT/IND 95529)* – Just like daddy.

— In Apr'97, 2PAC & SNOOP DOGGY DOGG had a combined UK No.16 hit 'WANTED DEAD OR ALIVE'. 2PAC then guested on the SCARFACE single 'Smile' which hit No.12 US.

Aug 97. (c-s) *(INC 95521)* **TOSS IT UP / (album mix)** [15] [ ]
(12"+=) *(INT 95521)* – ('A'-instrumental).
(cd-s++=) *(IND 95521)* – ('A'-video).

Feb 98. (c-s) *(INC 95575)* **HAIL MARY / (album mix)** [43] [ ]
(12"+=) *(INT 95575)* – ('A'-instrumental).
(cd-s++=) *(IND 95575)* – Life of an outlaw.

□ TYRANNOSAURUS REX

(see under ⇒ BOLAN, Marc)

UB40

Formed: Mosley, Birmingham, England ... early 1979 by ALI and ROBIN, sons of Scots folk singer, IAN CAMPBELL. The self-taught brothers built around them a multi-racial ensemble, who, due to their own jobless status and the country's unemployment figures, decided to name themselves after the dole card form, UB40. BRIAN TRAVERS, EARL FALCONER and JIM BROWN had been in their band while at Art College in 1977 and around two years later (including a lengthy stint playing in local pubs and clubs), they signed to David and Susan Virr's new label, 'Graduate'. Their protest reggae style was introduced to a wider audience as the group embarked on a prestigious tour with The PRETENDERS and 1980 saw UB40 hitting the UK Top 5 with the classic double A-side, 'FOOD FOR THOUGHT' / 'KING'. A Top 10 follow-up, 'THE EARTH DIES SCREAMING', was preceded by a Bob Lamb-produced debut album, appropriately enough titled 'SIGNING OFF' (as one does after procuring employment). In 1981, they formed their own label, 'DEP International' and recording studio, 'The Abbatoir', where they laid down the material for a second album, 'PRESENT ARMS'. The cosmopolitan reggae conglomerate continued to have massive hits throughout the 80's, including two chart topping covers, 'RED RED WINE' (from the pen of NEIL DIAMOND) and the CHRISSIE HYNDE collaboration, 'I GOT YOU BABE' (previously a 60's No.1 for SONNY & CHER). The former was taken from their album of cover versions, 'LABOUR OF LOVE' (1983) and marked their first real inroads into the lucrative US market. UB40 consolidated their position as Britain's foremost mainstream reggae act with an impressive run of hit singles and albums, continuing to translate traditional Jamaican stylings into more chart friendly pop. A temporary change in personnel was required in July 1988 when bassist FALCONER was jailed for six months on a drink driving charge. Upon his return UB40 went on to achieve further success in the 90's, their version of the ELVIS PRESLEY hit 'CAN'T HELP FALLING IN LOVE' topping the charts and a definite highlight of their equally successful long player, 'PROMISES AND LIES' (1993). ALI went solo in 1995, releasing the 'BIG LOVE' album before returning to the band for UB40's umpteenth outing, 'GUNS IN THE GHETTO' (1997). While 'LABOUR OF LOVE III' (1998) featured the usual set of covers, although a third instalment was perhaps milking the cash cow just a bit too hard and there were precious few moments of inspiration to refute that conclusion. After an extended break punctuated by a millennial 'BEST OF ...' detailing their 20-year career, Birmingham's veteran reggae revivalists returned with 'COVER UP' (2001), the title track a reference to AIDS prevention rather than an indication of a covers set. 'HOMEGROWN' (2003) was notable mainly for the inclusion of UB40's highly unlikely contribution to England's Rugby World Cup hopes, 'SWING LOW SWEET CHARIOT', although there were hints at the brooding brilliance of old on the likes of 'YOUNG GUNS', a swipe at hip-hop's culture of violence. 'WHO YOU FIGHTING FOR?' (2005) saw UB40 get back to their observational best, the UK Top 20 set a mixture of self-penned numbers and reggae-fied covers such as Dennis Bovell's 'AFTER TONIGHT', the Beatles' 'I'LL BE ON MY WAY' and hit single 'KISS AND SAY GOODBYE' once a smash for the Manhattans.

• **Songwriters:** ALI penned most material except singles I THINK IT'S GOING TO RAIN TODAY (Randy Newman) / MANY RIVERS TO CROSS (Jimmy Cliff) / CHERRY OH BABY (Eric Donaldson) / PLEASE DON'T MAKE ME CRY (Junior Tucker) / SMALL AXE + SOUL REBEL (Bob Marley) / KEEP ON MOVING (Mayfield-Marley) / JOHNNY TOO BAD (Wilson, Bedford, Bailey & Crooks) / VERSION GIRL (R.Thompson aka-Dandy Livingstone) / BREAKFAST IN BED (Dusty Springfield) / HOMELY GIRL (Chi-Lites) / KINGSTON TOWN (Andy Patrick) / HERE I AM (Al Green) / THE WAY YOU DO THE THINGS YOU DO (Smokey Robinson) / HOLLY HOLY (Neil Diamond). LABOUR OF LOVE and LABOUR OF LOVE II & III were cover albums featuring some already mentioned. ALI CAMPBELL covered HAPPINESS (Stevie Wonder-Syreeta) / SOMETHIN' STUPID (hit; Frank & Nancy Sinatra) / THAT LOOK IN YOUR EYE (Starks-Grey) / YOU CAN CRY ON MY SHOULDER (Berry Gordy) / LET YOUR YEAH BE YEAH (Jimmy Cliff) / DRIVE IT HOME (Ernest Ranglin) / GOOD SITUATION (Davis & Lewis) / THINGS YOU SAY YOU LOVE (Jamaicans).

Album rating: SIGNING OFF (*8) / PRESENT ARMS (*7) / PRESENT ARMS IN DUB (*5) / THE SINGLES ALBUM compilation (*7) / UB44 (*6) / LABOUR OF LOVE (*8) / GEFFREY MORGAN (*7) / BAGGARIDDIM (*6) / RAT IN THE KITCHEN (*7) / CCCP: LIVE IN MOSCOW (*4) / THE BEST OF UB40 VOLUME 1 compilation (*7) / UB40 (*7) / LABOUR OF LOVE II (*6) / PROMISES AND LIES (*6) / THE BEST OF UB40 VOL.2 compilation (*7) / GUNS IN THE GHETTO (*6) / LABOUR OF LOVE III (*5) / THE VERY BEST OF UB40 1980-2000 compilation (*8) / COVER UP (*5) / ...PRESENT THE FATHERS OF REGGAE (*5) / HOMEGROWN (*4) / WHO ARE YOU FIGHTING FOR? (*6)

ALI CAMPBELL (b. ALISTAIR, 15 Feb'59) – vocals, guitar / **ROBIN CAMPBELL** (b.25 Dec'54) – guitar, vocals / **ASTRO** (b. TERENCE WILSON, 24 Jun'57) – toaster/**vocals** repl. YOMI BABAYEMI / **MICHAEL VIRTUE** (b.19 Jan'57) – keyboards repl. JIMMY LYNN / **EARL FALCONER** (b.23 Jan'59) – bass / **BRIAN TRAVERS** (b. 7 Feb'59) – saxophone / **JIM BROWN** (b.20 Nov'57) – drums / **NORMAN HASSAN** (b.26 Jan'58) – percussion

		Graduate	Sound
Jan 80.	(7") *(GRAD 6)* **FOOD FOR THOUGHT. / KING**	4	
Jun 80.	(7"/12") *(GRAD/12GRAD 8)* **MY WAY OF THINKING. / I THINK IT'S GOING TO RAIN TODAY**	6	
Aug 80.	(lp/c) *(GRAD LP/C 2)* **SIGNING OFF** – Tyler / King / 12 bar / Burden of shame / Adella / I think it's going to rain today / 25% / Food for thought / Little by little / Signing off. *(free-12"ep w.a.)* **MADAM MEDUSA. / STRANGE FRUIT / REEFER MADNESS** *(cd-iss. 1986 on 'Target')*	2	
Oct 80.	(7"/12") *(GRAD/12GRAD 10)* **THE EARTH DIES SCREAMING. / DREAM A LIE** *(all above 45's re-iss. 1984)*	10	
		DEP Inter.	A & M
May 81.	(7"/12") *(DEP 1/112)* **DON'T LET IT PASS YOU BY. / DON'T SLOW DOWN**	16	–
May 81.	(lp/c) *(LP/CA DEP 1)* **PRESENT ARMS** – Present arms / Sardonicus / Don't let it pass you by / Wild cat / One in ten / Don't slow down / Silent witness / Lambs bread. *(free 12" w.a.)* **DON'T WALK ON THE GRASS. / DOCTOR X** *(lp re-iss. Jan83) (cd-iss. Apr88 on 'Virgin')*	2	–
Jul 81.	(7") *(DEP 2)* **ONE IN TEN. / PRESENT ARMS IN DUB**	7	–

Oct 81. (lp/c) *(LP/CA DEP 2)* **PRESENT ARMS IN DUB** [38] [–]
– Present arms / Smoke it / B-line / Kings Row / Return of Doctor X / Walk out / One in ten / Neon haze. *(re-iss. Jan83)*

Feb 82. (7"/12") *(DEP 3/+12)* **I WON'T CLOSE MY EYES. / FOLITICIAN** [32] [–]

May 82. (7") *(DEP 4)* **LOVE IS ALL IS ALRIGHT. / HOT-CROSS DUB** [29] [–]
(12"+=) *(DEP 412)* – ('A'live version).

Aug 82. (7") *(DEP 5)* **SO HERE I AM. / SILENT WITNESS** [25] [–]
(12"+=) *(DEP 512)* – Doctor X (live).

Sep 82. (lp/c) *(LP/CA DEP 3)* **UB44** [4] [–]
– So here I am / I won't close my eyes / Forget the cost / Love is all is alright / The piper calls the tune / The key / Don't do the crime / Folitician / The prisoner. *(re-iss. Jan83) (re-iss. +cd.remixed Apr86)*

—— DEP International were now distributed by 'Virgin'.

Jan 83. (7") *(DEP 6)* **I'VE GOT MINE. / DUBMOBILE** [45] [–]
(12"+=) *(DEP 612)* – Forget the cost.

Feb 83. (lp/c) *(LPCA DEP 4)* **UB40 LIVE (live in Ireland)** [44] [–]
– Food for thought / Sardonicus / Don't slow down / Folitician / Tyler / Present arms / The piper calls the tune / Love is all is alright / Burden of shame / One in ten. *(re-iss. Aug84) (cd-iss. 1988)*

Aug 83. (7"/12") *(DEP 7/+12) <2600>* **RED RED WINE. / SUFFERING** [1] Nov 83 [34]
(US re-iss. Aug88, hit No.1) (at same time, below album hits US No.14)

Sep 83. (lp/c) *(LP/CA DEP 5) <4980>* **LABOUR OF LOVE** [1] Nov 83 [39]
– Cherry oh baby / Keep on moving / Please don't make me cry / Sweet sensation / Johnny too bad / Red red wine / Guilty / She caught the train / Version girl / Many rivers to cross. *(cd-iss. Jul86)*

Oct 83. (7"/12") *(DEP 8/+12)* **PLEASE DON'T MAKE ME CRY. / SUFFERING (featuring NYA & NATTY)** [10] [–]

Dec 83. (7") *(DEP 9)* **MANY RIVERS TO CROSS. / FOOD FOR THOUGHT (live)** [16] [ ]
(12"+=) *(DEP 9-12)* – Johnny Too Bad (version).

Feb 84. (7") **CHERRY OH BABY. / FOOD FOR THOUGHT** [–] [ ]

Mar 84. (7"/12")(10"pic-d) *(DEP 10/+12)(DEPY 10)* **CHERRY OH BABY. / FRILLA** [12] [ ]

Apr 84. (7") **PLEASE DON'T MAKE ME CRY. / FOOD FOR THOUGHT** [–] [ ]

Sep 84. (7"/12") *(DEP 11/+12)* **IF IT HAPPENS AGAIN. / NKOMO A GO-GO** [9] [ ]

Oct 84. (lp/c)(cd) *(LP/CA DEP 6)(DEPCD 6) <5033>* **GEFFERY MORGAN** [3] [60]
– Riddle me / As always you were wrong again / If it happens again / D.U.B. / The pillow / Nkomo a go-go / Seasons / You're not an army / I'm not fooled so easily / Your eyes were open.

Nov 84. (7"/12") *(DEP 15/+12)* **RIDDLE ME. / D.U.B. (dub)** [59] [ ]

—— In Feb85, they appeared on charity single STARVATION with various BEAT members, etc. Released on 'Zarjazz' label, it hit UK No.33.

Mar 85. (7"/12") *(DEP 16/+12)* **I'M NOT FOOLED. / THE PILLOW** [ ] [ ]

Jul 85. (7"; UB40 & CHRISSIE HYNDE) *(DEP 20)* **I GOT YOU BABE. / THEME FROM LABOUR OF LOVE** [1] [–]
(12"+=) *(DEP 2012)* – Up and coming MC.

Jul 85. (7"; UB40 & CHRISSIE HYNDE) *<2758>* **I GOT YOU BABE. / NKOMO A GO-GO** [–] [28]

Aug 85. (m-lp/c)(cd) *<5090>* **LITTLE BAGGARIDM** [–] [40]
– Don't break my heart / I got you babe / Hip hop lyrical robot / One in ten.

Sep 85. (lp/c)(cd) *(LP/CA DEP 10)(DEPCD 10)* **BAGGARIDDIM** [14] [–]
– The king step mk.1 / The buzz feeling / Lyric officer mk.2 / Demonstrate / Two in a one mk.1 / Hold your position mk.3 / Hip hop lyrical robot / Style mk.4 / Fight fe come in mk.2 / V's version. (12"w.a.) **DON'T BREAK MY HEART. / I GOT YOU BABE / MI SPLIFF** *(re-iss. Apr90)*

Oct 85. (7"/12") *(DEP 22/+12)* **DON'T BREAK MY HEART. / MEK YA ROK** [3] [ ]

Jun 86. (7"/12") *(DEP 23/+12)* **SING OUR OWN SONG. / ('A' instrumental)** [5] [ ]

Jul 86. (lp/c)(cd) *(LP/CA DEP 11)(DEPCD 11) <5137>* **RAT IN THE KITCHEN** [8] [53]
– All I want to do / You could meet somebody / Tell it like this / The elevator / Watchdogs / Rat in me kitchen / Looking down at my reflection / Don't blame me / Sing our own song.

Sep 86. (7"/12") *(DEP 24/+12)* **ALL I WANT TO DO. / ('A'version)** [41] [ ]

Jan 87. (7"/12") *(DEP 25/+12)* **RAT IN MI KITCHEN. / ('A' long version)** [12] [ ]

Apr 87. (7") *(DEP 26)* **WATCHDOGS. / DON'T BLAME ME** [39] [ ]
(12"+=) *(DEP 26-12)* – ('A'live version).

Aug 87. (lp/c/cd) *<5168>* **CCCP: LIVE IN MOSCOW (live)** [–] [ ]
– All I want to do / Cherry oh baby / Keep on moving / Watchdogs / Don't blame me / Tell it like it is / Please don't make me cry / Johnny too bad / I got you babe / Don't break my heart / If it happens again / Rat in me kitchen / Sing our own song.

Sep 87. (7") *(DEP 27)* **MAYBE TOMORROW. / DREAD DREAD TIME** [14] [ ]
(12"+=)(c-s+=) *(DEP 27-12)(DEPC 27)* – Anything mi chat.

May 88. (7"; UB40 & CHRISSIE HYNDE) *(DEP 29)* **BREAKFAST IN BED. / ('A'instrumental)** [6] [ ]
(12"+=)(cd-s+=) *(DEP 29-12)(DEPX 29)* – ('A'other versions).

May 88. (lp/c)(cd) *(LP/CA DEP 13)(DEPCD 13) <5213>* **UB40** [12] [44]
– Dance with the Devil / Come out to play / Breakfast in bed / You're always pulling me down / I would do for you / 'Cause it isn't true / Where did I go wrong / Contaminated minds / Matter of time / Music so nice / Dance with the Devil (reprise). *(pic-cd.Dec88)*

Aug 88. (7") *(DEP 30)* **WHERE DID I GO WRONG. / ('A'instrumental)** [26] [–]
(12"+=) *(DEP 3012)* – Contaminated dub.
(cd-s++=) *(DEPX 30)* – Hit it (instrumental).

Nov 88. (7") *<>* **WHERE DID I GO WRONG. / DANCE WITH THE DEVIL** [–] [ ]

—— **LARRY BUSHELL** – bass temp.repl. EARL for 4 mths. Jul88.

Nov 88. (7"/c-s) *(DEP/+C 31)* **COME OUT TO PLAY. / CONTAMINATED MINDS** [ ] [ ]
(12"+=) *(DEP 31-12)* – Sing our own song (live).
(10"++=) *(DEP 31-10)* – ('A'instrumental).
(cd-s+=) *(DEPX 31)* – Dance with the Devil / Rat in mi kitchen.

Jun 89. (7"/c-s) *(DEP/+C 32)* **I WOULD DO FOR YOU. / HIT IT** [45] [ ]
(12"+=)(3"cd-s+=) *(DEP 32-12)(DEPX 32)* – ('B'version).

DEP Int. Virgin

Nov 89. (7"/c-s) *(DEP/+C 33)* **HOMELY GIRL. / GATOR** [6] [ ]
(12"+=)(3"cd-s+=) *(DEP 33-12)(DEPX 33)* – ('A'extended).

Dec 89. (lp/c)(cd) *(LP/CA DEP 14)(DEPCD 14) <91324>* **LABOUR OF LOVE II** [4] [30]
– Here I am (come and take me) / Tears from my eyes / Groovin' / The way you do the things you do / Wear you to the ball / Singer man / Kingston Town / Baby / Wedding day / Sweet Cherrie / Stick by me / Just another girl / Homely girl / Impossible love.

Jan 90. (7"/c-s) *(DEP/+C 34)* **HERE I AM (COME AND TAKE ME). / CRISIS** [46] [–]
(12"+=)(cd-s+=) *(DEP 34-12)(DEPX 34)* – ('B'dub version).

Mar 90. (7"/c-s) *(DEP/+C 35)* **KINGSTON TOWN. / LICKWOOD** [4] [ ]
(12"+=)(cd-s+=) *(DEP 35-12)(DEPXT 35)* – ('A'extended mix).

Jul 90. (7"/c-s) *(DEP/+C 36)* **WEAR YOU TO THE BALL. / SPLUGIN** [35] [ ]
(12"+=)(cd-s++=) *(DEP 36-12)(DEPXT 36)* – ('A'extended)./ / ('A'dub version).

Sep 90. (c-s,cd-s) *<98978>* **THE WAY YOU DO THE THINGS YOU DO** [–] [6]

—— in Oct'90, they teamed up with ROBERT PALMER on UK No.6, 'I'LL BE YOUR BABY TONIGHT'

Nov 90. (7"/c-s) *(DEP/+C 37)* **IMPOSSIBLE LOVE. / FIRST SHOT** [47] [ ]
(12"+=)(cd-s+=) *(DEP 37-12)(DEPXT 37)* – Council house.

Jan 91. (7"/c-s) *(DEP/+C 38)* **THE WAY YOU DO THE THINGS YOU DO. / MISSPENT YOUTH** [49] [–]
(cd-s+=) *(DEPXT 38)* – ('A'remix).

Mar 91. (c-s,cd-s) *<99141>* **HERE I AM (COME AND TAKE ME) / GATOR** [–] [7]

Nov 91. (7"/c-s) *(DEP/+C 39)* **BABY. / SHE CAUGHT THE TRAIN** [ ] [ ]
(12"+=)(cd-s+=) *(DEP 39-12)(DEPXT 39)* – Here I am (come and take me) (mix) / Dubmobile (live).

Nov 91. (c-s,cd-s) *<98654>* **GROOVIN' / COUNCIL HOUSE** [–] [90]

—— In Nov'92, teamed up with 808 STATE on a UK Top 20 version of 'ONE IN TEN'.

May 93. (7"/c-s) *(DEP/+C 40) <12653>* **(I CAN'T HELP) FALLING IN LOVE WITH YOU. / JUNGLE LOVE** [1] [1]
(12"+=)/ /(cd-s++=) *(DEP 40-12)/ /(DEPDG 40)* – ('A'extended)./ / Red red wine.

Jul 93. (cd/c)(lp) *(LP/CA DEP 15)(DEPCD 15) <88229>*
PROMISES AND LIES [1] [6]
– C'est la vie / Desert sand / Promises and lies / Bring me your cup / Higher ground / Reggae music / Can't help falling in love / Now and then / Things ain't what they used to be / It's a long long way / Sorry.

Aug 93. (7"/c-s) *(DEP/+C 41) <12681>* **HIGHER GROUND. / CHRONIC** [8] Oct93 [45]
(12"+=)(cd-s+=) *(DEP 4112)(DEPD 41)* – Punjab dub (mix).

Nov 93. (7"/c-s) *(DEP/+C 42)* **BRING ME YOUR CUP. / BAD EKKO** [24] [ ]
(cd-s+=) *(DEPD 42)* – ('A'mixes).

Mar 94. (7"/c-s) *(DEP/+C 43)* **C'EST LA VIE. / PROMISES AND LIES (live)** [37] [ ]
(12"+=)(cd-s+=) *(DEP 43-12)(DEPD 43)* – Tyler.

Aug 94. (7"/c-s) *(DEP/+C 44)* **REGGAE MUSIC. / MATTER OF TIME** [28] [ ]
(cd-s+=) *(DEPDG 44)* – Things ain't like they used to be.

— In Oct94, they featured on UK No.1 'Baby Come Back' by PATO BANTON.

Oct 95. (c-s) *(DEPC 45)* **UNTIL MY DYING DAY / ('A'instrumental)** [15] [ ]
(cd-s+=) *(DEPD 45)* – Sorry (live) / Bring me your cup (live).
(cd-s+=) *(DEPDX 45)* – ('A'-C.J.'s closet mix).

Oct 95. (cd/c) *(DUBTV/UBTVC 2)* **THE BEST OF UB 40 VOL.2** (compilation) [12] [–]
– Breakfast in bed / Where did I go wrong / I would do for you / Homely girl / Here I am (come and take me) / Kingston Town / Wear you to the ball / Can't help falling in love / Higher ground / Bring me your cup / C'est la vie / Reggae music / Superstition / Until my dying day.

Jul 97. (cd/c) *(DEPCD/CADEP/LPDEP 16) <44402>* **GUNS IN THE GHETTO** [7] [ ]
– Always there / Hurry come on up / I love it when you smile / I've been missing you / Guns in the ghetto / Tell me is it true / Oracabessa moonshine / Friendly fire / I really can't say / Lisa.

Aug 97. (c-s/cd-s) *(DEP C/DE 48)* **TELL ME IS IT TRUE / IT'S TRUE** [14] [ ]
(12"+=/cd-s+=) *(DEP X/D 48)* – ('A'mixes; Fugees / Sly & Robbie).

Nov 97. (cd-s) *(DEPDE 49)* **ALWAYS THERE / MAGIC CARPET (pincers)** [53] [–]
(c-s+=) *(DEPC 49)* – ('A'-remixed by Gogglehead).
(cd-s++=) *(DEPDC 49)* – Hills and valley (Ninjaman).

May 98. (cd/c) *(DEP CD/C 17)* **UB40 present THE DANCEHALL ALBUM** [ ] [–]
– Magic carpet (with PINCHERS) / Force ripe (with MERCILESS) / Smile for me (with GENERAL DEGREE) / Waw waw waw (with Lt. STITCHIE) / More opportunity (with ANTHONY B) / Oh no baby don't go (with PETER METRO) / Love that I need (with BEENIE MAN) / Ladda bay (with MAD COBRA) / More love (with RED DRAGON) / Nuff love (with LADY SAW) / Who (SPRAGGA BENZ) / Hills and valley (with NINJA MAN) / No stray (with ROUNDHEAD).

Sep 98. (c-s) *(DEPC 50)* **COME BACK DARLING / IN THE PARK** [10] [–]
(cd-s+=) *(DEPD 50)* – ('A'instrumental).

Oct 98. (cd/c) *(DEPCD/CADEP 18) <48469>* **LABOUR OF LOVE III** [8] [ ]
– Holly holy / It's my delight / Come back darling / Never let you go / Soul rebel / My best girl / Good ambition / The train is coming / Blood and fire / Mr. Fix it / Stay a little bit longer / Someone like you / The time has come / Crying over you / Legalise it.

Dec 98. (c-s) *(DEPC 51)* **HOLLY HOLY / KING OF THE HILL** [31] [–]
(cd-s+=) *(DEPD 51)* – Legalise it (mixes) / Now you see it.
(cd-s+=) *(DEPX 51)* – Legalise it (high grade mix).

Apr 99. (c-s/cd-s) *(DEP C/D 52)* **THE TRAIN IS COMING / MISPENT YOUTH / THE WAY YOU DO THE THINGS YOU DO (remix)** [30] [–]
(cd-s) *(DEPDX 52)* – ('A'side) / Tyler / King.

Oct 00. (cd/c) *(DUBTVX/UBTVCX 3) <50525>* **THE VERY BEST OF UB40 – 1980-2000** (compilation) [7] Nov00 [ ]
– One in ten / Red red wine / Kingston town / Higher ground / King / Cherry oh baby / I got you babe / Come back darling / The Earth dies screaming / If it happens again / Don't break my heart / Can't help falling in love / Watchdogs / Tell me it is true / Rat in mi kitchen / Homely girl / Light my fire / Bring me your cup / Food for thought / Sing our own song. *(d-lp iss.Nov00 on 'Simply Vinyl'; SVLP 274)*

Nov 00. (cd-s) *(DEPD 53)* **LIGHT MY FIRE / KING (snipers remix) / HIGH ON A BREEZE** [63] [–]
(12") *(DEP 53-12)* – ('A'side) / King (instrumental).

DEP Int. E.M.I.

Oct 01. (cd-s; by UB40 featuring LADY SAW) *(DEPD 55)*
SINCE I MET YOU LADY / SPARKLE OF MY EYES / SINCE I MET YOU LADY (Oracabessa original) [38] [–]

Oct 01. (cd) *(DEPCD 19) <811298>* **COVER UP** [29] [ ]
– Rudie / Sparkle of my eyes / Really / The day I broke the law / Let me know / Cover up / Walk on me land / Something more than this / Everytime / I'm on the up / Look at me / Since I met you lady / Walked in the rain / Write off the debt.

Feb 02. (cd-s) *(DEPD 56)* **COVER UP / COUVRE LA / DON'T FORGET TO SMELL THE ROSES** [54] [–]

Aug 02. (cd) *(DEPCD 20) <812675>* **UB40 PRESENT THE FATHERS OF REGGAE** [ ] Sep02 [ ]
– You could meet somebody (with MIGHTY DIAMONDS) / You're always pulling me down (with FREDDIE McGREGOR) / Bring me your cup (with GREGORY ISAACS) / Silent witness (with BRENT DOWE) / Always there (with HONEY BOY) / I love it when you smile (with ANTON ELLIS) / Don't do the crime (with JACKIE ROBINSON) / Watchdogs (with MAX ROMEO) / Love is all is alright (with BOB ANDY) / The earth dies screaming (with KEN BOOTHE) / Don't slow down (with WINSTON GROOVY) / Higher ground (with LEROY SIBBLES) / Pillow (with JOHN HOLT) / C'est la vie (with TOOTS HIBBERT).

Oct 03. (cd-s; by UB40 & UNITED COLOURS OF SOUND)
(DEPD 54) **SWING LOW SWEET CHARIOT / SO DESTRUCTIVE (dub)** [17] [–]
(cd-s) *(DEPX 54)* – ('A'-stadium mix) / ('A'-acappella mix) / ('A'-video).

Nov 03. (cd) *(DEPCD 22) <593124>* **HOMEGROWN** [49] [ ]
– So destructive / I knew you / Drop on by / Someone like me / Freestyler / Everything is better now / Just be good / Young guns / Hand that rocks the cradle / Nothing without you / Nothing without you (dub). *(UK+=)* – Swing low sweet chariot.

Jun 05. (cd-s) *(DEPD 59)* **KISS AND SAY GOODBYE / GOTTA TELL SOMEONE** [19] [–]
(cd-s+=) *(DEPDX 59)* – Shotta dub / ('A'-video).

Jun 05. (cd) *(DEPCD 23) <121140>* **WHO YOU FIGHTING FOR?** [20] Jul05 [ ]
– Who you fighting for? / After tonight / Bling bling / Plenty more / War poem / Sins of the fathers / Good situation / Gotta tell someone / Reasons / One woman man / I'll be on my way / Kiss and say goodbye / Things you say you love. *(ltd-cd w/dvd+=; DEPCDX 23)* – (DVD tracks).

Aug 05. (cd-s; w/ HUNTERZ & the DHOLL BLASTERS)
(DEPD 60) **REASONS / (dub)** [75] [–]
(cd-s+=) *(DEPDX 60)* – One woman man / ('A'-video).

– compilations, others, etc. –

Aug 82. (lp/c) *Graduate; (GRAD LP/C 3)* **THE SINGLES ALBUM** [17] [–]
– Food for thought / King / My way of thinking / I think it's going to rain today / Dream a lie / Tyler / Adella / Little by little / The earth dies screaming.

Feb 83. (12"m) *Graduate; (12GRAD 15)* **TYLER. / ADELLA / LITTLE BY LITTLE** [ ] [–]
(re-iss. 1984)

Mar 85. (d-lp/c) *Graduate; (VGD/+C 3511)* **THE UB40 FILE** [ ] [–]
(cd-iss. Jul86; VGDCD 3511)

Oct 87. (lp/c/cd) *Virgin TV; (UBTV/UBTVC/DUBTV 1)* **THE BEST OF UB40 VOLUME 1** [3] [–]
– Red red wine / I got you babe / One in ten / food for thought / Rat in mi kitchen / Don't break my heart / Cherry oh baby / Many rivers to cross / Please don't make me cry / If it hapens again / Sing our own song / Maybe tomorrow / My way of thinking / King. (cd+=extra tracks) *(re-iss. +cd.Jan89) (re-iss. cd+c Aug93, hit UK No.51)*

Oct 94. (3xcd-box) *Virgin;* **THE COMPACT COLLECTION** [ ] [–]

Nov 94. (d-cd) *Virgin; (DEPDDX 1)* **LABOUR OF LOVE VOLUMES I & II** [5] [ ]

Jun 03. (3xcd-box) *DEP Int.; (DEPCDX 21)* **LABOUR OF LOVE VOL.1-3** [7] [–]

Nov 05. (d-cd) *DEP int.; (DEPDDX 2)* **THE BEST OF – VOLUMES 1 & 2** [47] [–]

□ UGLY CASANOVA (see under ⇒ MODEST MOUSE)

ULTRAVOX

Formed: London, England . . . mid '76 out of TIGER LILY (whose one and only single was a bizarre cover of Fats Waller's 'AIN'T MISBEHAVIN'', subsequently withdrawn from release) comprising frontman JOHN FOXX, CHRIS CROSS, STEVE SHEARS, BILLY CURRIE and WARREN CANN. With the addition of violin (courtesy of CURRIE) and added synth power, the group became ULTRAVOX, initially with a ! at the end!. The fact that the band were picked up by 'Island' records and their eponymous 1977 debut album produced by BRIAN ENO says a lot about where ULTRAVOX! were coming from; artsy avant-pop combining elements of a punked-up ROXY MUSIC, the group were something of a cult live act. This didn't translate into sales, however, and despite an improved second effort, 'HA! HA! HA!' (1977), the group languished in relative obscurity. With ROBIN SIMON replacing SHEARS, they decamped to Germany to begin work on a third set under the auspices of electronic maestro, CONNY PLANK. The underwhelming result, 'SYSTEMS OF ROMANCE' (1978), failed to change the group's fortunes and by the Spring of '79, FOXX had abandoned ship for a solo career while SIMON went on to join MAGAZINE. The ubiquitous MIDGE URE was brought in as lead man, the singer having already cut his music business teeth in such diverse outfits as SLIK, The RICH KIDS and THIN LIZZY. He was also an integral part of moody synth-poppers, VISAGE, co-writing some of their material alongside mainman, STEVE STRANGE. Ironically, all this upheaval seemed to work wonders for all concerned, FOXX going his experimental electronic way and scoring a Top 40 hit almost immediately with the brilliant 'UNDERPASS' (early '80), while the newly revamped ULTRAVOX (now without a ! and signed to 'Chrysalis') broke the Top 30 that summer with 'SLEEPWALK'. 'VIENNA' (1980; again produced by CONNY PLANK) was released later that year, its Top 5 placing indicating that the new-look outfit had effectively cornered the burgeoning new romantic/electropop market. This was confirmed early in '81 when the album's title track narrowly missed the UK No.1 spot, its chilly, grandiose Euro feel and indelible melody managing to combine pretentiousness with mass public appeal. This was a talent which was to serve the group well over the ensuing five years, ULTRAVOX scoring an impressive run of seven Top 10 albums and a string of Top 30 hits. 'RAGE IN EDEN' (1981) was another Top 5 success, spawning three Top 20 singles including the po-faced 'ALL STOOD STILL'. The album also marked the end of the group's tenure with PLANK, GEORGE MARTIN overseeing production duties on 'QUARTET' (1982). The result was a markedly warmer sound and more commercial appeal, evident on the preceding single, 'REAP THE WILD WIND'. By the release of 'LAMENT' (1984), ULTRAVOX were a fully fledged pop band, the evocative heartbreak of 'DANCING WITH TEARS IN MY EYES' giving the group their biggest hit since 'VIENNA'. A bonus new track on the best selling compilation, 'THE COLLECTION' (1984), 'LOVE'S GREAT ADVENTURE', was another pop odyssey, its rolling synth crescendos a taster for the latest chapter in URE's solo career. Strangely enough, ULTRAVOX's last hit single was the sombre 'ALL FALL DOWN', its subject matter the war-torn Northern Ireland, an almost militaristic rhythm and uillean pipes utilised for greater effect. The track was lifted from the 'U-VOX' (1986) set, an album featuring the drumming talents of BIG COUNTRY's MARK BRZEZICKI. Realising they'd reached a creative impasse, ULTRAVOX disbanded the following year, URE taking up the solo career that had begun so successfully in 1982 with a Top 10 cover of Tom Rush's 'NO REGRETS' (made famous by the WALKER BROTHERS) and continued with the soaring pop of 'IF I WAS', a No.1 single in summer '85 (URE had also helped to mastermind the Band Aid single, 'Do They Know It's Christmas). He struggled, however, to resurrect his flagging solo career, the 1988 set, 'ANSWERS TO NOTHING' barely scraping into the Top 40 while a Spring '89 single, 'SISTERS AND BROTHERS' was withdrawn by 'Chrysalis'. Subsequently securing a new contract with 'Arista', URE returned in 1991 with the Top 20 hit, 'COLD COLD HEART' and a Top 40 album, 'PURE'. While ULTRAVOX made a low-key comeback in 1993 with a new singer, TONY FENELLE, and a new album, 'REVELATION', URE was conspicuous by his absence from the charts for most of the 90's.

• **Songwriters:** FOXX and group until URE replaced FOXX. Covered only KING'S LEAD HAT (Brian Eno). MIDGE URE's solo career included THE MAN WHO SOLD THE WORLD (David Bowie) / STRANGE BREW (Cream).

Album rating: ULTRAVOX! (*5) / HA! HA! HA! (*5) / SYSTEMS OF ROMANCE (*5) / THREE INTO ONE compilation (*7) / VIENNA (*7) / RAGE IN EDEN (*6) / QUARTET (*5) / MONUMENT – THE SOUNDTRACK (*4) / LAMENT (*5) / THE COLLECTION compilation (*7) / U-VOX (*4) / REVELATION (*3) / INGENUITY (*2) / Midge Ure: THE GIFT (*6) / ANSWERS TO NOTHING (*5) / PURE (*4) / IF I WAS: THE VERY BEST OF MIDGE URE & ULTRAVOX compilation (*7) / BREATHE (*5)

TIGER LILY

DENNIS LEIGH (JOHN FOXX) – vocals / **STEVE SHEARS** – guitar / **BILLY CURRIE** (b. 1 Apr'52, Huddersfield, Yorkshire, England) – keyboards / **WARREN CANN** (b.20 May'52, Victoria, Canada) – drums / **CHRIS ST. JOHN** (b. CHRISTOPHER ALLEN, 14 Jul'52) – bass

Gull | not iss.

Mar 75. (7") *(GULS 12)* **AIN'T MISBEHAVIN'. / MONKEY JIVE** [–] w-drawn [–]
(re-iss. Oct77; GULS 54) (re-iss. Oct80 on 'Dead Good'; DEAD 11)

ULTRAVOX!

LEIGH became **JOHN FOXX** and ST.JOHN now **CHRIS CROSS.** (CURRIE now added violin, synthesizers.)

Island | Antilles

Feb 77. (7") *(WIP 6375)* **DANGEROUS RHYTHM. / MY SEX** [ ] [–]

Mar 77. (lp/c) *(ILPS/ICT 9449)* **ULTRAVOX!** [ ] [–]
– Saturday night in the city of the dead / Life at Rainbow End (for all the tax exiles on Main Street) / Slip away / I want to be a machine / Wide boys / Dangerous rhythm / The lonely hunter / The wild the beautiful and the damned / My sex. *(cd-iss. Jul92; IMCD 146)*

May 77. (7") *(WIP 6392)* **YOUNG SAVAGE. / SLIPAWAY** [ ] [–]

Oct 77. (7") *(WIP 6404)* **ROCKWROK. / HIROSHIMA MON AMOUR** [ ] [–]
(all 3 ULTRAVOX! singles were re-iss. Jul81)

Oct 77. (lp/c) *(ILPS/ICT 9505)* **HA! HA! HA!** [ ] [–]
– Rockwrok / The frozen ones / Fear in the western world / Distant smile / The man who dies every day / Artificial life / While I'm still alive / Hiroshima mon amour. *(free-7"w.a.)–* **QUIRKS. / MODERN LOVE (live).** *(cd-iss. Jul92; IMCD 147)*

Feb 78. (7"ep) *(IEP 8)* **RETRO E.P. (live)** [ ] [–]
– The wild the beautiful and the damned / Young savage / My sex / The man who dies every day.

— **ROBIN SIMON** – guitar (ex-NEO) repl. SHEARS to COWBOYS INTERNATIONAL

Aug 78. (7"/12"violet) *(WIP/12WIP 6454)* **SLOW MOTION. / DISLOCATION** [ ] [ ]

Sep 78. (lp/c) *(ILPS/ICT 9555)* *<7069>* **SYSTEMS OF ROMANCE** [ ] [ ]
– Slow motion / I can't stay long / Someone else's clothes / Blue light / Some of them / Quiet men / Dislocation / Maximum acceleration / When you walk through me / Just for a moment. *(cd-iss. Aug92; IMCD 148)*

Oct 78. (7"/12"white) *(WIP/12WIP 6459)* **QUIET MEN. / CROSS FADE** [ ] [ ]

— (Apr79) **MIDGE URE** (b.JAMES, 10 Oct'53, Cambuslang, Scotland) – vocals, guitar (ex-SLIK, ex-RICH KIDS, ex-THIN LIZZY, ex-VISAGE) repl. JOHN FOXX who went solo. ROBIN also departed to MAGAZINE. Now as ULTRAVOX, after dropping the exclamation mark!

Chrysalis Chrysalis

Jun 80. (7",7"clear) *(CHS 2441)* **SLEEPWALK. / WAITING** 29

Sep 80. (7",7"clear/12") *(CHS 2457/122457)* **PASSING STRANGERS. / SOUND ON SOUND** 57

Oct 80. (lp/c) *(CHR/ZCHR 1296)* <1296> **VIENNA** 3
– Astradyne / New Europeans / Private lives / Passing strangers / Sleepwalk / Mr. X / Western promise / Vienna / All stood still. *(cd-iss. 1985; CCD 1296) (re-iss. Dec92 on 'Fame' cd/c; CDFA/TCFA 3283) (re-iss. cd Mar94 + Jul94; same) (cd re-iss. Apr00 on 'EMI Gold'; 5255230)*

Jan 81. (7",7"clear) *(CHS 2481)* **VIENNA. / PASSIONATE REPLY** 2
(12"+=) *(CHS 122481)* - *Herr X.*

Apr 81. (7",7"clear) *(CHS 2457)* **PASSING STRANGERS. / FACE TO FACE** –
(12"+=) *(CHA 122457)* – King's lead hat.

May 81. (7",7"clear) *(CHS 2522)* **ALL STOOD STILL. / ALLES KLAR** 8
(12"+=) *(CHS 122522)* – Keep talking.

Aug 81. (7",7"clear/ext-12") *(CHS 2549/122549)* **THE THIN WALL. / I NEVER WANTED TO BEGIN** 14

Sep 81. (lp/c) *(CHR/ZCHR 1338)* <1338> **RAGE IN EDEN** 4
– The voice / We stand alone / Rage in Eden / I remember (death in the afternoon) / The thin wall / Stranger within / Accent on youth / The ascent / Your name has slipped my mind again. *(cd-iss. Jun87; CPCD 1338) (cd re-iss. Sep97 on 'EMI Gold'; CDGOLD 1097)*

Nov 81. (7",7"clear) *(CHS 2559)* **THE VOICE. / PATHS AND ANGELS** 16
(12"+=,12"clear+=) *(CHS 122559)* – All stood still (live) / Private lives (live).

Sep 82. (7",7"clear/c-s/12") *(CHS 2639/122639)* <42682> **REAP THE WILD WIND. / HOSANNA (IN EXCELIS DEO)** 12 Mar 83 71

Oct 82. (lp/c/pic-lp) *(CDL/ZCDL/PCDL 1394)* <1394> **QUARTET** 6 Mar83 61
– Reap the wild wind / Serenade / Mine for life / Hymn / Visions of blue / When the scream subsides / We came to dance / Cut and run / The song (we go). *(cd-iss. 1988; CCD 1394) (cd re-iss. Sep98 on 'EMI Gold'; 496823-2)*

Nov 82. (7",7"clear) *(CHS 2557)* **HYMN. / MONUMENT** 11
(12"+=,12"clear+=) *(CHS 122557)* – The thin wall.

Mar 83. (7",7"clear,7"pic-d) *(CHS 2676)* **VISIONS IN BLUE. / BREAK YOUR BACK** 15
(12"+=,12"clear+=) *(CHS 122676)* – Reap the wild wind.

May 83. (7",7"pic-d,7"clear/12",12"clear) *(VOX/+X 1)* **WE CAME TO DANCE. / OVERLOOK** 18

Oct 83. (lp/c) *(CUX/ZCUX 1452)* **MONUMENT – THE SOUNDTRACK (live)** 9
– Monument / Reap the wild wind / The voice / Vienna / Mine for life / Hymn. *(cd-iss. 1986 +=; CCD 1452)* – Passing strangers / Visions in blue. *(cd re-iss. Jul96 on 'EMI Gold'; CDGOLD 1025)*

Feb 84. (7",7"clear/12") *(VOX/+X 2)* **ONE SMALL DAY. / EASTERLY** 27

Apr 84. (lp/c/pic-lp/cd) *(CDL/ZCDL/PCDL/CCD 1459)* *<41459>* **LAMENT** 8
– White China / One small day * / Dancing with tears in my eyes / Lament * / Man of two worlds / Heart of the country / When the time comes / A friend I called Desire. *(c+=/cd+=)* – (tracks * remixed). *(cd re-iss. Sep99 on 'EMI Gold'; 521834-2)*

May 84. (7",7"clear/12") *(UV/+X 1)* **DANCING WITH TEARS IN MY EYES. / BUILDING** 3

Jul 84. (7",7"clear) *(UV 2)* **LAMENT. / HEART OF THE COUNTRY** 22
(12"+=) *(UVX 2)* – ('A'instrumental).

Oct 84. (7",7"clear,7"pic-d/12") *(UV/+X 3)* **LOVE'S GREAT ADVENTURE. / WHITE CHINA** 12

Nov 84. (lp/c/cd) *(UTV/ZUTV 1)(CCD 1490)* **THE COLLECTION** (compilation) 2
– Dancing with tears in my eyes / Hymn / The thin wall / The voice / Vienna / Passing strangers / Sleepwalk / Reap the wild wind / All stood still / Visions in blue / We came to dance / One small day / Love's great adventure / Lament. *(w/ free 12")*

— guest **MARK BRZEZICKI** (b.21 Jun'57) – drums (of BIG COUNTRY) repl. CANN to HELDEN

Sep 86. (7",7"clear,7"pic-d) *(UV 4)* **SAME OLD STORY. / 3** 31
(12",12"clear) *(UVX 4)* – ('A'side) / All in one day.

Oct 86. (lp/c/cd) *(CDL/ZCDL/CCD 1545)* <207934> **U-VOX** 9
– Same old story / Sweet surrender / Dream on / The prize / All fall down / Time to kill / Moon madness / Follow your heart / All in one day. *(cd re-iss. Oct00 on 'EMI Gold'; 525611-2)*

Nov 86. (7",7"clear) *(UV 5)* **ALL FALL DOWN. / DREAM ON** 30
(12"+=) *(UVX 5)* – ('A'version).

May 87. (7",7"clear) *(UV 6)* **ALL IN ONE DAY. / THE PRIZE (live)** –
(12"+=) *(UVX 6)* – Stateless.

— disbanded 1987, although U-VOX was formed by BILLY CURRIE, ROBIN SIMON and MARCUS O'HIGGINS – vocals; they toured 1989 playing ULTRAVOX songs

— **TONY FENELLE** – vocals; repl. MIDGE URE who was by now continuing solo

D.S.B. not iss.

May 93. (cd/c/lp) *(DSB 3098-2/-4/-1)* **REVELATION** –
– I am alive / Revelation / Systems of love / Perfecting the art of common ground / The great outdoors / The closer I get to you / No turning back / True believer / Unified / The new frontier. *(cd re-iss. Sep02 on 'Puzzle'; PZLCD 106)*

Jun 93. (7"/c-s/7"clear) *(DSB 3097-7/-3/-1)* **I AM ALIVE. / SYSTEMS OF LOVE**
(cd-s+=) *(DSB 30975)* – ('A'extended).

— line-up: **CURRIE / BLUE / BURNS**

Resurgence not iss.

Nov 95. (cd) *(RES 109CD)* **INGENUITY** –
– Ingenuity / There goes a beautiful world / Give it all back / Future picture forever / The silent cries / Distance / Ideals / Who'll save you / A way out, a way through / Majestic. *(re-iss. Mar02 on 'Puzzle'; PZLCD 105)*

– compilations, others, etc. –

Jun 80. (lp/c) *Island/ US= Antilles; (ILPS/ICM 9614) <7079>* **THREE INTO ONE**
– Young savage / Rockwrok / Dangerous rhythm / The man who dies every day / The wild the beautiful and the damned / Slow motion / Just for a moment / My sex / Quiet men / Hiroshima mon amour. *(re-iss. Nov86, cd-iss. 1989; IMCD 30)*

Mar 81. (12"ep,12"clear-ep) *Island; (DWIP 6691)* **SLOW MOTION / DISLOCATION. / QUIET MEN / HIROSHIMA MON AMOUR** 33 –

Dec 82. (d-c) *Chrysalis; (ZCDP 109)* **VIENNA / RAGE IN EDEN** –

Feb 87. (7") *Old Gold; (OG 9675)* **VIENNA. / THE VOICE** –

Apr 87. (7") *Old Gold; (OG 9698)* **DANCING WITH TEARS IN MY EYES. / REAP THE WILD WIND** *(12"-iss.Jan88)* –

Apr 88. (12"ep) *Strange Fruit; (SFPS 047)* **THE PEEL SESSIONS** (21.7.77) –
– My sex / Artificial life / Young savage.

Sep 93. (cd/c) *Spectrum; (550112-2/-4)* **SLOW MOTION** –

Aug 94. (cd) *Chrysalis; (CDCHR 6053)* **RARE VOLUME 2** –

Jun 95. (cd) *Receiver; (RRCD 199)* **FUTURE PICTURE** –

Aug 95. (cd-s) *Old Gold;* **VIENNA / REAP THE WILD WIND** –

Oct 95. (cd) *MFP; (CDMFP 6175)* **DANCING WITH TEARS IN MY EYES** –

Nov 95. (3xcd-box) *Island; (5241522)* **ULTRAVOX! / HA! HA! HA! / SYSTEMS OF ROMANCE** –

Feb 98. (cd) *EMI Gold; (493465-2)* **EXTENDED – A COLLECTION OF 12" REMIXES** –

Nov 98. (d-cd) *Disky; (HR 85380-2)* **ORIGINAL GOLD** –

Mar 99. (cd) *Spectrum; (554898-2)* **THE ISLAND YEARS** –

Jul 00. (cd) *Disky; (SI 25080-2)* **THE BEST OF THE 80'S** –

Aug 01. (cd) *Armoury; (ARMCD 043)* **GREATEST HITS LIVE (live)** –

MIDGE URE

— had already started own solo career. Debut w / ex-COCKNEY REBEL **STEVE HARLEY** – dual vocals

Chrysalis Chrysalis

Mar 82. (7") **I CAN'T EVEN TOUCH YOU. / I CAN'T BE ANYONE** –

Jun 82. (7"/12") *(CHS 2618/122618)* **NO REGRETS. / MOOD MUSIC** 9

Jul 83. (7"/12") *(FEST/+X 1)* **AFTER A FASHION ("MIDGE URE & MICK KARN"). / TEXTURES** 39 –
Above 45 on 'Musicfest' w / ex-JAPAN bassist

— Dec'84 saw MIDGE co-write and create BAND AID with BOB GELDOF (BOOMTOWN RATS). They hit UK No.1 with famine relief single DO THEY KNOW IT'S CHRISTMAS.

Aug 85. (7",7"clear) *(URE 1)* **IF I WAS. / PIANO** [1] [ ]
(12"+=,12"clear+=) *(UREX 1)* – The man who sold the world.
Oct 85. (lp/c/cd) *(CHR/ZCHR/CCD 1508)* **THE GIFT** [2] [ ]
– If I was / When the winds blow / Living in the past / That certain smile / The gift / Antilles / Wastelands / Edo / The chieftain / The gift (reprise). *(re-iss. cd+c Apr93)*
Nov 85. (7",7"clear/7"pic-d) *(URE/+P 2)* **THAT CERTAIN SMILE. / THE GIFT** [28] [ ]
(12"+=,d12"+=,12"clear+=) *(UREX 2)* – ('A'instrumental) / Fade to grey.
Jan 86. (7",7"clear) *(URE 3)* **WASTELANDS. / THE CHIEFTAIN** [46] [ ]
(12"+=,12"clear+=) *(UREX 3)* – Dancer.
May 86. (7",7"clear) *(URE 4)* **CALL OF THE WILD. / WHEN THE WIND BLOWS** [27] [ ]
(12"+=,12"clear+=) *(UREX 4)* – After a fashion (w/ MICK KARN).
Aug 88. (7",7"clear) *(URE 5)* **ANSWERS TO NOTHING. / HONORARE** [49] [ ]
(12"+=,12"clear+=) *(UREX 5)* – Oboe.
(cd-s++=) *(URECD 5)* – (excerpts from lp below).
Sep 88. (lp/c/cd) *(CDL/ZCHR/CCD 1649)* *<41649>* **ANSWERS TO NOTHING** [30] [88]
– Answers to nothing / Take me home / Sister and brother / Dear God / The leaving (so long) / Just for you / Hell to Heaven / Lied / Homeland / Remembrance day. *<US cd re-iss. Aug98 on 'EMI'; 96824>*
Nov 88. (7",7"clear) *(URE 6)* *<43319>* **DEAR GOD. / MUSIC 1** [55] [95]
(12"+=) *(UREX 6)* – All fall down (live) / Strange brew (live).
(cd-s+=) *(URECD 6)* – Remembrance day.

— In Apr'89, SISTERS AND BROTHERS single was withdrawn.

— **URE** now with **MARK BRZEZICKI** – drums / **STEVE BRZEZICKI** + **JEREMY MEEHAN** – bass / **ROBBIE KILGORE** – keys / **SIMON PHILLIPS** – drums / **STEVE WILLIAMS** – perc./ etc

Arista / R.C.A.

Aug 91. (7") *(114 555)* **COLD COLD HEART. / FLOWERS** [17] [ ]
(12"+=/cd-s+=) – Supernatural *(written by GREEN; SCRITTI POLITTI)*
Sep 91. (cd/lp) *(261/211 922)* *<61010>* **PURE** [36] [ ]
– I see hope in the morning light / Cold, cold heart / Pure love / Sweet 'n' sensitive thing / Let it go? / Rising / Light in your eyes / Little one / Hands around my heart / Waiting days / Tumbling down.
Oct 91. (7"/c-s) **I SEE HOPE IN THE MORNING LIGHT. / THE MAN I USED TO BE** [ ] [ ]
(12"+=/cd-s+=) – Madame de Sade.
May 96. (c-s) *(74321 37117-4)* **BREATHE / COLD COLD HEART (live)** [70] [ ]
(cd-s+=) *(74321 37117-2)* – No regrets / Trail of tears (live).
Jun 96. (cd/c) *(74321 34629-2/-4)* **BREATHE** [ ] [–]
– Breathe / Fields of fire / Fallen angel / Free / Guns and arrows / Lay my body down / Sinner man / Live forever / Trail of tears / May your good Lord / Maker.
Oct 96. (c-s) *(74321 42316-4)* **GUNS & ARROWS / TRAIL OF TEARS (demo)** [ ] [–]
(cd-s+=) *(74321 42316-2)* – Trail of tears (demo) / Man of the world (live).

not iss. / Orchard

Oct 00. (cd) *<7226>* **WENT TO CONEY ISLAND ON A MISSION FROM GOD . . . BE BACK BY FIVE** (instrumental soundtrack) [–] [ ]
– The Gabby variations / High noon on 103rd Street / Surgery / Stan's disco / Stealing candy / Arriving at Coney / Midday suite / Bumper cars – Locket stealing / Pawnshop – Jerry Mahoney / Finding Richie again / Allegra / Richie calls his mom / Wedding / Lost point / Return to Skeeball.

Curb / Arista-MI5

May 01. (cd) *(CURCD 100)* *<03484>* **MOVE ME** [ ] [ ]
– You move me / Beneath a Spielberg sky / Words / Strong / Let me go / Alone / Monster / Absolution sometime! / The refugee song / Four / Somebody. *(ltd-bonus disc)*
Jul 01. (cd-s) *(CUBC 070)* **BENEATH A SPIELBERG SKY** [ ] [–]

– (MIDGE URE & ULTRAVOX) compilations, etc. –

on 'Chrysalis' unless mentioned otherwise

Jan 93. (7"/c-s) *(TCCHS 3936)* **VIENNA. / WASTELANDS** [13] [ ]
(cd-s+=) *(CDCHS 3936)* – Answers to nothing / The voice.
(cd-s) *(CDCHSS 3936)* – ('A'side) / Call of the wild / One small day / Hymn.
Feb 93. (cd/c/lp) *(CD/TC/+CHR 1987)* **IF I WAS: THE VERY BEST OF MIDGE URE & ULTRAVOX** [10] [ ]
– If I was / No regrets / Love's great adventure / Dear God / Cold cold heart / Vienna / Call of the wild / Dancing with tears in my eyes / All fall down / Yellow pearl / Fade to grey / Reap the wild wind / Answers to nothing / Do they know it's Christmas? (BAND AID). *(cd+=)* – After a fashion (with MICK KARN) / That certain smile.
Oct 01. (cd) *(535811-2)* **THE VERY BEST OF MIDGE URE & ULTRAVOX** [45] [ ]

UNCLE TUPELO

Formed: Belleville, Illinois, USA . . . 1987 by schoolmates JEFF TWEEDY and JAY FARRAR (who had played in punk outfit, The PRIMITIVES – US), MIKE HEIDORN completing the line-up. A band that have achieved almost legendary status among alternative country afficionados, UNCLE TUPELO christened a whole movement with the release of their seminal debut album, 'NO DEPRESSION' (1990). Issued on the small 'Rockville' label, the record translated the raw expression and sonic assault of punk into a contemporary country context; the spirit of what TWEEDY and FARRAR were trying to do was best illustrated on the title track, an impressive excavation of an ancient CARTER FAMILY song yearning for the sanctuary of Heaven, performed with as much conviction as any bonafide gospel act. Follow-up set, 'STILL FEEL GONE' (1991) continued in the same vein, developing and updating country in a fashion a damn sight closer to GRAM PARSONS' cosmic vision than the polished dross coming out of Nashville. Yet it was the stark testimony of the PETER BUCK-produced 'MARCH 16-20' (1992) that really cut to the heart of American roots tradition, a breathtaking album of grainy originals and hard-bitten folk covers. While the quality of the songwriting arguably outstripped almost anything released under the banner of country/alt-country in the past twenty years, it was the bruised beauty of the vocals (especially FARRAR) that really brought on the goose-bumps and belied UNCLE TUPELO's relative youthfulness. The likes of 'GRINDSTONE', 'BLACK EYE' and the traditional 'MOONSHINER' resonated with what sounded like the careworn resignation of a lifetime's toil and trouble, the whole album religious in its rawness. Released to rave reviews, it didn't take long for word to spread and with major labels eager for a piece of the action, FARRAR and TWEEDY opted to sign for 'Reprise' (home to spiritual forefathers PARSONS and NEIL YOUNG amongst others). With FARRAR and TWEEDY maintaining a hard-drinking, volatile relationship at the best of times, 'ANODYNE' (1993) proved to be the final product of their mercurial partnership. A return to more upbeat material, the album featured a rousing cover of Doug Sahm's 'GIVE BACK THE KEY TO MY HEART' (featuring the cult Texan roots man on guitar) alongside more reflective fare like the gorgeously plaintive 'SLATE', one of the most perfectly formed compositions in the FARRAR/TWEEDY canon with fiddle arrangements to break the hardest heart. While many mourned the band's passing, fans could look forward to the prospect of two solo projects, FARRAR's SON VOLT and TWEEDY's WILCO.

• **Songwriters:** All compositions FARRAR – TWEEDY except arrangements of traditional tunes, plus covers: I WANNA DESTROY YOU (Soft Boys) / NO DEPRESSION (Carter Family) / JOHN HARDY (Leadbelly) / ATOMIC POWER (Louvin Brothers) / BLUE EYES (Gram Parsons) / SIN CITY (Flying Burrito Brothers) / I WANNA BE YOUR DOG (Stooges) / EFFIGY (Creedence Clearwater Revival).

Album rating: NO DEPRESSION (*8) / STILL FEEL GONE (*9) / MARCH 16-20 (*7) / ANODYNE (*8) / 1989-1993: AN ANTHOLOGY (*8)

JEFF TWEEDY (b.25 Aug'67) – vocals, guitar, bass / **JAY FARRAR** (b.26 Dec'66) – vocals, guitar / **MICHAEL HEIDORN** – drums

Rockville / Rockville

Aug 90. (lp) *<ROCK 6050-1>* **NO DEPRESSION** [–] [ ]
– Graveyard shift / That year / Before I break / No depression / Factory belt / Whiskey bottle / Outdone / Train / Life worth livin' / Flatness / So called friend / Screen door / John Hardy. *(UK cd-iss. Sep97; ROCK 6050-2)*
Sep 90. (7") *<ROCK 6055-7>* **I GOT DRUNK. / SIN CITY** [–] [ ]

Sep 91. (7") *<ROCK 6069-7>* **GUN. / I WANNA DESTROY YOU** –

Sep 91. (lp) *<ROCK 6070-1>* **STILL FEEL GONE** –
– Gun / Looking for a way out / Fall down easy / Nothing / Still be around / Watch me fall / Punch drunk / Postcard / D. Boon / True to life / Cold shoulder / Discarded / If that's alright. *(UK-iss.cd Nov92 on 'Yellow Moon'; BUFF 001CD)*

Nov 92. (7") *<(ROCK 6089-7)>* **SAUGET WIND. / LOOKING FOR A WAY OUT (acoustic) / TAKE MY WORD**

Mar 93. (cd/c/lp) *<(ROCK 6110-2/-4/-1)>* **MARCH 16-20, 1992** Aug92
– Grindstone / Coalminers / Wait up / Criminals / Shaky ground / Satan, your kingdom must come down / Black eye / Moonshiner / I wish my baby was born / Atomic power / Lilli Schull / Warfare / Fatal wound / Sandusky / Wipe the clock.

— **KEN COOMER** – drums + **JOHN STIRRATT** – bass; repl. HEIDORN

Warners Sire

Oct 93. (cd/c) *(9362 45330-2/-4) <45424>* **ANODYNE**
– Slate / Acuff-Rose / The long cut / Give back the key to my heart / Chickamauga / New Madrid / Anodyne / We've been had / Fifteen keys / High water / No sense in lovin' / Steal the crumbs.

— arguments arose, FARRAR subsequently forming SON VOLT with MICHAEL HEIDORN, TWEEDY took STIRRATT + COOMER and formed WILCO

– compilations, etc. –

May 95. (c) *Dutch East; <6110>* **STILL FEEL GONE / MARCH 16-20, 1992** –

May 02. (cd) *Sony; (507612-2) <62223>* **1989-1993: AN ANTHOLOGY** Mar02
– No depression / Screen door / Graveyard shift / Whiskey bottle / Outdone / I got drunk / I wanna be your dog / Gun / Still be around / Looking for a way out (acoustic) / Watch me fall / Sauget wind / Black eye / Moonshiner / Fatal wound / Grindstone / Effigy / The long cut / Chickamuuga / New Madrid / We've been had (live). *<(d-lp-iss.Jun02 on 'Sundazed'; SCLP 5153)>*

the UNDERTONES

Formed: Londonderry, N. Ireland ... late '75 by the O'NEILL brothers, DAMIAN and JOHN, alongside FEARGAL SHARKEY, MIKE BRADLEY and BILLY DOHERTY. Taking up the offer of a one-off singles deal with Belfast label, 'Good Vibrations', they released a debut EP in September '78 with the seminal 'TEENAGE KICKS' as the lead track. Immediately championed by DJ John Peel, this compelling slice of adolescent angst reached the collective ear of 'Sire' records leading to a prestigious deal. Their major label debut, 'GET OVER YOU', scraped into the Top 60 although they eventually cracked the chart later that Spring with 'JIMMY JIMMY', a boisterous post-punk stomper reminiscent of a wittier, more laid-back SHAM 69. This was closely followed by an eponymous debut album, establishing The UNDERTONES as one of the most promising and intelligent new-wave punk/pop bands in the UK. Like a more hyperactive KINKS, the band chronicled the nitty gritty, highs and lows of everyday life in such unforgettable pop nuggets as 'HERE COMES THE SUMMER', 'TRUE CONFESSIONS' and 'FAMILY ENTERTAINMENT'. Arguably, 'YOU'VE GOT MY NUMBER (WHY DON'T YOU USE IT), remains The UNDERTONES' finest moment, a jarring, insistent riff marking it out from the group's standard pop rush. While the song barely made the UK Top 40, The UNDERTONES were back in the Top 10 the following year with the sneering 'MY PERFECT COUSIN', a humorous tale of a goody-two-shoes relative which obviously struck a chord with more than a few disaffected youngsters. The accompanying album, 'HYPNOTISED' (1980), consolidated the group's standing, critically and commercially, a more assured set which also spawned another classic single in 'WEDNESDAY WEEK'. Inevitably, however, along with many of their contemporaries, The UNDERTONES increasingly moved away from the roughshod charm of old to a more refined sound. This was evident in the group's third album, 'THE POSITIVE TOUCH' (1981), only one track making the Top 20 ('IT'S GOING TO HAPPEN') despite such enduring material as the lovely 'JULIE OCEAN'. By 1983's 'THE SIN OF PRIDE', FEARGAL's quavering vocals and the group's boy-next-door image had been shelved for a blend of "alternative soul". Predictably, this didn't sit well with the group's more traditional fans who were unsurprisingly becoming increasingly critical of The UNDERTONES newfound sophistication. The imminent split eventually came in mid '83 with SHARKEY initially hooking up with VINCE CLARKE in The ASSEMBLY before launching a solo career. The O'NEILL brothers, meanwhile, formed the critically acclaimed THAT PETROL EMOTION, alongside with CIARAN McLAUGHLIN, REAMANN O'GORMAN and US-born frontman, STEVE MACK. Basing themselves in London from the mid-80's onwards, the TPE made their vinyl debut in summer '85 with the independently released 'KEEN'. A further indie single, 'V2' followed a few months later before 'Demon' took them on for a critically acclaimed ROLI MOSSIMAN-produced debut album, 'MANIC POP THRILL' (1986). Strikingly different from The UNDERTONES' three-chord rush, THAT PETROL EMOTION dealt in a more caustic, politicised brand of alternative pop/rock which embraced elements of 60's garage and psychedelia, their potential subsequently recognised by 'Polydor'. The major label backing paid almost immediate dividends as the band narrowly missed the UK Top 40 with their next single, 'BIG DECISION'. A follow-up album, 'BABBLE' (1987) appeared a couple of months later and landed the band their first and only Top 30 success; despite vocal support from the likes of John Peel and the NME, THAT PETROL EMOTION seemed unable to convert their potential into sales. Moving on to 'Virgin', they came up with the more experimental 'END OF THE MILLENNIUM PSYCHOSIS BLUES' (1988), featuring O'NEILL's political coup de grace, 'CELLOPHANE'. Yet he was unhappy with the life of a professional musician and subsequently moved back to Derry. A potentially fatal blow was overcome with the recruitment of JOHN MARCHINI and the songwriting development of McLAUGHLIN, the group attempting a final shot at pop glory with the 'SENSITIZE' and 'HEY VENUS' singles. Both were culled from 1990's 'CHEMICRAZY' album and both fell cruelly short of the Top 40 to the exasperation of the band, their label and their many advocates in the media. Dropped by 'Virgin', the band stuck it out for one final set, 'FIREPROOF' (1993) on their own 'Koogat' label before finally throwing in the towel. The O'NEILL's continued with the short-lived project, RARE. Following that band's demise, the pair, together with DOHERTY, BRADLEY and newly installed frontman, PAUL McLOONE, re-formed The UNDERTONES and released 'GET WHAT YOU NEED' (2003), the Derry outfit's first album of new material in two decades. Despite the absence of SHARKEY's petulant yelp, the new look band proved they could still bang out two-minute blasts of hormonal, adrenalised pop despite nudging their mid-forties.

• **Songwriters:** O'NEILL brothers except UNDER THE BOARDWALK (Drifters) / ME AND BABY BROTHER (War) / FOR WHAT IT'S WORTH (Buffalo Springfield) / NON-ALIGNMENT PACT (Pere Ubu) / ZIGZAG WANDERER (Captain Beefheart) / HEY BULLDOG (Beatles) / CINNAMON GIRL (Neil Young) / FUNTIME (Iggy Pop).

Album rating: THE UNDERTONES (*9) / HYPNOTISED (*7) / POSITIVE TOUCH (*6) / THE SIN OF PRIDE (*5) / ALL WRAPPED UP compilation (*7) / CHER O'BOWLES – THE PICK OF THE UNDERTONES compilation (*8) / That Petrol Emotion: MANIC POP THRILL (*7) / BABBLE (*8) / END OF THE MILLENNIUM PSYCHOSIS BLUES (*6) / CHEMICRAZY (*5) / FIREPROOF (*6) / Undertones: TEENAGE KICKS – THE BEST OF . . . compilation (*9) / GET WHAT YOU NEED (*7)

FEARGAL SHARKEY (b.13 Aug'58) – vocals / **DAMIAN O'NEILL** (b.15

The UNDERTONES

Jan'61, Belfast, N.Ireland) – guitar, bass / **JOHN O'NEILL** (b.26 Aug'57) – guitar / **MIKE BRADLEY** (b.13 Aug'59) – bass / **BILLY DOHERTY** (b.10 Jul'58, Larne, N.Ireland) – drums

Good Vibrations — not iss.

Sep 78. (7"ep) *(GOT 4)* **TEENAGE KICKS / TRUE CONFESSIONS. / SMARTER THAN U / EMMERGENCY CASES** [ ] [–]
(re-iss. Oct78 on 'Sire'; SIR 4007) – hit No.31 *(re-iss. Jul83 on 'Ardeck';* ARDS 1) – hit 60 *(re-iss. on 7"ep/cd-ep Apr94 on 'Dojo'; TONES/+CD 1)*

Sire — Sire

Jan 79. (7"m) *(SIR 4010)* **GET OVER YOU. / REALLY REALLY / SHE CAN ONLY SAY NO** [57] [ ]
Apr 79. (7",7"lime green) *(SIR 4015)* **JIMMY JIMMY. / MARS BARS** [16] [ ]
May 79. (lp/c) *(SRK/+C 6071)* <6081> **THE UNDERTONES** [13] Jan 80 [ ]
– Family entertainment / Girls don't like it / Male model / I gotta getta / Teenage kicks / Wrong way / Jump boys / Here comes the summer / Get over you / Billy's third / Jimmy Jimmy / True confessions / She's a runaround / I know a girl / Listening in. *(re-iss. Jul83 on 'Ardeck'; ARDM 164739-1) (re-iss. Oct87 on 'Fame' lp/c/cd; FA/TCFA/CDFA 3188) (re-iss. May94 on 'Dojo' cd/c/lp; DOJO CD/MC/LP 190)* – Smarter than u / Emergency cases / Top twenty / Really really / Mars Bars / She can only say no / One way love. *(cd re-iss. Mar97 on 'Essential'; ESMCD 484) (re-iss. Feb00; ESMCD 831)*
Jul 79. (7"m) *(SIR 4022)* **HERE COMES THE SUMMER. / ONE WAY LOVE / TOP TWENTY** [34] [ ]
Sep 79. (7") *(SIR 4024)* **YOU'VE GOT MY NUMBER (WHY DON'T YOU USE IT). / LET'S TALK ABOUT GIRLS** [32] [ ]
Mar 80. (7"m) *(SIR 4038)* **MY PERFECT COUSIN. / HARD LUCK / I DON'T WANNA SEE YOU AGAIN** [9] [ ]
(d7"+=) *(SIR 4038)* – Here comes the summer.
Apr 80. (lp/c) *(SRK/+C 6088)* <6088> **HYPNOTISED** [6] [ ]
– More songs about chocolate and girls / There goes Norman / Hypnotised / See that girl / Whizz kids / Under the boardwalk / The way girls talk / Hard luck / My perfect cousin / Boys will be boys / Tearproof / Wednesday week / Nine times out of ten / Girls that don't talk / What's with Terry?. *(re-iss. Jul83 on 'Ardeck'; ARDM 164742-1) (re-iss. Mar86 on 'Fame' lp/c; FA/TCFA 3145) (re-iss. May94 on 'Dojo' cd+=/c/lp; DOJO CD/MC/LP 192)* – You've got my number (why don't you use it?) / Hard luck (again) / Let's talk about girls / I told you so / I don't want to see you again. *(cd re-iss. Mar97 on 'Essential'; ESMCD 486) (cd re-iss. Feb00; ESMCD 832)*
Jun80. (7") *(SIR 4042)* **WEDNESDAY WEEK. / I TOLD YOU SO** [11] [ ]

Ardeck-EMI — Rykodisc

Apr 81. (7") *(ARDS 8)* **IT'S GOING TO HAPPEN. / FAIRLY IN THE MONEY NOW** [18] [–]
May 81. (lp/c) *(ARD/TCARD 103)* <12159> **THE POSITIVE TOUCH** [17] [ ]
– Fascination / Life's too easy / You're welcome / The positive touch / Julie Ocean / Crisis of mine / His good looking friend / When Saturday comes / It's going to happen / Sigh and explode / I don't know / Hannah Doot / Boy wonder / Forever Paradise. *(re-iss. Apr84 on 'E.M.I.' lp/c; ATAK/TCATAK 46) (re-iss. May94 on 'Dojo' cd+=/c/lp; DOJO CD/MC/LP 193)* – Kiss in the dark / Beautiful friend / Life's too easy / Fairly in the money now. *(cd re-iss. Mar97 on 'Essential'; ESMCD 485) (cd re-mast.Apr00; ESMCD 853)*
Jul 81. (7") *(ARDS 9)* **JULIE OCEAN. / KISS IN THE DARK** [41] [ ]
Feb 82. (7") *(ARDS 10)* **BEAUTIFUL FRIEND. / LIFE'S TOO EASY** [ ] [–]
Jan 83. (7") *(ARDS 11)* **THE LOVE PARADE. / LIKE THAT** [ ] [–]
(12"+=) *(12ARDS 11)* – You're welcome / Family entertainment / Crises of mine.
Mar 83. (7") *(ARDS 12)* **GOT TO HAVE YOU BACK. / TURNING BLUE** [ ] [–]
(12"+=) *(12ARDS 12)* – Bye bye baby blue.
Mar 83. (lp/c) *(ARD/TCARD 104)* **THE SIN OF PRIDE** [43] [–]
– Got to have you back / Valentine's treatment / Luxury / Love before romance / Untouchable / Bye bye baby blue / Conscious / Chain of love / Soul seven / The love parade / Save me / The sin of pride. *(re-iss. Aug85 on 'E.M.I.' lp/c; ATAK/TCATAK 47) (re-iss. May94 on 'Dojo' cd+=/c/lp; DOJO CD/MC/LP 194)* – Turning blue / Like that / Window shopping for new clothes / Bitter sweet / You stand so close (but you're never there) / I can only dream. *(cd re-iss. Mar97 on 'Essential'; ESMCD 487) (cd re-mast.Apr00; ESMCD 854)*
Apr 83. (7") *(ARDS 13)* **CHAIN OF LOVE. / WINDOW SHOPPING FOR NEW CLOTHES** [ ] [–]

— split mid '83 with FEARGAL SHARKEY joining The ASSEMBLY; (see YAZOO) before going solo. The O'NEILL brothers formed THAT PETROL EMOTION

THAT PETROL EMOTION

STEVE MACK (b.19 May'63, New York City, USA) – vocals / (ex-EAGER SIN BABIES) / **SEAN O'NEILL** – guitar / **DAMIAN O'NEILL** – bass, keyboards / **REAMANN O'GORMAIN** (b. 7 Jun'61) – guitar / **CIARAN McLAUGHLIN** (b.18 Nov'62) – drums

Pink — not iss.

Jun 85. (7") *(PINKY 004)* **KEEN. / A GREAT DEPRESSION ON SLUM NIGHT** [ ] [–]
(re-iss. Oct86; PINKY 13T)

Noise A Noise — not iss.

Oct 85. (7") *(NAN 1)* **V2. / THE GONEST THING** [ ] [–]
(12"+=) *(NAN 1T)* – Happiness drives me round the bend.

Demon — Demon

Apr 86. (7") *(D 1042)* **IT'S A GOOD THING. / THE DEADBEAT** [ ] [–]
(12"+=) *(D 1042T)* – Mine.
May 86. (lp/c/cd)<US-orange-lp> *(<FIEND/+CASS/+CD 70>)* **MANIC POP THRILL** [84] [ ]
– Fleshprint / Can't stop / Lifeblood / Natural kind of joy / It's a good thing / Circusville / Mouth crazy / Tight lipped / A million miles away / Lettuce / Cheepskate / Blind spot. *(cd+=)* – V2 / Jesus said / The deadbeat. *(cd re-iss. Mar97 on Diabolo'; DIAB 823)*
Jul 86. (7") *(D 1043)* **NATURAL KIND OF JOY. / CAN'T STOP** [ ] [–]
(12"+=) *(D 1043T)* – Non-alignment pact / Jesus said.

Polydor — Polydor

Mar 87. (7"/12") *(TPE/+X 1)* **BIG DECISION. / SOUL DEEP** [43] [–]
(ext.10"+=) *(TPE/+T 1)* – Split!
May 87. (lp/c/cd) *(TPELP/+MC/+CD 1) <833132-1/-4/-2>* **BABBLE** [30] [ ]
– Swamp / Spin cycle / For what it's worth / Big decision / Static / Split! / Belly bugs / In the playpen / Inside / Chester Burnette / Creeping to the cross. *(cd re-mast.Feb01 +=; 549565-2)* – Big decision (12" mix) / Swamp (12" mix) / Creeping to the cross (7" mix) / Soul deep / Dance your ass off.
Jun 87. (7") *(TPE 2)* **SWAMP. / DANCE YOUR ASS OFF** [64] [–]
(12"+=) *(TPEX 2)* – Creeping to the cross (live).
(7"ep++=) *(TPEE 2)* – Me and baby brother (live).

Virgin — Virgin

Oct 87. (7") *(VS 1022)* **GENIUS MOVE. / PARTY GAMES** [65] [–]
(12"+=) *(VST 1022)* – Mouthcrazy.
Sep 88. (lp/c/cd) *(V/TCV/CDV 2550) <91019-1/-4/-2>* **END OF THE MILLENNIUM PSYCHOSIS BLUES** [53] [ ]
– Sooner or later / Every little bit / Cellophane / Candy love satellite / Here it is . . . take it! / The price of my soul / Groove check / The bottom line / Tension / Tired shattered man / Goggle box / Under the sky.
Oct 88. (7") *(VS 1116)* **CELLOPHANE. / THINK OF A WOMAN** [ ] [–]
(12"+=/cd-s+=) *(VST/VSCD 1116)* – Hot head / Fast 'n' bullbous.

— **JOHN MARCHINI** – bass; repl. SEAN O'NEILL (only temporary until 1989 then full-time)

Feb 89. (10"ep/3"cd-ep) *(VSA/VSCD 1159)* **GROOVE CHECK / CHEMICRAZY. / TENSION (live) / UNDER THE SKY (live)** [ ] [ ]
Mar 90. (7") *(VS 1242)* **ABANDON. / FAT MOUTH CREED** [73] [–]
(12"+=) *(VST 1242)* – Jewel.
(cd-s+=) *(VSCD 1242)* – ('A'-Boys own mix) / Headstaggered.
Apr 90. (cd/c/lp) *(CD/TC+/V 2618) <91354-2/-4/-1>* **CHEMICRAZY** [62] [ ]
– Hey Venus / Blue to black / Mess of words / Sensitize / Another day / Gnaw mark / Scum surfin' / Compulsion / Tingle / Head staggered / Abandon / Sweet shiver burn.
May 90. (7") *(VS 1261)* **SENSITIZE. / CHEMICRAZY (revitalized)** [ ] [–]
(10"+=/12"+=/cd-s+=) *(VSAX/VST/VSCDT 1261)* – Abandon (Boys Own mix) / Groove check this groove.
Aug 90. (7") *(VS 1290)* **HEY VENUS. / ('A'-Mad Thatcher mix)** [49] [–]
(12"+=/cd-s+=) *(VST/VSCD 1290)* – (2-'A'mixes).

— **FRANK TREISCHLER** – bass (ex-YOUNG GODS) repl. MARCHINI

Jan 91. (7") *(VS 1312)* **TINGLE. / ('A'-Hard bop edit)** [49] [–]
(12"+=) *(VST 1312)* – ('A'mix).
(cd-s+=) *(VSCD 1312)* – Light and shade / Hey Bulldog.
(12") *(VSTX 1312)* – ('A'-Christmas mix) / 'A'-Jazz tup mix).

Apr 91. (7"ep/12"ep) *(VS/+T 1261)* **SENSITIZE. / ABANDON (mix) / GROOVE CHECK** [55] [–]
(10"ep+=/c-ep+=/cd-ep+=) *(VS X/C/CD 1261)* – Cinnamon girl.

— **MARCHINI** now returned to substitute TREICHE who went back to the YOUNG GODS

Koogat Rykodisc

Mar 93. (12"ep/cd-ep) *(GAT 1 T/CDS)* **DETONATE MY DREAMS. / BLUE TO BLACK (extended) / BIG HUMAN THING** [ ] [–]

Apr 93. (cd/c/lp) *(GAT 1 CD/MC/LP)* *<RCD/RAC+/10289>* **FIREPROOF** [ ] Feb94 [ ]
– Detonate my dreams / Catch a fire / Last of the true believers / Too late blues / 7th wave / Infinite thrill / Speed of light / Shangri-la / Heartbeat mosaic / Metal mystery. *(cd re-mast.Aug00 on 'Essential'; ESMCD 903)*

Jul 93. (12"ep/cd-ep) *(GAT 2 T/CDS)* **CATCH A FIRE (re-mix). / FUN TIME / LITTLE BIKINI / CHROME** [ ] [–]

— disbanded at the end of April 1994; the O'NEILL brothers formed RARE

– compilations, others, etc. –

Oct 87. (12"ep) *Strange Fruit; (SFPS 038)* **THE PEEL SESSIONS** [ ] [–]
– Blind spot / Lettuce / V2 / Can't stop.

Dec 89. (m-lp/m-cd) *Strange Fruit; (SFPMA/+CD 205) / Dutch East India; <DEI 8401>* **DOUBLE PEEL SESSIONS II** [ ] [ ]

Aug 00. (cd) *Essential; (ESMCD 902)* **LIVE (live)** [ ] [–]

the UNDERTONES

re-formed **PAUL McLOONE** – vocals (not FEARGAL!)

Sanctuary Sanctuary

Oct 03. (cd) *(SANCD 210) <84646>* **GET WHAT YOU NEED** [ ] [ ]
– Thrill me / I need your love the way it used to be / Everything but you / Ride the rough escalator / You can't say that / Enough / Touch / Girl like you / The cruellest thing / Oh please / Winter sun / Joyland / Shut down.

– compilations, others, etc. –

Nov 83. (d-lp)(c) *Ardeck-EMI; (ARD 1654283)(1654289)* **ALL WRAPPED UP** [67] [–]
– Teenage kicks / Get over you / Jimmy Jimmy / Here comes the summer / You've got my number (why don't you use it) / My perfect cousin / Wednesday week / It's going to happen / Julie Ocean / Beautiful friend / The love parade / Got to have you back / Chain of love.

— (note: all singles were re-iss. on 'Ardeck-EMI')

May 86. (lp/c) *Ardeck-EMI; (EMS/TCEMS 1172)* **CHER O'BOWLIES – THE PICK OF THE UNDERTONES** [96] [–]
– Teenage kicks / True confessions / Get over you / Family entertainment / Jimmy Jimmy / Here comes the Summer / You got my number (why don't you use it) / My perfect cousin / See that girl / Tearproof / Wednesday week / It's going to happen / Julie Ocean / You're welcome / Forever Paradise / Beautiful friend / Save me / The love parade / Valentine's treatment / Love before romance. *(re-iss. Oct89 on 'Fame' cd/c/lp; CD/TC+/FA 3226)*

Jun 86. (7") *Ardeck-EMI; (ARDS 14)* **SAVE ME. / TEARPROOF** [ ] [–]
(12"+=) *(12ARDS 14)* – I know a girl.

Dec 86. (12"ep) *Strange Fruit; (SFPS 016)* **THE PEEL SESSIONS** (21.1.79) [ ] [–]
– Listening in / Family entertainment / Here comes the summer / Billy's third. *(cd-ep iss.Mar88)*

Dec 89. (lp/c/cd) *Strange Fruit; (SFR LP/MC/CD 103)* **DOUBLE PEEL SESSIONS** [ ] [–]
(re-iss. cd Mar94 as 'THE PEEL SESSIONS ALBUM'; same)

Sep 93. (cd/c) *Castle; (CTV CD/MC 121) / Rykodisc; <RCD 20297>* **THE BEST OF THE UNDERTONES – TEENAGE KICKS** [45] [ ]
(cd re-iss. Jan97 on 'Renaissance'; CCSCD 808)

Jul 95. (cd-ep) *Dojo; (TONESCD 1)* **HERE COMES THE SUMMER / GET OVER YOU / JIMMY JIMMY / YOU'VE GOT MY NUMBER (WHY DON'T YOU USE IT)** [ ] [–]

Sep 99. (d-cd) *Essential; (ESDCD 788)* **TRUE CONFESSIONS: SINGLES A's & B's** [ ] [–]

Jun 00. (12xcd-s) *Essential; (ESFCD 893)* **THE SINGLES BOX SET** [ ] [–]

Sep 03. (cd) *Sanctuary; (TVSAN 005)* **TEENAGE KICKS – THE BEST OF THE UNDERTONES** [35] [–]

UNDERWORLD

Formed: Romford, London, England . . . 1987 by RICK SMITH, KARL HYDE, ALFIE THOMAS and BRYN BURROWS, who had all been in Cardiff outfit FREUR (which was actually a symbol translated into a word!; no, PRINCE wasn't the first!). Even before this, RICK and KARL had played in synth-pop band, The SCREEN GEMS. In 1987, they took on the more conventional moniker, UNDERWORLD and hit America in the late 80's after signing for Seymour Stein's 'Sire' records. After a No.1 smash, 'RADAR', in Australia, they toured the States supporting EURYTHMICS, but it was clear this was not the direction for them. After recruiting DJ DARREN EMERSON, the band signed with the 'Boys Own' label, releasing the seminal techno crescendo of 'REZ' in February '93. They followed this up with the critically acclaimed, early '94 album, 'DUBNOBASSWITHMYHEADMAN', a nouveau-psychedelic classic climaxing with the delirious trance-athon of 'COWGIRL'. However, their big break came with the track 'BORN SLIPPY', a song featured on the 'Trainspotting' soundtrack. When re-released as a single in 1996, the track stormed to No.2, boosting sales of their recently released follow-up album, 'SECOND TOUGHEST IN THE INFANTS'. The band remain one of Britain's best loved techno acts, and with the Stateside success of The PRODIGY, there was still a chance that the band might break in America. Indeed, 1999's long-awaited 'BEAUCOUP FISH' took them into the US Top 100 having already made Top 3 in Britain. Highlights from the set were undoubtably hit singles, 'PUSH UPSTAIRS', 'JUMBO' and 'SHUDDER – KING OF SNAKE', while 'MOANER' (theme from 1997's 'Batman & Robin' movie) was its 10-star pièce de resistance. The first live album of their decade+ career, 'EVERYTHING, EVERYTHING' (2000) was as thrilling a recreation of UNDERWORLD's unique techno meets rock'n'roll concert experience as you could hope for, featuring a fair clutch (with some notable omissions nevertheless) of their best loved dancefloor marathons including 'REZ' and 'BORN SLIPPY'. EMERSON officially departed in spring 2000. The first post-EMERSON album, 'A HUNDRED DAYS OFF', followed in 2002, a strangely muted affair undoubtedly affected by the alteration in group chemistry. There were still touches of the sly genius of old, notably on the marathon, near 10-minute 'TWO MONTHS OFF'.

• **Songwriters:** SMITH / HYDE / THOMAS then SMITH / HYDE / EMERSON. • **Trivia:** Produced by RUPERT HINES in 1988. HYDE worked on a 1991 'Paisley P.' album with TERRI NUNN (ex-Berlin). GEOFF DUGMORE (ex-ART OF NOISE) was a guest on 1989 album. Also appeared on WILLIAM ORBIT's 'Watch From A Vine Leaf' & ORBITAL's 'Lush 3' and remixed BJORK's 'Human Behaviour'.

Album rating: Freur: DOOT DOOT (*4) / GET US OUT OF HERE (*4) / Underworld: UNDERNEATH THE RADAR (*5) / CHANGE THE WEATHER (*4) / DUBNOBASSWITHMYHEADMAN (*8) / SECOND TOUGHEST IN THE INFANTS (*8) / BEAUCOUP FISH (*8) / A HUNDRED DAYS OFF (*4) / 1992-2002 compilation (*8)

FREUR

RICK SMITH (b.25 May'59, Ammanford, Wales) – keyboards, vocals / **KARL HYDE** (b.10 May'57, Worcester, England) – vocals, guitar / **ALFIE THOMAS** – guitar, vocals / **JOHN WARWICKER LE BRETON** – synthesizers / **BRYN B. BURROWS** – drums

C.B.S. Epic

Mar 83. (7"pic-d/ext.12") *(WA/A13 3141)* **DOOT DOOT. / HOLD ME MOTHER** [59] [ ]

Jun 83. (7"/7"pic-d) *(A/WA 3456)* **MATTERS OF THE HEART. / YOU'RE A HOOVER** [ ] [ ]
(12"+=) *(TA 3456)* – ('A'extended).
Sep 83. (7"/12") **RUNAWAY. / YOU'RE A HOOVER** [–] [ ]
Nov 83. (lp/c) *(CBS/40 25522)* *<81566>* **DOOT DOOT** [ ] [ ]
– Doot doot / Runaway / Riders in the night / Theme from the film of the same name / Tender surrender / Matters of the heart / My room / Steam machine / Whispering / All too much.
Jan 84. (7"/ext.12") *(A/TA 4073)* **DOOT DOOT. / HOLD ME MOTHER** [ ] [ ]
Apr 84. (7") *(A 4333)* **RIDERS IN THE NIGHT. / INNOCENCE** [ ] [ ]
(12"+=) *(TA 4333)* – This is the way I like to live my life.

—— added **JAKE BOWIE** – bass
Oct 84. (7") *(A 4726)* **DEVIL AND DARKNESS. / JAZZ 'N' KING** [ ] [ ]
(12"+=) *(TX 4726)* – ('A'extended).
Feb 85. (7") *(A 4983)* **LOOK IN THE BACK FOR ANSWERS. / HEY HO AWAY WE GO** [ ] [ ]
(12"+=) *(TX 4983)* – Uncle Jeff.
Feb 85. (lp/c/cd) **GET US OUT OF HERE** [ ] [ ]
– Look in the back for answers / Emeralds and pearls / Kiss me / A.O.K.O. / The Devil and darkness / The piano song / Happiness / Endless groove / This is the way I'd like to live my life / Bella Donna.

UNDERWORLD

—— **BAZ ALLEN** – bass; repl. JOHN

Sire Sire

Mar 88. (lp/c/cd) *(<925627-1/-4/-2>)* **UNDERNEATH THE RADAR** [ ] [ ]
– Glory! glory! / Call me No.1 / Rubber ball (space kitchen) / Show some emotion / Underneath the radar / Miracle party / I need a doctor / Bright white flame / Pray / The God song.
Jul 88. (7") *(W 7968)* *<27968>* **UNDERNEATH THE RADAR. / BIG RED X** [ ] Apr88 [74]
(12"+=) *(W 7968T)* – ('A'dub version).
Aug 88. (7") **SHOW SOME EMOTION. / SHOCK THE DOCTOR** [–] [ ]

—— **PASCAL CONSOLI** – percussion, drums repl. BURROWS who joined WORLDWIDE ELECTRIC
Aug 89. (7"/c-s) *(W 2854/+C)* *<22852>* **STAND UP. / OUTSKIRTS** [ ] [67]
(12") *(W 2854T)* – Stand up (and dance) / Stand up (ya house) / Outskirts.
(cd-s) *(W 2854CD)* – (all mixes & B-side)
Sep 89. (lp/c)(cd) *(WX 289/+C)(K 925945-2)* *<25945>* **CHANGE THE WEATHER** [ ] [ ]
– Change the weather / Stand up / Fever / Original song / Mercy / Mr. Universe / Texas / Thrash / Sole survivor / Beach.
Nov 89. (7") **CHANGE THE WEATHER. / TEXAS** [–] [ ]

—— ALLEN + CONSOLI became D-INFLUENCE

—— **SMITH** + **HYDE** brought in **DARREN EMERSON** (b.30 Apr'71, Hornchurch, Essex, England) – keyboards

Tomato not iss.

1992. (12") *(PLUM 2001)* **MOTHER EARTH / MOTHER EARTH (FM mix). / THE HUMP / THE HUMP (groove without a doubt mix)** [ ] [–]

Boys Own not iss.

Jan 93. (12"ep/cd-ep) *(BOI X/CD 13)* **MMM . . . SKYSCRAPER I LOVE YOU. / ('A'-Telegraph mix 6.11.92) / ('A'-Jamscraper mix)** [ ] [–]
1993. (12"/12"pink) *(Collect 002/+P)* **REZ. / WHY WHY WHY** [ ] [–]

Junior Boys Own Wax Trax!

1993. (12"; as LEMON INTERRUPT) *(JBO 12-002)* **ECLIPSE. / BIGMOUTH** [ ] [–]
1993. (12"; as LEMON INTERRUPT) *(JBO 7-12)* **DIRTY / MINNEAPOLIS. / MINNEAPOLIS (AIRWAVES)** [ ] [–]
Sep 93. (12"/cd-s) *(JBO 13/+CD)* **COWGIRL. / REZ** [ ] [–]
(re-iss. Aug95 on 'Junior Boys Own'; JBO 1001)
Dec 93. (12"/cd-s) *(JBO 17/+CD)* **SPIKEE. / DOGMAN GO WOOF** [60] [ ]
Feb 94. (cd/c/d-lp) *(JBO CD/CS/LP 1)* *<7217>* **DUBNOBASSWITHMYHEADMAN** [12] [ ]
– Dark and long / Mmm . . . skyscraper I love you / Surf boy / Spoon man / Tongue / Dirty epic / Cowgirl / River of bass / M.E. *(cd re-iss. May97; same)*
Jun 94. (cd-ep) *(JBO 19CDS)* **DARK & LONG (mixes)** [57] [–]
– Hall's mix / Dark train / Most 'ospitable / 215 miles.
(12") *(JB 019)* – ('A'-spoon deep mix) / ('A'-thing in a back mix).
(12") *(JB 019X)* – ('A'-dark train mix) / ('A'-Burt's mix).
(re-iss. Sep99 12"/cd-s; JBO 501027-3/-6)
Dec 94. (cd-ep) *<8722>* **DIRTY EPIC (mixes; dirty guitar / dirty mix / album) / COWGIRL (mixes; Irish pub in Kyoto / winjer / album) / REZ / RIVER OF BASS** [–] [ ]
Jan 95. (12") *<8724-0>* **COWGIRL (mixes; album / Winjer / Irish pub in Kyoto)** [–] [ ]
May 95. (12") *(JBO 29)* **BORN SLIPPY (telenatic). / COWGIRL (Vinjer mix)** [52] [ ]
(12") *(JBO 29R)* – ('A'side) / ('A'-Nuxx mix).
(cd-s) *(JBO 29CDS)* – (above 2) / ('A'side again).
Mar 96. (cd/c/d-lp) *(JBO CD/MC/LP 4)* *<7240>* **SECOND TOUGHEST IN THE INFANTS** [9] [ ]
– Juanita – Kiteless – To dream of love / Banstyle – Sappys curry / Confusion the waitress / Rowla / Pearls girl / Air towel / Blueski / Stagger. *(cd re-iss. May97; same)*
May 96. (12"ep) *(JBO 38)* **PEARLS GIRL. / MOSAIC / DEEP ARCH** [24] [–]
(cd-ep) *(JBO 38CDS1)* – ('A'-Carp Dreams . . . Koi) / Oich oich / Cherry pie.
(cd-ep) *(JBO 38CDS2)* – ('A'mixes).

Junior Boys Own TVT

Jun 96. (12") *<8737>* **ROWLA. / JUANITA** [–] [ ]
Jul 96. (12"/cd-s) *(JBO 44/+CDS1)* *<8731>* **BORN SLIPPY. / ('A'mixes)** [2] [ ]
(cd-s) *(JBO 38CDS2)* – ('A'side) / ('A'-Deep pan mix) / ('A'-Darren Price mix) / ('A'-Darren Price remix).
(re-iss. Apr99 on 'Junior Boys Own-V2' 12"/cd-s/cd-s; JBO 50056 2-6/0-3/1-3)
Oct 96. (12"/cd-s) *(JBO 45/+CDS1)* *<8748>* **PEARLS GIRL. / ('A'mixes; Puppies / Oich oich / Cherry Pie)** [22] Feb97 [ ]
(cd-s) *(JBO 45CDS2)* – ('A'mixes; Mosaic / Deep arch).
1997. (cd-ep) *(9362 43905-2)* **MOANER (short) / (album) / (relentless legs) / (long)** [ ] [ ]
(above from the Warners movie, 'Batman & Robin')

Junior Boys Own – V2 V2

Mar 99. (cd/c/d-lp) *(JBO 100543-2/-4/-1)* *<27042>* **BEAUCOUP FISH** [3] [93]
– Cups / Push upstairs / Jumbo / Shudder – King of snake / Winjer / Skym / Bruce Lee / Kittens / Push downstairs / Something like a mama / Moaner.
Mar 99. (12"/cd-s) *(JBO 500544-6/-3)* **PUSH UPSTAIRS (mixes; The Large Unit / Darren Price) / PLEASE HELP ME** [12] [ ]
(cd-s) *(JBO 500617-3)* – ('A'mixes).
May 99. (12"/cd-s) *(JBO 500719-6/-3)* **JUMBO (mixes; edit / Rob Rives & Francois K Main Dish / Jedis Electro dub)** [21] [ ]
(cd-s) *(JBO 500720-3)* – ('A'mixes).
Aug 99. (cd-s) *(JBO 500879-3)* **KING OF SNAKE (mixes; Straight (Mate) / Fatboy Slim / Slam)** [17] [ ]
(12"/cd-s) *(JBO 500879-6/-8)* – ('A'mixes) / Shudder – King of snake.
Nov 99. (12"/cd-s) *(JBO 501003-6/-3)* **BRUCE LEE (Micronauts remixes) / CUPS (Salt City Orchestra mix)** [ ] [–]
Aug 00. (12"/cd-s) *(JBO 501251-6/-3)* **COWGIRL (mixes; radio / Bedrock / Futureshock) / REZ – COWGIRL (live)** [24] [–]
(cd-s) *(JBO 501251-8)* – (mixes).
Sep 00. (cd/c) *(JBO 101254-2/-4)* *<27078>* **EVERYTHING, EVERYTHING (live)** [22] [ ]
– Juanita – Kiteless / Cups / Push upstairs / Pearls girl / Jumbo / Shudder – King of snake / Born slippy nuxx / Rez – Cowgirl.

—— EMERSON left in April 2000
Sep 02. (cd-s) *(JBO 502009-3)* **TWO MONTHS OFF / TWO MONTHS OFF (KIng Unique sunspots – vocal) / HEADSET** [12] [ ]
(cd-s) *(JBO 502009-8)* – ('A'side) / ('A'-John Ciafone vocal) / Tiny clicks.
(12") *(JBO 502009-6)* *<27764-1>* – (2 'A'-mixes).
Sep 02. (cd/d-lp) *(JBO 102010-2/-1)* *<27137>* **A HUNDRED DAYS OFF** [16] [ ]
– Mo move / Two months off / Twist / Sola sistim / Little speaker / Trim / Ess Gee / Dinosaur adventure 3D / Ballet lane / Luetin.
Jan 03. (cd-s) *(JBO 502052-3)* **DINOSAUR ADVENTURE 3D / ANSUM** [34] [–]
(12"/cd-s) *(JBO 502052-6/-8)* – ('A'mixes).

Oct 03. (cd-s) *(JBO 502470-3)* **BORN SLIPPY NUXX (mixes; Rick Smith / Atomic Hooligan / Paul Oakenfold)** 27 –
(12") *(JBO 502470-0)* – ('A'-mixes; Atomic Hooligan / London Elektricity).

Nov 03. (d-cd/q-lp) *(JBO 102469-2/-1)* <27175> **1992-2002** (compilation) 43 Dec03
– Big mouth / Dirty / Mmm skyscraper I love you / Rez / Spikee / Dirty epic / Dark and long (dark train) // Cowgirl / Born slippy NUXX / Pearls girl / Jumbo / Push upstairs / Moaner / Shudder – King of snake / 8 ball / Two months off.

– compilations, etc. –

Oct 97. (cd) *April; <002>* **DARK & LONG** –

Mar 99. (cd-s) *TVT; (8722-2)* **DIRTY EPIC / COWGIRL / REZ** –

Sep 02. (12") *T.V.T.; (TVT 87180)* **COWBOY. / REX** –
(12") *(TVT 87420)* – ('A'-mixes; album / Winjer / Irish pub in Kyoto).

U.N.K.L.E.

Formed: London, England . . . 1994 by JAMES LAVELLE (head honcho of 'Mo Wax'), along with TIM GOLDSWORTHY (from New York) and Japanese label boss KUDO (of 'Major Force' and psychedelic electronic outfit SKYLAB). The collective – not so much of a band – gathered acclaim due to their classy remixes, which included the likes of TORTOISE and The JON SPENCER BLUES EXPLOSION. LAVELLE, already a renowned producer and label boss, was planning a special "all-star" concept album to go under the UNKLE banner. He enlisted the help of DJ SHADOW, moved out to a studio in Los Angeles and effectively began work on his epic 'PSYENCE FICTION' set. KUDO, due to work commitments had left the project, leaving SHADOW to do most of the work on the sampling and the music side of things. They enlisted some of the in-demand musicians of the moment – noteably THOM YORKE who had just delivered RADIOHEAD's groundbreaking album 'OK Computer', RICHARD ASHCOFT (ex-of THE VERVE) and MIKE D (of the BEASTIE BOYS). The resulting aforementioned set was a cross-breed of jazz, electronica, hip-hop and trip-hop with the standout track being YORKE's contribution 'RABBIT IN YOUR HEADLIGHTS', a strange off-kilter, free-jazz time signature, with a mellow piano and memorable voice sample from the movie 'Jacob's Ladder'. LAVELLE toured the album, not with SHADOW, but with the not-so-well-known SCRATCH PERVERTS and set to work on its follow-up. Fans had a long time to wait as it eventually arrived in 2003 under the title 'NEVER, NEVER, LAND'. It featured guests IAN BROWN, 3D (from MASSIVE ATTACK) and JOSH HOMME (of the QUEENS OF THE STONE AGE). However, unlike its Top 5 predecessor, the set went practically unnoticed, although it did hit the UK Top 30.

Album rating: PSYENCE FICTION (*8) / NEVER, NEVER, LAND (*6)

JAMES LAVELLE plus **DJ SHADOW** + **TIM GOLDSWORTHY** + **MASAYUKI KUDO** (Major Force West)

Mo' Wax Universal

Jan 95. (12"/12"pic-d) <*(MW 028/+P)*> **THE TIME HAS COME (mixes)** –
(re-iss. May96 w/cd-ep; MW 028CD)

Feb 97. (12"/cd-s) <*(MW 069/+CD)*> **BERRY MEDITATION (mixes; original / last ever / the darker the berry . . .)** –
(12"clear) *(MW 069L)* – ('A'remixes).

Mar 97. (12"/cd-s) <*(MW 070/+CD)*> **ROCK ON (mixes)** –

— **LAVELLE** + **DJ SHADOW** with guests vocalists **THOM YORKE** (Radiohead) / **RICHARD ASHCROFT** (Verve) / **MIKE D** (Beastie Boys) / **MARK HOLLIS** (ex-Talk Talk) / **ALICE TEMPLE** (Eg And Alice) / **BADLY DRAWN BOY** + **KOOL G RAP**

Aug 98. (lp/c/cd) *(MW 085/+MC/CD)* <540970> **PSYENCE FICTION** 4
– Intro – Guns blazing (drums of death, pt.1) / UNKLE main title theme / Blood stain / Unreal / Lonely soul / Getting ahead in the field of artistic management / Nursery rhyme – Breather / Celestial annihilation / The knock (drums of death, pt.2) / Chaos / Rabbit in your headlights / Outro. *(also ltd;d-cd/d-lp; MW 085 CDS/S)*

Oct 98. (12"ep/cd-ep) *(MW 103/+CD)* **RABBIT IN YOUR HEADLIGHTS / (instrumental) / (Underdog mix) / (Underdog instrumental) / (30 mix 'reverse light') / (30 mix 'reverse light' instrumental) / (Suburban hell remix)** – nochart –

Feb 99. (12"/cd-s; UNKLE featuring IAN BROWN) *(MW 108/+CD1)* **BE THERE (mixes; original / Underdog / Underdog instrumental)** 8 –
(cd-s) *(MW 108CD2)* – ('A'side) / The knock (drums of Zep) (Noel Gallagher mix) / Rabbit in your headlights (video).

— DJ SHADOW was now not part of the UNKLE set-up

— **LAVELLE** + **RICHARD FILE** + **ANTHONY GLENN** recruited numerous guests (see biog)

Aug 03. (cd-s) *(CID 826)* **AN EYE FOR AN EYE (mixes)** 31 –
(12"/cd-s) *(12IS/CIDX 826)* – ('A'mixes).
(12"/12"/12"/12") *(12IS W/X/Y/Z 826)* – (various mixes).
(above on 'Island' records)

Sep 03. (cd) *(MWU 001CD)* <986554> **NEVER, NEVER, LAND** 24 Oct04
– Back and forth / Eye for an eye / In a state / Safe in mind (UNKLE & JOSH HOMME) / I need something stronger / What are you to me? / Panic attack / Invasion (UNKLE & 3D) / Reign (UNKLE & IAN BROWN) / Glow (UNKLE & JOE CADBURY) / Inside. *(d-lp-iss.Nov03 +=; MWU 001LP)* – Awake the unkind. <*US*+=> – Eye for an eye backwards / Safe in the mind (please take this gun from out of my face).

Nov 03. (12") *(MWU 002TX)* **IN A STATE. / (Sasha remix)** 44 –
(12") *(MWU 002TY)* – ('A'-DFA remix) / ('A'-Meat Katie & Elite Force remix).
(cd-s) *(CID 839)* – (all above +).

Nov 04. (12"; as UNKLE feat. IAN BROWN) *(GUSIN 007)* **REIGN (Way Out West remix). / REIGN (Evil 9 remix)** 40
(cd-s+=) *(GUSIN 007CDS)* – (edit) / (Morgan Geist delayed gratification mix) / (UNKLE reconstruction).
(12") *(GUSIN 007US)*> – (mixes; RJD2 vocal / Three AM's Black Swan vocal / Morgan Geist delayed gratification / Beat Pharmacy's better to reign in hell than to serve in heaven).

☐ Midge URE (see under ⇒ ULTRAVOX)

the USED

Formed: Orem, Utah, USA . . . 2000 by JEPH HOWARD (then vocalist), BRANDEN STEINECKERT, QUINN ALLMAN and BERT McCRACKEN. Adept at going from a pleading PERRY FARRELL-esque whimper to a godless grunt, McCRACKEN went some way to defining the USED's screamo balladry. Channelling their societal struggles (homelessness included) into their lyrics/music, the quartet made good with a major label deal courtesy of 'Reprise'. A recording/production relationship with GOLDFINGER's John Feldmann was initiated with their eponymous 2002 debut, a middling breakthrough in itself in America and the source of minor UK hit, 'THE TASTE OF INK'. Their corporate backers took the increasingly common option of milking the situation with a live/demos/videos CD/DVD named after debut opener, 'MAYBE MEMORIES' (2003). A Feldmann-produced sophomore set proper, 'IN LOVE AND DEATH', finally arrived in September 2004, wrapped in an indulgently gothic sleeve depicting a disembodied strung-up heart. This pretty much summed up the musical content, a tortured, genre-splintering trip through their own scarred hearts. While many critics weren't entirely convinced, the band still managed to pick up a Metal Hammer award and a US Top 10 placing. A collaborative (download) cover of Bowie & Queen's 'UNDER PRESSURE' with gloom buddies MY CHEMICAL ROMANCE (in aid of Hurricane Katrina disaster) almost reached the Top 40 the following September.

Album rating: THE USED (*6) / MAYBE MEMORIES collection w/dvd (*4) / IN LOVE AND DEATH (*5)

BERT McCRACKEN (b. ROBERT.., 25 Feb'82) – vocals (+ piano, keyboards) / **QUINN ALLMAN** (b.18 Jan'82) – guitar, vocals / **JEPH HOWARD** (b. JEPHAREE.., 4 Jan'79) – bass, vocals / **BRANDEN STEINECKERT** (b.21 Apr'78) – drums, vocals

Reprise Reprise

Nov 02. (cd) *<9362 48287-2>* **THE USED** [ ] Jun02 [63]
– Maybe memories / The taste of ink / Bulimic / Say days ago / Poetic tragedy / Buried myself alive / A box full of sharp objects / Blue and yellow / Greener with the scenery / Noise and kisses / On my own / Pieces mended.

Mar 03. (7") *(W 601)* **THE TASTE OF INK. / JUST A LITTLE** [52] [ ]
(cd-s+=) *(W 601CD)* – Alone this holiday / ('A'-video).

Jul 03. (cd w/dvd) *<9362 48503-2>* **MAYBE MEMORIES** (collection) [–] [84]
– Maybe memories (live) / A box full of sharp objects (live) / On my own (live) / Say days ago (live) / Just a little / It could be a good excuse (home demo) / Zero mechanism (home demo) / Bulimic (home demo) / Alone this holiday (KROQ Christmas) / Sometimes I just go for it (piano solo) / 801 underground // (the video diary & DVD tracks).

Sep 04. (cd) *<(9362 48789-2)>* **IN LOVE AND DEATH** [ ] [6]
– Take it away / I caught fire / Let it bleed / All that I've got / Cut up angels / Listening / Yesterday's feelings / Light with a sharpened edge / Sound effects and overdramatics / Hard to say / Lunacy fringe / I'm a fake. *(re-iss. Jan05 +=; same)* – Under pressure.

Jan 05. (7"red/cd-s) *(W 662/+CD1) <868963>* **TAKE IT AWAY. / ALL THAT I'VE GOT (live at Soma)** [44] Apr05 [ ]
(cd-s) *(W 662CD2) <242785>* – ('A') / The taste of ink (live at Soma) / ('A'-live at Soma).

Jul 05. (cd-s) *(W 678CD1)* **ALL THAT I'VE GOT / I'M A FAKE (live at Soma)** [ ] [–]
(cd-s) *(W 678CD2)* – ('A') / A box full of sharp objects (live at Soma) / I caught fire (live at Soma) / ('A'-video).

Sep 05. (dl-s; w/ MY CHEMICAL ROMANCE) *<net>* **UNDER PRESSURE** [–] [41]

Nov 05. (cd-s) *(W 690CD1)* **I CAUGHT FIRE / ALONE THIS HOLIDAY** [ ] [–]
(cd-s) *(W 690CD2)* – ('A') / All that I've got (acoustic) / Lunacy fringe (acoustic).

□ UTOPIA (see under ⇒ RUNDGREN, Todd)

U2

Formed: Dublin, Ireland . . . 1977 by BONO, THE EDGE, ADAM CLAYTON and LARRY MULLEN. Indisputably one of the biggest and the most talked about 'musical phenomenon's of the last two decades, U2 nevertheless graduated from humble beginnings as a covers band. Finally adopting the U2 moniker in 1978, they subsequently attracted the attention of Paul McGuinness, one of the most respected managers in the business. It wasn't long before they found themselves signed to 'C.B.S.' Ireland via A&R man, Jackie Hayden, releasing a debut single, 'U2-3' in late '79. The track scaled the Irish charts, as did a follow-up, 'ANOTHER DAY', the group subsequently snapped up by 'Island' records for a worldwide deal. Initially, U2 made little impact, singles '11 O'CLOCK TICK TOCK' and 'A DAY WITHOUT ME' failing to chart. By the release of the Steve Lillywhite-produced debut album, 'BOY' (1980), however, U2 were already assuming the mantle of cult status. Strikingly original, the group carved out their own plot of fertile territory within the suffocatingly oversubscribed rock format, cultivating a watertight, propulsive minimalism to partner their politically direct lyrics. Carried equally by BONO's crusading vocal theatrics, THE EDGE's serrated guitar cascades and the ryhthmic drive of CLAYTON and MULLEN, the likes of 'I WILL FOLLOW' was a blueprint for the U2 formula. And it was a formula which seemed to command devotion; those who followed the band did so with the same zeal as U2 set out their humanitarian agenda, the group eschewing party politics for a more expansive but no less focused commentary on the world's ills with an overriding religious/spiritual bent. Live, the group were also being hailed as one of the most innovative and exciting acts to emerge from the post-punk morass. Though 'OCTOBER' (1981) almost broke into the Top 10, the album failed to spawn any major hits, the clarion call of 'GLORIA' surprisingly stiffing outside the Top 50. So it was then, that U2 seemed to come out of nowhere in early '83 with a Top 10 single, the highly emotive 'NEW YEAR'S DAY' (inspired by the Lech Walenska's Polish Solidarity Union) and a No.1 album, 'WAR'. U2's first masterstroke, the album was consistently compelling, through the rousing rhythmic militarism of 'SUNDAY BLOODY SUNDAY' (interpreted by many as a republican rebel song, BONO famously declared otherwise when introducing the track live) and the celebratory 'TWO HEARTS BEAT AS ONE' to the more meditative acoustics of 'DROWNING MAN'. The record's anthemic Irish qualities also appealed to the Americans, 'WAR' almost making the US Top 10; from the electric atmosphere of the live 'UNDER A BLOOD RED SKY' (1983), it certainly seemed U2's sound could galvanise a transatlantic audience, probably (and eventually) a world audience. Previewed by perhaps U2's most anthemic, politically pointed song, 'PRIDE (IN THE NAME OF LOVE)' (a tribute to assassinated black civil rights hero, Martin Luther King), 'THE UNFORGETTABLE FIRE' (1984) consolidated the band's commerical and creative maturity. For the most part, however, the record took a completely different approach, BRIAN ENO presiding over a collection of more exploratory, occasionally near-ambient excursions, the highlight arguably being the epic atmospherics of the stunning title track. Equally evocative was 'BAD', an almost hymn-like incantation with which U2 entranced the world at Live Aid in summer '85. One of the key events in the band's career, their celebrated performance undoubtedly won them a massive new audience almost overnight, much in the same way as QUEEN rejuvenated their career through the concert. Understandably, then, the anticipation for U2's next album, 'THE JOSHUA TREE' (1987), was fevered. Fortunately it was also justified, U2 delivering what was undeniably the most accomplished set of their career and probably one of the greatest rock albums ever released. Like many such masterworks, U2 scaled this pinnacle of creativity by means of a subtle balance, between panoramic euphoria and hushed reflection, between the personal and the political and between insinuation and crystal clarity. The record's undertow of spiritual soul searching evident on the likes of 'I STILL HAVEN'T FOUND WHAT I'M LOOKING FOR' (a US No.1) obviously struck a chord in a decade more concerned with ruthless material gain, while the air of soft-focus melancholy permeating 'WITH OR WITHOUT YOU' and 'RUNNING TO STAND STILL' further enhanced the album's almost tangible warmth. Even the more full-on tracks such as 'WHERE THE STREETS HAVE NO NAME' and 'IN GOD'S COUNTRY' seemed to emanate from a deep-seated yearning through the shards of THE EDGE's guitar scree. 'THE JOSHUA TREE' was a transatlantic No.1 (a worldwide No.1), facilitating U2's move to the top of the world premier league. As well as being a formidable commercial proposition, U2 were hailed by some commentators as the most 'important' rock group on the planet, both lyrically and musically. Of course, such inflated claims were matched by equally vociferous critics of the group's perceived pomposity and preaching self-importance. Such criticism was nothing new, although it reached its height in the aftermath of 'THE JOSHUA TREE' and its attendant tour, when BONO was being hailed as some kind of messiah. The sight of the singer charging around the stage with a floodlight and a white flag, together with his increasingly politicised between song (or even half-way through) speeches became too much for some, although in a music scene bereft of direction or purpose, BONO probably made up for the prevailing insipidness. Attempting to follow up this musical landmark, U2 released a kind of stop-

Bono of U2

gap half-live/half-studio affair, 'RATTLE AND HUM' (1988). A soundtrack to the rockumentary of the same name which marked the culmination of the group's obsession with America, the album was accused of being half-baked in parts. Possibly, but the gut-level punch of 'GOD PART II' and the bleakly beautiful 'VAN DIEMEN'S LAND' were unquestionably full-baked, if oddities nonetheless. Following the poignant love song, 'ALL I WANT IS YOU' (a UK Top 5) in summer '89, U2 went to ground, hard at work on a new strategy. Sporting wraparound shades and skin-tight black leather, BONO finally emerged in late '91 with 'THE FLY', a grinding guitar groove with urgent, hoarsely whispered lyrics. The track entered the UK chart at No.1, paving the way for the massively successful 'ACHTUNG BABY' (1991). Stylistically diverse, the album marked the beginnings of U2's flirtation with dance culture, a sign that the band were wary of falling into the rock dinosaur mould. BONO had also obviously been listening to his critics, changing his persona from earnest poet to lounge lizard sophisticate. Though the likes of 'WHO'S GONNA RIDE YOUR WILD HORSES' and the deeply affecting 'ONE' (probably the most intimate song the group have ever penned) signalled a move into more personal lyrical territory, the album's attendant 'Zoo TV' tour was themed around political events in Europe, albeit with a more post-modern, multi-media stoked irony. Inspired by the tour, 'ZOOROPA' (1993) was U2's most contemporary release to date, a fractured, dance-orientated affair which rather unfairly received a bit of a pasting from more short-sighted critics. Following on from the celebrated dance mixes of 'EVEN BETTER THAN THE REAL THING' (from 'ACHTUNG BABY'), the 12' remix of 'LEMON' was hot property when originally released in limited lemon coloured vinyl. As well as catering for dance trainspotters, U2 even recorded a duet with JOHNNY CASH, the darkly brilliant 'THE WANDERER', in effect kickstarting the aging country star's career. In the ensuing two years, BONO popped up with GAVIN FRIDAY on the theme to the acclaimed 'IN THE NAME OF THE FATHER', while U2 scored a UK No.2 hit with 'HOLD ME, THRILL ME, KISS ME, KILL ME' from the huge box office smash, 'Batman Forever'. This fascination with soundtrack music continued via the PASSENGERS project, a collaboration between U2, BRIAN ENO, italian opera singer PAVAROTTI and Glaswegian beatz guru HOWIE B. Entitled 'ORIGINAL SOUNDTRACKS VOL.1' (1995), a few of the album's tracks (highlight being the hit single, 'MISS SARAJEVO') were actually written as themes to avant-garde films while the remainder were written for obscure celluloid pieces. As low-key as U2 have ever dared go, the album passed by without much fuss, its ambient noodlings not really indicating a new direction as such but proving that the group were firmly committed to constant experimentation. For their next album proper, U2 retained HOWIE B as co-producer, crafting an album that once again used dance music as a touchstone. Preview single, 'DISCOTHEQUE', sounded like a watered-down 'FLY' although the accompanying VILLAGE PEOPLE-pastiche video showed, shock horror!, U2 having a right old laugh! Despite this newfound sense of humour, the 'POP' (1996) album met with mixed reviews, some hailing it as a bold new dawn, others accusing the band of treading water. The record certainly had its moments, the searing desolation of 'STARING AT THE SUN' and the apocalyptic 'LAST NIGHT ON EARTH' (the video featuring an appearance from counter-culture guru, William Burroughs, just weeks before his death, U2 having previously persuaded the voraciously anti-rock Charles Bukowski to attend a gig, no mean feat!) for example, but there was a feeling of incompleteness to the whole affair. Likewise, the accompanying 'Pop Mart' tour which got off to a shaky start in Las Vegas, its consumerist theme carried by another media extravaganza, albeit downscaled from the Zoo TV era. While U2 undoubtedly lead the way in terms of stadium rock, constantly innovative in new ways to keep the medium fresh, they arguably need to rediscover themselves musically and give up recycling second hand ideas. Whether they have either the willingness or ability to do this is another matter, although being past masters of coming out fighting in the face of adversity, it's highly likely. With a new decade, a new millennium and a new album, 'ALL THAT YOU CAN'T LEAVE BEHIND' (2000), U2 arguably did rediscover themselves although only in terms of the strident, open sound which defined their approach during the 80's. This revisionism works (often spectacularly) well within a modern – or even post-modern – context, most obviously on the massive singles, 'BEAUTIFUL DAY' and 'ELEVATION'. BONO's recently stated intention to reclaim U2's position as the world's top dogs matched the overarching reach of the album, resuming normal service for the Irish veterans. The inevitable best-of surfaced in 2002 although it could've been much more thoughtfully put together. While classics like 'THE FLY' and 'LEMON' were missing altogether, the tendency to replace original songs with inferior – and usually pointless – remixes only underlined a missed opportunity. 'HOW TO DISMANTLE AN ATOMIC BOMB' (2004) hammered home a ruthlessly back to basics policy and a complete disavowal of production flash (an economy they might've well applied to the clunky title). Lead single – and UK No.1 – 'VERTIGO' dropped like a scud missile from wars long forgotten, the hardest, grungiest U2 single since 'THE FLY' more than a decade earlier, but ultimately more bluster than substance. Follow-up 'SOMETIMES YOU CAN'T MAKE IT ON YOUR OWN' was likewise their most earnest power ballad for years, the album's standout track and another – more deserved – UK No.1. 'LOVE AND PEACE OR ELSE' mixed politics with BOLAN stomp, but it was perhaps the swooning 'CITY OF BLINDING LIGHTS' which most convincingly reprised their 80s pomp, a UK Top 5 alongside the disturbingly DEEP PURPLE-esque 'ALL BECAUSE OF YOU'.

• **Songwriters:** All written by BONO / THE EDGE, except HELTER SKELTER (Beatles) / ALL ALONG THE WATCHTOWER (Bob Dylan) (hit; Jimi Hendrix) / STAR SPANGLED BANNER (US National anthem) / DANCING BAREFOOT (Patti Smith) / NIGHT AND DAY (Cole Porter) / PAINT IT BLACK (Rolling Stones) / FORTUNATE SON (Creedence Clearwater Revival) / HALLELUJAH (Leonard Cohen) by BONO / NEON LIGHTS (Kraftwerk). • **Trivia:** BONO contributed vox to BAND AID single late '84. That year, the band also started own record label, mainly for other Irish groups and was a starter for HOTHOUSE FLOWERS, CACTUS WORLD NEWS etc. In 1988, BONO and THE EDGE co-wrote for ROY ORBISON on his last living studio album, 'Mystery Girl'. They wrote the theme for the James Bond film 'GoldenEye', which became a hit for TINA TURNER in 1995.

Album rating: BOY (*8) / OCTOBER (*6) / WAR (*9) / UNDER A BLOOD RED SKY (*6) / THE UNFORGETTABLE FIRE (*9) / WIDE AWAKE IN AMERICA (*6) / THE JOSHUA TREE (*10) / RATTLE AND HUM (*8) / ACHTUNG BABY (*8) / ZOOROPA (*9) / ORIGINAL SOUNDTRACKS 1 (*6; as the Passengers) / POP (*6) / THE BEST OF 1980-1990 compilation (*9) / ALL THAT YOU CAN'T LEAVE BEHIND (*7) / THE BEST OF 1990-2000 + THE B-SIDES compilation (*7) / HOW TO DISMANTLE AN ATOMIC BOMB (*7)

BONO (b. PAUL HEWSON, 10 May'60, Dublin) – vocals / **THE EDGE** (b. DAVID EVANS, 8 Aug'61, Barking, Essex) – guitar, keyboards / **ADAM CLAYTON** (b.13 Mar'60, Chinnor, Oxfordshire, England) – bass / **LARRY MULLEN** (b. LAURENCE MULLEN, 31 Oct'61, Dublin) – drums

C.B.S. | not iss.

Oct 79. (7"ep/12"ep) *(CBS/+12 7951)* **U2: THREE** | – Irish | –
– Out of control / Stories for boys / Boy-girl. *(re-iss. 1980 7"orange,yellow,white; same) (re-iss. c-ep 1985; CBS 40-7951)*

Feb 80. (7",7"yellow,7"orange,7"white) *(CBS 8306)* **ANOTHER DAY. / TWILIGHT (demo)** | – Irish | –

Island | Island

May 80. (7") *(WIP 6601)* **11 O'CLOCK TICK TOCK. / TOUCH** | | –

Aug 80. (7") *(WIP 6630)* **A DAY WITHOUT ME. / THINGS TO MAKE AND DO** | | –

Oct 80. (7") *(WIP 6656)* **I WILL FOLLOW. / BOY-GIRL (live)** | | –

Nov 80. (lp/c) *(ILPS/ICT <9646>)* **BOY** | 52 Feb81 | 63
– I will follow / Twilight / An cat dubh / Into the heart / Out of control /

Stories for boys / The ocean / A day without me / Another time, another place / The Electric Co. / Shadows and tall trees. *(cd-iss. May86; CID 110) (re-iss. May95 cd)(c)(lp; IMCD 211)(ILPM 9646)*

Apr 81. (7") **I WILL FOLLOW. / OUT OF CONTROL** [–] [ ]

Jul 81. (7") *(WIP 6679)* **FIRE. / J. SWALLO** [35] [ ]
(d7"+=) *(U-WIP 6679)* – 11 o'clock tick tock (live) / The ocean (live) / Cry (live) / The Electric Co. (live).

Sep 81. (7") *(WIP 6733)* **GLORIA. / I WILL FOLLOW (live)** [55] [ ]

Oct 81. (lp/c) *(ILPS/ICT <9680>)* **OCTOBER** [11] [ ]
– Gloria / I fall down / I threw a brick through a window / Rejoice / Fire / Tomorrow / October / With a shout / Stranger in a strange land / Scarlet / Is that all?. *(cd-iss. May86; CID 111) (re-dist.Jun92; same) (cd re-iss. Mar96; IMCD 223)*

Mar 82. (7") *(WIP 6770)* **A CELEBRATION. / TRASH, TRAMPOLENE AND THE PARTY GIRL** [47] [ ]

Jan 83. (7") *(WIP 6848)* *<99915>* **NEW YEAR'S DAY. / TREASURE (WHATEVER HAPPENED TO PETE THE CHOP)** [10] [53]
(d7"+=/12"+=) *(U-WIP/12WIP 6848)* – Fire (live) / I threw a brick through the window (live) / A day without me (live).

Feb 83. (lp/c) *(ILPS/ICT 9733)* *<90067>* **WAR** [1] [12]
– Sunday bloody Sunday / Seconds / Like a song / New Year's day / Two hearts beat as one / The refugee / Drowning man / Red light / '40' / Surrender. *(cd-iss. Dec85; CID 112) (re-iss. Aug91 cd/c; IMCD/ICT 141; hit No.51 Jun92, hit UK No.38 Aug93)*

Mar 83. (7") *(IS 109)* *<99861>* **TWO HEARTS BEAT AS ONE. / ENDLESS DEEP** [18] [ ]
(d7"+=) *(ISD 109)* – Two hearts beat as one (U.S. remix) / New Year's day (U.S. remix).
(12") *(12IS 109)* – ('A'-club mix) / New Year's day (U.S. remix) / ('A'-U.S. remix).

Nov 83. (lp/c) *(IMA/IMC 3)* *<90127>* **UNDER A BLOOD RED SKY (live)** [2] [28]
– Gloria / 11 o'clock tick tock / I will follow / Party girl / Sunday bloody Sunday / The Electric Co. / New Year's day / '40'. *(cd-iss. May86; CID 113) (re-dist.Jun92; same)*

Dec 83. (7") *<99789>* **I WILL FOLLOW (live). / TWO HEARTS BEAT AS ONE (live)** [–] [81]

Sep 84. (7"/7"pic-d) *(IS/+P 202)* *<99704>* **PRIDE (IN THE NAME OF LOVE). / BOOMERANG 2** [3] [33]
(d7"+=/c-s+=/12"white+=) *(ISD/CIS/12IS 202)* – 4th of July / Boomerang 1.
(12"blue+=) *(12ISX 202)* – Boomerang 1 / 11 o'clock tick tock (extended) / Touch.

Oct 84. (lp/c)(cd) *(U2/+C 5)(CID 102)* *<90231>* **THE UNFORGETTABLE FIRE** [1] [12]
– A sort of homecoming / Pride (in the name of love) / Wire / The unforgettable fire / Promenade / 4th of July / Bad / Indian summer sky / Elvis Presley and America / MLK. *(re-dist.Jun92 hit No.38 UK; same)*

May 85. (7"/7"sha-pic-d) *(IS/+P 220)* **THE UNFORGETTABLE FIRE. / A SORT OF HOMECOMING (live)** [6] [ ]
(12"+=) *(12IS 220)* – The three sunrises / Bass trap / Love comes tumbling.
(d7"+=) *(ISD 220)* – The three sunrises / Love comes tumbling / 60 seconds in kingdom come.

May 85. (m-lp/c) *(ISSP/+C 22)* *<90279>* **WIDE AWAKE IN AMERICA** [11] [37]
– Bad (live) / A sort of homecoming (live) / The three sunrises / Love comes tumbling. *(cd-iss. Oct87; CIDU 22) (cd re-iss. Nov89; IMCD 75)*

— Later in the year, BONO guested for CLANNAD on hit 'IN A LIFETIME'.

— In Sep'86, THE EDGE issued soundtrack album 'CAPTIVE' (see below).

Mar 87. (7"/c-s/12"/cd-s) *(IS/CIS/12IS/CID 319)* *<99469>* **WITH OR WITHOUT YOU. / LUMINOUS TIMES (HOLD ON TO LOVE) / WALK TO THE WATER** [4] [1]

Mar 87. (lp/c)(cd) *(U2/+C 6)(CIDU 26)* *<90581>* **THE JOSHUA TREE** [1] [1]
– Where the streets have no name / I still haven't found what I'm looking for / With or without you / Bullet the blue sky / Running to stand still / Red Hill mining town / In God's country / Trip through your wires / One tree hill / Exit / Mothers of the disappeared. *(also on 4x7"box) (re-charted UK Jan92, peaked Jun92 at No.19) (re-iss. Aug93 cd/c/lp, hit UK No.27; same)*

May 87. (7"/c-s/12") *(IS/CIS/12IS 328)* *<99430>* **I STILL HAVEN'T FOUND WHAT I'M LOOKING FOR. / SPANISH EYES / DEEP IN THE HEART** [6] [1]

Sep 87. (7") *(IS 340)* *<99408>* **WHERE THE STREETS HAVE NO NAME. / SILVER AND GOLD / SWEETEST THING** [4] [13]
(c-s+=/12"+=/cd-s+=) *(CIS/12IS/CID 340)* – Race against time.

Jan 88. (7"-US-imp) *<7-99385>* **IN GOD'S COUNTRY. / BULLET THE BLUE SKY / RUNNING TO STAND STILL** [48] Nov87 [44]

Sep 88. (7") *(IS 400)* *<99250>* **DESIRE. / HALLELUJAH (HERE SHE COMES)** [1] [3]
(12"+=/12"g-f+=/pic-cd-s+=) *(12IS/12ISG/CIDP 400)* – ('A'-Hollywood remix).

Oct 88. (d-lp/c)(cd) *(U2/+C 7)(CIDU 27)* *<91003>* **RATTLE AND HUM** (some live) [1] [1]
– Helter skelter (live) / Van Diemen's land / Desire / Hawkmoon 269 / All along the watchtower (live) / I still haven't found what I'm looking for (live) / Freedom for my people / Silver and gold (live) / Pride (in the name of love) (live) / Angel of Harlem / Love rescue me / When love comes to town / Heartland / God part II / The star spangled banner / Bullet the blue sky (live) / All I want is you. *(re-charted UK No.37 on Jun92) (re-iss. Aug93, hit UK No.34)*

Dec 88. (7") *(IS 402)* *<99254>* **ANGEL OF HARLEM. / A ROOM AT THE HEARTBREAK HOTEL** [9] [14]
(12"+=/pic-cd-s+=/US-3"cd-s+=) *(12IS/CIDP/CIDX 402)* – Love rescue me (live with KEITH RICHARDS & ZIGGY MARLEY).

Apr 89. (7"/c-s; U2 & B.B. KING) *(IS 411)* *<99225>* **WHEN LOVE COMES TO TOWN. / DANCING BAREFOOT** [6] Mar89 [68]
(12"+=/pic-cd-s+=/US-3"cd-s+=) *(12IS/CIDP/CIDX 411)* – ('A'-live from the kingdom mix) / God part II (the hard metal dance mix).

Jun 89. (7"/7"box/c-s) *(IS/ISB/CIS 422)* *<99199>* **ALL I WANT IS YOU. / UNCHAINED MELODY** [4] [83]
(ext;12"+=/12"box+=) *(12IS/+B 422)* – Everlasting love.
(pic-cd-s++=) *(CIDP 422)* – ('A'extended).

Oct 91. (c-s/7") *(C+/IS 500)* *<868885>* **THE FLY. / ALEX DESCENDS INTO HELL FOR A BOTTLE OF MILK / KOROVA 1** [1] [61]
(12"+=/cd-s+=) *(12IS/CID 500)* – The Lounge Fly mix.

Nov 91. (cd)(lp/c) *(CIDU 28)(U2/+C 8)* *<10347>* **ACHTUNG BABY** [2] [1]
– Zoo station / Even better than the real thing / One / Until the end of the world / Who's gonna ride your wild horses / So cruel / The fly / Mysterious ways / Tryin' to throw your arms around the world / Ultra violet (light my way) / Acrobat / Love is blindness. *(re-iss. Aug93, hit UK No.17; same)*

Dec 91. (c-s/7") *(C+/IS 509)* *<866188>* **MYSTERIOUS WAYS. / ('A'-solar plexus magic hour remix)** [13] Nov91 [9]
(12"+=) *(12IS 509)* – ('A'-Apollo 440 remix) / ('A'-Tabla Motown remix).
(pic-cd-s++=) *(CID 509)* – ('A'-Solar Plexus extended club mix).
(12") *(12ISX 509)* – ('A'-Perfecto mix) / ('A'-Ultimatum mix) / ('A'-Apollo 400 Magic Hour remix) / ('A'-Solar Plexus extended club mix).

Feb 92. (c-s/7") *(C+/IS 515)* *<866533>* **ONE. / LADY WITH THE SPINNING HEAD (UVI)** [7] [10]
(12"+=) *(12IS 515)* – Satellite of love.
(cd-s++=) *(CID 515)* – Night and day (steel string remix).

Jun 92. (c-s/7") *(C+/IS 525)* *<866977>* **EVEN BETTER THAN THE REAL THING. / SALOME** [12] [32]
(12"+=/cd-s+=) *(12IS/CID 525)* – Where did it all go wrong (demo) / Lady with the spinning head (UVI) (extended dance mix).

Jul 92. (12") *(REAL U2)* **EVEN BETTER THAN THE REAL THING (the perfecto mix) / ('A'-trance mix) / ('A'-sexy dub mix)** [8] [–]
(cd-s) *(CREAL 2)* – (first 2) / ('A'-Apollo 440 Stealth Sonic remix) / ('A'-V16 Exit Wound remix) / ('A'-Apollo 440 vs. U2 instrumental remix).

Nov 92. (c-s/7") *(C+/IS 550)* *<864521>* **WHO'S GONNA RIDE YOUR WILD HORSES. / PAINT IT BLACK** [14] [35]
(cd-s+=) *(CID 550)* – Fortunate son / ('A'version).
(pic-cd-s+=) *(CIDX 550)* – Salome (Zooromancer remix) / Can't help falling in love (Triple Peaks remix).

Jun 93. (12"ltd-promo) *(12LEMDJ 1)* **LEMON. / SALOME (Boys Own Mix)** [–] [–]

Jul 93. (cd)(lp/c) *(CIDU 29)(U2/+C 9)* *<518047>* **ZOOROPA** [1] [1]
– Zooropa / Babyface / Numb / Lemon / Stay (faraway, so close!) / Daddy's gonna pay for your crashed car / Some days are better than others / The first time / Dirty day / The wanderer.

Aug 93. (video-ep) *(088 162-3)* **NUMB / NUMB (video remix) / LOVE IS BLINDNESS** [–] [–]

Nov 93. (c-s/7") *(C+/IS 578)* *<858076>* **STAY (FARAWAY, SO CLOSE!). / FRANK SINATRA WITH BONO: I'VE GOT YOU UNDER MY SKIN** [4] [61]
(cd-s+=) *(CID 578)* – Lemon (Bad Yard club) / Lemon (Perfecto mix).

(pic-cd-s) *(CIDX 578)* – ('A'side) / Slow dancing / Bullet the blue sky (live) / Love is blindness (live).

— In Mar 94, BONO teamed up with GAVIN FRIDAY (Virgin Prunes) on single 'IN THE NAME OF THE FATHER' from the film of the same name. It made No.46 in UK and was taken from soundtrack album. (below from the 'Batman Forever' movie released on 'Atlantic' UK)

Jun 95. (7"red/c-s) *(A 7131/+C) <87131>* **HOLD ME, THRILL ME, KISS ME, KILL ME / (other artist)** 2 16
(cd-s+=) *(A 7131CD)* – (other artist).

PASSENGERS

— aka U2, ENO + guests incl. vocalists PAVAROTTI + HOLI

Island Island

Nov 95. (cd/c/lp) *(CID/ICT/ILPS 8043) <524166>* **ORIGINAL SOUNDTRACKS 1** 12 76
– United colours / Slug / Your blue room / Always forever now / A different kind of blue / Beach sequence / Miss Sarajevo / Ito Okashi / One minute warning / Corpse (these chains are way too long) / Elvis ate America / Plot 180 / Theme from The Swan / Theme from Let's Go Native.

Nov 95. (c-s/7") *(C+/IS 625)* **MISS SARAJEVO. / ONE (live)** 6 –
(cd-s+=) *(CID 625)* – Bottoms (Watashitachi No Ookina Yume) (Zoo Station remix) / Viva Davidoff.

U2

Feb 97. (c-s) *(CIS 649) <7316>* **DISCOTHEQUE / HOLY JOE (Garage mix)** 1 10
(cd-s+=) *(CID 649)* – Holy Joe (Guilty mix).
(cd-s) *(CIDX 649)* – ('A'-DM Deep Club mix) / ('A'-Howie B, hairy mix) / ('A'-Hexidecimal mix) / ('A'-DM Tec radio mix).
(3x12"box) *(12IST 649)* – 1:- (David Morales mixes; 4) // 2:- (12"version & David Holmes mix) // 3:- (Howie B & Steve Osborne's Hexidecimal mix).

Mar 97. (cd/c/d-lp) *(CIDU/UC/U 210) <524334>* **POP** 1 1
– Discotheque / Do you feel loved / Mofo / If God will send his angels / Staring at the sun / Last night on Earth / Gone / Miami / The Playboy mansion / If you wear that velvet dress / Please / Wake up dead man.

Apr 97. (c-s) *(CIS 658) <854972>* **STARING AT THE SUN / NORTH AND SOUTH (OF THE RIVER)** 3 26
(cd-s+=) *(CID 658)* – Your blue room.
('A'-Monster Truck mix; cd-s+=) *(CIDX 658)* – ('A'-Sad bastards mix) / ('A'-Lab rat mix).

Jul 97. (c-s) *(CIS 664) <572053>* **LAST NIGHT ON EARTH / POP MUZIK (Pop Mart mix)** 10 57
(cd-s+=) *(CID 664)* – Happiness is a warm gun (the gun mix).
('First Night In Hell mix; cd-s+=) *(CIDX 664)* – Numb (the Soul Assassins mix) / Happiness is a warm gun (the Danny Saber mix).
(12") *(12IS 664)* – ('A'mixes).

Sep 97. (c-s) *(CIS 673) <572195>* **PLEASE / DIRTY DAY (JUNK DAY)** 7 Nov97 –
(cd-s+=) *(CID 673)* – Dirty day (bitter kiss) / I'm not your baby (Sky splintered mix).
(cd-ep) **POPHEART EP** *(CIDX 673)* – ('A'live) / Where the streets have no name (live) / With or without you (live) / Staring at the sun (live).

Dec 97. (c-s) *(CIS 684) <572189>* **IF GOD WILL SEND HIS ANGELS / MOFO (Romin remix)** 12 Mar98 –
(cd-s) *(CID 684)* – ('A'side) / Slow dancing (with WILLIE NELSON) / Two shots of happy, one shot of sad / Sunday bloody Sunday (live with THE EDGE on vox).
(cd-s) *(CIDX 684)* – ('A'-The Grand Jury mix) / Mofo (Phunk Phorce mix) / Mofo (Mother's mix).
(12") *(12IS 684)* – Mofo (Funk Force mix) / (Black hole dub) / (Mothers mix) / (House flava mix) / (Roamin' mix).

Oct 98. (c-s) *(CIS 727) <radio cut>* **SWEETEST THING / STORIES FOR BOYS (live 1981)** 3 63
(cd-s+=) *(CIDX 727)* – Out of control (live 1981).
(cd-s) *(CID 727)* – ('A'side) / Twilight (live 1983) / An cat dubh (live 1983).

Nov 98. (cd/c/d-lp) *(CIDU/UC/U 211) <524612>* **THE BEST OF 1980-1990** (compilation) 1 2
– Pride (in the name of love) / New years day / With or without you / I still haven't found what I'm looking for / Sunday bloody Sunday / Bad / Where the streets have no name / I will follow / The unforgettable fire / Sweetest thing (new recording) / Desire / When love comes to town / Angel of Harlem / All I want is you. *(also on d-cd; CIDDU 211)<524613>* – (hit UK No.8 & US No.45).

— In March 2000, BONO, U2, ENO & The MDH BAND contributed the bulk of songs from 'The Million Dollar Hotel' soundtrack

Oct 00. (c-s) *(CIS 766) <562972>* **BEAUTIFUL DAY / SUMMER RAIN** 1 Sep00 21
(cd-s+=) *(CID 766)* – Always.
(cd-s) *(CIDX 766)* – ('A'side) / Discotheque (live) / If you wear that velvet dress (live).

Oct 00. (cd/c/lp) *(CIDU/UC/U 212) <524653>* **ALL THAT YOU CAN'T LEAVE BEHIND** 1 Nov00 3
– Beautiful day / Stuck in a moment you can't get out of / Elevation / Walk on / Kite / In a little while / Wild honey / Peace on Earth / When I look at the world / New York / Grace / Ground beneath her feet.

Jan 01. (c-s) *(CIS 770) <radio cut>* **STUCK IN A MOMENT YOU CAN'T GET OUT OF / BIG GIRLS ARE BEST** 2 Sep01 52
(cd-s+=) *(CID 770)* – Beautiful day (Quincey & Sonance remix).
(cd-s) *(CIDX 770)* – ('A'side) / Beautiful day (live) / New York (live).

Jul 01. (cd-s) *(CID 780)* **ELEVATION (Tomb Raider mix) / ELEVATION (escalation mix) / ELEVATION (Bandit club mix)** 3 –
(cd-s) *(CIDX 780)* – ('A'side) / Last night on Earth (live) / Don't take your guns to town.
(d12"+=) *(12ISD 780)* – Beautiful day (remixes).

Nov 01. (cd-s) *(CID 788)* **WALK ON / WHERE THE STREETS HAVE NO NAME (live) / STAY (FARAWAY SO CLOSE) (live)** 5 –
(cd-s) *(CIDX 788)* – ('A'side) / Stuck in a moment you can't get out of (acoustic) / Stuck in a moment you can't get out of (CD-Rom).

Oct 02. (cd-s) *(CID 808) <radio>* **ELECTRICAL STORM (William Orbit mix) / NEW YORK NEW YORK (nice mix) / NEW YORK NEW YORK (nasty mix)** 5 77
(cd-s) *(CIDX 808)* – ('A'side) / Bad – 40 – Where the streets have no name (medley live).

Nov 02. (cd/c/d-lp) *(CIDU/UC/U 213) <063438>* **THE BEST OF 1990-2000 / THE B-SIDES** (compilation) 2 3
– Even better than the real thing / Mysterious ways / Beautiful day / Electrical storm (William Orbit mix) / One / Miss Sarajevo (PASSENGERS) / Stay (faraway, so close!) / Stuck in a moment you can't get out of / Gone (Mike Hedges mix) / Until the end of the world / The hands that built America (theme from Gangs Of New York) / Discotheque (Mike Hedges mix) / Hold me, thrill me, kiss me, kill me / Staring at the sun (Mike Hedges mix) / Numb (Mike Hedges mix) / The first time / Fly *[UK cd+=]. (THE B-SIDES d-cd+=; CIDTU 213)* – Lady with the spinning head (extended dance mix) / Dirty day / Summer rain / Electrical storm / North and south of the river / Your blue room / Happiness is a warm gun / Salome (Zooromancer remix) / Even better than the real thing / Numb (gimme some more dignity mix) / Mysterious ways (solar plexus club mix) / If God will send his angels / Lemon (jeep mix) / Discotheque (hexidecimal mix). *(dvd++=)* – (videos, etc.)

Nov 04. (cd-s) *(CID 878) <9868184>* **VERTIGO / ARE YOU GONNA WAIT FOREVER?** 1 Dec04 31
(cd-s) *(CIDX 878) <9868183>* – ('A'-Jacknife Lee mix) / Neon lights.
(12") *(12IS 878)* – ('A'-Redanka power mix) / ('A'-Trent Reznor remix).
(dvd-s) *(CIDV 878)* – ('A'-HQ video) / ('A') / Are you gonna wait forever? / ('A'-Jacknife Lee mix – Lisbon video).

Nov 04. (cd/d-lp) *(CID+/U 214) <36130-2>* **HOW TO DISMANTLE AN ATOMIC BOMB** 1 1
– Vertigo / Miracle drug / Sometimes you can't make it on your own / Love and peace or else / City of blinding lights / All because of you / A man and a woman / Crumbs from your table / One step closer / Original of the species / Yahweh. *(ltd-cd w/dvd+=; CIDX 214)* – (DVD tracks).

Feb 05. (cd-s) *(CID 886)* **SOMETIMES YOU CAN'T MAKE IT ON YOUR OWN / FAST CARS (Jacknife Lee mix)** 1 97
(cd-s) *(CIDX 886)* – ('A') / Ave Maria (Jacknife Lee mix with PAVAROTTI) / Vertigo (Redanka power mix).
(dvd-s) *(CIDV 886)* – ('A'-live at Hanover Quay, 16 Nov 2004 video) / Vertigo (video) / ('A') / Vertigo (Trent Reznor remix).

Jun 05. (cd-s) *(CID 890)* **CITY OF BLINDING LIGHTS / ALL BECAUSE OF YOU (killahurtz mix)** 2 –
(cd-s) *(CIDX 890)* – ('A') / The fly (live from the Stop Sellafield concert) / Even better than the real thing (live from the Stop Sellafield concert).
(dvd-s) *(CIDV 890)* – ('A'-live at Brooklyn Bridge video) / Sometimes you can't make it on your own (live local video) / ('A').

Oct 05. (cd-s) *(CID 906)* **ALL BECAUSE OF YOU / SHE'S A MYSTERY TO ME (live from Brooklyn)** 4 –
(cd-s) *(CIDX 906)* – ('A') / Miss Sarajevo (live from Milan) / A man and a woman (acoustic).
(dvd-s) *(CIDV 906)* – ('A'-video) / City of blinding lights (video) / ('A').

☐ the VALENTINOS (see under ⇒ WOMACK, Bobby)

VAN DER GRAAF GENERATOR

Formed: Manchester, England ... 1967 by PETER HAMMILL, CHRIS 'JUDGE' SMITH and NICK PEAME, who met at Manchester University. A one-off 45, 'THE PEOPLE YOU WERE GOING TO', surfaced in 1968, before they disbanded. Re-grouping soon after with a slightly modified line-up, HAMMILL and SMITH enlisted the more experienced KEITH ELLIS, GUY EVANS and NICK BANTON. However, it wasn't long before SMITH left HAMMILL as the focal point and sole remaining founder member. This line-up recorded what was initially intended to be a HAMMILL solo album, 'AEROSOL GREY MACHINE', which surprisingly only saw a full release in the States. It was a remarkable debut, showcasing cuts such as 'NECROMANCER', 'RUNNING BACK' and 'AFTERWARDS', in which HAMMILL exercised his wide-ranging vocal talent to startling effect. A change of line-up ensued, with NIC POTTER (like EVANS, he had played in The MISUNDERSTOOD) replacing the JUICY LUCY bound ELLIS. Signing to 'Charisma', they released their conceptual follow-up, 'THE LEAST WE CAN DO IS WAVE TO EACH OTHER', which dented the UK Top 50 in early 1970. The album saw the band developing a hybrid of pseudo-gothic lyrics and progressive rock styles, the stand-out tracks being 'REFUGEEES' and 'AFTER THE FLOOD'. POTTER departed during their next project, 'H TO HE', a record which featured the services of the (then) in-demand guitarist ROBERT FRIPP (KING CRIMSON). He also contributed session work to their subsequent effort, 'PAWN HEARTS' (1971), which included the 20-minute piece, 'A PLAGUE OF LIGHTHOUSE KEEPERS'. The composition traversed a varying degree of moods and tempos, hitting a breathtaking finale. After a GEORGE MARTIN (yes, that one!) penned 45, 'THEME ONE', failed to sell, they disbanded for the second time in the summer of '72. With the help of some VAN DER GRAAF members, HAMMILL had previously recorded a solo album, 'FOOL'S MATE', returning to the studio once again for a follow-up, 'CHAMELEON IN THE SHADOW OF THE NIGHT', released in 1972. For a few years, HAMMILL continued in an increasingly experimental and inventive vein, much in evidence on his 1975 album, 'NADIR'S BIG CHANCE'. VAN DER GRAAF reformed around this time, releasing three albums during the next two years, one of which was the highly regarded 'WORLD RECORD' (1976). After the plug was finally pulled on the 'GENERATOR, HAMMILL went to work on a series of solo albums, bringing in his group K. His work was quite prolific in the 80's and was virtually VAN DER GRAAF in all but name. He has been an inspiration to many alternative acts, JOHN LYDON citing HAMMILL's vocal technique as a guiding influence. Still going strong with a string of albums behind him (including 1988's 'SITTING TARGETS'), PETER moved into the millennium with three further sets, 'NONE OF THE ABOVE' (2000), 'WHAT, NOW?' (2001) and return to form 'CLUTCH' (2002). What else could a poor boy do? yes, re-form VAN DER GRAAF GENERATOR after over a quarter of a century in the dark. Along with JACKSON, EVANS and BANTON, the 4-piece ventured into the studio early in 2004, double-disc 'PRESENT' surfacing the following summer. VDGG never sounded so claustrophobically great.

• **Trivia:** Named after a generator built by Dr. Robert Jemison Van Der Graaf.

Album rating: AEROSOL GREY MACHINE (*8) / THE LEAST WE CAN DO IS WAVE TO EACH OTHER (*7) / H TO HE, WHO AM THE ONLY ONE (*6) / PAWN HEARTS (*6) / Peter Hammill: FOOL'S MATE (*6) / CHAMELEON IN THE SHADOW OF THE NIGHT (*6) / THE SILENT CORNER AND THE EMPTY STAGE (*6) / IN CAMERA (*5) / NADIR'S BIG CHANCE (*7) / Van Der Graaf Generator: GODBLUFF (*6) / STILL LIFE (*6) / WORLD RECORD (*7) / Van Der Graaf: THE QUIET ZONE – THE PLEASURE DOME (*6) / VITAL (*5) / REPEAT PERFORMANCE posthumous collection (*7) / Peter Hammill: OVER (*6) / THE FUTURE NOW (*6) / pH7 (*6) / A BLACK BOX (*6) / SITTING TARGETS (*7) / ENTER K (*6) / LOOPS AND REELS (*5) / PATIENCE (*6) / THE LOVE SONGS collection (*6) / THE MARGIN – LIVE (*6) / SKIN (*6) / AND CLOSE AS THIS (*6) / SPUR OF THE MOMENT with Guy Evans (*5) / IN A FOREIGN TOWN (*6) / OUT OF WATER (*6) / THE FALL OF THE HOUSE OF USHER (*3) / FIRESHIPS (*4) / THE NOISE (*4) / THE CALM (AFTER THE STORM) compilation (*6) / THE STORM (BEFORE THE CALM) compilation (*6) / THERE GOES THE DAYLIGHT (*6) / ROARING FORTIES (*6) / ROOM TEMPERATURE LIVE (*6) / X MY HEART (*6) / SONIX (*5) / EVERYONE YOU HOLD (*5) / THIS (*5) / TYPICAL (*6) / NONE OF THE ABOVE (*5) / WHAT, NOW? (*5) / CLUTCH (*7) / Van Der Graaf Generator: PRESENT (*6)

PETER HAMMILL (b. 5 Nov'48, London, England) – vocals, guitar, piano / **NICK PEAME** – organ / **CHRIS JUDGE SMITH** – drums, vocals, oricanos

Polydor Mercury

Jan 69. (7") *(56758)* **PEOPLE YOU WERE GOING TO. / FIREBRAND** ☐ [-]

— **HUGH BANTON** – keyboards; repl. PEAME

— added **KEITH ELLIS** – bass (ex-KOOBAS) / **GUY EVANS** – drums (ex-MISUNDERSTOOD)

— now a quartet when CHRIS formed HEEBALOB. He later wrote for HAMMILL

not iss. Mercury

Jan 69. (lp) *<SR 61238>* **AEROSOL GREY MACHINE** [-] ☐
– Afterwards / Orthenthian St. (part 1 & 2) / Running back / Into a game / Aerosol grey machine / Black smoke yen / Aguarian / Necromancer / Octopus. *(UK-iss.Feb75 on 'Fontana'; 6430 083) (cd-iss. Mar97 on 'Repertoire'+=; RR 4647)* – People you were going to / Firebrand. *(cd re-iss. May97 on 'Fie!'+=; FIE 9116)* – Ferret / Featherbird / Giant squid.

Apr 69. (7") *<72979>* **AFTERWARDS. / NECROMANCER** [-] ☐

— **NIC POTTER** – bass (ex-MISUNDERSTOOD) repl. ELLIS who joined JUICY LUCY / added **DAVE JACKSON** – saxophone (ex-HEEBALOB)

Charisma Dunhill

Feb 70. (lp) *(CAS 1007)* **THE LEAST WE CAN DO IS WAVE TO EACH OTHER** [47] ☐
– Darkness / Refugees / White hammer / Whatever would Robert have said / Out of my book / After the flood. *(re-iss. Aug82 lp/c; CHC/+MC 5) (cd-iss. Apr87; CASCD 1007)*

Apr 70. (7") *(CB 122)* **REFUGEES. / THE BOAT OF MILLIONS OF YEARS** ☐ ☐

— A quartet again, when POTTER left only completing half of next album. Guest on next 2 albums **ROBERT FRIPP** – guitar (of KING CRIMSON)

Dec 70. (lp) *(CAS 1027) <50097>* **H TO HE, WHO AM THE ONLY ONE**
– Killer / House with no door / The emperor in his war-room: The emperor – The room / Lost: Dance in sand and sea – Dance in frost / The pioneers over C. *(re-iss. Jun81 & Sep83 on 'Polydor'; 6321 126) (cd-iss. Nov88; CASCD 1027)*

Charisma Mercury

Oct 71. (lp) *(CAS 1051)* **PAWN HEARTS** –
– Lemmings / Man-erg / A plague of lighthouse keepers: 1) Eyewitness – 2) Pictures – Lighthouse – 3) Eyewitness – 4) S.H.M. – 5) Presence of the night – 6) Kosmos tours – 7) (Custards) Last stand – 8) The clot chickens – 9) Lands End – 10) We go now. *(re-iss. Oct86; CHC 54) (cd-iss. Apr88; CASCD 1051)*

Feb 72. (7") *(CB 175)* **THEME ONE. / W**

PETER HAMMILL

had by this time gone solo when VAN DER GRAAF split. He continued to use VDGG members.

Charisma Charisma

Jul 71. (lp) *(<CAS 1037>)* **FOOL'S MATE**
– Imperial zeppelin / Candle / Happy / Solitude / Vision / Re-awakening / Sunshine / Child / Summer song (in the autumn) / Viking / The birds / I once wrote some poems. *(re-iss. Sep83 lp/c; CHC/+MC 2) (cd-iss. Oct88; CASCD 1037)*

May 73. (lp) *(<CAS 1067>)* **CHAMELEON IN THE SHADOW OF THE NIGHT**
– German overalls / Slender threads / Rock and role / In the end / What's it worth / Easy to slip away / Dropping the torch / In the black room / The tower. *(cd-iss. Apr89; CASCD 1067)*

Feb 74. (lp) *(<CAS 1083>)* **THE SILENT CORNER AND THE EMPTY STAGE**
– Modern / Wilhemina / The lie (Bernini's Saint Teresa) / Forsaken gardens / Red shift / Rubicon / A louse is not a home. *(re-iss. Oct86; CHC 61) (cd-iss. Nov88; CASCD 1083)*

Sep 74. (lp) *(<CAS 1089>)* **IN CAMERA**
– Ferret and featherbed / (No more) The sub-mariner / Tapeworm / Again / Faintheart and the sermon / The comet, the course. the tail / Gog Magog (in bromine chambers). *(re-iss. Nov80 on 'Polydor'; 9198 770) (re-iss. Aug88 lp/c; CHC/+MC 33) (cd-iss. Nov88; CASCD 1089)*

Feb 75. (lp) *(<CAS 1099>)* **NADIR'S BIG CHANCE**
– Nadir's big chance / The institute of mental health's burning / Open your eyes / Nobody's business / Been alone so long / Pompeii / Shingle song / Airport / People you were going to / Birthday special / Two or three spectres. *(re-iss. Mar83 lp/c; CHC/+MC 19) (cd-iss. Nov88; CASCD 1099)*

Apr 75. (7") *(CB 245)* **BIRTHDAY SPECIAL. / SHINGLE SONG**

— **HAMMILL, BANTON, JACKSON + EVANS** reformed

VAN DER GRAAF GENERATOR

Charisma Mercury

Oct 75. (lp) *(CAS 1109) <1069>* **GODBLUFF**
– The undercover man / Scorched Earth / Arrow / The sleepwalkers. *(re-iss. Mar83 lp/c; CHC/+MC 13) (cd-iss. Apr88; CASCD 1109)*

Apr 76. (lp)(c) *(CAS 1116)(7208 605) <1096>* **STILL LIFE**
– Pilgrims / Still life / La rossa / My room (waiting for Wonderland) / Childlike faith in childhood's end. *(re-iss. Oct86; CHC 55) (cd-iss. Apr87; CASCD 1116)*

Oct 76. (lp)(c) *(CAS 1120)(7208 610) <1116>* **WORLD RECORD**
– When she comes / A place to survive / Masks / Meurglys III (the songwriters guild) / Wondering. *(re-iss. Aug88; CHC 62) (cd-iss. 1988; CASCD 1120)*

Oct 76. (7") *(CB 297)* **WONDERING. / MEURGLYS III**

VAN DER GRAAF

GRAHAM SMITH – violin (ex-STRING DRIVEN THING) repl. JACKSON / **NIC POTTER** – bass returned after US session work to repl. BANTON

Sep 77. (lp) *(CAS 1131)* **THE QUIET ZONE – THE PLEASURE DOME**
– Lizard play / The habit of the broken heart / The siren song / Last frame / The wave / Yellow fever (running) / The sphinx in the face / Chemical world / The sphinx returns. *(re-iss. 1987 lp/c; CHC/+MC 32) (cd-iss. 1987; CASCD 1131)*

— added **DAVE JACKSON** who returned w / **CHARLES DICKIE** – cello, piano

Charisma P.V.C.

Jul 78. (d-lp) *(CVLD 101)* **VITAL (live)**
– Ship of fools / Still life / Mirror images / Medley: Parts of A plague of lighthouse keepers and Sleepwalkers / Pioneers over C / Door / Urban / Nadir's big chance. *(cd-iss. Apr89; CVCLD 101) (re-iss. cd Mar94 on 'Virgin';)*

– compilations, etc. –

Aug 72. (lp) *Charisma; (CS 2)* **68-71** –
Aug 80. (lp/c) *Charisma; (BG/+C 3)* **REPEAT PERFORMANCE** –
– Afterwards / Refugees / The boat of millions of years / W / White hammer / Necromancer / The Emperor in his war room / The empereor / The room / Manerg. *(c+=)* – The clot thickens (extended).
Mar 83. (d-c) *Charisma; (CASMC 106)* **PAWN HEARTS / STILL LIFE** –
May 85. (lp) *Demi-Monde; (DM 003)* **TIME VAULTS** (rare) –
(cd-iss. Apr97 on 'Spalax'; 14847)
Feb 87. (cd) *Virgin; (COMCD 2)* **FIRST GENERATION** –
Feb 87. (cd) *Virgin; (COMCD 3)* **SECOND GENERATION** –
May 88. (lp/cd) *Thunderbolt; (THBL/CDTB 042)* **NOW AND THEN** –
Sep 93. (cd) *Virgin; (CDVM 9026)* **I PROPHESY DISASTER** –
Jun 94. (cd) *Band Of Joy; (BOJCD 008)* **MAIDA VALE** –

PETER HAMMILL

went solo after the VDGG split

Charisma Charisma

Sep 76. (lp) *(<CAS 1125>)* **OVER**
– Crying wolf / Autumn / Time heals / Alice (letting go) / This side of the looking-glass / Betrayed (on Tuesdays she used to) / Yoga / Lost and found. *(cd-iss. Feb91; CASCD 1125)*

Charisma P.V.C.

Sep 78. (lp) *(CAS 1137) <2202>* **THE FUTURE NOW**
– The future now / Still in the dark / Mediaevil / A motor-bike in Africa / The cut / Palinurus / Pushing thirty / The second hand / Trappings / The mousetrap (caught in) / Energy vampires / If I could. *(re-iss. Oct86; CHC 59) (cd-iss. Nov88; CASCD 1137)*

Nov 79. (lp) *(CAS 1146) <2205>* **pH7**
– My favourite / Careering / Porton Down / Mirror images / Handicap and equality / Not for Keith / The old school tie / Time for a change / Imperial walls / Mr. X gets tense / Faculty X. *(cd-iss. Apr89; CASCD 1146)*

Nov 79. (7"; as RICKY NADIR) *(CB 339)* **THE POLAROID. / THE OLD SCHOOL TIE** –

Mercury not iss.

1980. (lp) *(6302 067)* **A BLACK BOX** – Europe –
– Golden promise / Losing faith in words / The Jargon king / Fog walking / The spirit / In slow time / The wipe / Flight: Flying blind – White cave fandango – Control – Cockpit – Silk worm wings / Nothing is nothing – A black box. *(UK-iss.Jun83; same) (re-iss. Aug88 on 'Virgin' lp/cd; OVED/CDOVD 140)*

Virgin not iss.

May 81. (7") *(VS 424)* **MY EXPERIENCE. / GLUE** –
Jun 81. (lp) *(V 2205)* **SITTING TARGETS** –
– Breakthrough / My experience / Ophelia / Empress's clothes / Glue / Hesitation / Sitting targets / Stranger still / Sign / What I did for love / Central hotel. *(re-iss. Aug88; OVED 139) (cd-iss. Oct88; CDV 2205)*

— **HAMMILL** with **GUY EVANS / NIC POTTER** plus **JOHN ELLIS** – guitar (ex-VIBRATORS), formed **K**

Naive not iss.

Sep 82. (7") *(NAV 3)* **PARADOX DRIVE. / NOW MORE THAN EVER** –
Oct 82. (lp/c) *(NAV L/C 1)* **ENTER K** –
– Paradox Drive / The unconscious life / Accidents / The great experiments / Don't tell me / She wraps it up / Happy hour / Seven wonders. *(cd-iss. May92 on 'Fie!'; FIE 9101)*

Sep 83. (lp) *(NAVL 3)* **PATIENCE** –
– Labour of love / Film noir / Just good friends / Jeunesse D'Oree / Traintime / Now more than ever / Comfortable / Patient. *(cd-iss. May92 on 'Fie!'; FIE 9102) (above 2 re-iss. Jan86 on 'Spartan' d-lp/d-c; SPD P/C 1)*

Sep 83. (7") *(NAV 8)* **FILM NOIR. / SEVEN WONDERS** –

Foundry not iss.

Feb 85. (d-lp) *(FONDL 1)* **THE MARGIN (live)** –
– Future now / Porton Down / Stranger still / Sign / The Jargon king / The second hand / Empress's clothes / The sphinx in the face / Labour of love / Sitting targets / Patience / Flight. *(cd-iss. Feb91 on 'Virgin'; CDOVD 345)*

Mar 86. (lp/c) *(FOND L/C 3)* **SKIN**
– Skin / After the show / Painting by numbers / Shell / All said and done / A perfect date / Four pails / New lover. *(cd-iss. Nov87 on 'Line'; DACD 900145) (cd re-iss. Feb91 on 'Virgin'; CDOVD 344)*

Mar 86. (7") *(FOUND 3)* **PAINTING BY NUMBERS. / YOU HIT ME WHERE I LIVE**
(ext.12"+=) *(FOUND 3-12)* – Shell.

Virgin not iss.

Nov 86. (lp/c) *(V/TCV 2409)* **AND CLOSE AS THIS**
– Too many of my yesterdays / Faith / Empire of delight / Silver / Beside the one you love / Other old cliches / Confident / Sleep now. *(cd-iss. Nov88; CDV 2409) (cd re-iss. 1989 on 'Line'; DACD 900254)*

Red Hot not iss.

Jun 88. (c/cd; PETER HAMMILL & GUY EVANS) *(ZCRH/CDR 102)* **SPUR OF THE MOMENT**
– Sweating it out / Little did he know / Without a glitch / Anatol's proposal / You think not? / Multiman / Deprogramming Archie / Always so polite / An imagined brother / Bounced / Roger and out. *(re-iss. May93; same)*

Enigma Restless

Nov 88. (lp/c/cd) *(ENVLP/TCENV/CDENV 512)* <72337> **IN A FOREIGN TOWN**
– Hemlock / Invisible ink / Sci-finance (re-visited) / This book / Time to burn / Auto / Vote brand X / Sun City night life / The play's the thing / Under cover names. *(c+=/cd+=)* – Smile / Time to burn (instrumental). *(cd re-iss. Jun95 on 'Fie!'; FIE 9108)*

Feb 90. (cd/c/lp) *(CDENV/TVENVENVLP 1003)* <73540> **OUT OF WATER**
– Evidently goldfish / Not the man / No Moon in the water / Our oyster / Something about Ysabel's dance / Green fingers / On the surface / A way out. *(cd re-iss. Jun95 on 'Fie!'; FIE 9109)*

Some Bizzare not iss.

Nov 91. (cd/c/lp) *(SBZ CD/MC/LP 007)* **THE FALL OF THE HOUSE OF USHER**
– An unenviable role / That must be the house / Architecture / The sleeper / One thing at a time / I shun the light / Leave this house / Dreaming / A chronic catalepsy / The herbalist / The evil that is done / Five years ago / It's over now / An influence / No rot / She is dead / Beating of the heart / The haunted palace / I dared not speak / She comes towards the door / The fall. *(cd re-iss. Nov99 on 'Fie!'; FIE 9121)*

Fie! Fie!

Mar 92. (cd/c) *(FIE/+C 9103)* **FIRESHIPS**
– I will find you / Curtains / His best girl / Oasis / Incomplete surrender / Fireship / Given time / Reprise / Gaia.

Mar 93. (cd/c) *(FIE/+C 9104)* **THE NOISE**
– A kick to kill the kiss / Like a shot / The entertainer / Noise / Celebrity kissing / Where the mouth is / Great European department store / Planet Coventry / Primo on the carpet.

Nov 93. (cd; as PETER HAMMILL & THE NOISE) *(FIE 9106)* **THERE GOES THE DAYLIGHT (live)**
– Sci-finance (revisited) / The habit of a broken heart / Sign / I will find you / Lost and found / Planet Coventry / Empress's clothes / Cat's eye – Yellow fever / Primo on the parapet / Central hotel.

Sep 94. (cd) *FIE 9107)* **ROARING FORTIES**
– Sharply unclear / The gift of fire / You can't want what you always get / A headlong stretch / Your tall ship.

Jun 95. (d-cd) *(FIE 9110)* **ROOM TEMPERATURE (live)**
– Wave / Just good friends / Vision / Time to burn / Four pails / The comet, the course, the tail / Ophelia / Happy hour / If I could / Something about Ysabel's dance / Patient / Cat's eye, yellow fever (running) / Running / Skin / Hemlock / Our oyster / Unconscious life / After the snow / Way out / Future now / Traintime / Modern.

Mar 96. (cd) *(FIE 9111)* **X MY HEART**
– Better time / Amnesiac / Ram origami / Forest of pronouns / Earthbound / Narcissus (bar & grill) / Material possession / Come clean.

Nov 96. (cd) *(FIE 9114)* **SONIX**
– Emmene moi bare theme / Walk in the dark / In the Polish house / Dark matter / Hospital silence / Four to the floor / Exercise for Louise / Labyrinthe dreams / Emmene moi full theme.

Oct 97. (cd) *(<FIE 9117>)* **EVERYONE YOU HOLD**
– Everyone you hold / Personality / Nothing comes / From the safe house / Phosphorescence / Falling open / Bubble / Can do / Tenderness.

Oct 98. (cd) *(FIE 9118)* **THIS**
– Frozen in place (fragment) / Unrehearsed / Stupid / Since the kids / Nightman / Fallen (the city of night) / Unready (fragment) / Always is next / Unsteady (fragment) / The light continent.

Apr 99. (d-cd) *(FIE 9119)* **TYPICAL (live 1992)**
– My room / Curtains / Just good friends / Too many of my yesterdays / Vision / Time to burn / The comet, the course, the tail / I will find you / Ophelia / Given time / Modern / Time for a change / Patient / Stranger still / Our oyster / Shell / A way out / Traintime / The future now.

May 00. (cd) *(FIE 9122)* **NONE OF THE ABOVE**
– Touch and go / Naming the rose / Hoe far I fell / Somebody bad enough / Tango for one / Like Veronica / In a bottle / Astart.

Jun 01. (cd) *(FIE 9123)* **WHAT, NOW?**
– Here come the talkies / Far-flung (across the sky) / The American girl / Wendy and the lost boy / Lunatic in knots / Edge of the road / Fed to the wolves / Enough.

Oct 02. (cd) *(FIE 9127)* **CLUTCH**
– We are written / Crossed wires / Driven / Once you called me / Ice hotel / This is the fall / Just a child / Skinny / Bareknuckle trade.

– compilations, etc. –

1978. (lp) *G.I.R.; <9211 1016>* **VISION**

1983. (c) *Sofa;* **LOOPS AND REELS**
(cd-iss. Nov93 on 'Fie!'; FIE 9105)

Aug 84. (lp) *Charisma; (CAS 1166)* **THE LOVE SONGS** (remixes)
– Just good friends / My favourite / Been alone so long / Ophelia / Again / If I could / Vision / Don't tell me / The birds / (THis side of) The looking glass. *(re-iss. Jun88 lp/c; CHC/+MC 69) (cd-iss. Nov88; CASCD 1166)*

May 85. (7") *Charisma; (CB 414)* **JUST GOOD FRIENDS. / ('A'instrumental)**

Jul 93. (cd) *Virgin; (CDVM 9017)* **THE CALM (AFTER THE STORM)**

Jul 93. (cd) *Virgin; (CDVM 9018)* **THE STORM (BEFORE THE CALM)**

Jan 95. (cd) *Golden Hind; (GH 70112)* **OFFENSICHTLLICH GOLDFISCH**
– Offensichtilich goldfisch / Dich zu finden / Die kalte killt den kub / Favorit / Kaufhaus Europa / Der larm / Oase / Die prominenz kubt sich / Die tunte verlischt / Auto (wieder im wagen) / Gaia / Schlaft nun.

Nov 95. (cd) *Strange Fruit; (SFRCD 136)* **THE PEEL SESSIONS**

Jan 96. (cd) *Virgin; (CDOVD 460)* **AFTER THE SHOW**

Sep 96. (cd) *Fie!; (FIE 9112)* **PAST GO: COLLECTED**
– A kick to kill the kiss / I will find you / Accidents / His best girl / Sharply unclear / Patient / Planet Coventry / A ritual mask / The noise / The gift of fire / Traintime / Gaia / Your tall ship.

Sep 96. (cd) *Sine; (SINE 006)* **TIDES**
– My room / Too many yesterdays / Just good friends / Mirror images / Time to burn / Untitled / Stranger / Where the actors go.

May 02. (cd) *Fie!; (<FIE 9126>)* **THE THIN MAN SINGS BALLADS** Feb04

VAN DER GRAAF GENERATOR

PETER HAMMILL, DAVE JACKSON, GUY EVANS + HUGH BANTON

Virgin E.M.I.

Apr 05. (d-cd) *(CDVD 2999)* <73679> **PRESENT** Jun05
– Every bloody emperor / Boleas panic / Nutter alert / Abandon ship! / In Babelsberg / On the beach / Vulcan meld / Double bass / Slo moves / Architectural hair / Spanner / Crux / Manuelle / 'Eavy mate / Homage to Teo / The price of admission.

VAN HALEN

Formed: Pasadena, California, USA ... 1975 by brothers ALEX and EDDIE VAN HALEN. Recruiting blonde-maned high priest of metal cool, DAVE LEE ROTH, and bass player MICHAEL ANTHONY, the quartet initially traded under the MAMMOTH moniker. As VAN HALEN, the group built up a solid reputation as a covers outfit on L.A.'s Sunset Strip, gradually introducing original material into their set. Eventually signed to 'Warners' after being spotted by in-house producer, Ted Templeman, the group released their eponymous debut album in 1977. Coming at a time when hard rock was in seemingly terminal stagnation with punk snapping at its heels, 'VAN HALEN' redefined the boundaries of the genre; from the back cover shot of a shirtless ROTH (chest-wig de rigueur!) sporting leather flares to the opening three chord mash-up of The KINKS' 'YOU REALLY GOT ME', VAN HALEN dripped effortless cool, the golden elixir of sun-bleached California coursing through their collective veins. Then there was 'AIN'T TALKIN' 'BOUT LOVE', EDDIE casually reeling off the razor-edged, caterwauling riff (recently resurrected by dance bods, APOLLO FOUR FORTY) while ROTH drawled his most lascivious, sneering drawl. And basically, this was what set VAN HALEN apart from the spandex pack; ROTH actually sang rather than screeching like an asphyxiated budgie, while in EDDIE VAN HALEN, the group boasted one of the most inventive and single-mindedly talented guitarists in the history of metal. O.K., 'ERUPTION' may be responsible for countless fret-wank crimes but it's still impossible not to be impressed by the man's vision, his innovations (flying-fingered hammer-ons, leaving a still smoking cigarette nudged in at the top of the fretboard etc.) becoming base material for any aspiring 80's guitar hero. Essentially, VAN HALEN were glamourous as opposed to glam, and for a few heady years they made heavy metal desirable. Though the debut album barely nudged into the US Top 20, it would go on to sell in excess of five million copies and remains one of THE classic hard-rock releases. A follow-up, 'VAN HALEN II' (1979) didn't pack quite the same punch, although it made the US Top 10 and spawned the group's first hit single, the dreamy 'DANCE THE NIGHT AWAY'. 'WOMEN AND CHILDREN FIRST' (1980) and 'FAIR WARNING' (1981) consolidated the band's standing, both commercially and critically although it wasn't until 'DIVER DOWN' (1982) that VAN HALEN began to cast their net wider. A cover of Roy Orbison's 'PRETTY WOMAN' gave them another US Top 20 hit, the album going Top 5 as a result. The following year, EDDIE famously flashed his fretboard skills on MICHAEL JACKSON's 'Beat It', gaining valuable crossover exposure although by this point, VAN HALEN were already one of the biggest hard rock acts in the world. This was proved with the massive success of the '1984' (released in 1984, funnily enough!) opus and attendant synth-heavy No.1 single, 'JUMP'. For many people, especially in Britain, this was the first time they'd witnessed "Diamond" DAVE in action, the loose-limbed singer, as ever, performing death-defying feats of stage acrobatics in the accompanying video. While the album saw VAN HALEN successfully tackling obligatory 80's experimentation (which did for many of their peers), the likes of 'HOT FOR TEACHER' carried on the grand tradition of tongue-in-cheek lewdness and six-string trickery. Incredibly, at the peak of their success, ROTH buggered off for a solo career, taking his not inconsiderable wit, charisma and sly humour with him. Though VAN HALEN chose to rumble on, it was a rather different beast which reared its head in early '86 with the single, 'WHY CAN'T THIS BE LOVE'. With ex-MONTROSE man, SAMMY HAGAR on vocals, VAN HALEN had created their most consistently accessible and musically ambitious set to date in '5150' (1986), although the absence of ROTH's cheeky innuendo was glaringly obvious. If not gone completely, the group chemistry had been irrevocably altered, in effect, making VAN HALEN just another hard rock band, albeit highly professional and massively successful. '5150' gave the revamped group their first US No.1 album, the record not doing too badly in the UK either. 'OU812' (1988) was another multi-million selling No.1, VAN HALEN now virtually a US institution guaranteed multi-platinum sales with every successive release. 'FOR UNLAWFUL CARNAL KNOWLEDGE' (1991), or 'F.U.C.K.' in its abbreviated form (very clever, lads) saw the group adopt a heavier approach although this didn't prevent it from selling in bucketloads, VAN HALEN holding their own in the age of grunge when many of their contemporaries suddenly seemed embarrassingly outdated. A long overdue live album, 'RIGHT HERE, RIGHT NOW', finally appeared in 1993, while a rare European tour no doubt helped boost UK sales of 'BALANCE' (1995), yet another US No.1 album and their first Top 10 placing in Britain. DAVE LEE ROTH returned during the same year; however after a compilation set in which he appeared on a few new songs, the man departed once more, this time to be replaced by ex-EXTREME frontman, GARY CHERRONE. In 2004, EDDIE re-formed VAN HALEN yet again, this time chosing HAGAR as frontman to spearhead and promote US Top 3 (UK Top 2) anthology set, 'THE BEST OF BOTH WORLDS'.

• **Covered:** FAIR WARNING (Aerosmith) / A POLITICAL BLUES (Little Feat) / WON'T GET FOOLED AGAIN (Who). • **Trivia:** In April '81, EDDIE married actress Valerie Bertinelli.

Album rating: VAN HALEN (*8) / VAN HALEN II (*7) / WOMEN AND CHILDREN FIRST (*7) / FAIR WARNING (*6) / DIVER DOWN (*6) / 1984 (*7) / 5150 (*5) / OU812 (*6) / FOR UNLAWFUL CARNAL KNOWLEDGE (*6) / LIVE: RIGHT HERE, RIGHT NOW (*6) / BALANCE (*5) / THE BEST OF: VOLUME ONE compilation (*8) / VAN HALEN III (*5) / THE BEST OF BOTH WORLDS double compilation (*8)

EDDIE VAN HALEN (b.26 Jan'57, Nijmegen, Netherlands) – guitar / **DAVID LEE ROTH** (b.10 Oct'55, Bloomington, Indiana) – vocals / **MICHAEL ANTHONY** (b.20 Jun'55, Chicago, Illinois) – bass / **ALEX VAN HALEN** (b. 8 May'55, Nijmegen) – drums

Warners Warners

Feb 78. (7") *(K 17107)* <8515> **YOU REALLY GOT ME. / ATOMIC ROCK PUNK** [ ] Jan78 [36]

Apr 78. (lp/c) *(K/K4 56470)* <3075> **VAN HALEN** [34] Feb78 [19]
– Runnin' with the Devil / Eruption / You really got me / Ain't talkin' 'bout love / I'm the one / Jamie's cryin' / Atomic punk / Feel your love tonight / Little dreamer / Ice cream man / On fire. *(cd-iss. Jul86; K2 56470) (cd re-iss. Feb95; K2 56470) (cd re-iss. Jan01; 9362 47737-2)*

Apr 78. (7") *(K 17162)* <8556> **RUNNIN' WITH THE DEVIL. / ERUPTION** [ ] [84]

Jul 78. (7") *<8631>* **JAMIE'S CRYIN'. / I'M THE SAME** [–] [ ]

Sep 78. (7") *<8707>* **AIN'T TALKIN' BOUT LOVE. / FEEL YOUR LOVE TONIGHT** [–] [ ]

Apr 79. (lp/c) *(K/K4 56616)* <3312> **VAN HALEN II** [23] [6]
– You're no good / Dance the night away / Somebody get me a doctor / Bottoms up! / Outta love again / Light up the sky / Spanish fly / D.O.A. / Women in love / Beautiful girls. *(cd-iss. Mar87; K2 56616) (cd re-iss. Jan01; 9362 47738-2)*

May 79. (7"/7"pic-d) *(K 17371/+P)* <8823> **DANCE THE NIGHT AWAY. / OUTTA LOVE AGAIN** [ ] Apr79 [15]

Sep 79. (7") *<49035>* **BEAUTIFUL GIRLS. / D. O. A.** [–] [84]

Apr 80. (lp/c) *(K/K4 56793)* <3415> **WOMEN AND CHILDREN FIRST** [15] [6]
– And the cradle will rock . . . / Everybody wants some / Fools / Romeo delight / Tora! Tora! / Loss of control / Take your whiskey home / Could this be magic? / In a simple rhyme. *(cd-iss. Jun89; K 923415-2) (cd re-iss. Jan01; 9362 47739-2)*

Apr 80. (7") *<49501>* **AND THE CRADLE WILL ROCK. / COULD THIS BE MAGIC** [–] [55]

Jun 80. (7") *(HM 10)* **RUNNIN' WITH THE DEVIL. / D.O.A.** [52] [–]
(above on 'Atlantic')

Aug 80. (7") *(K 17645)* **AND THE CRADLE WILL ROCK. / EVERYBODY WANTS SOME!!** [ ] [–]

May 81. (7") *<49751>* **SO THIS IS LOVE. / HEAR ABOUT IT LATER** [–] [ ]

May 81. (lp/c) *(K/K4 56899)* *<3540>* **FAIR WARNING** [49] [6]
– Mean street / Dirty movies / Sinner's swing / Hear about it later / Unchained / Push comes to shove / So this is love? / Sunday afternoon in the dark / One foot out of the door. *(cd-iss. Jun89; K 923540-2) (cd re-iss. Jan01; 9362 47740-2)*

Feb 82. (7") *(K 17909)* <50003> **(OH) PRETTY WOMAN. / HAPPY TRAILS** [ ] Jan82 [12]

May 82. (7") *<29986>* **DANCING IN THE STREET. / THE BULL BUG** [–] [38]

May 82. (lp/c) *(K/K4 57003)* *<3677>* **DIVER DOWN** [36] [3]
– Where have all the good times gone / Hang 'em high / Cathedral / Secrets / Intruder / (Oh) Pretty woman / Dancing in the street / Little guitars (intro) / Little guitars / Big bad Bill (is sweet William now) / The bull bug / Happy trails. *(cd-iss. Jan84; K2 57003) (cd re-iss. Jan01; 9362 47718-2)*

May 82. (7") *(K 17957)* **DANCING IN THE STREET. / BIG BAD BILL (IS SWEET WILLIAM NOW)** [ ] [–]

Aug 82. (7") *<29929>* **BIG BAD BILL (IS SWEET WILLIAM NOW). / SECRETS** [–] [ ]

Jan 84. (lp/c/cd) *(923985-1/-4/-2) <23985>* **1984 (MCMLXXXIV)** [15] [2]
– 1984 / Jump / Panama / Top Jimmy / Drop dead legs / Hot for teacher / I'll wait / Girl gone bad / House of pain. *(re-iss. cd/c Feb95; same) (cd re-iss. Jan01; 9362 47741-2)*

Jan 84. (7") *<29384>* **JUMP. / HOUSE OF PAIN** [–] [1]

Jan 84. (7") *(W 9384)* **JUMP. / RUNNIN' WITH THE DEVIL** [7] [–]
(12"+=) *(W 9384T)* – House of pain.

Apr 84. (7") *<29307>* **I'LL WAIT. / GIRL GONE BAD** [–] [13]

Apr 84. (7") *(W 9273) <29250>* **PANAMA. / GIRL GONE BAD** [61] Jun84 [13]
(12"+=) *(W 9273T)* – Dance the night away.

Jun 84. (7") *(W 9213)* **I'LL WAIT. / DROP DEAD LEGS** [ ] [–]
(12"+=) *(W 9213T)* – And the cradle will rock / (Oh) Pretty woman.

Jun 85. (7") *(W 9199) <29199>* **HOT FOR TEACHER. / LITTLE PREACHER** [ ] Oct84 [56]
(12"+=) *(W 9199T)* – Hear about it later.

— (Jun'85) trimmed to a trio, when DAVID LEE ROTH went solo full-time

— early '86 added **SAMMY HAGAR** (b.13 Oct'47, Monterey, Calif.) – vocals (ex-MONTROSE, ex-Solo Artist)

Mar 86. (7"/7"sha-pic-d/12") *(W 8740/+P/T) <28740>* **WHY CAN'T THIS BE LOVE. / GET UP** [8] [3]

Apr 86. (lp/c)(cd) *(W 5150/+C)(925394-2) <25394>* **5150** [16] [1]
– Good enough / Why can't this be love / Get up / Dreams / Summer nights / Best of both worlds / Love walks in / "5150" / Inside. *(re-iss. cd/c Feb95; same)*

Jun 86. (7"/7"sha-pic-d/12") *(W 8642/+P/T) <28702>* **DREAMS. / INSIDE** [62] May86 [22]

Aug 86. (7") *<28626>* **LOVE WALKS IN. / SUMMER NIGHTS** [–] [22]

Oct 86. (7") *<28505>* **BEST OF BOTH WORLDS. / ('A'live)** [–] [ ]

May 88. (7"/12") *(W 7891/+T) <27891>* **BLACK AND BLUE. / APOLITICAL BLUES** [ ] [34]

Jun 88. (lp/c)(cd) *(WX 177/+C)(K 925732-2) <25732>* **OU812** [16] [1]
– Mine all mine / When it's love / A.F.U. (naturally wired) / Cabo wabo / Source of infection / Feels so good / Finish what ya started / Black and blue / Sucker in a 3-piece. *(cd+=)* – Apolitical blues.

Jul 88. (7") *<27827>* **WHEN IT'S LOVE. / CABO WABO** [–] [5]

Jul 88. (7") *(W 7816)* **WHEN IT'S LOVE. / APOLITICAL BLUES** [28] [–]
(12"+=/12"pic-d+=/cd-s+=) *(W 7816 T/TP/CD)* – Why can't this be love.

Sep 88. (7") *<27746>* **FINISH WHAT YA STARTED. / SUCKER IN A 3-PIECE** [–] [13]

Feb 89. (7") *(W 7565) <27565>* **FEELS SO GOOD. / SUCKER IN A 3 PIECE** [63] Jan89 [35]
(12"+=/cd-s+=) *(W 7565 T/CD)* – Best of both worlds (live).

Jun 91. (7"/c-s) *(W 0045/+C)* **POUNDCAKE. / PLEASURE DOME** [74] [–]
(12"+=/cd-s+=) *(W 0045 T/CD)* – (interview).

Jul 91. (cd)(lp/c) *(7599 26594-2)(WX 420/+C) <26594>* **FOR UNLAWFUL CARNAL KNOWLEDGE** [12] [1]
– Poundcake / Judgement day / Spanked / Runaround / Pleasure dome / In 'n' out / Man on a mission / The dream is over / Right now / 316 / Top of the world.

Sep 91. (7") *<19151>* **TOP OF THE WORLD. / POUNDCAKE** [–] [27]

Oct 91. (7"/c-s) *(W 0066/+C)* **TOP OF THE WORLD. / IN 'N' OUT** [63] [–]
(cd-s+=) *(W 0066CD)* – Why can't this be love (extended) / When it's love / Dreams.

Feb 92. (c-s,cd-s) *<19059>* **RIGHT NOW / MAN ON A MISSION** [–] [55]

Feb 93. (d-cd/d-c) *<(9362 45198-2/-4)>* **LIVE: RIGHT HERE, RIGHT NOW** (live) [24] [5]
– Poundcake / Judgement day / When it's love / Spanked / Ain't talkin' 'bout love / In'n'out / Dreams / Man on a mission / Ultra bass / Pressure dome – Drum solo / Panama / Love walks in / Runaround/ / Right now / One way to rock / Why can't this be love / Give to love / Finished what ya started / Best of both worlds / 316 / You really got me – Cabo wabo / Won't get fooled again / Jump / Top of the world.

Mar 93. (7"/c-s/cd-s) *(W 0155/+C/CD)* **JUMP (live). / LOVE WALKS IN (live)** [26] [–]
(cd-s+=) *(W 0155CDX)* – Eagles fly (live) / Mine, all mine (live).

Jan 95. (7"purple/c-s) *(W 0280 X/C)* **DON'T TELL ME (WHAT LOVE CAN DO). / BALUCHITHERIUM** [27] [–]
(cd-s+=) *(W 0280CD)* – Why can't this be love (live) / Poundcake (live) / Panama (live).
(cd-s) *(W 0280CDX)* – ('A') / Judgement day (live) / Dreams (live)/ Top of the world (live).

Jan 95. (cd/c/lp) *<(9362 45760-2/-4/-1)>* **BALANCE** [8] [1]
– The seventh seal / Can't stop lovin' you / Don't tell me (what love can do) / Amsterdam / Big fat money / Strung out / Not enough / Aftershock / Doin' time / Baluchitherium / Take me back (deja vu) / Feelin'.

Mar 95. (7"/c-s) *(W 0288/+C) <17909>* **CAN'T STOP LOVIN' YOU. / CROSSING OVER** [33] [30]
(cd-s+=) *(W 0288CD)* – Man on a mission / Right now.
(cd-s) *(W 0288CDX)* – ('A') / Best of both worlds (live) / One way to rock (live) / When it's love (live).

Jun 95. (c-s) *(W 0302C)* **AMSTERDAM / RUNAROUND (live)** [ ] [–]
(cd-s) *(W 0302CDX)* – ('A') / Finish what ya started (live).

Aug 95. (c-s,cd-s) *<17810>* **NOT ENOUGH / AMSTERDAM** [–] [97]

— **DAVID LEE ROTH** returned on 2 tracks below ('Me Wise Magic' & 'Can't Get This Stuff No More') to repl. HAGAR

Oct 96. (cd/c) *(9362 46474-2/-4) <46332>* **THE BEST OF: VOLUME ONE** (compilation) [45] [1]
– Eruption / Ain't talkin' 'bout love / Runnin' with the Devil / Dance the night away / And the cradle will rock . . . / Unchained / Jump / Panama / Why can't this be love / Dreams / When it's love / Poundcake / Right now / Can't stop lovin' you / Humans being / Can't get this stuff no more / Me wise magic.

— ROTH's ego led to the old reunion failing. **GARY CHERONE** (ex-EXTREME) became frontman and co-writer.

Mar 98. (cd/c) *<(9362 46662-2/-4)>* **VAN HALEN III** [43] [4]
– Neworld / Without you / One I want / From afar / Dirty water dog / Once / Fire in the hole / Josephina / Year to the day / Primary / Ballot or the bullet / How many say I.

— re-formed for tour in 2004 with **HAGAR** as frontman

Jul 04. (d-cd) *(8122 76515-2) <78961>* **THE BEST OF BOTH WORLDS** (compilation) [15] [3]
– Eruption / It's about time / Up for breakfast / Learning to see / Ain't talkin' 'bout love / Finish what ya started / You really got me / Dreams / Hot for teacher / Poundcake / And the cradle will rock . . . / Black and blue / Jump / Top of the world / Oh, pretty woman / Love walks in / Beautiful girls / Can't stop lovin' you / Unchained // Panama / Best of both worlds / Jamie's cryin' / Runaround / I'll wait / Why can't this be love / Runnin' with the Devil / When it's love / Dancing in the street / Not enough / Feels so good / Right now / Everybody wants somw!! / Dance the night away / Ain't talkin' 'bout love (live) / Panama (live) / Jump (live).

☐ Alan VEGA (see under ⇒ SUICIDE)

Suzanne VEGA

Born: 12 Aug'59, Upper West Side, New York, USA. Studying dance at the High School of Performing Arts, VEGA spent her spare time gaining valuable musical experience in the folk clubs of New York's Greenwich Village. Hooking up with managers Ron Fierstein and Steve Addabbo, VEGA eventually secured a contract with 'A&M', Addabbo and LENNY KAYE (ex-PATTI SMITH GROUP and 'Nuggets' curator) overseeing production duties on her eponymous 1985 debut album. Critically acclaimed, this starkly compelling folk set saw VEGA hailed as the new JONI MITCHELL with some observers drawing comparisons with LAURA NYRO and even DORY PREVIN. Highly intelligent and acutely observed, VEGA's musings were reminiscent of LEONARD COHEN although she possessed a distinctive lyrical voice with a delicately understated vocal to match. Buoyed by the UK success (on its second release) of 'MARLENE ON THE WALL', the album almost made the British Top 10 although it struggled to penetrate the US Top 100. A couple of months later, she scored another UK Top 40 with the moodily intense 'LEFT OF CENTER', written for the soundtrack of 80's movie, 'Pretty In Pink' and featuring JOE JACKSON on piano. VEGA finally broke through in her home country with 'LUKA', a poignant character portrayal of an abused child which made No.3

in the American charts. The accompanying album, 'SOLITUDE STANDING' (1987) consolidated VEGA's standing as one of the most promising young talents in the new singer/songwriter movement alongside the likes of TRACY CHAPMAN etc. One track, the acappella 'TOM'S DINER', only a minor UK hit upon its original release in 1987, was later reworked by dance act, D.N.A., its success prompting a remixed version credited to SUZANNE VEGA & D.N.A. This in turn was even more successful, going Top 5 in Britain and America and leading to an album of the same name featuring interpretations of various VEGA tracks by such esteemed artists as R.E.M. A third album proper, 'DAYS OF OPEN HAND' (1990), met with mixed reactions however, its more ambitious jazz arrangements and enigmatic lyrics standing in contrast to the economical simplicity of her earlier work. No hit singles were forthcoming although the success of the aforementioned 'TOM'S DINER' track made sure VEGA's career stayed on the commercial straight and narrrow. No doubt indspired by the rhythmic innovation applied to the track, her fourth set, '99.9F' (1992) saw VEGA experimenting with all manner sound effects. The result was arguably her most consistent set since the debut, the likes of 'BLOOD MAKES NOISE' and 'FAT MAN & DANCING GIRL' fastening spiky rhythmic structures to VEGA's trademark sound, while the more traditional 'WHEN HEROES GO DOWN' showed VEGA could still pen affecting folk-pop. In 1997, SUZANNE was back with her most accessible work to date, 'NINE OBJECTS OF DESIRE', one of tracks featured on the record, NO CHEAP THRILL' even appearing on Britain's lottery show! While the 90's were characterised by an experimentalism in large part due to the influence of husband/producer Mitchell Froom, her subsequent divorce made for both rich songwriting material and a back to basics approach on the Rupert Hine-produced 'SONGS IN RED AND GRAY' (2001). Very much a return to the sparse, confessional style which made her name back in the 80's, the record analysed the breakdown of her marriage in oblique yet emotionally loaded style.

• **Covered:** CHINA DOLL (Grateful Dead) / STORY OF ISAAC (Leonard Cohen). • **Trivia:** In 1987, she contributed two song lyrics for a PHILIP GLASS album, 'Songs From Liquid Days'.

Album rating: SUZANNE VEGA (*8) / SOLITUDE STANDING (*7) / DAYS OF OPEN HAND (*5) / 99.9 F (*6) / NINE OBJECTS OF DESIRE (*6) / THE BEST OF SUZANNE VEGA – TRIED AND TRUE compilation (*8) / SONGS IN RED AND GRAY (*6) / RETROSPECTIVE: THE BEST OF . . . double compilation (*8)

SUZANNE VEGA – vocals, guitar with **JIM GORDON** – guitar / **FRANK CHRISTIAN** – guitar / **PAUL DUGAN** + **FRANK GRAVIS** – bass / **SUE EVANS** – drums / **C.P. ROTH** – synth She replaced above with touring + studio band from mid'85-late 80's. **MARC SHULMAN** – guitar / **MIKE VISCEGLIA** – bass / **ANTON SANKO** – keyboards / **STEPHEN FERRARA** – percussion / **SUE EVANS** – drums

A&M A&M

Jul 85. (lp/c) <*(AMA/AMC 5072)*> **SUZANNE VEGA** 11 Jun85 91
– Cracking / Freeze tag / Marlene on the wall / Small blue thing / Straight lines / Undertow / Some journey / The queen and the soldier / Knight moves / Neighborhood girls. *(cd-iss. Feb86 & Mar93; CDA 5072) (lp re-iss. Apr00 on 'Vivante'; VPLP 006)*

Aug 85. (7") *(AM 275)* <2759> **MARLENE ON THE WALL. / NEIGHBORHOOD GIRLS**

Jan 86. (7") *(AM 294)* **SMALL BLUE THING. / THE QUEEN AND THE SOLDIER** 65 –
(d7"+=) *(DAM 294)* – Some journey / Black widow station.

Feb 86. (7") <2834> **SMALL BLUE THING. / LEFT OF CENTER** –

Mar 86. (7") *(AM 309)* **MARLENE ON THE WALL. / SMALL BLUE THING** 21 –
(10"+=) *(AMY 309)* – Neighborhood girls / Straight lines (live).

May 86. (7") *(AM 320)* **LEFT OF CENTER. / UNDERTOW** 32 –
(10"+=) *(AMX 320)* – ('A'live) / Freeze tag (live).
(cd-s+=) *(CDQ 320)* – Cracking.
(above 'A'side featured JOE JACKSON – piano). SUE EVANS had now left.

Oct 86. (7") *(AM 349)* **GYPSY. / CRACKING (live)** –
(12"+=) *(AMY 349)* – Knight movies (live).

May 87. (lp/c/cd) *(SUZ LP/MC/CD 2)* <5136> **SOLITUDE STANDING** 2 11
– Tom's diner / Luka / Ironbound / Fancy poultry / In the eye / Night vision / Solitude standing / Calypso / Language / Gypsy / Wooden horse.

May 87. (7") <2937> **LUKA. / NIGHT VISION** – 3

May 87. (7") *(VEGA 1)* **LUKA. / STRAIGHT LINES (live)** 23 –
(12"+=) *(VEGA 12)* – Neighbourhood girls.
(10"+=/c-s+=) *(VEGA 10/C10)* – Cracking (alternative mix).

Jul 87. (7") *(VEGA 2)* **TOM'S DINER. / LEFT OF CENTER** 58 –
(10"+=/12"+=) *(VEGA 210/212)* – Luka (live).
(cd-s+=) *(VEGCD 2)* ('A'live).

Sep 87. (7") <2960> **SOLITUDE STANDING. / TOM'S DINER** – 94

Nov 87. (7") <2888> **GYPSY. / LEFT OF CENTER** –

Nov 87. (7"/c-s) *(VEGA/+C 3)* **SOLITUDE STANDING. / LUKA** –
(12"+=) *(VEGA 3-12)* – Ironbound – Fancy poultry.
(10"/cd-s) *(VEG A3-10/CD 3)* – ('A'side) / Marlene on the wall (live) / Some journey (live).

— **FRANK VILARDI** – drums repl. FERRARA

— added **MICHAEL BLAIR** – percussion

Apr 90. (cd/c/lp) *(CDA/AMC/AMA 5293)* <15293> **DAYS OF OPEN HAND** 7 50
– Tired of sleeping / Men in a war / Rusted pipe / Institution green / Book of dreams / Those whole girls (run in grace) / Room off the street / Big space / Predictions / Fifty-fifty chance / Pilgrimage. *(re-iss. cd May95; 395293-2)*

Apr 90. (7"/c-s) *(AM/+MC 559)* **BOOK OF DREAMS. / BIG SPACE** 66
(cd-s+=) *(AMCD 559)* – Marlene on the wall (live) / Ironbound (live).
(10"++=) *(AMX 559)* – Fancy poultry.

Jun 90. (7") *(AM 565)* **TIRED OF SLEEPING. / THOSE WHOLE GIRLS (RUN IN GRACE)**
(10"+=/cd-s+=) *(AM X/CD 565)* – Left of center / Room off the street.

Jul 90. (7"/c-s; D.N.A. featuring SUZANNE VEGA) *(AM/+MC 592)* <1592> **TOM'S DINER. / ('A'version)** 2 Sep90 5
(12"+=/cd-s+=) *(AM X/CD 592)* – (2 other mixes by the Bristol duo).

Sep 90. (7"/c-s) *(AM/+MC 584)* **MEN IN A WAR. / UNDERTOW (live)**
(12"+=/cd-s+=) *(AM X/CD 584)* – ('A'live).

Aug 92. (7"/c-s) *(AM/+C 0029)* **IN LIVERPOOL. / SOME JOURNEY** 52
(cd-s+=) *(AMCD 0029)* – The Queen and the soldier / Luka.

Sep 92. (cd/c/lp) *(540012-2/-4/-1)* <0005> **99.9 F** 20 86
– Rock in this pocket (song of David) / Blood makes noise / In Liverpool / 99.9 F / Blood sings / Fat man & dancing girl / (If you were) In my movie / As a child / Bad wisdom / When heroes go down / As girls go / Songs of sand / Private goes public.

Oct 92. (7"/c-s) *(AM/+C 0085)* **99.9 F. / MEN WILL BE MEN** 46 –
(cd-s+=) *(AMCD 0085)* – Rock in this pocket (acoustic) / In Liverpool (acoustic).
(cd-s) *(AMCDX 0085)* – ('A'side) / Tired of sleeping / Straight lines / Tom's diner (all live).

Dec 92. (7"/c-s) *(AM/+C 0112)* **BLOOD MAKES NOISE. / TOM'S DINER** 60 –
(cd-s) *(AMCD 0112)* – ('A'side) / Neighbourhood girls / Predictions / China doll.
(12") *(AMY 0112)* – ('A'side) / ('A'-Mitchell Froom remix) / ('A'house mix) / ('A'master mix).

Feb 93. (7"/c-s) *(AM/+C 0158)* **WHEN HEROES GO DOWN. / KNIGHT MOVES (live)** 58 –
(cd-s+=) *(AMCD 0158)* – Men in a war (live) / Gypsy (live).
(cd-s) *(AMCDX 0158)* – ('A'side) / Marlene on the wall / Luka / Left of center.

Feb 97. (c-ep/cd-ep) *(581869-4/-2)* **NO CHEAP THRILL / LUKA / MARLENE ON THE WALL / TOM'S DINER** 40 –

Feb 97. (cd/c) *(540583-2/-4)* **NINE OBJECTS OF DESIRE** 43 Sep96 92
– Birth-day (love made real) / Headshots / Caramel / Stockings / Casual match / Thin man / No cheap thrill / World before Colombus / Lolita / Honeymoon suite / Tombstone / My favorite plum.

Jun 97. (c-s) *(582269-4)* **BIRTH-DAY (LOVE MADE REAL) / WOMEN ON A TIER** –
(cd-s) *(582267-2)* – ('A'side) / Caramel / Small blue thing / Blood makes noise.
(cd-s) *(582269-2)* – ('A'side) / Casual match / World before Columbus.

Oct 98. (cd/c) *<(540945-2/-4)>* **THE BEST OF SUZANNE VEGA – TRIED AND TRUE** (compilation) 46
– Luka / Tom's diner (DNA featuring SUZANNE VEGA) / Marlene on the wall / Caramel / 99.9f / Small blue thing / Blood makes noise / Left of the center / In Liverpool / Gypsy / Book of dreams / No cheap thrill / World before Columbus / When heroes go down / The queen and the soldier / Book & a cover / Rosemary.

Sep 01. (cd) *<(493111-2)>* **SONGS IN RED AND GRAY**
– Penitent / Widow's walk / (I'll never be) Your Maggie May / It makes me wonder / Soap and water / Songs in red and gray / Last year's troubles / Priscilla / If I were a weapon / Harbor song / Machine ballerina / Solitaire / St. Clare.

Universal Universal

Jul 03. (cd) *(9808884) <493670>* **RETROSPECTIVE: THE BEST OF . . .** (compilation) 27 Apr03
– Luka / Tom's diner (DNA featuring SUZANNE VEGA) / Marlene on the wall / Caramel / 99.9F / Tired of sleeping / Small blue thing / Blood makes noise / Left of center / (I'll never be) Your Maggie May / In Liverpool / Gypsy / Book of dreams / No cheap thrill / Calypso / World before Columbus / Solitude standing / Penitent / Rosemary / The queen and the soldier (live) / Woman on the tier (I'll see you through). *(UK cd w/bonus cd+=)* – Caramel (live) / Widow's talk (live) / Solitude standing (live) / Blood makes noise (live) / In Liverpool (a short reading from The Passionate Eye) / In Liverpool (live) / Anniversary (demo) / Tom's diner (original).

– more compilations, others, etc. –

Oct 88. (cd-ep) *A&M; (AMCD 912)* **COMPACT HITS** –
– Luka / Left of center / Neighbourhood girls / The queen and the soldier.

Sep 91. (cd/c/lp; Various Artists) *A&M; (395363-2/-4/-1)* **TOM'S ALBUM**
– (contained re-workings by other artists of the track TOM'S DINER)

□ VELVET REVOLVER (see under ⇒ GUNS N' ROSES)

the VELVET UNDERGROUND

Formed: New York City, New York, USA . . . early 1965, by LOU REED and JOHN CALE, who nearly hit as The PRIMITIVES with the single, 'The Ostrich'. They met modern pop artist, ANDY WARHOL, who invited German chanteuse NICO to join the set-up alongside STERLING MORRISON and MO TUCKER. Early in 1966, they signed to 'MGM-Verve', and soon began work on what was to be their debut album, 'THE VELVET UNDERGROUND AND NICO'. The album was a revelation, strikingly different from the love and peace psychedelia of the day, The VELVETS vision was decidedly darker and more disturbing. Combining sublime melodies and nihilistic noise, it featured eleven superb ahead-of-their-time classics, notably the brutally frank and frenetic 'HEROIN', the S&M 'VENUS IN FURS' and the garage raunch of 'WAITING FOR THE MAN'. It also contained three NICO sung beauties, 'FEMME FATALE', 'ALL TOMORROW'S PARTIES' and 'I'LL BE YOUR MIRROR'. The record only managed a brief stay in the US Top 200, as did the 1967 follow-up, 'WHITE LIGHT, WHITE HEAT', which included the 17-minute white noise freak-out of 'SISTER RAY'. With CALE now out of the picture, the focus fell on REED's songwriting for the self-titled third album. An altogether mellower set of more traditionally structured songs, the highlight was undoubtedly REED's beautiful lullaby, 'PALE BLUE EYES'. The band's last studio album, 'LOADED', was the closest The VELVET UNDERGROUND ever came to mainstream rock and an indicator of the direction REED would take in his solo career. 'SWEET JANE' and 'ROCK 'N' ROLL' marked his creative peak, a final glorious burst of guitar noise before the group disbanded and the myth started to crystallise. And that was that. Except it wasn't, not come 1992 anyway, when many a precious, pasty faced obsessive went even whiter with horror as The VELVET UNDERGROUND reformed. Many more fans, however, eagerly shelled out their hard earned cash for a reunion tour and album as CALE and REED became buddies once more. The live shows were apparently rather joyous and the accompanying vinyl document, 'LIVE MCMXCIII' (1993), was an enjoyable romp through all the favourites. After the death of STERLING MORRISON in 1995, however, the prospect of further VELVETS activity looked doubtful. Yet despite the reunion, despite LOU REED's dodgy hairdo, despite everything, The VELVET UNDERGROUND of the 60's remain perennially cool and insidiously influential. Basically, alternative music begins and ends with VU and they have been cited as the inspiration for punk rock. A decade after that, a generation of indie groups (i.e. JESUS & MARY CHAIN, early PRIMAL SCREAM, MY BLOODY VALENTINE, etc.) paid barely disguised homage to their heroes.

• **Songwriters:** REED compositions, except some by group. Many rock acts have covered their material, but so far not surprisingly, none have managed to score a major chart hit yet. • **Miscellaneous:** In 1990, REED and CALE re-united on a tribute album to the deceased ANDY WARHOL. NICO had earlier died on the 18th of July '88 after suffering a brain haemorrhage due to a fall from her bike while on holiday in Ibiza. • **Trivia:** Their debut LP sleeve featured a gimmick peeling-banana-skin sticker. They reformed for a gig in Paris, 15 June 1990. UK's Channel 4 featured a night-long session of all their previous work.

Album rating: THE VELVET UNDERGROUND AND NICO (*10) / WHITE LIGHT – WHITE HEAT (*9) / THE VELVET UNDERGROUND (*8) / LOADED (*8) / ANDY WARHOL'S VELVET UNDERGROUND FEATURING NICO compilation (*7) / LIVE AT MAX'S KANSAS CITY exploitation (*2) / SQUEEZE (*3) / THE VELVET UNDERGROUND AND LOU REED compilation (*6) / 1969 – THE VELVET UNDERGROUND LIVE exploitation (*7) / GREATEST HITS compilation (*6) / V.U. unreleased set (*7) / ANOTHER VIEW exploitation (*4) / THE BEST OF THE VELVET UNDERGROUND (THE WORDS AND MUSIC OF LOU REED) compilation (*7) / LIVE MCMXCIII reunion (*5)

LOU REED (b. LOUIS FIRBANK, 2 Mar'44, Long Island, N.Y.) – vocals, guitar (ex-JADES, ex-PRIMITIVES) / **JOHN CALE** (b. 9 Dec'42, Garnant, Wales) – bass, viola, vocals, etc. / **STERLING MORRISON** – guitar / **MAUREEN TUCKER** – drums / plus **NICO** (b. CHRISTA PAFFGEN, 16 Oct'38, Cologne, Germany) – vocals (also – Solo artist)

Verve Verve

Oct 66. (7") *<10427>* **ALL TOMORROW'S PARTIES. / I'LL BE YOUR MIRROR** –

Dec 66. (7") *<10466>* **SUNDAY MORNING / FEMME FATALE** –

Oct 67. (lp; stereo/mono) *(S+/VLP 9184) <5008>* **THE VELVET UNDERGROUND AND NICO** Dec66
– Sunday morning / I'm waiting for the man / Femme fatale / Venus in furs / Run run run / All tomorrow's parties / Heroin / There she goes again / I'll be your mirror / Black angel's death song / European son to Delmore Schwartz. *(re-iss. Oct71 on 'M.G.M.; 2315 056) (re-iss. Aug83 on 'Polydor' lp/c; SPE LP/MC 20) (cd-iss. 1986 on 'Polydor'; 823 290-2) (cd re-iss. May96 on 'Polydor'; 531 250-2) (lp re-iss. Jun99 on 'Simply Vinyl'; SVLP 90) <(d-cd-iss. Apr02 on 'Polydor'+=; MLST 756)>* – (NICO tracks) / (mono versions) / (various versions). *(hit UK No.59)*

— trimmed to a quartet when NICO preferred the solo life

Jan 68. (7") *<10543>* **WHITE LIGHT – WHITE HEAT. / HERE SHE COMES NOW** –

Mar 68. (7") *<10560>* **I HEARD HER CALL MY NAME. / HERE SHE COMES NOW** –

Jun 68. (lp; stereo/mono) *(S+/VLP 9201) <5046>* **WHITE LIGHT / WHITE HEAT** Dec67
– White light – white heat / The gift / Lady Godiva's operation / Here she comes now / I heard her call my name / Sister Ray. *(re-iss. Oct71 on 'MGM Select'; 2353 024) (re-iss. Apr84 on 'Polydor' lp/c; SPE LP/MC 73) (cd-iss. 1986 on 'Polydor'; 825 119-2) (cd re-iss. May96 on 'Polydor'; 531 251-2) (lp re-iss. Apr00 on 'Simply Vinyl'; SVLP 200)*

— **DOUG YULE** – bass, vocals, keyboards, guitar; repl. CALE who went solo

M.G.M. M.G.M.

Apr 69. (lp) *(CS 8108) <4617>* **THE VELVET UNDERGROUND** Mar 69
– Candy says . . . / What goes on / Some kinda love / Pale blue eyes / Jesus / Beginning to see the light / I'm set free / That's the story of my life /

Lou Reed of The VELVET UNDERGROUND

The murder mystery / Afterhours. *(re-iss. Nov71 on 'MGM Select'; 2353 022) (re-iss. Mar76;) (re-iss. Sep83 on 'Polydor'; SPE LP/MC 39) <US re-iss. Apr85; 815454> (cd-iss. May96 on 'Polydor'; 531 252-2)*

May 69. (7") *<14057>* **JESUS. / WHAT GOES ON** –

— **BILLY YULE** – drums repl. TUCKER who had a baby. **MO TUCKER** returned in 1970 and BILLY only appeared on MAX's live album (see compilations)

Atlantic Cotillion

Jan 71. (7") *<44107>* **WHO LOVES THE SUN? / OH! SWEET NUTHIN'** –

Apr 71. (lp) *(2400 111) <9034>* **LOADED** Aug70
– Who loves the sun? / Sweet Jane / Rock and roll / Cool it down / New age / Head held high / Lonesome cowboy Bill / I found a reason / Train around the bend / Oh! sweet nuthin'. *(re-iss. 1972 lp/c; K/K4 40113) (cd-iss. Jun88 & Feb93 on 'Warners'; 7567 90367-2) (d-cd-iss. May97 as 'LOADED (THE FULLY LOADED EDITION)' on 'Rhino'+=; 8122 72563-2)* – (diff.mixes & demos, etc.) *(lp re-iss. Oct97 on 'Simply Vinyl'; SVLP 22)*

Apr 71. (7") *(2091 008)* **WHO LOVES THE SUN. / SWEET JANE** –

— (Aug70) now with no originals The **YULE's** brought in newcomers **WALTER POWERS** – bass repl. LOU REED who went solo in 1971. (1971) **WILLIE ALEXANDER** – guitar repl. MORRISON who took a doctorate in English. MO TUCKER finally departed to raise her new family and eventually had five children in total, before going solo in 1980.

Polydor not iss.

Feb 73. (lp) *(2383 180)* **SQUEEZE** –
– Little Jack / Mean old man / She'll make you cry / Wordless / Dopey Joe / Crash / Friends / Jack and Jane / Send no letter / Louise.

— Folded soon after above, DOUG sessioned for ELLIOTT MURPHY and later joined AMERICAN FLYER.

— they re-formed early in 1993; **REED, CALE, MORRISON + TUCKER**

Sire Sire

Oct 93. (d-cd/d-c) *<(9362 45464-2/-4)>* **LIVE MCMXCIII (live 1993)** 70
– We're gonna have a good time together / Venus in furs / Guess I'm falling in love / After hours / All tomorrow's parties / Some kinda love / I'll be your mirror / Beginning to see the light / The gift / I heard her call my name / Femme fatale / Hey Mr. Rain / Sweet Jane / Velvet nursery rhyme / White light – white heat / I'm sticking with you / Black angel's death song / Rock'n'roll / I can't stand it / I'm waiting for the man / Heroin / Pale blue eyes / Coyote.

Feb 94. (7"/c-s) *(W 0224/+C)* **VENUS IN FURS (live). / I'M WAITING FOR THE MAN (live)** 71
(cd-s+=) *(W 0224CD)* – Heroin (live) / Sweet Jane (live).

— On the 30th August 1995, STERLING MORRISON died of lymphoma.

— Group inducted into the Rock'n'roll Hall Of Fame, and performed 'LAST NIGHT I SAID GOODBYE TO A FRIEND', REED's tribute to recently deceased STERLING.

– compilations, others, etc. –

Dec 71. (d-lp) *M.G.M.; (2683 006)* **ANDY WARHOL'S VELVET UNDERGROUND FEATURING NICO** –
– I'm waiting for the man / Candy says / Run, run, run / White light – white heat / All tomorrow's parties / Sunday morning / I heard her call my name / Femme fatale / Heroin / Here she comes now / There she goes again / Sister Ray / Venus in furs / European son / Pale blue eyes / Black angel's death song / Beginning to see the light.

Aug 72. (lp) *Atlantic; (K 30022) / Cotillion; <9500>* **LIVE AT MAX'S KANSAS CITY (live 22 Aug'70)** May72
– I'm waiting for the man / Sweet Jane / Lonesome Cowboy Bill / Beginning to see the light / I'll be your mirror / Pale blue eyes / Sunday morning / New age / Femme fatale / After hours. *(cd-iss. Jun93 on 'Warners'; 7567 90370-2)*

Jun 73. (7"m; as LOU REED & VELVET UNDERGROUND) *M.G.M.; (2006 283)* **CANDY SAYS. / I'M WAITING FOR THE MAN / RUN RUN RUN** –

Aug 73. (7") *Atlantic; (K 10339)* **SWEET JANE (live). / ROCK AND ROLL** (live) –

Oct 73. (lp) *Verve; (2315 258) / Pride; <0022>* **THE VELVET UNDERGROUND AND LOU REED**

1974. (lp) *M.G.M.; <4950>* **ARCHETYPES** –

1976. (ltd-7"m) *A.E.B.;* **FOGGY NOTION – INSIDE YOUR HEART. / I'M STICKING WITH YOU / FERRYBOAT BILL** –

Feb 79. (d-lp) *Mercury; (6643 900) <SRM2 7504>* **1969 – THE VELVET UNDERGROUND LIVE (live)** Apr74
– I'm waiting for the man / Lisa says / What goes on / Sweet Jane / We're gonna have a real good time together / Femme fatale / New age / Rock and roll / Beginning to see the light / Ocean / Pale blue eyes / Heroin / Some kinda love / Over you / Sweet Bonnie Brown – It's just too much / I'll be your mirror / White light – white heat. *(re-iss. Nov84; PRID 7) (re-iss. 1987; 834 823-1) (re-iss. 1988 as 'VOL.1' & 'VOL.2' cd/c; 834823-2/-4 & 834824-2/-4)*

Nov 80. (d-lp)(d-c) *Polydor; (2664 438)(3578 485)* **GREATEST HITS** –

Oct 82. (12"ep) *Polydor; (POSPX 603)* **HEROIN / VENUS IN FURS. / I'M WAITING FOR THE MAN / RUN RUN RUN** –

Feb 85. (lp/c) *Polydor; (POLD/+C 5167) <823721>* **V.U.** (rare rec.68-69) 47 85
– I can't stand it / Stephanie says / She's my best friend / Lisa says / Ocean / Foggy notion / Temptation inside your heart / One of these days / Andy's chest / I'm sticking with you. *(cd-iss. Jun87; 825 092-2)*

May 86. (5xlp-box)(5xcd-box) *Polydor; (VUBOX 1)(815 454-2)* **BOXED SET**
– (first 3 albums, plus V.U. & ANOTHER VIEW)

Aug 86. (lp/c/cd) *Polydor; (829 405-1/-4/-2)* **ANOTHER VIEW**
– We're gonna have a good time together / I'm gonna move right in / Hey Mr. Rain (version 1) / Ride into the Sun / Coney Island steeplechase / Guess I'm falling in love / Hey Mr. Rain (version 2) / Ferryboat Bill / Rock and roll (original).

Feb 88. (12") *Old Gold; (OG 4049)* **I'M WAITING FOR THE MAN. / HEROIN** –

Mar 88. (12") *Old Gold; (OG 4051)* **VENUS IN FURS. / ALL TOMORROW'S PARTIES** –

Sep 88. (lp) *Plastic Inevitable; <FIRST 1>* **THE VELVET UNDERGROUND ETC.** –
– The ostrich / Cycle Annie / Sneaky Pete / Noise.

Sep 88. (lp) *Plastic Inevitable; <SECOND 1>* **THE VELVET UNDERGROUND AND SO ON** –
– It's alright (the way you live) / I'm not too sorry / Stephanie says.

Oct 89. (lp/c/cd) *Verve; <(841 164-1/-4/-2)>* **THE BEST OF THE VELVET UNDERGROUND (THE WORDS AND MUSIC OF LOU REED)**
– I'm waiting for the man / Femme fatale / Run run run / Heroin / All tomorrow's parties / I'll be your mirror / White light – white heat / Stephanie says / What goes on / Beginning to see the light / Pale blue eyes / I can't stand it / Lisa says / Sweet Jane / Rock and roll.

Oct 95. (cd/c) *Global; (RAD CD/MC 21)* **THE BEST OF LOU REED & VELVET UNDERGROUND** 56

Oct 95. (4xcd-box) *Polydor; <(527887-2)>* **PEEL SLOWLY AND SEE** Sep95

Oct 00. (cd) *Universal; <(AA314 549133-2)>* **THE MILLENNIUM COLLECTION: THE BEST OF . . .**

Jul 01. (cd) *Polydor; (549690-2)* **ROCK AND ROLL: AN INTRODUCTION TO THE VELVET UNDERGROUND** –

Aug 01. (4xcd-box) *Captain Trip; (CTCD 35053)* **FINAL VU 1971-1973 (live)** –
– (LIVE IN LONDON 1971 / LIVE IN THE NETHERLANDS 1971 / LIVE IN WALES 1972 / MASSACHUSETTS 1973).

Oct 01. (3xcd-box) *Polydor; <(557665-2)>* **BOOTLEG SERIES VOL.1: THE QUINE TAPES**

— (see also LOU REED discography for other tracks on comps & B's)

— Also tribute albums 'HEAVEN AND HELL' 1, 2 & 3 were issued Oct'90-Feb'92, all on 'Imaginary' records, as was another '15 MINUTES'.

□ Tom VERLAINE (see under ⇒ TELEVISION)

the VERVE

Formed: Wigan, England . . . 1990 by local college lads RICHARD ASHCROFT (the main writer), NICK McCABE, SIMON JONES and PETER SALISBURY. They were soon supporting the likes of RIDE and SPIRITUALIZED, signing to 'Hut' in 1991. The following year, they released three singles, the spiralling psychedelia of 'ALL IN THE MIND', 'SHE'S A SUPERSTAR' & 'GRAVITY GRAVE'. In early summer of '93, they had a minor hit with 'BLUE', a taster for the debut album, 'A STORM IN HEAVEN', which made the UK Top 30. The album delivered on the promise of the early singles; an amorphous melange of trippy rock and liquid space-jazz ambience. Ambitious and cocksure, they toured the States, subsequently coming unstuck with US label 'Verve', who forced them to slightly change their name to The VERVE. In 1995, they unleashed a second album, 'A NORTHERN SOUL', a much darker, more intense affair featuring more conventional song structures. Although the album went Top 20, they announced they were splitting several months later, the 'HISTORY' single apparently their swan song. Just when the band were poised to enter the big league, it looked as if they'd missed the boat, McCABE and ASHCROFT's quarreling, together with well documented drug problems, seemingly to blame for the band's demise. By February '97, however, they got it together sufficiently to reform and their first single of the year was to many, their best song yet, the grandiose, string-laden 'BITTER SWEET SYMPHONY' (written by MICK JAGGER and KEITH RICHARDS for The ANDREW LOOG OLDHAM ORCHESTRA). The song crashed into the UK chart at No.2 thanks to a glorious video featuring a tense, jaywalking ASHCROFT barging into everyone in sight! A follow-up, 'THE DRUGS DON'T WORK', went straight in at No.1, as did parent album, 'URBAN HYMNS' (1997). It seemed THE VERVE could do no wrong, although tensions between ASHCROFT and the others were coming to a head; McCABE would subsequently announce his retirement from stage work in July '98 (veteran pedal steel man BJ COLE was enlisted). The Americans had already taken the band into their hearts by this time, the aforementioned third set hitting the Top 30 and going platinum in the process. However by May 1999, THE VERVE were history, "astral man" ASHCROFT opting for a solo career with his SPIRITUALIZED wife KATE RADLEY in tow. And what a picture of domestic bliss he painted on 'ALONE WITH EVERYBODY' (2000), his first solo set and a marked transition from the anguished soul-searching of his best work with THE VERVE. Eloquent string arrangements, folky strumming and contented musings on life's basic essentials made for one of the best solo debuts in years. A lucky man? It certainly seemed so. ASHCROFT returned in 2002 to deliver 'HUMAN CONDITIONS', a slighty bitter sophomore record, that seemed to isolate VERVE fans even more. Reverting into a world of deliberate melancholy, ASHCROFT even dabbled with the world's smallest violin. Themes of God, lost love and difficult relationships have all been explored before by ASHCROFT et al, nevertheless it reached UK No.3. Yet its only saving grace remained in the brilliant closing track 'NATURE IS THE LAW' (excuse the cheesy title), which featured BRIAN WILSON on backing harmonies. Newly signed to 'Parlophone' and back within sniffing distance of No.1, the man prone to overstatement returned with the underrated 'KEYS TO THE WORLD' (2006), its title perhaps a subtle reference to CURTIS MAYFIELD, one of whose productions he sampled on Top 20 hit, 'MUSIC IS POWER' (shades of 'BITTERSWEET SYMPHONY's string pomp), and whose Windy City soul perhaps provided a spiritual – if not literal – compass to the album's symphonic roots sound. 'WHY NOT NOTHING' was the most visceral opening to any ASHCROFT record, a NEIL DIAMOND-phlemgy, veteran-wise acoustic rocker which might have cleaned up as a lead single. The more typical 'BREAK THE NIGHT WITH COLOUR' went Top 3 anyway, all layered angst and straining martyrdom. The title track sailed close to the VERVE and 'SWEET BROTHER MALCOLM' sounded like the obligatory levee-side ballad from a mid-period BLACK CROWES album (one that he actually managed to bring off), yet it was the swelling 'SIMPLE SONG' which perhaps supplied the most finely-cut key to ASHCROFT's world, a penultimate manifesto for better times ahead.

Album rating: A STORM IN HEAVEN (*7) / NO COME DOWN collection (*6) / A NORTHERN SOUL (*8) / URBAN HYMNS (*9) / THIS IS MUSIC – THE SINGLES 92-98 compilation (*8) / Richard Ashcroft: ALONE WITH EVERYBODY (*7) / HUMAN CONDITIONS (*6) / KEYS TO THE WORLD (*6)

VERVE

RICHARD ASHCROFT (b.11 Sep'71) – vocals, guitar / **NICK McCABE** (b.14 Jul'71) – lead guitar / **SIMON JONES** (b.29 Jul'72) – bass / **PETER SALISBURY** (b.24 Sep'71) – drums

Hut | Vernon Yard

Mar 92. (7") *(HUT 12)* **ALL IN THE MIND. / ONE WAY TO GO** [ ] [–]
(12"+=/cd-s+=) *(HUT T/CD 12)* – A man called Sun.

Jun 92. (7"/ext-12"/ext-cd-s) *(HUT/+H/CD 16)* **SHE'S A SUPERSTAR. / FEEL** [66] [–]

Oct 92. (10"ep) *(HUTEN 21)* **GRAVITY GRAVE EP** [ ] [–]
– Gravity grave / Endless life / She's a superstar (live).
(12"+=/cd-s++) *(HUT T/CD 21)* – ('A'extended) / Endless life / A man called Sun (live).

Jan 93. (m-cd) *(<HUTUS 1>)* **THE VERVE E.P.** (compilation) [–] [ ]
– Gravity grave / A man called Sun / She's a superstar / Endless life / Feel. *(UK-iss.Sep97 on 'Vernon Yard'; YARDCD 001)*

May 93. (12"ep) *(HUTT 29)* **BLUE. / TWILIGHT / WHERE THE GEESE GO** [69] [–]
(10"ep+=/cd-ep+=) *(HUT EN/CD 29)* – No come down.

Jun 93. (cd/c/lp) *(CDHUT/HUTMC/HUTLP 10) <87950>* **A STORM IN HEAVEN** [27] [ ]
– Star sail / Slide away / Already there / Beautiful mind / The sun, the sea / Virtual world / Make it 'til Monday / Blue / Butterfly / See you in the next one (have a good time).

Sep 93. (7"pink) *(HUT 35)* **SLIDE AWAY. / 6 O'CLOCK** [ ] [–]
(12"/cd-s) *(HUT T/CD 35)* – ('A'side) / Make it 'til Monday (acoustic) / Virtual world (acoustic).

May 94. (cd) *(CDHUT 18)* **NO COMEDOWN** (rare / b-sides) [ ] [–]
– No come down / Blue (USA mix) / Make it 'til Monday (acoustic) / Butterfly (acoustic) / Where the grease go / 6 o'clock / One way to go / Gravity grave (live) / Twilight. *(re-iss. Sep97 on 'Vernon Yard'; YARDCD 007) (re-iss. Jun05; CDHUTX 18)*

the VERVE

Apr 95. (7"burgundy) *(HUT 54)* **THIS IS MUSIC. / LET THE DAMAGE BEGIN** [35] [–]
(12"+=/cd-s+=) *(HUT T/CD 54)* – You and me.

Jun 95. (7"green/c-s) *(HUT/+C 55)* **ON YOUR OWN. / I SEE THE DOOR** [28] [–]
(cd-s+=) *(HUTCD 55)* – Little gem / Dance on your bones.

Jul 95. (cd/c/d-lp) *(CDHUT/HUTMC/HUTLP 27) <40437>* **A NORTHERN SOUL** [13] [ ]
– A new decade / This is music / On your own / So it goes / A northern soul / Brainstorm interlude / Drive you home / History / No knock on my door / Life's an ocean / Stormy clouds / Stormy clouds (reprise).

Sep 95. (c-s) *(HUTC 59)* **HISTORY / BACK ON MY FEET AGAIN** [24] [–]
(cd-s+=) *(HUTCD 59)* – On your own (acoustic) / Monkey magic (Brainstorm mix).
(cd-s) *(HUTDX 59)* – ('A'extended) / Grey skies / Life's not a rehearsal.

—— originals re-formed adding **SIMON TONG** – guitar, keyboards

Hut | Virgin

Jun 97. (7") *(HUTLH 82) <38634>* **BITTER SWEET SYMPHONY. / SO SISTER** [2] Mar98 [12]
('A'extended; cd-s+=) *(HUTDX 82)* – Echo bass.
(c-s/cd-s) *(HUT C/DG 82)* – ('A'side) / Lord I guess I'll never know / Country song / ('A'radio version).

Sep 97. (c-s/cd-s) *(HUT C/DG 88)* **THE DRUGS DON'T WORK / THREE STEPS / THE DRUGS DON'T WORK (original demo)** [1] [–]
(cd-s) *(HUTDX 88)* – ('A'extended) / Bitter sweet symphony (James Lavelle remix) / The crab / Stamped.

Sep 97. (cd/c/lp) *(<44913-2/-4/-1>)* **URBAN HYMNS** [1] [23]
– Bitter sweet symphony / Sonnet / The rolling people / The drugs don't work / Catching the butterfly / Neon wilderness / Space and time / Weeping willow / Lucky man / One day / This time / Velvet morning / Come on.

Nov 97. (c-s/cd-s) *(HUT C/DG 92)* **LUCKY MAN / NEVER WANNA SEE YOU CRY / HISTORY** [7] [–]

(cd-s) *(HUT DX 92)* – ('A'side) / MSG / The longest day / Lucky man (happiness more or less).

Feb 98. (cd-ep) *<13112-2>* **FIVE BY FIVE** [–] [ ]
– Come on / The rolling people / Lucky man (radio edit) / Catching the butterfly / Space and time.

—— the VERVE announced their demise in '99; JONES (and later TONG) formed the SHINING

– compilations, etc. –

Mar 98. (ltd-12"ep) **BITTER SWEET SYMPHONY (original) / LORD I GUESS I'LL NEVER KNOW. / BITTER SWEET SYMPHONY (James Lavelle mix) / COUNTRY SONG** [ ] [–]

Mar 98. (ltd-12"ep) **THE DRUGS DON'T WORK / THREE STEPS. / THE DRUGS DON'T WORK (demo) / THE CRAB** [ ] [–]

Mar 98. (ltd-12"ep) **LUCKY MAN / NEVER WANNA SEE YOU CRY. / MSG / THE LONGEST DAY** [ ] [–]

Mar 98. (ltd-12"ep) **SONNET / STAMPED. / SO SISTER / ECHO BASS** [ ] [–]
(the import cd-single version of the above single <895075-2> actually hit UK No.74 in May'98)

Nov 04. (cd) *Virgin; (CDV 2991) / E.M.I.; <863689-2>* **THIS IS MUSIC – THE SINGLES 92-98** [15] [ ]
– This is music / Slide away / Lucky man / History / She's a superstar / On your own / Blue / Sonnet / All in the mind / The drugs don't work / Gravity grave / Bitter sweet symphony / This could be my moment / Monte Carlo.

RICHARD ASHCROFT

—— with various session people incl. **PETER SALISBURY**

Hut Virgin

Apr 00. (c-s) *(HUTC 128)* **A SONG FOR THE LOVERS / PRECIOUS STONE** [3] [–]
(12"+=/cd-s+=) *(HUT T/CD 128)* – Could be a country thing city thing blues thing.

Jun 00. (c-s) *(HUTC 136)* **MONEY TO BURN / XXYY** [17] [–]
(12"+=/cd-s+=) *(HUT T/CD 136)* – Leave me high.

Jun 00. (cd/c/lp) *(CDHUTX/HUTMCX/HUTDLP 63) <49494>* **ALONE WITH EVERYBODY** [1] Jul00 [ ]
– A song for the lovers / I get my beat / Brave new world / New York / You on my mind in my sleep / Crazy world / On a beach / Money to burn / Slow was my heart / C'mon people (we're making it now) / Everybody.

Sep 00. (c-s) *(HUTC 138)* **C'MON PEOPLE (WE'RE MAKING IT NOW) / A SONG FOR THE LOVERS (remix)** [21] [–]
(12"+=/cd-s+=) *(HUT T/CD 138)* – Make a wish.

Oct 02. (7") *(HUT 161)* **CHECK THE MEANING. / MIRACLE** [11] [–]
(cd-s+=) *(HUTCD 161)* – ('A'-Chris Potter remix) / ('A'-video).

Oct 02. (cd/d-lp) *(CDHUT/HUTDLP 77) <13383>* **HUMAN CONDITIONS** [3] [ ]
– Check the meaning / Buy it in bottles / Bright lights / Paradise / God in the numbers / Science of silence / Man on a mission / Running away / Lord I've been trying / Nature is the law.

Jan 03. (7") *(HUT 163)* **SCIENCE OF SILENCE. / GET UP NOW** [14] [–]
(cd-s+=) *(HUTCD 163)* – Check the meaning (freelance hellraiser remix) / ('A'-video).

Apr 03. (7") *(HUT 167)* **BUY IT IN BOTTLES. / DON'T TAKE ME IN** [26] [–]
(cd-s+=) *(HUTCD 167)* – The journey's just begun / ('A'-video).

Parlophone E.M.I.

Jan 06. (cd-s/7") *(CD+/R 6680)* **BREAK THE NIGHT WITH COLOUR. / THE DIRECTION** [3] [–]
(dvd-s) *(DVDR 6680)* – ('A') / Slip sliding / ('A'-video) / (making of the video).

Jan 06. (cd) *(354520-2) <8373>* **KEYS TO THE WORLD** [2] [ ]
– Why not nothing? / Music is power / Break the night with colour / Words just get in the way / Keys to the world / Sweet brother Malcolm / Cry 'til the morning / Why do lovers? / Simple song / World keeps turning. *(ltd-cd w/dvd+=; 350381-2)* – (DVD tracks).

Apr 06. (cd-s/7") *(CD+/R 6688)* **MUSIC IS POWER. / LONG WAY DOWN** [20] [–]
(dvd-s) *(DVDR 6688)* – ('A') / Break the night with colour (live) / ('A'-live) / ('A'-video) / (making of . . . video).

☐ VICTOR (see under ⇒ RUSH)

Gene VINCENT

Born: EUGENE VINCENT CRADDOCK, 11 Feb'35, Norfolk, Virginia, USA. In 1955, he left the US Navy after suffering leg injuries in a serious motor-cycle crash. Incidentally, this never fully healed, and after a year in plaster, he had a leg-brace fitted and took up singing during his recuperation, often sitting in with WCMS Radio house band, The VIRGINIANS. Early in 1956, he briefly married 15 year-old Ruth Ann Hand, also gaining a contract for 'Capitol' in April. He formed The BLUE CAPS (name taken from President Eisenhower's favourite blue golf cap) for tour work, his live commitments becoming more extensive after the US Top 10 success of his debut single (B-side), 'BE-BOP-A-LULA' (which ELVIS PRESLEY's mother reportedly thought was her own son singing). VINCENT subsequently became a cult star in the 50's, his black leather-clad image and sporadic chart appearances (his last US chart single was 'DANCE TO THE BOP' in January 1958) fueling the myth. Later that year, the media attention focused on his recent drinking bouts which made him irritable to everyone bar his great friend, EDDIE COCHRAN; late in 1959, he toured the UK with EDDIE, resurrecting his chart status in the process with 'PISTOL PACKIN MAMA' (with GEORGIE FAME on piano) and 'SHE SHE LITTLE SHEILA'. Tragedy struck however, on the 17th of April 1960, when EDDIE was killed in a London cab, with GENE and EDDIE's fiancee sustaining injuries. Shaken but vowing to continue, he had a short series of UK hits that year although success soon eluded him and his last UK chart single was 1961's 'I'M GOING HOME'. The following year, he appeared on a bill at The Cavern Club with an up and coming beat combo, The BEATLES, although his 'Capitol' contract expired in '63 and was not renewed. He married for a fourth time in 1965, signing to US label 'Challenge', although his move into country rock'n'roll in 1966 was treated with apathy. In the early 70's, his career took off again when UK BBC Radio DJ John Peel contracted him to his newly formed 'Dandelion' imprint, releasing 'I'M BACK AND I'M PROUD' in the same year. VINCENT then signed to 'Kama Sutra' in the US and released his final albums, 'GENE VINCENT' and 'THE DAY THE WORLD TURNED BLUE', and although critically well received, the records failed to sell. After more hard-living and domestic problems, GENE VINCENT died on the 12th of October 1971 (of a burst stomach ulcer) in Newall hospital California. Many had copied his image including The BEATLES and ALVIN STARDUST and there were many tributes, none more poignant than IAN DURY's 'SWEET GENE VINCENT'.

• **Songwriters:** His first hit, was written by fellow hospital patient in the same ward. He then wrote own material, except covers OVER THE RAINBOW (Judy Garland) / SUMMERTIME (Gershwin) / FRANKIE & JOHNNY (?) / ANOTHER SATURDAY NIGHT (Sam Cooke) / SLIPPIN' AND SLIDIN' + LONG TALL SALLY + GOOD GOLLY MISS MOLLY (Little Richard) / SUSIE Q (Dale Hawkins) / YOU ARE MY SUNSHINE (hit; Ray Charles) / WHITE LIGHTNING (Big Bopper) / etc. • **Trivia:** He and his BLUE CAPS made appearances in the film 'The Girl Can't Help It' & 'Hot Rod Gang'.

Best CD compilation: THE SCREAMING END: THE BEST OF . . . (*8)

GENE VINCENT & HIS BLUE CAPS

GENE VINCENT – vocals, guitar / **CLIFF GALLUP** – lead guitar / **WILLIE WILLIAMS** – acoustic rhythm guitar / **JACK NEAL** – upright bass / **DICKIE HARRELL** – drums

Capitol Capitol

Jun 56. (7",78) *(CL 14599) <3450>* **BE BOP A LULA. / WOMAN LOVE** [16] May 56 [7]
(above B-side, was originally the A, until BE BOP . . . was radio playlisted)

Aug 56. (7",78) *(CL 14628) <3530>* **RACE WITH THE DEVIL. / GONNA BACK UP MY BABY** 28 Jul 56 96

Oct 56. (7",78) *(CL 14637) <3558>* **BLUE JEAN BOP. / WHO SLAPPED JOHN?** 16 Sep 56 49

Nov 56. (lp) *<(T 764)>* **BLUE JEAN BOP** Sep 56 16
– Blue jean bop / Jezebel / Who slapped John / Ain't she sweet / I flipped / Waltz of the wind / Jump back, honey, jump back / That old gang of mine / Jumps, giggles and shouts / Up a lazy river / Bop street / Peg o' my heart. *(re-iss. 1983 on 'E.M.I.') (cd-iss. Jan03 on 'E.M.I.'+=; 540685-2)* – Woman love / Be-bop-a-lula / Race with the Devil / Gonna back up my baby / Well I knocked him bam bam / Crazy legs.

— **PAUL PEAK** – rhythm guitar, vocals repl. WILLIAMS. (NEAL now on bass)

Mar 57. (7",78) *(CL 14693) <3617>* **CRAZY LEGS. / IMPORTANT WORDS** Nov 56

Jan 57. (7",78) *(CL 14681)* **JUMPS, GIGGLES AND SHOUTS. / WEDDING BELLS** –

Apr 57. (lp) *<(T 811)>* **GENE VINCENT AND HIS BLUE CAPS**
– Red blue jeans and a pony tail / Hold me, hug me, rock me / Unchained melody / You told a fib / Cat man / You better believe / Cruisin' / Double talkin' baby / Blues stay away from me / Pink Thunderbird / I sure miss you / Pretty, pretty baby. *(re-iss. 1983 on 'E.M.I.') (cd-iss. Jan03 on 'E.M.I.'+=; 540684-2)* – Important words (version 1) / Bi-bickey-bi-bo-bo-go / Five days, five days / Teenage partner (version 1) / Five feet of lovin' (version 1).

— On tour **RUSSELL WILAFORD** then **TEDDY CRUTCHFIELD** had repl. GALLUP

May 57. (7",78) *(CL 14722) <3678>* **BI-BICKEY-BI-BO-BO-GO. / FIVE DAYS, FIVE DAYS**

— **JOHNNY MEEKS** – lead guitar repl. GALLUP **BOBBY LEE JONES** – bass repl. BILLY MACK who had repl. NEAL (PEEK was now relegated to clapper boy alongside TOMMY FACIENDA)

Sep 57. (7",78) *(CL 14763) <3763>* **LOTTA LOVIN'. / WEAR MY RING** Jul 57 13

Nov 57. (7",78) *(CL 14808) <3839>* **DANCE TO THE BOP. / I GOT IT** 23

Dec 57. (lp) *<(T 970)>* **GENE VINCENT ROCKS AND THE BLUE CAPS ROLL**
– Brand new beat / By the light of the silvery Moon / You'll never walk alone / Frankie and Johnny / In my dreams / Flea brain / Rollin' Dany / You belong to me / Your cheatin' heart / Time will bring you everything / Should I ever love again / It's no lie. *(cd-iss. Oct00 on 'Magic'; 499271-2)*

— briefly on tour **DUDE KAHN** – drums had repl. HARRELL until quick return. / added **MAX LIPSCOMB** – rhythm guitar, piano

Feb 58. (7",78) *(CL 14830) <3874>* **I GOT A BABY. / WALKING HOME FROM SCHOOL WITH YOU**

— **CLIFF SIMMONS** – piano + GRADY OWEN – drums repl. MAX, PAUL & TOMMY

Apr 58. (7") *(CL 14868) <3959>* **BABY BLUE. / TRUE TO YOU**

1958. (lp) *<(T 1059)>* **A GENE VINCENT RECORD DATE**
– Five feet of lovin' / The wayward mind / Somebody help me / Keep it a secret / Hey good lookin' / Git it / Teenage partner / Peace of mind / Look what you gone and done to me / Summertime / I can't help it / I love you. *(cd-iss. Nov99 on 'Magic'; 520757-2)*

— on tour **JUVEZ GOMEZ** – drums repl. HARRELL

— **BLUE CAPS:- HOWARD REED** – lead guitar / **BILL MACK** – bass / **MAX LIPSCOMB** – rhythm guitar / **CLIFF SIMMONS** – piano / **GRADY OWEN** – bass / **DUDE KAHN** – drums

Aug 58. (7") *(CL 14908) <4010>* **ROCKY ROAD BLUES. / YES I LOVE YOU BABY**

— (Sep58) **JOHNNY MEEKS** – lead guitar returned to repl. REED / **CLYDE PENNINGTON** – drums repl. KAHN and D.J.FONTANA. (sax – **JACKIE KELSO**)

Oct 58. (7") *(CL 14935) <4051>* **GIT IT. / LITTLE LOVER**

Oct 58. (lp)*<(T 1207)>* **SOUNDS LIKE GENE VINCENT**
–] My baby don't 'low / I can't believe you wanna leave / I might have known / In love again / You are the one for me / Ready Teddy / I got to you yet / Vincent's blues / Now is the hour / My heart / Maybelline.

Jan 59. (7") *(CL 14974) <4105>* **SAY MAMA. / BE BOP BOOGIE BOY**

Mar 59. (7") *(CL 15000) <4153>* **WHO'S PUSHIN' YOUR SWING. / OVER THE RAINBOW**

Jun 59. (7") *(CL 15035)* **SUMMERTIME. / FRANKIE AND JOHNNY** –

— The BLUE CAPS had already disbanded late 1958,

GENE VINCENT

now solo augmented by **JACKIE MERRITT** – guitar / **SANDY NELSON** – drums / **JACKIE KELSO** – sax

Aug 59. (7") *(CL 15053) <4237>* **RIGHT NOW. / THE NIGHT IS LONELY**

Dec 59. (7") *(CL 15099) <4313>* **WILD CAT. / RIGHT HERE ON EARTH** 21

Feb 60. (7") *(CL 15115) <7P 159>* **MY HEART. / I'VE GOT TO GET TO YOU YET** 16

May 60. (7") *(CL 15136)* **PISTOL PACKIN' MAMA. / WEEPING WILLOW** 15 –

May 60. (lp) *<(T 1342)>* **CRAZY TIMES** 12 Sep 59
– Crazy times / She she little Sheila / Darlene / Everybody's got a date but me / Why don't you people learn how to drive / Green back dollar / Big fat Saturday night / Mitchiko from Tokyo / Hot dollar / Accentuate the postive / Blue eyes crying in the rain / Pretty Pearly. *(re-iss. +c.1970's on 'M.F.P.', re-iss. Oct87 on 'Tower')*

Oct 60. (7") *<4442>* **ANNA ANNABELLE. / PISTOL PACKIN' MAMA** –

Nov 60. (7") *(CL 15169)* **ANNA ANNABELLE. / ACCENT-TCHUATE THE POSITIVE** –

Jan 61. (7") *(CL 15179)* **JEZEBEL. / MAYBE**

Feb 61. (7") *(CL 15185) <4525>* **IF YOU WANT LOVIN'. / MISTER LONELINESS**

May 61. (7") *(CL 15202)* **SHE SHE LITTLE SHEILA. / HOT DOLLAR** 22 Jul 60

Aug 61. (7") *(CL 15215)* **I'M GOING HOME. / LOVE OF A MAN** 36

Nov 61. (7") *(CL 15231)* **BRAND NEW BEAT. / UNCHAINED MELODY**

Mar 62. (7") *(CL 15243)* **LUCKY STAR. / BABY DON'T BELIEVE HIM**

Aug 62. (7") *(CL 15264)* **KING OF FOOLS. / BE BOP A LULA 2 (with The CHARLES BLACKWELL ORCHESTRA)**

Feb 63. (7") *(CL 15290)* **HELD FOR QUESTIONING. / YOU'RE STILL IN MY HEART**

Jul 63. (7") *(CL 15307)* **CRAZY BEAT. / HIGH BLOOD PRESSURE**

Aug 63. (lp) *<(T 20453)>* **THE CRAZY BEAT OF GENE VINCENT**
– Crazy beat / Important words / It's been nice / Lonesome boy / Good lovin' / I'm gonna catch me a rat / Rip it up / High blood pressure / That's the trouble with love / Weeping willow / Tear drops / Gone, gone, gone. *(re-iss. 1983 as 'CRAZY BEAT' on 'E.M.I.') (cd-iss. Nov99 on 'Magic'; 523015-2)*

— now w / **TIM BATES** – guitar, vocals / **JOHN REECE** – bass, vocals / **JEM FIELD** – tenor sax, vocals / **ERIC BAKER** – keyboards / **VICTOR CLARK** – drums, percussion

Columbia Columbia

Nov 63. (7") *(DB 7174)* **WHERE HAVE YOU BEEN ALL MY LIFE. / TEMPTATION BABY**

Apr 64. (7") *(DB 7218)* **HUMPITY DUMPITY. / LOVE 'EM LEAVE 'EM KINDA GUY**

Jul 64. (7") *(DB 7293)* **LA DEN LA DEN DA DA. / BEGINNING OF THE END**

Sep 64. (7") *(DB 7343)* **PRIVATE DETECTIVE. / YOU ARE MY SUNSHINE**

Oct 64. (lp) *(33SX 1646)* **SHAKIN' UP A STORM**
– Hey-hey-hey-hey / Lavender blue / Private detective / Shimmy shammy shingle / Someday (you'll want me to want you) / Another Saturday night / Slippin' and slidin' / Long tall Sally / Send me some lovin' / Love love love / Good golly, miss Molly / Baby blue / Susie Q / You are my sunshine. *(re-iss. +c.Jun83 as 'PLAYIN' UP A STORM' on 'E.M.I.') (cd-iss. Aug97 on 'E.M.I.'; DORIG 124) (cd re-iss. Feb02 on 'Magic'; 3930159)*

London Challenge

Sep 66. (7") *(HLH 10079)* **BIRD DOGGIN'. / AIN'T THAT MUCH TO DO**

Dec 66. (7") *(HLH 10099* **LONELY STREET. / I'VE GOT MY EYES ON YOU**

Sep 67. (lp) *(HAH 8333)* **GENE VINCENT**
– I've got my eyes on you / Ain't that too much / Bird doggin' / Love is a bird / Lonely street / Hurtin' for you baby / Poor man's prison / Born to be a rolling stone / Hi lili hi lo / I'm a lonesome fugitive. *(re-iss. +c.Aug82 as 'BIRD-DOGGIN'' on 'Bulldog')*

1967. (7") **BORN TO BE A ROLLING STONE. / HURTIN' FOR YOU BABY** [–] [ ]
(re-iss. later on 'Playground')

not iss. Forever

1968. (7") **STORY TO THE ROCKERS. / PICKIN' POPPIES** [–] [ ]

— w / **MARS BONFIRE** – guitar / **GRANT JOHNSON** – keyboards / **RED RHODES** – steel guitar / **SKIP BATTIN** – bass / **JIM GORDON** – drums

Dandelion Elektra

1969. (7") *(S 4596)* **BE BOP A LULA '69. / RUBY BABY** [ ] [–]
Jan 70. (7") *(S 4974)* **WHITE LIGHTNING. / SCARLET RIBBONS** [ ] [–]
Jan 70. (lp) *(63754) <102>* **I'M BACK AND I'M PROUD** [ ] [–]
– Rockin' Robin / In the pines / Be bop a lula / Rainbow at midnight / Black letter / White lightning / Sexy ways / Ruby baby / Lotta lovin' / Circle never broken / I heard that lonesome whistle / Scarlet ribbons. *(cd-iss. 1987 on 'Nightlife Communications') (cd-iss. Dec94 on 'See For Miles')*

— now w/several musicians incl. **CHRIS DARROW**

Kama Sutra Kama Sutra

1970. (lp) *(2361009) <2019>* **IF ONLY YOU COULD SEE ME TODAY** [ ] [ ]
– Sunshine / I need woman's love / Slow times comin' / Danse Colinda / Geese / 500 miles / Listen to the music / If only you could see me today / A million shades of blue.
Jan 70. (7") **SUNSHINE. / GEESE** [–] [ ]
above was recorded with UK band KANSAS HOOK early in Oct'71.
Nov 70. (7") *(2013 018)* **THE DAY THE WORLD TURNED BLUE. / HIGH OF LIFE** [ ] [–]
Jan 71. (lp) *<(KSBS2027)>* **THE DAY THE WORLD TURNED BLUE** [ ] [ ]
– How I love them old songs / High on life / North Carloina line / You can make it if you try / Our souls / Looking back / The day the world turned blue / Boppin' the blues / There is something on your mind / Oh lonesome me / The woman in black.
Jan 71. (7") **THE DAY THE WORLD TURNED BLUE. / HOW I LOVE THEM OLD SONGS** [–] [ ]

— Sadly on the 12th Oct'71, GENE VINCENT died of a bleeding ulcer. He was just 36.

– (selective) compilations, etc. –

all below on 'Capitol' unless otherwise stated

Oct 85. (lp/c) *(EG 260760-/-4)* **THE BEST OF GENE VINCENT AND HIS BLUE CAPS** [ ] [ ]
– Race with the Devil / Be-bop-a-lula / Woman love / I sure miss you / Crazy legs / Gonna back up baby / Who slapped John / Important words / Rollin' Dany / In my dreams / Baby blues '57 / Git it / Somebody help me / Summertime / Beautiful brown eyes / Say mama. *(cd-iss. Jul88)*
Jul 88. (lp/c/cd) *See For Miles; (SEE/+K/+CD 233)* **INTO THE SEVENTIES** [ ] [–]
(cd re-iss. Sep00; same) (below cd re-iss. May02; same)
May 89. (lp/c/cd) *See For Miles; (SEE/+K/+CD 253)* **THE EP COLLECTION** [ ] [–]
Aug 90. (6xcd-box) *(CDS 7945932)* **THE GENE VINCENT CD BOXED SET: THE COMPLETE CAPITOL & COLUMBIA RECORDINGS 1956-64** [ ] [ ]
– (BE BOP A LULA / DANCE TO THE BOP / GIT IT / SAY MAMA / WILD CAT / KING OF . . .)
Nov 92. (cd) *Magnum Force; (CDMF 087)* **REBEL HEART VOL.1** [ ] [ ]
Apr 95. (cd) *Magnum Force; (CDMF 093)* **REBEL HEART VOL.2** [ ] [ ]
Apr 96. (cd) *Magnum Force; (CDMF 096)* **REBEL HEART VOL.3** [ ] [ ]
Feb 97. (cd) *Razor & Tie; <(RE 2123)>* **THE SCREAMING END: THE BEST OF GENE VINCENT** [ ] Jan97 [ ]
Mar 97. (cd) *Magnum Force; (CDMF 097)* **REBEL HEART VOL.4** [ ] [ ]
Jan 98. (cd) *Camden; (74321 55844-2)* **500 MILES** [ ] [ ]
Feb 98. (cd) *Disky; (TO 86094-2)* **THE ORIGINAL** [ ] [ ]
Mar 98. (cd) *Eagle; (EDMCD 028)* **THE MASTERS** [ ] [–]
Apr 98. (cd) *Rollercoaster; (RCCD 3031)* **THE LOST DALLAS SESSIONS 1957-1958** [ ] [ ]
Apr 98. (cd) *Magnum Force; (CDMF 099)* **REBEL HEART VOL.5** [ ] [ ]
Jun 98. (cd) *See For Miles; (SEECD 492)* **THE EP COLLECTION** [ ] [ ]
Apr 99. (cd) *Magnum Force; (CDMF 101)* **REBEL HEART VOL.6** [ ] [ ]
Jan 00. (cd) *Magnum Force; (CDMF 020)* **ON THE ROAD AGAIN** [ ] [ ]
Mar 00. (cd) *Magnum Force; (CDMF 089)* **THE LEGENDARY BLUE CAPS** [ ] [ ]
Apr 00. (cd) *Magnum Force; (CDMF 102)* **REBEL HEART VOL.7** [ ] [ ]
Oct 00. (cd) *Members Edition; (UAE 31292)* **GENE VINCENT** [ ] [ ]
Feb 01. (cd) *EMI Plus; (5761420)* **THE STORY** [ ] [ ]
Mar 01. (cd/c) *Castle Pulse; (PLS CD/MC 383)* **BE-BOP-A-LULA** [ ] [ ]
Jul 01. (cd) *E.M.I.; (533632-2)* **BLUE JEAN BOP / GENE VINCENT ROCKS** [ ] [ ]
Oct 01. (10"lp) *Stomper Time; (STEN 7)* **THE BE BOP BOOGIE BOY** [ ] [–]
May 02. (cd) *Magnum Force; (CDMF 109)* **BIRD DOGGIN': THE COMPLETE CHALLENGE SESSIONS** [ ] [ ]
Jul 03. (cd) *Magnum Force; (CDMF 108)* **REBEL HEART VOL.8** [ ] [ ]

the VINES

Formed: Sydney, Australia . . . late 1999 by frontman CRAIG NICHOLLS, a NIRVANA-obsessed McDonalds worker who pulled together PATRICK MATTHEWS, RYAN GRIFFITHS and DAVID OLLIFFE. Named after NICHOLLS' dad's band from the 60's (although they were called the VYNES), the group began performing at house parties where they would amuse the guests with NIRVANA and MUDHONEY covers. It wasn't until 2001 that they issued their debut single, a roaring number entitled 'FACTORY', which sounded like a lost song from COBAIN and crew, with screeching vocals aplenty and a chorus to die for. This led to their signing with 'Heavenly' in the UK, and the VINES were shipped off to L.A. to record their debut album, all the while being compared to Jesus by the ever reliable NME. It wasn't until summer 2002 that the ensemble would return, clutching a handful of admittedly great rock songs with the unfettering of the album 'HIGHLY EVOLVED'. 'GET FREE', the debut single was grunge from the very first note, with NICHOLLS even singing in unison with his guitar – just like COBAIN. The hollowed out sound of 'OUTTATHAWAY' was much more intense, and the 90-minute pop/punk blast of 'HIGHLY EVOLVED' was just a smack in the face. However it was not all grind-core grunge; the group also showed their 'sensitive' side (with NICHOLLS basically saying "look how tortured I am") with such trite stuff as 'AUTUMN SHADE' and the cringeworthy 'HOMESICK', all pianos and welling tears. During interviews with the group NICHOLLS also admitted that his two favourite things were "a McDonalds meal and a SUEDE album". McDonalds was bad enough, but SUEDE! The Australian grunge evangelists returned in 2004 with 'WINNING DAYS', a transatlantic Top 30 that critics roundly panned as showcasing the flimsiest of musical progressions without the debut's hooks. The Cod-psyche cover art was a clue to their latest prop, a nod to the quasi-lysergic melodies of 'TV PRO' and 'EVIL TOWN', even if more familiar sounding opener 'RIDE' was lifted – along with minor hit 'WINNING DAYS' – as a lead single, making the UK Top 30. CRAIG NICHOLLS' behaviour subsequently became increasingly unpredictable, culminating in his being charged with assaulting a photographer after a promotional appearance in Sydney. While the charges were later dropped, he was diagnosed as suffering from a type of autism known as Asperger's Syndrome. While NICHOLLS' looks likely to preclude any further full scale touring, it didn't stop him recording and the VINES finally returned – with ANDY KENT of YOU AM I filling in on bass following the departure of MATTHEWS for YOUTH GROUP – on 'VISION VALLEY' (2006). Critics still weren't ready to be won over by their magpie concoctions, which ranged from the bile-spitting likes of 'GROSS OUT' and 'DOPE TRAIN', to the handclap stomp of self-fulfilling non-hit 'DON'T LISTEN TO THE RADIO' and psych-lite of 'SPACESHIP'.

• **Covers:** I'M ONLY SLEEPING (Beatles).

Album rating: HIGHLY EVOLVED (*7) / WINNING DAYS (*4) / VISION VALLEY (*6)

CRAIG NICHOLLS (b.31 Aug'77) – vocals, guitar / **PATRICK MATTHEWS** – bass, vocals / **DAVID OLLIFFE** – drums

Illustrious Artists — not iss.

2001. (ltd-7"+green) *(IARC 002)* **HOT LEATHER. / SUNCHILD** — [–] Austra [–]

Rex — not iss.

Oct 01. (ltd-7") *(REKD 195)* **FACTORY. / AIN'T NO ROOM / DROWN THE BAPTISTS** — [ ] [–]

Heavenly — Capitol

Apr 02. (7"/cd-s) *(HVN 112/+CD)* **HIGHLY EVOLVED. / SUN CHILD** — [32] [–]

— **HAMISH ROSSER** – drums; repl. OLLIFFE

— added **RYAN GRIFFITHS** – guitar

Jun 02. (7") *(HVN 113)* **GET FREE. / BLUES RIFF** — [24] Jul02 [ ]
(cd-s) *(HVN 113CD)* <550942> – ('A') / Down at the club / Hot leather.

Jul 02. (lp/cd) *(HVNLP 36/+CD)* <537527> **HIGHLY EVOLVED** — [3] [ ]
– Highly evolved / Autumn shade / Outtathaway / Sunshinin' / Homesick / Get free / Country yard / Factory / In the jungle / Mary Jane / Ain't no room / 1969.

Oct 02. (7") *(HVN 120)* **OUTTATHAWAY. / MS. JACKSON** — [20] [ ]
(cd-s+=) *(HVN 120CDS)* <551223> – Country yard (live) / ('A'-David LaChapelle video).
(cd-s) *(HVN 120CD)* <551215> – ('A') / Don't go (demo) / Get free (live) / ('A'-Alastair McKevitt US film video).

2003. (7"white) <53784> **FUCK THE WORLD. / (same)** — [–] [ ]

Mar 04. (7") *(HVN 137)* **RIDE. / DROWN THE BAPTISTS** — [25] [–]
(cd-s) *(HVN 137CD)* – ('A') / Give up, give out, give in.

Mar 04. (lp/cd) *(HVNLP 48/+CD)* <84338> **WINNING DAYS** — [29] [23]
– Ride / Animal machine / TV pro / Autumn shade II / Evil town / Winning days / She's got something to say to me / Rainfall / Amnesia / Sun child / F.T.W.

May 04. (7") *(HVN 139)* **WINNING DAYS. / LANDSLIDE (demo)** — [42] [–]
(cd-s+=) *(HVN 139CDS)* – Ride (XFM live session) / ('A'-video) / (making of Ride video footage).
(cd-s) *(HVN 139CD)* – ('A') / Watch the world (demo).

— revert to a trio when MATTHEWS left to join YOUTH GROUP

Apr 06. (lp/cd) *(HVNLP 56/+CD)* <31817-2> **VISION VALLEY** — [71] [ ]
– Anysound / Nothin's comin' / Candy daze / Vision valley / Don't listen to the radio / Gross out / Take me back / Going gone / Fuk yeh / Futuretarded / Dope train / Atmos / Spaceship.

– compilations, etc. –

Sep 04. (d-cd) *Heavenly; (EBX 18)* **HIGHLY EVOLVED / WINNING DAYS** — [ ] [–]

☐ VIOLET INDIANA (see under ⇒ COCTEAU TWINS)

□ the WAILERS (see under ⇒ MARLEY, Bob)

Rufus WAINWRIGHT

Born: 22 Jul'73, Rhinebeck, New York, USA. The son of LOUDON WAINWRIGHT III and KATE McGARRIGLE, RUFUS was raised in Canada following his parents' divorce. Steeped in music from an early age, by the time he reached his teens RUFUS was touring with his folk singing family. It'd be the lure of classic torch singing, cabaret and opera, however, which was to really fire the piano player through his formative years. These were influences which he carried over to his pop career, which received an early boost after his father passed (via the legendary VAN DYKE PARKS) a demo to an impressed 'DreamWorks' head Larry Waronker. The label subsequently issued WAINWRIGHT's eponymous 1998 debut album to almost unanimous critical acclaim, RUFUS' incredible voice investing the record's intimate, baroque chamber pop (arrangements by that man PARKS) with a profound emotional charge. Sophomore set, 'POSES' (2001) featured contributions from his sister MARTHA and another second generation musician TEDDY THOMPSON (son of RICHARD and LINDA) as well as the likes of PROPELLERHEADS' ALEX GIFFORD. Less personal then, than his debut but cut from the same singular cloth and basking in that same neo-operatic glow which surrounds RUFUS' songs. 'WANT ONE' followed in 2003, confirming his unique position in contemporary pop. Originally intended to be released as a part of a double set with its predecessor, 'WANT TWO' (2004) was pretty much a continuation of the same, quasi-religious, soul-scouring themes: conflicted sexuality, love lost and found, sin and redemption. Opener 'AGNUS DEI' was a Latinate plea for slate-cleaning communion with God, executed as a Gypsy lament, 'LITTLE SISTER' dressed his projections up in classical garb and 'GAY MESSIAH' addressed the vagaries of homosexual iconicity like a profligate THOM YORKE. Not your average singer/songwriter album, then, but another rakish, regal minor masterpiece from a man who's still more appreciated in the UK than his homeland: released in Britain some months later in March 2005, the record narrowly missed the UK Top 20.

• **Covered:** ACROSS THE UNIVERSE (Beatles).

Album rating: RUFUS WAINWRIGHT (*8) / POSES (*7) / WANT ONE (*5) / WANT TWO (*7)

RUFUS WAINWRIGHT – vocals, acoustic guitar / w/ session people

DreamWorks DreamWorks

Aug 98. (cd) <(DRD 50039)> **RUFUS WAINWRIGHT** [ ] May98 [ ]
– Foolish love / Danny boy / April fools / In my arms / Millbrook / Baby / Beauty mark / Barcelona / Matinee idol / Damned ladies / Sally Ann / Imaginary love.

Jun 01. (cd) <(450237-2)> **POSES** [ ] [ ]
– Cigarettes and chocolate milk / Greek song / Poses / Shadows / California / The tower of learning / Grey gardens / Rebel prince / The consort / One man guy / Evil angel / In a graveyard / Cigarettes and chocolate milk (reprise). *<re-iss. Feb02 +=; 450369-2>* – Across the universe (remix).

Sep 03. (cd) *(4505041) <89612>* **WANT ONE** [ ] [60]
– Oh what a world / I don't know what it is / Vicious world / Movies of myself / Pretty things / Go or go ahead / Vibrate / 14th street / Natasha / Harvester of hearts / Beautiful child / Want / 11:11 / Dinner at eight. *(UK+=)* – Es mus sein / Velvet curtain rag.

Jul 04. (cd-s) *(9863229)* **I DON'T KNOW WHAT IT IS / L'ABSENCE (live at the Fillmore) / 14TH STREET (live at the Fillmore)** [74] [–]

Mar 05. (cd) *(210309-2) <371600>* **WANT TWO** [21] Nov04 [ ]
– Agnus dei / The one you love / Peach trees / Little sister / The art teacher (live) / Hometown waltz / This love affair / Gay messiah / Memphis skyline / Waiting for a dream / Crumb by crumb / Old whore's diet. *(UK+=)* – Coeur de Parisienne – reprise d'Arletty (live) / Quand vous mourez de nos amours (live). *(ltd-cd w/dvd+=; 9880444)* – (DVD tracks). *<US lp-iss.Oct05 on 'Zoe'; ZOE 1075> (d-cd-iss. Nov05++; 9887273)* – WANT ONE

Tom WAITS

Born: 7 Dec'49, Pomona, California, USA. Signed to 'Asylum' in 1973, after being spotted at the Troubadour club. His debut album 'CLOSING TIME' produced by Jerry Yester (ex-LOVIN' SPOONFUL), didn't sell greatly, but it did contain 'OL '55' which was soon covered by The EAGLES on their album 'On The Border'. 'THE HEART OF SATURDAY NIGHT' (1974) was more proficient, his downtrodden JACK KEROUAC meets CHARLES BUKOWSKI persona beginning to develop. With his distinctive Billy Goat Gruff vocals he sounded frighteningly like he'd been drinking industrial strength paint stripper since childhood. A born raconteur, his sharply observed tales of American lowlife were set against a musical backdrop of smokey blues and jazz stylings. The live album 'NIGHTHAWKS AT THE DINER' (1975) was WAITS in his element, reeling off wry vignettes with casual ease. 'SMALL CHANGE' (1976) was a confident step forward, his booze-sodden recollections more focused and his songwriting more complex on tracks like 'TOM TRAUBERT'S BLUES'. He even attempted to cultivate his parched vocals on 'FOREIGN AFFAIR' (1977), duetting with BETTE MIDLER for 'I NEVER TALK TO STRANGERS'. With 'BLUE VALENTINE' (1978) and 'HEARTATTACK AND VINE' (1980), WAITS opted for a combination of supple R&B tracks and heartbroken love ballads, the latter set spawning the haunting 'JERSEY GIRL' which was later covered by BRUCE SPRINGSTEEN. This was the end of an era for the maverick singer/songwriter as he signed to 'Island' and employed a more experimental strategy. The gloriously titled 'SWORDFISHTROMBONES' (1983) introduced the new WAITS sound, a surrealistic cut up of mutant jazz, skewed rhythms, jarring guitar and wildly inspired lyrics. 'RAIN DOGS' (1985) advanced this formula, again employing an array of session musicians to realise his eccentric musical vision. Adapted from a song on 'SWORDFISH..', 'FRANKS WILD YEARS' (1987) was set to a musical stage show that included the brilliant horn-driven weirdness of 'HANG ON ST. CHRISTOPHER'. Live soundtrack 'BIG TIME' (1988) was similar in tone, taking material from all his 'Island' recordings to date. With a string of acting credits

TOM WAITS

already behind him as well as 1982's 'ONE FROM THE HEART' (with soundtrack CRYSTAL GAYLE), he scored Jim Jarmusch's 'NIGHT ON EARTH' in 1992. His next album proper was 'BONE MACHINE', released later the same year. The title was apt, a stark collection of minimalistic clankings and dark, muted musings. 'BLACK RIDER' (1993) held the musical fruits of a collaboration between director ROBERT WILSON and uber-Beat poet WILLIAM BURROUGHS. It was six long years before WAITS returned to the fold, the 'Epitaph' label (more identified with today's hardcore/punk scene) astonishingly taking up the reins for his marvellous comeback set, 'MULE VARIATIONS' (1999); if his gruff vox could be singled out as one type of music, it would indeed be "hard core". Now nearly fifty years of age (and looking every part of it!), WAITS had his first UK Top 10 success with 'MULE . . .', and even more importantly, his debut into the American Top 30. WAITS is an artist with defiantly singular vision and is a rare commodity in a marketplace where so often the blind lead the blind in a musical wild goose chase for the next trend. Why bother with a double set when two simultaneously-released single albums will do, May 2002's 'BLOOD MONEY' and 'ALICE', gave WAITS another cross-Atlantic success. Some might claim that WAITS has been 'REAL GONE' for decades, but if the title of his umpteenth album (released 2004) was stating the obvious, the music wasn't. Shorn of frippery, disassembled, distorted and scar-naked, it roared to the gun-metal rhythms of MARC RIBOT and LES CLAYPOOL (ex-PRIMUS), as WAITS barked out agit-surrealist protest: 'SINS OF MY FATHER' howled against cancerous politics to a chain-gang lurch; 'DAY AFTER TOMORROW' was a heroic rasp for sanity, 'HOIST THAT RAG' a death-growl bolero, an anti-social club for embattled guerillas. That this kind of in-house subversion managed to breach the US Top 30 (UK Top 20) must be proof of something; if not a popular revelation, then at least evidence that music hasn't drowned in market-slop just yet.

• **Songwriters:** Pens own songs except; WHAT KEEPS MAN ALIVE (Kurt Weill) / HEIGH-HO (from 'Snow White') / IT'S ALL RIGHT WITH ME (Cole Porter). From 1987, his material was co-written with wife and Irish playwright Kathleen Brennan, whom he married on the 31st December '81.
• **Trivia:** In the late 70's, he parted company with girlfriend/singer RICKIE LEE JONES. In 1991, he sued a radio ad company for using a soundalike in a chips commercial and won nearly $2.5 million.

Album rating: CLOSING TIME (*7) / THE HEART OF SATURDAY NIGHT (*6) / NIGHTHAWKS AT THE DINER (*6) / SMALL CHANGE (*8) / FOREIGN AFFAIRS (*6) / BLUE VALENTINE (*6) / HEARTATTACK AND VINE (*7) / BOUNCED CHECKS compilation (*6) / ONE FROM THE HEART soundtrack with Crystal Gayle (*6) / SWORDFISHTROMBONES (*9) / THE ASYLUM YEARS compilation (*8) / RAIN DOGS (*9) / FRANKS WILD YEARS (*7) / BIG TIME live soundtrack (*7) / NIGHT ON EARTH soundtrack (*5) / BONE MACHINE (*8) / THE BLACK RIDER (*5) / BEAUTIFUL MALADIES – THE ISLAND YEARS compilation (*8) / MULE VARIATIONS (*7) / BLOOD MONEY (*7) / ALICE (*7) / REAL GONE (*6)

TOM WAITS – vocals, piano, accordion

Asylum Elektra

May 73. (lp) *(SYL 9007)* *<SD 5061>* **CLOSING TIME**
– Ol' 55 / I hope that I don't fall in love with you / Virginia Ave/ Old shoes (and picture postcards) / Midnight lullaby / Martha / Rosie / Lonely / Ice cream man / Little trip to Heaven (on the wings of your love) / Grapefruit moon / Closing time. *(re-iss. Jun76; K 53030) (cd-iss. Feb93 on 'WEA'; 960836-2)*

May 73. (7") **OL '55. / MIDNIGHT LULLABY** –

Jan 74. (lp) *(K 53035)* *<7E 1015>* **THE HEART OF SATURDAY NIGHT**
– New coat of paint / San Diego serenade / Semi suite / Shiver me timbers / Diamonds on my windshield / (Looking for) The heart of Saturday night / Fumblin' with the blues / Please call me baby / Depot, depot / Drunk on the Moon / The ghosts of Saturday night (after hours at Napoleon's pizza house). *(re-iss. Jun76; same) (cd-iss. 1989 on 'WEA'; 960 597-2)*

Mar 74. (7") *<45213>* **DIAMONDS ON MY WINDSHIELD. / SAN DIEGO SERENADE** –

Jun 75. (7") *<45233>* **NEW COAT OF PAINT. / BLUE SKIES** –

Oct 75. (7") *<45262>* **(LOOKING FOR) THE HEART OF SATURDAY NIGHT. / DIAMONDS ON MY WINDSHIELD** –

— with **MIKE MELVOIN** – piano / **JIM HUGHART** – bass / **BILL GOODWIN** – drums

Dec 75. (d-lp) *(SYSP 903)* *<7E 2008>* **NIGHTHAWKS AT THE DINER (live)** Oct75
– (opening intro) / Emotional weather report / (intro) / On a foggy night / (intro) / Eggs and sausage / (intro) / Better off without a wife / Nighthawk postcards (from Easy street) / (intro) / Warm beer and cold women / (intro) / Puttnam County / Spare parts 1 (a nocturnal emission) / Nobody / (intro) / Big Joe and Phantom 309 / Spare parts 2 and closing. *(re-iss. Jun76; K 63002) (cd-iss. 1989 on 'WEA'; 960 620-2)*

— retained **HUGHART** + new **SHELLY MANNE** – drums / **LEW TABACKIN** – tenor sax

Nov 76. (7") *<45371>* **STEP RIGHT UP. / THE PIANO HAS BEEN DRINKING (NOT ME)** –

May 77. (lp) *(K 52050)* *<7E 1078>* **SMALL CHANGE** Nov 76 89
– Tom Traubert's blues / Step right up / Jitterbug boy / I wish I was in New Orleans / The piano has been drinking (not me) / Invitation to the blues / Pasties and a g-string / Bad liver and a broken heart / The one that got away / Small change / I can't wait to get off work. *(cd-iss. 1989 on 'WEA'; 960 612-2)*

— **FRANK VICARI** – tenor sax / **JACK SHELDON** – trumpet repl. TABACKIN

Oct 77. (lp) *(K 53068)* *<7E 1117>* **FOREIGN AFFAIRS**
– Cinny's waltz / Muriel / I never talk to strangers / Jack and Neal – California here I come / A sight for sore eyes / Potter's field / Burma shave / Barber shop / Foreign affair. *(cd-iss. Mar95 on 'WEA'; 7559 60618-2)*

— **RICK LAWSON** – drums repl. MANNE / added **ROLAND BAUTISTA** + **RAY CRAWFORD** – guitar / **BYRON MILLER** – bass / **DA WILLIE CONGA** – piano / **HAROLD BATTISTE** – piano

Apr 79. (7") *<45539>* **SOMEWHERE. / RED SHOES BY THE DRUGSTORE** –

Aug 79. (lp) *(K 53088)* *<6E 162>* **BLUE VALENTINE**
– Somewhere / Red shoes by the drugstore / Christmas card from a hooker in Minneapolis / Romeo is bleeding / Wrong side of the road / Whistlin' past the graveyard / Kentucky Avenue / A sweet little bullet from a pretty blue gun / Blue valentines. *(cd-iss. Feb93; 7559 60533-2)*

— retained **HUGHART** + **BAUTISTA** + new **LARRY TAYLOR** – upright bass / **RONNIE BARRON** – organ / **GREG COHEN** – bass / **PLAS JOHNSON** – sax / **BIG JOHN THOMASSIE** – drums

Oct 80. (lp/c) *(K/K4 52252)* *<6E 295>* **HEARTATTACK AND VINE** 96
– Saving all my love for you / On the nickel / In shades / Downtown / Jersey girl / Til the money runs out / Mr. Segal / Ruby's arms. *(cd-iss. 1989 on 'WEA') (re-iss. cd May93; 7559 60547-2)*

Dec 80. (7") *<47077>* **JERSEY GIRL. / HEARTATTACK AND VINE** –

Nov 81. (lp/c) *(K/K4 52316)* **BOUNCED CHECKS** (compilation, some live) –
– Heartattack and vine / Jersey girl / Eggs and sausage / I never talk to strangers / The piano has been drinking (not me) / Whistlin' past the graveyard / Mr. Henry / Diamonds on my windshield / Burma shave / Tom Traubert's blues.

— now with many session people from above incl. **VICTOR FELDMAN** – percussion

C.B.S. Columbia

Feb 83. (lp/c; by TOM WAITS & CRYSTAL GAYLE) *(CBS/40 70215)* *<37703>* **ONE FROM THE HEART** (soundtrack)
– Opening montage: Tom's piano intro – Once upon a town – The wages of love / (CRYSTAL GAYLE solo track) / Picking up after you / (CRYSTAL GAYLE solo track) / Broken bicycles (TOM WAITS solo) / I beg your pardon (TOM WAITS solo) / Little boy blue (TOM WAITS solo) / Instrumental montage: The tango – Circus girl / You can't unring a bell (TOM WAITS solo) / This one's from the heart / (CRYSTAL GAYLE solo track) / Presents. *(re-iss. Jan91 cd/c/lp; 467609-2/-4/-1) <cd re-mast.Jan04 on 'Legacy-Columbia'+=; CK 85813>* – Candy apple red (**) / Once upon a town – Empty rockets (**).

— **FRED TACKETT** – guitar + **STEPHEN TAYLOR HODGES** – drums repl. BAUTISTA + LAWSON / added **FRANCIS THUMM** – pump organ / **RANDY ALDCROFT** – horns

Island Island

Sep 83. (lp/c) *(ILPS/ICM 9762)* *<90095>* **SWORDFISHTROMBONES** 62

– Underground / Shore leave / Dave the butcher / Johnsburg, Illinois / 16 shells from a thirty-ought-six / Town with no cheer / In the neighbourhood / Just another sucker on the vine / Frank's wild years / Swordfishtrombones / Down, down, down / Soldier's things / Gin soaked boy / Trouble's braids / Rainbirds. *(re-iss. Sep86 lp/c; same) (cd-iss. Nov87; CID 9762) (re-iss. cd Jun89; IMCD 48) (re-iss. lp Jan94 + May94; ILPM 9762)*

Oct 83. (7") *(IS 141)* **IN THE NEIGHBOURHOOD. / FRANK'S WILD YEARS** ☐ ☐

— **MARC RIBOT** – guitar + **MICHAEL BLAIR** – drums, percussion repl. TACKETT, THUMM + HODGES / **WILLIAM SCHIMMEL** – piano / **RAPLH CARNEY** – sax, clarinet + **BOB FUNK** – trombone repl. FELDMAN + ALDCROFT

Oct 85. (lp/c)(cd) *(ILPS/ICT 9803)(CID 131) <90299>* **RAIN DOGS** 29 ☐
– Singapore / Clap hands / Cemetery polka / Jockey full of bourbon / Tango till they're sore / Big black Mariah / Diamonds and gold / Hang down your head / Time / Rain dogs / Midtown / Ninth and headpin / Gun Street girl / Union square / Blind love / Walking Spanish / Downtown train / Bride of Rain dog / Anywhere I lay my head. *(re-iss. cd.Aug89 & Apr91; IMCD 49)*

Nov 85. (7"/12") *(IS/12IS 253)* **DOWNTOWN TRAIN. / TANGO 'TILL THEY'RE SORE** ☐ ☐

Feb 86. (7") *(IS 260)* **IN THE NEIGHBOURHOOD. / SINGAPORE** ☐ ☐
(d7"+=) *(ISD 260)* – Tango till they're sore (live) / Rain dogs (live).
(12") *(12IS 260)* – ('A'side) / Jockey full of bourbon / Tango till they're sore (live) / 16 shells from a thirty-ought-six (live).

— Past live group **FRED TACKETT** – guitar / **RICHIE HAYWARD** – drums / **LARRY TAYLOR** – upright bass. Retained only **TAYLOR, CARNEY, SCHIMMEL** / new: **MORRIS TEPPER** – guitar / **FRANCIS THUMM** – pump organ (on some) / guest **DAVID HIDALGO** – accordion

Aug 87. (lp/c/cd) *(ITW/+C/CD 3) <90572>* **FRANKS WILD YEARS** 20 ☐
– Hang on St. Christopher / Straight to the top (rhumba) / Blow wind blow / Temptation / Innocent when you dream (barroom) / I'll be gone / I'll take New York / Telephone call from Istanbul / Cold cold ground / Train song / Yesterday is here / Please wake me up / Frank's theme / More than rain / Way down in the hole / Straight to the top (Vegas). *(re-iss. cd.Jun89 & Apr91; IMCD 50)*

— 1988 live band **WILLIE SCHWARZ** – keyboards, accordion repl. SCHIMMEL + TEPPER

Sep 88. (lp/c/cd) *(ITW/+C/CD 4) <90987>* **BIG TIME** (live soundtrack) 84 ☐
– 16 shells from a thirty-ought-six / Red shoes / Underground *[cd-only]* / Cold cold ground / Straight to the top *[cd-only]* / Yesterday is here *[cd-only]* / Way down in the hole / Falling down / Strange weather / Big black Mariah / Rain dogs / Train song / Johnsburg, Illinois *[cd-only]* / Ruby's arms *[cd-only]* / Telephone call from Istanbul / Clap hands *[cd-only]* / Gun street girl / Time. *(cd-iss. Mar97; IMCD 249)*

Sep 88. (7") *(IS 370)* **16 SHELLS FROM A THIRTY-OUGHT-SIX (live). / BIG BLACK MARIAH (live)** ☐ ☐
(12"+=) *(12IS 370)* – Ruby's arms (live).

May 92. (cd/c) *<(510929-2/-4)>* **NIGHT ON EARTH** (soundtrack) ☐ ☐
– Back in the good old world / Los Angeles mood (chromium descensions) / Los Angeles theme (another private dick) / New York theme (hey, you can have that heart attack outside, buddy) / New York mood (a new haircut and a busted lip) / Baby, I'm not a baby anymore (Beatrice theme) / Good old world (waltz) / Carnival (Brunello del Montalcino) / On the old side of the world (vocal) / Good old world (gypsy instrumental) / Paris mood (un de fromage) / Dragging a dead priest / Helsinki mood / Carnival Bob's confession / Good old world (waltz vocal) / On the other side of the world (instrumental).

Aug 92. (7") *(IS 537)* **GOIN' OUT WEST. / A LITTLE RAIN** ☐ –
(10"+=/cd-s+=) *(10IS/CID 537)* – The ocean doesn't want me / Back in the good old world (gypsy).

Sep 92. (cd/c/lp) *(CID/ICT/ILPS 9993) <512580>* **BONE MACHINE** 26 ☐
– Earth died screaming / Dirt in the ground / Such a scream / All stripped down / Who are you / The ocean doesn't want me / Jesus gonna behave / A little rain / In the Colosseum / Goin' out west / Murder in the red barn / Black wings / Whistle down the wind / I don't wanna grow up / Let me get up on it / That feel.

Nov 93. (cd/c/lp) *(CID/ICT/ILPS 8021) <518559>* **THE BLACK RIDER** 47 ☐
– Lucky day overture / The black rider / November / Just the right bullets / Black box theme / 'T ain't no sin / Flash pan hunter intro / That's the way / The briar and the rose / Russian dance / Gospel train-orchestra / I'll shoot the Moon / Flash pan hunter / Crossroads / Gospel train / Interlude / Oily night / Lucky day / The last rose of summer / Carnival.

— 3 of above tracks were co-written with author WILLIAM S. BURROUGHS

Epitaph Epitaph

Apr 99. (cd/c/lp) *<(8 6547-2/-4/-1)>* **MULE VARIATIONS** 9 30
– Big in Japan / Lowside of the road / Hold on / Get behind the mule / House where nobody lives / Cold water / Pony / What's he building? / Black market baby / Eyeball kid / Picture in a frame / Chocolate Jesus / Georgia Lee / Filipino box spring hog / Take it with me / Come on up to the house.

Jun 99. (cd-s) *(1020-2)* **HOLD ON / BIG IN JAPAN / FLEDDERJON** ☐ ☐

Anti- Anti-

May 02. (cd/lp) *<(8 6629-2/-1)>* **BLOOD MONEY** 21 32
– Misery is the river of the world / Everything goes to hell / Coney Island baby / All the world is green / God's away on business / Another man's vine / Knife chase / Lullaby / Starving in the belly of a whale / The part you throw away / Woe / Calliope / A good man is hard to find.

May 02. (cd/lp) *<(8 6632-2/-1)>* **ALICE** 20 33
– Alice / Everything you can think / Flower's grave / No one knows I'm gone / Kommienezuspadt / Poor Edward / Table top Joe / Lost in the harbour / We're all mad here / Watch her disappear / Reeperbahn / I'm still here / Fish & bird / Barcarolle / Fawn.

Oct 04. (cd) *<(8 6678-2)>* **REAL GONE** 16 28
– Top of the hill / Hoist that rag / Sins of my father / Shake it / Don't go into that barn / How's it gonna end / Metropolitan glide / Dead and lovely / Circus / Trampled rose / Green grass / Baby gonna leave me / Clang boom steam / Make it rain / Day after tomorrow.

– compilations, etc. –

Apr 84. (d-lp/c) *Asylum; (960 321-1/-4)* **THE ASYLUM YEARS** ☐ ☐
– Diamonds on my windshield / (Looking for) The heart of Saturday night / Martha / The ghosts of Saturday night / Grapefruit Moon / Small change / Burma slave / I never talk to strangers / Tom Traubert's blues / Blue valentine / Potter's field / Kentucky avenue / Somewhere / Ruby's arms. *(cd-iss. Oct86; 960 494-2)* – (omitted 9 tracks but added 3 others).

Jul 91. (cd/c/lp) *Edsel; (ED/C+/ED 332)* **THE EARLY YEARS** (rare & demos) ☐ –
– Goin' down slow / Poncho's lament / I'm your late night evening prostitute / Had me a girl / Ice cream man / Rockin' chair / Virginia Ave. / Midnight lullabye / When you ain't got nobody / Little trip to Heaven / Frank's song / Looks like I'm up shit creek again / So long I'll see you. *(re-iss. Feb97 & Mar98 on 'Manifesto'; PT 340601)*

Nov 92. (d-cd) *Island; (ITSCD 5)* **SWORDFISHTROMBONES / RAIN DOGS** ☐ ☐

Feb 93. (cd/c) *Edsel; (ED CD/MC 371)* **THE EARLY YEARS VOL.2** ☐ –
– Hope I don't fall in love with you / Ol' 55 / Mockin bird / In between love / Blue skies / Nobody / I want you / Shiver me timbers / Grapefruit moon / Diamonds on my windshield / Please call me, baby / So it goes / Old shoes. *(re-iss. Feb97 & Mar98 on 'Manifesto'; PT 340602)*

Mar 93. (7"/c-s) *Elektra; (EKR 162/+C)* **HEARTATTACK AND VINE. / BLUE VALENTINES** ☐ ☐
(cd-s+=) *(EKR 162CD)* – On a foggy night (live) / Intro to a foggy night (live).

Jun 98. (d-cd) *Island; (524 519-2)* **BEAUTIFUL MALADIES – THE ISLAND YEARS** 63 ☐
– Hang on St. Christopher / Temptation / Clap hands / The back rider / Underground / Jockey full of bourbon / Earth died screaming / Innocent when you dream (78) / Straight to the top / Frank's wild years / Singapore / Shore leave / Johnsburg, Illinois / Way down in the hole / Strange weather (live) / Cold, cold ground (live) / November / Downtrain train / 16 shells from a thirty-ought six / Jesus gonna be here / Good old world (waltz) / I don't wanna grow up / Time.

Nov 01. (cd) *Burning Airlines; (PILOT 082)* **DIME STORE NOVELS VOL.1** ☐ –

Mar 02. (cd) *Rhino; <(8122 78351-2)>* **USED SONGS 1973-1980** ☐ ☐

Rick WAKEMAN

Born: 18 May'49, Perivale, Middlesex, England. Aged 16, he attended The Royal College of Music, although interest in playing live and doing sessions led to him dropping out. His in-demand pop session work (i.e. WHITE PLAINS, EDISON LIGHTHOUSE, etc.), saw him working on albums by CAT STEVENS, DAVID BOWIE, T.REX, etc. In 1970, he joined The STRAWBS, but the following year he couldn't turn down YES, as they matched his classical ambitions. He was an on-off YES member during the 70's, subsequently starting his own solo career on 'A&M' records. Prior to this, he had augmented The JOHN SCHROEDER ORCHESTRA on the 1971 'Polydor lp, 'PIANO VIBRATIONS'; (2460 135). Taking themes of history, fiction and legend, he released three well-received (at the time) Top 10 albums between 1973-1975. His second album, 'JOURNEY TO THE CENTRE OF THE EARTH' (an adaptation of the Jules Verne classic), was premiered live at The Royal Festival Hall in January '74, topping the UK charts upon its release that year. With orchestra and choir in tow, he performed it at an open-air Crystal Palace Garden Party, subsequently touring the show around major US venues. His virtuoso, exhibitionist keyboard-playing and flash-rock image (long blonde hair and ankle-length silver capes) was perfectly suited to the live arena, a comparison that could be made with the other famous keys-basher of the era, KEITH EMERSON. Nevertheless, this gruelling tour took its toll, when RICK suffered a minor heart attack nearing the end of the pocket-draining extravaganza. On his recovery, he released the third of these epics, 'KING ARTHUR' in 1975, regarded by many as overblown pomp-rock, although it did have its redeeming moments (i.e. 'MERLIN THE MAGICIAN' and 'SIR LANCELOT & THE BLACK KNIGHT'). Following a move into soundtrack work, notably on Ken Russell's 'LISZTOMANIA' (starring ROGER DALTREY) and 'WHITE ROCK' (a docu-film focussing on the 1976 Winter Olympics), he found time to squeeze in his fourth studio set, 'NO EARTHLY CONNECTION', a record that still managed a Top 10 placing. WAKEMAN returned in 1977 with his '. . . CRIMINAL RECORD', which was a failure both critically and commercially, leading to public attention drifting somewhat, thus his steady decline. He continued to release a plethora of albums, most taking a neo-classical rock/pop or new-age stance. He will probably be remembered in the next century, not for his theatrical rock indulgence, but for the romantic classical style he helped revive.

• **Songwriters:** All his own work, interspersed with little snatches of past classical works. • **Trivia:** Most distinguished session work included; LIFE ON MARS (David Bowie) / CHANGES (Black Sabbath) / MORNING HAS BROKEN (Cat Stevens) / LOU REED's debut album. WAKEMAN was married in the 70's to Ros and settled down in a Buckingham mansion alongside his collection of Rolls Royce's. The couple had three children before their divorce. In the 80's, RICK married ex-model, NINA CARTER, (also of twin-sister outfit, BLONDE ON BLONDE). He fathered another two kids (so far), later finding Christianity. BILL ODDIE (of the GOODIES TV programme) contributed vocals on WAKEMAN's 'JOURNEY' and 'CRIMINAL RECORD'.

Album rating: THE SIX WIVES OF HENRY VIII (*8) / JOURNEY TO THE CENTRE OF THE EARTH (*7) / THE MYTHS & LEGENDS OF KING ARTHUR . . . (*6) / LISTZOMANIA soundtrack (*4) / NO EARTHLY CONNECTION (*5) / WHITE ROCK soundtrack (*6) / RICK WAKEMAN'S CRIMINAL RECORD (*4) / RHAPSODIES (*4) / 1984 (*4) / THE BURNING soundtrack (*5) / ROCK'N'ROLL PROPHET (*3) / G'OLE! soundtrack (*3) / THE COST OF LIVING (*4) / SILENT NIGHTS (*3) / LIVE AT HAMMERSMITH (*4) / COUNTRY AIRS (*5) / THE GOSPELS (*3) / CRIMES OF PASSION soundtrack (*4) / THE FAMILY ALBUM (*4) / A SUITE OF GODS with Ramon Remedios (*4) / ZODIAQUE with Tony Fernandez (*4) / TIME MACHINE (*4) / SEA AIRS (*4) / NIGHT AIRS (*4) / ASPIRANT SUNSET (*4) / ASPIRANT SUNRISE (*4) / BLACK KNIGHTS IN THE COURT OF FERNINAND IV with Mario Fasciano (*4) / PHANTOM POWER soundtrack (*4) / SOFTSWORD: KING JOHN AND THE MAGNA CHARTER (*4) / A WORLD OF WISDOM with Norman Wisdom (*3) / 2000 A.D. INTO THE FUTURE (*4) / AMBIENT SUNSHADOWS (*4) / WAKEMAN WITH WAKEMAN with Adam Wakeman (*4) / HERITAGE SUITE (*4) / AFRICAN BACH (*4) / NO EXPENSE SPARED with Adam (*4) / ROMANCE OF THE VICTORIAN AGE with Adam (*4) / THE SEVEN WONDERS OF THE WORLD (*3) / CIRQUE SURREAL – STATE CIRCUS OF IMAGINATION (*6) / VISIONS (*4) / VOYAGE: THE VERY BEST RICK WAKEMAN compilation (*7) / HUMMINGBIRD w/ Dave Cousins (*5) / OUT THERE . . . (*5)

RICK WAKEMAN – keyboards (a member of YES; Aug71-Jun74, Nov76-Mar80, 1990+)

—— now used various YES people on sessions plus numerous choirs & ensembles.

A&M A&M

Feb 73. (lp/c) *(AMLH/CAM 64361)* **THE SIX WIVES OF HENRY VIII** 7 30
– Catherine of Aragon / Anne of Cleves / Catherine Howard / Jane Seymour / Anne Boleyn / Catherine Parr. *(quad-lp; QU-84361) (cd-iss. 1988; CDA 3229) (re-iss. cd Aug89; 393 229-2) (re-iss. cd Jan92; CDMID 136)*

Mar 73. (7") *(AMS 7061)* **CATHERINE. / ANNE** -
(below A-side was an excerpt of 'CATHERINE PARR')

—— Introduced **ASHLEY HOLT** – vocals / **ROGER NEWELL** – bass / **BARNEY JAMES** – drums / plus The ENGLISH ROCK ENSEMBLE with The LONDON SYMPHONY ORCHESTRA. Narration by actor DAVID HEMMINGS.

May 74. (lp/c) *(AMLH/CAM 63621)* **JOURNEY TO THE CENTRE OF THE EARTH** 1 3
– The journey / Recollections / The battle / The forest. *<US quad-lp 1974; SPQU 3621> (re-iss. Feb85 on 'Hallmark' lp/c; SHM/HSC 3164) (cd-iss. Jan88; CDA 3156) <US cd-iss. 1988 on 'Mobile Fidelity'; MFCD 848> (re-iss. cd Jan92; CDMID 161) (re-iss. May93 on 'Spectrum' cd/c; 550 061-2/-4)*

Oct 74. (7") **THE JOURNEY. / THE RETURN** -

Dec 74. (7") **THE BATTLE. / AND NOW A WORD FROM OUR SPONSOR** -

Apr 75. (lp/c) *(AMLH/CAM 64515)* **THE MYTHS AND LEGENDS OF KING ARTHUR AND THE KNIGHTS OF THE ROUND TABLE** 2 21
– Arthur / Lady of the lake / Guinevere / Sir Lancelot & the Black Knight / Merlin the magician / Sir Galahad / The last battle. *<US quad-lp 1975; SPQU 54515> (cd-iss. 1988; CDA 3230) (re-iss. cd; CDMID 135)*

Jun 75. (7") **MERLIN THE MAGICIAN. / SIR GALAHAD** -
(below 1975 releases with ROGER DALTREY on vocals)

Nov 75. (lp) *(AMLH 64546) <SP 4546>* **LISZTOMANIA** (soundtrack)
– Rienzi – Chopsticks – Fantasia / Love's dream / Dante period / Orpheus song / Hell / Hibernation / Excelsior song / Master race / Rape, pillage and clap / Funerailles / Free song / Peace at last.

Nov 75. (7") *(AMS 7206)* **ORPHEUS SONG. / LOVE'S DREAM**

—— For North & South American tour he trimmed his ENGLISH ROCK ENSEMBLE down to **ASHLEY HOLT** – vocals / **JOHN DUNSTERVILE** – guitar / **ROGER NEWELL** – bass / **TONY FERNANDEZ** – drums / **REG BROOKS + MARTYN SHIELDS** – brass section

Apr 76. (lp/c) *(AMLK/CLK 64583)* **NO EARTHLY CONNECTION** 9 67
– Music reincarnate: (part 1) The warning – (part 2) The maker – (part 3) The spaceman – (part 4) The realization – (part 5) The reaper / The prisoner / The lost cycle.

Jan 77. (lp/c) *(AMLH/CAM 64614)* **WHITE ROCK** (soundtrack) 14
– White rock / Searching for gold / The loser / The shoot / Lax'x / After the ball / Montezuma's revenge / Ice run. *(cd-iss. 1988; CDA 4614)*

Jun 77. (7") *<1937>* **AFTER THE BALL. / WHITE ROCK** -

Nov 77. (lp/c) *(AMLH/CAM 64660)* **RICK WAKEMAN'S CRIMINAL RECORD** 25
– Statute of justice / Crime of passion / Chamber of horrors / Birdman of Alcatraz / The breathalizer / Judas Iscariot. *(re-iss. Mar82 lp/c; AMID/CMID 125)*

Apr 79. (7") *(AMS 7435)* **BIRDMAN OF ALCATRAZ (theme from My Son My Son). / FALCONS DE NEIGE** -

Apr 79. (7") *<2010>* **BIRDMAN OF ALCATRAZ. / AND NOW A WORD FROM OUR SPONSOR** -

May 79. (d-lp/c) *(AMLX/CXM 68508)* **RHAPSODIES** 25
– Pedra da Gavea / Front line / Bombay duck / Animal showdown / Big Ben / Rhapsody in blue / Wooly Willy tango / The pulse / Swan lager / March of the gladiators / Flacons de Neige / The flasher / The palais / Stand by / Sea horses / Half holiday / Summertime.

May 79. (7"/7"pic-d) *(AMS/+P 7436)* **ANIMAL SHOWDOWN. / SEA HORSES** [ ] [–]
Nov 79. (7") *(AMS 7497)* **SWAN LAGER. / WOOLLY WILLY TANGO** [ ] [–]
Feb 80. (7") *(AMS 7510)* **I'M SO STRAIGHT I'M A WEIRDO. / DO YOU BELIEVE IN FAIRIES?** [ ] [–]

WEA — not iss.

Oct 80. (7") *(K 18354)* **THE SPIDER. / DANIELLE** [ ] [–]
featured **FERNANDEZ / STEVE BARNACLE** – bass / **GARY BARNACLE** – sax / **TIM STONE** – guitar / etc.

Charisma — Varese Sarabande

Jun 81. (lp)(c) *(CDS 4022)(7144 136)* **1984** [24] [ ]
– 1984 overture – part 1 & 2 / War games / Julia / The hymn / The room – part 1 & 2 / Robot man / Sorry / No name / 1984 / Forgotten memories / The proles / 1984. *(re-iss. Jun88; CHC 41)*
(below vocals by; CORI JOSIAS)
Jul 81. (7"; by The RICK WAKEMAN BAND) *(CB 384)* **JULIA. / SORRY** [ ] [–]
Nov 81. (7"; by The RICK WAKEMAN BAND) *(CB 392)* **ROBOT MAN. / 1984 OVERTURE (part 1)** [ ] [–]
Jan 82. (lp) *(CLASS 12)* *<STV 81162>* **THE BURNING** (soundtrack) [ ] [ ]
– Theme from 'The Burning' / The chase continues (Po's plane) / Variations on the fire / Shear terror and more / The burning end title theme / Campfire story *[UK-only]* / The fire / Doin' it / Devils creek breakdown / The chase / Shear terror. *(UK re-iss. Jan89; some tracks switched; same as US)*

Moon — not iss.

Nov 82. (7") *(LUNA 6)* **I'M SO STRAIGHT I'M A WEIRDO. / MAYBE '80 (edit)** [ ] [–]
Dec 82. (lp/c) *(LUNLP/ZCLUN 1)* **ROCK'N'ROLL PROPHET** (rec.1979) [ ] [–]
– I'm so straight I'm a weirdo / The dragon / Dark / Maybe '80 / Early warning / Spy of '55 / Do you believe in fairies? / Rock'n'roll prophet. *(cd-iss. Apr93 on 'President'; RWCD 12)(+=)* – Return of the prophet / Alpha sleep / March of the child soldiers / Stalemate.

Charisma — not iss.

Apr 83. (7") *(CB 411)* **LATIN REEL (theme from G'OLE!). / NO POSSIBLA** [ ] [–]
Apr 83. (lp/c) *(CAS/+MC 1162)* **G'OLE!** (soundtrack) [ ] [–]
– International flag / The dove (opening ceremony) / Wayward spirit / Latin reel (theme from G'ole) / Red island / Spanish holiday / No possibla / Shadows / Black pearls / Frustration / Spanish montage / G'ole!
Jun 83. (lp) *(CAS 1163)* **THE COST OF LIVING** [ ] [ ]
– Twij / Pandomonia / Gone but not forgotten / One for the road / Bedtime stories / Happening man / Shakespeare's run / Monkey nuts / Elegy (written in a country church yard). *(re-iss. Aug88; CHC 63) (cd-iss. Jun97 on 'Griffin'; GCDWR 1892)*

— Oct '84, WAKEMAN collaborated on album BEYOND THE PLANETS by KEVIN PEEK (Sky); hit UK No.64

— His spring 1985 tour band: **TONY FERNANDEZ** – drums / **CHAS CRONK** – bass / **RICK FENN** – lead guitar / **GORDON NEVILLE** – vocals / **LYNN SHEPHERD** – b.vocals

President — not iss.

Dec 84. (7") *(WAKE 1)* **GLORY BOYS. / GHOST OF A ROCK AND ROLL STAR** [ ] [–]
(12"+=) *(12WAKE 1)* – Elgin mansions.
Mar 85. (lp/c) *(RW/+K 1)* **SILENT NIGHTS** [ ] [–]
– Tell 'em all you know / The opening line / The opera / Man's best friend / Glory boys / Silent nights / Ghost of a rock and roll star / The dancer / That's who I am. *(cd-iss. Jan87; RWCD 1)* – Elgin mansions.
Jun 85. (7"/12") *(WAKE/12WAKE 2)* **THE THEME FROM 'LYTTON'S DIARY'. / DATABASE** [ ] [–]
Dec 85. (lp) *(RW 2)* **LIVE AT HAMMERSMITH (live)** [ ] [–]
– Arthur / Three wives of Henry VIII / The journey / Merlin the magician. *(cd-iss. Jan87; RWCD 2) (re-iss. Nov93)*

Coda — not iss.

Apr 86. (lp/c)(cd) *(NAGE/+C 10)(NAGE 10CD)* **COUNTRY AIRS** [ ] [–]
– Dandelion dreams / Stepping stones / Ducks and drakes / Morning haze / Waterfalls / Quite valleys / Nature trail / Heather carpets / Wild moors / Lakeland walks. *(re-iss. Oct92 on 'Art Of Language' cd/c; NAGE 102CD) (re-iss. re-recorded cd Dec92 on 'President'; RWCD 10)* – The spring / Green to gold / Harvest festival / The glade.
Apr 86. (7") *(CODS 19)* **WATERFALLS. / HEATHER CARPETS** [ ] [–]

Stylus — not iss.

Nov 86. (d-lp/d-c/d-cd) *(SMR/SMC/SMD 729)* **THE GOSPELS** [94] [–]
– The baptism / The welcoming / The sermon on the mount / The Lord's Prayer / The way / The road to Jerusalem / Trial and error / Galilee / The gift / The magnificat / Welcome a star / Power (the acts of the apostles) / The word / The hour / The children of mine / The last verse. *(re-iss. d-cd Mar94 on 'Fragile'; BM 2-3)*

President — Edel Screen

Mar 87. (lp/c/cd) *(RW/+K/CD 3)* *<CD 5404>* **CRIMES OF PASSION** (1984 soundtrack) [ ] Dec84 [ ]
– It's a lovely life (MAGGIE BELL) / Eastern shadows / Joanna / The stretch / Policeman's ball / Stax / Taken in hand / Paradise lost / The box / Web of love. *(cd+=)* – Dangerous woman (MAGGIE BELL). *(cd re-iss. Nov93 +=; same) (cd re-iss. Mar95 on 'Silva Screen'; CIN 2202-2)*
Aug 87. (lp/c/cd) *(RW/+K/CD 4)* **THE FAMILY ALBUM** [ ] [–]
– Adam (Rick's second son) / Black Beauty (black rabbit) / Jemma (Rick and Nina's daughter) / Benjamin (Rick's third son) / Oscar (Rick & Nina's son) / Oliver (Rick's eldest son) / Nina (Rick's wife) / Chloe (German shepherd) / Rookie (cat) / Tilly (Golden Retriever) / Mum / Dad. *(c+=)* – Wiggles (black & white rabbit). *(cd++=)* – The day after the fair / Mackintosh.
Feb 88. (lp/c/cd; RICK WAKEMAN & RAMON REMEDIOS) *(RW/+K/CD 5)* **A SUITE OF GODS** [ ] [–]
– Dawn of time / The oracle / Pandora's box / Chariot of the sun / The flood / The voyage of Ulysses / Hercules.
Apr 88. (lp/c/cd; RICK WAKEMAN & TONY FERNANDEZ) *(RW/+K/CD 6)* **ZODIAQUE** [ ] [–]
– Sagittarius / Capricorn / Gemini / Cancer / Pisces / Aquarius / Aries / Libra / Leo / Virgo / Taurus / Scorpio.

— retained **FERNANDEZ** + recruited **DAVEY PATON** – bass / **JOHN KNIGHTSBRIDGE** – guitar (2) / guest vocals **TRACEY ACKERMAN** + **ASHLEY HOLT**
below vocals by ROY WOOD (A-side) / JOHN PARR (B-side)

Jul 88. (7") *(WAKE 3)* **CUSTER'S LAST STAND. / OCEAN CITY** [ ] [–]
Jul 88. (lp/c/cd) *(RW/+K/CD 7)* **TIME MACHINE** [ ] [–]
– Custer's last stand / Ocean city / Angel of time * / Slaveman * / Ice / Open up your eyes * / Elizabethan rock / Make me a woman * / Rock age *. *(cd has extended versions of *)*
Nov 89. (lp/c/cd) *(RW/+K/CD 8)* **SEA AIRS** [ ] [–]
– Harbour lights / The pirate / Storm clouds / Last at sea / The mermaid / Waves / The fisherman / Flying fish / The Marie Celeste / Time and tide / The lone sailor / The sailor's lament.
Nov 90. (lp/c/cd) *(RW/+K/CD 9)* **NIGHT AIRS** [ ] [–]
– The sad dream / Twilight / The sleeping child / Mr. Badger / Jack Frost / The lone star / Rain shadows / Fox by night / Night owls / An evening romance.

— (in the US; he released cd 'IN THE BEGINNING' for 'Asaph'; *<AR-1049>*, which received a UK date Dec91). In 1991, the 'Badger' label issued cassette 'THE SUN TRILOGY'; *AMB 4MC)*

Ambient — not iss.

Nov 90. (cd) *(AMB1-MCD)* **ASPIRANT SUNSET** [ ] [–]
– Floating clouds / Still waters / The dream / The sleeping village / Sea of tranquility / Peace / Sunset / Dying embers / Dusk / Evening moods. *(re-iss. 1992 on 'Rio Digital'; RIOCD 1008) (re-iss. Jun93 on 'President'; RWCD 18)*
Nov 90. (cd) *(AMB2-MCD)* **ASPIRANT SUNRISE** [ ] [–]
– Thoughts of love / Gentle breezes / Whispering cornfields / Peaceful beginnings / Dewy morn / Musical dreams / Distant thoughts / The dove / When time stood still / Secret moments / Peaceful. *(re-iss. 1992 on 'Rio Digital'; RIOCD 1009) (re-iss. Jun93 on 'President'; RWCD 17)*
Jan 91. (lp/cd; by RICK WAKEMAN & MARIO FASCIANO) *(A-IOM-2/+CD)* **BLACK KNIGHTS IN THE COURT OF FERNINAND IV** [ ] [–]
(re-iss. cd Nov92 on 'Rio Digital'; RIOCD 1002) (re-iss. cd Jun94 on 'West Coast'; WCPCD 1009)
Feb 91. (lp/cd) *(A-IOM-2/+CD)* **PHANTOM POWER** (soundtrack to 1925 movie!) [ ] [–]
– The visit / Heaven / The rat / The stiff / Evil love / The voice of love / Heat of the moment / Fear of love / The love trilogy:- One night – The dream sequence – One night of love / The hangman / The sand-dance / You can't buy my love / Phantom power / Rock pursuit. *(cd re-iss. Nov92 on 'Rio Digital'; RIOCD 1003) (cd re-iss. Jun01 on 'President'; RWCD 35)*
May 91. (lp/cd) *(A-IOM-3/+CD)* **SOFTSWORD: KING JOHN AND THE MAGNA CHARTER** [ ] [–]
– Magna charter / After prayers / Battle sonata / The siege / Rochester

college / The story of love (King John) / March of time / Don't fly away / Isabella / Softsword / Hymn of hope. *(re-iss. cd Nov92 on 'Rio Digital'; RIOCD 1001) (re-iss. cd Feb94 on 'President'; RWCD 24)*

Sep 91. (lp/cd) *(A-IOM-5/+CD)* **A WORLD OF WISDOM** –
(re-iss. cd Feb94 on 'D-Sharp'; DSHCD 7013)
(above credited to veteran English comedian/singer NORMAN WISDOM)

Oct 91. (7"; by RICK WAKEMAN featuring CHRISSIE HAMMOND) *(A-IOMS 1)* **DON'T FLY AWAY. / AFTER PRAYERS** –

Nov 91. (cd) **2000 A.D. INTO THE FUTURE** –
– Into the future / Toward peace / 2000 A.D. / A.D rock / The time tunnel / Robot dance / A new beginning / Forward past / The seventh dimension. *(re-iss. Dec92 on 'Rio Digital'; RIOCD 1007) (re-iss. Sep93 on 'President'; RWCD 21)*

Rio Digital — not iss.

1992. (cd) *(RIOCD 1010)* **AMBIENT SUNSHADOWS** –
– The nightwind / Churchyard / Tall shadows / Shadowlove / Melancholy mood / Mount Fuji by night / Hidden reflections / The evening harp / The moonraker pond / The last lamplight / Japanese sunshadows. *(re-iss. Jul93 as 'ASPIRANT SUNSHADOWS' on 'President'; RWCD 19)*

Nov 92. (cd; RICK WAKEMAN & ADAM WAKEMAN) *(RIOCD 1011)* **WAKEMAN WITH WAKEMAN** –
– Lure of the wild / The beach comber / Meglomania / Raga and rhyme / Sync or swim / Jigajig / Caesarea / After the atom / The suicide shuiffle / Past and present / Paint it black. *(re-iss. Feb93 on 'President'; RWCD 11)*
(above was with son ADAM)

Myrrh — not iss.

May 93. (cd) *(MYRCD 1296)* **PRAYERS** –

President — not iss.

May 93. (cd) *(RWCD 16)* **HERITAGE SUITE** –
– The chasms / Thorwald's cross / St.Michael's isle / Spanish head / The Ayres / Mona's isle / The Dhoon / The bee orchid / Chapel Hill / The Curraghs / The painted lady / The Peregrine falcon.

Aug 93. (cd) *(RWCD 17)* **AFRICAN BACH** (rec.& rel.South Africa 1991) –
– African Bach / Message of mine / My homeland / Liberty / Anthem / Brainstorm / Face in the crowd / Just a game / Africa east / Don't touch the merchandise.

Nov 93. (cd; by WAKEMAN WITH WAKEMAN) *(RWCD 22)* **NO EXPENSE SPARED** –

May 94. (cd-ep; by RICK WAKEMAN & HIS BAND) *(WAKEY 4)* **LIGHT UP THE SKY / SIMPLY FREE / STARFLIGHT / THE BEAR**

Nov 94. (cd; by WAKEMAN WITH WAKEMAN) *(RWCD 25)* **ROMANCE OF THE VICTORIAN AGE** –
– Burlington arcade / If only / The last teardrop / Still dreaming / Memories of the Victorian age / Lost in words / A tale of love / Mysteries unfold / Forever in my heart / Days of wonder / The swans / Another mellow day / Dance of the elves.

Jun 95. (cd) *(RWCD 27)* **THE SEVEN WONDERS OF THE WORLD** (with narration) –
– The Pharoahs Of Alexandria / The Colossus Of Rhodes / The Pyramids Of Egypt / The Gardens Of Babylon / The Temples Of Artemis / The Statue Of Zeus / The Mausoleum At Halicarnassus.

Jul 95. (cd) *(DSHLCD 7018)* **CIRQUE SURREAL – STATE CIRCUS OF IMAGINATION** –
– Gnash / Balance of power / Wings of fortune / Static / Party / Wired for sound / Juliet / Tubular balls / Carlos / Love that I know / The jig.
(above released on 'D-Sharp' label)

Oct 95. (cd) *(RWCD 28)* **VISIONS** –
– Fantasy / Peace of mind / Innermost thoughts / Vision of light / Higher planes / Astral traveller / Dream on / Thought waves / Drifting patterns / Future patterns / Levitation / Moondreams.

Nov 96. (cd; by RICK & ADAM WAKEMAN) *(RWCD 30)* **VIGNETTES** –
– Waiting alone / Wish I was you / Sun comes crying / A breath of Heaven / Moment in time / Artist's dream / Change of face / Madman blues / A painting of our love / Riverside / Need you / Simply acoustic / Just another tear.

Hope — not iss.

Mar 97. (cd) *(HRHCD 004)* **LIGHT AT THE END OF THE TUNNEL** –

Mar 97. (cd) *(HRHCD 005)* **CAN YOU HEAR ME?** –

EMI Classics — EMI Classics

Mar 99. (cd/lp) *(<CDC/EX 556763-2/-1>)* **RETURN TO THE CENTRE OF THE EARTH** 34
– A vision / The return overture / Mother Earth: Shadow of June – Gallery – Avenue of prismed light – Earthquake / Buried alive (with OZZY OSBOURNE) / The enigma / Is anybody there? (with BONNIE TYLER) / The ravine / Dance of a thousand lights / The shephard / Mr Slow / Bridge of time / Never is a long time (with TREVOR RABIN) / Tales of the Lidenbrook sea – River of hope – Hunter and hunted – Fight for life / The kill / Timeless history / Still waters run deep (with JUSTIN HAYWARD) / Time within time / The ebbing tide – Electric storm / Ride of your life (with KATRINA LESKANICH) / Globes of fire – Cascades of fear / Floodflames / The volcano: Tongues of fire – Blue mountains / The end of the return.

Music Fusion — Musea

Jun 99. (cd) *(MFCD 004)* *<4396>* **WHITE ROCK II** (soundtrack re-scored) 2001
– Oriental iceman / Ice pie / Dancing on snowflakes / Nine ice groove / In the frame / Harlem slalom / Frost in space.

— next with **DAVE COUSINS** (ex-STRAWBS)

Witchwood — Witchwood

Sep 02. (cd; as WAKEMAN & COUSINS) *(WRCD 2007)* *<50001>* **HUMMINGBIRD** Feb03
– The young pretender / Hummingbird / So shall our love die / Steppes / October to May / Ice maiden / Higher Germanie / Stone cold is the woman's heart / Crie du coeur / All in vain / Can you believe / Via Bencini / Forever ocean blue.

— next with the New English Rock Ensemble

Music Fusion — not iss.

Apr 05. (cd) *(MFW 6093X)* **OUT THERE . . .** (rec. 2003) –
– Out there (w/ T. TEXAS TYLER) / The mission / To be with you / Universe of sound / Music of love / The cathedral of the sky. *(bonus+=)* – single mixes:- To be with you / The mission / Music of love.

– compilations, others, etc. –

1978. (lp) *A&M; (AMLX 68447)* **THE ROYAL PHILHARMONIC ORCHESTRA PERFORMING BEST KNOWN WORKS OF RICK WAKEMAN** –

May 81. (d-c) *A&M; (CAMCR 8)* **THE SIX WIVES OF HENRY VIII / THE MYTHS AND LEGENDS OF KING ARTHUR . . .** –

Feb 89. (4xcd-box) *A&M; (RWCD 20)* **20th ANNIVERSARY** –
– (THE SIX WIVES OF HENRY VIII / JOURNEY TO THE CENTRE OF THE EARTH / THE MYTHS AND LEGENDS OF KING ARTHUR AND THE KNIGHTS OF THE ROUND TABLE / WHITE ROCK)

Mar 83. (d-c) *Charisma; (CASMC 111)* **1984 / THE BURNING** –

May 91. (cd) *Ambient; (A-IOM-4CD)* **THE PRIVATE COLLECTION** –
(re-iss. Nov92 on 'Rio Digital'; RIOCD 1004) (re-iss. Feb94 on 'President'; RWCD 23)

Oct 91. (d-cd) *Ambient; (AMB5-MCD)* **THE CLASSICAL CONNECTION** –
(re-iss. Dec92 on 'Rio Digital'; RIOCD 1005) (re-iss. 1-cd May93 on 'President'; RWCD 13)

Oct 91. (cd) *Ambient; (A-IOM-6MCD)* **THE CLASSICAL CONNECTION II** –
(re-iss. Dec92 on 'Rio Digital'; RIOCD 1006) (re-iss. May93 on 'President'; RWCD 14)

Sep 93. (cd) *Icon; (ICONCD 005)* **THE VERY BEST OF RICK WAKEMAN – CHRONICLES** –
– (see below cd for tracks, although not YES songs)

Dec 93. (d-cd) *Fragile; (CDFRL 001)* **RICK WAKEMAN'S GREATEST HITS** (some with YES) –
– Roundabout / Wondrous stories / Don't kill the whale / Going for the one / Siberian khatru / Madrigal / Starship trooper/ / Overture / The journey / The Hansbach / Lost in time / The recollection / Stream of voices / The battle / Liddenbrook / The forest / Mount Etna / Journey's end / Sea horses / Catherine of Aragon / Gone but not forgotten / Merlin the magician.

Apr 94. (cd/c) *Prestige; (CDSGP 115)* **THE CLASSIC TRACKS** –

Jun 94. (d-cd; WAKEMAN WITH WAKEMAN) *Cyclops; (CYCLD 006)* **THE OFFICIAL LIVE BOOTLEG** –
(re-iss. Mar95 on 'Griffin'; GCDRW 156)

Dec 94. (cd; as RICK WAKEMAN & THE ENGLISH ROCK ENSEMBLE) *Windsong; (WHISCD 007)* **LIVE ON THE TEST (live)** –

Jun 95. (cd) *Disky; (RPCD 13)* **ROCK AND POP LEGENDS** –

Sep 95. (d-cd) *Hope; (HR 001)* **THE NEW GOSPELS** –

Oct 95. (cd) *Essential; (ESSCD 322)* **THE PIANO ALBUM – LIVE (live)** [ ] [–]
Nov 96. (cd) *A&M; <5852>* **VOYAGE: THE VERY BEST OF RICK WAKEMAN** [–] [ ]
– Catherine of Aragon / Catherine Howard / Jane Seymour / Anne Boleyn / Arthur / Merlin the magician / The last battle / White rock / Searching for gold / After the ball / Ice run / March of the gladiators / Summertime / Temperament of mind / Journey – Recollection / The battle – The forest / Crime of passion / Judas Iscariot / Hibernation / Free song / Maker.
May 97. (cd) *RP Media; (CDRPM 0018)* **TRIBUTE** [ ] [–]
May 99. (3xcd-box) *Music Fusion: (MFCD 001)* **NATURAL WORLD TRILOGY** [ ] [–]
May 99. (3xcd-box) *Music Fusion; (MFCD 002)* **ART IN MUSIC TRILOGY** [ ] [–]
– (THE SCULPTOR / THE WRITER / SKETCHES)
May 99. (2xcd-box) *Music Fusion; (MFCD 003)* **OFFICIAL LIVE BOOTLEG (live)** [ ] [–]
Jun 99. (cd) *Music Fusion; (MFCD 004)* **WHITE ROCK VOL.2** [ ] [–]
Jun 99. (d-cd) *Eagle; (EDMCD 086)* **THE MASTERS** [ ] [–]
Mar 05. (cd) *Heliopause; (HPVP 104CD) <528>* **AT LINCOLN CATHEDRAL** (live) [ ] May05 [ ]

Scott WALKER / the WALKER BROTHERS

Formed: Los Angeles, California, USA . . ..1964 as The WALKER BROTHERS by GARY LEEDS, SCOTT ENGEL and JOHN MAUS. LEEDS was a drummer for P.J. PROBY (previously a co-founder of The STANDELLS) and ENGEL and MAUS were playing bass and lead guitar respectively for The DALTON BROTHERS. After signing to 'Smash' Records, they were advised to try their luck in Britain and they subsequently relocated to London. Their debut single, 'PRETTY GIRLS EVERYWHERE' (with MAUS on lead vocal) flopped although their second, 'LOVE HER'(1965), scraped into the UK Top 20. After SCOTT took over on vocals they soon made No.1 twice in the UK with the 1965-66 cult easy-listening classics, 'MAKE IT EASY ON YOURSELF' (US Top 20) and 'THE SUN AIN'T GONNA SHINE ANYMORE' (also US Top 20 and written by FRANKIE VALLI). Their debut album, 'TAKE IT EASY WITH THE WALKER BROTHERS' (1966) hit the UK Top 5, followed by further smashes, 'PORTRAIT' (1966) and 'IMAGES' (1967). Later in '67, SCOTT WALKER left JOHN MAUS and GARY LEEDS (after some arguments with JOHN) and went solo, hitting the heights until the 70's (his melancholy ballads later influencing the likes of JULIAN COPE). SCOTT scored late 60's solo hits with the controversial 'JACKIE', 'JOANNA' and 'LIGHTS OF CINCINATTI' as well as the albums, 'SCOTT' (1967), 'SCOTT 2' (1968; a UK No.1) and 'SCOTT 3' (1969). He also contributed backing vocals to The BEATLES' 'All You Need Is Love' world broadcast in 1967, by this point even hosting his own TV show on BBC1. With the release of cult classic, 'SCOTT 4' (1969), however, he faded from popular stardom and languished in MOR hell for much of the early 70's. The man briefly re-emerged mid-decade as part of a reformed WALKER BROTHERS, enjoying a UK Top 10 with a cover of Tom Rush's 'NO REGRETS'. SCOTT eschewed the lure of the beckoning nostalgia circuit, however, leading the band in a radically different direction for 1978's 'NITE FLIGHTS' (the brothers' final album together). WALKER eventually resurfaced in solo mode with the tortured 'CLIMATE OF HUNTER' in 1984, hardly a record to kickstart his career. 'Virgin' were suitably unimpressed with the commercial returns and he subsequently signed to 'Fontana' in 1985. Although he recorded with BRIAN ENO, the project was never completed; similarly, SCOTT's collaborative work with former JAPAN warbler, DAVID SYLVIAN produced no concrete results. It would be a further eleven years before he came out with new work in the form of 1995's 'TILT'. As out-there as WALKER has yet ventured, fans and critics alike agreed that while he mightn't be the most prolific artist, his darkly compelling experiments are worth waiting for. More than a decade in birthing pains, 'THE DRIFT' (2006) was met with almost universal shock, horror, awe and admiration as one of the most gratuitously, beautifully unnerving listening experiences ever released. Against Dante-esque screeds of Eraserhead ambience and nerve-flaying industrio-tronics, WALKER picked his metaphors with the delectation of a deranged hangman, dropping them into traumatic treatise on the likes of 9/11, ELVIS PRESLEY's stillborn brother, and the fate of Italian dictator, Benito Mussolini.

• **Songwriters:** WALKER BROTHERS covered (45's only); LOVE HER (Mann-Weill) / MAKE IT EASY ON YOURSELF (Jerry Butler) / MY SHIP IS COMING IN (Jimmy Radcliffe) / THE SUN AIN'T GONNA SHINE ANYMORE (Frankie Valli) / LOVE MINUS ZERO (Bob Dylan) / ANOTHER TEAR FALLS (Gene McDaniels) / STAY WITH ME BABY (Lorraine Ellison) / WALKING IN THE RAIN (Ronettes) / NO REGRETS (Tom Rush) / etc. SCOTT WALKER covers; JACKIE and others from 'SCOTT 2' lp (Jacques Brel). JOANNA (Tony Hatch & Jackie Trent). On his 'STRETCH' country roots album, several songs were written by BILLY JOE SHAVER. • **Trivia:** In 1987, SCOTT appeared in TV ads for Britvic juice.

Best CD compilation(s): Walker Brothers: AFTER THE LIGHTS GO OUT: THE BEST OF 1965-1967 (*7) / NO REGRETS: THE BEST OF . . . (*6; shared with Scott Walker) / THE SUN AIN'T GONNA SHINE: THE BEST OF SCOTT WALKER & THE WALKER BROTHERS (*8)

Album rating: SCOTT (*7) / SCOTT 2 (*8) / SCOTT (*7) / . . .SINGS SONGS FROM HIS TV SERIES special (*4) / SCOTT 4 (*8) / 'TIL THE BAND COMES IN (*6) / THE MOVIEGOER (*4) / ANY DAY NOW (*4) / STRETCH (*4) / WE HAD IT ALL (*4) / FIRE ESCAPE IN THE SKY: THE GODLIKE GENIUS OF SCOTT WALKER compilation (*7) / SCOTT WALKER SINGS JACQUES BREL collection (*6) / CLIMATE OF HUNTER (*7) / BOY CHILD; THE BEST OF SCOTT WALKER 1967-1970 compilation (*8) / TILT (*5) / POLA X soundtrack (*6) / THE DRIFT (*7)

SCOTT ENGEL

(aka SCOTT WALKER) – vocals

Vogue / Orbit

Aug 58. (7") *<511>* **CHARLIE BOP. / ALL I DO IS DREAM OF YOU** [–] [ ]
Oct 58. (7") *(V 9125)* **BLUEBELL. / PAPER DOLL** [ ] [ ]
Jun 59. (7") *(V 9145) <506>* **THE LIVIN' END. / GOOD FOR NOTHIN'** [ ] Jun58 [ ]
Sep 59. (7") *<537>* **SUNDAY. / GOLDEN RULE OF LOVE** [–] [ ]
Nov 59. (7") **I DON'T WANNA KNOW. / COMIN' HOME** [–] [ ]

— Continued to do session work until 1962 when he joined The ROUTERS alongside JOHN STEWART. They released 2 singles late 62-early 63, 'LET'S GO WITH THE ROUTERS' & 'MAKE IT SNAPPY'. After a spell with the SANDY NELSON band, he and JOHN joined The MOONGOONERS. They issued singles MOONGOON STOMP and MOONGOON TWIST in 1963. The following year, they became The DALTONS duo releasing one 45, 'I ONLY CAME TO DANCE WITH YOU'. SCOTT was now part of the famous trio.

the WALKER BROTHERS

SCOTT ENGEL (WALKER)(b. 9 Jan'44, Hamilton, Ohio) – vocals, bass, keyboards / **JOHN MAUS** (WALKER)(b.12 Nov'43, New York City, N.Y.) – vocals, guitar / **GARY LEEDS** (WALKER) (b. 3 Sep'44, Glendale, Calif.) – drums, vocals

Philips / Smash

Feb 65. (7") *<1952>* **PRETTY GIRLS EVERYWHERE. / DOIN' THE JERK** [–] [ ]
Apr 65. (7") *(BF 1409) <1976>* **LOVE HER. / THE SEVENTH DAWN** [20] [ ]
Aug 65. (7") *(BF 1428) <2000>* **MAKE IT EASY ON YOURSELF. / BUT I DO** [1] Jul65 [ ]
Sep 65. (7") *<2009>* **MAKE IT EASY ON YOURSELF. / DOIN' THE JERK** [–] [16]

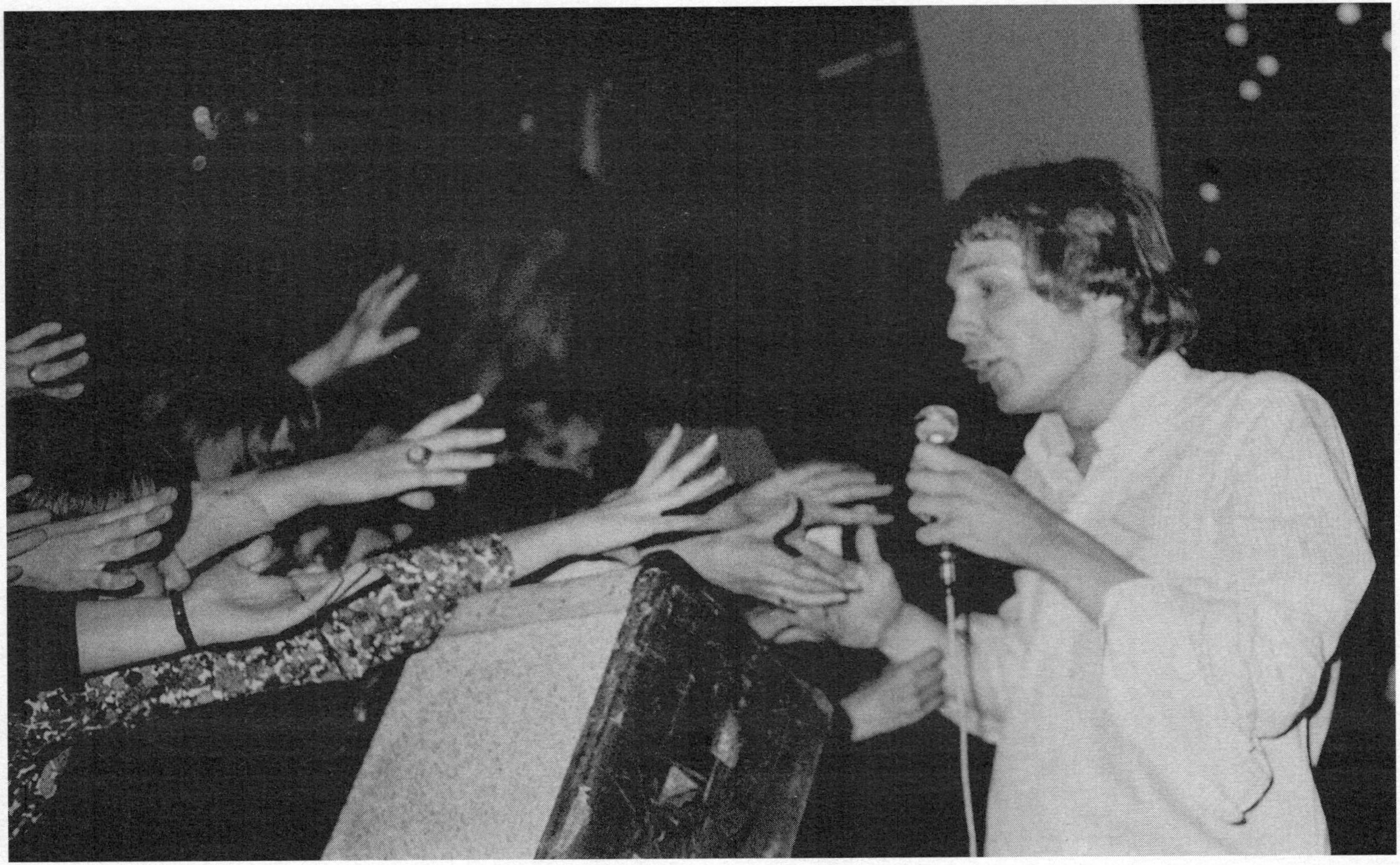

SCOTT WALKER

Nov 65. (7") *(BF 1454) <2016>* **MY SHIP IS COMING IN. / YOU'RE ALL AROUND ME** [3] [63]

Dec 65. (lp) *(SBL 7691)* **TAKE IT EASY WITH THE WALKER BROTHERS** [4] [–]
– Make it easy for yourself / There goes my baby / First love never dies / Dancing in the street / Lonely winds / The girl I lost in the rain / Land of 1000 dances / You're all around me / Love minus zero / I don't want to hear it anymore / Here comes the night / Tell the truth.

Feb 66. (7") *(BF 1473) <2032>* **THE SUN AIN'T GONNA SHINE ANYMORE. / AFTER THE LIGHTS GO OUT** [1] [13]

Jul 66. (7") *(BF 1497) <2048>* **(BABY) YOU DON'T HAVE TO TELL ME. / MY LOVE IS GROWING** [13] [ ]

Aug 66. (lp) *(SBL 7732)* **PORTRAIT** [3] [ ]
– In my room / Saturday's child / Just for a thrill / Hurting each other / Old folks / Summertime / People get ready / I can see it now / Where's the girl / Living above your head / Take it like a man / No sad songs for me.

Sep 66. (7") *(BF 1514) <2063>* **ANOTHER TEAR FALLS. / SADDEST NIGHT IN THE WORLD** [12] [ ]

Nov 66. (7") *(BF 1537)* **DEADLIER THAN THE MALE (theme from the film). / ARC ANGEL** [34] [–]

Jan 67. (7") *(BF 1548)* **STAY WITH ME BABY. / TURN OUT THE MOON** [26] [–]

Mar 67. (lp) *(SBL 7770)* **IMAGES** [6] [ ]
– Everything under the sun / Once upon a summertime / Experience / Blueberry Hill / Orpheus / Stand by me / I wanna know / I willwait for you / It makes no difference now / I can't let it happen to you / Genevieve / Just say goodbye.

May 67. (7") *(BF 1576)* **WALKING IN THE RAIN. / BABY MAKE IT THE LAST TIME** [26] [–]

—— disbanded May '67

SCOTT WALKER

re-issued old recordings

Liberty Liberty

1966. (7"ep; as SCOTT ENGEL) *(LEP 2261)* **SCOTT ENGEL** [ ] [–]
– I broke my own heart / What do you say / Are these really mine / Crazy in love with you.

Capitol Capitol

May 66. (7"; with JOHN STEWART) *(CL 15440)* **I ONLY CAME TO DANCE WITH YOU. / GREENS** [ ] [ ]

Philips not iss.

Dec 66. (7"ep; 1-side by JOHN MAUS) *(BE 12597)* **SOLO SCOTT – SOLO JOHN** [ ] [–]
– (SCOTT WALKER:- The gentle rain / Mrs. Murphy.

—— solo after the WALKER BROTHERS split

Philips Smash

Aug 67. (lp; stereo/mono) *(S+/BL 7816)* **SCOTT** [3] [ ]
– Mathilde / Montague Terrace (in blue) / Angelica / Lady came from Baltimore / When Joanna loved me / My death / Through a long and sleepless night / The big hurt / Such a small love / You're gonna hear from me / Always coming back to me / Amsterdam. *(re-iss. Mar92 & Jun00 on 'Fontana' cd/c; 510 879-2/-4)*

Nov 67. (7") *(BF 1628) <2156>* **JACKIE. / THE PLAGUE** [22] [ ]

Mar 68. (lp; stereo/mono) *(S+/BL 7840)* **SCOTT 2** [1] [ ]
– Jackie / Best of both worlds / The amorous Humphrey Plugg / Black sheep boy / Next / The girls from the street / Plastic palace people / Wait until dark / The girls and the dogs / Windows of the world / The bridge / Come next Spring. *(re-iss. Aug92 & Jun00 on 'Fontana' cd/c; 510 880-2/-4)*

Apr 68. (7") *(BF 1662) <2168>* **JOANNA. / ALWAYS COMING BACK TO YOU** [7] [ ]

Mar 69. (lp) *(SBL 7882)* **SCOTT 3** [3] [ ]
– It's raining today / Copenhagen / Rosemary / Big Louise / We came through / Butterfly / Two ragged soldiers / 30th century man / Winter night / Two weeks since you've gone / Sons of / Funeral tango / If you go away. *(re-iss. Aug92 & Jun00 on 'Fontana' cd/c; 510 881-2/-4)*

Jun 69. (7") *(BF 1793) <2228>* **LIGHTS OF CINCINNATI. / TWO WEEKS SINCE YOU'VE GONE** [13] [ ]

Jun 69. (lp) *(SBL 7900)* **. . . SINGS SONGS FROM HIS TV SERIES** [7] [ ]
– I have dreamed / The impossible dream / Will you still be mine / When the world was young / Who (will take my place) / If she walked into my life / The song is you / The look of love / Country girl / Someone to light up my life / Only the young / Lost in the stars.

Nov 69. (lp; as NOEL SCOTT ENGEL) *(SBL 7913)* **SCOTT 4** [ ] [ ]
– The seventh seal / On your own again / World's strongest man / Angels of ashes / Boy child / The old man's back again / Hero of the war / Duchess / Get behind me / Rhymes of goodbye. *(re-iss. Aug92 & Jun00 on 'Fontana' cd/c; 510 882-2/-4)*

Dec 70. (lp) *(6308 035)* **'TIL THE BAND COMES IN** [ ] [ ]
– Prologue / Little things (that keep us together) / Jean the machine / Joe / Thanks for Chicago, Mr. James / Long about now / Time operator / Cowbells shakin' / 'Til the band comes in / The war is over / Stormy / The hills of yesterday / What are you doing the rest of your life / Rueben James / It's over. *(cd-iss. Aug96 on 'Beat Goes On'; BGOCD 320)*

Oct 71. (7") *(6006 168)* **I STILL SEE YOU. / MY WAY HOME** [ ] [–]

Oct 72. (lp) *(6308 127)* **THE MOVIEGOER** [ ] [–]
– This way Mary / Speak softly love / Glory road / That night / The summer of '42 / Easy come easy go / The ballad of Sacco and Vanzetti (here's to you) / Face in the crowd / Joe Hill / All his children / Come Saturday morning / The look of love. *(re-iss. on 'Contour'; 6870 633)*

May 73. (7") *(6006 311)* **THE ME I NEVER KNEW. / THIS WAY MARY** [ ] [ ]

May 73. (lp) *(6308 148)* **ANY DAY NOW** [ ] [ ]
– Any day now / All my love's laughter / Do I love you / Ain't no sunshine / Maria Bethania / Cowboy / When you get right down to it / The me I never knew / If ships were made to sail / We could be flying.

C.B.S. Columbia

Oct 73. (7") *(1795)* **A WOMAN LEFT LONELY. / WHERE LOVE HAS DIED** [ ] [ ]

Nov 73. (lp) *(65725)* **STRETCH** [ ] [ ]
– Sunshine / Just one smile / A woman left lonely / No easy way down / That's how I got to Memphis / Use me / Frisco depot / Someone who cared / Where does brown begin / Where love has died / I'll be home.

Jul 74. (7") *(2521)* **DELTA DAWN. / WE HAD IT ALL** [ ] [–]

Aug 74. (lp) *(80254)* **WE HAD IT ALL** [ ] [ ]
– Low down freedom / We had it all / Black rose / Ride me down easy / You're young and you'll forget / The house song / Old five and dimers like me / Whatever happened to Saturday night / Sundown / Delta dawn.

—— SCOTT shelved solo career when the WALKERS re-formed in 1975

the WALKER BROTHERS

—— (SCOTT, JOHN & GARY) / on session were **BIG JIM SULLIVAN** – guitar / **ALAN SKIDMORE / BRIAN BENNETT + CHRIS MERCER**

G.T.O. G.T.O.

Oct 75. (lp) *(GTLP 007)* **NO REGRETS** [49] [ ]
– No regrets / Hold an old friend's hand / I've got to have you / Boulder to Birmingham / Lover's lullaby / Walkers' in the Sun / Half break your heart / Everything that touches you / Lovers / Burn our bridges. *(re-iss. Jul77; same) (re-iss. May94 on 'Sony' cd/c; 983276-2/-4) (cd re-iss. Sep94 on 'Rewind'; 477354-2)*

Nov 75. (7") *(GT 42)* **NO REGRETS. / REMEMBER ME** [7] [ ]

Jul 76. (lp) *(GTLP 014)* **LINES** [ ] [ ]
– Lines / Taking it all in stride / Inside of you / Have you seen my baby / We're all alone / Many rivers to cross / Hard to be friends / First day / Brand new Tennessee waltz / Dreaming as one. *(cd-iss. Mar96 on 'Columbia'; 483674-2)*

Sep 76. (7") *(GT 67)* **LINES. / FIRST DAY** [ ] [–]

Jun 77. (7") *(GT 78)* **WE'RE ALL ALONE. / HAVE YOU SEEN MY BABY** [ ] Nov76 [ ]

Jul 78. (7") *(GT 230)* **THE ELECTRICIAN. / DEN HAAGUE** [ ] [–]

Jul 78. (lp) *(GTLP 033)* **NITE FLIGHTS** [ ] [–]
– Shutout / Fat mama kick / Nite flights / The electrician / Death of romance / Den Haague / Rhythms of vision / Child of flames / Disciples of death / Fury and the fire. *(cd-iss. Jul96 on 'Epic'; 484438-2)*

—— split again in 1978 for the last time

– (selected WALKERs) compilations, etc. –

Sep 67. (d-lp) *Philips; (DBL 002)* **THE WALKER BROTHERS STORY** [9] [ ]

Dec 91. (cd/c/lp) *Fontana; (510831-2/-4/-1)* **NO REGRETS – THE BEST OF SCOTT WALKER AND THE WALKER BROTHERS 1965-1976** [4] [ ]
– (* denotes SCOTT WALKER track) – No regrets / Make it easy on yourself / The sun ain't gonna shine anymore / My ship is comin' in / * Joanna / * Lights of Cincinatti / Another tear falls / * Boy child / * Montague Terrace in blue / * Jackie / Stay with me baby / * If you go away / First love never dies / Love her / Walking in the rain / (Baby) You don't have to tell me / Deadlier than the male / We're all alone. *(re-dist.Jul00)* – hit UK No.55

May 06. (cd) *Universal TV; (9839598)* **THE SUN AIN'T GONNA SHINE: THE BEST OF SCOTT WALKER & THE WALKER BROTHERS** [24] [–]
– (virtually a variation of above tracks).

SCOTT WALKER

went solo again in '84

Virgin Virgin

Mar 84. (7") *(VS 666)* **TRACK 3. / BLANKET ROLL BLUES** [ ] [ ]

Mar 84. (lp/c) *(T/TCV 2303)* **CLIMATE OF HUNTER** [60] [ ]
– Rawhide / Dealer / Track 3 / Sleepwalker's woman / Track 5 / Track 6 / Track 7 / Blanket roll blues. *(re-iss. Aug88 lp/c; OVED/+C 149) (cd-iss. Nov89; CDV 2303)*

—— retired from music until . . .

Fontana Drag City

May 95. (cd/lp) *(526 859-2/-1)* *<DC 134CD>* **TILT** [27] Nov97 [ ]
– Farmer in the city / The cockfighter / Bouncer see bouncer . . . / Manhattan / Face on breast / Bolivia '95 / Patriot (a single) / Tilt / Rosary.

Barclay not iss.

Jun 00. (cd) *(547608-2)* **POLA X** (1999 soundtrack) [–] French [–]
– The time is out of joint / Light / Meadow / The darkest forest / Extra blues (by SMOG) / Never again / Iza kana zanbi (by FAIRUZ) / Trang mo ben suo / Zai na yao yuan de di fang / The church of the apostles / Bombupper / River of blood / Blink (by SONIC YOUTH) / Running / Closing / Isabel.

4 a.d. 4 a.d.

May 06. (d-lp/cd) *(CAD 2603/+CD)* *<72603>* **THE DRIFT** [ ] Jun06 [ ]
– Cossacks are / Clara / Jesse / Jolson and Jones / Cue / Hand me ups / Buzzers / Psoriatic / The escape / A lover loves.

– (selective SCOTT) compilations, etc. –

on 'Philips' unless otherwise stated

Dec 67. (lp) *Ember; (EMB 3393)* **LOOKING BACK WITH SCOTT WALKER** [ ] [–]
(cd-iss. Nov00 & Jul02 on 'Repertoire'; REP 4604)

Jan 70. (lp) *(SBL 7910)* **THE BEST OF SCOTT WALKER** [ ] [–]
(re-iss. Nov71 as 'THIS IS SCOTT WALKER'; 6382 007) (re-iss. Jun82; 6381 073) (re-iss. Oct83; PRICE 43)

Oct 72. (lp) *(6382 052)* **THIS IS SCOTT WALKER – VOL.2** [ ] [–]

Nov 81. (lp) *(6359 090)* **SINGS JAQUES BREL** [ ] [–]
(cd-iss. Sep92 on 'Fontana' cd/c; 838212-2/-4)

Sep 81. (lp) *Zoo; (ZOO 2)* **FIRE ESCAPE IN THE SKY – THE GODLIKE GENIUS OF SCOTT WALKER** [ ] [–]

Jun 90. (cd/c/lp) *Fontana; <(842832-2/-4/-1)>* **BOY CHILD: 67-70** [ ] 1992 [ ]
– Montague Terrace (in blue) / Such a small love / The amorous Humphrey Plugg / The girl from the streets / Plastic palace people / The bridge / It's raining today / Copenhagen / Big Louise / We came through / The seventh seal / On your own again / Boy child / The old man's back again (dedicated to the neo-Stalinist regime) / Angels of ashes / Prologue / Little things (that keep us together) / Time operator / Epilogue, the war is over (sleepers). *(re-iss. Jun00; 542705-2)*

Dec 96. (cd) *Razor & Tie; (RE 2120-2)* **IT'S RAINING TODAY: THE SCOTT WALKER STORY 1967-1970** [ ] [–]

May 97. (cd) *Beat Goes On; <(BGOCD 358)>* **STRETCH / WE HAD IT ALL** [ ] [ ]

Dec 97. (cd) *Spalax; (14566)* **EARLY TEN YEARS** [ ] [–]

Mar 99. (cd) *Fontana; (538609-2)* **SCOTT ON SCREEN** [ ] [–]

Mar 01. (cd/c) *Castle Pulse; (PLS CD/MC 367)* **IN THE BEGINNING** [ ] [–]

Jul 01. (cd) *Platinum; (PLATCD 672)* **14 ORIGINAL RECORDINGS** [ ] [–]

the WATERBOYS

Formed: London, England . . . 1982 by Scots-born MIKE SCOTT, Englishman ANTHONY THISTLETHWAITE and Welshman KARL WALLINGER. SCOTT had previously fronted Edinburgh new wave outfit, ANOTHER PRETTY FACE, along with old Ayr school pals, JOHN CALDWELL and JIM GEDDES. Taking their name from a track on LOU REED's sleaze-noir masterpiece, 'Berlin', The WATERBOYS soon secured a deal with the Irish-run label, 'Ensign', following the release of a self-financed debut single in Spring '83, 'A GIRL CALLED JOHNNY'. A tribute to punk priestess, PATTI SMITH (an obvious early influence), the track received a fair amount of airplay and almost broke into the lower regions of the charts. An eponymous debut album followed later that summer, an esoteric set of avant folk/rock which drew comparisons with TIM BUCKLEY's more ambitious meanderings and introduced SCOTT as a promising singing/songwriting seer. Embellished by additional instrumentation such as horns and violin, 'A PAGAN PLACE' (1984) was a confident follow-up, SCOTT venturing ever further out on his spiritual journey with the likes of 'THE BIG MUSIC' and 'CHURCH NOT MADE WITH HANDS'. A burgeoning live reputation and gushing critical praise saw The WATERBOYS' third set, 'THIS IS THE SEA' (1985) break into the UK Top 40, its centerpiece epic, 'THE WHOLE OF THE MOON', becoming the group's first Top 30 single. Despite this overdue success, WALLINGER subsequently departed to form his own outfit, WORLD PARTY. Relocating to Galway, Ireland for an extended sabbatical at the behest of fiddler, STEVE WICKHAM (who'd played on 'THIS..'), SCOTT and THISTLETHWAITE increasingly infused their music with traditional Irish folk influences. It was an earthier WATERBOYS, then, who eventually emerged in late '88 with the acclaimed 'FISHERMAN'S BLUES', SCOTT seemingly having at last found his true musical calling. From the strident Celtic clarion call of the title track to the soulful cover of Van Morrison's 'SWEET THING', it sounded as if The WATERBOYS had been playing this music for centuries. The record almost made the UK Top 10, an album which established The WATERBOYS as a major league act and which remains their biggest seller. 'ROOM TO ROAM' (1990) continued in the same vein, making the UK Top 5 although it lacked the depth of its predecessor. Bang on cue, 'Ensign' re-released 'THE WHOLE OF THE MOON' to massive success (Top 3), the track being played to death by radio all over again. By this point, however, the original WATERBOYS line-up had splintered following a final UK tour (wherein the group drew criticism for their return to an all-out rock sound), THISTLETHWAITE forming the BLUE STARS while SCOTT eventually moved to New York and gathered together a new group of musicians. Now signed to 'Geffen', he recorded 'DREAM HARDER' (1993), the sixth WATERBOYS album but a SCOTT solo set in all but name. Exploring many familiar themes, the album spawned two Top 30 singles in 'THE RETURN OF PAN' and 'GLASTONBURY SONG', even boasting a brief contribution from Scots comedy legend, BILLY CONNOLLY. Although SCOTT released two solo albums, 'BRING 'EM ALL IN' (1995) and 'STILL BURNING' (1997), the WATERBOYS had been out of action nigh on seven years. 'A ROCK IN THE WEARY LAND', put this to rights. Fusing psychedelia, folk-rock and pop, the album was a lacklustre attempt to break back into the mainstream, although it did have its moments. SCOTT harboured the current trend of rock'n'roll nihilism on opening track 'LET IT HAPPEN', while 'CROWN' remained quietly poignant. It's easy to see why SCOTT still carries on despite critical disapproval from some of the press. He at least enjoys what he does as do his dedicated fanbase who'll never forget what the man and his group have achieved. An odds'n'sods collection of outtakes and unreleased material from the band's early days, 'TOO CLOSE TO HEAVEN' (2001) was a fascinating document of MIKE SCOTT's genesis from punk beat poet to fledgling folk mystic. Named after a theatre run by Scotland's very own Findhorn Foundation (which remains very much a place of inspiration for SCOTT), 'UNIVERSAL HALL' (2003) was markedly different from its predecessor. Heavily accented with spiritual and religious concerns, albeit not in the dogmatic fashion that such themes can be in lesser hands, the record was closest in spirit – if not exactly in feel – to VAN MORRISON's (an obvious comparison but one which continues to be relevant) latter day quasi-religious searching. The following few years saw the WATERBOYS tour all around Britain, a live document of this, 'KARMA TO BURN' (2005), was SCOTT and co's first official concert set.

• **Covered:** LOST HIGHWAY (Hank Williams) / DEATH IS NOT THE END (Bob Dylan) / WAYWARD WIND (Lebawsky-Newman) / BECAUSE THE NIGHT (Patti Smith – Bruce Springsteen) / PURPLE RAIN (Prince) / COME LIVE WITH ME (Roy Carr) / A SONG FOR LIFE (Rodney Crowell) / and a several traditional renditions.

Album rating: THE WATERBOYS (*6) / A PAGAN PLACE (*6) / THIS IS THE SEA (*7) / FISHERMAN'S BLUES (*6) / ROOM TO ROAM (*6) / THE BEST OF THE WATERBOYS compilation (*9) / DREAM HARDER (*5) / THE SECRET LIFE OF THE WATERBOYS early stuff (*4) / A ROCK IN THE WEARY LAND (*7) / TOO CLOSE TO HEAVEN collection (*5) / UNIVERSAL HALL (*6) / KARMA TO BURN (*6) / Mike Scott: BRING 'EM ALL IN (*6) / STILL BURNING (*5)

ANOTHER PRETTY FACE

MIKE SCOTT (b.14 Dec'58, Edinburgh, Scotland) – vocals, guitar, piano / **JOHN CALDWELL** – guitar / **JIM GEDDES** – bass / **CRIGG** (b.IAN WALTER GREIG) – drums

New Pleasures not iss.

May 79. (7") *(Z1)* **ALL THE BOYS LOVE CARRIE. / THAT'S NOT ENOUGH** –

Virgin not iss.

Feb 80. (7") *(VS 320)* **WHATEVER HAPPENED TO THE WEST?. / GODDBYE 1970's** –

— trimmed to basic duo of **SCOTT + CALDWELL** plus **MAIRI ROSS** – bass / added **ADRIAN JOHNSON** – drums

Chicken Jazz not iss.

Dec 80. (7") *(JAZZ 1)* **ONLY HEROES LIVE FOREVER. / HEAVEN GETS CLOSER EVERY DAY** –

Mar 81. (c-ep) *(JAZZ 2)* **I'M SORRY THAT I BEAT YOU, I'M SORRY THAT I SCREAMED, FOR A MOMENT THERE I REALLY LOST CONTROL(live)** –
– This could be Hell / My darkest hour / Lightning that strikes twice / Graduation day / Carrie. *(on most copies, studio tracks +=)* – Another kind of circus / Only heroes live forever / Out of control.

Apr 81. (7") *(JAZZ 3)* **SOUL TO SOUL. / A WOMAN'S PLACE / GOD ON THE SCREEN** –

— now just **SCOTT + CALDWELL**

Ensign not iss.

Feb 82. (7"/ext.12"; as FUNHOUSE) *(ENY/+T 222)* **OUT OF CONTROL. / THIS COULD BE HELL** –

the WATERBOYS

MIKE SCOTT plus **ANTHONY THISTLETHWAITE** (b. 8 Aug'55, Leicester, England) – saxophone (ex-ROBYN HITCHCOCK / of SOFT BOYS) / **KARL WALLINGER** (b.19 Oct'57, Prestatyn, Wales) – keyboards, bass

Chicken Jazz not iss.

May 83. (7") *(CJ 1)* **A GIRL CALLED JOHNNY. / THE LATE TRAIN TO HEAVEN** –
(12") *(CJT 1)* – ('A'side) / Ready for the monkey house / Somebody might wave back / Out of control (APF; John Peel session).

Ensign Chrysalis

Jul 83. (lp/c) *(ENC L/C 1)* **THE WATERBOYS** –
– December / A girl called Johnny / The three day man / Gala / I will not follow / It should have been you / The girl in the swing / Savage Earth heart. *(re-iss. Aug86 on 'Chrysalis-Ensign' lp/c; CHEN/ZCHEN 1) (cd-iss. Feb87; CCD 1541) <US cd-iss. 1987; 21541> (cd re-mast.Mar02 on 'Chrysalis'+=; 537703-2)* – (extra tracks).

Sep 83. (7") *(ENY 506)* **DECEMBER. / WHERE ARE YOU NOW WHEN I NEED YOU** –
(12") *(12ENY 506)* – ('A'side) / Red army blues / The three day man (Peter Powell session).

— added **KEVIN WILKINSON** – drums / **RODDY LORIMER** (b. Glasgow, Scotland) – trumpet / **TIM BLANTHORN** – violin

Apr 84. (7") *(ENY 508)* **THE BIG MUSIC. / THE EARTH ONLY ENDURES** –
(12"+=) *(12ENY 508)* – Bury my heart.

May 84. (lp/c) *(ENC L/C 3)* **A PAGAN PLACE** 100 –
– Church not made with hands / All the things she gave me / The thrill is gone / Rags / Somebody might wave back / The big music / Red army blues / A pagan place. *(re-iss. Aug86 on 'Chrysalis-Ensign' lp/c; CHEN/ZCHEN 2) (cd-iss. Feb87 & Jul94; CCD 1542) <US cd-iss. 1987; 21542> (cd re-mast.Mar02 on 'Chrysalis'+=; 537704-2)* – (extra tracks).

— (Oct84) **MIKE + KARL** recruited new people for tour/lp **TERRY MANN** – bass / **CHARLIE WHITTEN** – drums / **STEVE WICKHAM** (b. Dublin, Ireland) – violin / **LORIMER / DELAHAYE** – organ

Sep 85. (lp/c) *(ENC L/C 5)* **THIS IS THE SEA** 37 –
– Don't bang the drum / The whole of the Moon / Spirit / The pan within / Medicine bow / Old England / Be my enemy / Trumpets / This is the sea. *(re-iss. Aug86 on 'Chrysalis-Ensign' lp/c; CHEN/ZCHEN 3) (cd-iss. Feb87; CCD CCD 1543) (re-iss. cd Mar94;) <US cd-iss. 1987; 21543> (lp re-iss. Aug00 on 'Simply Vinyl'; SVLP 234)*

Oct 85. (7") *(ENY 502)* **THE WHOLE OF THE MOON. / MEDICINE BOW** 26
(ext.12"+=) *(12ENY 520)* – Spirit (extended) / The girl in the swing (live).

— **MIKE SCOTT** now only original survivor (retained THISTLETHWAITE + HUTCHISON), when KARL formed WORLD PARTY.

— additional band **STEVE WICKHAM** – violin (ex-IN TUA NUA) / **J.D. DOHERTY** – drums / **COLIN BLAKEY** (b. Falkirk, Scotland) – flute (ex-WE FREE KINGS) /('88) added **SHARON SHANNON** (b. Ireland) – accordion / **NOEL BRIDGEMAN** (b. Dublin, Ireland) – drums repl. DOHERTY

Nov 88. (lp/c)(cd) *(CHEN/ZCHEN 5)(CCD 1589) <41589>* **FISHERMAN'S BLUES** 13 76
– Fisherman's blues / We will not be lovers / Strange boat / World party / Sweet thing / And a bang on the ear / Has anybody here seen Hank? / When we will be married? / When ye go away / The stolen child. *(cd+=)* – The lost highway. *(lp re-iss. Sep00 on 'Simply Vinyl'; SVLP 245)*

Dec 88. (7"/12"/cd-s) *(ENY/+X/CD 621)* **FISHERMAN'S BLUES. / THE LOST HIGHWAY** 32 –

Jun 89. (7"/c-s/12"/cd-s) *(ENY/+MC/X/CD 624)* **AND A BANG ON THE EAR. / THE RAGGLE TAGGLE GYPSY** 51 –

— **MIKE SCOTT / THISTLETHWAITE / HUTCHISON / + KEV BLEVINS** – drums repl. last additional band members

Sep 90. (cd)(c/lp) *(CCD 1768)(Z+/CHEN 16) <21768>* **ROOM TO ROAM** 5
– In search of a rose / Songs from the edge of the world / A man is in love / Bigger picture / Natural bridge blues / Something that is gone / The star and the sea / Life on Sundays / Island man / The raggle taggle gypsy / How long will I love you? / Upon the wind and waves / Spring rooms to Spiddal / Further up, further in / Trip to Broadford / Room to roam. *(cd+=)* – The kings of Kerry. *(re-iss. Sep94 cd/c;)*

Mar 91. (7"/c-s) *(ENY/+MC 642) <Alex; 1516>* **THE WHOLE OF THE MOON. / A GOLDEN AGE** 3 Jul91
(12"+=/cd-s+=) *(ENY X/CD 642)* – Higher in time / High far soon / Soon as I get home.

Apr 91. (cd)(c/lp) *(CCD 1845)(Z+/CHEN 19) <21845>* **THE BEST OF THE WATERBOYS ('81-'90)** (compilation) 2
– A girl called Johnny / The big music / All the things she gave me / The whole of the Moon / Spirit / Don't bang the drum / Fisherman's blues / Killing my heart / Strange boat / And a bang on the ear / Old England / A man is in love. *(cd re-iss. Aug00; same)*

May 91. (7"/c-s) *(ENY/+MC 645) <Alex; 1581>* **FISHERMAN'S BLUES. / LOST HIGHWAY** 75 Jun91
(12"+=/cd-s+=) *(ENY X/CD 645)* – Medicine bow (live).

— disbanded soon after last studio album above. In mid'91, MIKE SCOTT re-formed group and signed for US-based label 'Geffen'. THISTLETHWAITE formed The BLUE STARS.

— **MIKE SCOTT** with **CHRIS BRUCE** – guitars / **SCOTT THUNES** – bass / **CARLA AZAR** – drums / **BASHIRI JOHNSON** – percussion / **LJUBISA 'Lubi' RISTIC** – sitar / **GEORGE STATHOS** – Greek clarinet / **JAMES CAMPAGNOLA** – saxophone / **JERE PETERS** – rattles / **PAL SHAZAR + JULES SHEAR** – backing vox / **BILLY CONNOLLY**– guest 10 second voiceover

Geffen Geffen

May 93. (7"/c-s) *(GFS/+C 42)* **THE RETURN OF PAN. / KARMA** 24
(12"+=/cd-s+=) *(GFS T/CD 42)* – Mister Powers / ('A'demo).

May 93. (cd/c/lp) *(<GED/GEC/GEF 24476>)* **DREAM HARDER** 5
– The new life / Glastonbury song / Preparing to fly / The return of Pan / Corn circles / Suffer / Winter winter / Love and death / Spiritual city / Wonders of Lewis / The return of Jimi Hendrix / Good news. *(cd re-iss. Jul96; GFLD 19318)*

Jul 93. (7"/c-s) *(GFS/+C 49)* **GLASTONBURY SONG. / CHALICE HILL** [29] [–]
(12"+=/cd-s+=) *(GFS T/CD 49)* – Burlington Bertie – Accrington Stanley / Corn circle symphony (extended).

— MIKE SCOTT split the band after above

MIKE SCOTT

— mostly all solo with some guests

Chrysalis Chrysalis

Sep 95. (c-s/7") *(TC+/CHS 5025)* <58503> **BRING 'EM ALL IN. / CITY FULL OF GHOSTS (DUBLIN)** [56] Nov95 [ ]
(cd-s+=) *(CDCHS 5025)* – Mother Cluny / Beatles reunion blues.

Sep 95. (cd/c/lp) *(<CD/TC+/CHR 6108>)* **BRING 'EM ALL IN** [23] [ ]
– Bring 'em all in / Iona song / Edinburgh Castle / What do you want me to do? / I know she's in the building / City full of ghosts (Dublin) / Wonderful disguise / Sensitive children / Learning to love him / She is so beautiful / Wonderful disguise (reprise) / Long way to the light / Building the city of light.

Nov 95. (7") *(CHS 5026)* **BUILDING THE CITY OF LIGHT. / WHERE DO YOU WANT THE BOOMBOX, BUDDY** [60] [–]
(cd-s+=) *(CDCHSS 5026)* – Goin' back to Glasters (live) / The whole of the Moon (live).
(cd-s) *(CDCHS 5026)* – ('A'side) / Two great waves / My beautiful guide / Building the city of light (Universal Hall demo).

— now with **CHRIS BRUCE** – lead guitar / **PINO PALLADINO** – bass / **JIM KELTNER** – drums / **JAMES HALLAWELL** – organ / etc

Sep 97. (c-s) *(TCCHS 5064)* **LOVE ANYWAY / KING OF STARS** [50] [–]
(cd-s) *(CDCHS 5064)* – ('A'side) / King electric (including Moonage Daydream) / Blues is my business.
(cd-s) *(CDCHSS 5064)* – ('A'side) / Big lover / Careful with the mellotron, Eugene / Since I found my school.

Oct 97. (cd/c) *(<CD/TC CHR 6122>)* **STILL BURNING** [34] [ ]
– Questions / My dark side / Open / Love anyway / Rare, precious and gone / Dark man of my dreams / Personal / Strawberry man / Sunrising / Everlasting arms.

Feb 98. (cd-ep) *(CDCHSS 5073)* **RARE, PRECIOUS AND GONE / KISS THE WIND / WHEN WILL WE BE MARRIED (live) / LOVE ANYWAY (demo)** [74] [–]
(cd-ep) *(CDCHS 5073)* – ('A'side) / All things she gave me (live) / She is so beautiful (live) / Nectar (7 days).

the WATERBOYS

MIKE SCOTT re-formed the band with **LIVINGSTON BROWN** + **MARK SMITH** – bass / **JEREMY STACEY** – drums / **ANTHONY THISTLETHWAITE** – electric slide mandolin / + others on session

R.C.A. R.C.A.

Sep 00. (cd/c) *(<74321 78305-2/-4>)* **A ROCK IN THE WEARY LAND** [47] Nov00 [ ]
– Let it happen / My love is my rock in the weary land / It's all gone / Is she conscious? / We are Jonah / Malediction / Dumbing down the world / His word is not his bond / Night falls on London / The charlatan's lament / The wind in the wires / Crown.

Oct 00. (7") *(74321 79417-7)* **MY LOVE IS MY ROCK IN THE WEARY LAND. / YOUR BABY AIN'T YOUR BABY ANYMORE (with the Half Mast Flag Country & Western Band)** [ ] [–]
(cd-s) *(74321 79417-2)* – ('A'side) / Lucky day – Bad advice / Time space and the bride's bed.
(cd-s) *(74321 79418-2)* – ('A'side) / Trouble down yonder / Send him down to Waco.

Feb 01. (m-cd) *(74321 83649-2)* **IS SHE CONSCIOUS?** [ ] [–]
– Is she conscious? (album version) / Sad procession / Faeries prisoner / Is she conscious? / Savage earth heart / My Lord what a morning / Is she conscious (video).

Apr 01. (7") *(74321 84870-7)* **WE ARE JONAH. / TIME, SPACE AND THE BRIDE'S BED** [ ] [–]
(cd-s) *(74321 84870-2)* – ('A'side) / Lucky day – Bad advice / Dumbing down the world (live at Glastonbury 2000).
(cd-s) *(74321 84871-2)* – ('A'side) / Martin descent / Send him down to Waco.

Sep 01. (cd) *(<74321 88152-2>)* **TOO CLOSE TO HEAVEN** (rarities) [ ] Jan02 [ ]
– On my way to heaven / Higher in time / The ladder / Too close to Heaven / Good man gone / Blues for your baby / Custer's blues / A home in the meadow / Tenderfootin' / Lonesome old wind.

— **SCOTT** brought back **STEVE WICKHAM** – fiddle / + new **RICHARD NAIFF** – flute, piano

Puck Minty Fresh

Jun 03. (cd) *(PUCK 1)* <70053> **UNIVERSAL HALL** [74] May03 [ ]
– This light is for the world / The Christ in you / Silent fellowship / Every breath is yours / Peace of Iona / Ain't no words for the things I'm feeling / Seek the light / I've lived here before / Always dancing, never getting tired / The dance at the crossroads / E.B.O.L. / Universal hall.

Sep 05. (cd) *(PUCK 4)* **KARMA TO BURN** (live) [ ] [–]
– Long way to the light / Peace of Iona / Glastonbury song / Medicine bow / The Pan within / Open / The return of Jimi Hendrix / My dark side / A song for the life / Bring 'em all in / The whole of the moon / Fisherman's blues / Come live with me.

– compilations, etc. –

Oct 94. (cd/c) *Ensign; (CD/TC CHEN 35)* **THE SECRET LIFE OF THE WATERBOYS** (81-85 material) [ ] [ ]
(cd re-iss. Sep97; same)

Aug 98. (d-cd) *Griffin; <40>* **LIVE ADVENTURES OF THE WATERBOYS (live)** [–] [ ]
– Death is not the end / Earth only endures / Medicine bow / Fisherman's blues / This is the sea / Meet me at the station / We will not be lovers / Wayward wind / A girl called Johnny / Purple rain / Be my enemy / Old England / The thrill is gone – And the healing has begun / Pain within (including Because the night) / Whole of the moon / Spirit / Savage earth heart / Saints and angels. *(UK-iss.Jul00 on 'Burning Airlines' d-cd/t-lp; PILOT 040/+LP)*

Sep 98. (cd) *Chrysalis; (496505-2)* **THE WHOLE OF THE MOON – THE BEST OF MIKE SCOTT & THE WATERBOYS** [ ] [–]

Sep 00. (3xcd-box) *EMI; (528661-2)* **A PAGAN PLACE / THIS IS THE SEA / FISHERMAN'S BLUES** [ ] [–]

Mar 03. (cd) *E.M.I.; (582226-2)* **THE ESSENTIAL WATERBOYS** [ ] [–]

Muddy WATERS

Born: McKINLEY MORGANFIELD, 4th April 1915, Rolling Fork, Mississippi, USA. While perhaps not as widely celebrated as his peers, JOHN LEE HOOKER and BB KING, it was WATERS who was the main catalyst in converting blues to urban electric and then to rock'n'roll. Brought up by his mother in Clarksdale (birthplace of HOOKER), he began singing and playing harmonica at the age of 7, acquired his nickname due to his fondness for playing in a nearby muddy creek. By his late teens, WATERS had switched to guitar and was supplementing his wages as a cotton picker (although he had ambitions beyond that – in his late teens he was running his own whisky still!) by playing at local juke joints and parties. Initially, his style was a combination of CHARLEY PATTON, SON HOUSE (his mentor and tutor) and his hero, ROBERT JOHNSON (although he never met him, he once saw him play, the experience apparently changing his life) although he had evolved his own approach to the blues by the time he'd moved to Chicago in 1943. Another turning point came in 1941 when ALAN LOMAX visited the plantation where MUDDY worked; LOMAX had already recorded SON HOUSE and wanted to record ROBERT JOHNSON for the Library Of Congress, unaware that JOHNSON was already dead. When he found out, he asked about ELMORE JAMES and finally ended up recording the young MUDDY WATERS, both solo and in a band with the SON SIMS FOUR (the recorded songs were 'I BE'S TROUBLED' and 'COUNTRY BLUES'). WATERS was suitably impressed with the sound of the recordings to decide on a career as a professional musician. In Chicago he worked in a paper mill by day and played in clubs at night (encouraged by BIG BILL BROONZY and SUNNYLAND SLIM), quickly discovering that his acoustic guitar wasn't loud enough for these venues and subsequently going electric. WATERS gradually assembled the finest blues band of the era, featuring, at various times, MARVIN 'LITTLE WALTER' JACOBS (harmonica/vocals), OTIS SPANN (piano) and WILLIE DIXON (bass), among others; his bands attracted the greatest talents, WATERS giving them a platform to develop their reputations (even allowing them to record their own music during his studio time) and training them to be leaders in their own right. When LITTLE WALTER, JIMMY ROGERS, OTIS SPANN and JAMES COTTON set off on their own he wished them the best and simply replaced them. He recorded briefly for 'Columbia' in 1946 ('HARD DAY BLUES' displayed signs of what was to come) before signing to 'Aristocrat' (later 'Chess' in 1950) although he didn't start recording under his own name until 1948. Such was the strength of WATERS' reputation that his first single, 'I CAN'T BE SATISFIED' sold out its first pressing within 24 hours while the follow up, 'I FEEL LIKE GOING HOME' saw him making his R&B chart debut. WATERS' first 'Chess' single was 'ROLLIN STONE' in 1950, the bluesman achieving his second major R&B success with 'LOUISIANA BLUES' (WATERS had a further thirteen R&B hits up to 1956) the following year. His band toured the UK in 1958 and although critics weren't so supportive, viewers of the shows were taken aback by the power of the performances which effected an incalculable impact upon a future generation of British performers including ALEXIS KORNER and CYRIL DAVIES, who were inspired to form BLUES INCORPORATED. Songs like 'HOOCHIE COOCHIE MAN', 'ROLLIN' AND TUMBLIN', 'BABY PLEASE DON'T GO', 'I GOT MY MOJO WORKING', 'I JUST WANT TO MAKE LOVE TO YOU' and 'MANNISH BOY', many written by WILLIE DIXON, became standards among early UK R&B bands while The ROLLING STONES, The MOJOS, The HOOCHIE COOCHIE MEN and The MANNISH BOYS even took their name from WATERS songs. He also had a direct influence on JUNIOR WELLS, BUDDY GUY, JIMI HENDRIX and ERIC CLAPTON. Yet it took a long time for him to reap the financial benefits (he was often out-sold by JIMMY REED, JIMMY ROGERS and LITTLE WALTER) and at the end of the 50's Chess decided to market WATERS as an album based performer, released two albums in 1960 including 'MUDDY WATERS AT NEWPORT' (arguably his finest live album). When the 'STONES arrived to record at the Chess studios in 1964 (the year that saw the release of the all-acoustic 'MUDDY WATERS, FOLK SINGER') they famously found WATERS up a ladder, painting the studio(!); some of the musicians he had inspired subsequently recorded collaborative albums with him. They were of inconsistent quality, but they did, at least, get WATERS noticed outwith blues circles. 'FATHERS & SONS' was a joint effort with MIKE BLOOMFIELD, PAUL BUTTERFIELD, DONALD 'DUCK' DUNN, BUDDY MILES and OTIS SPANN, marking his only entry to the US Top 100. 'THE LONDON MUDDY WATERS SESSIONS' featuring RORY GALLAGHER, GEORGIE FAME, MITCH MITCHELL, RICK GRECH and STEVE WINWOOD also helped him break out of the blues ghetto. In an attempt to keep WATERS in the public eye, 'Chess' rather ill-advisedly persuaded him to record such projects as the psychedelic 'ELECTRIC MUD' (which included a version of The STONES' 'LET'S SPEND THE NIGHT TOGETHER') album in the late 60's. Nevertheless, he won Grammy's in 1972 for 'THEY CALL ME MUDDY WATERS' and 'LONDON SESSIONS' although tragedy struck the following year when he was seriously injured in a car crash; the accident left three people dead and put him into semi-retirement for two years. The guitarist returned with the Grammy Award winning 'MUDDY WATERS WOODSTOCK ALBUM' and performed 'MANNISH BOY' at The BAND's farewell concert. WATERS left 'Chess' (after the CHESS brothers sold out to a New York corporation) in 1977 and signed to STEVE PAUL's 'Blue Sky' (PAUL was the manager of JOHNNY WINTER) imprint. WINTER, who had long idolised WATERS, jumped at the chance to work with his hero and set about recreating the veteran bluesman's 50's recording sound aided by the likes of JAMES COTTON, WALTER HORTON, LUTHER JOHNSON, JIMMY ROGERS, PINETOP PERKINS and WILLIE 'BIG EYES' SMITH. Four albums, 'HARD AGAIN', 'I'M READY', 'MUDDY MISSISSIPPI WATERS' (all Grammy winners) and 'I'M A KING BEE' were released between 1977 and 1980. 'HARD AGAIN' was recorded amid a great atmosphere, lots of excitement at the end of each track as the band went through classics like 'I WANT TO BE LOVED', 'I CAN'T BE SATISFIED' (with WINTER on slide guitar), 'DEEP DOWN IN FLORIDA' and 'MANNISH BOY'. Incidentally, it was this recording of 'MANNISH BOY' that was used for a Levi jeans TV advert in 1988 and was subsequently released as a single, becoming WATERS' only UK chart entry at number 51. By 1980, he had moved from the south side to a comfortable home in the suburbs with his 25 year old wife and numerous grandchildren. WATERS died peacefully in his sleep on the 30th of April 1983 (only after his death it was discovered that he had contracted cancer), receiving a posthumous induction to the Rock And Roll Hall Of Fame in 1987 and a Lifetime Achievement Award at the Grammy's in 1992.

Best CD compilation: MUDDY WATERS – THE CHESS BOX box-set (*9)

MUDDY WATERS – vocals, guitar; with **SUNNYLAND SLIM** – piano

		not iss.	Aristocrat
1948.	(78) *<1302>* **GYPSY WOMAN. / LITTLE ANNA MAE**	-	
1948.	(78) *<1305>* **I CAN'T BE SATISFIED. / FEEL LIKE GOIN' HOME**		
1948.	(78) *<1306>* **TRAIN FARE HOME. / SITTIN' HERE AND DRINKIN'**	-	
1949.	(78) *<1307>* **YOU'RE GONNA MISS ME. / MEAN RED SPIDER**	-	
1949.	(78) *<1310>* **STREAMLINE WOMAN. / MUDDY JUMPS ONE**	-	
1949.	(78) *<1311>* **LITTLE GENEVA. / CANARY BIRD**	-	
1949.	(78) *<406>* **SCREAMIN' AND CRYIN'. / WHERE'S MY WOMAN BEEN**	-	
1951.	(78) *<412>* **ROLLIN' AND TUMBLIN'. / (pt. 2)**	-	

— with band **JIMMY RODGERS** – guitar / **WILLIE DIXON** – bass / **LITTLE WALTER** – harmonica / **LEONARD CHESS** – drums / **ERNEST CRAWFORD** – bass

		not iss.	Chess
1950.	(78) *<1434>* **YOU'RE GONNA NEED MY HELP I SAID. / SAD LETTER BLUES** *(UK-iss.May52 on 'Vogue Coral'; V 2101)*	-	
1951.	(78) *<1441>* **LOUISIANA BLUES. / EVAN'S SHUFFLE**	-	
1951.	(78) *<1452>* **LONG DISTANCE CALL. / TOO YOUNG TO KNOW** *(UK-iss.Nov54 on 'Vogue Coral'; V 2273)*	-	
1951.	(7") *<1468>* **HONEY BEE. / APPEALING BLUES** *(UK-iss.May56 on 'Vogue Coral'; V 2372)*	-	
1951.	(78) *<1480>* **MY FAULT. / STILL A FOOL**	-	
—	ELGIN EVANS – drums repl. CHESS		
1952.	(78) *<1490>* **SHE MOVES ME. / EARLY MORNING BLUES**	-	
1952.	(78) *<1509>* **ALL NIGHT LONG. / COUNTRY BOY**	-	
1952.	(78) *<1514>* **PLEASE HAVE MERCY. / I CAN'T BE SATISFIED (LOOKING FOR MY BABY)**	-	
1952.	(78) *<1526>* **STANDING AROUND CRYING. / GONE TO MAIN STREET**	-	
1953.	(78) *<1537>* **SHE'S ALL RIGHT. / SAD, SAD DAY**	-	
1953.	(78) *<1542>* **TURN THE LAMP DOWN LOW. / WHO'S GONNA BE YOUR SWEET MAN**	-	
1953.	(78) *<1550>* **BLOW WIND BLOW. / MAD LOVE (I JUST WANT YOU TO LOVE ME)**	-	
—	**OTIS SPANN** – piano (to mid-60's) repl. SLIM		
1954.	(78) *<1560>* **HOOCHIE COOCHIE MAN. / SHE'S SO PRETTY**	-	
1954.	(78) *<1571>* **I JUST WANT TO MAKE LOVE TO YOU. / OH YEAH**	-	
1954.	(78) *<1579>* **I'M READY. / I DON'T KNOW WHY**	-	

1954. (78) *<1585>* **I'M A NATURAL BORN LOVER. / LOVING MAN**

Mar 55. (7"ep) *Vogue; (EPV 1046)* **MUDDY WATERS WITH LITTLE WALTER**
– I can't be satisfied / Louisiana blues / Evans shuffle / I feel like going home.

1955. (78) *<1596>* **I WANT TO BE LOVED. / MY EYES (KEEP ME IN TROUBLE)**

1955. (78) *<1602>* **MANNISH BOY. / YOUNG FASHIONED WAYS**

1955. (78) *<1612>* **SUGAR SWEET. / TROUBLE NO MORE**

1956. (78) *<1620>* **40 DAYS AND 40 NIGHTS. / ALL ABOARD**

1956. (78) *<1630>* **DON'T GO NO FURTHER. / DIAMONDS AT YOUR FEET**

1956. (78) *<1644>* **JUST TO BE WITH YOU. / I GOT TO FIND MY BABY**

London Chess

Oct 56. (7"ep) *(RU-E 1060)* **MISSISSIPPI BLUES**
– All aboard / 40 days and 40 nights / Mannish boy / Young fashioned ways.

1957. (7") *<1652>* **GOT MY MOJO WORKING. / ROCK ME**

1957. (7") *<1667>* **GOOD NEWS. / COME HOME BABY**

1957. (7") *<1680>* **EVIL. / I LIVE THE LIFE I LOVE**

1958. (7") *<1692>* **I WON'T GO. / SHE'S GOT IT**

1958. (7") *<1704>* **SHE'S 19 YEARS OLD. / CLOSE TO YOU**

1958. (7") *<1718>* **WALKING THRU THE PARK. / MEAN MISTREATER**

1958. (7") *<1724>* **CLOUDS IN MY HEART. / OOH WEE**

1959. (7") *<1733>* **TAKE THE BITTER WITH THE SWEET. / SHE'S INTO SOMETHING**

1959. (7") *<1739>* **TELL ME BABY. / LOOK WHAT YOU'VE DONE**

1959. (7") *<1748>* **WHEN I GET TO THINKING. / I FEEL SO GOOD**

1960. (7") *<1752>* **I'M YOUR DOCTOR. / READ WAY BACK**

1960. (7") *<1758>* **LOVE AFFAIR. / RECIPE FOR LOVE**

— **WALTER HORTON** – repl. LITTLE WALTER until **JAMES COTTON** repl. HORTON / **PAT HARE** came in on drums and ROGERS departed. He toured in the UK.

Mar 59. (lp) *(LJZ-M 15152)* **THE BEST OF MUDDY WATERS** (compilation)
– I just want to make love to you / Long distance call / Louisiana blues / Honey bee / Rollin' stone / I'm ready / Hoochie coochie / She moves me / I want you to love me / Standing around crying / Still a fool / I can't be satisfied. *(re-iss. Oct87 lp/c; GCH/+K7 8044) (cd-iss. Jun88; CDCHESS 1012)*

— toured now with **FRANCIS CLAY** – drums / **ANDREW STEPHENSON** – bass / **PAT HARE** – guitar / **SPANN + COTTON**

Jun 60. (7") *<1765>* **TIGER IN YOUR TANK. / MEANEST WOMAN**

Aug 60. (7") *<1774>* **GOT MY MOJO WORKING (pt.1). / WOMAN WANTED**

1961. (7") *<1796>* **LONESOME ROOM BLUES. / MESSIN' WITH THE MAN**

Pye Jazz Chess

Sep 61. (lp) *(NJL 34) <1449>* **MUDDY WATERS AT NEWPORT (live 1960)** 1960
– Tiger in your tank / I've got my mojo working / I got my brand on you / Baby, please don't go / Soon forgotten / I feel so glad / Goodbye Newport blues. *(re-iss. Nov65 on 'Chess'; CRL 4513) (re-iss. Jan67 on 'Marble Arch'; MAL 661) (re-iss. 1973 on 'Checker') (cd-iss. Jun96 on 'Beat Goes On'; BGOCD 314)*

1962. (7") *<1819>* **TOUGH TIMES. / GOING HOME**

1962. (7") *<1827>* **YOU SHOOK ME. / MUDDY WATERS TWIST**

1962. (7") *<1839>* **YOU NEED LOVE. / LITTLE BROWN BIRD**

1963. (7") *<1862>* **FIVE LONG YEARS. / TWENTY FOUR HOURS**

1964. (7") *<1895>* **THE SAME THING. / YOU CAN'T LOSE WHAT YOU NEVER HAD**

Pye Inter. Chess

May 64. (lp) *(NPL 28038) <1483>* **MUDDY WATERS – FOLK SINGER**
– My home is my delta / Long distance / My captain / Good morning little schoolgirl / You're gonna need my help / Cold weather blues / Peg leg woman / Country boy / Feel like going home. *(re-iss. Aug87 on 'Chess'; GCH/+K7 8040)*

Sep 64. (lp) *(NPL 28040)* **MUDDY WATERS**
– I got my brand on you / Baby, please don't go / Tiger in your tank / I've got my mojo working (part 1) / Goodbye Newport blues / The same thing / Sittin' and thinkin' / 19 years old / I'm your hoochie coochie man / Soon forgotten / I feel so good / I've got my mojo working (part 2) / Long distance call / Wee wee baby / Clouds in my heart. *(cd-iss. Mar90 on 'Roots'; RTS 33018)*

Chess Chess

Feb 65. (7") *(CRS 8001) <1914>* **MY JOHN THE CONQUER ROOT. / SHORT DRESS WOMAN**

1965. (7") *<1921>* **PUT ME IN YOUR LAY-A-WAY. / STILL A FOOL**

Aug 65. (7"ep) *(CRE 6006)* **I'M READY**
– She moves me / I can't be satisfied / I want you to love me.

Aug 65. (7") *(CRS 8019) <1937>* **I GOT A RICH MAN'S WOMAN. / MY DOG CAN'T BARK**

Jan 66. (lp) *(CRL 4515) <1501>* **THE REAL FOLK BLUES**
– Mannish boy / Screamin' and cryin' / Just to be with you / Walking in the park / Same thing / Walking blues / Canary bird / Gypsy women / Rollin' and tumblin' / Forty days and forty nights / You can't lose what you never had / Little Geneva.

May 66. (7"ep) *(CRE 6022)* **THE REAL FOLK BLUES VOL.4**
– I just want to make love to you / Louisiana blues / Still a fool / Standing around crying.

1966. (7") *<1973>* **CORINA, CORINA. / HOOTCHI KOOTCHIE MAN**

Jan 67. (lp) *(CRL 4525) <1507>* **MUDDY, BRASS AND THE BLUES**
– Corrine, Corrina / Piney brown blues / Black night / Trouble in mind / Goin' back to Memphis / Betty and Dupree / Sweet little angel / Take me advice / Trouble / Hard loser.

Aug 67. (lp; MUDDY WATERS, BO DIDDLEY & LITTLE WALTER) *(CRL 4529)* **SUPERBLUES**

1967. (7") *<2018>* **BIRDNEST ON THE GROUND. / WHEN THE EAGLE FLIES**

May 68. (lp; MUDDY WATERS, BO DIDDLEY & HOWLIN' WOLF) *(CRL 4537) <LPS 3010>* **THE SUPER BLUES BAND**

Chess Cadet

Jan 69. (lp) *(CRL 4542) <314>* **ELECTRIC MUD** Nov68
– I just want to make love to you / Hoochie coochie man / Let's spend the night together / She's all right / I'm a man / Herbert Harper's free press / Tom cat / Same thing. *(cd-iss. Apr97 on 'Chess-MCA'; MCD 09364)*

Jan 69. (7") *(CRS 8083)* **LET'S SPEND THE NIGHT TOGETHER. / I'M A MAN**

Aug 69. (lp) *(CRL 4553) <320>* **AFTER THE RAIN**
– I a the blues / Ramblin' mind / Rollin and tumblin' / Bottom of the sea / Honey bee / Blues and trouble / Hurtin' soul / Screamin' and cryin'

Oct 69. (d-lp) *(CRL 4556) <127>* **FATHERS AND SONS (live with PAUL BUTTERFIELD & MIKE BLOOMFIELD)** Sep69 **70**
– All aboard / Mean disposition / Blow wind blow / Can't lose what you ain't never had / Walking through the park / 40 days and 40 nights / Standin' round crying / I'm ready / Twenty four hours / Sugar sweet / Long distance call / Baby, please don't go / Honey bee / The same thing / Got my mojo working (pt.1 & 2). *(cd-iss. Oct01 on 'Universal'+=; AA8811 2648-2)* – (extra tracks).
(above also featured **BUDDY MILES + PHIL UPCHURCH**)

1970. (7") *<2085>* **GOING HOME. / I FEEL SO GOOD**

Chess Chess

1972. (7") *<2107>* **MAKING FRIENDS. / TWO STEPS FORWARD**

Jul 72. (lp) *(6310 121) <60013>* **THE LONDON MUDDY WATERS SESSIONS**
– Blind man blues / Key to the highway / Walkin' blues / I'm gonna move to the outskirts of town / Who's gonna be your sweet man when I'm gone / Young fashioned ways / Sad sad day / I don't know why. *(re-iss. Apr82 on 'Charly'; CXMP 2005) (re-iss. May92 on 'Chess-MCA'; CHLD/CHLC 19105)*

— On 11 Oct'73, he was involved in a car accident which 3 people were killed. After releasing one more album, he went into semi-retirement for 2 years. Released 'LONDON REVISITED' Jan74 with HOWLIN' WOLF.

Nov 73. (7") *<2143>* **CAN'T GET NO GRINDIN'. / GARBAGE MAN** –
Jan 74. (lp) *(6310 129) <50023>* **CAN'T GET NO GRINDIN'**
– Can't get no grindin' / Mothers bad luck / Funky butt / Sad letter / Someday I'm gonna kitch you / Love weapon / Garbage man / After hours / Whiskey ain't no good / Muddy Waters' shuffle. *(re-iss. Sep90 lp/cd; CH/+D 9319)*
Mar 74. (lp) *<60031>* **"UNK" IN FUNK** –

Blue Sky Blue Sky

Apr 77. (lp) *(SKY 81853) <34449>* **HARD AGAIN** Feb77
– Mannish boy / Bus driver / I want to be loved / Jealous-hearted man / I can't be satisfied / The blues had a baby, and they named it rock'n'roll / Deep down in Florida / Crosseyed cat / Little girl. *(re-iss. Sep83; 32357) (cd-iss. Mar91) (re-iss. Feb94 on 'Columbia' cd/c; CD/40 32357)*
Feb 78. (lp) *(SKY 82235) <34928>* **I'M READY**
– I'm ready / 33 years / Who do you trust / Cooper Brown / I'm your hoochie coochie man / Mame / Rock me / Screamin' and cryin' / Good morning little schoolgirl. *(cd-iss. Nov91 on 'Beat Goes On';)*
Jan 79. (lp) *(SKY 83422) <35712>* **MUDDY MISSISSIPPI WATERS LIVE (live)**
– Mannish boy / She's 19 years old / Nine below zero / Streamline woman / Howling wolf / Baby please don't go / Deep down in Florida. *(cd-iss. Mar91 on 'Beat Goes On';)*
May 81. (lp) *(SKY 84918) <37064>* **KING BEE**
– I'm a king bee / Too young to know / Mean old Frisco blues / Forever lonely / I feel like goin' home / Champagne and reefer / Sad sad day / My eyes keep me in trouble / Deep down in Florida / No escape from the blues.

— On the 30th Apr'83, MUDDY died of a heart attack in his Chicago home.

– (selective) compilations, etc. –

Nov 64. (lp) *Pye; (NPL 28048)* **MUDDY SINGS BIG BILL (BROONZY)**
(re-iss. Nov67 on 'Marble Arch'; MAL 723)
Jan 67. (lp) *Chess; <1511>* **MORE REAL FOLK BLUES** –
May 70. (lp) *Syndicate/ US= Chess; (SC 002) <002>* **GOOD NEWS**
– Trouble no more / Don't go no further / Diamonds at your feet / Evil / All aboard / I love the life I live / Mean mistreater / Recipe for love / Good news / Come home baby / I won't go / She's got it / Close to you. *(re-iss. 1979)*
Jun 70. (lp) *Syndicate; (SC 005) / Chess; <005>* **WE THREE KINGS ("with HOWLIN' WOLF & LITTLE WALTER")**
(re-iss. Sep82)
Feb 71. (lp) *Chess; <1553>* **THEY CALL ME MUDDY WATERS** –
(cd-iss. Jan98 on 'Summit'; SUMCD 4173)
Aug 92. (9xcd-box) *Chess; (CDREDBOX 3)* **THE COMPLETE MUDDY WATERS: 1947-1967**
Jan 92. (cd) *Quality; (QSCD 6004)* **THE ESSENTIAL RECORDINGS** –
Aug 92. (cd) *Columbia; (4768922)* **BLUE SKIES**
(re-iss. Nov02; 509315-2)
Nov 92. (cd/c) *Charly; (CD/TC BM 10)* **ROCK ME** –
Feb 93. (cd/c) *Charly; (CD/TC BM 39)* **FUNKY BUTT** –
Feb 93. (cd) *Charly; (CDCD 1039)* **GOT MY MOJO WORKING** –
Jul 93. (cd) *Charly; (CDCD 1100)* **HOOCHIE COOCHIE MAN** –
Sep 93. (cd) *See For Miles; (SEECD 379)* **THE EP COLLECTION (1-side by HOWLIN' WOLF)** –
May 94. (cd) *Charly; (CDTT 3)* **TWO ON ONE (w/JOHN LEE HOOKER)** –
Aug 94. (cd) *Charly;* **LIVE AT NEWPORT (live w/OTIS SPANN)** –
Nov 94. (cd) *Charly;* **CHICAGO 1979 (live)** –
Apr 95. (cd) *Charly; (CDRB 15)* **ELECTRIC MUD & MORE** –
Apr 95. (4xcd-box+book) *Charly; (CDDIG 9)* **THE KING OF CHICAGO BLUES** –
Apr 96. (cd) *Imp; (IMP 305)* **BABY PLEASE DON'T GO (live)**
(re-iss. May01 on 'I.T.M.'; ITM 960006)
Apr 97. (cd) *Chess-MCA; (MCD 09344)* **THE COMPLETE PLANTATION RECORDINGS**
Apr 97. (cd) *Chess-MCA; (MCD 09348)* **ONE MORE MILE**
Jul 97. (cd) *Chess-MCA; (MCD 09370)* **THE BEST OF MUDDY WATERS 1947-1955**
Feb 98. (cd) *Just A Memory; (JAM 9130-2)* **GOIN' WAY BACK**
Aug 98. (cd) *Beat Goes On; (BGOCD 397)* **MUDDY WATERS SINGS BILL BROONZY / FOLK SINGER**
Jan 99. (cd) *Beat Goes On; (BGOCD 436)* **REAL FOLK BLUES / MORE REAL FOLK BLUES**
Sep 99. (cd) *Just A Memory; (JAM 9142-2)* **HOOCHIE COOCHIE MAN: LIVE AT THE RISING CLUB 1977**
Jan 00. (cd) *I.T.M.; (ITM 960014)* **AFTER HOURS**
Mar 00. (d-cd) *Snapper; (SMDCD 249)* **TAKE A WALK WITH ME**
May 00. (cd) *Music Club; (MCCD 425)* **MOJO**
Jul 00. (cd) *Zircon Bleu; (BLEU 506)* **ARISTOCRAT OF THE BLUES 1946-1948**
Oct 00. (cd) *Play Me..; (PBCD 20510)* **PLAY ME THE BLUES VOL.10: THE LEGENDARY BLUES SINGERS**
Nov 00. (3xcd-box) *Golden Stars; (GSS 5293)* **BLUES LEGEND**
Jan 01. (cd) *Catfish; (KATCD 117)* **STREAMLINED WOMAN**
Feb 01. (cd) *Pablo; (PACD 5302-2)* **PARIS 1972**
Sep 01. (d-cd) *M.C.A.; (112649-2)* **THE ANTHOLOGY: 1947-1972**
Jul 02. (cd/c) *Castle Pulse; (PLS CD/MC 594)* **KINGS OF THE BLUES**
Jul 03. (cd) *Apreggio Blues; (ARB 001)* **OL' MAN MUD**

Roger WATERS

Born: 6 Sep'44, Great Bookham, Cambridge, England. A founding member of PINK FLOYD in 1965, WATERS became the outfit's mainman in 1968 following SYD BARRETT's break with reality. PINK FLOYD's frontman and main contributor until his departure in 1983, he put together the soundtrack to the film 'THE BODY' in 1970 together with synth/keys man, RON GEESIN. With PINK FLOYD absent from the recording front in the mid-80's, fans locked onto WATERS for worthwhile material. His debut album, 'PROS & CONS OF HITCH HIKING' (1984) didn't exactly set the world alight but managed a UK Top 20 placing. Not straying too far from latter day PF territory, WATERS carried on in even more lugubrious fashion with two sets, 'WHEN THE WIND BLOWS' (1986) – a shared animation soundtrack album with Various Artists – and 'RADIO KAOS' (1987). Come the turn of the decade, with The BERLIN WALL being dismantled, ROGER thought it necessary to revive the 1979 PINK FLOYD album, 'THE WALL'. With an array of famous guests, he played there to a live audience of 200,000, plus TV millions all contributing to The Disaster Relief Fund. Almost ten years on from the release of studio set, 'AMUSED TO DEATH', WATERS released concert set, 'IN THE FLESH LIVE' (2000), a document of his turn of the decade American tour. For the first time since his break with PINK FLOYD – save his Berlin effort – WATERS revisited his favourite tracks from the band's glory heyday. 2005's 'CA IRA' (sub-titled THERE IS HOPE) was strictly classical and an album that saw composer WATERS invite a full orchestra and opera singer, Bryn Terfel – not for fans of PINK FLOYD.

• **Songwriters:** WATERS wrote all material. • **Trivia:** In 1987, WATERS took the existing members of PINK FLOYD to court, for their use of group name.

Album rating: THE BODY soundtrack with Ron Geesin (*6) / THE PROS AND CONS OF HITCH HIKING (*7) / WHEN THE WIND BLOWS soundtrack with V/A (*4) / RADIO K.A.O.S. (*5) / THE WALL: LIVE IN BERLIN (*4) / AMUSED TO DEATH (*5) / IN THE FLESH – LIVE (*5) / FLICKERING FLAME compilation (*7) / CA IRA with Various Artists (*4)

ROGER WATERS – vocals, bass, etc. (ex-PINK FLOYD) with **ERIC CLAPTON** – guitar / **ANDY NEWMARK** – drums / **RAY COOPER** – percussion / **MADELINE BELL** – vocals

Harvest Columbia

Apr 84. (7") *(HAR 5228)* **5:01 a.m. (THE PROS AND CONS OF HITCH HIKING). / 4:30 a.m. (APPARENTLY THEY WERE TRAVELLING ABROAD)**
(12"+=) *(12HAR 5228)* – 4:33 a.m. (Running shoes).

May 84. (lp/c/cd) *(SHVL 240105-1/-4/-2)* <39290> **THE PROS AND CONS OF HITCH HIKING** 13 31
– 4:30 a.m. (Apparently they were travelling abroad) / 4:33 a.m. (Running shoes) / 4:37 a.m. (Arabs with knives and West German skies) / 4:39 a.m. (For the first time today) / 4:41 a.m. (Sexual revolution) / 4:47 a.m. (The remains of our love) / 4:50 a.m. (Go fishing) / 4:56 a.m. (For the first time today pt.2) / 4:58 a.m. (Dunroamin' duncarin' dunlivin') / 5:06 a.m. (Every strangers eyes) / 5:11 a.m. (The moment of clarity).

Jun 84. (7") *(HAR 5230)* **5:06 a.m. (EVERY STRANGERS EYES). / 4:39 a.m. (FOR THE FIRST TIME TODAY)**
next with his BLEEDING HEART BAND

Virgin not iss.

Oct 86. (cd/c/lp; w/ the BLEEDING HEART BAND) *(CD/TC+/V 2406)* **WHEN THE WIND BLOWS** (soundtrack w/ Various Artists) -
– (side 1 – Various Artists) / The Russian missile / Towers of faith / Hilda's dream / The American bomber / The Anderson shelter / The British submarine / The attack / The fallout / Hilda's hair / Folded flags. *(re-iss. 1989 lp/c; OVED/+C 259)*

—— His new band: **ANDY FAIRWEATHER-LOW** – guitar / **JAY STAPLEY** – electric guitar / **MEL COLLINS** – sax / **IAN RITCHIE** – keyboards, drum prog. / **GRAHAM BROAD** – drums

E.M.I. Columbia

May 87. (7") *(EM 6)* **RADIO WAVES (edit). / GOING TO LIVE IN L.A.** 74
(12"+=/cd-s+=) *(12/CD EM 6)* – ('A'demo version).

Jun 87. (cd/c/lp) *(CD/TC+/KAOS 1)* <40795> **RADIO KAOS** 25 50
– Radio waves / Who needs information / Me or him / The powers that be / Sunset Strip / Home / Four minutes / The tide is turning.

Nov 87. (7") *(EM 37)* **THE TIDE IS TURNING (After Live Aid). / GET BACK ON THE RADIO (demo)** 54
(12"+=/cd-s+=) *(12/CD EM 37)* – Money (live).

Mercury Mercury

Sep 90. (d-cd/d-c/d-lp) *(<846611-2/-4/-1>)* **THE WALL: LIVE IN BERLIN (live)** 27 56
– In the flesh? (SCORPIONS) / The thin ice (UTE LEMPER) / Another brick in the wall – part 1 / The happiest days of our lives (JOE CHEMAY) / Another brick in the wall – part 2 (CYNDI LAUPER) / Mother (SINEAD O'CONNOR) / Goodbye blue sky (JONI MITCHELL) / Empty spaces + Young lust (BRYAN ADAMS) / One of my turns / Don't leave me now / Another brick in the wall – part 3 / Goodbye cruel world / Hey you (PAUL CARRACK) / Is there anybody out there? (MICHAEL KAMEN /The RUNDFUNK ORCHESTRA +*) / Nobody home / Vera (*) / Bring the boys back home / Comfortably numb (VAN MORRISON) / In the flesh? (*) / Run like Hell / Waiting for the worms (*) / Stop to / The trial (TIM CURRY & THOMAS DOLBY) / The tide is turning (The COMPANY). *(re-iss. d-cd Sep95)*

Sep 90. (7") *(MER 332)* **ANOTHER BRICK IN THE WALL PART 2. / RUN LIKE HELL (Potsdamer mix)** -
(12"+=/cd-s+=) *(MER X/CD 332)* – ('A'-full version).

Jan 91. (7") *(MER 336)* **THE TIDE IS TURNING. / NOBODY HOME** -
(12"+=/cd-s+=) *(MER X/CD 336)* – ('A'-lp version).

Columbia Columbia

Aug 92. (7"/c-s) *(658 139-7/-4)* **WHAT GOD WANTS, PART 1. / ('A'video edit)** 35
(cd-s+=) *(658 139-2)* – What God wants, part III.

Sep 92. (cd/c/lp) *(468761-2/-4/-1)* <47127> **AMUSED TO DEATH** 8 21
– The ballad of Bill Hubbard / What God wants, part 1 / Perfect sense, part I & II / The bravery of being out of range / Late home tonight, part I & II / Too much rope / What God wants, part II & III / Watching TV / Three wishes / It's a miracle / Amused to death. *(cd re-iss. Jan99; same)*

Dec 92. (7"/c-s) *(658 819-7/-4)* **THE BRAVERY OF BEING OUT OF RANGE. / WHAT GOD WANTS (part 1)**
(cd-s+=) *(658 819-2)* – Perfect sense (part 1).

—— ROGER semi-retired for several years

Dec 00. (d-cd) *(501137-2)* <85235> **IN THE FLESH – LIVE** (live)
– In the flesh / The happiest days of our lives / Another brick in the wall (part 2) / Mother / Get your filthy hands off my desert / Southampton dock / Pigs on the wing (part 1) / Dogs / Welcome to the machine / Wish you were here / Shine on you crazy diamond (parts 1-8) / Set the controls for the heart of the sun / Breathe (in the air) / Time / Money / The pros and cons of hitch hiking (part 2) / Perfect sense (parts 1 & 2) / The bravery of being out of range / It's a miracle / Amused to death / Brain damage / Eclipse / Comfortably numb / Each small candle.

Sony Sony

Sep 05. (d-cd) *(52K 96439)* <86762> **CA IRA** (Opera w/ Various Artists) Oct05
– (an opera in three acts).

– compilations, etc. –

May 02. (cd) *Columbia; (<5 07906-2>)* **FLICKERING FLAME: THE SOLO YEARS VOLUME 1**
– Knockin' on Heaven's door / Too much rope / The tide is turning / Perfect sense (pts.1 & 2) / Three wishes / 5.06 a.m. (every stranger's eyes) / Who needs information / Each small candle / Flickering flame / Towers of faith / Radio waves / Lost boys calling (original demo).

the WEDDING PRESENT

Formed: Leeds, England . . . 1984 by ex-teachers DAVID GEDGE and PETE SOLOWKA (from Ukrainian stock) along with KEITH GREGORY and SHAUN CHARMAN. They gained a deal with local indie label, 'Reception', in 1985 and, with appearances on John Peel's radio 1 show, quickly grew into a cult act. Debut album, 'GEORGE BEST' (1987) was one of the key 80's indie releases, GEDGE's tunefully challenged monotone combining with the fast and furious punk-jangle racket to somehow create something more than the sum of its parts. Towards the end of the decade, they were finally signed to a major record company, 'R.C.A.', their first release on the label, 'UKRAINSKI . . .', surprising many with its marriage of Ukranian folk styles and indie-rock. GEDGE reverted to his trademark lovelorn lyrical fashion for follow-up proper, 'BIZARRO', a record that disappointed many longtime fans. Nevertheless, The WEDDING PRESENT were nothing if not prolific, even achieving the accolade of a Guinness Book Of Records entry in 1992 when every one of their monthly single (7"only) releases hit the UK Top 30 (The 12 hits also contained an unusual cover version on the B-side, see below). Despite the departure of all founding members save GEDGE (SALOWKA left in the early 90's to form The UKRAINIANS), 1994's 'WATUSI' again found the band in favour with the critics if not commanding the fanbase they once had. In 1998, GEDGE re-invented himself as a SERGE GAINSBOURG or BURT BACHARACH-type crooner in the project/duo, CINERAMA, alongside SALLY MURRELL, his sort of JANE BIRKIN, you could say. An album, 'VA VA VOOM', was a marked change of direction from the WEDDOES bust-a-gut blasts, into EDWYN COLLINS glutty vocals. CINERAMA completed their second batch, 'DISCO VOLANTE' (2000), while the romantic GEDGE and MURRELL returned all 'STARRY EYED' (one of the tracks incidentally) on 2002's 'TORINO'. With CINERAMA out of the way, GEDGE re-formed the WEDDING PRESENT in 2004, kicking off with minor UK hit, 'INTERSTATE 5', the opening track on the following year's comeback set, 'TAKE FOUNTAIN'. Suitably fitting was a final session (in October 2004) for the late, great John Peel, who was probably the band's biggest fan.

• **Songwriters:** GEDGE compositions, except GETTING NOWHERE FAST (Girls At Our Best) / WHAT BECOME OF THE BROKEN HEARTED (Jimmy Ruffin) / I FOUND THAT ESSENCE RARE (Gang Of Four) / IT'S NOT UNUSUAL (hit; Tom Jones) / FELICITY (Orange Juice) / MAKE ME SMILE (COME UP AND SEE ME) (Steve Harley & Cockney Rebel) / BOX ELDER (Pavement) / SHE'S MY BEST FRIEND (Velvet Underground) / MOTHERS (Jean Michel Satre) / CUMBERLAND GAP (Leadbelly) / CATTLE AND CANE (Go-Betweens) / DON'T CRY NO TEARS (Neil Young) / THINK THAT IT MIGHT (Altered Images) / FALLING (Julee Cruise) / PLEASANT VALLEY SUNDAY (Monkees) / LET'S MAKE SOME PLANS (Close Lobsters) / ROCKET (Mud) / THEME FROM SHAFT

(Isaac Hayes) / CHANT OF THE EVER CIRCLING SKELETAL FAMILY (Bowie) / GO WILD IN THE COUNTRY (Bow Wow Wow) / U.F.O. (Barry Gray) / STEP INTO CHRISTMAS (Elton John) / JUMPER CLOWN (Marc Riley). CINERAMA covered: LONDON (Smiths) / ELENORE (Turtles) / YESTERDAY ONCE MORE (Carpenters) / DIAMONDS ARE FOREVER (John Barry) / ERINNER DICH (Klee). • **Trivia:** STEVE ALBINI (ex-BIG BLACK) produced their early 90s material.

Album rating: GEORGE BEST (*9) / TOMMY collection (*8) / UKRAINSKI VISTUPU V JOHNA PEELA (*5) / BIZARRO (*7) / SEAMONSTERS (*7) / THE HIT PARADE 1 compilation (*7) / THE HIT PARADE 2 compilation (*6) / WATUSI (*5) / MINI (*4) / SATURNALIA (*5) / TAKE FOUNTAIN (*5) / Cinerama: VA VA VOOM (*6) / DISCO VOLANTE (*5) / THIS IS CINERAMA collection (*6) / JOHN PEEL SESSIONS collection (*5) / TORINO (*5) / CINERAMA HOLIDAY collection (*5)

DAVID GEDGE (b.23 Apr'60) – vocals, guitar / **PETE SOLOWKA** (b. Manchester) – guitar / **KEITH GREGORY** (b. 2 Jan'63, County Durham) – bass / **SHAUN CHARMAN** (b.Brighton) – drums

Reception — not iss.

May 85. (7") *(REC 001)* **GO OUT AND GET 'EM BOY. / (THE MOMENT BEFORE) EVERYTHING'S SPOILED AGAIN** — –
(re-iss. Sep85 on 'City Slang'; CSL 001)

Feb 86. (7") *(REC 002)* **ONCE MORE. / AT THE EDGE OF THE SEA** — –

Apr 86. (12"ep) *(REC 002-12)* **DON'T TRY AND STOP ME MOTHER** — –
– Go out and get 'em boy / (The moment before) Everything's spoiled again / Once more / At the edge of the sea.

Jul 86. (7") *(REC 003)* **THIS BOY CAN'T WAIT. / YOU SHOULD ALWAYS KEEP IN TOUCH WITH YOUR FRIENDS** — –
(ext.12"+=) *(REC 003-12)* – Living and learning.

Feb 87. (7",7"white/12") *REC 005/+12)* **MY FAVOURITE DRESS. / EVERY MOTHER'S SON / NEVER SAID** — –
(2,000 copies of above single were also given free with debut lp)

Sep 87. (7") *(REC 006)* **ANYONE CAN MAKE A MISTAKE. / ALL ABOUT EVE** — –
(c-s+=/12"+=) *(REC 006 C/12)* – Getting nowhere fast.

Oct 87. (lp/c/cd) *(LEEDS 001/+C/CD)* **GEORGE BEST** 47 –
– Everyone thinks he looks daft / What did your last servant die of? / Don't be so hard / A million miles / All this and more / Getting nowhere fast * / My favourite dress / Shatner / Something and nothing / It's what you want that matters / Give my love to Kevin / Anyone can make a mistake / You can't moan can you / All about Eve *. *(c+=/cd+= * tracks) (<cd re-iss. Oct97 on 'Cooking Vinyl' 4x10"lp-box++/cd+=; COOK/+CD 134>)* – Nobody's twisting your arm / Nothing comes easy / Don't laugh / I'm not always so stupid / Why are you being so reasonable now? / Not from where I'm standing / Give my love to Kevin / Getting better / Pourquoi es tu devenue si raisonnable?

— **SIMON SMITH** (b. 3 May'65, Lincolnshire) – drums repl. SHAUN to POPGUNS

Feb 88. (7") *(REC 009)* **NOBODY'S TWISTING YOUR ARM. / I'M NOT ALWAYS SO STUPID** 46 –
(12"+=/cd-s+=) *(REC 009 12/CD)* – Nothing comes easy / Don't laugh.

Jul 88. (lp/c/cd) *(LEEDS 002/+C/CD)* **TOMMY** (compilation 4 singles + Peel sessions) 42 –
– Go out and get 'em boy / (The moment before) Everything's spoiled again / Once more / At the edge of the sea / Living and learning / This boy can't wait / You should always keep in touch with your friends / Felicity / What becomes of the broken hearted? / Never said / Every mother's son / My favourite dress. *(<cd-iss. Oct97 on 'Cooking Vinyl'; COOKCD 135>)*

Sep 88. (7") *(REC 011)* **WHY ARE YOU BEING SO REASONABLE NOW?. / NOT FROM WHERE I'M STANDING** 42 –
(12"+=) *(REC 011-12)* – Give my love to Kevin (acoustic) / Getting better.
(c-s++=/cd-s++=) *(REC 011 C/CD)* – Pourquoi es tu devenue si raisonable?.
(s7") *(REC 011F)* – Pourquoi es tu devenue si raisonable?. / Give my love to Kevin (acoustic).

— added guest **LEN LIGGINS** – vocals, violin (ex-SINISTER CLEANERS, Solo artist) others played assortment of instruments in Ukrainian style.

R.C.A. — R.C.A.

Apr 89. (lp/c/cd) *(PL/PK/PD 74104)* **UKRAINSKI VISTUPI V JOHNA PEELA** (Ukrainian style John Peel sessions) 22 –
– Davny chasy / Yikhav kozak za dunai / Tiutiunyk / Zadmav didochok svitit misyats / Katrusyai Vasya vasyl'ok / Hude dn ipro hude Verkhovyno. *(was to have been issued as 10"m-lp, Nov88 on 'Reception'; REC 010) (cd re-iss. Sep00 as 'UKRAINIAN JOHN PEEL SESSIONS' on 'Fresh Air'; FRESHCD 100)*

— reverted to usual 4-piece & style

Sep 89. (7"/c-s) *(PB/PK 43117)* **KENNEDY. / UNFAITHFUL** 33 –
(c-s+=/12"+=/cd-s+=) *(PT/PK/PD 43118)* – One day all this will all be yours / It's not unusual.

Oct 89. (lp/c/cd) *(PL/PK/PD 74302)* *<2173>* **BIZARRO** 22
– Brassneck / Crushed / No / Thanks / Kennedy / What have I said now / Granadaland / Bewitched / Take me / Be honest. *(cd+=)* – Brassneck (extended) / Box elder / Don't talk, just kiss / Gone. *(cd re-mast.Aug01 on 'Camden'++=; 74321 86965-2)* – One day this will all be yours / Unfaithful / It's not unusual.

Feb 90. (7"/c-s) *(PB/PK 43403)* **BRASSNECK. / DON'T TALK, JUST KISS** 24 –
(c-s+=/12"+=/cd-s+=) *(PK/PT/PD 43404)* – Gone / Box elder.

Sep 90. (7"ep/c-ep)(12"ep/cd-ep) *(PB/PK 44021)(PT/PD 44022)* **THE 3 SONGS EP** 25 –
– Corduroy / Make me smile (come up and see me) / Crawl.
(10"+=) *(PJ 44022)* – Take me (live).

R.C.A. — First Warning

Apr 91. (7") *(PB 44495)* **DALLIANCE. / NIAGARA** 29 –
(c-s+=)(12"+=/cd-s+=) *(PK 44495)(PT/PD 44496)* – She's my best friend.
(10"++=) *(PJ 44495)* – What have I said now? (live).

May 91. (cd/c/lp) *(PD/PK/PL 75012)* *<75708>* **SEAMONSTERS** 13
– Dalliance / Dare / Suck / Blonde / Rotterdam / Lovenest / Corduroy / Carolyn / Heather / Octopussy. *(cd+=)* – Niagara / Dan Dare / Fleshworld. *(cd re-mast.Aug01 on 'Camden'++=; 74321 86966-2)* – Make me smile (come up and see me) / She's my best friend.

Jul 91. (12"ep/cd-ep) *(PT/PD 44750)* **LOVENEST (edit) / MOTHERS. / DAN DARE / FLESHWORLD** 58 –

— **PAUL DORRINGTON** – guitar (ex-TSE TSE FLY, ex-AC TEMPLE) repl. SOLOWKA to UKRAINIANS

Jan 92. (7") *(PB 45185)* **BLUE EYES. / CATTLE AND CANE** 26 –

Feb 92. (7") *(PB 45183)* **GO-GO DANCER. / DON'T CRY NO TEARS** 20 –

Mar 92. (7") *(PB 45181)* **THREE. / THINK THAT IT MIGHT** 14 –

Apr 92. (7") *(PB 45311)* **SILVER SHORTS. / FALLING** 14 –

May 92. (7") *(PB 45313)* **COME PLAY WITH ME. / PLEASANT VALLEY SUNDAY** 10 –

Jun 92. (7") *(PB 45313)* **CALIFORNIA. / LET'S MAKE SOME PLANS** 16 –

Jun 92. (cd/c/lp) *(PD/PK/PL 75343)* *<75711>* **THE HIT PARADE 1** (compilation of last 6 singles) 22
(cd re-iss. Sep96 on 'Camden'; 74321 40073-2)

Jul 92. (7") *(PB 10115)* **FLYING SAUCER. / ROCKET** 22 –

Aug 92. (7") *(PB 10117)* **BOING!. / THEME FROM SHAFT** 19 –

Sep 92. (7") *(PB 10116)* **LOVESLAVE. / CHANT OF THE EVER CIRCLING SKELETAL FAMILY** 17 –

Oct 92. (7") *(PB 11691)* **STICKY. / GO WILD IN THE COUNTRY** 17 –

Nov 92. (7") *(PB 11692)* **THE QUEEN OF OUTER SPACE. / U.F.O.** 23 –

Dec 92. (7"red) *(PB 11693)* **NO CHRISTMAS. / STEP INTO CHRISTMAS** 25 –

— The above 12 singles, were limited to 15,000 copies, and hit peak chart position on its first week of issue.

Jan 93. (cd/c/lp) *(PD/PK/PL 74321)* *<75711>* **THE HIT PARADE 2** 19
– (all last 6 'A'&'B' singles above) (free lp w/lp+=) **BBC SESSIONS** – (all 12 of the years' A-sides).

— **DARREN BELK** – guitar, bass; repl. GREGORY who later formed CHA CHA COHEN

Island — Polygram

Sep 94. (c-ep/12"ep/cd-ep) *(CIS/12IS/CID 585)* **YEAH YEAH YEAH YEAH YEAH / THE BIKINI / FLAME ON / HIM OR ME (WHAT'S IT GONNA BE)** 51 –
(cd-ep) *(CIDX 585)* – ('A'side) / Gazebo / So long baby / Spangle.

Sep 94. (cd/c/lp) *(CID/ICT/ILPS 8014)* *<524044>* **WATUSI** 47
– So long, baby / Click click / Yeah yeah yeah yeah yeah / Let him have it / Gazebo / Shake it / Spangle / It's a gas / Swimming pools, movie stars / Big rat / Catwoman / Hot pants.

Nov 94. (c-s/7") *(C+/IS 591)* **IT'S A GAS. / BUBBLES** –
(12"purple+=/cd-s+=) *(12IS/CID 591)* – ('A'acoustic) / Jumper clown.

— SMITH was another turn up in CHA CHA COHEN

Cooking Vinyl | Cooking Vinyl

Jan 96. (10"m-lp/m-cd) *(<COOK/+CD 094>)* **MINI** ☐ ☐
– Drive / Love machine / Go, man, go / Mercury / Convertible / Sports car. *(cd+=)* – Sucker / Waiting on the guns / Jet girl.

— line-up now **DAVID GEDGE** + **SIMON SMITH** plus newcomers **SIMON CLEAVE** – guitar (ex-TSE TSE FLY) / + guest on last mini-cd **JAYNE LOCKEY** – bass, vocals (ex-TSE TSE FLY)

Aug 96. (7") *(FRY 048)* **2, 3, GO. / UP** 67 –
(cd-s+=) *(FRYCD 048)* – Jet girl / Real thing.

Sep 96. (2x10"lp/c/cd) *(<COOK/+C/CD 099>)* **SATURNALIA** 36 ☐
– Venus / Real thing / Dreamworld / 2, 3, go / Snake eyes / Hula doll / Big boots / Montreal / Skin diving / Jet girl / Kansas / 50s.

Jan 97. (7") *(FRY 063) <5053>* **MONTREAL. / PROJECT CENZO** 40 ☐
(7") *(FRY 053X)* – ('A') / Where everybody knows your name.
(cd-s) *(FRYCD 053)* – ('A') / Sports car / My favourite dress (live) / Brassneck (live).

— they officially split after above

CINERAMA

DAVID LEWIS GEDGE – vocals, guitar / **SALLY MURRELL** – vocals, programming / with **DARE MASON** – guitar, theremin / **MARTY WILLSON-PIPER** – guitar (of The CHURCH) / **ANTHONY COOTE** – bass (of ANIMALS CAN SWIM) / **DAVEY RAY MOORE** – keyboards (of PUSHA) / **RICHARD MARKANGELO + CHE ALBRIGHTON** – drums, percussion / **JULIA PALMER + ABIGAIL TRUNDLE** – cello / **RACHEL DAVIES** – violin / **DUNCAN BRIDGEMAN** – flute / **THIBAULT DE MONTFORT** – oboe / **DEREK CRABTREE** – trumpet / **EMMA POLLOCK** – vocals (of DELGADOS)

Cooking Vinyl | SpinArt

Jul 98. (7") *(FRY 072)* **KERRY KERRY. / 7X** 71 –
(7") *(FRY 072X)* – ('A'side) / Mr Kiss Kiss Bang Bang.
(cd-s) *(FRYCD 072)* – ('A'side) / Love / Au pair.

Aug 98. (lp/cd) *(COOK/+CD 150) <68>* **VA VA VOOM** ☐ Oct98 ☐
– Maniac / Comedienne / Hate / Kerry Kerry / Barefoot in the park / You turn me on / Ears / Me next / Hard, fast and beautiful / Dance, girl, dance / Honey rider.

Oct 98. (7") *(FRY 077)* **DANCE, GIRL, DANCE. / EARS (acoustic version)** ☐ –
(cd-s) *(FRYCD 077)* – ('A'side) / Crusoe / Model spy.
(cd-s) *(FRYCD 077X)* – Pacific / King's Cross.

Elefant | not iss.

Aug 99. (ltd-7") *(ER 210)* **PACIFIC. / KING'S CROSS** ☐ –

— **SIMON CLEAVE** – guitar (ex-TSE TSE FLY) was added to duo

— + added **TERRY DE CASTRO** – bass (ex-GOYA DRESS) / **SIMON PEARSON** – drums (ex-GOYA DRESS)

Scopitones | Manifesto

Feb 00. (cd-s) *(TONECD 001)* **MANHATTAN / LONDON / FILM** ☐ –

Jun 00. (cd-s) *(TONECD 002)* **WOW / 10 DENIER / GIGOLO** ☐ –

Aug 00. (cd-s) *(TONECD 003)* **LOLLOBRIGIDA / SEE THRU / SLY CURL** ☐ –

Sep 00. (cd/lp) *(TONE CD/LP 004) <42401>* **DISCO VOLANTE** ☐ Oct00 ☐
– 146 degrees / Lollobrigida / Your charms / Heels / Unzip / Apres ski / Superman / Because I'm beautiful / Let's pretend / Wow (extended) / Your time startys here.

Nov 00. (cd-s) *(TONECD 005)* **YOUR CHARMS / REEL 2 DIALOGUE / GIRL ON A MOTORCYCLE** ☐ –

Apr 01. (cd) *(TONECD 006) <42402>* **JOHN PEEL SESSIONS** (1998-2000) ☐ ☐
– Comedienne / Maniac / You turn me on / Honey rider / Pacific / Dance, girl, dance (acoustic) / 146 degrees / Reel 2 dialogue 2 / Film / Elenore / Kerry Kerry (live) / Hard fast and beautiful (live).

Apr 01. (7"m) *(TONE 007)* **SUPERMAN. / SUPERMAN (Spanish version) / HARD FAST AND BEAUTIFUL (Spanish version)** ☐ –
(cd-s) *(TONECD 007)* – ('A'side) / Starry eyed / Yesterday once more.

— session strings repl. PEARSON

Oct 01. (7"m) *(TONE 008)* **HEALTH AND EFFICIENCY. / HEALTH AND EFFICIENCY (French version) / LOLLOBRIGIDA (French version)** ☐ –
(cd-s) *(TONECD 008)* – ('A'side) / Swim / Diamonds are forever.

Jun 02. (cd-s) *(TONECD 010)* **QUICK BEFORE IT MELTS / EARS (acoustic) / AS IF** ☐ –

Jul 02. (cd) *(TONECD 011) <42404>* **TORINO** ☐ ☐
– And when was she bad / Two girls / Estrella / Cat girl tights / Airborne / Quick, before it melts (extended) / Tie me up / Careless / Close up / Starry eyed / Get up and go / Get smart / Health and efficiency.

Aug 02. (cd-s) *(TONECD 012)* **CARELESS / THIS ISN'T WHAT IT LOOKS LIKE / SPARKLE LIPSTICK** ☐ –

Oct 03. (cd-s) *(TONECD 016)* **DON'T TOUCH THAT DIAL / THE ONE THAT GOT AWAY / ON/OFF / CARELESS (video)** ☐ –

– compilations, etc. –

Oct 00. (cd) *Cooking Vinyl; (COOKCD 180) / SpinArt; <SPIN 82>* **THIS IS CINERAMA** ☐ ☐
– Kerry Kerry / Love / Au pair / 7x / Mr. kiss kiss bang bang / Dance, girl, dance / Model spy / Crusoe / Pacific / King's Cross / Manhattan / Film / London / Ears.

Sep 02. (cd) *Scopitones; (TONECD 013)* **CINERAMA HOLIDAY** ☐ –
– Wow / 10 denier / Gigolo / Lollobrigida / See thru / Sly curls / Your charms / Reel 2 dialogue 2 / Girl on a motorcycle / Superman / Starry eyed / Yesterday one more / Superman (Spanish version) / Dura rapida y hermosa.

Apr 03. (cd) *Scopitones; (TONE 014CD)* **JOHN PEEL SESSIONS: SEASON 2** ☐ –
– Your charms / Heels / Apres ski / Superman / Because I'm beautiful / Lollobrigida (French version) / Sly curl / Yesterday once more / Careless / Get smart / Quick, before it melts / Health and efficiency.

2004. (7"cream) *GoMetric!; (mm 001)* **IT'S NOT YOU, IT'S ME. / ERINNER DICH** ☐ –

the WEDDING PRESENT

DAVID GEDGE – vocals, guitar, keyboards / **SIMON CLEAVE** – guitar / **TERRY DE CASTRO** – bass / **SIMON PEARSON** – drums

Scopitones | Manifesto

Nov 04. (cd-s) *(TONECD 018)* **INTERSTATE 5 / BAD THING / SNAPSHOTS** 62 –

Feb 05. (7") *(TONECD 019)* **I'M FROM FURTHER NORTH THAN YOU. / NICKELS AND DIMES** 34 –
(cd-s) *(TONECD 019)* – ('A') / Rekindling / The girl with the curious smile.
(dvd-s) *(TONEDVD 019)* – ('A'-video) / Interstate 5 (video) / Perfect blue (3 minute film).

Feb 05. (cd) *(TONECD 020)* **TAKE FOUNTAIN** 68 ☐
– Interstate / Always the quiet one / I'm from further north than you / Mars sparkles down on me / Ringway to Seatac / Don't touch that dial / It's for you / Larry's / Queen Anne / Perfect blue.

Oct 05. (cd-s) *(TONECD 022)* **RINGWAY TO SEATAC / SHIVERS / AMERICAN TAN** ☐ –

May 06. (cd) *(TONECD 023)* **SEARCH FOR PARADISE: SINGLES 2004-5** (compilation) ☐ –

– compilations, etc. –

Oct 86. (12"ep) *Strange Fruit; (SFPS 009)* **THE PEEL SESSIONS** (26.2.86) ☐ –
– What becomes of the broken hearted / This boy can't wait / Felicity / You should always keep in touch with your friends. *(c-ep iss.Jun87; SFPSC 009) (cd-ep iss.Aug88; SFPSC 009)*

Nov 88. (12"ep/cd-ep) *Nighttracks; (SFNT/+CD 016)* **THE EVENING SHOW SESSIONS** (20.4.86) ☐ –
– Everyone thinks he looks daft / I found that essence rare / Shatner / My favourite dress.

Oct 93. (lp/cd) *Strange Fruit; (SFR LP/CD 122)* **JOHN PEEL SESSIONS 1987-1990** ☐ –
– Give my regards to Kevin / Getting nowhere fast / A million miles / Something and nothing / Take me I'm yours / Unfaithful / Why are you being so reasonable now? / Happy birthday / Dalliance / Heather Blonde / Niagara.

Jun 97. (cd) *Strange Fruit; (<SFRSCD 029>)* **THE EVENING SESSIONS 1986-1994** ☐ ☐

Apr 98. (cd) *Cooking Vinyl; (<COOKCD 146>)* **JOHN PEEL SESSIONS 1992-1995** ☐ ☐

Sep 99. (cd) *Cooking Vinyl; (COOKCD 184) / SpinArt; <SPIN 78>* **SINGLES 1995-1997** ☐ Oct99 ☐

Nov 99. (4xcd-box) *Cooking Vinyl; (COOKCD 117) / SpinArt; <SPIN 75>* **REGISTRY** [ ] [ ]
– (GEORGE BEST / TOMMY / MINI / SATURNALIA)

WEEZER

Formed: Los Angeles, California, USA ... early 2002 by Connecticut-raised songwriter RIVERS CUOMO, MATT SHARP and PATRICK WILSON. Signing to 'Geffen' and recruiting final member, BRIAN BELL (who replaced JASON CROPPER), the group released their eponymous RIC OCASEK-produced debut album in September '94. Helped by the transatlantic success of singles such as 'UNDONE – THE SWEATER SONG' and the pogo-pop of 'BUDDY HOLLY', the album became one of the year's biggest sellers. Often described as the PIXIES meeting the BEACH BOYS, their blaring college 'nerd'-rock saw WEEZER riding the crest of an American 'new wave' triggered by the likes of GREEN DAY and the OFFSPRING. Meanwhile, MATT SHARP was also busy with a side project, the RENTALS (also comprising CHERIELYNN WESTRICH, ROD CERVERA, PETRA HADEN, PAT WILSON and JIM RICHARDS), releasing an album of New Wave-esque songs in 'RETURN OF (THE RENTALS)' (1995/96). A second WEEZER album, 'PINKERTON' (1996), was much of the same, although it brought the band a bit of grief when the American security firm of the same name brought legal action. Now without SHARP (who was replaced by MIKEY WELSH), WEEZER released their third long-awaited set, 'THE GREEN ALBUM', in May 2001, bringing back geek-rock to the masses. After a year of touring, self-produced 'MALADROIT' (2002), a sort of companion piece to 'THE GREEN ALBUM' was released into the US Top 5. Short, sweet and very melodic (as always), CUOMO and crew (PAT WILSON, BRIAN BELL and SCOTT SHRINER) had created another half-an-hour blast of guitar pop that was impossible not to like. Reasons why? Well, the faux-thrash metal piss-take 'DEATH AND DESTRUCTION', or jangling opener 'AMERICAN GIGOLO' or the catchy head-bopping single 'KEEP FISHING', which featured the entire cast of the Muppets in its video. Reasons to be cheerful, 1, 2, 3! Older, wiser and, dare one say it, a little less angst-ridden with their lot, the kings of geek-pop returned in 2005 with 'MAKE BELIEVE', a Rick Rubin-produced tidal new wave of an album whose US No.2 chart position spoke fondly of how much folks had missed them. Opener 'BEVERLEY HILLS' welded a Hollywood Babylon lyric and STEVE MILLER-time charm onto an 'I LOVE ROCK'N'ROLL'-esque stomp, while 'THIS IS SUCH A PITY' bemoaned its failings with quintessentially – and fortunately fashionable – 80s pop-histrionica.

• **Trivia:** WILSON and BELL are also part of own outfits, the SPECIAL GOODNESS and SPACE TWINS respectively.

Album rating: WEEZER (*7) / PINKERTON (*7) / THE GREEN ALBUM (*8) / MALADROIT (*6) / MAKE BELIEVE (*6)

RIVERS CUOMO (b.13 Jun'70, New York City) – vocals, guitar / **BRIAN BELL** (b. 9 Dec'68, Iowa City, Iowa) – rhythm guitar, vocals (ex-CARNIVAL ART) repl. JASON CROPPER (left 1993) / **MATT SHARP** (b.22 Sep'69, Bangkok, Thailand) – bass, vocals / **PATRICK WILSON** (b. 1 Feb'69, Buffalo, New York) – drums

Geffen D.G.C.

Jan 95. (7"blue) *(GFS 85) <19378>* **UNDONE – THE SWEATER SONG. / HOLIDAY** [35] Sep94 [57]
(c-s+=/cd-s+=) *(GFS C/TD 85)* – Mykel & Carli / Susanne.

Feb 95. (cd/c/lp) *<(GED/GEC/GEF 24629)>* **WEEZER** [23] Aug94 [16]
– My name is Jonas / No one else / The world has turned and left me here / Buddy Holly / Undone – the sweater song / In the garage / Holiday / Only in dreams. *(lp re-iss. Mar02 on 'Universal'; AA694 93045-1) (cd re-iss. May04 +=; 9861907)* – (B-sides, etc.)

Apr 95. (7"/c-s) *(GFS/+C 88)* **BUDDY HOLLY. / JAMIE** [12] [–]
(cd-s+=) *(GFSTD 88)* – My name is Jonas / Surf wax America.

Jul 95. (10"ep/c-ep/cd-ep) *(GFS V/C/TD 95)* **SAY IT AIN'T SO (remix). / NO ONE ELSE (live acoustic) / JAMIE (live acoustic)** [37] [–]

—— MATT SHARP sidelined with the RENTALS on 'Return Of (The Rentals')

Sep 96. (7"/c-s) *(GFS/+C 22167)* **EL SCORCHO. / YOU GAVE YOUR LOVE TO ME SOFTLY** [50] [–]
(cd-s+=) *(GFSTD 22167)* – Devotion.

Oct 96. (cd/c) *<(GED/GEC 25007)>* **PINKERTON** [43] [19]
– Tired of sex / Getchoo / No other one / Why bother / Across the sea / Good life / El Scorcho / Pink triangle / Falling for you / Butterfly.

—— MATT SHARP left after above set; recorded second set and went solo

—— (1998) **MIKEY WELSH** (b.20 Apr'71, Syracuse, NY) repl. SHARP

Geffen Interscope

May 01. (cd) *(493061-2) <493045>* **THE GREEN ALBUM** [31] [4]
– Don't let go / Photograph / Hash pipe / Island in the sun / Crab / Knock-down drag-out / Smile / Simple pages / Glorious days / O girlfriend / I do *[UK-only]*.

Jul 01. (7") *(497567-7)* **HASH PIPE. / TEENAGE VICTORY SONG** [21] [–]
(c-s) *(497567-4)* – ('A') / Starlight.
(cd-s+=) *(497564-2)* – ('A'-Jimmy Pop remix) / ('A'-video).

Oct 01. (7") *(497616-7)* **ISLAND IN THE SUN. / ALWAYS** [31] [–]
(cd-s+=) *(497610-2)* – Oh Lisa / ('A'-video).
(cd-s) *(297616-2)* – ('A') / Sugar booger / My best friends are gone.

—— **SCOTT SHRINER** (b.11 Jul'65, Toledo, Ohio) repl. WELSH

May 02. (cd) *(493325-2) <493241>* **MALADROIT** [16] [3]
– American gigolo / Dope noise / Keep fishin' / Take control / Death and destruction / Slob / Burndt jamb / Space rock / Slave / Fall together / Possibilities / Love explosion / December *(UK+=)* – Living without you (version) / Island in the sun (version). *(lp-iss.May02; same as US)*

Sep 02. (7") *(497771-7)* **KEEP FISHIN'. / PHOTOGRAPH (live)** [29] [–]
(cd-s+=) *(497771-2)* – Death and destruction (live) / ('A'-video).
(cd-s) *(497792-2)* – ('A') / Slob (live) / Knockdown drag out (live).

Sep 02. (cd-ep) *<493458>* **THE LION AND THE WITCH** (live) [–] [ ]
– Dope nose / Island in the sun / Falling for you / Death and destruction / El scorcho / Holiday.

May 05. (7"pic-d) *(9881793)* **BEVERLY HILLS. / BUTTERFLY (live)** [9] [10]
(cd-s+=) *<(9881791)>* – Island in the sun (live) / ('A'-video).

May 05. (cd) *(9882166) <4520>* **MAKE BELIEVE** [11] [2]
– Beverly Hills / Perfect situation / This is such a pity / Hold me / Peace / We are all on drugs / The damage in your heart / Pardon me / My best friend / The other way / Freak me out / Haunt you every day. *(ltd-cd+=; 9881718)* – Butterfly (live) / Island in the sun (live).

Aug 05. (7"pink-marble) *(9883498)* **WE ARE ALL ON DRUGS. / BEVERLY HILLS (Urbanix mix)** [47] [–]
(cd-s+=) *(9883495)* – Burndt jamb (live) / ('A'-video).

Aug 05. (-) *<radio>* **PERFECT SITUATION** [–] [51]

☐ Scott WEILAND

(see under ⇒ STONE TEMPLE PILOTS)

Paul WELLER

Born: 25 May'58, Woking, Surrey, England. (see the JAM for further details). Formed the STYLE COUNCIL in early '83 with former MERTON PARKAS keys player, MICK TALBOT, and talented young sticksman, STEVE WHITE. Though it was merely a matter of months since WELLER had folded the JAM, the STYLE COUNCIL followed a radical new direction, taking the agit-soul of CURTIS MAYFIELD as their inspiration and fashioning a very 80's hybrid of cocktail jazz, breezy pop and white funk. Scoring immediately with the Top 5 'SPEAK LIKE A CHILD', the group went Top 3 later that year with the 'LONG HOT SUMMER' EP, its sultry lead track arguably the best the group ever penned and the creative pinnacle of what they were trying to achieve. Previewing The STYLE COUNCIL's debut album, 'CAFE BLEU' (1984), the mellow atmospherics of 'MY EVER CHANGING MOODS' gave

WEEZER

the group another huge hit in early '84. The album itself was a lush fusion of summery jazz and easy soul, the keening strum of 'YOU'RE THE BEST THING' making the Top 5. WELLER became increasingly political as the decade wore on, the rousing soul/funk of 'SHOUT TO THE TOP' and 'WALLS COME TUMBLING DOWN' an indication of the direction The JAM may have taken had they still been in existence. With the miners strike in full effect, politics were very much still an issue in rock/pop and WELLER and Co. released a benefit single, 'SOUL DEEP', at Christmas '84 under the COUNCIL COLLECTIVE banner. With production handled by HEAVEN 17's MARTYN WARE, the project included the likes of JIMMY RUFFIN, JUNIOR (GISCOMBE), VAUGHN TOULOUSE, DIZZY HEIGHTS and DEE C. LEE. The latter became not only WELLER's other half but a full-time backing singer for the STYLE COUNCIL, her sweet soul tones helping make 'OUR FAVOURITE SHOP' (1985) a mid-80's classic. The overall sound was more satisfying and the writing was sharper; 'COME TO MILTON KEYNES' was WELLER's most cutting slice of social commentary since The JAM heyday. Come 1986, the STYLE COUNCIL became heavily involved in the 'Red Wedge' movement alongside the likes of the COMMUNARDS and BILLY BRAGG, attempting to educate music fans into voting for the right party in the upcoming elections i.e. Labour. Such an openly party political stance was probably doomed to failure from the start, the attendant tour floundering and the Tories of course, predictably romping home. It was the last time WELLER would lay his beliefs on the line and the failure of the project seemed to lie at the heart of the lugubrious meanderings of the double set, 'THE COST OF LOVING' (1987). The following year's 'CONFESSIONS OF A POP GROUP' (1988) was similarly lacking in focus, its string arrangements and classical pretensions seeing the STYLE COUNCIL sinking in a mire of self-indulgence. The record failed to spawn any major hits and didn't even make the Top 10; when 'Polydor' refused to release a proposed fifth set, WELLER finally adjourned the 'COUNCIL and retired to re-evaluate his career. Now without a band or a recording deal, WELLER eventually regained his thirst for music via the low-key PAUL WELLER MOVEMENT, a band comprising STEVE WHITE, JACKO PEAKE, PAUL FRANCIS, MAX BEESLEY, DAMON BROWN, CHRIS LAWRENCE and DJ PAULO HEWITT along with backing singers DEE C.LEE, DR. ROBERT and CAMELLE HINDS. The subsequent early late 1990/early 1991 shows saw the singer once again armed with a guitar and suggested that he'd been reacquainting himself with his record collection, more specifically late 60's R&B and psychedelia. The 'MOVEMENT released a sole single, 'INTO TOMORROW' on the DIY 'Freedom High' label. It squeezed into the Top 40 nonetheless and WELLER eventually whittled down the bulk of the group for a more basic sound, signing with 'Go! Discs' and debuting with 'UH HUH OH YEH' in late summer '92. Hailed as the best thing he'd done in years, the single went into the Top 20 and the PAUL WELLER revival was up and running. The music press had given the singer a wide berth since the heyday of the STYLE COUNCIL and as the plaudits began to roll in for his eponymous debut album, were eventually forced to admit that, yes, WELLER was undergoing something of a creative rebirth. Matching the visceral, emotional punch of the music, the lyrics were of a decidedly more personal nature, eschewing politics for matters of the soul and the heart. With the ebullient 'SUNFLOWER' single and the attendant 'WILD WOOD' (1993) album, WELLER's star was most definately in the ascendant. Characterised by a crisp, uncluttered Brendan Lynch production, the record saw WELLER distill his influences into vintage singer/songwriter maturity. With his voice now sufficiently rough around the edges to complement such material, the likes of the resonating, meditative folkiness of the title track assumed a greater depth. The album reached No.2, featuring in many end of year polls (Mercury Prize), the chino wearing ghost of the STYLE COUNCIL now finally laid to rest. While the UK music press were still largely fixated on US grunge, WELLER was nothing if not instrumental in the upcoming Brit-pop debacle. Cited by the likes of OASIS as a guiding influence, the Modfather, as WELLER came to be known, was everything that the hordes of mop-topped chancers aspired to. It was a role that WELLER fitted into naturally, OCEAN COLOUR SCENE's STEVE CRADOCK was already a regular musical collaborator, while NOEL GALLAGHER would guest on WELLER's forthcoming No.1 album, 'STANLEY ROAD'. Released in spring '95 as Brit-pop was reaching its zenith, the album was earthier than anything WELLER had recorded in his career to date. Again produced by LYNCH, the record was previewed by the blistering single, 'THE CHANGINGMAN', its lyrics signalling an even more personal bent to WELLER's writing as the looking-good-for-30-something star even began appearing in the British style press. Elsewhere on the album, WELLER covered Dr. John's 'I WALK ON GILDED SPLINTERS' although it was the spirit of ERIC CLAPTON or NEIL YOUNG that most often came to mind. WELLER was at his most affecting on the ballads, the deeply felt 'YOU DO SOMETHING TO ME', the beautiful gospel-soul of album closer 'WINGS OF SPEED' and the brilliantly evocative hammond/wurlitzer musings of 'BROKEN STONES'. Of course, a backlash was inevitable, and certain sections of the music press derided WELLER's new material as tired 'Dad-rock', an incestuous Brit-pop conspiracy which continually looked to the past instead of breaking new ground. While this may have been true to a certain degree, and WELLER was partly responsible for the vexing success of the terminally workmanlike OCEAN COLOUR SCENE, the man was simply integrating retro influences into his muse as he'd done all the way through his career; it's the fact that these influences changed which seems to annoy some writers. Keeping his profile high with various festival appearances (as well as a predictable guest spot at OASIS' Knebworth show), WELLER (now signed to 'Island' following the demise of 'Go! Discs' eventually returned to the fray in summer '97 with the storming 'BRUSHED' single. Arguably standing among the best of WELLER's work to date, the track was propelled by a stone solid/funky as hell rhythmic thrust (courtesy of WHITE), combining mod, psychedelia and rock in a fashion that he's only previously hinted at. 'Raw' is probably the best word to describe it and the best word to describe the accompanying album, 'HEAVY SOUL' (1997), WELLER's voice as impressive as ever on a set which nevertheless too often relies on 'authentic' sound over songwriting. 1998, saw the release of two Top 30 singles, 'BRAND NEW DAY' and the 'WILD WOOD' remixes EP, mainly to complement the delivery of his best of package, 'MODERN CLASSICS – THE GREATEST HITS'. Come the new millennium the doggedly determined WELLER underwent yet another creative renaissance with the acclaimed 'HELIOCENTRIC' (2000). The record mightn't have struck a zeitgeist-style chord like 'STANLEY ROAD' but it confirmed his ever changing muse was still as fertile as ever. It was also one of the most PAUL WELLER-sounding albums he'd ever done, a rich, life affirming blend of soulful, occasionally psychedelic retro influences. That very richness was the key ingredient of 'DAYS OF SPEED' (2001), a document of WELLER's recent solo tour which – in its pared down acoustica (and included old JAM numbers!) – served to underline the sheer breadth and consistency of the man's songwriting. Just to note, PAUL was cleared of all rape charges in October 2000 (from four years previous) and stated at the time the unfairness of the anonymity law not protecting the innocently accused. On the music front once again, WELLER released his umpteenth solo set, 'ILLUMINATION' (No.1 in September 2002), a soulful and back to basics album that featured the Top 10 single, 'IT'S WRITTEN IN THE STARS'. The modfather was back in 2004 with a full-blown covers set, 'STUDIO

150', almost making it two No.1's in succession but never straying far from his time honoured soul/folk/pop predilections. Three of the album's four spin-off singles covered soul/disco territory: Rose Royce's 'WISHING ON A STAR', Gil Scott-Heron's 'THE BOTTLE' and Sister Sledge's 'THINKING OF YOU', Top 20 hits all. He also just scraped the Top 40 with Gordon Lightfoot's 'EARLY MORNING RAIN', previously covered by the likes of George Hamilton IV amongst others. WELLER had long expressed his fondness for writers like Tim Hardin and Neil Young, so nor was it much of a surprise to see him doing 'DON'T MAKE PROMISES' and 'BIRDS', or even Noel Gallagher's previously unrecorded 'ONE WAY ROAD'. The Top 5 'AS IS NOW' (2005) showcased harder hitting originals, acknowledging the current crop of JAM devotees on singles, 'COME ON/LET'S GO' (Top 20) and especially 'FROM THE FLOOR BOARDS UP', his spikiest Top 10 in decades. Save for its FRED WESLEY-esque brass, 'HERE'S THE GOOD NEWS', was more familiar WELLER, and a Top 30 to boot. Summer 2006 saw the man release live at the Alexandra Palace set, 'CATCH – FLAME!' and appear at T In The Park in Balado, Scotland.

• **Songwriters:** WELLER penned except for TALBOT's STYLE COUNCIL instrumentals. They also covered MOVE ON UP (Curtis Mayfield) / PROMISED LAND (Joe Smooth) / OHIO (Neil Young). WELLER solo:- FEELIN' ALRIGHT (Traffic) / SEXY SADIE (Beatles) / I'M ONLY DREAMING (Small Faces) / I SHALL BE RELEASED + CORRINA CORRINA (Bob Dylan) / COCONUT GROVE (John Sebastian) / FAMILY AFFAIR (Sly & The Family Stone) / LET IT BE ME (Everly Brothers) / DON'T GO TO STRANGERS (Joni MItchell) / NEEDLES AND PINS (Searchers) + see 'Studio 150' set.

Album rating: Style Council: CAFE BLEU (*5) / OUR FAVOURITE SHOP (*6) / HOME AND ABROAD – LIVE (*4) / THE COST OF LOVING (*5) / CONFESSIONS OF A POP GROUP (*3) / THE SINGULAR ADVENTURES OF THE STYLE COUNCIL compilation (*7) / HERE'S SOME THAT GOT AWAY collection (*4) / Paul Weller: PAUL WELLER (*6) / WILD WOOD (*9) / LIVE WOOD (*6) / STANLEY ROAD (*8) / HEAVY SOUL (*7) / MODERN CLASSICS – THE GREATEST HITS compilation (*8) / HELIOCENTRIC (*7) / DAYS OF SPEED (*6) / ILLUMINATION (*6) / FLY ON THE WALL – B-SIDES & RARITIES compilation (*5) / STUDIO 150 (*4) / AS IS NOW (*6) / CATCH – FLAME! (*6)

the STYLE COUNCIL

PAUL WELLER – vocals, guitar (ex-JAM) / **MICK TALBOT** (b.11 Sep'58) – keyboards (ex-MERTON PARKAS) / **STEVE WHITE** – drums / plus various guests

Polydor Polydor

Mar 83. (7") *(TSC 1)* **SPEAK LIKE A CHILD. / PARTY CHAMBERS** 4

May 83. (7") *(TSC 2)* **MONEY GO ROUND. / (part 2)** 11
(12") *(TSCX 2)* – ('A'side) / Headstart for happiness / Mick's up.

Aug 83. (7"ep/12"ep) *(TSC/+X 3)* **LONG HOT SUMMER / PARTY CHAMBERS. / PARIS MATCH / LE DEPART** 3

Nov 83. (7") *(TSC 4)* **SOLID BOND IN YOUR HEART. / IT JUST CAME TO PIECES IN MY HAND / ('A'instrumental)** 11

Oct 83. (m-lp) *<815277>* **INTRODUCING THE STYLE COUNCIL** –
– (above songs)

Polydor Geffen

Feb 84. (7") *(TSC 5) <29359>* **MY EVER CHANGING MOODS. / MICK'S COMPANY** 5 29
(12"+=) *(TSCX 5)* – Spring, Summer, Autumn.

Mar 84. (lp/c)(cd) *(TSC LP/MC 1)(817535-2) <4029>* **CAFE BLEU** <US-title 'MY EVER CHANGING MOODS'> 2 56
– Mick's blessings / My ship came in / Blue cafe / The Paris match / My ever changing moods / Dropping bombs on the Whitehouse / A gospel / Strength of your nature / You're the best thing / Here's the one that got away / Headstart for happiness / Council meetin'. *(cd+=)* – The whole point of no return. *(re-iss. cd Sep95; same)*

May 84. (7") *(TSC 6) <29248>* **YOU'RE THE BEST THING. / BIG BOSS GROOVE** 5 76
(12") *(TSCX 6)* – ('A'dub version).

Oct 84. (7") *(TSC 7)* **SHOUT TO THE TOP. / GHOSTS OF DACHAU** 7
(12"+=) *(TSCX 7)* – Piccadilly trail / ('A'instrumental).

Dec 84. (7"; as COUNCIL COLLECTIVE) *(MINE 1)* **SOUL DEEP. / (part 2)** 24 –
(12"+=) *(MINEX 1)* – ('A'version) / (striking miner's interview).
(above single gave proceeds to miner's strike & the deceased miner David Wilkie's widow) The COLLECTIVE featured guests JIMMY RUFFIN, JUNIOR GISCOMBE, VAUGHN TOULOUSE, DEE C.LEE and DIZZY HEIGHTS. Production handled by MARTYN WARE (Heaven 17).

May 85. (7"ep/12"ep) *(TSC/+X 8)* **WALLS COME TUMBLING DOWN. / THE WHOLE POINT II / BLOODSPORTS** 6 –

Jun 85. (lp/c)(cd) *(TSC LP/MC 2)(825700-2) <24061>* **OUR FAVOURITE SHOP** <US title 'INTERNATIONALISTS'> 1
– Homebreakers / All gone away / Come to Milton Keynes / Internationalists / A stone's throw away / The stand up comic's instructions / Boy who cried wolf / A man of great promise / Down in the Seine / The lodgers / Luck / With everything to lose / Our favourite shop / Walls come tumbling down. *(cd+=)* – Shout to the top. *(c+=)* – (interview). *(cd re-iss. Aug90; same)*

Jun 85. (7") *(TSC 9)* **COME TO MILTON KEYNES. / WHEN YOU CALL ME** 23 –
(12"+=) *(TSCG 9)* – Our favourite shop / ('A'club) / The lodgers (club mix).

Aug 85. (7") *<28941>* **OUR FAVOURITE SHOP. / BOY WHO CRIED WOLF** –

Sep 85. (7") *(TSC 10)* **THE LODGERS (remix). / YOU'RE THE BEST THING (live)** 13
(d7"+=) *(TSCDP 10)* – Big boss groove (live) / Long hot summer (live).
(12"+=) *(TSC?? 10)* – Big boss groove (live) / Move on up (live).
(12"+=) *(TSCX 10)* – Medley: Money go round – Soul deep – Strength of your nature.

Mar 86. (7"/12") *(CINEX 1/+12)* **HAVE YOU EVER HAD IT BLUE. / MR. COOL'S DREAM** 14 –

May 86. (lp/c)(cd) *(TCS LP/MC 3)(829143-2)* **HOME AND ABROAD – LIVE (live)** 8 –
– The big boss groove * / My ever changing moods / The lodgers / Headstart for happiness / (When you) Call me / The whole point of no return / Our favourite shop * / With everything to lose / Homebreakers / Shout to the top / Walls come tumbling down / Internationalists. *(cd+= *) (cd re-iss. Aug90; same)*

Jun 86. (7") *<28674>* **INTERNATIONALISTS. / (WHEN YOU) CALL ME** –

Polydor Polydor

Jan 87. (7"/12") *(TSC/+X 12)* **IT DIDN'T MATTER. / ALL YEAR ROUND** 9

Feb 87. (2x12"lp/c)(cd) *(TSC LP/MC 4)(<831433-2>)* **THE COST OF LOVING** 2
– It didn't matter / Right to go / Waiting / Walking the night / The cost of loving / Heaven's above / Fairy tales / Angel / A woman's song. *(re-iss. Oct90)*

Mar 87. (7") *(TSC 13)* **WAITING. / FRANCOISE** 52
(12"+=) *(TCSX 13)* – Theme from 'Jerusalem'.

Oct 87. (7") *(TSC 14)* **WANTED (FOR WAITER). / THE COST OF LOVING** 20
(12"+=/c-s+=) (TSC X/CS 14) – There's soup in my flies.
(cd-s++=) – The cost.

May 88. (7") *(TSC 15)* **LIFE AT A TOP PEOPLE'S HEALTH FARM. / SWEET LOVING WAYS** 28
(12"+=/cd-s+=) *(TSC X/CD 15)* – Spark (live) / ('A'version).

Jun 88. (lp/c)(cd) *(TSC LP/MC 5)(<835785-2>)* **CONFESSIONS OF A POP GROUP** 15
– It's a very deep sea / The story of someone's shoe / Changing of the guard / The little boy in a castle – A dove flew down from the elephant / The gardener of Eden (a three piece suite):- In the beginning – The gardener of Eden – Mourning the passing of time / Life at a top people's health farm / Why I went missing / How she threw it all away / I was a doledads toyboy / Confessions of a pop group (parts 1, 2 & 3) / Confessions of a pop group. *(cd re-iss. Oct90; same)*

Jul 88. (7"ep/12"ep) *(TSC 16)* **HOW SHE THREW IT ALL AWAY / IN LOVE FOR THE FIRST TIME. / LONG HOT SUMER / I DO LIKE TO BE B-SIDE THE A-SIDE** 41

Feb 89. (7") *(TSC 17)* **PROMISED LAND. / CAN YOU STILL LOVE ME** 27
(12") *(TSCXS 17)* – ('A'-Joe Smooth's alternate club) / ('B'club) / ('B'dub).
(cd-s) *(TSCCD 17)* – ('A'-Juan Atkins mix) / ('A'-Pianopella mix) / ('B'-dub).
(cd-s) *(TSCD 17)* – ('A'side) / ('A'extended) / ('B'vocal) / ('B'dub).
(7"box) *(TSCB 17)* – ('A'-Juan Atkins mix) / ('B'side).

Mar 89. (lp/c)(cd) *(TSC TV/TC 1)(837896-2)* **THE SINGULAR ADVENTURES OF THE STYLE COUNCIL** (compilation) 3 –
– You're the best thing / Have you ever had it blue (extended) / Money go round (parts 1 & 2) / My ever changing moods (extended) / Long hot summer (extended) / The lodgers / Walls come tumbling down / Shout to the top / Wanted / It didn't matter / Speak like a child / A solid bond in your heart / Life at a top people's health farm / Promised land. *(c+=/cd+=)* – How she threw it all away / Waiting.

May 89. (7") *(LHS 1)* **LONG HOT SUMMER ('89 mix). / EVERYBODY'S ON THE RUN** 48 –
(12"+=/cd-s+=) *(LHS X/CD 1)* – ('A'&'B' different mixes).

—— Disbanded Mar'90. WELLER went solo, see below.

– compilations, etc. –

on 'Polydor' unless mentioned otherwise

Nov 87. (cd-ep) *(TSCCD 101)* **CAFE BLEU** –
– Headstart for happiness / Here's one that got away / Blue cafe / Strength of your nature.

Nov 87. (cd-ep) *(TSCCD 102)* **BIRDS AND BEES** –
– Piccadilly trail / It just came to pieces in my hands / Spin drifting / Spring, Summer, Autumn.

Nov 87. (cd-ep) *(TSCCD 103)* **MICK TALBOT IS AGENT '88** –
– Mick's up / Party chambers / Mick's blessing / Mick's company.

Jan 90. (7") *Old Gold; (OG 9924)* **LONG HOT SUMMER. / SPEAK LIKE A CHILD** –

Jan 90. (7") *Old Gold; (OG 9929)* **YOU'RE THE BEST THING. / MY EVER CHANGING MOODS** –

Jul 93. (cd/c) *(519 372-2/-4)* **HERE'S SOME THAT GOT AWAY** 39 –

Feb 96. (cd/c) *(529 483-2/-4)* **THE STYLE COUNCIL COLLECTION** 60 –

Aug 00. (cd)(d-lp) *(557900-2)(549134-1)* **GREATEST HITS** 28 –

PAUL WELLER

with **STEVE WHITE** – drums, percussion / **JACKO PEAKE** – sax, flute, b.vox / **DEE C.LEE, DR.ROBERT + CAMELLE HINDS** – b.vox

Freedom High London

May 91. (7"/c-s; as PAUL WELLER MOVEMENT) *(FHP/+C 1)* **INTO TOMORROW. / HERE'S A NEW THING** 36 1992
(12"+=/cd-s+=) *(FHP T/CD 1)* – That spiritual feeling / ('A'demo).

Go! Discs London

Aug 92. (7"/c-s) *(GOD/+MC 86)* **UH HUH OH YEH. / FLY ON THE WALL** 18 –
(12"+=/cd-s+=) *(GOD X/CD 86)* – Arrival time / Always there to fool you.

Sep 92. (cd/c/lp) *(<828 343-2/-4/-1>)* **PAUL WELLER** 8 Oct92
– Uh huh oh yeh / I didn't mean to hurt you / Bull-rush / Round and round / Remember how we started / Above the clouds / Clues / Into tomorrow / Amongst butterflies / The strange museum / Bitterness rising / Kosmos. *(re-iss. Apr94; same)*

Oct 92. (7"/c-s) *(GOD/+MC 91)* **ABOVE THE CLOUDS. / EVERYTHING HAS A PRICE TO PAY** 47 –
(12"+=/cd-s+=) *(GOD X/CD 91)* – All year round (live) / Feelin' alright.

—— now with **STEVE WHITE** – drums, percussion / **MARCO NELSON** – bass

Go! Discs Go! Discs

Jul 93. (7"/c-s) *(GOD/+MC 102)* **SUNFLOWER. / BULL-RUSH – MAGIC BUS (live)** 16 –
(12"+=/cd-s+=) *(GOD X/CD 102)* – Kosmo's sxdub 2000 / That spiritual feeling (new mix).

Aug 93. (7"/c-s/10"/cd-s) *(<GOD/+MC/T/CD 104>)* **WILD WOOD. / ENDS OF THE EARTH** 14

Sep 93. (cd/c/lp) *(<828 435-2/-4/-1>)* **WILD WOOD** 2 Oct93
– Sunflower / Can you heal us (holy man) / Wild wood – instrumental (pt.1) / All the pictures on the wall / Has my fire really gone out? / Country / 5th season / The weaver – instrumental (pt.2) / Foot of the mountain / Shadow of the Sun – Holy man (reprise) / Moon on your pyjamas. *(re-iss. Apr94 +=; same)* – Hung up.

Nov 93. (7"ep/c-ep/10"ep/cd-ep) *(GOD/+MC/T/CD 107)* **THE WEAVER EP** 18 –
– The weaver / This is no time / Another new day / Ohio (live).

Mar 94. (7"ep/c-ep/12"ep/cd-ep) *(GOD/+MC/X/CD 111)* **HOME OF THE CLASSIC EP** 11 –
– Hung up / Foot of the mountain (live from Albert Hall) / The loved / Kosmos (Lynch Mob bonus beats).

Sep 94. (cd/c/lp) *(828 561-2/-4/-1) <00601>* **LIVE WOOD (live)** 13
– Bull rush – Magic bus / This is no time / All the pictures on the wall / Remember how we started? / Dominoes / Above the clouds / Wild wood / Shadow of the Sun / (Can you hear us) Holy man – War / 5th season / Into tomorrow / Fool of the mountains / Sunflower / Has the fire really gone out?.

Oct 94. (7"ep/c-ep/12"ep/cd-ep) *(GOD/+MC/X/CD 121)* **OUT OF THE SINKING. / SUNFLOWER (Lynch Mob dub) / SEXY SADIE** 20 –

—— with **STEVE WHITE** – drums / **DR.ROBERT** – bass, vocals (ex-BLOW MONKEYS) / **STEVE CRADDOCK** – guitar / **MARK NELSON** – bass / **HELEN TURNER** – strings, organ / **BRENDAN LYNCH** – organ, co-producer / + guests **MICK TALBOT / CARLEEN ANDERSON / STEVE WINWOOD / NOEL GALLAGHER / YOLANDA CHARLES / CONSTANTINE WEIR**

Apr 95. (12"ep/c-ep/cd-ep) *(GOD X/MC/CD 127)* **THE CHANGINGMAN / I'D RATHER GO BLIND / IT'S A NEW DAY, BABY / I DIDNT MEAN TO HURT YOU (live)** 7

May 95. (cd/c/lp)(6x7"pack) *(<828 619-2/-4/-1>)(850070-7)* **STANLEY ROAD** 1
– The changingman / Porcelain gods / I walk on gilded splinters / You do something to me / Woodcutter's son / Time passes / Stanley Road / Broken stones / Out of the sinking / Pink on white walls / Whirlpool's end / Wings of speed.

Jul 95. (7"ep/c-ep/cd-ep) *(GOD/+MC/CD 130)* **YOU DO SOMETHING TO ME / A YEAR LATE. / MY WHOLE WORLD IS FALLING DOWN / WOODCUTTER'S SON** 9 –

Sep 95. (7"/c-s) *(GOD/+MC 132)* **BROKEN STONES. / STEAM** 20
(cd-s+=) *(GODCD 132)* – Whirlpool's end / Porcelain gods.

—— WELLER was also part of one-off supergroup The SMOKIN' MOJO FILTERS alongside PAUL McCARTNEY and NOEL GALLAGHER. They had a Top 20 hit late '95 with 'COME TOGETHER'.

Feb 96. (7"ep/cd-ep) *(GOD/+CD 143)* **OUT OF THE SINKING EP** 16 –
– Out of the sinking / I shall be released / Porcelain gods / Broken stones.

Aug 96. (7"/c-s/cd-s) *(GOD/+MC/CD 149)* **PEACOCK SUIT. / EYE OF THE STORM** 5 –

Island Polygram

Jun 97. (cd/c/lp) *(CID/ICT/ILPS 8058) <524277>* **HEAVY SOUL** 2 Aug97
– Heavy soul / Peacock suit / Up in Suzie's room / Brushed / Driving nowhere / I should have been there to inspire you / Heavy soul (part 2) / Friday Street / Science / Golden sands / As you lean into the light / Mermaids.

Aug 97. (7"ep/c-ep/cd-ep) *(IS/CIS/CID 666)* **BRUSHED EP** 14 –
– Brushed / Ain't no love in the heart of the city / Shoot the dove / As you lean into the light.

Oct 97. (7"ep/c-ep/cd-ep) *(CIS/IS/CID 676)* **FRIDAY STREET EP** 21 –
– Friday street / Sunflower (live) / Brushed (live) / Mermaids (live).

Nov 97. (c-s/cd-s/7") *(CIS/CID/IS 683)* **MERMAIDS. / EVERYTHING HAS A PRICE TO PAY ('97 version) / SO YOU WANT TO BE A DANCER** 30 –

Nov 98. (c-s/7") *(C+/IS 711)* **BRAND NEW START. / RIGHT UNDERNEATH IT** 16
(cd-s+=) *(CID 711)* – The riverbank (new version).

Nov 98. (cd/c/d-lp) *(CID/ICT/ILPSD 8080) <524558>* **MODERN CLASSICS – THE GREATEST HITS** (compilation) 7
– Out of the sinking / Peacock suit / Sunflower / The weaver / Wild wood / Above the clouds / Uh huh oh yeh / Brushed / The changingman / Friday Street / You do something to me / Brand new start / Hung up / Mermaids / Broken stones / Into tomorrow. *(lp-box; IBX 8080) (d-cd; CIDD 8080)*

Dec 98. (7"ep/12"ep/cd-ep) *(IS/12IS/CID 734)* **WILD WOOD EP** 22 –
– Wild wood (mixes; original / Portishead / Science (Psychonauts).

Apr 00. (cd/c/lp) *(CID/ICT/ILPS 8093) <542394>* **HELIOCENTRIC** 2 May00
– He's the keeper / Frightened / Sweet pea, my sweet pea / A whale's tale / Back in the fire / Dust and rocks / There is no drinking after you're dead / With time and temperance / Picking up sticks / Love-less.

May 00. (12"/cd-s) *(12IS/CID 760)* **HE'S THE KEEPER. / HELIOCENTRIC / BANG-BANG** –

Aug 00. (12"/cd-s) *(12IS/CID 764)* **SWEET PEA, MY SWEET PEA. / BACK IN THE FIRE (BBC session) / THERE IS NO DRINKING AFTER YOU'RE DEAD (noonday underground mix)** [44] [–]

Independiente Epic

Oct 01. (cd/d-lp) *(ISOM 26 CD/LP)* <80703> **DAYS OF SPEED** (live) [3] [ ]
– Brand new start / Loved / Out of the sinking / Clues / English rose / Above the clouds / You do something to me / Amongst butterflies / Science / Back in the fire / Down in the Seine / That's entertainment / Love-less / There's no drinking after you're dead / Everything has a price to pay / Wild wood / Headstart for happiness / A town called Malice. *(cd re-iss. Aug02; same)*

— in summer 2002, WELLER featured on NOONDAY UNDERGROUND's single, 'I'll Walk Right In'.

Sep 02. (10"m/cd-s) *(ISOM 63 TE/MS)* **IT'S WRITTEN IN THE STARS. / HORSESHOE DRAMA / PUSH BUTTON AUTOMATIC** [7] [–]
(cd-s) *(ISOM 63SMS)* – ('A') / The butterfly collector / Carnation.

Sep 02. (cd/lp) *(ISOM 33 CD/LP)* <892000> **ILLUMINATION** [1] [ ]
– Going places / A bullet for everyone / Leafy mysteries / It's written in the stars / Who brings joy / Now the night is here / Spring (at last) / One x one / Bag man / All good books / Call me No.5 / Standing out in the universe / Illumination.

Nov 02. (cd-s) *(ISOM 65S)* **LEAFY MYSTERIES / TALISMAN / WILD WOOD (live)** [23] [–]
(cd-s) *(ISOM SMS)* – ('A') / Broken stones (live) / Peacock suit (live).

V2 V2

Jun 04. (7"/cd-s) *(VVR 502691-0/-3)* **THE BOTTLE. / CORRINA CORRINA / COCONUT GROVE** [13] [–]
(7") *(VVR 502691-7)* – ('A'-Big Boss Man vocal) / (instrumental).

Aug 04. (7") *(VVR 502692-7)* **WISHING ON A STAR. / FAMILY AFFAIR** [11] [–]
(cd-s) *(VVR 502692-3)* – ('A') / Let it be me.
(cd-s+=) *(VVR 502692-8)* – (all 3 tracks).

Sep 04. (cd/lp) *(VVR 102690-2/-1)* <27211> **STUDIO 150** [2] [ ]
– If I could only be sure / Wishing on a star / Don't make promises / The bottle / Black is the colour / Close to you / Early morning rain / One way road / Hercules / Thinking of you / All along the watchtower / Birds. *(ltd-cd w/dvd+=; VVR 102690-8)* – (DVD tracks). *(d-cd iss.Mar05 +=; VVR 103213-2)* – LIVE AT RBB SENDESSAL BERLIN:- Thinking of you / The bottle / One way road / Wishing on a star / If I could only be sure / Come together.

Nov 04. (7"/cd-s) *(VVR 502846-7/-3)* **THINKING OF YOU. / DON'T GO TO STRANGERS / NEEDLES AND PINS** [18] [–]
(dvd-s) *(VVR 802846-9)* – ('A'-live video) / Wishing on a star (Beta Band remix) / Early morning rain (live video).

Feb 05. (7"red) *(VVR 503059-7)* **EARLY MORNING RAIN. / COME TOGETHER** [40] [–]

V2 Yep Roc

Jul 05. (7"orange/green) *(VVR 503341-7)* **FROM THE FLOOR BOARDS UP. / ORANGES & ROSEWATER** [6] [–]
(cd-s+=) *(VVR 503341-3)* – ('A'-video).
(7") *(VVR 503341-0)* – ('A') / (Lynchmob remix – instrumental).

Sep 05. (7") *(VVR 503322-7)* **COME ON – LET'S GO. / GOLDEN LEAVES** [15] [–]
(7"orange/red) *(VVR 503322-0)* – ('A'-acoustic) / Into tomorrow (live at the Guilfest).
(cd-s) *(VVR 503322-3)* – ('A') / Shine on / ('A'-video).

Oct 05. (cd/lp) *(VVR 103320-2/-1)* <2112> **AS IS NOW** [4] [ ]
– Blink and you'll miss it / Paper smile / Come on – Let's go / Here's the good news / The start of forever / Pan / All on a misty morning / From the floor boards up / I wanna make it alright / Savages / Fly little bird / Roll along summer / Bring back the funk (pts.1 & 2) / The pebble and the boy. *(ltd-cd w/dvd+=; VVR 5013320-8)* – (DVD tracks). *(d-cd iss.Feb06 +=; VVR 103823-2)* – Come on – Let's go (live) / From the floor boards up (live) / Changing man (live) / A town called Malice (live).

Dec 05. (7"blue/pink) *(VVR 503460-7)* **HERE'S THE GOOD NEWS. / PAPER SMILE (audio twitch remix)** [21] [–]
(cd-s) *(VVR 503460-3)* – ('A') / Alone / Super Lekker stoned.
(7") *(VVR 503460-0)* – ('A') / Super Lekker stoned (Richard Fearless remix).

Feb 06. (7"ep) *(VVR 503626-7)* **AS IS NOW EP** [—] non-ch [–]
– Blink & you'll miss it / From the floor boards up / Here's the good news / Come on – Let's go.

Jun 06. (d-cd) *(VVR 1039391)* <2126> **CATCH – FLAME!** (live at the Alexandra Palace) [17] [ ]
– The weaver / Out of the sinking / Blink & you'll miss it / Paper smile / Peacock suit / From the floorboards up / The changing man / Savages / Going places / Up in Suzi's room / Porcelain god – I walk on guilded splinters // In the crowd / Come on – Let's go / Foot of the mountain / You do something to me / Wishing on a star / Wild wood / The pebble & the boy / That's entertainment / Long hot summer / Shout to the top / A town called Malice.

– compilations, etc. –

Aug 03. (t-cd) *Polydor-Universal; (<063527-2>)* **FLY ON THE WALL – B-SIDES & RARITIES** (1991-2000) [22] [ ]

Kanye WEST

Born: 8 Jun'77, Atlanta, Georgia, USA. The son of a photo-journalist father and academic mother, KANYE WEST bucked the ghetto-superstar trend by becoming the first brainy black, middle class hip-hop icon of the noughties. Already moonlighting as an RZA-influenced producer while studying at Chicago State University, he subsequently dropped out and worked his way up the production pecking order. Pitching up at 'Roc-A-Fella', he contributed to JAY-Z's millennial set, 'Roc La Familia – The Dynasty' (2000), but only really made his mark with follow-up, 'The Blueprint' (2001), masterminding the DOORS-sampling 'Takeover' and the JACKSON 5-borrowing 'Izzo (H.O.V.A.)', a US Top 10 single. Inspired – if that's the right word – by a near-fatal car crash on 23rd October 2002, WEST penned what was to be his first single, 'THROUGH THE WIRE', a fortnight after the accident, his mouth still trussed up in wire. Further successes for ALICIA KEYS' (the Grammy moninated-'You Don't Know My Name'), TALIB KWELI ('Get By') and LUDACRIS ('Stand Up') held back its release, and while 'Roc-A-Fella' had initially been reluctant to market him as a solo artist in his own right, the single finally appeared in late 2003, making the US Top 20 and – eventually – the UK Top 10. Hot on its heels was his collaboration with TWISTA and actor/comedian Jamie Foxx, 'SLOW JAMZ', the first of two Foxx features to make the US No.1. With their treated samples – Chaka Khan's 'THROUGH THE FIRE' and Luther Vandross' 'A HOUSE IS NOT A HOME' respectively – both tracks were indicative of WEST's highly distinctive, pop-orientated style, showcased in more depth on his Grammy-winning, US No.2 debut album, 'THE COLLEGE DROPOUT' (2004). Further singles, 'ALL FALLS DOWN' (which re-worked a line of the gorgeous 'MYSTERY OF INIQUITY', from Lauryn Hill's underrated 'MTV Unplugged') and the Grammy-winning (Best Rap Song) 'JESUS WALKS' went transatlantic Top 20/Top 10 respectively, and while WEST wasn't exactly a revolutionary, his wry, contradictory rhymes – on subject matter that'd be considered high brow for most rappers – at least began to question his place in hip-hop's monolithic temples of bling. While his ego swelled in line with his fame, the blanket media coverage on everything from his controversial Live8 appearance to anti-Bush comments fired anticipation for sophomore set, 'LATE REGISTRATION' (2005). Almost universally acclaimed, the album topped the charts in America and came within a whisker of doing the same in Britain. The familiar lyrical tone was set by a Shirley Bassey-sampling lead single (UK Top 10), 'DIAMONDS FROM SIERRA LEONE'; WEST might've been telling some people what they didn't already know, but the song – or at least its delivery – remained the same. With producer of the moment Jon Brion smoothing WEST's sonic horizons, the effect was a classy gloss on the debut, most effective when tackling issues long since abandoned in hip-hop: on the Gil Scott-Heron-sampling 'MY WAY HOME' (hingeing on a slowed-down refrain from 'HOME IS WHERE THE HATRED IS'), and the Scott-Heron namechecking 'CRACK MUSIC'. Foxx popped up again on the US No.1, 'GOLD DIGGER', a track which – appropriately enough given Foxx's turn as Brother

KANYE WEST

Ray in the Hollywood biopic – featured a sample from Ray Charles' 'I Got A Woman'. While some within the rap community were sceptical about WEST's prowess on the mic, his status as a maverick hip-hop messiah (he even appeared on the cover of Rolling Stone in controversial, crown-of-thorns pose) looks assured: a live, orchestrated hip-hop album recorded at Abbey Road? WEST delivered; 'LATE ORCHESTRATION' (2006) came complete with the by now time-honoured Abbey Road mock-up sleeve.

Album rating: THE COLLEGE DROPOUT (*8) / LATE REGISTRATION (*7) / LATE ORCHESTRATION (*6)

KANYE WEST – vocals, etc. / with various guests, etc.

—— late in 2003, TWISTA (feat. KANYE WEST & JAMIE FOXX) hit US No.1 (UK No.3) with the single, 'Slow Jamz'

Roc-A-Fella Roc-A-Fella

Feb 04. (cd) *(9862061)* *<20300>* **THE COLLEGE DROPOUT** 12 2
– Intro / We don't care / Graduation day / All falls down (feat. SYLEENA JOHNSON) / I'll fly away / Spaceship (feat. GLC & CONSEQUENCE) / Jesus walks / Never let me down (feat. JAY-Z & J. IVY) / Get em high (feat. TALIB KEWLI & COMMON) / Workout plan / The new workout plan / Slow jamz (feat. TWISTA & JAMIE FOXX) / Breathe in breathe out (feat. LUDACRIS) / School spirit skit 1 / School spirit / School spirit skit 2 / Lil Jimmy skit / Two words (feat. MOS DEF, FREEWAY & the HARLEM CHOIR CHOIR) / Through the wire / Family business / Last call. *<(ltd-cd w/dvd+= iss.Mar05; B0004214)>* – (DVD video anthology).

Mar 04. (cd-s) *(9862117)* **THROUGH THE WIRE / TWO WORDS (with MOS DEF & FREEWAY)** 9 15
(12"+=) *(9862202)* – ('A'-version).
(cd-s++=) *(9862270)* – ('A'-video).

Jun 04. (cd-s; feat. SYLEENA JOHNSON) *(9862669)* **ALL FALLS DOWN / (clean version)** 10 Jul04 7
(12") *(9862671)* – ('A'-clean) / ('A'-heavy hitters dirty version) / ('A'-heavy hitters a capella).
(cd-s+=) *(9862670)* – ('A'-video).

—— in Jun'04, KANYE feat. on BRANDY's Top 10 hit, 'Talk About Our Love'

Aug 04. (cd-s) *(9863964)* **JESUS WALKS / (live in Paradiso 2004)** 16 May04 11
(12") *(9863965)* *<27091-1>* – ('A') / Through the wire (live in Paradiso 2004) / ('A'-Ma$e mix) / ('A'-heavy hitters mixes).
(cd-s+=) *(9863962)* – ('A'-video 1) / ('A'-video 2).

Jul 05. (cd-s) *(9883228)* **DIAMONDS FROM SIERRA LEONE / (instrumental)** 8 43
(cd-s) *(9883229)* – ('A') / Jesus walks (remix) / New workout plan (remix).
(12"+=) *(9883549)* – (all above).

Aug 05. (cd) *(9885153)* *<B00053250-2>* **LATE REGISTRATION** 2 1
– Wake up Mr. West / Heard 'em say (feat. ADAM LEVINE of MAROON 5) / Touch the sky (feat. LUPE FIASCO) / Gold digger (feat. JAMIE FOXX) / Skit #1 / Drive slow (feat. PAUL WALL & GLC) / My way home (feat. COMMON) / Crack music (feat. the GAME) / Roses / Bring me down (feat. BRANDY) / Addiction / Skit #2 / Diamonds from Sierra Leone (remix feat. JAY-Z) / We major (feat. NAS & REALLY DOE) / Skit #3 / Hey mama / Celebration / Skit #4 / Gone (feat. CAM'RON & CONSEQUENCE). *(bonus+=)* – Diamonds from Sierra Leone. *(hidden+=)* – Late. *(ltd-cd w/dvd+=; 9885282)* – (DVD tracks). *(d-lp iss.Sep05; 9885652)*

Sep 05. (12"/cd-s; feat. JAMIE FOXX) *(988569 6/9)* **GOLD DIGGER / (instrumental)** 2 1
(cd-s) *(9885694)* – ('A') / Diamonds from Sierra Leone (remix with JAY-Z) / We can make it better.

Dec 05. (12"/cd-s; feat. ADAM LEVINE) *(988841 4/5)* **HEARD 'EM SAY / (instrumental) / (call out)** 22 26
(cd-s) *(9888416)* – ('A') / ('A'-feat. JOHN LEGEND live at Abbey Road) / Back to basics.

Mar 06. (cd-s; feat. LUPE FIASCO) *(9852115)* **TOUCH THE SKY / GOLD DIGGER (AOL session)** 6 42
(cd-s) *(9852115)* – ('A') / Jesus walks (remix) / Diamonds from Sierra Leone (AOL session) / ('A'-video).
(12") *(9852116)* – ('A') / Jesus walks (remix) / ('A'-instrumental) / Jesus walks (version).

May 06. (cd) *(9878399)* **LATE ORCHESTRATION** (live at Abbey Road Studios) 59 –
– Diamonds from Sierra Leone / Touch the sky / Crack music / Drive slow / Through the wire / Workout plan / Heard 'em say / All falls down / Bring me down / Gone / Late / Jesus walks. *(bonus+=)* – Gold digger (AOL session).

☐ Paul WESTERBERG (see under ⇒ REPLACEMENTS)

☐ Alan WHITE (see under ⇒ YES)

the WHITE STRIPES

Formed: Detroit, Michigan, USA ... 1997 by husband and wife duo JACK and MEG WHITE; JACK (aka JOHN GILLIS) took his wife's surname when they married in October 1996. Mystery surrounding their relationship (many including myself and other biographers were fooled) thought that they were brother and sister! JACK began his musical career in Michigan's local outfit GO, before recruiting his partner MEG to play percussion in what would ultimately become The WHITE STRIPES. Clad in matching red and white clothes (apparently they even smoke Embassy Royals because of their clever color scheme), the duo debuted with the single 'LET'S SHAKE HANDS' (1997), issued on the 'Italy' imprint, after whipping up a storm on the local garage/underground rock circut. Two more singles followed and the group flitted to champions of the independent scene 'Sympathy For The Record Industry', where their self-titled album was released in 1999. It was good enough to generate column inches and critics seemed most impressed with covers of blues classics 'STOP BREAKING DOWN BLUES' and 'ST. JAMES INFIRMARY BLUES'. Whilst still borrowing a variation of sounds from the likes of The WHO and MC5, JACK's love for the blues was apparent: he continuously cited giant of the genre CHARLEY PATTON as his immediate influence, and frequently covered some of his songs in The STRIPES' live sets. This love of country blues was even more obvious come the sophomore LP 'DE STIJL' (2000), named after the abstract art movement led by Dutch artist Gerrit Rietveld. Stand-out tracks included the rock-steady 'LITTLE BIRD', 'TRUTH DON'T MAKE A NOISE' and a worthy Son House cover 'DEATH LETTER'. A break was imminent and JACK took to producing some of the scene's most promising acts during the period between 1999-2000. Shortly before the release of 'DE STIJL' – March 2000, to be precise – the couple officially divorced having lived separately for just over a year. The VON BONDIES and the SOLEDAD BROTHERS were just two of the groups that had impressed him, and judging by the cover of the latter's debut album, he was happy to dress up as Uncle Sam, get propped up against a wall and shot by a firing squad (but don't worry, ladies and gents, he didn't really suffer for his art). That aside, it was time for him and MEG to venture back into the studio to record what was to become their breakthrough album, 'WHITE BLOOD CELLS' (2001). On the eve of its premiere, the NME claimed that the WHITE STRIPES, along with fellow garage rockers the STROKES, were destined to become the future of rock music. Even the tabloids caught on, with the Sun hailing them as "Stripe-tastic". Meanwhile, normally MOR radio station Radio 4 caught the STRIPE's buzz, as did John Peel, who casually compared them to the SEX PISTOLS. Rolling Stone magazine reckoned that Detroit was the new Seattle, but JACK STRIPE was unfazed, claiming he'd rather hang-out with fellow musicians the VON BONDIES than pay attention to the hype. A sold-out tour followed, plus a reputed $1m move to 'X.L.' records, once home to the PRODIGY. Singles 'HOTEL YOBA'- named after a "doss-house" – and 'FELL IN LOVE WITH A GIRL' followed, both charting in the Top 20. Going from strength to strength, the WHITE STRIPES' trail-blazing success saw them entering the US Top 10 and the UK No.1 spot with their indispensable set 'ELEPHANT' (2003). A stonking mix of blues, acoustic folk and downright dirty riffage, it saw the duo initiate a worldwide anthem with the single 'SEVEN NATION ARMY'. Hinged solely on one guitar hook and

The WHITE STRIPES

MEG WHITE's booming drum kit, it was the envy of all guitarists and probably the song which will replace 'Smells Like Teen Spirt' when kids test out new guitars in music shops (much to the annoyance of the employees). That aside, the album had much more on offer; the BACHARACH cover of 'I JUST DON'T KNOW WHAT TO DO WITH MYSELF' (coupled with a Kate Moss pole-dancing video), the start/stop ferocity of 'HARDEST BUTTON TO BUTTON' and the complex blues jam 'BALL AND BISCUIT'. Dark, moody and slightly harsh on the ears, 'ELEPHANT' also had its fun moments, most notably the warm three-way acoustic stop of 'IT'S TRUE THAT WE LOVE ONE ANOTHER', with MEG and first lady of Garage rock HOLLY GOLIGHTLY sharing vocal duties with JACK. Mostly recorded live by Liam Watson on reel-to-reel tape at his studio in London's Abbey Road, 'ELEPHANT' is as punk as it comes with a band who are were literally in the throes of international and critical acclaim. Darlings they ain't! JACK's subsequent extra curricular activites – contributions to the soundtrack 'Cold Mountain' (2003) and a production credit on Nashville legend LORETTA LYNN's 'Van Lear Rose' (2004) – as well as the 'STRIPES' cover of Dolly Parton's 'JOLENE' (a Top 20 UK hit in late 2004), suggested that he and MEG might well be goin' up country. 'GET BEHIND ME SATAN' (2005), a transatlantic Top 3, wasn't going to trouble Vince Gill or Kenny Chesney but – from its cannily ambiguous biblical title to its ramshackle setlist – it did document the band's most intimate love affair with Americana to date. Comparisons to 'Exile On Main St.' were obvious and oft-stated – right down to lead single (UK Top 10) and foot-stomping opener, 'BLUE ORCHID'. For once, the comparisons were on the nail: the likes of successive Top 10s, 'MY DOORBELL', 'THE DENIAL TWIST' and especially 'FOREVER FOR HER (IS OVER FOR ME)' were some of the loosest 'Exile..-updates yet conceived, with the same primitive production, soul-strafed vocals and candle-in-the-basement aura. 'THE NURSE', meanwhile, sounded like it'd been crooned over a marimba session in downtown Guadalajara. That sense of sprawl was carried over to WHITE's most high profile moonlight to date, the RACONTEURS. Primarily a meeting of the minds of WHITE and fellow Detroit-based songwriter BRENDAN BENSON, together with the GREENHORNES rhythm section, JACK LAWRENCE and PATRICK KEELER, the band formed in 2005, releasing a debut, limited edition 7", 'STEADY, AS SHE GOES', in January 2006. An album, 'BROKEN BOY SOLDIERS', appeared in early spring to glowing reviews, a lads-together appreciation of their favourite records rather than a JACK WHITE ego trip (although he did give the title track the most cock-rocking, PLANT-howling welly heard since the DARKNESS last touched down). More importantly, their endlessly gratifying spin on various 60s/70s references, from the BEATLES to BOB DOROUGH to the SMALL FACES, sounded borne of happy coincidence rather than big-budget graft.

• **Covers:** LOOK ME OVER CLOSELY (Marlene Dietrich) / ONE MORE CUP OF COFFEE (Bob Dylan) / STOP BREAKING DOWN (Robert Johnson) / ST. JAMES INFIRMARY BLUES (Cab Calloway) / LORD, SEND ME AN ANGEL + YOUR SOUTHERN CAN IS MINE (Blind Willie McTell) / DEATH LETTER (Son House) / PARTY OF SPECIAL THINGS TO DO + CHINA PIG + ASHTRAY HEART (Captain Beefheart) / RATED X (Loretta Lynn) / BLACK JACK DAVEY (trad.) / GOOD TO ME (Brendan Benson) / WHO'S TO SAY? (Blanche) / ST. IDES OF MARCH (Soledad Brothers) / SHELTER OF YOUR ARMS (Greenhornes).

Album rating: THE WHITE STRIPES (*7) / DE STIJL (*7) / WHITE BLOOD CELLS (*8) / ELEPHANT (*9) / GET BEHIND ME SATAN (*8) / the Raconteurs: BROKEN BOY SOLDIERS (*6)

JACK WHITE (b. JOHN ANTHONY GILLIS, 9 Jul'75) – vocals, guitar, piano, etc / **MEG WHITE** (b. MEGAN MARTHA WHITE, 10 Dec'74) – drums, tambourine

not iss. — Italy

1997. (7"red,7") <*IR 003*> **LET'S SHAKE HANDS. / LOOK ME OVER CLOSELY** [–] [ ]

1998. (7"white,7") <*IR 006*> **LAFAYETTE BLUES. / SUGAR NEVER TASTED SO GOOD** [–] [ ]

Sympathy F — Sympathy F

Jun 99. (lp/cd) <*(SFTRI 577/+CD)*> **THE WHITE STRIPES** [ ] [ ]
– Jimmy the exploder / Stop breaking down / The big three killed my baby *[cd-only]* / Suzy Lee / Sugar never tasted so good *[cd-only]* / Wasting my time / Cannon / Astro / Broken bricks / When I hear my name / Do / Screwdriver / One more cup of coffee *[cd-only]* / Little people / Slicker drips / St. James infirmary blues / I fought piranhas. *(UK re-iss. Apr01; same)* <*(re-iss. Sep01 on 'X.L.' lp/cd; XLLP/XLCD 149)*>

Jun 99. (7"red) <*SFTRI 578*> **THE BIG THREE KILLED MY BABY. / RED BOWLING BALL RUTH** [–] [ ]
(UK-iss.Jan02; same as US)

Jun 00. (lp/cd) <*(SFTRI 609/+CD)*> **DE STIJL** [ ] [ ]
– You're pretty good looking / Hello operator / Little bird / Apple blossom / I'm bound to pack it up / Death letter / Sister, do you know my name? / Truth doesn't make a noise / A boy's best friend / Let's build a home / Jumble, jumble / Why can't you be nicer to me? / Your southern can is mine. *(UK re-iss. Apr01; same)* <*(re-iss. Sep01 on 'X.L.' lp/cd; XLLP/XLCD 150)*>

Aug 00. (7"pic-d,7") <*SFTRI 619*> **HELLO OPERATOR. / JOLENE** [–] [ ]
(UK-iss.Jan02; same as US)

Nov 00. (7"red,7"; tour) <*SFTRI 645*> **LORD, SEND ME AN ANGEL. / YOU'RE PRETTY GOOD LOOKING (trendy American remix)** [–] Austra [–]
(UK-iss.Jan02; same)

Jan 01. (7") <*SP 527*> **PARTY OF SPECIAL THINGS TO DO. / CHINA PIG / ASHTRAY HEART** [–] [ ]

— <above issued for 'Sub Pop' singles club>

Jul 01. (lp/cd) <*(SFTRI 660/+CD)*> **WHITE BLOOD CELLS** [55] [ ]
– Dead leaves and the dirty ground / Hotel Yorba / I'm finding it harder to be a gentleman / Fell in love with a girl / Expecting / Little room / The union forever / The same boy you've always known / We're going to be friends / Offend in every way / I think I smell a rat / Aluminium / I can't wait / Now Mary / I can learn / This protector. <*(re-iss. Sep01 on 'X.L.' lp/cd; XLLP/XLCD 151)*> <*US cd re-iss. 2002 on 'V2'; 27124*> – hit No.61

X.L. — X.L.

Nov 01. (7") <*(XLS 139)*> **HOTEL YORBA (live at the Hotel Yorba). / RATED X (live at the Hotel Yorba)** [26] [ ]
(cd-s+=) <*(XLS 139CD)*> – ('A'-video).

Feb 02. (7") *(XLS 142)* **FELL IN LOVE WITH A GIRL. / I JUST DON'T KNOW WHAT TO DO WITH MYSELF** [21] [–]
(cd-s+=) *(XLS 142CD2)* – Lovesick (live) / ('A'-video).
(cd-s) *(XLS 142CD)* – ('A'side) / Let's shake hands / Lafayette blues.

Sep 02. (7") *(XLS 148)* **DEAD LEAVES AND THE DIRTY GROUND. / STOP BREAKING DOWN** [25] [–]
(cd-s+=) *(XLS 148CD)* – Suzy Lee.

X.L. — V2

Mar 03. (cd/d-lp) *(XLCD/XLLP 162)* <*27148*> **ELEPHANT** [1] Apr03 [6]
– Seven nation army / Black math / There's no home for you here / I just don't know what to do with myself / In the cold, cold night / I want to the boy to warm your mother's heart / You've got her in your pocket / Ball and biscuit / The hardest button to button / Little acorns / Hypnotize / The air near my fingers / Girl, you have no faith in medicine / Well it's true that we love each other.

Apr 03. (7") *(XLS 162)* <*radio*> **SEVEN NATION ARMY. / GOOD TO ME** [7] [76]
(cd-s+=) *(XLS 162CD)* – Black Jack Davey.

Sep 03. (7") *(XLS 166)* **I JUST DON'T KNOW WHAT TO DO WITH MYSELF. / WHO'S TO SAY** [13] [–]
(cd-s+=) *(XLS 166CD)* – I'm finding it harder to be a gentlemen.

Nov 03. (7") *(XLS 173)* **THE HARDEST BUTTON TO BUTTON. / ST IDES OF MARCH** [23] [–]
(cd-s+=) *(XLS 173CD)* – ('A'-video).

— in 2003, JACK WHITE contributed several songs/tracks to the movie, 'Cold Mountain'

Nov 04. (7") *(XLS 207)* **JOLENE (live under Blackpool Lights). / DO (live under Blackpool Lights)** [16] [–]
(cd-s) *(XLS 207CD)* – ('A') / Black math (live under..).

May 05. (7") *(XLS 216)* <*63881-27832-7*> **BLUE ORCHID. / THE NURSE** [9] [43]
(cd-s) *(XLS 216CD1)* – ('A') / Though I hear you calling I will not answer.
(cd-s) *(XLS 216CD2)* – ('A') / Who's a big baby? / You've got her in your pocket (live).

Jun 05. (cd) *(XLCD 191) <27256>* **GET BEHIND ME SATAN** [3] [3]
– Blue orchid / The nurse / My doorbell / Forever for her (is over for me) / Little ghost / The denial twist / White moon / Instinct blues / Passive manipulation / Take, take, take / As ugly as I seem / Red rain / I'm lonely (but I ain't that lonely yet).

Sep 05. (7"white) *(XLS 218)* **MY DOORBELL. / SAME BOY YOU'VE ALWAYS KNOWN (live in Manaus, Brazil 1st June 2005)** [10] [–]
(cd-s) *(XLS 218CD)* – ('A') / Screwdriver (live in Manaus..)
(12") *(XLT 218)* – ('A') / Blue orchid (high contrast remix).

Nov 05. (7"/cd-s) *(XLS 223 A/CD)* **THE DENIAL TWIST. / SHELTER OF YOUR ARMS** [10] [–]
(7") *(XLS 223B)* – ('A'-live) / As ugly as I seem (live).

the RACONTEURS

JACK WHITE – vocals, guitars, keyboards / **BRENDAN BENSON** – vocals, guitars, keyboards (solo artist) / **JACK LAWRENCE** – bass (of GREENHORNES) / **PATRICK KEELER** – drums (of GREENHORNES)

X.L. V2

Jan 06. (ltd-7") *<(XLS 227)>* **STEADY, AS SHE GOES. / STORE BOUGHT BONES** [–] Mar06 [–]

Apr 06. (7") *(XLS 229A)* **STEADY, AS SHE GOES. / STORE BOUGHT** [4] [ ]
(cd-s) *(XLS 229CD)* – ('A') / The Bane rendition.
(7") *(XLS 229B)* – ('A'-acoustic) / Call it a day.

May 06. (cd/lp) *(XLCD/XLLP 196) <27306>* **BROKEN BOY SOLDIERS** [2] [7]
– Steady, as she goes / Hands / Broken boy soldier / Intimate secretary / Together / Level / Store bought bones / Yellow sun / Call it a day / Blue veins.

WHITE ZOMBIE

Formed: New York City, New York, USA ... early 1985 by frontman ROB ZOMBIE and female bassist SEAN YSEULT. Guitarist TOM GUAY and drummer IVAN DePRUME were drafted in a few years later after early members (ENA KOSTABI, PETER LANDAU and TIM JEFFS) had departed. Fresh from an unhealthy diet of BLACK SABBATH and horror B-movies, this cartoon-esque bunch of schlock-rockers set out on their demonic trail in 1987 with a debut mini-set, 'PSYCHO-HEAD BLOWOUT', for the US indie 'Silent Explosion'. A year later, their first full-length album, 'SOUL CRUSHER', was unleashed to an unsuspecting public, although the British still awaited their landing party by early '89. A third set, 'MAKE THEM DIE SLOWLY' came out around this time, produced by the seasoned BILL LASWELL and released on 'Caroline' records, its funky death-metal slowly unearthing itself and finding underground success from both metal and alternative rock audiences. J (JOHN RICCI) had replaced GUAY at this point, although his stay was short-lived when he was in turn superseded by JAY YUENGER. In the early 90's and now on the bulging, money-spinning roster of 'Geffen', WHITE ZOMBIE went to work on a new album with producer, ANDY WALLACE. The results were mindblowing in every conceivable sense, 'LA SEXORCISTO: DEVIL MUSIC VOLUME 1' (1992), being the musical carcass that The STOOGES and KISS once spewed out. Inevitably, twisted tracks such as 'WELCOME TO PLANET MOTHERFUCKER (PSYCHOHOLIC SLAG)', 'THUNDERKISS '65', etc. (lyrics, care of the warped brain of ROB), saw the band reach the American Top 30, cracking open the skull of any youth into terror-metal (even "real" cartoon pair, Beavis & Butt-head loved them, 'ZOMBIE being a highlight on the duo's various artists album). The band were rewarded with a heavy metal Grammy the following year as the band went on a mighty touring schedule across the globe, only halting to find a replacement for the departing DePLUME. In 1995, having substituted temp P[illegible]ith (ex-TESTAMENT) drummer JOEY TEMPESTA, they rooted out a second long-player for the label, 'ASTROCREEP 2000: SONGS OF LOVE, DESTRUCTION, AND OTHER SYNTHETIC DELUSIONS OF THE ELECTRIC HEAD' (whew!). Conceptual and groundbreaking yet again, it duly scurried up the charts and into the Top 10 (also cracked the UK Top 30), demented titles such as 'EL PHANTASMO AND THE CHICKEN-RUN BLAST-O-RAMA' carrying off where the predecessor left off. During the summer of '96, they surprised many by issuing some danceable remixes of earlier tracks going under the title of 'SUPER SEXY SWINGIN' SOUNDS', a Top 20 hit in their own country. WHITE ZOMBIE split in 1997, although the solo ROB ZOMBIE (retaining TEMPESTA) released an album, 'HELLBILLY DELUXE' (1998) and after failing to come up with the score for 'The Crow 3' movie, launched his own label, 'Zombie A Go-Go'. Meanwhile, YSEULT resurrected her moonlighting project, FAMOUS MONSTERS, releasing a second CRAMPS/B-52's style 45, 'KNOCK KNOCK HALLOWEEN' (the first, 'MONSTER GIRLS – ARE GO!', was issued a few years previously) and a debut album, 'IN THE NIGHT' (1998). Following on from 1999's 'HELLBILLY DELUXE' remix set, 'AMERICAN MADE MUSIC TO STRIP BY', the undead one was back with 'THE SINISTER URGE' (2001). If that urge is to keep on making music as menacingly camp, humourously twisted and downright swinging as he managed here then we can only hope it's never satisfied. The likes of OZZY OSBOURNE and SLAYER's KERRY KING put in their tuppence worth although as ever, ROB ZOMBIE was the undisputed star of his own freakshow. Despite being turned down by 'Universal', ZOMBIE's gorefest of a directorial debut, 'House Of 1000 Corpses', finally saw a release in 2003 through 'Lion's Gate', a self-administered soundtrack appearing the same year. While it hardly set the box office alight, prudent budgeting saw an equally uncompromising sequel, 'The Devil's Rejects', appear in summer 2005 in tandem with another soundtrack. Having established himself as a revisionist auteur, the man returned to the metal scene in 2006 with 'EDUCATED HORSES', appropriately enough a more cinematic, experimental dose of cuban-heel stomping splatter-rock that made the US Top 5.

• **Covers:** STRAKER/ZOMBIE except CHILDREN OF THE GRAVE (Black Sabbath) / GOD OF THUNDER (Kiss). FM covered CLOCK STRIKES TEN (Cheap Trick).

Album rating: PSYCHO-HEAD BLOWOUT mini (*4) / SOUL CRUSHER (*4) / LA SEXORCISTO: DEVIL MUSIC VOLUME 1 (*7) / ASTROCREEP 2000: SONGS OF LOVE AND DESTRUCTION ... (*6) / SUPER SEXY SWINGIN' SOUNDS dance remixes (*7) / Rob Zombie: HELLBILLY DELUXE (*6) / THE SINISTER URGE (*7) / HOUSE OF 1000 CORPSES soundtrack w/ Scott Humphrey (*6) / PAST, PRESENT & FUTURE compilation (*7) / EDUCATED HORSES (*6)

ROB ZOMBIE (b. ROBERT CUMMINGS, 12 Jan'66, Haverhill, Mass.) – vocals, guitar / **ENA KOSTABI** – guitar / **SEAN YSEULT** (b. 6 Jun'66) – bass / **PETER LANDAU** – drums

not iss. Silent Explosion

Feb 86. (7"ep) *<none>* **GODS ON VOODOO MOON** [–] [ ]
– Gentlemen junkie / King of souls / Tales from the scarecrow man / Cat's eye resurrection / Black Friday / Dead or alive.

— **IVAN DePRUME** – drums; repl. PETER

— **TIM JEFFS** – guitar; repl. ENA

Dec 86. (7") *<none>* **SLAUGHTER THE GREY. / PIG HEAVEN** [–] [ ]

Feb 87. (m-lp) *<SILENT 001>* **PSYCHO-HEAD BLOWOUT** [–] [ ]
– Eighty eight / Fast jungle / Gun crazy / Kick / Memphis / Magdalen / True crime / God of thunder.

— **TOM GUAY** – guitar; repl. TIM

Jan 88. (lp) *<(SILENT 002)>* **SOUL CRUSHER** [ ] [ ]
– Ratmouth / Shack of hate / Drowning the collosus / Crow III / Die, zombie, die / Skin / Truck on fire / Future shock / Scum-kill / Diamond ass.

— **J** (b. JOHN RICCI) – guitar; repl. TOM

Caroline Caroline

Feb 89. (lp/c/cd) *<(CAR LP/C/CD 3)>* **MAKE THEM DIE SLOWLY** [ ] [ ]
– Demonspeed / Disaster blaster / Murderworld / Revenge / Acid flesh / Power hungry / Godslayer.

Mar 89. (7") **GOD OF THUNDER. / LOVE RAZOR / DISASTER BLASTER** [–] [ ]

— **JAY YUENGER** (b.1967, Chicago, Illinois) – guitar; repl. RICCI

Jul 89. (12"ep) *(CLNT 1)* **GOD OF THUNDER. / LOVE RAZOR / DISASTER BLASTER 2** [ ] [ ]

Geffen Geffen

Mar 92. (lp/c/cd) *<(GEF/+C/D 24460)>* **LA SEXORCISTO: DEVIL MUSIC VOL.1** [ ] [26]
– Welcome to Planet Motherfucker (psychoholic slag) / Knuckle duster (Radio 1-A) / Thunderkiss '65 / Black sunshine / Soul-crusher / Cosmic monsters inc. / Spiderbaby (yeah-yeah-yeah) / I am legend / Knuckle duster (Radio 2-B) / Thrust! / One big crunch / Grindhouse (a go-go) / Starface / Warp asylum.

— **JOHN TEMPESTA** – drums (ex-TESTAMENT, ex-EXODUS) repl. PHILO (PHIL BUERSTATTE), who had briefly repl. DePRUME

May 95. (c-s) *(GFSC 92)* **MORE HUMAN THAN HUMAN / BLOOD, MILK AND SKY (KERO KERO KEROPFI AND THE SMOOTH OPERATOR)** [51] [–]
(10"+=/cd-s+=) *(GFST/+D 92)* – ('A'-Jeddak of the Tharks super mix).

May 95. (cd/c/lp) *(GED/GEC/GEF 24806)>* **ASTROCREEP 2000: SONGS OF LOVE AND DESTRUCTION AND OTHER SYNTHETIC DELUSIONS OF THE ELECTRIC HEAD** [25] [6]
– Electric head part I (the agony) / Super charger Heaven / Real solution No.9 / Creature of the wheel / Electric head part II (the ecstasy) / Grease paint and monkey brains / I, zombie / More human than human / El Phantasmo and the chicken-run blast-o-rama / Blur the technicolor / Blood, milk and sky. *(c+=/cd+=)* – The sidewalk ends where the bug parade begins.

May 96. (12"ep) *(GFST 22140)* **ELECTRIC HEAD PART II (THE ECSTASY) / EL PHANTASMO AND THE CHICKEN-RUN BLAST-O-RAMA. / SUPER CHARGER HEAVEN / MORE HUMAN THAN HUMAN (The Warlord Of Mars mega mix)** [31] [–]
(cd-ep) *(GFSTD 22140)* – (first 2 tracks) / More human than human (Princess of Helium ultra) / Blood, milk & sky (Im-Ho-Tep 3,700 year old boogie mix).
(cd-ep) *(GFSXD 22140)* – (tracks except second) / Thunder kiss '65 (Swinging Lovers extended mix).

Oct 96. (cd/c) *<(GED/GEC 24976)>* **SUPERSEXY SWINGIN' SOUNDS** (dance remixes!) [ ] Aug96 [17]
– Phantasmo / Blood, milk & sky / Real solution / Electronic head pt.1 / I'm your boogie man / Electronic head pt.2 / More human than human / I, zombie / Grease paint & monkey brains / Blur the technicolour / Super charger Heaven.

— WHITE ZOMBIE looked to have split, J YUENGER went on to produce FU MANCHU while YSEULT moonlighted in the all-girl surf-rock act, FAMOUS MONSTERS

ROB ZOMBIE

— with **TEMPESTA** + **DANNY LOHNER** – guitar (ex-NINE INCH NAILS, ex-SKREW) / **BLASKO** – bass

Aug 98. (cd/c) *<(GED/GEC 25212)>* **HELLBILLY DELUXE** [37] [5]
– Call of the zombie / Superbeast / Dragula / Living dead girl / Perversion / Demonoid phenomenon / Spookshow baby / How to make a monster / Meet the creeper / The ballad of resurrection Joe and Rosa Whore / What lurks on Channel X? / Return of the phantom stranger / Beginning of the end.

Dec 98. (7"pic-d) *(GFS 22367) <1213>* **DRAGULA. / DRAGULA (Hot Rod Herman mix)** [44] [ ]
(cd-s+=) *(GFSTD 22367)* – ('A'-video).
(7"pic-d) *(GFX 22367)* – ('A'side) / Halloween (she's so mean).

Interscope Interscope

Oct 99. (cd) *<(490349-2)>* **AMERICAN MADE MUSIC TO STRIP BY** (HELLBILLY DELUXE remixed) [ ] [38]

Nov 01. (cd) *<(493147-2)>* **THE SINISTER URGE** [ ] [8]
– Sinners Inc. / Demon speeding / Dead girl superstar / Never gonna stop / Iron head / (Go to) California / Feel so numb / Transylvania transmissions (pt.1) / Bring her down (to Crippletown) / Scum of the earth / House of 1000 corpses.

Universal Geffen

Mar 03. (cd) *<(493634-2)>* **HOUSE OF 1000 CORPSES** (soundtrack [solo *] +w/ Scott Humphrey) [ ] [53]
– Howdy punks / House of 1000 corpses (*) / Saddle up the mule / Everybody scream (*) / Stuck in the mud / Holy Miss Moley / Who's gonna mow your grass? (BUCK OWENS) / Run, rabbit, run (*) / Into the pit / Something for you men / I wanna be loved by you (HELEN KANE) / Pussy liquor (*) / Scarecrow attack / My baby boy / Now I wanna sniff some glue (RAMONES) / Investigation and the smokehouse / The bigger the cushion / I remember you (SLIM WHITMAN) / Drive out the rabbit / Mary's escape / Little piggy (*) / Ain't the only thing tasty / Dr. Satan / Brick house 2003 (* w/ LIONEL RICHIE & TRINA) / To the house.

Sep 03. (cd) *<(104100)>* **PAST, PRESENT & FUTURE** (compilation) [ ] [11]
– Thunder kiss '65 (WHITE ZOMBIE) / Black sunshine (WHITE ZOMBIE & IGGY POP) / Feed the gods (WHITE ZOMBIE) / More human than human (WHITE ZOMBIE) / Super charger heaven (WHITE ZOMBIE) / I'm your boogieman (WHITE ZOMBIE) / Hands of death (burn baby burn) (with ALICE COOPER) / The great American nightmare (with HOWARD STERN) / Dragula / Living dead girl / Superbeast / Feel so numb / Never gonna stop (the red red kroovy) / Demon speeding / Brick house 2003 (with LIONEL RICHIE & TRINA) / Pussy liquor / Blitzkrieg bop. *(ltd-cd w/dvd+=; 98612090)* – (bonus tracks).

Mar 06. (cd) *(9852647) <63310-2>* **EDUCATED HORSES** [ ] [5]
– Sawdust in the blood / American witch / Foxy foxy / 17 year locust / The scorpion sleeps / 100 ways / Let it all bleed out / Death of it all / Ride / The Devil's rejects / The lords of Salem.

WHITESNAKE

Formed: London, England ... late 70's by ex-DEEP PURPLE vocalist, DAVID COVERDALE (b.22 Sep'49, Saltburn-On-Sea, Yorkshire, England). After leaving 'PURPLE, COVERDALE recorded two fine sets of bluesy hard-rock, 'DAVID COVERDALE'S WHITESNAKE' (1977) and 'NORTHWINDS' (1978), taking the name for his new outfit from the former and retaining a core of musicians which included such seasoned veterans as MICKY MOODY, BERNIE MARSDEN and NEIL MURRAY. Signing to 'EMI International', he/they debuted with the 'SNAKEBITE' EP in summer '78, the record's highlight being a smoky cover of Bobby Bland's 'AIN'T NO LOVE IN THE HEART OF THE CITY'. The group subsequently hit the UK Top 50 with their debut album, 'TROUBLE' (1978), the record adding the keyboard skills of ex-DP man, JON LORD. While they followed it up with the overlooked 'LOVE HUNTER' in 1979, they only really broke through with the 'READY AN' WILLING' (1980) set, the success of its attendant single pushing the album into the UK Top 10. The band were certainly ready, willing and able to fill the gap in the market left by the now defunct DEEP PURPLE, their musical prowess securing them an enviable live reputation if not quite measuring up in the songwriting department. Consequently then, the band's only official concert set, 'LIVE ... IN THE HEART OF THE CITY' (1980), ranks as one of the most consistent recordings of their career. However their most successful album to date (narrowly missing No.1), 'COME AN' GET IT' (1981) was something of a disappointment, the group moving away from their bluesy roots towards a neutered hard-rock sound. Critics also rounded on COVERDALE's notoriously sexist, cliche-ridden lyrics, complaints which were water off a duck's back to the blonde-maned, mouth-full-of-plums cock-rocker. Despite personnel shuffles which saw new faces such as MEL GALLEY, COLIN 'Bomber' HODGKINSON and COZY POWELL, 'SAINTS AN' SINNERS' (1982) failed to remedy matters although it went Top 10 nevertheless. With the addition of ex-TYGERS OF PAN TANG guitarist, JOHN SYKES, COVERDALE had finally found a sympathetic writing partner as evidenced on the much improved 'SLIDE IT IN' (1984). Blatant innuendo was still high on the agenda, but then again, that's what COVERDALE excelled at, his panting and moaning all over the shop on the epic climax-blues stomp, 'SLOW AN' EASY', actually as effective as it was hilarious. Never the most stable of bands, the tour that followed saw WHITESNAKE eventually reduced to SYKES and COVERDALE, even LORD bogging off to join the reformed DEEP PURPLE. Recruiting TONY FRANKLIN and CARMINE APPICE, the group eventually returned with the eponymous 'WHITESNAKE 1987' (1987, funnily enough), sleeker, (some might say) sexier, and considerably more commercial than ever before. Previewed by the Top 10 LED ZEPELLIN-esque, 'STILL OF THE NIGHT', the album stormed both the British and US charts. The latter track was the hardest fare on offer, however, the bulk of the album made up of limp MTV ballads like 'IS THIS LOVE' and ravamps of old songs, the infectious reworking of 'HERE I GO AGAIN' (the original can be found on 'SAINTS AN' SINNERS') giving the group their first and only No.1. While the album no doubt alienated many of their previously loyal older fans, it sold millions, finally giving COVERDALE the success he'd long been after. It didn't do much for the group's stability, however, as SYKES split for BLUE MURDER and COVERDALE once again recruited a whole new line-up numbering ADRIAN VANDENBURG, RUDY SARZO, TOMMY ALDRIDGE and VIVIAN CAMPBELL. Guitar wizard STEVE VAI subsequently replaced CAMPBELL and this line-up gave a rather lacklustre headlining performance at the 1989 Monsters Of Rock Festival, the highly anticipated 'SLIP OF THE TONGUE' (1989) equally uninspiring. Unsurprisingly, the record failed to match the giddy commercial heights of its predecessor and COVERDALE put the band on ice while he subsequently hooked up with JIMMY PAGE for the successful 'COVERDALE ° PAGE' album in 1993. Last sighted on a tour of Europe in support of a 1994 greatest hits collection, DAVID COVERDALE & WHITESNAKE delivered a UK Top 40 comeback album, 'RESTLESS HEART' in 1997. With the metal/hard-rock scene changing almost beyond recognition, it looks unlikely that WHITESNAKE can repeat the glory days of the late 80's . . . the nostalgia circuit beckons. Well, maybe not quite yet, it seems there's life in the old dog yet. While his new image may shock a few of his older fans, not to mention a few small children, the song, basically remains the same on COVERDALE's 2000 solo set, 'INTO THE LIGHT'. His first since 'NORTHWINDS' back in '78, the record featured a solid if unadventurous selection of the man's trademark bluesy hard rock and histrionic balladry, co-written largely with veteran guitarist EARL SLICK.

• **Trivia:** On the 17th of February '89, COVERDALE married actress Tawny Kittaen, who had previously featured on their video of 'IS THIS LOVE'.

Album rating: NORTHWINDS (*7; by David Coverdale) / TROUBLE (*5) / LOVEHUNTER (*6) / READY AN' WILLING (*6) / LIVE . . . IN THE HEART OF THE CITY (*6) / COME AND GET IT (*6) / SAINTS 'N' SINNERS (*4) / SLIDE IN IT (*5) / 1987 (*5) / SLIP OF THE TONGUE (*5) / WHITESNAKE'S GREATEST HITS compilation (*8) / STARKERS IN TOKYO (*5) / BEST OF compilation (*7) / COVERDALE – PAGE (*5) / RESTLESS HEART (*5) / David Coverdale: INTO THE LIGHT (*5)

DAVID COVERDALE

(solo) – vocals (ex-DEEP PURPLE) with **MICK MOODY** – guitar (ex-JUICY LUCY, ex-SNAFU) / **TIM HINKLEY** – keyboards / **SIMON PHILLIPS** – drums / **DELISLE HARPER** – bass / plus **RON ASPERY** – sax / **ROGER GLOVER** – producer, bass, keyboards

Purple — not iss.

May 77. (lp) *(TPS 3509)* **DAVID COVERDALE'S WHITESNAKE** □ –
– Lady / Blindman / Goldie's place / Whitesnake / Time on my side / Peace lovin' man / Sunny days / Hole in the sky / Celebration. *(cd-iss. Aug00 on 'Connoisseur'+=; VSOPCD 313)* – Peace lovin' man (version) / Sunny days (version).

May 77. (7") *(PUR 133)* **HOLE IN THE SKY. / BLINDMAN** □ –

— **COVERDALE** retained only **MOODY** and recruited **BERNIE MARSDEN** – guitar (ex-PAICE, ASHTON & LORD, ex-UFO, ex-WILD TURKEY) / **NEIL MURRAY** [illegible] (ex-COLOSSEUM, ex-NATIONAL HEALTH) / **BRIAN JOHNSON** – keyboards + **DAVID DOWELL** – drums (both ex-STREETWALKERS)

Feb 78. (7") *(PUR 136)* **BREAKDOWN. / ONLY MY SOUL** □ –

Mar 78. (lp) *(TPS 3513)* **NORTHWINDS** □ –
– Keep on giving me love / Northwinds / Give me kindness / Time & again / Queen of hearts / Only my soul / Say you love me / Breakdown. *(re-iss. Apr84 on 'Fame' lp/c; FA41 3097-1/-4) (cd-iss. Aug00 on 'Connoisseur'+=; VSOPCD 314)* – Shame the Devil / Sweet mistreater.

Jun 78. (7") **BREAKDOWN. / BLOODY MARY** – □

DAVID COVERDALE'S WHITESNAKE

PETE SOLLEY – keyboards repl. JOHNSTON

EMI Int. — Sunburst

Jun 78. (lp) *<5C 062-61290>* **SNAKEBITE** □ –
– Come on / Bloody Mary / Ain't no love in the heart of the city / Steal away / Keep on giving me love / Queen of hearts / Only my soul / Breakdown.

Jun 78. (7"ep,7"white-ep) *(INEP 751) <915>* **SNAKEBITE EP** 61 □
– Bloody Mary / Steal away / Come on / Ain't no love in the heart of the city.

— **JON LORD** (b. 9 Jun'41, Leicester, England) – keyboards (ex-PAICE, ASHTON & LORD, ex-DEEP PURPLE) repl. SOLLEY

Oct 78. (7") *(INT 568)* **LIE DOWN. / DON'T MESS WITH ME** □ –

Oct 78. (lp) *(INS 3022) <937>* **TROUBLE** 50 □
– Take me with you / Love to keep you warm / Lie down (a modern love song) / Day tripper / Night hawl (vampire blues) / The time is right for love / Trouble / Belgian Tom's hat trick / Free flight / Don't mess with me. *(re-iss. Sep80 on 'United Artists'; UAG 30305) (re-iss. May82 on 'Fame' lp/c; FA/TCFA 3002) (re-iss. May90 cd/c/lp; CD/TC+/FA 3234) (re-iss. Jun87 on 'E.M.I.' lp/c; EMS/TCEMS 1257) (cd-iss. Apr88 on 'E.M.I.'; CZ 9)*

Mar 79. (7") *(INT 578)* **THE TIME IS RIGHT FOR LOVE. / COME ON (live)** □ –

Apr 79. (7") **THE TIME IS RIGHT FOR LOVE. / BELGUIN TOM'S HAT TRICK** – □

U.A. — U.A.

Oct 79. (lp/c) *(UAG 30264) <981>* **LOVE HUNTER** 29 □
– Long way from home / Walking in the shadow of the blues / Help me thro' the day / Medicine man / You 'n' me / Mean business / Love hunter / Outlaw / Rock'n'roll women / We wish you well. *(re-iss. Apr84 on 'Fame' lp/c; FA/TCFA 3095) (cd-iss. Apr88; CDFA 3095) (cd re-iss. Jul94 on 'E.M.I.'; CDEMS 1529)*

Oct 79. (7"m) *(BP 324)* **LONG WAY FROM HOME. / TROUBLE (live) / AIN'T NO LOVE IN THE HEART OF THE CITY (live)** 55 –

Nov 79. (7") **LONG WAY FROM HOME. / WE WISH YOU WELL** – □

WHITESNAKE

— with **IAN PAICE** (b.29 Jun'48, Nottingham, England) – drums (ex-PAICE, ASHTON & LORD, ex-DEEP PURPLE) repl. DOWELL

U.A. — Mirage-Atlantic

Apr 80. (7"m) *(BP 352)* **FOOL FOR YOUR LOVING. / MEAN BUSINESS / DON'T MESS WITH ME** 13 –

Jun 80. (lp/c) *(UAG 30302) <19276>* **READY AN' WILLING** 6 90
– Fool for your loving / Sweet talker / Ready an' willing / Carry your load / Blindman / Ain't gonna cry no more / Love man / Black and blue / She's a woman. *(re-iss. Sep85 on 'Fame' lp/c; FA/TCFA 3134) (cd-iss. Apr88; CDFA 3134) (cd re-iss. Jul94 on 'E.M.I.'; CDEMS 1526) (cd re-iss. Feb00 on 'Axe Killer';* **AXE 305526CD***)*

Jul 80. (7"m) *(BP 363)* **READY AN' WILLING. / NIGHT HAWK (VAMPIRE BLUES) / WE WISH YOU WELL** 43 –

Jul 80. (7") *<3672>* **FOOL FOR YOUR LOVING. / BLACK AND BLUE** – 53

Oct 80. (7") *<3766>* **SWEET TALKER. / AIN'T GONNA CRY NO MORE** – □

Nov 80. (d-lp/d-c) *(SNAKE/TC2SNAKE 1) <19292>* **LIVE . . . IN THE HEART OF THE CITY (live)** 5 □
– Come on * / Sweet talker / Walking in the shadow of the blues / Love hunter / Fool for your loving / Ain't gonna cry no more / Ready an' willing / Take me with you * / Might just take your life / Lie down * / Ain't no love in the heart of the city / Trouble * / Mistreated. *<cd-iss. Jul88 on 'Underdog'; CDS 790860-2>* – *<omits *> (re-iss. Nov91 on 'Fame' cd/c; CD/TC FA 3265) (re-iss. Jul94 on 'E.M.I.' cd/c; CD/TC EMS 1525)*

Nov 80. (7"/12") *(BP/12BP 381)* *<3794>* **AIN'T NO LOVE IN THE HEART OF THE CITY (live). / TAKE ME WITH YOU (live)** [51] [ ]

Liberty Atlantic

Apr 81. (7") *(BP 395)* **DON'T BREAK MY HEART AGAIN. / CHILD OF BABYLON** [17] [–]

Apr 81. (lp/c) *(LBG/TCLBG 30327)* *<16043>* **COME AN' GET IT** [2] [ ]
– Come an' get it / Hot stuff / Don't break my heart again / Lonely days, lonely nights / Wine, women an' song / Child of Babylon / Would I lie to you / Girl / Hit an' run / Till the day I die. *(re-iss. May89 on 'Fame' cd/c/lp; CD/TC+/FA 3219) (re-iss. Jul94 on 'E.M.I.' cd/c; CD/TC EMS 1528)*

May 81. (7") *(BP 399)* **WOULD I LIE TO YOU. / GIRL** [37] [–]

Jun 81. (7") *<3844>* **DON'T BREAK MY HEART AGAIN. / LONELY DAYS, LONELY NIGHTS** [–] [ ]

—— **COVERDALE** retained **MOODY + LORD** and brought in **MEL GALLEY** – guitar (ex-TRAPEZE) repl. MARSDEN who formed ALASKA / **COLIN 'Bomber' HODGKINSON** (b.14 Oct'45) – bass (ex-BACK DOOR) repl. MURRAY to GARY MOORE / **COZY POWELL** (b.29 Dec'47, Cirencester, England) – drums (ex-JEFF BECK, ex-RAINBOW, Solo Artist, ex-BEDLAM) repl. PAICE who joined GARY MOORE

Liberty Geffen

Oct 82. (7"pic-d) *(BP 416)* **HERE I GO AGAIN. / BLOODY LUXURY** [34] [–]

Nov 82. (lp/c/pic-lp) *(LBG/TCLBG/LBGP 30354)* *<2-24173>* **SAINTS AN' SINNERS** [9] [ ]
– Young blood / Rough an' ready / Blood luxury / Victim of love / Crying in the rain / Here I go again / Love an' afection / Rock'n'roll angels / Dancing girls / Saints an' sinners. *(re-iss. 1985 lp/c; ATAK/TCATAK 10) (re-iss. May87 on 'Fame' lp/c; FA/TCFA 3177) (cd-iss. Apr88; CDFA 3177) (cd re-iss. Jul94 & Jul98 on 'E.M.I.'; CDEMS 1521)*

Aug 83. (7"/7"sha-pic-d) *(BP/+P 420)* **GUILTY OF LOVE. / GAMBLER** [31] [–]

—— now a quintet, when MICK MOODY departed

Jan 84. (7"/12") *(BP/12BP 422)* **GIVE ME MORE TIME. / NEED YOUR LOVE SO BAD** [29] [–]

—— **NEIL MURRAY** – bass returned to repl. HODGKINSON / added **JOHN SYKES** (b.29 Jul'59) – guitar (ex-TYGERS OF PAN TANG)

Feb 84. (lp/c) *(WHITE/TCWHITE 1)* *<4018>* **SLIDE IT IN** [9] Aug84 [40]
– Gambler / Slide it in / Standing in the shadow / Give me more time / Love ain't no stranger / Slow an' easy / Spit it out / All or nothing / Hungry for love / Guilty of love. *(cd-iss. Apr88 on 'E.M.I.'; CZ 88) (pic-lp 1984 w/extra US mixes; LBGP 240-000-0)*

Apr 84. (7"/7"pic-d) *(BP/+P 423)* **STANDING IN THE SHADOWS. / ALL OR NOTHING (US mix)** [62] [–]
(12"+=) – ('A'-US remix).

Aug 84. (7") *<29171>* **LOVE AIN'T NO STRANGER. / GUILTY OF LOVE** [–] [ ]

Feb 85. (7"/12") *(BP/12BP 424)* **LOVE AIN'T NO STRANGER. / SLOW AN' EASY** [44] [–]
(12"white+=) *(BP12 424)* – Slide it in.

—— split for a while in 1984 when JON LORD re-joined DEEP PURPLE. **WHITESNAKE** were re-formed by **COVERDALE + SYKES** and new musicians **TONY FRANKLIN** – bass (ex-The FIRM) repl. MURRAY and GALLEY / **CARMINE APPICE** – drums (ex-BECK, BOGERT & APPICE) repl. POWELL to E.L.P.

EMI Int. Geffen

Mar 87. (7"/7"white) *(EMI/+W 5606)* **STILL OF THE NIGHT. / HERE I GO AGAIN (1987)** [16] [–]
(12"+=/12"pic-d+=) *(12EMI/+P 5606)* – You're gonna break my heart again.

Apr 87. (cd/c/lp) *(CD/TC+/EMC 3528)* *<24099>* **WHITESNAKE 1987** [8] [2]
– Still of the night / Bad boys / Give me all your love / Looking for love / Crying in the rain / Is this love / Straight for the heart / Don't turn away / Children of the night. *(also on pic-lp; EMCP 3528) (cd+=)* – Here I go again '87 / You're gonna break my heart again. *(re-iss. Jul94 cd/c; CD/TC EMS 1531)*

May 87. (7"/7"sha-pic-d) *(EM/+P 3)* **IS THIS LOVE. / STANDING IN THE SHADOWS** [9] [–]
(12"+=/12"white+=) *(12EM/+P 3)* – Need your love so bad.
(cd-ep++=/7"ep++=) *(EMX/CDEM 3)* – Still of the night.

Jun 87. (7") *<28331>* **STILL OF THE NIGHT. / DON'T TURN AWAY** [–] [79]

Jul 87. (7") *<28339>* **HERE I GO AGAIN. / CHILDREN OF THE NIGHT** [–] [1]

Oct 87. (7") *<28233>* **IS THIS LOVE. / BAD BOYS** [–] [2]

Oct 87. (c-s/12"/7") *(TC/12+/EM 35)* **HERE I GO AGAIN '87 (US mix). / GUILTY OF LOVE** [9] [–]
(7"etched/10"white/cd-s) *(EMP/10EM/CDEM 35)* – ('A'side) / ('A'-US remix).

Jan 88. (7"/7"white) *(EM/+W 23)* **GIVE ME ALL YOUR LOVE. / FOOL FOR YOUR LOVING** [18] [–]
(12"+=/12"white) *(12EMP/+W 23)* – Don't break my heart again.
(3"cd-s+=) *(CDEM 23)* – Here I go again (USA remix).

Jan 88. (7") *<28103>* **GIVE ME ALL YOUR LOVE. / STRAIGHT FROM THE HEART** [–] [48]

—— **COVERDALE** completely re-modelled line-up when SYKES formed BLUE MURDER. He was replaced by **ADRIAN VANDENBURG** (b. Netherlands) – guitar (ex-VANDENBERG) / **RUDY SARZO** (b. 9 Nov'52, Havana, Cuba) – bass (ex-OZZY OSBOURNE, ex-QUIET RIOT) repl. FRANKLIN / **TOMMY ALDRIDGE** – drums (ex-OZZY OSBOURNE, ex-BLACK OAK ARKANSAS) repl. APPICE (Dec88) / **STEVE VAI** (b. 6 Jun'60, Carle Place, N.Y.) – guitar (solo Artist, ex-FRANK ZAPPA, DAVID LEE ROTH) repl. VIVIAN CAMPBELL

Nov 89. (cd/c/lp) *(CD/TC+/EMD 1013)* *<24249>* **SLIP OF THE TONGUE** [10] [10]
– Slip of the tongue / Cheap an' nasty / Fool for your loving / Now you're gone / Kitten's got claws / Wings of the storm / The deeper the love / Judgement day / Slow poke music / Sailing ships. *(re-iss. Jul94 cd/c; CD/TC EMS 1527)*

Nov 89. (7"/7"s)<US-c-s> *(EM/+P 123)* *<22715>* **FOOL FOR YOUR LOVING ('89). / SLOW POKE MUSIC** [43] [37]
(c-s+=) *(TCEM 123)* – ('A'version).
(12"+=/12"white+=) *(12EM+/P 1243)* – Walking in the shadow of the blues.

Jan 90. (7") *<19951>* **THE DEEPER THE LOVE. / SLIP OF THE TONGUE** [–] [28]

Feb 90. (c-s/7"/7"pic-d) *(TC+/EM/+PD 128)* **THE DEEPER THE LOVE. / JUDGEMENT DAY** [35] [–]
(12"white+=) *(12EMS 128)* – Sweet lady luck.
(12"++=/cd-s++=) *(12/CD EM 128)* – Fool for your lovin' (Vai voltage mix).

Aug 90. (c-s/7"/7"sha-pic-d) *(TC+/EM+/PD 150)* *<19976>* **NOW YOU'RE GONE (remix). / WINGS OF THE STORM** [31] May90 [96]
(12"+=/12"pic-d+=/cd-s+=) *(12EM/12EMPS/CDEM 150)* – Kittens got claws / Cheap an' nasty.

DAVID COVERDALE

Epic Epic

Sep 90. (7"/c-s) *(656 292-7/-4)* **THE LAST NOTE OF FREEDOM. / (track by HANS ZIMMER)** [ ] [ ]
(12"+=) *(656 292-6)* – (track by other artist).
(cd-s++=) *(656 292-2)* – ('A'version).

COVERDALE• PAGE

DAVID COVERDALE – vocals / **JIMMY PAGE** – guitar (ex-LED ZEPPELIN, ex-solo artist) / **JORGE CASAS** – bass / **DENNY CARMASSI** – drums (ex-MONTROSE) / **RICKY PHILIPS** – bass / **LESTER MENDEL** – keyboards / **JOHN HARRIS** – acoustic harmonica / **TOMMY FUNDERBUCK** – backing vocals

E.M.I. Geffen

Mar 93. (cd/c/lp) *(CD/TC+/EMD 1041)* *<24487>* **COVERDALE• PAGE** [4] [5]
– Shake my tree / Waiting on you / Take me for a little while / Pride and joy / Over now / Feeling hot / Easy does it / Take a look at yourself / Don't leave me this way / Absolution blues / Whisper a prayer for the dying *(re-iss. Jul94 cd/c; same)*

Jun 93. (c-s/12"pic-d) *(12EMPD/TCEM 270)* **TAKE ME FOR A LITTLE WHILE. / EASY DOES IT** [29] [ ]
(cd-s) *(CDEM 270)* – ('A'side) / ('A'acoustic) / Shake my tree (the crunch mix) / ('A'edit).

Sep 93. (7"pic-d/c-s) *(EMPD/TCEM 279)* **TAKE A LOOK AT YOURSELF. / WAITING ON YOU** [ ] [ ]
(cd-s+=) *(CDEM 279)* – ('A'acoustic) / ('A'girls version).

DAVID COVERDALE & WHITESNAKE

E.M.I. E.M.I.

May 97. (c-s/cd-s) *(TC/CD EM 471)* **TOO MANY TEARS / THE DEEPER THE LOVE / IS THIS LOVE** [46] [–]

(cd-s) *(CDEMS 471)* – ('A'part 1) / Can't stop now / ('A'part 2).

Jun 97. (cd/c) *(CD/TCEMD 1104)* <56806> **RESTLESS HEART** [34] Jun98 [ ]
– Don't fade away / All in the name of love / Restless heart / Too many tears / Crying / Stay with me / Can't go on / You're so fine / Your precious love / Take me back again / Woman trouble blues.

Oct 97. (c-s) *(TCEM 495)* **DON'T FADE AWAY / OI** [ ] [–]
(cd-s+=) *(CDEM 495)* – Anything you want / Don't fade away.

WHITESNAKE

— **COVERDALE, VANDENBERG**, etc.

E.M.I. E.M.I.

Mar 99. (cd) *(4 99508-2)* <23788> **STARKERS IN TOKYO** (live) [ ] Jul98 [ ]
– Sailing ships / Too many tears / The deeper the love / Love ain't no stranger / Can't go on / Give me all your love / Don't fade away / Is this love / Here I go again / Soldier of fortune.

DAVID COVERDALE

— with various session people

E.M.I. Dragonfly

Sep 00. (cd-s) *(CDEM 574)* **LOVE IS BLIND / LOVE IS BLIND (radio) / SHE GIVE ME** [ ] [–]

Sep 00. (cd) *(528124-2)* <12251> **INTO THE LIGHT** [75] Oct00 [ ]
– Into the light / River song / She give me / Don't you cry / Love is blind / Slave / Cry for love / Living on love / Midnight blue / Too many tears / Don't lie to me / Where you may go.

– compilations, etc. –

Apr 88. (d-lp/c/cd) *Connoisseur; (VSOP LP/MC/CD 118)* **THE CONNOISSEUR COLLECTION** [ ] [–]
– (DAVID COVERDALE's first 2 solo albums)

Jun 88. (d-lp) *Polydor; <9244/5>* **GREATEST HITS** [–] [ ]

Jul 94. (cd/c/lp) *E.M.I.; (CD/TC+/EMD 1065) / Geffen; <24620>* **WHITESNAKE'S GREATEST HITS** [4] [ ]
– Still of the night / Here I go again / Is this love / Love ain't no stranger / Looking for love / Now you're gone / Slide it in / Slow an' easy / Judgement day / You're gonna break my heart again / The deeper the love / Crying in the rain / Fool for your loving / Sweet lady luck.

Jul 94. (7"/7"white/c-s) *E.M.I.; (EM/EMS/TCEM 329)* **IS THIS LOVE. / SWEET LADY LUCK** [25] [ ]
(cd-s+=) *(CDEM 329)* – Now you're gone.

Nov 95. (3xcd-box) *E.M.I.; (CDOMB 016)* **SLIDE IT IN / 1987 / SLIP OF THE TONGUE** [ ] [ ]

Jun 00. (d-cd) *Axe Killer; (AXE 3055482CD)* **1987 / SLIP OF THE TONGUE** [ ] [ ]

Mar 03. (cd) *E.M.I.; (581245-2)* **BEST OF** [44] [–]
– Fool for your loving / Don't break my heart again / Love ain't no stranger / Is this love / Now you're gone / Give me all your love / Ready and willing / Guilty of love / Would I lie to you / Long way from home / The deeper the love / Ain't no love in the heart of the city / Too many tears / Give me more time / Standing in the shadow / Here I go again / Still of the night.

Apr 03. (cd) *Polydor; <2580>* **BEST!** [–] [ ]

May 03. (d-cd) *E.M.I.; (<581694-2>)* **THE SILVER ANNIVERSARY COLLECTION** [ ] [ ]

the WHO

Formed: Chiswick & Hammersmith, London, England ... 1964 as The HIGH NUMBERS, by ROGER DALTREY, PETE TOWNSHEND, JOHN ENTWISTLE and DOUG SANDOM. After making his impromptu mid-set debut at an early gig, manic sticksman, KEITH MOON, was immediately recruited in favour of the struggling SANDERS. At his first show proper, MOON reportedly mystified colleagues by roping his drums to some pillars before the show. All became clear when the drummer proceeded to knock seven shades of proverbial shit out of them during a solo, the kit actually bouncing off the floor! And thus was completed the line-up that would make their mark as one of the most pivotal, not to mention aggressive bands in rock history. Manager PETE MEADON introduced the band to the burgeoning "Mod" scene and shaped their image accordingly as a musical voice for the sharply dressed, scooter-riding young rebels, a movement that TOWNSHEND in particular felt a strong affinity with, and whose frustrations he'd document in his early, indignant blasts of raw rock'n'roll. A strutting, gloriously arrogant piece of R&B, the band's debut one-off 45 for 'Fontana', 'I'M THE FACE', was released the same month as the experienced managerial team of KIT LAMBERT and CHRIS STAMP took the reins from MEADON and began a concerted campaign for chart domination. Later that year, the band were re-christened The WHO and by this time had begun to perfect their powerful stageshow, TOWNSHEND developing his ferocious "windmilling" power-chord guitar style while the band courted controversy and delighted crowds by smashing their instruments in a cathartic rage. Rejected by major labels, they eventually secured a deal with 'Decca' US, through producer SHEL TALMY. Released in Britain via 'Decca's' UK subsidiary, 'Brunswick', 'I CAN'T EXPLAIN' (1965) introduced a more melodic sound and gave the band their first chart hit. The single climbed into the top 10 after TV appearances on 'Ready Steady Go' (which later adopted the track as its theme tune) and Top Of The Pops, 'ANYWAY, ANYHOW, ANYWHERE' following it later that summer. For most people however, The WHO really arrived with the seminal rebel anthem, 'MY GENERATION'. A stuttering, incredibly focused piece of amphetamine aggression, it galvanised legions of disaffected youths and only The SEX PISTOLS ever equalled it for sheer snide factor. It reached No.2 and was closely followed by the similarly titled debut album which included 'THE KIDS ARE ALRIGHT', probably TOWNSHEND's most explicit alignment with his "Mod" following. But if the kids were alright, The WHO's deal with SHEL TALMY certainly wasn't, or at least that's what the band thought, and after releasing their next single, 'SUBSTITUTE' (1966), on a new label, they became embroiled in a court battle over TALMY's right to produce the group. Despite TALMY winning a royalty on all the band's recordings for another five years, The WHO came out fighting, releasing a string of hits including 'I'M A BOY' (1966), 'HAPPY JACK' (1966) and the wistful ode to masturbation, 'PICTURES OF LILY' (1967). The title track from 'A QUICK ONE' (1966) was a patchy, prototype of the rock opera concept TOWNSHEND would later refine towards the end of the decade. Elsewhere on the album, tracks like ENTWISTLE's 'BORIS THE SPIDER' and TOWNSHEND's 'HAPPY JACK' possessed the same quirky Englishness that was the essence of The KINKS, and The WHO only really began to make some headway in America after their incendiary performance at The Monterey Pop Festival in the summer of '67. 'THE WHO SELL OUT' (1967), a mock concept album, contained the sublime 'I CAN SEE FOR MILES', a spiralling piece of neo-psychedelia that had a spiritual partner in the equally trippy 'ARMENIA CITY IN THE SKY'. With 'TOMMY' (1969), TOWNSHEND ushered in the dreaded concept of the 'Rock Opera'. Yet with his compelling story of a "deaf, dumb and blind kid" who finds release through pinball, he managed to carry the whole thing off. 'PINBALL WIZARD' and 'SEE ME, FEEL ME' were classic TOWNSHEND. The album was even made into a film by maverick director Ken Russell and later into a successful West End show. After this artful tour de force, the band released the legendary 'LIVE AT LEEDS' (1970) album while they worked on TOWNSHEND's latest idea, the 'LIFEHOUSE' project. An ambitious attempt at following up 'TOMMY', the venture was later aborted, although some of the material was used as the basis for the landmark 'WHO'S NEXT' album. Released in 1971, the record heralded a harder rocking sound with the anthemic 'WON'T GET FOOLED AGAIN' and 'BABA O'REILLY'. Immaculately produced, it still stands as The WHO's most confident and cohesive work and only No.1 album. TOWNSHEND finally created a follow-up

The WHO

to TOMMY with 'QUADROPHENIA' in 1973. A complex, lavishly embellished piece that saw him retrospectively examining the Mod sub-culture he'd so closely identified with. The project was later made into a film, inspiring a whole new wave of neo-Mod bands at the turn of the decade. 'THE WHO BY NUMBERS' (1975) was exactly that, a confused set that found the band treading water while trying to find direction in a music scene that was to become increasingly dominated by punk rock. While 'WHO ARE YOU' (1978) sounded more assured, the album's release was marred by the death of KEITH MOON, whose hard drinking and drugging ways finally proved his undoing. Speculation of a split was rife but ex-FACE, KENNY JONES, was drafted in and the band eventually came up with 'FACE DANCES' in 1981. Neither this album, nor 1982's 'IT'S HARD' were successful in rekindling The WHO spark of old and, already demoralised after a number of fans were crushed at a gig in Cincinatti, the band finally called it a day in 1983. The WHO have since occasionally reformed for one-off live appearances including 'Live Aid' and as DALTREY has mainly concentrated on his acting career, TOWNSHEND is the only ex-WHO member who's maintained a serious solo career. His most recent release was the critically acclaimed 'PSYCHODERELICT' (1993) album which was a rock opera of sorts updated for the 90's and included material from the shelved 'LIFEHOUSE' project. 1999's 'PETE TOWNSHEND LIVE: A BENEFIT FOR MARYVILLE ACADEMY' documented a 1998 charity concert at Chicago's House Of Blues with the WHO veteran giving it large on a selection of golden oldies and a few oddities including a cover of Canned Heat's 'ON THE ROAD AGAIN'. More interesting, at least for diehard WHO fans was 'THE OCEANIC CONCERTS' (2001), a document of obscure late 70's live material performed for TOWNSHEND's spiritual guru, Meher Baba. The album was co-credited to RAPHAEL RUDD (of RENAISSANCE fame) who accompanied PETE on meditative, stripped down covers of WHO classics performed for a select audience of Baba devotees. Meanwhile, The WHO (featuring ZAK STARKEY on drums) were still filling stadiums all around the world. 'LIVE AT THE ROYAL ALBERT HALL' (2003), a one-off charity concert reunion, featured a line-up of DALTREY, TOWNSHEND, ENTWISTLE, STARKEY and JOHN 'RABBIT' BUNDRICK, belting out the cream of the band's back catalogue with surprising verve and vitality, and featuring guest spots from the likes of PAUL WELLER and EDDIE VEDDER. It was to be the last time ENTWISTLE would appear on record with the band, the bassist dying in a hotel room in Las Vegas on the 22nd of July 2002. On another rather sour note, TOWNSHEND was arrested in January 2003 on child pornography charges, his website computers confiscated by police who found nothing incriminating – although he did use his credit card – that he was only looking at indecent images for novel research purposes. His autobiography should resolve the matter. Meanwhile, the WHO were still doing the odd venue all around the world, the new line-up even getting out a few songs on the retrospective set, 'THEN AND NOW: 1964-2004' (2004).

• **Songwriters:** TOWNSHEND wrote most of material except, I'M THE FACE (Slim Harpo's 'Got Live If You Want It') / I'M A MAN (Bo Diddley) / IN THE CITY (Speedy Keen; aka of Thunderclap Newman) / BARBARA ANN (Beach Boys) / BABY DON'T YOU DO IT (Marvin Gaye) / THE LAST TIME + UNDER MY THUMB (Rolling Stones) / SUMMERTIME BLUES (Eddie Cochran). KEITH MOON's only album was comprised wholly of cover versions. DALTREY's solo career started with songs written for him by LEO SAYER and DAVE COURTNEY. • **Trivia:** DALTREY continues to run a trout farm in Dorset. The WHO were inducted into the Guinness Book Of Records after performing the loudest concert (120 decibels) at Charlton Athletic's Football Club.

Album rating: MY GENERATION (*7) / A QUICK ONE (*6) / THE WHO SELL OUT (*7) / MAGIC BUS – THE WHO ON TOUR (*5) / TOMMY (*8) / THE WHO LIVE AT LEEDS (*8) / WHO'S NEXT (*10) / MEATY, BEATY, BIG AND BOUNCY compilation (*9) / QUADROPHENIA (*9) / ODDS AND SODS collection (*5) / THE WHO BY NUMBERS (*5) / THE STORY OF THE WHO compilation (*7) / WHO ARE YOU (*6) / THE KIDS ARE ALRIGHT soundtrack (*7) / FACE DANCES (*5) / IT'S HARD (*4) / selective compilations:- WHO'S BETTER WHO'S BEST (*8) / MY GENERATION – THE VERY BEST OF THE WHO (*9) / THE ULTIMATE COLLECTION (*9) / LIVE AT THE ROYAL ALBERT HALL (*5) / THEN AND NOW: 1964-2004 (*7) / Pete Townshend: WHO CAME FIRST (*6) / ROUGH MIX with Ronnie Lane (*6) / EMPTY GLASS (*7) / ALL THE BEST COWBOYS HAVE CHINESE EYES (*4) / SCOOP rarities (*4) / WHITE CITY – A NOVEL (*4) / PETE TOWNSHEND'S DEEP END LIVE! (*3) / THE IRON MAN a musical (*4) / ANOTHER SCOOP rarities (*3) / PSYCHODERELICT (*5) / THE BEST OF PETE TOWNSHEND – COOLWALKINGSMOOTH . . . compilation (*7) / Roger Daltrey: DALTREY (*5) / RIDE A ROCK HORSE (*6) / ONE OF THE BOYS (*5) / McVICAR soundtrack (*5) / THE BEST OF . . . compilation (*6) / PARTING SHOULD BE PAINLESS (*4) / UNDER A RAGING MOON (*5) / CAN'T WAIT TO SEE THE MOVIE (*3)

ROGER DALTREY (b. ROGER HARRY DALTREY, 1 Mar'45) – vocals / **PETE TOWNSHEND** (b.19 May'45) – guitar, vocals / **JOHN ENTWISTLE** (b. 9 Oct'44) – bass, vocals / **KEITH MOON** (b.23 Aug'47) – drums, vocals repl. DOUG SANDOM

Fontana — not iss.

Jul 64. (7"; as The HIGH NUMBERS) *(TF 480)* **I'M THE FACE. / ZOOT SUIT** [ ] [-]
(re-iss. Feb65) (re-iss. Mar80 on 'Back Door', hit UK No.49) (US re-iss. Mar80 as The WHO on 'Mercury')

Brunswick — Decca

Jan 65. (7") *(05926)* *<31725>* **I CAN'T EXPLAIN. / BALD HEADED WOMAN** [8] Feb65 [93]
(US re-iss. 1973 on 'MCA')

May 65. (7") *(05935)* **ANYWAY ANYHOW ANYWHERE. / DADDY ROLLING STONE** [10] [-]

Jun 65. (7") *<31801>* **ANYWAY ANYHOW ANYWHERE. / ANYTIME YOU WANT ME** [-] [ ]

Oct 65. (7") *(05944)* **MY GENERATION. / SHOUT & SHIMMY** [2] [-]

Nov 65. (7") *<31877>* **MY GENERATION. / OUT IN THE STREET** [-] [74]

Dec 65. (lp) *(LAT 8616)* *<74664>* **MY GENERATION** [5] [ ]
– Out in the street / I don't mind / The good's gone / La-la-la-lies / Much too much / My generation / The kid's are alright / Please please please / It's not true / I'm a man / A legal matter / The ox. *(US title 'THE WHO SING MY GENERATION') (UK re-iss. Oct80 on 'Virgin' lp/c; V/TCV 2179)* – (hit UK No.20) *(cd-iss. 1990;) (deluxe d-lp edition iss.Sep02 +=; 133981-1)* – Circles / I can't explain / Bald headed woman / Daddy rolling stone / Leaving here / Lubie (come back home) / Shout and shimmy / Love is like a heat wave / Motoring / Anytime you want it / Anyhow anywhere anyway / Instant party mixture / I don't mind / Good's gone / My generation (instrumental) / Anytime you want me. *(deluxe d-cd edition ++=; 112926-2)* – A legal matter / My generation (mono). *(hit UK No.47)*

Reaction — Decca

Mar 66. (7") *(591 001)* *<6409>* **SUBSTITUTE. / WALTZ FOR A PIG ("The WHO ORCHESTRA")** [5] [ ]

—— (some copies 'INSTANT PARTY' or 'CIRCLES' on b-side)
<above on US 'Atco'; re-iss. Aug67; 6509>

Aug 66. (7") *(591 004)* *<32058>* **I'M A BOY. / IN THE CITY** [2] Dec66 [ ]

Dec 66. (7") *(591 010)* **HAPPY JACK. / I'VE BEEN AWAY** [3] [-]

Dec 66. (lp) *(593 002)* *<74892>* **A QUICK ONE** <US-title 'HAPPY JACK'> [4] May67 [67]
– Run run run / Boris the spider / Whiskey man / I need you / Heatwave / Cobwebs and strange / Don't look away / See my way / So sad about us / A quick one, while he's away. *(re-iss. Aug88 on 'Polydor' lp/c)(cd); (SPE LP/MC 114)(835 782-2) (cd re-iss. Jun95 & Apr97; 527758-2)*

Mar 67. (7") *<32114>* **HAPPY JACK. / WHISKEY MAN** [-] [24]

Track — Decca

Apr 67. (7") *(604 002)* *<32156>* **PICTURES OF LILY. / DOCTOR DOCTOR** [4] Jun67 [51]

Jul 67. (7") *(604 006)* **THE LAST TIME. / UNDER MY THUMB** [44] [-]

Oct 67. (7") *(604 011)* **I CAN SEE FOR MILES. / SOMEONE'S COMING** [10] [-]

Oct 67. (7") *<32206>* **I CAN SEE FOR MILES. / MARY ANN WITH THE SHAKY HANDS** [-] [9]

Jan 68. (lp; mono/stereo) *(612/613 002)* *<74950>* **THE WHO SELL OUT** [13] [48]
– Armenia, city in the sky / Heinz baked beans / Mary Anne with the shaky hands / Odorono / Tattoo / Our love was, is / I can see for miles / I can't

reach you / Medac / Silas Stingy / Sunrise / Tattoo / Rael (1 and 2). *(re-iss. Aug88 on 'Polydor' lp/c)(cd; (SPE LP/MC 115) (cd re-iss. Jun95 & Apr97 on 'Polydor'; 527 759-2)*

Mar 68. (7") *<32288>* **CALL ME LIGHTNING. / DR. JEKYLL & MR. HIDE** – 40

Jun 68. (7") *(604 023)* **DOGS. / CALL ME LIGHTNING** 25 –

Jul 68. (7") *<32362>* **MAGIC BUS. / SOMEONE'S COMING** – 25

Oct 68. (7") *(604 024)* **MAGIC BUS. / DR. JEKYLL & MR. HIDE** 26 –

Oct 68. (lp) *<75064>* **MAGIC BUS – (THE WHO ON TOUR) (live)** – 39
– Disguises / Run run run / Dr. Jekyll & Mr. Hyde / I can't reach you / Our love was, is / Call me Lightning / Magic bus / Someone's coming / Doctor doctor / Bucket T. / Pictures of ily.

Nov 68. (lp; mono/stereo) *(612/613 006)* **DIRECT HITS** (compilation) –
– Bucket T. / I'm a boy / Pictures of Lily / Doctor doctor / I can see for miles / Substitute / Happy Jack / The last time / In the city / Call me Lightning / Mary-Anne with the shaky hand / Dogs.

Mar 69. (7") *(604 027) <32465>* **PINBALL WIZARD. / DOGS (part 2)** 4 19
<US re-iss. 1973 on 'MCA'>

May 69. (d-lp) *(613 013-014) <7205>* **TOMMY** 2 4
– Overture / It's a boy / 1921 / Amazing journey / Sparks / Eyesight for the blind / Miracle cure / Sally Simpson / I'm free / Welcome / Tommy's holiday camp / We're not gonna take it / Christmas / Cousin Kevin / The acid queen / Underture / Do you think it's alright / Fiddle about / Pinball wizard / There's a doctor / Go to the mirror / Tommy can you hear me / Smash the mirror / Sensation. *(re-iss. Jul84 on 'Polydor'; 2486 161/2) (d-cd-iss. Apr89; 800 077-2)*

Jul 69. (7") *<32519>* **I'M FREE. / WE'RE NOT GONNA TAKE IT** – 37

Mar 70. (7") *(604 036) <32670>* **THE SEEKER. / HERE FOR MORE** 19 44

May 70. (lp) *(2406 001) <79175>* **LIVE AT LEEDS (live)** 3 4
– Young man / Substitute / Summertime blues / Shakin' all over / My generation / Magic bus. *(re-iss. Nov83 on 'Polydor' lp/c; SPE LP/MC 50) (cd-iss. May88 on 'Polydor'; 825 339-2) (cd re-iss. Feb95 on 'Polydor', hit No.59 & Apr97; 527 169-2)*

Jul 70. (7") *(2094 002)* **SUMMERTIME BLUES (live). / HEAVEN AND HELL** 38 –

Jul 70. (7") *<32708>* **SUMMERTIME BLUES (live). / HERE FOR MORE** – 27

Sep 70. (7") *<32729>* **SEE ME, FEEL ME. / WE'RE NOT GONNA TAKE IT / OVERTURE FROM TOMMY** – 12
<US re-iss. 1973 on 'MCA'>

Sep 70. (7"w-drawn) *(2094 004)* **SEE ME, FEEL ME. / OVERTURE FROM TOMMY** – –

Jul 71. (7") *(2094 009) <32846>* **WON'T GET FOOLED AGAIN. / I DON'T EVEN KNOW MYSELF** 9 15

Sep 71. (lp) *(2408 102) <79182>* **WHO'S NEXT** 1 Aug71 4
– Baba O'Riley / Bargain / Love ain't for keeping / My wife / Song is over / Getting in tune / Going mobile / Behind blue eyes / Won't get fooled again. *(re-iss. Nov83 on 'Polydor' lp/c)(cd; SPE LP/MC 49)(813 651-2) (cd re-iss. Aug96; 527760-2)*

Oct 71. (7") *(2094 012)* **LET'S SEE ACTION. / WHEN I WAS A BOY** 16 –

Nov 71. (7") *<32888>* **BEHIND BLUE EYES. / MY WIFE** – 34

Dec 71. (lp/c) *(2406/3191 006) <79184>* **MEATY, BEATY, BIG AND BOUNCY** (compilation) 9 Nov71 11
– I can't explain / The kids are alright / Happy Jack / I can see for miles / Pictures of Lily / My generation / The seeker / Anyway, anyhow, anywhere / Pinball wizard / A legal matter / Boris the spider / Magic bus / Substitute / I'm a boy. *(re-iss. 1974)*

Jun 72. (7") *(2094 102) <32983>* **JOIN TOGETHER. / BABY DON'T YOU DO IT** 9 17

— In Oct72, PETE TOWNSHEND was another like ENTWISTLE to issue debut solo album 'WHO CAME FIRST'. It scraped into UK Top30. He issued more throughout 70's-80's (see . . .) In Apr'73, ROGER DALTREY hit the singles chart with GIVING IT ALL AWAY. It was a cut from debut album DALTREY.

Jan 73. (7") *(2094 106) <33041>* **RELAY. / WASPMAN** 21 Dec72 39

Track M.C.A.

Oct 73. (7") *(2094 115)* **5:15. / WATER** 20 –

Oct 73. (7") *<40152>* **5:15. / LOVE REIGN O'ER ME** –

Nov 73. (d-lp) *(2657 002) <10004>* **QUADROPHENIA** 2 2
– I am the sea / The real me / Quadrophenia / Cut my hair / The punk and the godfather / I'm one / Dirty jobs / Helpless dancer / Is it in my head? / I've had enough / 5:15 / Sea and sand / Drowned / Bell boy / Doctor Jimmy / The rock / Love, reign o'er me. *(re-iss. Sep79 on 'Polydor' d-lp)(d-c; 2657013)(3526001) (d-cd-iss. Jan87 on 'Polydor'; 831074-2)*

Nov 73. (7") *<40152>* **LOVE, REIGN O'ER ME. / WATER** – 76

Jan 74. (7") *<40182>* **THE REAL ME. / I'M ONE** – 92

— In Apr75, KEITH MOON was the last WHO member to release solo vinyl. The dismal 'TWO SIDES OF THE MOON' sold poorly.

Polydor M.C.A.

Oct 75. (lp/c) *(2490/3194 129) <2161>* **THE WHO BY NUMBERS** 7 8
– Slip kid / However much I booze / Squeeze box / Dreaming from the waist / Imagine a man / Success story / They are all in love / Blue, red and grey / How many friends / In a hand or a face. *(re-iss. Mar84 lp/c; SPE LP/MC 68) (cd-iss. Jul89; 831552-2)*

Jan 76. (7") *(2121 275) <40475>* **SQUEEZE BOX. / SUCCESS STORY** 10 Nov75 16

Aug 76. (7") *<40603>* **SLIP KID. / DREAMING FROM THE WAIST** –

Sep 76. (d-lp)(d-c) *(2683 069)(3519 020)* **THE STORY OF THE WHO** (compilation) 2 –
– Magic bus / Substitute / Boris the spider / Run run run / I'm a boy / Heatwave / My generation / Pictures of Lily / Happy Jack / The seeker / I can see for miles / Bargain / Squeeze box / Amazing journey / The acid queen / Do you think it's alright / Fiddle about / Pinball wizard / I'm free / Tommy's holiday camp / We're not gonna take it / See me, feel me / Summertime blues / Baba O'Riley / Behind blue eyes / Slip kid / Won't get fooled again.

Jul 78. (7") *(WHO 1) <40948>* **WHO ARE YOU?. / HAD ENOUGH** 18 14

— On 5th Aug'78, manager PETE MEADON committed suicide.

Sep 78. (lp/c)<US-red/pic-lp> *(WHOD/+C 5004) <3050>* **WHO ARE YOU** 6 2
– New song / Had enough / 905 / Sister disco / Music must change / Trick of the light / Guitar and pen / Love is coming down / Who are you. *(re-iss. Aug84 lp/c; SPE LP/MC 77) (cd-iss. Jul89; 831557-2)*

— After a party on 7th Sep'78, KEITH MOON died on an overdose of heminevrin.

Dec 78. (7") *<40978>* **TRICK OF THE LIGHT. / 905** –

— Early'79, **KENNY JONES** (b.16 Sep'48) – drums (ex-SMALL FACES, ex-FACES) took place of KEITH. Added 5th tour member **JOHN 'Rabbit' BUNDRICK** – keyboards

Polydor Warners

Feb 81. (7") *(WHO 4) <49698>* **YOU BETTER YOU BET. / THE QUIET ONE** 9 18

Mar 81. (lp/c) *(WHOD/+C 5037) <3516>* **FACE DANCES** 2 4
– You better you bet / Don't let go the coat / Cache cache / The quiet one / Did you steal my money / How can you do it alone / Daily records / You / Another tricky day. *(re-iss. May88 lp/c; SPE LP/MC 112) (re-iss. cd Jun93;) (cd re-iss. May97; 537695-2)*

May 81. (7") *(WHO 5) <49743>* **DON'T LET GO THE COAT. / YOU** 47 84

Sep 82. (lp/c) *(WHOD/+C 5066) <23731>* **IT'S HARD** 11 8
– Athena / It's your turn / Cooks county / It's hard / Dangerous / Eminence front / I've known no war / One life's enough / One at a time / Why did I fall for that / A man is a man / Cry if you want. *(cd-iss. 1983 & Jun93; 800 106-2) (cd re-iss. May97; 537696-2)*

Sep 82. (7"/7"pic-d) *(WHO/+P 6)* **ATHENA. / A MAN IS A MAN** 40 –
(12"+=/12"pic-d+=) *(WHO X/PX 6)* – Won't get fooled again.

Sep 82. (7") *<29905>* **ATHENA. / IT'S YOUR TURN** – 28

Dec 82. (7") *<29814>* **EMINENCE FRONT. / ONE AT A TIME** – 68

Feb 83. (7") *<29731>* **IT'S HARD. / DANGEROUS** –

— They officially split late 1983 from studio work. They occasionally returned for one-off live work.

– (selective) compilations, etc. –

below 4 on 'Brunswick' label.

Mar 66. (7") *(05956)* **A LEGAL MATTER. / INSTANT PARTY** 32 –

Aug 66. (7") *(05965)* **THE KIDS ARE ALRIGHT. / THE OX** 41 –

Aug 66. (7") *<31988>* **THE KIDS ARE ALRIGHT. / A LEGAL MATTER** –

Nov 66. (7") *(05968)* **LA LA LA LIES. / THE GOOD'S GONE** –

Nov 66. (7"ep) *Reaction; (592 001)* **READY STEADY WHO** –
– Circles / Disguises / Batman / Bucket 'T' / Barbara Ann. *(re-iss. Nov83 on 'Reaction-Polydor'; WHO 7); hit 58*

Oct 74. (lp/c) *Track; (2406/3191 116)* <2126> **ODDS AND SODS** (rarities) [10] [15]
– Postcard / Now I'm a farmer / Put the money down / Little Billy / Too much of anything / Glow girl / Pure and easy / Faith in something bigger / I'm the face / Naked eye / Long live rock. *(cd-iss. Jun93; 517946-2)*
below with guest singers ELTON JOHN, TINA TURNER, OLIVER REED, ANN-MARGRET, etc

Aug 75. (d-lp/d-c) *Polydor; (2657/5326 002)* <9502> **TOMMY** (soundtrack) [30] Mar75 [2]
– Overture / Prologue – 1945 / Captain Walker – It's a boy / Bernie's holiday camp / 1951 – What about the boy? / Amazing journey / Christmas / Eyesight to the blind / The Acid queen / Do you think it's alright / Cousin Kevin / Do you think it's alright / Fiddle about / Do you think it's alright / Sparks / Extra, extra, extra / Pinball wizard / Champagne / There's a doctor / Go to the mirror / Tommy can you hear me / Smash the mirror / I'm free / Mother and son / Sensation / Miracle cure / Sally Simpson / Welcome / T.V. studio / Tommy's holiday camp / We're not gonna take it / Listening to you – See me, feel me.

— Note; below on 'Polydor' UK/ 'MCA' US, unless mentioned otherwise

Oct 76. (7"m) *(2058 803)* **SUBSTITUTE. / I'M A BOY / PICTURES OF LILY** [7] [–]

Apr 79. (7"m) *(WHO 2)* <41053> **LONG LIVE ROCK. / I'M THE FACE / MY WIFE** [48] Jun79 [54]

Jun 79. (d-lp)(d-c)<US-pic-d-lp> *(2675 179)(3577 343)* *<11005>* **THE KIDS ARE ALRIGHT** (live soundtrack) [26] [8]
– My generation / I can't explain / Happy Jack / I can see for miles / Magic bus / Long live rock / Anyway, anyhow, anywhere / Young man blues / Baba O'Riley / My wife / A quick one while he's away / Tommy can you hear me? / Sparks / Pinball wizard / See me, feel me / Join together – Roadrunner – My generation blues / Won't get fooled again. *(cd-iss. Jun93; 517947-2)*

Sep 79. (7") *(WHO 3)* <2022> **5:15. / I'M ONE** [ ] [45]

Sep 79. (d-lp)(d-c) *(2625 037)(3577 352)* <6235> **QUADROPHENIA (Film Soundtrack)** [23] [46]
– I am the sea / The real me / I'm one / 5:15 / Love reign o'er me / Bell boy / I've had enough / Helpless dancer / Doctor Jimmy / Zoot suit (HIGH NUMBERS) / Hi heel sneakers (CROSS SECTION) / Get out and stay out / Four faces / Joker James / The punk and the godfather / (+ tracks by other artists) / I'm the face (HIGH NUMBERS). *(d-cd iss.1988; 831074-2) (cd re-iss. Jun96; 531971-2)*

Feb 81. (lp)(c) *(2486 140)(3195 235)* **MY GENERATION (compilation)** [ ] [–]

Oct 81. (lp/c) *<MCA/+C 212001>* **HOOLIGANS** [–] [52]
(UK-iss.Dec88; same)

May 83. (lp) *<5408>* **WHO'S GREATEST HITS** [–] [94]

Nov 84. (d-lp/d-c) *(WHO/+C 1)* *<8018>* **WHO'S LAST** [48] [81]
(cd-iss. Dec88; DWHO 1)

Oct 85. (d-lp/d-c) *Impression; (IMDP/IMDK 1)* **THE WHO COLLECTION** [44] [–]
(d-cd-iss. Oct88; IMCD 41)

Feb 88. (7") *(POSP 907)* **MY GENERATION. / SUBSTITUTE** [68] [ ]
(12"+=/c-s+=/cd-s+=) *(POSPX/POSPC/POCD 907)* – Baba O'Riley / Behind blue eyes.

Mar 88. (lp/c)(cd) *(WTV/+C 1)(835 389-2) <MCAD 8031>* **WHO'S BETTER WHO'S BEST** [10] Nov88 [ ]
– My generation / Anyway, anyhow, anywhere / The kids are alright / Substitute / I'm a boy / Happy Jack / Pictures of Lily / I can see for miles / Who are you / Won't get fooled again / Magic bus / Pinball wizard / I'm free / I can't explain / See me feel me / Squeeze box / Join together / You better you bet. *(cd+=)* – Baba O'Riley.

Mar 90. (cd/d-c/d-lp) *Virgin; (CD/TC+/VDT 102) / M.C.A.;* *<19501>* **JOIN TOGETHER** [59] [ ]
– (contains some solo material)

Jul 94. (4xcd-box) *(521751-2)* *<11020>* **THIRTY YEARS OF MAXIMUM R&B** [48] [ ]

Jul 96. (7"/c-s) *(863918-7/-4)* **MY GENERATION. / PINBALL WIZARD (live)** [31] [–]
(cd-s+=) *(854637-2)* – Boris the spider.

Aug 96. (cd/c) *(533150-2/-4)* *<11462>* **MY GENERATION – THE VERY BEST OF** [11] [ ]
– I can't explain / Anyway, anyhow, anywhere / My generation / Substitute / I'm a boy / Boris the spider / Hapy Jack / Pictures of Lily / I can see for miles / Magic bus / Pinball wizard / The seeker / Baba O'Riley / Won't get fooled again / Let's see action / 5.15 / Join together / Squeeze box / Who are you / You better you bet.

Feb 00. (cd/c/d-lp) *(547727-2/-4/-1)* *<111960>* **BBC SESSIONS** (1965-73) [24] [ ]
– My generation / Anyway, anyhow, anywhere / Good lovin' / Just you and me, darling / Leaving here / My generation / The good's gone / La-la lies / Substitute / Dancing in the street / Disguises / I'm a boy / Run run run / Boris the spider / Happy Jack / See my way / Pictures of Lily / A quick one, while he's away / Substitute / The seeker / I'm free / Shakin' all over / The relay / Long live rock / Boris the spider (Radio 1 jingle).

Oct 02. (d-cd) *Universal TV; (065234-2)* *<112877>* **THE ULTIMATE COLLECTION** [17] Jun02 [31]
– I can't explain / Anyway, anyhow, anywhere / My generation / The kids are alright / A legal matter / Substitute / I'm a boy / Boris the spider / Happy Jack / Pictures of Lily / I can see for miles / Call me lightning / Magic bus / Pinball wizard / I'm free / See me feel me / The seeker / Summertime blues (live) / My wife / Baba O'Riley / Bargain / Behind blue eyes / Won't get fooled again / Let's see action / Pure and easy / Join together / Long live rock / The real me / 5.15 / Love reign o'er me / Squeeze box / Who are you / Had enough / Sister disco / You better you bet / Don't let go the coat / The quiet one / Another tricky day / Athena / Eminence front. *(t-cd+=; 0655300-2)* – Substitute (rare US single version) / I'm a boy (early version) / Happy Jack (acoustic) / Magic bus (UK single) / Baba O'Riley (CD-Rom) / Substitute (CD-Rom).

Jun 03. (3xcd-box) *S.P.V.; (<093 7488-2>)* **LIVE AT THE ROYAL ALBERT HALL** (live in November 2000) [72] Jul03 [ ]
– I can't explain / Anyway anyhow anywhere / Pinball wizard / Relay / My wife / The kids are alright / Mary Anne with the shaky hand / Bargain / Magic bus / Who are you / Baba O'Riley / Drowned / A heart to hang onto / So sad about us / I'm one / Getting in tune / Behind blue eyes / You better you bet / The real me / 5.15 / Won't get fooled again / Substitute / Let's see action / My generation / See me feel me / Listening to you / I'm free / I don't even know myself / Summertime blues / Young man blues.

the WHO

(final 2 songs feat. **RABBIT BUNDRICK + ZAK STARKEY**

Polydor Geffen

May 04. (cd) *(9866577)* *<B00018360-2>* **THEN AND NOW: 1964-2004** (part compilation) [5] Mar04 [57]
– I can't explain / My generation / The kids are alright / Substitute / I'm a boy / Happy Jack / I can see for miles / Magic bus / Pinball wizard / See me, feel me / Summertime blues (live) / Behind blue eyes / Won't get fooled again / 5:15 / Love, reign o'er me / Squeeze box / Who are you / You better you bet / Real good looking boy / Old red wine.

PETE TOWNSHEND

(solo). Before his 1972 official debut, TOWNSHEND issued 2 lp's on 'Universal'; HAPPY BIRTHDAY (1970) & I AM (1972).

Track Track

Oct 72. (lp) *(2408 201)* *<79189>* **WHO CAME FIRST** [30] [69]
– Pure and easy / Evolution / Forever's no time at all / Let's see action / Time is passing / There's a heartache followin' me / Sheraton Gibson / Content / Parvardigar. *(cd-iss. Oct92 & Mar97 on 'Rykodisc'; RCD 20246)*

— next collaboration with Solo artist and ex-SMALL FACES bassman and singer.

PETE TOWNSHEND & RONNIE LANE

Polydor M.C.A.

Sep 77. (7") *<40818>* **MY BABY GIVES IT AWAY. / APRIL FOOL** [–] [ ]

Sep 77. (lp) *(2442 147)* *<2295>* **ROUGH MIX** [44] [45]
– My baby gives it away / Nowhere to run / Rough mix / Annie / Keep me turning / Catmelody / Misunderstood / April fool / Street in the city / Heart to hang on to / Till the rivers all run dry. *(re-iss. Nov80 & Nov83)*

Nov 77. (7") *(2058 944)* **STREET IN THE CITY. / Ronnie Lane: ANNIE** [ ] [–]

Nov 77. (7") *<40878>* **NOWHERE TO RUN . / KEEP ME TURNING** [–] [ ]

PETE TOWNSHEND

Island / not iss.

Dec 79. (12"ep) *(12WIP 6598)* **THE SECRET POLICEMAN'S BALL** (the songs) [ ] [–]
– Drowned / Pinbal wizard / Won't get fooled again.

Atco / Atco

Mar 80. (7") *(K 11460) <7318>* **ROUGH BOYS. / AND I MOVED** [39] Nov80 [89]

Apr 80. (lp/c) *(K/K4 50699) <32100>* **EMPTY GLASS** [11] [5]
– Rough boys / I am an animal / And I moved / Let my love open your door / Jools and Jim / Keep on working / Cat's in the cupboard / A little is enough / Empty glass / Gonna get ya. *(cd-iss. 1984; K 250 699) (cd re-iss. Nov93 & Oct95; 7567 9038-2-2)*

Jun 80. (7") *<7217>* **LET MY LOVE OPEN THE DOOR. / AND I LOVED** [–] [9]

Jun 80. (7"m) *(K 11486)* **LET MY LOVE OPEN THE DOOR. / CLASSIFIED / GREYHOUND GIRL** [46] [–]

Sep 80. (7") *<7312>* **A LITTLE IS ENOUGH. / CAT'S IN THE CUPBOARD** [–] [72]

Oct 80. (7") *(K 11609)* **KEEP ON WORKING. / JOOLS AND JIM** [ ] [–]

May 82. (7") *(K 11734) <99989>* **FACE DANCES (pt.2). / MAN WATCHING** [ ] [ ]

Jun 82. (lp/c) *(K/K4 50889) <38149>* **ALL THE BEST COWBOYS HAVE CHINESE EYES** [32] [26]
– The sea refuses no river / Communication / Exquisitely bored / North country girl / Slit skirts / Uniforms / Prelude / Somebody saved me / Face dances 2 / Stardom in action / Stop hurting people. *(cd-iss. 1984; K 250 699) (cd re-iss. Nov93 & Oct95 & Jul00; 7567 82812-2)*

Aug 82. (7",7"pic-d) *(K 11751)* **UNIFORMS (CORPS D'ESPRIT). / DANCE IT ALL AWAY** [48] [–]
(12",12"pic-d) *(K 11751T)* – ('A'side) / Stop hurting people.

Aug 82. (7") *<99973>* **UNIFORMS (CORPS D'ESPRIT). / SLIT SKIRTS** [–] [ ]

Apr 83. (7") *<99884>* **BARGAIN. / DIRTY WATER** [–] [ ]

Oct 85. (7"/12") *(U/UT 8859)* **FACE THE FACE. / HIDING OUT** [ ] [26]

Nov 85. (lp/c/cd) *(252392-1/-4/-2) <90473>* **WHITE CITY – A NOVEL** [70] [26]
– Give blood / Brilliant blues / Face the face / Hiding out / Secondhand love / Crashing by design / I am secure / White City fighting Come to mama. *(re-iss. cd Nov93; same)*

Jan 86. (7") *<99553>* **SECOND HAND LOVE. / WHITE CITY FIGHTING** [–] [ ]

Apr 86. (7") *(U 8744)* **GIVE BLOOD. / MAGIC BUS (live)** [ ] [–]
(12"+=) *(UT 8744)* – Won't get fooled again.

May 86. (7") *<99499>* **BEHIND BLUE EYES. / BAREFOOTIN'** [–] [ ]

Oct 86. (lp,c,cd) *<90553>* **PETE TOWNSEND'S DEEP END LIVE! (live)** [–] [98]
– Barefootin' / After the fire / Behind blue eyes / Stop hurtin' people / I'm one / I put a spell on you / Save it for later / Pinball wizard / Little is enough / Eyesight to the blind.

— Next featured singers JOHN LEE HOOKER (Iron Man) / NINA SIMONE (The Dragon) / DALTREY + JOHN ENTWISTLE who play on 2 new WHO tracks.

Virgin / Atlantic

Jun 89. (lp/c/cd) *(CD/TC+/V 2592) <81996>* **THE IRON MAN (The Musical)** [ ] [58]
– I won't run anymore / Over the top / Man machines / Dig / A friend is a friend / I eat heavy metal / All shall be well / Was there life / Fast food / A fool says . . . / Fire / New life (reprise). *(re-iss. Mar91 lp/c; OVED/+C 355)*

Jul 89. (7"/c-s) *(VS/+C 1198)* **A FRIEND IS A FRIEND. / MAN MACHINES** [ ] [ ]
(12"+=/12"g-f+=/3"cd-s+=) *(VS T/TG/CD 1198)* – Real world.

Nov 89. (7"/12"/12"g-f) *(VS/+T/TG 1209)* **I WON'T RUN ANYMORE. / A FOOL SAYS . . .** [ ] [ ]

Atlantic / Atlantic

Jul 93. (cd/c) *<(7567 82494-2/-4)>* **PSYCHODERELICT** [ ] [ ]
– English boy / Meher Baba M3 / Let's get pretentious / Meher Baba M4 (signal box) / Early morning dreams / I want that thing / Introduction to outlive the dinosaur / Outlive the dinosaur / Flame (demo) / Now and then / I am afraid / Don't try to make me real / Introduction to predictable / Predictable / Flame / Meher Baba M5 (Vivaldi) / Fake it / Introduction to now and then (reprise) / Now and then (reprise) / Baba O'Riley (demo) / English boy (reprise). *(cd re-iss. Jan97; same)*

Jul 93. (7"/c-s) *(A 7370/+C)* **ENGLISH BOY. / ('A'-dialogue mix)** [ ] [–]
(cd-s+=) *(A 7370CD1)* – Fake it / Psycho montage.
(cd-s+=) *(A 7370CD2)* – ('A'dialogue version) / Fake it / Flame / Early morning dreams.

May 96. (cd/c) *<(7567-82712-2/-4)>* **THE BEST OF PETE TOWNSHEND – COOLWALKINGSMOOTHSTRAIGHTSMOKINGFIRESTOKING** (compilation) [ ] [ ]
– Rough boys / Let my love open the door / Mis understood / Give blood / A friend is a friend / Sheraton Gibson / English boy / Street in the city / Pure and easy / Slit skirts / The sea refuses no river / A little is enough / Face the face / Uneasy street / Let my love open the door (E. Cola mix).

Jun 96. (c-s) *(A 5511C)* **LET MY LOVE OPEN THE DOOR / ROUGH BOYS** [ ] [–]
(cd-s+=) *(A 5511CD)* – ('A'-E. Cola mix; long version).

Platinum / Platinum

Jun 00. (cd) *(<15095 9555-2>)* **LIVE: A BENEFIT FOR MARYVILLE ACADEMY – HOUSE OF THE BLUES CHICAGO** [ ] Sep99 [ ]
– On the road again / Anyway, anyhow, anywhere / A little is enough / Drowned / Now and then / North country girl / Let my love open the door / Won't get foled again / Magic bus / I'm one / Magic bus / Heart to hang onto.

Rhino / Rhino

Oct 01. (cd; by PETE TOWNSHEND & RAPHAEL RUDD) *(<8122 74289-2>)* **OCEANIC CONCERTS (live)** [ ] [ ]
– Raga / Drowned / The seeker / Magic grace / Who is Meher Baba? / The ferryman / Kitty's theme / A little is enough / Contact in solitude / Sleeping dog / Sound barrier / Bargain / Longing for the beloved / Tattoo / Let my love open the door / Awakening / Western (American) Arti / O'Parvardigar.

– (other PETE TOWNSHEND compilations, etc.) –

Apr 83. (d-lp) *Atco; (B 0063) <90063>* **SCOOP** [ ] [35]
– (unfinished WHO demos and solo rarities)

Jul 89. (d-lp/d-c) *Polydor; (839350-1/-4)* **ANOTHER SCOOP** [ ] [ ]

Jun 00. (cd) *Redline; (70001)* **LIFEHOUSE ELEMENTS (SAMPLER)** [ ] [ ]

Dec 01. (cd) *Compact; <13>* **SCOOP3** [–] [ ]

ROGER DALTREY

Track / Track

Apr 73. (7") *(2094 110) <40053>* **GIVING IT ALL AWAY. / THE WAY OF THE WORLD** [5] [83]

Apr 73. (lp) *(2406 207) <328>* **DALTREY** [ ] [45]
– One man band / The way of the world / You are yourself / Thinking / You and me / It's a hard life / Giving it all away / The story so far / When the music stops / Reasons. *(re-iss. Aug82 lp/c; 2485/3201 219) (cd-iss. Apr95 on 'Polydor') (cd re-iss. Mar00 on 'Repertoire'; REP 4636)*

Jun 73. (7") *(ODS 66302) <Ode; 66040>* **I'M FREE. / (OVERTURE)** [13] [ ]

Sep 73. (7") *(2094 014) <40084>* **THINKING. / THERE IS LOVE** [ ] [ ]

Nov 73. (7") *(2094 016)* **IT'S A HARD LIFE. / ONE MAN BAND** [ ] [ ]

Polydor / M.C.A.

Mar 75. (7") *(2001 561)* **LISTENING TO YOU. / (OVERTURE)** [ ] [–]

May 75. (7") **COME AND GET YOUR LOVE. / THE WORLD OVER** [ ] [–]

Jul 75. (lp)(c) *(2442 135)(2660 111) <2147>* **RIDE A ROCK HORSE** [14] [28]
– Come and get your love / Hearts right / Oceans away / Proud / The world over / Near to surrender / Feeling / Walking the dog / Milk train / I was to sing your song. *(cd-iss. Mar00 on 'Repertoire'; REP 4642)*

Jul 75. (7") *(2058 628)* **WALKING THE DOG. / PROUD** [ ] [–]

Sep 75. (7") *<40453>* **COME AND GET YOUR LOVE. / FEELING** [–] [68]

Nov 75. (7") *<40512>* **OCEANS AWAY. / FEELING** [–] [ ]

Oct 75. (7") *<1779>* **ORPHEUS SONG. / LOVE'S DREAM** [ ] [ ]

— (above from the Ken Russell film LISTZOMANIA. Released at the same time, it was scored by RICK WAKEMAN for 'A&M' *(AMLH 64546)* and featured some with DALTREY vocals).

Apr 77. (7") *(2121 319)* **WRITTEN ON THE WIND. / DEAR JOHN** [46] [–]

May 77. (7") *<40761>* **ONE OF THE BOYS. / DOING IT ALL AGAIN** –

May 77. (lp) *(2441 146) <2271>* **ONE OF THE BOYS** 45 46
– Parade / Single man's dilemma / Avenging Annie / The prisoner / Leon / One of the boys / Giddy / Written on the wind / Satin and lace / Doing it all again. *(cd-iss. Mar00 on 'Repertoire'; REP 4643)*

Jun 77. (7") *(2058 896)* **ONE OF THE BOYS. / TO PUT SOMETHING BETTER INSIDE ME** –

Jul 77. (7") *<40765>* **SAY IT ISN'T SO, JOE. / SATIN AND LACE** –

Sep 77. (7") *<40800>* **AVENGING ANNIE. / THE PRISONER** – 88

Jan 78. (7") *<40862>* **THE PRISONER. / LEON** –

Feb 78. (7") *(2058 986)* **SAY IT AIN'T SO, JOE. / THE PRISONER** –

Polydor Polydor

Jul 80. (7") *(2001 980) <2105>* **FREE ME. / McVICAR** 39 Jun80 53

Jul 80. (lp/c) *(POLD/+C 5034) <6284>* **McVICAR (Soundtrack)** 39 22
– Bitter and twisted / Just a dream away / Escape (part 1) / White City lights / Free me / My time is gonna come / Waiting for a friend / Escape (part 2) / Without your love / McVicar. *(cd-iss. Apr95; 527341-2)*

Sep 80. (7") *<2121>* **WITHOUT YOUR LOVE. / ESCAPE (part 2)** – 20

Oct 80. (7") *(POSP 181)* **WITHOUT YOUR LOVE. / SAY IT AIN'T SO, JOE. / FREE ME** 55 –

Jan 81. (7") *<2153>* **WAITING FOR A FRIEND. / BITTER AND TWISTED** –

Polydor M.C.A.

Mar 82. (lp/c) *(2490/3194 162) <5301>* **THE BEST OF ROGER DALTREY** <US-title 'BEST BITS'>(compilation)
– Martyrs and madmen / Say it isn't so, Joe / Oceans away / Treasury / Free me / Without your love / It's a hard life / Giving it all away / Avenging Annie / Proud / You put something better inside me. *(UK cd-iss. May91)*

Apr 82. (7") *<52051>* **MARTYRS AND MADMEN. / AVENGING ANNIE** –

WEA Atlantic

Feb 84. (7") *(U 9686) <89704>* **WALKING IN MY SLEEP. / SOMEBODY TOLD ME** 56 62
(12"+=) *(U 9686T)* – Gimme some lovin'.

Feb 84. (lp) *(2502 981) <80128>* **PARTING SHOULD BE PAINLESS**
– Walking in my sleep / Parting would be painless / Is there anybody out there / Would a stranger do / Going strong / Looking for you / Somebody told me / How does the cold wind cry / Don't wait on the stairs.

Jun 84. (7") *(U 9541) <89667>* **PARTING SHOULD BE SO PAINLESS. / IS THERE ANYBODY OUT THERE**
(12"+=) *(U 9541T)* – I won't be the one to say goodbye.

Ten-Virgin Atlantic

Sep 85. (7") *(TEN 69) <89491>* **AFTER THE FIRE. / IT DON'T SATISFY ME** 50 48
(12"+=) *(TEN 69-12)* – Love me like you do.

Oct 85. (lp/c/cd) *(DIX/CDIX/DIXCD 17) <81269>* **UNDER A RAGING MOON** 52 42
– After the fire / Don't talk to strangers / Breaking down Paradise / The pride you hide / Move better in the night / Let me down easy / Fallen angel / It don't satisfy me / Rebel / Under a raging moon. *(cd+=)* – Behind blue eyes / 5:15 / Won't get fooled again. *(re-iss. 1989 lp/c; XID/CXID 22)*

Dec 85. (7") *<89471>* **LET ME DOWN EASY. / FALLEN ANGEL** – 86

Feb 86. (7"/12") *(TEN 81/+12)* **UNDER A RAGING MOON. / MOVE BETTER IN THE NIGHT** 43 –
(d7"+=) *(TEND 81)* – Behind blue eyes / 5:15 / Won't get fooled again.

Apr 86. (7") *<89457>* **QUICKSILVER LIGHTNING. / LOVE ME LIKE YOU DO** –

May 86. (7") *(TEN 103)* **THE PRIDE YOU HIDE. / BREAK OUT** –
(d7"+=/12"+=) *(TEN D/T 103)* – Don't talk to strangers (live) / Pictures of Lily (live).

Jun 86. (7") *<89419>* **UNDER A RAGING MOON. / THE PRIDE YOU HIDE** –

Jun 87. (7") *(TEN 147)* **HEARTS OF FIRE. / LOVERS STORM**
(12"+=) *(TENT 147)* – Quick silver lightning.

Jul 87. (lp/c/cd) *(DIX/CDIX/DIXCD 54) <81759>* **CAN'T WAIT TO SEE THE MOVIE**
– Hearts of fire / When the thunder comes / Ready for love / Balance on wires / Miracle of love / The price of love / The heart has its reasons / Alone in the night / Lover's storm / Take me home.

Jul 87. (7") *(TEN 202)* **DON'T LET THE SUN GO DOWN ON ME. / THE HEART HAS ITS REASONS**
(12"+=) *(TENT 202)* – ('A'extended).

—— next featured **GERARD McMANN**

not iss. Rhino

Jul 92. (cd) *<72846>* **ROCKS IN THE HEAD** –
– Who's gonna walk on water / Before my time is up / Times changed / You can't call it love / Mirror mirror / Perfe t world / Love is / Blues man's road / Everything a heart could ever want / Days of light / Unforgettable opera.

not iss. Continuum

1994. (cd) *<19402>* **A CELEBRATION: THE MUSIC OF PETE TOWNSHED & THE WHO** –

– compilations, etc. –

Jul 97. (cd) *Rhino;* **MARTYRS & MADMEN: THE BEST OF ROGER DALTREY** –

Mar 00. (cd) *Repertoire; (REP 4670)* **ANTHOLOGY**

WILCO

Formed: Belleville, Illinois, USA . . . 1994 out of UNCLE TUPELO members JEFF TWEEDY, JAY BENNETT, JOHN STIRRATT and veterans MAX JOHNSTON and KEN COOMER. WILCO were off the starting block with 1994's 'A.M.', an enjoyable enough set of uptempo country-rock. It was nevertheless eclipsed by the 1996 follow-up, 'BEING THERE', a sprawling double set drawing comparisons with The 'STONES 'Exile On Main Street' and hailed as one of the albums of the year. Reaching far beyond TWEEDY's patented musical boundaries to encompass everything from bar-room belters to Spector-esque rock/pop, the record proved conclusively that FARRAR's other half was blessed with his own distinct musical vision. While former writing partner JAY FARRAR continued to come up with the goods, the prospect of an UNCLE TUPELO reunion was (at the time) still tantalisingly within reach. However, WILCO returned in the summer of '98, an unlikely collaboration with English bard BILLY BRAGG on a memorable WOODY GUTHRIE tribute album, 'MERMAID AVENUE', kept the duo ticking over fine style. The following March, the leaders of the alt-country/folk scene released their long-awaited third set, 'SUMMERTEETH' (1999), a UK Top 40 record (Top 100 in the US) that boasted some breezy old tales opening with minor UK hit, 'CAN'T STAND IT'. A second volume of GUTHRIE re-writes, 'MERMAID AVENUE VOL.2' (2000) couldn't come up with anything quite as affecting as say, 'CALIFORNIA STARS' but it had its moments. WILCO's penchant for uptempo roots-rock wasn't always the best vehicle for presenting the legendary socialist's humourous protest-folk, BRAGG often stealing the limelight. TWEEDY moved even further from both his old sparring partner and his musical roots with 'YANKEE HOTEL FOXTROT' (2002), a record the band believed in so much they spent a hefty sum buying it back from 'Reprise'. While JIM O'ROURKE's off-kilter production opened up angles seemingly irreconcilable with their limited roots-rock sound of yore, the results were never less than intriguing and often brilliantly conceived. Released around the same time was the soundtrack to actor Ethan Hawke's 'CHELSEA WALLS' (2002), composed in large part by TWEEDY and new WILCO drummer GLENN KOTSCHE. While the bulk of the music consisted of pared-down, instrumental mood pieces well out of WILCO's normal orbit, there were a couple of previously unreleased offcuts: one from 'MERMAID AVENUE' ('WHEN THE ROSES BLOOM AGAIN') and one from the WILCO vaults ('PROMISING'). Add those to a cover of John Lennon's 'Jealous Guy' by Jimmy Scott, and you had a mixed bag to say the least. Seemingly in thrall to his newly expanded musical horizons, TWEEDY went on to

WILCO

cut an album's worth of off-kilter experiments with O'ROURKE and KOTSCHE. An eponymous set released under the LOOSE FUR banner in early 2003, the record spliced the various musical personalities in intriguing and often frustrating fashion. 'A GHOST IS BORN' (2004) was another thoughtful, multi-faceted meta-pop record, further proof – if needed – of TWEEDY's determination to unshackle his inner changeling (and with a US Top10/UK Top 50 showing, proof that WILCO's new muse is better appreciated in the States). With O'ROURKE still sculpting the production, the balance between hook, white noise and tangent was ever-wavering, occasionally vexing, but almost always worthy of perseverance. TWEEDY sometimes sounds like a refugee from a lost BEATLES session, tarrying in the studio and tinkering with the afterthoughts; yet for every idea that doesn't quite come off, there's always several that surprise by degrees: 'THE LATE GREATS' ranks as one of the wryest vignettes he's yet penned, 'THE THEOLOGIANS' one of his most immediate. The subsequent tour saw the replacement of LEROY BACH (who himself had replaced JAY BENNET during the 'YANKEE HOTEL FOXTROT' sessions) with PAT SANSONE and NELS CLINE, with the latter especially, mainlining much of the invention in concert set, 'KICKING TELEVISION: LIVE IN CHICAGO' (2005). In lieu of another WILCO studio album, fans could take heart in a LOOSE FUR follow-up, 'BORN AGAIN IN THE USA' (2006), altogether a much less uptight, more humorous and generally rootsier take on WILCO-arcana, from its tongue-in-cheek title to the toe-tapping irreverence of 'THE RULING CLASS' and 'THOU SHALT WILT'.

• Other info: TWEEDY was also an integral part of y'allternative supergroup, GOLDEN SMOG, alongside members of the JAYHAWKS, SOUL ASYLUM, RUN WESTY RUN and BIG STAR.

Album rating: A.M. (*8) / BEING THERE (*8) / SUMMERTEETH (*8) / YANKEE HOTEL FOXTROT (*6) / A GHOST IS BORN (*7) / KICKING TELEVISION: LIVE IN CHICAGO (*6) / Jeff Tweedy: CHELSEA WALLS soundtrack (*5) / Loose Fur: LOOSE FUR (*6) / BORN AGAIN IN THE USA (*6)

JEFF TWEEDY – vocals, guitar (ex-UNCLE TUPELO) / **JOHN STIRRATT** – organ, guitars, bass, vocals (ex-UNCLE TUPELO) / **KEN COOMER** – drums (ex-UNCLE TUPELO) / with others

Warners Reprise

Apr 95. (cd) *<(9362 45857-2)>* **A.M.** ☐ ☐
– I must be high / Casino queen / Box full of letters / Shouldn't be ashamed / Pick up the change / I thought IU held you / That's not the issue / It's just that simple / Should've been in love / Passenger side / Dash 7 / Blue eyed soul / Too far apart.

Jul 95. (c-s) *(W 0306MC)* **BOX FULL OF LETTERS / I AM NOT WILLING** ☐ [-]
(cd-s+=) *(W 0306)* – Who were you thinking of (live).

— added **JAY BENNETT** – guitar

Feb 97. (d-cd) *<(9362 46236-2)>* **BEING THERE** ☐ Nov96 [73]
– Misunderstood / Forget the flowers / I got you (at the end of the century) / Red eyed and blue / (Was I) In your dreams / Dreamer in my dreams / Lonely one / Why would you wanna live / Kingpin / Someone else's song / Outta mind (outta sight) / Someday soon / Sunken treasure / Say you miss me / Hotel Arizona / What's the world got in store / Far far away / Monday.

Apr 97. (cd-ep) *(W 0397CD)* **OUTTA SIGHT (OUTTA MIND) / OUTTA MIND (OUTTA SIGHT) / THIRTEEN / A LASTING FONDER** ☐ [-]

— In the middle of '98, WILCO collaborated with BILLY BRAGG on a tribute album ('MERMAID AVENUE') to WOODY GUTHRIE

Mar 99. (cd/c/lp) *<(9362 47282-2/-4/-1)>* **SUMMERTEETH** [38] [78]
– Can't stand it / She's a jar / A shot in the arm / We're just friends / I'm always in love / Nothing'severgonnastandinmyway (again) / Pieholden suite / How to fight loneliness / Via Chicago / ELT / My darling / When you wake up feeling old / Summer teeth / In a future age.

Apr 99. (cd-s) *(W 475CD1)* **CAN'T STAND IT / STUDENT LOAN ZERO / TRIED AND TRUE** [67] [-]
(cd-s) *(W 475CD2)* – ('A'side) / Sunken treasure (solo acoustic) / I'm always in love (solo acoustic).

Jun 99. (c-s/cd-s) *(W 496 C/CD2)* **A SHOT IN THE ARM / VIA CHICAGO (demo) / SHE'S A JAR** ☐ ☐
(cd-s) *(W 496CD1)* – ('A'side) / ELT (demo) / True love will find you in the end.

— a 2nd 'MERMAID AVENUE' (VOL.2) was issued with BILLY BRAGG in mid'00

— **GLENN KOTCHE** – drums; repl. COOMER

— **LEROY BACH** – multi; repl. BENNETT

Nonesuch Nonesuch

Apr 02. (cd) *<(7559 79669-2)>* **YANKEE HOTEL FOXTROT** [40] [13]
– I am trying to break your heart / Kamera / Radio cure / War on war / Jesus, etc. / Ashes of American flags / Heavy metal drummer / I'm the man who loves you / Pot kettle black / Poor places / Reservations. *(d-lp-iss.Nov02 on 'Sundazed'; SCLP 5161)>*

May 02. (cd-s) *(NONE 001CD)* **WAR ON WAR / THE GOOD PART / I'M THE MAN WHO LOVES YOU (live)** ☐ [-]

— added **MIKAEL JORGENSEN** – keyboards + **NELS CLINE** – guitar

Jun 04. (cd) *<(7559 79809-2)>* **A GHOST IS BORN** [50] [8]
– At least that's what you said / Hell is chrome / Spiders (kidsmoke) / Muzzle of bees / Hummingbird / Handshake drugs / Wishful thinking / Company in my back / I'm a wheel / Theologians / Less than you think / The late greats. *(ltd d-cd.Apr05 +=; 7559 79892-2)* – Panthers / At least that's what you said (live) / The late greats (live) / Handshake drugs / Kicking television.

Jul 04. (7") *(WILCO 1)* **I'M A WHEEL. / KICKING TELEVISION** ☐ [-]

— **PAT SANSONE** – guitar, keyboards (of AUTUMN DEFENSE) repl. BACH

Nov 05. (d-cd) *<(7559 79903-2)>* **KICKING TELEVISION: LIVE IN CHICAGO** (live) ☐ [47]
– Misunderstood / Company in my back / The late greats / Hell is chrome / Handshake drugs / I am trying to break your heart / Shot in the arm / At least that's what you said / Wishful thinking / Jesus, etc. / I'm the man who loves you / Kicking television // Via Chicago / Hummingbird / Muzzle of bees / One by one / Airline to Heaven / Radio cure / Ashes of American flags / Heavy metal drummer / Poor places / Spiders (kidsmoke) / Comment (if all men are truly brothers).

JEFF TWEEDY

with **GLENN KOTCHE** – drums, percussion

Rykodisc Rykodisc

Apr 02. (cd) *<(RCD 10624)>* **CHELSEA WALLS** (soundtrack) ☐ ☐
– Opening titles / Red elevator / Promising / Frank's dream / When the roses bloom again / Jealous guy / The wallman / The lonely 1 / Hello, are you there? / Softly and tenderly Jesus is calling / Finale / End credits.

LOOSE FUR

JEFF TWEEDY + GLENN KOTCHE + JIM O'ROURKE

Domino Drag City

Jan 03. (lp/cd) *(WIG LP/CD 119) <DC 203/+CD>* **LOOSE FUR** ☐ ☐
– Laminated cat / Elegant transaction / So long / You were wrong / Liquidation totale / Chinese apple.

Drag City Drag City

Mar 06. (lp/cd) *<(DC 309/+CD)>* **BORN AGAIN IN THE USA** ☐ ☐
– Hey chicken / The ruling class / Answers to your questions / Apostolic / Stupid as the sun / Pretty sparks / An ecumenical matter / Thou shalt wilt / Wreckroom / WAnted.

☐ the WILDBUNCH (see under ⇒ ELECTRIC SIX)

☐ Pharrell WILLIAMS (see under ⇒ N.E.R.D.)

Robbie WILLIAMS

Born: 13 Feb'74, Stoke-On-Trent, England. As the cheeky chappy of legendary Manchester boy band TAKE THAT, WILLIAMS enjoyed massive chart success from the early innocence of the 'Take That And Party' era through to the more risqué bare-arsed antics of the band's latter days. Yet even the adoration of schoolgirl legions wasn't enough to tether the boy wonder to the restrictions of the manufactured pop industry; as WILLIAMS embarked on an extended booze-athon with rock'n'roll bad boys OASIS etc., his position as a boy band popster was deemed untenable and he soon found himself looking at solo prospects. After eventually recovering from his much publicised indulgences, the singer launched his revamped career with a hugely successful cover of George Michael's 'FREEDOM', subsequently hooking up with songwriter GUY CHAMBERS to pen the likes of 'OLD BEFORE I DIE' and 'LAZY DAYS'. While the former was a sunny, vaguely humorous stab at deflating the rock'n'roll myth, the latter showed our ROBBIE could be mean'n'moody when he wanted to be. Along with fourth single, 'SOUTH OF THE BORDER', all the tracks (save 'FREEDOM') were included on his 1997 debut album, 'LIFE THRU A LENS', the general critical concensus being that WILLIAMS was having the last laugh, beating his former TAKE THAT cronies hands down (both GARY BARLOW and MARK OWEN were taking the solo road with middling success) and winning over a cross section of musical palates with his irrepressible style. He sealed his success that Christmas with the tearjerking ballad, 'ANGELS', a massive Top 5 hit which proved conclusively, if any further proof was needed, that the lad was most definitely back for good. 'LET ME ENTERTAIN YOU' (complete with QUEEN/KISS-style video) was ROBBIE'S next single to reach the Top 3 (America still took a backseat for a while). In September '98, the classy JOHN BARRY ('You Only Live Twice')-styled 'MILLENNIUM', deservedly topped the UK chart for a week – ROBBIE now kitted out in James Bond tin flute. The track was also one of the highlights on his sophomore set, 'I'VE BEEN EXPECTING YOU' (1998), a record that boasted three further Top 5 hits, 'NO REGRETS', 'STRONG' and 'SHE'S THE ONE'. The latter was a recent WORLD PARTY track, having failed to be issued as a single by KARL WALLINGER and Co it was now a No.1 smash all around Europe. 1999 was not all party-time for the reformed Mr. WILLIAMS, celebrations were probably subdued a little when he lost a court battle with former TAKE THAT manager, Nigel Martin-Smith; the £90,000 claim would turn into £1 million adding of course legal fees, commission, interest and probably a counter damage claim. Still, there was no holding down the roguish heart-throb for long, 'SING WHEN YOU'RE WINNING' (2000) sticking to the well established blueprint. Thus we were treated to the infectious but ultimately turgid 'ROCK DJ', the even more turgid 'SUPREME' and a string of "heartfelt" album tracks baring the star's manly but oh-so sensitive side. Anyone suffering from ROBBIE overkill no doubt blanched when they heard of his next conceit, an easy listening tribute to Rat Pack stars like FRANK SINATRA and DEAN MARTIN. 'SWING WHEN YOU'RE WINNING' (2001) was tailor-made to please his simpering fans, ROBBIE'S swell guy persona gorging itself on chestnuts like 'WELL, DID YOU EVAH' and 'SOMETHIN' STUPID' (the latter a Xmas No.1 duet with actress NICOLE KIDMAN). We await the American-networked ROBBIE soap with glazed eyes. If his work had been tiresome if admittedly professional up to this point, 2002's 'ESCAPOLOGY' signalled that even the sheen of songwriting polish which had kept him in the charts thus far was beginning to dull. Save for the trite 'SOMETHING BEAUTIFUL' hit single, there were no stadium singalongs to speak of. Even his formidable force of personality couldn't mask the tiredness in these songs. Despite the album's lack of lighter waving anthems, ROBBIE persisted in trundling out a selection on 'LIVE AT KNEBWORTH' (2003), a document of those mammoth summer gigs which even eclipsed his old pals' OASIS' former record at the English country estate. In pop life years, 'GREATEST HITS' (2004) was long overdue, a package featuring all WILLIAMS' major hits (itself a tally stretching well into double figures). It was also an opportunity to raise the curtain on his new writing partner, none other than STEPHEN "formerly TIN TIN" DUFFY: the embarrassingly 80s 'RADIO' netted the pair yet another No.1, while 'MISUNDERSTOOD' was another quavering ballad and yet another UK Top 10. There were more 80s throwback flavours on the chart-topping 'INTENSIVE CARE' (2005), not least the falsetto pop-reggae of 'TRIPPING', possibly one of the most satisfying, least cloying singles (No.2) of his career, even if it did come on like the bastard child of the LONDON BOYS and 10CC. Top 10 follow-up, 'ADVERTISING SPACE', was the requisite ballad, although hardly as memorable.

• **Songwriters:** Self-penned except collaborations and covers; MAKING PLANS FOR NIGEL (Xtc) / KOOKS (David Bowie) / I WOULDN'T NORMALLY DO THIS KIND OF THING (Pet Shop Boys) / EV'RY TIME WE SAY GOODBYE (Cole Porter) / ANT MUSIC (Adam & The Ants) / etc.

Album rating: LIFE THRU A LENS (*7) / I'VE BEEN EXPECTING YOU (*7) / SING WHEN YOU'RE WINNING (*7) / SWING WHEN YOU'RE WINNING (*5) / ESCAPOLOGY (*6) / LIVE AT KNEBWORTH (*5) / GREATEST HITS compilation (*8) / INTENSIVE CARE (*5)

Chrysalis Capitol

Aug 96. (c-s) *(TCFREE 1)* **FREEDOM '96 / ('A'-The Next Big Gen mix) / ('A'-Arthur Baker's Shake and Bake mix)** 2 –
(cd-s+=) *(CDSFREE 1)* – (interview part 2).
(cd-s) *(CDFREE 1)* – ('A'side) / ('A'-Arthur Baker mix) / ('A'instrumental) / (interview part 1).

Apr 97. (c-s/cd-s) *(TCCHS/CDCHSS 5055)* **OLD BEFORE I DIE / KOOKS / MAKING PLANS FOR NIGEL** 2 –
(cd-s) *(CDCHS 5055)* – ('A'side) / Better days / Average B side.

Jun 97. (c-s/cd-s) *(TC/CD CHS 5063)* **LAZY DAYS / TEENAGE MILLIONAIRE / FALLING IN BED (AGAIN)** 8 –
(cd-s) *(CDCHSS 5063)* – ('A'side) / She makes me high / Everytime we say goodbye..

Sep 97. (c-s/cd-s) *(TC/CD CHS 5068)* **SOUTH OF THE BORDER / ('A'-Mother's milkin' it mix) / CHEAP LOVE SONG** 14 –
(cd-s) *(CDCHSS 5068)* – ('A'side) / Cheap love song / ('A'-187 Lockdown mix) / ('A'-Phil "The Kick Drum" Dane & Mart Smith's nosebag dub).

Oct 97. (cd/c) *(CD/TC CHR 6127)* **LIFE THRU A LENS** 1 –
– Lazy days / Life thru a lens / Ego a go go / Angels / South of the border / Old before I die / One of God's better people / Let me entertain you / Killing me / Clean / Baby girl window. *(lp-iss.Jun01 on 'Simply Vinyl'; SVLP 329)*

Dec 97. (7") *(CHSLH 5072)* **ANGELS. / SOUTH OF THE BORDER** 4 –
(c-s/cd-s) *(TC/CD CHS 5072)* – ('A'side) / Back for good (live) / Walk this sleigh.
(cd-s) *(CDCHSS 5072)* – ('A'side) / Karaoke overkill / ('A'acoustic) / Get the joke.

Mar 98. (7") *(CHSLH 5080)* **LET ME ENTERTAIN YOU. / LAZY DAYS** 3 –
(c-s/cd-s) *(TCCHS/CDCHSS 5080)* – The Full Monty medley: Make me smile (come up and see me) – You can leave your hat on – Land of a 1000 dances) / I wouldn't normally do this kind of thing / I am the (res)erection.
(cd-s) *(CDCHS 5080)* – ('A'extended) / ('A'-Stretch'n'Vern's rock'n'roll mix) / ('A'-Amethyst's dub) / ('A'-Robbie loves his mother mix) / ('A'-The Bizarro mix).

Sep 98. (c-s/cd-s) *(TC/CD CHS 5099)* *<radio cut>* **MILLENNIUM / LAZY DAYS (original) / ANGELS (live)** 1 May99 72
(cd-s) *(CDCHSS 5099)* – ('A'side) / Love cheat (demo) / Rome Munich Rome (demo).

Oct 98. (cd/c) *(497837-2/-4)* **I'VE BEEN EXPECTING YOU** 1 –
– Strong / No regrets / Millennium / Phoenix from the flames / Win some lose some / Grace / Jesus in a camper van / Heaven from here / Karma killer / She's the one / Man machine / These dreams. *(cd+=)* – Stand your ground / Stalker's day.

Nov 98. (7") *(CHS 5100)* **NO REGRETS. / ANTMUSIC** 4 –
(c-s+=/cd-s+=) *(TCCHS/CDCHSS 5100)* – Deceiving is believing.
(cd-s) *(CDCHS 5100)* – ('A'side) / There she goes / Sexed up.

Mar 99. (c-s/cd-s) *(TC/CD CHS 5107)* **STRONG / LET ME ENTERTAIN YOU (live at The Brit Awards) / HAPPY SONG** 5 –

Jul 99. (cd) *<97726-2>* **THE EGO HAS LANDED** (compilation) – 63

Nov 99. (-) *<album cut>* **ANGELS** – 53

Nov 99. (c-s) *(TCCHS 5112)* **SHE'S THE ONE / IT'S ONLY US / MILLENNIUM (live)** 1 –
(cd-s+=) *(CDCHS 5112)* – ('A'-video).
(cd-s) *(CDCHSS 5112)* – ('A') / Coke and tears / It's only us / It's only us (video).

Jul 00. (c-s) *(TCCHS 5112)* **ROCK DJ / TALK TO ME** 2 –
(cd-s+=) *(CDCHS 5112)* – ('A'-Player One remix).
Aug 00. (cd/c/d-lp) *(528125-2/-4/-1)* *<29024>* **SING WHEN YOU'RE WINNING** 1 Oct00
– Let love be your energy / Better man / Rock DJ / Supreme / Kids / If it's hurting you / Singing for the lonely / Love calling Earth / Knutsford city limits / Forever Texas / By all means necessary / The road to Mandalay. *(cd re-iss. Dec00 +=; 528125-0)* – live:- Often / Sing when you're winning / Phoenix from the flames.
Oct 00. (c-s; by ROBBIE WILLIAMS & KYLIE MINOGUE) *(TCCHS 5119)* **KIDS / JOHN'S GAY / OFTEN** 2 –
(cd-s+=) *(CDCHS 5119)* – ('A'-video).
(cd-s) *(CDCHSS 5119)* – ('A') / Karaoke star / Kill me or cure me.
Dec 00. (c-s/cd-s) *(TC/CD CHS 5120)* **SUPREME / DON'T DO LOVE / COME TAKE ME OVER** 4 –
(cd-s) *(CDCHSS 5120)* – ('A') / United / ('A'-live).
Apr 01. (c-s) *(TCCHS 5124)* **LET LOVE BE YOUR ENERGY / MY WAY / ROLLIN' STONE** 10 –
(cd-s+=) *(CDCHS 5124)* – My way (video).
Jul 01. (c-s/cd-s) *(TC/CD CHS 5126)* **ETERNITY / THE ROAD TO MANDALAY / TOXIC** 1 –
Nov 01. (cd/c/lp) *(<536826-2/-4/-1>)* **SWING WHEN YOU'RE WINNING** 1
– I will talk and Hollywood will listen / Mack the knife / Somethin' stupid / Do nothin' 'til you hear from me / It was a very good year / Straighten up and fly right / Well, did you evah / Mr. Bojangles / One for my baby / Things / Ain't that a kick in the head / They can't take that away from me / Have you met Miss Jones? / Me and my shadow / Beyond the sea.
Dec 01. (c-s; by ROBBIE WILLIAMS & NICOLE KIDMAN) *(TCCHS 5132)* **SOMETHIN' STUPID / ETERNITY (orchestral version) / MY WAY (live at the Royal Albert Hall)** 1 –
(cd-s+=) *(CDCHS 5132)* – ('A'-video).
(dvd-s) *(DVDCHS 5132)* – ('A'-video) / Let's face the music and dance / That's life / (video clips).
Chrysalis Virgin
Nov 02. (cd/c/lp) *(543994-2/-4/-1)* *<81777>* **ESCAPOLOGY** 1 Apr03 43
– How peculiar / Feel / Something beautiful / Monsoon / Sexed up / Get a little high *[US-only]* / Love somebody / Revolution / Handsome man / Come undone / One fine day *[US-only]* / Me and my monkey / World's most handsome man *[US-only]* / Song 3 *[UK-only]* / Hot fudge *[UK-only]* / Cursed *[UK-only]* / Nan's song / How peculiar (reprise) / I tried love *[UK-only]*.
Dec 02. (cd-s) *(CDCHS 5150)* **FEEL / NOBODY SOMEDAY (demo) / YOU'RE HISTORY / (video footage)** 4 –
(dvd-s) *(DVDCHS 5150)* – ('A'-video) / (as above).
Apr 03. (cd-s) *(CDCHS 5151)* **COME UNDONE / ONE FINE DAY / HAPPY EASTER (WAR IS COMING) / (video clips)** 4 –
(dvd-s) *(DVDCHS 5151)* – ('A'-video) / (as above..).
Jul 03. (cd-s) *(CDCHS 5152)* **SOMETHING BEAUTIFUL / BERLINER STAR / COFFEE TEA AND SYMPATHY** 3 –
(dvd-s) *(DVDCHS 5152)* – ('A'-interactive video) / (tracks 2 & 3) / (video clips).
Sep 03. (cd) *(594637-2)* **LIVE AT KNEBWORTH** (live) 2 –
– Let me entertain you / Let love be your energy / We will rock you / Monsoon / Come undone / Me and my monkey / Hot fudge / Mr. Bojangles / She's the one / Kids / Better man / Nan's song / Feel / Angels.
Nov 03. (cd-s) *(CDCHS 5153)* **SEXED UP / GET A LITTLE HIGH / APPLIANCE OF SCIENCE** 10 –
(dvd-s) *(DVDCHS 5153)* – (tracks first & third) / Big beef / (trailer for Live At Knebworth).
Oct 04. (cd-s) *(CDCHS 5156)* **RADIO / (Maloney mix)** 1 –
(cd-s) *(CDCHSS 5156)* – ('A') / Northern town / ('A'-Sam La More jumpin' radio mix) / (video clips).
(12") *(12CHS 5156)* – ('A'-mixes; Maloney / Sam La More jumpin' radio / Sam La More thumpin' club / Graham Massey).
(dvd-s) *(DVDCHS 5156)* – ('A'-video) / 1974 / ('A'-Massey mix) / (video clips).
Oct 04. (cd) *(<866819-2>)* **GREATEST HITS** (compilation) 1
– Old before I die / Lazy days / Angels / Let me entertain you / Millennium / No regrets / Strong / She's the one / Rock DJ / KIds / Supreme / Let love be your energy / Eternity / The road to Mandalay / Feel / Come undone / Sexed up / Radio / Misunderstood.
Dec 04. (cd-s) *(CDCHS 5157)* **MISUNDERSTOOD / DO ME NOW (demo)** 8 –
(cd-s) *(CDCHSS 5157)* – ('A') / Please please / (I feel it but) I can't explain / Sometimes I go by the name Roberta (video clip).
(dvd-s) *(DVDCHS 5157)* – ('A') / Chemical devotion / The postcard / Are you tryin' to be funny Mr. Williams? (video clip).
Oct 05. (cd-s) *(CDCHS 5158)* **TRIPPING / MAKE ME PURE** 2 –
(cd-s+=) *(CDCHSS 5158)* – Meet the stars / (2-min. video clip).
(dvd-s) *(DVDCHS 5158)* – ('A'-video) / ('B'-video) / Bag full of silly / (2-min. video clip, & photos).
Oct 05. (cd/d-lp) *(<341823-2/-1>)* **INTENSIVE CARE** 1 Nov05
– Ghosts / Tripping / Make me pure / Spread your wings / Advertising space / Please don't die / Your gay friend / Sin sin sin / Random acts of kindness / A place to crash / Kind of bloke and bird. *(ltd-cd w/dvd+=; 343706-2)* – (DVD tracks + making of..).
Dec 05. (cd-s) *(CDCHS 5159)* **ADVERTISING SPACE / FAMILY COACH** 8 –
(cd-s) *(CDCHSS 5159)* – ('A') / Twist / Don't say no / (making of video).
(dvd-s) *(DVDCHS 5159)* – ('A') / Don't say no / Overture for Berlin / ('A'-video).

□ Brian WILSON (see under ⇒ BEACH BOYS)

□ WINGS (see under ⇒ McCARTNEY, Paul)

Steve WINWOOD

Born: 12 May'48, Birmingham, Warwickshire, England. The young WINWOOD had his first encounter with rock'n'roll via his music loving uncle before beginning his illustrious career with his father's band. At the age of 15 (already an accomplished vocalist, guitarist and keyboard player), he joined The SPENCER DAVIS GROUP with brother MUFF, where he had three massive hits on the fledgling 'Island' records between 1963 and April 1967; the brilliant 'KEEP ON RUNNING', 'SOMEBODY HELP ME' and 'GIMME SOME LOVING'. Around this time he formed TRAFFIC and scored three more, newly psychedelicised UK Top 10 smashes, 'PAPER SUN', 'HOLE IN MY SHOE' and 'HERE WE GO ROUND THE MULBERRY BUSH'. In 1969, (still only 21) WINWOOD joined ERIC CLAPTON, GINGER BAKER and RIC GRECH in the short-lived supergroup, BLIND FAITH. Early the following year, he joined GINGER BAKER's AIRFORCE, subsequently returning to TRAFFIC in 1971. WINWOOD's first solo album was to have been 'MUD SHADOWS' in 1970 although it eventually surfaced as TRAFFIC album, 'JOHN BARLEYCORN MUST DIE', following the input of JIM CAPALDI and CHRIS WOOD. After leaving TRAFFIC, he made session appearances for TOOTS & THE MAYTALS, The SUTHERLAND BROTHERS and SANDY DENNY plus a guest spot on 'GO' by STOMU YAMASHTA. Having re-signed to 'Island' in 1976, his first solo venture (released at the onset of punk) was an undistinguished eponymous effort in 1977. His second release (taking two years to complete) 'ARC OF A DIVER' (1981) was produced, engineered and performed by WINWOOD himself with excellent results (the album and the extracted single 'WHILE YOU SEE A CHANCE' both reached US Top 10 while the album hit the UK Top 20). 'TALKING BACK TO THE NIGHT' (1982) was similar to the preceding album and had, in 'VALERIE', an outstanding highlight. 1986 saw WINWOOD joining the 80's tasteful coffee table elite with 'BACK IN THE HIGH LIFE', a record which sold three million copies in the US alone. One of the set's standouts, 'HIGHER LOVE' (with guest vocals by CHAKA KHAN), topped the US singles chart and earned him a Grammy. His contract with 'Island' expired shortly after and the label were outbid by 'Virgin', who reportedly secured WINWOOD's artistic services with an offer worth 13 million. His first release for the label, 'ROLL WITH IT', saw him teaming up with The MEMPHIS HORNS, such enduring songs as 'DANCING SHOES' and the fantastic title track ensured that WINWOOD would enjoy the fruits of his first No.1 album. The 1990 follow-up, 'REFUGEES OF THE

HEART' was extremely disappointing, however, and together with CAPALDI, WINWOOD re-formed TRAFFIC for one set in 1994. It seemed that the short-lived TRAFFIC reformation hadn't exactly rejuvenated WINWOOD's muse judging by the insipid blandness of 'JUNCTION SEVEN' (1997). Co-produced by veteran knob-twiddler Narada Michael Walden, the album was coffee table soul-pop without the soul. It was a much more natural sounding WINWOOD who emerged in 2003 with 'ABOUT TIME', the first album for his own 'Wincraft' label. The downscaling seemed to have done him good, presumably inspiring him to also pare things back both in terms of arrangements and production. In place of the airbrushed fodder of his last effort was an easy going selection of jazzy, small-band R&B influenced by the chops of his latin sidemen: if it wasn't quite a VAN MORRISON, it does seem as if WINWOOD is headed back to his roots as he gets older.

• **Songwriters:** For his debut in 1977, he co-wrote with JIM CAPALDI (an ex-member of TRAFFIC). He collaborated on some further releases with lyricist VIV STANSHALL, WILL JENNINGS and JOE WALSH. • **Trivia:** He was also a renowned session man, having played on albums by JIMI HENDRIX (1968 + 1970) / JOE COCKER (1969) / McDONALD & GILES (1970) / LEON RUSSELL (1970) / HOWLIN' WOLF (1971) / ALVIN LEE (1973) / JOHN MARTYN (1973) / AMAZING BLONDEL (1973) / JADE WARRIOR (1975) / TOOTS & THE MAYTALS (1976) / SANDY DENNY (1977) / VIVIAN STANSHALL (1978) / GEORGE HARRISON (1979) / MARIANNE FAITHFULL (1979) / PIERRE MOERLEN'S GONG (1979) / etc. (see other 'Island' label artists).

Album rating: STEVE WINWOOD (*7) / ARC OF A DIVER (*8) / TALKING BACK TO THE NIGHT (*6) / BACK IN THE HIGH LIFE (*8) / CHRONICLES compilation (*7) / ROLL WITH IT (*6) / REFUGEES OF THE HEART (*6) / THE FINER THINGS boxed-set compilation/history (*8) / JUNCTION SEVEN (*4) / ABOUT TIME (*5)

STEVE WINWOOD (debut solo recording was actually compiled from his past bands' work)

Island U.A.

May 71. (d-lp) *(ILPS 9964) <9950>* **WINWOOD** [ ] [93]
– (tracks by SPENCER DAVIS GROUP / TRAFFIC / BLIND FAITH / AIRFORCE)

— Later that year, WINWOOD reformed TRAFFIC and went into numerous session work mainly for 'Island' artists. In 1976, he and ex-SANTANA drummer MIKE SHRIEVE collaborated with solo classical percussionist STOMU YAMASH'TA. As **"GO"**, they issued eponymous live album in Jun76. When WINWOOD was releasing solo albums, GO also issued live 12" CROSSING THE LINE. Another album GO LIVE IN PARIS (live), was given light in Spring'78. (see STOMU YAMASH'TA discography)

STEVE WINWOOD

STEVE WINWOOD – vocals, keyboards solo with **WILLIE WEEKS** – bass / **ANDY NEWMARK** – drums / **REEBOP KWAKU BANU** – congas

Island Island

Jun 77. (7")*(WIP 6394)* **TIME IS RUNNING OUT. / PENULTIMATE ZONE** [ ] [–]
Jul 77. (7") **TIME IS RUNNING OUT. / HOLD ON** [–] [ ]
Jul 77. (lp/c) *(ILPS/ZCI <9494>)* **STEVE WINWOOD** [12] [22]
– Hold on / Time is running out / Midland maniac / Vacant chair / Luck's in / Let me make something in your life. *(cd-iss. May87; CID 9494) (re-iss. cd Mar93; IMCD 161)*

— His next projects/albums featured WINWOOD on all instruments, vocals

Dec 80. (lp/c) *(ILPS/ICT <9576>)* **ARC OF A DIVER** [13] [3]
– While you see a chance / Arc of a diver / Second-hand woman / Slowdown sundown / Spanish dancer / Night train / Dust. *(cd-iss. May87; CID 9576)*
Dec 80. (7"/c-s) *(WIP/CWIP 6655) <49656>* **WHILE YOU SEE A CHANCE. / VACANT CHAIR** [45] [7]
Mar 81. (7"/12") *(WIP/12WIP 6680)* **SPANISH DANCER (remix). / HOLD ON** [ ] [ ]
May 81. (7") *<49726>* **ARC OF A DIVER. / DUST** [–] [48]
Sep 81. (7"/12") *(WIP/12WIP 6710)* **NIGHT TRAIN. / ('A'instrumental)** [ ] [ ]
Nov 81. (7") *(WIP 6747)* **THERE'S A RIVER. / TWO WAY STRETCH** [ ] [ ]
Jul 82. (7") *(WIP 6786) <29940>* **STILL IN THE GAME. / DUST** [ ] [47]
Aug 82. (lp/c) *(ILPS/ICT <9777>)* **TALKING BACK TO THE NIGHT** [6] Jul82 [28]
– Valerie / Big girls walk away / And I go / While there's a candle burning / Still in the game / It was happiness / Help me angel / Talking back to the night / There's a river. *(cd-iss. May87; CID 9777)*
Sep 82. (7"/12") *(WIP/12WIP 6818) <29879>* **VALERIE. / SLOWDOWN SUNDOWN** [51] [70]
Jun 83. (7") *(WIP 6849)* **YOUR SILENCE IS YOUR SONG. / ('A'instrumental)** [ ] [ ]

— Around the mid-80's, his work took a back seat as his marriage broke down. In 1986, he brought in session musicians to augment.

Jun 86. (7") *(IS 288) <28710>* **HIGHER LOVE. / AND I GO** [13] [1]
(ext.12"+=) *(12IS 288)* – ('A'instrumental).
(c-s+=) *(CIS 288)* – Valerie / While you see a chance / Talking back to the night.
Jul 86. (lp/c/cd) *(ILPS/ICT/CID 9844) <25448>* **BACK IN THE HIGH LIFE** [8] [3]
– Higher love / Take it as it comes / Freedom overspill / Back in the high life again / The finer things / Wake me up on judgement day / Split decision / My love's leavin'.
Aug 86. (7") *<28595>* **FREEDOM OVERSPILL. / HELP ME ANGEL** [–] [20]
Aug 86. (7") *(IS 294)* **FREEDOM OVERSPILL. / SPANISH DANCER** [69] [–]
(some w/ c-s+=) *(IS 294)* – (last lp excerpts & interview).
(12"+=) *(12IS 294)* – ('A'-Liberty mix).
(12"w/ free 7") *(ISG 294)* – Low spark of high heeled boys / Gimme some lovin'.
(d7"+=) *(ISD 294)* – Higher love / And I go.
Jan 87. (7") *(IS 303)* **BACK IN THE HIGH LIFE AGAIN. / HELP ME ANGEL** [53] [–]
(12"+=) *(12IS 303)* – Night train (instrumental).
Feb 87. (7") *<28498>* **THE FINER THINGS. / NIGHT TRAIN** [–] [8]
May 87. (7") *<28472>* **BACK IN THE HIGH LIFE AGAIN. / NIGHT TRAIN (instrumental)** [–] [13]
Sep 87. (7") *(IS 336) <28231>* **VALERIE (remix). / TALKING BACK TO THE NIGHT (instrumental)** [19] [9]
(c-s+=/12"+=/cd-s+=) *(CIS/12IS/CID 336)* – The finer things.
Oct 87. (lp)(c)(cd) *(SSW/+MC/CD 1) <25660>* **CHRONICLES (compilation)** [12] [26]
– Wake me up on judgement day / While you see a chance / Vacant chair / Help me angel / My love's leavin' / Valerie / Arc of a diver / Higher love / Spanish dancer / Talking back to the night.
Feb 88. (7") *<28122>* **TALKING BACK TO THE NIGHT. / THERE'S A RIVER** [–] [57]

Virgin Virgin

May 88. (7"/ext.12") *(VS/+T 1085) <99326>* **ROLL WITH IT. / THE MORNING SIDE** [53] [1]
(cd-s+=) *(VSCD 1085)* – ('A'extended).
(c-s+=) *(VSTC 1085)* – ('A'dub version).
Jun 88. (cd/c/lp) *(CD/TC+/V 2532) <90946>* **ROLL WITH IT** [4] [1]
– Roll with it / Holding on / The morning side / Put on your dancing shoes / Don't you know what the night can do? / Hearts on fire / One more morning / Shining song.
Aug 88. (7") *(VS 1107) <99290>* **DON'T YOU KNOW WHAT THE NIGHT CAN DO? (remix). / ('A'instrumental)** [ ] [6]
(12"+=) *(VST 1107)* – ('A'extended).
(cd-s+=) *(VSCD 1107)* – Roll with it.
Oct 88. (7") *(VS 1135) <99261>* **HOLDING ON. / ('A'instrumental)** [ ] [11]
(3"cd-s+=/12"+=) *(VS T/CD 1135)* – ('A'dance version) / Go Juan.
Mar 89. (7") *<99234>* **HEARTS ON FIRE. / (instrumental)** [–] [53]
Oct 90. (7") *(VS 1299) <98892>* **ONE AND ONLY MAN. / ALWAYS** [ ] [18]
(12"+=/cd-s+=) *(VST/+CD 1299)* – ('A'extended).
Nov 90. (cd/c/lp) *(CD/TC+/V 2650) <91405>* **REFUGEES OF THE HEART** [26] [27]
– You'll keep on searching / Every day (oh Lord) / One and only man / I will be here / Another deal goes down / Running on / Come out and dance / In the light of day.
Apr 91. (7"/12") *(VS/+T 1317)* **I WILL BE HERE. / IN THE LIGHT OF DAY (Instrumental)** [ ] [–]
Mar 97. (c-s/cd-s) *(VSC/+DT 1642)* **SPY IN THE HOUSE OF LOVE / COME OUT AND DANCE** [ ] [–]
Jun 97. (cd/c) *(CDV/TCV 2832) <44059>* **JUNCTION SEVEN** [32] [ ]

– Spy in the house of love / Angel of mercy / Just wanna have some fun / Let your love come down / Real love / Fill me up / Gotta get back to my baby / Someone like you / Family affair / Plenty lovin' / Lord of the street.

Sanctuary Wincraft

Jun 03. (cd) *(SANCD 130) <1>* **ABOUT TIME** ☐ ☐
– Different light / Cigano (for the gypsies) / Take it to the final hour / Why can't we live together / Domingo morning / Now that you're alive / Bully / Phoenix rising / Horizon / Walking on / Silvia (who is she?).

– compilations, others –

May 65. (7"; by ANGLOS) *Fontana; (TF 589)* **INCENSE. / YOU'RE FOOLING ME** ☐ -
(re-iss. May69 on 'Island'; WIP 6061)

Aug 91. (cd/c/lp) *Island; (CID/ICT/ILPS 9975)* **KEEP ON RUNNING** ☐ ☐
– (tracks by SPENCER DAVIS GROUP / TRAFFIC / BLIND FAITH / + 2 solo) *(re-iss. cd Mar96; IMCD 224)*

Mar 95. (4xcd-box) *Island; (IBXCD 2)* **THE FINER THINGS** ☐ ☐
– (tracks by SPENCER DAVIS GROUP / ERIC CLAPTON & POWERHOUSE / BLIND FAITH / TRAFFIC / STOMU YAMASH'TA's GO / solo)

WIRE

Formed: London, England . . . October '76, by GRAHAM LEWIS, COLIN NEWMAN, BRUCE GILBERT and ROBERT GOTOBED. WIRE made their vinyl debut in April '77 when safety pin-pierced ears were subjected to their punk anthems, '12XU' and 'LOWDOWN' on the seminal Various Artists lp, 'Live At The Roxy'. The EMI backed label 'Harvest', desperate for some hip punk credibility, decided to give WIRE a contract and although unsuccessful with their first single attempt ('MANNEQUIN'), unleashed the Mike Thorne-produced 'PINK FLAG' at the end of '77. The record contained 21 short, sharp shocks of minimalist punk rock/new wave, possessed of a musical intelligence that dwarfed their more retro-fixated contemporaries. Early in 1978, they followed this with the classic 'I AM THE FLY', lyrically a simple piece of what can only be described as progressive punk. After another fruitless stab at the charts with 'DOT DASH', they returned with an even more engaging second set, the oblique, atmospheric 'CHAIRS MISSING'. This record surely deserved better than its Top 50 placing, featuring as it did the classy avant-punk tunes, 'PRACTICE MAKES PERFECT', 'I FEEL MYSTERIOUS TODAY' and the "minor" hit 45, 'OUTDOOR MINER'. In the Autumn of '79, WIRE's third set, '154' hit the Top 40, effectively displaying an even more experimental side to the one-time three-chord wonders. Sadly, however, it was their final outing for 'Harvest', the group moving on to the more appropriate indie label, 'Rough Trade', who released the 1981 single, 'OUR SWIMMER'. An anti-commercial, unproduced live set appeared around the same time, the band members having already taken off for solo projects. One of these, DOME (aka GILBERT & LEWIS), had been in the pipeline for some time, while NEWMAN went on to indie success with several albums. In 1986, the much-in-demand WIRE returned, completing a few EP's for top indie, 'Mute' before the following year's 'THE IDEAL COPY' album. They continued to enjoy cult success, which even spread across the Atlantic, the band signing to US label, 'Enigma'. In 1991, GOTOBED retired (to Bedfordshire, no doubt?!) and the band became WIR, releasing the disappointing 'THE FIRST LETTER' that year. For the remainder of the 90's, each took on individual projects, all fairly obscure of course. With the nasty 90's out of the way, WIRE were back with the internet-friendly series releases, 'READ & BURN 01' (2002), a record that opened with the basic and incisive 'IN THE ART OF STOPPING'. This track was the opener on their long-awaited full-set, 'SEND' (2003), a transitional, energetic return to form which also included new greats such a 'SPENT' and 'MR. MARX'S TABLE'.

• **Songwriters:** Group compositions. • **Trivia:** COLIN NEWMAN producec The VIRGIN PRUNES in 1982 and FAD GADGET in 1984. He moved to India at this time, returning after a few years to live in Belgium where he founded 'Crammed Discs' records.

Album rating: PINK FLAG (*8) / CHAIRS MISSING (*9) / 154 (*7) / DOCUMENT AND EYEWITNESS: ELECTRIC BALLROOM (*3) / THE IDEAL COPY (*7) / A BELL IS A CUP . . . UNTIL IT IS STRUCK (*5) / ON RETURNING (1977-1979) compilation (*8) / IT'S BEGINNING TO & BACK AGAIN (*6) / MANSCAPE (*5) / THE FIRST LETTER (*4; as Wir) / SEND (*7)

COLIN NEWMAN (b.16 Sep'54, Salisbury, England) – vox, guitar, keyboards / **BRUCE GILBERT** (b.18 May'46, Watford, England) – guitar, vocals, synths. / **GRAHAM LEWIS** (b.22 Feb'53, Grantham, England) – bass, vocals, synthesizers / **ROBERT GOTOBED** (b. MARK FIELD, 1951, Leicester, England) – drums, percussion (ex-SNAKES, ex-ART ATTACKS) / **GEORGE GILL** – guitar (left before debut)

Harvest Harvest

Nov 77. (7"m) *(HAR 5144)* **MANNEQUIN. / 12XU / FEELING CALLED LOVE** ☐ -

Nov 77. (lp/c) *(SHSP/TC-SHSP 4076) <11757>* **PINK FLAG** ☐ ☐
– Reuters / Field day for the Sundays / Three girl rhumba / Ex-lion tamer / Lowdown / Start to move / Brazil / It's so obvious / Surgeon's girl / Pink flag / The commercial / Straight line / 106 beats that / Mr. Suit / Strange / Fragile / Mannequin / Different to me / Champs / Feeling called love / 12XU. *(cd-iss. 1990 on 'Restless'+=; 72360)* – Options R. *(re-iss. cd Aug94 on 'E.M.I.'; CDGO 2063) <cd-iss. 1995 on 'Capitol'; 29857-2>*

Feb 78. (7") *(HAR 5151)* **I AM THE FLY. / EX-LION TAMER** ☐ -

Jun 78. (7") *(HAR 5161)* **DOT DASH. / OPTIONS R** ☐ -

Sep 78. (lp/c) *(<SHSP/TC-SHSP 4093>)* **CHAIRS MISSING** 48 ☐
– Practice makes perfect / French film blurred / Another the letter / Men 2nd / Marooned / Sand in my joints / Being sucked in again / Heartbeat / Mercy / Outdoor miner / I am the fly / I feel mysterious today / From the nursery / Used to / Too late. *(cd-iss. 1990 on 'Restless'+=; 72361)* – Go ahead / A question of degree / Former airline. *(re-iss. cd Aug94 on 'E.M.I.'; CDGO 2065) <cd-iss. 1995 on 'Capitol'; 29858-2>*

Jan 79. (7",7"white) *(HAR 5172)* **OUTDOOR MINER. / PRACTICE MAKES PERFECT** 51 -

Harvest Warners

Jun 79. (7") *(HAR 5187)* **A QUESTION OF DEGREE. / FORMER AIRLINE** ☐ -

Sep 79. (lp/c) *(SHSP/TC-SHSP 4105) <3398>* **154** 39 ☐
– I should have known better / Two people in a room / The 15th / The other window / Single k.o. / A touching display / On returning / A mutual friend / Blessed state / Once is enough / Map reference 41°N, 93°W / Indirect enquiries / 40 versions. *(free-7"ep w.a) (Dome; PSR 444)* – Song 2 / Get down (parts 1 & 2) / Let's panic / Later / Small electric piece. *(cd-iss. 1990 on 'Restless'+= 72362)* – (7"ep above). *(re-iss. cd Aug94 on 'E.M.I.'; CDGO 2064) <cd-iss. 1995 on 'Capitol'; 39859> (cd re-iss. Jul99; CDGO 2064)*

Oct 79. (7") *(HAR 5192)* **MAP REFERENCE 41°N 93°W. / GO AHEAD** ☐ -

— In 1980, WIRE also diverged into own activities; GILBERT & LEWIS became CUPOL and DOME, etc. The pair also joined THE THE. COLIN NEWMAN went solo taking ROBERT GOTOBED with him. The latter also became member of FAD GADGET. (see further on for these activities)

Rough Trade not iss.

May 81. (7") *(RT 079)* **OUR SWIMMER. / MIDNIGHT BAHNHOF CAFE** ☐ -

Jul 81. (lp) *(ROUGH 29)* **DOCUMENT AND EYEWITNESS: ELECTRIC BALLROOM (live)** ☐ -
– 5 10 / 12XU (fragment) / Underwater experiences / Zegk hoqp / Everything's going to be nice / Instrumental (thrown bottle) / Piano tuner (keep strumming those guitars) / And then . . . / We meet under tables / Revealing trade secrets / Eels sang lino / Eastern standard / Coda. *(free 12"m-lp)* **DOCUMENT AND EYEWITNESS: NOTRE DAME HALL (live)** – Underwater experiences / Go ahead / Ally in exile / Relationship / Our swimmer / Witness to the fact / 2 people in a room / Heartbeat. *(re-iss. 1984 lp/c; same/ COPY 004) (cd-iss. Apr91 on 'Grey Area-Mute'; WIRE 80CD)*

Mar 83. (12"m) *(RTT 123)* **CRAZY ABOUT LOVE. / SECOND LENGTH (OUR SWIMMER) / CATAPULT 30** ☐ -

— WIRE were now back to full-time membership.

WIRE

Mute | Enigma

Nov 86. (12"ep) *(12MUTE 53) <72245>* **SNAKEDRILL** [ ] [ ]
– A serious of snakes / Advantage in height / Up to the sun / Drill.

Mar 87. (7") *(MUTE 57)* **AHEAD. / FEED ME (live)** [ ] [–]
(12"+=) *(12MUTE 57)* – Ambulance chasers (live) / Vivid riot of red (live).

Apr 87. (cd/c/lp) *(CD/C+/STUMM 42) <273270>* **THE IDEAL COPY** [87] [ ]
– Points of collapse / Ahead / Madman's honey / Feed me / Ambitious / Cheeking tongues / Still shows / Over theirs. *(cd+=)* – Ahead II / SNAKEDRILL EP tracks.

Mar 88. (7") *(MUTE 67)* **KIDNEY BONGOS. / PIETA** [ ] [ ]
(3"cd-s+=) *(CDMUTE 67)* – Drill (live).
(12"++=) *(12MUTE 67)* – Over theirs (live).

May 88. (cd/c/lp) *(CD/C+/STUMM 54) <73314-1>* **A BELL IS A CUP . . . UNTIL IT IS STRUCK** [ ] [ ]
– Silk skin paws / The finest drops / The queen of Ur and the king of Um / Free falling divisions / It's a boy / Boiling boy / Kidney bongos / Come back in two halves / Follow the locust / A public place. *(cd+=)* – The queen of Ur and the king of Um (alternate take) / Pieta / Over theirs (live) / Drill (live).

Jun 88. (7") *(MUTE 84)* **SILK SKIN PAWS. / GERMAN SHEPHERDS** [ ] [ ]
(12"+=) *(12MUTE 84)* – Ambitious (remix).
(3"cd-s+=) *(CDMUTE 84)* – Come back in two halves.

Apr 89. (7"clear; withdrawn) *(MUTE 87)* **EARDRUM BUZZ. / THE OFFER** [68] [ ]
(12"+=) *(12MUTE 87)* – It's a boy (instrumental).
(cd-s) *(CDMUTE 87)* – ('A'side) / Silk skin paws / A serious of snakes / Ahead (extended).
(live-12") *(LMUTE 87)* – BUZZ BUZZ BUZZ – Eardrum buzz / Ahead / Kidney bongos.

Mute | Mute

May 89. (cd/c/lp) *(CD/C+/STUMM 66) <73516-2>* **IT'S BEGINNING TO AND BACK AGAIN (live)** [ ] [ ]
– Finest drops / Eardrum buzz / German shepherds / Public place / It's a boy / Illuminated / Boiling boy / Over theirs / Eardrum buzz (12"version) / The offer / In vivo.

Jul 89. (7") *(MUTE 98)* **IN VIVO. / ILLUMINATED** [ ] [ ]
(12"+=/cd-s+=) *(12/CD MUTE 98)* – Finest drops (live).

May 90. (7"; w-drawn) *(MUTE 107)* **LIFE IN THE MANSCAPE. / GRAVITY WORSHIP** [–] [ ]
(12"+=/cd-s+=) *(12/CD MUTE 107)* – Who has wine.

May 90. (cd/c/lp) *(CD/C+/STUMM 80) <73559-2>* **MANSCAPE** [ ] [ ]
– Patterns of behaviour / Goodbye ploy / Morning bell / Small black reptile / Torch it / Other moments / Sixth sense / What do you see? / Where's the deputation? / You hung your lights in the trees – A craftman's touch. *<US cd+=>* – Life in the manscape / Stampede / Children of groceries.

Apr 91. (cd/c/lp) *(CD/C+/STUMM 74)* **DRILL** [ ] [ ]
– (7 versions of out-takes from last album)

WIR

— slightly different name when GOTOBED left

Sep 91. (7") *(MUTE 107)* **SO AND SLOW IT GOES. / NICE FROM HERE** [ ] [–]
(12") *(12MUTE 107)* – ('A'side) / ('A'-Orb mix) / Take it (LFO mix)
(cd-s+=) *(CDMUTE 107)* – (all 4 tracks).

Oct 91. (cd/c/lp) *(CD/C+/STUMM 87) <61238>* **THE FIRST LETTER** [ ] [ ]
– Take it (for greedy) / So and slow it goes (extended) / A bargain at 3 and 20 yeah! / Rootsi-rootsy / Ticking mouth / It continues / Looking at me (stop!) / Naked, whooping and such-like / Tailor made / No cows on the ice / A big glue canal.

— all 4 members were back again

pinkflag | pinkflag

Nov 00. (7") *(VPF 3)* **TWELVE TIMES YOU. / X U (version)** [ ] [–]

May 02. (m-cd) *(<PF 4>)* **READ & BURN 01** [ ] [ ]
– In the art of stopping / I don't understand / Comet / Germ ship / 1st fast / The Agfers of Kodack.

Apr 03. (cd) *(<PF 6CD>)* **SEND** [ ] May03 [ ]
– In the art of stopping / Mr Marx's table / Being watched / Comet / The Agfers of Kodack / Nice streets above / Spent / Read and burn / You can't leave now / Half eaten / 99.9.

– compilations, others, etc. –

Mar 86. (m-lp) *Pink; (PINKY 7)* **PLAY POP** [ ] [–]

Aug 86. (lp) *Dojo; (DOJOLP 36)* **IN THE PINK (live)** [ ] [–]

Nov 87. (12"ep) *Strange Fruit; (SFPS 041)* **THE PEEL SESSIONS** (18.1.78) [ ] [–]
– I am the fly / Culture vultures / Practice makes perfect / 106 beats that.

Jul 89. (cd)(c/lp) *Harvest; (CDP 792 535-2)(TC+/SHSP 4127) / Restless; <72358-1>* **ON RETURNING (1977-1979)** [ ] [ ]
– 12XU / It's so obvious / Mr. Suit / Three girl rhumba / Ex lion tamer / Lowdown / Strange / Reuters / Feeling called love / I am the fly / Practise makes perfect / French film blurred / I feel mysterious today / Marooned / Sand in my joints / Outdoor miner / A question of degree / I should have known better / The other window / 40 versions / A touching display / On returning. *(cd+=)* – Straight line / 106 beats that / Field day for the Sundays / Champs / Dot dash / Another the letter / Men 2nd / Two people in a room / Blessed state. *(cd re-iss. Feb00; same)*

Feb 90. (cd/c/lp) *Strange Fruit; (SFR CD/MC/LP 108)* **DOUBLE PEEL SESSIONS** [ ] [–]
(cd re-iss. May96; same)

May 93. (cd/c/d-lp) *Mute; (CD/C+/STUMM 116)* **1985-1990 THE A LIST** [ ] [–]

Sep 94. (cd; w/book) *Audioglobe; (SCONC 25)* **EXPLODING VIEWS** [ ] [–]

May 95. (cd) *E.M.I.; (CDGO 2066)* **BEHIND THE CURTAIN** [ ] [–]

Dec 95. (12"; WIRE with HAFLER TRIO) *Touch; (TONE 5)* **THE FIRST LETTER / THE LAST LAST NUMBER** [ ] [–]

May 96. (cd) *W.M.O.; (WMO 004CD)* **TURNS AND STROKES** [ ] [–]
– Safe / Lorries / Panamanian craze / Remove for improvement / Spare one / Over my head / 12XU / Inventory / Ritual view / Part of our history / Second length (our swimmer) / Catapult 30.
(d-lp-iss.Apr97; same)

Oct 97. (cd) *W.M.O.; (WMO 014CD) / World Domination; <67>* **COATINGS** [ ] [ ]
– Ambulance chasers / Series of snakes / Ambitious / Madman's honey / Kidney bongos / It's a boy / German shepherds / Boling boy / Drill / In vivo / Who has nine? / It can't be true can it? / Gravity worship. *(w/ free cd-s)* – AMBITIOUS

Sep 00. (3xcd-box) *E.M.I.; (528357-2)* **PINL FLAG / CHAIRS MISSING / 154** [ ] [–]

☐ WIZZARD (see under ⇒ MOVE)

Bobby WOMACK

Born: 4 Mar'44, Cleveland, Ohio, USA. Along with his four siblings, CECIL, CURTIS, HARRIS, FRIENDLY Jnr and BOBBY formed The WOMACK BROTHERS as a gospel quintet in 1959. It wasn't long before he met SAM COOKE who subsequently snapped him up to play guitar in his own gospel outfit, The SOUL STIRRERS. In early 1960, COOKE formed the L.A.-based 'SAR' label with manager J.W. Alexander and promptly added the brothers to his roster, renaming them The VALENTINOS after the following year's debut single, 'SOMEBODY'S WRONG'. A handful of classy R&B singles followed while two of them, 'IT'S ALL OVER NOW' and 'LOOKIN' FOR A LOVE' became major hits for The ROLLING STONES and The J.GEILS BAND respectively. After SAM COOKE's controversial death in 1964, Alexander had a dispute with COOKE's widow, Barbara (whom BOBBY married three months later) and subsequently shut down 'SAR'. Although The VALENTINOS soon followed suit, BOBBY's songwriting and performing credentials were already well established and although he began recording for new label, 'Him', most of his time was taken up by session work for the likes of ARETHA FRANKLIN, RAY CHARLES and WILSON PICKETT. As well as playing on the latter's 'Funky Broadway' single, WOMACK penned a series of tracks for PICKETT including 'I'M IN LOVE' and 'I'M A MIDNIGHT MOVER'. The two also became great buddies and it isn't difficult to hear similarities in their gritty soul-shout vocal style; WOMACK himself was nicknamed 'The

PREACHER'. After a brief spell at 'Chess', he signed to Liberty's R&B subsidiary, 'Minit', where he cut a series of fair to middling solo singles, none of which were big hits. His final effort for the label was 'THE WOMACK LIVE (LIVE '68)', a Hollywood-recorded concert set that pitted masterful interpretations of soul classics like Sam Cooke's 'LAUGHING AND CLOWNING' and Percy Mayfield's 'TO LIVE THE PAST' against his characteristic penchant for seemingly incongruous cover material i.e. The Mamas And The Papas' 'CALIFORNIA DREAMIN' and Fred Neil's 'Everybody's Talkin''. The square-spectacled soul man had more success with his 'United Artists' (who took over over 'Liberty') recordings which he kicked off in late 1971 with his first (US) Top 30 hit, 'THAT'S THE WAY I FEEL ABOUT 'CHA'. WOMACK's impressive development as both a singer and songwriter was illustrated the following year with the release of two great albums, 'COMMUNICATION' and 'UNDERSTANDING', the latter featuring BOBBY's fond ode to his brother HARRY (who was subsequently stabbed to death by his own wife in 1978), 'HARRY HIPPIE'. 1972 was also the year of SLY & THE FAMILY STONE's seminal 'There's A Riot Goin' On', to which WOMACK added his famous wah-wah guitar; his well documented friendship with the wayward SLY STONE led them both off the rails in the early 70's as they became increasingly dependent on drugs and the high-rolling L.A. lifestyle. Following the lead of contemporaries MARVIN GAYE and CURTIS MAYFIELD, WOMACK cut a blaxploitation soundtrack in 1973 for the movie, 'ACROSS 110th STREET' and although the classic title track remains arguably one of the finest marriages of soul and pop ever committed to vinyl, the project failed to bring BOBBY the same fame as ISAAC HAYES' 'Shaft' which was screened around the same time. A series of back to basics Muscle Shoals-recorded efforts followed in the form of 'FACTS OF LIFE' (1973), 'LOOKIN' FOR A LOVE AGAIN' (1974), 'I DON'T KNOW WHAT THE WORLD IS COMING TO' (1975) and 'SAFETY ZONE' (1976) although only the old VALENTINOS song, 'LOOKIN' FOR A LOVE' was a major hit (US Top 10) in 1974. 1976, meanwhile saw the release of his brave country-soul set, 'B.W. GOES C & W', one of the poorest selling albums of his career. Things didn't get much better as he recorded another couple of flop albums for 'Columbia', 'HOME IS WHERE THE HEART IS' (1977) and 'PIECES' (1978), closing the decade with a patchy one-off set for 'Arista', 'ROADS OF LIFE' (1979) as he tried to come to terms with the cot death of his baby son. Salvation came in the form of CRUSADERS man, WILTON FELDER who asked WOMACK to sing on his solo album, 'Inherit The Wind'; the title track was a UK hit and its success provided the impetus for BOBBY's creative and critical rebirth with 'THE POET' (1982). One of that sterile decade's few soul records of any lasting worth, WOMACK had succeeded in updating his classic soulman stance without being swamped by new technology, singing his pain on the massive R&B hit, 'IF YOU THINK YOU'RE LONELY NOW'. Yet more strife followed however as he fought a protracted court battle with his new label, 'Beverly Glen' over non-payment of royalties. Nevertheless, a second instalment, 'THE POET II' (1984), finally emerged on 'Motown', hitting the UK Top 40 and enjoying further critical acclaim due in part to some stunning duets with PATTI LaBELLE. Following another collaboration with FELDER, WOMACK returned to his Memphis roots for 'WOMAGIC' (1986), hooking up with veteran country-soul man, Chips Moman. For the remainder of the decade, WOMACK kept a low profile, occasionally popping up on other artist's albums (notably the ROLLING STONES' 'Dirty Work'). The 90's brought another period of personal upheaval before the true soul survivor finally re-emerged with 'RESURRECTION' (1994).

• **Songwriters:** All his own work, except covers:- CALIFORNIA DREAMIN' (Mamas & The Papas) / SWEET CAROLINE (Neil Diamond) / I WISH IT WOULD RASIN (Temptations) / LIVING IN A BOX (Living In A Box) / etc.

• **Trivia:** His brother CECIL became part of WOMACK & WOMACK team with wife LINDA.

Album rating: FLY ME TO THE MOON (*6) / MY PRESCRIPTION (*6) / THE WOMACK "LIVE" (*5) / COMMUNICATION (*6) / UNDERSTANDING (*6) / ACROSS 110th STREET soundtrack (*8) / FACTS OF LIFE (*6) / LOOKIN' FOR A LOVE AGAIN (*5) / BOBBY WOMACK'S GREATEST HITS compilation (*6) / I DON'T KNOW WHAT THE WORLD IS COMING TO (*5) / SAFETY ZONE (*5) / BW GOES C&W (*4) / HOME IS WHERE THE HEART IS (*4) / PIECES (*4) / ROADS OF LIFE (*4) / THE POET (*7) / THE POET II (*8) / SOMEDAY WE'LL ALL BE FREE (*4) / SO MANY RIVERS (*5) / WOMAGIC (*4) / THE SOUL MAN (*4) / MIDNIGHT MOVER: THE BOBBY WOMACK COLLECTION compilation (*8)

the VALENTINOS

BOBBY, CECIL, CURTIS, HARRY + FRIENDLY Jnr

		not iss.	S.A.R.
Nov 61.	(7"; as WOMACK BROTHERS) *<118>* **SOMEBODY'S WRONG. / YIELD NOT TO TEMPTATION**	–	
Jul 62.	(7") *<132>* **LOOKIN' FOR A LOVE. / SOMEWHERE THERE'S A GIRL**	–	72
Sep 62.	(7") *<137>* **I'LL MAKE IT ALRIGHT. / DARLING COME BACK HOME**	–	97
Feb 63.	(7") *<144>* **SHE'S SO GOOD TO ME. / BABY, LOT'S OF LUCK**	–	
Jun 64.	(7") *<152>* **IT'S ALL OVER NOW. / TIRED OF LIVING IN THE COUNTRY** *(UK-iss.1968 on 'Soul City'; SC 106)*	–	94
Sep 64.	(7") *<155>* **EVERYBODY WANTS TO FALL IN LOVE. / BITTER DREAMS**	–	

— they split later in the year. On February '65, BOBBY married SAM COOKE's widow, BARBARA. That year, he recorded for new label 'Him', but time was mostly taken up by session work for RAY CHARLES, WILSON PICKETT and other 'Atlantic' artists. In 1966, he signed for the label, but he mainly wrote for PICKETT before briefly moving to 'Chess'.

BOBBY WOMACK

		Minit	Minit
Sep 67.	(7") *<32024>* **TRUST ME. / BABY, I CAN'T STAND IT**	–	
Feb 68.	(7") *(MLF 11001) <32030>* **BROADWAY WALK. / SOMEBODY SPECIAL**		
Apr 68.	(7") *(MLF 11005) <32037>* **WHAT IS THIS. / WHAT YOU GONNA DO (WHEN YOUR LOVE HAS GONE)**		
Sep 68.	(7") *(MLF 11010) <32048>* **FLY ME TO THE MOON. / TAKE ME**		Aug68 52
Dec 68.	(lp) *<24014>* **FLY ME TO THE MOON** – Fly me to the Moon / Baby, you oughta think it over / I'm a midnight mover / What is this / Somebody special / Take me / Moonlight in Vermont / Love, the time is now / I'm in love / California dreamin' / No money in my pocket / Lillie-Mae.	–	
Jan 69.	(7") *(MLF 11012) <32055>* **CALIFORNIA DREAMIN'. / BABY! YOU OUGHTA THINK IT OVER**		Nov68 43
Apr 69.	(7") *<32059>* **I LEFT MY HEART IN SAN FRANCISCO. / LOVE, THE TIME IS NOW**	–	
Jul 69.	(7") *<32071>* **IT'S GONNA RAIN. / THANK YOU**	–	
Nov 69.	(7") *<32081>* **HOW I MISS YOU BABY. / TRIED AND CONVICTED**	–	93
Feb 70.	(lp) *<24027>* **MY PRESCRIPTION** – How I miss you baby / More than I can stand / It's gonna rain / Everyone's gone to the Moon / I can't take it like a man / I left my heart in San Francisco / Arkansas state prison / I'm gonna forget about you / Don't look back / Tired and convicted / Fly me to the Moon / Thank you.	–	
Apr 70.	(7") *<32093>* **MORE THAN I CAN STAND. / ARKANSAS STATE PRISON**	–	90
		not iss.	Liberty
Jun 70.	(7") *<56186>* **I'M GONNA FORGET ABOUT YOU. / DON'T LOOK BACK**	–	
Dec 70.	(7") *<56206>* **SOMETHING (live). / EVERYBODY'S TALKIN' (live)**	–	
Apr 71.	(lp) *<7645>* **THE WOMACK "LIVE" (live '68)** – Intro – Let it out / Oh how I miss you baby / California dreamin' / Something / Everybody's talking / Laughin' and clownin' / To live the	–	

past / I'm a midnight mover / More than I can stand. *(UK-iss.Feb89 on 'Charly' lp/c; CRB/TCCRB 1201) (cd; CDCHARLY 155)*

— with a number of exceptions, his band over the 70's included **ROGER HAWKINS** – drums / **CLAYTON IVEY** – keyboards / **JIMMY JOHNSON** – guitar / **BARRY BECKETT** – keyboards / **TRUMAN THOMAS** – bass

U.A. U.A.

Feb 72. (7") *(UP 35339) <50847>* **THAT'S THE WAY I FEEL ABOUT CHA. / COME L'AMORE** Nov71 27

Jun 72. (lp) *(UAS 29306) <5539>* **COMMUNICATION** Nov71 83
– Communication / Come l'amore / Fire and rain / (If you don't want my love) Give it back / (They long to be) Close to you / Everything is beautiful / That's the way I feel about cha / Held not to temptation.

Jul 72. (7") *(UP 35375) <50902>* **WOMAN'S GOT TO HAVE IT. / (IF YOU DON'T WANT MY LOVE) GIVE IT BACK** Apr72 60

Sep 72. (lp) *(UAG 29365) <5577>* **UNDERSTANDING** Jun72 43
– I can understand it / Woman's gotta have it / And I love her / Got to get you back / Simple man / Ruby Dean / A thing called love / Sweet Caroline (good times never seemed so good) / Harry hippie. *(re-iss. Jan75 as 'I CAN UNDERSTAND IT'; UAG 29715)*

Aug 72. (7") *<50946>* **SWEET CAROLINE (GOOD TIMES NEVER SEEMED SO GOOD). / HARRY HIPPIE** – 51 / 31

Dec 72. (7") *(UP 35456)* **HARRY HIPPIE. / I CAN UNDERSTAND IT** –
(re-iss. Jan75 but flipped over; UP 36462)

Apr 73. (7") *(UP 35512) <196>* **ACROSS 110th STREET. / HANG ON IN THERE** Mar73 56

May 73. (lp) *(UAS 29451) <UAS 5225>* **ACROSS 110th STREET** (soundtrack + J.J. JOHNSON & ORCHESTRA *) Jan73 50
– Across 110th Street / Harlem clavinette (*) / (If you don't want my love) Give it back / Hang on in there (*) / Quicksand / Harlem love theme (*) / Across 110th Street – instrumental (*) / Do it right / Hang on in there / If you don't want my love (*) / Across 110th Street part II. *<(cd-iss. Jan98 on 'Rykodisc'+=; RCD 10706)>* – (original dialogue). *(cd re-iss. May98 original on 'Charly'; CPCD 8340) <(cd re-iss. Oct03 as 'RUBARE ALLA MAFIA E'UN SUICIDIO' on 'Dagored'; RED 123CD)>*

Jul 73. (7") *(UP 35565) <255>* **NOBODY WANTS YOU WHEN YOU'RE DOWN AND OUT. / I'M THROUGH TRYING TO PROVE MY LOVE TO YOU** Jun73 29

Sep 73. (lp) *(UAS 29456) <LA 043>* **FACTS OF LIFE** Jun73 37
– Nobody wants you when you're down and out / I'm through trying to prove my love to you / If you can't give her love give her up / That's Heaven to me / Holdin' on to my baby's love / Nobody (reprise) / Facts of life / He'll be there when the sun goes down / Can't stop a man in love / The look of love / Natural man / All along the watchtower / Interlude No.1.

Mar 74. (7") *(35644) <375>* **LOOKIN' FOR A LOVE. / LET IT ALL HANG OUT** Jan74 10

Apr 74. (lp) *(UAS 29574) <LA 199>* **LOOKIN' FOR A LOVE AGAIN** Jan74 85
– Lookin' for a love / I don't wanna be hurt by your love again / Doing it my way / Let it all hang out / Point of no return / You're welcome, stop on by / You're messing up a good thing / Don't let me down / Copper kettle / There's one thing that beats falling. *(re-iss. Aug88 on 'Edsel'; ED 291) (re-iss. Jan89 on 'Charly' lp/c; CRB/TCRB 1193) (cd; CDCHARLY 153)*

Jun 74. (7") *<439>* **YOU'RE WELCOME, STOP ON BY. / I DON'T WANNA BE HURT BY YA LOVE AGAIN** – 59

Nov 74. (lp) *<LA 346>* **BOBBY WOMACK'S GREATEST HITS** (compilation) –

May 75. (lp) *(UAG 29762) <LA 353>* **I DON'T KNOW WHAT THE WORLD IS COMING TO**
– I don't know – (interlude 1 & 2) / Superstar / I want my love, put something down on it / Git it / What's your world / Check it out / Interlude No.2 / Jealous love / It's all over now / Yes Jesus loves me.

Jun 75. (7") *(UP 35859) <621>* **CHECK IT OUT. / INTERLUDE No.2** Apr75 91

Jul 75. (7") *<674>* **GIT IT. / IT'S ALL OVER NOW** –

Jan 76. (7") *(UP 36042) <735>* **WHERE THERE'S A WILL THERE'S A WAY. / EVERYTHING'S GONNA BE ALRIGHT** Nov75

Feb 76. (lp) *(UAG 29907) <LA 544>* **SAFETY ZONE** Jan76
– Everything's gonna be alright / I wish it would rain / Trust me / Where there's a will there's a way / Love ain't something you can get for free / Something you got / Daylight / I feel a groove comin' on / Don't make this the last date for you and me.

Mar 76. (7") *(UP 36098) <763>* **DAYLIGHT. / TRUST ME**

Aug 76. (lp) *(UAS 29979) <LA 638>* **B.W. GOES C & W** Apr76
– Behind closed doors / Bouquet of roses / Tired of living in the country / Tarnished rings / Big bayou / Song of the mockingbird / I'd be ahead if I could quit while I'm behind / You / I take it on home.

Sep 76. (7") *<804>* **TRUST ME. / I FEEL A GROOVE COMIN' ON** –

C.B.S. Columbia

Jan 77. (7"; as BOBBY WOMACK & BROTHERHOOD) *(CBS 4827) <10437>* **HOME IS WHERE THE HEART IS. / WE'VE ONLY JUST BEGUN** Oct76

Feb 77. (lp/c) *(CBS/40 81693) <34384>* **HOME IS WHERE THE HEART IS** Sep76
– Home is where the heart is / A little bit salty / Standing in the safety zone / One more chance on love / How long (has this been goin' on) / I could never be satisfied / Something for my head / A change is gonna come / We've only just begun. *(re-iss. Feb86 on 'Edsel' lp/c; ED/CED 172) (cd-iss. Feb91; EDCD 172)*

Mar 77. (7"; as BOBBY WOMACK & BROTHERHOOD) *<10493>* **STANDING IN THE SAFETY ZONE. / A CHANGE IS GONNA COME** –

Apr 78. (7") *<10672>* **TRUST YOUR HEART. / WHEN LOVE BEGINS, FRIENDSHIP ENDS** –

Jun 78. (7") *<10732>* **WIND IT UP. / STOP BEFORE WE START** –

Jul 78. (lp) *<39083>* **PIECES** –
– It's party time / Trust your heart / Stop before we start / When love begins, friendship ends / Wind it up / Is this the thanks I get / Caught up in the middle / Never let nothing get the best of you.

Arista Arista

Jun 79. (7") *<0421>* **I HONESTLY LOVE YOU. / HOW COULD YOU BREAK MY HEART** –

Jul 79. (lp) *(ARTY 165) <4222>* **ROADS OF LIFE**
– Roads of life / How could you break my heart / Honey dripper boogie / Roots in me / What are you doin' / Give it up / Mr. D.J. don't stop the music / I honestly love you. *(cd-iss. Aug97 on 'Razor & Tie'; RE 2140)*

Aug 79. (7") *<0446>* **ROADS OF LIFE. / GIVE IT UP** –

— took time out to stifle increasing drug intake, re-actifying again after his brother Harris was murdered. Oct'80, he provided the vocals for WILTON FELDER's (of The CRUSADERS) hit single 'INHERIT THE WIND'.

Motown Beverly Glen

Jun 82. (lp) *(STML 12168) <BG 10000>* **THE POET** Dec81 29
– So many sides of you / Lay your lovin' on me / Secrets / Just my imagination / Stand up / Games / If you think you're lonely now / Where do we go from here. *(cd-iss. Jul87 on 'Pacific'; BGD 10000) (re-iss. Sep94 on 'M.C.I.' cd/c; MUS CD/MC 505) (cd re-iss. Jun96 on 'Razor & Tie'; RE 2029) (cd-iss. May99 on 'Charly'; CPCD 8054) (cd re-iss. Jul99 on 'Sequel'; NEMCD 437)*

Jul 82. (7"/12") *(TMG/+T 1267)* **SO MANY SIDES OF YOU. / JUST MY IMAGINATION** –

Sep 82. (7") *(TMG 1278) <2000>* **SECRETS. / STAND UP** Feb82

Sep 82. (7") *<2001>* **WHERE DO WE GO FROM HERE. / JUST MY IMAGINATION** –

— In 1982, BOBBY took 'Beverly Glen' label owner Otis Smith to court, fighting literally over non-payment of royalties.

Mar 84. (7"; by BOBBY WOMACK and PATTI LaBELLE) *<2012>* **LOVE HAS FINALLY COME AT LAST. / AMERICAN DREAM** – 88

Apr 84. (lp/c) *(ZL/ZK 72205) <BG 10003>* **THE POET II** 31 Mar84 60
– Love has finally come at last / It takes a lot of strength to say goodbye / Through the eyes of a child / Surprise surprise / Tryin' to get over you / Tell me why / Who's foolin' who / I wish I had someone to go home to / American dream. *(cd-iss. Jul87 on 'Pacific'; BGD 10003) (re-iss. Sep94 on 'M.C.I.' cd/c; MUS CD/TC 506) (cd re-iss. Jun96 on 'Razor & Tie'; RE 2030) (cd re-iss. Jul99 on 'Sequel'; NEMCD 438)*

Jun 84. (7"/12") *(TMG/+T 1339) <2014/2015>* **TELL ME WHY. / THROUGH THE EYES OF A CHILD** 60

Sep 84. (7") *(TMG 1353)* **SURPRISE SURPRISE. / AMERICAN DREAM** –
(12"+=) *(TMGT 1353)* – If you think you're lonely now.

Sep 84. (7"; by BOBBY WOMACK and PATTI LaBELLE) *<2018>* **IT TAKES A LOT OF STRENGTH TO SAY GOODBYE / WHO'S FOOLIN' WHO** –

Jan 85. (7") *<2021>* **I WISH I HAD SOMEONE TO GO HOME TO. / SOMEDAY WE'LL ALL BE FREE** –

Feb 85. (lp) *<BG 10006>* **SOMEDAY WE'LL ALL BE FREE** –
– I'm so proud / Someday we'll all be free / Gifted one / Falling in love

again / Searching for my love / In over my heart / I wish I had someone to go home to / Someday we'll all be free (acoustic) / Gifted one (acoustic). *(cd-iss. Jul99 as 'THE POET VOL.3' on 'Sequel; NEMCD 439)*

Mar 85. (7") *<2023>* **SEARCHING FOR MY LOVE. / I'M SO PROUD** [–] [ ]

— early in 1985, he re-united with WILTON FELDER on 7+12" '(NO MATTER HOW HIGH I GET) I WILL STILL BE LOOKING UP TO YOU'.

M.C.A. M.C.A.

Sep 85. (lp/c) *(MCF/+C 3282) <5617>* **SO MANY RIVERS** [ ] [66]
– I wish he didn't trust me so much / So baby don't leave home without it / So many rivers / Got to be with you tonight / Whatever happened to the times / Let me kiss it where it hurts / The only survivor / That's where it's at / Check it out / Gypsy woman. *(cd-iss. 1986; DMCF 3282) (cd re-iss. Aug89; DMCL 1894) (cd-iss. Mar93; MCLD 19136)*

Sep 85. (7"/12") *(MCA/+T 944)* **I WISH HE DIDN'T TRUST ME SO MUCH. / GOT TO BE WITH YOU TONIGHT** [64] [ ]

May 86. (7"/12") *(MCA/+T 1050)* **GYPSY WOMAN. / WHATEVER HAPPENED TO THE TIMES** [ ] [ ]

Nov 86. (lp/c) *(MCG/+C 6020) <5899>* **WOMAGIC** [ ] [Jul86]
– I wanna make love to you / When the weekend comes / All the things you do / I can't stay mad too long / Hear the music / Outside myself / I ain't got to live nobody else / More than love / It ain't me. *(cd-iss. Nov87; DMCG 6020)*

Jan 87. (7"/12") *(MCA/+T 1108)* **I WANNA MAKE LOVE TO YOU. / WHATEVER HAPPENED TO THE TIMES** [ ] [ ]

Oct 87. (7") *(MCA 1210)* **LIVING IN A BOX. / ('A'instrumental)** [70] [ ]
(12"+=) *(MCAT 1210)* – ('A'-Another box) / ('A'-Hacienda mix).

Nov 87. (lp/c/cd) *(MCF/MCFC/DMCF 3408) <42097>* **THE LAST SOUL MAN** [ ] [ ]
– Living in a box / When the weekend comes / I still love you / Gina / A world where no one cries / A woman likes to hear that / Real love please stand up / The things we do (when we're lonely) / Falling in love again / Outside myself.

— In Nov'89, WOMACK teamed up with SHIRLEY BROWN on the single, 'AIN'T NOTHIN' LIKE THE LOVIN' WE GOT' on 'Chrysalis' ('Cooltempo' US)

— In Mar'93, he was credited on the LULU single, 'I'm Back For More', which hit the UK Top 30

Continuum Continuum

Aug 94. (c-s/12"/cd-s) *(T/12/CD CTUM 105)* **FOREVER LOVE / COLOUR HIM FATHER / (other mixes)** [ ] [–]

Sep 94. (cd/c) *(CD/T CTUM 8) <19401>* **RESURRECTION** [ ] [ ]
– Good ole days / You made me love again / So high on your love / Don't break your promise (too soon) / Forever love / Please change your mind / Trying not to break down / Cousin Henry / Centerfield / Goin' home / Walking on the wildside / Cry myself to sleep / Wish / Color him father.

— In May'95, he collaborated with JEANIE TRACY on the single, 'IT'S A MAN'S MAN'S WORLD' on 'Pulse'.

not iss. Capitol

Jul 99. (cd) *<98584>* **BACK TO MY ROOTS** (gospel) [–] [ ]

– (selective) compilations, etc. –

Nov 89. (d-lp/c)(cd) *Charly; (CDX/TCCDX 47)(CDCHARLY 199)* **SAFETY ZONE / B.W. GOES C&W** [ ] [–]

May 91. (cd/c/lp) *Essential; (ESD CD/MC/LP 141)* **SUPER SOUL SEDUCTION** [ ] [–]

Jun 91. (cd/c) *Music Club; (MC CD/TC 018)* **THE VERY BEST OF BOBBY WOMACK** [ ] [–]
– I can understand it / Harry hippie / I'm a midnight mover / What is this / Somebody special / That's the way I feel about cha / Communication / California dreaming / If you don't want my love give it back / I wish it would rain / Nobody wants you when you're down and out / Across 110th Street / If you want my love, put something down on it / Lookin' for a love / I don't wanna be hurt by ya love again / Got to get you back / Woman's gotta have it / There's one thing that beats failing / You're messing up a good thing / Love ain't something you can get for free.

Mar 94. (d-cd) *E.M.I.; (CDEM 1514)* **MIDNIGHT MOVER – THE BOBBY WOMACK STORY** [ ] [ ]

Apr 94. (cd/c) *Castle; (CCS CD/MC 404)* **THE COLLECTION** [ ] [–]
(re-iss. May03 on 'Spectrum'; 113125-2)

Jul 94. (3xcd-box) *Charly; (CPCD 80803)* **THE POET TRILOGY** [ ] [–]

Jun 96. (cd) *Razor & Tie; (RE 2009)* **LOOKIN' FOR A LOVE (THE BEST OF BOBBY WOMACK 1968-1975)** [ ] [–]

Nov 96. (d-cd) *Charly; (CPCD 8255-2)* **THE VERY BEST OF BOBBY WOMACK** [ ] [–]

Apr 97. (cd) *M.C.A.; (MCLD 19355)* **THE ONLY SURVIVOR (THE M.C.A. YEARS)** [ ] [–]

Sep 97. (cd) *Charly; (CDGR 165)* **FLY ME TO THE MOON / MY PRESCRIPTION** [ ] [–]

Nov 97. (d-cd) *Eagle; (EDMCD 020)* **THE MASTERS** [ ] [–]

Nov 97. (cd) *Charly; (CDGR 179)* **LOOKIN' FOR A LOVE / B.W. GOES C.W.** [ ] [–]

Jan 98. (cd) *Sequel; (NEMCD 996)* **SOUL SENSATION** [ ] [–]

Feb 98. (cd) *Charly; (CDGR 183)* **UNDERSTANDING / COMMUNICATION** [ ] [ ]

Mar 98. (cd) *Charly; (CDGR 208)* **FACTS OF LIFE / I DON'T KNOW WHAT THE WORLD IS COMING TO** [ ] [ ]

Jun 98. (cd) *Charly; (CDGR 237)* **SAFETY ZONE / THE WOMACK "LIVE"** [ ] [ ]

Jun 98. (cd) *Charly; (CDGR 255)* **GREATEST HITS** [ ] [–]

Aug 98. (cd) *Columbia; (487394-2)* **AT HOME IN MUSCLE SHOALS** [ ] [ ]

Jul 99. (d-cd) *Sequel; (NXTCD 319)* **THE BEST OF THE POETS** [ ] [ ]

Oct 99. (cd) *Sequel; (NEMCD 453)* **SAVE THE CHILDREN** [ ] [ ]

Nov 99. (d-cd) *Charly; (CDVAL 1092)* **THE ULTIMATE COLLECTION** [ ] [ ]

Feb 00. (cd) *Castle Pie; (PIESD 189)* **SOUL BROTHER** [ ] [ ]

Mar 00. (cd) *Neon; (NE 3452-2)* **THE VERY BEST OF BOBBY WOMACK** [ ] [ ]

Sep 00. (cd) *Music Club; (MCCD 432)* **THE BEST OF THE POET TRILOGY** [ ] [ ]

Nov 00. (cd) *Indigo; (IGOXCD 525)* **THE CHRISTMAS ALBUM** [ ] [ ]

Nov 02. (cd) *Disky; (SI 905178)* **LOOKIN' FOR A LOVE** [ ] [ ]

Feb 03. (d-cd) *Black Box; (BB 256)* **HOW I MISS YOU BABY** [ ] [ ]

Jun 03. (d-cd) *Excellence; (EXCEL 2114)* **TWENTY LEGENDARY R&B MASTERPIECES** [ ] [–]

Jun 03. (cd) *Castle; (CMRCD 652)* **THE BEST OF BOBBY WOMACK** [ ] [ ]

Jul 03. (cd) *E.M.I.; (584936-2)* **LOOKIN' FOR A LOVE: THE BEST OF BOBBY WOMACK 1068-1976** [ ] [ ]

Jun 04. (cd-s) *E.M.I.; (WOMACK 001)* **CALIFORNIA DREAMIN' /** [59] [–]
(above was from a Saab cars commercial)

Nov 04. (cd) *Charly; (B00063342-2)* **CHECK IT OUT – THE BEST OF BOBBY WOMACK** [ ] [ ]

Stevie WONDER

Born: STEVELAND JUDKINS MORRIS, 13 May'50, Saginaw, Michigan, USA. Blind since birth, he became a member of his local Baptist choir, and in 1960 he also formed a duo with JOHN GLOVER, who recommended him to his cousin; MIRACLES singer RONNIE WHITE. He in turn contacted, BERRY GORDY, who immediately signed STEVIE for a long-term contract to 'Tamla Motown' and gave him the famous title of (LITTLE) STEVIE WONDER. After two albums and a few flop 45's, STEVIE broke through in 1963 with US chart-topper, 'FINGERTIPS – Pt.2', an updated version of a track from his debut album that featured STEVIE's dazzling harmonica playing. This preceded the No.1 album, 'RECORDED LIVE – THE 12 YEAR OLD GENIUS' (1963), a record which featured the child prodigy in concert playing an array of instruments with breathtaking ease. After a few years of mediocre fortunes, and now somewhat older, he emerged as simply STEVIE WONDER, notching up a top 3 hit with the high-octane soul of 'UPTIGHT' (1966). The album of the same name was released later the same year and included an early indication of WONDER's developing social awareness and eclectic diversity with a cover of Bob Dylan's 'BLOWIN' IN THE WIND'. 'I WAS MADE TO LOVE HER' (1968) contained some passionately executed covers, while the goose-bump gem of a title track was a Top 10 hit in its own right. The celebratory title track from 'FOR ONCE IN MY LIFE' (1969) was similarly successful while

STEVIE WONDER

the sun-ripened loveliness of 'MY CHERIE AMOUR' went Top 5 on both sides of the Atlantic. 'SIGNED, SEALED, DELIVERED (I'M YOURS)' (1970) saw WONDER begin taking more control of his affairs in the studio, handling the whole operation almost single-handedly. This self-determination was consolidated in 1971 when he turned 21 and renegotiated his contract with 'Motown'. Setting up his own publishing operation, WONDER made sure that he'd never be on the wrong end of a bum deal again, especially one where he received only one million dollars out of the thirty million he'd earned at 'Motown' in his youth. 'MUSIC OF MY MIND' (1972) was the first album to fully realise WONDER's kaleidoscopic vision, fusing jazz, rock and soul with pioneering synthesizer sounds and ethnic rhythms while still maintaining an overt pop sensibility. That summer he toured with The ROLLING STONES, bringing his music to a predominantly white rock audience who subsequently lapped up WONDER's heaviest offering to date, the taut funk of 'SUPERSTITION' (1973). The album 'TALKING BOOK' was released the same month and was the first of STEVIE's mercurial 70's masterpieces. From the heart-melting opening chords of 'YOU ARE THE SUNSHINE OF MY LIFE' to the gospel-like closer, 'I BELIEVE (WHEN I FALL IN LOVE IT WILL BE FOREVER)', WONDER had created one of the most accomplished, searching albums in the soul pantheon. It was a hard act to follow but follow it he did, in fine style with 'INNERVISIONS' (1973), a similarly spiritual journey of epic proportions. 'HIGHER GROUND' kept the funk intact while 'VISIONS' and 'JESUS CHILDREN OF AMERICA' were meditative quests for truth. 'LIVING FOR THE CITY' was a hard-bitten knot of genius while the closing 'HE'S MISSTRA KNOW-IT-ALL' featured some beautifully careworn piano playing. These themes were developed on 'FULFILLINGNESS' FIRST FINALE' (1974), an album that repeated 'INNERVISIONS' Grammy Award winning success and included the defiantly anti-Nixon 'YOU HAVEN'T DONE NOTHIN' as well as a rare nod to sexuality on 'BOOGIE ON REGGAE WOMAN'. WONDER completed this quadruple whammy with his groundbreaking double album, 'SONGS IN THE KEY OF LIFE' (1976). A breathtaking summation of all that WONDER had been working towards up to that point, it embraced everything from jazz and funk ('SIR DUKE' and 'I WISH' respectively, both American No.1's) to charming MOR with 'ISN'T SHE LOVELY'. The ominously chiding 'PASTIME PARADISE' was later reinterpreted by rapper COOLIO to massive success. In many ways, releasing another double album, especially one as esoteric and lacking in focus as 'JOURNEY THROUGH THE SECRET LIFE OF PLANTS' (1979) was commercial suicide. The album – using music from an obscure documentary a year earlier – was a moderate success however, but still outshone WONDER's contemporaries. Returning to more commercial fare with a vengeance on 'HOTTER THAN JULY' (1980), WONDER offered up the reggae-flavoured 'MASTERBLASTER (JAMMIN')' (1980) and the anthemic Martin Luther King tribute, 'HAPPY BIRTHDAY' (1980). A string of singles followed, among them the duet with PAUL McCARTNEY, 'EBONY AND IVORY' (1982) and the similarly radio-friendly 'I JUST CALLED TO SAY I LOVE YOU' (1984) – taken from the movie/album 'THE WOMAN IN RED' – which won an Oscar the following year. While 1985's 'IN SQUARE CIRCLE' produced the No.1 hit 'PART-TIME LOVER', it was generally inconsistent and along with 'CHARACTERS' (1987) and his soundtrack to Spike Lee's 'JUNGLE FEVER' (1991) failed to capture the pioneering spirit of his 70's work. 1995's 'CONVERSATION PEACE' contained flashes of brilliance but fans are still waiting (probably in vain) for another 'TALKING BOOK' or 'INNERVISIONS'. Live, WONDER is still worth selling your granny for the ticket price, his charismatic energy rarely failing to deliver the goods. As well as being a tireless promoter of worthy causes he remains one of the most respected figures in the music industry, and his influence on the course of popular music is incalculable. 'A TIME TO LOVE' was the closest he'd come for a long, long time, a record which – seemingly forever delayed – finally emerged in late 2005. It wasn't quite the exhilarating squelch-funk-fest promised by lead single, 'SO WHAT THE FUSS' – the toughest, most soulful STEVIE vocal in decades, and the man's first Top 20 hit since the mid-80's – but it proved there was still fire behind those famous shades. It was also his highest US charting album (Top 5) since 'IN SQUARE CIRCLE', with a massive guestlist taking their own little share of the credit: rock royalty like BONNIE RAITT, PAUL McCARTNEY and PRINCE, as well as less famous faces INDIA.ARIE, onetime GIL SCOTT-HERON sideman HUBERT LAWS, and even his own daughter – as almost every commentator without exception couldn't resist pointing out, the same who gurgled through 'ISN'T SHE LOVELY' back in the mid-70's; here, she sang a little more conventionally, alternating lead vocals with her pop on 'HOW WILL I KNOW'.

• **Songwriters:** STEVIE wrote all his own work except, when in the 60's he collaborated with producer HENRY COSBY. His cover versions were; MR. TAMBOURINE MAN (Bob Dylan) / WE CAN WORK IT OUT (Beatles) / SIXTEEN TONS (Ernie Ford) / CAN I GET A WITNESS (Marvin Gaye) / PLEASE, PLEASE, PLEASE (James Brown) / RESPECT (Otis Redding) / MY GIRL (Temptations) / LIGHT MY FIRE (Doors) / GOD BLESS THE CHILD (Billie Holiday) / BRIDGE OVER TROUBLED WATER (Simon & Garfunkel). The album 'TRIBUTE TO UNCLE RAY', had many covers of RAY CHARLES' songs. • **Miscellaneous:** On the 14th September '70, STEVIE married singer, SYREETA WRIGHT, who became his co-writer in the early 70's. They split-up 4 years later and STEVIE found new girlfriend, YOLANDA SIMMONS, who moved with him and their new daughter, to Manhattan. On the 6th August '73, STEVIE was nearly killed in a serious road accident. He recovered from head injuries, after spending a few days in a coma. STEVIE also wrote million sellers for Minnie Riperton (LOVIN' YOU) & Rufus (TELL ME SOMETHING GOOD).

Album rating: TRIBUTE TO UNCLE RAY (*5) / THE JAZZ SOUL OF LITTLE STEVIE (*5) / THE 12 YEAR OLD GENIUS (RECORDED LIVE) (*6) / WITH A SONG IN MY HEART (*4) / AT THE BEACH (HEY HARMONICA MAN) (*4) / UP-TIGHT EVERYTHING'S ALRIGHT (*6) / DOWN TO EARTH (*5) / I WAS MADE TO LOVE HER (*7) / GREATEST HITS compilation (*8) / FOR ONCE IN MY LIFE (*7) / MY CHERIE AMOUR (*7) / STEVIE WONDER LIVE (AT THE TALK OF THE TOWN) (*6) / SIGNED SEALED & DELIVERED (*7) / WHERE I'M COMING FROM (*7) / STEVIE WONDER'S GREATEST HITS, VOL.2 compilation (*8) / MUSIC OF MY MIND (*7) / TALKING BOOK (*9) / INNERVISIONS (*10) / FULFILLINGNESS' FIRST FINALE (*7) / SONGS IN THE KEY OF LIFE (*8) / LOOKING BACK (aka ANTHOLOGY) compilation (*8) / JOURNEY THROUGH THE SECRET LIFE OF PLANTS soundtrack (*7) / HOTTER THAN JULY (*7) / ORIGINAL MUSIQUARIUM 1 compilation (*9) / THE WOMAN IN RED soundtrack (*4) / IN SQUARE CIRCLE (*5) / CHARACTERS (*4) / JUNGLE FEVER soundtrack (*5) / CONVERSATION PEACE (*4) / NATURAL WONDER – LIVE IN CONCERT (*4) / THE DEFINITIVE COLLECTION double compilation (*8) / A TIME TO LOVE (*6)

LITTLE STEVIE WONDER

– vocals, piano, harmonica

		Oriole	Tamla
Aug 62.	(7") *<54061>* **I CALL IT PRETTY MUSIC (BUT OLD PEOPLE CALL IT THE BLUES). / (part 2)**	–	
1962.	(lp) *<232>* **TRIBUTE TO UNCLE RAY**	–	
	– Hallelujah I love her so / Ain't that love / Don't you know / Sunset / Frankie and Johnny / Drown in my own tears / Come back baby / Mary Ann / My baby's gone / (I'm afraid) The masquerade is over. *(UK-iss.Aug63 on 'Oriole'; PS 40049) (re-iss. May82 on 'Motown') (cd-iss. Sep95)*		
Oct 62.	(7") *<54070>* **LITTLE WATER BOY (w/ CLARENCE PAUL). / LA LA LA LA LA**	–	
1963.	(lp) *<233>* **THE JAZZ SOUL OF LITTLE STEVIE**	–	
	– Fingertips / Square / Soul bongo / Manhattan at six / Some other time / Wandering / Session number 112 / Bam. *(UK-iss.May64 on 'Stateside'; SL 10078) (re-iss. Mar82 on 'Motown')*		
Dec 62.	(7") *<54074>* **CONTRACT ON LOVE. / SUNSET**	–	
Aug 63.	(7") *(CBA 1853) <54080>* **FINGERTIPS (part 2). / FINGERTIPS (part 1)**		Jun63 1

Aug 63. (lp) *(PS 40050) <240>* **THE 12 YEAR OLD GENIUS (RECORDED LIVE) (live)** Jul63 1
– Fingertips / Soul bongo / Drown in my own tears / La la la la / (I'm afraid) The masquerade is over / Hallelujah I love her so / Don't you know. *(re-iss. Oct81 on 'Motown')*

Stateside Tamla

Nov 63. (7") *(SS 238) <54086>* **WORKOUT STEVIE, WORKOUT. / MONKEY TALK** Oct63 33

Jan 64. (lp) *<250>* **WITH A SONG IN MY HEART** –
– Dream / With a song in my heart / Get happy / Put on a happy face / When you wish upon a star / Smile / Make someone happy / Without a song / On the sunny side of the street / Give your heart a chance. *(UK-iss.Oct81 on 'Motown')*

Apr 64. (7") *(SS 285) <54090>* **CASTLES IN THE SAND. / THANK YOU (FOR LOVING ME ALL THE WAY)** Feb64 52

STEVIE WONDER

Aug 64. (7") *(SS 323) <54096>* **HEY HARMONICA MAN. / THIS LITTLE GIRL** Jun64 29

Sep 64. (7") *<54103>* **SAD BOY. / HAPPY STREET** –

Jan 65. (lp) *(SL 10108)* **AT THE BEACH (HEY HARMONICA MAN)**
– Red sails in the sunset / Party at the beach house / Happy Street / Beachcomber / Castles in the sand / Beyond the sea / Sad boy / Beach stomp / Hey, harmonica man.

Tamla Motown Tamla

Jan 65. (7") *<54108>* **PRETTY LITTLE ANGEL. / TEARS IN VAIN** –

Mar 65. (7") *(TMG 505)* **KISS ME BABY. / TEARS IN VAIN**

Sep 65. (7") *(TMG 532) <54119>* **HIGH HEEL SNEAKERS. / MUSIC TALK** Aug65 59

Jan 66. (7") *(TMG 545) <54124>* **UPTIGHT (EVERYTHING'S ALRIGHT). / PURPLE RAINDROPS** 14 Dec65 3

Apr 66. (7") *(TMG 558) <54130>* **NOTHING'S TOO GOOD FOR MY BABY. / WITH A CHILD'S HEART** Mar66 20

Aug 66. (7") *(TMG 570) <54136>* **BLOWIN' IN THE WIND. / AIN'T THAT ASKING FOR TROUBLE** 36 Jun66 9

Nov 66. (lp) *(TML 11036)* **UP-TIGHT EVERYTHING'S ALRIGHT** Jun 66 33
– Love a go-go / Hold me / Blowin' in the wind / Nothing's too good for my baby / Teach me tonight / Uptight (everything's alright) / Ain't that asking for trouble / I want my baby back / Pretty little angel / Music talk / Contract on love / With a child's heart. *(re-iss. Oct81) (re-iss. 1973 on 'M.F.P.')*

Dec 66. (7") *(TMG 588) <54139>* **A PLACE IN THE SUN. / SYLVIA** 20 Oct66 9

Dec 66. (7") *<54142>* **SOME DAY AT CHRISTMAS. / THE MIRACLE OF CHRISTMAS** –

Apr 67. (lp) *(TML 11045) <272>* **DOWN TO EARTH** Jan67 92
– A place in the Sun / Bang bang / Thank you love / Mr. Tambourine man / Hey love / Sixteen tons / Down to Earth / Sylvia / Lonesome road / The world is empty without you / Angel baby (don't you ever leave me) / Be cool, be calm (and keep yourself together). *(re-iss. Oct81)*

Apr 67. (7") *(TMG 602) <54147>* **TRAVELLIN' MAN. / HEY LOVE** 32
Mar67 90

Jul 67. (7") *(TMG 613) <54151>* **I WAS MADE TO LOVE HER. / HOLD ME** 5 Jun 67 2

Oct 67. (7") *(626) <54157>* **I'M WONDERING. / EVERY TIME I SEE YOU I GO WILD** 22 12

Apr 68. (lp) *(TML 11059) <279>* **I WAS MADE TO LOVE HER** Sep67 45
– I was made to love her / Send me some lovin' / I'd cry / Everybody needs somebody (I need you) / Respect / My girl / Baby don't you do it / A fool for you / Can I get a witness / I pity the fool / Please, please, please / Every time I see you I go wild. *(re-iss. Oct81)*

Apr 68. (7") *(TMG 653) <54165>* **SHOO-BE-DOO-BE-DOO-DA-DAY. / WHY DON'T YOU LEAD ME TO LOVE** 46 9

Aug 68. (lp) *(TML 11075) <282>* **STEVIE WONDER'S GREATEST HITS** (compilation) 25 Apr68 37
– Shoo-be-doo-be-doo-da-day / A place in the Sun / Uptight (everything's alright) / Travellin' man / High heel sneakers / Sad boy / Kiss me, baby / Workout Stevie, workout / Fingertips (part 2) / Hey, harmonica man / Contract on love / Castles in the sand / Nothing's too good for my baby / I was made to love her / Blowin' in the wind / I'm wonderin'. *(re-iss. Oct81 & 1986) (cd-iss. 'VOL.1' Sep89) (cd-iss. Nov93 & Oct98; 530941-2)*

Aug 68. (7") *(TMG 666) <54168>* **YOU MET YOUR MATCH. / MY GIRL** Jul68 35

Dec 68. (7") *(TMG 679) <54174>* **FOR ONCE IN MY LIFE. / ANGIE GIRL** 3 Oct68 2
(re-iss. Oct81)

Feb 69. (lp) *(TML 11098) <291>* **FOR ONCE IN MY LIFE** Oct68 50
– For once in my life / Shoo-be-ddo-be-doo-da-day / You met your match / I wanna make her love me / I'm more than happy (I'm satisfied) / I don't know why (I love you) / Sunny / I'd be a fool right now / Ain't no lovin' / God bless the child / Do I love her / The house on the hill. *(re-iss. Oct81) (cd-iss. Aug88) (cd re-iss. Mar03; AA374635234-2)*

Mar 69. (7") *(TMG 690) <54180>* **I DON'T KNOW WHY (I LOVE YOU). / MY CHERIE AMOUR** 14 Feb69 39
(above flipped over Jun69 hit both UK + US No.4) (re-iss. Oct81)

Nov 69. (7") *(TMG 717) <54188>* **YESTER-ME, YESTER-YOU, YESTERDAY. / I'D BE A FOOL RIGHT NOW** 2 Oct69 7

Nov 69. (lp) *(TML 11128) <296>* **MY CHERIE AMOUR** 17 Oct69 34
– My Cherie amour / Hello young lovers / At last / Light my fire / The shadow of your smile / You and me / Pearl / Somebody knows, somebody cares / Yester-me, yester-you, yesterday / Angie girl / Give your love / I've got you. *(re-iss. Oct81 & Apr84, cd-iss. Aug88)*

Mar 70. (7") *(TMG 731) <54191>* **NEVER HAD A DREAM COME TRUE. / SOMEBODY KNOWS, SOMEBODY CARES** 6 Feb70 26

Mar 70. (lp) *(TML 11164) <298>* **LIVE (AT THE TALK OF THE TOWN)** Apr70 81
– Pretty world / Never had a dream come true / Shoo-be-doo-be-doo-da-day / My Cherie amour / Alfie / (drum solo) / Bridge over troubled water / I was made to love her / Yester-me, yester-you, yesterday / For once in my life / Signed, sealed, delivered (I'm yours). *(re-iss. Oct81)*

Jun 70. (7") *(TMG 744) <54196>* **SIGNED, SEALED, DELIVERED (I'M YOURS). / I'M MORE THAN HAPPY (I'M SATISFIED)** 15 3

Nov 70. (lp) *(TML 11169) <304>* **SIGNED, SEALED, DELIVERED (I'M YOURS)** Aug70 25
– Never had a dream come true / We can work it out / Signed, sealed, delivered (I'm yours) / Heaven help us all / You can't judge a book by it's cover / Sugar / Don't wonder why / Anything you want me to do / I can't let my Heaven walk away / Joy (takes over me) / I gotta have a song / Something to say. *(re-iss. Oct81, re-iss. +cd.Aug88)*

Nov 70. (7") *(TMG 757) <54200>* **HEAVEN HELP US ALL. / I GOTTA HAVE A SONG** 29 Oct70 9

Mar 71. (7") *<54202>* **WE CAN WORK IT OUT. / NEVER DREAMED YOU'D LEAVE ME IN SUMMER** – 13
78

May 71. (7") *(TMG 772)* **WE CAN WORK IT OUT. / DON'T WONDER WHY** 27 –

Jul 71. (7") *(TMG 779)* **NEVER DREAMED YOU'D LEAVE ME IN SUMMER. / IF YOU REALLY LOVE ME** –

Jul 71. (lp) *(TML 11183) <308>* **WHERE I'M COMING FROM** May71 62
– Look around / Do yourself a favour / Think of me as your soldier / Something out of the blue / If you really love me / I wanna talk to you / Take up a course in happiness / Never dreamed you'd leave me in Summer / Sunshine in their eyes. *(re-iss. Jul81) (re-iss. +cd.Apr91) (cd-iss. Sep93)*

Nov 71. (7") *<54214>* **WHAT CHRISTMAS MEANS TO ME. / BEDTIME FOR TOYS** –

Jan 72. (7") *(TMG 798) <54208>* **IF YOU REALLY LOVE ME. / THINK OF ME AS YOUR SOLDIER** 20 Aug71 8

Jan 72. (lp) *(STML 11196) <313>* **GREATEST HITS VOL.2** (compilation) 30 Nov71 69
– Signed, sealed, delivered (I'm yours) / We can work it out / For once in my life / If you really love me / You met your match / My Cherie amour / Yester-me, yester-you, yesterday / Never had a dream come true / Heaven help us all / Don't know why I love you / Never dreamed you'd leave in Summer. *(re-iss. Oct81 & 1986) (cd-iss. Sep89 as 'VOL.2') (cd-iss. Nov93 & Oct98; 530942-2)*

May 72. (7") *<54216>* **SUPERWOMAN (WHERE WERE YOU WHEN I NEEDED YOU). / I LOVE EVERY LITTLE THING ABOUT YOU** –

May 72. (lp/c) *(STMA/TC-STMA 8002) <314>* **MUSIC OF MY MIND** Mar72 21
– Love having you around / Superwoman (where were you when I needed you) / I love every thing about you / Sweet little girl / Happier than the morning sun / Girl blue / Seems so long / Keep on running / Evil. *(re-iss. Oct81) (cd-iss. Nov87 & Jul92 & May00; 157353-2) (lp re-iss. Apr01 on 'Simply Vinyl'; SVLP 228)*

Sep 72. (7") *(TMG 827)* **SUPERWOMAN (WHERE WERE YOU WHEN I NEEDED YOU). / SEEMS SO LONG** [ ] [–]

Sep 72. (7") *<54223>* **KEEP ON RUNNING. / EVIL** [–] [90]

Jan 73. (7") *(TMG 841) <54226>* **SUPERSTITION. / YOU'VE GOT IT BAD GIRL** [11] Nov72 [1]

Jan 73. (lp/c) *(STMA/TC-STMA 8007) <319>* **TALKING BOOK** [16] Nov72 [3]
– You are the sunshine of my life / Maybe your baby / You and I / Tuesday heartbreak / You've got it bad girl / Superstition / Big brother / Blame it on the sun / Lookin' for another pure love / I believe (when I fall in love it will be forever). *(re-iss. Oct81) (cd-iss. May86 & Jul92 & May00; 157354-2) (lp re-iss. Apr01 on 'Simply Vinyl'; SVLP 229)*

Mar 73. (7") *<54232>* **YOU ARE THE SUNSHINE OF MY LIFE. / TUESDAY HEARTBREAK** [–] [1]

May 73. (7") *(TMG 852)* **YOU ARE THE SUNSHINE OF MY LIFE. / LOOK AROUND** [7] [–]
(re-iss. Oct81)

Aug 73. (lp/c) *(STMA/TC-STMA 8011) <326>* **INNERVISIONS** [8] [4]
– Too high / Visions / Living for the city / Golden lady / Higher ground / Jesus children of America / All in love is fair / Don't you worry 'bout a thing / He's a misstra know-it-all. *(re-iss. Oct81) (cd-iss. Oct87 & Jul92 & May00; 157355-2) (lp re-iss. Apr01 on 'Simply Vinyl'; SVLP 230)*

Sep 73. (7") *(TMG 869) <54235>* **HIGHER GROUND. / TOO HIGH** [29] Aug73 [4]

Dec 73. (7") *(TMG 881) <54242>* **LIVING FOR THE CITY (edit). / VISIONS** [15] Nov73 [8]

Apr 74. (7") *(TMG 892)* **HE'S MISSTRA KNOW IT ALL. / YOU CAN'T JUDGE A BOOK BY IT'S COVER** [10] [–]
(re-iss. Oct81)

Apr 74. (7") *<54245>* **DON'T YOU WORRY 'BOUT A THING. / BLAME IT ON THE SUN** [–] [16]

Jul 74. (7") *(TMG 908)* **DON'T YOU WORRY 'BOUT A THING. / DO YOURSELF A FAVOUR** [ ] [–]

Aug 74. (lp/c) *(STMA/TCSTMA 8019)* **FULFILLINGNESS' FIRST FINALE** [5] [1]
– Smile please / Heaven is 10 zillion light years away / Too shy to say / Boogie on reggae woman / Creepin' / You haven't done nothin' / It ain't no use / They won't go when I go / Bird of beauty / Please don't go. *(re-iss. Oct81) (cd-iss. Oct87 & Nov93 & May00; 157356-2)*

Aug 74. (7") *<54252>* **YOU HAVEN'T DONE NOTHIN? / BIG BROTHER** [–] [1]

Oct 74. (7") *(TMG 921)* **YOU HAVEN'T DONE NOTHIN'. / HAPPIER THAN THE MORNING SUN** [30] [–]

Nov 74. (7") *<54254>* **BOOGIE ON REGGAE WOMAN. / SEEMS SO LONG** [–] [3]

Dec 74. (7") *(TMG 928)* **BOOGIE ON REGGAE WOMAN. / EVIL** [12] [–]

Oct 76. (d-lp/d-c) *(TMPS/TC-TMSP 6002) <340>* **SONGS IN THE KEY OF LIFE** [2] [1]
– Love's in need of love today / Have a talk with God / Village ghetto land / Confusion / Sir Duke / Isn't she lovely / Joy inside my tears / Black man / I wish / Knocks me off my feet / Pastime Paradise / Summer soft / Ordinary pain / Ngiculela es una historia – I am singing / If it's magic / As / Another star. *(7"ep w.a.) (re-iss. Oct81, d-cd-iss. 1988 & Jul92 & May00; 157357-2)*

Dec 76. (7") *(TMG 1054) <54274>* **I WISH. / YOU AND I** [5] Nov76 [1]

Mar 77. (7") *<54281>* **SIR DUKE. / HE'S MISSTRA KNOW-IT-ALL** [–] [1]

Mar 77. (7") *(TMG 1068)* **SIR DUKE. / TUESDAY HEARTBREAK** [2] [–]

Aug 77. (7") *(TMG 1083) <54286>* **ANOTHER STAR. / CREEPIN'** [29] [32]

Nov 77. (7") *(TMG 1091) <54291>* **AS. / CONFUSION** [ ] [36]
(last 5 singles, except Aug77 re-iss. Oct81)

Jan 79. (t-lp) *<M-804 LP3>* **LOOKING BACK** (compilation) [–] [34]

— In Feb'79, STEVIE WONDER teamed up with DIANA ROSS, MARVIN GAYE & SMOKEY ROBINSON on minor hit single POPS WE LOVE YOU.

Nov 79. (d-lp/d-c) *(TMSP/+TC-TMSP 6009) <371>* **STEVIE WONDER'S JOURNEY THROUGH THE SECRET LIFE OF PLANTS** [8] [4]
– Earth's creation / The first garden / Voyage to India / Same old story / Venus' flytrap and the bug / Ai no, sono / Seasons / Power flower / Send one your love (instrumental) / Race babbling / Send one your love (vocal) / Outside my window / Black orchid / Ecclesiates / Kesse ye lolo de ye / Come back as a flower / A seed's a star – Tree (medley) / The secret life of plants / Tree / Finale. *<(d-cd-iss. 1986 & Sep95; 530106-2)>*

Nov 79. (7") *(TMG 1146) <54303>* **SEND ONE YOUR LOVE. / ('A'instrumental)** [52] [4]

Jan 80. (7") *(TMG 1173)* **BLACK ORCHID. / BLAME IT ON THE SUN** [63] [–]

Mar 80. (7") *(TMG 1179) <54308>* **OUTSIDE MY WINDOW. / SAME OLD STORY** [52] Feb80 [52]

Sep 80. (7")(12") *(TMG 1204) <54317>* **MASTERBLASTER (JAMMIN'). / MASTERBLASTER (dub)** [2] [5]
(last 3 singles re-iss. Oct81)

Oct 80. (lp/c) *(STMA/TC-STMA 8035) <373>* **HOTTER THAN JULY** [2] [3]
– Did I hear you say you love me / All I do / Rocket love / I ain't gonna stand for it / As if you read my mind / Masterblaster (jammin') / Do like you / Cash in your face / Lately / Happy birthday. *(re-iss. Oct81) (cd-iss. Oct87 & Apr00; E 157363-2)*

Dec 80. (7") *(TMG 1215) <54320>* **I AIN'T GONNA STAND FOR IT. / KNOCKS ME OFF MY FEET** [10] [11]

Feb 81. (7") *(TMG 1226) <54323>* **LATELY. / IF IT'S MAGIC** [3] [64]
(re-iss. Oct81)

May 81. (7") *<54328>* **DID I HEAR YOU SAY YOU LOVE ME. / AS IF YOU READ MY MIND** [–] [ ]

Jul 81. (7"/12") *(TMG/+T 1235)* **HAPPY BIRTHDAY. / HAPPY BIRTHDAY (SINGALONG)** [2] [–]

Jan 82. (7") *(TMG 1254) <1602>* **THAT GIRL. / ALL I DO** [39] [4]

— In Mar82, hit UK/US No.1 with PAUL McCARTNEY on single EBONY AND IVORY.

May 82. (7"/12") *(TMG/+T 1269/) <1612>* **DO I DO. / ROCKET LOVE** [10] [13]

May 82. (d-lp/d-c) *(TMSP/TC-TMSP 6012) <6002>* **ORIGINAL MUSIQUARIUM 1** (compilation) [8] [ ]
– Superstition / You haven't done nothin' / Living for the city / Front line / Superwoman (where were you when I needed you) / Send one your love / You are the sunshine of my life / Ribbon in the sky / Higher ground / Sir Duke / Master blaster / Boogie on reggae woman / That girl / I wish / isn't she lovely / Do I do. *(re-iss. +d-cd-'2 VOLUMES' Nov84 & Jul92)*

Sep 82. (7"/12") *(TMG/+T 1280)* **RIBBON IN THE SKY. / THE SECRET LIFE OF PLANTS** [45] [–]

Sep 82. (7") *<1639>* **RIBBON IN THE SKY. / BLACK ORCHID** [–] [54]
Dec 82, he & other Motown artist CHARLENE had US Top50 hit with USED TO BE.

Jan 83. (7"/12") *(TMG/+T 1289)* **FRONT LINE. / ('A'instrumental)** [ ] [–]

— In Aug'83, STEVIE co-wrote and sang on GARY BYRD's UK Top 10 hit 12" 'The CROWN'. Early next year, he guested on ELTON JOHN's 'I Guess That's Why They Call It The Blues'.

Aug 84. (7"/12") *(TMG/+T 1349) <1745>* **I JUST CALLED TO SAY I LOVE YOU. / ('A'instrumental)** [1] [1]

— singer **DIONNE WARWICK** features on below soundtrack

Sep 84. (lp/c) *(ZL/ZK 72285) <6108>* **THE WOMAN IN RED** (soundtrack) [2] [4]
– The woman in red / It's you (w/ DIONNE WARWICK) / It's more than you (instrumental) / I just called to say I love you / Love light in flight / Moments aren't moments (DIONNE WARWICK solo) / Weakness (w/ DIONNE WARWICK) / Don't drive drunk. *(cd-iss. Oct87; ZD 72285)*

Nov 84. (7"/12") *(TMG/+T 1364) <1769>* **LOVE LIGHT IN FLIGHT. / IT'S MORE THAN YOU** [44] [17]

Dec 84. (7"/12") *(TMG/+T 1372)* **DON'T DRIVE DRUNK. / ('A'instrumental)** [62] [–]

— In Mar'85, STEVIE featured on USA FOR AFRICA charity single, 'We Are The World'

Aug 85. (7"/12") *(ZB/ZT 40351) <1808>* **PART-TIME LOVER. / ('A'instrumental)** [3] [1]

Sep 85. (lp/c/cd) *(ZL/ZK/ZD 72005) <6134>* **IN SQUARE CIRCLE** [5] [5]
– Part-time lover / I love you too much / Whereabouts / Stranger on the shore of love / Never in the sun / Spiritual walkers / Land of la la / Go home / Overjoyed / It's wrong (apartheid). *(re-iss. cd.Nov92 & Mar96; 530046-2)*

Nov 85. (7"/12") *(ZB/ZT 40501) <1817>* **GO HOME. / ('A'instrumental)** [67] [10]

Feb 86. (7"/12") *(ZB/ZT 40567) <1832>* **OVERJOYED. / ('A'instrumental)** [17] [24]

Jun 86. (7"/12") *(WOND/+T 1) <1846>* **LAND OF LA LA. / ('A'instrumental)** [ ] [86]

Jan 87. (7"/12") *(WOND/+T 2)* **STRANGER ON THE SHORE OF LOVE. / DID I HEAR YOU SAY YOU LOVE ME** [55] [–]

Oct 87. (7"/12"/c-s) *(ZB/ZT/ZC 41439)* *<1907>* **SKELETONS. / ('A'instrumental)** [59] [19]

Nov 87. (lp/c/cd) *(ZL/ZK/ZD 72001)* *<6248>* **CHARACTERS** [33] [17]
– You will know / Dark 'n' lovely / In your corner / With each part of my heart / One of a kind / Skeletons / Get it / Galaxy Paradise / Cryin' through the night. *(c+=/cd+=)* – Come let me make your love come down / My eyes don't cry.

Jan 88. (7"/12") *(ZB/ZT 41723)* *<1919>* **YOU WILL KNOW. / ('A'instrumental)** ☐ [77]
(cd-s+=) *(ZD 41723)* – (interview).

—— In Feb88, collaborated with JULIO IGLESIAS on single MY LOVE.

May 88. (7"/12"; STEVIE WONDER & MICHAEL JACKSON) *(ZB/ZT 41883)* *<1930>* **GET IT. / GET IT (instrumental)** [37] [80]

Oct 88. (7") *(ZB 42259)* **MY EYES DON'T CRY. / ('A'instrumental)** ☐ ☐
(12"/cd-s) *(ZT/ZD 42260)* – ('A'side) / ('A'dub) / ('A'radio edit).

May 89. (7"/c-s) *(ZB/ZK 42855)* **FREE. / HAPPY BIRTHDAY** [49] ☐
(12"+=/cd-s+=) *(ZT/ZD 42856)* – It's wrong (aparteid).

Oct 90 (7"/c-s) **KEEP YOUR LOVE ALIVE. / ('A'instrumental)** ☐ ☐
(12"+=)(cd-s+=) – ('A'version).

May 91. (cd/c/lp) *(ZD/ZK/ZL 71750)* *<6291>* **JUNGLE FEVER** (soundtrack) [56] [24]
– Fun day / Queen in the black / These three words / Each other's throat / If she breaks your heart / Gotta have you / Make sure you're sure / Jungle fever / I go sailing / Chemical love / Lighting up the candles.

Jun 91. (7"/c-s) *<2081>* **GOTTA HAVE YOU. / FEEDING OFF THE LOVE OF THE LAND** ☐ [92]
(12"+=/cd-s+=) – ('A'extended mix).

Sep 91. (7"/c-s) *(ZB/ZK 44957)* **FUN DAY. / ('A'instrumental)** [63] ☐
(12"+=/cd-s+=) *(ZT/ZD 44958)* – ('A'remix) / ('A'club mix).

Feb 95. (7"/c-s) *(TMG/+CS 1437)* *<0290>* **FOR YOUR LOVE. / ('A'mix)** [23] [53]
(cd-s+=) – My Cherie amour/ Uptight (everything's alright).

Mar 95. (cd/c) *(530238-2/-4)* *<0238>* **CONVERSATION PEACE** [8] [16]
– Rain your love down / Edge of eternity / Taboo to love / Take the time out / I'm new / My love is with you / Treat myself / Tomorrow Robins will sing / Sensuous whisper / For your love / Cold chill / Sorry / Conversation peace.

Jul 95. (c-s) *(860 356-4)* **TOMORROW ROBINS WILL SING / ('A'-Wonder West side version)** [71] ☐
(12") *(860 373-1)* – ('A'-Ronin smooth) / ('A'-Dance Hall) / ('A'-Slo jungle).
(cd-s) *(860 373-2)* – ('A'side) / (above 3 tracks).

Oct 95. (c-s) *(860 464-4)* **COLD CHILL / ('A'mix)** ☐ ☐
(12"+=/cd-s+=) *(860 465-1/-2)* – ('A'mixes).

Oct 95. (d-cd/d-c) *(530546-2/-4)* *<0546>* **NATURAL WONDER – LIVE IN CONCERT** (live) ☐ ☐
– Love's in need of love today / Master blaster (jammin') / Higher ground / Rocket love / Ribbon in the sky / Pastime paradise / If it's magic / Village ghetto land / Tomorrow robins will sing / Overjoyed / My Cherie amour / Signed, sealed, delivered (I'm yours) / Living for the city / Sir Duke / I wish / You are the sunshine of my life / Superstition / I just called to say I love you / For your love / Another star / Stevie Ray blues / Ms. and Mr. little ones / Stay gold.

—— in mid 1996, STEVIE provided songs/versions ('Kiss Lonely Good-Bye' & 'Hold On To Your Dream') for the children's fantasy movie, 'The Adventures Of Pinocchio'.

—— in Dec'03, STEVIE (& ANGIE STONE) featured on BLUE's No.11 UK hit cover of 'Signed, Sealed, Delivered (I'm Yours)'

May 05. (7"/cd-s) *(TMG/+CD 1510)* **SO WHAT THE FUSS. / (remix feat. Q-TIP)** [19] [96]
(cd-s+=) *(TMGCDX 1510)* – ('A'-Global soul radio mix).
(12"+=) *<B0005140-11>* – Signed, sealed, delivered, I'm yours.

Oct 05. (cd) *(9882094)* *<2402>* **A TIME TO LOVE** [24] [5]
– If your love cannot be moved / Sweetest somebody I know / Moon blue / From the bottom of my heart / Please don't hurt my baby / How will I know / My love is on fire / Passionate raindrops / Tell your heart I love you / True love / Shelter in the rain / So what the fuss / Can't imagine love without you / Positivity / A time to love.

Nov 05. (7") *(TMG 1512)* **POSITIVITY. / IF YOU REALLY LOVE ME** [54] [-]
(cd-s) *(TMGCD 1512)* – ('A') / Master blaster (jammin') – 12" version / Happy birthday – 12" version.

Feb 06. (7") *(TMG 1513)* **FROM THE BOTTOM OF MY HEART. / EVERY TIME I SEE YOU I GO WILD** ☐ Nov05 ☐
(cd-s) *(TMGCD 1513)* – ('A') / Pastime paradise / Part-time lover (12" version).
(cd-s) *<B0004964-32>* – ('A') / ('A'-version).

– (selective) compilations, etc. –

note; on 'Tamla Motown' until otherwise stated

Dec 77. (d-lp/d-c) *(M9 804)* *<804>* **ANTHOLOGY** ☐ ☐
(both above re-iss. Oct81)

Oct 86. (cd) *(ZD 72489)* **FOR ONCE IN MY LIFE / UPTIGHT** ☐ ☐

Oct 86. (cd) *(ZD 72453)* **MY CHERIE AMOUR / SIGNED, SEALED, DELIVERED, I'M YOURS** ☐ ☐

Jun 87. (d-lp/d-c/d-cd) *(WL/WK/ZD 72585)* **THE ESSENTIAL** ☐ ☐
(d-cd re-iss. Jan93; 530047-2)

Jul 87. (cd) *(ZD 72558)* **DOWN TO EARTH / I WAS MADE TO LOVE YOU** ☐ ☐

Nov 84. (lp/c) *Telstar; (STA R/C 2251)* **LOVE SONGS – 16 CLASSIC HITS** [20] [-]
(re-iss. +cd.Jul86 & Jan 93 as '20 CLASSIC HITS' on 'Motown'; 530037-2) – (4 extra tracks).

Nov 96. (cd/c) *(530757-2/-4)* **SONG REVIEW – A GREATEST HITS COLLECTION** [19] ☐

Jan 00. (cd) *(153928-2)* **THE BALLAD COLLECTION** ☐ ☐

Jan 00. (cd) *Universal; (E 157261-2)* **UNIVERSAL MASTERS COLLECTION** ☐ ☐

Feb 00. (cd) *Spectrum; (544211-2)* **MOTOWN EARLY CLASSICS** ☐ ☐

Mar 00. (4xcd-box) *(153992-2)* **AT THE CLOSE OF THE CENTURY** ☐ ☐

Oct 00. (d-cd) *Universal; (E 159048-2)* **INNERVISIONS / FULFILLINGNESS FIRST FINALE** ☐ ☐

Oct 00. (d-cd) *Universal; (E 159049-2)* **TALKING BOOK / MUSIC OF MY MIND** ☐ ☐

Oct 02. (d-cd) *Universal TV; <(066502-2)>* **THE DEFINITIVE COLLECTION** [16] ☐
– Superstition / Sir Duke / I wish / Masterblaster (jammin') / Isn't she lovely / I just called to say I love you / Ebony and ivory (with PAUL McCARTNEY) / As / Never had a dream come true / I was made to love her / Heaven help us all / Overjoyed / Lately / For your love / If you really love me / Higher ground / Do I do / Living for the city / Part-time lover / For once in my life / Uptight (everything's alright) / We can work it out / Signed, sealed, delivered (I'm yours) / Yester-me, yester-you, yesterday / I'm wondering / My cherie amour / You are the sunshine of my life / I don't know why (I love you) / A place in the sun / Blowin' in the wind / Send one your love / Pastime paradise / I ain't gonna stand for it / Fingertips (parts 1-2) / Boogie on reggae woman / You haven't done nothin' / He's misstra know it all / Happy birthday.

Oct 02. (cd) *<AA440 066164-2>* **THE DEFINITIVE COLLECTION** [-] [35]
– Fingertips part 2 (live) / Uptight (everything's alright) / Hey love / I was made to love her / For once in my life / My cherie amour / Signed, sealed, delivered (I'm yours) / You are the sunshine of my life / Superstition / Higher ground / Living for the city / You haven't done nothin' / Boogie on reggae woman / I wish / Sir Duke / Masterblaster (jammin') / That girl / Do I do / I just called to say I love you / Overjoyed / Part-time lover.

☐ Roy WOOD (see under ⇒ MOVE)

☐ Richard WRIGHT (see under ⇒ PINK FLOYD)

WU-TANG CLAN

Formed: Staten Island, New York, USA . . . 1992 by the RZA (aka THE ABBOT) and a posse of several young rappers under the pseudonyms; METHOD MAN, GENIUS/GZA, CHEF RAEKWON, OL' DIRTY BASTARD, GHOSTFACE KILLAH and U-GOD. The RZA was originally a solo artist (who at one point stood trial for murder) and the man responsible for forming GRAVEDIGGAZ, a gothic hip hop outfit who later worked with TRICKY. All chess-loving, blunt-smoking wordsmiths, the 'CLAN were highly influenced by martial art movies and took their name from the WU-TANG or SHAOLIN sword. In 1991, GENIUS released a debut album for 'Cold Chillin'', 'WORDS FROM THE GENIUS', followed a year later by the 'CLAN's first single, the self-financed, 'PROTECT YA NECK'. The following year, the conglomerate signed for 'R.C.A.', although each member was allowed to retain his separate contract, if he had one. In 1993, complete with Kung-Fu style movie samples, WU-TANG CLAN's acclaimed debut 'ENTER THE WU-TANG (36 CHAMBERS)', scaled the US charts and showed the socially aware, wise-cracking gang in full flow. With their lavish use of sampled jazz/soul, loping beats and breathtaking, expletive-filled spitfire rapping, the crew opened up a whole new chapter of the ever unfolding hip hop saga and, for a while at least, breathed some spliff-heavy air into a stagnant scene. However, in March the following year, tragedy struck when U-GOD's toddler son, Dante, was seriously injured by a bullet in a crossfire battle. 1995 proved to be a busy and commercially fruitful year for most of the gang, especially OL' DIRTY BASTARD, METHOD MAN, CHEF RAEKWON and GENIUS/GZA, the latter unleashing the highly praised 'LIQUID SWORDS' set later that year. WU-TANG themselves made a belated return in 1997 with the feverishly anticipated 'WU-TANG FOREVER', an album which broke records by gatecrashing/topping both the US and UK charts simultaneously, an incredible feat for a hip hop act. Even more surprisingly, the set was a double; on reflection, the material could have been pared down to a blistering single disc although the schizophrenic combination of melodic but hard-bitten soul and frenetic rapping was rarely less engaging. Early in '98, GHOSTFACE KILLAH was jailed for three months on a 1995! attempted robbery charge, while on June 30th, OL' DIRTY BASTARD was wounded in the back and arm after being shot by an intruder (in his cousin's New York apartment); he er, discharged himself a day later! ODB was up on a number of separate charges the following year in which he was alleged to have threatened security guards then (a few months later) his girlfriend before topping it all off with a shoot-out with the police; the latter would see him charged with attempted murder, although after a short-stay in jail (a six-figure bail was paid) this case – and later the others – was thrown out due to lack of evidence. Were they out to get 'im, who knows? The rapper (who was admitted to a drug rehabilitation center in August '99) was back on the record front soon after, 'N***A PLEASE' (1999) the RICK JAMES-meets-IGGY POP-stylings making it the best WU-TANG platter for some time. In fact, mostly all the 'CLAN were at the solo game in the last few years, INSPECTAH DECK philosophising with his 'UNCONTROLLED SUBSTANCE' (in September also), the GENIUS/GZA swordsman with 'BENEATH THE SURFACE' (in July '99) and master CLANsman RZA with their 'HITS' package (also in July) – RZA, wrote, produced, directed and starred in his own movie, 'BOBBY DIGITAL', which also featured WU-TANG members and was released late in '98. Around the same time, METHOD MAN made a re-appearance with 'TICAL 2000: JUDGEMENT DAY', while KILLAH PRIEST (via 'HEAVY MENTAL') and CAPPADONNA (via 'THE PILLAGE') were both out and about in March of 1998 – note also that GHOSTFACE KILLAH issued his solo 'IRONMAN' in October '96. Phew! and is if that wasn't enough, towards the end of the decade, CHEF RAEKWON added 'IMMOBILARITY' to WU-TANG's stock-pile release schedule, while METHOD MAN (and "outsider" REDMAN) had their 'BLACKOUT!' collaboration – all albums, monster sellers in the big U.S. of A. Come the new millennium, it was only fitting that the apocalyptically inclined CLAN get back together for another dose of street-poet doom-mongering. 'THE W' (2000) pared both the running time and sound back to a digestible level, resulting in a tighter, tougher and ultimately more menacing rhythmic and lyrical flow. It also focused and concentrated their brooding essence, which had arguably been dispersed in the avalanche of solo projects. The surfeit of guest collaborators (everyone from SNOOP DOGG to JUNIOR REID) may have detracted from RZA's sonic originality but when it resulted in such gutter-scarred ferocity as 'LET MY NIGGAS LIVE', this seemed a minor quibble. GHOSTFACE KILLAH released his feisty sophomore effort, 'SUPREME CLIENTELE' (2000), the same year, utilising a raft of producers to create a comfortingly belligerent sound absent on the tarted-up 'BULLETPROOF WALLETS' (2001). The WU-TANG CLAN no doubt surprised even themselves by getting their shit together two years in a row. Even more surprising, perhaps, 'IRON FLAG' (2001) – with ODB – was another focused effort, RZA keeping the production frills to a minimum on a set that was closer in spirit to their East Coast roots. Solo outings in 2001 came courtesy of RZA's BOBBY DIGITAL ('DIGITAL BULLET'), while the same man brought out two sets, the Various Artists 'THE WORLD ACCORDING TO RZA' and the "real" solo 'BIRTH OF A PRINCE'; he also contributed to Quentin Tarantino's 'Kill Bill Vol.1' martial arts movie. A year previous to this saw ODB branch out on his own label 'D-3' (having been dissed by 'Elektra' after his drug busts) for the extremely disappointing 'THE TRIALS AND TRIBULATIONS OF RUSSELL JONES' (2002); sadly the man would be dead by the 13th of November 2004. The WU-TANG members continued a run of solo outings, namely 'LEGEND OF THE LIQUID SWORD' (2002) – by GZA/GENIUS, 'THE MOVEMENT' (2003) – by INSPECTAH DECK, 'THE LEX DIAMOND STORY' – by RAEKWON, 'THE PRETTY TONEY ALBUM' (2003) – by GHOSTFACE, 'TICAL 0: THE PREQUEL' (2004) – by METHOD MAN, before they all teamed up in July 2004 to release the live 'DISCIPLES OF THE 36 CHAMBERS: CHAPTER 1' that September. Having had a string of hits, collaborations, etc., etc., GHOSTFACE KILLAH once again er, scaled the US Top 10 with the excellent, 'FISHSCALE' (2006).

Album rating: ENTER THE WU-TANG (36 CHAMBERS) (*8) / WU-TANG FOREVER (*7) / WU-TANG RECORDS PRESENTS: WU-CHRONICLES various artists compilation (*5) / Genius/GZA: WORDS FROM THE GENIUS (*6) / LIQUID SWORDS (*8) / BENEATH THE SURFACE (*7) / LEGEND OF THE LIQUID SWORD (*5) / Ol' Dirty Bastard: RETURN TO THE 36 CHAMBERS (*7) / N***A PLEASE (*8) / THE DIRTY STORY compilation (*6) / THE TRIALS AND TRIBULATIONS OF RUSSELL JONES (*4) / OSIRUS: THE OFFICIAL MIXTAPE (*6) / FREE TO BE DIRTY: LIVE! (*3) / Method Man: TICAL (*7) / TICAL 2000: JUDGEMENT DAY (*7) / BLACKOUT! with Redman (*6) / HOW HIGH soundtrack with Redman (*6) / TICAL 0: THE PREQUEL (*4) / Raekwon: ONLY BUILT 4 CUBAN LINX (*7) / IMMOBILARITY (*5) / THE LEX DIAMOND STORY (*6) / Ghostface Killah: IRONMAN (*7) / SUPREME CLIENTELE (*6) / BULLETPROOF WALLETS (*4) / THE PRETTY TONEY ALBUM (*6) / FISHSCALE (*7) / RZA: RZA AS BOBBY DIGITAL IN STEREO (*6) / THE RZA HITS various artists compilation (*7) / GHOST DOG: THE WAY OF THE SAMURAI soundtrack (*6) / DIGITAL BULLET (*6) / THE WORLD ACCORDING TO RZA Various Artists (*4) / BIRTH OF A PRINCE (*5) / Inspectah Deck: UNCONTROLLED SUBSTANCE (*7) / THE MOVEMENT (*6) / Wu-Tang Clan: THE W (*7) / IRON FLAG (*6) / DISCIPLES OF THE 36 CHAMBERS: CHAPTER 1 (*4) / LEGEND OF THE WU-TANG CLAN: WU-TANG CLAN'S GREATEST HITS compilation (*7)

RZA (b. ROBERT DIGGS, 22 Aug'66) – producer, mixer / rappers **GENIUS** (aka GZA and MAXIMILLIAN) (b. GARY PRICE, 22 Aug'66) **METHOD MAN** (aka JOHNNY BLAZE and SHAQUAN) (b. CLIFFORD SMITH, 1 Apr'71) / **OL' DIRTY BASTARD** (aka DIRT McDIRT and OSIRIS) (b. RUSSELL JONES, 15 Nov'68) / **RAEKWON** (aka CHEF and LEX DIAMONDS) (b. COREY WOODS) / **GHOSTFACE KILLAH** (aka TONY STARKS) (b. DENNIS COLES, 9 May'70) / **U-GOD** (aka GOLDEN ARMS) (b. LAMONT HAWKINS) / **INSPECTAH DECK** (aka REBEL INS) (b. JASON HUNTER) / **CAPPADONNA** (aka CAPPUCCINO and TRACK SLASHER) (b. DARRYL HILL) / with other early members **MASTA KILLAH** (aka NOODLES and JAMAL) (b. ELGIN TURNER) / **SHYLEIM THE RUGGED PRINCE (PAUL) / DOLLY FINGERS / DREDDY KRUGER / KILLAH PRIEST** (b. WILLIAM REED) (of SUNZ OF MAN) / **4th DISCIPLE**

		Loud-RCA	Loud-RCA
May 93.	(c-s)(12",cd-s) *<62544>* *<62530>* **PROTECT YA NECK. / (mixes)**	–	

Sep 93. (c-s,cd-s) <62544> **METHOD MAN / PROTECT YA NECK** [-] [69]
Feb 94. (c-s,12",cd-s) <62829> **C.R.E.A.M. (CASH RULES EVERYTHING AROUND ME). / DA MYSTERY OF CHESSBOXIN'** [-] [60]
May 94. (cd/c) *(74321 20367-2/-4)* <66336> **ENTER THE WU-TANG (36 CHAMBERS)** [ ] Nov93 [41]
– Bring da ruckus / Shame on a nigga / Clan in da front / Wu-Tang: 7th chamber / Can it all be so simple / (intermission) / Da mystery of chessboxin' / Wu-Tang Clan ain't nuthing ta f'wit / C.R.E.A.M. / Method Man / Protect ya neck / Tearz / Wu-Tang: 7th chamber – part II. *(cd+=)* – Method Man (skunk mix) / (conclusion).

— were back (**RZA The Abbott / GZA The Genius / DIRTY Osirus / U-GOD Golden Arms / METHOD MAN Hott Nikkels / RAEKWON Lex Diamonds / GHOSTFACE KILLAH Ironman / INSPECTAH DECK Fifth Brother / MASTA KILLAH High Chief / CAPPADONNA Jaybird,** plus STREET LIFE, TEKITHA or POPPA WU and UNCLE PETE / **TRUEMASTER** (b. DAVID HARRIS) a new member now on tour

Jun 97. (d-cd/d-c) *(74321 45769-2/-4)* <66905> **WU-TANG FOREVER** [1] [1]
– Wu-revolution / Reunited / For Heaven's sake / Cash still rules – Scary hours (still don't nothing move but the money) / Visionz / As high as Wu-Tang get / Severe punishment / Older gods / Maria / A better tomorrow / It's yourz / / Intro / Triumph / Impossible / Little ghetto boys / Deadly melody / The city / The projects / Bells of war / The M.G.M. / Dog sh*t / Duck seazon / Hellz wind staff / Heaterz / Black shampoo / Second coming / The closing / Sunshower / Projects international remix.
Aug 97. (12"/cd-s) *(74321 49678-1/-2)* **TRIUMPH. / PROJECTS INTERNATIONAL** [ ] [ ]
(cd-s+=) *(74321 51021-2)* – Diesel.
(above featured CAPPADONNA)

— In Mar'98, the WU-TANG CLAN featured on TEXAS's new UK Top 5 version of 'SAY WHAT YOU WANT'

Aug 98. (cd/c/d-lp; as RZA presents WU-TANG KILLA BEES) <*(50013)*> **THE SWARM VOLUME 1** [ ] Jul98 [4]
– (Various cuts from some of the WU-TANG CLAN and new talents including SUNZ OF MAN and BLACK KNIGHTS OF THE NORTH STAR)
Mar 99. (cd/d-lp) *(WT 004 CD/LP)* <51143> **WU-TANG RECORDS PRESENTS: WU-CHRONICLES** (V/A compilation) [ ] [25]
(above 2 issued on 'Wu-Tang Records')
Nov 00. (c-s) *(670518-4)* **GRAVEL PIT / PROTECT YA NECK (THE JUMP OFF) (dirty)** [6] [ ]
(12"+=) *(670518-6)* – Protect ya neck (the jump off) (Dirty DJ mix).
(cd-s++=) *(670518-2)* – ('A'-video).
Nov 00. (cd/c/d-lp) *(499576-2/-4/-1)* <62193> **THE W** [19] [5]
– Intro (Shaolin finger jab) – Chamber music / Careful (click, click) / Hollow bones / Redbull (with REDMAN) / One blood under W (with JUNIOR READ) / Conditioner (with SNOOP DOGG) / Protect ya neck (the jump off) / Let my niggas live (with NAS) / I can't go to sleep (with ISAAC HAYES) / Do you really (thang, thang) (with ISAAC HAYES) / Monument (with BUSTA RHYMES) / Gravel pit / Jah world (with JUNIOR READ).
Dec 01. (cd) *(504752-2)* <86236> **IRON FLAG** [ ] [32]
– In the hood / Rules / Chrome wheels / Soul power (black jungle) / Uzi (pinky ring) / One of these days / Ya'll been warned / Babies / Radioactive (four assassins) / Back in the game (with RON ISLEY) / Iron flag / Dashing (reasons).

Sanctuary Sanctuary

Oct 04. (cd) *(SANCD 314)* <84727> **DISCIPLES OF THE 36 CHAMBERS: CHAPTER 1** (live) [ ] [82]
– Bring da ruckus / Da mystery of chessboxin' / Clan in da front / C.R.E.A.M. / Wu-Tang Clan ain't nuthin' ta f' wit / Shame on a nigga / Ghost Deini / Re-united / For heaven's sake / Criminology / Incarcerated scarfaces / Brooklyn zoo / Bring the pain / It's yourz / Liquid swords / One blood under W / Ice cream / Triumph / Hood / Run / Run / Tearz / Method Man / Dog shit / Shimmy shimmy ya / Y'all been warned / Gravel pit.

B.M.G. B.M.G.

Oct 04. (cd) *(82876 61645-2)*> **LEGEND OF THE WU-TANG CLAN: WU-TANG CLAN'S GREATEST HITS** (compilation) [ ] [72]
– C.R.E.A.M. / Method Man / Pretoct ya neck / Can it all be so simple / Shame on a nigga / Da mystery of chessboxin' / Reunited / It's yourz / Triumph / Gravel pit / Protect ya neck (the jump off) / Sucker M.C.'s / Uzi (pinky ring) / Shaolin worldwide / Diesel.

– other associated releases, etc. –

OL' DIRTY BASTARD

Elektra Elektra

Feb 95. (c-s,cd-s) <64477> **BROOKLYN ZOO / ('A'remix)** [-] [54]
Mar 95. (cd/c) <*(7559 61659-2/-4)*> **RETURN TO THE 36 CHAMBERS** (dirty version) [ ] [7]
– Intro / Shimmy shimmy ya / Baby c'mon / Brooklyn zoo / Hippa to da hoppa / Raw hide / Damage / Don't u know / The stomp / Goin' down / Drunk game (sweet sugar pie) / Snakes / Brooklyn zoo II (tiger crane) / Proteck ya neck II the zoo / Cuttin' headz / Dirty dancin' / Harlem world. *(cd+=)* – (2 extra).
May 95. (c-s,12"/cd-s) <66419> **SHIMMY SHIMMY YA. / ('A'version)** [-] [62]

— In Jun'97, ODB featured on The ALKOHOLIKS minor US hit, 'Hip Hop Drunkies'. A month later, he was also on the BLACKstreet hit single, 'Fix'.

Sep 99. (cd/c) <*(7559 62414-2/-4)*> **N***A PLEASE** [ ] [10]
– Recognize / I can't wait / Cold blooded / Got your money / Rollin' wit' you / Getting high / You don't want to fuck with me / Nigga please / Dirt dog / I want pussy / Good morning heartache / All in together now.
Nov 99. (c-s/12"/cd-s; as OL' DIRTY BASTARD featuring KELIS) *(E 3719 C/T/CD)* <*radio cut*> **GOT YOUR MONEY / ROLLIN' WITH YOU** [ ] Oct99 [33]
Jun 00. (c-s/12"/cd-s; by OL' DIRTY BASTARD feat. KELIS) *(E 7077 C/T/CD)* **GOT YOUR MONEY (mixes)** [11] [ ]
Oct 01. (cd/lp) <*(7559 62683-2/-1)*> **THE DIRTY STORY: THE BEST OF OL' DIRTY BASTARD** (compilation) [ ] [ ]

— he left the CLAN before 'IRON FLAG'; ODB hit US No.33 with his next set, 'THE TRIALS AND TRIBULATIONS OF RUSSELL JONES' (2002).

METHOD MAN

— with RZA on co-writing credits

Def Jam Def Jam

Nov 94. (c-s,cd-s) <*85-3964*> **BRING THE PAIN / ('A'radio version)** [-] [45]
Apr 95. (12") *(12DEF 6)* <*85-4184*> **RELEASE YO' DELF / (3 'A'mixes)** [46] Feb95 [98]
(cd-s+=) *(DEFCD 6)* – (2 'A'mixes) / Bring the pain (remix).
Jul 95. (cd-s; METHOD MAN featuring MARY J. BLIGE) *(DEFDX 11)* <*85-1878*> **I'LL BE THERE FOR YOU / YOU'RE ALL I NEED TO GET BY** [10] Apr95 [3]
(12"+=) *(12DEF 11)* – Bring the pain (remix).
(cd-s++=) *(DEFCD 11)* – Release yo' delf.
Aug 95. (cd/c) *(529 174-2/-4)* <523839> **TICAL** [ ] [4]
– Tical / Biscuits / Bring the pain / All I need / What the blood clot / Meth Vs. Chef / Sub crazy / Release yo' delf / P.L.O. style / I get my thang in action / Mr. Sandman / Stimulation / Method Man (remix) / I'll be there for you – You're all I need to get by (featuring MARY J. BLIGE).

— In Aug'95, METHOD MAN was credited with REDMAN on the single, 'HOW HIGH', which hit US No.13. In Oct'95, MM featured on CAPLETON's minor hit 'Wings Of The Morning'. Below from the movie, 'Batman Forever' on 'Atlantic' records.

Oct 95. (c-s,cd-s) <*87100*> **THE RIDDLER / ('A'-Riddler Hide-Out mix)** [-] [56]
Nov 98. (cd/d-lp) <*(558 920-2/-1)*> **TICAL 2000: JUDGEMENT DAY** [49] [2]
– 1999: Judgement day (intro) / Perfect world / Cradle rock (featuring LEFT EYE) / Dangerous grounds (featuring STREETLIFE) / Sweet love (skit) / Sweet love (featuring CAPPADONNA & STREETLIFE) / Shaolin what (skit) / Torture / Where's Method Man? (skit featuring ED LOVER) / Suspect chin music (featuring STREETLIFE) / Retro godfather / Dooney boy / Spazzola (featuring STREETLIFE, RAEKWON, MASTA KILLA, KILLER SIN & INSPECTAH DECK) / Check writer (skit) / 2000: You play too much (CHRIS ROCK & METHOD MAN) / Party crasher / Grid iron rap (featuring STREETLIFE) / Step by step / Play IV keeps (featuring INSPECTAH DECK, STREETLIFE & MOBB DEPP) / Donald Trump / Snuffed out (skit featuring STREETLIFE) / Elements (featuring STAR & POLITE) / Killin' fields / Big dogs (featuring REDMAN) / Break ups 2 make ups (featuring D'ANGELO) / Message from Penny / Judgement day / C.E.O.utro.
Feb 99. (c-s/cd-s; as METHOD MAN featuring D'ANGELO) <563405> **BREAK UPS 2 MAKE UPS / DANGEROUS GROUNDS (featuring Streetlife) / I'LL BE THERE FOR YOU – YOU'RE ALL I NEED TO GET BY** [-] [98]
Mar 99. (12"/cd-s) *(566 851-1/845-2)* **JUDGEMENT DAY / (mixes)** [ ] [ ]

May 99. (12"/cd-s; by METHOD MAN featuring D'ANGELO) *(870927-1/-2)* **BREAK UPS 2 MAKE UPS (mixes).** [33] [–]
(cd-s) *(870929-2)* – (mixes).

Sep 99. (cd/lp; by METHOD MAN & REDMAN) <*(546609-2/-1)*> **BLACKOUT!** [45] [3]
– A special joint (intro) / Tear it off / Mi casa / Maaad crew / The? / Cheka / 1, 2, 1, 2 / Da rockwilder / Run 4 cover / 4 seasons / Dat's dat shit / Blackout / Y.O.U. / Cereal killer / Fire ina hole / Where we at (skit) / Well all rite cha / Big dogs / How high.

— in Nov'99, METHOD MAN featured on US singles by D'ANGELO ('Left & Right') and LIMP BIZKIT ('N 2 Gether Now')

Dec 01. (cd-s; by METHOD MAN & REDMAN) <*588891*> **PART II** [–] [72]

Dec 01. (cd/c; by METHOD MAN & REDMAN) <*(586628-2/-4)*> **HOW HIGH** (soundtrack w/ Various Artists) [ ] [ ]
– (intro) / Part II / Round & round – remix (solo w/ JONELL) / Cisco kid (feat. WAR & CYPRESS HILL) / America's most wanted / Let's do it / (REDMAN track) / N2gether (solo w/ LIMP BIZKIT) / (other artists) / Da Rockwilder / Bring da pain (solo) / (REDMAN track) / All I need (solo w/ MARY J. BLIGE) / Big dogs / How high.
also in Dec'01, METHOD MAN featured on JONELL's hit, 'Round & Round'
in Sep'03, he feat. on MARY J. BLIGE's hit, 'Love @ First Sight'

May 04. (cd-s; feat. BUSTA RHYMES) *(9862517)* **WHAT'S HAPPENIN'** [17] [ ]

May 04. (cd) <*(548405-2)*> **TICAL 0: THE PREQUEL** [29] [2]
– Intro / The prequel / Say what / What's happenin' (feat. BUSTA RHYMES) / The motto / We some dogs / The turn / Tease / Rodeo / Baby come on / Who ya rollin wit / Never hold back / The show / Act right / Afterparty / Crooked letter I / Ridin' for outro.

RAEKWON

Loud-RCA Loud-RCA

Jul 95. (c-s,cd-s) <*64375*> **GLACIERS OF ICE / CRIMINOLOGY** [–] [43]

Aug 95. (cd/c; as CHEF RAEKWON) <*(07863 66663-2/-4)*> **ONLY BUILT 4 CUBAN LINX . . .** [ ] [4]
– Striving for perfection / Knuckleheadz / Knowledge god / Criminology / Incarcerated scarfaces / Rainy dayz / Guillotine (swordz) / Can it all be so simple (remix) / Shark niggas (biters) / Ice water / Glaciers of ice / Verbal intercourse / Wisdom body / Spot rusherz / Ice cream / Wu-Gambinos / Heaven G Hell. *(cd+=)* – North Star (jewels).

Oct 95. (c-s,cd-s) <*64426*> **INCARCERATED SCARFACES / ICE CREAM** [–] [37] [71]

— RAEKWON featured on FAT JOE's minor US hit 'FIREWATER' / 'ENVY'

Loud-Epic Loud-Columbia

Nov 99. (cd/c/lp) *(496361/-2/-4/-1)* <*63844*> **IMMOBILARITY** [ ] [9]
– Intro / Yae yo / Casablanca / 100 rounds / Real life / Power / Skit No.1 / All I got is you pt.II / Jury / Fuck them / Skit No.2 / Live from New York / My favourite dred / Friday / The table / Sneakers / Raw / Pop shit / Heart to heart / Forecast / Outro.

Universal Universal

Dec 03. (cd) <*(B000 17160-2)*> **THE LEX DIAMOND STORY** [ ] [ ]
– The Lex Diamond intro / Pit bull fights / (hitman salary – skit) / King of kings / Missing watch / All over again / Clientele kidd / Smith Bros. / (restaurant skit) / Robbery / (f**k you skit) / Pa-blow Escablow / Musketeers of pig alley / Ices cream part 2 / The hood / (wild chimpanzees slit) / Planet of the apes / Wyld in da club / Once upon a time / Lex Diamond story outro.

GENIUS/GZA

with some of the posse

Geffen Geffen

Oct 95. (c-s)(cd-s) <*19390*> **LIQUID SWORDS / LABELS** [–] [48]

Nov 95. (cd/c/lp) <*(GED/GEC/GEF 24813)*> **LIQUID SWORDS** [73] [9]
– Killah Hills 10304 / Liquid swords / Living in the world today / Investigative reports / Duel of the Iron Mic / Labels / Cold world / Gold / I gotcha back / Swordsman / 4th chamber / Shadowboxin' / B.I.B.L.E. (Basic Instructions Before Leaving Earth) / Hell's wind staff / Unexplained.

Feb 96. (c-s; GENIUS/GZA featuring Inspektah Deck a.k.a. Rollie Fingers) *(GFSC 2214)* <*19391*> **COLD WORLD (RZA mix) / COLD WORLD (power mix)** [40] Dec95 [97]
(12"+=/cd-s+=) *(GFST/+D 2214)* – B.I.B.L.E.
above featuring D'ANGELO

Mar 96. (c-s,cd-s; GENIUS/GZA featuring METHOD MAN) <*19396*> **SHADOWBOXIN' / (instrumental) / SHADOWBOXIN' (2 versions)** [–] [67]

M.C.A. M.C.A.

Jul 99. (cd/d-lp as GZA) <*(MCD/MCA 11969)*> **BENEATH THE SURFACE** [56] [9]
– Intro / Amplified sample / Beneath the surface / Skit 1 / Skit 2 / Crash your crew / Breaker breaker / High price small reward / Hip hop fury / Skit 3 / 1112 / Skit 4 / Victim / Publicity / Feel like an enemy / Stingplay (like dis – like dat) / Mic trippin' / Outro.

Dec 02. (cd) <*(113083-2)*> **LEGEND OF THE LIQUID SWORD** [ ] [ ]
– Intro / Auto bio / Did ya say that / Silent / Knock, knock / Stay in line / Animal planet / Fam (members only) / Legend of the Liquid Sword / Fame / Highway robbery / Luminal / Sparring minds / Rough cut / Uncut material.

RZA

not iss. Big Beat

Aug 96. (c-s,cd-s; RZA featuring METHOD MAN & CAPPADONNA) <*98045*> **WU-WEAR: THE GARMENT RENAISSANCE / GET DOWN FOR MINE (REAL LIVE)** [–] [60]
(above from the film, 'High School High')

Gee Street V2

Nov 98. (cd/d-lp) *(GEE 100380-2/-1)* <*32521*> **RZA AS BOBBY DIGITAL IN STEREO** [70] [16]
– Intro / B.O.B.B.Y. / Unspoken word / Slow grind African / Airwaves / Love Jones / N.Y.C. everything / Mantis / Slow grind French / Holocaust (silkworm) / Terrorist / Bobby did it (Spanish fly) / Handwriting on the wall / Kiss of a black widow / Slow grindi Italian / My lovin' is digi / Domestic violence / Project talk / Lab drunk / Fuck what you think / Daily routine.

Epic Epic

Jun 99. (cd/c) *(492542-2/-4)* <*69610*> **THE RZA HITS** (V/A compilation) [ ] [61]
– RZA: (narration) / WU-TANG CLAN: Wu-Tang Clan ain't nothin' to fuck with / Protect ya neck / OL' DIRTY BASTARD: Shimmy / GENIUS/GZA: Liquid swords / METHOD MAN: Method man / RAEKWON THE CHEF: Incarcerated surfaces / Ice cream / RZA: (narration) / METHOD MAN: Bring the pain / GHOSTFACE KILLAH; Winter warz / OL' DIRTY BASTARD: Brooklyn zoo / METHOD MAN: All I need / WU-TANG CLAN: Cream / GHOSTFACE KILLAH: All that I got is you / RZA: (narration) / WU-TANG CLAN: Wu wear the garment renaissance.

not iss. Victor

Dec 99. (cd) <*VICP 60944*> **GHOST DOG: THE WAY OF THE SAMURAI** (soundtrack) [–] Japan [–]
– Ghost Dog theme (WITH DOGS & EFX) / Opening theme (raise your sword) instrumental / Flying birds / Samurai theme / Gangsters theme / Dead birds / Fast shadow – version 1 (WU-TANG CLAN) / RZA #7 / Funky theme / RZA's theme / Samurai showdown (raise your sword) / Ghost Dog theme / Fast shadow – version 2 (WU-TANG CLAN) / Untitled #8 *[not in film]* / Untitled #12 – free jazz *[not in film]* / Wu-world order – version 1 (WU-TANG CLAN) *[not in film]. <re-iss. Nov01 on 'J.V.C.'; 81047>*

Koch Int. Koch Int.

Sep 01. (cd-s; as BOBBY DIGITAL) *(KOCDS 8335)* **LA RHUMBA / LA RHUMBA (dirty) / LA RHUMBA (instrumental) / LA RHUMBA (acappella) / SHOW U LOVE (dirty)** [ ] [ ]

Sep 01. (cd/lp; RZA as BOBBY DIGITAL) <*(KOC CD/LP 8182)*> **DIGITAL BULLET** [ ] [24]
– Show U love / Can't loose / Glocko pop / Must be Bobby / Brooklyn babies / Domestic violence (part 2) / Do U / Fools / La rhumba / Black widow (part 2) / Shady / Break bread / Bong bong / Throw your flag up / Be a man / Righteous way / Build strong / Sickness.

Virgin E.M.I.

Apr 03. (cd/d-lp; Various Artists) *(CD/LP VIR 207)* <*584255*> **THE WORLD ACCORDING TO RZA** [ ] [ ]

Sanctuary Sanctuary

Oct 03. (cd) *(SANCD 231)* <*84652*> **THE BIRTH OF A PRINCE** [ ] [49]
– Bob n' L / The grunge / We pop / Grits / Fast cars / Chi kung / You'll never know / Drink, smoke + fcuk / The whistle / The drop off / Wherever I go / Koto chotan / A day to God is 1,000 years / Cherry range / The birth / See the joy.

Nov 03. (cd-s; by RZA & OL' DIRTY BASTARD) *(SANXD 241)* <*9934*> **WE POP (mixes)** [ ] [ ]

GHOSTFACE KILLAH

Razor Sharp – Epic | Razor Sharp – Epic

Oct 96. (cd/c) *(485389-2/-4) <67729>* **IRONMAN** [38] [2]
– Iron maiden / Wildflower / Faster blade / 260 / Assassination day / Poisonous darts / Winter warz / Box in hand / Fish / Camay / Daytona 500 / Motherless child / Black Jesus / After the smoke is clear / All that I got is you / Soul controller / Marvel. *(cd re-iss. Apr00; same)*

Jun 97. (c-s) *(664684-4)* **ALL THAT I GOT IS YOU / DAYTONA 500** [11] [ ]
(12"+=/cd-s+=) *(664684-6/-2)* – Camay.

Feb 00. (cd/lp) *(491955-2/-1) <69325>* **SUPREME CLIENTELE** [ ] [7]
– Intro / Nutmeg (with RZA) / One / Saturday nite / Ghost Deini (with SUPERB) / Apollo kids (with RAEKWON) / The grain (with RZA) / Buck 50 / Mighty healthy / Woodrow the base head / Stay true (with 60 SECOND ASSASSIN) / We made it (with SUPERB) / Stroke of death / Iron's theme / Malcolm / Who would you fuck / Child's play / Cherchez LaGhost / Wu banga / Clyde Smith (skit) / Iron's theme (conclusion).

Jul 00. (cd-s) *<79464>* **CHERCHEZ LaGHOST (mixes; clean / instrumental / album)** [–] [98]

—— in 2000, KILLAH featured on the MOS DEF hit single, 'Miss Fat Booty – part II'

Nov 01. (cd) *(501941-2)* **BULLETPROOF WALLETS** [ ] [ ]
– (intro) / Maxine / Flowers (with RAEKWON, METHOD MAN & SUPERB) / Never be the same again (with CARL THOMAS & RAEKWON) / (Teddy skit) / Theodore (with TRIFE & TWITZ) / Ghostshowers / Strawberry (with KILLAH SIN) / The forest / The juks (pop your collar) (with TRIFE & SUPERB) / Walking thru darkness (with TAKITHA) / Jealousy / The Hilton (with RAEKWON) / (interlude) / Love session (with RUFF ENDZ) / Street chemistry.

Apr 04. (cd) *<(210690-2)>* **THE PRETTY TONEY ALBUM** [ ] [6]
– Intro / Biscuits / Kunta fly shit / Beat the clock / Metal lungies / Bathtub – skit / Save me dear / It's over / Keisha's house – skit / Tush / Last night – skit / Holla / Ghostface / Be this way / The letter – skit / Tooken back / Run / Love.

Mar 06. (cd) *<(615502)>* **FISHSCALE** [ ] [4]
– The return of Clyde Smith – skit / Shakey dog / Kilo / The champ / Major operation – skit / 9 Milli Bros / Beauty Jackson / Heart street directions – skit / Columbus exchange / R.A.G.U. / Bad mouth kid – skit / Whip you with a strap / Back like that / Be easy / Clipse of doom / Jellyfish / Dogs of war / Barbershop / Ms. Sweetwater – skit / Big girl / Underwater / The Ironman takeover – skit / Momma. *(bonus +=)* – Three bricks.

INSPECTAH DECK

Loud-Epic | Loud-Columbia

Oct 99. (cd/c) *(496180-2/-4) <1865>* **UNCONTROLLED SUBSTANCES** [ ] [19]
– Intro / Movas & shakers / 9th chamber / Uncontrolled substance / Femme fatale / Grand prix / Forget me not / Longevity / Word on the street / Elevation / Lovin you / Trouble man / R.E.C. room / Friction / Hyperdermix / Show n prove / Cause.

Koch | Koch

May 03. (cd) *<(KOCD 8660)>* **THE MOVEMENT** [ ] [ ]
– Intro / City high / That shit / Get right / The movement / Who got it / It's like that / Shorty right there / U wanna be / Framed / Bumpin and grindin / Vendetta / The stereotype / The nigga / Big city / Cradle to the grave.

Robert WYATT

Born: ROBERT ELLIDGE, 28 Jan'45, Bristol, England. While at school he formed The WILDE FLOWERS with the HOPPER brothers, which soon spliced into two groups, CARAVAN and SOFT MACHINE. The latter was the band WYATT joined in 1966, but after four albums ('THE SOFT MACHINE', 'VOLUME 2', 'THIRD' & 'FOURTH'), he estranged himself from the group in '71, forming his own MATCHING MOLE. The previous year, his record label 'C.B.S.', had issued his first solo album, 'THE END OF THE EAR', which was assisted by fellow SOFT MACHINE members supplying the jazz-rock feel. In the summer of '73, WYATT was paralysed from the waist down after falling from a window, convalescing for several months at Stoke Mandeville hospital. He returned the following year (now confined to a wheel-chair), his single, a version of The MONKEES' 'I'M A BELIEVER' hitting the Top 30. Richard Branson had given him a break on 'Virgin' records earlier in the year, WYATT subsequently critically heralded for his NICK MASON-produced album, 'ROCK BOTTOM' (1974). The set featured such gems as 'SEA SONG' and 'LITTLE RED RIDING HOOD HITS THE ROAD' (in two parts). His second for the label, 'RUTH IS STRANGER THAN RICHARD' (1975), showed an even deeper side, WYATT covering CHARLIE HAYDEN's jazz track, 'SONG FOR CHE'. In 1977, he had another stab at the pop charts, a dire cover version of CHRIS ANDREWS' 'YESTERDAY MAN' being his final recording for some time. He signed to indie, 'Rough Trade' in 1980, releasing a number of singles prior to his comeback album, 'NOTHING CAN STOP US NOW' (1982). This featured his classy re-working of ELVIS COSTELLO and CLIVE LANGER's 'SHIPBUILDING'. In 1983, through constant airplay by Radio 1 DJ John Peel, the anti-Falklands war song gained a Top 40 placing. He continued to spread his political messages through his music, although he has never been one to preach, his songs retaining an intensely personal quality. He returned to penning his own material with a vengeance on 1985's 'OLD ROTTENHAT', titles such as 'THE UNITED STATES OF AMNESIA', 'VANDALUSIA' and 'EAST TIMOR' pretty much indicative of the record's brooding political atmospherics. While 'DONDESTAN' (1991) also had its quota of skeletal, subtly barbed commentaries, there were a clutch of co-writing credits for his wife Alfreda Benge, whose more abstruse poetic sensibilities lent the album's somber keyboard-led minimalism some balance. 'DONDESTAN (REVISITED)' (1998), meanwhile, was a remixed version of the record which attempted to flesh out the sparest songs and, in slightly rearranging the running order, sandwich the collaborations with his wife between the political commentary. The result was a less oppressive listen, one which drew out more of the record's quiet humour. 1997's 'SHLEEP' continued the songwriting collaboration with Benge, lending the record even more of a phantasmagorical sheen than usual. PAUL WELLER was also among the songwriting credits, penning the brief but memorable coda 'WHOLE POINT OF NO RETURN'. The WELLER association carried over into the brilliant 'CUCKOOLAND' (2003), where WYATT was also joined by the likes of BRIAN ENO, DAVID GILMOUR, PHIL MANAZANERA and ANNIE WHITEHEAD. If the compelling avant-jazz wiles of 'TRICKLE DOWN' and 'OLD EUROPEAN' were anything to go by, fans should probably be grateful that WYATT's record collection apparently doesn't stretch much beyond the post-bop era. Ditto the searching cover of the Tom Jobim/Víncius de Moraes bossa classic, 'INSENSATEZ', as graceful in its own way as his reading of the Boudleaux Bryant's tearjerker 'RAINING IN MY HEART'.

• **Songwriters:** WYATT penned except: GRASS (Ivor Cutler) / STRANGE FRUIT (Billie Holiday) / AT LAST I AM FREE (Chic) / STALIN WASN'T STALLIN' (Golden Gate Quartet) / BIKO (Peter Gabriel). • **Trivia:** WYATT also provided session drums for SYD BARRETT (1969) / KEVIN AYERS (early 70's) / HENRY COW (1975) / NICK MASON (1981) / RAINCOATS (1981 and '83).

Album rating: THE END OF AN EAR (*6) / Matching Mole: MATCHING MOLE (*6) / MATCHING MOLE'S LITTLE RED RECORD (*6) / Robert Wyatt: ROCK BOTTOM (*7) / RUTH IS STRANGER THAN RICHARD (*6) / NOTHING CAN STOP US (*8) / ANIMALS mini (*4) / OLD ROTTENHAT (*6) / DONDESTAN (*6) / A SHORT BREAK mini (*5) / FLOTSAM JETSAM collection (*5) / GOING BACK A BIT: A LITTLE HISTORY OF ROBERT WYATT compilation (*8) / SHLEEP (*7) / DONDESTAN (REVISTED) (*6) / EPS BY ROBERT WYATT compilation (*6) / CUCKOOLAND (*8) / SOLAR FLARES BURN FOR YOU collection (*7)

ROBERT WYATT

ROBERT WYATT (solo) – vocals, drums (ex-SOFT MACHINE) w / **DAVID SINCLAIR** – oboe (of CARAVAN) / **MARK CHARIG** – cornet (of SOFT MACHINE) / **ELTON DEAN** – sax / plus **NEVILLE WHITEHEAD** – bass / **CYRIL AYERS** – percussion

C.B.S. Columbia

Oct 70. (lp) *(64189) <31846>* **THE END OF AN EAR**
– Las Vegas tango (part 1) / To Mark everywhere / To saintly Bridget / To Oz alien Daevyd and Gilly / To Nick everyone / To caravan and Brother Jim / To the old world (thank you for the use of your body) / To Carla, Marsha and Caroline (for making everything beautifuller) / Las Vegas tango (part 2). *(re-iss. Aug80 on 'Embassy' lp/c; CBS/40 31846) (cd-iss. Apr93 on 'Sony Europe') (cd re-iss. Nov02 on 'Columbia'; 493342-2)*

MATCHING MOLE

WYATT with retained guest **D.SINCLAIR** and band **DAVE McRAE** – keyboards / **BILL McCORMICK** – bass (ex-QUIET SUN) / **PHIL MILLER** – guitar (ex-DYBLE, COXHILL & THE MB's) (same label)

Apr 72. (lp) *(64850) <32148>* **MATCHING MOLE**
– O Caroline / Instant pussy / Signed curtain / Part of the dance / Instant kitten / Dedicated to Hugh, but you weren't listening / Beer as in braindeer / Immediate curtain. *(re-iss. Mar82; CBS 32105) (cd-iss. Mar93 on 'Beat Goes On'; BGOCD 175)*

Apr 72. (7") *(8101)* **O CAROLINE. / SIGNED CURTAIN** –

Oct 72. (lp) *(65260)* **MATCHING MOLE'S LITTLE RED RECORD**
– Gloria gloom / God song / Flora fidgit / Smoke signal / Starting in the middle of the day we can drink all our politics away / Marchides / Nan's true hole / Righteous rumba / Brandy as in Benji. *(cd-iss. Jul93 on 'Beat Goes On'; BGOCD 174) (cd re-iss. Mar97 on 'Columbia Rewind'; 471488-2)*

— In the summer of '73, WYATT was paralysed from the waist down after falling from a window. After a year convalescing, but still in a wheelchair;

ROBERT WYATT

returned as solo vocalist. He was augmented by guests/friends **FRED FRITH** – percussion / **HUGH HOPPER** – bass / **GARY WINDO** – wind / **LAURIE ALLEN** – drums / **MIKE OLDFIELD** – guitar / **RICHARD SINCLAIR** – bass / **IVOR CUTLER** – vox, keyboards / **ALFREDA BENGE** – vocals

Virgin Virgin

Jul 74. (lp/c) *(V/TCV 2017) <13112>* **ROCK BOTTOM**
– Sea song / A last straw / Little Red Riding Hood hits the road (part 1) / Alifib / Alife / Little Red Riding Hood hit the road (part 2). *(cd-iss. Feb89; CDV 2017)*

Sep 74. (7") *(VS 114)* **I'M A BELIEVER. / MEMORIES** 29

— **WYATT** retained **FRITH, ALLEN & WINDO** and contributions from **PHIL MANZANERA** – guitar / **BILL McCORMICK** – bass / **BRIAN ENO** – synthesizers / **JOHN GREAVES** – bass / **MONEZI FEZI** – trumpet / **GEORGE KHAN** – saxophone

May 75. (lp/c) *(V/TCV 2034)* **RUTH IS STRANGER THAN RICHARD**
– SIDE RICHARD:- Muddy house (a) / Solar flares / Muddy mouse (b) / 5 black notes and 1 white note / Muddy mouse (c) – Muddy mouth / SIDE RUTH:- Soup song / Sonia / Team spirit / Soup for Che. *(cd-iss. Feb89; CDV 2034)*

Apr 77. (7") *(VS 115)* **YESTERDAY MAN. / SONIA** –

— accompanied only by **McCORMICK** – bass / **HARRY BECKETT** – flugelhorn (B-side)

Rough Trade not iss.

Mar 80. (7") *(RT 037)* **ARAUCO. / CAIMENERA** –

— now used only **MOGOTSI MOTHLE** – double bass / **FRANK ROBERTS** – keyboards

Nov 80. (7") *(RT 052)* **AT LAST I AM FREE. / STRANGE FRUIT** –

Feb 81. (7") *(RT 046)* **STALIN WASN'T STALLIN'. / STALINGRAD (P. Blackman)** –

— now with **ESMAIL SHEK** – tabla / **KADIR DURUESH** – shenzi

Aug 81. (7") *(RT 81)* **GRASS. / TRADE UNION (Dishari featuring Abdus Salique)** –

Apr 82. (lp) *(ROUGH 35)* **NOTHING CAN STOP US** –
– Born again cretin / At last I am free / Quantanera / Grass / Stalin wasn't stalling / The red flag / Strange fruit / Arauco / Strange fruit / Trade union / Stalingrad. *(re-iss. Apr83 lp+=/c+=; ROUGH/+C 35)* – Shipbuilding. *(cd-iss. May87; ROUGHCD 35)*

— Above album featured musicians as 1980-82.

— In Apr'82, WYATT was credited on BEN WATT ep 'SUMMER INTO WINTER'.

— guests **STEVE NIEVE** – piano / **MARK BEDDERS** – double bass / **MARTIN HUGHES** – drums / **CLIVE LANGER** – organ / **ELVIS COSTELLO** – b.vox

Aug 82. (7") *(RT 115)* **SHIPBUILDING. / MEMORIES OF YOU** –
(12"-iss.Nov82+=; RTT 115) – Round midnight. *(re-iss. Apr83; same); hit No.35)*

— now with ? plus **HUGH HOPPER,** etc.

May 84. (m-lp) *(ROUGH 40)* **THE ANIMAL FILM (Soundtrack)** –
– (no tracks listed) *(cd-iss. Jul94)*

Aug 84. (12"ep) *(RTT 149)* **WORK IN PROGRESS** –
– Biko / Amber and the amberines / Yolanda / Te rescuerdo Amanda.

Oct 85. (7"/12"; ROBERT WYATT with The SWAPO SINGERS) *(RT/+T 168)* **THE WIND OF CHANGE. / NAMIBIA** –

Rough Trade Gramavision

Dec 85. (lp/c) *(ROUGH/+C 69) <18 8604-1/-4>* **OLD ROTTENHAT**
– Alliance / The United States of amnesia / East Timor / Speechless / The age of self / Vandalusia / The British road / Mass medium / Gharbzadegi / P.L.A. *(cd-iss. Nov86; ROUGHCD 69) (cd re-iss. Jun98 on 'Hannibal'; HNCD 1434)*
below with one side by/with BENGE

Sep 91. (cd/c/lp) *(R 274-2/-4/-1)* **DONDESTAN**
– Costa / The sight of the wind / Worship / Catholic architecture / Shrink rap / Left on man / Lisp service / CP jeebies / Dondestan.

Blueprint not iss.

Nov 92. (cd+book) *(BP 108CD)* **A SHORT BREAK** –
– A short break / Tubab / Kutcha / Ventilatir / Unmasked. *(re-iss. Apr96; same)*

Trade 2 not iss.

— the next A-side featured **PAUL WELLER** – guitars, vocals

Sep 97. (7") *(TRDSC 010)* **FREE WILL AND TESTAMENT. / THE SIGHT OF THE WIND** –

Hannibal Thirsty Ear

Sep 97. (cd) *(HNCD 1418) <57040>* **SHLEEP** Nov97
– Heaps of sheeps / The duchess / Maryan / Was a friend / Free will and testament / September the ninth / Alien / Out of season / A Sunday in Madrid / Blues in Bob minor / The whole point of no return.

Oct 98. (cd) *(HNCD 1436) <57057>* **DONDESTAN (REVISITED)** Nov98
– CP jeebies / N.I.O. (New Information Order) / Donestan / Sight of the wind / Shrinkwrap / Catholic architecture / Worship / Costa (memories of under-development) / Left on man / Lisp service.

Hannibal Hannibal

Sep 03. (cd) *(<HNCD 1468>)* **CUCKOOLAND** Oct03
– Just a bit / Old Europe / Tom Hay's fox / Forest / Beware / Cuckoo madame / Raining in my heart / Lullaby for Hamza – Silence / Trickle down / Insensatez / Mister E / Lullaloop / Life is sheep / Foreign accents / Brian the fox / La ahada yalam (No-one knows).

– compilations, others, etc. –

Mar 81. (d-lp) *Virgin; (VGD 3505)* **ROCK BOTTOM / RUTH IS STRANGER THAN RICHARD** –

Apr 82. (7"ep; ROBERT WYATT & MEMBERS OF CAST) *Virgin; (VS 499)* **FROM MAN TO WOMAN** –

Dec 84. (lp) *Rough Trade; (RTSP 25)* **1982-1984** –

Feb 85. (12") *Recommended; (RE 1984)* **THE LAST NIGHTINGALE. / ON THE BEACH AT CAMBRIDGE** –

— next 'B'side by "The GRIMETHORPE COLLIERY BAND".

Sep 85. (7") *T.U.C.;* **THE AGE OF SELF. / RAISE YOUR BANNERS HIGH** –

Sep 87. (12"ep) *Strange Fruit; (SFPS 037)* **THE PEEL SESSIONS (10.9.74)** –
– Soup song / Sea song / Alife / I'm a believer.

Jan 93. (cd) *Rough Trade; (R 2952)* **MID EIGHTIES**

Jul 94. (cd; by MATCHING MOLE) *Windsong; (WINCD 063)* **BBC RADIO 1 LIVE IN CONCERT (live)** –

Jul 94. (d-cd) *Virgin; (CDVM 9031)* **GOING BACK A BIT: A LITTLE HISTORY OF . . .** –

Aug 94. (cd) *Rough Trade; (R 3112)* **FLOTSAM AND JETSAM** (rare 1968-1990) ☐ [–]

Feb 99. (5xcd-ep;box) *Hannibal; (HNCD 1440) / Thirsty Ear; <57062> EPS BY ROBERT WYATT* ☐ ☐

Sep 03. (cd) *Cuniform; (RUNE 175)* **SOLAR FLARES BURN FOR YOU** (sessions) ☐ ☐

XTC

Formed: Swindon, Wiltshire, England . . . 1976 after 3 years of calling themselves The HELIUM KIDZ. Not an early version of acid house as the name might suggest, XTC traded in a quirky blend of pop that owed more to quintessential English psychedelia than the nihilistic three chord assault of their punk peers. Nevertheless, they were picked up by 'Virgin' in the signing scramble that followed The SEX PISTOLS early success in 1977. The debut album, 'WHITE MUSIC' (1978), introduced their tentative art-pop sound, PARTRIDGE's songwriting talent much in evidence even at this early stage. The JOHN LECKIE produced 'GO 2' (1978) was a more sonically adventurous follow-up, heavily influenced by BRIAN ENO and moulding their pop with quirky electronica. Soon after the record's release, ANDREWS left to join ROBERT FRIPP's 'LEAGUE OF GENTLEMEN' and was replaced by DAVE GREGORY. The new improved unit cut the successful 'DRUMS AND WIRES' (1979) album which spawned a top 20 hit single, the hypnotic, MOULDING-penned 'MAKING PLANS FOR NIGEL'. The rest of the tracks were just as catchy in their distinctive, left-of-centre way. This signalled the onset of a punishing touring/recording schedule during which time the band released a succession of impressive singles, some of which went top 20 and an album, 'BLACK SEA' (1980), that hinted at the psychedelic nostalgia which would characterise their later output. 'ENGLISH SETTLEMENT' (1982) is generally held to be band's finest hour. A double set, the record artfully blended rustic folk, ethnic rhythms and synthesizer pop, all shot through with the spectral hue of psychedelia. Although the stellar single, 'SENSES WORKING OVERTIME' was one of the band's biggest hits and XTC looked to be headed for the big time, PARTRIDGE, never comfortable with live performance, was dreading the inevitable round of touring. In the event, after a few disastrous shows he decided he could suffer it no longer and shortly after, announced that the band would never tour again. CHAMBERS promptly left, unhappy with such a prospect and although PARTRIDGE was now suffering from Agoraphobia, the band struggled on. With no full-time drummer and a string of producers, 'MUMMER' (1983) and 'THE BIG EXPRESS' (1983) were inconsistent and lacking in direction although 'EVERYDAY STORY OF SMALLTOWN' from the latter set was a charming piece of nostalgia-pop. It was clear the band needed some fresh inspiration and with the help of JOHN LECKIE they cut the '25 O'CLOCK' mini-album in 1985 under the pseudonym DUKES OF STRATOSPHERE. More overtly psychedelic than any previous XTC material, PARTRIDGE was given free range to indulge his obvious passions. Re-energised, the band were paired with TODD RUNDGREN for 'SKYLARKING' (1986) and although there were some well documented clashes between PARTRIDGE and the maverick American, the resultant album was a triumphant return to form. Embellishing the gentle hybrid of 'ENGLISH SETTLEMENT' with a 'PET SOUNDS'-like sonic richness, the album spawned the sultry single 'GRASS'. Its B-side, the semi-acoustic sweep of 'DEAR GOD' was picked up by American radio, with the end result that 'SKYLARKING' was a considerable stateside success. After a final DUKES OF STRATOSPHERE album, 'PSONIC PSUNSPOT', XTC began work on the 'ORANGES AND LEMONS' set. Released in 1989, the album was another resounding success, creatively at least, and spawned the charming 'MAYOR OF SIMPLETON' single. While the album was a relative success in America, it failed to make any lasting impact in the UK and after 'NONESUCH' (1992) stiffed completely, XTC faded into obscurity. Although sightings are rare, PARTRIDGE has surfaced occasionally, notably on the HAROLD BUDD collaboration, 'THROUGH THE HILL', in 1994. Without even an inkling that songwriters PARTRIDGE and MOULDING were about to unleash a new episode of quirky pop tunes, the public were happy to find out XTC were once again planning their comeback. Delivered early '99 for 'Cooking Vinyl', 'APPLE VENUS VOLUME 1' saw Swindon's finest regain the ground they had lost while securing a Top 30 entry in the process. The record's swelling, organic orchestrations delighted many longtime fans and whetted appetites for a follow-up. In the event, 'WASP STAR (APPLE VENUS, PT.2)' (2000) was a more straightforward XTC album rather than a continuation of its predecessor's grandiose pop, concentrating on the kind of nuts and bolts material that the band have long made their own.

• **Covered:** ALL ALONG THE WATCHTOWER (Bob Dylan) / ELLA GURU (Captain Beefheart).

Album rating: WHITE MUSIC (*8) / GO 2 (*4) / DRUMS AND WIRES (*8) / BLACK SEA (*7) / ENGLISH SETTLEMENT (*8) / WAXWORKS (SOME SINGLES 1977-82) compilation (*8) / BEESWAX (SOME B-SIDES 1977-82) compilation (*5) / MUMMER (*7) / THE BIG EXPRESS (*7) / SLYLARKING (*8) / THE COMPACT XTC – THE SINGLES 1978-1985 (*8) / ORANGES AND LEMONS (*7) / EXPLODE TOGETHER (THE DUB EXPERIMENTS '78-'80) exploitation (*4) / RAG 'N' BONE BUFFET collection (*5) / NONESUCH (*8) / FOSSIL FUEL: THE XTC SINGLES 1977-1992 compilation (*8) / APPLE VENUS VOLUME 1 (*7) / WASP STAR – APPLE VENUS VOLUME 2 (*6) / Andy Partridge: TAKE AWAY (THE LURE OF SALVAGE) (*5) / Dukes Of Stratosfear: 25 O'CLOCK mini (*4) / PSONIC PSUNSPOT (*5)

ANDY PARTRIDGE (b.11 Dec'53) – vocals, guitar / **COLIN MOULDING** (b.17 Aug'55) – bass, vocals / **BARRY ANDREWS** (b.12 Sep'56, London) – keyboards repl. JONATHAN PERKINS / **TERRY CHAMBERS** (b.18 Jul'55) – drums

		Virgin	Virgin-Epic
Oct 77.	(7") *(VS 188)* **SCIENCE FRICTION. / SHE'S SO SQUARE**		–
	(12"ep+=) *(VS 188-12)* **3-D** – Dance band.		
Jan 78.	(7") *(VS 201)* **STATUE OF LIBERTY. / HANG ON TO THE NIGHT**		–
Feb 78.	(lp/c) *(<V/TCV 2095>)* **WHITE MUSIC**	38	
	– Radios in motion / Cross wires / This is pop? / Do what you do / Statue of liberty / All along the watchtower / Into the atom age / I'll set myself on fire / I'm bugged / New town animal in a furnished cage / Neon shuffle. *(re-iss. Mar84 lp/c; OVED/+C 60) (cd-iss. Mar87 +=; CDV 2095)* – Science friction / She's so square / Dance band / Hang on to the night / Heatwave / Traffic light rock / Instant tunes. *(cd re-iss. Jun01 +=; CDVX 2095) <US cd-iss. May02 on 'Caroline'+=; 50691>*		
Apr 78.	(7") *(VS 209)* **THIS IS POP?. / HEATWAVE**		–
Oct 78.	(7") *(VS 231)* **ARE YOU RECEIVING ME. / INSTANT TUNES**		–

XTC

Oct 78. (lp/c) *(<V/TCV 2108>)* **GO 2** [21] [ ]
– Mekanic dancing (oh we go!) / Battery brides / Buzzcity talking / Crowded room / The rhythm / Beatown / My weapon / Life is good in the greenhouse / Jumping in Gomorrah / My weapon / Super-tuff. *(free-12"ep w/ lp)* **GO +** – Dance with me Germany / Beat the bible / A dictionary of modern marriage / Clap, clap, clap / We kill the beast. *(re-iss. Mar84 lp/c; OVED/+C 61) (cd-iss. Jul87 +=; CDV 2108)* – Are you receiving me. *(cd re-iss. Jun01 +=; CDVX 2108) <US cd-iss. Jun02 on 'Caroline'+=; 50666>*

— **DAVE GREGORY** – synthesizers, guitar repl. ANDREWS who joined LEAGUE OF GENTLEMEN (w/ ROBERT FRIPP). He later went solo and formed SHRIEKBACK

May 79. (7",7"clear) *(VS 259)* **LIFE BEGINS AT THE HOP. / HOMO SAFARI** [54] [–]

Virgin | Virgin Atlantic

Aug 79. (lp/c) *(V/TCV 2129) <VA 13134>* **DRUMS AND WIRES** [34] [ ]
– Making plans for Nigel / Helicopter / Life begins at the hop / When you're near me I have difficulty / Ten feet tall / Roads girdle the globe / Reel by reel / Millions / That is the way / Outside world / Scissor man / Complicated game. *(free-7"w/ lp)* – LIMELIGHT. / CHAIN OF COMMAND *(re-iss. 1986 lp/c; OVED/+C 113) (cd-iss. Jun88 +=; CDV 2129)* – Limelight / Chain of command. *(cd re-mast.Jun01 +=; CDVX 2129) <US cd-iss. Aug02 on 'Caroline'; 50653>*

Sep 79. (7"m) *(VS 282)* **MAKING PLANS FOR NIGEL. / BUSHMAN PRESIDENT (HSS 2) / PULSING, PULSING** [17] [–]

Nov 79. (7") **TEN FEET TALL. / HELICOPTER / THE SOMNAMBULIST** [–] [ ]

Feb 80. (7"m) *<VA 67009>* **MAKING PLANS FOR NIGEL. / THIS IS POP? / MEKANIC DANCING (OH WE GO!)** [–] [ ]

Mar 80. (7") *(VS 322)* **WAIT TILL YOUR BOAT GOES DOWN. / TEN FEET TALL (U.S. version)** [ ] [ ]

Aug 80. (7") *(VS 365)* **GENERALS AND MAJORS. / DON'T LOSE YOUR TEMPER** [32] [ ]
(d7"+=) *(VS 365)* – Smokeless zone. / The somnambulist.

Sep 80. (lp/c) *(V/TCV 2173) <VA 13147>* **BLACK SEA** [16] [41]
– Respectable Street / General and majors / Living through another Cuba / Love at first sight / Rocket from a bottle / No language in our lungs / Towers of London / Paper and iron (notes and coins) / Burning with optimism's flames / Sgt. Rock (is going to help me) / Travels in Nihilon. *(re-iss. 1986 lp/c; OVED/+C 83) (cd-iss. Mar87 +=; CDV 2172)* – Smokeless zone / Don't lose your temper / The somnambulist. *(cd re-mast.Jun01 +=; CDVX 2173) <US cd-iss. Jun02 on 'Caroline'+=; 50636>*

Oct 80. (7") *(VS 372)* **TOWERS OF LONDON. / SET MYSELF ON FIRE (live)** [31] [ ]
(d7"+=) *(VS 372)* – Battery brides (live) / Scissor man.

Oct 80. (7"; as The COLONEL) *(VS 380)* **TOO MANY COOKS IN THE KITCHEN. / I NEED PROTECTION** [ ] [–]
(above by The COLONEL; aka MOULDING + CHAMBERS)

Nov 80. (7") *(RSO 71)* **TAKE THIS TOWN. / (b-side by The Ruts)** [ ] [ ]
(above single was from 'Times Square' film soundtrack on 'R.S.O.')

Dec 80. (7") **LOVE AT FIRST SIGHT. / ROCKET FROM A BOTTLE** [–] [ ]

Jan 81. (7"m) *(VS 384)* **SGT. ROCK (IS GOING TO HELP ME). / LIVING THROUGH ANOTHER CUBA (live) / GENERALS AND MAJORS (live)** [16] [ ]

Mar 81. (7"m) *(VS 407)* **RESPECTABLE STREET. / STRANGE TALES, STRANGE TAILS / OFFICER BLUE** [ ] [ ]

Virgin | Epic

Jan 82. (7"m) *(VS 462)* **SENSES WORKING OVERTIME. / BLAME THE WEATHER / TISSUE TIGERS** [10] [–]
(12"+=) *(VS 462-12)* – Egyptian solution (HSS 3).

Feb 82. (d-lp/c)<US-lp> *(V/TCV 2223) <37943>* **ENGLISH SETTLEMENT** [5] Mar82 [48]
– Runaways / Ball and chain / Senses working overtime / Jason and the Argonauts / No thugs in our house / Yacht dance / All of a sudden (it's too late) / Melt the guns / ** Leisure * / It's nearly Africa * / Knuckle down * / Fly on the wall * / ** Down in the cockpit * / English roundabout / Snowman. *<US single-lp version omits *> (cd-iss. Jun88; CDV 2223)*; omits tracks **) *(cd re-iss. Jun01 +=; CDVX 2223)*

Mar 82. (7"m) *(VS 482)* **BALL AND CHAIN. / PUNCH AND JUDY / HEAVEN IS PAVED WITH BROKEN GLASS** [58] [ ]
(12"+=) *(VS 482-12)* – Cockpit dance mixture.

May 82. (7"ep,9"ep) *(VS 490)* **NO THUGS IN OUR HOUSE / CHAIN OF COMMAND. / LIMELIGHT / OVER RUSTY WALLS** [ ] [–]

May 82. (7") **SENSES WORKING OVERTIME. / ENGLISH ROUNDABOUT** [–] [ ]

Nov 82. (lp/c) *(V/TCV 2251)* **WAXWORKS (SOME SINGLES 1977-82)** (compilation) [54] [–]
(free lp w/ above) **BEESWAX (SOME B-SIDES 1977-82)** (re-iss. Dec82 lp/c; *OVED/+C 9)*

— trimmed to basic trio of **PARTRIDGE, MOULDING + GREGORY** plus on session **PETER PHIPPES** – drums (ex-GLITTER BAND) (CHAMBERS emigrated to Australia)

Virgin | Geffen

Apr 83. (7") *(VS 553)* **GREAT FIRE. / GOLD** [ ] [–]
(12"+=) *(VS 553-12)* – Frost circus (HSS 5) / Procession towards learning land (HSS 6).

Jul 83. (7"/7"pic-d) *(VS/+Y 606)* **WONDERLAND. / JUMP** [ ] [ ]

Aug 83. (lp/c) *(V/TCV 2264) <4027>* **MUMMER** [51] [ ]
– Beating of hearts / Wonderland / Love on a farmboy's wages / Great fire / Deliver us from the elements / Human alchemy / Ladybird / In loving memory of a name / Me and the wind / Funk pop a roll. *(re-iss. 1986 lp/c; OVED/+C 142) (cd-iss. Mar87 +=; CDV 2264)* – Frost circus (HSS 5) / Jump / Toys / Gold / Procession towards learning land (HSS 6) / Desert island. *(cd re-iss. Jun01 +=; CDVX 2264) <US cd-iss. Aug02 on 'Caroline'+=; 50672>*

Sep 83. (7") *(VS 613)* **LOVE ON A FARMBOY'S WAGES. / IN LOVING MEMORY OF A NAME** [50] [ ]
(d7"+=) *(VS 613)* – Desert island / Toys.
(12") *(VS 613-12)* – ('A'side) / Burning with optimism's flames (live / English roundabout (live) / Cut it out (live).

Nov 83. (7"; as THREE WISE MEN) *(VS 642)* **THANKS FOR CHRISTMAS. / COUNTDOWN TO CHRISTMAS PARTYTIME** [ ] [–]

Sep 84. (7") *(VS 709)* **ALL YOU PRETTY GIRLS. / WASHAWAY** [55] [–]
(12"+=) *(VS 709-12)* – Red brick dream.

Oct 84. (lp/c) *(V/TCV 2325) <24054>* **THE BIG EXPRESS** [38] [ ]
– Wake up / All you pretty girls / Shake you donkey up / Seagulls screaming kiss her, kiss her / This world over / The everyday story of Smalltown / I bought myself a liarbird / Reign of blows / You're the wish you are I had / I remember the sun / Train running low on soul coal. *(cd-iss. 1987 +=; CDV 2325)* – Red brick dreams / Washaway / Blue overall. *(re-iss. 1988 lp/c; OVED/+C 182) (cd re-iss. Jun01 +=; CDVX 2325)*

Oct 84. (7"/12") *(VS 721/+12)* **THIS WORLD OVER. / BLUE OVERALL** [ ] [ ]

Jan 85. (7"m) *(VS 746)* **WAKE UP. / TAKE THIS TOWN / MANTIS ON PAROLE (HSS 4)** [ ] [ ]
(12"+=) *(VS 746-12)* – Making plans for Nigel / Sgt. Rock (is going to help me) / Senses working overtime.

— **IAN GREGORY** (DAVE's brother) – drums repl. PHIPPES

DUKES OF STRATOSPHEAR

Apr 85. (7") *(VS 763)* **THE MOLE FROM THE MINISTRY. / MY LOVE EXPLODES** [ ] [–]

Apr 85. (m-lp/c) *(WOW/+C 1)* **25 O'CLOCK** [ ] [ ]
– 25 o'clock / Bike ride to the Moon / My love explodes / What in the world . . . / Your gold dress / The mole from the ministry.

XTC

Aug 86. (7") *(VS 882)* **GRASS. / DEAR GOD** [ ] [ ]
(12"+=) *(VS 882-12)* – Extrovert.

Oct 86. (lp/c/cd) *(V/TCV/CDV 2399) <24117>* **SKYLARKING** [90] [70]
– Summer's cauldron / Grass / The meeting place / That's really super, Supergirl / Ballet for a rainy day / 1000 umbrellas / Season cycle / Earn enough for us / Big day / Another satellite / Mermaid smiled * / The man who sailed around his soul / Dying / Sacrificial bonfire. *<re-iss. 1987; 'Dear God' repl. *> (cd re-iss. Jun01 +=; CDVX 2399)*

Jan 87. (7"/7"clear) *(VS/+Y 912)* **THE MEETING PLACE. / THE MAN WHO SAILED AROUND HIS SOUL** [ ] [ ]
(12"+=) *(VS 912-12)* – Terrorism.

Jun 87. (7") *(VS 960)* **DEAR GOD. / BIG DAY** [ ] [–]
(12"+=) *(VS 960-12)* – Another satellite (live).
(cd-s) *(CDEP 3)* – ('A'side) / Homo safari series (HSS 1-6):- Homo safari / Bushman president / Egyptian solution / Mantis on parole / Frost circus / Procession towards learning land.

Jul 87. (7") **DEAR GOD. / MERMAID SMILED** [–] [ ]

the DUKES OF STRATOSPHEAR

Jul 87. (7"/7"colrd) *(VS/+Y 982)* **YOU'RE A GOOD MAN ALBERT BROWN (CURSE YOU RED BARREL). / VANISHING GIRL** □ [–]
(12"+=) *(VS 982-12)* – The mole from the ministry / My love explodes.
Aug 87. (lp/colrd-lp/c) *(V/VP/TCV 2440)* **PSONIC PSUNSPOT** □ □
– Vanishing girl / Have you seen Jackie? / Little lighthouse / You're a good man Albert Brown (curse you red barrel) / Collideascope / You're my drug / Shiny cage / Brainiac's daughter / The affiliated / Pale and precious.
1989. (cd) *(COMCD 11)* **CHIPS FROM THE CHOCOLATE FIREBALL** □ □
– (25 O'CLOCK / PSONIC PSUNSPOT)

XTC

—— **PAT MASTELOTTO** – drums (of MR. MISTER) repl. IAN
Jan 89. (7") *(VS 1158)* **THE MAYOR OF SIMPLETON. / ONE OF THE MILLIONS** [46] [72]
(12"+=) *(VST 1158)* – Ella guru.
(3"cd-s) *(VSCD 1158)* – ('A'side) / Ella guru / Living in a haunted heart / The good thing.
(12") *(VSR 1158)* – ('A'side) / Dear God / Senses working overtime / Making plans for Nigel.
Feb 89. (d-lp/c/cd) *(V/TCV/CDV 2581)* *<24218>* **ORANGES AND LEMONS** [28] [44]
– Garden of earthly delights / The Mayor of Simpleton / King for a day / Here comes President Kill again / The loving / Poor skeleton steps out / One of the millions / Scarecrow people / Merely a man / Cynical days / Across this antheap / Hold me my daddy / Pink thing / Miniature sun / Chalkhills and children. *(re-iss. Oct89, 3xcd-ep-box; CDVT 2581) (cd re-iss. Jun01; CDVX 2581)*
Apr 89. (7") *(VS 1177)* **KING FOR A DAY. / HAPPY FAMILIES** □ [–]
(12"+=) *(VST 1177)* – ('A'extended).
(c-s+=) *(VSC 1177)* – Generals and majors / Towers of London.
(3"cd-s) *(VSCD 1177)* – ('A'extended) / ('A'side) / My paint heroes (home demo) / Skeletons (home demo).
Aug 89. (7") *(VS 1201)* **THE LOVING. / CYNICAL DAYS** □ [–]
(c-s) *(VSC 1201)* – ('A'side) / The world is full of angry young men.
(12"/cd-s) *(VS T/CD 1201)* – (all 3 tracks).
Sep 89. (cd-ep) *<9-21236-2>* **KING FOR A DAY (Czar mix) / ('A' Versailles mix) / TOYS / DESERT ISLAND** [–] □
Mar 92. (7"/c-s) *(VS/+C 1404)* **THE DISAPPOINTED. / THE SMARTEST MONKEYS** [33] [–]
(10"+=) *(VST 1404)* – Humble Daisy.
(cd-s++=) *(VSCD 1404)* ('B'demo).
May 92 (cd/c/d-lp) *(CD/TC+/V 2699)* *<24474>* **NONESUCH** [28] [97]
– The ballad of Peter Pumpkinhead / My bird performs / Dear Madam Barnum / Humble Daisy / The smartest monkeys / The dismal / Holly up on poppy / Crocodile / Rook / Omnibus / That wave / Then she appeared / War dance / Wrapped in grey / The ugly underneath / Bungalow / Books are burning. *(cd re-iss. Jun01; CDVX 2699)*
Jun 92. (7"/c-s) *(VS/+C 1415)* **THE BALLAD OF PETER PUMPKINHEAD. / WAR DANCE** [71] [–]
(cd-s+=) *(VSCD1 1415)* – Down a peg (demo) / ('A'demo).
(cd-s+=) *(VSCD2 1415)* – My bird performs (demo) / Always winter never Christmas (demo).

—— **PARTRIDGE + MOULDING** re-formed six years later

—— additional musicians **DAVE GREGORY, PRAIRIE PRINCE**, etc

Cooking Vinyl T.V.T.

Feb 99. (lp/c/cd) *(COOK/+C/CD 172)* *<3250>* **APPLE VENUS VOLUME 1** [42] □
– River of orchids / I'd like that / Easter theatre / Knights in shining karma / Frivolous tonight / Greenman / Your dictionary / Fruit nut / I can't own her / Harvest festival / Last balloon.
Apr 99. (cd-s) *(FRYCD 080)* **EASTER THEATRE / EASTER THEATRE (home demo) / HOW EASTER THEATRE CAME TO BE** □ [–]
Jun 99. (cd-s) *(FRYCD 083)* **I'D LIKE THAT / I'D LIKE THAT (home demo) / HOW I'D LIKE THAT CAME TO B** □ [–]
Sep 99. (lp/cd) *(COOK/+CD 188)* **HOMESPUN (APPLE VENUS VOLUME 1 HOME DEMOS)** □ [–]
May 00. (lp/c/cd) *(COOK/+C/CD 194)* *<3260>* **WASP STAR – APPLE VENUS VOLUME 2** [40] □
– Playground / Stupidly happy / In another life / My brown guitar / Boarded up / I'm the man who murdered love / We're all light / Standing in for Joe / Wounded horse / You and the clouds will still be beautiful / Church of women / The wheel and the maypole.
Jul 00. (cd-s) *(FRYCD 095)* **I'M THE MAN WHO MURDERED LOVE (mixes) / DIDN'T HURT A BIT** □ [–]

– compilations, others, etc. –

on 'Virgin' unless otherwise mentioned
Jan 87. (cd) *(CDV 2251)* **THE COMPACT XTC – THE SINGLES 1978-1985** □ [–]
– Science friction / Statue of liberty / This is pop? / Are you receiving me / Life begins at the hop / Making plans for Nigel / Wait till your boat goes down / Generals and majors / Towers of London / Sgt. Rock (is going to help me) / Senses working overtime / Ball and chain / Great fire / Wonderland / Love on a farmboy's wages / All you pretty girls / This world over / Wake up.
Jul 88. (3"cd-ep) *(VSCDT 9)* **SENSES WORKING OVERTIME / BLAME THE WEATHER / TISSUE TIGERS** □ [–]
Nov 88. (7") *Old Gold; (OG 9819)* **MAKING PLANS FOR NIGEL. / SENSES WORKING OVERTIME** □ [–]
Aug 90. (cd) *(CDOVD 308)* **EXPLODE TOGETHER (THE DUB EXPERIMENTS 78-80)** □ [–]
– (included the ANDY PARTRIDGE album below)
Aug 90. (cd) *(CDOVD 311) / Geffen; <24417>* **RAG & BONE BUFFET** (rare) □ □
Nov 94. (cd) *Night Tracks; (CDNT 008)* **DRUMS AND WIRELESS: BBC RADIO SESSIONS 77-89** □ [–]
Jun 96. (d-cd) *Geffen; <25137>* **UPSY DAISY ASSORTMENT (A SELECTION OF SWEETEST HITS)** [–] □
Sep 96. (cd/c) *(CD/TC VD 2811)* **FOSSIL FUEL: THE XTC SINGLES 1977-92** [33] □
– (nearly same tracks as 1987 collection + add more recent) *(d-cd; CDVDX 2811)*
Nov 98. (4xcd-box) *Cooking Vinyl; (COOKCD 152) / TVT; <3240>* **TRANSISTOR BLAST: BEST OF THE BBC SESSIONS** □ □
Mar 02. (4xcd-box) *Virgin; (XTCBOX 1) / Caroline; <CAROL 11900>* **A COAT OF MANY CUPBOARDS** □ □

☐ Y KANT TORI READ
(see under ⇒ AMOS, Tori)

the YARDBIRDS

Formed: Richmond, Surrey, England . . . 1963, by KEITH RELF and PAUL SAMWELL-SMITH (both ex-METROPOLITAN BLUES QUARTET) together with JIM McCARTY, CHRIS DREJA and ANTHONY TOPHAM. The latter was soon replaced by ERIC CLAPTON and after a residency at Richmond's 'Crawdaddy' club backing bluesman, SONNY BOY WILLIAMSON, the YARDBIRDS were signed up by EMI's 'COLUMBIA' label in early '64. After two well received singles that year, 'I WISH YOU WOULD' and 'GOOD MORNING LITTLE SCHOOLGIRL', the band released the acclaimed 'FIVE LIVE YARDBIRDS' the following year. Recorded at London's Marquee club, the album was a thrilling snapshot of the group's pioneering, souped-up blues and R&B sound. Although it contained no original material, the band marked interpretations of standards like 'SMOKESTACK LIGHTNING' and 'RESPECTABLE' with an indelible stamp. But this line-up promptly came to an end upon the release of the classic 'FOR YOUR LOVE' (1965) single. Considering the record a betrayal of the band's blues roots, CLAPTON upped sticks and left for JOHN MAYALL'S BLUESBREAKERS. Enter JEFF BECK, another supremely gifted guitarist, and the band embarked upon the most successful period of their career, notching up hits with the likes of 'HEART FULL OF SOUL', 'EVIL HEARTED YOU', 'STILL I'M SAD' and 'SHAPES OF THINGS'. BECK had brought a new spirit of experimentation to the band and employed such psychedelic tactics as Eastern-style guitar mantras, distortion and Gregorian Chant. With 'THE YARDBIRDS' (1966), the band further embraced psychedelia and the album stands as a career pinnacle, innovative while maintaining the essence of their R&B heritage. This was especially evident on the single, 'OVER UNDER SIDEWAYS DOWN' (1966), which was backed by another of the album's best tracks, the self explanatory 'JEFF'S BOOGIE'. SAMWELL-SMITH, who'd produced the album, departed soon after and was replaced by yet another future guitar God, JIMMY PAGE. Soon shifting from bass to co-lead alongside BECK, the new line-up cut the electrifying psychedelia of 'HAPPENINGS TEN YEARS AGO' (1966). This honeymoon period was short-lived however, as BECK parted ways with the band during a particularly laborious US tour. 'LITTLE GAMES' (1967) was an ill-advised attempt at commerciality while covers of MANFRED MANN's 'HA! HA! SAID THE CLOWN' and NILSSON's 'TEN LITTLE INDIANS' were equally puzzling. Though these releases achieved a modicum of success in America, the band split in mid '68, PAGE and DREJA going on to form The NEW YARDBIRDS which in turn evolved into LED ZEPPELIN. The inevitable reunion took place in the mid-80's and under the BOX OF FROGS moniker, a line-up of BECK, McCARTY, DREJA, SAMWELL-SMITH, RORY GALLAGHER and MAX MIDDLETON cut a self-titled album in 1984 and the 'STRANGE LAND' lp in 1986. After a recording gap that made TERRY CALLIER's sabbatical look like a lunch break, the YARDBIRDS – or at least the rhythm section of JIM McCARTY and CHRIS DREJA, plus sundry newbies – returned with 'BIRDLAND' (2003), their first album since the late 60s split. Taking the opportunity to spruce up what they considered an inferior production on their old classics, the reconvened 'BIRDS cranked out digital-era versions of 'SHAPES OF THINGS' and 'FOR YOUR LOVE' amongst others, as well as a batch of surprisingly sturdy originals that included a RELF tribute, 'AN ORIGINAL MAN (A SONG FOR KEITH)'.

• **Songwriters:** RELF wrote some, except covers, I WISH YOU WOULD (Billy Boy Arnold) / SMOKESTACK LIGHTNING (Howlin' Wolf) / A CERTAIN GIRL (Ernie K-Doe) / GOOD MORNING LITTLE SCHOOLGIRL (Don & Bob) / TRAIN (Johnny Burnette) / FOR YOUR LOVE + HEART FULL OF SOUL (c. Graham Gouldman, ⇒ 10cc) / I'M A MAN (Bo Diddley) / THE SUN IS SHINING (Elmore James) / plus loads of other blues greats. • **Trivia:** Made two group appearances in the 66/67 films 'SWINGING LONDON' & 'BLOW-UP'. Early in 1966, manager GIORGIO GOMELSKY was replaced by SIMON NAPIER-BELL.

Album rating: FIVE LIVE YARDBIRDS (*8) / FOR YOUR LOVE (*6) / HAVING A RAVE UP WITH THE YARDBIRDS (*5) / SONNY BOY WILLIAMSON & THE YARDBIRDS exploitation (*5) / THE YARDBIRDS (aka OVER UNDER SIDEWAYS DOWN) (*5) / GREATEST HITS compilation (*7) / LITTLE GAMES (*(*5) / THE VERY BEST OF THE YARDBIRDS (*9) / BIRDLAND (*4)

KEITH RELF (b.22 Mar'43, Richmond) – vocals, harmonica / **ERIC CLAPTON** (b.30 Mar'45, Ripley, England) – lead guitar, vocals repl. ANTHONY TOPHAM / **CHRIS DREJA** (b.11 Nov'45, Surbiton, Surrey) – rhythm guitar / **PAUL SAMWELL-SMITH** (b. 8 May'43, Richmond) – bass / **JIM McCARTY** (b.25 Jul'43, Liverpool) – drums

		Columbia	Epic
Jun 64.	(7") *(DB 7283)* <9709> **I WISH YOU WOULD. / A CERTAIN GIRL**		Oct64
Oct 64.	(7") *(DB 7391)* **GOOD MORNING LITTLE SCHOOLGIRL. / I AIN'T GOT YOU**	44	–
Feb 65.	(lp) *(33SX 1677)* **FIVE LIVE YARDBIRDS (live)**		–

– Too much monkey business / I got love if you want it / Smokestack lightning / Good morning little schoolgirl / Respectable / Five long years / Pretty girl / Louise / I'm a man / Here 'tis. *(re-iss. Aug79 on 'Charly' lp)(c; CR 30173)(CFK 1017) (re-iss. Aug89; LIK 55) (cd-iss. on 'Charly'; CDCHARLY 182)*

		Columbia	Epic
Mar 65.	(7") *(DB 7499)* <9790> **FOR YOUR LOVE. / GOT TO HURRY**	3	May65 6

(re-iss. Aug76 on 'Charly'; CYS 1012)

		Columbia	Epic
Jul 65.	(lp; mono/stereo) <LN24/BN26 167> **FOR YOUR LOVE**	–	96

– For your love / I'm not talking / Putty (in your hands) / I ain't got you / Got to hurry / I ain't done wrong / I wish you would / A certain girl / Sweet music / Good morning little schoolgirl / My girl Sloopy.

—— (Mar65) **JEFF BECK** (b.24 Jun'44, Surrey) – lead guitar repl. CLAPTON who joined JOHN MAYALL's BLUESBREAKERS. He later formed CREAM and went solo

		Columbia	Epic
Jul 65.	(7") *(DB 7594)* <9823> **HEART FULL OF SOUL. / STEELED BLUES**	2	9
Oct 65.	(7") *(DB 7706)* **EVIL HEARTED YOU. / STILL I'M SAD**	3	–

(re-iss. Jul82 on 'Old Gold'; OG 9111)

		Columbia	Epic
Nov 65.	(7") <9857> **I'M A MAN. / STILL I'M SAD**	–	17

Jan 66. (lp; mono/stereo) *(export; SCXC 28)* <LN24/BN26 177>
HAVING A RAVE UP WITH THE YARDBIRDS (live) – Dec65 53
– You're a better man than I / Evil hearted you / I'm a man / Still I'm sad / Heart full of soul / The train kept a-rollin' / Smokestack lightning / Respectable / I'm a man / Here 'tis. *(last 4 tracks from 'FIVE LIVE YARDBIRDS')*

Feb 66. (7") *(DB 7848)* **SHAPES OF THINGS. / YOU'RE A BETTER MAN THAN I** 3 –

Mar 66. (7") *<10006>* **SHAPES OF THINGS. / NEW YORK CITY BLUES** – 11

—— (Feb66) **JIMMY PAGE** (b. 9 Jan'44, Middlesex, England) – guitar (ex-session man, solo artist) repl. SAMWELL-SMITH who became producer. (DREJA moved to bass) KEITH issued solo 45 in May.

May 66. (7") *(DB 7928) <10035>* **OVER, UNDER, SIDEWAYS, DOWN. / JEFF'S BOOGIE** 10 Jun66 13

Jul 66. (lp; mono/stereo) *(SX/SCX 6063) <LN24/BN26 210>*
THE YARDBIRDS (US title 'OVER UNDER SIDEWAYS DOWN') 20 52
– Lost women / Over, under, sideways, down / The Nazz are blue / I can't make your way / Rack my mind / Farewell / Hot house of Omagarashid / Jeff's boogie / He's always there / Turn into earth / What do you want / Ever since the world began. *(re-iss. Feb83 as 'ROGER THE ENGINEER' on 'Edsel' lp; mono/stereo)(c; ED 116 M/S)(CED 116) (cd-iss. 1986+=; EDCD 116)* – Happenings ten years time ago / Psycho daisies. *(cd-iss. Feb92 on 'Raven-Topic' US version;)*

Oct 66. (7") *(DB 8024)* **HAPPENINGS TEN YEARS TIME AGO. / PSYCHO DAISIES** 43 –

Nov 66. (7") *<10094>* **HAPPENINGS TEN YEARS TIME AGO. / THE NAZZ ARE BLUE** – 30

—— (Oct66) Trimmed to a quartet when JEFF BECK left to go solo.

Apr 67. (7") *(DB 8165) <10156>* **LITTLE GAMES. / PUZZLES** 51

Apr 67. (lp; mono/stereo) *<LN24/BN26 246>* **GREATEST HITS** (compilation) – 28
– Shapes of things / Still I'm sad / New York City blues / For your love / Over, under, sideways, down / I'm a man / Happenings ten years time ago / Heart full of soul / Smokestack lightning / I'm not talking.

Jun 67. (7") *<10204>* **HA HA SAID THE CLOWN. / TINKER, TAILOR, SOLDIER, SAILOR** – 45

Aug 67. (lp; mono/stereo) *<LN24/BN26 313>* **LITTLE GAMES** – 80
– Little games / Smile on me / White summer / Tinker, tailor, soldier, sailor / Glimpses / Drinking muddy water / No excess baggage / Stealing, stealing / Only the black rose / Little soldier boy. *(UK-iss.May85 on 'Fame' lp/c; FA 41 3124-1/-4) (re-iss. Apr91 on 'E.M.I.'; CDEMS 1389) (cd re-iss. Oct96 on 'Gold'; CDGOLD 1068)*

Oct 67. (7") *<10248>* **TEN LITTLE INDIANS. / DRINKIN' MUDDY WATER** – 96

Mar 68. (7"w-drawn) *(DB 8368) <10303>* **GOODNIGHT SWEET JOSEPHINE. / THINK ABOUT IT** –

—— Disbanded mid'68. PAGE and DREJA formed NEW YARDBIRDS, but when DREJA departed, PAGE formed LED ZEPPELIN. RELF and McCARTY formed the original RENAISSANCE. On 14 May'76, RELF was electrocuted when touching a faulty amp. In the early 90s, McCARTY was also part of PRETTY THINGS / YARDBIRD BLUES BAND collaboration

—— **the YARDBIRDS** re-formed with **CHRIS DREJA + JIM McCARTY** plus **JOHN IDAN** – vocals + guests **JEFF BECK, JEFF BAXTER, STEVE VAI, JOE SATRIANI, BRIAN MAY + JOHNNY RZEZNIK**

Favored Nations Favored Nations

Apr 03. (cd) *(<FN2280-2>)* **BIRDLAND**
– I'm not talking / Crying out of love / The nazz are blue / For your love / Please don't tell me 'bout the news / Train kept a rollin' / Mr. Sabateur / Shapes of things / My blind life / Over, under, sideways, down / Mr. you're a better man than I / Mystery of being / Dream within a dream / Happenings ten years time ago / An original man (a song for Keith).

– (selective) compilations, etc. –

Jan 66. (lp; mono/stereo) *Fontana; (TL 5277) / Mercury; <MG2/SR6 1071>* **SONNY BOY WILLIAMSON AND THE YARDBIRDS (live)** Feb66
– Bye bye bird / Mr. Downchild / The river Rhine / 23 hours too long / Out on the water coast / Baby don't worry / Pontiac blues / Take it easy baby / I don't care no more / Do the Weston. *(re-iss. 1968; SFJL 960) (re-iss. Jun75 on 'Philips'; 6435 011)*

Aug 77. (lp) *Charly; (CR 30013)* **THE YARDBIRDS FEATURING JEFF BECK** –
(re-iss. Mar83; CR 30195) (re-iss. Feb85 on 'Cambra'; CR 107)

Nov 84. (lp-box) *Charly; (BOX 104)* **SHAPES OF THINGS – COLLECTION OF CLASSIC RECORDINGS 1964-66** –
– (lp's) THE FIRST RECORDINGS / SONNY BOY WILLIAMSON & . . . / FIVE LIVE YARDBIRDS / FOR YOUR LOVE / HAVING A RAVE . . . / SHAPES OF THINGS / ODDS AND SODS *(4xcd-box Jun91 on 'Decal'; CDLIKBOX 1)*

Jun 91. (cd) *Music Club; (MCCD 023)* **THE VERY BEST OF THE YARDBIRDS** –
– For your love / Heart full of soul / Good morning little schoolgirl / Still I'm sad / Evil hearted you / A certain girl / Jeff's blues / I wish you would / New York City / I'm not talking / You're a better man than I / Shapes of things / I'm a man / Boom boom / Smokestack lightning (live) / Let it rock (live) / You can't judge a book by it's cover (live) / Who do you love (live) / Too much monkey business (live) / Respectable (live) / Pretty girl (live) / Stroll on.

Apr 91. (cd/c/lp) *Band Of Joy; (BOJ CD/MC/LP 20)* **ON AIR** (65-67) –

Apr 93. (4xcd-box) *Decal; (CDLIKBOX 3)* **THE BLUES WAILING YARDBIRDS – THE COMPLETE GIORGIO GOMELSKY SESSIONS** –

Mar 97. (cd) *Nectar; (NTMCD 527)* **THE BEST OF THE LEGENDARY YARDBIRDS** –

YEAH YEAH YEAHS

Formed: New York City, New York, USA . . . 2000 by South Korean-born KAREN O, a student from Ohio who flitted to NY and subsequently met guitarist NICK ZINNER and drummer BRAIN CHASE. Dubbed the "Strokes' favourite new band" (Christ, isn't everyone!), because one of them wore a YEAH YEAH YEAHS' badge while playing on an American chatshow, this 3-piece outfit didn't deserve being introduced like that in the wake of NYC's other trendy garage rockers. However, if one could describe the sound of O and her cohorts, it would most likely include a ROYAL TRUX's rock-out sludginess and POLLY JEAN HARVEY's precise eroticism mixed with garage guts and slut-chic. After a handful of support gigs with the likes of the WHITE STRIPES and BOSS HOG, they recorded and issued their self-titled EP in 2001, which was produced by JERRY TEEL, himself a member of BOSS HOG. After touring even more, another EP arrived on 'Touch and Go' records, entitled 'MACHINE' (in 2002), and displayed KAREN O's raw, sexually driven grind-house stompers (barely backed by only guitar and drums), which were harshly reminiscent of early BIKINI KILL, especially on screamers such as 'ART STAR' and 'BANG'. It was all worth the hype when the band issued their debut album 'FEVER TO TELL' in 2003. Backed by the hit single 'PIN', the no-wave funky garage of the YEAH YEAH YEAHS was a million miles away from the LOU REED-esque narcissism of The STROKES. Hit single 'DATE WITH THE NIGHT''s abruptness was startling, while elsewhere, 'COLD LIGHT''s heavy drone was very much reminiscent of fellow rockers the KILLS. Much like their partners-in-ennui the STROKES, New York's razor-sharpest hipsters YEAH YEAH YEAHS mooched back in 2006 with 'SHOW YOUR BONES', a UK Top 10 (US Top 20) album critically chided for its lack of promise fulfillment. Kicking off with the unmistakably SIOUXSIE-esque falsetto frippery of 'GOLD LION' (a UK Top 20 single), the album found KAREN O earthing some of that livewire spark, absorbing and assimilating both emotional and musical shock-tactics into a work of typically sophomoric reflection. When it worked – check the sing-song, 'Mocking Bird'-meets-the MISSION vibe of 'DUDLEY, or the brittle consonants of 'PHENOMENA' (even if they'd been enunciated years earlier by LL COOL J) – it suggested that YEAH YEAH YEAHS hadn't sighed their last just yet.

Album rating: FEVER TO TELL (*8) / SHOW YOUR BONES (*7)

KAREN O (b. KAREN LEE ORZOLEK, 20 Nov'78, South Korea) – vocals / **NICK ZINNER** – guitar / **BRIAN CHASE** (b. 2 Dec'78) – drums

Wichita Shifty

Apr 02. (12"ep/cd-ep) *(WEBB 029 T/CD)* <05> **YEAH YEAH YEAHS EP** [ ] Nov01 [ ]
– Bang / Mystery girl / Art star / Miles away / Our time. *<(US re-iss. Mar02 + UK-iss.Jan03 on 'Touch & Go'; T&G 238)>*

Wichita Touch & Go

Nov 02. (7"ep/cd-ep) *(WEBB 036 S/CD)* *<T&G 244/+CD>* **MACHINE EP** [37] [ ]
– Machine / Graveyard / Pin (remix). *(UK-iss.May03; same)*

Polydor Interscope

Apr 03. (7") *(65744-7)* **DATE WITH THE NIGHT. / YEAH! NEW YORK / BANG (remix)** [16] [–]
(cd-s+=) *(65744-2)* – ('A'-video).

Apr 03. (cd/lp) *(76061-2/-1)* *<03490-2/-1>* **FEVER TO TELL** [13] May03 [55]
– Rich / Date with the night / Man / Tick / Black tongue / Pin / Cold light / No no no / Maps / Y control / Modern romance. *(hidden tracks+=)* – Yeah! New York / Date with the night (video).

Jun 03. (7"red) *(9808086)* **PIN. / RICH (Pandaworksforthecops remix) / MR. YOU'RE ON FIRE MR.** [29] [–]
(cd-s+=) *(9808085)* – ('A'-video).

Sep 03. (7")<10"red> *(9811414)* *<B0002074-11>* **MAPS. / COUNTDOWN / MILES AWAY (Radio 1 John Peel session)** [26] Feb04 [87]
(cd-s+=) *(9811413)* *<B0002073-22>* – ('A'-video).

Nov 04. (7") *(9868816)* **Y CONTROL. / (Faint remix)** [54] [–]

Mar 06. (7"pic-d) *(9877352)* **GOLD LION. / LET ME KNOW (demo)** [18] Feb06 [88]
(cd-s+=) *(9877351)* *<B00063363-2>* – ('A'-Diplo remix) / ('A'-video).

Mar 06. (cd)(lp) *(9877235)(9852956)* *<B00063370-2/-1>* **SHOW YOUR BONES** [7] [11]
– Gold lion / Way out / Fancy / Phenomena / Honeybear / Cheated hearts / Dudley / Mysteries / The sweets / Warrior / Turn into. *(UK cd+=)* – Deja vu.

YES

Formed: London, England . . . mid '68 by veterans of the 60's beat era; JON ANDERSON and CHRIS SQUIRE. They added BILL BRUFORD, PETE BANKS and TONY KAYE, soon signing to 'Atlantic' after opening for CREAM at their farewell concert at London's Royal Albert Hall. In the summer of 1969, their self-titled debut album was released, a set of original material such as 'SURVIVAL', interspersed with two covers ('I SEE YOU' – Byrds & 'EVERY LITTLE THING' – Beatles). In 1970, the follow-up, 'TIME AND A WORD', also included a version of Stephen Stills' 'NO OPPORTUNITY NECESSARY', alongside the more accomplished title track and the single, 'SWEET DREAMS'. A UK Top 50 hit, it was surpassed early the next year by 'THE YES ALBUM', their first release to feature the innovative guitar-work of STEVE HOWE; BANKS having moved on to the group FLASH. The record featured four meticulously-crafted tracks, 'YOURS IS NO DISGRACE', 'STARSHIP TROOPER', 'PERPETUAL CHANGE' and 'I'VE SEEN ALL GOOD PEOPLE', which went some way to crystallising the typical YES sound, ANDERSON's high-pitched choirboy vocals providing the focal point. The more stylish and flamboyant keyboard-wizard, RICK WAKEMAN was then drafted in to replace KAYE on their 4th album, 'FRAGILE'. A little self-indulgent, it nonetheless garnered widespread critic acclaim and was the first to feature ROGER DEAN's fantasy sleeve artwork. The record's sales were boosted by the Top 20 smash, 'ROUNDABOUT', a US-only single in 1972. Later in the year, they unleashed their progressive tour de force, 'CLOSE TO THE EDGE', an exuberant, atmospheric set which utilised a high-tech multi-layered sound. A triple live set, 'YESSONGS', peaked at No.1 in the UK, also hitting Top 20 in America. During this period, they returned with a double studio concept piece, 'TALES FROM TOPOGRAPHIC OCEANS' which was subsequently lambasted by certain sections of the music press for its overly long tracks. This, and other minor details (such as WAKEMAN not toeing the vegetarian line and being partial to a few beers), led to his departure (he had already released a solo album 'THE SIX WIVES OF HENRY VIII'). His replacement was PATRICK MORAZ (ex-REFUGEE) who took over in time for the 1974 album, 'RELAYER'. Each of the individual group members then took the opportunity to have their own solo outing (see below for details). In 1977, when punk rock was king, YES re-grouped once more with RICK WAKEMAN back in the fold for comeback album, 'GOING FOR THE ONE'. By this stage, the pomp-rock excesses had been slimmed down somewhat to accommodate a more commercial sound, much in evidence on the hit single (first in the UK), 'WONDROUS STORIES'. They failed to emulate this success, critically at least, on their follow-up, 'TORMATO', although it did provide a minor hit, 'SAVE THE WHALE'. In the early 80's, two of their most fundamental creative forces, WAKEMAN and ANDERSON, split ranks, leaving YES to pick up the pieces. However, fans were aghast at the pieces they picked up, i.e. The BUGGLES (TREVOR HORN and GEOFFREY DOWNES), who had previously topped the pop charts with the novelty hit, 'Video Killed The Radio Star'. Despite the initial shock, fans still parted with their hard-earned cash for the resultant 'DRAMA' album. YES split again in 1982, when HOWE and DOWNES joined the soon-to-be successful British supergroup ASIA. ANDERSON returned from a solo career (including a lucrative collaboration with VANGELIS on the hit 45 'I Hear You Now') to a newly reformed YES the following year. The new line-up also included old hands TONY KAYE, CHRIS SQUIRE, ALAN WHITE and a new guitarist, the South African born TREVOR RABIN. Retaining TREVOR HORN on production duties only, they recorded the '90125' album, which spawned the US No.1, 'OWNER OF A LONELY HEART. After RABIN dominated the songwriting on their 1987 set, 'THE BIG GENERATOR', ANDERSON departed yet again. Over the next two years, a bitter dispute was fought over the rights to the YES name. SQUIRE and the last remaining members in 1987 won, while ANDERSON, BRUFORD, WAKEMAN & HOWE were forced to record a surprisingly successful album under their own surnames. Come 1991, the two opposing camps had reconciled their differences, recording the appropriately-titled 'UNION' together. The '90125' line-up was then resurrected for the 1994 'TALK' album, a more lightweight affair which was yet another pointless exercise in dinosaur rock. The second half of the 90's have seen YES deliver some well below par recordings, the concert pair 'KEYS TO ASCENSION' 1 & 2 (1996/97), 'OPEN YOUR EYES' (1997) and Top 40 entry! 'THE LADDER' (1999). With the millennial 'MAGNIFICATION' (2001), YES went for broke and did what they've always probably secretly wanted to do, record a whole album in conjunction with a full blown symphony orchestra. A lowly chart placing of UK Top75 suggested that fans weren't exactly thrilled with the results.

• **Other covers:** I'M DOWN (Beatles) / SOMETHING'S COMING (Sondheim-Bernstein) / AMERICA (Simon & Garfunkel) / AMAZING GRACE (trad).

Album rating: YES (*6) / TIME AND A WORD (*6) / THE YES ALBUM (*9) / FRAGILE (*8) / CLOSE TO THE EDGE (*10) / YESSONGS (*7) / TALES FROM TOPOGRAPHIC OCEANS (*7) / RELAYER (*6) / YESTERDAYS collection (*5) / GOING FOR THE ONE (*7) / TORMATO (*3) / DRAMA (*4) / YESSHOWS (*4) / CLASSIC YES compilation (*8) / 90125 (*6) / 90125 – THE SOLOS (*3) / BIG GENERATOR (*5) / ANDERSON BRUFORD WAKEMAN HOWE (*5) / UNION (*4) / TALK (*5) / KEYS TO ASCENSION (*5) / KEYS TO ASCENSION, VOL.2 (*3) / OPEN YOUR EYES (*4) / THE LADDER (*4) / MAGNIFICATION (*4) / THE ULTIMATE YES double compilation (*5) / Steve Howe: BEGINNINGS (*5) / THE STEVE HOWE ALBUM (*3) / TURBULENCE (*4) / THE GRAND SCHEME OF THINGS (*4) / VOYAGERS (*4) / Chris Squire: FISH OUT OF WATER (*4) / Alan White: RAMSHACKLED (*2) / Jon Anderson: OLIAS OF SUNHILLOW (*6) / SONG OF SEVEN (*7) / ANIMATION (*6) / 3 SHIPS (*3) / IN THE CITY OF ANGELS (*4) / CHANGE WE MUST (*4)

JON ANDERSON (b.25 Oct'44, Accrington, England) – vocals (ex-WARRIORS, ex-MABEL GREER'S TOY SHOP) / **TONY KAYE** (b.11 Jan'46, Leicester, England) – keyboards (ex-FEDERALS, ex-BITTER SWEET) / **PETER BANKS** (b. 7 Jul'47, Barnet, England) – guitar (ex-SYN, ex-MABEL GREER'S TOYSHOP) / **CHRIS SQUIRE** (b. 4 Mar'48, Nth. London) – bass, vocals (ex-SYN, ex-MABEL GREER'S TOYSHOP) / **BILL BRUFORD** (b.17 May'48, Seven Oaks, London, England) – drums, percussion (ex-SAVOY BROWN BLUES BAND)

Atlantic Atlantic

Jun 69. (7") *(584 280)* **SWEETNESS. / SOMETHING'S COMING** [ ] [–]

Jul 69. (lp) *(588 190) <8243>* **YES** [ ] Oct69 [ ]
– Beyond and before / I see you / Yesterday and today / Looking around / Harold land / Every little thing / Sweetness / Survival. *(re-iss. Dec71 lp/c; K/K4 40034) (cd-iss. Oct94 on 'East West'; 7567 82680-2)*

Oct 69. (7"w-drawn) *(584 298)* **LOOKING AROUND. / EVERYDAYS** [–] [–]

Jan 70. (7") *<2709>* **SWEETNESS / EVERY LITTLE THING** [–] [ ]

Mar 70. (7") *(584 323)* **TIME AND A WORD. / THE PROPHET** [ ] [–]

Jun 70. (lp) *(2400 006) <8273>* **TIME AND A WORD** [45] Nov70 [ ]
– No opportunity neccessary, no experience needed / Then / Everydays / Sweet dreams / The prophet / Clear days / Astral traveller / Time and a word. *(re-iss. Dec71 lp/c; K/K4 40085) (cd-iss. Oct94 on 'East West'; 7567 82681-2)*

Jun 70. (7") *(2091 004)* **SWEET DREAMS. / DEAR FATHER** [ ] [–]

—— **STEVE HOWE** (b. 8 Apr'47) – guitar (ex-TOMORROW, ex-IN CROWD, ex-SYNDICATS, ex-BODAST) repl. BANKS who joined BLODWYN PIG and later FLASH

Mar 71. (lp) *(2400 101) <8283>* **THE YES ALBUM** [7] May71 [40]
– Yours is no disgrace / The clap / Starship trooper; (a) Life seeker – (b) Disiilusion – (c) Wurm / I've seen good people (a) Your move – (b) All good people / A venture / Perpetual change. *(re-iss. Dec71 lp/c; K/K4 40106) (cd-iss. Jul87; SD 19131-2) (cd re-iss. Aug94 on 'East West'; 7567 82665-2)*

Aug 71. (7") *<2819>* **YOUR MOVE. / THE CLAP** [–] [40]
<re-iss. 1974; 3141>

—— **RICK WAKEMAN** (b.18 May'49) – keyboards (ex-STRAWBS) repl. KAYE who formed BADGER

Nov 71. (lp) *(2401 019) <7211>* **FRAGILE** [7] Jan72 [4]
– Roundabout / Cans and Brahms / We have Heaven / South side of the sky / Five per cent of nothing / Long distance runaround / The fish (Shindleria Praematurus) / Mood for a day / Heart of the sunrise. *(re-iss. Dec71 lp/c; K/K4 50009) (cd-iss. Dec86; K2 50009) (cd re-iss. Aug94 on 'East West'; 7567 82667-2)*

Jan 72. (7") *<2854>* **ROUNDABOUT. / LONG DISTANCE RUNAROUND** [–] [13]

Jul 72. (7") *<2899>* **AMERICA. / TOTAL MASS RETAIN** [–] [46]

Sep 72. (lp/c) *(K/K4 50012) <7244>* **CLOSE TO THE EDGE** [4] [3]
– Close to the edge; (a) The solid time of change – (b) Total mass retain – (c) I get up I get down – (d) Seasons of man / And you and I; (a) Cord of life – (b) Eclipse – (c) The preacher the teacher – (d) The apocalypse / Siberian Khatru. *(cd-iss. Dec86; K2 50012) (cd re-iss. Aug94 on 'East West'; 7567 82666-2)*

Oct 72. (7") *<2920>* **AND YOU AND I (part II). / (part I)** [–] [42]

—— (Aug72) **ANDERSON, HOWE, WAKEMAN + SQUIRE** brought in **ALAN WHITE** (b.14 Jun'44, Pelton, Durham, England) – drums (ex-John Lennon's PLASTIC ONO BAND, ex-HAPPY MAGAZINE) repl. BRUFORD who joined KING CRIMSON, etc. (both appeared on live album below)

May 73. (t-lp/d-c) *(K/K4 60045) <100>* **YESSONGS (live)** [1] [12]
– (opening excerpt from 'Firebird Suite') / Siberian Khatru / Heart of the sunrise / Perpetual change / And you and I; (a) Cord of life – (b) Eclipse – (c) The preacher the teacher – (d) The apocalypse / Mood for a day / (excerpts from 'The Six Wives Of Henry VIII') / Roundabout / I've seen all good people; Your move – All good people / Long distance runaround / The fish (Shindleria Praematurus) / Close to the edge (a) The solid time of change – (b) Total mass retain – (c) I get up I get down – (d) Seasons of man / Yours is no disgrace / Starship trooper (a) Life seeker – (b) Disillusion – (c) Wurm. *(d-cd-iss. Feb87; K2 60045) (re-iss. d-cd Oct94 on 'East West'; 7567 82682-2)*

Dec 73. (d-lp/c) *(K/K4 80001) <2908>* **TALES FROM TOPOGRAPHIC OCEANS** [1] [6]
– The revealing science of God / The remembering / The ancient / Ritual. *(cd-iss. Sep89; K 781325) (re-iss. d-cd Oct94 on 'East West'; 7567 82683-2)*

Jan 74. (7") *(K 10407)* **ROUNDABOUT (live). / AND YOU AND I (live)** [ ] [–]

—— **PATRICK MORAZ** (b.24 Jun'48, Morges, Switzerland) – keyboards (ex-REFUGEE) repl. WAKEMAN who continued solo

Nov 74. (lp/c) *(K/K4 50096) <18122>* **RELAYER** [4] Dec74 [5]
– The gates of delirium / Sound chaser / To be over. *(cd-iss. Jul88; K2 50096) (re-iss. cd Oct94 on 'East West'; 7567 82664-2)*

Dec 74. (7") *<3222>* **SOON (from 'Gates of Delirium'). / SOUND CHASER** [–] [ ]

—— temporarily disbanded to release solo albums

STEVE HOWE

augmented by **WHITE, BRUFORD, MORAZ** + many including **GRAEME TAYLOR** – guitar / **MALCOLM BENNETT + COLIN GIBSON** – bass / **DAVID OBERLE** – drums

Atlantic Atlantic

Nov 75. (lp/c) *(K/K4 50151) <SD 18154>* **BEGINNINGS** [22] [63]
– Doors of sleep / Australia / The nature of the sea / The lost symphony / Beginnings / Will o' the wisp / Ram / Pleasure stole the night / Break away from it all. *(cd-iss. Oct94 on 'East West'; 7567 80319-2)*

CHRIS SQUIRE

augmented by **BILL BRUFORD** – drums / **ANDREW BRYCE JACKMAN + BARRY ROSE** – keyboards / **MEL COLLINS** – sax / **PATRICK MORAZ** – keyboards, synthesizers / **JIMMY HASTINGS** – flute

Atlantic Atlantic

Nov 75. (lp/c) *(K/K4 50203) <SD 18159>* **FISH OUT OF WATER** [25] [69]
– Hold out your hand / You by my side / Silently falling / Lucky seven / Safe (canon song). *(cd-iss. Feb96 on 'WEA'; 7567 81500-2)*

ALAN WHITE

augmented by **PETER KIRTLEY** – guitar, vocals / **COLIN GIBSON** – bass / **KENNY CRADDOCK** – keyboards, vocals / **ANDY PHILIPS** – steel drums / **ALAN MARSHALL** vocals / **HENRY LOWTHER** – trumpet / **STEVE GREGORY + BUD BEADLE** – wind

Atlantic Atlantic

Mar 76. (lp/c) *(K/K4 50217) <SD 18167>* **RAMSHACKLED** [41] [ ]
– Oooh! baby (going to pieces) / One way rag / Avakak / Spring – Song of innocence / Giddy / Silly woman / Marching into a bottle / Everybody / Darkness (parts 1, 2 & 3). *(cd-iss. Jan96 on 'WEA'; 7567 80396-2)*

Apr 76. (7") *(K 10747)* **OOOH! BABY (GOING TO PIECES). / ONE WAY RAG** [ ] [–]

JON ANDERSON

augmented **BRIAN GAYLOR** – synths / **KEN FREEMAN** – strings

Atlantic Atlantic

Jun 76. (lp/c) *(K/K4 50261) SD 18180>* **OLIAS OF SUNHILLOW** [8] [47]
– Ocean song / Meeting (Garden of Geda) – Sound of the galleon / Dance of Ranyart – Olias (to build the Moorglade) / Qoquag en transic – Naon – Transic to / Flight of the Moorglade / Solid space / Moon Ra – Chords – Song of search / To the runner. *(cd-iss. Feb96 on 'WEA'; 7567 80273-2)*

Oct 76. (7") *(K 10840)* **FLIGHT OF THE MOORGLADE. / TO THE RUNNER** [ ] [–]

—— PATRICK MORAZ also hit UK Top 30 with his 'I, PATRICK MORAZ' album for 'Charisma'. He had now departed YES to continue solo work & join MOODY BLUES.

YES

re-formed the 1973 line-up w / **RICK WAKEMAN** returning, to repl. MORAZ

Jul 77. (lp/c/3x12") *(K/K4/DSK 50379) <19106>* **GOING FOR THE ONE** [1] [8]
– Going for the one / Turn of the century / Parallels / Wondrous stories / Awaken. *(cd-iss. Jul88; K2 50379) (cd re-iss. Aug94 on 'East West'; 7567 82670-2)*

Sep 77. (12"blue) *(K 10999)* **WONDROUS STORIES. / PARALLELS** [7] [–]

Sep 77. (7") *<3416>* **WONDEROUS STORIES. / AWAKEN** [–] [ ]

Nov 77. (12") *(K 11047)* **GOING FOR THE ONE. / AWAKEN (part 1)** [24] [–]

Sep 78. (7") *(K 11184)* **DON'T KILL THE WHALE. / ABILENE** [36] [–]

Sep 78. (lp/c) *(K/K4 50518) <19202>* **TORMATO** [8] [10]
– Future times / Rejoice / Don't kill the whale / Madrigal / Release, release / Arriving UFO / Circus of Heaven / Onward / On the silent wings of freedom. *(cd-iss. Aug94 on 'East West'; 7567 82671-2)*

Nov 78. (7") *<3534>* **RELEASE, RELEASE. / DON'T KILL THE WHALE** [–] [ ]

— They shocked their fans, when they replaced (solo seeking once more) WAKEMAN and ANDERSON with (ex-BUGGLES duo) :-**TREVOR HORN** (b.15 Jul'49, Hertfordshire, England) – vocals, bass / + **GEOFF DOWNES** – keyboards

Aug 80. (lp/c) *(K/K4 50736) <16019>* **DRAMA** [2] [18]
– Machine messiah / White car / Does it really happen? / Into the lens / Run through the light / Tempus fugit. *(cd-iss. Oct94 on 'East West'; 7567 82685-2)*

Oct 80. (7") *(K 11622) <3767>* **INTO THE LENS. / DOES IT REALLY HAPPEN?** [ ] [ ]

Jan 81. (7") *<3801>* **RUN THROUGH THE LIGHT. / WHITE CAR** [–] [ ]

— YES split again.

Nov 81. (7"; CHRIS SQUIRE & ALAN WHITE / or / CAMERA) *(K 11695)* **RUN WITH THE FOX. / RETURN OF THE FOX** [ ] [–]
above partnership brought back **ANDERSON + KAYE**, plus newcomer **TREVOR RABIN** (b.13 Jan'54, Johannesburg, South Africa) – guitar, vocals. They repl. DOWNES + HOWE (to ASIA) / and HORN who was retained as producer.

Atco Atco

Nov 83. (7"/7"colrd-sha-pic-d/c-s) *(B9817/+P/C) <99817>* **OWNER OF A LONELY HEART. / OUR SONG** [28] [1]

Nov 83. (lp/c/cd) *(790 125-1/-4/-2) <90125>* **90125** [16] [5]
– Owner of a lonely heart / Hold on / It can happen / Changes / Cinema / Leave it / Our song / City of love / Hearts.

Mar 84. (7") *(B 9787) <99787>* **LEAVE IT. / LEAVE IT (acappella)** [56] [24]
(12"+=) *(B 9787T)* – ('A'version).
(c-s+=)<US cd-s+=> *<B 9789C>* – ('A'-hello goodbye mix) / Owner of a lonely heart.

Jun 84. (7") *(B 9745) <99745>* **IT CAN HAPPEN. / IT CAN HAPPEN (live)** [ ] [51]

Mar 86. (m-lp/c) *(790 474-1/-4) <90474>* **9012LIVE – THE SOLOS (live)** [44] Dec85 [81]
– Hold on / Si / Solly's beard / Soon / Changes / Amazing Grace / Whitefish.

Sep 87. (7") *(A 9449) <99449>* **LOVE WILL FIND A WAY. / HOLY LAMB** [73] [30]
(ext.12"+=) *(A 9449T)* – ('A'-Rise & fall mix).

Sep 87. (lp/c)(cd) *(WX 70/+C)(790 522-2) <90522>* **BIG GENERATOR** [17] [15]
– Rhythm of love / Big generator / Shoot high aim low / Almost like love / Love will find a way / Final eyes / I'm running / Holy love.

Dec 87. (12"ep) *<99419>* **RHYTHM OF LOVE (dance mix) – ('A'move mix) / ('A'dub) / CITY OF LOVE** (live) [–] [40]

— In-house squabbles led to splinter of YES . . .

ANDERSON BRUFORD WAKEMAN HOWE

Arista Arista

Jun 89. (lp/c/cd) *(209/409/259 970) <90126>* **ANDERSON BRUFORD WAKEMAN HOWE** [14] [30]
– Themes: Sound – Second attention – Soul warrior / Fist of fire / Brother of mine: The big dream – Nothing can come between us – Long lost brother of mine / Quartet: I wanna learn – She gives me love – Who was the first – I'm alive / Birthright / The meeting / Teakbois / Order of the universe: Order theme – Rock gives courage – It's so hard to grow – The universe / Let's pretend. *(lp tracks edited) (re-iss. Dec91 cd/c; 262/412 155)*

Jun 89. (7") *(112444)* **BROTHER OF MINE. / THEMES: SOUND** [63] [–]
(12"+=) *(612379)* – Themes: Second attention – Soul warrior.
(3"cd-s+=/5"cd-s+=)(10"+=)(c-s+=) *(1/6 62379)(260018)(410017)* – Vultures (in the city).

Jun 89. (cd-s) *<9852>* **BROTHER OF MINE: THE BIG DREAM – NOTHING CAN COME BETWEEN US – LONG LOST BROTHER OF MINE / VULTURES** [–] [ ]

Aug 89. (7") *<9898>* **LET'S PRETEND. / QUARTET: I'M ALIVE** [–] [ ]

Nov 89. (7"/c-s) *(112618)* **ORDER OF THE UNIVERSE. / FIST OF FIRE** [ ] [–]
(12"+=)(cd-s+=) *(612618)(662693)* – ('A'extended).

YES

now settled dispute by combining last line-up of **ANDERSON, BRUFORD, HOWE, WAKEMAN** with present YES men **SQUIRE, WHITE, RABIN + KAYE**

Arista Arista

May 91. (cd/c/lp) *(261/411/211 558) <8643>* **UNION** [7] [15]
– I would have waited forever / Shock to the system / Masquerade / Lift me up / Without hope you cannot start the day / Saving my heart / Miracle of life / Silent talking / The more we live-let go / Dangerous / Holding on / Evensong. *(c+=/cd+=)* – Angkor wat / Take the water to the mountain / Give and take.

Jun 91. (7") *(114 553)* **SAVING MY HEART. / LIFT ME UP (edit)** [ ] [–]
(cd-s+=) *(664 553)* – America.

Aug 91. (c-s) *<2218>* **LIFT ME UP / AMERICA** [–] [86]
(cd-s+=) *<2218>* – Give and take.

Nov 91. (c-s) **SAVING MY HEART. / THE MORE WE LIVE – LET GO** [–] [ ]

Victory London

Mar 94. (cd/c) *(828 489-2/-4) <480033>* **TALK** [20] [33]
– Calling / I am waiting / Real love / State of play / Walls / Where will you be / Endless dream (Silent spring – Talk – Endless dream).

Essential CMC Int.

Oct 96. (cd/c) *(EDF CD/MC 417) <86204>* **KEYS TO ASCENSION (live)** [48] [99]
– Siberia / Revealing science / America / Onward / Awaken / Roundabout / Starship trooper / Be the one / That, that is.

Essential Cleopatra

Nov 97. (d-cd/d-c) *(EDF CD/MC 457) <159>* **KEYS TO ASCENSION (2) (live)** [62] [ ]
– All good people / Going for the one / Time and a word / Close to the edge / Turn of the century / And you and I / Mind drive / Foot prints / Bring to the power / Lightning / Children of the light / Lifeline / Sign language.

Eagle Beyond

Nov 97. (cd/c) *(EAG CD/MC 013) <3074>* **OPEN YOUR EYES** [ ] [ ]
– New state of mind / Open your eyes / Universal garden / No way we can lose / Fortune seller / Man in the moon / Wonderlove / From the balcony / Love shine / Somehow . . . someday / The solution.

— **ANDERSON, HOWE, SQUIRE, WHITE / + BILLY SHERWOOD** – guitar, vocals + **IGOR KHOROSHEV** – keyboards, vocals

Eagle Damian

Sep 99. (cd/d-lp) *(EAG CD/12 088) <78046>* **THE LADDER** [36] [ ]
– Homeworld (the ladder) / It will be a good day (the river) / Lightning strikes / Can I? / Face to face / If only you knew / To be alive (hep yadda) / Finally / The messenger / New language / Nine voices (longwalker).

— **ANDERSON, HOWE, SQUIRE + WHITE**

Eagle Beyond

Sep 01. (cd) *(EAGCD 189) <578205>* **MAGNIFICATION** [71] [ ]
– Magnification / Spirit of survival / Don't go / Give love each day / Can you imagine / We agree / Soft as a dove / Dreamtime / In the presence of: 1. Deeper – 2. Death of . . . / Time is time.
in May'05, MAX GRAHAM vs YES had a club anthem UK Top 10 hit with 'OWNER OF A LONELY HEART'

– compilations, others, etc. –

Note; on 'Atlantic' unless otherwise stated.

Feb 75. (lp/c) *(K/K4 50048) <18103>* **YESTERDAYS** (early rare) [27] [17]
– America / Looking around / Time and a word / Sweet dreams / Then / Survival / Astral traveller / Dear father. *(re-iss. cd Oct94)*

Dec 81. (lp/c) *(K/K4 50842) <19320>* **CLASSIC YES** [ ] [ ]
– Heart of the sunrise / Wondrous stories / Yours is no disgrace / Roundabout / Starship trooper (a) Life seeker (b) Disillusion (c) Wurm / Long distance runaround / The fish (schindleria praematurus) / And you and I; (a) Cord of life (b) Eclipse (c) The preacher the teacher (d) The apocalypse / I've seen all good people; (a) Your move (b) All good people. *(w/ free 7")* ROUNDABOUT (live). / I'VE SEEN ALL GOOD PEOPLE (live) *(cd-iss. Dec86; 250842-2) (re-iss. cd Oct94 on 'East West'; 7567 82687-2)*

Dec 80. (d-lp/c) *Atco; (K 60142) <510>* **YESSHOWS (live 1976-1978)** [22] [43]
(cd-iss. Oct94; 7567 91747-2)

Oct 82. (d-c) *(K4 60166)* **FRAGILE / CLOSE TO THE EDGE** [ ] [–]

Aug 91. (4xcd-box) *Atco; (<7567 91644-2>)* **YESYEARS** [ ] [ ]

Oct 91. (d-cd/d-c/t-lp) *East West; (<7567 91747-2/-4/-1>)* **THE YES STORY**

Nov 91. (7"/c-s) *East West; (B 8713/+C)* **OWNER OF A LONELY HEART. / ('A'-wonderous mix)**
(12"/cd-s) *(B 8713 T/CD)* – ('A'side) / ('A'-Not Fragile mix) / ('A'-Move Yourself mix) / ('A'-Close To The Edge mix).

Sep 93. (cd) *Connoiseur; (VSOPCD 190)* **FAMILY ALBUM AFFIRMATIVE** (YES family tree) –
– Small beginnings (FLASH) / Feels good to me (BRUFORD) / Catherine Howard / Merlin the magician (RICK WAKEMAN) / Ocean song / All in a matter of time (JON ANDERSON) / I HEAR YOU NOW (JON & VANGELIS) / SPRING SONG OF INNOCENCE (ALAN WHITE) / Nature of the sea / Ram (STEVE HOWE) / Cahcaca (PATRICK MORAZ) / Hold out your hand (CHRIS SQUIRE) / Wind of change (BADGER) / Etoile noir (TREVOR RABIN).

Sep 93. (cd/c) *(7567 82517-2/-4)* **HIGHLIGHTS – THE VERY BEST OF YES**

Dec 93. (d-cd/video) *Fragile;* **AN EVENING OF YES MUSIC . . . PLUS**

Jul 03. (d-cd) *WEA; (8122 73702-2)* **THE ULTIMATE YES – 35th ANNIVERSARY COLLECTION** 10 Jan04

JON ANDERSON

with more solo releases. Earlier in the year 1980, he (JON) and VANGELIS ⇒ had hit UK No.8 with single 'I HEAR YOU NOW', and 'SHORT STORIES' lp hit No.4.

—— with a plethera of session people.

Atlantic Atlantic

Sep 80. (7") *(K 11619)* **SOME ARE BORN. / DAYS**

Nov 80. (lp/c) *(K/K4 50756) <16021>* **SONG OF SEVEN** 38
– For you for me / Some are born / Don't forget (nostalgia) / Heart of the matter / Hear it / Everybody loves you / Take your time / Days / Song of seven. *(cd-iss. May96 on 'WEA'; 7567 81475-2)*

Nov 80. (7") *(K 11641)* **TAKE YOUR TIME. / HEART OF THE MATTER**

—— Around mid'81, JON & VANGELIS released album 'THE FRIENDS OF MR. CAIRO' which hit UK No.6. Lifted from it 'I'LL FIND MY WAY HOME' also managed to hit UK No.6 / US No.51 in Nov '81. These and his next solo releases were issued on

Polydor Mercury

Apr 82. (7") *(POSP 393)* **SURRENDER. / SPIDER**

May 82. (lp/c) *(POLD/+C 5044) <19355>* **ANIMATION** 43
– Olympia / Animation / All in a matter of time / Unlearning / Boundaries / Pressure point / Much better reason / All Gods children.

Nov 82. (7") *(POSP 465)* **ALL IN A MATTER OF TIME. / SPIDER**

—— May83, sees another JON & VANGELIS album 'PRIVATE COLLECTION' hit UK No.22. Their compilation album 'THE BEST OF . . . ' hit UK No.42 in Aug84.

Elektra Elektra

Nov 85. (7"/12") *(EKR 31/+T* **EASIER SAID THAN DONE. / DAY OF DAYS**

Dec 85. (lp/c) *(EKT/+C 22)* **3 SHIPS** –
– Save all your love / Easier said than done / 3 ships / Forest of fire / Ding dong merrily on high / Save all your love (reprise) / The holly and the ivy / Day of days / 2,000 years / Where were you / Oh holy night / How it hits you / Jingle bells.

—— In 1986, he guested on MIKE OLDFIELD'S album 'SHINE'.

Epic Atlantic

Jun 88. (7"/12") *(651514-7/-1)* **HOLD ON TO LOVE. / SUN DANCING (FOR THE HOPI-NAVAJO ENERGY)**
(cd-s+=) *(651514-2)* – In a lifetime.

Jun 88. (lp/c/cd) *(460693-1/-4/-2) <40910>* **IN THE CITY OF ANGELS**
– Hold on to love / If it wasn't for love (oneness family) / Sun dancing (for the Hopi-Navajo energy) / Is it me / In a lifetime / For you / New civilization / It's on fire / Betcha / Top of the world (the glass bead game) / Hurry home (soon from the Pleiades).

Aug 88. (7") *(652947-7)* **IS IT ME. / TOP OF THE WORLD (GLASS BEAD GAME)**
(12"+=/cd-s+=) *(652947-6/-2)* – For you.

—— Later that year he provided vocals for charity 45 'WHATEVER YOU BELIEVE' accompanying STEVE HARLEY & MIKE BATT.

E.M.I. not iss.

Oct 94. (c-s/7") *(TC+/JON 1)* **CHANGE WE MUST. / STATE OF INDEPENDENCE**
(cd-s+=) *(CDJON 1)* – ('A'mixes) / (interview).

Oct 94. (cd/c) *(CDL/EL 555088-2/-4)* **CHANGE WE MUST**
– State of independence / Shaker loops / Hearts / Alive and wel / Kiss / Chagall duet / Run on, Jon / Candle song / View from the coppice / Hurry home / Under the sun / Change we must.

STEVE HOWE

with in 1979; **PATRICK MORAZ** – keyboards / **ALAN WHITE** + **BILL BRUFORD** + **CLIVE BUNKER** – drums / **RONNIE LEAHY** – keyboards / **GRAHAM PRESKETT** – violin / **CLAIRE HAMILL** – vocals

Atlantic Atlantic

Oct 79. (lp/c) *(K/K4 50621) <19243>* **THE STEVE HOWE ALBUM** 68
– Pennants / Cactus boogie / All's a chord / Look over your shoulder / Diary of a man who disappeared / Meadow rag / The continental / Surface tension / Double rondo / Concerto in D (second movement). *(cd-iss. Oct94 on 'East West'; 7567 81559-2)*

Roadrunner Roadrunner

Jan 92. (cd/c/lp) *(RR 9233-2/-4/-1)* **TURBULENCE**
– Turbulence / Hint hint / Running the human race / The inner battle / Novalis / Fine line / Sensitive chaos / Corkscrew / While Rome's burning / From a place where time runs slow.

Sep 93. (cd/c) *(RR 9086-2/-4)* **THE GRAND SCHEME OF THINGS**
– The grand scheme of things / Desire comes first / Blinded by science / Beautiful ideas / The valley of rocks / At the gates of the new world / Wayward course / Reaching the point / Common ground / Luck of the draw / The fall of civilization / Passing phase / Georgia's theme / Too much is taken and not enough is given / Maiden voyage / Road to one's self.

– others, etc –

Apr 90. (cd; with BODAST) *C5; (C5 528)* **THE EARLY YEARS** –

Jun 95. (cd) *Thunderbird-R.P.M.; (CSA 104)* **NOT NECESSARILY ACOUSTIC** –

Mar 96. (cd; STEVE HOWE & PAUL SUTIN) *S.P.V.; (SPV 0768956-2)* **SEREAPHIM** –

Mar 96. (cd) *S.P.V.; (SPV 0768957-2)* **VOYAGERS** –

Jun 96. (cd) *R.P.M.; (RPM 164)* **HOMEBREW** –

—— For RICK WAKEMAN releases, see under own solo entry.

Neil YOUNG

Born: NEIL PERCIVAL YOUNG, 12 Nov'45, Toronto, Canada. He was raised in Winnipeg until 1966, when he drove to America in his Pontiac hearse. NEIL had cut his teeth in local instrumental outfit, The SQUIRES, who released one '45 'THE SULTAN'. / 'AURORA' for 'V' records in September '63. The following year, NEIL formed The MYNHA BIRDS and joined forces with RICKY JAMES MATTHEWS (later to become RICK JAMES). Although many songs were recorded, only one saw the light of day; 'MYNHA BIRD HOP' for 'Columbia' Canada. They signed to 'Motown' (first white people to do so) but were soon dropped when they found out that RICKY had dodged the draft. He subsequently met up with past acquaintance, STEPHEN STILLS, and formed BUFFALO SPRINGFIELD. Constant rivalry led to YOUNG departing for a solo venture after signing for new label, 'Reprise', in Spring '68. His eponymous debut with arranger/producer JACK NITZSCHE, then DAVID BRIGGS, was finally issued in early 1969. A fragile, acoustic affair, the album was a tentative start to YOUNG's mercurial solo career, songs like 'THE OLD LAUGHING LADY' and 'THE LONER' hinting at the genius to come. The album was also a guinea pig for 'Warners' (then) new 'CSG' recording process, YOUNG later complaining bitterly about the resulting sound quality. 'EVERYBODY KNOWS THIS IS NOWHERE' (1969), however, was the sound of YOUNG in full control. Hooking up

NEIL YOUNG

with a bunch of hard-bitten rockers going by the name of CRAZY HORSE, the record marked the beginning of a long and fruitful partnership that's still going strong almost thirty years on. With 'CINNAMON GIRL', DOWN BY THE RIVER' and 'COWGIRL IN THE SAND', this bruising musical synergy saw YOUNG scaling cathartic new heights and the guitar interplay would become a template for the primal improvisation of YOUNG's live work. Although 'AFTER THE GOLDRUSH' (1970) was partly recorded with CRAZY HORSE and featured the blistering 'SOUTHERN MAN', most of the album was by turns melancholy, bittersweet and charming in the style of the gorgeous ballad, 'HELPLESS', he'd contributed some months earlier to the CSN&Y album, 'DEJA VU'. 'BIRDS' and 'I BELIEVE IN YOU' stand as two of the most poignant love songs of YOUNG's career while the title track was a compelling lament of surreal poetry, based on a script written by actor DEAN STOCKWELL. The album gave YOUNG his breakthrough, going Top 10 in Britain and America but it was the 1972 single, 'HEART OF GOLD' and subsequent album, 'HARVEST', which made YOUNG a household name. Most of the tracks were recorded in Nashville with a band called The STRAY GATORS, piano and production duties falling to JACK NITZSCHE. His biggest selling album to date, the finely crafted country crooning of 'OUT ON THE WEEKEND' and 'HEART OF GOLD' was the closest YOUNG ever came to MOR and true to his contrary style, the next few years saw him trawling the depths of his psyche for some of the most uncompromising and uncommercial material of his career. After the fierce sonic assault of the live 'TIME FADES AWAY' (1973) album, YOUNG went back into the studio with CRAZY HORSE to record a tribute to DANNY WHITTEN, their sad-voiced singer who'd overdosed on heroin the previous year. Just as YOUNG was due to begin recording, another of his friends, BRUCE BERRY (STEPHEN STILLS' guitar roadie), succumbed to smack the morose, drunken confessionals that resulted from those sessions eventually appeared a couple of years later as the 'TONIGHT'S THE NIGHT' (1975) album. Arguably YOUNG's most essential release, this darkly personal chronicle of drug oblivion veered from the resigned melancholy of 'ALBUQUERQUE' to the detached, twisted country of 'TIRED EYES', while the visceral catharsis of 'COME ON, BABY, LET'S GO DOWNTOWN' (an earlier live recording with a WHITTEN vocal) cranked up the guitars to match the unrelenting intensity level. Following 'Warners' reluctance to release the album, YOUNG set about writing yet another batch of hazy confessionals upon his return from touring the 'TONIGHT'S THE NIGHT' material. Deeply troubled by his increasing estrangement from actress CARRIE SNODGRASS (with whom he'd had a son, ZEKE), he shacked himself up in his new Malibu pad and penned 'ON THE BEACH' (1974). When every other rock star in L.A. was desperately trying to forget they'd ever hung out with CHARLES MANSON, YOUNG wrote 'REVOLUTION BLUES' in response to the Manson Family killings. 'AMBULANCE BLUES' was just as darkly compelling and the album remains an obscure classic. After a brief, ill-starred reunion with CROSBY, STILLS & NASH, YOUNG came up with a set entitled 'HOMEGROWN', which 'Warners' deemed too downbeat to release. Instead, they relented to the belated issue of 'TONIGHT'S THE NIGHT'. Come 1975, YOUNG was back in the studio with CRAZY HORSE, who'd recently recruited FRANK 'PANCHO' SAMPEDRO on guitar as a permanent replacement for WHITTEN. The resulting album, 'ZUMA' (1975), bore the first raw fruits of this new guitar partnership, the lucid imagery and meditative ruminations of 'CORTEZ THE KILLER' bringing the album to a darkly resonant climax while 'DON'T CRY NO TEARS' and 'BARSTOOL BLUES' found YOUNG more animated then he'd sounded for years. Following a disappointing album, 'LONG MAY YOU RUN' (1976), and aborted tour with STEPHEN STILLS, YOUNG cut the 'AMERICAN STARS 'N' BARS' (1977) album. A competent set of country rock, the record featured one of his best loved songs, an aching, soaring testament to the power of romantic obsession entitled 'LIKE A HURRICANE'. With 'COMES A TIME' (1978), he reverted to 'HARVEST'-style mellow country, duetting with then girlfriend, NICOLETTE LARSON. But YOUNG's more abrasive side couldn't be suppressed for long and, rejuvenated by the energy of the punk explosion, YOUNG reunited with CRAZY HORSE once more for the 'RUST NEVER SLEEPS' (1979) album. An electrifying set of passionate rockers and lean acoustic songs, it included such enduring live favourites as 'MY MY, HEY HEY (OUT OF THE BLUE)/(INTO THE BLACK)' (written about SEX PISTOL, JOHNNY ROTTEN) and the wounded 'POWDERFINGER'. The former was YOUNG's own comment on the "live fast, die young" rock'n'roll school of thought (it came back to haunt him when KURT COBAIN quoted the song in his suicide note). 'LIVE RUST' (1979) was the corrosive companion album capturing NEIL YOUNG & CRAZY HORSE live in all their frayed magnificence. Towards the end of 1978, YOUNG's new love, PEGI MORTON, had borne him a second child, BEN. While YOUNG's first son, ZEKE, had been born with cerebral palsy, BEN was a spastic. A stunned YOUNG began to clam up emotionally, with the result that much of his 80's work sounded confused and directionless. After 'REACTOR' (1981) stiffed, YOUNG moved to 'Geffen' where he recorded 'TRANS' (1983), an album that attempted to reflect his son's communication problems. Using a vocoder, YOUNG succeeded in rendering the lyrics almost unintelligible and while the album was almost universally panned, tracks like 'TRANSFORMER MAN' remain oddly affecting. The remainder of his time at 'Geffen' marked an all-time low in his career, both commercially and creatively, during which time he made ill-advised forays into rockabilly and stagnant, MOR country as well as making embarrassing pro-Reagan statments in interviews. Testing his fans to the limit, he was eventually sued by 'Geffen' for making records that didn't sound like NEIL YOUNG! He didn't really get back on track until 1989's 'FREEDOM' album, 'ROCKIN' IN THE FREE WORLD' (on 'Reprise') and 'CRIME IN THE CITY' marking YOUNG's return to searing rock'n'roll. With CRAZY HORSE, he cut 'RAGGED GLORY' (1990) the following year, a frenetic guitar mash-up that was staggering in its intensity for such an elder statesman of rock. 'WELD' (1991), a live document of the subsequent tour, saw YOUNG championed by the new "grunge" vanguard and revered once more by the indie/rock press as the epitome of guitar cool. Influenced by SONIC YOUTH (who supported him for part of the tour), he even recorded a CD collage of feedback, 'ARC', available in a limited quantity as a bonus disc with the 'WELD' double set. His critical rebirth now complete, 'HARVEST MOON' (1992) gave him his biggest commercial success since the 70's. A lilting, careworn set of country-folk, it was billed as a belated follow-up to 1972's 'HARVEST'. Of course, the MTV 'UNPLUGGED' (1993) set was now obligatory, but rather than give the audience a predictable run through of acoustic numbers, he presented radically altered versions of old numbers like 'TRANSFORMER MAN' and 'LIKE A HURRICANE'. 'SLEEPS WITH ANGELS' (1994) was a downbeat elegy for KURT COBAIN while 'MIRRORBALL' (1995) was a misguided collaboration with grunge band, PEARL JAM. The 'DEAD MAN' soundtrack was interesting although 'BROKEN ARROW' (1996) and the live 'YEAR OF THE HORSE' (1997) were given short shrift by the press. In truth, the records were far too inconsistent to warrant parting with hard earned cash. The man's long awaited 'SILVER & GOLD' (2000) went some way towards redressing the balance although it wasn't quite the dazzling return to form many had hoped for. Much of the album meandered along in a similar fashion to the trio of acoustic songs YOUNG had contributed to the previous year's CSN&Y

reunion set, 'Looking Forward'. Bearing in mind that these tracks were by far the most memorable, it follows that 'SILVER & GOLD' is an enjoyable enough listen without ever hitting those plateaus of inspiration integral to YOUNG's best work. A less obvious comparison than 'HARVEST MOON' might be his transitional 1978 effort, 'COMES A TIME'. New fans could do worse than starting with the 'DECADE' (1977) compilation, a stunning triple set (double CD) gathering the best of YOUNG's earlier work and including such obscure gems as the beautiful 'WINTERLONG'. With 2002's 'ARE YOU PASSIONATE', YOUNG extended his relationship with BOOKER T & THE MG's to the studio, cutting a straight-up Southern soul set. While this might've confounded his more rock-centric converts, it came as little surprise to long time fans who've learned to take YOUNG's stylistic whims in their stride. Like VAN MORRISON, the ageing troubadour seems more and more content to indulge lifelong passions than keep on top of his muse. The result was pleasant if unstartling; it all seemed a long way away from his feedback experimentation of the early 90's. More than a decade after 'WELD', YOUNG & CRAZY HORSE finally tried his hand at something more ambitious with 'GREENDALE' (2003), a bizarre quasi-concept, film musical set which, if not exactly holding together as a narrative (the convoluted plot centres on a fictional American town of the title, and more specifically on the troubles of one of the community's families) at least found the singer flexing his creative muscle for a change. Shearing the peerless 'DECADE' of 1977 down to a single disc, with the addition of a few more classic picks, the long, long, long-time-comin' 'GREATEST HITS' (2004) was pretty superfluous for most YOUNG fans, if a Top 30 treasure trove for uninitiates. The biggest news in years was 'PRAIRIE WIND' (2005), touted as tracing a post-millennial arc through 'HARVEST' and HARVEST MOON'. Lyrically elegiac with a title track reprising the latter's folksy picking and breeze-tousled female harmonies, the album in general was nevertheless just too diverse and Memphis Horn-brassy to function as a country-rock trilogy closer. In the likes of 'FALLING OFF THE FACE OF THE EARTH' and 'THIS OLD GUITAR', it did, however, feature some of YOUNG's most wraith-like songwriting in years, refracting grief and mortality more convincingly than almost all of his peers. No sooner had fans digested its subtleties, than YOUNG was back with a bullet: the splenetic 'LIVING WITH WAR' (2006) ranked as his most aggravated volte-face since 'RUST NEVER SLEEPS' trailed 'COMES A TIME'. Recorded inside a two-week burst of indignation and wrapped in the starkest packaging of his career, the album was the most overt anti-Bush statement yet conceived by any artist. Burning with the conviction that this was a record that had to be made by someone sooner or later, its torrent of distorted guitar and Mount Rushmore choruses was one part 'OHIO', one part 'WELD' (check the blistering, mariachi-seared 'SHOCK AND AWE'), and one part the small town/big problems of 'GREENDALE', as subtle as a jackboot but aflame with the freedom of believing that the concept of protest/redemption song was still viable: 'FLAGS OF FREEDOM' made no bones about its 'Chimes Of Freedom' inspiration, even mentioning DYLAN by name. The song titles told their own story; YOUNG – like most of the rest of the world – was still reeling from Bush's re-election, but 'LET'S IMPEACH THE PRESIDENT' was the boldest move by any American (naturalised or not) artist to confront him directly.

• **Songwriters:** As said, 99% of material is his own with contributions from CRAZY HORSE members, except; FARMER JOHN (Harris-Terry). The album 'EVERYBODY'S ROCKIN'' was full of covers.

Album rating: NEIL YOUNG (*7) / EVERYBODY KNOWS THIS IS NOWHERE (*8; with Crazy Horse) / AFTER THE GOLD RUSH (*10) / HARVEST (*9) / JOURNEY THROUGH THE PAST soundtrack (*3) / TIME FADES AWAY (*6) / ON THE BEACH (*9) / TONIGHT'S THE NIGHT (*8) / ZUMA (*8; with Crazy Horse) / AMERICAN STARS 'N BARS (*5) / DECADE compilation (*8) / COMES A TIME (*6) / RUST NEVER SLEEPS (*9; with Crazy Horse) / LIVE RUST (*7; with Crazy Horse) / HAWKS & DOVES (*6) / RE-AC-TOR (*5; with Crazy Horse) / TRANS (*5) / EVERYBODY'S ROCKIN' (*4; as Neil & The Shocking Pinks) / OLD WAYS (*5) / LANDING ON WATER (*3) / LIFE (*4; with Crazy Horse) / THIS NOTE'S FOR YOU (*6; as Neil Young & The Bluenotes) / FREEDOM (*7) / RAGGED GLORY (*8; with Crazy Horse) / WELD (*8; with Crazy Horse) / HARVEST MOON (*8) / LUCKY THIRTEEN compilation (*6) / UNPLUGGED (*6) / SLEEPS WITH ANGELS (*8; with Crazy Horse) / MIRRORBALL (*6) / DEAD MAN soundtrack (*4) / BROKEN ARROW (*5; with Crazy Horse) / THE YEAR OF THE HORSE (*5; with Crazy Horse) / SILVER & GOLD (*6) / ROAD ROCK VOL.1: FRIENDS & RELATIVES (*5) / ARE YOU PASSIONATE? (*5) / GREENDALE (*6; with Crazy Horse) / GREATEST HITS compilation (*10) / PRAIRIE WIND (*5) / LIVING WITH WAR (*7)

NEIL YOUNG – vocals, guitar (ex-BUFFALO SPRINGFIELD) with **JIM MESSINA** – bass / session men, etc.

Reprise Reprise

Jan 69. (lp) *<(RSLP 6317)>* **NEIL YOUNG** [ ] [ ]
– The Emperor of Wyoming / The loner / If I could have her tonight / I've been waiting for you / The old laughing lady / String quartet from Whiskey Boot Hill / Here we are in the years / What did I do to my life / I've loved her so long / The last trip to Tulsa. *(re-iss. 1971 lp/c; K/K4 44059) (cd-iss. 1987; K2 44059)*

Mar 69. (7") *<0785>* **THE LONER. / SUGAR MOUNTAIN** [–] [ ]

Sep 69. (7") *(RS 23405)* **THE LONER. / EVERYBODY KNOWS THIS IS NOWHERE** [ ] [–]

NEIL YOUNG with CRAZY HORSE

— with **DANNY WHITTEN** – guitar / **BILLY TALBOT** – bass / **RALPH MOLINA** – drums / **BOBBY NOTKOFF** – violin

Jul 69. (lp) *<(RSLP 6349)>* **EVERYBODY KNOWS THIS IS NOWHERE** [ ] May69 [24]
– Cinnamon girl / Everybody knows this is nowhere / Round and round (it won't be long) / Down by the river / The losing end (when you're on) / Running dry (requiem for the rockets) / Cowgirl in the sand. *(re-iss. 1971 lp/c; K/K4 44073) (cd-iss. 1988; K2 44059)*

Jul 69. (7") *<0836>* **DOWN BY THE RIVER (edit). / THE LOSING END (WHEN YOU'RE ON)** [–] [ ]

— Late 1969, NEIL YOUNG was also added to CROSBY, STILLS, NASH (& YOUNG).

Aug 70. (7") *(RS 23462)* **DOWN BY THE RIVER (edit). / CINNAMON GIRL (alt.take)** [ ] [–]

NEIL YOUNG

— with **NILS LOFGREN** – guitar (of GRIN) repl. NOTKOFF

Aug 70. (7") *<0898>* **OH LONESOME ME (extended). / I'VE BEEN WAITING FOR YOU (alt.mix)** [–] [ ]

Sep 70. (lp) *<(RSLP 6383)>* **AFTER THE GOLD RUSH** [7] [8]
– Tell me why / After the gold rush / Only love can break your heart / Southern man / Till the morning comes / Oh lonesome me / Don't let it bring you down / Birds / When you dance I can really love / I believe in you / After the goldrush / Cripple Creek ferry. *(re-iss. 1971 lp/c; K/K4 44088) (cd-iss. Jul87; K2 44088)*

Sep 70. (7") *(RS 20861)* **OH LONESOME ME (extended). / SUGAR MOUNTAIN** [ ] [–]

Jun 70. (7") *<0911>* **CINNAMON GIRL (alt.mix). / SUGAR MOUNTAIN** [–] [55]

Oct 70. (7") *(RS 20958) <0958>* **ONLY LOVE CAN BREAK YOUR HEART. / BIRDS** [ ] [33]

Jan 71. (7") *<0992>* **WHEN YOU DANCE I CAN REALLY LOVE. / SUGAR MOUNTAIN** [–] [93]

Feb 71. (7") *(RS 23488)* **WHEN YOU DANCE I CAN REALLY LOVE. / AFTER THE GOLDRUSH** [ ] [–]

— solo with The STRAY GATORS. (CRAZY HORSE now recorded on their own). NEIL's musicians: **JACK NITZSCHE** – piano / **BEN KEITH** – steel guitar / **TIM DRUMMOND** – bass / **KENNY BUTTREY** – drums. guests included **CROSBY, STILLS & NASH, LINDA RONSTADT, JAMES TAYLOR** plus The LONDON SYMPHONY ORCHESTRA

Feb 72. (7") *(K 14140) <1065>* **HEART OF GOLD. / SUGAR MOUNTAIN** [10] [1]

Mar 72. (lp/c) *(K/K4 54005) <MS 2032>* **HARVEST** [1] [1]
– Out on the weekend / Harvest / A man needs a maid / Heart of gold / Are you ready for the country? / Old man / There's a world / Alabama / The needle and the damage done / Words (between the lines of age). *(cd-iss. May83; K 244131)*

Apr 72. (7") *(K 14167)* *<1084>* **OLD MAN. / THE NEEDLE AND THE DAMAGE DONE** [ ] [31]

Jun 72. (7"; by NEIL YOUNG & GRAHAM NASH) *<1099>* **WAR SONG. / THE NEEDLE AND THE DAMAGE DONE** [–] [61]

— **JOHNNY BARBATA** – drums (ex-CROSBY, STILLS & NASH) repl. BUTTREY

Sep 73. (lp/c) *(K/K4 54010)* *<MS 2151>* **TIME FADES AWAY (live)** [20] [22]
– Time fades away / Journey through the past / Yonder stands the sinner / L.A. / Love in mind / Don't be denied / The bridge / Last dance.

Oct 73. (7") *<1184>* **TIME FADES AWAY (live). / LAST TRIP TO TULSA (live)** [–] [ ]

— now used session people including **CRAZY HORSE** members **BEN KEITH** – steel guitar; had now repl. WHITTEN who o.d.'d August 1972

Jul 74. (7") *(K/K4 54014)* *<R 2180>* **ON THE BEACH** [42] [16]
– Walk on / See the sky about to rain / Revolution blues / For the turnstiles / Vampire blues / On the beach / Motion pictures (for Carrie) / Ambulance blues. *<(cd-iss. Jul03; 9362 48497-2)>* – hit UK No.42

Jul 74. (7") *(K 14360)* *<1209>* **WALK ON. / FOR THE TURNSTILES** [ ] [69]

— Had just earlier in 1974, re-united with CROSBY, STILLS & NASH

— recorded solo lp in '73. Musicians: **NILS LOFGREN / BEN KEITH / BILLY TALBOT / RALPH MOLINA**

Jun 75. (lp/c) *(K/K4 54040)* *<MS 2221>* **TONIGHT'S THE NIGHT** [48] [25]
– Tonight's the night (part I) / Speakin' out / World on a string / Borrowed tune / Come on baby let's go downtown / Mellow my mind / Roll another number (for the road) / Albuquerque / New mama / Lookout Joe / Tired eyes / Tonight's the night (part II). *(cd-iss. Jul93; 7599 27221-2)*

NEIL YOUNG with CRAZY HORSE

— (Mar'75) **FRANK 'Poncho' SAMPEDRO** – guitar, vocals repl. KEITH + LOFGREN The latter earlier went solo, and later joined BRUCE SPRINGSTEEN band.

Nov 75. (lp/c) *(K/K4 54057)* *<MS 2242>* **ZUMA** [44] [25]
– Don't cry no tears / Danger bird / Pardon my heart / Lookin' for a love / Barstool blues / Stupid girl / Drive back / Cortez the killer / Through my sails. *(cd-iss. Jul93; 7599 27222-2)*

Mar 76. (7") *<K 14416>* *<1344>* **LOOKIN' FOR A LOVE. / SUGAR MOUNTAIN** [ ] Dec75 [ ]

Mar 76. (7") *<1350>* **DRIVE BACK. / STUPID GIRL** [–] [ ]

May 76. (7") *(K 14431)* **DON'T CRY NO TEARS. / STUPID GIRL** [ ] [–]

— Mid 1976, he teamed up as STILLS-YOUNG BAND with STEPHEN STILLS on album 'LONG MAY YOU RUN'; *K/K4 54081* *<MS 2253>*

Jun 77. (lp/c) *(K/K4 54088)* *<MSK 2261>* **AMERICAN STARS 'N BARS** [17] [21]
– The old country waltz / Saddle up the Palomino / Hey babe / Hold back the tears / Bite the bullet / Star of Bethlehem / Will to love / Like a hurricane / Homegrown. *(cd-iss. Dec96; 7599 27234-2)*

Jul 77. (7") *<1390>* **HEY BABE. / HOMEGROWN** [–] [ ]

Sep 77. (7") *(K 14482)* *<1391>* **LIKE A HURRICANE (edit). / HOLD BACK THE TEARS** [ ] [ ]

NEIL YOUNG

— solo with loads on session incl.**NICOLETTE LARSON** – vox

Oct 78. (7") *<1395>* **COMES A TIME. / MOTORCYCLE MAMA** [–] [ ]

Oct 78. (lp/c) *(K/K4 54099)* *<2266>* **COMES A TIME** [42] [7]
– Goin' back / Comes a time / Look out for my love / Lotta love / Peace of mind / Human highway / Already one / Field of opportunity / Motorcycle mama / Four strong winds. *(cd-iss. Jul93; 7599 27235-2)*

Nov 78. (7") *(K 14493)* **FOUR STRONG WINDS. / MOTORCYCLE MAMA** [57] [–]

Dec 78. (7") *<1396>* **FOUR STRONG WINDS. / HUMAN HIGHWAY** [–] [61]

NEIL YOUNG with CRAZY HORSE

— (YOUNG w / **SAMPEDRO, TALBOT & MOLINA**)

Jun 79. (lp/c) *(K/K4 54105)* *<2295>* **RUST NEVER SLEEPS** [13] [8]
– My my, hey hey (out of the blue) / Thrasher / Ride my llama / Pocahontas / Sail away / Powderfinger / Welfare mothers / Sedan delivery / Hey hey, my my (into the black). *(cd-iss. Jul93; 7599 27249-2)*

Aug 79. (7") *(K 14498)* *<49031>* **HEY HEY, MY MY (INTO THE BLACK). / MY MY, HEY HEY (OUT OF THE BLUE)** [ ] [79]

Nov 79. (d-lp/d-c) *(K/K4 64041)* *<2296>* **LIVE RUST (live)** [55] [15]
– Sugar mountain / I am a child / Comes a time / After the gold rush / My my, hey hey (out of the blue) / When you dance I can really love / The loner / The needle and the damage done / Lotta love / Sedan delivery / Powderfinger / Cortez the killer / Cinnamon girl / Like a hurricane / Hey hey, my my (into the black) / Tonight's the night. *(re-iss. cd Jul93; 7599 27250-2)*

Dec 79. (7") *<49189>* **CINNAMON GIRL (live). / THE LONER (live)** [–] [ ]

— 1980's 'Where The Buffalo Roam' movie contained several YOUNG songs

NEIL YOUNG

— solo with **TIM DRUMMOND + DENNIS BELFIELD** – bass / **LEVON HELM + GREG THOMAS** – drums / **BEN KEITH** – steel, dobro / **RUFUS THIBODEAUX** – fiddle

Oct 80. (lp/c) *(K/K4 54109)* *<2297>* **HAWKS & DOVES** [34] [30]
– Little wing / The old homestead / Lost in space / Captain Kennedy / Stayin' power / Coastline / Union power / Comin' apart at every nail / Hawks & doves.

Nov 80. (7") *(K 14508)* *<49555>* **HAWKS & DOVES. / UNION MAN** [ ] [ ]

Feb 81. (7") *<49641>* **STAYIN' POWER. / CAPTAIN KENNEDY** [–] [ ]

NEIL YOUNG with CRAZY HORSE

— (see last CRAZY HORSE line-up)

Oct 81. (lp/c) *(K/K4 54116)* *<2304>* **RE• AC• TOR** [69] [27]
– Opera star / Surfer Joe and Moe the sleaze / T-bone / Get back on it / Southern Pacific / Motor city / Rapid transit / Shots.

Nov 81. (7"/10"shaped-red) *<498 70/95>* **SOUTHERN PACIFIC. / MOTOR CITY** [–] [70]

Jan 82. (7") *<50014>* **OPERA STAR. / SURFER JOE AND MOE THE SLEAZE** [–] [ ]

NEIL YOUNG

— solo adding synthesizers, drum machine (sessioners) **BRUCE PALMER** – bass (ex-BUFFALO SPRINGFIELD)

Geffen Geffen

Jan 83. (7") *(GEF 2781)* *<29887>* **LITTLE THING CALLED LOVE. / WE R IN CONTROL** [ ] Dec82 [71]

Jan 83. (lp/c) *(GEF/+C 25019)* *<2018>* **TRANS** [29] [19]
– Little thing called love / Computer age / We r in control / Transformer man / Computer cowboy (aka Syscrusher) / Hold on to your love / Sample and hold / Mr. Soul / Like an Inca. *(re-iss. Sep86 lp/c; 902018-1/-4) (cd-iss. Apr97; GFLD 19357)*

Jan 83. (12") *<20105>* **SAMPLE AND HOLD (extended). / MR SOUL (extended) / SAMPLE AND HOLD** [–] [ ]

Feb 83. (7") *<29707>* **MR. SOUL. / MR. SOUL (part 2)** [–] [ ]

— w / **BEN KEITH** – guitar / **TIM DRUMMOND** – bass / **KARL HIMMEL** – drums / **LARRY BYROM** – piano, vocals / **RICK PALOMBI + ANTHONY CRAWFORD** – b.vocals

Sep 83. (lp/c; as NEIL & THE SHOCKING PINKS) *(GEF/+C 25590)* *<4013>* **EVERYBODY'S ROCKIN'** [50] Aug83 [46]
– Betty Lou's got a new pair of shoes / Rainin' in my heart / Payola blues / Wonderin' / Kinda fonda Wanda / Jellyroll man / Bright lights, big city / Cry, cry, cry / Mystery train / Everybody's rockin'. *(re-iss. Sep86 lp/c/cd; 904013-1/-4/-2)*

Sep 83. (7") *(GEF 3581)* *<29574>* **WONDERIN'. / PAYOLA BLUES** [ ] [ ]

Oct 83. (7") *<29433>* **CRY, CRY, CRY. / PAYOLA BLUES** [–] [ ]

— Jul85, with country singer WILLIE NELSON he duets on his ARE THERE ANY MORE REAL COWBOYS single issued on 'Columbia'.

— solo again with loads of session people.

Aug 85. (lp/c) *(GEF/40 26377)* *<24068>* **OLD WAYS** [39] [75]
– The wayward wind / Get back to the country / Are there any more real cowboys? / Once an angel / Misfits / California sunset / Old ways / My boy / Bound for glory / Where is the highway tonight? *(cd-iss. Apr97; GFLD 19356)*

Sep 85. (7") *<28883>* **BACK TO THE COUNTRY. / MISFITS** [–] [ ]

Nov 85. (7") *<28753>* **OLD WAYS. / ONCE AN ANGEL** [–] [ ]

— w / **STEVE JORDAN** – drums, synths, vox / **DANNY KORTCHMAR** – guitar, synth

Aug 86. (lp/c/cd) *(924109-1/-4/-2) <24109>* **LANDING ON WATER** [52] [46]
– Weight of the world / Violent side / Hippie dream / Bad news beat / Touch the night / People on the street / Hard luck stories / I got a problem / Pressure / Drifter. *(re-iss. Apr91;) (cd-iss. Nov96; GED 24109)*

Sep 86. (7"/12") *(GEF/+T 7) <28623>* **WEIGHT OF THE WORLD. / PRESSURE** [ ] Jul86 [ ]

NEIL YOUNG & CRAZY HORSE

— (see last **CRAZY HORSE, + BRYAN BELL** – synth)

May 87. (lp/c)(cd) *(WX 108/+C)(924154-2) <24154>* **LIFE** [71] [75]
– Mideast vacation / Long walk home / Around the world / Inca queen / Too lonely / Prisoners of rock'n'roll / Cryin' eyes / When your lonely heart breaks / We never danced.

Jun 87. (7") *<28196>* **MIDEAST VACATION. / LONG WALK HOME** [–] [ ]

Jun 87. (7") *(GEF 25)* **LONG WALK HOME. / CRYIN' EYES** [ ] [–]

NEIL YOUNG & THE BLUENOTES

— with **SAMPEDRO** – keyboards plus others **CHAD CROMWELL** – drums / **RICK ROSAS** – bass / **STEVE LAWRENCE** – tenor sax / **BEN KEITH** – alto sax / **LARRY CRAIG** – baritone sax / **CLAUDE CAILLIET** – trombone / **JOHN FUMO** – trumpet / **TOM BRAY** – trumpet

Reprise Reprise

Apr 88. (7") *<27908>* **TEN MEN WORKIN'. / I'M GOIN'** [–] [ ]

May 88. (lp/c/cd) *(WX 168/+C)(925719-2) <25719>* **THIS NOTE'S FOR YOU** [56] [61]
– Ten men workin' / This note's for you / Coupe de ville / Life in the city / Twilight / Married man / Sunny inside / Can't believe you're lyin' / Hey hey / One thing. *(re-iss. cd Feb95)*

May 88. (7") *<27848>* **THIS NOTE'S FOR YOU (live). / THIS NOTE'S FOR YOU** [–] [ ]

— Nov88, NEIL re-joined CROSBY, STILLS, NASH & YOUNG for 'AMERICAN DREAM' lp.

NEIL YOUNG

— solo again with **SAMPEDRO, ROSAS, CROMWELL,** etc.

Oct 89. (lp/c/cd) *(WX 257/+C)(K 925899-2) <25899>* **FREEDOM** [17] [35]
– Rockin' in the free world / Crime in the city (sixty to zero part 1) / Don't cry / Hangin' on a limb / Eldorado / The ways of love / Someday / On Broadway / Wreckin' ball / No more / Too far gone / Rockin' in the free world (live). *(re-iss. cd/c Feb95)*

Apr 90. (7") *(W 2776) <22776>* **ROCKIN' IN THE FREE WORLD. / ('A'live)** [ ] Aug89 [ ]
(12"+=/cd-s+=) *(W 2776 T/CD)* – Cocaine eyes.

NEIL YOUNG & CRAZY HORSE

— with **SAMPEDRO, TALBOT + MOLINA**

Sep 90. (cd)(lp/c) *<(7599-26315-2)>(WX 374/+C)* **RAGGED GLORY** [15] [31]
– Country home / White line / Fuckin' up / Over and over / Love to burn / Farmer John / Mansion on the hill / Days that used to be / Love and only love / Mother Earth (natural anthem). *(re-iss. cd/c Feb95)*

Sep 90. (cd-s) *<7599-21759-2>* **MANSION ON THE HILL (edit) / MANSION ON THE HILL / DON'T SPOOK THE HORSE** [–] [ ]

Oct 91. (d-cd/d-c/d-lp) *<(7599 26671-2/-4/-1)>* **WELD (live)** [20] [ ]
– Hey hey, my my (into the black) / Crime in the city / Blowin' in the wind / Live to burn / Welfare mothers / Cinnamon girl / Mansion on the hill / F+!#in' up / Farmer John / Cortez the killer / Powderfinger / Love and only love / Roll another number / Rockin' in the free world / Like a hurricane / Tonight's the night. *(free-cd-ep w.a.+=)* – ARC EP – (feedback).

NEIL YOUNG

solo, with The STRAY GATORS (**KENNY BUTTREY, TIM DRUMMOND, BEN KEITH & SPOONER OLDHAM**) plus **JAMES TAYLOR, LINDA RONSTADT, NICOLETTE LARSON, ASTRID YOUNG & LARRY CRAGG** – backing vocals

Oct 92. (cd/c/lp) *<(9362 45057-2/-4/-1)>* **HARVEST MOON** [9] [16]
– Unknown legend / From Hank to Hendrix / You and me / Harvest moon / War of man / One of these days / Such a woman / Old king / Dreamin' man / Natural beauty.

Feb 93. (7"/c-s) *(W 0139/+C)* **HARVEST MOON. / WINTERLONG** [36] [ ]
(cd-s+=) *(W 0139CD)* – Deep forbidden lake / Campaigner.
(cd-s) *(W 0139CDX)* – ('A'side) / Old king / The needle and the damage done / Goin' back.

Jun 93. (cd/c/lp) *<(9362 45310-2/-4/-1)>* **UNPLUGGED** [4] [23]
– The old laughing lady / Mr. Soul / World on a string / Pocahontas / Strongman / Like a hurricane / The needle and the damage done / Helpless / Harvest Moon / Transformer man / Unknown legend / Look out for my love / Long may you run / From Hank to Hendrix.

Jul 93. (7"/c-s) *(W 0191/+C)* **THE NEEDLE AND THE DAMAGE DONE (live). / YOU AND ME** [75] [ ]
(cd-s+=) *(W 0191CD)* – From Hank to Hendrix.

Oct 93. (7"/c-s) *(W 207/+C)* **LONG MAY YOU RUN (live). / SUGAR MOUNTAIN (live)** [71] [ ]
(cd-s+=) *(W 0207CD)* – Cortez the killer (live) / Cinnamon girl (live).

Feb 94. (7"/c-s) *(W 0231/+C)* **ROCKIN' IN THE FREE WORLD. / ('A'mixes)** [ ] [ ]
(cd-s+=) *(W 0231CD)* – Weld.

Apr 94. (7"/c-s) *(W 0242/+C)* **PHILADELPHIA. / SUCH A WOMAN** [62] [ ]
(12"+=/cd-s+=) *(W 0242 T/CD)* – Stringman (unplugged).

— Above 'A'side was another to be taken from the film 'Philadelphia'.

NEIL YOUNG & CRAZY HORSE

Aug 94. (cd/c/d-lp) *<(9362 45749-2/-4/-1)>* **SLEEPS WITH ANGELS** [2] [9]
– My heart / Prime of life / Drive by / Sleeps with angels / Western hero / Change your mind / Blue Eden / Safeway cart / Train of love / Trans Am / Piece of crap / A dream that can last. *(re-iss. Jan97; same)*

Aug 94. (c-s/cd-s) *(W 0261 C/CD)* **PIECE OF CRAP / TONIGHT'S THE NIGHT** [ ] [–]

Oct 94. (c-s) *(W 0266C)* **MY HEART / ROLL ANOTHER NUMBER (FOR THE ROAD)** [ ] [ ]
(cd-s+=) *(W 0266CD)* – Tired eyes.

Nov 94. (c-s) *(W 0276C)* **CHANGE YOUR MIND / SPEAKIN' OUT** [ ] [–]
(cd-s+=) *(W 0276CD)* – ('A'-full 14 minute version).

NEIL YOUNG

— with backing from all of PEARL JAM; 8th track written w/ EDDIE VEDDER

Jun 95. (cd/c/lp) *<(9362 45934-2/-4/-1)>* **MIRRORBALL** [4] [5]
– Song X / Act of love / I'm the ocean / Big green country / Truth be known / Downtown / What happened yesterday / Peace and love / Throw your hatred down / Scenery / Fallen angel.

Sep 95. (c-s) *(W 0314C)* **DOWNTOWN / BIG GREEN COUNTRY** [ ] [ ]
(cd-s+=) *(W 0314CD)* – ('A'-lp version).

Feb 96. (cd) *<(9362 46171-2)>* **DEAD MAN** (soundtrack) [ ] [ ]
– Guitar solo, No.1 / The round stones beneath the earth / Guitar solo, No.2 / Why does thou hide thyself, clouds / Organ solo / Do you know how to use this weapon? / Guitar solo, No.3 / Nobody's story / Guitar solo, No.4 / Stupid white men / Guitar solo, No.5 / Time for you to leave, William Blake / Guitar solo, No.6.
above was instrumental YOUNG, and based on Jim Jarmusch's film starring Johnny Depp.

NEIL YOUNG WITH CRAZY HORSE

Jun 96. (cd/c) *<(9362 46291-2/-4)>* **BROKEN ARROW** [17] [31]
– Big time / Loose change / Slip away / Changing highways / Scattered (let's think about livin') / This town / Music arcade / Baby what you want me to do.

Jun 97. (cd/c) *<(9362 46652-2/-4)>* **THE YEAR OF THE HORSE (live)** [36] [57]
– When you dance / Barstool blues / When your lonely heart breaks / Mr. Soul / Big time / Pocahontas / Human highway / Slip away / Scattered / Danger bird / Prisoners / Sedan delivery.

NEIL YOUNG

— with **BEN KEITH, JIM KELTNER, DONALD "DUCK" DUNN, SPOONER OLDHAM**

Apr 00. (cd/c) <*(9362 47305-2/-4)*> **SILVER & GOLD** [10] [22]
– Good to see you / Silver and gold / Daddy went walkin' / Buffalo Springfield again / The great divide / Horseshoe man / Red sun / Distant camera / Razor love / Without rings.

Nov 00. (cd) <*(9362 48036-2)*> **ROAD ROCK VOL.1: FRIENDS & RELATIVES** (live 2000) [ ] [ ]
– Cowgirl in the sand / Walk on / Fool for your love / Peace of mind / Words (between the lines of age) / Motorcycle mama / Tonight's the night / All along the watchtower.

— next with backing from **BOOKER T & THE MG'S** (house band), etc.

Apr 02. (cd) <*(9362 48111-2)*> **ARE YOU PASSIONATE?** [24] [10]
– You're my girl / Mr. Disappointment / Differently / (Quit) Don't say you love me / Let's roll / Are you passionate? / Goin' home / When I hold you in my arms / Be with you / Two old friends / She's a healer. *(d-lp-iss.May02; 9362 48111-1)*

NEIL YOUNG & CRAZY HORSE

Aug 03. (cd) <*(9362 48543-2)*> **GREENDALE** (soundtrack) [24] [22]
– Falling from above / Double E / Devil's sidewalk / Leave the driving / Carmichael / Bandit / Grandpa's interview / Bringin' down dinner / Sun Green / Be the rain. <*(ltd-cd w/dvd+=; 9362 48543-2)*> – LIVE AT VICAR ST., DUBLIN, IRELAND

NEIL YOUNG

Sep 05. (cd/d-lp) <*(9362 49593-2/-1)*> **PRAIRIE WIND** [22] [11]
– The painter / No wonder / Falling off the face of the earth / Far from home / It's a dream / Prairie wind / Here for you / This old guitar / He was the king / When God made me. <*US d-lp+=*> – (interview). *(ltd-cd w/dvd+=; 9362 49494-2)* – (DVD footage).

May 06. (cd) <*(9362 44335-2)*> **LIVING WITH WAR** [14] [15]
– After the garden / Living with war / The restless consumer / Shock and awe / Families / Flags of freedom / Let's impeach the President / Lookin' for a leader / Roger and out / America the beautiful.

– compilations, others, etc. –

Note; on 'Reprise' until otherwise stated.

1971. (7") <*0746*> **CINNAMON GIRL (alt.mix). / ONLY LOVE CAN BREAK YOUR HEART** [-] [ ]

Jan 73. (d-lp) *(K 64015)* <*2XS 6480*> **JOURNEY THROUGH THE PAST** (soundtrack; live & rare) [ ] Nov72 [45]
– For what it's worth – Mr. Soul / Rock & roll woman / Find the cost of freedom / Ohio / Southern man / Are you ready for the country / Let me call you sweetheart / Alabama / Words (between the lines of age) / Relativity invitation / Handel's Messiah / The king of kings theme / Soldier / Let's go away for awhile. <*(cd-iss. Jun94; 7599 26123-2)*>

Jan 73. (7") <*1152*> **HEART OF GOLD. / OLD MAN** [-] [ ]

Mar 74. (7") *(K 14319)* **ONLY LOVE CAN BREAK YOUR HEART. / AFTER THE GOLDRUSH** [ ] [-]

May 74. (7"ep) *(K 14350)* **SOUTHERN MAN / TILL MORNING COMES. / AFTER THE GOLDRUSH / HEART OF GOLD** [ ] [-]

Nov 77. (t-lp) *(K 54088)* <*3RS 2257*> **DECADE** [46] [43]
– Down to the wire + Burned + Mr.Soul + Broken arrow + Expecting to fly (BUFFALO SPRINGFIELD) / Sugar mountain / I am a child / The loner / The old laughing lady / Cinnamon girl / Down by the river / Cowgirl in the sand / I believe in you / After the goldrush / Southern man / Helpless + Ohio (CROSBY, STILLS, NASH & YOUNG) / A man needs a maid / Harvest / Heart of gold / Star of Bethlehem / The needle and the damage done / Tonight's the night (part 1) / Turnstiles / Winterlong / Deep forbidden lake / Like a hurricane / Love is a rose / Cortez the killer / Campaigner / Long may you run (with STEPHEN STILLS). *(re-iss. d-cd Jul93; 7559 27233-2) (d-cd-iss. Jul02 as 'DECADE – THE VERY BEST OF 1968-1976'; same)* – hit UK No.15

Jan 78. (7") <*1393*> **SUGAR MOUNTAIN. / THE NEEDLE AND THE DAMAGE DONE** [-] [ ]

Oct 82. (d-c) *(K4 64043)* **NEIL YOUNG / EVERYBODY KNOWS THIS IS NOWHERE** [ ] [-]

Oct 82. (d-c) *(K4 64044)* **AFTER THE GOLDRUSH / HARVEST** [ ] [-]

Feb 87. (cd) *(925271-2)* **THE BEST OF NEIL YOUNG** [ ] [ ]

Jan 93. (cd) *Movieplay Gold; (MPG 74011)* **THE LOST TAPES** [ ] [-]

Jan 93. (cd/c) *Geffen; (GED/GEC 24452)* **LUCKY THIRTEEN** (80's material) [69] [ ]
– Sample and hold / Transformer man / Depression blues / Get gone / Don't take your love away from me / Once an angel / Where is the highway tonight / Hippie dream / Pressure / Around the world / East vacation / Ain't it the truth / This note's for you. *(cd re-iss. Sep96; GFLD 19328)*

Nov 04. (cd) <*(9362 48935-2)*> **GREATEST HITS** [45] [27]
– Down by the river / Cowgirl in the sand / Cinnamon girl / Helpless / After the gold rush / Only love can break your heart / Southern man / Ohio / The needle and the damage done / Old man / Heart of gold / Like a hurricane / Comes a time / Hey hey, my my (into the black) / Rockin' in the free world / Harvest moon. *(ltd-cd w/dvd+=; 9362 48944-2)* – (DVD tracks).

□ Robin ZANDER (see under ⇒ CHEAP TRICK)

Frank ZAPPA

Born: FRANK VINCENT ZAPPA, 21 Dec'40, Baltimore, Maryland, USA, from Sicilian and Greek parents, who moved to California in 1950. In 1956, he formed The BLACKOUTS with school chum DON VAN VLIET (aka CAPTAIN BEEFHEART). After marrying in the late 50's, he wrote a soundtrack for B-movie, 'The World's Greatest Sinner'. In 1963, after writing another B-movie soundtrack, 'Run Home Slow', he set up his own Studio Z. He also initiated local groups, The MASTERS and The SOUL GIANTS, who recorded some extremely rare 45's. In 1964, he was arrested and sentenced to 10 days in prison and put on probation for 3 years, having made a pornographic tape. He moved to Los Angeles and reformed The SOUL GIANTS, who soon evolved into The MOTHERS OF INVENTION. Early in 1966, after a residency at The Whiskey A-Go-Go, they were signed to 'M.G.M.' by producer Tom Wilson. Their debut album (a double!), 'FREAK OUT!', peaked at No.130 in the States, an avant-garde, satirical piece, that combined psych-pop/rock of songs such as, 'WHO ARE THE BRAIN POLICE' and 'HELP, I'M A ROCK'. The following year (1967), FRANK and his MOTHERS, unleashed another set of weird but wonderful songs on the 'ABSOLUTELY FREE' album. This contained seminal work with equally bizarre titles, 'CALL ANY VEGETABLE', 'SON OF SUZY CREAMCHEESE' and 'BROWN SHOES DON'T MAKE IT', the album nearly scratching the surface of the Top 40. On the 23rd of September '67, The MOTHERS played London's Albert Hall with a 15-piece orchestra, an arrangement he would take further on future albums. His third album, 'WE'RE ONLY IN IT FOR THE MONEY' was an obvious swipe at The BEATLES and their sleeve design for 'Sgt. Pepper's'. This was certainly FRANK and the band's most inventive work to date, the album taking a uniquely anti-drug/hippie stance. The tracks 'LET'S MAKE THE WATER TURN BLACK', 'MOM AND DAD' and 'FLOWER PUNK' being his swipe at America and the 60's counter-cultural establishment. His work continued apace, 'LUMPY GRAVY', 'CRUISING WITH RUBEN AND THE JETS' and 'UNCLE MEAT' all hitting the shelves in the space of a year. Late in 1969, FRANK released his first solo album, 'HOT RATS', which gave him deserved widespread critical acclaim, hitting Top 10 in Britain! The album forsook doo-wop and sardonic pastiche, for a more rock-based guitar extravaganza, the tracks 'PEACHES EN REGALIA' and the BEEFHEART-led 'WILLIE THE WIMP', becoming future ZAPPA jewels. For a few years to come, he combined MOTHERS albums with solo releases (normally with his entourage anyway), the best of these came in the form of live sets, including the double, 'FILLMORE EAST – JUNE 1971'. His commercial fortunes declined however, until The MOTHERS (who had just re-united) came back with the almost pornographic, 'OVERNITE SENSATION', which included the squealing, 'DINAH MOE HUMM'. A year later in 1974, he attacked the US charts once more with the Top 10 return to form, 'APOSTROPHE (')', which featured the cautionary, 'DON'T EAT THE YELLOW SNOW'. His work was now gaining more attention and a live album with his old buddy CAPTAIN BEEFHEART, reconciled their egotistical differences. In 1976, after securing a new deal with 'Warners', he unleashed another fine effort, 'ZOOT ALLURES', which contained some more risqué ditties in the shape of the rocking, 'DISCO BOY' and 'FRIENDLY LITTLE FINGER'. After releasing a few instrumental albums, he was back again in 1979 with the 'SHEIK YERBOUTI' set, which included another dig at dance music, 'DANCIN' FOOL' and the cheeky 'BOBBY BROWN GOES DOWN'. The album 'JOE GARAGE' (ACTS 1, II & III) was split over two albums and a lot more was to come in the 80's. Although his work was still quite excellent during this period (i.e. 'SHIP ARRIVING TOO LATE TO SAVE A DROWNING WITCH' and 'THE MAN FROM UTOPIA' being his best), he returned to his favourite pastime of jazz and classical. In the early 90's, he was diagnosed with prostate cancer, and sadly he was to die on the 4th of December '93.

• **Songwriters:** ZAPPA compositions, augmented by MOTHERS. Covered WHIPPING POST (Allman Brothers Band) / STAIRWAY TO HEAVEN (Led Zeppelin) / etc. • **Trivia:** In 1969, he married for a second time and was soon the father of sons, DWEEZIL (who became a guitarist in the 80's), AHMET RODAN, and daughters MOON UNIT and DIVA. In 1976, ZAPPA produced GRAND FUNK on their lp, 'Good Singin', Good Playin'.

Album rating: FREAK OUT (*8) / ABSOLUTELY FREE (*8) / WE'RE ONLY IN IT FOR THE MONEY (*8) / LUMPY GRAVY (*6) / CRUISING WITH RUBEN AND THE JETS (*6) / MOTHERMANIA – THE BEST OF THE MOTHERS compilation (*8) / UNCLE MEAT soundtrack (*7) / HOT RATS (*8) / BURNT WEENY SANDWICH (*6) / WEASELS RIPPED MY FLESH (*7) / CHUNGA'S REVENGE (*7) / FILLMORE EAST: JUNE 1971 (*6) / 200 MOTELS soundtrack (*5) / JUST ANOTHER BAND FROM L.A. (*5) / WAKA – JAWAKA (*6) / THE GRAND WAZOO (*6) / OVER-NITE SENSATION (*8) / APOSTROPHE (') (*8) / ROXY & ELSEWHERE (*6; by Frank Zappa – Mothers) / ONE SIZE FITS ALL (*8; as Frank Zappa & The Mothers Of Invention) / BONGO FURY (*6; as Frank Zappa, Captain Beefheart & The Mothers) / ZOOT ALLURES (*7) / ZAPPA IN NEW YORK (*6) / STUDIO TAN (*5) / SLEEP DIRT (*4) / SHEIK YERBOUTI (*6) / ORCHESTRAL FAVORITES (*4) / JOE'S GARAGE, ACT I (*7) / JOE'S GARAGE, ACTS II & III (*6) / TINSEL TOWN REBELLION (*7) / YOU ARE WHAT YOU IS (*7) / SHIP ARRIVING TO LATE TO SAVE A DROWNING WITCH (*6) / SHUT UP 'N PLAY YER GUITAR (*6) / THE MAN FROM UTOPIA (*5) / THEM OR US (*8) / THING FISH (*6) / DOES HUMOR BELONG IN MUSIC (*6) / FRANK ZAPPA MEETS THE MOTHERS OF PREVENTION (*5) / JAZZ FROM HELL (*4) / THE LONDON SYMPHONY ORCHESTRA VOL.II out-takes (*3) / GUITAR exploitation (*4) / YOU CAN'T DO THAT ON STAGE ANYMORE, VOL.1 collection (*6) / YOU CAN'T DO THAT ON STAGE ANYMORE, VOL.2 collection (*6) / BROADWAY THE HARD WAY (*5) / BABY SNAKES soundtrack (*3) / YOU CAN'T DO THAT ON STAGE ANYMORE, VOL.3 collection (*6) / THE BEST BAND YOU NEVER HEARD IN YOUR LIFE collection (*6) / MAKE A JAZZ NOISE HERE collection (*4) / YOU CAN'T DO THAT ON STAGE ANYMORE, VOL.4 collection (*6) / BEAT THE BOOTS boxed bootlegs (*5) / BEAT THE BOOTS #2 boxed bootlegs (*5) / YOU CAN'T DO THAT ON STAGE ANYMORE, VOL.5 collection (*6) / YOU CAN'T DO THAT ON STAGE ANYMORE, VOL.6 collection (*6) / AHEAD OF THEIR TIME early stuff (*5) / THE YELLOW SHARK (*7) / STRICTLY COMMERCIAL – THE BEST OF FRANK ZAPPA (*9) / LOST EPISODES (*7) / LATHER (*5) / HAVE I OFFENDED SOMEONE collection (*7) / STRICTLY GENTEEL: A CLASSICAL INTRODUCTION collection (*7)

FRANK ZAPPA

the MOTHERS OF INVENTION

FRANK ZAPPA – guitar, vocals / with **RAY COLLINS** – vocals (had been temp.repl. by JIM GUERCIO; later a producer) / **ELLIOTT INGBER** – guitar repl. JIM FIELDER + STEVE MANN who had repl. HENRY VESTINE. Before he moved onto CANNED HEAT he had repl. MOTHERS original ALICE STUART. / **ROY ESTRADA** – bass / **JIM BLACK** – drums

Verve Verve-MGM

1966. (7") *<10418>* **HELP, I'M A ROCK. / HOW COULD I BE SUCH A FOOL?** [–] [ ]

Nov 66. (7") *(VS 545)* **IT CAN'T HAPPEN HERE. / HOW COULD I BE SUCH A FOOL?** [ ] [–]

1966. (7") *<10458>* **TROUBLE EVERY DAY. / WHO ARE THE BRAIN POLICE?** [–] [ ]

Mar 67. (lp; stereo/mono) <US; d-lp+=*> *(S+/VLP 9154)* *<5005>* **FREAK OUT!** [ ] Aug66 [ ]
– Hungry freaks, daddy / I ain't got no heart / Who are the brain police? / Go cry on somebody else's shoulder * / Motherly love / How could I be such a fool * / Wowie Zowie / You didn't try to call me / Any way the wind blows * / I'm not satisfied / You're probably wondering why I'm here / Trouble comin' every day / Help, I'm a rock / The return of the son of monster magnet. *(UK re-iss. Dec71 on 'Verve-Polydor' d-lp; 2683 004) (cd-iss. Oct87 on 'Zappa'; CDZAP 1) <Rykodisc'US> (cd re-iss. May95 on 'Rykodisc'; RCD 10501)*

— **JIM 'MOTORHEAD' SHERWOOD** – sax repl. INGBER who joined FRATERNITY OF MAN. He later changed his name and joined CAPTAIN BEEFHEART / added **BILLY MUNDI** – drums / **DON PRESTON** – keyboards / **BUNK GARDNER** – horns

Apr 67. (7") *(VS 557)* **BIG LEG EMMA. / WHY DON'T YOU DO ME RIGHT?** [ ] [–]

Oct 67. (lp; stereo/mono) *(S+/VLP 9174) <5013>* **ABSOLUTELY FREE** [ ] May67 [41]
– Plastic people / The duke of prunes / Amnesia vivace / The Duke regains his chops / Call any vegetable / Invocation and ritual dance of the young pumpkin / Soft-cell conclusion and ending of side 1 / America drinks / Status back baby / Uncle Bernie's farm / Son of Suzy Creamcheese / Brown shoes don't make it / America drinks and goes home. *(re-iss. Jun72 on 'Verve-Polydor'; 2317 035) (cd-iss. Jan89 on 'Zappa'; CDZAP 12) ('Rykodisc' US version +=) (cd re-iss. May95 on 'Rykodisc'+=; RCD 10502)* – Big leg Emma / Why don'tcha do me right?.

— **ZAPPA, ESTRADA, MUNDI, PRESTON, GARDNER & JIMMY CARL BLACK** plus **IAN UNDERWOOD** – piano, wind repl. COLLINS

Dec 67. (7") *<10570>* **MOTHER PEOPLE. / LONELY LITTLE GIRL (version)** [–] [ ]

Jun 68. (lp; stereo/mono) *(S+/VLP 9199) <5045>* **WE'RE ONLY IN IT FOR THE MONEY** [32] Jan68 [30]
– Are you hung up? / Who needs the peace corps? / Concentration Moon / Mom and dad / Telephone conversation / Bow tie daddy / Harry, you're a beast / What's the ugliest part of your body? / Absolutely free / Flower punk / Hot poop / Nasal retentive calliope music / Let's make the water turn black / The idiot bastard son / Lonely little girl / Take your clothes off when you dance / What's the ugliest part of your body (reprise) / Mother people / The chrome plated megaphone of destiny. *(re-iss. Jun72 on 'Verve-Polydor'; 2317 034) (re-iss. cd/c/lp Apr95 on 'Rykodisc'; RCD/RAC/RALP 10503)*

— (now with The ABNUCEALS EMUUKHA ELECTRIC SYMPHONY ORCHESTRA & CHORUS; a 50+ piece orchestra incl. GARDNER + GUERIN + some other MOTHERS in choir)

Oct 68. (lp; stereo/mono; by FRANK ZAPPA) *(S+/VLP 9223)* *<8741>* **LUMPY GRAVY** [ ] May68 [ ]
– Lumpy gravy (part one): The way I see it, Barry – Duodenum – Oh no – Bit of nostalgia – It's from Kansas – Bored out 90 over – Almost Chinese – Switching girls – Oh no again – At the gas station – Another pickup – I don't know if I can go through this again / Lumpy gravy (part two): Very distrautening – White ugliness – Amen – Just one more time – A vicious circle – King Kong – Drums are too noisy – Kangaroos – Envelopes the bath tub – Take your clothes off. *(re-iss. Jun72 on 'Verve-Polydor'; 2317 046) (cd-iss. Apr95 on 'Rykodisc'; RCD 10504)*

— **ARTHUR TRIPP III** – drums repl. MUNDI who formed RHINOCEROS / added again **RAY COLLINS** – vocals

Dec 68. (7") **DESERI. / JELLY ROLL GUM DROP** [–] [ ]

Feb 69. (lp; stereo/mono) *(S+/VLP 9237) <5055>* **CRUISING WITH RUBEN & THE JETS** [ ] Nov68 [ ]
– Cheap thrills / Love of my life / How could I be such a fool / Deseri / I'm not satisfied / Jelly roll gum drop / Anything / Later that night / You didn't try to call me / Fountain of love / No no no / Anyway the wind blows * / Stuff up the cracks. *(re-iss. Jun73 on 'Verve-Polydor'; 2317 069) (cd-iss. Oct87 on 'Zappa'; CDZAP 4) ('Rykodisc'US) (re-iss. cd May95 on 'Rykodisc'; RCD 10505)*

Apr 69. (lp; stereo/mono) *(S+/VLP 9239) <5068>* **MOTHERMANIA: THE BEST OF THE MOTHERS** (compilation) [ ] Mar68 [ ]
– Brown shoes don't make it / Mother people / Duke of prunes / Call any vegetable / The idiot bastard son / It can't happen here / You're probably wondering why I'm here / Who are the brain police? / Plastic people / Hungry freaks, daddy / America drinks and goes home. *(re-iss. Feb72 on 'Verve-Polydor'; 2317 047) (re-iss. Jul73 on 'Verve-Polydor'; 2352 017)*

— added **RUTH KOMANOFF** (UNDERWOOD) – marimba, vibes / **NELCY WALKER** – soprano vocals (on 2)

Transatla. Bizarre

Sep 69. (d-lp) *(TRA 197) <2024>* **UNCLE MEAT** [ ] Apr69 [43]
– Uncle Meat: main title theme / The voice of cheese / Nine types of industrial pollution / Zolar Czakl / Dog breath, in the year of the plague / The legend of the golden arches / Louie Louie (at the Royal Albert Hall in London) / The dog breath variations / Sleeping in a jar / Our bizarre relationship / The Uncle Meat variations / Electric Aunt Jemima // Prelude to King Kong / God bless America (live at the Whisky A Go Go) / A pound for a brown on the bus / Ian Underwood whips it out (live on stage in Copenhagen) / Mr. Green genes / We can shoot you / "If we'd all been living in California" / The air / Project X / Cruising for burgers // Uncle Meat film excerpt part I * / Tengo na minchia tanta * / Uncle Meat film excerpt part II * / King Kong itself / King Kong II / King Kong III / King Kong IV / King Kong V / King Kong VI. *(d-cd-iss. Oct87 on 'Zappa' += *; CDZAP 3) (cd-iss. May95 on 'Rykodisc' += *; RCD 10506-7)*

Sep 69. (7") *<0840>* **MY GUITAR. / DOG BREATH** [–] [ ]

FRANK ZAPPA

— solo guitar w/ **UNDERWOOD** plus **CAPTAIN BEEFHEART** – vocals / **JEAN-LUC PONTY + SUGAR-CANE HARRIS** – violin / **MAX BENNETT + SHUGGY OTIS** – bass / **PAUL HUMPHREY + RON SELICO + JOHN GUERIN** – drums

Reprise Reprise

Jan 70. (7") *<0889>* **PEACHES EN REGALIA. / LITTLE UMBRELLAS** [–] [ ]

Feb 70. (lp) *(RSLP <6356>)* **HOT RATS** [9] Oct69 [ ]
– Peaches en regalia / Willie the pimp / Son of Mr. Green genes / Little umbrellas / The Gumbo variations / It must be a camel. *(re-iss. Jul71; K 44078) (remixed cd-iss. Oct87 on 'Zappa'; CDZAP 2) (cd-iss. May95 on 'Rykodisc'; RCD 10508)*

the MOTHERS OF INVENTION

— (see last MOTHERS line-up) + add **BUZZ GARDNER** – horns / **SUGAR-CANE HARRIS** – violin (now without KOMANOFF)

Mar 70. (lp) *(RSLP <6370>)* **BURNT WEENY SANDWICH** [17] Feb70 [94]
– WPLJ / Igor's boogie – phase 1 / Overture to a holiday in Berlin / Theme from Burnt Weenie Sandwich / Igor's boogie – phase 2 / Holiday in Berlin, full blown / Aybe sea / The little house I used to live in / Valarie. *(re-iss. Jul71; K 44083) (cd-iss. Nov91 on 'Zappa'; CDZAP 35) (re-iss. cd May95 on 'Rykodisc'; RCD 10509)*

Mar 70. (7") *<0892>* **WPLJ. / MY GUITAR** [–] [ ]
(below album used rare material from 1967-69, as The MOTHERS OF INVENTION officially disbanded Oct69) guest LOWELL GEORGE – guitar

Sep 70. (lp) *(RSLP <2028>)* **WEASELS RIPPED MY FLESH** [28] [ ]
– Didja get any onya? / Directly from my heart to you / Prelude to the afternoon of a sexually aroused gas mask / Toads of the short forest / Get a little / Eric Dolphy memorial barbecue / Dwarf Nebula processional march and dwarf Nebula / My guitar wants to kill your mama / oh no / The Orange County lumber truck / Weasels ripped my flesh. *(re-iss. Jul71; K 44019) (cd-iss. May95 on 'Rykodisc'; RCD 10510)*

— LOWELL and ROY formed LITTLE FEAT. ART TRIPP became ED MARIMBA and joined CAPTAIN BEEFHEART & HIS MAGIC BAND. BUNK GARDNER and JIMMY CARL BLACK formed GERONIMO BLACK.

FRANK ZAPPA

— formed solo band with **IAN UNDERWOOD, SUGAR-CANE HARRIS & MAX BENNETT**. He introduced **JEFF SIMMONS** – bass / **JOHN GUERIN** – drums / **AYNSLEY DUNBAR** – drums / **GEORGE DUKE** –

keyboards, trombone / **MARK VOLMAN + HOWARD KAYLAN** (aka The PHLORESCENT LEECH AND EDDIE) – vocals (ex-TURTLES)

Nov 70. (lp) *(RSLP <2030>)* **CHUNGA'S REVENGE** [43] [ ]
– Transylvania boogie / Road ladies / Twenty small cigars / The Nancy and Mary music (part 1, 2 & 3) / Tell me you love me / Would you go all the way? / Chunga's revenge / The clap / Rudy wants to buy yez a drink / Sharleena. *(re-iss. Jul71; K 44020) (cd-iss. Jun90 on 'Zappa'; CDZAP 23) (cd-iss. May95 on 'Rykodisc'; RCD 10511)*

Nov 70. (7") *<0967>* **TELL ME YOU LOVE ME. / WOULD YOU GO ALL THE WAY?** [–] [ ]

the MOTHERS

— re-formed early 1971 and retained **DON PRESTON** – mini moog / **DUNBAR / VOLMAN & KAYLAN** and recruited **JIM PONS** – bass (ex-TURTLES) / **BOB HARRIS** – keyboards

Aug 71. (lp) *(K 44150) <2042>* **FILLMORE EAST – JUNE 1971 (live)** [ ] [38]
– Little house I used to live in / The mud shark / What kind of girl do you think we are? / Bwana Dik / Latex solar beef / Willie the pimp (part 1) / Do you like my new car? / Happy together / Lonesome electric turkey / Peaches en regalia / Tears began to fall. *(cd-iss. Jun90 on 'Zappa'; CDZAP 29) (cd re-iss. May95 on 'Rykodisc'; RCD 10512)*

Aug 71. (7") *(K 14100) <1052>* **TEARS BEGAN TO FALL. / JUNIER MINTZ BOOGIE** [ ] [ ]

FRANK ZAPPA

— solo, with MOTHERS:- **IAN + RUTH UNDERWOOD / GEORGE DUKE / AYNSLEY DUNBAR / VOLMAN + KAYLAN / MARTIN LICKERT** – bass / guests were **JIM PONS + JIMMY CARL BLACK / THEODORE BIKEL** – narrator + ROYAL PHILHARMONIC ORCHESTRA

U.A. U.A.

Oct 71. (d-lp) *(UDF 50003) <9956>* **200 MOTELS (live studio soundtrack)** [ ] [59]
– Semi-fraudulent – Direct-from-Hollywood overture / Mystery roach / Dance of the rock & roll interviewers / This town is a sealed tuna sandwich (prologue) / Tuna fish promenade / Dance of the just plain folks / This town is a sealed tuna fish sandwich (reprise) / The sealed tuna bolero / Lonesome cowboy Burt / Touring can make you crazy / Would you like a snack? / Redneck eats / Centerville / She painted up her face / Janet's big dance number / Half a dozen provocative squats / Mysterioso / Shove it right in / Lucy's seduction of a bored violinist & postlude / I'm stealing the towels / Dental hygeine dilemma / Does this kind of life look interesting to you? / Daddy, daddy, daddy / Penis dimension / What will this evening bring me this morning / A nun suit painted on some old boxes / Magic fingers / Motorhead's midnight ranch / Dew on the newts we got / The lad searches the night for his newts / The girl wants to fix him some broth / The girl's dream / Little green scratchy sweaters & corduroy ponce / Strictly genteel (the finale). *(re-iss. Jan89 on 'M.C.A.' d-lp/c; MCA/+C 24183) <(d-cd-iss. Oct97 on 'Rykodisc'+=; RCD 10513)>* – (extra cuts).

Oct 71. (7") *<50857>* **MAGIC FINGERS. / DADDY, DADDY, DADDY** [–] [ ]

Nov 71. (7") *(UP 35319)* **WHAT WILL THIS EVENING BRING ME THIS MORNING?. / DADDY, DADDY, DADDY** [ ] [–]

— now with a plethera of musicians (see next solo also), including some MOTHERS

Reprise Reprise

Aug 72. (lp) *(K 44203) <2094>* **WAKA/JAWAKA: HOT RATS** [ ] [ ]
– Big Swifty / Your mouth / It just might be a one-shot deal / Waka-Jawaka. *(cd-iss. Jan89 on 'Zappa'; CDZAP 10) (re-iss. cd May95 on 'Rykodisc'; RCD 10516)*
(above featured **PRESTON, DUNBAR, DUKE, SIMMONS** & others also on next).

the MOTHERS

— recorded live 7th August'71. (see last ZAPPA line-up) Re-formed earlier that year minus BOB HARRIS

Reprise Bizarre

Jun 72. (lp) *(K 44179) <2075>* **JUST ANOTHER BAND FROM L.A.** [ ] [85]
– Billy the mountain / Call any vegetable / Eddie, are you kidding? / Magdalena / Dog breath. *(cd-iss. Jun90 on 'Zappa'; CDZAP 10515) (cd re-iss. May95 on 'Rykodisc'; RCD 10515)*

— The MOTHERS added **TONY DURAN** – slide guitar / **ERRONEOUS** – bass repl. SIMMONS / **KEN SHROYER** – trombone / **JOEL PESKIN** – tenor saxophone / **SAL MARQUEZ** – timpani / **BILL BYERS** – trombone / **MIKE ALTSCHUL** – wind / **JANET NEVILLE-FERGUSON** – vocals / **CHUNKY** – vocals / **EARL DUMLER, FRED JACKSON + TONY ORTEGA** – wind / **ERNIE WATTS** – sax / **ERNIE TACK + MALCOLM McNABB** – horns / **JOHNNY ROTELLA, BOB ZIMMITTI + LEE CLEMENT** – percussion / **JOANNE CALDWELL McNABB** – violin

Dec 72. (lp) *(K 44209)* **THE GRAND WAZOO** [ ] [–]
– The grand Wazoo / For Calvin (and his next two hitch-hikers) / Cletus-awreetus-awrightus / Eat that question / Blessed relief. *(cd-iss. Sep90 on 'Zappa'; CDZAP 31) (cd re-iss. May95 on 'Rykodisc'; RCD 10517)*

Dec 72. (7") *<1127>* **CLETUS-AWREETUS-AWRIGHTUS. / EAT THAT QUESTION** [–] [ ]

— **ZAPPA** brought back **IAN + RUTH UNDERWOOD** (They were on '72 tour) / **GEORGE DUKE / JEAN-LUC PONTY / SAL MARQUEZ.** He introduced **TOM FOWLER** – bass / **BRUCE FOWLER** – trombone / **RALPH HUMPHREY** – drums

DiscReet DiscReet

Jan 73. (lp) *(K 41000) <2149>* **OVERNITE SENSATION** [ ] [32]
– Camarillo brillo / I'm the slime / Dirty love / Fifty-fifty / Zomby woof / Dinah-Moe humm / Montana. *<cd-iss. Oct87 w / 'APOSTROPHE' tracks on 'Rykodisc'> (cd-iss. Jul90 on 'Zappa'; CDZAP 36) (re-iss. cd/c Apr95 on 'Rykodisc'; RCD/RAC 10518)*

Feb 73. (7") *<1180>* **I'M THE SLIME. / MONTANA** [–] [ ]

FRANK ZAPPA

— solo retaining current MOTHERS. He also brought back past MOTHERS: **AYNSLEY DUNBAR / RAY COLLINS / ERRONEOUS / JOHN GUERIN / SUGAR CANE HARRIS / RUBEN GUEVARA + ROBERT CAMARENA** – b.vocals (of RUBEN &..JETS) **NAPOLEON BROCK** – saxophone / guest **JACK BRUCE** – bass (ex-CREAM)

May 74. (lp/c) *(K/K4 59201) <2175>* **APOSTROPHE (')** [ ] Apr74 [10]
– Don't eat the yellow snow / Nanook rubs it / St. Alfonzo's pancake breakfast / Father O'Blivion / Cosmik debris / Excentrifugal forz / Apostrophe' / Uncle Remus / Stink-foot. *(re-iss. cd/c Apr95 on 'Rykodisc'; RCD/RAC 10519) (cd-version-iss.Jun96; RCD 80519)*

Aug 74. (7") *<1312>* **DON'T EAT THE YELLOW SNOW. / COSMIK DEBRIS** [–] [86]

Aug 74. (7") *(K 19201)* **COSMIK DEBRIS. / UNCLE REMUS** [ ] [–]

Sep 74. (7") *(K 19202)* **DON'T EAT THE YELLOW SNOW. / CAMARILLO BRILLO** [ ] [–]

— were now basically **GEORGE DUKE / TOM FOWLER / NAPOLEON / RUTH UNDERWOOD** and new drummer **CHESTER THOMPSON.** Temp. old members were also used **DON PRESTON / BRUCE + WALT FOWLER / JEFF SIMMONS + RALPH HUMPHREY**

Oct 74. (d-lp/c; ZAPPA / MOTHERS) *(K/K4 69201) <2202>* **ROXY & ELSEWHERE (live + unreleased)** [ ] Sep74 [27]
– Preamble / Penguin in bondage / Pygmy twylyte / Dummy up / Preamble / Village of the sun / Echidna's arf (of you) / Don't you ever wash that thing? / Preamble / Cheepnis / Son of Orange County / More trouble every day / Be-bop tango (of old Jazzmen's church). *(cd-iss. Feb92 on 'Zappa'; CDZAP 39) (re-iss. cd/c May95 on 'Rykodisc'; RCD/RAC 10520)*

— temp.members above repl. by **JOHNNY GUITAR WATSON** – vocals / **JAMES YOUMAN** – bass / **BLOODSHOT ROLLIN RED** (DON WATSON) – harmonica

Aug 75. (lp; by FRANK ZAPPA & THE MOTHERS OF INVENTION) *(K 59207) <2216>* **ONE SIZE FITS ALL** [ ] [26]
– Inca roads / Can't afford no shoes / Sofa No.1 / Po-jama people / Florentine pogen / Evelyn, a modified dog / San Ber'dino / Andy / Sofa No.2. *<(cd-iss. Jan89 on 'Zappa'; RCD 10095 / CDZAP 11)> (re-iss. cd May95 on 'Rykodisc'; RCD 10521)*

Sep 75. (7"; by FRANK ZAPPA & THE MOTHERS OF INVENTION) *(K 19205)* **STINK-FOOT. / DU BIST MEIN SOFA** [ ] [–]

— next a collaboration with **CAPTAIN BEEFHEART** with also **DUKE / FOWLER's / BROCK / THOMPSON** plus **TERRY BOZZIO** – drums / **DENNY WALLEY**– slide guitar

Nov 75. (lp; by FRANK ZAPPA, CAPTAIN BEEFHEART & THE MOTHERS) *(K 59209; w-drawn) <2234>* **BONGO FURY (live + 2 studio)** [–] [66]
– Debra Kadabra / Caroline hard-core ecstasy / Sam with the showing scalp flat top / Poofter's froth Wyoming plans ahead / 200 years old / Cucamonga / Advance romance / Man with the woman head / Muffin man. *(cd-iss. Jan89 on 'Zappa'; CDZAP 15) <US 'Rykodisc'; RY 10097> (re-iss. cd May95 on 'Rykodisc'; RCD 10522)*

FRANK ZAPPA

— finally disbanded The MOTHERS and went solo. Augmented by **TERRY BOZZIO** – drums / **ROY ESTRADA, DAVE PARLATO + RUTH UNDERWOOD** – marimba, synth / **DAVEY MOIRE** – b.vocals / **LU ANN NEIL** – harp / **ANDRE LEWIS** – backing vocals

Warners Warners

Oct 76. (7") *<8296>* **FIND HER FINER. / ZOOT ALLURES** [–] [ ]

Nov 76. (lp/c) *(K/K4 56298) <2970>* **ZOOT ALLURES** [ ] [61]
– Wind up workin' in a gas station / Black napkins / The torture never stops / Ms. Pinky / Find her finer / Friendly little finger / Wonderful wino / Zoot allures / Disco boy. *(cd-iss. Jun90 on 'Zappa'; CDZAP 22) (re-iss. cd May95 on 'Rykodisc'; RCD 10523)*

Dec 76. (7") *<8342>* **DISCO BOY. / MS. PINKY** [–] [ ]

— His basic band were **EDDIE JOBSON** – keyboards, violin (ex-ROXY MUSIC) / **RAY WHITE** – guitar, vocals / **PATRICK O'HEARN** – bass / **RUTH UNDERWOOD** – / **TERRY BOZZIO** – drums. Plus brass section – **RANDY + MICHAEL BRECKER / LOU MARINI / RONNIE CUBER / TOM MALONE / DAVID SAMUELS** – percussion

DiscReet DiscReet

Jun 78. (d-lp) *(K 69204) <2290>* **ZAPPA IN NEW YORK (live 1976)** [55] [57]
– Titties & beer / Cruisin' for burgers * / I promise not to come in your mouth / Punky's whips *[not on some]* / Honey, don't you want a man like me? / The Illinois enema bandit // I'm the slime * / Pound for a brown * / Manx needs women / The black page drum solo – Black page #1 / Big leg Emma / Sofa / Black page #2 / The torture never stops * / The purple lagoon – approximate. *(d-cd-iss. Sep91 on 'Zappa'; CDDZAP 37) (cd re-iss. May95 on 'Rykodisc'+= *; RCD 10524-5)*

Nov 78. (lp/c) *(K/K4 59210) <2291>* **STUDIO TAN** (2 instrumental 74-76) [ ] [ ]
– The adventures of Greggery Peccary / Revised music for guitar and low budget orchestra / Lemme take you to the beach / RDNZL. *(cd-iss. May95 on 'Rykodisc'; RCD 10526)*

Feb 79. (lp/c) *(K/K4 59211) <2292>* **SLEEP DIRT** (mostly instrumental 74-76) [ ] [ ]
– Filthy habits / Flambay / Spider of destiny / Regyptian strut / Time is money / Sleep dirt / The ocean is the ultimate solution. *(cd-iss. Oct91 on 'Zappa'; CDZAP 43) (cd re-iss. May95 on 'Rykodisc'; RCD 10527)*

— He retained only **BOZZIO + O'HEARN,** bringing back **NAPOLEON, ANDRE LEWIS + MOIRE.** New musicians:- **ADRIAN BELEW** – rhythm guitar, some lead vox / **TOMMY MARS** – keyboards, vocals / **PETER WOLF** – keyboards / **ED MANN** – percussion, vocals / **RANDY THORNTON** – b.vocals / **DAVID OCKER** – clarinet (1)

Zappa-CBS Zappa

Mar 79. (d-lp/d-c) *(CBS/40 88339) <1501>* **SHEIK YERBOUTI** [32] [21]
– I have been in you / Flakes / Broken hearts are for assholes / I'm so cute / Jones crusher / What ever happened to all the fun in the world / Rat tomago / Wait a ninute / Bobby Brown goes down / Rubber shirt / The Sheik Yerbouti tango / Baby snakes / Tryin' to grow a chin / City of tiny lites / Dancin' fool / Jewish princess / Wild love / Yo' mama. *(re-iss. Feb86 on 'E.M.I.' d-lp/d-c; EN/TCEN 5001) (cd-iss. Apr88; CDEN 5001) (cd re-iss. Jun91 on 'Zappa'; CDZAP 28) (re-iss. cd/c May95 on 'Rykodisc'; RCD/RAC 10528)*

Apr 79. (7") *(SCBS 7261) <10>* **DANCIN' FOOL. / BABY SNAKES** [ ] [45]

— **WARREN CUCURULLO** – rhythm guitar repl. BELEW (later to BOWIE + TALKING HEADS) /**IKE WILLIS** – lead vocals / **ARTHUR BARROW** – bass repl. O'HEARN / **VINNIE COLAIUTA** – drums repl. TERRY BOZZIO. Others in line-up **DALE BOZZIO** – vocals / **DENNIS WALLEY** – slide guitar / **MARGINAL CHAGRIN** – sax / **WOLF + MANN.**

Sep 79. (lp/c) *(CBS/40 86101) <1603>* **JOE'S GARAGE ACT I** [62] [27]
– Central scrutinizer / Joe's garage / Catholic girls / Crew slut / Fembot in a wet T-shirt / On the bus / Why does it hurt when I pee? / Lucille has messed my mind up / Scrutinizer postlude. *<d-cd-iss. Oct87 on 'Rykodisc'; RCD 10060> (UK d-cd-iss. Sep90 on 'Zappa'; CDZAP 20) (d-cd re-iss. May95; RCD 10530-31)*

Jan 80. (7") **JOE'S GARAGE. / CENTRAL SCRUTINIZER** [–] [ ]

Jan 80. (7") *(SCBS 7950)* **JOE'S GARAGE. / CATHOLIC GIRLS** [ ] [–]

— now without DALE, MARS + CHAGRIN

Jan 80. (d-lp/d-c) *(CBS/40 88475) <1502>* **JOE'S GARAGE ACT II & III** [75] [53]
– ACT II:- A token of my extreme / Stick it out / Sy Borg / Dong work for Yuda / Keep it greasey / Outside now / ACT III:- He used to cut the grass / Packard goose / Watermelon in Easter hay / A little green Rosetta. *<US d-cd-iss. Oct87 on 'Rykodisc'; RCD 10061>*

Jun 80. (7") *(SCBS 8652) <ZR 1001>* **I DON'T WANT TO GET DRAFTED. / ANCIENT ARMAMENTS** [ ] [ ]

— now with **STEVE VAI + RAY WHITE + IKE WILLIS** – rhythm guitar, vocals / **TOMMY MARS** – keyboards / **BOB HARRIS** – keyboards, trumpet, high vox / **ED MANN / BARROW** – bass / **COLAIUTA / WOLF**

CBS CBS

May 81. (d-lp/d-c) *(CBS/40 88516) <37336>* **TINSELTOWN REBELLION (live)** [55] [66]
– Fine girl / Easy meat / For the young sophisticate / Love of my life / I ain't got no heart / Panty rap / Tell me you love me / Now you see it – now you don't / Dance contest / The blue light / Tinseltown rebellion / Pick me, I'm clean / Bamboozled by love / Brown shoes don't make it / Peaches III. *(re-iss. Feb86 on 'E.M.I.' d-lp/d-c; EN/TCEN 5002) (d-cd-iss. Apr88; CDEN 5002) (cd-iss. Jun90 on 'Zappa'; CDZAP 26) (re-iss. cd May95 on 'Rykodisc'; RCD 10532)*

— **JIMMY CARL BLACK** – guest vocals returned (+ daughter MOON, son AHMET) to repl. CUCURULLO / WOLF / COLAIUTA and O'HEARN. new members:- **DAVID OCKER** – – clarinet / **PATRICK O'HEARN** – bass / **SHERWOOD** – sax (returned) / **DAVID LOGEMAN** – drums

Oct 81. (d-lp/d-c) *(CBS/40 88560) <37537>* **YOU ARE WHAT YOU IS** [51] [93]
– Teenage wind / Harder than your husband / Doreen / Goblin girl / Theme from the 3rd movement of sinister footwear / Society pages / I'm a beautiful guy / Beauty knows no pain / Charlie's enormous mouth / Any downers? / Conehead / You are what you is / Mudd club / The meek shall inherit nothing / Dumb all over / Heavenly bank account / Suicide chump / Jumbo go away / If only she woulda / Drafted again. *(re-iss. Feb86 on 'E.M.I.' d-lp/d-c; EN/TCEN 5000) (d-cd-iss. Apr88; CDEN 5000) (cd-iss. Jun90 on 'Zappa'; CDZAP 27) (re-iss. cd May95 on 'Rykodisc'; RCD 10536)*

Nov 81. (12"pic-d) *<BPRP 114>* **GOBLIN GIRL. / PINK NAPKINS** [–] [ ]

Feb 82. (7") *(A 1622)* **YOU ARE WHAT YOU IS. / HARDER THAN YOUR HUSBAND** [ ] [ ]
(12"pic-d+=) *(A12 1622)* – Pink napkins / Soup'n'old clothes.

— added **SCOTT THUNES** – bass / **CHAD WACKERMAN** – drums / **BOBBY MARTIN** – keyboards, sax / vocalists ROY ESTRADA, LISA POPIEL / MOON, who replaced WALLEY, LOGEMAN, SHERWOOD, OCKER, STEWART, BLACK + AHMET

Jun 82. (lp/c) *(CBS/40 85804) <38066>* **SHIP ARRIVING TOO LATE TO SAVE A DROWNING WITCH** [61] [23]
– No not now / Valley girl / I come from nowhere / Drowning witch / Envelopes / Teen-age prostitute. *(free 7"w.a.) (XPS 147)* – SHUT UP 'N' PLAY YER GUITAR. / VARIATION ON THE C. SANTANA SECRET *(re-iss. Feb86 on 'E.M.I.' lp/c; EMC/TCEMC 3501) (re-iss. Jun87 on 'Fame' lp/c; FA/TCFA 3180) (cd-iss. Aug91 on 'Zappa'; CDZAP 42) (re-iss. cd May95 on 'Rykodisc'; RCD 10537)*

Jul 82. (7")(12") *<02972><03069>* **VALLEY GIRL. / YOU ARE WHAT YOU IS** [–] [32]

Aug 82. (7"; by FRANK & MOON ZAPPA) *(A 2412) <02972>* **VALLEY GIRL. / TEENAGE PROSTITUTE** [ ] [–]

— **MYRTY KRYSTALL** – sax repl.MOON + POPIEL / **DICK FEGY** – mandolin / also added **CRAIG STEWARD** – harmonica

Jun 83. (lp/c) *(CBS/40 25251) <38403>* **THE MAN FROM UTOPIA** [87] [ ]
– Cocaine decisions / Sex / Tink walks amok / The radio is broken / We are not alone / The dangerous kitchen / The man from Utopia meets Mary Lou / Stick together / The jazz discharge party hats / Luigi & the wise guys * / Moggio. *(re-iss. Feb86 on 'E.M.I.' lp/c; EMC/TCEMC 3500) (re-iss. Apr88 on 'Fame' lp/c)(cd; FA/TCFA 3203)(CDP 790074-2) (cd-iss. Feb93 on 'Zappa'+= *; CDZAP 53) (re-iss. cd May95 on 'Rykodisc'; RCD 10538)*

— **JOHNNY GUITAR WATSON + NAPOLEON MURPHY BROCK** – vocals repl. STEWARD, FEGY, KRISTALL (+ COLAIUTA) other guest his son DWEEZIL ZAPPA – guitar solos (2)

E.M.I. Rykodisc

Sep 84. (7") *(EMI 5499)* **BABY TAKE YOUR TEETH OUT. / STEVIE'S SPANKING** [ ] [ ]

Oct 84. (d-lp/d-c) *(FZD/+TC 1) <R 40027>* **THEM OR US** [53] [ ]
– The closer you are / In France / Ya hozna / Sharleena / Sinister footwear II / Truck driver divorce / Stevie's spanking / Baby take your teeth out / Marqueson's chicken / Planet of my dreams / Be in my video / Them or us / Frogs with dirty, little lips / Whippin' post. *(cd-iss. Apr88; CDEN 24) (cd re-iss. Apr91 on 'Zappa'; CDZAP 30) (re-iss. cd May95 on 'Rykodisc'; RCD 10543)*

1984. (lp) **FRANCESCO ZAPPA** (classical) [-] [ ]
(UK cd-iss. May92 on 'Zappa'; CDZAP 48) (cd re-iss. May95 on 'Rykodisc'; RCD 10546)
(above was conducted by FRANK, and taken from pieces of music from an Italian musician circa 1973-1988)

— **ZAPPA** with band: **VAI, MARS, WHITE, MANN, WACKERMAN, BARROW, THUNES** plus **STEVE DE FURIA & DAVID OCKER** – synclavier programmer. Characters: **IKE WILLIS** (Thing Fish) / **TERRY BOZZIO** (Harry) / His wife **DALE BOZZIO** (Rhonda) / **NAPOLEON MURPHY BROCK** (Evil Prince) / **BOB HARRIS** (Harry as a boy) / **JOHNNY GUITAR WATSON** (Brown Moses) / **RAY WHITE** (Owl Gonkwin Jane Cowhoon)

E.M.I. Capitol

Mar 85. (t-lp/d-c) *(EX240294-1/-4)* <*R 10020*> **THING FISH** [ ] [ ]
– Prologue / The mammy nuns / Harry & Rhonda / Galoot up-date / The 'torchum' never stops / That evil prince / You are what you is / Mudd club / The meek shall inherit nothing / Clowns on velvet / Harry-as-a-boy / He's so gay / The massive improve'lence / Artificial Rhonda / The crab-grass baby / The white boy troubles / No not now / Briefcase boogie / Brown Moses / Wistful wit a fist-full / Drop dead / Won ton on. *(d-cd-iss. Apr88; CDFZ 3) (d-cd-iss. Feb90 on 'Zappa'; CDDZAP 21) (re-iss. d-cd May95 on 'Rykodisc'; RCD 10544-45)*

— In Jun'85, PIERRE BOULEZ released his versions of ZAPPA, under the title 'THE PERFECT STRANGER – BOULEZ CONDUCTS ZAPPA'. Later issued in the UK on cd on 'Rykodisc'; *RCD 10542)*

— musicians; as last but without BOZZIO's, BARROW, BROCK, HARRIS

— **BOBBY MARTIN** – vocals, keyboards repl. DE FURIA + OCKER

Mar 86. (lp/c) *(EMC/TCEMC 3507)* <*ST 74203*> **FRANK ZAPPA MEETS THE MOTHERS OF PREVENTION** [ ] [ ]
– Porn wars / We're turning again / Alien orifice / Aerobics in bondage / I don't even care * / Little beige sambo / What's new in Baltimore / One man, one vote * / H.R. 2911 *. *(cd-iss. Sep90 on 'Zappa'; CDZAP 33)* – repl. Porn wars; w/ *) *(cd-iss. May95 on 'Rykodisc' all tracks; RCD 10547)*

— now ZAPPA on synclavier only + one live from '82. others:- **VAI, WHITE, MARS, MARTIN, MANN, THUNES, WACKERMAN**

E.M.I. Barking P.

Dec 86. (lp/c) *(EMC/TCEMC 3521)* <*74205*> **JAZZ FROM HELL** [ ] [ ]
– Night school / The Beltway bandits / While you were art II / Jazz from Hell / G-spot tornado / Damp ankles / St.Etienne / Massaggio galore. *(cd-iss. Sep90 on 'Zappa'; CDZAP 32) (cd-iss. May95 on 'Rykodisc'; RCD 10549)*

— **FRANK** still with **WILLIS, WACKERMAN, THUNES, MANN, MARTIN,** plus new **MIKE KENEALLY** – guitar, synth., vocals repl. VAI who went solo, etc. / **WALT FOWLER** – trumpet / **BRUCE FOWLER** – trombone / **PAUL CARMAN** – alto sax / **ALBERT WING** – tenor sax / **KURT McGETTRICK** – baritone sax / guest vox – **ERIC BUXTON**

Zappa Zappa

Dec 88. (lp/c/cd) <*(ZAPPA/TZAPPA/CDZAP 14)*> **BROADWAY THE HARD WAY (live)** [ ] [ ]
– Elvis has just left the building / Planet of the baritone women / Any kind of pain / Dickie's such an asshole / When the lie's so big / Rhymin' man / Promiscuous / The untouchables / Why don't you like me? * / Bacon fat * / Stolen moments * / Murder by numbers * / Jezebel boy * / Outside now * / Hot plate heaven at the green hotel * / What kind of a girl? * / Jesus thinks you're a jerk. *(cd+= *) (re-iss. cd May95 on 'Rykodisc'; RCD 10552)*

— Late '91, it was announced FRANK had been diagnosed with prostrate cancer. He was to die of this on 4th Dec'93.

Feb 93. (12"/cd-s) *(12/CD FRANK 101)* **STAIRWAY TO HEAVEN. / BOLERO** [ ] [-]

— next with the ENSEMBLE MODERN, conducted by himself & PETER RUNDEL

Oct 93. (cd/c) <*(CDZAP/TZAPPA 57)*> **YELLOW SHARK (live)** [ ] [ ]
– Intro / Dog breath variations / Uncle Meat / Outrage at Valdez / Times beach II / III revised / The girl in the magnesium dress / Be bop tango / Ruth is sleeping / None of the above / Pentagon afternoon / Questi cazzi di piccione / Times beach III / Food gathering in post industrial America 1992 / Welcome to the united States / Pound for a brown / Exercise 4 / Get Whitey / G-spot tornado. *(re-iss. cd/c May95 on 'Rykodisc'; RCD/RAC 40560)*

— an opera-pantomime with pre-recorded voices and music supplied by THE PIANO PEOPLE: **F.Z. / SPIDER / JOHN / MOTORHEAD / LARRY / ROY / LOUIS / MONICA / GILLY / GIRL 1 / GIRL 2 / MOON / MIKE / ALI / TODD / DARYL / JESUS**

Feb 95. (d-cd/d-c) <*(CDDZAP/TZAPPA 56)*> **CIVILIZATION PHAZE III** [ ] [ ]
– ACT ONE; This is phaze III / Put a motor in yourself / Oh-umm / They made me eat it / Reagan at Bitburg / A very nice body / Navanax / How the pigs' music works / Xmas values / Dark water / Amnerika / Have you ever heard their band / Religious superstition / Saliva can only take so much / Buffalo voice / Someplace else right now / Get a life / A kayak (on snow) / N-lite (I) Negative light (II) Venice submerged (III) The new world order (IV) The lifestyle you deserve (V) Creationism (VI) He is risen / / ACT TWO; I wish Motorhead would come back / Secular humanism / Attack! attack! attack! / I was in a drum / A different octave / This ain't CNN / The pigs' music / A pig with wings / This is all wrong / Hot & putrid / Flowing inside-out / I had a dream about that / Gross man / A tunnel into muck / Why not? / Put a little motor in 'em / You're just insultin' me, aren't you! / Cold light generation / Dio fa / That would be the end of that / Beat the reaper / Waffenspiel.

– compilations, others, etc. –

1975. (lp; by ZAPPA & THE MOTHERS) *Verve-Polydor; (2352 057)* **ROCK FLASHBACKS** [ ] [-]

Jun 79. (lp/c) *DiscReet; (K/K4 59212)* <*2294*> **ORCHESTRAL FAVORITES (live 1975)** [ ] [ ]
– Strictly genteel / Pedro's dowry / Naval aviation in art? / Duke of prunes / Bogus pomp. *(cd-iss. May95 on 'Rykodisc')*

— Next vocal-less **ZAPPA** – lead guitar plus usual ensemble.

Aug 82. (t-lp) *Barking Pumpkin-CBS; (66368)* **SHUT UP 'N PLAY YER GUITAR** (rec.1977-80 live) [ ] [ ]
– Five, five, five / Hog heaven / Pink napkins / Stucco homes / Variations on the C. Santana secret chord progression / Gee I like your pants / Soup 'n old clothes / The deathless horsie / Shut up 'n play yer guitar (x2) / Heavy duty Judy / The return of shut up 'n play yer guitar / Canard du joir / While you were out / Pinocchio's furniture / Beat it with your fist / Why Johnny can't read / Canarsie / Treacherous cretins. *(re-iss. Apr88 on 'E.M.I.' t-lp/d-cd; FZAP/CDFZ 2) (d-cd-re-iss. Jan90 on 'Zappa'; CDDZAP 19) (re-iss. t-cd May95 on 'Rykodisc'; RCD 10533-34-35)*

Mar 83. (lp) *Barking Pumpkin;* <*1115*> **BABY SNAKES** (1979 soundtrack; live October 1976) [-] [ ]
– Intro rap / Baby snakes / Titties and beer / Black page No.2 / Jones crusher / Disco boy / Dinah-Moe Humm / Punky's whips. <*(cd-iss. Jan89 on 'Zappa'; CDZAP 16)*> <*(cd re-iss. May95 on 'Rykodisc'; RCD 10539)*>

Feb 86. (cd) *E.M.I.; (CDP 746188-2)* **DOES HUMOR BELONG IN MUSIC** [ ] [ ]
(re-iss. Apr95 on 'Rykodisc' cd/c; RCD/RAC 10548)

Jul 87. (lp-box) *Barking Pumpkin; (BPR 7777)* **OLD MASTERS – BOX ONE** [ ] [ ]
– FREAK OUT / ABSOLUTELY FREE / WE'RE ONLY IN IT FOR THE MONEY / LUMPY GRAVY / CRUISIN' WITH RUBEN & THE JETS / (Mystery Disc – rare).

Jul 87. (lp-box) *Barking Pumpkin; (BPR 8888)* **OLD MASTERS – BOX TWO** [ ] [ ]
– UNCLE MEAT / HOT RATS / BURNT WEENIE SANDWICH / WEASELS RIPPED MY FLESH / CHUNGA'S REVENGE / LIVE AT THE FILLMORE EAST / JUST ANOTHER BAND FROM L.A. / (Mystery Disc – live in London 1968).

Oct 87. (cd) *Rykodisc;* <*RCD 40025*> **APOSTROPHE / OVERNIGHT SENSATION** [-] [ ]

Oct 87. (3"cd-ep) *Rykodisc;* **PEACHES EN REGALIA / I'M NOT SATISFIED / LUCILLE HAS MESSED UP MY MIND** [-] [ ]

Nov 87. (lp-box) *Barking Pumpkin; (BPR 9999)* **OLD MASTERS – BOX THREE** [ ] [ ]
– OVERNITE SENSATION / ONE SIZE FITS ALL / WAKA JAWAKA / THE GRAND WAZOO / APOSTROPHE / BONGO FURY / ZOOT ALLURES / ROXY AND ELSEWHERE.

Jan 88. (lp/c/cd) *Zappa; (ZAPPA/TZAPPA/CDDZAP 5)* **THE LONDON SYMPHONY ORCHESTRA VOL.II** (out-takes from '200 MOTELS') [ ] [ ]
– Bob in Dacron / Strictly genteel / Bogus bomp. *(cd+=)* – (2 extra tracks).

Apr 88. (d-lp/c/cd) *Zappa/ US= Barking Pumpkin; (ZAPPA/TZAPPA/CDDZAP 6)* **GUITAR** (rec.live 1979-84) [82] [ ]
– Sexual harassment in the workplace / Which one is it? * / Republicans / Do not pass go / Chalk pie * / In-a-gadda-Stravinsky * / That's not

really reggae / When no one was no one / Once again, without the net / Outside now (original solo) / Jim and Tammy's upper room / Were we ever really safe in San Antonio? / That ol' G minor thing again / Hotel Atlanta incidentals * / That's not really a shuffle * / Move it or park it / Sunrise redeemer // Variations on sinister #3 * / Orrin Hatch on skis * / But who was Fulcanelli? / For Duane / Goa / Winos do not march / Swans? what swans? * / Too ugly for show business * / Systems of edges / Do not try this at home * / Things that look like meat / Watermelon in Easter hay / Canadian customs * / Is that all there is? * / It ain't necessarily the St. James Infirmary *. *(cd+= *) (re-iss. cd May95 on 'Rykodisc'; RCD 10550-51)*

Apr 88. (cd) *EMI/ US= Capitol;* **THE MAN FROM UTOPIA / SHIP ARRIVING TOO LATE TO SAVE THE DROWNING WITCH** ☐ [-]

Apr 88. (2xt-lp-box) *E.M.I.; (FZAP 1)* **JOE'S GARAGE ACTS I / II / III / SHUT UP AND PLAY YER GUITAR** ☐ ☐

Apr 88. (d-lp) *Zappa; (ZAPPA 7)* **YOU CAN'T DO THAT ON STAGE ANYMORE SAMPLER** ☐ ☐
(d-cd-iss. Jan90; CDZAP 7)

Apr 88. (3"cd-s) *Rykodisc;* **SEXUAL HARASSMENT IN THE WORKPLACE / WATERMELON IN EASTER HAY** [-] ☐

May 88. (3"cd-s) *Rykodisc;* **ZOMBY WOOF / YOU DIDN'T TRY TO CALL ME** [-] ☐

May 88. (3"cd-s) *Rykodisc;* **MONTANA (WHIPPING FLOSS) / CHEEPNIS** [-] ☐

May 88. (d-cd) *Zappa; (CDZAP 8)* **YOU CAN'T DO THAT ON STAGE ANYMORE VOL.2** ☐ ☐
(re-iss. Jul95 on 'Rykodisc'; RCD 10561-62)

May 88. (cd) *E.M.I.; (CDP 790078-2)* **ZAPPA MEETS THE MOTHERS OF PREVENTION / JAZZ FROM HELL** ☐ [-]

Oct 88. (d-cd) *Zappa; (CDDZAP 9)* **YOU CAN'T DO THAT ON STAGE ANYMORE VOL.2** ☐ ☐
(re-iss. May95 on 'Rykodisc'; RCD 10563-64)

Dec 88. (d-cd) *Zappa; (CDZAP 13) / Rykodisc; <RCD 40024>* **WE'RE ONLY IN IT FOR THE MONEY / LUMPY GRAVY** ☐ ☐

Jan 90. (t-cd) *Zappa; (CDDZAP 20)* **JOE'S GARAGE ACT I / II / III** ☐ [-]

— FRANK decided to bootleg the bootleggers by releasing 10 best sellers that had fleeced him in the past. They were limited on 'Rhino'.

Apr 91. (d-cd/d-c) *Zappa; (CDDZAP/TZAPPA 38)* **THE BEST BAND YOU NEVER HEARD IN YOUR LIFE** (live 1988) ☐ ☐
(re-iss. May95 on 'Rykodisc'; RCD 10653-54)

Jun 91. (d-cd/d-c) *Zappa; (CDDZAP/TZAPA 41)* **MAKE A JAZZ NOISE HERE** (live 1988) ☐ ☐
(re-iss. d-cd May95 on 'Rykodisc'; RCD 10555-56)

Jun 91. (d-cd) *Zappa; (CDDZAP 17)* **YOU CAN'T DO THAT ON STAGE ANYMORE VOL.3** ☐ ☐
(re-iss. d-cd May95 on 'Rykodisc'; RCD 10565-66)

Jun 91. (d-cd/d-c) *Zappa; (CDDZAP/TZAPPA 40)* **YOU CAN'T DO THAT ON STAGE ANYMORE VOL.4** ☐ ☐
(re-iss. May95 on 'Rykodisc'; RCD 10567-68)
Note; below former bootleg releases on 'Essential-Zappa' UK/ 'Rykodisc' US. Released Aug91 as 'BEAT THE BOOTS' 10-lp box; *70907*

Sep 91. (cd) *(ESMCD 956) <70537>* **AS AN AM (live 1981)** ☐ ☐

Sep 91. (cd) *(ESMCD 957) <70538>* **THE ARK (live Boston 1968)** ☐ ☐

Sep 91. (cd) *(ESMCD 958) <70539>* **FREAKS & MOTHERFU*£'%!** ☐ ☐

Sep 91. (cd) *(ESMCD 959) <70540>* **UNMITAGATED AUDACITY** ☐ ☐

Sep 91. (d-cd) *(ESMCD 960) <70541>* **ANYWAY THE WIND BLOWS** ☐ ☐

Sep 91. (cd) *(ESMCD 961) <70542>* **'TIS THE SEASON TO BE JELLY** ☐ ☐

Sep 91. (cd) *(ESMCD 962) <70543>* **SAARBRUCKEN 1978** ☐ ☐

Sep 91. (cd) *(ESMCD 963) <70544>* **PIQUANTIQUE** ☐ ☐
(above 'Essential' releases of 1991 were re-iss. May97; same)

May 92. (cd) *Zappa; (CDZAP 49)* **BOULEZ CONDUCTS ZAPPA: THE PERFECT STRANGER** (Various Artists) ☐ ☐
(re-iss. May95 on 'Rykodisc'; RCD 10542)

Jul 92. (8xcd-box/ 7xc-box/ 11xlp-box) *Rykodisc; <R2/R4/R1 70372>* **BEAT THE BOOTS II** [-] ☐
– (DISCONNECTED SYNAPSES / TENGO NA MINCHIA TANTA / ELECTRIC AUNT JEMIMA / AT THE CIRCUS / SWISS CHEESE (double) / FIRE (double) / OUR MAN IN NIRVANA / CONCEPTUAL CONTINUITY)

Nov 92. (d-cd) *Zappa; (CDDZAP 55)* **PLAYGROUND PSYCHOTICS** (live 1971) ☐ ☐
(re-iss. May95 on 'Rykodisc'; RCD 10557-58)

Nov 92. (d-cd) *Zappa; (CDDZAP 46)* **YOU CAN'T DO THAT ON STAGE ANYMORE VOL.5** ☐ ☐
(re-iss. May95 on 'Rykodisc'; RCD 10569-70)

Nov 92. (d-cd) *Zappa; (CDDZAP* **YOU CAN'T DO THAT ON STAGE ANYMORE VOL.6** ☐ ☐
(re-iss. May95 on 'Rykodisc'; RCD 10571-72)

Mar 93. (cd) *Zappa; (CDZAP 51)* **AHEAD OF THEIR TIME** (live 1968) ☐ ☐
(re-iss. May95 on 'Rykodisc'; RCD 10559)

Jul 93. (12"/cd-s) *Zappa; (12/CD FRANK 102)* **VALLEY GIRLS. / YOU ARE WHAT YOU IS** ☐ ☐

Apr 95. (d-cd) *Rykodisc; (RCD 10540-41)* **LONDON SYMPHONY ORCHESTRA VOLUMES 1 & 2** ☐ ☐

May 95. (cd; w/mag) *Sonora;* **MAGAZINE & CD** ☐ ☐

Aug 95. (cd/c/d-lp) *Rykodisc; (RCD/RAC/RALP 40600)* **STRICTLY COMMERCIAL (THE BEST OF FRANK ZAPPA)** [45] ☐
– Peaches en regalia / Don't eat the yellow snow / Dancin' fool / San Ber'dino / Dirty love / My guitar wants to kill your mama / Cosmik debris / Trouble every day / Disco boy / Fine girl / Sexual harassment in the workplace / Let's make the water turn black / I'm the slime / Joe's garage / Bobby Brown goes down / Montana / Valley girl / Be in my video / Muffin man.

Feb 96. (cd/c) *Rykodisc; (RCD/RAC 40573)* **THE LOST EPISODES** ☐ ☐

Sep 96. (t-cd) *Rykodisc; (RCD 10574-75)* **LATHER** ☐ ☐

Apr 97. (cd) *Rykodisc; (RCD 10577)* **HAVE I OFFENDED SOMEONE?** ☐ [-]

Nov 99. (7"; as FRANK ZAPPA & JOHN TRUBEE) *Musical Tragedies; (efa 126047)* **LETTER FROM JEEPERS** ☐ [-]

ZERO 7

Formed: North London, England . . . 1997 by HENRY BINNS and SAM HARDAKER. Both began working in a London studio making tea for producers and visiting artists. They watched engineers work the desks and soon picked up the procedures for recording, testing their trade with a few low-key remixes; RADIOHEAD's 'Climbing Up The Walls' and TERRY CALLIER's ' . . .Spartacus'. The duo assembled a collection of songs, issued in early 2000 as 'EP1'. The record sold its limited pressing of 1000 in days. With support from Radio One DJ GILLES PETERSON, the band issued the highly anticipated second EP, the aptly titled 'EP2'. This preceded their debut set, 'SIMPLE THINGS', in May 2001. The album boasted a light and breezy psychedelic take-on of jazz, funk and lounge, with inevitable comparisons to AIR, although the album came across more like a hybrid mix of GROOVE ARMADA, BOARDS OF CANADA and the loungey musings of JIM O'ROURKE's recent material, all backed by chilled-out beats and the occasional soaring female vocal. The record featured the Top 30 hit 'DESTINY' plus sophomore single 'IN THE WAITING LINE' and, as well as winning the Mercury Music Award, went gold in September 2001. The pair also remixed LAMBCHOP's immortal 'UP WITH PEOPLE', turning it from a choir-driven country/soul classic, to a sparkling laid-back summer anthem with looped guitars, horns and climbing cresendos over thick drawn-out beats. ZERO 7 weren't in any way "Britain's answer to AIR", nor were they the next generation's MASSIVE ATTACK, they simply were two very talented, like-minded producers whose futures were the next beat. Delivered in a sleeve that STEVIE WONDER would've sold at least one of his braids for back in the 70s, the Top 3 'WHEN IT FALLS' (2004) reprised at least some of STEVIE's spirit if not his genius, skinny dipping in strum-dappled pools of electric piano and singer-songwriterly rumination. Vocals came from at least two of the same hired sirens that graced their last album, namely SIA FURLER, whose late night burr inflamed both 'SOMERSAULT' and 'SPEED DIAL No.2', and SOPHIE BARKER who guested on 'PASSING BY' and the cosmic folk-stroll of 'IN TIME'. Newcomer TINA DICO, meanwhile, got her own brace: the syncopated drift of 'HOME' and 'THE SPACE BETWEEN'. Third album, 'THE GARDEN' (2006), hit the UK Top 5 (US Top 100), although it didn't have the same appeal as its predecessor.

Album rating: SIMPLE THINGS (*8) / WHEN IT FALLS (*6) / THE GARDEN (*5)

HENRY BINNS – electronics / **SAM HARDAKER** – electronics

Zero 7 / not iss.

Jan 00. (12"ltd) **EP 1** [ ] [-]
– Out of town / This world / Likufanele (Zero 7 remix) / Low / One arm break.

Ultimate Dilemma / Palm Pictures

Mar 01. (12"ep/cd-ep) *(UDR/+CDS 040)* **EP 2** [ ] [-]
– Give it away / Polaris / Distractions / Monday night.

—— with also vocals from:- SIA FURLER, SOPHIE BARKER + MOZEZ

May 01. (cd/lp) *(UDR CD/LP 016)* <5007> **SIMPLE THINGS** [28] Jun01 [ ]
– I have seen / Polaris / Destiny / Give it away / Simple things / Red dust / Distractions / In the waiting line / Out of town / This world / Likufanele / End theme / Salt water sound / Spining.

Jun 01. (12"/cd-s) *(UDR/+CDS 041)* **I HAVE SEEN. / SALT WATER SOUND / SPINNING** [ ] [-]

Aug 01. (12"/cd-s; by ZERO 7 featuring SIA & SOPHIE) *(UDR/+CDS 043)* **DESTINY. / DESTINY (Photek mix) / END THEME (Roni Size remix)** [30] [-]
(cd-s) *(UDRCDSX 043)* – ('A'extended) / ('A'-Hefner's destiny chill mix) / ('A'-Simian remix).

Oct 01. (ltd-12") *(UDR 042)* **END THEME (Roni Size tear it up remix). / END THEME (Roni Size tear it down remix)** [ ] [-]

Nov 01. (12"/cd-s) *(UDR/+CDS 045)* **IN THE WAITING LINE. / IN THE WAITING LINE (Dorfmeister con Madrid de los Austrias dub) / SIMPLE THINGS (live)** [47] [-]
(cd-s) *(UDRCDSX 045)* – ('A'-original) / This world / Likufanele.

Mar 02. (12"/cd-s) *(UDR/+CDR 046)* **DISTRACTIONS (mixes; radio / Bugz in the attic / DJ Spinna)** [45] [-]
(12"/cd-s) *(UDRX/+CDS 046)* – ('A'-mixes; radio / idjut / Madlib / Block 16).

—— with **SOPHIE BARKER, TINA DICO + SIA FURLER**

Warners / Elektra

Feb 04. (12"/cd-s) *(EW 282 T/CD)* **HOME. / HOME (Stereolab remix) / HOME (Ben Watt remix)** [ ] [-]

Mar 04. (cd) *(5046 709875)* <61558-2> **WHEN IT FALLS** [3] [ ]
– Warm sound / Home / Somersault / Over our heads / Passing by / When it falls / The space between / Look up / In time / Speed dial No.2 / Morning song.

May 04. (cd-s) *(EW 290CD)* **SOMERSAULT / LIGHT BLUE MOVERS** [56] [-]
(cd-s) *(EW 290DVD)* – ('A') / ('A'-video) / Home (video).

—— next feat. **JOSE GONZALEZ** + **SIA**

Atlantic / Atlantic

Mar 06. (7") *(ATUK 026)* **FUTURES. / DREAMING** [ ] [-]
(12"+=) *(ATUK 026T)* – ('A') / Seeing things (extended).

May 06. (cd/d-lp) *(510112857-5/-1)* <63380> **THE GARDEN** [4] Jun06 [94]
– Futures / Throw it all away / Seeing things / The pageant of the bizarre / You're my flame / Left behind / Today / This fine social scene / Your place / If I can't have you / Crosses / Waiting to die.

May 06. (7") *(ATUK 028)* **THROW IT ALL AWAY. / INAMINUTE** [ ] [-]
(12"+=) *(ATUK 028T)* – Thistles.
(cd-s++=) *(ATUK 028CD)* – ('A'-video).

□ Rob ZOMBIE (see under ⇒ WHITE ZOMBIE)

the ZOMBIES

Formed: St. Albans, England . . . 1963 by ROD ARGENT, COLIN BLUNSTONE, HUGH GRUNDY and PAUL ATKINSON. In early 1964, after winning a local band competition, they signed to 'Decca' and soon had a massive worldwide hit with the classic 'SHE'S NOT THERE'. With its distinctive churning organ and portentous overtones, the single instantly marked the band out from the rest of the Brit-Beat pack, especially in America where the song climbed to No.2. The equally classy 'TELL HER NO', again reaped success across the Atlantic but strangely stiffed in the UK. Despite a fine debut album, 'BEGIN HERE' (1965) and a string of well-crafted singles, the band met with zero success in the UK and even their early success in America wasn't repeated. 'Decca' duly declined to renew their contract and they signed to 'C.B.S.' in 1967. Although The ZOMBIES split in frustration before its release, 'ODESSEY AND ORACLE' (deliberate spelling mistake!) was their masterstroke. A concept album of sorts, the record boasted an exquisitely arranged combination of sublime harmonies and jazz-inflected instrumentation, BLUNSTONE's unmistakable high vocals floating overhead. Though the album barely scraped into the top 100, it was an ironic twist of fate when the compelling 'TIME OF THE SEASON' single became an American million seller. The band reformed briefly (minus BLUNSTONE and WHITE) and released a couple of singles without success, ARGENT going on to form, funnily enough, ARGENT, while BLUNSTONE carved out a fairly successful solo career. ARGENT and BLUNSTONE finally reunited for a joint album, 'OUT OF THE SHADOWS' (2002), following it up with a set under the ZOMBIES moniker: 'AS FAR AS I CAN SEE' (2004) and citing their reasons as songs being written for BLUNSTONE's voice. As far as critics could see, the album was a schlocky slight on the band's hallowed name and a waste of BLUNSTONE's talent, although that didn't stop them from continuing to tour together, releasing 'LIVE AT BLOOMSBURY THEATRE, LONDON' (2005).

• **Songwriters:** ARGENT-WHITE penned, except for the ubiquitous covers; GOT MY MOJO WORKING (Muddy Waters) / YOU'VE REALLY GOT A HOLD ON ME (Smokey Robinson) / ROADRUNNER (Bo Diddley) / SUMMERTIME (Gershwin) / GOIN' OUT OF MY HEAD (Little Anthony & The Imperials) / etc. • **Trivia:** Early in 1966, they made a cameo appearance in the film, 'Bunny Lake Is Missing'. They were known as the most intelligent pop group of the mid-60's, after leaving school with over fifty 'O' and 'A' levels between them.

Album rating: BEGIN HERE (*6) / ODESSEY & ORACLE (*8) / NEW WORLD (*3) / THE BEST OF THE ZOMBIES compilation (*8) / AS FAR AS I CAN SEE.. (*4)

COLIN BLUNSTONE (b.24 Jun'45, Hatfield, England) – vocals / **ROD ARGENT** (b.14 Jun'45, St.Albans) – piano, keyboards, vocals / **PAUL ATKINSON** (b.19 Mar'46, Cuffley, England) – guitar / **CHRIS WHITE** (b. 7 Mar'43, Barnet, England) – bass repl. PAUL ARNOLD / **HUGH GRUNDY** (b. 6 Mar'45, Winchester, England) – drums

Decca / Parrot

Jul 64. (7") *(F 11940)* <9695> **SHE'S NOT THERE. / YOU MAKE ME FEEL GOOD** [12] Oct64 [2]

Oct 64. (7") *(F 12004)* **LEAVE ME BE. / WOMAN** [ ] [-]

Jan 65. (7") *(F 12072)* <9723> **TELL HER NO. / WHAT MORE CAN I DO** [42] [6]

Mar 65. (7") *(F 12125)* <9747> **SHE'S COMING HOME. / I MUST MOVE** [ ] [58]

Apr 65. (lp) *(LK 4679)* <7001> **BEGIN HERE** <US-title 'THE ZOMBIES'> [ ] Feb65 [39]
– Roadrunner / Summertime / I can't make up my mind / The way I feel inside / Work 'n' play / You've really got a hold on me / She's not there / Sticks and stones / Can't nobody love you / Woman / I don't want to know / I remember when I loved her / What more can I do / I got my mojo working. *(re-iss. Nov84; DOA 4) (re-iss. Jul86 on 'See For Miles' US version) (cd-iss. Aug92 & May01 on 'Repertoire'+=; REP 4939)* – You make me feel

good / Leave me be / Tell her no / She's coming home / I must move / Kind of girl / It's alright with me / Sometimes / Whenever you're ready / I love you / Is this the dream / Don't go away / Remember you / Just out of reach / Indication / How we were before / I'm going home. *(cd re-iss. Apr99 on 'Big Beat'; CDWIKD 191)*

Jun 65. (7") *<9769>* **I WANT YOU BACK AGAIN. / ONCE UPON A TIME** – 95

Sep 65. (7") *(F 12225) <9786>* **WHENEVER YOU'RE READY. / I LOVE HER**

Nov 65. (7") *(F 12296) <9821>* **IS THIS A DREAM. / DON'T GO AWAY** Apr66

Jan 66. (7") *(F 12322) <9797>* **REMEMBER YOU. / JUST OUT OF REACH**

Jun 66. (7") *(F 12426) <3004>* **INDICATION. / HOW WE WERE BEFORE**

Nov 66. (7") *(F 12495)* **GOTTA GET A HOLD ON MYSELF. / THE WAY I FEEL INSIDE** –

Mar 67. (7") *(F 12584)* **GOIN' OUT OF MY HEAD. / SHE DOES EVERYTHING FOR ME** –

May 67. (7") *(F 12798)* **I LOVE YOU. / THE WAY I FEEL INSIDE** –

C.B.S. Columbia

Sep 67. (7") *(2960)* **FRIENDS OF MINE. / BEECHWOOD PARK** –

Nov 67. (7") *(3087) <44363>* **CARE OF CELL 44. / MAYBE AFTER HE'S GONE**
(re-iss. Mar74 on 'Epic';)

— disbanded late '67; posthumous release below resurrected group in '69

C.B.S. Date

Apr 68. (lp; stereo/mono) *(S+/BPG 63280) <4013>* **ODYSSEY AND ORACLE** Mar69 95
– Care of Cell 44 / A rose for Emily / Maybe after he's gone / Beechwood park / Brief candles / Hung up on a dream / Changes / I want her she wants me / This will be our year / Butcher's tale (Western Front 1914) / Friends of mine / Time of the season. *(re-iss. Dec86 on 'Razor';) (cd-iss. Aug92 & Sep02 on 'Repertoire'+=; REP 4940)* – I call you mine / She loves the way they love her / Imagine the swan / Smokey day / If it don't work out / I know she will / Don't cry for me / Walking in the sun / Conversation off Floral Street / I want you back again / Gotta get hold of myself / Goin' out of my head / She does everything for me / Nothing's changed / I could spend the day / Girl help me. *(re-iss. Apr98 on 'Big Beat' cd/lp; CD+/WIKD 181)*

Apr 68. (7") *(3380) <1604>* **TIME OF THE SEASON. / I'LL CALL YOU MINE**

Jul 68. (7") *<1612>* **THIS WILL BE OUR YEAR. / BUTCHERS TALE (WESTERN FRONT 1914)** –

Feb 69. (7") *<1628>* **TIME OF THE SEASON. / FRIENDS OF MINE** – 3

— (Mar'69) With them riding high in US Top 3, they decided to re-form but without BLUNSTONE (who went solo) / WHITE (who went into producing) + ATKINSON. ARGENT + GRUNDY recruited **RICK BIRKETT** – guitar / **JIM RODFORD** – bass

May 69. (7") *<1644>* **IMAGINE THE SWAN. / CONVERSATIONS OF FLORAL STREET** –

Jul 69. (7") *<1648>* **IF IT DON'T WORK OUT. / DON'T CRY FOR ME** –

— Didn't last long, when ROD and JIM decided to form ARGENT. The ZOMBIES reformed for one-off in the early 90's

Essential not iss.

Apr 91. (cd/c/lp) *(ESS CD/MC/LP 131)* **NEW WORLD** –
– New world (my America) / Love breaks down / I can't be wrong / Lula Lula / Heaven's gate / Time of the season / Moonday morning dance / Blue / Losing you / Alone in Paradise / Knowing you / Love conquers all / Nights on fire. *(cd re-iss. Jun94 on 'Castle'; CLACD 348) (cd re-iss. Aug03 on 'Ace'; CDWIKM 234)*

— **the ZOMBIES** were re-formed; **ROD ARGENT + COLIN BLUNSTONE**

Redhouse Redhouse

May 04. (cd) *(<REDHCD 3>)* **AS FAR AS I CAN SEE..**
– In my mind a miracle / Memphis / Southside of the street / I want to fly / Time to move / I don't believe in miracles / As far as I can see / With you not here / Wings against the sun / Together / Look for a better way.

Aug 04. (cd-s) *(CDREDH 104)* **SOUTHSIDE OF THE STREET** –

Jun 05. (d-cd) *(REDHCD 4)* **LIVE AT BLOOMSBURY THEATRE, LONDON** (live) –
– Andorra / This will be our year / I love you / What becomes of the broken hearted / Mystified / A rose for Emily / Beechwood park / Time of the season / I want to fly / In my mind a miracle / Keep on rolling / Hold your head up // Sanctuary / Pleasure / Say you don't mind / Misty roses / I don't believe in miracles / Old & wise / Care of cell 44 / Indication / Tell her no / She's not there / Just out of reach / God gave rock'n'roll to you / Summertime.

– (selective) compilations, etc. –

Feb 86. (lp) *Rhino; (RNLP 120)* **LIVE ON THE BBC 1965-67 (live)** –

Sep 87. (lp/c) *See For Miles; (SEE/K 30)* **THE SINGLES A's & B's** –
(cd-iss. Sep88 & May97; SEECD 30)

Aug 88. (d-lp/c/cd) *Castle; (CCS LP/MC/CD 196)* **THE COLLECTION** –
– Goin' out of my head / Leave me be / Gotta get a hold on myself / I can't make up my mind / Kind of girl / Sticks and stones / Summertime / Woman / I got my mojo working / Roadrunner / You really got a hold on me / Nothing's changed / You make me feel good / She's not there / Don't go away / How we were before / Tell her no / Whenever you're ready / Just out of reach / Remember you / Indication / She does everything for me / Time of the season / I love you.

Feb 91. (cd/c) *Music Club; (MC CD/TC 002)* **BEST OF THE ZOMBIES** –

Jul 91. (3xcd-box) *Razor; (RAZCDBOX 1)* **THE ZOMBIES** –

Nov 92. (cd) *See For Miles; (SEECD 358)* **THE EP COLLECTION** –

Feb 95. (cd/c) *More Music; (MO CD/MC 3009)* **THE ZOMBIES 1964-67** –

Apr 96. (cd) *Disky; (DC 86272-2)* **THE ZOMBIES**

Nov 97. (4xcd-box) *Big Beat; (ZOMBOX 7)* **ZOMBIE HEAVEN**

Jul 99. (cd) *Varese Sarabande; (VSD 1039)* **ABSOLUTELY THE BEST**

Jan 00. (cd) *Chiswick; (CDWIKD 200)* **THE SINGLES**

Apr 00. (cd) *Disky; (SI 99076-2)* **THE BEST OF THE SIXTIES**

Sep 02. (d-cd) *Repertoire; (REP 4985)* **SINGLES A'S AND B'S**

Nov 02. (d-cd) *Big Beat; (CDWIK2 225)* **THE DECCA STEREO ANTHOLOGY**

Mar 03. (cd) *Disky; (EMI 760160)* **THE STORY OF THE ZOMBIES**

Apr 03. (cd) *Repertoire; (REP 4790)* **LIVE AT THE BBC**

the ZUTONS

Formed: Liverpool, England . . . 2001 by DAVE McCABE, BOYAN CHOWDHURY, RUSSELL PRITCHARD and SEAN PAYNE, making the latter's girlfriend ABI HARDING one of the gang after her sax playing became integral to their stage shows. The very fact that their moniker was inspired by former CAPTAIN BEEFHEART/MAGIC BAND member ZOOT HORN ROLLO, suggested the ZUTONS were coming from a freakier place than their peers. While most British bands were referencing the homegrown class of '77, the Scouse quintet clearly had their heads stuck in the outer limits of West Coast psychedelia, patenting a sound haunted by the echoes of the aforementioned MAGIC BAND, SPIRIT, LOVE and early STEVE MILLER BAND. Sharing a label ('Deltasonic') and a retro sensibility with fellow Liverpudlians, the CORAL, the ZUTONS' career got off to a fairly humble beginning via two singles, 'DEVIL'S DEAL' and 'CREEPIN' AN' A CRAWLIN''. In early 2004, however, the Northern space cadets zapped their way into the mainstream with the stress-heavy, cosmic rock of 'PRESSURE POINT', making a serious dent in the UK Top 30. The "Dropout Boogie"-esque 'YOU WILL YOU WON'T', hurtled into a similar position and paved the milky way for Mercury-nominated Top 10 debut album, 'WHO KILLED . . . . . . THE ZUTONS' (2004). Produced by IAN BROUDIE and opening with the sax-psychotic 'ZUTON FEVER' (worth playing back to back with ELECTRIC SIX's inimitable 'Gay Bar'), cramming in the hits and generating further singles, 'REMEMBER ME', 'DON'T EVER THINK (TOO MUCH)' and 'CONFUSION', the LP was picked up by 'Epic' Stateside. The album also got a boost from

TV ad licensing, with both 'PRESSURE POINT' and the ozone lullaby of 'CONFUSION' soundtracking Levi jeans and Peugeot cars respectively. Taking a breath of fresh air in 2005, the ZUTONS returned the following year with Stephen Street-produced sophomore set 'TIRED OF HANGING AROUND' (2006). Less paranoid and more contemporary friendly, the Top 3 album carried its usual quota of hits, kicking off with 'WHY WON'T YOU GIVE ME YOUR LOVE?' and 'VALERIE'.

Album rating: WHO KILLED...... THE ZUTONS (*8) / TIRED OF HANGING AROUND (*7)

DAVID McCABE – vocals, guitar / **BOYAN CHOWDHURY** – lead guitar / **RUSSELL PRITCHARD** – bass (ex-BIG KIDS) / **SEAN PAYNE** – drums (ex-BIG KIDS) / **ABI HARDING** – saxophone

		Deltasonic	Epic
Sep 02.	(cd-s) *(DLTCD 007)* **DEVIL'S DEAL / SIX FOOT MAN / ZUTONKHAMUUN**		–
May 03.	(7"/cd-s) *(DLT/+CD 011)* **CREEPIN' AN' A CRAWLIN'. / RUMBLIN' RAMBLIN'**		–
Jan 04.	(7") *(DLT 016)* **PRESSURE POINT. / ZUTONKHAMUUN**	19	–
	(cd-s) *(DLTCD 016)* – ('A') / Beggars and choosers.		
	(cd-s) *(DLTCV 016)* – ('A') / Over the hill / Zuton fever (acoustic).		
Apr 04.	(7") *(DLT 020)* **YOU WILL YOU WON'T. / NIGHTMARE PART 1**	22	–
	(cd-s) *(DLTCD 020)* – ('A') / Nobody loves me / Times of trouble / ('A'-video) / (late night documentary).		
Apr 04.	(lp/cd) *(DLT/+CD 019) <92836>* **WHO KILLED...... THE ZUTONS**	9	Oct04
	– Zuton fever / Pressure point / You will you won't / Confusion / Havana gang brawl / Railroad / Long time coming / Nightmare part II / Not a lot to do / Remember me / Dirty dancehall / Moons and horror shows. *(ltd d-cd+=; DLTCD 023)* – Long time coming (alt.) / You will you won't (alt.) / Remember me (alt.) / Creepin' an a crawlin' (alt.). *(cd re-iss. Oct04 +=; DLTCDX 019)* – Don't ever think (too much).		
Jun 04.	(7") *(DLT 024)* **REMEMBER ME. / ZUTON FEVER (live)**	39	–
	(cd-s) *(DLTCD 024)* – ('A') / Long time coming (live).		
	(cd-s) *(DLTCD2 024)* – ('A') / Have I lost you / Havana gang brawl (demo) / ('A'-video).		
Oct 04.	(7") *(DLT 026)* **DON'T EVER THINK (TOO MUCH). / CREEPIN' AN A CRAWLIN'**	15	–
	(cd-s+=) *(DLTCD2 026)* – Haunts me / ('A'-video).		
	(cd-s) *(DLTCD 026)* – ('A') / Rumblin' ramblin'.		
Dec 04.	(7") *(DLT 030)* **CONFUSION. / YOU WILL YOU WON'T**	37	–
	(cd-s) *(DLTCD 030)* – ('A') / Jump sturdy.		
Apr 06.	(7"pic-d) *(DLT 046)* **WHY WON'T YOU GIVE ME YOUR LOVE? / LOVE'S LITTLE LIES**	9	–
	(cd-s) *(DLTCD 046)* – ('A') / I want you.		
	(cd-s) *(DLTCD2 046)* – ('A') / Are we friends or lovers / What's my heart for? / ('A'-video).		
Apr 06.	(cd/lp) *(DLT CD/LP 040) <68227-2>* **TIRED OF HANGING AROUND**	2	
	– Tired of hanging around / It's the little things we do / Valerie / Someone watching over me / Secrets / How does it feel / Why won't you give me your love? / Oh Stacey (look what you've done) / You've got a friend in me / Hello conscience / I know I'll never leave.		
Jun 06.	(7") *(DLT 047)* **VALERIE. / GET UP AND DANCE**	9	–
	(cd-s) *(DLTCD 047)* – ('A') / April fool.		
	(cd-s) *(DLTCD2 047)* – ('A') / I will be your pockets / In the city / ('A'-video).		

□ ZWAN (see under ⇒ SMASHING PUMPKINS)

ZZ TOP

Formed: Houston, Texas, USA . . . as garage band, THE MOVING SIDEWALKS by BILLY GIBBONS, the now infamous trio/line-up finally emerging in 1970 with the addition of DUSTY HILL and FRANK BEARD. Having initially released a debut single on manager Billy Ham's new 'Scat' label (prior to the arrival of messrs. BEARD and HILL), ZZ TOP subsequently secured a deal with 'London' records. 'FIRST ALBUM' appeared in 1971, its stark title matching the raw simplicity of the southern blues/boogie contained within the grooves. This straightforward approach also extended to the group's music biz masterplan; ZZ TOP were first and foremost a live band, their punishing touring schedule, largely in the American South initially, would eventually turn grassroots support into record sales as well as honing their musical skills for future glories. A follow-up set, 'RIO GRANDE MUD' (1972) spawned the group's first (US) hit single in 'FRANCENE' although ZZ TOP only really began to make an impact with 1973's 'TRES HOMBRES'. Occasionally reminiscent of 'EXILE . . .'-era 'STONES (see the the smokin' 'LA GRANGE' single), the group had begun to perfect their combination of boot-leather riffing and Texas blues drawl, GIBBONS' nifty axe-work oiling the beast nicely (he'd previously drawn public praise from none other than JIMI HENDRIX). By 1976, the group were popular enough to take their 'Wordwide Texas Tour' on the road, a mammoth operation which certainly equalled The ROLLING STONES in terms of stage set and ticket sales, ZZ TOP now one of America's biggest grossing homegrown acts. The classic 70's grind of 'TUSH' was the group's highest charting single of the decade (Top 20 in '75), although ZZ TOP didn't really garner widespread critical acclaim until the release of 'DEGUELLO' in 1979, their first album for 'Warners'. The record's gristly blues licks and knowing, often surreal sense of humour demonstrating that ZZ TOP were considerably more sussed than the backwoods caricatures which they were often portrayed as (a perception which they often perpetuated), the deadpan 'CHEAP SUNGLASSES' a blistering cover of ELMORE JAMES' 'DUST MY BROOM' and a version of Isaac Hayes' 'I THANK YOU' proving highlights. 'EL LOCO' (1981) was almost as good, the boys insisting that what a woman really wanted was, ahem . . . a 'PEARL NECKLACE'. The tongue-in-cheek smut only really got underway with 'ELIMINATOR' (1983), however, the gleaming videos for the likes of the pounding 'GIMME ALL YOUR LOVIN', 'SHARP DRESSED MAN' and of course, 'LEGS', featuring more leggy lovelies than a ROBERT PALMER video. These MTV staples also introduced ZZ TOP's famous red Ford coupe, the fearsome motor becoming as much of an 80's icon as FRANKIE GOES TO HOLLYWOOD t-shirts. Musically, the album was almost a complete departure, turbo-charging the guitars way up in the mix and boosting the overall sound with a synthesized throb. This trademark electro-boogie would see ZZ TOP through the best part of a decade. Deservedly, the record was a massive worldwide success, a multi-million seller which marked the first instalment in a three-album semi-concept affair, built around the 'Eliminator' car. For 'AFTERBURNER' (1985), the car, don't laugh!, had turned into a space rocket flying high above the earth although it seemed as if they'd also jettisoned the cocksure stomp of old. 'SLEEPING BAG' and 'VELCRO FLY' were competent enough, the videos ensuring another MTV bonanza and healthy sales. 'RECYCLER' (1990) continued in much the same vein, although relatively poor sales subsequently saw the group parting with 'Warners' and starting afresh with 'R.C.A.'. Never the most prolific band, ZZ TOP only released a further four albums in the 90's, the compilation 'ZZ TOP GREATEST HITS' (1992; and including 'VIVA LAS VEGAS' made famous by Elvis), 'ANTENNA' (1994), 'RHYTHMEEN' (1996) and 'XXX' (1999), at last abandoning their outdated 80's sound in favour of a leaner, meaner return to their roots. The 'TOP strode boldly into the new millennium with 'MESCALERO' (2003), not quite the ever anticipated return to tequila-swilling cross-border boogie which its title suggested but at least another tentative step in the right direction. They mightn't sell as many records these days but they've still got beards (save FRANK BEARD, that is!) as long and grizzly as a DEEP PURPLE guitar solo, and that's what counts!

• **Songwriters:** Group penned (plus some early with manager BILL HAM) except; FRANCINE (trad.) / JAILHOUSE ROCK (hit; Elvis Presley)

Album rating: FIRST ALBUM (*6) / RIO GRANDE MUD (*6) / TRES HOMBRES (*8) / FANDANGO (*7) / TEJAS (*6) / THE BEST OF ZZ TOP compilation (*8) / DEGUELLO (*8) / EL LOCO (*6) / ELIMINATOR (*8) / AFTERBURNER (*6) / RECYCLER (*5) / ZZ TOP'S GREATEST HITS compilation (*9) / ANTENNA (*5) / ONE FOOT IN THE BLUES collection (*4) / RHYTHMEEN (*4) / XXX (*3) / MESCALERO (*4)

the MOVING SIDEWALKS

BILLY GIBBONS (b.12 Dec'49) – vocals, guitar / **TOM MOORE** – keyboards / **DON SUMMERS** – bass / **DAN MITCHELL** – drums

not iss. — Tantara

1967. (7") <3101> **99th FLOOR. / WHAT ARE YOU GOING TO DO?** [–] [ ]
<re-iss. 1967 on 'Wand'; 1156>

not iss. — Wand

1967. (7") <1167> **NEED ME. / EVERY NIGHT A NEW SURPRISE** [–] [ ]
<above tracks were re-iss. 1980 as EP on 'Moxie'; 1030>

— **LANIER GREIG** – keyboards repl. MOORE

not iss. — Tantara

1968. (7") <3108> **I WANT TO HOLD YOUR HAND. / JOE BLUES** [–] [ ]
1968. (lp) <6919> **FLASH** [–] [ ]
– Flashback / Crimson witch / Pluto – Sept.31 / Eclipse / Scoun da be / No good to cry / You don't know the life / You make me shake / Reclipse.
1969. (7") <3113> **FLASHBACK. / NO GOOD TO CRY** [–] [ ]

ZZ TOP

(GIBBONS, MITCHELL & GREIG)

not iss. — Scat

1970. (7") <45-500> **SALT LICK. / MILLER'S FARM** [–] [ ]
<re-iss. later 1970 on 'London'; 45-131>

— **GIBBONS** now sole survivor when LANIER and DAN departed. Newcomers were **DUSTY HILL** (b.JOE, 1949) – bass, vocals (ex-WARLOCKS, ex-AMERICAN BLUES) / **FRANK BEARD** (b.10 Dec'49) – drums (ex-CELLAR DWELLARS)

London — London

Jan 71. (lp) <PS 584> **FIRST ALBUM** [–] [ ]
– (Somebody else been) Shaking your tree / Brown sugar / Squank / Goin' down to Mexico / Old man / Neighbor, neighbor / Certified blues / Bedroom thang / Just got back from baby's / Backdoor love affair. *<re-iss. 1980 on 'Warners'; WB 3268> (UK-iss.Sep84 on 'Warners' lp/c; K/K4 56601) (cd-iss. Jan87; K2 56601)*

Feb 71. (7") <45-138> **(SOMEBODY ELSE BEEN) SHAKING YOUR TREE. / NEIGHBOR, NEIGHBOR** [–] [ ]

May 72. (7") <45-179> **FRANCENE. / FRANCENE (Spanish)** [–] [69]

Jul 72. (lp) *(SHU 8433)* <PS 612> **RIO GRANDE MUD** [ ] Apr72 [ ]
– Francene / Just got paid / Mushmouth shoutin' / Ko ko blue / Chevrolet / Apologies to Pearly / Bar-b-q / Sure got cold after the rain fell / Whiskey'n mama / Down Brownie. *<US re-iss. 1980 on 'Warners'; BSK 3269> (re-iss. Sep84 on 'Warners' lp/c; K/K4 56602) (cd-iss. Jan87; K2 56602) (cd re-iss. Mar94 on 'Warners'; 7599 27380-2)*

Jul 72. (7") *(HLU 10376)* **FRANCENE. / DOWN BROWNIE** [ ] [–]

Nov 73. (lp) *(SHU 8459)* <PS 631> **TRES HOMBRES** [ ] Aug73 [8]
– Waitin' for the bus / Jesus just left Chicago / Beer drinkers & Hell raisers / Master of sparks / Hot, blue and righteous / Move me on down the line / Precious and Grace / La Grange / Sheik / Have you heard?. *<US re-iss. 1980 on 'Warners'; BSK 3270> (re-iss. Nov83 on 'Warners' lp/c; K/K4 56603)*

Jun 74. (7") *(HLU 10458)* **BEER DRINKERS & HELL RAISERS. / LA GRANGE** [ ] [–]

Jan 75. (7") *(HLU 10475)* <45-179> **LA GRANGE. / JUST GOT PAID** [ ] Mar74 [41]

Jun 75. (lp) *(SH 8482)* <PS 656> **FANDANGO! (live Warehouse, New Orleans + studio)** [60] May75 [10]
– Thunderbird / Jailhouse rock / Back door medley: Backdoor love affair – Mellow down easy – Backdoor love affair No.2 – Long distance boogie / Nasty dogs and funky kings / Blue jean blues / Balinese / Mexican blackbird / Heard it on the X / Tush. *<US re-iss. 1980 on 'Warners'; BSK 3271> (re-iss. Nov83 on 'Warners' lp/c; K/K4 56604) (cd-iss. Jan87; K2 56604)*

Jul 75. (7") *(HLU 10495)* <5N-220> **TUSH. / BLUE JEAN BLUES** [ ] [20]

Aug 76. (7") *(HLU 10538)* <5N-241> **IT'S ONLY LOVE. / ASLEEP IN THE DESERT** [ ] [44]

Feb 77. (lp) *(LDU 1)* <PS 680> **TEJAS** [ ] Jan77 [17]
– It's only love / Arrested for driving while blind / El Diablo / Snappy kakkie / Enjoy and get it on / Ten dollar man / Pan Am highway blues / Avalon hideaway / She's a heartbreaker / Asleep in the desert. *<US re-iss. 1980 on 'Warners'; BSK 3272> (re-iss. Sep84 on 'Warners' lp/c; K/K4 56605) (cd-iss. Mar87; K2 56605) (cd re-iss. Mar94 on 'Warners'; 7599 27383-2)*

Mar 77. (7") <5N-251> **ARRESTED FOR DRIVING WHILE BLIND. / IT'S ONLY LOVE** [–] [91]

Apr 77. (7") *(HLU 10547)* **ARRESTED FOR DRIVING WHILE BLIND. / NEIGHBOUR, NEIGHBOUR** [ ] [–]

May 77. (7") <5N-252> **EL DIABLO. / ENJOY AND GET IT ON** [–] [ ]

Dec 77. (lp) <PS 706> **THE BEST OF ZZ TOP** (compilation) [–] [94]
– Tush / Waitin' for the bus / Jesus just left Chicago / Francene / Just got paid / La grange / Blue jean blues / Backdoor love affair / Beer drinkers and Hell raisers / Heard it on the X. *<re-iss. 1980 on 'Warners'; BSK 3273> (UK-iss.Dec83 on 'Warners' lp/c; K/K4 56598) cd-iss. Jan86; K2 56598)*

Warners — Warners

Dec 79. (lp/c) *(K/K4 56701)* <HS 3361> **DEGUELLO** [ ] Nov79 [24]
– I thank you / She loves my automobile / I'm bad, I'm nationwide / A fool for your stockings / Manic mechanic / Dust my broom / Lowdown in the street / Hi fi mama / Cheap sunglasses / Esther be the one. *(re-iss. Jan85 lp/cd; same/K2 56701) (re-iss. Mar94 on 'Warners' cd/c; K2/K4 56701)*

Mar 80. (7") *(K 17516)* <WB 49163> **I THANK YOU. / A FOOL FOR YOUR STOCKINGS** [ ] Jan80 [34]

Jun 80. (7") <WB 49220> **CHEAP SUNGLASSES. / ('A'live)** [–] [89]

Jun 80. (7") *(K 17647)* **CHEAP SUNGLASSES. / ESTHER BE THE ONE** [ ] [–]

Jul 81. (7") <WB 49782> **LEILA. / DON'T TEASE ME** [–] [77]

Jul 81. (lp/c) *(K/K4 56929)* <BSK 3593> **EL LOCO** [88] [17]
– Tube snake boogie / I wanna drive you home / Ten foot pole / Leila / Don't tease me / It's so hard / Pearl necklace / Groovy little hippy pad / Heaven, Hell or Houston / Party on the patio. *(cd-iss. Mar87; K2 56929) (cd re-iss. Mar94 on 'Warners'; 7599 23593-2)*

Jan 82. (7") <WB 49865> **TUBE SNAKE BOOGIE. / HEAVEN, HELL OR HOUSTON** [–] [ ]

Jun 83. (7"/7"sha-pic-d) *(W 9693/+P)* <WB 29693> **GIMME ALL YOUR LOVIN'. / IF I COULD ONLY FLAG HER DOWN** [61] Mar83 [37]
(12") *(W 9693T)* – ('A'side) / Jesus just left Chicago / Heard it on the x / Arrested for driving while blind.

Jun 83. (lp/c) *(W 3774/+4)* <23774-1/-4> **ELIMINATOR** [3] Apr83 [9]
– Gimme all your lovin' / Got me under pressure / Sharp dressed man / I need you tonight / I got the six / Legs / Thug / TV dinners / Dirty dog / If I could only flag her down / Bad girl. *(cd-iss. 1984; 9-3774-2) (pic-lp Aug85; W 3774P)*

Nov 83. (7") *(WB 9576)* <WB 29576> **SHARP DRESSED MAN. / I GOT THE SIX** [53] Jul83 [56]
(12"+=) *(WB 9576T)* – La Grange.

Mar 84. (7") *(WB 9334)* **TV DINNERS. / CHEAP SUNGLASSES** [67] [–]
(c-s+=/d12"+=) *(W 9334 C/T)* – A fool for your stockings.

Sep 84. (single re-issue) *(same)* **GIMME ALL YOUR LOVIN'** [10] [–]

Dec 84. (single re-issue) *(same)* **SHARP DRESSED MAN** [22] [–]

Feb 85. (7") *(W 9272)* <WB 29272> **LEGS (remix). / BAD GIRL** [16] May84 [8]
('A'-Metal mix-12") *(W 9272T)* – A fool for your stockings.

Jul 85. (7"ep/c-ep/12"ep) *(W 8946/+C/T)* **THE ZZ TOP SUMMER HOLIDAY EP** [51] [–]
– Tush / Got me under pressure / Beer drinkers and hell raisers / I'm bad, I'm nationwide.

Oct 85. (7"/7"sha-pic-d/7"interlocking jigsaw pic-d pt.1) *(W 2001/+P/DP)* <WB 28884> **SLEEPING BAG. / PARTY ON THE PATIO** [27] [8]
(12"+=) *(W 2001T)* – Blue jean blues.
(d7+=) *(W 2001D)* – Sharp dressed man / I got the six.

Nov 85. (lp/c)(cd) *(WX 27/+C)(925342-2)* <25342> **AFTERBURNER** [2] [4]
– Sleeping bag / Stages / Woke up with wood / Rough boy / Can't stop rockin' / Planet of women / I got the message / Velcro fly / Dipping low (in the lap of luxury) / Delirious.

Feb 86. (7"/7"jigsaw pic-d pt.2) <US-12"> *(W 2002/+BP)* <*WB 28810T*> **STAGES. / HI-FI MAMA** 43 Jan86 21
(12"+=) *(W 2002T)* – ('A'extended).

Apr 86. (7"/7"pic-d,7"jigsaw pic-d pt.3) *(W 2003/+FP)* <*WB 28733*> **ROUGH BOY. / DELIRIOUS** 23 Mar86 22
(12"shrinkwrapped w/ free jigsaw 'SLEEPING BAG' pic-d+=) – Legs (mix).

Jul 86. (7") <*WB 28650*> **VELCRO FLY. / CAN'T STOP ROCKIN'** – 35

Sep 86. (7") *(W 8515)* **VELCRO FLY. / WOKE UP IN WOOD** 54 –
(12"+=) *(W 8515T)* – Can't stop rockin' ('86 remix).

Jul 90. (7"/c-s/12") *(W 9812/+C/T)* <*19812*> **DOUBLEBACK. / PLANET OF WOMEN** 29 May90 50
(cd-s+=) *(W 9812CD)* – ('A'-AOR mix).

Oct 90. (cd)(lp/c) *(7599 26265-2)(WX 390/+C)* <*26265*> **RECYCLER** 8 6
– Concrete and steel / Lovething / Penthouse eyes / Tell it / My head's in Mississippi / Decision or collision / Give it up / 2000 blues / Burger man / Doubleback. *(re-iss. Mar94 cd/c)*

Nov 90. (7"/c-s) *(W 9509/+C)* **GIVE IT UP. / SHARP DRESSED MAN** –
(12"+=/cd-s+=) *(W 9509 T/CD)* – Cheap sunglasses (live).

Jan 91. (c-s,cd-s) <*19470*> **GIVE IT UP / CONCRETE AND STEEL** – 79

Apr 91. (7"/7"sha-pic-d/c-s) *(W 0009/+P/C)* **MY HEAD'S IN MISSISSIPPI. / A FOOL FOR YOUR STOCKINGS** 37 –
(12"+=/cd-s+=) *(W 0009 T/CD)* – Blue Jean blues.

Mar 92. (7"/c-s) *(W 0098/+C)* <*18979*> **VIVA LAS VEGAS. / 2000 BLUES** 10
(cd-s+=) *(W 0098CD)* – Velcro fly / Stages / Legs.

May 92. (cd/c/lp) <*(7599 26846-2/-4/-1)*> **GREATEST HITS** (compilation) 5 9
– Gimme all your lovin' / Sharp dressed man / Rough boy / Tush / My head's in Mississippi / Pearl necklace / I'm bad, I'm nationwide / Viva Las Vegas / Doubleback / Gun love / Got me under pressure / Give it up / Cheap sunglasses / Sleeping bag / Planet of women / La Grange / Tube snake boogie / Legs.

Jun 92. (7"/c-s) *(W 0111/+C)* **ROUGH BOY. / VIVA LAS VEGAS (remix)** 49 –
(cd-s+=) *(W 0111CD)* – Velcro fly (extended) / Doubleback (AOR mix).
(cd-s) *(W 0111CDX)* – ('A'side) / TV dinners / Jesus has just left Chicago / Beer drinkers and Hell raisers.

R.C.A. R.C.A.

Jan 94. (7"/c-s/cd-s) *(74321 18473-7/-4/-2)* **PINCUSHION. / CHERRY RED** 15
(cd-s+=) *(74321 18261-2)* – ('A'mix).

Jan 94. (cd/c/lp) *(74321 18260-2/-4/-1)* <*66317*> **ANTENNA** 3 14
– Pincushion / Breakaway / World of swirl / Fuzzbox voodoo / Girl in a T-shirt / Antenna head / PCH / Cherry red / Cover your rig / Lizard life / Deal goin' down / Everything.

Apr 94. (c-s/12"/cd-s) *(74321 19228-4/-1/-2)* **BREAKAWAY. / MARY'S / BREAKAWAY (version)** 60

Jun 96. (7"m) *(74321 39482-7)* **WHAT'S UP WITH THAT. / STOP BREAKIN' DOWN BLUES (live) / NASTY DOGS AND FUNKY KINGS (live)** 58
(cd-s+=) *(74321 39482-2)* – ('A'version).

Sep 96. (cd/c) *(74321 39466-2/-4)* <*66958*> **RHYTHMEEN** 32 29
– Rhythmeen / Bang bang / Black fly / What's up with that / Vincent Price blues / Zipper job / Hairdresser / She's just killing me / My mind is gone / Loaded / Prettyhead / Hummbucking, part 2.

— ZZ were back in the UK Top 30 in Oct'99, albeit credited on MARTAY's version of their 'GIMME ALL YOUR LOVIN' 2000'

May 00. (cd/c) *(74321 69377-2)* <*67850-2*> **XXX** Sep99 100
– Poke chop sandwich / Crucifixx-a-flatt / Fearless boogie / 36-22-36 / Made into a movie / Beatbox / Trippin' / Dreadmonboogaloo / Introduction by Ross Mitchell / Sinpusher / (Let me be your) Teddy bear / Hey Mr. Millionaire / Belt buckle.

Apr 03. (cd) *(82876 51654-2)* <*51168*> **MESCALERO** 57
– Mescalero / Two ways to play / Alley-gator / Buck nekkid / Goin' so good / Me so stupid / Piece / Punk ass boyfriend / Stackin' paper / What would you do / What it is kid / Que lastima / Tramp / Crunchy / Dusted / Liquor.

– compilations, others, etc. –

on 'Warners' unless mentioned otherwise

Nov 83. (d-c) *(K4 66121)* **TRES HOMBRES / FANDANGO** –

1987. (3xcd-box) *(K 925661-2)* **FIRST ALBUM / RIO GRANDE MUD / / TRES HOMBRES / FANDANGO! / / TEJAS / EL LOCO**

Nov 94. (cd/c) <*(9362 45815-2/-4)*> **ONE FOOT IN THE BLUES**

Dec 02. (3xcd-box) *R.C.A.; (74321 95370-2)* **ANTENNA / RHYTHMEEN / XXX**